NEW AGE INTERNATIONAL

WEBSTER'S STUDENT DICTIONARY

OF THE ENGLISH LANGUAGE

INTERNATIONAL ENCYCLOPEDIC EDITION

NEW ENLARGED EDITION

Sidney I. Landau

Editor in Chief

NEW AGE INTERNATIONAL PUBLISHERS

First Indian Sub-Continent Edition : 2009
by New Age International (P) Ltd., Publishers

This special low-priced edition is for sale in India, Bangladesh, Bhutan, Myanmar (Burma), Sri Lanka, Nepal and Maldives only.
Originally Published in United States of America.

Printed in India at L.B. Enterprises, Delhi.
C-10-03-4403

ISBN: 978-81-224-2684-7
Indian Edition Price Rs. 325.00

PUBLISHING FOR ONE WORLD
NEW AGE INTERNATIONAL (P) LIMITED, PUBLISHERS
4835/24, Ansari Road, Daryaganj, New Delhi- 110002
Visit us at **www.newagepublishers.com**

Contents

Pronunciation Key	vii
Formation of Plurals and Participles	vii
Terms Used in the *Guide to the Use of This Dictionary*	viii
Guide to the Use of This Dictionary	ix
Usage *by Albert H. Marckwardt*	xii
Punctuation *by Harold B. Allen*	xvii
Canadian English *by H. Rex Wilson*	xxiii
Abbreviations and Symbols Used in This Dictionary	xxvi
A DICTIONARY OF THE ENGLISH LANGUAGE	**1**

Dictionary Advisory Committee

Albert H. Marckwardt *Chairman*
Professor Emeritus of English and Linguistics
Princeton University

Harold B. Allen
Professor Emeritus of English and Linguistics
University of Minnesota

S. I. Hayakawa
President Emeritus
San Francisco State University

Rudolph C. Troike
Director
Center for Applied Linguistics

H. Rex Wilson
Associate Professor of English (Linguistics)
University of Western Ontario

Editorial Staff

EDITOR IN CHIEF
Sidney I. Landau

MANAGING EDITOR
Ronald J. Bogus

EDITORS
Sheila C. Brantley, Samuel Davis,
Barbara Nolan, Kathleen D. Shafer

CONTRIBUTING EDITORS
Myrna Breskin, Olga Coren, Helene MacLean,
Harold A. Rodgers, Karin Whiteley

CLERICAL ASSISTANTS
Lurlene Scott, Lynn Tricarico, Martha Adams

ART DIRECTOR
Marian Hurd Manfredi

CARTOGRAPHER
Rafael Palacios

ARTISTS
Robert Byrd, Kiyoshi Kanai, Mary Suzuki, Jean Taylor

Special acknowledgment is gratefully made of the contributions of Diana Klemin, Associate Art Director of Doubleday & Company, Inc., in acquiring new illustrations for this work.

Pronunciation Key

The primary stress mark (ʹ) is placed after the syllable bearing the heavier stress or accent; the secondary stress mark (ʹ) follows a syllable having a somewhat lighter stress, as in **com·men·da·tion** (kom′ən·dāʹshən).

a	add, map	g	go, log	o	odd, hot	t	talk, sit	v	vain, eve
ā	ace, rate	h*	hope, hate	ō	open, so	th	thin, both	w	win, away
â(r)	care, air	i	it, give	ô	order, jaw	t͟h	this, bathe	y*	yet, yearn
ä	palm, father	ī	ice, write	oi	oil, boy	u	up, done	z	zest, muse
b	bat, rub	j	joy, ledge	ou	pout, now	û(r)	burn, term	zh	vision, pleasure
ch	check, catch	k	cool, take	o͝o	took, full	yo͞o	fuse, few		
d	dog, rod	l	look, rule	o͞o	pool, food				
e	end, pet	m	move, seem	p	pit, stop				
ē	even, tree	n	nice, tin	r	run, poor				
f	fit, half	ng	ring, song	s	see, pass				
				sh	sure, rush				

ə the schwa, an unstressed vowel representing the sound of
a in *above* *o* in *melon*
e in *sicken* *u* in *focus*
i in *clarity*

Superscript *h,* as in *white* (ʰwīt) or *whale* (ʰwāl), and *y,* as in *due* (dʸo͞o) or *Tuesday* (tʸo͞ozʹdā) represent sounds that commonly occur in certain regions but are commonly omitted in others.

FOREIGN SOUNDS

à as in French *ami, patte.* This is a vowel midway in quality between (a) and (ä).

œ as in French *peu,* German *schön.* Round the lips for (ō) and pronounce (ā).

ü as in French *vue,* German *grün.* Round the lips for (o͞o) and pronounce (ē).

kh as in German *ach,* Scottish *loch.* Pronounce a strongly aspirated (h) with the tongue in position for (k) as in *cool* or *keep.*

ṅ This symbol indicates that the preceding vowel is nasal. The nasal vowels in French are œṅ *(brun),* aṅ *(main),* äṅ *(chambre),* ôṅ *(dont).*

ʼ This symbol indicates that a preceding (l) or (r) is voiceless, as in French *débâcle* (dā·bäʹklʼ) or *fiacre* (fyàʹkrʼ), or that a preceding (y) is pronounced consonantly in a separate syllable followed by a slight schwa sound, as in French *fille* (fēʹyʼ).

Formation of Plurals and Participles

Basically, plurals in English are formed by the addition of *-s* or *-es* (depending on the preceding sound) to the complete word; past participles are formed by the addition of *-ed,* and present participles by adding *-ing.* There are, however, many exceptions. In this dictionary, all such exceptions (the "irregular" inflected forms) are indicated within the entry, in boldface immediately following the part-of-speech label.

fly (flī) *n. pl.* **flies** . . .
sheep (shēp) *n. pl.* **sheep** . . .
cal·ci·fy (kalʹsə·fī) *v.t. & v.i.* **·fied, ·fy·ing** . . .
go (gō) *v.* **went, gone, go·ing** .

Some rules for the spelling of these forms (with the exception of nouns which form their plurals by some internal change and the so-called strong verbs) are listed below:

PLURALS

1. Nouns ending in *y* preceded by a consonant change *y* to *i* and add *-es.*
   baby babies story stories
2. Nouns ending in *y* preceded by a vowel add *-s* without change.
   chimney chimneys valley valleys
   Note, however, that *money* may have either form in the plural—*moneys, monies.*
3. Some nouns ending in *f* or *fe* change this to *v* and add *-es.*
   knife knives shelf shelves
   But: roof roofs safe safes
   Some words may have alternate plural forms.
   scarf scarfs or scarves
4. Most words ending in *o* add *-s* without change.
   cameo cameos folio folios

A few words ending in *o* (*echo, hero, Negro,* etc.) form the plural only in *-oes (echoes, heroes, Negroes),* but many others in this category have alternative plurals in both forms.

mosquito mosquitos or mosquitoes
volcano volcanoes or volcanos

PAST AND PRESENT PARTICIPLES

1. The final consonant is doubled for monosyllables or words accented on the final syllable when they end in a *single* consonant preceded by a *single* vowel.
   control, controlled, controlling
   hop, hopped, hopping
   occur, occurred, occurring
   But: help, helped, helping *(two consonants)*
   seed, seeded, seeding *(two vowels)*
   Some words *not* accented on the final syllable have a variant participial form with a doubled consonant; the single consonant form is preferred in the United States.
   travel, traveled or travelled, traveling or travelling
   worship, worshiped or worshipped, worshiping or worshipping
2. Words ending in silent or mute *e* drop the *e* before *-ed* and *-ing,* unless it is needed to avoid confusion with another word.
   change, changed, changing love, loved, loving
   singe, singed, singeing dye, dyed, dyeing
3. Verbs ending in *ie* usually change this to *y* before adding *-ing.*
   die, died, dying lie, lied, lying
4. Verbs ending in *c* add a *k* before *-ed* and *-ing.*
   mimic, mimicked, mimicking
   picnic, picnicked, picnicking

Terms Used in the Guide to the Use of This Dictionary

cross-reference to illustration	**ser·rate** (ser′āt, -it) *adj.* Having sawlike teeth, as the margins of certain leaves. Also **ser′rat·ed.** [< L *serra* a saw] • See LEAF.
inflected forms	**skin·ny** (skin′ē) *adj.* **-ni·er, -ni·est** 1 Consisting of or like skin. 2 Without sufficient flesh; too thin. 3 Lacking the
	skip (skip) *v.* **skipped, skip·ping** *v.i.* 1 To move with springing steps, esp. by a series of light hops on alternate feet.
homographs	**skip·per¹** (skip′ər) *n* 1 One who or that which skips. 2 Any of various insects that make erratic, skipping movements.
	skip·per² (skip′ər) *n.* 1 The master or captain of a vessel, esp. of a small ship or boat.
definition number	2 One who is in charge of any endeavor. —*v.t.* To act as the skipper of (a vessel, etc.) [< Du. *schip* ship]
abbreviation	**Skt.** Sanskrit.
variant form	**sku·a** (skyōō′ə) *n.* A predatory sea bird. Also **skua gull.** [< ON *skūfr*]
	slice (slīs) *n.* 1 A thin, broad piece cut off from a larger * * * such a course. —*v.* **sliced, slic·ing** *v.t.* 1 To cut or remove
usage information	from a larger piece: often with *off, from,* etc. 2 To cut,
cross-reference	**slide fastener** ZIPPER.
	splen·did (splen′did) *adj.* 1 Magnificent; imposing. 2 Conspicuously great or illustrious; glorious: a *splendid* achievement. 3 Giving out or reflecting brilliant light; * * *
synonym list	*n.* —**Syn.** 1 majestic, dazzling, sublime, superb, grand. 2 outstanding, renowned, celebrated, marvelous.
part-of-speech labels	**splin·ter** (splin′tər) *n.* 1 A thin, sharp piece of wood, glass, metal, etc., split or torn off lengthwise; a sliver. 2 SPLINTER GROUP. —*v.t.* & *v.i.* 1 To split into thin sharp pieces or
usage note	**split infinitive** A verbal phrase in which the sign of the infinitive "to" is separated from its verb by an intervening word, usu. an adverb, as in "to quickly return." • Although this construction is often condemned by purists, it is sometimes justified to avoid ambiguity or awkwardness.
syllabic dots	**stra·to·cu·mu·lus** (strāt′ō·kyōō′myə·ləs, strat′-) *n. pl.* **·li**
subject label	(-lī) *Meteorol.* A type of dark, low-lying cloud, characterized by horizontal bases and high, rounded summits.
main entry	**strength** (strength) *n.* 1 The quality or property of being physically strong: the *strength* of a weight lifter. 2 The capacity to sustain the application of force without yielding or breaking. 3 Effectiveness: the *strength* of an argument. 4 Binding force or validity, as of a law. 5 Vigor or
illustrative example	force of style: a drama of great *strength.* 6 Available numerical force in a military unit or other organization. 7 Degree of intensity, as of color, light, or sound. 8 Potency, as of a drug, chemical, or liquor; concentration. 9
idiomatic phrase	A support; aid: He is our *strength.* —**on the strength of** Relying on; on the basis of. [< OE *strang* strong] —**Syn.** 1 force, power, vigor. 2 solidity, tenacity, toughness.
run-on derivatives	**stren·u·ous** (stren′yōō·əs) *adj.* Necessitating or marked by strong effort or exertion. [< L *strenuus*] —**stren′u·ous·ly** *adv.* —**stren′u·ous·ness** *n.*
pronunciation	**strep·to·coc·cus** (strep′tə·kok′əs) *n. pl.* **·coc·ci** (-kok′sī, -sē, -ī, -ē) Any of a large group of spherical bacteria that
etymology	**strep·to·my·cin** (strep′tō·mī′sin) *n.* A potent antibiotic isolated from a mold. [< Gk. *streptos* twisted + *mykēs* fungus]
cross-reference to map	**Swit·zer·land** (swit′sər·lənd) *n.* A republic of CEN. Europe, 15,940 sq. mi., cap. Bern. • See map at ITALY.

Guide to the Use of This Dictionary

1. Main entries are in large, bold-faced type and are listed alphabetically by letter, regardless of whether composed of one or more words.

blue·jack·et
blue jay

2. Syllabication is indicated by syllabic dots dividing main-entry words. **blue·jack·et** may be hyphenated at the end of a line after *blue-* or after *bluejack-*. Phrasal entries are not syllabified when each element is entered elsewhere.

3. Homographs These words, identical in spelling but differing in meaning and origin (and sometimes in pronunciation), are separately entered and differentiated by a superior figure, as **bear**[1] (to support or endure) and **bear**[2] (the animal).

4. Pronunciations are shown in parentheses immediately following the main entry, as **di·chot·o·my** (dī-kot′ə·mē). When more than one pronunciation is recorded, the first given is usually the most widely used wherever it has been possible to determine extent of usage; often, however, usage may be almost equally divided. The order of the pronunciations is not intended to be an indication of preference; all pronunciations shown are valid for educated American speech.

The syllabication of the pronunciations follows, in general, the syllabic breaks heard in speech rather than the conventional division of the main entry, as **ju·di·cial** (jōō·dish′əl), **an·es·the·tize** (ə·nes′thə·tīz).

When a variant pronunciation differs merely in part from the first pronunciation recorded, only the differing syllable or syllables are shown, provided that there is no possibility of misinterpretation, as **eq·ua·ble** (ek′wə·bəl, ē′kwə-). Phrasal entries are not pronounced if the individual elements are separately entered in proper alphabetic place.

5. Part-of-speech labels are shown in italics following the pronunciation for main entries, and are abbreviated as follows: *n.* (noun), *v.* (verb), *pron.* (pronoun), *adj.* (adjective), *adv.* (adverb), *prep.* (preposition), *conj.* (conjunction), *interj.* (interjection). When more than one part of speech is entered under a main entry, the additional labels are run in and preceded by a bold-faced dash, as **cor·ner** (kôr′nər) *n.* . . . — *v.t.* . . . —*v.i.* . . . —*adj.* . . .

Verbs used transitively are identified as *v.t.*, those intransitively as *v.i.;* those used both transitively and intransitively in all senses are designated *v.t. & v.i.*

6. Inflected forms include the past tense, past participle, and present participle of verbs, the plural of nouns, and the comparative and superlative of adjectives and adverbs. The inflected forms are entered wherever there is some irregularity in spelling or form. They are shown in bold-faced type with syllabication immediately after the part-of-speech label. Only the syllable affected is shown, provided there is no ambiguity possible, as **com·pute** (kəm·pyōōt′) *v.t.* **·put·ed, ·put·ing.** An inflected form that requires pronunciation or is alphabetically distant from the main entry may also be separately entered and pronounced in its proper vocabulary place.

a *Principal parts of verbs* The order in which the principal parts are shown is past tense, past participle, and present participle, as **come** (kum) *v.* **came, come, com·ing.** Where the past tense and past participle are identical, only two forms are entered, as **bake** (bāk) *v.* **baked, bak·ing.** When alternative forms are given, the first form indicated is usually the one preferred, as **grov·el** (gruv′əl, grov′-) *v.i.* **grov·eled** or **grov·elled, grov·el·ing** or **grov·el·ling.** Variant forms not in the standard vocabulary are shown in parentheses and labeled, as **drink** (dringk) *v.* **drank** (*Archaic* **drunk**), **drunk** (*Archaic* **drunk·en**), **drink·ing.** Principal parts entirely regular in formation—those that add *-ed* and *-ing* directly to the infinitive without spelling modification—are not shown.

b *Plural of nouns* Irregular forms are here preceded by the designation *pl.*, as **a·lum·nus** (ə·lum′-nəs) *n. pl.* **·ni** (-nī); **deer** (dir) *n. pl.* **deer.** When alternative plurals are given, the first shown is the preferred form, as **buf·fa·lo** (buf′ə·lō) *n. pl.* **·loes** or **·los** or **·lo.**

c *Comparison of adjectives and adverbs* The comparatives and superlatives of adjectives and adverbs are shown immediately after the part of speech when there is some spelling modification or a complete change of form, as **mer·ry** (mer′ē) *adj.* **-ri·er, -ri·est; bad** (bad) *adj.* **worse, worst.**

7. Definition In entries for words having several senses, the order in which the definitions appear is, wherever possible, that of frequency of use, rather than semantic evolution. Each such definition is distinguished by a bold-faced number, the numbering starting anew after each part-of-speech label when it is followed by more than one sense. Closely related meanings, especially those within a specific field or area of study, may be defined under the same number and set apart by small bold-faced letters. Illustrative examples are provided when necessary to supplement definitions.

> **strength** (strength) *n.* **1** The quality or property of being physically strong: the *strength* of a weight lifter.

8. Restrictive labels Entries or particular senses of words and terms having restricted application are variously labeled according to:

a usage level, as *Slang, Informal* (colloquial)

b localization, as *Regional* (restricted in usage to a particular region of the U.S.), *Brit.* (British), *Can.* (Canadian), *Austral.* (Australian), etc.; *U.S.* (United States) is used only to avoid confusion with another meaning of the same word not restricted to the U.S. It is understood that many unlabeled definitions are current chiefly or only in the U.S.

c field or subject, as *Astron.* (astronomy), *Ecol.* (ecology), *Med.* (medicine), *Naut.* (nautical), etc.

d language of origin, as *French, German, Latin,* etc. These entries, although used in English speech and writing, have not yet undergone the process of Anglicization of pronunciation, meaning, or usage, and are usually italicized in writing.

e *Nonstand.* (nonstandard) is applied to those usages which are not accepted as standard English by most native speakers.

Restrictive labels that apply to only one sense of a word are entered after the definition number. Restrictive labels entered immediately after the part-of-speech label apply to all the senses for that part of speech; those shown before the first part-of-speech label refer to the entire entry.

9. Cross-references Small capital letters are used to identify:

a A cross-reference from a variant form to the entry where the term is defined.

> **es·thet·ic** (es·thet′ik) *adj.* AESTHETIC.

b A cross-reference to a synonymous meaning or term where a full definition will be found.

> **slide fastener** ZIPPER.

c A cross-reference to an illustration, map, or usage note. These cross-references are preceded by •.

d A cross-reference in an etymology. See *Etymologies* below.

Variant forms that do not require cross-reference are shown after the definition or definitions to which they apply, and appear in bold-faced type with syllabication, stress marks, and, when necessary, pronunciation. When they apply to one sense only of an entry having more than one definition, they are linked to the appropriate definition with a colon.

10. Spelling variations between U.S. and British usage are noted by the label *Brit. sp.*, followed by the usual British spelling or that part of it that differs from the U.S. spelling.

> **hon·or** . . . *Brit. Sp.* **-our.**

11. Idiomatic phrases, as those formed by a verb and preposition or adverb (*carry on, put down, set off,* etc.) appear in bold-faced type within the entry for the principal word in the phrase, following the definitions for the principal part of speech involved.

> **car·ry** . . . *v.t.* . . . *v.i.* **19** . . . **20** . . . **21** . . . **—carry on 1** To keep going; continue. **2** To behave in a free, frolicsome manner. **3** To continue, as a tradition. . . . **—***n.* . . . .

12. Etymologies are shown in brackets after the definitions. The following examples show the manner of entry and the use of cross-references:

a special [<L *species* kind, species] means: ultimately derived from (<) the Latin (L) word *species,* meaning "kind, species."

b arroyo [Sp.] means that *arroyo* was borrowed directly from a Spanish (Sp.) word of the same form and meaning.

c cloche [F, lit., bell]; like *arroyo* above, *cloche* exists in the same form and meaning in another language, French (F), from which English borrowed it, but in this case the foreign word has a literal meaning (lit.), "bell," that elucidates its English meaning.

d hassle [?< HAGGLE + TUSSLE] means: possibly (?) derived from (<) a blending of "haggle" and (+) "tussle."

e decency [<L *decens.* See DECENT.]; "See" directs attention to the etymology under "decent" for further information.

13. Run-on derivatives Words that are actually or ostensibly derived from other words by the addition or replacement of a suffix, and whose sense can be inferred from the meaning of the main word, are run on in smaller bold-faced type at the end of the appropriate main entries. The run-on derivatives are preceded by a heavy dash and followed by a part-of-speech label. They are syllabified and stressed, and, when necessary, a full or partial pronunciation is provided.

14. Usage information, when an integral part of definition, is included, following a colon, after the particular sense of a word to which it applies, as:

> **slice** . . . *v.t.* **1** To cut or remove from a larger piece: often with *off, from,* etc.

More extensive notes consisting of supplementary information on accepted usage, style, grammar, status of variant forms, etc., are entered at the end of the relevant entries and prefaced with the symbol •. (See *anyone, Asia, shop, split infinitive.*)

15. Synonym lists are appended to many entries following the abbreviation **Syn.** In entries having more than one sense, synonyms are keyed by definition number, and, if necessary, by part of speech, to the appropriate sense.

16. Word lists The meaning of many combinations of words is easily apparent by combining the senses of their component parts. Such self-explaining compounds have been entered in six lists under the respective first elements: *in-*, *multi-*, *non-*, *over-*, *re-*, and *un-*. These lists serve to indicate the preferred form of a compound—whether written solid, with a hyphen, or as a two-word phrase. The listings are not intended to be all-inclusive; the prefixes and combining forms so entered combine freely in English in the formation of new compounds based on existing forms.

17. Trade names Some words used to identify trademarked or proprietary articles, drugs, processes, and services have been entered and defined because these terms are so familiar that their omission would be remarkable. In every case the word is identified with the notation "a trade name," and no treatment of any such term should be construed as affecting its status as a trademark.

18. Abbreviations commonly used in English are entered in their respective alphabetic places in the main section of this dictionary.

Usage

BY ALBERT H. MARCKWARDT

Every society places its stamp of approval upon certain forms or modes of social behavior and looks askance upon deviations from them. In our culture, applause for a fine musical performance would be considered out of place at a church service, but entirely appropriate and in fact praiseworthy in a concert hall. The particular mode of behavior which is accorded such prestige may vary according to geography and social class. The English and European continentals recognize one manner of manipulating a knife and fork to convey food to the mouth; Americans employ a quite different technique. The American way seems needlessly awkward to the European; the European way seems crude to the Americans. When they entertain at dinner, upper middle-class Americans are likely to eat by candlelight and to have flowers on the table. This is regarded as ostentatious, or at best superfluous, in working-class circles.

The use of language is one of many kinds of social behavior. Here, as in other matters, certain forms of speech and writing have acquired prestige, whereas others are looked upon with disfavor. Moreover, differentiations on the basis of geography and social class are readily apparent. The past tense of the verb *eat (et),* used by many speakers of British English of unquestioned social standing, would be considered rustic or uneducated by most Americans; conversely, the Americanism *donate* has not yet gained thorough acceptance in Britain. "Bring them crates over here," is a sentence calculated to produce cooperation and a speedy result when addressed to a group of factory workmen; the substitution of *those containers* in that particular social context would produce suspicion, resentment, and probably not the desired result.

Standard English

That form of the English language which has acquired prestige from its use by those educated persons who are carrying on the affairs of the English-speaking community (whether narrowly or broadly conceived) is known as Standard English. In short, the standard language is that which possesses social utility and social prestige. History bears out this observation with remarkable fidelity. All we know of the earliest stage of our language, that which we refer to as Old English, spoken on the island between the mid-fifth century incursions of Germanic-speaking Angles, Saxons, and Jutes and the mid-11th century Norman Conquest, was that there were decided regional differences, resulting in four major dialects. During the first two of these six centuries the center of power was clearly in the kingdom of Northumbria, and that dialect constituted the standard. At the time of the powerful King Offa, political and cultural influence shifted southward, and the dialect of Mercia acquired prestige. From the mid-ninth century onward, the West Saxon dynasty assumed political leadership; King Alfred fathered a cultural renaissance and a major educational program; and this time the standard moved westward, remaining there through the period of religious reform, also centered in the same area. Thus it is that most of the Old English literature which has come down to us is in West Saxon. Even the early selections originally written in other dialects were finally recopied in the prestige dialect.

The development of the language during the Middle English period (1050–1475) bears out the same principle. By the time the English language had recovered from its temporary subjugation to Norman French, London was firmly established as the political, economic, and cultural center of the island. It is interesting to observe that by the end of the 14th century the dialect of London was used by many of the major literary figures irrespective of where they were born. Chaucer, a native Londoner, employed it in his poetry, which is possibly no surprise, but so too did Gower, born in Kent, and Wycliffe, who hailed from Lincolnshire. One acute observer has pointed out that Standard English had its origin in the kind of language employed in the courts of law and the governmental offices at Westminster, that it was essentially administrative English. This is another telling bit of evidence of the close relationship between the standard language and the bases of influence.

The emergence of the London dialect as a standard for the entire country first won formal recognition in

Puttenham's *The Arte of English Poesie* (1589) in which the language of London and of the shires within a radius of sixty miles, "and not much beyond," was recommended as a model for aspiring writers to follow. This was accompanied by the statement that educated gentlemen in the outlying portions of England had adopted London English as a standard and were speaking it as well as people living in the capital.

It was just at this point in time that the English language entered on its worldwide career. It was transported first across the Atlantic to the American mainland and the Caribbean islands. The spread to the Asian subcontinent followed in the 18th century; to Australia and South Africa in the 19th. At the outset the colonies were generally willing and eager to follow the standard of the mother country, even though it was at times less than ideally suited to all aspects of the local situation, but as they acquired more and more independence, economic and cultural as well as political, new national forms of the language tended to emerge and to develop their own standard norms.

Today English is spoken as a native language by vast numbers of people—approximately 275,000,000—distributed over four continents of the globe. The standard reveals a considerable amount of variation from one country to another, and even in one part of some countries as compared with another. Thus, Standard West Indian English differs from both Standard British and Standard American English, and Standard South African differs from all of these. Standard Canadian English is distinct from Standard Australian. It is even possible to speak of standard forms of English in areas where it is not the native language, notably India and the Philippines. In the United Kingdom itself there is a standard form of Scots and a standard Northern English, both of which differ from the Received Standard of the London area.

The Role of the Dictionary

Ideally a dictionary is an accurate record of a language as it is employed by those who speak and write it. But as we have already seen, the English language, even in terms of just its present use, to say nothing of its past, exists on such a vast scale that no single work is likely to do justice to it in its entirety. Inevitably the task has had to be broken up into smaller segments. Some dictionaries deal with pronunciation only, at times even confined to a particular country—England or America. Others confine themselves to particular segments of the language: dialect, slang, or one or another technical vocabulary. More ambitious is the attempt by the historical dictionary to include within the bounds of a single work evidence of both the present and earlier stages of the language, although sometimes a dictionary may be confined to just one early period—Old or Middle English, for example. There are dictionaries which concentrate on the language as it is, and has been, used in England, in Scotland, in the United States, and in Canada. Consequently, in the face of this inescapable specialization and division of labor, a dictionary which purports to be general in its purpose must of necessity exercise a high degree of selective reporting on those aspects of the language which will best serve the needs of those who consult it.

The editors of this dictionary have assumed that it will be used principally in the United States, by persons who are familiar with American English. Only rarely have they felt it necessary to identify features of the language which are characteristic of this country. For example, the past participial form *gotten* is identified in a note as an American usage, and the peculiarly American use of *integrate* as used in "to integrate schools" bears the label *U.S.* The editors have taken on the responsibility of identifying usages peculiar to Britain, Canada, or Australia, indicating these with the appropriate label. Any item not so identified is in current use in the United States. In this connection it should be realized that despite all that has been said here about differences throughout the world, the unity of the English language in the many countries in which it is spoken far outweighs the diversity.

The obligation of the dictionary to record the state of the language or some segment of it as accurately as possible has already been mentioned. This may properly be termed a descriptive function, and it reflects the way in which the editors approach their task. But the nonprofessional, the layman who consults the dictionary, does so from other motives. Either he is seeking information on some particular facet of the language about which he knows nothing—the most obvious instance being the meaning of a word he has not previously encountered—or to discover which of several possible uses of the language, relative to spelling, pronunciation, word division, word meaning, or grammatical form, has acquired a sufficient degree of prestige and propriety to justify his employment of it. In short, his view of the dictionary function is essentially prescriptive. He hopes to be told what to say and to write, or more accurately perhaps, how to say and how to write.

In the light of all that has been said up to this point, these two concepts, the descriptive and the prescriptive, should not be in conflict with each other. It has already been pointed out that the standard language *is* the language of the socially and culturally dominant group within a speech community. There can be no other source upon which to base it. Accordingly, if the dictionary records that language accurately and faithfully, it should constitute a reliable guide and preceptor.

Unfortunately, the problem is not so simple as it seems on the surface. For a number of reasons too complicated to explain here, many people, Americans in particular, are reluctant to accept this simple and straightforward view of the matter. For one thing, experience has taught them that some persons of position and influence have little feeling for or command of the niceties of the language, and accordingly they are led to question the reliability and usefulness of an accurate exercise of the descriptive technique. Second, they are committed to a rigid and monolithic view of what constitutes the standard language and expect to find a single answer as to what is linguistically approved or appropriate, irrespective of the circumstances in which it may occur. The facts of the case are quite at variance with this assumption. Again, language like any form of social behavior varies in response to the demands of the particular social situation. Many of us would not hesitate to pick up a chicken drumstick with our fingers at a picnic but would feel constrained to use a knife and fork at a formal dinner. Neither form of behavior is superior or inferior to the other; it is a question of adaptation to the circumstances. Differences in regional standards prevail as well. In some parts of the country, for the host at a cocktail party to employ a bartender smacks of ostentation, whereas a hired caterer is accepted as the norm. Elsewhere just the reverse set of values prevails.

Varieties of Usage

It is precisely for this reason that dictionaries find it necessary to employ various kinds of labels to indicate the sphere of usage in which a particular word or expression is or is not acceptable. Those labels which are most often misunderstood have to do with the degree of formality which characterizes the communication. No dictionary has found it possible to recognize more than a dichotomy here, namely a formal and an informal type of speech. Clearly, each one of us in the course of a day's use of the language communicates much more in an informal manner than in a formal. The differences are pervasive, including pronunciation and structure as well as vocabulary. To take just a few obvious instances: the clipped form *dorm* is a frequent informal equivalent for *dormitory;* the phrase *all in* often serves for *exhausted, catch on* for *understand,* to cover at least three of the four major parts of speech. There is a whole battery of adverbs such as *consequently* and *accordingly* which may find *so* as their normal equivalent in less formal discourse. The same distinction extends to such phrase structures as *at all events* and *needless to say.* In the negative-interrogative form of the verb, *isn't he, can't he, won't he* are the informal expressions corresponding to *is he not, can he not, will he not,* a consideration affecting both syntax and pronunciation.

Actually we are faced with more than a dichotomy here. Some observers recognize at least four distinct linguistic styles, including the formal *(This is not the man whom we seek),* the consultative *(This is not the man we're looking for),* the casual *(He's not our man)* and the intimate *('Fraid you picked a lemon).* It is beyond the bounds of practicality or serviceability for the dictionary to recognize more than two broad types of situation, the formal and the informal. Moreover, in terms of the expectations of most of the people who consult a dictionary, it is more to the point to label the justifiably informal than it would be to signalize the formal. Generally the length and stylistic aura of a word will identify it as being primarily confined to formal use.

Distinctions drawn on the basis of formality often cut across differences in the mode of communication, speech or writing. Much, but not all, of our speech activity in the course of a day is informal. Some of our writing at least is more likely to be formal, although many personal letters, memoranda, the private writing contained in diaries and journals, may well fall into the informal category.

The point is that these are matters of the function of language, not of acceptability or correctness. A person whose informal speech may be characterized as "talking like a book" or "talking as if he had swallowed the dictionary," has simply failed to sort out the styles properly. One may rest assured that whatever a dictionary labels as *informal* is not less correct than an unlabeled item but that it is appropriate to an informal situation or purpose. Dictionaries usually do not affix a label to those words appropriate only for formal use on the ground that the social penalties for excessive formality of speech, though very real, seem somehow less onerous than those for misplaced informality.

Slang

Somewhat akin to informality, but differing from it in several important respects, is the use of language we have come to call slang. Slang is difficult to define, partly because the term itself has changed in meaning over the centuries. Originally it referred to thieves' argot, and today the term is still applied to the special terminology of certain occupations and other groups, including oil drillers, baseball players, rock or jazz musicians, college students, shoe salesmen, tramps, drug addicts, and prison inmates, but it has also taken on a much broader application. It includes clipped forms like *benny* and *frag,* echoic terms like *slurp,* meaningless tag phrases of the class of *twenty-three skidoo* from the early years of the century, *so's your old man, and how, you better believe it,* all of which have had their fleeting currency, only to be replaced by what will undoubtedly be the equally temporary *got to (He's got to be the best ball player in the league)* and the interjection *Wow!* which appears to be the stock in trade of the younger generation and the mindless consumer pictured on television commercials.

Not included in the concept of slang are dialect, localisms, profanity, and the so-called four-letter words once taboo in polite society, now increasingly accepted. It is also important to recognize that most slang is colloquial in nature in that it occurs in speech much more frequently than in writing; on the other hand, it would be a grave error to think of all colloquial or informal language as slang. Nor is slang to be confused with nonstandard language; it is at times consciously employed for a particular effect by persons of unquestioned cultivation.

Dictionaries are far from uniform in what they label as slang; even the special dictionaries of slang include many entries which do not at all fit the concept as it has been set forth here. The label *slang* after a word or a particular meaning of a word is an indication of its general unsuitability for formal communication; it suggests moreover that when used informally, it may have something of a slight shock value in a serious context; at the very least it will call attention to itself. This would be true, for example, of *boss* used adjectivally in the sense of "great, wonderful," of *bug off* for "go away!" and of *bug out,* "to escape, run away." Each country where English is a native language has its own variety of slang. *Wizard* is often used in England as a blanket term of approval; *dinkum* is confined to Australia. Both are relatively unknown in the United States. In this dictionary, slang terms found in other English-speaking countries will be labeled as to their place of origin. If an item is simply characterized as *slang* with no additional qualifying term, it may be assumed to be current in this country.

Regional Variation

In no English-speaking country is the language uniform over the entire area. In certain fields of the vocabulary, terminology differs from one part of the country to the other. This is especially true of words having to do with the more homelike and intimate aspects of life: the physical environment, the home, foods and cooking, the farm and farm operations, the fauna and flora. The literary term *earthworm* is called an *angleworm* in certain regions and a *fishworm* or *fishing worm* in others, and in addition there are several terms which have a much more restricted currency: *eaceworm, angle dog,* and *dewworm. Skillet* and *spider,* though now somewhat old-fashioned, are still used for *frying pan* or *fry pan* in some areas. Limited access highways have developed a highly varied terminology: *turnpike, freeway, expressway, parkway,* to mention only a few.

It is impossible in a general dictionary such as this to include all such variants, nor would it be helpful to label as *Regional* every term limited to extensive regions. Nevertheless, in terms of its function as an accurate recorder of the language, the dictionary must inform its users when a term, limited geographically, differs from a more commonly preferred synonym. There is a problem here in that dialect research in this country is still going on and that reliable information about the regional incidence of many terms is not yet readily available. In general the policy of this dictionary will be to indicate that a word is regional when that is known to be the case and when the word is not likely to be familiar to others outside the region of its use, but there will be no attempt to delimit the precise areas of its occurrence.

Nonstandard English

The very fact that a painstaking attempt has been made to clarify the concept of Standard English should be evidence in itself that there are features of the language which do not meet these requirements. Most of the aberrations are matters of grammatical form: *hisself* instead of *himself, hisn* instead of *his, growed* instead of *grew* or *grown, anyways* instead of *anyway,* and so on. Occasionally these are matters which pertain wholly to the vocabulary, like *irregardless,* or to the pronunciation, as with the dropping of the first *r* in *secretary* and *library.*

At one time it was the custom for dictionaries to employ the label *illiterate* for such deviations from standard usage. For several reasons the term is far from satisfactory. The percentage of actual illiterates in the United States is relatively small, even if so-called functional illiteracy is to be used as a criterion. The type of expressions so labeled often extended to many persons who had experienced some schooling. Because of these and other considerations dictionaries have recently tended to use *nonstandard* as the preferred designation for deviations from the linguistic norm which tend to be matters of social rather than regional dialect. It is rare, of course, for anyone to consult the dictionary for the meanings of words so labeled. The principal service that the dictionary performs is to indicate their status.

Usage Notes

It must be recognized, however, that there is no immediately definable hard-and-fast line separating the standard from the nonstandard. There is, indeed, a gray area, a zone of disputed items about which there may be considerable difference of opinion, even among authorities of equal experience and eminence. In connection with some of the locutions falling within this zone of uncertainty, not only must the extent of use by speakers of the standard language be considered but also the attitude toward the word or construction in question. For example, there can be no doubt about the extent to which the verb *finalize* has been used in American English by speakers and writers of unquestioned prestige. It is by no means a new coinage. It has appeared in magazines and newspapers with high editorial standards. It conforms to an active and long-standing pattern of converting adjectives to verbs by the addition of the *-ize* suffix, one which has been present in the language for some four centuries, evident in words like *fertilize, brutalize,* and *solemnize,* the propriety of which is never questioned. Yet the fact remains that a fair number of persons who can use the language with skill and discrimination react negatively to this single *-ize* formation. To them it suggests the awkwardness and bombast of bureaucratic language, administrators' jargon. Logical or illogical, informed or uninformed, this fairly widespread feeling is part of the total record, the total history of the word, and as such, it is the function of the dictionary to take note of that fact. Clearly no single label would suffice in this instance; an explanation of some sort is called for. This dictionary, along with many other reference works on language, copes with problems such as this through the device of a usage note, which, though necessarily brief and concise, does explain the nature of the problem that has arisen in connection with this particular word.

Further issues about usage may arise from mistaken grammatical analysis on the one hand, or the failure to distinguish what is current in informal as opposed to the formal standard language on the other. An instance of the latter is the use of *like* as a conjunction introducing a subordinate clause ("He didn't work like his father worked."). Reliable measures of the incidence of this construction indicate that it has a high frequency in informal English but that it occurs only rarely in the formal written language. But again there are some who are reluctant to accept it. Labeling the construction *informal* would probably satisfy the purely factual requirements of the situation, but it would fail to warn the reader of the dictionary that his use of the construction might give offense in some quarters. Again a brief statement is more helpful than a single unmodified categorization.

The usual ground for objecting to *hopefully* in a context such as "Hopefully, the project will be finished by the end of the year," is that *hopefully* as an adverb cannot properly modify the verb phrase *will be finished* and is therefore grammatically unacceptable. Again the facts are simple enough. The word, used in this manner, is widely current among those who employ Standard English. Moreover, the grammatical argument is unsound since in this instance the word modifies the entire clause and not just the verb phrase. This time the usage note serves to clarify a grammatical misconception.

As one compares the usage notes in various dictionaries, he is likely to find a wide divergence of attitude and philosophy, ranging from a fairly broad permissiveness to a nervous reluctance to admit any deviation from the most rigid adherence to approved formal usage of a century ago. It is the considered opinion of the editors of this work that neither of these extremes is well calculated to serve the needs of those who look to the dictionary for help in matters of this kind.

Language changes from century to century and from generation to generation. To the extent that these changes have affected the usage of Standard English it is the responsibility of the dictionary to acknowledge them. There is often a discrepancy, as well, between what is in actual fact current as Standard English and what many opinionated or ill-informed persons believe that usage to be. The responsibility of the dictionary here is to set the record straight, to report and interpret the facts as accurately as possible. At the same time the dictionary must be equally perceptive in distinguishing, for the person who consults it, between standard usage which is acceptable beyond a shadow of doubt and that about which there is some qualification or question. Unfortunately, there is a great lack of awareness on the part of the general public about the services which dictionaries do perform with respect to matters of usage. As dictionaries improve in their faithfulness to fact and the nicety of their discrimination, it is reasonably certain that readers will take fuller advantage of the service which only a carefully and conscientiously edited dictionary is capable of offering.

Punctuation

BY HAROLD B. ALLEN

Punctuation is the art of using special marks to make written or printed material more easily understood, just as pause and stress and intonation or pitch change are needed to make speech understood.

Punctuation uses can be grouped, somewhat loosely, into two kinds. The first kind is structural, since it principally includes those uses that reveal the external structure of what is written, that show how its parts relate meaningfully to one another. In these uses punctuation marks do often correspond to the spoken signals of pause and intonation, so that generally that relationship is a useful clue to choice of punctuation. But it is not safe to rely unthinkingly upon that correspondence. A person who habitually pauses for emphasis after the adversative conjunctions *but* and *yet* can thus be misled into inserting an unnecessary comma, as in *We expected the shipment yesterday but, it did not come* or *Yet, the weather has remained too wet for planting.* A safer reliance is upon correspondence between the punctuation and the grammatical structure.

In ordinary communication the structural uses of punctuation typically conform to accepted conventions, although it is true that, as with the comma, options exist that the skilled writer can utilize in order to indicate more precisely his particular emphasis and shades of meaning. But punctuation is one area where individualism is likely to be self-defeating. Since the purpose of writing is to communicate, punctuation should help and not hinder the attainment of the objective—communication.

The second kind of punctuation use is essentially arbitrary, like that of a period after an abbreviation. Although some variation does occur in printers' styles, once a writer has memorized the arbitrary uses they should cause no problems.

Some marks are employed in different ways in other countries and in other languages. The uses described here are those common in the United States and Canada. They are treated in the following order. Three punctuation marks serve principally to end sentences. These are the period (.), called full stop in Britain; the question mark or interrogation point (?); and the exclamation point (!). The others are the comma (,); the semicolon (;); the quotation marks, both single and double, (' ') and (" "); parentheses, known as brackets in Britain, ( ); the brackets, known as square brackets in Britain, ([ ]); the hyphen (-); the apostrophe ('); and the virgule, also called the slant, slash, diagonal, or solidus (/). In each section structural uses are given first, under 1, and arbitrary uses next, under 2.

THE PERIOD

1. Put a period at the end of every sentence not signaled by a question word or intonation pattern as a question or exclamation.

   The faucet leaked all night.
   Please ship the remaining goods at once.
   The chairman asked us to be seated.

Sometimes the sentence intonation justifies the use of a period with a word or words constituting less than a complete grammatical sentence.

No, sir. Thanks.
Just as you like. All right.

Especially in business correspondence a request in the form of a question may be followed by a period instead of a question mark. Spoken, such a request has a falling intonation pattern.

May we obtain a list of possible suppliers.

2. Use three periods in a row, called an ellipsis, to show omission within a quoted passage.

   Housewares include a wide range of items from silverware to . . . stainless steel fixtures. . . .

The second ellipsis of three periods is followed by a fourth period to denote the end of the sentence.

Use a period after an abbreviation.

J. O. Morton, M.D. etc. Ms. Anne Janis

Omission of the period is common with frequent and familiar abbreviations.

YMCA rpm FBI

In Britain the period is now generally omitted after these:

Dr Mr Mrs

A period after an abbreviation may be followed by any other required punctuation mark except another period.

B. D., our dog, is a three-year-old schnauzer.
But: We named our dog B.D.

Use a period with decimals, with cents, when the dollar sign is present, and with parts or divisions, as in a section of a book.

7.3% $9.46   Section 3.7

THE QUESTION MARK

1. Use a question mark at the end of any sentence signaled as a question

By a question word, i.e., a *wh-* word.

When will the meeting be held?

By inverted word order.

Are nonmembers allowed to attend?

By rising intonation.

You said Harry won the election?

Use a question mark after a nonsentence marked by a *wh-* word or a rising question intonation.

Why not?
What if the truth were known?
At three-thirty then?

2. Use a question mark to indicate doubt about a specific item, such as a spelling or a number.

Cyrus was born in (?)424 B.C.

Use only one question mark if a question ends with a quoted question, and put it inside the quotation marks.

Did he actually ask, "Is your mother married?"

After a quoted question within a sentence, use no other punctuation such as a comma or semicolon.

Because the manager asked her specifically, "Why weren't you at work yesterday?" Miss Fleming felt that she had a just complaint.

If a question ends with a quoted declarative sentence, put the question mark outside the quotation marks.

Who said, "All the world's a stage"?

THE EXCLAMATION POINT

Use an exclamation point after heavily stressed, often high-pitched, short sentences, commands, phrases, or single words and interjections that convey intense feeling.

Yes, and a damnable war it was!
"How exquisite!" Jean exclaimed sarcastically.

Use only the exclamation point when otherwise a comma or semicolon would be required.

Before she is finished there are shouts of "Thunder!" "Lightning!" "Twister!"

THE COMMA

Although most of its uses are conventional, the comma responds more sensitively than other punctuation marks to the needs of the individual writer. Its use or nonuse in certain situations enables a writer to communicate subtle meanings and relationships not readily shown in words alone. But generally its uses are governed by accepted basic principles common in ordinary social and business writing. The structural uses of the comma usually correlate in speech with the level or the rising intonation accompanied by pause, and in writing with definable grammatical structures.

1. A major structural use of the comma is to set off certain language units from the rest of the sentence. If any such unit is at the beginning or the end of a sentence, usually one comma is needed; if it is within the sentence, then usually two commas are needed.

Use commas to set off nonrestrictive elements. A nonrestrictive element is one that adds information without limiting or cutting down the idea of the main clause. It may be identified by your supplying the testing clue, "and by the way," as well as by the pause following level or rising intonation. Suppose you have written "Suburban residents who object to the wheelage tax are expected to petition the metropolitan council." If you can say to yourself, "Suburban residents—and, by the way, they object to the wheelage tax—are expected to petition the metropolitan council," then you have a nonrestrictive clause, and you should set it off with commas, representing the intonation pattern and pause. But if you find that now the sentence does not say what you mean it to say, and if you can say to yourself, "Those particular residents who object to the wheelage tax, etc.", then the included element restricts the meaning of the main clause and no commas are needed, and, spoken aloud, the sentence would not have a pause both after "residents" and after "tax."

Use commas to set off a nonrestrictive clause.

William James, who was a pioneer in psychology, developed the philosophical idea of pragmatism.

But not a restrictive clause:

Only staff members who are teachers will go to the convention.

Use commas to set off a nonrestrictive phrase.

It was also raining here when the senator's plane landed, at the end of his trip.

But not a restrictive phrase:

Other members of the senator's party were making different kinds of news on his first morning back.

Use commas to set off that special nonrestrictive word or phrase usually called an appositive.

I called the press officer, David Kelsey.

Do not use commas with close apposition, which is not marked by the intonation plus pause.

I called press officer David Kelsey.

Use commas to set off a negative appositive.

It is paid for in local currency, not gold.

Use commas to set off parenthetical words and phrases.

Had he been back home, of course, he would have gone by jet or car.

Use commas to set off transitional words and phrases.

Nevertheless, man still has not learned to fly like a bird.

Consider, for example, the invention of one of the world's all-time best-selling games.

But not when a transitional word or phrase is an integral part of the sentence.

The next man to speak was a local politician.

Use commas to set off an adverbial clause at the beginning or in the middle of a sentence.

It also seems very likely that, where obscenity laws continue to be constitutionally applicable, the Supreme Court will give the law relatively broad scope.

However, a short introductory clause may occur without the comma if the meaning is quite clear, as when both clauses have the same subject.

When he saw the sun he shouted for joy.

Use commas to set off an adverbial phrase out of its expected position after the verb.

The doors slid silently shut, and, without so much as a slight jerk, the train sped away.

Use commas to set off words in direct address.

"Can you spare him for a few minutes, Shirley?"

Use commas to prevent ambiguity or misunderstanding.

What is needed are investment funds to start up the service network, and assured means for paying for continuing home service.

(The comma prevents the reader from taking both "network" and "means" as objects of "start up.")

2. Commas are often used to separate coordinate or correlative sentence parts, especially when such separation is indicated in speech by level or rising intonation pattern plus pause.

Except when the clauses are short and the meaning quite clear, use a comma before a conjunction that precedes the second clause of a compound sentence. The comma is most necessary before *for*.

It's very hard work, for the children have led quite pampered lives up till now.
The public schools have been open to all since before the Civil War, and some public colleges have admitted virtually all applicants.

But not in:

Karla withdrew the doll and the child released it with a sigh.

Between short main clauses you may use a comma without a conjunction when it represents a rising or level intonation with pause. Note that this use is not the objectionable "sentence fault" or "comma splice" that occurs with a falling intonation.

Décor is part of the dining experience. People like it, people demand it.
She left early, she had such a bad headache.

Use commas to separate words, phrases, and clauses that constitute a series.

I had a lunch of sauerbraten, red cabbage, lentils, pumpernickel, and dark beer.

Newspapers and some other publications tend to omit the comma before *and* on the assumption that the comma represents the absence of a conjunction and thus is not needed when the conjunction is present. Actually, it represents a perceptible rising or level intonation pattern with pause, which occurs before the final member of the series regardless of the presence or absence of *and*. It is best to use a comma there consistently, so that inadvertently you do not produce such a result as this:

Berle can sing, dance, juggle, act, do card tricks, imitations and acrobatics, ride a unicycle and mug under water.

You may use a comma to separate long predicative constructions even when a conjunction is present.

Even the newest bones were now crusted with moss and lichen, and were scarred with the teeth marks of foxes.

Use a comma to separate two or more adjectives that independently modify a noun, as would be signaled by an intonation pattern with pause.

Please enclose a stamped, self-addressed envelope.
They were not like the lounging, bossy owners.

The owners were both lounging and bossy. Compare a "bright blue dress," with punctuation indicating a dress that is bright blue, not a dress that is both bright and blue.

Use a comma to indicate the omission of an element that, if present, would parallel the same element in a preceding part of the sentence.

Most of the young climbers had come by motor scooters; the older ones, by train.

3. Certain uses of the comma are nonstructural—arbitrary and mechanical rather than related to the syntax.

Use a comma to set off a direct quotation.

"I eat too much," Adler confessed.

Use commas to separate place names.

Bernard came from Astoria, Oregon.
My new address is 1737 Fillmore Avenue, Philadelphia, PA 19146.

No punctuation mark is used between the official post office abbreviation and the ZIP code number.

Use commas in dates.

On September 3, 1939, the judge offered him the choice between prison and the Army.

There is a tendency not to use the comma when the date of the month is not given, and also to omit it after the year even if the date is given.

Steller and his companions abandoned ship on Bering Island in November 1741.

THE SEMICOLON

The semicolon is essentially a mark of coordination. Its use indicates that the grammatical construction before it is equivalent to the construction after it. It correlates with rising, sometimes level, intonation pattern with pause.

1. Use a semicolon between main clauses when no conjunction is present and the clauses are not very short.

I was unprepared for the sight of the main dining room without its bright bustle and white linen; the place looked as forlorn as an abandoned house with windows broken and shutters hanging loose.

Use a semicolon between main clauses when the second clause is introduced by a conjunctive adverb, such as *however, moreover, nevertheless, furthermore, consequently*.

The strike left a residue of ill feeling on both sides; moreover, the terms of the settlement were bound to cause trouble in the future.

2. Use a semicolon between main clauses when commas break up one or both of them, even if a conjunction is present.

They wandered over the dunes, hand in hand, often shouting in sheer exuberance as the salt breezes whipped their hair; and then, suddenly overwhelmed by the emptiness of the island, they sat on the top of a dune and looked around for a long time, silent and somewhat sad.

3. Use a semicolon between clauses or other constructions in a series when the constructions themselves are subdivided by commas.

Schools may make you suspicious, not curious; cynical, not skeptical; passive and bored, not calm.

4. Use a semicolon before a word or phrase, abbreviated or not, such as *namely, i.e., for example, e.g., for instance*, that introduces an illustration, example, or explanation.

Most student clubs can't survive without a strong leader; for example, the Ornithology Club folded when its founder graduated.

THE COLON

1. Structurally the colon indicates suspense in anticipation of something to follow and hence corresponds to a level intonation pattern with a long pause. It is more common in formal writing than in informal writing, where its function is often assumed by the dash.

   Use a colon to introduce a long statement or question, whether quoted or not.

   As the certifying agent from the Maine Board of Education put it: "We can't figure out exactly what you folks are up to, but I reckon you should have a right to try."

   Use a colon to introduce a series of formal items or phrases.

   Karate can be done at three speeds: slow for grace, medium for skill, and fast for the kill.

   Use a colon before a long explanatory passage.

   Seismologists disagree on the significance of creep: some believe that it reduces the strain on faults, reducing the likelihood of a major quake.

2. The colon has several purely arbitrary functions.

   Use a colon at the end of a formal salutation in a letter.

   Dear Dr. Fenton: Gentlemen: Dear Madam:

   Use a colon between the numerals for the hour and the minutes.

   If you get the 7:30 flight, you'll be home in time.

   Use a colon in the title of a book or article before a supplementary phrase.

   Rattlesnakes: Their Habits, Life Histories, and Influence on Mankind

   Use a colon after the name of a speaker in a play or other long dialogue.

   HAMLET: Are you fair?
   OPHELIA: What means your lordship?

QUOTATION MARKS

Quotation marks, both single and double, are essentially arbitrary rather than structural; certain uses, however, such as those denoting a sarcastic or humorous repetition of another's word, do correspond with a special intonation pattern.

1. The primary function of quotation marks is to indicate matter that is taken verbatim from some source, spoken or written.

   Use double quotation marks to set off a simple direct quotation.

   "Wait a minute," the girl said.

   Do not enclose an indirect quotation. Compare:

   Jim asked what she was doing.

   If the quotation is longer than a single paragraph, use quotation marks at the beginning of each paragraph but at the end of the last quoted paragraph only.

   Use quotation marks to designate words or phrases quoted directly within a sentence. Some editors prefer single quotation marks for this purpose.

   The manufacturers prefer to describe the effect as a "tingling sensation."

   Use single quotation marks to indicate quoted material within other quoted material. In England the reverse practice is common, the double marks occurring within the single marks.

   "What does 'decisional' mean?" the boy asked.

   Use quotation marks to set off words or phrases quoted derisively or humorously or with other special attitudinal meaning associated with the source of the word or phrase. This device should not be overused.

   The owners of the Lobster were "the boys"—two very tall men in their early fifties.

2. Several conventional uses of quotation marks do not correspond with written or spoken structural units.

   Quotation marks are used, usually double, to distinguish titles of stories, articles, plays, songs, and the like incorporated in a longer work, such as a book or opera.

   Oddly enough, the editor has seen fit to omit "Macbeth" from the anthology.

   Some editors use double quotation marks or, less frequently, italics (indicated by underlining the typewritten copy) for the title of the entire work.

   The opera "Der Junge Lord," first performed in Berlin, in 1965. . . .

   Use double quotation marks to designate names of trains, ships, planes, and the like. Italics may serve the same purpose.

   Now ships like the "Volendam" are devoted to the cruise business.

   Use single or double quotation marks to set off words considered as items. In books italics often serve this function.

   But "nice" is a double-edged word.

3. Use quotation marks appropriately with other marks.

   For aesthetic reasons American printers customarily put the period and the comma inside the closing quotation marks, illogical though the practice is.

   Harris put on a new recording he had bought of Mahler's "Songs of a Wayfarer."
   "It's raining," he said.

   Other punctuation marks are put either before or after the closing marks, according to whether they are required by the quoted passage or by the entire sentence.

   "Do you like that?" we asked. "Others imitating you?"
   He asked, "Have you read 'The Necklace'?"
   "What a riot!" a girl exclaimed.

   If you put a terminal punctuation mark before closing quotation marks, do not put another one after them. No period is required with the following:

   She couldn't compare with Carol Burnett in "Who's Been Sleeping in My Bed?"
   "I saw a flying saucer! It was—" She interrupted him, her hands still in the water.

THE DASH

Structurally, the dash represents some kind of break or interference in the normal flow of language and hence corresponds usually to a level intonation, sometimes rising, plus pause, with the implication that more is to follow. With a typewriter a dash is made with two unspaced hyphens.

1. Use a dash to set off with emphasis any parenthetical material considered so close or relevant to the thought that commas are inadequate.

   Some are mainly for hauling oil; others—known as LNG carriers—are for liquefied natural gas.

Use a dash to set off appositional elements more emphatically or more clearly than could be done with commas.

Actually, there were only two—a pair of good-sized corn snakes.

Use a dash to mark an abrupt break in speech, as denoting an unfinished or interrupted sentence.

CLARA: But she—
ROBERT: I will never believe it.

Use a dash to mark an abrupt break in the grammatical structure.

I've heard of cases—What am I saying?—I've known them: cases of immorality. . . .

Somewhat less formally, use a dash instead of a colon before a list or explanation.

The Ashanti have kept their gold sculptures largely within the tribe, bringing them out only for the most solemn ceremonies—coronations, weddings, funerals.

Informally, use a dash after the salutation in a personal letter.

Dear Connie— Hi, Dad—

2. Use a dash to indicate omission of letters, euphemistically to avoid spelling out a possibly offensive term, to withhold information, or to indicate lack of information.

The h— you say!
The mysterious Lawrence M— who brought the letter has never been identified.

PARENTHESES

1. Use parentheses to set off an element that supplies comment or additional information and that is usually less relevant to the main thought than would be suggested by commas.

The idiocy is made worse by journalists and politicians (also divines, academics, bank presidents, and union organizers) who, for reasons of their own, require an opaque use of the language.

Use parentheses to enclose an explanatory element that is not structurally a part of the sentence.

On the day in 1853 on which they were introduced, Robert Schumann noted in his diary: "Brahms to see me (a genius)."

2. Use parentheses to enclose letters or numbers in a series or outline. The use of only the closing parenthesis, common in Europe and sometimes found in the United States, is illogical and in a sentence context can lead to misunderstanding.

The Committee's functions will be (1) to facilitate the orderly consideration of proposals and (2) to make an equitable apportionment of available time for discussion.

Use parentheses to enclose a numeral equivalent to a preceding spelled-out number.

As an initial payment I enclose a check for thirty-five dollars ($35.00).

3. Use no punctuation before an opening parenthesis.

Put a comma, semicolon, or colon only after the closing parenthesis. Put a question mark, exclamation point, or quotation marks inside the closing parenthesis only if the parenthetical element requires their use.

She is forced to wade in Scots dialect ("I dinna ken the wor-rd").
(Why should one minor blunder disqualify him forever from holding public office?)

BRACKETS

1. Use brackets to set off an explanatory word or phase inserted by a writer or editor into context written by someone else.

It was a spring evening [1908].
The integrity and authority of the Supreme Court has been flaunted [sic!].

Use brackets to enclose a word or phrase inserted to complete the syntax of quoted material.

". . . special instruments and techniques [are] taken to be the method itself."

2. Use brackets as parentheses within a parenthesis. This use is largely restricted to bibliographical entries and footnotes.

Problems in Lexicography. (RCAFL-P 21; IJAL, 28[2], Part IV, Bloomington.)

THE HYPHEN

The first two uses of the hyphen listed below are structural insofar as they relate to word or phrase structure and do correspond to a level intonation pattern with slight pause. The remaining uses are arbitrary printers' conventions.

1. Use hyphens to separate words in a phrase that functions as a single adjective before a noun.

A 51-foot-long, 65,000-pound prototype is now being tested.

Use a hyphen after the first part of a compound when the second part is to be inferred from its occurrence in a following compound in the same construction.

The hotel never used anything brighter than 40- and 60-watt bulbs.

2. Use a hyphen to separate the parts of spelled-out fractions and the parts of both cardinal and ordinal numerals between twenty-one and ninety-nine.

That makes twenty-eight present already. When the twenty-ninth comes, we'll have a quorum.

You may use a hyphen to separate the parts of a compound noun when it is so treated in this dictionary or other current dictionaries. The punctuation of compounds is too inconsistent to be generalized in a rule; dictionaries themselves vary with respect to particular compounds. Some compounds appear with a space between the parts, as *income tax, appropriations committee, measuring cup, surprise party;* some appear with a hyphen, as *hanky-panky, one-sided, awe-inspiring;* and some are written solid, as *football, typewriter, secondhand.* The modern tendency, stronger in America than in Britain, is to avoid the use of the hyphen.

Use a hyphen to distinguish two similarly spelled words having different pronunciations and different meanings. Usually the word requiring the hyphen is a recent formation.

I commend James Lawton for his bravery in rescuing a four-year-old child from a burning house and re-commend him for rescuing and resuscitating an invalid overcome by gas fumes, and therefore recommend him for the department's citation for valor in the line of duty.

Use a hyphen to represent a missing part of a word, one element of which is treated as an item.

He was such a poor speller that he could never get beyond the *Miss-* in "Mississippi" without making a mistake.

Use a hyphen at the end of a line to indicate that part of a word is at the beginning of the next line. Always divide at a syllable break. Consult your dictionary if you are uncertain about the syllabication.

Use hyphens to indicate the letter-by-letter spelling of a word.

Ron carefully spelled it for her: "p-t-a-r-m-i-g-a-n."

Use hyphens to indicate stammering or hesitation or prolongation of a sound.

"I never s-s-stuttered b-b-before," he said.

Use a hyphen after a prefix when otherwise confusion or misreading might result, as with similar letters or an internal capital letter.

semi-inspired un-American non-English

Use a hyphen to indicate a time stretch between two inclusive dates.

The conference is scheduled for May 14-18.

In printed matter, a slightly longer dash (en-dash) is often used in place of the hyphen between numerals.

His dates were 1841–1903.

THE APOSTROPHE

The apostrophe is structural only in that the uses under 1 are related to grammatical functions, but without correspondence with a spoken feature.

1. Use an apostrophe in the singular possessive or genitive form of a noun or indefinite pronoun. This use reflects an early loss of *e* from the *-es* ending some genitives had. Illogically, the personal pronouns *hers, its, ours, yours,* and *theirs* are not written with an apostrophe.

   the chairman's prerogative
   someone's coat
   the river's edge
   It was John's money, not hers.

   If the addition of the possessive *-s* to a noun already ending in the sound of *s* or *z* makes too much hissing, some speakers prefer not to pronounce it and hence omit it in spelling. The present tendency, however, is both to pronounce the added *s* and to add the letter.

   Harry Sparks's car (*or* Harry Sparks' car)
   Jesus's parables (*or* Jesus' parables)

   Use only an apostrophe at the end of a regular plural noun to denote the possessive or genitive case, since the pronounced *-s* of the possessive has merged with the *-s* of the plural.

   the players' unanimous vote

   However, if the plural is irregular, not ending in *-s*, then use the apostrophe with *-s*.

   Where is the men's room?

   Note these special uses.

   her father-in-law's present
   both fathers-in-law's presents
   someone else's idea
   Gilbert and Sullivan's popularity

   Use the apostrophe with *-s* in forming the plural of letters, numerals, symbols, abbreviations, and words used as items. The current trend, however, is to omit the apostrophe when no loss of clarity results.

   She never dots her i's.
   (*but compare* . . . adding "t"s and "s"s . . .)
   In the 1730's (*or* 1730s)
   The reporter asked how many ICBM's are in the nation's stockpile.

2. Use an apostrophe to show the omission of a letter or letters and the omission of numerals.

   two o'clock (two of the clock)
   it's (it is)
   Class of '34 (1934)

THE VIRGULE

1. You may use a virgule as equivalent to a hyphen in indicating a correspondence between two terms used as a single modifier.

   Price/earnings ratios show equally glaring disparities.

2. Use a virgule to indicate a contrasting or alternative relation between two or more words.

   An Art/Information/Science Issue

3. You may use a virgule to show a choice between an alternative and an additive relationship.

   For sale: pick-up truck and/or house trailer.

4. You may use a virgule between year dates to indicate overlapping.

   Post-Impressionist exhibits of 1910/1911 and 1912/1913.

5. Use a virgule when in quoting poetry or a long prose passage you want to indicate a line-ending in the original.

   Do you remember what comes after "Stone walls do not a prison make / Nor iron bars a cage"?

Canadian English

BY H. REX WILSON

As the language of the greatest colonizing nation in modern times, English has spread to widely separated parts of the world and has evolved on its own as the first language of the dominant peoples of several now-independent nations. The largest of these is the United States, but just as inhabitants of both sides of the Atlantic recognize the difference between American English and that of the Old Country, so Canadians are conscious of respectable varieties of English within their boundaries which differ in various degrees and ways from the language used by the residents of Great Britain or the United States.

Scholarly interest in Canadian English has developed real strength only since World War II, although the bibliography of writings on the English spoken in Canada goes back over a hundred years. This literature is disproportionately loaded with alarm and indignation over the unfortunate spread of "Americanisms." Because Canada evolved by gradual stages from a group of colonies to an independent nation, the long-held British connection has led to false linguistic expectations on the part of some Englishmen and Canadians, and even of a few residents of the United States. To the majority of visitors from the U.S. who come from the states just south of the border from New York and on westward, Canadians speak "just like us." And indeed even the most exacting students of Canadian English would have to admit that superficially this remark is justified.

Origins of Canadian English

In its origins Canadian English is predominantly American. It descends directly from the language of pre-Revolutionary War settlers on the seaboard and immediate hinterland of the present United States. In the uprootings, both forced and voluntary, which followed the Revolution, Canada received an English-speaking population drawn almost entirely from the old American colonies. It is estimated that by 1830 eighty percent of the English-speaking population of Canada could be traced back to the United States. Upon the language of this majority the relative handful of governors, administrators, military officers and clergy of English origin could not be expected to make any substantial impression, although as members of a highly prestigious group they were bound to have some effect.

Some time before the settlement of the American colonies, some groups in England began to lose the *r*-sound between a vowel and a following consonant (as in *art*). This sort of pronunciation and the one which retained the older *r* were rivals both in England and in some of the settlement areas of the U.S. The "*r*-droppers" prevailed in eastern New England and in the coastal South, but the *r*-sound was retained throughout the rest of the colonies, and it was largely from these areas that the basic post-Revolutionary population of Canada was drawn. Meanwhile, the *r*-dropping became the dominant speech fashion in England. These easily-noted features are the main ones which cause superficial observers from England to identify Canadian speakers as "American" and U.S. visitors to find that Canadians talk "just like us."

But subsequent settlement, independent patterns of pronunciation, the distinctive experience of the physical environment, contact with other linguistic groups, and the prestige of the colonial administration have imposed upon Canadian English features which set it off from other types of English.

Pronunciation

The first difference in language that most people notice when they meet someone from another speech area is in pronunciation. Strangers have accents. But this is just what Canadians seem to lack when they are first heard by many residents of the U.S., and even visitors from the South and Southwest will find Canadian speech little different from that of the "Yankees." The origins of Canadian English just mentioned will help account for this.

Sooner or later the visitor to Canada will notice that Canadians say *oot* and *aboot* for *out* and *about*, but if he asks about it Canadians will deny it. And, strictly speaking, they are right. However, what has been heard is something different from the vowel in *down* and *mountain*. This tendency to have a different vowel before sounds like *t* and *s* than before sounds like *d, z, n* is very widespread. In the verb *house* (where the vowel is followed by a *z* sound) the vowel sound will be the same as the one in *down,* and although it may sound different in various places in Canada the range of difference will be about the same as in the U.S. But the vowel sound of the noun *house* (where the vowel is followed by an *s* sound) is different. This pronunciation varies quite a bit from place to place and even in the pronunciations of one speaker, but the general characteristic of most Canadian speech is to have a difference between the vowels in these different situations, and Americans are left with the impression that Canadians say *oot* and *aboot.*

The pronunciation of vowels varying on the basis of the following sound is not unique and can be found in scattered parts of the United States. In these areas and in Canada the vowels of *write* and *ride* show a similar pattern.

The pronunciation of a few individual words may also catch the visitor's ear. The words *either* and *neither* have first syllables which rhyme with *eye* with far greater frequency than is found in the United States. Some longer words, such as *controversy,* may have the main stress on the second rather than the first syllable, reflecting the prestige of British pronunciation supported by private schools set up on the British model and by returning Canadians who have studied at British universities. Although not unknown before World War II, the British pronunciation of *schedule* (shed′yo͞ol) has gained ground in recent years, apparently under the influence of the Canadian Broadcasting Corporation.

The pronunciation of the word *clerk* like that of the family name *Clark,* once a striking feature of Ontario speech, has now died out except in official usage *(County Clerk)* and in the Presbyterian Church *(Clerk of Session).*

Regional accents are not prominent in Canada, probably because of a large amount of movement within the country and relatively few isolated homogeneous settlements of native speakers of English. The island provinces of Newfoundland and Prince Edward Island are notable exceptions, while the imprint of New England continues to set parts of Nova Scotia and New Brunswick off from Ontario and from the Scottish-settled areas of Nova Scotia. Some areas originally settled by non-English-speakers have produced distinctive varieties of English as the result of earlier bilingualism.

Spelling Differences

For the most part, differences in spelling between England and the United States are traceable to Noah Webster, America's first great lexicographer. Canadians understandably did not come under the influence of Webster's spelling reforms in the early 19th century, and British spelling conventions have persisted. Words like *traveller* and *jeweller* continued to have double *l,* and *-our* spellings persisted in words like *honour* and *flavour.* The noun *practice* continued to be set off from the verb *practise.* Today these spellings are no longer insisted upon in most school systems, although consistency in usage by the individual is expected. This "loss of standards," especially in the *-our* spellings, can still raise furious condemnation in the editorial pages of some newspapers in Canada. In their own style these pages and the advertisements in the paper may tend to be conservative, while the news columns tend toward "American" spellings.

The spellings *tyre* and *kerb(stone)* are as strange to Canadians as to Americans and must be explained in Canadian dictionaries as *Brit.* for *tire* and *curb(stone).* The spelling *gaol* for *jail* was once common in newspapers but began disappearing even before World War II.

Vocabulary

The words which a nation uses to conduct its business are great reflectors of its discovery of its environment and its historical development. In 1967 a group of scholars under Professor Walter S. Avis produced *A Dictionary of Canadianisms on Historical Principles* which provides a comprehensive view of the growing and changing vocabulary of Canadian life. This vocabulary has been drawn from many sources, and much of it belongs to experiences shared with settlers of the northern states in the common development of North America. It is not surprising, therefore, that many words reflecting this early experience have passed out of use or are found only in writings referring to specific historical periods.

An American would be puzzled, to say the least, by a reference to an alligator in the forests of Ontario. In the movement of logs by water the lumber industry was greatly helped by *alligators,* amphibious paddle-wheel scows, equipped with a winching arrangement for travel overland.

An equally puzzling term, but in this case a contemporary one, might be found in the statement, "We went to separate schools together." In many parts of Canada religious groups have the legal right to set up their own schools supported by public funds. These are usually referred to as *separate schools,* and a statement such as the one mentioned may be made without suspicion of humorous intent or mental deficiency.

In the Arctic (usually pronounced *Artic*) the term *white-out* has been formed on the model of *black-out* to describe a condition where reflected light from snow or haze or fine blowing snow obscures the horizon and features of the landscape.

Canadian coiners of words have sometimes shown a fine sense of irony as in the now obsolete *Nova Scotia nightingale* for a "singing" marsh frog, and *CPR strawberries* for prunes, which were a prominent item of diet during the building of the Canadian Pacific Railway. On the whole, Canadians have not been distinguished in coining regional names. Most are obviously derivative, like Winipegger or Newfie (Newfoundlander), but Maritimers may be called *Bluenoses* (from Nova Scotia), *Herringchokers* (from New Brunswick) and *Spud Islanders* (a reference to the importance of the potato in the economy of Prince Edward Island).

The *Dictionary of Canadianisms* shows a surprising number of words which have long been accepted in the United States but apparently first gained currency in Canada. In recent times the most striking exports have been in the vocabulary of lacrosse and hockey. *Lacrosse* is of Canadian French origin from a fancied resemblance between the stick used in the game and a Bishop's crozier. While U.S. fans are familiar with the whole standard terminology of hockey, including the penitential seat known as the *penalty box,* they may not know the journalistic coinage *sin bin.*

Because of an administrative history different from that of the United States, Canadian government offers a large number of distinctive terms of British origin. The title *Prime Minister* is, of course, widely used in other countries, but the names of some other positions may be surprising and even a little quaint, such as the term *Reeve* for the council chairman of a village, township, or municipal district council in Ontario and the West. In Ontario the County Council composed of Reeves and Deputy Reeves is presided over by a *Warden.* The familiar title *Sheriff* in Canada signifies a court officer and not a man charged with general law enforcement and peacekeeping duties. A Lieutenant- (pronounced *leftenant*) Governor is not a person who acts for a Governor but the official and ceremonial head of the government of a Province, representing the Crown.

Since colonial times Canadian English has imported virtually its whole technological vocabulary from the United States. Visitors from England have problems in discussing automobile maintenance until they have learned the American words for parts of their motor cars. Canadian railroading, established in large part by American engineers, uses the terminology they brought augmented by later imports. The term *sleeper* for a railway tie held its own until the 1920's at least, but now is rarely heard and one Canadian dictionary labels it *British.*

Canada made its first contribution to the jet age in 1854 by the invention and naming of kerosene in Nova Scotia. Oddly, in Ontario a term of apparent Pennsylvania origin, *coal oil,* is preferred. So widely accepted has *kerosene* become in the U.S. that it has even raised objections in New Zealand as an "Americanism" displacing the British *paraffin (oil).*

Canadians have borrowed words from languages with which they have had contact. *Woodchuck,* although it looks and sounds English, is derived from an Algonquian word which was first imitated by English speakers as *wejack.* The Canada jay has a name that goes one step further. A Cree name was first imitated as *Whisky John* and then familiarized to *whisky-jack.*

Naturally the long French sojourn in Canada before English settlement has left its marks and, as far as place names go, this extends beyond the border of Canada. The word *portage* is classically representative of the early years, and it has never been displaced by *carry* or *carrying place.* In politics the old terms *Bleu* (or *Parti Bleu,* Conservative) and *Rouge* (or *Parti Rouge,* Liberal) may occasionally appear in English newspaper accounts of politics in Quebec. Sometimes these are Anglicized to *Blue* and *Red.*

Influenced by the special economics of printing in a bilingual country, no passenger train of the Canadian National Railways has "left" its station for many years, although most have "departed" fairly close to schedule. The abbreviations *Arr.* and *Dep.* in the timetable require no translation. Similarly, the two telegraph companies in the country have settled on *telecommunications* in their names.

In its modest space program Canada has named its first communications satellite *Alouette* (French, lark) and a more recent one *anik* (Eskimo, brother).

Abbreviations and Symbols Used in This Dictionary

abbr.	abbreviation
abl.	ablative
A.D.	year of our Lord
adj.	adjective
adv.	adverb
Aeron.	Aeronautics
AF	Anglo-French
Agric.	Agriculture
Alg.	Algebra
Algon.	Algonquian
alt.	alternative
alter.	alteration
Amer.	American
Am. Ind.	American Indian
Am. Sp.	American Spanish
Anat.	Anatomy
Anthropol.	Anthropology
appar.	apparently
Ar.	Arabic
Archeol.	Archeology
Archit.	Architecture
Astron.	Astronomy
aug.	augmentative
Austral.	Australian
b.	born
Bacteriol.	Bacteriology
B.C.	before Christ
Belg.	Belgian
Biochem.	Biochemistry
Biol.	Biology
Bot.	Botany
Brit.	British
c.	century
ca.	circa
Can.	Canadian
cap.	capital, capitalized
CEN.	central
cf.	compare
Chem.	Chemistry
Chin.	Chinese
compar.	comparative
conj.	conjunction
d.	died
Dan.	Danish
def(s).	definition(s)
Dent.	Dentistry
dial.	dialect, dialectal
dim.	diminutive
Du.	Dutch
E	east
E	English
Eccl.	Ecclesiastical
Ecol.	Ecology
Econ.	Economics
Egypt.	Egyptian
Electr.	Electricity
Eng.	English
Engin.	Engineering
Entomol.	Entomology
esp.	especially
F	French
fem.	feminine
Fr.	French
freq.	frequentative
G	German
Gael.	Gaelic
Geog.	Geography
Geol.	Geology
Geom.	Geometry
Ger.	German
Gk.	Greek, Greek (Homer–A.D. 200)
Gmc.	Germanic
Govt.	Government
Gram.	Grammar
Heb.	Hebrew
Her.	Heraldry
HG	High German
Hind.	Hindustani
Hung.	Hungarian
Icel.	Icelandic
Illit.	Illiterate
imit.	imitative
incl.	including
infl.	influence, influenced
intens.	intensive
interj.	interjection
Ir.	Irish
Ital.	Italian
Jap.	Japanese
L, Lat.	Latin (Classical, 80 B.C.–A.D. 200)
LG	Low German
LGk.	Late Greek (200–600)
Ling.	Linguistics
lit.	literally
LL	Late Latin (200–600)
M	Middle
masc.	masculine
Math.	Mathematics
MD, MDu.	Middle Dutch
ME	Middle English (1150–1500)
Mech.	Mechanics
Med.	Medicine, Medieval
Med. Gk.	Medieval Greek (600–1500)
Med. L	Medieval Latin (600–1500)
Metall.	Metallurgy
Meteorol.	Meteorology
MF	Middle French (1400–1600)
MHG	Middle High German (1100–1450)
Mil.	Military
Mineral.	Mineralogy
MLG	Middle Low German (1100–1450)
Myth.	Mythology
n.	noun
N	north
N. Am. Ind.	North American Indian
Naut.	Nautical
Nav.	Naval
NE	northeast
neut.	neuter
NF	Norman French
NL	New Latin (after 1500)
Nonstand.	Nonstandard
Norw.	Norwegian
NW	northwest
O	Old
Obs.	Obsolete
ODan.	Old Danish (before 1400)
OE	Old English (before 1150)
OF	Old French (before 1400)
OHG	Old High German (before 1100)
ON	Old Norse (before 1500)
orig.	original, originally
Ornithol.	Ornithology
OSp.	Old Spanish (before 1500)
Paleontol.	Paleontology
Pers.	Persian
Pg.	Portuguese
Philos.	Philosophy
Phonet.	Phonetics
Phot.	Photography
Physiol.	Physiology
pl.	plural
Pol.	Polish
p.p., pp.	past participle
prec.	preceding
prep.	preposition
pres.	present
prob.	probably
pron.	pronoun
Prov.	Provençal
pr.p.	present participle
pseud.	pseudonym
Psychoanal.	Psychoanalysis
Psychol.	Psychology
pt.	preterit
p.t.	past tense
redupl.	reduplication
ref.	reference
Rom.	Roman
Russ.	Russian
S	south
S. Am. Ind.	South American Indian
Scand.	Scandinavian
Scot.	Scottish
Scot. Gael.	Scottish Gaelic
SE	southeast
sing.	singular
Skt.	Sanskrit
Sociol.	Sociology
sp.	spelling
Sp.	Spanish
sq. mi.	square miles
Stat.	Statistics
superl.	superlative
Surg.	Surgery
Sw.	Swedish
SW	southwest
syn.	synonyms
Technol.	Technology
Telecom.	Telecommunication
Theol.	Theology
trans.	translation
Trig.	Trigonometry
ult.	ultimate, ultimately
U.S.	United States
usu.	usually
v.	verb
var.	variant
v.i.	verb intransitive
v.t.	verb transitive
W	west
WGmc.	West Germanic
Zool.	Zoology

• Introduces a usage note or marks a cross-reference to a note, illustration, or map

< means "from"

+ means "plus"

? (preceding etymology) means "possibly"; (preceding date) means "approximately"

[?] means "origin uncertain or unknown"

Biblical abbreviations are listed alphabetically in the main section. Abbreviations used in the Gazetteer are listed at the beginning of that section.

A Dictionary of the English Language

A

A, a (ā) *n. pl.* **A's, a's, As, as** (āz) **1** The first letter of the English alphabet. **2** Any spoken sound representing the letter *A* or *a*. **3** First in a series, class, or order. **4** The highest grade in quality. **5** *Music* The sixth tone in the diatonic scale of C major. **6** Something shaped like an A. —*adj.* Shaped like an A.

a[1] (ə, *stressed* ā) *indefinite article* or *adj.* In each; to each; for each: twice *a* year. [< OE *an, on* in, on, at]

a[2] (ə, *stressed* ā) *indefinite article* or *adj.* **1** One; one type or kind of: I saw *a* bird. **2** Each; any: *A* fish swims. **3** Some: to have *a* fear of height. **4** The same: birds of *a* feather. [Reduced form of AN] • **a, an** *A* is used before a word beginning with a consonant or a consonant sound, now including *h* when pronounced: *a* history. *a* hotel (*Brit.* often *an* hotel). Before a vowel sound or silent *h, an* is used: *an* egg, *an* opera, *an* honor. Before an unaccented syllable beginning with *h* some writers prefer the older usage: *an* historical novel, *an* hysterical cry.

a-[1] *prefix* On; in; at: *aboard, atop.* [< OE *an, on* in, on, at]

a-[2] *prefix* Used as an intensive or without added meaning: *arise, abide.* [< OE *ā-*]

a-[3] *prefix* Of; from: *athirst, akin, anew.* [< OE *of* off, of]

a-[4] *prefix* **1** Without; not: *achromatic.* **2** Apart from; unconcerned with: *amoral.* [Reduced form of AN- used before consonant sounds]

a. about; alto; ampere; are (measure); area; before (L *ante*); in the year (L *anno*).

AA, A.A. Alcoholics Anonymous.

AAA, A.A.A. American Automobile Association.

aard·vark (ärd′värk′) *n.* A burrowing, ant-eating African mammal about the size of the pig. Also **ant bear.** [< Afrikaans, lit., earth pig]

Aardvark

aard·wolf (ärd′wo͝olf′) *n.* A hyenalike, nocturnal mammal of southern Africa. [< Afrikaans, lit., earth wolf]

Aar·on (âr′ən, ar′ən) The first Jewish high priest; brother of Moses.

ab- *prefix* Off; from; away: *absolve, abduct.* [< L *ab* from]

A.B. Bachelor of Arts (L *Artium Baccalaureus*).

A.b., a.b. able-bodied (seaman).

a·ba (ä′bə) *n.* **1** Fabric woven of camel's or goat's hair. **2** A sleeveless garment worn in Arabia, Syria, etc. [< Ar. *'abā'*]

ABA American Bar Association.

ab·a·ca (ab′ə·kä, ä′bə·kä′) *n.* **1** A bananalike Philippine plant. **2** The inner fiber of this plant, used for cordage. Also **ab′a·ka.** [< Tagalog]

a·back (ə·bak′) *adv.* So as to be pressed or blown backward against the mast: said of sails. —**taken aback** Startled, surprised, or disconcerted. [< OE *on bæc* to or on the back]

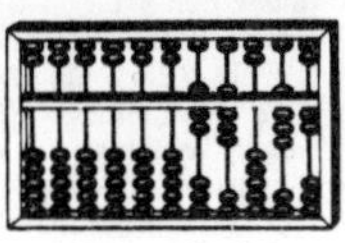
Abacus *def. 1*

ab·a·cus (ab′ə·kəs) *n. pl.* **cus·es** or **·ci** (-sī) **1** A calculating device with counters sliding on wires or in grooves. **2** *Archit.* A slab forming the top of a capital. [L< Gk. *abax* counting table]

a·baft (ə·baft′, ə·bäft′) *adv.* At or toward the stern. —*prep.* Behind; to the rear of. [< OE *on* on, at + *be* about + *æftan,* adv., behind, back]

ab·a·lo·ne (ab′ə·lō′nē) *n.* An edible shellfish having an ear-shaped shell lined with mother-of-pearl. [< Sp.]

a·ban·don (ə·ban′dən) *v.t.* **1** To desert; forsake. **2** To surrender or give up. **3** To yield (oneself) without restraint, as to a feeling or pastime. —*n.* Utter surrender to one's feelings or natural impulses. [< OF *a bandon* under one's own control]. —**a·ban′don·er, a·ban′don·ment** *n.*

a·ban·doned (ə·ban′dənd) *adj.* **1** Deserted; forsaken. **2** Unrestrained. **3** Immoral; dissolute.

a·base (ə·bās′) *v.t.* **a·based, a·bas·ing** To humiliate, humble, or degrade. [< L *ad-* to + LL *bassus* low] —**a·bas·ed·ly** (ə·bā′sid·lē) *adv.* —**a·bas′ed·ness, a·base′ment, a·bas′er** *n.*

a·bash (ə·bash′) *v.t.* To make ashamed, confused, or ill at ease. [< L *ex-* out of + *batare* to gape] —**a·bash·ed·ly** (ə·bash′id·lē) *adv.* —**a·bash′ment** *n.* —**Syn.** disconcert, discompose, bewilder, embarrass.

a·bate (ə·bāt′) *v.* **a·bat·ed, a·bat·ing** *v.t.* **1** To make less; reduce in quantity, degree, force, etc. **2** To deduct. **3** *Law* **a** To put an end to. **b** To annul. —*v.i.* **4** To become less, as in strength, degree, force, etc.: After six hours, the storm *abated.* [< L *ad-* to + *batuere* to beat] —**a·bat′a·ble** *adj.* —**a·bate′ment, a·bat′er** *n.*

ab·at·toir (ab′ə·twär′) *n.* A slaughterhouse. [F]

ab·ba·cy (ab′ə·sē) *n. pl.* **·cies** The office, term, or jurisdiction of an abbot.

ab·bé (ab′ā, *Fr.* à·bā′) *n.* In France, a title of respect given to any male entitled to wear ecclesiastical dress. [< LL *abbas* abbot]

ab·bess (ab′is) *n.* A female superior of a community of nuns connected with an abbey.

ab·bey (ab′ē) *n. pl.* **ab·beys** **1** A monastery under the jurisdiction of an abbot or a convent under an abbess. **2** The church or buildings of an abbey.

ab·bot (ab′ət) *n.* The superior of a community of monks. [< LGk. *abbas* < Aramaic *abba* father] —**ab′bot·cy, ab′·bot·ship** *n.*

abbr., abbrev. abbreviation.

ab·bre·vi·ate (ə·brē′vē·āt) *v.t.* **·at·ed, ·at·ing** **1** To condense or make briefer. **2** To shorten, as a word or expression, esp. by omission or contraction. [< L *ad-* to + *breviare* shorten] —**ab·bre′vi·a′tor** *n.*

ab·bre·vi·a·tion (ə·brē′vē·ā′shən) *n.* **1** A shortened form or contraction, as of a word or phrase. **2** A making shorter, or the state of being shortened. **3** *Music* A notation indicating repeated notes, chords, etc., by a single symbol.

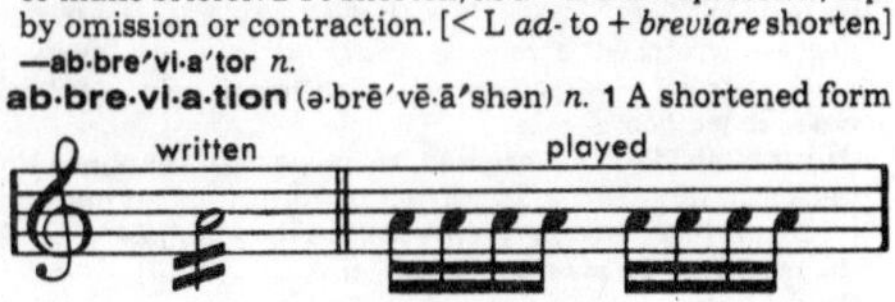

Abbreviation *def. 3*

ABC (ā′bē′sē′) *pl.* **ABC's** *Usu. pl.* **1** The alphabet. **2** The rudiments, elements, or basic facts (of a subject).

ABC American Broadcasting Company.

ab·di·cate (ab′də·kāt) *v.* **·cat·ed, ·cat·ing** *v.t.* **1** To give up formally; renounce, as a throne, power, or rights. —*v.i.* **2** To surrender or relinquish a throne, a right, responsibility, etc. [< L *ab-* away + *dicare* proclaim] **—ab·di·ca·ble** (ab′di·kə·bəl), **ab′di·ca′tive** *adj.* **—ab′di·ca′tion, ab′di·ca′tor** *n.*

ab·do·men (ab′də·mən, ab·dō′mən) *n.* **1** In mammals, the visceral cavity between the diaphragm and the pelvic floor; the belly. **2** In vertebrates other than mammals, the region or cavity that contains the viscera. **3** In insects, crabs, etc., the hindmost part of the body. [< L] **—ab·dom·i·nal** (ab·dom′ə·nəl) *adj.* **—ab·dom′i·nal·ly** *adv.*

Abdomen
def. 3

ab·duct (ab·dukt′) *v.t.* **1** To carry away wrongfully, as by force or fraud; kidnap. **2** To draw (a part of the body) away from the median axis of the body or from a neighboring part. [< L *ab-* away + *ducere* lead] **—ab·duc′tion, ab·duc′tor** *n.*

a·beam (ə·bēm′) *adv.* At right angles to the line of a vessel's keel.

a·bed (ə·bed′) *adv.* In bed; on a bed; to bed.

A·bel (ā′bəl) Second son of Adam.

ab·er·rant (ab·er′ənt, ab′ər·ənt) *adj.* **1** Straying from the right way or usual course. **2** Varying from type; abnormal; deviant. [< L *ab-* from + *errare* wander] **—ab·er′rance, ab·er′ran·cy** *n.*

ab·er·ra·tion (ab′ə·rā′shən) *n.* **1** Deviation from a right, customary, prescribed, or natural course or condition. **2** Partial mental derangement.

a·bet (ə·bet′) *v.t.* **a·bet·ted, a·bet·ting** To encourage and support, esp. to support wrongdoing. [< OF *abeter* incite, arouse] **—a·bet′ment, a·bet′tal, a·bet′ter, a·bet′tor** *n.*

a·bey·ance (ə·bā′əns) *n.* Suspension or temporary inaction. Also **a·bey′an·cy.** [< OF *abaer* to gape at, yearn for] **—a·bey′ant** *adj.*

ab·hor (ab·hôr′) *v.t.* **ab·horred, ab·hor·ring** To regard with repugnance, horror, or disgust. [< L *ab-* from + *horrere* shrink] **—ab·hor′rer** *n.* **—Syn.** loathe, detest, despise, abominate.

ab·hor·rence (ab·hôr′əns, -hor′-) *n.* **1** The act of abhorring. **2** That which is abhorred.

ab·hor·rent (ab·hôr′ənt, -hor′-) *adj.* **1** Detestable or horrible. **2** Feeling abhorrence: with *of.* **3** Opposed; not in accord: with *to.* **—ab·hor′rent·ly** *adv.*

a·bide (ə·bīd′) *v.* **a·bode** or **a·bid·ed, a·bid·ing** *v.i.* **1** To continue, last, or endure. **2** To continue in a place; stay; dwell; reside. —*v.t.* **3** To look for; wait for. **4** To endure; put up with. **—abide by 1** To behave in accordance with, as a promise or rule. **2** To accept the consequences of; submit to. [< OE *ābīdan*] **—a·bid′ance, a·bid′er** *n.* **—a·bid′ing** *adj.* **—a·bid′ing·ly** *adv.*

a·bil·i·ty (ə·bil′ə·tē) *n. pl.* **·ties 1** The condition or power of being able. **2** Talent or skill. [< L *habilitas*]

ab·i·o·gen·e·sis (ab′ē·ō·jen′ə·sis) *n.* The springing up of living from nonliving matter. [< A-⁴ + BIO- + GENESIS]

ab·ir·ri·tant (ab·ir′ə·tənt) *n.* A soothing agent; a medicine that eases irritation. —*adj.* Relieving irritation; soothing.

ab·ir·ri·tate (ab·ir′ə·tāt) *v.t.* **·tat·ed, ·tat·ing** To diminish sensibility in; relieve irritation in. **—ab·ir′ri·ta′tion** *n.*

ab·ject (ab′jekt, ab·jekt′) *adj.* **1** Of the lowest kind or degree; wretched. **2** Servile; cringing. [< L *ab-* away + *jacere* throw] **—ab·jec′tive** *adj.* **—ab′ject·ly** *adv.* **—ab′ject·ness, ab·jec′tion** *n.*

ab·jure (ab·jŏŏr′) *v.t.* **ab·jured, ab·jur·ing 1** To renounce under oath; forswear. **2** To retract or recant, as an opinion. [< L *abjurare* deny on oath] **—ab·jur·a·to·ry** (ab·jŏŏr′a·tôr′ē, -tō′rē) *adj.* **—ab′ju·ra′tion, ab·jur′er** *n.*

abl. ablative.

ab·la·tion (ab·lā′shən) *n.* The act or process of wearing away or eroding. [< L *ablatus* carried away]

ab·la·tive (ab′lə·tiv) *Gram. adj.* In Latin, Sanskrit, and certain other languages, designating a grammatical case expressing separation, deprivation, direction away from, or instrumentality. —*n.* **1** The ablative case. **2** A word in this case. [< L *ablatus* carried away]

a·blaze (ə·blāz′) *adj.* **1** On fire. **2** Brilliantly glowing with light. **3** Zealous; ardent.

a·ble (ā′bəl) *adj.* **a·bler** (ā′blər), **a·blest** (ā′blist) **1** Having adequate power; competent. **2** Having superior abilities; talented. [< L *habilis* manageable, fit < *habere* have, hold] **—a′bly** *adv.*

-able *suffix* **1** Given to; tending to: *changeable.* **2** Fit to; able to; capable of; worthy of: *eatable, solvable.* Also **-ble, -ible.** [< L *-abilis*]

a·ble-bod·ied (ā′bəl·bod′ēd) *adj.* Having a sound, strong body; robust.

able-bodied seaman An experienced and skilled seaman. Also **able seaman.**

a·bloom (ə·blōōm′) *adj. & adv.* Blooming.

ab·lu·tion (ab·lōō′shən) *n.* **1** A washing or cleansing of the body; a bath. **2** *Eccl.* **a** A washing of the priest's hands or of the chalice during the Mass. **b** The liquid used to do this. [< L *abluere* wash away] **—ab·lu′tion·ar′y** *adj.*

-ably *suffix* Like; in the manner of: *peaceably.*

ABM antiballistic missile.

ab·ne·gate (ab′nə·gāt) *v.t.* **·gat·ed, ·gat·ing.** To renounce or give up, as a right or privilege. [< L *ab-* away + *negare* deny] **—ab′ne·ga′tion, ab′ne·ga′tor** *n.*

ab·nor·mal (ab·nôr′məl) *adj.* Not according to what is normal, usual, or average; unnatural; irregular. [< Gk. *anōmalos* irregular] **—ab·nor′mal·ly** *adv.*

ab·nor·mal·i·ty (ab′nôr·mal′ə·tē) *n. pl.* **·ties 1** The state of being abnormal. **2** That which is abnormal.

a·board (ə·bôrd′, ə·bōrd′) *adv.* **1** On board; into, in, or on a ship, airplane, etc. **2** Alongside. **—all aboard!** Get on board or in!: a warning to passengers. —*prep.* On board of; upon or within.

a·bode (ə·bōd′) *p.t. & p.p.* of ABIDE. —*n.* **1** A place of abiding; dwelling; home. **2** A sojourn; stay. [< ME *abiden* to abide]

a·bol·ish (ə·bol′ish) *v.t.* To do away with; put an end to. [< L *abolere* destroy] **—a·bol′ish·a·ble** *adj.* **—a·bol′ish·er, a·bol′ish·ment** *n.* **—Syn.** destroy, eradicate, annul, end.

ab·o·li·tion (ab′ə·lish′ən) *n.* **1** The act of abolishing or the state of being abolished. **2** *Sometimes cap.* The abolishing of slavery in the United States. **—ab′o·li′tion·al, ab′o·li′tion·ar′y** *adj.* **—ab′o·li′tion·ism, ab′o·li′tion·ist** *n.*

ab·o·ma·sum (ab′ə·mā′səm) *n. pl.* **·sa** (-sə) The fourth or true digestive stomach of a ruminant. [< L *ab-* away from + *omasum* bullock's tripe]

A-bomb (ā′bom′) *n.* ATOMIC BOMB.

a·bom·i·na·ble (ə·bom′ə·nə·bəl) *adj.* **1** Very hateful; loathsome. **2** Very bad or unpleasant. **—a·bom′i·na·bly** *adv.*

a·bom·i·nate (ə·bom′ə·nāt) *v.t.* **·nat·ed, ·nat·ing 1** To regard with horror or loathing; abhor. **2** To dislike strongly. [< L *abominari* abhor as an ill omen] **—a·bom′i·na′tion, a·bom′i·na′tor** *n.*

ab·o·rig·i·nal (ab′ə·rij′ə·nəl) *adj.* **1** Of or pertaining to aborigines. **2** Existing from the beginning; indigenous; primitive. —*n. pl.* **·nes** (-nēz) An aborigine. **—ab′o·rig′i·nal·ly** *adv.*

ab·o·rig·i·ne (ab′ə·rij′ə·nē) *n.* **1** One of the original native inhabitants of a country. **2** *pl.* Flora and fauna indigenous to a geographical area. [< L *ab origine* from the beginning]

a·bort (ə·bôrt′) *v.i.* **1** To bring forth young prematurely; miscarry. **2** To remain rudimentary. **3** To conclude prematurely or fail, as a mission. —*v.t.* **4** To cause to have a miscarriage. **5** To bring to a premature or unsuccessful conclusion. [< L *aboriri* miscarry < *ab-* off, away + *oriri* arise, be born]

a·bor·tion (ə·bôr′shən) *n.* **1** The expulsion of a fetus prematurely; miscarriage. **2** The defective result of a premature birth; a monstrosity. **3** A person or thing that fails to progress or develop normally or as expected. **—a·bor′tion·al** *adj.* **—a·bor′tion·ist** *n.*

a·bor·tive (ə·bôr′tiv) *adj.* **1** Brought forth or born prematurely. **2** Imperfectly developed. **3** Coming to naught; failing, as an effort. **4** Causing abortion. **—a·bor′tive·ly** *adv.* **—a·bor′tive·ness** *n.*

a·bound (ə·bound′) *v.i.* **1** To be in abundance; be plentiful. **2** To have plenty of; be rich: with *in.* **3** To be full of; teem: with *with.* [< L *abundare* overflow]

a·bout (ə·bout′) *adv.* **1** In every direction; on every side: Look *about.* **2** In any direction; here and there: to wander *about.* **3** Almost: *about* finished. **4** Nearly; approximately: in *about* an hour. **5** To a reversed position; around: It turned *about.* **6** In the area; near. **7** In rotation: spinning *about* on its axis. —*prep.* **1** On every side of; encircling. **2** Here and there in or upon. **3** Somewhere near or within:

Stay *about* the house. **4** Attached to as an attribute: an aura of sanctity *about* him. **5** Approximating to, as in measure: *about* 500 miles. **6** Engaged in; concerned with: Go on *about* your business. **7** In reference to; concerning: a book *about* Napoleon. **8** With: I have no money *about* me. *—adj. Used only predicatively* **1** Astir; moving: to be up and *about.* **2** Nearby. [< OE *onbūtan, abūtan*]

a·bout-face (ə·bout′fās′) *n.* **1** A pivoting about to face in exactly the opposite direction. **2** A sudden reversal, as of opinion or point of view. *—v.i.* (ə·bout′fās′) **-faced, -fac·ing** To perform an about-face.

a·bove (ə·buv′) *adv.* **1** To or in a higher place; overhead; up. **2** Superior in rank, position, etc. **3** In a previous place of something written. **4** In heaven. *—adj.* Given, said, placed, etc., in what is above: the *above* names. *—n.* Something above. *—prep.* **1** Vertically over; higher than. **2** Beyond or farther north than: the town *above* ours. **3** In excess of; more than. **4** In preference to; over: We chose her *above* all others. **5** Surpassing or superior to in any way. [< OE *abufen*]

a·bove·board (ə·buv′bôrd′ -bōrd′) *adj. & adv.* Without concealment, fraud, or trickery; honest.

abr. abridged; abridgment.

ab·ra·ca·dab·ra (ab′rə·kə·dab′rə) *n.* **1** A word used as a preventive or curative charm. **2** A spell. **3** Any jargon or nonsensical words. [< LL]

a·brade (ə·brād′) *v.t.* **a·brad·ed, a·brad·ing** To rub or wear off; scrape away. [< L *ab-* away + *radere* scrape] **—a·bra′·dant** *adj., n.* **—a·brad′er** *n.*

A·bra·ham (ā′brə·ham) The progenitor of the Hebrews.

a·bran·chi·ate (ə·brang′kē·it, -āt′) *adj. Zool.* Without gills. Also **a·bran·chi·al** (ə·brang′kē·əl). [< A-⁴ without + Gk. *branchia* gills]

a·bra·sion (ə·brā′zhən) *n.* **1** The act or result of abrading. **2** An abraded place, as on the skin.

a·bra·sive (ə·brā′siv, -ziv) *adj.* **1** Abrading or tending to abrade. **2** Harshly irritating: an *abrasive* person. *—n.* An abrasive substance.

a·breast (ə·brest′) *adv.* Side by side. **—abreast of** (or **with**) Side by side with.

a·bridge (ə·brij′) *v.t.* **a·bridged, a·bridg·ing** **1** To give the substance of in fewer words; condense. **2** To shorten, as in time. **3** To curtail or lessen, as rights. [< L *abbreviare.* See ABBREVIATE.] **—a·bridg′a·ble, a·bridge′a·ble** *adj.*

a·bridg·ment (ə·brij′mənt) *n.* **1** The act of abridging or the state of being abridged. **2** A condensation, as of a book. Also **a·bridge′ment.**

a·broad (ə·brôd) *adv.* **1** Out of one's home; outdoors. **2** Out of one's own country; in or to foreign lands. **3** Broadly; widely. **4** At large; in circulation. **—from abroad** From a foreign country or countries.

ab·ro·gate (ab′rə·gāt) *v.i.* **·gat·ed, ·gat·ing** To annul by authority, as a law. [< L *ab-* away + *rogare* ask, propose] — **ab·ro·ga·ble** (ab′rə·gə·bəl), **ab′ro·ga′tive** *adj.* **—ab′ro·ga′tion, ab′ro·ga′tor** *n.* **—Syn.** abolish, repeal, cancel, nullify.

a·brupt (ə·brupt′) *adj.* **1** Beginning, ending, or happening suddenly. **2** Brusque or curt, as in speech. **3** Changing subject suddenly; unconnected, as style. **4** Steep, as a cliff. [< L *ab-* off + *rumpere* break] **—a·brupt′ly** *adv.* **—a·brupt′·ness** *n.* **—Syn. 1** sudden, unexpected. **4** sheer, precipitous.

abs. absent; absolute; absolutely; abstract.

Ab·sa·lom (ab′sə·ləm) The favorite and rebellious son of David.

ab·scess (ab′ses) *n.* A collection of pus within a body tissue, usu. painfully inflamed. *—v.i.* To form an abscess. [< L *abscedere* go away]

ab·scis·sa (ab·sis′ə) *n. pl.* **ab·scis·sas** or **ab·scis·sae** (-ē) The distance of any point from the Y-axis in a two-dimensional coordinate system, measured on a line parallel to the X-axis. [< L *(linea) abscissa* (line) cut off]

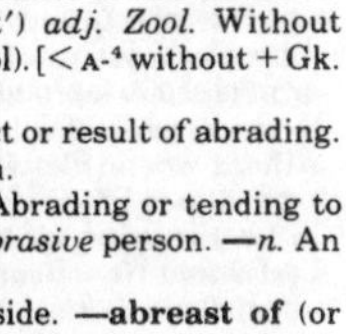

Abscissa
AB: axis of abscissas (X-axis). AC: axis of ordinates (Y-axis). df or Ae: abscissa of point f.

ab·scond (ab·skond′) *v.i.* To depart suddenly and secretly, esp. to hide oneself. [< L *ab-* away + *condere* store] **—ab·scond′er** *n.*

ab·sence (ab′səns) *n.* **1** The state, fact, or time of being absent. **2** Lack; want.

ab·sent (ab′sənt) *adj.* **1** Not present. **2** Nonexistent; missing. **3** Inattentive; absentminded. *—v.t.* (ab·sent′) To take or keep (oneself) away; not be present. [< L *ab-* away + *esse* be] **—ab·sent′er, ab′sent·ness** *n.* **—ab′sent·ly** *adv.*

ab·sen·tee (ab′sən·tē′) *n.* One who is absent, as from a job. *—adj.* **1** Designating or for a person qualified to vote by mail. **2** Nonresident. **—ab′sen·tee′ism** *n.*

ab·sent-mind·ed (ab′sənt·mīn′did) *adj.* **1** Inattentive to one's immediate environment or duties because the mind is occupied elsewhere. **2** Constantly forgetful. **—ab′·sent-mind′ed·ly** *adv.* **—ab′sent-mind′ed·ness** *n.*

ab·sinthe (ab′sinth) *n.* **1** A green, bitter liqueur having the flavor of licorice and wormwood. **2** Wormwood. Also **ab′sinth.** [< L *absinthium* wormwood]

ab·so·lute (ab′sə·lo͞ot) *adj.* **1** Free from restriction; unlimited; unconditional. **2** Complete or perfect. **3** Unadulterated; pure. **4** Positive; unquestionable. **5** Not dependent on or relative to anything else; independent. **6** Relating to or describing a form of government in which the power of the ruler is complete and unchecked, as by any constitutional restraint: *absolute* monarchy. **7** *Gram.* **a** Free from the usual relations of syntax, as *It being late* in *It being late, we started home.* **b** Of a transitive verb, having no object expressed but implied, as *She is one who really gives.* **c** Of an adjective or pronoun, standing alone with the noun understood, as *Ours is first.* **8** *Physics* **a** Not dependent on any arbitrary standard. **b** Of, pertaining to, or measured on the absolute temperature scale. *—n.* That which is absolute or perfect. **—the Absolute** The ultimate basis of all being. [< L *absolvere.* See ABSOLVE.] — **ab′so·lute·ly** *adv.* **—ab′so·lute′ness** *n.*

absolute pitch **1** The pitch of a musical tone determined by its frequency. **2** The ability to remember pitch.

absolute temperature Temperature reckoned from absolute zero.

absolute zero That temperature at which a body would be wholly deprived of heat, equivalent to about −273°C. or −459°F.

ab·so·lu·tion (ab′sə·lo͞o′shən) *n.* **1** An absolving, or a being absolved; forgiveness. **2** *Eccl.* In certain churches: **a** The sacramental remission of sin, or the penalties attached to it. **b** The formula pronounced by a priest declaring the sins to be remitted.

ab·so·lu·tism (ab′sə·lo͞o·tiz′əm) *n.* In government, the doctrine or practice of unlimited authority and control; despotism. **—ab′so·lu·tist** *n.* **—ab′so·lu·tis′tic** *adj.*

ab·solve (ab·solv′, -zolv′) *v.t.* **ab·solved, ab·solv·ing** **1** To pronounce free from the penalties or consequences of an action. **2** To release from an obligation, liability, or promise. **3** *Eccl.* To grant a remission of sin. [< L *ab-* from + *solvere* loosen] **—ab·solv′a·ble** *adj.* **—ab·sol′vent** *adj., n.* — **ab·solv′er** *n.*

ab·sorb (ab·sôrb′, -zôrb′) *v.t.* **1** To drink in or suck up, as through or into pores. **2** To engross completely; occupy wholly. **3** *Physics* To take up or in with no reflection or transmission. **4** To take in and incorporate; assimilate. **5** To assume or defray (costs). **6** To receive the force or action of; intercept. [< L *ab-* from + *sorbere* suck in] **—ab·sorb′a·bil′i·ty, ab·sorb′er** *n.* **—ab·sorb′a·ble, ab·sorb′ing** *adj.* **—ab·sorb′ing·ly** *adv.*

ab·sorbed (ab·sôrbd′, -zôrbd′) *adj.* **1** Deeply engrossed; rapt. **2** Sucked up, assimilated, etc.

ab·sor·bent (ab·sôr′bənt, -zôr′-) *adj.* Absorbing or tending to absorb. *—n.* A substance, duct, etc., that absorbs. — **ab·sor′ben·cy** *n.*

ab·sorp·tion (ab·sôrp′shən, -zôrp′-) *n.* **1** The act of absorbing or the condition of being absorbed. **2** Engrossment of the mind; preoccupation. **3** Assimilation, as by the digestive process. **—ab·sorp′tive** *adj.* **—ab·sorp′tive·ness, ab′sorp·tiv′i·ty** *n.*

ab·stain (ab·stān′) *v.i.* To refrain voluntarily; with *from.* [< L *ab-* from + *tenere* hold] **—ab·stain′er** *n.*

ab·ste·mi·ous (ab·stē′mē·əs) *adj.* 1 Eating and drinking sparingly. 2 Characterized by abstinence. [< L *abstemius* temperate] **—ab·ste′mi·ous·ly** *adv.* **—ab·ste′mi·ous·ness** *n.*

ab·sten·tion (ab·sten′shən) *n.* An abstaining. **—ab·sten′·tious** *adj.*

ab·sti·nence (ab′stə·nəns) *n.* The act or practice of abstaining, as from alcoholic beverages, food, pleasure, etc. **—ab′sti·nent** *adj.* **—ab′sti·nent·ly** *adv.* **—Syn.** continence, self-denial, temperance, fasting.

abstr. abstract.

ab·stract (ab·strakt′, ab′strakt) *adj.* 1 Considered apart from particular examples or concrete objects; general, as opposed to particular. 2 Theoretical; ideal, as opposed to practical. 3 Expressing a quality or relation that is thought of apart from any specific object or particular instance: Redness is an *abstract* noun. 4 Difficult to understand; abstruse. 5 Designating art that uses as subject matter the relationship of formal elements rather than the depiction or representation of recognizable objects. —*n.* (ab′strakt) 1 A summary or epitome, as of an article, book, report, etc. 2 Something abstract. **—in the abstract** Apart from actual, concrete examples or experience. —*v.t.* (ab·strakt′) 1 To take away; remove. 2 To take away secretly or dishonestly; steal. 3 To withdraw or disengage (the attention, interest, etc.). 4 To consider apart from particular or material instances. 5 (ab′strakt) To make an abstract of, as a book or treatise; summarize. [< L *ab-* away + *trahere* draw] **—ab·stract′er, ab·stract′ness** *n.* **—ab·stract′ly** *adv.*

ab·stract·ed (ab·strak′tid) *adj.* 1 Absentminded; preoccupied. 2 Separated from all else; apart. **—ab·stract′ed·ly** *adv.* **—ab·stract′ed·ness** *n.*

ab·strac·tion (ab·strak′shən) *n.* 1 The act of removing or summarizing; also, the result of this. 2 The forming of an idea or concept without reference to actual objects or specific examples. 3 An abstract idea or a term to express it. 4 Absence of mind; preoccupation. 5 An abstract work of art. **—ab·strac′tive** *adj.* **—ab·strac′tive·ly** *adv.* **—ab·strac′tive·ness** *n.*

ab·struse (ab·stro͞os′) *adj.* Hard to understand. [< L *abstrudere* to hide] **—ab·struse′ly** *adv.* **—ab·struse′ness** *n.*

ab·surd (ab·sûrd′, -zûrd′) *adj.* 1 Irrational; preposterous; ridiculous. 2 Of or pertaining to the absurd. —*n.* The state of man's existence in what appears to be an unreasonable, meaningless universe: a thesis dealing with the literature of the *absurd.* [< L *absurdus* out of tune, incongruous]—**ab·surd′ism, ab·surd′ness** *n.* **—ab·surd′ist** *adj., n.* **—ab·surd′ly** *adv.*

ab·surd·i·ty (ab·sûr′də·tē, -zûr′-) *n. pl.* **·ties** 1 The quality of being absurd. 2 Something absurd.

a·bun·dance (ə·bun′dəns) *n.* 1 A plentiful supply. 2 Affluence; wealth.

a·bun·dant (ə·bun′dənt) *adj.* 1 More than enough; ample. 2 Well supplied; abounding. [< L *abundare* to overflow] **—a·bun′dant·ly** *adv.*

a·buse (ə·byo͞oz′) *v.t.* **a·bused, a·bus·ing** 1 To use improperly or injuriously; misuse. 2 To hurt by treating wrongly; injure. 3 To speak in coarse or bad terms of or to; revile; malign. —*n.* (ə·byo͞os′) 1 Improper or injurious use; misuse. 2 Ill-treatment; injury. 3 An immoral or dishonest practice or act. 4 Harsh, abusive language. [< L *abuti* misuse] **—a·bus′er** *n.*

a·bu·sive (ə·byo͞o′siv) *adj.* 1 Of or characterized by abuse or misuse; mistreating. 2 Insulting or vituperative. **—a·bu′sive·ly** *adv.* **—a·bu′sive·ness** *n.*

a·but (ə·but′) *v.* **a·but·ted, a·but·ting** *v.i.* 1 To touch or join at the end or side; border: with *on, upon,* or *against.* —*v.t.* 2 To border on; end at. [< OF *abouter* to border on] **—a·but′ter** *n.* **—a·but′ting** *adj.*

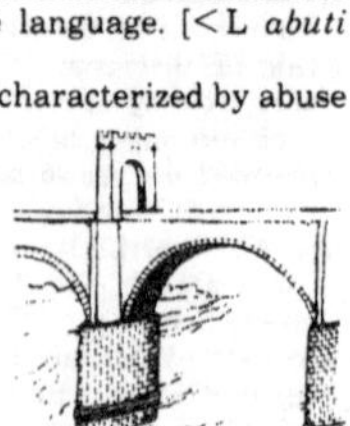

Abutments

a·but·ment (ə·but′mənt) *n.* 1 The act of abutting. 2 That which abuts. 3 The point at which one thing abuts another thing. 4 A supporting structure or buttress, as at the end of a bridge or wall.

a·bysm (ə·biz′əm) *n.* An abyss. [< L *abyssus* abyss]

a·bys·mal (ə·biz′məl) *adj.* 1 Bottomless. 2 Immeasurably great or terrible: *abysmal* ignorance. **—a·bys′mal·ly** *adv.*

a·byss (ə·bis′) *n.* 1 A deep chasm or gulf. 2 Any bottomless void or depth: the *abyss* of infinity. 3 The lowest depths of the sea. [< Gk. *a-* without + *byssos* bottom] **—a·bys′sal** *adj.*

Ab·ys·sin·i·a (ab′ə·sin′ē·ə) ETHIOPIA. **—Ab′ys·sin·i·an** *adj., n.* • See map at AFRICA.

-ac *suffix* 1 Having; affected by: *demoniac.* 2 Like or pertaining to: *cardiac.* [< Gk. *-akos* or L *-acus* or F *-aque*]

A.C., a.c. alternating current.

A/C, a/c account; account current.

Ac actinium.

a·ca·cia (ə·kā′shə) *n.* 1 Any of a genus of usu. evergreen leguminous trees and shrubs found in warm regions, having yellow or white flowers. 2 GUM ARABIC. 3 The common locust tree. [< Gk. *akakia* a thorny tree of Egypt]

acad. academic; academy.

ac·a·dem·i·a (ak′ə·dē′mē·ə) *n. Often cap.* Academic institutions, collectively; the academic world. [L]

ac·a·dem·ic (ak′ə·dem′ik) *adj.* 1 Pertaining to an academy, college, or university. 2 In education, classical and literary rather than technical or vocational. 3 Theoretical rather than practical: What he might have done is *academic.* 4 Scholarly; pedantic. 5 Conventional; traditional. Also **ac′a·dem′i·cal.** —*n.* A college or university teacher or student. **—ac′a·dem′i·cal·ly** *adv.*

a·cad·e·mi·cian (ə·kad′ə·mish′ən, ak′ə·də-) *n.* A member of a society for the advancement of an art or science.

a·cad·e·my (ə·kad′ə·mē) *n. pl.* **·mies** 1 A secondary school, usu. private. 2 A school for special studies, as in art or music. 3 A learned society for the advancement of arts or sciences. [< Gk. *Akadēmeia,* name of the grove in Athens where Plato taught]

A·ca·di·a (ə·kā′dē·ə) A former French colony that settled in 1604 in what are now the Canadian provinces of Nova Scotia and New Brunswick. **—A·ca′di·an** *adj., n.*

a·can·thus (ə·kan′thəs) *n. pl.* **·thus·es** or **·thi** (-thī) 1 Any of several related plants having large, lobed, usu. spiny leaves, common in the Mediterranean region. 2 *Archit.* A decorative representation of its leaf, characteristic of the Corinthian capital. Also **acanthus leaf.** [< Gk. *akanthos* < *akē* thorn]

Acanthus *def. 2*

a cap·pel·la (ä′ kə·pel′ə, *Ital.* ä′ käp·pel′lä) *Music* Without instrumental accompaniment. [< L *ad* according to + *cappella* chapel]

acc. accompanied; account; accountant; accusative.

ac·cede (ak·sēd′) *v.i.* **ac·ced·ed, ac·ced·ing** 1 To give one's consent or adherence; agree; assent: with *to.* 2 To come into or enter upon an office or dignity: with *to.* [< L *ad-* to + *cedere* yield, go]

ac·cel·er·an·do (ak·sel′ə·ran′dō; *Ital.* ät·che′le·rän′dō) *adj. & adv. Music* With a gradually accelerating tempo. [Ital., lit., accelerating]

ac·cel·er·ate (ak·sel′ə·rāt) *v.* **·at·ed, ·at·ing** *v.t.* 1 To cause to act or move faster; increase the speed of. 2 *Physics* To increase or change the velocity of. 3 To hasten the natural or usual course of: to *accelerate* a schedule. 4 To cause to happen ahead of time. —*v.i.* 5 To move or become faster: The car suddenly *accelerated.* [< L *ad-* to + *celerare* hasten] **—ac·cel′er·a′tive** *adj.*

ac·cel·er·a·tion (ak·sel′ə·rā′shən) *n.* 1 The act of accelerating, or the process of being accelerated. 2 *Physics* The rate at which the velocity of a body changes per unit of time.

ac·cel·er·a·tor (ak·sel′ə·rā′tər) *n.* 1 One who or that which accelerates. 2 The throttle control of an automobile, etc. 3 *Physics* Any of several devices for accelerating various subatomic particles, as a cyclotron.

ac·cent (ak′sent) *n.* 1 A vocal stress or emphasis given to a word. 2 A mark used to indicate such stress: the **primary accent** (′), noting the chief stress, and the **secondary accent** (′), noting a weaker stress. 3 In certain languages, a mark used to indicate the quality of a vowel or diphthong, as in French, the acute (´), grave (`), and circumflex (ˆ) accents. 4 *Music* a Rhythmic prominence, as of a tone. b A characteristic, esp. greater loudness, that causes this. 5 A modulation of the voice. 6 A particular manner of speech or pronunciation: a British *accent.* 7 *pl. Archaic* Speech. 8 In prosody, the stress determining the rhythm of poetry. 9 A distinguishing feature or characteristic. 10 An object, color, etc., that provides interest or contrast. 11 Special emphasis: He put an *accent* on clarity. —*v.t.* (ak′sent, ak·sent′) 1 To speak, pronounce, or produce with an accent; stress. 2 To write or print with a mark indicating accent or stress. 3 To call attention to; emphasize. [< L *accentus,* lit., song added to speech]

ac·cen·tu·al (ak·sen′cho͞o·əl) *adj.* Of, pertaining to, having, or made by accent. —**ac·cen′tu·al·ly** *adv.*

ac·cen·tu·ate (ak·sen′cho͞o·āt) *v.t.* **·at·ed, ·at·ing** 1 To strengthen or heighten the effect of; emphasize. 2 To speak or pronounce with an accent. [< L *accentus.* See ACCENT.] —**ac·cen′tu·a′tion** *n.*

ac·cept (ak·sept′) *v.t.* 1 To receive with favor or willingness, as a gift. 2 To give an affirmative answer to. 3 To agree to; admit: to *accept* an apology. 4 To take with good grace; submit to: to *accept* the inevitable. 5 To agree to pay, as a draft. 6 To believe in. —*v.i.* 7 To agree or promise to fulfill an engagement; receive favorably. [< L *ad-* to + *capere* take] —**ac·cept′er** *n.*

ac·cept·a·ble (ak·sep′tə·bəl) *adj.* Worthy or capable of being accepted. —**ac·cept′a·ble·ness, ac·cept′a·bil′i·ty** *n.* —**ac·cept′a·bly** *adv.* —**Syn.** adequate, satisfactory, agreeable.

ac·cep·tance (ak·sep′təns) *n.* 1 The act of accepting or the state of being accepted. 2 Approval. 3 Belief in something. 4 A written agreement to pay; also, the paper itself when endorsed "accepted." Also **ac·cep′tan·cy.** —**ac·cep′·tant** *adj.*

ac·cep·ta·tion (ak′sep·tā′shən) *n.* The accepted meaning of a word or expression.

ac·cept·ed (ak·sep′tid) *adj.* Commonly recognized, believed, approved, etc.

ac·cess (ak′ses) *n.* 1 The act of approaching; approach. 2 A means of approaching, using, knowing, etc. 3 The right to approach, use, etc. 4 Increase. 5 An attack; onset, as of a disease. 6 An outburst. [< L *accedere.* See ACCEDE.]

ac·ces·si·ble (ak·ses′ə·bəl) *adj.* 1 Capable of being approached or reached. 2 Easy to approach or reach. 3 That can be obtained or used: *accessible* funds. 4 Open to the influence of: with *to*: *accessible* to pity. —**ac·ces′si·bil′i·ty** *n.* —**ac·ces′si·bly** *adv.*

ac·ces·sion (ak·sesh′ən) *n.* 1 The attainment of or the succession to an office, throne, right, etc. 2 Assent; agreement; consent. 3 An increase by adding something; also, that which is added. —*v.t.* To record, as additions to a library or museum. [< L *accedere.* See ACCEDE.] —**ac·ces′·sion·al** *adj.*

ac·ces·so·ry (ak·ses′ər·ē) *n. pl.* **·ries** 1 Something added as an aid, convenience, decorative item, etc. 2 *Law* A person who, even if not present during the perpetration of a felony, knowingly instigates or assists the felony beforehand (**accessory before the fact**) or assists or conceals the felon afterwards (**accessory after the fact**). —*adj.* 1 Aiding the principal design, or assisting subordinately the chief agent, as in the commission of a crime. 2 Supplemental; additional. Also, esp. in law, **ac·ces′sa·ry.** [< L *accessus* access] —**ac·ces′so·ri·ly** *adv.* —**ac·ces′so·ri·ness** *n.*

ac·ci·dent (ak′sə·dənt) *n.* 1 Anything that happens unexpectedly, undesignedly, or without known cause. 2 Any unpleasant or unfortunate occurrence involving injury, loss, suffering, or death. 3 Chance; fortune. 4 Any nonessential circumstance or attribute. [< L *ad-* upon + *cadere* fall]

ac·ci·den·tal (ak′sə·den′təl) *adj.* 1 Happening or coming by chance or without design. 2 Nonessential; subordinate; incidental. 3 *Music* Of or indicating an accidental. —*n.* 1 A casual, incidental, or nonessential feature or property. 2 *Music* A sharp, flat, or natural elsewhere than in the signature. —**ac′ci·den′tal·ly** *adv.* —**ac′ci·den′tal·ness** *n.*

ac·claim (ə·klām′) *v.t.* 1 To proclaim or receive with approval; hail. 2 To show enthusiasm for; welcome with applause or praise. 3 *Can.* To elect by acclamation. —*v.i.* 4 To applaud or shout approval. —*n.* Great approval, demonstrated by applause, shouting, etc. [< L *ad-* to + *clamare* shout] —**ac·claim′a·ble** *adj.* —**ac·claim′er** *n.*

ac·cla·ma·tion (ak′lə·mā′shən) *n.* 1 An expression of approval, as by applause, shouting, etc. 2 An enthusiastic vocal vote. 3 *Can.* An election in which the candidate has no opposition. —**ac·clam·a·to·ry** (ə·klam′ə·tôr′ē, -tō′rē) *adj.*

ac·cli·mate (ak′lə·māt, ə·klī′mit) *v.t. & v.i.* **·mat·ed, ·mat·ing** To adapt or become adapted to a different climate, environment, or situation. [< F *à* to + *climat* climate] —**ac·cli·ma·ta·ble** (ə·klī′mə·tə·bəl) *adj.* —**ac·cli·ma·tion** (ak′lə·mā′shən), **ac·cli·ma·ta·tion** (ə·klī′mə·tā′shən) *n.*

ac·cli·ma·tize (ə·klī′mə·tīz) *v.t. & v.i.* **·tized, ·tiz·ing** To acclimate. —**ac·cli′ma·tiz′a·ble** *adj.* —**ac·cli′ma·ti·za′tion** *n.*

ac·cliv·i·ty (ə·kliv′ə·tē) *n. pl.* **·ties** An upward slope. [< L *acclivitas* steepness] —**ac·cliv′i·tous, ac·cli·vous** (ə·klī′vəs) *adj.*

ac·co·lade (ak′ə·lād′, -läd′) *n.* 1 Anything done or given to show praise, honor, or approval. 2 *Archit.* A curved ornamental molding. 3 In conferring knighthood, the light blow with a sword. [< Ital. *accollare* embrace about the neck]

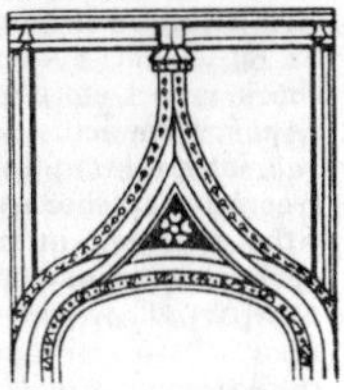

Accolade *def. 2*

ac·com·mo·date (ə·kom′ə·dāt) *v.* **·dat·ed, ·dat·ing** *v.t.* 1 To do a favor for; oblige; help. 2 To provide for; give lodging to. 3 To be suitable or have space for. 4 To adapt or modify; adjust. 5 To reconcile or settle, as conflicting opinions. —*v.i.* 6 To be or become adjusted or conformed, as the eye to distance. [< L *ad-* to + *commodare* make fit, suit] —**ac·com′mo·da′tive** *adj.* —**ac·com′mo·da′tive·ness** *n.*

ac·com·mo·dat·ing (ə·kom′ə·dā′ting) *adj.* Disposed to accommodate; obliging. —**ac·com′mo·dat′ing·ly** *adv.*

ac·com·mo·da·tion (ə·kom′ə·dā′shən) *n.* 1 An adaptation or adjustment. 2 A reconciliation, as of conflicts. 3 *pl.* Lodging, board, etc. 4 *pl.* A seat, berth, etc., on a train, airplane, or the like. 5 A disposition to help or oblige. 6 A loan. 7 A convenience. 8 The adjustment of the eye to vision at different distances.

ac·com·pa·ni·ment (ə·kum′pə·ni·mənt, ə·kump′ni-) *n.* 1 Anything that accompanies. 2 *Music* A part that sounds along with a main or leading part.

ac·com·pa·nist (ə·kum′pə·nist, ə·kump′nist) *n.* A musician who provides an accompaniment.

ac·com·pa·ny (ə·kum′pə·nē) *v.t.* **·nied, ·ny·ing** 1 To go with; attend; escort. 2 To be or occur with; coexist with: Weakness often *accompanies* disease. 3 To supplement with. 4 *Music* a To provide with an accompaniment. b To be the accompaniment to or for. [< LL *ad-* to + *companio* companion] —**ac·com′pa·ni·er** *n.*

ac·com·plice (ə·kom′plis) *n.* An associate in wrong or crime, whether as principal or accessory. [< *a,* indefinite article + LL *complex* accomplice]

ac·com·plish (ə·kom′plish) *v.t.* To do, perform, effect, or finish. [< L *ad-* to + *complere* fill up, complete] —**ac·com′·plish·a·ble** *adj.* —**ac·com′plish·er** *n.*

ac·com·plished (ə·kom′plisht) *adj.* 1 Completed; finished. 2 Skilled; proficient. 3 Socially polished or polite.

ac·com·plish·ment (ə·kom′plish·mənt) *n.* 1 A completion or fulfillment. 2 Something acquired or attained, as a skill. 3 Something done, as a task.

ac·cord (ə·kôrd′) *v.t.* 1 To render as due; grant; concede. 2 To bring into agreement, as opinions. —*v.i.* 3 To agree; harmonize. —*n.* 1 Harmony, agreement, or conformity. 2 An agreement between governments. —**of one's own accord** By one's own choice; voluntarily. [< LL *accordare* be of one mind, agree] —**ac·cord′a·ble** *adj.* —**ac·cord′er** *n.*

ac·cord·ance (ə·kôr′dəns) *n.* Agreement; conformity. —**ac·cord′ant** *adj.* —**ac·cord′ant·ly** *adv.*

ac·cord·ing (ə·kôr′ding) *adj.* Being in agreement; harmonizing. —*adv.* Accordingly. —**according as** 1 In proportion as. 2 Depending on whether. —**according to** 1 In accordance with. 2 As stated or believed by; on the authority of. 3 In proportion to.

ac·cord·ing·ly (ə·kôr′ding·lē) *adv.* 1 In a conformable manner; suitably. 2 Consequently.

ac·cor·di·on (ə·kôr′dē·ən) *n.* A portable reed organ using air from a self-contained bellows operated by the performer. [< Ital. *accordare* accord, harmonize] —**ac·cor′di·on·ist** *n.*

Accordion

ac·cost (ə·kôst′, ə·kost′) *v.t.* To speak to first; address. [< LL *accostare* be side to side]

ac·couche·ment (ə·kōōsh′·mənt, *Fr.* à·kōōsh·mäṅ′) *n.* The act of childbirth; confinement. [F < *accoucher* put to bed, give birth]

ac·count (ə·kount′) *v.t.* 1 To hold to be; consider; estimate. —*v.i.* 2 To provide a reckoning, as of funds paid or received: with *to* or *with* (someone) *for* (something). 3 To give a rational explanation: with *for.* 4 To be responsible; answer: with *for.* 5 To cause death, capture, or incapacitation: with *for.* —*n.* 1 An explanation, statement, report, or description. 2 Importance; value. 3 A reckoning or calculation. 4 A record of financial transactions, as of debits, credits, etc. 5 A bank account. 6 A charge account. 7 A customer or client. —**give a good account of oneself** To do well. —**on account** 1 On credit. 2 As partial payment. —**on account of** Because of; for the sake of. —**on no account** Under no circumstances. —**take into account** To take into consideration. [< L *ad-* to + *computare* count]

ac·count·a·ble (ə·koun′tə·bəl) *adj.* 1 Liable to be called to account; responsible. 2 Capable of being accounted for or explained. —**ac·count′a·bil′i·ty** *n.* —**ac·count′a·bly** *adv.*

ac·count·ant (ə·koun′tənt) *n.* One whose business is to keep or examine accounts, as of a business or bank. —**ac·count′an·cy** *n.*

ac·count·ing (ə·koun′ting) *n.* The occupation or system of recording, classifying, and interpreting financial accounts; also, an item so recorded, classified, etc.

ac·cou·ter (ə·kōō′tər) *v.t.* To outfit or equip, esp. for military service. [< F *accoutrer*]

ac·cou·ter·ment (ə·kōō′tər·mənt) *n.* Equipment or furnishings, esp. the equipment of a soldier other than arms and dress.

ac·cou·tre (ə·kōō′tər) *v.t.* **·tred, ·tring** (ə·kōō′tə·ring, -kōō′·tring) ACCOUTER. —**ac·cou′tre·ment** (-trə·mənt, -tər-) *n.*

ac·cred·it (ə·kred′it) *v.t.* 1 To furnish or send with credentials, as an ambassador. 2 To certify as fulfilling requirements. 3 To give credit for. 4 To attribute to. 5 To accept as true; believe. 6 To confer acceptance or favor on. [< F *à* to + *crédit* credit]

ac·cre·tion (ə·krē′shən) *n.* 1 Growth or increase in size, as by external additions. 2 The result of such growth or increase; also, that which is added to effect such a result. 3 An accumulation, as of soil on a seashore. [< L *accrescere* to grow to] —**ac·cre′tive** *adj.*

ac·crue (ə·krōō′) *v.i.* **·crued, ·cru·ing** 1 To come as a natural result or increment, as by growth: with *to.* 2 To accumulate, as the interest on money: with *from.* [< L *accrescere* to grow to] —**ac·cru′al, ac·crue′ment** *n.*

ac·cu·mu·late (ə·kyōōm′yə·lāt) *v.t.* & *v.i.* To gather; collect; heap or pile up. [< L < *ad-* to + *cumulare* heap] —**ac·cu·mu·la·ble** (ə·kyōōm′yə·lə·bəl) *adj.*

ac·cu·mu·la·tion (ə·kyōōm′yə·lā′shən) *n.* 1 The act or process of accumulating. 2 That which has accumulated.

ac·cu·mu·la·tive (ə·kyōōm′yə·lā′tiv) *adj.* 1 Tending to accumulate. 2 Resulting from accumulation. —**ac·cu′mu·la′tive·ly** *adv.* —**ac·cu′mu·la′tive·ness** *n.*

ac·cu·mu·la·tor (ə·kyōōm′yə·lā′tər) *n.* 1 A person that accumulates. 2 *Brit.* A storage battery.

ac·cu·ra·cy (ak′yər·ə·sē) *n.* The quality or condition of being accurate. —**Syn.** correctness, precision, exactness.

ac·cu·rate (ak′yər·it) *adj.* 1 Conforming exactly to truth or to a standard; without error: an *accurate* measurement. 2 Careful; precise. [< L *accurare* take care of] —**ac′cu·rate·ly** *adv.* —**ac′cu·rate·ness** *n.*

ac·curs·ed (ə·kûr′sid, ə·kûrst′) *adj.* 1 Doomed to be under a curse. 2 Deserving a curse; detestable. Also **ac·curst′.** —**ac·curs′ed·ly** *adv.* —**ac·curs′ed·ness** *n.*

ac·cu·sa·tion (ak′yōō·zā′shən) *n.* 1 The act of accusing or the state of being accused. 2 The crime or act of which one is accused. Also **ac·cu·sal** (ə·kyōō′zəl). —**ac·cu·sa·to·ry** (ə·kyōō′zə·tôr′ē, -tō′rē) *adj.*

ac·cu·sa·tive (ə·kyōō′zə·tiv) *Gram. adj.* Denoting, in inflected languages, the case of the noun, pronoun, etc., that is the direct object of a verb or preposition. —*n.* 1 The accusative case. 2 A word in this case. [< L *(casus) accusativus* (the case) indicating accusation] —**ac·cu′sa·tive·ly** *adv.*

ac·cuse (ə·kyōōz′) *v.t.* **ac·cused, ac·cus·ing** 1 To charge with fault or error; blame. 2 To bring charges against, as of a crime or an offense: with *of.* [< L *accusare* call to account] —**ac·cus′er** *n.* —**ac·cus′ing·ly** *adv.*

ac·cused (ə·kyōōzd′) *n. Law* The defendant or defendants in a criminal case.

ac·cus·tom (ə·kus′təm) *v.t.* To make familiar by use; habituate or inure: with *to.* [< OF *a-* to + *costume* custom]

ac·cus·tomed (ə·kus′təmd) *adj.* 1 Habitual; usual: his *accustomed* haunts. 2 Used; wont: with *to*: He is *accustomed* to rising early.

ace (ās) *n.* 1 A playing card, die, etc., marked with a single spot; also, the single spot. 2 One who excels in any field. 3 A military pilot who has destroyed five or more enemy aircraft. 4 In tennis and similar games, a point won by a single serve; also, such a serve. —*adj. Informal* First-rate; excellent. —*v.t.*, **aced** (āst), **ac·ing** To score an ace against, as in tennis. [< L *as* unity, unit]

-acea *suffix Zool.* Used in forming names of classes and orders of animals. [< L]

-aceae *suffix Bot.* Used in forming names of families of plants. [< L]

a·cen·tric (ā·sen′trik) *adj.* Without a center; off-center.

-aceous *suffix* Of the nature of; belonging or pertaining to; like: used in botany and zoology to form adjectives corresponding to nouns in *-acea, -aceae.* [< L *-aceus* of the nature of]

ac·er·bate (as′ər·bāt) *v.t.* **·bat·ed, ·bat·ing** To exasperate.

a·cerb·ic (ə·sûr′bik) *adj.* 1 Sour and astringent to the taste, as unripe fruit. 2 Harsh or sharp in tone: an *acerbic* rejoinder. Also **a·cerb** (ə·sûrb′). [< L *acerbus* sharp] —**a·cer′bi·ty** *n.*

ac·e·tab·u·lum (as′ə·tab′yə·ləm) *n. pl.* **·la** (-lə) The socket in the hip into which the thighbone fits. [< L, a small vinegar cup < *acetum* vinegar]

ac·et·an·i·lide (as′ə·tan′ə·līd, -lid) *n.* A derivative of aniline, used as an analgesic and antipyretic.

ac·e·tate (as′ə·tāt) *n.* A salt or ester of acetic acid.

a·ce·tic (ə·sē′tik, ə·set′ik) *adj.* Pertaining to or like vinegar; sour. [< L *acetum* vinegar]

acetic acid A colorless sour liquid, found in vinegar.

a·cet·i·fy (ə·set′ə·fī) *v.t.* & *v.i.* **·fied, ·fy·ing** To make into or become acid or vinegar. —**a·cet′i·fi·ca′tion, a·cet′i·fi′er** *n.*

aceto- *combining form* Of, pertaining to, or from acetic acid. Also, before vowels, **acet-.** [< L *acetum* vinegar]

ac·e·tone (as′ə·tōn) *n.* A clear, flammable liquid produced industrially and used as a solvent. [< ACET(O)- + -ONE] —**ac·e·ton·ic** (as′ə·ton′ik) *adj.*

a·cet·y·lene (ə·set′ə·lēn) *n.* A colorless hydrocarbon gas, used as an illuminant and for welding. [< ACET- + -YL + -ENE]

a·ce·tyl·sal·i·cyl·ic acid (ə·set′əl·sal′ə·sil′ik, ə·sē′təl-) Aspirin.

A·chae·an (ə·kē′ən) *adj.* Pertaining to Achaea, its people, or their culture. —*n.* 1 A member of one of the four major tribes of ancient Greece. 2 A Greek. Also **A·cha′·ian** (ə·kā′ən, -kī′-).

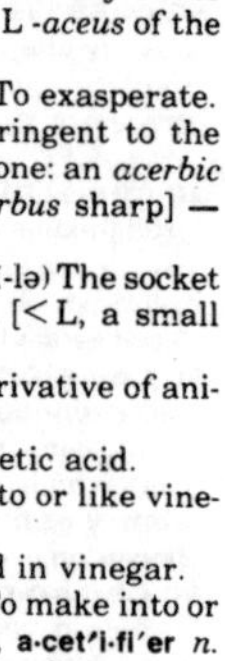

Achenes of dandelion

ache (āk) *v.i.* **ached** (ākt), **ach·ing** 1 To suffer dull, continued pain. 2 To feel sympathy or distress: with *for.* 3 To be anxious or distressed. 4 To yearn; be eager: followed by *for* or the infinitive. —*n.* A local, dull, and protracted pain. [< OE *ācan*]

a·chene (ə·kēn′) *n.* A small, dry fruit having one seed, as the dandelion. [< A-[4] not + Gk. *chainein* to gape, recoil]

Ach·e·ron (ak′ə·ron) *Gk. & Rom. Myth.* 1 The river of woe, one of the five rivers surrounding Hades. 2 HADES.

a·chieve (ə·chēv′), *v.* **a·chieved, a·chiev·ing** *v.t.* 1 To accomplish; do successfully. 2 To win or attain, as by effort or skill. —*v.i.* 3 To accomplish something; to attain an object. [< LL *ad caput (venire)* (come) to a head] —**a·chiev′a·ble** *adj.* —**a·chiev′er** *n.*

a·chieve·ment (ə·chēv′mənt) *n.* 1 The act of achieving. 2 Something achieved.

A·chil·les (ə·kil′ēz) In the *Iliad,* the foremost Greek hero of the Trojan War, who killed Hector and was killed by the arrow Paris shot into his right heel, the only vulnerable spot on his body.

Achilles' heel A vulnerable point.

Achilles tendon The tendon that connects the muscles of the calf of the leg to the bone of the heel.

ach·ro·mat·ic (ak′rə·mat′ik) *adj.* 1 *Optics* Transmitting light without separating it into its constituent colors, as a lens. 2 Having lightness or darkness only, with no hue, as a gray color. [< Gk. *a-* without + *chrōma* color] —**ach′·ro·mat′i·cal·ly** *adv.*

ac·id (as′id) *adj.* 1 Sharp and biting to the taste, as vinegar; sour. 2 *Chem.* Having properties of or pertaining to an acid. 3 Sharp; biting; sarcastic. —*n.* 1 *Chem.* A compound which in aqueous solution produces hydrogen ions which have a sour taste, turn blue litmus red, and may be replaced by another positive ion to form a salt. 2 Any sour substance. 3 *Slang* LSD. [< L *acidus* sour] —**ac′id·ly** *adv.* —**ac′id·ness** *n.*

acid head *Slang* A habitual user of LSD.

a·cid·ic (ə·sid′ik) *adj.* 1 Tending to form acid. 2 Acid.

a·cid·i·fy (ə·sid′ə·fī) *v.t. & v.i.* **·fied, ·fy·ing** To make or become acid. —**a·cid′i·fi′a·ble** *adj.* —**a·cid′i·fi·ca′tion, a·cid′i·fi′er** *n.*

a·cid·i·ty (ə·sid′ə·tē) *n.* 1 The state or quality of being acid; sourness; tartness. 2 Degree of acid strength. 3 HYPERACIDITY. Also **ac′id·ness.**

ac·i·do·sis (as′ə·dō′sis) *n.* A deficiency of sodium bicarbonate in the blood, characteristic of certain diseases. —**ac·i·dot·ic** (as′ə·dot′ik) *adj.*

acid test A final, severe test revealing the genuineness or worth of something.

a·cid·u·late (ə·sij′o͞o·lāt) *v.t.* **·lat·ed, ·lat·ing** To make somewhat acid or sour. —**a·cid′u·la′tion** *n.*

a·cid·u·lous (ə·sij′o͞o·ləs) *adj.* Slightly acid, as in taste or manner. Also **a·cid′u·lent.** —**Syn.** sour, biting, caustic, tart.

-acious *suffix of adjectives* Abounding in; characterized by; given to: *pugnacious, vivacious.* [< L *-ax, -acis* + OUS]

-acity *suffix* Quality or state of: used to form abstract nouns corresponding to adjectives in *-acious.* [< L *-acitas*]

ack-ack (ak′ak′) *n. Slang* Antiaircraft fire. [British radio operator's code for *A.A.* (antiaircraft)]

ac·knowl·edge (ak·nol′ij) *v.t.* **·edged, ·edg·ing** 1 To own or admit as true; confess. 2 To declare or admit the validity of, as a claim or right. 3 To show appreciation of; thank for. 4 To recognize and respond to, as a greeting. 5 To respond to the arrival of: to *acknowledge* a letter. [< OE *oncnāwan* recognize] —**ac·knowl′edge·a·ble** *adj.* —**ac·knowl′edg·er** *n.*

ac·knowl·edg·ment (ak·nol′ij·mənt) *n.* 1 The act of acknowledging. 2 Something done, given, or said in acknowledging a greeting, favor, etc. 3 A legal certificate or avowal. Also **ac·knowl′edge·ment.**

ac·me (ak′mē) *n.* The highest point or summit. [< Gk. *akmē* point]

ac·ne (ak′nē) *n.* A skin disease causing pimples on the face, chest, and back, and caused by clogging or inflammation of the sebaceous glands. [Alter. of Gk. *akmē* point]

ac·o·lyte (ak′ə·līt) *n.* 1 An attendant or assistant. 2 ALTAR BOY. 3 In the Roman Catholic Church, a member of the highest of the four minor orders. [< Gk. *akolouthos* follower, attendant]

ac·o·nite (ak′ə·nīt) *n.* 1 Any of a genus of usu. poisonous plants with a helmet-shaped petal on the flowers, as monkshood. 2 An extract made from an aconite, formerly used in medicine. [< Gk. *akoniton*]

a·corn (ā′kôrn, ā′kərn) *n.* The fruit of the oak, a one-seeded nut, fixed in a woody cup. [< OE *æcern*]

Acorns
a. red oak. b. pin oak. c. black oak.

a·cous·tic (ə·ko͞os′tik) *adj.* 1 Pertaining to the act or sense of hearing, sound, or the science of sound. 2 Adapted for modifying sound or hearing. Also **a·cous′ti·cal.** [< Gk. *akoustikos* < *akouein* hear] —**a·cous′ti·cal′ly** *adv.*

ac·ous·ti·cian (ak′o͞os·tish′ən) *n.* A specialist in acoustics.

a·cous·tics (ə·ko͞os′tiks) *n. pl. (construed as sing. in def. 1)* 1 The branch of physics that deals with the phenomena of sound. 2 The sound-transmitting properties of a place, as an auditorium.

ac·quaint (ə·kwānt′) *v.t.* 1 To make familiar or conversant; inform: with *with: Acquaint* yourself with the court routine. 2 To cause to know, esp. socially. [< LL *adcognitare* make known]

ac·quain·tance (ə·kwān′təns) *n.* 1 Knowledge of any person or thing. 2 A person whom one knows, but not closely. 3 The state of being acquainted. —**ac·quain′tance·ship** *n.*

ac·qui·esce (ak′wē·es′) *v.i.* **·esced** (-est′), **·esc·ing** To consent or concur quietly or passively; comply: usu. with *in*: The candidate *acquiesced* in all his party's plans. [< L *acquiescere* to remain at rest] —**ac′qui·es′cence** *n.* —**ac′qui·es′cent** *adj.* —**ac′qui·es′cent·ly** *adv.*

ac·quire (ə·kwīr′) *v.t.* **·quired, ·quir·ing** 1 To obtain by one's own endeavor or purchase. 2 To gain or possess as one's own. [< L *ad-* to + *quaerere* seek] —**ac·quir′a·ble** *adj.* —**ac·quir′er** *n.*

ac·quire·ment (ə·kwīr′mənt) *n.* 1 The act of acquiring. 2 Something acquired, as a skill.

ac·qui·si·tion (ak′wə·zish′ən) *n.* 1 The act of acquiring. 2 Anything acquired, as by purchase or trade.

ac·quis·i·tive (ə·kwiz′ə·tiv) *adj.* Eager or inclined to acquire; greedy. —**ac·quis′i·tive·ly** *adv.* —**ac·quis′i·tive·ness** *n.*

ac·quit (ə·kwit′) *v.t.* **ac·quit·ted, ac·quit·ting** 1 To free or clear, as from an accusation. 2 To relieve, as of an obligation. 3 To conduct (oneself): He *acquitted* himself nobly. [< L *ad-* to + *quietare* settle, quiet] —**ac·quit′ter** *n.*

ac·quit·tal (ə·kwit′l) *n.* 1 The act of setting free or the state of being set free by legal process. 2 The performance of a duty.

ac·quit·tance (ə·kwit′əns) *n.* Release or discharge from indebtedness or obligation.

a·cre (ā′kər) *n.* 1 A measure of area equal to 4,840 square yards. 2 *pl.* Lands. 3 *pl. Informal* A great many; lots. [< OE *æcer* field]

a·cre·age (ā′kər·ij) *n.* Area in acres; acres collectively.

ac·rid (ak′rid) *adj.* 1 Sharp, burning, or bitter to the taste or smell. 2 Bitterly sarcastic or satirical. [< L *acer*] —**a·crid·i·ty** (ə·krid′ə·tē), **ac′rid·ness** *n.* —**ac′rid·ly** *adv.*

ac·ri·mo·ni·ous (ak′rə·mō′nē·əs) *adj.* Bitterly sarcastic; caustic; sharp. —**ac′ri·mo′ni·ous·ly** *adv.* —**ac′ri·mo′ni·ous·ness** *n.*

ac·ri·mo·ny (ak′rə·mō′nē) *n.* Sharpness or bitterness of speech or temper. [< L *acrimonia* < *acer* sharp] —**Syn.** acridity, acerbity, sharpness, tartness.

acro- *combining form* 1 At the top, tip, or end of. 2 Pertaining to the extremities of the body. [< Gk. *akros* at the top or end]

ac·ro·bat (ak′rə·bat) *n.* One who is skilled in feats requiring muscular coordination, as in tightrope walking, tumbling, trapeze performing, etc.; a gymnast. [< Gk. *akrobatos* walking on tiptoe] —**ac′ro·bat′ic** or **·i·cal** *adj.* —**ac′·ro·bat′i·cal·ly** *adv.*

ac·ro·bat·ics (ak′rə·bat′iks) *n. pl (construed as sing. or pl.)* 1 The art or feats of an acrobat. 2 Anything requiring or demonstrating unusual agility.

ac·ro·gen (ak′rə·jən) *n.* A plant growing at the tip only, as ferns, mosses, etc. [< ACRO- + -GEN] —**ac′ro·gen′ic** *adj.*

ac·ro·meg·a·ly (ak′rō·meg′ə·lē) *n. Pathol.* A pituitary disorder characterized by enlargement of the extremities, thorax, and face. [< ACRO- + Gk. *megas, megalon* big] — **ac·ro·me·gal·ic** (ak′rō·mi·gal′ik) *adj.*

ac·ro·nym (ak′rə·nim) *n.* A word formed by the combining of initial letters *(UNESCO)* or syllables and letters *(radar, sonar)* of a series of words or a compound term. [< ACRO- + *-nym* name, as in HOMONYM]

ac·ro·pho·bi·a (ak′rə·fō′bē·ə) *n.* A fear of high places.

a·crop·o·lis (ə·krop′ə·lis) *n.* The fortified upper section of various ancient Greek cities. —**the Acropolis** Such a section in Athens, site of the Parthenon and other temples. [< Gk. *akros* top, highest part + *polis* city]

a·cross (ə·krôs′, ə·kros′) *adv.* **1** From one side to the other. **2** On or at the other side. **3** Crosswise; crossed. —*prep.* **1** From one side to the other side of. **2** On or to the other side of. **3** Into an encounter with or discovery of: I came *across* the book today. [< A-[1] on, in + CROSS]

a·cross-the-board (ə·krôs′t͟hə·bôrd′, ə·kros′-, -bōrd′) *adj.* **1** In horse racing, designating a bet in which equal amounts are placed on the same horse to win, place, or show. **2** That includes or affects all people, categories, etc.

a·cros·tic (ə·krôs′tik, ə·kros′-) *n.* A poem or other composition in which initial or other letters, taken in order, form a word or phrase. [< Gk. *akros* end + *stichos* line of verse] —**a·cros′ti·cal·ly** *adv.*

a·cryl·ic (ə·kril′ik) *adj.* Pertaining to or derived from an organic acid that polymerizes to form various commercially important transparent resins and plastics. —*n.* **1** Any of a class of clear, transparent resins and plastics derived from acrylic acid, as lucite, plexiglass, etc. **2** A substance derived from an acrylic resin, as a paint medium, a fiber, etc. **3** A painting done in such a medium. [< ACR(ID + OLEIN) + -YL + -IC]

act (akt) *v.t.* **1** To play the part of; impersonate. **2** To perform on the stage, as a play. **3** To perform as if on a stage; feign: Don't *act* the martyr. **4** To behave as suitable to: *Act* your age. —*v.i.* **5** To behave or conduct oneself: He knows how to *act* in society. **6** To carry out a purpose or function: The test *acted* as a check. **7** To do something: You must *act* immediately. **8** To produce an effect: often with *on:* The poison *acted* on his stomach at once. **9** To serve temporarily or as a substitute, as in some office or capacity: with *for.* **10** To perform on or as on the stage: She *acts* for a living. **11** To pretend so as to appear: She concealed her real feelings and *acted* friendly. —**act up** *Informal* **1** To behave mischievously. **2** To become troublesome, painful, etc. —*n.* **1** Something done; a deed. **2** An action; a doing: caught in the *act.* **3** An enactment, law, decree, or edict, as of a legislative body. **4** A formal written statement, as of a law or decree. **5** A main section or division of a play or opera. **6** A separate, specialty performance: a circus *act.* **7** Insincere behavior; pose. [< L *actus* a doing, and *actum* a thing done < *agere* do]

act·a·ble (ak′tə·bəl) *adj.* That can be acted, as a role in a play. —**act′a·bil′i·ty** *n.*

ACTH A pituitary hormone that stimulates hormone production in the cortical area of the adrenal glands; adrenocorticotropic hormone.

act·ing (ak′ting) *adj.* **1** Operating or officiating, esp. in place of another: *acting* secretary. **2** Functioning; in working order. **3** Containing directions for actors: the *acting* script. —*n.* The art or occupation of an actor.

ac·tin·i·a (ak·tin′ē·ə) *n. pl.* **·i·ae** (-i·ē) or **·i·as** A sea anemone. [< Gk. *aktis* ray] —**ac·tin′i·an** *adj., n.*

ac·tin·ic (ak·tin′ik) *adj.* Of or exhibiting actinism. Also **ac·tin′i·cal.** —**ac·tin′i·cal·ly** *adv.*

ac·ti·nide series (ak′ti·nīd) A series of chemically similar radioactive elements within the periodic table, from actinium, element 89, through lawrencium, element 103. • See PERIODIC TABLE OF ELEMENTS.

ac·tin·ism (ak′tin·iz′əm) *n.* **1** The property of radiant energy which effects chemical changes. **2** The production of such change. [< Gk. *aktis* ray + -ISM]

ac·tin·i·um (ak·tin′ē·əm) *n.* A radioactive element (symbol Ac) occurring in pitchblende.

ac·ti·noid (ak′ti·noid) *adj.* Having the form of rays; radiate, as a starfish.

ac·ti·no·zo·an (ak′ti·nə·zō′ən) *n.* ANTHOZOAN.

ac·tion (ak′shən) *n.* **1** The doing of something by the use of power, movement, energy, etc. **2** The thing done; deed. **3** *pl.* Behavior; conduct. **4** Energy, initiative, and decisiveness: a man of *action.* **5** The result or effect of something: the medicine's *action.* **6** The movement or manner of movement of a body organ, mechanism, etc.: the *action* of the heart. **7** The parts that move in a mechanism, as in a gun, piano, etc. **8** An event or series of events in a novel, play, etc. **9** *Law* A lawsuit. **10** A military conflict or encounter. **11** *Slang* Lively or exciting social activity; excitement: to find out where the *action* is. [< L *actio* < *agere* do]

ac·tion·a·ble (ak′shən·ə·bəl) *adj. Law* Affording ground or cause for a lawsuit.

ac·ti·vate (ak′tə·vāt) *v.t.* **·vat·ed, ·vat·ing 1** To make active. **2** To put into action, as a military unit. **3** To make radioactive. **4** To promote chemical reaction in. **5** To make pure by aeration, as sewage. —**ac′ti·va′tion, ac′ti·va′tor** *n.*

ac·tive (ak′tiv) *adj.* **1** Abounding in action; busy. **2** Being in or capable of action, movement, performance, etc.: an *active* volcano. **3** Causing or promoting action, change, movement etc. **4** Agile; lively; quick. **5** Characterized by actual participation, contribution, etc.: an *active* member. **6** Producing profit or bearing interest: *active* funds. **7** *Gram.* **a** Designating a voice of the verb which indicates that the subject of the sentence is performing the action. **b** Describing verbs expressing action as distinguished from being and state, as *run, hit, jump.* —*n. Gram.* The active voice. [< L *activus* < *agere* do] —**ac′tive·ly** *adv.* —**ac′tive·ness** *n.*

active duty Full military or naval duty. Also **active service.**

ac·tiv·ism (ak′tə·viz′əm). The doctrine or practice of active engagement in pursuit of a social or political goal. —**ac′tiv·ist** *adj., n.*

ac·tiv·i·ty (ak·tiv′ə·tē) *n. pl.* **·ties 1** The state or quality of being active; action. **2** Lively action or movement. **3** A specific action, project, pursuit, etc.: school *activities.* **4** *Physics* The degree of emission from a radioactive source.

act of God *Law* An event occurring by reason of the operations of nature unmixed with human agency or human negligence.

ac·tor (ak′tər) *n.* **1** A performer on the stage, in motion pictures, etc. **2** Any person who actively participates in something.

ac·tress (ak′tris) *n.* A woman who acts, as on the stage, in television, motion pictures, etc.

Acts of the Apostles The fifth book of the New Testament. Also **Acts.**

ac·tu·al (ak′cho͞o·əl) *adj.* **1** Existing in fact; real. **2** Being in existence or action now; existent; present. [< LL *actualis* < L *actus* a doing. See ACT.]

ac·tu·al·i·ty (ak′cho͞o·al′ə·tē) *n. pl.* **·ties 1** The quality of being actual; reality. **2** *pl.* Actual facts or conditions.

ac·tu·al·ize (ak′cho͞o·əl·īz) *v.t.* **·ized, ·iz·ing 1** To make real; realize in action, as a possibility. **2** To make seem real; represent realistically. —**ac′tu·al·i·za′tion** *n.*

ac·tu·al·ly (ak′cho͞o·əl·ē) *adv.* As a matter of fact; in reality; really; truly.

ac·tu·ar·y (ak′cho͞o·er′ē) *n. pl.* **·ar·ies** One who specializes in the mathematics of insurance; esp., an official statistician of an insurance company. [< L *actuarius* clerk < *actus.* See ACT.] —**ac·tu·ar·i·al** (ak′cho͞o·âr′ē·əl) *adj.* —**ac′tu·ar′i·al·ly** *adv.*

ac·tu·ate (ak′cho͞o·āt) *v.t.* **·at·ed, ·at·ing 1** To set into action or motion. **2** To incite or influence to action: [< Med.L *actuare* < L *actus* a doing. See ACT.] —**ac′tu·a′tion, ac′tu·a′tor** *n.*

a·cu·i·ty (ə·kyo͞o′ə·tē) *n.* Acuteness; sharpness. [< L *acus* needle]

a·cu·men (ə·kyo͞o′mən, ak′yo͞o·mən) *n.* Quickness of insight or discernment; keenness of intellect. [< L, sharpness (of the mind) < *acuere* sharpen] —**Syn.** acuteness, cleverness, keenness, insight.

a·cu·mi·nate (ə·kyo͞o′mə·nāt) *v.t.* **·nat·ed, ·nat·ing** To sharpen; make pointed. —*adj.* (ə·kyo͞o′mə·nit, -nāt) Ending in a long tapering point, as a leaf, feather, fin, etc. Also **a·cu′mi·nat′ed.** [< L *acumen.* See ACUMEN.] —**a·cu′mi·na′tion** *n.* • See LEAF.

ac·u·punc·ture (ak′yo͞o·pungk′chər) *n.* The Chinese art of traditional medicine in which needles are inserted at specific points through the skin to treat disease and induce anesthesia. [<L *acus* needle + PUNCTURE]

a·cute (ə·kyo͞ot′) *adj.* 1 Keenly discerning or sensitive. 2 Affecting keenly; poignant; intense. 3 Critical; crucial: an *acute* lack of power. 4 Coming to a crisis quickly: *acute* appendicitis. 5 Shrill; of high pitch. 6 Less than 90° in measure: an *acute* angle. 7 Sharply pointed; not blunt. [< L *acuere* sharpen] **—a·cute′ly** *adv.* **—a·cute′ness** *n.* • See ANGLE.

acute accent A mark (′) used to indicate: 1 Primary stress of a sound or syllable. 2 Rhythmical stress, as in poetry. 3 Vowel quality or length.

-acy *suffix* Quality, state or condition: *fallacy, celibacy.* [<L *-acia,* or <Gk. *-ateia*]

a·cy·clo·vir (ā·sī′klə·vir) *n.* An antiviral drug used in the treatment of genital herpes.

ad (ad) *n. Informal* 1 An advertisement. 2 In tennis, advantage.

ad- *prefix* To; toward; near: *adhere, advert.* Also **a-, ab-, ac-, af-, ag-, al-, an-, ap-, ar-, as-, at-,** before various consonants. [<L *ad-* <*ad* to]

A.D. year of our Lord (L *anno Domini*).

A.D.A. American Dental Association; Americans for Democratic Action.

ad·age (ad′ij) *n.* A saying or proverb. [<L *adagium*]

a·da·gio (ə·dä′jō, -zhē·ō) *Music adj.* Slow. —*n.* An adagio composition, movement, etc. —*adv.* Slowly. [<Ital. *adagio,* lit., at ease]

Ad·am (ad′əm) The first man, progenitor of the human race. **—the old Adam** Unregenerate or depraved human nature. **—A·dam·ic** (ə·dam′ik) *adj.*

ad·a·mant (ad′ə·mant, -mənt) *n.* In legends, a very hard but imaginary mineral. —*adj.* 1 Very hard. 2 Immovable and unyielding, as in purpose. [<Gk *adamas* the hardest metal (hence, unyielding)] **—ad·a·man·tine** (ad′a·man′tin, -tēn, -tīn) *adj.*

Adam's apple The projection of the thyroid cartilage at the front of the neck, conspicuous in men.

a·dapt (ə·dapt′) *v.t.* 1 To make suitable, as by changing: to *adapt* a novel for the theater. 2 To modify (oneself) to conform to a situation or environment. —*v.i.* 3 To become adjusted to a circumstance or environment. [<L *ad-* to + *aptare* fit]

a·dapt·a·ble (ə·dap′tə·bəl) *adj.* 1 Capable of being adapted. 2 Able to adapt, as to new circumstances. **—a·dapt′a·bil′i·ty, a·dapt′a·ble·ness** *n.*

ad·ap·ta·tion (ad′əp·tā′shən) *n.* 1 The act of adapting or the state of being adapted. 2 Something adapted.

a·dapt·er (ə·dap′tər) *n.* 1 A person or thing that adapts. 2 Any device designed to connect two pieces of apparatus, or to broaden the use or application of another device. Also **a·dap′tor.**

a·dap·tive (ə·dap′tiv) *adj.* Capable of, fit for, or manifesting adaptation. **—a·dap′tive·ly** *adv.* **—a·dap′tive·ness** *n.*

A.D.C., a.d.c., aide-de-camp.

add (ad) *v.t.* 1 To join or unite, so as to increase the importance, size, quantity or number: with *to.* 2 To find the sum of, as a column of figures; unite in a total. 3 To say or write further. —*v.i.* 4 To produce an increase in: with *to:* His new duties *added* to his worries. 5 To perform the arithmetical operation of addition. **—add up** 1 To accumulate to a total. 2 *Informal.* To make sense. **—add up to** *Informal* To signify; mean. [<L *ad-* to + *dare* give] **—add′a·ble, add′i·ble** *adj.*

add. addendum; addition; additional; address.

ad·dax (ad′aks) *n.* A North African and Arabian antelope. [<L <native African word]

ad·dend (ad′end, ə·dend′) *n. Math.* A number or element to be added to another.

ad·den·dum (ə·den′dəm) *n. pl.* **·da** (-də) A thing added, or to be added. [<L *addere* add]

ad·der[1] (ad′ər) *n.* 1 A viper, esp. the common European viper. 2 One of various other snakes, as the puff adder, the milk snake, etc. [<OE *nædre* (*a nadder* in ME becoming *an adder*)]

add·er[2] (ad′ər) *n.* One who or that which performs addition, esp. a computer circuit.

ad·der's-tongue (ad′ərz·tung′) *n.* 1 Any of a genus of ferns having a single sterile frond and a spore-bearing spike. 2 Dog's-tooth violet.

ad·dict (ə·dikt′) *v.t.* 1 To give or devote (oneself) persistently or habitually: usu. used in the passive voice with *to:* He is *addicted* to drugs. 2 To cause to pursue or practice continuously: with *to:* This task *addicted* him to obscure research. —*n.* (ad′ikt) One who is addicted to some habit, esp. to the use of narcotic drugs. [<L *addicere* assign, devote to] **—ad·dict′ed·ness** *n.*

ad·dic·tion (ə·dik′shən) *n.* The state of being addicted to a habit, as to the taking of narcotic drugs.

ad·dic·tive (ə·dik′tiv) *adj.* Of, pertaining to, causing, or characterized by addiction.

ad·di·tion (ə·dish′ən) *n.* 1 The act of adding. 2 That which is added, esp. a room, annex, etc. 3 *Math.* An operation defined for every pair of elements or numbers of a set, whereby each pair is associated with a unique element of the same set called the sum. **—ad·di′tion·al** *adj.* **—ad·di′tion·al·ly** *adv.*

ad·di·tive (ad′ə·tiv) *n.* A substance added or to be added to a product or device. —*adj.* 1 That is to be added. 2 *Math.* Pertaining to addition. **—ad′di·tive·ly** *adv.*

ad·dle (ad′l) *v.t.* & *v.i.* **ad·dled, ad·dling** 1 To make or become spoiled. 2 To make or become muddled or mixed up. —*adj.* 1 Spoiled, as eggs; rotten. 2 Confused; mixed up. [<OE *adela* liquid filth]

ad·dle·brained (ad′l·brānd′) *adj.* Confused; mixed up. Also **ad′dle·head′ed, ad′dle·pat′ed.**

ad·dress (ə·dres′) *v.t.* **ad·dressed, ad·dress·ing** 1 To speak to. 2 To deliver a set discourse to. 3 To direct, as spoken or written words, to the attention of: with *to:* He *addressed* his prayers to his God. 4 To direct the attention, energy, or force of (oneself): with *to:* He *addressed* himself to the task. 5 To mark with a destination, as a letter. 6 To consign, as a cargo to a merchant. 7 To aim or direct the club at (a golf ball). —*n.* (ə·dres′, *esp. for defs. 3 & 4* ad′. res) 1 The act of addressing or speaking to a person or persons. 2 A formal speech. 3 The writing on an envelope, etc., directing something to a person or place. 4 The name, place, residence, etc., of a person. 5 Consignment, as of a vessel or cargo. 6 Conversational manner or delivery. 7 *Usu. pl.* Any courteous or devoted attention; wooing. 8 Adroitness; tact. 9 In the memory or storage element of a computer, a particular location or its designation. [<L *ad-* to + *directus* straight] **—ad·dress′er, ad·dres′sor** *n.*

ad·dress·ee (ad′res·ē′, ə·dres′ē′) *n.* One to whom mail, etc., is addressed.

ad·duce (ə·dʸo͞os′) *v.t.* **ad·duced, ad·duc·ing** To bring forward for proof or consideration, as an example. [<L *ad-* to + *ducere* lead] **—ad·duce′a·ble, ad·duc′i·ble** *adj.* **—Syn.** cite, allege, advance.

ad·duct (ə·dukt′) *v.t. Physiol.* To draw a part of the body toward the median axis of the body or toward a neighboring part. [<L *adducere.* See ADDUCE.] **—ad·duc′tion** *n.* **—ad·duc′tive** *adj.*

ad·duc·tor (ə·duk′tər) *n. Physiol.* An adducting muscle.

-ade *suffix of nouns* 1 Act or action of: *cannonade.* 2 A person or group concerned in an action or process: *cavalcade.* 3 Product of: *pomade.* 4 Drink made from: *lemonade.* [<L *-ata,* fem. pp. ending]

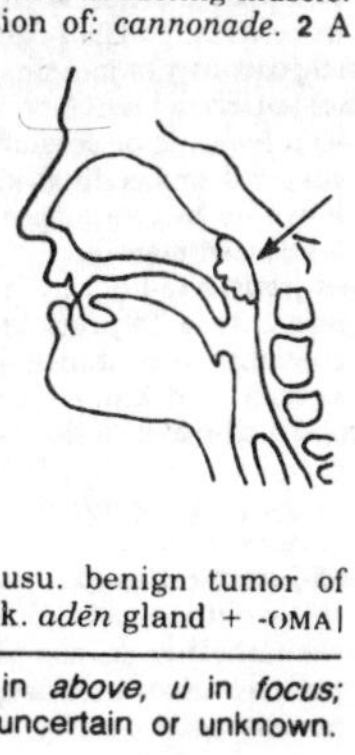

A·den (äd′n, ād′n) A former British colony, part of the People's Democratic Republic of Yemen since 1968.

ad·e·noid (ad′ə·noid) *adj.* Of or like a gland; glandular: also **ad′e·noi′dal.** —*n. Usu. pl.* An enlarged lymphoid growth behind the pharynx. [<Gk. *adēn* gland + -OID]

ad·e·no·ma (ad′ə·nō′mə) *n.* A usu. benign tumor of glandular origin or structure. [<Gk. *adēn* gland + -OMA]

a·dept (ə·dept′) *adj.* Highly skillful; proficient. **—ad·ept** (ad′ept, ə·dept′) *n.* One fully skilled in any art; an expert. [< L *adeptus* pp. of *adipisci* attain] **—a·dept′ly** *adv.* **—a·dept′ness** *n.*

ad·e·quate (ad′ə·kwit) *adj.* **1** Equal to what is required; suitable; sufficient. **2** Barely acceptable or sufficient. [< L *ad-* to + *aequus* equal] **—ad·e·qua·cy** (ad′ə·kwə·sē), **ad′e·quate·ness** *n.* **—ad′e·quate·ly** *adv.*

ad·here (ad·hir′) *v.i.* **ad·hered, ad·her·ing 1** To stick fast or together. **2** To be attached or devoted, as to a party or faith. **3** To follow closely or without deviation. [< L *ad-* to + *haerere* stick] **—ad·her′ence** *n.*

ad·her·ent (ad·hir′ənt) *adj.* Clinging or sticking fast. —*n.* One who is devoted or attached, as to a cause or leader; a follower: also **ad·her′er. —ad·her′ent·ly** *adv.*

ad·he·sion (ad·hē′zhən) *n.* **1** The act of sticking together or the state of being stuck together. **2** Assent; concurrence. **3** Close connection, as of ideas. **4** *Physics* The force of attraction between molecules of unlike substances in contact. **5** *Med.* Abnormal surface union of dissimilar tissues as a result of inflammation, etc. [< L *adhaerere.* See ADHERE.]

ad·he·sive (ad·hē′siv) *adj.* **1** Tending to adhere; sticky; clinging. **2** Prepared to adhere; gummed. —*n.* A substance that promotes adhesion. **—ad·he′sive·ly** *adv.* **—ad·he′sive·ness** *n.*

ad hoc (ad hok′, hōk′) With respect to this (particular thing); for this purpose. [L]

ad·i·a·bat·ic (ad′ē·ə·bat′ik, ā′dē·ə-) *adj. Physics* Without gain or loss of heat, as a thermodynamic system or reaction. [< Gk. *adiabatos* impassable]

a·dieu (ə·dyōō′; *Fr.* á·dyœ′) *n. pl.* **a·dieus,** *Fr.* **a·dieux** (á·dyœ′) A farewell. —*interj.* Good-by; farewell: literally, "to God (I commend you)." [< F < *à* to + *dieu* God]

ad in·fi·ni·tum (ad in′fə·nī′təm) Endlessly; limitlessly. [L]

ad in·ter·im (ad in′tər·im) In the meantime. [L]

a·di·os (ä′dē·ōs′, ad′ē·ōs′; *Sp.* ä·dyōs′) *interj.* Farewell; good-by: literally, "to God (I commend you)." [Sp. < *a* to + *dios* God]

ad·i·pose (ad′ə·pōs) *adj.* Of or pertaining to fat; fatty: also **ad·i·pous** (ad′ə·pəs). —*n.* Fat. [< L *adeps* fat] **—ad′i·pose′ness, ad·i·pos·i·ty** (ad′ə·pos′ə·tē) *n.*

adj. adjective; adjunct; adjustment; adjutant.

ad·ja·cent (ə·jā′sənt) *adj.* Lying near or close at hand. [< L *ad-* near + *jacere* lie] **—ad·ja′cence, ad·ja′cen·cy,** *n.* **—ad·ja′cent·ly** *adv.* **—Syn.** adjoining, contiguous, abutting, bordering.

adjacent angle Either of a pair of angles having a common vertex and a common side. See ANGLE.

ad·jec·ti·val (aj′ik·tī′vəl, aj′ik·ti·vəl) *adj.* Of or like an adjective. **—ad′jec·ti′val·ly** *adv.*

ad·jec·tive (aj′ik·tiv) *n.* **1** *Gram.* A word used to limit or qualify a noun or other substantive. **2** A phrase or clause used similarly. —*adj.* Of, pertaining to, or functioning as an adjective. [< L *adjectivus* that is added < *adjicere* add to] **—ad′jec·tive·ly** *adv.*

ad·join (ə·join′) *v.t.* **1** To be next to; border upon. **2** To join to; append; unite: with *to.* —*v.i.* **3** To lie close together; be in contact. [< L *ad-* to + *jungere* join]

ad·join·ing (ə·join′ing) *adj.* Lying next; contiguous.

ad·journ (ə·jûrn′) *v.t.* **1** To put off to another day or place, as a meeting or session; postpone. —*v.i.* **2** To postpone or suspend proceedings for a specified time. **3** *Informal* To move or go to another place. [< LL *adjurnare* set a day] **—ad·journ′ment** *n.*

ad·judge (ə·juj′) *v.t.* **1** To determine or decide judicially, as a case. **2** To pronounce or order by law; find; rule. **3** To condemn or sentence: with *to.* **4** To award by law, as damages. **5** To deem; regard. [< L *ad-* to + *judicare* judge]

ad·ju·di·cate (ə·jōō′də·kāt) *v.* **·cat·ed, ·cat·ing** *v.t.* **1** To determine judicially, as a case; adjudge. —*v.i.* **2** To act as a judge. [< L *adjudicare.* See ADJUDGE.] **—ad·ju′di·ca′tion, ad·ju′di·ca′tor** *n.*

ad·junct (aj′ungkt) *n.* **1** Something connected to another thing but in a subordinate position. **2** A person associated with another person in an auxiliary or subordinate relation; an associate; assistant. **3** *Gram.* A modifier. **4** Any nonessential quality or property. —*adj.* Joined subordinately; auxiliary. [< L *adjungere.* See ADJOIN.] **—ad·junc·tive** (ə·jungk′tiv) *adj.* **—ad·junc′tive·ly** *adv.*

ad·jure (ə·jŏŏr′) *v.t.* **ad·jured, ad·jur·ing 1** To charge or entreat solemnly, as under oath or penalty. **2** To appeal to earnestly. [< L *ad-* to + *jurare* swear] **—ad·ju·ra·tion** (aj′ŏŏ·rā′shən), **ad·jur′er, ad·ju′ror** *n.* **—ad·jur·a·to·ry** (ə·jŏŏr′ə·tor′ē, -tō′rē) *adj.*

ad·just (ə·just′) *v.t.* **1** To arrange or regulate so as to produce a desired accuracy, condition, fit, etc. **2** To harmonize or compose, as differences. **3** To arrange in order; systematize. **4** To determine an amount to be paid, as in settling an insurance claim. —*v.i.* **5** To adapt oneself; conform, as to a new environment: to *adjust* to civilian life. [< L *ad-* to + *juxta* near] **—ad·just′a·ble** *adj.* **—ad·just′er, ad·jus′tor** *n.* **—ad·jus′tive** *adj.*

ad·just·ment (ə·just′mənt) *n.* **1** The act of adjusting or the condition of being adjusted. **2** A means or device whereby something may be adjusted. **3** A determining of an amount to be paid, as in an insurance claim.

ad·ju·tant (aj′ə·tənt) *n.* **1** *Mil.* A staff officer who assists and issues the administrative orders of a commanding officer. **2** A large stork of India and Africa. [< L *adjutare* to assist] **—ad′ju·tan·cy, ad′ju·tant·ship** *n.*

adjutant general *pl.* **adjutants general** The adjutant of a division or larger military unit.

ad-lib (ad′lib′) *Informal v.t. & v.i.* **-libbed, -lib·bing** To improvise, as words, gestures, or music not called for in the original script or score. —*n.* An instance of this. [< AD LIBITUM]

ad lib·i·tum (ad lib′ə·təm) **1** At will; as one pleases. **2** *Music* Freely; at the discretion of the performer: also **ad lib.** [L]

Adm. Admiral; Admiralty.

ad·meas·ure (ad·mezh′ər) *v.t.* **·ured, ·ur·ing** To apportion. [< LL *ad-* to + *mensurare.* See MEASURE.] **—ad·meas′ure·ment, ad·meas′ur·er** *n.*

ad·min·is·ter (ad·min′is·tər) *v.t.* **1** To have the charge or direction of; manage. **2** To provide with; apply, as medicine or treatment. **3** To inflict; dispense, as punishment. **4** *Law* To act as executor of, as an estate. **5** To tender, as an oath. —*v.i.* **6** To be helpful; minister: with *to.* **7** To carry out the functions of an administrator. [< L *administrare* minister to] **—ad·min·is·te·ri·al** (-min′is·tir′ē·əl), **ad·min·is·tra·ble** (-min′is·trə·bəl) *adj.* **—ad·min′is·trant** *adj., n.*

ad·min·is·trate (ad·min′is·trāt) *v.t.* **·trat·ed, ·trat·ing** To administer.

ad·min·is·tra·tion (ad·min′is·trā′shən) *n.* **1** The act of administering, or the state of being administered. **2 a** The executive department of a government, school, etc. **b** Their policies. **c** Their term of office.

ad·min·is·tra·tive (ad·min′is·trā′tiv) *adj.* Pertaining to administration; executive. **—ad·min′is·tra′tive·ly** *adv.*

ad·min·is·tra·tor (ad·min′is·trā′tər) *n.* **1** One who administers something; an executive. **2** *Law* One commissioned by a competent court to administer the personal property of a deceased or incompetent person. **—ad·min′is·tra′tor·ship** *n.* **—ad·min·is·tra·trix** (ad·min′is·trā′triks) *n. Fem.* (*pl.* **·tra·trix·es** or **·tra·tri·ces**)

ad·mi·ra·ble (ad′mər·ə·bəl) *adj.* Worthy of admiration or praise; excellent. [< L *admirari.* See ADMIRE.] **—ad′mi·ra·bil′i·ty, ad′mi·ra·ble·ness** *n.* **—ad′mi·ra·bly** *adv.*

ad·mi·ral (ad′mər·əl) *n.* See GRADE. [< Ar. *amīr-al* commander of the]

ad·mi·ral·ty (ad′mər·əl·tē) *n. pl.* **·ties 1** The office or functions of an admiral. **2** The branch of the judiciary in charge of maritime affairs.

ad·mi·ra·tion (ad′mə·rā′shən) *n.* **1** Wonder combined with pleasure and approval in view of anything rare, great, excellent, etc. **2** That which excites pleased approval.

ad·mire (ad·mīr′) *v.* **ad·mired, ad·mir·ing** *v.t.* **1** To regard with wonder, pleasure, and approval. **2** To have respect or esteem for. —*v.i.* **3** To feel or express admiration. [< L *ad-* at + *mirari* wonder] **—ad·mir′er** *n.* **—ad·mir′ing** *adj.* **—ad·mir′ing·ly** *adv.* **—Syn. 1** approve, applaud, enjoy. **2** honor, revere.

ad·mis·si·ble (ad·mis′ə·bəl) *adj.* **1** Such as may be admitted; allowable. **2** Worthy of being considered. **—ad·mis′si·bil′i·ty** *n.* **—ad·mis′si·bly** *adv.*

ad·mis·sion (ad·mish′ən) *n.* **1** The act of admitting, or the state of being admitted. **2** A right to enter. **3** An entrance fee. **4** An acknowledging or confessing. **5** That which is acknowledged or confessed. **—ad·mis′sive** *adj.*

ad·mit (ad·mit′) *v.* **ad·mit·ted, ad·mit·ting** *v.t.* **1** To grant entrance to. **2** To be the means or channel of admission to; let in: This key will *admit* you. **3** To have room for; contain. **4** To leave room for; permit: His impatience *admits* no delay. **5** To concede or grant. **6** To acknowledge or avow. **7** To allow to join. *—v.i.* **8** To give scope or warrant: with *of:* This problem *admits* of several solutions. **9** To afford entrance; open on: with *to.* [<L *ad-* to + *mittere* send, let go]

ad·mit·tance (ad·mit′əns) *n.* **1** The act of admitting or the state or fact of being admitted. **2** The right or permission to enter.

ad·mit·ted·ly (ad·mit′id·lē) *adv.* Confessedly.

ad·mix (ad·miks′) *v.t.* **ad·mixed** or **ad·mixt, ad·mix·ing** To mix with something else.

ad·mix·ture (ad·miks′chər) *n.* **1** A mixture. **2** The thing added in mixing.

ad·mon·ish (ad·mon′ish) *v.t.* **1** To scold or reprove gently. **2** To caution against danger or error; warn. **3** To exhort; urge. [<L *ad-* to + *monere* warn] **—ad·mon′ish·er** *n.* **—Syn. 1** rebuke, reprimand, censure. **2** counsel, advise.

ad·mo·ni·tion (ad′mə·nish′ən) *n.* **1** The act of admonishing. **2** A gentle reproof. Also **ad·mon′ish·ment.**

ad·mon·i·tor (ad·mon′ə·tər) *n.* One who admonishes. **—ad·mon′i·to′ry** (-tôr′ē, -tō′rē) *adj.*

ad nau·se·am (ad nô′zē·əm, -sē-) So as to nauseate or produce disgust. [L]

a·do (ə·do͞o′) *n.* Bustling activity; fuss; trouble. [ME *at do* to do]

a·do·be (ə·dō′bē) *n.* **1** A sun-dried brick. **2** The mixed earth or clay of which such bricks are made. **3** A building made of such bricks. *—adj.* Composed of adobe. [<Sp. *adobar* to plaster]

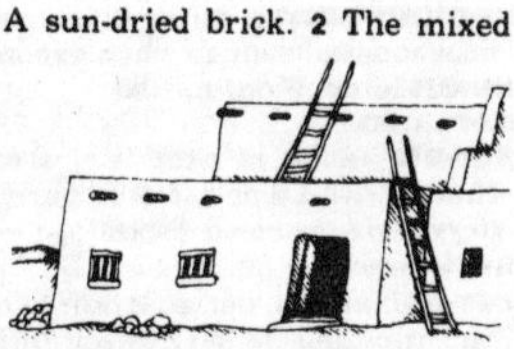

Adobe house

ad·o·les·cence (ad′ə·les′əns) *n.* **1** The condition or quality of being adolescent. **2** The period of growth from puberty to maturity.

ad·o·les·cent (ad′ə·les′ənt) *adj.* **1** Approaching maturity. **2** Characteristic of or pertaining to youth. *—n.* A person in the period of adolescence. [<L *adolescere* grow up]

A·don·is (ə·don′is, ə·dō′nis) *Gk. Myth.* A youth beloved by Venus for his beauty. *—n.* Any very handsome youth or man.

a·dopt (ə·dopt′) *v.t.* **1** To take into a new relationship, esp. to take legally and raise as one's own child. **2** To take (a course of action) and follow as one's own. **3** To use as one's own, as a phrase, practice, etc. **4** To vote to accept. [<L *ad-* to + *optare* choose] **—a·dopt′a·ble** *adj.* **—a·dopt′er, a·dop·tion** (ə·dop′shən) *n.*

a·dop·tive (ə·dop′tiv) *adj.* **1** Pertaining to adoption. **2** Related by adoption. **—a·dop′tive·ly** *adv.*

a·dor·a·ble (ə·dôr′ə·bəl, ə·dōr′-) *adj. Informal* Attractive; pretty; charming. **—a·dor′a·bil′i·ty, a·dor′a·ble·ness** *n.* **—a·dor′a·bly** *adv.*

ad·o·ra·tion (ad′ə·rā′shən) *n.* **1** The act of worshiping a divine being. **2** Profound love and devotion.

a·dore (ə·dôr′, ə·dōr′) *v.t.* **a·dored, a·dor·ing 1** To worship as divine. **2** To love or honor with intense devotion. **3** *Informal* To like very much. [<L *ad-* to + *orare* speak, pray] **—a·dor′er** *n.*

a·dorn (ə·dôrn′) *v.t.* **1** To be an ornament to; increase the beauty of. **2** To decorate with ornaments. [<L *ad-* to + *ornare* furnish] **—a·dorn′er, a·dorn′ment** *n.*

ad·re·nal (ə·drē′nəl) *adj.* **1** Near the kidneys. **2** Of or from the adrenal glands. *—n.* An adrenal gland. [<AD- + L *renes* kidneys]

adrenal gland Either of two small ductless glands situated above each kidney.

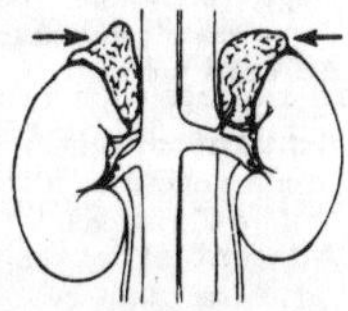

Adrenal glands

Ad·ren·a·lin (ə·dren′ə·lin) *n.* EPINEPHRINE: a trade name. Also **ad·ren′a·lin, ad·ren′a·line.**

ad·re·no·cor·ti·co·tro·pic (ə·drē′nō·kôr′ti·kō·trō′pik) *adj.* Acting on the cortex of the adrenal gland.

a·drift (ə·drift′) *adv.* & *adj.* **1** Without moorings. **2** Without a goal or purpose.

a·droit (ə·droit′) *adj.* Skillful; dexterous; expert. [<F *à* to + *droit* right] **—a·droit′ly** *adv.* **—a·droit′ness** *n.* **—Syn.** clever, deft, apt, handy.

ad·sorb (ad·sôrb′, -zôrb′) *v.t.* To hold by adsorption. [<AD- + L *sorbere* suck in] **—ad·sor′bent** *n.*

ad·sorp·tion (ad·sôrp′shən, -zôrp′-) *n.* Retention of a gas or soluble substance upon the surface of a solid. [<ADSORB] **—ad·sorp′tive** *adj.*

ad·u·late (aj′ə·lāt) *v.t.* **·lat·ed, ·lat·ing** To flatter or praise extravagantly. [<L *adulari* to fawn] **—ad′u·la′tion, ad′u·la′tor** *n.* **—ad·u·la·to·ry** (aj′ə·lə·tôr′ē, -tō′rē) *adj.*

a·dult (ə·dult′, ad′ult) *n.* **1** A person who has attained the age of maturity or legal majority. **2** *Biol.* A fully developed animal or plant. *—adj.* **1** Pertaining to mature life; full-grown. **2** Of or for adults. [<L *adolescere* grow up] **—a·dult′·hood, a·dult′ness** *n.*

a·dul·ter·ant (ə·dul′tər·ənt) *n.* An adulterating substance. *—adj.* Adulterating.

a·dul·ter·ate (ə·dul′tər·āt) *v.t.* **·at·ed, ·at·ing** To make impure or inferior by adding other or baser ingredients; corrupt. *—adj.* (ə·dul′tər·it) **1** Adulterated; corrupted. **2** Adulterous. [<L *adulterare* corrupt < *ad-* to + *alter* other, different] **—a·dul′ter·a′tion, a·dul′ter·a′tor** *n.*

a·dul·ter·ous (ə·dul′tər·əs) *adj.* Of, pertaining to, or given to adultery; illicit. **—a·dul′ter·ous·ly** *adv.*

a·dul·ter·y (ə·dul′tər·ē) *n. pl.* **·ter·ies** The voluntary sexual intercourse of two persons, either or both of whom are married but not to each other. [<L *adulterare* to adulterate] **—a·dul′ter·er** *n.* **—a·dul′ter·ess** *n. Fem.*

ad·um·brate (ad′əm·brāt, ə·dum′-) *v.t.* **·brat·ed, ·brat·ing 1** To outline sketchily. **2** To foreshadow; prefigure. **3** To obscure or overshadow. [<L *ad-* to + *umbrare* shade] **—ad′um·bra′tion** *n.* **—ad·um′bra·tive** (-brə·tiv) *adj.*

adv. adverb; adverbial; advertisement.

ad va·lo·rem (ad və·lôr′əm, -lō′rəm) According to value. [L]

ad·vance (ad·vans′, -väns′) *v.* **ad·vanced, ad·vanc·ing** *v.t.* **1** To move forward in position or place. **2** To put in a better or more advantageous situation. **3** To further; promote. **4** To make occur earlier; accelerate. **5** To offer; propose. **6** To raise in rate or price. **7** To pay (money) before due. **8** To lend. *—v.i.* **9** To move or go forward: The armies *advance* on all fronts. **10** To make progress; rise or improve. *—adj.* Being ahead or before in time or place. *—n.* **1** The act of advancing. **2** Progress; improvement. **3** An increase or rise, as of prices. **4** Anything paid beforehand; also, a loan. **5** An overture; proposal: His *advances* were rejected. **—in advance 1** In front. **2** Before due; beforehand. [<L *ab-* away + *ante* before] **—ad·vanc′er** *n.*

ad·vanced (ad·vanst′, -vänst′) *adj.* **1** Being in advance of others, as in progress, degree of difficulty, thought, etc. **2** Far on, as in time. **3** Higher: *advanced* prices.

ad·vance·ment (ad·vans′mənt, -väns′-) *n.* **1** The act of advancing, or the state of being advanced. **2** Progression; furtherance; promotion. **3** A payment of money before it is due.

ad·van·tage (ad·van′tij, -vän′-) *n.* **1** Anything favorable to success. **2** Superiority, as of position, rank, etc. **3** Gain or benefit. **4** In tennis, the first point scored after deuce. **—take advantage of 1** To use so as to benefit. **2** To use or impose upon for selfish purposes. **—to advantage** So as to bring about the best results. *—v.t.* **·taged, ·tag·ing** To be a benefit or service to. [<OF *avant* before <L *ab ante* from before]

---

add, āce, câre, pälm; end, ēven; it, īce; odd, ōpen, ôrder; to͝ok, po͞ol; up, bûrn; ə = *a* in *above, u* in *focus;* yo͞o = *u* in *fuse;* oil; pout; check; go; ring; thin; this; zh, *vision.* < derived from; ? origin uncertain or unknown.

ad·van·ta·geous (ad′vən·tā′jəs) *adj.* Affording advantage; profitable; beneficial. **—ad′van·ta′geous·ly** *adv.* **—ad′van·ta′geous·ness** *n.*

ad·vent (ad′vent) *n.* A coming or arrival. [<L *ad-* to + *venire* come]

Ad·vent (ad′vent) *n.* **1** The birth of Christ. **2** The second coming of Christ. **3** The season including the four Sundays before Christmas.

Ad·vent·ist (ad′ven·tist, ad·ven′-) *n.* A member of a religious sect that believes the second coming of Christ is near at hand. **—Ad′vent·ism** *n.*

ad·ven·ti·tious (ad′vən·tish′əs) *adj.* Not inherent; extrinsic; accidental. [<L *adventicius* coming from abroad, foreign] **—ad′ven·ti′tious·ly** *adv.* **—ad′ven·ti′tious·ness** *n.*

ad·ven·ture (ad·ven′chər) *n.* **1 a** A hazardous or exciting experience. **b** A daring feat. **2** A commercial venture; a speculation. *—v.i.* **·tured, ·tur·ing** To run risks. [<L *adventura (res)* (a thing) about to happen <*advenire* to come to]

ad·ven·tur·er (ad·ven′chər·ər) *n.* **1** A seeker of adventures. **2** A speculator in finance. **3** A person who tries to gain wealth, social position, etc., by questionable means.

ad·ven·tur·ism (ad·ven′chər·iz′əm) *n.* Aggressive and incautious action or conduct often involving grave risk, esp. in the execution of national policy. **—ad·ven′tur·ist** *adj., n.*

ad·ven·tur·ous (ad·ven′chər·əs) *adj.* **1** Disposed to seek adventures or take risks. Also **ad·ven′ture·some** (-səm). **2** Attended with risk; hazardous. **—ad·ven′tur·ous·ly** *adv.* **—ad·ven′tur·ous·ness** *n.*

ad·verb (ad′vûrb) *n.* Any of a class of words used to modify the meaning of a verb, adjective, or other adverb, in regard to time, place, manner, means, cause, degree, etc. [<L *ad-* to + *verbum* verb] **—ad·ver·bi·al** (ad·vûr′bē·əl) *adj.* **—ad·ver′bi·al·ly** *adv.*

ad·ver·sar·y (ad′vər·ser′ē) *n. pl.,* **·sar·ies** An opponent or enemy. [<L *adversarius,* lit., one turned towards]

ad·ver·sa·tive (ad·vûr′sə·tiv) *adj.* Expressing opposition or antithesis. **—ad·ver′sa·tive·ly** *adv.*

ad·verse (ad·vûrs′, ad′vûrs) *adj.* **1** Opposing or opposed. **2** Unfriendly. **3** Harmful; detrimental. **4** Opposite. [<L *ad-* to + *vertere* turn] **—ad·verse′ly** *adv.* **—ad·verse′ness** *n.*

ad·ver·si·ty (ad·vûr′sə·tē) *n. pl.,* **·ties 1** A condition of hardship or misfortune. **2** *Usu. pl.* An instance of misfortune. **—Syn. 2** calamity, disaster, mishap, affliction, blow.

ad·vert (ad·vûrt′) *v.i.* To take notice; refer: with *to.* [<L *ad-* to + *vertere* turn] **—ad·ver′tence, ad·ver′ten·cy** *n.*

ad·ver·tent (ad·vûr′tənt) *adj.* Giving attention; heedful. **—ad·ver′tent·ly** *adv.*

ad·ver·tise (ad′vər·tīz, ad′vər·tīz′) *v.* **·tised, ·tis·ing** *v.t.* **1** To or proclaim the qualities of, as by publication or broadcasting, generally in order to sell. **2** To call attention to. *—v.i.* **3** To inquire by public notice, as in a newspaper: with *for:* to *advertise* for a house. **4** To distribute or publish advertisements. [<MF *advertir* warn, give notice to <L *advertere.* See ADVERT.] **—ad′ver·tis′er** *n.*

ad·ver·tise·ment (ad′vər·tīz′mənt, ad·vûr′tis·mənt, -tiz-) *n.* A public notice, as of products for sale, events, etc.

ad·ver·tis·ing (ad′vər·tī′zing) *n.* **1** Any system or method of attracting public notice to an event or product. **2** The business of preparing advertisements. Also **ad′ver·tiz′ing.**

ad·ver·tor·i·al (ad·vər·tôr′e·əl, -to·re-) *n.* An editorial that includes elements of a commercial advertising message. [ADVERT(ISING)+(EDIT)ORIAL]

ad·vice (ad·vīs′) *n.* **1** Counsel or a suggestion as to a course of action. **2** *Often pl.* Information; notification. [<L *ad-* to + *visum,* p.p. of *videre* see]

ad·vis·a·ble (ad·vī′zə·bəl) *adj.* Recommended; expedient. **—ad·vis′a·bil′i·ty, ad·vis′a·ble·ness** *n.* **—ad·vis′a·bly** *adv.*

ad·vise (ad·vīz′) *v.* **ad·vised, ad·vis·ing** *v.t.* **1** To give advice to; counsel. **2** To recommend: to *advise* a course of action. **3** To notify; inform, as of a transaction: with *of.* *—v.i.* **4** To take counsel: with *with:* He *advised* with his lawyer. **5** To give advice. **—ad·vis′er, ad·vis′or** *n.*

ad·vised (ad·vīzd′) *adj.* **1** Done with deliberation and forethought. **2** Counseled. **3** Informed.

ad·vis·ed·ly (ad·vī′zid·lē) *adv.* With forethought or advice; not hastily.

ad·vise·ment (ad·vīz′mənt) *n.* Consultation; deliberation.

ad·vi·so·ry (ad·vī′zər·ē) *adj.* **1** Having power to advise. **2** Containing or given as advice.

ad·vo·ca·cy (ad′və·kə·sē) *n.* The act of advocating or pleading a cause; a defense.

ad·vo·cate (ad′və·kāt) *v.t.* **·cat·ed, ·cat·ing** To speak or write in favor of. *—n.* (ad′və·kit, -kāt) One who defends or supports something or someone. [<L *advocatus* one summoned to another] **—ad′vo·ca′tor** *n.* **—ad·voc·a·to·ry** (ad·vok′ə·tôr′ē, -tō′rē) *adj.*

advt. advertisement.

adz (adz) *n.* A hand cutting tool having its usu. curved blade at right angles with its handle, used for dressing timber, etc. Also **adze.** [<OE *adesa*]

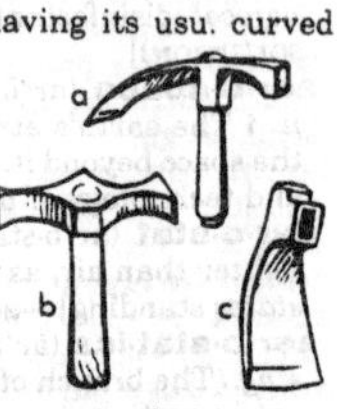

Adzes
a. sculptor's.
b. cooper's.
c. carpenter's.

ae- For words not entered below, see under E-.

æ A ligature of Latin origin, sometimes retained in Greek and Latin proper names and used in certain scientific terms, but in modern spelling usu. represented by *e.*

AEC, A.E.C. Atomic Energy Commission.

AEF, A.E.F. American Expeditionary Force.

ae·gis (ē′jis) *Gk. Myth.* The shield of Zeus, used also by Athena. *—n.* **1** Any protection. **2** Patronage; sponsorship.

-aemia -EMIA.

Ae·ne·as (i·nē′əs) *Gk. & Rom. Myth.* A Trojan who, after the sack of Troy, wandered for seven years before settling in Italy.

Ae·ne·id (i·nē′id) *n.* A Latin epic poem by Virgil narrating the adventures of Aeneas.

ae·o·li·an (ē·ō′lē·ən) *adj.* EOLIAN.

aeolian harp A stringed instrument constructed to produce musical sounds when exposed to a current of air.

ae·on (ē′ən, ē′on) *n.* EON.

aer- AERO-.

aer·ate (âr′āt, ā′ə·rāt) *v.t.* **·at·ed, ·at·ing 1** To supply or charge with air or gas. **2** To purify by exposure to air. **3** To oxygenate, as blood. [<AER(O)-] **—aer·a′tion, aer′a·tor** *n.*

aeri- AERO-.

aer·i·al (âr′ē·əl, ā·ir′ē·əl) *adj.* **1** Of, in, or by the air. **2** Like air; atmospheric. **3** Growing in the air: an *aerial* root. **4** Not real; imaginary; unsubstantial. **5** Existing or performed in the air. **6** Of, by, or for aircraft: *aerial* bombardment. *—n.* (âr′ē·əl) ANTENNA (def. 2). [<L *aer* air] **—aer′i·al·ly** *adv.* • See AIRPLANE.

aer·i·al·ist (âr′ē·əl·ist, ā·ir′ē·əl-) *n.* One who performs on a tightrope, trapeze, etc.

aer·ie (âr′ē, ir′ē) *n.* **1** The nest of a predatory bird, as the eagle, on a crag. **2** The brood or young of such a bird. **3** A house or fortress built on a high place. [<L *area* open space] **—aer′ied** *adj.*

aer·i·fy (âr′ə·fī, ā′ər·ə·fī) *v.t.* **·fied, ·fy·ing 1** To aerate. **2** To change into a gaseous form. **—aer′i·fi·ca′tion** *n.*

aero- *combining form* **1** Air; of the air: *aerodynamics.* **2** Of aircraft or flying. **3** Gas; of gases. [<Gk. *aēr* air]

aer·obe (âr′ōb, ā′ər·ōb) *n.* A microorganism which cannot live without free oxygen. [<AERO- + Gk. *bios* life] **—aer·o′bic** *adj.*

aer·o·bics (âr′ō′biks) *n.pl.* Exercises that involve a workout for the lungs and heart.

aer·o·dy·nam·ics (âr′ō·dī·nam′iks, ā′ər·ō-) *n.pl. (construed as sing.)* The branch of physics that deals with the motion of gases, esp. with the effects of bodies moving through the atmosphere. **—aer′o·dy·nam′ic** *adj.*

aer·o·foil (âr′ə·foil, ā′ər·ə-) *n.* AIRFOIL.

aer·o·me·chan·ics (âr′ō·mə·kan′iks, ā′ər·ō-) *n. pl. (construed as sing.)* The mechanics of air and gases. **—aer′o·me·chan′ic** *adj., n.*

aer·o·naut (âr′ə·nôt, ā′ər·ə-) *n.* The pilot of any aircraft. [<AERO- + Gk. *nautēs* sailor]

aer·o·nau·tics (âr′ə·nô′tiks, ā′ər·ə-) *n.pl. (construed as sing.)* The science and technology that deal with the design, construction, and operation of aircraft. **—aer′o·nau′tic** or **·ti·cal** *adj.*

aer·o·pause (âr′ə·pôz, ā′ər·ə-) *n. Meteorol.* The uppermost region of the atmosphere.

aer·o·plane (âr′ə·plān, ā′ər·ə-) *Chiefly Brit.* AIRPLANE.

aer·o·sol (âr′ə·sōl, -sol, ā′ər·ə-) *n.* A colloidal dispersion of a solid or liquid in a gas. —*adj.* **1** Pertaining to a method of packaging a product under pressure in a valved container so that on release of the valve the contents escape in a spray or foam. **2** Describing a product so packaged: an *aerosol* disinfectant. [< AERO- + SOL(UTION)]

Aerosol bomb

aer·o·space (âr′ō·spās, ā′ər·ō-) *n.* **1** The earth's atmosphere and the space beyond it. **2** The science and technology of aeronautics and space flight.

aer·o·stat (âr′ə·stat, ā′ər·ə-) *n.* Any aircraft which is lighter than air, as a balloon or dirigible. [< AERO- + Gk. *statos* standing] —**aer′o·stat′ic** or **·i·cal** *adj.*

aer·o·stat·ics (âr′ə·stat′iks, ā′ər·ə) *n. pl. (construed as sing.)* The branch of physics that deals with air and gases not in motion.

aer·y (âr′ē, ir′ē)*n.* AERIE.

Aes·cu·la·pi·us (es′kyə·lā′pē·əs) *Rom. Myth.* The god of medicine. —**Aes′cu·la′pi·an** *adj.*

aes·thete (es′thēt) *n.* **1** A person who appreciates beauty, culture, and art. **2** A person possessing an excessive refinement of taste and a pretentious sensibility to art and culture. —**aes·thet·i·cism** (es·thet′ə·siz′əm) *n.*

aes·thet·ic (es·thet′ik) *adj.* **1** Of aesthetics. **2** Of, pertaining to, or appreciating beauty and art. **3** Having or characterized by fine taste. [< Gk. *aisthētikos* of sense perception] Also **aes·thet′i·cal.** —**aes·thet′i·cal·ly** *adv.*

aes·thet·ics (es·thet′iks) *n. pl. (construed as sing.)* The philosophy or study of beauty and art, and the responses they engender. —**aes·the·ti·cian** (es′thə·tish′ən) *n.*

af- AD-.

AF Anglo-French.

AF, A.F. Air Force.

AF, A.F. a.f., a-f audio frequency.

a·far (ə·far′) *adv.* At, from, or to a distance; remotely.

a·feard (ə·fird′) *adj. Regional* Afraid. Also **a·feared′.**

af·fa·ble (af′ə·bəl) *adj.* Easy and courteous in manner; friendly; approachable. [< L *affabilis,* lit., able to be spoken to] —**af′fa·bil′i·ty, af′fa·ble·ness** *n.* —**af′fa·bly** *adv.* —**Syn.** amicable, cordial, genial, sociable, kind.

af·fair (ə·fâr′) *n.* **1** Anything done or to be done; business. **2** *pl.* Matters of business or concern. **3** Any matter, event, or thing. **4** A social event. **5** An object or device. **6** A romantic and usu. sexual relationship between two people not married to each other.

af·fect[1] (ə·fekt′) *v.t.* **1** To act upon or have an effect upon. **2** To touch or move emotionally. —*n.* (af′ekt) *Psychol.* Emotion, as distinguished from thought or perception. [< L *afficere* influence, attack < *ad-* to + *facere* do] • **affect**[1], **effect** To *effect* means to produce, accomplish, or bring about a definite, specific result, whereas to *affect* means merely to influence or act upon: The disease *affected* the patient's eyesight until her doctor *effected* a cure.

af·fect[2] (ə·fekt′) *v.t.* **1** To have a liking for; show a preference for. **2** To imitate or counterfeit for effect or show: to *affect* a British accent. [< L *affectare* aim at, freq. of *afficere.* See AFFECT[1].]

af·fec·ta·tion (af′ek·tā′shən) *n.* **1** A studied pretense; shallow display: with *of.* **2** Artificiality of manner. [< L < *affectare.* See AFFECT[2].]

af·fect·ed[1] (ə·fek′tid) *adj.* **1** Acted upon, as by a drug. **2** Moved emotionally; influenced. **3** Attacked, as by disease. [p.p. of AFFECT[1]]

af·fect·ed[2] (ə·fek′tid) *adj.* **1** Artificial or mannered, as in behavior. **2** Assumed falsely or for outward show only. [p.p. of AFFECT[2]] —**af·fect′ed·ly** *adv.* —**af·fect′ed·ness** *n.*

af·fect·ing (ə·fek′ting) *adj.* Having power to move the feelings. —**af·fect′ing·ly** *adv.*

af·fec·tion (ə·fek′shən) *n.* **1** Good, kind, or loving feelings, as towards another. **2** A particular mental state or disposition. **3** A disease. **4** A property or attribute. [< L *afficere* to influence, affect]

af·fec·tion·ate (ə·fek′shən·it) *adj.* Having or expressing affection; loving; fond. —**af·fec′tion·ate·ly** *adv.* —**af·fec′tion·ate·ness** *n.*

af·fec·tive (ə·fek′tiv) *adj. Psychol.* Of or arising from emotion rather than from thought.

af·fer·ent (af′ər·ənt) *adj.* Conducting inward: said of those nerve processes which transmit sensory stimuli to the central nervous system. [< L *ad-* to + *ferre* bear]

af·fi·ance (ə·fī′əns) *v.t.* **·anced, ·anc·ing** To promise in marriage; betroth. [< L *ad-* to + *fidus* faithful]

af·fi·da·vit (af′ə·dā′vit) *n.* A sworn declaration, in writing, made before an official authority. [< Med.L, he has stated on oath]

af·fil·i·ate (ə·fil′ē·āt) *v.* **·at·ed, ·at·ing** *v.t.* **1** To associate or unite, as a member or branch: with *to* or *with.* **2** To join or associate (oneself): with *with.* **3** To determine the origins of. —*v.i.* **4** To associate or ally oneself: with *with.* —*n.* (ə·fil′ē·it) An affiliated person or thing. [< L *affiliare* adopt] —**af·fil′i·a′tion** *n.*

af·fin·i·ty (ə·fin′ə·tē) *n. pl.* **·ties** **1** Any natural liking or inclination. **2** Likenesses indicating a common origin. **3** Physical or chemical attraction. **4** Connection through certain relations formed, as by marriage. **5** An attraction held to exist between certain persons. [< L *affinis* adjacent, related]

af·firm (ə·fûrm′) *v.t.* **1** To declare positively; assert to be true. **2** To confirm or ratify, as a judgment or law. —*v.i.* **3** *Law* To make a formal judicial declaration, but not under oath. [< L *ad-* to + *firmare* make firm] —**af·firm′a·ble** *adj.* —**af·firm′a·bly** *adv.* —**af·firm′ant** *adj., n.* —**af·firm′er** *n.* —**Syn. 1** maintain, propound, avow, advance, insist.

af·fir·ma·tion (af′ər·mā′shən) *n.* **1** The act of affirming. **2** That which is affirmed. **3** A solemn declaration made before a competent officer, in place of a judicial oath.

af·firm·a·tive (ə·fûr′mə·tiv) *adj.* **1** Asserting or confirming that something is so. **2** Positive. Also **af·firm·a·to·ry** (ə·fûr′mə·tôr′ē, -tō′re). —*n.* **1** A word or expression of affirmation or assent. **2** That side in a debate which affirms the proposition debated. —**af·firm′a·tive·ly** *adv.*

af·fix (ə·fiks′) *v.t.* **1** To fix or attach; fasten. **2** To put at the end; append, as a signature. **3** To attribute, as blame. —*n.* (af′iks) **1** That which is attached, appended, or added. **2** *Ling.* A prefix, suffix, or infix. [< L *ad-* to + *figere* fasten]

af·fla·tus (ə·flā′təs) *n.* Any creative inspiration or impulse. [< L *afflare* blow on]

af·flict (ə·flikt′) *v.t.* To distress with continued suffering; trouble. [< L *affligere* dash against, strike down] —**af·flict′·er** *n.* —**af·flic′tive** *adj.* —**af·flic′tive·ly** *adv.*

af·flic·tion (ə·flik′shən) *n.* **1** The state of being afflicted. **2** A misfortune; calamity.

af·flu·ence (af′lo͞o·əns, ə·flo͞o′-) *n.* Riches; wealth. [< L *affluere.* See AFFLUENT.]

af·flu·ent (af′lo͞o·ənt, ə·flo͞o′-) *adj.* **1** Abounding; abundant. **2** Wealthy; opulent. —*n.* A stream that flows into another. [< L *ad-* to + *fluere* flow] —**af′flu·ent·ly** *adv.*

af·ford (ə·fôrd′, ə·fōrd′) *v.t.* **1** To have sufficient means for: usu. preceded by *can* or *be able to.* **2** To be able to do, say, etc., without detriment: usu. preceded by *can:* He can *afford* to laugh now. **3** To provide or furnish: It *affords* me great delight. [< OE *geforthian* further, promote] —**af·ford′a·ble** *adj.*

af·fray (ə·frā′) *n.* A public brawl or fight; a disturbance of the peace. [< OF *esfrei*]

af·fri·cate (af′ri·kit) *n. Phonet.* A sound consisting of a stop followed by the fricative release of breath at the point of contact, as *ch* in *match.* [< L *ad-* against + *fricare* rub] —**af·fric·a·tive** (ə·frik′ə·tiv) *adj., n.*

af·front (ə·frunt′) *v.t.* **1** To insult openly; offend by word or act. **2** To confront in defiance; accost. —*n.* An open insult or indignity. [< OF *afronter* strike on the forehead] —**af·front′er** *n.* —**af·fron′tive** *adj.* —**Syn. 1** aggravate, annoy, provoke, irritate, vex.

Afg., Afgh. Afghanistan.

af·ghan (af′gən, -gan) *n.* A soft wool coverlet, knitted or crocheted.

Af·ghan (af′gən, -gan) *adj.* Of or pertaining to Afghanistan, its people, or their language. —*n.* 1 A native or citizen of Afghanistan. 2 The language spoken by the Afghans.

Af·ghan·i·stan (af·gan′ə·stan) *n.* A republic of sw Asia, 250,000 sq. mi., cap. Kabul.

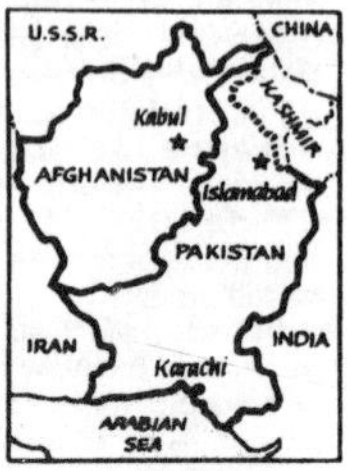

a·fi·cio·na·do (ə·fish′ə·nä′dō, ə·fis′ē·ə-, ə·fē′sē·ə-, *Sp.* äfē·thyō·nä′thō, -fē·syō-) *n. pl.* **·dos** (-dōz, *Sp.* -thōs) An avid follower or fan, as of a sport or activity; devotee. [Sp.]

a·field (ə·fēld′) *adv.* 1 In or to the field. 2 Away; abroad. 3 Off the track; astray.

a·fire (ə·fīr′) *adv. & adj.* On fire.

AFL, A.F.L., A.F. of L. American Federation of Labor.

a·flame (ə·flām′) *adv. & Adj.* 1 Flaming; glowing. 2 Very much excited or aroused.

AFL-CIO, A.F.L.-C.I.O. American Federation of Labor-Congress of Industrial Organizations: a labor organization formed by a merger in 1955.

a·float (ə·flōt′) *adv. & adj.* 1 On the water. 2 In circulation, as a rumor. 3 Adrift. 4 Flooded, as the deck of a ship. 5 Out of trouble or difficulties.

a·foot (ə·fo͝ot′) *adv.* 1 On foot. 2 Able to walk. 3 In motion or progress; on the move. [ME *on fot*]

a·fore (ə·fôr′, ə·fōr′) *adv., prep., & conj. Chiefly Naut.* Before [<OE *onforan*]

a·fore·men·tioned (ə·fôr′men′shənd, a·fōr′-) *adj.* Mentioned before.

a·fore·said (ə·fôr′sed′, ə·fōr′-) *adj.* Said or mentioned before.

a·fore·thought (ə·fôr′thôt′, ə·fōr′-) *adj.* Intended or planned beforehand.

a·fore·time (ə·fôr′tīm′, ə·fōr′-) *adv.* At a previous time.

a for·ti·o·ri (ä fôr′tē·ôr′ē, ā fôr′tē·ō′rī, ā fôr′shē·ôr′ī, -ôr′ē) For a stronger reason; all the more. [L]

a·foul (ə·foul′) *adv. & adj.* In collision; entangled. **—run** (or **fall**) **afoul of** To get into difficulties with.

Afr. Africa; African.

a·fraid (ə·frād′) *adj.* Filled with fear or apprehension. [<ME *affrayen* to fear <OF *esfrei* affray]

A-frame (ā′frām′) *n.* A framework in the shape of the letter A, as that supporting a slanted roof.

a·fresh (ə·fresh′) *adv.* Once more; anew; again.

Af·ri·ca (af′ri·kə) *n.* The second largest continent, located

in the E hemisphere south of Europe and joined to Asia by the Sinai peninsula, 11,500,000 sq. mi.

Af·ri·can (af′ri·kən) *adj.* Of Africa, its peoples and their languages, culture, etc. —*n.* 1 A native or naturalized inhabitant of Africa. 2 One of the indigenous peoples of Africa, esp. a Negro.

African American An American of black African descent.

Af·ri·can·ize (af′rə·kən·īz′) *v.t.* **·ized, ·iz·ing** 1 To make African in character. 2 To place under the control of Africans, esp. black Africans. **—Af′ri·can·i·za′tion** *n.*

Af·ri·kaans (af′ri·käns′, -känz′) *n.* A language spoken in South Africa, evolved from 17th-century Dutch.

Af·ri·ka·ner (af′ri·kä′nər) *n.* An Afrikaans-speaking South African descended from the early Dutch settlers.

Af·ro (af′rō) *n. pl.* **Af·ros** A hair style in which bushy hair is shaped into a full, rounded mass. —*adj.* Of, pertaining to, or influenced by African culture, style, etc. Also **af′ro.**

Afro- *combining form* Africa; African.

Af·ro-Amer·i·can (af′rō·ə·mer′ə·kən) *adj.* Of or pertaining to Americans of black African descent. —*n.* An Afro-American person.

aft (aft, äft) *adj.* Of or near the stern, or rear, of a vessel. —*adv.* Toward the rear; astern. [<OE *æftan* behind]

A.F.T. American Federation of Teachers.

af·ter (af′tər, äf′-) *prep.* 1 In the rear of; following. 2 At a later period than. 3 In succession to; following repeatedly. 4 As a result of; subsequently to. 5 Notwithstanding. 6 Next below in order or importance. 7 In search or pursuit of: to strive *after* wisdom. 8 According to the nature, wishes, or customs of. 9 In the manner of: a painting *after* Vermeer. 10 In honor, remembrance, or observance of: I was named *after* Lincoln. 11 In relation to: to inquire *after* someone's health. —*conj.* Following the time that. —*adj.* 1 Following in time or place. 2 *Naut.* Farther aft. —*adv.* 1 At a later time. 2 In the rear; behind. [<OE *æfter* behind]

af·ter·birth (af′tər·bûrth′, äf′-) *n.* The placenta and fetal membranes expelled from the uterus after childbirth.

af·ter·burn·er (af′tər·bûr′nər, äf′-) *n. Aeron.* A device that injects extra fuel into the exhaust of a jet engine to increase its thrust.

af·ter·deck (af′tər·dek′, äf′-) *n. Naut.* That part of a deck toward the stern.

af·ter·ef·fect (af′tər·ə·fekt′, äf′-) *n.* An effect succeeding its cause after an interval.

af·ter·glow (af′tər·glō, äf′-) *n.* 1 A glow left after a light has disappeared. 2 An agreeable feeling occurring after a pleasant or profitable experience.

af·ter·im·age (af′tər·im′ij, äf′-) *n.* An image or sensation that persists after the direct stimulation has been withdrawn.

af·ter·math (af′tər·math, äf′-) *n.* Results; consequences. [<AFTER + OE *mæth* a mowing]

af·ter·most (af′tər·mōst, äf′-) *adj.* 1 *Naut.* Nearest the stern: also **aft′most.** 2 Last.

af·ter·noon (af′tər·no͞on′, äf′-) *n.* That part of the day between noon and sunset. —*adj.* Of, for, or occurring in the afternoon.

af·ter·taste (af′tər·tāst′, äf′-) *n.* 1 A taste persisting in the mouth, as after eating or drinking. 2 A feeling or reaction that comes after an experience.

af·ter·thought (af′tər·thôt′, äf′-) *n.* 1 A later or more deliberate thought, as after decision or action. 2 A thought occurring too late to affect action.

af·ter·ward (af′tər·wərd, äf′-) *adv.* In time following; subsequently. Also **af′ter·wards.**

AG, A.G. Adjutant General; Attorney General.

Ag silver (L *argentum*).

Ag. August.

a·gain (ə·gen′, *esp. Brit.* ə·gān′) *adv.* 1 Once more; anew. 2 Once repeated: half as much *again.* 3 In or to the same or former place or condition: to be ill *again.* 4 Further; moreover. 5 On the other hand; from another point of view. [<OE *ongegn*]

a·gainst (ə·genst′, esp. Brit. ə·gānst′) *prep.* 1 In contact with and pressing upon. 2 In collision with. 3 In front of; directly opposite: *against* a background. 4 In anticipation of; in preparation for. 5 In opposition to; contrary to. 6 In a counter or opposite direction to. 7 In hostility to. 8 To the debit of. 9 In comparison with; contrasted with. [< OE *ongegn* again]

Ag·a·mem·non (ag′ə·mem′non, -nən) *Gk. Myth.* The king of Mycenae and leader of the Greek army in the Trojan War.

a·gape (ə·gāp′, ə·gap′) *adv. & adj.* 1 In a state of wonder or astonishment, usu. with the mouth wide open. 2 Wide open; gaping.

a·gar (ä′gär, ā′gär, ag′ər) *n.* A gelatinous substance obtained from seaweed, employed as a laxative, emulsifier, and bacterial culture medium. [< Malay *agar-agar*]

ag·a·ric (ag′ə·rik, ə·gar′ik) *n.* Any fungus of the mushroom group. [< Gk. *agarikon*] • See MUSHROOM.

ag·ate (ag′it) *n.* 1 A variegated, waxy, usu. banded quartz or chalcedony. 2 A child's playing marble. 3 *Printing* 5½ point type [< Gk. *achatēs*]

a·ga·ve (ə·gä′vē) *n.* An American desert plant with fleshy leaves and a single spike of flowers; the century plant. [< Gk. *agauos* noble]

age (āj) *n.* 1 The entire period of life or existence, as of a person, thing, nation, etc. 2 A period or stage of life: a good *age* to be married. 3 The closing period of life. 4 A generation or lifetime. 5 *Often cap.* Any great or distinct period in history: the Atomic *Age.* 6 *Often pl. Informal* A long time. **—of age** To or at the age of full legal responsibility: to be *of age.* —*v.* **aged, ag·ing** or **age·ing** *v.t.* 1 To cause to become mature. 2 To cause to grow or seem to grow old. —*v.i.* 3 To become or seem to become old. 4 To ripen or mature. [< L *aetas* age, a span of life]

-age *suffix of nouns* 1 Collection or aggregate of: *baggage.* 2 Condition, office, service, or other relation or connection of: *pilgrimage.* [< L *-aticum,* neut. adj. suffix]

a·ged (ā′jid *for defs. 1 & 2;* ājd *for def. 3*) *adj.* 1 Advanced in years; old. 2 Of, like, or characteristic of old age. 3 Of or at the age of: a child, *aged* five. **—a′ged·ness** *n.*

age·ism (ā′jiz·əm) *n.* Discrimination or prejudice, esp. as directed against elderly people. **—age′ist** *n., adj.*

age·less (āj′lis) *adj.* 1 Not seeming to grow old. 2 Having no limits of duration.

age·long (āj′lông′) *adj.* Lasting a long time.

a·gen·cy (ā′jən·sē) *n. pl.* **·cies** 1 Active power or force. 2 Means; instrumentality. 3 Any establishment where business is done for others. 4 The office or offices of such an establishment. 5 A specific division of governmental administration. [< L *agere* do]

a·gen·da (ə·jen′də) *n. pl.* **·das** A list or program of things to be done, as at a meeting. [< L < *agere* to do]

a·gen·dum (ə·jen′dəm) *n. pl.* **·dums** or **·da** An agenda.

a·gent (ā′jənt) *n.* 1 One who acts or has power to act. 2 Any force or substance having power to cause change: a chemical *agent.* 3 A person, business, etc., who represents or acts for another: an actor's *agent.* 4 A means by which something is done. 5 *Informal* A traveling salesman. [< L *agere* do] **—a·gen·tial** (ā·jen′shəl) *adj.* **—Syn.** 1 actor, doer, operator, mover. 3 representative, proxy, deputy. 4 factor, cause, instrument.

age of consent The age at which a girl may legally consent to have sexual intercourse.

ag·e·ra·tum (aj′ə·rā′təm, ə·jər′ə·təm) *n.* Any of a genus of plants having long-lasting, usu. blue, composite flowers. [< Gk. *agēraton,* a kind of plant < *agēratos* ageless]

ag·gior·na·men·to (ə·jôr′nə·men′tō, *It.* ad·jōr′nä·men′·tō) *n.* A bringing up to date, esp. of the ideas, rituals, or policies of the Roman Catholic Church. [It.]

ag·glom·er·ate (ə·glom′ə·rāt) *v.t. & v.i.* **·at·ed, ·at·ing** To gather, form, or grow into a ball or rounded mass. —*adj.* (ə·glom′ər·it, -ə·rāt) Gathered into a mass or heap; clustered densely. —*n.* (ə·glom′ər·it, -ə·rāt) A heap or mass of things thrown together indiscriminately. [< L *ad-* to + *glomerare* gather into a ball] **—ag·glom′er·a′tion** *n.*

ag·glu·ti·nant (ə·glo͞o′tə·nənt) *adj.* Tending to cause adhesion; uniting. —*n.* Any sticky substance.

ag·glu·ti·nate (ə·glo͞o′tə·nāt) *v.t. & v.i.* **·nat·ed, ·nat·ing** 1 To unite, as with glue; join by adhesion. 2 *Ling.* To form (words) by combining into compounds. 3 *Biol.* To come together in clumps, as blood corpuscles, etc. —*adj.* (ə·glo͞o′·tə·nit, -nāt) Joined by adhesion. [< L *ad-* to + *glutinare* to glue] **—ag·glu′ti·na′tion** *n.* **—ag·glu′ti·na′tive** *adj.*

ag·gran·dize (ə·gran′dīz, ag′rən·dīz) *v.t.* **·dized, ·diz·ing** 1 To make great or greater. 2 To make appear greater; exalt. [< L *ad-* to + *grandire* make great or large] **—ag·gran′dize·ment, ag·gran′diz·er** *n.*

ag·gra·vate (ag′rə·vāt) *v.t.* **·vat·ed, ·vat·ing** 1 To make worse. 2 To make heavier or more burdensome, as a duty. 3 *Informal* To provoke or exasperate. [< L *ad-* to + *gravare* make heavy] **—ag′gra·vat′ing, ag′gra·va′tive** *adj.* **—ag′gra·vat′ing·ly** *adv.* **—ag′gra·va′tion** *n.*

ag·gre·gate (ag′rə·gāt) *v.t.* **·gat·ed, ·gat·ing** 1 To bring or gather together, as into a mass, sum, or body. 2 To amount to; form a total of. —*adj.* (ag′rə·git) Collected into a sum, mass, or total; gathered into a whole. —*n.* (ag′rə·git) 1 The entire number, sum, mass, or quantity of something; amount; total. 2 Material, as sand or pebbles, used in making concrete. **—in the aggregate** Collectively; as a whole. [< L *aggregare,* lit. bring to the flock] **—ag′gre·ga′tive** *adj.* **—ag′gre·ga′tion, ag′gre·ga′tor** *n.*

ag·gress (ə·gres′) *v.i.* To undertake an attack; begin a quarrel. [< L *aggredi* approach, attack]

ag·gres·sion (ə·gresh′ən) *n.* 1 An unprovoked attack. 2 Aggressive action or practices.

ag·gres·sive (ə·gres′iv) *adj.* 1 Characterized by or inclined to begin an attack or encroachment; hostile. 2 Disposed to vigorous activity; energetic and forceful. **—ag·gres′sive·ly** *adv.* **—ag·gres′sive·ness** *n.*

ag·gres·sor (ə·gres′ər) *n.* One who commits an aggression or begins a quarrel.

ag·grieve (ə·grēv′) *v.t.* **ag·grieved, ag·griev·ing** 1 To cause sorrow to; distress or afflict. 2 To give cause for just complaint. [< L *aggravare.* See AGGRAVATE.]

a·ghast (ə·gast′, ə·gäst′) *adj.* Struck with horror or amazement; shocked. [< A-[2] + *gæstan* terrify]

ag·ile (aj′əl, aj′il) *adj.* 1 Able to move quickly and easily; nimble. 2 Alert; lively: an *agile* mind. [< L *agilis* < *agere* do, move] **—ag′ile·ly** *adv.* **—ag′ile·ness, a·gil·i·ty** (ə·jil′ə·tē) *n.*

ag·i·tate (aj′ə·tāt) *v.* **·tat·ed, ·tat·ing** *v.t.* 1 To shake or move irregularly. 2 To set or keep moving, as a fan. 3 To excite or endeavor to excite, as a crowd. 4 To discuss publicly and incessantly, as a controversial question. —*v.i.* 5 To excite public interest in a cause by continuous discussion, writing, etc. [< L *agitare* set in motion, freq. of *agere* do, move] **—ag′i·ta′tion** *n.*

ag·i·ta·tor (aj′ə·tā′tər) *n.* 1 One who or that which agitates. 2 One who seeks to stimulate public opinion and response to controversial issues: usu. derogatory.

ag·it·prop (aj′it·prop′) *n.* 1 Communist political propaganda, esp. in a play, film, etc. 2 Any political propaganda. —*adj.* Pertaining to or of the nature of agitprop. [Russ., Communist Party agency for agitation and propaganda]

a·gleam (ə·glēm′) *adv. & adj.* Bright; gleaming.

a·glow (ə·glō′) *adv. & adj.* In a glow; glowing.

ag·no·men (ag·nō′mən) *n. pl.* **ag·nom·i·na** (ag·nom′ə·nə) A nickname. [< L *ad-* to + *(g)nomen* name]

ag·nos·tic (ag·nos′tik) *adj.* Of or pertaining to agnosticism or agnostics. —*n.* One who believes in agnosticism. [< Gk. *agnōstos* unknowing, unknown]

ag·nos·ti·cism (ag·nos′tə·siz′əm) *n.* The theory that man can neither prove nor disprove the existence of God nor know with certainty the nature of ultimate truth.

Ag·nus De·i (ag′nəs dē′ī, dā′ē) 1 A figure of a lamb, as an emblem of Christ. 2 *Eccl.* **a** A prayer in the Mass, beginning with the words *Agnus Dei.* **b** A musical setting for this prayer. [LL, Lamb of God]

a·go (ə·gō′) *adv.* In the past; since. —*adj.* Gone by; past. [OE *āgān* past, gone away]

a·gog (ə·gog′) *adv. & adj.* In a state of eager interest or expectation. [< MF *en gogues* in a merry mood]

à go-go (ä gō′gō) *adj.* GO-GO. Also **a go′-go′, a-go′go′.** [F, lit., joyfully]

-agogue *combining form* Leading, promoting, or inciting; *demagogue, pedagogue.* Also **-agog.** [< Gk. *agōgos* leading]

ag·o·nize (ag′ə·nīz) *v.* **·nized, ·niz·ing** *v.i.* **1** To be in or suffer extreme pain or anguish. **2** To make convulsive efforts, as in wrestling; strive. —*v.t.* **3** To subject to agony; torture. [<Gk. *agōnizesthai* contend, strive]

ag·o·ny (ag′ə·nē) *n. pl.* **·nies 1** Intense suffering of body or mind. **2** Any violent emotion. **3** Violent striving or effort. **4** The struggle that sometimes precedes death. [<Gk. *agōnia* <*agon* contest]

ag·o·ra (ag′ər·ə) *n. pl.* **ag·o·rae** (-ər·ē) or **ag·o·ras 1** In ancient Greece, a popular assembly. **2** A place of popular assembly.

a·gou·ti (ə·gōō′tē) *n. pl.* **·tis** or **·ties** A large, burrowing rodent of tropical America with dark, gray-flecked fur. Also **a·gou′ty.**[<Sp.*aguti*<Tupian]

Agouti

agr. agricultural; agriculture; agriculturist.

a·grar·i·an (ə·grâr′ē·ən) *adj.* **1** Pertaining to land or its distribution. **2** Agricultural. —*n.* One who advocates a more equitable distribution of land or farm income. [<L *ager* field] —**a·grar′i·an·ism** *n.*

a·gree (ə·grē′) *v.* **a·greed, a·gree·ing** *v.i.* **1** To give consent; accede: with *to.* **2** To be in harmony or in accord. **3** To be of one mind; concur: with *with.* **4** To come to terms, as in the details of a transaction: with *about* or *on.* **5** To be acceptable; suit: with *with.* **6** *Gram.* To correspond in person, number, case, or gender. —*v.t.* **7** To grant as a concession: with a noun clause: I *agree* that it is difficult. [<L *ad* to + *gratus* pleasing] —**Syn. 1** acquiesce, assent. **2** coincide, harmonize. **3** approve, accept.

a·gree·a·ble (ə·grē′ə·bəl) *adj.* **1** Pleasing; pleasurable. **2** Ready or inclined to agree: He is *agreeable* to your proposal. **3** Being in accordance or conformity. —**a·gree′·a·bil′i·ty, a·gree′a·ble·ness** *n.* —**a·gree′a·bly** *adv.*

a·greed (ə·grēd′) *adj.* **1** In agreement; united. **2** Settled by consent or contract. **3** Admitted or conceded; granted.

a·gree·ment (ə·grē′mənt) *n.* **1** The act of agreeing. **2** The state of being agreed or in accord; conformity. **3** An arrangement or understanding between two or more people, countries, etc. **4** A contract. **5** Correspondence between words as to number, person, gender, or case.

ag·ri·bus·i·ness (ag′rə·biz′·nis, -niz) *n.* All those commercial activities associated with agriculture, including the production, processing, and distribution of farm products and the manufacture of farm equipment. [<AGRI(CULTURE) + BUSINESS]

ag·ri·cul·ture (ag′rə·kul′chər) *n.* The act or science of cultivating the soil and of raising food crops and livestock; farming. [<L *ager* field + *cultura* cultivation] —**ag′ri·cul′·tur·al** *adj.* —**ag′ri·cul′tur·al·ly** *adv.*

ag·ri·cul·tur·ist (ag′rə·kul′chər·ist) *n.* One who studies or practices agriculture. Also **ag′ri·cul′tur·al·ist.**

ag·ri·mo·ny (ag′rə·mō′nē) *n. pl.* **·nies** A perennial herb with small yellow flowers and bristly fruit. [<Gk. *argemōnē*]

agro- *combining form* Of or pertaining to fields or agriculture: *agronomy.* [<Gk. <*agros* field]

a·gron·o·my (ə·gron′ə·mē) *n.* The application of scientific principles to the cultivation of land. [<Gk. *agronomos* an overseer of lands] —**ag·ro·nom·ic** (ag′rə·nom′ik) or **·i·cal** *adj.* —**a·gron′o·mist** *n.*

a·ground (ə·ground′) *adv. & adj.* On the shore or bottom, as a vessel; stranded.

agt. agent; agreement.

a·gue (ā′gyōō) *n.* Intermittent fever or chills and fever. [<L *(febris) acuta* an acute fever] —**a′gu·ish** *adj.*

ah (ä) *interj.* An exclamation expressive of various emotions, as surprise, triumph, satisfaction, contempt, etc.

a·ha (ä·hä′) *interj.* An exclamation expressing surprise, triumph, or mockery.

a·head (ə·hed′) *adv.* **1** At the head or front. **2** In advance. **3** Onward; forward. —**ahead of** In advance of. —**get ahead** To succeed socially, financially, etc.

a·hoy (ə·hoi′) *interj.* Ho there! a call used in hailing: ship *ahoy!* [<AH + HOY]

aid (ād) *v.t. & v.i.* To render assistance (to). —*n.* **1** Help; assistance. **2** A person or thing that helps. **3** An aide. [<L *adjuvare* give help to] —**aid′er** *n.*

aide (ād) *n.* **1** An assistant. **2** AIDE-DE-CAMP. [F]

aide-de-camp (ād′də·kamp′) *n. pl.* **aides-de-camp** An officer in the army, navy, etc., acting as a confidential assistant to a superior officer. Also **aid′-de-camp′.** [<F *aide de camp*, lit., field assistant]

AIDS (ādz) *n.* An infectious disease that attacks the human immune system, caused by a retrovirus, spread by transfer of infected blood or by sexual contact, usually fatal. [<A(CQUIRED) I(MMUNO) D(EFICIENCY) S(YNDROME)]

ai·gret (ā′gret, ā·gret′) *n.* An ornamental tuft of feathers or gems. Also **ai′grette.** [<F *aigrette* an egret]

ail (āl) *v.t.* **1** To cause uneasiness or pain to; trouble; make ill. —*v.i.* **2** To be somewhat ill; feel pain. [<OE *eglan*] —**ail′ing** *adj.*

ai·lan·thus (ā·lan′thəs) *n.* Any of several tall deciduous trees of Asiatic origin; tree of heaven. [<native Indonesian name]

ai·le·ron (ā′lə·ron) *n.* Any of several types of control surfaces of an airplane, usu. near the trailing edge of the wing, used to produce rolling on the longitudinal axis. [<L *ala* wing] • See AIRPLANE.

ail·ment (āl′mənt) *n.* Any illness of body or mind, esp. a minor one.

aim (ām) *v.t.* **1** To direct, as a missile, blow, weapon, word, or act, toward or against some thing or person. —*v.i.* **2** To have a purpose; endeavor: with an infinitive: to *aim* to please. **3** To direct a missile, weapon, etc. —*n.* **1** The act of aiming. **2** The line of direction of anything aimed. **3** Design; purpose; intention. [<L *ad-* to + *aestimare* estimate] —**Syn.** *n.* **3** goal, end, aspiration, endeavor, intent.

aim·less (ām′lis) *adj.* Wanting in aim or purpose. —**aim′·less·ly** *adv.* —**aim′less·ness** *n.*

ain't (ānt) *Nonstand. & Regional* Contraction of *am not;* also used for *are not, is not, has not,* and *have not.*

Ai·nu (ī′nōō) *n.* **1** One of a primitive, aboriginal people of Japan, now found only in the northern parts. **2** The language of the Ainu.

air (âr) *n.* **1** The gaseous envelope of the earth, consisting chiefly of nitrogen and oxygen; the atmosphere. **2** The open space around and above the earth. **3** A wind; breeze. **4** Utterance or publicity: to give *air* to one's opinions. **5** Peculiar or characteristic appearance or impression: an *air* of mystery. **6** *pl.* Artificial manners or affectations: to put on *airs.* **7** Travel or transportation by aircraft. **8** *Music* A melody or tune. —**in the air 1** Prevalent; abroad, as gossip. **2** Not finally decided or settled: also **up in the air.** —*v.t.* **1** To expose to the air, so as to dry, ventilate, etc. **2** To make public; display; exhibit. [<Gk. *aēr* air, mist] —**Syn** *n.* **5** demeanor, look, mien, manner, way.

air base A base for operations by aircraft.

air bladder A sac filled with air, found in many aquatic animals and plants. Also **air cell.**

air·borne (âr′bôrn′, -bōrn′) *adj.* **1** Transported through the air, esp. in aircraft. **2** Not on the ground; aloft.

air brake A brake operated by compressed air.

air·brush (âr′brush′) *n.* An implement for spraying liquids, esp. paint, by compressed air.

air·burst (âr′bûrst′) *n.* An explosion in the air, as of a bomb or projectile.

air·bus (âr′bus′) *n.* A large airplane designed to accommodate several hundred passengers.

air-con·di·tion (âr′kən·dish′ən) *v.t.* To equip with or ventilate by air conditioning. —**air′-con·di·tioned** *adj.*

air conditioner A machine to provide air conditioning.

air conditioning A system for controlling the temperature, purity, and humidity of air in buildings, cars, etc.

air-cool (âr′kōōl′) *v.t.* To cool, as engine cylinders, with a flow of air. —**air′-cooled′** *adj.*

air·craft (âr′kraft′, -kräft′) *n.* Any form of craft designed for flight through the air, as airplanes, dirigibles, etc.

aircraft carrier A large ship designed to carry aircraft, with a level upper flight deck usu. extending beyond the bow and stern.

air·drome (âr′drōm′) *n.* An airport.

air·drop (âr′drop′) *n.* Personnel, food, equipment, and other supplies dropped by parachute from an aircraft. —*v.t. & v.i.* **·dropped, ·drop·ping** To drop (personnel, supplies, etc.) by parachute from an aircraft.

Aire·dale (âr′dāl) *n.* A large terrier with a wiry tan coat and black markings. [< *Airedale,* the valley of the Aire River in Yorkshire, England]

Airedale

air·field (âr′fēld′) *n.* An airport or landing strip.

air·foil (âr′foil′) *n.* A part of an aircraft, as a wing, rudder, etc., designed to produce or be subject to certain forces when in motion through the air.

air force The air arm of a country's defense forces.

air gun 1 A gun impelling a missile by compressed air. 2 A device for spraying liquids by compressed air.

air hole 1 A hole for the flow of air. 2 An opening in the ice over a body of water. 3 AIR POCKET.

air·i·ly (âr′ə·lē) *adv.* In a light or airy manner; jauntily.

air·i·ness (âr′ē·nis) *n.* The quality of being airy.

air·ing (âr′ing) *n.* 1 An exposure to the air, as for drying. 2 Public exposure or discussion. 3 A walk or drive outdoors.

air lane An established route for air traffic.

air·less (âr′lis) *adj.* 1 Destitute of air. 2 Destitute of fresh air, a breeze, etc.; close. **—air′less·ness** *n.*

air letter 1 An airmail letter. 2 An international airmail letter consisting of a single folded sheet.

air·lift (âr′lift′) *n.* The operation of transporting foodstuffs, other commodities, and personnel by airplane during land blockade. *—v.t. & v.i.* To transport (food and supplies) by airplane.

air·line (âr′līn′) *n.* 1 A regular route traveled by aircraft carrying freight and passengers. 2 The business organization operating such a system. *—adj.* Of or for an airline.

air·lin·er (âr′lī′nər) *n.* A large, passenger aircraft operated by an airline.

air·lock (âr′lok′) *n.* An airtight chamber for adjusting the air pressure between regions of different atmospheric pressure.

air·mail (âr′māl′) *n.* 1 Mail carried by airplane. 2 A postal system of carrying mail by airplane. *—v.t.* To send by airmail.

air·man (âr′mən) *n. pl.* **air·men** 1 Any person who is occupied with flying, maintaining, or servicing aircraft. 2 An enlisted man or woman in the U.S. Air Force.

air mass *Meteorol.* Any large portion of the atmosphere having little variation of temperature, pressure, moisture, etc.

air mile A nautical mile by air.

air·plane (âr′plān′) *n.* A heavier-than-air flying craft,

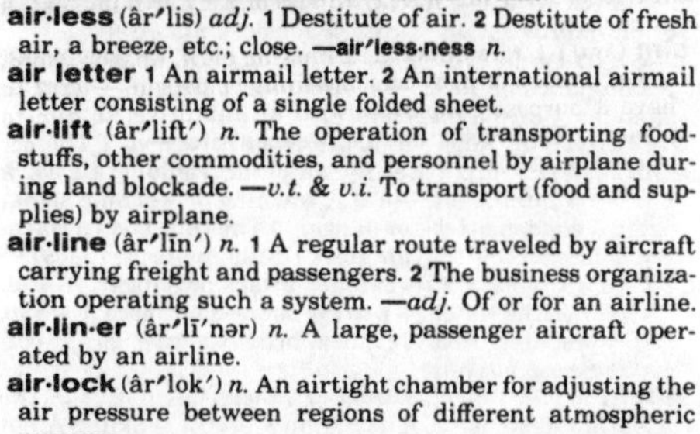

Airplane

supported by aerodynamic forces and propelled by an engine or engines.

air pocket An atmospheric condition that causes an airplane to have a sudden brief drop in altitude.

air·port (âr′pôrt′, -pōrt′) *n.* An area for aircraft takeoffs and landings, together with buildings for maintenance, storage, and passenger service.

air pressure The pressure of the atmosphere or of compressed air.

air raid An attack by military aircraft, esp. bombers.

air rifle A rifle utilizing compressed air to propel a pellet.

air sac Any of the hollow cavities in the body and bones of a bird and communicating with its lungs.

air shaft A shaft intended to secure ventilation of a building, tunnel, etc.

air·ship (âr′ship′) *n.* A lighter-than-air aircraft having means for propulsion and steering; dirigible.

air·sick·ness (âr′sik′nis) *n.* Nausea due to varied motions of an aircraft in which one is traveling. **—air′sick′** *adj.*

air·space (âr′spās′) *n.* The part of the atmosphere over a designated geographical area that is subject to territorial jurisdiction or international law in respect to use by aircraft, rockets, etc.

air speed The speed of an aircraft with respect to the air rather than to the ground.

air·strip (âr′strip′) *n.* A runway for airplanes, usu. for temporary use.

air·tight (âr′tīt′) *adj.* 1 Not allowing air to escape or enter. 2 Having no weak places; flawless: an *airtight* argument.

air·waves (âr′wāvz′) *n. pl.* The medium for transmitting radio or television signals.

air·way (âr′wā′) *n.* 1 Any passageway for air, as an air shaft. 2 AIR LANE. 3 *pl.* AIRWAVES.

air·wor·thy (âr′wûr′thē) *adj.* Being in fit condition for flight. **—air′wor′thi·ness** *n.*

air·y (âr′ē) *adj.* **air·i·er, air·i·est** 1 Of the air. 2 In the air. 3 Open to the air; breezy. 4 Light or delicate, as air. 5 Vivacious; gay. 6 Lightly nonchalant or flippant. 7 Without reality; visionary.

aisle (īl) *n.* 1 A passageway to or between rows of seats. 2 A similar passageway, as between trees. 3 An interior division of a church, alongside the main part or nave. [< OF *aile, ele* wing (of a building)] **—aisled** (īld) *adj.*

a·jar[1] (ə·jär′) *adv. & adj.* Partly open, as a door. [ME *a-* on + *char* a turning]

a·jar[2] (ə·jär′) *adv. & adj.* In a jarring or discordant condition; wanting in harmony.

AK Alaska (P.O. abbr.).

a·kim·bo (ə·kim′bō) *adv.* With the hands on hips and the elbows outward. [ME *in kenebowe* in a sharp bow]

a·kin (ə·kin′) *adj. & adv.* 1 Of the same kin; related by blood. 2 Of similar nature or qualities.

al-[1] *prefix* The: Arabic definite article, as in *algebra.*

al-[2] Var. of AD-.

-al[1] *suffix of adjectives and nouns* Of or pertaining to; characterized by: *personal, musical.* [< L *-alis*]

-al[2] *suffix of nouns* The act or process of: used with a verb stem, as in *betrayal, refusal.* [< L *-alia,* neut. pl. of *-alis*]

AL Alabama (P.O. abbr.).

Al aluminum.

à la (ä′lä, ä′lə; *Fr.* à là) After the manner or in the style of. Also **a la.** [F]

Ala. Alabama.

al·a·bas·ter (al′ə·bas′tər, -bäs′-) *n.* 1 A white or delicately tinted fine-grained gypsum. 2 A banded variety of calcite. *—adj.* 1 Made of or like alabaster. 2 Smooth and white. [< Gk. *alabast(r)os*] **—al′a·bas′trine** (-trin) *adj.*

à la carte (ä′ lə kärt′) According to the menu: said of meals, menus, etc., in which each item of food has a separate price. [F, lit., by the bill of fare]

a·lack (ə·lak′) *interj. Archaic* An exclamation of regret or sorrow. Also **a·lack·a·day** (ə·lak′ə·dā′). [< *ah* oh + *lack* failure, lack]

a·lac·ri·ty (ə·lak′rə·tē) *n.* 1 Cheerful willingness: She accepted the challenging assignment with *alacrity.* 2 Prompt and lively action: to respond to the taunt with *alacrity.* [< L *alacer* lively] **—a·lac′ri·tous** *adj.*

à la mode (ä′ lə mōd′, al′ə mōd′) 1 According to the mode; in the fashion. 2 Served with ice cream: pie *à la mode.* 3 Cooked in a rich sauce with vegetables: beef *à la mode.* [F, lit., in the fashion]

a·larm (ə·lärm′) *n.* 1 Sudden fear or apprehension. 2 Any sound or signal to warn of danger or arouse from sleep. 3 A mechanism, as of a clock, giving such a signal. *—v.t.* 1

To strike with sudden fear. 2 To arouse to a sense of danger; give warning to. [< Ital. *all' arme* to arms]

alarm clock A clock that can be set to sound an alarm at a predetermined hour.

a·larm·ing (ə·lär′ming) *adj.* Causing alarm or apprehension. **—a·larm′ing·ly** *adv.*

a·larm·ist (ə·lär′mist) *n.* One who needlessly excites or tries to excite alarm. *—adj.* Provoking unnecessary alarm. **—a·larm′ism** *n.*

a·las (ə·las′, ə·läs′) *interj.* An exclamation of disappointment, regret, sorrow, etc. [< OF *a* ah! + *las* wretched]

Alas. Alaska.

alb (alb) *n. Eccl.* A white linen vestment, reaching to the ankles and girded at the waist, worn by a priest celebrating Mass. [< L *alba (vestis)* white (garment)]

Alb. Albania; Albanian.

al·ba·core (al′bə·kôr, -kōr) *n.* Any of various tunas or related fish. [< Ar. *al* the + *bukr* young camel]

Al·ba·ni·a (al·bā′nē·ə, -bān′yə) *n.* A Balkan republic s of Yugoslavia, 10,629 sq. mi., cap. Tirana. **—Al·ba′ni·an** *adj., n.* • See map at BALKAN STATES.

al·ba·tross (al′bə·trôs, -tros) *n. pl.* **·tros·ses** or **·tross** A large, web-footed sea bird with long narrow wings and a hooked beak. [< Pg. *alcatraz* pelican]

Albatross

al·be·it (ôl·bē′it) *conj.* Even though; although. [ME *al be it* although it be completely]

al·bi·no (al·bī′nō) *n. pl.* **·nos** 1 A person having a genetic deficiency of normal pigmentation, resulting in a very pale skin, whitish hair, and a pale or pinkish eye coloration. 2 An animal or plant lacking normal pigmentation. [< L *albus* white] **—al·bin·ic** (al·bin′ik) *adj.* **—al·bin·ism** (al′bə·niz′əm) *n.*

al·bum (al′bəm) *n.* 1 A blank book for holding photographs, autographs, stamps, etc. 2 A long-playing phonograph record or records encased in a jacket or box. 3 A booklike container for a number of phonograph records. 4 A bound anthology, as of musical compositions. [< L, white tablet]

al·bu·men (al·byo͞o′mən) *n.* 1 The white of an egg. 2 The nutritive material surrounding the embryo in a seed. 3 ALBUMIN. [< L< *albus* white]

al·bu·min (al·byo͞o′mən) *n.* Any of a class of protein substances found in many animal and vegetable fluids and tissues. [< L *albumen.* See ALBUMEN.] **—al·bu′mi·nous** (-nəs), **al·bu′mi·nose** (-nōs) *adj.*

al·caz·ar (al·kaz′ər, al′kə·zär; *Sp.* äl·kä′thär) *n.* A Moorish castle in Spain; esp. **the Alcazar,** a Moorish palace in Seville. [< Sp. < Ar. *al-qasr* the castle]

al·che·my (al′kə·mē) *n.* 1 The primitive chemistry of the Middle Ages, characterized by the search for a way to change base metals into gold. 2 Any mysterious changing of the structure or appearance of things. Also **al′chy·my.** [< Ar. *al-kīmiyā* < L Gk. *chēmeia* transmutation of metals] **—al·chem·ic** (al·kem′ik) *adj.* **—al·chem′i·cal·ly** *adv.* **—al·che·mist** (al′kə·mist) *n.*

al·co·hol (al′kə·hôl, -hol) *n.* 1 A volatile, flammable, colorless, potable but intoxicating liquid obtained from fermentation of the sugars in grain, grapes, etc., by yeast; ethyl alcohol. 2 Any potable liquor containing ethyl alcohol, as brandy, gin, etc. 3 A very toxic liquid similar chemically to ethyl alcohol, obtained from wood tar or synthetically; methanol. 4 Any of a large group of organic compounds in which one or more hydrogen atoms in a hydrocarbon have been replaced by a hydroxyl group. [< Med.L, orig., fine powder < Ar. *al-koh'l* the powdered antimony]

al·co·hol·ic (al′kə·hôl′ik, -hol′-) *adj.* 1 Of or containing alcohol. 2 Caused by alcohol or alcoholism. 3 Suffering from alcoholism. *—n.* One who suffers from alcoholism.

al·co·hol·ism (al′kə·hôl′iz·əm, -hol′-) *n.* The habitual and compulsive use of alcoholic beverages.

al·cove (al′kōv) *n.* 1 A recess connected with or at the side of a larger room. 2 Any embowered or secluded spot. 3 A niche in the face of a cliff or the wall of a building. [< Ar. *al-qobbah* the vaulted chamber]

Al·deb·a·ran (al·deb′ə·rən) *n.* A bright, red, double star in the constellation Taurus. [< Ar. *al-dabarān* the follower (i.e., of the Pleiades)]

al·de·hyde (al′də·hīd) *n.* Any of a group of organic compounds derived from the alcohols by gentle oxidation. [< AL(COHOL) + DEHYD(ROGENIZED)]

al·der (ôl′dər) *n.* Any of various shrubs or small trees related to the birch. [< OE *alor*]

al·der·man (ôl′dər·mən) *n. pl.* **·men** 1 A member of a municipal legislative body who often exercises certain judicial functions. 2 In England and Ireland, a member of the higher branch of a town council. [< OE *ealdorman* head man] **—al′der·man′ic** (-man′ik) *adj.*

Al·der·ney (ôl′dər·nē) *n.* One of a breed of cattle originally peculiar to the island of Alderney of the Channel Islands.

ale (āl) *n.* A beverage resembling beer made from a fermented infusion of malt, usu. flavored with hops. [< OE *ealu*]

a·le·a·tor·ic (ā′lē·ə·tôr′ik, -tō′rik) *adj.* 1 Based on chance or on improvisation: *aleatoric* music. 2 ALEATORY.

a·le·a·to·ry (ā′lē·ə·tôr′ē, -tō′rē) *adj.* Of or dependent upon chance or luck. *—n.* Aleatoric music. [< L *aleator* gambler < *alea* a die, chance]

ale·house (āl′hous′) *n.* A saloon or tavern.

a·lert (əlûrt′) *adj.* 1 Keenly watchful; vigilant. 2 Lively; nimble. 3 Intelligent. *—n.* 1 A warning or warning signal against sudden attack or danger. 2 The time such a warning is in effect. **—on the alert** On the lookout; ready. *—v.t.* To warn, as of a threatened attack or danger. [< Ital. *all' erta* on the watch] **—a·lert′ly** *adv.* **—a·lert′ness** *n.* **—Syn.** *adj.* 1 prepared, ready. 2 quick, brisk. 3 active, quick, perceptive, responsive.

A·leut (ə·lo͞ot′) *n. pl.* **A·leuts** or **A·leut** 1 A native of the Aleutian Islands. 2 A subfamily of the Eskimo-Aleut family of languages. **—A·leu·tian** (ə·lo͞o′shən) *adj., n.*

ale·wife (āl′wīf′) *n. pl.* **·wives** A small North American fish related to the herring. [?]

Al·ex·an·dri·an (al′ig·zan′drē·ən, -zän′-) *adj.* 1 Of or pertaining to Alexander the Great. 2 Of or pertaining to Alexandria. 3 ALEXANDRINE. *—n.* 1 A native or inhabitant of Alexandria. 2 An Alexandrine verse.

Al·ex·an·drine (al′ig·zan′drin, -drēn, -zän′-) *n.* A line of verse having six iambic feet with the caesura generally after the third. *—adj.* Composed of Alexandrines.

al·fal·fa (al·fal′fə) *n.* A cloverlike plant used as forage. [< Sp. < Ar. *al-fasfasah* the best kind of fodder]

al·fres·co (al·fres′kō) *adv.* In the open air. *—adj.* Occurring outdoors, as a meal. Also **al fresco.** [< Ital.]

Alg. Algeria; Algerian.

alg. algebra.

al·ga (al′gə) *n. pl.* **·gae** (-jē) Any of a large variety of primitive chlorophyll-bearing plants widely distributed in aquatic and moist habitats, and including the seaweeds, kelps, diatoms, etc. [< L, seaweed] **—al·gal** (al′gəl) *adj.*

al·ge·bra (al′jə·brə) *n.* 1 A generalized arithmetic in which symbols representing any of a set of numbers are used in calculations. 2 A defined set of elements with various operations defined on the set. [< Ital. < Ar. *al-jebr* the reunion of broken parts, bone-setting] **—al′ge·bra′ic** (-brā′ik) *adj.* **—al′ge·bra′i·cal·ly** *adv.* **—al′ge·bra′ist** *n.*

Al·ge·ri·a (al·jir′ē·ə) *n.* A republic of NW Africa, 919,352 sq. mi., cap. Algiers. **—Al·ge′ri·an** *adj., n.* • See map at AFRICA.

-algia *suffix* Pain or disease of: *neuralgia.* [< Gk. *algos* pain]

Algon. Algonquian.

Al·gon·qui·an (al·gong′kē·ən, -kwē·ən) *n.* 1 A large family of languages used by many tribes of North American Indians, including the Algonquin, Blackfoot, Cheyenne, Cree, Ojibwa, Shawnee and other tribes. 2 A member of one of the tribes belonging to this language family. *—adj.* Of or pertaining to the Algonquian family of languages.

Al·gon·quin (al·gong′kin, -kwin) *n.* 1 A member of a tribe of Algonquian Indians. 2 The language spoken by this tribe. Also **Al·gon·kin** (al·gong′kin).

Al·ham·bra (al·ham′brə) *n.* The medieval palace of the Moorish kings at Granada, Spain. [< Ar. *al-hamrā'* the red (house)]

a·li·as (ā′lē·əs) *n. pl.* **a·li·as·es** An assumed name: She used an *alias* to cash the stolen checks. —*adv.* Called by the assumed name of: Horace Jones, *alias* Howard Smith. [L, at another time or place]

al·i·bi (al′ə·bī) *n. pl.* **·bis 1** A form of defense by which the accused undertakes to show that he was elsewhere when the crime was committed. **2** *Informal* Any excuse. —*v.i.* **·bied, ·bi·ing** *Informal* To make excuses for oneself. [< L, elsewhere]

al·i·en (ā′lē·ən, āl′yən) *adj.* **1** Of another country or people; foreign. **2** Opposed; contrary; inconsistent: with *to:* actions *alien* to his character. —*n.* **1** A foreign-born person who is not a citizen of the country in which he resides. **2** A person of another race, country, religion, etc. **3** One excluded; an outsider. [< L *alienus*] —**Syn.** *adj.* **2** contradictory, foreign, unlike.

al·ien·a·ble (āl′yən·ə·bəl, ā′lē·ən-) *adj.* That can be transferred, as property, to the ownership of another. —**al′ien·a·bil′i·ty** *n.*

al·ien·ate (āl′yən·āt, ā′lē·ən-) *v.t.* **·at·ed, ·at·ing 1** To make indifferent or unfriendly; estrange. **2** To cause to feel estranged or withdrawn from society. **3** To transfer, as property, to the ownership of another. —**al′ien·a′tion, al′ien·a′tor** *n.*

a·light[1] (ə·līt′) *v.i.* **a·light·ed** or **a·lit, a·light·ing 1** To descend and come to rest, as after flight. **2** To dismount. **3** To come by accident: with *on* or *upon.* [< OE *ā-* out, off + *līhtan* alight, orig., make light]

a·light[2] (ə·līt′) *adj. & adv.* Lighted; on fire. [ME *alihten* light up]

a·lign (ə·līn′) *v.t.* **1** To place or bring into a straight line. **2** To bring (oneself, a group, etc.) to the support of an idea, cause, etc. —*v.i.* **3** To come into line. [< F *a-* to + *ligne* line] —**a·lign′ment** *n.*

a·like (ə·līk′) *adj.* Having resemblance; like one another. —*adv.* In like manner. [< OE *gelīc*] —**a·like′ness** *n.*

al·i·ment (al′ə·mənt) *n.* Nourishment; food. [< L *alimentum* < *alere* nourish] —**al·i·men·tal** (al′ə·men′təl) *adj.* —**al′i·men′tal·ly** *adv.*

al·i·men·ta·ry (al′ə·men′tər·ē) *adj.* **1** Supplying nourishment. **2** Of or pertaining to food or nutrition.

alimentary canal The digestive tract between the mouth and the anus, including esophagus, stomach, and intestines.

al·i·men·ta·tion (al′ə·men·tā′shən) *n.* **1** The act or process of supplying nutrition. **2** Maintenance; support. —**al′·i·men′ta·tive** (-men′tə·tiv) *adj.*

al·i·mo·ny (al′ə·mō′nē) *n.* The allowance made to a woman from her husband's estate or income, for her maintenance after her divorce or legal separation. [< L *alimonia* food, support < *alere* nourish]

a·line (ə·līn′) *v.* **a·lined, a·lin·ing** ALIGN. —**a·line′ment** *n.*

a·lit (ə·lit′) A *p.t. & p.p.* of ALIGHT[1].

a·live (ə·līv′) *adj.* **1** In a living state; having life. **2** In existence, operation, etc. **3** In an animated state; lively. —**alive to** Aware of; alert to. —**alive with** Abounding in (living things). [< OE *on līfe* in life] —**Syn. 3** active, alert, vivacious.

a·liz·a·rin (ə·liz′ə·rin) *n.* An orange-red synthetic compound formerly obtained from madder, used as a red dye and to manufacture other dyes. Also **a·liz·a·rine** (ə·liz′ə·rin, -rēn). [< F *alizari* madder]

al·ka·li (al′kə·lī) *n. pl.* **·lis** or **·lies 1** Any of various highly reactive compounds that dissolve readily in water to form hydroxyl ions, neutralize acids, saponify fats, and turn red litmus blue. **2** Any compound that will neutralize an acid, as sodium carbonate, magnesia, etc. **3** Mineral matter found in soil and natural water and capable of neutralizing acid. [< Ar. *al-qalīy* the ashes of saltwort] —**al·ka·line** (al′kə·līn, -lin) *adj.* —**al′ka·lin′i·ty** (-lin′ə·tē) *n.*

al·ka·lize (al′kə·līz) *v.t. & v.i.* **·lized, ·liz·ing** To make or become like an alkali. —**al′ka·li·za′tion** *n.*

al·ka·loid (al′kə·loid) *n.* A nitrogenous organic base, usu. of vegetable origin, toxic in effect on animals and man, as strychnine, caffeine, morphine, etc. —**al′ka·loi′dal** *adj.*

Al·ko·ran (al′kō·rän′, -ran′) *n.* The Koran. —**Al′ko·ran′ic** (-ran′ik) *adj.*

all (ôl) *adj.* **1** The entire substance or extent of: *all* wisdom. **2** The entire number of. **3** The greatest possible: in *all* haste. **4** Any whatever: beyond *all* doubt. **5** Every: used in phrases with *manner, sorts,* and *kinds.* **6** Nothing except; only: He was *all* skin and bones. —*n.* **1** Everything that one has. **2** Whole being; totality. —*pron.* **1** Everyone: *All* are condemned. **2** Each one. **3** Everything: *All* is in readiness. **4** Every part, as of a whole: *All* of it is gone. —**above all** Primarily. —**after all 1** On the other hand. **2** In spite of everything. —**all in all** All things considered. —**at all 1** In any way: I can't come *at all.* **2** To any degree or extent: no luck *at all.* —**for all** To the degree that: *For all* I care, you can go without me. —**in all** Including everything; all told. —*adv.* **1** Wholly; entirely; traveling *all* through the night. **2** Exclusively; only: That portion is *all* for me. **3** For each; on each side: a score of three *all.* —**all along** All the time: I knew it *all along.* —**all but 1** Almost: I was *all but* drowned. **2** Every one except: He took *all but* six. —**all in** *Informal* Wearied. —**all of** No less than; quite: It's *all of* ten miles. —**all out** Making every effort. —**all over 1** Finished; past and gone. **2** Everywhere. **3** *Informal* Typically; in every way: That's George *all over.* —**all the** (**better, more,** etc.). So much the (better, more, etc.) [< OE]

Al·lah (al′ə, ä′lə) In the Muslim religion, the one supreme being; God. [< Ar.]

all-A·mer·i·can (ôl′ə·mer′ə·kən) *adj.* **1** Composed of or considered as representing the best in America: an *all-American* football team; an *all-American* boy. **2** Of or composed of Americans or products made in America. —*n.* **1** A hypothetical team, as of football players, selected from U.S. college players considered best in a season. **2** A player selected for such a team.

all-a·round (ôl′ə·round′) *adj.* **1** Having many uses. **2** Excelling in many things; versatile.

al·lay (ə·lā′) *v.t.* **1** To lessen the violence or reduce the intensity of. **2** To lay to rest, as fears; pacify; calm. [< OE *ā-* away + *lecgan* lay] —**al·lay′er** *n.*

all-clear (ôl′klir′) *n.* The signal indicating that an air raid is over. Also **all clear.**

al·le·ga·tion (al′ə·gā′shən) *n.* **1** The act of alleging. **2** That which is alleged. **3** Something alleged without proof. **4** *Law* The assertion that a party to a suit undertakes to prove.

al·lege (ə·lej′) *v.t.* **al·leged, al·leg·ing 1** To assert to be true without proving; affirm. **2** To plead as an excuse, in support of or in opposition to a claim or accusation. [?< L *allegare* to send on a mission, dispatch] —**al·lege′a·ble** *adj.* —**al·leg′er** *n.*

al·leged (ə·lejd′, ə·lej′id) *adj.* So represented but not proven: his *alleged* crime. —**al·leg′ed·ly** (-lej′id-) *adv.*

al·le·giance (ə·lē′jəns) *n.* Loyalty, or an obligation of loyalty, to a government, a superior, a cause, etc. [< OF *ligeance* < *liege.* See LIEGE.]

al·le·gor·ic (al′ə·gôr′ik, -gor′-) *adj.* Pertaining to or containing allegory. Also **al′le·gor′i·cal.** —**al′le·gor′i·cal·ly** *adv.*

al·le·go·rize (al′ə·gə·rīz) *v.* **·rized, ·riz·ing** *v.t.* **1** To relate or explain as or in the manner of an allegory. —*v.i.* **2** To make or use allegory. —**al·le·go·ri·za·tion** (al′ə·gôr′ə·zā′·shən, -gor′-), **al′le·go·riz′er** *n.*

al·le·go·ry (al′ə·gôr′ē, -gō′rē) *n. pl.* **·ries 1** A story or narrative that teaches a moral or truth by using people, animals, events, etc., as symbols of that moral or truth. **2** Any symbolic representation in literature or art. [< Gk. *allēgoria,* lit., a speaking otherwise] —**al′le·go′rist** (-gôr′ist, -gō′·rist, -gər·ist) *n.*

al·le·gret·to (al′ə·gret′o, *Ital.* ä′lā·gret′tō) *adj. & adv. Music* Somewhat slower than allegro. —*n. pl.* **·tos** An allegretto movement or passage. [Ital.]

al·le·gro (ə·lā′grō, ə·leg′rō; *Ital.* äl·lā′grō) *adj. & adv. Music* Quick; lively. —*n. pl.* **·gros** An allegro passage or movement. [Ital.]

al·le·lu·ia (al′ə·lo͞o′yə) *n. & interj.* HALLELUJAH.

al·ler·gen (al′ər·jən) *n.* Any substance capable of producing allergy. —**al·ler·gen·ic** (al′ər·jen′ik) *adj.*

al·ler·gic (ə·lûr′jik) *adj.* **1** Of or caused by allergy. **2** Highly susceptible to. **3** *Informal* Having an aversion.

al·ler·gist (al′ər·jist) *n.* A doctor specializing in allergies.

al·ler·gy (al′ər·jē) *n. pl.* **·gies** A condition of heightened susceptibility to a substance, as smoke or pollen. [<G *Allergie,* lit., altered reaction]

al·le·vi·ate (ə·lē′vē·āt) *v.t.* **·at·ed, ·at·ing** To make lighter or easier to bear; relieve. [< L *alleviare* < *ad-* to + *levis* light] —**al·le′vi·a′tion, al·le′vi·a′tor** *n.* —**al·le·vi·a·tive** (a·le′vē·ā′tiv, ə·lē′vē·ə·tiv) *adj.* —**Syn.** allay, assuage, lessen, mitigate.

al·ley (al′ē) *n. pl.* **·leys 1** A narrow passageway, esp. one behind or between city buildings. **2** A walk or lane bordered by trees, flowers, etc. **3** A bowling lane. [<OF *alee* a going, passage < *aler* go]

al·ley·way (al′ē·wā′) *n.* An alley (def. 1).

All Fools' Day APRIL FOOLS' DAY.

all fours The four legs of a quadruped, or the arms and legs of a person.

All·hal·lows (ôl′hal′ōz) *n.* All Saints' Day, Nov. 1.

al·li·ance (ə·lī′əns) *n.* **1** A formal treaty or agreement between countries, states, parties, etc; also, those involved in such an agreement. **2** Any union or relationship, as by blood, marriage, interests, etc. **3** Any similarity or affinity. [<L *alligantia* < *alligare.* See ALLY.]

al·lied (ə·līd′) *adj.* **1** United, as by treaty, relationship, etc. **2** Similar in nature or qualities.

Al·lies (al′īz, ə·līz′) **1** In World War I, Russia, France, Great Britain, and, later, the U.S., Italy, Japan, etc., the nations allied against Germany, Austria-Hungary, Bulgaria, and Turkey. **2** In World War II, Great Britain, the U.S.S.R., the U.S., and the other nations that fought the Axis. —**Al′lied** *adj.*

al·li·ga·tor (al′ə·gā′tər) *n.* **1** A large crocodilian reptile, found only in the southern U.S. and in China, having a shorter, blunter snout than the crocodile. **2** Leather made from the skin of the alligator. [<Sp. *el lagarto* the lizard <L *lacertus*]

alligator pear AVOCADO.

all-im·por·tant (ôl′im·pôr′tənt) *adj.* Very important; crucial; necessary.

all-in·clu·sive (ôl′in·klo͞o′siv) *adj.* Including everything.

al·lit·er·ate (ə·lit′ə·rāt) *v.* **·at·ed, ·at·ing** *v.i.* **1** To use alliteration. **2** To constitute alliteration. —*v.t.* **3** To make alliterative. [<L *ad-* to + *littera* a letter (of the alphabet)]

al·lit·er·a·tion (ə·lit′ə·rā′shən) *n.* The use or repetition of a succession of words with the same initial letter or sound, as in "The river running round the rock." —**al·lit·er·a·tive** (ə·lit′ər·ə·tiv, ə·rā′tiv) *adj.* —**al·lit′er·a·tive·ly** *adv.*

al·lo·cate (al′ə·kāt) *v.t.* **·cat·ed, ·cat·ing 1** To set apart for a special purpose, as funds. **2** To apportion; assign, as a share or in shares. **3** To locate or localize, as a person or event. [<L *ad-* to + *locare* to place] —**al′lo·ca′tion** *n.*

al·lo·path (al′ə·path) *n.* One who practices or approves of allopathy. Also **al·lop·a·thist** (ə·lop′ə·thist).

al·lop·a·thy (ə·lop′ə·thē) *n.* The system of treating disease by producing conditions different from or incompatible with the effects of the disease. [<Gk. *allos* other + *pathos* suffering] —**al·lo·path·ic** (al′ə·path′ik) *adj.* —**al′lo·path′i·cal·ly** *adv.*

al·lot (ə·lot′) *v.t.* **al·lot·ted, al·lot·ting 1** To assign or distribute by lot. **2** To apportion or assign: with *to.* [<OF *a-* to + *lot* a portion, lot]

al·lot·ment (ə·lot′mənt) *n.* **1** The act of allotting or that which is allotted. **2** A portion or share.

al·lo·trope (al′ə·trōp) *n.* Any of the forms assumed by an allotropic element.

al·lot·ro·py (ə·lot′rə·pē) *n.* The occurrence of certain chemical elements, as carbon, oxygen, etc., in two or more forms exhibiting different properties. Also **al·lot′ro·pism′** (-rə·piz′əm). —**al·lo·trop·ic** (al′ə·trop′ik) *adj.* —**al′lo·trop′i·cal·ly** *adv.* [<Gk. *allotropia* variation <*allos* other + *tropos* turn, manner]

all-out (ôl′out′) *adj.* Done with maximum effort; unrestrained. —*adv.* Without stint; with maximum effort.

al·low (ə·lou′) *v.t.* **1** To permit to occur, do, have, enter, etc. **2** To admit; acknowledge as true or valid. **3** To make provision for: *Allow* one yard for waste. **4** To grant; allot, as a share or portion. **5** *Regional* To maintain; declare. —**allow for** To make provision for; bear in mind: *Allow for* traffic. —**allow of** To permit or be subject to: Your remark *allows of* several interpretations. [<OF *alouer* place, use, assign <Med.L *allocare* to allocate and OF *alouer, aloer* approve <L *allaudare* extol] —**al·lowed′** *adj.*

al·low·a·ble (ə·lou′ə·bəl) *adj.* Permissible; admissible. —**al·low′a·ble·ness** *n.* —**al·low′a·bly** *adv.*

al·low·ance (ə·lou′əns) *n.* **1** The act of allowing. **2** That which is allowed. **3** An amount or portion, as of money or food, granted at regular intervals, for a specific purpose, etc. **4** A discount given, as for buying in volume, exchanging a used article, etc. **5** A compensation or consideration, as for circumstances, etc.: an *allowance* for late delivery. —*v.t.* **·anced, ·anc·ing 1** To put on an allowance. **2** To supply in limited or meager quantities.

al·low·ed·ly (ə·lou′id·lē) *adv.* Admittedly.

al·loy (al′oi, ə·loi′) *n.* **1** A substance having metallic properties and consisting of a metal and at least one other element, usu. another metal. **2** Anything that reduces purity. —*v.t.* (ə·loi′) **1** To reduce the purity of, as a metal, by mixing with an alloy. **2** To mix (metals) so as to form into an alloy. **3** To modify or debase, as by mixture with something inferior. [<L *alligare* to bind to]

all-pur·pose (ôl′pûr′pəs) *adj.* Generally useful; answering every purpose.

all-right (ôl′rīt′) *adj. Slang* Honest, good, excellent, etc.: an *all-right* guy.

all right 1 Satisfactory: His work is *all right.* **2** Correct. **3** Uninjured; not hurt. **4** *Informal* Certainly; without a doubt: I'll be there *all right!* **5** Yes: usu. in answer to a question: May I leave now? *All right.*

all-round (ôl′round′) *adj.* ALL-AROUND.

All Saints' Day A Christian festival commemorative of all saints, occurring Nov. 1.

All Souls' Day In certain Christian churches, a day of commemoration for the dead, usu. Nov. 2.

all·spice (ôl′spīs′) *n.* **1** The berry of a West Indian tree; the pimento. **2** The fragrant spice made from it. **3** The tree itself. [So called because it seems to combine the flavors of several spices]

all-star (ôl′stär′) *adj.* Consisting wholly of star performers, as the cast of a play.

all-time (ôl′tīm′) *adj.* Of or for all time.

al·lude (ə·lo͞od′) *v.i.* **al·lud·ed, al·lud·ing** To make indirect or casual reference: with *to.* [<L *alludere* play with, joke] —**Syn.** hint, imply, insinuate, intimate, suggest.

al·lure (ə·lo͝or′) *v.t. & v.i.* **al·lured, al·lur·ing** To attract attention and interest; entice. —*n.* The ability to attract or fascinate. [<OF *a-* to + *leurre* a lure] —**al·lur′er, al·lure′·ment** *n.*

al·lur·ing (ə·lo͝or′ing) *adj.* Attractive; fascinating. —**al·lur′ing·ly** *adv.* —**al·lur′ing·ness** *n.*

al·lu·sion (ə·lo͞o′zhən) *n.* **1** The act of alluding. **2** An indirect reference or mention. [<L *allusus,* p.p. of *alludere.* See ALLUDE.]

al·lu·sive (ə·lo͞o′siv) *adj.* Containing allusions. —**al·lu′sive·ly** *adv.* —**al·lu′sive·ness** *n.*

al·lu·vi·al (ə·lo͞o′vē·əl) *adj.* Pertaining to or composed of alluvium. —*n.* Alluvial soil.

al·lu·vi·um (ə·lo͞o′vē·əm) *n. pl.* **·vi·a** (-vē·ə) or **·vi·ums** *Geol.* Any deposit, as of sand or mud, transported and left by flowing water. [<L]

al·ly (ə·lī′) *v.* **al·lied, al·ly·ing** *v.t.* **1** To unite or combine by some relationship: usu. used in the passive or reflexively. —*v.i.* **2** To enter into alliance; become allied. —*n.* (al′ī, ə·lī′) *pl.* **al·lies 1** A country, sovereign, group, etc., leagued with another or others, as by treaty. **2** Any friend, associate, or helper. [<L *ad-* to + *ligare* bind]

al·ma ma·ter (al′mə mä′tər, al′mə mā′tər, äl′mə mä′tər) The institution of learning that one has attended. [L, fostering mother]

al·ma·nac (ôl′mə·nak) *n.* **1** A yearly calendar giving weather forecasts, astronomical information, times of high and low tides, and other data. **2** An annual book containing facts and statistics on a large variety of subjects. [<Ar. *al-manākh*]

al·might·y (ôl·mī′tē) *adj.* **1** Able to do all things; omnipotent. 2 *Informal* Great; extreme: an *almighty* defeat. —*adv. Slang* Exceedingly: *almighty* mad. —**the Almighty** God. [< OE < *eall* all + *mihtig* mighty] —**al·might′i·ly** *adv.* —**al·might′i·ness** *n.*

al·mond (ä′mənd, am′ənd) *n.* 1 A small tree related to the plum, cultivated in warm regions. 2 The edible, nutlike kernel of the fruit of this tree. [< Gk. *amygdalē*]

al·mon·er (al′mən·ər, ä′mən-) *n.* An official dispenser of alms. [< L *eleemosyna* alms]

al·most (ôl′mōst, ôl·mōst′) *adv.* Approximately; very nearly; all but: *Almost* everyone attended; *almost* time for supper. [< OE *eall* all + *mǣst* most]

alms (ämz) *n. sing. & pl.* Money or gifts for the poor. [< Gk. *eleēmosynē* < *eleos* pity]

alms·house (ämz′hous′) *n.* A poorhouse.

al·oe (al′ō) *n. pl.* **·oes** Any of various liliaceous plants with fleshy leaves, mostly native to Africa. [< Gk. *aloē*]

al·oes (al′ōz) *n. pl. (construed as sing.)* A bitter cathartic made from certain species of aloe.

a·loft (ə·lôft′, ə·loft′) *adv.* 1 In or to a high or higher place; on high; high up. 2 *Naut.* At or to the higher parts of a ship's rigging. [< ON *a lopt* in (the) air]

a·lo·ha (ə·lō′ə, ä·lō′hä) *n. Hawaiian* Love: used also as a salutation and a farewell.

a·lone (ə·lōn′) *adv. & adj.* 1 Without company; solitary. 2 Without equal; unique. 3 Excluding all other people or things; only: She *alone* understood. [ME *al* all + *one* one]

a·long (ə·lông′, ə·long′) *adv.* 1 Following the length of; lengthwise. 2 Progressively onward. 3 In company or association: with *with*: I came *along* with my cousins. 4 As a companion, necessary object, etc.: Bring a sweater *along.* 5 Advanced: well *along* in years. 6 *Informal* Near; approaching: with *about: along* about sundown. —**all along** The whole time; from the outset. —**get along** 1 To go forward. 2 To manage in spite of difficulties. 3 To be successful. 4 To exist together in harmony. 5 *Informal* To go away. —*prep.* 1 In the line of; through or over the length of: *along* the coast. 2 In agreement or harmony with: *along* certain principles. [< OE *andlang*]

a·long·shore (ə·lông′shôr′, ə·long′-, -shōr′) *adv.* Along the shore.

a·long·side (ə·lông′sīd′, ə·long′-) *adv.* Close to or along the side. —*prep.* Side by side with.

a·loof (ə·lōōf′) *adj.* Distant or reserved, as in manner, interest, etc. —*adv.* At a distance. [< A-[1] + earlier *loof* luff] —**a·loof′ly** *adv.* —**a·loof′ness** *n.*

a·loud (ə·loud′) *adv.* Loudly or audibly.

alp (alp) *n.* 1 Any peak of the Alps. 2 A high mountain. [< L *Alpes* the Alps]

al·pac·a (al·pak′ə) *n.* 1 A domesticated ruminant of South America, resembling the llama. 2 Its long, silky wool. 3 A cloth made of this wool. [< Sp.]

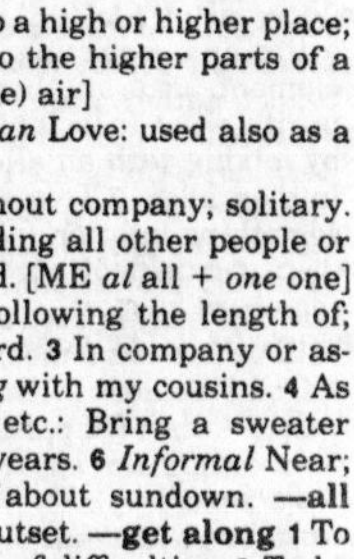

Alpaca

al·pen·horn (al′pən·hôrn′) A very long, wooden horn, used by herdsmen in the Alps.

al·pen·stock (al′pən·stok′) *n.* A long, iron-pointed staff, used by mountain-climbers. [< G, lit., alps stick]

al·pha (al′fə) *n.* 1 The first letter and vowel of the Greek alphabet (Α, α). 2 The beginning or first of anything.

al·pha·bet (al′fə·bet) *n.* 1 The letters that form the elements of written language, in an order as fixed by usage. 2 Any system of characters or symbols representing the sounds of speech. 3 The simplest elements of anything. [< Gk. *alpha* alpha + *bēta* beta]

al·pha·bet·i·cal (al′fə·bet′i·kəl) *adj.* 1 Of or expressed by an alphabet. 2 Arranged in the order of the alphabet. Also **al′pha·bet′ic.** —**al′pha·bet′i·cal·ly** *adv.*

al·pha·bet·ize (al′fə·bə·tīz′) *v.t.* **·ized, ·iz·ing** 1 To put in alphabetical order. 2 To express by or furnish with an alphabet. —**al·pha·bet·i·za·tion** (al′fə·bet′ə·zā′shən) *n.*

Alpha Cen·tau·ri (sen·tôr′ē) *Astron.* The stellar system nearest to the solar system, a bright double star about 4.4 light-years away.

al·pha·nu·mer·ic (al′fə·nyōō·mer′ik) *adj.* Consisting of or using the letters of the alphabet and numerals, as in a computer code. Also **al′pha·nu·mer′i·cal.** [< ALPHA(BET) + NUMERIC(AL)] —**al′pha·nu·mer′i·cal·ly** *adv.*

alpha particle *Physics* The nucleus of a helium atom, consisting of two protons and two neutrons.

alpha ray *Physics* A stream of alpha particles.

al·pine (al′pīn, -pin) *adj.* 1 Like an alp or mountain; lofty and towering. 2 *Biol.* Inhabiting or growing in mountain regions.

Al·pine (al′pīn, -pin) *adj.* Pertaining to or characteristic of the Alps. [< L *Alpinus*]

al·read·y (ôl·red′ē) *adv.* Before or by this time; even now: He has *already* left.

al·right (ôl·rīt′) All right: a spelling not yet considered acceptable.

Al·sa·tian (al·sā′shən) *adj.* Of or pertaining to Alsace. —*n.* 1 A native or citizen of Alsace. 2 A German shepherd dog.

al·so (ôl′sō) *adv. & conj.* 1 Besides; in addition. 2 In like manner; likewise. [< OE *alswā, ealswā* all so]

al·so-ran (ôl′sō·ran′) *n. Informal* One who loses a race, election, or any competition.

alt. alteration; alternate; altitude; alto.

Alta. Alberta (Canada).

Al·ta·ir (al·tä′ir, al·târ′) A double star, one of the 20 brightest stars. [< Ar. *al-ṭā′ir* the bird]

al·tar (ôl′tər) *n.* 1 Any raised place or structure on which sacrifices may be offered or incense burned as an act of worship. 2 *Eccl.* The structure of wood or stone on which the elements are consecrated in the Eucharist. —**lead to the altar** To marry. [< L *altare*]

altar boy A boy or man who assists the celebrant of a religious service.

al·tar·piece (ôl′tər·pēs′) *n.* A painting, mosaic, or bas-relief for display over and behind an altar.

al·ter (ôl′tər) *v.t.* 1 To cause to be different; change; modify. 2 To fit (a garment) by recutting, resewing, etc. 3 To castrate. —*v.i.* 4 To change, as in character or appearance. [< Med.L *alterare* < L *alter* other] —**al′ter·a·ble** *adj.* —**al′ter·a·bly** *adv.*

al·ter·a·tion (ôl′tə·rā′shən) *n.* 1 The act of altering or the state of being altered. 2 The result of this; change.

al·ter·a·tive (ôl′tə·rā′tiv, -tər·ə·tiv) *adj.* 1 Tending to produce change. 2 *Med.* Gradually returning the body to a normal state. —*n. Med.* An alterative medicine. Also **al·ter·ant** (ôl′tər·ənt).

al·ter·cate (ôl′tər·kāt, al′-) *v.i.* **·cat·ed, ·cat·ing** To dispute vehemently; wrangle. [< L *altercari* to dispute with one another < *alter* other]

al·ter·ca·tion (ôl′tər·kā′shən, al′-) *n.* Angry controversy; disputing; wrangling.

al·ter e·go (ôl′tər ē′gō, al′tər eg′ō) 1 Another self; a double. 2 An intimate friend. [L, lit., other I]

al·ter·nate (ôl′tər·nāt, al′-) *v.* **·nat·ed, ·nat·ing** *v.t.* 1 To arrange, use, or perform by turns. 2 To cause to follow in turns. —*v.i.* 3 To occur or appear in turns. 4 To take turns: to *alternate* on a job. 5 To pass repeatedly back and forth from one thing or condition to another —*adj.* (ôl′tər·nit, al′-) 1 Existing, occurring, or following by turns; reciprocal. 2 Referring to every second or every other (of a series). 3 Alternative: an *alternate* method. 4 *Bot.* **a** Placed singly at intervals on either side of the stem, as leaves. **b** Disposed at intervals between other parts. —*n.* (ôl′tər·nit, al′-) A substitute or second. [< L *alternare* < *alternus* every second one < *alter* other] —**al′ter·nate·ly** *adv.* —**al′ter·nate·ness** *n.*

alternating current An electric current that undergoes cyclic changes in direction or polarity.

al·ter·na·tion (ôl′tər·nā′shən, al′-) *n.* Occurrence or change from one place, state, or condition to another and back again.

al·ter·na·tive (ôl·tûr′nə·tiv, al-) *adj.* Being or affording a choice between two or, loosely, more than two things. —

n. 1 A choice between two things or, loosely, more than two. 2 One of the things to be chosen. 3 Something still to be chosen or decided: What is the *alternative* to war? **—al·ter′na·tive·ly** *adv.* **—al·ter′na·tive·ness** *n.*

al·ter·na·tor (ôl′tər·nā′tər, al′-) *n.* A mechanical generator of alternating current.

al·though (ôl·thō′) *conj.* Admitting or granting that; though. Also **al·tho′.** [< ALL + THOUGH]

al·tim·e·ter (al·tim′ə·tər, al′tə·mē′tər) *n.* Any of various instruments for measuring altitude, esp. of aircraft.

al·ti·tude (al′tə·tyōōd) *n.* 1 Vertical elevation above any given reference point, esp. above mean sea level; height. 2 *Astron.* Angular elevation above the horizon. 3 *Geom.* The vertical distance from the base of a figure to its highest point. 4 A high or the highest point. [< L *altus* high] **—al′ti·tu′di·nal** (-də·nəl) *adj.*

al·to (al′tō) *adj.* Having a range immediately below the highest or between soprano and tenor: an *alto* saxaphone. *—n. pl.* **·tos** 1 The lowest female voice; contralto. 2 The highest male voice; countertenor. 3 An alto singer, instrument, or part. [< Ital. < L *altus* high]

al·to·geth·er (ôl′tə·geth′ər, ôl′tə·geth′ər) *adv.* 1 Completely; wholly; entirely. 2 With everything included; all told. *—n.* A whole.

al·tru·ism (al′trōō·iz′əm) *n.* Unselfish devotion to the welfare of others. [< L *alter* other] **—al′tru·ist** *n.* **—al′tru·is′tic** *adj.* **—al′tru·is′ti·cal·ly** *adv.*

al·um (al′əm) *n.* 1 A double sulfate of aluminum and potassium, used as a styptic and astringent. 2 Any of a class of double sulfates containing both a univalent and a trivalent metal. [< L *alumen*]

a·lu·mi·na (ə·lōō′mə·nə) *n.* An oxide of aluminum occurring abundantly in clay and bauxite and as corundum in emery, sapphires, rubies, etc. [< L *alumen* alum]

a·lu·mi·num (ə·lōō′mə·nəm) *n.* A lightweight, silvery, metallic element (symbol Al) very abundant in minerals in the earth's crust and having countless technological uses, esp. as a structural and packaging material. *Brit. sp.* **al·u·min·i·um** (al′yə·min′ē·əm). [< L *alumen* alum] **—a·lu′mi·nous** *adj.*

a·lum·na (ə·lum′nə) *n. pl.* **·nae** (-nē) A woman who has attended or graduated from a college or school. [< L, fem. of *alumnus*] • See ALUMNUS.

a·lum·nus (ə·lum′nəs) *n. pl.* **·ni** (-nī) A person, esp. a male, who has attended or graduated from a college or school. [< L, foster son < *alere* nourish] • In referring to graduates or former students of a coeducational school, the plural form *alumni* often is used to include both men and women.

al·ve·o·lar (al·vē′ə·lər) *adj.* 1 Denoting that part of the jaws in which the teeth are set. 2 *Phonet.* Formed with the tongue touching or near the alveolar ridge, as (t), (d), and (s) in English. *—n. Phonet.* A sound so produced.

alveolar ridge *Anat.* The bony ridge of the jaw just above the upper front teeth.

al·ve·o·late (al·vē′ə·lit, al′vē·ə-) *adj.* Deeply pitted. **—al·ve′o·la′tion** *n.*

al·ve·o·lus (al·vē′ə·ləs) *n. pl.* **·li** (-lī) 1 A small cavity or pit, as an air cell of a lung, a tooth socket, etc. 2 *Usu. pl.* The alveolar ridge. [< L, dim. of *alveus* a hollow]

al·ways (ôl′wāz, -wiz) *adv.* 1 Perpetually; for all time. 2 At every time; on all occasions. [< OE *ealne weg* all the way]

a·lys·sum (ə·lis′əm) *n.* Any of a large genus of plants related to mustard and often grown in gardens, as sweet alyssum. [< Gk. *alysson*, name of a plant]

am (am, *unstressed* əm) Present tense, first person singular, of BE. [< OE *eom, am*]

AM, A.M., a.m., a-m, amplitude modulation.

A.M. Air Mail; Master of Arts (L *Artium Magister*).

A.M., a.m. before noon (L *ante meridiem*).

Am americium.

Am. America; American.

A.M.A. American Medical Association.

a·mah (ä′mə, am′ə) *n.* In India and the Orient, a female attendant for children. Also **a′ma.**

a·mal·gam (ə·mal′gəm) *n.* 1 An alloy of mercury with another metal. 2 Any mixture or combination. [< Med.L *amalgama*]

a·mal·ga·mate (ə·mal′gə·māt) *v.t. & v.i.* **·mat·ed, ·mat·ing** 1 To form an amalgam. 2 To unite or combine: to *amalgamate* several small government agencies. **—a·mal′ga·ma′tion, a·mal′ga·ma′tor** or **a·mal′ga·ma′ter** *n.*

a·man·u·en·sis (ə·man′yōō·en′sis) *n. pl.* **·ses** (-sēz) One who copies manuscript or takes dictation; a secretary. [< L *ab-* from, by + *manus* hand]

am·a·ranth (am′ə·ranth) *n.* 1 Any of various plants with dry flowers that do not readily fade. 2 An imaginary, never-fading flower. 3 A purplish red. [< Gk. *amarantos*, lit., unfading] **—am·a·ran·thine** (am′ə·ran′thin) *adj.*

am·a·ryl·lis (am′ə·ril′is) *n.* A bulbous South African plant with large white, red, or purplish flowers, superficially resembling the lily. [< Gk. *Amaryllis*, fem. personal name]

a b

Amaryllis
a. bulb. b. flower.

a·mass (ə·mas′) *v.t.* To heap up; accumulate, esp. wealth or possessions. [< OF *a-* to + *masser* pile up] **—a·mass′a·ble** *adj.* **—a·mass′er, a·mass′ment** *n.* **—Syn.** collect, gather, acquire.

am·a·teur (am′ə·chōōr, -tyōōr, -tər, am′ə·tûr′) *n.* 1 One who practices an art, science, skill, etc., for his own pleasure and not as a paid professional. 2 An athlete who has not used any athletic skill or fame as a means of profit. 3 One who does something without professional skill or ease. *—adj.* 1 Of, pertaining to, or done by an amateur or amateurs. 2 Not expert. [< L *amator* lover < *amare* love] **—am′a·teur·ism** *n.*

am·a·teur·ish (am′ə·chōōr′ish, -tyōōr′-, -tûr′-) *adj.* Lacking the skill or perfection of an expert or professional. **—am′a·teur′ish·ly** *adv.* **—am′a·teur′ish·ness** *n.*

am·a·to·ry (am′ə·tôr′ē, -tō′rē) *adj.* Of, characterized by, or exciting love, esp. sexual love. [< L *amare* love]

a·maze (ə·māz′) *v.t.* **a·mazed, a·maz·ing** To overwhelm, as by wonder or surprise; astonish greatly: explorers *amazed* to discover a flourishing civilization. [< OE *āmasian*] **—a·maz·ed·ly** (ə·mā′zid·lē), **a·maz′ing·ly** *adv.*

a·maze·ment (ə·māz′mənt) *n.* Wonder; surprise; astonishment.

Am·a·zon (am′ə·zon, -zən) *Gk. Myth.* One of a race of female warriors. *—n.* Any large, strong, or athletic woman or girl: also **am′a·zon.**

am·bas·sa·dor (am·bas′ə·dər, -dôr) *n.* 1 An accredited diplomatic agent of the highest rank, appointed as the representative of one government to another. 2 Any personal representative or messenger. 3 A person considered as a representative, as of his homeland: visiting athletes serving as *ambassadors* of good will. [< Ital. *ambasciatore*] **—am·bas·sa·do·ri·al** (am·bas′ə·dôr′ē·əl, -dō′rē-) *adj.* **—am·bas′sa·dor·ship** *n.* **—am·bas′sa·dress** (-drəs) *n. Fem.*

am·ber (am′bər) *n.* 1 A translucent, yellow or brownish yellow fossil resin, used in the arts, jewelry, etc. 2 The color of amber. *—adj.* Pertaining to, like, or of the color of amber. [< Ar. *'anbar* ambergris]

am·ber·gris (am′bər·grēs, -gris) *n.* An opaque, gray, waxy secretion from the intestines of the sperm whale, used in certain perfumes. [< F *ambre gris* gray amber]

ambi- *combining form* Both: *ambidextrous.* [< L *ambo* both]

am·bi·ance (am′bē·əns, *Fr.* äṅ·byäṅs′) *n.* The environment or pervading atmosphere of a place, situation, etc. Also **am·bi·ence.** [F< L *ambi-* around + *ire* go]

am·bi·ant (am′bē·ənt) *adj.* Surrounding; encompassing. Also **am′bi·ent.**

am·bi·dex·ter·i·ty (am′bə·dek·ster′ə·tē) *n.* 1 The state or quality of being ambidextrous. 2 Duplicity; trickery.

am·bi·dex·trous (am′bə·dek′strəs) *adj.* 1 Able to use both hands equally well. 2 Very dexterous or skillful. 3 Dissembling; double-dealing. **—am′bi·dex′trous·ly** *adv.* **—am′bi·dex′trous·ness** *n.*

am·bi·gu·i·ty (am′bə·gyōō′ə·tē) *n. pl.* **·ties** 1 The quality of being ambiguous. 2 Something ambiguous.

am·big·u·ous (am·big′yōō·əs) *adj.* 1 Capable of being understood in more senses than one. 2 Doubtful or uncertain. [< L *ambigere* wander about] **—am·big′u·ous·ly** *adv.* **—am·big′u·ous·ness** *n.*

am·bi·tion (am·bish′ən) *n.* 1 A strong desire to achieve something, as success, power, wealth, etc. 2 An object so desired or striven for. 3 A desire to work, or energy for work. [< L *ambitio* a going about (to solicit votes) < *ambire* to go about]

am·bi·tious (am·bish′əs) *adj.* 1 Actuated or characterized by ambition. 2 Greatly desiring; eager for: with *of* or the infinitive. 3 Demanding; difficult: an *ambitious* plan. **—am·bi′tious·ly** *adv.* **—am·bi′tious·ness** *n.*

am·biv·a·lence (am·biv′ə·ləns) *n.* The existence of contradictory emotions or ideas about a person or thing. [< AMBI- + L *valere* be strong, be worth] **—am·biv′a·lent** *adj.*

am·ble (am′bəl) *v.i.* **am·bled** (-bəld), **am·bling** 1 To move, as a horse, by lifting the two feet on one side together, alternately with the two feet on the other. 2 To proceed leisurely. —*n.* An ambling movement, like that of a horse. [< L *ambulare* walk] **—am′bler** *n.* **—am′bling·ly** *adv.*

am·bro·sia (am·brō′zhə, -zhē·ə) *n.* 1 *Gk. & Rom. Myth.* The food of the gods, giving immortality. 2 Any very delicious food or drink. [< Gk. *ambrotos* immortal] **—am·bro′·sial, am·bro′sian** *adj.* **—am·bro′sial·ly** *adv.*

am·bu·lance (am′byə·ləns) *n.* A vehicle for conveying the sick and wounded. [< F *(hôpital) ambulant* walking (hospital)]

am·bu·lant (am′byə·lənt) *adj.* Walking or moving about. [< L *ambulare* walk]

am·bu·late (am′byə·lāt) *v.i.* **·lat·ed, ·lat·ing** To walk about; move from place to place. [< L *ambulare* walk] **—am′bu·la′tion** *n.* **—am·bu·la·tive** (am′byə·lā′tiv, -lə·tiv) *adj.*

am·bu·la·to·ry (am′byə·lə·tôr′ē, -tō′rē) *adj.* 1 Of or for walking or walkers. 2 Able to walk, as an invalid. 3 Shifting; not fixed or stationary.

am·bus·cade (am′bəs·kād′, am′bəs·kād′) *n.* AMBUSH. —*v.t. & v.i.* **·cad·ed, ·cad·ing** AMBUSH. [< Ital. *imboscata* an ambush]

am·bush (am′boosh) *n.* 1 The act of lying in wait to surprise or attack an enemy. 2 The hiding place or the persons hidden. Also **am′bush·ment.** —*v.t. & v.i.* To hide in or attack from ambush. [< Ital. *imboscare* place in a bush, set an ambush] **—am′bush·er** *n.*

a·me·ba (ə·mē′bə) *n. pl.* **·bas** or **·bae** (-bē) AMOEBA.

a·me·boid (ə·mē′boid) *adj.* AMOEBOID.

a·meer (ə·mir′) *n.* EMIR.

a·mel·io·rate (ə·mēl′yə·rāt) *v.t & v.i.* **·rat·ed, ·rat·ing** To make or become better; improve. [< L *ad-* to + *miliorare* to better] **—a·mel′io·rant** (-rənt), **a·mel′io·ra′tion** *n.* **—a·mel·io·ra·tive** (ə·mēl′yə·rā′tiv, -rə·tiv) *adj.*

a·men (ā′men′, ä′-) *interj.* So it is; so be it; used at the end of a prayer or to express agreement. —*adv.* Verily; truly. —*n.* The word *amen* or its use. [< Heb. *āmēn* verily]

A·men (ä′mən) *Egypt. Myth.* The god of life and procreation. Also **A′men-Ra′** (-rä′).

a·me·na·ble (ə·mē′nə·bəl, ə·men′ə-) *adj.* 1 Agreeable; tractable. 2 Accountable or responsible, as to authority. 3 Capable of being tested by rule or law. [< L *ad-* to + *minare* drive (with threats)] **—a·me′na·bil′i·ty, a·me′na·ble·ness** *n.* **—a·me′na·bly** *adv.*

a·mend (ə·mend′) *v. t.* 1 To change for the better; improve. 2 To free from faults. 3 To change or alter by authority; to *amend* a bill. —*v.i.* 4 To become better in conduct. [< L *emendare* to free from faults] **—a·mend′a·ble, a·mend′a·to′ry** *adj.* **—a·mend′a·ble·ness, a·mend′er** *n.* **—Syn.** 1 ameliorate, better, mitigate. 2 correct, rectify, reform, repair, restore.

a·mend·ment (ə·mend′mənt) *n.* 1 Change for the better. 2 A removal of faults; correction. 3 The changing, as of a law, bill, or motion. 4 The statement of such a change.

a·mends (ə·mendz′) *n. pl.* Reparation, as in satisfaction for loss, insult, etc.

a·men·i·ty (ə·men′ə·tē, ə·mēn′-) *n. pl.* **·ties** 1 Agreeableness; pleasantness. 2 *Usu. pl.* Any of the pleasant acts and courtesies of polite behavior. [< L *amoenus* pleasant]

Amer. America; American.

Am·er·a·sian (am′ər·ā′zhən, -shən) *adj.* Of American and Asian descent. —*n.* A person of mixed American and Asian parentage.

a·merce (ə·mûrs′) *v.t.* **a·merced, a·merc·ing** 1 To punish by an assessment or fine. 2 To punish, as by deprivation. [< AF *a merci* at the mercy of] **—a·merce′a·ble** *adj.*

A·mer·i·ca (ə·mer′ə·kə) *n.* 1 The United States of America. 2 North America. 3 South America. 4 Both of these continents considered together: also **the Americas.**

A·mer·i·can (ə·mer′ə·kən) *adj.* 1 Of or pertaining to the United States of America, its history, government, people, etc. 2 Of, in, near, or pertaining to North America or South America. —*n.* 1 A native or citizen of the U.S. 2 English as used in the U.S.; American English.

A·mer·i·ca·na (ə·mer′ə·kä′nə, -kan′ə, -kā′nə) *n. pl.* Things or materials relating to or characteristic of America, its history, traditions, etc.

American cheese Any of several mild Cheddar cheeses popular in the U.S.

American English The English language as used in the U.S.

American Expeditionary Forces The U.S. Army troops sent to Europe during World War I.

American Federation of Labor A federation of trade unions, founded in 1886, which merged in 1955 with the Congress of Industrial Organizations.

American Indian 1 A member of one of the aboriginal races of North or South America or the West Indies. 2 Any of the native languages spoken by American Indians.

A·mer·i·can·ism (ə·mer′ə·kən·iz′əm) *n.* 1 A word, phrase, usage, or a trait, custom, or tradition peculiar to the people of the U.S. 2 Attachment to America, its institutions and traditions.

A·mer·i·can·ize (ə·mer′ə·kən·īz) *v.t. & v.i.* **·ized, ·iz·ing** To become or cause to become American in spirit, speech, customs, etc. **—A·mer′i·can·i·za′tion** *n.*

American Legion An organization of U.S. war veterans, founded in 1919.

American plan At a hotel, a system in which meals and services are included in the price for the room.

American Revolution The war (1775–83) by which the British colonies in North America won their independence.

American Spanish The Spanish language as it is used in the Western Hemisphere.

am·er·ic·i·um (am′ə·rish′ē·əm) *n.* An artificially produced radioactive element (symbol Am). [< *America*]

Am·er·ind (am′ə·rind) *n.* An American Indian or Eskimo. **—Am′er·in′di·an** *adj., n.* **—Am′er·in′dic** *adj.*

am·e·thyst (am′ə·thist) *n.* 1 Quartz with purple or violet color; a semiprecious stone. 2 A purple variety of sapphire or corundum used as a gem. 3 A purplish violet color. [< Gk. *amethystos* not intoxicated, from the ancient belief that the stone prevented intoxication]

Am·har·ic (am·har′ik, äm·hä′rik) *n.* A Semitic language, the official language of Ethiopia.

a·mi (á·mē′) *n. pl.* **a·mis** (á·mē′) *French* A friend.

a·mi·a·ble (ā′mē·ə·bəl) *adj.* Friendly and good-natured. [< L *amicus* friend.] **—a′mi·a·bil′i·ty, a′mi·a·ble·ness** *n.* **—a′mi·a·bly** *adv.* **—Syn.** agreeable, kind, pleasant, pleasing.

am·i·ca·ble (am′i·kə·bəl) *adj.* Friendly; peaceable. [< L *amicus* friend] **—am·i·ca·bil·i·ty** (am·i·kə·bil′ə·tē), **am′i·ca·ble·ness** *n.* **—am′i·ca·bly** *adv.*

am·ice (am′is) *n.* A rectangular piece of white linen worn around the shoulders by a priest celebrating Mass. [< L *amictus* cloak]

a·mid (ə·mid′) *prep.* In the midst of; among. [< OE *on middan* in the middle]

am·ide (am′īd, -id) *n.* A derivative of ammonia having one or more hydrogen atoms replaced by an organic radical or a metal. Also **am·id** (am′id). [< AM(MONIA) + -IDE] **—am·ic** (am′ik), **a·mid·ic** (ə·mid′ik) *adj.*

am·i·dol (am′ə·dol, -dōl) *n.* A white crystalline powder used in photography as a developer.

a·mid·ships (ə·mid′ships) *adv. Naut.* Halfway between stem and stern of a ship.

a·midst (ə·midst′) *prep.* AMID.

---

a·mi·go (ə·mē′gō) *n. pl.* **·gos** *Spanish* A friend.

Am. Ind. American Indian.

am·ine (am′ēn, ə·mēn′) *n.* One of numerous organic compounds derived from ammonia by replacement of hydrogen by one or more univalent hydrocarbon radicals. [< AM(MONIA) + -INE]

a·mi·no (ə·mē′nō, am′ə·nō) *adj.* Pertaining to an amine or amines.

amino acid Any of a group of amines having both acidic and basic properties and forming the constituents of protein molecules.

a·mir (ə·mir′) *n.* EMIR.

Am·ish (am′ish, ä′mish) *n.* A sect of Mennonites, founded in the 17th century. —*adj.* Of this sect. [after Jacob *Ammann,* the founder]

a·miss (ə·mis′) *adj.* Out of order; wrong; improper: used predicatively: Something is *amiss.* —*adv.* In a wrong, improper, or defective way or manner. —**take amiss** To take offense at. [< ME *a-* at + *missen* to miss]

am·i·to·sis (ā′mī·tō′sis) *n.* Cell division without preliminary formation of chromosomes. [< A-[4] without + MITOSIS] —**am·i·tot·ic** (ā′mī·tot′ik) *adj.* —**am′i·tot′i·cal·ly** *adv.*

am·i·ty (am′ə·tē) *n. pl.* **·ties** Peaceful relations; friendship. [< L *amicus* friend]

am·me·ter (am′mē′tər) *n. Electr.* An instrument for measuring an electric current. [< AM(PERE) + -METER]

am·mo·nia (ə·mōn′yə, ə·mō′nē·ə) *n.* **1** A colorless, pungent, suffocating gas composed of nitrogen and hydrogen. **2** A solution of this gas in water: also **ammonia water.** [< SAL AMMONIAC] —**am·mo′ni·ac, am·mo·ni·a·cal** (am′ə·nī′ə·kəl) *adj.*

am·mo·ni·ac (ə·mō′nē·ak) *n.* A gum resin obtained from a plant related to the carrot. [< Gk. *ammōniakon,* a resinous gum said to come from a plant growing near the temple of *Amen* in Libya]

am·mon·ite (am′ən·īt) *n.* A spiral fossil cephalopod shell, commonly found in Mesozoic rocks. [< L *cornu Ammonis* horn of Amen]

Ammonite

am·mo·ni·um (ə·mō′nē·əm) *n.* The univalent cation formed by the solution of ammonia in water.

ammonium chloride A white, crystalline, soluble compound formed by the replacement of hydrogen in hydrochloric acid by ammonium; sal ammoniac, used in medicine and industry.

ammonium hydroxide The alkaline solution of ammonia in water.

am·mu·ni·tion (am′yə·nish′ən) *n.* **1** Any one of various articles used in the discharge of firearms and ordnance, as cartridges, shells, rockets, grenades, etc. **2** Any resources for attack or defense. [< L *munitio* < *munire* fortify]

am·ne·sia (am·nē′zhə, -zhē·ə) *n.* Loss or impairment of memory. [< Gk. *amnēsia* forgetfulness] —**am·ne′si·ac** (-zhē·ak′, -zē-) *adj., n.* —**am·ne′sic** (-sik, -zik), **am·nes′tic** (-nes′tik) *adj.*

am·nes·ty (am′nəs·tē) *n. pl.* **·ties** An act of pardon on the part of a government or authority, absolving offenders or groups of offenders. —*v.t.* **·tied, ·ty·ing** To grant amnesty to. [< Gk. *amnēstia* < *a-* not + *mnasthai* remember]

am·ni·o·cen·te·sis (am′nē·ō·sen·tē′sis) *n. Med.* The sampling of amniotic fluid of a pregnant woman, as to detect chromosomal anomalies or determine the sex of the fetus. [< AMNION + Gk. *kentein* to prick]

am·ni·on (am′nē·ən) *n. pl.* **·ni·ons** or **·ni·a** (-nē·ə) *Biol.* A membranous sac enclosing the embryo in mammals, birds, and reptiles. [< Gk. *amnion* sac] —**am·ni·on·ic** (am′·nē·on′ik), **am·ni·ot·ic** (am′nē·ot′ik) *adj.*

a·mok (ə·muk′) *adj.* Possessed with murderous frenzy. —*adv.* In a violent or frenzied manner. —**run** (or **go**) **amok** **1** To run around attacking everybody one meets. **2** To exceed all bounds of restraint; go wild. Also **a·mock′.** [< Malay *amoq* engaging furiously in battle]

a·moe·ba (ə·mē′bə) *n. pl.* **·bas** or **·bae** (bē) Any of a genus of unicellular organisms found in soil, water, and as parasites in other animals, of an indefinite shape that changes in the process of moving. [< Gk. *amoibē* change] —**a·moe′·bic, a·moe′boid** *adj.*

A·mon (ä′mən) AMEN.

a·mong (ə·mung′) *prep.* **1** In the midst of. **2** In the class, number, or company of: She is *among* the best. **3** In company or association with: working *among* the poor. **4** Of or with a number of: a custom *among* the French. **5** In portions for each of: Divide this *among* the sick. **6** In comparison with: He was just one *among* hundreds. **7** Reciprocally with or between: quarrels *among* friends. **8** Through the joint effort of: *Among* us, we can get the money. Also **a·mongst′.** [< OE *on gemang* in the crowd] • See BETWEEN.

a·mon·til·la·do (ə·mon′tə·lä′dō, *Sp.* ä·môn′tē·lyä′thō) *n.* A pale, dry sherry. [< *Montilla,* a town in southern Spain]

a·mor·al (ā·môr′əl, ā·mor′əl) *adj.* **1** Not subject to or concerned with moral or ethical distinctions. **2** Lacking a sense of right and wrong. —**a·mo·ral·i·ty** (ā′mə·ral′ə·tē) *n.* —**a·mor′al·ly** *adv.* • See UNMORAL.

am·o·rous (am′ə·rəs) *adj.* **1** Full of or desiring love, esp. sexual love. **2** Showing, springing from, or exciting to love or sexual desire: an *amorous* look. **3** In love; enamored: usu. with *of.* [< OF < LL *amorosus* < L *amor* love] —**am′·o·rous·ly** *adv.* —**am′o·rous·ness** *n.*

a·mor·phous (ə·môr′fəs) *adj.* **1** Without definite form or shape; structureless. **2** Without definite characteristics or organization; anomalous. **3** Lacking definite crystalline structure. [< Gk. *a-* without + *morphē* form] —**a·mor′·phism, a·mor′phous·ness** *n.* —**a·mor′phous·ly** *adv.*

am·or·tize (am′ər·tīz, ə·môr′tīz) *v.t.* **·tized, ·tiz·ing** To pay off (a debt) by installments or by payments to a sinking fund. *Brit. sp.* **·tise.** [< OF *amortir* extinguish < L *ad-* to + *mors* death] —**am·or·tiz·a·ble** (am′ər·tīz′ə·bəl, a·môr′·tiz·ə·bəl) *adj.* —**am·or·ti·za·tion** (am′ər·tə·zā′shən, ə·môr′·tə·zā′shən), **a·mor·tize·ment** (ə·môr′tiz·mənt) *n.*

A·mos (ā′məs) A minor Hebrew prophet of the eighth century B.C. —*n.* The Old Testament book bearing his name.

a·mount (ə·mount′) *n.* **1** A sum of two or more quantities; total. **2** The principle sum with the interest included, as in a loan. **3** The entire significance, value, or effect. **4** Quantity: a considerable *amount* of discussion. —*v.i.* **1** To total or add up: with *to:* to *amount* to ten dollars. **2** To be equivalent in effect or importance: with *to:* Their actions *amounted* to nothing. [< OF *amont* upward < *a mont* to the mountain]

a·mour (ə·mŏŏr′) *n.* A love affair. [F]

amp. ampere; amperage.

am·pe·lop·sis (am′pə·lop′sis) *n.* Any of a genus of ornamental woody vines related to the grape. [< Gk. *ampelos* vine + *opsis* appearance]

am·per·age (am′pər·ij, am·pir′ij) *n.* The measure of an electric current in amperes.

am·pere (am′pir, am·pir′) *n.* A unit of electric current, defined as the steady current that produces a force of 2×10^{-7} newtons per meter of length when flowing through parallel wires of negligible cross section and infinite length one meter apart in free space. [< A. M. *Ampère,* 1775–1836, French physicist]

am·per·sand (am′pər·sand, am′pər·sand′) *n.* The character (usu. &) meaning *and.* [< *and per se and,* lit., & by itself equals and]

am·phet·a·mine (am·fet′ə·mēn, -min) *n.* A synthetic organic compound used as a stimulant. [< A(LPHA)-M(ETHYL)-PH(ENYL)-ET(HYL)-AMINE]

amphi- *prefix* **1** On both or all sides: amphitheater. **2** Of both kinds; in two ways: *amphibious.* [< Gk. *amphi* around]

am·phib·i·an (am·fib′ē·ən) *n.* **1** One of a class of cold-blooded, chiefly egg-laying, scaleless vertebrates that breathe with lungs or gills or both at different stages of development, as salamanders, newts, frogs, and toads. **2** An amphibious plant. **3** An airplane constructed to rise from and land on water or land. **4** A vehicle capable of operating on land and water. —*adj.* Of or pertaining to an amphibian. [< Gk. *amphibios.* See AMPHIBIOUS.]

am·phib·i·ous (am·fib′ē·əs) *adj.* **1** Living or adapted to life both on land and in water. **2** Capable of operating on or from land or water, as a vehicle or aircraft. **3** Of a mixed nature. [< Gk. *amphibios* having a double life] —**am·phib′·i·ous·ly** *adv.* —**am·phib′i·ous·ness** *n.*

am·phi·bole (am′fə·bōl) *n. Mineral.* Any of a class of variously colored silicate minerals, as asbestos or hornblende. [< Gk. *amphibolos* ambiguous]

am·phi·the·a·ter (am′fə·thē′ə·tər) *n.* 1 A round or oval structure consisting of tiers of seats rising upward from a central open space or arena. 2 Any structure of similar shape. 3 Any arena or place of contest.

am·pho·ra (am′fə·rə) *n. pl.* **·rae** (-rē) In ancient Greece, a tall, two-handled earthenware jar for wine or oil, narrow at the neck and the base. [< Gk. *amphoreus* < AMPHI- + *phoreus* bearer] **—am′pho·ral** *adj.*

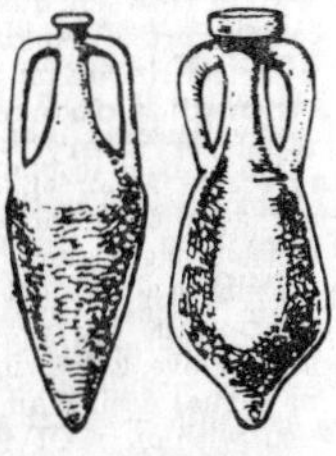

Amphorae

am·ple (am′pəl) *adj.* 1 Large in size, capacity, amount, etc. 2 More than enough; abundant. 3 Sufficient to meet all needs or requirements; adequate. [< L *amplus* large, abundant] **—am′ple·ness** *n.*

am·pli·fi·ca·tion (am′plə·fi·kā′·shən) *n.* 1 An amplifying or being amplified. 2 Details or other matter added to amplify a subject, statement, etc. 3 An increase in the power of a signal, esp. an electric signal.

am·pli·fi·er (am′plə·fī′ər) *n.* 1 One who or that which amplifies or increases. 2 Any device that increases the power of a signal, esp. an electric signal.

am·pli·fy (am′plə·fī) *v.* **·fied, ·fy·ing** *v.t.* 1 To enlarge or increase in scope, significance, or power. 2 To add to so as to make more complete, as by examples, data, etc. 3 To exaggerate; magnify. 4 To increase the power of a signal, esp. an electric signal. *—v.i.* 5 To make additional remarks; expatiate. [< L *amplus* large + *facere* make] **—am·pli·fi·ca·tive** (am′plə·fi·kā′tiv, am·plif′i·kə·tiv), **am·plif·i·ca·to·ry** (am·plif′i·kə·tôr′ē, -tō′rē) *adj.*

am·pli·tude (am′plə·tōōd) *n.* 1 The quality of being ample; largeness; breadth. 2 Fullness or completeness; abundance; richness. 3 Broad range or scope, as of mental capacity. 4 *Physics* The difference between the peak and mean values of an oscillating variable. [< L *amplus* large]

amplitude modulation Modulation of a carrier wave so that its amplitude is at any instant proportional to the value of another signal, as in radio transmission.

am·ply (am′plē) *adv.* In an ample manner; largely; liberally; sufficiently.

am·poule (am·pōōl′) *n.* A sealed glass vial used as a sterile container for one dose of a hypodermic injection. Also **am·pule** (am′pyōōl), **am·pul** (am′pul). [< L *ampulla* ampulla (def. 2)]

am·pul·la (am·pul′ə) *n. pl.* **am·pul·lae** (-pul′ē) 1 *Eccl.* The cruet used for the wine or water at Mass. 2 An ancient Roman bottle used to hold perfumes, oils, or wine. [< L, dim. of *amphora* amphora] **—am·pul′lar** *adj.*

am·pu·tate (am′pyŏŏ·tāt) *v.t.* **·tat·ed, ·tat·ing** To remove by cutting, as a limb. [< L < *ambi-* around + *putare* trim, prune] **—am′pu·ta′tion, am′pu·ta′tor** *n.*

am·pu·tee (am′pyŏŏ·tē′) *n.* One who has had a limb or limbs removed by amputation.

amt. amount.

Am·trak (am′trak) *n.* A private corporation, administered by the Federal Government, that manages passenger service on selected U.S. railroads.

amu atomic mass unit.

a·muck (ə·muk′) *adj. & adv.* AMOK.

am·u·let (am′yə·lit) *n.* Anything worn about one's person to protect from accident or ill luck; a charm. [< L *amuletum* charm]

a·muse (ə·myōōz′) *v.t.* **a·mused, a·mus·ing** 1 To occupy pleasingly; entertain; divert. 2 To cause to laugh or smile. [< OF *a* to + *muser* to muse] **—a·mus′er** *n.*

a·muse·ment (ə·myōōz′ment) *n.* 1 The state of being amused. 2 That which amuses.

a·mus·ing (ə·myōō′zing) *adj.* 1 Entertaining. 2 Arousing laughter. **—a·mus′ing·ly** *adv.*

am·yl (am′il) *n.* A univalent radical composed of carbon and hydrogen. [< Gk. *amylon* starch + -YL]

am·y·la·ceous (am′ə·lā′shəs) *adj.* Pertaining to or like starch; starchy.

am·y·lase (am′ə·lās) *n.* Any of several digestive enzymes that promote the conversion of starch into simple sugars. [< AMYL + -ASE]

am·y·loid (am′ə·loid) *n.* A starchlike substance. *—adj.* Like or containing starch. **—am′y·loi′dal** *adj.*

am·y·lum (am′ə·ləm) *n.* Starch. [< Gk. *amylon*]

Am·y·tal (am′ə·tal, -tôl) *n.* A barbiturate: a trade name.

an (an, *unstressed* ən) *indefinite article & adj.* 1 Each or any. 2 One; one kind of. 3 For each: The price is ten cents *an* apple. [< OE *ān* one] • See A².

an-¹ *prefix* Without; not: *anastigmatic.* [< Gk.]

an-² Var. of ANA-: *anode.*

an-³ Var. of AD-.

-an *suffix* Used to form adjectives and nouns denoting connection with a country, person, group, doctrine, etc., as follows: 1 Pertaining to; belonging to: *human, sylvan.* 2 Originating in; living in: *Italian.* 3 Adhering to; following: *Lutheran.* 4 *Zool.* Belonging to a class or order: *amphibian.* [< L *-anus*]

an. anonymous; in the year (L *anno*).

ana- *prefix* 1 Up; upward: *anadromous.* 2 Back; backward: *anapest.* 3 Anew: sometimes capable of being rendered *re-*, as *Anabaptism.* 4 Throughout; thoroughly: *analysis.* [< Gk. *ana* on]

-ana *suffix* Pertaining to: added to the names of notable persons, places, etc., to indicate a collection of materials, such as writings or anecdotes, about the subject: *Americana.* Also *-iana.* [< L *-anus*]

An·a·bap·tist (an′ə·bap′tist) *n.* One of a 16th-century, Protestant sect that opposed infant baptism, believing only adults could validly be baptized. [< Gk. *ana-* anew + *baptizein* baptize] **—An′a·bap′tism** *n.*

a·nab·o·lism (ə·nab′ə·liz′əm) *n.* Constructive metabolism; the process by which nutrients are built up into the living organism. [< ANA- up + (META)BOLISM] **—an·a·bol·ic** (an′ə·bol′ik) *adj.*

a·nach·ro·nism (ə·nak′rə·niz′əm) *n.* 1 The representation of something existing or occurring out of its proper time. 2 Anything placed out of its proper time. [< Gk. *anachronizein* refer to a wrong time] **—a·nach′ro·nis′tic, a·nach′ro·nis′ti·cal, a·nach′ro·nous** *adj.*

an·a·con·da (an′ə·kon′də) *n.* 1 A very large nonvenomous tropical serpent that crushes its prey in its coils. 2 Any similar snake, as the boa constrictor or python. [?]

Anaconda *def. 1*

a·nad·ro·mous (ə·nad′rə·məs) *adj.* Running up: said of fishes, as the salmon, that go up rivers to spawn. [< Gk. *ana-* up + *dromos* a running]

a·nae·mi·a (ə·nē′mē·ə) *n.* ANEMIA.

an·aer·obe (an′ə·rōb, an·âr′ōb, an·ā′ə·rōb) *n.* A microorganism which flourishes without free oxygen. [See ANAEROBIUM] **—an·aer·o·bic** (an′âr·ō′bik, -ob′ik, an·ā′ə·rō′bik, -rob′ik) *adj.*

an·aer·o·bi·um (an′âr·ō′bē·əm, an′ā·ə·rō′-) *n. pl.* **·bi·a** (-bē·ə) An anaerobe. [< AN-¹ without + AERO- + Gk. *bios* life]

an·aes·the·sia (an′is·thē′zhə, -zhē·ə) *n.* ANESTHESIA.

an·a·gram (an′ə·gram) *n.* 1 A word or phrase formed by transposing the letters of another word or phrase. 2 *pl.* *(construed as sing.)* A game in which the players make words by transposing or adding letters. [< ANA- back + Gk. *gramma* a letter] **—an·a·gram·mat·ic** (an′ə·grə·mat′ik) or **·i·cal** *adj.* **—an′a·gram·mat′i·cal·ly** *adv.*

a·nal (ā′nəl) *adj.* Of, pertaining to, or situated in the region of the anus. **—a′nal·ly** *adv.*

an·al·ge·si·a (an′əl·jē′zē·ə, -sē·ə) *n.* Insensibility to pain. [< Gk. *an-* without + *algos* pain]

an·al·ge·sic (an′əl·jē′zik, -sik) *n.* A drug that alleviates pain. *—adj.* Pertaining to or promoting analgesia.

a·nal·o·gous (ə·nal′ə·gəs) *adj.* 1 Similar in certain respects. 2 *Biol.* Having a similar function but different in origin and structure. —**a·nal'o·gous·ly** *adv.*

an·a·logue (an'ə·lôg, -log) *n.* Anything analogous to something else. Also **an'a·log.**

a·nal·o·gy (ə·nal'ə·jē) *n. pl.* **·gies** 1 A similarity or resemblance between things not otherwise identical. 2 *Biol.* A similarity in function but not in origin or structure. 3 *Logic* The assumption that things similar in some respects are probably similar in others.

a·nal·y·sis (ə·nal'ə·sis) *n. pl.* **·ses** (-sēz) 1 The separation of a whole into its parts or elements. 2 A statement of the results of this. 3 A method of determining or describing the nature of a thing by separating it into its parts. 4 *Chem.* The identification of some or all constituents forming a compound or substance. 5 PSYCHOANALYSIS. [<Gk. *analysis* a releasing]

an·a·lyst (an'ə·list) *n.* 1 One who analyzes or is skilled in analysis. 2 PSYCHOANALYST.

an·a·lyt·ic (an'ə·lit'ik) *adj.* 1 Pertaining to, skilled in, or proceeding by analysis. 2 Separating into constituents or first principles. Also **an'a·lyt'i·cal.** —**an'a·lyt'i·cal·ly** *adv.*

an·a·lyt·ics (an'ə·lit'iks) *n. pl. (construed as sing.)* The science or use of logical analysis.

an·a·lyze (an'ə·līz) *v.t.* **·lyzed, ·lyz·ing** 1 To separate into constituent parts or elements. 2 To make an analysis of, as a chemical compound. 3 *Gram.* To separate (a sentence) into its grammatical elements. 4 To examine minutely or critically, as a text. *Brit. sp.* **an'a·lyse.** —**an'a·lyz'a·ble** *adj.* —**an'a·ly·za'tion, an'a·lyz'er** *n.*

an·a·pest (an'ə·pest) *n.* 1 In prosody, a metrical foot consisting of two short or unaccented syllables followed by one long or accented syllable. 2 A line of verse made up of or characterized by such feet. Also **an'a·paest.** [<Gk. *anapaistos*<*ana-* back + *paiein* strike] —**an'a·pes'tic** *adj.*

an·a·phy·lac·tic (an'ə·fə·lak'tik) *adj.* Of or pertaining to a severe reaction to a usually harmless drug when injected the second time, often resulting in shock or death. [<Gk. *ana* on + *phylaxis* a guarding]

an·ar·chism (an'ər·kiz'əm) *n.* 1 The theory that all forms of government are incompatible with individual and social liberty and should be replaced by voluntary cooperation and mutual aid. 2 The methods, esp. terroristic ones, of anarchists.

an·ar·chist (an'ər·kist) *n.* 1 One who believes in anarchism. 2 One who encourages or furthers anarchy. —**an'·ar·chis'tic** *adj.*

an·ar·chy (an'ər·kē) *n. pl.* **·chies** 1 Absence of government. 2 Lawless confusion and political disorder. 3 General disorder. [<Gk. *an-* without + *archos* leader] —**an·ar·chic** (an·är'kik), **an·ar'chi·cal** *adj.* —**an·ar'chi·cal·ly** *adv.*

an·as·tig·mat·ic (an·as'tig·mat'ik) *adj.* Not astigmatic; esp., corrected for astigmatism, as a lens. [<AN-[1] + ASTIGMATIC]

anat. anatomical; anatomy.

a·nath·e·ma (ə·nath'ə·mə) *n. pl.* **·mas** or **·ma·ta** (-mə·tə) 1 A formal ecclesiastical ban or curse, excommunicating a person or damning something, as a book or heresy. 2 A person or thing so banned or cursed. 3 Any curse or imprecation. 4 A person or thing greatly disliked or detested. [<Gk. *anathema* an offering]

a·nath·e·ma·tize (ə·nath'ə·mə·tīz) *v.* **·tized, ·tiz·ing** *v.t.* To pronounce an anathema against. —*v.i.* To utter or express anathemas. —**a·nath'e·ma·ti·za'tion** *n.*

an·a·tom·i·cal (an'ə·tom'i·kəl) *adj.* 1 Of or pertaining to anatomy. 2 Structural. Also **an'a·tom'ic.** —**an'a·tom'i·cal·ly** *adv.*

a·nat·o·mist (ə·nat'ə·mist) *n.* One skilled in or a student of anatomy.

a·nat·o·mize (ə·nat'ə·mīz) *v.t.* **·mized, ·miz·ing** 1 To dissect (an animal or plant) for the purpose of investigating its structure. 2 To examine critically or minutely; analyze.

a·nat·o·my (ə·nat'ə·mē) *n. pl.* **·mies** 1 The structure of a plant or animal. 2 The science of the structure of organisms. 3 The art or practice of dissection in order to investigate structure. 4 The human body. [<Gk. *anatomē* dissection]

-ance *suffix of nouns* Forming nouns of action, quality, state, or condition from adjectives in *-ant,* and also from verbs, as in *ignorance, resistance, forbearance.* [<L *-antia*]

an·ces·tor (an'ses·tər) *n.* 1 One from whom a person is descended; progenitor; forebear. 2 Anything regarded as an earlier model or forerunner. 3 An earlier organism from which later organisms have been derived. [<L *ante-* before + *cedere* go] —**an·ces·tress** (an'ses·tris) *n. Fem.*

an·ces·tral (an·ses'trəl) *adj.* Of, pertaining to, or inherited from an ancestor. —**an·ces'tral·ly** *adv.*

an·ces·try (an'ses·trē) *n. pl.* **·tries** 1 Ancestors collectively. 2 Descent; ancestral lineage.

an·chor (ang'kər) *n.* 1 A heavy implement, usu. metal, attached to a chain or cable and used, when lowered into the water, to hold a ship or boat in place by its weight or its hooks or flukes that grip the bottom. 2 Anything or anyone giving support or security. —**at anchor** Anchored, as a ship. —**cast** (or **drop**) **anchor** To put down the anchor in order to hold fast a vessel. —**ride at anchor** To be anchored, as a ship. —**weigh anchor** To take up the anchor so as to sail away. —*v.t.* 1 To secure or make secure by an anchor. 2 To fix firmly. —*v.i.* 3 To lie at anchor, as a ship. 4 To be or become fixed. [<Gk. *ankyra*]

Anchor

an·chor·age (ang'kər·ij) *n.* 1 A place used for anchoring. 2 A lying at anchor. 3 The fee charged for anchoring. 4 Any means of support or security.

an·cho·rite (ang'kə·rīt) *n.* A religious recluse or hermit. Also **an'cho·ret** (-rit, -ret). [<Gk. *anachōreein* retire, retreat] —**an·cho·rit·ic** (ang'kə·rit'ik) *adj.*

anchor man 1 An athlete, as in a relay race, who competes last for his team. 2 A television or radio broadcaster who coordinates the coverage of an event or program.

an·cho·vy (an'chō·vē, -chə·vē, an·chō'vē) *n. pl.* **·vies** Any of several small, herringlike fish found in warm seas, used as food. [<Sp., Pg. *anchova,*? <Basque *anchua*]

an·cient (ān'shənt) *adj.* 1 Existing or occurring in times long gone by, esp. before the fall of the Roman Empire. 2 Having existed a long time; of great age. —*n.* 1 One who lived in ancient times. 2 A very old person. —**an'cient·ly** *adv.*

an·cil·lar·y (an'sə·ler'ē) *adj.* Subordinate; auxiliary. [<L *ancilla* maidservant]

an·con (ang'kon) *n. pl.* **an·co·nes** (ang·kō'nēz) *Archit.* An elbow-shaped projection. Also **an·cone** (ang'kōn). [<Gk. *ankōn* a bend, the elbow]

-ancy Var. of -ANCE: *infancy.* [<L *-antia*]

and (and, *unstressed* ənd, ən) *conj.* 1 Also; added to; as well as. 2 As a result or consequence: Speak one word *and* you are a dead man! 3 Although; but: One day is cold *and* the next is warm. 4 *Informal* To: Try *and* stop me. [<OE]

and. andante.

an·dan·te (an·dan'tē, än·dän'tā) *adj. & adv. Music* Moderately slow or slowly. —*n.* An andante passage, movement, etc. [<Ital., lit., walking]

an·dan·ti·no (an'dan·tē'nō, än'dän-) *adj. & adv. Music* Slightly quicker than andante. —*n.* An andantino passage, movement, etc. [<Ital., dim. of *andante*]

and·i·ron (and'ī'ərn) *n.* One of two metal supports for wood to be burned in an open fireplace. [<OF *andier*]

and/or Either *and* or *or,* according to the meaning intended.

An·dor·ra (an·dôr'ə, -dor'ə) *n.* A principality located in the Pyrenees between France and Spain, 179 sq. mi., cap. Andorra la Vella.

andro- *combining form* 1 Man; male; *androgen.* 2 *Bot.* Stamen; anther: *androecium.* [<Gk. *anēr, andros* man]

an·droe·ci·um (an·drē'shē·əm, -sē·əm) *n. pl.* **·ci·a** (-shē·ə, -sē·ə) The stamens of a flower collectively. [<ANDRO- + Gk. *oikos* house] —**an·droe·cial** (an·drē'shəl) *adj.*

an·dro·gen (an'drə·jən) *n.* Any of various hormones that control the appearance and development of male characteristics. —**an·dro·gen·ic** (an'drə·jen'ik) *adj.*

an·drog·y·nous (an·droj'ə·nəs) *adj.* 1 Uniting the characteristics of both sexes; hermaphrodite. 2 Having male and female flowers on the same spike. Also **an·drog'y·nal, an·dro·gyn·ic** (an'drə·jin'ik). [<Gk.<ANDRO- + *gynē* woman] —**an·drog'y·ny** (-ə·nē) *n.*

An·drom·a·che (an·drom'ə·kē) *Gk. Myth.* The wife of Hector, taken captive after the fall of Troy.

An·drom·e·da (an·drom′ə·də) *Gk. Myth.* An Ethiopian princess rescued from a sea monster and married by Perseus. —*n.* A northern constellation.

an·dros·ter·one (an·dros′tə·rōn) *n.* An androgen present in the urine of men and women. [< ANDRO- + STER(OL) + -ONE]

-androus *suffix Bot.* Having a stamen or stamens. [< Gk. *anēr, andros* man]

-ane *suffix Chem.* Denoting a hydrocarbon compound of the methane series.

an·ec·do·tal (an′ik·dōt′l) *adj.* Pertaining to, characterized by, or consisting of anecdotes. —**an′ec·do′tal·ly** *adv.*

an·ec·dote (an′ik·dōt) *n.* A short narrative of an interesting or entertaining nature. [< Gk. *anekdotos* unpublished] —**an′ec·dot′ic** (-dot′ik) or **·i·cal** *adj.* —**an′ec·dot′ist** (-dō′tist) *n.*

a·ne·mi·a (ə·nē′mē·ə) *n.* A deficiency in the amount or quality of red blood corpuscles or of hemoglobin in the blood. [< Gk. *an-* without + *haima* blood] —**a·ne′mic** *adj.*

a·nem·o·graph (ə·nem′ə·graf, -gräf) *n. Meteorol.* An anemometer that produces a graphic record. [< Gk *anemos* wind + -GRAPH] —**a·nem′o·graph′ic** *adj.*

an·e·mom·e·ter (an′ə·mom′ə·ter) *n. Meteorol.* An instrument for measuring the force or velocity of wind. [< Gk. *anemos* wind + -METER] —**an·e·mo·met·ric** (an′ə·mō·met′rik) or **·ri·cal** *adj.*

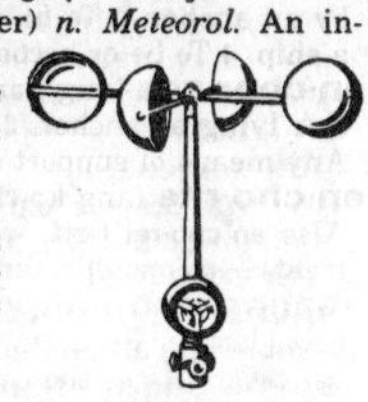

Anemometer

a·nem·o·ne (ə·nem′ə·nē) *n.* **1** Any of various small herbs related to buttercups, having flowers with no petals but showy sepals. **2** SEA ANEMONE. [< Gk. *anemos* wind]

an·er·oid barometer (an′ə·roid) An instrument that indicates atmospheric pressure by the movements of the elastic top of a chamber from which almost all the air has been removed. [< Gk. *a-* not + *nēron* water + -OID]

an·es·the·sia (an′is·thē′zhə, -zhē·ə) *n.* **1** Partial or total loss of physical sensation, due to disease. **2** Local insensibility to pain or general unconsciousness induced by an anesthetic. Also **an·es·the·sis** (an′is·thē′sis). [< Gk. *an-* without + *aisthēsis* sensation]

an·es·thet·ic (an′is·thet′ik) *adj.* **1** Pertaining to or like anesthesia. **2** Producing anesthesia; making insensible to pain. —*n.* A drug that causes unconsciousness or deadens sensation, as during surgery, etc.

an·es·the·tist (ə·nes′thə·tist) *n.* A person trained to administer anesthetics.

an·es·the·tize (ə·nes′thə·tīz) *v.t.* **·tized, ·tiz·ing** To render insensible, esp. to pain, by means of an anesthetic. —**an·es·the·ti·za·tion** (ə·nes′thə·tə·zā′shən, an′is·thet′ə-) *n.*

an·eu·rysm (an′yə·riz′əm) *n.* A sac formed by localized dilation of the wall of an artery, due to disease or injury. Also **an′eu·rism.** [< Gk. *ana-* throughout + *eurys* wide] —**an·eu·rys·mal** (an′yə·riz′məl) or **·ris′mal** *adj.*

a·new (ə·nyōō′) *adv.* **1** Again. **2** Again in a different way.

an·gel (ān′jəl) *n.* **1** *Theol.* **a** One of an order of spiritual beings attendant upon the Deity; a heavenly messenger. **b** A fallen spiritual being. **2** A conventional representation of an angel, usu. a youthful winged human figure in white robes with a halo. **3** A person thought of as being angelically beautiful, pure, kind, etc. **4** A guardian spirit or attendant. **5** *Informal* The financial backer of a play or of any enterprise. [< Gk. *angelos* messenger]

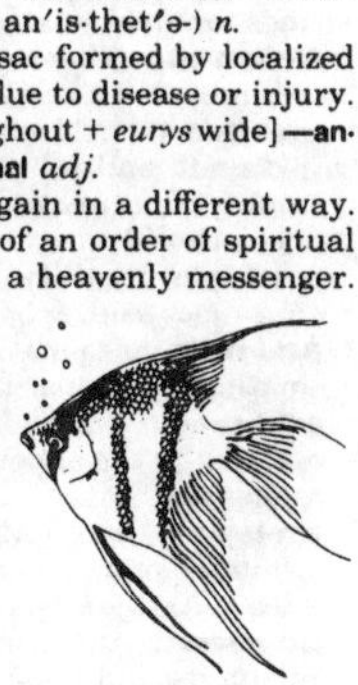

Angelfish *def. 2*

an·gel·fish (ān′jəl·fish′) *n.* **1** A raylike shark of temperate seas, having very large winglike pectoral fins. **2** A fish of warm seas having brilliant coloration, as the porgy.

angel food cake A delicate, spongy cake made with egg whites and no shortening. Also **angel cake.**

an·gel·ic (an·jel′ik) *adj.* **1** Pertaining to, of, or consisting of angels. **2** Like an angel; pure; beautiful; saintly. Also **an·gel′i·cal.** —**an·gel′i·cal·ly** *adv.*

an·gel·i·ca (an·jel′i·kə) *n.* **1** Any of various aromatic plants related to celery. **2** The stalks of this plant, often candied and used as a flavoring. [< Med.L *(herba) angelica* the angelic (herb)]

an·ge·lus (an′jə·ləs) *n.* **1** A prayer to commemorate the Annunciation. **2** A bell rung at morning, noon, and night as a call to recite this prayer. Also **An′ge·lus.** [< L, angel]

an·ger (ang′gər) *n.* Violent and strong displeasure, as a result of opposition, mistreatment, etc.; wrath; ire. —*v.t.* **1** To make angry; enrage. —*v.i.* **2** To become angry. [< ON *angr* grief]

an·gi·na (an·jī′nə, an′jə·nə) *n.* **1** Inflammation of the throat characterized by spasmodic suffocation, as quinsy, croup, etc. **2** Angina pectoris. [< L, quinsy]

angina pec·to·ris (pek′tə·ris) A condition characterized by pain in the chest and usu. the left arm, due to insufficient blood supply to the heart muscle. [< NL, angina of the chest]

an·gi·o·ma (an′jē·ō′mə) *n. pl.* **·mas** or **·ma·ta** (-mə·tə) A tumor composed of dilated blood or lymph vessels. [< Gk. *angeion* vessel + *ōma,* a noun ending] —**an·gi·om·a·tous** (an′jē·ōm′ə·təs) *adj.*

an·gi·o·sperm (an′jē·ə·spûrm′) *n.* One of a class comprising all flowering plants, in which the seeds are contained within a pericarp. [< Gk. *angeion* vessel + SPERM] —**an′gi·o·sper′mal, an′gi·o·sper′ma·tous** (-spûr′mə·təs), **an′·gi·o·sper′mous** *adj.*

Angl. Anglican; Anglicized.

an·gle[1] (ang′gəl) *v.i.* **an·gled, an·gling** **1** To fish with a hook and line. **2** To seek deviously; fish: to *angle* for compliments. [< OE *angel* fish hook]

an·gle[2] (ang′gəl) *n.* **1** *Geom.* **a** The figure formed by the intersection of two lines or of two planes. **b** The inclination of either of these lines or planes with respect to the other. **2** A corner or sharp bend. **3** A position from which something may be regarded; viewpoint. —*v.t. & v.i.* **an·gled, an·gling** **1** To move or turn at an angle or by angles. **2** To present with or show a particular bias or interpretation, as a story or report. [< L *angulus* a corner, angle] —**an′gled** *adj.*

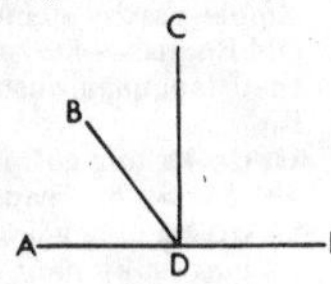

Angle
ADB: acute, adjacent. ADC: right. BDE: obtuse.

An·gle (ang′gəl) *n.* A member of a Germanic tribe that migrated from southern Denmark to Britain in the fifth and sixth centuries and founded the kingdoms of East Anglia, Mercia, and Northumbria. [< L *Anglus,* sing. of *Angli* < Gmc.]

angle iron A piece of metal in the form of an angle, especially a right angle, for joining or strengthening beams, girders, etc.

angle of incidence *Physics* The angle between a beam of radiant energy and a perpendicular to a surface at the point of incidence.

an·gler (ang′glər) *n.* **1** One who fishes by angling. **2** An anglerfish.

an·gler·fish (ang′glər·fish′) *n., pl.* **·fish** or **·fish·es** One of a family of fishes having antennalike filaments attached to the head with which it lures its prey.

an·gle·worm (ang′gəl·wûrm′) *n.* An earthworm, esp. one used as fishing bait.

An·gli·can (ang′glə·kən) *adj.* **1** Of or pertaining to the Church of England or the churches derived from it. **2** Of or pertaining to England; English. —*n.* A member of the Church of England or of any church derived from it. [< Med.L *Anglicus* English] —**An′gli·can·ism′** *n.*

An·gli·cism (ang′glə·siz′əm) *n.* **1** A word, phrase, or idiom typical of English, esp. British English. **2** A typically English trait, quality, etc.

An·gli·cize (ang′glə·sīz) *v.t. & v.i.* **·cized, ·ciz·ing** To give or acquire a characteristically English use, style, quality, etc. *Brit. sp.* **An′gli·cise.** **—An·gli·ci·za·tion** (ang′glə·sə·zā′·shən, -sī·zā′shən) *n.*

an·gling (ang′gling) *n.* The act or art of fishing with a hook, line, and rod.

An·glo (ang′glō) *n. pl.* **·glos** An Anglo-American.

Anglo- *combining form* English; English and: *Anglo-American.* [< L *Angli* the English]

An·glo-A·mer·i·can (ang′glō·ə·mer′ə·kən) *adj.* Of, pertaining to, or between England and America. **—***n.* A U.S. citizen of English origin.

An·glo-French (ang′glō·french′) *adj.* Of, pertaining to, or between England and France or the English and French. **—***n.* The Norman dialect of Old French current in England from the Norman Conquest to the end of the 13th century.

An·glo·ma·ni·a (ang′glō·mā′nē·ə) *n.* A passion for English customs, speech, etc. **—An′glo·ma′ni·ac** (-ak) *n.*

An·glo-Nor·man (ang′glō·nôr′mən) *adj.* Pertaining to the Normans who settled in England after the Norman Conquest in 1066. **—***n.* **1** One of the Norman settlers in England after the Norman Conquest. **2** Anglo-French.

An·glo·phile (ang′glə·fīl, -fil) *n.* A devotee of England and its people, institutions, etc. **—***adj.* Of or like Anglophiles. Also **An′glo·phil** (-fil).

An·glo·phobe (ang′glə·fōb) *n.* One who dislikes or distrusts England or its people, institutions, etc. **—***adj.* Of or like Anglophobes. Also **An·glo·pho·bi·ac** (ang′glə·fō′bē·ak). **—An·glo·pho·bi·a** (ang′glə·fō′bē·ə) *n.* **—An′glo·pho′bic** (-fō′bik, -fob′ik) *adj.*

An·glo-Sax·on (ang′glō·sak′sən) *n.* **1** A member of one of the Germanic tribes that conquered Britain in the fifth and sixth centuries. **2** A member of the nation descended from these peoples. **3** Their West Germanic language. See OLD ENGLISH. **4** One of English origin or descent. **5** The simple, earthy elements of modern English retained from Old English. **—***adj.* Of or pertaining to the Anglo-Saxons, their language, customs, or descendants. **—An′glo-Sax′on·ism** *n.*

An·go·la (ang·gō′lə) *n.* A Portuguese colony in sw Africa, 481,351 sq. mi., cap. Luanda. • See map at AFRICA.

An·go·ra (ang·gôr′ə, -gō′rə) *n.* **1** A type of goat bred for its long, silky hair. **2** The long, silky hair of this goat, or cloth made from it. **3** A type of cat having long hair. [< *Angora,* former name of Ankara]

an·gos·tu·ra bark (ang′gəs·t^y^ōōr′ə) The bark of a South American tree used in the preparation of a tonic and as a flavoring in bitters. Also **angostura.** [< *Angostura,* former name of Ciudad Bolivar]

an·gry (ang′grē) *adj.* **an·gri·er, an·gri·est** **1** Feeling, showing, or excited by anger. **2** Appearing to threaten: *angry* skies. **3** Badly inflamed: an *angry* sore. **—an·gri·ly** (ang′grə·lē) *adv.* **—an·gri·ness** *n.* **—Syn.** **1** furious, enraged, irate, wrathful. **2** stormy, turbulent. **3** sore, painful, burning.

angst (ängst) *n.* Anxiety; dread. [G]

ang·strom (ang′strəm) *n. Often cap.* A unit of length equal to 10^{-8} meter. Also **Ångstrom, angstrom unit.** [< A. J. *Ångström,* 1814–74, Swedish physicist]

an·guish (ang′gwish) *n.* Severe mental or physical distress. [< L *angustus* narrow, tight] **—an·guished** *adj.* **—Syn.** agony, torment, torture, suffering.

an·gu·lar (ang′gyə·lər) *adj.* **1** Of, having, or forming an angle or angles. **2** Measured by an angle: *angular* motion. **3** Bony; gaunt. **4** Awkwardly stiff: *angular* gestures. **—an′·gu·lar·ly** *adv.*

an·gu·lar·i·ty (ang′gyə·lar′ə·tē) *n. pl.* **·ties** **1** The state or condition of being angular. **2** *pl.* Angular contours. Also **an′gu·lar·ness.**

an·hy·dride (an·hī′drīd, -drid) *n.* **1** Any compound from which the elements of water have been removed. **2** An oxide which reacts with water to form an acid or a base. [See ANHYDROUS]

an·hy·drous (an·hī′drəs) *adj.* Without water, esp. water of crystallization. [< Gk. *anydros* waterless]

an·il (an′il) *n.* **1** A West Indian plant. **2** The indigo dye made from it. [< Ar. *al-nīl*]

an·ile (an′īl, ā′nīl, an′il) *adj.* Like an old woman; infirm. [< L *anus* old woman] **—a·nil·i·ty** (ə·nil′ə·tē) *n.*

an·i·line (an′ə·lin, -līn) *n.* A colorless oily compound derived from benzene, used in the production of many dyes, resins, and varnishes. **—***adj.* Of, derived from, or pertaining to aniline. Also **an·i·lin** (an′ə·lin). [< ANIL + -INE]

an·i·mad·ver·sion (an′ə·mad·vûr′zhən, -shən) *n.* An unfavorably critical comment: with *on* or *upon.* [See ANIMADVERT.] **—an′i·mad·ver′sive** (-siv) *adj.* **—an′i·mad·ver′sive·ness** *n.*

an·i·mad·vert (an′ə·mad·vûrt′) *v.i.* To comment with adverse criticism: with *on* or *upon.* [< L *animadvertere* take notice of]

an·i·mal (an′ə·məl) *n.* **1** Any member of a primary subdivision of organisms distinguished from plants by inability to produce nutrients by photosynthesis and by various other characteristics. **2** Any such creature as distinguished from man, esp. a mammal. **3** A bestial human being. **—***adj.* **1** Of or pertaining to animals. **2** Like an animal; bestial. [< L *animalis* living < *animus* breath]

an·i·mal·cule (an′ə·mal′kyōōl) *n.* A microscopically small animal. **—an′i·mal′cu·lar** (-kyə·lər) *adj.*

animal husbandry The breeding, raising, and care of farm animals.

an·i·mal·ism (an′ə·məl·iz′əm) *n.* **1** Existence dominated by animal instincts, appetites, etc. **2** The doctrine that man is entirely animal, having no soul or spirit. **—an′i·mal·ist** *n.* **—an′i·mal·is′tic** *adj.*

an·i·mal·i·ty (an′ə·mal′ə·tē) *n.* **1** Animal nature or qualities. **2** Animal life.

an·i·mal·ize (an′ə·məl·īz′) *v.t.* **·ized, ·iz·ing** To make bestial, inhuman, etc.; brutalize. **—an·i·mal·i·za·tion** (an′ə·məl·ə·zā′shən) *n.*

animal kingdom One of the three divisions of nature, embracing all animals.

animal magnetism **1** MESMERISM. **2** Magnetic personal qualities.

animal spirits Vivaciousness or buoyancy of good health.

an·i·mate (an′ə·māt) *v.t.* **·mat·ed, ·mat·ing** **1** To impart life to; make alive. **2** To make lively, energetic, vivacious, etc. **3** To move to action; incite; inspire. **4** To impart lifelike motion to. **—***adj.* (an′ə·mit) **1** Possessing animal life; living. **2** Animated. [< L *animare* to fill with breath, make alive] **—an′i·ma′tor, an′i·ma′ter** *n.*

an·i·mat·ed (an′ə·māt′id) *adj.* Full of life, spirit, etc. **—an′i·mat′ed·ly** *adv.* **—Syn.** lively, spirited, vivacious, energetic.

animated cartoon A motion-picture film made by photographing a series of drawings, each changed slightly from the preceding one to produce an effect of motion.

an·i·ma·tion (an′ə·mā′shən) *n.* **1** The act or process of animating. **2** The state of being animated; liveliness; vivacity. **3** The process and technique of preparing drawings for an animated cartoon.

a·ni·ma·to (ä′nē·mä′tō) *adv. Music* With animation; in an animated manner. [< Ital.]

an·i·mism (an′ə·miz′əm) *n.* The belief that inanimate objects and natural phenomena possess a personal life or soul. [< L *anima* soul] **—an′i·mist** *n.* **—an′i·mis′tic** *adj.*

an·i·mos·i·ty (an′ə·mos′ə·tē) *n. pl.* **·ties** Active, intense enmity or hostility. [< L *animositas* high spirit, boldness < *animus* soul, spirit]

an·i·mus (an′ə·məs) *n.* **1** Hostile feeling; animosity. **2** Animating purpose or intention. [< L mind, soul]

an·i·on (an′ī′ən) *n.* A negatively charged ion; the ion migrating to the anode in electrolysis. [< Gk. *anion* (thing) going up]

an·ise (an′is) *n.* **1** A plant related to parsley, having small white or yellow flowers and seeds with a flavor like licorice. **2** Aniseed. [< Gk. *anison*]

an·i·seed (an′i·sēd) *n.* The fragrant seed of the anise plant, used in cookery and medicine.

an·i·sette (an′ə·zet′, -set′) *n.* A cordial flavored with aniseed. [F]

an·kle (ang′kəl) *n.* **1** The joint connecting the foot and the leg. **2** The part of the leg between the foot and the calf near the ankle joint. [< OE *ancleōw*]

an·kle·bone (ang′kəl·bōn′) *n.* TALUS.

an·klet (ang′klit) *n.* **1** An ornament or fetter for the ankle. **2** A short sock reaching just above the ankle.

an·ky·lose (ang′kə·lōs) *v.t. & v.i.* **·losed, ·los·ing** To unite or join together into a single unit.

an·ky·lo·sis (ang'kə·lō'sis) *n.* **1** The consolidation of two bones or other parts. **2** The abnormal cohesion of bones, esp. those forming a joint; stiffening of a joint. [<Gk. *ankylōsis* joint stiffening] **—an'ky·lot'ic** (-lot'ik) *adj.*

ann. annals; annual; annuity.

an·na (an'ə) *n.* A former monetary unit and copper coin of India, equal to 1/16 of a rupee. [<Hind. *ānā*]

an·nals (an'əlz) *n. pl.* **1** A year-by-year record of events in chronological order. **2** History or records in general. **3** A periodical publication of discoveries, transactions, etc. [<L *annales (libri)* yearly (record)] **—an'nal·ist** *n.*

an·neal (ə·nēl') *v.t.* To toughen (brittle metal, glass, etc.) by heating and then slowly cooling. [<OE *onælan* to burn] **—an·neal'er** *n.*

an·ne·lid (an'ə·lid) *n.* Any of a phylum of worms having bodies segmented into a series of rings, including earthworms, leeches, etc. *—adj.* Of or pertaining to this phylum. [<F *anneler* arrange in rings] **—an·nel·i·dan** (ə·nel'ə·dən) *adj., n.*

an·nex (ə·neks') *v.t.* **1** To add or append, esp. to something larger. **2** To incorporate as territory. **3** To attach, as an attribute, condition, etc. *—n.* (an'eks) **1** An addition to a building, or a nearby auxiliary building. **2** An addition to a document. *Brit. sp.* **annexe** (*n.*) [<L *annectere* tie together] **—an·nex'a·ble, an·nex'ive** *adj.*

an·nex·a·tion (an'ek·sā'shən) *n.* **1** An annexing or being annexed. **2** That which is annexed. Also **an·nex'ment.**

An·nie Oak·ley (an'ē ōk'lē) *Slang* A free ticket or pass to a theater, etc. [From resemblance of a punched ticket to a target used by *Annie Oakley,* 1860–1926, U.S. markswoman]

an·ni·hi·late (ə·nī'ə·lāt) *v.t.* **·lat·ed, ·lat·ing** To destroy absolutely. [<L *ad-* to + *nihil* nothing] **—an·ni·hi·la·ble** (ə·nī'ə·lə·bəl) *adj.* **—an·ni'hi·la'tion, an·ni'hi·la'tor** *n.* **—Syn.** demolish, wipe out, exterminate.

an·ni·ver·sa·ry (an'ə·vûr'sər·ē) *n. pl.* **·ries 1** A day or occasion recurring on the same date each year as a past event. **2** An observance or celebration on such a day. *—adj.* **1** Recurring on the same date every year. **2** Of or marking an anniversary. [<L *annus* year + *versus,* p.p. of *vertere* turn]

Anniversary Day Australia Day.

an·no Dom·i·ni (an'ō dom'ə·nī) *Latin* In the year of the Lord; in a specified year of the Christian era.

an·no·tate (an'ō·tāt) *v.t. & v.i.* **·tat·ed, ·tat·ing** To make explanatory or critical notes on or provide a commentary for (a text, etc.). [<L *ad-* to + *notare* note, mark<*nota* a mark] **—an'no·ta'tion, an'no·ta'tor** *n.* **—an'no·ta'tive** *adj.*

an·nounce (ə·nouns') *v.t.* **an·nounced, an·nounc·ing 1** To make known publicly or officially. **2** To give notice of the approach or appearance of, as by a signal. **3** To serve as the announcer for, as a radio program [<L<*ad-* to + *nuntiare* report]

an·nounce·ment (ə·nouns'mənt) *n.* **1** An announcing or being announced. **2** That which is announced. **3** A printed declaration or publication.

an·nounc·er (ə·noun'sər) *n.* One who announces, esp. one who introduces performers, provides station identification, etc., on radio or television broadcasts.

an·noy (ə·noi') *v.t.* To be troublesome to; bother; vex. [<LL *inodiare* to make odious] **—an·noy'er** *n.* **—Syn.** irk, irritate, harass, pester, bedevil, plague.

an·noy·ance (ə·noi'əns) *n.* **1** An annoying or being annoyed. **2** One who or that which annoys.

an·noy·ing (ə·noi'ing) *adj.* Vexatious; troublesome. **—an·noy'ing·ly** *adv.* **—an·noy'ing·ness** *n.*

an·nu·al (an'yōō·əl) *adj.* **1** Returning, performed, or occurring every year. **2** Of or for a year; reckoned by the year. **3** *Bot.* Lasting or living only one year. *—n.* **1** A book or pamphlet issued once a year. **2** *Bot.* A plant living for a single year or season. [<L *annus* year] **—an'nu·al·ly** *adv.*

an·nu·i·ty (ə·nʸōō'ə·tē) *n. pl.* **·ties 1 a** An annual allowance or income. **b** The right to receive such an allowance. **c** The duty to pay it. **2** The return from an investment of capital, in a series of yearly payments. [<L *annus* year]

an·nul (ə·nul') *v.t.* **an·nulled, an·nul·ling** To make or declare void or invalid, as a law or marriage. [<L *ad-* to + *nullus* none] **—an·nul'la·ble** *adj.* **—an·nul'ment** *n.*

an·nu·lar (an'yə·lər) *adj.* Formed like a ring; ring-shaped. [<L *annulus* ring] **—an'nu·lar·ly** *adv.*

annular eclipse *Astron.* A solar eclipse in which a circular strip of the sun is visible.

an·nu·lus (an'yə·ləs) *n. pl.* **·li** (-lī) or **·lus·es** A ringlike part, marking, etc. [<L, a ring]

an·nun·ci·ate (ə·nun'shē·āt, -sē-) *v.t.* **·at·ed, ·at·ing** To announce [<L *annuntiare.* See ANNOUNCE.]

an·nun·ci·a·tion (ə·nun'sē·ā'shən, -shē-) *n.* The act of announcing; a proclamation.

An·nun·ci·a·tion (ə·nun'sē·ā'shən, -shē-) *n.* **1** The announcement of the Incarnation to the Virgin by an angel. *Luke* 1:28–38. **2** The festival (March 25) commemorating this event.

an·nun·ci·a·tor (ə·nun'shē·ā'tər, -sē-) *n.* An electrical indicator that identifies the caller when a bell is rung.

an·ode (an'ōd) *n.* **1** The electrode of a polarized device through which current enters. **2** In an electrolytic cell, the positive pole at which oxidation of anions occurs. [<Gk. *anodos* a way up] **—an·od·ic** (an·od'ik) *adj.*

an·o·dize (an'ə·dīz) *v.t.* **·dized, ·diz·ing** To treat the surface of (a metal) by making it the anode of an electrolytic bath.

an·o·dyne (an'ə·dīn) *adj.* Having power to allay pain; soothing. *—n.* Anything that relieves pain or soothes. [<Gk. *an-* without + *odynē* pain]

a·noint (ə·noint') *v.t.* **1** To rub with oil, ointment, etc. **2** To put oil on as a sign of consecration. [<L *inungere*<*in-* on + *ungere* smear] **—a·noint'er, a·noint'ment** *n.*

a·nom·a·lous (ə·nom'ə·ləs) *adj.* Deviating from the usual or normal; irregular; abnormal. [<Gk. *an-* not + *homalos* even] **—a·nom'a·lous·ly** *adv.* **—a·nom'a·lous·ness** *n.*

a·nom·a·ly (ə·nom'ə·lē) *n. pl.* **·lies 1** Deviation from rule, type, or form; irregularity; abnormality. **2** Something anomalous. [<Gk. *anōmalos* uneven] **—a·nom'a·lism** *n.* **—a·nom·a·lis·tic** (ə·nom'ə·lis'tik) or **·ti·cal** *adj.*

an·o·mie (an'ə·mē) *n.* An anxious awareness of the irrelevance of society's values to oneself; also, a condition of society marked by the absence of moral standards. Also **an'o·my.** [F<Gk. *anomia* lawlessness] **—a·nom·ic** (ə·nom'ik) *adj.*

a·non (ə·non') *adv.* **1** In a little while; soon; presently. **2** At another time; again. **—ever and anon** From time to time; now and then. [<OE *on ān* in one]

Anon., anon. anonymous.

an·o·nym (an'ə·nim) *n.* **1** An anonymous person or writer. **2** A pseudonym.

a·non·y·mous (ə·non'ə·məs) *adj.* **1** Of unknown authorship or agency. **2** Bearing no name. [<Gk. *an-* without + *onoma, onyma* name] **—an·o·nym·i·ty** (an'ə·nim'ə·tē), **a·non'y·mous·ness** *n.* **—a·non'y·mous·ly** *adv.*

a·noph·e·les (ə·nof'ə·lēz) *n.* Any of a genus of mosquitoes that carry the malaria parasite. [<Gk. *anōphelēs* harmful] **—a·noph·e·line** (ə·nof'ə·līn, -lin) *adj.*

an·o·rex·i·a (an'ə·rek'sē·ə) *n. Med.* A chronic condition marked by extreme avoidance of food, often resulting in near-starvation.

an·oth·er (ə·nuth'ər) *adj.* **1** An additional; one more. **2** Not the same; different. *—pron.* **1** One more. **2** A different one; a substitute. **3** One of the same or similar character. [<ME *an other*]

an·ox·i·a (an·ok'sē·ə) *n.* Oxygen deficiency; insufficient oxidation of body tissues. [<AN-[1] + OX(YGEN)]

ans. answer.

an·ser·ine (an'sə·rīn, -sər·in) *adj.* Of or like a goose; gooselike. [<L *anser* a goose]

an·swer (an'sər, än'-) *v.i.* **1** To reply or respond, as by words or actions. **2** To prove successful. **3** To be accountable: with *for:* I will *answer* for his honesty. **4** To correspond or match, as in appearance: with *to:* He *answers* to your description. *—v.t.* **5** To speak, write, or act in response or reply to: to *answer* a letter. **6** To be sufficient for; fulfill: This rod *answers* the purpose. **7** To conform or correspond to: to *answer* a description. **—answer back** To talk back, as in contradiction. *—n.* A reply, as to a question, message, request, etc. 2 Any action in return or in kind; retaliation. 3 The result or solution, as of a problem in mathematics. 4 *Music* The restatement of a musical theme or phrase by a different voice or instrument. [<OE *andswaru* an answer] **—an'swer·er** *n.* **—Syn.** *v.* reply, respond, react. *n.* 1 response, rejoinder, acknowledgment. 2 reaction.

an·swer·a·ble (an'sər·ə·bəl, än'-) *adj.* 1 Responsible; accountable. 2 Capable of being answered. 3 Adequate; suitable. **—an'swer·a·ble·ness** *n.* **—an'swer·a·bly** *adv.*

answering service A business that answers telephone calls and takes messages for its clients.

ant (ant) *n.* Any of a large family of typically wingless insects living in colonies having an elaborate social organization. [<OE *æmete*]

Ant

-ant *suffix* 1 In the act or process of doing: *exultant.* 2 One who or that which does: *servant.* [<L *-ans (-antis)* present participial suffix]

ant. antenna; antonym.

ant·ac·id (ant·as'id) *adj.* Counteracting acidity. *—n.* An antacid substance. Also **an'ti-ac'id.**

an·tag·o·nism (an·tag'ə·niz'əm) *n.* Mutual opposition or hostility.

an·tag·o·nist (an·tag'ə·nist) *n.* 1 An adversary; opponent. 2 Anything that acts in an opposite direction, as a muscle, drug, etc.

an·tag·o·nis·tic (an·tag'ə·nis'tik) *adj.* 1 Opposed; hostile. 2 Counteractive. Also **an·tag'o·nis'ti·cal.—an·tag'o·nis'ti·cal·ly** *adv.*

an·tag·o·nize(an·tag'ə·nīz) *v.t.* **·nized, ·niz·ing** 1 To oppose, contend with, or struggle against. 2. To make unfriendly; to make an antagonist of. [<Gk. *antagōnizesthai* struggle against]

Ant·arc·tic (ant·ärk'tik, -är'tik) *n.* 1 The region south of the Antarctic Circle: used with *the.* 2 The Antarctic Ocean. *—adj.* Of, in, or pertaining to the Antarctic or the Antarctic Ocean, [<Gk. *antarktikos* southern <*anti-* opposite + *arktos* the Bear (a northern constellation), the north]

antartic circle *Often cap.* The parallel at about 66.5 south latitude that encircles the southern frigid zone.

An·tar·es (an·târ'ēz) *n.* A bright giant red star in the constellation Scorpio.

ant bear (ant' bâr') 1 A giant anteater of tropical America having a shaggy, black-banded coat. 2. AARDVARK.

an·te (an'tē) *v.t. & v.i.* **an·teed or an·ted, an·te·ing** 1 To put up (a poker stake) before the cards are dealt. 2 *Slang* To pay (one's share). **—ante up** *Slang* To ante. *—n.* 1 The stake put up in a game of poker. 2 *Slang* The share one must pay. [<L, before]

ante- *prefix* Before in time, order, or position: *antedate, anteroom.* [<L *ante* before]

ant·eat·er (ant'ē'tər) *n.* Any of several mammals that have a long snout and sticky tongue adapted to feeding on ants, as the echidna, aardvark, etc.

Anteater

an·te·bel·lum (an'tē·bel'əm) *adj.* Before the war, esp. the U.S. Civil War. [<L *ante bellum* before the war]

an·te·cede (an'tə·sēd') *v.t. & v.i.* **·ced·ed, ·ced·ing** To go or come before; precede. [<L *ante* before + *cedere* go]

an·te·ce·dence (an'tə·sēd'əns) *n.* 1 Precedence; priority. 2 *Astron.* The apparent retrograde motion of a planet. Also **an'te·ce'den·cy.**

an·te·ce·dent (an'tə·sēd'ənt) *adj.* Going before; prior in time, place, or order. *—n.* 1 One who or that which precedes or goes before. 2. *pl.* One's ancestry or past background. 3 *Gram.* The word, phrase, or clause referred to by a pronoun. 4 *Math.* The first term of a ratio; numerator. **—an'te·ce'dent·ly** *adv.*

an·te·cham·ber (an'ti·chām'bər) *n.* A room serving as an entranceway to another.

an·te·date (an'ti·dāt') *v.t.* **·dat·ed, ·dat·ing** 1 To come before in time; precede. 2 To assign to a date earlier than the actual one.

an·te·di·lu·vi·an (an'ti·di·lōō'vē·ən) *adj.* 1 Of the times, events, etc., before the Flood. 2 Antiquated; primitive. *—n.* Someone or something antediluvian. [<ANTE- + L *diluvium* deluge]

an·te·lope (an'tə·lōp) *n. pl.* **·lope** or **·lopes** 1 Any of various swift-running, long-horned bovines, including the gazelle, chamois, gnu, etc. 2 Leather made from the hide of such an animal. 3 PRONGHORN. [<LGk. *antholops*]

an·te me·rid·i·em (an'tē mə·rid'ē·em) *Latin* Before noon.

an·ten·na (an·ten'ə) *n. pl.* **·ten·nae** (-ten'ē) *for def. 1,* **·ten'nas** *for def. 2.* 1 One of the paired, movable, sensory appendages on the head of an insect or other arthropod; a feeler. 2 Any of various devices designed to project or receive electromagnetic waves, as in television or radio. [<L, a yard on which a sail is spread] • See INSECT.

an·te·pe·nult (an'ti·pē'nult, -pi·nult') *n.* The syllable before the next to the last syllable, as *pol* in *anthropology.*

an·te·pe·nul·ti·mate (an'ti·pi·nul'tə·mit) *adj.* The last but two of any series. *—n.* ANTEPENULT.

an·te·ri·or (an·tir'ē·ər) *adj.* 1 In front or forward. 2 Preceding in time; earlier. [<L, compar. of *ante* before] **—an·te'ri·or·ly** *adv.* **—Syn.** 1 front, fore, forward, foremost. 2 prior, preceding, antecedent.

an·te·room (an'ti·rōōm', -rōōm') *n.* A waiting room; antechamber.

an·them (an'thəm) *n.* 1 A song of praise or triumph, as one officially adopted by a nation. 2 A choral composition, usually on a religious text. [<Gk. *antiphōna*, lit., things sounding in response]

an·ther (an'thər) *n.* The pollen-bearing part of a stamen. [<Gk. *antherōs* flowery <*anthos* flower] • See STAMEN.

an·ther·id·i·um (an'thə·rid'ē·əm) *n. pl.* **·i·a** (-ē·ə) The organ in which male cells are developed in mosses, fungi, etc., the analog of the anther in flowering plants. [<Gk. *anthēros* flowery] **—an'ther·id'i·al** *adj.*

ant hill The earth heaped by ants or termites at the entrance to their nest.

an·thol·o·gize (an·thol'ə·jīz) *v.i. & v.t.* **·gized, ·giz·ing** To make or include in an anthology. **—an·thol'o·gist** *n.*

an·thol·o·gy (an·thol'ə·jē) *n. pl.* **·gies** A collection of selected poems, stories, etc. [<Gk. *anthologia* a garland, collection of poems] **—an·tho·log·i·cal** (an'thə·loj'i·kəl) *adj.*

an·tho·zo·an (an'thə·zō'ən) *n.* One of a class of sessile marine coelenterates, including the sea anemones and corals; a polyp. *—adj.* Of or pertaining to anthozoans. Also **an'tho·zo'on** (-on). [<Gk. *anthos* flower + *zōon* animal] **—an'tho·zo'ic** *adj.*

an·thra·cene (an'thrə·sēn) *n.* A fluorescent crystalline compound derived from coal tar and used in the manufacture of dyes and to detect radiation. [<Gk. *anthrax* coal + -ENE]

an·thra·cite (an'thrə·sīt) *n.* Coal that burns with much heat and little flame; hard coal. [<Gk. *anthrax* coal] **—an·thra·cit·ic** (an'thrə·sit'ik) *adj.*

an·thrac·nose (an·thrak'nōs) *n.* Any one of many plant diseases often producing dark lesions or blisters. [<Gk. *anthrax* coal+*nosos* disease]

an·thrax (an'thraks) *n. pl.* **·thra·ces** (-thrə·sēz) 1 A malignant febrile disease of sheep, swine, and other animals, sometimes transmitted to man by the resistant spores of the causative bacillus. 2 A pustule due to the disease. [<Gk., coal, carbuncle]

anthropo- *combining form* Man; human: *anthropology.* [<Gk. *anthrōpos* man]

an·thro·po·cen·tric (an'thrə·pō·sen'trik) *adj.* Regarding mankind and human values as the central fact or focus of the universe, life, etc. **-an'thro·po·cen'tri·cal·ly** *adv.*

an·thro·pog·e·ny(an'thrə·poj'ə·nē) *n.* The branch of anthropology that deals with the origin and development of human beings. Also **an·thro·po·gen·e·sis** (an'thrə·pō·jen'ə·sis).

an·thro·poid (an'thrə·poid) *adj.* 1 Resembling a human being: said of the highest apes, as the gorilla, chimpanzee, and orang-utan. 2 Apelike: long, *anthropoid* arms. Also **an'thro·poid'al.** *—n.* An anthropoid ape.

an·thro·pol·o·gy (an'thrə·pol'ə·jē) *n.* The scientific study of human beings and their physiscal, social, material, and cultural development. **—an·thro·po·log·i·cal** (an'thrə·pə·loj'i·kəl) or **·log'ic** *adj.* **—an'thro·po·log'i·cal·ly** *adv.* **—an'thro·pol'o·gist** *n.*

an·thro·pom·e·try (an'thrə·pom'ə·trē) *n.* The science and technique of measuring anatomical and physiological features of human beings. **—an·thro·po·met·ric** (an'thrə·pō·met'rik) or **·met'ri·cal** *adj.*

an·thro·po·mor·phism (an′thrə·pō·môr′fiz·əm) *n.* The ascription of human attributes, feelings, motives, or characteristics to nonhuman objects, beings, or phenomena. —**an′thro·po·mor′phic** *adj.* —**an′thro·po·mor′phi·cal·ly** *adv.* —**an′thro·po·mor′phist** *n.*

an·thro·po·mor·phize (an′thrə·pō·môr′fīz) *v.t. & v.i.* **·phized, ·phiz·ing** To attribute human characteristics (to).

an·thro·po·mor·phous (an′thrə·pō·môr′fəs) *adj.* Having or resembling human form.

an·thro·poph·a·gous (an′thrə·pof′ə·gəs) *adj.* Feeding on human flesh; cannibalistic. [< Gk. *anthrōpos* man + *phagein* eat] —**an·thro·poph·a·gy** (an′thrə·pof′ə·jē) *n.*

an·ti (an′tī, an′tē) *n. pl.* **·tis** *Informal* One opposed to a policy, group, etc.

anti- *prefix* **1** Against; opposed to: *anti-Semitic.* **2** Opposite to; reverse: *antisocial.* **3** Rivaling; spurious: *Antichrist.* **4** Counteracting: *antibiotic.* [< Gk. *anti* against]

an·ti·air·craft (an′tē·âr′kraft′, -âr′kräft′) *adj.* Used defensively against aircraft.

an·ti·bal·lis·tic missile (an′tē·bə·lis′tik) A missile designed to intercept and destroy hostile ballistic missiles as soon as possible.

an·ti·bi·ot·ic (an′ti·bī·ot′ik) *n.* Any of certain substances, as penicillin and streptomycin, produced by various fungi, bacteria, etc., that destroy or arrest the growth of other microorganisms, used in the treatment of infectious diseases. —*adj.* Of or acting as an antibiotic. [< ANTI- + Gk. *bios* mode of life]

an·ti·bod·y (an′ti·bod′ē) *n. pl.* **·bod·ies** A protein in the blood serum formed in response to a specific foreign protein and conferring immunity to that foreign protein.

an·tic (an′tik) *n.* A ludicrous or clownish action; a prank; caper. —*adj.* Odd; ludicrous; incongruous. —*v.i.* **an·ticked, an·tick·ing** To perform antics. [< Ital. *antico* old, grotesque]

An·ti·christ (an′ti·krīst′) *n.* An opponent or enemy of Christ.

an·tic·i·pate (an·tis′ə·pāt) *v.t.* **·pat·ed, ·pat·ing 1** To count on in advance; expect; foresee. **2** To be in advance of or earlier than. **3** To act so as to prevent; forestall. **4** To foresee and act on beforehand. **5** To take or make use of beforehand, as income not yet available. [< L *ante-* before + *capere* take] —**an·tic′i·pa′tor** *n.* —**an·tic·i·pa·to·ry** (-tis′ə·pə·tôr′ē, -tō′rē) *adj.*

an·tic·i·pa·tion (an·tis′ə·pā′shən) *n.* **1** The act of anticipating. **2** Something anticipated or expected. **3** The act of awaiting expectantly; expectation. **4** A presentiment; foretaste.

an·ti·cler·i·cal (an′ti·kler′i·kəl) *adj.* Opposed to clerical influence, esp. that of the Roman Catholic Church.

an·ti·cli·max (an′ti·klī′maks) *n.* **1** A sudden shift from the serious, lofty, etc., to the trivial or ludicrous. **2** Any sudden and disappointingly contrasting shift. —**an′ti·cli·mac′tic** (-klī·mak′tik) *adj.* —**an′ti·cli·mac′ti·cal·ly** *adv.*

an·ti·cline (an′ti·klīn) *n.* A rock stratum or group of strata forming a bend with the convex side upward. [< ANTI- + Gk. *klinein* to slope] —**an′ti·cli′nal, an′ti·clin′ic** (-klin′ik) *adj.*

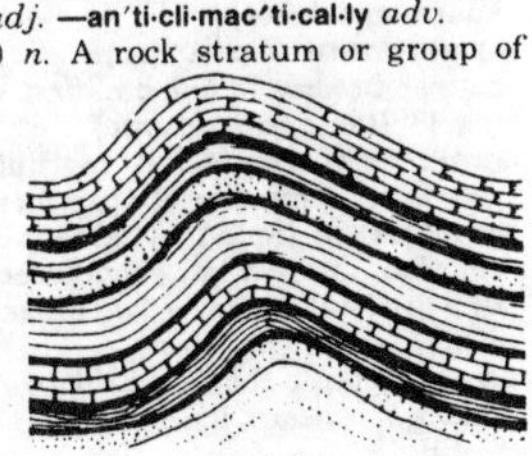

Anticline

an·ti·cy·clone (an′ti·sī′klōn) *n.* An atmospheric condition of high pressure relative to the surrounding area, with clockwise horizontal currents in the northern hemisphere, and counterclockwise ones in the southern. —**an·ti·cy·clon·ic** (an′ti·sī·klon′ik) *adj.*

an·ti·dote (an′ti·dōt) *n.* **1** Anything that neutralizes or counteracts the effects of a poison. **2** Something that counteracts a harmful effect. [< Gk *antidotos* given against] —**an′ti·do′tal** *adj.* —**an′ti·do′tal·ly** *adv.*

an·ti·freeze (an′ti·frēz′) *n.* A liquid added to or substituted for the water in a cooling or heating system to prevent freezing.

an·ti·gen (an′tə·jən) *n.* Any substance that stimulates the development of antibodies. Also **an′ti·gene** (-jēn). —**an·ti·gen·ic** (an′tə·jen′ik) *adj.*

An·tig·o·ne (an·tig′ə·nē) *Gk. Myth.* A daughter of Oedipus who was sentenced to death for performing forbidden funeral rites for her brother.

an·ti·he·ro (an′tē·hē′rō, an′tī-) *n.* A protagonist, as of a novel or play, who lacks traditional qualities attributed to a hero, as courage, gallantry, etc. —**an·ti·he·ro·ic** (an′tē·hi·rō′ik, an′tī-) *adj.*

an·ti·his·ta·mine (an′ti·his′tə·mēn, -min) *n.* Any of certain drugs that neutralize the action of histamine in allergic conditions and colds. —**an′ti·his′ta·min′ic** (-min′ik) *adj.*

an·ti-knock (an′ti·nok′) *adj.* Preventing detonation in an engine. —*n.* An agent, as tetraethyl lead, that prevents knock or detonation when added to the fuel of an internal-combustion engine.

an·ti·log·a·rithm (an′ti·lôg′ə·rith′əm, -log′-) *n.* The number corresponding to a given logarithm.

an·ti·ma·cas·sar (an′ti·mə·kas′ər) *n.* A small covering to prevent soiling of the backs or arms of chairs or sofas. [< ANTI- + *Macassar* a kind of hair oil]

an·ti·mat·ter (an′ti·mat′ər) *n.* A theoretical form of matter composed of antiparticles.

an·ti·mo·ny (an′tə·mō′nē) *n.* A metallic element (symbol Sb) used chiefly in alloys, as type metal, etc. [< Med. L *antimonium*]

an·ti·par·tic·le (an′ti·par′ti·kəl) *n.* Either of a pair of subatomic particles, as an electron and positron, that are equal in mass but opposite in charge and in magnetic properties. Contact between a particle and its opposite results in mutual annihilation and the release of energy.

an·ti·pas·to (än′tē·päs′tō) *n.* An appetizer of assorted meats, fish, vegetables, etc. [< Ital. *anti-* before + *pasto* food]

an·tip·a·thet·ic (an·tip′ə·thet′ik, an′ti·pə-) *adj.* Having antipathy; opposed; averse. Also **an·tip′a·thet′i·cal.** —**an·tip′a·thet′i·cal·ly** *adv.*

an·tip·a·thy (an·tip′ə·thē) *n. pl.* **·thies 1** A feeling of aversion or dislike. **2** The cause of such feeling. [< Gk. *anti-* against + *pathein* feel, suffer] —**Syn.** repugnance, abhorrence, antagonism, hostility.

an·ti·per·son·nel (an′ti·pûr′sə·nel′) *adj.* Used as a weapon against individuals rather than against defenses or equipment.

an·ti·per·spi·rant (an′ti·pûr′spə·rənt) *n.* A preparation applied to the skin to retard or prevent perspiration. —*adj.* Preventing or retarding perspiration.

an·ti·phon (an′tə·fon) *n.* **1** A hymn or liturgical chant sung by alternating choirs. **2** A versicle chanted before, and often after, a psalm or canticle. [< Gk. *antiphona.* See ANTHEM.] —**an·tiph·o·nal** (an·tif′ə·nəl), **an′ti·phon′ic** or **·i·cal** *adj.* —**an·tiph′o·nal·ly** *adv.*

an·tiph·o·ny (an·tif′ə·nē) *n.* Antiphonal singing, form, etc.

an·ti·pode (an′ti·pōd) *n.* An exact opposite.

an·tip·o·des (an·tip′ə·dēz) *n. pl.* **1** A place or region on the opposite side of the earth. **2** *(often construed as sing.)* Something diametrically opposed to another; an opposite extreme. [< Gk. *antipous* having the feet opposite] —**an·tip′o·dal, an·tip′o·de′an** *adj.*

an·ti·py·ret·ic (an′ti·pī·ret′ik) *adj.* Alleviating fever. —*n.* A medicine to allay fever. [< ANTI- + Gk. *pyretos* fever]

an·ti·quar·i·an (an′ti·kwâr′ē·ən) *adj.* Pertaining to antiquity or to expertise in antiquities. —*n.* An antiquary. —**an′ti·quar′i·an·ism** *n.*

an·ti·quar·y (an′ti·kwer′ē) *n. pl.* **·quar·ies** One who collects, deals in, or studies antiquities. [< L *antiquarius* < *antiquus* ancient]

an·ti·quate (an′ti·kwāt) *v.t.* **·quat·ed, ·quat·ing 1** To make old or obsolete. **2** To cause to appear old-fashioned. —**an′ti·qua′tion** *n.*

an·ti·quat·ed (an′ti·kwā′tid) *adj.* **1** Out of date; obsolete. **2** Ancient. —**Syn.** old-fashioned, passé, superannuated, archaic.

an·tique (an·tēk′) *adj.* **1** Of or pertaining to ancient times, esp. ancient Greece or Rome. 2 Of or in the style of an earlier time. 3 Old; ancient. —*n.* 1 An object, esp. a work of art or handicraft, valued because of its age. 2 The style of ancient art. —*v.t.* **an·tiqued, an·ti·quing** To cause to resemble an antique. [< L *antiquus* ancient] **—an·tique′ly** *adv.* **—an·tique′ness** *n.*

an·tiq·ui·ty (an·tik′wə·tē) *n. pl.* **·ties** 1 The condition of being ancient; great age. 2 Ancient times. 3 *Usu. pl.* A relic of ancient times.

an·ti·scor·bu·tic (an′ti·skôr·byo͞o′tik) *adj.* Relieving or preventing scurvy. —*n.* A remedy for scurvy.

an·ti-Sem·i·tism (an′ti·sem′ə·tiz′əm) *n.* Hostility toward or prejudice against Jews. **—an′ti-Sem′ite** *n.* **—an′ti-Se·mit′ic** (-sə·mit′ik) *adj.* **—an′ti-Se·mit′i·cal·ly** *adv.*

an·ti·sep·sis (an′tə·sep′sis) *n.* The prevention of infection by destroying the causative organisms. [< ANTI- + Gk. *sēpsis* putrefaction]

an·ti·sep·tic (an′tə·sep′tik) *adj.* 1 Of, pertaining to, or used in antisepsis. 2 Destructive of organisms causing infection, fermentation, or putrefaction. Also **an′ti·sep′ti·cal.** —*n.* An antiseptic substance. **—an′ti·sep′ti·cal·ly** *adv.*

an·ti·slav·er·y (an′ti·slā′vər·ē, -slāv′rē) *adj.* Opposed to human slavery.

an·ti·so·cial (an′ti·sō′shəl) *adj.* 1 Opposed to or disruptive of social order. 2 Avoiding social contact; not sociable. **—an′ti·so′cial·ly** *adv.*

an·tis·tro·phe (an·tis′trə·fē) *n.* In ancient Greek dramatic poetry, the verses sung by the chorus while moving from left to right in answer to the strophe. [< Gk. *antistrephein* turn against.] **—an·ti·stroph·ic** (an′ti·strof′ik) *adj.*

an·ti·tank (an′ti·tangk′) *adj.* Designed to combat mechanized equipment, as tanks.

an·tith·e·sis (an·tith′ə·sis) *n. pl.* **·ses** (-sēz) 1 The balancing of contrasted words, ideas, etc., against each other. 2 The direct contrary or opposite. [< Gk. *antitithenai* oppose] **—an·ti·thet·i·cal** (an′tə·thet′i·kəl), **an′ti·thet′ic** *adj.* **—an′ti·thet′i·cal·ly** *adv.*

an·ti·tox·in (an′ti·tok′sin) *n.* 1 An antibody formed in response to a specific toxin. 2 A preparation of a serum containing an antitoxin, used in treating certain diseases. **—an′ti·tox′ic** *adj.*

an·ti·trades (an′ti·trādz′) *n. pl.* The upper air currents in the tropics, moving contrary to the trade winds.

an·ti·trust (an′ti·trust′) *adj.* Regulating or opposing trusts, monopolies, etc., that are in restraint of trade.

ant·ler (ant′lər) *n.* One of the paired, deciduous, solid, bony outgrowths on the head of various members of the deer family. [< OF *antoillier,* < L *ante-* before + *oculus* eye] **—ant′lered** *adj.*

Antlers

ant lion An insect resembling a dragonfly, esp. its louselike larva, which preys on ants and other insects.

an·to·nym (an′tə·nim) *n.* A word opposite to another in meaning. [< Gk. *anti-* opposite + *onoma, onyma* name]

an·trum (an′trəm) *n. pl.* **·tra** (-trə) A cavity, usu. in a bone. [< Gk. *antron* cave]

a·nus (ā′nəs) *n.* The opening at the lower end of the alimentary canal. [< L, orig. a ring]

an·vil (an′vil) *n.* 1 A heavy block of iron or steel on which metal may be forged. 2 *Anat.* The incus of the inner ear. [< OE *anfilt*]

anx·i·e·ty (ang·zī′ə·tē) *n. pl.* **·ties** 1 Distress of mind; uneasiness; worry. 2 Strained or intent eagerness. 3 A neurotic state of great tension or dread. **—Syn.** 1 concern, misgiving, apprehension, disquiet, care. [< L *anxius* anxious]

anx·ious (angk′shəs, ang′-) *adj.* 1 Troubled in mind; uneasy; worried. 2 Fraught with or causing anxiety: an *anxious* wait. 3 Intently eager or desirous: *anxious* to succeed. [< L *anxius* < *angere* choke, distress] **—anx′ious·ly** *adv.* **—anx′ious·ness** *n.*

anxious seat *U.S.* The bench at a revival meeting for those who fear they may not be saved.

an·y (en′ē) *adj.* 1 One or some of several or many: Choose *any* item. Have *any* eggs hatched? 2 Some, no matter what: at *any* price. 3 Every: *Any* fool knows that. —*pron.* One or more persons, things, etc., of a number. —*adv.* At all: Are you *any* better today? [< OE *ān* one]

an·y·bod·y (en′i·bod′ē, -bud′ē) *pron.* Any person; anyone. —*n.* A person of importance: He isn't *anybody.*

an·y·how (en′i·hou′) *adv.* 1 In any way whatever; by any means. 2 Notwithstanding; in any case. 3 Carelessly.

an·y·more (en′ē·môr′, -mōr′) *adv.* Now; at present: used only in the negative and in questions: He's not welcome *anymore.* Do you see her *anymore?* Also **any more.**

an·y·one (en′i·wun′, -wən) *pron.* Any person. • **any one, anyone** *Any one* is used to distinguish one individual from others in the same group or class: *Any one* of these men may be guilty. *Anyone* means any person at all: Can *anyone* identify the culprit?

any·place (en′ē·plās′) *adv.* In or to any place.

an·y·thing (en′i·thing′) *pron.* Any thing or matter of any sort. —*n.* A thing of any kind. —*adv.* At all; in any way: not *anything* like that. **—anything but** By no means: *anything but* safe.

an·y·way (en′i·wā′) *adv.* 1 No matter what happens; in any event. 2 Nevertheless; anyhow. 3 Carelessly.

an·y·where (en′i·hwâr′) *adv.* In, at, or to any place.

an·y·wise (en′i·wīz′) *adv.* In any manner.

An·zac (an′zak) *n.* A soldier from Australia or New Zealand.

A/O, a/o account of.

A-OK (ā′ō·kā′) *adj. Informal* Perfectly all right; just fine. Also **A′-o·kay′.**

A-one (ā′wun′) *adj. Informal* Excellent; first-rate. Also **A-1.**

a·or·ta (ā·ôr′tə) *n. pl.* **·tas** or **·tae** (-tē) The great artery leading from the left ventricle of the heart and distributing oxygenated blood to the body. [< NL < Gk. *aortē* < *aeirein* to raise, heave] **—a·or′tal, a·or′tic** *adj.* • See HEART.

a·ou·dad (ä′o͞o·dad) *n.* A wild sheep of northern Africa. [< Berber *audad*]

AP, A.P. Associated Press.

a·pace (ə·pās′) *adv.* Rapidly; swiftly. [< *a-* on + PACE]

a·pache (ə·päsh′, ə·pash′; *Fr.* à·pàsh′) *n.* A Parisian hoodlum or gangster. [< *Apache*]

A·pach·e (ə·pach′ē) *n. pl.* **A·pach·es** or **A·pach·e** A member of a tribe of North American Indians of Athapascan stock.

ap·a·nage (ap′ə·nij) *n.* APPANAGE.

a·part (ə·pärt′) *adv.* 1 At a distance or interval: placed two feet *apart.* 2 So as to be isolated or separated: set *apart.* 3 Away or aside: held *apart.* 4 Separately; independently: considered *apart.* 5 In or to pieces: torn *apart.* **—apart from** Other than; with the exception of. —*adj.* Separated. [< L *ad* to + *pars* part]

a·part·heid (ə·pärt′hīt, -hāt) *n.* The racial segregation decreed by law in the Republic of South Africa. [Afrikaans, apartness]

a·part·ment (ə·pärt′mənt) *n.* One of several rooms or suites of rooms in one building, equipped for housekeeping. [< Ital. *appartamento*]

apartment house A multiple-dwelling building divided into a number of apartments.

ap·a·thet·ic (ap′ə·thet′ik) *adj.* Feeling or showing no emotion, interest, etc.; indifferent. Also **ap′a·thet′i·cal.** **—ap′a·thet′i·cal·ly** *adv.* **—Syn.** unfeeling, unconcerned, sluggish, listless, spiritless.

ap·a·thy (ap′ə·thē) *n.* 1 Lack of emotion, motivation, etc. 2 Lack of concern; indifference. [< Gk. *a-* without + *pathos* feeling]

ape (āp) *n.* 1 A large, tailless primate, as a gorilla or chimpanzee. 2 Loosely, any monkey. 3 A mimic. —*v.t.* **aped, ap·ing** To imitate; mimic. [< OE *apa*]

a·pe·ri·ent (ə·pir′ē·ənt) *adj.* Acting as a laxative. —*n.* An aperient remedy. Also **a·per·i·tive** (ə·per′ə·tiv). [< L *aperire* open]

a·pe·ri·tif (ä′per·ə·tēf′, ə·per-, *Fr.* à·pā·rē·tēf′) *n.* An alcoholic drink, esp. of fortified wine, taken as an appetizer. [< F *apéritif*]

ap·er·ture (ap′ər·cho͝or, -chər) *n.* 1 An opening; hole. 2 An opening through which radiation is captured, as by a lens or antenna. [< L *apertus,* pp. of *aperire* open] **—ap′er·tur·al** *adj.* **—ap′er·tured** *adj.*

a·pet·al·ous (ā·pet′əl·əs) *adj.* Without petals.

a·pex (ā′peks) *n. pl.* **a·pex·es** or **ap·i·ces** (ap′ə·sēz, ā′pə-) **1** The highest point; tip; top. **2** The vertex of an angle. **3** Climax. [< L]

a·pha·sia (ə·fā′zhə, -zhē·ə) *n.* Partial or total loss of the power to use language, due to brain injury or disease. [< Gk. *aphatos* speechless] **—a·pha·sic** (ə·fā′zik, -sik), **a·pha·si·ac** (ə·fā′zē·ak) *adj., n.*

a·phe·li·on (ə·fē′lē·ən) *n. pl.* **·li·a** (-lē·ə) The point in an orbit, as of a planet, farthest from the sun. [< Gk. *apo* away from + *hēlios* sun] **—a·phe′li·an** (-ən) *adj.*

a·phid (ā′fid, af′id) *n.* Any of a family of numerous, small, juice-sucking insects, injurious to plants; a plant louse.

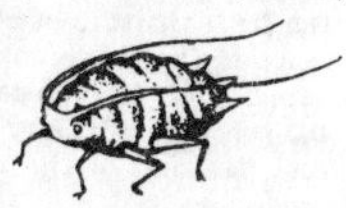
Aphid

a·phis (ā′fis, af′is) *n. pl.* **aph·i·des** (af′ə·dēz) APHID. [?]

aph·o·rism (af′ə·riz′əm) *n.* A brief, pithy statement of a truth or principle; maxim. [< Gk. *aphorismos* definition] **—aph·o·rist** (af′ə·rist) *n.* **—aph′o·ris′tic** or **·ti·cal** *adj.* **—aph′o·ris′ti·cal·ly** *adv.*

aph·ro·dis·i·ac (af′rə·diz′ē·ak) *adj.* Arousing or increasing sexual desire or potency. —*n.* An aphrodisiac drug, food, etc. [< Gk. *Aphroditē* goddess of love]

Aph·ro·di·te (af′rə·dī′tē) *Gk. Myth.* The goddess of love and beauty, identified with the Roman Venus.

a·pi·an (ā′pē·ən) *adj.* Of or pertaining to bees.

a·pi·ar·i·an (ā′pē·âr′ē·ən) *adj.* Of or relating to bees or beekeeping. —*n.* An apiarist.

a·pi·a·rist (ā′pē·ə·rist) *n.* One who tends bees and collects honey.

a·pi·ar·y (ā′pē·er′ē) *n. pl.* **·ar·ies** A place where bees are kept. [< L *apis* bee]

ap·i·cal (ap′i·kəl, ā′pi-) *adj.* Of, at, or forming an apex. [< L *apex* tip] **—ap′i·cal·ly** *adv.*

ap·i·ces (ap′ə·sēz, ā′pə-) *n.pl.* of APEX.

a·pi·cul·ture (ā′pi·kul′chər) *n.* The raising and care of bees, esp. on a large scale. [< L *apis* bee + CULTURE]

a·piece (ə·pēs′) *adv.* For or to each one; each.

ap·ish (ā′pish) *adj.* **1** Of or like an ape. **2** Foolishly imitative. **3** Sly; tricky. **—ap′ish·ly** *adv.* **—ap′ish·ness** *n.*

a·plen·ty (ə·plen′tē) *adv. Informal* In plentiful supply.

a·plomb (ə·plom′, ə·plum′) *n.* Assurance; self-confidence. [F, perpendicularity, assurance] **—Syn.** poise, self-assurance, self-possession, equanimity.

apo- *prefix* Off; from; away: *apogee.* [< Gk. *apo* from, off]

APO, A.P.O. Army Post Office.

Apoc. Apocalypse; Apocrypha; Apocryphal.

a·poc·a·lypse (ə·pok′ə·lips) *n.* A prophetic revelation. [< L < Gk. *apokalyptein* disclose] **—a·poc′a·lyp′tic** (-lip′tik) or **·ti·cal** *adj.* **—a·poc′a·lyp′ti·cal·ly** *adv.*

A·poc·a·lypse (ə·pok′ə·lips) *n.* The book of Revelation, the last book of the New Testament.

a·poc·o·pe (ə·pok′ə·pē) *n.* A cutting off or elision of the last sound or syllable of a word. [< Gk. *apokoptein* cut off]

a·poc·ry·pha (ə·pok′rə·fə) *n. pl.* Any writings or accounts of questionable authorship or doubtful authenticity. [< Gk. *apokryphos* hidden]

A·poc·ry·pha (ə·pok′rə·fə) *n. pl.* **1** Fourteen books of the Septuagint, eleven of which are accepted in the Roman Catholic canon, but none of which is accepted by Protestants or included in the Hebrew Scriptures. **2** Any of various unauthenticated early Christian writings. **—A·poc′ry·phal** *adj.*

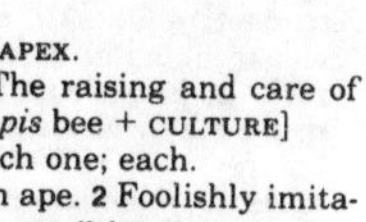

a. apogee. p. perigee.

a·poc·ry·phal (ə·pok′rə·fəl) *adj.* Of doubtful authenticity. **—a·poc′ry·phal·ly** *adv.*

ap·o·gee (ap′ə·jē) *n.* **1** The point in the orbit of the moon or of an artificial satellite that is farthest from the earth. **2** The highest point; climax. [< Gk. < *apo-* away from + *gē, gaia* earth] **—ap·o·ge·al** (ap′ə·jē′əl), **ap′o·ge′an** *adj.*

a·po·lit·i·cal (ā′pə·lit′i·kəl) *adj.* Not associated with or interested in politics. **—a′po·lit′i·cal·ly** *adv.*

A·pol·lo (ə·pol′ō) *Gk. & Rom. Myth.* The god of music, poetry, prophecy, and medicine. —*n.* Any handsome young man.

A·pol·lyon (ə·pol′yən) The devil. *Rev.* 9:11.

a·pol·o·get·ic (ə·pol′ə·jet′ik) *adj.* **1** Making or implying an apology. **2** Defending or explaining. Also **a·pol′o·get′i·cal.** [< Gk. *apologia* a speech in defense] **—a·pol′o·get′i·cal·ly** *adv.*

a·pol·o·get·ics (ə·pol′ə·jet′iks) *n. pl. (construed as sing.)* The branch of theology that deals with the defense of Christianity.

ap·o·lo·gi·a (ap′ə·lō′jē·ə) *n.* A justification or defense. [< Gk.]

a·pol·o·gist (ə·pol′ə·jist) *n.* One who argues in defense of a person or cause.

a·pol·o·gize (ə·pol′ə·jīz) *v.i.* **·gized, ·giz·ing 1** To express regret for an offense or wrongdoing. **2** To make a formal justification or defense. **—a·pol′o·giz′er** *n.*

ap·o·logue (ap′ə·lôg) *n.* A moral tale; a fable. Also **ap′o·log.** [< Gk. *apologos* < *apo-* from + *logos* speech]

a·pol·o·gy (ə·pol′ə·jē) *n. pl.* **·gies 1** A formal expression of regret for an offense, incivility, etc. **2** A poor substitute. [< Gk. *apologia* a speech in defense < *apo-* from + *logos* speech]

ap·o·phthegm (ap′ə·them) *n.* APOTHEGM.

ap·o·plec·tic (ap′ə·plek′tik) *adj.* **1** Of, affected with, or tending toward apoplexy. **2** Causing or likely to cause apoplexy. **3** Wildly excited, as with rage; beside oneself. Also **ap′o·plec′ti·cal.** —*n.* A person subject to apoplexy. **—ap′o·plec′ti·cal·ly** *adv.*

ap·o·plex·y (ap′ə·plek′sē) *n.* Sudden loss of sensation and voluntary motion, due to hemorrhage or impaired circulation in the brain; a stroke. [< Gk. *apoplēxia* < *apoplēssein* disable by a stroke]

a·port (ə·pôrt′, ə·pōrt′) *adv. Naut.* On or toward the port or left side.

a·pos·ta·sy (ə·pos′tə·sē) *n. pl.* **·sies** Desertion of one's religious faith, party, or principles, etc. [< Gk. *apostasia* a standing off, desertion]

a·pos·tate (ə·pos′tāt, -tit) *n.* One guilty of apostasy. —*adj.* Guilty of apostasy.

a·pos·ta·tize (ə·pos′tə·tīz) *v.i.* **·tized, ·tiz·ing** To forsake one's faith, principles, etc.

a pos·te·ri·o·ri (ā′ pos·tir′ē·ôr′ī, -ō′rī) **1** Reasoning from facts to principles or from effect to cause. **2** Inductive; empirical. [L, from what comes after]

a·pos·tle (ə·pos′əl) *n.* **1** *Often cap.* One of the twelve disciples originally chosen by Christ to preach the gospel. **2** A missionary or preacher in the early Christian church. **3** A Christian missionary who first evangelizes a nation or place. **4** An early or chief advocate of a cause. [< Gk. *apostolos* one sent forth, a messenger] **—a·pos′tle·ship, a·pos·to·late** (ə·pos′tə·lit, -lāt) *n.*

Apostles' Creed A traditional Christian confession of faith.

ap·os·tol·ic (ap′ə·stol′ik) *adj.* **1** Of or pertaining to an apostle, the Apostles, or their times. **2** According to the doctrine or practice of the Apostles. **3** *Often cap.* Papal. Also **ap′os·tol′i·cal. —ap′os·tol′i·cal·ly** *adv.* **—ap′os·tol′i·cism** (-ə·siz′·əm) *n.*

Apostolic See The see of Rome, regarded as having been founded by St. Peter.

a·pos·tro·phe[1] (ə·pos′trə·fē) *n.* A symbol (′) shown above the line, to indicate the omission of a letter or letters, the possessive case, or certain plurals, esp. of numbers *(4's)* or letters *(i's).* [< Gk. *(prosōidia) apostrophos* (accent) of turning away] **—ap·os·troph·ic** (ap′ə·strof′ik) *adj.*

a·pos·tro·phe[2] (ə·pos′trə·fē) *n.* A digression from a discourse, esp. to speak to an imaginary or absent person. [< Gk. *apostrophē* a turning away] **—ap·os·troph·ic** (ap′ə·strof′ik) *adj.*

a·pos·tro·phize[1] (ə·pos′trə·fīz) *v.t. & v.i.* **·phized, ·phiz·ing** To mark with or use the apostrophe in writing.

a·pos·tro·phize[2] (ə·pos′trə·fīz) *v.t. & v.i.* **·phized, ·phiz·ing** To address by or use a rhetorical apostrophe.

apothecaries' measure A system of liquid measure used in pharmacy. • See MEASURE.

apothecaries' weight A system of weights used in pharmacy. • See MEASURE.

a·poth·e·car·y (ə·poth′ə·ker′ē) *n. pl.* **·car·ies** A druggist; pharmacist. [< Gk. *apothēkē* storehouse]

ap·o·thegm (ap′ə·them) *n.* A terse, instructive, practical saying; a maxim. [< Gk. *apophthegma* a thing uttered] — **ap·o·theg·mat·ic** (ap′ə·theg·mat′ik) or **·i·cal** *adj.*

a·poth·e·o·sis (ə·poth′ē·ō′sis, ap′ə·thē′ə·sis) *n. pl.* **·ses** (-sēz) **1** Elevation to divine status; deification. **2** Supreme exaltation or idealization; essence. [< Gk. *apo-* from + *theos* a god]

a·poth·e·o·size (ə·poth′ē·ə·sīz′, ap′ə·thē′ə·sīz) *v.t.* **·sized, ·siz·ing 1** To deify. **2** To glorify.

app. apparatus; appendix; apprentice.

ap·pall (ə·pôl′) *v.t.* **ap·palled, ap·pal·ling** To fill with dismay or horror; horrify; shock. Also **ap·pal (ap·palled, ap·pal·ling).** [< OF *apallir* become or make pale]

ap·pall·ing (ə·pô′ling) *adj.* Causing dismay; shocking; frightful. —**ap·pall′ing·ly** *adv.*

ap·pa·loo·sa (ap′ə·lōō′sə) *n. Often cap.* A breed of western saddle horses having a mottled appearance. [Prob. after *Palouse* Indians of the NW U.S.]

ap·pa·nage (ap′ə·nij) *n.* **1** Land, property, etc., for the maintenance of a ruler's younger offspring. **2** One's due; a perquisite. **3** A natural attribute or adjunct. [< OF *apaner* nourish]

ap·pa·rat (ap′ə·rat, äp′ə·rät′) *n.* APPARATUS (def. 4). [Russ.]

ap·pa·ra·tchik (äp′ə·rä′chik) *n. pl.* **·ra·tchi·ki** (-rä′chə·kē) or **·ra·tchiks** A political functionary in a Communist bureaucracy. [Russ.]

ap·pa·ra·tus (ap′ə·rā′təs, -rat′əs) *n. pl.* **·tus** or **·tus·es 1** A complex device or machine for a particular purpose. **2** An assembly of devices designed to achieve a specified result. **3** The organs and parts of the body involved in a specific function. **4** The organization or bureaucratic formula for accomplishing a political purpose, as maintaining a party in power. [L, preparation]

ap·par·el (ə·par′əl) *n.* Garments; clothing. —*v.t.* **·eled** or **·elled, ·el·ing** or **·el·ling** To clothe; dress. [< OF *apareiller* prepare] —**Syn.** *n.* dress, attire, raiment, garb.

ap·par·ent (ə·par′ənt, ə·pâr′-) *adj.* **1** Evident; obvious. **2** Seeming rather than actual. [< OF *aparoir* appear] —**ap·par′ent·ly** *adv.* —**ap·par′ent·ness** *n.*

ap·pa·ri·tion (ap′ə·rish′ən) *n.* **1** A specter; phantom; ghost. **2** An eerie or startlingly unusual sight. **3** An appearance. [< L *apparere* to appear] —**ap′pa·ri′tion·al** *adj.*

ap·peal (ə·pēl′) *n.* **1** An earnest entreaty for aid, sympathy, etc. **2** A quality or manner that attracts. **3** A resort to some higher power or final means. **4** *Law* **a** The carrying of a cause from a lower to a higher tribunal for a rehearing. **b** The right or request to do this. **c** A case so carried. —*v.i.* **1** To make an earnest supplication or request. **2** To be interesting or attractive. **3** To resort or have recourse: to *appeal* to reason. **4** To request that a case be moved to a higher court. —*v.t.* **5** To refer or transfer (a case) to a higher court. [< L *appellare* call upon] —**ap·peal′a·ble** *adj.* —**ap·peal′er** *n.* —**ap·peal′ing·ly** *adv.*

ap·pear (ə·pir′) *v.i.* **1** To become visible; come into view. **2** To seem: He *appeared* tired and out of sorts. **3** To be on public view. **4** To be published or issued, as a book. **5** To present oneself formally in a law court. [< L *ad-* to + *parere* come forth, appear]

ap·pear·ance (ə·pir′əns) *n.* **1** The act of appearing; a coming into view, notice, etc. **2** External aspect: her stern *appearance.* **3** Semblance: an *appearance* of diligence. **4** *pl.* Circumstances or indications. **5** A visible phenomenon, as an apparition.

ap·pease (ə·pēz′) *v.t.* **ap·peased, ap·peas·ing 1** To placate or pacify, as by yielding to demands. **2** To satisfy; allay. [< OF *a-* to + *pais* peace] —**ap·peas′a·ble** *adj.* —**ap·peas′a·bly, ap·peas′ing·ly** *adv.* —**ap·peas′er** *n.* —**Syn. 1** calm, soothe, mollify, propitiate. **2** relieve, assuage, alleviate, quench.

ap·pease·ment (ə·pēz′mənt) *n.* **1** An appeasing or being appeased. **2** The policy of making concessions to a potential aggressor in order to maintain peace.

ap·pel·lant (ə·pel′ənt) *adj. Law* Of or pertaining to an appeal. —*n.* One who appeals.

ap·pel·late (ə·pel′it) *adj. Law* Pertaining to or having jurisdiction of appeals: an *appellate* court. [< L *appellare* to entreat, appeal to]

ap·pel·la·tion (ap′ə·lā′shən) *n.* **1** A name or title. **2** The act of calling or naming.

ap·pel·la·tive (ə·pel′ə·tiv) *adj.* Serving to designate or name. —*n.* A title; appellation. —**ap·pel′la·tive·ly** *adv.*

ap·pend (ə·pend′) *v.t.* **1** To add, as something supplemental. **2** To attach; affix. [< L *ad-* to + *pendere* hang]

ap·pend·age (ə·pen′dij) *n.* **1** Anything appended. **2** *Biol.* A part attached to the main body, as a limb, tail, leaf, etc.

ap·pen·dant (ə·pen′dənt) *adj.* **1** Attached; adjunct. **2** Associated by cause; consequent. —*n.* Something attached or appended. Also **ap·pen′dent.**

ap·pen·dec·to·my (ap′ən·dek′tə·mē) *n. pl.* **·mies** Surgical excision of the vermiform appendix. Also **ap·pen·di·cec·to·my** (ə·pen′də·sek′tə·mē). [< APPENDIX + Gk. *ex-* out + *-tomos* a cutting]

ap·pen·di·ci·tis (ə·pen′də·sī′tis) *n.* Inflammation of the vermiform appendix.

ap·pen·dix (ə·pen′diks) *n. pl.* **·dix·es** or **·di·ces** (-də·sēz) **1** An addition, as of supplementary matter at the end of a book. **2** An outgrowth or prolongation, esp. the vermiform appendix. [< L, an appendage] • See INTESTINE.

ap·per·cep·tion (ap′ər·sep′shən) *n.* **1** Perception in which the mind is conscious of perceiving. **2** The ability to acquire and utilize knowledge; understanding. [< L *ad-* to + *percipere* perceive] —**ap′per·cep′tive** *adj.* —**ap′per·cep′tive·ly** *adv.*

ap·per·tain (ap′ər·tān′) *v.i.* To relate or be relevant; pertain; belong: with *to.* [< LL *ad-* to + *pertinere* pertain]

ap·pe·tence (ap′ə·təns) **1** Strong craving or desire. **2** Natural propensity or tendency. Also **ap′pe·ten·cy.** [< L *appetere.* See APPETITE.] —**ap′pe·tent** *adj.*

ap·pe·tite (ap′ə·tīt) *n.* **1** A desire for food or drink. **2** Any strong liking or desire. [< L *appetitus* < *appetere* strive for] —**ap·pe·ti·tive** (ap′ə·tī′tiv, ə·pet′ə·tiv) *adj.*

ap·pe·tiz·er (ap′ə·tī′zər) *n.* **1** A food or drink served before a meal to stimulate the appetite. **2** A sample, foretaste, etc., that stimulates further desire or interest. *Brit. sp.* **ap′pe·tis′er.**

ap·pe·tiz·ing (ap′ə·tī′zing) *adj.* **1** Arousing the appetite. **2** Temptingly attractive. *Brit. sp.* **ap′pe·tis′ing.** —**ap′pe·tiz′ing·ly** *adv.*

ap·plaud (ə·plôd′) *v.t. & v.i.* **1** To express approval (of) by clapping the hands. **2** To commend; praise. [< L *ad-* to + *plaudere* clap hands, strike] —**ap·plaud′a·ble** *adj.* —**ap·plaud′a·bly, ap·plaud′ing·ly** *adv.* —**ap·plaud′er** *n.*

ap·plause (ə·plôz′) *n.* **1** Approval shown by clapping the hands. **2** General acclaim. [< L *applaudere* to applaud]

ap·ple (ap′əl) *n.* **1** The fleshy, edible, round fruit of any variety of a widely cultivated tree. **2** A tree that bears apples. **3** Any of various fruits or plants with more or less resemblance to the apple. [< OE *æppel*]

ap·ple·jack (ap′əl·jak′) *n.* Brandy made from fermented cider.

ap·ple-pie order (ap′əl·pī′) *Informal* Neat or excellent condition.

apple polisher *Slang* One who seeks favor by obsequious behavior, flattery, etc.

ap·ple·sauce (ap′əl·sôs′) *n.* **1** Apples sweetened and stewed to a pulp. **2** *Slang* Nonsense; bunk.

ap·pli·ance (ə·plī′əns) *n.* A machine or device, esp. one used in the home. [< APPLY]

Appliance
(electric skillet)

ap·pli·ca·ble (ap′li·kə·bəl, ə·plik′ə-) *adj.* Capable of or suitable for application; relevant; fitting. —**ap′pli·ca·bil′i·ty, ap′pli·ca·ble·ness** *n.* —**ap′pli·ca·bly** *adv.*

ap·pli·cant (ap′li·kənt) *n.* One who applies, as for employment or admission.

ap·pli·ca·tion (ap′li·kā′shən) *n.* **1** The act of applying. **2** That which is applied, as a medical remedy. **3** That by which one applies, as a written request or form. **4** Appropriation or relevance to a particular use. **5** Close and continuous attention. —**ap·pli·ca·tive** (ap′li·kā′tiv), **ap′pli·ca·to′ry** *adj.*

applications software Computer software for a specific job or problem, such as word processing.

ap·pli·ca·tor (ap′li·kā′tər) *n.* An object used to apply medication, adhesives, etc.

ap·plied (ə·plīd) *adj.* Put in practice; used practically: *applied* science.

ap·pli·qué (ap′li·kā′) *n.* Ornamentation made from pieces cut out from one material and sewed or fastened to the surface of another. —*v.t.* **·quéd** (-kād′), **·qué·ing** (-kā′·ing) To decorate with appliqué. [F < L *applicare* apply]

ap·ply (ə·plī′) *v.* **ap·plied, ap·ply·ing** *v.t.* **1** To put or spread on: to *apply* paint. **2** To put to a particular use: to *apply* steam to navigation. **3** To connect, as an epithet, with a person or thing. **4** To devote (oneself): to *apply* oneself to study.—*v.i.* **5** To make a formal request, as for employment or admission. **6** To be relevant or appropriate. [< L *applicare* join to < *ad-* to + *plicare* fold]

ap·pog·gia·tu·ra (ə·poj′ə·tyŏŏr′ə, *Ital.* äp·pōd′jä·tōō′rä) *n. Music* An accented ornamental tone followed, usu. stepwise, by a tone that fits the harmony. [Ital. < *appoggiare* lean upon, rest]

ap·point (ə·point′) *v.t.* **1** To designate or select, as a person for a position. **2** To name or decide upon, as a time or place for a meeting. **3** To ordain; decree. **4** To fit out; equip: a *well-appointed* office. [<OF *apointer* arrange, lit., bring to a point]

ap·point·ee (ə·poin′tē′) *n.* One appointed to an office or position.

ap·poin·tive (ə·poin′tiv) *adj.* Filled by appointment: *appointive* office.

ap·point·ment (ə·point′mənt) *n.* The act of appointing or the condition of being appointed, as to a position. **2** A position to which one may be appointed. **3** An agreement to meet at a given time; an engagement. **4** *pl.* Accessories; equipment.

ap·por·tion (ə·pôr′shən, ə·pōr′-) *v.t.* To divide and assign proportionally; allot. [<L *ad-* to + *portio* position] —**ap·por′tion·ment** *n.*

ap·pose (ə·pōz′) *v.t.* **ap·posed, ap·pos·ing 1** To apply or put one thing to another. **2** To arrange side by side. [<F *à-* to + *poser* put] —**ap·pos′a·ble** *adj.*

ap·po·site (ap′ə·zit) *adj.* Appropriate; pertinent. [<L *apponere* put near to] —**ap′po·site·ly** *adj.* —**ap′po·site·ness** *n.*

ap·po·si·tion (ap′ə·zish′ən) *n.* **1** *Gram.* A construction in which one substantive is placed beside another to add to or explain the first, as in *John, president* of the class. **2** A placing or being in contact or side by side. —**ap′po·si′tion·al** *adj.* —**ap′po·si′tion·al·ly** *adv.*

ap·pos·i·tive (ə·poz′ə·tiv) *adj.* In or of apposition. —*n.* A word or phrase in apposition. —**ap·pos′i·tive·ly** *adv.*

ap·prais·al (ə·prā′zəl) *n.* **1** An appraising. **2** An official valuation. Also **ap·praise′ment.**

ap·praise (ə·prāz′) *v.t.* **ap·praised, ap·prais·ing 1** To make an official valuation of. **2** To estimate the amount, quality, or worth of; judge. [<AD- + PRAISE] —**ap·prais′er** *n.*

ap·pre·ci·a·ble (ə·prē′shē·ə·bəl, -shə·bəl) *adj.* Sufficient to be noticed and evaluated. —**ap·pre′ci·a·bly** *adv.*

ap·pre·ci·ate (ə·prē′shē·āt) *v.* **·at·ed, ·at·ing** *v.t.* **1** To be fully aware of the worth of; regard or value highly. **2** To be keenly sensitive to. **3** To enjoy deeply or fully. **4** To be grateful for. **5** To raise the price or value of. —*v.i.* **6** To rise in value. [<L *appretiare* appraise] —**ap·pre′ci·a·tor** *n.* —**Syn. 1** value, esteem, prize, treasure.

ap·pre·ci·a·tion (ə·prē′shē·ā′shən) *n.* **1** High or adequate valuation or regard. **2** Keen awareness or enjoyment. **3** Recognition or gratitude. **4** Increase in value.

ap·pre·ci·a·tive (ə·prē′shē·ə′tiv, -shə·tiv, -shē·ā′-) *adj.* Feeling or showing appreciation. Also **ap·pre·ci·a·to·ry** (ə·prē′shē·ə·tôr′ē, -tō′rē, -shə-). —**ap·pre′ci·a·tive·ly** *adv.* —**ap·pre′ci·a·tive·ness** *n.*

ap·pre·hend (ap′ri·hend′) *v.t.* **1** To seize; arrest. **2** To grasp mentally; understand. **3** To expect with fear or anxiety. [<L *ad-* to + *prehendere* seize] —**ap′pre·hend′er** *n.*

ap·pre·hen·si·ble (ap′ri·hen′sə·bəl) *adj.* Capable of being apprehended. —**ap′pre·hen′si·bil′i·ty** *n.* —**ap′pre·hen′si·bly** *adv.*

ap·pre·hen·sion (ap′ri·hen′shən) *n.* **1** Fearful anxiety; foreboding. **2** Seizure; arrest. **3** Ability to apprehend; understanding. **4** An estimate; opinion. [<L *apprehendere* to seize]

ap·pre·hen·sive (ap′ri·hen′siv) *adj.* **1** Anxiously fearful. **2** Of or pertaining to understanding or perception. —**ap′pre·hen′sive·ly** *adv.* —**ap′pre·hen′sive·ness** *n.*

ap·pren·tice (ə·pren′tis) *n.* **1** One who is legally bound to serve another in order to learn a trade or business. **2** Any learner or beginner. —*v.t.* **·ticed, ·tic·ing** To place as an apprentice. [<OF *aprendre* teach < L *apprehendere* comprehend] —**ap·pren′tice·ship** *n.*

ap·prise (ə·prīz′) *v.t.* **ap·prised, ap·pris·ing** To notify, as of an event; inform. [<F *apprendre* teach, inform] —**ap·prise′ment, ap·pris′er** *n.*

ap·proach (ə·prōch′) *v.i.* **1** To draw near or nearer. —*v.t.* **2** To draw near or nearer to. **3** To come close to; approximate. **4** To begin to treat or deal with: to *approach* a new subject. **5** To make a proposal, advances, etc., to. —*n.* **1** The act of approaching. **2** Nearness; approximation. **3** A way of approaching; access. **4** A way of treating or dealing with something: Try a new *approach.* **5** A golf stroke made toward the putting green after teeing off. [<LL *appropiare* < L *ad-* to + *prope* near]

ap·proach·a·ble (ə·prōch′ə·bəl) *adj.* **1** Capable of being approached. **2** Easy to speak to or get to know. —**ap·proach′a·bil′i·ty** *n.*

ap·pro·ba·tion (ap′rə·bā′shən) *n.* **1** Approval; commendation. **2** Official approval; sanction. [<L *approbare* approve] —**ap·pro·ba·tive** (ap′rə·bā′tiv), **ap·pro′ba·to′ry** (ə·prō′bə·tôr′ē) *adj.*

ap·pro·pri·ate (ə·prō′prē·it) *adj.* Suitable; fitting; proper; relevant. —*v.t.* (ə·prō′prē·āt) **·at·ed, ·at·ing 1** To set apart for a particular use. **2** To take for one's own use. [<L *appropriare* to make one's own] —**ap·pro′pri·ate·ly** *adv.* —**ap·pro′pri·ate·ness, ap·pro′pri·a′tor** *n.* —**ap·pro′pri·a′tive** *adj.*

ap·pro·pri·a·tion (ə·prō′prē·ā′shən) *n.* **1** The act of appropriating. **2** Funds, etc., set apart for a special use.

ap·prov·al (ə·prōō′vəl) *n.* **1** An approving or being approved; approbation. **2** Official consent; sanction. **3** Favorable opinion; praise. —**on approval** For a customer's examination without obligation to purchase.

ap·prove (ə·prōōv′) *v.* **ap·proved, ap·prov·ing** *v.t.* **1** To regard as worthy, proper, or right. **2** To confirm formally or authoritatively. **3** To show or state approval: often with *of.* [<L *ad-* to + *probare* approve, prove] —**ap·prov′er** *n.* —**ap·prov′ing·ly** *adv.*

approx. approximate; approximately.

ap·prox·i·mate (ə·prok′sə·mit) *adj.* Nearly exact, accurate, complete, etc. —*v.* (ə·prok′sə·māt) **·mat·ed, ·mat·ing**— *v.t.* **1** To be almost the same as or very close to. **2** To bring close to or cause to approach closely. **3** *Math.* To calculate an approximation of. —*v.i.* **4** To come close; be similar. [<L *approximare* come near] —**ap·prox′i·mate·ly** *adv.*

ap·prox·i·ma·tion (ə·prok′sə·mā′shən) *n.* **1** The process or result of approximating. **2** *Math.* A result sufficiently exact for a specified purpose.

ap·pur·te·nance (ə·pûr′tə·nəns) *n.* **1** Something added or attached as an accessory or adjunct. **2** *pl.* Accessory equipment, fittings, etc. [<L *appertinere* to pertain to]

ap·pur·te·nant (ə·pûr′tə·nənt) *adj.* Appertaining or belonging. —*n.* APPURTENANCE.

Apr, Apr. April.

a·pri·cot (ā′pri·kot, ap′ri·kot) *n.* **1** A yellowish, cultivated fruit resembling a small peach. **2** The tree bearing this fruit. **3** A yellow-orange color. [<Ar. *al-barqūq* < Med. Gk. *praikokion* early ripe]

A·pril (ā′prəl) *n.* The fourth month of the year, containing 30 days. [<L *Aprilis*]

April Fools' Day April 1, traditionally a day for playing practical jokes.

a pri·o·ri (ā′prī·ō′rī, ä′ prē·ôr′ē) **1** Proceeding from cause to effect, or from an assumption to its logical conclusion. **2** Based on theory and not supported by experience. [L, from what is before] —**a′pri·or′i·ty** *n.*

a·pron (ā′prən, ā′pərn) *n.* 1 A garment, usu. tied at the waist, worn to cover the front of a person's clothes. 2 Any of various pieces protecting parts of machines. 3 A paved area surrounding a hangar or aircraft shelter. 4 The part of a theater stage in front of the curtain. [< OF *naperon,* dim. of *nape* cloth]

ap·ro·pos (ap′rə·pō′) *adj.* Suited to the time, place, or occasion; pertinent. —*adv.* 1 With reference or regard: with *of.* 2 Pertinently; appropriately. 3 By the way; incidentally. [< F *à* to + *propos* purpose]

apse (aps) *n.* A usu. semicircular recess with a half dome, forming the eastern or altar end of a church. [< Gk. *hapsis* a fastening, loop, wheel]

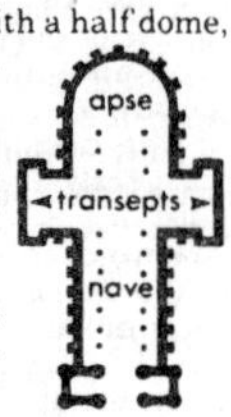

apt (apt) *adj.* 1 Likely; liable; 2 Quick to learn. 3 Pertinent; appropriate. [< L *aptus* fitted, suited] **—apt′ly** *adv.* **—apt′ness** *n.*

apt. (*pl.* **apts.**) apartment.

ap·ter·ous (ap′tər·əs) *adj.* Lacking wings or winglike expansions. [< Gk. *a-* without + *pteron* wing]

ap·ter·yx (ap′tər·iks) *n.* A New Zealand bird, the kiwi. [< Gk. *a-* without + *pteryx* wing]

ap·ti·tude (ap′tə·t(y)ōōd) *n.* 1 A natural ability or gift. 2 Quickness in learning or understanding. 3 Fitness; suitability. [< L *aptus* fitted, suited] **—Syn.** 1 endowment, talent, skill.

aptitude test A test designed to gauge ability to learn or to perform a skill.

aq·ua (ak′wə-, äk′-, ā′kwə) *n. pl.* **aq·uas,** or *for def. 1* **aq·uae** (ak′wē, ā′kwē) 1 Water. 2 A light bluish green color. —*adj.* Light bluish green. [L]

aqua for·tis (fôr′tis) Commercial nitric acid. [L, strong water]

Aq·ua-lung (ak′wə·lung′) *n.* An underwater breathing apparatus or scuba: a trade name. Also **aq′ua·lung′.**

aq·ua·ma·rine (ak′wə·mə·rēn′) *n.* 1 A bluish green variety of precious beryl. 2 A bluish green color. —*adj.* Bluish green. [< L *aqua marina* sea water]

aq·ua·naut (ak′wə·nôt) *n.* One trained and equipped to live, work, or explore underwater over a period of time. [< L *aqua* water + *-naut* < Gk. *nautēs* sailor]

aq·ua·plane (ak′wə·plān′) *n.* A board on which one stands while being towed over water by a motorboat. —*v.i.* **·planed, ·plan·ing** To ride an aquaplane.

aqua re·gi·a (rē′jē·ə) A mixture of concentrated nitric and hydrochloric acids which dissolves gold and platinum. [L, royal water]

a·quar·i·um (ə·kwâr′ē·əm) *n. pl.* **·i·ums** or **·i·a** (-ē·ə) 1 A tank, pond, etc., for the exhibition or study of aquatic animals or plants. 2 A public building containing such an exhibition. [< L *aquarius* pertaining to water]

A·quar·i·us (ə·kwâr′ē·əs) *n.* A constellation and the eleventh sign of the zodiac; the Water Bearer. **—A·quar′i·an** *adj., n.* • See ZODIAC.

a·quat·ic (ə·kwat′ik, ə·kwot′-) *adj.* 1 Of, living, or growing in water. 2 Done in or on water: *aquatic* sports. —*n.* 1 An aquatic animal or plant. 2 *pl.* Aquatic sports. [< L *aqua* water] **—a·quat′i·cal·ly** *adv.*

aq·ua·tint (ak′wə·tint′) *n.* 1 A form of engraving differing from an etching in which spaces instead of, or as well as, lines are etched by acid. 2 An engraving printed from a plate so prepared. —*v.t.* To etch by this process. [< Ital. *acqua tinta* dyed water]

a·qua·vit (ä′kwə·vēt) *n.* A colorless Scandinavian liquor flavored with caraway seed. Also **ak·va·vit** (äk′vä·vēt).

aqua vi·tae (vī′tē) 1 Alcohol. 2 Whiskey, brandy, etc. [< L, water of life]

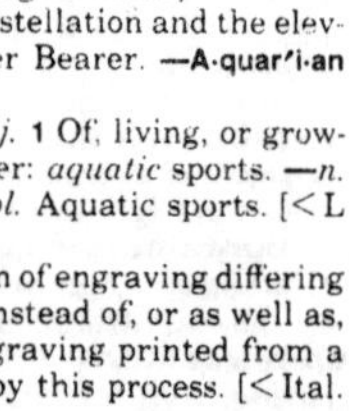
Aqueduct

aq·ue·duct (ak′wə·dukt) *n.* 1 A water conduit, esp. one for supplying a community from a distance. 2 A structure supporting such a conduit across a river or over low ground. 3 *Anat.* Any of several canals through which body liquids are conducted. [< L *aqua* water + *ductus,* p.p. of *ducere* lead]

a·que·ous (ā′kwe·əs, ak′we-) *adj.* Of, resembling, or containing water. [< L *aqua* water]

aqueous humor The limpid fluid that fills the anterior chamber of the eye from the cornea to the crystalline lens.

aq·ui·line (ak′wə·līn, ·lin) *adj.* 1 Of or like an eagle. 2 Hooked like an eagle's beak: an *aquiline* nose. [< L *aquila* eagle]

-ar *suffix* 1 Pertaining to; like: *regular, singular.* 2 A person having to do with: *scholar.* [< L *-aris*]

AR Arkansas (P.O. abbr.).

Ar Argon.

Ar., Arab. Arabian; Arabic.

Ar·ab (ar′əb) *n.* 1 A native or inhabitant of Arabia. 2 One of an Arabic-speaking people. 3 One of a Semitic people inhabiting Arabia from ancient times. 4 A horse of a swift-running, graceful breed originally native to Arabia. —*adj.* Arabian.

ar·a·besque (ar′ə·besk′) *n.* 1 An ornament or design of intertwined scrollwork, conventionalized leaves or flowers, etc. 2 In ballet, a position in which the dancer extends one leg straight backward, one arm forward, and the other arm backward. —*adj.* Of, resembling, or forming an arabesque. [< F < Ital. *arabesco,* lit., Arabic]

A·ra·bi·an (ə·rā′bē·ən) *adj.* Of or pertaining to Arabia or the Arabs. —*n.* 1 A native or inhabitant of Arabia. 2 An Arab horse.

Arabian Nights A collection of stories from Arabia, India, Persia, etc., dating from the tenth century A.D.

Ar·a·bic (ar′ə·bik) *adj.* Of or pertaining to Arabia, the Arabs, their language, culture, etc. —*n.* The Semitic language of the Arabians.

Arabic numerals The characters 0, 1, 2, 3, 4, 5, 6, 7, 8, 9.

ar·a·ble (ar′ə·bəl) *adj.* Capable of being plowed or cultivated. [< L *arare* plow] **—ar′a·bil′i·ty** *n.*

Arab League A confederation formed originally by Egypt, Iraq, Jordan, Lebanon, Saudi Arabia, Syria, and Yemen, and later joined by Kuwait, Libya, Morocco, Sudan, and Tunisia.

Ar·a·by (ar′ə·bē) *n. Archaic* Arabia.

a·rach·nid (ə·rak′nid) *n.* Any of a class of eight-legged arthropods, including the spiders, scorpions, mites, etc. [< NL < Gk. *arachnē* spider] **—a·rach′ni·dan** *adj., n.*

Aram. Aramaic.

Ar·a·ma·ic (ar′ə·mā′ik) *n.* Any of a group of Semitic languages, including the language of the Jews in Palestine at the time of Jesus.

ar·ba·lest (är′bə·list) *n.* A medieval crossbow having a steel bow. Also **ar′ba·list.** [< L *arcus* a bow + *ballista* < Gk. *ballein* throw] **—ar′ba·lest′er** *n.*

ar·bi·ter (är′bə·tər) *n.* 1 A person chosen to settle a dispute. 2 One who is authorized to judge or decide or whose decisions are considered final. [< L, one who goes to see, a witness] **—Syn.** 1 judge, referee, umpire, moderator. 2 authority, expert, master, specialist.

ar·bit·ra·ment (är·bit′rə·mənt) *n.* 1 The act of arbitration. 2 The decision of an abritrator. 3 The power or right to make such decision. Also **ar·bit′re·ment.**

ar·bi·trar·y (är′bə·trer′ē) *adj.* 1 Based on mere opinion or prejudice; capricious. 2 Absolute; despotic. [< L *arbiter.* See ARBITER.] **—ar′bi·trar′i·ly** *adv.* **—ar′bi·trar′i·ness** *n.*

ar·bi·trate (är′bə·trāt) *v.t. & v.i.* **·trat·ed, ·trat·ing** 1 To submit (a dispute) to or have (a dispute) settled by an arbiter. 2 To act as arbiter in (a dispute). [< L *arbiter.* See ARBITER.] **—ar·bi·tra·ble** (är′bə·trə·bəl), **ar′bi·tra′tive** *adj.*

ar·bi·tra·tion (är′bə·trā·shən) *n.* The hearing and settlement of a dispute between two parties by the decision of a third party to which the matter is referred.

ar·bi·tra·tor (är′bə·trā′tər) *n.* 1 A person chosen to decide a dispute, as in arbitration. 2 An arbiter (def. 2). [< L]

ar·bor[1] (är′bər) *n.* A bower, as of latticework, supporting vines or trees; a place shaded by trees. [< L *herbarium* a collection of herbs]

ar·bor[2] (är′bər) *n. pl.* **ar·bo·res** (är′bər·ēz) *for def.* **1, ar·bors** *for def.* **2.** 1 A tree: used chiefly in botanical names. 2 *Mech.* a A shaft, mandrel, spindle, or axle for a rotary part. b A support for a cutting tool. [< L, tree]

Arbor Day A U.S. spring holiday observed in some States by planting trees.

ar·bo·re·al (är·bôr′ē·əl, -bō′rē) *adj.* **1** Of or pertaining to a tree or trees; arborescent. **2** Living or situated among trees. Also **ar·bor′e·ous.**

ar·bo·res·cent (är′bə·res′ənt) *adj.* Treelike in appearance or growth. **—ar′bo·res′cence** *n.*

ar·bo·re·tum (är′bə·rē′təm) *n. pl.* **·tums** or **·ta** (-tə) A botanical garden exhibiting trees for their scientific and educational value. [< L *arbor* tree]

ar·bor·vi·tae (är′bər·vī′tē) *n.* An evergreen shrub or tree of the pine family. [< L, tree of life]

ar·bu·tus (är·byōō′təs) *n.* **1** Any of several evergreen trees or shrubs related to heath. **2** TRAILING ARBUTUS. [< L, strawberry tree]

arc (ärk) *n.* **1** Anything in the shape of an arch, of a curve, or of a part of a circle. **2** A part of any curve, esp. of a circle. **3** *Electr.* The light caused by an electric discharge in a gas. **—*v.i.*** **arcked** or **arced** (ärkt), **arck·ing** or **arc·ing** (är′king) *Electr.* To form an arc. [< L *arcus* bow, arch]

ARC, A.R.C. American Red Cross

ar·cade (är·kād′) *n.* **1** A series of arches with their supporting columns or piers. **2** An arched or covered passageway or street, esp. one having shops, etc. opening from it. **—*v.t.*** **·cad·ed, ·cad·ing** To furnish with or form into an arcade. [< L *arcus,* arch]

Ar·ca·di·a (är·kā′dē·ə) *n.* **1** An ancient pastoral region in the Peloponnesus. **2** Any region of rustic simplicity and peace. Also **Ar·ca·dy** (är′kə·dē). **—Ar·ca′di·an** *adj., n.*

ar·cane (är·kān′) *adj.* Secret; hidden; mysterious. [< L *arcanus.* See ARCANUM.]

ar·ca·num (är·kā′nəm) *n. pl.* **·na** (-nə) A secret or mystery. [< L *arcanus* hidden < *arca* chest]

arch[1] (ärch) *n.* **1** A curved structure spanning an opening, formed of wedge-shaped parts resting on supports at the two extremities. **2** Any similarly shaped structure, object, or part: the dental *arch.* **3** The form of an arch; a bowlike curve. **—*v.t.*** **1** To cause to form into an arch. **2** To furnish with an arch or arches. **—*v.i.*** **3** To form an arch or arches. [< L *arcus* bow, arch]

Arch

arch[2] (ärch) *adj.* **1** Roguish; sly. **2** Artificially playful; forced. **3** Most eminent; chief. [< ARCH-] **—arch′ly** *adv.* **—arch′ness** *n.*

arch- *prefix* Chief; principal: *archbishop.* [< Gk. *archos* ruler]

Arch., Archbp. Archbishop.

arch. archaic; archipelago; architect; architecture.

ar·chae·ol·o·gy (är′kē·ol′ə·jē) The scientific search for and study of artifacts and relics of past human cultures. [< Gk. *archaios* ancient + -LOGY] **—ar·chae·o·log·i·cal** (är′kē·ə·loj′i·kəl) or **·log′ic** *adj.* **—ar′chae·ol′o·gist** (-jist) *n.*

Ar·chae·o·zo·ic (är′kē·ə·zō′ik) ARCHEOZOIC.

ar·cha·ic (är·kā′ik) *adj.* **1** Belonging to a former period; ancient or antiquated. **2** Characterizing a verbal form or phrase no longer in current use except for special purposes, as poetry, the law, and church ritual. Also **ar·cha′i·cal.** [< Gk. *archaios* ancient]

ar·cha·ism (är′kē·iz′əm, -kā-) *n.* **1** An archaic word, idiom, or expression. **2** Archaic style or usage. **—ar′cha·ist** *n.* **—ar′cha·is′tic** *adj.*

arch·an·gel (ärk′ān′jəl) *n.* An angel of highest rank. **—arch·an·gel·ic** (ärk′an·jel′ik) or **·i·cal** *adj.*

arch·bish·op (ärch′bish′əp) *n.* The chief bishop of an ecclesiastical province.

arch·bish·op·ric (ärch′bish′əp·rik) *n.* The office, rank, term of office, or jurisdictional province of an archbishop.

arch·dea·con (ärch′dē′kən) *n.* A church official next in rank below a bishop. **—arch·dea·con·ate** (ärch′dē′kən·it), **arch′dea′con·ship** *n.*

arch·dea·con·ry (ärch′dē′kən·rē) *n. pl.* **·ries** The office, rank, jurisdiction, or residence of an archdeacon.

arch·di·o·cese (ärch′dī′ə·sis, -sēs′) *n.* The diocese of an archbishop.

arch·du·cal (ärch′dyōō′kəl) *adj.* Of or pertaining to an archduke or an archduchy.

arch·duch·ess (ärch′duch′is) *n.* **1** A princess of the former imperial family of Austria. **2** The wife or widow of an archduke.

arch·duch·y (ärch′duch′ē) *n. pl.* **·duch·ies** The territory under the control of an archduke or an archduchess. Also **arch′duke′dom.**

arch·duke (ärch′dyōōk′) *n.* A sovereign prince, esp. a prince of the former imperial family of Austria.

arch·en·e·my (ärch′en′ə·mē) *n. pl.* **·mies** **1** A chief enemy. **2** Satan.

ar·che·ol·o·gy (är′kē·ol′ə·jē) *n.* ARCHAEOLOGY. **—ar·che·o·log·i·cal** (är′kē·ə·loj′i·kəl) or **·log′ic** *adj.* **—ar′che·ol′o·gist** (-jist) *n.*

Ar·che·o·zo·ic (är′kē·ə·zō′ik) *n. & adj.* See GEOLOGY. [< Gk. *archaios* ancient + *zōion* animal]

arch·er (är′chər) *n.* One who shoots with a bow and arrow. [< L *arcus* bow]

Arch·er (är′chər) *n.* SAGITTARIUS.

arch·er·y (är′chər·ē) *n.* **1** The art or sport of shooting with bow and arrow. **2** The gear of the archer. **3** Archers collectively.

ar·che·type (är′kə·tīp) *n.* An original or standard pattern or model. [< Gk. *arche-* first + *typos* stamp, pattern] **—ar′che·typ′al** *adj.* **—ar′che·typ′ic** (-tip′ik) or **·i·cal** *adj.* **—Syn.** prototype, example, ideal, paradigm.

arch·fiend (ärch′fēnd′) *n.* A chief fiend; specifically, Satan.

archi- *prefix* Principal; chief: *architrave.*

ar·chi·e·pis·co·pal (är′kē·i·pis′kə·pəl) *adj.* Of or pertaining to an archbishop.

ar·chi·pel·a·go (är′kə·pel′ə·gō) *n. pl.* **·goes** or **·gos** A sea studded with many islands, or the islands collectively. [< ARCHI- + *pelagos* sea] **—ar·chi·pe·lag·ic** (är′kə·pə·laj′ik) *adj.*

ar·chi·tect (är′kə·tekt) *n.* **1** One whose profession is to design and draw up the plans for buildings, etc., and supervise their construction. **2** A planner; creator; designer. [< Gk. *archi-* chief + *tektōn* worker]

ar·chi·tec·ton·ics (är′kə·tek·ton′iks) *n. pl. (construed as sing.)* **1** The science of architecture. **2** *Philos.* The scientific arrangement and construction of systems of knowledge. **3** Structural design, as in works of art.

ar·chi·tec·ture (är′kə·tek′chər) *n.* **1** The science, art, or profession of designing and constructing buildings or other structures. **2** A style or system of building. **3** Construction or structure generally; any ordered arrangement of the parts of a system. **4** A building, or buildings collectively. **—ar′chi·tec′tur·al** *adj.* **—ar′chi·tec′tur·al·ly** *adv.*

ar·chi·trave (är′kə·trāv) *n. Archit.* **1** A chief beam; that part of an entablature which rests upon the column heads and supports the frieze. **2** A molded ornament, as that skirting the head and sides of a door or window. [< ARCHI- + L *trabs* beam] • See ENTABLATURE, FRIEZE.

ar·chives (är′kīvz) *n. pl.* **1** A place where public records and historical documents are kept. **2** The records and documents themselves. [< Gk. *archeion* a public office < *archē* government] **—ar·chi′val** *adj.* **—ar′chi·vist** (-kə·vist) *n.*

arch·priest (ärch′prēst′) *n.* Formerly, the priest serving as chief assistant to a bishop. **—arch′priest′hood, arch′priest′ship** *n.*

arch·way (ärch′wā′) *n.* A passage under an arch.

-archy *combining form* Rule; government: *patriarchy.* [< Gk. *archos* ruler]

arc light A lamp in which intense light is produced directly by a continuous electric discharge. Also **arc lamp.**

arc·tic (ärk′tik, är′tik) *adj.* Extremely cold; frigid. **—*n.*** A warm, waterproof overshoe.

Arc·tic (ärk′tik, är′tik) *n.* **1** The region north of the Arctic Circle: used with *the.* **2** The Arctic Ocean. **—*adj.*** Of, in, or pertaining to the Arctic or the Arctic Ocean. [< Gk. *arktikos* of the Bear (the northern constellation *Ursa Major*) < *arktos* bear]

Arc·tu·rus (ärk·tyōōr′əs) *n.* A bright, orange star located in the constellation Boötes. [< Gk. *Arktouros* guardian of the bear]

-ard *suffix of nouns* One who does something to excess or who is to be disparaged: *drunkard.* Also **-art:** *braggart.* [< G *-hard, -hart* hardy]

ar·dent (är′dənt) *adj.* **1** Passionate; zealous; intense. **2** Red; glowing; flashing. **3** Fiery; burning. [< L *ardere* burn] **—ar′den·cy** *n.* **—ar′dent·ly** *adv.*

ar·dor (är′dər) *n.* **1** Warmth or intensity of feeling; eagerness; zeal. **2** Great heat, as of fire, sun, or fever. *Brit. sp.* **ar′dour.** [< L, a flame, fire]

ar·du·ous (är′jo͞o·əs) *adj.* **1** Involving great labor or hardship; difficult. **2** Toiling strenuously; energetic. **3** Steep. [< L *arduus* steep] **—ar′du·ous·ly** *adv.* **—ar′du·ous·ness** *n.*

are[1] (är) *v.* First, second, and third person plural, present indicative, of the verb BE; also used as second person singular. [< OE *aron*]

are[2] (âr, är) *n.* A metric unit of area equal to one hundred square meters. [< L *area* area]

ar·e·a (âr′ē·ə) **1** An open space, often devoted to a special purpose. **2** A tract or portion of the earth's surface; region; section. **3** The measure of a surface. **4** A yard of a building; areaway. **5** Extent; scope. [< L, an open space of level ground] **—ar′e·al** *adj.*

ar·e·a·way (âr′ē·ə·wā) *n.* **1** A small sunken passageway to a basement door. **2** A passageway, as from one building to another.

a·re·na (ə·rē′nə) *n.* **1** The central space for contestants in a Roman amphitheater. **2** Any place like this: the boxing *arena.* **3** A sphere of action or contest. [< L, sand, sandy place]

ar·e·na·ceous (ar′ə·nā′shəs) *adj.* Sandy.

aren't (ärnt) Contraction of *are not.*

a·re·o·la (ə·rē′ə·lə) *n. pl.* **·lae** (-lē) or **·las 1** A small space in a network of veins or vessels, as on leaves. **2** *Anat.* The colored circle about a nipple or about a vesicle. Also **ar·e·ole** (âr′ē·ōl). [< L, dim. of *area* open space] **—a·re′o·lar** *adj.*

Ar·es (âr′ēz) *Gk. Myth.* The god of war.

Arg. Argentina.

ar·ga·li (är′gə·lē) *n. pl.* **·lis** or **·li** An Asiatic wild sheep with large, curved horns [< Mongolian]

ar·gent (är′jənt) *n. Archaic* Silver. *—adj.* Silvery: also **ar·gen·tal** (är·jen′təl). [< L *argentum* silver]

Ar·gen·ti·na (är′jən·tē′nə) *n.* A republic of sw South America, 1,084,362 sq. mi., cap. Buenos Aires.

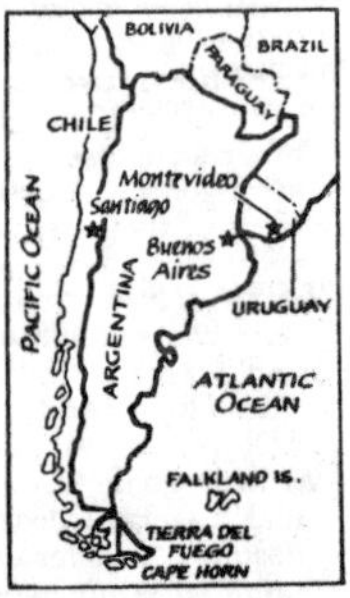

ar·gen·tine (är′jən·tin, -tīn) *n.* Silver. *—adj.* Silvery. [< L *argentum* silver]

Ar·gen·tine (är′jən·tēn′, -tīn′) *adj.* Of or pertaining to Argentina. *—n.* A native or citizen of Argentina: also **Ar·gen·tin·e·an** (är′jən·tin′ē·ən). **—the Argentine** *Brit.* Argentina.

ar·gil (är′jil) *n.* Potters' clay; white clay. [< Gk. *argos* white]

Ar·go (är′gō) *Gk. Myth.* The ship in which Jason sailed for the Golden Fleece.

ar·gon (är′gon) *n.* A colorless, odorless, chemically inactive, gaseous element (symbol Ar), constituting almost one percent of the atmosphere, and used chiefly to fill electric light bulbs. [< Gk. *argos* idle, inert]

ar·go·sy (är′gə·sē) *n. pl.* **·sies 1** A large merchant ship. **2** A fleet of merchant vessels. [< *Ragusa,* Italian name of Dubrovnik]

ar·got (är′gō, -gət) *n.* The specialized or secret language peculiar to a class or group, as to the underworld. [< F] **—ar·got·ic** (är·got′ik) *adj.*

ar·gue (är′gyo͞o) *v.* **ar·gued, ar·gu·ing** *v.i.* **1** To give reasons to support or contest a measure or opinion. **2** To dispute or quarrel. *—v.t.* **3** To give reasons for or against; discuss. **4** To contend or maintain. **5** To prove or indicate, as from evidence. **6** To influence or convince, as by argument. [< L *arguere* make clear, prove] **—ar′gu·a·ble** *adj.* **—ar′gu·er** *n.*

ar·gu·ment (är′gyə·mənt) *n.* **1** A reason offered for or against something. **2** The act of reasoning to establish or refute a position. **3** A disagreement, dispute, or quarrel. **4** A summary or synopsis of a plot, subject, etc. [< L *arguere* make clear, prove]

ar·gu·men·ta·tion (är′gyə·men·tā′shən) *n.* **1** The methodical setting forth of premises and the drawing of conclusions therefrom. **2** Discussion; debate.

ar·gu·men·ta·tive (är′gyə·men′tə·tiv) *adj.* **1** Consisting of or marked by argument. **2** Given to arguing. **—ar′gu·ment′ta·tive·ly** *adv.* **—ar′gu·men′ta·tive·ness** *n.* **—Syn. 1** controversial, debatable, disputable, controvertible. **2** disputatious, contentious, quarrelsome, combative.

ar·gyle (är′gīl) *n.* **1** A design of varicolored diamonds on a solid-color background. **2** A knit sock of this design. Also **Ar′gyle, ar′gyll, Ar′gyll.** [from the tartan of the clan Campbell of *Argyll,* Scotland] • See PLAID.

a·ri·a (ä′rē·ə, âr′ē·ə) *n.* **1** An air; melody. **2** An elaborate solo for voice, as in an opera. [< L *aer* air]

-aria *suffix* Used in forming new Latin names, esp. in zoological and botanical classifications. [< L *-arius*]

Ar·i·ad·ne (ar′ē·ad′nē) *Gk. Myth.* The daughter of Minos, who gave Theseus the thread by which he found his way out of the Labyrinth.

Ar·i·an (âr′ē·ən, ar′-, är-, är′yən) *adj., n.* ARYAN.

-arian *suffix* Used in forming adjectives and adjectival nouns denoting occupation, age, sect, beliefs, etc.: *nonagenarian, seminarian.* [< L *-arius* -ary + *-anus* -an]

ar·id (ar′id) *adj.* **1** Lacking enough moisture to support vegetation; barren. **2** Without interest; dull. [< L *arere* be dry] **—a·rid·i·ty** (ə·rid′ə·tē), **ar′id·ness** *n.* **—ar′id·ly** *adv.*

Ar·ies (âr′ēz, âr′ē·iz) *n.* **1** A constellation and the first sign of the zodiac; the Ram. [< L, the Ram] • See ZODIAC.

a·right (ə·rīt′) *adv.* In a right way; correctly.

-arious *suffix of adjectives* Connected with; pertaining to: *gregarious.* [< L *-arius* -ary + -OUS]

a·rise (ə·rīz′) *v.i.* **a·rose** (ə·rōz′), **a·ris·en** (ə·riz′ən), **a·ris·ing 1** To get up, as from a prone position. **2** To rise; ascend. **3** To come into being; originate. **4** To result or proceed: with *from.* [OE *ā-* up + *rīsan* rise]

ar·is·toc·ra·cy (ar′is·tok′rə·sē) *n. pl.* **·cies 1** A hereditary nobility or privileged class. **2** Government by a privileged upper class. **3** A country having such a government. **4** Any group made up of the best: an *aristocracy* of musicians. [< Gk. *aristos* best + -CRACY]

a·ris·to·crat (ə·ris′tə·krat, ar′is·tə·krat′) *n.* **1** A member of an aristocracy. **2** A person who has the tastes, ideas, manners, etc., associated with the aristocracy. **—a·ris′to·crat′ic** or **·i·cal** *adj.* **—a·ris′to·crat′i·cal·ly** *adv.*

Ar·is·to·te·li·an (ar′is·tə·tē′lē·ən, -tə·tēl′yən, ə·ris′tə-) *adj.* Of or pertaining to Aristotle or his philosophy. *—n.* An adherent of Aristotle. **—Ar′is·to·te′li·an·ism′** *n.*

a·rith·me·tic (ə·rith′mə·tik) *n.* The use and study of integers under the operations of addition, subtraction, multiplication, division. [< Gk. *(hē) arithmetikē (technē)* (the) counting (art)] **—ar·ith·met·ic** (ar′ith·met′ik) or **·i·cal** *adj.* **—ar′ith·met′i·cal·ly** *adv.*

a·rith·me·ti·cian (ə·rith′mə·tish′ən, ar′ith-) *n.* One who uses or is skilled in arithmetic.

arithmetic mean The sum of a set of measures, observations, scores, etc., divided by the number of items in the set.

arithmetic progression A sequence of terms such that each except the first is equal to the sum of its predecessor and a given constant, as 3, 7, 11, 15, 19, etc.

-arium *suffix of nouns* **1** A place for: *herbarium.* **2** Connected with: *honorarium.* [< L< *-arius.* See -ARY.]

Ariz. Arizona.

ark (ärk) *n.* **1** In the Bible: **a** The ship of Noah (*Gen.* 6). **b** The chest containing the stone tablets on which were inscribed the Ten Commandments: also **ark of the covenant** (*Ex.* 25:10). **2** A place of refuge. **3** A large, usu. flat-bottomed boat. [< L *arca* chest]

Ark. Arkansas.

arm[1] (ärm) *n.* **1** The upper limb of the human body, from the shoulder to the hand or wrist. **2** The fore limb of vertebrates other than man. **3** An armlike part or appendage. **4** The part in contact with or covering the human arm: *arm* of a chair. **5** Anything branching out like an arm, usu. considered as a distinct part or branch: an *arm* of the sea. **6** Strength; might: the *arm* of the law. **—at**

arm's length At a distance, so as to preclude intimacy. [< OE *arm, earm*]

arm² (ärm) *n.* **1** *Usu. pl.* A weapon. **2** A distinct branch of the naval or military service: the air *arm.* —*v.t.* **1** To supply with instruments of warfare. **2** To provide with whatever is necessary for action, struggle, protection, etc. —*v.i.* **3** To equip oneself with weapons. **4** To supply oneself with the means necessary for an undertaking. [See ARMS]

Arm. Armenia; Armenian.

ar·ma·da (är·mä′də, -mā′-) *n.* A fleet of war vessels or war planes. —**the Armada** The fleet sent against England by Spain in 1588 and defeated by the English navy: also **Spanish Armada.** [< L< *armare* to arm]

ar·ma·dil·lo (är′mə·dil′ō) *n. pl.* **·los** An American burrowing nocturnal mammal having an armorlike covering of jointed plates. [< Sp. *armado* armed]

Armadillo

Ar·ma·ged·don (är′mə·ged′n) *n.* **1** In the Bible, the scene of a great battle between the forces of good and evil, to occur at the end of the world. *Rev.* 16:16. **2** Any great or decisive conflict. [< Heb. *Megiddon* the plain of Megiddo, a battlefield]

ar·ma·ment (är′mə·mənt) *n.* **1** *Often pl.* The whole of a nation's military forces and equipment. **2** The guns, munitions, and other military equipment of a fortification, military unit, airplane, etc. **3** The body of naval, air, and ground forces equipped for war. **4** The act of arming for war. [< L *armamenta* implements < *armare* to arm]

ar·ma·ture (är′mə·chŏŏr) *n.* **1** A piece of soft iron joining the poles of a magnet to prevent the loss of magnetic power. **2** *Electr.* **a** The rotor of a generator or motor, carrying coils of insulated wire on iron cores. **b** The part of a relay, buzzer, or bell that moves when activated. **3** *Biol.* Protective devices for defense or offense, as quills, thorns, etc. **4** In sculpture, a framework to support the clay or other modeling substance. **5** Arms; armor. —*v.t.* **·tured, ·turing** To furnish with an armature. [< L *armatura* armor]

arm·band (ärm′band′) *n.* A band worn around the upper arm to identify the wearer, indicate bereavement, etc.

arm·chair (ärm′châr′) *n.* A chair with side supports for the arms or elbows. —*adj.* Describing one who offers opinions or advice about matters with which he is not involved or not conversant: an *armchair* critic.

armed (ärmd) *adj.* Provided with that which aids in an offensive action, affords defense, gives security, etc.

armed forces The combined military and naval forces of a nation.

Ar·me·ni·a (är·mē′nē·ə, -mēn′yə) *n.* A former country of w Asia, now in Turkey, Iran, and the Soviet Union. —**Ar·me′ni·an** *adj., n.*

arm·ful (ärm′fŏŏl′) *n. pl.* **·fuls** That which is held, or as much as can be held, in the arm.

arm·hole (ärm′hōl′) *n.* An opening for the arm in a garment.

ar·mi·stice (är′mə·stis) *n.* A temporary cessation, by mutual agreement, of hostilities; a truce. [< L *arma* arms + *-stitium* a stoppage]

Armistice Day VETERANS DAY.

arm·let (ärm′lit) *n.* **1** A little arm, as of the sea. **2** An ornamental band worn around the upper arm.

ar·moire (är·mwär′) *n.* A large, movable wardrobe or cabinet. [< L *armarium* a chest, orig., place to store arms]

ar·mor (är′mər) *n.* **1** A defensive covering, as of mail for a warrior, or of metallic plates for a war vessel, a tank, etc. **2** *Biol.* Any protective covering on a plant or animal. —*v.t.* & *v.i.* To furnish with or put on armor. *Brit. sp.* **ar′mour.** [< L *armatura* < *armare* to arm] • See MAIL².

ar·mored (är′mərd) *adj.* **1** Protected by armor. **2** Equipped with armored vehicles, as a military unit.

ar·mor·er (är′mər·ər) *n.* **1** A maker or repairer of armor. **2** A manufacturer of arms. **3** *Mil.* An enlisted man in charge of small arms. *Brit. sp.* **ar′mour·er.**

ar·mo·ri·al (är·môr′ē·əl, -mō′rē-) *adj.* Pertaining to heraldry or heraldic arms.

armor plate A protective covering of a special steel alloy, used on warships, tanks, etc. —**ar′mor-plat′ed** *adj.*

ar·mor·y (är′mər·ē) *n. pl.* **·mor·ies** **1** A place for the storage of arms. **2** A building for the use of a body of militia, including storage for arms and equipment, drill-rooms, etc. **3** A factory for making firearms. *Brit. sp.* **ar′mour·y.** [< ARMOR]

arm·pit (ärm′pit′) *n.* The cavity under the arm at the shoulder; axilla.

arms (ärmz) *n. pl.* **1** Weapons collectively. **2** Warfare. **3** The official insignia or device of a state, person, or family. **4** Heraldic symbols. —**under arms** Ready for war. —**up in arms** Aroused and ready to fight. [< L *arma* weapons]

ar·my (är′mē) *n. pl.* **ar·mies** **1** A large organized body of men armed for military service on land. **2** The whole of the military land forces of a country. [< L *armata* < *armare* to arm]

ar·ni·ca (är′ni·kə) *n.* **1** Any of a genus of plants bearing heads of yellow-rayed composite flowers. **2** A tincture prepared from this plant, once used for sprains and bruises. [< NL]

a·ro·ma (ə·rō′mə) *n.* **1** Fragrance, as from plants; agreeable odor. **2** Characteristic quality or style. [< Gk. *arōma* spice]

ar·o·mat·ic (ar′ə·mat′ik) *adj.* Having an aroma; fragrant; spicy. Also **ar′o·mat′i·cal.** —*n.* Any vegetable or drug of agreeable odor. —**ar′o·mat′i·cal·ly** *adv.*

a·ro·ma·tize (ə·rō′mə·tīz) *v.t.* **·tized, ·tiz·ing** To make fragrant or aromatic.

a·rose (ə·rōz′) p.t. of ARISE.

a·round (ə·round′) *adv.* **1** On all sides; in every direction. **2** In a circle or a circular manner or course. **3** In or to the opposite way, belief, attitude, etc. **4** From place to place; here and there. **5** From beginning to end: the year *around.* **6** For every person, part, etc.: enough to go *around.* **7** *Informal* To a usual or desired condition. **8** *Informal* Nearby; in the vicinity: Wait *around* until I call. **9** In or to a particular place: Come *around* to see us again. —**have been around** *Informal* To be experienced in the ways of the world. —*prep.* **1** About the circumference or outer part of; encircling. **2** On all or many sides of. **3** So as to encircle or envelop. **4** In or to various parts of. **5** On the other side of: *around* the corner. **6** About the center or axis of: to rotate *around* a shaft. **7** Close to: We leave *around* midnight. [< A-¹ on + ROUND]

a·rouse (ə·rouz′) *v.* **a·roused, a·rousing** *v.t.* **1** To stir from or as if from sleep. **2** To excite, as to a state of high emotion. —*v.i.* **3** To become aroused from or as if from sleep. [< ROUSE, on analogy with *arise*] —**a·rous′al, a·rous′er** *n.* —**Syn. 1, 3** wake, waken, awake, awaken. **2** incite, provoke, stimulate, stir up.

ar·peg·gi·o (är·pej′ē·ō, -pej′ō) *n. pl.* **·gi·os** *Music* **1** The sounding or playing of the notes of a chord in rapid succession instead of simultaneously. **2** A chord so played. [< Ital. *arpeggiare* play on a harp]

Arpeggio

ar·que·bus (är′kwə·bəs) *n.* HARQUEBUS.

arr. arranged; arrangement(s); arrival; arrive.

ar·rack (ar′ək) *n.* A strong Oriental liquor distilled from rice, molasses, etc. [< Ar. *'araq* sweat, juice]

ar·raign (ə·rān′) *v.t.* **1** To call into court to answer to an indictment. **2** To call upon for an answer; accuse. [< LL *arrationare* call to account] —**ar·raign′ment** *n.*

ar·range (ə·rānj′) *v.* **ar·ranged, ar·rang·ing** *v.t.* **1** To put in definite or proper order. **2** To adjust, as a conflict or dispute; settle. **3** To make plans or prepare for. **4** To change or adapt, as a musical composition, for performers other than those originally intended. —*v.i.* **5** To come to an agreement or understanding: often with *with.* **6** To see about the details; make plans. [< OF *a-* to + *rangier* put in order]

ar·range·ment (ə·rānj′mənt) *n.* **1** An arranging or a being arranged. **2** That which is arranged. **3** *Usu. pl.* A preparation or plan. **4** The style or manner in which something is arranged. **5** Settlement, as of a dispute. **6** *Music* **a** The adaptation of a composition to performers or instruments other than those originally intended. **b** The composition so adapted.

ar·rant (ar'ənt) *adj.* Notoriously bad; unmitigated. [Var. of ERRANT] —**ar'rant·ly** *adv.*

ar·ras (ar'əs) *n.* **1** A tapestry. [*Arras,* France]

ar·ray (ə·rā') *n.* **1** Regular or proper order, esp. of troops. **2** A military force. **3** Clothing; fine dress. **4** An impressive gathering or arrangement, as of people or things. —*v.t.* **1** To draw up in order of battle, as troops. **2** To adorn; dress, as for display. [<OF <*a-* to + *rei* order]

ar·ray·al (ə·rā'əl) *n.* **1** The act or process of arraying. **2** Anything arrayed; an array.

ar·rear·age (ə·rir'ij) *n.* **1** The state of being in arrears. **2** The amount in arrears.

ar·rears (ə·rirz') *n. pl.* Debts, obligations, etc., not met on time. —**in arrears** (or **arrear**) Behind in meeting payment, fulfilling an obligation, etc. [<L *ad-* to + *retro* backward]

ar·rest (ə·rest') *v.t.* **1** To stop suddenly; check, as the course, movement, or development of. **2** To take into custody by legal authority. **3** To attract and fix, as the attention; engage. —*n.* **1** An arresting or being arrested. **2** A device for arresting motion, as in a machine. [<L *ad-* to + *restare* stop, remain] —**ar·rest'er, ar·res'tor** *n.*

ar·rest·ing (ə·res'ting) *adj.* Notable; compelling attention. —**ar·rest'ing·ly** *adv.*

ar·rhyth·mi·a (ə·rith'mē·ə) *n.* Variation from the normal heartbeat. —**ar·rhyth'mic** *adj.*

ar·ri·val (ə·rī'vəl) *n.* **1** The act of arriving. **2** One who or that which arrives or has arrived.

ar·rive (ə·rīv') *v.i.* **ar·rived, ar·riv·ing 1** To reach or come to a destination or place. **2** To come at length, by any stage or process; often with *at:* to *arrive* at an idea. **3** To attain worldly success or fame. [<LL *arripare* come to shore <L *ad-* to + *ripa* shore]

ar·ri·viste (a·rē·vēst', *Fr.* á-) One newly arrived at social position, wealth, etc., disparaged as an upstart. [F]

ar·ro·gance (ar'ə·gəns) *n.* The quality or state of being arrogant. Also **ar'ro·gan·cy.**

ar·ro·gant (ar'ə·gənt) *adj.* Full of or characterized by excessive pride or self-esteem; overbearing; haughty. [<L *arrogare.* See ARROGATE.] —**ar'ro·gant·ly** *adv.*

ar·ro·gate (ar'ə·gāt) *v.t.* **·gat·ed, ·gat·ing 1** To claim, demand, or take presumptuously; assume; usurp. **2** To attribute or ascribe without reason. [<L *arrogare* claim for oneself] —**ar'ro·ga'tion** *n.*

ar·row (ar'ō) *n.* **1** A straight, slender shaft, usu. feathered at one end and with a pointed head at the other, to be shot from a bow. **2** Anything resembling an arrow in shape, speed, etc. **3** A sign or figure in the shape of an arrow, used to indicate directions. [<OE *earh, arwe*] —**ar'row·y** *adj.*

ar·row·head (ar'ō·hed') *n.* **1** The sharp-pointed head of an arrow. **2** Something resembling an arrowhead. **3** Any of various water plants with arrow-shaped leaves.

ar·row·root (ar'ō·ro͞ot', -ro͝ot') *n.* **1** A starch obtained from the roots of a tropical American plant. **2** The plant.

ar·roy·o (ə·roi'ō) *n. pl.* **·os** (-ōz) *sw U.S.* **1** A brook. **2** A dry gully. [Sp.]

ar·se·nal (är'sə·nəl) *n.* **1** A place for making or storing arms and munitions. **2** Any supply or stock. [<Ar. *dār aṣ-ṣinā'ah* workshop]

ar·se·nic (är'sə·nik) *n.* **1** An element (symbol As) chemically similar to phosphorus, used chiefly to make insecticides. **2** The highly poisonous, white, crystalline trioxide of arsenic. —**ar·sen·ic** (är·sen'ik) *adj.* Of or containing arsenic: also **ar·sen'i·cal.** [<L *arsenicum*]

ar·son (är'sən) *n.* The crime of deliberately setting fire to another's building, property, etc., or to one's own, esp. for a criminal or fraudulent purpose. [<L *arsus,* pp. of *ardere* burn] —**ar'son·ist** *n.*

art[1] (ärt) *n.* **1** The ability of man to arrange or adapt natural things or conditions to his own uses. **2** The creation of works that are, in form, content, and execution, esthetically pleasing and meaningful, as in music, painting, sculpture, literature, architecture, dance, etc. **3** The principles and techniques governing the creation of such works. **4** The works so created, esp. paintings, drawings, and sculpture. **5** Skilled workmanship; craft. **6** Any specific skill, craft, trade, or profession: the *art* of cooking; a teacher's *art.* **7** *Printing* Any illustrative or decorative material that accompanies the text. **8** *Usu. pl.* The liberal arts. **9** Craft; cunning. **10** *Usu. pl.* A trick, stratagem, or wile. —*adj.* Of or for artists or their works. [<L *ars* skill]

art[2] (ärt) Archaic or poetic second person singular present tense of BE: used with *thou.* [<OE *eart*]

-art *suffix* Var. of -ARD.

Ar·te·mis (är'tə·mis) *Gk. Myth.* The goddess of the chase and of the moon; twin sister of Apollo.

ar·te·ri·al (är·tir'ē·əl) *adj.* **1** Of, like, or carried in the arteries. **2** Pertaining to the bright red blood which has been aerated in the lungs. **3** Constituting a main channel or route: an *arterial* highway.

ar·te·ri·o·scle·ro·sis (är·tir'ē·ō·sklə·rō'sis) *n.* Thickening and loss of elasticity of the walls of an artery, as in old age. —**ar·te'ri·o·scle·rot'ic** (-rot'ik) *adj.*

ar·ter·y (är'tər·ē) *n. pl.* **·ter·ies 1** Any of the numerous muscular vessels and their branches that convey blood from the heart to every part of the body. • See HEART. **2** Any main channel or route. [<L *arteria* artery, windpipe]

ar·te·sian well (är·tē'zhən) A well bored down to a water-bearing stratum in which the water pressure is great enough to force a flow of water to the surface. [<F *artésien,* from *Artois,* town in France]

art·ful (ärt'fəl) *adj.* **1** Crafty; cunning. **2** Artificial; imitative. **3** Skillful; ingenious. —**art'ful·ly** *adv.* —**art'ful·ness** *n.*

ar·thri·tis (är·thrī'tis) *n.* Inflammation of a joint or joints. [<Gk. *arthron* joint + -ITIS] —**ar·thrit·ic** (är·thrit'ik) *adj.*

ar·thro·pod (är'thrə·pod) *n.* Any of a large group of invertebrate animals characterized by jointed legs and segmented body parts, as insects, spiders, crabs, etc. [<Gk. <*arthron* joint + *podos* foot] —**ar·throp·o·dous** (är·throp'ə·dəs), **ar·throp'o·dal** *adj.*

ar·thro·scope (är'thrə·skōp) *n.* A small endoscope for the examination and repair of a shoulder or knee joint. [<ARTHRO- + SCOPE]

Ar·thur (är'thər) A legendary British king of the sixth century A.D., hero of the Round Table. —**Ar·thu·ri·an** (är·tho͝or'ē·ən) *adj.*

ar·ti·choke (är'tə·chōk) *n.* **1** A thistlelike garden plant. **2** Its succulent flower head, used as a vegetable. **3** The Jerusalem artichoke. [<Ar. *al-kharshūf*]

Artichoke *def. 2*

ar·ti·cle (är'ti·kəl) *n.* **1** A particular object or thing. **2** A member of a class of things. **3** A composition written for or appearing in a newspaper, magazine, etc. **4** A distinct proposition, statement, or stipulation in a series of such, as in a constitution, treaty, etc. **5** A complete item of religious belief; a point of doctrine. **6** *Gram.* One of the three words *a, an* (**indefinite articles**) or *the* (**definite article**), used as modifiers. —*v.* **·cled, ·cling** *v.t.* **1** To bind to service by a written contract. **2** To specify. **3** To accuse by formal articles. —*v.i.* **4** To make accusations: with *against.* [<L *articulus,* dim. of *artus* a joint]

ar·tic·u·lar (är·tik'yə·lər) *adj.* Pertaining to a joint or the joints.

ar·tic·u·late (är·tik'yə·lit) *adj.* **1** Jointed; segmented: also **ar·tic'u·lat'ed** (-lā'tid). **2** Able to speak. **3** Able to speak clearly, easily, and effectively. **4** Divided into syllables or words so as to be intelligible. **5** Clear and logically coherent. —*v.* (är·tik'yə·lāt) **·lat·ed, ·lat·ing** *v.t.* **1** To utter distinctly; enunciate. **2** To express clearly in words. **3** *Phonet.* To produce, as a speech sound, by the movement of the organs of speech. **4** To unite by joints. —*v.i.* **5** To speak distinctly. **6** *Phonet.* To produce a speech sound. **7** *Anat.* To form a joint: used with *with.* [<L *articulare* divide into joints, utter distinctly] —**ar·tic'u·late·ly** *adv.* —**ar·tic'u·late·ness, ar·tic'u·lat·or** *n.* —**ar·tic'u·la'tive** *adj.*

ar·tic·u·la·tion (är·tik'yə·lā'shən) *n.* **1** A jointing or being jointed together; also the manner or method of this. **2** A joint between two bones. **3** The utterance of articulate sounds; enunciation. **4** A speech sound, esp. a consonant. **5** *Bot.* A joint between two separable parts; a node.

ar·ti·fact (är′tə·fakt) *n.* Anything made by human work or art. Also **ar′te·fact.** [<L *ars* art, skill + *factus,* p.p. of *facere* make]

ar·ti·fice (är′tə·fis) *n.* 1 Subtle or deceptive craft; trickery. 2 Skill; ingenuity. 3 An ingenious expedient; stratagem. [<L *artificium* handicraft, skill]

ar·tif·i·cer (är·tif′ə·sər) *n.* 1 A skilled craftsman. 2 An inventor or designer of things.

ar·ti·fi·cial (är′tə·fish′əl) *adj.* 1 Produced by human art rather than by nature. 2 Made in imitation of or as a substitute for something natural. 3 Not genuine or natural; affected. [See ARTIFICE.] **—ar′ti·fi′ci·al′i·ty, ar′ti·fi′cial·ness** *n.* **—ar′ti·fi′cial·ly** *adv.*

artificial insemination Impregnation of the female with semen from the male without direct sexual contact.

ar·til·ler·y (är·til′ə·rē) *n.* 1 Guns of larger caliber than machine guns. 2 Military units armed with such guns. 3 Branches of the U.S. Army composed of such units. 4 *Informal* Any small firearm. 5 The science of gunnery. [<OF *artiller* fortify] **—ar·til′ler·y·man** *n.* (*pl.* **·men**).

ar·ti·san (är′tə·zən) *n.* A trained or skilled workman. [<L *ars* art]

art·ist (är′tist) *n.* 1 One who is skilled in or who makes a profession of any of the fine arts or the performing arts. 2 One who does anything with artistry. [<L *ars* art]

ar·tiste (är·tēst′) *n.* A professional entertainer: usu. a humorous usage. [<F]

ar·tis·tic (är·tis·tik) *adj.* 1 Of or pertaining to art or artists. 2 Esthetically pleasing; tastefully executed. 3 Fond of or sensitive to art. **—ar·tis·ti·cal·ly** *adv.*

art·ist·ry (är′tis·trē) *n.* Artistic ability, quality, or workmanship. **—Syn.** talent, skill, invention, genius.

art·less (ärt′lis) *adj.* 1 Without guile or deceit; innocent. 2 Natural; simple. 3 Without art or skill; clumsy. 4 Without taste; ignorant. **—art′less·ly** *adv.* **—art′less·ness** *n.*

Art Nou·veau (ärt nōō·vō′, *Fr.* ar nōō·vō′) A style of art and design of the late 19th and early 20th centuries characterized by curved and twisting shapes often representing natural objects. [F, lit., new art]

art·y (är′tē) *adj.* **art·i·er, art·i·est** Affectedly or ostentatiously artistic. **—art′i·ness** *n.*

ar·um (âr′əm) *n.* Any of various plants having small flowers on a thick spike surrounded by a spathe, as the jack-in-the-pulpit. [<Gk. *aron*]

-ary *suffix of adjectives and nouns* 1 Connected with or pertaining to what is expressed in the root word: *elementary.* 2 A person engaged in: *apothecary.* 3 A thing connected with or a place dedicated to: *dictionary.* [<L *-arius, -arium*]

Ar·y·an (âr′ē·ən, ar′-, är′yən) *n.* 1 A member or descendant of a prehistoric people who spoke Indo-European. 2 In Nazi ideology, a Caucasian gentile, esp. one of Nordic stock. *—adj.* Of or pertaining to Aryans. [<Skt. *ārya* noble]

as (az, *unstressed* əz) *adv.* 1 To the same extent or degree; equally: Do I look *as* pretty? 2 For instance; thus: to release, *as* prisoners, from confinement. *—conj.* 1 To the same amount or degree that: He became gentler *as* he grew older. 2 In the way that: Do *as* I tell you. 3 At the same time that; while: They sang *as* we left. 4 Because: *As* the weather was bad, the game was postponed. 5 However; though: Bad *as* it was, it might have been worse. 6 That the result is: The play is so bad *as* not to merit discussion. 7 *Informal* That: I don't know *as* I told you. *—prep.* 1 In the role, capacity, or sense of: I'll act *as* referee. 2 In the manner of; like: to dress *as* a witch. *— pron.* 1 That: used after *such* and *same:* the same pen *as* you have. 2 A fact that: She is a genius, *as* everyone knows. **—as . . . as** A correlative construction that indicates identity or equality of two things: *as* much *as, as* good *as.* **—as for** Concerning; in the case of. **—as if** (or **as though**) 1 As it would if. 2 That: It seems *as if* he'll never win. **—as is** *Informal* Just as it is: said of an article somewhat damaged. **—as it were** So to speak. **—as to** Concerning. **—As yet** Up to the present time. [<OE *ealswa* entirely so, also] • See LIKE.

AS, A.S., AS. Anglo-Saxon.

As arsenic.

as·a·fet·i·da (as′ə·fet′ə·də) *n.* A fetid gum resin obtained from certain plants related to parsley, formerly used in medicine. [<Med.L *asa* mastic + L *foetida* ill-smelling]

as·bes·tos (as·bes′təs, az-) *n.* A white or gray mineral silicate of calcium and magnesium which may be woven or shaped into acid-resisting, nonconducting, and fireproof articles. *—adj.* Of asbestos. [<Gk., unquenchable]

ASCAP, A.S.C.A.P. American Society of Composers, Authors, and Publishers.

as·cend (ə·send′) *v.i.* 1 To go or move upward; rise. 2 To go from a lower to a higher degree, pitch, etc. 3 To slope upward. *—v.t.* 4 To move or climb upward on. 5 To succeed to (a throne). [<L *ad-* to + *scandere* climb] **—as·cend′a·ble** or **·i·ble** *adj.* **—as·cen′der** *n.*

as·cen·den·cy (ə·sen′dən·sē) *n.* The state of being in the ascendent; domination; supremacy. Also **as·cen′dan·cy.**

as·cen·dent (ə·sen′dənt) *adj.* 1 Ascending; rising. 2 Superior; dominant. *—n.* 1 A position of supreme power; preeminence. 2 In astrology, the sign of the zodiac that is rising above the eastern horizon at any given instant. Also **as·cen′dant. —in the ascendent** Approaching or having controlling power, fame, influence, etc.

as·cen·sion (ə·sen′shən) *n.* The act of ascending **—the Ascension** *Theol.* The bodily ascent of Christ into heaven after the Resurrection, commemorated on **Ascension Day,** the fortieth day after Easter. **—as·cen′sion·al** *adj.*

as·cent (ə·sent′) *n.* 1 The act of ascending, rising, or climbing. 2 The method or way of ascending. 3 The measure or degree of upward slope: an *ascent* of 30°. 4 A rise in rank or station; advancement [<ASCEND]

as·cer·tain (as′ər·tān′) *v.t.* To learn with certainty about; find out. [<OF *a-* to + *certain* certain] **— as′cer·tain′a·ble** *adj.* **—as′cer·tain′a·bly** *adv.* **—as′cer·tain′ment** *n.*

as·cet·ic (ə·set′ik) *n.* 1 A religious hermit or recluse. 2 One who leads a very austere and self-denying life. *—adj.* Given to or involving severe self-denial and austerity: also **as·cet′i·cal.** [<Gk. *askētēs* one who exercises (self-denial), a monk] **—as·cet′i·cal·ly** *adv.*

as·cet·i·cism (ə·set′ə·siz′əm) *n.* Ascetic practices and conduct, esp. as a way to greater spirituality.

ASCII (as′kē) *n.* American Standard Code for Information Interchange, a coding scheme for representing information digitally so that different kinds of computers can communicate with each other.

a·scor·bic acid (ə·skôr′bik) A white, odorless, crystalline compound, present in citrus fruits and other foods, and also made synthetically; vitamin C. [<Gk. *a-* not + SCORB(UT)IC]

as·cot (as′kət, -kot) *n.* A kind of scarf or necktie, knotted so that the broad ends are laid one across the other. [<*Ascot,* England]

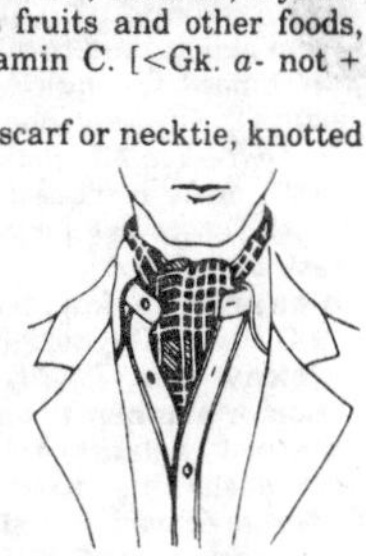

Ascot

as·cribe (ə·scrīb′) *v.t.* **as·cribed, as·crib·ing** 1 To attribute, as to a cause, source, author, etc. 2 To assign as a quality or attribute. [<L *ad-* to + *scribere* write] **— as·crib·a·ble** (ə·skrī′bə·bəl) *adj.*

as·crip·tion (ə·skrip′shən) *n.* An ascribing or being ascribed.

-ase *suffix Chem.* Used in naming enzymes; sometimes added to the name of the compound which the enzyme decomposes: *amylase, casease,* etc. [<(DIAST)ASE]

a·sep·sis (ə·sep′sis, ā-) *n.* 1 An aseptic condition. 2 The prevention of infection by maintaining sterile conditions. [A- (not) + SEPSIS]

a·sep·tic (ə·sep′tik, ā-) *adj.* Free from or doing away with microorganisms that produce disease or putrefaction. **— a·sep′ti·cal·ly** *adv.*

a·sex·u·al (ā·sek′shōō·əl) *adj.* 1 Having no distinct sexual organs; without sex. 2 Occurring or performed without union of the sexes. **—a·sex·u·al·i·ty** (ā·sek′shōō·al′ə·tē) *n.* **— a·sex′u·al·ly** *adv.*

ash[1] (ash) *n.* The powdery, whitish gray residue of a substance that has been burnt. [< OE *asce*]

ash[2] (ash) *n.* 1 Any of a genus of hardy deciduous trees related to the olive and valued as a shade and timber tree. 2 Its light, tough, elastic wood. —*adj.* Made of ash wood. [< OE *æsc*]

a·shamed (ə·shāmd′) *adj.* 1 Feeling shame. 2 Deterred by the anticipation of shame. [< obs. *ashame* to shame or feel shame] —**a·sham·ed·ly** (ə·shā′mid·lē) *adv.* —**Syn.** 1 embarrassed, mortified, abashed, humiliated.

ash·en[1] (ash′ən) *adj.* 1 Of, pertaining to, or like ashes. 2 Pale and grayish in color.

ash·en[2] (ash′ən) *adj.* Pertaining to or made of the wood of the ash tree.

ash·es (ash′iz) *n. pl.* 1 The grayish white, powdery particles remaining after something has been burned. 2 The remains of the human body after cremation. 3 Any dead body; corpse. 4 Remains or ruins, as after destruction.

ash·lar (ash′lər) *n.* 1 A rough-hewn block of stone. 2 A thin, dressed, squared stone, used for facing a wall. 3 Masonwork made of ashlar. Also **ash′ler.** [< L *axilla*, dim. of *axis* board, plank]

a·shore (ə·shôr′, ə·shōr′) *adv.* 1 To or on the shore. 2 On land; aground.

Ash Wednesday The first day of Lent.

ash·y (ash′ē) *adj.* **ash·i·er, ash·i·est** 1 Of, pertaining to, or like ashes. 2 Very pale.

A·sia (ā′zhə, ā′shə) *n.* The world's largest continent, bounded by Europe and the Pacific, Arctic, and Indian Oceans; 16,900,000 square miles. —**A′sian, A·si·at·ic** (ā′zhē·at′ik, ā′shē-) *adj., n.* • In most cases, esp. in the ethnic sense, *Asian* is now preferred to *Asiatic.*

Asia Minor The peninsula of extreme western Asia between the Black and the Mediterranean seas, comprising most of Turkey in Asia.

Asiatic cholera An acute, infectious, often epidemic disease marked by severe diarrhea and high mortality.

a·side (ə·sīd′) *adv.* 1 On or to one side; apart. 2 Out of thought or use. 3 Notwithstanding; apart: all kidding *aside.* 4 In reserve. —**aside from** 1 Excepting. 2 Apart from. —*n.* 1 The words spoken by an actor and supposed to be heard by the audience but not by the other actors. 2 A digression. [< A- on + SIDE]

as·i·nine (as′ə·nīn) *adj.* 1 Of or like an ass. 2 Silly, thoughtless, stupid, etc. [< L *asinus* ass] —**as′i·nine′ly** *adv.* —**as·i·nin·i·ty** (as′ə·nin′ə·tē) *n.*

ask (ask, äsk) *v.t.* 1 To put a question to. 2 To put a question about; inquire after. 3 To make a request for; solicit. 4 To need or require: This job *asks* too much of me. 5 To state the price of; demand. 6 To invite: Were many guests *asked?* —*v.i.* 7 To make inquiries: with *for, after,* or *about.* 8 To make a request. 9 To act as if inviting something: with *for:* to *ask* for trouble. [< OE *āscian*] —**ask′er** *n.* —**ask′ing** *n.*

a·skance (ə·skans′) *adv.* 1 With a side glance; sidewise. 2 Disdainfully; distrustfully. Also **a·skant′.** [?]

a·skew (ə·skyōō) *adj.* Oblique. —*adv.* In an oblique position or manner; to one side. [< A- on + SKEW]

a·slant (ə·slant′, ə·slänt′) *adj.* Slanting; oblique. —*adv.* In a slanting direction or position; obliquely. —*prep.* Across or over in a slanting direction or position.

a·sleep (ə·slēp′) *adj.* 1 Sleeping. 2 Dormant; inactive. 3 Numb or prickly. 4 Dead. —*adv.* Into a sleeping condition.

a·slope (ə·slōp) *adj.* Sloping. —*adv.* In a sloping position.

a·so·cial (ā·sō′shəl) *adj.* Avoiding society; not gregarious.

asp[1] (asp) *n.* Any of several small poisonous snakes of Africa and Europe, as the horned viper. [< Gk. *aspis*]

asp[2] (asp) *n.* ASPEN.

as·par·a·gus (ə·spar′ə·gəs) *n.* 1 The edible shoots of a cultivated plant of the lily family. 2 Any plant of this genus. [< Gk. *asparagos, aspharogos*]

as·pect (as′pekt) *n.* 1 The look a person has; expression of countenance. 2 Appearance presented to the eye by something; look. 3 Appearance presented to the mind by circumstances, etc.; interpretation. 4 A facing in a given direction. 5 The side or surface facing in a certain direction. 6 In astrology, the configuration of the planets in relation to each other or to the observer, as a supposed influence on human affairs. [< L *aspicere* to look at]

asp·en (as′pən) *n.* Any of several kinds of poplar with leaves that flutter in the slightest breeze. —*adj.* 1 Of the aspen. 2 Quivering; shaking. [< OE *aspe*]

as·per·i·ty (as·per′ə·tē) *n. pl.* **·ties** 1 Roughness or harshness, as of surface, sound, weather, etc. 2 Bitterness or sharpness of temper [< L *asper* rough]

as·perse (ə·spûrs′) *v.t.* **as·persed** (ə·spûrst′), **as·pers·ing** To spread false charges against; slander. [< L *aspergere* sprinkle on] —**as·pers′er, as·per′sor** *n.*

as·per·sion (ə·spûr′zhən, -shən) *n.* 1 A slandering. 2 Slander; a slanderous report or charge.

as·phalt (as′fôlt) *n.* 1 A dark brown, semisolid, bituminous substance obtained from natural deposits or as a residue in refining petroleum; mineral pitch. 2 A mixture of this with sand or gravel, used for paving, etc. Also **as·phal·tum** (as·fôl′təm). —*v.t.* To pave or cover with asphalt. [< Gk. *asphaltos*] —**as·phal·tic** (as·fôl′tik) *adj.*

as·pho·del (as′fə·del) *n.* A plant of the lily family, bearing white or yellow flowers. [< Gk. *asphodelos*]

as·phyx·i·a (as·fik′sē·ə) *n.* Loss of consciousness, usu. resulting from suffocation caused by too little oxygen and too much carbon dioxide in the blood. [< Gk. *asphyxia* stopping of the pulse] —**as·phyx′i·ant** *adj., n.*

as·phyx·i·ate (as·fik′sē·āt) *v.* **·at·ed, ·at·ing** *v.t.* 1 To cause asphyxia in. 2 To suffocate, as by drowning or breathing noxious gases. —*v.i.* 3 To undergo asphyxia. —**as·phyx′i·a′tion, as·phyx′i·a′tor** *n.*

as·pic (as′pik) *n.* A savory jelly of meat or vegetable juices, served as a relish or mold for meat, vegetables, etc. [< F]

as·pi·dis·tra (as′pə·dis′trə) *n.* Any of a small genus of stemless Asian plants of the lily family, with large, glossy, evergreen leaves. [< Gk. *apis* shield + *astron* star]

as·pir·ant (as′pər·ənt, ə·spīr′ənt) *n.* One who aspires after something. —*adj.* Aspiring.

as·pi·rate (as′pə·rāt) *v.t.* **·rat·ed, ·rat·ing** 1 To utter with a breathing or as if preceded by the letter *h.* 2 To follow (a consonant, esp. (p), (t), and (k)) with an explosive release of breath. 3 To draw off by suction. —*n.* An aspirated sound. —*adj.* (as′pər·it) Uttered with an aspirate: also **as′pi·rat′ed.** [< L *aspirare* to breathe on]

as·pi·ra·tion (as′pə·rā′shən) *n.* 1 Exalted desire; high ambition. 2 The act of breathing. 3 The use of an aspirator. 4 *Phonet.* **a** The pronunciation of a consonant with an aspirate. **b** An aspirate.

as·pi·ra·tor (as′pə·rā′tər) *n.* An appliance producing suction, as for drawing off fluid matter or gases from the body.

as·pir·a·to·ry (ə·spīr′ə·tôr′ē, -tō′rē) *adj.* Of, pertaining to, or adapted for breathing or suction.

as·pire (ə·spīr′) *v.i.* **as·pired, as·pir·ing** 1 To have an earnest desire or ambition: with *to.* 2 To long for: with *after.* [< L *aspirare* breathe on, attempt to reach] —**as·pir′er** *n.*

as·pi·rin (as′pər·in) *n.* A white crystalline synthetic compound, used to allay pain and fever and to treat rheumatism. [< A(CETYL) + *spir(aeic acid)* former name of salicylic acid + -IN]

a·squint (ə·skwint′) *adj. & adv.* With sidelong glance.

ass[1] (as) *n. pl.* **ass·es** 1 Any of a genus of animals, including the donkey, resembling but smaller than the horse, and with longer ears. 2 A stubborn or stupid person. [< L *asinus*]

ass[2] (as) *n.* The buttocks: *usu. considered vulgar.* [ME < OE *assa*]

ass. assistant; association.

as·sail (ə·sāl′) *v.t.* To attack violently, as by force, argument, or censure; assault. [< LL *assalire* leap upon] —**as·sail′a·ble** *adj.* —**as·sail′a·ble·ness, as·sail′er** *n.*

as·sail·ant (ə·sā′lənt) *n.* One who assails or attacks.

as·sas·sin (ə·sas′in) *n.* A murderer, esp. one who murders a politically prominent person. [< Ar. *hashshāshīn* hashish-eaters, from hashish-eating Muslims who murdered Christians during the Crusades]

as·sas·si·nate (ə·sas′ə·nāt) *v.t.* **·nat·ed, ·nat·ing** 1 To kill by secret assault. 2 To destroy or harm by treachery, as a reputation. —**as·sas′si·na′tion, as·sas′si·na′tor** *n.*

as·sault (ə·sôlt′) *n.* 1 Any violent physical or verbal attack. 2 *Law* An unlawful attempt or offer to do bodily injury to another. 3 A rape. 4 *Mil.* A violent attack by troops, as upon a fortified place. —*v.t. & v.i.* To make an assault (upon). [< L *ad-* to + *salire* leap] —**as·sault'er** *n.*

assault and battery *Law* The carrying out of an assault with force and violence; a beating.

as·say (ə·sā', as'ā) *n.* **1** The analysis of an alloy, etc., to ascertain the ingredients and their proportions. **2** The substance to be so examined. **3** The result of such a test. **4** Any examination or testing. —*v.t.* (ə·sā') **1** To make an assay of. **2** To test. —*v.i.* **3** To show by analysis a certain value or proportion, as of a precious metal. [< L *exagium* a weighing < *exigere* prove] —**as·say'er** *n.*

as·sem·blage (ə·sem'blij) *n.* **1** An assembling or being assembled. **2** Any gathering of persons or things; assembly. **3** A fitting together, as parts of a machine. **4** A work of art created by assembling materials and objects; also, the technique of making such works.

as·sem·ble (ə·sem'bəl) *v.t. & v.i.* **·bled, ·bling 1** To collect or convene; congregate. **2** To fit together, as the parts of a mechanism. [< L *assimulare* < *ad-* to + *simul* together] —**as·sem'bler** *n.*

as·sem·bly (ə·sem'blē) *n. pl.* **·blies 1** An assembling or being assembled. **2** A number of persons met together for a common purpose. **3** The act or process of fitting together the parts of a machine, etc.; also, the parts themselves. **4** *Mil.* The signal calling troops to form ranks.

As·sem·bly (ə·sem'blē) *n.* In some states of the U.S., the lower house of the legislature.

assembly line In some factories, an arrangement in which workers perform specialized operations on a unit of work as it passes before them.

as·sem·bly·man (ə·sem'blē·mən) *n. pl.* **·men** (-men', -mən) *U.S.* A member of a legislative assembly.

as·sent (ə·sent') *v.i.* To express agreement; concur: usu. with *to.* —*n.* Concurrence or agreement. [< L *assentire* < *ad-* to + *sentire* feel] —**as'sen·ta'tion, as·sent'er** *n.*

as·sert (ə·sûrt') *v.t.* **1** To state positively; affirm. **2** To maintain as a right or claim. —**assert oneself** To state and defend firmly one's rights, opinions, etc. [< L *asserere* bind to, claim] —**as·sert'er, as·ser'tor** *n.*

as·ser·tion (ə·sûr'shən) *n.* **1** The act of asserting. **2** A positive statement or declaration.

as·ser·tive (ə·sûr'tiv) *adj.* Characterized by confidence and positiveness, often excessively so. —**as·ser'tive·ly** *adv.* —**as·ser'tive·ness** *n.* —**Syn.** positive, decided, dogmatic, aggressive.

as·sess (ə·ses') *v.t.* **1** To charge with a tax, fine, etc., as a person or property. **2** To determine the amount of, as a tax or fine, on a person or property. **3** To put a value on, as property, for taxation. **4** To take stock of; evaluate. [< LL *assessare* fix a tax] —**as·sess'a·ble** *adj.*

as·sess·ment (ə·ses'mənt) *n.* **1** An assessing. **2** The amount assessed.

as·ses·sor (ə·ses'ər) *n.* One who makes assessments, as for taxation. [< L, lit., one who sits beside as assistant judge] —**as·ses·so·ri·al** (as'ə·sôr'·ē·əl, -sō'rē-) *adj.*

as·set (as'et) *n.* **1** An item of property. **2** A person, thing, or quality regarded as useful or valuable to have. **3** *pl.* In accounting, the entries in a balance sheet showing all the property or resources of a person or business, as cash, accounts receivable, equipment, etc. **4** *pl. Law* **a** The property of a deceased person which can be used to pay debts or legacies. **b** All the property, real or personal, of a person or corporation. [< L *ad-* to + *satis* enough]

as·sev·er·ate (ə·sev'ə·rāt) *v.t.* **·at·ed, ·at·ing** To affirm or aver emphatically or solemnly. [< L < *ad-* to + *severus* serious] —**as·sev'er·a'tion** *n.*

as·si·du·i·ty (as'ə·dyōō'ə·tē) *n.* The quality or state of being assiduous; diligence.

as·sid·u·ous (ə·sij'ōō·əs) *adj.* Carefully attentive and diligent. [< L *assidere* sit by] —**as·sid'u·ous·ly** *adv.* —**as·sid'u·ous·ness** *n.*

as·sign (ə·sīn') *v.t.* **1** To set apart, as for a particular function; designate. **2** To appoint, as to a post. **3** To give out or allot, as a lesson. **4** To ascribe or attribute, as a motive. **5** *Law* To make over or transfer, as personal property, to another. —*n. Law Usu. pl.* Assignee. [< L *ad-* to + *signare* make a sign] —**as·sign'a·bil'i·ty, as·sign'er,** *Law* **as·sign'or** *n.* —**as·sign'a·ble** *adj.*

as·sig·na·tion (as'ig·nā'shən) *n.* **1** An appointment for meeting, esp. a secret or illicit one as made by lovers; a tryst. **2** An assignment.

as·sign·ee (ə·sī'nē', as'ə·nē') *n. Law* A person to whom property, rights, or powers are transferred by another.

as·sign·ment (ə·sīn'mənt) *n.* **1** An assigning or being assigned. **2** Anything assigned, as a lesson or task. **3** *Law* **a** The transfer of a claim, right, or property or the instrument or writing of transfer. **b** The claim, right, or property transferred.

as·sim·i·la·ble (ə·sim'ə·lə·bəl) *adj.* Capable of being assimilated. —**as·sim'i·la·bil'i·ty** *n.*

as·sim·i·late (ə·sim'ə·lāt) *v.* **·lat·ed, ·lat·ing** *v.t.* **1** To absorb and incorporate (food) into the body. **2** To make part of one's own thinking. **3** To absorb (a different culture, group, etc.) into the main social or cultural body. **4** To make alike; cause to resemble. —*v.i.* **5** To become alike or similar. **6** To become absorbed or assimilated. [< L *ad-* to + *similare* make like] —**as·sim'i·la'tion** *n.* —**as·sim'i·la'tive, as·sim·i·la·to·ry** (ə·sim'ə·lə·tôr'ē, -tō'rē) *adj.*

as·sist (ə·sist') *v.t.* **1** To give succor or support to; help; relieve. **2** To act as an assistant to. —*v.i.* **3** To give help or support. **4** In baseball, to aid a teammate or partner in a play. —**assist at** To be present at (a ceremony, etc.). —*n.* **1** An act of helping. **2** In baseball, a play that helps to put out a runner. [< L *ad-* to + *sistere* cause to stand] —**as·sist'er** *n.*

as·sis·tance (ə·sis'təns) *n.* Help; aid; support.

as·sis·tant (ə·sis'tənt) *n.* A subordinate or helper. —*adj.* **1** Holding a subordinate or auxiliary place, office, or rank. **2** Affording aid; assisting.

as·size (ə·sīz') *n.* In England, one of the regular sessions of a superior court. [< L *assidere* sit at, settle]

assn. association.

assoc. associate; association.

as·so·ci·ate (ə·sō'shē·it, -āt, -sē-) *n.* **1** A companion. **2** A co-worker; colleague. **3** Anything that accompanies or is associated with something else; a concomitant. **4** One admitted to partial membership in an association, society, etc. —*adj.* **1** Joined with another or others; united; allied. **2** Having subordinate or secondary status: an *associate* professor. —*v.* (ə·sō'shē·āt) **·at·ed, ·at·ing** *v.t.* **1** To bring into company or relation; combine together. **2** To unite (oneself) with another or others, as in friendship. **3** To connect mentally: to *associate* poetry with madness. —*v.i.* **4** To join or be in company or relation: with *with.* **5** To unite, as nations. [< L *associare* join to]

as·so·ci·a·tion (ə·sō'sē·ā'shən, -shē-) *n.* **1** The act of associating. **2** The state of being associated; fellowship; companionship. **3** A body of persons associated for some common purpose. **4** *Ecol.* A grouping of many plant species over a wide area, sharing a common habitat and similar geographic conditions. **5** A connection or relation in the mind of ideas, feelings, etc., with each other or with external objects or symbols. —**as·so'ci·a'·tion·al** *adj.*

association football SOCCER.

as·so·ci·a·tive (ə·sō'shē·ā'tiv, -shē·ə-, -sē-) *adj.* **1** Of, pertaining to, or characterized by association. **2** Causing association. —**as·so'ci·a'tive·ly** *adv.*

as·so·nance (as'ə·nəns) *n.* Resemblance in sound; specifically, in prosody, correspondence of the accented vowels, but not of the consonants, as in *main, came.* [< L *assonare* sound to, respond to] —**as'so·nant** *adj., n.*

as·sort (ə·sôrt') *v.t.* **1** To distribute into groups or classes according to kinds; classify. **2** To furnish, as a warehouse, with a variety of goods, etc. —*v.i.* **3** To fall into groups or classes of the same kind. **4** To associate; consort: with *with.* [< OF *a-* to + *sorte* sort, kind] —**as·sort·a·tive** (ə·sôr'·tə·tiv) *adj.*

as·sort·ed (ə·sôr'tid) *adj.* **1** Varied; miscellaneous. **2** Sorted out; classified. **3** Matched; suited.

as·sort·ment (ə·sôrt'mənt) *n.* **1** The act of assorting; classification. **2** A collection or group of various things; miscellany.

asst. assistant.
as·suage (ə·swāj′) *v.* **as·suaged, as·suag·ing** *v.t.* **1** To lessen or reduce the intensity of. **2** To reduce to a quiet or peaceful state. **3** To end by satisfying. [< L *ad-* to + *suavis* sweet] **—as·suage′ment** *n.* **—Syn. 1** ease, alloy, mitigate. **2** calm, pacify, mollify. **3** appease, slake, quench.
as·sume (ə·sōōm′) *v.t.* **as·sumed, as·sum·ing 1** To take up or adopt, as a style of dress, aspect, or character. **2** To undertake, as an office or duty. **3** To arrogate to oneself; usurp, as powers of state. **4** To take for granted; suppose to be true. **5** To affect; pretend to have. [< L *assumere* to take up, adopt] **—as·sum·a·ble** (ə·sōō′mə·bəl) *adj.*
as·sumed (ə·sōōmd′) *adj.* **1** Taken for granted. **2** Pretended; fictitious.
as·sum·ing (ə·sōō′ming) *adj.* Presumptuous; arrogant.
as·sump·tion (ə·sump′shən) *n.* **1** The act of assuming. **2** Something taken for granted; supposition. **3** Presumption; arrogance. **—the Assumption 1** The doctrine that the Virgin Mary was bodily taken up into heaven at her death. **2** A church feast, observed on August 15, commemorating this event. **—as·sump′tive** *adj.*
as·sur·ance (ə·shōōr′əns) *n.* **1** The act of assuring. **2** A positive or encouraging declaration. **3** Full confidence; certainty. **4** Self-confidence; firmness of mind. **5** Boldness; effrontery. **6** *Brit.* Insurance.
as·sure (ə·shōōr′) *v.t.* **as·sured, as·sur·ing 1** To make sure or secure; establish. **2** To give confidence to; convince. **3** To guarantee, as something risky. **4** To promise confidently. **5** *Brit.* To insure. [< L *ad-* to + *securus* safe] **—as·sur′a·ble** *adj.*
as·sured (ə·shōōrd′) *adj.* **1** Made certain and sure. **2** Self-possessed; confident. **3** Insured. **—***n.* An insured person or persons. **—as·sur·ed·ly** (ə·shōōr′id·lē) *adv.* **—as·sur′ed·ness** *n.*
As·syr·i·a (ə·sir′ē·ə) *n.* An ancient empire of western Asia, cap. Nineveh. **—As·syr′i·an** *adj., n.*
As·tar·te (as·tär′tē) In Phoenician mythology, the goddess of love and fertility.
as·ta·tine (as′tə·tēn, -tin) *n.* An artificially produced radioactive element (symbol At) chemically similar to iodine. [< Gk. *astatos* unstable + -INE]
as·ter (as′tər) *n.* Any of a large group of related plants having composite flowers with white, purple, or blue rays and yellow disk. [< Gk. *astēr* star]
-aster *suffix* A contemptuous diminutive: *poetaster, criticaster.* [< L]
as·ter·isk (as′tər·isk) *n.* A starlike figure (*) used to indicate omissions, footnotes, references, etc. **—***v.t.* To mark with an asterisk. [< Gk. *astēr* star]
a·stern (ə·stûrn′) *adv. Naut.* **1** In or at the stern. **2** In the rear; at any point behind a vessel. **3** To the rear; backward.
as·ter·oid (as′tə·roid) *n.* **1** Any of several hundred small, planetlike bodies with orbits mainly between Mars and Jupiter. **2** A starfish. **—***adj.* Resembling a star. [< Gk. *astēr* star + -OID] **—as′ter·oi′dal** *adj.*
asth·ma (az′mə, as′-) *n.* A chronic disorder characterized by recurrent breathing difficulty and bronchial spasms. [< Gk. *azein* breathe hard] **—asth·mat·ic** (az·mat′ik, as-) *adj., n.* **—asth·mat′i·cal** *adj.* **—asth·mat′i·cal·ly** *adv.*
a·stig·ma·tism (ə·stig′mə·tiz′əm) *n.* A defect of the eye or a lens such that the rays of light from an object do not converge to a perfect focus. [< A-[4] without + Gk. *stigma* mark] **—as·tig·mat·ic** (as′tig·mat′ik) *adj.*
a·stir (ə·stûr′) *adv. & adj.* Stirring; moving about.
a·ston·ish (ə·ston′ish) *v.t.* To affect with wonder and surprise; amaze; confound. [< L *ex-* out + *tonare* thunder] **—a·ston′ish·ing** *adj.* **—a·ston′ish·ing·ly** *adv.*
a·ston·ish·ment (ə·ston′ish·mənt) *n.* **1** The state of being astonished; surprise; amazement. **2** An object or cause of such emotion.
a·stound (ə·stound′) *v.t.* To overwhelm or shock with wonder or surprise; confound. [ME *astoned* stunned, pp. of *astonien* astonish] **—a·stound′ing** *adj.* **—a·stound′ing·ly** *adv.*
a·strad·dle (ə·strad′l) *adv. & adj.* Astride.
as·tra·khan (as′trə·kan, -kən) *n.* **1** The pelts of very young lambs, with tightly curled wool, from the region near Astrakhan. **2** A fabric imitating this.
as·tral (as′trəl) *adj.* **1** Of, coming from, or like the stars. **2** In theosophy, pertaining to or consisting of a supersensible substance supposed to pervade all space. [< Gk. *astron* star] **—as′tral·ly** *adv.*
a·stray (ə·strā′) *adv.* **1** Away from the right path. **2** Wandering in or into error or evil. [< L *extra-* beyond + *vagare* wander]
a·stride (ə·strīd′) *adv.* **1** With one leg on each side. **2** With the legs far apart. **—***prep.* With one leg on each side of.
as·trin·gent (ə·strin′jənt) *adj.* **1** Causing contraction of body tissue; styptic. **2** Harsh; stern; austere. **—***n.* A substance that arrests perspiring or bleeding. [< L *astringere* bind together] **—as·trin′gen·cy** *n.* **—as·trin′gent·ly** *adv.*
astro- *combining form* Star: *astrophysics.* [< Gk. *astron* star]
astrol. astrologer; astrological; astrology.
as·tro·labe (as′trə·lāb) *n.* An ancient instrument for determining altitudes of planets and stars. [< Gk. *astrolabon*, orig., star-taking]
as·trol·o·gy (ə·strol′ə·jē) *n.* **1** Originally, the practical application of astronomy to human uses. **2** The study professing to interpret the influence of the heavenly bodies upon the destinies and behavior of men. [< Gk. < ASTRO- + -LOGY] **—as·trol′o·ger** *n.* **—as·tro·log·ic** (as′trə·loj′ik), **as·tro·log·i·cal** *adj.* **—as′tro·log′i·cal·ly** *adv.*
astron. astronomer; astronomy.
as·tro·naut (as′trə·nôt) *n.* One who travels in space. [< ASTRO- + Gk. *nautēs* sailor]
as·tro·nau·tics (as′trə·nô′tiks) *n. pl. (construed as sing.)* The science of space travel.
as·tron·o·mer (ə·stron′ə·mər) *n.* One learned or expert in astronomy.
as·tro·nom·ic (as′trə·nom′ik) *adj.* **1** Of or pertaining to astronomy. **2** Enormously or inconceivably large. Also **as′tro·nom′i·cal.** **—as′tro·nom′i·cal·ly** *adv.*
astronomical year Solar year.
as·tron·o·my (ə·stron′ə·mē) *n.* The science that studies stars, planets, and other bodies in space and the phenomena that involve them. [< Gk. *astronomia* < *astron* star + *nomos* law]
as·tro·phys·ics (as′trō·fiz′iks) *n. pl. (construed as sing.)* The branch of astronomy that deals with the physical constitution and properties of bodies in space. **—as′tro·phys′i·cal** *adj.* **—as·tro·phys·i·cist** (as′trō·fiz′ə·sist) *n.*
as·tute (ə·styōōt′) *adj.* Having or showing keen intelligence or shrewdness: an *astute* businessman. [< L *astus* cunning] **—as·tute′ly** *adv.* **—as·tute′ness** *n.* **—Syn.** acute, sagacious, cunning, crafty.
a·sun·der (ə·sun′dər) *adv.* **1** In or into a different place or direction. **2** Apart; into pieces. [< OE *on sundran*]
a·sy·lum (ə·sī′ləm) *n.* **1** An institution for the care of the aged, the mentally disturbed, the poor, etc. **2** A place of refuge. **3** An inviolable shelter from arrest or punishment, as a temple or church in ancient times. **4** The protection afforded by a sanctuary or refuge. [< Gk. *a-* without + *sylon* right of seizure]
a·sym·met·ric (ā′si·met′rik, as′i-) *adj.* Not symmetrical. Also **a′sym·met′ri·cal.** **—a′sym·met′ri·cal·ly** *adv.*
a·sym·me·try (ā·sim′ə·trē) *n.* Lack of symmetry or proportion. [< Gk. *a-* without + *symmetria* symmetry]
as·ymp·tote (as′im·tōt) *n. Math.* A straight line which is a limit of the set of lines tangent to a curve as the point of tangency approaches infinity. [< Gk. *asymptōtos* not falling together] **—as′ymp·tot′ic** (-tot′ik) or **·i·cal** *adj.* **—as′ymp·tot′i·cal·ly** *adv.*
at (at, *unstressed* ət) *prep.* **1** On; in; near; upon: *at* the door; *at* the center. **2** On or near the age or time of: the train leaving *at* two; a man *at* sixty. **3** During the course or lapse of: *at* the moment. **4** To or toward: Look *at* that sunset! **5** Through; by way of: smoke coming out *at* the windows. **6** From: Get gas *at* the pump. **7** Engaged or occupied in: to be *at* work. **8** Attending: He was *at* the party. **9** In the state or condition of: a nation *at* war. **10** Viewed from; with an interval of: a target *at* sixty paces. **11** As a result of: He winced *at* the thought. **12** In the manner of: *at* a trot. **13** In pursuit or quest of; in the direction of: to catch *at* straws. **14** Dependent upon: to be *at* an enemy's mercy. **15** According to: Proceed *at* your discretion. **16** To or for the extent, amount, degree, price, etc., of: pencils *at*

a dime apiece. 17 With reference to: to be good *at* baking cakes. [< OE *æt*]

At·a·brine (at′ə·brin, -brēn) *n.* A synthetic antimalarial drug: a trade name.

at·a·vism (at′ə·viz′əm) *n.* 1 Reversion to an earlier or primitive type. 2 *Biol.* a The occurrence in an individual of a characteristic present in remote ancestors. b An instance of such an occurrence. [< L *atavus* ancestor] —**at′·a·vist** *n.* —**at′a·vis′tic** *adj.*

a·tax·i·a (ə·tak′sē·ə) *n.* 1 Absence or failure of muscular coordination. 2 Locomotor ataxia. Also **a·tax·y** (ə·tak′sē). [< Gk. *ataxia* lack of order] —**a·tax′ic** *adj., n.*

ate (āt, *chiefly Brit.* et) *p.t.* of EAT.

-ate[1] *suffix* Forming: 1 Participial adjectives equivalent to those in *-ated: separate.* 2 Adjectives meaning "possessing or characterized by": *foliate.* 3 Verbs formed by analogy: *assassinate.* 4 *Chem.* Verbs with the meaning "combine or treat with": *chlorinate.* [< L *-atus,* pp. ending of 1st conjugation verbs]

-ate[2] *suffix* Forming: 1 Nouns denoting office, function, or agent: *magistrate.* 2 Nouns denoting the object or result of an action: *mandate.* [< L *-atus,* suffix of nouns]

-ate[3] *suffix Chem.* Used to form the names of salts and esters derived from acids whose names end in *-ic: carbonate, nitrate.* [< L *-atum,* neut. of *-atus* -ATE[1]]

at·el·ier (at′əl·yā, *Fr.* à·tə·lyā′) *n.* A workshop; studio. [< F, orig., pile of chips]

a tem·po (ä tem′pō) *Music* In the tempo originally indicated. [< Ital.]

a·the·ism (ā′thē·iz′əm) *n.* The belief that there is no God. [< Gk. *a-* without + *theos* god] —**a′the·ist** *n.* —**a′the·is′tic** or **·ti·cal** *adj.* —**a′the·is′ti·cal·ly** *adv.*

A·the·na (ə·thē′nə) *Gk. Myth.* The goddess of wisdom, war, and patroness of arts and crafts. Also **A·the·ne** (ə·thē′nē). [< Gk. *Athēnē*]

ath·e·ne·um (ath′ə·nē′əm) *n.* 1 A literary or scientific club. 2 A reading room or library. Also **ath′e·nae′um.** [< Gk. *Athēnaion* the temple of Athena]

A·the·ni·an (ə·thē′nē·ən) *adj.* Of or pertaining to Athens, or to its art or culture. —*n.* A native or citizen of Athens.

a·thirst (ə·thûrst′) *adj.* 1 Wanting water; thirsty. 2 Having a strong desire. —**Syn.** 2 eager, anxious, avid, longing.

ath·lete (ath′lēt) *n.* A person trained or skilled in acts or games requiring physical strength, agility, speed, etc. [< Gk. *athlētēs* a contestant in the games]

athlete's foot Ringworm of the foot.

ath·let·ic (ath·let′ik) *adj.* 1 Of, pertaining to, or like an athlete. 2 Strong; vigorous; muscular. —**ath·let′i·cal·ly** *adv.* —**ath·let·i·cism** (ath·let′ə·siz′əm) *n.*

ath·let·ics (ath·let′iks) *n. pl. (sometimes construed as sing.)* Athletic games and exercises collectively.

at-home (ət·hōm′) *n.* An informal party or reception given at one's home.

a·thwart (ə·thwôrt′) *adv.* 1 From side to side; across. 2 So as to thwart; perversely. —*prep.* 1 Across the course of; from side to side of. 2 Contrary to; in opposition to. [< *a-* on + THWART]

-atic *suffix* Of; of the kind of: *erratic.* [< Gk. *-atikos*]

a·tilt (ə·tilt′) *adv. & adj.* Tilted.

-ation *suffix* 1 Act or process of: *creation.* 2 Condition or quality of: *affectation.* 3 Result of: *reformation.* [< L *-atio, -ationis*]

-ative *suffix* 1 Of, like, or pertaining to: *qualitative* 2 Tending to: *talkative.* [< L *-ativus*]

At·lan·tic (at·lan′tik) *adj.* 1 Of, near, in, on, or pertaining to the Atlantic Ocean. 2 Of, near, on, or pertaining to the E coast of the U.S. —*n.* The Atlantic Ocean. [< Gk. *Atlantikos* pertaining to Atlas]

Atlantic Charter A statement issued in August 1941 by Churchill and Roosevelt, setting forth the basic aims of the Allied Nations for peace after World War II.

At·lan·tis (at·lan′tis) *n.* A legendary island continent supposed to have existed west of Gibraltar and to have been engulfed by the Atlantic Ocean.

at·las (at′ləs) *n.* 1 A book of maps. 2 A collection of charts, tables, etc. illustrating any subject.

At·las (at′ləs) 1 *Gk. Myth.* A Titan supporting the pillars of heaven on his shoulders. 2 *n.* An intercontinental ballistic missile of the U.S. Air Force. [< Gk. *Atlas* < *tlaein* bear]

atm. atmosphere; atmospheric.

at·mos·phere (at′məs·fir) *n.* 1 The envelope of gases that surrounds the earth or any body in space. 2 The particular climatic condition of any place or region regarded as dependent on the air. 3 Any surrounding or pervasive element or influence: an *atmosphere* of gloom. 4 *Physics* A unit of pressure equal to 14.69 pounds per square inch or 1.01325 x 10^5 newtons per square meter. [< Gk. *atmos* vapor + *sphaira* sphere]

at·mos·pher·ic (at′məs·fer′ik) *adj.* 1 Of, pertaining to, or existing in atmosphere. 2 Dependent on, caused by, or producing atmosphere. Also **at′mos·pher′i·cal.** —**at′mos·pher′i·cal·ly** *adv.*

at. no. atomic number.

at·oll (at′ôl, -ol, ə·tol′) *n.* A ring-shaped coral island and its associated reef, nearly or totally enclosing a lagoon. [< Malayalam *atolu*]

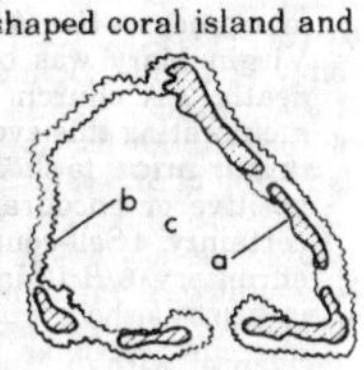

Atoll

a. islet. b. reef. c. lagoon.

at·om (at′əm) *n.* 1 The smallest unit of an element capable of existing, consisting of the electrically neutral combination of a nucleus and its complement of electrons. 2 An exceedingly small quantity or particle; iota. [< Gk. *atomos* indivisible]

a·tom·ic (ə·tom′ik) *adj.* 1 Of or pertaining to an atom or atoms: also **a·tom′i·cal.** 2 Minute; infinitesimal. 3 Nuclear: an *atomic* power plant. —**a·tom′i·cal·ly** *adv.*

atomic bomb A bomb whose explosive power is derived from nuclear fission.

atomic energy The energy released from an atom, as by nuclear fission or nuclear fusion.

atomic mass unit A unit of mass, equal to 1/12 of the mass of an atom of the most abundant isotope of carbon, or about 1.6604 × 10^{-24} gram.

atomic number A number which represents the unit positive charges (protons) in the atomic nucleus of each element.

atomic theory The concept that all matter is composed of atoms, and that the properties of matter are ultimately to be understood in terms of the properties and interactions of the component atoms.

atomic weight The weight of an atom of an element relative to that of an atom of carbon, expressed in atomic mass units.

at·om·ize (at′əm·īz) *v.t.* **·ized, ·iz·ing** 1 To reduce to or separate into atoms; pulverize. 2 To reduce to a spray.

at·om·iz·er (at′əm·ī′zər) *n.* An apparatus for reducing a liquid, esp. medicine or perfume, to a spray.

a·to·nal (ā·tō′nəl) *adj. Music* Without tonality; lacking key. —**a·to·nal·i·ty** (ā′tō·nal′ə·tē) *n.* —**a·to′nal·ly** *adv.*

a·tone (ə·tōn′) *v.* **a·toned, a·ton·ing** *v.i.* To make amends, as for sin. [< earlier *at one* in accord, short for *to set at one,* reconcile] —**a·ton′a·ble, a·tone′a·ble** *adj.* —**a·ton′er** *n.*

a·tone·ment (ə·tōn′mənt) *n.* 1 Satisfaction made, as for wrong or injury. 2 *Theol. Usu. cap.* The reconciliation between God and man effected by Christ's life, passion, and death. —**Syn.** 1 reparation, amends, compensation.

a·top (ə·top′) *adv. & adj.* On or at the top. —*prep.* On the top of.

-atory *suffix* Of or pertaining to, produced by, characterized by: *exclamatory.* [< L *-atorius* adj. suffix]

at·ra·bil·ious (at′rə·bil′yəs) *adj.* 1 Disposed to melancholy; gloomy. 2 Peevish; surly. Also **at′ra·bil′i·ar** (-bil′ē·ər) [< L *atra bilis* black bile] —**at′ra·bil′ious·ness** *n.*

a·tri·um (ā′trē·əm) *n. pl.* **a·tri·a** (ā′trē·ə) 1 In ancient Roman houses, the central hall or court. 2 A hall or open court. 3 *Anat.* A chamber or sac, esp. one of the upper chambers of the heart through which venous blood is transmitted to the ventricles. [< L] • See HEART.

a·tro·cious (ə·trō′shəs) *adj.* 1 Outrageously wicked, criminal, cruel, etc. 2 *Informal.* Very bad or in bad taste: an *atrocious* remark. [< L *atrox* harsh, cruel < *ater* black] —**a·tro′cious·ly** *adv.* —**a·tro′cious·ness** *n.*

a·troc·i·ty (ə·tros′ə·tē) *n. pl.* **·ties** 1 The state or quality of being atrocious. 2 An atrocious deed or act; cruelty, wickedness, etc. 3 *Informal.* Something that is very bad or in bad taste.

at·ro·phy (at′rə·fē) *n. pl.* **·phies** 1 A wasting away of the body or any of its parts. 2 A stoppage of growth or development, as of a part. —*v.* **·phied, ·phy·ing** *v.t.* 1 To affect with atrophy. —*v.i.* 2 To waste away; wither. [< Gk. *atrophas* poorly nourished] —**a·troph·ic** (ə·trof′ik).

at·ro·pine (at′rə·pēn, -pin) *n.* A poisonous alkaloid found in belladonna and other plants, used in medicine as an antispasmodic, to enlarge the pupil of the eye, etc. [< Gk. *atropos* inflexible]

att. attorney.

at·tach (ə·tach′) *v.t.* 1 To make fast to something; fasten on. 2 To connect, join on, or bind: He *attached* himself to the expedition. 3 To add or append, as a word or signature. 4 To attribute; ascribe: to *attach* great importance to the outcome of an event. 5 *Law* To secure for legal jurisdiction; seize or arrest by legal process: to *attach* an employee's salary. 6 *Mil.* To order to serve temporarily or as a nonintegral part: The regiment *attached* a medical officer. —*v.i.* 7 To belong, as a quality or circumstance; be incidental: with *to:* Much interest *attaches* to this opinion. [< OF *atachier* < *a-* to + *tache* nail] —**at·tach′a·ble** *adj.*

at·ta·ché (at′ə·shā′, *esp. Brit.* ə·tash′ā) n. A person assigned to a diplomatic mission or staff. [< F *attacher* attach]

attaché case A slender rectangular case with a hard exterior, for carrying papers, documents, etc.

at·tach·ment (ə·tach′mənt) *n.* 1 An attaching or a being attached. 2 Something that is attached, as an accessory for an appliance. 3 That by which anything is attached. 4 Affection; devoted regard. 5 *Law* a Seizure of a person or property. b The writ commanding this.

at·tack (ə·tak′) *v.t.* 1 To set upon suddenly; assault or begin conflict with. 2 To assail with hostile words; criticize, censure. 3 To begin work on, esp. with vigor. 4 To begin to affect seriously or injuriously: Acid *attacks* metal; Disease *attacks* a person. —*v.i.* 5 To make an attack. —*n.* 1 The act of attacking. 2 The first movement toward any undertaking. 3 Any hostile, offensive movement or action, as with troops. 4 A seizure, as by disease. [< Ital. *attaccare*]

at·tain (ə·tān′) *v.t.* 1 To achieve, accomplish or gain. 2 To come to; arrive at. —**attain to** To arrive at with effort; succeed in reaching. [< L *attingere* reach] —**at·tain′a·bil′i·ty, at·tain′a·ble·ness** *n.* —**at·tain′a·ble** *adj.*

at·tain·der (ə·tān′dər) *n.* The loss of all civil rights of a person sentenced to death or outlawed. [< OF *ataindre* attain, strike, accuse]

at·tain·ment (ə·tān′mənt) *n.* 1 The act of attaining. 2 That which is attained, as a skill. —**Syn.** 1, 2 accomplishment, acquisition, acquirement, achievement.

at·taint (ə·tānt′) *v.t.* 1 To inflict attainder upon; condemn. 2 To disgrace; taint; sully. —*n.* Attainder.

at·tar (at′ər) *n.* A perfume or essential oil extracted from the petals of flowers, esp. roses. [< Ar. *'itr* perfume]

at·tempt (ə·tempt′) *v.t.* To make an effort to perform, get, etc.; endeavor; try. —*n.* 1 A putting forth of effort; trial; endeavor; essay. 2 An attack. [< L *attemptare* try] —**at·tempt′a·bil′i·ty** *n.* —**at·tempt′a·ble** *adj.*

at·tend (ə·tend′) *v.t.* 1 To wait upon; minister to; visit or care for professionally. 2 To be present at or in, as a meeting. 3 To follow as a result. 4 To accompany. 5 *Archaic* To give heed; listen. [< L *attendere* give heed to, consider]

at·ten·dance (ə·ten′dəns) *n.* 1 An attending. 2 Those who attend; an audience or congregation; retinue.

at·ten·dant (ə·ten′dənt) *n.* 1 One who attends, as a servant. 2 One who is present at a ceremony. 3 A concomitant; consequent. —*adj.* Following or accompanying; waiting upon.

at·ten·tion (ə·ten′shən) *n.* 1 The act or faculty of concentrating on something. 2 Observation; notice: to get someone's *attention.* 3 *Usu. pl.* An act of courtesy, gallantry, or devotion. 4 Practical or thoughtful consideration or care. 5 *Mil.* a The prescribed position of readiness to obey orders. b The order to assume this position. [< L *attendere* to attend]

at·ten·tive (ə·ten′tiv) *adj.* 1 Giving or showing attention; observant. 2 Courteous; gallant; polite. —**at·ten′tive·ly** *adv.* —**at·ten′tive·ness** *n.*

at·ten·u·ate (ə·ten′yo͞o·āt) *v.* **·at·ed, ·at·ing** *v.t.* 1 To make thin, small, or fine. 2 To reduce in value, quantity, severity, strength, etc.; weaken. 3 To reduce in density; rarefy, as a liquid or gas. 4 To weaken the virulence of a microorganism. —*v.i.* 5 To become thin, weak, rarefied, etc. —*adj.* (a·ten′yo͞o·it) Attenuated. [< L *ad-* + *tenuare* make thin] —**at·ten′u·a·ble** *adj.* —**at·ten′u·a′tion** *n.*

at·test (ə·test′) *v.t.* 1 To confirm as accurate, true, or genuine; vouch for. 2 To certify, as by signature or oath. 3 To be proof of. 4 To put upon oath. —*v.i.* 5 To bear witness; testify: with *to.* [< L *ad-* to + *testari* bear witness]

at·tes·ta·tion (at′es·tā′shən) *n.* 1 The act of attesting. 2 Testimony.

at·tic (at′ik) *n.* 1 A usu. low story or room beneath the roof; a garret. 2 A low structure above a cornice or entablature. [< F *attique* Attic (in style)]

At·tic (at′ik) *adj.* 1 Of Attica. 2 Of or characteristic of Athens or the Athenians. —*n.* The dialect of Attica.

At·ti·ca (at′i·kə) An ancient Greek kingdom that included Athens.

at·tire (ə·tīr′) *v.t.* **at·tired, at·tir·ing** To dress; array; adorn. —*n.* Dress or clothing. [< OF *atirer* arrange, adorn]

at·ti·tude (at′ə·tʸo͞od) *n.* 1 Position of the body, as suggesting some thought, feeling, or action. 2 State of mind, behavior, or conduct, as indicating one's feelings, opinion, or purpose. [< LL *aptitudo* fitness, aptitude] —**at·ti·tu·di·nal** (at′ə·tʸo͞o′də·nəl) *adj.*

at·ti·tu·di·nize (at′ə·tʸo͞o′də·nīz) *v.i.* **·nized, ·niz·ing** To pose for effect; strike an attitude. *Brit. sp.* **at′ti·tu′di·nise.**

at·tor·ney (ə·tûr′nē) *n. pl.* **·neys** A person empowered by another to act in his stead, esp. a lawyer. —**by attorney** By proxy. —**power of attorney** Legal written authority to transact business for another. [< OF *atorner* turn to, assign] —**at·tor′ney·ship** *n.*

attorney at law A lawyer.

attorney general *pl.* **attorneys general, attorney generals** The chief law officer of a state or national government.

Attorney General The head of the U.S. Department of Justice and a member of the President's cabinet.

at·tract (ə·trakt′) *v.t.* 1 To draw to or cause to come near by some physical force, without apparent mechanical connection. 2 To draw the admiration, attention, etc. of. [< L *ad-* toward + *trahere* draw, drag] —**at·tract′a·ble** *adj.* —**at·tract′a·ble·ness, at·tract′a·bil′i·ty, at·tract′er, at·trac′tor** *n.*

at·trac·tion (ə·trak′shən) *n.* 1 The act of attracting. 2 Power to attract. 3 Something that attracts. 4 A physical force exerted between or among bodies, tending to draw them together or prevent their separation.

at·trac·tive (ə·trak′tiv) *adj.* 1 Having the power or quality of attracting. 2 Pleasing, winning, pretty, etc. —**at·trac′tive·ly** *adv.* —**at·trac′tive·ness** *n.*

attrib. attribute; attributive; attributively.

at·trib·ute (ə·trib′yo͞ot) *v.t.* **·ut·ed, ·ut·ing** To ascribe as belonging to, resulting from, or created or caused by. —**at·tri·bute** (at′rə·byo͞ot) *n.* 1 A quality or characteristic. 2 *Gram.* An adjective or its equivalent. 3 In art and mythology, a distinctive mark or symbol. [< L *ad-* to + *tribuere* allot, give over] —**at·trib′u·ta·ble** *adj.* —**Syn.** *v.* assign, impute, associate. *n.* 1 property, trait, feature, peculiarity.

at·tri·bu·tion (at′rə·byo͞o′shən) *n.* 1 An attributing or being attributed. 2 An ascribed characteristic or quality; attribute.

at·trib·u·tive (ə·trib′yə·tiv) *adj.* 1 Pertaining to or of the nature of an attribute. 2 So ascribed, as a work of art: That canvas is an *attributive* Vermeer. 3 *Gram.* Designating an adjective or its equivalent which stands before the noun it modifies. —*n. Gram.* An attributive word or phrase. —**at·trib′u·tive·ly** *adj.* —**at·trib′u·tive·ness** *n.*

at·tri·tion (ə·trish′ən) *n.* 1 A rubbing out or grinding down, as by friction. 2 A gradual wearing down or weakening. [< L *atterere* rub away]

at·tune (ə·t^{y}ōōn') *v.t.* **at·tuned, at·tun·ing 1** To bring into accord with; harmonize. **2** To adjust to the right pitch; tune. [<AD- + TUNE]

atty. attorney.

at. wt. atomic weight.

a·typ·i·cal (ā·tip'i·kəl) *adj.* Not typical. Also **a·typ'ic.** **—a·typ'i·cal·ly** *adv.*

A.U., A.u., a.u. angstrom unit.

Au gold (L *aurum*).

au·burn (ô'bûrn) *adj.* & *n.* Reddish brown. [<LL *alburnus* whitish]

au cour·rant (ō kōō·räṅ') Up to date; well or fully informed. [F, lit., in the current]

auc·tion (ôk'shən) *n.* **1** A public sale in which the price offered for individual items is increased by bids, until the highest bidder becomes the purchaser. **2** The bidding in bridge. **—***v.t.* To sell by or at auction: usu. with *off.* [<L *auctio* an increase, a public sale (with increasing bids)]

auc·tion·eer (ôk'shən·ir') *n.* One who conducts an auction, usu. as a business. **—***v.t.* To sell by auction.

au·da·cious (ô·dā'shəs) *adj.* **1** Fearless; bold. **2** Defiant of convention, decorum, etc.; brazen; insolent. [<L *audax* bold] **—au·da'cious·ly** *adv.* **—au·da'cious·ness** *n.*

au·dac·i·ty (ô·das'ə·tē) *n. pl.* **·ties 1** Boldness; fearlessness. **2** Insolence; shamelessness. **3** An audacious act, remark, etc. [<L *audax* bold, rash <*audere* dare]

au·di·bil·i·ty (ô'də·bil'ə·tē) *n.* Capability of being heard.

au·di·ble (ô'də·bəl) *adj.* Perceptible by the ear. [<L *audire* hear] **—au'di·ble·ness** *n.* **—au'di·bly** *adv.*

au·di·ence (ô'dē·əns) *n.* **1** An assembly gathered to hear and see, as at a concert. **2** Those who are reached by a book, television program, etc. **3** A formal hearing, interview, or conference. **4** Opportunity to be heard. [<L *audientia* a hearing]

au·di·o (ô'dē·ō) *adj. Telecom.* **1** Of or pertaining to characteristics, esp. frequency, associated with sound waves. **2** Designating devices used in transmission or reception of sound. [<L *audire* hear]

au·di·o·cas·ette (ô'dē·ō·kə·set', -ka·set') *adj.* A cassette for the storage of audio material.

audio frequency A frequency of electrical, sound, or other wave vibrations coming within the range of normal human hearing, or from about 20 to 20,000 hertz.

au·di·o-vis·u·al (ô'dē·ō·vizh'ōō·əl) *adj.* **1** Relating to both hearing and sight. **2** Pertaining to instructional materials other than books, as filmstrips, motion pictures, television, and recordings.

au·dit (ô'dit) *v.t.* **1** To examine, adjust, and certify, as accounts. **2** To attend (a college course) as a listener only without receiving credit. **—***n.* **1** An examination of financial accounts to establish their correctness. **2** A prepared statement concerning such an examination. **3** An adjustment and settlement of accounts. [<L *auditus* a hearing]

au·di·tion (ô·dish'ən) *n.* **1** The act or sense of hearing. **2** A trial test or hearing, as of an actor or singer. **—***v.t.* **1** To give an audition to. **—***v.i.* **2** To give an audition. [<L *auditio* a hearing]

au·di·tor (ô'də·tər) *n.* **1** One who audits accounts. **2** One who listens. **3** One who audits classes.

au·di·to·ri·um (ô'də·tôr'ē·əm, -tō'rē·əm) *n. pl.* **·to·ri·ums** or **·to·ri·a** (-tôr'ē·ə, -tō'rē·ə) **1** The room or part of a building, as a church, theater, etc., occupied by the audience. **2** A building for concerts, public meetings, etc. [<L, lecture room, courtroom]

au·di·to·ry (ô'də·tôr'ē, -tō'rē) *adj.* Of or pertaining to hearing or the organs or sense of hearing. [<L *audire* hear] **—au'di·to'ri·ly** *adv.*

auditory canal *Anat.* The passage in the ear leading from the auricle to the tympanic membrane. • See EAR.

Aug. August.

au·gend (ô'jend) *n. Math.* A number or element to which another is to be added. [<L *augere* to increase]

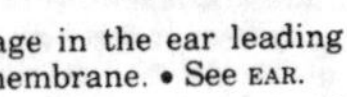

Auger

au·ger (ô'gər) *n.* A large tool with a spiral groove for boring holes in wood, etc. [<OE *nafugār*, lit., nave-borer]

aught[1] (ôt) *n.* Anything; any part or item. **—***adv.* By any chance; at all. [<OE *ā* ever + *wiht* thing]

aught[2] (ôt) *n.* The figure 0; cipher; nothing. [*a naught* taken as *an aught*]

aug·ment (ôg·ment') *v.t.* & *v.i.* To make or become greater, as in size, number, or amount. [<L *augere* to increase] **—aug·ment'a·ble** *adj.* **—aug·ment'er** *n.* **—Syn.** enlarge, intensify, increase, expand.

aug·men·ta·tion (ôg'men·tā'shən) *n.* **1** An augmenting or being augmented. **2** An addition or increase.

aug·men·ta·tive (ôg·men'tə·tiv) *adj.* **1** Having the quality or power of augmenting. **2** *Gram.* Denoting greater size or intensity. **—***n. Gram.* An augmentative suffix, prefix, etc. Also **aug·men'tive.**

au gra·tin (ō grät'n, grat'n; *Fr.* ō grà·taṅ') Sprinkled with bread crumbs or grated cheese and baked until brown. [F, lit., with the burnt part]

au·gur (ô'gər) *n.* A prophet; soothsayer. **—***v.t.* **1** To be an omen of. **—***v.i.* **2** To be an augury or omen. [<L]

au·gu·ry (ô'g^{y}ə·rē) *n. pl.* **·ries 1** The art or practice of divination. **2** A portent or omen.

au·gust (ô·gust') *adj.* Majestic; grand; imposing. [<L *augere* increase, exalt] **—au·gust'ly** *adv.* **—au·gust'ness** *n.*

Au·gust (ô'gəst) *n.* The eighth month of the year, containing 31 days. [<L, after *Augustus* Caesar, 63 B.C.-A.D. 14, Roman emperor]

Au·gus·tan (ô·gus'tən) *adj.* **1** Of or pertaining to Augustus Caesar or to his times. **2** Classical; refined.

Augustan age 1 The period of the reign of Augustus Caesar, the golden age of Roman literature. **2** A period in English literature during the reign of Queen Anne in the early 18th century.

Au·gus·tin·i·an (ô'gəs·tin'ē·ən) *adj.* **1** Of or pertaining to St. Augustine or his doctrines. **2** Belonging to a monastic order named after St. Augustine or following his rule.

auk (ôk) *n.* Any of various short-winged, web-footed diving birds of northern seas. [<ON *ālka*]

au lait (ō le') With milk. [F]

auld lang syne (ôld' lang sīn', zīn') Literally, old long since; hence, long ago. [Scot.]

aunt (ant, änt) *n.* The sister of one's father or mother, or the wife of one's uncle. [<L *amita* paternal aunt]

aunt·ie (an'tē, än'-) *n.* A familiar, diminutive form of aunt. Also **aunt'y.**

au pair (ō pâr) *Chiefly Brit.* **1** An arrangement whereby one receives room and board in a foreign household in exchange for doing certain chores: often used attributively: *au pair* girls. **2** *Informal* A girl participating in such an arrangement. [<F, lit., at par]

au·ra (ôr'ə) *n. pl.* **au·ras** or **au·rae** (ôr'ē) **1** An invisible emanation or exhalation. **2** A distinctive air or quality enveloping or characterizing a person or thing. [<Gk. *aurē* breath] **—au'ral** *adj.*

au·ral (ôr'əl) *adj.* Pertaining to the ear or the sense of hearing. [<L *auris* ear + -AL]

au·re·ate (ôr'e·it) *adj.* **1** Of the color of gold; golden. **2** Florid, grandiloquent. [<L *aurum* gold]

au·re·ole (ôr'ē·ōl) *n.* **1** A halo that appears to surround the image of a brilliant body, as the corona of the sun. **2** A radiant glow around the head or body, as of a saint. Also **au·re·o·la** (ô·rē'ə·lə). [<L *aureolus* golden]

Au·re·o·my·cin (ôr'ē·ō·mī'sin) *n.* An antibiotic effective against bacteria and certain viruses: a trade name.

au re·voir (ō rə·vwär') Good-by; till we meet again. [F, lit., to the seeing again]

au·ri·cle (ôr'i·kəl) *n.* **1** The external ear. **2** Any ear-shaped appendage or part. **3** An atrium of the heart. [<L *auris* ear] **—au'ri·cled** *adj.*

au·ric·u·lar (ô·rik'yə·lər) *adj.* **1** Of or pertaining to the ear or the sense of hearing. **2** Intended for the ear; confidential. **3** Ear-shaped. **4** Of or pertaining to an auricle.

au·rif·er·ous (ô·rif'ər·əs) *adj.* Containing gold. [<L *aurum* gold + *ferre* bear] **—au·rif'er·ous·ly** *adv.*

au·ri·form (ôr'ə·fôrm) *adj.* Ear-shaped. [<L *auris* ear + -FORM]

au·rochs (ôr'oks) *n.* **1** The extinct European wild ox. **2** A rare or extinct bison of Europe. [< OHG *ūr* bison + *ohso* ox]

au·ro·ra (ô·rôr′ə, ô·rō′rə) *n.* **1** The dawn. **2** *Meteorol.* A luminous display seen in the skies of high northern and southern latitudes, caused by electrical disturbances in the atmosphere. [< L, dawn]

Au·ro·ra (ô·rôr′ə, ô·rō′rə) *Rom. Myth.* The goddess of the dawn.

aurora aus·tra·lis (ôs·trā′lis) *Meteorol.* The aurora as seen in far southern latitudes. [< NL, southern aurora]

aurora bo·re·al·is (bôr′ē·al′is, -ā′lis, bō′rē-) *Meteorol.* The aurora as seen in the high northern latitudes. [< NL, northern aurora]

au·ro·ral (ô·rôr′əl, ô·rō′rəl) *adj.* **1** Pertaining to or like the dawn. **2** Of, like, or caused by an aurora. Also **au·ro·re·an** (ô·rôr′ē·ən, ô·rō′rē-), **au·ro′ric.** **—au·ro′ral·ly** *adv.*

aus·cul·tate (ôs′kəl·tāt) *v.t. & v.i.* **·tat·ed, ·tat·ing** *Med.* To examine by listening, as with a stethoscope, for sounds produced in the chest, abdomen, etc. [< L *auscultare* listen, give ear to] **—aus·cul·ta·tion** (ôs′kəl·tā′shən) *n.* **—aus·cul·ta·tive** (ôs·kul′tə·tiv), **aus·cul′ta·to′ry** *adj.*

aus·pice (ôs′pis) *n. pl.* **aus·pi·ces** (ôs′pə·sēz) **1** *Usu. pl.* Patronage; sponsorship: under the *auspices* of the alumni association. **2** An omen or sign. [< L *auspex* a bird augur]

aus·pi·cious (ôs·pish′əs) *adj.* **1** Favoring or conducive to future success. **2** Attended by good fortune; fortunate; successful. **—aus·pi′cious·ly** *adv.* **—aus·pi′cious·ness** *n.* **—Syn. 1** propitious, favorable, hopeful, promising.

aus·tere (ô·stir′) *adj.* **1** Severe, grave, or stern, as in look or conduct. **2** Abstemious; ascetic. **3** Severely simple; unadorned. [< Gk. *austēros* harsh, bitter] **—aus·tere′ly** *adv.*

aus·ter·i·ty (ô·ster′ə·tē) *n. pl.* **·ties 1** The quality or condition of being austere. **2** An austere act, practice, or manner. **3** Extreme or rigid economy. Also **aus·tere′ness.**

aus·tral (ôs′trəl, os′-) *adj.* Southern; southerly. [< L *auster* south wind]

Aus·tral·a·sian (ôs′trəl·ā′zhən, -ā′shən) *n.* An inhabitant of Australasia. *—adj.* Of Australasia or its people.

Aus·tra·lia (ô·strāl′yə, o-) *n.* A country, a member of the Commonwealth of Nations, occupying a continent SE of Asia, 2,971,081 sq. mi., cap. Canberra.

Australia Day January 26, an Australian holiday marking the landing of the British in 1788.

Aus·tra·lian (ô·strāl′yən, o-) *n.* A native or citizen of Australia. *—adj.* Of or pertaining to Australia or its people.

Australian ballot A ballot bearing the names of all the candidates of all parties, given out only at the polls where it is marked in secret by the voter.

Aus·tri·a (ôs′trē·ə) *n.* A republic of CEN. Europe, 32,375 sq. mi., cap. Vienna. **—Aus′tri·an** *adj., n.*

Aus·tri·a-Hun·ga·ry (ôs′trē·ə·hung′gə·rē) *n.* A former monarchy of CEN. Europe. **—Aus·tro-Hun·gar·i·an** (ôs′trō·hung·gâr′ē·ən) *adj.*

Aus·tro·ne·sian (ôs′trō·nē′·zhən, -shən) *adj.* Of or pertaining to Austronesia, its inhabitants, or their languages. *—n.* A family of languages spoken throughout the Pacific and divided into three subfamilies: Indonesian or Malayan, Oceanic (including the Melanesian and Micronesian languages), and Polynesian.

au·tar·chy (ô′tär·kē) *n.* **1** Absolute rule or sovereignty or a country under such rule. **2** Self-government. **3** AUTARKY. [< Gk. *autarchos* absolute ruler] **—au·tar·chic** (ô·tär′kik) or **·chi·cal** *adj.*

au·tar·ky (ô′tär·kē) *n.* National economic self-sufficiency. [< Gk. *autarkeia* self-sufficiency] **—au·tar·ki·cal** (ô·tär′ki·kəl) *adj.*

au·teur (ō·tœr′) *n.* A film director whose work is the product of personal vision and total production control. [F, lit., author]

au·then·tic (ô·then′tik) *adj.* **1** Authoritative; trustworthy; reliable. **2** Genuine; real. **3** *Law* Duly executed before the proper officer. Also **au·then′ti·cal.** [< Gk. *authentikos*] **—au·then′ti·cal·ly** *adv.*

au·then·ti·cate (ô·then′ti·kāt) *v.t.* **·cat·ed, ·cat·ing 1** To make genuine, credible, or authoritative. **2** To give legal force or validity to. **3** To establish or certify as genuine or authentic. **—au·then′ti·ca′tion, au·then′ti·ca′tor** *n.*

au·then·tic·i·ty (ô′thən·tis′ə·tē, ô′then′-) *n.* The state or quality of being authentic or authoritative.

au·thor (ô′thər) *n.* **1** The writer of a book, article, etc. **2** A person who writes as a profession. **3** A person who originates or creates something. *—v.t. Informal* To be the author of. [< L *auctor* originator, producer] **—au′thor·ess** *n. Fem.* **—au·tho·ri·al** (ô·thôr′ē·əl, ô·thō′rē-) *adj.*

au·thor·i·tar·i·an (ô·thor′ə·târ′ē·ən, -thôr′-, ə-) *adj.* Encouraging and upholding absolute obedience to some authority as against individual freedom. *—n.* A person who favors or enforces such obedience. **—au·thor′i·tar′i·an·ism** *n.*

au·thor·i·ta·tive (ô·thor′ə·tā′tiv, ô·thôr′-, ə-) *adj.* **1** Possessing or proceeding from proper or reliable authority; duly sanctioned. **2** Exercising authority, esp. in a dictatorial manner. **—au·thor′i·ta′tive·ly** *adv.* **—au·thor′i·ta′tive·ness** *n.*

au·thor·i·ty (ə·thor′ə·tē, ə·thôr′-, ô-) *n. pl.* **·ties 1** The right to command, enforce obedience, make decisions, etc. **2** Such a right given to another; authorization. **3** *pl.* Persons having the right to command or govern. **4** Personal power or expertness that commands influence, respect, or confidence. **5** That which may be appealed to in support of action or belief, as an author, volume, etc. **6** One who has special skill, knowledge, etc.; expert. **7** An authoritative opinion, decision, or precedent. [< L *auctoritas* power, authority < *augere* increase]

au·thor·i·za·tion (ô′thər·ə·zā′shən) *n.* **1** The act of conferring legality. **2** Formal legal power; sanction.

au·thor·ize (ô′thər·īz) *v.t.* **·ized, ·iz·ing 1** To confer authority upon; empower; commission. **2** To warrant; justify. **3** To sanction; approve. **—au′thor·i·za′tion, au′thor·iz′er** *n.*

au·thor·ized (ô′thər·īzd) *adj.* **1** Endowed with authority; accepted as authoritative. **2** Formally or legally sanctioned.

au·thor·ship (ô′thər·ship) *n.* **1** The profession or occupation of an author. **2** Origin or source, esp. of a literary work.

au·tism (ô′tiz·əm) *n. Psychol.* A mental disorder, esp. in children, marked by lack of response to external activities. [< AUT(O)- + -ISM] **—au·tis·tic** (ô·tis′tik) *adj.*

au·to (ô′tō) *Informal n. pl.* **·tos** An automobile. *—v.i.* To ride in or travel by an automobile.

auto-[1] *combining form* **1** Arising from some process or action within; as in *autism.* **2** Acting, directed upon, or of the self; as in *autobiography, autosuggestion.* Also, before vowels, **aut-.** [< Gk. *autos* self]

auto-[2] *combining form* Self-propelled. [< AUTOMOBILE]

au·to·bi·og·ra·phy (ô′tə·bī·og′rə·fē, -bē·og′-) *n. pl.* **·phies** The story of a person's life written by that same person. **—au′to·bi·og′ra·pher** *n.* **—au·to·bi·o·graph·ic** (ô′tə·bī′ə·graf′·ik) or **·i·cal** *adj.* **—au′to·bi′o·graph′i·cal·ly** *adv.*

au·to·clave (ô′tə·klāv) *n.* A container designed to contain superheated steam under pressure, used for the sterilization of surgical instruments, etc. [< AUTO-[1] + L *clavis* a key]

au·toc·ra·cy (ô·tok′rə·sē) *n. pl.* **·cies 1** Absolute government or rule by an autocrat. **2** A state ruled by an autocrat. **3** Complete power or dominance over others.

au·to·crat (ô′tə·krat) *n.* **1** A supreme ruler of unrestricted power. **2** An arrogant, dictatorial person. [< Gk. *autokratēs* self-ruling, independent] **—au′to·crat′ic** or **·i·cal** *adj.* **—au′to·crat′i·cal·ly** *adv.*

au·to-da-fé (ô′tō·də·fā′, ou′-) *n. pl.* **au·tos-da-fé** (ô′tōz-, ou′tōz-) The public announcement and execution of the sentence of the Inquisition, as the burning of heretics at the stake, etc. [< Pg., lit., act of the faith]

au·to·gi·ro (ô′tə·jī′rō) *n. pl.* **·ros** An aircraft that is propelled forward by a propeller, but which receives its lift and support from freely revolving, horizontal rotors. Also **au′to·gy′ro.** [< *Autogiro* former trade name]

au·to·graph (ô′tə·graf, -gräf) *n.* **1** A person's own handwriting or signature. **2** Something written in a person's own handwriting, as a manuscript. *—v.t.* **1** To write one's name in or affix one's signature to. 2 To write in one's own handwriting. —*adj.* Written by one's own hand, as a will. [<Gk. *autographos* written with one's own hand] —**au'to·graph'ic** or **·i·cal** *adj.* —**au'to·graph'i·cal·ly** *adv.*

au·to·im·mune (ô'tō·i·myōōn) *adj.* Caused by antibodies that operate against the body's own tissues: *autoimmune* diseases. —**au'to·im·mu'ni·ty** *n.*

au·to·in·tox·i·ca·tion (ô'tō·in·tok'sə·kā'shən) *n.* The poisoning of an organism by a toxin produced within the organism.

au·to·mat (ô'tə·mat) *n.* U.S. A restaurant in which certain foods are automatically made available from a receptacle when money is deposited in a slot alongside.

au·to·mate (ô'tə·māt) *v.t.* **·mat·ed, ·mat·ing** To operate or adapt (a factory, process, etc.) for automation.

au·to·mat·ic (ô'tə·mat'ik) *adj.* 1 Done as from force of habit or without conscious intent or volition; involuntary; reflex. 2 Capable of moving, operating, etc., at least partly, without human control or attention, as a machine. 3 Accomplished by such movements or operations. Also **au'to·mat'i·cal, au·tom·a·tous** (ô·tom'ə·təs). —*n.* An automatic machine, device, or firearm. [<Gk. *automatos* acting of oneself] —**au'to·mat'i·cal·ly** *adv.*

automatic pilot A device that automatically keeps a moving aircraft or other vehicle on a stable course.

au·to·ma·tion (ô'tə·mā'shən) *n.* 1 The automatic performance or control of an operation, system, device, etc. 2 The equipment or devices used to accomplish this. 3 The design and installation of such devices. [<AUTOM(ATIC) + (OPER)ATION] —**au'to·ma'tive** *adj.*

au·tom·a·tism (ô·tom'ə·tiz'əm) *n.* 1 The state or quality of being automatic. 2 The functioning or action of muscular or other processes independent of conscious control. —**au·tom'a·tist** *n.*

au·tom·a·ton (ô·tom'ə·ton, -tən) *n. pl.* **·tons** or **·ta** (-tə) 1 A contrivance or apparatus that functions automatically, esp. a robot. 2 Any living being whose actions are or appear to be involuntary or mechanical. 3 Anything capable of spontaneous movement or action. [<Gk. *automatos* acting of oneself, independent]

au·to·mo·bile (ô'tə·mə·bēl', ô'tə·mə·bēl', ô'tə·mō'bēl) *n.* A usu. four-wheeled vehicle for a small number of passengers, driven by an engine or motor and independent of rails or tracks; a motorcar. —*adj.* (ô'tə·mō'bil) Of or for automobiles. [<AUTO-[1] + MOBILE]

au·to·mo·tive (ô'tə·mō'tiv) *adj.* 1 Self-propelling. 2 Of or for automobiles or similar vehicles.

au·to·nom·ic (ô'tə·nom'ik) *adj.* 1 Autonomous. 2 *Biol.* Functioning spontaneously or independently. Also **au'to·nom'i·cal.** —au'to·nom'i·cal·ly *adv.*

autonomic nervous system The part of the nervous system that activates and controls tissues and organs not subject to voluntary control, as the heart, blood vessels, smooth muscle, glands, stomach, and intestines.

au·ton·o·mous (ô·ton'ə·məs) *adj.* 1 Functioning or existing independently. 2 Of or having self-government, as a state, group, etc. [<Gk. *autos* self + *nomos* law, rule] —**au·ton'o·mous·ly** *adv.*

au·ton·o·my (ô·ton'ə·mē) *n. pl.* **·mies** 1 The condition or quality of being autonomous; esp., the power or right of self-government. 2 A self-governing state, community, or group. —**au·ton'o·mist** *n.* —**Syn.** 1 independence, freedom, self-rule, self-determination.

au·top·sy (ô'top·sē, ô'təp-) *n. pl.* **·sies** Post-mortem examination of a human body, esp. to determine the cause of death. [<Gk. *autopsia* a seeing for oneself]

au·to·sug·ges·tion (ô'tō·səg·jes'chən, -sə·jes'-) *n.* The process of dwelling upon an idea to induce a change in one's behavior or physical condition. —**au'to·sug·ges'tive** *adj.*

au·tumn (ô'təm) *n.* 1 The season between summer and winter; fall. 2 A time of maturity and incipient decline. —*adj.* Of, in, or like autumn. [<L *autumnus*] —**au·tum·nal** (ô·tum'nəl) *adj.* —**au·tum'nal·ly** *adv.*

autumnal equinox The equinox that occurs near the end of September.

aux·il·ia·ry (ôg·zil'yər·ē, -zil'ər-) *adj.* 1 Giving or furnishing aid. 2 Subsidiary; subordinate. 3 Supplementary; additional. —*n. pl.* **·ries** 1 An auxiliary person, group, ship, etc. 2 *pl.* Foreign troops helping those of a nation at war. 3 AUXILIARY VERB. [<L *auxilium* a help]

auxiliary verb A verb that helps to express the tense, mood, voice, or aspect of another verb, as *be, have, do, will, shall, can, may, must.*

A.V. Authorized Version (of the Bible).

A/V, a.v., a/v according to value (L *ad valorem*).

av. average; avoirdupois.

a·vail (ə·vāl') *n.* 1 Use or advantage; benefit; good. 2 *pl.* Proceeds. —*v.t.* 1 To assist or aid; profit. —*v.i.* 2 To be of value or advantage; suffice. —avail oneself of To take advantage of; utilize. [<L *ad-* to + *valere* be strong] —**a·vail'ing** *adj.* —**a·vail'ing·ly** *adv.*

a·vail·a·ble (ə·vā'lə·bəl) *adj.* 1 At hand or at one's disposal, as funds. 2 That can be contacted, had, used, etc. —**a·vail'a·bil'i·ty, a·vail'a·ble·ness** *n.* —**a·vail'a·bly** *adv.*

av·a·lanche (av'ə·lanch, -länch) *n.* 1 A large mass of snow, ice, rocks, etc., sliding down a mountain slope. 2 Something like an avalanche, as in power, destructiveness, etc. —*v.* **·lanched, ·lanch·ing** —*v.i.* 1 To fall or slide like an avalanche. —*v.t.* 2 To fall or come down upon like an avalanche. [F]

a·vant-garde (ə·vänt'gärd', *Fr.* å·väṅ·gård') *n.* A group, as of artists or writers, who support or use the most advanced or unconventional ideas, techniques, etc.; vanguard. —*adj.* Of this group or their ideas, techniques, etc. [<F, lit., advance guard] —**a·vant-gard'ism** *n.* —**a·vant-gard'ist** *adj.*, n.

av·a·rice (av'ə·ris) *n.* Passion for riches; covetousness; greed. [<L *avarus* greedy] —**av·a·ri·cious** (av'ə·rish'əs) *adj.* —**av'a·ri'cious·ly** *adv.* —**av'a·ri'cious·ness** *n.*

a·vast (ə·vast', ə·väst') *interj.* Naut. Stop! hold! cease! [<Du. *hou' vast, houd vast* hold fast]

av·a·tar (av'ə·tär') *n.* 1 In Hindu mythology, the incarnation of a god. 2 Any embodiment or manifestation, as of a quality. [<Skt. *avatāra* descent]

a·ve (a'vē, ä'vā) *interj.* 1 Hail! 2 Farewell! —*n.* The salutation *ave.* [<L, hail or farewell]

ave. avenue.

A·ve Ma·ri·a (ä'vā mə·rē'ə, ä'vē) 1 A prayer to the Virgin Mary. 2 Hail Mary, the first words of this prayer. [<Med. L, hail, Mary]

a·venge (ə·venj') *v.t.* **a·venged, a·veng·ing** 1 To take vengeance or exact punishment for (a crime, insult, etc.) or on behalf of (a person or persons). —*v.i.* 2 To take vengeance. [<L *ad-* to + *vindicare* avenge] —**a·veng'er** *n.*

av·e·nue (av'ə·nyōō) *n.* 1 A broad street. 2 A way of approach, as to an estate, often bordered with trees or statues. 3 A way of attaining something. [<F *avenir* to approach]

a·ver (ə·vûr') *v.t.* **a·verred, a·ver·ring** 1 To declare confidently as fact; affirm. 2 *Law* To assert formally; prove or justify (a plea). [<L *ad-* to + *verus* true] —**a·ver'ment** *n.* —**a·ver'ra·ble** *adj.*

av·er·age (av'rij, av'ər·ij) *n.* 1 *Math.* A number representing a set of numbers of which it is a function, esp. an arithmetic mean. 2 A symbol, ratio, etc., representing such a number: a B *average.* 3 The normal or ordinary quality, amount, kind, degree, etc.: This meal is above *average.* 4 In marine law: **a** The loss arising by damage to a ship or cargo. **b** The proportion of such loss falling to a single person in an equitable distribution among those interested. —*adj.* 1 Obtained by calculating the mean of several. 2 Normal; ordinary. —*v.* **·aged, ·ag·ing** *v.t.* 1 To fix or calculate as the mean. 2 To amount to or obtain an average of: He *averages* three dollars profit every hour. 3 To apportion on the average. —*v.i.* 4 To be or amount to an average. 5 To sell or purchase more of something so as to increase the average price. [<OF *avarie* damage to a ship or its cargo] —**av'er·age·ly** *adv.*

a·verse (ə·vûrs') *adj.* Opposed; unfavorable; reluctant: with *to.* [<L *avertere* turn aside] —**a·verse'ly** *adv.* —**a·verse'ness** *n.*

a·ver·sion (ə·vûr′zhən, -shən) *n.* **1** Extreme dislike; repugnance; antipathy. **2** A cause of extreme dislike. —**a·ver′sive** *adj.*

a·vert (ə·vûrt′) *v.t.* **1** To turn or direct away: to *avert* one's eyes. **2** To prevent or ward off, as a danger. [< L *avertere* turn aside] —**a·vert′ed·ly** *adv.* —**a·vert′i·ble, a·vert′a·ble** *adj.*

A·ves·ta (ə·ves′tə) *n.* The sacred writings of Zoroastrianism, written in an ancient Iranian language. **A·ves·tan** (ə·ves′tən).

avg. average.

a·vi·ar·y (ā′vē·er′ē) *n. pl.* **·ar·ies** An enclosure or large cage for birds. [< L *avis* bird] —**a·vi·ar·ist** (ā′vē·er′ist, -ər·ist) *n.*

a·vi·a·tion (ā′vē·ā′shən, av′ē-) *n.* The operation or production of heavier-than-air aircraft. [< L *avis* bird]

a·vi·a·tor (ā′vē·ā′tər, av′ē-) *n.* One who flies airplanes or similar aircraft; a pilot. —**a′vi·a′tress** (-tris) or **a·vi·a·trix** (ā′vē·ā′triks, av′ē-) *n. Fem.*

av·id (av′id) *adj.* Having or showing an intense desire or interest. [< L *avere* crave] —**av′id·ly** *adv.* —**av′id·ness, a·vid·i·ty** (ə·vid′ə·tē) *n.* —**Syn.** desirous, greedy, eager, anxious.

a·vi·on·ics (ā·vē·on′iks, av′ē-) *n. pl. (construed as sing.)* The study of the applications of electricity and electronics to aviation. [< AVI(ATION ELECTR)ONICS] —**a′vi·on′ic** *adj.*

av·o·ca·do (av′ə·kä′dō, ä′və-) *n. pl.* **·dos** **1** A pear-shaped, edible fruit with a green skin and buttery flesh; alligator pear. **2** The tree bearing this fruit. [< Nahatl *ahuacatl*]

av·o·ca·tion (av′ə·kā′shən) *n.* An occupation or hobby that one has in addition to one's regular work or profession. [< L *ab-* away + *vocare* to call]

av·o·cet (av′ə·set) *n.* A long-legged shore bird having webbed feet and slender up-curved bill. Also **av′o·set.** [< Ital. *avocetta*]

a·void (ə·void′) *v.t.* **1** To keep away or at a distance from; shun; evade. **2** *Law* To make void. [< L *ex-* out + *viduare* empty, deprive] —**a·void′a·ble** *adj.* —**a·void′a·bly** *adv.* —**a·void′ance, a·void′er** *n.*

av·oir·du·pois (av′ər·də·poiz′) *n.* **1** Avoirdupois weight. **2** *Informal.* Weight; corpulence. —*adj.* Measured or expressed in avoirdupois weight. [< OF *avoir de pois* goods of (i.e., sold by) weight]

avoirdupois weight The ordinary U.S. system of weight in which 16 ounces make a pound. • See MEASURE.

a·vouch (ə·vouch′) *v.t.* **1** To vouch for; guarantee. **2** To affirm positively; proclaim. **3** To acknowledge; avow. [< L *advocare* call to one's aid, summon]

a·vow (ə·vou′) *v.t.* To declare openly, as facts; own; acknowledge. [< L *advocare* summon] —**a·vow′a·ble** *adj.* —**a·vow′a·bly** *adv.* —**a·vow′er** *n.*

a·vow·al (ə·vou′əl) *n.* Frank admission or acknowledgment.

a·vowed (ə·voud′) *adj.* Openly acknowledged; plainly declared. —**a·vow·ed·ly** (ə·vou′id·lē) *adj.* —**a·vow′ed·ness** *n.*

a·vun·cu·lar (ə·vung′kyə·lər) *adj.* Of or pertaining to an uncle. [< L *avunculus* maternal uncle]

a·wait (ə·wāt′) *v.t.* **1** To wait for; expect. **2** To be ready or in store for. [< OF *awaitier* watch for]

a·wake (ə·wāk′) *adj.* **1** Not asleep. **2** Alert; vigilant. —*v.* **a·woke** (or **a·waked**), **a·waked** (or **a·woke** or **a·wok·en**), **a·wak·ing** *v.t.* **1** To arouse from sleep. **2** To stir up; excite. —*v.i.* **3** To cease to sleep; become awake. **4** To become alert or aroused. **5** To become aware of something: with *to.* [< OE *ā-* A-² + *wacian* watch]

a·wak·en (ə·wā′kən) *v.t. & v.i.* To awake. [< OE *onwæcnan* arise] —**a·wak′en·er** *n.*

a·wak·en·ing (ə·wā′kən·ing) *adj.* Stirring; exciting. —*n.* **1** The act of waking. **2** An arousing of attention or interest.

a·ward (ə·wôrd′) *v.t.* **1** To adjudge as due, as by legal decisions. **2** To bestow as the result of a contest or examination, as a prize. —*n.* **1** A decision, as by a judge or arbitrator. **2** That which is awarded. [< OF *es-* out + *guarder* watch] —**a·ward′a·ble** *adj.* —**a·ward′er** *n.*

a·ware (ə·wâr′) *adj.* Knowing or conscious of something; cognizant. [< OE *gewær* watchful] —**a·ware′ness** *n.*

a·wash (ə·wosh′, ə·wôsh′) *adv. & adj.* **1** Level with or just above the surface of the water. **2** Tossed or washed about by waves. **3** Covered or flooded with water.

a·way (ə·wā′) *adv.* **1** From a given place; off. **2** Far; at or to a distance. **3** In another direction; aside. **4** Out of existence; at an end. **5** On and on continuously: to peg *away* at a task. **6** From one's keeping, attention, or possession. **7** At once, without hesitation: Fire *away!* —**do** (or **make**) **away with** **1** To get rid of. **2** To kill. —*adj.* **1** Absent. **2** At a distance. —*interj.* Begone! [< OE *on weg* on (one's) way]

awe (ô) *n.* **1** Wonder and veneration somewhat mixed with fear. **2** Overwhelming admiration or appreciation. —*v.t.* **awed, aw·ing** or **awe·ing** to fill with awe. [< ON *agi* fear]

a·weigh (ə·wā′) *adv. Naut.* Hanging with the flukes just clear of the bottom: said of an anchor. [< A- (on) + WEIGH]

awe·some (ô′səm) *adj.* **1** Inspiring awe: an *awesome* display of strength. **2** Characterized by or expressing awe. —**awe′some·ly** *adv.* —**awe′some·ness** *n.*

awe·struck (ô′struk′) *adj.* Filled with awe. Also **awe·strick·en** (ô′strik′ən).

aw·ful (ô′fəl) *adj.* **1** Exceedingly bad, unpleasant, etc.: an *awful* man. **2** Terrible; dreadful: an *awful* accident. **3** Great: an *awful* egotist. **4** Very bad, as in quality, performance, taste, etc.: an *awful* play. —**aw′ful·ness** *n.*

aw·ful·ly (ô′fəl·ē) *adv.* **1** In an awful manner. **2** (ô′flē) *Informal* Excessively; very.

a·while (ə·ʰwīl′) *adv.* For a brief time. • Since the word "for" is part of the meaning of *awhile,* it is redundant to say or write "He will be here for awhile." The correct sentence would be either "He will be here awhile" or "He will be here for a while."

awk·ward (ôk′wərd) *adj.* **1** Ungraceful in bearing. **2** Unskillful in action; bungling. **3** Embarrassing or perplexing. **4** Difficult or dangerous to deal with, as an opponent. **5** Inconvenient for use; uncomfortable. [< ON *afug* turned the wrong way + -WARD] —**awk′ward·ly** *adv.* —**awk′ward·ness** *n.* —**Syn. 1** ungainly, gawky. **2** clumsy, inept.

awl (ôl) *n.* A pointed instrument for making small holes. [< OE *al, awel*]

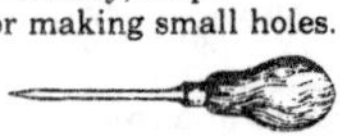

Awl

awn (ôn) *n.* A bristlelike appendage of certain grasses; beard, as of barley, etc. [< ON *ögn* chaff]

awn·ing (ô′ning) *n.* A rooflike cover, as of canvas, for protection from sun or rain. [?]

a·woke (ə·wōk′) *p.t.* of AWAKE.

a·wok·en (ə·wō′kən) A *p.p.* of AWAKE.

AWOL *(as an acronym pronounced* ā′wôl) *Mil.* Absent or absence without leave. Also **awol, A.W.O.L., a.w.o.l.**

a·wry (ə·rī′) *adj. & adv.* **1** Toward one side; crooked; askew. **2** Out of the right course; erroneously [< A- (on) + WRY]

ax (aks) *n. pl.* **ax·es** A tool with a bladed head mounted on a handle, used for chopping, hewing, etc. —**get the ax** *Informal* **1** To be beheaded. **2** To be fired from one's job. —**have an ax to grind** *Informal* To have a private purpose or interest to promote. —*v.t.* **1** To cut or shape with an ax. **2** *Informal* To dismiss or delete. Also **axe.** [OE *æx, eax*]

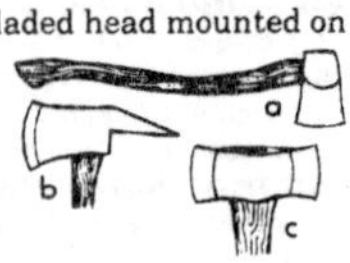

Axes
a. common.
b. fireman's.
c. double-bitted.

ax·es¹ (ak′sēz) *n.* Plural of AXIS.

ax·es² (ak′siz) *n.* Plural of AX.

ax·i·al (ak′sē·əl) *adj.* **1** Of, pertaining to, or constituting an axis. **2** On or along an axis.

ax·il (ak′sil) *n.* The angle between the upper side of a leafstalk, branch, etc., and a stem or branch. [< L *axilla* armpit] —**ax′il·lar′y** *adj.*

ax·il·la (ak·sil′ə) *n. pl.* **ax·il·las** or **ax·il·lae** (-sil′ē) The armpit [< L] —**ax′il·lar′y** *adj.*

ax·i·om (ak′sē·əm) *n.* **1** A self-evident or universally recognized truth. **2** An established principle or rule. **3** *Logic & Math.* A proposition assumed to be true. [< Gk. *axiōma* a thing thought worthy]

ax·i·o·mat·ic (ak′sē·ə·mat′ik) *adj.* **1** Of, pertaining to, or resembling an axiom. **2** Full of axioms; aphoristic, as a literary style. Also **ax′i·o·mat′i·cal.** —**ax′i·o·mat′i·cal·ly** *adv.*

ax·is (ak′sis) *n. pl.* **ax·es** (ak′sēz) **1** A line around which a turning body rotates or may be supposed to rotate. **2** *Geom.* **a** A straight line through the center of a figure, esp. one with respect to which the figure is symmetrical. **b** A line along which distances are measured or to which positions are referred. **3** A real or imaginary central line about which things or parts are symmetrically arranged.

4 An affiliation or coalition of two or more nations to promote mutual interest, cooperation, etc. **—the Axis** In World War II, the coalition between Germany, Italy, and later Japan and other countries that opposed the United Nations. [<L, axis, axle]

ax·le (ak'səl) *n.* **1** A shaft or spindle on which a wheel is mounted and on or with which it turns. **2** AXLETREE. [<ON *öxull*] **—ax'led** *adj.*

ax·le·tree (ak'səl·trē) *n.* A crossbar that connects the opposite wheels of an automobile, wagon, etc., and on which the wheels revolve.

ax·man (aks'man) *n. pl.* **·men** (-mən) One who wields an ax; a woodman. Also **axe'man.**

ax·on (ak'sän) *n.* A nerve-cell structure that usu. conducts impulses away from the cell body.

a·yah (ä'yə) *n.* India, a native nurse or lady's maid. [<Hind. *āya* <Pg. *aia* nurse]

a·ya·tol·lah (ä'yə·tō'lə) *n.* Title of the highest-ranking teacher of religion in Iran. [<Ar., sign of God]

aye (ī) *n.* An affirmative vote or voter. *—adv.* Yes; yea. Also **ay.** [?]

AZ Arizona (P.O. abbr.).

a·zal·ea (ə·zāl'yə) *n.* Any of various usu. deciduous shrubs with showy flowers, related to rhododendrons. [<Gk. *azein* parch, from its preference for dry soil]

az·i·muth (az'ə·məth) *n.* Direction to or toward an object, measured as an angle in the horizontal plane. [<Ar. *as-sumūt* the ways] **—az·i·muth·al** (az'ə·muth'əl) *adj.* **—az'i·muth'al·ly** *adv.*

az·o (az'ō, ā'zō) *adj.* Containing nitrogen. [<F *azote* nitrogen]

Az·tec (az'tek) *n.* **1** A member of a tribe of Mexican Indians, founders of an empire at its height when Cortés invaded the country in 1519. **2** NAHUATL. *—adj.* Of or pertaining to the Aztec Indians, their language, culture, or empire: also **Az·tec·an** (az'tek·ən).

az·ure (azh'ər, ā'zhər) *adj.* Sky-blue. *—n.* **1** A clear sky-blue color or pigment. **2** The sky. [<Ar. *al-lāzward* lapis lazuli]

az·u·rite (azh'ə·rīt) *n.* A blue, glassy, mineral carbonate of copper sometimes used as a gem.

az·y·gous (az'i·gəs, ā·zī'gəs) *adj.* Having no mate; not paired. [<Gk. *azygos* unpaired]

B

B, b (bē) *n. pl.* **B's, b's, Bs, bs** (bēz) **1** The second letter of the English alphabet. **2** Any spoken sound representing the letter *B* or *b.* **3** Second in a series, class, or order. **4** Something shaped like a B. **5** *Music* The seventh tone in the diatonic scale of C. *—adj.* **1** Shaped like a B. **2** Second-class.

B *chess* bishop; boron.

B. bacillus; Bible; British; Brotherhood.

B., b. bachelor; base; bass; basso; bat; battery; book; born.

b, b. base; base hit; baseman.

B.A. Bachelor of Arts; British Academy.

Ba barium.

baa (bä, ba) *v.i.* **baaed, baa·ing** To bleat, as a sheep. *— n.* The bleat, as of a sheep. [Imit.]

Ba·al (bā'əl, bāl) *n. pl.* **Ba·al·im** (bā'əl·im) **1** Any of several ancient Semitic gods of fertility. **2** An idol or false god. [<Heb. *Ba'al* lord] **—Ba'al·ish** *adj.*

Bab·bitt metal (bab'it) A soft, white, antifriction alloy of tin, copper, and antimony, used in making bearings. [after Isaac *Babbitt*, 1799–1862, U.S. metallurgist]

bab·ble (bab'əl) *n.* **1** A murmuring sound, as of a stream. **2** Prattle, as of an infant. **3** A confusion of sounds, as of a crowd. *—v.* **bab·bled, bab·bling** *—v.t.* **1** To utter unintelligibly. **2** To blurt out thoughtlessly *—v.i.* **3** To utter inarticulate or meaningless noises. **4** To murmur, as a brook. **5** To talk unwisely or foolishly. [ME *babelen*] **—bab'bler** *n.*

babe (bāb) *n.* **1** A baby. **2** *Informal* One lacking worldly experience. **3** *Slang* A girl. [ME]

ba·bel (bā'bəl, bab'əl) *n.* A confusion of many voices or languages; tumult. Also **Ba'bel.**

Ba·bel (bā'bəl, bab'əl) *n.* In the Bible, an ancient city now thought to be Babylon. **—Tower of Babel** A tower built in Babel and intended to reach to heaven. God punished such presumption by preventing the workers from understanding each other and from completing the tower. *Gen.* 11:1–9.

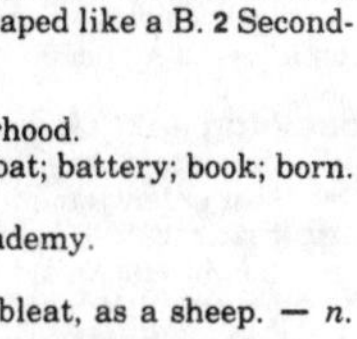

Baboon

ba·bies' breath BABY'S BREATH.

ba·boon (ba·bōōn') *n.* A large, terrestrial monkey of Africa and Asia having large bare callosities on the buttocks, and usu. a short tail. [<OF *babuin*] **—ba·boon'ish** *adj.*

ba·bush·ka (bə·bōōsh'kə) *n.* A woman's scarf for the head. [<Russ., grandmother]

ba·by (bā'bē) *n. pl.* **ba·bies** **1** An infant. **2** The youngest or smallest member of a family or group. **3** A very timid person. **4** *Slang* **a** A girl or woman. **b** Anything one likes or is interested in. *—adj.* **1** For a baby. **2** Childish; infantile. **3** Small; diminutive. *—v.t.* **ba·bied, ba·by·ing** To treat or handle with care or affection. **—ba'by·hood** *n.* **—ba'by·like'** *adj.* [ME]

baby carriage A padded carriage for a baby, often with a collapsible top.

ba·by·ish (bā'bē·ish) *adj.* Childish; infantile **—ba'by·ish·ly** *adv.* **—ba'by·ish·ness** *n.*

Bab·y·lon (bab'ə·lən, -lon) **1** An ancient city of Mesopotamia, capital of Babylonia and celebrated as a seat of wealth, luxury, and vice. **2** Any city or place of great wealth, luxury, or vice.

Bab·y·lo·ni·a (bab'ə·lō'nē·ə) An ancient empire (*circa* 2100–538 B.C.) of sw Asia; capital, Babylon. **—Bab'y·lo'ni·an** *adj., n.*

baby's breath **1** A tall plant with clusters of small, white or pink, fragrant flowers. **2** Any of several similar plants.

ba·by-sit (bā'bē·sit') *v.* **-sat, sit·ting** To act as a baby sitter.

baby sitter A person employed to take care of young children during the hours when the parents are absent.

baby tooth Any of the first, temporary set of teeth in children, normally 20 in all; milk tooth.

bac·ca·lau·re·ate (bak'ə·lôr'ē·it) *n.* **1** The degree of bachelor of arts, bachelor of science, etc. **2** An address to a graduating class at commencement; also **baccalaureate sermon.** [<Med. L *baccalaurius* a squire]

bac·ca·rat (bak'ə·rä', bak'ə·rä) *n.* A card game of chance. Also **bac'ca·ra'.** [<F *baccara*]

Bac·chae (bäk'ē, -ī) *n. pl.* The female followers or priestesses of the god Bacchue; BACCHANAL (def. 1).

bac·cha·nal (bak'ə·nəl) *n.* **1** A votary of Bacchus. **2** A drunken reveler. **3** *pl.* BACCHANALIA. *—adj.* Bacchanalian. [<L *bacchanalis* of Bacchus]

bac·cha·na·li·a (bak'ə·nā'lē·ə, -nāl'yə) *n. pl.* **1** Drunken revelries; orgies. **2** *Usu. cap.* An ancient Roman festival in honor of Bacchus. **—bac'cha·na'li·an** *adj., n.*

Bac·chus (bak'əs) *Rom. Myth.* The god of wine and revelry.

bach·e·lor (bach'ələr, bach'lər) *n.* **1** An unmarried man. **2** One who has a baccalaureate degree. *—adj.* Of or for a bachelor. [<Med. L *baccalaurius* a squire] **—bach'e·lor·hood', bach'e·lor·ship'** *n.*

Bachelor of Arts (of Science, of Engineering, etc.) **1** A degree given by a college or university to a person who has completed a four-year course or its equivalent in one of the (specified) academic disciplines. **2** A person who has received this degree.

bachelor's button Any of several plants with composite flowers having a flasklike involucre, esp. the cornflower.

ba·cil·lus (bə·sil′əs) *n. pl.* **ba·cil·li** (-sil′ī) **1** Any of a genus of aerobic, rod-shaped, spore-forming bacteria often growing linked together. **2** Any rod-shaped bacterium. [<L *baculum* rod] **—ba·cil′lar, bac·il·lar·y** (bas′ə·ler′ē) *adj.* • See BACTERIUM.

bac·i·tra·cin (bas′ə·trā′sin) *n.* An antibiotic produced from a bacillus, used in the treatment of some bacterial skin infections.

back[1] (bak) *n.* **1** The part of the body nearest the spine; in man the hinder, in quadrupeds the upper part, extending from the neck to the base of the spine. **2** The backbone or spine. **3** A part touching or supporting the back: the *back* of a dress. **4** The rear or posterior part: the *back* of the car. **5** The part opposite in position to the part most used, seen, etc.: the *back* of a knife; the *back* of the hand. **6** The part of the pages of a book stitched or glued together; also, the part of the binding around this part. **7** In certain sports: **a** A position behind the front line of players. **b** A player in this position. **8** Physical strength or energy. **—at one's back** Following closely. **—behind one's back 1** Secretly. **2** Treacherously. **—be (flat) on one's back** To be helplessly ill. **—in back of** Behind; to the rear of. **—turn one's back on 1** To turn away from, as in contempt or criticism. **2** To ignore or refuse to help. **3** To renounce. **—with one's back to the wall** Cornered. *—v.t.* **1** To cause to move or go backwards or to the rear: often with *up*. **2** To form the back of. **3** To strengthen at the back. **4** To support, assist, or uphold: often with *up*. **5** To bet on the success or chances of. *—v.i.* **6** To move or go backward: often with *up*. **7** To have the back facing in a certain direction: It *backs* onto the woods. **8** To shift counterclockwise: said of the wind. **—back down** To withdraw from a position, abandon a claim, etc. **—back off** To retreat, as from contact. **—back out (of)** To withdraw from or refuse to carry out an engagement, contest, etc. *—adj.* **1** In the rear; behind: a *back* room. **2** Distant; remote: the *back* country. **3** Of or for a previous date. **4** In arrears; overdue, as a debt. **5** In a backward direction: a *back* thrust. [<OE *bæc* back]

back[2] (bak) *adv.* **1** At, to, or toward the rear. **2** In, to, or toward a former place, condition, etc. **3** To or towards times past. **4** In return or retort: to talk *back*. **5** In reserve or concealment: to keep something *back* [<ABACK]

back·bench·er (bak′ben′chər) *n.* A new, inexperienced, or unimportant member of a legislature, esp. of the British House of Commons or the Canadian Parliament.

back·bite (bak′bīt) *v.t. & v.i.* **·bit, ·bit·ten** (or *Informal* **·bit**), **·bit·ing** To revile behind one's back; slander. **—back′bit′er, back′bit′ing** *n.*

back·blocks (bak′bloks′) *n.pl. Austral.* Inland farming areas.

back·bone (bak′bōn′) *n.* **1** The spine or vertebral column. **2** Any main support. **3** Firmness; resolution; courage.

back·break·ing (bak′brā′king) *adj.* Physically exhausting; fatiguing.

back·door (bak′dôr′, -dōr′) *adj.* Underhand; indirect; secret.

back·drop (bak′drop′) *n.* The curtain hung at the rear of a stage, often painted to represent a scene. Also **back cloth.**

backed (bakt) *adj.* Having a specified kind of back or backing: used in combination: *low-backed; steel-backed.*

back·er (bak′ər) *n.* **1** One who supports with money; a patron. **2** One who bets on a contestant.

back·field (bak′fēld′) *n.* In football, the players behind the line of scrimmage, including the quarterback.

back·fill (bak′fil′) *n.* Soil and other material used to refill an excavation. *—v.t.* To refill (an excavation).

back·fire (bak′fīr′) *n.* **1** A fire built to check an advancing forest or prairie fire by creating a barren area in its path. **2** Premature explosion in the cylinder of an internal-combustion engine. *—v.i.* **·fired, ·fir·ing 1** To set or use a backfire. **2** To explode in a backfire. **3** To have an unexpected and unfavorable result or conclusion.

back formation *Ling.* **1** The creation, by analogy, of one word from another in cases where the original word would seem to be the derivative, as *emote* from *emotion.* **2** A word so formed.

back·gam·mon (bak′gam′ən, bak′gam′ən) *n.* **1** A board game for two players, the moves of the pieces being determined by dice throws. **2** A victory in this game. *—v.t.* To win a backgammon from. [ME *back gamen* back game]

back·ground (bak′ground′) *n.* **1** That part in a picture which forms a setting for the main elements. **2** The surface, area, object, etc. that is behind something, usu. of a contrasting color, texture, or shape. **3** A subordinate or obscure place or position. **4** The whole of one's experiences, training, cultural environment, etc. **5** Music or sound effects accompanying a motion picture, play, etc. **6** The events leading up to or causing a situation. **7** Information explaining a situation, person, etc.

back·hand (bak′hand′) *adj.* Backhanded. *—n.* **1** Handwriting that slopes toward the left. **2** A stroke, as in tennis, made with the back of the hand moving forward. *—adv.* With a backhand.

back·hand·ed (bak′han′did) *adj.* **1** In sports: **a** Made with the back of the hand moving forward. **b** Made with the back of the hand turned toward the body, as a catch in baseball. **2** Having elements of criticism and sarcasm: a *backhanded* compliment. *—adv.* With a backhand. **—back′hand′ed·ly** *adv.* **—back′hand′ed·ness** *n.*

back·ing (bak′ing) *n.* **1** Support or assistance given to a person, cause, etc. **2** Supporters collectively. **3** Something added at the back for extra support or strength. **4** *Informal* Musical accompaniment.

back·lash (bak′lash′) *n.* **1** A sudden, usu. violent backward movement. **2** In angling, a snarl or tangle of the line on a reel. **3** A sudden, violent reaction, as of public opinion.

back·log (bak′lôg, -log′) *n. U.S.* **1** A large log at the back of a fireplace. **2** Any reserve or accumulation, as of funds, business orders, etc.

back number 1 An old issue of a magazine or newspaper. **2** *Informal* An old-fashioned person or thing.

back·pack (bak′pak′) *n.* A pack or knapsack carried on the back, as by campers. *—v.t. & v.i.* To carry (equipment) in a backpack. **—back′pack′er** *n.*

back seat Status or position of little or no importance.

back-seat driver (bak′sēt′) A passenger in a vehicle who, unasked, offers advice about driving.

back·side (bak′sīd′) *n.* **1** The back part. **2** The rump or buttocks.

back·slide (bak′slīd′) *v.i.* **·slid, ·slid** or **slid·den, ·slid·ing** To return to former ways or opinions after reformation or conversion; relapse. **—back′slid′er** *n.*

back·spin (bak′spin′) *n.* Reverse rotation of a round object that is moving forward, causing it to rebound.

back·stage (bak′stāj′) *adv.* In or toward the portion of a theater behind the stage, including the wings, dressing rooms, etc. *—n.* The back portion of the stage. *—adj.* (bak′stāj′) Placed backstage, so as to be hidden.

back·stop (bak′stop′) *n.* A fence or screen to stop the ball from going too far in certain games, as baseball, tennis, etc.

back·stretch (bak′strech′) *n.* That part of a race course farthest from the spectators and opposite the homestretch.

back·stroke (bak′strōk′) *n.* In swimming, a stroke executed while on one's back.

back talk Impudent answering back.

back·track (bak′trak′) *v.i.* **1** To retrace one's steps. **2** To withdraw from a position.

back·up (bak′up′) *adj.* **1** Held in readiness for use as a substitute: a *backup* plan. **2** Supporting. *—n.* A substitute.

back·ward (bak′wərd) *adj.* **1** Turned to the back or rear; reversed. **2** Done the reverse way. **3** Shy; bashful. **4** Slow in growth or development; retarded. *—adv.* **1** In the direction of the back; to the rear. **2** Into time past; toward earlier times. **3** With the back foremost. **4** In reverse order. **5** From better to worse. **—back′ward·ly** *adv.* **—back′ward·ness** *n.*

back·wards (bak′wardz) *adv.* Backward.

back·wash (bak′wosh′, -wôsh) *n.* **1** The water moved

backward, as by a boat, oars, etc. 2 A backward current of air, as set up by aircraft propellers. 3 An aftermath.

back·wa·ter (bak′wô′tər, -wot′ər) *n.* 1 Water set, thrown, or held back, as by a dam. 2 Any place or condition regarded as stagnant, backward, etc.

back·woods (bak′wŏŏdz′) *n.pl.* Remote, heavily wooded, or sparsely settled districts. —*adj.* In, from, or like the backwoods: also **back′wood′.** —**back′woods′man** *n.*

ba·con (bā′kən) *n.* The salted and dried or smoked back and sides of the hog. —**bring home the bacon** *Informal* 1 To provide a living. 2 To succeed. [< OF]

bact., bacteriol. bacteriologist; bacteriology.

bac·te·ri·a (bak·tir′ē·ə) Plural of BACTERIUM.

bac·te·ri·cide (bak·tir′ə·sīd) *n.* An agent destructive of bacteria. —**bac·te′ri·ci′dal** *adj.*

bac·te·ri·ol·o·gy (bak·tir′ē·ol′ə·jē) *n.* The branch of science that deals with bacteria. —**bac·te·ri·o·log·i·cal** (bak·tir′ē·ə·loj′i·kəl) *adj.* —**bac·te′ri·o·log′i·cal·ly** *adv.* —**bac·te′ri·ol′o·gist** *n.*

bac·te·ri·o·phage (bak·tir′ē·ə·fāj′) *n.* A virus having the power to destroy bacteria. [< BACTERIA + Gk. *phagein* eat]

bac·te·ri·um (bak·tir′ē·əm) *n. pl.* **·te·ri·a** (-tir′·ē·ə) One of numerous unicellular microorganisms that exhibit both plant and animal characteristics, and range from the harmless and beneficial to the intensely virulent and lethal. [< Gk. *baktērion,* dim. of *baktron* staff, stick] —**bac·te′ri·al** *adj.* —**bac·te′ri·al·ly** *adv.*

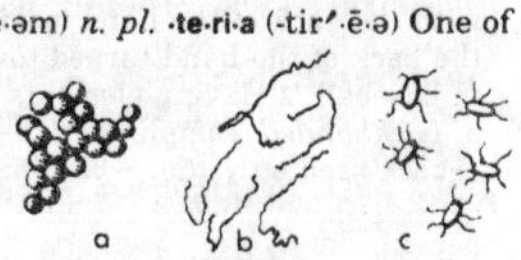

Bacteria
a. staphylococcus. b. species of spirochete. c. bacillus typhosus.

bad (bad) *adj.* **worse, worst** 1 Not good in any manner or degree. 2 Inadequate or defective: *bad* lighting. 3 Lacking skill or proficiency: a *bad* musician. 4 Disagreeable; unpleasant: a *bad* odor; *bad* manners. 5 Rotten; decomposed. 6 Incorrect: *bad* grammar. 7 Immoral; corrupt; wicked. 8 Naughty: a *bad* child. 9 Injurious; harmful: a *bad* habit. 10 Severe: a *bad* sprain. 11 Sick; in poor health. 12 Sorry: to feel *bad* about it. —**in bad** *Informal* 1 In difficulty. 2 In disfavor. —**not bad** Rather good: also **not half bad, not so bad.** —*n.* 1 That which is bad. 2 Those who are bad. 3 A bad state or condition; wickedness. —*adv. Informal* Badly. [ME *badde*] —**bad′ness** *n.* —**Syn.** *adj.* 2 imperfect, unsatisfactory. 3 inferior, mediocre. 4 offensive, displeasing, nasty, disgusting, revolting, repulsive. 7 evil, vile, sinful. 8 mischievous, disobedient, troublesome. 9 hurtful, detrimental. • *Bad* is an adjective and *badly* an adverb. Their use is confusing only when they come after one of the linking verbs, as feel, seem, appear, look, etc. It is correct to say *I feel bad* (ill), because *bad* describes or refers back to the pronoun *I* and not to the verb. *I feel badly* is correct only if one's sense of touch is defective. In like manner, it is correct to say *That egg smells bad; This meat tastes bad,* because *bad* is obviously describing the noun in each case and not the verb. However, because *badly* is so often, although incorrectly, used in such instances, it is becoming somewhat acceptable, esp. in casual, informal speech.

bade (bad) *p.t.* of BID.

badge (baj) *n.* 1 A token, decoration, or emblem of office, rank, attainment, etc. 2 Any distinguishing mark or symbol. —*v.t.* **badged, badg·ing** To decorate or provide with a badge. [ME *bagge*]

badg·er (baj′ər) *n.* 1 A small, burrowing, nocturnal, carnivorous mammal, with a broad body, short legs, and long clawed forefeet. 2 The fur of a badger. —*v.t.* To worry persistently; nag. [?]

bad·i·nage (bad′ə·näzh′, bad′ə·nij) *n.* Playful raillery; banter. —*v.t.* **·naged, ·nag·ing** To tease with badinage. [< F *badin* silly, jesting]

bad·lands (bad′landz′) *n.* A barren area characterized by numerous ridges, peaks, and mesas cut into unusual shapes by erosion.

Bad·lands (bad′landz′) *n.* The badlands of western U.S., esp. in sw South Dakota. Also **Bad Lands.**

bad·ly (bad′lē) *adv.* 1 Improperly; imperfectly; incorrectly. 2 Unpleasantly. 3 Harmfully. 4 *Informal* Very much; greatly. • See BAD.

bad·min·ton (bad′min·tən) *n.* A game played by batting a shuttlecock back and forth over a high narrow net with a light racket. [< *Badminton,* an estate in England.]

bad-tem·pered (bad′tem′pərd) *adj.* Irritable.

baf·fle (baf′əl) *v.* **baf·fled, baf·fling** *v.t.* 1 To confuse or perplex. 2 To thwart or frustrate; defeat. 3 To block with or as with a baffle. —*v.i.* 4 To struggle to no avail. —*n.* A plate or partition acting as a barrier to sound, motion of a fluid, etc. —**baf′fling** *adj.* —**baf′fling·ly** *adv.* —**baf′fle·ment, baf′fler** *n.*

bag (bag) *n.* 1 A flexible container open at one end and made of paper, plastic, etc.; a sack or pouch. 2 A purse. 3 A suitcase. 4 A bagful. 5 The amount of game caught or killed. 6 A bulging, wrinkled, or puffy condition: *bags* under one's eyes. 7 An animal sac or udder. 8 *Slang* An interest, skill, profession, etc.: What's your *bag?* 9 In baseball, a base. —**a mixed bag** *Informal* A heterogeneous collection. —**be in the bag** *Informal* To be assured of a success. —**be left holding the bag** *Informal* To be left to assume full responsibility. —*v.* **bagged, bag·ging** *v.t.* 1 To put into a bag or bags. 2 To cause to bulge like a bag. 3 To capture or kill, as game. —*v.i.* 4 To bulge or swell like a bag. 5 To hang loosely. [< ON *baggi* pack, bundle]

ba·gasse (bə·gas′) *n.* The dry refuse of sugarcane after the juice has been expressed. Also **ba·gass′.** [< Sp. *bagazo* refuse, dregs]

bag·a·telle (bag′ə·tel′) *n.* 1 A trifle. 2 A game similar to billiards. [< Ital. *bagatella*]

ba·gel (bā′gəl) *n.* A doughnut-shaped hard-baked roll of unsalted yeast dough. [< Yiddish]

bag·ful (bag′fŏŏl′) *n. pl.* **·fuls** The amount a bag will hold.

bag·gage (bag′ij) *n.* 1 The trunks, packages, etc., of a traveler. 2 *Archaic* A prostitute. [< OF *bague* bundle]

bag·ging (bag′ing) *n.* A coarse material for making bags.

bag·gy (bag′ē) *adj.* **bag·gi·er, bag·gi·est** 1 Loose or ill-fitting. 2 Wrinkled. 3 Puffy. —**bag′gi·ly** *adv.* —**bag′gi·ness** *n.*

bag·pipe (bag′pīp′) *n. Often pl.* A reed musical instrument in which the several drone pipes and the melody pipe with its finger stops are supplied with air from a windbag filled by the player's breath. —**bag′pip′er** *n.*

Bagpipe

ba·guette (bag·get′) *n.* 1 A gem cut in long, narrow, rectangular form. 2 This form. Also **ba·guet′.** [< Ital. *bacchetta,* dim. of *bacchio* staff, stick]

bah (bä, ba) *interj.* A scornful exclamation.

Bah·rain (bä·rān′) *n.* A sheikdom under British protection, located on an archipelago in the Persian Gulf, 213 sq. mi., cap. Manama. Also **Bah·rein′, Bah·rayn′.** • See map at SAUDI ARABIA.

bail[1] (bāl) *n.* A scoop or bucket for dipping out fluids, as from a boat. —*v.t. & v.i.* 1 To dip (water), as from a boat. 2 To clear (a boat) of water by dipping out. —**bail out** To parachute from an aircraft. [< OF *baille*] —**bail′er** *n.*

bail[2] (bāl) *n.* In cricket, one of the crosspieces of the wicket. [< OF *baile* barrier]

bail[3] (bāl) *Law n.* 1 Money or security given to a court to secure the release of an arrested person on the proviso that the person will be present later to stand trial. 2 Such a release. 3 The person or persons who give such money or security. —*v.t.* 1 To release (an arrested person) on bail: often with *out.* 2 To obtain the release of (an arrested person) on bail: usu. with *out.* 3 To help out of any difficulty: usu. with *out.* —**go** (or **stand**) **bail for** To provide bail for. [< OF *baillier* guard, carry] —**bail′a·ble** *adj.*

bail[4] (bāl) *n.* 1 The semicircular handle of a pail, kettle, etc. 2 An arch-shaped support, as for a canopy. [ME *baile*]

bai·liff (bā′lif) *n.* 1 An officer of court having custody of prisoners under arraignment. 2 A sheriff's deputy. 3 A custodian of an estate; overseer. 4 *Brit.* A subordinate magistrate. [< L *bajulus* porter, manager]

bai·li·wick (bā′lə·wik) *n.* 1 The office, jurisdiction, or district of a bailiff. 2 One's own special place. [< OF *baillif* bailiff + OE *wic* village]

bails·man (bālz′mən) *n. pl.* **·men** (-mən) One who provides bail for another.

bait (bāt) *n.* 1 Food or other lure in a trap, on a hook, etc. 2 Any allurement or enticement. —*v.t.* 1 To put food or some other lure on or in. 2 To torment, as by setting dogs upon, for sport: to *bait* a bear. 3 To harass; heckle. 4 To lure; entice. [< ON *beita* food] —**bait′er** *n.*

baize (bāz) *n.* A cotton or woolen feltlike, usu, green fabric, used to cover pool tables, etc. [< OF *baies*, fem. pl. of *bai* chestnut-brown]

bake (bāk) *v.* **baked, bak·ing** *v.t.* 1 To cook by dry heat, as in an oven. 2 To harden or vitrify by heat, as bricks or pottery. —*v.i.* 3 To bake bread, pastry, meat, or other food. 4 To become baked or hardened by heat, as soil. —*n.* A baking or the amount baked. [< OE *bacan*] —**bak′er** *n.*

Ba·ke·lite (bā′kə·līt) *n.* Any of a group of thermosetting plastics derived from phenol and formaldehyde: a trade name.

baker's dozen Thirteen.

bak·er·y (bā′kər·ē, bāk′rē) *n. pl.* **′·er·ies** 1 A place for baking bread, cake, etc. 2 A shop where baked goods are sold: also **bake′shop′**.

bak·ing powder (bā′king) A mixture of baking soda and an acid salt, acting as a leavening agent by releasing carbon dioxide when moistened in a batter.

baking soda SODIUM BICARBONATE.

bal. balance; balancing.

Ba·laam (bā′ləm) A prophet, reproached by the ass he rode for cursing the Israelites. *Num. 22–24.*

bal·a·lai·ka (bal′ə·lī′kə) *n.* A Russian instrument with a triangular body, a guitar neck, and three strings.

Balalaika

bal·ance (bal′əns) *n.* 1 An instrument for measuring weights, often a bar pivoted on a central point with matched pans at either end; scales. 2 The imaginary scales of destiny; a symbol of justice. 3 The power to decide fate, value, etc., as by a balance. 4 A state of equilibrium or equality, as in value, importance, etc. 5 Equilibrium of the body. 6 Mental or emotional stability; sanity. 7 Harmonious proportion, as in the design or arrangement of parts. 8 Something used to produce an equilibrium; counteracting influence; counterpoise. 9 The act of balancing. 10 a Equality between the credit and debit totals of an account. b A difference between such totals; the excess on either the debit or credit side. 11 *Informal* Whatever is left over; remainder: the *balance* of the week. 12 A balance wheel. —**in the balance** Being judged; not yet settled. —**strike a balance** To compromise. —*v.* **·anced, ·anc·ing** *v.t.* 1 To bring into or keep in equilibrium; poise. 2 To weigh in a balance. 3 To compare or weigh in the mind. 4 To offset or counteract. 5 To bring into harmony, proportion, etc. 6 To be equal to. 7 To compute the difference between the debit and credit sides of (an account). 8 To reconcile, as by making certain entries, the debit and credit sides of (an account). 9 To adjust (an account) by paying what is owed. —*v.i.* 10 To be or come into equilibrium. 11 To be equal. 12 To hesitate or waver; tilt: to *balance* on the edge of a chasm. [< L *bilanx* having two plates or scales < *bis* two + *lanx* plate] —**bal′ance·a·ble** *adj.* —**bal′an·cer** *n.*

balance of payments The difference in payments made and received between a country and other countries, including costs of exports and imports of goods and services and the exchange of gold and capital.

balance of power A distribution of forces among nations such that no single nation or combination of nations will dominate or endanger any other.

balance of trade The difference in value between exports and imports of a country.

balance sheet A statement in tabular form to show assets and liabilities, profit and loss, etc., of a business at a specified date.

balance wheel The oscillating wheel of a watch or chronometer, which determines its rate of motion.

bal·brig·gan (bal·brig′ən) *n.* 1 A fine, knitted cotton fabric, used for hosiery, underwear, etc. 2 Clothing made of this. [< *Balbriggan*, Ireland]

bal·co·ny (bal′kə·nē) *n. pl.* **·nies** 1 A platform with balustrade or railing projecting from a wall of a building. • See BALUSTRADE. 2 A projecting gallery inside a theater, auditorium, etc. [< Ital. *balco* a beam]

bald (bôld) *adj.* 1 Without hair on the head. 2 Without natural growth, as a mountain. 3 Unadorned; without embellishments; plain. 4 Without disguise: *bald* jealousy. 5 Having white feathers or fur on the head: the *bald* eagle. [ME *ballede*] —**bald′ly** *adv.* —**bald′ness** *n.*

bald eagle A large eagle of N America, dark brown, with the head, neck, and tail white.

Bald eagle

Bal·der (bôl′dər) *Norse Myth.* The god of sunlight, spring, and joy. Also **Bal′dr.**

bal·der·dash (bôl′dər·dash) *n.* A meaningless flow of words; nonsense. [?]

bald·head (bôld′hed′) *n.* One whose head is bald. —**bald′head′·ed** *adj.*

bald·pate (bôld′pāt′) *n.* A baldheaded person. —**bald′·pat′ed** *adj.*

bal·dric (bôl′drik) *n.* A belt worn over one shoulder to support a sword, bugle, etc. [< OF *baudrei*]

Bald·win (bôld′win) *n.* A red winter apple. [< Col. L. *Baldwin*, 1740–1807, U.S. soldier]

bale (bāl) *n.* A large package of bulky material, as hay or cotton, corded or otherwise prepared for transportation. —*v.t.* **baled, bal·ing** To make into a bale or bales. [< OF] —**bal′er** *n.*

ba·leen (bə·lēn′) *n.* Whalebone. [< L *balaena whale*]

bale·ful (bāl′fəl) *adj.* Hurtful; malignant; 2 Sorrowful: a *baleful* look. [< OE *bealu* evil + -FUL] —**bale′ful·ly** *adv.* —**bale′ful·ness** *n.*

balk (bôk) *v.t.* 1 To render unsuccessful; thwart; frustrate. —*v.i.* 2 To stop short and refuse to proceed. 3 To refuse to consider or act upon: with *at:* He *balked* at every idea. 4 In baseball, to make a balk. —*n.* 1 a hindrance, disappointment, defeat, etc. 2 An error; blunder. 3 In baseball, an illegal, uncompleted motion by a pitcher when there are men on base. 4 A ridge left unplowed between furrows. 5 A squared beam or timber. [< OE *balca* bank, ridge]

Bal·kan (bôl′kən) *adj.* 1 Of or pertaining to the Balkan Peninsula, to the people of this region, their customs, etc. 2 Of or pertaining to the Balkan Mountains.

bal·kan·ize (bôl′kən·īz) *v.t.* **·ized, ·iz·ing** *Often cap.* To subdivide (a nation or region) into small and often incompatible units, as the Balkans after World War I. —**bal′kan·i·za′tion** *n.*

Balkan Peninsula A peninsula of SE Europe, bounded by the Black, Aegean, Mediterranean, Ionian, and Adriatic Seas.

Balkan States The countries occupying the Balkan Peninsula; Albania, Bulgaria, Greece, Romania, Yugoslavia, and the western part of Turkey. Also **the Balkans.** • See map next page.

balk·y (bô′kē) *adj.* **balk·i·er, balk·i·est** Disposed to stop suddenly or refuse to go: a *balky* mule. —**balk′i·ly** *adv.* —**balk′i·ness** *n.*

ball[1] (bôl) *n.* 1 A spherical body. 2 Such a body, of any size and made of various substances, used in a number of games. 3 Any of several such games, esp. baseball. 4 The manner of throwing or pitching a ball: a slow *ball.* 5 In baseball, a pitch in which the ball fails either to pass over home plate or between the batter's shoulder and knees and is not struck at by him. 6 A roundish part of something: the *ball* of the foot. 7 A planet or star, esp. the earth. —*v.t. & v.i.* To form into a ball. [< ON *böllr*]

ball[2] (bôl) *n.* 1 A large, formal gathering for dancing. 2 *Slang* A very good time. —*v.i. Slang* To have a very good time. [< LL *ballare* dance]

bal·lad (bal′əd) *n.* 1 A narrative poem or song of popular

Balkan States

origin in short stanzas, often with a refrain. **2** A popular song, usu. slow in tempo and sentimental in nature. [< OF *ballade* dancing song] **—bal·lad·eer** (bal′ə·dir′), **bal′lad·ry** *n.*

bal·lade (bə·läd′, ba-) *n.* **1** A verse form. **2** A musical composition of romantic nature, usu. for piano. [< OF *ballade* dancing song]

bal·last (bal′əst) *n.* **1** Any heavy substance carried in a vessel or vehicle to stablize it or, in a balloon, to control altitude. **2** Gravel or broken stone laid down as a railroad bed. **3** That which gives stability to character, morality, etc. *—v.t.* **1** To provide with ballast. **2** To stabilize. [< ODan. *barlast* bare load]

ball bearing *Mech.* **1** A bearing in which the shaft rests upon small metal balls that turn freely as it revolves. **2** Any of the metal balls in such a bearing.

bal·le·ri·na (bal′ə·rē′nə) *n.* A female ballet dancer. [< LL *ballare* to dance]

bal·let (bal′ā, ba·lā′) *n.* **1** An elaborate group dance using conventionalized movements, often for narrative effects. **2** This style of dancing. **3** Music for a ballet. **4** A company of ballet dancers. [< LL *ballare* to dance] **—bal·let·ic** (ba·let′ik) *adj.*

ball game **1** A game played with a ball, esp. a baseball game. **2** *Informal* **a** Any collective effort or its purpose. **b** A set of circumstances; situation: It's a whole new *ball game.*

bal·lis·ta (bə·lis′tə) *n. pl.* **·tae** (-tē) An engine used in ancient and medieval warfare for hurling missiles. [< Gk. *ballein* throw]

bal·lis·tic (bə·lis′tik) *adj.* Pertaining to projectiles or to ballistics.

ballistic missile A missile that is powered and guided at launch and through the early part of its trajectory, and in free fall thereafter.

bal·lis·tics (bə·lis′tiks) *n. pl. (construed as sing.)* The science that deals with the motion of projectiles. **—bal·lis·ti·cian** (bal′ə·stish′ən) *n.*

bal·loon (bə·lo͞on′) *n.* **1** A large, airtight bag, inflated with gas lighter than air, designed to rise and float in the atmosphere, often carrying passengers, instruments, etc. **2** A small inflatable rubber bag, used as a toy. **3** In comic strips, the outline containing the dialogue. *—v.i.* **1** To increase quickly in scope or magnitude; expand. **2** To swell out like a balloon. **3** To ascend in a balloon. *—v.t.* **4** To inflate or swell with air. [< Ital. *balla* ball, sphere] **—bal·loon′ist** *n.*

bal·lot (bal′ət) *n.* **1** A written or printed slip or ticket used in secret voting. **2** The total number of votes cast in an election. **3** The act or system of voting secretly by ballots or by voting machines. **4** The list of candidates in an election. *—v.* **bal·lot·ed, bal·lot·ing** *—v.i.* **1** To vote or decide by ballot. *—v.t.* **2** To vote for or decide on by means of a ballot: to *ballot* the players in selecting a captain. [< Ital. *ballotta,* dim. of *balla* ball]

ball·play·er (bôl′plā′ər) *n.* A baseball player.

ball-point pen (bôl′point′) A pen having for a point a ball bearing that rolls against an ink cartridge. Also **ball′point′, ball point.**

ball·room (bôl′ro͞om′, -ro͝om′) *n.* A large room or public hall for dancing.

bal·ly·hoo (bal′ē·ho͞o) *n. Informal* **1** Noisy talk or patter. **2** Immoderate or sensational advertising or propaganda. *—v.t. & v.i.* **·hooed, ·hoo·ing** To publicize sensationally or with much fanfare. [?]

balm (bäm) *n.* **1** An aromatic gum resin from various trees or shrubs. **2** Any of a genus of fragrant herbs. **3** Any oil or resin used as ointment, esp. if fragrant. **4** Anything that soothes or heals. [< L *balsamum* balsam]

balm of Gilead **1** Any of several Asian evergreen trees. **2** The fragrant resin obtained from them. **3** The balsam fir.

balm·y (bä′mē) *adj.* **balm·i·er, balm·i·est** **1** Very pleasant and mild. **2** Soothing. **3** *Slang* Insane; crazy; foolish. **—balm′i·ly** *adv.* **—balm′i·ness** *n.*

ba·lo·ney (bə·lō′nē) *n.* **1** *Slang* Nonsense. **2** Bologna sausage. [< BOLOGNA]

bal·sa (bôl′sə, bäl′-) *n.* **1** A tree of tropical America; also, its very lightweight wood. **2** A raft. [< Sp. *balza*]

bal·sam (bôl′səm) *n.* **1** Any of a group of fragrant oleoresins obtained from various trees. **2** Any such tree. **3** Any fragrant ointment. **4** The balsam fir. *—v.t.* To anoint with balsam; salve. [< L *balsamum* < Gk. *balsamon* balsam tree]

balsam fir A North American tree of the pine family, yielding Canada balsam.

Bal·tic (bôl′tik) *adj.* Of or pertaining to the Baltic Sea or the Baltic States.

Bal·ti·more oriole (bôl′tə·môr, -mōr) An American oriole with orange and black feathers in the male. [< George Calvert, Lord *Baltimore's* coat-of-arms' colors]

Baltimore oriole

bal·us·ter (bal′əs·tər) *n.* One of a set of small pillars that support a hand rail. [< Ital. < *balaustra* pomegranate flower < the resemblance in shape of the post]

bal·us·trade (bal′ə·strād′) *n.* A hand rail supported by balusters.

bam·bi·no (bam·bē′nō) *n. pl.* **·ni** (-nē) *Ital.* **1** A little child; a baby. **2** A figure of the child Jesus.

bam·boo (bam·bo͞o′) *n.* **1** A tall shrubby grass of tropical and semi-tropical regions. **2** The tough, hollow, jointed stem of this plant. [< Malay *bambu*]

Balustrade on balcony

bam·boo·zle (bam·bo͞o′zəl) *v.* **·zled, ·zling** *v.t. Informal* **1** To mislead; cheat. **2** To perplex. *—v.i.* **3** To practice deception. [?] **—bam·boo′zle·ment** *n.* **—bam·boo′zler** *n.*

ban (ban) *v.t.* To forbid or prohibit, esp. officially. *—n.* **1** An official prohibition. **2** Disapproval or prohibition, as by public opinion. **3** An ecclesiastical edict of excommunication or interdiction. [< ME *bannen* to summon & OF *ban* a summoning]

ba·nal (bā′nəl, bə·nal′, ban′əl) *adj.* Trite; commonplace. [< OF, ordinary, common] **—ba·nal·i·ty** (bə·nal′ə·tē) *n.* **—ba′nal·ly** *adv.* **—Syn.** hackneyed, stale, boring, dull.

ba·nan·a (bə·nan′ə) *n.* **1** A large, tropical, treelike plant cultivated for its fruit. **2** The edible, pulpy fruit of this plant. [< native w African name]

banana oil Amyl acetate, a sweet-smelling, colorless liquid, used as a solvent and a flavoring.

band[1] (band) *n.* **1** A flat flexible strip of any material, used for binding, securing, etc. **2** Any strip of fabric used to finish, strengthen, or trim an article of dress: a *neckband.* **3** *pl.* A pair of linen strips hanging from the front of the neck, worn with certain clerical or academic garments. **4** Any broad stripe of contrasting color, material, or surface. **5** *Physics* An interval of some variable, such as frequency, wavelength, energy, etc. **6** A ring. —*v.t.* **1** To unite or tie with a band; encircle. **2** To mark with a band, as birds. [< OF *bande* ribbon]

band[2] (band) *n.* **1** A company of persons associated together for some purpose. **2** A group of musicians performing together, esp. on wind and percussion instruments. **3** A drove of animals wandering together. **4** *Can.* A group of Indians living as a recognized unit on a reservation. —*v.t.* To join or unite, as in a league or company: often with *together.* —*v.i.* To confederate. [< OF *bande* a troop]

band·age (ban′dij) *n.* A strip, usu. of soft cloth, used in dressing wounds, etc. —*v.t.* **·aged, ·ag·ing** To bind or cover with a bandage. [< F *bande* band]

Band-Aid (band′ād′) *n.* A gauze patch attached to an adhesive strip, used to cover minor wounds: a trade name. —*adj.* Makeshift or improvised. Also **band′-aid′.**

ban·dan·na (ban·dan′ə) *n.* A large, bright-colored handkerchief with spots or figures. Also **ban·dan′a.** [< Hind. *bāndhnū* method of dyeing]

band·box (band′boks′) *n.* A light round or oval box, for carrying hats, collars, etc.

ban·deau (ban·dō′) *n. pl.* **·deaux** (-dōz′) **1** A narrow band, esp. one worn about the hair. **2** A brassière. [< OF *bande* ribbon]

ban·di·coot (ban′di·kŏŏt) *n.* **1** A very large rat of India and Ceylon. **2** A small marsupial of Australia, Tasmania, etc. [< Telugu *pandikokku*]

ban·dit (ban′dit) *n. pl.* **ban·dits** or **ban·dit·ti** (ban·dit′ē) **1** A robber. **2** Any outlaw. [< Ital. *bandire* to join together in a band] —**ban′dit·ry** *n.*

band·mas·ter (band′mas′tər, -mäs′tər) *n.* The conductor of a musical band.

ban·do·leer (ban′də·lir′) *n.* A broad, canvas band, with loops for holding cartridges, worn over the shoulder. Also **ban′do·lier′.** [< F *bandoulière*]

band saw *Mech.* A saw consisting of a toothed endless belt on wheels.

band shell A concave, hemispherical bandstand for concerts.

band·stand (band′stand′) *n.* An outdoor or indoor platform for a band of musicians.

band·wag·on (band′wag′ən) *n.* A high, decorated wagon to carry a band in a parade. —**climb (get, hop,** etc.) **on the bandwagon** To support those principles, candidates, etc., that are most popular or most likely to succeed.

ban·dy (ban′dē) *v.t.* **ban·died, ban·dy·ing** **1** To give and take; exchange, as blows, quips, or words. **2** To pass along; circulate: to *bandy* stories. [?]

ban·dy-leg·ged (ban′dē·leg′id, -legd′) *adj.* Bowlegged. [< earlier *bandy* crooked]

bane (bān) *n.* **1** Anything destructive or ruinous. **2** A deadly poison. [< OE *bana* murderer, destruction]

bane·ful (bān′fəl) *adj.* Injurious; deadly; ruinous. —**bane′ful·ly** *adv.* —**bane′ful·ness** *n.*

bang[1] (bang) *n.* **1** A sudden or noisy blow, thump, whack, or explosion. **2** *Informal* A sudden spurt of energy, activity, etc. **3** *Slang* Thrill; excitement. —*v.t.* **1** To beat, slam, or strike loudly. —*v.i.* **2** To make a heavy, loud sound. **3** To strike noisily. —*adv.* **1** Loudly and with force. **2** Suddenly. [< ON *banga* hammer, beat]

bang[2] (bang) *n. Usu. pl.* Front hair cut straight across. [?< BANG[1]]

bang[3] (bang) *n.* BHANG.

Bang·la Desh (bäng′glä·desh′) A nation situated on the NE part of the Indian subcontinent, coextensive with the former East Pakistan, 55,126 sq. mi., cap. Dacca. Also **Bang′la·desh′.** • See map at INDIA.

ban·gle (bang′gəl) *n.* A decorative bracelet or anklet. [< Hind. *bangrī* glass bracelet]

bang-up (bang′up′) *adj. Slang* Excellent.

ban·ish (ban′ish) *v.t.* **1** To compel to leave a country by political decree; exile. **2** To expel; drive away; dismiss, as a thought from one's mind. [< LL *banire*] —**ban′ish·er, ban′ish·ment** *n.*

ban·is·ter (ban′is·tər) *n. Often pl.* The railing on a staircase. [Alter. of BALUSTER]

ban·jo (ban′jō) *n. pl.* **·jos** A long-necked, stringed musical instrument having a circular body covered on top with stretched skin and played by plucking. [Alter. of *mbanza,* a similar instrument of Africa] —**ban′jo·ist** *n.*

Banjo

bank[1] (bangk) *n.* **1** Any moundlike formation or mass, as of ground, clouds, etc. **2** A steep rising, as of ground. **3** The slope of land at the edge of a body of water. **4** A large, raised portion of the bed of an ocean; also, a shallow; sandbar; shoal. **5** An upward lateral slope, as on the curve of a race track. **6** The cushioned edge of a billiard table. **7** *Aeron.* The sidewise inclination of an airplane in making a turn. —*v.t.* **1** To enclose, cover, or protect by a bank, dike, or border; embank. **2** To heap up into a bank or mound. **3** To cover (a fire) with fuel, ashes, etc., to keep it alive but burning low. **4** To give an upward lateral slope to, as the curve of a road. **5** To incline (an airplane) laterally. **6** In billiards and pool, to cause (a ball) to rebound at an angle from a cushion. —*v.i.* **7** To form or lie in banks. **8** To incline an airplane laterally. [ME *banke*]

bank[2] (bangk) *n.* **1** An institution for lending, borrowing, exchanging, issuing, or storing money. **2** An office or building used for such purposes. **3** The funds of a gaming establishment or the fund held by the dealer or banker in some gambling games. **4** A reserve supply of anything needed for future use: a blood *bank.* —*v.t.* **1** To deposit in a bank. —*v.i.* **2** To do business as or with a bank or banker. **3** In gambling, to keep the bank. —**bank on** *Informal* To rely or count on. [< Ital. *banca* money-changer's table] —**bank′er, bank′ing** *n.*

bank[3] (bangk) *n.* **1** A set of like articles grouped together in a line. **2** A rowers' bench in a galley. **3** A horizontal row of keys, as on a typewriter or organ. **4** In journalism, a subhead under a headline; deck. —*v.t.* To bring together in a bank. [< OF *banc* bench]

bank account Money deposited in a bank and subject to the withdrawal of the depositor.

bank·book (bangk′bŏŏk′) *n.* A book held by the depositor and serving as a record of deposits; passbook.

bank·note (bangk′nōt′) *n.* A promissory note, issued by a bank, payable on demand, and serving as a form of currency.

bank·rupt (bangk′rupt) *n.* **1** A person unable to pay his debts. **2** *Law* One judicially declared insolvent, whose property is administered for and divided among his creditors. **3** A person who has failed in or totally lacks something. —*adj.* **1** Being a bankrupt; insolvent. **2** Destitute or depleted: spiritually *bankrupt.* **3** Utterly ruined. —*v.t.* To make bankrupt. [< Ital. *banca rotta* bankruptcy, lit., broken counter] —**bank′rupt·cy** *n.* (*pl.* **·cies**).

ban·ner (ban′ər) *n.* **1** A piece of cloth, often long, bearing a design, motto, advertisement, etc. **2** Any flag or standard. **3** In journalism, a headline extending across a newspaper page. —*v.t.* To furnish with a banner. —*adj.* Leading; foremost; outstanding. [< LL *bandum* banner]

ban·nis·ter (ban′is·tər) *n.* BANISTER.

banns (banz) *n. pl. Eccl.* A public announcement of an intention to marry, usu. made on three successive Sundays. [< BAN]

ban·quet (bang′kwit) *n.* **1** A sumptuous feast. **2** A formal or ceremonial dinner, often followed by speeches. —*v.t. & v.i.* To entertain at a banquet; feast sumptuously. [< F *banc* bench, table] —**ban′quet·er** *n.*

ban·quette (bang·ket′) *n.* **1** *Mil.* A gunner's raised platform behind an earthwork. **2** An upholstered bench along a wall, as in a restaurant. **3** S *U.S.* A sidewalk. [<F *banc* bench]

ban·shee (ban′shē, ban·shē′) *n.* In Gaelic folklore, a supernatural being whose wailing foretold a death. Also **ban′shie.**

ban·tam (ban′təm) *n.* **1** Any of various breeds of small domestic fowl. Also **Ban′tam. 2** A small, pugnacious person. —*adj.* Like a bantam; small; combative. [<*Bantam*, a town in Java]

ban·tam·weight (ban′təm·wāt′) *n.* A boxer who weighs between 113 and 118 pounds.

ban·ter (ban′tər) *n.* Good-humored joking or repartee. —*v.t.* **1** To tease good-naturedly. —*v.i.* **2** To exchange good-natured repartee.[?] —**ban′ter·er** *n.* —**ban′ter·ing·ly** *adv.* —**Syn.** *n.* badinage, raillery.

Ban·tu (ban′tōō) *n. pl.* **Ban·tu** or **Ban·tus** (-tōōz) **1** A member of any of numerous Negro tribes of central and southern Africa. **2** A family of languages spoken by these tribes.

ban·tu·stan (ban′tōō·stan) *n. Usu. cap.* One of a number of enclaves for black South Africans within the Republic of South Africa.

ban·yan (ban′yən) *n.* An East Indian fig-bearing tree which sends down from its branches roots that become new trunks. [<Skt. *vanija* merchant, from the use of the ground under the tree as a market place]

ba·o·bab (bā′ō·bab, bä′ō-) *n.* An African tree with a thick trunk, bearing edible, gourdlike fruit. [<native African name]

bap·tism (bap′tiz·əm) *n.* **1** The act of baptizing or of being baptized. **2** Any initiatory or purifying experience. [<Gk. *baptismos* immersion] —**bap·tis·mal** (bap·tiz′məl) *adj.* —**bap·tis′mal·ly** *adv.*

Bap·tist (bap′tist) *n.* A member of a Protestant denomination holding that baptism should be given only to adult believers, and by immersion rather than by sprinkling. —**the Baptist** John the Baptist.

bap·tis·ter·y (bap′tis·tər·ē, -tis·trē) *n. pl.* **·ter·ies** A part of a church set apart for baptism. Also **bap′tis·try** (-trē).

bap·tize (bap·tīz′, bap′tīz) *v.* **·tized, ·tiz·ing** *v.t.* **1** *Eccl.* To immerse in water or pour water on, symbolizing purification and admission into a specific church. **2** To christen or name at baptism. **3** To purify or cleanse. **4** To initiate. —*v.i.* **5** To administer baptism. [<Gk. *baptizein* immerse, wash] —**bap·tiz′er** *n.*

bar (bär) *n.* **1** A piece of solid material, evenly shaped and long in proportion to its width and thickness. **2** Any barrier or obstruction. **3** Any hindrance. **4** A sandbar. **5** The enclosed place in court occupied by counsel; also, the place where a prisoner stands to plead. **6** A court or any place of justice. **7** Lawyers collectively or the legal profession. **8** A room, establishment, or a counter where liquors or refreshments are dispensed. **9** A stripe; a band, as of color. **10** *Mil.* Small metal or cloth strips showing rank. **11** *Music* **a** Any of the vertical lines that mark off measures. **b** A double bar. **c** The unit of music between two bars; measure. **12** A handrail for certain ballet exercises; also, the exercises done at a bar. —*v.t.* **barred, bar·ring 1** To fasten, lock, or secure with or as with a bar. **2** To confine or shut out with or as with bars. **3** To obstruct or hinder. **4** To exclude or except. **5** To mark with bars. —*prep.* Excluding; excepting: *bar* none. [<LL *barra* bar] —**Syn.** *v.* **3** block, impede, thwart, check. **4** prohibit, reject, prevent, boycott.

BAR, B.A.R. Browning automatic rifle.

bar. barometer; barometric; barrel; barrister.

barb (bärb) *n.* **1** A backward-projecting point on a sharp weapon, as on an arrow, fish hook, etc. **2** A beard, as in certain grains and grasses; awn. **3** One of the threadlike outgrowths from the shaft of a feather. **4** A cutting remark. **5** Sting: the *barb* of his wit. —*v.t.* To provide with a barb or barbs. [<L *barba* beard] —**barbed, bar′bate** *adj.*

bar·bar·i·an (bär·bâr′ē·ən, -bar′-) *n.* **1** A member of a tribe or race thought of as uncivilized. **2** Any rude, brutal, or coarse person. **3** A person lacking culture. **4** Originally, a non-Greek, non-Roman, or non-Christian. —*adj.* **1** Uncivilized; cruel; barbarous. **2** Foreign; alien.

bar·bar·ic (bär·bar′ik) *adj.* **1** Of or characteristic of barbarians. **2** Wild; crude; uncouth.

bar·ba·rism (bär′bə·riz′əm) *n.* **1** The use of words or forms not standard in a language; also, an instance of this. **2** Rudeness, cruelty, or coarseness of manner, speech, acts, etc.; also, an instance of this. **3** An uncivilized state or condition.

bar·bar·i·ty (bär·bar′ə·tē) *n. pl.* **·ties 1** Brutal or barbarous conduct. **2** A cruel deed. **3** Crudeness or coarseness in taste or behavior; also, an instance of this.

bar·ba·rize (bär′bə·rīz) *v.* **·rized, ·riz·ing** *v.t.* To make barbarous; corrupt, as language. —*v.i.* To become barbarous.

bar·ba·rous (bär′bər·əs) *adj.* **1** Uncivilized. **2** Uncultivated; crude. **3** Cruel; savage. **4** Marked by barbarisms in speech; unpolished. **5** Rude or harsh in sound. [<Gk. *barbaros* non-Hellenic, foreign, rude] —**bar′ba·rous·ly** *adv.* —**bar′ba·rous·ness** *n.* —**Syn. 2** uncouth, unrefined, vulgar, coarse, gross. **3** brutal, inhuman, ferocious.

Barbary ape A tailless monkey of North Africa and Gibraltar.

bar·be·cue (bär′bə·kyōō) *n.* **1** An outdoor meal for which the food is roasted over an open fire. **2** Any meat roasted over an open fire. —*v.t.* **·cued, ·cu·ing 1** To roast (meat, fowl, etc.) over an open fire or in a trench. **2** To cook (meat) with a highly seasoned sauce. [<Taino *barbacoa* framework of sticks]

barbed wire Fence wire having sharp points or barbs at intervals.

bar·bel (bär′bəl) *n.* **1** One of the threadlike appendages on the jaws and mouth of certain fishes: an organ of touch. **2** A European fish having such appendages. [<L *barba* beard]

bar·bell (bär′bel′) *n.* A bar with circular weights attached to each end, used for weightlifting exercises.

bar·ber (bär′bər) *n.* One who cuts the hair, shaves the beard, etc., as a business. —*v.t.* To cut or dress the hair of; shave or trim the beard of. [<L *barba* beard]

bar·ber·ry (bär′ber′ē, -bər·ē) *n.* **1** A thorny shrub bearing yellow flowers and red berries. **2** Its fruit. [<Ar. *barbārīs*]

bar·ber·shop (bär′bər·shop′) *n.* The place of business of a barber. —*adj.* Characterized by close harmony, esp. of male voices in sentimental songs.

bar·bit·u·rate (bär·bich′ər·it, bär′bə·tyŏŏr′it) *n.* Any of various derivatives of barbituric acid used in medicine to induce sedation or sleep.

bar·bi·tu·ric acid (bär′bə·tyŏŏr′ik) A synthetic organic compound from which barbiturates are derived.[?]

bar·ca·role (bär′kə·rōl) *n.* **1** A Venetian gondolier's song. **2** A melody in imitation of this. Also **bar′ca·rolle.** [<F<Ital. *barca* boat]

bar code A code made up of a set of short vertical lines and spaces printed on something, designed to be machine-readable to yield a price, an address, etc.

bard (bärd) *n.* **1** A Celtic poet and minstrel. **2** A poet. —**bard′ic** *adj.*

bare[1] (bâr) *adj.* **1** Lacking its natural or usual covering. **2** Without clothes; naked. **3** Poorly supplied or unfurnished. **4** Destitute: *bare* of all comforts. **5** Without arms or equipment: with his *bare* hands. **6** Unadorned; undisguised: *bare* facts. **7** Not more than just suffices; mere. **8** Threadbare, —*v.t.* **bared, bar·ing** To make or lay bare; reveal; expose. [<OE *bær*] —**bare′ness** *n.*

bare[2] (bâr) Obsolete *p.t.* of BEAR.

bare·back (bâr′bak′) *adj.* Riding a horse without a saddle. —*adv.* Without a saddle. —**bare′backed′** *adj.*

bare·faced (bâr′fāst′) *adj.* **1** Having the face bare. **2** Unconcealed; open. **3** Impudent; audacious. —**bare·fac·ed·ly** (bâr′fā′sid·lē, -fāst′lē) *adv.* —**bare′fac′ed·ness** *n.*

bare·foot (bâr′fŏŏt′) *adj.* & *adv.* With the feet bare. Also **bare′foot′ed** *adj.*

bare·hand·ed (bâr′han′did) *adj.* & *adv.* **1** With the hands uncovered. **2** Without weapons, tools, etc.

bare·head·ed (bâr′hed′id) *adj.* & *adv.* With the head bare.

bare·leg·ged (bâr′leg′id, -legd′) *adj.* & *adv.* With the legs bare.

bare·ly (bâr′lē) *adv.* 1 Only just; scarcely. 2 Meagerly. 3 Openly; boldly; plainly.

bar·gain (bär′gən) *n.* 1 An agreement between persons, esp. one to buy or sell goods. 2 That which is agreed upon or the terms of the agreement. 3 The agreement as it affects one of the parties: a bad *bargain.* 4 An article bought or offered at a price favorable to the buyer. *—v.i.* 1 To discuss terms for selling or buying. 2 To make a bargain; reach an agreement. *—v.t.* 3 To barter or sell by bargaining. **—bargain for** (or **on**) To expect; count on: usu. in the negative: We didn't *bargain on* getting twins. [< OF *bargaine*]

barge (bärj) *n.* 1 A flat-bottomed freight boat for harbors and inland waters. 2 A large boat, for pleasure, state occasions, etc. *—v.* **barged, barg·ing** *v.t.* 1 To transport by barge. *—v.i.* 2 To move clumsily and slowly. 3 *Informal* To collide with: with *into.* 4 *Informal* To intrude; enter rudely: with *in* or *into.* [< OF] **—barge′man** *n.*

bar graph A graph in which parallel bars represent, by their lengths, numerical variations in a set of data.

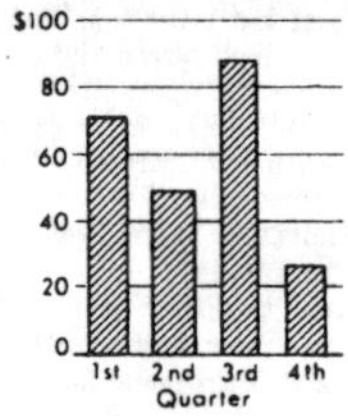

Bar graph

bar·ite (bar′īt, bâr′-) *n.* A crystalline barium sulfate mineral.

bar·i·tone (bar′ə·tōn) *n.* 1 A male voice higher than bass and lower than tenor. 2 One having such a voice. 3 A small tuba, used chiefly in military bands. *—adj.* 1 Of, like, or pertaining to a baritone. 2 Having the range of a baritone. [< Gk. *barytonos* deep-sounding]

bar·i·um (bar′ē·əm) *n.* A metallic element (symbol Ba) similar in properties to calcium but forming certain compounds that are poisonous.

barium sulfate An insoluble white salt, used in paints and in X-ray diagnosis.

bark[1] (bärk) *n.* 1 The short, explosive sound made by a dog. 2 Any sound like this. *—v.i.* 1 To utter a bark, as a dog, or to make a sound like a bark. 2 *Informal* To cough. 3 To speak loudly and sharply. 4 *Slang* To announce the attractions of a show at its entrance. *—v.t.* 5 To say roughly and curtly. [< OE *beorcan* to bark]

bark[2] (bärk) *n.* The covering of the stems, branches, and roots of a woody plant. *—v.t.* 1 To remove the bark from. 2 To rub off the skin of. 3 To tan or treat with an infusion of bark. [< Scand.]

bark[3] (bärk) *n.* 1 A three-masted vessel square-rigged except for the mizzenmast, which is fore-and-aft rigged. 2 Any vessel or boat. [< LL *barca* boat]

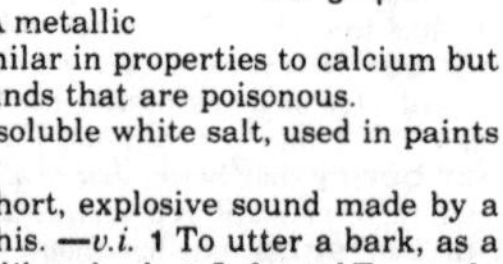
Bark

bar·keep·er (bär′kē′pər) *n.* 1 One who owns or manages a bar where alcoholic liquors are served. 2 A bartender. Also **bar′keep′.**

bar·ken·tine (bär′kən·tēn) *n.* A three-masted vessel square-rigged on the foremast and fore-and-aft rigged on the other two masts. [? < BARK[3] + (BRIG)ANTINE]

bark·er (bär′kər) *n.* 1 One who barks. 2 A person stationed at the entrance to a store, a show, etc., to attract patrons by loud, animated patter.

bar·ley (bär′lē) *n.* 1 A hardy, bearded cereal grass. 2 Its grain. [< OE *bærlic*]

bar·ley·corn (bär′lē·kôrn) *n.* A grain of barley. **—John Barleycorn** A humorous personification of intoxicating liquors.

barm (bärm) *n.* The froth rising on fermented malt liquors. [< OE *beorma* yeast]

bar·maid (bär′mād) *n.* A woman who tends bar.

bar mitz·vah (bär mits′və) *Often cap.* In Judaism, a boy commencing his thirteenth year, the age of religious duty; also, the ceremony celebrating this. Also **bar miz′vah.**

barm·y (bär′mē) *adj.* **barm·i·er, barm·i·est** 1 Full of barm; frothy. 2 *Brit. Slang* Silly.

barn (bärn) *n.* A building for storing hay, stabling livestock, etc. [< OE *bern*]

bar·na·cle (bär′nə·kəl) *n.* 1 A marine shellfish that attaches itself firmly to rocks, ship bottoms, etc. 2 Something or someone that clings tenaciously. [ME *bernacle*] **—bar′na·cled** *adj.*

barn dance A party, originally held in a barn, for square dancing, etc.

barn owl An owl with brownish back and white breast flecked with black, often found in barns.

Barn owl

barn·storm (bärn′stôrm′) *v.i.* To tour rural districts, giving plays, making political speeches, giving exhibitions of stunt flying, etc. **—barn′storm′er, barn′storm′ing** *n.*

barn swallow A common swallow that frequently nests in the eaves of barns.

barn·yard (bärn′yärd′) *n.* An enclosed space adjoining a barn.

baro- *combining form* Pressure, esp. atmospheric pressure: *barometer.* [< Gk. *baros* weight]

bar·o·gram (bar′ə·gram) *n.* The record of a barograph.

bar·o·graph (bar′ə·graf, -gräf) *n.* A recording barometer. **—bar′o·graph′ic** *adj.*

ba·rom·e·ter (bə·rom′ə·tər) *n.* 1 An instrument for measuring atmospheric pressure. 2 Anything that indicates changes. **—bar·o·met·ric** (bar′ə·met′rik) or **·ri·cal** *adj.* **—bar′o·met′ri·cal·ly** *adv.* **—ba·rom′e·try** *n.*

bar·on (bar′ən) *n.* 1 A member of the lowest order of hereditary nobility in Great Britain, Japan, and several European countries; also, the dignity or rank itself. 2 One who has great power in a commercial field: a coal *baron.* [< LL *baro*] **—ba·ro·ni·al** (bə·rō′nē·əl) *adj.*

bar·on·age (bar′ən·ij) *n.* 1 Barons collectively. 2 The dignity or rank of a baron.

bar·on·ess (bar′ən·is) *n.* 1 The wife or widow of a baron. 2 A woman holding a barony.

bar·on·et (bar′ən·it, -ə·net) *n.* 1 An inheritable English title, below that of baron. 2 The bearer of the title, who is not a member of the nobility. **—bar′on·et·cy** (-sē) *n.*

bar·o·ny (bar′ə·nē) *n. pl.* **·nies** The rank, dignity, or domain of a baron.

ba·roque (bə·rōk′) *adj.* 1 Of, like, or characteristic of a style of art, architecture, and music that flourished in 16th- and 17th-century Europe, characterized by elaboration and profuse ornamentation. 2 Excessively elaborate and decorative. 3 Irregularly shaped: said of pearls. *—n.* 1 The baroque style. 2 An object, composition, or design in this style. [< Ital. *barroco*]

ba·rouche (bə·rōōsh′) *n.* A four-wheeled, low-bodied carriage with folding top, two inside seats, and an outside seat for the driver. [< Ital. *baroccio*]

barque (bärk) *n.* BARK[3].

bar·quen·tine (bär′kən·tēn) *n.* BARKENTINE.

bar·rack (bar′ək) *n.* 1 *pl.* A structure or group of structures for the housing of soldiers. 2 *pl.* A temporary or rough shelter for a gang of laborers, etc. *—v.t. & v.i.* To house in barracks. [< Ital. *baracca* soldiers' tent]

barracks bag A soldier's cloth bag for holding clothing and equipment. Also **barrack bag.**

bar·ra·cu·da (bar′ə·kōō′də) *n. pl.* **·da** or **·das** A voracious fish of tropical seas. [< Sp.]

bar·rage (bə·räzh′) *n.* 1 A curtain of artillery fire designed to prevent enemy advancement, protect one's own advancing troops, etc. 2 Any overwhelming attack, as of words or blows. *—v.t. & v.i.* **·raged, ·rag·ing** To lay down a barrage (against) or subject to a barrage. [< F *(tir de) barrage* barrage (fire)]

bar·ran·ca (bə·rang′kə) *n.* SW *U.S.* A deep ravine or gorge. [< Sp.]

bar·ra·tor (bar′ə·tər) *n.* One guilty of barratry. Also **bar′ra·ter.**

bar·ra·try (bar′ə·trē) *n. pl.* **·tries** 1 Any willful and unlawful act committed by the master or crew of a ship, whereby the owners suffer a loss. 2 *Law* The offense of habitually exciting lawsuits, quarrels, etc. [< OF *barat* fraud] **—bar′ra·trous** *adj.*

barred (bärd) *adj.* 1 Having or made of bars. 2 Obstructed by bars. 3 Striped. 4 Prohibited; not allowed.

bar·rel (bar′əl) *n.* 1 A large, round, wooden vessel, made with staves and hoops, having a flat base and top and slightly bulging sides. 2 As much as a barrel will hold; in liquid measure varying from 31 to 42 U.S. gallons. 3 Something resembling a barrel, as the rotating drum of a windlass, capstan, etc. 4 In firearms, the tube through which the projectile is discharged. • See REVOLVER. —*v.* **·reled** or **·relled, ·rel·ing** or **·rel·ling** —*v.t.* 1 To put or pack in a barrel. —*v.i.* 2 *Slang* To move at high speed. [<OF *baril*]

barrel organ HAND ORGAN.

bar·ren (bar′ən) *adj.* 1 Incapable of producing offspring; sterile. 2 Not producing crops, fruit, etc. 3 Unprofitable, as an enterprise. 4 Lacking in interest or attractiveness; dull. 5 Devoid; lacking: *barren* of any new ideas. —*n. Usu. pl.* A tract of level, usu. sandy, barren land. [<OF *baraigne*] **—bar′ren·ly** *adv.* **—bar′ren·ness** *n.*

Barren Grounds The tundra of northern Canada. Also **Barren Lands, Barrens.**

bar·rette (bə·ret′) *n.* A small bar or comb with a clasp, used for keeping a girl's or woman's hair in place. [<F *barre* bar]

bar·ri·cade (bar′ə·kād, bar′ə·kād′) *n.* 1 A barrier hastily built for obstruction or for defense. 2 Any obstruction or barrier closing a passage. —*v.t.* **·cad·ed, ·cad·ing** To enclose, obstruct, or defend with a barricade. [<Sp. *barricada* barrier < *barrica* barrel]

bar·ri·er (bar′ē·ər) *n.* 1 Something that prevents entrance, obstructs passage, etc., as a fence. 2 Anything that tends to separate or retard progress: a language *barrier.* 3 A boundary or limit. [<OF *barre* bar]

barrier reef A long, narrow ridge of rock or coral parallel to the coast and close to or above the surface of the sea.

bar·ring (bär′ing) *prep.* Excepting; apart from.

bar·ri·o (bär′rē·ō) *n. pl.* **·os** 1 In Spanish-speaking countries, a district or ward of a town or city. 2 *U.S.* A section of a city or town populated largely by Spanish-speaking people. [Sp.]

bar·ris·ter (bar′is·tər) *n.* In English law, a member of the legal profession who argues cases in the courts, as distinguished from a solicitor, who prepares them. [<BAR]

bar·room (bär′ro͞om′, -ro͝om′) *n.* A room where alcoholic liquors are served across a bar.

bar·row[1] (bar′ō) *n.* 1 WHEELBARROW. 2 HANDBARROW. 3 A two-wheeled pushcart, as that of a street vendor. [<OE *bearwe*]

bar·row[2] (bar′ō) *n.* 1 A burial mound. 2 A hill. [<OE *beorg*]

bar sinister BEND SINISTER.

Bart. Baronet.

bar·tend·er (bär′ten′dər) *n.* One who serves liquors over a bar.

bar·ter (bär′tər) *v.i.* 1 To exchange goods or services without use of money. —*v.t.* 2 To trade (one thing) for another of equal value. —*n.* 1 The act of bartering. 2 Something bartered. [<OF *barater* exchange] **—bar′ter·er** *n.*

bar·ti·zan (bär′tə·zən, bär′tə·zan′) *n.* A small turret jutting out from a tower or wall. [Alter. of *bratticing,* planking]

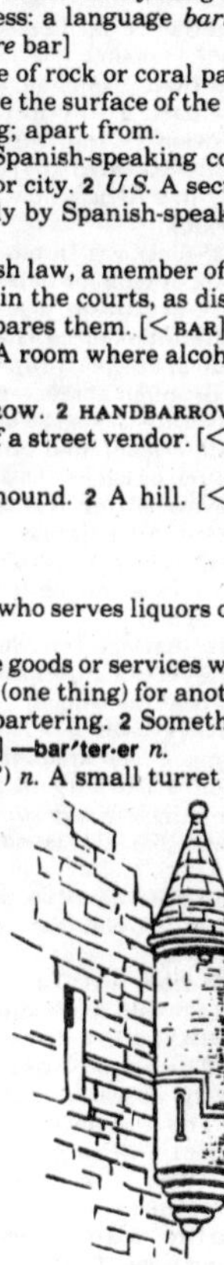

Bartizan

Bart·lett (bärt′lit) *n.* A variety of large, juicy pear. Also **Bartlett pear.** [<E. *Bartlett,* 1779–1860, U.S. merchant]

ba·ry·tes (bə·rī′tēz) *n.* BARITE.

ba·sal (bā′səl) *adj.* 1 Of, at, or being the base. 2 Basic; fundamental. **—ba′sal·ly** *adv.*

basal metabolism The energy, measured in calories, used by the body at rest in maintaining essential vital activities.

ba·salt (bə·sôlt′, bas′ôlt) *n.* A fine-grained, volcanic rock of high density and dark color. [<L *basaltes*] **—ba·sal′tic** *adj.*

bas·cule (bas′kyo͞ol) *n.* A mechanical apparatus of which each end counterbalances the other, used in a kind of drawbridge **(bascule bridge)** operated by a counterpoise. [<F, see-saw]

base[1] (bās) *n.* 1 The lowest or supporting part of anything; bottom; foundation. 2 The essential or main part or element of anything: the *base* of our plan. 3 The essential ingredient or bottom layer of something: a tar *base.* 4 Any point, line, or quantity from which a measurement, inference, or conclusion is made; basis. 5 In certain games, a starting point or goal; esp. in baseball, any one of the four points of the diamond. 6 A place from which operations proceed, supplies are stored, etc.: a military *base.* 7 The point of attachment of a bodily organ. 8 *Archit.* The lowest part of a column, wall, etc. 9 *Chem.* **a** A compound capable of reacting with an acid to form a salt. **b** Any molecule or radical that takes up positive ions. 10 *Geom.* The side or face of a figure on which it appears to rest. 11 *Math.* A number whose powers are used as the various orders of units in a numeration system. 12 *Ling.* The form of a word used in making derivatives, as by adding prefixes or suffixes; root. 13 *Her.* The lower part of a shield. **—off base** 1 In baseball, not on the base one should be on. 2 *Informal* In error. —*v.t.* **based, bas·ing** 1 To put on a logical basis, as an argument, decision, or theory: with *on* or *upon.* 2 To make or form a base for. 3 To assign to a base: with *in* or *at.* —*adj.* Serving as a base. [<Gk. *basis* step, pedestal]

base[2] (bās) *adj.* 1 Vile; low; contemptible: *base* conduct. 2 Menial; degrading: *base* employment. 3 Inferior, as in quality. 4 Debased or counterfeit, as money. 5 Having comparatively little value: said of metals. [<LL *bassus* low] **—base′ly** *adv.* **—base′ness** *n.* **—Syn.** 1 ignoble, infamous, mean, sordid, despicable. 2 miserable, wretched.

base·ball (bās′bôl′) *n.* 1 A game played with a wooden bat and a hard ball by two teams of nine players each, one team being at bat and the other in the field, alternately, for a minimum of nine innings. The game is played on a field having four bases in a diamond formation. 2 The ball used in this game.

base·board (bās′bôrd′, -bōrd′) *n.* 1 A board skirting the wall of a room, next to the floor. 2 A board forming a base.

base·born (bās′bôrn′) *adj.* 1 Born out of wedlock. 2 Of low birth. 3 Mean.

base hit In baseball, a hit by which the batter reaches base without help of an opposing player's error or without forcing out a runner previously on base.

base·less (bās′lis) *adj.* Without foundation in fact; unfounded; groundless. **—base′less·ness** *n.*

base line 1 In baseball, a path of a certain width connecting the bases. 2 In tennis, the line behind which the players serve. 3 Any line acting as a base.

base·ment (bās′mənt) *n.* 1 The lowest floor of a building, usu. underground. 2 The substructure of any building, structure, or member.

base runner In baseball, a member of the team at bat who has reached base.

bas·es[1] (bā′siz) *n.pl.* of BASE[1].

ba·ses[2] (bā′sēz) *n.pl.* of BASIS.

bash (bash) *v.t. Informal* To strike heavily; smash in. —*n.* 1 *Informal* A smashing blow. 2 *Slang* A gala party or gathering. [?]

bash·ful (bash′fəl) *adj.* Shy; timid; modest. [<ABASH + -FUL] **—bash′ful·ly** *adv.* **—bash′ful·ness** *n.*

ba·sic (bā′sik) *adj.* 1 Pertaining to, forming, or like a base or basis. 2 Essential; fundamental. 3 *Chem.* Having properties of a base; alkaline. —*n. Usu. pl.* The essential or fundamental principles, techniques, etc.: to learn the *basics* of good design. **—ba′si·cal·ly** *adv.*

bas·il (baz′əl) *n.* Any of certain aromatic plants of the mint family, used as a culinary herb. [<Gk. *basilikon (phyton)* royal (plant), basil]

bas·i·lar (bas′ə·lər) *adj.* At the base, esp. of the skull. Also **bas·i·lar·y** (bas′ə·ler′ē).

ba·sil·i·ca (bə·sil′i·kə) *n.* 1 In ancient Rome, a rectangular building divided into nave and aisles, used as a hall of justice, etc. 2 A church shaped like a Roman basilica. 3 A Roman Catholic church accorded certain liturgical privileges. [<Gk. *basilikos* royal] **—ba·sil′i·can** *adj.*

bas·i·lisk (bas′ə·lisk) *n.* **1** A fabled reptile whose breath and look were supposedly fatal. **2** A tropical American lizard having an erectile crest. [< Gk. *basiliskos,* dim. of *basileus* king]

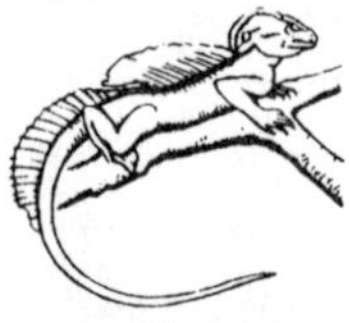
Basilisk *def. 2*

ba·sin (bā′sən) *n.* **1** A round, wide, shallow vessel for holding liquids. **2** The amount that a basin will hold. **3** A sink or wash bowl. **4** A depression in the earth's surface, as a valley. **5** The region drained by a river. **6** A partially enclosed harbor or bay. **7** A bowllike depression in the floor of the ocean. [< LL *bacca*] **—ba′sined** *adj.*

ba·sis (bā′sis) *n. pl.* **ba·ses** (bā′sēz) **1** That on which anything rests; support; foundation. **2** Fundamental principle. **3** The main component of a thing. [< Gk., base, pedestal] **—Syn. 1** base, groundwork. **2** theory, premise.

bask (bask, bäsk) *v.i.* **1** To lie in and enjoy a pleasant warmth, as of the sun. **2** To enjoy a pleasing circumstance: to *bask* in the affection of a friend. [< Scand.]

bas·ket (bas′kit, bäs′-) *n.* **1** A container made of interwoven twigs, rushes, strips, etc. **2** Something resembling a basket, as the structure under a balloon for carrying passengers or ballast. **3** The amount a basket will hold. **4** In basketball, either of the goals, consisting of a cord net suspended from a metal ring; also, the point or points made by throwing the ball through the basket. [ME]

bas·ket·ball (bas′kit·bôl′, bäs′-) *n.* **1** A game played by two teams of five players each, in which the object is to throw the ball through the elevated goal (basket) at the opponent's end of a zoned, oblong court. **2** The inflated ball used in this game.

bas·ket·ry (bas′kit·rē, bäs′-) *n.* **1** Baskets collectively. **2** The art of making baskets.

bas·ket·weave (bas′kit·wēv′, bäs′-) *n.* A fabric weave that resembles the plaiting of a basket.

bas·ket·work (bas′kit·wûrk′, bäs′-) *n.* Work that is woven or textured like a basket; wickerwork.

basque (bask) *n.* A woman's closely fitting bodice, separate from the skirt. [F]

Basque (bask) *n.* **1** One of a people of unknown origin living in the w Pyrenees. **2** The language of the Basque people, unrelated to any other language. *—adj.* Of or pertaining to the Basques.

bas-re·lief (bä′ri·lēf′) *n.* Sculpture in which the figures project only slightly from the background. [F< Ital. *basso* low + *rilievo* relief]

bass[1] (bas) *n.* Any of various unrelated marine and freshwater food fishes having spiny fins. [< OE *bærs*]

bass[2] (bās) *n.* **1** The lowest-pitched male singing voice. **2** A deep, low sound, as of this voice or of low-pitched instruments. **3** The lowest of two or more musical parts. **4** A low-pitched musical instrument, esp. a double bass. *—adj.* **1** Low in pitch or range. **2** Pertaining to, for, or able to play bass. [< OF *bas* low, base]

bass[3] (bas) *n.* **1** LINDEN. **2** BAST. [Alter. of BAST]

bass drum (bās) A large drum producing a sound of low frequency. • See DRUM.

bas·set (bas′it) *n.* A hound with a long, low body, long head and nose, and short, heavy, crooked forelegs. Also **bas′set-hound′** (-hound′). [< OF *bas* low]

basset horn A tenor clarinet. [< Ital. < *bassetto,* dim. of *basso* low + *corno* horn]

bass horn (bās) TUBA.

bas·si·net (bas′ə·net′) *n.* **1** A partly hooded basket, used as a cradle. **2** A small basket for holding the clothing of an infant. [< F *bassin* basin]

bas·so (bas′ō, *Ital.* bäs′sō) *n. pl.* **bas·sos** (bas′ōz) or *Ital.* **bas·si** (bäs′sē) **1** A bass singer. **2** The bass part. [Ital., low]

bas·soon (ba·so͞on′, bə-) *n.* A large, double-reed woodwind instrument with a long, curved mouthpiece. [< F *bas* low]

Bassoon

bass viol (bās vī′əl) *Music* DOUBLE BASS.

bass·wood (bas′wo͝od′) *n.* LINDEN.

bast (bast) *n. Bot.* **1** The food-conducting tissue of vascular plants; phloem. **2** Fibrous vegetable material used for making cordage, etc. [< OE *bæst*]

bas·tard (bas′tərd) *n.* **1** An illegitimate child. **2** Any hybrid plant, tree, or animal. **3** Any irregular, inferior, or counterfeit thing. *—adj.* **1** Born out of wedlock. **2** False; spurious. **3** Resembling but not typical of the genuine thing. **4** Abnormal or irregular in size, shape, or proportion. [< OF *fils de bast* packsaddle child] **—bas′tard·ly** *adv.* **—bas′tar·dy** *n.*

bas·tard·ize (bas′tər·dīz) *v.* **-ized, -iz·ing** *v.t.* **1** To prove to be, or stigmatize as, a bastard. **2** To debase. *—v.i.* **3** To become debased. **—bas′tard·i·za′tion** *n.*

baste[1] (bāst) *v.t.* **bast·ed, bast·ing** To sew together with long, temporary stitches. [< OF *bastir*]

baste[2] (bāst) *v.t.* **bast·ed, bast·ing** To moisten (meat or fish) with drippings, butter, etc., while cooking. [?]

baste[3] (bāst) *v.t. Informal.* **1** To thrash. **2** To attack verbally; abuse. [prob. < Scand.]

bas·tille (bas·tēl′) *n.* A prison. Also **bas·tile′. —the Bastille** A fortress in Paris serving as a prison until its destruction July 14, 1789 in the French Revolution. [< OF]

bas·ti·na·do (bas′tə·nā′dō) *n. pl.* **·does 1** A beating with a stick, usu. on the soles of the feet. **2** A stick or cudgel. *—v.t.* **·doed, ·do·ing** To beat with a stick, usu. on the soles of the feet. Also **bas′ti·nade′.** [< Sp. *bastón* cudgel]

bast·ing (bās′ting) *n.* **1** The act of sewing loosely together. **2** *pl.* Loose, temporary stitches. **3** The thread used. [< BASTE[1]]

bas·tion (bas′chən, -tē·ən) *n.* **1** In fortifications, a projecting part. **2** Any fortified or strongly defended place or position. [< Ital. *bastione*] **—bas′tioned** *adj.*

Ba·su·to·land (bə·so͞o′tō·land′) *n.* A former British colony in s Africa, now the nation of Lesotho. • See map at AFRICA.

bat[1] (bat) *n.* **1** In baseball, cricket, and other games: **a** A stick or club for batting the ball. **b** The act of batting. **c** A turn at batting. **d** A racket or paddle, as in table tennis, badminton, etc. **e** The batsman, as in cricket. **2** Any heavy club or cudgel. **3** *Informal* A blow, as with a stick. **4** *Slang* A drunken spree. **—go to bat for** *Informal* To defend or advocate the cause of. *—v.* **bat·ted, bat·ting** *—v.i.* **1** In baseball, cricket, and other games: **a** To use a bat. **b** To take a turn at bat. *—v.t.* **2** To strike with or as with a bat. **3** To have a batting average of. **—bat around** *Slang* **1** To travel about. **2** To discuss. [< OE *batt* cudgel]

bat[2] (bat) *n.* A nocturnal flying mammal having elongated forelimbs and digits that support a thin wing membrane. [< Scand.]

bat[3] (bat) *v.t. Informal* To wink; flutter. **—not bat an eye** or **eyelash** *Informal* To fail to show surprise. [< F *battre* to beat (as wings)]

batch (bach) *n.* **1** The quantity of bread, etc., baked at one time. **2** The amount of material required for one operation. **3** The amount produced at one operation. **4** Persons or things in a group; lot. [< OE *bacan* to bake]

bate (bāt) *v.t.* **bat·ed, bat·ing** To lessen; moderate. [Var. of ABATE]

ba·teau (ba·tō′) *n. pl.* **·teaux** (-tōz′) **1** A light, flat-bottomed boat. **2** A pontoon for a floating bridge. [F < OF *batel,* ult. < Gmc.]

bat·fish (bat′fish′) *n.* Any of various marine fishes having broad, flat bodies suggestive of a bat's wings.

bath (bath, bäth) *n. pl.* **baths** (ba*th*z, bä*th*z; baths, bäths) **1** The act of washing or immersing something, esp. the body, in water or other liquid. **2** The liquid used for this. **3** The container for such a liquid, as a bathtub. **4** A bathroom. **5** *Often pl.* A set of rooms or a building for bathing. **6** *Often pl.* A resort where bathing is part of a medical treatment. *—v.t. Brit.* To bathe. [< OE *bæth*]

bathe (bā*th*) *v.* **bathed, bath·ing** *v.t.* **1** To place in liquid; immerse. **2** To wash; wet. **3** To apply liquid to, as for comfort or healing. **4** To cover or suffuse as with liquid: The hill was *bathed* in light. *—v.i.* **5** To take a bath. **6** To go into or remain in water so as to swim or cool off. **7** To be covered or suffused as if with liquid: to *bathe* photographic prints in a fixer solution. *—n. Brit.* The act of bathing, as in the sea. [< OE *bathian*] **—bath′er** *n.*

bath·house (bath′hous′, bäth′-) *n.* **1** A building for taking baths. **2** A dressing room or rooms for bathers.
bath·ing suit (bāth′ing) A garment worn for swimming.
ba·thos (bā′thos) *n.* **1** A descent from the lofty to the trite in discourse. **2** Insincere pathos; sentimentality. [< Gk. *bathys* deep] —**ba·thet·ic** (bə·thet′ik) *adj.*
bath·robe (bath′rōb′, bäth′-) *n.* A long, loose garment for wear before and after bathing.
bath·room (bath′rōōm′, -rōōm′, bäth′-) *n.* **1** A room in which to bathe. **2** A toilet.
bath·tub (bath′tub′, bäth′-) *n.* A tub in which to bathe, esp. one in a bathroom.
bathy- *combining form* Deep: of the ocean depths: *bathysphere.* [< Gk. *bathys* deep]
bath·y·scaph (bath′ə·skaf) *n.* A self-propelled diving ship for deep-sea exploration. Also **bath·y·scaphe** (-skaf, -skāf). [< BATHY- + Gk. *skaphē* bowl]
bath·y·sphere (bath′ə·sfir) *n.* A spherical, cable-lowered, diving chamber with windows for deep-sea observations. [< BATHY- + SPHERE]
ba·tik (bə·tēk′, bat′ik) *n.* **1** A process for dyeing fabrics in which those areas not to be dyed are covered with wax. **2** A fabric so dyed. —*adj.* Of batik. [< Malay]
ba·tiste (bə·tēst′) *n.* A sheer, cotton fabric. [< Jean *Baptiste,* 13th c. French linen weaver]
ba·ton (bə·ton′, ba·ton′) *n.* **1** A short staff borne as an emblem of authority or privilege. **2** *Music* A slender stick or rod used for conducting. **3** A short stick passed from one runner to another in relay racing. **4** A hollow metal rod, knobbed at one end, twirled as by a drum majorette. [< LL *bastum* stick]
ba·tra·chi·an (bə·trā′kē·ən) *adj.* Of frogs and toads. [< Gk. *batrachos* frog]
bat·tal·ion (bə·tal′yən) *n.* **1** *Mil.* **a** A regimental unit, consisting of a headquarters and two or more companies, batteries, or comparable units. **b** A body of troops. **2** *Usu. pl.* A large group or number. [< Ital. *battaglione*]
bat·ten[1] (bat′n) *v.i.* **1** To grow fat or thrive. **2** To live well, esp. at another's expense. —*v.t.* **3** To make fat, as cattle. [< ON *batna* grow better, improve]
bat·ten[2] (bat′n) *n.* **1** A narrow strip of wood, often nailed across parallel boards as reinforcement. **2** *Naut.* A thin strip of wood placed in a sail to keep it flat or used to fasten down a tarpaulin covering on a hatchway. —*v.t.* To strengthen or fasten with battens. [Var. of BATON]
bat·ter[1] (bat′ər) *v.t.* **1** To strike with repeated, violent blows. **2** To break or injure with or as with such blows. —*v.i.* **3** To beat with blow after blow. [< L *battuere* beat]
bat·ter[2] (bat′ər) *n.* In baseball and cricket, the player whose turn it is to bat.
bat·ter[3] (bat′ər) *n.* A liquid mixture of eggs, flour, milk, etc., used for making pancakes, cakes, etc. [< OF *battre* beat]
bat·ter·ing-ram (bat′ər·ing·ram′) *n.* **1** A long, stout beam, used in ancient warfare for forcing gates and making breaches in walls. **2** Any similar device used to make forced entrance.
bat·ter·y (bat′ər·ē) *n. pl.* **·ter·ies** **1** Any group or array of similar things used or connected together to serve a common end or purpose. **2** *Electr.* **a** An array of similar parts or devices, esp. primary or secondary cells, connected together. **b** A primary cell: a flashlight *battery.* **3** *Mil.* **a** A unit of an artillery regiment equivalent to an infantry company. **b** A group of heavy artillery, as guns, missiles, etc. **4** *Law* The illegal beating or touching of another person. **5** In baseball, the pitcher and catcher together. **6** *Music* The percussion instruments of an orchestra. [< F *battre* beat]
bat·tik (bə·tēk′, bat′ik) *n.* BATIK.
bat·ting (bat′ing) *n.* Wadded cotton or other fiber prepared in sheets or rolls.
bat·tle (bat′l) *n.* **1** An extensive combat between hostile armies or fleets. **2** Any fighting, dispute, or conflict. —*v.* **bat·tled, bat·tling** —*v.i.* **1** To contend in or as in battle; struggle. —*v.t.* **2** To fight. [< LL *battuere* beat] —**bat′tler** *n.* —**Syn.** *n.* **1** engagement, encounter. *v.* **1** vie.
bat·tle-ax (bat′l·aks′) *n.* **1** A large ax formerly used in battle; a broad-ax. **2** *Slang* An aggressively contentious woman. Also **bat′tle-axe′.**
battle cruiser A war vessel less heavily armored but faster than a battleship.
battle cry **1** A shout used by troops in battle. **2** A rallying slogan or identifying phrase.
bat·tle·dore (bat′l·dôr, -dōr) *n.* **1** A paddle or bat, used to drive a shuttlecock. **2** The game in which a shuttlecock is so batted: also **battledore and shuttlecock.** [?< Provençal *batedor* an implement for beating]
battle fatigue A psychoneurotic condition occurring among soldiers engaged in prolonged combat.
bat·tle·field (bat′l·fēld′) *n.* The ground on which a battle is fought. Also **bat′tle·ground′** (-ground′).
bat·tle·ment (bat′l·mənt) *n.* A parapet indented along its upper line. —**bat·tle·ment·ed** (bat′l·men′·tid) *adj.* [< OF *batailler* fortify]

Battlement

battle royal **1** A fight involving numerous combatants. **2** A protracted, rigorous dispute.
bat·tle·ship (bat′l·ship′) *n. Nav.* A large warship having heavy armor and powerful guns.
bat·ty (bat′ē) *adj.* **·ti·er, ·ti·est** *Slang* Crazy; odd.
bau·ble (bô′bəl) *n.* A worthless, showy trinket or trifle. [< OF *baubel* toy]
baulk (bôk) *v.* BALK.
baux·ite (bôk′sīt, bō′zīt) *n.* A claylike mineral of varying composition, the principal ore of aluminum. [< Les *Baux,* town in southern France]
bawd (bôd) *n.* The keeper of a brothel; a procuress. [ME *bawde*]
bawd·y (bô′dē) *adj.* **bawd·i·er, bawd·i·est** Obscene; indecent. —**bawd′i·ly** adv. —**bawd′i·ness** *n.* —**Syn.** improper, lewd, immodest, salacious, lascivious.
bawd·y-house (bô′dē·hous′) *n.* A brothel.
bawl (bôl) *v.t.* **1** To proclaim or call out noisily; bellow. —*v.i.* **2** To weep or sob noisily. —**bawl out** *Slang* To scold; berate. —*n.* A loud outcry. [< Scand.] —**bawl′er** *n.*
bay[1] (bā) *n.* A body of water partly enclosed by land; an inlet of a sea or lake. [< LL *baia*]
bay[2] (bā) *n.* **1** A space or compartment separated from others in a structure, as in an aircraft. **2** *Archit.* **a** BAY WINDOW. **b** A wing of a building. [< F *baie* < *bayer* gape]
bay[3] (bā) *adj.* Reddish brown: said esp. of horses. —*n.* **1** A horse or other animal of this color. **2** This color. [< L *badius*]
bay[4] (bā) *n.* **1** A deep bark or cry, as of dogs in hunting. **2** The situation of or as of a hunted creature compelled to turn on its pursuers. —**at bay** **1** Cornered; with no escape. **2** Held off: He kept his attackers *at bay.* —**bring to bay** To force into a position from which there is no escape. —*v.i.* **1** To utter a deep-throated, prolonged bark, as a hound. —*v.t.* **2** To utter as with this bark: to *bay* defiance. **3** To bring to bay. [< OF *abai* a barking]
bay[5] (bā) *n.* **1** A laurel wreath, bestowed as a token of honor. **2** *pl.* Fame; poetic renown. **3** BAYBERRY. **4** Any of several trees and shrubs resembling the laurels. [< L *baca* berry]
bay·ber·ry (bā′ber′ē, -bər·ē) *n. pl.* **·ber·ries** **1** Any of various trees, as the wax myrtle or laurel, or its fruit. **2** A tropical American tree whose leaves are used in making bay rum. [< BAY[5] + BERRY]
bay·o·net (bā′ə·nit, -net′, bā′ə·net′) *n.* A daggerlike weapon attachable to the muzzle of a rifle, for close fighting. —*v.t.* **·net·ed, ·net·ing** To stab or pierce with a bayonet. [< *Bayonne,* France, where first made]

Bayonets

bay·ou (bī′ōō) *n.* A marshy inlet or outlet of a lake, bay, river, etc. [< Choctaw *bayuk* small stream]

bay rum An aromatic liquid used in medicines and cosmetics. [< BAY[5]]

bay window 1 A window structure projecting from the wall of a building. 2 *Slang* A protruding abdomen.

ba·zaar (bə·zär′) *n.* 1 An Oriental market place or range of shops. 2 A shop or store for the sale of miscellaneous wares. 3 A sale of miscellaneous articles, as for charity. Also **ba·zar′**. [< Pers. *bāzār* market]

ba·zoo·ka (bə·zo͞o′kə) *n. Mil.* A long, tubular launcher which fires an explosive rocket at short range. [< the *bazooka,* a comical musical instrument]

BB A standard, commercial size of lead shot, 0.18 in. in diameter.

B.B.A., B. Bus. Ad. Bachelor of Business Administration.

BBC, B.B.C. British Broadcasting Corporation.

bbl, bbl. barrel; barrels.

B.C. before Christ; British Columbia.

bch. bunch.

B.D. Bachelor of Divinity.

B/D., b.d. bank draft; bills discounted.

bd. board; bond; bound; bundle.

bd. ft. board feet.

bdl., bdle. bundle.

be (bē, *unstressed* bi) *v.i.* **been, be·ing** Present indicative: I **am**, he, she, it **is**, we, you, they **are**; past indicative: I, he, she, it **was**, we, you, they **were**; present subjunctive: **be**; past subjunctive: **were**; archaic forms: thou **art** (present); thou **wast** or **wert** (past). 1 As a substantive verb, *be* is used to mean: **a** To have existence, truth, or actuality: There *are* bears in the zoo. **b** To take place; happen: The party *is* next week. **c** To stay or continue: She *was* here for one week. **d** To belong; befall: often with *to* or *unto:* Joy *be* unto you. 2 As a copulative verb, *be* forms a link between the subject and the predicate noun, pronoun, or adjective: This *is* Charles; I *am* he; they both *are* sick; it also forms infinitive and participial phrases: the pleasure of *being* here. 3 As an auxiliary verb, *be* is used: **a** With the present participle of other verbs to express continuous or progressive action: I *am* working. **b** With the past participle of transitive verbs to form the passive voice: He *was* injured. **c** With the past participle of intransitive verbs to form the perfect tense: I *am* finished. **d** With the infinitive or present participle to express purpose, duty, possibility, futurity, etc.: We *are* to start on Monday. [< OE *bēon*]

be- *prefix* Used to form words from nouns, adjectives, and verbs with the following meanings: 1 (from verbs) Around; all over; throughout: *besmudge, besprinkle.* 2 (from verbs) Completely; thoroughly: *bemuddle; beset.* 3 (from verbs) Off; away: *behead.* 4 (from intransitive verbs) About; at; on; over; against; for: *beswarm; beweep.* 5 (from adjectives and nouns) To make; cause to be: *befoul.* 6 (from nouns) To provide with; affect by; cover with: *bejewel; begloom.* 7 (from adjectives usu. in past participial forms) Furnished or covered with, usu. excessively: *bespangled; beribboned.* [< OE *be-*, *bi-*]

B.E. Bachelor of Education; Bachelor of Engineering; Bank of England; Board of Education.

BE, B/E bill of exchange.

Be beryllium.

beach (bēch) *n.* 1 The shore of a body of water, as of a lake or sea, esp. when covered with sand or pebbles. 2 Loose pebbles on the shore; shingle. —*v.t.* & *v.i.* To drive or haul up (a boat or ship) on a beach; strand. [?]

beach·comb·er (bēch′kō′mər) *n.* 1 A vagrant living on what he can find or beg around the wharves and beaches of ports. 2 A long wave rolling upon the beach.

beach·head (bēch′hed′) *n. Mil.* A landing position on a hostile shore established by an advance invasion force.

bea·con (bē′kən) *n.* 1 A signal fire or light on a hill, tower, or the like. 2 A lighthouse or other warning signal on a coast or shoreline. 3 Something that serves as a conspicuous warning or a guide. 4 *Aeron.* A radio device used to establish and plot flight courses. —*v.t.* 1 To furnish with a beacon. —*v.i.* 2 To shine or serve as a beacon. [< OE *bēacen* sign, signal]

bead (bēd) *n.* 1 Any small, usu. round piece of glass, wood, stone, etc., perforated and intended to be strung or attached to a fabric. 2 *pl.* A string of beads. 3 *pl.* A rosary. 4 Froth; foam. 5 A liquid drop, as of sweat. 6 A small spherical knob used as the front sight of a gun. 7 *Archit.* A molding composed of a row of half-oval ornaments. —**draw a bead on** To take careful aim at. —*v.t.* 1 To decorate with beads or beading. —*v.i.* 2 To collect in beads or drops. [< OE *gebed* prayer]

bead·ing (bē′ding) *n.* 1 Ornamentation of beads. 2 Any narrow trimming. 3 A decorative work made with beads.

bea·dle (bēd′l) *n.* In the Church of England, a minor parish officer who ushers, etc. [< OE *bydel* messenger]

beads·man (bēdz′mən) *n. pl.* **·men** (-mən) One who prays for another, esp. when hired to do so. —**beads′wom′an** *n. Fem.*

bead·y (bē′dē) *adj.* **bead·i·er, bead·i·est** 1 Small and glittering, like beads. 2 Decorated with beads. 3 Foamy.

bea·gle (bē′gəl) *n.* A small, short-coated hound with short legs and drooping ears. [ME *begle*]

Beagle

beak (bēk) *n.* 1 The horny projecting mouth parts of birds; the bill. 2 A beaklike part or organ, as the horny jaws of turtles. 3 *Slang* The nose of a person. 4 Something shaped like a beak, as the spout of a pitcher. [< L *beccus*] —**beaked** (bēkt, bē′kid) *adj.*

beak·er (bē′kər) *n.* 1 A large, wide-mouthed cup or goblet. 2 A cylindrical, flat-bottomed vessel with a pouring lip, used in laboratories. 3 The contents or capacity of a beaker. [< ON *bikarr*]

beam (bēm) *n.* 1 A long, horizontal piece of material forming part of a structure. 2 *Naut.* **a** One of the heavy pieces of timber or iron set transversely across a vessel. **b** The greatest width of a vessel. 3 The widest part of anything. 4 The bar of a balance; also, the balance. 5 *Slang* The hips. 6 A ray or a group of nearly parallel rays of light or other radiant energy. 7 A radiant smile. 8 *Aeron.* A continuous radio signal used as a beacon: also **radio beam.** —**off the beam** 1 *Aeron.* Not following the radio beam. 2 *Informal* On the wrong track; wrong. —**on the beam** 1 *Aeron.* Following the radio beam. 2 *Informal* **a** Functioning well or quickly. **b** In the right direction; correct. —*v.t.* 1 To send out in or as in beams or rays. 2 *Telecom.* To aim or transmit (a signal) in a specific direction. 3 *Aeron.* To guide (an airplane) by a radio beam. —*v.i.* 4 To emit light. 5 To smile or grin radiantly. [< OE *bēam* tree]

beam·ing (bē′ming) *adj.* Radiant; bright; cheerful. —**beam′ing·ly** *adv.*

beam·y (bē′mē) *adj.* **beam·i·er, beam·i·est** 1 Sending out beams of light; radiant. 2 Like a beam; massive; broad.

bean (bēn) *n.* 1 The oval edible seed of various leguminous plants. 2 A plant that bears beans. 3 One of several beanlike seeds or plants. 4 *Slang* The head. —*v.t. Slang* To hit on the head. [< OE *bēan*]

bear[1] (bâr) *v.* **bore** (*Archaic* **bare**), **borne** or **born, bear·ing** *v.t.* 1 To support; hold up. 2 To carry; convey. 3 To show visibly; carry: to *bear* a scar. 4 To conduct or guide. 5 To spread: to *bear* tales. 6 To hold in the mind: to *bear* a grudge. 7 To suffer or endure; undergo. 8 To accept or assume, as responsibility. 9 To give birth to (see note below). 10 To conduct or comport (oneself). 11 To manage or carry (oneself or a part of oneself). 12 To render; give: to *bear* witness. 13 To be able to withstand; allow: His story will not *bear* investigation. 14 To have or stand (in comparison or relation): with *to:* What relation does this *bear* to the other? 15 To possess as a right or power: to *bear* title. —*v.i.* 16 To carry burdens; convey. 17 To rest heavily; lean; press. 18 To endure patiently; suffer: often with *with.* 19 To produce fruit or young. 20 To move, point, or lie in a certain direction: Later, we *bore* west. 21 To be relevant; have reference: with *on* or *upon.* —**bear down upon** 1 To approach. 2 To put pressure on. —**bear out** To confirm; justify. [< OE *beran*] • In def. 9, meaning *to give birth to, borne* is the participle used when speaking of the mother or when followed by *by:* She has *borne* twins; The twins were *borne* by her. When speaking of the offspring, *born* is used: He was *born* today. In all other meanings, the participle *borne* is the only one used: They have *borne* their troubles well; *air-borne* bacteria.

bear[2] (bâr) *n.* 1 Any of various large carnivorous or omnivorous mammals with massive thick-furred body and short tail. 2 An ill-mannered, grumpy, or clumsy person. 3 A speculator who sells shares of stock, etc., in the belief that prices will decline and he can buy later at a profit. —*adj.* Of or favorable to bears (def. 3). [< OE *bera*]

Bear

Bear (bâr) *n.* Either of two constellations, the Great Bear or the Little Bear.

bear·a·ble (bâr′ə·bəl) *adj.* Capable of being borne or endured. **—bear′a·ble·ness** *n.* **—bear′a·bly** *adv.*

beard (bird) *n.* 1 The hair on a man's face, esp. on the chin. 2 The long hair on the chin of some animals, as the goat. 3 Any similar growth or appendage. 4 *Bot.* A tuft of hairlike processes; an awn. • See WHEAT. —*v.t.* 1 To defy courageously. 2 To furnish with a beard. [< OE] **—beard′·ed** *adj.*

bear·er (bâr′ər) *n.* 1 One who or that which bears, carries, or has in possession. 2 A person who presents a check, money order, etc., for payment. 3 A tree or vine producing fruit. 4 PALLBEARER.

bear·ing (bâr′ing) *n.* 1 Manner of conducting or carrying oneself. 2 The act, capacity, or period of producing. 3 That which is produced; yield. 4 Endurance. 5 A direction in relation to the compass or another point or place. 6 *Usu. pl.* The position or attitude of something relative to that of another. 7 *pl.* An awareness of one's position or surroundings. 8 Relevance; connection. 9 *Mech.* That part of a machine on which something moves, turns, etc.

bear·ish (bâr′ish) *adj.* 1 Like a bear; rough; surly. 2 Tending to depress the price of stocks by offering to sell. **—bear′ish·ly** *adv.* **—bear′ish·ness** *n.*

bear·skin (bâr′skin′) *n.* The skin of a bear or a garment or rug made of it.

beast (bēst) *n.* 1 Any animal except man. 2 Any large quadruped. 3 Animal characteristics or animal nature. 4 A cruel, rude, or filthy person. [< L *bestia* beast]

beast·ly (bēst′lē) *adj.* **beast·li·er, beast·li·est** 1 Resembling a beast; brutish; vile. 2 *Informal* Disagreeable or unpleasant; nasty; abominable. —*adj. Brit. Slang* Very. **—beast′·li·ness** *n.*

beat (bēt) *v.* **beat, beat·en** (*Informal* **beat**), **beat·ing** *v.t.* 1 To strike repeatedly; pound. 2 To punish in this way; thrash. 3 To dash or strike against. 4 To make, as a path, by repeated walking, blows, pushing, etc. 5 To forge or shape by hammering. 6 To walk on for a long time. 7 To defeat or outdo. 8 To flap; flutter, as wings. 9 *Music* To mark (time or rhythm) with or as with a baton. 10 To hunt over; search. 11 To sound (a signal) as on a drum. 12 To whip (ingredients) so as to make lighter or frothier. 13 *Informal* To baffle; perplex: It *beats* me. 14 *Slang* To defraud; swindle. —*v.i.* 15 To strike repeated blows. 16 To strike or pound as with blows. 17 To throb; pulsate. 18 To give forth sound, as when struck. 19 To sound a signal, as on a drum. 20 *Physics* To fluctuate periodically in intensity. 21 To be adaptable to beating: The yolk *beats* well. 22 To hunt through underbrush, etc., as for game. 23 To win a victory or contest. **—beat around the bush** To be evasive. —**beat it** *Slang* To go hastily. **—beat up** *Informal* To thrash thoroughly. —*n.* 1 A stroke or blow. 2 A pulsation or throb, as of the pulse. 3 *Physics* A periodic reinforcement and cancellation that results when waves of slightly different frequencies interact. 4 *Naut.* A tack. 5 *Music* a One of a series of pulses used to mark time in music. b The gesture or symbol for this. 6 A round, line, or district regularly traversed, as by a sentry or a policeman. 7 *Slang* A scoop for a newspaper. 8 *Slang* A deadbeat. 9 *Informal* A beatnik. —*adj.* 1 *Informal* Fatigued; worn out. 2 Of or pertaining to the Beat Generation. [< OE *bēatan*]

beat·en (bēt′n) *adj.* 1 Struck by repeated blows; thrashed. 2 Shaped or made thin by beating. 3 Worn by use or much travel. 4 Defeated. 5 Utterly discouraged or fatigued.

Beat Generation A group of young people who, esp. in the 1950's, expressed a growing social disillusionment by adopting unconventional modes of dress and behavior, Eastern philosophies, etc.

be·a·tif·ic (bē′ə·tif′ik) *adj.* Showing or imparting great joy or blessedness. **—be′a·tif′i·cal·ly** *adv.*

be·at·i·fy (bē·at′ə·fī) *v.t.* **·fied, ·fy·ing** 1 To make supremely happy. 2 In the Roman Catholic Church, to declare as blessed and worthy of public honor by an act of the Pope. 3 To exalt above others. [< L *beatus* happy, blessed + *facere* make] **—be·at·i·fi·ca·tion** (bē·at′ə·fi·kā′shən) *n.*

beat·ing (bē′ting) *n.* 1 The action of one who or that which beats. 2 A flogging. 3 Pulsation; throbbing. 4 A defeat.

be·at·i·tude (bē·at′ə·t^yo͞od) *n.* Supreme blessedness. —**the Beatitudes** The declarations of special blessedness in the Sermon on the Mount. *Matt.* 5:3–11. [< L *beatitudo* blessedness]

beat·nik (bēt′nik) *n.* A member of the Beat Generation. [< BEAT, *adj.* def. 2 + -NIK]

beau (bō) *n. pl.* **beaus** or **beaux** (bōz) 1 A lover or suitor of a girl or woman. 2 An escort. [< F < L *bellus* fine, pretty]

Beau·fort scale (bō′fərt) *Meteorol.* A scale of wind velocities, ranging from 0 (calm) to 12 (hurricane). [< Sir Francis *Beaufort*, 1774–1857, British admiral]

beau·te·ous (byo͞o′tē·əs) *adj.* Beautiful. **—beau′te·ous·ly** *adv.* **—beau′te·ous·ness** *n.*

beau·ti·cian (byo͞o·tish′ən) *n.* One who works in a beauty parlor, or a person trained in hairdressing, manicuring, massaging, etc.

beau·ti·ful (byo͞o′tə·fəl) *adj.* Possessing beauty. **—beau′ti·ful·ly** *adv.* **—Syn.** attractive, comely, exquisite, fair, handsome, lovely, pretty.

beau·ti·fy (byo͞o′tə·fī) *v.t.* & *v.i.* **·fied, ·fy·ing** To make or grow beautiful; embellish; adorn. **—beau′ti·fi·ca′tion, beau′ti·fi′er** *n.*

beau·ty (byo͞o′tē) *n. pl.* **·ties** 1 Any of those attributes of form, sound, color, execution, character, behavior, etc., which give pleasure and gratification to the senses or to the mind. 2 A person or thing that is beautiful, esp. a woman. 3 Physical attractiveness. 4 Any special or compelling feature. [< OF *beaute* < L *bellus* handsome, fine, pretty]

beauty parlor A place for the hairdressing, manicuring, cosmetic treatment, etc., of women. Also **beauty salon, beauty shop.**

beauty spot 1 A small black patch put on the face to enhance the brilliance of the complexion. 2 A mole or other natural mark resembling this.

beaux (bōz) *n.pl.* of BEAU.

beaux-arts (bō·zär′) *n. pl. French* The fine arts, as music, painting, sculpture, etc.

bea·ver[1] (bē′vər) *n.* 1 An aquatic rodent with a scaly, broad tail and webbed hind feet, noted for skill in damming shallow streams. 2 The fur of the beaver. 3 A high silk hat, originally made of this fur. [< OE *beofor*]

bea·ver[2] (bē′vər) *n.* 1 A movable piece of medieval armor covering the lower part of the face. 2 The visor of a helmet. 3 *Slang* A beard. [< OF *bavière* child's bib]

bea·ver·board (bē′vər·bôrd′, -bōrd′) *n.* A light, stiff building material made of compressed or laminated wood pulp, used chiefly for walls and partitions. [< *Beaverboard*, a trade name]

Beaver

be-bop (bē′bop′) *n.* A variety of jazz; bop.

be·calm (bi·käm′) *v.t.* 1 To make quiet or calm; still. 2 To cause to be motionless for lack of wind, as a ship: used in the passive: *becalmed* off the coast of Spain.

be·came (bi·kām′) *p.t.* of BECOME.

be·cause (bi·kôz′) *conj.* For the reason that; since. —

—because of On account of; by reason of. [ME *bi cause* by cause]

be·chance (bi·chans′, -chäns′) *v.t. & v.i.* **be·chanced, be·chanc·ing** To befall; happen by chance.

Bech·u·a·na·land (bech′o͞o·ä′nə·land, bek′yo͞o-) A former British protectorate in s Africa, now the nation of Botswana. • See map at AFRICA.

beck (bek) *n.* A nod or other gesture of summons. **—at one's beck and call** Subject to one's slightest wish. [Var. of BECKON]

beck·on (bek′ən) *v.t. & v.i.* **1** To signal, direct, or summon by sign or gesture. **2** To entice or lure. *—n.* A summoning gesture; beck. [<OE *biecnan, beacnian* to make signs]

be·cloud (bi·kloud′) *v.t.* **1** To make cloudy; darken. **2** To confuse, as an issue.

be·come (bi·kum′) *v.* **be·came, be·come, be·com·ing** *v.i.* **1** To grow to be: The chick *becomes* the chicken. **2** To come to be: The land *became* dry. *—v.t.* **3** To suit or befit. **4** To show to advantage: Your dress *becomes* you. **—become of** To be the fate of: What *became of* him? [<OE *becuman* happen, come about]

be·com·ing (bi·kum′ing) *adj.* **1** Appropriate; suitable. **2** Pleasing; adorning. **—be·com′ing·ly** *adv.*

bed (bed) *n.* **1** An article of furniture to rest or sleep in or on, usu. consisting of the bedstead, springs, mattress, and bedclothes. **2** Any place or thing used for resting or sleeping. **3** Conjugal cohabitation or the right to it. **4** The ground at the bottom of a body of water. **5** Something serving as a foundation or support: a *bed* of gravel. **6** A garden plot or the plants, etc., growing therein. **7** A pile of something resembling a bed. **8** *Geol.* Any layer in a mass of stratified rock; a seam. **—bed and board 1** Accommodations for sleeping and for meals. **2** The marriage state. **—put** (or **go**) **to bed 1** To prepare for sleeping. **2** To prepare (a newspaper, etc.) for printing; go to press. *—v.* **bed·ded, bed·ding** *v.t.* **1** To furnish with a sleeping place. **2** To put to bed. **3** To set out or plant in a bed of earth. **4** To have sexual intercourse with. **5** To lay flat or arrange in layers: to *bed* oysters. **6** EMBED. *—v.i.* **7** To go to bed. **8** To form a closely packed layer; stratify. **—bed down** To prepare a sleeping place for: to *bed down* cattle. [<OE] **—bed′der** *n.*

be·daub (bi·dôb′) *v.t.* **1** To smear or oil. **2** To load with vulgar ornament or flattery.

be·daz·zle (bi·daz′əl) *v.t.* **·zled, ·zling 1** To blind by too much light. **2** To bewilder; stun.

bed·bug (bed′bug′) *n.* A flat, wingless, bloodsucking insect of reddish brown color, infesting houses, esp. beds, and usu. active only at night.

bed·cham·ber (bed′chām′bər) *n.* A bedroom.

bed·clothes (bed′klōz′, -klōt͟hz′) *n.pl.* Covering for a bed, as sheets, blankets, quilts, etc.

bed·ding (bed′ing) *n.* **1** Mattress and bedclothes. **2** Straw or other litter for animals to sleep on. **3** That which forms a bed or foundation. **4** *Geol.* Stratification of rocks.

be·deck (bi·dek′) *v.t.* To deck; adorn.

be·dev·il (bi·dev′əl) *v.t.* **·iled** or **·illed, ·il·ing** or **·il·ling 1** To harass; worry. **2** To torment diabolically; plague. **3** To spoil; corrupt. **4** To bewitch. **—be·dev′il·ment** *n.*

be·dew (bi·dʸo͞o′) *v.t.* To moisten with or as with dew.

bed·fel·low (bed′fel′ō) *n.* **1** One who shares a bed with another. **2** A companion, cohort, etc.

be·dight (bi·dīt′) *adj. Archaic* Adorned.

be·dim (bi·dim′) *v.t.* **be·dimmed, be·dim·ming** To make dim; obscure.

be·di·zen (bi·dī′zən, -diz′ən) *v.t.* To dress or adorn in a gaudy way. **—be·di′zen·ment** *n.*

bed·lam (bed′ləm) *n.* **1** An excited crowd. **2** An incoherent uproar. **3** A lunatic asylum. [<*Bedlam,* a former London asylum]

bed linen Sheets, pillow cases, etc., for beds.

Bed·ou·in (bed′o͞o·in, -ēn) *n.* **1** One of the nomadic Arabs of Syria, Arabia, etc. **2** Any nomad or vagabond. *—adj.* **1** Of or pertaining to the Bedouins. **2** Roving; nomadic. [<Ar. *badāwī* desert dweller]

bed·pan (bed′pan′) *n.* **1** A vessel used for urination or defecation by a bedridden person. **2** A warming pan.

be·drag·gle (bi·drag′əl) *v.t. & v.i.* **·gled, ·gling** To make or become wet or soiled, as by dragging through mire.

bed·rid·den (bed′rid′ən) *adj.* Confined to bed, as by sickness. Also **bed′rid′**. [<OE *bed* bed + *rida* rider]

bed·rock (bed′rok′) *n.* **1** The solid rock underlying the looser materials of the earth's surface. **2** Any solid foundation. **3** The bottom or lowest limit. **4** Basic principles; fundamentals.

bed·roll (bed′rōl′) *n.* Bedding compactly rolled to facilitate carrying.

bed·room (bed′ro͞om′, -ro͝om′) *n.* A room for sleeping in.

bed·side (bed′sīd′) *n.* The space beside a bed. *—adj.* **1** Beside a bed. **2** Suitable for the sick: a *bedside* manner.

bed-sit·ter (bed′sit′ər) *n. Brit.* A one-room apartment consisting of a combined bedroom and living room. Also **bed′-sit′ting room.**

bed·sore (bed′sôr′, -sōr′) *n.* An ulcer due to prolonged pressure on a small area of a bedridden person's body.

bed·spread (bed′spred′) *n.* A piece of fabric, usu. ornamental, for covering a bed.

bed·spring (bed′spring′) *n.* The framework of springs supporting the mattress of a bed.

bed·stead (bed′sted′) *n.* A framework for supporting the springs and mattress of a bed.

bed·time (bed′tīm′) *n.* The time for retiring to bed. *—adj.* Of or for this time.

bed-wet·ting (bed′wet′ing) *n.* Involuntary urination during sleep.

bee (bē) *n.* **1** Any of a large number of hymenopterous insects that feed largely upon nectar and pollen, esp. the common honeybee. **2** A social gathering for work or competitive activity. [<OE *bēo*]

bee·bread (bē′bred′) *n.* A mixture of pollen and honey, made and stored by bees for food.

beech (bēch) *n.* **1** Any of a family of trees of temperate regions with smooth, ash-gray bark, and bearing an edible nut. **2** The wood of this tree. [<OE *bēce*] **—beech′en** *adj.*

beech·mast (bēch′mast′) *n.* Beechnuts.

beech·nut (bēch′nut′) *n.* The edible nut of the beech.

beef (bēf) *n. pl.* **beeves** (bēvz) or **beefs** *for def. 2;* **beefs** *for def. 4* **1** The flesh of a slaughtered adult bovine animal. **2** Any adult bovine animal, as an ox, cow, steer, bull, etc., fattened for the butcher. **3** *Informal* Muscular power; brawn. **4** *Slang* A complaint. *—v.i. Slang* To complain. **—beef up** *Slang* To strengthen. [<L *bos, bovis* ox]

beef·cake (bēf′kāk′) *n. Slang* The display of a male's legs or torso, as in photographs.

beef·steak (bēf′stāk′) *n.* A slice of beef suitable for broiling or frying.

beef tea A beverage made by boiling lean beef or from a beef extract.

beef·y (bē′fē) *adj.* **beef·i·er, beef·i·est 1** Like an ox; fat; dull. **2** *Informal* Brawny; muscular. **—beef′i·ness** *n.*

bee·hive (bē′hīv′) *n.* **1** A hive for a colony of honeybees. **2** A place of great activity.

bee·keep·er (bē′kē′pər) *n.* APIARIST. **—bee′keep′ing** *n.*

bee·line (bē′līn′) *n.* The shortest course from one place to another, as of a bee to its hive.

Be·el·ze·bub (bē·el′zə·bub) The devil. *—n.* Any devil.

been (bin, *Brit.* bēn) *p.p.* of BE.

beep (bēp) *n.* A short, usu. high-pitched mechanical or electronic sound used as a signal or warning. *—v.i.* **1** To make such a sound. *—v.t.* **2** To sound (a horn). **3** To transmit (a message) by a beep or beeps. [Imit.]

beer (bir) *n.* **1** An undistilled alcoholic liquor made from fermented grain, esp. from malted barley flavored with hops. **2** A beverage made from the roots, etc., of plants, as sassafras, ginger, etc. [<OE *bēor*]

beer·y (bir′ē) *adj.* **beer·i·er, beer·i·est 1** Affected by beer. **2** Like beer in taste or smell. **3** Maudlin. **—beer′i·ly** *adv.* **—beer′i·ness** *n.*

beest·ings (bēs′tingz) *n.pl. (construed as sing.)* The first milk from a cow after calving. [<OE *bēost*]

bees·wax (bēz′waks′) *n.* A wax secreted by honey bees, from which they make their honeycomb. *—v.t.* To smear with beeswax; wax.

beet (bēt) *n.* **1** The fleshy red or white root of a biennial herb, eaten as a vegetable and used as a source of sugar. **2** The plant. [<OE *bēte* <L *beta*]

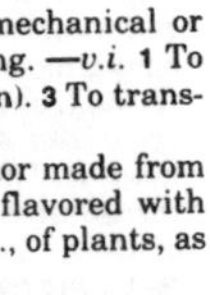

Carpet beetle

bee·tle[1] (bēt′l) *n.* **1** Any of a large order of insects having biting mouth parts and hard front wings that cover the membranous hind wings when at rest. 2 Loosely, any insect resembling a beetle. —*adj.* Shaggy; overhanging: a *beetle* brow: also **bee'tling.** —*v.i.* **·tled, ·tling** To jut out; overhang. [< OE *bitula* < *bītan* bite]

bee·tle² (bēt'l) *n.* 1 A heavy wooden hammer or mallet. 2 A pestle or mallet for pounding, mashing, etc. —*v.t.* **·tled, ·tling** To beat or stamp with or as with a beetle. [< OE *bīetel* mallet]

bee·tle-browed (bēt'l·broud') *adj.* 1 Having prominent, overhanging eyebrows. 2 Scowling; frowning. [< BEETLE¹]

beeves (bēvz) A *n.pl.* of BEEF.

be·fall (bi·fôl') *v.* **be·fell, be·fall·en, be·fall·ing** *v.i.* 1 To come about; happen. —*v.t.* 2 To happen to. [< OE *bef(e)allan* fall]

be·fit (bi·fit') *v.t.* **be·fit·ted, be·fit·ting** To be suited to; be appropriate for. **—be·fit'ting** *adj.* **—be·fit'ting·ly** *adv.*

be·fog (bi·fôg', -fog') *v.t.* **be·fogged, be·fog·ging** 1 To envelop in or as in fog. 2 To confuse; obscure.

be·fore (bi·fôr', -fōr') *adv.* 1 In front; ahead. 2 Preceding in time; previously. 3 Earlier; sooner. —*prep.* 1 In front of; ahead of, as in time, place, rank, sequence, etc. 2 In or into the presence, sight, attention, etc. of: He stood *before* the court. 3 Under the judgment or consideration of: The bill is *before* the senate. 4 In preference to; rather than. —*conj.* 1 Previous to the time when. 2 Sooner than: They would die *before* they yielded. [< OE *beforan* in front of]

be·fore·hand (bi·fôr'hand', -fōr'-) *adv. & adj.* In anticipation or advance; ahead of time.

be·foul (bi·foul') *v.t.* 1 To make foul or dirty. 2 To slander; defame.

be·friend (bi·frend') *v.t.* 1 To be a friend to; stand by. 2 To become a friend to; make friends with.

be·fud·dle (bi·fud'l) *v.t.* **·dled, ·dling** To confuse, as with liquor or glib arguments.

beg (beg) *v.* **begged, beg·ging** *v.t.* 1 To ask for or solicit in charity. 2 To entreat of; beseech. —*v.i.* 3 To ask alms or charity. 4 To entreat politely or humbly. **—beg off** To ask to be excused from. **—beg the question** 1 To take for granted the matter in dispute. 2 To avoid the question or issue; equivocate. [?] **—Syn.** 2 implore, plead, supplicate.

be·gan (bi·gan') *p.t.* of BEGIN.

be·get (bi·get') *v.t.* **be·got** (*Archaic* **be·gat**), **be·got·ten** or **be·got, be·get·ting** 1 To procreate; be the father of. 2 To cause to be; occasion. [< OE *begitan*] **—be·get'ter** *n.*

beg·gar (beg'ər) *n.* 1 One who asks alms, esp. one who lives by begging. 2 An impoverished person. 3 A fellow; rogue. —*v.t.* 1 To impoverish. 2 To exhaust the resources of: It *beggars* analysis. **—beg'gar·dom, beg'gar·hood** *n.*

beg·gar·ly (beg'ər·lē) *adj.* Miserably poor, mean, sordid, etc. **—beg'gar·li·ness** *n.*

beg·gar's-lice (beg'ərz·līs') *n.* Any of various plants bearing burs which adhere to clothes. Also **beg·gar·ticks** (beg'ər·tiks'), **beg'gar's-ticks'.**

be·gin (bi·gin') *v.* **be·gan, be·gun, be·gin·ning** *v.i.* 1 To take a first step in doing something; start. 2 To come into being; arise. 3 To have the essentials or the ability: It doesn't *begin* to compare with the original painting. —*v.t.* 4 To enter upon; commence. 5 To give origin to; start. [< OE *beginnan*]

be·gin·ner (bi·gin'ər) *n.* 1 A founder; originator. 2 One beginning to learn a new skill, subject, etc.; a novice.

be·gin·ning (bi·gin'ing) *n.* 1 The starting point in space, time, or action; origin. 2 The first stage or part. 3 The source or first cause. 4 *Usu. pl.* An early phase.

be·gone (bi·gôn', -gon') *interj.* Go away!

be·gon·ia (bi·gōn'yə) *n.* Any of various tropical plants widely cultivated for their showy leaves and flowers. [< Michel *Begon,* 1638–1710, French colonial administrator]

be·got (bi·got') *p.t. & p.p.* of BEGET.

be·got·ten (bi·got'n) A *p.p.* of BEGET.

be·grime (bi·grīm') *v.t.* **be·grimed, be·grim·ing** To soil; make dirty with grime.

be·grudge (bi·gruj') *v.t.* **be·grudged, be·grudg·ing** 1 To envy one the possession of (something). 2 To give or grant reluctantly. **—be·grudg'ing·ly** *adv.*

be·guile (bi·gīl') *v.t.* **be·guiled, be·guil·ing** 1 To deceive; mislead by guile. 2 To cheat; defraud: with *of* or *out of.* 3 To while away pleasantly, as time. 4 To charm; divert. —**be·guile'ment, be·guil'er** *n.* **—be·guil'ing·ly** *adv.*

be·gum (bē'gəm) *n.* A Muslim princess, or woman of rank in India.

be·gun (bi·gun') *p.p.* of BEGIN.

be·half (bi·haf', -häf') *n.* The interest or defense (of anyone): preceded by *in, on,* or *upon.* [< OE *be healfe* by the side (of)]

be·have (bi·hāv') *v.* **be·haved, be·hav·ing** *v.i.* 1 To comport oneself properly. 2 To act; conduct oneself or itself: The car *behaves* well. 3 To react to stimuli or environment. —*v.t.* 4 To conduct (oneself) properly or suitably. [ME *be-* thoroughly + *haven* hold oneself, have]

be·hav·ior (bi·hāv'yər) *n.* 1 Manner of one's conduct; deportment. 2 Manner or action of a machine, substance, organism, etc. 3 Any observable response of an organism to stimuli. *Brit. sp.* **be·hav'iour. —be·hav'ior·al** (-yər·əl) *adj.* **—Syn.** 1 comportment, manner, actions, ways.

behavioral science Any science dealing with some aspect of human activity, as psychology, sociology, anthropology, etc.

be·hav·ior·ism (bi·hāv'yər·iz'əm) *n.* A school of psychology that confines its studies to observable phenomena, holding that subjective factors, as thought and feelings, are beyond scientific investigation. **—be·hav'ior·ist** *adj., n.* **—be·hav'ior·is'tic** *adj.*

be·head (bi·hed') *v.t.* To cut off the head of; decapitate. **—be·head'ing** *n.*

be·held (bi·held') *p.t. & p.p.* of BEHOLD.

be·he·moth (bi·hē'məth, bē'ə-) *n.* 1 In the Bible, a colossal beast. 2 Anything huge. [< Heb. *behēmāh* beast]

be·hest (bi·hest') *n.* An authoritative request; command. [< OE *behæs* promise, vow]

be·hind (bi·hīnd') *adv.* 1 In, toward, or at the rear. 2 In a previous place, condition, etc.: They left their regrets *behind.* 3 In time gone by. 4 In arrears. 5 Retarded in time, as a train or clock. —*prep.* 1 At the back or farther side of. 2 To or toward the rear. 3 No longer existing for: His troubles are *behind* him. 4 Remaining after. 5 Later than. 6 Sustaining; supporting. 7 Inferior to, as in rank, achievement, etc. 8 Not yet revealed or made known about: something strange *behind* that remark. —*adj.* 1 Following: the car *behind.* 2 In arrears. —*n. Informal* The buttocks. [< OE *behindan*]

be·hind·hand (bi·hīnd'hand') *adv. & adj.* 1 Behind time; late. 2 In arrears. 3 In a backward state; not sufficiently advanced.

be·hold (bi·hōld') *v.t.* **be·held, be·hold·ing** To look at or upon. —*interj.* Look! See! [< OE *beh(e)aldan* hold] **—be·hold'er** *n.*

be·hold·en (bi·hōl'dən) *adj.* Under obligation; indebted.

be·hoof (bi·hōōf') *n.* That which benefits; advantage; use. [< OE *behōf* advantage]

be·hoove (bi·hōōv') *v.t.* **be·hooved, be·hoov·ing** To be fit, needful, or right for: used impersonally: It *behooves* me to leave. *Brit. sp.* **be·hove** (bi·hōv'). [< OE *behōfian*]

beige (bāzh) *n.* The light, grayish tan color of natural wool. —*adj.* Of this color. [F]

be·ing (bē'ing) *p.p.* of BE. —*n.* 1 The state or quality of existing, either materially or immaterially: when art came into *being.* 2 One who exists or is conceived of as existing. 3 Any living thing. 4 Essential nature or substance: His whole *being* is musical.

Be·ing (bē'ing) *n.* God: the Supreme *Being.*

be·la·bor (bi·lā'bər) *v.t.* 1 To beat; thrash soundly. 2 To assail verbally. 3 To repeat, explain, etc., endlessly.

be·lat·ed (bi·lā'tid) *adj.* Late; tardy. **—be·lat'ed·ly** *adv.* **—be·lat'ed·ness** *n.*

be·lay (bi·lā') *v.* **be·layed, be·lay·ing** *v.t.* 1 *Naut.* To make fast (a rope) by winding on a pin **(belaying pin)**, cleat, etc. —*v.i.* 2 *Informal* To stop or hold; cease: *Belay* there. [< OE *belecgan*]

belch (belch) *v.t. & v.i.* 1 To eject forcibly or violently. 2 To eject (gas) noisily from the stomach through the mouth. —*n.* The act of belching or the thing belched. [< OE *bealcian*] —**belch′er** *n.*

bel·dam (bel′dəm) *n.* An old woman, esp. a hag or crone. Also **bel·dame** (bel′dəm, -dām′). [ME, grandmother]

be·lea·guer (bi·lē′gər) *v.t.* **1** To surround or shut in with an armed force. **2** To harass or annoy, as if from all directions at once. [< Du. *belegeren*] —**be·lea′guered** *adj.*

bel·fry (bel′frē) *n. pl.* **·fries 1** A tower in which a bell is hung. **2** The part of such a tower containing the bell. [< OF *berfrei*] —**bel′fried** *adj.*

Belg. *n.* Belgian; Belgium.

Bel·gium (bel′jəm, -jē·əm) *n.* A constitutional monarchy of northwestern Europe, 11,775 sq. mi., cap. Brussels. —**Bel′gian** (-jən) *adj., n.*

be·lie (bi·lī′) *v.t.* **be·lied, be·ly·ing 1** To misrepresent; disguise. **2** To contradict: Her actions *belied* her words. **3** To fail to fulfill: to *belie* hopes. **4** To slander. [< OE *belēogan*] —**be·li′er** *n.*

be·lief (bi·lēf′) *n.* **1** The acceptance of something as true or actual. **2** That which is believed true, as a creed. **3** Religious faith. **4** Confidence; trust. **5** An opinion.

be·lieve (bi·lēv′) *v.* **be·lieved, be·liev·ing** *v.t.* **1** To accept as true or real. **2** To accept the word of (someone). **3** To think; assume: with a clause as object. —*v.i.* **4** To accept the truth, existence, worth, etc., of something: with *in.* **5** To have confidence: with *in:* The country *believes* in you. **6** To have religious faith. [< OE *gelēfen* believe] —**be·liev′a·ble** *adj.* —**be·liev′a·bly** *adv.* —**be·liev′er** *n.*

be·lit·tle (bi·lit′l) *v.t.* **·tled, ·tling** To cause to seem small or less; disparage; minimize. —**Syn.** run down, depreciate, deride, ridicule, malign, criticize, sneer at.

bell (bel) *n.* **1** A hollow, usu. cuplike metallic instrument which rings when struck. **2** The sound of a bell. **3** Anything in the shape of or suggesting a bell. **4** The flaring end of a tubular musical instrument. **5** *Naut.* **a** A stroke on a bell to mark the time on shipboard. **b** *pl.* With a numeral prefixed, the time so marked in half-hours. —*v.t.* **1** To put a bell on. **2** To shape like a bell. —*v.i.* **3** To flare out, as a bell. [< OE *belle*]

bel·la·don·na (bel′ə·don′ə) *n.* **1** A poisonous plant with purple-red flowers and shining black berries; deadly nightshade. **2** A drug derived from this plant; atropine. [< Ital. *bella donna* beautiful lady]

bell·boy (bel′boi′) *n.* BELLMAN.

belle (bel) *n.* **1** A beautiful woman or girl. **2** The reigning beauty of a city, social function, etc. [F, beautiful]

belles-let·tres (bel′let′rə) *n. pl. (construed as sing.)* Literary works, as poetry, drama, fiction, etc., as distinguished from technical or didactic writings. [F, fine letters] —**bel·let·rist** (bel′let′rist) *n.* —**bel·le·tris·tic** (bel′lə·tris′tik) *adj.*

bel·li·cose (bel′ə·kōs) *adj.* Pugnacious; warlike. [< L *bellum* war] —**bel′li·cose′ly** *adv.* —**bel′li·cos′i·ty** (-kos′ə·tē) *n.*

bel·lig·er·ent (bə·lij′ər·ənt) *adj.* **1** Warlike. **2** Engaged in or pertaining to war. **3** Aggressively quarrelsome. —*n.* A belligerent nation or person. [< L *belligare* wage war] —**bel·lig′er·ence, bel·lig′er·en·cy,** *n.* —**bel·lig′er·ent·ly** *adv.*

bell·man (bel′mən) *n. pl.* **·men** (-mən) A man or boy employed by a hotel to carry luggage, run errands, etc., for the guests. Also **bell·hop** (bel′hop′).

bel·low (bel′ō) *v.i.* **1** To utter a loud, hollow sound; roar, as a bull. **2** To roar, usu. with anger. —*v.t.* **3** To utter with a loud, roaring voice. —*n.* A loud, hollow cry or roar. [ME *belwen*] —**bel′low·er** *n.*

bel·lows (bel′ōz, *earlier* bel′əs) *n.* **1** An instrument with flexible sides, for drawing in air and expelling it under pressure through a tube. **2** The expansible portion of a camera. **3** *Informal* The lungs. [< OE *belg, belig* bag]

Bellows *def. 1*

bell·weth·er (bel′weth′ər) *n.* **1** The male sheep that wears a bell and leads a flock of sheep. **2** One who leads a group, esp. a sheeplike group.

bel·ly (bel′ē) *n. pl.* **bel·lies 1** The soft ventral part of a vertebrate body between ribs and pelvis; abdomen. **2** The thick, middle part of a muscle. **3** The stomach. **4** Anything resembling a belly: the *belly* of a flask; the *belly* of a wind-filled sail. **5** The front surface of the sounding box of a violin, viola, etc. —*v.t. & v.i.* **bel·lied, bel·ly·ing** To swell out or fill, as a sail. [< OE *belg, belig* bag]

bel·ly·ache (bel′ē·āk′) *n.* Pain in the abdomen; colic. —*v.i.* **·ached, ·ach·ing** *Slang* To complain petulantly.

bel·ly·band (bel′ē·band′) *n.* A strap passing beneath a draft animal, as to fasten the saddle, harness, etc.

bel·ly·but·ton (bel′ē·but′n) *n. Informal* The navel.

be·long (bi·lông′, -long′) *v.i.* **1** To be in the possession of someone: with *to.* **2** To be a part of or an appurtenance to something: with *to:* The screw *belongs* to this fan. **3** To be suitable: That lamp *belongs* in this room. **4** To have relation or be a member: with *to.* [< ME *be-* completely + *longen* to suit, go along with]

be·long·ing (bi·lông′ing, -long′-) *n.* **1** That which belongs to a person or thing. **2** *pl.* Possessions; effects. **3** Rapport; relationship: a sense of *belonging.*

be·lov·ed (bi·luv′id, -luvd′) *adj.* Greatly loved; dear to the heart. —*n.* One greatly loved.

be·low (bi·lō′) *adv.* **1** In or to a lower place. **2** To a place under the floor or deck: Get *below!* **3** Farther along, as on a page, list, etc. **4** On earth. **5** In or to hell. **6** Lower in rank or authority. —*prep.* **1** Farther or lower down than. **2** Inferior to in degree, rank, value, etc. **3** Unworthy of. [< BY- + LOW]

belt (belt) *n.* **1** A band worn around the waist, as to hold up clothing, secure tools, etc. **2** Any encircling band, highway, etc. **3** *Mech.* **a** A flexible band passing over two or more wheels and serving to transmit motion from one part to another. **b** A moving assembly line in a factory. **4** *Ecol.* A zone or stretch of country having some distinct characteristic: a corn *belt.* **5** A girdle of armor plates protecting a warship along the water line. **6** *Informal* A blow, as with the fist. **7** *Slang* A drink of liquor. —**below the belt** Unfairly. —*v.t.* **1** To gird with or as with a belt. **2** To fasten with a belt. **3** *Informal* To strike with force. **4** *Informal* To sing or play loudly: usu. with *out.* **5** *Slang* To have one or more drinks of liquor: usu. with *down.* [< OE] —**belt′ed** *adj.* —**belt′er** *n.*

belt·ing (bel′ting) *n.* **1** Belts collectively, or the material for belts. **2** *Slang* A beating.

be·lu·ga (bə·lo͞o′gə) *n. pl.* **·ga** or **·gas 1** A large, white dolphin of arctic seas. **2** The great white sturgeon of the Caspian Sea and the Black Sea; its roe is **beluga caviar.** [< Russ., whale, white whale]

be·mire (bi·mīr′) *v.t.* **be·mired, be·mir·ing 1** To soil with mud or mire. **2** To stall in mud.

be·moan (bi·mōn′) *v.t. & v.i.* To mourn or lament. [< OE *bemænan*]

be·muse (bi·myo͞oz′) *v.t.* **·mused, ·mus·ing 1** To muddle or stupefy. **2** To engross; preoccupy. —**be·mused′** *adj.*

bench (bench) *n.* **1** A long, wooden seat, with or without a back. **2** A stout worktable. **3** The judges' seat in court. **4** The judge or the judges collectively; also, the court. **5** The office or status of a judge. **6** In sports: **a** The seat or seats for the players not playing. **b** Such players collectively. —**on the bench 1** Presiding, as a judge. **2** In sports, not playing, as a substitute player. —*v.t.* **1** To furnish with benches. **2** To seat on a bench. **3** In sports, to remove (a player) from a game. [< OE *benc*]

bench·mark (bench′märk′) *n.* **1** A permanent reference mark fixed in the ground for use in surveys, tidal observations, etc. **2** A reference point serving as a standard for comparing or judging other things. Also **bench mark.**

bench warrant A warrant issued by a presiding judge for the arrest of a person.

bend[1] (bend) *v.* **bent** (*Archaic* **bend·ed**), **bend·ing** *v.t.* **1** To make curved or different in shape. **2** To direct or turn, as one's course, in a certain direction. **3** To subdue; cause to yield, as to one's will. **4** To direct or concentrate, as the mind. **5** To resolve: used in the passive: with *on:* They were *bent* on winning. **6** *Naut.* To tie; make fast. —*v.i.* **7** To take or assume a new or different shape. **8** To take a new or different direction; swerve. **9** To bend over; stoop. **10** To yield or conform. —*n.* **1** A curve or crook. **2** A bending or being bent. **3** Any of various knots used to fasten a rope to something. [< OE *bendan*]

bend[2] (bend) *n. Her.* A band drawn diagonally from the upper left to the lower right of a shield. [< OE *bend* band]

Bend

bend·er (ben′dər) *n.* **1** A person or thing that bends. **2** *Slang* A drinking spree.

bends (bendz) *n.pl.* DECOMPRESSION SICKNESS.

bend sinister *Her.* A band drawn diagonally from the lower left to the upper right of a shield, a mark of bastardy.

be·neath (bi·nēth′) *adv.* **1** At a lower point; below. **2** On the underside of; underneath. —*prep.* **1** In a lower place or position than. **2** Underneath. **3** Influenced or controlled by. **4** Inferior to or lower in rank, quality, etc., than. **5** Unworthy of. [<OE *beneathan*]

Ben·e·dic·tine (ben′ə·dik′tin, -tēn) *adj.* Of St. Benedict or his order. —*n.* **1** A monk or nun following St. Benedict's monastic rules. **2** A liqueur originally made by Benedictines in France.

ben·e·dic·tion (ben′ə·dik′shən) *n.* **1** The act of blessing. **2** The invocation of divine favor upon a person. **3** Any of various formal ecclesiastical ceremonies of blessing. [<L *benedicere* bless] **—ben′e·dic′tive, ben′e·dic′to·ry** *adj.*

ben·e·fac·tion (ben′ə·fak′shən) *n.* **1** The act of giving or doing something for charitable reasons. **2** That which is given or done. [<L *benefacere* do well]

ben·e·fac·tor (ben′ə·fak′tər, ben′ə·fak′-) *n.* A friendly and generous helper; a patron. **—ben′e·fac′tress** *n. Fem.*

ben·e·fice (ben′ə·fis) *n.* **1** A church office, as for a rector, parson, etc., endowed with funds or property. **2** The revenue from such funds or property. —*v.t.* **·ficed, ·fic·ing** To invest with a benefice. [<L *beneficium* favor] **—ben′e·ficed** *adj.*

be·nef·i·cence (bə·nef′ə·səns) *n.* **1** The quality of being charitable and good. **2** A charitable act or gift. [<L *beneficus* generous] **—be·nef′i·cent** *adj.* **—be·nef′i·cent·ly** *adv.*

ben·e·fi·cial (ben′ə·fish′əl) *adj.* Benefiting or tending to benefit; advantageous; helpful; useful; salutary. [<L *beneficium* favor] **—ben′e·fi′cial·ly** *adv.*

ben·e·fi·ci·ar·y (ben′ə·fish′ē·er′ē, -fish′ər·ē) *n. pl.* **·ar·ies** **1** One who receives benefit. **2** The holder of a benefice or church living. **3** The person designated to receive the income from an insurance policy, annuity, inheritance, etc. [<L *beneficium* favor]

ben·e·fit (ben′ə·fit) *n.* **1** Something helpful; profit; advantage. **2** A special public event, as a performance, bazaar, etc., the proceeds of which are donated to a charitable cause. **3** *Usu. pl.* Payments made by a government, employer, insurance company, etc., to the aged, unemployed, sick, etc. —*v.* **·fit·ed, ·fit·ing** *v.t.* **1** To be helpful or useful to. —*v.i.* **2** To profit; gain advantage. [<L *benefacere* do well] **—Syn.** *v.* **1** help, serve, assist, profit, improve, aid, better.

benefit of clergy Churchly approval or sanction: married without *benefit of clergy.*

Ben·e·lux (ben′ə·luks) *n.* The economic union of Belgium, the Netherlands, and Luxembourg. [<BE(LGIUM) + NE(THERLANDS) + LUX(EMBOURG)]

be·nev·o·lence (bə·nev′ə·ləns) *n.* **1** Good will; charitableness. **2** Any act of kindness or charity.

be·nev·o·lent (bə·nev′ə·lənt) *adj.* **1** Characterized by benevolence. **2** Kindly; charitable. [<L *bene* well + *volens*, pr.p. of *velle* wish] **—be·nev′o·lent·ly** *adv.*

Beng. Bengal; Bengali.

Ben·ga·li (ben·gô′lē, beng-) *adj.* Of or pertaining to Bengal. —*n.* **1** A native of Bengal. **2** The modern Indic language of Bengal.

ben·ga·line (beng′gə·lēn, beng′gə·lēn′) *n.* A ribbed fabric of silk, wool, etc. [<BENGAL]

be·night·ed (bi·nī′tid) *adj.* **1** Morally or intellectually unenlightened; ignorant. **2** Overtaken by nightfall. **—be·night′ed·ness** *n.*

be·nign (bi·nīn′) *adj.* **1** Kindly; genial. **2** Mild; temperate. **3** Beneficial; favorable. **4** *Pathol.* Not likely to worsen; harmless: a *benign* tumor. [<L *benignus* kindly] **—be·nign′ly** *adv.* **—Syn.** **1** kind, gentle, gracious, amiable, affable. **3** salutary, salubrious, wholesome.

be·nig·nant (bi·nig′nənt) *adj.* **1** Gentle; gracious. **2** Beneficial; benign. [<BENIGN] **—be·nig′nant·ly** *adv.*

be·nig·ni·ty (bi·nig′nə·tē) *n. pl.* **·ties** Benign quality, influence, behavior, etc. Also **be·nig·nan·cy** (bi·nig′nən·sē).

Be·nin (be·nēn′) *n.* A republic of w Africa, 44,696 sq. mi., cap. Porto-Novo. • See map at Africa.

ben·i·son (ben′ə·zən, -sən) *n.* A benediction; blessing [<LL *benedictio* benediction]

Ben·ja·min (ben′jə·mən) In the Old Testament, the youngest son of Jacob and Rachel. —*n.* The tribe of Israel descended from him.

ben·ny (ben′ē) *n. pl.* **·nies** *Slang* An amphetamine pill or capsule. [<BENZEDRINE]

bent[1] (bent) *p.t. & p.p.* of BEND. —*adj.* **1** Not straight; crooked. **2** Set; determined: *bent* on having her own way. —*n.* Inclination; tendency; penchant: following one's natural *bent.* **—to** (or **at**) **the top of one's bent** To the limit of capacity or endurance.

bent[2] *n.* **1** Any of various grasses having flower heads of branched spikelets: also **bent grass. 2** The stiff flower stalk of various grasses. [<OE *beonet*]

Ben·tham·ism (ben′thəm·iz′əm) *n.* The philosophy of Jeremy Bentham, which equates good with happiness and maintains that the greatest good for the greatest number is the chief social and moral goal. [<Jeremy *Bentham,* 1748–1832, English philosopher] **—Ben′tham·ite** *n.*

be·numb (bi·num′) *v.t.* **1** To make numb. **2** To make incapable of feeling or responding; deaden: He was *benumbed* with grief. [<OE *benumen,* p.p. of *benuman* deprive]

Ben·ze·drine (ben′zə·drēn, -drin) *n.* A brand of amphetamine: a trade name.

ben·zene (ben′zēn, ben·zēn′) *n.* A flammable liquid hydrocarbon obtained from coal tar and used in the manufacture of various synthetic chemicals. [<BENZOIN]

ben·zine (ben′zēn, ben·zēn′) *n.* A mixture of hydrocarbons derived from petroleum by fractional distillation and used as a solvent and fuel. [<BENZOIN]

ben·zo·ate (ben′zō·it, -āt) *n.* A salt of benzoic acid.

ben·zo·caine (ben′zo·kān′) *n.* A white compound used in some ointments as a local anesthetic for minor burns.

ben·zo·ic (ben·zō′ik) *adj.* Pertaining to or derived from benzoin.

benzoic acid An aromatic compound used as a food preservative and antiseptic.

ben·zo·in (ben′zō·in, -zoin) *n.* **1** A resin from various East Indian plants used in medicine and as a perfume. **2** A crystalline chemical compound. [<Ar. *lubān jāwī* incense of Java]

ben·zol (ben′zōl, -zol) *n.* A grade of crude benzene.

Be·o·wulf (bā′ə·wo͝olf) The hero of the eighth-century Anglo-Saxon epic poem of the same name.

be·queath (bi·kwēth′, -kwēth′) *v.t.* **1** *Law* To give (personal property) by will. **2** To hand down, as to posterity. [<OE *becwethan*] **—be·queath′al, be·queath′ment** *n.*

be·quest (bi·kwest′) *n.* **1** The act of bequeathing. **2** Something bequeathed. [ME *biqueste*]

be·rate (bi·rāt′) *v.t.* **·rat·ed, ·rat·ing** To scold harshly. **—Syn.** upbraid, castigate, revile.

Ber·ber (bûr′bər) *n.* **1** A member of a group of Muslim tribes inhabiting northern Africa. **2** The Hamitic language of the Berbers. —*adj.* Of or pertaining to the Berbers or their language.

ber·ceuse (bâr·sœz′) *n. pl.* **·ceuses** (-sœz′) A cradle song; a lullaby. [F]

be·reave (bi·rēv′) *v.t.* **·reaved** or **·reft** (bi·reft′), **·reav·ing** **1** To leave saddened by someone's death. **2** To deprive, as of hope or happiness. [<OE *berēafian*] **—be·reave′ment** *n.*

be·reft (bi·reft′) A *p.t. & p.p.* of BEREAVE. —*adj.* Deprived: *bereft* of all hope.

be·ret (bə·rā′, ber′ā) *n.* A soft, flat, visorless cap, usu. of wool or felt. [F]

Beret

berg (bûrg) *n.* An iceberg.

ber·ga·mot (bûr′gə·mot) *n.* **1** A citrus tree bearing pear-shaped fruit. **2** Its fruit, furnishing an oil used as a perfume. **3** Any of several herbs of the mint family. [<Ital. *bergamotta*]

Berg·son·ism (berg′sən·iz′əm) *n.* The philosophy of Henri Bergson, which holds that reality is the expression of the creative or vital force inherent in all organisms. [< Henri Bergson, 1859–1941, French philosopher] **—Berg′·son·ist** *adj., n.*

ber·i·ber·i (ber′ē·ber′ē) *n.* A disease affecting the nervous system and due to a deficiency of thiamine in the diet. [<Singhalese *beri* weakness]

berke·li·um (bûrk′lē·əm) *n.* An artificially produced radioactive element (symbol Bk) of atomic number 97. [< *Berkeley,* California]

Berk·shire (bûrk′shir, -shər) *n.* One of a breed of medium-sized black swine from Berkshire, England.

berm (burm) *n.* A ledge or bank along the side of a road, canal, etc. Also **berme.** [<F *berme*]

Ber·mu·da onion (bər·myōō′də) A large, mild-flavored variety of onion.

Bermuda shorts Shorts reaching to just above the knees.

ber·ry (ber′ē) *n. pl.* **ber·ries** **1** Any small, succulent fruit, as the blackberry or strawberry. **2** *Bot.* A fruit with seeds in a juicy pulp, as the grape or tomato. **3** A dry seed or kernel of various plants, as the coffee bean. *—v.i.* **·ried, ·ry·ing** **1** To form or bear berries. **2** To gather berries. [< OE *berie*]

ber·serk (bər·sûrk′, -zûrk′) *adj. & adv.* In or into a violent, destructive frenzy. *—n.* BERSERKER. [<BERSERKER]

ber·serk·er (bər·sûrk′ər, -zûrk′-) *n.* In Norse legend, a warrior who battled with frenzied fury. [<ON *berserkr* bearskin]

berth (bûrth) *n.* **1** A bunk or bed in a ship, sleeping car, etc. **2** A place where a ship may anchor or dock. **3** A job; employment. **—give a wide berth to** To keep out of the way of. *—v.t.* **1** To bring (a ship) to a berth. **2** To provide with a berth. *—v.i.* **3** To come to or occupy a berth. [?]

ber·tha (bûr′thə) *n.* A deep, capelike collar. [<Queen *Bertha,* Charlemagne's mother]

Bertha

Ber·til·lon system (bûr′tə·lon, *Fr.* ber·tē·yôn′) A system of coded physical measurements and personal characteristics used as a means of identifying people, esp. criminals. [<Alphonse *Bertillon,* 1853–1914, French anthropologist]

ber·yl (ber′əl) *n.* A vitreous mineral of various colors, consisting of silicate of aluminum and beryllium, and used as a gem, esp. in the green and blue varieties. [<Gk. *bēryllos*] **—ber·yl·line** (ber′ə·lin, -līn) *adj.*

be·ryl·li·um (bə·ril′ē·əm) *n.* A rigid, lightweight, metallic element (symbol Be), having important technological uses in alloys, etc. [<L *beryllus* beryl]

be·seech (bi·sēch′) *v.t.* **·sought, ·seech·ing** To entreat or beg for earnestly; implore. [<OE *besēcan*] **—be·seech′er** *n.* **—be·seech′ing·ly** *adv.* **—Syn.** entreat, implore, plead, supplicate.

be·seem (bi·sēm) *v.t.* To be fitting or appropriate to; befit.

be·set (bi·set′) *v.t.* **·set, ·set·ting** **1** To trouble persistently; plague. **2** To attack on all sides. **3** To hem in; encircle. **4** To set or stud, as with gems. [<OE *besettan*] **—be·set′ment** *n.* **—Syn. 1** harass, annoy, pester.

be·set·ting (bi·set′ing) *adj.* Constantly present and troublesome; a *besetting* sin.

be·shrew (bi·shrōō′) *v.t. Archaic* To curse. [<ME *beshrewen* to curse]

be·side (bi·sīd′) *prep.* **1** At the side of; close to. **2** In comparison with. **3** Away or apart from: This discussion is *beside* the point. **4** Other than. **—beside oneself** Out of one's senses, as from anger, fear, etc. *—adv.* In addition; besides. [<OE *be sīdan* by the side (of)]

be·sides (bi·sīdz′) *adv.* **1** In addition; as well. **2** Moreover; furthermore. **3** Otherwise; else. *—prep.* **1** In addition to. **2** Except for; apart from.

be·siege (bi·sēj′) *v.t.* **·be·sieged, be·sieg·ing** **1** To lay siege to, as a castle or city. **2** To crowd around; block. **3** To overwhelm, as with requests. **—be·siege′ment, be·sieg′er** *n.*

be·smirch (bi·smûrch′) *v.t.* **1** To soil; stain. **2** To sully; dishonor. **—be·smirch′er, be·smirch′ment** *n.*

be·som (bē′zəm) *n.* **1** A bundle of twigs used as a broom. **2** The broom plant. [<OE *besma*]

be·sot (bi·sot′) *v.t.* **·sot·ted, ·sot·ting** **1** To stupefy, as with drink. **2** To make foolish or stupid. **3** To infatuate. **—be·sot′ted** *adj.* **—be·sot′ted·ly** *adv.* **—be·sot′ted·ness** *n.*

be·sought (bi·sôt′) *p.t. & p.p.* of BESEECH.

be·spat·ter (bi·spat′ər) *v.t.* **1** To soil by spattering. **2** To sully; dishonor.

be·speak (bi·spēk′) *v.t.* **·spoke** (*Archaic* **·spake**), **·spoke** or **·spo·ken, ·speak·ing** **1** To give evidence of; indicate. **2** To arrange for in advance; reserve. **3** To foretell; foreshadow.

be·spec·ta·cled (bi·spek′tə·kəld) *adj.* Wearing eyeglasses.

be·spoke (bi·spōk′) *p.t. &* a *p.p.* of BESPEAK. *—adj. Brit.* Made to order, as clothing.

Bes·se·mer converter (bes′ə·mər) A large pear-shaped container for molten iron to be converted into steel by the Bessemer process.

Bessemer process A process for oxidizing excess carbon, silicon, etc. in pig iron and converting it to steel by forcing a blast of air through the molten metal. [<Sir Henry *Bessemer,* 1813–98, British engineer]

best (best) Superlative of GOOD and WELL. *—adj.* **1** Excelling all others. **2** Most advantageous, suitable, desirable, etc. **3** Largest; greatest: the *best* part of an hour. *—adv.* **1** In the best way or with the best result. **2** To the greatest degree; most. **—had best** Ought to; should. *—n.* **1** One who or that which is best. **2** Best condition, effort, etc. **3** One's best clothes. **—at best** Given the most favorable conditions, interpretation, etc. **—get** (or **have**) **the best of** To defeat or outwit. **—make the best of** To do as well as one can under the circumstances. *—v.t.* To defeat or outdo. [<OE *betst*]

bes·tial (bes′chəl, bēs′-, best′yəl, bēst′) *adj.* **1** Of or typical of a beast. **2** Having the undesirable qualities of an animal; brutish. [<L *bestia* beast] **—bes′ti·al′i·ty** (-chē·al′·ə·tē, -tē·al′-) *n.* **—bes′tial·ly** *adv.*

bes·tial·ize (bes′chəl·īz, bēs′-, best′yəl-, bēst′-) *v.t.* **·ized, ·iz·ing** To make bestial; brutalize.

bes·ti·ar·y (bes′tē·er′ē) *n. pl.* **·ar·ies** A medieval allegory or treatise on animals.

be·stir (bi·stûr′) *v.t.* **·stirred, ·stir·ring** To rouse to activity.

best man The bridegroom's chief attendant at a wedding.

be·stow (bi·stō′) *v.t.* **1** To present as a gift or honor; confer: with *on* or *upon.* **2** To expend; apply. **3** To give in marriage. [ME *bi-* to, upon + *stowen* place] **—be·stow′al, be·stow′ment** *n.*

be·strew (bi·strōō′) *v.t.* **·strewed, ·strewed** or **·strewn, ·strew·ing** **1** To cover or strew (a surface). **2** To scatter about. **3** To lie scattered over. [<OE *bestreowian*]

be·stride (bi·strīd′) *v.t.* **·strode, ·strid·den, ·strid·ing** **1** To stand or sit astride of; straddle. **2** To stride over or across.

best-sell·er (best′sel′ər) *n.* A product, esp. a book, that sells better than most others of its kind. **—best′-sell′er·dom** *n.* **—best′-sell′ing** *adj.*

bet (bet) *n.* **1** An offer or agreement to risk winning or losing money or something of value on an uncertain outcome. **2** The wager thus risked. **3** A contestant, event, etc. on which a bet is made. **4** Anything to be risked or chanced. *—v.* **bet** or **bet·ted, bet·ting** *v.t.* **1** To stake or pledge (money, etc.) in a bet. **2** To declare as in a bet: I'll *bet* he doesn't come. *—v.i.* **3** To place a wager. **—you bet** *Informal* Certainly. [?]

bet. between.

be·ta (bā′tə, bē′-) *n.* **1** The second letter of the Greek alphabet (Β, β). **2** The second in a series.

beta blocker A drug useful in slowing the heartbeat by blocking the effect of adrenal hormones on the heart's action.

be·take (bi·tāk′) *v.t.* **·took, ·tak·en, ·tak·ing** **1** To take (oneself); go: used reflexively with *to.* **2** To resort or have recourse: used reflexively with *to.*

beta particle An electron.

beta rays A stream of high-energy electrons, esp. as emitted by radioactive substances.

be·ta·tron (bā'tə·tron) *n.* An accelerator designed to operate on electrons, raising them to high velocities. [<BETA (RAY) + (ELEC)TRON]

be·tel (bēt'l) *n.* An Asian plant of the pepper family, the leaves of which are chewed in some parts of Asia. [<Pg. *betel* <Malay *vettila*]

Be·tel·geuse (bē'təl·jo͞oz, bet'əl·jœz) *n.* A giant red star in the constellation Orion. Also **Be'tel·geux.** [<Ar. *bat al-jauza,* shoulder of the giant]

be·tel·nut (bēt'l·nut') *n.* The seed of an East Indian palm, the **betel palm,** used for chewing with betel leaves.

bête noire (bāt'nwär', *Fr.* bet nwär') An object of hate or dread. [<F, black beast]

beth·el (beth'əl) *n.* **1** A seamen's church or chapel. **2** A hallowed place. [<Heb. *bēth-ēl* house of God]

be·think (bi·thingk') *v.t.* **·thought, ·think·ing** To remind (oneself); remember: used reflexively.

be·tide (bi·tīd') *v.t. & v.i.* **·tid·ed, ·tid·ing** To happen (to); befall.

be·times (bi·tīmz') *adv.* In good time; soon enough. [ME *betymes* in time, seasonably]

be·to·ken (bi·tō'kən) *v.t.* **1** To be a sign of; indicate. **2** To portend. **—be·to'ken·er** *n.* **—Syn. 1** signify, denote, bespeak. **2** bode, presage, foreshadow, augur.

be·took (bi·to͝ok') *p.t.* of BETAKE.

be·tray (bi·trā') *v.t.* **1** To commit treason against; be a traitor to. **2** To be faithless or disloyal to. **3** To disclose, as secret information. **4** To reveal unwittingly. **5** To seduce and desert; wrong. **6** To indicate; show. [<ME *bi* over, to + OF *trair* <L *tradere* deliver, give up] **—be·tray'al, be·tray'er** *n.*

be·troth (bi·trōth', -trôth') *v.t.* **1** To engage to marry. **2** To contract to give in marriage. [<ME *bi* to + *treuthe* truth]

be·troth·al (bi·trō'thəl, -trôth'əl) *n.* The state of being betrothed; an engagement to marry. Also **be·troth'ment.**

be·trothed (bi·trōthd', -trôtht') *adj.* Engaged to be married. —*n.* A person engaged to be married.

bet·ter[1] (bet'ər) Comparative of GOOD and WELL. —*adj.* **1** Of greater excellence. **2** More advantageous, suitable, desirable, etc. **3** Larger; greater: the *better* part of a week. **4** Improved in health. —*adv.* **1** In a better way or with a better result. **2** To a greater degree. **3** More usually, correctly, etc. **4** More: lasted *better* than a day. **—better off** In more advantageous circumstances. **—had better** Should. **—think better of** To reconsider and change one's mind. —*n.* **1** That which is better. **2** *Usu. pl.* A superior, as in ability, rank, etc. **—get** (or **have**) **the better of 1** To gain an advantage over. **2** To overcome. —*v.t.* **1** To improve. **2** To surpass. —*v.i.* **3** To grow better. [<OE *betera*]

bet·ter[2] (bet'ər) *n.* BETTOR.

bet·ter·ment (bet'ər·mənt) *n.* Improvement.

bet·tor (bet'ər) *n.* One who bets.

betw. between.

be·tween (bi·twēn') *prep.* **1** In a space or interval separating two persons, things, times, events, etc. **2** In an intermediate state, quantity, etc. **3** From one point to another in time or space. **4** In joint or reciprocal relationship or action. **5** One or the other of. **6** As a combined result of. **—between you and me** Confidentially. —*adv.* In an intervening space, position, relationship, etc. **—in between** In an intermediate state or relationship. [<OE *betwēonan*] • **between, among** In strict usage, the preposition *between* is used only of two objects, *among* of more than two: Divide the money *between* the two, *among* the three. *Between,* however, may be used of more than two when some reciprocal relation is denoted: a treaty *between* the three powers.

be·twixt (bi·twikst') *adv. & prep. Archaic* Between. **—betwixt and between** In an intermediate state; neither one nor the other. [<OE *betwēohs* twofold]

bev·el (bev'əl) *n.* **1** An inclination of two surfaces other than 90°, as the edge of a timber, etc. **2** An adjustable instrument for measuring angles: also **bevel square.** —*adj.* Oblique; slanting; beveled. —*v.* **bev·eled** or **bev·elled, bev·el·ing** or **bev·el·ling** *v.t.* To cut or form a bevel on. —*v.i.* To slant. [?]

bevel gear A gear having beveled teeth.

bev·er·age (bev'rij, bev'ər·ij) *n.* Any kind of drink. [<L *bibere* to drink]

beverage room *Can.* A public room in a hotel licensed to sell only beer.

bev·y (bev'ē) *n. pl.* **·ies 1** A flock of quail, grouse, etc. **2** A small group, usu. of girls or women. [ME]

be·wail (bi·wāl') *v.t. & v.i.* To lament.

be·ware (bi·wâr') *v.t. & v.i.* To be wary (of); look out (for): used in the imperative and infinitive. [ME *be ware* be on guard, be wary]

be·wil·der (bi·wil'dər) *v.t.* To confuse utterly; perplex. [<BE- + archaic English *wilder*] **—be·wil'dered·ly, be·wil'der·ing·ly** *adv.* **—be·wil'der·ment** *n.*

be·witch (bi·wich') *v.t.* **1** To gain power over by witchcraft. **2** To charm; fascinate. **—be·witch'ment, be·witch'er·y** *n.* **—Syn. 2** captivate, entrance, enchant, beguile.

be·witch·ing (bi·wich'ing) *adj.* Charming; captivating. **—be·witch'ing·ly** *adv.*

bey (bā) *n.* **1** The governor of a Turkish province or district. **2** Formerly, a ruler of Tunis. **3** A Turkish title of respect. [<Turkish *beg* lord]

be·yond (bi·yond') *prep.* **1** Farther than; on or to the far side of. **2** Extending past. **3** After; later than. **4** Out of the reach or scope of. **5** Surpassing; exceeding: *beyond* description. —*adv.* Farther on or away. **—the (great) beyond** Whatever comes after death. [<OE *begeondan*]

bez·el (bez'əl) *n.* **1** A bevel on the edge of a cutting tool. **2** The upper part of a cut gem. **3** A groove and flange made to receive a beveled edge. [?]

be·zique (bə·zēk') *n.* A game of cards similar to pinochle. [<F *bésigue*]

B/F, b.f. brought forward.

bf., b.f. *Printing* bold face.

bhang (bang) *n.* **1** The hemp plant. **2** The dried leaves and capsules of hemp, used as an intoxicant and narcotic. [<Skt. *bhangā* hemp]

Bhu·tan (bo͞o·tän') *n.* A small state in the E Himalayas, associated with India in its external affairs, 18,000 sq. mi., cap. Thimpu. **—Bhu'tan·ese'** *adj., n.* • See map at INDIA.

bi- *prefix* **1** Two; doubly: *bicycle; bifurcate.* **2** Occurring twice or at intervals of two: *biannual; bicentennial.* **3** *Chem.* **a** Having two equivalents of: *bichloride.* **b** Indicating the named component in double the ordinary proportion, or the doubling of a radical, etc., in an organic compound. [<L *bis* twice]

Bi bismuth.

bi·a·ly (bē·ä'lē) *n. pl.* **·lys** A flat, onion-topped roll. [<*Byalystok,* city in Poland]

bi·an·nu·al (bī·an'yo͞o·əl) *adj.* Occurring twice a year; semiannual. **—bi·an'nu·al·ly** *adv.*

bi·as (bī'əs) *n. pl.* **bi·as·es 1** A line crossing the weave of a fabric obliquely: sewn on the *bias.* **2** A personal inclination, esp. one based on fixed attitudes unresponsive to persuasion or influence. **3** A personal preference. **4** A fixed or steady force, voltage, current, etc., impressed on a device or system to set its conditions of operation. —*adj.* Diagonal; slanting: *bias* seams. —*adv.* Diagonally. —*v.t.* **bi·ased** or **bi·assed, bi·as·ing** or **bi·as·sing 1** To influence unduly or unfairly; prejudice. **2** To impose a fixed condition of operation on. [<F *biais* oblique]

Bib

bi·ath·lon (bī·ath'lon) *n.* A contest in the winter Olympics that combines cross-country ski racing with rifle marksmanship. [<BI- + Gk. *athlon* a contest]

bib (bib) *n.* **1** A cloth worn under the chin by children while eating to protect against spillage. **2** The upper portion of an apron, overalls, etc. [<L *bibere* to drink]

Bib. Bible; Biblical.
bib and tucker *Informal* Clothes.
bib·cock (bib′kok′) *n.* A faucet having the nozzle bent downward.
bibe·lot (bib′lō, *Fr.* bĕb·lō′) *n.* A small, decorative or valued object; a curio or trinket. [F]
Bibl., bibl. Biblical; bibliographical.
bi·ble (bī′bəl) *n.* Any authoritative text or writing.
Bi·ble (bī′bəl) *n.* **1** The sacred writings of Christianity; the Old Testament and the New Testament. **2** The Holy Scriptures of Judaism; the Old Testament. **3** The sacred text or writings of any religion. [<Gk. *biblion* book]
bib·li·cal (bib′li·kəl) *adj. Often cap.* **1** Of, in, or derived from the Bible. **2** In harmony with the Bible. **—bib′li·cal·ly** *adv.*
Bib·li·cist (bib′lə·sist) *n.* **1** One well versed in the Bible. **2** A literal adherent of the Bible.
biblio- *combining form* Of or pertaining to books or to the Bible; *bibliophile.* [<Gk. *biblion* book]
bib·li·og·ra·phy (bib′lē·og′rə·fē) *n. pl.* **·phies 1 a** A list of the works of an author. **b** A list of writings on a particular subject, esp. one of sources consulted by an author. **2** The study of books, their history, authorship, etc. **—bib′li·og′·ra·pher** *n.* **—bib·li·o·graph·ic** (bib′lē·ə·graf′ik) or **·i·cal** *adj.*
bib·li·o·ma·ni·a (bib′lē·ō·mā′nē·ə) *n.* A passion for acquiring books. **—bib′li·o·ma′ni·ac** (-ak) *n., adj.*
bib·li·o·phile (bib′lē·ə·fīl′, -fil′) *n.* One who loves books. Also **bib·li·oph·i·list** (bib′lē·of′ə·list). **—bib′li·oph′i·lism** *n.*
bib·u·lous (bib′yə·ləs) *adj.* **1** Given to drinking alcoholic liquor. **2** Absorbent. [<L *bibere* to drink]
bi·cam·er·al (bī·kam′ər·əl) *adj.* Consisting of two chambers or houses, as a legislature. [<BI- + L *camera* chamber]
bi·car·bo·nate (bī·kär′bə·nit, -nāt) *n.* A salt of carbonic acid in which one of the hydrogen atoms is replaced by a metal: sodium *bicarbonate.*
bicarbonate of soda SODIUM BICARBONATE.
bi·cen·ten·ni·al (bī′sen·ten′ē·əl) *adj.* **1** Of a 200th anniversary. **2** Occurring once in 200 years. **—***n.* A 200th anniversary. Also **bi·cen·ten·a·ry** (bī′sen·ten′ər·ē, bī·sen′tə·ner′ē) (*pl.* **·ries**)
bi·ceps (bī′seps) *n. pl.* **bi·ceps** A muscle having two points or origin, esp. the large flexor muscle of the upper arm or of the back of the thigh. [<L, two headed]
bi·chlo·ride (bī·klôr′īd, -id, -klō′rīd, -rid) *n.* **1** A salt having two atoms of chlorine per atom of another element. **2** Bichloride of mercury, or corrosive sublimate.
bick·er (bik′ər) *v.i.* **1** To dispute petulantly; wrangle. **2** To flow noisily, as a brook. **—***n.* A petulant dispute; a petty squabble. [ME *bikeren*] **—bick′er·er** *n.*
bi·coast·al (bī′kō′stəl) *adj.* Of or pertaining to both the east and west coasts of the United States: a *bicoastal* production company.
bi·col·or (bī′kul′ər) *adj.* Having two colors. Also **bi′col′·ored.**
bi·con·cave (bī·kon′kāv, -kong′-, bī′kon·kāv′) *adj.* Concave on both sides. • See LENS.
bi·con·vex (bī·kon′veks, bī′kon·veks′) *adj.* Convex on both sides. • See LENS.
bi·cron (bī′kron) *n.* The one-billionth part of a meter.
bi·cus·pid (bī·kus′pid) *adj.* Having two cusps or points. Also **bi·cus′pi·dal** (-dəl), **bi·cus′pi·date** (-dāt). **—***n.* Any of the eight teeth with two cusps in the normal human jaw. [< L *bi-* two + *cuspis* point] • See TOOTH.
bi·cy·cle (bī′sik·əl) *n.* A two-wheeled vehicle with the wheels in tandem, a seat or seats, a steering handle, and propelled by pedals or a motor. **—***v.i.* **·cled, ·cling** To ride a bicycle. [<BI- + Gk. *kyklos* wheel] **—bi′cy·cler, bi′cy·clist** *n.* • See TANDEM.
bid (bid) *v.* **bade** (bad, bād) *for defs. 1,2,3* or **bid** *for defs. 4,5,6* **bid·den** (bid′ən), **bid·ding** *v.t.* **1** To command; order. **2** To invite. **3** To say (to) in greeting or farewell. **4** To offer (a price), as in an auction. **5** In card games, to declare (the number of tricks one intends to make in a specified trump suit). **—***v.i.* **6** To make a bid, as in cards or at an auction. **—bid fair** To seem probable. **—bid up** To increase the price of by offering higher bids. **—***n.* **1 a** An offer to pay or accept a price. **b** The amount offered. **2 a** In card games, the number of tricks or points that a player engages to make. **b** A player's turn to bid. **3** An effort to win or attain. **4** An invitation to join. [Fusion of OE *biddan* ask, demand and *bēodan* proclaim, command] **—bid′der** *n.*
bid·da·ble (bid′ə·bəl) *adj.* **1** Of sufficient value to bid on. **2** Docile; obedient.
bid·ding (bid′ing) *n.* **1** A behest; command. **2** A request or invitation. **3** The making of a bid or bids.
bid·dy (bid′ē) *n. pl* **·dies 1** A hen. **2** A gossipy woman. [?]
bide (bīd) *v.* **bid·ed** or **bode** (bōd), **bid·ing —***v.i.* **1** To remain; stay. **2** To dwell; abide. **—***v.t.* **3** To await. **—bide one's time** To await the most favorable opportunity. [<OE *bīdan* wait, stay]
bi·den·tate (bī·den′tāt) *adv.* Having two teeth or toothlike processes.
bi·det (bē·dā′) *n.* A fountainlike fixture used for washing the anus and genitals. [<F]
bi·en·ni·al (bī·en′ē·əl) *adj.* **1** Occurring every second year. **2** Lasting or living for two years. **—***n.* **1** A plant that normally dies after two seasons of growth. **2** An event occurring once in two years. [<L *bi-* two + *annus* year] **—bi·en′ni·al·ly** *adv.*
bien·ve·nue (byaṅ·və·nü′) *n. French* A welcome.
bier (bir) *n.* A framework for supporting a corpse or coffin. [<OE *bǣr*]
biff (bif) *Slang v.t.* To give a blow. **—***n.* A whack; blow. [Imit.]
bi·fid (bī′fid) *adj.* Cleft in two; forked. [<L *bifidus*]
bi·fo·cal (bī·fō′kəl) *adj.* Having two foci; said of a lens ground for both near and far vision. [<BI- + L *focus* hearth, focus of a lens]
bi·fo·cals (bī·fō′kəlz, bī′fō·kəlz) *n. pl.* Eyeglasses with bifocal lenses ground for distant and near vision.
bi·fur·cate (bī′fər·kāt, bī·fûr′kāt) *v.t. & v.i.* **·cat·ed, ·cat·ing** To divide into two branching parts; fork. **—***adj.* (bī′·fər·kāt, bī·fûr′kit) Forked: also **bi′fur·cat′ed.** [<BI- + L *furca* fork] **—bi′fur·cate·ly** (-kit·lē) *adv.* **—bi′fur·ca′tion** *n.*
big (big) *adj.* **big·ger, big·gest 1** Of great size, amount, etc.; large. **2** Of great intensity, degree, etc. **3** Fully grown. **4** Pregnant. **5** Important. **6** Pompous; self-important. **7** Generous; magnanimous. **8** Loud. **—***adv. Informal* **1** Boastfully; extravagantly; to talk *big.* **2** On a grand scale. [ME] **—big′gish** *adj.* **—big′ly** *adv.* **—big′ness** *n.*
big·a·my (big′ə·mē) *n.* The crime of marrying another person while still legally married. [<BI- + Gk. *gamos* wedding] **—big′a·mist** *n.* **—big′a·mous** *adj.* **—big′a·mous·ly** *adv.*
Big Ben 1 The bell of a clock which strikes the hour in the tower of the Houses of Parliament, London. **2** The clock itself.
Big Dipper A dipper-shaped group of seven stars in the constellation Ursa Major.
big game 1 Large wild animals hunted for sport. **2** *Informal* An important objective, esp. if difficult.
big-heart·ed (big′här′tid) *adj.* Generous; charitable. **—big′heart′ed·ly** *adv.* **—big·heart′ed·ness** *n.*
big·horn (big′hôrn′) *n. pl.* **·horns.** or **·horn** A wild sheep of the Rocky Mountains, having large horns.

Bighorn

bight (bīt) *n.* **1** A loop or turn in a rope. **2** A bend in a shoreline, river, etc. **3** A shallow bay formed by such a bend. **—***v.t.* To secure with a bight. [<OE *byht* corner, bay]
big·no·ni·a (big·nō′nē·ə) *n.* Any of a genus of tropical American vines bearing large, trumpet-shaped flowers. [<A. J. *Bignon,* 1711–72, librarian to Louis XV]
big·ot (big′ət) *n.* One intolerant of or prejudiced against those of differing religious beliefs, political opinions, etc. [<F] **—big′ot·ed** *adj.* **—big′ot·ed·ly** *adv.* **—big′ot·ry** *n.*
big shot *Slang* A person of importance.
big time *Slang* The highest or best-paid level in an occupation or field. **—big′time′** *adj.* **—big′tim′er** *n.*
big top *Informal* **1** The main tent of a circus. **2** The circus.
big tree The giant sequoia of California.
big wheel *Slang* A person of importance.
big·wig (big′wig′) *n. Informal* A person of importance.

bi·jou (bē′zhōō, bē·zhōō′) *n. pl.* **bi·joux** (bē′zhōōz, bē·zhōōz′) A jewel; trinket. [F]

bike (bīk) *n. Informal* A bicycle.

bi·ki·ni (bi·kē′nē) *n. pl.* **·nis** A very scanty two-piece bathing suit for women. [< *Bikini* atoll in the Pacific]

bi·la·bi·al (bī·lā′bē·əl) *adj.* **1** Articulated with both lips, as certain consonants. **2** Having two lips. —*n.* A bilabial speech sound. **—bi·la′bi·al·ly** *adv.*

bi·la·bi·ate (bī·lā′bē·āt, -it) *adj.* Two-lipped: said of a flower.

bi·lat·er·al (bī·lat′ər·əl) *adj.* **1** Two-sided. **2** On or of two corresponding sides. **3** Undertaken by two sides: a *bilateral* agreement. **—bi·lat′er·al·ly** *adv.* **—bi·lat′er·al·ness** *n.*

bil·ber·ry (bil′ber′ē, -bər·ē) *n. pl.* **·ries** **1** A European shrub with edible blue-black berries; whortleberry. **2** Its fruit. [< Scand.]

bile (bīl) *n.* **1** A bitter, golden brown or greenish digestive fluid secreted by the liver. **2** Anger; peevishness. [< L *bilis* bile, anger] **—bil·i·ar·y** (bil′ē·er′ē) *adj.*

bilge (bilj) *n.* **1** The lower, rounded part of a ship's bottom. **2** The foul water that collects there: also **bilge water. 3** The bulge of a barrel. **4** *Slang* Stupid nonsense. —*v.t. & v.i.* **bilged, bilg·ing** To leak or cause to leak in the bilge. [Var. of BULGE] **—bilg′y** *adj.* **(·i·er, ·i·est)**

bi·lin·gual (bī·ling′gwəl) *adj.* **1** Written or expressed in two languages. **2** Fluent in two languages. **—bi·lin′gual·ism** *n.* **—bi·lin′gual·ly** *adv.*

bil·ious (bil′yəs) *adj.* **1** Suffering from malaise attributed to a disorder of the liver. **2** Of or suggestive of bile. **3** Ill-natured; cross. [< L *bilis* bile] **—bil′ious·ly** *adv.* **—bil′·ious·ness** *n.*

bilk (bilk) *v.t.* To cheat; swindle. —*n.* **1** A swindler. **2** A trick; a hoax. [?] **—bilk′er** *n.*

bill[1] (bil) *n.* **1** A statement of payment due for goods or services. **2** A piece of paper money. **3** A list of items: a *bill* of fare. **4** The draft of a proposed law. **5** An advertising poster. **6** A theater program. **7** *Law* A formal statement of a case, charge, etc. **—fill the bill** *Informal* To meet the needs. **—foot the bill** *Informal* To pay the costs. —*v.t.* **1** To enter in a bill; charge. **2** To present a bill to. **3** To advertise by bills or placards. [< L *bulla* document, seal] **—bill′er** *n.*

bill[2] (bil) *n.* A beak, as of a bird. —*v.i.* To join bills, as birds. **—bill and coo** To kiss and murmur lovingly. [< OE *bile*]

bill[3] (bil) *n.* **1** A hook-shaped gardening instrument: also **bill′hook′. 2** A weapon with a hook-shaped blade. [< OE *bill* sword, ax]

bil·la·bong (bil′ə·bong) *n. Austral.* A stagnant pool or backwater. [< native Australian *billa* water + *bong* dead]

bill·board (bil′bôrd′, -bōrd′) *n.* A board or panel for displaying posters or placards.

bil·let[1] (bil′it) *n.* **1** A lodging for soldiers in a household or nonmilitary building. **2** A requisition for such lodging. **3** A job; position. —*v.t. & v.i.* To lodge (soldiers) in a private household or other billet. [< L *bulla* seal, document] **—bil′let·er** *n.*

bil·let[2] (bil′it) *n.* **1** A short, thick stick, as of firewood. **2** A mass of iron or steel forming a small bar. [< OF *bille* log]

bil·let-doux (bil′ā·dōō′, -ē·dōō′, *Fr.* bē·ye·dōō′) *n. pl.* **bil·lets-doux** (bil′ā·dōōz′, -ē·dōōz′, *Fr.* bē·ye·dōō′) A love letter. [F, lit., sweet note]

bill·fold (bil′fōld′) *n.* A folding wallet.

bill·head (bil′hed′) *n.* **1** A heading on paper used for making out bills. **2** A sheet of such paper.

bil·liard (bil′yərd) *adj.* Of or pertaining to billiards. —*n.* A carom in billiards.

bil·liards (bil′yərdz) *n.* A game played with a cue and hard balls **(billiard balls)** on an oblong, cloth-covered table with cushioned edges. [< OF *bille* log] **—bil′liard·ist** *n.*

bill·ing (bil′ing) *n.* The order in which performers or acts are listed on a theater billboard, playbill, etc.

bil·lings·gate (bil′ingz·gāt) *n.* Vulgar and abusive language. [< *Billingsgate* fish market, London]

bil·lion (bil′yən) *n.* See NUMBER. [< F] **—bil·lionth** (bil′·yənth) *adj., n.*

bil·lion·aire (bil′yən·âr′) *n.* One who owns wealth worth a billion dollars.

bill of attainder Formerly, a legal act making certain actions punishable by attainder.

bill of exchange A written order to pay a particular amount of money to a specified person.

bill of fare A menu.

bill of health An official certificate of the crew's health issued to a ship's master on departure from a port.

bill of lading A written acknowledgment of goods received for transportation.

bill of rights **1** A formal summary and declaration of the fundamental rights of individuals. **2** *Often cap.* The first ten amendments to the U.S. Constitution.

bill of sale A document transferring title to personal property by sale.

bil·low (bil′ō) *n.* **1** A great wave or surge of the sea. **2** A swell or surge, as of sound. —*v.i.* To form billows; surge. [< ON *bylgja*] **—bil′low·y** *adj.* **—bil′low·i·ness** *n.*

bill·post·er (bil′pōs′tər) *n.* One who posts advertising bills on walls, fences, etc. **—bill′post′ing** *n.*

bil·ly[1] (bil′ē) *n. pl.* **bil·lies** A short bludgeon, esp. a policeman's club. [< *Billy,* a nickname for William]

bil·ly[2] (bil′ē) *n. Austral.* A can used for heating water. [< native Australian *billa* water]

billy goat A male goat.

bi·lo·bate (bī·lō′bāt) *adj.* Divided into or having two lobes. Also **bi·lo′bat·ed.**

bi·man·u·al (bī·man′yōō·əl) *adj.* Employing both hands. **—bi·man′u·al·ly** *adv.*

bi·me·tal·lic (bī′mə·tal′ik) *adj.* **1** Consisting of or relating to two metals. **2** Of or pertaining to bimetallism. [< F *bimétallique*]

bi·met·al·lism (bī·met′əl·iz′əm) *n.* The concurrent use of both gold and silver as the standard of currency and value. **—bi·met′al·list** *n.*

bi·month·ly (bī·munth′lē) *adj.* **1** Occurring once every two months. **2** Semimonthly. —*adv.* **1** Every two months. **2** Semimonthly. —*n.* A publication issued bimonthly. • In strict usage, *bimonthly, biweekly,* and *biyearly* are used only to mean once in every interval of two months, two weeks, etc., while *semimonthly, semiweekly,* etc., are used to mean twice a month, twice a week, etc.

bin (bin) *n.* An enclosed place for holding foods, coal, etc. —*v.t.* **binned, bin·ning** To store or deposit in a bin. [< OE *binn* basket, crib]

bi·na·ry (bī′nə·rē) *adj.* **1** Of, characterized by, or consisting of two; double; paired. **2** Denoting a pair of stars revolving about a common center. **3** Of or denoting the binary numeration system. —*n. pl.* **·ries** A paired or double entity, esp. a binary star. [< L *bini* two, double]

binary numeration system A system of numeration based on two, capable of expressing any integer as a numeral using only the characters 0 and 1.

bi·nate (bī′nāt) *adj.* Growing in pairs. [< L *bini* double, two by two] **—bi′nate·ly** *adv.* • See LEAF.

bin·au·ral (bī·nôr′əl, bin·ôr′əl) *adj.* **1** Hearing with both ears. **2** Designating a device for presenting sounds, esp. different sounds simultaneously to both ears. **—bin·au′ral·ly** *adv.*

bind (bīnd) *v.* **bound, bind·ing** *v.t.* **1** To tie together; make fast by tying; secure. **2** To encircle, as with a belt. **3** To bandage. **4** To cause to cohere or adhere. **5** To strengthen or ornament at the edge, as in sewing. **6** To fasten together within a cover, as a book. **7** To make irrevocable, as a bargain. **8** To oblige, as by moral or legal authority. **9** To make constipated. —*v.i.* **10** To tie up anything. **11** To cohere; stick together. **12** To have binding force; be obligatory. **13** To become stiff, hard, or tight. **—bind over** *Law* To hold under bond for appearance at a future time. —*n.* **1** *Informal* A difficult or constraining situation. **2** That which fastens, ties, or binds. [< OE *bindan*]

bind·er (bīn′dər) *n.* **1** One who binds, esp. a bookbinder. **2** Something that binds; a device, substance, etc., used for binding. **3** A loose-leaf notebook cover. **4** A payment or written statement given as a pledge pending the completion of a contract. **5** A device on a reaper for binding grain.

bind·er·y (bīn′dər·ē) *n. pl.* **·er·ies** A place where books are bound.

bind·ing (bīn′ding) *adj.* **1** Something that binds or is used to bind. **2** The act of one who or that which binds. **3** The cover holding together the pages of a book. **4** A strip sewed or fastened over an edge for protection. —*adj.* **1** Obligatory. **2** Uncomfortably tight or confining.

bind·weed (bīnd′wēd′) *n.* Any of various plants with twining stems.

bine (bīn) *n.* **1** A twining or climbing stem. **2** A plant with such stems, as the hop, woodbine, etc. [<ME *binden* to bind]

Bi·net-Si·mon scale (bi·nā′sī′mən, *Fr.* bē·ne′sē·môn′) A system of rating the mental development of children according to norms established by a series of tests given previously to many children at given ages. [<Alfred *Binet*, 1857–1911, and Théodore *Simon*, 1873–1961, French psychologists]

binge (binj) *n. Slang* **1** A drunken carousal. **2** Any uncontrolled bout; a spree. [?]

bin·go (bing′gō) *n.* A game in which players cover numbers on a printed card as they are called out, the first to cover five numbers in a row being the winner. [?]

bin·na·cle (bin′ə·kəl) *n.* A stand or case for a ship's compass, usu. placed before the steering wheel. [<Pg. *bitacola* <LL *habitaculum* little house]

bin·oc·u·lar (bə·nok′yə·lər, bī-) *adj.* Of, for, or using eyes at once. —*n. Often pl.* A telescope, opera glass, etc., adapted for use by both eyes at once. [<BI + OCULAR] —**bin·oc′u·lar′i·ty** (-lar′ə·tē) *n.* —**bin·oc′u·lar·ly** *adv.*

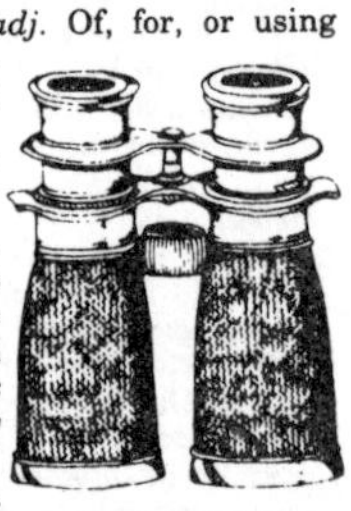

Binoculars

bi·no·mi·al (bī·nō′mē·əl) *adj.* Consisting of or using two names or terms. —*n. Math.* An algebraic expression in the form of a sum of two terms. [<Med. L *binomius* having two names] —**bi·no′mi·al·ly** *adv.*

bio- *combining form* Life: *biology.* [<Gk. *bios* life]

bi·o·chem·is·try (bī′ō·kem′is·trē) *n.* The branch of chemistry relating to life processes, their mode of action, and their products. —**bi′o·chem′i·cal** *adj.* —**bi′o·chem′i·cal·ly** *adv.* —**bi′o·chem′ist** *n.*

bi·o·de·grad·a·ble (bī′ō·di′grā′də·bəl) *adj.* Capable of being broken down by natural processes, such as bacterial action, etc. [<BIO- + DEGRADABLE]

bi·o·e·col·o·gy (bī′ō·ē·kol′ə·jē) *n.* That branch of ecology having to do with the mutual relationships between organisms and the environment.

bi·o·e·lec·tric·i·ty (bī′ō·i·lek′tris′ə·tē) *n.* Electric phenomena associated with and characteristic of living matter. —**bi′o·e·lec′tri·cal** *adj.*

bi·o·eth·ics (bī′ō·eth′iks) *n. pl. (construed as sing.)* The study of the ethical implications of medical practice, esp. in regard to the preservation of human life. —**bi′o·eth′i·cal** *adj.* —**bi′o·eth′i·cist** (-eth′ə·sist) *n.*

bi·o·feed·back (bī′ō·fēd′bak) *n.* Voluntary control by feedback of involuntary functions, as heart rate.

biog. biographer; biographical; biography.

bi·o·gen·e·sis (bī′ō·jen′ə·sis) *n.* **1** The doctrine that life is generated from living organisms only. **2** Such generation itself. Also **bi·og·e·ny** (bī·oj′ə·nē). —**bi·o·ge·net·ic** (bī′ō·jə·net′ik) or **·i·cal** *adj.* —**bi′o·ge·net′i·cal·ly** *adv.*

bi·og·ra·phy (bī·og′rə·fē, bē-) *n. pl.* **·phies 1** A written account of a person's life. **2** Such writing as a literary form or practice. [<Gk. *bios* life + *graphein* write] —**bi·og′raph·er** *n.* —**bi·o·graph·ic** (bī′ə·graf′ik) or **·i·cal** *adj.* —**bi′o·graph′i·cal·ly** *adv.*

biol. biological; biologist; biology.

bi·o·log·i·cal (bī′ə·loj′i·kəl) *adj.* **1** Of or pertaining to vital functions, structures, and processes. **2** Used for or produced by research in biology. Also **bi′o·log′ic.** —bi′o·log′i·cal·ly *adv.*

biological warfare The use of disease-producing microorganisms, toxins, etc., in waging war.

bi·ol·o·gy (bī·ol′ə·jē) *n.* The science of life and the origin, structure, reproduction, growth, and development of living organisms. [<BIO- + -LOGY] —**bi·ol′o·gist** *n.*

bi·o·lu·mi·nes·cence (bī′ō·lōō′mə·nes′əns) *n.* **1** The emission of light by living organisms. **2** The light so emitted. —**bi′o·lu′mi·nes′cent** *adj.*

bi·o·mass (bī′ō·mas′) *n.* All the plant material in a given area, esp. when considered as an energy source.

bi·ome (bī′ōm) *n.* Any major ecosystem, such as a desert, that has its own particular climate and plant and animal life.

bi·om·e·try (bī·om′ə·trē) *n.* The application of statistics to biological data. Also **bi·o·met·rics** (bī′ə·met′riks). [<BIO + -METRY] —**bi′o·met′ric** or **·ri·cal** *adj.*

bi·o·phys·ics (bī′ō·fiz′iks) *n. pl. (construed as sing.)* The study of the physics of living organisms. —**bio′o·phys′i·cal** *adj.* —**bi′o·phys′i·cist** *n.*

bi·op·sy (bī′op·sē) *n. pl.* **·sies** The excision and examination of tissue from a living subject for diagnostic purposes. [<BIO- + Gk. *opsis* sight] —**bi·op·sic** (bī·op′sik) *adj.*

bi·o·sphere (bī′ə·sfir) *n.* The envelope of soil, water, and air to which life on earth is confined.

bi·o·ta (bī·ō′tə) *n.* The combined fauna and flora of an area or period. [<Gk. *biotē* life <*bios* life]

bi·o·tech·nol·o·gy (bī′ō·tek·nol·ə·jē) *n.* **1** The use of technology in biological science. **2** The use of microorganisms in the production of valuable products.

bi·ot·ic (bī·ot′ik) *adj.* Of or pertaining to living organisms.

bi·o·tin (bī′ə·tin) *n.* A constituent of the vitamin B complex. [<Gk. *bios* life]

bi·par·ti·san (bī·pär′tə·zən) *adj.* Of or supported by two political parties. —**bi·par′ti·san·ship** *n.*

bi·par·tite (bī·pär′tīt) *adj.* Consisting of two usu. corresponding parts. —**bi·par′tite·ly** *adv.*

bi·ped (bī′ped) *n.* A two-footed animal. —*adj.* Two-footed: also **bi·pe·dal** (bī·ped′əl, bī′pə·dəl). [<L *bipes* two-footed]

bi·pin·nate (bī·pin′āt) *adj.* Twice or doubly pinnate, as a leaf. Also **bi·pin′nat·ed.** —**bi·pin′nate·ly** *adv.*

bi·plane (bī′plān′) *n. Aeron.* An airplane having two parallel wings, one above the other.

bi·po·lar (bī·pō′lər) *adj.* **1** Relating to or having two poles. **2** Found in both polar regions of the earth.

birch (bûrch) *n.* **1** Any of a genus of hardy trees and shrubs usu. having the outer bark separable in thin layers. **2** A rod from such a tree, used as a whip. **3** The tough, close-grained wood of the birch. —*v.t.* To whip with a birch rod. [<OE *birce*] —**birch·en** (bûr′chən) *adj.*

bird (bûrd) *n.* **1** Any of a class of warm-blooded, feathered, egg-laying vertebrates having the forelimbs modified as wings. **2** GAME BIRD. **3** A shuttlecock used in the game of badminton. **4** CLAY PIGEON. **5** *Slang* A peculiar or remarkable person. **6** *Slang* A derisive sound of disapproval. —**for the birds** *Slang* Worthless. —*v.i.* **1** To be a bird watcher. **2** To trap or shoot birds. [<OE *bridd*]

bird·call (bûrd′kôl′) *n.* A bird's characteristic note or song. **2** A device for imitating this.

bird dog A dog trained to assist in hunting game birds.

bird·ie (bûr′dē) *n.* **1** *Informal* A small bird. **2** In golf, a score of one stroke less than par in playing a hole.

bird·lime (bûrd′līm′) *n.* A sticky substance smeared on twigs to catch small birds.

bird of paradise A bird of New Guinea noted for its colorful plumage.

bird of prey Any of various predacious birds, as an eagle, hawk, etc.

bird·seed (bûrd′sēd′) *n.* A mixture of seeds used to feed birds.

bird's-eye (bûrdz′ī) *adj.* **1** Marked with spots resembling birds' eyes: *bird's-eye* maple. **2** Seen at a distance and from above: a *bird's-eye* view. —*n.* A fabric woven in a pattern of small, eyelike indentations.

bird watcher One who observes birds in their natural state, esp. as a hobby. —**bird watching.**

bi·reme (bī′rēm) *n.* An ancient galley having two banks of oars. [<L *bi-* two + *remus* oar]

bi·ret·ta (bi·ret′ə) *n.* A stiff, square cap with three or four upright projections on the crown, worn by clerics of the Roman Catholic Church. [<LL *birretum* cap]

birl (bûrl) *v.t.* **1** To rotate (a floating log) rapidly with the feet. —*v.i.* **2** To spin with a humming sound. [Blend of earlier *birr*, whirring sound + WHIRL] —**birl′er** *n.*

birl·ing (bûr′ling) *n.* A contest in which opponents try to outstay each other while balanced on a floating log rotated by their feet. [?]

birth (bûrth) *n.* 1 The act or fact of being born. 2 The bringing forth of offspring; parturition. 3 Beginning; origin. 4 Ancestry or descent. 5 Inborn or inherent tendency. **—give birth to** 1 To bear as offspring. 2 To give rise to. [<ON *byrth*]

birth control The use of preventive methods or devices to regulate conception; contraception.

birth·day (bûrth′dā′) *n.* The day of one's birth or its anniversary.

birth·mark (bûrth′märk′) *n.* A mark or blemish existing on the body from birth.

birth·place (bûrth′plās′) *n.* 1 The place of one's birth. 2 A place of origin: the *birthplace* of freedom.

birth rate The number of births in a given population during a given time, usu. births per 1,000 persons per year.

birth·right (bûrth′rīt′) *n.* A right or privilege due by virtue of one's birth or origin.

birth·stone (bûrth′stōn′) *n.* A jewel identified with the particular month of one's birth.

bis·cuit (bis′kit) *n.* 1 Bread in the form of a small cake leavened with baking powder or soda. 2 *Brit.* A cracker or cooky. 3 Fired, unglazed pottery. 4 A pale brown. [<L *bis* twice + *coquere* to cook]

bi·sect (bī′sekt, bī·sekt′) *v.t.* 1 To cut into two parts; halve. 2 *Geom.* To divide into two equal parts. *—v.i.* 3 To fork, as a road. [<BI- + L *sectus* cut] **—bi·sec′tion, bi·sec′tor** *n.* **—bi·sec′tion·al** *adj.* **—bi·sec′tion·al·ly** *adv.*

bi·sex·u·al (bī·sek′shōō·əl) *adj.* 1 Pertaining to both sexes. 2 Having both male and female organs; hermaphroditic. 3 Attracted sexually by both sexes. **—bi·sex′u·al·ism, bi·sex′u·al′i·ty** (-shōō·al′ə·tē) *n.* **—bi·sex′u·al·ly** *adv.*

bish·op (bish′əp) *n.* 1 In various Christian churches, a clergyman of the highest order, usu. head of a diocese. 2 A chessman which may be moved only diagonally. [<LL *episcopus*]

bish·op·ric (bish′əp·rik) *n.* The office or diocese of a bishop.

bis·muth (biz′məth) *n.* A brittle, reddish white metallic element (symbol Bi) of atomic number 83, used chiefly as a constituent of alloys. [G] **—bis′muth·al** *adj.*

bi·son (bī′sən, -zən) *n. pl.* **bi·son** 1 A bovine mammal of western North America, having a dark, shaggy mane; buffalo. 2 A similar European animal. [<L *bison* wild ox]

North American bison

bisque[1] (bisk) *n.* A thick, rich, cream soup made from shellfish, vegetables, etc. [F]

bisque[2] (bisk) *n.* BISCUIT (def. 3). [<BISCUIT]

bis·sex·tile (bi·seks′təl, -tīl) *adj.* 1 Pertaining to the extra day occurring in a leap year. 2 Pertaining to a leap year. *—n.* A leap year. [<L *bisextilis* intercalary day in the Julian calendar]

bis·ter (bis′tər) *n.* 1 A yellowish brown pigment made from soot. 2 A dark brown. Also **bis′tre.** [F *bistre* dark brown] **—bis′tered** *adj.*

bis·tro (bis′trō, *Fr.* bē·strō′) *n. pl.* **·tros** *Informal* A small night club, bar, or café. [F]

bi·sul·fate (bī·sul′fāt) *n.* An acid sulfate.

bit[1] (bit) *n.* 1 A small piece, amount, etc. 2 A short time: Wait a *bit.* 3 A very small part, as in a play. 4 *Informal* An amount worth 12½ cents: now used mostly in the expression *two bits.* **—a bit of** To some degree; somewhat: *a bit of* a nuisance. **—do one's bit** To contribute one's share of work, money, etc. [<OE *bita* piece bitten off] **—Syn.** 1 morsel, fragment, scrap, mite, iota.

bit[2] (bit) *n.* 1 A boring tool adapted to be used with a stock or brace. • See BRACE. 2 The metallic mouthpiece of a bridle. 3 Something that curbs or restrains. 4 The part of a key that engages the bolt or tumblers of a lock. *—v.t.* **bit·ted, bit·ting** 1 To put a bit in the mouth of. 2 To curb; restrain. [<OE *bite* a biting]

bit[3] (bit) *p.t. & alt. p.p.* of BITE.

bit[4] (bit) *n.* 1 A binary digit; a 0 or 1. 2 A unit of information equivalent to the choice between a pair of alternatives of equal probability. [<B(INARY) + (DIG)IT]

bitch (bich) *n.* 1 A female dog, coyote, etc. 2 *Slang* A woman regarded as hateful, sluttish, mean, etc. 3 *Slang* Something difficult or troublesome to accomplish. *—v.i. Slang* To complain. **—bitch up** *Slang* To botch. [<OE *bicce*]

bitch·y (bich′ē) *adj.* **bitch·i·er, bitch·i·est** *Slang* 1 Quick to find fault or complain; captious. 2 Mean-spirited; malicious; spiteful. **—bitch′i·ly** *adv.* **—bitch′i·ness** *n.*

bite (bīt) *v.* **bit, bit·ten** (bit′n) or **bit, bit·ing** *v.t.* 1 To seize, cut, tear, or wound with the teeth. 2 To cut, tear, etc., as if with teeth. 3 To pierce with a sting, fangs, etc. 4 To cause to smart; sting. 5 To corrode, as acid. 6 To grip or hold, as by traction. *—v.i.* 7 To seize or cut into something with or as if with the teeth. 8 To have a stinging effect. 9 To take firm hold. 10 To take bait, as fish. 11 To be taken in by a trick. **—bite the dust** To fall dead or wounded, as in battle. *—n.* 1 The act of biting. 2 An injury inflicted by biting. 3 A smarting sensation or effect. 4 An amount taken by or as by biting. 5 A quick, light meal; snack. 6 A grip or hold, as of a tool. 7 The way in which the jaws meet. [<OE *bītan*] **—bit′a·ble, bite′a·ble** *adj.* **—bit′er** *n.*

bit·ing (bī′ting) *adj.* 1 Sharp; stinging. 2 Mordant; sarcastic. **—bit′ing·ly** *adv.* **—bit′ing·ness** *n.* **—Syn.** 2 caustic, cutting, incisive, acrimonious.

bitt (bit) *n.* A post on a ship's deck, to which cables, etc., are made fast. *—v.t.* To wind (a cable) around a bitt. [?]

bit·ter (bit′ər) *adj.* 1 Having an acrid, usu. unpleasant taste. 2 Causing acute physical discomfort or mental anguish. 3 Feeling or showing resentment, animosity, etc. 4 Hard to bear or accept. *—v.t. & v.i.* To make or become bitter. [<OE *biter*] **—bit′ter·ly** *adv.* **—bit′ter·ness** *n.*

bit·tern (bit′ərn) *n.* Any of various small herons noted for sounding a booming note in the breeding season. [<OF *butor*]

bit·ter·root (bit′ər·rōōt′, -rŏŏt′) *n.* A perennial herb of w North America with showy flowers and an edible root.

bit·ters (bit′ərs) *n. pl.* A usu. alcoholic liquor containing bitter herbs, bark, roots, etc., used as a tonic or flavoring agent.

bit·ter·sweet (bit′ər·swēt′) *n.* 1 A climbing shrub having orange seed pods that open to display a red aril. 2 A trailing plant of the nightshade family, having poisonous red berries. *—adj.* Both bitter and sweet or pleasant and unpleasant.

bi·tu·men (bi·tʸōō′mən, bich′ōō·mən) *n.* A mixture of solid and semisolid hydrocarbons, as naphtha or asphalt. [<L] **—bi·tu·mi·noid** (bi·tʸōō′mə·noid), **bi·tu′mi·nous** *adj.*

bi·tu·mi·nize (bi·tʸōō′mə·nīz) *v.t.* **·ized, ·iz·ing** To treat with bitumen. **—bi·tu′mi·ni·za′tion** *n.*

bituminous coal Coal containing volatile hydrocarbons and burning with a smoky flame.

bi·va·lent (bī·vā′lənt, biv′ə-) *adj.* 1 *Chem.* a Having a valence of two. b Having two valences. 2 *Biol.* Composed of or characterizing two similar chromosomes joined together or in close proximity. *—n.* A double chromosome. [<BI- + L *valens,* pr.p. of *valere* have power] **—bi·va′lence, bi·va′len·cy** *n.*

bi·valve (bī′valv′) *n.* A mollusk having a shell of two hinged valves. *—adj.* Having two valves, as a mollusk: also **bi′valved′, bi·val·vous** (bī·val′vəs), **bi·val·vu·lar** (bī·val′vyə·lər).

biv·ou·ac (biv′ōō·ak, biv′wak) *n.* A temporary field encampment with little or no shelter, esp. for soldiers. *—v.i.* **biv·ou·acked, biv·ou·ack·ing** To encamp in a bivouac. [<G *Beiwacht* guard]

bi·week·ly (bī·wēk′lē) *adj.* 1 Occurring every two weeks. 2 Semiweekly. *—adv.* 1 Every two weeks. 2 Semiweekly. *—n.* A biweekly publication. • See BIMONTHLY.

bi·year·ly (bī·yir′lē) *adj.* 1 Occurring once every two years. 2 Biannual. *—adv.* 1 Every two years. 2 Biannually. • See BIMONTHLY.

bi·zarre (bi·zär′) *adj.* Startingly odd. [F] **—bi·zarre′ly** *adv.* **—bi·zarre′ness** *n.* **—Syn.** outré, outlandish, fantastic, grotesque, freakish.

Bk berkelium.
bk. blank; block; book.
bkg. banking.
B.L., B.LL. Bachelor of Laws.
B/L, b.l. bill of lading.
bl. bale; barrel; black; blue.
blab (blab) *v.t. & v.i.* **blabbed, blab·bing 1** To reveal (a secret or confidence) indiscreetly. **2** To prattle. —*n.* **1** One who blabs. **2** Idle chatter. [ME *blabblen*]
blab·ber (blab′ər) *v.i.* To chatter; babble —*n.* One who blabs.
blab·ber·mouth (blab′ər·mouth′) *n. Informal* One who talks too much and can't be trusted to keep secrets.
black (blak) *adj.* **1** Reflecting little or no light; of the darkest color, as of coal or jet. **2** Without light; very dark. **3 a** Belonging to a dark-skinned ethnic group; esp., Negroid. **b** Of or relating to members of such a group: *black* power; *black* studies. **4** Soiled; stained. **5** Gloomy; dismal. **6** Disastrous; unlucky. **7** Indicating or deserving disgrace, censure, etc. **8** Evil; wicked. **9** Angry; scowling. **10** Dressed in black clothing. **11** Without cream or milk: *black* coffee. —*n.* **1** The darkest of all colors. **2** Something black, esp. black clothing. **3** A dark-skinned person, esp. a Negro. —**in the black** Ahead in business or finance; prospering. —*v.t. & v.i.* **1** To make or become black. **2** To polish with blacking. —**black out 1** To extinguish or screen all light. **2** To become temporarily unconscious. **3** To delete by scoring through. [< OE *blæc*] —**black′ish** *adj.* —**black′ly** *adv.* —**black′ness** *n.*
black·a·moor (blak′ə·mŏŏr′) *n. Archaic* A dark-skinned person, esp. a Negro.
black-and-blue (blak′ən·blōō′) *adj.* Discolored: said of skin that has been bruised.
black and white Writing or printing.
black art Necromancy; magic.
black·ball (blak′bôl′) *v.t.* **1** To vote against and ban from membership. **2** To exclude or ostracize. —*n.* **1** A negative vote resulting in the rejection of an application for membership. **2** A willful act of ostracism. [< BLACK + BALL, a black ball to signify a negative vote during balloting] —**black′ball′er** *n.*
black bass Any of a genus of fresh-water fishes of the eastern United States and Canada.
black bear 1 The common North American bear. **2** A dark-colored bear of Asia.
black·ber·ry (blak′ber′ē, -bər·ē) *n. pl.* **·ries 1** The black, edible fruit of certain shrubs of the rose family. **2** Any of the plants producing it.

Blackberries

black·bird (blak′bûrd′) *n.* **1** One of various black or blackish North American birds related to the orioles. **2** A common European thrush, the male of which is black.
black·board (blak′bôrd′, -bōrd′) *n.* A slate or black surface on which chalk is used to write or draw.
black body An ideal body that is uniformly and completely absorptive of radiation at all frequencies.
black·cap (blak′kap′) *n.* **1** Any of several birds having a black crown. **2** A variety of raspberry bearing black fruit.
Black Death A bubonic plague of exceptional virulence prevalent in the 14th century.
black·en (blak′ən) *v.t.* **1** To make black or dark. **2** To slander; defame. —*v.i.* **3** To become black; darken. —**black′·en·er** *n.*
black eye 1 A discolored bruise near the eye. **2** *Informal* A bad reputation.
black-eyed Susan (blak′īd′) A composite flower having a dark, conical center and yellow ray florets.
black·face (blak′fās′) *n.* **1** Dark, often grotesquely exaggerated make-up worn by someone portraying a Negro, esp. in a minstrel show. **2** Someone so made up.
Black·foot (blak′fŏŏt) *n. pl.* **·feet** or **·foot** A member of a confederacy of Algonquian North American Indian tribes formerly living E of the Rocky Mountains, now on reservations in Alberta and Montana.
black·guard (blag′ərd, -ärd) *n.* A despicable scoundrel. —*v.t.* **1** To vilify. —*v.i.* **2** To act like a blackguard. —*adj.* Of or like a blackguard: also **black′guard·ly.** [< *black guard*, orig., a group of low menials.] —**black′guard·ism** *n.*
Black Hand A secret organization in the U.S., esp. of Sicilians, for the purpose of vengeance or blackmail.
black·head (blak′hed′) *n.* **1** A plug of fatty material in a pore of the skin. **2** SCAUP, a duck. **3** An infectious disease of domestic fowl.
black-heart·ed (blak′här′tid) *adj.* Villainous; wicked.
black hole A hypothetical region characterized by an intense gravitational field that causes infinite curvature of the space within it allowing no matter or electromagnetic energy to escape, believed to result as the final stage of gravitational collapse of stellar material too massive to reach any stable state short of infinite density.
black·ing (blak′ing) *n.* A black polish used on shoes, stoves, etc.
black·jack (blak′jak′) *n.* **1** A small bludgeon with a flexible handle. **2** JOLLY ROGER. **3** A card game won by the player holding cards whose face value totals 21 or less but is higher than that of the dealer, popular as a gambling game. **4** A large drinking cup, formerly of leather. —*v.t.* **1** To strike with a blackjack. **2** To coerce by threat.
black·leg (blak′leg′) *n.* **1** An infectious, often fatal disease of cattle and sheep. **2** A professional swindler or gambler; sharper. **3** *Brit.* A strikebreaker.
black letter A type face with heavy, angular letters.

This line is in black letter

black·list (blak′list′) *n.* A list of persons or groups to be censured, refused membership, excluded from employment, etc. —*v.t.* To place on a blacklist.
black lung disease A form of pneumoconiosis caused by prolonged exposure to and inhalation of coal dust.
black magic Sorcery with an evil intention.
black·mail (blak′māl′) *n.* **1** The extortion of payment by threats of public exposure. **2** Money, etc. obtained by such extortion. —*v.t.* **1** To subject to blackmail. **2** To coerce, as by threats. [< BLACK + obs. *mail* tribute] —**black′mail′er** *n.*
Black Ma·ri·a (mə·rī′ə) *Informal* A police patrol wagon.
black market A place or business in which merchandise is sold in amounts or at prices contrary to legal restrictions. —**black mar·ket·eer** (mar′kə·tir′)
Black Muslim A member of a U.S. Negro sect (the **Nation of Islam**) which follows the practices of Islam and rejects integration with whites.
black nightshade The common nightshade, having black, poisonous berries.
black·out (blak′out′) *n.* **1** The hiding or extinguishing of all lights, esp. as a precautionary measure against air attack. **2** A temporary loss of consciousness or vision. **3** The sudden darkening of the stage in a theatrical performance. **4** A ban or suppression, as of news, a television broadcast, etc.
black sheep A person regarded as a disreputable member of a family or group.
Black Shirt A member of a fascist group having uniforms with black shirts, as the Italian Fascist Party.
black·smith (blak′smith′) *n.* One who shapes metal using an anvil and forge, esp. one who makes horseshoes and shoes horses.
black·snake (blak′snāk′) *n.* **1** Any of various black or nearly black snakes. **2** A heavy, pliant whip of braided leather or rawhide.
black spruce 1 A small conifer abundant in boggy northern areas of North America. **2** Its soft wood.
black·thorn (blak′thôrn′) *n.* **1** A thorny European shrub of the rose family; the sloe. **2** A cane made from its wood.
black tie 1 A black bow tie. **2** A dinner jacket and its correct accessories.
black walnut 1 A large walnut tree native to North America, having hard, dark brown wood. **2** Its wood. **3** Its oily, edible nut. • See WALNUT.

black widow An American spider of which the venomous female has a black body marked with red.

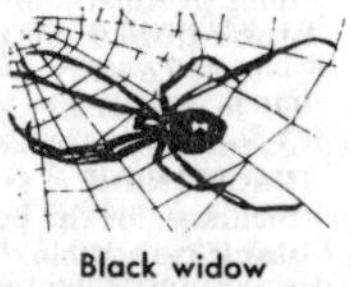

Black widow

blad·der (blad′ər) *n.* **1** A distensible sac for the temporary retention of urine. **2** Any similar part or organ for retaining fluid or gas. **3** An air vessel or float in some seaweeds. [< OE *blǣdre*] **—blad′·der·y** *adj.*

blad·der·wort (blad′ər·wûrt′) *n.* Any of a genus of usu. aquatic plants having little bladders in which minute organisms are trapped and digested.

blade (blād) *n.* **1** The flat cutting part of an edged tool or weapon. **2** A thin, flat part, as of an oar, propeller, plow, etc. **3** **a** The expanded part of a leaf. **b** A narrow leaf having no petiole: a *blade* of grass. **4** **a** A sword. **b** A swordsman. **5** A rakish young man. [< OE *blæd* blade of a leaf] **—blad′ed** *adj.*

blah (blä) *Slang n.* Blather; nonsense. *—adj.* Lacking interest or animation.

blain (blān) *n.* A small inflamed area; a blister. [< OE *blegen*]

blam·a·ble (blā′mə·bəl) *adj.* Deserving blame; culpable. **—blam′a·bly** *adv.*

blame (blām) *v.t.* **blamed, blam·ing** **1** To accuse of fault: often with *for.* **2** To find fault with; reproach. **3** To hold responsible for something undesirable. **—be to blame** To be at fault. *—n.* **1** Responsibility for a fault, error, wrongdoing, etc. **2** Censure; condemnation. [< OF *blasmer* < LL *blasphemare* revile, reproach] **—blame′ful** *adj.* **—blame′ful·ly** *adv.* **—blame′ful·ness** *n.* **—blame′less** *adj.* **—blame′less·ly** *adv.* **—blame′less·ness** *n.* **—Syn.** *v.* **1** censure, condemn, damn, charge, indict.

blamed (blāmd) *adj. & adv. Regional* Damned: a *blamed* fool; *blamed* hot.

blame·wor·thy (blām′wûr′t͟hē) *adj.* Deserving of blame. **—blame′wor′thi·ness** *n.*

blanch (blanch, blänch) *v.t.* **1** To remove the color from; bleach. **2** To cause to turn pale. **3** To plunge (food) briefly into boiling water, as to remove the skin or in preparation for freezing. *—v.i.* **4** To turn or become white or pale. [< F *blanc* white] **—blanch′er** *n.*

blanc·mange (blə·mänzh′, -mänzh′) *n.* A whitish, jelly-like dessert of milk, eggs, sugar, cornstarch, flavoring, etc. [< OF *blanc-manger* white food]

bland (bland) *adj.* **1** Smooth; suave; unctuous. **2** Mild; gentle; temperate. **3** Not stimulating or irritating. **4** Insipid; flat. [< L *blandus* mild] **—bland′ly** *adv.* **—bland′ness** *n.*

blan·dish (blan′dish) *v.t.* To wheedle; flatter; cajole. [< OF *blandir* flatter] **—blan′dish·er, blan′dish·ment** *n.*

blank (blangk) *adj.* **1** Having no writing, printing, decoration, etc. **2** Not completed or filled out: a *blank* check. **3** Vacant; empty: a *blank* stare. **4** Utter; complete: *blank* terror. **5** Useless; fruitless: *blank* efforts. **6** Not finished, as with cuts or grooves: a *blank* key. *—n.* **1** An empty area, condition, etc.; a void. **2** A space left empty, as in printed matter. **3** A printed form to be filled out. **4** A piece, as of metal or wood, ready to be formed into a finished object, as a key, button, etc. **5** A cartridge loaded with powder only: also **blank cartridge.** **—draw a blank** **1** To draw a lottery ticket that does not win. **2** *Informal* To fail in an effort. **3** *Informal* To be unable to remember something. *—v.t.* **1** To delete; invalidate: often with *out.* **2** In games, to prevent (an opponent) from scoring. [< OF *blanc* white] **—blank′ly** *adv.* **—blank′ness** *n.*

blan·ket (blang′kit) *n.* **1** A large cloth covering used esp. for warmth, as on a bed. **2** Any thick, extensive covering: a *blanket* of snow. *—adj.* Covering a wide range of conditions, needs, items, etc.: a *blanket* injunction. *—v.t.* **1** To cover with or as with a blanket. **2** To have uniform application to. **3** To obscure or suppress as with a blanket. [< OF *blankete,* dim. of *blanc* white]

blank verse Unrhymed verse, esp. of iambic pentameter as used in English epic and dramatic poetry.

blare (blâr) *v.t. & v.i.* **blared, blar·ing** **1** To sound loudly and harshly, as a trumpet. **2** To exclaim loudly and stridently. *—n.* **1** A loud, brazen sound. **2** Brightness or glare, as of color. [Prob. imit.]

blar·ney (blär′nē) *n.* Coaxing flattery. *—v.t. & v.i.* To flatter or cajole. [< BLARNEY STONE]

Blarney Stone A stone in a castle in Blarney, Ireland, which, when kissed, reputedly endows one with invincible eloquence.

bla·sé (blä·zā′, blä′zā) *adj.* Sated or bored, as by excessive indulgence, experience, etc. [< F *blaser* satiate]

blas·pheme (blas·fēm′) *v.* **·phemed, ·phem·ing** *—v.t.* **1** To speak in an impious or irreverent manner of (God or sacred things). **2** To speak ill of; malign. *—v.i.* **3** To utter blasphemy. [< Gk. *blasphēmein* revile] **—blas·phem′er** *n.*

blas·phe·my (blas′fə·mē) *n. pl.* **·mies** **1** Words or action showing impious irreverence toward God or sacred things. **2** Any irreverent act or utterance. **—blas′phe·mous** *adj.* **—blas′phe·mous·ly** *adv.*

blast (blast, bläst) *v.t.* **1** To shatter, destroy, etc., by or as by explosion. **2** To cause to wither or fail to mature. **3** To attack or criticize with intense force. *—v.i.* **4** To make a loud, harsh sound. **—blast off** To begin a flight with explosive force, as a rocket. *—n.* **1** A strong or sudden wind. **2** The strong jet of air in a blast furnace. **3** The discharge of an explosive, or its effect. **4** A loud, sudden sound, as of a trumpet. **5** A blight or blighting influence **—at full blast** At maximum speed or capacity. [< OE *blǣst* a blowing] **—blast′er** *n.*

blast·ed (blas′tid, bläs′-) *adj.* **1** Withered or destroyed. **2** Damned; confounded: a euphemistic oath.

blast furnace A smelting furnace in which the fire is intensified by an air blast.

blast·off (blast′ôf, -of) *n.* The launching of a rocket, space vehicle, etc.

blas·tu·la (blas′cho͞o·lə) *n. pl.* **·lae** (-lē) or **·las** An early stage of embryonic development, consisting of a hollow sphere enclosed by one or more layers of cells. [< Gk. *blastos* sprout] **—blas′tu·lar** *adj.*

blat (blat) *v.* **blat·ted, blat·ting** *v.t.* **1** *Informal* To blurt out. *—v.i.* **2** To bleat, as a sheep. [Imit.]

bla·tant (blā′tənt) *adj.* **1** Offensively loud or clamorous. **2** Obtrusively obvious; glaring: a *blatant* lie. [? < L *blatire* babble] **—bla′tan·cy** *n.* **—bla′tant·ly** *adv.*

blath·er (blat͟h′ər) *v.t. & v.i.* To talk or say foolishly. *—n.* Foolish talk. [< ON *blathra* talk stupidly]

blath·er·skite (blat͟h′ər·skīt) *n.* A blustering, noisy fellow. [< BLATHER + SKATE (fish)]

blaze[1] (blāz) *v.i.* **blazed, blaz·ing** **1** To burn brightly. **2** To burn as with emotion: to *blaze* with anger. **3** To shine; be resplendent. **—blaze away** **1** To keep on firing. **2** To attack persistently. *—n.* **1** A brightly burning fire. **2** Intense light or glare. **3** A brilliant display. **4** A burst, as of emotion. **5** *pl.* Hell: a euphemism in oaths. [< OE *blæse* firebrand] **—blaz′ing·ly** *adv.*

blaze[2] (blāz) *v.t.* **blazed, blaz·ing** **1** To mark (a tree) by chipping off a piece of bark. **2** To indicate (a trail) by making such marks. *—n.* **1** A white spot on the face of an animal. **2** A mark made by blazing a tree. [?]

blaze[3] (blāz) *v.t.* **blazed, blaz·ing** To publicize or noise about. [< ON *blāsa* blow]

blaz·er (blā′zər) *n.* A lightweight jacket, often vividly colored or patterned.

bla·zon (blā′zən) *n.* **1** A coat of arms. **2** A technical description or a graphic representation of a coat of arms. **3** Ostentatious display. *—v.t.* **1** To inscribe or adorn, as with names or symbols. **2** To describe technically or paint (coats of arms). **3** To proclaim; publish. [< OF *blason* coat of arms, shield] **—bla′zon·er, bla′zon·ment, bla′zon·ry** *n.*

bldg., blg. building.

bleach (blēch) *v.t. & v.i.* To make or become colorless, pale, or white. *—n.* **1** An act of bleaching. **2** A fluid or powder used as a bleaching agent. [< OE *blǣcean*]

bleach·er (blē′chər) *n.* **1** One who or that which bleaches. **2** *pl.* Outdoor, uncovered seats or benches for spectators, as of a sports event.

bleak (blēk) *adj.* **1** Exposed to wind and weather; bare. **2**

Cold; cutting. **3** Dreary; gloomy. [< ON *bleikja* pale] —**bleak′ly** *adv.* —**bleak′ness** *n.* —**Syn. 1** barren, unsheltered, windswept, withered. **3** melancholy, miserable.

blear (blir) *adj.* Bleary. —*v.t.* **1** To dim or inflame (the eyes). **2** To obscure; blur. [ME *blere*]

blear·y (blir′ē) *adj.* **·i·er, ·i·est 1** Made dim, as by tears. **2** Blurry; hazy: *bleary* vision. —**blear′i·ly** *adv.* —**blear′i·ness** *n.*

blear·y-eyed (blir′ē·īd′) *adj.* Having bleary eyes or vision. Also **blear′-eyed′**.

bleat (blēt) *v.i.* **1** To cry, as a sheep or goat. **2** To speak with such a sound, as in complaint. —*v.t.* **3** To utter with the sound of a bleat. **4** To babble foolishly; prate. —*n.* The act or sound of bleating. [< OE *blǣtan*] —**bleat′er** *n.*

bleed (blēd) *v.* **bled, bleed·ing** *v.i.* **1** To lose or shed blood. **2** To exude sap or other fluid. **3** To suffer wounds or die, as in battle. **4** To feel grief or sympathy. —*v.t.* **5** To draw blood from. **6** To exude (sap, blood, etc.). **7** To draw sap or other fluid from. **8** *Informal* To extort money from. —**bleed white** To deplete of all resources, as if by draining of blood. [< OE *blēdan*]

bleed·er (blē′dər) *n.* A person who bleeds profusely, esp. a hemophiliac.

bleeding heart 1 Any of various plants having pink, drooping flowers. **2** *Informal* One whose political views are unduly influenced by sympathy for alleged suffering.

blem·ish (blem′ish) *v.t.* To mar the perfection of; sully. —*n.* **1** A spot or surface defect, as on the skin. **2** A fault or shortcoming. [< OF *blemir* make livid] —**blem′ish·er** *n.*

blench[1] (blench) *v.i.* To shrink back; flinch. [< OE *blencan* deceive] —**blench′er** *n.*

blench[2] (blench) *v.t.* & *v.i.* To make or become pale; blanch.

blend (blend) *v.* **blend·ed** or **blent, blend·ing** *v.t.* **1** To mix or combine so as to obtain a product of a desired quality, taste, color, or consistency. —*v.i.* **2** To mix; intermingle. **3** To pass or shade imperceptibly into each other, as colors. **4** To harmonize. —*n.* The act or result of blending. [< ON *blanda* mingle]

blende (blend) *n.* Any of several shiny minerals, esp. a compound of sulfur with a metal. [< G *blendendes erz* deceptive ore]

blend·er (blen′dər)*n.* **1** One who or that which blends. **2** Any of various electrical devices that mix and blend substances, as foods, paints, cement, etc.

blen·ny (blen′ē) *n. pl.* **blen·nies** Any of various small, elongated marine fishes. [< Gk. *blennos* slime]

bless (bles) *v.t.* **blessed** or **blest, bless·ing 1** To consecrate; make holy by religious rite. **2** To glorify. **3** To make the sign of the cross over or upon. **4** To invoke divine favor upon (a person or thing). **5** To make happy. **6** To endow, as with a gift: She was *blessed* with a beautiful face. **7** To guard; protect: *Bless* me! [< OE *blētsian* consecrate (with blood)] —**bless′er** *n.*

bless·ed (bles′id, blest) *adj.* **1** Made holy by a religious rite. **2** In heavenly bliss; beatified. **3** Characterized by or causing great happiness. **4** Confounded; damned: used euphemistically or ironically: not a *blessed* cent. Also **blest** (blest). —**bless′ed·ly** *adv.* —**bless′ed·ness** *n.* —**Syn. 1** consecrated, sanctified, sacred. **3** joyous, joyful, rapturous.

blessed event *Informal* The birth of a baby.

bless·ing (bles′ing) *n.* **1** A benediction. **2** A grace said at mealtime. **3** Approval. **4** Good wishes. **5** Anything that gives happiness, prosperity, etc.

blest (blest) A *p.t.* & *p.p.* of BLESS. —*adj.* Blessed.

bleu (blo͞o) *Can. n.* A member of the Conservative party in Quebec. —*adj.* Of or pertaining to the Conservative party.

blew (blo͞o) *p.t.* of BLOW.

blight (blīt) *n.* **1** Any of a number of destructive plant diseases, as rust, smut, etc. **2** An environmental factor injurious to a specific group or groups of plants or animals. **3** A person or thing that withers hopes, destroys prospects, etc. **4** A blighted condition. —*v.t.* **1** To cause to decay. **2** To ruin; frustrate. —*v.i.* **3** To suffer blight. [?]

blimp (blimp) *n.* *Informal* A small, nonrigid dirigible. [< Type *B-Limp,* a kind of British dirigible]

blind (blīnd) *adj.* **1** Without the power of seeing. **2** Of or for blind persons. **3** Lacking in perception, sound judgment, or logic. **4** Done without preparation, plan, or control: a *blind* effort. **5** Impossible to control or foresee: *blind* fate. **6** Having no opening or outlet: a *blind* ditch. **7** Open at one end only: a *blind* alley. **8** Hard to see; hidden: a *blind* driveway. **9** Using instruments only: *blind* flying. —*n.* **1** Something that obstructs vision or shuts off light, as a window shade. **2** A person or thing meant to deceive; decoy. **3** A hiding place, esp. for hunters. —**the blind** Blind people. —*v.t.* **1** To make blind. **2** To dazzle. **3** To deprive of judgment. **4** To darken; obscure. **5** To outshine; eclipse. —*adv.* **1** By using instruments only. **2** So as to be insensible. [< OE] —**blind′ly** *adv.* —**blind′ness** *n.*

blind date 1 A social engagement arranged for a man and woman who have not previously met. **2** Either of the two persons involved.

blind·er (blīn′dər) *n.* **1** One who or that which blinds. **2** A flap on both sides of a horse's bridle, used to obstruct his side view.

Blinders

blind·fold (blīnd′fōld′) *v.t.* **1** To cover or bandage the eyes of. **2** To hoodwink; mislead. —*n.* A bandage, etc., over the eyes. —*adj.* **1** Having the eyes bandaged. **2** Reckless; rash. [< ME *blindfelden* < *blind* blind + *fellen* to strike]

blind spot 1 A small area on the retina occupied by optic nerve connections and hence insensible to light. **2** A subject or area of thought about which one is ignorant or prejudiced.

blink (blingk) *v.i.* **1** To wink rapidly. **2** To squint, as in sunlight. **3** To twinkle; glimmer; also, to flash on and off. **4** To ignore or disregard something: He *blinked* at the corruption in politics. —*v.t.* **5** To cause to wink. **6** To shut the eyes to; evade. **7** To send (a message) by a flashing light. —*n.* **1** A blinking of the eye. **2** A gleam of light. —**on the blink** *Informal* Out of order; not working. [ME *blinken*]

blink·er (blingk′ər) *n.* **1** A light that flashes on and off, used as a warning, to send messages, etc. **2** *pl.* Goggles. **3** A horse's blinder.

blin·tze (blin′tsə) *n.* A thin pancake folded about a filling, as of cheese. Also **blintz** (blınts). [Yiddish]

blip (blip) *n.* **1** *Telecom.* A visual display of a radar echo. **2** A short, sharp sound. —*v.i.* **blipped, blip·ping 1** To make blips. —*v.t.* **2** To delete (speech) from a videotape, as in censoring, thus creating a discontinuity. [Imit.]

bliss (blis) *n.* **1** Superlative happiness and joy. **2** A cause of delight. [< OE *bliths*] —**bliss′ful** *adj.* —**bliss′ful·ly** *adv.*

blis·ter (blis′tər) *n.* **1** A raised sac under the epidermis, containing watery matter, as from a burn or irritation. **2** Something that resembles a blister, as on a plant, on a painted surface, etc. —*v.t.* **1** To produce a blister or blisters upon. **2** To rebuke harshly. —*v.i.* **3** To become blistered. [OF *blestre*] —**blis′ter·y** *adj.*

blithe (blī*th*) *adj.* Joyous; gay; carefree. [< OE] —**blithe′ly** *adv.* —**blithe′ness** *n.*

blithe·some (blī*th*′səm) *adj.* Blithe; merry. —**blithe′·some·ly** *adv.* —**blithe′some·ness** *n.*

blitz (blits) *v.t.* To attack with sudden and overwhelming force. —*n.* A sudden, overwhelming attack. [G, lightning]

blitz·krieg (blits′krēg) *n.* A sudden, overwhelming attack. [G, lit., lightning war]

bliz·zard (bliz′ərd) *n.* **1** A severe storm with heavy snow. **2** Anything resembling a blizzard, as in the swirl or rush of great numbers of things. [?]

blk. black; block; bulk.

bloat (blōt) *v.t.* **1** To cause to swell, as with fluid or gas. **2** To make proud or vain. —*v.i.* **3** To swell; become puffed up. [< ME *blout* swollen]

blob (blob) *n.* A soft, globular mass, as of viscous liquid. —*v.t.* **blobbed, blob·bing** To smear with ink or color. [Imit.]

bloc (blok) *n.* A group, as of politicians, nations, etc., combined to foster special interests. [F]

block (blok) *n.* **1** A solid piece of wood, stone, etc., usu. with flat

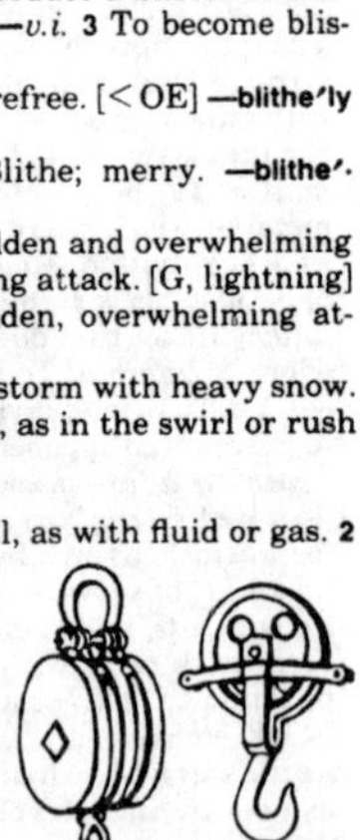

a b

Blocks *def. 8*
a. tackle. b. gin.

surfaces. 2 An obstacle, obstruction, or hindrance. 3 The act of obstructing or the condition of being obstructed. 4 A wooden log or cube on which chopping is done: a butcher's *block;* a headsman's *block.* 5 In sports, an interference with an opponent's movements. 6 An auctioneer's stand. 7 The mold on which something is shaped: a hat *block.* 8 A pulley, or set of pulleys, in a frame or shell. 9 A toy building cube, usu. of wood. 10 A piece of wood, linoleum, etc., for engraving a design to be printed. 11 A city square bounded by streets; also, the distance along any of such streets. 12 A large group of adjacent buildings. 13 A group acting or considered as a unit: a *block* of theater seats; the Asian *block* of nations. 14 A section of a railroad track controlled by signals. 15 An interruption of normal physical or mental functioning: a nerve *block;* a memory *block.* 16 *Austral.* An area of farming land. —*v.t.* 1 To obstruct; impede the progress of. 2 To fill (an area or space) so as to prevent movement into or through. 3 In sports: a To hinder the movements of (an opposing player). b To stop (a ball, etc.) with the body. 4 To shape on a block, as a hat. 5 To put up on blocks. —*v.i.* 6 To act so as to hinder. —**block out** 1 To obscure from view. 2 To plan broadly without details: to *block out* a design. [< OF *bloc*] —**block′age, block′er** *n.*

block·ade (blo·kād′) *n.* 1 A military or naval closing of an enemy port, coast, etc., to traffic or communication. 2 The forces that set up a blockade. 3 Any hindrance or obstruction to action or traffic. —**run the blockade** To elude a blockade. —*v.t.* **·ad·ed, ·ad·ing** To subject to a blockade. [< F *bloquer* obstruct]

block and tackle An arrangement of pulleys and ropes for hoisting heavy objects.

block·bust·er (blok′bus′tər) *n.* 1 An aerial bomb capable of devastating a large area. 2 *U.S.* One who engages in blockbusting.

block·bust·ing (blok′bust′ing) *n. U.S.* The practice of inducing home owners to sell hastily and often at a loss by arousing the fear that the sale of nearby homes to members of a minority group will lower the values of their houses.

block·head (blok′hed′) *n.* A stupid person. —**Syn.** ass, dolt, dunce, fool.

block·house (blok′hous′) *n.* 1 A fortification, formerly of logs and heavy timbers, having loopholes from which to fire guns. 2 A heavily reinforced shelter offering protection and observation at missile launchings, nuclear bomb testings, etc. 3 *U.S.* A house made of hewn logs set square.

block·ish (blok′ish) *adj.* Like a block; stupid; dull. —**block′ish·ly** *adv.* —**block′ish·ness** *n.*

block·y (blok′ē) *adj.* **·i·er, ·i·est** 1 Unequally shaded, as if printed in blocks. 2 Short and stout; stocky.

bloke (blōk) *n. Brit. Slang* A fellow; guy.

blond (blond) *adj.* 1 Having flaxen or yellowish brown hair, fair skin and light eyes. 2 Flaxen, golden, or yellowish brown: said of hair. 3 Light-colored. —*n.* A blond person. [< Med.L *blondus*]

blonde (blond) *adj. (feminine only)* BLOND (def. 1). —*n.* A blond woman or girl. • In modern usage the final *-e* is usu. kept in the noun when it refers to a fair-haired woman or girl and in the adjective describing such a woman or girl.

blood (blud) *n.* 1 The usu. red fluid that circulates throughout the bodies of vertebrates, delivering oxygen and nutrients to the cells and tissues and removing waste products. 2 A fluid resembling blood, as in certain invertebrates. 3 The shedding of blood, esp. murder. 4 Temperament; disposition: cool *blood.* 5 Vitality; life; lifeblood. 6 Relationship by descent from a common ancestor; kinship. 7 Ancestry; lineage. 8 Royal or noble lineage. —**in cold blood** Without passion or mercy; deliberately. —**make one's blood boil** To make one very angry. —**make one's blood run cold** To terrify one. [< OE *blōd*]

blood bank A reserve of processed blood from various donors for clinical use.

blood bath A massacre; slaughter.

blood count The number and proportion of red cells, platelets, etc., in a given sample of blood.

blood·cur·dling (blud′kurd′ling) *adj.* Terrifying; horrible; chilling.

blood·ed (blud′id) *adj.* 1 Having blood or temper of a specified character: cold-*blooded.* 2 Having pure blood or lineage; thoroughbred.

blood group One of several classes to which any sample of human blood is assignable according to genetic factors identified by agglutination reactions.

blood·hound (blud′hound′) *n.* 1 A large hound with an unusual ability to follow a scent, often used to track fugitives, etc. 2 A person who pursues relentlessly.

Bloodhound

blood·less (blud′lis) *adj.* 1 Having no blood. 2 Without bloodshed. 3 Without vitality; lifeless. 4 Cold-hearted. —**blood′less·ly** *adv.* —**blood′less·ness** *n.*

blood·let·ting (blud′let′ing) *n.* 1 Drawing blood for a therapeutic purpose. 2 Bloodshed.

blood money 1 Money paid to a hired murderer. 2 Money paid as compensation to the next of kin of a murdered man. 3 Money obtained at the expense of another's death, suffering, etc.

blood plasma The liquid part of blood in which corpuscles and other particles are suspended.

blood platelet One of the minute circular bodies found in the blood of higher vertebrates, essential to clotting.

blood poisoning The presence of bacteria in the blood; septicemia.

blood pressure The pressure of the blood on the walls of the arteries.

blood relation A person related by birth.

blood·root (blud′rōōt′, -rōōt′) *n.* A perennial North American herb having a fleshy rootstalk with red sap.

blood·shed (blud′shed′) *n.* The shedding of blood; slaughter; carnage.

blood·shot (blud′shot′) *adj.* Red and inflamed or irritated: said of the eye.

blood·stained (blud′stānd′) *adj.* Stained or spotted with blood.

blood·stone (blud′stōn′) *n.* A green chalcedony flecked with red jasper, often cut as a gem.

blood stream The blood in motion in a living body.

blood·suck·er (blud′suk′ər) *n.* 1 An animal that sucks blood, as a leech. 2 A person who takes excessively from or sponges on others.

blood·thirst·y (blud′thûrs′tē) *adj.* Thirsting for blood; murderous; cruel. —**blood′thirst′i·ly** *adv.* —**blood′thirst′i·ness** *n.*

blood type BLOOD GROUP.

blood vessel Any tubular canal in which the blood circulates; an artery, vein, or capillary.

blood·y (blud′ē) *adj.* **blood·i·er, blood·i·est** 1 Covered or stained with blood: also **blood′ied.** 2 Of, containing, or mixed with blood. 3 Involving bloodshed. 4 Bloodthirsty. 5 Red like blood. 6 *Brit. Slang* Damned; confounded. —*adv. Brit. Slang* Very; exceedingly. —*v.t.* **blood·ied, blood·y·ing** To smear or stain with blood. —**blood′i·ly** *adv.* —**blood′i·ness** *n.*

bloom (blōōm) *n.* 1 A flower; blossom. 2 Flowers collectively. 3 The state of being in flower. 4 A time of freshness, vigor, and health; prime. 5 A fresh flush or glow, as on the cheeks. 6 A whitish, powdery coating on certain fruits and leaves. —*v.i.* 1 To bear flowers; blossom. 2 To glow with health and vigor. 3 To flourish; be in a prime condition. —*v.t.* 4 To bring into bloom; cause to flourish. [< ON *blōm* flower, blossom] —**bloom′er** *n.*

bloom·er (blōō′mər) *n.* 1 Formerly, a woman's costume of loose trousers gathered at the ankles and worn under a short skirt. 2 *pl.* Loose, wide knickerbockers gathered at the knees, formerly worn by women in athletic practice; also, an undergarment resembling this. [< Amelia *Bloomer,* 1818–94, U.S. feminist reformer who first proposed it]

bloom·ing (blōō′ming) *adj.* 1 Coming into flower. 2 Fresh and vigorous. 3 Flourishing. 4 *Brit. Informal* Utter; veritable. —**Syn. 3** prosperous, successful, thriving.

bloop·er (blōō′pər) *n. Slang* 1 An error or blunder. 2 In baseball: **a** A weakly hit fly ball reaching just beyond the infield. **b** A high, softly thrown pitch. [Imit.]

blos·som (blos′əm) *n.* 1 A flower, esp. one of a plant yielding edible fruit. 2 The state or period of flowering; bloom. —*v.i.* 1 To come into blossom; bloom. 2 To prosper; thrive. [OE *blōstma*] —**blos′som·y** *adj.*

blot (blot) *n.* 1 A spot or stain, as of ink. 2 A moral fault or disgrace. 3 Something unattractive; blemish. —*v.* **blot·ted, blot·ting** *v.t.* 1 To spot, as with ink; stain. 2 To disgrace; sully. 3 To obliterate, as writing, a memory, etc.: often with *out.* 4 To dry with blotting paper. 5 To obscure; darken: usu. with *out.* —*v.i.* 6 To spread in a blot or blots, as ink. 7 To become blotted; acquire spots. 8 To absorb: This paper *blots* well. [ME *blotte*]

blotch (bloch) *n.* 1 A spot or blot. 2 An eruption on the skin. —*v.t.* To mark or cover with blotches. [Blend of BLOT and BOTCH] —**blotch′y** *adj.* **(-i·er, -i·est)**

blot·ter (blot′ər) *n.* 1 A sheet or pad of blotting paper. 2 The daily record of arrests and charges in a police station.

blotting paper Unsized paper for absorbing excess ink.

blouse (blous, blouz) *n.* 1 A loose garment extending from the neck to the waist or below, worn by women and children. 2 A loose, knee-length shirt usu. belted at the waist, worn chiefly by French workmen. 3 A U.S. Army service coat. —*v.t. & v.i.* **bloused** (bloust, blouzd), **blous·ing** To drape at the waistline. [F]

blow[1] (blō) *v.* **blew, blown, blow·ing** *v.t.* 1 To move by a current of air. 2 To cause air to be released from (a bellows, etc.). 3 To emit, as air or smoke, from the mouth. 4 To force air upon, as for cooling, drying, warming, etc. 5 To empty or clear by forcing air through, as pipes. 6 To cause to sound, as a bugle or horn. 7 To sound (a signal) by blowing. 8 To form or shape, as by inflating: to *blow* glass. 9 To put out of breath, as a horse. 10 To shatter or destroy by or as by explosion: usu. with *up, down, out, through,* etc.: to *blow* a hole through a wall; to *blow* up a house. 11 To melt (a fuse). 12 To lay eggs in, as flies in meat. 13 *Informal* To spend (money) lavishly; also, to treat or entertain: I'll *blow* you to a meal. 14 *Informal* To forget (one's lines) in a play, etc. 15 *Slang* To leave; go out of. 16 *Slang* To handle badly; bungle. —*v.i.* 17 To be in motion, usu. with some force: said of wind or air. 18 To move in a current of air; be carried by the wind. 19 To emit a current or jet of air, water, steam, etc. 20 To sound by being blown: The bugle *blew* at dawn. 21 To fail or become useless, as by melting: The fuse *blew.* 22 To explode: usu. with *up, down, to,* etc. 23 To pant; gasp for breath. 24 *Informal* To talk boastfully. 25 *Slang* To leave; go. —**blow hot and cold** *Informal* To vacillate. —**blow off** 1 To let off steam, as from a boiler. 2 *Informal* To speak in anger, as to relieve pent-up emotion. —**blow out** 1 To extinguish (a fire or flame) by blowing. 2 To be extinguished by air or wind. 3 To explode, as a tire. 4 To subside: The storm will *blow* itself *out.* —**blow over** 1 To overturn by blowing. 2 To be forgotten. 3 To pass, as a storm; subside. —**blow up** 1 To inflate. 2 To enlarge, as a photographic print. 3 To explode. 4 *Informal* To lose self-control; become enraged. 5 To arise, as a storm. 6 To exaggerate (an incident, etc.). —*n.* 1 The act of blowing. 2 A gale. 3 *Slang* Boastfulness. 4 *Slang* A braggart. [<OE *blāwan*]

blow[2] (blō) *n.* 1 A hard hit or punch, as with the fist or a weapon. 2 A sudden misfortune. 3 A hostile or combative act. —**come to blows** To start fighting. [<ME *blaw*]

blow·er (blō′ər) *n.* 1 One who or that which blows. 2 A device for forcing a draft of air through a building, furnace, machinery, etc.

blow·fly (blō′flī′) *n. pl.* **·flies** Any of several flies that lay eggs in carrion or in open wounds.

blow·gun (blō′gun′) *n.* A long tube through which a missile may be blown by the breath.

blow·hole (blō′hōl′) *n.* 1 The breathing opening in the heads of whales, etc. 2 A vent for the release of gas or air. 3 A hole in the ice to which seals, etc., come to breathe.

blown[1] (blōn) *p.p.* of BLOW[1]. —*adj.* 1 Winded from overexertion. 2 Spoiled, as food, by exposure to flies or other organisms. 3 Inflated or swollen. 4 Made with a blowpipe: *blown* glass.

blown[2] (blōn) *adj.* In full flower or bloom.

blow·out (blō′out′) *n.* 1 *Electr.* The opening of a fuse due to excess current. 2 *Slang* An elaborate social function or meal. 3 A sudden bursting of a tire. 4 A flameout.

blow·pipe (blō′pīp′) *n.* 1 A tube by which air or gas is blown through a flame to increase its temperature. 2 BLOWGUN.

blow·torch (blō′tôrch′) *n.* A device that burns a jet of air and gasoline vapor to make an intensely hot flame.

blow·up (blō′up′) *n.* 1 An explosion. 2 An enlarged photograph, page of print, etc. 3 *Informal* Loss of self-control.

blow·y (blō′ē) *adj.* **blow·i·er, blow·i·est** Windy.

blowz·y (blou′zē) *adj.* **·i·er, ·i·est** 1 Unkempt; slovenly. 2 Coarse, fat, and ruddy-faced. Also **blows·y** (blou′zē). [?]

blub·ber[1] (blub′ər) *v.t.* 1 To utter sobbingly. —*v.i.* 2 To weep and sob noisily. [ME *blubren*] —**blub′ber·er** *n.*

blub·ber[2] (blub′ər) *n.* The layer of fat beneath the skin of whales and other sea mammals. [ME *bluber*] —**blub′·ber·y** *adj.*

bludg·eon (bluj′ən) *n.* A short club, commonly loaded at one end, used as a weapon. —*v.t.* 1 To strike with or as with a bludgeon. 2 To coerce; bully. [?]

blue (blōō) *adj.* **blu·er, blu·est** 1 Having the color of the clear, daytime sky. 2 Livid: said of the skin. 3 Sad; melancholy. 4 Depressing; discouraging. 5 Puritanic; strict: *blue* laws. 6 *Informal* Risqué. 7 *Can.* BLEU. —*n.* 1 The color of the clear, daytime sky; azure. 2 Any blue coloring matter or pigment. 3 BLUING. 4 *Often pl.* Blue clothing. 5 *Sometimes cap.* A person who wears a blue uniform. 6 *pl.* See BLUES. 7 *Can.* BLEU. —**out of the blue** From an unsuspected source; completely unforeseen. —*v.t.* **blued, blu·ing** 1 To make blue. 2 To treat with bluing. [<OF *bleu*] —**blue′ly** *adv.* —**blue′ness** *n.*

Blue·beard (blōō′bird′) In folklore, a man who married and then murdered one wife after another.

blue·bell (blōō′bel′) *n.* Any of various plants that bear blue, bell-shaped flowers.

blue·ber·ry (blōō′ber′ē, -bər·ē) *n. pl.* **·ries** 1 A many-seeded, edible, blue-black berry. 2 The plant that bears it.

blue·bird (blōō′bûrd′) *n.* Any of various small North American songbirds with blue plumage.

blue blood 1 Descent from a noble or aristocratic family. 2 A person of noble or aristocratic family. Also **blue′blood′.** —**blue′-blood′ed** *adj.*

blue·bon·net (blōō′bon′it) *n.* 1 A lupine with blue flowers. 2 Any of various herbs having blue flowers.

blue book 1 A government report or register: also **Blue Book.** 2 A register of socially prominent persons. 3 A blue-covered, blank notebook for writing college examinations.

blue·bot·tle (blōō′bot′l) *n.* 1 A large blowfly with a metallic-blue or -green abdomen. 2 Any of various blue flowers with bottle-shaped parts, as the cornflower.

blue cheese A cheese marbled with bluish mold.

blue·coat (blōō′kōt′) *n.* A policeman.

blue-col·lar (blōō′kol′ər) *adj.* Of, pertaining to, or designating employees engaged in physical or manual work that requires them to wear rough-textured, dark, or special clothing for protection or as a uniform.

blue·fish (blōō′fish′) *n. pl.* **·fish** or **·fish·es** A food fish common along the Atlantic Coast of North America.

blue flag An iris having blue flowers.

blue·grass (blōō′gras′, -gräs′) *n.* Any of a genus of forage and lawn grasses.

blue·gum (blōō′gum′) *n.* A species of eucalyptus tree.

blue·ing (blōō′ing) BLUING.

blue·ish (blōō′ish) BLUISH.

blue·jack·et (blōō′jak′it) *n.* An enlisted man in the U.S. Navy.

blue jay A crested corvine bird of North America.

Blue jay

blue law Any of various puritanical laws, esp. one prohibiting certain activities and entertainments on Sunday.

blue·nose (blōō′nōz′) *n.* A puritanical person.

blue-pen·cil (blōō′pen′səl) *v.t.* 1 To edit or revise. 2 *Informal* To veto or censor.

blue·print (bloo͞′print′) *n.* 1 A photographic print of a plan or drawing showing in white lines on a blue ground. 2 Any detailed plan. —*v.t.* To make a blueprint of.
blue ribbon In competitions, a first prize.
blues (bloo͞z) *n.pl.* (*construed as sing. or pl.*) 1 Depression; melancholy: with *the.* 2 A type of song written in minor keys, and characterized by slow jazz rhythms and melancholy words: usu. with *the.*
blue-sky (bloo͞′skī′) *adj.* 1 Without value; worthless. 2 *Informal* Highly speculative in nature; impractical. —*v.* **-skied, -sky·ing** *Informal v.i.* 1 To engage in impractical or visionary speculation. —*v.t.* 2 To speculate about impractically.
blue-sky laws Laws enacted to prevent the sale of worthless stocks and bonds.
blue·stock·ing (bloo͞′stok′ing) *n.* A learned or literary woman, usu. pretentiously so.
blu·et (bloo͞′it) *n.* Any of various plants with blue flowers.
bluff[1] (bluf) *v.t.* 1 To deceive by putting on a bold front. 2 To frighten with empty threats. —*v.i.* 3 To pretend to knowledge, ability, strength, etc., which one does not have. —**bluff one's way** To obtain (an objective) by bluffing. —*n.* 1 The act of bluffing. 2 One who bluffs. [?< Du. *bluffen* deceive, mislead] —**bluff′er** *n.*
bluff[2] (bluf) *n.* A high, steep cliff or bank. —*adj.* 1 Blunt, frank, and hearty. 2 Having an upright, broad, flattened front. [?< Du. *blaf* flat, as in *blaf aensicht* broad flat face] —**bluff′ly** *adv.* —**bluff′ness** *n.* —**Syn.** 1 abrupt, brusque, open, plain-spoken.
blu·ing (bloo͞′ing) *n.* The blue coloring matter used in laundering white fabrics to counteract yellowing.
blu·ish (bloo͞′ish) *adj.* Somewhat blue. —**blu′ish·ness** *n.*
blun·der (blun′dər) *n.* A stupid mistake. —*v.t.* 1 To move carelessly or awkwardly. 2 To make a stupid and awkward mistake. —*v.t.* 3 To say clumsily or thoughtlessly: often with *out.* 4 To bungle. [ME *blondren* mix up, confuse] —**blun′der·er** *n.* —**blun′der·ing·ly** *adv.*
blun·der·buss (blun′dər·bus) *n.* 1 An old-fashioned, short gun with a large bore and flaring mouth. 2 One who blunders. [Blend of BLUNDER and Du. *donderbus* thunder box]
blunt (blunt) *adj.* 1 Having a thick or dull end or edge. 2 Abrupt and plain-spoken in manner. 3 Slow of wit; dull. —*v.t.* & *v.i.* 1 To make or become blunt or dull. 2 To make or become less keen or poignant. [ME *blunt;* origin unknown] —**blunt′ly** *adv.* —**blunt′ness** *n.*
blur (blûr) *n.* 1 A smeared or indistinct marking. 2 Something vague or indistinct to the sight or mind. —*v.t.* & *v.i.* **blurred, blur·ring** *v.t.* 1 To stain, smear, or smudge. 2 To make or become obscure or indistinct in outline. 3 To make or become dim or cloudy. [?] —**blur′ry** *adj.* (**·ri·er, ·ri·est**)
blurb (blûrb) *n.* A brief, commendatory statement, as on a book jacket, that serves as publicity for a book, author, etc. [Coined by Gelett Burgess, 1866–1951, U.S. humorist]
blurt (blûrt) *v.t.* To utter abruptly, as if on impulse: usu. with *out.* [?]
blush (blush) *v.i.* 1 To redden in the face, as from embarrassment. 2 To be or become red or rosy. 3 To feel shame or regret: usu. with *at* or *for.* —*v.t.* 4 To make red. —*n.* 1 A reddening of the face, as from modesty, etc. 2 A red or rosy tint; flush. [< OE *blyscan* redden] —**blush′er** *n.* —**blush′ful** *adj.*
blus·ter (blus′tər) *n.* 1 Boisterous talk or swagger. 2 A noisy blowing of the wind. —*v.i.* 1 To blow gustily, as the wind. 2 To act or speak noisily and aggressively. —*v.t.* 3 To utter noisily and boisterously. 4 To force or bully by blustering. [ME *blusteren*] —**blus′ter·er** *n.* —**blus′ter·y, blus′ter·ous** *adj.*
blvd. boulevard.
Bn., bn. battalion.
b.o. box office; branch office.
bo·a (bō′ə) *n. pl.* **bo·as** 1 Any of several nonvenomous serpents that crush their prey, as the anaconda, python, and esp. the **boa constrictor.** 2 A long feather or fur neckpiece for women. [< L]

boar (bôr, bōr) *n. pl.* **boars** or **boar** 1 An uncastrated male hog. 2 The wild hog of Europe, North Africa, and Asia. [< OE *bār*]

Boar *def. 2*

board (bôrd, bōrd) *n.* 1 A flat piece of sawed wood whose length is much greater than its width. 2 A slab of wood or other material prepared for a specific purpose: a diving *board.* 3 Pasteboard or other material, often used for book covers. 4 A table, spread for serving food. 5 Meals regularly furnished for pay. 6 An organized official body: a *board* of directors. 7 A table around which meetings are held. —**on board** On or in a vessel or other conveyance. —**tread the boards** To appear as an actor. —*v.t.* 1 To cover or enclose with boards: often with *up.* 2 To furnish with meals or meals and lodging for pay. 3 To place (someone) where meals are provided, as in a boarding school. 4 *Naut.* To come alongside or go on board of (a ship). 5 To enter, as a ship or train. —*v.i.* 6 To take meals or meals and lodging for pay. (< OE *bord*]
board·er (bôr′dər, bōr′-) *n.* 1 A person who receives regular meals, or meals and lodging, for pay. 2 One detailed to board an enemy's ship.
board foot *pl.* **board feet** The measure of a board 1 foot square and 1 inch thick; 144 cubic inches.
board·ing (bôr′ding, bōr′-) *n.* 1 Boards collectively. 2 A structure of boards.
boarding house A house for keeping boarders.
boarding school A school in which pupils are boarded.
board measure A system of measure for boards, based on the board foot.
board·walk (bôrd′wôk′, bōrd′-) *n.* 1 A promenade along a beach, usu. raised and made of boards. 2 Any walk made of boards.
boast (bōst) *v.i.* 1 To extol the deeds or abilities of oneself or of another; brag. 2 To be excessively proud: with *of.* —*v.t.* 3 To brag about. 4 To be proud to possess; take pride in. —*n.* 1 A boastful speech. 2 A source of pride. [ME *bosten*] —**boast′er** *n.* —**Syn.** *v.* 1 crow, flaunt, swagger, vaunt.
boast·ful (bōst′fəl) *adj.* Tending to brag. —**boast′ful·ly** *adv.* —**boast′ful·ness** *n.*
boat (bōt) *n.* 1 A small, open watercraft propelled by oars, sails, or an engine. 2 A large, seagoing vessel; ship: a nautically incorrect usage. 3 A dish resembling a boat. —**be in the same boat** To be in the same situation. —*v.i.* 1 To travel by boat. 2 To go boating for pleasure. —*v.t.* 3 To transport or place in a boat. [< OE *bāt*]
boat·house (bōt′hous′) *n.* A building for storing boats.
boat·ing (bō′ting) *n.* Rowing, cruising, or sailing.
boat·load (bōt′lōd′) *n.* 1 The full amount that a boat can hold. 2 The load carried by a boat.
boat·man (bōt′mən) *n. pl.* **·men** One who manages, rows, or works on a boat. —**boat′man·ship** *n.*
boat·swain (bō′sən, *rarely* bōt′swān′) *n.* On a ship, a warrant officer or petty officer in charge of the deck crew, the rigging, anchors, etc.
bob[1] (bob) *n.* 1 In fishing: **a** A cork or float on a line. **b** A ball-shaped bait of angleworms, rags, etc. 2 A small, pendent object or weight: a plumb *bob.* 3 A jerky bow or curtsy. 4 Any short, jerky movement. 5 A short style of haircut. 6 The docked tail of a horse. —*v.* **bobbed, bob·bing** *v.t.* 1 To move up and down: to *bob* the head. 2 To cut short, as hair. —*v.i.* 3 To move up and down with an irregular motion. 4 To curtsy. 5 To fish with a bob. —**bob up** To appear or emerge suddenly. [ME *bobbe* a hanging cluster] —**bob′ber** *n.*
bob[2] (bob) *v.t.* **bobbed, bob·bing** To strike lightly; tap. [ME *bobben*]
bob[3] (bob) *n. pl.* **bob** *Brit. Informal* A shilling. [?]
bob·bin (bob′in) *n.* A spool or reel to hold weft or thread in spinning, weaving, or in machine sewing. [F *bobine*]
bob·ble (bob′əl) *n.* 1 A bobbing motion. 2 One of the small decorative balls forming an edge of a tablecloth, etc. 3 *Informal* A blunder; esp., in sports, the mishan-

dling of a ball upon trying to field or catch it. —*v.* **bob·bled, bob·bling** *v.i.* 1 To move with a bobbing motion. —*v.t.* *Informal* To mishandle; fumble. [Freq. of BOB[1]] —**bob′·bler** *n.*

bob·by (bob′ē) *n. pl.* **·bies** *Brit. Informal* A policeman. [after Sir Robert *(Bobby)* Peel, 1788–1850, Brit. statesman]

bobby pin A metal hairpin so shaped as to hold the hair tightly. Also **bobbie pin.**

bobby socks *Informal* Ankle-length socks worn by girls.

bob·by-sox·er (bob′ē·sok′sər) *n. Informal* An adolescent girl, esp. in the 1940's.

bob·cat (bob′kat′) *n.* The American lynx.

bob·o·link (bob′ə·lingk) *n.* An American songbird with black and white or buff plumage. [Imit. of its call]

bob·sled (bob′sled′) *n.* 1 A racing sled having a set of runners in front, another set in back, and controlled by a steering apparatus and brakes. 2 A sled made of two short sleds or pairs of runners connected tandem by a top plank. —*v.i.* **·sled·ded, ·sled·ding** To ride on a bobsled.

bob·tail (bob′tāl′) *n.* 1 A short tail or a tail cut short. 2 An animal with such a tail. —*adj.* 1 Having the tail docked. 2 Incomplete. —*v.t.* To cut the tail of; dock. —**bob′·tailed′** *adj.*

bob·white (bob′hwīt′) *n.* A small North American quail. [Imit. of its call]

bock beer (bok) An extra strong beer brewed in the winter and served in early spring. Also **bock.** [< *Einbeck,* town in Germany]

bode[1] (bōd) Archaic *p.t. & p.p.* of BIDE.

bode[2] (bōd) *v.* **bod·ed, bod·ing** *v.t.* 1 To be a token of; presage, as good, evil, etc. —*v.i.* 2 To presage good or ill. [< OE *bodian* announce] —**bode′ment** *n.* —**Syn. 1, 2** augur, forebode, foretell, predict.

bod·ice (bod′is) *n.* 1 The part of a woman's dress from waist to shoulder. 2 A woman's ornamental laced waist. [Var. of *bodies,* pl. of BODY]

bod·ied (bod′ēd) *adj.* 1 Having a body. 2 Having a specified kind of body: used in combination: *able-bodied.*

bod·i·less (bod′i·lis) *adj.* Having no body; incorporeal.

bod·i·ly (bod′ə·lē) *adj.* 1 Of or pertaining to the body. 2 Physical rather than mental. —*adv.* 1 In the body; in person. 2 All together; wholly; completely.

bod·kin (bod′kin) *n.* 1 A thick needle for drawing tape through a hem. 2 A pointed instrument for piercing holes in cloth, etc. 3 A pin for fastening the hair. 4 *Obs.* A stiletto. [ME *boydekin* dagger]

bod·y (bod′ē) *n. pl.* **bod·ies** 1 The entire physical structure of a person, animal, or plant. 2 A corpse. 3 The trunk of a person or animal. 4 *Informal* A person. 5 A collection of persons or things considered as a unit. 6 The principal part or mass of anything. 7 Any mass of matter: a celestial *body;* a *body* of water. 8 Density or substance: a fabric with *body.* 9 Fullness and richness, as of a wine. —*v.t.* **bod·ied, bod·y·ing** To give shape or form to; embody; represent: usu. with *forth.* [< OE *bodig*]

bod·y·guard (bod′ē·gärd′) *n.* A person or persons designated to guard or protect someone.

body politic The people of a state or nation viewed as an organized political body.

Boe·o·tia (bē·ō′shə, -shē·ə) *n.* An ancient province of Greece, cap. Thebes. —**Boe·o′tian** *adj., n.*

Boer (bōr, bôr, bŏŏr) *n.* A Dutch colonist, or person of Dutch descent in South Africa. [Du., farmer]

bog (bog, bôg) *n.* Wet and spongy ground; marsh; morass, —*v.t. & v.i.* **bogged, bog·ging** To sink or stick in or as in a bog: often with *down.* [< Ir., soft] —**bog′gish** *adj.*

bo·gey (bō′gē) *n. pl.* **bo·geys** In golf: 1 An estimated standard score. 2 One stroke over par on a hole. Also **bo′gie.** [?]

bog·gle (bog′əl) *v.* **bog·gled, bog·gling** *v.i.* 1 To hesitate, as from doubt or scruples: often with *at.* 2 To be startled or amazed. 3 To bungle. —*v.t.* 4 To startle. 5 To bungle. [?]

bog·gy (bog′ē, bôg′ē) *adj.* **bog·gi·er, bog·gi·est** Swampy; miry. —**bog′gi·ness** *n.*

bo·gus (bō′gəs) *adj.* Counterfeit; spurious; fake. [?]

bo·gy (bō′gē) *n. pl.* **bo·gies** A goblin; bugbear. Also **bo′gie, bo′gey.** [?]

Bo·he·mi·an (bō·hē′mē·ən) *adj.* 1 Of or pertaining to Bohemia. 2 Leading the life of a Bohemian; unconventional. —*n.* 1 A native or inhabitant of Bohemia. 2 A gypsy. 3 A person, usu. of artistic or literary tastes, who lives in a more or less unconventional manner. Also (for *adj.* def. 2 and *n.* def. 3) **bo·he′mi·an.** —**Bo·he′mi·an·ism** *n.*

boil[1] (boil) *v.i.* 1 To be agitated, as a liquid when heated, by gaseous bubbles rising to the surface. 2 To reach the boiling point. 3 To undergo the action of a boiling liquid. 4 To be agitated: The water *boiled* with sharks. 5 To be stirred, as by violent anger. —*v.t.* 6 To bring to the boiling point. 7 To cook or cleanse by boiling. —**boil away** To evaporate in boiling. —**boil down** 1 To reduce in bulk by boiling. 2 To condense; edit. —**boil over** 1 To overflow while boiling. 2 To become enraged. —*n.* The act or state of boiling. [< L *bullire* to boil]

boil[2] (boil) *n.* A pussy and painful swelling in the skin, of bacterial origin. [< OE *bӯl, bӯle*]

boil·er (boi′lər) *n.* 1 A utensil in which food or liquid is boiled. 2 A closed vessel generating steam, as for motive power. 3 A receptacle for heating and storing hot water.

boiling point The temperature at which the vapor pressure in a liquid equals the external pressure; at normal atmospheric pressure the boiling point of water is 212°F or 100°C.

bois·ter·ous (bois′tər·əs) *adj.* 1 Noisy; rowdy; unrestrained. 2 Violent; turbulent. [ME *boistous*] —**bois′ter·ous·ly** *adv.* —**bois′ter·ous·ness** *n.*

bo·la (bō′lə) *n.* A weapon consisting of balls fastened to cords and used, when thrown, to entangle the legs of cattle and large game. Also **bo·las** (bō′ləs). [< Sp., a ball]

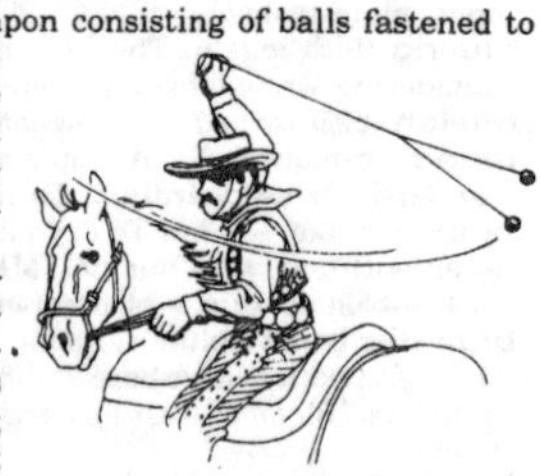

Bola

bold (bōld) *adj.* 1 Possessing courage; fearless. 2 Showing or requiring courage. 3 Shameless; forward; brazen. 4 Striking; vigorous, as language. 5 Clear; prominent: *bold* outlines. 6 Abrupt; steep, as a cliff. —**make bold** To take the liberty; venture. [< OE *bald*] —**bold′ly** *adv.* —**bold′ness** *n.* —**Syn. 1** audacious, brave, daring, valiant. 3 brassy, immodest, impudent.

bold·face (bōld′fās′) *n. Printing* A type in which the lines have been thickened to give a very heavy impression. —**bold′-faced′** *adj.*

bole (bōl) *n.* The trunk of a tree. [< ON *bolr*]

bo·le·ro (bō·lâr′ō) *n. pl.* **·ros** 1 A short jacket open at the front. 2 A Spanish dance, usu. accompanied by castanets; also, the music for it. [Sp.]

bol·i·var (bol′ə·vər, *Sp.* bō·lē′vär) *n. pl.* **bol·i·vars,** Sp. **bo·li·va·res** (bō′lē·vä′rās) A monetary unit of Venezuela. [< Simón *Bolivar,* 1783–1830, South American liberator]

Bo·liv·i·a (bə·liv′ē·ə) *n.* A republic of CEN. South America, 424,162 sq. mi., caps. Sucre and La Paz. —**Bo·liv′i·an** *adj. & n.* • See map at BRAZIL.

boll (bōl) *n.* A round seed capsule, as of flax or cotton. —*v.i.* To form pods. [< MDu. *bolle*]

boll weevil A small weevil whose larvae destroy cotton bolls.

boll·worm (bōl′wûrm′) *n.* The very destructive moth larva that feeds on cotton bolls, corn ears, and other plants.

bo·lo (bō′lō) *n. pl.* **·los** (-lōz) A heavy, single-edged weapon used in the Philippine Islands. [Sp.]

bo·lo·gna (bə·lō′nē, -lo′nə, -lōn′yə) *Sometimes cap.* A highly seasoned sausage of mixed meats. Also **bologna sausage.** [< *Bologna,* Italy]

bo·lo·ney (bə·lō′nē) *n.* BALONEY.

Bol·she·vik (bōl′shə·vik, bol′-) *n. pl.* **Bol·she·viks** or **Bol·she·vi·ki** (bōl′shə·vē′kē, bol′-) 1 A member of the dominant branch of the Russian Social Democratic Party or, since the 1917 Revolution, of the Russian Communist Party. 2 A Communist. 3 Loosely, any radical. Also **bol′she·vik.** [Russ., a member of the majority (group in the party)]

Bol·she·vism (bōl′shə·viz′əm, bol′-) *n.* 1 The Marxian doctrines and policies of the Bolsheviki. 2 A government based on these policies. Also **bol′she·vism.** —**Bol′she·vist** *n.* —**Bol′she·vis′tic** *adj.*

bol·ster (bōl′stər) *n.* 1 A long, narrow pillow as wide as a bed. 2 A pad used as a support or for protection. 3 Anything shaped like or used as a bolster. —*v.t.* To prop up, as something ready to fall. [< OE] —**bol′ster·er** *n.*

bolt[1] (bōlt) *n.* 1 A sliding bar or piece for fastening a door, etc. 2 In a lock, the movable bar or piece that is operated by the key. 3 A metal pin or rod usu. threaded and having a head at one end, used with a nut for holding anything in its place. 4 A sliding bar that closes the breech in certain firearms. 5 An arrow for a crossbow. 6 A lightning flash. 7 A sudden start or departure. 8 A roll of cloth, wall paper, etc. —**bolt from the blue** A sudden and wholly unexpected event. —*v.i.* 1 To move, go, or spring suddenly: usu. with *out* or *from*: He *bolted* from the room. 2 *U.S.* To break away, as from a political party. —*v.t.* 3 To fasten with or as with bolts. 4 *U.S.* To break away from, as a political party. 5 To gulp, as food. 6 To blurt out. —*adv.* Rigidly; erectly: to sit *bolt* upright. [< OE, arrow for a crossbow]

bolt[2] (bōlt) *v.t.* 1 To sift. 2 To examine as by sifting. [< OF *buleter*]

bo·lus (bō′ləs) *n. pl.* **bo·lus·es** 1 A large pill. 2 Any rounded mass. [< Gk. *bōlos* clod of earth, lump]

bomb (bom) *n.* 1 A hollow projectile containing explosive, incendiary, or chemical material to be discharged by concussion or by a time fuse. 2 An unexpected occurrence. 3 *Slang* A flop; failure; dud. 4 *Informal* In football, a long forward pass. —*v.t.* 1 To attack or destroy with or as with bombs. —*v.i.* 2 *Slang* To fail utterly. [< L *bombus* loud sound]

bom·bard (bom·bärd′) *v.t.* 1 To attack with bombs or shells. 2 To attack or press as with bombs: to *bombard* with questions. 3 To expose to the effect of radiation or to the impact of high-energy atomic particles. [< MF *bombarde* a cannon] —**bom·bard′er, bom·bard′ment** *n.*

bom·bar·dier (bom′bər·dir′) *n.* The member of the crew of a bomber who operates the bombsight and releases bombs.

bom·bast (bom′bast) *n.* Pompous, high-flown language. [< OF *bombace* cotton padding] —**bom·bas′tic, bom·bas′ti·cal** *adj.* —**bom·bas′ti·cal·ly** *adv.* —**Syn.** grandiloquence, prolixity, verbosity, wordiness.

bomb bay A compartment in military aircraft in which bombs are carried and from which they are dropped.

bombed (bombd) *adj. Slang* Drunk.

bomb·er (bom′ər) *n.* 1 One who attacks with bombs. 2 An airplane employed in bombing.

bomb·proof (bom′pro͞of′) *adj.* So constructed as to resist damage from bombs.

bomb·shell (bom′shel′) *n.* BOMB (def. 1). 2 *Informal* Something astounding or shocking.

bomb·sight (bom′sīt′) *n.* An instrument for aiming aerial bombs.

bo·na fide (bō′nə·fīd′, -fī′dē) 1 Acting or carried out in good faith. 2 Authentic; real. [< L, in good faith]

bo·nan·za (bə·nan′zə) *n.* 1 A rich mine, vein, or find of ore. 2 Any profitable operation. [Sp., success]

bon·bon (bon′bon′, *Fr.* bôṅ·bôṅ′) *n.* A small piece of candy coated with fondant or chocolate. [< F *bon* good]

bond (bond) *n.* 1 Something that binds, holds, or fastens. 2 The union thus formed. 3 A tie, link, or union: a family *bond.* 4 An obligation, promise, or agreement. 5 *pl.* a Fetters. b Captivity. 6 An interest-bearing certificate sold by a government or business to raise money and carrying the promise to repay the purchaser by a specified date. 7 An insurance policy covering losses suffered through the acts of an employee. 8 The condition of goods stored in a warehouse until duties are paid. 9 *Law* a An obligation in writing under seal. b One who furnishes bail. c Bail. 10 *Chem.* A force that holds together the atoms of a molecule. —**bottled in bond** Bottled after storage in a bonded warehouse for a specified amount of time, as some whiskies. —*v.t.* 1 To put a certified debt upon; mortgage. 2 To furnish bond for; be surety for (someone). 3 To place, as goods or an employee, under bond. 4 To unite or bind tightly together. —*v.i.* 5 To hold or cohere with or as with a bond. [< ON *band*]

bond·age (bon′dij) *n.* 1 Compulsory servitude; slavery. 2 Subjection to any force or influence. —**Syn.** 1 captivity, serfdom, thralldom.

bond·ed (bon′did) *adj.* 1 Subject to a bond. 2 Stored in a warehouse until duties are paid. 3 Held close together, as by a strong adhesive or by chemical action.

bond·hold·er (bond′hōl′dər) *n.* One owning or holding bonds. —**bond′hold′ing** *adj., n.*

bond paper A strong paper of superior fiber, used in printing bonds and paper money, for business letters, etc.

bond·ser·vant (bond′sûr′vənt) *n.* One in servitude without wages; slave. Also **bond′slave′.**

bonds·man (bondz′mən) *n. pl.* **·men** (-mən) A person who furnishes bond or surety for another.

bone (bōn) *n.* 1 A separate piece of the skeleton of a vertebrate animal. 2 The hard tissue of which a skeleton is composed. 3 One of various objects made of bone or similar material, as a corset stay. 4 A material resembling bone, as whalebone. 5 *pl. Slang* Dice. —**feel in (one's) bones** To have an intuition of. —**have a bone to pick** To have grounds for complaint or dispute. —**make no bones about** To be totally frank or honest about. —*v.* **boned, bon·ing** *v.t.* 1 To remove the bones from. 2 To stiffen with whalebone. —*v.i.* 3 *Slang* To study intensely: often with *up.* [< OE *bān*]

bone·head (bōn′hed′) *n. Informal* A slow-witted, stupid person. —**bone′head′ed** *adj.*

bone meal Pulverized bone, used as fertilizer or animal feed.

bon·er (bō′nər) *n. Slang* An error; faux pas.

bone·set (bōn′set′) *n.* Any of various herbs of the composite family thought to have curative properties.

bon·fire (bon′fīr′) *n.* A large fire in the open air. [< BONE + FIRE; formerly a fire for calcining bones]

bon·go drums (bong′gō) A pair of drums played with the hands, originally from Africa. Also **bon′gos.** [Am. Sp.] • See DRUM.

bo·ni·to (bə·nē′tō) *n. pl.* **·tos** or **·toes** Any of various large, tunalike marine food and game fishes. [Sp., beautiful]

bon jour (bôṅ zho͞or′) *French* Good day.

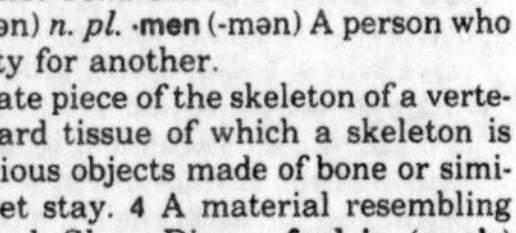

Bonito

bon mot (bôṅ mō′) *pl.* **bons mots** (bôṅ mōz′, *Fr.* mō′) A clever saying; terse witticism. [F]

bon·net (bon′it) *n.* 1 An outdoor headdress for women and children, usu. tied under the chin. 2 A brimless cap for men and boys, worn esp. in Scotland. 3 An American Indian headdress of feathers. 4 Any of various metal hoods protecting machinery, etc. 5 *Brit.* The hood of an automobile. —*v.t.* To cover with or as with a bonnet. [< OF *bonet*]

bon·ny (bon′ē) *adj.* **·ni·er, ·ni·est** *Chiefly Brit. & Scot.* 1 Pretty and sweet. 2 Robust; healthy. 3 Fine; good. Also **bon′nie.** [< F *bon* good] —**bon′ni·ly** *adv.* —**bon′ni·ness** *n.*

bon·sai (bon′sī, bōn′-) *n. pl.* **·sai** 1 A decorative dwarfed tree grown in a pot. 2 The art of creating such trees. [Jap.]

bon soir (bôṅ swâr′) *French* Good evening.

bo·nus (bō′nəs) *n. pl.* **bo·nus·es** Something given, as a sum of money, over and above what is usual, current, or stipulated. [L, good]

bon vi·vant (bôṅ vē·väṅ′) *pl.* **bons vi·vants** (bôṅ vē·väṅ′) A person who enjoys the pleasurable things of life. [F] —**Syn.** sybarite, voluptuary, epicure.

bon vo·yage (bôṅ vwȧ·yȧzh′) *French* A phrase wishing a traveler a pleasant voyage or trip.

bon·y (bō′nē) *adj.* **bon·i·er, bon·i·est** 1 Of, like, or consisting of bone. 2 Having prominent bones. 3 Thin; gaunt. —**bon′i·ness** *n.*

boo (bo͞o) *n. & interj.* A vocal sound made to indicate contempt or frighten. —*v.* **booed, boo·ing** *v.i.* To utter boos. —*v.t.* To shout boo at.

boob (bo͞ob) *n. Slang* A stupid or gullible person, simpleton. [Short for BOOBY]

boo-boo (bo͞o'bo͞o') *n. pl.* **-boos** *Slang* A mistake or blunder. Also **boo'boo'**.

boob tube *Slang* Television or a television set.

boo·by (bo͞o'bē) *n. pl.* **boo·bies** 1 A dull fellow; dunce. 2 In some games, the person who makes the poorest score. 3 Any of several gannets of warm seas. [Sp. *bobo* fool <L *balbus* stammering]

booby prize A mock award for the worst score or performance in a contest, game, etc.

booby trap 1 A concealed bomb, mine, etc., designed to explode when inadvertently disturbed. 2 Any scheme for catching a person off guard.

boo·dle (bo͞od'l) *n. Slang* 1 A bribe; graft. 2 Loot; plunder. 3 A crowd; caboodle. —*v.i.* **·dled, ·dling** To bribe or receive bribes. [<Du. *boedel* property] —**boo'dler** *n.*

boog·ie-woog·ie (bo͝og'ē·wo͝og'ē) *n.* A style of jazz piano playing characterized by a repeated, rhythmic bass with melodic inventions in the treble. —*adj.* Of, in, or pertaining to this style. [?]

boo·hoo (bo͞o·ho͞o') *v.i.* **·hooed, ·hoo·ing** To weep loudly. —*n. pl.* **·hoos** Noisy sobbing. [Imit.]

book (bo͝ok) *n.* 1 A number of printed or written sheets of paper bound together, usu. between covers. 2 A literary or other written composition or treatise so bound and usu. of some length. 3 A subdivision of a literary composition or treatise: one of the *books* of the Bible. 4 A business record or ledger. 5 LIBRETTO. 6 A script for a play, musical comedy, etc. 7 A booklike pack of matches, etc. 8 A list of bets made. —**by the book** According to rule. —**like a book** Thoroughly. —**the Book** The Bible. —*v.t.* 1 To enter or list in a book. 2 To arrange for beforehand, as accommodations or seats. 3 To engage, as actors or a play, for performance. 4 To make a record of charges against (someone) on a police blotter. [<OE *bōc*]

book·bind·ing (bo͝ok'bīn'ding) *n.* The art or trade of binding books. —**book'bind'er** *n.*

book·case (bo͝ok'kās') *n.* A case containing shelves for holding books.

book club An organisation that sells books at reduced prices to its members.

book·end (bo͝ok'end') *n.* A support or prop used to hold upright a row of books.

book·ie (bo͝ok'ē) *n. Informal* BOOKMAKER (def. 2).

book·ish (bo͝ok'ish) *adj.* 1 Fond of reading and learning. 2 Pedantic. —**book'ish·ly** *adv.* —**book'ish·ness** *n.*

book jacket DUST JACKET.

book·keep·ing (bo͝ok'kē'ping) *n.* The art, method, or practice of recording business transactions systematically. —**book'keeper'er** *n.*

book·let (bo͝ok'lit) *n.* A small, thin book.

book·mak·er (bo͝ok'mā'kər) *n.* 1 One who compiles, prints, or binds books. 2 One whose business is accepting and paying off bets, esp. in horse racing.

book·mark (bo͝ok'märk') *n.* Any object to be placed between the leaves of a book to mark a place.

book·plate (bo͝ok'plāt') *n.* A printed label placed in a book to indicate ownership.

book·rack (bo͝ok'rak') *n.* 1 A frame to hold an open book: also **book'rest'**. 2 A framework to hold books, as on a table.

book review An article or essay discussing or critically examining a book.

book·sell·er (bo͝ok'sel'ər) *n.* One who sells books.

book·stack (bo͝ok'stak') *n.* A tall rack containing shelves for books, as in a library.

book·stall (bo͝ok'stôl) *n.* A stall or stand where books are sold.

book·stand (bo͝ok'stand') *n.* 1 A rack for books. 2 BOOKSTALL.

book·store (bo͝ok'stôr', -stōr') *n.* A store for the sale of books.

book·worm (bo͝ok'wûrm') *n.* 1 A person devoted to books and study. 2 Any of various insect larvae destructive to books.

boom[1] (bo͞om) *n.* 1 A spar used to extend or support the foot of a sail. 2 A chain of logs to intercept or retard the advance of a vessel, to confine timbers, sawlogs, etc. 3 A long mobile beam projecting upward from the foot of a derrick to carry or guide a load suspended from its outer end. 4 A long, mobile arm with a microphone attached at one end. [<Du. *boom* tree, beam]

boom[2] (bo͞om) *v.i.* 1 To emit a deep, resonant sound, as cannon. 2 To grow rapidly; flourish. —*v.t.* 3 To utter or sound in a deep, resonant tone. 4 To praise or advertise vigorously. —*n.* 1 A deep, reverberating sound, as of a cannon. 2 Any sudden or rapid growth or popularity. [Imit.] —**Syn.** *v.* 1 resound, reverberate, roar. 2 increase, prosper, succeed, thrive.

boom box (bo͞om'boks') *n. Slang* A portable combination of radio and tape player.

boom·e·rang (bo͞o'mə·rang) *n.* 1 A curved, wooden missile weapon originated in Australia, one form of which will return to the thrower. 2 Any act or statement that works to the disadvantage of its originator. —*v.i.* To react harmfully on the doer or user. [<native Australian name]

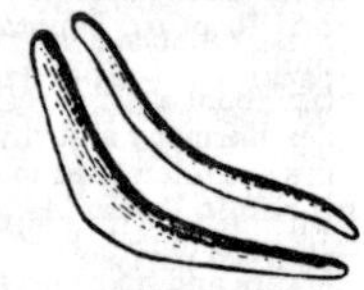

Boomerangs

boom town A town that has suddenly increased in population, as from a discovery of gold or oil.

boon[1] (bo͞on) *n.* 1 A good thing; blessing. 2 *Archaic* A petition. [<ON *bōn* petition]

boon[2] (bo͞on) *adj.* Genial; jovial: now only in **boon companion**. [<L *bonus* good]

boon·docks (bo͞on'doks') *n. pl. Informal* An out-of-the-way or backwoods area: used with *the.* [<Tagalog *bundok* mountain]

boon·dog·gle (bo͞on'dôg'əl) *v.i.* **·dog·gled, ·dog·gling** *Informal* To work on wasteful or unnecessary projects. —*n.* A wasteful or worthless project. [?] —**boon'dog'gler, boon'dog'gling** *n.*

boor (bo͝or) *n.* A rude, coarse, or unpleasant person. [<Du. *boer* farmer, rustic] —**boor'ish** *adj.* —**boor'ish·ly** *adv.* —**boor'ish·ness** *n.*

boost (bo͞ost) *v.t.* 1 To raise by or as by pushing from beneath or behind. 2 To speak in praise of; help by speaking well of. 3 To increase: to *boost* prices. —*n.* 1 A lift; help. 2 An increase. [?]

boost·er (bo͞os'tər) *n.* 1 Any device for increasing the output of another device or system. 2 One who gives enthusiastic support to a person, organization, community, or cause. 3 The first stage of a multistage rocket, the source of thrust during takeoff. 4 BOOSTER SHOT.

booster shot Another injection, as of a vaccine, to reinforce immunity, administered at an interval after the initial dose.

boot[1] (bo͞ot) *n.* 1 A shoelike covering, as of leather, rubber, etc., for the foot and all or part of the leg. 2 A shoe reaching to or above the ankle. 3 An overshoe. 4 A medieval instrument of torture for crushing the foot and leg. 5 A kick. 6 *Informal* In the U.S. Navy or Marine Corps, a new recruit. —**die with one's boots on** To die fighting or working. —**get the boot** *Slang* To be discharged. —*v.t.* 1 To put boots on. 2 To kick; also, in football, to punt. 3 *Slang* To dismiss; fire. —*v.i.* To load a program into a computer. [<OF *bote*]

boot[2] (bo͞ot) *n. Obs.* Advantage; resource. —**to boot** In addition; over and above. [<OE *bōt* profit]

boot·black (bo͞ot'blak') *n.* One who cleans and shines shoes or boots.

boot camp The primary training station for naval or marine recruits.

boo·tee (bo͞o·tē', bo͞o'tē) *n.* 1 A woman's or child's short, light boot. 2 A knitted woolen boot for a baby.

Bo·ö·tes (bō·ō'tēz) *n.* A northern constellation, whose brightest star is Arcturus.

booth (bo͞oth, bo͞o*th*) *n.* 1 A stall at a fair, market, etc. 2 A small compartment or enclosure: a voting *booth.* 3 A stationary table and seating compartment, as in a restaurant. [<Scand.]

boot·jack (bo͞ot'jak') *n.* A forked device for holding the heel of a boot while the wearer withdraws his foot.

boot·leg (bo͞ot'leg') *v.t.* & *v.i.* **·legged, ·leg·ging** To make, sell, or carry for sale (liquor, etc.) illegally; smuggle. —*adj.* Unlawful: *bootleg* whisky. —*n.* 1 The part of a boot above the instep. 2 Something bootlegged, esp. liquor. [With ref. to the smuggling of liquor in bootlegs] —**boot′leg′ger, boot′leg′ging** *n.*

boot·less (bo͞ot′lis) *adj.* Profitless; useless; unavailing. —**boot′less·ly** *adv.* —**boot′less·ness** *n.*

boot·lick (bo͞ot′lik′) *v.t. & v.i.* To flatter servilely; to toady. —**boot′lick′er** *n.* —**boot′lick′ing** *adj., n.*

boo·ty (bo͞o′tē) *n. pl.* **boo·ties** 1 The spoils of war. 2 Any plunder. 3 Any prize or gain. [< MLG *būte* exchange]

booze (bo͞oz) *n. Informal* 1 Strong drink; liquor. 2 A drunken spree. —*v.i.* **boozed, booz·ing** To drink to excess. [< MDu. *busen* drink, tipple] —**booz′er** *n.*

booz·y (bo͞o′zē) *adj.* Somewhat intoxicated. —**booz′i·ly** *adv.* —**booz′i·ness** *n.*

bop[1] (bop) *v.t.* **bopped, bop·ping** *Slang* To hit or strike. [Imit.]

bop[2] (bop) *n.* A type of jazz having characteristically complex harmony and rhythm and in which nonsense syllables are often used in singing. [Short for BE-BOP]

bo·rac·ic (bə·ras′ik) *adj.* BORIC.

bor·age (bûr′ij, bôr′-, bor′-) *n.* An edible herb with blue flowers and hairy leaves. [< Med. L *borrago*]

bo·rate (bôr′āt, bō′rāt) *n.* A salt of boric acid. —**bo′rat·ed** *adj.*

bo·rax (bôr′aks, bō′raks) *n.* A white crystalline borate of sodium having various uses, as in soap and glass manufacture. [< Ar. *bōraq* < Pers. *būrah*]

Bor·deaux (bôr·dō′) *n.* A white or red wine produced in the vicinity of Bordeaux, France.

Bordeaux mixture A fungicide composed of copper sulfate, water, and lime.

bor·der (bôr′dər) *n.* 1 A margin or edge. 2 The peripheral line or district of a country or state; a boundary or frontier. 3 A surrounding or enclosing strip or edge. 4 A decorative edge or margin. —*adj.* Of, on, forming, or pertaining to a border. —*v.t.* 1 To put a border or edging on. 2 To lie next to; form a boundary to. —**border on** (or **upon**) 1 To resemble; have the appearance: That *borders on* piracy. 2 To touch or abut. [< OF *bord* edge] —**bor′der·er** *n.*

bor·der·land (bôr′dər·land′) *n.* 1 Land on or near the border of two adjoining countries. 2 A debatable or indeterminate area or condition.

bor·der·line (bôr′dər·līn′) *n.* 1 A boundary line. 2 An indeterminate line or condition. Also **border line.** —*adj.* Difficult to classify; indeterminate.

bore[1] (bôr, bōr) *v.* **bored, bor·ing** *v.t.* 1 To make a hole in or through, as with a drill. 2 To make (a tunnel, hole, well, etc.) by or as by drilling. 3 To advance or force (one's way). 4 To weary by monotony, dullness, etc. —*v.i.* 5 To make a hole, etc., by or as by drilling. 6 To admit of being drilled: This wood *bores* easily. 7 To force one's way. —*n.* 1 A hole made by or as if by boring. 2 The interior diameter of a firearm or cylinder. 3 A tiresome person or thing. [< OE *borian*]

bore[2] (bôr, bōr) *n.* A high crested wave caused by the rush of flood tide up a river. [< ON *bāra* billow]

bore[3] (bôr, bōr) *p.t.* of BEAR.

bo·re·al (bôr′ē·əl, bō′rē-) *adj.* Pertaining to the north or the north wind. [< LL *borealis* < BOREAS]

Bo·re·as (bôr′ē·əs, bō′rē-) *n. Gk. Myth.* The north wind.

bore·dom (bôr′dəm, bōr′-) *n.* The condition of being bored; fatigue. —**Syn.** ennui, tedium, weariness.

bor·er (bôr′ər, bō′rər) *n.* 1 One who or that which bores. 2 A larva or worm that burrows in plants, wood, etc.

bo·ric (bôr′ik, bō′rik) *adj.* Of, pertaining to, or derived from boron.

boric acid A white crystalline compound of hydrogen, boron, and oxygen, used as a mild antiseptic.

born (bôrn) *adj.* 1 Brought forth or into being, as offspring. 2 Natural; innate: a *born* musician. [< OE *boren,* p.p. of *beran* bear]

borne (bôrn, bōrn) *p.p.* of BEAR.

bo·ron (bôr′on, bō′ron) *n.* A nonmetallic element (symbol B), occurring in nature only in compounds, as borax. [< BOR(AX) + (CARB)ON]

bor·ough (bûr′ō) *n.* 1 An incorporated village or town. 2 One of the five administrative divisions of New York, N.Y. 2 *Brit.* a A town having a municipal corporation endowed by royal charter with certain privileges. b A town, whether corporate or not, entitled to representation in Parliament. [< OE *burg, burh* fort, town]

bor·row (bôr′ō, bor′ō) *v.t. & v.i.* 1 To take or obtain (something) on a promise to return it or its equivalent. 2 To adopt for one's own use: to *borrow* an idea. 3 *Math.* In subtraction, to perform the operation inverse of carrying, in addition. [< OE *borgian* give a pledge, borrow] —**bor′row·er** *n.*

borscht (bôrsht) *n.* A Russian beet soup, often served with sour cream and eaten hot or cold. Also **borsch** (bôrsh). [Russ.]

bor·stal (bôr′stəl) *n. Often cap.* Any of a number of correctional schools for delinquent boys and girls in England. [after *Borstal,* an English village]

bort (bôrt) *n.* A poor diamond, used for cutting and polishing. Also **bortz** (bôrts). [?< OF *bort* bastard]

bor·zoi (bôr′zoi) *n.* A breed of Russian hounds, generally resembling the greyhound, but with a long, silky coat; a Russian wolfhound. [< Russ., swift]

bosh (bosh) *n. Informal* Empty words; nonsense. [< Turkish, empty, worthless]

bo's'n (bō′sən) *n.* BOATSWAIN.

Bos·ni·an (boz′nē·ən) *adj.* Of or belonging to Bosnia: also **Bos·ni·ac** (boz′nē·ak). —*n.* 1 A native of Bosnia, esp. one inhabiting the region on the northern Adriatic. 2 Their Serbo-Croatian language.

bos·om (bo͝oz′əm, bo͞o′zəm) *n.* 1 The breast of a human being, esp. of a woman. 2 That portion of a garment covering the breast, as a shirt front. 3 The breast thought of as the seat of emotion or thought. 4 The central part; midst. —*adj.* Close; intimate; cherished: a *bosom* friend. —*v.t.* 1 To have or cherish in the bosom; embrace. 2 To hide; conceal. [< OE *bōsm*]

boss[1] (bôs, bos) *n.* 1 A person who employs workers or supervises their work. 2 One who controls a political party or organization. —*v.t.* 1 To control or supervise. 2 *Informal* To order or control in a domineering manner: often with *around.* —*adj.* 1 *Informal* Chief. 2 *Slang* Great; excellent. [< Du. *baas* master]

boss[2] (bôs, bos) *n.* 1 A circular prominence; a knob. 2 A raised ornament on a surface. 3 *Mech.* An enlargement of a shaft to couple with a wheel or another shaft. —*v.t.* To ornament with bosses. [< OF *boce* bump, knob]

boss·ism (bôs′iz·əm, bos′-) *n.* Political control or management by bosses.

boss·y (bôs′ē, bos′ē) *adj.* **boss·i·er, boss·i·est** *Informal* Domineering; dictatorial. —**boss′i·ly** *adv.* —**bos′si·ness** *n.*

Boston terrier Any of a breed of small terriers having a smooth dark-brown or black coat with white markings. Also **Boston bull.**

Boston terrier

bo·sun (bō′sən) *n.* BOATSWAIN.

bot (bot) *n.* The larva of a botfly. [?]

bot. botanical; botanist; botany; bottle.

bo·tan·i·cal (bə·tan′i·kəl) *adj.* Of or pertaining to botany or plants. Also **bo·tan′ic.** [< Gk. *botanē* plant] —**bo·tan′i·cal·ly** *adv.*

bot·a·nist (bot′ə·nist) *n.* A specialist in botany.

bot·a·nize (bot′ə·nīz) *v.* **·nized, ·niz·ing** *v.i.* 1 To study botanical specimens. 2 To gather plants for study. —*v.t.* 3 To explore in search of botanical specimens. —**bot′a·niz′er** *n.*

bot·a·ny (bot′ə·nē) *n. pl.* **·nies** 1 That division of biology which treats of plants with reference to their structure, functions, classification, etc. 2 The plant life of a region. 3 The common characteristics of a group of plants: the *botany* of orchids.

botch (boch) *v.t.* 1 To patch or mend clumsily. 2 To do ineptly; bungle. —*n.* A bungled piece of work. [ME *bocchen*] —**botch′er** *n.* —**botch′er·y** *n.*

botch·y (boch′ē) *adj.* **botch·i·er, botch·i·est** Imperfect; botched; poorly done. —**botch′i·ly** *adv.* —**botch′i·ness** *n.*

bot·fly (bot′flī) *n.* Any of various flies whose larvae are parasitic in horses, sheep and other animals.

both (bōth) *adj. & pron.* The two; the one and the other: *Both* girls laughed; *Both* were there. —*adv. & conj.* Equally; as well: with *and:* He is *both* thin and pale. [< ON *badhir*]

bother (both′ər) *v.t.* **1** To give trouble to; pester; annoy. **2** To confuse; fluster. —*v.i.* **3** To trouble or concern oneself. —*n.* A source or condition of annoyance. [?]

both·er·a·tion (both′ə-rā′shən) *n. Informal* Annoyance; vexation.

both·er·some (both′ər·səm) *adj.* Causing bother.

Bot·swa·na (bot′swä′nä) *n.* A republic in s Africa, 222,000 sq. mi., cap. Gaberones. • See map at AFRICA.

bott (bot) *n.* BOT.

bot·tle (bot′l) *n.* **1** A vessel for holding, carrying, and pouring liquids, having a relatively narrow neck and mouth. **2** As much as a bottle will hold: also **bot′tle·ful.** —**hit the bottle** *Slang* To drink alcoholic beverages to excess. —*v.t.* **·tled, ·tling 1** To put into a bottle or bottles. **2** To restrain; shut in: with *up.* [< LL *buticula* flask, dim. of *butis* vat, vessel] —**bot′tler** *n.*

bot·tle·neck (bot′l·nek′) *n.* **1** A narrow or congested way. **2** Any condition that retards progress.

bot·tle·nose (bot′l·nōz′). One of various dolphins.

bot·tom (bot′əm) *n.* **1** The lowest part of anything. **2** The undersurface or base of something. **3** The last or lowest place. **4** The seat of a chair. **5** The ground beneath a body of water. **6** *Often pl.* BOTTOM LAND. **7** The real meaning, cause, or source of something. **8** The part of a ship's hull below the water line. **9** *Informal* The buttocks. **10** Endurance; stamina; grit. —**at bottom** Basically; fundamentally. —*adj.* Lowest; fundamental; basal. —*v.t.* **1** To provide with a bottom. **2** To base or found: with *on* or *upon.* **3** To fathom; comprehend. —*v.i.* **4** To be founded; rest. **5** To touch or rest upon the bottom. [< OE *botm*]

bottom land Lowland along a river.

bottom line 1 *Informal* The line of a business accounting statement showing net profit or loss: with *the.* **2** *Slang* The condition or status of any enterprise after assets and liabilities have been calculated: with *the.*

bot·tom·ry (bot′əm·rē) *n.* A contract whereby the owner of a ship borrows money, pledging the vessel as security.

bot·u·lism (boch′o͞o·liz′əm) *n.* An often fatal form of food poisoning due to a toxin formed by a species of anaerobic bacteria. [< L *botulus* sausage; the bacteria were first isolated from spoiled sausage]

bou·clé (bo͞o·klā′) *n.* **1** A curly yarn of wool, silk, or cotton. **2** Fabric made with such yarn. Also **bou′cle.** [< F *boucler* to buckle, curl]

bou·doir (bo͞o′dwär, bo͞o·dwär′) *n.* A lady's private dressing room or bedroom. [< F, lit., pouting room]

bough (bou) *n.* A limb of a tree. [< OE *bog* shoulder, bough]

bought (bôt) *p.t. & p.p.* of BUY.

bought·en (bôt′n) *adj. Regional* Bought at a store rather than being homemade.

bouil·la·baisse (bo͞ol′yə·bās′, *Fr.* bo͞o·yà·bes′) *n.* A chowder made of several varieties of fish. [< Prov. *boui* boil + *abaisso* settle, go down]

bouil·lon (bo͞ol′yon, -yən; Fr. bo͞o·yôn′) *n.* Clear broth made from meat, as beef or chicken. [< F *bouillir* boil]

boul·der (bōl′dər) *n.* A large stone moved, as by a glacier, from its original location. [< Scand.]

boul·e·vard (bo͞ol′ə·värd, bo͞o′lə-) *n.* A broad avenue, often planted with trees. [< MHG *bolwerc* bulwark]

bounce (bouns) *v.* **bounced, bounc·ing** *v.t.* **1** To cause to bound or rebound. **2** *Slang* To eject forcibly. **3** *Slang* To discharge from employment. —*v.i.* **4** To bound or rebound. **5** To move suddenly and violently; jump or spring. **6** *Informal* To be returned because of insufficient funds: said of a check. —*n.* **1** A sudden spring or leap. **2** A bounding or elastic motion; rebound. [ME *bunsen*]

bounc·er (boun′sər) *n. Informal* A strong man employed in a bar, etc., to throw out objectionable customers.

bounc·ing (boun′sing) *adj.* **1** Strong and active. **2** Large; strapping.

bound[1] (bound) *v.i.* **1** To strike and spring back from a surface, as a ball. **2** To leap. —*v.t.* **3** To cause to bound. —*n.* **1** A leap or spring. **2** A rebound. [< F *bondir* leap]

bound[2] (bound) *v.t.* **1** To set limits to; restrict. **2** To form the boundary of. **3** To describe or name the boundaries of. —*v.i.* **4** To adjoin. —*n.* **1** A limit or boundary. **2** *pl.* An area near or within a boundary. [< LL *bodina* limit]

bound[3] (bound) *p.t. & p.p.* of BIND. —*adj.* **1** Made fast; tied. **2** Obligated legally or morally. **3** Connected; related. **4** Certain: *bound* to fail. **5** Having a cover or binding. **6** *Informal* Determined; resolved.

bound[4] (bound) *adj.* Having one's course directed; on the way: with *for* or *to.* [< ON *būinn* < *būa* prepare]

bound·a·ry (boun′də·rē, -drē) *n. pl.* **·ries** Anything forming or serving to indicate a limit or end. —**Syn.** border, confines, edge, margin.

bound·en (boun′dən) *adj.* **1** Obligatory; necessary: *bounden* duty. **2** Under obligations; obliged. [Obs. p.p. of BIND]

bound·er (boun′dər) *n. Chiefly Brit. Informal* A man whose behavior is offensive; cad.

bound·less (bound′lis) *adj.* Having no limit; measureless; infinite. —**bound′less·ly** *adv.* —**bound′less·ness** *n.*

boun·te·ous (boun′tē·əs) *adj.* **1** Bountiful; generous. **2** Plentiful. —**boun′te·ous·ly** *adv.* —**boun′te·ous·ness** *n.*

bounti·ful (boun′tə·fəl) *adj.* **1** Giving freely; generous. **2** Abundant; plentiful. —**boun′ti·ful·ly** *adv.*

boun·ty (boun′tē) *n. pl.* **·ties 1** Liberality in giving. **2** Gifts or favors generously bestowed. **3** A reward paid by a government for the killing of predatory animals, raising certain crops, etc. [< L *bonitas* goodness]

bou·quet (bō·kā′, bo͞o·kā′ *for def. 1;* bo͞o·kā′ *for def. 2*) *n.* **1** A bunch of flowers. **2** The distinctive aroma of a wine. [< OF *boschet,* dim. of *bosc* wood]

bour·bon (bûr′bən) *n.* A whiskey distilled from corn or partly from corn. Also **bourbon whiskey.** [< *Bourbon* County, Ky., where originally made]

Bour·bon (bo͝or′bən) **1** A ruling family of French origin which ruled, for certain periods, over France, Spain, Naples, and Sicily. **2** One who is stubbornly conservative in politics. —**Bour′bon·ism, Bour′bon·ist** *n.*

bour·geois (bo͝or′zhwä, bo͝or·zhwä′) *n. pl* **·geois** A member of the middle class as distinguished from the aristocracy or the working class. —*adj.* **1** Of the middle class. **2** Regarded as typically middle-class; conventional, smug, etc. [< OF *burgeis*] —**bour·geoise** (-zhwäz′) *n. Fem.*

bour·geoi·sie (bo͝or′zhwä·zē′) *n.* **1** The middle class as distinguished from the aristocracy or the working class. **2** In Marxist philosophy, the social class in conflict with the proletariat. [< F *bourgeois* middle class]

bourn[1] (bôrn, bōrn, bo͝orn) *n.* **1** A boundary; limit. **2** An end; goal. **3** Realm; domain. Also **bourne.** [< LL *bodina* limit]

bourn[2] (bôrn, bōrn, bo͝orn) *n.* A brook or rivulet. Also **bourne.** [< OE *burna* spring]

bourse (bo͝ors) *n. Often cap.* An exchange or money market, esp. the Paris stock exchange. [< LL *bursa* bag]

bout (bout) *n.* **1** A contest or match, as in boxing. **2** An active period; spell: a *bout* of illness [Var. of ME *bought* bending, turn]

bou·tique (bo͞o·tēk′) *n.* A small shop in which dress accessories, gifts, etc., are sold. [F]

bou·ton·niere (bo͞o′tə·nyâr′) *n.* A flower or small bouquet worn in the button hole of a lapel. [< F *bouton* button] Also **bou·ton·nière.**

bou·zou·ki (bə·zo͞o′kē) *n.* A mandolinlike instrument with a very long neck. [< New Gk. *mpouzouki*]

bo·vine (bō′vīn, -vin) *adj.* **1** Of, related to, or characteristic of cattle, oxen, etc. **2** Patient and dull; stolid. —*n.* A bovine animal, as an ox, cow, etc. [< L *bos* ox]

bow[1] (bou) *v.i.* **1** To bend the body or head, as in greeting, reverence, assent, etc. **2** To bend or incline downward. **3** To submit; yield. —*v.t.* **4** To bend (the head, knee, etc.) in reverence, assent, etc. **5** To express by bowing. **6** To escort or direct while bowing. **7** To cause to bend, stoop, etc., as by weighting down. **8** To cause to yield or submit. —**bow out** To withdraw or resign. —*n.* **1** A bending of the body or head, as in greeting. **2** An indication of polite acknowledgment. [< OE *bugan* bow, bend, flee] **—Syn.** *v.* **3** capitulate, surrender, acquiesce. *n.* **1** obeisance, curtsey, salaam.

bow[2] (bō) *n.* **1** A weapon for shooting arrows, made from a flexible strip of wood, etc., strung from end to end with a cord. **2** A rod with hairs stretched between the ends, used to vibrate the strings of a violin, cello, etc., by friction. **3** A knot tied with a loop or loops. **4** Something bent or curved. **5** A rainbow. *—adj.* Bent; curved. *—v.t. & v.i.* **1** To bend into the shape of a bow. **2** To play (a stringed instrument) with a bow. [< OE *boga*]

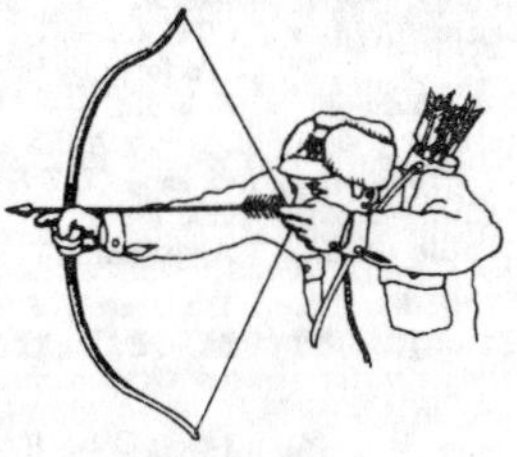

Bow *def. 1*

bow[3] (bou) *n.* **1** The forward part of a ship or boat. **2** The forward oarsman of a boat. [< MLG *boog*]

bowd·ler·ize (boud'lər·īz) *v.t.* **·ized, ·iz·ing** To expurgate or edit prudishly. [< Thomas *Bowdler,* 1754–1825, Brit. editor of a "family" edition of Shakespeare] **—bowd'ler·ism, bowd'ler·i·za'tion** *n.*

bow·el (bou'əl, boul) *n.* **1** An intestine. **2** *pl.* The intestines collectively. **3** *pl.* The inner part of anything: the *bowels* of the earth. **4** *pl. Archaic* Inmost or deepest feelings. *—v.t.* **·eled** or **·elled, ·el·ing** or **·el·ling** To disembowel. [< L *botellus,* dim. of *botulus* sausage]

bow·er (bou'ər) *n.* **1** A shady, usu. leafy shelter. **2** *Archaic* A private apartment; boudoir. *—v.t.* To enclose in or as in a bower. [< OE *būr* chamber] **—bow'er·y** *adj.*

Bow·er·y (bou'ər·ē), **the** A street in downtown New York City noted for its seedy bars, hotels, etc.

bow·fin (bō'fin') *n.* A freshwater fish of eastern North America, having a long dorsal fin.

bow·ie knife (bō'ē, bōō'ē) A hunting knife with a long, single-edged blade. [< James Bowie, died 1836, American soldier]

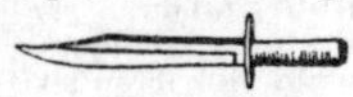

Bowie knife

bow·knot (bō'not') *n.* An ornamental slipknot with one or more loops. • See KNOT.

bowl[1] (bōl) *n.* **1** A deep, rounded container or dish. **2** The amount held by a bowl. **3** Something rounded and hollow that resembles a bowl. **4** A bowl-shaped amphitheater or stadium. [< OE *bolla*]

bowl[2] (bōl) *v.i.* **1** To engage in the game of bowling. **2** To roll a ball or similar object in or as in this game. **3** To move swiftly and smoothly. *—v.t.* **4** To throw (a ball) with a rolling motion. **—bowl over 1** To knock down. **2** To dumbfound; astound. *—n.* **1** A large ball used for bowling or similar games. **2** A throw of the ball in or as in bowling. [< F *boule* ball]

bowl·der (bōl'dər) *n.* BOULDER.

bow·leg (bō'leg') *n.* A leg bent in an outward curve. **—bow'leg'ged** (-leg'id) *adj.*

bowl·er[1] (bō'lər) *n.* One who bowls.

bowl·er[2] (bō'lər) *n. Brit.* A derby hat. [< John *Bowler,* 19th c. Brit. hatter]

bow·line (bō'lin, -līn') *n.* **1** A knot that forms a loop and that does not slip. Also **bowline knot. 2** A rope to keep the edge of a vessel's square sail forward when sailing close-hauled.

bowl·ing (bō'ling) *n.* **1** A game played on a narrow lane along which a ball is rolled in an attempt to knock down ten pins at the far end of the lane. **2** Any of various similar games. **3** The playing of any of these games.

bowling alley 1 A narrow, wood-surfaced lane used in the game of bowling. **2** A building containing such alleys.

bowls (bōlz) *n.pl. (construed as sing.)* Any of various bowling games, esp. one played outdoors with weighted balls rolled at a stationary ball.

bow·man (bō'mən) *n. pl.* **·men** (-mən) An archer.

bow·shot (bō'shot') *n.* The distance which an arrow may be shot from a bow.

bow·sprit (bou'sprit', bō'-) *n.* A spar projecting forward from the bow of a vessel.

bow·string (bō'string') *n.* The string of a bow.

bow·tie (bō'tī') *n.* A necktie tied in a bow.

bow window (bō) A projecting curved window.

box[1] (boks) *n.* **1** A container of wood, cardboard, metal, etc., usu. rectangular and having a cover or top. **2** The amount held by a box. **3** Something resembling a box, as a rectangular space or enclosed compartment. **4** A separate, enclosed seating space, as in a theater. **5** A raised seat for the driver of a coach or carriage. **6** A casing or enclosure for a mechanical part or device. **7** A space on a baseball field designated for the pitcher, batter, etc. *—v.t.* **1** To put or enclose in a box. **2** To confine as if in a box; trap or block, esp. to impede movement: often with *in* or *up*. **—box the compass 1** To recite in order the 32 points of the compass. **2** To make a complete turn or revolution. [< OE < LL *buxis*] **—box'er** *n.* **—box'ful'** *adj.*

box[2] (boks) *v.t.* **1** To hit with the hand; cuff. **2** To engage in a boxing match with. *—v.i.* **3** To fight with one's fists; engage in boxing. *—n.* A cuff or blow, esp. on the ear. [ME]

box[3] (boks) *n.* **1** An evergreen shrub with small, glossy leaves, often used for hedges. **2** Its hard wood. [< OE < L *buxus*]

box·car (boks'kär') *n.* An enclosed railway car for carrying freight.

box elder A maple tree having compound leaves.

box·er[1] (bok'sər) *n.* A man who fights in boxing matches; pugilist.

box·er[2] (bok'sər) *n.* A breed of medium-sized dog related to the bulldog. [< G < E BOXER[1]]

Box·er (bok'sər) *n.* A member of a Chinese secret society, active in 1900, which aimed to rid China of foreigners by force. [From their practice of traditional posture boxing]

box·ing (bok'sing) *n.* The sport or practice of fighting with one's fists; pugilism.

boxing glove A thickly padded leather mitten used for boxing.

box office 1 The ticket office of a theater, etc. **2** Success rated according to volume of tickets sold.

box score A tabular record of a baseball game, giving statistical information for each player.

box seat A seat in a box at a theater, stadium, etc.

box·wood (boks'wŏŏd') *n.* **1** The hard, close-grained, durable wood of the box shrub. **2** The shrub.

boy (boi) *n.* **1** A male child or youth. **2** *Informal* A fellow; man. **3** A male servant or worker. *—interj. Informal* An exclamation of pleasure, wonder, etc. [ME *boi*] **—boy'ish** *adj.* **—boy'ish·ly** *adv.* **—boy'ish·ness** *n.*

boy·cott (boi'kot) *v.t.* **1** To combine together in refusing to deal or associate with, so as to punish or coerce. **2** To refuse to use or buy. *—n.* An act or instance of boycotting. [< Capt. C. *Boycott,* 1832–1897, Irish landlord's agent]

boy friend *Informal* **1** A girl's or woman's sweetheart, favorite male companion, etc. **2** A male friend. Also **boy'·friend'**.

boy·hood (boi'hŏŏd') *n.* **1** The state or period of being a boy. **2** Boys collectively.

boy scout A member of the **Boy Scouts,** an organization giving boys training and experience in self-reliance, citizenship, outdoor activities, etc.

boy·sen·ber·ry (boi'zən·ber'ē) *n. pl.* **·ries 1** A hybrid plant obtained by crossing the blackberry, raspberry, and loganberry. **2** Its edible fruit. [< Rudolph *Boysen,* 20th c. U.S. horticulturist, the originator]

B/P, b.p. bill of parcels; bills payable.

bp, b.p. boiling point.

bp. birthplace; bishop.

B.P.O.E. Benevolent and Protective Order of Elks.

B/R, b.r. bills receivable.

Br bromine.

Br. Breton; Britain; British.

br. branch; brand; bridge; bronze; brother.

bra (brä) *n.* A brassiere.

brace (brās) *v.* **braced, brac·ing** *v.t.* 1 To make firm or steady; strengthen with or as with a prop or support. 2 To make ready to withstand pressure, impact, assault, etc. 3 To stimulate; enliven. —*v.i.* 4 To strain against pressure. —**brace up** *Informal* To rouse one's courage or resolution. —*n.* 1 A support, as of wood or metal, to hold something firmly in place. 2 A clasp or clamp used for connecting, fastening, etc. 3 A cranklike handle for turning a bit or other boring tool. 4 *Often pl.* A wire device attached to the teeth to correct malformation. 5 A pair: a *brace* of ducks. 6 A doubly curved line, { or }, used to connect printed or written lines, staves of music, etc. 7 *pl. Brit.* Suspenders. [< L *brachia,* pl. of *brachium* arm] —**Syn.** *v.* 1 support, prop, shore, buttress.

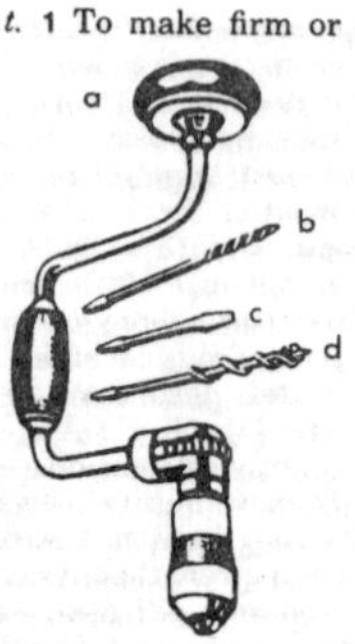

Brace *(def. 3)* and bits a. brace. b. drill bit. c. screwdriver bit. d. auger bit.

brace·let (brās′lit) *n.* 1 An ornamental band worn around the wrist or arm. 2 *Informal* A handcuff. [< L *brachium* arm]

brac·er (brā′sər) *n.* 1 One who or that which braces or steadies. 2 *Informal* A stimulating drink.

bra·ce·ro (brə·sâr′ō) *n. pl.* **·ros** A Mexican laborer brought into the U.S. under contract for seasonal farm work. [< Sp., day laborer]

bra·chi·o·pod (brā′kē·ə·pod′, brak′ē-) *n.* Any of a phylum of marine animals having a bivalve shell and a pair of armlike appendages near the mouth. [< Gk. *brachiōn* arm + *pous* foot]

bra·chi·um (brā′kē·əm, brak′ē-) *n. pl.* **·chi·a** (brā′kē·ə, brak′ē-) 1 The upper arm, or a homologous part. 2 Any armlike appendage. [< L] —**bra′chi·al** *adj.*

brach·y·ce·phal·ic (brak′i·sə·fal′ik) *adj.* Having a short, relatively broad skull; round-headed. Also **brach·y·ceph·a·lous** (brak′ē·sef′ə·ləs). [< Gk. *brachys* short + *kephalē* head] —**brach′y·ceph′a·lism, brach′y·ceph′a·ly** *n.*

brac·ing (brā′sing) *adj.* Invigorating.

brack·en (brak′ən) *n.* 1 A large, coarse, weedy fern. 2 A place covered with such ferns. [< Scand.]

brack·et (brak′it) *n.* 1 A piece projecting from a wall to support a shelf or other weight. 2 A projecting fixture, as for a lamp. 3 A brace used to strengthen an angle. 4 One of two marks, [ ], used to enclose part of a text. 5 A part within a graded grouping or category: the high-income *bracket.* —*v.t.* 1 To provide or support with a bracket. 2 To enclose within brackets. 3 To group or categorize together. [< L *bracae,* pl., breeches]

brack·ish (brak′ish) *adj.* 1 Somewhat saline; briny. 2 Unpleasant to taste. [< Du. *brak* salty] —**brack′ish·ness** *n.*

bract (brakt) *n.* A modified leaf growing near and sometimes seemingly part of a flower. [< L *bractea* thin metal plate] —**brac·te·al** (brak′tē·əl), **brac′te·ate** (-tē·it, -āt) *adj.*

brad (brad) *n.* A slender nail with a small head. [< ON *broddr* spike]

brad·awl (brad′ôl′) *n.* A short awl with a chisellike end.

brag (brag) *v.* **bragged, brag·ging** *v.t.* & *v.i.* To say or talk boastfully. —*n.* 1 Boastfulness; boastful language. 2 Something bragged of. 3 A person who brags. [ME *braggen*] —**brag′ger** *n.*

brag·ga·do·ci·o (brag′ə·dō′shē·ō) *n. pl.* **·ci·os** 1 Pretentious boasting. 2 A swaggering braggart. [< *Braggadochio,* a boastful character in Spenser's *Faerie Queene*]

brag·gart (brag′ərt) *n.* A bragging showoff. —*adj.* Boastful.

Brah·ma (brä′mə) *n.* In Hinduism: 1 The supreme soul of the universe. 2 The supreme creator conceived of as forming a trinity together with Vishnu and Siva. [< Skt. *Brahmā*]

Brah·man (brä′mən) *n. pl.* **·mans** 1 A member of the highest, or priestly, Hindu caste. 2 One of a breed of humped cattle developed from stock from India. [< Skt. *brahman* praise, worship] —**Brah·man·i** (brä′mən·ē) *n. Fem.* —**Brah·man·ic** (brä·man′ik) or **·i·cal** *adj.*

Brah·man·ism (brä′mən·iz′əm) *n.* The religious and social system of the Brahmans. —**Brah′man·ist** *n.*

Brah·min (brä′min) *n.* 1 BRAHMAN. 2 An aristocratic, highly cultured person, esp. one of an old New England family. —**Brah′min·ism** *n.*

braid (brād) *v.t.* 1 To interweave or intertwine several strands of; plait. 2 To form by braiding: to *braid* a mat. 3 To ornament with braid. —*n.* 1 Anything braided or plaited: a *braid* of hair. 2 A flat tape or strip for binding or ornamenting fabrics. [< OE *bregdan* brandish, weave, braid] —**braid′er, braid′ing** *n.*

Braille (brāl) *n.* 1 A system of printing or writing for the blind in which the characters consist of raised dots to be read by feeling with the fingers. 2 The characters themselves. Also **braille.** [< Louis *Braille,* 1809–52, French educator, who invented it]

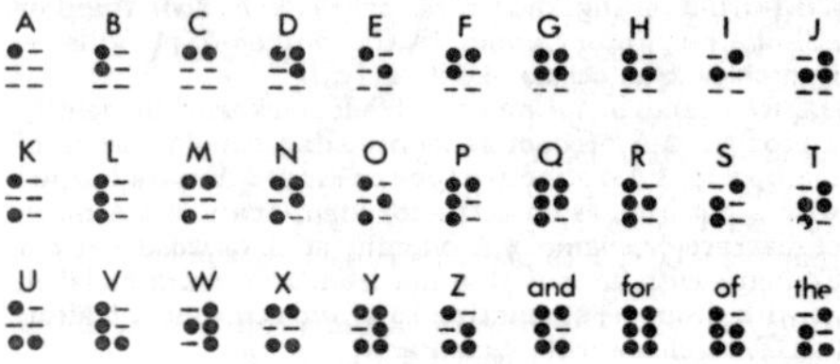

Braille alphabet

brain (brān) *n.* 1 The mass of nerve tissue contained within the cranium of vertebrates and continuous with the spinal cord. 2 The chief focal area of the nervous system in any animal. 3 *Often pl.* Mind; intellect. 4 *Informal* A notably intelligent person. —**have on the brain** To be obsessed by —*v.t.* 1 To dash out the brains of. 2 *Slang* To strike on the head. [< OE *brægen*]

brain·child (brān′chīld′) *n.* An idea, project, or other product of the mind considered as belonging to its creator.

brain·less (brān′lis) *adj.* Lacking brains or intelligence; senseless. —**brain′less·ly** *adv.* —**brain′less·ness** *n.*

brain·pan (brān′pan′) *n.* The part of the skull enclosing the brain; cranium.

brain·sick (brān′sik′) *adj.* Mentally disordered. —**brain′·sick′ness** *n.*

brain·storm (brān′stôrm′) *n. Informal* A burst of inspiration.

brain trust *Informal* A group of experts who advise, plan policy, etc.

brain·wash (brān′wosh′, -wôsh′) *v.t.* To alter the convictions, beliefs, etc., of by systematic indoctrination. —**brain′wash·ing** *n.*

brain wave 1 A rhythmic fluctuation of electrical potential in the brain. 2 *Informal* A sudden inspiration.

brain·y (brā′nē) *adj.* **brain·i·er, brain·i·est** *Informal* Intelligent; smart. —**brain′i·ly** *adv.* —**brain′i·ness** *n.*

braise (brāz) *v.t.* **braised, brais·ing** To cook by browning quickly and then simmering in a covered pan. [< F *braise* charcoal]

brake[1] (brāk) *n.* 1 A device for retarding or arresting the motion of a vehicle, a wheel, etc. 2 *Often pl.* Anything that checks or slows an action or process. 3 An instrument for separating the fiber of flax, hemp, etc., by bruising. —*v.* **braked, brak·ing** *v.t.* 1 To apply a brake to. 2 To bruise and crush, as flax. —*v.i.* 3 To operate a brake or brakes. 4 To be retarded or stopped by a brake. [< MDu. *braeke* brake for flax]

brake[2] (brāk) *n.* A fern; bracken.

brake[3] (brāk) *n.* A thicket. [< OE *(fearn) braca* bed of (fern)]

brake[4] (brāk) *Archaic p.t. of* BREAK.

brake·man (brāk′mən) *n. pl.* **·men** (-mən) A railroad employee who assists the conductor on a train.

brake shoe A part that presses on a wheel or associated structure in order to stop or slow it.

bram·ble (bram′bəl) *n.* A prickly plant or shrub, as the raspberry, blackberry, etc. [< OE *bræmble*] —**bram′bly** *adj.* **(·bli·er, ·bli·est)**

bran (bran) *n.* The coarse, outer coat of cereals, separated from the flour. [< OF *bran, bren*]

branch (branch, bränch) *n.* **1** A secondary stem growing from the trunk or main limb of a tree, shrub, etc. **2** A similar division or part, as of a deer's antler. **3** A part or subdivision of a comprehensive whole. **4** A separate unit, department, etc., as of a business organization or institution. **5** A division of a family, tribe, etc. **6** A subdivision of a linguistic family. **7** A tributary of a river or main stream. **8** A small stream or creek. —*v.i.* **1** To put forth branches. **2** To divide into branches or subdivisions; diverge. —*v.t.* **3** To separate into branches. —**branch out** To extend or diversify, as one's business or interests. [< LL *branca* paw]

bran·chi·a (brang'kē·ə) *n. pl.* **·chi·ae** (-ki·ē) *Zool.* A gill or gill-like respiratory organ. [< Gk. *branchia,* pl., gills] —**bran'chi·al, bran'chi·ate** (-kē·it, -āt) *adj.*

brand (brand) *n.* **1** A name or trademark used to identify a product. **2** A product so identified: a popular *brand* of toothpaste. **3** A distinctive type or kind. **4** A mark burned with a hot iron, as on cattle for identification. **5** A mark of disgrace or shame. **6** A burning stick of wood. —*v.t.* **1** To mark with or as with a hot iron. **2** To mark or label, as with disgrace; stigmatize: to *brand* someone a traitor. [< OE, torch, sword] —**brand'er** *n.*

bran·dish (bran'dish) *v.t.* To wave or flourish triumphantly, menacingly, etc. —*n.* A flourish, as with a weapon. [< OF *brand* sword] —**brand'ish·er** *n.*

brand-new (bran'nʸōō') *adj.* Quite new; not yet used. Also **bran-new** (bran'-).

bran·dy (bran'dē) *n. pl.* **·dies** An alcoholic liquor distilled from the fermented juice of grapes or other fruits. —*v.t.* **·died, dy·ing** To mix, flavor, or preserve with brandy. [< Du. *brandewijn* brandy, lit., distilled wine]

brant (brant) *n. pl.* **brants** or **brant** A small, dark, wild goose of Europe and North America. [? < Scand.]

brash[1] (brash) *adj.* **1** Hasty and thoughtless; rash. **2** Impudent; bold. [?] —**brash'ly** *adv.* —**brash'ness** *n.* —**Syn. 1** reckless, impetuous. **2** impertinent, pert, cheeky, saucy.

brash[2] (brash) *adj.* Brittle: said of wood or timber. [?]

bra·sier (brā'zhər) *n.* BRAZIER.

brass (bras, bräs) *n.* **1** A yellow alloy of copper and zinc. **2** *Sometimes pl.* Brass ornaments, utensils, etc. **3** The brass wind instruments of an orchestra or band, collectively. **4** *Informal* Impudence; effrontery. **5** *Slang* High-ranking military officers, executives, etc. —*adj.* Made of brass. [< OE *bræs*]

bras·sard (bras'ärd, brə·särd') *n.* **1** A cloth arm band worn as a badge. **2** A piece of armor for the arm: also **bras·sart** (bras'ərt). [< F *bras* arm]

brass band A band of musicians using mostly brass instruments.

brass hat *Slang* A high-ranking military officer or official.

bras·sie (bras'ē, bräs'ē) *n.* A wooden golf club with a brass plate on the sole. Also **brass'y.**

bras·siere (brə·zir') *n.* A woman's undergarment shaped to support the breasts. Also **bras·sière'.** [< F *brassière* shoulder strap < *bras* arm]

brass knuckles A metal device that slips over the fingers and is used as a weapon in fist fighting.

brass tacks *Informal* Concrete or essential facts.

brass winds *Music* The wind instruments that sound by a buzzing of the player's lips into a mouthpiece, as the trumpet, horn, trombone, and tuba.

brass·y (bras'ē, bräs'ē) *adj.* **brass·i·er, brass·i·est 1** Of or decorated with brass. **2** Resembling brass. **3** Blaring; harsh-sounding. **4** Flashy; tawdry. **5** Bold and shameless. —**brass'i·ly** *adv.* —**brass'i·ness** *n.*

brat (brat) *n.* An objectionable child. [?] —**brat'ti·ness** *n.* —**brat'ty** *adj.*

bra·va·do (brə·vä'dō) *n. pl.* **·dos** or **·does 1** Affectation of reckless bravery; bluster. **2** A show of false courage or daring. [< Sp. *bravo* brave]

brave (brāv) *adj.* **brav·er, brav·est 1** Having or showing courage. **2** Showy; splendid. —*v.t.* —**braved, brav·ing 1** To face with courage and fortitude. **2** To defy; challenge. —*n.* A North American Indian warrior. [< L *barbarus* wild, fierce] —**brave'ly** *adv.* —**brave'ness** *n.* —**Syn.** *adj.* **1** courageous, fearless, bold, intrepid, valorous.

brav·er·y (brā'vər·ē) *n.* **1** Courage; valor. **2** Showy or splendid appearance.

bra·vo[1] (brä'vō) *interj.* Good! well done! —*n. pl.* **·vos** A shout of "bravo!" [< Ital., brave]

bra·vo[2] (brä'vō, brā'-) *n. pl.* **·voes** or **·vos** A hired assassin or ruffian. [< Ital., brave]

bra·vu·ra (brə·vʸōōr'ə, *Ital.* brä·vōō'rä) *n.* **1** A brilliant style of musical execution. **2** Any dashing or daring style. [< Ital., dash, daring < *bravo* brave]

brawl (brôl) *n.* **1** A noisy quarrel or fight; a row. **2** *Slang* A noisy celebration. —*v.i.* **1** To quarrel or fight noisily. **2** To move noisily, as water. [ME *braulen*] —**brawl'er** *n.*

brawn (brôn) *n.* **1** Strong, well-developed muscles. **2** Muscular strength; physical power. [< OF *braon* slice of flesh] —**brawn'y** *adj.* **(·i·er, ·i·est)** —**brawn'i·ness** *n.*

bray (brā) *v.i.* **1** To utter a loud, harsh cry, as a donkey. **2** To sound harshly, as a trumpet. —*v.t.* **3** To utter loudly and harshly. —*n.* **1** The loud, harsh cry of a donkey. **2** A sound resembling this. [< OF *braire* cry out] —**bray'er** *n.*

Braz. Brazil; Brazilian.

braze (brāz) *v.t.* **brazed, braz·ing** To join the surfaces of metals with a solder that melts at a high temperature. [< F *braser* to solder] —**braz'er** *n.*

bra·zen (brā'zən) *adj.* **1** Made of or resembling brass. **2** Trumpetlike; blaring. **3** Bold and shameless. —*v.t.* To face with bold or defiant self-assurance: with *out.* —**bra'zen·ly** *adv.* —**bra'zen·ness** *n.*

bra·zier[1] (brā'zhər) *n.* An open pan for holding burning coals. [< F *braise* hot coals]

bra·zier[2] (brā'zhər) *n.* A worker in brass.

Bra·zil (brə·zil') *n.* A republic of CEN. and E South America, 3,287,951 sq.mi., cap. Brasilia. —**Bra·zil'ian** *adj., n.*

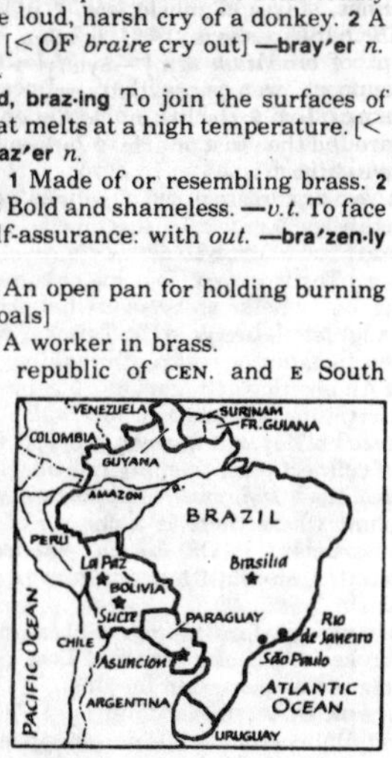

Brazil nut An oily, hard-shelled, edible seed of a South American tree.

breach (brēch) *n.* **1** Violation or infraction of a law, legal obligation, promise, etc. **2** A gap or break, as in a wall. **3** A break in friendly relations; an estrangement. —*v.t.* To make a breach in; break through. [< OE *bryce* a breaking]

bread (bred) *n.* **1** A food made with flour or meal mixed with a liquid, usu. raised with yeast, kneaded, and baked. **2** Food in general. **3** The necessities of life. **4** *Slang* Money. —*v.t.* To coat with bread crumbs before cooking. [< OE *brēad*]

bread-and-but·ter (bred'ən·but'ər) *adj.* Expressing thanks for hospitality: a *bread-and-butter* letter.

bread and butter *Informal* Subsistence; livelihood

bread·fruit (bred'frōōt') *n.* **1** The fruit of a tree of the South Sea Islands which, when roasted, resembles bread. **2** The tree.

bread line A line of persons waiting for charitable donations of food.

bread·stuff (bred'stuf') *n.* **1** Grain, flour, etc., for making bread. **2** Bread.

breadth (bredth, bretth) *n.* **1** Measure or distance from side to side; width. **2** A piece of something, as cloth, of full or standard width. **3** Comprehensive range or scope. **4** Freedom from bias or restriction. [< OE < *brad* broad]

breadth·wise (bredth'wīz', bretth'-) *adv.* In the direction of the breadth. Also **breadth'ways'** (-wāz').

bread·win·ner (bred'win'ər) *n.* One whose earnings support one's wife, husband, or family.

break (brāk) *v.* **broke** (*Archaic* **brake**), **bro·ken** (*Archaic* **broke**), **break·ing** *v.t.* **1** To separate into pieces by or as by force, a blow, etc. **2** To crack; fracture. **3** To pierce or part the surface of. **4** To cause to burst. **5** To make useless or inoperative. 6 To make a way through by force. 7 To escape from: to *break* jail. 8 To end by force or opposition: to *break* a strike. 9 To destroy the order, continuity, or completeness of: to *break* step; to *break* the silence. 10 To diminish the force of; moderate: to *break* a fall. 11 To interrupt (an electric circuit, a journey, etc.). 12 To violate: to *break* a law. 13 a To discontinue (a habit). b To cause to discontinue a habit. 14 To train or tame, as a horse. 15 To demote in rank. 16 To subdue or destroy; crush. 17 To surpass; excel: to *break* a record. 18 To make known, as news. 19 To exchange for smaller units: to *break* a dollar. 20 To invalidate (a will) by court action. 21 To solve or decipher. 22 To bankrupt. 23 To overwhelm with grief: It *broke* his heart. —*v.i.* 24 To become separated into pieces or fragments; come or fall apart. 25 To burst. 26 To become unusable or inoperative. 27 To move apart or away; disperse: The crowd *broke.* 28 To move or escape suddenly: He *broke* from the crowd. 29 To come into being or evidence: Dawn *broke.* 30 To collapse or crash. 31 To diminish or fall abruptly: The fever *broke.* 32 To change suddenly, as the voice. 33 To be overwhelmed with grief: Her heart *broke.* 34 In baseball, to curve near the plate, as a pitched ball. —**break down** 1 To become inoperative. 2 To have a physical or nervous collapse. 3 To give way as to grief. 4 To decompose. 5 To analyze. —**break in** 1 To enter by force. 2 To interrupt. 3 To train. 4 To adapt to use or wear. —**break off** 1 To stop suddenly, as in speaking. 2 To sever relations. —**break out** 1 To start suddenly. 2 To develop a rash, pimples, etc. —**break up** 1 To disperse. 2 To bring or come to an end. 3 *Informal* To overwhelm or be overwhelmed, as with distress or laughter. —**break with** To sever connection with. —*n.* 1 An instance or result of breaking; a fracture, crack, etc. 2 An opening, rift, gap, etc. 3 A breach or interruption of continuity. 4 A pause or interval. 5 A beginning; start: the *break* of day. 6 A dash or run, esp. to escape. 7 A severing of connection or friendly relations. 8 A sudden change or decline. 9 *Informal* An opportunity or piece of luck. 10 A point where there is a change of register of a voice or instrument. [< OE *brecan*] —**break′a·ble** *adj.* —**Syn.** *v.* 1 shatter, smash, fragment, shiver, disintegrate, splinter, dash.

break·age (brā′kij) *n.* 1 A breaking, or the state of being broken. 2 Articles broken. 3 Loss or damage due to breaking. 4 Compensation for this.

break·down (brāk′doun′) *n.* 1 The act of breaking down; a failure, as of a machine, one's health, etc. 2 A systematic analysis. 3 *Chem.* Decomposition or analysis of compounds.

break·er (brā′kər) *n.* 1 One who or that which breaks. 2 A wave that breaks into foam on the shore, on rocks, etc. 3 *Can.* ICEBREAKER.

break·fast (brek′fəst) *n.* The first meal of the day. —*v.i.* To eat breakfast. —**break′fast·er** *n.*

break·front (brāk′frunt′) *n.* A high, wide bookcase or cabinet with a slightly projecting center part.

break·neck (brāk′nek′) *adj.* Headlong and recklessly dangerous: *breakneck* speed.

break·through (brāk′thrōō′) *n.* 1 A decisive or dramatic advance, as in research, knowledge, etc. 2 An attack that penetrates an enemy's defensive system.

break·up (brāk′up′) *n.* 1 The act or process of breaking up. 2 A rift or dissolution, as of a relationship.

break·wa·ter (brāk′wô′tər, -wot′ər) *n.* A structure for protecting a harbor or beach from the force of waves.

bream (brēm) *n. pl.* **breams** or **bream** 1 A European freshwater fish. 2 Any of various freshwater sunfishes. [< OF *bresme*]

breast (brest) *n.* 1 The front of the body from the neck to the abdomen. 2 One of the two milk-secreting organs on the upper front part of a woman's torso. 3 A similar organ in any mammal. 4 The part of a garment that covers the breast. 5 The seat of the emotions. 6 Anything likened to the human breast. —**make a clean breast of** To confess. —*v.t.* To face or advance against boldly or resolutely. [< OE *brēost*]

breast·bone (brest′bōn′) *n.* STERNUM.

breast-feed (brest′fēd′) *v.t.* & *v.i.* **-fed, -feed·ing** To feed (a baby) with milk from the breast; suckle.

breast·plate (brest′plāt′) *n.* A piece of armor covering and protecting the breast.

Breastplate

breast stroke A swimming stroke in which the arms are simultaneously thrust forward from the breast, then brought laterally back to the sides.

breast·work (brest′wûrk′) *n.* A low, temporary defensive structure, usu. breast-high.

breath (breth) *n.* 1 Air inhaled or exhaled in respiration. 2 An act of respiration, esp. an inhalation. 3 Ability to breathe or breathe freely. 4 The moisture of exhaled air condensed by cooling. 5 The time of a single respiration; an instant. 6 A slight breeze or motion of air. 7 A slight indication, suggestion, etc. 8 A whisper. —**hold one's breath** To prevent oneself from breathing temporarily. —**in the same breath** At the same moment. —**out of breath** Panting, as from exertion. —**take one's breath away** To awe, astonish, etc. —**under one's breath** In a whisper. [< OE *brǣth* vapor]

breath·a·lyz·er (breth′ə·lī′zər) *n.* A device that measures the alcoholic content of blood, used esp. to test motorists for intoxication. *Brit. sp.* **-lys·er.** [< BREATH + (AN)ALYZER]

breathe (brē<u>th</u>) *v.* **breathed** (brē<u>th</u>d), **breath·ing** *v.i.* 1 To inhale and exhale air. 2 To be alive; live. 3 To pause for breath. 4 To move gently, as a breeze. 5 To allow air to penetrate: said of a fabric or garment. —*v.t.* 6 To inhale and exhale, as air. 7 To take in or emit by inhaling or exhaling. 8 To infuse or impart, as by breathing. 9 To evince; manifest. 10 To utter; whisper. 11 To allow to rest. [ME *brethren* < *breth* breath] —**breath′a·ble** *adj.*

breath·er (brē′<u>th</u>ər) *n.* *Informal* A brief rest period.

breath·less (breth′lis) *adj.* 1 Out of breath. 2 Intense or eager, as if holding the breath. 3 Causing or filled with tension or excitement. 4 Dead. 5 Having no breeze; oppressive. —**breath′less·ly** *adv.* —**breath′less·ness** *n.*

breath·tak·ing (breth′tā′king) *adj.* Very exciting, moving, etc. —**breath′tak′ing·ly** *adv.*

breath·y (breth′ē) *adj.* **breath·i·er, breath·i·est** Characterized by audible breathing.

bred (bred) *p.t.* & *p.p.* *of* BREED.

breech (brēch) *n.* 1 The buttocks. 2 The rear end of a gun barrel, cannon bore, etc. —*v.t.* (brēch, brich) *Archaic* To clothe with breeches. [< OE *brec,* pl., breeches]

breech·cloth (brēch′klôth, -kloth′) *n.* LOINCLOTH. Also **breech′clout′** (-klout′).

breech·es (brich′iz) *n. pl.* 1 Trousers, usu. close-fitting, that reach to or just below the knee. 2 *Informal* Trousers. [< OE *brec*]

breeches buoy A life-saving apparatus consisting of canvas breeches attached to a life buoy and run upon a rope stretched from a ship to the shore or another ship.

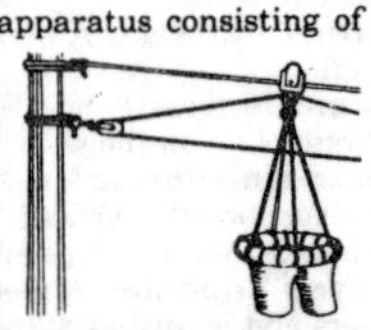

Breeches buoy

breech·load·er (brēch′lō′dər) *n.* A firearm that is loaded at the breech. —**breech′load′ing** *adj.*

breed (brēd) *v.* **bred, breed·ing** *v.t.* 1 To produce (offspring). 2 To control the reproduction of (animals or plants), often to develop new strains in. 3 To cause; give rise to. 4 To bring up; train. —*v.i.* 5 To procreate. 6 To originate or be caused. —*n.* 1 A strain or type, esp. of an animal, produced by selective mating. 2 A sort or kind. [< OE *brēdan*] —**breed′er** *n.*

breeder reactor A nuclear reactor that produces power and acts on nonfissionable elements to produce more fissionable material than it uses.

breed·ing (brē′ding) *n.* 1 The production of offspring. 2 Ancestry; descent. 3 Training, as in good manners; upbringing. 4 The selective production of desired strains of animals or plants.

breeze (brēz) *n.* 1 A moderate current of air; a gentle wind. 2 *Informal* An easily accomplished thing or action. —*v.i.* **breezed, breez·ing** *Informal* To go quickly and blithely. [< Sp. and Pg. *brisa, briza* northeast wind]

breeze·way (brēz′wā′) *n.* A roofed, open passageway between two buildings, as a house and a garage.

breez·y (brē′zē) *adj.* **breez·i·er, breez·i·est** 1 Having a breeze; slightly windy. 2 Jaunty; light-hearted. **—breez′i·ly** *adv.* **—breez′i·ness** *n.*

breth·ren (breth′rən) *n. Alternative pl. of* BROTHER: now used chiefly in formal and religious contexts.

Bret·on (bret′n) *adj.* Of or pertaining to Brittany, its inhabitants, or their language. —*n.* 1 A native of Brittany. 2 The Celtic language of the Bretons.

breve (brev, brēv) *n.* 1 A mark (˘) placed over a vowel to indicate that it has a short sound. 2 *Music* A note equal in time to two whole notes. [< L *brevis* short]

bre·vet (brə·vet′, *esp. Brit.* brev′it) *n.* A commission advancing an officer in honorary rank without advance in pay. —*v.t.* **bre·vet·ted** or **bre·vet·ed, bre·vet·ting** or **bre·vet·ing** To raise in rank by brevet. —*adj.* Held or conferred by brevet. [< OF *brevet,* dim. of *bref* letter, document] **—bre·vet′cy** *n.*

bre·vi·ar·y (brē′vē·er′ē, brev′ē-) *n. pl.* **·ar·ies** A book of daily prayers, etc., for the canonical hours. [< LL *breviarium* abridgment]

brev·i·ty (brev′ə·tē) *n.* 1 Shortness of duration or time. 2 Condensation of language; conciseness. [< L *brevis* short]

brew (broo͞) *v.t.* 1 To make, as beer or ale, by steeping, boiling, and fermentation of malt, hops, etc. 2 To make (a beverage) by boiling, steeping, etc. 3 To concoct; devise. —*v.i.* 4 To make ale, beer, etc. 5 To be imminent. —*n.* A beverage, etc., made by brewing. [< OE *breōwan*] **—brew′·er** *n.*

brew·er·y (broo͞′ər·ē) *n. pl.* **·er·ies** An establishment for brewing beer, etc.

brew·ing (broo͞′ing) *n.* 1 The process of making beer, ale, etc. 2 An amount brewed at one time.

bri·ar[1] (brī′ər) *n.* 1 A European shrub of the heath family, having a hard, woody root. 2 A tobacco pipe made from this root. [< F *bruyère*]

bri·ar[2] (brī′ər) *n.* BRIER[1].

bri·ar·root (brī′ər·ro͞ot′, -ro͞ot′) *n.* The woody root of the briar.

bri·ar·wood (brī′ər·wo͝od′) *n.* The wood of the briarroot.

bribe (brīb) *n.* 1 Something of value given or offered as an inducement to do something wrong. 2 Anything that seduces or allures. —*v.* **bribed, brib·ing** *v.t.* 1 To offer or give a bribe to. 2 To gain or influence by means of bribery. —*v.i.* 3 To give bribes. [< OF, piece of bread given a beggar] **—brib′a·ble** *adj.* **—brib′er** *n.*

brib·er·y (brī′bər·ē) *n. pl.* **·er·ies** The giving, offering, or accepting of a bribe.

bric-a-brac (brik′ə·brak) *n.* Small objects displayed as ornaments; knickknacks. Also **bric-à-brac.** [F]

brick (brik) *n.* 1 A molded block of baked or fired clay, used for building, paving, etc. 2 Bricks collectively. 3 An object shaped like a brick. 4 *Informal* An admirable fellow. —*v.t.* 1 To build or line with bricks. 2 To cover or close with bricks: with *up* or *in.* [< OF *brique* fragment, bit]

brick·bat (brik′bat′) *n.* 1 A piece of a brick, esp. when used as a missile. 2 A critical or unflattering comment.

brick·lay·er (brik′lā′ər) *n.* One who builds walls, etc., with bricks. **—brick′lay′ing** *n.*

brick red Dull brownish red. **—brick-red** (brik′red′) *adj.*

brick·work (brik′wûrk′) *n.* Construction with or a structure of bricks.

brick·yard (brik′yärd′) *n.* A place where bricks are made.

bri·dal (brīd′l) *adj.* Of a bride or a wedding; nuptial. —*n.* A wedding. [< OE *brȳdeala* wedding feast]

bri·dal·wreath (brīd′l·rēth′) *n.* A cultivated shrub with small white flowers.

bride (brīd) *n.* A woman newly married or about to be married. [< OE *brȳd*]

bride·groom (brīd′gro͞om′, -gro͝om′) *n.* A man newly married or about to be married. [< OE *brȳd* bride + *guma* man]

brides·maid (brīdz′mād′) *n.* A usu. young, unmarried woman who attends a bride at her wedding.

bridge[1] (brij) *n.* 1 A structure built to span and afford passage across a waterway, railroad, ravine, etc. 2 Something that spans or connects in the manner of a bridge. 3 An observation platform across and above a ship's deck for the use of the officers, the pilot, etc. 4 The bony upper portion of the nose. 5 The part of a pair of eyeglasses resting on this part of the nose. 6 A block for raising the strings of a musical instrument, as a violin or guitar. • See VIOLIN. 7 A mounting for holding false teeth, attached to adjoining teeth on each side. 8 *Music* A transitional passage. **—burn one's bridges (behind one)** To cut off all possibility of retreat. —*v.t.* **bridged, bridg·ing** 1 To construct a bridge over. 2 To span or connect as by a bridge. [< OE *brycg*] **—bridge′a·ble** *adj.*

bridge[2] (brij) *n.* A card game derived from whist, in which a trump suit is determined by bidding. [?]

bridge·head (brij′hed′) *n.* An advance military position on or near a river bank, pass, etc., in enemy territory.

bridge·work (brij′wûrk′) *n.* A dental bridge or bridges.

bri·dle (brīd′l) *n.* 1 The head harness of a horse, including bit and reins. 2 Anything that restrains or checks. —*v.* **bri·dled, bri·dling** *v.t.* 1 To put a bridle on. 2 To check or control with or as with a bridle. —*v.i.* 3 To raise the head and draw in the chin, as in resentment, pride, etc. [< OE *brīdel*] **—bri′dler** *n.*

bri·dle·path (brīd′l·path′, -päth′) *n.* A path for horseback riding.

brief (brēf) *adj.* 1 Short in duration or extent. 2 Of few words; concise. 3 Curt; abrupt. —*n.* 1 A concise statement or summary. 2 A written summary of the relevant facts, points of law, etc., in a legal case. 3 *pl.* Short, close-fitting underpants. **—in brief** Briefly; in short. **—hold a brief for** To champion. —*v.t.* 1 To make a summary of. 2 To instruct or advise in advance. [< L *brevis* short] **—brief′ly** *adv.* **—brief′ness** *n.* **—Syn.** *adj.* 2 condensed, succinct, terse, laconic.

brief·case (brēf′kās′) *n.* A soft-sided case, as of leather, for carrying papers, books, etc.

brief·ing (brē′fing) *n.* Final instructions, advice, etc., given in preparation for an action or undertaking.

bri·er[1] (brī′ər) *n.* A prickly bush or shrub, esp. of the rose family. [< OE *brēr*] **—bri′er·y** *adj.*

bri·er[2] (brī′ər) *n.* BRIAR[1].

bri·er·root (brī′ər·ro͞ot′, -ro͞ot′) *n.* BRIARROOT.

bri·er·wood (brī′ər·wo͝od′) *n.* BRIARWOOD.

brig[1] (brig) *n.* A two-masted ship, square-rigged on both masts. [Short for BRIGANTINE]

brig[2] (brig) *n.* 1 A prison on shipboard. 2 *Slang* A guardhouse. [?< BRIG[1]]

Brig. brigade; brigadier.

bri·gade (bri·gād′) *n.* 1 A U.S. Army unit of varying size, together with its headquarters and supporting units. 2 Any of various large military units. 3 A group of persons organized to work together: a fire *brigade.* —*v.t.* **·gad·ed, ·gad·ing** To form into a brigade. [< Ital. *brigata* crew < *brigare* to brawl]

brig·a·dier (brig′ə·dir′) *n.* BRIGADIER GENERAL.

brigadier general See GRADE.

brig·and (brig′ənd) *n.* A bandit; esp. one of a roving band of outlaws. [< Ital. *brigare* to brawl, fight] **—brig′and·age** (-ij), **brig′and·ism** *n.*

brig·an·tine (brig′ən·tēn, -tīn) *n.* A two-masted vessel, square-rigged on the foremast, and fore-and-aft rigged on the mainmast. [< MF *brigandin* a fighting vessel < Ital. *brigare* to fight]

Brig. Gen. Brigadier General.

bright (brīt) *adj.* 1 Emitting or reflecting much light; shining. 2 Full of light. 3 Brilliant, as in color or tone; vivid. 4 Intelligent; quick-witted. 5 Cheerful; gay. 6 Promising; auspicious. —*adv.* In a bright manner. [< OE *beorht, briht*] **—bright′ly** *adv.* **—bright′ness** *n.* **—Syn.** 1 radiant, luminous, glowing, gleaming, effulgent.

bright·en (brīt′n) *v.t.* & *v.i.* To make or become bright or brighter. **—bright′en·er** *n.*

Bright's disease Any of various forms of nephritis, an inflammation of the kidney. [< Richard *Bright,* 1789–1858, English physician]

bril·liant (bril′yənt) *adj.* 1 Very bright or vivid: a *brilliant* light. 2 Splendid; dazzling: a *brilliant* performance. 3 Strikingly intelligent or extraordinarily able or talented. —*n.* A diamond cut with many facets. [< MF *briller* to sparkle] —**bril′liance, bril′lian·cy** *n.* —**bril′liant·ly** *adv.*

bril·lian·tine (bril′yən·tēn) *n.* A perfumed hair oil. [< F *brillant* brilliant]

brim (brim) *n.* 1 The rim or uppermost edge of a cup, bowl, etc. 2 A projecting rim, as of a hat. —*v.t.* & *v.i.* **brimmed, brim·ming** To fill or be filled to the brim. —**brim over** To overflow. [ME *brimme*]

brim·ful (brim′fo͞ol′) *adj.* Full to the brim.

brim·stone (brim′stōn′) *n.* SULFUR. [< OE *brynstān,* lit., burning stone]

brin·dle (brin′dəl) *adj.* BRINDLED. —*n.* 1 A brindled color. 2 A brindled animal.

brin·dled (brin′dəld) *adj.* Tawny or grayish with darker streaks or spots. [< ME *brende*]

brine (brīn) *n.* 1 Water saturated with salt. 2 The sea; the ocean. —*v.t.* **brined, brin·ing** To steep in brine. [< OE *brȳne*] —**brin′i·ness** *n.* —**brin′y** *adj.* **(·i·er, ·i·est)**

bring (bring) *v.t.* **brought, bring·ing** 1 To convey or cause (a person or thing) to come with oneself to or toward a place. 2 To cause to come about; result in. 3 To cause to appear, come to mind, etc. 4 To persuade or induce, as to a course of action. 5 To sell for: The house *brought* a good price. 6 To institute (a lawsuit, charge, etc.). —**bring about** 1 To cause to happen. 2 *Naut.* To turn, as a ship. —**bring around** (or **round**) 1 To cause to adopt an opinion, course of action, etc. 2 To restore to consciousness. —**bring down** 1 To cause to fall. 2 To fell. —**bring forth** 1 To give birth to. 2 To produce. —**bring in** 1 To render or submit (a verdict). 2 To yield or produce, as profits. —**bring off** To do successfully. —**bring on** To cause; lead to. —**bring out** 1 To reveal; cause to be evident. 2 To publish or produce. 3 To introduce, as a young girl to society. —**bring to** 1 To restore to consciousness. 2 *Naut.* To cause (a ship) to lie to. —**bring up** 1 To raise and train during childhood; rear. 2 To mention or introduce, as a subject. 3 To cough or vomit up. [< OE *bringan*] —**bring′er** *n.* • In strict usage, *bring* (def. 1) means to convey or accompany to a place, while *take* means to remove or go with from a place: *Take* the books from the shelf and *bring* them to the office.

brink (bringk) *n.* 1 The upper edge of a steep place. 2 The edge; verge: the *brink* of despair. [< Scand.]

brink·man·ship (bringk′mən·ship) *n.* A policy of following a course of action to a point bordering on disaster.

bri·oche (brē·ōsh′, -osh′) *n.* A soft, sweet roll. [F]

bri·quette (bri·ket′) *n.* A block of compressed coal dust or charcoal, used as fuel. Also **bri·quet′.** [< F *brique* brick]

brisk (brisk) *adj.* 1 Quick; energetic; spirited. 2 Zestful; stimulating. 3 Active: *brisk* sales. [? < F *brusque* abrupt, sudden] —**brisk′ly** *adv.* —**brisk′ness** *n.*

bris·ket (bris′kit) *n.* 1 The breast of an animal. 2 A cut of meat from this part. [? < Scand.]

bris·tle (bris′əl) *n.* A short, stiff hair or similar part. —*v.* **·tled, ·tling** —*v.i.* 1 To erect the bristles. 2 To stand up stiffly, as bristles. 3 To be thickly set as if with bristles. 4 To show anger, irritation, etc. —*v.t.* 5 To erect as or like bristles. [< OE *byrst*] —**bris·tli·ness** (bris′lē·nis) *n.* —**bris·tly** (bris′lē) *adj.* **(·i·er, ·i·est)**

Brit. Britain; British.

Brit·ain (brit′n) *n.* GREAT BRITAIN.

Bri·tan·ni·a (bri·tan′yə, -tan′ē·ə) *n.* 1 Great Britain or the British Empire. 2 A female personification of Great Britain or the British Empire. [< L]

Bri·tan·nic (bri·tan′ik) *adj.* Of Great Britain; British.

britch·es (brich′iz) *n. pl. Informal* BREECHES.

Brit·i·cism (brit′ə·siz′əm) *n.* A verbal usage characteristic of the British.

Brit·ish (brit′ish) *adj.* Of or pertaining to Great Britain or the United Kingdom. —*n.* 1 The people of Great Britain: used with *the.* 2 The English language as used in Great Britain.

British America 1 Canada: also **British North America.** 2 Sometimes, all British possessions in or near North or South America.

Brit·ish·er (brit′ish·ər) *n.* A native or subject of Great Britain.

British thermal unit The quantity of heat required to raise the temperature of one pound of water one degree Fahrenheit.

Brit·on (brit′n) *n.* 1 A member of one of the Celtic tribes of ancient Britain. 2 A native or subject of Great Britain.

brit·tle (brit′l) *adj.* 1 Likely to break or snap; fragile. 2 Stiff or tense in manner. —*n.* A crisp candy made with sugar and nuts. [ME *britel*] —**brit′tle·ness** *n.*

bro. (*pl.* **bros.**) brother.

broach (brōch) *v.t.* 1 To introduce or mention for the first time, as a subject. 2 To pierce (a cask, etc.) to draw off liquid. —*n.* A pointed, tapering tool for boring or reaming. [< OF *broche* a spit] —**broach′er** *n.*

broad (brôd) *adj.* 1 Extended in lateral dimensions; wide. 2 Extensive; spacious. 3 Clear; full: *broad* daylight. 4 Wide in scope or range; comprehensive. 5 Liberal; tolerant. 6 Obvious; plain: a *broad* hint. 7 Not detailed or specific; general. 8 Coarse; ribald. 9 Strongly dialectal. 10 *Phonet.* Formed with the oral passage wide open and the tongue low and flat, as the *a* in *calm.* —*n.* 1 The broad part of anything. 2 *Slang* A woman: a disparaging term. —*adv.* Completely; fully. [< OE *brād*] —**broad′ly** *adv.* —**broad′·ness** *n.*

broad·ax (brôd′aks′) *n.* An ax with a broad edge and short handle. Also **broad′axe′.**

broad·cast (brôd′kast′, -käst′) *v.* **·cast** or **·casted, ·cast·ing** *v.t.* 1 To transmit over an area by radio or television. 2 To make known; disseminate. 3 To scatter, as seed, over a wide area. —*v.i.* 4 To transmit or take part in a broadcast program. —*adj.* 1 Of or for transmission by broadcasting. 2 Scattered widely, as seed. —*n.* 1 The transmitting of a radio or television program. 2 A program so transmitted. —*adv.* Over an extended area. —**broad′cast′er** *n.*

broad·cloth (brôd′klôth′, -kloth′) *n.* 1 A fine, smooth-surfaced wool cloth. 2 A closely woven fabric of silk, cotton, etc.

broad·en (brôd′n) *v.t.* & *v.i.* To make or become broad or broader.

broad-gauge (brôd′gāj′) *adj.* Having railroad tracks more than the standard 56½ inches apart. Also **broad′-gauged′.**

broad jump A jump for distance in an athletic contest.

broad·loom (brôd′lo͞om′) *n.* Carpeting woven on a wide loom. —*adj.* Woven on a wide loom.

broad-mind·ed (brôd′mīn′did) *adj.* Liberal or tolerant in beliefs and opinions. —**broad′-mind′ed′ly** *adv.* —**broad′-mind′ed·ness** *n.*

broad·side (brôd′sīd′) *n.* 1 **a** All the guns on one side of a man-of-war. **b** The simultaneous firing of such guns. 2 An abusive attack or denunciation. 3 A ship's side above the water line. 4 A large sheet of paper printed on one side: also **broad′sheet′.** —*adv.* With the side facing or turned toward something: The shell struck the ship *broadside.*

broad·sword (brôd′sôrd′, -sōrd′) *n.* A sword with a broad cutting blade.

broad·tail (brôd′tāl′) *n.* Fur made from the flat, glossy pelts of very young karakul lambs.

Broad·way (brôd′wā′) *n.* A street running north from lower Manhattan through New York City, famous for its entertainment district.

bro·cade (brō·kād′) *n.* A rich fabric with a raised interwoven design. —*v.t.* **·cad·ed, ·cad·ing** To weave (cloth) with a raised design. [< Med. L *broccare* embroider]

broc·co·li (brok′ə·lē) *n.* A plant related to cauliflower, having green, edible buds and stalks. [< Ital., pl. of *broccolo* cabbage sprout]

bro·chure (brō·sho͞or′) *n.* A pamphlet. [< F *brocher* to stitch]

bro·gan (brō′gən) *n.* A heavy ankle-high shoe. [< Ir. *brōg* shoe]

brogue[1] (brōg) *n.* A dialectal accent, esp. an Irish accent, in speaking English. [? < BROGUE[2]]

brogue[2] (brōg) *n.* 1 A heavy oxford shoe with decorative perforations. 2 A shoe of untanned hide formerly worn in Ireland and Scotland. [< Ir. *brōg* brogue (def. 2)]

broil[1] (broil) *v.t.* 1 To cook, as meat, by subjecting to direct heat. 2 To expose to great heat. —*v.i.* 3 To become cooked by broiling. 4 To be exposed to great heat. —*n.* 1 Something broiled. 2 A broiling heat. [< OF *bruller*]

broil[2] (broil) *n.* A noisy quarrel; brawl. —*v.i.* To engage in a broil; brawl. [< OF *brouiller* confuse]

broil·er (broi′lər) *n.* **1** A device for broiling. **2** A chicken suitable for broiling.

broke (brōk) *p.t. & archaic p.p.* of BREAK. —*adj. Informal* Without money; bankrupt.

bro·ken (brō′kən) *p.p.* of BREAK. —*adj.* **1** Shattered; fractured. **2** Not working; out of order. **3** Violated; disregarded: *broken* oaths. **4** Not continuous; interrupted. **5** Incomplete: a *broken* set. **6** Disordered; disrupted. **7** Rough or irregular. **8** Crushed, as in spirit. **9** Weakened; infirm. **10** Tamed; trained. **11** Imperfectly spoken: *broken* English. —**bro′ken·ly** *adv.* —**bro′ken·ness** *n.*

bro·ken-heart·ed (brō′kən·här′tid) *adj.* Overwhelmed by grief, despair, etc. —**bro′ken-heart′ed·ly** *adv.*

bro·ker (brō′kər) *n.* One who acts as a commissioned agent in negotiating contracts, buying and selling stocks, real estate, etc. [ME, peddler]

bro·ker·age (brō′kər·ij) *n.* The business or commission of a broker.

bro·mide (brō′mīd, -mid) *n.* **1** Any of various compounds of bromine with a metallic or organic radical, used in medicine, photography, anti-knock gasoline, etc. **2** A medicine, esp. a sedative, containing a bromide. **3** *Informal* A dull remark; platitude. —**bro·mid·ic** (brō·mid′ik) *adj.* [< BROM(INE) + -IDE]

bro·mine (brō′mēn) *n.* A reddish brown, heavy, liquid element (symbol Br) of the halogen group, with irritating fumes. [< Gk. *brōmos* stench + -INE] —**bro′mic** *adj.*

bron·chi (brong′kī) *pl.* of BRONCHUS.

bron·chi·al (brong′kē·əl) *adj.* Of or pertaining to the chief air passages of the lungs.

bronchial tubes The subdivisions of the trachea conveying air into the lungs.

bron·chi·tis (brong·kī′tis) *n.* Inflammation of the bronchial tubes, or, loosely, of the bronchi or trachea. [< Gk. *bronchos* windpipe + -ITIS] —**bron·chit·ic** (brong·kit′ik) *adj.*

bron·cho·scope (brong′kə·skōp) *n.* An instrument for inspecting or treating the interior of the bronchi.

bron·chus (brong′kəs) *n. pl.* **·chi** (-kī) One of the two forked branches of the trachea. [< Gk. *bronchos* windpipe]

bron·co (brong′kō) *n. pl.* **·cos** A small, wild, or partly broken horse of the w U.S. Also **bron′cho.** [< Sp., rough]

bron·co·bust·er (brong′kō·bus′tər) *n. Informal* One who breaks a bronco to the saddle. Also **bron′cho·bust′er.**

bron·to·sau·rus (bron′tə·sôr′əs) *n.* A huge, herbivorous

Brontosaurus

dinosaur of the Jurassic period. Also **bron′to·saur′.** [< Gk. *brontē* thunder + *sauros* lizard]

Bronx cheer *Slang* A derisive sound made by sticking out the tongue and vibrating the nearly closed lips by forcibly expelling breath.

bronze (bronz) *n.* **1** A reddish brown alloy of copper, esp. with tin. **2** The color of bronze. **3** A sculpture cast in bronze. —*v.* **bronzed, bronz·ing** *v.t.* **1** To color like or cover with bronze. —*v.i.* **2** To become brown or tan. [< Ital. *bronzo*] —**bronz′y** *adj.* **(·i·er, ·i·est)**

Bronze Age A period between the Stone Age and the Iron Age during which implements were made of bronze.

Bronze Star A U.S. military decoration awarded for heroic or meritorious achievement.

brooch (brōch, brōōch) *n.* An ornamental pin fastened with a clasp. [Var. of BROACH, *n.*]

brood (brōōd) *n.* **1** All the young birds of a single hatching. **2** The children of a household. —*v.t.* **1** To sit upon or incubate (eggs). **2** To protect (young) by or as by covering with the wings. —*v.i.* **3** To sit on eggs; incubate. **4** To think about gloomily and persistently; ponder moodily. —*adj.* Kept for breeding: a *brood* mare. [< OE *brod*]

brood·er (brōō′dər) *n.* **1** A warmed shelter for chicks reared without a hen. **2** One who broods.

brood·y (brōō′dē) *adj.* **brood·i·er, brood·i·est** **1** Inclined to sit on eggs, as a hen. **2** Moody.

brook[1] (brŏŏk) *n.* A small, natural stream. [< OE *brōc*]

brook[2] (brŏŏk) *v.t.* To put up with; tolerate: He will *brook* no disobedience. [< OE *brūcan* use, enjoy]

brook·let (brŏŏk′lit) *n.* A little brook.

brook trout A speckled freshwater game fish of North America.

broom (brōōm, brŏŏm) *n.* **1** A brush with a long handle, used for sweeping. **2** Any of various leguminous shrubs with flexible shoots and usu. yellow flowers. —*v.t.* To sweep with a broom. [< OE *brōm*]

broom·corn (brōōm′kôrn′, brŏŏm′-) *n.* A grass used to make brooms and brushes.

broom·stick (brōōm′stik′, brŏŏm′-) *n.* The handle of a broom.

broth (brôth, broth) *n.* Thin soup consisting of the water in which meat, vegetables, etc., have been boiled. [< OE]

broth·el (broth′əl, broth′-, brôth′əl, brôth′-) *n.* A house of prostitution. [< OE *brēothan* to ruin, decay]

broth·er (bruth′ər) *n. pl.* **broth·ers** or *esp. in formal or religious use* **breth·ren** **1** A male person having the same parents as another person. **2** A male of the lower animals having one parent in common with another. **3 a** HALF BROTHER. **b** BROTHER-IN-LAW. **c** A foster brother. **4** A fellow man. **5** A man or boy allied to another or others by race, creed, membership in a society, etc. **6** A lay member of a male Christian religious order. [< OE *brōthor*]

broth·er·hood (bruth′ər·hŏŏd) *n.* **1** The condition or relationship of being brothers. **2** A group or organization of men having a close relationship, common interests, etc.

broth·er-in-law (bruth′ər·in·lô′) *n. pl.* **broth·ers-in-law** **1** The brother of one's husband or wife. **2** One's sister's husband. **3** The husband of one's husband's or wife's sister.

broth·er·ly (bruth′ər·lē) *adj.* Of or typical of a brother or brothers; fraternal; affectionate. —**broth′er·li·ness** *n.*

brougham (brōōm, brōō′əm, brō′əm) *n.* A closed, four-wheeled carriage or automobile with an uncovered driver's seat. [< Lord Henry *Brougham,* 1778–1868, British statesman]

Brougham

brought (brôt) *p.t. & p.p.* of BRING.

brow (brou) *n.* **1** The forehead. **2** An eyebrow. **3** The countenance in general. **4** The upper edge of a cliff, precipice, etc. [< OE *brū*]

brow·beat (brou′bēt′) *v.t.* **·beat, ·beat·en, ·beat·ing** To intimidate by an overbearing manner. —**Syn.** cow, bully, hector.

brown (broun) *n.* **1** A color, as of coffee or chocolate, combining red, yellow, and black. **2** A pigment, dye, etc., of this color. —*adj.* **1** Of the color brown. **2** Tanned by the sun. —*v.t. & v.i.* **1** To make or become brown. **2** To cook until brown. [< OE *brūn*] —**brown′ish** *adj.* —**brown′·ness** *n.*

brown Betty A baked pudding made with bread crumbs, apples, sugar, etc.

Brown·i·an movement (brou′nē·ən) The rapid random movement of small particles suspended in fluids. Also **Brownian motion.** [< Robert *Brown,* 1773–1858, English botanist, who discovered it]

brown·ie (brou′nē) *n.* **1** A good-natured elflike sprite. **2** A small, flat, usu. square chocolate cake. [< BROWN]

Brown·ie (brou′nē) *n.* A junior girl scout of the age group seven through nine.

brown-out (broun′out′) *n.* A partial dimming of lights or loss of electric power.

brown rice Unpolished rice grains.

Brown Shirt **1** A member of the storm troops in Germany under Hitler. **2** A Nazi.

brown·stone (broun′stōn′) *n.* 1 A brownish red sandstone. 2 A house built of or faced with this.
brown study A state of deep, preoccupied thought.
brown sugar Partly or wholly unrefined sugar.
browse (brouz) *v.* **browsed, brows·ing** —*v.i.* 1 To feed on leaves, twigs, etc. 2 To read or inspect casually. —*v.t.* 3 To nibble at (leaves, twigs, etc.). —*n.* Leaves, twigs, etc., eaten by animals. [< MF *broust* bud, sprout] —**brows′er** *n.*
bru·in (brōō′in) *n.* A bear. [< Du., brown]
bruise (brōōz) *v.* **bruised, bruis·ing** *v.t.* 1 To injure, as by a blow, without breaking the surface of the skin. 2 To dent or mar the surface of. 3 To hurt or offend slightly, as feelings. 4 To crush, as with a mortar and pestle. —*v.i.* 5 To become discolored as the result of a blow. —*n.* A surface injury, usu. with discoloration of the skin. [Fusion of OE *brȳsan* crush and OF *bruisier* break, shatter]
bruis·er (brōō′zər) *n.* A powerfully built fellow.
bruit (brōōt) *v.t.* To noise abroad; talk about. [< OF *bruit* noise]
brunch (brunch) *n.* A meal combining breakfast and lunch. [Blend of BREAKFAST and LUNCH]
Bru·nei (brōō·nī′) *n.* A sultanate under British protection on the N part of Borneo, 2,226 sq. mi., cap. Brunei.
bru·net (brōō·net′) *adj.* 1 Dark in color, as the hair or complexion. 2 Having dark hair and often dark complexion and eyes. —*n.* A man or boy with dark hair, complexion, etc. [< F *brun* brown]
bru·nette (brōō·net′) *adj.* BRUNET. —*n.* A woman or girl with dark hair, complexion, etc. [< F *brun* brown]
brunt (brunt) *n.* The main force or impact of a blow, attack, etc. [?]
brush[1] (brush) *n.* 1 An implement having bristles, hair, wires, etc., fixed in a handle or a back, and used for applying paint, removing dirt, grooming the hair, etc. 2 The act of brushing. 3 A light, grazing touch. 4 A short, brisk fight; skirmish. 5 Something resembling a brush, as the bushy tail of a fox. 6 An electrical conductor bearing on the commutator of a dynamo or motor. —*v.t.* 1 To sweep, polish, smooth, paint, etc., with a brush. 2 To remove with or as with a brush. 3 To touch lightly in passing. 4 To refuse to consider; dismiss: used with *aside, away,* or *off.* —*v.i.* 5 To move with a slight contact: to *brush* past someone. —**brush up** To refresh one's knowledge or skill. [< OF *brosse*]
brush[2] (brush) *n.* 1 A growth of small trees and shrubs. 2 Wooded country sparsely settled; backwoods. 3 Cut or broken-off branches; brushwood. [< OF *broche*]
brush-off (brush′ôf′, -of′) *n. Informal* An abrupt or contemptuously quick refusal or dismissal.
brush·wood (brush′wōōd′) *n.* 1 Cut or broken-off branches. 2 A dense, thicketlike growth.
brusque (brusk, *esp. Brit.* brōōsk) *adj.* Blunt or gruff, esp. so as to cause offense; rudely abrupt. Also **brusk.** [< Ital. *brusco* rough, rude] —**brusque′ly** *adv.* —**brusque′ness** *n.* —**Syn.** curt, short, bluff.
Brus·sels sprouts (brus′əlz) 1 A cultivated variety of cabbage having stems covered with sprouts like little cabbages. 2 The small edible heads of this plant.
bru·tal (brōōt′l) *adj.* 1 Of or typical of a brute; savagely cruel; unfeeling. 2 Harsh; insufferable; punishing: *brutal* weather; He maintained a *brutal* pace. [< L *brutus* stupid] —**bru′tal·ly** *adv.* —**Syn.** bestial, barbarous, inhuman, savage.
bru·tal·i·ty (brōō·tal′ə·tē) *n. pl.* **·ties** 1 The state or quality of being brutal. 2 A brutal act.
bru·tal·ize (brōō′təl·īz) *v.t. & v.i.* **·ized, ·iz·ing** To make or become brutal. —**bru′tal·i·za′tion** *n.*
brute (brōōt) *n.* 1 An animal as distinguished from a human being. 2 A brutal person. —*adj.* 1 Of or typical of a brute; animal. 2 Merely physical: *brute* force. [< L *brutus* stupid]
brut·ish (brōō′tish) *adj.* Resembling or characteristic of a brute; gross; coarse. —**brut′ish·ly** *adv.* —**brut′ish·ness** *n.*
bry·ol·o·gy (brī·ol′ə·jē) *n.* The branch of botany that treats of bryophytes. [< Gk. *bryon* moss + -LOGY] —**bry·o·log·i·cal** (brī′ə·loj′i·kəl) *adj.* —**bry·ol′o·gist** *n.*
bry·o·phyte (brī′ə·fīt) *n.* Any moss or liverwort. [< Gk. *bryon* moss + *phyton* plant] —**bry′o·phyt′ic** (-fit′ik) *adj.*
B.S., B. Sc. Bachelor of Science.
B/S bags; bales.
B/S, b.s. bill of sale.
b.s. balance sheet.
B.S.A. Boy Scouts of America.
B.S. Ed. Bachelor of Science in Education.
B.T., B. Th. Bachelor of Theology.
Bt. Baronet.
Btry. Battery.
BTU, B.T.U., Btu, B.th.u. British thermal unit.
bu. bureau; bushel; bushels.
bub·ble (bub′əl) *n.* 1 A rounded film of cohesive liquid filled with air or other gas. 2 A globule of air or other gas confined in a liquid or solid. 3 A usu. transparent glass or plastic dome. 4 Something insubstantial or delusive. 5 The process or sound of bubbling. —*v.* **·bled, ·bling** *v.i.* 1 To form or rise in bubbles. 2 To move or flow with a gurgling sound. 3 To behave in a lively, irrepressible manner. —*v.t.* 4 To cause to bubble. 5 To utter as by bubbling. [ME *buble*] —**bub′bly** *adj.* (**·i·er, ·i·est**)
bubble gum Chewing gum that can be blown into bubbles.
bu·bo (byōō′bō) *n. pl.* **bu·boes** An inflammatory swelling of a lymph gland, esp. in the groin or armpit. [< Gk. *boubōn* groin] —**bu·bon·ic** (byōō·bon′ik) *adj.*
bubonic plague A contagious, often fatal disease, characterized by fever, vomiting, diarrhea, and buboes, caused by a bacterium transmitted by fleas from infected rats.
buc·cal (buk′əl) *adj.* Of or pertaining to the cheek or mouth cavity. [< L *bucca* cheek]
buc·ca·neer (buk′ə·nir′) *n.* A pirate or freebooter. [< F *boucanier*]
buck[1] (buk) *n.* 1 A male deer, rabbit, etc. 2 A sudden upward leap, as of a horse. 3 A dashing young fellow. —*v.i.* 1 To leap upward suddenly, as a horse trying to dislodge a rider. 2 To charge with the head down. 3 To move with jerks and jolts. —*v.t.* 4 To throw by bucking. 5 To butt with the head. 6 To resist stubbornly; struggle against. 7 To charge into (the opposing line in football). —**buck for** *Slang* To strive for (a raise, promotion, etc.). —**buck up** *Informal* To cheer up. —*adj.* Being of the lowest grade within a class: *buck* sergeant. [Fusion of OE *buc* he-goat and *bucca* male deer] —**buck′er** *n.*
buck[2] (buk) *n. Slang* A dollar. [< BUCKSKIN]
buck[3] (buk) *n.* A marker formerly used in poker to indicate the next dealer. —**pass the buck** *Informal* To shift responsibility, blame, etc., to someone else. [?]
buck and wing An intricate, fast tap dance.
buck·a·roo (buk′ə·rōō′, buk′ə·rōō) *n.* A cowboy. [< Sp. *vaquero* cowboy]
buck·board (buk′bôrd′, -bōrd′) *n.* A four-wheeled open carriage with the seat resting on a flexible floorboard. [< BUCK, *v.* + BOARD]
buck·et (buk′it) *n.* 1 A cylindrical container with a curved handle at the top; a pail. 2 As much as a bucket will hold: also **buck′et·ful′**. 3 A scooplike part, as of a steam shovel. —*v.t.* 1 To draw or carry in a bucket. —*v.i.* 2 To move along rapidly. —**kick the bucket** *Slang* To die. [< OF *buket* kind of tub]
bucket seat A single seat with a rounded, usu. padded back, as in a sports car or airplane.
buck·eye (buk′ī′) *n.* 1 Any of several North American species of horse chestnut. 2 The glossy brown nut of such a tree. [< BUCK[1] + EYE]
buck·le[1] (buk′əl) *n.* 1 A metal clasp for fastening together ends of a strap, belt, etc. 2 An ornament resembling this, as on a shoe. —*v.t. & v.i.* **·led, ·ling** To fasten or be fastened with a buckle. —**buckle down** To apply oneself vigorously or industriously. [< F *boucle* cheek strap, boss of a shield]
buck·le[2] (buk′əl) *v.t. & v.i.* **·led, ·ling** 1 To bend, warp, or crumple, as under pressure. 2 To give way; collapse. —*n.* A bend, bulge, wrinkle, etc. [< F *boucler* bulge]
buck·ler (buk′lər) *n.* 1 A small, round shield. 2 Something that defends or protects. [< OF *boucler* having a boss]
buck private *Informal* A private of the lowest rank in the U.S. Army.
buck·ram (buk′rəm) *n.* A coarse, stiffened cotton fabric, used for bookbinding, lining garments, etc. [< OF *boquerant*]

buck·saw (buk′sô′) *n.* A saw set in an adjustable H-shaped frame.

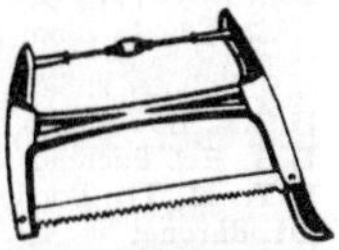

Bucksaw

buck·shot (buk′shot′) *n.* Shot of a large size, used in hunting deer and other large game.

buck·skin (buk′skin′) *n.* **1** Soft, strong, yellowish leather made from the skins of deer or sheep. **2** *pl.* Breeches, etc., made from this leather.

buck·thorn (buk′thôrn′) *n.* Any of several sometimes thorny trees and shrubs with small greenish flowers.

buck·tooth (buk′to͞oth′) *n. pl.* **·teeth** A projecting front tooth. **—buck′toothed′** *adj.*

buck·wheat (buk′ʰwēt′) *n.* **1** A plant with triangular seeds used as fodder and for flour. **2** Its seeds. **3** The flour. [< OE *bōc* beech + WHEAT]

bu·col·ic (byo͞o·kol′ik) *adj.* **1** Of or concerning shepherds; pastoral. **2** Rustic; rural. —*n.* A pastoral poem. [< Gk. *boukolos* herdsman] **—bu·col′i·cal·ly** *adv.*

bud (bud) *n.* **1 a** An undeveloped stem, branch, or shoot of a plant, with rudimentary leaves or unexpanded flowers. **b** The state or stage of budding. **2** A budlike projection or part. **3** An early or undeveloped state. **—nip in the bud** To stop in the initial stage. —*v.* **bud·ded, bud·ding** *v.i.* **1** To put forth buds. **2** To begin to grow or develop. —*v.t.* **3** To cause to bud. **4** To graft by inserting a bud of (a plant) into another plant. [ME *budde*] **—bud′der** *n.*

Bud·dhism (bo͝od′iz·əm, bo͞o′diz-) *n.* A mystical and ascetic religious faith of E Asia, founded in northern India by Buddha in the sixth century B.C., teaching that the ideally perfect and happy state of Nirvana can be attained by mental and sensory discipline and purification. **—Bud′dhist** *adj., n.* **—Bud·dhis′tic** or **·ti·cal** *adj.*

bud·dy (bud′ē) *n. pl.* **·dies** *Informal* Pal; chum.

budge (buj) *v.t. & v.i.* **budged, budg·ing 1** To move or stir slightly. **2** To give in or cause to give in. [< F *bouger* stir, move]

budg·et (buj′it) *n.* **1** A statement of probable revenue and expenditure and of financial proposals for the ensuing year. **2** A summary of probable income for a given period, with approximate allowances for certain expenditures. **3** A collection or stock of items. —*v.t.* **1** To determine in advance the expenditure of (time, money, etc.) over a period of time. **2** To put on or into a budget. —*v.i.* **3** To make a budget. [< L *bulga* leather bag] **—budg·et·ar·y** (buj′ə·ter′ē) *adj.* **—budg′et·er** *n.*

buff[1] (buf) *n.* **1** A soft, flexible, undyed leather, made from the skins of buffalo, elk, oxen, etc. **2** Its color, a light yellow. **3** A coat made of buff leather. **4** *Informal* The bare skin; the nude. **5** A stick or wheel covered with leather, velvet, etc., and used in polishing. —*adj.* **1** Made of buff. **2** Light brownish yellow. —*v.t.* To clean or polish with or as with a buff. [< OF *buffle* buffalo]

buff[2] (buf) *v.t.* **1** To deaden the shock of. —*v.i.* **2** To act as a buffer; absorb or reduce shock. [< OF *buffe* blow]

buff[3] (buf) *n. Informal* An enthusiast or devotee: a theater *buff.* [< BUFF[1], after the buff coats worn by certain volunteer firemen]

buf·fa·lo (buf′ə·lō) *n. pl.* **·loes** or **·los** or **·lo 1** Any of several wild or domesticated oxlike mammals, as the water buffalo, etc. **2** The North American bison. —*v.t. Slang* To overawe; hoodwink. [< Gk. *boubalos* buffalo]

Cape buffalo

buffalo grass A low, creeping, prairie grass, used for forage.

buff·er[1] (buf′ər) *n.* One who or that which cleans or polishes with a buff.

buff·er[2] (buf′ər) *n.* **1** Something that lessens or absorbs the shock of an impact. **2** A person or thing that reduces friction, as between antagonists. **3** A substance that tends to prevent change in acidity or alkalinity. —*v.t.* To stabilize (a solution) by adding a buffer. **—buff′ered** *adj.*

buffer state A small country situated between two larger rival powers and regarded as lessening the possibility of open hostilities between them.

buf·fet[1] (bo͞o·fā′, bə·fā′, *Brit.* buf′it) *n.* **1** A sideboard for china, glassware, etc. **2** A counter for serving refreshments. **3** An informal meal in which guests serve themselves from a table or buffet. [F]

buf·fet[2] (buf′it) *v.t.* **1** To strike or cuff, as with the hand. **2** To strike again and again; knock about, as if by blows: *buffeted* by high winds. **3** To force (a way) by pushing or striking. —*v.i.* **4** To struggle. **5** To force a way. —*n.* A blow; cuff. [< OF *buffe* blow, slap] **—buf′fet·er** *n.*

buf·foon (bu·fo͞on′, bə-) *n.* **1** One given to jokes, coarse pranks, etc.; a clown. **2** A loutish or inept person. [< Ital. *buffone* clown] **—buf·foon′er·y** *n.* **—buf·foon′ish** *adj.*

bug (bug) *n.* **1** Any of a large variety of insects with piercing and sucking mouth parts. **2** Loosely, any insect. **3** *Informal* A pathogenic microorganism. **4** *Informal* Any small but troublesome defect in a motor, machine, etc. **5** *Slang* An enthusiast. **6** *Informal* A miniature electronic microphone, used in wiretapping, etc. —*v.* **bugged, bug·ging** *v.i.* **1** To stare; stick out: said of eyes. —*v.t.* **2** *Informal* To fix an electronic eavesdropping device in (a room, etc.) or to (a wire, etc). **3** *Slang* To annoy or anger; also to bewilder or puzzle. **—bug off** *Slang* Go away! Get lost! **—bug out** *Slang* To quit, esp. hastily or ignominiously. [?]

bug·a·boo (bug′ə·bo͞o) *n. pl.* **·boos** BUGBEAR. [< ME *bugge* scarecrow + BOO]

bug·bear (bug′bâr′) *n.* An imaginary object of terror; a specter. [< ME *bugge* scarecrow + BEAR[2]]

bug·gy[1] (bug′ē) *n. pl.* **·gies 1** A light, horse-drawn vehicle. **2** A baby carriage. [?]

bug·gy[2] (bug′ē) *adj.* **·gi·er, ·gi·est 1** Infested with bugs. **2** *Slang* Crazy. **—bug′gi·ness** *n.*

bug·house (bug′hous′) *Slang n.* An asylum for the insane. —*adj.* Crazy; insane.

bu·gle (byo͞o′gəl) *n.* A brass, trumpetlike instrument, usu. without keys or valves. —*v.t. & v.i.* **bu·gled, bu·gling 1** To summon with a bugle. **2** To sound a bugle. [< L *buculus,* dim. of *bos* ox; because first made from the horns of oxen] **—bu′gler** *n.*

buhl (bo͞ol) *n.* Metal or tortoise shell inlaid in furniture; also, cabinetwork so decorated. Also **buhl′work′**. [< A. C. *Boule,* 1642–1732, French cabinetmaker]

build (bild) *v.* **built** (*Archaic* **build·ed**), **build·ing** *v.t.* **1** To construct, erect, or make by assembling separate parts or materials. **2** To establish and increase: often with *up:* to *build* up a business. **3** To make a basis for; found: immigrants who *built* a new life. —*v.i.* **4** To construct a house, building, etc. **5** To be in the business of building. **6** To grow in intensity, force, etc.: often with *up.* **7** To base or form an idea, theory, etc.: with *on* or *upon.* **—build up 1** To renew or strengthen, as health. **2** To fill, as an area, with houses. —*n.* The manner in which a person or thing is shaped or formed; form; figure: a good *build;* a slight or husky *build.* [< OE *byldan*]

build·er (bil′dər) *n.* **1** One who or that which builds. **2** One whose occupation is building.

build·ing (bil′ding) *n.* **1** A structure, usu. having walls and a roof, as a house, a place of work, etc. **2** The occupation, business, or art of constructing.

build·up (bild′up′) *n.* **1** A gradual accumulation or increase. **2** *Informal* An enhancement of reputation, as by praise or favorable publicity. Also **build′-up′**.

built-in (bilt′in′) *adj.* **1** Part of or permanently attached to the structure: *built-in* bookcases. **2** By the nature of things; inherent: a *built-in* advantage.

bulb (bulb) *n.* **1** An underground plant stem having a cluster of thickened leaves above and sending down roots, as in the onion, lily, etc. **2** An underground stem resembling a bulb, as a corm, tuber, or rhizome. **3** An enlargement resembling a plant bulb, as the end of a thermometer tube. **4** An incandescent electric lamp. [< Gk. *bolbos* bulbous root] —**bul·ba·ceous** (bul·bā′shəs), **bul′bar, bul′bous** *adj.* • See INCANDESCENT.

Bul·gar·i·a (bul·gâr′ē·ə, bo͝ol-) *n.* A republic of SE Europe, 42,796 sq. mi., cap. Sofia. • See map at BALKAN STATES.

Bul·gar·i·an (bul·gâr′ē·ən, bo͝ol-) *adj.* Of or pertaining to Bulgaria, its people, or their language. —*n.* **1** A native or citizen of Bulgaria. **2** The Slavic language of Bulgaria.

bulge (bulj) *v.t.* & *v.i.* **bulged, bulg·ing** To swell out; make or be protuberant. —*n.* Something that swells out or protrudes. [<OF *boulge*] —**bulg′y** *adj.* —**bulg′i·ness** *n.*

bu·lim·i·a (byo͞o·lim′ē·ə) *n.* A psychological disorder marked by alternating periods of uncontrolled eating and induced vomiting. [<Gk. *boulimia* great hunger]

bulk (bulk) *n.* **1** Mass, volume, or size, esp. if large or great. **2** A large body, esp. a human body. **3** The largest or principal part. —**in bulk** Loose; not boxed or packaged. —*v.i.* **1** To have an appearance of largeness or weight. **2** To be of importance: to *bulk* large in his thought. —*v.t.* **3** To cause to expand or grow large. [<ON *būlki* heap, cargo]

bulk·head (bulk′hed′) *n.* **1** Any of various partitions in a ship, airplane, etc., used as a protection against the spread of water, fire, etc. **2** A partition of stone or wood to keep back earth, gas, etc., as in a mine. **3** A framework opening into a staircase or shaft. —**bulk′head′ed** *adj.*

bulk·y (bul′kē) *adj.* **bulk·i·er, bulk·i·est 1** Marked by great bulk; massive. **2** Clumsy; ungainly.

bull[1] (bo͝ol) *n.* **1** The male of cattle or of some other animals, as of the elephant, moose, giraffe, whale, seal, etc. **2** A dealer who seeks or expects higher prices, and buys stocks or bonds accordingly. **3** One whose actions or looks suggest a bull. **4** *Slang* A policeman. **5** *Slang* Exaggerated or nonsensical talk. —*v.t.* **1** To attempt to raise the price of or in. **2** To push or force (a way). —*v.i.* **3** To go up in price: said of stocks, etc. —*adj.* **1** Male. **2** Large; bull-like. **3** Going up or advancing: a *bull* market. [OE *bola*]

bull[2] (bo͝ol) *n.* An official edict or decree issued by the Pope. [<L *bulla* edict, seal]

Bull (bo͝ol) *n.* TAURUS.

bull·dog (bo͝ol′dôg′, -dog′) *n.* A medium-sized, short-haired, powerful dog, originally bred to bait bulls. —*adj.* Resembling a bulldog; tenacious. —*v.t.* *Informal* To throw (a steer) by gripping its horns and twisting its neck.

bull·doze (bo͝ol′dōz′) *v.t.* **·dozed, ·doz·ing 1** *Slang* To intimidate; bully. **2** To clear, dig, scrape, etc., with a bulldozer. **3** *Slang* To force in a coarse, pushing manner. [?<BULL, *adj.* + DOSE]

bull·doz·er (bo͝ol′dō′zər) *n.* **1** A powerful tractor with a heavy plowing blade, used for moving soil, cleaning debris, etc. **2** *Slang* One who bulldozes.

bul·let (bo͝ol′it) *n.* **1** A small projectile for a firearm. **2** Any small ball. [<F *boule* ball]

bul·le·tin (bo͝ol′ə·tən) *n.* **1** A brief news item, usu. of special or immediate interest. **2** A periodical publication, as of the proceedings of a society. —*v.t.* To make public by bulletin. [<L *bulla* edict] —**bul′le·tin·ist** *n.*

bul·let·proof (bo͝ol′it·pro͞of′) *adj.* Not penetrable by bullets: a *bulletproof* vest.

bull·fight (bo͝ol′fīt′) *n.* A spectacle held in an arena and marked by combat between men and a bull, which is goaded and usu. killed, traditional in Hispanic countries. —**bull′fight′ing, bull′fight′er** *n.*

bull·finch (bo͝ol′finch′) *n.* A European songbird having a short, stout bill and red breast. [<BULL, *adj.* + FINCH]

bull·frog (bo͝ol′frog′, -frôg′) *n.* A large frog with a deep hoarse voice.

bull·head (bo͝ol′hed′) *n.* **1** Any of various catfishes, as the horned pout. **2** An obstinate person.

bull·head·ed (bo͝ol′hed′id) *adj.* Obstinate; stubborn.

bull·horn (bo͝ol′hôrn′) *n.* An electrical, hand-held voice amplifier resembling a megaphone.

bul·lion (bo͝ol′yən) *n.* Gold or silver uncoined or in mass, as in ingots. [<AF *bullion*]

bull·ish (bo͝ol′ish) *adj.* **1** Like a bull, as in size. **2** Characterized by or suggesting a trend toward higher prices, as in the stock market; also, hopeful of such a trend. **3** Confidently optimistic. —**bull′ish·ly** *adv.* —**bull′ish·ness** *n.*

bul·lock (bo͝ol′ək) *n.* A gelded bull; a steer or an ox. [<OE *bulluc*]

bull·pen (bo͝ol′pen′) *n.* **1** An enclosure for bulls. **2** *Informal* A large room for temporary detention of prisoners. **3** In baseball, an area near the playing field where pitchers who may be called upon to enter a game can practice.

bull·ring (bo͝ol′ring′) *n.* A circular enclosure for bullfights.

bull session *Informal* An informal discussion.

bull's-eye (bo͝olz′ī′) *n.* **1** The center of a target, or a shot that hits it. **2** Anything that exactly achieves a specific goal or result. **3** A thick, circular, glass window.

bull terrier A short-haired white terrier crossbred from bulldog, terrier, and pointer breeds.

bull·whip (bo͝ol′hwip′) *n.* A long, tough whip used by teamsters.

bul·ly[1] (bo͝ol′ē) *n. pl.* **bul·lies** A person who likes to hurt or intimidate those weaker than himself. —*adj.* **bul·li·er, bul·li·est 1** *Informal* Excellent, admirable, **2** Jolly; dashing; gallant. —*interj.* Well done! —*v.* **bul·lied, bul·ly·ing** *v.t.* **1** To coerce by threats; intimidate. —*v.i.* **2** To be quarrelsome and blustering. [?]

bul·ly[2] (bo͝ol′ē) *n.* Canned or pickled beef. Also **bul′ly·beef′** (-bēf′). [?<F *bouillir* boil]

bul·rush (bo͝ol′rush′) *n.* **1** Any of various tall marsh plants having brown spikes of tiny flowers, as the cattail and certain sedges. **2** Papyrus. *Exodus* 2:3. [<BULL[1], *adj.* + RUSH]

bul·wark (bo͝ol′wərk) *n.* **1** A defensive wall or rampart. **2** A person or thing considered as a strong support or defense. **3** *Usu. pl.* The raised side of a ship, above the upper deck. —*v.t.* To fortify with, or as with, a bulwark. [<MHG *bolwerc*]

bum (bum) *n.* *Informal* **1** A shiftless, often drunken loafer or beggar. **2** A hobo; tramp. **3** An irresponsible devotee: a ski *bum.* —*adj.* **bum·mer, bum·mest** *Slang* **1** Bad; inferior. **2** Ailing. —*v.* **bum·med, bum·ming** *Informal* *v.i.* **1** To live by sponging from others. **2** To loaf. —*v.t.* **3** To get by begging. [Short for *bummer*, alter. of G *bummler* loafer, dawdler] —**bum′mer** *n.*

bum·ble·bee (bum′bəl·bē′) *n.* Any of certain large, hairy, social bees.

bum·bling (bum′bling) *adj.* Awkward and inept. [<BUNGLE]

Bumblebee

bump (bump) *v.t.* **1** To come into contact with; knock into. **2** To cause to knock into or against. **3** *Informal* To displace, as from a position or seat. —*v.i.* **4** To come into contact; collide. **5** To move with jerks and jolts. **6** *Slang* To do a bump (def. 3). —*n.* **1** An impact or collision; a jolt. **2** A swelling, protuberance, or rough part. **3** *Slang* A sharp forward movement of the pelvis, as in a striptease. [Imit.]

bump·er[1] (bum′pər) *n.* A guard on the front or rear of an automobile to absorb the shock of collision.

bump·er[2] (bum′pər) *n.* A cup or glass filled to the brim. —*adj.* Unusually full or large: a *bumper* crop. [?]

bump·kin (bump′kin) *n.* An awkward, unsophisticated person from the country. [?<Du. *boomkin* little tree, block]

bump·tious (bump′shəs) *adj.* Aggressively and offensively conceited.[?] —**bump′tious·ly** *adj.* —**bump′tious·ness** *n.*

bump·y (bum′pē) *adj.* **bump·i·er, bump·i·est 1** Having bumps. **2** Producing jolts or bounces: a *bumpy* ride. —**bump′i·ly** *adv.* —**bump′i·ness** *n.*

bun (bun) *n.* **1** A small bread roll, usu. sweetened or spiced. **2** A roll of hair worn at the nape of the neck. [ME *bunne*]

bunch (bunch) *n.* **1** A group of usu. like objects growing or fastened together. **2** *Informal* A group or cluster, as of people. —*v.t.* & *v.i.* **1** To make into or form bunches or groups. **2** To gather, as in pleats or folds. [ME *bonche, bunche*]

bun·co (bung′kō) *n. pl.* **·cos** *Informal* A swindling game in which confederates join to rob a stranger. —*v.t.* **·coed, ·co·ing** To swindle or bilk. [Prob.<Sp. *banco*, a card game]

bun·combe (bung′kəm) *n.* Empty, bombastic talk or speechmaking; humbug. [<*Buncombe* County, N.C., whose Congressman (1819–21) often insisted on making empty, unimportant speeches "for Buncombe"]

bun·dle (bun′dəl) *n.* 1 A number of things or a quantity of anything bound together. 2 A parcel or package. 3 A group; collection. 4 *Slang* A large sum of money. —*v.* **·dled, ·dling** *v.t.* 1 To tie, roll, or otherwise secure in a bundle. 2 To send away in haste: with *away, off, out,* or *into.* —*v.i.* 3 To leave or move hastily. 4 To practice bundling. — **bundle up** To dress warmly for outdoors. [< MDu. *bond* group] —**bun′dler** *n.*

bun·dling (bun′dling) *n.* An old courting custom, prevalent in New England, in which sweethearts lay or slept together in bed without undressing.

bung (bung) *n.* 1 A stopper for the hole in a keg, barrel, etc. 2 BUNGHOLE. —*v.t.* 1 To close with or as with a bung. 2 *Slang* To damage; maul: with *up.* [< MDu. *bonghe*]

bun·ga·low (bung′gə·lō) *n.* 1 In India, a one-storied house with wide verandas. 2 A small house or cottage. [< Hind. *banglā* Bengalese]

bung·hole (bung′hōl′) *n.* A hole in a keg or barrel from which liquid is tapped.

bun·gle (bung′gəl) *v.t. & v.i.* **·gled, ·gling** To do (something) badly; botch. —*n.* An imperfect job or performance; botch. —**bun′gler** *n.* [? < Scand.]

bun·ion (bun′yən) *n.* A painful swelling of the bursa at the base of the great toe. [? <OF *bugne* swelling]

bunk[1] (bungk) *n.* 1 A small compartment, shelf, or recess, used as a sleeping place. 2 *Informal* Any bed, esp. a small one. —*v.i.* 1 To sleep in a bunk or bed. 2 *Informal* To sleep overnight, esp. in makeshift accommodations. —*v.t.* 3 To provide with a bunk or place to sleep. [?]

bunk[2] (bungk) *n. Slang* Inflated or empty speech; balderdash. [Short for BUNCOMBE]

bun·ker (bung′kər) *n.* 1 A large bin or tank, as for fuel on a ship. 2 In golf, a sandy hollow or a mound of earth serving as an obstacle. 3 A steel and concrete fortification, usu. underground. —*v.i.* 1 To fill the bunkers of a ship. — *v.t.* 2 In golf, to drive (a ball) into a bunker. [?]

bunk·house (bungk′hous′) *n.* A structure used as sleeping quarters.

bun·ko (bung′kō) *n. pl.* **·kos** BUNCO.

bun·kum (bung′kəm) *n.* BUNCOMBE.

bun·ny (bun′ē) *n. pl.* **·nies** A rabbit. [?]

Bun·sen burner (bun′sən) An adjustable gas burner used in laboratories to produce a small, hot flame. [<R. W. E. *Bunsen,* 1811–99, German inventor]

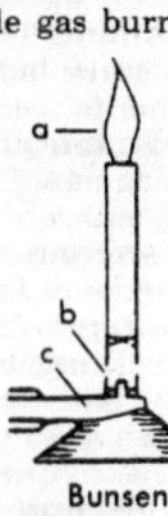

Bunsen burner a. flame. b. air. c. gas.

bunt (bunt) *v.t. & v.i.* 1 To butt, as with horns. 2 In baseball, to bat (the ball) lightly to the infield, without swinging the bat. —*n.* 1 A push or butt. 2 In baseball: a The act of bunting. b A bunted ball. [? < Celtic]

bunt·ing[1] (bun′ting) *n.* 1 A light fabric used for flags. 2 Flags. 3 Lengths of fabric decorated as a flag. 4 A hooded, outer garment for a baby. [?]

bunt·ing[2] (bun′ting) *n.* Any of various brightly colored, small birds related to the finches. [ME *bountyng*]

buoy (boi, bo͞o′ē) *n.* 1 A float moored near a dangerous rock or shoal or at the edge of a channel, as a guide to navigators. 2 LIFE BUOY. —*v.t.* 1 To keep from sinking in a liquid; keep afloat. 2 To sustain the courage or heart of; encourage: usu. with *up.* 3 To mark, as a channel, with buoys. [< MDu. *boeie*]

buoy·an·cy (boi′ən·sē, bo͞o′yən·sē) *n.* 1 The property of being able to float in liquid or air. 2 The power of a liquid or gas to keep an object afloat. 3 Cheerfulness; liveliness. Also **buoy′ance.**

buoy·ant (boi′ənt, bo͞o′yənt) *adj.* 1 Having buoyancy. 2 Vivacious; cheerful; hopeful. [Prob. < Sp. *boyar* float] — **buoy′ant·ly** *adv.*

bur[1] (bûr) 1 A rough, prickly, clinging seedcase, as of the chestnut or burdock. 2 A plant that bears burs. 3 Something resembling a bur. 4 A dentist's drilling bit. —*v.t.* **burred, bur·ring** To remove burs from. [< Scand.]

bur[2] (bûr) 1 BURR[1] (defs. 1 and 2). 2 BURR[2].

bur·ble (bûr′bəl) *v.i.* **·bled, ·bling** 1 To bubble; gurgle. 2 To talk excitedly and confusedly. [ME]

bur·bot (bûr′bət) *n. pl.* **·bots** or **·bot** A freshwater fish with barbels on the nose and chin. [< L *barbata* bearded]

bur·den[1] (bûr′dən) *n.* 1 Something carried; a load. 2 Something difficult to bear, as a worry, responsibility, etc. 3 The carrying of loads: beasts of *burden.* 4 *Naut.* a The carrying capacity of a vessel. b The weight of the cargo. —*v.t.* 1 To load or overload. 2 To oppress, as with care. [< OE *byrthen* load]

bur·den[2] (bûr′dən) *n.* 1 The prevailing idea or tone: the *burden* of a speech. 2 A refrain of a song. [<F *bourdon* bass]

burden of proof The obligation to prove something to be true or genuine.

bur·den·some (bûr′dən·səm) *adj.* Hard or heavy to bear; oppressive. —**bur′den·some·ly** *adv.* —**bur′den·some·ness** *n.*

bur·dock (bûr′dok) *n.* A coarse weed having large leaves and prickly burs. [< BUR[1] + DOCK]

bu·reau (byo͝or′ō) *n. pl.* **bu·reaus** or **bu·reaux** (byo͝or′ōz) 1 A chest of drawers for clothing. 2 A government department or subdivision of a department. 3 Any agency providing specialized information and services: travel *bureau.* [<F, cloth-covered desk]

bu·reauc·ra·cy (byo͝o·rok′rə·sē) *n. pl.* **·cies** 1 Government by bureaus managed by officials who are appointed rather than elected. 2 Such officials collectively. 3 Excessively rigid and arbitrary governmental regulations and routines.

bu·reau·crat (byo͝or′ə·krat) *n.* 1 A member of a bureaucracy. 2 An official who governs by rigid routine. —**bu′reau·crat′ic** or **·i·cal** *adj.* —**bu′reau·crat′i·cal·ly** *adv.*

bu·reau·cra·tize (byo͞o·rok′rə·tīz) *v.t.* **·tized, ·tiz·ing** To make into a bureaucracy. —**bu·reau′cra·ti·za′tion** *n.*

bu·rette (byo͞o·ret′) *n.* A graduated glass tube with a stopcock for drawing off precise quantities of liquid. Also **bu·ret′.** [<F *buire* vase]

burg (bûrg) *n. Informal* A town or city, usu. considered somewhat backward. [< OE *burg*]

bur·geon (bûr′jən) *v.t. & v.i.* 1 To put forth buds; sprout. 2 To grow or develop rapidly. [< OF *burjon* a bud]

bur·gess (bûr′jis) *n.* 1 A citizen or officer of a borough. 2 In colonial Maryland and Virginia, a member of the lower house of the legislature. [< OF *bourg* town]

burgh (bûrg, *Scot.* bûr′ō, -ə) *n.* A chartered town or borough in Scotland. [Var. of BOROUGH] —**burgh·al** (bûr′gəl) *adj.*

burgh·er (bûr′gər) *n.* An inhabitant of a borough or town. [< Du. *burg* town]

bur·glar (bûr′glər) *n.* One who commits a burglary. [< Med.L *burglator*]

bur·glar·ize (bûr′glə·rīz) *v.t.* **·ized, ·iz·ing** To commit burglary in or upon.

bur·gla·ry (bûr′glər·ē) *n. pl.* **·ries** The breaking and entering of a building to steal something or commit some other felony.

bur·gle (bûr′gəl) *v.t. & v.i.* **·gled ·gling** *Informal* To burglarize or commit burglary. [Back formation < BURGLAR]

bur·go·mas·ter (bûr′gə·mas′tər, -mäs′-) *n.* A mayor in the Netherlands, Germany, or Austria. [< Du. *burgemeester*]

Bur·gun·dy (bûr′gən·dē) *n. pl.* **·dies** 1 A red or white wine made in Burgundy. 2 A similar wine made elsewhere.

bur·i·al (ber′ē·əl) *n.* The burying of a dead body. [< OE *byrgels* tomb]

bu·rin (byo͝or′in) *n.* A pointed engraver's tool. [F]

burl (bûrl) *n.* 1 A knot or lump in yarn or cloth. 2 A large, wartlike excrescence, formed on the trunks of trees. 3 A veneer made from wood having burls. —*v.t.* To dress (cloth) by removing burls. [< LL *burra* shaggy hair] — **burled** *adj.* —**burl′er** *n.*

bur·lap (bûr′lap) *n.* A coarse fabric made of jute or hemp, used for wrapping, bagging, etc. [?]

bur·lesque (bər·lesk′) *n.* 1 Broad, satirical imitation or caricature; parody. 2 A product of such imitation, as a literary work. 3 A theatrical entertainment marked by low comedy, striptease, etc. —*v.* **·lesqued, ·les·quing** *v.t.* 1 To imitate or parody by using burlesque. —*v.i.* 2 To use burlesque. [< Ital. *burla* joke] —**bur·les′quer** *n.*

bur·ley (bûr′lē) *n. Often cap.* A fine, light tobacco grown principally in Kentucky. [? < *Burley,* name of a grower]

bur·ly (bûr′lē) *adj.* **bur·li·er, bur·li·est** 1 Large and muscular of body; stout. 2 Rough and lusty in manner. [ME *borlich*] —**bur′li·ly** *adv.* —**bur′li·ness** *n.*

Bur·ma (bûr′mə) *n.* A republic of SE Asia, 261,789 sq. mi., cap. Rangoon. —**Bur·mese** (bər·mēz′, -mēs′) *adj., n.* • See map at INDOCHINA.

burn (bûrn) *v.* **burned** or **burnt, burn·ing** *v.t.* 1 To destroy or consume by fire. 2 To set afire; ignite. 3 To injure or kill by fire. 4 To injure or damage by friction, heat, steam, etc.; scald; wither. 5 To produce by fire, as a hole in a suit. 6 To brand; also, to cauterize. 7 To finish or harden by intense heat; fire. 8 To use or employ so as to give off light, heat, etc. 9 To cause a feeling of heat in. 10 To sunburn. 11 To transform into energy, as fat in body tissues. 12 *Slang* To electrocute. 13 *Slang* To cheat. —*v.i.* 14 To be on fire; blaze. 15 To be destroyed, damaged, or changed by fire. 16 To give off light, heat, etc.; shine. 17 To die by fire. 18 To appear or feel hot. 19 To be eager, excited, or inflamed. 20 To oxidize; undergo combustion. 21 *Slang* To be electrocuted. —**burn out** 1 To become extinguished through lack of fuel. 2 To destroy or wear out by heat, friction, etc. —**burn up** 1 To consume by fire. 2 *Slang* To make or become irritated or enraged. —*n.* 1 An effect or injury from burning; a burnt place. 2 The process or result of burning. 3 *Aerospace* A single firing of a space rocket. [Fusion of OE *beornan* be on fire and OE *bærnan* set afire]

burn·er (bûr′nər) *n.* 1 One who or that which burns. 2 The light-giving or heat-giving part of a lamp, stove, etc.

burn·ing (bûr′ning) *adj.* 1 Consuming or being consumed by fire. 2 Extremely important or controversial.

bur·nish (bûr′nish) *v.t. & v.i.* To polish by friction; make or become brilliant or shiny. —*n.* Polish; luster. [< OF *burnir* polish] —**bur′nish·er, bur′nish·ment** *n.*

bur·noose (bər·no͞os′, bûr′no͞os) *n.* A cloak with hood, worn by Arabs and Moors. Also **bur·nous′**. [< Ar. *burnus*]

burn·sides (bûrn′sīdz) *n. pl.* Side whiskers and mustache worn with closely shaven chin. [< Ambrose E. *Burnside,* 1824–81, U.S. major general]

burnt (bûrnt) A *p.t. & p.p.* of BURN.

burp (bûrp) *n. Informal* BELCH. —*v.i.* 1 *Informal* BELCH. —*v.t.* 2 To cause (a baby) to belch, esp. after a meal, by rubbing or patting the back. [Imit.]

burr[1] (bûr) 1 A roughness or rough edge, esp. one left on metal in casting or cutting. 2 A rotary cutting tool. 3 BUR[1]. —*v.t.* 1 To form a rough edge on. 2 To remove a rough edge from. [Var. of BUR[1]]

burr[2] (bûr) *n.* 1 A rough guttural sound of *r* caused by the vibration of the uvula, as in the dialectal pronunciation of Scotland. 2 A whirring sound; a buzz. —*v.t.* 1 To pronounce with a burr. —*v.i.* 2 To speak with a burr. 3 To whir. [Imit.]

bur·ro (bûr′ō, bo͝or′ō) *n. pl.* **·ros** A small donkey, used as a pack animal. [Sp.]

bur·row (bûr′ō) *n.* A hole or tunnel made in the ground, as by an animal, for shelter, etc. —*v.t.* 1 To make by burrowing. 2 To perforate with burrows. —*v.i.* 3 To live or hide in or as in a burrow. 4 To make a burrow. [ME *borow*] —**bur′row·er** *n.*

bur·sa (bûr′sə) *n. pl.* **·sas** or **·sae** (-sē) A closed sac within the body, esp. one containing a viscid fluid and located at a joint. [< Med. L, sack, pouch] —**bur′sal** *adj.*

bur·sar (bûr′sər, -sär) *n.* A treasurer, as of a college. [< Med. L *bursarius* treasurer] —**bur·sar·i·al** (bər·sâr′ē·əl) *adj.*

bur·sa·ry (bûr′sər·ē) *n. pl.* **·ries** 1 The treasury, as of a public institution. 2 A grant; scholarship.

bur·si·tis (bər·sī′tis) *n.* Inflammation of a bursa.

burst (bûrst) *v.* **burst, burst·ing** *v.i.* 1 To break open or come apart suddenly and violently; explode, as from internal force. 2 To be full of something to the breaking point. 3 To issue forth or enter suddenly or violently. 4 To appear or begin; become audible or evident, etc. 5 To give sudden expression to passion, grief, etc. —*v.t.* 6 To cause to break open suddenly or violently; puncture. 7 To fill or cause to swell to the point of breaking open. —*n.* 1 The act or result of bursting. 2 A sudden eruption, as of feeling. 3 A sudden effort; spurt. 4 A series of shots fired. [< OE *berstan*] —**burst′er** *n.* —**Syn.** *v.* 1, 6 rupture, shatter, tear, rip, rend.

Bu·run·di (bo͞o·ro͞on′dē) *n.* A republic in CEN. Africa, 10,747 sq. mi., cap. Usumbura. • See map at AFRICA.

bury (ber′ē) *v.t.* **bur·ied, bur·y·ing** 1 To put (a dead body) in a grave, etc.; inter. 2 To conceal in the ground. 3 To cover, as for concealment. 4 To sink or embed. 5 To end; put out of mind: to *bury* a quarrel. 6 To occupy deeply; engross: He *buried* himself in study. [< OE *byrgan*]

burying ground A cemetery.

bus (bus) *n. pl.* **bus·es** or **bus·ses** 1 A large motor vehicle that carries passengers; an omnibus. 2 *Informal* An automobile. —*v.* **bused** or **bussed, bus·ing** or **bus·sing** *v.t.* 1 To transport by bus. —*v.i.* 2 To go by bus. 3 *Informal* To do the work of a bus boy. [Short form of OMNIBUS]

bus boy A waiter's helper who sets and clears tables, fills water glasses, etc.

bus·by (buz′bē) *n. pl.* **·bies** A tall fur cap worn as part of the full-dress uniform of British hussars, artillerymen, and engineers. [?]

Busby

bush[1] (bo͝osh) *n.* 1 A low, thickly branching shrub. 2 A thick growth of shrubs. 3 Land that is unsettled, remote, often arid, and covered with a scrubby undergrowth, esp. such land in Australia: with *the.* 4 A bushy tail. —*v.i.* 1 To grow or branch like a bush. —*v.t.* 2 To protect or support with bushes. —*adj. Slang* Bush-league; small-time. [ME *bussche*]

bush[2] (bo͝osh) *v.t.* To line with a bushing, as an axle bearing, a pivot hole, etc. —*n.* BUSHING. [< MDu. *busse* box]

bushed (bo͝osht) *adj. Informal* 1 Exhausted; worn out. 2 *Austral.* Lost; confused.

bush·el (bo͝osh′əl) *n.* 1 A measure of capacity; four pecks, 35.238 liters, or 2150.42 cubic inches. 2 A vessel holding that amount. 3 *Informal* A large amount. [< OF *boissel*]

bu·shi·do (bo͞o′shē·dō) *n. Often cap.* The code of conduct for the medieval Japanese samurai.

bush·ing (bo͝osh′ing) *n.* 1 A protective lining for a hole, as in the hub of a wheel. 2 A tube for insertion into another to reduce the diameter.

bush league *Slang* 1 In baseball, a minor league. 2 Anything minor or second-rate. —**bush′-league′** *adj.* —**bush′-lea′guer** *n.*

bush·man (bo͝osh′mən) *n. pl.* **·men** (-mən) *Austral.* A dweller or farmer in the bush.

Bush·man (bo͝osh′mən) *n. pl.* **·men** (-mən) 1 One of a nomadic people of South Africa, related to the Pygmies. 2 The language of the Bushmen, characterized by clicks.

bush·mas·ter (bo͝osh′mas′tər, -mäs′-) *n.* A large, poisonous viper of Central and South America.

bush·rang·er (bo͝osh′rān′jər) *n.* 1 One who lives in the bush. 2 *Austral.* A robber.

bush·whack (bo͝osh′hwak′) *v.i.* 1 To cut one's way through bushes or underbrush. 2 To ride or range in the bush. 3 To fight from ambush, as a guerrilla. —*v.t.* 4 To ambush. [< Du. *boschwachter* forest-keeper; infl. by WHACK] —**bush′whack′er, bush′whack′ing** *n.*

bush·y (bo͝osh′ē) *adj.* **bush·i·er, bush·i·est** 1 Covered with or full of bushes. 2 Thick and shaggy. —**bush′i·ly** *adv.* —**bush′i·ness** *n.*

bus·ied (biz′ēd) *p.t. & p.p.* of BUSY.

bus·i·ly (biz′ə·lē) *adv.* In a busy manner.

busi·ness (biz′nis, -niz) *n.* 1 One's occupation, trade, or profession. 2 A function or province. 3 Legitimate interest or concern. 4 An activity, matter, or affair. 5 Commercial affairs in general. 6 A commercial enterprise or establishment, as a store. 7 Amount of commercial trade or patronage. 8 Commercial policy or practices. 9 The actions on a stage, in a movie, etc., other than dialogue. —*adj.* Of or for business. [< OE *bysignis* < *bysig* active] —**Syn.** 1 employment, work, calling, vocation, career. 5 commerce, industry. 7 volume, traffic.

busi·ness·like (biz′nis·līk′, -niz-) *adj.* Methodical and efficient, as in matters of business.

busi·ness·man (biz′nis·man′, -niz-) *n. pl.* **·men** (-men′)

One engaged in commerical business. —**busi′ness·wom′an** *n. Fem.* (*pl.* **·wom′en**)

bus·ing (bus′ing) *n.* The transporting of pupils in schoolbuses from one school district to another to approximate racial balance in schools.

bus·kin (bus′kin) *n.* **1** A high shoe or half boot reaching halfway to the knee, esp. one worn in ancient times by actors in Greek or Roman tragedies. **2** Tragedy.[?]

buss (bus) *Informal n.* A kiss; smack. —*v.t. & v.i.* To kiss heartily. [Imit.]

buss·es (bus′iz) A plural of BUS.

bust[1] (bust) *n.* **1** The human chest or breast. **2** A statue of the human head, shoulders, and breast. [<Ital. *busto* trunk of the body]

bust[2] (bust) *Slang v.t.* **1** To burst. **2** To tame; train, as a horse. **3** To make bankrupt or short of funds. **4** To reduce in rank; demote. **5** To arrest. **6** To hit; strike. —*v.i.* **7** To burst. **8** To become bankrupt or short of funds. —*n.* **1** Failure; bankruptcy. **2** A spree. **3** An arrest. [Alter. of BURST]

bus·tard (bus′tərd) *n.* Any of a family of large Old World game birds related to the plovers and cranes. [<OF *bistarde, oustarde*<L *avis tarda,* lit., slow bird]

bus·tle[1] (bus′əl) *n.* Excited activity; noisy stir; fuss. —*v.t. & v.i.* **·tled, ·tling** To hurry noisily; make a stir or fuss.[?]

bus·tle[2] (bus′əl) *n.* A frame or pad formerly worn by women on the back below the waist to distend the skirts.[?]

bus·y (biz′ē) *adj.* **bus·i·er, bus·i·est 1** Intensely active; constantly occupied. **2** Temporarily engaged; not at leisure. **3** Prying; meddling. **4** In use, as a telephone. **5** Full of varied designs, colors, etc., usu. excessively so. —*v.t.* **bus·ied, bus·y·ing** To make or be busy. [<OE *bysig* active]

bus·y·bod·y (biz′ē·bod′ē) *n. pl.* **·bodies** One who intrudes upon others' privacy or interferes with their affairs.

but (but, *unstressed* bət) *conj.* **1** However; yet: He seemed honest, *but* he was lying. **2** Unless; if not: It never rains *but* it pours. **3** Excepting: Nothing would satisfy him *but* I come along. **4** Other than; otherwise than: I cannot choose *but* hear. **5** On the other hand: You are right, *but* he's also right. **6** That: We don't doubt *but* matters will improve. **7** That . . . not: He is not so strong *but* a little exercise will do him good. —*prep.* Except for; save: owning nothing *but* his clothes. —*adv.* **1** Only; just: If I had *but* thought. **2** Merely: She is *but* a child. —**all but** Almost: He is *all but* well. —**but for** Were it not for: *But for* me, how would you have succeeded? —*n.* An objection; exception; condition: without any ifs or *buts* [<OE *būten*]

bu·ta·di·ene (byo͞o′tə·dī′ēn, -dī·ēn′) *n.* A hydrocarbon obtained from petroleum and used to manufacture synthetic rubber. [<BUTA(NE) + DI- + -ENE]

bu·tane (byo͞o′tān, byo͞o·tān′) *n.* A flammable, gaseous hydrocarbon. [<L *butyrum* butter].

butch (bo͝och) *adj. Slang* Masculine, as in appearance or manner: said of one who adopts a masculine role, esp. a female homosexual. —*n.* **1** A closely cropped haircut for boys or men. **2** *Slang* A butch woman, esp. a lesbian. [Prob.<*Butch,* a boy's nickname]

butch·er (bo͝och′ər) *n.* **1** One who slaughters animals or deals in meats for food. **2** A bloody or cruel murderer. **3** A vendor of candy, cigarettes, etc., on trains, in theaters, etc. —*v.t.* **1** To slaughter or dress (animals) for market. **2** To kill (people or game) barbarously or brutally. **3** *Slang* To botch. [<OF *bouchier*<*boc* buck, he-goat]

butch·er·bird (bo͝och′ər·bûrd′) *n.* Any of various shrikes.

butch·er·broom (bo͝och′ər·bro͞om′, -bro͝om′) *n.* A low, evergreen shrub with leathery stems bearing scarlet berries: also **butch′er's-broom′**.

butch·er·y (bo͝och′ər·ē) *n. pl.* **·er·ies 1** Wanton slaughter. **2** A slaughterhouse. **3** The trade of a butcher.

but·ler (but′lər) *n.* The chief male servant in a household, usu. in charge of the dining room, wine, plate, etc. [<OF *bouteillier* bottle-bearer<Med. L] —**but′ler·ship** *n.*

butler's pantry A serving room between the kitchen and the dining room.

butt[1] (but) *v.t.* **1** To strike with or as with the head or horns; ram. **2** To touch or bump against. **3** To cause to abut. **4** To abut on. **5** To make a butting motion. **6** To project; jut out. **7** To abut. —*n.* **1** A stroke, thrust, or push with or as with the head. **2** A thrust in fencing. [<OF *abouter* strike]

butt[2] (but) *n.* **1** A target, as for a rifle range. **2** *Often pl.* The range itself. **3** The retaining wall placed behind a target to stop the bullets. **4** A target for ridicule or criticism. [< OF *but* end, goal]

butt[3] (but) *n.* **1** The larger or thicker end of anything, as of a rifle stock. **2** The remaining end or edge of something, esp. the unused end of a cigar or cigarette. **3** *Slang* The buttocks. [ME *butte*]

butt[4] (but) *n.* **1** A large cask. **2** A measure of wine, 126 U.S. gallons. [<OF *boute*]

butte (byo͞ot) *n.* An isolated hill, esp. one with steep sides and a flattened top. [<F]

but·ter (but′ər) *n.* **1** The fatty constituent of milk, separated by churning into a soft, whitish yellow solid, processed for cooking and table use. **2** A substance like butter. —*v.t.* **1** To put butter on. **2** *Informal* To flatter: usu. with *up.* [<OE *butere,* ult.<Gk. *boutyron* lit. cow cheese]

butter bean Wax bean.

but·ter·cup (but′ər·kup′) *n.* **1** A species of crowfoot with yellow, cup-shaped flowers. **2** The flower.

but·ter·fat (but′ər·fat′) *n.* The fat component of milk of which butter is made.

but·ter·fin·gers (but′ər·fing′gərz) *n. pl. (construed as sing.)* One who drops things easily. —**but′ter·fin′gered** *adj.*

but·ter·fish (but′ər·fish′) *n. pl.* **·fish** or **·fish·es** One of various marine food fishes of the North Atlantic.

but·ter·fly (but′ər·flī′) *n. pl.* **·flies 1** A diurnal lepidopterous insect with large, often brightly colored wings, knobbed antennae, and slender body. **2** One who lives frivolously. [<OE *buttor flēoge*]

butter knife A small, blunt-edged knife for cutting or spreading butter.

but·ter·milk (but′ər·milk′) *n.* The sour liquid left after the butterfat has been separated from milk or cream.

but·ter·nut (but′ər·nut′) *n.* **1** The oily, edible nut of the North American white walnut. **2** The tree, or its inner bark.

but·ter·scotch (but′ər·skoch′) *n.* **1** Hard, sticky candy made with brown sugar, butter, and flavoring. **2** A syrup having a butterscotch flavor. —*adj.* Made of or flavored with butterscotch.

but·ter·y[1] (but′ər·ē) *adj.* Containing, like, flavored, or smeared with butter.

but·ter·y[2] (but′ər·ē, but′rē) *n. pl.* **·ter·ies** A pantry or a wine cellar. [<LL *botaria*<*butta* bottle]

but·tock (but′ək) *n.* **1** Either of the two fleshy prominences that form the rump, on which a person sits. **2** *pl.* The rump. [?<OE *buttuc* end]

but·ton (but′n) *n.* **1** A knob or disk, as of bone, metal, leather, etc., used as an ornament or fastening. **2** Anything like a button. **3** A knob or protuberance, as for operating an electric switch, etc. **4** *Slang* The point of the jaw. —*v.t.* **1** To fasten with or as with a button or buttons. **2** To provide with buttons. —*v.i.* **3** To admit of being buttoned. [<OF *boton* button, bud] —**but′ton·er** *n.*

but·ton·hole (but′n·hōl′) *n.* A slit to receive and hold a button. —*v.t.* **·holed, ·hol·ing 1** To work buttonholes in. **2** To detain by conversation. —**but′ton·hol′er** *n.*

but·ton·wood (but′n·wo͝od′) *n.* The sycamore or plane tree of the U.S.; also, its wood. Also **but′ton·ball′**.

but·tress (but′ris) *n.* **1** A structure built against a wall to strengthen it. **2** Any support or prop. **3** Any formation suggesting a buttress. —*v.t.* **1** To support with a buttress. **2** To prop up; sustain. [<OF *bouter* push, thrust] • See FLYING BUTTRESS.

bu·tyr·ic (byo͞o·tir′ik) *adj.* Of, pertaining to, or derived from butter or butyric acid. [<L *butyrum* butter]

butyric acid Either of two isomeric acids, esp. one found as an ester in butter and certain oils, and free in rancid butter, perspiration, etc.

bux·om (buk′səm) *adj.* **1** Attractively plump and well-proportioned: said of women. **2** Having a large bosom. [< OE *būhsum* pliant) —**bux′om·ly** *adv.* —**bux′om·ness** *n.*

buy (bī) *v.* **bought, buy·ing** *v.t.* **1** To obtain for a price; purchase. **2** To be a price for. **3** To obtain by an exchange or sacrifice: to *buy* wisdom with experience. **4** To bribe; corrupt. **5** *Slang* To accept as true, possible, etc. —*v.i.* **6** To make purchases; be a purchaser. —**buy off** To bribe. —**buy out** To purchase the stock, interests, etc., of, as in a business. —*n. Informal* **1** A purchase. **2** A bargain. [<OE *bycgan*] —**buy'a·ble** *adj.* —**buy'er** *n.*

buy out (bī'out') *n.* The purchase of a business or stock shares in it by its management or its employees.

buzz (buz) *v.i.* **1** To make a vibrating hum, as a bee. **2** To discuss or gossip excitedly. **3** To bustle about. —*v.t.* **4** To utter or gossip about in a buzzing manner. **5** To cause to buzz, as wings. **6** To fly an airplane low over. **7** To summon with a buzzer. **8** *Informal* To telephone. —*n.* **1** A low vibrating hum, as of bees, of talk, or of distant sounds. **2** Rumor; gossip. **3** Activity; bustle. **4** The sound of a buzzer. **5** *Informal* A telephone call. [Imit.]

buzzard (buz'ərd) *n.* **1** One of several large, slow-flying hawks. **2** TURKEY BUZZARD. [<OF *busart* <L *buteo* hawk]

buzz bomb A self-propelled, guided missile used by the Germans in World War II.

buzz·er (buz'ər) *n.* An electric signal making a buzzing sound.

buzz saw A motor-driven, circular saw.

by (bī) *prep.* **1** Next to; near: the house *by* the road. **2** Toward: west *by* north. **3** Past or beyond: The train flashed *by* us. **4** In the course of; during: birds flying *by* night. **5** Not later than: Be here *by* four tomorrow. **6** For the period of; according to: They work *by* the day. **7** As a result of the effort, means, or action of: a play written *by* Shakespeare. **8** With the perception of: a loss felt *by* all. **9** By means of: leading a child *by* the hand. **10** In consequence of: a case won *by* default. **11** As a means of conveyance; via: Mail your letters *by* air. **12** To the extent or amount of: insects *by* the thousands. **13** On the basis of: four miles long *by* actual measurement. **14** Considered according to: advancing step *by* step; reading word *by* word. **15** With reference to: to do well *by* one's friends. **16** And; and in another dimension: used in numerical measurements and processes: to divide 9 *by* 3; a room ten *by* twelve. **17** In the name of: swearing *by* all that is sacred. —*adv.* **1** At hand; near: to keep one's sword *by*. **2** Up to and beyond something; past: the train roared *by*. **3** Apart; aside: to lay something *by*. **4** At or into a person's house, store, etc.: to stop *by*. —*adj.* & *n.* BYE. [<OE *bī* near, about]

by- *combining form* **1** Secondary; inferior; incidental: *by-product.* **2** Near; close: *bystander.* **3** Aside; out of the way: *byway.*

bye (bī) *n.* **1** Something of minor or secondary importance. **2** The position of a person who is assigned no opponent and automatically advances to the next round, as in the preliminary pairings of a tennis tournament. —*adj.* Not principal or main; secondary. [Var. of BY]

bye-bye (bī'bī') *interj.* Good-bye.

by-e·lec·tion (bī'i·lek'shən) *n. Brit.* A parliamentary election between general elections, held to fill a vacancy.

Bye·lo·rus·sian (byel'ō·rush'ən) *adj.* Of or pertaining to the Byelorussian SSR, its people, or their language. —*n.* **1** A native or citizen of the Byelorussian SSR. **2** The Slavic language of the Byelorussian SSR. Also **Be·lo·rus·sian** (bel'ō·rush'ən).

by·gone (bī'gôn', -gon') *adj.* Gone by; former. —*n. Usu. pl.* Something past; that which has gone by.

by·law (bī'lô) *n.* A rule or law adopted by an association, a corporation, etc., which is subordinate to a constitution or charter. [ME *by, bi* village + *lawe* law]

by-line (bī'līn') *n.* The line at the head of a newspaper article, giving the name of the writer.

by·pass (bī'pas', -päs') *n.* Any road, channel, duct, or route that is auxiliary to the one normally used; a detour. —*v.t.* **1** To go around (an obstacle). **2** To provide with a bypass. **3** To pay no attention to.

by·path (bī'path', -päth') *n.* A side, secluded, or secondary path.

by·play (bī·plā') *n.* Any action that is secondary or incidental to the main action, as in a play.

by·prod·uct (bī'prod'əkt) *n.* **1** Any material or product produced in the making of something else. **2** A secondary result or effect.

by·road (bī'rōd') *n.* A secondary road.

by·stand·er (bī'stan'dər) *n.* One who stands by; an onlooker.

by·street (bī·strēt') *n.* A side street; a byway.

byte (bīt) *n.* A group of eight bits in a computer memory that form a character symbol, or keyboard function. [<B(INAR)Y (DIGI)T E(IGHT)]

by·way (bī'wā') *n.* A side road.

by·word (bī'wûrd') *n.* **1** A proverb, common saying, etc. **2** Something that has become an object of derision. [<OE *biword* proverb]

Byz·an·tine (biz'ən·tēn, -tīn, bi·zan'tin) *adj.* **1** Of or pertaining to Byzantium. **2** Of or designating a style of architecture developed in the Byzantine Empire, characterized by round arches, domes, and colorful mosaics. —*n.* A native or inhabitant of Byzantium. [<L *Byzantinus* <*Byzantium*]

Byzantine architecture

Byzantine Empire The eastern part of the later Roman Empire (395–1453).

By·zan·ti·um (bi·zan'shē·əm, -tē·əm) *n.* **1** An ancient city on the site of what is now Istanbul. **2** BYZANTINE EMPIRE.

C

C, c (sē) *n. pl.* **C's, c's, Cs, cs** (sēz) **1** The third letter of the English alphabet. **2** Any spoken sound representing the letter *C* or *c*. **3** In Roman notation, the symbol for 100. **4** *Music* The first tone in the diatonic scale of C major. **5** Something shaped like a C. **6** A grade of average in quality. **7** *Slang* One hundred dollars. —*adj.* Shaped like a C.

C Carbon.

C, C., c, c. Celsius or centigrade; centimeter.

C. Catholic; Chancellor; Congress; Conservative; Church; Court.

C., c. capacity; carton; cent; century; chapter; church; circa; copyright.

CA California (P.O. abbr.).

Ca calcium.

ca. circa; cathode.

cab (kab) *n.* **1** TAXICAB. **2** A one-horse public carriage. **3** The part of a locomotive, truck, crane, etc., where the controls are operated. [Short form of CABRIOLET]

CAB Civil Aeronautics Board.

ca·bal (kə·bal') *n.* **1** A number of persons secretly united, as in a plot or conspiracy. **2** Intrigue; conspiracy. —*v.i.* **ca·balled, ca·bal·ling** To form a cabal; plot. [<Med. L *cabbala* cabala]

cab·a·la (kab'ə·lə, kə·bä'lə) *n.* **1** The mystic theosophy of the Hebrews. **2** Any secret, occult, or mystic system. [<Heb. *qabbālāh* tradition] —**ca·bal'ic, cab'a·lis'tic** *adj.* —**cab·a·lism** (kab'ə·liz'əm), **cab'a·list** *n.*

cab·al·le·ro (kab′əl·yâr′ō) *n. pl.* **·ros** A Spanish gentleman; cavalier; knight.
ca·ba·na (kə·bä′nə, -ban′ə) *n.* **1** A small cabin. **2** A small bathhouse, as on a beach. Also **ca·ba′ña** (-bän′yə, -ban′yə). [< Sp.]
cab·a·ret (kab′ə·rā′) *n.* **1** A restaurant or café with singing, dancing, etc., as entertainment. **2** Entertainment of this type.
cab·bage (kab′ij) *n.* **1** A plant having a rounded, dense head of leaves eaten as a vegetable. **2** The head of such a plant. **3** *Slang* Money, esp. paper money. *—v.i.* **·baged, ·bag·ing** To form a head, as cabbage. [< OF *caboche*]
cabbage palm A palm with a terminal leaf bud used as a vegetable.
cab·by (kab′ē) *n. pl.* **·bies** *Informal* A taxicab driver.
cab·in (kab′in) *n.* **1** A small, crudely built house; hut. **2** A compartment in a vessel, aircraft, etc., for crew or passengers. *—v.t. & v.i.* To shut up or dwell in or as in a cabin. [< LL *capanna*]
cabin boy A boy who waits on the officers and passengers of a vessel.
cabin cruiser A powerboat with an equipped cabin.
cab·i·net (kab′ə·nit) *n.* **1** A piece of furniture, case, etc., with shelves, drawers, or compartments. **2** *Often cap.* The body of official advisers of a chief of state. **3** A private council room or study. *—adj.* Of or suitable for a cabinet. [< OF *cabine*]
cab·i·net·mak·er (kab′ə·nit·mā′kər) *n.* A craftsman who makes fine wooden furniture, etc.
cab·i·net·work (kab′ə·nit·wûrk′) *n.* The work of a cabinetmaker; expert woodwork.
ca·ble (kā′bəl) *n.* **1** A heavy rope of wire strands, hemp, etc. **2** A unit of nautical measure, 720 feet in the U.S. and 608 feet in England. Also **cable length, cable's length. 3** An insulated electrical conductor or group of conductors protected by an outer covering. **4** CABLEGRAM. *—v.* **·bled, ·bling** *v.t.* **1** To send a cablegram to. **2** To fasten with a cable. *—v.i.* **3** To send a cablegram. [< LL *capulum* rope]
cable car A car pulled along rails by a cable.
ca·ble·gram (kā′bəl·gram) *n.* A telegraphic message sent by undersea cable.
ca·ble-tel·e·vi·sion (kā′bəl·tel′ə·vizh′ən) *n.* A system utilizing cables or wires to transmit television signals. Also **cable-TV** (kā′bəl·tē′vē′).
cab·man (kab′mən) *n. pl.* **·men** (-mən) The driver of a cab.
cab·o·chon (kab′ə·shon, *Fr.* kȧ·bô·shôṅ′) *n.* **1** An unfaceted gemstone cut convex and highly polished. **2** This style of cutting. [< F *caboche* head]
ca·boo·dle (kə·bo͞od′l) *n. Informal* Lot; collection: usu. in the phrase **the whole (kit and) caboodle.** [Prob. < KIT + BOODLE]
ca·boose (kə·bo͞os′) *n.* A railroad car, usu. the last of a freight train, equipped for the use of the crew. [< MDu. *cabuse* cook's galley]
cab·ri·o·let (kab′rē·ə·lā′, -let′) *n.* **1** An automobile of the coupé type, having a collapsible top. **2** A one-horse carriage with two seats and a usu. collapsible top. [< L *capreolus* wild goat]
cab·stand (kab′stand′) *n.* A place where cabs are stationed for hire.
ca·ca·o (kə·kā′ō, -kä′ō) *n. pl.* **·ca·os 1** A tropical American tree bearing large seed pods. **2** The seeds of this tree, from which chocolate and cocoa are obtained. [< Nah. *cacauatl* cacao]
cach·a·lot (kash′ə·lot, -lō) *n.* SPERM WHALE. [F]
cache (kash) *v.t.* **cached, cach·ing** To store or hide in a secret place. *—n.* **1** A place for hiding or storing provisions. **2** Supplies stored or hidden in such a place. [< F *cacher* hide]
ca·chet (ka·shā′, kash′ā) *n.* **1** A seal, as on a document or letter. **2** A distinctive mark of individuality. **3** A mark, slogan, etc., stamped or printed on mail. [< F *cacher* hide]
cach·in·nate (kak′ə·nāt) *v.i.* **·nat·ed, ·nat·ing** To laugh immoderately or noisily. [< L *cachinnare*] **—cach′in·na′tion** *n.*
ca·cique (kə·sēk′) *n.* An Indian chief of the West Indies or Latin America. [< Sp. < Arawakan]
cack·le (kak′əl) *v.* **·led, ·ling** *v.i.* **1** To make a shrill cry, as a hen that has laid an egg. **2** To laugh or talk with a sound resembling this. *—v.t.* **3** To utter in a cackling manner. *—n.* **1** The shrill, broken cry made by a hen after laying an egg. **2** A laugh or sound resembling this. **3** Idle talk. [Imit.] **—cack′ler** *n.*
caco- *combining form* Bad; unpleasant. [< Gk. *kakos* bad]
ca·cog·ra·phy (ka·kog′rə·fē) *n.* Bad handwriting or spelling.
ca·coph·o·ny (kə·kof′ə·nē) *n. pl.* **·nies** A harsh, disagreeable, discordant sound. **—ca·coph′o·nous** *adj.* **—ca·coph′on·ous·ly** *adv.*
cac·tus (kak′təs) *n. pl.* **·tus·es** or **·ti** (-tī) Any of a family of plants native to arid regions of America, having fleshy, usu. leafless and spiny stems and often showy flowers. [< Gk. *kaktos* a prickly plant]
cad (kad) *n.* A contemptible, ungentlemanly man. [Short form of CADDIE] **—cad′dish** *adj.* **—cad′dish·ly** *adv.* **—cad′dish·ness** *n.* **—Syn.** bounder, rotter, scoundrel, heel.

Cactus

ca·dav·er (kə·dav′ər, -dā′vər) *n.* A dead body, esp. a human corpse intended for dissection. [< L]
ca·dav·er·ous (kə·dav′ər·əs) *adj.* Of or resembling a corpse; pale; ghastly; gaunt. **—ca·dav′er·ous·ly** *adv.* **—ca·dav′er·ous·ness** *n.*
cad·die (kad′ē) *n.* One paid to carry clubs for golf players. *—v.i.* **·died, ·dy·ing** To act as a caddie. [< CADET]
cad·dis fly (kad′is) Any of certain four-winged insects having an aquatic larva, the **caddis worm,** enclosing itself in a cylindrical case covered with sand, gravel, etc. [?]
cad·dy[1] (kad′ē) *n. pl.* **·dies** A small box or receptacle, esp. for tea. [< Malay *kati,* a measure of weight]
cad·dy[2] (kad′ē) *n. pl.* **·dies** CADDIE. *—v.i.* **·died, ·dy·ing** CADDIE.
ca·dence (kād′ns) *n.* **1** Rhythmic flow, as of poetry. **2** Rhythmic beat or measure, as of marching. **3** Modulation or inflection, as of the voice. **4** A formula for ending a phrase, section, etc. Also **ca′den·cy.** [< LL *cadentia* a falling]
ca·den·za (kə·den′zə, *Ital.* kä·dent′sä) *n. Music* An elaborate display passage, often improvised, inserted into a composition for a solo voice or instrument. [Ital.]
ca·det (kə·det′) *n.* **1** A student at a military or naval school who is training for commissioning as an officer. **2** A younger son or brother. [F, ult. < dim. of L *caput* head, chief] **—ca·det′ship** *n.*
cadge (kaj) *v.t.* **cadged, cadg·ing** *Informal* To get by begging or sponging. [?] **—cadg′er** *n.*
ca·di (kä′dē, kā′-) *n. pl.* **·dis** A Muslim judge or magistrate. [< Ar. *qādī*]
cad·mi·um (kad′mē·əm) *n.* A bluish white metallic element (symbol Cd), occurring in small quantities in ores of zinc and used in fusible alloys, in electroplating, etc. [< L *cadmia* zinc ore] **—cad′mic** *adj.*
cad·re (kad′rē) *n.* **1** A framework. **2** The nucleus of trained personnel necessary to establish and manage a larger organization, as a military unit. [< Ital. *quadro* < L *quadrum* square]
ca·du·ce·us (kə·dyo͞o′sē·əs) *n. pl.* **·ce·i** (-sē·ī) The winged, snake-entwined staff of the god Hermes, now used as a symbol of the medical profession. [< Gk. *karykion* herald's staff] **—ca·du′ce·an** *adj.*
cae·cum (sē′kəm) *n.* CECUM.
Cae·sar (sē′zər) **1** The title of the Roman emperors from Augustus to Hadrian. **2** A dictator or despot.

Caduceus

Cae·sar·e·an (si·zâr′ē·ən) *adj.* Pertaining to Caesar. *—n.* CAESAREAN SECTION. Also **Cae·sar′i·an.**
Caesarean section The delivery of a child through a surgical incision in the abdominal wall. Also **Caesarean operation.**

cae·si·um (sē′zē·əm) *n.* CESIUM.

cae·su·ra (si·zhŏŏr′ə, -zyŏŏr′ə) *n. pl.* **·su·ras** or **·su·rae** (-zhŏŏr′ē, -zyŏŏr′ē) 1 A pause within a line or foot of verse, usu. near the middle. 2 *Music* A pause at a division point of an air or melody. [< L, a cutting, caesura < *caedere* to cut] **—cae·su′ral** *adj.*

ca·fé (ka·fā′, ka-) *n.* 1 A coffee house, restaurant, barroom, etc. 2 Coffee. Also **ca·fé**. [F]

ca·fé au lait (kȧ·fā′ ō lā′) *French* 1 Coffee with scalded milk. 2 A light brown.

ca·fé noir (kȧ·fā′ nwȧr′) *French* Black coffee.

caf·e·te·ri·a (kaf′ə·tir′ē·ə) *n.* A restaurant where the patrons wait upon themselves. [< Am. Sp., coffee store]

caf·feine (kaf′ēn, ka·fēn′, kaf′ē·in) *n.* An alkaloid found in coffee, tea, and cola and used as a stimulant. Also **caf′·fein.** [< F *café* coffee]

caf·tan (kaf′tən, käf·tän′) *n.* A loose, long-sleeved robe worn in E Mediterranean countries. [< Turkish *qaftān*]

cage (kāj) *n.* 1 A structure enclosed with bars or wires, for confining birds, animals, etc. 2 A structure or enclosure resembling this. 3 In baseball, a backstop used for batting practice. 4 In hockey, the frame and network forming the goal. 5 In basketball, the basket. *—v.t.* **caged, cag·ing** To confine in or as in a cage. [< L *cavea* an enclosure < *cavus* empty, hollow]

ca·gey (kā′jē) *adj.* **·gi·er, ·gi·est** *Informal* Shrewd; wary. Also **ca′gy. —ca′gi·ly** *adv.* **—ca′gi·ness** *n.*

ca·hoots (kə·hōōts′) *n. pl. Informal* Partnership; collusion: used in the phrase **in cahoots.**

cai·man (kā′mən) *n.* A tropical American crocodilian related to the alligator. [< Cariban]

Cain (kān) The eldest son of Adam and slayer of his brother Abel. *—n.* A murderer. **—raise Cain** *Slang* To make a noisy disturbance.

ca·ique (kä·ēk′) *n.* A long, narrow skiff used on the Bosporus. [< Turkish *qāyiq*]

cairn (kârn) *n.* A mound of stones placed as a memorial or marker. [< Celtic] **—cairned** *adj.*

cais·son (kā′sən, -son) *n.* 1 An ammunition chest. 2 A two-wheeled vehicle carrying such a chest. 3 A watertight chamber within which work is done under water, as on a bridge pier. 4 A watertight box or other apparatus for floating a sunken vessel. [< F *caisse* box, chest]

caisson disease DECOMPRESSION SICKNESS.

cai·tiff (kā′tif) *n.* A base wretch or coward. *—adj.* Vile or cowardly. [< AF *caitif* weak, wretched < L *captivus* captive]

ca·jole (kə·jōl) *v.t. & v.i.* **·joled, ·jol·ing** To persuade or coax with flattery; wheedle. [< F *cajoler*] **—ca·jole′ment, ca·jol′·er, ca·jol′er·y** *n.* **—ca·jol′ing·ly** *adv.*

Ca·jun (kā′jən) *n.* A descendant of the Acadian French in Louisiana. [Alter. of ACADIAN]

cake (kāk) *n.* 1 A baked mixture of flour, eggs, milk, sugar, etc. 2 A thin mass of dough or batter, etc., baked or fried: *pancake.* 3 A patty or shaped mass, as of fish or meat. 4 A hardened mass: a *cake* of soap, etc. **—take the cake** *Informal* To deserve a prize; be the best. *—v.t. & v.i.* **caked, cak·ing** To form into a hardened mass. [< ON *kaka*]

cakes and ale A carefree way of life.

cake·walk (kāk′wôk′) *n.* 1 Originally, a promenade in which the couple performing the most original dance steps won a cake as a prize. 2 a A dance based on this. b Music for such a dance. *—v.i.* To do a cakewalk. **—cake′·walk′er** *n.*

Cal calorie (large).

Cal. California.

cal calorie (small).

cal. calendar; caliber.

cal·a·bash (kal′ə·bash) *n.* 1 A tropical American tree bearing gourdlike fruit. 2 A vine of Africa and Asia having bottle-shaped, hard-shelled fruit. 3 The fruit of a calabash tree or vine. 4 An object, as a pipe, rattle, etc., made from a calabash gourd. [< Sp. *calabaza* pumpkin]

cal·a·boose (kal′ə·bōōs) *n. Slang* A jail. [< Sp. *calaboza*]

ca·la·di·um (kə·lā′dē·əm) *n.* A tropical American plant with large, variegated leaves. [< NL < Malay *kēlādy*]

cal·a·mine (kal′ə·mīn, -min) *n.* 1 A white zinc silicate mineral, often colored by impurities. 2 A native zinc carbonate, a pink powder used in lotions and ointments. *—v.t.* **·mined, ·min·ing** To apply calamine to. [< LL *calamina* < L *cadmia* zinc ore]

ca·lam·i·tous (kə·lam′ə·təs) *adj.* Causing or resulting in a calamity. **—ca·lam′i·tous·ly** *adv.* **—ca·lam′i·tous·ness** *n.* **—Syn.** disastrous, catastrophic, ruinous.

ca·lam·i·ty (kə·lam′ə·tē) *n. pl.* **·ties** 1 An event causing great suffering, grief, or misery; disaster. 2 A state or time of affliction, distress, etc. [< L *calamitas*]

cal·a·mus (kal′ə·məs) *n. pl.* **·mi** (-mī) 1 SWEET FLAG. 2 The quill of a feather. [< Gk. *kalamos* reed]

ca·lash (kə·lash′) *n.* 1 A low-wheeled carriage with a folding top. 2 A folding carriage top. 3 A folding hoodlike bonnet of the 18th century. [< F *calèche*]

Calash *def. 3*

cal·ca·ne·us (kal·kā′nē·əs) *n. pl.* **·ne·i** (-nē·ī) The heel bone. Also **cal·ca′ne·um.** [< L < *calx* heel]

cal·car·e·ous (kal·kâr′ē·əs) *adj.* Composed of, containing, or of the nature of limestone; chalky. [< L *calx* lime]

cal·ces (kal′sēz) *n.pl.* of CALX.

calci- *combining form* Lime. [< L *calx, calcis* lime]

cal·cif·er·ol (kal·sif′ər·ōl, -ol) *n.* Vitamin D as formed by the irradiation of ergosterol. [< CALCIFER(OUS) + (ERGOSTER)OL]

cal·cif·er·ous (kal·sif′ər·əs) *adj.* Yielding or containing calcium carbonate, as rocks.

cal·ci·fi·ca·tion (kal′sə·fi·kā′shən) *n.* 1 Hardening of tissue by deposition of calcium salts, as in bone formation. 2 Such hardened tissue.

cal·ci·fy (kal′sə·fī) *v.t. & v.i.* **·fied, ·fy·ing** To make or become hard by the deposit of lime salts.

cal·ci·mine (kal′sə·mīn, -min) *n.* A white or tinted wash of zinc white, glue, and water, for ceilings, walls, etc. *—v.t.* **·mined, ·min·ing** To apply calcimine to. [< L *calx* lime]

cal·cine (kal′sīn, -sin) *v.* **·cined, ·cin·ing** *v.t.* 1 To expel volatile matter from (a substance) by heat. 2 To reduce to powder by roasting. *—v.i.* 3 To become changed by the action of heat into a powder. [< L *calx* lime] **—cal·ci·na·tion** (kal′sə·nā′shən) *n.*

cal·cite (kal′sīt) *n.* Any of various mineral forms of calcium carbonate, usu. colorless or whitish, as chalk, limestone, and marble. **—cal·cit·ic** (kal·sit′ik) *adj.*

cal·ci·um (kal′sē·əm) *n.* A silver-white, malleable, metallic element (symbol Ca) widely distributed in combination, as in chalk, gypsum and limestone. [< L *calx* lime]

calcium carbide A compound of calcium and carbon which when treated with water yields acetylene.

calcium carbonate The chief natural compound of calcium, occurring as chalk, marble, limestone, etc., and as a constituent of bones, teeth, shells, etc.

calcium chloride A white, deliquescent salt, used as a drying agent, refrigerant, etc.

calcium hydroxide A white, crystalline powder used to make bleaches, cement, etc.; slaked lime.

calcium phosphate Any of a class of phosphates found in various animal tissues and prepared commercially for use as an antacid, polishing agent, etc.

cal·cu·la·ble (kal′kyə·lə·bəl) *adj.* 1 Capable of being calculated. 2 Reliable. **—cal′cu·la·bly** *adv.*

cal·cu·late (kal′kyə·lāt) *v.* **·lat·ed, ·lat·ing** *v.t.* 1 To determine by arithmetical means. 2 To ascertain beforehand; determine by estimation. 3 To adapt to a purpose; intend: used chiefly in the passive: *calculated* to carry a two-ton load. 4 *Regional* To suppose; believe. *—v.i.* 5 To compute. 6 *Informal* To rely; depend. [< LL *calculatus,* pp. of *calculare* reckon < *calculus* a pebble used in reckoning] **—Syn.** 1 compute, figure, reckon. 2 estimate, surmise, presume, conjecture.

cal·cu·lat·ed (kal′kyə·lā′tid) *adj.* 1 Arrived at by calculation. 2 Thoughtfully estimated: a *calculated* risk. 3 Intentional; deliberate: a *calculated* insult.

cal·cu·lat·ing (kal′kyə·lā′ting) *adj.* 1 Shrewdly self-interested; scheming. 2 Designed for computation: a *calculating* machine. **—cal′cu·lat′ing·ly** *adv.*

cal·cu·la·tion (kal′kyə·lā′shən) *n.* 1 The act, process, or result of calculating. 2 A shrewd forethought; prudence.

cal·cu·la·tor (kal′kyə·lā′tər) *n.* 1 One who calculates. 2 A mechanical or electronic device, usu. having a keyboard, for doing mathematical computations.

cal·cu·lus (kal′kyə·ləs) *n. pl.* **·li** (-lī) or **·lus·es** 1 *Pathol.* Any abnormal hard mass formed in the body. 2 *Math.* **a** A method of calculating by the use of a highly specialized system of symbols. **b** Analysis based on determination of rates of change of functions and the determination of a set of functions having a given rate of change, and their study and application. [<L, a pebble (used in counting)]

cal·de·ra (kôl·dir′ə, kal-) *n.* Crater formed by the collapse of, or outward explosion from, the cone of a volcano [<Sp.]

cal·dron (kôl′drən) *n.* A large kettle or boiler. [<L *caldaria* kettle <*calidus* hot]

ca·lèche (kȧ·lesh′) *n.* CALASH.

Cal·e·do·ni·a (kal′ə·dō′nē·ə, -dōn′yə) *n.* Scotland. —**Cal′·e·do′ni·an** *adj., n.*

cal·en·dar (kal′ən·dər) *n.* 1 A systematic arrangement of subdivisions of time, as years, months, days, weeks, etc. 2 A table showing such subdivisions, esp. of a single year. 3 A schedule or list: a *calendar* of events. —*v.t.* To register in a calendar or list. [<L *calendae* calends]

cal·en·der (kal′ən·dər) *n.* A machine for giving a gloss to cloth, paper, etc., by pressing between rollers. —*v.t.* To press (cloth, paper, etc.) in a calender. [<Gk. *kylindros* roller] —**cal′en·der·er** *n.*

cal·ends (kal′əndz) *n. pl. (often construed as sing.)* The first day of the month in the ancient Roman calendar. [<L *calendae*]

ca·len·du·la (kə·len′jo͞o·lə) *n.* A plant related to the daisies, having yellow or orange flowers. [<NL *calendae* calends; because it blooms almost every month]

calf[1] (kaf, käf) *n. pl.* **calves** (kavz, kävz) 1 The young of cattle. 2 The young of certain mammals, as the elephant, whale, etc. 3 Leather made from the skin of a calf. 4 *Informal* An awkward young fellow. [<OE *cealf*]

calf[2] (kaf, käf) *n. pl.* **calves** (kavz, kävz) The muscular back part of the human leg below the knee. [<ON *kālfi*]

calf·skin (kaf′skin′, käf′-) *n.* 1 The skin of a calf. 2 Leather made from this.

cal·i·ber (kal′ə·bər) *n.* 1 The internal diameter of a tube or of the barrel of a gun, cannon, etc. 2 The diameter of a bullet, shell, etc. 3 Degree of personal ability or quality. Also **cal′i·bre.** [<Ar. *qālib* mold, form]

cal·i·brate (kal′ə·brāt) *v.t.* **·brat·ed, ·brat·ing** 1 To graduate or adjust (a measuring instrument). 2 To ascertain the caliber of. —**cal′i·bra′tion** *n.* —**cal′i·bra′tor** *n.*

cal·i·co (kal′i·kō) *n. pl.* **·coes** or **·cos** A cotton cloth printed in bright colors. —*adj.* 1 Made of calico. 2 Resembling calico; dappled or spotted: a *calico* cat. [<*Calicut,* India]

Calif. California.

Cal·i·for·nia poppy (kal′ə·fôrn′yə, -fôr′nē·ə) A plant of the poppy family, having finely divided leaves and usu. yellow-orange flowers.

cal·i·for·ni·um (kal′ə·fôr′nē·əm) *n.* An artificially produced radioactive element (symbol Cf). [<the University of *California,* where first produced]

cal·i·per (kal′ə·pər) *n. Usu. pl.* Any of various instruments for making precise measurements of dimensions. —*v.t. & v.i.* To measure by using calipers. [Var. of CALIBER]

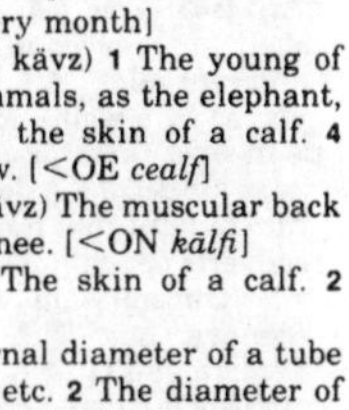

Calipers
a. inside. b. outside.

ca·liph (kā′lif, kal′if) *n.* The spiritual and civil head of a Muslim state. Also **ca′lif.** [<Ar. *khalīfah* successor] —**cal·i·phate** (kal′ə·fāt, -fit) *n.*

cal·is·then·ics (kal′is·then′iks) *n. pl.* 1 Light gymnastic exercises to promote physical fitness. 2 *(construed as sing.)* The art of practice of such exercises. [<Gk. *kallos* beauty + *sthenos* strength] —**cal′is·then′ic** *adj.*

calk[1] (kôk) *v.t.* CAULK.

calk[2] (kôk) *n.* 1 A spur on a horse's shoe to prevent slipping. 2 A plate with sharp points worn on the sole of a boot or shoe to prevent slipping. —*v.t.* To furnish with calks. [<L *calx* heel]

call (kôl) *v.t.* 1 To utter loudly. 2 To address or appeal to by such utterance. 3 To read or enumerate aloud: to *call* the roll. 4 To summon. 5 To communicate with by telephone. 6 To waken. 7 To convoke; convene. 8 To bring to action or being, as by order. 9 To name or designate. 10 To consider to be; estimate as. 11 To insist on payment of: to *call* a loan. 12 To predict in advance, as a shot in pool. 13 To stop or suspend (a game). 14 To judge on (a play, pitched ball, etc.), as in baseball. 15 In poker, to demand that (a player) show his hand by equaling his bet. —*v.i.* 16 To shout or raise the voice, as to attract attention. 17 To telephone. 18 To make a brief visit: often with *on.* 19 In poker, to demand a show of hands by equaling an opponent's bet. —**call down** 1 To invoke. 2 *Informal* To reprimand. —**call for** 1 To go to get; stop by for. 2 To require; demand. —**call forth** To evoke. —**call in** To remove from circulation, as currency. —**call off** To cancel. —**call on** 1 To ask to speak. 2 To visit briefly. —**call up** 1 To telephone. 2 To summon for active military service. 3 To bring to memory. —*n.* 1 A shout or cry. 2 A summons, appeal, or command. 3 A telephone communication or message. 4 A sounded signal: a bugle *call.* 5 A brief visit. 6 A demand; need. 7 Occasion; reason: no *call* for such behavior. 8 A claim or obligation. 9 A religious vocation. 10 **a** The characteristic cry of a bird or animal. **b** A device for imitating such a sound. 11 A sports decision, as by an umpire. —**on call** 1 Ready when summoned or requested. 2 Payable on demand. [<ON *kalla*]

cal·la (kal′ə) *n.* Any of several plants of the arum family, having a showy, usu. white petallike leaf surrounding a club-shaped flower stalk. Also **calla lily.** [<NL *calla,* a plant name]

call·board (kôl′bôrd′, -bōrd′) *n.* A backstage theater bulletin board for posting notices.

call·boy (kôl′boi′) *n.* 1 A boy who calls actors to go on stage. 2 BELLMAN.

call·er (kô′lər) *n.* 1 One who calls, esp. one who calls out the steps in square dancing. 2 One making a brief visit.

call girl *Informal* A prostitute who makes assignations in response to telephone calls.

cal·lig·ra·phy (kə·lig′rə·fē) *n.* 1 Beautiful penmanship. 2 The art of fine handwriting. [<Gk. *kalos* beautiful + -GRAPHY] —**cal·lig′ra·pher, cal·lig′ra·phist** *n.* —**cal·li·graph·ic** (kal′ə·graf′ik) *adj.*

call·ing (kô′ling) *n.* 1 A profession or occupation. 2 A vocation or inner urge, esp. of a religious nature.

calling card A small card bearing one's name, used when paying a business or social call, etc.

cal·li·o·pe (kə·lī′ə·pē, kal′ē·ōp) *n.* A musical instrument having steam whistles played by means of a keyboard. [<L<Gk. *Kalliopē* Calliope, lit., the beautiful-voiced]

Cal·li·o·pe (kə·lī′ə·pē) *Gk. Myth.* The Muse of eloquence and epic poetry.

cal·li·per (kal′ə·pər) *n.* CALIPER.

call letters The code letters identifying a radio or television transmitting station.

call number A number employed by libraries to classify and locate a book.

cal·los·i·ty (kə·los′ə·tē) *n. pl.* **·ties** 1 A thickened, hardened area of skin, produced by or as by pressure or friction. 2 Hardness; insensibility.

cal·lous (kal′əs) *adj.* 1 Thickened and hardened, as the skin by friction or pressure. 2 Coldly or cruelly unfeeling. —*v.t. & v.i.* To make or become callous. [<L *callus* hard skin] —**cal′lous·ly** *adv.* —**cal′lous·ness** *n.* —**Syn.** 2 insensitive, thick-skinned, hard, heartless, hardhearted.

cal·low (kal′ō) *adj.* 1 Inexperienced; youthful. 2 Unfledged, as a bird. [<OE *calu* bare, bald] —**cal′low·ness** *n.*

cal·lus (kal′əs) *n. pl.* **·lus·es** 1 A thickened, hardened area of skin. 2 The new tissue formed around the ends of a broken bone when reuniting. —*v.t. & v.i.* To develop callus (on). [<L, hard skin]

calm (käm) *adj.* **1** Free from agitation; unruffled; composed. **2** Not turbulent; quiet; still. —*n.* **1** Lack of turbulence, wind, or motion. **2** Serenity; peacefulness. —*v.t.* & *v.i.* To make or become calm. [<LL *cauma* heat of the day, rest at midday] —**calm'ly** *adv.* —**calm'ness** *n.* —**Syn.** *adj.* **1** tranquil, serene, placid, peaceful, untroubled.

cal·o·mel (kal'ə·mel, -məl) *n.* A white, tasteless compound of mercury and chlorine, a strong purgative now used chiefly in prophylactic ointments. [<Gk. *kalos* beautiful + *melas* black]

ca·lor·ic (kə·lôr'ik, -lor'-) *adj.* Of or pertaining to heat. [<L *calor* heat]

cal·o·rie (kal'ə·rē) *n.* **1** One of two units of heat. The **great, large,** or **kilogram calorie** is the amount of heat required to raise the temperature of one kilogram of water 1°C. The **small** or **gram calorie** is the amount of heat required to raise one gram of water 1° C. **2** The large calorie, used as a measure of the energy value of foods or the heat output of organisms. [<F *calorie* <L *calor* heat]

cal·o·rif·ic (kal'ə·rif'ik) *adj.* Of or producing heat. [<L *calorificus* heat-producing]

cal·o·rim·e·ter (kal'ə·rim'ə·tər) *n.* Any apparatus for measuring heat. [<L *calor* heat + -METER] —**ca·lor·i·met·ric** (kə·lôr'ə·met'rik, -lor'-) *adj.* —**cal'o·rim'e·try** *n.*

cal·u·met (kal'yə·met, kal'yə·met') *n.* A tobacco pipe with a long, ornamented stem, used by American Indians in various ceremonies. [<L *calamus* reed]

Calumet

ca·lum·ni·ate (kə·lum'nē·āt) *v.t.* **·at·ed, ·at·ing** To make false and damaging statements about; slander. [<L *calumnia* slander] —**ca·lum'ni·a'tion, ca·lum'ni·a'tor** *n.*

ca·lum·ni·ous (kə·lum'nē·əs) *adj.* Slanderous; defamatory. —**ca·lum'ni·ous·ly** *adv.*

cal·um·ny (kal'əm·nē) *n. pl.* **·nies** **1** A false accusation or report made with malicious or injurious intent. **2** The making of such statements; defamation. [<L *calumnia* slander]

Cal·va·ry (kal'vər·ē) *n.* The place where Christ was crucified; Golgotha. *Luke* 23:33. [<L *calvaria* skull]

calve (kav, käv) *v.t.* & *v.i.* **calved, calv·ing** To give birth to (a calf). [<OE *cealf* calf]

calves (kavz, kävz) *n. pl.* of CALF.

Cal·vin·ism (kal'vin·iz'əm) *n.* The religious system or doctrines of John Calvin, characterized by an austere moral code. —**Cal'vin·ist** *adj., n.* —**Cal'vin·is'tic** or **·ti·cal** adj. —**Cal'vin·is'ti·cal·ly** *adv.*

calx (kalks) *n. pl.* **calx·es** or **cal·ces** (kal'sēz) The residue from the calcination of minerals. [<L, lime]

ca·lyp·so (kə·lip'sō) *n. pl.* **·sos** A type of improvised, often topical song that originated in Trinidad. [<Calypso]

Ca·lyp·so (kə·lip'sō) In the *Odyssey,* a nymph who detained Odysseus for seven years on an island.

ca·lyx (kā'liks, kal'iks) *n. pl.* **ca·lyx·es** or **cal·y·ces** (kal'ə·sēz, kā'lə-) *Bot.* The outermost part of a flower, made up of usu. green, leaflike sepals. [<Gk. *kalyx* husk, pod]

cam (kam) *n.* A rotating wheel of irregular shape, used to change the direction of the motion of another part moving against it. [? <F *came*]

ca·ma·ra·de·rie (kä'mə·rä'dər·ē) *n.* Friendly good will; comradeship. [F]

cam·a·ril·la (kam'ə·ril'ə, *Sp.* kä'mä·rē'lyä) *n.* A group or clique of unofficial political advisers; a cabal. [<Sp. *camara* chamber]

cam·as (kam'əs) *n.* Any of several North American plants related to lilies, having an edible bulb. Also **cam'ass.** [<Chinook jargon]

cam·ber (kam'bər) *v.t.* & *v.i.* To shape with or have a slight upward convex curve. —*n.* A slight upward bend or convex curve. [<L *camera* curved roof, vault]

cam·bi·um (kam'bē·əm) *n.* A layer of growing and dividing cells between the phloem and xylem in the stems and roots of many plants, from which new tissues are developed. [<LL, exchange]

Cam·bo·di·a (kam·bō'dē·ə) *n.* A country of SW Indochina, 69,844 sq. mi., cap. Phnom Penh. • See map at INDOCHINA.

Cam·bri·a (kam'brē·ə) *n.* The Latin name for Wales.

Cam·bri·an (kam'brē·ən) *n.* & *adj.* See GEOLOGY.

cam·bric (kām'brik) *n.* A fine white linen or cotton fabric. [<Flemish *Kameryk* Cambrai, city in France]

cambric tea A drink made of sweetened hot water, milk, and often a little tea.

cam·cor·der (kam'kôr'dər) *n.* A combination of a portable TV camera and a videotape recorder.

came (kām) *p.t.* of COME.

cam·el (kam'əl) *n.* Either of two species of domesticated ruminants used as beasts of burden in arid regions of Africa and Asia: the **Arabian camel,** or dromedary, having one hump on the back, and the **Bactrian camel,** having two. [<Gk. *kamēlos* <Semitic]

Bactrian camel

ca·mel·lia (kə·mēl'yə, -mēl'ē·ə) *n.* A tropical tree or shrub with glossy evergreen leaves and showy flowers. [<George Joseph *Kamel,* 1661–1706, Jesuit missionary]

ca·mel·o·pard (kə·mel'ə·pärd) *n. Archaic* The giraffe. [<Gk. *kamēlos* camel + *pardalis* leopard]

Cam·e·lot (kam'ə·lot) In Arthurian legend, the seat of King Arthur's court.

camel's hair **1** The hair of a camel. **2** A warm, soft, usu. yellowish-tan cloth made from this. Also **camel hair.** —cam'el-hair', cam'el's-hair' *adj.*

Cam·em·bert (kam'əm·bâr, *Fr.* kȧ·mäṅ·bâr') *n.* A rich, creamy, soft, cheese. [<*Camembert,* town in NW France]

cam·e·o (kam'ē·ō) *n. pl.* **·e·os** **1** A gem of onyx, agate, shell, etc., carved in relief with design and background of different colors. **2** A small part, as in a movie or TV show, played by a well-known performer. [<Ital. *cammeo*]

cam·er·a (kam'ər·ə, kam'rə) *n. pl.* **·er·as** *for defs. 1 & 2,* **·er·ae** *for def. 3* **1** A device for exposing a sensitized plate or film to light that forms an image thereon. **2** A device that converts optical images into electrical impulses for television transmission. **3** *Law* A judge's private room. —**in camera** *Law* Not in public court; privately. [<Gk. *kamara* vault]

cam·er·a·man (kam'ər·ə·man', kam'rə-) *n. pl.* **·men** (-men') The operator of a camera, esp. a motion-picture camera.

Cam·e·roon (kam'ə·ro͞on') *n.* A republic of CEN. Africa, 183,376 sq. mi., cap. Yaoundé. Also **Cam'e·roun'.** • See map at AFRICA.

cam·i·sole (kam'ə·sōl) *n.* A woman's sleeveless, often lace-trimmed undergarment. [<Sp. *camisa* shirt]

cam·o·mile (kam'ə·mīl) *n.* CHAMOMILE.

cam·ou·flage (kam'ə·fläzh) *n.* **1** A protective disguise that matches, blends in with, or imitates natural surroundings. **2** Any disguise or pretense. —*v.t.* **·flaged, ·flag·ing** To hide or obscure with or as with camouflage. [<F *camoufler* disguise] —**cam'ou·flag'er** *n.*

camp[1] (kamp) *n.* **1 a** A place where a group of people, as soldiers, hunters, miners, or vacationers, live in tents or other temporary or informal shelters. **b** The tents or shelters of such a place. **2** A body of persons who support a doctrine or cause: the opposing political *camp.* —*v.i.* **1** To set up a camp. **2** To live temporarily in or as in a camp. **3** To sleep outdoors in a tent: often with *out.* —*v.t.* **4** To shelter or station in a camp. [<L *campus* level plain]

camp[2] (kamp) *n.* Something so banal, flamboyant, out-of-date, or artificial as to be thought humorous or appealing. —*adj.* Characterized by camp: also **camp'y (·i·er, ·i·est).** [?]

cam·paign (kam·pān') *n.* **1** A series of military operations conducted for a particular objective. **2** A series of related political or other activities designed to bring about a result. —*v.i.* To conduct or take part in a campaign. [<L *campus* open field] —**cam·paign'er** *n.*

cam·pa·ni·le (kam'pə·nē'lē, *Ital.* -nē'lā) *n. pl.* **·les** or **·li** (-lē) A tower that houses and supports a bell, esp. a tower near but not attached to a church. [<LL *campana* bell]

cam·pan·u·la (kam·pan'yə·lə) *n.* Any of a genus of plants having flowers with a bell-shaped, usu. blue corolla. [<LL *campana* bell]

camp chair A light, folding chair.

camp·er (kamp′pər) *n.* **1** One who camps out or stays in a summer camp, as for children. **2** A vehicle equipped as a shelter for travelers, vacationers, etc.
camp·fire (kamp′fīr′) *n.* **1** A fire in an outdoor camp, for cooking, warmth, etc. **2** A gathering around such a fire.
camp follower 1 A civilian who follows an army about, esp. a prostitute. **2** An adherent or hanger-on who is not officially a member of a group.
camp·ground (kamp′ground′) *n.* An area used for a camp or a camp meeting.
cam·phor (kam′fər) *n.* A crystalline compound with a penetrating odor and pungent taste, obtained synthetically or from the wood of an Asian tree, and used as a moth repellant, in medicine, etc. [< Ar. *kāfūr* < Malay *kāpūr*] **—cam·phor·ic** (kam·fôr′ik, -for′-) *adj.*
cam·phor·ate (kam′fə·rāt) *v.t.* **·at·ed, ·at·ing** To treat or saturate with camphor.
camphor ball A moth ball.
camphor ice An ointment containing camphor, used for chapped skin, etc.
camp·ing (kamp′ing) *n.* The act or practice of living outdoors, as in tents or without shelter, esp. for recreation.
cam·pi·on (kam′pē·ən) *n.* One of various flowering plants related to the pinks. [?]
camp meeting A series of religious meetings held outdoors or in a tent.
camp·site (kamp′sīt′) *n.* An outdoor site for camping.
camp stool A light, folding stool or seat.
cam·pus (kam′pəs) *n.* The grounds of a school, college, etc. [L, field, plain]
can¹ (kan, *unstressed* kən) *v., present* **can,** *past* **could 1** To be able to. **2** To know how to. **3** To have the right to. **4** *Informal* To be permitted to; may. [< OE *cunnan* know, be able] • Although there is a formal distinction made between *can* to express ability to do something and *may* to express permission, in informal usage *can* is generally acceptable to express permission, esp. in questions or negative statements.
can² (kan) *n.* **1** A usu. metal container in which foods, beverages, etc., are sealed for preserving. **2** A usu. large metal container for garbage, milk, etc. **3** The contents of a can. **4** *Slang* **a** A jail. **b** A toilet. **c** The backside. *—v.t.* **canned, can·ning 1** To preserve in a sealed can, jar, etc. **2** *Slang* To dismiss; fire. **3** *Informal* To record the sound of. [< OE *canne* cup] **—can′ner** *n.*
Can. Canada; Canadian.
Ca·naan (kā′nən) *n.* The part of Palestine between the Jordan and the Mediterranean; the Promised Land of the Israelites.
Ca·naan·ite (kā′nən·īt) *n.* A dweller in Canaan prior to the Israelite conquest.
Can·a·da (kan′ə·də) *n.* A member of the Commonwealth

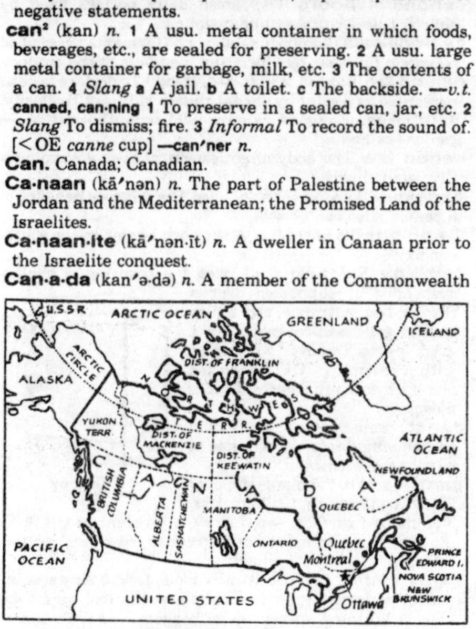

of Nations in N North America, 3,851,809 sq. mi., cap. Ottawa. **—Ca·na·di·an** (kə·nā′dē·ən) *adj., n.*
Canada goose A grayish wild goose of North America, having a black head and neck.
Canadian bacon Bacon from the loin of a pig, having the flavor of ham.
Ca·na·di·en (kə·nā′dē·en′, *Fr.* kä·nä·dyen′) *n.* FRENCH CANADIAN.
ca·naille (kə·nāl′, *Fr.* kȧ·nä′y′) *n.* The rabble; mob. [< Ital. *canaglia* pack of dogs < L *canis* dog]
ca·nal (kə·nal′) *n.* **1** An artificial waterway for navigation, irrigation, etc. **2** *Anat.* A duct, tube, or groove. **3** One of the faint lines visible on the planet Mars. **3** *Zool.* A groove. *—v.t.* **ca·nalled** or **ca·naled, ca·nal·ling** or **ca·nal·ing** To make a canal in or through. [< L *canalis* groove.]
ca·nal·ize (kə·nal′īz, kan′əl·īz) *v.t.* **·ized, ·iz·ing 1** To convert into a canal. **2** To furnish with a canal or canals. **3** To furnish with an outlet. **—ca·nal·i·za·tion** (kə·nal′ə·zā′shən, kan′ə·lə-) *n.*
can·a·pé (kan′ə·pē, -pā; *Fr.* kȧ·nȧ·pā′) *n.* A piece of bread, cracker, etc., topped with any of various relishes. [< F, lit., couch]
ca·nard (kə·närd′, *Fr.* kȧ·när′) *n.* A false or baseless story or rumor. [F, lit., duck]
ca·nar·y (kə·nâr′ē) *n. pl.* **·nar·ies 1** A small, usu. yellow songbird native to the Canary Islands, popular as a cage bird. **2** A bright yellow color: also **canary yellow. 3** A sweet, white wine from the Canary Islands. [< L *Canaria (Insula)* Dog (Island) < the dogs found there]
ca·nas·ta (kə·nas′tə) *n.* A card game similar to rummy, using two decks. [< Sp., basket]
canc. cancel; cancellation; canceled.
can·can (kan′kan′, *Fr.* käṅ·käṅ′) *n.* A lively dance characterized by high kicking. [F]
can·cel (kan′səl) *v.t.* **can·celed** or **·celled, can·cel·ing** or **·cel·ling 1** To strike out, as by marking lines through; cross off. **2** To countermand or call off. **3** To stamp or mark, as a postage stamp, to prevent reuse. **4** To make up for; counterbalance. **5** *Math.* To eliminate (a common factor) by dividing the numerator and denominator of a fraction, or both sides of an equation. *—v.i.* **6** To be canceled or counterbalanced: with *out.* *—n.* A cancellation. [< L *cancellare* cross out] **—can′cel·a·ble, can′cel·la·ble** *adj.* **—can′cel·er, can′cel·ler** *n.* **—Syn. 1** delete, expunge, obliterate. **2** repeal, annul, abrogate.
can·cel·la·tion (kan′sə·lā′shən) *n.* **1** The act of canceling. **2** That which is canceled. **3** A mark that cancels.
can·cer (kan′sər) *n.* **1** A malignant neoplasm, as carcinoma, sarcoma, etc. **2** Any baneful and spreading evil. [< L, crab, ulcer] **—can′cer·ous** *adj.*
Can·cer (kan′sər) *n.* A constellation and the fourth sign of the zodiac; the Crab. • See TROPIC and ZODIAC.
can·del·a (kan·del′ə) *n.* A unit of luminous intensity, equal to that of 1/60 of one square centimeter of the surface of a black body radiating at 1773.5°C.
can·de·la·brum (kan′də·lä′brəm, -lā′-) *n. pl.* **·bra** (-brə) or **·brums** A large, branched candlestick. [< L *candela* candle]
can·des·cence (kan·des′əns) *n.* INCANDESCENCE. [< L *candere* to glow] **—can·des′cent** *adj.*
can·did (kan′did) *adj.* **1** Frank, open, and sincere. **2** Impartial; fair. **3** Unposed; natural or informal: a *candid* snapshot. [< L *candidus* white, pure] **—can′did·ly** *adv.* **—can′did·ness** *n.* **—Syn. 1** straightforward, outspoken, ingenuous, guileless.
can·di·date (kan′də·dāt, -dit) *n.* One seeking or considered for an elective office, position, honor, etc. [< L *candidatus* wearing white < the white togas of Roman candidates] **—can·di·da·cy** (kan′də·də·sē), **can·di·da·ture** (kan′də·də·chŏŏr, -dā′chər) *n.*
candid camera A small camera with a fast lens, used for taking informal pictures of unposed subjects.
can·died (kan′dēd) *adj.* Cooked, glazed or permeated with sugar, syrup, etc.
can·dle (kan′dəl) *n.* **1** A usu. cylindrical stick of wax, tallow, etc., containing a wick ignited to give light. **2** Something resembling this. **3** CANDELA. **—burn the candle at both ends** To expend one's energy or resources excessively. **—hold a candle to** To compare with favorably: usu. used in the negative. *—v.t.* **·dled, ·dling** To test (eggs) for freshness by holding between the eye and a light. [< L *candela* < *candere* shine, gleam] **—can′dler** *n.*

can·dle·ber·ry (kan′dəl·ber′ē) *n. pl.* **·ries** BAYBERRY.

can·dle·light (kan′dəl·līt′) *n.* 1 Light given by a candle. 2 Early evening; dusk.

Can·dle·mas (kan′dəl·məs) *n.* February 2, a church festival marking the purification of the Virgin and the presentation of Christ in the temple. [OE *candel* candle + *mæsse* mass]

can·dle·pow·er (kan′dəl·pou′ər) *n.* Illuminating power as expressed in candelas.

can·dle·stick (kan′dəl·stik′) *n.* A holder for a candle or candles.

can·dor (kan′dər) *n.* 1 Openness; frankness. 2 Freedom from prejudice; impartiality; fairness. *Brit. sp.* **can′dour.** [< L, sincerity, purity, whiteness]

can·dy (kan′dē) *n. pl.* **·dies** 1 Any of numerous confections made from sugar, syrup, etc., often combined with chocolate, fruit, nuts, etc. 2 A single piece of this. 3 Sugar or syrup crystallized by boiling or evaporation. —*v.* **·died, ·dy·ing** *v.t.* 1 To cook, coat, or preserve with sugar or syrup. 2 To cause to form sugar crystals. 3 To make pleasant; sweeten. —*v.i.* 4 To form sugar crystals; turn to sugar. [< Ar. *qandī* made of sugar]

can·dy·tuft (kan′dē·tuft′) *n.* A garden plant with white, pink, or purple flowers.

cane (kān) *n.* 1 A stick carried or used as an aid in walking. 2 A similar rod, esp. one used for flogging. 3 A plant, as bamboo, rattan, or sugar cane, having jointed, woody stems. 4 The stem of certain of these plants, often split and woven, as for furniture. 5 The woody stem of a raspberry, blackberry, rose, etc. —*v.t.* **caned, can·ing** 1 To strike or beat with a cane. 2 To weave or repair with cane, as a chair seat. [< Gk. *kanna* reed < Semitic] —**can′er** *n.*

cane·brake (kān′brāk′) *n.* An area densely overgrown with canes.

cane sugar Sucrose made from sugar cane.

ca·nine (kā′nīn) *adj.* Of, resembling, or characteristic of a dog or related animal. —*n.* 1 A dog or related animal, as a wolf, coyote, etc. 2 Any of the four conical teeth adjoining the incisors at the front of the upper and lower jaws: also **canine tooth.** [< L < *canis* dog] • See TOOTH.

Ca·nis Ma·jor (kā′nis mā′jər) A northern constellation that contains the bright star Sirius.

Canis Mi·nor (mī′nər) A northern constellation containing the star Procyon.

can·is·ter (kan′is·tər) *n.* 1 A usu. metal container, as for tea, coffee, or spices. 2 A metal cylinder containing shot, etc., that shatters when fired, as from a cannon. [< L *canistrum* basket]

can·ker (kang′kər) *n.* 1 An ulcerous sore in the mouth. 2 A plant disease marked by dead tissue. 3 Any secret or spreading evil. —*v.t.* 1 To infect with canker. 2 To decay or corrupt. —*v.i.* 3 To be affected by a canker. [< L *cancer* crab, ulcer] —**can′ker·ous** *adj.*

can·ker·worm (kang′kər·wûrm′) *n.* Any of several moth larvae that destroy trees.

can·na (kan′ə) *n.* Any of a genus of tropical plants with broad leaves and red or yellow irregular flowers. [< Gk. *kanna* reed]

can·na·bis (kan′ə·bis) *n.* MARIHUANA. [< Gk. *kannabis* hemp]

canned (kand) *adj.* 1 Preserved in a can or jar. 2 *Informal* Recorded: *canned* music.

can·nel (kan′əl) *n.* A bituminous coal that burns with a bright flame. Also **cannel coal.** [Alter. of *candle coal*]

can·ner·y (kan′ər·ē) *n. pl.* **·ner·ies** A processing plant where foods are canned.

can·ni·bal (kan′ə·bəl) *n.* 1 A human being who eats human flesh. 2 An animal that devours members of its own species. [< Sp. *Canibales*, var. of *Caribes* Caribs] —**can′ni·bal·ism** *n.* —**can′ni·bal·is′tic** *adj.* —**can′ni·bal·is′ti·cal·ly** *adv.*

can·ni·bal·ize (kan′ə·bəl·īz′) *v.t.* **·ized, ·iz·ing** To take parts from (inoperative equipment) to repair other equipment and vehicles. —**can′ni·bal·i·za′tion** *n.*

can·ni·kin (kan′ə·kin) *n.* A small can or drinking cup.

can·ning (kan′ing) *n.* The process or business of preserving food, etc., in sealed cans or jars.

can·non (kan′ən) *n. pl.* **·nons** or **·non** 1 A large, usu. mounted tubular weapon for discharging a heavy projectile. 2 The large bone between the fetlock and knee of a horse or related animal: also **cannon bone.** 3 *Brit.* CAROM. —*v.t.* & *v.i.* 1 To fire or attack with cannon. 2 *Brit.* To carom or cause to carom.

can·non·ade (kan′ən·ād′) *v.* **·ad·ed, ·ad·ing** *v.t.* 1 To attack with cannon shot. —*v.t.* 2 To fire cannon repeatedly. —*n.* A continued attack with or discharge of cannon.

cannon ball A large spherical shot for firing from a cannon.

can·non·eer (kan′ən·ir′) *n.* An artillery man.

cannon fodder Soldiers regarded as expendable in warfare.

can·non·ry (kan′ən·rē) *n.* 1 Artillery. 2 Cannon fire.

can·not (ka′not) *v.i.* Can not. —**cannot but** Have no alternative except to.

can·ny (kan′ē) *adj.* **can·ni·er, can·ni·est** 1 Shrewd; astute. 2 Prudent; thrifty. [< CAN (to know how)] —**can′ni·ly** *adv.* —**can′ni·ness** *n.* —**Syn.** 1 clever, sharp, smart, wise.

ca·noe (kə·nōō′) *n.* A light, narrow boat, pointed at both ends and propelled by paddles. —*v.t.* & *v.i.* To travel or convey by canoe. [< Sp. *canoa* boat] —**ca·noe′ist** *n.*

Canoe

can·on[1] (kan′ən) *n.* 1 A law, rule, or body of rules of a church. 2 An established rule or principle; standard; criterion. 3 Writings, as books of the Bible, considered holy or authoritative by a church, sect, etc. 4 An official list or catalogue. 5 *Often cap.* A portion of the Mass following the Sanctus. 6 *Music* A composition in which each voice or part in turn takes up the melody and all combine in counterpoint. [< Gk. *kanōn* rule, straight rod]

can·on[2] (kan′ən) *n.* A clergyman belonging to the chapter of a cathedral or collegiate church. [< LL *canon* rule]

cañ·on (kan′yən, *Sp.* kä·nyōn′) *n.* CANYON.

ca·non·i·cal (kə·non′i·kəl) *adj.* 1 Of or according to church law. 2 Accepted or approved; authoritative. Also **ca·non′ic.** —**ca·non′i·cal·ly** *adv.*

canonical hours The seven daily periods fixed by church rule for prayer and devotion.

ca·non·i·cals (kə·non′i·kəlz) *n. pl.* Garments prescribed by canon for wear by officiating members of the clergy.

can·on·ize (kan′ən·īz) *v.t.* **·ized, ·iz·ing** 1 To declare (a dead person) to be a saint by official church ruling. 2 To glorify: 3 To make or regard as canonical or authoritative. —**can′on·i·za′tion** *n.*

canon law The body of ecclesiastical laws governing a Christian church.

can·on·ry (kan′ən·rē) *n. pl.* **·ries** The office or benefice of a canon. Also **can′on·ship.**

Ca·no·pus (kə·nō′pəs) *n.* A very bright star in the southern sky. [L]

can·o·py (kan′ə·pē) *n. pl.* **·pies** 1 A covering or shelter suspended or supported over a throne, bed, entrance, etc. 2 Any similar overhead covering. —*v.t.* **·pied, ·py·ing** To cover with or as with a canopy. [< Gk. *kōnōpeion* bed with mosquito net < *kōnōps* mosquito]

Canopy

canst (kanst) *Archaic* Second person singular present tense of CAN[1]: used with *thou.*

cant[1] (kant) *n.* 1 A slant, slope, or tilt. 2 A motion that tilts or tips. 3 A slanted surface. —*v.t.* & *v.i.* 1 To slant or tilt. 2 To move or cause to move with a sudden, swerving motion. [< L *cantus*, rim of a wheel]

cant[2] (kant) *n.* 1 Hypocritically pious talk. 2 Any specialized or esoteric jargon or vocabulary: thieves' *cant;* legal *cant.* 3 Whining speech, as of beggars. —*v.i.* To use or speak in cant. [< L *cantus* song] —**cant′er** *n.*

can't (kant, känt) Contraction of *cannot.*

Cantab. of Cambridge (Univ.) (L *Cantabrigiensis*).

can·ta·bi·le (kän·tä′bē·lā) *Music adj.* & *adv.* In a flowing, songlike style. —*n.* A composition or passage in this style. [Ital.]

can·ta·loupe (kan′tə·lōp) *n.* A variety of muskmelon with a hard, rough rind and orange flesh. Also **can′ta·loup.** [< *Cantalupo*, a villa near Rome]

can·tank·er·ous (kan·tang′kər·əs) *adj.* Bad-tempered; quarrelsome. [ME *contak* strife] **—can·tank′er·ous·ly** *adv.* **—can·tank′er·ous·ness** *n.* **—Syn.** irritable, irascible, snappish, testy, cranky.

can·ta·ta (kən·tä′tə) *n.* A vocal composition in several movements. [Ital. < *cantare* to sing]

can·teen (kan·tēn′) *n.* **1** A usu. metal flask for carrying drinking water, etc. **2** A shop at a military base where soldiers buy provisions, refreshments, etc. **3** A cafeteria, recreation center, etc., usu. operated by an institution. [< Ital. *cantina* cellar]

can·ter (kan′tər) *n.* A moderate, easy gallop. *—v.t. & v.i.* To ride or go at a canter. [Short for *Canterbury gallop;* with ref. to the pace of pilgrims riding to Canterbury]

Can·ter·bur·y bells (kan′tər·ber′ē) A garden plant having bell-shaped usu. blue flowers.

cant hook A pole with a hinged hook, used for handling logs.

can·ti·cle (kan′ti·kəl) *n.* A chant or hymn, esp. one with words taken directly from the Bible. [< L *cantus* song]

can·ti·lev·er (kan′tə·lev′ər) *n.* **1** A projecting structural member supported at only one end. **2** A similar arrangement consisting of a projecting part supported only at its point of balance. *—v.t.* To build or design (a structural part) to extend as a cantilever. [?]

cantilever bridge A bridge formed by two counterbalanced projecting parts each supported at one end.

can·tle (kan′təl) *n.* The upward-curving rear part of a saddle. [< LL *cantus* corner]

can·to (kan′tō) *n. pl.* **·tos** A division of an extended poem. [< L *cantus* song]

can·ton (kan′tən, -ton, kan·ton′) *n.* A political division of Switzerland. *—v.t.* **1** To divide into cantons. **2** To assign to quarters, as military troops. [< LL *cantus* corner] **—can·ton·al** (kan′tən·əl) *adj.*

Can·ton·ese (kan′tən·ēz′, -ēs′) *n. pl.* **·ese 1** A native of Canton, China. **2** The Chinese language spoken in and around Canton. *—adj.* Of Canton.

can·ton·ment (kan·ton′mənt, -tōn′-) *n.* **1** A group of buildings used as temporary housing for troops. **2** The assignment or troops to such housing.

can·tor (kan′tər, -tôr) *n.* **1** A liturgical singer serving as soloist and leader of prayer in a synagogue. **2** A leader of church choral music. [< L]

Ca·nuck (kə·nuk′) *n. Slang* **1** A Canadian. **2** FRENCH CANADIAN. *Sometimes disparaging.*

can·vas (kan′vəs) *n.* **1** Strong, close-woven cloth of cotton, flax, or hemp, used for sails, tents, etc. **2** A piece of such cloth used for a painting. **3** A painting on such cloth. **4** A sail or sails. **—under canvas 1** With sails set. **2** In tents. [< L *cannabis* hemp]

can·vas·back (kan′vəs·bak′) *n.* A North American wild duck with a grayish white back.

can·vass (kan′vəs) *v.t.* **1** To go about (an area) or to (persons) to solicit opinions, votes, orders, etc. **2** To examine or discuss thoroughly. *—v.i.* **3** To go about seeking votes, information, etc. *—n.* **1** A survey, poll, etc., as to ascertain opinion or solicit votes. **2** A detailed examination or discussion. [< CANVAS] **—can′vass·er** *n.*

can·yon (kan′yən) *n.* A deep gorge or narrow valley with high, steep sides. [< Sp. *cañón*]

caout·chouc (kou·chōōk′, kōō′chōōk) *n.* Rubber; esp. crude rubber. [F]

cap (kap) *n.* **1** A close-fitting head covering, usu. with a visor or brimless. **2** A distinctive head covering denoting status, occupation, etc. **3** A cover, top part, etc., resembling or suggestive of a cap. **4** A metal case, small paper container, etc., enclosing an explosive. **—set one's cap for** To try to win as a suitor or husband. *—v.t.* **capped, cap·ping 1** To put a cap or cover on. **2** To cover as with a cap; top. **3** To add the final touch to. **4** To surpass. [< LL *cappa* hooded cloak, cap]

cap. (*pl.* **caps.**) capacity; capital; capitalize.

ca·pa·bil·i·ty (kā′pə·bil′ə·tē) *n. pl.* **·ties 1** The quality of being capable; ability. **2** *Often pl.* A feature, quality, etc., that may be used or developed; potential.

ca·pa·ble (kā′pə·bəl) *adj.* Having suitable ability; competent. **—capable of 1** Having the required ability or capacity for. **2** Open to; susceptible of. [< LL *capabilis* < L *capere* take, receive] **—ca′pa·ble·ness** *n.* **—ca′pa·bly** *adv.*

ca·pa·cious (kə·pā′shəs) *adj.* Able to contain or receive much. [< L *capax* able to hold, roomy < *capere* take] **—ca·pa′cious·ly** *adv.* **—ca·pa′cious·ness** *n.* **—Syn.** ample, roomy, commodious, spacious.

ca·pac·i·tance (kə·pas′ə·təns) *n.* The ratio of electrical charge on a system of conductors to the resulting potential. [< CAPACI(TY) + (REAC)TANCE] **—ca·pac′i·tive** *adj.*

ca·pac·i·tate (kə·pas′ə·tāt) *v.t.* **·tat·ed, ·tat·ing** To render capable or qualified.

ca·pac·i·ty (kə·pas′ə·tē) *n. pl.* **·ties 1** Ability to receive or contain. **2** A measure of the ability to receive or contain; volume. **3** Maximum ability to contain, perform, etc. **4** Ability to do something; power. **5** Specific position, role, etc. **6** Legal qualification. **7** *Electr.* **a** CAPACITANCE. **b** The maximum output of an electric generator. [< L *capax* able to hold]

cap-a-pie (kap′ə·pē′) *adv.* From head to foot. Also **cap′-à-pie′.** [< OF]

ca·par·i·son (kə·par′ə·sən) *n.* **1** A decorative covering for a horse. **2** Showy or sumptuous apparel. *—v.t.* **1** To put ornamental trappings on. **2** To clothe richly. [< OF *caparasson* < Sp. *caparazón* < LL *cappa* cape]

cape[1] (kāp) *n.* A point of land extending into the sea or other body of water. [< L *caput* head]

cape[2] (kāp) *n.* A sleeveless outer garment falling loosely over the shoulders. [< LL *cappa*]

cap·e·lin (kap′ə·lin) *n. pl.* **·lin** or **·lins** A small, edible, smeltlike fish of northern seas. [< F *capelan*]

ca·per[1] (kā′pər) *v.i.* To leap or skip playfully; frisk. *—n.* **1** A playful skip or jump. **2** A prank; antic. **—cut a caper** (or **capers**) To caper; frolic. [Short for CAPRIOLE] **—ca′·per·er** *n.* **—Syn.** *v.* gambol, frolic, prance, cavort.

ca·per[2] (kā′pər) *n.* **1** The flower bud of a Mediterranean shrub, pickled and used as a condiment. **2** The shrub. [< Gk. *kapparis*]

cape·skin (kāp′skin′) *n.* Leather made from sheepskins, used esp. for gloves. [< *Cape* of Good Hope]

ca·pi·as (kā′pē·əs, kap′ē·əs) *n. Law* A judicial writ ordering an arrest by an officer. [< L, you may take]

cap·il·lar·i·ty (kap′ə·lar′ə·tē) *n.* **1** The state or quality of being capillary. **2** *Physics* The interaction between adjoining surfaces of a liquid and a solid that constrains it.

cap·il·lar·y (kap′ə·ler′ē) *n. pl.* **·lar·ies 1** Any of the microscopic blood vessels connecting the arterial and venous systems. **2** Any tube with a fine, hairlike bore. *—adj.* **1** Of or resembling a hair; fine; slender. **2** Having a slender, hairlike opening, as a tube or vessel. **3** Of capillarity. [< L *capillus* hair]

cap·i·tal[1] (kap′ə·təl) *n.* **1** A city that is the seat of government of a country, state, etc. **2** CAPITAL LETTER. **3** Wealth or property assets available for producing more wealth, as through investment. **4** The assets of a business after deduction of liabilities. **5** Capitalists or wealthy people as a class. **6** A quality, resource, etc., that can be used to advantage. *—adj.* **1** Chief; principal; foremost. **2** Serving as the seat of government. **3** Excellent; first-rate. **4** Of or pertaining to financial capital. **5** Involving or punishable by the death penalty. [< MF < L *caput* head]

cap·i·tal[2] (kap′ə·təl) *n.* The top part of a column or pillar. [< L *caput* head]

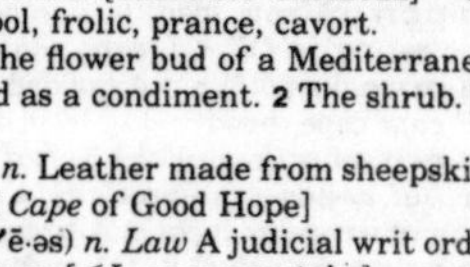

a b c

Capitals. a. Doric. b. Ionic. c. Corinthian.

capital gain Profit from the sale of capital investments, such as stocks, real estate, etc.

cap·i·tal·ism (kap′ə·təl·iz′əm) *n.* **1** An economic system in which the means of production and distribution are privately owned and operated for private profit. **2** The principles, power, results, etc., of this system.

cap·i·tal·ist (kap′ə·təl·ist) *n.* **1** An owner of capital, esp. one with considerable wealth invested in business. **2** A supporter of capitalism. **3** Loosely, any very wealthy person. **—cap′i·tal·is′tic** *adj.* **—cap′i·tal·is′ti·cal·ly** *adv.*

cap·i·tal·ize (kap′ə·təl·īz) *v.t.* **·ized, ·iz·ing 1** To begin with a capital letter, or write or print in capital letters. **2** To convert into capital or cash. **3** To invest for profit; use to provide capital. **4** To organize on a basis of capital. **5** To profit by: used with *on.* **—cap′i·tal·i·za′tion** *n.*

capital letter A letter, as A, B, or Z, printed or written larger than and often in different form from that of the corresponding small letter.

cap·i·tal·ly (kap′ə·təl·ē) *adv.* Excellently; very well.

capital punishment The death penalty for a crime.

capital ship A large warship, as an aircraft carrier.

capital stock The amount of negotiable shares of stock owned by an individual or a corporation.

cap·i·ta·tion (kap′ə·tā′shən) *n.* An individual assessment or tax; a poll tax. [< LL *capitatio* poll tax < L *caput* head]

cap·i·tol (kap′ə·təl) *n.* The building in which a State legislature convenes.

Cap·i·tol (kap′ə·təl) *n.* **1** The official building of the U.S. Congress in Washington. **2** The temple of Jupiter in ancient Rome. [< L *Capitolium*]

Capitol Hill 1 The site of the Capitol in Washington, D.C. **2** The U.S. Congress. **—on Capitol Hill** or **on the Hill** In the U.S. Congress.

ca·pit·u·late (kə·pich′o͞o·lāt) *v.i.* **·lat·ed, ·lat·ing 1** To surrender on stipulated conditions. **2** To give in; yield. [< L *capitulare* draw up in chapters, arrange terms] **—ca·pit′·u·la′tor** *n.* **—ca·pit′u·la·to′ry** *adj.*

ca·pit·u·la·tion (kə·pich′o͞o·lā′shən) *n.* **1** The act of capitulating; surrender. **2** A statement of the terms of surrender. **3** A summary or outline of main points.

ca·pon (kā′pon, -pən) *n.* A rooster castrated and raised for eating. [< OE < L *capo, -onis*]

ca·pote (kə·pōt′) *n.* **1** A hooded coat or cloak. **2** A bonnet. [F *cape* cape, hood]

ca·pric·ci·o (kə·prē′chē·ō, *Ital.* kä·prēt′chō) *n. pl.* **·ci·os** or *Ital.* **ca·pric·ci** (kä·prēt′chē) **1** A lively musical composition of irregular form. **2** A prank or whim. [Ital., caprice]

ca·price (kə·prēs′) *n.* **1** A sudden, unreasonable impulse or change of mind; a whim. **2** A tendency to such acts or impulses. **3** *Music* CAPRICCIO. [< Ital. *capriccio*]

ca·pri·cious (kə·prish′əs) *adj.* **1** Characterized by or resulting from caprice. **2** Liable to sudden changes or impulses; fickle. **—ca·pri′cious·ly** *adv.* **—ca·pri′cious·ness** *n.*

Cap·ri·corn (kap′rə·kôrn) *n.* A constellation and the tenth sign of the zodiac; the Goat. [< L *caper* goat + *cornu* horn] • See TROPIC and ZODIAC.

cap·ri·ole (kap′rē·ōl) *n.* An upward leap in place with feet off the ground, made by a trained horse. *—v.i.* **·oled, ·ol·ing** To do a capriole. [< Ital. *capriola* leap of a goat]

cap·si·cum (kap′si·kəm) *n.* **1** Any of various plants of the nightshade family producing many-seeded pods from which red pepper is obtained. **2** The fruit of these plants. [< L *capsa* box (from the shape of the fruit)]

cap·size (kap′sīz, kap·sīz′) *v.t. & v.i.* **·sized, ·siz·ing** To upset or overturn. [?]

cap·stan (kap′stən) *n.* A drumlike apparatus for hoisting anchors, etc., by exerting traction upon a cable. [< L *capistrum* halter < *capere* to hold]

capstan bar A lever used in turning a capstan.

cap·stone (kap′stōn′) *n.* COPESTONE.

cap·sule (kap′səl, -syo͞ol) *n.* **1** A small gelatinous case for containing a dose of a drug. **2** *Bot.* A dry seed vessel or spore case, esp. one that splits open when ripe. **3** A membrane enclosing an organ or structure. **4** The cargo or passenger container of a space vehicle. [< L *capsula,* dim. of *capsa* box] **—cap′su·lar** *adj.*

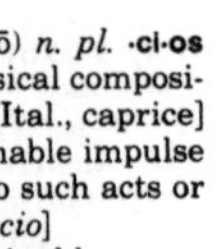

a b

Capsules
a. iris.
b. carnation.

Capt. Captain.

cap·tain (kap′tən, -tin) *n.* **1** One at the head of or in command; chief; leader. **2** The master or commander of a vessel. **3** See GRADE. *—v.t.* To be captain of; command; [< LL *capitaneus* < L *caput* head] **—cap′tain·cy** (-sē), **cap′tain·ship** *n.*

cap·tion (kap′shən) *n.* **1** A heading of a chapter, section, document, etc. **2** The title and explanatory material accompanying an illustration. **3** A subtitle in a motion picture. *—v.t.* To provide a caption for. [< L *captio* deception, sophism < *capere* take]

cap·tious (kap′shəs) *adj.* **1** Apt to find fault. **2** Intended to confuse or trip up: *captious* questions. [< L *captiosus* fallacious] **—cap′tious·ly** *adv.* **—cap′tious·ness** *n.* **—Syn. 1** critical, carping, caviling.

cap·ti·vate (kap′tə·vāt) *v.t.* **·vat·ed, ·vat·ing** To charm; fascinate. [< L *captivus.* See CAPTIVE.] **—cap′ti·vat′ing·ly** *adv.* **—cap′ti·va′tion, cap′ti·va′tor** *n.*

cap·tive (kap′tiv) *n.* **1** One captured and held; a prisoner. **2** One who is captivated or enthralled. *—adj.* **1** Taken or held as a prisoner. **2** Held under constraint or control. **3** Unable to avoid being present or listening: a *captive* audience. **4** Captivated; enthralled. [< L *captivus* < *capere* take]

cap·tiv·i·ty (kap·tiv′ə·tē) *n. pl.* **·ties** The state of being held captive.

cap·tor (kap′tər) *n.* One who takes or holds a captive.

cap·ture (kap′chər) *v.t.* **·tured, ·tur·ing 1** To seize and hold, as by force, skill, etc. **2** To win possession of; gain. **3** To succeed in preserving an impression or image of. *—n.* **1** The act of capturing or of being captured. **2** One who or that which is captured. [< L *captura* < *capere* take]

cap·u·chin (kap′yo͞o·chin, -shin) *n.* **1** A hooded cloak. **2** A long-tailed South American monkey with a hoodlike growth of hair. [< Ital. *cappuccino* hooded one]

Cap·u·chin (kap′yo͞o·chin, -shin) *n.* A monk of a Franciscan order wearing a habit with a pointed hood.

cap·y·ba·ra (kap′i·bä′rə) *n.* A large, short-tailed aquatic rodent of South America. [< Tupi]

car (kär) *n.* **1** An automobile. **2** A wheeled vehicle that moves on rails. **3** An enclosure for passengers, as of an elevator. **4** A chariot. [< L *carrus* wagon]

ca·ra·ba·o (kä′rə·bä′ō) *n. pl.* **·ba·os** WATER BUFFALO. [< Malay *karbau*]

car·a·bin (kar′ə·bin), **car·a·bine** (-bīn) *n.* CARBINE.

car·a·bin·eer, car·a·bin·ier (kar′ə·bin·ir′) *n.* CARBINEER.

car·a·cal (kar′ə·kal) *n.* A wild cat of sw Asia and Africa, having light brown fur and pointed, black-tipped ears. [< Turkish *qarah* black + *qulaq* ear]

Caracal

ca·ra·ca·ra (kä′rə·kä′rə) *n.* A large, vulturelike hawk of South America. [< Tupian]

car·a·cole (kar′ə·kōl) *n.* A sudden half turn to the right or left made by a horse and rider. *—v.i.* **·coled, ·col·ing** To make a caracole or caracoles. [< Ital. *caracollo*]

car·a·cul (kar′ə·kəl) *n.* KARAKUL.

ca·rafe (kə·raf′, -räf′) *n.* A glass bottle for serving water, wine, etc. [< Ar. *gharafa* draw water]

car·a·mel (kar′ə·məl, -mel, kär′məl) *n.* **1** A chewy candy made with butter, sugar, etc. **2** A brown syrup made by heating sugar, used to flavor and color foods. [Prob. < L *calamus* reed]

car·a·pace (kar′ə·pās) *n.* The hard, horny shield on the back of a turtle, lobster, etc. [< Sp. *carapacho*]

car·at (kar′ət) *n.* **1** A unit of weight for gems, equal to 200 milligrams, or 3.086 grains. **2** Loosely, a karat. [< Ar. *qīrāt* weight of 4 grains < Gk. *keration* seed, small weight]

car·a·van (kar′ə·van) *n.* **1** A company of people traveling together, as across a desert. **2** A group of vehicles traveling together. **3** VAN[1] (def. 1). **4** *Brit.* TRAILER (def. 3). [< Pers. *kārwān* caravan]

car·a·van·sa·ry (kar′ə·van′sə·rē) *n. pl.* **·ries** A hostelry or inn. [< Pers. *kārwān* caravan + *sarāī* inn]

car·a·vel (kar′ə·vel) *n.* A fleet vessel of Spain and Portugal in the 15th and 16th centuries. [< Gk. *korabus* light ship]

car·a·way (kar′ə·wā) *n.* **1** A biennial herb related to parsley. **2** Its small aromatic seeds **(caraway seeds)** used for flavoring. [< Sp. *alcarahueya* < Arabic *al* the + *karwīyā* caraway < Gk. *karon*]

car·bide (kär′bīd, -bid) *n.* A compound of carbon with a metal or other element.

car·bine (kär′bīn, -bēn) *n.* **1** A light short-barreled rifle originally devised for mounted troops. **2** A magazine-fed, gas-operated .30-caliber rifle used by the U.S. armed forces in World War II. [< F *carabine*] **—car′bi·neer′** *n*

carbo- *combining form* Carbon: *carbohydrate.* Also **carb-**.

car·bo·hy·drate (kär′bō·hī′drāt) *n.* Any of a group of compounds synthesized by plants from carbon dioxide and water, including sugars, starches, and cellulose.

car·bol·ic acid (kär·bol′ik) A poisonous, caustic organic compound with a distinctive odor, derived from coal tar and used as a disinfectant. [< CARB- + L *oleum* oil]

car·bon (kär′bən) *n.* **1** A nonmetallic element (symbol C) that occurs in three allotropic forms and as a constituent of all organisms and in many inorganic minerals and in atmospheric gases. **2** *Electr.* A rod of carbon, used as an electrode in an arc light. **3** A piece of carbon paper. **4** CARBON COPY. **—*adj.*** **1** Of, pertaining to, or like carbon. **2** Treated with carbon. [< L *carbo* coal]

car·bo·na·ceous (kär′bə·nā′shəs) *adj.* Of, pertaining to, or yielding carbon.

car·bon·ate (kär′bə·nāt) *v.t.* **·at·ed, ·at·ing** **1** To charge with carbonic acid. **2** CARBONIZE. **—*n.*** (kär′bə·nāt, -nit) A salt or ester of carbonic acid. **—car′bo·na′tion** *n.*

carbon copy **1** A copy of a typewritten letter, etc., made by means of carbon paper. **2** Someone or something closely resembling another.

carbon dating The assignment of approximate age to fossils by measuring the residual radioactivity of the carbon 14 incorporated in a specimen during its lifetime.

carbon dioxide A heavy, colorless, nonflammable gas, comprising about 0.04 percent of the atmosphere, utilized by plants in photosynthesis of carbohydrates, and released by respiration of plants and animals.

carbon 14 A radioactive isotope of carbon, having a half-life of 5,700 years.

car·bon·ic (kär·bon′ik) *adj.* Of, pertaining to, or obtained from carbon.

carbonic acid A weak, unstable acid, existing only in solution and readily dissociating into water and carbon dioxide.

car·bon·ic-ac·id gas (kär·bon′ik·as′id) CARBON DIOXIDE.

car·bon·if·er·ous (kär′bə·nif′ər·əs) *adj.* Of, pertaining to, containing, or yielding carbon or coal.

Car·bon·if·er·ous (kär′bə·nif′ər·əs) *adj.* & *n.* See GEOLOGY.

car·bon·ize (kär′bən·īz) *v.t.* **·ized, ·iz·ing** **1** To reduce to carbon; char. **2** To coat with carbon, as paper. **3** To combine with carbon. **—car′bon·i·za′tion** *n.*

carbon monoxide A colorless, odorless, poisonous gas, formed by the incomplete oxidation of carbon.

carbon paper A tissuelike paper coated on one side with carbon or other material for transferring impressions made, as by a typewriter, from a sheet placed over it to another facing the carbon, etc.

carbon tetrachloride A colorless, nonflammable, volatile, poisonous liquid.

Car·bo·run·dum (kär′bə·run′dəm) *n.* An abrasive of silicon carbide: a trade name.

car·boy (kär′boi) *n.* A large glass bottle enclosed in a crate or in wickerwork, used as a container for corrosive acids, etc. [< Pers. *qarāba* demijohn]

car·bun·cle (kär′bung·kəl) *n.* **1** A skin eruption resembling a boil but larger and more painful. **2** A garnet or other red gemstone cut without facets. [< L *carbunculus,* dim. of *carbo* coal] **—car·bun·cu·lar** (kär·bung′kyə·lər) *adj.*

car·bu·re·tor (kär′byə·rā′tər) *n.* A device for mixing a liquid fuel with air to form an explosive mixture, as in internal-combustion engines, *Brit. sp.* **car·bu·ret·tor** (kär′·byə·ret′ər).

car·ca·jou (kär′kə·jōō, ·zhōō) *n.* WOLVERINE. [< native Algon. name]

car·cass (kär′kəs) *n.* **1** The dead body of an animal. **2** The human body: a contemptuous use. **3** Something lifeless or worthless. **4** A framework or skeleton, Also **car′case.** [< MF *carcasse* a corpse]

car·cin·o·gen (kär′sin′ə·jen) *n.* A cancer-producing substance. **—car′cin·o·gen′ic** *adj.*

car·ci·no·ma (kär′sə·nō′mə) *n. pl.* **·ma·ta** (-mə·tə) or **·mas** A malignant tumor; cancer. [< Gk. *karkinos* cancer] **—car′ci·nom′a·tous** (-nom′ə·təs, -nō′mə-) *adj.*

card[1] (kärd) *n.* **1** A usu. small and rectangular piece of stiff paper or cardboard. **2** One of a pack of playing cards. **3** *pl.* Any of various games played with cards. **4** CALLING CARD. **5** GREETING CARD. **6** POSTAL CARD. **7** A card used for identification, supplying information, etc.: a library *card.* **8** A program of events: a boxing *card.* **9** *Informal* A witty or humorous person. **—*v.t.*** **1** To put or list on a card or cards. **2** To provide with a card. [< F *carte* < Ital. *carta* card, sheet of paper < L *charta* paper < Gk. *chartēs*]

card[2] (kärd) *n.* **1** A wire-toothed brush for combing and cleansing fibers, as wool. **2** A similar instrument for currying cattle and horses. **—*v.t.*** To comb, dress, or cleanse with a card. [< MF *carde* < Ital. *carda* < Med. L *cardus* < L *carduus* thistle] **—card′er** *n.*

car·da·mom (kär′də·məm) *n.* **1** An Asian plant related to ginger. **2** Its aromatic seeds, used as a flavoring. Also, **car′da·mon** (-mən), **car′da·mum.** [< Gk. *kardamon* cress + *amōmon* spice]

card·board (kärd′bôrd′, -bōrd′) *n.* A thin, stiff pasteboard used for making cards, boxes, etc.

car·di·ac (kär′dē·ak) *adj.* **1** Of or pertaining to the heart. **2** Of or designating the upper part of the stomach. **—*n.*** **1** One suffering from a heart disease. **2** A cardiac stimulant. [< Gk. *kardia* heart]

car·di·gan (kär′də·gən) *n.* A knitted sweater opening down the front. [< the seventh Earl of *Cardigan,* 1797–1868]

car·di·nal (kär′də·nəl) *adj.* **1** Of prime importance. **2** Of a deep scarlet color. **—*n.*** **1** In the Roman Catholic Church, a member of the Sacred College whose members elect and advise the Pope. **2** A North American, bright red, crested finch. **3** A deep scarlet. **4** CARDINAL NUMBER. [< L *cardinalis* important < *cardo* hinge] **—car′di·nal·ly** *adv.*

Cardinal

car·di·nal·ate (kär′də·nəl·āt′) *n.* The rank, dignity, or term of office of a cardinal.

cardinal flower A perennial North American lobelia having scarlet flowers.

cardinal number A number, esp. an integer, indicating how many (as ten, 48, etc.).

cardinal point Any one of the four principal points of the compass, north, south, east, or west.

card·ing (kär′ding) *n.* The combing of wool, flax, or cotton fibers before spinning.

cardio- *combining form* Heart: *cardiogram.* Also **cardi-**. [< Gk. *kardia* heart]

car·di·o·gram (kär′dē·ə·gram′) *n.* The record produced by a cardiograph.

car·di·o·graph (kär′dē·ə·graf′, -gräf′) *n.* An instrument for recording the activity of the heart. **—car′di·o·graph′ic** *adj.* **—car·di·og·ra·phy** (kär′dē·og′rə·fē) *n.*

car·di·o·pul·mo·nar·y (kär′dē·ō·pōōl′mə·ner′e) *adj.* Pertaining to or or affecting the heart and lungs.

card·sharp (kärd′shärp′) *n.* One who cheats at cards, esp. as a profession.

care (kâr) *v.i.* **cared, car·ing** **1** To have or show regard, interest or concern. **2** To mind or be concerned. **—*v.t.*** **3** To want; desire: used with an infinitive: Do you *care* to go? **4** To be interested in or concerned about: I don't *care* what he said. **—care for** **1** To protect or provide for; watch over. **2** To feel love or affection for. **3** To want; desire. **4** To be interested in: to *care* for music. **—*n.*** **1** Anxiety, concern, or worry. 2 A cause of anxiety or worry. 3 Watchful attention or regard; heed. 4 Charge; custody. 5 An object of solicitude or guardianship. [< OE *carian*] **—car′er** *n.* —**Syn.** *n.* 1 solicitude. 3 precaution, forethought, vigilance, watchfulness, prudence.

CARE Cooperative for American Relief Everywhere.

ca·reen (kə·rēn′) *v.i.* 1 To lurch or twist from side to side. 2 To lean sideways. *—v.t.* 3 To cause (a ship) to turn over to one side, as for repairing. 4 To clean, repair, or calk (a careened ship). 5 To tilt; tip. *—n.* A careening. [< L *carina* keel of a ship]

ca·reer (kə·rir′) *n.* 1 One's lifework or employment. 2 The course or progress of one's life or lifework. 3 A swift course or run. *—adj.* Pursuing the (stated) occupation as a lifework: a *career* diplomat. *—v.i.* To move with a swift, free, and headlong motion. [< LL *carraria (via)* road for carriages] **—ca·reer′er** *n.*

ca·reer·ist (kə·rir′ist) *n.* A person chiefly or excessively concerned with advancing himself professionally. **—ca·reer′ism** *n.*

care·free (kâr′frē′) *adj.* Free of troubles or responsibilities; light-hearted.

care·ful (kâr′fəl) *adj.* 1 Exercising, marked by, or done with care and attention. 2 Prudent; circumspect. **—care′·ful·ly** *adv.* **—care′ful·ness** *n.* —**Syn.** 1 heedful, thoughtful, painstaking, particular. 2 guarded, cautious, alert.

care·less (kâr′lis) *adj.* 1 Not attentive or careful. 2 Done without attention, precision, etc. 3 Indifferent; unconcerned: *careless* about his appearance. 4 Not studied or constrained; easy: a *careless* attitude. 5 Free from worry or anxiety. **—care′less·ly** *adv.* **—care′less·ness** *n.*

ca·ress (kə·res′) *n.* An expression of affection by patting, embracing, or stroking. *—v.t.* To touch or handle lovingly. [< L *carus* dear] **—ca·ress′er** *n.* **—ca·ress′ive** *adj.* —**Syn.** *v.* fondle, embrace, pet, cuddle.

car·et (kar′ət) *n.* A sign (^) placed below a line to denote an omission. [< L, it is missing]

care·tak·er (kâr′tā′kər) *n.* One who takes care of a place, thing, or person.

care·worn (kâr′wôrn′) *adj.* Harassed with troubles or worries.

car·fare (kär′fâr′) *n.* The charge for a ride on a bus, subway train, etc.

car·go (kär′gō) *n. pl.* **·goes** or **·gos** Goods and merchandise taken on board a vessel, aircraft, etc. [< LL *carricum* load]

car·hop (kär′hop′) *n. Informal* A waiter or waitress at a drive-in restaurant.

Car·ib (kar′ib) *n.* One of an Indian people of N South America and the Lesser Antilles. *—adj.* Of or pertaining to the Caribs.

Car·ib·an (kar′ə·bən) *n.* The language family comprising the languages of the Caribs. *—adj.* Of or pertaining to Cariban.

Car·ib·be·an (kar′ə·bē′ən, kə·rib′ē·ən) *n.* The Caribbean Sea and the islands in it. *—adj.* Of, in, or pertaining to the Caribbean Sea or its islands.

Caribbean Sea

Caribbean Sea An arm of the Atlantic between the West Indies and Central and South America.

car·i·bou (kar′ə·bōō) *n.* Any of several large North American deer having antlers projecting forward in both sexes. [< Algon.]

car·i·ca·ture (kar′i·kə·chŏŏr, -chər) *n.* 1 A picture or description using gross exaggeration or distortion, as for humorous effect or in ridicule. 2 The act or art of caricaturing. 3 A poor imitation. *—v.t.* **·tured, ·tur·ing** To represent so as to make ridiculous; travesty. [< Ital. *caricatura,* lit., an overloading] **—car′i·ca·tur′al** *adj.* **—car′i·ca·tur′ist** *n.*

car·ies (kâr′ēz, -i·ēz) *n.* Decay of a bone or tooth. [< L]

car·il·lon (kar′ə·lon) *n.* 1 A set of bells sounding the tones of the chromatic scale, now usu. played by a keyboard. 2 A tune played on such bells. *—v.i.* **·lonned, ·lon·ning** To play a carillon. [< Med. L *quadrilio* set of four bells]

car·il·lon·neur (kar′ə·lə·nûr′) *n.* One who plays a carillon. [F]

car·i·ole (kar′ē·ōl) *n.* A small carriage. [< F < Ital. *carra* wagon]

car·i·ous (kâr′ē·əs) *adj.* Affected with caries; decayed. Also **car·ied** (-ēd). **—car′i·os′i·ty** (-os′ə·tē), **car′i·ous·ness** *n.*

car·load (kär′lōd′) *n.* The amount a car can carry or is carrying.

Car·mel·ite (kär′məl·īt) *n.* A member of the religious order of Our Lady of Mt. Carmel.

car·min·a·tive (kär·min′ə·tiv, kär′mə·nā′tiv) *adj.* Tending to relieve flatulence. *—n.* A remedy for flatulence. [< L *carminare* cleanse]

car·mine (kär′min, -mīn) *n.* A rich purplish red pigment prepared mainly from cochineal. *—adj.* Having the color of carmine. [< Med. L *carminium*]

car·nage (kär′nij) *n.* Extensive and bloody slaughter; massacre. [< L *caro* flesh, meat]

car·nal (kär′nəl) *adj.* 1 Pertaining to bodily appetites; not spiritual. 2 Sensual; sexual. [< L *caro, carnis* flesh] **—car′·nal·ist, car·nal·i·ty** (kär·nal′ə·tē) *n.* **—car′nal·ly** *adv.*

car·na·tion (kär·nā′shən) *n.* 1 Any of many cultivated varieties of plants related to the pink, having fragrant, usu. double, flowers. 2 A light pink, bright rose, or scarlet color. [< L *carnatio* fleshiness < *caro* flesh]

car·nel·ian (kär·nēl′yən) *n.* A clear red chalcedony, often cut as a gem. [< MF *corneline*]

car·ni·val (kär′nə·vəl) *n.* 1 A period of festival and gaiety immediately preceding Lent. 2 Any gay festival, esp. one featuring sports contests or other amusements. 3 A traveling amusement show. [< Ital. *carnivale,* lit., the putting away of flesh]

car·ni·vore (kär′nə·vôr, -vōr) *n.* 1 A flesh-eating mammal. 2 An insectivorous plant.

car·niv·o·rous (kär·niv′ə·rəs) *adj.* Eating or living on flesh. [< L *caro* flesh + *vorare* eat, devour] **—car·niv′o·rous·ly** *adv.* **—car·niv′o·rous·ness** *n.*

car·ol (kar′əl) *v.* **·oled** or **·olled, ·ol·ing** or **·ol·ling** *v.t.* 1 To sing, as a bird. 2 To celebrate in song. *—v.i.* 3 To sing, esp. in a joyous strain. *—n.* A song of joy; esp., a Christmas song. [< L *choraules* a flutist] **—car′o·ler, car′ol·ler** *n.*

car·om (kar′əm) *v.t.* & *v.i.* To make or cause to make a rebounding movement. *—n.* In billiards, the impact of one ball against two others in succession. [< Sp. *carambola* a kind of fruit]

car·o·tene (kar′ə·tēn) *n.* A deep yellow plant pigment that is changed in the body to vitamin A. Also **car′o·tin** (-tin). [< L *carota* carrot]

ca·rot·id (kə·rot′id) *adj.* Of, pertaining to, or near one of the two major arteries on each side of the neck. Also **ca·rot′i·dal.** [< Gk. *karoein* stupefy; so called because pressure on them can cause unconsciousness]

ca·rou·sal (kə·rou′zəl) *n.* A boisterous or drunken party.

ca·rouse (kə·rouz′) *v.i.* **ca·roused, ca·rous·ing** To drink heavily and boisterously with others. *—n.* CAROUSAL. [< G *gar aus (trinken)* (drink) all out] **—ca·rous′er** *n.*

car·ou·sel (kar′ə·sel′, -zel′) *n.* MERRY-GO-ROUND (def. 1). [< F *carrousel* < Ital. *carosello* tournament]

carp[1] (kärp) *v.i.* To nag or find fault excessively. [< ON *karpa* boast] **—carp′er** *n.*

carp[2] (kärp) *n. pl.* **carp** or **carps** 1 Any of a group of related freshwater food fish. 2 Any of various similar fishes, as minnows and goldfish. [< LL *carpa*]

Carp *def. 1*

-carp *combining form* Fruit; fruit (or seed) vessel: *pericarp.* [< Gk. *karpos* fruit]

car·pal (kär′pəl) *adj.* Of, to, or near the wrist. *—n.* A wrist bone. [< L *carpus* wrist]

car·pel (kär′pəl) *n.* A simple pistil or one member of a compound pistil. [< Gk. *karpos* fruit] **—car·pel·lar·y** (kär′pə·ler′ē) *adj.*

car·pen·ter (kär′pən·tər) *n.* One who builds or repairs houses, ships, etc., with timber or wood. *—v.t.* 1 To make by carpentry. *—v.i.* 2 To work with wood. [< LL *carpentarius* carpenter, wagon-maker] **—car′pen·try** (-trē) *n.*

car·pet (kär′pit) *n.* 1 A heavy, usu. ornamental fabric for covering a floor. 2 Any smooth surface upon which one may walk. —*v.t.* To cover with or as with a carpet. [< LL *carpita* thick woolen covering < L *carpere* pluck]

car·pet·bag (kär′pit·bag′) *n.* A suitcase of carpeting.

car·pet·bag·ger (kär′pit·bag′ər) *n.* Any of the Northern political or profit-seeking adventurers in the South after the Civil War.

carpet beetle A beetle whose larvae feed on fur and woolen fabrics. • See BEETLE.

car·pet·ing (kär′pit·ing) *n.* 1 Fabric used for carpets. 2 Carpets collectively.

carpet sweeper A hand-operated apparatus for sweeping carpets.

carp·ing (kär′ping) *adj.* Apt to find fault or criticize without sufficient cause. —**carp′ing·ly** *adv.*

car·port (kär′pôrt′, -pōrt′) *n.* A roof projecting from the side of a building, used as a shelter for motor vehicles.

car·pus (kär′pəs) *n. pl.* **·pi** (-pī) The wrist. [< Gk. *karpos* wrist]

car·riage (kar′ij) *n.* 1 A wheeled, usu. horse-drawn vehicle for carrying persons. 2 BABY CARRIAGE. 3 A wheeled or moving mechanical part for supporting or carrying something. 4 One's physical posture; bearing. 5 The act or cost of transporting something. [< AF *carier* to carry]

car·ri·er (kar′ē·ər) *n.* 1 One who or that which carries something, as a mailman, bus, airplane, etc. 2 A device, mechanical part, conduit, etc., in or on which something is carried. 3 AIRCRAFT CARRIER. 4 A person or animal who is immune to a disease but transmits it to others. 5 *Telecom.* A flow of energy that changes in some way with time, so as to carry information.

carrier pigeon HOMING PIGEON.

car·ri·ole (kar′ē·ōl) *n.* CARIOLE. [F]

car·ri·on (kar′ē·ən) *n.* Dead and putrefying flesh. —*adj.* 1 Feeding on carrion. 2 Like or pertaining to carrion; putrefying. [< L *caro* flesh]

car·rom (kar′əm) *n.* CAROM.

car·rot (kar′ət) *n.* 1 A widely cultivated plant related to parsley. 2 Its reddish yellow edible root. [< L *carota* < Gk. *karōton*]

car·rot·y (kar′ət·ē) *adj.* 1 Like a carrot, esp in color. 2 Having red hair.

car·rou·sel (kar′ə·sel′, -zel′) *n.* MERRY-GO-ROUND (def. 1). [F]

car·ry (kar′ē) *v.* **·ried, ·ry·ing** *v.t.* 1 To bear from one place to another; transport; convey. 2 To have or bear upon or about one's person or in one's mind. 3 To serve as a means of conveyance or transportation: The wind *carries* sounds. 4 To lead; urge; move; influence: Love for art *carried* him abroad. 5 To have or bear as a feature, quality, consequence, etc. 6 To bear up; hold in position. 7 To conduct (oneself) or move or hold (oneself) in a specified manner. 8 To transfer, as a number or figure, to the column of next highest order, as in adding. 9 To keep on the account books. 10 To have or keep on hand: We *carry* a full stock. 11 To have as part of its program, contents, etc.: This radio station does not *carry* the news. 12 To win, as an election; also, to win the majority of votes in (a state, city, etc.). 13 To win the support of (a group, audience, etc.). 14 To gain the acceptance or adoption of (a cause, law, etc.). 15 To support or sustain, esp. financially. 16 To be pregnant with. 17 To extend or continue: to *carry* a joke too far. 18 *Music* To sing or play (a melody or part). —*v.i.* 19 To act as bearer or carrier. 20 To have a specified range, propelling power, etc.: The sound *carried* nearly a mile. 21 To gain acceptance or adoption. —**carry off** 1 To cause to die. 2 To win, as a prize or honor. 3 To face or handle (an embarrassment, etc.) well. —**carry on** 1 To keep going; continue. 2 To behave in a free, frolicsome manner. 3 To continue, as a tradition. —**carry out** To accomplish; bring to completion. —**carry through** 1 To carry to completion or success. 2 To sustain or support to the end. —*n. pl.* **·ries** 1 The act or manner of carrying. 2 A portage, as between navigable steams. 3 The range of, or the distance covered by, a gun, projectile, golf ball, etc. [< LL *carricare* < L *carrus* cart] —**Syn.** *v.* 1 move, transfer, haul, ship. 4 impel. 5 show, display, harbor.

carrying charge In installment buying, the interest charged on the unpaid balance.

carrying place *Can.* PORTAGE (def. 2).

car·ry-o·ver (kar′ē·ō′vər) *n.* Something left over or repeated, as an entry brought forward in bookkeeping.

cart (kärt) *n.* 1 A two-wheeled vehicle, for carrying loads. 2 Loosely, any two- or four-wheeled vehicle. —*v.t.* 1 To convey or carry in or as in a cart. —*v.i.* 2 To drive or use a cart. [< OE *cræt*] —**cart′er** *n.*

cart·age (kär′tij) *n.* The act or cost of carting.

carte blanche (kärt′ blänsh′, *Fr.* kȧrt bläṅsh′) *n. pl.* **cartes blanches** (kärts′ blänsh′, *Fr.* kȧrt bläṅsh′) Unrestricted authority or freedom to act. [F, white card]

car·tel (kär·tel′, kär′təl) *n.* 1 An association of businesses aiming at monopolistic control of the market. 2 A written official agreement between governments at war, as for the exchange of prisoners. [< Ital. *carta* paper]

Car·te·sian (kär·tē′zhən) *adj.* Of or pertaining to Descartes, or to his philosophy, doctrines, and methods. —*n.* A follower of Descartes. [< NL *Cartesius,* Latinized form of *Descartes*] —**Car·te′sian·ism** *n.*

Car·thage (kär′thij) *n.* An ancient city-state in North Africa near modern Tunis, destroyed by the Romans in 146 B.C. —**Car·tha·gin·i·an** (kär′thə·jin′ē·ən) *adj., n.*

Car·thu·sian (kär·tho͞o′zhən) *n.* A monk or nun of a religious order founded in 1086 in Chartreuse in the French Alps. —*adj.* Of or pertaining to this order. [< Med. L *Carturissium* Chartreuse]

car·ti·lage (kär′tə·lij) *n.* 1 A tough, elastic supporting tissue in animals; gristle. 2 A structure or part consisting of cartilage. [< L *cartilago* gristle]

car·ti·lag·i·nous (kär′tə·laj′ə·nəs) *adj.* 1 Of or like cartilage; gristly. 2 Having a gristly skeleton, as sharks.

car·tog·ra·phy (kär·tog′rə·fē) *n.* The science or art of drawing or compiling maps or charts. [< L *charta* + -GRAPHY] —**car·tog′ra·pher** *n.* —**car′to·graph′ic** or **·i·cal** *adj.*

car·ton (kär′tən) *n.* 1 A pasteboard box. 2 A heavyweight paper container for liquids. [< L *charta* paper]

car·toon (kär·to͞on′) *n.* 1 A humorously critical or satirical drawing or caricature, as in a periodical. 2 A sketch for a fresco or mosaic. 3 COMIC STRIP. 4 ANIMATED CARTOON. —*v.t.* 1 To make a caricature or cartoon of; satirize pictorially. —*v.i.* 2 To make cartoons. [< Ital. *cartone* pasteboard < *carta* card] —**car·toon′ist** *n.*

car·tridge (kär′trij) *n.* 1 An explosive charge for a small arm, consisting of primer, gunpowder, cardboard or metal case, and projectile or projectiles. 2 *Phot.* A roll of protected sensitized films. 3 A small case attached to the arm of a phonograph and containing the stylus and pickup. 4 CASSETTE. [< F *cartouche*]

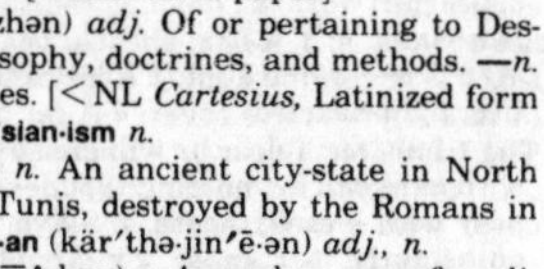

Cartridge
a. powder. b. wad. c. shot.

cart·wheel (kärt′hwēl′) *n.* 1 *Informal* A silver dollar. 2 A sideways handspring.

carve (kärv) *v.* **carved, carv·ing** *v.t.* 1 To cut figures or designs upon. 2 To make by cutting or chiseling. 3 To cut up, as cooked meat. —*v.i.* 4 To make carved work or figures. 5 To cut up meat. [< OE *ceorfan*] —**carv′er, carv′ing** *n.*

car·vel (kär′vəl) *n.* CARAVEL.

car·y·at·id (kar′ē·at′id) *n. pl.* **·ids** or **·i·des** (-ə·dēz) *Archit.* A supporting column in the form of a sculptured female figure. [< Gk. *Karyiatis* a priestess of Artemis at Karyai, town of Laconia, Greece]

ca·sa·ba (kə·sä′bə) *n.* A melon with sweet white flesh and yellow rind. Also **casaba melon.** [< *Kasaba,* in w Turkey]

ca·sa·va (kə·sä′və) *n.* CASSAVA.

Cas·bah (käz′bä) *n.* The native quarter of Algiers or of other cities with a large Arab population.

cas·cade (kas·kād′) *n.* 1 A fall of water over steeply slanting rocks, or one of a series of such falls. 2 Anything resembling a waterfall. —*v.i.* **·cad·ed, ·cad·ing** To fall in the form of a waterfall; form cascades. [< Ital. *cascare* to fall]

cas·car·a (kas·kâr′ə) *n.* A buckthorn of the NW U.S. whose bark yields **cascara sa·gra·da** (sə·grä′də), used as a laxative. Also **cascara buckthorn.** [< Sp. *cáscara* bark]

case[1] (kās) *n.* **1** An instance, example, or condition: a *case* of fraud. **2** The actual fact or facts: Such is not the *case.* **3** A person or matter being given aid, undergoing investigation, treatment, etc. **4** *Law* **a** A suit or action. **b** The facts or arguments presented in a legal action. **5** Any facts or arguments that support a belief or action. **6** A question or dilemma: a *case* of conscience. **7** *Gram.* **a** The syntactical relationship of a noun, pronoun, or adjective to other words in a sentence. **b** The form of a word indicating this relationship. **8** *Informal* A peculiar or exceptional person. **9** *Informal* An infatuation. —**in any case** No matter what; regardless. —**in case** In the event that; if. —**in no case** Not under any circumstances. [< L *casus* event < *cadere* fall]

case[2] (kās) *n.* **1** A box, sheath, bag, etc., in which something is or may be kept. **2** A box and the items contained in it. **3** A protective cover. **4** A set or pair, as of pistols. **5** The frame for a door or window. **6** *Printing* A tray, with compartments for holding type. —*v.t.* **cased, cas·ing 1** To cover with a case; incase. **2** *Slang* To look over; inspect, esp. secretly. [< L *capsa* box < *capere* take, hold]

case·hard·en (kās′här′dən) *v.t.* **1** *Metall.* To harden the surface of (iron). **2** To make callous or unfeeling.

case history The record of an individual, as compiled by hospitals, social agencies, insurance companies, etc.

ca·se·in (kā′sē·in, -sēn) *n.* The protein found in milk and constituting the principal ingredient in cheese, also used in manufacturing adhesives, plastics, etc. [< L *caseus* cheese] —**ca·se·ic** (kā′sē·ik) *adj.*

case·mate (kās′māt) *n.* **1** A bombproof shelter from which guns fire through openings. **2** An armored bulkhead on shipboard, with openings for guns. [< F < Ital. *casamatta,* ? < Gk. *chasmata,* pl. of *chasma* opening]

case·ment (kās′mənt) *n.* **1** A window arranged to open on hinges at the side. **2** A case; covering. [< OF *encassement*] —**case′ment·ed** *adj.*

ca·se·ous (kā′sē·əs) *adj.* Of or like cheese; cheesy.

case·work (kās′wûrk′) *n.* The investigation and guidance by a social worker of maladjusted individuals and families. —**case′work′er** *n.*

cash (kash) *n.* **1** Current money in hand or readily available. **2** Money paid down; immediate payment. —*v.t.* To convert into ready money, as a check. —**cash in 1** In gambling, to receive cash in exchange for. **2** *Slang* To die. —**cash in on** *Informal* To turn to advantage; make a profit from. [< F *caisse* cash box, cash < L *capsa* box]

cash-and-car·ry (kash′ən·kar′ē) *adj.* Operated on a system of cash purchase and no delivery.

cash·book (kash′bŏŏk′) *n.* A book in which money received or paid out is recorded.

cash discount A discount from a purchase price contingent on payment within a stipulated period.

cash·ew (kash′ōō, kə·shōō′) *n.* **1** A tropical evergreen tree. **2** Its small, kidney-shaped, edible fruit, the **cashew nut.** [< Tupi]

cash·ier[1] (ka·shir′) *n.* **1** A person who has charge of accepting and recording the payment of bills, as in a restaurant. **2** A bank official who has charge of the receipts, disbursements, cash on hand, etc.

cash·ier[2] (ka·shir′) *v.t.* **1** To dismiss in disgrace, as a military officer. **2** To discard. [< L *quassare* destroy]

cash·mere (kash′mir) *n.* **1** A fine wool obtained from goats native to Kashmir. **2** A soft fabric made from this. **3** Something made of cashmere. [< *Kashmir,* India]

cash register A mechanical device having a cash drawer and recording, adding, and displaying the amount of each sale.

cas·ing (kā′sing) *n.* **1** A protective cover or covering. **2** The framework around a door or window. **3** The outer covering of an automobile tire. **4** *pl.* The intestines of cattle, hogs, etc., used as sausage containers.

ca·si·no (kə·sē′nō) *n. pl.* **·nos 1** A room or building for public amusement, dancing, gambling, etc. **2** A game of cards. [Ital., dim. of *casa* house]

cask (kask, käsk) *n.* **1** A barrel made of staves, used for liquids, nails, etc. **2** The quantity a cask will hold. [< Sp. *casco* skull, cask]

cas·ket (kas′kit, käs′-) *n.* **1** A coffin. **2** A small box or chest. —*v.t.* To enclose in or as in a casket. [< F *casse* chest]

casque (kask) *n.* A helmet.

cas·sa·ba (kə·sä′bə) *n.* CASABA.

Cas·san·dra (kə·san′drə) *Gk. Myth.* A daughter of Priam whose prophecies were never believed. —*n.* Anyone who utters unheeded prophecies of disaster.

cas·sa·va (kə·sä′və) *n.* **1** One of several tropical American plants cultivated for their edible roots. **2** The root or starch made from it, used to make tapioca, bread, etc. [< native West Indian language]

cas·se·role (kas′ə·rōl) *n.* **1** A baking dish of earthenware, glass, etc., in which food may be baked and served. **2** The food so prepared and served. [F]

cas·sette (kə·set′, ka-) *n.* **1** A lightproof, quick-loading case for holding film in a camera. **2** A small cartridge containing magnetic tape for use in a tape recorder. [F, lit., small box]

cas·sia (kash′ə) *n.* **1** A variety of cinnamon obtained from a species of Asian laurel. **2** The tree yielding it. **3** Any of a genus of usu. tropical leguminous shrubs or herbs yielding pods whose pulp contains a laxative. [< Gk. *kasia*]

cas·si·no (kə·sē′no) *n.* CASINO (def. 2).

cas·sock (kas′ək) *n.* A close-fitting garment, reaching to the feet, worn by many clergymen, altar boys, or choristers. [< Ital. *casacca* greatcoat] —**cas·socked** (kas′əkt) *adj.*

cas·so·war·y (kas′ə·wer′ē) *n. pl.* **·war·ies** Any of a genus of large, flightless, ostrichlike birds of Australia and New Guinea. [< Malay *kasuārī*]

cast (kast, käst) *v.* **cast, cast·ing** *v.t.* **1** To throw with force; fling; hurl. **2** To place with violence or force, as by the sea. **3** To throw up, as with a shovel. **4** To put into some form or system; formulate. **5** To deposit; give: He *cast* his vote. **6** To draw by chance; throw, as dice. **7** To cause to fall upon or over; direct: to *cast* a shadow. **8** To throw out or forth; get rid of. **9** To let down; put out; let drop: to *cast* anchor. **10** To discard or shed, as in the process of growth. **11** To give birth to, esp. prematurely; drop. **12** *Metall.* To shape in a mold; make a cast of; found. **13** *Printing* To stereotype or electroplate. **14** To assign roles, as in a play; assign to a part. **15** To add; total, as a column of figures. **16** To calculate (a horoscope, tides, etc.). **17** *Naut.* To veer. —*v.i.* **18** To throw or throw out something, as dice or a fishing line. **19** To calculate a horoscope, tides, etc. **20** To take shape in a mold. **21** To add up a column of figures. **22** *Naut.* To veer; tack. —**cast about 1** To consider ways and means; scheme. **2** To search for. —**cast away** To discard; reject. —**cast down 1** To overthrow; destroy. **2** To discourage; depress. —**cast off 1** To reject or discard. **2** To let go, as a ship from a dock. —*n.* **1** The act of throwing or casting. **2** The manner of casting; also the distance thrown or cast. **3** A throw of dice; also, the number or total thrown. **4** Anything thrown out or off, as an insect's skin. **5** The material run into molds at one operation. **6** An object formed in a mold; also, the mold. **7** An impression taken of something and usu. forming a mold. **8** An electrotype plate. **9** A hardened plaster support for a broken limb. **10** An appearance or type: a man of his *cast.* **11** Shade; tinge: a bluish *cast.* **12** A twisting of the eye to one side. **13** A glance; look. **14** The actors in a play, movie, etc. [< ON *kasta* throw]

cas·ta·net (kas′tə·net′) *n.* One of a pair of small concave disks of wood or ivory, clapped together with the fingers, as an accompaniment to song or dance. [< L *castanea* chestnut]

Castanets

cast·a·way (kast′ə·wā′, käst′-) *adj.* **1** Adrift; shipwrecked. **2** Thrown away; discarded. —*n.* **1** One who is shipwrecked. **2** An outcast.

caste (kast, käst) *n.* **1** One of the hereditary classes into which Hindu society is traditionally divided in India. **2** Any rigidly exclusive social class. **3** Any system of such class distinctions. **4** Social standing or prestige. [< L *castus* pure]

cas·tel·lat·ed (kas′tə·lā′tid) *adj.* Having battlements and turrets. **—cas′tel·la′tion** *n.*
cast·er (kas′tər, käs′-) *n.* **1** One who or that which casts. **2** A cruet for condiments. **3** A swiveling, wheellike roller fastened under an article of heavy furniture, etc.
cas·ti·gate (kas′tə·gāt) *v.t.* **·gat·ed, ·gat·ing** To punish or scold severely; chastise. [< L *castigare* chasten] **—cas′ti·ga′tion, cas′ti·ga′tor** *n.* **—cas·ti·ga·to·ry** (kas′ti·gə·tôr′ē, -tō′rē) *adj.*
Cas·tile soap (kas·tēl′, kas′tēl) A pure, mild soap made with olive oil. [< *Castile,* Spain]
Cas·til·ian (kas·til′yən) *n.* **1** A citizen of Castile. **2** The official and literary form of Spanish. *—adj.* Pertaining to Castile, its language, and inhabitants.
cast·ing (kas′ting, käs′-) *n.* **1** The act of one who or that which casts. **2** Something cast in a mold.
cast-i·ron (kast′ī′ərn, käst′-) *adj.* **1** Made of cast iron. **2** Like cast iron; rigid; unyielding. **3** Tough; strong: a *cast-iron* stomach.
cast iron A hard, brittle iron produced in a blast furnace and containing a large proportion of carbon, manganese, silicon, and other impurities.
cas·tle (kas′əl, käs′-) *n.* **1** The fortified dwelling of a feudal noble. **2** Any massive or imposing dwelling. **3** Any place of security or refuge. **4** In chess, a rook. *—v.t. & v.i.* **·tled, ·tling** In chess, to move (the king) two squares to the right or left, at the same time bringing the rook to the square over which the king has passed. [< L *castellum,* dim. of *castrum* camp, fort]
castle in the air A fanciful, impractical scheme. Also **castle in Spain.**
cast·off (kast′ôf′, -of′, käst′-) *adj.* Thrown aside; discarded. *—n.* A person or thing no longer wanted or used.
cas·tor[1] (kas′tər, käs′-) *n.* **1** A hat of beaver or other fur. **2** An oily, odorous secretion of beavers, used in perfumery: also **cas·to·re·um** (kas·tôr′ē·əm, -tō′rē·əm). [< Gk. *kastōr* beaver]
cas·tor[2] (kas′tər, käs′-) *n.* CASTER (defs. 2 & 3).
Cas·tor (kas′tər, käs′-) *Gk. Myth.* The mortal twin of Pollux. *—n.* One of the two brightest stars in the constellation Gemini.
castor bean The seed of the castor-oil plant.
castor oil A viscous oil extracted from castor beans, used as a cathartic and lubricant.
cas·tor-oil plant (kas′tər·oil′, käs′-) A herbaceous plant of warm climates, yielding the castor bean.
cas·trate (kas′trāt) *v.t.* **·trat·ed, ·trat·ing 1** To remove the testicles from; emasculate; geld. **2** To remove the ovaries from; spay. **3** To make less vigorous, forceful, significant, etc. [< L *castrare*] **—cas′trat·er, cas·tra′tion** *n.*
cas·u·al (kazh′o͞o·əl) *adj.* **1** Occurring by chance; not planned; accidental. **2** Irregular; occasional. **3** Nonchalant. **4** Careless; haphazard. **5** Slight: a *casual* acquaintance. **6** Informal: *casual* clothes. *—n.* **1** A casual laborer. **2** *pl.* Informal clothes and accessories. [< L *casus* accident < *cadere* fall] **—cas′u·al·ly** *adv.* **—cas′u·al·ness** *n.* **—Syn.** *adj.* **1** random; incidental. **2** haphazard, cursory. **3** dispassionate, unconcerned, offhand. **4** negligent, slovenly.
cas·u·al·ty (kazh′o͞o·əl·tē) *n. pl.* **·ties 1** A fatal or serious accident. **2** A person killed or severely injured in an accident. **3** Any person or thing badly harmed or damaged. **4** *Mil.* **a** A soldier missing in action or removed from active duty by death, wounds, or capture. **b** *pl.* Losses arising from death, etc.
cas·u·ist (kazh′o͞o·ist) *n.* A person given to casuistry. [< L *casus* event, case] **—cas·u·is·tic** (kazh′o͞o·is′tik) or **·ti·cal** *adj.* **—cas′u·is′ti·cal·ly** *adv.*
cas·u·ist·ry (kazh′o͞o·is·trē) *n. pl.* **·ries 1** The resolving of questions of right and wrong according to standard ethical principles. **2** Overly refined or false reasoning, esp. about matters of conscience.
cat (kat) *n.* **1** A small, domesticated, carnivorous mammal with retractile claws. **2** Any animal of the cat family, as a lion, tiger, lynx, ocelot, etc. **3** *Informal* A spiteful woman given to gossip. **4** CAT-O'-NINE-TAILS. **5** *Slang* CATERPILLAR. **6** *Slang* **a** A person, esp. a man. **b** A jazz musician or devotee. **7** *Naut.* A device used for hoisting an anchor. [< OE]
cat. catalog; catechism.
cata- *prefix* **1** Down; against; upon. **2** Back; over. Also **cat-.** [< Gk. *kata* down, against, back]
ca·tab·o·lism (kə·tab′ə·liz′əm) *n.* The destructive aspect of metabolism, by which living matter breaks down into simpler substances. [< Gk. *katabolē* destruction] **—cat·a·bol·ic** (kat′ə·bol′ik) *adj.* **—cat′a·bol′i·cal·ly** *adv.*
cat·a·chre·sis (kat′ə·krē′sis) *n.* The misuse of a word. [< Gk. *katachrēsis*] **—cat·a·chres·tic** (kat′ə·kres′tik) or **·ti·cal** *adj.* **—cat′a·chres′ti·cal·ly** *adv.*
cat·a·clysm (kat′ə·kliz′əm) *n.* **1** An overwhelming flood. **2** Any violent change or upheaval, as a war or earthquake. [< Gk. *kataklysmos* flood] **—cat·a·clys·mal** (kat′ə·kliz′məl), **cat′a·clys′mic** *adj.*
cat·a·comb (kat′ə·kōm) *n. Usu. pl.* A long underground gallery with excavations in its sides for tombs or human remains. [< LL *catacumbas*]
cat·a·falque (kat′ə·falk) *n.* A temporary raised structure that supports the coffin of a deceased personage lying in state. [< Ital. *catafalco*]
Cat·a·lan (kat′ə·lan, -lən) *adj.* Of Catalonia, its people, or their language. *—n.* **1** One of Catalonian descent or blood. **2** The Romance language of Catalonia and Valencia.
cat·a·lep·sy (kat′ə·lep′sē) *n.* An abnormal condition of muscular rigidity and lack of response to stimuli. [< Gk. *kata-* upon + *lēpsis* seizure] **—cat′a·lep′tic** (-lep′tik) *adj., n.*
cat·a·log (kat′ə·lôg, -log) *n.* **1** A systematic list or enumeration of names, persons, or things, bound in book form, printed on cards, etc. **2** A publication listing wares for sale by a commercial establishment. *—v.* **·loged, ·log·ing** *v.t.* **1** To make a catalog of. *—v.i.* **2** To work on or make a catalog. [< Gk. *kata-* down + *legein* select, choose] **—cat′a·log′er, cat′a·log′ist** *n.*
cat·a·logue (kat′ə·lôg, -log) *n., v.t. & v.i.* **·logued, ·logu·ing** CATALOG. **—cat′a·logu′er, cat′a·logu′ist** *n.*
ca·tal·pa (kə·tal′pə) *n.* A hardy, deciduous tree having large, ovate leaves, large, fragrant bell-shaped flowers, and long slender pods. [< N. Am. Ind.]
ca·tal·y·sis (kə·tal′ə·sis) *n. pl.* **·ses** (-sēz) An alteration in the speed of a chemical reaction effected by an agent that itself remains unchanged. [< Gk. *katalysis* dissolution] **—cat·a·lyt·ic** (kat′ə·lit′ik) *adj., n.*
cat·a·lyst (kat′ə·list) *n.* **1** A substance that effects catalysis. **2** Any factor providing impetus for change.
cat·a·lyze (kat′ə·līz) *v.t.* **·lyzed, ·lyz·ing** To submit (a reaction) to catalysis. **—cat′a·lyz′er** *n.*
cat·a·ma·ran (kat′ə·mə·ran′) *n. Naut.* **1** A boat having twin hulls. **2** A long, narrow raft of logs, often with an outrigger. [< Tamil *katta-maram* tied wood]

Catamaran

cat·a·mount (kat′ə·mount) *n.* Any of various wildcats, as a cougar or lynx. [Short form of *cat of the mountain*]
cat·a·pult (kat′ə·pult, -po͝olt) *n.* **1** An engine of ancient warfare for throwing stones, spears, or arrows. **2** A slingshot. **3** *Aeron.* A device for launching an airplane at flight speed, as from the deck of a ship. *—v.t.* **1** To hurl from or as from a catapult. *—v.i.* **2** To hurtle through the air as if from a catapult. [< Gk. *kata-* down + *pallein* to hurl]
cat·a·ract (kat′ə·rakt) *n.* **1** A waterfall. **2** *Pathol.* Opacity of the crystalline lens of the eye. **3** A deluge; downpour. [< Gk. *kata-* down + *arassein* fall headlong]
ca·tarrh (kə·tär′) *n.* Inflammation of mucous membrane, esp. of the throat and nose. [< Gk. *kata-* down + *rheein* flow] **—ca·tarrh′al, ca·tarrh′ous** *adj.*
ca·tas·tro·phe (kə·tas′trə·fē) *n.* **1** Any great and sudden misfortune; disaster. **2** A sudden, violent change. **3** A ruinous failure. [< Gk. *kata-* over, down + *strephein* turn] **—cat·a·stroph·ic** (kat′ə·strof′ik) *adj.* **—Syn. 1** calamity, mishap, débacle. **2** cataclysm, convulsion, upheaval.

add, āce, câre, pälm; end, ēven; it, īce; odd, ōpen, ôrder; to͝ok, po͞ol; up, bûrn; ə = *a* in *above, u* in *focus;* yo͞o = *u* in *fuse;* oil; pout; check; go; ring; thin; this; zh, *vision.* < derived from; ? origin uncertain or unknown.

Ca·taw·ba (kə·tô′bə) *n.* **1** One of a tribe of North American Indians. **2** An American red grape. **3** A dry white wine made from it.

cat·bird (kat′bûrd′) *n.* A small slate-colored North American songbird, having a catlike cry.

cat·boat (kat′bōt′) *n. Naut.* A small sailboat, having its mast well forward and carrying a single fore-and-aft sail.

cat·call (kat′kôl′) *n.* A shrill, discordant call or whistle indicating impatience or derision. —*v.t. & v.i.* To deride with or utter catcalls.

catch (kach) *v.* **caught, catch·ing** *v.t.* **1** To take or seize; capture. **2** To entrap; ensnare. **3** To captivate, gain, or hold. **4** To apprehend or perceive clearly. **5** To surprise; detect, as in a misdeed. **6** To contract; incur, as a disease. **7** To arrive at or take, as a train or boat. **8** To arrest the motion of; entangle. **9** To grasp and retain. **10** To perceive, as something fleeting: to *catch* sight of. **11** To reach, as a person, with a blow: She *caught* him a box on the ear. —*v.i.* **12** To close and remain fastened: The lock didn't *catch*. **13** In baseball, to act as catcher. **14** To become entangled or fastened. **15** To be communicated or communicable, as a disease or enthusiasm. **16** To take fire; kindle; ignite. —**catch on** *Informal* **1** To understand. **2** To become popular or fashionable. —**catch up 1** To seize or snatch quickly. **2** To discover (someone) to be in error. **3** To overtake. **4** To regain lost ground, as by extra work. **5** To become involved or engrossed in something: *caught up* in his studies. **6** To fasten loosely or with loops. —*n.* **1** The act of catching. **2** That which catches or fastens. **3** A person or thing caught. **4** The amount caught. **5** A person worth obtaining, as in marriage. **6** A brief bit or scrap, as of a song. **7** *Informal* Something deceitful or misleading: a *catch* in that bargain sale. **8** An impediment; a break, as in the voice or breathing. —*adj.* **1** Attracting or meant to attract notice: a *catch* phrase. **2** Meant to test or trick: a *catch* question. [<LL *captiare,* freq. of L *capere* take, hold]

catch-all (kach′ôl′) *n.* A bag or other container to hold odds and ends.

catch·er (kach′ər) *n.* **1** One who or that which catches. **2** In baseball, the player stationed behind home plate to catch balls that pass the batter.

catch·ing (kach′ing) *adj.* **1** Infectious. **2** Captivating; attractive.

catch·pen·ny (kach′pen′ē) *adj.* Cheap, poor, and showy. —*n. pl.* **·nies** An inferior article.

catch·up (kach′əp, kech′-) *n.* KETCHUP.

catch·word (kach′wûrd′) *n.* **1** A much-repeated word, phrase, or slogan. **2** A word at the head of a page or column, as of a dictionary, encyclopedia, etc.

catch·y (kach′ē) *adj.* **·i·er, ·i·est 1** Interesting; infectious. **2** Deceptive; puzzling. **3** Broken; fitful. —**catch′i·ness** *n.*

cat·e·chet·ic (kat′ə·ket′ik) *adj.* Of or pertaining to oral instruction by question and answer. Also **cat′e·chet′i·cal.**

cat·e·chism (kat′ə·kiz′əm) *n.* **1** A short manual of instruction in religious doctrine, usu. in the form of questions and answers. **2** Any similar manual of instruction. [<Gk. *katēchizein* instruct]

cat·e·chist (kat′ə·kist) *n.* One who catechizes. —**cat·e·chis·tic** (kat′ə·kis′tik) or **·ti·cal** *adj.*

cat·e·chize (kat′ə·kīz) *v.t.* **·chized, ·chiz·ing 1** To teach, esp. religious doctrine, by questions and answers. **2** To question closely and fully. Also **cat′e·chise.** [<Gk. *katēchizein* to instruct] —**cat′e·chi·za′tion** *n.*

cat·e·chu·men (kat′ə·kyōō′mən) *n.* **1** One who is under instruction in the elements of Christianity. **2** One learning the elements of any subject or skill. [<Gk. *katēchoumenos*]

cat·e·gor·i·cal (kat′ə·gôr′i·kəl, -gor′-) *adj.* **1** Without qualification; absolute; unequivocal. **2** Of, relating to, or in a category. —**cat′e·gor′i·cal·ly** *adv.* —**cat′e·gor′i·cal·ness** *n.*

cat·e·go·rize (kat′ə·gə·rīz′) *v.t.* **·rized, ·riz·ing** To put into a category; classify.

cat·e·go·ry (kat′ə·gôr′ē, -gō′rē) *n. pl.* **·ries** A class, division, or group in any system of classification. [<Gk. < *katēgoreein* allege, predicate]

ca·ter (kā′tər) *v.i.* **1** To furnish food or entertainment. **2** To provide for the gratification of any need or taste. —*v.t.* **3** To furnish food for. [<LL *acceptare* buy, procure, accept] —**ca′ter·er** *n.*

cat·er-cor·nered (kat′ər·kôr′nərd) *adj.* Diagonal. —*adv.* Diagonally. Also **cat′er-cor′ner.** [<F *quatre* four + CORNERED]

cat·er·pil·lar (kat′ər·pil′ər) *n.* The larva of certain insects, esp. of a butterfly or moth. [<L *catta* cat + *pilum* hair]

Cat·er·pil·lar (kat′ər·pil′ər) *n.* A tractor whose wheels drive continuous treads or tracks: a trade name.

cat·er·waul (kat′ər·wôl) *v.i.* **1** To utter the discordant cry peculiar to cats at rutting time. **2** To make any discordant screeching. —*n.* Such a sound. [ME *caterwawen*]

cat·fish (kat′fish′) *n. pl.* **·fish** or **·fish·es** Any of various fishes having no scales and having barbels around the mouth suggestive of a cat's whiskers.

Catfish

cat·gut (kat′gut′) *n.* A very tough cord made from the intestines of certain animals and used for stringing musical instruments, making surgical ligatures, etc.

ca·thar·sis (kə·thär′sis) *n.* **1** *Med.* A purgation, esp. of the alimentary canal. **2** A purifying or relieving of the emotions. [<Gk. <*katharos* pure] —**ca·thar′tic** *adj., n.*

ca·the·dral (kə·thē′drəl) *n.* **1** The church containing the official chair of the bishop. **2** Any large or important church. —*adj.* Of, pertaining to, or like a cathedral. [<Gk. *kata-* down + *hedra* seat]

cath·e·ter (kath′ə·tər) *n.* A slender tube for drawing off fluid from a body cavity, esp. urine from the bladder. [<Gk. *kata-* down + *hienai* send, let go]

cath·e·ter·ize (kath′ə·tər·īz′) *v.t.* **·ized, ·iz·ing** To introduce a catheter into.

cath·ode (kath′ōd) *n. Electr.* The electrode through which negative charges leave a nonmetallic conductor and toward which positive ions flow from the anode. [<Gk. *kata-* down + *hodos* road, way]

cathode rays *Physics* A stream of electrons that pass from a cathode of an electron tube.

cath·ode-ray tube (kath′ōd·rā′) *Electronics* A type of electron tube in which a beam of electrons is focused and deflected so as to make a trace or image on a screen, as in a television receiver.

cath·o·lic (kath′ə·lik, kath′lik) *adj.* **1** Broadminded, as in belief, tastes, or views; liberal; comprehensive. **2** Universal in reach; general. [<Gk. *katholikos* universal] —**ca·thol·i·cal·ly** (kə·thol′ik·lē) *adv.* —**cath·o·lic·i·ty** (kath′ə·lis′ə·tē) *n.*

Cath·o·lic (kath′ə·lik, kath′lik) *adj.* **1** Of or pertaining to the Roman Catholic Church. **2** Of or pertaining to the ancient, undivided Christian Church or its later divisions, as the Anglican or Eastern Orthodox. —*n.* A member of any Catholic Church. —**Cath·o·lic·i·ty** (kath′ə·lis′ə·tē) *n.*

Catholic Church 1 ROMAN CATHOLIC CHURCH. **2** Any of several Christian churches, as the Anglican or Eastern Orthodox.

Ca·thol·i·cism (kə·thol′ə·siz′əm) *n.* The doctrine, system, and practice of a Catholic Church, esp. the Roman Catholic Church.

ca·thol·i·cize (kə·thol′ə·sīz) *v.t. & v.i.* **·cized, ·ciz·ing** To make or become catholic or Catholic.

cat·house (kat′hous′) *n. Slang* A house of prostitution.

cat·i·on (kat′ī′ən) *n. Chem.* A positive ion. [<Gk. *kata-* down + *ienai* go] —**cat·i·on·ic** (kat′ī·on′ik) *adj.*

cat·kin (kat′kin) *n.* A dense, deciduous scaly spike of flowers, as in the willow, birch, etc. [<MDu. *katteken* kitten]

cat·nap (kat′nap′) *n.* A short doze.

cat·nip (kat′nip) *n.* An aromatic herb of the mint family, of which cats are fond. Also **cat′mint′** (-mint′).

cat-o′-nine-tails (kat′ə·nīn′tālz′) *n.* A whip with nine lashes.

CAT scan An electronic scanning procedure in which the body is x-rayed from many angles as it revolves.

cat's-eye (kats′ī′) *n.* A gemstone that shows a line of light across the dome resembling that in the eye of a cat.

cat's-paw (kats′pô′) *n.* **1** A person used as a tool or dupe. **2** A light wind that barely ruffles the water. Also **cats′·paw′.**

cat·sup (kat′səp, kech′əp) *n.* KETCHUP.

cat·tail (kat′tāl′) *n.* A tall, marsh plant with long, straplike leaves and flowers in dense, brown terminal spikes.

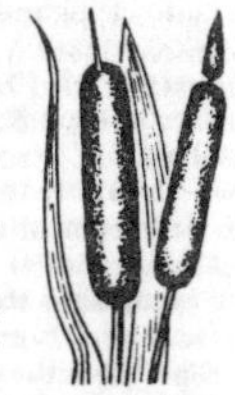
Cattail

cat·tle (kat′l) *n.* **1** Domesticated cows, bulls, steers, and oxen. **2** Formerly, all livestock. **3** Human beings: a contemptuous term. [< L *capitale* capital, wealth]

cat·tle·man (kat′l·mən) *n. pl.* **·men** (-mən) One who raises cattle.

cat·ty (kat′ē) *adj.* **·ti·er, ·ti·est 1** Of cats. **2** Malicious; spiteful. **—cat′ti·ly** *adv.* **—cat′ti·ness** *n.*

CATV community antenna television.

cat·walk (kat′wôk′) *n.* Any narrow walking space, as at the side of a bridge, in an aircraft, near the ceiling of the stage in a theater, etc.

Cau·ca·sian (kô·kā′zhən) *n.* **1** A Caucasoid person. **2** A native of the Caucasus region. *—adj.* **1** Of the Caucasus region, its inhabitants, or their languages. **2** CAUCASOID. Also **Cau·cas·ic** (kô·kas′ik). [< *Caucasus,* the region where the "white" race was once thought to have originated]

Cau·ca·soid (kô′kə·soid) *adj.* Of or pertaining to the so-called white race, believed to have originally inhabited Europe, N Africa, India, and parts of E Asia, and characterized by a skin color varying from very light to dark brown. *—n.* A member of this racial group.

cau·cus (kô′kəs) *n.* A meeting of members of a political party to select candidates or plan a campaign. *—v.i.* **cau·cused** or **·cussed, ·cus·ing** or **·cus·sing** To meet in or hold a caucus. [< Algon.]

cau·dal (kôd′l) *adj.* **1** Of, pertaining to, or near the tail or posterior part of the body. **2** Resembling a tail. [< L *cauda* tail] **—cau′dal·ly** *adj.*

cau·date (kô′dāt) *adj.* Having a tail or taillike appendage. Also **cau′dat·ed.** [< L *cauda* tail]

cau·dle (kôd′l) *n.* A warm drink of gruel with wine, eggs, etc., for invalids. [< Med. L *caldum, calidum* warm, hot]

caught (kôt) *p.t. & p.p.* of CATCH.

caul (kôl) *n.* The amniotic sac, esp. if it envelops the head of a newborn child. [Prob. < OF *cale* cap]

caul·dron (kôl′drən) *n.* CALDRON.

cau·li·flow·er (kô′lə·flou′ər, kol′i-) *n.* **1** A vegetable consisting of the dense, white, flower head of a plant related to cabbage. **2** The plant bearing this. [< NL *cauliflora* flowering cabbage]

caulk (kôk) *v.t.* To make watertight, as a boat, window frame, pipe, etc., by using some waterproof substance. [< L *calcare* to tread] **—caulk′er** *n.*

caus·al (kô′zəl) *adj.* **1** Of, being, or expressing a cause. **2** Having to do with cause and effect. **—caus′al·ly** *adv.*

cau·sal·i·ty (kô·zal′ə·tē) *n. pl.* **·ties 1** The principle that all that exists or happens depends upon a cause. **2** Causal action or agency.

cau·sa·tion (kô·zā′shən) *n.* **1** The act of causing. **2** That which causes an effect. **3** CAUSALITY.

caus·a·tive (kô′zə·tiv) *adj.* **1** Effective as a cause. **2** *Gram.* Expressing cause or agency. *—n.* A causative word or form. **—caus′a·tive·ly** *adv.* **—caus′a·tive·ness** *n.*

cause (kôz) *n.* **1** Any person, thing, event, etc., that produces an effect or result. **2** Any rational ground for choice or action; reason. **3** Any great enterprise, movement, principle, or aim. **4** *Law* An action or suit to be settled in court. *—v.t.* **caused, caus·ing** To be the cause of; produce; effect; induce; compel. [< L *causa* cause, legal case] **—caus′a·ble** *adj.* **—caus′er** *n.* **—Syn. 1** agent, principle, origin, source.

cause cé·lè·bre (kōz′sə·leb′r′, *Fr.* kōz′sā·leb′r′) **1** A famous legal case. **2** A controversial issue or event. [F, lit., celebrated case]

cause·way (kôz′wā′) *n.* **1** A raised road or way, as over marshy ground. **2** A highway. [< LL *calciata* paved]

caus·tic (kôs′tik) *adj.* **1** Capable of corroding or eating away tissue. **2** Stinging; biting; sarcastic. *—n.* A caustic substance. [< Gk. *kausos* burning < *kaiein* to burn] **—caus′ti·cal·ly** *adv.* **—caus·tic′i·ty** (-tis′ə·tē) *n.*

caustic potash POTASSIUM HYDROXIDE.

caustic soda SODIUM HYDROXIDE.

cau·ter·ize (kô′tər·īz) *v.t.* **·ized, ·iz·ing** To destroy dead or abnormal tissue by applying a caustic, intense heat or cold, etc. [< L *cauterium* branding iron] **—cau′ter·i·za′tion** *n.*

cau·ter·y (kô′tər·ē) *n. pl.* **·ter·ies 1** The process of cauterizing. **2** A cauterizing substance or instrument. [< L *cauterium* branding iron]

cau·tion (kô′shən) *n.* **1** Care to avoid injury or misfortune; prudence; wariness. **2** An admonition or warning. **3** *Informal* A person or thing that alarms, astonishes, provokes, etc. *—v.t.* To advise to be prudent; warn. [< L *cautio* < *cavere* beware, take heed]

cau·tion·ar·y (kô′shən·er′ē) *adj.* Constituting or conveying a warning; admonitory.

cau·tious (kô′shəs) *adj.* Exercising or manifesting caution; wary; prudent. **—cau′tious·ly** *adv.* **—cau′tious·ness** *n.* **—Syn.** careful, discreet, circumspect, heedful, chary.

cav·al·cade (kav′əl·kād, kav′əl·kād′) *n.* **1** A procession or parade, esp. of horsemen. **2** A series or procession of events. [< Ital. *cavalcare* to ride on horseback]

cav·a·lier (kav′ə·lir′) *n.* **1** A horseman; knight. **2** GALLANT. *—adj.* **1** Free and easy; offhand. **2** Haughty; supercilious. **—cav′a·lier′ly** *adj., adv.*

cav·al·ry (kav′əl·rē) *n. pl.* **·ries** Mobile ground troops, originally mounted on horses, but now using mechanized or motorized units. [< LL *caballarius* horseman < L *caballus* horse] **—cav′al·ry·man** *n.*

cave (kāv) *n.* A natural cavity beneath the earth's surface or in a mountain. *—v.i.* **caved, cav·ing** To fall in or down; give way, as ground. **—cave in 1** To fall in or down, as by undermining. **2** *Informal* To yield utterly; give in. [< L *cava* < *cavus* hollow]

ca·ve·at (kā′vē·at, kav′ē·at, käv′-) *n.* **1** *Law* A formal notification to a court or officer not to take a certain step until the person giving notice can be heard. **2** A caution, esp. to avoid misinterpretation. [< L, let him beware]

cave-in (kāv′in′) *n.* A collapse or falling in, as of a mine or tunnel; also, the site of such a collapse.

cave man 1 A cave dweller, esp. of prehistoric times. **2** *Informal* A rough and brutal man.

cav·ern (kav′ərn) *n.* A large cave.

cav·ern·ous (kav′ər·nəs) *adj.* **1** Full of caverns. **2** Like a cavern, esp. hollow. **—cav′ern·ous·ly** *adv.*

cav·i·ar (kav′ē·är, kä′vē-) *n.* The salted roe of sturgeon or other related fish, considered a delicacy. Also **cav′i·are.** [< Turkish *khavyar*]

cav·il (kav′əl) *v.i.* **cav·iled** or **·illed, cav·il·ing** or **·il·ling** To pick flaws or raise trivial objections; quibble: with *at* or *about.* *—n.* A trivial objection. [< L *cavilla* a jeering, a scoffing] **—cav′il·er, cav′il·ler** *n.*

cav·i·ty (kav′ə·tē) *n. pl.* **·ties 1** A hollow or depression. **2** A natural hollow in the body. **3** A hollow place in a tooth, esp. one caused by decay. [< L *cavus* hollow, empty]

ca·vort (kə·vôrt′) *v.i.* **1** To act up; cut up. **2** To prance and show off, as a horse. [?]

CAVU ceiling and visibility unlimited.

ca·vy (kā′vē) *n. pl.* **·vies** Any of various South American burrowing rodents, as the guinea pig. [< Cariban]

caw (kô) *n.* The harsh cry of crows, ravens, etc. *—v.i.* To make this cry. [Imit.]

cay (kā, kē) *n.* A coastal reef or sandy islet. [< Sp. *cayo* shoal]

cay·enne pepper (kī·en′, kā-) A hot, red pepper made from the fruit of various pepper plants; red pepper. Also **cay·enne′.**

cay·man (kā′mən) *n. pl.* **·mans** CAIMAN.

Ca·yu·ga (kā·yōō′gə, kī-) *n. pl.* **·ga** or **·gas** A member of a tribe of North American Indians of Iroquoian linguistic stock formerly dwelling in w New York State.

cay·use (kī·yōōs′) *n.* A small horse native to w U.S. [< the *Cayuse* Indians, formerly living in Oregon.]

Cb columbium.

CBC Canadian Broadcasting Corporation.

CBS Columbia Broadcasting System.

C.C., c.c. carbon copy; cashier's check; city council; county clerk.

cc, cc., c.c. cubic centimeter(s).
CCCP A Russian acronym for SSSR, Soyuz (Union) Soviet Socialist Republic.
C clef See CLEF.
Cd cadmium.
cd candela.
c.d. cash discount, compact disc.
Ce cerium.
cease (sēs) *v.* **ceased, ceas·ing** *v.t.* 1 To leave off or discontinue. —*v.i.* 2 To come to an end; stop; desist. —**Without cease** Without end. [<L *cessare* stop <*cedere* withdraw, yield] —**cease′less** *adj.* —**cease′less·ly** *adv.* —**cease′less·ness** *n.* —**Syn.** *v.* 1 conclude, end, finish, terminate, quit, stop, break off.
cease-fire (sēs′fīr′) *n.* A temporoary truce, esp. in warfare.
ce·cum (sē′kəm) *n. pl.* **ce·ca** (sē′kə) A cavity with a single opening, esp. the blind pouch between the large and small intestines. [<L *caecus* blind] —**ce′cal** *adj.*
ce·dar (sē′dər) *n.* 1 Any of a genus of large, Old World conifers, having needlelike leaves and fragrant wood. 2 Any of a large variety of similar evergreen trees. 3 The wood of any of these trees. —*adj.* Pertaining to or made of cedar. [<Gk *kedros*]
ce·dar·bird (sē′dər·bûrd′) *n.* A common American waxwing. Also **cedar waxwing.** • See WAXWING
cede (sēd) *v.t.* **ced·ed, ced·ing** 1 To yield or give up: to *cede* disputed territory to avoid war. 2 To surrender title to; transfer. [<L *cedere* withdraw, yield]
ce·dil·la (si·dil′ə) *n.* A mark put under the letter *c* (ç) to indicate that it is to be sounded as (s). [<Sp., dim of *ceda*, the letter *z*]
ceil·ing (sē′ling) *n.* 1 The overhead covering of a room. 2 The top limit or maximum, as of prices, wages, etc. 3 *Aeron.* a The maximum height attainable by a given aircraft. b The upward limit of visibility for flying. [ME *celing*]
cel·an·dine (sel′ən·dīn) *n.* Any of several weedy plants with yellow flowers. [<Gk. *chelidōn* a swallow]
cel·e·brant (sel′ə·brənt) *n.* 1 One who celebrates. 2 The officiating priest at a mass.
cel·e·brate (sel′ə·brāt) *v.* **·brat·ed, ·brat·ing** *v.t.* 1 To observe, as a festival or occasion: to *celebrate* an anniversary. 2 To make known or famous; extol. 3 To perform a ceremony publicly and as ordained: to *celebrate* the mass. —*v.i.* 4 To observe or commemorate a day or event. 5 *Informal* To have a lively and happy time. [<L *celebrare* <*celeber* famous] —**cel′e·brat′er** or **·bra′tor** *n.* —**Syn.** *v.* 1 commemorate, keep. 2 glorify, exalt, commend. 3 solemnize. 5 rejoice, make merry.
cel·e·brat·ed (sel′ə·brā′tid) *adj.* 1 Famous; renowned. 2 Performed or observed with customary rites.
cel·e·bra·tion (sel′ə·brā′shən) *n.* 1 The act or an instance of celebrating. 2 Things done in commemoration of any event.
ce·leb·ri·ty (sə·leb′rə·tē) *n. pl.* **·ties** 1 A famous or much publicized person. 2 Fame; renown.
ce·ler·i·ty (sə·ler′ə·tē) *n.* Quickness of motion; speed; rapidity. [<L *celer* swift]
cel·er·y (sel′ər·ē) *n.* An herb related to parsley, having long, crisp, edible leafstocks. [<Gk *selinon* parsley]
ce·les·ta (sə·les′tə) *n.* A musical instrument having a keyboard of five octaves and hammers that strike steel plates. [<F *celeste* celestial]
ce·les·tial (sə·les′chəl) *adj.* 1 Of or pertaining to the sky or heavens. 2 Heavenly; divine. [<L *caelum* sky, heaven] —**ce·les′tial·ly** *adv.*
celestial equator *Astron.* The great circle in which the plane of the earth's equator cuts the celestial sphere.
celestial sphere The spherical surface on which the positions of bodies in space are projected.
ce·li·ac (sē′lē·ak) *adj.* Of or pertaining to the abdomen. [<Gk. *koilia* belly, abdomen]
cel·i·ba·cy (sel′ə·bə·sē) *n.* 1 The state of being unmarried, esp. in accordance with religious vows. 2 Abstinence from sexual intercourse. [<L *caelebs* unmarried]
cel·i·bate (sel′ə·bit, -bāt) *adj.* Unmarried or sexually abstinent, esp. by vow. —*n.* One who practices celibacy.
cell (sel) *n.* 1 A small room, as in a prison or monastery. 2 Any small area or space, as a chamber in a seedcase, a single compartment in a honeycomb, an area bounded by veins on an insect's wing. 3 *Biol* One of the fundamental structural units of which all living tissue is composed, typically consisting of a cell membrane enclosing a mass of cytoplasm that contains a nucleus and various ultramicroscopic structures. 4 *Electr.* A device consisting of electrodes in contact with an electrolyte. 5 A body of persons forming a single unit in an organization of similar groups. —**dry cell** A voltaic cell with its electrolyte in the form of a paste. [<L *cella*]

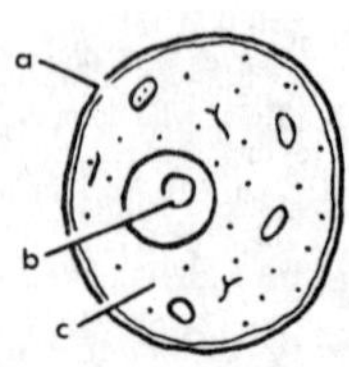

Cell. a. cell wall. b. nucleus. c. cell body.

cel·lar (sel′ər) *n.* 1 An underground room usu. under a building. 2 A room for storing wines. 3 The wines so stored. —*v.t.* To put or keep in or as in a cellar. [<L *cellarium* pantry <*cella* cell, small room]
cel·lar·er (sel′ər·ər) *n.* The keeper of a cellar, as in a monastery.
cel·lo (chel′ō) *n. pl.* **·los** A stringed instrument of the violin family, usu. tuned an octave below the viola and held between the knees when played; violoncello. Also **′cel′lo.** [Short for VIOLONCELLO] —**cel′list** *n.*
cel·lo·phane (sel′ə·fān) *n.* A specially treated cellulose in transparent sheets, used as a wrapping. [<CELL(ULOSE) + -PHANE]
cel·lu·lar (sel′yə·lər) *adj.* 1 Of, pertaining to, or like a cell or cells. 2 Consisting of or containing cells.
cellular telephone A portable radiotelephone, as in an automobile, connected to the regular telephone system. A system of cells, each equipped with a radiotransmitter and a receiver, allows the phone to operate as it moves from one place to another.
cel·lule (sel′yo͞ol) *n.* A very small cell.
Cel·lu·loid (sel′yə·loid) *n.* A flammable synthetic solid derived from cellulose: a trade name.
cel·lu·lose (sel′yə·lōs) *n.* A complex carbohydrate forming the cell walls of plants and the principal component of wood, paper, cotton, etc. [<L *cella* cell]
ce·lom (sē′ləm) *n.* COELOM.
Cel·si·us (sel′sē·əs) *adj.* Of or designating a temperature scale in which the freezing point of water is 0° and the boiling point 100°. [<Anders *Celsius*, 1701–44, Swedish astronomer]
Celt (selt, kelt) *n.* A person of Celtic linguistic stock, now represented by the Irish, Welsh, Highland Scots, Manx, Cornish, and Bretons.
Celt·ic (sel′tik, kel′-) *n.* A subfamily of the Indo-European family of languages, including Cornish, Welsh, Breton, Irish, Scottish Highland Gaelic, and Manx. —*adj.* Of or pertaining to the Celtic peoples, their languages, or culture.
ce·ment (si·ment′) *n.* 1 A powdery substance, usu. of burned lime and clay, that when mixed with water or with water, sand, and gravel produces mortar or concrete. 2 Any gluelike substance. 3 A dental filling for cavities. • See TOOTH. 4 Any bond or union, as between persons. —*v.t.* 1 To unite or join with or as with cement. 2 To cover or coat with cement. —*v.t.* 3 To become united by cement; cohere. [<L *caementum* rough stone, stone chip <*caedere* cut] —**ce·men·ta·tion** (sē′mən·tā′shən, sem′ən-), **ce·ment′er** *n.* • *Cement* is often used as a synonym for *concrete*. This is technically incorrect, since cement is only one, although the principal, ingredient of concrete.
cem·e·ter·y (sem′ə·ter′ē) *n. pl.* **·ter·ies** A place for the burial of the dead. [<Gk. *koimaein* put to sleep]
cen., cent. central; century.
-cene *suffix* Recent; new; *pleistocene*. [Gk. *kainos* new]
cen·o·taph (sen′ə·taf, -täf) *n.* A monument to a dead person whose remains are elsewhere. [<Gk. *kenos* empty + *taphos* tomb]
Ce·no·zo·ic (sē′nə·zō′ik, sen′ə-) *adj.* & *n.* See GEOLOGY [<Gk. *kainos* new + *zōē* life]
cen·ser (sen′sər) *n.* A vessel for burning incense. [<Med. L *incensum* incense]
cen·sor (sen′sər) *n.* 1 An official examiner of manu-

scripts, plays, movies, etc., empowered to delete or suppress whatever is considered offensive or objectionable. 2 An official who deletes from letters, dispatches, etc., any secret or forbidden information. 3 Anyone who censures or criticizes. 4 In Ancient Rome, one of two magistrates who took the census and supervised public morals. —*v.t.* To act as censor of. [<L *censere* judge] —**cen·so·ri·al** (sen·sôr′ē·əl, -sō′rē-) *adj.*

cen·so·ri·ous (sen·sôr′ē·əs, -sō′rē-) *adj.* Given to or expressing censure; critical. —**cen·so′ri·ous·ly** *adv.* —**cen·so′ri·ous·ness** *n.*

cen·sor·ship (sen′sər·ship) *n.* 1 The office or power of a censor. 2 The act or process of censoring.

cen·sur·a·ble (sen′shər·ə·bəl) *adj.* Deserving censure; blameworthy. —**cen′sur·a·bly** *adv.*

cen·sure (sen′shər) *n.* Condemnation or blame; disapproval. —*v.t.* **·sured, ·sur·ing** To express disapproval of; condemn. [<L *censere* judge] —**cen′sur·er** *n.*

cen·sus (sen′səs) *n. pl.* **cen·sus·es** An official count of the people of a country or district, including age, sex, employment, etc. [<L *censere* assess]

cent (sent) *n.* 1 The hundredth part of a dollar. 2 The hundredth part of a standard unit of other money systems. 3 A coin of this value. [<L *centum* hundred]

cent. centered; centigrade; centimeter; century.

cen·taur (sen′tôr) *Gk. Myth.* One having the head, arms, and torso of a man and the body and legs of a horse.

cen·ta·vo (sen·tä′vō) *n. pl.* **·vos** (-vōz, *Sp.* -vōs) A small coin of the Philippines, Mexico, and other Latin American countries, usu. equal to the hundredth part of a peso. [Sp.]

cen·te·nar·i·an (sen′tə·nâr′ē·ən) *n.* One who is one hundred or more years old.

cen·te·nary (sen′tə·ner′ē, sen·ten′ə·rē) *n. pl.* **·nar·ies** 1 A hundredth anniversary. 2 A period of a hundred years. [<L *centum* hundred]

cen·ten·ni·al (sen·ten′ē·əl) *adj.* Of a hundred or a hundredth anniversary. —*n.* A hundredth anniversary. [<L *centum* hundred + *annus* a year] —**cen·ten′ni·al·ly** *adv.*

cen·ter (sen′tər) *n.* 1 *Geom.* The point within a circle or sphere equally distant from any point on the circumference or surface. 2 The middle: the *center* of the town. 3 The point, object, person, or place about which things cluster or revolve or from which they emanate: a *center* of interest. 4 Any hub of a specified activity: a manufacturing *center*. 5 *Mech.* A point on or by which an object is secured or rotated. 6 The person who takes the middle position in certain games, as football, basketball, etc. 7 *Often cap.* a The moderate position of a political group neither conservative nor liberal but sharing some views with both. b Such a group. —*v.t.* 1 To place in or at the center. 2 To supply with a center. 3 To draw to or direct toward one place; concentrate. —*v.i.* 4 To be in or at the center. 5 To have a focal point; concentrate. —*adj.* Central; middle. [<Gk. *kentron* point (i.e., around which a circle is described)]

center of gravity That point, if it exists, at which the weight of a body appears to be concentrated regardless of the position of the body.

cen·ter·piece (sen′tər·pēs′) *n.* 1 An ornament for the center of a table. 2 Any object conspicuously displayed.

cen·tes·i·mal (sen·tes′ə·məl) *adj.* 1 Hundredth. 2 Divided into hundredths. [<L *centesimus* hundredth]

centi- *combining form* 1 Hundred: *centipede.* 2 Hundredth. [<L *centum* hundred]

cen·ti·grade (sen′tə·grād) *adj.* 1 Graduated to a scale of a hundred. 2 CELSIUS. [<L *centum* hundred + *gradus* step, degree]

cen·til·lion (sen·til′yən) *n.* See NUMBER.

cen·time (sän′tēm, *Fr.* sän·tēm′) *n.* A hundredth of a franc. [F < OF *centisme* < L *centesimus* hundredth]

cen·ti·me·ter (sen′tə·mē′tər) *n.* The hundredth part of a meter.

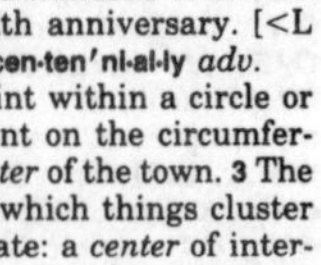

Centipede

cen·ti·pede (sen·tə·pēd) *n.* Any of a class of elongated arthropods having a pair of legs to each segment. [<L *centum* hundred + *pes, pedis* foot]

cen·tral (sen′trəl) *adj.* 1 Of, in, near, or from the center. 2 Being the center. 3 Being a dominant or controlling factor, element, point, etc.; chief. —*n. Informal.* 1 A telephone exchange. 2 The operator in charge of it. [<L *centrum* center] —**cen′tral·ly** *adv.* —**cen·tral·i·ty** (sen′tral′ə·tē), **cen′tral·ness** *n.*

Central African Republic A republic in CEN. Africa, 238,234 sq. mi., cap. Bangui. • See map at AFRICA.

Central America A narrow, winding strip of land between Mexico and South America.

Central America

cen·tral·ize (sen′trəl·īz) *v.* **·ized, ·iz·ing** *v.t.* 1 To make central; bring to a center. 2 To concentrate (power or control) in one authority. —*v.i.* 3 To come to a center. —**cen′tral·i·za′tion, cen′tral·iz′er** *n.*

central processing unit A microprocessor that directs a computer to execute instructions and performs basic mathematical functions.

cen·tre (sen′tər) *n., adj., v.t. & v.i.* **·tred, ·tring** *Brit.* CENTER.

cen·tric (sen′trik) *adj.* 1 In, at, or near the center. 2 Being or having a center. Also **cen′tri·cal.** —**cen′tri·cal·ly** *adv.* —**cen·tric·i·ty** (sen·tris′ə·tē) *n.*

cen·trif·u·gal (sen·trif′yə·gəl, -ə·gəl) *adj.* 1 Directed or tending away from a center; radiating. 2 Employing centrifugal force: a *centrifugal* pump. [<L *centrum* center + *fugere* flee] —**cen·trif′u·gal·ly** *adv.*

centrifugal force *Physics* The force that makes a rotating body tend to pull away from the center around which it rotates.

cen·tri·fuge (sen′trə·fyōōj) *n.* A rotary machine employing centrifugal force to separate substances having different densities.

cen·trip·e·tal (sen·trip′ə·təl) *adj.* 1 Directed, tending, or drawing toward a center. 2 Employing centripetal force: a *centripetal* pump. [<L *centrum* center + *petere* seek]

centripetal force *Physics* A force attracting a body toward a center around which it revolves.

cen·tro·some (sen′trə·sōm) *n. Biol.* A small body situated near the nucleus. [<Gk *kentron* center + *sōma* body]

cen·tro·sphere (sen′trə·sfir′) *n.* 1 *Geol.* The central portion of the earth. 2 *Biol.* The sphere which surrounds the centrosome.

cen·tu·ple (sen′tə·pəl, sen·tyōō′pəl) *v.t.* **·pled, ·pling** To increase a hundredfold. —*adj.* Increased a hundredfold. [<L *centuplus* hundredfold].

cen·tu·ri·on (sen·tyōōr′ē·ən) *n.* The commander of a century in the ancient Roman army. [<L *centurio*]

cen·tu·ry (sen′chə·rē) *n. pl.* **·ries** 1 A period of 100 years in any system of chronology, esp. in reckoning from the first year of the Christian era. 2 A body of Roman foot soldiers (at one time 100 men). [<L *centum* hundred]

century plant An American agave that flowers after twenty to thirty years and then dies.

ce·phal·ic (sə·fal′ik) *adj.* Of, pertaining to, on, in, or near the head. [<Gk. *kephalē* head]

cephalic index The ratio of the greatest breadth of the skull to the greatest length, multiplied by 100.

ceph·a·lo·pod (sef′ə·lə·pod′) *n.* Any of a class of mollusks such as squids, cuttlefishes, octopuses, etc., having a clearly defined head and eyes, ink sac, and tentacles or arms. —*adj.* Of or pertaining to cephalopods. [<Gk. *kephalē* head + *pous, podis* foot]

-cephalous *combining form* Headed; *hydrocephalous.* [<Gk. *kephalē* head]

ce·ram·ic (sə·ram′ik) *adj.* Of or pertaining to earthenware, pottery, porcelain, etc., or to their manufacture. —*n.* An article of ceramic manufacture. [<Gk. *keramos* potters' clay]

ce·ram·ics (sə·ram′iks) *n.pl. (construed as sing.)* The art or technique of making ceramic articles. **—ce·ra′mist, ce·ram′i·cist** *n.*

Cer·ber·us (sûr′bər·əs) *Gk. & Rom. Myth.* The three-headed dog guarding the portals of Hades.

cere (sir) *n.* In parrots, eagles, etc., a waxlike, fleshy area about the bill. [< L *cera* wax]

ce·re·al (sir′ē·əl) *n.* 1 The grain of certain grasses used as food, as rice, wheat, etc. 2 Any of the plants yielding such grains. 3 A breakfast food made from a cereal —*adj.* Pertaining to edible grain. [< CERES]

cer·e·bel·lum (ser′ə·bel′əm) *n. pl.* **·bel·lums** or **·bel·la** (-bel′ə) The part of the brain that acts as the coordination center of voluntary movement, posture, and equilibrium. [< L *cerebrum* brain] **—cer′e·bel′lar** *adj.*

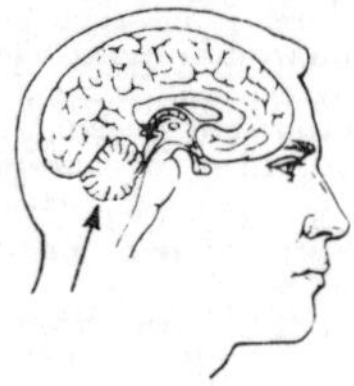

Cerebellum

cer·e·bral (ser′ə·brəl, sə·rē′-) *adj.* 1 Of or pertaining to the cerebrum or the brain. 2 Appealing to or requiring the intellect; intellectual.

cerebral palsy Paralysis and inability to control movement due to brain injury.

cer·e·brate (ser′ə·brāt) *v.i.* **·brat·ed, ·brat·ing** To think. [< L *cerebrum* brain] **—cer′e·bra′tion** *n.*

cer·e·bro·spi·nal (ser′ə·brō·spī′nəl) *adj.* Of the brain and the spinal cord.

cer·e·brum (sə·rē′brəm, ser′ə·brəm) *n. pl.* **·bra** (-brə) The upper part of the brain consisting of two hemispheres connected at the base. [< L] **—cer·e·bric** (sə·rē′brik, ser′ə-) *adj.*

cere·cloth (sir′klôth′, -kloth′) *n.* A cloth treated with wax, formerly used to cover the dead. [< obs. *cere* to cover with wax < L *cera* wax]

cere·ment (sir′mənt) *n. Usu. pl.* SHROUD.

cer·e·mo·ni·al (ser′ə·mō′nē·əl) *adj.* Of, pertaining to or characterized by ceremony; ritual; formal. —*n.* 1 A system of rules of ceremony; ritual. 2 A ceremony. **—cer′e·mo′ni·al·ism, cer′e·mo′ni·al·ist** *n.* **—cer′e·mo′ni·al·ly** *adv.*

cer·e·mo·ni·ous (ser′ə·mō′nē·əs) *adj.* 1 Observant of or conducted with ceremony; formal. 2 Studiously polite. **—cer′e·mo′ni·ous·ly** *adv.* **—cer′e·mo′ni·ous·ness** *n.*

cer·e·mo·ny (ser′ə·mō′nē) *n. pl.* **·nies** 1 A formal act, or a series of them, as on religious and state occasions. 2 The performance of such acts. 3 Mere outward form. 4 Formal civility; formality. [< L *caerimonia* awe, veneration]

Ce·res (sir′ēz) *Rom. Myth.* The goddess of grain and harvests.

ce·rise (sə·rēz′, -rēs′) *adj., n.* Bright, cherry red. [< F, cherry]

ce·ri·um (sir′ē·əm) *n.* A shiny, gray, rare-earth element (symbol Ce). [< the asteroid *Ceres*]

cert. certificate; certify; certified.

cer·tain (sûr′tən) *adj.* 1 Established as fact or truth; beyond doubt or question; true. 2 Absolutely sure; convinced. 3 Definitely settled; fixed; determined. 4 Inevitable: Death is *certain.* 5 Sure in its workings or results; reliable. 6 Appreciable; limited: to a *certain* extent. 7 Indefinite, but assumed to be determinable: a *certain* man. **—for certain** Without doubt. [< L *certus,* p.p. of *cernere* determine] **—Syn.** 1 undeniable, indisputable, incontestable, irrefutable. 2 positive. 3 assured, decided. 4 unavoidable.

cer·tain·ly (sûr′tən·lē) *adv.* Without a doubt; surely.

cer·tain·ty (sûr′tən·tē) *n. pl.* **·ties** 1 The quality or fact of being certain. 2 Something definite and certain.

cer·tif·i·cate (sər·tif′ə·kit) *n.* A document or written statement declaring something to be true, genuine, or legally valid. —*v.t.* (-kāt) **·cat·ed, ·cat·ing** To furnish with or attest by a certificate. [< Med.L *certificare* certify]

cer·ti·fi·ca·tion (sûr′tə·fi·kā′shən) *n.* 1 The act of certifying. 2 The state of being certified. 3 A certified statement.

certified check A check drawn on an account having sufficient funds for the bank to guarantee in writing its payment.

cer·ti·fy (sûr′tə·fī) *v.t.* **·fied, ·fy·ing** 1 To guarantee (something) to be true, genuine, etc., usu. in a formal, written statement. 2 To issue a certificate to. 3 To give assurance of; vouch for. 4 To declare to be legally insane. [< L *certus* certain + *facere* make] **—cer′ti·fi′a·ble** *adj.* **—cer′ti·fi′er** *n.*

cer·ti·o·ra·ri (sûr′shē·ə·râr′ē, -râr′ī) *n. Law* A writ from a superior to an inferior court, directing that a record of a designated case be sent up for review. [< LL, to be certified]

cer·ti·tude (sûr′tə·tʸōōd) *n.* Perfect assurance; certainty. [< L *certus* certain]

ce·ru·le·an (sə·rōō′lē·ən) *n.* Sky blue. —*adj.* Sky-blue. [< L *caeruleus* dark blue]

cer·vi·cal (sûr′vi·kəl) *adj. Anat.* Of or pertaining to the neck or a necklike part. [< L CERVIX]

cer·vine (sûr′vīn, -vin) *adj.* Of or similar to deer. [< L *cervus* deer]

cer·vix (sûr′viks) *n. pl.* **cer·vix·es** or **cer·vi·ces** (sər·vī′sēz, sûr′və·sēz) 1 The neck. 2 Any necklike part, as the constricted end of the uterus, etc. [< L]

Ce·sar·e·an (si·zâr′ē·ən) *adj.* CAESAREAN. Also **Ce·sar′i·an.**

ce·si·um (sē′zē·əm) *n.* A soft, silvery, and very reactive metallic element (symbol Cs) chemically similar to potassium and used in photoelectric cells. [< L *caesius* bluish gray]

ces·sa·tion (se·sā′shən) *n.* A ceasing; stop; pause. [< L *cessare* stop]

ces·sion (sesh′ən) *n.* The act of ceding; surrender. [< L *cessus* p.p. of *cedere* yield]

cess·pool (ses′pōōl′) *n.* 1 A covered well or pit for the drainage from sinks, etc. 2 Any repository of filth. [?]

ce·su·ra (si·zhōōr′ə, -zyōōr′ə) *n.* CAESURA.

ce·ta·cean (sə·tā′shən) *adj.* Of or belonging to an order of aquatic mammals, as the whales, dolphins, and porpoises. Also **ce·ta′ceous.** —*n.* A cetacean mammal. [< Gk. *kētos* whale]

Cey·lon (si·lon′) *n.* SRI LANKA.

C.F., c.f. cost and freight.

C/F, c/f carried forward.

Cf californium.

cf. compare (L *confer*).

C.F.I., c.f.i. cost, freight, and insurance.

cfm., c.f.m. cubic feet per minute.

cfs., c.f.s. cubic feet per second.

C.G. Coast Guard.

cg, cg., cgm. centigram(s).

cgs, c.g.s., C.G.S. centimeter-gram-second.

C.H., c.h. courthouse; customhouse.

Ch. Chaldean; Chaldea; China; Chinese.

ch. champion; chapter; check; chief; children; church.

cha·blis (sha·blē′) *n.* 1 A dry, white, Burgundy wine made in the region of Chablis, France. 2 Any of various similar wines.

Chad (chad) *n.* A republic in CEN. Africa, 495,752 sq. mi., cap. Fort-Lamy. • See map at AFRICA.

chafe (chāf) *v.* **chafed, chaf·ing** *v.t.* 1 To abrade or make sore by rubbing. 2 To make warm by rubbing. 3 To irritate; annoy. —*v.i.* 4 To rub. 5 To be irritated; fret. —*n.* 1 Soreness or wear from friction. 2 Irritation or vexation. [< OF *chaufer* warm < L *calere* be warm + *facere* make] **—chaf′er** *n.*

chaf·er (chā′fər) *n.* The cockchafer or other scarabaeid beetle. Also **chaf·fer** (chaf′ər). [< OE *ceafor*]

chaff[1] (chaf, chäf) *n.* 1 The husks of grain. 2 Worthless matter; refuse. [OE *ceaf*] **—chaff′y** *adj.*

chaff[2] (chaf, chäf) *v.t.* To poke fun at; ridicule. —*n.* Good-natured banter. [?]

chaf·fer (chaf′ər) *v.i.* To haggle about price; bargain. —*n.* The act of chaffering; bargaining. [< OE *cēap* bargain + *faru* going] **—chaf′fer·er** *n.*

chaf·finch (chaf′inch) *n.* A European song finch, popular as a cage bird. [< CHAFF[1] + FINCH]

chaf·ing dish (chā′fing) *n.* A vessel with a heating apparatus beneath, to cook or keep hot its contents at table.

cha·grin (shə·grin′) *n.* Distress or embarrassment caused by disappointment, failure, etc.; mortification. —*v.t.* To humiliate; mortify. [F, sad] **—Syn.** *n.* confusion, dismay, humiliation, vexation.

chain (chān) *n.* 1 A series of connected rings or links, serving to bind, drag, hold, or ornament. 2 *pl.* Shackles; bonds. 3 *pl.* Bondage; captivity. 4 Any connected series: a *chain* of events. 5 A range of mountains. 6 A unit of linear measure equal to 66 or 100 feet. 7 *Chem.* A series of atoms linked together. 8 A series of associated stores, banks, etc. —*v.t.* 1 To fasten, as with a chain. 2 To bring into or hold in subjection. [< L *catena*]

chain gang A gang of convicts chained together while doing hard labor.

chain mail Flexible armor made of joined metal links. • See MAIL[2].

chain of command A hierarchy of persons in command according to rank.

chain reaction A series of reactions each of which develops from the energy or products released by its predecessor.

chain stitch A sewing stitch of loops connected in a chain, used in embroidery, etc.

chain store A retail store that is a member of a chain of stores.

chair (châr) *n.* 1 A seat, usu. with four legs and a back and for one person. 2 A seat of office, as of a professor or moderator. 3 A person holding such an office. 4 A chairman. 5 ELECTRIC CHAIR. —*v.t.* 1 To put into a chair; install in office. 2 To preside over (a meeting). [< F *chaiere* < L *cathedra*]

chair·man (châr′mən) *n. pl.* **·men** (-mən) One who presides over an assembly, committee, etc. —**chair′man·ship** *n.*

chair·per·son (châr′pûr′sən) *n. pl.* **·sons** One who presides over an assembly, committee, etc.

chair·wom·an (châr′wŏŏm′ən) *n. pl.* **·wom·en** (-wim′ən) A woman who presides over an assembly, committee, etc.

chaise (shāz) *n.* 1 A light, four-wheeled carriage, usu. with an open top. 2 CHAISE LONGUE. [F, var. of *chair* chair]

chaise longue (shāz′ lông′, *Fr.* shez lông′) *n.* A chair having a backrest at one end and the seat prolonged to support the sitter's outstretched legs. [F, lit., long chair]

cha·la·za (kə·lā′zə) *n. pl.* **·zas** or **·zae** (-zē) Either of the two ropes of dense albumen attached to the lining membrane of an egg. [< Gk., hailstone, small lump]

chal·ced·o·ny (kal·sed′ə·nē, kal′sə·dō′nē) *n. pl.* **·nies** A waxy, translucent variety of quartz. [< *Chalcedon,* an ancient Greek port]

Chal·de·a (kal·dē′ə) *n.* In Biblical geography, the southernmost part of the valley of the Tigris and the Euphrates, sometimes extended to include Babylonia. Also **Chal·dae′a.** —**Chal·de′an** *adj. & n.*

cha·let (sha·lā′, shal′ā) *n.* 1 A Swiss cottage having a gently sloping and projecting roof. 2 Any house built in this style. [F]

chal·ice (chal′is) *n.* 1 A consecrated cup used in the celebration of the Eucharist. 2 Any cup or goblet. 3 A cup-shaped flower. [< L *calix* cup]

chalk (chôk) *n.* 1 A soft, grayish white or yellowish limestone, largely composed of minute sea shells. 2 A piece of chalk or chalklike material used for marking or drawing. 3 A score or reckoning, as one recorded with chalk. —*v.t.* 1 To mark or draw with chalk. 2 To put chalk on or in. 3 To make pale. —**chalk up** 1 To score. 2 To give credit. —*adj.* Made with chalk. [< OE *cealc* < L *calx* limestone] —**chalk′i·ness** *n.* —**chalk′y** *adj.* **(·i·er, ·i·est)**

chalk·board (chôk′bôrd′, -bōrd′) *n.* A hard, flat surface for writing on with chalk, used for classroom instruction.

chal·lenge (chal′ənj) *v.* **·lenged, ·leng·ing** *v.t.* 1 To dare or invite to a duel, contest, etc. 2 To stop and demand identification. 3 To call in question; object to: to *challenge* a decision, voter, juror, etc. 4 To stimulate: to *challenge* the imagination. 5 To call for; claim as due. —*v.i.* 6 To utter or make a challenge. —*n.* 1 A call or dare to fight, esp. to fight a duel. 2 A formal objection or exception to a person or thing. 3 A sentry's call, requiring one to halt and give identification. 4 Something that stimulates a person or persons to greater effort, dedication, etc. [< LL *calumniare* accuse falsely < *calumnia* slander] —**Syn.** *v.* 3 dispute, query, contest, doubt. 4 excite, arouse, animate, spur, stir. —**chal′lenge·a·ble** *adj.* —**chal′leng·er** *n.*

chal·lis (shal′ē) *n.* A light printed dress fabric. [?]

cham·ber (chām′bər) *n.* 1 A room in a house, esp. a bedroom. 2 *pl.* A suite of rooms or offices for the use of one person, as a judge's office. 3 a A hall where an assembly or council meets. b The council or assembly itself. 4 An enclosed space, as one of the cavities in the cartridge cylinder of a revolver. 5 *Anat.* A cavity or compartment, as in the heart, eyeball, etc. —*v.t.* To make chambers in, as a gun. [< L *camera* vaulted room < Gk. *kamara*]

cham·ber·lain (chām′bər·lin) *n.* 1 A high court official. 2 An official who manages a royal household. 3 A treasurer. [< L *camera.* See CHAMBER.]

cham·ber·maid (chām′bər·mād′) *n.* A woman who cleans bedrooms in a hotel.

chamber music Music for a small ensemble.

chamber of commerce An association of businessmen for the protection and regulation of commerce.

chamber pot A portable receptacle used in a bedroom as a toilet.

cham·bray (sham′brā) *n.* A cotton fabric woven with colored warp crossed by white threads. [< *Cambrai,* France]

cha·me·le·on (kə·mē′lē·ən, -mēl′yən) *n.* 1 Any of various lizards having the power to change its color. 2 A person of changeable character or habits. [< Gk. < *chamai* on the ground + *leōn* lion] —**cha·me·le·on·ic** (kə·mē′lē·on′ik) *adj.*

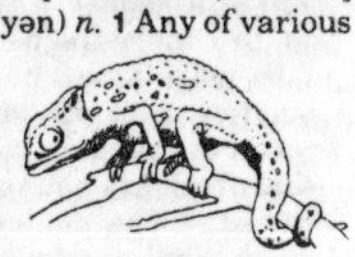

Chameleon

cham·fer (cham′fər) *v.t.* 1 To cut a channel or groove in. 2 To bevel. —*n.* A groove or channel. [< F *chanfrein* < OF *chanfraindre* to cut off an edge]

cham·ois (sham′ē, *Fr.* sha·mwä′) *n. pl.* **·ois** 1 A small mountain antelope of Europe and western Asia. 2 A soft leather originally prepared from the skin of the chamois, now from sheep, goats, deer, etc. [F]

cham·o·mile (kam′ə·mīl) *n.* A strongly scented, bitter herb with daisylike flowers, used to make a medicinal tea. [< Gk. *chamai* on the ground + *mēlon* apple]

champ[1] (champ) *v.t.* 1 To crush and chew noisily; munch. 2 To bite upon restlessly. —*n.* The action of champing.

champ[2] (champ) *n. Slang* Champion.

cham·pagne (sham·pān′) *n.* 1 A sparkling white wine made in the region of Champagne, France. 2 Any sparkling white wine. 3 A pale, tawny or greenish yellow.

cham·paign (sham·pān′) *n.* Flat and open country; a plain. —*adj.* Level and open. [< L *campus,* plain, field]

cham·pi·on (cham′pē·ən) *n.* 1 The victor in a contest. 2 One who defends a person, principle, etc. —*adj.* Acknowledged superior to all competitors; holding the first prize. —*v.t.* To stand up for the rights of; defend. [< LL *campio* fighter < L *campus* field]

cham·pi·on·ship (cham′pē·ən·ship′) *n.* 1 A contest held to determine a champion. 2 The position of a champion. 3 The act of championing; advocacy.

chance (chans, chäns) *n.* 1 The unknown or the undefined cause of events; luck; fortune. 2 An unknown agency, assumed to be the cause of events. 3 The likelihood of something; probability. 4 A fortuitous event; an accident. 5 An opportunity. 6 A risk. 7 A ticket in a lottery, raffle, etc. —*v.* **chanced, chanc·ing** *v.i.* 1 To occur accidentally; happen. —*v.t.* 2 To risk; hazard. —*adj.* Occurring by chance. [< LL *cadentia* < L *cadere* to fall]

chan·cel (chan′səl, chän′-) *n.* The space in a church for the clergy and choir, often separated from the rest of the church by a screen or railing. [< LL < *cancelli,* pl., lattice]

chan·cel·ler·y (chan′sə·lər·ē, chän′-, chans′lər·ē, chäns′-) *n. pl.* **·ries** 1 The office or position of a chancellor. 2 The building or room in which a chancellor has his office. 3 The office of an embassy or legation.

chan·cel·lor (chan′sə·lər, chän′-, chans′lər, chäns′-) *n.* 1 In certain universities, the president. 2 In certain countries, the head of state or prime minister. 3 A judicial officer sitting in a court of chancery or equity. [< LL *cancellarius* one who stands at the bar in a court < *cancelli,* pl., railing] —**chan′cel·lor·ship′** *n.*

chan·cer·y (chan′sər·ē, chän′-) *n. pl.* **·cer·ies 1** In the U.S., a court of equity. **2** In Great Britain, one of the five divisions of the High Court of Justice. **3** A court of records; archives. **4** CHANCELLERY (def. 3). **—in chancery 1** Pending in a court of chancery. **2** In a hopeless predicament. [< LL *cancellarius.* See CHANCELLOR.]

chan·cre (shang′kər) *n.* A primary syphilitic lesion. [< L *cancer* crab, ulcer] **—chan·crous** (shang′krəs) *adj.*

chan·croid (shang′kroid) *n.* A nonsyphilitic venereal sore.

chanc·y (chan′sē, chän′-) *adj.* **·i·er, ·i·est** *Informal.* Subject to chance; risky.

chan·de·lier (shan′də·lir′) *n.* A branched light fixture. [< L *candela* candle]

chan·dler (chan′dlər, chän′-) *n.* **1** A retailer or supplier of groceries, provisions, etc. **2** One who makes or sells candles. [< F *chandelier* chandler, candlestick]

change (chānj) *v.* **changed, chang·ing** *v.t.* **1** To make different; alter. **2** To exchange; interchange: to *change* places. **3** To replace, substitute, or abandon (something) for another thing: to *change* plans. **4** To give or get the equivalent of, as money. **5** To put other garments, coverings, etc., on: to *change* the bed. **—***v.i.* **6** To become different; vary. **7** To make an exchange. **8** To transfer from one train to another. **9** To put on other garments. **—***n.* **1** The act or result of changing. **2** A substitution or something used in substitution: a *change* of clothes. **3** Something different or varied. **4** The money returned to a purchaser who has given a bill or coin of greater value than his purchase. **5** Money of smaller denomination given in exchange for money of larger denomination. **6** Small coins. **7** An exchange for the transaction of business: also **'change. — ring the changes 1** To operate a chime of bells so as to produce a variety of tuneful combinations. **2** To repeat something with much variation. [< LL *cambiare* exchange] **—change′ful** *adj.* **—change′ful·ly** *adv.* **—chang′er, change′ful·ness** *n.* **—Syn.** *v.* **1** transmute, transform, vary, modify.

change·a·ble (chān′jə·bəl) *adj.* **1** Capable of being changed; alterable. **2** Likely to change or vary; inconstant. **3** Reflecting light so as to appear of different color from different points of view. **—change·a·bil·i·ty** (chān′jə·bil′ə·tē), **change′a·ble·ness** *n.* **—change′a·bly** *adv.*

change·less (chānj′lis) *adj.* Without change; constant; enduring. **—change′less·ly** *adv.* **—change′less·ness** *n.*

change·ling (chānj′ling) *n.* A child believed to have been substituted secretly for another.

change of life MENOPAUSE.

chan·nel (chan′əl) *n.* **1** The bed of a stream. **2** A wide strait: the English *Channel.* **3** The deep part of a river, harbor, strait, etc. **4** A groove or tubular passage, as for liquids. **5** *pl.* A usu. official course or route through which communications, requests, etc., are handled or transmitted. **6** *Telecom.* **a** A path for the transmission of telegraph, telephone, and radio communications. **b** A wave band of specified frequency over which radio and television programs are transmitted. **—***v.t.* **chan·neled** or **·nelled, chan·nel·ing** or **·nel·ling 1** To cut or wear channels in. **2** To convey through or as through a channel. [< L *canalis* groove]

chant (chant, chänt) *n.* **1** A vocal melody sung in free rhythm, usu. unaccompanied, and with a series of words sung at a single pitch. **2** A psalm or canticle so recited. **3** A song; melody. **4** Any measured monotonous singing or speaking. **—***v.t.* **1** To sing to a chant. **2** To celebrate in song. **3** To say repetitiously and monotonously. **—***v.i.* **4** To sing chants. **5** To sing. **6** To talk monotonously and continuously. [< L *cantare,* freq. of *canere* sing] **—chant′er** *n.*

chant·ey (shan′tē, chan′-) *n. pl.* **·eys** A rhythmical working song of sailors. [Alter. of F *chantez,* imperative of *chanter* sing]

chan·ti·cleer (chan′tə·klir) *n.* COCK[1] (defs. 1, 2). [< OF < *chanter* sing, crow + *cler* aloud]

Cha·nu·kah (khä′nōō·kä) *n.* HANUKKAH.

cha·os (kā′os) *n.* **1** A condition of utter disorder and confusion. **2** *Often cap.* The primal, formless condition said to have existed before the creation of the universe. [< Gk., abyss < *chainein* gape, yawn]

cha·ot·ic (kā·ot′ik) *adj.* Of or like chaos; completely disordered. **—cha·ot′i·cal·ly** *adv.*

chap[1] (chap) *n. Informal* A fellow; lad. [< OE *cēap* trade + *man*]

chap[2] (chap) *v.t. & v.i.* **chapped** or **chapt, chap·ping** To split, crack, or redden. **—***n.* A chapped place in the skin. [ME *chappen*]

chap[3] (chap, chop) *n.* A jaw or cheek.

chap. chaplain; chapter.

cha·pa·re·jos (chä′pä·rā′hos) *n. pl.* CHAPS. Also **cha·pa·ra·jos** (chä′pä·rä′hōs) [< Sp.]

chap·ar·ral (chap′ə·ral′) *n.* A thicket of dwarf oak, low thorny shrubs, etc. [< Sp. *chaparra* evergreen oak]

chap·book (chap′bŏŏk′) *n.* A cheap popular book formerly sold on the street.

cha·peau (sha·pō′, *Fr.* shȧ·pō′) *n. pl.* **·peaux** (-pōz′, *Fr.* -pō′) or **·peaus** (-pōz′) A hat. [F < LL *cappa* head covering]

chap·el (chap′əl) *n.* **1** A building for Christian worship, but smaller than a church. **2** A room for worship, as in a hospital, etc. **3** A building for religious services on a campus; also, the services. **4** A compartment or recess in a church where independent services may be held. [< Med. L *cappa* cloak; orig., a sanctuary where the cloak of St. Martin was kept as a relic]

chap·er·on (shap′ə·rōn) *n.* **1** A woman who acts as attendant to a young unmarried woman in public. **2** An older person who attends a social function to maintain its decorum and propriety. **—***v.t.* To act as chaperon to. Also **chap′er·one.** [F < *chape* cape; because she protects her charges from harm] **—chap·er·on·age** (shap′ə·rō′nij) *n.*

chap·lain (chap′lin) *n.* A clergyman authorized to conduct religious services in a legislative assembly, in a regiment, on board a ship, at court, etc. [< Med. L *cappella* CHAPEL] **—chap′lain·cy, chap′lain·ship** *n.*

chap·let (chap′lit) *n.* **1** A wreath for the head. **2** A string of beads. **3** A third of a rosary. [< LL *cappa* hooded cape]

chaps (shaps, chaps) *n. pl.* Leather overalls without a seat, worn over trousers by cowboys to protect the legs. [Short for CHAPAREJOS]

Chaps

chap·ter (chap′tər) *n.* **1** A division of a book or treatise, usu. marked by a number and heading. **2** Any period or a sequence of episodes. **3** The canons of a cathedral or other collegiate church. **4** A meeting of such canons or of monks or nuns. **5** A branch of a club, fraternity, etc. **—***v.t.* To divide into chapters, as a book. [< L *caput* head, capital, chapter]

char[1] (chär) *n. Brit.* A chore; an odd job. **—***v.i.* **charred, char·ring** To clean and scrub for pay. [OE *cerr* turn of work]

char[2] (chär) *v.* **charred, char·ring** *v.t.* **1** To burn or scorch. **2** To convert into charcoal. **—***v.i.* **3** To become charred. **—***n.* Charcoal. [? < CHARCOAL]

char. character; charter.

char·ac·ter (kar′ik·tər) *n.* **1** The combination of qualities or traits distinguishing any person or class of persons. **2** Any distinguishing or essential quality or property. **3** Moral excellence. **4** A good reputation. **5** Position; status. **6** A person in a novel, play, etc. **7** A person of note. **8** Any person. **9** A humorous or eccentric person. **10** A written or printed figure, as a letter, mark, sign, etc. **11** *Genetics* A structural or functional trait in a plant or animal. **—***v.t.* **1** To write or print. **2** To describe. [< Gk. *charaktēr* stamp, mark < *charassein* engrave]

char·ac·ter·is·tic (kar′ik·tə·ris′tik) *adj.* Distinguishing or distinctive; typical. **—***n.* **1** A distinctive feature; peculiarity. **2** The integral part of a logarithm; index. **—char′ac·ter·is′ti·cal·ly** *adv.*

char·ac·ter·ize (kar′ik·tə·rīz′) *v.t.* **·ized, iz·ing 1** To describe or portray by qualities or peculiarities. **2** To be a mark or peculiarity of; distinguish. **—char′ac·ter·i·za′tion, char′ac·ter·iz′er** *n.*

cha·rade (shə·rād′) *n.* A guessing game in which a word or each syllable of a word is acted in pantomime. [< Prov. *charrado* chatter]

char·coal (chär′kōl′) *n.* **1** An impure carbon obtained by driving off volatile compounds of organic matter, as of wood, used as a fuel, a filter, etc. **2** A drawing pencil or crayon of charcoal. **3** A drawing made in charcoal. **—***v.t.* To write, draw, or mark with charcoal. [ME *charcole*]

chard (chärd) *n.* A variety of beet having large leaves and leafstalks, which are used as a vegetable. [< L *carduus* thistle]

chare (char) *n. & v.* CHAR[1].

charge (chärj) *v.* **charged, charg·ing** *v.t.* **1** To lay or impose a load, burden, responsibility, etc. upon. **2** To put something into or upon. **3** To put carbon dioxide into (water, etc.). **4** *Electr.* To replenish, as a storage battery. **5** To load (a firearm, etc.). **6** To command or instruct authoritatively: to *charge* a jury. **7** To accuse: with *with.* **8** To make an onset against or attack upon, as a fort. **9** To set or state, as a price. **10** To set down or record, as a debt to be paid later; also, to purchase (something) by this method. —*v.i.* **11** To demand or fix a price. **12** To make an onset: *Charge!* —**charge off** To regard or write off as a loss. —*n.* **1** The quantity of gunpowder, fuel, etc., put or to be put into a firearm, a furnace etc. **2** A quantity of electricity, as in a storage battery or carried by an atomic particle. **3** Care, custody, responsibility, etc. **4** The person or thing for which one is responsible. **5** Instruction or command: the *charge* to a jury. **6** An accusation. **7** A price or cost. **8** A debt; expense. **9** An entry in an account of indebtedness. **10** A charge account. **11** An attack or onslaught; also, the signal for it. [< LL *carricare* carry] —**charge′a·ble** *adj.*

charge account An account against which the purchase of merchandise in a store is charged.

char·gé d'af·faires (shär·zhā′ də·fâr′, *Fr.* shár·zhā′ da·fâr′) *pl.* **char·gés d'af·faires** (shär·zhāz′də·fâr′, *Fr.* shár·zhā′ da·fâr′) **1** A person who temporarily assumes the command of a diplomatic mission. **2** A diplomat ranking below an ambassador or minister.

charg·er (chär′jər) *n.* **1** One who or that which charges. **2** A horse used for battle and in parades. **3** An apparatus for charging electric storage batteries.

char·i·ly (châr′ə·lē) *adv.* In a chary manner; warily.

char·i·ness (châr′ē·nis) *n.* The quality of being chary.

char·i·ot (char′ē·ət) *n.* An ancient two-wheeled vehicle used in war and in racing. —*v.t. & v.i.* To convey, ride, or drive in a chariot. [< L *carrus* cart, wagon] —**char′i·o·teer′** *n.*

Chariot

cha·ris·ma (kə·riz′·mə) *n.* A quality that enables a person, esp. a leader, to capture the interest, devotion, and confidence of others. [< Gk., grace, favor] —**char·is·mat·ic** (kar′iz·mat′ik) *adj.*

char·i·ta·ble (char′ə·tə·bəl) *adj.* **1** Of or characterized by charity. **2** Generous in giving gifts to the poor. **3** Tolerant; benevolent; kindly. —**char′i·ta·ble·ness** *n.* —**char′i·ta·bly** *adv.*

char·i·ty (char′ə·tē) *n. pl.* **·ties 1** The giving of aid to the poor. **2** The aid given. **3** An institution, organization, or fund for the help of the needy. **4** A feeling of good will or kindness towards others. **5** An act of good will or kindness. **6** Tolerance; leniency. [< L *caritas* love < *carus* dear]

char·la·tan (shär′lə·tən) *n.* A person who claims to possess a knowledge or skill he does not have; a fake; quack. —**char′la·tan·ry, char′la·tan·ism** *n.* [< Ital. *ciarlatano* babbler]

Charles·ton (chärlz′tən) *n.* A fast dance in four-four time. [< *Charleston,* S.C.]

char·ley horse (chär′lē) *Informal* A cramp in the muscles of the leg or arm, caused by excessive exertion. [?]

char·lock (chär′lək) *n.* Wild mustard, often a troublesome weed. [< OE *cerlic*]

charm (chärm) *v.t.* **1** To attract irresistibly; delight; enchant. **2** To influence as by magic power. **3** To protect as by a spell: a *charmed* life. —*v.i.* **4** To be pleasing or fascinating. **5** To act as a charm; work as a spell. —*n.* **1** The power to allure or delight; fascination. **2** Something that delights or fascinates. **3** A small ornament worn on a bracelet, etc. **4** Something worn or used to avert evil or bring good luck. [< L *carmen* song, incantation] —**charm′·er** *n.* —**Syn.** *v.* **1** bewitch, captivate, entrance, fascinate.

charm·ing (chär′ming) *adj.* Enchanting; fascinating; bewitching. —**charm′ing·ly** *adv.* —**charm′ing·ness** *n.*

char·nel house (chär′nəl) A room or building where bones or bodies of the dead are placed. [< L *caro, carnis* flesh]

Char·on (kâr′ən) *Gk. Myth.* The ferryman who carried the dead over the river Styx to Hades.

chart (chärt) *n.* **1** A map; esp., one for the use of navigators, aviators, and meteorologists. **2** A sheet showing facts graphically or in tabular form. —*v.t.* To map out; lay out on a chart. [< Gk. *chartē* leaf of paper]

char·ter (chär′tər) *n.* **1** A document, given by a ruler or government, granting special rights or privileges to a person, institution, etc. **2** *Usu. cap.* A document outlining the aims or purposes of a group: *Charter* of the United Nations. **3** A permit to establish a branch or chapter of a society. **4** The leasing or renting of a vessel, airplane, bus, etc. —*v.t.* **1** To hire or rent. **2** To give a charter to. [< L *charta* paper] —**char′ter·er** *n.*

charter member An original member of an organization or society.

char·treuse (shár·trœz′) *n.* **1** A yellow, pale green, or white liqueur made by the Carthusian monks. **2** (*also* shär·tro͞oz′) A pale yellowish green. —*adj.* Pale, yellowish green. [< *Chartreuse,* a monastery in France.]

char·wom·an (chär′wo͝om′ən) *n. pl.* **·wom·en** A woman employed to do cleaning, scrubbing, etc., as in office buildings.

char·y (châr′ē) *adj.* **char·i·er, char·i·est 1** Cautious; wary. **2** Slow to give; sparing. [< OE *cearig* sorrowful, sad]

Cha·ryb·dis (kə·rib′dis) *Gk. Myth.* A whirlpool off the Sicilian coast opposite the rock Scylla.

chase[1] (chās) *v.* **chased, chas·ing** *v.t.* **1** To pursue with intent to catch, capture, or molest. **2** To drive away; dispel: often with *away, out* or *off.* **3** To hunt, as deer. —*v.i.* **4** To follow in pursuit. **5** *Informal* To rush; go hurriedly. —*n.* **1** Earnest pursuit. **2** That which is pursued. **3** The sport of hunting: usu. with *the.* [< LL *captiare,* freq. of *capere* take, hold]

chase[2] (chās) *n.* **1** *Printing* A metal frame into which pages of type are fastened for printing. **2** A groove or slot. —*v.t.* **chased, chas·ing** To ornament by embossing, indenting, etc. [< L *capsa* box]

chas·er (chā′sər) *n.* **1** One who chases or pursues. **2** *Informal* Water or some mild beverage taken with or after a drink of liquor.

chasm (kaz′əm) *n.* **1** A deep gorge. **2** A gap or void. **3** A difference, as of opinions, feelings, etc. [< Gk. *chasma* < *chainein* gape] —**chas·mal** (kaz′məl) *adj.*

Chas·si·dim (khä·sē′dim) *n. pl.* of **Chas·sid** (khä′sid) A sect of Jewish mystics. [< Heb., pious] —**Chas·si·dic** (khä·sē′dik) *adj.*

chas·sis (shas′ē, chas′ē) *n. pl.* **chas·sis** (shas′ēz, chas′-) **1** The frame, suspension, wheels, brakes, and steering assembly of an automobile or similar vehicle. **2** The landing gear of an aircraft. **3 a** The metal framework supporting the parts of a radio, television set, etc. **b** The assembled framework and components. [< L *capsa* box]

chaste (chāst) *adj.* **1** Free from unlawful sexual activity; virtuous. **2** Sexually abstinent. **3** Pure and modest, as in conduct. **4** Pure and simple in style; not ornate. [< L *castus* pure] —**chaste′ly** *adv.* —**chaste′ness** *n.*

chast·en (chā′sən) *v.t.* **1** To discipline by punishment or affliction; chastise. **2** To moderate; soften; temper. [< L *castigare* castigate] —**chast′en·er** *n.* —**chast′en·ing** *n.*

chas·tise (chas·tīz′) *v.t.* **·tised, ·tis·ing 1** To punish, esp. by whipping. **2** To scold sharply. [< L *castigare* castigate] —**chas·tise·ment** (chas′tiz·mənt, chas·tīz′-), **chas·tis′er** *n.*

chas·ti·ty (chas′tə·tē) *n.* The state or quality of being chaste. [< L *castus* pure]

chas·u·ble (chaz′yə·bəl, chas′-) *n.* The sleeveless, outer vestment worn by a priest in celebrating the Mass or Eucharist. [< Med. L *casula* cloak < L, dim. of *casa* house]

chat (chat) *v.i.* **chat·ted, chat·ting** To converse in an easy, familiar manner. —*n.* **1** An informal conversation. **2** Any of several singing birds. [Short for CHATTER]

cha·teau (sha·tō′, *Fr.* shä·tō′) *n. pl.* **·teaux** (-tōz′, *Fr.* -tō′) **1** A French castle or manor house. **2** A house on a country estate. [F< L *castellum* CASTLE]

chat·e·laine (shat′ə·lān) *n.* **1** The mistress of a chateau or castle. **2** A clasp or chain hung from a woman's belt to hold small articles. [F]

chat·tel (chat′l) *n.* An article of personal property that is movable, such as furniture, livestock, etc. [< L *capitale* property < *caput* head]

chat·ter (chat′ər) *v.i.* **1** To click together rapidly, as the teeth in shivering. **2** To talk rapidly and trivially. **3** To make rapid and indistinct sounds, as a monkey or squirrel. —*v.t.* **4** To utter in a trivial or chattering manner. —*n.* **1** Idle prattle. **2** Jabbering, as of a monkey. [Imit.] **—chat′ter·er** *n.*

chat·ter·box (chat′ər·boks′) *n.* A person who talks incessantly.

chat·ty (chat′ē) *adj.* **·ti·er, ·ti·est 1** Given to chatting. **2** Familiar; informal: a *chatty* writing style. **—chat′ti·ly** *adv.* **—chat′ti·ness** *n.*

chauf·feur (shō′fər, shō·fûr′) *n.* One employed to drive an automobile for someone else. —*v.t.* To serve as a chauffeur for. [F< *chauffer* warm]

chaunt (chônt, chänt) *n. & v.* CHANT.

chau·vin·ist (shō′vən·ist) *n.* One who believes excessively and often belligerently in the superiority of his own country, race, sex, etc.: a male *chauvinist.* [< Nicolas *Chauvin,* an overzealous supporter of Napoleon Bonaparte] **—chau′vin·ism** *n.* **—chau′vin·is′tic** *adj.* **—chau′vin·is′ti·cal·ly** *adv.*

chaw (chô) *v.t. & n. Regional* CHEW.

Ch.E., Che.E. Chemical Engineer.

cheap (chēp) *adj.* **1** Low in price; inexpensive. **2** Lower in price than the going rate or the real value. **3** Demanding little effort: a *cheap* victory. **4** Of little value. **5** Inferior in quality. **6** Low; vulgar; contemptible. **7** Stingy; tight. **8** Embarrassed; sheepish. **9** *Econ.* Obtainable at a low interest rate; also, depreciated: said of money. —*adv.* **1** At a low cost. **2** In a cheap manner. [Earlier *good cheap* a bargain < OE *ceap* business, trade] **—cheap′ly** *adv.* **—cheap′ness** *n.*

cheap·en (chē′pən) *v.t. & v.i.* To make or become cheap or cheaper. **—cheap′en·er** *n.*

cheap·skate (chēp′skāt′) *n. Slang* A miserly person.

cheat (chēt) *v.t.* **1** To deceive or defraud. **2** To delude; trick. **3** To elude or escape; foil: to *cheat* the hangman. —*v.i.* **4** To practice fraud or act dishonestly. **—cheat on** *Slang* To be sexually unfaithful to. —*n.* **1** An act of cheating. **2** One who cheats. [ME *chete,* short for *achete* escheat] **—cheat′er** *n.* **—cheat′ing·ly** *adv.*

check (chek) *n.* **1** A sudden stopping or halt. **2** Any control or restraint. **3** Any person or thing that controls or restrains. **4** Any examination, test, comparison, etc., for quality, verification, or identification. **5** A mark to show verification, approval, identification, etc. **6** A numbered tag used in duplicate to identify the owner of something. **7** A bill, as in a restaurant. **8** A written order for money drawn upon one's account in a bank. **9** A single square in a checkered surface. **10** A checkered pattern or a fabric having a checkered pattern. **11** In chess, an attack upon or menace to a king. **12** A slight crack. **—check in 1** To register, as at a hotel. **2** To report, as for work. **—check into** To investigate. **—check out 1** To vacate one's lodging and settle the bill, as at a hotel. **2** To calculate the cost of and collect payment for (merchandise), as in a supermarket. **3** To examine and approve. **4** To prove, upon examination, to be accurate, in good condition, etc. **—in check 1** Under control. **2** In danger: said of the king in chess. —*v.t.* **1** To stop or restrain forcibly or suddenly. **2** To curb; hold in restraint. **3** To ascertain the correctness, completeness, etc., of. **4** To investigate. **5** To mark with a check or checks. **6** To mark with a pattern of squares, as cloth. **7** To cause to crack; to make checks or chinks in. **8** To rebuke; rebuff; repulse: They *checked* the attack. **9** In chess, to put (an opponent's king) in check. **10** To deposit temporarily for safekeeping: to *check* one's luggage. —*v.i.* **11** To agree item for item: My figures *check* with yours. **12** To investigate: often with *on.* **13** To crack, as paint. **14** In chess, to put an opponent's king in check. —*interj.* **1** In chess, an exclamation proclaiming that the opponent's king is in check. **2** Correct; I understand; OK. —*adj.* **1** Having a checked pattern. **2** Serving to verify or confirm. [< Ar. *shāh* king (in chess) < Pers.] **—check′a·ble** *adj.*

check·book (chek′bo͝ok′) *n.* A book of blank bank checks.

checked (chekt) *adj.* **1** Marked with squares: *checked* gingham. **2** Kept in check; restrained. **3** Stopped.

check·er (chek′ər) *n.* **1** A piece in the game of checkers, usu. a small disk. **2** One of the squares in a checkered surface. **3** One who checks, esp. one who inspects, counts, or supervises the disposal of merchandise. —*v.t.* **1** To mark with squares or crossed lines. **2** To vary or diversify, as with changes in fortune, etc. [< OF *eschequier* chessboard < Ar. *shāh* king (in chess)]

check·er·board (chek′ər·bôrd′, -bōrd′) *n.* A board divided into 64 squares, used in playing checkers or chess.

check·ered (chek′ərd) *adj.* **1** Divided into squares. **2** Showing alternating spaces of color or of light and darkness. **3** Varied or diversified, as by changes in fortune.

check·ers (chek′ərz) *n. pl. (construed as sing.)* A game played by two persons with 24 pieces on a checkerboard.

checking account A bank account against which a depositor may draw checks.

check·mate (chek′māt′) *v.t.* **·mat·ed, mat·ing 1** In chess, to put (an opponent's king) in check from which no escape is possible, thus winning the game. **2** To defeat by a skillful maneuver. —*n.* **1** The act of checkmating. **2** The situation of a king that has been checkmated. **3** Complete defeat. [< Ar. *al-shāh māt* the king is dead]

check·off (chek′ôf′, -of′) *n.* The collection of trade-union dues by deduction from the pay of each employee.

check·out (chek′out′) *n.* The action or an instance of checking out.

check·rein (chek′rān′) *n.* A rein from the bit of the bridle to the saddle of a harness to keep a horse's head up.

check·up (chek′up′) *n.* **1** A medical examination. **2** Any examination or investigation.

Ched·dar (ched′ər) *n.* Any of several types of mild or sharp, white to yellow, hard, smooth cheese. Also **ched′·dar.** [< *Cheddar,* Somersetshire, England]

cheek (chēk) *n.* **1** Either side of the face below the eye and above the mouth. **2** A side or part analogous to the side of a face. **3** *Informal* Impudent boldness. [< OE *cēce, cēace*]

cheek·bone (chēk′bōn′) *n.* Either of two bones in the upper cheek, just below the eye.

cheek·y (chē′kē) *adj.* **cheek·i·er, cheek·i·est** *Informal* Impudent; brazen. **—cheek′i·ly** *adv.* **—cheek′i·ness** *n.*

cheep (chēp) *v.t. & v.i.* To chirp faintly or shrilly. —*n.* A weak chirp, as of a young bird. [Imit.] **—cheep′er** *n.*

cheer (chir) *n.* **1** A shout of approval or encouragement. **2** Cheerfulness; gaiety. **3** Something that promotes cheerfulness. **4** Food or drink. —*v.t.* **1** To make cheerful; comfort: often with *up.* **2** To applaud or salute with cheers. **3** To encourage; incite: often with *on.* —*v.i.* **4** To become cheerful, happy or glad: with *up.* **5** To utter cheers. [< OF *chere* face, countenance < LL *cara*] **—cheer′er** *n.*

cheer·ful (chir′fəl) *adj.* **1** Joyous; happy. **2** Willing. **3** Attractively bright, sunny, etc. **—cheer′ful·ly** *adv.* **—cheer′ful·ness** *n.*

cheer·i·o (chir′ē·ō) *interj. & n. Brit.* **1** Hello! **2** Goodbye!

cheer·less (chir′lis) *adj.* Bleak; gloomy. **—cheer′less·ly** *adv.* **—cheer′less·ness** *n.*

cheer·y (chir′ē) *adj.* **cheer·i·er, cheer·i·est** Joyous; bright; cheerful. **—cheer′i·ly** *adv.* **—cheer′i·ness** *n.*

cheese (chēz) *n.* **1** The pressed curd of milk, variously prepared and flavored. **2** A cake or mass of this substance. [< L *caseus* cheese]

cheese·cake (chēz′kāk′) *n.* **1** A cake containing cheese, sugar, eggs, milk, etc.: also **cheese cake. 2** *Slang* A photograph of a pretty girl's legs or figure.

cheese·cloth (chēz′klôth′, -kloth′) *n.* A thin, loosely woven, white cotton fabric.

chees·y (chē′zē) *adj.* **·i·er, ·i·est 1** Like cheese, as in texture, taste, etc. **2** *Slang* Of inferior quality; second-rate.

chee·tah (chē′tə) *n.* A swift feline resembling the leopard, native to Asia and Africa. [< Hind. *chītā* leopard]

chef (shef) *n.* **1** A head cook. **2** Any cook. [< OF *chef* chief]

chef-d'oeu·vre (she·dœ′vr′) *n. pl.* **chefs-d'oeu·vre** (she-) *French* A masterpiece, as of an artist, writer, etc.

che·la (kē′lə) *n. pl.* **·lae** (-lē) *Zool.* A terminal pincerlike claw, as in lobsters and scorpions. [< Gk. *chēlē* claw] **—che·late** (kē′·lāt) *adj.*

Chelae of scorpion

chem. chemical; chemist; chemistry.

chem·i·cal (kem′i·kəl) *adj.* **1** Of or pertaining to chemistry. **2** Obtained by or used in chemistry. —*n.* A substance obtained by or used in a chemical process. — **chem′i·cal·ly** *adv.*

chemical energy Energy released from substances by chemical reaction, as in the detonation of explosives, burning of fuel, etc.

chemical engineering The application of chemistry to industrial processes.

chemical warfare The military use of chemical agents, such as poisonous gases, incendiary materials, etc.

che·mise (shə·mēz′) *n.* **1** A woman's undergarment resembling a short slip. **2** A dress that hangs straight from the shoulders. [< LL *camisia* shirt]

chem·ist (kem′ist) *n.* **1** One versed in chemistry. **2** *Brit.* A druggist. [< Med. L *alchymista* alchemist]

chem·is·try (kem′is·trē) *n.* **1** That science which treats of the structure, composition, and properties of substances and of the transformations which they undergo. **2** Chemical composition or processes.

chem·o·ther·a·py (kem′ō·ther′ə·pē) *n.* The treatment of disease with chemicals. Also **chem′o·ther′a·peu′tics.** — **chem′o·ther′a·peu′tic** *adj.* **—chem′o·ther′a·pist** *n.*

chem·ur·gy (kem′ər·jē) *n.* The utilization of organic raw materials, esp. agricultural products, in the development of new products. **—chem·ur·gic** (kem·ûr′jik) or **·gi·cal** *adj.*

che·nille (shə·nēl′) *n.* **1** A soft, fluffy cord or yarn having a fuzzy pile on all sides, used for embroidery, tassels, etc. **2** Any fabric made with such yarn. [F, lit., caterpillar < L *canicula,* dim. of *canis* dog]

cheque (chek) *n. Brit.* CHECK (def. 8). **—cheq′uer** *n.*

cher·ish (cher′ish) *v.t.* **1** To care for kindly. **2** To hold dear. **3** To entertain fondly, as a hope or an idea. [< F *cher* dear < L *carus*] **—cher′ish·er** *n.*

Cher·o·kee (cher′ə·kē, cher′ə·kē′) *n. pl.* **·kee** or **·kees 1** A member of a tribe of Iroquoian Indians now dwelling in Oklahoma. **2** The language of this tribe.

Cherokee rose An evergreen, trailing rose having large, fragrant white flowers.

che·root (shə·ro͞ot′) *n.* A cigar cut square at both ends. [< Tamil *shuruttu* roll, cigar]

cher·ry (cher′ē) *n. pl.* **·ries 1** Any of various trees related to the plum and bearing small, round or heart-shaped drupes enclosing a smooth pit. **2** The wood or fruit of a cherry tree. **3** A bright red color: also **cherry red.** —*adj.* **1** Bright red. **2** Made of cherry wood. **3** Made with or from cherries. **4** Having a cherrylike flavor. [< Gk. *kerasos* cherry tree]

cher·ub (cher′əb) *n. pl.* **cher·ubs** *for defs. 1 & 2,* **cher·u·bim** (cher′ʸə·bim) *for def. 3.* **1** In art, the representation of a beautiful winged child. **2** Any beautiful child or infant. **3** One of an order of angelic beings ranking second to the seraphim. [< Heb. *kerūbh,* an angelic being] **—che·ru·bic** (chə·ro͞o′·bik) *adj.* **—che·ru′bi·cal·ly** *adv.*

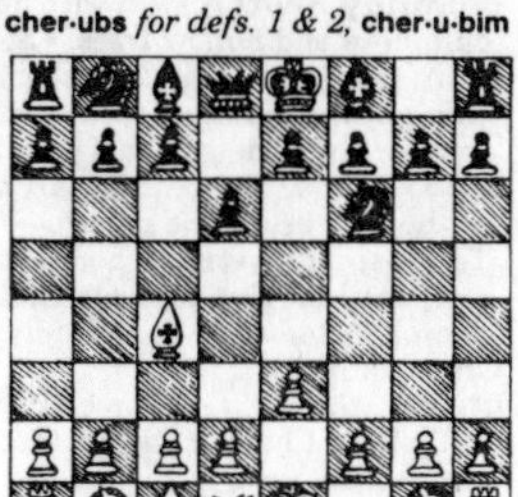

Chess game in progress. The horizontal rows are *ranks;* the vertical rows are *files.*

cher·vil (chûr′vəl) *n.* A garden herb related to parsley. [< Gk. *chairephyllon*]

chess (ches) *n.* A game played by two persons on a checkered board, with 16 pieces on each side, the object being to checkmate an opponent's king. [< OF *eschec* check (at chess)]

chest (chest) *n.* **1** The part of the body enclosed by the ribs; the thorax. **2** A box usu. having a hinged lid, used for tools, personal possessions, etc. **3** A chest of drawers. **4 a** A public treasury or fund. **b** The funds contained there. [< Gk. *kistē* basket, box]

ches·ter·field (ches′tər·fēld) *n.* A single-breasted topcoat, usu. with concealed buttons and a velvet collar. [< an Earl of *Chesterfield* of the 19th c.]

chest·nut (ches′nut′, -nət) *n.* **1** A smooth-shelled, edible nut. **2** Any of various trees related to the beech that bear this nut. **3** One of certain other trees: the horse *chestnut.* **4** A reddish brown. **5** A horse of this color. **6** *Informal* **a** A trite joke. **b** Anything trite. —*adj.* Reddish brown. [< Gk. *kastanea* + NUT]

chest of drawers A piece of furniture containing a set of drawers for storing linens, wearing apparel, etc.

chest·y (ches′tē) *adj.* **chest·i·er, chest·i·est** *Informal* **1** Having a large chest. **2** Proud; self-important.

che·tah (chē′tə) *n.* CHEETAH.

chev·a·lier (shev′ə·lir′) *n.* **1** A French knight or nobleman. **2** A gallant gentleman. **3** A member of the French Legion of Honor. [< LL *caballarius* cavalier]

chev·i·ot (shev′ē·ət) *n.* A sturdy woolen or cotton cloth of twill weave, used for suits, overcoats, etc.

Chev·i·ot (chev′ē·ət, chē′vē-) *n.* One of a breed of sheep, much esteemed for their wool.

chev·ron (shev′rən) *n.* A V-shaped insignia worn on the sleeve of a military or police uniform to show rank or length of service. [< Med. L *capro* rafter < L *caper* goat]

Chevrons

chev·y (chev′ē) *v.t.* **chev·ied, chev·y·ing** CHIVY.

chew (cho͞o) *v.t. & v.i.* **1** To cut or grind with the teeth. **2** To consider carefully. **—chew out** *Slang* To scold or reprimand severely. —*n.* **1** The act of chewing. **2** Something chewed or made for chewing. [< OE *cēowan*] **—chew′er** *n.*

chewing gum A sweetened, gummy substance, usu. chicle, for chewing.

che·wink (chi·wingk′) *n.* A towhee having red-brown sides and a black hood and back.

chew·y (cho͞o′ē) *adj.* **chew·i·er, chew·i·est** Relatively soft and requiring chewing: Caramels are *chewy.*

Chey·enne (shī·en′) *n. pl.* **·enne** or **·ennes 1** A member of an Algonquian tribe of North American Indians now dwelling in Montana and Oklahoma. **2** The language of this tribe.

chg. charge.

chgd. charged.

chi (kī) The twenty-second letter of the Greek alphabet (Χ, χ), transliterated into English by *ch.*

Chian·ti (kyän′tē) *n.* A dry, red Italian wine; also, any similar wine. [< Monti *Chianti,* a region in Italy]

chi·a·ro·scu·ro (kē·är′ə·skyo͝or′ō) *n. pl.* **·ros 1** The distribution and treatment of light and shade in a picture. **2** A technique of painting or drawing using only light and shade to achieve its effects. **3** A painting or drawing using this technique. Also **chi·a·ro·o·scu·ro** (kē·är′ə·ō·skyo͝or′ō). [Ital. < *chiaro* clear + *oscuro* dim, obscure]

chic (shēk, shik) *adj.* Smart; stylish; elegant. —*n.* Elegance and taste; style. [F < G *Schick* skill]

chi·can·er·y (shi·kā′nər·ē) *n. pl.* **·er·ies 1** The use of tricky or deceptive talk or action. **2** An instance of this. [< F *chicaner* to quibble]

Chi·ca·no (chi·kä′nō) *n. pl.* **·nos** A Mexican-American.

chi·chi (shē′shē) *adj. Informal* Ostentatiously chic, elegant, or sophisticated. [F]

chick (chik) *n.* **1** A young chicken or other bird. **2** *Slang* A young woman.

chick·a·dee (chik′ə·dē) *n.* A North American titmouse with the top of the head and the throat dark-colored. [Imit. of its cry]

Chick·a·saw (chik′ə·sô) *n. pl.* **·saw** or **·saws 1** A member of a tribe of Muskhogean North American Indians now dwelling in Oklahoma. 2 The language of this tribe.

chick·en (chik′ən) *n.* 1 The young of the common domestic fowl. 2 Loosely, a fowl of any age. 3 Its flesh used as food. 4 *Informal* A young or inexperienced person. —*adj.* 1 Of chicken. 2 Small. 3 *Slang* Cowardly. [< OE *cȳcen*]

chick·en-heart·ed (chik′ən·här′tid) *adj.* Timid or cowardly; faint-hearted.

chicken pox An infectious, viral disease of childhood, characterized by skin eruptions.

chick·weed (chik′wēd′) *n.* Any of several common low-growing weeds related to pinks.

chic·le (chik′əl) *n.* 1 The milky juice of the sapodilla tree. 2 A gum prepared from it, used in making chewing gum. Also **chicle gum.** [< Nah. *chictli*]

chic·o·ry (chik′ə·rē) *n. pl.* **·ries** 1 Any of several species of perennial edible salad herbs of the composite family. 2 The dried, ground roots of a chicory plant, sometimes used with or instead of coffee. [< Gk. *kichora*]

chide (chīd) *v.t. & v.i.* **chid·ed** or **chid** (chid), **chid·ed** or **chid·den** (chid′n), **chid·ing** To scold or reprove. [< OE *cidan*] —**chid′er** *n.* —**chid′ing·ly** *adv.*

chief (chēf) *n.* 1 A ruler, leader, head, etc., of an organization, group, or establishment. 2 *Usu. cap. Naut.* a A chief petty officer. b A chief engineer. 3 *Slang* A boss. —*adj.* 1 Highest in rank or authority. 2 Principal, most important, or most eminent. [< L *caput* head]

Chief Executive The President of the U.S.

chief justice The presiding judge of a court composed of several justices.

Chief Justice The official head of the U.S. Supreme Court.

chief·ly (chēf′lē) *adv.* 1 Most of all or above all. 2 Generally; mostly.

Chief of Staff The ranking officer of a staff, assisting the officer in command, as, in the U.S. Army or Air Force, the officer immediately under the Secretary of his department.

chief·tain (chēf′tən) *n.* 1 The head of a tribe or clan. 2 Any chief.

chif·fon (shi·fon′) *n.* A sheer fabric of silk, nylon, etc. [F < *chiffe* rag]

chif·fo·nier (shif′ə·nir′) *n.* A high chest of drawers. Also **chif′fon·nier′.** [F < *chiffon* chiffon]

chig·ger (chig′ər) *n.* 1 The tiny larvae of certain mites that burrow under the skin. 2 CHIGOE (def. 1). [Alter. of CHIGOE]

chi·gnon (shēn′yon, *Fr.* shē·nyôṅ′) *n.* A roll of hair worn at the back of a woman's head. [F< OF *chaignon* chain]

chig·oe (chig′ō) *n.* 1 A flea of tropical Africa and South America whose female causes sores by burrowing under the skin. 2 CHIGGER (def. 1). [< Cariban]

Chi·hua·hua (chi·wä′wä) *n.* One of an ancient Mexican breed of very small, smooth-coated dogs with large, pointed ears. [< *Chihuahua,* Mexico]

chil·blain (chil′blān) *n.* A painful inflamed area on the hands or feet, due to exposure to cold. [< CHILL + BLAIN] —**chil′blained** *adj.*

child (chīld) *n. pl.* **chil·dren** 1 An offspring of either sex of human parents. 2 A young person, usu. one between infancy and youth. 3 A descendant. 4 A childish or immature person. 5 A person or thing considered as an offspring or product: Poems are the *children* of fancy. [< OE *cild*]

child·bear·ing (chīld′bâr′ing) *n.* The act or process of bearing children. —*adj.* Of or relating to childbearing.

child·birth (chīld′bûrth′) *n.* The act of bearing a child; parturition.

child·hood (chīld′ho͝od′) *n.* The state or time of being a child.

child·ish (chīl′dish) *adj.* 1 Of, pertaining to, or characteristic of a child. 2 Immature; petty. —**child′ish·ly** *adv.* —**child′ish·ness** *n.* —**Syn.** 2 babyish, infantile, puerile, foolish, trivial, silly. • See CHILDLIKE.

child·like (chīld′līk′) *adj.* 1 Like a child. 2 Innocent; naive. • The word *childish,* when applied to an adult, is never complimentary. If one wishes to describe a grown-up who possesses a certain innocence, charm, candor, etc., ascribed to children, the word to use is *childlike.*

chil·dren (chil′drən) *n. pl.* of CHILD.

chil·e (chil′ē) *n.* CHILI.

Chil·e (chil′ē, *Sp.* chē′lā) *n.* A republic of w South America, 286,397 sq. mi., cap. Santiago. —**Chil′e·an** *adj., n.* • See map at ARGENTINA.

Chile saltpeter A mineral sodium nitrate found in Chile and Peru.

chil·i (chil′ē) *n. pl.* **chil′ies** 1 A tropical species of capsicum. 2 The dried pod of this plant, a hot red pepper. 3 CHILI CON CARNE. Also **chil′e, chil′li.** [< Nah. *chilli*]

chil·i con car·ne (chil′ē kon kär′nē) A Mexican dish of red peppers, with meat, beans, spices, etc. Also **chil′e con car′ne.**

chili sauce A spicy sauce made with tomatoes, sweet peppers, etc. Also **chile sauce.**

chill (chil) *n.* 1 A sensation of cold, often with shivering or shaking. 2 A disagreeable feeling of coldness, as from fear. 3 A dampening of enthusiasm, joy, etc. 4 A distant or unfriendly manner. —*v.t.* 1 To reduce to a low or lower temperature. 2 To make chilly; seize with a chill. 3 To discourage; dampen, as joy. —*v.i.* 4 To become cold. 5 To be stricken with a chill. —*adj.* CHILLY. [< OE *ciele, cyle*] —**chill′er, chill′ness** *n.* —**chill′ing·ly** *adv.*

chill·y (chil′ē) *adj.* **chill·i·er, chill·i·est** 1 Producing or feeling cold. 2 Disheartening; depressing. 3 Not genial; unfriendly. —**chill′i·ly** *adv.* —**chill′i·ness** *n.*

chime (chīm) *n.* 1 *Often pl.* A set of bells tuned to a scale. 2 A single bell, as in a clock. 3 *Often pl.* The sounds produced by a chime or chimes. 4 Accord; harmony. —*v.* **chimed, chim·ing** *v.t.* 1 To cause to ring musically, as by striking. 2 To announce, as the hour, by the sound of bells. 3 To summon, welcome, or send by chiming. 4 To recite in unison or cadence. —*v.i.* 5 To ring musically, as bells. 6 To harmonize; agree: with *with.* 7 To recite or intone in cadence. [< L *cymbalum* cymbal] —**chim′er** *n.*

chi·me·ra (kə·mir′ə, kī-) *n.* 1 An impractically fanciful or absurd hope, plan, or conception. 2 Any fabulous creature composed of incongruous parts 3 *Biol.* An organism or mass of living cells incorporating diverse genetic patterns. Also **chi·mae′ra.** [See CHIMERA.]

Chi·me·ra (kə·mir′ə, kī-) *Gk. Myth.* A fire-breathing monster having a lion's head, a goat's body, and a serpent's tail. [< Gk. *chimaira* she-goat]

chi·mer·i·cal (kə·mer′i·kəl, kī-) *adj.* 1 Not realizable or possible; impracticable; visionary. 2 Imaginary; fanciful. Also **chi·mer′ic.** —**chi·mer′i·cal·ly** *adv.*

chim·ney (chim′nē) *n. pl.* **·neys** 1 A pipe or tube for the escape of smoke or gases from a fire. 2 A structure containing such a pipe or tube, often extending above a roof. 3 A tube for enclosing a flame, as of a lamp. 4 *Geol.* A rock formation or a volcano vent resembling a chimney. [< Gk. *kaminos* furnace]

chimney corner The space between the sides of a large, old-fashioned fireplace and the fire, where one might sit.

chim·ney·sweep (chim′nē·swēp′) *n.* One who cleans the soot from chimneys.

chimney swift A swift with dark plumage that nests in chimneys and hollow trees. • See SWIFT.

chim·pan·zee (chim′pan·zē′, chim·pan′zē) *n.* An African anthropoid ape with large ears and black hair, smaller than the gorilla. [< native w African name]

chin (chin) *n.* The central part of the lower jaw; the part of the face below the mouth. —*v.* **chinned, chin·ning** *v.t.* 1 To grasp an overhead horizontal support and lift (oneself) until the chin is level with the hands. —*v.i.* 2 To chin oneself. 3 *Informal* To talk idly. [< OE *cin*]

Chin. Chinese.

chi·na (chī′nə) *n.* 1 Porcelain or similar pottery, originally from China. 2 Dishes, etc., made of such ware. Also **chi′na·ware′** (-wâr′).

Chi·na (chī′nə) *n.* 1 A republic of E and CEN. Asia, 3,768,-377 sq. mi., cap. Peking. 2 A republic located on Taiwan and nearby islands, 13,890 sq. mi., cap. Taipei. • See map next page.

chi·na·ber·ry (chī′nə·ber′ē) *n. pl.* **·ries** 1 A tree common in s North America, having purple flowers and yellowish, ball-like fruit. Also **China tree.** 2 The fruit of this tree.

Chi·na·town (chī′nə·toun′) *n.* The Chinese quarter of any city outside China.

chin·ca·pin (ching′kə·pin) *n.* CHINQUAPIN.

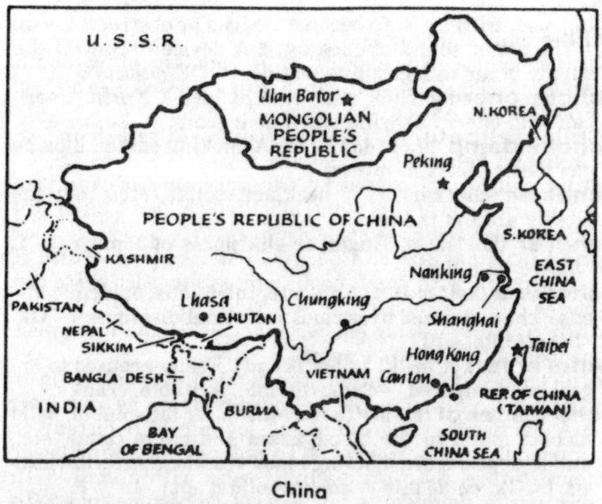

China

chinch (chinch) *n.* BEDBUG. [<L *cimex* bug]

chinch bug A small black and white insect destructive to grain.

chin·chil·la (chin·chil′ə) *n.* **1** A small South American rodent having soft pearl-gray fur. **2** Its highly valued fur. **3** A heavy wool fabric with a nubbed surface, used esp. for overcoats. [<Sp.]

chine (chīn) *n.* **1** The spine, backbone, or back. **2** A cut of meat including vertebrae. [<OF *eschine* backbone]

Chi·nese (chī·nēz′, -nēs′) *n. pl.* **·nese 1** A native or citizen of China. **2** A person whose ancestry is Chinese. **3** Any of a group of related languages spoken in China, esp. the official language. —*adj.* Of or pertaining to China, its peoples, or any of their languages.

Chinese lantern A collapsible lantern made of thin, usu. brightly colored paper.

chink[1] (chingk) *n.* A small, narrow cleft; crevice. —*v.t.* **1** To make cracks or fissures in. **2** To fill the cracks of, as a wall. [?<OE *cine* crack]

chink[2] (chingk) *n.* A short, sharp, metallic sound. —*v.t.* & *v.i.* To make or cause to make such a sound. [Imit.]

chi·no (chē′nō) *n. pl.* **·nos 1** A strong, twilled cotton fabric. **2** *pl.* Trousers made of this fabric. [<Sp., toasted; with ref. to the original tan color]

chi·nook (chi·no͞ok′, -no͝ok′) *n.* **1** A warm, moist wind of the Oregon and Washington coasts. **2** A warm, dry wind that descends the eastern slopes of the Rocky Mountains in the NW United States and W Canada.

Chi·nook (chi·no͞ok′, -no͝ok′) *n. pl.* **·nook** or **·nooks 1** A member of a tribe of North American Indians formerly occupying the Columbia River valley. **2** The language of this tribe. —**Chi·nook′an** *adj., n.*

Chinook jargon A language comprised of words from Chinook and other Indian languages, mixed with English and French, once used by traders and Indians from Oregon to Alaska.

chin·qua·pin (ching′kə·pin) *n.* **1** A dwarf chestnut tree of the E U.S. **2** A related tall tree of NW North America. **3** The edible nut of any of these trees. Also **chink′a·pin.** [<N.Am. Ind.]

chintz (chints) *n.* A usu. glazed, brightly printed cotton fabric. [<Skt. *chitra* variegated]

chintz·y (chint′sē) *adj.* **chintz·i·er, chintz·i·est 1** Of or like chintz. **2** *Informal* Tacky; cheap.

chip (chip) *n.* **1** A small piece cut or broken off. **2** A mark where such a piece has broken off. **3** A small disk used as a counter in games, as poker. **4** A thin crisp morsel: potato *chips.* **5** *pl. Brit.* French-fried potatoes. **6** An integrated circuit in a computer. —**a chip off the old block** A child who closely resembles either parent. —**a chip on one's shoulder** A tendency to quarrel. —*v.* **chipped, chip·ping** *v.t.* **1** To break or cut a small piece or pieces from. —*v.i.* **2** To become broken in this way. —**chip in** To contribute, as money. [<OE *cippe* piece cut off a beam]

chip·munk (chip′mungk) *n.* Any of various squirrellike striped North American rodents. [<N.Am. Ind.]

Chipmunk

chipped beef Smoked beef sliced thin.

Chip·pen·dale (chip′ən·dāl) *adj.* Of or designating a rococo style of 18th-century furniture. [<Thomas *Chippendale,* 1718–79, English cabinetmaker]

chip·per (chip′ər) *adj.* Brisk; cheerful. [<earlier *chip* chirp] —**Syn.** lively, spry, sprightly, cheery.

Chip·pe·wa (chip′ə·wä, -wā, -wə) *n. pl.* **·wa** or **·was** OJIBWA. Also **Chip·pe·way** (chip′ə·wā).

chiro- *combining form* Hand. [<Gk. *cheir* hand]

chi·rog·ra·phy (kī·rog′rə·fē) *n.* Handwriting; penmanship. —**chi·rog′ra·pher** *n.*

chi·rop·o·dy (kə·rop′ə·dē, kī-) *n.* PODIATRY. [<CHIRO- + Gk. *pous, podos* foot] —**chi·rop′o·dist** *n.*

chi·ro·prac·tic (kī′rə·prak′tik) *n.* Therapeutic treatment involving manipulation of the body, esp. the spine. [<CHIRO + Gk. *praktikos* effective<*prattein* do, act] —**chi′ro·prac′tor** *n.*

chirp (chûrp) *v.i.* **1** To give a short, sharp cry, as a small bird or cricket. **2** To talk in a quick, high-pitched manner. —*v.t.* **3** To utter with a quick, sharp sound. —*n.* A sound made by chirping. [ME *chirpen,* var. of *chirken*]

chirr (chûr) *v.i.* To make a sharp trilling sound, as of a grasshopper. —*n.* The sound of chirring. [Imit.]

chir·rup (chir′əp) *v.i.* To chirp continuously or repeatedly. —*n.* A series of chirps. [<CHIRP]

chis·el (chiz′əl) *n.* A tool with a sharp, beveled edge, used for cutting or shaping metal, stone, or wood. —*v.t.* & *v.i.* **chis·eled** or **·elled, chis·el·ing** or **·el·ling 1** To cut, engrave, or carve with or as with a chisel. **2** *Informal.* To cheat; swindle. [<L *caesus* pp. of *caedere* cut] —**chis′el·er** or **chis′el·ler** *n.*

chit[1] (chit) *n.* A voucher of a small sum owed, as for food. [<Hind. *chitthī* note]

chit[2] (chit) *n.* A pert girl. [ME *chitte*]

chit-chat (chit′chat′) *n.* Informal talk or gossip. [Redupl. of CHAT]

chi·tin (kī′tin) *n.* A tough, horny substance forming the principal constituent of the hard covering of insects, crustaceans, etc. [<Gk. *chitōn* tunic] —**chi′ti·nous** *adj.*

chit·ter·lings (chit′ər·lingz) *n. pl.* The small intestines of pigs, prepared as food. Also **chit′lings, chit′lins.** [ME *chiterling*]

chiv·al·rous (shiv′əl·rəs) *adj.* **1** Having the qualities of the ideal knight; courteous, honorable, brave, etc. **2** Of or pertaining to chivalry. Also **chi·val·ric** (shi·val′rik, shiv′·əl-). —**chiv′al·rous·ly** *adv.* —**chiv′al·rous·ness** *n.* —**Syn.** gallant, knightly, courtly, valiant.

chiv·al·ry (shiv′əl·rē) *n.* **1** The system or spirit of medieval knighthood. **2** The idealized qualities of knighthood, as courtesy, magnanimity, bravery, etc. **3** An instance of such qualities. [<LL *caballarius* cavalier]

chive (chīv) *n.* An herb related to the onion, having slender, hollow leaves used as flavoring in cooking. [<L *cepa* onion]

chiv·y (chiv′ē) *v.t.* **chiv·ied, chiv·y·ing** To harass; hound. Also **chiv′vy.** [<*Chevy* Chase, old English ballad]

chla·myd·i·a (klə·mid′ē·ə) *n.* A venereal disease affecting the genitals and urinary tract, caused by a parasitic organism. [<NL<Gk. *chlamys* short cloak]

chlo·ral (klôr′əl, klō′rəl) *n.* **1** A colorless, oily liquid with a penetrating odor, obtained by the action of chlorine on alcohol. **2** A white, toxic, crystalline compound, used medicinally as a hypnotic, etc.: also **chloral hydrate.** [<CHLOR(INE) + AL(COHOL)]

chlor·am·phen·i·col (klôr′am·fen′i·kol, -kol, klō′ram-) *n.* An antibiotic used in the treatment of typhoid fever and various other diseases. [<CHLOR- + AM(IDE) + PHE(NOL) + NI(TROGEN) + (GLY)COL]

chlo·rate (klôr′āt, klō′rāt) *n.* A salt of chloric acid.

chlor·dane (klôr′dān, klōr′-) *n.* A colorless, odorless, poisonous liquid compound, used as an insecticide.

chlo·ric (klôr′ik, klō′rik) *adj.* Of, pertaining to, or combined with chlorine: said specifically of relatively unstable compounds containing oxygen.

chloric acid An unstable acid with great oxidizing power.

chlo·ride (klôr′īd, -id, klō′rīd, -rid) *n.* A compound of chlorine with another element or radical. **—chlo·rid·ic** (klə·rid′ik) *adj.*

chloride of lime A disinfecting and bleaching agent made by the action of chlorine gas on slaked lime.

chlo·rin·ate (klôr′ə·nāt, klō′rə-) *v.t.* **·at·ed, ·at·ing** To treat, impregnate, or cause to combine with chlorine, as in disinfecting sewage, etc. **—chlo′rin·a′tion, chlo′rin·a′tor** *n.*

chlo·rine (klôr′ēn, -in, klō′rēn, -rin) *n.* A greenish yellow, poisonous, gaseous element (symbol Cl) of the halogen group, occurring abundantly in combination with other elements and widely used in industry, medicine, etc. [< Gk. *chlōros* green]

chloro- *combining form* **1** Light green: *chlorophyll.* **2** Chlorine: *chloroform.* Also **chlor-**. [< Gk. *chlōros* green]

chlo·ro·form (klôr′ə·fôrm, klō′rə-) *n.* A colorless, volatile, sweetish liquid compound, used as an anesthetic and a solvent. *—v.t.* To anesthetize or kill with chloroform. [< CHLORO- + FORM(YL)]

Chlo·ro·my·ce·tin (klôr′ə·mī·sē′tən, klō′rə-) *n.* CHLORAMPHENICOL: a trade name.

chlo·ro·phyll (klôr′ə·fil, klō′rə-) *n.* The green pigment of plants, essential to photosynthesis. Also **chlo′ro·phyl.** [< CHLORO- + Gk. *phyllon* leaf] **—chlo′ro·phyl′lose** (-fil′·ōs), **chlo′ro·phyl′lous** (-fil′əs) *adj.*

chlo·ro·plast (klôr′ə·plast, klō′rə-) *n.* One of the small chlorophyll-bearing bodies found in the cytoplasm of plant cells. [< CHLORO- + Gk. *plastos* molded]

chlor·pro·ma·zine (klôr·prō′mə·zēn, -zin, klōr-) *n.* A synthetic drug used as a tranquilizer in treating mental illness. [A composite word from di*m*ethyl amino*pro*pyl *chlor*ophenothi*azine* hydrochloride]

chm., chmn. chairman.

chock (chok) *n.* **1** A block or wedge placed so as to prevent or limit motion. **2** *Naut.* A heavy piece of metal or wood fastened to a deck, etc., and having jaws through which a rope or cable may pass. *—v.t.* To wedge or hold in place with or as with chocks. *—adv.* As completely or as close as possible. [< AF *choque* log]

chock-a-block (chok′ə·blok′) *adj.* Close together; crowded. *—adv.* Close; very near.

chock-full (chok′fo͝ol′) *adj.* Completely full. [ME *chokkeful*]

choc·o·late (chôk′lit, chôk′ə·lit, chok′-) *n.* **1** Roasted and ground cacao seeds, often sweetened or flavored. **2** A beverage or confection made from this. **3** A dark brown. *—adj.* **1** Flavored or made with chocolate. **2** Dark brown. [< Nah. *chocólatl*]

Choc·taw (chok′tô) *n. pl.* **·taw** or **·taws** **1** A member of a tribe of North American Indians of Muskhogean linguistic stock now dwelling in Oklahoma. **2** The language of this tribe.

choice (chois) *n.* **1** The act of choosing; selection. **2** The right or power to choose; option. **3** Something or someone chosen. **4** A number or a variety from which to choose. **5** An alternative. **6** The best or preferred part. *—adj.* **choic·er, choic·est** **1** Of special quality; excellent. **2** Carefully selected. [< OF *choisir* choose] **—choice′ly** *adv.* **—choice′·ness** *n.*

choir (kwīr) *n.* **1** A body of trained singers, esp. in a church. **2** The part of a church used by such a group. **3** A group of musicians, as instrumentalists. *—v.t. & v.i.* To sing in a choir or in chorus. [< L *chorus* chorus]

choke (chōk) *v.* **choked, chok·ing** *v.t.* **1** To stop or obstruct the breathing of; strangle. **2** To keep back; suppress. **3** To obstruct or close up by filling. **4** To retard the progress, growth, or action of. **5** To lessen the air intake in order to enrich the fuel mixture of (a gasoline engine). *—v.i.* **6** To become suffocated or stifled. **7** To have difficulty in breathing. **8** To be so affected by emotion, fright, etc., that one's behavior is noticeably constrained or one's speech faltering: usu. with *up.* **9** To become clogged or obstructed. *—n.* **1** The act or sound of choking. **2** A device to control the supply of air to a gasoline engine. [< OE *acēocian*]

choke·cher·ry (chōk′cher′ē) *n. pl.* **·ries** A North American wild cherry bearing astringent fruit.

choke·damp (chōk′damp′) *n.* A choking carbon dioxide gas that collects in mines.

chok·er (chō′kər) *n.* A necklace, collar, etc., that fits closely around the neck.

chol·er (kol′ər) *n.* Anger or sharpness of temper. [< L *cholera* jaundice]

chol·er·a (kol′ər·ə) *n.* An acute, infectious, epidemic disease, characterized by serious intestinal disorders. [< Gk. < *cholē* bile, gall]

chol·er·ic (kol′ər·ik, kə·ler′ik) *adj.* Easily aroused to anger; bad-tempered. **—Syn.** irascible, irritable, cranky.

cho·les·ter·ol (kə·les′tə·rôl, -rōl) *n.* A fat-soluble, solid alcohol found in the blood, brain and nerve tissue, etc., and in deposits constricting blood vessels in arteriosclerosis. [< Gk. *cholē* bile + *stereos* solid + -OL]

chomp (chomp) *v.t. & v.i.* To chew or bite upon (something). [Alter. of CHAMP[1]] **—chomp′er** *n.*

choose (cho͞oz) *v.* **chose, cho·sen, choos·ing** *v.t.* **1** To select among others or as an alternative. **2** To desire or prefer (to do something). *—v.i.* **3** To make a selection or decision. [< OE *cēosan*] **—choos′er** *n.*

choos·y (cho͞o′ze) *adj.* **choos·i·er, choos·i·est** *Informal* Particular or fussy in one's choices. **—choos′i·ness** *n.*

chop[1] (chop) *v.* **chopped, chop·ping** *v.t.* **1** To cut or make by strokes of a sharp tool; hew. **2** To cut up in small pieces; mince. **3** To utter jerkily. *—v.i.* **4** To make cutting strokes, as with an ax. **5** To move with a sudden, jerky motion. *—n.* **1** A small cut of meat, usu. containing a rib. **2** The act of chopping. **3** A short, swift blow. **4** A sudden choppy motion, as of a wave. [ME *choppen* var. of *chappen* to chap]

chop[2] (chop) *v.i.* To veer suddenly; shift, as the wind. [< OE *cēapian* to barter, exchange]

chop·house (chop′hous′) *n.* A restaurant specializing in steaks and chops.

chop·per (chop′ər) *n.* **1** One who or that which chops. **2** *pl. Slang* Teeth. **3** *Slang* A helicopter.

chop·py (chop′ē) *adj.* **·pi·er ·pi·est** **1** Full of short, rough waves. **2** Jerky; irregular; shifting. **—chop′pi·ly** *adv.* **—chop′pi·ness** *n.*

chops (chops) *n. pl.* **1** The jaws. **2** The mouth, or the area of the face near the mouth. [?]

chop·sticks (chop′stiks′) *n. pl.* Paired, slender sticks used as eating implements in China, Japan, etc. [< Pidgin English *chop* quick + STICK]

chop su·ey (chop′ so͞o′ē) A Chinese-American dish of meat and vegetables cooked together and served with rice. [< Chin. *tsa sui*, lit., mixed pieces]

cho·ral (kôr′əl, kō′rəl) *adj.* **1** Of a chorus or choir. **2** Written for or sung by a chorus. **—cho′ral·ly** *adv.*

cho·rale (kə·ral′) *n.* A hymn, esp. a German Protestant hymn. Also **cho·ral′**. [< G *choral* choral]

chord[1] (kôrd) *n.* A combination of three or more musical tones sounded together. [Earlier *cord*, short for ACCORD]

chord[2] (kôrd) *n.* **1** A string of a musical instrument. **2** An emotional response or reaction. **3** *Geom.* A straight line connecting the ends of an arc. **4** *Anat.* A cordlike structure, as a tendon or ligament. [< Gk. *chordē* string of a musical instrument] **—chord′al** *adj.*

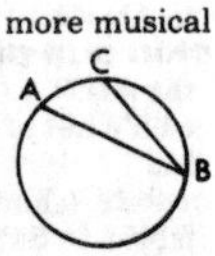

Chord[2]
AB and CB are chords.

chore (chôr, chōr) *n.* **1** A small or routine task. **2** An unpleasant or hard task. [Var. of CHAR[1]]

cho·re·a (kô·rē′ə, kō-) *n.* A nervous disease characterized by involuntary spasms of muscular contraction. [< Gk. *choreia* dance] **—cho·re′al** *adj.*

cho·re·o·graph (kôr′ē·ə·graf, kō′rē-, -gräf) *v.t.* To devise dance steps and movements for (a ballet, etc.). **—cho·re·og·ra·pher** (kôr′ē·og′rə·fər, kō′rē-)

cho·re·og·ra·phy (kôr′ē·og′rə·fē, kō′rē-) *n.* **1** The art of devising ballets and dances. **2** The art of dancing, esp. for theatrical performance. **3** The written representation of figures and steps of dancing. [< Gk. *choreia* dance + -GRAPHY] **—cho·re·o·graph·ic** (kôr′ē·ə·graf′ik, kō′rē-) *adj.*

cho·ric (kôr′ik) *adj.* Of or pertaining to a chorus, as in Greek drama.

chor·is·ter (kôr′is·tər, kor′-) *n.* A singer in a choir.

cho·roid (kôr′oid, kō′roid) *adj.* Of or pertaining to certain highly vascular membranes. —*n.* The middle or vascular layer covering the eyeball. Also **cho·ri·oid** (kôr′ē·oid, kō′rē-). [< Gk. *chorion* afterbirth, membrane]

chor·tle (chôr′təl) *v.t. & v.i.* **·tled, ·tling** To utter or say with a loud, exuberant, chuckling sound. —*n.* A loud, exuberant chuckle. [Blend of CHUCKLE and SNORT; coined by C. L. Dodgson (Lewis Carroll), 1832–98, Eng. author]

cho·rus (kôr′əs, kō′rəs) *n.* **1** A group of singers who perform together. **2** A musical composition or section for such a group. **3** A group of dancers and singers who perform together in supporting roles in musical comedy, etc. **4** Any group uttering something simultaneously. **5** Something uttered by such a group. **6** A repeated section of a song; refrain. **7** In Greek drama, a body of actors who comment upon and sometimes take part in the main action of a play. —**in chorus** All together; in unison. —*v.t. & v.i.* **cho·rused** or **·russed, ·rus·ing** or **·rus·sing** To sing or utter in chorus. [< L < Gk. *choros* dance]

chorus girl A woman in the chorus of a musical comedy, cabaret, etc.

chose (chōz) *p.t.* of CHOOSE.

cho·sen (chō′zən) *p.p.* of CHOOSE. —*adj.* Accorded or worthy of special choice or preference.

chow (chou) *n.* **1** A medium-sized dog having a thick brownish or black coat and a blue-black tongue: also **chow chow.** **2** *Slang* Food. [< Pidgin English]

chow·chow (chou′chou′) *n.* A relish of chopped pickles in mustard. [< Pidgin English]

chow·der (chow′dər) *n.* A thick soup of clams, other seafood, or vegetables, often with milk. [< L *caldaria* cauldron]

chow mein (chou′mān′) A Chinese-American dish of pieces of meat and various vegetables served with fried noodles. [< Chin. *ch'ao mien* fried noodles]

Chr. Christ; Christian.

chrism (kriz′əm) *n.* Oil used for anointing at baptism, confirmation, unction, etc. [< Gk. *chrisma* < *chriein* anoint]

Christ (krīst) *n.* **1** The founder of Christianity; Jesus. **2** MESSIAH (def. 1). [< Gk. *Christos* < *chriein* anoint] —**Christ′li·ness** *n.* —**Christ′ly** *adj.* • The *Christ* means the Anointed, or the divinely chosen one, and was originally used as a title identifying Jesus as the Messiah. Now it is commonly used as part of the name *Jesus Christ.*

chris·ten (kris′ən) *v.t.* **1** To name in baptism. **2** To baptize. **3** To give a name to in some ceremony: to *christen* a ship. **4** *Informal* To use for the first time. [< OE *cristnian* < *cristen* Christian]

Chris·ten·dom (kris′ən·dəm) *n.* **1** Christians collectively. **2** The Christian world.

chris·ten·ing (kris′ən·ing) *n.* A baptismal ceremony, esp. the baptizing of an infant.

Chris·tian (kris′chən) *adj.* **1** Professing or following the religion of Christ. **2** Of or derived from Christ or his doctrine. **3** Manifesting the spirit of Christ or of his teachings. **4** Of Christianity or Christendom. **5** *Informal* Human; decent. —*n.* **1** One who believes in or professes belief in Jesus as the Christ; a member of a Christian church. **2** *Informal* A civilized, decent, or respectable person. [< LL *christianus* < *Christus* Christ] —**Chris′tian·ly** *adv.*

Christian era The period beginning with the birth of Christ.

Chris·ti·an·i·ty (kris′chē·an′ə·tē) *n.* **1** The Christian religion. **2** Christians collectively. **3** The state of being a Christian.

Chris·tian·ize (kris′chən·īz) *v.* **·ized, ·iz·ing** *v.t.* **1** To convert to Christianity. **2** To imbue with Christian ideas, principles, and faith. —*v.i.* **3** To adopt Christianity. —**Chris′tian·i·za′tion** *n.* —**Chris′tian·iz′er** *n.*

Christian name A baptismal name; first or given name.

Christian Science A religious system embodying metaphysical healing, founded in 1866 by Mary Baker Eddy, and practiced in the *Church of Christ, Scientist.* —**Christian Scientist**

Christ·like (krīst′līk′) *adj.* **1** Resembling Christ. **2** Having or showing the spirit of Christ. —**Christ′like′ness** *n.*

Christ·mas (kris′məs) *n.* December 25, a holiday marking the birth of Jesus Christ. Also **Christmas Day.** [< CHRIST + MASS]

Christmas Eve The evening or day before Christmas.

Christ·mas·tide (kris′məs·tīd) *n.* The Christmas season, esp. from December 24 to January 6.

Christmas tree An evergreen or artificial tree decorated with ornaments at Christmas.

chro·ma (krō′mə) *n.* The shade and intensity of a color other than white, black, or gray. [< Gk. *chrōma* color]

chro·mate (krō′māt) *n.* A salt of chromic acid.

chro·mat·ic (krō·mat′ik) *adj.* **1** Of color or colors. **2** *Music* Using or proceeding by semitones. —**chro·mat′i·cal·ly** *adv.*

chro·mat·ics (krō·mat′iks) *n. pl. (construed as sing.)* The science of colors.

chromatic scale The musical scale made up of semitones. • See SCALE.

chro·ma·tin (krō′mə·tin) *n.* The deeply staining material in the nucleus of a living cell, that forms the chromosomes during cell division. [< Gk. *chrōma, -atos* color]

chro·ma·tog·ra·phy (krō′mə·tog′rə·fē) *n.* A method of separating the constituents of a solution by their differing adsorption by various substances. —**chro·mat·o·graph·ic** (krō·mat′ə·graf′ik) *adj.*

chrome (krōm) *n.* **1** Chromium, or an alloy of chromium, esp. as used in plating. **2** Any of certain chromium compounds used as pigments. —*v.t.* **chromed, chrom·ing** To plate with chromium. [< Gk. *chrōma* color]

chro·mic (krō′mik) *adj.* Of, from, or pertaining to chromium, esp. in its higher valency.

chromic acid A hypothetical acid known only in solution and forming chromates.

chro·mi·um (krō′mē·əm) *n.* A hard, gray, metallic element (symbol Cr) having resistance to corrosion and forming highly colored compounds. [< Gk. *chrōma* color]

chro·mo (krō′mō) *n. pl.* **·mos** CHROMOLITHOGRAPH.

chromo- *combining form* **1** Color. **2** Chromium. [< Gk. *chrōma* color]

chro·mo·lith·o·graph (krō′mō·lith′ə·graf, -gräf) *n.* A print reproduced in color by lithography. —**chro·mo·li·thog·ra·pher** (krō′mō·li·thog′rə·fər), **chro′mo·li·thog′ra·phy** *n.* —**chro′mo·lith′o·graph′ic** *adj.*

chro·mo·some (krō′mə·sōm) *n.* One of the rodlike bodies formed from chromatin in the nucleus during cell division, acting as a carrier of the genes or units of heredity. [< CHROMO- + Gk. *sōma* body]

chro·mo·sphere (krō′mə·sfir′) *n.* The envelope of incandescent gas surrounding the sun beyond the photosphere. —**chro·mo·spher·ic** (krō′mə·sfer′ik) *adj.*

Chron. Chronicles.

chron., chronol. chronological; chronology.

chron·ic (kron′ik) *adj.* **1** Continuing for a long period, as a disease. **2** Inveterate; habitual: a *chronic* complainer. [< Gk. *chronos* time] —**chron′i·cal·ly** *adv.*

chron·i·cle (kron′i·kəl) *n.* A record of events chronologically arranged. —*v.t.* **·cled, ·cling** To record in or as a chronicle. [< Gk. *chronikos* of time] —**chron′i·cler** *n.*

Chron·i·cles (kron′i·kəlz) *n. pl.* Either of two books of the Old Testament, I and II Chronicles.

chrono- *combining form* Time. [< Gk. *chronos* time]

chron·o·log·i·cal (kron′ə·loj′i·kəl) *adj.* **1** Occurring or recorded in sequential time order. **2** Of the science of time. Also **chron′o·log′ic.** —**chron′o·log′i·cal·ly** *adv.*

chro·nol·o·gy (krə·nol′ə·jē) *n. pl.* **·gies** **1** The science that treats of the measurement of time or the order of events. **2** An arrangement of events in the order of the time of their occurrence. **3** A table or list so arranged. [< CHRONO- + -LOGY] —**chro·nol′o·ger, chro·nol′o·gist** *n.*

chro·nom·e·ter (krə·nom′ə·tər) *n.* A timekeeping instrument of high precision and accuracy. [< CHRONO- + -METER] —**chron·o·met·ric** (kron′ə·met′rik) or **·ri·cal** *adj.* —**chron′o·met′ri·cal·ly** *adv.*

chro·nom·e·try (krə·nom′ə·trē) *n.* The science, method, or process of measuring time.

chrys·a·lid (kris′ə·lid) *n.* CHRYSALIS. —*adj.* Of or like a chrysalis.

chrys·a·lis (kris′ə·lis) *n. pl.* **chrys·a·lis·es** or **chry·sal·i·des** (kri·sal′ə·dēz) **1** The capsule-enclosed pupal stage of a butterfly or moth, from which the winged adult emerges. **2** Anything in an undeveloped stage. [<Gk. *chrysallis* < *chrysos* gold]

Chrysalis

chrys·an·the·mum (kri·san′thə·məm) *n.* **1** Any of several varieties of plants cultivated for their showy, composite flowers. **2** The flower. [<Gk. *chrysanthemon,* lit., golden flower]

chrys·o·lite (kris′ə·līt) *n.* A vitreous, olive-green mineral used as a gem. [<Gk. *chrysolithos,* lit., gold stone]

chrys·o·prase (kris′ə·prāz) *n.* A green variety of chalcedony, used as a gem. [< Gk. *chrysos* gold + *prason* leek]

chub (chub) *n. pl.* **chub** or **chubs** **1** A fresh-water fish related to the carp. **2** One of various other fishes. [ME *chubbe*]

chub·by (chub′ē) *adj.* **·bi·er, ·bi·est** Plump. [<CHUB] —**chub′bi·ness** *n.*

chuck[1] (chuk) *v.t.* **1** To pat or tap lightly, esp. under the chin. **2** To throw; toss. **3** *Informal* To throw out or away. —*n.* **1** A playful pat. **2** A throw or toss. [?]

chuck[2] (chuk) *n.* **1** A cut of beef extending from the neck to the shoulder blade. **2** A clamp, etc., used to hold a tool or piece of work. [Var. of CHOCK]

chuck-full (chuk′fŏŏl′) *adj.* CHOCK-FULL.

chuck·le (chuk′əl) *v.i.* **·led, ·ling** **1** To laugh quietly, as to oneself. **2** To cluck, as a hen. —*n.* A low, quiet laugh. [? Imit.] —**chuck′ler** *n.*

chuck·le·head (chuk′əl·hed′) *n. Informal* A stupid person; blockhead. —**chuck′le·head′ed** *adj.*

chuck wagon A wagon that carries provisions and cooking equipment for cowboys, harvest hands, etc.

chug (chug) *n.* A short, dull, explosive sound, as of an engine. —*v.i.* **chugged, chug·ging** To make or move with such sounds. [Imit.]

chuk·ker (chuk′ər) *n.* One of the periods of play in a polo game. Also **chuk′kar.** [<Hind. *chakkar* circle]

chum[1] (chum) *n.* An intimate companion. —*v.i.* **chummed, chum·ming** To be close friends. [? Short for *chamber fellow* (roommate)] —**Syn.** *n.* crony, pal, buddy.

chum[2] (chum) *n.* Cut-up fish, etc., scattered as bait. —*v.i.* **chummed, chum·ming** To fish with chum. [?]

chum·my (chum′ē) *adj.* **·mi·er, ·mi·est** *Informal* Friendly; intimate. —**chum′mi·ly** *adv.* —**chum′mi·ness** *n.*

chump (chump) *n. Informal* A gullible person; fool. [? Var. of CHUNK]

chunk (chungk) *n.* **1** A thick piece, lump, etc. **2** A goodly amount. [Var. of CHUCK[2]]

chunk·y (chung′kē) *adj.* **chunk·i·er, chunk·i·est** **1** Short and thickset; stocky. **2** In a chunk or chunks. —**chunk′i·ly** *adv.* —**chunk′i·ness** *n.*

church (chûrch) *n.* **1** A building for Christian worship. **2** Religious services in a church. **3** A congregation of Christians. **4** *Usu. cap.* A body of Christians having a common faith; a denomination. **5** Christians collectively. **6** Ecclesiastical organization and authority: separation of *church* and state. **7** The clerical profession. [<Gk. *kyriakon (dōma)* the Lord's (house)]

church·go·er (chûrch′gō′ər) *n.* One who goes to church regularly. —**church′go′ing** *adj., n.*

church·ly (chûrch′lē) *adj.* Of or suitable for a church. —**church′li·ness** *n.*

church·man (chûrch′mən) *n. pl.* **·men** (-mən) **1** A clergyman. **2** A male member of a church. —**church′man·ly** *adj.* —**church′man·ship** *n.*

Church of Christ, Scientist The official name of the Christian Science Church.

Church of England The national church of England.

Church of Jesus Christ of Latter-Day Saints The official name of the Mormon Church.

church·war·den (chûrch′wôr′dən) *n.* **1** In the Church of England or the Protestant Episcopal Church, a lay officer who assists in the administration of a parish. **2** A long-stemmed clay pipe.

church·wom·an (chûrch′wŏŏm′ən) *n. pl.* **·wom·en** (wim′·in) A female member of a church.

church·yard (chûrch′yärd′) *n.* Ground adjacent to a church, esp. a graveyard.

churl (chûrl) *n.* **1** A surly, boorish fellow. **2** A peasant, esp. in medieval England. [<OE *ceorl*] —**churl′ish** *adj.* —**churl′ish·ly** *adv.* —**churl′ish·ness** *n.*

churn (chûrn) *n.* A vessel in which milk or cream is agitated to produce butter. —*v.t.* **1** To stir or agitate (cream or milk) in or as in a churn. **2** To make (butter) in a churn. **3** To agitate violently. —*v.i.* **4** To use a churn. **5** To be in violent agitation. [<OE *cyrin*] —**churn′er** *n.*

churr (chûr) *n.* The whirring sound made by certain birds or insects. —*v.i.* To make such a sound. [Imit.]

chute (shōōt) *n.* **1** An inclined trough, slide, or passageway, as for grain, ore, coal, etc. **2** A waterfall or a rapid in a river. **3** *Informal* A parachute.

chut·ney (chut′nē) *n.* A piquant relish of fruit, spices, etc. Also **chut′nee.** [<Hind. *chatnī*]

chutz·pah (hŏŏts′pə, khŏŏts′-) *n. Informal* Brazen effrontery; gall. [Yiddish] —**Syn.** nerve, cheek, impudence.

chyle (kīl) *n.* The milky emulsion of lymph and fat taken up from the intestines by the lacteals during digestion. [<Gk. *chylos* juice <*cheein* pour] —**chy·la·ceous** (kī·lā′·shəs), **chy·lous** (kī′ləs) *adj.*

chyme (kīm) *n.* Partly digested food in liquid form as it passes from the stomach into the small intestine. [<Gk. *chymos* juice < *cheein* pour] —**chy·mous** (kī′məs) *adj.*

CIA Central Intelligence Agency.

ci·bo·ri·um (si·bôr′ē·əm, -bō′rē-) *n. pl.* **·bo·ri·a** (-bôr′ē·ə, -bō′rē·ə) **1** An arched canopy over an altar. **2** A receptacle for the wafers of the Eucharist. [<Gk. *kibōrion* cup]

ci·ca·da (si·kā′də, -kä′-) *n. pl.* **·das** or **·dae** (-dē) A large transparent-winged insect of which the male has vibrating membranes that produce a loud, shrill sound. [<L]

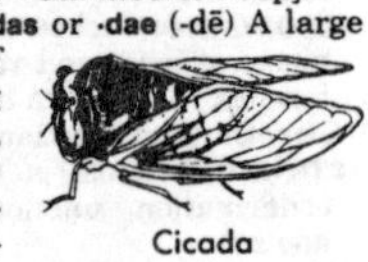

Cicada

cic·a·trix (sik′ə·triks) *n. pl.* **cic·a·tri·ces** (sik′ə·trī′sēz) **1** A scar remaining after a wound has healed. **2** A scar marking a former attachment of a leaf, etc. [<L] —**cic·a·tri·cial** (sik′ə·trish′əl) *adj.*

cic·a·trize (sik′ə·trīz) *v.t. & v.i.* **·trized, ·triz·ing** To heal or become healed by the formation of a scar. —**cic·a·tri·za·tion** (sik′ə·trə·zā′shən) *n.*

cic·e·ro·ne (sis′ə·rō′nē, *Ital.* chē′chā·rô′nā) *n. pl.* **·nes,** *Ital.* **·ni** (-nē) A guide for sightseers. [<Ital., Cicero]

-cide *combining form* **1** Killer or destroyer of: *insecticide.* **2** Murder or killing of: *suicide.* [<L *caedere* kill]

ci·der (sī′dər) *n.* The juice of apples, used to make vinegar and as a beverage before fermentation **(sweet cider)** or after fermentation **(hard cider).** [<OF *sidre* <LL *sicera* strong drink <Heb. *shēkār*]

ci·gar (si·gär′) *n.* A small roll of tobacco leaves prepared for smoking. [<Sp. *cigarro*]

cig·a·rette (sig′ə·ret′, sig′ə·ret) *n.* A small roll of finely cut tobacco in thin paper, used for smoking. Also **cig′a·ret′.** [<F *cigare* cigar]

cil·i·a (sil′ē·ə) *n. pl.* of CILIUM.

cil·i·ar·y (sil′ē·er′ē) *adj.* Of, pertaining to, or like cilia.

cil·i·ate (sil′ē·it, -āt) *adj.* Having cilia. Also **cil′i·at′ed.** —*n.* One of a class of microscopic, single-celled organisms possessing cilia.

cil·i·um (sil′ē·əm) *n. pl.* **cil·i·a** (sil′ē·ə) **1** *Biol.* A microscopic, hairlike process on the surface of a cell, organ, plant, etc., capable of a vibrating or whiplike movement. **2** EYELASH. [<L, eyelid]

Cim·me·ri·an (si·mir′ē·ən) *adj.* Densely dark; gloomy. —*n.* A member of a mythical people said by Homer to live in perpetual darkness.

CINC, C in C, C. in C. Commander in Chief.

cinch (sinch) *n.* **1** A saddle girth. **2** *Slang* A sure or easy thing. —*v.t.* **1** To fasten a saddle girth around. **2** *Slang* To make sure of. [<L *cingula* girdle <*cingere* bind] • See SADDLE.

cin·cho·na (sin·kō′nə, -chō′-) *n.* **1** Any of various South

American trees and shrubs widely cultivated as a source of quinine and related alkaloids. **2** The bark of any of these trees. [< the Countess of *Chinchón,* 1576–1639, wife of the viceroy of Peru] **—cin·chon′ic** *adj.*

cin·cho·nize (sin′kə·nīz) *v.t.* **·nized, ·niz·ing** To dose with cinchona or quinine. **—cin′cho·ni·za′tion** *n.*

cinc·ture (singk′chər) *n.* **1** A belt, girdle, etc. **2** Anything that encircles or encloses. *—v.t.* **·tured, ·tur·ing** To gird with or as with a cincture. [< L *cingere* gird]

cin·der (sin′dər) *n.* **1** Any partly burned combustible substance not completely reduced to ashes. **2** A charred bit of wood, coal, etc. **3** *pl.* Ashes. [< OE *sinder*] **—cin′der·y** *adj.*

cinder block A hollow building block of concrete mixed with cinders.

Cin·der·el·la (sin′dər·el′ə) *n.* A fairy-tale heroine who is treated as a household drudge but who eventually marries a prince.

cin·e·ma (sin′ə·mə) *n.* **1** A theater exhibiting motion-picture films. **2** A motion-picture film. **—the cinema 1** Motion-picture films collectively. **2** The art or business of making such films. [Short for CINEMATOGRAPH] **—cin·e·mat·ic** (sin′·ə·mat′ik) *adj.* **—cin′e·mat′i·cal·ly** *adv.*

cin·e·mat·o·graph (sin′ə·mat′ə·graf, -gräf) *n.* **1** A camera for taking motion-picture films. **2** A projector for showing such films. [< Gk. *kinēma, -atos* movement + -GRAPH]

cin·e·ma·tog·ra·phy (sin′ə·mə·tog′rə·fē) *n.* The art and process of making motion-picture films. **—cin′e·ma·tog′ra·pher** *n.* **—cin·e·mat·o·graph·ic** (sin′ə·mat′ə·graf′ik) *adj.* **—cin′e·mat′o·graph′i·cal·ly** *adv.*

cin·e·rar·i·a (sin′ə·râr′ē·ə) *n.* A plant with showy clusters of blue, reddish, or white flowers widely grown as a house plant. [< L *cinerarius* ashy < *cinis* ash]

cin·e·rar·i·um (sin′ə·râr′ē·əm) *n. pl.* **·rar·i·a** (-râr′ē·ə) A place for the ashes of a cremated body. [L]

cin·na·bar (sin′ə·bär) *n.* **1** A crystallized red mercuric sulfide, an ore of mercury. **2** A mixture formed by subliming mercury and sulfur, used esp. as a pigment. [< Gk. *kinnabari*]

cin·na·mon (sin′ə·mən) *n.* **1** The aromatic inner bark of any of several tropical trees of the laurel family, used as a spice. **2** Any tree that yields cinnamon. **3** A light reddish brown. *—adj.* **1** Made with cinnamon. **2** Light reddish brown. [< Gk. *kinnamōmon* < Heb. *qinnāmōn*]

cinque·foil (singk′foil) *n.* **1** Any of several related plants having leaves with usu. five leaflets. **2** An architectural ornament composed of five converging arcs. [< L *quinque* five + *folium* leaf]

Cinquefoil

CIO, C.I.O. Congress of Industrial Organizations.

ci·on (sī′ən) *n.* SCION (def. 2).

ci·pher (sī′fər) *n.* **1** The character 0; zero. **2** Any Arabic numeral. **3 a** A written code in which letters of the alphabet are substituted for others or represented by symbols. **b** The key for solving such a code. **4** A person or thing of no significance. **5** A monogram. *—v.i.* **1** To do arithmetic. *—v.t.* **2** To calculate arithmetically. **3** To put into cipher; encode.[< Ar. *sifr*]

cir., circ. circa; circular; circumference.

cir·ca (sûr′kə) *prep.* About; around: used to indicate approximate dates, etc. [L]

Cir·cas·sian (sər·kash′ən, -kash′ē·ən) *n.* A member of a group of tribes of the Caucasus region. *—adj.* Of or pertaining to Circassia, the Circassians, or their language.

Cir·ce (sûr′sē) In the *Odyssey,* an enchantress who turned Odysseus's men into swine.

cir·cle (sûr′kəl) *n.* **1** A plane figure bounded by a curved line everywhere equally distant from a fixed point. **2** Something having the form of such a figure, as a ring, round object or enclosure, etc. **3** A course, cycle, series, etc., that ends at the starting point. **4** A group of persons sharing a common interest, occupation, or other tie. **5** A sphere or area of influence. **6** A tier of seats in a theater. *—v.* **·cled, ·cling** *v.t.* **1** To enclose with or as with a circle. **2** To move around, or over, as in a circle. *—v.i.* **3** To move in a circle. [< L *circulus,* dim. of *circus* ring] **—cir′cler** *n.* **—Syn.** *n.* **4** set, crowd, coterie, clique.

cir·clet (sûr′klit) *n.* A small ring or ring-shaped object, esp. an ornament.

cir·cuit (sûr′kit) *n.* **1** A more or less circular route, course, etc.; a round. **2** A journey from place to place through such a course, as by a judge or clergyman. **3** A district visited by or within the jurisdiction of one having such a route, esp. a judge. **4** An association, as of theaters or teams, in which performances, contests, etc., take place in turn. **5** A curve forming a closed circumference. **6 a** The entire course traversed by an electric current. **b** An assembly of parts and components that function together in an electric or electronic device or system. **7** A radio transmission and reception system. *—v.t. & v.i.* To go or move through in a circuit. [< F < L *circuitus,* pp of < *circumire* go around]

circuit breaker *Electr.* A switch or relay for breaking a circuit under specified or abnormal conditions of current flow.

circuit court A court that holds sessions at different places within its jurisdiction.

cir·cu·i·tous (sər·kyōō′ə·təs) *adj.* Roundabout; indirect. **—cir·cu′i·tous·ly** *adv.* **—cir·cu′i·tous·ness** *n.*

circuit rider A minister who preaches at churches on a circuit or district route.

cir·cuit·ry (sûr′kit·rē) *n.* The design or component parts of an electric circuit.

cir·cu·lar (sûr′kyə·lər) *adj.* **1** Shaped like a circle; round. **2** Of, forming, or moving in a circle. **3** Ending at the point of beginning. **4** Circuitous; indirect. *—n.* A communication or notice for general circulation. [< L *circulus* CIRCLE] **—cir·cu·lar·i·ty** (sûr′kyə·lar′ə·tē) *n.* **—cir′cu·lar·ly** *adv.*

cir·cu·lar·ize (sûr′kyə·lə·rīz′) *v.t.* **·ized, ·iz·ing 1** To issue circulars to. **2** To publicize with circulars. **—cir′cu·lar·i·za′·tion, cir′cu·lar·iz′er** *n.*

circular saw A disk-shaped saw having a toothed edge, rotated at high speed by a motor.

cir·cu·late (sûr′kyə·lāt) *v.* **·lat·ed, ·lat·ing** *—v.i.* **1** To move in a closed course. **2** To move or travel about. **3** To move or flow freely, as air. *—v.t.* **4** To cause to circulate. [< L *circulari*] **—cir′cu·la′tive, cir·cu·la·to·ry** (sûr′kyə·lə·tôr′ē, -tō′rē) *adj.* **—cir′cu·la′tor** *n.*

cir·cu·la·tion (sûr′kyə·lā′shən) *n.* **1** The act of circulating or the state of being circulated. **2** Motion in a closed course. **3** Transmission or dissemination, as from person to person. **4** The extent or amount of distribution, as the number of copies issued of a periodical.

circum- *prefix* About; around; on all sides: *circumscribe.* [< L *circus* circle]

cir·cum·am·bi·ent (sûr′kəm·am′bē·ənt) *adj.* Surrounding; encompassing. **—cir′cum·am′bi·ence, cir′cum·am′bi·en·cy** *n.*

cir·cum·cise (sûr′kəm·sīz) *v.t.* **·cised, ·cis·ing** To cut off the prepuce or clitoris of. [< L *circum-* around + *caedere* cut] **—cir′cum·cis′er** *n.* **—cir′cum·ci′sion** (-sizh′ən) *n.*

cir·cum·fer·ence (sər·kum′fər·əns) *n.* **1** The boundary line of a circle. **2** Distance or measurement around something. [< L *circumferentia* < *circum-* around + *ferre* bear] **—cir·cum·fer·en·tial** (sər·kum′fər·en′shəl) *adj.*

cir·cum·flex (sûr′kəm·fleks) *n.* A mark (û) used over a vowel to indicate a pronunciation. *—adj.* **1** Pronounced or marked with the circumflex accent. **2** Bent or curved. *—v.t.* To mark with a circumflex. [< L *circum-* around + *flectere* bend]

cir·cum·flu·ent (sər·kum′flōō·ənt) *adj.* Flowing around; surrounding. Also **cir·cum′flu·ous.** [< L pr.p. of *circumfluere* < *circum-* around + *fluere* flow]

cir·cum·fuse (sûr′kəm·fyōōz′) *v.t.* **·fused, ·fus·ing 1** To pour or spread about. **2** To surround, as with a liquid. [< L *circum-* around + *fundere* pour] **—cir·cum·fu·sion** (-fyōō′·zhən) *n.*

cir·cum·lo·cu·tion (sûr′kəm·lō·kyōō′shən) *n.* A long, roundabout way of saying or expressing something. [< L *circum-* around + *loqui* speak] **—cir·cum·loc·u·tory** (sûr′·kəm·lok′yə·tôr′ē, -tō′rē) *adj.*

cir·cum·nav·i·gate (sûr′kəm·nav′ə·gāt) *v.t.* **·gat·ed, ·gat·ing** To sail around. **—cir′cum·nav′i·ga′tion, cir′cum·nav′i·ga′tor** *n.*

cir·cum·po·lar (sûr′kəm·pō′lər) *adj.* **1** Near or surrounding one of the terrestrial poles. **2** Revolving about a celestial pole without setting, as a star.

cir·cum·scribe (sûr′kəm·skrīb′) *v.t.* **·scribed, ·scrib·ing 1** To draw a line around; encircle. **2** To confine within bounds; restrict. **3** *Geom.* **a** To surround with a figure that coincides at every possible point: to *circumscribe* a triangle with a circle. **b** To cause to surround a figure thus: to *circumscribe* a circle about a triangle. [< L *circum-* around + *scribere* write] **—cir′cum·scrib′er, cir·cum·scrip·tion** (sûr′·kəm·skrip′shen) *n.*

cir·cum·spect (sûr′kəm·spekt) *adj.* Attentive to all possibilities; cautious. [< L *circum-* around + *specere* look] **—cir′cum·spec′tion, cir′cum·spect′ness** *n.* **—cir′cum·spec′tive** *adj.* **—cir′cum·spect′ly** *adv.* **—Syn.** prudent, wary.

cir·cum·stance (sûr′kəm·stans) *n.* **1** A related or concomitant condition, fact, occurrence, etc. **2** Any condition, fact, etc. **3** *pl.* The situation a person is in relative to certain conditions, esp. financial conditions. **4** Formal display; ceremony: pomp and *circumstance.* **—under no circumstances** Never; under no conditions. **—under the circumstances** Such being the case or conditions. [< L *circum-* around + *stare* stand] **—cir′cum·stanced** *adj.*

cir·cum·stan·tial (sûr′kəm·stan′shəl) *adj.* **1** Pertaining to or dependent on circumstances. **2** Incidental; not essential. **3** Complete and detailed; minute. **—cir′cum·stan′ti·al′i·ty** (-shē·al′ə·tē) *n.* **—cir′cum·stan′tial·ly** *adv.*

circumstantial evidence *Law* Evidence based on circumstances which form reasonable grounds for determining facts relevant to a case.

cir·cum·stan·ti·ate (sûr′kəm·stan′shē·āt) *v.t.* **·at·ed, ·at·ing** To establish by circumstances or in detail. **—cir′cum·stan′ti·a′tion** *n.*

cir·cum·vent (sûr′kəm·vent′) *v.t.* **1** To avoid by or as by going around; bypass. **2** To get the better of by strategy or craft; outwit. [< L *circum-* around + *venire* come] **—cir′·cum·vent′er, cir′cum·vent′or, cir′cum·ven′tion** *n.* **—cir′cum·ven′tive** *adj.*

cir·cus (sûr′kəs) *n.* **1** A show in which acrobats, trained animals, clowns, etc., perform. **2** The circular, often tented enclosure in which such a show is held. **3** The members of such a show. **4** A large arena with tiers of seats around it, used in ancient Rome for contests or public spectacles. **5** *Brit.* A circular intersection of several streets. **6** *Informal* Something uproariously entertaining. [< L, a ring, racecourse]

cir·rho·sis (si·rō′sis) *n.* A chronic disease of the liver or other organ, marked by degeneration of tissue. [< Gk. *kirrhos* tawny < the color of the cirrhotic liver] **—cir·rhot·ic** (si·rot′ik) *adj.*

cirro- *combining form* CIRRUS: *cirrostratus.* [< L *cirrus* curl]

cir·ro·cu·mu·lus (sir′ō·kyōō′myə·ləs) *n.* A mass of small, fleecy clouds at an average height of 5 miles.

cir·ro·stra·tus (sir′ō·strā′təs) *n.* A fine, whitish cloud at an average height of 6 miles.

cir·rus (sir′əs) *n. pl.* **cir·ri** (sir′ī) A type of white, wispy cloud at an average height of 7 miles, seen in tufts or feathery bands. [< L, ringlet]

cis·co (sis′kō) *n. pl.* **·coes** or **·cos** A North American freshwater fish related to the whitefish. [< N. Am. Ind.]

Cis·ter·cian (sis·tûr′shən) *n.* A monk of a Benedictine order founded in France in 1098. *—adj.* Of this order. [< Med. L *Cistercium,* French abbey site]

cis·tern (sis′tərn) *n.* **1** A tank or receptacle for storing water. **2** *Anat.* A large lymph space; a sac. [< L *cisterna* < *cista* chest]

cit. citation; cited; citizen.

cit·a·del (sit′ə·dəl, -del) *n.* **1** A fortress commanding a city. **2** Any fortress. [< Ital. *cittadella,* dim. of *citta* city]

ci·ta·tion (sī·tā′shən) *n.* **1** The act of citing. **2** A passage or source cited. **3** A public commendation for exceptional achievement, bravery, etc. **4** A summons to appear in a law court. **—ci·ta·to·ry** (sī′tə·tôr′ē, -tō′rē) *adj.*

cite (sīt) *v.t.* **cit·ed, cit·ing 1** To quote or refer to for proof, support, etc. **2** To mention specifically, esp. in official commendation. **3** To summon to appear in a court of law. [< L *citare,* freq. of *ciēre* call] **—cit′a·ble, cite′a·ble** *adj.*

cith·a·ra (sith′ə·rə) *n.* An ancient Greek stringed instrument similar to a lyre. [< Gk. *kithara*]

Cithara

cith·er (sith′ər) *n.* CITTERN. Also **cith·ern** (sith′ərn).

cit·i·fied (sit′i·fīd) *adj.* Considered typical of city dwellers or city life.

cit·i·zen (sit′ə·zən) *n.* **1** A native or naturalized person owing allegiance to, and entitled to protection from, a government. **2** A member of a state. **3** A resident of a city or town. **4** One who is not a member of the military, police, etc.; a civilian. [< OF *citeain* < *cité* CITY] • The word *citizen* is generally applied to one whose national government derives its power from the people, as in a republic. A *subject* is one who owes allegiance to a monarch or other sovereign.

cit·i·zen·ry (sit′ə·zən·rē) *n.* Citizens collectively.

cit·i·zen·ship (sit′ə·zən·ship′) *n.* **1** The status of a citizen. **2** The activities or attitudes of a citizen, esp. with regard to obligations, rights, etc.

cit·rate (sit′rāt, -rit, sī′trāt) *n.* A salt of citric acid.

cit·ric (sit′rik) *adj.* Derived from citrus fruits.

citric acid A white, crystalline, organic acid found in various fruits and also made synthetically.

cit·rine (sit′rin) *n.* A light yellow variety of quartz resembling topaz. [< F *citrin*]

cit·ron (sit′rən) *n.* **1** A fruit like a lemon, but larger and less acid. **2** The tree producing this fruit. **3** A variety of watermelon with hard-fleshed fruit: also **citron melon. 4** The candied rind of either of these fruits. [< L *citrus* citron tree]

cit·ron·el·la (sit′rə·nel′ə) *n.* A s Asian grass yielding **citronella oil,** which is used in perfumery, insect repellents, etc. Also **citronella grass.** [< CITRON]

cit·rus (sit′rəs) *adj.* Of or pertaining to a genus of fruit-bearing trees or shrubs including the orange, lemon, lime, grapefruit, etc. Also **cit′rous.** *—n. pl.* **·rus·es** A citrus tree or fruit. [< L, citron tree]

cit·tern (sit′ərn) *n.* A 16th- to 17th-century musical instrument resembling a lute or guitar. [Blend of CITHER and GITTERN.]

cit·y (sit′ē) *n. pl.* **cit·ies 1** A place inhabited by a large, permanent, organized community. **2** In the U.S. and Canada, a municipality of the first class. **3** The people of a city, collectively. [< L *civitas* < *civis* citizen]

city hall 1 The municipal building of a city. **2** A municipal government. **3** Bureaucratic procedures or officials characterized as obstinately unresponsive: Go fight *city hall.*

city manager An administrator appointed to manage the municipal affairs of a city.

cit·y·scape (sit′ē·skāp′) *n.* **1** A view of a city. **2** The plan or arrangement of elements in a city.

cit·y-state (sit′ē·stāt′) *n.* A sovereign state consisting of a city and adjacent territories, as in ancient Greece.

civ. civil; civilian.

civ·et (siv′it) *n.* **1** Any of several catlike mammals of Africa and Asia, having scent glands secreting a fluid with a musky odor: also **civet cat. 2** The musky secretion of such an animal, used in perfume. [< Ar. *zabād*]

civ·ic (siv′ik) *adj.* Of or pertaining to a city, citizens, or citizenship. [< L *civis* citizen]

civ·ics (siv′iks) *n.pl. (construed as sing.)* The branch of social science dealing with government, citizens' rights and duties, etc.

civ·ies (siv′ez) *n.pl.* CIVVIES.

civ·il (siv′əl) *adj.* **1** Of or pertaining to citizens, esp. in relation to the state. **2** Of or pertaining to general public life as distinguished from military or ecclesiastical activities. **3** Of or involving internal relationships and affairs of a country. **4** Socially acceptable; polite. [< L *civis* citizen] **—civ′il·ly** *adv.* **—Syn. 4** courteous, well-bred, civilized, proper, well-mannered, attentive.

civil defense A civilian program of action by civilians for general protection and maintenance of essential services in case of enemy attack or widespread disaster.

civil disobedience Passive resistance to offensive laws or official policies.

civil engineer An engineer trained to design and build roads, bridges, tunnels, etc. —**civil engineering**

ci·vil·ian (sə·vil′yən) *n.* One who is not a member of the armed forces. —*adj.* Of civilians or civil life.

ci·vil·i·ty (sə·vil′ə·tē) *n. pl.* **·ties** 1 Courtesy; politeness. 2 A courteous act, expression, etc.

civ·i·li·za·tion (siv′ə·lə·zā′shən, -lī·zā′-) *n.* 1 A condition of human society characterized by a comparatively high degree of cultural and technical development. 2 A region or people considered to be in this stage. 3 A stage in the cultural development of a people, region, or period. 4 The process of civilizing or of becoming civilized. *Brit. sp.* **civ′·i·li·sa′tion.**

civ·i·lize (siv′ə·līz) *v.t.* **·lized, ·liz·ing** 1 To bring from a primitive to a culturally advanced state. 2 To train in social amenities. *Brit. sp.* **civ′i·lise.**

civ·i·lized (siv′ə·līzd) *adj.* 1 Having or characteristic of a state of civilization. 2 Cultured; refined.

civil law The branch of law dealing with the rights of citizens.

civil liberty A right, as freedom of speech or thought, guaranteed to individuals by law.

civil rights Private, nonpolitical rights of citizens, as those established by the 13th and 14th amendments to the U.S. Constitution.

civil servant One employed in the civil service.

civil service 1 The branches of government service that are neither military, legislative, or judicial. 2 The persons employed in these branches.

civil war War between factions or sections of a nation.

Civil War In the U.S., a war between the North (the Union) and the South (the Confederacy), 1861–65.

civ·vies (siv′ēz) *n. pl. Slang* Civilian dress as distinguished from military uniform.

ck. cask; check; cook.

Cl chlorine.

c.l. carload; center line; civil law.

cl. centiliter(s); claim; class; classification; clause; clearance; clergyman; clerk; cloth.

clab·ber (klab′ər) *n.* Milk curdled by souring. —*v.t. & v.i.* To curdle, as milk. [Short for earlier *bonnyclabber* <Ir. *bainne clabair* curdled milk]

clack (klak) *v.t. & v.i.* 1 To make or cause to make the sound of a short, sharp impact. 2 To chatter. —*n.* 1 A sharp, short sound. 2 Chatter. [Imit.] —**clack′er** *n.*

clad (klad) A *p.t. & pp.* of CLOTHE. —*adj.* Clothed.

claim (klām) *v.t.* 1 To demand as a right; assert ownership or title to. 2 To hold to be true. 3 To require or deserve. —*n.* 1 A demand for something due; assertion of a right. 2 The basis for such a demand or assertion. 3 An assertion, as of a fact. 4 Something claimed, as a piece of land for use by a settler or miner. [<L *clamare* declare] —**claim′a·ble** *adj.* —**claim′er** *n.*

claim·ant (klā′mənt) *n.* One who makes a claim.

clair·voy·ant (klâr·voi′ənt) *adj.* Having the ability to see or know things not perceptible to normal human senses. —*n.* A clairvoyant person. [F, lit., clear-seeing] —**clair·voy′ance** *n.*

clam (klam) *n.* 1 Any of numerous often edible bivalve mollusks. 2 *Informal* An uncommunicative person. —*v.i.* **clammed, clam·ming** To hunt for or dig clams. —**clam up** *Slang* To become silent. [<OE *clamm* a clamp]

clam·bake (klam′bāk′) *n.* A seashore picnic where clams and other food are baked.

clam·ber (klam′bər) *v.t. & v.i.* To climb clumsily or laboriously as by using the hands and feet. —*n.* A difficult climb. [<ON *klimbra* to grip] —**clam′ber·er** *n.*

clam·my (klam′ē) *adj.* **·mi er, ·mi·est** Damp and sticky or cold. [<OE *clæman* to stick] —**clam′mi·ly** *adv.* —**clam′mi·ness** *n.*

clam·or (klam′ər) *n.* 1 A loud, persistent outcry or noise. 2 A vehement general demand or protest. —*v.i.* 1 To make a clamor. —*v.t.* 2 To utter with loud outcry. *Brit. sp.* **clam′our.** [<L *clamare* cry out] —**clam′or·er** *n.* —**Syn.** *n.* 1 din, uproar, hubbub, racket.

clam·or·ous (klam′ər·əs) *adj.* Making or made with clamor; noisy. —**clam′or·ous·ly** *adv.* —**clam′or·ous·ness** *n.*

clamp (klamp) *n.* A device for holding or pressing together two or more parts. —*v.t.* To join or press with or as with a clamp. [<MDu. *klampe*]

clan (klan) *n.* 1 A group of families having a common ancestor, as in the Scottish Highlands. 2 A group of related or closely associated persons. [<Scot. Gael. *clānn*]

clan·des·tine (klan·des′tin) *adj.* Kept secret; surreptitious. [<L *clandestinus* <*clam* in secret] —**clan·des′tine·ly** *adv.* —**clan·des′tine·ness** *n.*

clang (klang) *v.t. & v.i.* 1 To make or cause to make a loud, ringing, metallic sound. 2 To strike together with such a sound. —*n.* A loud, ringing sound, as of metal struck. [<L *clangere*]

clan·gor (klang′gər, klang′ər) *n.* Repeated clanging. —*v.i.* To ring noisily; clang. *Brit. sp.* **clan′gour.** [<L *clangere* clang] —**clan′gor·ous** *adj.* —**clan′gor·ous·ly** *adv.*

clank (klangk) *n.* A short, harsh, metallic sound. —*v.t. & v.i.* To make or cause to make a clank. [Blend of CLANG and CLINK]

clan·nish (klan′ish) *adj.* 1 Of or typical of a clan. 2 Tending to associate only with members of the same group. —**clan′nish·ly** *adv.* —**clan′nish·ness** *n.*

clans·man (klanz′mən) *n. pl.* **·men** (-mən) A male member of a clan. —**clans′wom′an** (*pl.* **·wom′en**) *n. Fem.*

clap¹ (klap) *v.* **clapped, clap·ping** *v.i.* 1 To strike the palms of the hands together with a short, sharp sound. 2 To strike or come together with a sharp, explosive sound. —*v.t.* 3 To strike together, as the hands, with a sharp, explosive sound. 4 To applaud by striking the hands together. 5 To strike briskly. 6 To put quickly or suddenly: to *clap* someone into jail. —*n.* 1 The act of clapping, esp. the hands. 2 A loud, sudden noise, as of thunder. 3 A slap. [<OE *clæppan*]

clap² (klap) *n. Slang* Gonorrhea: usu. with *the.* [<OF *clapoir* a venereal sore]

clap·board (klab′ərd, klap′bôrd′, -bōrd′) *n.* An overlapping board, usu. with one edge thicker than the other, used on the outside of buildings. —*v.t.* To cover with clapboards. [<MDu *klappen* to split]

clap·per (klap′ər) *n.* 1 The tongue of a bell. 2 One who or that which claps.

clap·trap (klap′trap) *n.* Cheap, sensational, pretentious language, trappings, etc.

claque (klak) *n.* 1 People hired to applaud in a theater. 2 Any group of fawning followers. [<F *claquer* clap]

clar·et (klar′ət) *n.* 1 A red wine, esp. a Bordeaux. 2 A deep purplish red. [<OF *(vin) claret* clear (wine)]

clar·i·fy (klar′ə·fī) *v.* **·fied, ·fy·ing** *v.t.* 1 To make clear or understandable. 2 To free from impurities, as fats. —*v.i.* 3 To become clear. [<L *clarus* clear + *facere* make] —**clar·i·fi·ca·tion** (klar′ə·fə·kā′shən) *n.* —**clar′i·fi′er** *n.*

clar·i·net (klar′ə·net′) *n.* A cylindrical woodwind instrument with a bell mouth, having a single reed mouthpiece, finger holes, and keys. [<F *clarine* bell <L *clarus* clear] —**clar′i·net′ist** or **clar′i·net′tist** *n.*

Clarinet

clar·i·on (klar′ē·ən) *n.* 1 A small trumpet. 2 The sound of a trumpet or a similar sound. —*adj.* Shrill and clear. [<L *clarus* clear]

clar·i·ty (klar′ə·tē) *n.* The state or fact of being clear; clearness.

clash (klash) *v.i.* 1 To collide with a harsh, metallic sound. 2 To be in opposition; conflict. —*v.t.* 3 To strike together with a harsh, metallic sound. —*n.* 1 A loud, harsh sound, as of metal objects striking. 2 A marked conflict. [Imit.]

clasp (klasp, kläsp) *n.* 1 A fastener by which things are held together. 2 A firm grasp or embrace. —*v.t.* 1 To fasten with or as with a clasp. 2 To embrace. 3 To grasp firmly in or with the hand. [ME *claspe*] —**clasp′er** *n.*

class (klas, kläs) *n.* 1 A group having something in common; category. 2 A grouping based on social or economic status. 3 A rating according to quality, rank, etc. 4 a A group of students under one teacher or pursuing a study together. b A meeting of such a group. c A group of students of the same graduating year. 5 *Biol.* A group of plants or animals ranking below a phylum and above an order. 6 *Slang* Superiority; elegance. —*v.t.* To assign to a class; classify. [< L *classis* group, class] —**Syn.** 1 kind, sort, type, set.

clas·sic (klas′ik) *adj.* 1 Regarded as best or exemplary of its kind. 2 Of or pertaining to the art, literature, etc., of ancient Greece and Rome. 3 Considered typical of such art or literature; formal; regular. 4 Founded or celebrated in tradition. 5 Fashionable because of the simplicity of its style: said of wearing apparel, furniture, etc. —*n.* 1 An author, artist, or creative work generally regarded as of the highest excellence. 2 A traditional event, as in sports. 3 Something that is classic (def. 5). —**the classics** Ancient Greek and Roman literature. [< L *classicus* of the first rank < *classis* order, class]

clas·si·cal (klas′i·kəl) *adj.* 1 Of, pertaining to, or based on the art, literature, or culture of ancient Greece and Rome. 2 Of, in, or pertaining to the style of European music of the late 18th century. 3 Highly regarded, authoritative, or traditional; standard. 4 *Physics* Pertaining to or describing theories based upon or derived from Newtonian mechanics, esp. as distinguished from relativity theory and quantum mechanics. —**clas′si·cal′i·ty** *n.* —**clas′si·cal·ly** *adv.*

clas·si·cism (klas′ə·siz′əm) *n.* 1 Aesthetic qualities and principles characterized by formality, balance, restraint, etc., regarded as typical of ancient Greek and Roman art, literature, and culture. 2 Application of these principles. 3 Classical scholarship. 4 An idiom or expression typical of the classics. Also **clas′si·cal·ism.**

clas·si·cist (klas′ə·sist) *n.* 1 One versed in the classics. 2 A user of classical style.

clas·si·fi·ca·tion (klas′ə·fə·kā′shən) *n.* 1 The act, process, or result of classifying. 2 A category; class. 3 TAXONOMY. —**clas·si·fi·ca·to·ry** (klas′ə·fə·kə·tôr′ē, -tō′rē, klas′ə·fə·kā′tər·ē, klə·sif′ə·kə·tôr′ē, -tō′rē) *adj.*

classified advertisement One of a listing of brief advertisements printed under a variety of headings.

clas·si·fy (klas′ə·fī) *v.t.* **·fied, ·fy·ing** 1 To arrange systematically on the basis of class or category. 2 To restrict as to circulation or use, as a specially designated document or item of information. [< L *classis* class + -FY] —**clas′si·fi′a·ble** *adj.* —**clas′si·fi′er** *n.*

class·mate (klas′māt′, kläs′-) *n.* A member of the same class in school or college.

class·room (klas′rōōm′, -rŏŏm′, kläs′-) *n.* A room where classes are held, as in a school.

class·y (klas′ē) *adj. Slang* **class·i·er, class·i·est** Elegant.

clat·ter (klat′ər) *v.i.* 1 To make or move with a rattling noise. 2 To chatter noisily. —*v.t.* 3 To cause to make a rattling noise. —*n.* 1 A rattling noise. 2 Noisy chatter. [< OE *clatrung* a clattering noise] —**clat′ter·er** *n.*

clause (klôz) *n.* 1 *Gram.* A group of words containing a subject and predicate and usu. forming part of a compound or complex sentence. 2 A separate statement or proviso in a legal document, treaty, etc. [< L *clausus*, pp. of *claudere* close] —**claus′al** *adj.*

claus·tro·pho·bi·a (klôs′trə·fō′bē·ə) *n.* Morbid fear of enclosed or confined places. [< L *claustrum* a closed place + -PHOBIA] —**claus′tro·pho′bic** *adj.*

clav·i·chord (klav′ə·kôrd) *n.* A keyboard musical instrument whose tones are produced by brass pins striking horizontal strings. [< L *clavis* key + *chorda* string]

clav·i·cle (klav′ə·kəl) *n.* The bone connecting the shoulder blade and breastbone. [< L *clavicula*, dim. of *clavis* key] —**cla·vic·u·lar** (klə·vik′yə·lər) *adj.*

clav·i·er (klav′ē·ər, klə·vir′) *n.* Any keyboard stringed instrument, as a clavichord, piano, etc. [F, keyboard < L *clavis* key]

claw (klô) *n.* 1 A sharp, curved, horny nail on the toe of a bird, mammal, or reptile. 2 A pincer or chela at the end of an appendage, as in certain insects and crustaceans. 3 Anything sharp and hooked. —*v.t. & v.i.* To tear, scratch, pull, etc., with or as with claws. [< OE *clawu*]

claw hammer A hammer with one end of its head forked and curved for drawing nails. • See HAMMER.

clay (klā) *n.* 1 A fine-textured earth that is plastic when wet but hard and compact when dry, used to make ceramic ware, bricks, etc. 2 Earth in general. 3 The human body. [< OE *clæg*] —**clay·ey** (klā′ē) *adj.*

clay·more (klā′môr, -mōr) *n.* A double-edged sword used formerly by Scottish Highlanders. [< Scot. Gael. *claidheamh* sword + *mor* great]

clay pigeon A saucer-shaped disk of baked clay or other brittle material, projected as a flying target in trapshooting.

clean (klēn) *adj.* 1 Free from dirt, stain, impurity, etc. 2 Unblemished; pure. 3 Habitually avoiding dirt; neat. 4 Not marked; blank: *clean* paper. 5 Not rough, uneven, or irregular. 6 Complete; thorough. 7 Clear; unencumbered: a *clean* title to land. 8 Dexterous; skillful. 9 Sportsmanlike; fair. 10 Producing little radioactive contamination: a *clean* nuclear test. —*v.t.* 1 To free from dirt, impurities, etc. 2 To prepare (fowl, fish, etc.) for cooking. —*v.i.* 3 To undergo or perform the act of cleaning. —**clean out** 1 To empty (a place) of contents or occupants. 2 *Informal.* To leave without money. —**clean up** *Informal.* To win a large amount or make large profits. —*adv.* 1 In a clean manner. 2 *Informal* Completely; wholly. [< OE *clæne* clear, pure] —**clean′a·ble** *adj.* —**clean′ness** *n.*

clean-cut (klēn′kut′) *adj.* 1 Clear in outline; sharply defined. 2 Neat and pleasing in appearance: a *clean-cut* young man.

clean·er (klē′nər) *n.* 1 One who cleans, esp. one who does dry cleaning. 2 A substance or device that removes dirt.

clean·ly (klen′lē) *adj.* **·li·er, li·est** Habitually and carefully clean; neat. —*adv.* (klēn′lē) In a clean manner. —**clean·li·ness** (klen′lē·nis) *n.*

cleanse (klenz) *v.t.* **cleansed, cleans·ing** To free from dirt or defilement; clean; purge. [< OE *clænsian* < *clæne* clean]

cleans·er (klenz′ər) *n.* A substance, as a soap or abrasive, used for cleaning.

clean·up (klēn′up′) *n.* 1 A thorough cleaning. 2 *Informal* A sweeping profit.

clear (klir) *adj.* 1 Not clouded, dimmed, or obscured. 2 Transparent. 3 Free from obstruction. 4 Free from blemish. 5 Readily perceived; distinct. 6 Readily understood; intelligible. 7 Plain; evident. 8 Free from confusion or doubt. 9 Free from guilt. 10 Free from hindrance or entanglement. 11 Without deductions; net. —*v.t.* 1 To make clear; brighten. 2 To free from impurities, blemishes, etc. 3 To remove, as obstructions, in making clear. 4 To remove obstructions from. 5 To free of guilt or blame. 6 To free from doubt or ambiguity. 7 To free from debt by payment. 8 To pass by or over without touching: to *clear* a fence. 9 To obtain or give clearance, as for a ship or cargo. 10 To net or gain over and above expenses. 11 To pass through a clearing house, as a check. —*v.i.* 12 To become clear. 13 To pass away, as mist or fog. 14 To settle accounts by exchange of bills and checks, as in a clearinghouse. —**clear out** *Informal.* To leave; depart. —**clear the air** To dispel emotional tensions, misunderstanding, etc. —**clear up** 1 To grow fair, as the weather. 2 To free from confusion or mystery. 3 To tidy. —*adv.* 1 Clearly; plainly. 2 *Informal* Completely; entirely. —*n.* An unobstructed space. —**in the clear** 1 Free from limitations or obstructions. 2 Not open to blame or accusation. [< L *clarus* clear, bright] —**clear′a·ble** *adj.* —**clear′ly** *adv.* —**clear′ness** *n.* —**Syn.** *adj.* 2 limpid, crystalline, pellucid. 7 obvious, apparent, manifest.

clear·ance (klir′əns) *n.* 1 The act or process of clearing. 2 The space by which a moving vehicle, part, etc., clears something. 3 A sale to dispose of accumulated merchandise. 4 Permission for a vessel, aircraft, etc., to proceed. 5 Authorization, as for access to information.

clear-cut (klir′kut′) *adj.* **1** Distinctly and sharply outlined. **2** Clearly evident; definite.

clear cutting Nonselective felling of all trees in a stand of timber.

clear-head·ed (klir′hed′id) *adj.* Having a clear perception or understanding; not mentally confused; sensible. —**clear′-head′ed·ly** *adv.* —**clear′-head′ed·ness** *n.*

clear·ing (klir′ing) *n.* A tract of land cleared of trees, underbrush, etc.

clear·ing·house (klir′ing·hous′) *n.* An office where bankers exchange drafts and checks and adjust balances.

clear-sight·ed (klir′sī′tid) *adj.* **1** Having keen eyesight. **2** Having accurate perception and good judgment. —**clear′-sight′ed·ly** *adv.* —**clear′-sight′ed·ness** *n.*

clear·sto·ry (klir′stôr′ē, -stō′rē) *n. pl.* **·ries** CLERESTORY.

cleat (klēt) *n.* **1** A piece of wood, metal, etc., fastened to a surface to strengthen, support, or prevent slipping. **2** *Naut.* A piece of metal or wood on which to belay a rope. —*v.t.* **1** To furnish or strengthen with a cleat or cleats. **2** *Naut.* To fasten (rope, etc.) to or with a cleat. [ME *clete*]

cleav·age (klē′vij) *n.* **1** A cleaving or being cleft. **2** A split, cleft, or division. **3** A tendency in certain rocks or crystals to split in certain directions. **4** The hollowed space between a woman's breasts, esp. when exposed by a low-cut neckline.

cleave[1] (klēv) *v.* **cleft** or **cleaved** or **clove, cleft** or **cleaved** or **clo·ven, cleav·ing** *v.t.* **1** To split or sunder, as with an ax or wedge. **2** To make or achieve by cutting. **3** To pass through; penetrate. —*v.i.* **4** To split or divide. **5** To make one's way, as by cutting: with *through.* [< OE *clēofan*] —**cleav′a·ble** *adj.*

cleave[2] (klēv) *v.i.* **cleaved, cleaved, cleav·ing 1** To stick fast; adhere. **2** To be faithful: with *to.* [< OE *cleofian*]

cleav·er (klē′vər) *n.* A heavy, hatchetlike knife used by butchers.

clef (klef) *n. Music* A symbol placed upon the staff to de-

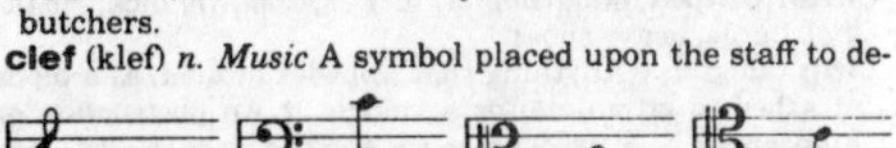

Clefs
Showing position of middle C on each.
1. Treble or G clef. 2. Bass or F clef.
3, 4. C clefs (alto, tenor).

termine the pitch of the notes, namely, the **treble** or **G clef, bass** or **F clef,** and the **C clef.** [< L *clavis* key]

cleft (kleft) *v.* A *p.t. & p.p.* of CLEAVE[1]. —*adj.* Divided partially or completely. —*n.* A fissure; crevice; crack.

cleft lip A congenital fissure of the upper lip.

cleft palate A congenital gap from front to back of the hard palate.

clem·a·tis (klem′ə·tis) *n.* A perennial shrub or woody vine related to the crowfoot. [< Gk. *klēma* vine]

clem·en·cy (klem′ən·sē) *n. pl.* **·cies 1** Leniency; mercy. **2** An act of leniency. **3** Mildness, as of weather. [< L *clemens* mild]

clem·ent (klem′ənt) *adj.* **1** Lenient; merciful. **2** Mild: said of weather. [< L *clemens* mild, merciful] —**clem′ent·ly** *adv.*

clench (klench) *v.t.* **1** To grasp or grip firmly. **2** To close tightly or lock, as the fist or teeth. **3** To clinch, as a nail. —*n.* **1** A firm grip. **2** A device that clenches. [< OE *beclencan* hold fast]

clere·sto·ry (klir′stôr′ē, -stō′rē) *n. pl.* **·ries 1** The highest story of the nave and choir of a church, with windows opening above the aisle roofs, etc. **2** A similar story in other structures. Also **clere′sto′rey.** [< earlier *clere* clear + STORY]

cler·gy (klûr′jē) *n. pl.* **·gies** The group of people ordained for service in a Christian church. [< OF *clerc* clerk, cleric < LL *clericus*]

cler·gy·man (klûr′jē·mən) *n. pl.* **·men** (-mən) One of the clergy; an ordained minister.

cler·ic (kler′ik) *adj.* CLERICAL (def. 1). —*n.* A member of the clergy.

cler·i·cal (kler′i·kəl) *adj.* **1** Of, pertaining to, or characteristic of a clergyman or the clergy. **2** Of or pertaining to workers or clerks in an office or to their work. —*n.* **1** A clergyman. **2** *pl.* The garb of a clergyman. —**cler′i·cal·ly** *adv.*

cler·i·cal·ism (kler′i·kəl·iz′əm) *n.* The policy of favoring or increasing the power of the clergy, esp. in politics. —**cler′i·cal·ist** *adj. & n.*

clerk (klûrk, *Brit.* klärk) *n.* **1** A person employed in an office to take care of records, filing, correspondence, etc. **2** An employee of a court, legislative body, etc. who has charge of records and accounts. **3** A salesperson in a store. **4** A hotel employee who assigns guests to their rooms. —*v.i.* To work or act as clerk. [< Gk. *klērikos* < *klēros* lot, portion] —**clerk′li·ness** *n.* —**clerk′ly** *adj.*

clev·er (klev′ər) *adj.* **1** Physically skillful; dexterous; adroit. **2** Mentally quick and intelligent; bright; keen; able. **3** Marked by ingenuity and originality. [? < Scand.] —**clev′er·ly** *adv.* —**clev′er·ness** *n.* —**Syn. 1** adept, expert, handy, deft. **2** sharp, shrewd, knowing, smart, talented. **3** inventive, ingenious, felicitous.

clev·is (klev′is) *n.* A U-shaped piece of iron with holes at both ends for a bolt, used to attach things together for hauling, pulling, etc. [? < Scand.]

clew (klo͞o) *n.* **1** In legends, a thread that guides through a maze. **2** A clue. **3** *pl.* The cords by which a hammock is slung. [< OE *cliewen* to roll into a ball]

cli·ché (klē·shā′) *n.* A trite saying, idea, etc. —*adj.* Being a cliché. [< F *clicher* to stereotype]

click (klik) *n.* **1** A short, sharp, metallic sound, as that made by the latch of a door. **2** *Phonet.* A speech sound occurring in certain African languages, produced by the sudden withdrawal of the tip of the tongue from the teeth or palate. —*v.t.* **1** To cause to make a click or clicks. —*v.i.* **2** To produce a click or clicks. **3** *Slang* To succeed. **4** *Slang* To agree or be in accord. [Imit.] —**click′er** *n.*

cli·ent (klī′ənt) *n.* **1** One in whose interest a lawyer acts. **2** One who engages the services of any professional adviser. **3** A customer. [< L *cliens* follower] —**cli·en·tal** (klī·en′təl, klī′ən·təl) *adj.*

cli·en·tele (klī′ən·tel′) *n.* A body of clients; a following.

cliff (klif) *n.* A high steep face of rock; a precipice. [< OE *clif*]

cliff·hang·er (klif′hang′ər) *n.* **1** A situation marked by suspense or uncertainty of outcome. **2** A serialized drama marked by suspense at the end of each episode. Also **cliff′-hang′er.** —**cliff′hang′ing** *adj., n.*

cli·mac·ter·ic (klī·mak′tər·ik, klī′mak·ter′ik) *n.* **1** A period of life characterized by physiological changes, esp. the menopause in women. **2** Any critical period of marked changes. —*adj.* Of or pertaining to a critical period of change: also **cli·mac·ter·i·cal** (klī′mak·ter′i·kəl). [< Gk. *klimaktēr* rung of a ladder]

cli·mac·tic (klī·mak′tik) *adj.* Of or constituting a climax. Also **cli·mac′ti·cal.** —**cli·mac′ti·cal·ly** *adv.*

cli·mate (klī′mit) *n.* **1** The weather and other meteorological conditions characteristic of a locality or region over an extended period of time. **2** A region as characterized by such conditions. **3** A prevailing or dominant trend in social affairs: *climate* of opinion. [< Gk. *klima* region, zone] —**cli·mat·ic** (klī·mat′ik) or **·i·cal** *adj.* —**cli·mat′i·cal·ly** *adv.*

cli·ma·tol·o·gy (klī′mə·tol′ə·jē) *n.* The science of climate. —**cli·ma·to·log·ic** (klī′mə·tə·loj′ik) or **·i·cal** *adj.* —**cli′·ma·tol′o·gist** *n.*

cli·max (klī′maks) *n.* **1** The highest point of intensity, interest, activity, etc.; culmination. **2** ORGASM. —*v.t. & v.i.* To reach or bring to a climax. [< Gk. *klimax* ladder]

climb (klīm) *v.t.* **1** To ascend or descend (something), esp. by means of the hands and feet. —*v.i.* **2** To mount, rise, or go up, esp. by using the hands and feet. **3** To rise, as in position or status: to *climb* to the top of one's profession. **4** To incline or slope upward. **5** To rise during growth, as certain vines, by clinging to a support. —*n.* **1** The act or process of climbing. **2** A place ascended by climbing. [< OE *climban*] —**climb′a·ble** *adj.* —**climb′er** *n.*

clime (klīm) *n.* A country; region; climate. [< L *clima* climate]

clinch (klinch) *v.t.* **1** To secure firmly, as a nail or staple, by bending down the protruding point. **2** To fasten together by this means. **3** To confirm or settle, as a bargain or agreement. —*v.i.* **4** To grip or grapple, as combatants. **5** *Slang* To embrace or hug. —*n.* **1** The act of clinching. **2** That which clinches; a clamp. **3** A grip or struggle at close quarters, as in boxing. **4** *Slang* A close embrace. [Var. of CLENCH]

clinch·er (klin′chər) *n.* **1** One who or that which clinches. **2** A nail made for clinching. **3** *Informal* A decisive argument, proof, etc.

cling (kling) *v.i.* **clung, cling·ing 1** To hold on to something firmly, as by grasping, embracing, or winding round. **2** To resist separation: with *together.* **3** To stick to tenaciously, as in the memory. [< OE *clingan*] **—cling′er** *n.* **—cling′y** *adj.* **(·i·er, ·i·est)**

cling·stone (kling′stōn′) *adj.* Having a stone to which the fleshy pulp adheres, as certain kinds of peach, plum, etc. —*n.* A fruit of this kind.

clin·ic (klin′ik) *n.* **1** The teaching of medicine and surgery by treatment of patients in the presence of a class. **2** A class receiving such instruction. **3** A medical establishment, often connected with a hospital, for the treatment of nonresident patients. **4** An organization that offers advice or instruction on certain problems: a drug *clinic.* [< Gk. *klinē* bed < *klinein* recline]

clin·i·cal (klin′i·kəl) *adj.* **1** Of or pertaining to a clinic or to the treatment of patients in clinics. **2** Scientific and impersonal; detached. **—clin′i·cal·ly** *adv.*

cli·ni·cian (kli·nish′ən) *n.* One who practices or is qualified to practice clinical medicine, psychiatry, or psychology.

clink[1] (klingk) *v.t. & v.i.* To make or cause to make a short, slight, ringing sound. —*n.* A short, slight, ringing sound. [< MDu. *klinken*]

clink[2] (klingk) *n. Slang* A prison. [< the *Clink,* a prison in London]

clink·er (kling′kər) *n.* **1** The stonelike residue left by coal in burning. **2** *Slang* **a** A mistake. **b** A failure. —*v.t. & v.i.* To form or cause to form a clinker. [< Du. *klinckaerd,* kind of brick]

cli·nom·e·ter (klī·nom′ə·tər, kli-) *n.* An instrument for determining angular inclination, as of guns, slopes, etc. [< Gk. *klinein* to bend + -METER]

Cli·o (klī′ō) *Gk. Myth.* The Muse of history.

clip[1] (klip) *n.* Any device that clasps, grips, or holds fast. —*v.t.* **clipped, clip·ping** To grip, fasten, or hold tightly. [< OE *clyppan* to clasp]

clip[2] (klip) *v.t.* **clipped, clip·ping 1** To cut or trim with shears or scissors, as hair. **2** To cut short; curtail: to *clip* the ends of words. **3** *Informal* To strike with a sharp blow. **4** *Slang* To cheat or defraud. —*v.i.* **5** To cut or trim. **6** *Informal* To run or move swiftly. —*n.* **1** The act of clipping, or that which is clipped. **2** The wool yielded at one shearing or season. **3** *Informal* A blow with the hand or fist. **4** *Informal* A quick pace. [< ON *klippa*]

clipped form A shortened form of a polysyllabic word, as *bus* for *omnibus.*

clip·per (klip′ər) *n.* **1** One who clips. **2** *Usu. pl.* An instrument for cutting or clipping hair, fleece, etc. **3** *Naut.* A 19th-century sailing vessel built for speed, with tall, raking masts: also **clipper ship.**

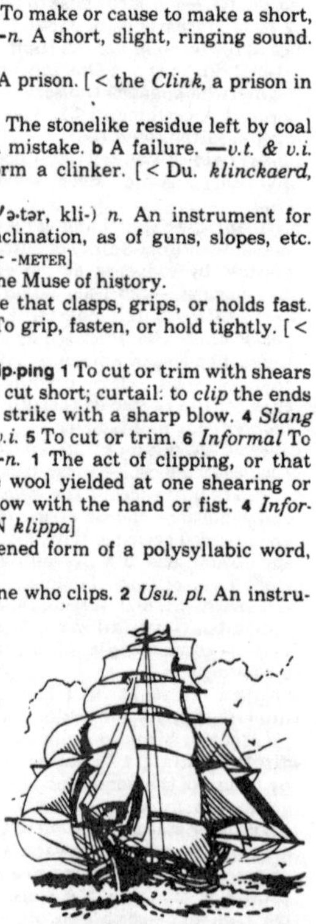

Clipper ship

clip·ping (klip′ing) *n.* **1** The act of one who or that which clips. **2** That which is cut off or cut by clipping: a newspaper *clipping.* —*adj.* That cuts or clips.

clique (klēk, klik) *n.* An exclusive or clannish group of people; coterie. —*v.i.* **cliqued, cli·quing** To unite in a clique; act clannishly. [< F *cliquer* click, clap]

cli·quish (klē′kish, klik′ish) *adj.* Inclined to form cliques; exclusive. Also **cli′quey, cli′quy. —cli′quish·ly** *adv.* **—cli′quish·ness** *n.*

cli·to·ris (klit′ə·ris, klī′tə-) *n.* A small, erectile organ at the upper part of the vulva, corresponding to the penis. [< Gk. *kleitoris*]

clk. clerk; clock.

clo·a·ca (klō·ā′kə) *n. pl.* **·cae** (-kē, -sē) **1** The common cavity into which the urinary, genital, and intestinal tracts lead in certain fishes, reptiles, birds, insects, etc. **2** A sewer or cesspool. [< L, a drain] **—clo·a′cal** *adj.*

cloak (klōk) *n.* **1** A loose outer garment. **2** Something that covers or hides; a pretext; disguise. —*v.t.* **1** To cover with a cloak. **2** To disguise; conceal. [< OF *cloque,* bell, cape]

cloak·room (klōk′rōōm′, -rōom′) *n.* A room where hats, coats, luggage, etc., are cared for temporarily.

clob·ber (klob′ər) *v.t. Slang* **1** To beat or trounce. **2** To defeat badly. [?]

cloche (klōsh) *n.* **1** A woman's closefitting, bell-shaped hat. **2** A portable translucent cover for the protection and forcing of young plants. [F, lit., bell]

clock[1] (klok) *n.* **1** An instrument for measuring and indicating time by mechanical movements; a timepiece. **2** Any clocklike recording device. **3** TIME CLOCK. —*v.t.* To time or measure by or as by means of a stopwatch. [< Med. L *cloca* bell]

clock[2] (klok) *n.* An embroidered ornament on the side of a stocking or sock. [?]

clock·wise (klok′wīz′) *adj. & adv.* In the direction traveled by the hands of a clock.

clock·work (klok′wûrk′) *n.* The machinery of a clock, or any similar mechanism.

clod (klod) *n.* **1** A lump of earth, clay, etc. **2** A dull, stupid fellow. [< OE *clott* lump, clot] **—clod′dish, clod′dy** *adj.*

clod·hop·per (klod′hop′ər) *n.* **1** *Informal* A hick; rustic. **2** *pl.* Large, heavy shoes.

clog (klog) *n.* **1** Anything that impedes motion, as a block attached to an animal or a vehicle. **2** An obstruction or hindrance. **3** A wooden-soled shoe. **4** CLOG DANCE. —*v.* **clogged, clog·ging** —*v.t.* **1** To choke up or obstruct. **2** To hinder. **3** To fasten a clog to; hobble. —*v.i.* **4** To become choked up. **5** To adhere in a mass; coagulate. **6** To perform a clog dance. [ME *clogge* block of wood] **—clog′gi·ness** *n.*

clog dance A dance performed by a person who wears clogs, using them to beat out a rhythm on the floor.

cloi·son·né (kloi′zə·nā′) *n.* **1** A method of producing designs in enamel by laying out the pattern with strips of flat wire and filling the interstices with enamel paste, which is then fused in place. **2** The ware so produced. —*adj.* Of, pertaining to, or made by this method. [< F *cloison* a partition]

clois·ter (klois′tər) *n.* **1** A covered walk along the inside walls of buildings enclosing a courtyard, as in a monastery or college. **2** A monastery or convent. **3** Monastic life. —*v.t.* **1** To seclude; confine, as in a cloister. **2** To provide with cloisters. [< L *claustrum* enclosed place] **—clois′ter·ed, clois′tral** *adj.*

clomb (klōm) Archaic *p.t. & p.p.* of CLIMB.

clone (klōn) *n.* **1** A group of organisms derived from a single individual by asexual means. **2** an exact genetic replica of an organism. Also **clon** (klōn, klon). —*v.t.* **cloned, clon·ing** To produce in the form of a clone. [< Gk. *klōn* sprout, twig] **—clon′al** *adj.* **—clon′al·ly** *adv.*

clon·ing (klōn′ing) *n.* The production of progeny that is genetically identical with a single progenitor.

clo·nus (klō′nəs) *n. Pathol.* A series of violent muscular spasms. [< Gk. *klonos* motion] **—clon·ic** (klon′ik) *adj.*

close (klōs) *adj.* **clos·er, clos·est 1** Near or near together in space, time, order, etc. **2** Compact; dense: a *close* weave. **3** Tight: a *close* fit. **4** Near to the surface; very short. **5** Affectionately associated; intimate: a *close* friend. **6** Near to the original; exact; literal: a *close* copy. **7** Thorough; strict: a *close* search. **8** Accurate. **9** Nearly even or equal in score, performance, etc.: said of contests or contestants. **10** Shut in or about. **11** Confined or encompassed by limits, walls, etc.: *close* quarters. **12** Carefully watched or guarded: *close* custody. **13** Secretive; reticent. **14** Not liberal; stingy. **15** Ill-ventilated; warm; stifling. **16** Difficult to obtain; tight: said of money, credit, etc. **17** Not open or free; restricted. **18** *Phonet.* Describing those vowels pronounced with a part of the tongue relatively near to the palate, as the (ē) in *seat.* —*v.* (klōz) **closed, clos·ing** *v.t.* **1** To shut, as a door. **2** To fill or obstruct, as an opening or passage. **3** To bring together; unite; join. **4** To bring to an end; terminate. **5** To shut in; enclose. —*v.i.* **6** To become shut or closed. **7** To come to an end. **8** To come to close quarters. **9** To join; coalesce; unite. **10** To come to an agreement. **11** To be worth at the end of a business day: Stocks *closed* three points higher. —*n.* (klōz) **1** The act of closing. **2** An end; conclusion. **3** (klōs) *Chiefly Brit.* Any place shut in or enclosed, esp. such a place adjoining a cathedral or abbey. —*adv.* (klōs) In a close manner or position. [< L *claudere* to close] —**close·ly** (klōs′lē) *adv.* —**close·ness** (klōs′nis) *n.* —**clos·er** (klō′zər) *n.*

close call (klōs) *Informal* A narrow escape. Also **close shave.**

closed circuit (klōzd) A system of transmitting a television program by cable only to those receivers connected to a special circuit. —**closed′-cir′cuit** *adj.*

closed shop An establishment in which all the employees are union members.

close·fist·ed (klōs′fis′tid) *adj.* Stingy; miserly. —**close′·fist′ed·ness** *n.*

close·fit·ting (klōs′fit′ing) *adj.* Fitting tightly.

close·hauled (klōs′hôld′) *adj. & adv. Naut.* With the sails set for sailing as close to the wind as possible.

close·mouthed (klōs′mouthd′, -moutht′) *adj.* Not given to imparting information; taciturn; uncommunicative.

clos·et (kloz′it) *n.* **1** A small room or recess for storage of clothes, linen, etc. **2** A room for privacy, esp. one used by a monarch as a council chamber. **3** WATERCLOSET. —*v.t.* **clos·et·ed, clos·et·ing** To shut up or conceal in or as in a closet: usu. used reflexively. —*adj.* **1** Private; confidential. **2** Based on theory rather than practice: *closet* strategy. [< L *clausus* closed]

close-up (klōs′up′) *n.* **1** In motion pictures and television, a picture taken at close range. **2** A personal or intimate look or view.

clo·sure (klō′zhər) *n.* **1** A closing or shutting up. **2** Something that closes or shuts. **3** A conclusion. **4** CLOTURE. —*v.t.* **clo·sured, clo·sur·ing** To cloture.

clot (klot) *n.* A thickened or coagulated mass, as of blood. —*v.t. & v.i.* **clot·ted, clot·ting** To form clots; coagulate. [< OE *clott* lump, mass] —**clot′ty, clot′ted** *adj.*

cloth (klôth, kloth) *n. pl.* **cloths** (klôthz, klothz, klôths, kloths) **1** A woven, knitted, or felted fabric of wool, cotton, rayon, etc. **2** A piece of cloth for a special use, as a tablecloth. —**the cloth** Clerical attire; also, the clergy. [< OE *clath*]

clothe (klōth) *v.t.* **clothed** or **clad, cloth·ing** **1** To cover or provide with clothes. **2** To cover as if with clothing; invest. [< OE *clathian*]

clothes (klōz, klōthz) *n. pl.* **1** Wearing apparel; garments. **2** BEDCLOTHES. [< OE *clath* cloth]

clothes·horse (klōz′hôrs′, klōthz′-) *n.* **1** A frame on which to hang or dry clothes. **2** *Slang* A person excessively concerned with dress.

clothes·line (klōz′līn′, klōthz′-) *n.* A cord, rope, or wire on which to hang clothes to dry.

clothes·pin (klōz′pin′, klōthz′-) *n.* A peg or clamp with which to fasten clothes on a line.

clothes·press (klōz′pres′, klōthz′-) *n.* A closet for clothes; wardrobe.

clothes tree An upright pole having arms or hooks on which to hang hats, coats, etc.

cloth·ier (klōth′yər) *n.* One who makes or sells cloths or clothing.

cloth·ing (klō′thing) *n.* **1** Dress collectively; apparel. **2** A covering.

clo·ture (klō′chər) *n.* A procedure to stop debate in a legislative body in order to secure a vote. —*v.t.* **·tured, ·tur·ing** To apply cloture to (a debate). [< OF *closure* closure]

cloud (kloud) *n.* **1** A mass of visible vapor or an aggregation of watery or icy particles floating in the atmosphere. **2** Any cloudlike mass, as of birds, dust, steam, etc. **3** Something that darkens, obscures, or threatens. **4** A milkiness or murkiness, as in a liquid. —**under a cloud** **1** Under suspicion. **2** Unhappy; depressed. —*v.t.* **1** To cover with or as with clouds; dim; obscure. **2** To render gloomy or troubled. **3** To bring disgrace on. —*v.i.* **4** To become overcast with clouds. **5** To be or appear sad or troubled. [< OE *clūd* rocky mass, hill] —**cloud′less** *adj.*

cloud·burst (kloud′bûrst′) *n.* A sudden, heavy rainfall.

cloud chamber A chamber containing a supersaturated vapor from which droplets condense along the tracks of charged atomic particles.

cloud·y (klou′dē) *adj.* **cloud·i·er, cloud·i·est** **1** Overspread with clouds. **2** Of or like a cloud or clouds. **3** Obscure; vague; confused. **4** Gloomy; troubled. **5** Not limpid or clear. **6** Marked with cloudlike spots. —**cloud′i·ly** *adv.* —**cloud′i·ness** *n.*

clout (klout) *n.* **1** *Informal* A heavy blow or cuff with the hand. **2** *Informal* In baseball, a long hit. **3** *Slang* Influence or power; pull. —*v.t. Informal* **1** To hit or strike; cuff. **2** To hit (a ball) hard. [< OE *clūt*]

clove[1] (klōv) *n.* A dried flower bud of a tropical evergreen tree, used as a spice. [< OF *clou (de girofle)* nail (of clove)]

clove[2] (klōv) *n.* A small, individual section of a bulb, as of garlic. [< OE *clufu*]

clo·ven (klō′vən) A *p.p.* of CLEAVE[1]. —*adj.* Parted; split.

cloven hoof **1** A divided hoof, as in cattle. **2** A symbol for Satan. Also **cloven foot.** —**clo′ven-hoofed′, clo′ven-foot′ed** (-fo͝ot′id) *adj.*

clo·ver (klō′vər) *n.* Any of several leguminous plants having dense flower heads and leaves divided into three leaflets; esp. the **red clover** used for forage. [< OE *clǣfre*]

clo·ver·leaf (klō′vər·lēf′) *n.* A highway intersection with curving ramps in the form of a four-leaf clover, designed to route traffic in four directions without interference.

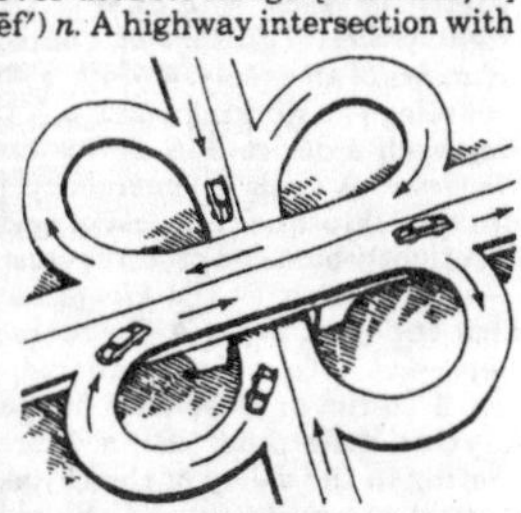

Cloverleaf

clown (kloun) *n.* **1** A professional buffoon in a play or circus who entertains by antics, jokes, tricks, etc. **2** A person who behaves like a clown. —*v.i.* To behave like a clown. [? < Scand.] —**clown′·er·y, clown′ish·ness** *n.* —**clown′ish** *adj.* —**clown′ish·ly** *adv.*

cloy (kloi) *v.t.* **1** To satiate with too much of something; surfeit. —*v.i.* **2** To cause satiation. [Var. of earlier *accloy* < OF *encloyer* nail up, block, overload] —**cloy′ing·ly** *adv.* —**cloy′ing·ness** *n.*

C.L.U. Chartered Life Underwriter.

club[1] (klub) *n.* **1** A stout stick or staff; cudgel. **2** In certain sports, a stick used to hit a ball, esp. a golf club. **3 a** A three-lobed spot used to identify one of the four suits in a deck of playing cards. **b** A card so marked. **c** *pl.* The suit so identified. —*v.* **clubbed, club·bing** *v.t.* To beat, as with a club. [< ON *klubba*]

club[2] (klub) *n.* **1** A group of persons organized for a particular purpose or activity. **2** A house or room reserved for the use of such a group. —*v.* **clubbed, club·bing** *v.t.* **1** To contribute for a common purpose. —*v.i.* **2** To unite for a particular purpose or activity: often with *together.* —*adj.* Of, pertaining to, or belonging to a club. [Special meaning of CLUB[1]]

club·by (klub′ē) *adj.* **·bi·er, ·bi·est** *Informal* Characteristic of a social club; friendly, congenial, or exclusive. —**club′bi·ness** *n.*

club car A railroad passenger car furnished with easy chairs, tables, a bar, etc.

club·foot (klub′fo͝ot′) *n. pl.* **·feet** **1** Congenital distortion of the foot; talipes. **2** A foot so affected. —**club′foot′ed** *adj.*

club·house (klub′hous′) *n.* **1** The building occupied by a club. **2** A dressing room or rooms for athletes.

club sandwich A sandwich containing three or more

slices of bread or toast filled with meat, lettuce, tomatoes, mayonnaise, etc.

club steak A small beefsteak cut from the loin.

cluck (kluk) *v.i.* 1 To make the noise of a hen calling her chicks. 2 To make any sound similar to a cluck. —*v.t.* 3 To call by clucking. 4 To express by clucking: to *cluck* disapproval. —*n.* The sound of clucking. [Imit.]

clue (klōō) *n.* A fact, object, idea, etc., that leads to the solution of a problem or mystery. —*v.t.* **clued, clu·ing** *Informal* To give a clue or information to: often with *in.* [Var. of CLEW]

clump (klump) *n.* 1 A thick cluster. 2 A heavy sound, as of tramping. 3 A lump or mass. —*v.t.* 1 To place or plant in a cluster or group. —*v.i.* 2 To walk clumsily and noisily. 3 To form clumps. [< LG] **—clump'y (·i·er, ·i·est), clump'ish** *adj.*

clum·sy (klum'zē) *adj.* **·si·er, ·si·est** 1 Lacking physical dexterity, ease, or grace; awkward. 2 Badly constructed; unwieldy. 3 Awkwardly worded, delivered, etc.; inept. [< ME *clumsen* be numb (with cold) < Scand.] **—clum'si·ly** *adv.* **—clum'si·ness** *n.* **—Syn.** 1 ungainly, unhandy, maladroit. 2 heavy, cumbersome, ungainly. 3 bungling, heavy-handed, gauche.

clung (klung) *p.t. & p.p. of* CLING.

clus·ter (klus'tər) *n.* 1 A group or bunch of objects or things joined together. 2 A group or assembly of persons or things close together. —*v.t. & v.i.* To be, form, or grow in a cluster or clusters. [< OE *clyster*] **—clus'tered** *adj.*

clutch[1] (kluch) *v.t.* 1 To snatch, as with hands or talons. 2 To grasp and hold firmly. —*v.i.* 3 To attempt to seize, snatch, or reach: with *at.* —*n.* 1 The act of clutching. 2 A tight, powerful grasp. 3 *pl.* Control; power: to fall into the *clutches* of an enemy. 4 *Mech.* **a** Any of various devices for coupling two working parts. **b** A pedal or lever for operating such a device. 5 A device for seizing and holding. 6 *Informal* A crisis or emergency. [< OE *clyccan* to grasp]

clutch[2] (kluch) *n.* 1 A nest of eggs. 2 A brood of chickens. 3 A tightly bunched group or cluster: a *clutch* of reporters. —*v.t.* To hatch. [< ON *klekja* hatch]

clut·ter (klut'ər) *n.* A disordered state or collection; litter. —*v.t.* 1 To make disordered; litter: often with *up.* —*v.i.* 2 To run or move with bustle. [ME *clotteren* to clot]

Clydes·dale (klīdz'dāl) *n.* A breed of draft horses originating in the valley of the Clyde, Scotland.

clyp·e·ate (klip'ē·āt) *adj.* Shield-shaped. Also **clyp'e·at'·ed.** [< L *clypeus* a shield]

clys·ter (klis'tər) *n. Med.* ENEMA. [< Gk. *klystēr* < *klyzein* wash out, rinse]

Cly·tem·nes·tra (klī'təm·nes'trə) *Gk. Myth.* The wife of Agamemnon who killed her husband and was herself killed by her son Orestes.

Cm. curium.

cm, cm. centimeter(s).

Cmdr. Commander.

cml. commercial.

CNO Chief of Naval Operations.

co- *prefix* 1 With; together; joint or jointly: *coexistence; coauthor.* 2 Of, pertaining to, or being the complement of an angle: *cosine.* [< L *cum* with]

CO Colorado (P.O. abbr.).

C.O. commanding officer; conscientious objector.

C/O, c/o, c.o. care of; carried over; cash order.

Co cobalt.

Co., co. (*pl.* **Cos., cos.**) company; county.

coach (kōch) *n.* 1 A large four-wheeled closed carriage; stagecoach. 2 A passenger bus. 3 The lowest-priced accommodations on a passenger train or airplane. 4 A trainer or director, as of athletes, singers, actors, etc. 5 A private tutor. —*v.t.* 1 To train or direct (athletes, singers, etc.). —*v.i.* 2 To study with or be trained by a coach. 3 To act as coach. [< *Kocs,* a Hungarian village where first used] **—coach'er** *n.*

coach-and-four (kōch'ən·fôr', -fōr') *n.* A coach drawn by four horses.

coach dog DALMATIAN.

coach·man (kōch'mən) *n. pl.* **·men** (-mən) One who drives a coach or a carriage.

co·ad·ju·tant (kō·aj'ə·tənt) *adj.* Cooperating. —*n.* An assistant. [< co- + L *adjutare* to help]

co·ad·ju·tor (kō·aj'ə·tər, kō'ə·jōō'tər) *n.* 1 An assistant. 2 A bishop's assistant, usu. another bishop.

co·ag·u·late (kō·ag'yə·lāt) *v.t. & v.i.* **·lat·ed, ·lat·ing** To change from a liquid state into a clot or jelly, as blood. [< L *coagulare* curdle] **—co·ag'u·la'tion, co·ag'u·la'tor** *n.* **—co·ag'u·la·ble, co·ag'u·la'tive** *adj.*

coal (kōl) *n.* 1 A black, brittle, amorphous mineral, resulting from the carbonization of prehistoric vegetation, used as fuel. 2 A piece of coal. 3 A glowing piece of wood, charcoal, or similar substance. —*v.t.* 1 To supply with coal. —*v.i.* 2 To take in coal. [< OE *col*]

co·a·lesce (kō'ə·les') *v.i.* **·lesced, ·lesc·ing** To grow or come together into one; fuse; blend. [< L *coalescere* unite] **—co'a·les'cence** *n.* **—co'a·les'cent** *adj.*

coal gas 1 The poisonous fumes produced by incomplete combustion of coal. 2 A fuel gas made by the distillation of bituminous coal.

co·a·li·tion (kō'ə·lish'ən) *n.* 1 An alliance, often temporary, of persons, parties, or states, usu. for a specific purpose. 2 A fusion or union. [< L *coalitio* < *coalescere* to coalesce] **—co'a·li'tion·ist** *n.*

coal oil 1 KEROSENE. 2 Crude petroleum.

coal tar A black viscid pitch obtained by heating bituminous coal in the absence of air and yielding a variety of compounds used in making dyestuffs, explosives, drugs, plastics, etc. **—coal'-tar'** *adj.*

coarse (kôrs, kōrs) *adj.* **coars·er, coars·est** 1 Composed of somewhat large or rough parts or particles. 2 Not fine or delicate in form, texture, etc. 3 Vulgar; indelicate; crude. [Adjectival use of COURSE, *n.,* def. 2] **—coarse'ly** *adv.* **—coarse'ness** *n.*

coarse-grained (kôrs'grānd', kōrs'-) *adj.* 1 Having a coarse texture. 2 Crude; indelicate.

coars·en (kôr'sən, kōr'-) *v.t. & v.i.* To make or become coarse.

coast (kōst) *n.* 1 The land next to the sea; the seashore. 2 A slope suitable for sliding, as on a sled; also, a slide down it. **—the Coast** That part of the United States bordering on the Pacific Ocean. —*v.t.* 1 To sail or travel along, as a coast or border. —*v.i.* 2 To slide or ride down a slope by force of gravity alone, as on a sled. 3 To continue moving on momentum after the source of power has been stopped. 4 To move or behave aimlessly. [< L *costa* rib, flank] **—coast'al** *adj.*

coast·er (kōs'tər) *n.* 1 One who or that which coasts. 2 A sled or toboggan. 3 A small disk on which to set a drinking glass.

coaster brake A clutch brake on a bicycle, operated by reversing the pressure on the pedals.

coast guard Any force used to guard or police the coasts of a country.

coast·line (kōst'līn') *n.* The boundary or shape of a coast.

coast·ward (kōst'wərd) *adj.* Directed or facing toward the coast. —*adv.* Toward the coast: also **coast'wards.**

coast·wise (kōst'wīz') *adj.* Along the coast. —*adv.* Along the coast: also **coast'ways'.**

coat (kōt) *n.* 1 A sleeved outer garment opening down the front, as an overcoat, suit jacket, etc. 2 Any outer covering, as the fur of an animal. 3 An outer layer, as of paint, ice, etc. —*v.t.* To cover with or as with a coat, as of paint. [< OF *cote*] **—coat'ed** *adj.*

coat·dress (kōt'dres') *n.* A dress buttoned along the full length of the front like a coat.

coat hanger A device of wood, plastic, etc., shaped to fit inside the shoulders of a coat or other garment, for hanging clothes when not in use.

co·a·ti (kō·ä'tē) *n. pl.* **·tis** A small, tree-dwelling, carnivorous, raccoonlike mammal of tropical America. Also **co·a'ti-mon'di, co·a'ti-mun'di** (-mun'dē). [< Tupi]

coat·ing (kō'ting) *n.* 1 A covering layer; coat. 2 Cloth for coats.

coat of arms The special armorial emblems and symbols of a person or family, as on a shield. • See CREST.

coat of mail *pl.* **coats of mail** A protective outer garment made of interlinked metal rings or scales; a hauberk.

coat·tail (kōt'tāl') *n.* 1 The back part of a coat below the waist. 2 *Usu. pl.* The divided, tapering, rear part of a man's formal or dress coat.

co·au·thor (kō·ô′thər) *n.* One who collaborates with another or others in writing a book, article, etc. —*v.t. Informal* To be a coauthor of.

coax (kōks) *v.t.* **1** To persuade or seek to persuade by gentleness, flattery, etc.; wheedle. **2** To obtain by coaxing. —*v.i.* **3** To use persuasion or cajolery. —*n.* One who coaxes. —**coax′er** *n.* [< earlier *cokes* a fool]

co·ax·i·al (kō·ak′sē·əl) *adj.* Having a common axis or coincident axes: also **co·ax·al** (kō·ak′səl).

coaxial cable An electric cable consisting of two insulated conductors, one of which surrounds the other.

cob (kob) *n.* **1** CORNCOB. **2** A male swan. **3** A thickset, short-legged horse. **4** A lump. [ME *cobbe*]

co·balt (kō′bôlt) *n.* A hard, gray, metallic element (symbol Co) related to iron and nickel, used in alloys and pigments. [< G *kobalt,* var. of *kobold* goblin]

cobalt blue **1** A deep blue pigment made from the oxides of cobalt and aluminum. **2** Dark blue.

cobalt 60 A radioactive isotope of cobalt emitting gamma rays, used chiefly in radiotherapy.

cob·ble[1] (kob′əl) *n.* COBBLESTONE. —*v.t.* **·bled, ·bling** To pave with cobblestones. [< ME *cobbe* lump, cob]

cob·ble[2] (kob′əl) *v.t.* **·bled, ·bling** **1** To make or repair, as boots or shoes. **2** To put together roughly. [?]

cob·bler[1] (kob′lər) *n.* **1** A shoemaker. **2** A clumsy workman. [< COBBLE[2]]

cob·bler[2] (kob′lər) *n.* **1** An iced drink made of wine, sugar, fruit juices, etc. **2** A deep-dish fruit pie with no bottom crust. [?]

cob·ble·stone (kob′əl·stōn′) *n.* A rounded stone formerly used for paving. [See COBBLE[1]]

cob coal Large round pieces of coal.

co·bel·lig·er·ent (kō′bə·lij′ər·ənt) *n.* A country fighting on the side of another or others but not bound by alliance.

co·bra (kō′brə) *n.* Any of various poisonous snakes of Asia and Africa that when excited dilate the loose skin at their necks into a hood. [< L *colubra* snake]

Cobra

cob·web (kob′web′) *n.* **1** The network of fine thread spun by a spider; also, a single thread of this. **2** Anything finespun or ensnaring. —*v.t.* **cob·webbed, cob·web·bing** To cover with or as with cobwebs. [< ME *coppe* spider + WEB] —**cob′web′by** *adj.*

co·ca (kō′kə) *n.* **1** The dried leaves of a South American shrub yielding cocaine and other alkaloids. **2** The shrub itself. [< Quechua]

co·caine (kō·kān′, kō′kān) *n.* A white, bitter, crystalline alkaloid, obtained from coca and used as a local anesthetic and as a narcotic. Also **co·cain′**. [< COCA]

-coccal *combining form* Of or produced by (a specified form of) coccus. Also **-coccic**.

coc·cus (kok′əs) *n. pl.* **coc·ci** (kok′sī) Any bacterium having an ovoid or spherical shape. [< Gk. *kokkos* berry] —**coc·coid** (kok′oid) *adj.*

-coccus *combining form* Ovoid or spherical in shape: used to indicate bacteria so shaped: *streptococcus.*

coc·cyx (kok′siks) *n. pl.* **coc·cy·ges** (kok·sī′jēz) The small, triangular bone at the caudal end of the spine. [< Gk. *kokkyx* cuckoo; from a fancied resemblance to a cuckoo's bill] —**coc·cyg·e·al** (kok·sij′ē·əl) *adj.* • See PELVIS.

coch·i·neal (koch′ə·nēl′, kōch′ə·nēl) *n.* A brilliant scarlet dye made from the dried bodies of the female of a scale insect. [< L *coccineus* scarlet < *coccus* a berry, grain of kermes]

coch·le·a (kok′lē·ə) *n. pl.* **·le·ae** (-li·ē) *Anat.* A spiral passage in the internal ear, containing the auditory nerve endings. [< L, snail] —**coch′le·ar** *adj.* • See EAR.

coch·le·ate (kok′lē·āt) *adj.* Spirally twisted like a snail shell. Also **coch′le·at′ed**.

cock[1] (kok) *n.* **1** A full-grown male of the domestic fowl. **2** Any male bird. **3** A leader; champion. **4** WEATHERCOCK. **5** A faucet, often with the nozzle bent downward. **6** In a firearm, the hammer; also, its position when ready to fire. **7** A jaunty, upward turn or position, as of a hat brim, the ears, eyes, etc. —*v.t.* **1** To raise the cock or hammer of (a firearm) preparatory to firing. **2** To turn up or to one side alertly, jauntily, or inquiringly, as the head, eye, ears, etc. —*v.i.* **3** To raise the hammer of a firearm. **4** To stick up; be prominent. —*adj.* Male. [< OE *cocc*]

cock[2] (kok) *n.* A small conical pile of straw or hay. —*v.t.* To arrange in cocks, as hay. [< OE *cocc*]

cock·ade (kok·ād′) *n.* A knot of ribbon, or the like, worn on the hat as a badge. [< MF *coq* cock] —**cock·ad′ed** *adj.*

cock·a·too (kok′ə·tōō′, kok′ə·tōō) *n. pl.* **·toos** Any of various bright-colored, crested parrots of the East Indies or Australia. [< Malay *kākatūa*]

Cockatoo

cock·a·trice (kok′ə·tris) *n.* A legendary serpent, said to be hatched from a cock's egg, deadly to those who felt its breath or met its glance. [< Med. L *calcatrix*]

cock·boat (kok′bōt′) *n.* A small boat, esp. a ship's tender. [< OF *coque* cockboat + BOAT]

cock·chaf·er (kok′chā′fər) *n.* A large, European beetle destructive to vegetation. [< COCK[1] + CHAFER]

cock·crow (kok′krō′) *n.* The early morning. Also **cock′crow′ing.**

cocked hat (kokt) A three-cornered hat with the brim turned up.

cock·er·el (kok′ər·əl) *n.* A rooster less than a year old. [Dim. of COCK[1]]

cock·er spaniel (kok′ər) A small, sturdy spaniel having long, silky hair of solid or various coloring and drooping ears.

cock·eye (kok′ī′) *n.* A squinting eye.

cock·eyed (kok′īd′) *adj.* **1** Cross-eyed. **2** *Slang* Off center; askew. **3** *Slang* Absurd; preposterous. **4** *Slang* Drunk.

cock·fight (kok′fīt′) *n.* A battle between gamecocks, usu. equipped with metal spurs on their legs. —**cock′·fight′ing** *adj. & n.*

cock·horse (kok′hôrs′) *n.* A child's rockinghorse or hobbyhorse.

cock·le[1] (kok′əl) *n.* **1** An edible European bivalve mollusk. **2** COCKLESHELL. **3** A wrinkle; pucker. —*v.t. & v.i.* **cock·led, cock·ling** To wrinkle; pucker. [< L *conchylium* shell]

cock·le[2] (kok′əl) *n.* Any of various weeds that grow among grain. [< OE *coccel*]

cock·le·boat (kok′əl·bōt′) *n.* COCKBOAT.

cock·le·bur (kok′əl·bûr′) *n.* A low-branching weed with burs about an inch long.

cock·le·shell (kok′əl·shel′) *n.* **1** The shell of a cockle. **2** A scallop shell. **3** A small, light boat.

cock·ney (kok′nē) *n. pl.* **·neys** **1** One born in the East End of London and speaking a characteristic dialect. **2** The characteristic dialect or accent of East End Londoners: also **cock′ney·ese′** (-ēz′, -ēs′). —*adj.* Of or like cockneys or their speech. [ME *cokeney,* lit., cock's egg, later, a soft or effeminate person, a city man] —**cock′ney·ish** *adj.*

cock·pit (kok′pit′) *n.* **1** A space in small airplanes for the pilot and a passenger or, in large airplanes, for the pilot and his crew. **2** A pit or ring for cockfighting. **3** In small ships or yachts, a space near the stern lower than the rest of the deck.

cock·roach (kok′rōch′) *n.* Any of a large group of swift-running, chiefly nocturnal insects having long feelers and flat, oval bodies, several species of which are household pests. [< Sp. *cucaracha*]

cocks·comb (koks′kōm′) *n.* **1** The comb of a rooster. **2** A plant with red or yellowish flowers. **3** COXCOMB.

cock·sure (kok′shŏŏr′) *adj.* **1** Absolutely sure. **2** Presumptuously self-confident or sure. —**cock′sure′ness** *n.*

cock·swain (kok′sən, -swān′) *n.* COXSWAIN.

cock·tail (kok′tāl′) *n.* **1** Any of various mixed alcoholic drinks. **2** Any of various appetizers, as diced fruits, fruit juices, sea food, etc. [?]

cock·y (kok′ē) *adj.* **cock·i·er, cock·i·est** *Informal* Jaunty and confident, esp. in a swaggering or conceited way. —**cock′i·ly** *adv.* —**cock′i·ness** *n.*

co·co (kō′kō) *n. pl.* **·cos** 1 The coconut palm tree. 2 Its fruit. [< Pg., coconut shell]

co·coa (kō′kō) *n.* 1 A powder made from the roasted, husked seed kernels of the cacao. 2 A beverage made from it. 3 A reddish brown color. [Alter. of CACAO]

co·co·nut (kō′kə·nut′, -nət) *n.* The fruit of the coconut palm, containing white meat enclosed in a hard shell, and a milky liquid. Also **co′coa·nut′**.

coconut oil Oil obtained from coconut meat, used in soaps, etc.

coconut palm A tropical palm tree that produces coconuts. Also **coco palm.**

co·coon (kə·ko͞on′) *n.* The envelope spun by the larvae of certain insects in which they are enclosed during the pupa stage. [< F *coque* shell]

cod (kod) *n. pl.* **cod** or **cods** An important food fish of the North Atlantic. [ME]

C.O.D., c.o.d. cash on delivery; collect on delivery.

co·da (kō′də) *n.* A musical passage used to conclude a movement. [< L *cauda* tail]

cod·dle (kod′l) *v.t.* **·dled, ·dling** 1 To cook gently in water. 2 To pamper, as a baby or an invalid. [? < CAUDLE] —**cod′dler** *n.*

code (kōd) *n.* 1 A systematized body of law. 2 Any system of rules or regulations. 3 A system of signals, characters, or symbols used in communication. 4 A set of prearranged symbols used for purposes of secrecy or brevity in transmitting messages. —*v.t.* **cod·ed, cod·ing** 1 To systematize as laws; make a digest of. 2 To put into the symbols of a code. [< L *codex* writing tablet]

co·deine (kō′dēn, kō′dē·in) *n.* An alkaloid derived from opium: used as an analgesic and in cough medicines. Also **co·de·in.** [< Gk. *kōdeia* head of a poppy]

co·dex (kō′deks) *n. pl.* **co·di·ces** (kō′də·sēz, kod′ə-) An ancient or medieval manuscript, as of the Scriptures or classics. [< L, writing tablet]

cod·fish (kod′fish′) *n.* COD.

codg·er (koj′ər) *n. Informal* A testy or eccentric old man. [Prob. var. of *cadger* < CADGE.]

cod·i·cil (kod′ə·səl) *n.* 1 A supplement to a will. 2 Any supplement or appendix. [< L *codex* writing tablet] —**cod·i·cil·la·ry** (kod′ə·sil′ə·rē) *adj.*

cod·i·fy (kod′ə·fī, kō′də-) *v.t.* **·fied, ·fy·ing** To systematize, as laws. —**cod′i·fi·ca′tion, cod′i·fi′er** *n.*

cod·ling[1] (kod′ling) *n.* 1 A young cod. 2 HAKE.

cod·ling[2] (kod′ling) *n.* 1 One of a variety of cooking apples, elongated and tapering. 2 A green or defective apple. Also **cod·lin** (kod′lin). [ME *querdling*]

codling moth A moth whose larvae bore into and feed on apples, pears, walnuts, etc. Also **codlin moth.**

cod-liv·er oil (kod′liv′ər) Oil from the livers of cod, esp. rich in vitamins A and D.

co·ed (kō′ed′) *Informal n.* A young woman being educated at a coeducational institution. —*adj.* Of, pertaining to, or devoted to coeducation. Also **co′-ed′.**

co·ed·u·ca·tion (kō′ej·o͝o·kā′shən) *n.* The education of both sexes in the same classes or institution. —**co′ed·u·ca′tion·al** *adj.*

coef., coeff. coefficient.

co·ef·fi·cient (kō′ə·fish′ənt) *n.* 1 *Math.* A number or symbol by which an algebraic expression is multiplied. 2 *Physics* A number indicating the degree of magnitude, or the kind and amount of change under given conditions.

coe·la·canth (sē′lə·kanth) *n.* Any of an order of primitive fossil fishes of which a few living specimens have been found. [< Gk. *koilos* hollow + *akantha* spine]

Coelacanth

coe·li·ac (sē′lē·ak) CELIAC.

coe·lom (sē′ləm) *n.* The body cavity occupied by the viscera. Also **coe·lome** (sē′lōm). [< Gk. *koilos* hollow]

coe·no·bite (sen′ə·bīt, sē′nə-) *n.* CENOBITE.

co·e·qual (kō·ē′kwəl) *adj.* Of the same value, age, size, importance, etc. —*n.* The equal of another or others.

co·erce (kō·ûrs′) *v.t.* **co·erced, co·erc·ing** 1 To constrain or force to do something. 2 To bring under control by force; repress. 3 To bring about by coercion: to *coerce* obedience. [< L *co-* together + *arcere* shut up, restrain] —**co·er′cer** *n.* —**co·er′ci·ble** *adj.*

co·er·cion (kō·ûr′shən) *n.* 1 Forcible constraint or restraint, moral or physical. 2 Government by force.

co·er·cive (kō·ûr′siv) *adj.* Serving or tending to coerce. —**co·er′cive·ly** *adv.* —**co·er′cive·ness** *n.*

co·e·val (kō·ē′vəl) *adj.* Of or belonging to the same age, time, or duration. —*n.* A contemporary. [< L *co-* together + *aevus* age] —**co·e′val·ly** *adv.*

co·ex·ist (kō′ig·zist′) *v.i.* To exist together, in the same place or at the same time. —**co′ex·ist′ence** *n.* —**co′ex·ist′·ent** *adj.*

C. of C. Chamber of Commerce.

cof·fee (kôf′ē, kof′ē) *n.* 1 The seeds (**coffee beans**) of a tropical evergreen shrub. 2 The shrub itself. 3 A beverage made from the roasted and ground seeds of this shrub. 4 The color of coffee containing cream. [< Turkish *qahveh* < Ar. *qahwah*]

coffee break A recess from work for the purpose of taking coffee or other refreshments.

coffee cake Any of several kinds of cake, usu. containing nuts, raisins, etc., and meant to be eaten with coffee.

coffee house A café where coffee and other refreshments are served.

coffee mill A hand mill for grinding roasted coffee beans. Also **coffee grinder.**

coffee pot A covered vessel in which coffee is prepared or served.

coffee shop A small restaurant, often in a hotel, where coffee and food are served. Also **coffee room.**

coffee table A low table, usu. placed in front of a sofa, for serving refreshments, etc.

cof·fer (kôf′ər, kof′-) *n.* 1 A chest or strongbox for valuables. 2 *pl.* Financial resources; funds. 3 A decorative, sunken panel in a dome or vault. 4 COFFERDAM. —*v.t.* 1 To place in a coffer. 2 To adorn with coffers, as a ceiling. [< L *cophinus*]

cof·fer·dam (kôf′ər·dam′, kof′-) *n.* A temporary enclosing dam or structure placed or built in the water and pumped dry, to protect workmen.

cof·fin (kôf′in, kof′-) *n.* The case or chest in which a corpse is buried. —*v.t.* To put into or as into a coffin. [< Gk. *kophinos* basket]

C. of S. Chief of Staff.

cog (kog) *n.* 1 A tooth or one of a series of teeth projecting from the surface of a wheel or gear to impart or receive motion. 2 COGWHEEL. 3 A person regarded as making a minor contribution to a large organization or process. [< Scand.]

co·gent (kō′jənt) *adj.* Compelling belief, assent, or action; forcible; convincing. [< L *cogere* compel] —**Syn.** forceful, persuasive, weighty, compelling, trenchant.

cog·i·tate (koj′ə·tāt) *v.t.* & *v.i.* **·tat·ed, ·tat·ing** To think carefully (about); ponder. [< L *co-* together + *agitare* consider] —**cog·i·ta·ble** (koj′ə·tə·bəl) *adj.* —**cog′i·ta′tor** *n.*

cog·i·ta·tion (koj′ə·tā′shən) *n.* Consideration; reflection; thought. —**cog′i·ta′tive** *adj.* —**cog′i·ta′tive·ly** *adv.* —**cog′i·ta′tive·ness** *n.*

co·gnac (kōn′yak, kon′-) *n.* 1 Brandy produced in the area of Cognac, France. 2 Any brandy.

cog·nate (kog′nāt) *adj.* 1 Allied by blood; kindred. 2 Belonging to the same stock or root: English *cold* and Latin *gelidus* are *cognate* words. 3 Having the same nature or quality. —*n.* A cognate person or thing. [< L *co-* together + *(g)natus*, pp. of *(g)nasci* be born] —**cog·na′tion** *n.*

cog·ni·tion (kog·nish′ən) *n.* 1 The act or faculty of apprehending, knowing, or perceiving. 2 Something known or perceived; a perception. [< L *co-* together + *(g)noscere* know] —**cog·ni′tion·al, cog·ni·tive** (kog′nə·tiv) *adj.*

cog·ni·zance (kog′nə·zəns) *n.* 1 Knowledge; perception; awareness. 2 *Law* a The hearing of a case in court. b Jurisdiction. [< L *cognoscere* to know]

cog·ni·zant (kog′nə·zənt) *adj.* Having knowledge; aware: with *of.*

cog·no·men (kog·nō′mən, kog′nə-) *n. pl.* **·no·mens** or **·nom·i·na** (-nom′ə·nə) **1** One's family name; surname. **2** Any name or nickname. [< L *co-* together + *(g)nomen* name] **—cog·nom·i·nal** (kog·nom′ə·nəl) *adj.*

cog·wheel (kog′hwēl′) *n.* A wheel with cogs.

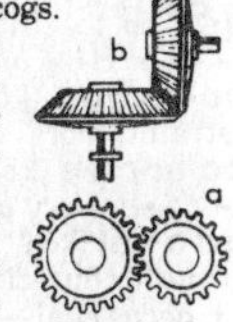

Cogwheels a. spur gears. b. bevel gears.

co·hab·it (kō·hab′it) *v.i.* To live together as husband and wife, esp. without legal marriage. [< L *co-* together + *habitare* live] **—co·hab′i·tant, co·hab′it·er, co·hab′i·ta′tion** *n.*

co·here (kō·hir′) *v.i.* **co·hered, co·her·ing 1** To stick or hold firmly together. **2** To be logically consistent or connected, as a piece of writing. [< L *co-* together + *haerere* stick]

co·her·ence (kō·hir′əns) *n.* **1** A sticking together; union; cohesion. **2** The quality of being consistent and intelligible, as in logic, thought, etc. **3** *Physics* That relation between two sets of waves, as light or sound waves, in which the phase of either can be determined from the other. Also **co·her′en·cy.**

co·her·ent (kō·hir′ənt) *adj.* **1** Cleaving or sticking together. **2** Logical, intelligible, or articulate, as in thought, speech, etc. **3** *Physics* Exhibiting coherence. **—co·her′ent·ly** *adv.*

co·he·sion (kō·hē′zhən) *n.* **1** The act or state of cohering. **2** *Physics* That force by which molecules of the same kind or of the same body are held together so that the substance or body resists separation.

co·he·sive (kō·hē′siv) *adj.* Having or causing cohesion. **—co·he′sive·ly** *adv.* **—co·he′sive·ness** *n.*

co·hort (kō′hôrt) *n.* **1** The tenth of an ancient Roman military legion, 300 to 600 men. **2** A band of soldiers. **3** A companion, colleague, or follower. [< L *cohors*]

coif (koif) *n.* **1** A close-fitting cap, hood, or headdress: a nun's *coif.* **2** (kwäf) A hair style. *—v.t.* **1** To cover with or as with a coif. **2** (kwäf) To style (hair). [< LL *cofia*]

coif·feur (kwȧ·fœr′) *n.* A male hairdresser. [F] **—coif·feuse** (kwȧ·fœz′) *n. Fem.*

coif·fure (kwä·fyŏŏr′, *Fr.* kwȧ·für′) *n.* **1** A style of arranging the hair. **2** HEADDRESS. *—v.t.* **·fured, ·fur·ing** To style (hair). [F< OF *coife* coif]

coign (koin) *n.* A projecting angle or corner. Also **coigne.** [< OF, wedge]

coign of vantage An advantageous position.

coil (koil) *n.* **1** A single ring or spiral, or a series of rings or spirals, formed by winding. **2** A series of pipes connected in rows or reversed windings. **3** An induction coil. *—v.t.* **1** To wind spirally or in rings. *—v.i.* **2** To form rings or coils. [< L *colligere* to collect] **—coil′er** *n.*

coin (koin) *n.* **1** A piece of metal stamped by government authority, for use as money. **2** Metal currency, collectively. **3** A corner; quoin. *—v.t.* **1** To stamp or mint (coins) from metal. **2** To make into coins, as metal. **3** To originate or invent, as a word or phrase. [< F, wedge, die < L *cuneus* wedge] **—coin′a·ble** *adj.* **—coin′er** *n.*

coin·age (koi′nij) *n.* **1** The making of coins or the coins made. **2** The system of coins of a country. **3** The act of fabricating or creating something, esp. a word or phrase. **4** An artificially created word or phrase.

co·in·cide (kō′in·sīd′) *v.i.* **·cid·ed, ·cid·ing 1** To be alike in parts, shape, space occupied, or position. **2** To agree exactly, as in opinions, interests, etc. **3** To occur at the same time. [< L *co-* together + *incidere* to happen]

co·in·ci·dence (kō·in′sə·dəns) *n.* **1** The fact or condition of coinciding; correspondence. **2** A remarkable occurrence of events, ideas, etc., at the same time or in the same way, apparently by mere accident.

co·in·ci·dent (kō·in′sə·dənt) *adj.* **1** Occurring at the same time. **2** Having the same shape, position, etc. **3** Exactly corresponding; identical. **—co·in′ci·dent·ly** *adv.*

co·in·ci·den·tal (kō·in′sə·den′təl) *adj.* Characterized by or involving coincidence. **—co·in′ci·den′tal·ly** *adv.*

coir (koir) *n.* Coconut-husk fiber, used in making ropes, matting, etc. [< Malay *kāyar* rope]

co·i·tus (kō′i·təs, kō·ēt′əs) *n.* Sexual intercourse. Also **co·i·tion** (kō·ish′ən). [< L *co-* together + *ire* go] **—co′i·tal** *adj.*

coke (kōk) *n.* A solid fuel obtained by heating coal so as to remove its gases. *—v.t. & v.i.* **coked, cok·ing** To change into coke. [ME]

Col. Colombia; Colonel; Colorado; Colossians.

col. collected; collector; college; colonial; colony; color; colored; column.

co·la (kō′lə) *n.* **1** A small, tropical tree bearing nuts which yield an extract used in the preparation of beverages and medicines. **2** A carbonated beverage flavored with this extract. **3** The extract itself. [< *kola* native African name]

col·an·der (kul′ən·dər, kol′-) *n.* A perforated vessel for draining off liquids. [< L *colare* strain]

cold (kōld) *adj.* **1** Of a relatively low temperature as compared with a normal or standard temperature. **2** Feeling chilled; chilly. **3** Without sufficient heat: *cold* coffee. **4** Dead. **5** Without feeling or enthusiasm; unmoved; indifferent. **6** Not cordial; unfriendly. **7** Without sexual desire; frigid. **8** Depressing or discouraging. **9** Objective; impersonal; detached: *cold* reasoning. **10** Lacking freshness, odor, etc.: a *cold* trail. **11** *Informal* Unconscious: to be out *cold.* **12** Distant from the object or answer sought: said of a guesser, etc. **13** In art, suggesting cold, as bluish or grayish colors. **14** *Informal* Unprepared. **15** *Slang* Perfectly prepared. *—adv. Slang* Completely; absolutely. *—n.* **1** A low temperature, esp. one below freezing. **2** Lack of heat, or the sensation caused by it. **3** A common viral infection marked by inflammation of the upper respiratory tract, chills, nasal discharge, etc. [< OE *cald*] **—cold′ly** *adv.* **—cold′ness** *n.*

cold·blood·ed (kōld′blud′id) *adj.* **1** Deliberately cruel; heartless. **2** Unfeeling; matter-of-fact. **3** Very sensitive to cold. **4** *Zool.* Having a temperature that fluctuates with that of the surrounding medium, as a fish or reptile. **—cold′blood′ed·ly** *adv.* **—cold′blood′ed·ness** *n.*

cold chisel A chisel of tempered steel for cutting cold metal.

cold cream A cleansing and soothing ointment for the skin.

cold front The forward edge of a cold air mass advancing against a warmer mass.

cold·heart·ed (kōld′här′tid) *adj.* Without sympathy, pity, or understanding; unfeeling. **—cold′heart′ed·ly** *adv.* **—cold′heart′ed·ness** *n.*

cold pack 1 *Med.* A wrapping of cold, wet blankets or sheets about a patient as a means of therapy. **2** A canning process in which raw food is packed in cans or jars, which are then heated for cooking and to destroy bacteria.

cold sore An eruption of small blisters, usu. about the mouth and accompanying a cold or fever.

cold turkey *Slang* **1** The abrupt and total deprivation of a substance, as a narcotic drug or cigarettes, from one addicted to its use. **2** Blunt, candid talk.

cold war Intense rivalry between nations in diplomacy, economic strategy, etc., falling just short of armed conflict.

cold wave A spell of unusually cold weather.

cole (kōl) *n.* Any of various plants related to cabbage, esp. rape. Also **cole·wort** (kōl′wûrt′). [< L *caulis* cabbage]

co·le·op·ter·ous (kō′lē·op′tər·əs, kol′ē) *adj.* Belonging to a large order of insects, including beetles and weevils, in which the front wings are modified to form a hard sheath. [< Gk. *koleos* sheath + *pteron* wing] **—co′le·op′ter, co′le·op′ter·an** *n.*

cole·slaw (kōl′slô′) *n.* A salad made of shredded, raw cabbage. [< Du. *kool sla* cabbage salad]

col·ic (kol′ik) *n.* Acute spasmodic pain in the abdomen. *—adj.* Pertaining to or like colic. [< Gk. *kolon* colon] **—col′ick·y** *adj.*

col·i·se·um (kol′ə·sē′əm) *n.* A large building or stadium for sports events, exhibitions, etc.

co·li·tis (kə·lī′tis) *n.* Inflammation of the colon.

coll. colleague; collect; collection; collector; college; colloquial.

col·lab·o·rate (kə·lab′ə·rāt) *v.i.* **·rat·ed, ·rat·ing 1** To labor or cooperate with another, esp. in literary or scientific pursuits. 2 To be a collaborationist. [< L *com-* with + *laborare* work] —**col·lab′o·ra′tion, col·lab′o·ra′tor** *n.* —**col·lab′o·ra′tive** *adj.*

col·lab·o·ra·tion·ist (kə·lab′ə·rā′shən·ist) *n.* A citizen of a country invaded or occupied by foreign troops who cooperates with the enemy.

col·lage (kə·läzh′) *n.* An artistic composition of objects and materials pasted on a surface. [< Gk. *kolla* glue]

col·lapse (kə·laps′) *v.* **·lapsed, ·laps·ing** *v.i.* 1 To give way; cave in. 2 To fail utterly. 3 To become compact by the folding in of parts. 4 To lose health, strength, value, etc., suddenly and completely. —*v.t.* 5 To cause to collapse. —*n.* 1 The act of collapsing. 2 Extreme prostration. 3 Utter failure; ruin. [< L *collapsus,* pp. of *collabi* fall together] —**col·laps′i·ble** or **·a·ble** *adj.* —**col·laps′i·bil′i·ty** *n.*

col·lar (kol′ər) *n.* 1 The part of a garment that circles the neck. 2 An article worn about the neck. 3 A band, part of a harness, etc., for the neck of an animal. 4 A growth of fur or ring of color about the neck of an animal. 5 *Mech.* Any of various cylindrical or ring-shaped devices used to limit or control motion. —*v.t.* 1 To grasp by the collar. 2 To provide with a collar. 3 *Informal* To detain or to capture. [< L *collum* neck]

col·lar·bone (kol′ər·bōn′) *n.* CLAVICLE.

col·lard (kol′ərd) *n.* A variety of cabbage with leaves that do not form a head. [Alter. of *colewort* < COLE]

collat. collateral.

col·late (kə·lāt′, kol′āt, kō′lāt) *v.t.* **·lat·ed, ·lat·ing** 1 To compare critically, as writings or facts. 2 To examine (pages, as those of an unbound book) to see that none are missing or out of order. 3 To assemble (mimeographed pages, etc.) in proper or consecutive order. [< L *collatus* carried together] —**col·la′tor** *n.*

col·lat·er·al (kə·lat′ər·əl) *adj.* 1 Subordinate; secondary. 2 Corroborating; confirmatory. 3 Being or lying alongside; parallel. 4 Descended from the same ancestor but in a different line. 5 Guaranteed by property, as stocks or bonds, deposited as security: a *collateral* loan. —*n.* 1 Property, stocks, bonds, etc. deposited as security for a loan or the like. 2 A collateral relative. [< L *com-* together + *latus, -eris* side] —**col·lat′er·al·ly** *adv.*

col·la·tion (kə·lā′shən, ko-, kō-) *n.* 1 The act or process of collating. 2 A light meal.

col·league (kol′ēg) *n.* A fellow worker, as in an office, or a fellow member of the same profession, etc. [< L *collega* one chosen simultaneously with another]

col·lect[1] (kə·lekt′) *v.t.* 1 To gather together; assemble. 2 To bring together as for a hobby. 3 To gather or obtain (payments of money). 4 To regain control of: to *collect* one's wits. —*v.i.* 5 To assemble or congregate, as people. 6 To accumulate, as dust. 7 To gather payments or donations. —*adj.* To be paid for by the receiver. —*adv.* So that the receiver pays. [< L *com-* together + *legere* gather] —**col·lect′a·ble** or **·i·ble** *adj.*

col·lect[2] (kol′ekt) *n.* In certain church services, a brief prayer varying with the season or occasion. [< L *collecta* a gathering together]

col·lect·ed (kə·lek′tid) *adj.* 1 Assembled; gathered. 2 Composed; self-possessed. —**col·lect′ed·ly** *adv.* —**col·lect′·ed·ness** *n.*

col·lec·tion (kə·lek′shən) *n.* 1 The act of collecting. 2 A group of collected objects or individuals. 3 An accumulation. 4 A sum of money that has been collected.

col·lec·tive (kə·lek′tiv) *adj.* 1 Formed or brought together by collecting. 2 Of, involving, or accomplished by a group of persons rather than individuals. —*n.* 1 A collective enterprise. 2 The people involved in such an enterprise. 3 COLLECTIVE NOUN. —**col·lec′tive·ly** *adv.* —**col·lec′·tive·ness, col′lec·tiv′i·ty** *n.*

collective bargaining Negotiation between organized workers and employers for reaching an agreement on working conditions, wages, hours, etc.

collective noun A singular noun naming a collection, or group of persons or things, as *jury, family, flock,* etc. • A *collective noun* takes either a singular or plural verb, according as it refers to the objects composing it as an aggregate or as separate individuals: The audience *was* large; The audience *were* divided in opinion.

col·lec·tiv·ism (kə·lek′tiv·iz′əm) *n.* An economic theory or system in which the people as a whole own or control the material and means of production and distribution. —**col·lec′tiv·ist** *adj., n.* —**col·lec′tiv·is′tic** *adj.*

col·lec·tiv·ize (kə·lek′tiv·īz) *v.t.* **·ized, ·iz·ing** To organize (an agricultural settlement, industry, economy, etc.) under a system of collectivism. —**col·lec′tiv·i·za′tion** *n.*

col·lec·tor (kə·lek′tər) *n.* One who or that which collects, as a person who receives taxes, duties, etc.

col·leen (kol′ēn, kə·lēn′) *n.* An Irish girl.

col·lege (kol′ij) *n.* 1 A school of higher learning, as an undergraduate school at a university, that offers a four-year course of study leading to a bachelor's degree. 2 A school, often a graduate school in a university, offering instruction in a specialized course of study: a *college* of medicine. 3 A building or buildings used by a college. 4 A body of associates or colleagues engaged in some definite work or duty: electoral *college.* [< L *collegium* body of associates] —**col·le·gi·al** (kə·lē′jē·əl) *adj.*

College of Cardinals In the Roman Catholic Church, the body of cardinals who elect the Pope, act as his council, and, in his absence, administer the Holy See.

col·le·gi·al·i·ty (kə·lē′jē·al′i·tē) *n.* 1 The relationship between colleagues. 2 In the Roman Catholic Church, the sharing of the power of government between the bishops and the Pope.

col·le·gian (kə·lē′jən, -jē·ən) *n.* A college student.

col·le·giate (kə·lē′jit, -jē·it) *adj.* Of, like, or for a college or college student.

col·lide (kə·līd′) *v.i.* **·lid·ed, ·lid·ing** 1 To come together with violent impact; crash. 2 To come into conflict; clash. [< L *com-* together + *laedere* strike]

col·lie (kol′ē) *n.* A breed of shepherd dogs which originated in Scotland, characterized by a long, narrow head and an abundant long-haired coat. [Prob. < Scot. Gael. *cuilean* puppy]

col·lier (kol′yər) *n. Chiefly Brit.* 1 A coal miner. 2 A vessel employed in carrying coal. [ME *colier* < *col* coal]

col·lier·y (kol′yər·ē) *n. pl.* **·lier·ies** *Chiefly Brit.* 1 A coal mine. 2 The coal trade.

col·li·mate (kol′ə·māt) *v.t.* **·mat·ed, ·mat·ing** 1 To bring into line. 2 To adjust the line of sight of, as of a telescope. 3 To make parallel, as refracted rays of light. [< L *com-* together + *lineare* align] —**col′li·ma′tion, col′li·ma′tor** *n.*

col·li·sion (kə·lizh′ən) *n.* 1 A violent impact or crash. 2 A conflict, as of views, interests, etc. [< L *collidere* to collide]

col·lo·cate (kol′ō·kāt) *v.t.* **·cat·ed, ·cat·ing** To place or arrange in certain order, as side by side. [< L *com-* together + *locare* place] —**col′lo·ca′tion** *n.*

col·lo·di·on (kə·lō′dē·ən) *n.* A flammable, quick-drying solution of cellulose, used to coat wounds, photographic plates, etc. Also **col·lo·di·um** (kə·lō′dē·əm). [< Gk. *kollōdēs* gluelike]

col·loid (kol′oid) *n.* Any system of mutually insoluble gaseous, liquid, or solid substances in which one component in very finely divided form remains dispersed in the other. —*adj.* Of, like, or pertaining to a colloid: also **col·loi·dal** (kə·loid′l). [< Gk. *kollōdēs* gluelike] —**col·loi·dal·i·ty** (kol′oi·dal′ə·tē) *n.*

colloq. colloquial.

col·lo·qui·al (kə·lō′kwē·əl) *adj.* 1 Characteristic of or suitable to the informal language of ordinary conversation or writing. 2 Of or pertaining to conversation; conversational. —**col·lo′qui·al·ly** *adv.* —**col·lo′qui·al·ness** *n.*

col·lo·qui·al·ism (kə·lō′kwē·əl·iz′əm) *n.* A colloquial style, usage, word, or expression.

col·lo·quy (kol′ə·kwē) *n. pl.* **·quies** A more or less formal conversation or conference. [< L *colloquium* conversation] —**col′lo·quist** *n.*

col·lude (kə·lo͞od′) *v.i.* **·lud·ed, ·lud·ing** To cooperate secretly; conspire; connive. [< L *com-* together + *ludere* play, trick] —**col·lud′er** *n.*

col·lu·sion (kə·lo͞o′zhən) *n.* Secret cooperation in fraud or in illegal activities. [< L *colludere* to collude] —**col·lu′sive** *adj.* —**col·lu′sive·ly** *adv.* —**col·lu′sive·ness** *n.*

co·logne (kə·lōn′) *n.* A toilet water consisting of alcohol scented with aromatic oils. Also **Cologne water.** [< *Cologne,* Germany]

Co·lom·bi·a (kə·lum′bē·ə, *Sp.* kō·lōm′byä) *n.* A republic in NW South America, 439,519 sq. mi., cap. Bogotá. —**Co·lom′bi·an** *adj., n.* • See map at VENEZUELA.

co·lon[1] (kō′lən) *n.* A punctuation mark (:) used to introduce a series or catalog of things, a speech, quotation, example, etc., and after the salutation in a formal letter. [<Gk. *kōlon* member, limb, clause]

co·lon[2] (kō′lən) *n. pl.* **co·lons** or **co·la** (kō′lə) The large intestine between the cecum and the rectum. [<Gk. *kolon*] —**co·lon·ic** (kə·lon′ik) *adj.* • See INTESTINE.

co·lon[2] (kō·lōn′) *n. pl.* **co·lons** (kō·lōnz′), *Sp.* **co·lo·nes** (kō·lō′nās) The monetary unit of Costa Rica and El Salvador.

colo·nel (kûr′nəl) *n.* See GRADE. [<Ital. *colonna* column of soldiers] —**colo′nel·cy, colo′nel·ship** *n.*

co·lo·ni·al (kə·lō′nē·əl) *adj.* **1** Of, possessing, like, or forming a colony or colonies. **2** *Often cap.* Of the Colonies. **3** *Often cap.* Of or like a style of architecture prevalent in the American colonies. —*n.* A citizen or inhabitant of a colony. —**co·lo′ni·al·ly** *adv.*

co·lo·ni·al·ism (kə·lō′nē·əl·iz′əm) *n.* The policy of a nation seeking to acquire, extend, or retain overseas dependencies. —**co·lo′ni·al·ist** *adj., n.* —**co·lo′ni·al·is′tic** *adj.*

col·o·nist (kol′ə·nist) *n.* **1** A member or inhabitant of a colony. **2** A founder of a colony.

col·o·nize (kol′ə·nīz) *v.* **·nized, ·niz·ing** *v.t.* **1** To settle a colony or colonies in. **2** To establish as colonists. —*v.i.* **3** To establish or unite in a colony or colonies. *Brit. sp.* **col′o·nise.** —**col′o·ni·za′tion, col′o·niz′er** *n.*

col·on·nade (kol′ə·nād′) *n. Archit.* A series of columns, usu. topped by an entablature. [<F *colonne* column] —**col′on·nad′ed** *adj.*

col·o·ny (kol′ə·nē) *n. pl.* **·nies 1** A body of emigrants who settle in a remote region but remain under the control of a parent country. **2** The region thus settled. **3** Any group of people having common ethnic backgrounds, interests, etc., and living in a particular area or region: the movie *colony.* **4** The area or region in which they live. **5** A discrete group of microorganisms growing in a culture medium. **6** A group of related plants or animals living or growing together. —**the Colonies** The British colonies that became the original thirteen states of the U.S.: Va., N.Y., Mass., Conn., R.I., N.H., Md., N.J., N.C., S.C., Pa., Del., and Ga. [<L *colonus* farmer]

col·o·phon (kol′ə·fon, -fən) *n.* A publisher's distinctive emblem, usu. printed on the title page of a book. [<Gk. *kolophon* summit]

col·or (kul′ər) *n.* **1** A visual attribute of bodies or substances distinct from their spatial characteristics and depending upon the spectral composition of the light emitted or reflected by them. **2** Any coloring matter, as a paint or pigment. **3** The hue or pigmentation of the human skin. **4** The pigmentation of the skin of a Negro or other non-Caucasian. **5** The complexion of the human face, esp. if ruddy or flushed. **6** *pl.* A flag or banner, as of a nation, military unit, etc. **7** *Usu. pl.* Any identifying color, ribbon, badge, etc.: our college *colors.* **8** *pl.* One's personal opinions, beliefs, etc.: Stick to your *colors.* **9** An outward appearance or semblance, often deceptive or false: under the *color* of truth. **10** General nature or character: the *color* of her thinking. **11** Liveliness or animation; vividness. **12** Justification; plausibility. **13** In art and literature, the use of realistic or characteristic details and effects. **14** In art, the effect produced by color. **15** *Music* TIMBRE. —*v.t.* **1** To apply or give color to, as by painting, staining, or dyeing. **2** To misrepresent by distortion or exaggeration. **3** To modify in nature or character. —*v.i.* **4** To take on or change color, as ripening fruit. **5** To blush or flush. *Brit. sp.* **col′our** [<L] —**col′or·er** *n.*

col·or·a·ble (kul′ər·ə·bəl) *adj.* **1** Capable of being colored. **2** Seemingly valid or plausible but actually specious; deceptive. —**col′or·a·bil′i·ty, col′or·a·ble·ness** *n.* —**col′or·a·bly** *adv.*

col·or·a·tion (kul′ə·rā′shən) *n.* **1** The state of being colored. **2** The choice or use of colors. **3** Arrangement or depth of color, as in an animal or plant.

col·or·a·tu·ra (kul′ər·ə·tʸŏŏr′ə) *n.* **1** Grace notes, runs, trills, or other florid decoration in vocal music. **2** A soprano who specializes in singing such music: also **coloratura soprano.** [<Ital., coloration]

col·or-blind (kul′ər·blīnd′) *n.* Totally or partially unable to distinguish between certain colors. —**col′or-blind′ness** *n.* or **color blindness**

col·ored (kul′ərd) *adj.* **1** Having color. **2** Of a (specified) color. **3** Of a race other than the Caucasoid race, esp. Negro. **4** Exaggerated, prejudiced, or influenced in some way: views *colored* by years of poverty.

col·or·fast (kul′ər·fast′, -fäst′) *adj.* Resistant to fading or running: *colorfast* fabrics.

col·or·ful (kul′ər·fəl) *adj.* **1** Full of colors, esp. contrasting colors. **2** Full of interest; picturesque: a *colorful* life. —**col′or·ful·ly** *adv.* —**col′or·ful·ness** *n.*

color guard The flagbearers and guards who conduct the colors in a ceremony.

col·or·ing (kul′ər·ing) *n.* **1** The imparting of color. **2** A source of color. **3** The natural color of something. **4** The effect produced by colors. **5** The tone, quality or style of something. **6** False or specious appearance.

col·or·ist (kul′ər·ist) *n.* **1** One who uses color. **2** An artist skilled in the use of color.

col·or·ize (kul′ər·īz) *v.t.* **·ized, ·iz·ing** To add color to movies that were originally black-and-white by means of computer-enhanced techniques. —**col′or·i·za′tion** *n.*

col·or·less (kul′ər·lis) *adj.* **1** Without color. **2** Dull; uninteresting. —**col′or·less·ly** *adv.* —**col′or·less·ness** *n.*

color line A social, political, or economic distinction drawn between the white and other races.

col·los·sal (kə·los′əl) *adj.* **1** Enormous; huge. **2** *Informal* Unbelievable; extraordinary: a *colossal* bore. —**co·los′sal·ly** *adv.*

Col·os·se·um (kol′ə·sē′əm) *n.* An amphitheater in Rome, built by Vespasian and Titus in A.D. 75–80.

Co·los·sian (kə·losh′ən) *n.* **1** A native or inhabitant of Colossae. **2** *pl.* Saint Paul's epistle to the Colossians, a book of the New Testament.

co·los·sus (kə·los′əs) *n. pl.* **co·los·si** (kə·los′ī) or **co·los·sus·es 1** A gigantic statue. **2** Any strikingly huge or important person or object. [<Gk. *kolossos*]

colt (kōlt) *n.* **1** A young horse, ass, etc., esp. a young male horse. **2** A frisky person. **3** An inexperienced person. [<OE] —**colt′ish** *adj.*

col·ter (kōl′tər) *n.* A blade or disk on the beam of a plow, to cut the sod. [<L *culter* knife]

col·um·bar·i·um (kol′əm·bâr′ē·əm) *n. pl.* **·bar·i·a** (-bâr′ē·ə) **1** A vault with recesses for urns containing ashes of the dead. **2** Such a recess. **3** DOVECOTE. [<L *columba* dove]

Co·lum·bi·a (kə·lum′bē·ə) *n.* The personification of the U.S. as a woman. [<Christopher *Columbus*]

col·um·bine (kol′əm·bīn) *n.* A herbaceous plant with variously colored flowers of five petals; esp. the **Colorado columbine.** [<L *columba* dove]

Columbus Day The second Monday in October, a U.S. holiday marking the discovery of America by Christopher Columbus in 1492, formerly celebrated October 12.

col·umn (kol′əm) *n.* **1** A vertical shaft or pillar, usu. having a base and a capital, and used as a support or as ornamentation. **2** Any object or structure resembling a column: the spinal *column.* **3** A vertical, usu. narrow section of printed matter separated from similar sections by a rule or a blank space. **4** A unit of troops, vehicles, ships, etc., arranged in single file or several abreast. **5** An article by a special writer or on a specific subject that appears regularly in a newspaper or periodical. [<L *columna*] —**co·lum·nar** (kə·lum′nər), **col·umned** (kol′əmd) *adj.*

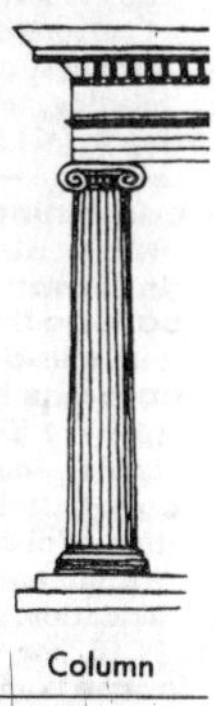

Column

co·lum·ni·a·tion (kə·lum′nē·ā′shən) *n.* The use or the grouping of columns, as in a building.

col·um·nist (kol′əm·nist, -əm·ist) *n.* A person who writes or conducts a special column for a newspaper or periodical.

col·za (kol′zə) *n.* The summer rape whose seeds yield rape oil. [< Du. *kool* cabbage + *zaad* a seed]

com- *prefix* With; together: *combine, compare.* Also: *col-* before *l,* as in *collide; con-* before *c, d, f, g, j, n, q, s, t, v,* as in *concur, confluence, connect, conspire; cor-* before *r,* as in *correspond.* [< L *cum* with]

Com. commander; commission; commissioner; committee; commodore; Communist.

com. comedy; comma; commerce; commercial; common; commonly; communication.

co·ma[1] (kō′mə) *n. pl.* **co·mas** 1 A state of deep, prolonged unconsciousness caused by disease, injury, etc. 2 Stupor; lethargy. [< Gk. *kōma* deep sleep] —**co′ma·tose** (-tōs) *adj.* —**co′ma·tose′ly** *adv.* —**co′ma·tose′ness** *n.*

co·ma[2] (kō′mə) *n. pl.* **co·mae** (kō′mē) 1 *Astron.* The nebulous mass surrounding the nucleus and constituting the head of a comet. 2 *Bot.* A tuft, as of hairs, at the end of certain seeds, etc. [< Gk. *komē* hair]

Co·man·che (kō·man′chē) *n. pl.* **·ches** A member of a tribe of North American Indians, formerly roaming between Kansas and northern Mexico, now in Oklahoma.

comb (kōm) *n.* 1 A firm piece of hard rubber, plastic, etc., with teeth, for dressing or fastening the hair. 2 Something resembling a comb, as a currycomb or card for dressing wool. 3 The fleshy crest on the head of a fowl. 4 The crest of a hill or wave. 5 HONEYCOMB. —*v.t.* 1 To dress, disentangle, etc., with or as with a comb. 2 To search carefully and exhaustively. —*v.i.* 3 To crest and break: said of waves. [< OE *camb*]

comb. combination; combining.

com·bat (kom′bat, kum′-) *n.* A battle or fight; struggle. —*v.* (kəm·bat′) **·bat·ed** or **·bat·ted, ·bat·ing** or **·bat·ting** *v.t.* 1 To fight or contend with. 2 To resist. —*v.i.* 3 To do battle; struggle: with *with* or *against.* [< L *com-* with + *battuere* fight, beat] —**com·bat′a·ble** *adj.* —**com·bat′er** *n.*

com·bat·ant (kəm·bat′ənt, kom′bə·tənt) *n.* One engaged in or prepared for combat. —*adj.* 1 Fighting; battling. 2 Ready for combat.

combat fatigue Severe anxiety, depression, etc., that can occur after prolonged exposure to combat in war.

com·bat·ive (kəm·bat′iv, kom′bə·tiv) *adj.* Inclined or eager to fight; pugnacious. —**com·bat′ive·ly** *adv.* —**com·bat′ive·ness** *n.* —**Syn.** warlike, bellicose, belligerent, hostile.

comb·er (kō′mər) *n.* 1 One who combs. 2 A long crested wave; a breaker.

com·bi·na·tion (kom′bə·nā′shən) *n.* 1 A combining or being combined. 2 That which is formed by combining. 3 A group of people, businesses, etc., allied for a common activity or purpose. 4 The series of numbers or letters used to open a combination lock. 5 *pl.* Underwear made in one piece. 6 *Math.* A set in which the order of elements is immaterial. [< LL *combinare* to combine]

combination lock A lock opened by turning a dial to a set sequence of letters or numbers.

com·bine (kəm·bīn′) *v.t. & v.i.* **·bined, ·bin·ing** 1 To bring or come into a close union; join; unite. 2 To unite chemically to form a compound. —*n.* (kom′bīn) 1 An association of persons united for political or business control, often by dishonest means. 2 A farm machine which combines the heading, threshing, and cleaning of grain while harvesting it. [< LL *com-* together + *bini* two by two] —**com·bin′a·ble** *adj.* —**com·bin′er** *n.*

combining form A word element used in combination with words or other forms to create compounds, as *over-* in *overeat.*

com·bo (kom′bō) *n. pl.* **·bos** *Informal* 1 A small group of jazz musicians performing together. 2 A combination.

com·bus·ti·ble (kəm·bus′tə·bəl) *adj.* 1 That burns easily. 2 Excitable; fiery. —*n.* Any substance that burns easily. —**com·bus′ti·ble·ness, com·bus′ti·bil′i·ty** *n.*

com·bus·tion (kəm·bus′chən) *n.* 1 The action or operation of burning. 2 The rapid combination of a substance with oxygen, accompanied by heat and usu. light. 3 Slow oxidation, as of food in the body. 4 Disturbance; tumult. [< LL *comburere* burn up] —**com·bus′tive** *adj.*

come (kum) *v.* **came, come, com·ing** *v.i.* 1 To move or go to or toward a position, place, or person. 2 To exist or occur at a specific place or point: Youth *comes* before maturity. 3 To occur mentally: A solution *came* to him. 4 To arrive as the result of motion or progress: They *came* to land. 5 To attain to a specific result or end. 6 To arrive at some state or condition; develop. 7 To appear: The static *comes* and goes. 8 To occur in time: when Christmas *comes.* 9 To become: The chain *came* loose. 10 To proceed or emanate as from a source. 11 To exist as an effect or result: This *comes* of trifling. 12 To happen or befall: *Come* what may, I'll do it. 13 To prove to be; become: The sign *came* true. 14 To reach or extend: with *to.* 15 To be offered, obtainable, or produced: The car *comes* in many colors. 16 To be descended. 17 To have lived or been born in: to *come* from Greece. 18 To amount: with *to:* This *comes* to two dollars. —**come about** To take place; happen. —**come across** To find or meet accidentally. —**come around** (or **round**) 1 To recover or revive. 2 To acquiesce or accede. —**come down** 1 To oppose or criticize: with *on* or *upon.* 2 To become ill: with *with.* —**come into** To inherit. —**come off** *Informal* 1 To occur; happen. 2 To be effective or successful. —**come out** 1 To become evident; transpire. 2 To make a debut in society. 3 To prove to be; turn out. 4 To declare oneself, esp. publicly: often with *for.* —**come through** To do what is wanted or needed. —**come to** To recover consciousness. —**come up** 1 To be mentioned or considered, as in discussion. 2 To occur. —**come up with** To suggest, propose, or produce: They had better *come up with* a new plan soon. [< OE *cuman*]

come·back (kum′bak′) *n.* 1 *Informal* A return to a former state or position. 2 *Slang* A smart retort.

co·me·di·an (kə·mē′dē·ən) *n.* 1 A comic actor or entertainer. 2 One who writes comedies. 3 One who is or tries to be amusing. —**co·me·di·enne** (kə·mē′dē·en′) *n. Fem.*

come·down (kum′doun′) *n.* A descent to a lower condition or position; downfall.

com·e·dy (kom′ə·dē) *n. pl.* **·dies** 1 Originally, a literary work with a nontragic view of life and a happy ending. 2 A play, motion picture, etc., characterized by a humorous treatment of characters, situation, etc., and having a happy ending. 3 Comedies collectively, esp. as a branch of the drama. 4 Any comic or ludicrous incident or series of incidents. [< Gk. *kōmos* revel + *aeidein* sing]

come-hith·er (kum′hith̲′ər) *adj. Slang* Alluring; inviting; able to attract: a *come-hither* look.

come·ly (kum′lē, kōm′lē) *adj.* **·li·er, ·li·est** Pleasing in appearance; attractive. [< OE *cȳmlic*] —**come′li·ness** *n.*

come-on (kum′on′) *n. Slang* Someone or something that attracts, interests, etc.

com·er (kum′ər) *n.* 1 One who comes or arrives. 2 *Informal* One showing great promise.

co·mes·ti·ble (kə·mes′tə·bəl) *adj.* Edible. —*n. Usu. pl.* Something that is eatable. [< L *comedere* to eat up]

com·et (kom′it) *n. Astron.* A celestial body consisting of a nucleus of condensed material surrounded by a luminous coma and accompanied by an elongated, luminous tail that always points away from the sun. [< Gk. *komētēs* long-haired] —**com·et·ar·y** (kom′ə·ter′ē), **co·met·ic** (kə·met′ik) *adj.*

come·up·pance (kum′up′əns) *n. Informal* Deserved punishment; deserts: to get one's *comeuppance.*

com·fit (kum′fit, kom′-) *n.* A sweetmeat; confection. [< L *confectus.* See CONFECTION]

com·fort (kum′fərt) *n.* 1 Freedom from pain, annoyance, want, etc. 2 Anything that contributes to such relief. 3 Relief from sorrow or distress. 4 One who or that which helps relieve sorrow or distress. 5 A bed comforter. —*v.t.* To give cheer or ease to; console; solace. [< LL *confortare* strengthen] —**com′fort·ing** *adj.* —**com′fort·ing·ly** *adv.*

com·fort·a·ble (kum′fər·tə·bəl, kumf′tə·bəl) *adj.* 1 Marked by or providing ease and comfort. 2 Not suffering in mind or body; at ease. 3 *Informal* Providing or enjoying security, well-being, etc.: a *comfortable* income. —**com′fort·a·ble·ness** *n.* —**com′fort·a·bly** *adv.*

com·fort·er (kum′fər·tər) *n.* 1 One who or that which comforts. 2 A thick, quilted bedcover.

comfort station A public restroom.

com·ic (kom′ik) *adj.* 1 Of, like, or connected with comedy. 2 Amusing, funny, ludicrous, etc. 3 Acting in or composing comedy. —*n.* 1 A comedian. 2 A comic book or comic strip. 3 The humorous side of art, life, etc. 4 *pl.* A newspaper section devoted to comic strips. [< Gk. *kōmos* revelry]

com·i·cal (kom′i·kəl) *adj.* Causing amusement, laughter, etc. —**com′i·cal·ly** *adv.* —**com′i·cal·ness** *n.*
comic book A magazine of comic strips.
comic strip A series of cartoons printed in a strip in newspapers, magazines, etc., and picturing a sequence of comic or adventurous incidents.
com·ing (kum′ing) *adj.* 1 Approaching; next: the *coming* year. 2 On the way to fame or note. —*n.* Arrival; advent.
com·i·ty (kom′ə·tē) *n.* Friendliness; good will; courtesy. [< L *comitas* courtesy]
com·ma (kom′ə) *n.* 1 A punctuation mark (,) indicating a slight separation in ideas or construction within a sentence. 2 Any pause or separation. [< Gk. *komma* short phrase < *koptein* cut]
comma bacillus The comma-shaped causative agent of Asiatic cholera.
com·mand (kə·mand′, -mänd′) *v.t.* 1 To order, require or enjoin with authority. 2 To control or direct; rule. 3 To have at one's disposal or use. 4 To overlook, as from a height. 5 To exact as being due or proper. —*v.i.* 6 To be in authority; rule. 7 To overlook, as from a height. —*n.* 1 The right to command; authority. 2 An order. 3 The troops or district under the command of one person. 4 Dominating power; control. 5 Mastery. 6 Range of view. [< L *com-* thoroughly + *mandare* order, charge]
com·man·dant (kom′ən·dant′, -dänt′) *n.* COMMANDING OFFICER.
com·man·deer (kom′ən·dir′) *v.t.* 1 To force into military service. 2 To take possession of for public use, esp. under military necessity. 3 To take over by force or by threat of force. [< Afrikaans *kommandeeren* command]
com·mand·er (kə·man′dər, -män′-) *n.* 1 One in command; a leader. 2 In the U.S. Army, the commanding officer of a post or unit. 3 See GRADE.
commander in chief *pl.* **commanders in chief** 1 *Often cap.* The officer commanding all the armed forces of a nation; in the U.S., the President. 2 The officer commanding all the armed forces in a certain area of war.
com·mand·ing (kə·man′ding, -män′-) *adj.* 1 Having power; in command. 2 Authoritative; impressive; dignified. 3 Having a wide, overlooking view or position. —**com·mand′ing·ly** *adv.*
commanding officer An officer in command, as of an army installation.
com·mand·ment (kə·mand′mənt, -mänd′-), *n.* An authoritative mandate, order, or law, esp. one of the Ten Commandments.
command module *Aerospace* A part of a space vehicle that houses the crew and navigational systems and is equipped for reentry.
com·man·do (kə·man′dō, -män′-) *n. pl.* **·dos** or **·does** 1 A special fighting force trained for quick raids into enemy territory. 2 A member of such a unit.
com·mem·o·rate (kə·mem′ə·rāt) *v.t.* **·rat·ed, ·rat·ing** To celebrate the memory of, as with a ceremony. [< L *com-* together + *memorare* remember] —**com·mem·o·ra·ble** (kə·mem′ə·rə·bəl), **com·mem′o·ra′tive, com·mem·o·ra·to·ry** (kə·mem′ə·rə·tôr′ē, -tō′rē) *adj.* —**com·mem′o·ra′tion** *n.*
com·mence (kə·mens′) *v.t.* & *v.i.* **·menced, ·menc·ing** To begin; initiate; start. [< L *com-* together + *initiare* begin]
com·mence·ment (kə·mens′mənt) *n.* 1 A beginning; origin. 2 A ceremony held at the completion of a school or college course, when degrees are conferred. 3 The day of such a ceremony.
com·mend (kə·mend′) *v.t.* 1 To express a favorable opinion of; praise. 2 To recommend. 3 To present the regards of. 4 To entrust. [< L *com-* thoroughly + *mandare* order, charge] —**com·mend′a·ble** *adj.* —**com·mend′a·bly** *adv.*
com·men·da·tion (kom′ən·dā′shən) *n.* 1 The act of commending; approbation. 2 Something that commends.
com·mend·a·to·ry (kə·men′də·tôr′ē, -tō′rē) *adj.* Expressing approval.
com·men·su·ra·ble (kə·men′shər·ə·bəl, -sər·ə-) *adj.* 1 Measurable by a common unit. 2 In proper proportion; proportionate. [< LL *com-* together + *mensurabilis* measurable] —**com·men′su·ra·bil′i·ty** *n.* —**com·men′su·ra·bly** *adv.*
com·men·su·rate (kə·men′shə·rit, -sə·rit) *adj.* 1 In proper proportion; proportionate. 2 COMMENSURABLE. 3 Equal in size or extent. [< LL *com-* together + *mensurare* measure] —**com·men′su·rate·ly** *adv.* —**com·men′su·rate·ness, com·men′su·ra′tion** *n.*
com·ment (kom′ent) *n.* 1 A note in explanation or criticism. 2 A remark made in observation or criticism. 3 Talk; conversation; gossip. —*v.i.* To make a comment or comments: with *on* or *upon.* [< L *comminisci* contrive]
com·men·tar·y (kom′ən·ter′ē) *n. pl.* **·tar·ies** 1 A series or body of comments; exposition. 2 Anything explanatory or illustrative.
com·men·ta·tor (kom′ən·tā′tər) *n.* 1 A writer of commentaries; an expounder. 2 One who discusses or analyzes news, politics, etc., as on television or radio.
com·merce (kom′ərs) *n.* 1 Exchange of goods, products, or property, as between states or nations. 2 Social intercourse. 3 SEXUAL INTERCOURSE. [< L *com-* together + *merx, mercis* wares]
com·mer·cial (kə·mûr′shəl) *adj.* 1 Of or belonging to trade or commerce; mercantile. 2 Made in large quantities for the market. 3 Having financial gain or popular appeal as an object: a *commercial* novel. —*n.* In radio and television, a paid advertisement. —**com·mer′cial·ly** *adv.*
com·mer·cial·ism (kə·mûr′shəl·iz′əm) *n.* The spirit, methods, or principles of commerce, esp. an excessive interest in profits.
com·mer·cial·ize (kə·mûr′shəl·īz) *v.t.* **·ized, ·iz·ing** 1 To put on a commercial basis. 2 To make or do mainly for profit. —**com·mer′cial·i·za′tion** *n.*
com·min·gle (kə·ming′gəl) *v.t.* & *v.i.* **·gled, ·gling** To mix together; mingle.
com·mi·nute (kom′ə·nyo͞ot) *v.t.* **·nut·ed, ·nut·ing** To reduce to minute particles; pulverize. [< L *com-* thoroughly + *minuere* lessen] —**com′mi·nu′tion** *n.*
com·mis·er·ate (kə·miz′ə·rāt) *v.* **·at·ed, ·at·ing** *v.t.* 1 To feel or manifest pity for; sympathize. —*v.i.* 2 To condole: with *with.* [< L *com-* with + *miserari* feel pity] —**com·mis′er·a′tive** *adj.* —**com·mis′er·a′tive·ly** *adv.* —**com·mis′er·a′tion, com·mis′er·a′tor** *n.*
com·mis·sar (kom′ə·sär, kom′ə·sär′) *n.* Formerly, an official in charge of a commissariat of the Soviet government. [< L *committere.* See COMMIT.]
com·mis·sar·i·at (kom′ə·sâr′ē·ət) *n.* 1 An army department supplying food and other necessaries. 2 Formerly, a major department of the government of the U.S.S.R.
com·mis·sar·y (kom′ə·ser′ē) *n. pl.* **·sar·ies** 1 A store selling food, supplies, etc., as at an army or lumber camp. 2 A restaurant for the employees of a movie studio, etc.
com·mis·sion (kə·mish′ən) *n.* 1 The act of entrusting or giving authority to perform certain acts or duties. 2 The acts or duties so entrusted. 3 An authorization or order to do something; also, a document conferring this. 4 *Mil.* a A document conferring rank and authority. b The rank or authority so conferred. 5 A body of persons authorized to perform certain duties. 6 The fee given an agent or salesperson for his or her services. 7 The act of committing or perpetrating, as a crime. —*v.t.* 1 To give rank or authority to, as an officer. 2 To put into active service, as a ship of war. 3 To give a commission to. 4 To appoint; delegate. 5 To order to be done: to *commission* a painting. [< L *committere.* See COMMIT.]
com·mis·sion·er (kə·mish′ən·ər) *n.* 1 A person commissioned to have certain powers or to perform certain acts. 2 A member of a commission. 3 A public official appointed as head of a state or municipal department. —**com·mis′sion·er·ship′** *n.*
com·mit (kə·mit′) *v.t.* **·mit·ted, ·mit·ting** 1 To do; perpetrate. 2 To place in an institution or prison. 3 To entrust or consign to any person, place, or use. 4 To devote or pledge (oneself) to the doing of something. 5 To consign for future reference, preservation, etc.: to *commit* a speech to memory. 6 To refer, as to a committee, for consideration or report. [< L *com-* together + *mittere* send]
com·mit·ment (kə·mit′mənt) *n.* 1 The act of committing, or the state of being committed. 2 An official

order committing someone to a prison or asylum. 3 A pledge; promise. Also **com·mit′tal** (kə·mit′l). **—Syn. 3** guarantee, word, obligation, compact, warrant.

com·mit·tee (kə·mit′ē) *n.* A group of persons organized or appointed to act upon some matter. [< COMMIT]

com·mit·tee·man (kə·mit′ē·mən) *n. pl.* **·men** (-mən) A member of a committee. **—com·mit′tee·wom′an** *n. Fem.*

com·mode (kə·mōd′) *n.* 1 A low chest of drawers. 2 A covered washstand. 3 A low chair or cabinet enclosing a chamber pot. 4 A toilet. [< L *commodus* convenient]

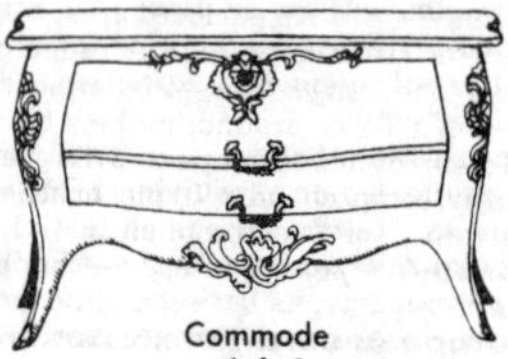

Commode *def. 1*

com·mo·di·ous (kə·mō′dē·əs) *adj.* Spacious; roomy. [< L *commodus* convenient] **—com·mo′di·ous·ly** *adv.* **—com·mo′di·ous·ness** *n.*

com·mod·i·ty (kə·mod′ə·tē) *n. pl.* **·ties** 1 Something bought and sold. 2 Something useful. [< L *commoditas* convenience]

com·mo·dore (kom′ə·dôr, -dōr) *n.* 1 In the U.S. Navy, an officer next below a rear admiral, a rank no longer in use since World War II. 2 In the British Navy, the commander of a squadron or division of a fleet. 3 A title given to the presiding officer of a yacht club. [< Du. *kommandeur* commander]

com·mon (kom′ən) *adj.* 1 Not unusual; ordinary; regular. 2 Of, pertaining to, or participated in by all or by others. 3 Belonging to the public: *common* facilities. 4 Widespread; general: *common* knowledge. 5 Coarse; vulgar; low. 6 Notorious: a *common* thief. 7 Having no special rank or privilege; not of the upper classes: the *common* people. 8 Having no rank: a *common* soldier. 9 *Gram.* **a** Of either gender. **b** Applicable to any individual of a class. 10 *Math.* Referring to a number or element related in a particular way to two or more other numbers or elements: a *common* denominator. *—n. Often pl.* Land owned by a town and open to the use of all. **—in common** Equally; jointly. [< L *communis* common] **—com′mon·ly** *adv.* **—com′mon·ness** *n.*

com·mon·al·ty (kom′ən·əl·tē) *n. pl.* **·ties** 1 The common people, as opposed to persons of title or rank. 2 The possession of qualities, characteristics, etc., in common.

common carrier An individual or company which, for a fee, provides public transportation.

com·mon·er (kom′ən·ər) *n.* One of the common people.

common fraction A fraction whose numerator and denominator are integers.

common law Law based on custom, usage, and legal precedent.

com·mon-law marriage (kom′ən·lô′) A marriage in which both parties agree to live as man and wife but without a church or civil ceremony.

Common Market EUROPEAN ECONOMIC COMMUNITY.

common noun A noun that represents any or all members of its class, as *plant, dog.*

com·mon·place (kom′ən·plās′) *adj.* Not remarkable or interesting; ordinary. *—n.* 1 A trite remark; platitude; truism. 2 Anything ordinary or common.

com·mons (kom′ənz) *n. pl.* 1 The common people; commonalty. 2 *(Often construed as sing.)* **a** Food served for many people. **b** The dining facilities for such food, as at a college.

Com·mons (kom′ənz) *n. pl.* HOUSE OF COMMONS.

common sense Practical understanding; sound judgment. **—com′mon-sense′** *adj.*

common stock Stock which entitles the owner to dividends only after all other obligations have been met and dividends paid to owners of preferred stock.

com·mon·weal (kom′ən·wēl′) *n.* The general welfare.

com·mon·wealth (kom′ən·welth′) *n.* 1 The people of a state or nation. 2 A state or nation in which the people rule; a republic. 3 Loosely, any State of the U.S. 4 A body of persons united by some common interest.

Commonwealth of Nations A political association comprising the United Kingdom, its dependencies, and certain of its former colonies that are now sovereign states.

com·mo·tion (kə·mō′shən) *n.* 1 A disturbance; fuss. 2 Violent agitation; tumult. [< L *com-* thoroughly + *movere* move]

com·mu·nal (kom′yə·nəl, kə·myo͞o′nəl) *adj.* 1 Of or pertaining to a commune. 2 Common; public. 3 Belonging to a community. **—com·mu′nal·ly** *adv.*

com·mune[1] (kə·myo͞on′) *v.i.* **·muned, ·mun·ing** 1 To converse or confer intimately. 2 To partake of the Eucharist. *—n.* (kom′yo͞on) Intimate conversation. [< OF *comun* common]

com·mune[2] (kom′yo͞on) *n.* 1 A small political division, as in France, Italy, and Spain. 2 A self-governing community. [< L *communis* common]

com·mu·ni·ca·ble (kə·myo͞o′nə·kə·bəl) *adj.* Capable of being communicated or transmitted. **—com·mu′ni·ca·bil′i·ty, com·mu′ni·ca·ble·ness** *n.* **—com·mu′ni·ca·bly** *adv.*

com·mu·ni·cant (kə·myo͞o′nə·kənt) *n.* 1 One who communicates or imparts, as information. 2 One who partakes of the Eucharist. *—adj.* Communicating.

com·mu·ni·cate (kə·myo͞o′nə·kāt) *v.* **·cat·ed, ·cat·ing** *v.t.* 1 To impart; transmit, as news, a disease, or an idea. *—v.i.* 2 To make or hold communication. 3 To be connected, as rooms. 4 To partake of the Eucharist. [< L *communicare* share < *communis* common] **—com·mu′ni·ca′tor** *n.*

com·mu·ni·ca·tion (kə·myo͞o′nə·kā′shən) *n.* 1 The act of communicating; exchange of ideas, conveyance of information, etc. 2 That which is communicated, as a letter or message. 3 *pl.* Means of communicating, as a highway, telephone, radio, television, etc.

com·mu·ni·ca·tive (kə·myo͞o′nə·kā′tiv, -kə·tiv) *adj.* 1 Ready to communicate; frank; talkative. 2 Of communication. **—com·mu′ni·ca′tive·ly** *adv.* **—com·mu′ni·ca′tive·ness** *n.*

com·mun·ion (kə·myo͞on′yən) *n.* 1 The act of communing or sharing. 2 A sympathetic, intimate relationship or conversation. 3 A body of Christians having a common faith and discipline. 4 *Usu. cap.* The Eucharist, or the act of celebrating or partaking of it.

com·mu·ni·qué (kə·myo͞o′nə·kā) *n.* An official message, announcement, etc. [F]

com·mu·nism (kom′yə·niz′əm) *n.* 1 A social system in which there are no classes and no private ownership of the means of production. 2 The theory of social change on which such a system is based. 3 *Often cap.* The system based on this theory in force in any state.

Com·mu·nist (kom′yə·nist) *n.* 1 A member of the Communist party. 2 Any person who endorses, supports, or advocates communism: also **communist. —com′mu·nis′tic** *adj.*

Communist party Any political party advocating communism.

com·mu·ni·ty (kə·myo͞o′nə·tē) *n. pl.* **·ties** 1 The people who reside in one locality and are subject to the same laws, have the same interests, etc. 2 The locality of such a group. 3 The public; society at large. 4 A group of plants and animals mutually reacting to create common habitat. 5 Common sharing, participation, or ownership. 6 Similarity or likeness: *community* of interest. [< L *communis* common]

community antenna television A television reception service in which a signal received at a master antenna is distributed to subscribers by cable.

com·mu·tate (kom′yə·tāt) *v.t.* **·tat·ed, ·tat·ing** *Electr.* To alter or reverse the direction of (a current). **—com′mu·ta′·tor** *n.*

com·mu·ta·tion (kom′yə·tā′shən) *n.* 1 A substitution, as of one kind of payment or service for another. 2 The payment or service substituted. 3 A reduction or change of a penalty. 4 *Electr.* The reversal of the direction of a current. 5 Daily or periodic travel on a commutation ticket. [< L *com-* thoroughly + *mutare* change]

commutation ticket A ticket issued at a reduced rate for a specified number of trips within a certain period of time.

com·mute (kə·myo͞ot′) *v.* **·mut·ed, ·mut·ing** *v.t.* 1 To exchange reciprocally for something else. 2 To change to something less severe: to *commute* a sentence. *—v.i.* 3 To serve as or be a substitute. 4 To travel as a commuter. —

n. Informal A commuter's trip, or its duration or distance: a two-hour *commute.* [<L *commutare.* See COMMUTATION] **—com·mut'a·ble** *adj.* **—com·mut'a·ble·ness, com·mut'a·bil'i·ty** *n.*
com·mut·er (kə·myōō'tər) *n.* One who daily or regularly travels for some distance between his or her home and place of work, school, etc.
comp. companion; comparative; compare; comparison; compiled; complete; composer; composition; compositor; compound; comprising.
com·pact[1] (kəm·pakt', kom'pakt) *adj.* **1** Closely and firmly united, pressed together; solid; dense. **2** Condensed; brief; terse. **3** Composed; made up: with *of.* **4** Relatively small: a *compact* car. *—v.t.* (kəm·pakt') To pack or press closely; condense. *—n.* (kom'pakt) **1** A small, hinged box for face powder and sometimes rouge. **2** A compact car. [<L *compactus,* pp. of *compangere* fasten together] **—com·pact'ly** *adv.* **—com·pact'ness** *n.*
com·pact[2] (kom'pakt) *n.* A covenant, agreement, or contract. [<L *compactus,* pp. of *compacisci* agree together]
compact disc A small digital disc on which recorded sound has been encoded so as to be replayed on an electronic device that utilizes a laser beam to reproduce the original sound with a very high level of fidelity.
com·pan·ion (kəm·pan'yən) *n.* **1** One who or that which accompanies; a comrade; associate. **2** One hired to live or travel with another. **3** A mate; one of a pair. *—v.t.* To be a companion to; accompany. [<LL *companio* <L *com-* together + *panis* bread] **—com·pan'ion·ship** *n.*
com·pan·ion·a·ble (kəm·pan'yən·ə·bəl) *adj.* Fitted for companionship; friendly. **—com·pan'ion·a·bil'i·ty** *n.* **—com·pan'ion·a·bly** *adv.*
com·pan·ion·ate (kəm·pan'yən·it) *adj.* Of companionship or association.
com·pan·ion·way (kəm·pan'yən·wā') *n.* A staircase from the deck of a ship to its cabins.
com·pa·ny (kum'pə·nē) *n. pl.* **·nies** **1** The society or presence of another or others. **2** One or more guests or visitors. **3** A business firm or corporation. **4** A number of persons associated for some common purpose. **5** The person or persons with whom one often associates: keeping bad *company.* **6** A body of soldiers, usu. a unit made up of two or more platoons and a headquarters. **7** A ship's crew, including officers. **8** A group of performers who work together: a ballet *company.* [<OF *compagnon* companion] **—Syn.** *n.* **1** companionship, fellowship. **4** assembly, group. **8** troupe.
compar. comparative; comparison.
com·pa·ra·ble (kom'pər·ə·bəl, kəm·par'-) *adj.* **1** Capable of being compared. **2** Worthy of comparison **—com'pa·ra·ble·ness, com'pa·ra·bil'i·ty** *n.* **—com'pa·ra·bly** *adv.*
com·par·a·tive (kəm·par'ə·tiv) *adj.* **1** Of, using, or resulting from comparison. **2** Not total or absolute; relative. **3** *Gram.* Expressing a degree of an adjective or adverb higher than the positive and lower than the superlative: "Better" is the *comparative* form of "good." *—n. Gram.* The comparative degree. **—com·par'a·tive·ly** *adv.*
com·pare (kəm·pâr') *v.* **·pared, ·par·ing** *v.t.* **1** To represent or speak of as similar, analogous, or equal: with *to.* **2** To examine so as to perceive and note similarity or dissimilarity: with *with.* **3** *Gram.* To form the degrees of comparison of (an adjective or adverb). *—v.i.* **4** To be worthy of comparison: with *with.* *—n.* Comparison: usu. in the phrase *beyond compare.* [<L *comparare* <*com-* together + *par* equal] • **compare to; compare with** Formal usage requires that one use *compare to* when noting a striking similarity between two things: The industrial potential of Japan *compares to* that of many larger nations. If the things being compared are similar in some aspects but dissimilar in others, *compare with* is preferred: to *compare* the physical discipline demanded of a classical ballet dancer *with* that required of a gymnast.
com·par·i·son (kəm·par'ə·sən) *n.* **1** An estimate or statement of relative likeness or unlikeness. **2** Similarity. **3** *Gram.* That inflection of adjectives or adverbs which indicates the positive, comparative, and superlative degrees.
com·part·ment (kəm·pärt'mənt) *n.* **1** One of the divisions or sections into which an enclosed space is subdivided. **2** Any separate section, category, division, etc. [<L *com-* together + *pars* a part]
com·pass (kum'pəs) *n.* **1** An instrument for determining direction, as from the earth's magnetic field. **2** *Often pl.* Any of various instruments having two legs hinged at the top, used for drawing circles, taking measurements, etc. **3** An enclosed area. **4** A boundary or circumference. **5** A range or scope, esp. the range of a voice or instrument. *—v.t.* **1** To go around; make a circuit of. **2** To surround; encompass. **3** To grasp mentally; comprehend. **4** To plot or scheme. **5** To attain or accomplish. [<L *com-* together + *passus* step] **—com'pass·a·ble** *adj.*

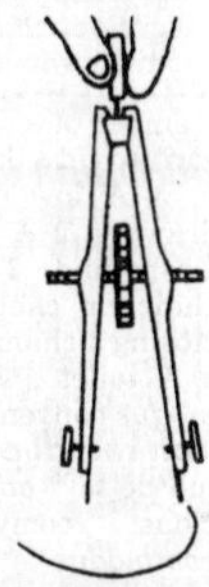
Compass *def. 2*

compass card The circular card or dial resting on the pivot of a mariner's compass, on which the 32 points of the compass and 360 degrees of the circle are marked. Also **compass dial.**
com·pas·sion (kəm·pash'ən) *n.* Pity for suffering, with desire to help; sympathy. [<L *com-* together + *pati* feel, suffer] **—Syn.** mercy, commiseration, empathy, clemency, charity.
com·pas·sion·ate (kəm·pash'ən·it) *adj.* Feeling compassion or pity; sympathetic. *—v.t.* (kəm·pash'ən·āt) **·at·ed, ·at·ing** To have compassion for; to pity. **—com·pas'sion·ate·ly** *adv.* **—com·pas'sion·ate·ness** *n.*
com·pat·i·ble (kəm·pat'ə·bəl) *adj.* **1** Capable of existing or living together; congruous; congenial. **2** Describing a television system in which broadcasts in color may be received in black and white on sets not adapted for color reception. [<L *com-* together + *pati* suffer] **—com·pat'i·bil'i·ty, com·pat'i·ble·ness** *n.* **—com·pat'i·bly** *adv.*
com·pa·tri·ot (kəm·pā'trē·ət, -pat'rē·ət) *n.* **1** A fellow countryman. **2** *Informal* A colleague.
com·pel (kəm·pel') *v.t.* **·pelled, ·pel·ling** **1** To drive or urge irresistibly; constrain. **2** To get or obtain by force. [<L *com-* together + *pellere* drive] **—com·pel'la·ble** *adj.* **—com·pel'la·bly** *adv.* **—com·pel'ler** *n.*
com·pel·ling (kəm·pel'ing) *adj.* Convincing; cogent: *compelling* evidence. **—com·pel'ling·ly** *adv.*
com·pen·di·ous (kəm·pen'dē·əs) *adj.* Briefly stated; succinct. [<L *compendiosus* brief] **—com·pen'di·ous·ly** *adv.* **—com·pen'di·ous·ness** *n.*
com·pen·di·um (kəm·pen'dē·əm) *n. pl.* **·di·ums** or **·di·a** (-dē·ə) A brief, comprehensive summary; abridgment. [<L *com-* together + *pendere* weigh]
com·pen·sa·ble (kəm·pen'sə·bəl) *adj.* Entitled to be or capable of being compensated.
com·pen·sate (kom'pən·sāt) *v.* **·sat·ed, ·sat·ing** *v.t.* **1** To make suitable amends to or for; remunerate. **2** To counterbalance or make up for; offset. *—v.i.* **3** To make compensation or amends: often with *for.* [<L *com-* together + *pensare,* freq. of *pendere* weigh] **—com·pen'sa·tive** (kəm·pen'sə·tiv), **com·pen·sa·to·ry** (kəm·pen'sə·tôr'ē, -tō'rē) *adj.* **—com'pen·sa'tor** *n.*
com·pen·sa·tion (kom'pən·sā'shən) *n.* **1** The act of compensating. **2** That which compensates or makes amends, as wages, unemployment benefits, etc. **3** *Biol.* The correction or counterbalancing of some organic defect or malfunction by a new or heightened activity in a different organ or an unimpaired part of the same organ. **4** *Psychol.* A mechanism by which a person attempts to compensate for feelings of inferiority or frustration in one area by achievement in another. **—com'pen·sa'tion·al** *adj.*
com·pete (kəm·pēt') *v.i.* **·pet·ed, ·pet·ing** To contend with another or others for a prize, superiority, etc.; vie. [<L *com-* together + *petere* seek]
com·pe·tence (kom'pə·təns) *n.* **1** The state of being competent. **2** Sufficient means for comfortable living. Also **com'pe·ten·cy.**
com·pe·tent (kom'pə·tənt) *adj.* **1** Sufficiently able or qualified; fit: a *competent* physician. **2** Sufficient; adequate. **3** Legally capable or qualified: *competent* to stand

trial. [<L *com-* together + *petere* go, seek] **—com'pe·tent·ly** *adv.* **—com'pe·tent·ness** *n.*

com·pe·ti·tion (kom'pə·tish'ən) *n.* **1** The act of competing; rivalry, as in business, athletics, etc. **2** The quality or degree of competitiveness or opposition. **3** Those persons against whom one competes. **4** A specific contest.

com·pet·i·tive (kəm·pet'ə·tiv) *adj.* Of or marked by competition. **—com·pet'i·tive·ly** *adj.* **—com·pet'i·tive·ness** *n.*

com·pet·i·tor (kəm·pet'ə·ter) *n.* One who competes; a rival: a business *competitor.*

com·pile (kəm·pīl') *v.t.* **·piled, ·pil·ing 1** To compose (a literary work, etc.) from other works or sources. **2** To gather (facts, data, etc.) into a volume or into orderly form. [<L *com-* thoroughly + *pilare* strip, plunder] **—com·pi·la·tion** (kom'pə·lā'shən) *n.*

com·pil·er (kəm·pī'lər) *n.* A computer program that translates instruction programs into machine language.

com·pla·cen·cy (kəm·plā'sən·sē) *n. pl.* **·cies 1** Satisfaction, esp. with oneself. **2** EQUANIMITY. Also **com·pla'cence.**

com·pla·cent (kəm·plā'sənt) *adj.* Feeling or showing complacency, esp. smugly self-satisfied. [<L *com-* thoroughly + *placere* to please] **—com·pla'cent·ly** *adv.*

com·plain (kəm·plān') *v.i.* **1** To express a sense of ill-treatment or of pain, grief, etc. **2** To find fault. **3** To make a formal accusation. [<L *com-* thoroughly + *plangere* beat (the breast in grief)] **—com·plain'er** *n.* **—com·plain'ing·ly** *adv.* **—Syn. 1** murmur, whine, lament. **2** grumble, deplore, gripe.

com·plain·ant (kəm·plā'nənt) *n.* One who complains, esp. before a magistrate or other authority.

com·plaint (kəm·plānt') *n.* **1** A statement of wrong, grievance, or injury. **2** The paper setting forth the plaintiff's cause of action. **3** A grievance. **4** A physical ailment; disease.

com·plai·sant (kəm·plā'sənt, -zənt) *adj.* Showing a desire to please; obliging. [<L *complacere* to please thoroughly] **—com·plai'sance** *n.* **—com·plai'sant·ly** *adv.*

com·plect·ed (kəm·plek'tid) *adj. Informal or Regional* COMPLEXIONED.

com·ple·ment (kom'plə·mənt) *n.* **1** That which fills up, completes, or makes perfect. **2** The number needed to fill or make complete. **3** Either of two parts that together form a whole; a counterpart. **4** Full number: the vessel has her *complement* of men. **5** *Geom.* The amount by which an angle or arc falls short of 90 degrees. **6** *Gram.* A word or phrase used after a verb to complete the meaning of the predicate, as *happy* in *She is happy.* —*v.t.* To supply a lack in; make complete; supplement. [<L *complere* complete] **—com·ple·men·tal** (kom'plə·men'təl) *adj.* • See SUPPLEMENT.

com·ple·men·ta·ry (kom'plə·men'tər·ē, -trē) *adj.* **1** Serving as a complement; completing. **2** Mutually providing each other's needs.

com·plete (kəm·plēt') *adj.* **·plet·er, ·plet·est 1** Having all needed or normal parts, elements, or details; lacking nothing; entire. **2** Thoroughly wrought; finished. **3** Perfect. —*v.t.* **·plet·ed, ·plet·ing 1** To make entire or whole. **2** To make perfect. **3** To finish; fulfill; end. [<L *com-* thoroughly + *plere* fill] **—com·plete'ly** *adv.* **—com·plete'ness** *n.* **—com·ple'tive** *adj.*

com·ple·tion (kəm·plē'shən) *n.* **1** The act of completing or the state of being completed. **2** Accomplishment; fulfillment.

com·plex (kəm·pleks', kom'pleks) *adj.* **1** Consisting of various parts or elements; composite. **2** Complicated; involved; intricate. —*n.* (kom'pleks) **1** A whole made up of interrelated parts or units. **2** *Psychoanal.* A group of interrelated and usu. repressed ideas with strong emotional content which distorts patterns of thought and behavior. **3** Loosely, an extreme or exaggerated fear or dislike. [<L *complexus,* pp. of *complectere* twist together] **—com·plex'ly** *adv.* **—com·plex'ness** *n.*

complex fraction A fraction having a fraction in its numerator or denominator, or in each.

com·plex·ion (kəm·plek'shən) *n.* **1** The color and appearance of the skin, esp. of the face. **2** General aspect; character; quality. [<L *complexio* the constitution of a body, a combination < *complectere* twist together] **—com·plex'ion·al** *adj.*

com·plex·ioned (kəm·plek'shənd) *adj.* Having a (specified) facial complexion.

com·plex·i·ty (kəm·plek'sə·tē) *n. pl.* **·ties 1** The state of being complex. **2** Something complex.

complex number A number of the form $a + bi$ in which a and b are real numbers and i is the square root of -1.

complex sentence A sentence having one main clause and one or more subordinate clauses.

com·pli·ance (kəm·plī'əns) *n.* **1** The act of complying, yielding, or acting in accord. **2** The disposition or willingness to please. Also **com·pli'an·cy.**

com·pli·ant (kəm·plī'ənt) *adj* Disposed or willing to comply. **—com·pli'ant·ly** *adv.*

com·pli·cate (kom'plə·kāt) *v.t. & v.i.* **·cat·ed, ·cat·ing** *v.t.* To make or become complex, difficult, or perplexing. —*adj.* (kom'plə·kit) Complicated; complex. [<L *com-* together + *plicare* to fold] **—com'pli·ca'tive** *adj.*

com·pli·cat·ed (kom'plə·kā'tid) *adj.* **1** Containing many parts or elements; intricate. **2** Difficult to analyze, understand, solve, etc. **—com'pli·cat'ed·ly** *adv.* **—com'pli·cat'ed·ness** *n.*

com·pli·ca·tion (kom'plə·kā'shən) *n.* **1** The act of complicating or the state of being complicated. **2** Anything that complicates, as an abnormal condition that aggravates a preexisting but unrelated disease.

com·plic·i·ty (kəm·plis'ə·tē) *n. pl.* **·ties** The act or state of being an accomplice, as in a crime.

com·pli·ment (kom'plə·mənt) *n.* **1** An expression of admiration, praise, congratulation, etc. **2** *pl.* A formal greeting or remembrance. —*v.t.* (kom'plə·ment) **1** To pay a compliment to. **2** To show regard for, as by a gift or other favor. [<Sp. *cumplimiento,* lit., completion of courtesy <L *complementum* completion]

com·pli·men·ta·ry (kom'plə·men'tər·ē, -trē) *adj.* **1** Expressing a compliment. **2** Given free. **—com'pli·men'ta·ri·ly** *adv.*

com·plin (kom'plin) *n.* The last of the canonical hours.

com·ply (kəm·plī') *v.i.* **·plied, ·ply·ing** To act in conformity; consent; obey: with *with.* [<Sp. *cumplir* complete an act of courtesy <L *complere* to complete] **—com·pli'er** *n.*

com·po·nent (kəm·pō'nənt) *n.* A constituent part. —*adj.* Forming a part or ingredient. [<L *componere* to place together]

com·port (kəm·pôrt', -pōrt') *v.t.* To conduct (oneself). —*v.i.* To be compatible; agree. [<L *com-* together + *portare* carry]

com·port·ment (kəm·pôrt'mənt, -pōrt'-) *n.* Behavior; deportment.

com·pose (kəm·pōz') *v.* **·posed, ·pos·ing** *v.t.* **1** To be the constituent elements or parts of; constitute; form. **2** To tranquilize; calm. **3** To reconcile, arrange, or settle, as differences. **4** To create artistically, as a literary or musical work. **5** To arrange (type) in lines; set. —*v.i.* **6** To engage in composition, as of a literary or musical work. **7** To set type. [<L *com-* together + *poser* to put]

com·posed (kəm·pōzd') *adj.* Free from agitation; calm. **—com·pos·ed·ly** (kəm·pō'zid·lē) *adv.* **—com·pos'ed·ness** *n.*

com·pos·er (kəm·pō'zər) *n.* One who composes, esp. one who composes music.

com·pos·ite (kəm·poz'it) *adj.* **1** Made up of separate parts or elements. **2** *Bot.* Belonging to a large family of plants, as the aster, sunflower, etc., having massed heads of modified florets that resemble single flowers. —*n.* That which is composed of parts; a compound. [<L *compositus,* pp. of *componere* to put together] **—com·pos'ite·ly** *adv.*

com·po·si·tion (kom'pə·zish'ən) *n.* **1** The act or art of composing a literary, musical, or artistic work. **2** The work so composed or its general arrangement or style. **3** Any putting together of separate elements or parts to form a whole; also, the whole so formed. **4** The general nature or makeup of a thing or person. **5** The act or skill of setting type.

com·pos·i·tor (kəm·poz'ə·tər) *n.* One who sets type; typesetter.

com·post (kom'pōst) *n.* A mixture of decomposed vegetable matter, used as fertilizer. [<L *compositus.* See COMPOSITE.]

com·po·sure (kəm·pō'zhər) *n.* Tranquility, as of manner; calmness; serenity.

com·pote (kom′pōt, *Fr.* kôṅ·pôt′) *n.* **1** Fruit stewed or preserved in syrup. **2** A dish for holding fruits, etc. [< L *compositus* put together. See COMPOSITE.]

com·pound[1] (kom′pound) *n.* **1** A combination of two or more elements, ingredients, or parts. **2** *Chem.* A substance composed of two or more elements combined chemically in definite proportions by weight. —*v.* (kom·pound′, kəm-) *v.t.* **1** To make by the combination of various elements or ingredients. **2** To mix (elements or parts); combine. **3** To settle for less than the sum due: to *compound* a debt. **4** To make more serious or complicated. **5** To compute (interest) on the principal and the interest that has accrued. —*v.i.* **6** To compromise or agree. —*adj.* (kom′pound, kom·pound′) Composed of or produced by the union of two or more elements, ingredients, or parts. [< L *componere* to put together] **—com·pound′a·ble** *adj.* **—com·pound′er** *n.*

com·pound[2] (kom′pound) *n.* An enclosed area of dwellings, as for prisoners of war. [< Malay *kampong*]

compound fracture A bone fracture in which a broken end of bone penetrates the skin.

compound interest Interest computed not only on the principal but also on the unpaid interest that has accrued.

compound sentence A sentence having at least two independent clauses.

com·pre·hend (kom′pri·hend′) *v.t.* **1** To grasp mentally; understand fully. **2** To include, take in, or comprise. [< L *com-* together + *prehendere* seize] **—com′pre·hend′i·ble** *adj.*

com·pre·hen·si·ble (kom′pri·hen′sə·bəl) *adj.* That can be comprehended; understandable. **—com′pre·hen′si·bil′i·ty, com′pre·hen′si·ble·ness** *n.* **—com′pre·hen′si·bly** *adv.*

com·pre·hen·sion (kom′pri·hen′shən) *n.* **1** The act of comprehending or understanding. **2** The ability to do this. **3** The knowledge so gained. **4** The state or quality of being comprehensive.

com·pre·hen·sive (kom′pri·hen′sive) *adj.* **1** Large in scope or content; broadly inclusive. **2** Able to understand fully. **—com′pre·hen′sive·ly** *adv.* **—com′pre·hen′sive·ness** *n.*

com·press (kəm·pres′) *v.t.* To press together or into smaller space; compact. —*n.* (kom′pres) **1** A device for compressing. **2** *Med.* A soft pad for applying pressure, heat, moisture, etc. to a part of the body. [< LL *compressare,* freq. of *comprimere* press together] **—com·press′i·ble, com·press′ive** *adj.* **—com·press′i·bil′i·ty, com·press′i·ble·ness** *n.*

com·pres·sion (kəm·presh′ən) *n.* The act of compressing or the state of being compressed.

com·pres·sor (kəm·pres′ər) *n.* **1** One who or that which compresses. **2** *Mech.* A machine for compressing a gas.

com·prise (kəm·prīz′) *v.t.* **·prised, ·pris·ing** To include and contain; consist of. [< L *comprehendere* comprehend] **—com·pris′a·ble** *adj.* **—com·pri′sal** *n.*

com·pro·mise (kom′prə·mīz) *n.* **1** A settlement by arbitration and mutual concession. **2** An adjustment or concession between conflicting courses, ideas, desires, etc. **3** An imperiling or surrender, as of character or reputation. —*v.* **·mised, ·mis·ing** *v.t.* **1** To adjust or settle by concessions. **2** To imperil or surrender. —*v.i.* **3** To make a compromise. [< L *com-* together + *promittere* promise] **—com′pro·mis′er** *n.*

comp·trol·ler (kən·trō′lər) *n.* CONTROLLER (def. 2). **—comp·trol′ler·ship** *n.*

com·pul·sion (kəm·pul′shən) *n.* **1** The act of compelling or the state of being compelled. **2** *Psychol.* An irresistible urge to perform some act without rational purpose. **—com·pul′sive** *adj.* **—com·pul′sive·ly** *adv.* **—com·pul′sive·ness** *n.*

com·pul·so·ry (kəm·pul′sər·ē) *adj.* **1** Employing compulsion; coercive. **2** Required by law or other rule. **—com·pul′so·ri·ly** *adv.* **—com·pul′so·ri·ness** *n.*

com·punc·tion (kəm·pungk′shən) *n.* **1** Self-reproach for wrong-doing; guilt. **2** A feeling of slight regret. [< L *com-* greatly + *pungere* to prick, sting] **—com·punc′tious** *adj.*

com·pu·ta·tion (kom′pyə·tā′shən) *n.* **1** The act of computing; calculation. **2** A computed amount or number.

com·pute (kəm·pyōōt′) *v.t.* **·put·ed, ·put·ing** To estimate numerically; calculate. [< L *com-* together + *putare* reckon] **—com·put′a·bil′i·ty** *n.* **—com·put′a·ble** *adj.*

com·put·er (kəm·pyōō′tər) *n.* **1** One who or that which computes. **2** An electronic machine capable of accepting data, manipulating or performing arithmetic on such data at high speed, and showing or printing the results.

com·put·er·ize (kəm·pyōō′tər·īz) *v.t.* **·ized, ·iz·ing** **1** To operate or process by or as if by computer. **2** To equip with computers. *Brit. sp.* **·ise.** **—com·put′er·i·za′tion** *n.*

Comr. Commissioner.

com·rade (kom′rad, -rid) *n.* **1** A friend or close companion. **2** A fellow member, as of a political party, esp. the Communist party. [< Sp. *camarada* roommate < L *camera* room] **—com′rade·ship** *n.*

com·sat (kom′sat′) *n.* Any of various artificial satellites employed to relay radio or television signals, etc. [< COM(MUNICATIONS) + SAT(ELLITE)]

con[1] (kon) *v.t.* **conned, con·ning** To peruse carefully; study. [< OE *cunnan* to know]

con[2] (kon) *adv.* Against. —*n.* Something opposed, as a reason, position, etc. [< L *contra* against]

con[3] (kon) *Slang adj.* Confidence: a *con* game. —*v.t.* **conned, con·ning** **1** To defraud; swindle. **2** To persuade, as by flattery.

con[4] (kon) *n. Slang* A convict.

con. against (L *contra*); concerto; conclusion; connection; conduct; consolidated; continued; wife (L *conjunx*).

con·cat·e·nate (kon·kat′ə·nāt) *v.t.* **·nat·ed, ·nat·ing** To join or link together; connect in a series. [< L *com-* together + *catena* chain] **—con·cat′e·na′tion** *n.*

con·cave (kon·kāv′, kon′kāv, kong′-) *adj.* Hollow and rounded, as the interior of a sphere or circle. —*n.* (kon′·kāv, kong′-) A concave surface. [< L *com-* thoroughly + *cavus* hollow] **—con·cave′ly** *adv.* • See CONVEX.

con·cav·i·ty (kon·kav′ə·tē) *n. pl.* **·ties** **1** The state of being concave. **2** A concave surface, object, line, etc.

con·ceal (kən·sēl′) *v.t.* To keep from sight, discovery, or knowledge; hide. [< L *com-* thoroughly + *celare* hide] **—con·ceal′a·ble** *adj.* **—con·ceal′er, con·ceal′ment** *n.*

con·cede (kən·sēd′) *v.* **·ced·ed, ·ced·ing** *v.t.* **1** To grant as a right or privilege. **2** To acknowledge as true, correct, or proper; admit. —*v.i.* **3** To make a concession. [< L *com-* thoroughly + *cedere* yield, go away] **—con·ced′er** *n.*

con·ceit (kən·sēt′) *n.* **1** Excessive self-esteem or vanity. **2** A fanciful or elaborate idea, expression, or metaphor. **3** Imagination. **4** A small, ingenious article or design. [< CONCEIVE]

con·ceit·ed (kən·sē′tid) *adj.* Having an excessively fine opinion of oneself; vain. **—con·ceit′ed·ly** *adv.* **—con·ceit′·ed·ness** *n.* **—Syn.** immodest, egotistic, haughty, arrogant.

con·ceive (kən·sēv′) *v.* **·ceived, ·ceiv·ing** *v.t.* **1** To become pregnant with. **2** To form in the mind; think of. **3** To believe or suppose. **4** To express in words. —*v.i.* **5** To form an idea or conception: with *of.* **6** To become pregnant. [< L *com-* thoroughly + *capere* take] **—con·ceiv′a·ble** *adj.* **—con·ceiv′a·bil′i·ty, con·ceiv′a·ble·ness, con·ceiv′er** *n.* **—con·ceiv′a·bly** *adv.*

con·cen·trate (kon′sən·trāt) *v.* **·trat·ed, ·trat·ing** *v.t.* **1** To bring or draw to a common center; focus. **2** To increase the strength or density of, as by condensation. **3** To fix or focus (one's thoughts, actions, etc.). —*v.i.* **4** To converge toward a center. **5** To fix or focus one's thoughts, actions, etc.: with *on* or *upon.* —*n.* A product of concentration. [< L *com-* together + *centrum* center] **—con·cen·tra·tive** (kon′sən·trā′tiv, kən·sen′trə·tiv) *adj.* **—con′cen·tra′tor** *n.*

con·cen·tra·tion (kon′sən·trā′·shən) *n.* **1** The act of concentrating or the state of being concentrated. **2** That which is concentrated. **3** The amount of one substance contained per unit volume of another substance; density.

Concentric tree rings

concentration camp A place of detention for prisoners of war, political prisoners, aliens, etc.

con·cen·tric (kən·sen′trik) *adj.* Having a common center: *concentric* circles. Also **con·**

cen′tri·cal. —**con·cen′tri·cal·ly** *adv.* —**con·cen·tric·i·ty** (kon′·sen·tris′ə·tē) *n.*

con·cept (kon′sept) *n.* An idea, thought, or opinion. [< L *conceptus* a conceiving]

con·cep·tion (kən·sep′shən) *n.* **1** The act of becoming pregnant. **2** An embryo or fetus. **3** The act of conceiving ideas or notions. **4** An idea, thought, or concept. —**con·cep′·tion·al, con·cep′tive** *adj.*

con·cep·tu·al (kən·sep′cho͞o·əl) *adj.* Of conception or a concept. —**con·cep′tu·al·ly** *adv.*

con·cern (kən·sûrn′) *v.t.* **1** To be of interest, relevance, or importance to. **2** To cause to be anxious or troubled. —*n.* **1** That which concerns one; something affecting one's interest or welfare. **2** Interest or regard. **3** Anxiety; worry. **4** Relation; reference. **5** A business establishment. [< Med. L. *com-* thoroughly + *cernere* to see, discern]

con·cerned (kən·sûrnd′) *adj.* **1** Involved or implicated. **2** Anxious; uneasy.

con·cern·ing (kən·sûr′ning) *prep.* In relation to; regarding; about.

con·cern·ment (kən·sûrn′mənt) *n.* **1** Bearing; importance. **2** Anxiety; solicitude. **3** Affair; concern; business.

con·cert (kon′sûrt) *n.* **1** A performance, as by a solo musician, an orchestra, dance group, etc. **2** Harmony; unity. —**in concert** Together. —*adj.* Of or for concerts. —*v.* (kən·sûrt′) *v.t. & v.i.* To arrange or contrive by mutual agreement. [< Ital. *concertare* agree]

con·cert·ed (kən·sûr′tid) *adj.* Arranged or agreed upon in concert. —**con·cert′ed·ly** *adv.*

con·cer·ti·na (kon′sər·tē′nə) *n.* A small, simple accordion. [< Ital. *concerto* a concert]

con·cert·mas·ter (kon′sərt·mas′tər, -mäs′-) *n.* The leader of the first violin section of an orchestra, who often serves as assistant to the conductor.

con·cer·to (kən·cher′tō) *n. pl.* **·tos, ·ti** (-tē) A composition, usu. having three movements, for performance by a solo instrument or instruments accompanied by an orchestra. [< Ital., concert]

con·ces·sion (kən·sesh′ən) *n.* **1** The act of conceding, or that which is conceded. **2** A privilege granted by a government, as the right to use land. **3** The right or a lease to operate a small business, as selling food, newspapers, etc., in office buildings, railroad stations, etc. **4** The space, land, etc., so leased, or the activity carried on there. [< L *concessus*, pp. of *concedere* to concede]

con·ces·sion·aire (kən·sesh′ən·âr′) *n.* One who holds a concession. Also **con·ces·sion·er** (kən·sesh′ən·ər).

conch (kongk, konch) *n. pl.* **conchs** (kongks) or **conch·es** (kon′chiz) The large, spiral shell of various marine mollusks. [< Gk. *konchē* shell]

con·ci·erge (kon′sē·ûrzh′, *Fr.* kôṅ·syârzh′) A doorkeeper or attendant, as of an apartment house or hotel, esp. in France. [F]

con·cil·i·ate (kən·sil′ē·āt) *v.t.* **·at·ed, ·at·ing 1** To overcome the enmity or hostility of; placate. **2** To secure or attract by reconciling measures; win. [< L *concilium* council] —**con·cil′i·a′tion, con·cil′i·a′tor** *n.* —**con·cil·i·a·to·ry** (kən·sil′ē·ə·tôr′ē, -tō′rē), **con·cil′i·a′tive** *adj.* —**con·cil′i·a·to′ri·ly** *adv.*

con·cise (kən·sīs′) *adj.* Expressing much in brief form; compact. [< L *concisus*, pp. of *concidere* to cut thoroughly] —**con·cise′ly** *adv.* —**con·cise′ness** *n.* —**Syn.** brief, terse, pithy, short, compact.

con·clave (kon′klāv, kong′-) *n.* **1** A secret council or meeting. **2 a** The apartments in the Vatican in which the college of cardinals meets to choose a pope. **b** The meeting itself. [< L, a place which can be locked up]

con·clude (kən·klo͞od′) *v.* **·clud·ed, ·clud·ing** *v.t.* **1** To come to a decision about; decide or determine. **2** To infer or deduce as a result or effect. **3** To arrange or settle finally. **4** To terminate. —*v.i.* **5** To come to an end. **6** To come to a decision. [< L *com-* thoroughly + *claudere* close, shut off] —**con·clud′er** *n.*

con·clu·sion (kən·klo͞o′zhən) *n.* **1** The act or an instance of concluding; termination. **2** A conviction reached by reasoning, inference, etc. **3** The last or closing part of something. **4** A result or outcome.

con·clu·sive (kən·klo͞o′siv) *adj.* **1** Putting an end to doubt; decisive. **2** Leading to a conclusion; final. —**con·clu′sive·ly** *adv.* —**con·clu′sive·ness** *n.*

con·coct (kon·kokt′, kən-) *v.t.* **1** To make by mixing ingredients, as a drink or soup. **2** To contrive; devise. [< L *com-* together + *coquere* to cook, boil] —**con·coct′er, con·coc′tor** *n.*

con·coc·tion (kon·kok′shən, kən-) *n.* **1** The act of concocting. **2** Something concocted.

con·com·i·tant (kon·kom′ə·tənt, kən-) *adj.* Existing or occurring together; attendant. —*n.* An attendant circumstance. [< L *com-* with + *comitari* accompany] —**con·com′·i·tance, con·com′i·tan·cy** *n.* —**con·com′i·tant·ly** *adv.*

con·cord (kon′kôrd, kong′-) *n.* **1** Unity of feeling or interest; agreement; accord. **2** A peace treaty. **3** *Music* A harmonious combination of simultaneous tones. **4** *Gram.* AGREEMENT (def. 5). [< L *concors* agreeing < *com-* together + *cor* heart]

con·cor·dance (kon·kôr′dəns, kən-) *n.* **1** An alphabetical list of the important words in a book or books, with reference to the passages in which each word is found. **2** Concord; agreement; harmony.

con·cor·dant (kon·kôr′dənt, kən-) *adj.* Harmonious; agreeing. —**con·cor′dant·ly** *adv.*

con·cor·dat (kon·kôr′dat) *n.* **1** An agreement between the papal see and a secular power for the settlement and regulation of ecclesiastical affairs. **2** Any public agreement.

con·course (kon′kôrs, -kōrs, kong′-) *n.* **1** An assembling or moving together; confluence. **2** An assembly; throng. **3** A large area for the passage of crowds, as a boulevard or a long passageway in a railroad station, subway, etc. [< L *concurrere* to run together]

con·crete (kon′krēt, kon·krēt′) *adj.* **1** Not general or abstract; specific. **2** Actually existing; real. **3** Made of concrete. **4** Joined into or being a solid mass. —*n.* **1** A material made of sand and gravel that is united by cement into a hardened mass, used for roads, foundations, etc. • See CEMENT. **2** Something concrete, as an idea, circumstance, etc. —*v.* (kon·krēt′; *usu. for def. 2* kon′krēt) **·cret·ed, ·cret·ing** *v.t.* **1** To unite together in one mass or body. **2** To treat or cover with concrete. —*v.i.* **3** To solidify. [< L *concretus*, pp. of *concrescere* to grow together] —**con·crete′ly** *adv.* —**con·crete′ness** *n.*

con·cre·tion (kon·krē′shən) *n.* **1** The act or an instance of concreting. **2** A solid mass. **3** *Geol.* An aggregate of rounded masses found in sedimentary rocks. —**con·cre′·tive** *adj.* —**con·cre′tive·ly** *adv.*

con·cre·tize (kon′kri·tīz, kong′-) *v.t.* **·tized, ·tiz·ing** To present in concrete terms; make actual or specific. —**con′cre·ti·za′tion** *n.*

con·cu·bine (kong′kyə·bīn, kon′-) *n.* **1** A woman who cohabits with a man without a marriage bond. **2** In certain polygamous societies, a secondary wife. [< L *com-* with + *cumbere* lie] —**con·cu′bi·nage** *n.*

con·cu·pis·cence (kon·kyo͞o′pə·səns) *n.* **1** Sexual desire; lust. **2** Any inordinate appetite or desire. [< L *com-* thoroughly + *cupere* to desire] —**con·cu′pis·cent** *adj.*

con·cur (kən·kûr′) *v.i.* **·curred, ·cur·ring 1** To agree, as in opinion or action: Three justices *concurred* in the finding. **2** To happen at the same time; coincide. **3** To act together: Many facts *concurred* to defeat him. [< L *com-* together + *currere* to run] —**con·cur′rence** *n.*

con·cur·rent (kən·kûr′ənt) *adj.* **1** Occurring or acting together. **2** In agreement. **3** Meeting at the same point. —**·cur′rent·ly** *adv.*

con·cus·sion (kən·kush′ən) *n.* **1** A violent shaking; shock. **2** Injury to soft tissue, esp. the brain, due to a violent shock or blow. [< L *concussus*, pp. of *concutere* to beat together] —**con·cus·sive** (kən·kus′iv) *adj.*

con·demn (kən·dem′) *v.t.* **1** To hold or prove to be wrong; censure. **2** To prove to be wrong or guilty, esp. to pronounce judicial sentence against. **3** To forbid the use of, commonly by official order, as something unfit. **4** To appropriate for public use by judicial decree. **5** To doom. [< L *com-* thoroughly + *damnare* condemn] —**con·dem·na·ble** (kən·dem′nə·bəl), **con·dem·na·to·ry** (kən·dem′nə·tôr′ē, -tō′rē) *adj.* —**con·demn·er** (kən·dem′ər) *n.* —**Syn. 1** blame, denounce, rebuke, vilify.

con·dem·na·tion (kon′dem·nā′shən) *n.* **1** The act of condemning or the state of being condemned. **2** The cause for condemning.

con·den·sa·tion (kon′den·sā′shən) *n.* **1** The act of condensing or the state of being condensed. **2** The reduction of a vapor or gas to a liquid or solid, or of a liquid to a solid or semisolid. **3** Any product of condensing.

con·dense (kən·dens′) *v.* **·densed, ·dens·ing** *v.t.* **1** To compress or make dense; subject to condensation. **2** To abridge or make concise. —*v.i.* **3** To become condensed. [< L *condensus* thick < *com-* together + *densus* crowded, close] —**con·dens′a·bil′i·ty** *n.* —**con·dens′a·ble** or **con·dens′i·ble** *adj.*

condensed milk Cow's milk, sweetened, and thickened by evaporation.

con·dens·er (kən·den′sər) *n.* **1** One who or that which condenses. **2** Any device for condensing a vapor. **3** *Electr.* A capacitor. **4** *Optics* A combination of lenses for focusing light rays.

con·de·scend (kon′di·send′) *v.i.* **1** To come down voluntarily to equal terms with a supposed inferior so as to do something; deign. **2** To behave towards others in a patronizing manner. [< L *com-* thoroughly + *descendere* to descend] —**con′de·scen′dence** *n.* —**con′de·scend′ing** *adj.* —**con′de·scend′ing·ly** *adv.*

con·de·scen·sion (kon′di·sen′shən) *n.* **1** An act or instance of condescending. **2** A patronizing manner.

con·dign (kən·dīn′) *adj.* Merited; deserved: said of punishment. [< L *com-* thoroughly + *dignus* worthy]

con·di·ment (kon′də·mənt) *n.* A sauce, relish, spice, etc. [< L *condimentum*]

con·di·tion (kən·dish′ən) *n.* **1** The state or mode in which a person or thing exists. **2** State of health. **3** A sound state of health or fitness. **4** *Informal* An ailment. **5** A modifying circumstance. **6** An event, circumstance, or fact necessary to the occurrence, completion, or fulfillment of something else: Luck is often a *condition* of success. **7** *Usu. pl.* Any circumstances that affect a person or activity: good working *conditions.* **8** Rank or social position. —**on condition that** Provided that; if. —*v.t.* **1** To place a stipulation upon; prescribe. **2** To be the prerequisite to. **3** To specify as a requirement. **4** To render fit. **5** *Psychol.* To train to a behavior pattern or conditioned response. **6** To accustom (a person or animal) to something. —*v.i.* **7** To stipulate. [< L *com-* together + *dicere* say] —**con·di′tion·er** *n.*

con·di·tion·al (kən·dish′ən·əl) *adj.* **1** Expressing or imposing conditions. **2** Not certain; indefinite. —**con·di·tion·al·i·ty** (kən·dish′ən·al′ə·tē) *n.* —**con·di′tion·al·ly** *adv.*

conditioned response *Psychol.* A learned response elicited by a stimulus which, though originally ineffective, has replaced the normal or natural stimulus after a period of close and repeated juxtaposition with it. Also **conditioned reflex.**

con·do (kon′dō) *n. U.S. Colloq.* Condominium (def. 3).

con·dole (kən·dōl′) *v.i.* **·doled, ·dol·ing** To grieve or express sympathy: with *with.* [< L *com-* together + *dolere* grieve] —**con·do·la·to·ry** (kən·dō′lə·tôr′ē, -tō′rē) *adj.* —**con·dol′er** *n.* —**con·dol′ing·ly** *adv.*

con·do·lence (kən·dō′ləns) *n.* Expression of sympathy with a person in pain, sorrow, or misfortune.

con·dom (kon′dəm, kun′-) *n.* A thin, impermeable sheath that is fitted over the penis to prevent conception and venereal disease. [? Alter. of *Conton,* an 18th c. English physician said to have invented it.]

con·do·min·i·um (kon′də·min′ē·əm) *n. U.S.* An apartment house in which the units are owned separately by individuals and not by a corporation or cooperative; also, an apartment in such a building. [< L *com-* together + *dominium* rule]

con·done (kən·dōn′) *v.t.* **·doned, ·don·ing** To overlook or forgive. [< L *com-* thoroughly + *donare* give] —**con·do·na·tion** (kon′dō·nā′shən), **con·don′er** *n.*

con·dor (kon′dər) *n.* **1** A very large vulture of the high Andes characterized by a bare head and white neck ruff. **2** A California vulture. [< Quechua *cuntur*]

con·duce (kən·dʸōōs′) *v.i.* **·duced, ·duc·ing** To help toward a result; contribute; with *to.* [< L *com-* together + *ducere* lead] —**con·duc′er** *n.*

con·du·cive (kən·dʸōō′siv) *adj.* Contributing; helping; with *to.* —**con·duc′ive·ly** *adv.* —**con·du′cive·ness** *n.*

con·duct (kən·dukt′) *v.t.* **1** To accompany and show the way; guide; escort. **2** To manage or control. **3** To direct and lead the performance of. **4** To serve as a medium of transmission for, as electricity. **5** To act or behave: used reflexively. —*v.i.* **6** To serve as a conductor. **7** To direct or lead. —*n.* (kon′dukt) **1** One's course of action; behavior. **2** Direction; control. **3** The act of leading. [< L *com-* together + *ducere* lead] —**con·duct′i·bil′i·ty** *n.* —**con·duct′i·ble, con·duct′ive** *adj.*

con·duc·tance (kən·duk′təns) *n. Electr.* The reciprocal of resistance.

con·duc·tion (kən·duk′shən) *n.* **1** *Physics* The transmission of heat, sound, or electricity through matter without motion of the conducting body as a whole. **2** Transmission or conveyance in general.

con·duc·tiv·i·ty (kon′duk·tiv′ə·tē) *n.* The capacity to transmit energy, as light, heat, or electricity.

con·duc·tor (kən·duk′tər) *n.* **1** One who conducts or leads. **2** One in charge of a railroad car, bus, etc. **3** The director of an orchestra or chorus. **4** Any medium, material, or device that conducts electricity, heat, etc. —**con·duc′tor·ship** *n.*

con·duit (kon′dit, -dōō·it) *n.* **1** A means for conducting something, as a tube or pipe for a fluid. **2** A passage for electric wires, underground cables, gas and water pipes, etc. [< L *conducere.* See CONDUCT.]

cone (kōn) *n.* **1** A solid figure that tapers uniformly from a circular base to a point. **2** *Geom.* A surface generated by a straight line passing always through a fixed point, called the *vertex,* and tracing a plane curve. **3** Something shaped like a cone, as a machine part or a pastry shell for ice cream. **4** *Bot.* A dry multiple fruit composed of scales, as of the pine or fir tree. —*v.t.* **coned, con·ing** To shape conically. [< Gk. *kōnos*]

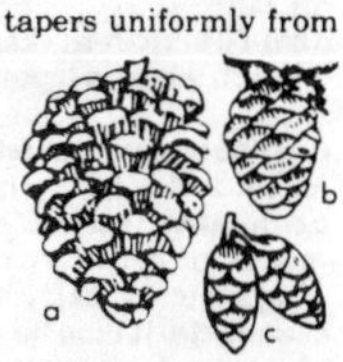

Cones. a. stone pine. b. California big tree. c. Eastern hemlock.

con·el·rad (kon′əl·rad) *n.* A technique for arranging radio signals from separate stations so as to prevent enemy aircraft from using the signals as a navigation aid or for information. [< *con(trol of) el(ectromagnetic) rad(iation)*]

Con·es·to·ga wagon (kon′is·tō′gə) A covered wagon with broad wheels. [< *Conestoga,* Pa., where first made]

co·ney (kō′nē, kun′ē) *n.* CONY.

con·fab (kon′fab) *Informal v.i.* **-fabbed, -fab·bing** To chat. —*n.* A chat. [< CONFABULATE]

con·fab·u·late (kən·fab′yə·lāt) *v.i.* **·lat·ed, ·lat·ing** To chat; gossip; converse. [< L *com-* together + *fabulari* chat < *fabula* story] —**con·fab′u·la′tion** *n.*

con·fec·tion (kən·fek′shən) *n.* Any sweet, such as candy. [< L *confectus,* pp. of *conficere* to prepare, make together] —**con·fec′tion·ar′y** *adj.*

con·fec·tion·er (kən·fek′shən·er) *n.* One who makes or sells confectionery.

con·fec·tion·er·y (kən·fek′shən·er′ē) *n. pl.* **·er·ies** **1** Candies, sweetmeats, etc., collectively. **2** A confectioner's shop or the business of a confectioner: sometimes **confectionary.**

Confed. Confederate; Confederation.

con·fed·er·a·cy (kən·fed′ər·ə·sē) *n. pl.* **·cies** **1** A number of states or persons in league with each other; league. **2** An unlawful conspiracy. —**the Confederacy** The 11 southern States that seceded from the U.S. in 1860–61.

con·fed·er·ate (kən·fed′ər·it) *n.* One united with another or others in an enterprise, plot, etc.; an associate; accomplice. —*adj.* Associated in a confederacy. —*v.t.* & *v.i.* (kən·fed·′ə·rāt) **·at·ed, ·at·ing** To form or join in a confederacy. [< LL *confoederare* join in a league < L *com-* together + *foedus* league] —**con·fed′er·a′tive** *adj.*

Con·fed·er·ate (kən·fed′ər·it) *adj.* Of or pertaining to the Confederacy. —*n.* An adherent of the Confederacy.

con·fed·er·a·tion (kən·fed′ə·rā′shən) *n.* **1** The act of confederating. **2** CONFEDERACY. —**the Confederation** The union of the American colonies, 1781–89, under the Articles of Confederation.

Con·fed·er·a·tion (kən·fed′ə·rā′shən) *n.* The union of Ontario, Quebec, Nova Scotia, and New Brunswick in 1867.

con·fer (kən·fûr′) *v.* **·ferred, ·fer·ring** *v.t.* **1** To give or grant; bestow. —*v.i.* **2** To hold a conference; consult. [< L *com-* together + *ferre* bring, carry] **—con·fer′ment, con·fer′rer** *n.* **—con·fer′ra·ble** *adj.*

con·fer·ee (kon′fə·rē′) *n.* **1** One who participates in a discussion. **2** One upon whom some honor, degree, etc., is conferred.

con·fer·ence (kon′fər·əns, -frəns) *n.* **1** A formal meeting for counsel or discussion. **2** A discussion or consultation. **3** A league or association, as of churches, schools, athletic teams, etc. [< L *conferre* to confer]

con·fess (kən·fes′) *v.t.* **1** To acknowledge or admit, as a fault, guilt, or debt. **2** To acknowledge belief or faith in. **3 a** To admit or make known (one's sins) to a priest, to obtain absolution. **b** To hear the confession of: said of a priest. **4** To concede or admit to be true. —*v.i.* **5** To make acknowledgment of, as a fault, crime, or error. **6** To make confession to a priest. [< L *confessus,* pp. of *confiteri* declare thoroughly] **—con·fess′ed·ly** *adv.*

con·fes·sion (kən·fesh′ən) *n.* **1** An avowal or admission, as of guilt. **2** That which is confessed or admitted. **3** *Eccl.* A contrite acknowledgment of one's sins to a priest in order to obtain absolution. **4** A formal declaration of belief or faith.

con·fes·sion·al (kən·fesh′ən·əl) *n.* A private booth in a church where a priest hears confessions. —*adj.* Of confession.

con·fes·sor (kən·fes′ər) *n.* **1** A priest who hears confessions. **2** One who confesses. Also **con·fess′er.**

con·fet·ti (kən·fet′ē) *n.pl. (construed as sing.)* Small pieces of brightly colored paper thrown about at weddings, etc. [< Ital. *confetto* confection]

con·fi·dant (kon′fə·dant′, -dänt′, kon′fə·dant′, -dänt′) *n.* A person to whom secrets are entrusted. [< L *confidere* to confide] **—con′fi·dante′** *n. Fem.*

con·fide (kən·fīd′) *v.* **·fid·ed, ·fid·ing** *v.t.* **1** To reveal in trust or confidence. **2** To put into one's trust or keeping. —*v.i.* **3** To reveal secrets in trust: often with *in.* [< L *com-* thoroughly + *fidere* to trust] **—con·fid′er** *n.*

con·fi·dence (kon′fə·dəns) *n.* **1** Trust in or reliance upon something or someone. **2** Assurance. **3** Self-reliance; courage or boldness. **4** A private conversation or a secret. **5** A relationship of trust: take into one's *confidence.*

confidence game A swindle in which the swindler first wins the confidence of his victim and then defrauds him.

confidence man One who practices or promotes a confidence game.

con·fi·dent (kon′fə·dənt) *adj.* Having or showing confidence; assured. —*n.* A confidant. **—con′fi·dent·ly** *adv.*

con·fi·den·tial (kon′fə·den′shəl) *adj.* **1** Trusted with secret or private information. **2** Imparted in confidence; secret: *confidential* information. **3** Of or marked by trust in others; confiding: a *confidential* manner. **—con′fi·den′tial·ly** *adv.* **—con′fi·den′tial·ness** *n.*

con·fid·ing (kən·fī′ding) *adj.* Trustful. **—con·fid′ing·ly** *adv.*

con·fig·u·ra·tion (kən·fig′yə·rā′shən) *n.* Structural arrangement; contour. **—con·fig′u·ra′tion·al** *adj.*

con·fine (kən·fīn′) *v.* **·fined, ·fin·ing** *v.t.* **1** To shut within an enclosure; imprison. **2** To restrain or oblige to stay within doors. **3** To keep within limits; restrict: to *confine* remarks. —*n. Usu. pl.* A boundary; limit; border. [< L *confinis* bordering < *com-* together + *finis* border] **—con·fin′a·ble** *adj.* **—con·fin′er** *n.*

con·fine·ment (kən·fīn′mənt) *n.* **1** The state of being confined. **2** Childbirth.

con·firm (kən·fûrm′) *v.t.* **1** To assure by added proof; verify; make certain. **2** To strengthen. **3** To ratify, as a bill, law, etc. **4** To receive into the church by confirmation. [< L *confirmare* strengthen < *com-* thoroughly + *firmus* strong] **—con·firm′a·ble, con·firm′a·tive, con·firm·a·to·ry** (kən·fûr′mə·tôr′ē, -tō′rē) *adj.* **—con·firm′er, con·firm′or** *n.* **—Syn.** **1** corroborate, prove, settle, substantiate, establish.

con·fir·ma·tion (kon′fər·mā′shən) *n.* **1** The act of confirming. **2** That which confirms; proof. **3** A rite administered to baptized persons, confirming or strengthening their faith, and admitting them to all the privileges of the church.

con·firmed (kən·fûrmd′) *adj.* **1** Verified; made certain. **2** Ratified. **3** Having received religious confirmation. **4** Firmly established; inveterate: a *confirmed* drunkard.

con·fis·cate (kon′fis·kāt) *v.t.* **·cat·ed, ·cat·ing** **1** To appropriate as forfeited to the public use or treasury, usu. as a penalty. **2** To appropriate by or as by authority. [< L *confiscare* < *com-* together + *fiscus* chest, treasury] **—con′fis·ca′tion** *n.* **—con′fis·ca′tor** *n.*

con·fla·gra·tion (kon′flə·grā′shən) *n.* A great or disastrous fire. [< L *com-* thoroughly + *flagrare* to burn]

con·flict (kon′flikt) *n.* **1** A struggle; battle. **2** A state or condition of opposition; antagonism. **3** Emotional disturbance due to opposed and contradictory impulses. —*v.i.* (kən·flikt′) **1** To come into collision; be in mutual opposition; clash. **2** To battle; struggle. [< L *com-* together + *fligere* strike] **—con·flic′tion** *n.* **—con·flic′tive** *adj.*

conflict of interest A situation in which the disinterested performance of official duties may be unduly influenced by considerations of private interest.

con·flu·ence (kon′floo·əns) *n.* **1** The flowing together of streams or the place where they meet. **2** The body of water so formed. **3** A flocking together, as of people; throng.

con·flu·ent (kon′floo·ənt) *adj.* Flowing together so as to form one. [< L *com-* together + *fluere* flow]

con·flux (kon′fluks) *n.* CONFLUENCE.

con·form (kən·fôrm′) *v.t.* **1** To make like or similar in form or character: with *to.* **2** To bring into agreement: often used reflexively. —*v.i.* **3** To be or act in accord; comply: with *to.* **4** To hold to or comply with the accepted modes of behavior, prevailing opinions, etc. [< L *com-* together + *formare* shape] **—con·form′er** *n.*

con·form·a·ble (kən·fôr′mə·bəl) *adj.* **1** In agreement. **2** Similar, as in form or character. **3** Adapted; suited. **4** Obedient; submissive. **—con·form′a·bil′i·ty, con·form′a·ble·ness** *n.* **—con·form′a·bly** *adv.*

con·form·ance (kən·fôr′məns) *n.* CONFORMITY.

con·for·ma·tion (kon′fôr·mā′shən) *n.* **1** The manner of formation of a body; general structure, form, or outline. **2** A symmetrical arrangement of parts.

con·form·ist (kən·fôr′mist) *n.* One who conforms or complies.

con·form·i·ty (kən·fôr′mə·tē) *n. pl.* **·ties** **1** Correspondence in form, manner, or use; agreement; harmony. **2** The act or habit of conforming; acquiescence.

con·found (kon·found′, kən-) *v.t.* **1** To amaze, confuse, or perplex. **2** To mingle or mix up (elements, things, ideas, etc.) indistinguishably. **3** (kon′found′) To damn: used as a mild oath. [< L *confundere.* See CONFUSE.] **—con·found′er** *n.*

con·found·ed (kon·foun′did, kən-) *adj.* **1** DAMNED (def. 2). **2** Perplexed; confused. **—con·found′ed·ly** *adv.*

con·front (kən·frunt′) *v.t.* **1** To stand face to face with. **2** To place or put face to face: with *with: Confront* him with the evidence. **3** To face defiantly. [< L *com-* together + *frons* face, forehead] **—con·front′er** *n.*

con·fron·ta·tion (kon′frən·tā′shən) *n.* **1** The act of confronting, or the state of being confronted. **2** A direct challenge, or the crisis resulting from it.

Con·fu·cian·ism (kən·fyoo′shən·iz′əm) *n.* The ethical system based on the teachings of Confucius and emphasizing ancestor worship, devotion to family and friends, and the maintenance of justice and peace. **—Con·fu·cian** *adj., n.* **—Con·fu′cian·ist** *n.*

con·fuse (kən·fyooz′) *v.t.* **·fused, ·fus·ing** **1** To perplex; confound; bewilder. **2** To mix indiscriminately. **3** To mistake (a person or thing) for another. **4** DISCONCERT. [< L *confusus,* pp. of *confundere* to pour together] **—con·fus·ed·ly** (kən·fyoo′zid·lē) *adv.* **—con·fus′ed·ness** *n.* **—con·fus′ing·ly** *adv.*

con·fu·sion (kən·fyoo′zhən) *n.* **1** The act of confusing or the state of being confused. **2** A state of disorder; jumble. **—con·fu′sion·al** *adj.*

con·fute (kən·fyoot′) *v.t.* **·fut·ed, ·fut·ing** **1** To prove to be false or invalid; refute successfully. **2** To prove (a person) to be in the wrong. [< L *confutare* check, restrain] **—con′·fu·ta′tion** *n.* **—con·fut′er** *n.*

Cong. Congress; Congressional.

con·ga (kong′gə) *n.* 1 A Latin-American dance in which the dancers form a winding line. 2 The music for this dance. —*v.i.* To dance the conga. [< Am. Sp.]

con·geal (kən·jēl′) *v.t.* 1 To solidify or thicken, as by cooling. 2 To curdle or coagulate. —*v.i.* 3 To become hard, stiff, or viscid. [< L *com-* together + *gelare* freeze < *gelum* frost] **—con·geal′a·ble** *adj.* **—con·geal′er, con·geal′ment** *n.*

con·gen·ial (kən·jēn′yəl) *adj.* 1 Having similar character or tastes. 2 Suited to one's disposition. [< CON- + GENIAL] **—con·ge·ni·al·i·ty** (kən·jē′nē·al′ə·tē) *n.* **—con·gen′ial·ly** *adv.* **—Syn.** 1 Sympathetic, kindred, congenial. 2 Agreeable, gratifying, pleasant.

con·gen·i·tal (kən·jen′ə·təl) *adj.* Existing at or from birth. [< L *com-* together + *genitus,* pp. of *gignere* bear, produce] **—con·gen′i·tal·ly** *adv.*

con·ger (kong′gər) *n.* Any of a family of large marine eels. Also **conger eel.** [< Gk. *gongros*]

Conger

con·gest (kən·jest′) *v.t.* 1 To collect or crowd together; overcrowd. 2 To cause excessive accumulation of blood in (an organ or tissue). —*v.i.* 3 To become congested. [< L *congestum,* pp. of *congerere* to carry together] **—con·ges′tion** *n.* **—con·ges′tive** *adj.*

con·glom·er·ate (kən·glom′ər·it) *adj.* 1 Massed or clustered. 2 *Geol.* Consisting of loosely cemented heterogeneous material. —*n.* 1 A heterogeneous collection. 2 *Geol.* A rock composed of fragments loosely cemented together. 3 A large corporation formed by merging a number of separate companies, often in unrelated fields. —*v.t. & v.i.* (kən·glom′ə·rāt) **·at·ed, ·at·ing** To gather into a cohering mass. [< L *com-* together + *glomus, glomeris* ball] **—con·glom′er·a′tion** *n.*

con·glu·ti·nate (kən·glōō′tə·nāt) *v.t. & v.i.* **·nat·ed, ·nat·ing** To glue or stick together; adhere. —*adj.* Glued together. [< L *com-* together + *glutinare* stick < *gluten* glue] **—con·glu′ti·na′tion** *n.*

con·go (kong′gō) *n.* An eellike salamander with rudimentary limbs, found in swamps of the SE U.S. Also **congo eel, congo snake.**

Con·go (kong′gō) *n.* A republic of CEN. Africa, 132,000 sq. mi., capital Brazzaville: also **Congo (Brazzaville).** **—Con·go·lese** (kong′gō·lēz′,-lēs′) *adj., n.* • See map at AFRICA.

con·grat·u·late (kən·grach′ōō·lāt) *v.t.* **·lat·ed, ·lat·ing** To express sympathetic pleasure in the joy, success, or good fortune of (another). [< L *com-* together + *gratulari* rejoice] **—con·grat′u·lant, con·grat′u·la·to′ry** *adj.* **—con·grat′u·la′tor** *n.*

con·grat·u·la·tion (kən·grach′ōō·lā′shən) *n.* 1 The act of congratulating. 2 *pl.* Expressions of pleasure and good wishes on another's fortune or success.

con·gre·gant (kong′grə·gənt) *n.* A member of a congregation.

con·gre·gate (kong′grə·gāt) *v.t. & v.i.* **·gat·ed, ·gat·ing** To bring or come together into a crowd; assemble. —*adj.* (kong′grə·git) Gathered together; collected. [< L *com-* together + *gregare* crowd, collect < *grex* flock] **—con′gre·ga′tive** *adj.* **—con′gre·ga′tor** *n.*

con·gre·ga·tion (kong′grə·gā′shən) *n.* 1 The act of congregating. 2 An assemblage of people or of things. 3 A group of people gathered for worship. 4 The body of persons who regularly attend a place of worship. **—con′gre·ga′tion·al** *adj.*

Con·gre·ga·tion·al (kong′grə·gā′shən·əl) *adj.* Belonging or pertaining to the **Congregational Christian Churches,** an evangelical Protestant denomination.

con·gre·ga·tion·al·ism (kong′grə·gā′shən·əl·iz′əm) *n.* A form of church polity in which each local congregation is autonomous in all ecclesiastical matters.

Con·gre·ga·tion·al·ism (kong′grə·gā′shən·əl·iz′əm) *n.* The beliefs and organizational form of an evangelical Protestant denomination that recognizes each member church as self-governing. **—Con′gre·ga′tion·al·ist** *n., adj.*

con·gress (kong′gris) *n.* 1 An assembly or conference; a gathering. 2 A coming together. [< L *congressus* a coming together < *congredi* to move together] **—con·gres·sive** (kən·gres′iv) *adj.*

Con·gress (kong′gris) *n.* The national legislative body of the U.S., consisting of the Senate and the House of Representatives. **—Con·gres·sion·al** (kən·gresh′ən·əl) *adj.*

con·gres·sion·al (kən·gresh′ən·əl) *adj.* Of or pertaining to a congress.

con·gress·man (kong′gris·mən) *n. pl.* **·men** (-mən) *Often cap.* A member of Congress, esp. of the House of Representatives.

Congress of Industrial Organizations A former affiliation of trade unions now merged with the American Federation of Labor.

con·gress·wom·an (kong′gris·wŏŏm′an) *n. pl.* **·wom·en** (-wim′in) *Often cap.* A female member of Congress, esp. of the House of Representatives.

con·gru·ence (kong′grōō·əns) *n.* Harmony; conformity; agreement. Also **con′gru·en·cy.**

con·gru·ent (kong′grōō·ənt) *adj.* 1 Having mutual agreement or conformity. 2 *Geom.* Describing two geometric figures that are identical part for part. [< L *congruere* agree] **—con′gru·ent·ly** *adv.*

con·gru·i·ty (kən·grōō′ə·tē) *n. pl.* **·ties** 1 Agreement; harmoniousness. 2 An example or case of harmoniousness.

con·gru·ous (kong′grōō·əs) *adj.* 1 Harmoniously related or combined. 2 Appropriate; consistent. 3 *Geom.* CONGRUENT. [< L *congruere* agree] **—con′gru·ous·ly** *adv.* **—con′gru·ous·ness** *n.*

con·ic (kon′ik) *adj.* 1 Cone-shaped. 2 Relating to or formed by or upon a cone. Also **con′i·cal.** —*n.* CONIC SECTION. **—con′i·cal·ly** *adv.*

conic section *Math.* A curve formed by the intersection of a plane with a right circular cone; a circle, ellipse, parabola, or hyperbola.

co·nid·i·um (kō·nid′ē·əm) *n. pl.* **co·nid·i·a** (kō·nid′ē·ə) An asexual spore produced by certain fungi. Also **co·nid·i·o·spore** (kō·nid′ē·ə·spôr′, -spōr′). [< Gk. *konis* dust] **—co·nid′i·al** *adj.*

con·i·fer (kon′ə·fər, kō′nə-) *n.* Any of an order of cone-bearing, usu. evergreen shrubs and trees, including pine, spruce, fir, cedar, etc. [< L *conus* cone + *ferre* bear] **—co·nif·er·ous** (kō·nif′ər·əs) *adj.*

conj. conjugation; conjunction; conjunctive.

con·jec·tur·al (kən·jek′chər·əl) *adj.* 1 Of or based on conjecture. 2 Given to conjecturing. **—con·jec′tur·al·ly** *adv.*

con·jec·ture (kən·jek′chər) *v.t.* **·tured, ·tur·ing** 1 To conclude or suppose from incomplete evidence; guess. —*v.i.* 2 To make a conjecture. —*n.* 1 An indecisive opinion; a guess. 2 The act of conjecturing. [< L *conjectura* < *conjicere* to throw together] **—con·jec′tur·a·ble** *adj.* **—con·jec′tur·a·bly** *adv.* **—con·jec′tur·er** *n.*

con·join (kən·join′) *v.t. & v.i.* To join together. **—Syn.** associate, connect, unite, combine.

con·joint (kən·joint′) *adj.* 1 Associated; conjoined. 2 Joint. **—con·joint′ly** *adv.*

con·ju·gal (kon′jōō·gəl) *adj.* Of or pertaining to marriage; matrimonial. [< L *conjungere* join in marriage] **—con·ju·gal·i·ty** (kon′jōō·gal′ə·tē) *n.* **—con′ju·gal·ly** *adv.*

con·ju·gate (kon′jōō·gāt, *for adj. & n., usu.* -git) *v.* **·gat·ed, ·gat·ing** *v.t.* 1 To give the inflections of: said of verbs. 2 To unite or join together. —*adj.* Joined in pairs; coupled; paired. —*n.* 1 A word closely related to another or others. 2 A member of a conjugate pair. [< L *com-* together + *jugare* to yoke] **—con′ju·ga′tive** *adj.* **—con′ju·ga′tor** *n.*

con·ju·ga·tion (kon′jōō·gā′shən) *n.* 1 CONJUNCTION (def. 1). 2 *Gram.* The inflection of a verb or the expression of such inflection. 3 A class of verbs with a similar inflection. **—con′ju·ga′tion·al** *adj.*

con·junc·tion (kən·jungk′shən) *n.* 1 The act of joining or the state of being joined together. 2 *Astron.* The position of a planet when it, the earth, and the sun lie on the same straight line. 3 Simultaneous occurrence of events. 4 *Gram.* A word used to connect words, phrases, clauses, or sentences. [< L *com-* together + *jungere* join]

con·junc·ti·va (kon′jungk·tī′və) *n. pl.* **·vas** or **·vae** (-vē) The mucous membrane lining the eyelids and covering the front of the eyeball. [< NL *(membrana) conjunctiva* connective (membrane)] —**con·junc·ti′val** *adj.*
con·junc·tive (kən·jungk′tiv) *adj.* **1** Joining; connective. **2** Joined together. **3** *Gram.* Serving as a conjunction: a *conjunctive* adverb. —*n. Gram.* A conjunctive word. —**con·junc′tive·ly** *adv.*
con·junc·ti·vi·tis (kən·jungk′tə·vī′tis) *n.* Inflammation of the conjunctiva.
con·junc·ture (kən·jungk′chər) *n.* **1** A combination of circumstances. **2** A crisis. **3** The act of joining; union.
con·ju·ra·tion (kon′jo͞o·rā′shən) *n.* **1** INCANTATION. **2** Magic or a magical expression used in incantation.
con·jure (kən·jo͝or′ *for def. 1,* kon′jər, kun′- *for defs. 2–5*) *v.* **·jured, ·jur·ing** *v.t.* **1** To appeal to solemnly. **2** To summon, bring, or drive away by incantation or spell, as a devil or spirit. **3** To accomplish or effect by or as by magic. —*v.i.* **4** To practice magic. **5** To summon a devil or spirit by incantation. [< L *com-* together + *jurare* swear] —**con′jur·er** *n.*
conk (kongk) *Slang n.* A blow, esp. on the head. —*v.t.* To hit on the head. —**conk out 1** To stall or fail, as a motor. **2** *Slang* To fall asleep, faint, or die.
con man (kon) *Slang* A confidence man.
Conn. Connecticut.
con·nect (kə·nekt′) *v.t.* **1** To join together, as by links; combine. **2** To associate mentally. **3** To close or complete, as an electric circuit or telephone connection. —*v.i.* **4** To unite or join; be in close relation. **5** To meet as scheduled, as buses or trains, for transference of passengers. [< L *com-* together + *nectere* bind] —**con·nect′er, con·nect′or** *n.*
connecting rod *Mech.* A rod that transmits motion by connecting a rotary with a reciprocating part.
con·nec·tion (kə·nek′shən) *n.* **1** The act of connecting or the state of being connected. **2** The means or place of connection. **3** That which connects or serves to connect. **4** *Often pl.* A relative, associate, or friend. **5** A direct transfer from one route to another, as in railway service. **6** Logical coherence or consistency. **7** *Slang* A contact for acquiring narcotics. *Brit. sp.* **con·nex′ion.**
con·nec·tive (kə·nek′tiv) *adj.* Capable of connection or serving to connect. —*n.* **1** That which connects. **2** *Gram.* A connecting word or particle, as a conjunction. —**con·nec′tive·ly** *adv.* —**con′nec·tiv′i·ty** *n.*
connective tissue The cellular tissue that serves to support muscle, nerve and epithelial tissues in the body, as cartilage, bone, tendon, etc.
con·ning tower (kon′ing) **1** The armored pilothouse on the deck of a warship. **2** In submarines, an observation tower serving also as an entrance.
con·nip·tion (kə·nip′shən) *n. Informal* A fit of hysteria, rage, etc. [?]
con·ni·vance (kə·nī′vəns) *n.* **1** The act of conniving. **2** *Law* Knowledge of a wrongful or criminal act during its occurrence. Also **con·ni′van·cy.**
con·nive (kə·nīv′) *v.i.* **·nived, ·niv·ing 1** To encourage or assent to a wrong by silence or feigned ignorance: with *at.* **2** To be in collusion: with *with.* [< L *conivere* shut the eyes] —**con·niv′er** *n.*
con·nois·seur (kon′ə·sûr′) *n.* A competent critical judge, esp. in matters of art and taste. [F < L *cognoscere* know thoroughly] —**con′nois·seur′ship** *n.*
con·no·ta·tion (kon′ə·tā′shən) *n.* **1** The emotional content or significance of a word in addition to its explicit literal meaning; implication. **2** The act of connoting. **3** The quality or qualities connoted. —**con′no·ta′tive** *adj.*
con·note (kə·nōt′) *v.t.* **·not·ed, ·not·ing** To indicate or imply along with the literal meaning. [< L *com-* together + *notare* mark]
con·nu·bi·al (kə·n^yo͞o′bē·əl) *adj.* Pertaining to matrimony. [< L *com-* together + *nubere* marry] —**con·nu·bi·al·i·ty** (kə·n^yo͞o′bē·al′ə·tē) *n.* —**con·nu′bi·al·ly** *adv.*
co·noid (kō′noid) *adj.* Cone-shaped. —*n.* Something having the form of a cone. —**co·noi′dal** *adj.*
con·quer (kong′kər) *v.t.* **1** To overcome or subdue by force, as in war. **2** To acquire or gain control of by or as by force. **3** To overcome by mental or moral force. —*v.i.* **4** To be victorious. [< L *conquirere* < *com-* thoroughly + *quaerere* seek] —**con′quer·a·ble, con′quer·ing** *adj.* —**con′quer·ing·ly** *adv.* —**con′quer·or** *n.*
con·quest (kon′kwest, kong′-) *n.* **1** The act of conquering. **2** That which is conquered by force. **3 a** The winning of the favor of a person. **b** The person whose favor is won. [< OF, pp. of *conquerre* conquer]
con·quis·ta·dor (kon·kwis′tə·dôr, *Sp.* kōng·kēs′tä·t͟hōr′) *n. pl.* **·dors,** *Sp.* **·do·res** (-t͟hō′rās) A conqueror, esp. any of the Spanish conquerors of Mexico and Peru in the 16th century. [< Sp. *conquistar* conquer]
Cons., cons. constable, constitution; consul.
cons. consonant.
con·san·guin·e·ous (kon′sang·gwin′ē·əs) *adj.* Descended from the same parent or ancestor; related. Also **con·san·guine** (kon·sang′gwin). [< L *com-* together + *sanguis* blood] —**con′san·guin′e·ous·ly** *adv.* —**con′san·guin′i·ty** *n.*
con·science (kon′shəns) *n.* The faculty by which distinctions are made between right and wrong; ethical judgment or sensibility. —**in (all) conscience 1** In reason and honesty. **2** Certainly; assuredly. [< L *conscientia* < *com-* together + *scire* know]
con·sci·en·tious (kon′shē·en′shəs) *adj.* **1** Governed or dictated by conscience. **2** Characterized by or done with care and attention. —**con′sci·en′tious·ly** *adv.* —**con′sci·en′tious·ness** *n.* —**Syn. 1** scrupulous, honest, principled, moral. **2** careful, thorough, meticulous, attentive.
conscientious objector One who refuses to perform military service on grounds of religious or moral convictions.
con·scion·a·ble (kon′shən·ə·bəl) *adj.* Conforming to conscience. —**con′scion·a·bly** *adv.*
con·scious (kon′shəs) *adj.* **1** Mentally aware of one's inner thoughts and feelings and also of things external to oneself. **2** In possession of one's mental faculties; awake. **3** Able to think, will, perceive, etc.; rational. **4** Felt or acknowledged by oneself: *conscious* guilt. **5** Self-conscious. **6** Deliberate; intentional: a *conscious* lie. —*n. Psychoanal.* That part of mental life of which an individual is aware. [< L *conscius* < *com-* together + *scire* know] —**con′scious·ly** *adv.*
con·scious·ness (kon′shəs·nis) *n.* **1** The state of being conscious. **2** The aggregate of the conscious states in an individual or a group of persons.
con·script (kon′skript) *n.* One who is compulsorily enrolled for military service; a draftee. —*v.t.* (kən·skript′) To force into military service; draft. —*adj.* (kon′skript) Compulsorily enlisted; drafted. [< L *conscriptus,* pp. of *conscribere* enroll < *com-* together + *scribere* write] —**con·scrip′tion** *n.*
con·se·crate (kon′sə·krāt) *v.t.* **·crat·ed, ·crat·ing 1** To set apart as sacred; dedicate to sacred uses. **2** To dedicate solemnly or devote: *consecrate* one's life to a cause. **3** To make reverend; hallow. [< L *com-* thoroughly + *sacer* holy] —**con′se·cra′tion, con′se·cra′tor** *n.* —**con·se·cra·to·ry** (kon′sə·krə·tôr′ē, -tō′rē) *adj.*
con·sec·u·tive (kən·sek′yə·tiv) *adj.* **1** Following in uninterrupted succession; successive. **2** Characterized by logical sequence. [< L *consequi* follow together] —**con·sec′u·tive·ly** *adv.* —**con·sec′u·tive·ness** *n.*
con·sen·sus (kən·sen′səs) *n.* A collective opinion; general agreement. [< L *com-* together + *sentire* feel, think]
con·sent (kən·sent′) *v.i.* To yield or accede; agree. —*n.* **1** A voluntary yielding to what is proposed or desired by another; acquiescence. **2** Agreement in opinion or sentiment. [< L *consentire.* See CONSENSUS.] —**con·sent′er** *n.*
con·se·quence (kon′sə·kwens, -kwəns) *n.* **1** That which naturally follows from a preceding action or condition; result. **2** A logical conclusion of an inference; deduction. **3** Distinction; note: a woman of *consequence.* **4** Significance; moment: an event of no *consequence.*
con·se·quent (kon′sə·kwent, -kwənt) *adj.* **1** Following as a natural result; resulting. **2** Characterized by correctness of reasoning; logical. —*n.* **1** That which follows something else. **2** An inference or conclusion.
con·se·quen·tial (kon′sə·kwen′shəl) *adj.* **1** Having or showing importance. **2** Self-important. **3** Following logically; consequent. —**con·se·quen·ti·al·i·ty** (kon′sə·kwen′shē·al′ə·tē), **con′se·quen′tial·ness** *n.* —**con′se·quen′tial·ly** *adv.*

con·se·quent·ly (kon′sə·kwent′lē, -kwənt·lē) *adv.* As a result; therefore.

con·ser·va·tion (kon′sər·vā′shən) *n.* 1 The act of keeping or protecting from loss of injury. 2 The preservation of natural resources. [< L *conservare.* See CONSERVE] —**con′ser·va′tion·al** *adj.* —**con′ser·va′tion·ist** *n.*

conservation of energy *Physics* The principle that in any closed material system the total amount of energy remains constant.

con·ser·va·tism (kən·sûr′və·tiz′əm) *n.* Conservative principles and practices.

con·ser·va·tive (kən·sûr′və·tiv) *adj.* 1 Adhering to and tending to preserve the existing order of things; opposed to change. 2 *Often cap.* Of, pertaining to, or characterizing a political party or philosophy that favors the preservation of the status quo and is critical of proposals for change. 3 Conserving; preservative. 4 Moderate; cautious: a *conservative* estimate or statement. —*n.* 1 A conservative person. 2 *Often cap.* A member of a conservative political party. —**con·ser′va·tive·ly** *adv.* —**con·ser′va·tive·ness** *n.*

con·ser·va·to·ry (kən·sûr′və·tôr′ē, -tō′rē) *n. pl.* **·ries** 1 A glass-enclosed room in which plants are grown and displayed. 2 A school of art, music, etc.

con·serve (kən·sûrv′) *v.t.* **·served, ·serv·ing** 1 To keep from loss, decay, or depletion; supervise and protect. 2 To preserve with sugar. —*n.* (kon′sûrv, kən·sûrv′) Often *pl.* A preserve made of several fruits stewed together in sugar, often with nuts, raisins, etc. [< L *com-* thoroughly + *servare* keep, save] —**con·serv′a·ble** *adj.* —**con·serv′er** *n.*

con·sid·er (kən·sid′ər) *v.t.* 1 To think about or deliberate upon. 2 To think to be. 3 To make allowance for. 4 To take into account: *consider* the feelings of others. —*v.i.* 5 To think closely; cogitate. [< L *considerare,* lit., to observe the stars]

con·sid·er·a·ble (kən·sid′ər·ə·bəl) *adj.* 1 Somewhat large in amount, extent, etc. 2 Worthy of consideration; significant. —**con·sid′er·a·bly** *adv.*

con·sid·er·ate (kən·sid′ər·it) *adj.* Showing consideration. —**con·sid′er·ate·ly** *adv.* —**con·sid′er·ate·ness** *n.* —**Syn.** mindful, thoughtful, kind, charitable.

con·sid·er·a·tion (kən·sid′ə·rā′shən) *n.* 1 The act of considering. 2 Something resulting from deliberation; a thought. 3 Thoughtful and kindly feeling or treatment. 4 A circumstance to be taken into account. 5 Something given in return for a service. 6 Importance; consequence.

con·sid·er·ing (kən·sid′ər·ing) *prep.* In view of. —*adv. Informal.* Taking all the facts into account: He came out quite well, *considering.*

con·sign (kən·sīn′) *v.t.* 1 To entrust or commit to the care of another. 2 To make over or relegate. 3 To forward or deliver, as merchandise, for sale or disposal. 4 To set apart, as for a specific purpose or use. [< L *com-* with + *signum* a seal] —**con·sign′a·ble** *adj.* —**con·sign·or** (kən·sī′nər, kon′sī·nôr′), **con·sign′er** *n.*

con·sign·ee (kon′sī·nē′) *n.* A person to whom property has been consigned.

con·sign·ment (kən·sīn′mənt) *n.* 1 The act of consigning. 2 The property consigned. —**on consignment** Sent to or in the possession of a retailer who pays the shipper after sale: said of merchandise.

con·sist (kən·sist′) *v.i.* 1 To be made up or constituted: with *of.* 2 To have as substance, quality, or nature: with *in.* 3 To exist in agreement: with *with.* [< L *com-* together + *sistere* stand]

con·sis·ten·cy (kən·sis′tən·sē) *n. pl.* **·cies** 1 Compatibility or harmony, as between things, acts, or statements. 2 Agreement with what has been previously done, expressed, etc. 3 Firmness, or density, as of a liquid. 4 Degree of firmness, thickness, or density. Also **con·sis′tence.**

con·sis·tent (kən·sis′tənt) *adj.* 1 Characterized by consistency. 2 In accord; compatible. —**con·sis′tent·ly** *adv.*

con·sis·to·ry (kən·sis′tər·ē) *n. pl.* **·ries** 1 A church council, esp. the council of Roman Catholic cardinals usu. presided over by the Pope. 2 The place where such a council meets, or the meeting itself. [< LL *consistorium* place of assembly] —**con·sis·to·ri·al** (kon′sis·tôr′ē·əl, -tō′rē-), **con′·sis·to′ri·an** *adj.*

con·so·la·tion (kon′sə·lā′shən) *n.* 1 The act of consoling or the state of being consoled; solace. 2 A comforting thought, person, or fact.

con·sol·a·to·ry (kən·sol′ə·tôr′ē, -tō′rē) *adj.* Providing comfort or solace.

con·sole[1] (kən·sōl′) *v.t.* **·soled, ·sol·ing** To comfort (a person) in grief or sorrow; solace. [< L *com-* together + *solari* solace] —**con·sol′a·ble** *adj.* —**con·sol′er** *n.*

con·sole[2] (kon′sōl) *n.* 1 A bracket, esp. an ornamental one. 2 CONSOLE TABLE. 3 The portion of an organ containing the manuals and stops. 4 A cabinet for a radio, phonograph, or television set, designed to rest on the floor. [F]

Console *def. 1*

console table A table supported by consoles or whose legs have the appearance of consoles.

con·sol·i·date (kən·sol′ə·dāt) *v.* **·dat·ed, ·dat·ing** *v.t.* 1 To make solid, firm, or coherent. 2 *Mil.* To secure and strengthen, as a newly captured position. 3 To form a union of. —*v.i.* 4 To become united, solid, or firm. [< L *com-* together + *solidus* solid] —**con·sol′i·da′tion, con·sol′i·da′tor** *n.*

consolidated school A school usu. consisting of several rural elementary schools merged into one.

con·som·mé (kon′sə·mā′, *Fr.* kôn·sô·mā′) *n.* A clear soup made from meat and sometimes vegetables boiled in water. [< F, pp. of *consommer* to concentrate]

con·so·nance (kon′sə·nəns) *n.* 1 Agreement; harmony. 2 *Music* A combination of tones regarded as pleasing and not requiring resolution. Also **con′so·nan·cy.**

con·so·nant (kon′sə·nənt) *adj.* 1 Being in agreement or harmony; consistent. 2 CONSONANTAL. 3 Having the quality of musical consonance. —*n.* 1 *Phonet.* A sound produced by partial blockage of the breath stream. 2 A letter representing such a sound. [< L *com-* together + *sonare* to sound] —**con′so·nant·ly** *adv.*

con·so·nan·tal (kon′sə·nan′təl) *adj.* Of the nature of or having a consonant or consonants.

con·sort (kon′sôrt) *n.* 1 A companion or associate. 2 A husband or wife; mate. 3 An accompanying vessel. —*v.t.* (kən·sôrt′) 1 To join; associate. —*v.i.* 2 To keep company; associate. 3 To be in agreement; harmonize. [< L *consors,* lit., one who shares the same fate]

con·sor·ti·um (kən·sôr′shē·əm) *n. pl.* **·ti·a** (-shē·ə) An association or agreement, often one entered into for international business or financial purposes. [L, fellowship]

con·spic·u·ous (kən·spik′yōō·əs) *adj.* 1 Clearly visible; prominent; obvious. 2 Unusual; striking. [< L *com-* together + *specere* look at] —**con·spic′u·ous·ly** *adv.* —**con·spic′u·ous·ness** *n.*

con·spir·a·cy (kən·spir′ə·sē) *n. pl.* **·cies** 1 The act of conspiring. 2 A plot, esp. one to do something harmful, illegal, or treasonable. 3 The persons engaged in such a plot. 4 A striking concurrence, as of circumstances or tendencies. —**con·spir·a·tor** (kən·spir′ə·tər) *n.* —**con·spir·a·to·ri·al** (kən·spir′ə·tôr′ē·əl, -tō′rē-) *adj.*

con·spire (kən·spīr′) *v.* **·spired, ·spir·ing** *v.t.* 1 To plot. —*v.i.* 2 To form a plot, especially secretly, for evil or unlawful purposes. 3 To concur in action or endeavor, as circumstances. [< L *com-* together + *spirare* breathe] —**con·spir·ant** (kən·spī′rənt) *adj., n.* —**con·spir′er** *n.*

con·sta·ble (kon′stə·bəl, kun′-) *n.* 1 An officer of the peace; a policeman. 2 A high military officer in medieval monarchies. [< LL *comes stabuli* count of the stable] —**con′sta·ble·ship′** *n.*

con·stab·u·lar·y (kən·stab′yə·ler′ē) *n. pl.* **·lar·ies** 1 Constables of an area, collectively. 2 A military police force.

con·stant (kon′stənt) *adj.* 1 Steady in purpose; resolute; persevering. 2 Steady in faithfulness; loyal. 3 Continually recurring. 4 Invariable; unchanging. —*n.* 1 That which is permanent or invariable. 2 *Math.* A quantity which retains a fixed value throughout a given discussion. **3** In the sciences, any characteristic of a substance, event, or phenomenon, numerically determined, that remains always the same under specified conditions, as gravitation, the velocity of light, etc. [< L *com-* together + *stare* stand] —**con′stan·cy** *n.* —**con′stant·ly** *adv.*

con·stel·late (kon′stə·lāt) *v.t. & v.i.* **·lat·ed, ·lat·ing** To group in constellations. [< LL *constellatus* studded with stars]

con·stel·la·tion (kon′stə·lā′shən) *n.* **1** *Astron.* Any of 88 apparent clusters of stars, each named for a mythological person, an animal, or some object that it suggests; also, the area in the heavens covering such a group. **2** Any assemblage of things or persons. **3** In astrology, the position of the planets, esp. at the time of one's birth.

CONSTELLATIONS

Explanation: GROUP N includes all constellations within 45 degrees of the North Pole. GROUP E includes all constellations within 45 degrees of each side of the equator. GROUP S includes all constellations within 45 degrees of the South Pole.

Name	*Group*	*On the Meridian at 9 p.m.*	*Name*	*Group*	*On the Meridian at 9 p.m.*
Andromeda	E	Nov.	Indus	S	Oct.
Antlia	E	April	Lacerta	N	Oct.
Apus	S	July	Leo	E	April
Aquarius	E	Oct.	Leo Minor	E	April
Aquila	E	Aug.	Lepus	E	Jan.
Ara	S	July	Libra	E	June
Aries	E	Dec.	Lupus	E	June
Auriga	E	Feb.	Lynx	N	Feb.
Boötes	E	June	Lyra	E	Aug.
Cælum	E	Jan.	Mensa	S	Jan.
Camelopardalis	N	March	Microscopium	E	Sept.
Cancer	E	March	Monoceros	E	March
Canes Venatici	E	May	Musca	S	May
Canis Major	E	Feb.	Norma	S	July
Canis Minor	E	March	Octans	S	.....
Capricornus	E	Sept.	Ophiuchus	E	July
Carina	S	March	Orion	E	Jan.
Cassiopeia	N	Nov.	Pavo	S	Aug.
Centaurus	E	May	Pegasus	E	Oct.
Cepheus	N	Nov.	Perseus	N	Dec.
Cetus	E	Dec.	Phœnix	S	Nov.
Chameleon	S	April	Pictor	S	Jan.
Columba	E	Feb.	Pisces	E	Nov.
Coma Berenices	E	May	Piscis Austrinus	E	Oct.
Corona Australis	E	Aug.	Puppis	E	Feb.
Corona Borealis	E	July	Pyxis	E	March
Corvus	E	May	Reticulum	S	Jan.
Crater	E	April	Sagitta	E	Aug.
Crux	S	May	Sagittarius	E	Aug.
Cygnus	E	Sept.	Scorpius	E	July
Delphinus	E	Sept.	Sculptor	E	Nov.
Dorado	S	Jan.	Scutum	E	Aug.
Draco	N	June	Serpens	E	July
Equuleus	E	Sept.	Sextans	E	April
Eridanus	E	Dec.	Taurus	E	Jan.
Fornax	E	Dec.	Telescopium	S	Aug.
Gemini	E	Feb.	Triangulum	E	Dec.
Grus	S	Oct.	Triangulum Australe	S	July
Hercules	E	July	Tucana	S	Oct.
Horologium	S	Dec.	Ursa Major	N	April
Hydra	E	April	Ursa Minor	N	.....
Hydrus	S	Dec.	Vela	E	March
			Virgo	E	June
			Volans	S	March
			Vulpecula	E	Sept.

The four constellations Carina, Puppis, Pyxis, and Vela were formerly considered as a single one, called Argo Navis.

con·ster·na·tion (kon′stər·nā′shən) *n.* Complete confusion or dismay. [< L *consternare* to stretch out, perplex] — **Syn.** amazement, astonishment, shock, distraction.

con·sti·pate (kon′stə·pāt) *v.t.* **·pat·ed, ·pat·ing** To cause constipation in. [< L *com-* together + *stipare* press, crowd] —**con′sti·pat′ed** *adj.*

con·sti·pa·tion (kon′stə·pā′shən) *n.* Infrequent or difficult evacuation of the bowels.

con·stit·u·en·cy (kən·stich′o͞o·ən·sē) *n. pl.* **·cies** **1** The voters or residents in an electoral district. **2** An electoral district.

con·stit·u·ent (kən·stich′o͞o·ənt) *adj.* **1** Serving to form or compose as a necessary part; constituting. **2** Entitled to vote for a public officer or representative. **3** Having the power to frame or modify a constitution. —*n.* **1** One represented politically; a voter. **2** An essential part; a component. [< L *constituere.* See CONSTITUTE.]

con·sti·tute (kon′stə·tyo͞ot) *v.t.* **·tut·ed, ·tut·ing** **1** To form or be the substance of; make up. **2** To establish or found, as a school. **3** To set up or enact, as a law. **4** To depute or appoint, as to an office or function. [< L *constituere* < *com-* together + *statuere* place, station] —**con′sti·tut′er** *n.*

con·sti·tu·tion (kon′stə·tyo͞o′shən) *n.* **1** The act of constituting. **2** A system of related parts; composition, esp. bodily make-up. **3** The fundamental laws and practices that normally govern the operation of a state or association. **4** A document containing these laws. —**the Constitution** The document drawn up in 1787 containing the laws by which the United States of America is governed.

con·sti·tu·tion·al (kon′stə·tyo͞o′shən·əl) *adj.* **1** Of, inherent in, or affecting the constitution of a person or thing. **2** Acting under and controlled by a constitution: a *constitutional* monarchy. **3** Loyal to the constitution of a government. **4** For one's health. —*n.* A walk taken for one's health. —**con·sti·tu·tion·al·i·ty** (kon′stə·tyo͞o′shən·al′ə·tē) *n.* —**con′sti·tu′tion·al·ly** *adv.*

constr. construction, construed.

con·strain (kən·strān′) *v.t.* **1** To compel; oblige. **2** To confine, as by bonds. **3** To restrain. [< L *com-* together + *stringere* bind tight] —**con·strain′a·ble** *adj.* —**con·strain′er** *n.*

con·strained (kən·strānd′) *adj.* Resulting from constraint; compulsory. —**con·strain′ed·ly** (-strā′nid·lē) *adv.*

con·straint (kən·strānt′) *n.* **1** The act of constraining or the state of being constrained. **2** Embarrassment. **3** Anything that constrains.

con·strict (kən·strikt′) *v.t.* To compress or draw together at some point; bind. [< L *constrictus,* pp. of *constringere* to bind together] —**con·stric′tive** *adj.*

con·stric·tion (kən·strik′shən) *n.* **1** A constricting. **2** That which constricts or is constricted. **3** A feeling of tightness, as in the chest.

con·stric·tor (kən·strik′tər) *n.* **1** That which constricts. **2** A muscle which contracts a part or organ of the body. **3** A snake that crushes its prey by coiling around it and squeezing.

con·struct (kən·strukt′) *v.t.* To put together and set up; build. —*n.* (kon′strukt) Anything systematically constructed or composed from simple elements, as a concept. [< L *constructus,* pp. of *construere* See CONSTRUE.] —**con·struct′er, con·struc′tor** *n.*

con·struc·tion (kən·struk′shən) *n.* **1** The act of constructing. **2** That which is constructed. **3** Style of building or composing. **4** An interpretation arrived at or deduced. **5** The arrangement of grammatical forms, as in sentences. —**con·struc′tion·al** *adj.*

con·struc·tion·ist (kən·struk′shən·ist) *n.* One who explains or interprets an instrument, as the Constitution, in a specified manner: a strict *constructionist.*

con·struc·tive (kən·struk′tiv) *adj.* **1** Involving the act or process of construction. **2** Tending toward or resulting in positive conclusions; affirmative. **3** *Law* Assumed or inferred. —**con·struc′tive·ly** *adv.* —**con·struc′tive·ness** *n.*

con·strue (kən·stro͞o′) *v.* **·strued, ·stru·ing** *v.t.* **1** To analyze the grammatical structure of (a clause or sentence) so as to determine the use and function of each word. **2** To translate orally. **3** To explain or interpret the meaning of. —*v.i.* **4** To construe a clause or sentence, esp. in translating. [< L *com-* together + *struere* build up] —**con·stru′a·ble** *adj.* —**con·stru′er** *n.*

con·sul (kon′səl) *n.* **1** An officer appointed to reside in a foreign city, chiefly as a representative of his country's commercial interests. **2** Either of two chief magistrates ruling in Ancient Rome. **3** Any of the three chief magistrates of the French republic, 1799-1804. [< L] —**con·su·lar** *adj.* —**con′sul·ship** *n.*

con·su·late (kon′sə·lit) *n.* **1** The offices and residence of a consul. **2** The position, duties and authority of a consul. **3** A consul's term of office.

consul general *pl.* **consuls general** A consular officer of the first rank.

con·sult (kən·sult′) *v.t.* **1** To ask advice or information of.

2 To consider. —*v.i.* 3 To ask advice. 4 To compare views: with *with.* [< L *consultare,* freq. of *consulere* seek advice] **—con·sult'a·ble** *adj.* **—con·sult'er** *n.*

con·sult·ant (kən·sul'tənt) *n.* 1 A person referred to for expert or professional advice. 2 One who consults.

con·sul·ta·tion (kon'səl·tā'shən) *n.* 1 The act of consulting. 2 A meeting for conference.

con·sume (kən·s^yo͞om') *v.* **·sumed, ·sum·ing** *v.t.* 1 To destroy, as by burning. 2 To eat or drink up. 3 To squander; use up, as money or time. 4 To hold the interest of; engross. —*v.i.* 5 To be wasted or destroyed. [< L *com-* thoroughly + *sumere* take up, use] **—con·sum'a·ble** *adj.*

con·sum·er (kən·s^yo͞o'mər) *n.* 1 One who or that which consumes. 2 One who uses economic goods or services.

con·sum·er·ism (kən·s^yo͞o'mər·iz'əm) *n.* The policy or program of protecting the interests of the consumer. [< CONSUMER + -ISM, on analogy with *capitalism,* etc.] **—con·sum'er·ist** *adj., n.*

con·sum·mate (kon'sə·māt) *v.t.* **·mat·ed, ·mat·ting** 1 To bring to completion or perfection; achieve. 2 To fulfill, as a marriage by the first act of sexual intercourse. —*adj.* (kən·sum'it) Of the highest degree; perfect. [< L *com-* together + *summa* sum, total] **—con·sum'mate·ly** *adv.* **—con'sum·ma'tion, con'sum·ma'tor** *n.* **—con'sum·ma'tive** *adj.*

con·sump·tion (kən·sump'shən) *n.* 1 The act or process of consuming. 2 The amount used up. 3 The using up of goods by consumers. 4 A wasting disease; specifically, pulmonary tuberculosis.

con·sump·tive (kən·sump'tiv) *adj.* 1 Tending to, causing, or designed for consumption. 2 Connected with or affected by pulmonary tuberculosis. —*n.* A person affected with pulmonary tuberculosis. **—con·sump'tive·ly** *adv.* **—con·sump'tive·ness** *n.*

cont. containing; contents; continent; continued.

con·tact (kon'takt) *n.* 1 The coming together, meeting, or touching of two bodies. 2 *Electr.* **a** The touching or joining of points or surfaces of conductors, permitting the passage or flow of a current. **b** One of two or more conductors that touch in this way. 3 Immediate proximity or association. 4 A useful or helpful acquaintance. —*v.t.* 1 To bring or place in contact; touch. 2 *Informal* To get or be in touch with (a person); communicate with. —*v.i.* 3 To be or come in contact. [< L *com-* together + *tangere* touch]

contact lens A thin, corrective lens of hard or soft plastic that fits against the eyeball.

contact print *Phot.* A positive print obtained by exposure of a photosensitive surface in direct contact with the negative.

con·ta·gion (kən·tā'jən) *n.* 1 The communication of disease by contact, direct or indirect. 2 A disease communicated in this way. 3 The medium of transmission of a disease. 4 A poison. 5 The transmission of an emotion, idea, etc., from person to person. [< L < *contingere*]

con·ta·gious (kən·tā'jəs) *adj.* 1 Transmissible by contact, as a disease. 2 Transmitting disease; pestilential. 3 Communicable from one person to another; catching; spreading. **—con·ta'gious·ly** *adv.* **—con·ta'gious·ness** *n.*

con·tain (kən·tān') *v.t.* 1 To hold or enclose. 2 To include or comprise. 3 To be able to hold. 4 To keep within bounds; restrain. 5 *Math.* To have as an exact factor. [< L *com-* together + *tenere* hold] **—con·tain'a·ble** *adj.* **—con·tain'er** *n.*

con·tain·er·i·za·tion (kən·tān'ər·i·zā'shən) *n.* The packing and shipping of freight in very large, sealed containers. **—con·tain'er·ized** *adj.*

con·tain·er·ship (kən·tān'ər·ship') *n.* A ship equipped to handle containerized cargo. Also **container ship.**

con·tain·ment (kən·tān'mənt) *n.* The forestalling or offsetting of territorial or ideological extension by an inimical power.

con·tam·i·nate (kən·tam'ə·nāt) *v.t.* **·nat·ed, ·nat·ing** To make impure by contact or admixture. [< L *com-* together + *tangere* touch] **—con·tam'i·nant, con·tam'i·na'tion, con·tam'i·na'tor** *n.* **—con·tam'i·na'tive** *adj.* **—Syn.** taint, defile, pollute, debase.

contd. continued.

con·temn (kən·tem') *v.t.* To despise; scorn. [< L *com-* thoroughly + *temnere* slight, scorn] **—con·temn·er** (kən·tem'ər, -tem'nər), **con·tem·nor** (kən·tem'nər) *n.*

con·tem·plate (kon'təm·plāt) *v.* **·plat·ed, ·plat·ing** *v.t.* 1 To look at attentively; gaze at. 2 To consider thoughtfully; ponder. 3 To intend or plan. 4 To treat as possible. —*v.i.* 5 To meditate; muse. [< L *contemplari* < *com-* together + *templum* temple; with ref. to the art of divination] **—con·tem·pla·ble** (kən·tem'plə·bəl) *adj.* **—con'tem·pla'tion, con'·tem·pla'tor** *n.*

con·tem·pla·tive (kən·tem'plə·tiv, kon'təm·plā'-) *adj.* Of or given to contemplating; meditative, thoughtful, etc. **—con'tem·pla'tive·ly** *adv.*

con·tem·po·ra·ne·ous (kən·tem'pə·rā'nē·əs) *adj.* Living or occurring at the same time. [< L *com-* together + *tempus, temporis* time] **—con·tem·po·ra·ne·i·ty** (kən·tem'pə·rə·nē'ə·tē), **con·tem'po·ra'ne·ous·ness** *n.* **—con·tem'po·ra'·ne·ous·ly** *adv.*

con·tem·po·rar·y (kən·tem'pə·rer'ē) *adj.* 1 Contemporaneous. 2 Having the same age. 3 Modern. —*n. pl.* **·rar·ies** A person or thing that is contemporary.

con·tempt (kən·tempt') *n.* 1 Disdain; scorn. 2 *Law* Willful disregard of authority, as of a court. 3 The state of being despised; disgrace; shame. [< L *contemptus* < *contemnere* despise, disdain. See CONTEMN.]

con·tempt·i·ble (kən·temp'tə·bəl) *adj.* Deserving of contempt; despicable; vile. **—con·tempt'i·bil'i·ty, con·tempt'i·ble·ness** *n.* **—con·tempt'i·bly** *adv.*

con·temp·tu·ous (kən·temp'cho͞o·əs) *adj.* Disdainful; scornful. **—con·temp'tu·ous·ly** *adv.* **—con·temp'tu·ous·ness** *n.*

con·tend (kən·tend') *v.t.* 1 To maintain or assert in argument. —*v.i.* 2 To debate earnestly; dispute. 3 To strive in competition: to *contend* for a prize. 4 To struggle or fight in opposition or combat. [< L *com-* together + *tendere* strive, strain] **—con·tend'er** *n.*

con·tent[1] (kon'tent) *n.* 1 *Usu. pl.* All that a thing contains or deals with. 2 The significance or basic meaning, as of a literary work. 3 Holding capacity; size. 4 Included area or space. 5 The quantity of a specified part: the silver *content* of a ton of ore. [< L *continere* contain]

con·tent[2] (kən·tent') *adj.* Satisfied with things as they are. —*v.t.* To satisfy. —*n.* Contentment; satisfaction. [< L *continere* contain]

con·tent·ed (kən·ten'tid) *adj.* Satisfied; content. **—con·tent'ed·ly** *adv.* **—con·tent'ed·ness** *n.*

con·ten·tion (kən·ten'shən) *n.* 1 The act of contending; strife, conflict, struggle, dispute, argument, etc. 2 An object or point in debate or controversy.

con·ten·tious (kən·ten'shəs) *adj.* 1 Of, pertaining to, or fond of contention; quarrelsome. 2 Full of or marked by contention. **—con·ten'tious·ly** *adv.* **—con·ten'tious·ness** *n.*

con·tent·ment (kən·tent'mənt) *n.* The condition or fact of being content.

con·ter·mi·nous (kən·tûr'mə·nəs) *adj.* 1 Having a common boundary line. 2 Having the same boundaries. [< L *com-* together + *terminus* limit]

con·test (kon'test) *n.* 1 A struggle to determine a winner; a competition. 2 Verbal conflict; controversy. —*v.t.* (kən·test') 1 To fight about; contend for; strive to win, keep, or control. 2 To argue about or challenge: to *contest* an election. —*v.i.* 3 To contend, struggle, or vie: with *with* or *against.* [< L *contestari* bring legal action against] **—con·test'a·ble** *adj.* **—con·test'er** *n.*

con·test·ant (kən·tes'tənt) *n.* One who enters a contest; a competitor.

con·text (kon'tekst) *n.* The portions of a discourse, treatise, etc., preceding and following a passage quoted or considered. [< L *com-* together + *texere* weave] **—con·tex·tu·al** (kən·teks'cho͞o·əl) *adj.* **—con·tex'tu·al·ly** *adv.*

con·ti·gu·i·ty (kon'tə·gyo͞o'ə·tē) *n.* The state of being contiguous.

con·tig·u·ous (kən·tig'yo͞o·əs) *adj.* 1 Touching or joining at the edge or boundary. 2 Adjacent; close. [< L *contingere* to contact] **—con·tig'u·ous·ly** *adv.* **—con·tig'u·ous·ness** *n.*

con·ti·nence (kon'tə·nəns) *n.* 1 Self-restraint; 2 Moderation, esp. in sexual passion; chastity. Also **con'ti·nen·cy.**

con·ti·nent (kon′tə·nənt) *n.* One of the great bodies of land on the globe, generally regarded as Africa, Antarctica, Asia, Australia, Europe, North America, and South America. —**the Continent** Europe, exclusive of the British Isles. —*adj.* Self-restrained; abstinent; chaste. [<L *continere* contain] —**con·ti·nen·tal** (kon′tə·nen′təl) *adj.* —**con′ti·nent·ly** *adv.*

Con·ti·nen·tal (kon′tə·nen′təl) *adj.* 1 European. 2 Pertaining to the United States during the Revolutionary War. —*n.* 1 A European. 2 A soldier of the regular forces under the control of Congress in the Revolutionary War. 3 A note of the rapidly depreciated paper money issued by Congress during the Revolution.

Continental Congress Either of two American legislative assemblies convened during the period 1774–1781.

Continental Divide In North America, the great ridge of Rocky Mountain summits separating westward-flowing streams from eastward-flowing streams.

continental drift *Geol.* The gradual alteration of the relative position of the land masses of the earth.

continental shelf *Geog.* The submerged border of a continent, of varying width and degree of slope, which separates the land mass from the ocean depths.

con·tin·gen·cy (kən·tin′jən·sē) *n. pl.* **·cies** 1 The condition of being contingent. 2 An unexpected, possible, or chance occurrence or condition. 3 Something incidental.

con·tin·gent (kən·tin′jənt) *adj.* 1 Not certain to happen; possible. 2 Accidental; fortuitous. 3 Dependent upon an uncertain occurrence or condition. —*n.* A contingency. 2 A representational group: the American *contingent* at the conference. 3 A quota of troops, laborers, etc. [<L *contingere* to contact] —**con·tin′gent·ly** *adv.*

con·tin·u·al (kən·tin′yōō·əl) *adj.* 1 Renewed in regular succession; often repeated. 2 Continuous (in time); uninterrupted. —**con·tin′u·al·ly** *adv.* • In careful usage *continual* refers to that which happens at intervals, *continuous* to that which goes on without interruption: the *continual* ticking of a clock; a *continuous* flow of oil.

con·tin·u·ance (kən·tin′yōō·əns) *n.* 1 The act of continuing. 2 The time during which something lasts; duration. 3 Uninterrupted succession. 4 A postponement of court proceedings to a future date. 5 A sequel, as of a novel.

con·tin·u·a·tion (kən·tin′yōō·ā′shən) *n.* 1 The act or state of continuing. 2 Something which continues, extends, increases, or carries on.

con·tin·ue (kən·tin′yōō) *v.* **·tin·ued, ·tin·u·ing** *v.t.* 1 To extend or prolong in space or time. 2 To persist in. 3 To cause to last or remain, as in a position or office. 4 To take up again after an interruption. 5 *Law* To postpone, as a judicial proceeding. —*v.i.* 6 To last; endure. 7 To keep on or persist. 8 To remain, as in a place or position. 9 To resume after an interruption. 10 To extend. [<L *continere* hold together, contain] —**con·tin′u·a·ble** *adj.* —**con·tin′u·er** *n.*

con·ti·nu·i·ty (kon′tə·nʸōō′ə·tē) *n.* 1 The state or quality of being continuous. 2 That which has or exhibits such a state or quality; an unbroken sequence or whole.

con·tin·u·ous (kən·tin′yōō·əs) *adj.* Connected, extended, prolonged, or going on without a break. —**con·tin′u·ous·ly** *adv.* —**con·tin′u·ous·ness** *n.* • See CONTINUAL.

con·tin·u·um (kən·tin′yōō·əm) *n. pl.* **·tin·u·a** (-tin′yōō·ə) 1 A total that is continuous and uninterrupted. 2 *Math.* A set of numbers or points such that between any two of them a third may be interpolated.

con·tort (kən·tôrt′) *v.t.* To twist or wrench out of shape or place. [<L *com-* together + *torquere* twist] —**con·tor′tion** *n.* —**con·tor′tive** *adj.* —**Syn.** bend, distort, deform.

con·tor·tion·ist (kən·tôr′shən·ist) *n.* An acrobat trained to contort his limbs into unusual positions.

con·tour (kon′tōōr) *n.* The line bounding a figure, land, etc.; outline. —*v.t.* To make or draw in outline or contour. —*adj.* Following the contour lines of land so as to avoid erosion. [<LL *comtogether* + *tornare* make round]

contour map A map designed to show the comparative elevation of topographic features.

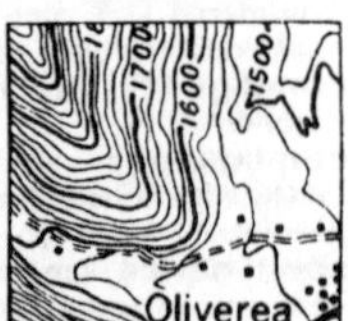

Contour map

contr. contract; contraction; control.

con·tra (kon′trə, kôn′-) *n.* A rebel counter- revolutionary, especially in Central America; guerrilla. [<Sp. *contra(revolucionario)*]

contra- *prefix* Against; opposite: *contraception*. [<L *contra* against]

con·tra·band (kon′trə·band) *adj.* Forbidden or excluded, as by law or treaty. —*n.* 1 Illegal or forbidden trade. 2 Contraband goods. 3 CONTRABAND OF WAR. [<LL *contra* against + *bannum* law, proclamation] —**con′tra·band′ist** *n.*

contraband of war Anything furnished by a neutral to a belligerent that is by the laws of war subject to seizure.

con·tra·bass (kon′trə·bās) *n.* DOUBLE BASS. —*adj.* Having its pitch an octave lower than a bass instrument of the same class; of deeper range: a *contrabass* horn.

con·tra·bas·soon (kon′trə·bə·sōōn′) *n.* DOUBLE BASSOON.

con·tra·cep·tion (kon′trə·sep′shən) *n.* The prevention of conception. [<CONTRA- + (CON)CEPTION]

con·tra·cep·tive (kon′trə·sep′tiv) *adj.* 1 Used to prevent conception. 2 Of or pertaining to contraception. —*n.* Any device or substance that inhibits conception.

con·tract (kən·trakt′ *for v. defs. 1, 3–6;* kon′trakt, kən·trakt′ *for v. def. 2*) *v.t.* 1 To reduce in size; shrink; narrow. 2 To arrange or settle by agreement; enter upon with reciprocal obligations. 3 To acquire or become affected with, as a disease or habit. 4 To shorten, as a word, by omitting or combining medial letters or sounds. —*v.i.* 5 To shrink. 6 To make a contract. —*n.* (kon′trakt) 1 An agreement between two or more parties, esp. when legally enforceable. 2 A formal document containing the terms of such an agreement. 3 The act of marriage. 4 A formal agreement of marriage; betrothal. 5 CONTRACT BRIDGE. 6 The highest bid in a hand of contract bridge. [<L *contractus*, pp. of *contrahere* pull together] —**con·tract′ed** *adj.* —**con·tract′i·bil′i·ty** *n.* **con·tract′a·ble** *adj.*

contract bridge A form of bridge in which the declarer, if successful, scores toward game only the tricks named in the bid.

con·trac·tile (kən·trak′təl) *adj.* Having the power to contract or inducing contraction. —**con·trac·til·i·ty** (kən·trak′til′ə·tē) *n.*

con·trac·tion (kən·trak′shən) *n.* 1 The act of contracting or the state of being contracted. 2 That which is contracted, as a word. 3 A shortening and thickening of a muscle in action.

con·trac·tor (kon′trak·tər, kən·trak′-) *n.* 1 One of the parties to a contract. 2 One who agrees to supply labor or materials or both.

con·trac·tu·al (kən·trak′chōō·əl) *adj.* Of, pertaining to, or implying a contract. —**con·trac′tu·al·ly** *adv.*

con·tra·dict (kon′trə·dikt′) *v.t.* 1 To maintain the opposite of (a statement); deny. 2 To be inconsistent with or opposed to. 3 To disagree with (someone). —*v.i.* 4 To dispute, deny, or maintain the opposite of something. [<L *contra-* against + *dicere* say, speak] —**con′tra·dict′a·ble, con′tra·dic′tive** *adj.* —**con′tra·dict′er** or **con′tra·dic′tor, con′tra·dic′tion** *n.*

con·tra·dic·to·ry (kon′trə·dik′tər·ē) *adj.* 1 Involving or of the nature of a contradiction. 2 Given or inclined to contradiction. —**con′tra·dic′to·ri·ly** *adv.*

con·tra·dis·tinc·tion (kon′trə·dis·tingk′shən) *n.* Distinction by contrast or by contrasting qualities. —**con′tra·dis·tinc′tive** *adj.*

con·trail (kon′trāl) *n.* The vapor trail sometimes left by an airplane flying at high altitudes, caused by the condensation of moisture from exhaust gases. [<CON(DENSATION) + TRAIL]

con·tra·in·di·cate (kon′trə·in′də·kāt) *v.t.* **·cat·ed, ·cat·ing** *Med.* To make (a given drug or method of treatment) dangerous or inadvisable. —**con′tra·in′di·ca′tion** *n.*

con·tral·to (kən·tral′tō) *n. pl.* **·tos** or **·ti** (-tē) 1 The lowest female voice, intermediate between soprano and tenor. 2 A part written for such a voice. 3 A singer with such a voice. —*adj.* Of or for a contralto. [<Ital.]

con·trap·tion (kən·trap′shən) *n.* *Informal* A contrivance or gadget. [?<CONTRIVE]

con·tra·pun·tal (kon′trə·pun′təl) *adj.* 1 Of, pertaining to, or according to the rules of counterpoint. 2 Characterized by the use of counterpoint. [< Ital. *contrapunto* counterpoint] —**con′tra·pun′tal·ly** *adv.* —**con′tra·pun′tist** *n.*

con·trar·i·wise (kon′trer·ē·wīz′; *for def. 3, also* kən·trâr′ē·wīz′) *adv.* 1 On the contrary; on the other hand. 2 In the reverse order; conversely. 3 In a contrary manner.

con·trar·y (kon′trer·ē; *for adj. def. 4, also* kən·trâr′ē) *adj.* 1 Totally different; opposed. 2 Adverse: *contrary* winds. 3 Opposite or other. 4 Inclined to opposition or contradiction; perverse —*n. pl.* **·trar·ies** 1 One of two opposing things. 2 The opposite. —**on the contrary** 1 On the other hand. 2 Just the opposite of what has been said. —**to the contrary** To the opposite effect. —*adv.* In a contrary manner. [< L *contra* against] —**con′trar·i·ly** *adv.* —**con′trar·i·ness** *n.*

con·trast (kən·trast′) *v.t.* 1 To place or set in opposition so as to show dissimilarities. —*v.i.* 2 To show dissimilarities when set in opposition. —*n.* (kon′trast) 1 The dissimilarity between two or more things or persons, as revealed by comparison. 2 A person or thing that contrasts with another. [< L *contra-* against + *stare* stand] —**con·trast′a·ble** *adj.*

con·tra·vene (kon′trə·vēn′) *v.t.* **·vened, ·ven·ing** 1 To act against or infringe upon, as a law. 2 To argue or disagree with. [< L *contra-* against + *venire* come] —**con′tra·ven′er, con·tra·ven·tion** (kon′trə·ven′shən) *n.* —**Syn.** 1 disregard, violate, disobey, defy. 2 dispute, contradict, contest, refute.

con·tre·danse (kôṅ·trə·däṅs′) *n.* COUNTRY-DANCE. Also **con·tre·dance** (kon′trə·dans′, -däns′). [< Alter. of COUNTRY-DANCE]

con·tre·temps (kôṅ·trə·taṅ′) *n. pl.* **·temps** (-täṅz′, *Fr.* -täṅ′) An embarrassing occurrence; awkward incident. [F, lit., against time]

con·trib·ute (kən·trib′yo͞ot) *v.* **·ut·ed, ·ut·ing** *v.t.* 1 To give or furnish (money, ideas, etc.), as for a common purpose. 2 To furnish, as an article or story, to a magazine or other publication. —*v.i.* 3 To share in effecting a result. 4 To make or give a contribution. [< L *com-* together + *tribuere* grant, allot] —**con·trib′ut·a·ble, con·trib′u·tive** *adj.* —**con·trib′u·tive·ly** *adv.* —**con·trib′u·tive·ness, con·trib′u·tor** *n.*

con·tri·bu·tion (kon′trə·byo͞o′shən) *n.* 1 The act of contributing. 2 Something contributed, as money, knowledge, etc. —**con′tri·bu′tion·al** *adj.*

con·trib·u·to·ry (kən·trib′yə·tôr′ē, -tō′rē) *adj.* 1 Contributing, as toward a result or action. 2 Involving or like a contribution. —*n. pl.* **·ries** One who or that which contributes.

con·trite (kən·trīt′, kon′trīt) *adj.* 1 Remorseful or guilty because of one's sins or shortcomings. 2 Proceeding from or showing remorse or guilt. [< L *contritus* bruised, pp. of *conterere* to rub together] —**con·trite′ly** *adv.* —**con·trite′ness, con·tri′tion** (-trish′ən) *n.*

con·tri·vance (kən·trī′vəns) *n.* 1 The act or manner of contriving. 2 Something contrived, as a device, tool, etc.

con·trive (kən·trīv′) *v.* **·trived, ·triv·ing** *v.t.* 1 To scheme or plan; devise. 2 To plot or conspire. 3 To make ingeniously; improvise; invent. 4 To manage or carry through, as by some device or scheme. —*v.i.* 5 To plan or plot. [< LL *contropare* represent figuratively] —**con·triv′a·ble** *adj.* —**con·triv′er** *n.*

con·trived (kən·trīvd′) *adj.* Overly planned or ingenious; artificial; labored.

con·trol (kən·trōl′) *v.t.* **·trolled, ·trol·ling** 1 To exercise authority over; govern. 2 To restrain; curb. 3 To direct, guide, or regulate, as a machine. 4 To verify, as an experiment, by comparison with a parallel experiment or other standard. 5 To check, as an account, by means of a duplicate register; verify or rectify. —*n.* 1 The act of controlling. 2 The power or ability to govern, regulate, or direct. 3 The condition of being controlled: The machine was out of *control.* 4 Something that directs, guides, or regulates, as a mechanical device. 5 A standard of comparison against which to check the results of an experiment. [< Med. L *contrarotulus* a check list < L *contra-* against + *rotulus* list] —**con·trol′la·bil′i·ty, con·trol′la·ble·ness** *n.* —**con·trol′la·ble** *adj.*

con·trol·ler (kən·trō′lər) *n.* 1 One who or that which controls. 2 An officer to examine and verify accounts; comptroller. —**con·trol′ler·ship** *n.*

con·tro·ver·sial (kon′trə·vûr′shəl) *adj.* 1 Of, causing, or characterized by controversy. 2 Given to controversy; disputatious. —**con′tro·ver′sial·ist** *n.* —**con′tro·ver′sial·ly** *adv.*

con·tro·ver·sy (kon′trə·vûr′sē) *n. pl.* **·sies** 1 Debate or disputation arising from conflicting attitudes and opinions. 2 A quarrel or dispute. [< L *contra-* against + *versus,* pp. of *vertere* turn]

con·tro·vert (kon′trə·vûrt, kon′trə·vûrt′) *v.t.* 1 To endeavor to disprove; argue against. 2 To argue about. [< L *controversus* turned against] —**con′tro·vert′er** *n.* —**con′tro·vert′i·ble** *adj.* —**con′tro·vert′i·bly** *adv.*

con·tu·ma·cy (kon′tyo͞o·mə·sē) *n. pl.* **·cies** Contemptuous disregard of authority; insolent and stubborn disobedience. Also **con·tu·mac·i·ty** (kon′tyo͞o·mas′ə·tē). [< L *contumax* stubborn] —**con·tu·ma·cious** (kon′tyo͞o·mā′shəs) *adj.* —**con′tu·ma′cious·ly** *adv.* —**con′tu·ma′cious·ness** *n.*

con·tu·me·ly (kon′tyo͞o·mə·lē, -mē′lē; kən·tyo͞o′mə·lē) *n. pl.* **·lies** 1 Insulting rudeness in speech or manner; scornful insolence. 2 An example of this. [< L *contumelia* reproach] —**con·tu·me·li·ous** (kon′tyo͞o·mē′lē·əs) *adj.* —**con′tu·me′li·ous·ly** *adv.* —**con′tu·me′li·ous·ness** *n.*

con·tuse (kən·tyo͞oz′) *v.t.* **·tused, ·tus·ing** To bruise by a blow. [< L *com-* together + *tundere* beat] —**con·tu·sive** (kən·tyo͞o′siv) *adj.*

con·tu·sion (kən·tyo͞o′zhən) *n.* A bruise.

co·nun·drum (kə·nun′drəm) *n.* 1 A riddle, often depending on a pun. 2 Any perplexing question or thing. [?]

con·va·lesce (kon′və·les′) *v.i.* **·lesced ·lesc·ing** To regain health after illness. [< L *com-* thoroughly + *valere* be strong] —**con·va·les·cent** (kon′və·les′ənt) *adj., n.*

con·va·les·cence (kon′və·les′əns) *n.* 1 Gradual recovery from illness. 2 The period of such recovery. Also **con′·va·les′cen·cy.**

con·vec·tion (kən·vek′shən) *n.* 1 The act of conveying. 2 *Physics* a The diffusion of heat through a liquid or gas by motion of its parts. b A process whereby atmospheric circulation is maintained through the transfer of air masses of different temperature. [< L *convectus,* pp. of *convehere* carry together] —**con·vec′tion·al, con·vec′tive** *adj.* —**con·vec′tive·ly** *adv.* —**con·vec′tor** *n.*

con·vene (kən·vēn′) *v.* **·vened, ·ven·ing** *v.t.* 1 To cause to assemble; convoke. 2 To summon to appear, as by judicial authority. —*v.i.* 3 To assemble. [< L *com-* together + *venire* come] —**con·ven′a·ble** *adj.* —**con·ven′er** *n.*

con·ven·ience (kən·vēn′yəns) *n.* 1 The quality of being convenient. 2 Personal comfort and ease. 3 Something which gives ease or comfort, as a labor-saving device.

con·ven·ient (kən·vēn′yənt) *adj.* 1 Conducive to comfort or ease; serviceable; handy. 2 Easy to get to; nearby. [< L *convenire.* See CONVENE.] —**con·ven′ient·ly** *adv.*

con·vent (kon′vent, -vənt) *n.* 1 A religious community, esp. of nuns. 2 The building or buildings occupied by such a body. [< L *conventus* meeting]

con·ven·ti·cle (kən·ven′ti·kəl) *n.* 1 A religious meeting, esp. a secret one. 2 The building in which such meetings are held. [< L *conventus.* See CONVENT.] —**con·ven′ti·cler** *n.*

con·ven·tion (kən·ven′shən) *n.* 1 A formal meeting of delegates, esp. for political or professional purposes. 2 The delegates themselves. 3 A generally accepted social custom or mode of behavior. 4 An established rule, form, or principle, as in art. 5 A formal agreement or compact.

con·ven·tion·al (kən·ven′shən·əl) *adj.* 1 Of or established by convention or custom; customary. 2 According to rule or custom; not natural, spontaneous, or unusual. 3 In art, stylized or simplified. 4 Nonnuclear: *conventional* warfare. 5 Of or pertaining to a convention of delegates. —**con·ven′tion·al·ism, con·ven′tion·al·ist** *n.* —**con·ven′tion·al·ly** *adv.*

con·ven·tion·al·i·ty (kən·ven′shən·al′ə·tē) *n. pl.* **·ties** 1 Adherence to established forms, customs, or usages. 2 A conventional act, principle, form, etc.

con·ven·tion·al·ize (kən·ven′shən·əl·īz) *v.t.* **·ized, ·iz·ing** **1** To make conventional. **2** *Art* To represent in a conventional manner. **—con·ven′tion·al·i·za′tion** *n.*

con·ven·tu·al (kən·ven′cho͞o·əl) *adj.* Belonging to a convent. —*n.* One who belongs to a convent.

con·verge (kən·vûrj′) *v.* **·verged, ·verg·ing** *v.t.* **1** To cause to tend toward one point. —*v.i.* **2** To move toward one point; come together by gradual approach. **3** To tend toward the same conclusion or result. [< L *com-* together + *vergere* bend]

con·ver·gence (kən·vûr′jəns) *n.* **1** The act or condition of converging. **2** Degree or point of convergence. Also **con·ver′gen·cy.** **—con·ver′gent** *adj.*

con·ver·sant (kon′vər·sənt, kən·vûr′sənt) *adj.* Familiar, as a result of study, experience, etc.: with *with* [< L *conversari.* See CONVERSE[1]] **—con′ver·sant·ly** *adv.*

con·ver·sa·tion (kon′vər·sā′shən) *n.* **1** The informal, verbal exchange of ideas, information, etc. **2** An instance of such an exchange. **—con′ver·sa′tion·al** *adj.* **—con′ver·sa′tion·al·ly** *adv.* **—Syn. 1,2** talk, communication, chat, dialogue.

con·ver·sa·tion·al·ist (kon′vər·sā′shən·əl·ist) *n.* A person skilled in conversation. Also **con′ver·sa′tion·ist.**

conversation piece Any article of furniture, decoration, etc., that arouses comment.

con·verse[1] (kən·vûrs′) *v.i.* **·versed, ·vers·ing** To speak together informally; engage in conversation. —*n.* (kon′·vûrs) **1** Conversation. **2** Close fellowship. [< L *conversari,* freq. of *convertere* to turn together] **—con·vers′a·ble** *adj.* **—con·vers′a·bly** *adv.* **—con·vers′er** *n.*

con·verse[2] (kən·vûrs′, kon′vûrs) *adj.* Turned about so that two parts are interchanged; transposed; reversed. —*n.* (kon′vûrs) That which exists in a converse relation; opposite. [< L *convertere* to turn around] **—con·verse·ly** (kən·vûrs′lē, kon′vûrs·lē) *adv.*

con·ver·sion (kən·vûr′zhən, -shən) *n.* **1** The act of converting, or the state of being converted, in any sense. **2** A change in one's opinions, way of life, etc., esp. the adoption of a religious belief. **—con·ver′sion·al** *adj.*

con·vert (kən·vûrt′) *v.t.* **1** To change into another state, form, or substance; transform. **2** To apply or adapt to a new or different purpose or use. **3** To change from one belief, doctrine, creed, opinion, or course of action to another. **4** To exchange for an equivalent value, as goods for money. **5** To exchange for value of another form, as preferred for common stock. **6** *Law* To assume possession of illegally. —*v.i.* **7** To become changed in character. **8** In football, to score the extra point after touchdown, as by kicking a field goal. —*n.* (kon′vûrt) A person who has been converted, as from one opinion, creed, etc., to another. [< L *convertere* to turn around]

con·vert·er (kən·vûr′tər) *n.* **1** One who or that which converts. **2** An apparatus for converting direct into alternating current. Also **con·ver′tor.**

con·vert·i·ble (kən·vûr′tə·bəl) *adj.* Capable of being converted. —*n.* **1** A convertible thing. **2** An automobile with a top that can be removed or folded back. **—con·vert′i·bil′·i·ty, con·vert′i·ble·ness** *n.* **—con·vert′i·bly** *adv.*

con·vex (kon·veks′, kon′veks) *adj.* Curving outward like a segment of a globe or of a circle viewed from outside; bulging out. —*n.* (kon′veks) A convex surface, body, line, etc. [< L *convexus* vaulted, curved] **—con·vex′i·ty, con·vex′ness** *n.* **—con·vex′ly** *adv.*

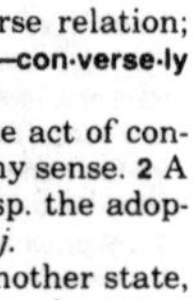

a. convex lens. b. concave lens.

con·vey (kən·vā′) *v.t.* **1** To carry from one place to another; transport. **2** To serve as a medium or path for; transmit. **3** To make known or impart; communicate. **4** To transfer ownership of, as real estate. [< L *com-* together + *via* road, way] **—con·vey′·a·ble** *adj.*

con·vey·ance (kən·vā′əns) *n.* **1** The act of conveying. **2** That by which anything is conveyed. **3** A vehicle. **4** *Law* **a** The transference of property ownership, esp. of real estate. **b** The document by which such transference is effected; deed. **—con·vey′anc·er, con·vey′anc·ing** *n.*

con·vey·er (kən·vā′ər) *n.* **1** One who or that which conveys. **2** A mechanical device, as a moving belt, that conveys materials. Also *(esp. for def. 2)* **con·vey′or** *n.*

con·vict (kən·vikt′) *v.t.* To prove or find guilty, esp. after a judicial trial. —*n.* (kon′vikt) One found guilty of or undergoing punishment for crime; a criminal. [< L *convictus,* pp. of *convincere.* See CONVINCE.] **—con·vic′tive** *adj.*

con·vic·tion (kən·vik′shən) *n.* **1** The act of convicting or the state of being convicted. **2** The act of convincing or the state of being convinced. **3** Something one firmly believes. **4** Fixed belief: He spoke with *conviction.* **—con·vic′tion·al** *adj.*

con·vince (kən·vins′) *v.t.* **·vinced, ·vinc·ing** To satisfy by evidence; persuade by argument. [< L *com-* thoroughly + *vincere* overcome, conquer] **—con·vinc′er** *n.* **—con·vinc′i·ble** *adj.*

con·vinc·ing (kən·vin′sing) *adj.* Having or marked by persuasive or satisfying evidence, arguments, or authority. **—con·vinc′ing·ly** *adv.*

con·viv·i·al (kən·viv′ē·əl) *adj.* Pertaining to or fond of feasting, drinking, or sociability; festive; jovial. [< L *convivium* a feast, banquet < *com-* together + *vivere* live] **—con·viv′i·al·ist, con·viv·i·al·i·ty** (kən·viv′ē·al′ə·tē) *n.* **—con·viv′i·al·ly** *adv.*

con·vo·ca·tion (kon′vō·kā′shən) *n.* **1** The act of summoning together an assembly. **2** The assembly thus summoned. [< L *convocare.* See CONVOKE.] **—con′vo·ca′tion·al** *adj.* **—con′vo·ca′tor** *n.*

con·voke (kən·vōk′) *v.t.* **·voked, ·vok·ing** To call together, as for a meeting. [< L *com-* together + *vocare* summon] **—con·vok′er** *n.* **—Syn.** summon, assemble, gather, muster.

con·vo·lute (kon′və·lo͞ot) *adj.* Rolled or coiled with one part turning inward upon another. —*v.t.* & *v.i.* **·lut·ed, ·lut·ing** To coil or twist around. [< L *convolvere.* See CONVOLVE.] **—con′vo·lute′ly** *adv.*

con·vo·lu·tion (kon′və·lo͞o′shən) *n.* **1** The act of convolving. **2** The state of being convolved. **3** A coil, twist, or fold, esp. one of the folds of the surface of the brain.

con·volve (kən·volv′) *v.* **·volved, ·volv·ing** *v.t.* To roll, twist, or wind around something. —*v.i.* To turn or wind upon itself. [< L *com-* together + *volvere* spin, twist]

con·vol·vu·lus (kən·vol′vyə·ləs) *n.* Any of a genus of twining herbs, as the morning glory, with trumpet-shaped flowers. [< L, bindweed]

con·voy (kon′voi) *n.* **1** A protecting force, as for accompanying ships at sea. **2** A group of vehicles, ships, etc., traveling together for protection. **3** The act of convoying. [< MF *convoi* < *convoyer*] —*v.t.* (kən·voi′, kon′voi) To act as convoy to. [< L *com-* together + *via* road]

con·vulse (kən·vuls′) *v.t.* **·vulsed, ·vuls·ing** **1** To affect with violent movements; agitate violently. **2** To cause to laugh violently. [< L *convulsus,* pp. of *convellere* to pull together] **—con·vul·sive** (kən·vul′siv) *adj.* **—con·vul′sive·ly** *adv.* **—con·vul′sive·ness** *n.*

con·vul·sion (kən·vul′shən) *n.* **1** A violent and abnormal muscular contraction of the body; spasm; fit. **2** An uncontrollable fit of laughter. **3** Any violent disturbance. **—con·vul·sion·ar·y** (kən·vul′shən·er′ē) *adj., n.*

co·ny (kō′nē, kun′ē) *n. pl.* **co·nies** **1** A rabbit. **2** Rabbit fur. [< L *cuniculus* rabbit]

coo (ko͞o) *v.* **cooed, coo·ing** *v.t.* **1** To utter with the soft murmuring sound of a dove or pigeon. —*v.i.* **2** To utter the coo of a dove, or a similar sound. **3** To speak in low, amorous tones: to bill and *coo.* —*n.* A murmuring sound, as of a dove. [Imit.] **—coo′er** *n.* **—coo′ing·ly** *adv.*

cook (ko͝ok) *v.t.* **1** To prepare (foodstuff) for eating by the action of heat. **2** *Slang* To ruin. —*v.i.* **3** To do the work of a cook. **4** To undergo cooking. **—cook up** *Informal* To concoct or invent, as a plot. [< L *coquere*] —*n.* One who prepares food for eating. **—cook′er** *n.*

cook·book (ko͝ok′bo͝ok′) *n.* A book containing recipes and instructions for cooking.

cook·er·y (ko͝ok′ər·ē) *n. pl.* **·er·ies** **1** The art or practice of cooking. **2** A place for cooking.

cook·out (ko͝ok′out′) *n. Informal* A picnic at which the meal is cooked out-of-doors; also, the meal itself.

cook·y (ko͝ok′ē) *n. pl.* **cook·ies** A small, flat, usu. crisp sweet cake. Also **cook′ey, cook′ie.** [< Du. *koek* cake]

cool (ko͞ol) *adj.* **1** Not warm; somewhat cold. **2** Serving to produce the effect of coolness: *cool* colors; a *cool* dress. **3** Self-controlled; self-possessed. **4** *Slang* Not involved or committed emotionally; detached. **5** Not friendly; chilling.

6 *Informal* Actual; not exaggerated: a *cool* million dollars. 7 *Slang* Very good; well done. —*v.t.* 1 To make cool. 2 To allay, as passion; calm. —*v.i.* 3 To become cool. 4 To become less ardent, angry, zealous, etc. —**cool it** *Slang* To become less angry, excited, emotional, etc.; calm down. —*n.* 1 A time, place, etc. that is cool. 2 *Slang* Self-possession: to lose one's *cool.* [< OE *col*] —**cool′ish** *adj.* —**cool′ly** *adv.* —**cool′ness** *n.*

cool·ant (ko͞o′lənt) *n.* Any substance used as a cooling medium, as for an internal-combustion engine.

cool·er (ko͞o′lər) *n.* 1 That which cools, as a vessel to cool liquids. 2 *Slang* A jail.

coo·lie (ko͞o′lē) *n.* 1 In the Orient, an unskilled laborer. 2 Any such person doing heavy work for low wages. Also **coo′ly.** [Prob. < Hind. *Kuli,* an aboriginal Gujarat tribe]

coon (ko͞on) *n.* RACCOON.

coop (ko͞op, ko͝op) *n.* 1 An enclosure, as for fowls or rabbits. 2 *Slang* A jail; prison. —**fly the coop** *Slang* To flee or escape. —*v.t.* To put into a coop; confine. [< MLG *kūpe* cask, basket]

co-op (kō′op, kō·op′) *n.* *Informal* A cooperative enterprise, as a store or apartment.

coop·er (ko͞o′pər, ko͝op′ər) *n.* One who makes or mends casks, barrels, etc. —*v.t.* & *v.i.* To make or mend (casks, barrels, etc.) [? < MLG *kūpe* a cask]

coop·er·age (ko͞o′pər·ij, ko͝op′ər-) *n.* The work of the cooper or the cost of such work.

co·op·er·ate (kō·op′ə·rāt) *v.i.* **·at·ed, ·at·ing** To work or operate together for a common purpose, effect, etc. —**co·op′er·a′tor** *n.*

co·op·er·a·tion (kō·op′ə·rā′shən) *n.* 1 Joint action or effort. 2 A union of laborers, farmers, small capitalists, etc., for mutual benefit. —**co·op′er·a′tion·ist** *n.*

co·op·er·a·tive (kō·op′ə·rə·tiv, -op′rə-, -op′ə·rā′tiv) *adj.* 1 Working together or inclined to work together. 2 Of, pertaining to, or set up as a cooperative. —*n.* An organization, store, apartment house, etc., owned in common by persons who use its services, facilities, etc. —**co·op′er·a·tive·ly** *adv.* —**co·op′er·a·tive·ness** *n.*

co·opt (kō·opt′) *v.i.* 1 To elect to fill a vacant membership. 2 To take or win over. [< L *co-* together + *optare* choose] —**co·op·ta·tive** (kō·op′tə·tiv) *adj.* —**co·op′tion, co′op·ta′tion** *n.* —**Syn.** 2 appropriate, preempt, assimilate, absorb, persuade, influence.

co·or·di·nate (kō·ôr′də·nit, -nāt) *adj.* 1 Of the same order, importance, or rank. 2 *Math.* Of or pertaining to coordinates. —*n.* 1 One who or that which is of the same order, rank, power, etc. 2 *Math.* Any of an ordered set of numbers that define the position of a point. —*v.* (kō·ôr′də·nāt) **·nat·ed, ·nat·ing** *v.t.* 1 To put in the same rank, class, or order. 2 To bring into harmonious relation or action. —*v.i.* 3 To be of the same order or rank. 4 To act in harmonious or reciprocal relation. [< L *co-* together + *ordinare* set in order] —**co·or′di·nate·ly** *adv.* —**co·or′di·nate·ness, co·or′di·na′tor** *n.* —**co·or′di·na′tive** *adj.*

co·or·di·na·tion (kō·ôr′də·nā′shən) *n.* 1 The act of coordinating. 2 The state of being coordinate. 3 The harmonious action of the various parts of a system.

coot (ko͞ot) *n.* 1 A dark, short-billed water bird. 2 *Informal* A simple-minded, usu. elderly fellow. [ME *cote*]

coot·ie (ko͞o′tē) *Slang* A body louse. [? < Indonesian *kutu,* parasitic insect]

cop (kop) *n.* *Informal* A policeman. —*v.t.* **copped, cop·ping** *Slang* 1 To steal. 2 To seize; take. —**cop out** *Slang* 1 To back down; renege. 2 To quit; give up. [Var. of *cap* to catch, take]

cop. copyright; copyrighted.

co·pal (kō′pəl) *n.* A hard, transparent resin exuded by various tropical trees, used in varnishes. [< Nah. *copalli* incense]

co·part·ner (kō·pärt′nər) *n.* An equal partner, as in a business. —**co·part′ner·ship** *n.*

cope[1] (kōp) *v.i.* **coped, cop·ing** To contend or deal successfully: often with *with.* [< OF *coup, colp* a blow < L *colaphus*]

cope[2] (kōp) *n.* 1 A semicircular ecclesiastical mantle worn on ceremonial occasions. 2 Something that arches or forms a canopy overhead.

Co·per·ni·can (kō·pûr′nə·kən) *adj.* Of or pertaining to the astronomical theories of Copernicus, who stated that the earth revolves on its axis and, with the other planets, revolves around the sun.

cope·stone (kōp′stōn′) *n.* 1 A top stone of a wall, as in a coping. 2 The finishing touch; culmination.

cop·i·er (kop′ē·ər) *n.* One who or that which copies.

co·pi·lot (kō′pī′lət) *n.* The assistant or relief pilot of an aircraft.

cop·ing (kō′ping) *n.* The top, usu. sloping course of a wall, roof, etc.

coping saw A narrow-bladed saw set in a frame and used for cutting curves in wood.

co·pi·ous (kō′pē·əs) *adj.* Ample in quantity; abundant. [< L *copia* abundance] —**co′pi·ous·ly** *adv.* —**co′pi·ous·ness** *n.* —**Syn.** plentiful, plenteous, profuse.

cop-out (kop′out′) *n.* *Slang* An act of or excuse for copping out; a quitting or backing down.

cop·per[1] (kop′ər) *n.* 1 A heavy, reddish metallic element (symbol Cu) with high thermal and electrical conductivity. 2 A coin made of this metal. 3 *Brit.* A large metal vat or pot. 4 A reddish brown. —*v.t.* To coat with copper. [< L *(aes) cyprium* Cyprian (metal)] —**cop′per·y** *adj.*

cop·per[2] (kop′ər) *n.* *Slang* A policeman. [< cop]

cop·per·as (kop′ər·əs) *n.* A green ferrous sulfate used in dyeing, inkmaking, photography, etc. [< Med. L *(aqua) cuprosa* copper (water)]

cop·per·head (kop′ər·hed′) *n.* A venomous North American snake with reddish brown markings.

Cop·per·head (kop′ər·hed′) *n.* During the Civil War, a Northerner who sympathized with the Confederate States.

Copperhead

cop·per·plate (kop′ər·plāt′) *n.* 1 An engraved or etched copper printing plate. 2 An impression printed from it.

cop·per·smith (kop′ər·smith′) *n.* One who makes utensils of copper.

cop·ra (kop′rə) *n.* Dried coconut meat, yielding coconut oil. Also **cop·per·ah** (kop′ər·ə), **cop′rah.** [< Malayalam *koppara*]

copse (kops) *n.* A thicket of small trees or bushes. Also **cop·pice** (kop′is) [< OF *coper* to cut]

Copt (kopt) *n.* 1 A native Egyptian descended from ancient Egyptian stock. 2 A member of the Coptic Church.

cop·ter (kop′tər) *n.* *Informal* HELICOPTER.

Cop·tic (kop′tik) *adj.* Of or pertaining to the Copts, or to their language. —*n.* The Hamitic language of the Copts, the liturgical language of the Coptic Church.

Coptic Church The principal Christian sect of Egypt, a separate body after 451.

cop·u·la (kop′yə·lə) *n.* *pl.* **·las** or **·lae** (-lē) *Gram.* A verb, as a form of *be, seem,* etc., that connects subject and predicate; a linking verb. [< L, a link, band] —**cop′u·lar** *adj.*

cop·u·late (kop′yə·lāt) *v.i.* **·lat·ed, ·lat·ing** To unite in sexual intercourse. [< L *copulare* fasten, link] —**cop′u·la′tion** *n.* —**cop·u·la·to·ry** (kop′yə·lə·tôr′ē, -tō′rē) *adj.*

cop·u·la·tive (kop′yə·lā′tiv) *adj.* 1 *Gram.* **a** Connecting coordinate words, clauses, etc., as a conjunction. **b** Serving as a copula. 2 Of or pertaining to copulation. —*n.* A copulative word. **cop′u·la′tive·ly** *adv.*

cop·y (kop′ē) *n.* *pl.* **cop·ies** 1 Something made to reproduce or imitate an original. 2 A single example of a printed edition, issue, etc. 3 Manuscript or other material to be reproduced in print. 4 A newsworthy or suitable subject for writing about. —*v.* **cop·ied, cop·y·ing** *v.t.* 1 To make a copy of; reproduce. 2 To follow as a model; imitate. —*v.i.* 3 To make a copy. [< L, supply, abundance]

cop·y·book (kop′ē·bo͝ok′) *n.* A book containing examples to be imitated in penmanship. —*adj.* Unimaginative; trite.

copy boy An errand boy in a newspaper office who carries copy.
cop·y·cat (kop′ē·kat′) *n. Informal* One who apes or imitates.
copy desk A desk in a newspaper office where copy is edited.
cop·y·ist (kop′ē·ist) *n.* **1** One who makes copies. **2** An imitator.
cop·y·right (kop′ē·rīt′) *n.* The exclusive statutory right to publish and dispose of a literary, musical, artistic, or dramatic work for a specified time. —*v.t.* To secure copyright for. —**cop′y·right′a·ble** *adj.* —**cop′y·right′er** *n.*
cop·y·writ·er (kop′ē·rī′tər) *n.* One who writes copy for advertisements. —**cop′y·writ′ing** *n.*
co·quet (kō·ket′) *v.* **co·quet·ted, co·quet·ing** *v.i.* **1** To flirt; play the coquette. **2** To act in a trifling manner; dally. [< F *coq* a cock; with ref. to its strutting] —**co·quet·ry** (kō′kə·trē, kō·ket′rē) *n.* (*pl.* **·ries**)
co·quette (kō·ket′) *n.* A woman or girl who flirts, esp. to gratify her vanity. [F< *coq* a cock] —**co·quet′tish** *adj.* —**co·quet′tish·ly** *adv.* —**co·quet′tish·ness** *n.*
co·qui·na (kō·kē′nə) *n.* **1** Any of a genus of small marine clams with varicolored shells. **2** A soft, porous limestone containing fragments of marine shells, used as building material. [Sp., shellfish]
Cor. Corinthians.
cor. corner; coroner; corpus; correct.
cor·a·cle (kôr′ə·kəl, kor′-) *n.* A small, rounded fishing boat of hide, etc., stretched on a wicker frame. [< Welsh *corwg* boat]
cor·al (kôr′əl, kor′-) *n.* **1** The calcareous skeletons secreted by various marine polyps and deposited in various forms and colors. **2** Any of numerous marine polyps that secrete coral. **3** A yellowish pink or red. —*adj.* **1** Made of coral. **2** Yellowish pink or red. [< Gk. *korallion*]

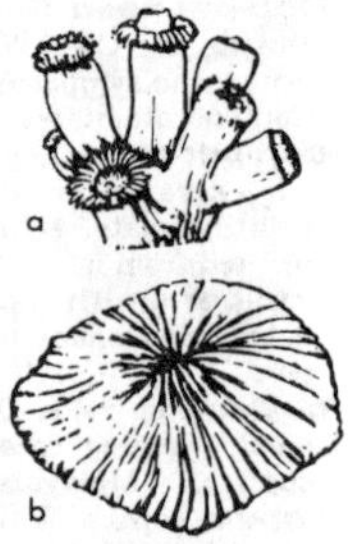

Corals
a. bud. b. mushroom.

coral reef A reef formed by the gradual deposit of coral skeletons.
coral snake A venomous snake of tropical America and the s U.S., having brilliant red, black, and yellow markings.
cor·bel (kôr′bəl, -bel) *n.* A bracketlike projection from the face of a wall, supporting a cornice or similar part. —*v.t.* **cor·beled** or **·belled, cor·bel·ing** or **·bel·ling** To supply or support with corbels. [< L *corvus* crow; from its shape]
cord (kôrd) *n.* **1** A string or thin rope of intertwined strands. **2** A flexible insulated electrical wire usu. having a plug at one end. **3** *Anat.* A cordlike structure: the spinal *cord.* **4** A measure for cut firewood equal to a pile of 128 cubic feet. **5 a** A raised rib in a fabric. **b** A fabric having such ribs. **6** *pl.* Corduroy trousers. **7** A force or influence acting as a bond. —*v.t.* **1** To bind or secure with cord. **2** To pile (firewood) by the cord. [< Gk. *chordē* string of a musical instrument] —**cord′ed** *adj.* —**cord′er** *n.*
cord·age (kôr′dij) *n.* **1** Ropes and cords collectively, esp. in the rigging of a ship. **2** The amount of wood in cords in a given area.
cor·date (kôr′dāt) *adj.* Heart-shaped. [< L *cor, cordis* heart] —**cor′date·ly** *adv.*
cor·dial (kôr′jəl) *adj.* Warm and sincere. —*n.* **1** A liqueur. **2** A medicine, etc., that stimulates or invigorates. [< L *cor, cordis* heart] —**cor·dial·i·ty** (kôr·jal′ə·tē, -jē·al′-, -dē·al′-), **cor′dial·ness** *n.* —**cor′dial·ly** *adv.* —**Syn.** *adj.* hearty, heartfelt, genial.
cor·dil·le·ra (kôr′dil·yâr′ə, kôr·dil′ər·ə) *n.* A system of mountain ranges extending through a large land mass. [< OSp. *cordilla,* dim. of *cuerda* rope, chain] —**cor′dil·le′·ran** *adj.*
cord·ite (kôr′dīt) *n.* A smokeless explosive. [< CORD; with ref. to its appearance]
cor·don (kôr′dən) *n.* **1** An extended line, as of men, ships, etc., enclosing or guarding an area. **2** A cord, ribbon, etc., esp. worn as a badge of honor. [< F *corde* cord]
cor·do·van (kôr′də·vən) *n.* A fine leather, usu. of split horsehide. —*adj.* Made of this leather. [< Sp. *Cordobán,* of Cordoba]
cor·du·roy (kôr′də·roi, kôr′də·roi′) *n.* **1** A durable usu. cotton fabric with ribs or wales of cut pile. **2** *pl.* Trousers made of corduroy. —*adj.* **1** Made of corduroy. **2** Formed from logs laid transversely; a *corduroy* road. [?]
cord·wood (kôrd′wo͝od′) *n.* Cut wood piled into cords or sold by the cord.
core (kôr, kōr) *n.* **1** The hard or fibrous central part of certain fruits, usu. containing the seeds. **2** The innermost or most important part of something. **3 a** The insulated conducting wires of an electric cable. **b** A ferromagnetic mass used to intensify or hold the magnetic field of a wire. —*v.t.* **cored, cor·ing** To remove the core of. [?]
CORE (kôr, kōr) Congress of Racial Equality.
co·re·lig·ion·ist (kō′ri·lij′ən·ist) *n.* A person having the same religion as another.
co·re·op·sis (kôr′ē·op′sis, kō′rē-) *n.* A plant of the composite family, having daisylike yellow or red and yellow flowers. [< Gk. *koris* bedbug + *opsis* appearance; with ref. to the shape of the seed]
cor·er (kôr′ər, kō′rər) *n.* A utensil for removing the cores of apples and other fruit.
co·re·spon·dent (kō′ri·spon′dənt) *n. Law* One charged with committing adultery with the husband or wife from whom a divorce is being sought. —**co′re·spon′den·cy** *n.*
co·ri·an·der (kôr′ē·an′dər, kō′rē-) *n.* **1** A plant related to parsley, having aromatic seeds used for seasoning. **2** The seeds of this plant. [< Gk. *koriannon*]
Co·rin·thi·an (kə·rin′thē·ən) *adj.* **1** Of or pertaining to Corinth, Greece. **2** Of or denoting an architectural order characterized by fluted columns having capitals decorated with stylized acanthus leaves. • See CAPITAL. —*n.* **1** A native or inhabitant of Corinth. **2** *pl.* Either of two books of the New Testament written by the apostle Paul as epistles to the Christians of Corinth. **3** A worldly, fashionable man. **4** An amateur yachtsman.
cork (kôrk) *n.* **1** The light, porous, elastic outer bark of a tree, the **cork oak,** of the Mediterranean region. **2** Something, esp. a bottle stopper, made from this bark. **3** A similar stopper, as of rubber. **4** *Bot.* The outer protective layer of the stems of woody plants. —*v.t.* **1** To stop with a cork. **2** To restrain; check. **3** To blacken with burnt cork. [< OSp. *alcorque* a cork slipper] —**cork′y** *adj.* (**·i·er, ·i·est**)
cork·er (kôr′kər) *n. Slang* An excellent or extraordinary person or thing.
cork·ing (kôr′king) *adj. Slang* Fine; excellent.
cork·screw (kôrk′skro͞o′) *n.* A spiral implement for drawing corks from bottles. —*v.t.* & *v.i.* To move or cause to move in a spiral; twist. —*adj.* Shaped like a corkscrew; twisted; spiral.
corm (kôrm) *n.* A bulblike underground enlargement of a plant stem. [< Gk. *kormos* tree trunk]
cor·mo·rant (kôr′mər·ənt) *n.* **1** A web-footed diving bird with dark plumage and a hooked bill. **2** A greedy or rapacious person. [< L *corvus marinus* sea crow]

Cormorant

corn[1] (kôrn) *n.* **1** A tall, widely cultivated cereal grass native to the New World, bearing edible kernels on large ears. **2** The kernels or ears of this plant. **3** *Brit.* **a** Any widely grown cereal plant, as wheat or rye. **b** The seeds of such a plant. **4** *Slang* Something regarded as trite, mawkish, etc. —*v.t.* To preserve in salt or in brine: to *corn* beef. [< OE]
corn[2] (kôrn) *n.* A horny thickening of the skin, esp. on a toe. [< L *cornu* horn]
corn borer A moth larva that infests and destroys corn and other plants.
corn bread Bread made from cornmeal.
corn·cob (kôrn′kob′) *n.* The hard central part of an ear of corn, on which the kernels grow.
corncob pipe A pipe whose bowl is cut from a corncob.
corn cockle A plant with purplish red flowers, often growing in grain fields.

cor·ne·a (kôr′nē·ə) *n.* The transparent outer coat of the eyeball, covering the iris and pupil. [< Med. L *cornea* horny] **—cor′ne·al** *adj.* • See EYE.

cor·nel (kôr′nəl) *n.* Any of several shrubs, trees, or plants belonging to the genus that includes the dogwood. [< L *cornus* cornel tree]

cor·nel·ian (kôr·nēl′yən) *n.* CARNELIAN.

cor·ner (kôr′nər) *n.* **1** The point or angle formed by the meeting of two lines or surfaces. **2** A space adjacent to the angle formed by converging surfaces or lines. **3** A place where two streets meet. **4** An area or region. **5** A remote or secluded place. **6** A position from which escape or extrication is difficult. **7** A piece placed on a corner for protection, decoration, etc. **8** Control of a commodity, stock, etc., acquired by buying up to force higher prices. **—cut corners** To reduce expenses; economize. *—v.t.* **1** To force or drive into a corner or difficult position. **2** To acquire control of (a commodity, stock, etc.) *—v.i.* **3** To turn a corner or corners, as a vehicle. **4** To form or abut with a corner. *—adj.* **1** Located at a corner. **2** Designed for a corner. [< L *cornu* horn, point]

cor·ner·stone (kôr′nər·stōn′) *n.* **1** A stone uniting two walls at the corner of a building. **2** Such a stone, often inscribed, laid ceremonially in a foundation. **3** Something fundamental or of primary importance.

cor·ner·wise (kôr′nər·wīz) *adv.* **1** With a corner in front. **2** Diagonally.

cor·net (kôr·net′) *n.* **1** A wind instrument like the trumpet but having a more flaring tube. **2** A cone-shaped paper wrapper, pastry shell, etc. [< L *cornu* a horn] **—cor·net′tist** or **cor·net′ist** *n.*

corn·flow·er (kôrn′flou′ər) *n.* A plant of the composite family having usu. blue flowers.

corn·husk·ing (kôrn′hus′king) *n.* A social gathering for the purpose of husking corn. **—corn′husk′er** *n.*

cor·nice (kôr′nis) *n.* **1** A horizontal projecting molding at the top of a wall, column, etc. **2** A framework or molding to conceal curtain rods, etc. *—v.t.* **·niced, ·nic·ing** To provide with a cornice. [< Gk. *korōnis* wreath, garland]

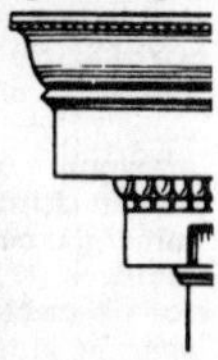

Cornice

Cor·nish (kôr′nish) *adj.* Of or pertaining to Cornwall, England, or its people. *—n.* The Celtic language formerly spoken in Cornwall. **—Corn′ish·man** *n.* (*pl* **·men**)

corn·meal (kôrn′mēl′) *n.* Meal made from corn. Also **corn meal.**

corn pone Bread made from cornmeal, usu. without milk and eggs.

corn silk The pale, lustrous, elongated styles which hang from an ear of corn.

corn·stalk (kôrn′stôk′) *n.* A stalk of the corn plant. Also **corn stalk.**

corn·starch (kôrn′stärch′) *n.* Starch obtained from corn, used in cooking, etc.

corn sugar Glucose obtained from cornstarch.

corn syrup Syrup obtained from cornstarch, containing glucose, maltose, etc.

cor·nu·co·pi·a (kôr′nə·kō′pē·ə) *n.* **1** A stylized representation of a goat's horn filled with fruit, grain, etc., symbolizing plenty or prosperity. **2** A cone-shaped container. [< L *cornu copiae* horn of plenty] **—cor′nu·co′pi·an** *adj.*

corn whiskey Whiskey made from corn.

corn·y (kôr′nē) *adj.* **corn·i·er, corn·i·est** *Slang* Trite, banal, sentimental, etc. **—corn′i·ness** *n.*

co·rol·la (kə·rol′ə) *n.* The inner envelope of a flower, consisting of separate petals or a single often tubelike or flaring part. [< L, dim. of *corona* crown]

cor·ol·lar·y (kôr′ə·ler′ē, kor′-; *Brit.* kə·rol′ər·ē) *n. pl.* **·lar·ies** **1** A proposition following so obviously from another that it requires little or no demonstration. **2** An inference; deduction. **3** A natural consequence. *—adj.* Deduced; resultant. [< L *corollarium* gift, orig. money paid for a garland]

co·ro·na (kə·rō′nə) *n. pl.* **·nas** or **·nae** (-nē) **1** A crownlike part, structure, or process. **2** *Astron.* A luminous circle around one of the heavenly bodies. **3** The luminous discharge at the surface of an electrical conductor under very high voltage. **4** *Bot.* A crownlike extension of the corolla, as in daffodils. [< L, crown]

cor·o·nar·y (kôr′ə·ner′ē, kor′-) *adj.* Pertaining to the two arteries that supply blood to the heart muscle. *—n. pl.* **·nar·ies** **1** A coronary artery. **2** CORONARY THROMBOSIS. [< L *corona* crown]

coronary thrombosis Blockage of a coronary artery by a blood clot.

cor·o·na·tion (kôr′ə·nā′shən, kor′-) *n.* The act or ceremony of crowning a monarch. [< L *coronare* to crown]

cor·o·ner (kôr′ə·nər, kor′-) *n.* A public officer who seeks to determine the cause of deaths not clearly due to natural causes. [< AF *coruner* officer of the crown]

cor·o·net (kôr′ə·net, -nit, kor′-) *n.* **1** A small crown, denoting noble rank below that of sovereign. **2** An ornamental band, wreath, etc., worn on the head. [< L *corona* crown]

Coronet

corp., corpn. corporation.

cor·po·ral[1] (kôr′pər·əl) *adj.* Of or relating to the body: *corporal* punishment. [< L *corpus* body] **—cor·po·ral·i·ty** (kôr′pə·ral′ə·tē) *n.* **—cor′po·ral·ly** *adv.* **—Syn.** physical, bodily.

cor·po·ral[2] (kôr′pər·əl) *n.* See GRADE. [< Ital. *caporale* < *capo* head]

cor·po·rate (kôr′pər·it) *adj.* **1** Constituting a corporation; incorporated. **2** Of or belonging to a corporation. **3** Combined; collective. [< L *corporare* make into a body < *corpus* body] **—cor′po·rate·ly** *adv.*

cor·po·ra·tion (kôr′pə·rā′shən) *n.* **1** A group of people having a legal charter that empowers them to transact business as a single body. **2** *Informal* A protuberant abdomen. **—cor·po·ra·tive** (kôr′pə·rā′tiv, -pər·ə·tiv′) *adj.* **—cor·po·ra·tor** (kôr′pə·rā′tər) *n.*

cor·po·re·al (kôr·pôr′ē·əl, -pō′rē·əl) *adj.* **1** Of or of the nature of the body. **2** Having physical or material existence. [< L *corpus* body] **—cor·po·re·al·i·ty** (kôr·pôr′ē·al′ə·tē, -pō′rē-), **cor·po′re·al·ness** *n.* **—cor·po′re·al·ly** *adv.*

corps (kôr, kōr) *n. pl.* **corps** (kôrz, kōrz) **1** *Mil.* **a** A special department or subdivision: the Quartermaster *Corps.* **b** A tactical unit consisting of two or more divisions. **2** An organized group of persons acting together. [< L *corpus* body]

corps de bal·let (kôr′də ba·lā′, *Fr.* bȧ·le′) The dancers of a ballet company who perform as a group rather than as soloists. [F]

corpse (kôrps) *n.* A dead body, esp. of a human being. [< L *corpus* body]

cor·pu·lent (kôr′pyə·lənt) *adj.* Having a fat body. [< L *corpulentus* < *corpus* body] **—cor′pu·lence, cor′pu·len·cy,** *n.* **—cor′pu·lent·ly** *adv.* **—Syn.** fat, obese, fleshy, stout.

cor·pus (kôr′pəs) *n. pl.* **·po·ra** (-pər·ə) **1** A large body or collection of written material of a specific nature. **2** The main mass or substance of anything. **3** A body of a person or animal. [L, body]

Cor·pus Chris·ti (kôr′pəs kris′tē, -tī) The first Thursday following Trinity Sunday, a Roman Catholic Church festival in honor of the Eucharist. [L, lit., body of Christ]

cor·pus·cle (kôr′pəs·əl, -pus·əl) *n.* **1** One of the particles forming part of the blood of vertebrates; an erythrocyte (**red corpuscle**) or a leukocyte (**white corpuscle**). **2** A minute particle. Also **cor·pus·cule** (kôr·pus′kyōōl). [< L *corpusculum,* dim. of *corpus* body] **—cor·pus·cu·lar** (kôr·pus′kyə·lər) *adj.*

corpus de·lic·ti (də·lik′tī) **1** *Law* The essential fact or material evidence proving the commission of a crime. **2** Loosely, the body of a murder victim. [L, lit., the body of the offense]

corr. corrected; correction; correspondence; correspondent.

cor·ral (kə·ral′) *n.* **1** An enclosed space or pen for livestock. **2** A space enclosed by wagons for protection against attack. *—v.t.* **·ralled, ·ral·ling** **1** To drive into and enclose in a corral. **2** *Informal* To seize or capture; secure. [Sp.]

cor·rect (kə·rekt′) *v.t.* **1** To remove errors from; make right. **2** To mark or indicate the errors of. **3** To rebuke or chastise. **4** To remedy or counteract, as a malfunction. **5** To make conformable to a standard: to *correct* a lens. —*adj.* **1** Free from fault or mistake. **2** True; right; accurate. **3** Proper; acceptable. [< L *com-* together + *regere* make straight] —**cor·rect′a·ble** or **·i·ble** *adj.* —**cor·rect′ly** *adv.* —**cor·rect′ness, cor·rec′tor** *n.* —**Syn.** *v.* **1** rectify, right, redress. **5** adjust, regulate.

cor·rec·tion (kə·rek′shən) *n.* **1** The act of correcting. **2** Something offered or substituted to correct an error. **3** Chastisement; punishment. —**cor·rec′tion·al** *adj.*

cor·rec·tive (kə·rek′tiv) *adj.* Tending or intended to correct. —*n.* Something that corrects or is intended to correct. —**cor·rec′tive·ly** *adv.*

correl. correlative.

cor·re·late (kôr′ə·lāt, kor′-) *v.* **·lat·ed, ·lat·ing** *v.t.* **1** To place or put in reciprocal relation. —*v.i.* **2** To be mutually or reciprocally related. —*adj.* Having mutual or reciprocal relations. —*n.* CORRELATIVE (def. 1). [< COM- + RELATE]

cor·re·la·tion (kôr′ə·lā′shən, kor′-) *n.* **1** Mutual or reciprocal relation. **2** The act or process of correlating. —**cor′re·la′tion·al** *adj.*

cor·rel·a·tive (kə·rel′ə·tiv) *adj.* **1** Having a corresponding or reciprocal relationship. **2** Used together and indicating a grammatical or logical relationship, as the conjunctions *either* and *or.* —*n.* **1** Either of two things in correlation. **2** A correlative term, as in grammar. —**cor·rel′a·tive·ly** *adv.* —**cor·rel′a·tive·ness, cor·rel′a·tiv′i·ty** *n.*

cor·re·spond (kôr′ə·spond′, kor′-) *v.i.* **1** To be in agreement, or conformity. **2** To be similar, equivalent, or analogous. **3** To communicate by letters. [< Med. L *com-* together + *respondere* to answer]

cor·re·spon·dence (kôr′ə·spon′dəns, kor′-) *n.* **1** Conformity; agreement. **2** Similarity; analogous relationship. **3 a** Communication by letters. **b** The letters themselves.

correspondence school A school that gives courses of instruction by mail.

cor·re·spon·dent (kôr′ə·spon′dənt, kor′-) *n.* **1** One who communicates by means of letters. **2** A reporter or writer, as for a newspaper, who sends news or articles from a distant place. **3** Something having a corresponding relationship. —*adj.* Having a corresponding relationship.

cor·re·spond·ing (kôr′ə·spon′ding, kor′-) *adj.* Reciprocal, analogous, or equivalent. —**cor′re·spond′ing·ly** *adv.*

cor·ri·dor (kôr′ə·dər, -dôr, kor′-) *n.* **1** A hallway or passageway usu. having rooms opening on it. **2** A strip of land belonging to one country crossing the territory of another. **3** A densely populated strip of territory including major cities. [< Ital. *corridore* < *correre* to run]

cor·ri·gen·dum (kôr′ə·jen′dəm, kor′-) *n. pl.* **·da** (-də) **1** An error to be corrected in a printed work. **2** *pl.* A list of corrected errors included in a book. [< L, gerundive of *corrigere.* See CORRECT.]

cor·ri·gi·ble (kôr′ə·jə·bəl, kor′-) *adj.* Capable of being corrected or reformed. [< L *corrigere* to correct] —**cor′ri·gi·bil′i·ty** *n.* —**cor′ri·gi·bly** *adv.*

cor·rob·o·rate (kə·rob′ə·rāt) *v.t.* **·rat·ed, ·rat·ing** To confirm or support (evidence, a statement, etc.) [< L *com-* together + *robur* strength] —**cor·rob′o·ra′tor, cor·rob′o·ra′tion** *n.* —**cor·rob·o·ra·tive** (kə·rob′ə·rā·tiv, -rob′ər·ə·tiv), **cor·rob·o·ra·to·ry** (kə·rob′ər·ə·tôr′ē, -tō′rē) *adj.* —**cor·rob′o·ra′tive·ly** *adv.*

cor·rode (kə·rōd′) *v.t. & v.i.* **·rod·ed, ·rod·ing** To wear away gradually, esp. by chemical action such as rusting. [< L *com-* thoroughly + *rodere* gnaw] —**cor·rod′i·ble, cor·ro·si·ble** (kə·rō′sə·bəl) *adj.*

cor·ro·sion (kə·rō′zhən) *n.* **1** The process of corroding. **2** A product of corrosive action.

cor·ro·sive (kə·rō′siv) *adj.* **1** Having the power of corroding. **2** Caustic; scathing. —*n.* Something that causes corrosion. —**cor·ro′sive·ly** *adv.* —**cor·ro′sive·ness** *n.*

corrosive sublimate MERCURIC CHLORIDE.

cor·ru·gate (kôr′ə·gāt, kor′-) *v.t. & v.i.* **·gat·ed, ·gat·ing** To form into alternating ridges and furrows. [< L *com-* together + *ruga* a wrinkle] —**cor′ru·ga′tion** *n.*

cor·rupt (kə·rupt′) *adj.* **1** Viciously immoral; depraved. **2** Capable of being bribed, improperly influenced, etc.; dishonest. **3** Altered or debased by errors, changes, etc., as a text. **4** Rotten; putrid. —*v.t. & v.i.* To make or become corrupt. [< L *com-* thoroughly + *rumpere* to break] —**cor·rupt′er, cor·rup′tor, cor·rupt′ness** *n.* —**cor·rupt′ly** *adv.* —**cor·rup′tive** *adj.*

cor·rupt·i·ble (kə·rup′tə·bəl) *adj.* Capable of being corrupted, as by bribery or improper influence. —**cor·rup′ti·bil′i·ty, cor·rup′ti·ble·ness.** *n.* —**cor·rup′ti·bly** *adv.*

cor·rup·tion (kə·rup′shən) *n.* **1** The act or process of corrupting or the condition of being corrupt. **2** An influence or action that corrupts, as bribery. **3** An alteration, as of a word or text, often to an incorrect or debased form.

cor·sage (kôr·säzh′) *n.* **1** A small bouquet of flowers for a woman to wear at the shoulder, waist, etc. **2** The bodice or waist of a woman's dress. [< OF < *cors* body < L]

cor·sair (kôr′sâr) *n.* **1** A pirate. **2** A pirate's vessel. **3** A privateer. [< Med. L *cursarius* < *cursus* inroad, raid]

corse·let (kôrs′lit *for def. 1;* kôr′sə·let′ *for def. 2*) **1** Armor for the upper part of the body: also **cors′let.** **2** A light corset: also **cor′se·lette′.** [< MF, dim. of *cors* body]

Corselet

cor·set (kôr′sit) *n.* A close-fitting under-garment, usu. reinforced by stays and sometimes tightened with laces, worn esp. by women to shape and support the body. —*v.t.* To enclose or dress in a corset. [< OF, dim. of *cors* body]

cor·tege (kôr·tezh′, -tāzh′) *n.* **1** A train of attendants. **2** A ceremonial procession. Also **cor·tège′.** [< Ital. *corte* court]

cor·tex (kôr′teks) *n. pl.* **·ti·ces** (-tə·sēz) **1** *Bot.* An outer layer, as the bark of trees or the rind of fruits. **2** *Anat.* **a** A distinctive outer layer of an organ, as the brain, kidney, etc. **b** The external portion of the adrenal glands. [< L, bark] • See KIDNEY.

cor·ti·cal (kôr′ti·kəl) *adj.* **1** Of, pertaining to, or consisting of a cortex. **2** Caused by or associated with the cerebral cortex. —**cor′ti·cal·ly** *adv.*

cor·ti·sone (kôr′tə·sōn, -zōn) *n.* A hormone secreted by the cortex of the adrenal gland and also made synthetically. [Short for *corticosterone* < L *cortex, -icis* cortex + STER(OID) + (HORM)ONE]

co·run·dum (kə·run′dəm) *n.* A hard aluminum oxide mineral occurring as sapphire or ruby and also used as an abrasive. [< Skt. *kuruvinda* ruby]

cor·us·cate (kôr′ə·skāt, kor′-) *v.i.* **·cat·ed, ·cat·ing** To sparkle; glitter; flash. [< L *coruscare* to glitter] —**cor′us·ca′tion** *n.*

cor·vette (kôr·vet′) *n.* **1** A small armed ship used chiefly as an antisubmarine escort vessel. **2** Formerly, a warship having sails and a single tier of guns. Also **cor·vet** (kôr·vet′, kôr′vet). [< MF]

cor·vine (kôr′vīn, -vin) *adj.* Of, related to, or resembling the crow. [< L *corvus* crow]

cor·ymb (kôr′imb, -im, kor′-) *n.* A flower cluster having stalks of different lengths growing to the same level. [< Gk. *korymbos* flower cluster] —**co·rym·bose** (kə·rim′bōs), **co·rym·bous** (kə·rim′bəs) *adj.* —**co·rym′bose·ly** *adv.*

co·ry·za (kə·rī′zə) *n.* Congestion of the nose and connecting sinuses; a cold in the head. [< Gk. *koryza* catarrh]

cos cosine.

cosec cosecant.

co·se·cant (kō·sē′kənt) *n. Trig.* The reciprocal of the sine of an angle.

co·sig·na·to·ry (kō·sig′nə·tor′ē, -tō′rē) *n. pl.* **·ries** One of two or more joint signers of a treaty, contract, or other document.

co·sine (kō′sīn) *n. Trig.* The sine of the complement of a given angle or arc.

cos·met·ic (koz·met′ik) *n.* A preparation applied to the skin, hair, etc., to beautify or improve appearance. —*adj.* **1** Used to beautify physical appearance. **2** Intended to improve appearance: *cosmetic* surgery. [< Gk. *kosmos* order, ornament] —**cos·met′i·cal·ly** *adv.*

cos·mic (koz′mik) *adj.* **1** Of or pertaining to the universe as a whole. **2** Immense; vast. Also **cos′mi·cal.** [< Gk. *kosmos* the universe] —**cos′mi·cal·ly** *adv.*

cosmic dust Fine particles of matter in or from space.

cosmic rays High-energy radiation that reaches the earth from space.

cosmo- *combining form* The universe: *cosmogony.* [< Gk. *kosmos* the universe]

cos·mog·o·ny (koz·mog′ə·nē) *n. pl.* **·nies 1** The origin of the universe. **2** A theory of the origin or creation of the world or universe. **—cos·mo·gon·ic** (koz′mə·gon′ik) or **·i·cal, cos·mog′o·nal** *adj.* **—cos·mog′o·nist** *n.*

cos·mog·ra·phy (koz·mog′rə·fē) *n. pl.* **·phies.** The science that describes the universe. **—cos·mog′ra·pher, cos·mog′ra·phist** *n.* **—cos·mo·graph·ic** (koz′mə·graf′ik) or **·i·cal** *adj.*

cos·mol·o·gy (koz·mol′ə·jē) *n. pl.* **·gies** The general science or philosophy of the universe. **—cos·mo·log·ic** (koz′mə·loj′ik) or **·i·cal** *adj.* **—cos·mol′o·gist** *n.*

cos·mo·naut (koz′mə·nôt) *n.* ASTRONAUT. [< COSMO- + Gk. *nautēs* sailor]

cos·mo·pol·i·tan (koz′mə·pol′ə·tən) *adj.* **1** Common to all the world; not local or limited. **2** At home in all parts of the world. **3** *Biol.* Widely distributed, as a plant or animal. **—***n.* A cosmopolitan person. **—cos′mo·pol′i·tan·ism** *n.*

cos·mop·o·lite (koz·mop′ə·līt) *n.* **1** A cosmopolitan person. **2** *Biol.* A plant or animal widely distributed over the world. [< Gk. *kosmopolites* world citizen]

cos·mos (koz′məs, -mos) *n.* **1** The world or universe considered as an orderly system. **2** Any orderly and complete system. **3** A plant with daisylike flowers of various colors. [< Gk. *kosmos* order, universe]

Cos·sack (kos′ak, -ək) *n.* One of a people of the s U.S.S.R., famous as cavalrymen.

cos·set (kos′it) *v.t.* To treat indulgently; pamper. **—***n.* A pet, esp. a pet lamb. [?]

cost (kôst, kost) *v.* **cost** (*for def. 3, also* **cost·ed**), **cost·ing** *v.t.* **1** To have or require as a price. **2** To cause to pay, lose, suffer, or exert. **3** To estimate the cost of production of. **—***n.* **1** The price paid for anything. **2** Loss; suffering; detriment. **3** *pl.* The charges in a lawsuit. **—at all costs** (or **at any cost**) No matter what price or effort is involved. [< L *constare* to stand at, cost]

cos·tal (kos′təl) *adj.* Of, pertaining to, or near a rib or ribs. [< L *costa* rib]

Cos·ta Ri·ca (kos′tə rē′kə, kôs′tə) A republic of Central America, 19,690 sq. mi., cap. San José. **—Costa Rican •** See map at CENTRAL AMERICA.

cos·ter·mon·ger (kos′tər·mung′gər, -mong′-, kôs′-) *n. Brit.* A street hawker of vegetables, fruits, etc. Also **cos′ter.** [Earlier *costardmonger* apple seller]

cos·tive (kos′tiv, kôs′-) *adj.* Constipated. [< L *constipare* constipate] **—cos′tive·ly** *adv.* **—cos′tive·ness** *n.*

cost·ly (kôst′lē, kost′-) *adj.* **·li·er, ·li·est 1** Of great cost; expensive. **2** Resulting in great loss, sacrifice, etc. **3** Splendid; sumptuous. **—cost′li·ness** *n.* **—Syn. 1** dear, high-priced, valuable, precious.

cost of living The average cost of the necessities of life, as food, clothing, shelter, etc.

cos·tume (kos′t^y^o͞om) *n.* **1** Clothing or style of dress characteristic of a particular country, period, etc. **2** Such clothing, or other distinctive dress, worn by a theatrical performer, to a masquerade, etc. **3** A set of clothing; ensemble; outfit. **—***v.t.* (kos·t^y^o͞om′) **·tumed, ·tum·ing** To furnish with costumes. [< Ital. *costuma* fashion, guise < L *consuetudo* custom]

costume jewelry Inexpensive jewelry made from nonprecious materials.

cos·tum·er (kos·t^y^o͞o′mər) *n.* One who makes or furnishes costumes, as for stage wear. Also **cos·tum·ier** (kos·t^y^o͞om′yər; *Fr.* kôs·tü·myā′).

co·sy (kō′zē) *adj.* **·si·er, ·si·est** COZY. **—co′si·ly** *adv.* **—co′si·ness** *n.*

cot[1] (kot) *n.* A light, narrow bed, usu. with a folding frame. [< Skt. *khatvā*]

cot[2] (kot) *n.* **1** A small house; cottage. **2** A protective sheath for a finger. [< OE]

cot cotangent.

co·tan·gent (kō·tan′jənt) *n. Trig.* The tangent of the complement of an angle. **—co·tan·gen·tial** (kō′tan·jen′shəl) *adj.*

cote (kōt) *n.* A small shelter for sheep or birds. [< OE]

co·te·rie (kō′tə·rē) *n.* A closely knit group of persons with shared interests. [< OF, group of landholding peasants < *cote* hut]

co·ter·mi·nous (kō·tûr′mə·nəs) *adj.* CONTERMINOUS.

co·til·lion (kō·til′yən, kə-) *n.* **1** A ballroom dance with many different figures. **2** A formal ball, esp. for debutantes. Also **co·til·lon** (kō·til′yən, kə-; *Fr.* kô·tē·yôn′). [< OF *cotillon* petticoat.]

cot·tage (kot′ij) *n.* **1** A small, unpretentious house. **2** A usu. small temporary residence, as at a vacation resort. [< OE *cote* hut]

cottage cheese A soft, white cheese made of strained milk curds.

cottage pudding Plain cake served with a sweet sauce.

cot·tag·er (kot′ij·ər) *n.* One who lives in a cottage.

cot·ter (kot′ər) *n.* A key or wedge used to fasten parts of machinery together. [?]

cotter pin A split metal pin for insertion in a nut, bolt, etc., to hold it in place.

cot·ton (kot′n) *n.* **1** A plant of warm regions cultivated for the fibrous material surrounding its seeds. **2** The soft, downy white fibers of this plant, used for textiles, etc. **3** Cloth or thread made from these fibers. **—***adj.* Of or made from cotton. **—***v.i. Informal* To become friendly; take a liking: used with *to.* **—cotton up to** *Informal* To flatter or make friendly overtures to. [< Ar. *quṭun*] **—cot′ton·y** *adj.*

cotton gin A machine used to separate the seeds from the fiber of cotton.

cot·ton·mouth (kot′n·mouth′) *n.* WATER MOCCASIN.

cot·ton·seed (kot′n·sēd′) *n.* The seed of the cotton plant, pressed to produce a yellow oil, **cottonseed oil,** used in cooking, paints, etc.

cot·ton·tail (kot′n·tāl′) *n.* Any of several common American rabbits having a tail with fluffy white fur.

cot·ton·wood (kot′n·wo͝od′) *n.* Any of several American poplar trees having seeds covered with cottony fibers.

cotton wool 1 Raw cotton. **2** A mass of cotton fibers used for padding, surgical dressing, etc.

cot·y·le·don (kot′ə·lēd′n) *n.* An embryonic leaf within a seed, often one of a pair appearing as the first sprouting leaves of a seedling plant. [< Gk. *kotylēdōn* socket] **—cot′y·le′do·nal; cot′y·le′do·nous** *adj.*

Cotyledons of Norway maple

couch (kouch) *n.* **1** A long, usu. upholstered piece of furniture on which one may sit or lie. **2** Any place for repose. **—***v.t.* **1** To cause to recline. **2** To put into words; phrase. **3** To hold in readiness for use, as a spear. **—***v.i.* **4** To lie down; recline. [< F *coucher* put to bed < L *collocare* to set, place] **—couch′er** *n.*

couch·ant (kou′chənt) *adj. Her.* Reclining with head uplifted. [F< *coucher* to put to bed]

couch grass (kouch, ko͞och) A weedy grass that spreads rapidly by means of long rootstocks. [< OE *cwice* couch grass + GRASS]

cou·gar (ko͞o′gər) *n.* MOUNTAIN LION. [< Tupian]

cough (kôf, kof) *v.i.* **1** To expel air from the lungs in a noisy or spasmodic manner. **—***v.t.* **2** To expel by coughing. **—cough up 1** To expel (phlegm, etc.) by coughing. **2** *Slang* To hand over, as money. **—***n.* **1** A sudden, harsh expulsion of breath. **2** An illness characterized by much coughing. [ME *coughen*] **—cough′er** *n.*

cough drop A small, medicated lozenge to relieve coughing.

could (ko͝od) *p.t.* of CAN[1].

could·n't (ko͝od′nt) Contraction of *could not.*

cou·lee (ko͞o′lē) *n.* **1** A deep, usu. dry gulch. **2** A sheet of solidified lava. [< F *couler* to flow]

cou·lomb (ko͞o′lom, -lōm, ko͞o·lom′) *n.* The unit of electric charge, the amount carried by a constant current of one ampere in one second. [< C. A. de *Coulomb,* 1736–1806, French physicist]

coul·ter (kōl′tər) *n.* COLTER.

coun·cil (koun′səl) *n.* **1** An assembly of persons convened for consultation or deliberation. **2** A body of persons elected or appointed to assist in the administration of government. **3** Deliberation or consultation among the members of a council. [< L *concilium*] • See COUNSEL.

coun·cil·man (koun′səl·mən) *n. pl.* **·men** (-mən) A member of a council, esp. the governing council of a city. —**coun′cil·wom′an** *n. Fem.* (*pl.* **·wom′en**)

coun·cil·or (koun′səl·ər, -slər) *n.* A council member. Also **coun′cil·lor.** —**coun′cil·or·ship′** *n.*

coun·sel (koun′səl) *n.* **1** Consultation for exchange of advice, opinions, etc. **2** Advice; opinion. **3** A lawyer or lawyers engaged for legal advice. —**keep one's (own) counsel** To keep one's ideas, plans, etc., to oneself. —*v.* **·seled** or **·selled, ·sel·ing** or **·sel·ling** *v.t.* **1** To advise; give advice to. **2** To advise in favor of; recommend. —*v.i.* **3** To confer; deliberate. [< L *consilium*] • The nouns *counsel* (def. 2) and *council* (def. 1) have related meanings, but are not interchangeable. *Council* in this sense is used chiefly in the phrase *in council,* while *counsel* is used in such expressions as *take counsel, heed someone's counsel,* etc.

coun·sel·or (koun′səl·ər, -slər) *n.* **1** One who gives counsel; an adviser. **2** An attorney. **3** One who supervises at a children's camp. Also **coun′sel·lor.**

count[1] (kount) *v.t.* **1** To list or call off the units of (a set or collection) in correspondence with a sequence of natural numbers. **2** To list numbers in a progressive sequence to: count *ten.* **3** To include in a reckoning. **4** To consider to be. —*v.i.* **5** To list numbers in sequence. **6** To rely; depend: with *on.* **7** To have importance; merit consideration. —**count in** To include. —**count out 1** To exclude. **2** To count to ten over (a downed boxer). —*n.* **1** The act of counting. **2** A number reached by counting. **3** A relevant item or point. **4** *Law* One of the charges in an indictment. **5** In boxing, the ten counted seconds during which a downed contestant must get up or lose the bout. [< L *computare*] —**count′a·ble** *adj.*

count[2] (kount) *n.* In some European countries, a nobleman having a rank corresponding to that of an earl in England. [< L *comes* an associate]

count·down (kount′doun′) *n.* A specified interval of time before an intended action, measured in descending units to zero.

coun·te·nance (koun′tə·nəns) *n.* **1** The face or features. **2** Expression; appearance. **3** Approval; support. **4** Composure; aplomb —**out of countenance** Disconcerted; abashed. —*v.t.* **·nanced, ·nanc·ing** To approve; give sanction to. [< L *continentia* behavior < *continere* to contain] —**coun′te·nanc·er** *n.* —**Syn.** *v.* condone, sanction, favor, abet.

coun·ter[1] (koun′tər) *adv.* In a contrary manner or direction. —*adj.* Opposing; opposite; contrary. —*v.t.* **1** To act so as to oppose or offset. **2** To return or parry, as a blow. —*v.i.* **3** To make an opposing or offsetting move or action. —*n.* **1** That which counters or opposes. **2** A parrying blow. **3** An outer piece of shoe leather that stiffens the heel. [< L *contra* against]

coun·ter[2] (koun′tər) *n.* **1** A narrow table or surface on which sales are transacted, food is served, etc. **2** A piece of wood, ivory, etc., used in counting or keeping score. [< L *computare,* to compute]

count·er[3] (koun′tər) *n.* One who or that which counts, esp. a machine for counting.

counter- *combining form* **1** In opposition; contrary: *counterclockwise.* **2** In exchange or retaliation: *counterattack.* **3** Complementing or corresponding: *counterpart.*

coun·ter·act (koun′tər·akt′) *v.t.* To act in opposition to; have an offsetting effect on. —**coun′ter·ac′tion** *n.* —**coun′ter·ac′tive** *adj.* —**coun′ter·ac′tive·ly** *adv.*

coun·ter·at·tack (koun′tər·ə·tak′) *n.* An attack in response to a previous attack. —*v.t. & v.i.* To attack in response to a previous attack.

coun·ter·bal·ance (koun′tər·bal′əns) *v.t.* **·anced, ·anc·ing** To oppose with an equal weight or force; offset. —*n.* (koun′tər·bal′əns) **1** Any power equally opposing another. **2** A weight that balances another.

coun·ter·claim (koun′tər·klām′) *n.* A claim, esp. a legal claim, made in opposition to another claim. —*v.t. & v.i.* To make or offer as a counterclaim. —**coun′ter·claim′ant** *n.*

coun·ter·clock·wise (koun′tər·clok′wīz′) *adj. & adv.* Contrary to the direction in which the hands of a clock move.

coun·ter·cul·ture (koun′tər·kul′chər) *n.* **1** The effort and methods used by certain alienated people to create a life style different from that of the Establishment. **2** The life style thus created. **3** The people who follow it.

coun·ter·es·pi·o·nage (koun′tər·es′pē·ə·nij, -näzh′) *n.* Activities intended to counteract enemy spying.

coun·ter·feit (koun′tər·fit) *v.t.* **1** To make a copy or imitation of (money, etc.) with intent to defraud. **2** To pretend; feign. **3** To imitate; resemble closely. —*v.i.* **4** To practice deception; dissemble. **5** To make counterfeits. —*n.* **1** A copy or imitation fraudulently intended to pass as genuine. **2** An imitation or close resemblence. —*adj.* **1** Fraudulently made to resemble something genuine. **2** Pretended; feigned. [< L *contra-* against + *facere* make] —**coun′ter·feit′er** *n.* —**Syn.** *adj.* false, spurious, fake, bogus.

coun·ter·in·tel·li·gence (koun′tər·in·tel′ə·jens) *n.* Activities intended to counteract or prevent espionage, subversion, sabotage, etc.

coun·ter·ir·ri·tant (koun′tər·ir′ə·tənt) *n.* An agent used to produce mild surface irritation so as to relieve more serious irritation elsewhere.

coun·ter·mand (koun′tər·mand′, -mänd′, koun′tər·mand, -mänd) *v.t.* **1** To cancel or revoke (an order, command, etc.). **2** To recall by a contradictory order. —*n.* (koun′tər·mand, -mänd) An order contrary to or revoking a previous one. [< L *contra-* against + *mandare* to order]

coun·ter·mea·sure (koun′tər·mezh′ər) *n.* An action taken to offset another.

coun·ter·of·fen·sive (koun′tər·ə·fen′siv, koun′tər·ə·fen′siv) *n.* A large-scale military action designed to stop an enemy offensive.

coun·ter·pane (koun′tər·pān′) *n.* A coverlet or quilt for a bed. [Alter. of obs. *counterpoint* < L *culcita puncta* a quilted coverlet]

coun·ter·part (koun′tər·pärt′) *n.* One having a close resemblance or corresponding relationship to another.

coun·ter·plot (koun′tər·plot′) *n.* A plot to oppose or frustrate another. —*v.t. & v.i.* (koun′tər·plot′) **·plot·ted, ·plot·ting** To oppose (a plot) by another plot.

coun·ter·point (koun′tər·point′) *n.* **1** The art of adding to a melody a part or parts related to but independent of it, according to fixed rules. **2** The part or parts so arranged. [< Med. L *(cantus) contrapunctus* (a melody) with contrasting notes]

coun·ter·poise (koun′tər·poiz′) *v.t.* **·poised, ·pois·ing** To balance by opposing with an equal weight or force; counterbalance. —*n.* (koun′tər·poiz) **1** A counterbalancing weight. **2** A force, influence, etc., that offsets another. **3** A state of equilibrium. [< L *contra-* against + *pensare* weigh]

coun·ter·pro·duc·tive (koun′tər·prə·duk′tiv) *adj.* Producing an effect opposite from that intended: The slurs on his opponent proved to be *counterproductive.*

coun·ter·rev·o·lu·tion (koun′tər·rev′ə·lo͞o′shən) *n.* An uprising against the government, policies, etc., established by a previous revolution. —**coun′ter·rev′o·lu′tion·ar′y** *adj., n.* —**coun′ter·rev′o·lu′tion·ist** *n.*

coun·ter·shaft (koun′tər·shaft′, -shaft′) *n. Mech.* An intermediate shaft driven by the main shaft and driving other parts.

coun·ter·sign (koun′tər·sīn′) *v.t.* To add one's signature to (a signed document) as authentication. —*n.* A password or secret signal to be given, as to a sentry. —**coun·ter·sig·na·ture** (koun′tər·sig′na·chər) *n.*

coun·ter·sink (koun′tər·singk′) *v.t.* **·sank** or **·sunk, ·sunk, ·sink·ing 1** To shape the opening of (a hole) to hold the head of a screw or bolt level with or below the surface. **2** To sink a bolt, screw, etc. into such a hole. —*n.* **1** A tool for countersinking. **2** A hole made by countersinking.

coun·ter·ten·or (koun′tər·ten′ər) *n.* **1** A man's voice with a range higher than that of a tenor. **2** A singer with such a voice.

coun·ter·weight (koun′tər·wāt′) *n.* Any counterbalancing weight, force, or influence. —**coun′ter·weight′ed** *adj.*

count·ess (koun′tis) *n.* **1** The wife or widow of a count, or, in Great Britain, of an earl. **2** A woman ranking equally with a count or earl.

count·ing·house (koun′ting·hous′) *n.* An office or building used by a business establishment for bookkeeping, correspondence, etc. Also **counting house, counting room.**

count·less (kount′lis) *adj.* Too numerous to be counted; innumerable. —**count′less·ly** *adv.*

coun·tri·fied (kun′tri·fīd) *adj.* Considered typical of country life; rural or rustic. Also **coun′try·fied.**

coun·try (kun′trē) *n. pl.* **·tries** 1 A land with its own government and geographic limits; a nation. 2 The land of one's birth or citizenship. 3 The people of a nation. 4 A tract or region of a specified nature. 5 A rural region. —*adj.* Of, pertaining to, or typical of rural regions. [<L *contra* on the opposite side]

country club A suburban club with facilities for outdoor sports and social activities.

coun·try-dance (kun′trē·dans′, -däns′) *n.* A folk dance in which partners are ranged in opposite lines.

coun·try·man (kun′trē·mən) *n. pl.* **·men** (-mən) 1 A man of the same country as another. 2 RUSTIC. —**coun′try·wom′an** *n. Fem.* (*pl.* **·wom′en**)

coun·try·side (kun′trē·sīd′) *n.* 1 A rural area. 2 Its inhabitants.

coun·ty (koun′tē) *n. pl.* **·ties** 1 A civil division of a nation or territory. 2 In most of the U.S., an administrative division of a state. 3 The inhabitants of a county. [<L *comes* count, companion]

county seat A municipality that is a county's center of government.

coup (kōō) *n. pl.* **coups** (kōōz, *Fr.* kōō) 1 A sudden and successful action; a masterstroke. 2 A coup d'état. [<L *colaphus* a blow with the fist]

coup de grâce (kōō′də gräs′) 1 A death stroke, as to one mortally wounded or suffering. 2 A finishing stroke. [F, lit., stroke of mercy]

coup d'é·tat (kōō′ dā·tä′)A forceful, unexpected political move, esp. a sudden overthrow of government and seizure of power. [F, lit., stroke of state]

cou·pé (kōō·pā′) *n.* 1 A small, closed, two-door automobile: also **coupe** (kōōp). 2 A closed carriage with two passenger seats and an outside seat. [<F *couper* to cut]

coup·le (kup′əl) *n.* 1 Two of a kind; a pair. 2 Two persons of opposite sex, married or otherwise paired. 3 *Informal* A few. —*v.* **coup·led, coup·ling** *v.t.* 1 To join, as one thing to another; link. 2 *Electr.* a To connect (two circuits). b To transfer (electricity), as by such connection. —*v.i.* 3 To copulate. 4 To form a pair or pairs. [<L *copula* a band, a bond]

coup·ler (kup′lər) *n.* 1 One who or that which couples. 2 A mechanical device by which objects are connected. 3 *Telecom.* A device for transferring signals from one circuit to another.

coup·let (kup′lit) *n.* Two successive lines of verse, usu. rhymed and of the same meter and length. [<F, dim. of *couple* a pair]

coup·ling (kup′ling) *n.* 1 The act of joining together. 2 A device for linking or connecting objects; a coupler.

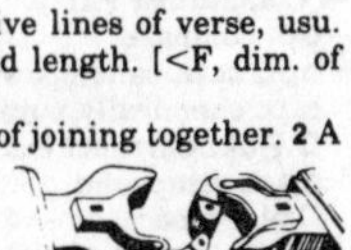
Coupling

cou·pon (kyōō′pon) *n.* 1 One of a number of dated certificates attached to a bond, representing interest payable at stated periods. 2 A certificate, detachable form, etc., entitling one to something in exchange. [<F *couper* to cut]

cour·age (kûr′ij) *n.* The capacity to meet danger or difficulty with firmness; bravery. [<L *cor* heart]

cou·ra·geous (kə·rā′jəs) *adj.* Possessing or characterized by courage. —**cou·ra′geous·ly** *adv.* —**cou·ra′geous·ness** *n.* —**Syn.** brave, fearless, intrepid, valorous, valiant.

cou·ri·er (kōōr′ē·ər, kûr′-) *n.* 1 A messenger, esp. one of official business. 2 An attendant who makes arrangements for travelers. [<Ital. *corriere* < *corre* to run]

course (kôrs, kōrs) *n.* 1 Onward motion or progress. 2 The way, direction, or duration of such progress. 3 A customary or expected procedure or development. 4 A line of conduct or action; policy. 5 A series of connected acts or events. 6 a A series of prescribed studies, as for a degree. b A series of classes in a specific subject. 7 A tract or area used for golf, racing, etc. 8 A part of a meal served at one time. 9 A row or layer, as of bricks. —**of course** 1 As one might expect; naturally. 2 Certainly. —*v.* **coursed, cours·ing** —*v.i.* 1 To move swiftly; run; race. 2 To hunt with hounds. —*v.t.* 3 To pursue, as in hunting. 4 To cause (hounds) to pursue game. 5 To traverse swiftly. [<L *cursus* a running]

cours·er (kôr′sər, kōr′-) *n.* A spirited or swift horse.

course·ware (kôrs′wâr′, kōrs′wâr′) *n.* Computer software used in teaching a subject, a skill, etc.

court (kôrt, kōrt) *n.* 1 An area enclosed by walls or buildings; a courtyard. 2 A short street or walled alley. 3 a A level area laid out for a game, as tennis or basketball. b A division of such an area. 4 The residence of a sovereign; palace. 5 The household, retinue, advisers, etc., of a sovereign. 6 A formal assembly held by or as by a sovereign. 7 a A tribunal for administering justice. b A judge or judges presiding at such a tribunal. c The place where such a tribunal meets. d A session of such a tribunal. 8 Attention paid to another to win affection, favor, etc. —**out of court** Without holding a trial. —*v.t.* 1 To attempt to acquire as a mate or lover; woo. 2 To try to get in the good graces of. 3 To attempt to gain: to *court* applause. 4 To invite, often unwisely: to *court* trouble. —*v.i.* 5 To conduct a courtship. —*adj.* Of or pertaining to a court. [<L *cohors, cohortis* yard, troop of soldiers]

cour·te·ous (kûr′tē·əs) *adj.* Showing courtesy; polite. —**cour′te·ous·ly** *adv.* —**cour′te·ous·ness** *n.*

cour·te·san (kôr′tə·zən, kōr′-, kûr′-) *n.* A prostitute who consorts with men of wealth or high status. Also **cour′te·zan.** [<Ital. *cortigiano* courtier]

cour·te·sy (kûr′tə·sē) *n. pl.* **·sies** 1 Gracious or considerate behavior; habitual politeness. 2 A courteous act. 3 Custom or indulgence rather than strict usage: He was called "Colonel" by *courtesy.* [<OF *corteisie*]

court·house (kôrt′hous′, kōrt′-) *n.* 1 A public building occupied by judicial courts. 2 A building for the offices of a county government.

court·i·er (kôr′tē·ər, -tyər, kōr′-) *n.* 1 An attendant at or frequenter of a royal court. 2 One who seeks favor by flattery.

court·ly (kôrt′lē, kōrt′-) *adj.* **·li·er, ·li·est** 1 Of or befitting a royal court. 2 Ceremonious and polite. —*adv.* In a courtly manner. —**court′li·ness** *n.*

court-mar·tial (kôrt′mär′shəl, kōrt′-) *n. pl.* **courts-mar·tial** 1 A military court convened to try persons subject to military law. 2 A trial by such a court. —*v.t.* —**mar·tialed** or **·tialled,** —**mar·tial·ing** or **·tial·ling** To try by court-martial.

court plaster An adhesive covering slight cuts, etc.

court·room (kôrt′rōōm′, -rŏŏm′, kōrt′-) *n.* A room in which judicial proceedings are held.

court·ship (kôrt′ship, kōrt′-) *n.* The act or period of courting or wooing.

court·yard (kôrt′yärd′, kōrt′-) *n.* An enclosed yard adjoining a building or surrounded by buildings.

cous·in (kuz′ən) *n.* 1 A child of one's aunt or uncle. 2 One collaterally related by descent from a common ancestor. 3 One of a kindred people or kind. [<L *consobrinus* child of a maternal aunt] —**cous′in·hood, cous′in·ship** *n.* —**cous′in·ly** *adj. adv.*

cou·tu·rier (kōō·tü·ryā′) *n.* A man who designs women's clothes. [F, lit., dressmaker] —**cou·tu·rière** (kōō·tü·ryâr′) *n. Fem.*

cove[1] (kōv) *n.* 1 A small, sheltered bay or inlet. 2 A recess or sheltered place. [OE *cofa* chamber, cave]

cove[2] (kōv) *n. Brit. Slang* A man; fellow. [<Romany *covo* that man]

cov·en (kuv′ən) *n.* An assembly of witches. [?<MF *covin* band]

cov·e·nant (kuv′ə·nənt) *n.* 1 A formal and binding agreement entered into by two or more persons or parties; a compact. 2 God's promises to mankind as set forth in the Bible. —*v.t.* & *v.i.* To promise by or in a covenant. [<L *convenire* meet together, agree] —**cov′e·nant·er** *n.*

cov·er (kuv'ər) *v.t.* 1 To place something over or upon, as to protect, conceal, etc. 2 To occupy the surface of. 3 To spread; overlay. 4 To clothe. 5 To hide; conceal. 6 To extend over. 7 To travel over. 8 To protect, as with insurance. 9 To provide for payment of (an expense, debt, etc.). 10 To treat of; include. 11 To keep within aim, as with a gun. 12 To report details of, as for a newspaper. 13 In sports, to guard (an opponent or position). 14 To incubate or sit on, as eggs. —*v.i.* 15 To substitute during someone's absence: with *for.* 16 To conceal an error, wrongdoing, crime, etc.: with *up.* —*n.* 1 Something that covers. 2 Shelter; protection. 3 Dense plant growth, underbrush, etc. 4 Something that masks, conceals, etc. 5 A table setting for one person. 6 COVER CHARGE. —**break cover** To come out from a hiding place. —**take cover** To seek shelter for protection. —**under cover** in secrecy; under concealment. [< L *cooperire* to hide thoroughly] —**cov'er·er** *n.*

cov·er·age (kuv'ər·ij) *n.* 1 The protection against risks extended by an insurance policy. 2 The extent to which a news story is covered.

cov·er·all (kuv'ər·ôl) *n. Often pl.* A one-piece garment worn over clothing as protection.

cover charge A fixed charge added to that for food and drink at a restaurant, nightclub, etc.

covered wagon A large wagon covered with canvas secured over arched supports, used esp. by American pioneers.

Covered wagon

cov·er·ing (kuv'ər·ing) *n.* Something that covers, conceals, etc.

cov·er·let (kuv'ər·lit) *n.* A bedspread.

cov·ert (kuv'ərt, kō'·vərt) *adj.* 1 Concealed; secret. 2 Sheltered. —*n.* 1 A place of shelter or concealment, as for hunters or game. 2 Any of the feathers overlying the bases of the quills of a bird's wings and tail. 3 A closely woven twilled cloth used for suits, coats, etc: also **covert cloth.** [< OF *covrir* to cover] —**cov'ert·ly** *adv.* —**cov'ert·ness** *n.*

cov·er-up (kuv'ər·up') *n.* 1 An act or effort designed to prevent the facts or truth, as of an embarrassing or illegal activity, from becoming known. 2 A means of covering up or concealing something.

cov·et (kuv'it) *v.t.* & *v.i.* To have an inordinate desire for (esp. something belonging to another). [< L *cupere* to desire] —**cov'et·a·ble** *adj.* —**cov'et·er** *n.*

cov·et·ous (kuv'ə·təs) *adj.* Overly desirous of something; greedy. —**cov'et·ous·ly** *adv.* —**cov'et·ous·ness** *n.*

cov·ey (kuv'ē) *n. pl.* **·eys** 1 A small flock of quails, partridges, etc. 2 A small group or band. [< OF *cover* hatch]

cow[1] (kou) *n. pl.* **cows** (*Archaic* **kine**) 1 The mature female of cattle and of some other animals, as the elephant. 2 Any domestic bovine regardless of sex or age. [< OE *cū*]

cow[2] (kou) *v.t.* To intimidate, as by instilling fear or awe; daunt. [< ON *kūga*]

cow·ard (kou'ərd) *n.* One lacking in courage; esp., one who gives in ignobly to fear. —*adj.* Cowardly. [< L *cauda* tail; with ref. to a dog with its tail between its legs]

cow·ard·ice (kou'ər·dis) *n.* Lack of courage; abject fearfulness.

cow·ard·ly (kou'ərd·lē) *adj.* 1 Lacking courage; abjectly fearful. 2 Of or typical of a coward. —*adv.* In the manner of a coward. —**cow'ard·li·ness** *n.*

cow·bell (kou'bel') *n.* A bell hung from the neck of a cow to show where she is by its sound.

cow·bird (kou'bûrd') *n.* An American blackbird that lays its eggs in the nests of other species of birds.

cow·boy (kou'boi') *n.* A man, usu. working on horseback, who herds and tends cattle, esp. in the w U.S. Also **cow'hand'.** —**cow'girl'** *n. Fem.*

cow·catch·er (kou'kach'ər) *n.* A metal frame on the front of a locomotive to remove obstructions from the track.

cow·er (kou'ər) *v.i.* To crouch or draw back tremblingly as in fear. [Prob. < Scand.] —**Syn.** cringe, quail, shrink, grovel.

cow·herd (kou'hûrd') *n.* One who herds cattle.

cow·hide (kou'hīd') *n.* 1 The hide of a cow. 2 Leather made from this. 3 A heavy, flexible leather whip. —*v.t.* **·hid·ed, ·hid·ing** To whip with or as with a cowhide.

cowl (koul) *n.* 1 A monk's hood or similar hooded garment. 2 A hood-shaped top for a chimney. 3 *Aeron.* COWLING. 4 The part of an automobile body to which the windshield, dash board, and the rear of the hood are attached. —*v.t.* To cover with or as with a cowl. [< L *cucullus* hood]

cow·lick (kou'lik') *n.* A tuft of hair that stands up stubbornly.

cowl·ing (kou'ling) *n. Aeron.* A metal covering for an airplane engine, etc. • See AIRPLANE.

cow·man (kou'mən) *n. pl.* **·men** (-mən) One who owns a cattle ranch.

co-work·er (kō'wûr'kər) *n.* A fellow worker.

cow·pea (kou'pē') *n.* 1 A twining leguminous plant cultivated in the s U.S. 2 The edible seed of this plant.

cow·poke (kou'pōk') *n. Informal* A cowboy.

cow pony A small horse used in herding cattle.

cow·pox (kou'poks') *n.* A contagious disease of cows, forming pustules containing a virus that is the source of vaccine for smallpox.

cow·punch·er (kou'pun'chər) *n. Informal* A cowboy.

cow·ry (kou'rē) *n. pl.* **·ries** Any of various tropical marine mollusks having a glossy shell. Also **cow'rie.** [< Hind. *kaurī*]

cow·slip (kou'slip') *n.* 1 A European wildflower related to the primrose. 2 MARSH MARIGOLD. [< OE *cū* cow + *slyppe* dung]

cox (koks) *Informal n.* COXSWAIN. —*v.t.* & *v.i.* To act as coxswain (for).

cox·comb (koks'kōm') *n.* 1 A vain, pretentious fellow; fop. 2 COCKSCOMB. [Var. of *cockscomb*] —**cox·comb·i·cal** (koks·kom'i·kəl, -kō'mi-) *adj.*

cox·swain (kok'sən, kok'swān') *n.* One who steers or has charge of a small boat or a racing shell. [< F *coque* a small boat + SWAIN]

coy (koi) *adj.* 1 Shy; diffident. 2 Pretending shyness or reluctance. [< L *quietus* quiet] —**coy'ly** *adv.* —**coy'ness** *n.*

coy·o·te (kī·ō'tē, kī'ōt) *n.* A wolflike North American animal common in the w U.S. [< Nah.]

coy·pu (koi'pōō) *n. pl.* **·pus** or **·pu** NUTRIA (def. 1). Also **coy'pou.** [Am. Sp.]

coz·en (kuz'ən) *v.t.* & *v.i.* To cheat in a petty way. [F *cousiner* deceive by claiming kinship < *cousin* cousin] —**coz·en·age** (kuz'ən·ij), **coz'en·er** *n.*

co·zy (kō'zē) *adj.* **co·zi·er, co·zi·est** Snug; comfortable. —*n. pl.* **·zies** A padded cover for a teapot to prevent the heat from escaping. [Scot. *cosie*] —**co'zi·ly** *adv.* —**co'zi·ness** *n.*

CP Command Post.

C.P. Chief Patriarch; Common Pleas; Common Prayer; Communist Party.

cp. compare.

cp., c.p. candlepower.

c.p. chemically pure.

C.P.A. Certified Public Accountant.

cpd. compound.

Cpl. corporal.

cpm, c.p.m. cycles per minute.

CPO, C.P.O. Chief Petty Officer.

cps, c.p.s. cycles per second.

C.R. Costa Rica.

Cr chromium.

cr. credit; creditor; crown.

crab[1] (krab) *n.* 1 Any of various crustaceans having eight legs, two pincers, a small abdomen, a flattened carapace, and short antennae. 2 HERMIT CRAB. 3 HORSESHOE CRAB. —*v.* **crabbed, crab·bing** *v.i.* To take or fish for crabs. [< OE *crabba*]

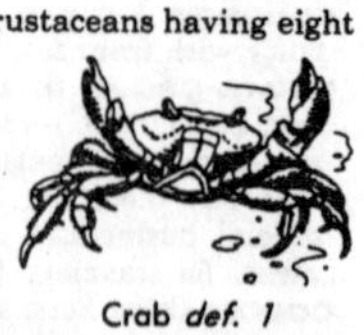

Crab *def. 1*

crab[2] (krab) *n.* 1 CRAB APPLE. 2 An ill-tempered person. —*v.* **crabbed, crab·bing** *Informal v.i.* 1 To complain; grumble. —*v.t.* 2 To ruin or spoil. [? < Scand.]

Crab *n.* CANCER.

crab apple 1 Any of various kinds of small, sour apples. 2 A tree bearing crab apples: also **crab tree.**

crab·bed (krab′id) *adj* 1 Sour-tempered; cross; peevish. 2 Hard to understand; abstruse. 3 Irregular in form; cramped. [< CRAB¹, *n.* (def. 1)] **—crab′bed·ly** *adv.* **—crab′·bed·ness** *n.*

crab·by (krab′ē) *adj.* **·bi·er, ·bi·est** Cross; ill-tempered. **—crab′bi·ly** *adv.* **—crab′bi·ness** *n.*

crab·grass (krab′gras′, -gräs′) *n.* A low-growing grass with freely rooting stems, a lawn pest.

crack (krak) *v.t.* 1 To cause to break open partially or completely. 2 To cause to give forth a short, sharp sound: to *crack* a whip. 3 *Slang* To open in order to drink, read, etc.: to *crack* a bottle or book. 4 *Informal* To break into, as a safe or building, in order to rob. 5 To solve, as a puzzle, crime, or code. 6 *Slang* To tell (a joke). 7 To destroy or crush: to *crack* one's spirit. 8 To cause (the voice) to break or change register. 9 *Informal* To strike sharply or with a sharp sound: He *cracked* him on the jaw. *—v.i.* 10 To split or break, esp. with suddenness. 11 To make a sharp snapping sound, as a whip or pistol. 12 To have a break in tone or to change register suddenly: said of the voice. 13 To become impaired or broken, as the spirit or will. **—crack down** To introduce severe disciplinary or corrective action. **—crack up** 1 To crash, as an airplane. 2 *Informal* To have a breakdown, nervous or physical. 3 *Informal* To break or cause to break into laughter. *—n.* 1 An incomplete separation into two or more parts; a fissure. 2 A narrow space, as between two boards. 3 A sudden sharp or loud sound. 4 *Informal* A blow that resounds. 5 A mental or physical defect or flaw. 6 A break in tone or change of register in the voice. 7 *Informal* An attempt. 8 An exact instant: the *crack* of dawn. 9 *Informal* A witty or sarcastic remark. *—adj. Informal* Of superior excellence; first-class. [< OE *cracian*]

crack·brain (krak′brān′) *n.* A weak-minded person. *—adj.* Weak-minded; crazy; odd: also **crack′-brained′**.

crack·down (krak′doun′) *n. Informal* Summary disciplinary or corrective action.

cracked (krakt) *adj.* 1 Having a crack or cracks; broken or split. 2 Hoarse or broken in tone, as the voice. 3 *Informal* Crazy; mentally unsound.

crack·er (krak′ər) *n.* 1 A person or thing that cracks. 2 A firecracker. 3 A thin brittle biscuit. 4 An impoverished white inhabitant of parts of the SE U.S.: a contemptuous term.

crack·er·jack (krak′ər·jak′) *Slang adj.* Of or pertaining to a person or thing of worth, merit, or the like. *—n.* A person or thing of exceptional skill or value. Also **crack′a·jack′**.

crack·ing (krak′ing) *n.* The process of splitting complex hydrocarbon molecules by heat, catalysts, etc., as in the production of gasoline from petroleum.

crack·le (krak′əl) *v.* **·led, ·ling** *v.i.* 1 To crack or snap repeatedly with light, sharp noises. *—v.t.* 2 To crush with such sounds. 3 To cover, as china, with a delicate network of cracks. *—n.* 1 A succession of light, cracking sounds. 2 The appearance produced in china, porcelain, etc., by the cracking of the glaze in all directions. 3 Such ware: also **crack′le·ware′**. [Freq. of CRACK] **—crack′ly** *adj.*

crack·ling (krak′ling) *n.* 1 The giving out of small sharp sounds. 2 The crisp browned skin of roasted pork. 3 *pl.* The crisp remains of rendered fat.

crack·pot (krak′pot′) *Slang n.* A weak-minded or eccentric person; crank. *—adj.* Eccentric; foolish; insane.

crack·up (krak′up′) *n.* 1 A serious accident in an aircraft or motor vehicle. 2 A mental or physical breakdown.

-cracy *combining form* Government or authority: *democracy.* [< Gk. *krateein* to rule]

cra·dle (krād′l) *n.* 1 A rocking or swinging bed for an infant. 2 A place of birth or origin. 3 A scythe with fingers that catch the grain when cut. 4 A frame or device for supporting an object or structure. 5 A support or holder for a handset telephone. *—v.* **·dled, ·dling** *v.t.* 1 To rock in or as in a cradle; soothe. 2 To cut or reap, as grain, with a cradle. 3 To place or support in or as in a cradle. *—v.i.* 4 To cut or reap with a cradle. [< OE *cradol*]

craft (kraft, kräft) *n.* 1 Any skill or art. 2 An occupation or trade demanding skill, esp. a manual skill. 3 The members of such a trade; guild. 4 Cunning or skill in deceiving; guile. 5 (*pl.* **craft**) A boat, ship, or airplane. [< OE *cræft* skill, art, strength, courage] **—Syn.** 1 expertness, artistry, mastery, facility. 2 business, job, employment. 4 trickery, deceitfulness, craftiness.

-craft *combining form* Skill; trade; art of: *woodcraft.*

crafts·man (krafts′mən, kräfts′-) *n. pl.* **·men** (-mən) A skilled workman or artist. **—crafts′man·ship** *n.*

craft union A labor union in which membership is limited to workers having the same trade or occupation.

craft·y (kraf′tē, kräf′-) *adj.* **craft·i·er, craft·i·est** Skillful in deception; cunning. **—craft′i·ly** *adv.* **—craft′i·ness** *n.*

crag (krag) *n.* A rough, steep, or broken rock rising or jutting out prominently. [ME *cragg* < Celtic]

crag·ged (krag′id) *adj.* Having numerous crags. Also **crag′gy. —crag′gi·ness** *n.*

crake (krāk) *n.* Any of several small, short-billed birds related to the rail. [< ON *krāka* crow]

cram (kram) *v.* **crammed, cram·ming** *v.t.* 1 To press or pack tightly together; crowd. 2 To feed to satiety. 3 To prepare hurriedly for an examination. *—v.i.* 4 To eat greedily; stuff oneself with food. 5 To force knowledge into the mind by hurried study. *—n.* 1 The act of cramming. 2 A crowded condition. [< OE *crammian* to stuff] **—cram′mer** *n.*

cramp¹ (kramp) *n.* 1 A metal bar with both ends bent into right angles, for holding together two stones, pieces of timber, etc.: also **cramp iron.** 2 An adjustable clamp. 3 Something that restrains or confines. *—v.t.* 1 To restrain or confine the action of; hinder. 2 To make fast; hold tightly, as with a cramp. 3 To turn (the wheels of an automobile, etc.) sharply to one side. [< MDu. *krampe* hook]

cramp² (kramp) *n.* 1 An involuntary, sudden, painful muscular contraction. 2 *pl.* Acute abdominal pains. *—v.t.* To affect with cramps. [< OF *crampe*]

cram·pon (kram′pən) *n.* A device of metal spikes attached to the shoe for walking on ice or to aid in climbing.

cran·ber·ry (kran′ber′ē, -bər·ē) *n. pl.* **·ries** 1 The edible, scarlet, acid berry of a woody, evergreen plant growing in marshy land. 2 The plant itself. [< Du. *kranebere,* lit., crane berry]

cranberry tree A shrub or small tree related to honeysuckle, having sour, edible fruit similar to the cranberry. Also **cranberry bush.**

crane (krān) *n.* 1 One of a family of large, long-necked, long-legged, heronlike birds allied to the rails. 2 Any of various similar birds, as a heron, stork, etc. 3 A hoisting machine having a movable arm for lifting, lowering, or shifting heavy weights. 4 An iron arm, swinging horizontally, attached to a fireplace, used for suspending pots or kettles. *—v.t. & v.i.* **craned, cran·ing** 1 To stretch out; elongate or be elongated. 2 To elevate or lift by or as if by a crane. [< OE *cran*]

Crane *def. 1*

crane fly A fly with very long, slender legs resembling a large mosquito.

cra·ni·ol·o·gy (krā′nē·ol′ə·jē) *n.* The branch of anatomy and medicine that treats of the structure and characteristics of skulls. [< ML *cranium* cranium + -LOGY] **—cra·ni·o·log·i·cal** (krā′nē·ə·loj′i·kəl) *adj.* **—cra′ni·ol′o·gist** *n.*

cra·ni·om·e·ter (krā′nē·om′ə·tər) *n.* An instrument for measuring skulls. **—cra·ni·o·met·ric** (krā′nē·ə·met′rik) or **·ri·cal** *adj.* **—cra′ni·o·met′ri·cal·ly** *adv.* **—cra′ni·om′e·try** *n.*

cra·ni·um (krā′nē·əm) *n. pl.* **·ni·ums** or **·ni·a** (-nē·ə) The skull, esp. the part that encloses the brain. [< Gk. *kranion* skull] **—cra′ni·al** *adj.*

crank (krangk) *n.* 1 A device, as a handle attached at right angles to a shaft, for transmitting motion or for converting reciprocating motion into rotary motion, or vice versa. 2 *Informal* a A person given to odd notions or actions; an eccentric. b A grouchy, ill-tempered person. —*v.t.* 1 To bend into the shape of a crank. 2 To operate or start by a crank. —*v.i.* 3 To turn a crank. [<OE *cranc,* as in *crancstæf* a weaving comb]

crank·case (krangk'kās') *n.* The case enclosing an engine crankshaft.

crank·shaft (krangk'shaft', -shäft') *n.* A shaft that bears one or more cranks or piston rods.

crank·y (krang'kē) *adj.* **crank·i·er, crank·i·est** 1 Irritable; peevish. 2 Eccentric; odd. 3 Loose and rickety. —**crank'i·ly** *adv.* —**crank'i·ness** *n.*

cran·ny (kran'ē) *n. pl.* **·nies** A narrow opening, fissure. [<OF *cran, cren* notch] —**cran'nied** *adj.*

crape (krāp) *n.* 1 CREPE (def. 1). 2 A piece of black crepe worn or hung as a sign of mourning. [Var. of CRÊPE]

crape myrtle A shrub having bright, rose-colored, purple, or white crumpled petals, native to China but often grown in the southeastern United States. Also *crepe myrtle.*

crap·pie (krap'ē) *n. pl.* **·pies** or **·pie** Any of a genus of edible freshwater sunfish.[?]

craps (kraps) *n. pl. (construed as sing.)* A game of chance, played with two dice. Also **crap game, crap'shoot'ing.** [obs. *crabs,* the lowest throw (two aces) in hazard]

crap·shoot·er (krap'shōō'tər) *n.* One who plays the game of craps.

crap·u·lence (krap'yōō·ləns) *n.* 1 Sickness by intemperance in eating or drinking. 2 Gross intemperance, as in drinking. [<Gk. *kraipalē* drunken headache]

crash[1] (krash) *v.t.* 1 To break in pieces noisily and with violence. 2 To proceed noisily and with violence: He *crashed* his way through the jungle. 3 *Informal* To enter uninvited or without paying admission: to *crash* a dance. 4 To cause, as an airplane, truck, or train, to fall to the earth or strike an obstacle with force. —*v.i.* 5 To break or fall in pieces with a violent sound. 6 To make a noise of clashing or breaking. 7 To move with such a noise. 8 To fall to the earth or violently strike an obstacle, as an airplane or automobile. 9 To fail or collapse; come to ruin. —*n.* A loud noise, as of something falling and breaking. 2 A breaking, colliding, or crashing. 3 A failure or collapse; ruin. [Imit.]

crash[2] (krash) *n.* A coarse fabric woven of thick uneven yarns: used for towels, curtains, etc. [<Russ. *krashenina*]

crash program An intensive emergency undertaking.

crass (kras) *adj.* Coarse or thick in structure; dense. 2 Dull; stupid. [<L *crassus* thick] —**crass'ly** *adv.* —**crass'·ness** *n.*

-crat *combining form* A supporter or member of a social class or a type of government: *democrat, aristocrat.* [<Gk. *krateein* govern]

crate (krāt) *n.* 1 a A large hamper or packing box for shipping or storing. b Its contents. 2 *Slang* An old or decrepit vehicle or airplane. —*v.t.* **crat·ed, crat·ing** To pack, store, or send in a crate. [<L *cratis* wickerwork]

cra·ter (krā'tər) *n.* 1 The bowl-shaped depression forming the outlet of a volcano or of a hot spring. 2 A pit made by an explosion or impact. 3 Any large bowl or cavity. [<Gk. *kratēr* bowl]

cra·vat (krə·vat') *n.* 1 A neckcloth or scarf. 2 A necktie. [<F *Cravate* a Croatian, with ref. to the neckcloths worn by Croatian soldiers]

crave (krāv) *v.* **craved, crav·ing** *v.t.* 1 To beg for humbly and earnestly. 2 To long for; desire greatly. 3 To be in need of; require. —*v.i.* 4 To desire or long: with *for* or *after.* [<OE *crafian*] —**crav'er** *n.* —**Syn.** 1 ask, solicit, seek, request, beseech, petition. 2 yearn for, wish, wish for, want.

cra·ven (krā'vən) *adj.* Lacking in courage; cowardly. —*n.* A base coward. [<L *crepare* to break] —**cra'ven·ly** *adv.*

crav·ing (krā'ving) *n.* An intense longing or need.

craw (krô) *n.* 1 The crop of a bird. 2 The stomach of any animal. [ME *crawe*]

craw·fish (krô'fish') *n. pl.* **·fish** or **·fish·es** CRAYFISH. [Var. of CRAYFISH]

crawl (krôl) *v.i.* 1 To move by dragging the body along a surface; creep. 2 To move slowly, feebly, or cautiously. 3 To have a sensation as of crawling things upon the body. 4 To have crawling things in or on the body, as a dead body. 5 To act with servility. —*n.* 1 The act of crawling. 2 An overarm swimming stroke. [<ON *krafla*] —**crawl'er** *n.* —**crawl'ing·ly** *adv.*

crawl·y (krô'lē) *adj.* **crawl·i·er, crawl·i·est** *Informal* Covered or filled with crawling things.

cray·fish (krā'fish') *n. pl.* **·fish** or **·fish·es** 1 A marine crustacean resembling a lobster but without claws. 2 Any of various small, fresh-water crustaceans resembling the lobster. [Earlier *crevice*<OF; infl. in form by *fish*]

cray·on (krā'ən, -on) *n.* 1 A small cylinder of colored wax, chalk, etc., used for coloring or drawing. 2 A drawing made with crayons. —*v.t.* To sketch or draw with a crayon or crayons. [<L *creta* chalk] —**cray'on·ist** *n.*

craze (krāz) *v.* **crazed, craz·ing** *v.t.* 1 To cause to become mentally ill. 2 To make full of minute cracks, as the glaze of pottery. —*v.i.* 3 To become insane. 4 To become full of minute cracks. —*n.* 1 A fad; rage. 2 An intense enthusiasm. 3 A flaw in the glaze of pottery. [<Scand. Cf. Sw. *krasa* break.] —**crazed** *adj.*

cra·zy (krā'zē) *adj.* **cra·zi·er, cra·zi·est** 1 Insane; mentally unbalanced. 2 Excessively emotional or disturbed as with rage. 3 *Informal* Impractical, illogical, etc.: a *crazy* plan. 4 *Informal* Inordinantly eager or enthusiastic: *crazy* about jazz. —**cra'zi·ly** *adv.* —**cra'zi·ness.** *n.*

crazy bone FUNNY BONE.

crazy quilt A patchwork bed quilt made of pieces of various sizes, shapes, and colors.

creak (krēk) *n.* A sharp, squeaking sound, as from friction. —*v.t. & v.i.* To make, or cause to make, a creak. [Imit.] —**creak'i·ly** *adv.* —**creak'i·ness** *n.* —**creak'y** *adj.* **(·i·er, ·i·est)**

cream (krēm) *n.* A thick, oily, light-yellow liquid contained in milk. 2 A food, candy, etc., containing or resembling cream. 3 A soft, oily cosmetic for the skin. 4 The best or choicest part. 5 A light yellow color, —*v.t.* 1 To skim cream from. 2 To take the best part from. 3 To add cream to, as coffee. 4 To beat (butter) until soft enough for mixing. 5 To cook or prepare (food) with cream or cream sauce. 6 *Slang* To defeat thoroughly. 7 To froth. 8 To form cream. [<LL *chrisma* ointment] —**cream'i·ness** *n.* **cream'y** *adj.* **(·i·er, ·i·est)**

cream cheese Soft, unripened cheese made of cream or a mixture of cream and milk.

cream·er (krē'mer) *n.* 1 A cream pitcher. 2 Any dish or machine in which cream is separated from milk.

cream·er·y (krē'mər·ē) *n. pl.* **·er·ies** 1 A store that sells mainly dairy products. 2 A place where butter and cheese are made, milk and cream are pasteurized, separated, bottled, etc.

cream of tartar A potassium salt of tartaric acid, used in baking powder.

cream puff 1 A shell of pastry filled with whipped cream or custard. 2 *Slang* An ineffectual or inconsequential person or thing.

crease[1] (krēs) *n.* 1 The mark of a wrinkle, fold, or the like. 2 In cricket, any of the lines limiting the position of the bowler or batsman. —*v.* **creased, creas·ing** *v.t.* 1 To make a crease or fold in; wrinkle. 2 To wound by a shot that grazes the flesh. —*v.i.* 3 To become wrinkled. [Var. of ME *creste* a crest, ridge] —**creas'er** *n.* —**creas'y** *adj.*

crease[2] (krēs) KRIS

cre·ate *(krē·āt')* *v.* **·at·ed, ·at·ing** *v.t.* 1 To cause to come into existence; originate. 2 To be the cause of; bring about: *create* interest. 3 To invest with a new rank, office, etc. 4 To be the first to portray, as a character in a play. [<L *creare*] —**Syn.** 1 fashion, make, form, produce, conceive, invent, build.

cre·a·tion (krē·ā'shən) *n.* 1 The act of creating or the fact of being created. 2 That which is created. 3 The universe or all things in it. —**the Creation** The act of God in creating the world. —**cre·a'tion·al** *adj.*

cre·a·tion·ism (krē·ā'shən·iz'əm) *n.* The belief that the Biblical story of the Creation in Genesis is as valid a theory as the theory of evolution.

cre·a·tive (krē·ā'tiv) *adj.* 1 Having the ability to create. 2 Having or characterized by imagination, originality, artistic skill, etc. 3 Productive: with *of.* —**cre·a'tive·ly** *adv.* —**cre·a'tive·ness, cre'a·tiv'i·ty (-ə·tē)** *n.*

cre·a·tor (krē·ā′tər) *n.* One who or that which creates. —**the Creator** God.

crea·ture (krē′chər) *n.* **1** Anything created. **2** Something living, esp. an animal. **3** A human being. **4** An imaginary being.

creature comfort Anything contributing to bodily comfort, as food and drink.

crèche (kresh, krāsh) *n.* **1** A group of figures representing the Nativity. **2** A foundling hospital. **3** *Brit.* A day nursery. [< F, crib]

cre·dence (krēd′ns) *n.* Confidence based upon external evidence; belief. [< L *credere* believe]

cre·den·tial (kri·den′shəl) *n.* **1** That which certifies one's authority, credit, or claim to confidence. **2** *pl.* Testimonials certifying a person's authority or claim to confidence or consideration.

cred·i·bil·i·ty (kred′ə·bil′ə·tē) *n.* **1** Capacity of being believed. **2** The capacity, as of a government or a public official, of maintaining the public's confidence that its report of the conduct of its affairs is worthy of belief. —**credibility gap 1** A lessening or loss of credibility, as in a government or public official. **2** The extent or degree of a decline in credibility: The official statement only widened the *credibility gap.*

cred·i·ble (kred′ə·bəl) *adj.* Capable of being believed; reliable. [< L *credibilis* < *credere* believe] —**cred′i·ble·ness** *n.* —**cred′i·bly** *adv.*

cred·it (kred′it) *n.* **1** Belief; trust; confidence. **2** Reputation for trustworthiness; character; repute. **3** Influence derived from trustworthiness, good opinion of others, etc. **4** Approval; praise: Give him *credit* for telling the truth. **5** One who or that which adds honor or reputation: a *credit* to his class. **6** *Usu. pl.* Acknowledgment of work done, as in the making of a motion picture. **7** In an account, the balance in one's favor. **8** An amount made available by a bank, against which a person or business may draw. **9** In bookkeeping: **a** The entry of any amount paid by a debtor. **b** The amount so entered. **c** The right-hand side of an account where such amounts are recorded. **10** Confidence in a firm's or person's solvency or ability to meet payments. **11** The time allowed for payment of a debt. **12** The amount to which a person or business may be financially trusted. **13** In education, official certification that a course of study has been finished; also, a recognized unit of school or college work. —**on credit** With a promise to pay later. —*v.t.* **1** To give credit for; accept as true. **2** To ascribe, as intelligence or honor, to: with *with.* **3** In bookeeping, to give credit for or enter as credit to. **4** In education, to give educational credits to (a student). [< L *credere* believe, trust] —**cred′it·a·bil′i·ty, cred′it·a·ble·ness** *n.* —**cred′it·a·ble** *adj.* —**cred′it·a·bly** *adv.*

credit card A card issued by a business, bank, etc., giving the owner the privilege to charge bills at certain stores, restaurants, etc.

cred·i·tor (kred′i·tər) *n.* One who gives credit or to whom another is indebted.

credit rating A rating given a person or business regarding financial status, reputation for paying bills, etc.

credit union A cooperative group for making loans to its members at low rates of interest.

cre·do (krē′dō, krā′-) *n. pl.* **·dos** CREED. [L, I believe; the opening word of the Nicene Creed.]

cre·du·li·ty (krə·dyōō′lə·tē) *n.* A disposition to believe on slight evidence. [< L *credulus* credulous]

cred·u·lous (krej′ōō·ləs) *adj.* **1** Apt or disposed to believe on slight evidence. **2** Arising from credulity. [< L *credere* believe] —**cred′u·lous·ly** *adv.* —**cred′u·lous·ness** *n.*

Cree (krē) *n. pl.* **Cree** or **Crees 1** One of a tribe of the Algonquian stock of North American Indians. **2** The language of this tribe.

creed (krēd) *n.* **1** A formal summary of religious belief. **2** Any statement of things believed, principles held, etc. [< L *credo* I believe]

creek (krēk, krik) *n.* **1** A stream between a brook and a river in size. **2** *Chiefly Brit.* A small inlet, bay, or cove. [< Scand.]

creel (krēl) *n.* **1** An angler's basket for carrying fish. **2** A cage for catching lobsters, etc. [< L *cratis* wickerwork]

creep (krēp) *v.i.* **crept, creep·ing 1** To move with the body close to a surface; crawl. **2** To move or change imperceptibly, slowly, secretly, or stealthily. **3** To exhibit servility; cringe. **4** To feel as if covered with creeping things. **5** To grow along a surface or support: *creeping* plants. **6** To slip out of place. —*n.* **1** The act of creeping. **2** *pl.* A sensation of uneasy apprehensiveness. **3** *Slang* A distasteful or obnoxious person. [< OE *crēopan*]

creep·er (krēp′ər) *n.* **1** One who or that which creeps. **2** A plant that trails on the ground or climbs on a support. **3** *pl.* A device worn on shoes to prevent one's slipping. **4** *pl.* A baby's one-piece garment.

creep·y (krē′pē) *adj.* **creep·i·er, creep·i·est** Having or producing a feeling of apprehension or disgust. —**creep′i·ly** *adv.* —**creep′i·ness** *n.*

creese (krēs) *n.* KRIS.

cre·mate (krē′māt, kri·māt′) *v.t.* **·mat·ed, ·mat·ing** To burn (a dead body) to ashes. [< L *cremare* burn to ashes] —**cre·ma′tion, cre′ma·tor** *n.*

cre·ma·to·ry (krē′mə·tôr′ē, -tō′rē, krem′-) *adj.* Related to cremation. —*n. pl.* **·ries** A place for cremating. Also **cre′ma·to′ri·um** (-tôr′ē·əm, -tō′rē-).

crème de ca·ca·o (də kə·kā′ō, -kä′ō) A sweet, chocolate-flavored liqueur. [F, lit., cream of cocoa]

crème de menthe (də mänt, menth) A green or white cordial with a strong flavor of mint. [F, lit., cream of mint]

cre·nate (krē′nāt) *adj.* Having a margin of rounded projections, as certain leaves. Also **cre′nat·ed.** [< LL *crena* a notch] —**cre·na′tion** *n.*

cren·e·late (kren′ə·lāt) *v.t.* **·lat·ed, ·lat·ing** To fortify or decorate with battlements. Also **cren′el·late.** [< LL *crena* notch] —**cren′e·la′tion, cren′el·la′tion** *n.*

cre·ole (krē′ōl) *adj.* Cooked with a savory sauce of peppers, tomatoes, onions, etc.

Cre·ole (krē′ōl) *n.* **1** A native of Spanish America or the West Indies, of European parentage. **2** A descendant of French, Spanish, or Portuguese settlers of the Gulf States. **3** The French patois of Louisiana. **4** Any person of both Creole and Negro descent. —*adj.* Of or relating to the Creoles.

cre·o·sol (krē′ə·sōl, -sol) *n.* A colorless, aromatic, oily compound derived from certain resins. [< CREOS(OTE) + -OL²]

cre·o·sote (krē′ə·sōt) *n.* An oily liquid mixture of phenols or hydrocarbons, obtained by the distillation of wood or coal tar, used to preserve timber. —*v.t.* **·sot·ed, ·sot·ing** To treat or impregnate with creosote, as shingles, etc. [< Gk. *kreas* flesh + *sōtēr* preserver]

crepe (krāp, *def. 4 also* krep) *n.* **1** A thin, crinkled fabric of silk, cotton, wool, etc. **2** Crape (def. 2). **3** CREPE PAPER. **4** A thin pancake. Also **crêpe.** [< F *crêpe* < L *crispus* curled]

crepe paper A crinkled, decorative paper.

crept (krept) *p.t.* of CREEP.

cre·pus·cu·lar (kri·pus′kyə·lər) *adj.* Of, pertaining to, or active during twilight. [< L *creper* dark, dusky]

cres., cresc. crescendo.

cres·cen·do (krə·shen′dō, -sen′-) *n. pl.* **·dos** *Music* A gradual increase in loudness. —*adj.* Slowly increasing in loudness. [< Ital. *crescere* to increase]

cres·cent (kres′ənt) *n.* **1** The visible part of the moon in its first quarter, having one concave edge and one convex edge. **2** Something crescent-shaped. —*adj.* **1** Increasing: said of the moon in its first quarter. **2** Shaped like the moon in its first quarter. [< L *crescere* to increase] • See MOON.

cre·sol (krē′sōl, -sol) *n.* Any one of three isomeric compounds obtained by the distillation of coal tar. [Var. of CREOSOL]

cress (kres) *n.* One of various plants of the mustard family having a pungent taste and used in salads. [< OE *cressa*] —**cress′y** *adj.*

cres·set (kres′it) *n.* An incombustible frame or vessel mounted to hold a torch or its fuel. [< OF *craicet, craisset*]

crest (krest) *n.* **1** A comb or tuft on the head of an animal or bird. **2** The decoration on the top of a helmet; a plume; tuft. **3** The ridge of a wave or of a mountain. **4** The highest point or maximum degree of anything. **5** A heraldic device placed above the shield in a coat of arms and also used on stationery, silverware, etc. —*v.t.* **1** To serve as a crest for; cap. **2** To furnish with or as with a crest. **3** To reach the crest of. **4** To adorn with a crest. —*v.i.* **5** To come to a crest, as a wave prior to breaking. [< L *crista* tuft] —**crest'ed** *adj.*

Crest *def. 5* above coat of arms

crest·fall·en (krest'fô'lən) *adj.* **1** Dejected; depressed. **2** Having the crest lowered.

cre·ta·ceous (kri·tā'shəs) *adj.* Of or like chalk; chalky. [< L *creta* chalk]

Cre·ta·ceous (kri·tā'shəs) *n. & adj.* See GEOLOGY.

cre·tin (krē'tin) *n.* A person afflicted with cretinism. [< F *crétin,* var. of *chrétien* Christian, human being, i.e., not an animal] —**cre'tin·ous** *adj.*

cre·tin·ism (krē'tən·iz'əm) *n.* A condition associated with thyroid deficiency during early development, marked by physical deformities and mental retardation.

cre·tonne (kri·ton', krē'ton) *n.* A heavy, unglazed patterned fabric used for draperies, chair coverings, etc. [< *Creton,* a village in Normandy]

cre·vasse (krə·vas') *n.* **1** A deep fissure, as in a glacier. **2** A break in a levee. —*v.t.* **·vassed, ·vass·ing** To split with crevasses. [< OF *crevace* crevice] —**cre·vassed'** *adj.*

crev·ice (krev'is) *n.* A small fissure or crack. [< L *crepare* to crack, creak] —**crev'iced** *adj.*

crew[1] (kroo͞) *n.* **1** All of the seamen manning a specific ship, usu. excluding officers. **2** All those manning an aircraft. **3** Any group of people organized for a particular work project. **4** A company of people in general; crowd. **5** The oarsmen and coxswain of a racing shell. [< OF *creue* an increase]

crew[2] (kroo͞) *p.t.* of CROW.

crew cut A closely cropped haircut.

crew·el (kroo͞'əl) *n.* A slackly twisted worsted yarn, used in fancywork. [?]

crew·el·work (kroo͞'əl·wûrk') *n.* Embroidery with crewel.

crib (krib) *n.* **1** A manger for fodder. **2** A stall for cattle. **3** A child's bed, with side railings. **4** A box, bin, or small building for grain. **5** A frame of wood or metal, used to support or retain earth, etc., as in a mine. **6** *Informal* PLAGIARISM. **7** A translation or other unauthorized aid in study. —*v.* **cribbed, crib·bing** *v.t.* **1** To enclose in or as in a crib; confine closely. **2** *Informal* To take and pass off as one's own, as an answer; plagiarize. **3** *Informal* To steal. **4** *Informal* To translate with a crib. —*v.i.* **5** *Informal* To use a crib in translating. [< OE *cribb*] —**crib'ber** *n.*

crib·bage (krib'ij) *n.* A game of cards for two, three, or four players in which the score is kept on a pegboard. [? < CRIB]

crick (krik) *n.* A spasmodic cramping of the muscles, as of the neck. —*v.t.* To turn or twist so as to produce a crick. [?]

crick·et[1] (krik'it) *n.* A leaping insect related to the grasshopper but having long antennae, the male of which makes a chirping sound by friction of the forewings. [< OF *criquet*]

crick·et[2] (krik'it) *n.* **1** An outdoor game played with bats, a ball, and wickets, between two opposing sides of eleven players each. **2** *Informal* Fair, gentlemanly behavior; sportsmanship. [< F *criquet* bat, stick] —**crick'et·er** *n.*

crick·et[3] (krik'it) *n.* FOOTSTOOL. [?]

cried (krīd) *p.t. & p.p.* of CRY.

cri·er (krī'ər) *n.* **1** One who cries. **2** One who makes public announcements in the street.

crime (krīm) *n.* **1** *Law* An act that subjects the doer to legal punishment. **2** Any grave offense against morality or social order. **3** *Informal* Any unjust or shameful action. [< L *crimen* accusation, charge]

crim·i·nal (krim'ə·nəl) *adj.* **1** *Law* **a** Of, relating to, or being a crime. **b** Dealing with penal as opposed to civil law. **2** Guilty of or involving crime. **3** *Informal* Regrettable; shameful. —*n.* One convicted of or guilty of a crime. —**crim·i·nal·i·ty** (krim'ə·nal'ə·tē), **crim'i·nal·ness** *n.* —**crim'i·nal·ly** *adv.*

crim·i·nol·o·gy (krim'ə·nol'ə·jē) *n.* The scientific study and investigation of crime and criminals. —**crim·i·no·log·i·cal** (krim'ə·nə·loj'i·kəl) *adj.* —**crim'i·nol'o·gist** *n.*

crimp (krimp) *v.t.* **1** To bend or press into ridges or folds; corrugate; flute. **2** To curl or wave: to *crimp* the hair. **3** To fold one edge of (paper, etc.) over another edge and press tightly together. **4** *Informal* To hinder or obstruct. —*n.* **1** The act of crimping. **2** Anything crimped. **3** *Informal* An obstruction or hindrance. [< MDu. *crimpen* wrinkle, draw together] —**crimp'er** *n.* —**crimp'y** *adj.*

crim·son (krim'zən) *n.* A deep red color. —*adj.* **1** Of a deep red color. **2** Bloody. —*v.t. & v.i.* To make or become crimson. [< Ar. *qirmiz* kermes (insect used in making a red dye)]

cringe (krinj) *v.i.* **cringed, cring·ing** **1** To crouch, wince, draw back, etc., as in fear. **2** To seek favor in a servile or flattering manner. —*n.* The act of cringing. [ME *cringen, crengen*] —**cring'er** *n.*

crin·kle (kring'kəl) *v.t. & v.i.* **·kled, ·kling** **1** To be or cause to be full of wrinkles or twists. **2** To make a crackling sound. —*n.* A wrinkle; ripple. [ME < *crenklen*] —**crin'kly** *adj.* **(·kli·er, ·kli·est)**

cri·noid (krī'noid, krin'oid) *adj.* Of or pertaining to various small, flowerlike sea animals attached by stalks to the sea bottom: also **cri·noi·dal** (kri·noid'l). —*n.* One of these animals. [< Gk. *krinon* lily + -OID]

crin·o·line (krin'ə·lin, -lēn) *n.* **1** A highly sized, stiff fabric, used in hems, interlinings, etc. **2** A skirt stiffened with such fabric. **3** HOOP SKIRT. [< L *crinis* hair + *linum* flax, thread]

crip·ple (krip'əl) *n.* A lame person or animal or one lacking the natural use of a limb or the body. —*v.t.* **·pled, ·pling** **1** To lame. **2** To impair or disable in some way. [< OE *crypel*] —**crip'pler** *n.*

cri·sis (krī'sis) *n. pl.* **cri·ses** (-sēz) **1** A decisive or crucial turning point in the progress of a series of events. **2** A dangerous or critical moment or development. **3** *Pathol.* A decisive change, favorable or unfavorable, in the course of a disease. [< Gk. *krisis* < *krinein* decide]

crisp (krisp) *adj.* **1** Firm and fresh. **2** Brittle or crumbling readily, as pastry. **3** Clean and neat. **4** Terse or pithy: a *crisp* reply. **5** Fresh and bracing. **6** Tightly curled or waved. —*v.t. & v.i.* To make or become crisp. [< L *crispus* curled] —**crisp'er, crisp'ness** *n.* —**crisp'ly** *adv.* —**crisp'y** *adj.*

criss·cross (kris'krôs', -kros') *v.t.* **1** To cross with interlacing lines. —*v.i.* **2** To move in crisscrosses. —*adj.* Characterized by crossing lines. —*n.* **1** The cross of one who cannot write. **2** A pattern of intersecting lines. —*adv.* Across; crosswise. [Alter. of *Christ-cross*]

crit. critic; critical; criticism.

cri·te·ri·on (krī·tir'ē·ən) *n. pl.* **·te·ri·a** (-tir'ē·ə) or **·te·ri·ons** A standard, rule, or test by which a correct judgment can be made. [< Gk. *kritēs* a judge]

crit·ic (krit'ik) *n.* **1** One who judges anything by some standard or criterion. **2** One whose profession is to judge or evaluate literary, theatrical, musical, or other artistic productions. **3** A faultfinder. —*adj.* Pertaining to criticism; critical. [< Gk. *kritēs* a judge]

crit·i·cal (krit'i·kəl) *adj.* **1** Faultfinding; censorious. **2** Characterized by careful, precise analysis or examination. **3** Of critics or criticism. **4** Risky; perilous. **5** Of, being, or contributing to a crisis; decisive. **6** *Pathol.* Of a crisis in a disease. **7** *Physics* Designating a value or point indicating a decisive change in a specified condition. —**crit'i·cal·ly** *adv.* —**crit'i·cal·ness** *n.* —**Syn.** **1** condemnatory, captious, carping, disapproving. **5** grave, serious, urgent, pressing.

crit·i·cism (krit'ə·siz'əm) *n.* **1** The act or art of criticizing. **2** A discriminating judgment; an evaluation. **3** A severe or unfavorable judgment. **4** The principles or rules for judging anything, esp. works of literature or art. **5** A review, article, etc., expressing a critical judgment.

crit·i·cize (krit'ə·sīz) *v.t. & v.i.* **·cized, ·ciz·ing** **1** To examine and judge as a critic. 2 To judge severely; censure. *Brit. sp.* **crit'i·cise. —crit'i·ciz'a·ble** *adj.* **—crit'i·ciz'er** *n.*

cri·tique (kri·tēk') *n.* 1 A critical review. 2 The art of criticism.

crit·ter (krit'ər) *n. Regional* 1 A domestic animal. 2 Any living creature. [Var. of CREATURE]

croak (krōk) *v.i.* 1 To utter a hoarse, low-pitched cry, as a frog or raven. 2 To speak in a low, hoarse voice. 3 To forbode evil; grumble. 4 *Slang* To die. —*v.t.* 5 To utter with a croak. 6 *Slang* To kill. —*n.* A hoarse vocal sound. [Imit.] **—croak'y** *adj.*

croak·er (krō'kər) *n.* 1 Any of various animals that croak. 2 One who forebodes evil.

Cro·at (krō'ăt, -ət) *n.* 1 A native or citizen of Croatia. 2 The language of the Croats; Serbo-Croatian. **—Cro·a·tian** (krō·ā'shən) *n., adj.*

cro·chet (krō·shā') *v.t. & v.i.* **·cheted** (-shād'), **·chet·ing** (-shā'ing) To form or ornament (a fabric) by interlacing thread with a hooked needle. —*n.* A kind of fancywork produced by crocheting. [< F *croche* a hook]

crock (krok) *n.* A earthenware pot or jar. [< OE *crocca*]

crock·er·y (krok'ər·ē) *n.* Earthenware; earthen vessels collectively.

croc·o·dile (krok'ə·dīl) *n.* A large, lizardlike, aquatic reptile of tropical regions, having the head longer and narrower than that of an alligator. [< Gk. *krokodilos* lizard, crocodile.] — **croc·o·dil·i·an** (krok'ə·dil'ē·ən), **croc'o·dil'e·an** *adj., n.*

Crocodile

crocodile tears Simulated weeping; hypocritical grief.

cro·cus (krō'kəs) *n. pl.* **cro·cus·es** or **cro·ci** (krō'sī) 1 Any of a genus of plants related to the iris with long grasslike leaves and large flowers. 2 The flower of this plant. 3 An orange-yellow or saffron color. [< Gk. *krokos* saffron]

crois·sant (krwä·säṅ') *n.* A small, buttery, crescent-shaped roll. [F]

Croix de Guerre (krwä də gâr') A French military decoration for bravery. [F lit., cross of war]

Cro-Mag·non (krō·mag'non, -man'yən) *n.* A member of a prehistoric race of men whose remains were found in France. —*adj.* Pertaining or relating to the Cro-Magnon race. [< *Cro-Magnon,* a cave in s France]

crom·lech (krom'lek) *n.* 1 DOLMEN. 2 An ancient monument of standing stones arranged in a circle. [< Welsh *crom* bent + *llech* flat stone]

crone (krōn) *n.* A withered old woman. [< OF *carogne* carcass]

cro·ny (krō'nē) *n. pl.* **·nies** A familiar friend. [< Gk. *chronios* long-lasting]

crook (kro͝ok) *n.* 1 A bend or curve. 2 The curved or bent part of a thing: the *crook* of a branch. 3 An implement with a crook in it: a shepherd's *crook.* 4 *Informal* A criminal; swindler; cheat. [< ON *krōkr*]

crook·ed (kro͝ok'id) *adj.* 1 Not straight; having angles or curves. 2 Tricky; dishonest. **—crook'ed·ly** *adv.* **—crook'ed·ness** *n.*

crook·neck (kro͝ok'nek') *n.* Any of several varieties of squash with a long, curved neck.

croon (kro͞on) *v.t. & v.i.* To sing or hum in a soft or romantic manner. —*n.* A low, humming sound. [< MDu. *krōnen* sing softly, lament] **—croon'er** *n.*

crop (krop) *n.* 1 Cultivated plants, grains, fruits, etc., collectively. 2 The plant product of a particular kind, place, or season. 3 The entire yield of anything. 4 A short haircut. 5 The first stomach of a bird; craw. 6 A hunting or riding whip with a leather loop for a lash. 7 A collection of things: a *crop* of lies. —*v.* **cropped, crop·ping** *v.t.* 1 To cut or eat off the stems or ends of. 2 To pluck or reap. 3 To cut off closely, as hair; trim, as a dog's ears or tail. 4 To raise a crop or crops on; cause to bear crops. —*v.i.* 5 To appear above the surface; sprout: with *up* or *out.* 6 To develop or come up unexpectedly: with *up* or *out:* A new problem *cropped* up. [< OE *cropp*]

crop·per[1] (krop'ər) *n.* 1 One who or that which crops. 2 SHARECROPPER.

crop·per[2] (krop'ər) *n.* A fall, as from a horse. **—come a cropper** 1 To fall headlong. 2 To fail disastrously. [? < *neck and crop* completely, thoroughly]

cro·quet (krō·kā') *n.* An outdoor game played by knocking wooden balls through a series of wire arches by means of mallets. [< AF *croquet*]

cro·quette (krō·ket') *n.* A ball or cake of previously cooked, minced food, fried in deep fat or baked. [F< *croquer* crunch]

cro·sier (krō'zhər) *n.* A staff surmounted by a crook or cross, borne by or before a bishop or archbishop on occasions of ceremony. [< Med. L *crocia* bishop's crook]

cross (krôs, kros) *n.* 1 A vertical post intersected by a horizontal bar near the top, used as an instrument of torture and death by the ancient Romans. 2 A representation of the cross on which Christ was crucified, a symbol of Christianity. 3 Any representation of a cross, used as a badge of honor, a grave marker, etc. 4 Any suffering, trial, or tribulation. 5 Any mark or design composed of two intersecting lines. 6 Such a mark used as a signature by one who cannot write. 7 Anything that combines the qualities of characteristics of two other things: a *cross* between poetry and prose. 8 The act of crossing, as from one side to another. 9 *Biol.* a A mixing of varieties or breeds of plants or animals. b The product of any such mixing; a hybrid. **—the Cross** 1 The cross on which Christ was crucified. 2 Christianity. —*v.t.* 1 To pass or move from one side to the other side of. 2 To extend from side to side of; span. 3 To intersect, as streets or lines. 4 To draw or put a line across. 5 To lay or place over or across: to *cross* the legs. 6 To transport across. 7 To make the sign of the cross upon or over. 8 To meet and pass: Your letter *crossed* mine. 9 To obstruct or hinder; thwart. 10 To cause, as plants or animals, to interbreed; hybridize. —*v.i.* 11 To intersect; lie across. 12 To pass, move, or extend from side to side. 13 To meet and pass. 14 To breed together; interbreed. —*adj.* 1 Lying or moving across or through; transverse: *cross* streets. 2 Contrary; opposed: *cross* purposes. 3 Ill-tempered; peevish. 4 HYBRID. —*adv.* Across; crosswise; traversely. [< L *crux*] **—cross'ly** *adv.* **—cross'ness** *n.*

Crosses
a. Celtic. b. Latin.
c. Maltese.

cross·bar (krôs'bär, kros'-) *n.* A transverse bar or line. —*v.t.* To secure or mark with transverse bars.

cross·beam (krôs'bēm', -kros'-) *n.* 1 A beam extending from wall to wall. 2 A beam that crosses another.

cross·bill (krôs'bil', kros'-) *n.* A finchlike bird having mandibles that cross each other when the beak is closed.

cross·bones (krôs'bōnz', kros'-) *n.* A symbol of death consisting of two arm or leg bones crossing each other, usu. surmounted by a skull.

cross·bow (krôs'bō', kros'-) *n.* A medieval missile weapon consisting of a bow fixed transversely on a grooved stock.

cross·breed (krôs'brēd', kros'-) *v.t. & v.i.* **·bred, ·breed·ing** *Biol.* HYBRIDIZE —*n.* A strain or animal so produced. **—cross'bred'** *adj.*

cross-coun·try (krôs'kun'trē, kros'-) *adj. & adv.* Across open country instead of by roads.

cross·cut (krôs'kut', kros'-) *v.t.* **·cut, ·cut·ting** To cut crosswise or through. —*adj.* Used or made for the purpose of cutting something across: a *crosscut* saw. —*n.* A cut across or a shortcut.

cross-ex·am·ine (krôs'ig·zam'in, kros'-) *v.t.* **·ined, ·in·ing** 1 To question anew (a witness already called by the opposing party) to test the reliability of his previous testimony. 2 To question thoroughly. **—cross'-ex·am'i·na'tion, cross'-ex·am'in·er** *n.*

cross-eye (krôs'ī', kros'-) *n.* STRABISMUS. **—cross'-eyed'** *adj.*

cross-fer·ti·li·za·tion (krôs′fûr′tə·lə·zā′shən, kros′-) *n.* **1** The union of male and female gametes from different individuals. **2** The fertilization of one plant or flower by the pollen from another.

cross-fer·ti·lize (krôs′fûr′tə·līz, kros′-) *v.t. & v.i.* **·lized, ·liz·ing** To fertilize or be fertilized by cross-fertilization.

cross-grained (krôs′grānd′, kros′-) *adj.* **1** Having the grain run across or irregularly: said of wood. **2** Difficult; stubborn; perverse.

cross·hatch (krôs′hach′, kros′-) *v.t.* To shade, as a picture, by crossed lines, either diagonal or rectangular. —**cross′-hatch′ing** *n.*

cross-in·dex (krôs′in′deks, kros′-) *v.t. & v.i.* To insert cross references in (an index, etc.).

cross·ing (krôs′ing, kros′-) *n.* **1** The place where a road, river, etc., may be crossed. **2** An intersection, as of roads. **3** The act of crossing.

cross·patch (krôs′pach′, kros′-) *n.* A cranky, ill-tempered person.

cross·piece (krôs′pēs′, kros′-) *n.* A piece of material of any kind crossing another.

cross-pol·li·nate (krôs′pol′ə·nāt, kros′-) *v.t.* **·nat·ed, ·nat·ing** To subject to cross-fertilization (def. 2). —**cross′-pol′li·na′tion** *n.*

cross-pur·pose (krôs′pûr′pəs, kros′-) *n.* A purpose which is contrary to or conflicts with another. —**at cross-purposes** In conflict as to means and aims.

cross-ques·tion (krôs′kwes′chən, kros′-) *v.t.* CROSS-EXAMINE.

cross-re·fer (krôs′ri·fûr′, kros′-) *v.* **·ferred, ·fer·ring** *v.t.* To refer to another passage or part. —*v.i.* To make a cross-reference.

cross-ref·er·ence (krôs′ref′rəns, kros′-) *n.* **1** A reference from one passage in a text to another in the same work. **2** In a library catalog, and in research and documentation, reference from one subject to another.

cross·road (krôs′rōd, kros′-) *n.* A road that crosses another, or that crosses from one main road to another. Also **cross′way′**.

cross·roads (krôs′rōdz′, kros′-) *n. pl. (construed as sing.)* **1** A place where roads cross. **2** A juncture in time where two cultures, eras, etc., meet. **3** A critical time or decision.

cross section **1** A section of any object cut at right angles to its length. **2** Any specimen or example typical of the whole.

cross-stitch (krôs′stich′, kros′-) *n.* **1** A double stitch in the form of an X. **2** Needlework made with this stitch. —*v.t.* To make or mark with a cross-stitch.

cross-town (krôs′toun′, kros′-) *adj.* Going across a city: a *cross-town* bus. —*adv.* Across a city: to go *cross-town.*

cross·tree (krôs′trē′, kros′-) *n. Usu. pl. Naut.* One of the pieces of wood or iron set crosswise at the head of a mast.

cross·walk (krôs′wôk′, kros′-) *n.* Any lane marked off, usu. by white lines, to be used by pedestrians in crossing a street.

cross·wise (krôs′wīz′, kros′-) *adv.* Across. Also **cross′·ways′**.

cross·word puzzle (krôs′wûrd′, kros′-) A puzzle consisting of black and white squares, the latter of which are numbered and are to be filled in with letters forming words to which clues are given in lists of definitions, synonyms, etc.

crotch (kroch) *n.* **1** A point of division or divergence; a fork. **2** The region of the human body where the legs separate from the pelvis. **3** A forked pole or stick. [?]

crotched (krocht) *adj.* Having a crotch.

crotch·et (kroch′it) *n.* **1** A whimsical notion; an eccentricity. **2** A small hook. [<OF *crochet* a hook]

crotch·et·y (kroch′ə·tē) *adj.* **1** Perverse; cantankerous; eccentric. **2** Like a crotchet. —**croch′et·i·ness** *n.*

cro·ton (krōt′n) *n.* **1** Any of a genus of widely dispersed trees and shrubs of the spurge family. **2** An ornamental plant with variegated foliage. [<Gk. *krotōn* a kind of plant]

Croton bug GERMAN COCKROACH. [<*Croton* River, New York]

croton oil A purgative obtained from the seeds of an East Indian croton.

crouch (krouch) *v.i.* **1** To stoop or bend low. **2** To cringe; cower. —*v.t.* **3** To bend low. —*n.* A crouching or the position taken in crouching. [<OF *croc* a hook]

croup[1] (kro͞op) *n.* A disease characterized by hoarse coughing, laryngeal spasm, and difficulty in breathing. [Imit.] —**croup′ous, croup′y** *adj.*

croup[2] (kro͞op) *n.* The rump of a horse, etc. Also **croupe.** [<OF *croupe*] • See HORSE.

crou·pi·er (kro͞o′pē·ər, *Fr.* kro͞o·pyā′) *n.* One in charge of collecting or paying out money at a gambling table. [F, lit., one who rides on the croup, an assistant]

crou·ton (kro͞o′ton, kro͞o·ton′; *Fr.* kro͞o·tôṅ′) *n.* Any of the small, toasted or fried cubes of bread used in soups, salads, etc. [<F *croûte* crust]

crow[1] (krō) *n.* **1** Any of various omnivorous, raucous birds with glossy black plumage. **2** Loosely, a rook or raven. [<OE *crāwe*]

crow[2] (krō) *v.i.* **crowed** or *(for def. 1) Chiefly Brit.* **crew, crowed, crow·ing** **1** To utter the cry of a rooster. **2** To exult; boast. **3** To utter sounds expressive of delight, as an infant. —*n.* A crowing sound of a rooster, infant, etc. [<OE *crāwan*]

Crow (krō) *n. pl.* **Crow** or **Crows** **1** A North American Indian of a Siouan tribe. **2** The language of this tribe.

crow·bar (krō′bär′) *n.* A straight iron or steel bar, with the point flattened and sometimes set at an angle, used as a lever.

crowd (kroud) *n.* **1** A large number of persons or things gathered closely together. **2** The populace in general; the masses. **3** *Informal* A particular set of people; a clique. —*v.t.* **1** To shove or push. **2** To fill to overflowing, as with a crowd; fill to excess. **3** To cram together; force into a confined space. **4** *Informal* To put pressure upon (a person), as by mental harassment. —*v.i.* **5** To gather in large numbers; throng together. **6** To push forward; force one's way. **7** To shove or push. [<OE *crūdan*] —**crowd′er** *n.*

crow·foot (krō′fo͝ot′) *n. pl.* **·foots** Any of numerous plants having variously lobed leaves and usu. yellow flowers.

crown (kroun) *n.* **1** A decorative circlet for the head, esp. as a mark of sovereign power. **2** *Often cap.* A sovereign ruler; also, sovereignty: with *the.* **3** A wreath or garland for the head. **4** A reward or prize for excellence or merit. **5** A complete or perfect state or type; acme. **6** The top or summit; crest. **7** The top of the head: a bald *crown.* **8** The head itself. **9** The upper portion of a hat. **10** *Dent.* **a** The part of a tooth exposed beyond the gum. **b** An artificial substitute for this. • See TOOTH. **11 a** A coin stamped with a crown or crowned head. **b** Formerly, a British five-shilling piece. **12** *Naut.* The outer point of junction of the two arms of an anchor. —*v.t.* **1** To place a crown or garland on the head of. **2** To enthrone; make a monarch of. **3** To be the topmost part of. **4** To form the ultimate ornament to or aspect of. **5** To endow with honor or dignity. **6** To bring to completion; consummate. **7** *Dent.* To put a crown on (a tooth). **8** *Slang* To hit, as a person, on the head. **9** In checkers, to make into a king. [<L *corona*] —**crown′er** *n.*

Crown

crown colony A colonial dependency of Great Britain in which the crown retains control of legislation.

crown glass Very hard, clear glass used in optical instruments.

crown land In some British dominions or colonies, land held under government control.

crown prince The heir apparent to a crown, a monarch's oldest living son.

crown princess **1** The wife of a crown prince. **2** The female heir apparent to a throne.

crow's-foot (krōz′fo͝ot′) *n. pl.* **-feet** One of the wrinkles diverging from the outer corner of the eye.

crow's-nest (krōz′nest′) *n.* **1** *Naut.* A small platform at a ship's masthead, used by the lookout. **2** Any similar lookout ashore.

cro·zier (krō′zhər) *n.* CROSIER.

crs. credits; creditors.

CRT cathode-ray tube.

cru·ces (kro͞o′sēz) A *n.pl.* of CRUX.

cru·cial (krōō′shəl) *adj.* 1 Of immense and decisive importance; critical. 2 Severely difficult and trying. [< L *crux, crucis* cross, torture] **—cru′cial·ly** *adv.*

cru·ci·ble (krōō′sə·bəl) *n.* 1 A pot or vessel made of a substance that will stand extreme heat. 2 The hollow place in the bottom of an ore furnace. 3 A trying and purifying test. [< Med. L *crucibulum* earthen pot]

cru·ci·fix (krōō′sə·fiks) *n.* A cross bearing an effigy of Christ crucified. [< L *crucifixus* one hanged on a cross]

Crucifix

cru·ci·fix·ion (krōō′sə·fik′shən) *n.* The act of crucifying or the state of being crucified. 2 Any representation of Christ's death. **—the Crucifixion** The death of Christ on the cross.

cru·ci·form (krōō′sə·fôrm) *adj.* Having the shape of a cross: a *cruciform* church. [< L *crux* cross + -FORM]

cru·ci·fy (krōō′sə·fī) *v.t.* **·fied, ·fy·ing** 1 To put to death by nailing or binding to a cross. 2 To torture; torment. [< L *crucifigere* fasten to a cross] **—cru′ci·fi′er** *n.*

crud (krud) 1 *Brit. Dial.* Curd. 2 A deposit or accretion of an undesirable substance, as grit. 3 *Slang* Worthless rubbish. **—crud′dy** *adj.* **(·di·er, ·di·est)**

crude (krōōd) *adj.* **crud·er, crud·est** 1 Not in a state ready for use; raw; unrefined: *crude* oil. 2 Lacking refinement, tact, good taste, etc. 3 Rough in workmanship, design, etc. 4 Not disguised; bare: a *crude* truth. [< L *crudus*] **—crude′ly** *adv.* **—crude′ness** *n.* **—Syn.** 2 coarse, gross, vulgar.

cru·di·ty (krōō′də·tē) *n. pl.* **·ties** 1 The state or quality of being crude. 2 A crude act, remark, etc.

cru·el (krōō′əl) *adj.* 1 Disposed to inflict suffering, pain, etc., on others. 2 Causing suffering, distress, etc.: a *cruel* fate. [< L *crudelis* severe] **—cru′el·ly** *adv.* **—Syn.** 1 pitiless, inhuman, merciless, sadistic, ruthless.

cru·el·ty (krōō′əl·tē) *n. pl.* **·ties** 1 The quality or condition of being cruel. 2 Something cruel, as an action.

cru·et (krōō′it) *n.* A small glass bottle, as for vinegar. [< OF *crue* pot]

cruise (krōōz) *v.* **cruised, cruis·ing** *v.i.* 1 To sail about, as for pleasure. 2 To drive about, as a taxi or police patrol car. 3 To move or proceed at a speed suitable for sustained travel. —*v.t.* 4 To cruise over or about. —*n.* The act of cruising, esp. at sea. [< Du. *kruisen*]

cruise missile A guided missile that flies like an airplane at low altitudes.

cruis·er (krōō′zər) *n.* 1 A person, vehicle, or ship that cruises. 2 A fast, maneuverable warship, having a long cruising radius. 3 CABIN CRUISER.

crul·ler (krul′ər) *n.* A small, twisted cake of sweetened fried dough. [< Du. *krullen* to curl]

crumb (krum) *n.* 1 A small bit, as of crumbled bread. 2 The soft inner part of a loaf. 3 A morsel. —*v.t.* 1 To break into small pieces. 2 In cooking, to cover with bread crumbs. [< OE *cruma*] **—crumb′y** *adj.* **(·i·er, ·i·est)**

crum·ble (krum′bəl) *v.t.* & *v.i.* **·bled, ·bling** To fall or cause to fall into small pieces; disintegrate. —*n.* 1 A crumb. 2 Any crumbly material. [Freq. of CRUMB, *v.*] **—crum′bly** *adj.*

crum·my (krum′ē) *adj.* **crum·mi·er, crum·mi·est** *Slang* Inferior, shoddy, cheap, etc. [< CRUMB] **—crum′mi·ness** *n.*

crum·pet (krum′pit) *n.* A thin, leavened batter cake baked on a griddle and then toasted. [< ME *crompid cake* curled cake]

crum·ple (krum′pəl) *v.t.* & *v.i.* **·pled, ·pling** 1 To become or cause to become wrinkled; rumple. 2 *Informal* To collapse. —*n.* A wrinkle, as in cloth or the earth. [Freq. of obs. *crump,* var. of CRIMP]

crunch (krunch) *v.t.* 1 To chew with a brittle, crushing sound. 2 To crush or grind noisily. —*v.i.* 3 To chew noisily. 4 To move or advance with a crushing sound. —*n.* 1 The act or sound of crunching. 2 *Slang* A critical time, as the moment of decision. [Imit.] **—crunch′y** *adj.* **(·i·er, ·i·est)**

crup·per (krup′ər) *n.* 1 The looped strap that goes under a horse's tail. 2 The rump of a horse; croup. [< OF *croupe* croup, rump]

cru·sade (krōō·sād′) *n.* 1 Any of the military expeditions undertaken by Christians from the 11th through the 13th century to recover the Holy Land from the Muslims. 2 Any similar expedition sanctioned by a church. 3 Any movement or cause conducted aggressively and vigorously, esp. against public evil. —*v.i.* **·sad·ed, ·sad·ing** To go on or engage in a crusade. [< Med. L. *cruciare* mark with a cross] **—cru·sad′er** *n.*

cruse (krōōz, krōōs) *n.* A small bottle, flask, or jug; cruet.

crush (krush) *v.t.* 1 To press or squeeze out of shape; mash. 2 To smash or grind into particles. 3 To obtain or extract by pressure. 4 To press upon; crowd. 5 To put down; subdue; overwhelm. 6 To oppress. —*v.i.* 7 To become broken or misshapen by pressure. 8 To crowd: with *into, against,* etc. —*n.* 1 The act of crushing. 2 A pressing or crowding together. 3 A fruit drink. 4 *Informal* An infatuation. [< OF *croissir* break] **—crush′er** *n.*

crust (krust) *n.* 1 A hard, thin coating over something softer. 2 **a** The outer part of bread. **b** A bit of stale, hard bread. 3 The pastry envelope of a pie or the like. 4 The cold, exterior portion of the earth. 5 *Slang* Insolence; impertinence. —*v.t.* & *v.i.* To cover with or acquire a crust. [< L *crusta*]

crus·ta·cean (krus·tā′shən) *n.* One of a class of arthropods having a hard shell, two pairs of antennae, and usu. gills, including lobsters, crabs, shrimps, etc. —*adj.* Of or pertaining to these animals. [< L *crusta* crust, shell]

crus·tal (krus′təl) *adj.* Of or derived from a crust, esp. of the moon, earth, or other planet.

crust·y (krus′tē) *adj.* **crust·i·er, crust·i·est** 1 Like a crust. 2 Having or hard as a crust. 3 Morosely curt in manner or speech; surly. **—crust′i·ly** *adv.* **—crust′i·ness** *n.*

crutch (kruch) *n.* 1 Any of various devices used as a support in walking, esp. a staff with a crosspiece fitting in the armpit. 2 Anything one feels to be necessary as a support or aid. 3 *Naut.* A forked support for a swinging boom when not in use. —*v.t.* To prop up, as on crutches. [< OE *crycc*]

crux (kruks) *n. pl.* **crux·es** or **cru·ces** (krōō′sēz) 1 A pivotal, fundamental, or vital point. 2 A tormenting or baffling problem. [L, a cross]

cry (krī) *v.* **cried, cry·ing** *v.t.* 1 To utter loudly or shout out; exclaim. 2 To proclaim loudly and publicly; advertise loudly. 3 To affect (one) in some specified way by weeping: to *cry* oneself to sleep. —*v.i.* 4 To speak, call, or appeal loudly; shout; yell. 5 To utter sounds of grief and sorrow; weep; sob. 6 To have or show a great need: with *for.* 7 To make characteristic calls: said of animals. —*n. pl.* **cries** 1 A loud call; shout; yell. 2 The act of weeping. 3 An earnest appeal; entreaty. 4 Advertisement by outcry. 5 General report or rumor; public opinion. 6 A word or phrase to rally men to action. 7 Public demand; outcry: a *cry* for clean streets. 8 The characteristic call of a bird or an animal. [< L *quiritare* call out]

cry·ba·by (krī′bā′bē) *n. pl.* **·bies** A person, esp. a child, given to crying or complaining over his circumstances.

cry·ing (krī′ing) *adj.* Calling for immediate action or redress: a *crying* shame.

cryo- *combining form* Cold; frost: *cryogenic.* [< Gk. *kyros* frost]

cry·o·gen·ic (krī′ə·jen′ik) *adj.* Pertaining to very low temperatures or their study. [< CRYO- + -GENIC]

cry·o·gen·ics (krī′ə·jen′iks) *n. pl. (construed as sing.)* The branch of physics dealing with very low temperatures.

cry·o·lite (krī′ə·līt) *n.* A vitreous, snow-white, translucent mineral fluoride of sodium and aluminum. [< CRYO- + Gk. *lithos* stone]

cry·o·sur·ger·y (krī′ō·sûr′jər·ē) *n.* Surgery utilizing extreme cold to destroy tissue. **—cry′o·sur′gi·cal** *adj.*

crypt (kript) *n.* A recess or vault, esp. one under some churches, used for burial, etc. [< Gk. *kryptos* hidden]

cryp·tic (krip′tik) *adj.* 1 Puzzling; ambiguous; mysterious. 2 Secret; arcane. Also **cryp′ti·cal.** [< Gk. *kryptos* hidden] **—cryp′ti·cal·ly** *adv.*

crypto- *combining form* Hidden; secret: *cryptogram.* [< Gk. *kryptos* hidden]

cryp·to·gam (krip′tə·gam) *n.* A plant having no flowers, but propagating by spores, as algae, fungi, lichens, and mosses. Also **cryp′to·phyte** (-fīt). [< CRYPTO- + Gk. *gamos* marriage] **—cryp′to·gam′ic, cryp·tog·a·mous** (krip·tog′ə·məs) *adj.*

cryp·to·gram (krip′tə·gram) *n.* A message whose meaning is hidden, as by use of a code.

cryp·to·graph (krip′tə·graf, -gräf) *n.* **1** CRYPTOGRAM. **2** A system of secret writing; a cipher. **—cryp·tog·ra·pher** (krip·tog′rə·fər), **cryp·tog′ra·phist** *n.* **—cryp′to·graph′ic** *adj.*

cryp·tog·ra·phy (krip·tog′rə·fē) *n.* The art or process of writing in secret characters.

cryst. crystalline; crystals.

crys·tal (kris′təl) *n.* **1** The solid form assumed by many minerals, esp. colorless transparent quartz, or rock crystal. **2** *Physics* A definite and symmetrical structure, based on a recurring unit cell, assumed by the atoms, molecules, or ions of a solid. **3** Flint glass, or any fine glass; also, tableware and decorative pieces made of such glass. **4** The transparent cover for a watch face. **5** Anything clear and transparent. *—adj.* **1** Composed of crystal. **2** Like crystal; extremely clear; limpid. [< Gk. *krystallos*] **—crys·tal·lic** (kris·tal′ik) *adj.*

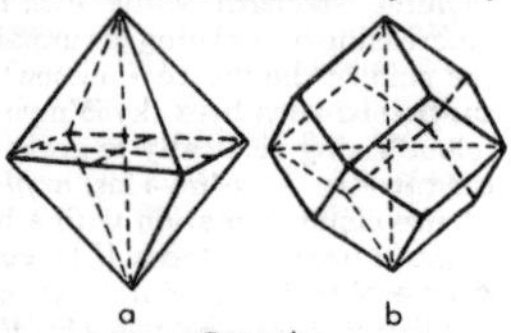

Crystals
a. tetragonal pyramid.
b. dodecahedron.

crys·tal·line (kris′tə·lin, -līn, -lēn) *adj.* **1** Of, pertaining to, or like crystal or crystals. **2** Transparent; clear.

crystalline lens A transparent, biconvex body situated behind the iris of the eye, serving to focus light on the retina. Also **crystalline humor.**

crys·tal·lize (kris′tə·līz) *v.* **·lized, ·liz·ing** *v.t.* **1** To cause to form crystals or become crystalline. **2** To bring to definite and permanent form. *—v.i.* **3** To assume the form of crystals. **4** To assume permanent form. **—crys′tal·liz′a·ble** *adj.* **—crys′tal·li·za′tion** *n.*

crys·tal·log·ra·phy (kris′tə·log′rə·fē) *n.* The science of crystals. **—crys′tal·log′ra·pher** *n.*

crys·tal·loid (kris′tə·loid) *adj.* Like, of, or pertaining to a crystal or crystals. *—n.* One of a class of substances, usu. crystallizable, whose solutions pass readily through animal or vegetable membranes. **—crys′tal·loi′dal** *adj.*

C.S. Christian Science; Christian Scientist.

C.S., c.s. capital stock; civil service.

Cs cesium.

CSC Civil Service Commission.

csc cosecant.

csk. cask.

CST, C.S.T., c.s.t. central standard time.

CT Connecticut (P.O. abbr.).

ct. cent; county; court.

ctn. carton, cotangent.

ctr. center.

cts. centimes; cents.

Cu copper (L *cuprum*).

cu, cu. cubic.

cub (kub) *n.* **1** The young of the bear, fox, wolf, and certain other carnivores; a whelp. **2** An awkward youth. **3** A beginner or learner. *—adj.* Young; inexperienced: a *cub* reporter; *cub* pilot. [?]

Cu·ba (kyo͞o′bə) *n.* A republic on an island in the Caribbean Sea, 44,217 sq. mi., cap. Havana. **—Cu′ban** *adj., n.*

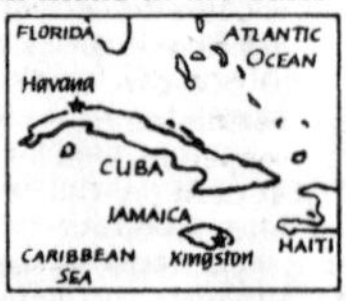

cub·by·hole (kub′ē·hōl′) *n.* A small, enclosed space. [< *cubby,* dim. of dial. E *cub* shed + HOLE]

cube (kyo͞ob) *n.* **1** *Geom.* A solid bounded by six equal squares and having all its angles right angles. **2** *Math.* The third power of a quantity; the product of three equal factors. *—v.t.* **cubed, cub·ing 1** To raise (a number or quantity) to the third power. **2** To find the cubic capacity of. **3** To form or cut into cubes or cubelike shapes. [< Gk. *kybos* cube, die[2]]

cu·beb (kyo͞o′beb) *n.* The berry of an East Indian species of pepper, formerly used to treat urinary and bronchial disorders. [< Ar. *kabābah*]

cube root A number which, taken three times as a factor, produces a given number.

cu·bic (kyo͞o′bik) *adj.* **1** Formed like a cube. **2** Being, or equal to, a cube whose edge is a given unit: a *cubic* foot. **3** *Math.* Of the third power or degree. Also **cu′bi·cal.** **—cu′bi·cal·ly** *adv.* **—cu′bi·cal·ness** *n.*

cu·bi·cle (kyo͞o′bi·kəl) *n.* **1** A partially enclosed section of a dormitory. **2** Any small, partially enclosed place, as a partitioned space for study. [< L *cubiculum* < *cubare* lie down]

cubic measure A unit or system of units for measuring volume.

cu·bism (kyo͞o′biz·əm) *n.* An early 20th-century school of art concerned with an abstract and geometric, rather than realistic, representation of things. **—cu′bist** *adj., n.*

cu·bit (kyo͞o′bit) *n.* An ancient measure equal to about 18 to 20 inches. [< L *cubitum* elbow]

cuck·old (kuk′əld) *n.* The husband of an unfaithful wife. *—v.t.* To make a cuckold of. [< OF *cucu* cuckoo, which lays its eggs in another bird's nest] **—cuck′old·ry** (-əl·drē) *n.*

cuck·oo (ko͝ok′o͞o) *n.* **1** Any of a large family of slender birds with slightly curved bills, long, narrow tails, and a call like the sound of its name. **2** A cuckoo's cry. **3** An imitation of this sound. *—v.* **·ooed, ·oo·ing** *v.t.* **1** To repeat without cessation. *—v.i.* **2** To utter or imitate the cry of the cuckoo. *—adj.* (*also* ko͞o′ko͞o) *Slang* Slightly deranged mentally. [< OF *cucu, coucou;* imit.]

cuckoo clock A clock in which a mechanical cuckoo announces the hours.

cu·cum·ber (kyo͞o′kum·bər) *n.* **1** The long, hard-rinded fruit of a creeping plant of the gourd family cultivated as a vegetable. **2** The plant. [< L *cucumis*]

cud (kud) *n.* Food forced up into the mouth from the first stomach of a ruminant and chewed over again. [< OE *cudu, cwidu*]

cud·dle (kud′l) *v* **·dled, ·dling** *v.t.* **1** To protect and caress fondly within a close embrace; hug. *—v.i.* **2** To hug one another; nestle together. *—n.* An embrace; caress. [?] **—cud′dle·some, cud·dly** (kud′lē) *adj.* **(·dli·er, ·dli·est)**

cudg·el (kuj′əl) *n.* A short, thick stick used as a club. *—v.t.* **·eled** or **·elled, ·el·ing** or **·el·ling** To beat with a cudgel. [< OE *cycgel*] **—cudg′el·er** or **cudg′el·ler** *n.*

cue[1] (kyo͞o) *n.* **1** A long, tapering rod, used to strike the cue ball in billiards, pool, etc. **2** A queue or line of persons. *—v.t.* **cued, cu·ing 1** In billiards, etc., to hit with a cue. *—v.i.* **2** To form a line of persons: usu. with *up.* [< F *queue* tail]

cue[2] (kyo͞o) *n.* **1** In the performing arts: **a** Any of various signals for an actor to speak or do something, as another actor's words or actions, a bit of music, etc. **b** Anything that initiates some action or change: a music *cue;* a lighting *cue.* **2** Any hint or suggestion. *—v.t.* **cued, cu·ing** To give a cue to. [?]

cue ball A white or whitish yellow ball struck by the cue in billiards or pool.

cuff[1] (kuf) *n.* **1** A band about the wrist, as a part of a sleeve. **2** The part of a long glove covering the wrist. **3** A turned-up hem on a trouser leg. **4** HANDCUFF. **—off the cuff** *Informal* Extemporaneous; unrehearsed. [ME *cuffe*]

cuff[2] (kuf) *v.t.* **1** To strike, as with the open hand; buffet. *—v.i.* **2** To scuffle or fight; box. *—n.* A blow, esp. with the open hand. [?]

cuff links A pair of linked buttons, etc., used to fasten shirt cuffs.

cu. ft. cubic foot; cubic feet.

cu. in. cubic inch(es).

cui·rass (kwi·ras′) *n.* **1** A piece of defensive armor consisting of a plate covering the breast and back. **2** The breastplate alone. [< OF *cuirasse*]

Cuirass

cui·sine (kwi·zēn′) *n.* **1** A particular style or manner of cooking. **2** The food prepared. [F< LL *coquina* kitchen]

cul-de-sac (kul′də·sak′, ko͝ol′-; *Fr.* kü′də·sȧk′) *n. pl.* **culs-de-sacs,** *Fr.* **culs·de·sac** (kü′-) **1** A passage open only at one end; blind alley. **2** Something having no way out. [F, lit., bottom of the bag]

-cule *suffix of nouns* Small; little: *animalcule.* [< L *-culus*]

cu·li·nar·y (kyōō′lə·ner′ē, kul′ə-) *adj.* Of or pertaining to cooking or the kitchen. [< L *culina* kitchen]

cull (kul) *v.t.* **culled, cull·ing 1** To pick or sort out; collect. **2** To select and gather. —*n.* Something picked or sorted out and rejected. [< L *colligere* collect] **—cull′er** *n.*

culm¹ (kulm) *n. Bot.* The jointed, usu. hollow, stem of certain grasses. [< L *culmus* stalk] **—cul·mif·er·ous** (kul·mif′ər·əs) *adj.*

culm² (kulm) *n.* **1** Coal dust. **2** An inferior anthracite coal. [ME *colme*]

cul·mi·nate (kul′mə·nāt) *v.i.* **·nat·ed, ·nat·ing 1** To attain the highest point or degree. **2** To come to a complete result; reach a final effect. [< L *culmen* top, highest point] **—cul′mi·nal** *adj.*

cul·mi·na·tion (kul′mə·nā′shən) *n.* The highest point, condition, or degree.

cu·lottes (kʸōō·lots′) *n.pl.* A woman's garment having trouser legs cut full to resemble a skirt. [F]

cul·pa·ble (kul′pə·bəl) *adj.* Deserving of blame or censure. [< L *culpa* fault] **—cul′pa·bil′i·ty, cul′pa·ble·ness** *n.* **—cul′pa·bly** *adv.*

cul·prit (kul′prit) *n.* **1** A guilty person. **2** A person charged with crime, but not yet convicted. [< AF *cul prit,* short for *culpable* guilty + *prit* ready for trial]

cult (kult) *n.* **1** A system of religious observances. **2** Extravagant devotion to a person, cause, or thing. **3** The object of such devotion. **4** A group of persons having an excessive interest in something. [< L *cultus,* pp. of *colere* worship]

cul·ti·va·ble (kul′tə·və·bəl) *adj.* Capable of cultivation. Also **cul′ti·vat′a·ble. —cul′ti·va·bil′i·ty** *n.*

cul·ti·vate (kul′tə·vāt) *v.t.* **·vat·ed, ·vat·ing 1** To prepare and use (land), as by plowing, fertilizing, sowing, etc. **2** To loosen the soil about (growing plants) with a cultivator, hoe, etc. **3** To plant and tend. **4** To improve or develop by study, exercise, training, etc.: to *cultivate* the mind. **5** To study carefully; pay special attention to: to *cultivate* philosophy. **6** To try to make friends with: to *cultivate* one's teacher. [< L *cultus,* pp. of *colere* care for, worship]

cul·ti·va·tion (kul′tə·vā′shən) *n.* **1** The act or result of cultivating. **2** Refinement; culture.

cul·ti·va·tor (kul′tə·vā′tər) *n.* **1** One who cultivates. **2** A tool or machine used to loosen the ground and destroy weeds.

cul·tur·al (kul′chər·əl) *adj.* **1** Of, pertaining to, or developing culture. **2** Resulting from breeding or artificial cultivation, as certain varieties of fruits or plants. **—cul′tur·al·ly** *adv.*

cul·ture (kul′chər) *n.* **1** The sum total of the attainments and activities of any specific period, race, or people; civilization: the *culture* of the ancient Greeks. **2** The knowledge, good taste, refinement, etc., acquired by training the mind and faculties. **3** Development or improvement, as of the mind or body, by special care, training, etc.: physical *culture;* voice *culture.* **4** *Bacteriol.* **a** The proliferation of a specific microorganism in a specially prepared nutrient, or **culture medium. b** The organisms so developed. **5** The cultivation or raising of a plant or animal. **6** Cultivation of the soil; tillage. —*v.t.* **·tured, ·tur·ing 1** CULTIVATE. **2** *Bacteriol.* To produce in a culture. [< L *cultura* < *cultus.* See CULTIVATE.]

cul·tured (kul′chərd) *adj.* **1** Having or characterized by culture and refinement. **2** Produced by cultivation; cultivated. **—Syn. 1** civilized, refined, polished, enlightened.

cul·vert (kul′vərt) *n.* An artificial, covered channel for water, as under a road. [?]

cum·ber (kum′bər) *v.t.* **1** To hinder, hamper, obstruct, or burden. **2** To trouble or inconvenience. [?< OF *encombrer* hinder]

cum·ber·some (kum′bər·səm) *adj.* Clumsy, unwieldy, or burdensome. **—cum′ber·some·ly** *adv.* **—cum′ber·some·ness** *n.*

cum·brance (kum′brəns) *n.* ENCUMBRANCE.

cum·brous (kum′brəs) *adj.* CUMBERSOME. **—cum′brous·ly** *adv.* **—cum′brous·ness** *n.*

cum·in (kum′in) *n.* **1** A small plant related to parsley. **2** Its aromatic seeds, used as flavoring. Also **cum′min.** [< Gk. *kyminon*]

cum lau·de (kum lô′dē, kŏŏm lou′de) With praise: to be graduated *cum laude.* [L]

cum·mer·bund (kum′ər·bund) *n.* A broad sash worn as a waistband. [< Pers. *kamar* loin + *band* band]

cum·quat (kum′kwot) *n.* KUMQUAT.

cu·mu·late (kyōō′myə·lāt) *v.i.* **·lat·ed, ·lat·ing** To collect into a heap; accumulate. —*adj.* (*also* kyōō′myə·lit) Massed; heaped; accumulated. [< L *cumulus* a heap] **—cu′mu·la′tion** *n.*

cu·mu·la·tive (kyōō′myə·lə·tiv, -lā′-) *adj.* **1** Gathering volume, strength, value, etc., by successive additions. **2** Increasing or accruing, as unpaid interest or dividends, to be paid in the future. **—cu′mu·la·tive·ly** *adv.*

cu·mu·lo·nim·bus (kyōō′myə·lō·nim′bəs) *n.* A massive cloud rising vertically to great heights; thundercloud.

cu·mu·lus (kyōō′myə·ləs) *n. pl.* **·li** (-lī) **1** A mass; pile. **2** A dense cloud formation with a horizontal base and dome-shaped upper surfaces. [L] **—cu′mu·lous** *adj.*

cu·ne·ate (kyōō′nē·it, -āt) *adj.* Wedge-shaped. [< L *cuneus* wedge] **—cu′ne·ate·ly** *adv.*

cu·ne·i·form (kyōō·nē′ə·fôrm, kyōō′nē·ə·fôrm′) *adj.* Wedge-shaped, as the characters in some ancient Assyrian, Babylonian, and Persian inscriptions. —*n.* Cuneiform writing. [< L *cuneus* wedge + -FORM]

cun·ni·lin·gus (kun′ə·ling′gəs) *n.* Oral stimulation of the vulva or clitoris. [L, lit., one who licks the vulva]

cun·ning (kun′ing) *n.* **1** Skill in deception; guile; artifice. **2** Proficiency; skill; dexterity. —*adj.* **1** Crafty; tricky; artful; guileful. **2** Appealing because of prettiness, charm, smallness, etc. **3** Showing ingenuity, skill, dexterity, etc. [< OE *cunnung* < *cunnan* know] **—cun′ning·ly** *adv.* **—cun′·ning·ness** *n.*

cup (kup) *n.* **1** A small open vessel, usu. with a handle, used chiefly for drinking. **2** CUPFUL. **3** The contents of a cup: another *cup* of tea. **4** The ornamental vessel used in administering wine at the Eucharist; also, the wine itself. **5** One's lot in life; portion. **6** A cup-shaped vessel awarded as a prize. **7** In golf, a hole, or its metal lining, into which the ball drops. **8** Any cup-shaped object or part. **9** A usu. iced beverage, as of wine mixed with fruit and spices. —*v.t.* **cupped, cup·ping 1** To subject to or treat by cupping. **2** To shape like or place in or as in a cup. [< LL *cuppa*]

cup·board (kub′ərd) *n.* **1** A closet or cabinet with shelves, as for tableware. **2** Any small cabinet or closet.

cup·cake (kup′kāk′) *n.* A small cake baked in a cup-shaped mold.

cup·ful (kup′fŏŏl) *n. pl.* **·fuls 1** The quantity held by a cup. **2** In cooking, half a pint.

cu·pid (kyōō′pid) *n.* A representation of Cupid as a naked, winged boy with a bow and arrow.

Cu·pid (kyōō′pid) *Rom. Myth.* The god of love.

cu·pid·i·ty (kyōō·pid′ə·tē) *n.* An inordinate wish for possession, esp. of wealth; avarice. [< L *cupidus* desirous]

cu·po·la (kyōō′pə·lə) *n.* **1** A dome-shaped roof or ceiling. **2** A small structure, often with a dome-shaped top, built on a roof. —*v.t.* **·laed, ·la·ing** To provide with a cupola. [< L *cupula,* dim. of *cupa* tub, cask]

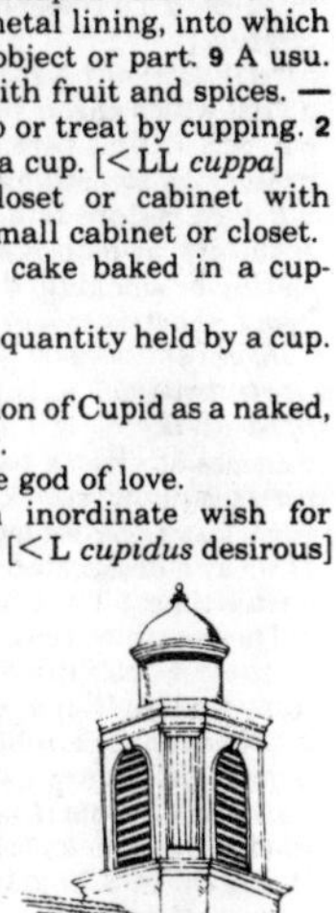

Cupola *def. 2*

cup·ping (kup′ing) *n.* The therapeutic application of a partial vacuum to an area of skin in order to draw blood to the surface.

cu·pre·ous (kyōō′prē·əs) *adj.* Of, pertaining to, containing, or like copper. [< L *cuprum* copper]

cu·pric (kyōō′prik) *adj.* Of, pertaining to, or containing bivalent copper.

cu·prous (kyōō′prəs) *adj. Chem.* Of, pertaining to, or containing univalent copper.

cu·prum (kyōō′prəm) *n.* COPPER. [L]
cur (kûr) *n.* **1** A mongrel dog. **2** A mean or malicious person. [Short for earlier *kur-dogge* snarling dog]
cur. currency; current.
cur·a·ble (kyŏŏr′ə·bəl) *adj.* Capable of being cured. —**cur′a·bil′i·ty, cur′a·ble·ness** *n.* —**cur′a·bly** *adv.*
cu·ra·cao (kyŏŏr′ə·sō′) *n.* A liqueur flavored with orange peel. [< *Curacao,* of the Netherlands Antilles]
cu·ra·cy (kyŏŏr′ə·sē) *n. pl.* **·cies** The position, duties, or term of office of a curate.
cu·ra·re (kyōō·rä′rē) *n.* **1** A toxic resinous extract of certain South American plants, originally used as an arrow poison, and in modern medicine as a muscle relaxant. **2** The plant from which this extract is obtained. Also **cu·ra·ra** (kyōō·rä′rə), **cu·ra′ri.** [<Tupian]
cu·rate (kyŏŏr′it) *n.* A clergyman assisting a parish priest, rector, or vicar. [<Med. L *cura* care or cure (of souls)] —**cu′rate·ship** *n.*
cur·a·tive (kyŏŏr′ə·tiv) *adj.* Pertaining to or used in the curing of disease. —**cur′a·tive·ly** *adv.*
cu·ra·tor (kyōō·rā′tər, kyōō′rā′tər) *n.* A person having charge, as of a museum or library; a superintendent. [< L *curare* care for < *cura* care] —**cu·ra·to·ri·al** (kyŏŏr′ə·tôr′·ē·əl, -tō′rē-) *adj.* —**cu·ra′tor·ship** *n.*
curb (kûrb) *n.* **1** A chain or strap to brace a bit against a horse's lower jaw, used to check the horse when the reins are pulled. **2** Anything that restrains or controls. **3** A raised border or edge, as that which forms a gutter along a street. **4** A market dealing in securities not listed on a stock exchange. —*v.t.* **1** To hold in check; control, with or as with reins. **2** To provide with a curb. **3** To lead (a dog) off a curb for defecation in the street. [< OF *courbe* curved < L *curvus*] —**Syn.** *v.* **1** restrain, subdue, repress, manage.
curb·ing (kûr′bing) *n.* **1** Material for making a curb. **2** A curb or a part of a curb.
curb·stone (kûrb′stōn′) *n.* A stone or a row of stones making up a curb.
curd (kûrd) *n. Often pl.* The solids separated from the watery whey of milk. —*v.t. & v.i.* CURDLE. [Metathetic var. of CRUD] —**curd′i·ness** *n.* —**curd′ly, curd′y** *adj.*
cur·dle (kûrd′l) *v.t. & v.i.* **·dled, ·dling** **1** To change or turn to curds. **2** To thicken; congeal. **3** To turn sour. [Freq. of CURD, *v.*]
cure (kyŏŏr) *n.* **1** A recovery from an unhealthy condition. **2** That which effects such a recovery, as a drug, treatment, etc. **3** Spiritual care: the *cure* of souls. **4** A manner of preserving something, as meat or fish. —*v.* **cured, cur·ing** *v.t.* **1** To restore to a healthy condition. **2** To remedy or eradicate, as a disease or bad habit. **3** To preserve, as by salting or smoking. **4** To vulcanize, as rubber. —*v.i.* **5** To bring about recovery. **6** To be preserved, as meat. [<L *cura* care]
cu·ré (kyōō·rā′) *n.* In France, a parish priest. [F, curate]
cure-all (kyŏŏr′ôl′) *n.* That which is asserted to cure all diseases or evils; a panacea.
cur·few (kûr′fyōō) *n.* **1** A regulation that specified persons leave the streets or that specified establishments close at a designated time. **2** The sounding of a signal at such a time. **3** The time at which a curfew goes into effect. **4** The length of time a curfew is in effect. [<OF *couvrir* to cover + *feu* fire]
cu·ri·a (kyŏŏr′ē·ə) *n. pl.* **·ae** (-ē) **1** A feudal court of justice. **2** *Often cap.* The collective body of officials that aids the pope in the government and administration of the Roman Catholic Church. [L] —**cu′ri·al** *adj.*
cu·rie (kyŏŏr′ē, kyōō·rē′) *n. Physics* A unit of radioactivity, equal to 3.70 x 10^{10} nuclear disintegrations per second. [<Marie *Curie,* 1867–1934, Polish-born Fr. chemist]
cu·ri·o (kyŏŏr′ē·ō) *n. pl.* **·os** An object considered rare or unusual. [Short for CURIOSITY]
cu·ri·os·i·ty (kyŏŏr′ē·os′ə·tē) *n. pl.* **·ties** **1** A desire for knowledge. **2** Inquisitive interest in things which are not of proper concern; nosiness. **3** A person or thing that excites interest or inquiry. [<L *curiosus.* See CURIOUS.]
cu·ri·ous (kyŏŏr′ē·əs) *adj.* **1** Eager for knowledge. **2** Too inquisitive; prying. **3** Novel; odd; strange; mysterious. [< L *curiosus* < *cura* care] —**cu′ri·ous·ly** *adv.* —**cu′ri·ous·ness** *n.* —**Syn.** **1** inquiring, inquisitive, questioning. **2** meddlesome, nosy, intrusive.

cu·ri·um (kyŏŏr′ē·əm) *n.* An artificially produced radioactive element (symbol Cm). [<Marie *Curie,* 1867–1934, and Pierre *Curie,* 1859–1906, Fr. chemists]
curl (kûrl) *v.t.* **1** To twist into ringlets or curves, as the hair. **2** To form into a curved or spiral shape. —*v.i.* **3** To become curved; take a spiral shape. **4** To play at the game of curling. —*n.* **1** Anything coiled or spiral, as a ringlet. **2** The act of curling or the condition of being curled. [< MDu. *crulle* curly]
cur·lew (kûr′lyōō) *n.* Any of a genus of shore birds with long legs and down-curved bills. [<OF *corlieu*]

Curlew

curl·i·cue (kûr′li·kyōō) *n.* An odd or fancy curl or twist, as a flourish with a pen. Also **curl′y·cue.** [< CURLY + CUE[1]]
curl·ing (kûr′ling) *n.* A game in which the players slide a heavy, round weight, or **curling stone,** along a narrow strip of ice toward a target circle.
curling iron An implement of metal, used when heated for curling the hair. Also **curling irons.**
curl·y (kûr′lē) *adj.* **curl·i·er, curl·i·est** **1** Having curls. **2** Tending to curl, as hair. **3** Marked by a wavy grain. —**curl′i·ness** *n.*
cur·mudg·eon (kər·muj′ən) *n.* A bad-tempered, ill-mannered man. [?] —**cur·mudg′eon·ly** *adj.*
cur·rant (kûr′ənt) *n.* **1** A small, round, acid berry, used for making jelly. **2** Any of a genus of hardy shrubs whose fruit is the red, white, or black currant. **3** A small seedless raisin from the Levant. [< AF *(raisins de) Corauntz* (raisins from) Corinth]
cur·ren·cy (kûr′ən·sē) *n. pl.* **·cies** **1** The money in general use in any country. **2** A circulation or passing from person to person. **3** General acceptance; prevalence; use.
cur·rent (kûr′ənt) *adj.* **1** Belonging to the present time; now in progress or in effect. **2** Generally accepted. **3** Circulating; going around. —*n.* **1** That part of any body of water or air which has a more or less steady flow in a definite direction. **2** *Electr.* **a** A flow of electricity through a conductor. **b** The measure of this flow. **3** Any general course, tendency, trend, or drift. [<L *currere* to run] —**cur′rent·ly** *adv.* —**cur′rent·ness** *n.*
cur·ric·u·lum (kə·rik′yə·ləm) *n. pl.* **·lums** or **·la** (-lə) **1** A regular or particular course of study, as in a college. **2** All of the courses offered by an educational institution. [<L, a race < *currere* run] —**cur·ric′u·lar** *adj.*
cur·rish (kûr′ish) *adj.* Like a cur; mean; nasty. —**cur′rish·ly** *adv.* —**cur′rish·ness** *n.*
cur·ry[1] (kûr′ē) *v.t.* **·ried, ·ry·ing** **1** To rub down and clean with a currycomb or other implement; groom (a horse, dog, etc). **2** To prepare (tanned hides) for use, as by soaking, beating, etc. —**curry favor** To seek favor, as by adulation and subserviency. [<OF *carreier, conreder* make ready, prepare]
cur·ry[2] (kûr′ē) *n. pl.* **·ries** **1** A cooked dish consisting of meats, fish, etc., seasoned with curry powder. **2** CURRY POWDER. **3** A sauce flavored with curry powder. —*v.t.* **·ried, ·ry·ing** To flavor with curry. [<Tamil *kari* sauce]
cur·ry·comb (kûr′ē·kōm′) *n.* A comb consisting of a series of upright serrated ridges, for grooming horses. —*v.t.* To comb with a currycomb.
curry powder A powdered condiment, prepared from turmeric, coriander, and other spices.
curse (kûrs) *v.* **cursed or curst, curs·ing** *v.t.* **1** To invoke evil or injury upon; damn. **2** To swear at. **3** To cause evil or injury to. —*v.i.* **4** To utter curses; swear; blaspheme. —*n.* **1** A blasphemous or profane oath. **2** A calling on a god to visit trouble or evil upon some person or thing. **3** A source of trouble or evil. **4** The evil which comes as a result of a curse. **5** A person or thing that is cursed. [<OE *cursian*]
curs·ed (kûr′sid, kûrst) *adj.* **1** Under a curse. **2** Deserving a curse; hateful; detestable. —**curs·ed·ly** (kûr′sid·lē) *adv.* —**curs′ed·ness** *n.*
cur·sive (kûr′siv) *adj.* Running; flowing: said of writing in which the letters are joined. —*n.* **1** A letter or character

used in cursive writing. 2 In printing, a type face that resembles handwriting. [<L *cursus* < *currere* to run] — **cur'sive·ly** *adv.* —**cur'sive·ness** *n.*

cur·sor (kûr'sər) *n.* A pointer on a computer screen that shows the position where an operation is taking place.

cur·so·ry (kûr'sər·ē) *adj.* Rapid and superficial; hasty, with no attention to detail. [<L *cursor* a runner < *currere* run] —**cur'so·ri·ly** *adv.* —**cur'so·ri·ness** *n.*

curst (kûrst) A *p.t.* & *p.p.* of CURSE. —*adj.* Cursed.

curt (kûrt) *adj.* 1 Concise; brief; terse. 2 Short and sharp in manner; brusque; abrupt. [<L *curtus* shortened] —**curt'ly** *adv.* —**curt'ness** *n.*

cur·tail (kər·tāl') *v.t.* To cut off or cut short; abbreviate; lessen; reduce. [<obs. *curtal* short; infl. in form by TAIL] —**cur·tail'er, cur·tail'ment** *n.*

cur·tain (kûr'tən) *n.* 1 A piece of fabric, often adjustable, hung for decoration, concealment, or to shut out light, as before a wall, window, doorway, etc. 2 Something that conceals, covers, or separates like a curtain. 3 In a theater, the drapery hanging at the front of a stage, drawn up or aside to reveal the stage. 4 *pl. Slang* The end; death. —*v.t.* 1 To supply or adorn with or as with a curtain or curtains. 2 To conceal or shut off as with a curtain; cover. [<LL *cortina*]

curtain call The appearance of a performer or performers to acknowledge applause from an audience.

curtain raiser A short play, sketch, etc., presented before a longer or more important work.

curt·sy (kûrt'sē) *n. pl.* **·sies** A gesture of civility or respect, made esp. by women, consisting of a slight lowering of the body with a bending of the knees. —*v.i.* **·sied, ·sy·ing** To make such a gesture. Also **curt'sey.** [Var. of COURTESY]

cur·va·ceous (kûr·vā'shəs) *adj. Informal* Having voluptuous curves; shapely in form: said of a woman.

cur·va·ture (kûr'və·chər) *n.* 1 The act of curving or the state of being curved. 2 A curve or curved part, often an abnormal one: *curvature* of the spine.

curve (kûrv) *n.* 1 A line continuously bent so that no portion of it is straight, as the arc of a circle. 2 The form, movement, or path of a curve. 3 Something having the form of a curve. 4 An instrument for drawing curves, used by draftsmen. 5 *Math.* A set of connected points having only length as a variable measure. 6 In baseball, a pitched ball so thrown that it veers to one side before crossing the plate. —*v.* **curved, curv·ing** *v.t.* 1 To cause to assume the form of a curve. —*v.i.* 2 To assume the form of a curve. 3 To move in a curve, as a projectile or ball; bend. [<L *curvus* bent]

cur·vet (kûr'vit) *n.* A light, low leap of a horse, with the forelegs and hind legs lifted and brought down an instant apart. —*v.t.* & *v.i.* (also kər·vet') **·vet·ted** or **·vet·ed, ·vet·ting** or **·vet·ing** To make or cause to make a curvet. [<Ital. *corva* bent]

cur·vi·lin·e·ar (kûr'və·lin'ē·ər) *adj.* Formed or enclosed by curved lines. Also **cur'vi·lin'e·al.**

cush·ion (ko͝osh'ən) *n.* 1 A flexible bag or casing filled with some soft or elastic material, as feathers, air, etc. 2 Anything resembling a cushion in appearance, construction, or application, as a device to deaden the jar or impact of parts. 3 The elastic rim of a billiard table. —*v.t.* 1 To place, seat, or arrange on or as on a cushion. 2 To provide with a cushion. 3 To cover or hide as with a cushion. 4 To absorb the shock or effect of. [<OF *coissin*]

Cush·it·ic (ko͝osh·it'ik) *n.* A group of Hamitic languages spoken in Ethiopia and Somaliland. —*adj.* Of this group of languages.

cush·y (ko͝osh'ē) *adj. Slang* **cush·i·er, cush·i·est** Comfortable; agreeable; easy; pleasant. [<CUSHION]

cusp (kusp) *n.* 1 A point or pointed end. 2 *Astron.* Either point of a crescent moon. 3 A prominence or point, as on the crown of a tooth. [<L *cuspis* a point]

cus·pate (kus'pāt, kus'pit) *adj.* 1 Having a cusp or cusps. 2 Cusp-shaped. Also **cus'pat·ed, cusped** (kuspt).

cus·pid (kus'pid) *n.* A canine tooth. —*adj.* CUSPIDATE.

cus·pi·date (kus'pə·dāt) *adj.* Having a cusp or cusps. Also **cus'pi·dat'ed, cus·pi·dal** (kus'pə·dəl).

cus·pi·dor (kus'pə·dôr) *n.* A spittoon. [<Pg. *cuspir* to spit <L *conspuere*]

cuss (kus) *Informal v.t.* & *v.i.* To curse. —*n.* 1 A curse. 2 A person or animal, often one that is odd or perverse. [Var. of CURSE]

cuss·ed (kus'id) *adj. Informal* 1 Cursed. 2 Mean; perverse. —**cuss'ed·ly** *adv.* —**cuss'ed·ness** *n.*

cus·tard (kus'tərd) *n.* A mixture of milk, eggs, sugar, and flavoring, either boiled or baked. [Alter. of earlier *crustade* a type of pie <L *crusta* crust]

cus·to·di·an (kus·tō'dē·ən) *n.* A guardian, caretaker, or janitor. —**cus·to'di·an·ship'** *n.*

cus·to·dy (kus'tə·dē) *n. pl.* **·dies** 1 A keeping; guardianship. 2 The state of being held in keeping or under guard; imprisonment. [<L *custos* guardian] —**cus·to·di·al** (kus·tō'dē·əl) *adj.*

cus·tom (kus'təm) *n.* 1 An ordinary or usual manner of doing or acting. 2 The habitual practice of a community or people; common usage. 3 *Law* An old and general usage that has obtained the force of law. 4 Business support; patronage. 5 *pl.* **a** A tariff or duty by a government upon goods imported or exported. **b** The government agency which collects such tariffs or duties. —*adj.* 1 Made to order. 2 Specializing in made-to-order goods: a *custom* tailor. [<L *consuetudo*]

cus·tom·ar·y (kus'tə·mer'ē) *adj.* 1 Conforming to or established by custom; habitual. 2 *Law* Holding or held by custom. —*n. pl.* **·ar·ies** A group of laws established by custom, as for a manor, district, etc. —**cus·tom·ar·i·ly** (kus'tə·mer'ə·lē) *adv.* —**cus'tom·ar'i·ness** *n.*

cus·tom-built (kus'təm·bilt') *adj.* Built to individual specifications.

cus·tom·er (kus'təm·ər) *n.* 1 One who gives his custom or trade; a purchaser. 2 *Informal* A person to be dealt with; a fellow: an ugly *customer.*

cus·tom·house (kus'təm·hous') *n.* The place where entries of imports are made, vessels cleared, and duties collected.

cus·tom-made (kus'təm·mād') *adj.* Made to order.

cut (kut) *v.* **cut, cut·ting** *v.t.* 1 To pierce, gash, or pass through with or as with a sharp edge. 2 To strike sharply, as with a whip. 3 To affect deeply; hurt the feelings of. 4 To divide, sever, or carve into parts or segments. 5 To fell, hew, or chop down, as a tree or timber: often with *down.* 6 To mow or reap, as grain. 7 To shape, prepare, or make, as gems or clothing. 8 To hollow out; excavate. 9 To trim, shear, or pare. 10 To excise; edit out. 11 To reduce or lessen: to *cut* prices. 12 To dilute or weaken: to *cut* whisky. 13 To dissolve or break down, as fat globules: to *cut* grease. 14 To cross or intersect. 15 *Slang* To discontinue; stop. 16 *Informal* **a** To ignore socially; snub. **b** To stay away from willfully, as work or classes. 17 To divide, as a pack of cards before dealing. 18 In racket sports, to chop (the ball) so it will spin and bound sharply and irregularly. 19 To turn the wheels of, as an automobile, so as to make the vehicle turn sharply. 20 To perform; present: to *cut* a caper. 21 To grow or acquire: to *cut* a tooth. —*v.i.* 22 To cut, cleave, or make an incision; do the work of a sharp edge. 23 To admit of being severed or cut. 24 To use an instrument for cutting. 25 To cause physical or mental distress: winds that *cut; cut* by his nastiness. 26 To divide a card pack before dealing. 27 In sports, to chop the ball. 28 To move or pass through by the shortest or most direct route. —**cut a figure** 1 To make a fine appearance. 2 To be of importance. 3 To make an impression. —**cut back** 1 To shorten by removing the end. 2 To curtail or cancel, as a contract, before fulfillment. 3 To run or dash erratically; change direction suddenly. —**cut down** To reduce the length or amount of; shorten; curtail. —**cut in** 1 To interrupt a dancing couple in order to take the place of one partner. 2 To interrupt, as a conversation. 3 To move into (a line or queue) out of turn. —**cut it fine** To make precise calculations or distinctions. —**cut loose** To speak or behave without restraint. —**cut off** 1 To put an end to; stop or shut off. 2 To interrupt. 3 To intercept. 4 To sever. 5 To disinherit. —**cut out** 1 *Informal* To leave quickly. 2

To displace (another); supplant, as a rival. **3** To quit or renounce, as smoking. **4** To form or make by or as if by cutting. **—cut up 1** To slice or cut into pieces. **2** *Slang* To behave in an unruly manner. *—n.* **1** The act of cutting. **2** An opening, cleft, or wound made by an edged instrument. **3** A groove, channel, or passage, as a road through a mountain. **4** A cutting motion or stroke. **5** A part or section removed by cutting. **6** That which cuts or hurts the feelings. **7** A direct way or route. **8** Fashion, form, or style: the *cut* of a suit. **9** An engraved block or plate used in printing; also, an impression made from it. **10** A reduction or decrease. **11** A refusal to recognize an acquaintance; snub. **12** *Informal* An intentional failure to attend a class, etc. **13** *Informal* A share. *—adj.* **1** That has been cut. **2** Formed or affected by cutting. **3** Reduced. [ME *cutten*]

cu·ta·ne·ous (kyōō·tā′nē·əs) *adj.* Of, pertaining to, affecting, or on the skin. [<L *cutis* skin]

cut·a·way (kut′ə·wā′) *n.* A man's coat with the front corners cut slopingly away from the waist down to the back. Also **cutaway coat.**

cut·back (kut′bak′) *n.* A reduction or cessation, as of production or in supply: a *cutback* in fuel.

cute (kyōōt) *adj.* **cut·er, cut·est** *Informal* **1** Pretty or dainty; attractive. **2** Clever or sharp. **3** Artificially striving for effect. [Var. of ACUTE] **—cute′ly** *adv.* **—cute′ness** *n.*

cut glass Glass ornamented by cutting or grinding and polishing.

cu·ti·cle (kyōō′ti·kəl) *n.* **1** The outer layer of cells that protect the true skin; epidermis. **2** The crescent of toughened skin around the base of a fingernail or toenail. [<L *cutis* skin] **—cu·tic′u·lar** *adj.*

cu·tin (kyōō′tin) *n.* A waxy, waterproof film on the leaves, stems, etc., of plants [<L *cutis* skin + -IN]

cut·lass (kut′ləs) *n.* A short, swordlike weapon, often curved, formerly used by sailors. Also **cut′·las.** [<F *couteau* knife]

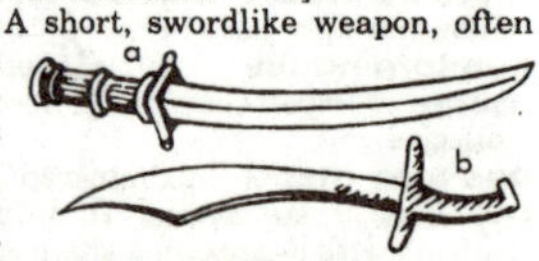

Cutlasses
a. British, 10th century.
b. German, 15th century.

cut·ler (kut′lər) *n.* One who manufactures or deals in cutlery. [<L *culter* knife]

cut·ler·y (kut′lər·ē) *n.* **1** Cutting instruments, as knives and shears, esp. those for use at the dinner table. **2** The occupation of a cutler. [<OF *coutelier* cutler]

cut·let (kut′lit) *n.* **1** A thin piece of meat from the ribs or leg, for broiling or frying. **2** A flat croquette of chopped meat, fish, etc. [<F *côte* rib <L *costa*]

cut·off (kut′ôf′, -of′) *n.* **1** The act of cutting off or terminating; cessation. **2** SHORT CUT. **3** A mechanism that cuts off the flow of a fuel or fluid. **3** The point at which flow is thus cut off. *—adj.* Terminating; ending.

cut·out (kut′out′) *n.* **1** *Electr.* A switch or other device for bypassing an element of a circuit. **2** A device to let the exhaust gases from an internal-combustion engine pass directly to the air without passing through the muffler. **3** Something that is or may be cut out of something else.

cut·o·ver (kut′ō′vər) *adj.* Having the timber cut: *cutover* land.

cut·purse (kut′pûrs′) *n.* A pickpocket.

cut-rate (kut′rāt′) *adj.* **1** Available at a reduced price or rate. **2** Offering goods or services at reduced prices or rates.

cut·ter (kut′ər) *n.* **1** One who cuts, shapes, or fits anything by cutting. **2** That which cuts, as a tool or a machine. **3** A boat carried by a large ship to transport passengers and supplies. **4** A small armed boat, esp. one in government service. **5** A sailboat or yacht having a single mast. **6** A small sleigh usu. drawn by one horse.

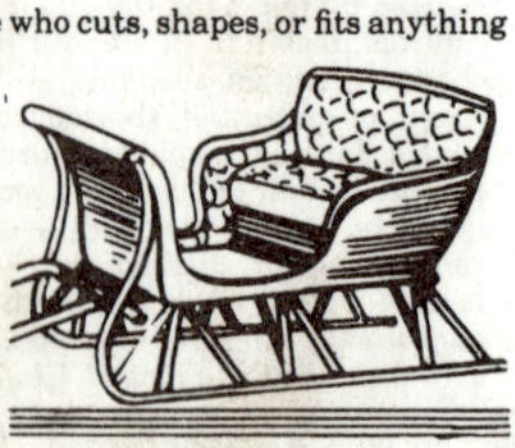

Cutter *def. 6*

cut·throat (kut′thrōt′) *adj.* **1** Murderous. **2** Ruinous; merciless: *cut-throat* competition. *—n.* A murderer.

cut·ting (kut′ing) *adj.* **1** Adapted to cut; sharp. **2** Piercing; penetrating; chilling. **3** Tending to wound the feelings; sarcastic; bitter. *—n.* **1** Something cut off or out. **2** *Bot.* A plant shoot cut off for rooting or grafting. **3** *Chiefly Brit.* A clipping from a newspaper or magazine.

cut·tle·bone (kut′l·bōn′) *n.* The internal calcareous plate of a cuttlefish, used as a dietary supplement for birds and, when powdered, as a polishing agent.

cut·tle·fish (kut′l·fish′) *n. pl.* **·fish** or **·fish·es** Any of various marine mollusks with lateral fins, ten sucker-bearing arms, and an internal calcareous skeleton. [<OE *cudele* + FISH]

cut·worm (kut′wûrm′) *n.* The larva of various moths that feeds on young plants, destroying the stems at ground level.

CWO, C.W.O. Chief Warrant Officer.

C.W.O., c.w.o. cash with order.

CWS Chemical Warfare Service.

cwt. hundredweight.

-cy *suffix* **1** Quality, state, or condition of being: *bankruptcy.* **2** Rank, order, or position of: *chaplaincy, baronetcy.* [<L *-cia* or <Gk. *-kia*]

cy·a·nate (sī′ə·nāt) *n.* A salt or ester of cyanic acid.

cy·an·ic (sī·an′ik) *adj.* **1** Of, pertaining to, or containing cyanogen. **2** Blue or bluish.

cyanic acid A volatile liquid compound with a pungent odor and caustic properties, that is stable at low temperatures only.

cy·a·nide (sī′ə·nīd) *n.* A compound of cyanogen with a metallic element or radical: potassium *cyanide.* *—v.t.* **·nid·ed, ·nid·ing** To subject to the action of cyanide: to extract gold by *cyaniding* the ore. **—cy′a·ni·da′tion** *n.*

cy·an·o·gen (sī·an′ə·jən) *n. Chem.* **1** A colorless, poisonous, gaseous compound of carbon and nitrogen, having an almondlike odor. **2** The univalent radical composed of carbon and nitrogen. [<Gk. *kyanos* dark blue + -GEN]

cy·a·no·sis (sī′ə·nō′sis) *n.* A blue color of the skin due to inadequate aeration of the blood. [<Gk. *kyanos* dark blue + -OSIS] **—cy·a·not·ic** (sī·ə·not′ik) *adj.*

cy·ber·nate (sī′bər·nāt) *v.t.* **·nat·ed, ·nat·ing** To subject to cybernation.

cy·ber·na·tion (sī′bər·nā′shən) *n.* Automation combined with computer control, requiring little or no human intervention. [< CYBERN(ETICS) + -ATION]

cy·ber·net·ics (sī′bər·net′iks) *n. pl. (construed as sing.)* The study of the control processes in physical and biological systems. [<Gk. *kybernētēs* steersman] **—cy′ber·net′ic** *adj.*

cy·cla·mate (sī′klə·māt) *n.* A synthetic organic salt, usu. of sodium or calcium, used as a nonnutritive sweetener.

cyc·la·men (sik′lə·mən, -men, sīk′-) *n.* An Old World plant related to the primrose, with showy white, pink, or crimson flowers. [<Gk. *kyklaminos*]

cy·cle (sī′kəl) *n.* **1** A period of time during which one sequence of a succession of regularly recurring phenomena or events is completed. **2** A sequence of phenomena or events that recur regularly in the same order. **3** A very long period of time; eon; age. **4** All of the legends, poems, romances, etc., relating to one period, person, event, etc. **5** A series of poems, songs, etc., dealing with a single theme. **6** A bicycle, tricycle, etc. *—v.i.* **cy·cled, cy·cling 1** To pass through or occur in cycles. **2** To ride a bicycle, tricycle, or the like. *—v.t.* **3** To put through a cycle or process. [<Gk. *kyklos* circle]

cy·clic (sī′klik, sik′lik) *adj.* **1** Of, pertaining to, or recurring in cycles. **2** *Chem.* Characterized by a closed chain or ring formation, as benzene. Also **cy′cli·cal. —cy′cli·cal·ly** *adv.*

cy·clist (sī′klist) *n.* One who rides a cycle, as a bicycle.

cyclo- *combining form* Circle or circular: *cyclometer.* [<Gk. *kyklos* circle]

cy·cloid (sī′kloid) *adj.* Circular. **—cy·cloi′dal** *adj.*

cy·clom·e·ter (sī·klom′ə·tər) *n.* An instrument for recording the rotations of a wheel, used to show the distance traveled by a vehicle. [<CYCLO- + -METER]

cy·clone (sī′klōn) *n.* **1** *Meteorol.* A storm or system of winds rotating clockwise in the southern hemisphere or counterclockwise in the northern hemisphere, about a center of low atmospheric pressure. 2 Loosely, any violent and destructive whirling windstorm. [<Gk. *kykloein* move in a circle] —**cy·clon·ic (sī·klon′ik) or ·i·cal** *adj.* —**cy·clon′i·cal·ly** *adv.*

cy·clo·pe·an (sī′klə·pē′ən) *adj.* 1 *Usu. cap.* Pertaining to the Cyclopes. 2 Huge; gigantic.

cy·clo·pe·di·a (sī′klə·pē′dē·ə) *n.* ENCYCLOPEDIA. Also **cy′·clo·pae′di·a.** [Short for ENCYCLOPEDIA] —**cy′clo·pe′dic, cy′·clo·pae′dic** *adj.* —**cy′clo·pe′dist, cy′clo·pae′dist** *n.*

Cy·clops (sī′klops) *pl.* **Cy·clo·pes** (sī·klō′pēz) *Gk. Myth.* Any of a race of one-eyed giants.

cy·clo·ram·a (sī′klə·ram′ə, -rä′mə) *n.* 1 A series of pictures on the interior of a cylindrical surface, appearing as in natural perspective to a spectator standing in the center. 2 A backdrop curtain or wall, often concave, used on theater stages to give the illusion of unlimited space. [< CYCLO- + Gk. *horama* a view] —**cy′clo·ram′ic** *adj.*

cy·clo·spo·rine (sī′klə·spôr′ēn, -spōr′-) *n.* A drug useful in reducing the body's natural rejection of organ transplants by partially repressing the immune system.

cy·clo·tron (sī′klə·tron) *n. Physics* An apparatus for accelerating charged particles to high energies in spiral paths by means of a fluctuating magnetic field. [<CYCLO- + (ELEC)TRON]

cyg·net (sig′nit) *n.* A young swan. [<Gk. *kyknos*]

Cyg·nus (sig′nəs) *n.* The Swan, a N constellation.

cyl. cylinder; cylindrical.

cyl·in·der (sil′in·dər) *n.* 1 *Geom.* A solid described by the circumference of a circle as its center moves along a straight line, the ends of the solid being parallel, equal circles. 2 Any object, container, etc., having this shape. 3 Any cylindrical portion of a machine, esp. one of a motor in which a piston moves. 4 The rotating chamber that holds the cartridges of a revolver. • See REVOLVER. [<Gk. *kylindros*<*kylindein* to roll]

cy·lin·dri·cal (si·lin′dri·kəl) *adj.* 1 Of or pertaining to a cylinder. 2 Having the form or shape of a cylinder. Also **cy·lin′dric.**—**cy·lin′dri·cal·ly** *adv.*—**cy·lin·dri·cal·i·ty** (si·lin′dri·kal′ə·tē) *n.*

cym·bal (sim′bəl) *n.* A platelike metallic musical instrument, played by being struck with a drumstick or brush or by striking one against another. [<Gk. *kymbē* cup, hollow of a vessel] —**cym′bal·ist** *n.*

cyme (sīm) *n.* A flat-topped flower cluster in which the central flowers bloom first. [<L *cyma* a wave, a sprout]—**cy·mose** (sī′mōs, sī·mōs′) *adj.*

Cym·ric (kim′rik, sim′-) *adj.* Relating to the Cymry. —*n.* The Welsh language.

Cym·ry (kim′rē, sim′-) *n.* A collective name for the Welsh and their Cornish and Breton kin.

cyn·ic (sin′ik) *n.* A person who tends to question the virtues, values, and sincerity of others. —*adj.* CYNICAL. [< Gk. *kynikos* doglike]

Cyn·ic (sin′ik) *n.* One of a sect of ancient Greek philosophers who held that virtue was the ultimate goal of life, their doctrine gradually coming to symbolize insolent self-righteousness. —*adj.* Belonging to or like the Cynics: also **Cyn′i·cal.**

cyn·i·cal (sin′i·kəl) *adj.* 1 Given to questioning people's virtues, values, and sincerity; skeptical; pessimistic. 2 Mocking; sarcastic; sneering. —**cyn′i·cal·ly** *adv.*

cyn·i·cism (sin′ə·siz′əm) *n.* 1 The state or quality of being cynical. 2 A cynical act, remark, etc.

cy·no·sure (sī′nə·shŏŏr, sin′ə-) *n.* An object of general interest or attention. [<Gk. *kynosoura* the constellation Ursa Minor<*kynos* dog + *oura* tail]

cy·pher (sī′fər) *n.* CIPHER.

cy·press (sī′prəs) *n.* 1 Any of a genus of evergreen conifers growing in warm climates. 2 Any of various similar trees, as the white cedar. 3 The wood of these trees. [<Gk. *kyparissos*]

Cyp·ri·an (sip′rē·ən) *adj.* Of or pertaining to Cyprus, its people, or their language. —*n.* CYPRIOT.

cyp·ri·noid (sip′rə·noid, si·prī′-) *adj.* Carplike. —*n.* Any of numerous freshwater fishes related to carp, as the minnow, dace, goldfish, etc. Also **cyp′ri·nid** (-nid). [<Gk. *kyprinos* carp]

Cyp·ri·ot (sip′rē·ət) *n.* A native or citizen of Cyprus. —*adj.* Of or pertaining to Cyprus. Also **Cyp′ri·ote** (-ōt).

Cy·prus (sī′prəs) *n.* A republic located on an island in the Mediterranean S of Turkey, 3,572 sq. mi., cap. Nicosia. • See map at TURKEY.

Cy·ril·lic (si·ril′ik) *adj.* Of or pertaining to the alphabet used in the Soviet Union, Bulgaria, and other Slavic countries.

cyst (sist) *n.* A saclike structure in a plant or animal containing liquid or semisolid material. [<Gk. *kystis* bladder] —**cys′tic** *adj.*

cystic fibrosis A hereditary disease marked by copious mucous secretion, breathing difficulty, enzyme deficiencies, and loss of weight.

cys·to·scope (sis′tə·skōp) *n.* A catheter with a device for viewing the interior of the urinary bladder. [<Gk. *kystis* bladder + -SCOPE] —**cys·to·scop·ic** (sis′tə·skop′ik) *adj.* —**cys·tos·co·py** (sis·tos′kə·pē) *n.*

-cyte *combining form* Cell: *phagocyte.* [<Gk. *kytos* hollow vessel]

cyto- *combining form* Cell: *cytology.* [<Gk. *kytos* hollow vessel]

cy·tol·o·gy (sī·tol′ə·jē) *n.* The branch of biology concerned with the structure and functions of cells. —**cy·to·log·ic** (sī′tə·loj′ik) or **·i·cal** *adj.* —**cy′to·log′i·cal·ly** *adv.* —**cy·tol′o·gist** *n.*

cy·to·plasm (sī′tə·plaz′əm) *n.* The colloidal substance surrounding the nucleus and other structures in living cells. —**cy′to·plas′mic** *adj.*

cy·to·plast (sī′tə·plast) *n.* The cytoplasm in a single cell. —**cy′to·plas′tic** *adj.*

C.Z. Canal Zone.

czar (zär) *n.* 1 An emperor or absolute monarch; esp., one of the former emperors of Russia. 2 A person having great power or authority. [<Russ. *tsare*, ult. <L *Caesar* Caesar] —**czar′ism** *n.* —**czar′ist** *adj., n.*

czar·e·vitch (zär′ə·vich) *n.* The eldest son of a czar of Russia.

cza·ri·na (zä·rē′nə) *n.* The wife of a czar of Russia. Also **cza·rit·za** (zä·rit′sə).

Czech (chek) *n.* 1 A native or citizen of Czechoslovakia. 2 The language of Czechoslovakia. —*adj.* Of Czechoslovakia, its people, or their language.

Czech·o·slo·va·ki·a (chek′ə·slō·vä′kē·ə, -vak′ē·ə) *n.* A republic of CEN. Europe, 49,368 sq. mi., cap. Prague. —**Czech′o·slo′vak, Czech′o·slo·va′ki·an** *adj., n.*

D

D, d (dē) *n. pl.* **D's, d's, Ds, ds** (dēz) **1** The fourth letter of the English alphabet. **2** Any spoken sound representing the letter *D* or *d*. **3** *Music* The second tone in the diatonic scale of C major. **4** Something shaped like a D. **5** In Roman notation, the symbol for 500. —*adj.* Shaped like a D.

D deuterium.

D. December; Democrat(ic); Dutch.

d. date; daughter; day(s); dead; degree; delete; died; dose; *Brit.* penny (L *denarius*) or pence (L *denarii*).

D.A. District Attorney.

dab[1] (dab) *n.* **1** One of various small flounders. **2** Any flatfish. [?]

dab[2] (dab) *n.* **1** A gentle blow; a pat. **2** A small amount of something. —*v.t. & v.i.* **dabbed, dab·bing 1** To strike softly; tap. **2** To peck. **3** To pat with something soft and damp. **4** To apply (paint, etc.) with light strokes. [Prob. < MDu. *dabben* fumble, dabble] —**dab'ber** *n.*

dab·ble (dab'əl) *v.* **·bled, ·bling** *v.i.* **1** To play, as with the hands, in a liquid; splash gently. **2** To do superficially or without serious involvement; to *dabble* in art. —*v.t.* **3** To wet slightly; bespatter. [Freq. of DAB[2]] —**dab'bler** *n.*

dab·chick (dab'chik) *n.* **1** A small grebe of Europe. **2** The pied-billed grebe of North America. [< DAB[2] + CHICK]

da ca·po (dä kä'pō) *Music* From the beginning. [Ital.]

dace (dās) *n. pl.* **dac·es** or **dace** Any of a genus of small freshwater fishes related to the carp. [< OF *dars*]

dachs·hund (däks'ho͝ont', daks'ho͝ond', dash'-) *n.* A breed of dog native to Germany, of medium size, with long, compact body and short legs, and reddish brown or black coat. [G < *Dachs* badger + *Hund* dog]

Dachshund

Da·cron (dā'kron, dak'ron) *n.* A strong synthetic fiber or washable fabric, resistant to stretching and wrinkling: a trade name. Also **da'cron.**

dac·tyl (dak'təl) *n.* In prosody, a measure consisting of one accented syllable followed by two short or unaccented ones (ōŏŏ). [< Gk. *daktylos* finger, dactyl] —**dac·tyl'ic** *adj.*

dad (dad) *n. Informal* Father: used familiarly, as by children. Also **dad'dy.**

da·da (dä'dä, -də) *n. Often cap.* An antirational movement in art and literature, about 1916–20, that rejected traditional aesthetic values and endorsed the absurd and incongruous. Also **da'da·ism.** [F] —**da'da·ist** *n.*

dad·dy-long·legs (dad'ē·lông'legz', -long'-) *n.* **1** A long-legged, insect-eating arachnid resembling a spider. **2** CRANE FLY.

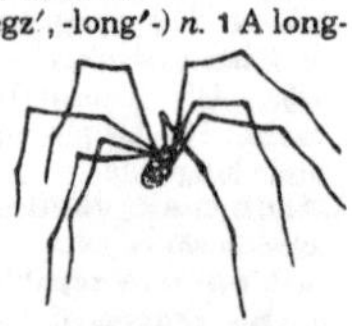

Daddy-longlegs *def. 1*

da·do (dā'dō) *n. pl.* **da·does** *Archit.* **1** A plain, flat surface at the base of a wall, as of a room, often decorated. **2** That part of a pedestal between the base and the surbase. [Ital., a die, a cube]

Daed·a·lus (ded'ə·ləs, *Brit.* dē'·də-) *Gk. Myth.* An architect and inventor who devised the Cretan Labyrinth in which he was later imprisoned with his son Icarus and from which they escaped by means of artificial wings.

dae·mon (dē'mən) *n.* DEMON.

daf·fo·dil (daf'ə·dil) *n.* A species of narcissus having yellow flowers with a long, trumpet-shaped corona. Also **daf'fa·dil'ly, daf'fa·down·dil'ly** (-doun·dil'ē), **daf'fy·down·dil'·ly.** [< L *asphodelus* asphodel]

daf·fy (daf'ē) *adj.* **·fi·er, ·fi·est** *Informal* Crazy; daft. [Prob. < DAFT]

daft (daft, däft) *adj.* **1** Silly; frolicsome. **2** Insane; crazy. [< OE *gedæfte* mild, meek] —**daft'ly** *adv.* —**daft'ness** *n.*

dag·ger (dag'ər) *n.* **1** A short, edged, and pointed weapon, for stabbing. **2** *Printing* A reference mark (†). —**double dagger** *Printing* A mark of reference (‡). —*v.t.* **1** To pierce with a dagger; stab. **2** *Printing* To mark with a dagger. [< OF *dague* dagger]

da·guerre·o·type (də·ger'ə·tīp, -ē·ə·tīp') *n.* **1** An early photographic process using light-sensitive metallic plates. **2** A picture made by this process. [< Louis J. M. *Daguerre*, 1789–1851, French inventor] —**da·guerre'o·typ'er, da·guerre'o·typ'ist** *n.* —**da·guerre'o·typ'y** *n.*

dahl·ia (dal'yə, däl'-, dāl'-) *n.* **1** A perennial plant having tuberous roots and large, composite flower heads of various colors. **2** Its flower or root. [< Anders *Dahl*, 18th c. Swedish botanist]

Dail Ei·reann (dôl âr'ən) The lower house of the legislature of Ireland.

dai·ly (dā'lē) *adj.* Occurring, appearing, or pertaining to every day. —*n. pl.* **·lies** A daily publication. —*adv.* Day after day; on every day. [< OE *dæg* day]

dain·ty (dān'tē) *adj.* **·ti·er, ·ti·est 1** Charmingly pretty or graceful. **2** Refined or delicate in tastes, manners, etc. **3** Overly nice or fastidious. **4** Delicious; tasty. —*n. pl.* **·ties** A choice bit of food. [< L *dignitas* dignity] —**dain'ti·ly** *adv.* —**dain'ti·ness** *n.*

dair·y (dâr'ē) *n. pl.* **dair·ies 1** A building or room where milk and cream are kept and made into butter and cheese. **2** A place for the sale of milk products. **3** DAIRY FARM. **4** DAIRY CATTLE. **5** DAIRYING. [< OE *dæge* dairymaid]

dairy cattle Cows of a breed adapted for milk production.

dairy farm A farm devoted to producing milk or milk products.

dair·y·ing (dâr'ē·ing) *n.* The business of conducting a dairy farm or a dairy.

dair·y·maid (dâr'ē·mād') *n.* A woman or girl who works in a dairy.

dair·y·man (dâr'ē·mən) *n. pl.* **·men** (-mən) A man who works in, or for, or keeps a dairy.

da·is (dā'is, dās) *n. pl.* **da·is·es** A raised platform in a room where speakers, distinguished guests, etc., may sit or stand. [< OF *deis* < LL *discus* disk]

dai·sy (dā'zē) *n. pl.* **dai·sies** Any of various small plants having composite flowers consisting of a yellow disk with white or rose-colored rays. [< OE *dæges ēage* day's eye]

Da·ko·ta (də·kō'tə) *n.* **1** A member of the largest division of the Siouan linguistic stock of North American Indians; a Sioux. **2** The Siouan language of the Dakotas. —**Da·ko'·tan** *adj., n.*

Da·lai La·ma (dä·lī' lä'mə) The principal priest of Lamaism in Tibet and Mongolia.

dale (dāl) *n.* A small valley. [< OE *dæl*]

dal·li·ance (dal'ē·əns) *n.* The act of dallying; frivolous or flirtatious action.

dal·ly (dal'ē) *v.* **dal·lied, dal·ly·ing** *v.i.* **1** To make love sportively; frolic. **2** To toy with; trifle; flirt: to *dally* with disaster. **3** To waste time. —*v.t.* **4** To waste (time): with *away*. [< OF *dalier* converse, chat] —**dal'li·er** *n.*

Dal·ma·tian (dal·mā'shən) *n.* **1** A native or citizen of Dalmatia. **2** A large, short-haired dog, white with black spots.

Dalmatian

dam[1] (dam) *n.* **1** A barrier to check the flow of a body of water. **2** The water held up by a dam. **3** Any obstruction. —*v.t.* **dammed, dam·ming 1** To erect a dam in; obstruct by a dam. **2** To restrain: with *up* or *in*. [< MDu. *damm*]

dam[2] (dam) *n.* A female parent: said of animals. [Var. of *dame*]

dam·age (dam'ij) *n.* **1** Destruction, injury, or harm to a person or thing. **2** *pl. Law* Money recoverable for a wrong or an injury. **3** *pl. Informal* Cost. —*v.* **dam·aged, dam·ag·ing**

v.t. 1 To cause damage to; impair the usefulness or value of. —*v.i.* 2 To be susceptible to damage. [< L *damnum* loss] —**dam'age·a·ble** *adj.* —**Syn.** *n.* 1 impairment, deterioration, loss. *v.* 1 injure, harm, ruin.

dam·as·cene (dam'ə·sēn, dam'ə·sēn') *v.t.* **·cened, ·cen·ing** To ornament (metal, iron, steel, etc.) with wavy or variegated patterns. Also **dam·as·keen** (dam'ə·skēn, dam'·ə·skēn'). —*adj.* Relating to damascening. —*n.* Work ornamented by damascening.

Da·mas·cus steel (də·mas'kəs) A steel decorated with wavy patterns, formerly used in making swords at Damascus.

dam·ask (dam'əsk) *n.* 1 A rich silk, linen, or wool fabric woven in elaborate patterns. 2 A fine, ornamentally patterned table linen. 3 Damascus steel or its patterns. 4 A deep-pink or rose color. —*adj.* 1 Of or from Damascus. 2 Made of damask steel or fabric. 3 Of the color of damask. —*v.t.* 1 DAMASCENE. 2 To weave with rich patterns. [< *Damascus,* Syria]

damask rose A large white, pink, or red rose noted for its fragrance.

dame (dām) *n.* 1 A married or mature woman. 2 *Slang* Any woman. 3 In Great Britain: **a** A title of address for a woman upon whom an order of knighthood has been conferred: used with the given name. **b** The title of the wife of a baronet or knight. [< L *domina* lady]

damn (dam) *v.t.* 1 To pronounce worthless, unfit, bad, a failure, etc. 2 To curse or swear at. 3 *Theol.* To condemn to eternal punishment. 4 To pronounce guilty; doom. —*v.i.* 5 To swear; curse. —**damn with faint praise** To praise so reluctantly as to imply adverse criticism. —*n.* 1 The saying of "damn" as an oath or curse. 2 *Informal* The least bit: not worth a *damn.* —*interj.* An expression of anger, disappointment, etc. —*adj. & adv. Informal* DAMNED. [< L *damnare* condemn to punishment]

dam·na·ble (dam'nə·bəl) *adj.* Meriting damnation; detestable; outrageous. [< OF < L *damnabilis* < *damnare* condemn] —**dam'na·ble·ness** *n.* —**dam'na·bly** *adv.*

dam·na·tion (dam·nā'shən) *n.* The act of damning or the state of the damned. —*interj.* DAMN. —**dam'na·to·ry** (-tôr'ē, -tō'rē) *adj.*

damned (damd) *adj.* 1 Judicially condemned; doomed, as to eternal punishment. 2 Damnable; detestable. —*adv. Informal* Very; extremely: *damned* funny.

Dam·o·cles (dam ə·klēz) *Gk. Myth.* A courtier who was forced to sit at a banquet under a sword suspended by a single hair to show him the perilous nature of a ruler's life. —**sword of Damocles** Any impending danger or calamity. —**Dam·o·cle·an** (dam'ə·klē'ən) *adj.*

Da·mon and Pyth·i·as (dā'mən; pith'ē·əs) *Rom. Myth.* Two friends so devoted that when the condemned Pythias wished to visit his home before dying, Damon volunteered to remain as hostage.

damp (damp) *n.* 1 Moisture; humidity; mist. 2 Foul air or gas, esp. in coal mines. 3 *Archaic* Depression of spirits. —*adj.* 1 Somewhat wet; moist. 2 Depressed in spirit. —*v.t.* 1 To moisten; make damp. 2 To check or lessen (energy, sound, flames, etc.). [< MDu., vapor, steam] —**damp'er, damp'ness.** *n.* —**damp'ly** *adv.*

damp·en (dam'pən) *v.t.* 1 To make or become damp; moisten. 2 To check; reduce, as ardor, sound, etc. —*v.i.* 3 To become damp. —**damp'en·er** *n.*

dam·sel (dam'zəl) *n. Archaic* A young girl; maiden. [< OF *dameisele,* ult. < L *domina* lady]

dam·son (dam'zən) *n.* 1 A small, purple plum. 2 The tree producing it. Also **damson plum.** [< L *(prunum) Damascenum* plum of Damascus]

Dan (dan) One of the twelve tribes of Israel.

Dan. Daniel; Danish.

Dan·a·id (dan'ē·id) *Gk. Myth.* One of the Danaides.

Da·na·i·des (də·nā'ə·dēz) *Gk. Myth.* The fifty daughters of a king, Danaus. All but one murdered their husbands at their father's command and were punished by having to draw water in a sieve forever.

dance (dans, däns) *v.* **danced, danc·ing** *v.i.* 1 To move the body and feet rhythmically, esp. to music. 2 To move excitedly; quiver. 3 To move about lightly and quickly. —*v.t.* 4 To perform or take part in the steps or figures of (a dance). 5 To cause to dance. —*n.* 1 A series of specified movements, usu. done to music. 2 A dancing party; ball. 3 A piece of music for dancing. 4 The art of dancing. [< OF *danser*] —**danc'er** *n.*

dan·de·li·on (dan'də·lī'ən) *n.* A weed with composite yellow flower heads and deeply toothed, edible leaves. [< F *dent de lion* lion's tooth; with ref. to the shape of the leaves]

dan·der (dan'dər) *Informal* Ruffled temper; anger. —**get one's dander up** *Informal* To become angry. [?]

dan·di·fy (dan'də·fī) *v.t.* **·fied, ·fy·ing** To cause to resemble a dandy. —**dan'di·fi·ca'tion** *n.*

dan·dle (dan'dəl) *v.t.* **·dled, ·dling** 1 To move up and down lightly on the knees, as an infant. 2 To fondle; caress. [?]

dan·druff (dan'drəf) *n.* Dead, scaly skin shed by the scalp; scurf. [?]

dan·dy (dan'dē) *n. pl.* **·dies** 1 A man overly refined in dress and affected in manner; a fop. 2 *Informal* A particularly fine specimen. —*adj.* 1 Like a dandy. 2 *Informal* Excellent; very fine. [?] —**dan'dy·ish** *adj.* —**dan'dy·ism** *n.*

Dane (dān) *n.* A native or citizen of Denmark.

dan·ger (dān'jər) *n.* 1 Exposure to chance of evil, injury, or loss; risk. 2 A cause of peril or risk. [< OF *dangier* power] —**Syn. 1, 2** peril, jeopardy, hazard.

dan·ger·ous (dān'jər·əs) *adj.* 1 Attended with danger; hazardous; perilous; unsafe. 2 Likely to or capable of causing injury or harm: a *dangerous* man. —**dan'ger·ous·ly** *adv.* —**dan'ger·ous·ness** *n.*

dan·gle (dang'gəl) *v.* **·gled, ·gling** *v.i.* 1 To hang loosely; swing to-and-fro. 2 To follow someone as a suitor or hanger-on. 3 *Gram.* To lack clear connection as a modifier in sentence construction: a *dangling* participle. —*v.t.* 4 To hold so as to swing loosely. [< Scand.] —**dan'gler** *n.*

Dan·iel (dan'yəl) A Hebrew prophet, saved by faith when imprisoned in a lion's den. —*n.* A book of the Old Testament attributed to him.

Dan·ish (dā'nish) *adj.* Of or pertaining to Denmark, the Danes, or their language. —*n. pl.* **Dan·ish** *for def. 3* 1 The North Germanic language of the Danes. 2 DANISH PASTRY. 3 A piece of Danish pastry.

Danish pastry A rich pastry made with raised dough.

dank (dangk) *adj.* Unpleasantly damp and chilly. [< Scand.] —**dank'ish** *adj.* —**dank'ish·ness** *n.* —**dank'ly** *adv.*

dan·seuse (dän·sœz') *n. pl.* **·seus·es** (-sœ'ziz, *Fr.* -sœz') Female dancer; esp., a ballerina. [F]

Daph·ne (daf'nē) *Gk. Myth.* A nymph who eluded Apollo by becoming a laurel tree.

dap·per (dap'ər) *adj.* 1 Smartly dressed; natty. 2 Small and active. [< MDu., strong, energetic] —**dap'per·ly** *adv.* —**dap'per·ness** *n.*

dap·ple (dap'əl) *v.t.* **·pled, ·pling** To spot or vary in color. —*adj.* Spotted; variegated: also **dap'pled.** —*n.* 1 A spot or dot, as on a horse. 2 A spotted animal. [?]

DAR, D.A.R. Daughters of the American Revolution.

dare (dâr) *v.* **dared** (*Archaic* **durst**), **dar·ing** *v.t.* 1 To have the courage or boldness for; venture on. 2 To challenge (someone) to do something dangerous or difficult. 3 To defy; oppose and challenge. —*v.i.* 4 To have the courage or boldness to do or attempt something; venture. —**I dare say** I am reasonably certain. —*n.* A challenge. [< OE *durran*] —**dar'er** *n.*

dare·dev·il (dâr'dev'əl) *n.* One who is recklessly bold. —*adj.* Venturesome; reckless. —**dare'dev'il·try** *n.*

dar·ing (dâr'ing) *adj.* Having or showing courage and boldness; lacking or putting aside restraints, as of fear or prudence. —*n.* Courage; boldness. —**dar'ing·ly** *adv.* —**dar'·ing·ness** *n.* —**Syn.** *adj.* courageous, fearless, venturesome.

dark (därk) *adj.* 1 Having or giving off little or no light. 2 Of a deep shade; black or almost black. 3 Of brunette complexion. 4 Not easily understood; obscure. 5 Ignorant; unenlightened. 6 Gloomy; dismal. 7 Angry; glum. 8 Evil; wicked. 9 Not known; hidden. 10 Deep and full in tone. —*n.* 1 Lack of light. 2 A place or state where there is little or no light. 3 Night. 4 A dark color or shade. —**in the**

dark Ignorant; uninformed. [<OE *deorc*] **—dark'ish** *adj.* **—dark'ly** *adv.* **—dark'ness** *n.*

Dark Ages 1 The period in European history from the fall of the Western Roman Empire in 476 to about 1000. 2 The Middle Ages, esp. the early part.

dark·en (där'kən) *v.t.* 1 To make dark or darker. 2 To obscure; confuse. *—v.i.* 3 To become dark or darker. **—dark'en·er** *n.*

dark horse One who unexpectedly wins a race, political nomination, etc.

dar·kling (därk'ling) *adj.* 1 Dim; obscure. 2 Occurring or being in the dark. *—adv.* In the dark.

dark·room (därk'ro͞om', -ro͝om') *n.* A room equipped for developing and treating photographic films, etc., in comparative darkness.

dar·ling (där'ling) *n.* 1 One tenderly beloved: often a term of direct address. 2 A favorite. *—adj.* Tenderly beloved; very dear. [<OE *dēor* dear]

darn[1] (därn) *v.t. & v.i.* To repair (a garment or a hole or rent) by filling the gap with interlacing stitches. *—n.* A place so mended. [<F *darner*] **—darn'er** *n.*

darn[2] (därn) *v.t., adj., n., & interj. Informal* Damn: a euphemism.

dar·nel (där'nəl) *n.* A weedy grass similar to rye, often found in grain fields. [ME]

darning needle 1 DRAGONFLY. 2 A large-eyed needle used in darning.

dart (därt) *n.* 1 A small, arrowlike, pointed missile, usu. thrown or shot. 2 Something resembling this. 3 A sudden and rapid motion. 4 A tapering tuck made in a garment to fit it to the figure. *—v.t. & v.i.* 1 To emit swiftly or suddenly. 2 To move swiftly and suddenly. [<OF]

dart·er (där'tər) *n.* 1 Any of various small American perchlike fish. 2 SNAKEBIRD.

darts (därts) *n. pl. (construed as sing.)* A game of skill in which small darts are thrown at a bull's-eye target.

Dar·win·ism (där'win·iz'əm) *n.* The biological theory of evolution by natural selection with variation, advanced by Charles Darwin. **—Dar·win·i·an** (där·win'ē·ən), **Dar'win·ist** *adj., n.* **—Dar'win·is'tic** *adj.*

dash (dash) *v.t.* 1 To strike with violence, esp. so as to break or shatter. 2 To throw, thrust, or knock suddenly and violently; usu. with *away, out, down,* etc. 3 To splash; bespatter. 4 To do, write, etc., hastily: with *off* or *down.* 5 To frustrate; confound: to *dash* hopes. 6 To daunt or discourage. 7 To put to shame; abash. 8 To adulterate; mix: with *with.* *—v.i.* 9 To strike; hit: The waves *dashed* against the shore. 10 To rush or move impetuously. *—n.* 1 A sudden advance or rush. 2 A short race. 3 A small addition or bit: a *dash* of humor. 4 Impetuosity; spirit; vigor. 5 Striking or ostentatious display. 6 A check or hindrance. 7 An impact or collision or its sound. 8 A quick stroke, as with a pen. 9 A horizontal line (—), as a mark of punctuation, etc. 10 The long element of the Morse code. 11 DASHBOARD. [<Scand.] **—dash'er** *n.*

dash·board (dash'bôrd', -bōrd') *n.* 1 A panel containing gauges and instruments, as in an automobile. 2 An upright screen on the front of a vehicle to intercept mud, etc.

da·shi·ki (dä·shē'kē) *n. pl.* **·kis** A loose-fitting garment of varying length, worn by men and women in West Africa and elsewhere. [<Yoruba]

dash·ing (dash'ing) *adj.* 1 Full of verve and spirit. 2 Stylishly showy or gay. **—dash'ing·ly** *adv.*

dash·y (dash'ē) *adj.* **dash·i·er, dash·i·est** Stylish; showy.

das·tard (das'tərd) *n.* A base coward; a sneak. [ME]

das·tard·ly (das'tərd·lē) *adj.* Contemptibly mean; base; cowardly. **—das'tard·li·ness** *n.*

dat. dative

da·ta (dā'tə, dat'ə, dä'tə) *n. pl.* of **da·tum** Facts or figures from which conclusions may be drawn. [L. neut. pl. of *datus,* pp. of *dare* give] • *Data,* although plural, is so frequently used with either a plural or singular verb that both forms have become acceptable, as in *Very little data is yet in; These data are not to be released.*

data bank An electronic library that contains information in database form.

da·ta base (dā'tə·bās') *n.* An extensive body of information organized and stored in a computer's memory for the quick retrieval of data in response to particular queries.

data processing The preparing, storing, or otherwise handling of information for or by computers.

date[1] (dāt) *n.* 1 A point of time, esp. the time of some event. 2 That part of a writing, inscription, coin, etc., which tells when it was written, published, etc. 3 The duration of something. 4 The day of the month. 5 A social engagement with a person, or the person with whom one has it. 6 An appointment: a *date* with a dentist. **—to date** Up to the present day or time; until now. *—v.* **dat·ed, dat·ing** *v.t.* 1 To furnish or mark with a date. 2 To ascertain the time or era of. 3 To reveal or betray as of a certain time or era. 4 To make an appointment with, as a member of the opposite sex. *—v.i.* 5 To have origin in or be in existence since an era or time: usu. with *from.* 6 To become obsolete or old-fashioned. 7 To have social engagements with persons of the opposite sex. [<L *datum* <*dare* give; from first word of Latin formula giving a letter's date and place of writing] **—dat'a·ble, date'a·ble** *adj.* **—dat'er** *n.*

date[2] (dāt) *n.* 1 The oblong, sweet, fleshy fruit of the date palm. 2 A lofty palm bearing this fruit: also **date palm.** [<Gk. *daktylos* finger; with ref. to its shape]

dat·ed (dā'tid) *adj.* 1 Marked with a date. 2 Antiquated; old-fashioned.

date·less (dāt'lis) *adj.* 1 Bearing no date. 2 Without end or limit. 3 Being beyond memory; immemorial. 4 Of permanent interest.

date·line (dāt'līn') *n.* The line containing the date and place of issue or publication, as of a newspaper, letter, etc.

date line A line approximately congruent with 180° longitude from Greenwich, separating points on the earth's surface which are by agreement a day apart in time. Also **International Date Line.**

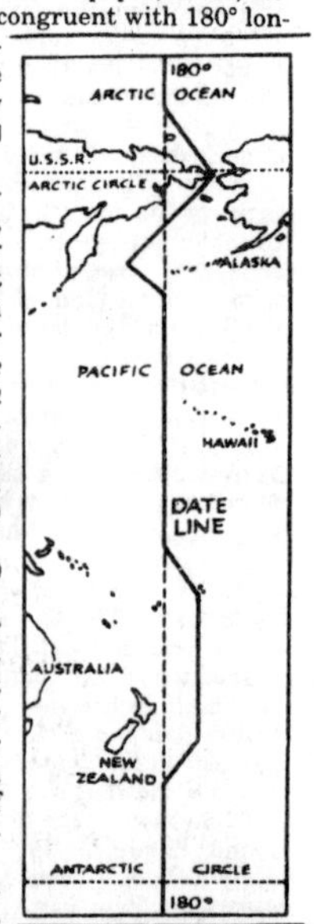

da·tive (dā'tiv) *n. Gram.* 1 In inflected Indo-European languages, that case of a noun, pronoun, or adjective denoting the indirect object. It is expressed in English by *to* or *for* with the objective or by word order, as in *I told the story to him, I told him the story.* 2 A word in this case. *—adj.* Pertaining to or designating the dative case or a word in this case. [<L *(casus) dativus* (the case of) giving] **—da'tive·ly** *adv.*

datum (dā'təm, dat'əm, dä'təm) Sing. of DATA. • See DATA.

daub (dôb) *v.t. & v.i.* 1 To smear or coat (something), as with plaster, grease, mud, etc. 2 To paint without skill or taste. *—n.* 1 Any sticky application. 2 A smear or spot. 3 A coarse, amateurish painting. 4 An instance or act of daubing. [<L *dealbare* whitewash] **—daub'er** *n.*

daugh·ter (dô'tər) *n.* 1 A female child considered in her relationship to one parent or both. 2 Any female descendant. 3 One who occupies the place of a daughter, as by adoption, marriage, or regard. 4 Any female regarded with reference to her origin: a *daughter* of Israel. [<OE *dohtor*] **—daugh'ter·ly** *adj.*

daugh·ter-in-law (dô'tər·in·lô') *n. pl.* **daugh·ters-in-law** The wife of one's son.

daunt (dônt, dänt) *v.t.* To dishearten or intimidate; cow; abash. [<L *domitare,* freq. of *domare* tame]

daunt·less (dônt'lis, dänt-) *adj.* Fearless; intrepid. **—daunt'less·ly** *adv.* **—daunt'less·ness** *n.*

dau·phin (dô'fin. *Fr.* dō·fan') *n.* The eldest son of a king of France. [F, lit., a dolphin, from a heraldic device]

dav·en·port (dav'ən·pôrt, -pōrt) *n.* A large sofa, often one that can be used as a bed. [Prob. after the name of the first manufacturer]

Da·vid (dā'vid) In the Old Testament, second king of Israel, reputed writer of the *Psalms.*

dav·it (dav′it, dā′vit) *n.* One of a pair of small cranes on a ship's side for hoisting its boats, stores, etc. [< *David,* proper name]
Da·vy Jones (dā′vē jōnz′) Sailors' name for the spirit of the sea.
Davy Jones's locker The bottom of the ocean, esp. as the grave of the drowned.
daw·dle (dôd′l) *v.t. & v.i.* **·dled, ·dling** To waste (time) in slow trifling; loiter. [Prob. var. of earlier *daddle* < DIDDLE] **—daw′dler** *n.* **—Syn.** linger, dally, trifle.
dawn (dôn) *v.i.* 1 To begin to grow light at the start of day. 2 To begin to be understood: with *on* or *upon.* 3 To begin to expand or develop. *—n.* 1 DAYBREAK. 2 An awakening or beginning. [Back formation < *dawning,* earlier *dawenyng* daybreak < Scand.]
day (dā) *n.* 1 The period of light from the sun's rising to its setting. 2 DAYLIGHT. 3 The 24-hour interval represented by one revolution of the earth upon its axis; also, this interval as a unit in computing time. 4 The period of rotation about its axis of any heavenly body. 5 A time or period; era; age: in Caesar's *day.* 6 A period of success, vigor, power, etc.: to have one's *day.* 7 A contest or battle: The liberals won the *day.* 8 The hours one works. 9 *Often cap.* A specified date: Independence *Day.* **—day after day** Every day. **—day by day** Each day. **—day in, day out** Every day. **—(from) day to day** From one day to the next; not long-range. [< OE *dæg*]
day·bed (dā′bed′) *n.* A lounge or couch convertible into a bed at night.
day·book (dā′bo͝ok′) *n.* 1 In bookkeeping, the book in which transactions are recorded in the order of occurrence. 2 DIARY.
day·break (dā′brāk′) *n.* The time of the sun's rising at the beginning of a day; dawn.
day-care center (dā′kâr′) A place for the care of young children during the day.
day coach A railroad car equipped for day-time travel only, as opposed to a sleeping-car.
day·dream (dā′drēm′) *n.* A usu. hopeful, dreamlike play of the imagination while awake; a reverie. *—v.i.* To have daydreams or indulge in wishful thinking. **—day′dream′er** *n.*
day laborer One who works for pay by the day, as at unskilled manual tasks.
day·light (dā′līt′) *n.* 1 Sunlight; the light of day. 2 The period of light during the day. 3 Insight; comprehension. 4 Exposure to view; publicity. 5 The end, as of a task.
day·light-sav·ing time (dā′līt′sā′ving) Time in which clocks are set one hour ahead of standard time.
day nursery DAY-CARE CENTER.
Day of Atonement YOM KIPPUR.
day school 1 A school that holds classes during the daytime only. 2 A private school attended by pupils living outside the school.
day·time (dā′tīm′) *n.* The time of daylight.
daze (dāz) *v.t.* **dazed, daz·ing** To stupefy or bewilder; stun. *—n.* The state of being dazed. [ME *dasen* < Scand.] **—daz·ed·ly** (dā′zid·lē) *adv.*
daz·zle (daz′əl) *v.* **·zled, ·zling** *v.t.* 1 To blind or dim the vision of by excess of light. 2 To bewilder or charm, as with brilliant display. *—v.i.* 3 To be blinded by lights or glare. 4 To excite admiration. *—n.* 1 The act of dazzling; dazzled condition. 2 Something that dazzles. [Freq. of DAZE] **—daz′zler** *n.* **—daz′zling·ly** *adv.*
db, db., decibel(s).
D. Bib. Douay Bible.
DC District of Columbia (P.O. abbr.).
DC, D.C. dc, d.c. direct current.
D.C. District of Columbia.
D.D. Doctor of Divinity.
D/D, d.d. demand draft.
D-day (dē′dā′) *n.* The unspecified day of the launching of a military attack, esp. June 6, 1944, the day France was invaded by the Allies in World War II. [< D, initial letter of DAY]
D.D.S. Doctor of Dental Surgery.
DDT A highly toxic derivative of chloral, widely used as an insecticide. [< *d(ichloro-)d(iphenyl-)t(richloroethane)*]
de- *prefix* 1 Away; off: *decapitate.* 2 Down: *decline.* 3 Completely: *denude.* 4 The reversing or ridding of (the action or condition expressed by the main element): *decoding, decentralization.* [< L *de* from, away, down]
DE Delaware (P.O. abbr.)
dea·con (dē′kən) *n.* 1 A lay church officer or subordinate minister. 2 In the Anglican, Greek, and Roman Catholic churches, a clergyman ranking next below a priest. [< Gk. *diakonos* servant, minister] **—dea′con·ry, dea′con·ship** *n.*
dea·con·ess (dē′kən·is) *n.* A woman appointed or chosen as a lay church worker or officer.
de·ac·ti·vate (dē·ak′tə·vāt) *v.t.* **·vat·ed, ·vat·ing** 1 To render inoperative or ineffective, as a bomb. 2 To release (a military unit, etc.) from active duty; demobilize. **—de·ac′ti·va′tion, de·ac′ti·va·tor** *n.*
dead (ded) *adj.* 1 Having ceased to live; lifeless. 2 In a state or condition resembling death. 3 Inanimate; inorganic: *dead* rocks. 4 Without interest, effectiveness, vitality, brillance, resonance, etc.: a *dead* color; a *dead* sound; a *dead* passage in a book. 5 Unresponsive; insensible: *dead* to feeling. 6 Motionless and unfeeling; numb: His arm felt *dead.* 7 Extinguished: *dead* cinders. 8 No longer productive or operative: *dead* capital; *dead* ground. 9 No longer used; obsolete: a *dead* language. 10 Without elasticity or resilience: These tennis balls are *dead.* 11 Unfailing; certain; sure: a *dead* shot. 12 Complete; absolute; utter: a *dead* stop; *dead* level. 13 *Informal* Exhausted; worn-out. 14 Not transmitting an electric current: a *dead* wire. 15 In sports, no longer in play: a *dead* ball. *—n.* 1 The part of most intense cold, darkness, etc.: the *dead* of night. 2 Dead persons collectively: with *the.* *—adv.* To the last degree; wholly; absolutely; exactly: *dead* right; *dead* straight. [< OE *dēad*] **—dead′ness** *n.*
dead·beat (ded′bēt′) *n.* 1 *Informal.* One who is notorious for not paying his bills. 2 *Slang* A sponger.
dead center *Mech.* Either of two positions of a crank and connecting rod in which the alignment is so perfect that the connecting rod has no power to turn the crank.
dead·en (ded′n) *v.t.* 1 To diminish the sensitivity, force, or intensity of. 2 To lessen or impede the velocity of; retard. 3 To render soundproof. 4 To make dull or less briliant in color. *—v.i.* 5 To become dead. **—dead′en·er** *n.*
dead end 1 An end of a street, road, etc., having no outlet. 2 A proposal, plan, or program that cannot develop or lead into something else. **—dead′-end′** *adj.*
dead·fall (ded′fôl′) *n.* A trap designed to drop a heavy weight upon its prey.
dead·head (ded′hed′) *n.* 1 One who receives gratis any service, admittance, or accommodation. 2 *Slang* A stupid person or a bore. *—v.i.* To make a trip, esp. by commercial carrier, without cargo.
dead heat A race in which two or more competitors finish together; a tie.
dead letter 1 A letter which can neither be delivered nor returned because of inadequate information on the envelope. 2 A statute or law not formally repealed but no longer enforced or active.
dead·line (ded′līn′) *n.* The time limit by which one must complete an assignment, a payment, etc.
dead·lock (ded′lok′) *n.* A cessation of activity or progress caused by the refusal of opposing parties to cooperate. *—v.t. & v.i.* To cause or come to a deadlock.
dead·ly (ded′lē) *adj.* **·li·er, ·li·est** 1 Liable or certain to cause death; fatal. 2 Mortal; implacable: *deadly* enemies. 3 Resembling death; deathly. 4 Excessive; extreme. 5 Extremely accurate or effective: a *deadly* wit; *deadly* aim. *—adv.* 1 In a way that suggests death. 2 Extremely; totally. **—dead′li·ness** *n.*
deadly nightshade BELLADONNA.
dead pan *Slang* A completely expressionless face. **—dead′-pan′** *adj., adv.*
dead point DEAD CENTER.
dead reckoning The determination of position by

means of log and compass without astronomical observations.

dead·weight (ded'wāt') *n.* 1 A completely inert weight or load. 2 The weight of a vehicle, as a railroad car, exclusive of its load.

dead·wood (ded'wŏŏd') *n.* 1 A useless or burdensome person or thing. 2 Wood dead upon the tree.

deaf (def) *adj.* 1 Partially or entirely unable to hear. 2 Determined not to listen or be persuaded. [<OE *dēaf*] — **deaf'ly** *adv.* —**deaf'ness** *n.*

deaf·en (def'ən) *v.t.* 1 To make deaf. 2 To stupefy or overwhelm, as with noise. 3 To drown (a sound) by a louder sound. 4 To make soundproof.

deaf-mute (def'myōōt') *n.* A person who is deaf and cannot speak. Also **deaf mute.**

deal (dēl) *v.* **dealt** (delt), **deal·ing** *v.t.* 1 To distribute; mete out, as playing cards. 2 To apportion to (one person) as a share. 3 To deliver, as a blow. —*v.i.* 4 To conduct oneself; behave towards: with *with:* to *deal* with an angry child. 5 To be concerned or occupied: with *in* or *with:* I *deal* in facts. 6 To consider, discuss, or administer; take action: with *with:* The court will *deal* with him. 7 To trade; do business: with *in, with,* or *at.* 8 In card games, to distribute the cards. —*n.* 1 In card games: **a** The act of distributing cards. **b** The cards so distributed. **c** The right or turn to distribute cards. **d** A single round of play. 2 An indefinite quantity, degree, or extent: a great *deal* of trouble. 3 A transaction or agreement, often secret: a political *deal.* 4 Treatment given or received: a square *deal.* [<OE *dǣlan* to divide] —**deal'er** *n.* —**Syn.** *n.* 3 scheme, arrangement, accommodation, understanding.

deal·ing (dē'ling) *n.* 1 *Usu. pl.* Any transaction with others. 2 The act of one who deals. 3 The method or manner of treatment.

dean (dēn) *n.* 1 The chief officer of a cathedral or of a collegiate church. 2 A college or university official having jurisdiction over a particular group of students, field of study, or acting as head of a faculty. 3 The senior or preeminent member of a group: the *dean* of American composers. [<LL *decanus* head of ten men <L *decem* ten] —**dean'ship** *n.*

dean·er·y (dē'nər·e) *n. pl.* **·er·ies** The office, jurisdiction, or place of residence of a dean.

dear (dir) *adj.* 1 Beloved; precious. 2 Esteemed: used in letter salutations: *Dear* Sir. 3 Expensive; costly. 4 Characterized by high prices. 5 Intense; earnest. —*n.* A beloved person. —*adv.* 1 With great affection. 2 At great cost. —*interj.* An exclamation of regret, surprise, etc. [<OE *dēore*] —**dear'ly** *adv.* —**dear'ness** *n.*

dearth (dûrth) *n.* Scarcity; lack; famine. [ME *derthe* costliness <*dere* dear] —**Syn.** paucity, want, absence, need.

death (deth) *n.* 1 The permanent cessation of physical life in a person, animal, or plant. 2 The condition of being dead. 3 Extinction of anything; destruction. 4 A cause or occasion of death. 5 Something similar to dying or being dead. 6 *Usu. cap.* The personification of death, usu. a skeleton holding a scythe. 7 Slaughter; bloodshed. —**to death** Very much: He frightened me *to death.* —**put to death** To kill; execute. [<OE *dēath*]

death·bed (deth'bed') *n.* 1 The bed on which one dies. 2 The last hours of life.

death·blow (deth'blō') *n.* 1 A fatal blow or shock. 2 Anything that causes something to end.

death·cup (deth'kup') *n.* A poisonous mushroom with a cuplike structure at the base of the stem.

death house The part of a prison in which prisoners condemned to death are confined. Also **death row.**

death·less (deth'lis) *adj.* Not liable to die; immortal; perpetual. —**death'less·ly** *adv.* —**death'less·ness** *n.*

death·ly (deth'lē) *adj.* 1 Like or suggestive of death: also **death'like'.** 2 Pertaining to death. 3 Deadly. —*adv.* In the manner of one dead or dying. —**death'li·ness** *n.*

death mask A cast of the face taken just after death.

death rate The number of persons per thousand of population dying in a given unit of time.

death's-head (deths'hed') *n.* A human skull or a representation of it, as a symbol of death.

death·trap (deth'trap') *n.* 1 An unsafe structure. 2 Any place or situation involving great peril.

death warrant 1 An official order for the execution of a person. 2 That which destroys, puts an end to hope, etc.

death·watch (deth'woch', -wôch') *n.* 1 The last vigil with the dying or with the body of one dead. 2 A guard set over a condemned man before his execution.

deb (deb) *n. Informal* A debutante.

de·ba·cle (dā·bä'kəl, -bak'əl, di-) *n.* 1 A sudden and disastrous overthrow or collapse; ruin. 2 The breaking up of ice in a river, etc. 3 A violent flood. [<F *débâcler* unbar, set free]

de·bar (di·bär') *v.t.* **·barred, ·bar·ring** 1 To shut out; exclude: usu. with *from.* 2 To prohibit; hinder. [<F *dé-* away + *barrer* to bar] —**de·bar'ment** *n.*

de·bark (di·bärk') *v.t. & v.i.* To put or go ashore from a ship or aircraft; disembark. [<F *dé-* away, from + *barque* a ship] —**de·bar·ka·tion** (dē'bär·kā'shən) *n.*

de·base (di·bās') *v.t.* **de·based, de·bas·ing** To lower in character, purity, value, etc.; degrade. [<DE- + ABASE] —**de·base'ment, de·bas'er** *n.* —**Syn.** abase, demean, devalue, cheapen.

de·bate (di·bāt') *v.* **de·bat·ed, de·bat·ing** *v.t.* 1 To discuss or argue about, as in a public meeting. 2 To discuss in formal argument. 3 To consider; deliberate upon in the mind. —*v.i.* 4 To argue; discuss. 5 To engage in formal argument. 6 To deliberate mentally; consider. —*n.* 1 The discussing of any question; dispute. 2 A formal argument conducted as a contest between opposing sides, usu. on a specific question. [<L *de-* down + *batuere* to strike] —**de·bat'a·ble** *adj.* —**de·bat'er** *n.*

de·bauch (di·bôch') *v.t.* 1 To corrupt in morals; deprave. —*v.i.* 2 To indulge in depravity. —*n.* 1 DEBAUCHERY. 2 An act or occasion of debauchery, as an orgy. [<F *débaucher* to lure from work <OF *desbaucher*] —**de·bauch'ed·ly** (-id·lē) *adv.* —**de·bauch'er, de·bauch'ed·ness** *n.*

deb·au·chee (deb'ô·chē', -shē') *n.* One habitually profligate, drunken, or lewd; a libertine.

de·bauch·er·y (di·bô'chər·ē) *n. pl.* **·er·ies** 1 Excessive gratification of all one's sensual appetites. 2 *pl.* Orgies. 3 *Archaic* Seduction from virtue, morality, fidelity, etc. Also **de·bauch'ment.**

de·ben·ture (di·ben'chər) *n.* An instrument, as a certificate, given as an acknowledgment of debt owed by the signer. [<L *debere* owe]

de·bil·i·tate (di·bil'ə·tāt) *v.t.* **·tat·ed, ·tat·ing** To make feeble; weaken. [<L *debilis* weak] —**de·bil'i·ta'tion** *n.* —**de·bil'i·ta'tive** *adj.*

de·bil·i·ty (di·bil'ə·tē) *n. pl.* **·ties** Bodily weakness; feebleness. [<L *debilis* weak]

deb·it (deb'it) *n.* 1 Something owed; a debt. 2 An item of debt. 3 The left-hand side of an account where debts are listed. —*v.t.* 1 To enter (a debt) in an account. 2 To charge (a customer) for goods. [<L *debitum,* p.p. of *debere* owe]

deb·o·nair (deb'ə·nâr') *adj.* 1 Suavely courteous and affable. 2 Carefree; gay. Also **deb'o·naire', deb'on·naire'.** [<OF *de bon aire* of good mien] —**deb'o·nair'ly** *adv.*

de·bouch (di·bouch', -bōōsh') *v.i.* 1 *Mil.* To emerge from a defile or a wood into the open. 2 To come forth. —*v.t.* 3 To cause to emerge. [<F *dé* from + *bouche* a mouth] —**de·bouch'ment** *n.*

de·brief (dē'brēf') *v.t.* To question or instruct (a pilot, agent, etc.) at the end of a mission or period of service. —**de'brief'ing** *n.*

de·bris (də·brē', dā'brē; *Brit.* deb'rē) *n.* 1 Accumulated fragments; rubbish; rubble. 2 An aggregation of detached fragments of rocks. Also **dé·bris'.** [<OF *des-* away + *brisier* to break]

debt (det) *n.* 1 That which one owes. 2 An obligation. 3 The condition of being indebted. 4 *Theol.* A sin. [<L *debitum.* See DEBIT.]

debt·or (det'ər) *n.* One who owes a debt. [<L *debitor* < *debere* owe]

de·bug (dē·bug') *v.t.* **·bugged, ·bug·ging.** To get rid of errors or other malfunctions in a computer or its software.

de·bunk (di·bungk') *v.t. Informal* To reveal the sham, false pretensions, etc., of [<BUNK[2]]

de·but (di·byōō', dā-, dā'byōō) *n.* 1 A first appearance, as in society or on the stage. 2 An opening or beginning. —*v.i. Informal* 1 To appear in a debut. 2 To open, as a show. Also **dé·but'.** [<F *débuter* begin, lead off]

deb·u·tante (deb′yo͞o·tänt, -yə-, -tant, deb′yo͞o·tänt′) *n.* A girl who makes a social debut. Also **dé′bu·tante′**. [< F *débuter* begin] **—deb′u·tant′** *n. Masc.*

Dec, Dec. December.

dec. deceased; decimeters; declension.

deca- *combining form* **1** Ten: *decapod.* **2** In the metric system, ten times (a specific unit of measure). Also **dec-**. [< Gk. *deka* ten]

dec·ade (dek′ād, de·kād′) *n.* **1** A period of ten years. **2** A group or set of ten. [< L *decas* a group of ten]

dec·a·dence (dek′ə·dəns, di·kād′ns) *n.* **1** A process of deterioration; decay. **2** A condition or period of decline, as in literature, art, morals, etc. [< L *de-* down + *cadere* to fall]

dec·a·dent (dek′ə·dənt, di·kād′nt) *adj.* Characterized by decadence. —*n.* A decadent person, esp. a decadent painter, writer, composer, etc. **—dec′a·dent·ly** *adv.*

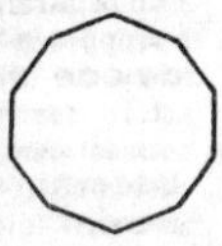
Decagon

dec·a·gon (dek′ə·gon) *n.* A plane figure with ten sides and ten angles. [< Gk. *deka* ten + -GON] **—de·cag·o·nal** (di·kag′ə·nəl) *adj.* **—de·cag′o·nal·ly** *adv.*

dec·a·gram (dek′ə·gram) *n.* A measure of weight equal to ten grams. Also **dec′a·gramme.**

dec·a·he·dron (dek′ə·hē′drən) *n.* A solid bounded by ten plane faces. [< DECA- + Gk. *hedra* seat] **—dec′a·he′dral** *adj.*

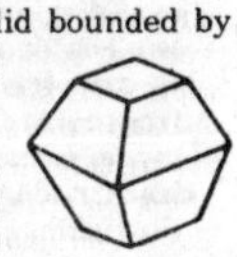
Decahedron

de·cal (dē′kal, di·kal′) *n.* A decorative picture or design on paper that is transferable, as to glass. [Short for DECALCOMANIA]

de·cal·ci·fy (dē·kal′sə·fī) *v.t.* **·fied, ·fy·ing** To deprive of calcium, as bones, teeth, etc. **—de·cal′ci·fi·ca′tion, de·cal′ci·fi·er** *n.*

de·cal·co·ma·ni·a (di·kal′kə·mā′nē·ə, -mān′yə) *n.* **1** A transferring of decorative pictures or designs from paper to glass, porcelain, etc. **2** DECAL. [< F *décalquer* transfer a tracing + *-manie* -MANIA]

Dec·a·logue (dek′ə·lôg, -log) *n.* TEN COMMANDMENTS. Also **Dec′a·log.** [< Gk. *deka* ten + *logos* word]

de·camp (di·kamp′) *v.i.* **1** To break camp or leave camp. **2** To leave suddenly or secretly. **—de·camp′ment** *n.*

de·cant (di·kant′) *v.t.* **1** To pour off gently so as not to disturb the sediment. **2** To pour from one container into another. [< L *de-* from + *canthus* lip of a jug] **—de·can·ta·tion** (dē′kan·tā′shən) *n.*

de·cant·er (di·kan′tər) *n.* An ornamental bottle for wine.

de·cap·i·tate (di·kap′ə·tāt) *v.t.* **·tat·ed, ·tat·ing** To cut off the head of; behead. [< L *de-* down + *caput* head] **—de·cap′i·ta′tion, de·cap′i·ta′tor** *n.*

dec·a·pod (dek′ə·pod) *adj.* Ten-footed or ten-armed. —*n.* **1** A crustacean having five pairs of legs, as a crab, lobster, etc. **2** A ten-armed cephalopod, as a cuttlefish or squid. [< Gk. *deka* ten + *pous* foot] **—de·cap·o·dal** (di·kap′ə·dəl), **de·cap′o·dous** *adj.*

de·car·bon·ize (di·kär′bə·nīz) *v.t.* **·ized, ·iz·ing** To remove carbon from (molten steel, the cylinders of an internal-combustion engine, etc.). **—de·car′bon·i·za′tion, de·car′bon·iz′er** *n.*

de·car·bu·rize (dē·kär′byə·rīz) *v.t.* **·rized, ·riz·ing** DECARBONIZE. **—de·car′bu·ri·za′tion** *n.*

dec·a·syl·la·ble (dek′ə·sil′ə·bəl) *n.* A line of verse having ten syllables. **—dec·a·syl·lab·ic** (dek′ə·si·lab′ik) *adj.*

de·cath·lon (di·kath′lon) *n.* An athletic contest consisting of ten different track and field events in all of which each contestant participates. [< DEC(A)- + Gk. *athlon* a contest]

de·cay (di·kā′) *v.i.* **1** To diminish slowly in health, power, beauty, quality, etc. **2** To rot; decompose. —*v.t.* **3** To cause to decay. —*n.* **1** A slow deterioration or weakening. **2** Decomposition; rottenness. **3** *Physics* The disintegration of a radioactive element. [< L *de-* down + *cadere* to fall]

decd. deceased.

de·cease (di·sēs′) *v.i.* **de·ceased, de·ceas·ing** To die. —*n.* Death. [< L *decessus* < *decedere* go away]

de·ceased (di·sēst′) *adj.* Dead. **—the deceased** The dead person or persons.

de·ce·dent (di·sēd′nt) *n.* A person deceased.

de·ceit (di·sēt′) *n.* **1** The act of deceiving. **2** A lie or other dishonest action. **3** The quality of being deceptive. [< OF *deceveir* deceive]

de·ceit·ful (di·sēt′fəl) *adj.* Characterized by deception; false; tricky; fraudulent. **—de·ceit′ful·ly** *adv.* **—de·ceit′ful·ness** *n.* **—Syn.** dishonest, disingenuous, two-faced.

de·ceive (di·sēv′) *v.* **de·ceived, de·ceiv·ing** *v.t.* **1** To mislead by or as by falsehood; delude. —*v.i.* **2** To practice deceit. [< L *decipere* < *de-* away, down + *capere* to take] **—de·ceiv′a·ble** *adj.* **—de·ceiv′a·bly** *adv.* **—de·ceiv′er** *n.*

de·cel·er·ate (dē·sel′ə·rāt) *v.t. & v.i.* **·at·ed. ·at·ing** To diminish in speed. [< DE- + L *celerare* hasten < *celer* quick] **—de·cel′er·a′tion, de·cel′er·a′tor** *n.*

De·cem·ber (di·sem′bər) *n.* The twelfth month of the year, having 31 days. [< L *decem* ten; because December was the tenth month in the old Roman calendar]

de·cen·cy (dē′sən·sē) *n. pl.* **·cies** **1** Propriety in conduct, speech, dress, etc. **2** *pl.* Actions that are socially proper or seemly. **3** *pl.* Things required for a proper manner of life. [< L *decens.* See DECENT.]

de·cen·ni·al (di·sen′ē·əl) *adj.* Continuing for or consisting of ten years; occurring every ten years. —*n.* A tenth anniversary. [< L *decem* ten + *annus* year] **—de·cen′ni·al·ly** *adv.*

de·cent (dē′sənt) *adj.* **1** Characterized by propriety of conduct, speech, manners, or dress; proper; respectable. **2** Modest; chaste. **3** Moderately good; satisfactory. **4** Kind; generous. **5** *Informal* Adequately clothed. [< L *decens,* pr.p. of *decere* be fitting, be proper] **—de′cent·ly** *adv.* **—de′cent·ness** *n.*

de·cen·tral·ize (dē·sen′trəl·īz) *v.t.* **·ized, ·iz·ing** To reorganize (a government, school system, etc.) by distributing authority to smaller or local units. **—de·cen′tral·i·za′tion** *n.*

de·cep·tion (di·sep′shən) *n.* **1** The act of deceiving. **2** The state of being deceived. **3** Anything deceptive; a delusion.

de·cep·tive (di·sep′tiv) *adj.* Having power or tendency to deceive. **—de·cep′tive·ly** *adv.* **—de·cep′tive·ness** *n.* **—Syn.** misleading, delusive, false.

dec·i·bel (des′ə·bel) *n.* A logarithmic unit defined so that an increase of 1 decibel represents multiplication of sound or signal power by about 1.258, with, for sound, 0 decibels representing a pressure of 0.0002 microbar. [< L *decem* ten + E *bel,* logarithmic unit < Alexander Graham *Bell,* 1847–1922, U.S. inventor]

de·cide (di·sīd′) *v.* **·cid·ed, ·cid·ing** *v.t.* **1** To determine; settle, as a dispute, contest, etc.; arbitrate. **2** To cause the outcome of; settle. **3** To bring (someone) to a decision. —*v.i.* **4** To give a decision. **5** To make a decision. [< MF *décider* < L *decidere* < *de-* down, away + *caedere* cut] **—de·cid′a·ble** *adj.* **—de·cid′er** *n.*

de·cid·ed (di·sī′did) *adj.* **1** Free from uncertainty; unquestionable. **2** Determined; resolute; emphatic. **—de·cid′ed·ly** *adv.* **—de·cid′ed·ness** *n.*

de·cid·u·ous (di·sij′o͞o·əs) *adj.* **1** Falling off or shed at specific seasons, as petals or leaves. **2** Characterized by such a falling off; not evergreen. [< L *de-* down, away + *cadere* to fall] **—de·cid′u·ous·ly** *adv.* **—de·cid′u·ous·ness** *n.*

de·cil·lion (de·sil′yən) *n. & adj.* See NUMBER. [< DEC(A)- + (M)ILLION] **—de·cil′lionth** *adj.*

dec·i·mal (des′ə·məl) *adj.* **1** Founded on the number 10. **2** Proceeding by powers of 10 or of one tenth. —*n.* A decimal fraction. [< L *decem* ten] **—dec′i·mal·ly** *adv.*

decimal fraction A fraction whose denominator is ten or a power of ten and is expressed by using a decimal point, as .8 = 8/10 or .08 = 8/100.

dec·i·mal·ize (des′ə·məl·īz) *v.t.* **·ized, ·iz·ing** To change to a decimal system, as currency. *Brit. sp.* **·ise.** **—dec′i·mal·i·za′tion** *n.*

decimal point A dot or period used before a decimal fraction.

dec·i·mate (des′ə·māt) *v.t.* **·mat·ed, ·mat·ing** **1** To destroy or kill a large proportion of. **2** To select by lot and kill one out of every ten of. [< L *decimare* take a tenth part from < *decem* ten] **—dec′i·ma′tion, dec′i·ma′tor** *n.*

de·ci·pher (di·sī′fər) *v.t.* **1** To figure out the sense of, as hieroglyphics, a scribble, etc. 2 To translate from cipher into ordinary characters; decode. [< DE- + CIPHER] —**de·ci′pher·a·ble** *adj.* —**de·ci′pher·er, de·ci′pher·ment** *n.*

de·ci·sion (di·sizh′ən) *n.* 1 The act of deciding or making up one's mind. 2 The result or conclusion arrived at by deciding. 3 The quality of being positive and firm; determination. 4 In boxing, a victory determined by points rather than by a knockout.

de·ci·sion-mak·ing (di·sizh′ən·mā′king) *n.* 1 The process by which decisions are made, esp. important decisions affecting others and made by virtue of one's office or position: a study of presidential *decision-making.* 2 The power or ability to make decisions of consequence: agitating for a voice in *decision-making.* —*adj.* Of, relating to, or requiring decision-making. —**de·ci′sion-mak′er** *n.*

de·ci·sive (di·sī′siv) *adj.* 1 Putting an end to uncertainty or debate; conclusive. 2 Prompt; positive; decided. 3 Crucially important; critical. —**de·ci′sive·ly** *adv.* —**de·ci′sive·ness** *n.*

deck (dek) *n.* 1 A platform covering or extending horizontally across a vessel. 2 Any similar flat surface. 3 A pack of cards. —**clear the deck** To prepare for activity. —**hit the deck** 1 *Slang* To rise from bed quickly. 2 *Slang* To prepare for activity. 3 *Slang* To drop to a prone position. —**on deck** 1 Present and available for action. 2 Next at bat in a baseball game. —*v.t.* 1 To array; adorn. 2 To put a deck on. [< MDu. *dek* roof, covering]

deck hand A sailor employed about the deck.

deck·le (dek′əl) *n.* 1 In papermaking by hand, a frame to confine the pulp to a definite width. 2 The ragged edge of hand-made paper: also **deckle edge.** Also **deck′el.** [< G *decke* cover]

de·claim (di·klām′) *v.i.* 1 To speak loudly and in a rhetorical manner. 2 To give a recitation. 3 To condemn or attack verbally and vehemently: with *against.* —*v.t.* 4 To utter aloud in a rhetorical manner. [< L *de-* completely + *clamare* shout] —**de·clam·a·to·ry** (di·klam′ə·tôr′ē, -tō′rē) *adj.* —**de·claim′er, dec·la·ma·tion** (dek′lə·mā′shən) *n.*

dec·la·ra·tion (dek′lə·rā′shən) *n.* 1 The act of declaring. 2 That which is declared. 3 In law, a formal presentation of facts by the plaintiff. 4 A statement of goods that can be taxed. 5 In bridge: **a** A meld. **b** The final or winning bid.

Declaration of Independence The manifesto of the Continental Congress adopted July 4, 1776, giving the reasons why the American colonies had declared their independence.

de·clar·a·tive (di·klar′ə·tiv) *adj.* Making a declaration or statement. Also **de·clar·a·to·ry** (di·klar′ə·tôr′ē, -tō′rē).

de·clare (di·klâr′) *v.* **·clared, ·clar·ing** *v.t.* 1 To assert positively or emphatically. 2 To announce or state formally and solemnly. 3 To reveal; manifest. 4 To make full statement of, as dutiable goods. 5 In bridge, to name, as a trump suit. —*v.i.* 6 To make a declaration. 7 To proclaim a choice or decision. [< L *de-* completely + *clarare* make clear < *clarus* clear] —**de·clar′er** *n.*

de·clas·si·fy (dē·klas′ə·fī) *v.t.* **·fied, ·fy·ing** To remove secrecy restrictions from (government documents, etc.).

de·clen·sion (di·klen′shən) *n.* 1 *Gram.* **a** The inflection of nouns, pronouns, and adjectives to indicate case, number, and gender. **b** A class of words similarly inflected. 2 A slope or descent. 3 A decline; deterioration. [< L *declinare.* See DECLINE.] —**de·clen′sion·al** *adj.*

dec·li·na·tion (dek′lə·nā′shən) *n.* 1 The act of inclining or sloping downward; descent; slope. 2 Deviation, as from a course or action. 3 A courteous refusal. 4 The angular distance of a heavenly body north or south from the celestial equator. 5 The angle between the direction in which a magnetic needle points and the true meridian: also **magnetic declination.**

de·cline (di·klīn′) *v.* **·clined, ·clin·ing** *v.i.* 1 To refuse to accept, comply with, or do something, esp. politely. 2 To lessen or fail, as in health. 3 To come to an end; wane. 4 To bend or incline downward or aside. 5 To degrade oneself, as to an unworthy action. —*v.t.* 6 To refuse to accept, comply with, or do, esp. politely. 7 To cause to bend or incline downward or aside. 8 To give the inflected forms of (a noun, pronoun, or adjective). —*n.* 1 The act or result of declining; deterioration; decay. 2 The period of such declining. 3 Any enfeebling disease, as tuberculosis. 4 A declivity; a slope. [< L *declinare* lean down] —**de·clin′a·ble** *adj.* —**de·clin′er** *n.*

de·cliv·i·ty (di·kliv′ə·tē) *n. pl.* **·ties** A downward slope; descending surface. [< L *de-* down + *clivus* hill, slope] —**de·cliv′i·tous, de·cli′vous** (-klī′vəs) *adj.*

de·coct (di·kokt′) *v.t.* To extract by boiling; condense. [< L *de-* down + *coquere* to cook] —**de·coc′tion** *n.*

de·code (dē·kōd′) *v.t.* **·cod·ed, ·cod·ing** To convert (a coded message) into plain language. —**de·cod′er** *n.*

dé·colle·té (dā′kol·tā′, *Fr.* dā·kôl·tā′) *adj.* 1 Cut low in the neck, as a gown. 2 Wearing a low-necked gown. [< F *décolleter* bare the neck] —**dé·colle·tage** (-täzh′) *n.*

de·com·pose (dē′kəm·pōz′) *v.t. & v.i.* **·posed, ·pos·ing** 1 To separate into constituent elements. 2 To decay. —**de′·com·pos′a·ble** *adj.* —**de′com·pos′er, de′com·po·si′tion** *n.*

de·com·press (dē′kəm·pres′) *v.t.* 1 To free of pressure. 2 To lessen the pressure on (caisson workers, etc.), as in an airlock. —**de′com·pres′sion** *n.*

decompression sickness A painful, sometimes fatal condition due to bubbles of nitrogen formed in the blood when a rapid reduction in pressure occurs, as when a diver returns directly to the surface after a period deep under water.

de·con·tam·i·nate (dē′kən·tam′ə·nāt) *v.t.* **·nat·ed, ·nat·ing** To rid of a noxious or dangerous substance. —**de′con·tam′i·na′tion** *n.*

de·con·trol (dē′kən·trōl′) *v.t.* **·trolled, ·trol·ling** To remove from control, esp. from government controls. —*n.* The removal of controls.

dé·cor (dā′kôr, dā·kôr′) *n.* 1 The plan or arrangement of furnishings and colors in an interior space, as a home or office. 2 In the theater, scenery. Also **de′cor.** [< F *décorer* decorate]

dec·o·rate (dek′ə·rāt) *v.t.* **·rat·ed, ·rat·ing** 1 To adorn; ornament. 2 To furnish, paint, refurbish (a dwelling, room, etc.). 3 To devise a décor, as for a home, and supervise its execution. 4 To confer a medal or decoration upon: *decorated* for valor. [< L *decorare* < *decus* embellishment] —**dec′o·ra′tor** *n.*

dec·o·ra·tion (dek′ə·rā′shən) *n.* 1 The act, process, or art of decorating. 2 Ornamentation; an ornament. 3 A badge or emblem conferred as a mark of honor; a medal.

Decoration Day MEMORIAL DAY.

dec·o·ra·tive (dek′ər·ə·tiv, dek′rə-, dek′ə·rā′-) *adj.* Of the nature of or used as decoration; ornamental. —**dec′o·ra·tive·ly** *adv.* —**dec′o·ra·tive·ness** *n.*

dec·o·rous (dek′ər·əs, di·kôr′əs, -kō′rəs) *adj.* Characterized by proper behavior and good taste. [< L *decus* grace, embellishment] —**dec′o·rous·ly** *adv.* —**dec′o·rous·ness** *n.* —**Syn.** becoming, suitable, seemly, correct.

de·co·rum (di·kôr′əm, -kō′rəm) *n.* 1 Propriety, as in manner, conduct, etc.; seemliness. 2 An act demanded by social custom. [< L *decorus* decorous]

de·coy (dē′koi, di·koi′) *n.* 1 A person or thing that lures others into danger or a snare. 2 A bird or animal, or the likeness of one, used to lure game within gunshot. 3 An enclosed place into which game may be lured. —*v.t. & v.i.* (dē′koi) To lure or be lured into danger, a snare, etc. [< Du. *de kooi* the cage] —**de′coy·er** *n.*

Decoy *def. 2*

de·crease (di·krēs′) *v.t. & v.i.* **·creased, ·creas·ing** To grow or cause to grow gradually less or smaller; abate; reduce. —*n.* (*usu.* dē′krēs) 1 The act, process, or state of decreasing. 2 The amount or degree of decreasing. [< L *decrescere* < *de-* down + *crescere* grow] —**de·creas′ing·ly** *adv.*

de·cree (di·krē′) *n.* 1 A formal order or ordinance, as of a civil or an ecclesiastical body. 2 Anything unalterably ordained. —*v.t.* 1 To order, adjudge, ordain, or appoint by law or edict. —*v.i.* 2 To issue an edict or decree. [< L *decretum,* neut. pp. of *decernere* decide]

dec·re·ment (dek′rə·mənt) *n.* 1 A decreasing; waning. 2 Amount of loss by decrease or waste. [< L *decrementum* < *decrescere.* See DECREASE.]

de·crep·it (di·krep′it) *adj.* Enfeebled by old age or overuse; broken down. [< L *decrepitus* < *de-* completely + *crepare* to creak] —**de·crep′it·ly** *adv.*

de·crep·i·tude (di·krep′ə·tyōōd) *n.* Enfeeblement through infirmity or old age.

de·cre·scen·do (dē′krə·shen′dō) *adj., adv., n.* DIMINUENDO. [< L *decrescere.* See DECREASE]

de·cre·tal (di·krēt′l) *n.* A decree, esp. one of the Pope determining some point in ecclesiastical law. —*adj.* Of or pertaining to a decree. [< L *decretum.* See DECREE.]

de·crim·i·nal·ize (dē·krim′ə·nəl·īz) *v.t.* **·ized, ·iz·ing** To abstain from applying criminal penalties to; regard as nonpunishable. **—de·crim′i·nal·i·za′tion** *n.*

de·cry (di·krī′) *v.t.* **·cried, ·cry·ing** 1 To condemn or disparage openly. 2 To depreciate, as foreign or obsolete coins. [< F *dé-* down + *crier* to cry] **—de·cri′al, de·cri′er** *n.*

de·cum·bent (di·kum′bənt) *adj.* 1 Lying down; recumbent. 2 *Bot.* Prostrate: said of stems, shoots, etc., growing along the ground. [< L *de-* down + *cumbere* lie, recline] **—de·cum′bence, de·cum′ben·cy** *n.*

ded·i·cate (ded′ə·kāt) *v.t.* **·cat·ed, ·cat·ing** 1 To set apart for sacred uses; consecrate. 2 To set apart for any special use, duty, or purpose. 3 To devote (oneself) to some special work, action, etc. 4 To open (a new building, park, etc.) with ceremonies. 5 To preface with a dedication, as a book. —*adj.* Dedicated; devoted. [< L *de-* down + *dicare* proclaim] **—ded′i·ca′tive** *adj.* **—ded′i·ca′tor** *n.*

ded·i·ca·tion (ded′ə·kā′shən) *n.* 1 A dedicating or being dedicated. 2 An inscription in a book, etc., as to a friend or cause.

de·duce (di·dyōōs′) *v.t.* **·duced, ·duc·ing** 1 To derive as a conclusion; infer. 2 To trace, as derivation or origin. [< L *deducere* < *de-* down + *ducere* to lead] **—de·duc′i·ble** *adj.*

de·duct (di·dukt′) *v.t.* To subtract; take away. [< L *deductus,* pp. of *deducere.* See DEDUCE.]

de·duct·i·ble (di·duk′tə·bəl) *adj.* That can be deducted, esp. in calculating taxable income. —*n.* In an insurance policy, a specified amount of damage or loss that the insured is responsible for before the insurer's coverage takes effect; also, such a provision in a policy. **—de′duct·i·bil′i·ty** *n.*

de·duc·tion (di·duk′shən) *n.* 1 The act of deducting or the sum or amount deducted. 2 Reasoning from stated premises to the formally valid conclusion; reasoning from the general to the particular. 3 An inference; conclusion. **—de·duc′tive** *adj.* **—de·duc′tive·ly** *adv.*

deed (dēd) *n.* 1 Anything done; an act. 2 A notable achievement or action. 3 Action performed, as opposed to words. 4 *Law* A written instrument under seal, whether a bond, agreement, or contract, but most frequently used in the conveyance of real estate. **—in deed** In fact; actually. —*v.t.* To convey or transfer by deed. [< OE *dǣd*]

deem (dēm) *v.t. & v.i.* To judge; think; regard; believe. [< OE *dēman* judge]

de·em·pha·size (dē·em′fə·sīz) *v.t.* **·sized, ·siz·ing** To place less emphasis on. **—de·em′pha·sis** (-sis) *n.*

deep (dēp) *adj.* 1 Extending or situated far below the surface. 2 Extending or situated far back, far in, or far from either side. 3 Having a (specified) depth, thickness, or distance: a box ten feet *deep.* 4 Far distant in time or space. 5 Hard to understand; abstruse. 6 Intellectually penetrating; profound. 7 Heartfelt and earnest: *deep* regrets. 8 Profound or great in degree, intensity, etc.: a *deep* coma. 9 Scheming; sly. 10 Of intense or dark hue. 11 Low in pitch; sonorous: a *deep* voice. —*n.* 1 That which has great depth; the sea. 2 The most profound part: the *deep* of night. —*adv.* 1 In a deep way or to a deep extent; deeply. 2 Far on; for a long time: *deep* into the night. [< OE *dēop*] **—deep′ly** *adv.* **—deep′ness** *n.*

deep·en (dē′pən) *v.t. & v.i.* To make or become deep or deeper.

deep-freeze (dēp′frēz′) *v.t.* **-froze** or **-freezed, -fro·zen** or **-freezed, -freez·ing** To freeze (foods) quickly to preserve natural flavor.

Deep·freeze (dēp′frēz′) *n.* A refrigerator for deep-freezing foods: a trade name.

deep-fry (dēp′frī′) *v.t.* **-fried, -fry·ing** To fry while submerged in fat or oil.

deep-root·ed (dēp′rōō′tid, -rŏŏt′id) *adj.* 1 Having deeply situated roots. 2 Firmly entrenched; hard to get rid of, overcome, etc.

deep-seat·ed (dēp′sē′tid) *adj.* 1 Deeply situated. 2 Difficult to overcome, get rid of, etc.

deer (dir) *n. pl.* **deer** A ruminant with deciduous antlers, usu. in the male only, as the moose, elk, and reindeer. [< OE *dēor* beast]

Deer

deer·hound (dir′hound′) *n.* A Scottish breed of sporting dog with a long, flat head, pointed muzzle, and a shaggy coat.

deer·skin (dir′skin′) *n.* A deer's hide, or leather made from it; buckskin.

de-es·ca·late (dē·es′kə·lāt) *v.t. & v.i.* **·lat·ed, ·lat·ing** To decrease or be decreased gradually, as in a conflict: to *de-escalate* a war. **—de-es′ca·la′tion** *n.*

def. defendant; defense; deferred; definition.

de·face (di·fās′) *v.t.* **·faced, ·fac·ing** To mar or disfigure the surface of. [< OF *des-* down, away + *face* face] **—de·face′a·ble** *adj.* **—de·face′ment, de·fac′er** *n.*

de fac·to (dē fak′tō) Actually or really existing, with or without legal sanction. [L]

de·fal·cate (di·fal′kāt) *v.i.* **·cat·ed, ·cat·ing** To embezzle money. [< Med. L *defalcare* lop off] **—de·fal·ca·tion** (dē′fal·kā′shən), **de·fal′ca·tor** *n.*

de·fame (di·fām′) *v.t.* **·famed, ·fam·ing** To attack the good name or reputation of. [< L *dis-* away, from + *fama* a report, reputation] **—def·a·ma·tion** (def′ə·mā′shən), **de·fam′er** *n.* **—de·fam·a·to·ry** (di·fam′ə·tôr′ē) *adj.* **—Syn.** revile, besmirch, slander, libel.

de·fault (di·fôlt′) *n.* A failure to fulfill an obligation or duty; failure to appear, as in a contest or a legal suit. **—in default of** Owing to lack or failure of. —*v.i.* 1 To fail or neglect to fulfill or do a duty, obligation, etc. 2 To fail to meet financial obligations. 3 *Law* To fail to appear in court. 4 In sports, to fail to compete or complete a game, etc. —*v.t.* 5 To fail to perform or pay. 6 In sports, to fail to compete in, as a game; also, to forfeit by default. [< L *de-* down + *fallere* deceive] **—de·fault′er** *n.*

de·feat (di·fēt′) *v.t.* 1 To overcome in any contest; vanquish. 2 To thwart or frustrate, as plans. 3 *Law* To make void; annul. —*n.* 1 The act of defeating. 2 A failure to win or succeed. [< OF *defaire* undo]

de·feat·ism (di·fē′tiz·əm) *n.* A too ready acceptance or anticipation of defeat. **—de·feat′ist** *adj., n.*

def·e·cate (def′ə·kāt) *v.* **·cat·ed, ·cat·ing** *v.i.* 1 To discharge excrement from the bowels. 2 To become free of dregs or impurities. —*v.t.* 3 To clear of dregs or impurities; purify. —*adj.* Clarified; refined. [< L < *de-* down, away + *faex* dregs] **—def′e·ca′tion, def′e·ca′tor** *n.*

de·fect (di·fekt′, dē′fekt) *n.* 1 Lack or absence of something essential; deficiency. 2 An imperfection; failing; fault. —*v.i.* (di·fekt′) To desert; go over to the enemy or opposition. [< L *deficere* fail] **—de·fec′tor** *n.* **—Syn.** *n.* 2 blemish, flaw, drawback.

de·fec·tion (di·fek′shən) *n.* Abandonment of allegiance or duty; desertion.

de·fec·tive (di·fek′tiv) *adj.* 1 Incomplete or imperfect; faulty. 2 *Gram.* Lacking one or more of the normal declensional or conjugational forms: Can is a *defective* verb. 3 *Psychol.* Having less than normal intelligence. —*n.* 1 One who is physically or mentally subnormal. 2 *Gram.* A defective word. **—de·fec′tive·ly** *adv.* **—de·fec′tive·ness** *n.*

de·fend (di·fend′) *v.t.* 1 To shield from attack; protect. 2 To justify or vindicate; support. 3 *Law* **a** To act in behalf of (an accused). **b** To contest, as a claim, charge, or suit. 4 In sports, to try to keep one's opponent from scoring at (a goal, etc.). —*v.i.* 5 To make a defense. [< L *de-* down, away + *fendere* to strike] **—de·fend′a·ble** *adj.* **—de·fend′er** *n.*

de·fen·dant (di·fen′dənt) *n.* *Law* A person against whom an action is brought. —*adj.* Defending.

de·fense (di·fens′) *n.* 1 The act of defending or guarding.

2 The state of being defended. 3 Anything that defends. 4 A plea or statement that supports or justifies something. 5 *Law* a The arguments brought forth by a defendant or his legal counsel. b A defendant and his lawyer or lawyers. 6 Protection of oneself, as in boxing, or of one's goal, as in team sports. 7 Any group that is defending, as in sports. *Brit. sp.* **de′fence.** **—de·fense′less** *adj.* **—de·fense′less·ly** *adv.* **—de·fense′less·ness** *n.*

defense mechanism 1 *Psychoanal.* An unconscious process for protecting the personality against unpleasant emotions, impulses, etc. 2 Any self-protective reaction of an organism.

de·fen·si·ble (di·fen′sə·bəl) *adj.* Capable of being defended or justified. **—de·fen′si·bil′i·ty, de·fen′si·ble·ness** *n.* **—de·fen′si·bly** *adv.*

de·fen·sive (di·fen′siv) *adj.* 1 Intended or suitable for defense. 2 Done in defense. 3 Excessively inclined to defend or justify one's conduct, opinions, etc. —*n.* An attitude or position of defense. **—de·fen′sive·ly** *adv.* **—de·fen′sive·ness** *n.*

de·fer[1] (di·fûr′) *v.t. & v.i.* **·ferred, ·fer·ring** To delay; put off to some other time; postpone. [<L *differre* to distract] —**de·fer′ra·ble** *adj.* **—de·fer′ment** *n.*

de·fer[2] (di·fûr′) *v.i.* **·ferred, ·fer·ring** To yield to the opinions or decisions of another. [<L *de-* down + *ferre* bear, carry] **—de·fer′rer** *n.*

def·er·ence (def′ər·əns) *n.* 1 Respectful yielding. 2 Polite respect; regard. **—def′er·ent** *adj.*

def·er·en·tial (def′ə·ren′shəl) *adj.* Marked by deference; respectful; courteous. **—def′er·en′tial·ly** *adv.*

de·fi·ance (di·fī′əns) *n.* 1 Bold opposition; disposition to oppose or resist. 2 The act of defying.

de·fi·ant (di·fī′ənt) *adj.* Showing or characterized by defiance; resisting boldly. [<OF, pr.p. of *defier.* See DEFY.] —**de·fi′ant·ly** *adv.*

de·fib·ril·late (dē·fib′rə·lāt, dē·fī′brə-) *v.t.* **·lat·ed, ·lat·ing** To stop fibrillation of (the heart muscle), as by jolting with an electric current. **—de·fib′ril·la′tion, de·fib′ril·la′tor** *n.*

de·fi·cien·cy (di·fish′ən·sē) *n. pl.* **·cies** 1 The state of being deficient. 2 A lack; insufficiency. Also **de·fi′cience.**

de·fi·cient (di·fish′ənt) *adj.* 1 Lacking an adequate or proper supply; insufficient. 2 Lacking some essential; incomplete. [<L *deficere* to lack] **—de·fi′cient·ly** *adv.*

def·i·cit (def′ə·sit) *n.* The amount of money lacking in a required or expected sum. [L, it is lacking]

de·fi·er (di·fī′ər) *n.* One who defies.

de·file[1] (di·fīl′) *v.t.* **·filed, ·fil·ing** 1 To make foul or dirty; pollute. 2 To corrupt the purity of. 3 To sully; profane (a name, reputation, etc.). 4 To render ceremonially unclean. [<OF *de-* down + *fouler* trample] **—de·file′ment, de·fil′er** *n.*

de·file[2] (di·fīl′, dē′fīl) *v.i.* **·filed, ·fil·ing** To march in a line. —*n.* 1 A long narrow pass or gorge, as between mountains. 2 A marching in file. [<MF *dé-* down + *file* a line, file]

de·fine (di·fīn′) *v.t.* **·fined, ·fin·ing** 1 To state the meaning of (a word, etc.). 2 To describe or give the characteristics of. 3 To determine and specify the limits of. 4 To determine and fix the boundaries of. 5 To show or bring out the form or outline of. [<L *de-* down + *finire* finish] **—de·fin′a·ble** *adj.* **—de·fin′er** *n.*

def·i·nite (def′ə·nit) *adj.* 1 Having precise limits. 2 Precise; clear, as in meaning. 3 Certain; sure. 4 *Gram.* Limiting; particularizing: The *definite* article in English is "the". **—def′i·nite·ly** *adv.* **—def′i·nite·ness** *n.*

def·i·ni·tion (def′ə·nish′ən) *n.* 1 A defining or being defined. 2 A statement of the meaning of a word, phrase, etc. 3 A statement describing or making clear an object, process, etc. 4 The state of being clear, definite, etc. 5 The determining of the outline, character, or limits of anything. 6 *Optics* The power of a lens to give a distinct image at whatever magnification. 7 In television and radio, the clarity of detail in the transmitted images or sounds.

de·fin·i·tive (di·fin′ə·tiv) *adj.* 1 Decisive and final; conclusive. 2 Most nearly accurate, complete, etc.: a *definitive* study. 3 Sharply defining or limiting; explicit. **—de·fin′i·tive·ly** *adv.* **—de·fin′i·tive·ness** *n.*

de·flate (di·flāt′) *v.t. & v.i.* **·flat·ed, ·flat·ing** 1 To collapse or cause to collapse by the removal of contained air or gas. 2 To take the conceit, confidence, or self-esteem out of. 3 To devaluate; lessen (currency or prices). [<L *de-* down + *flare* blow] **—de·fla′tor** *n.*

de·fla·tion (di·flā′shən) *n.* 1 The act of deflating or the condition of being deflated. 2 A decrease in the amount of currency in circulation in a country, resulting in a decline in prices. **—de·fla·tion·ar·y** (di·flā′shən·er′ē) *adj.*

de·flect (di·flekt′) *v.t. & v.i.* To turn aside; swerve or cause to swerve from a course. [<L *de-* down + *flectere* bend] **—de·flec′tion, de·flec′tor** *n.* **—de·flec′tive** *adj.*

de·flow·er (di·flou′ər) *v.t.* 1 To deprive (a woman) of virginity. 2 To violate; rob of beauty.

de·fo·li·ate (dē·fō′lē·āt) *v.t.* **·at·ed, ·at·ing** To deprive or strip of leaves. [<L *de-* down + *folium* leaf] **—de·fo′li·a′tion, de·fo′li·a′tor** *n.*

de·for·est (dē·fôr′ist, -for′-) *v.t.* To clear of forests or trees. **—de·for′es·ta′tion, de·for′est·er** *n.*

de·form (di·fôrm′) *v.t.* 1 To distort the form or shape of. 2 To make ugly or dishonorable. —*v.i.* 3 To become deformed or disfigured. **—def·or·ma·tion** (def′ər·mā′shən) *n.*

de·formed (di·fôrmd′) *adj.* 1 Misshapen; warped. 2 Unattractive; ugly. **—de·form·ed·ly** (di·fôr′mid·lē) *adv.*

de·form·i·ty (di·fôr′mə·tē) *n. pl.* **·ties** 1 A deformed or misshapen condition or part. 2 Unsightliness; ugliness. 3 Moral depravity. 4 One who or that which is deformed.

de·fraud (di·frôd′) *v.t.* To take or withhold property, etc., from by fraud; cheat. **—de·fraud·a·tion** (dē′frô·dā′shən), **de·fraud′er** *n.*

de·fray (di·frā′) *v.t.* To pay for; bear the expense of. [<OF *de-* away + *frai* cost, charge] **—de·fray′a·ble** *adj.* **—de·fray′al, de·fray′ment, de·fray′er** *n.*

de·frock (dē·frok′) *v.t.* UNFROCK.

de·frost (dē·frôst′, -frost′) *v.t.* 1 To remove ice or frost from. —*v.i.* 2 To be rid of ice or frost.

de·frost·er (dē·frôs′tər, -fros′-) *n.* A device for defrosting, as in a refrigerator.

deft (deft) *adj.* Skillful; adroit; dexterous. [<OE *gedæfte* meek, gentle] **—deft′ly** *adv.* **—deft′ness** *n.*

de·funct (di·fungkt′) *adj.* Having passed out of existence or life; no longer functioning or alive: a *defunct* publication. [<L *de-* not + *fungi* perform]

de·fy (di·fī′) *v.t.* **·fied, ·fy·ing** 1 To resist openly or boldly. 2 To challenge; dare: to *defy* a rival politician to make public his tax returns. 3 To resist successfully; baffle; obstruct: to *defy* definition. [<OF *defier* <Med. L *dis-* not + *fidare* be faithful]

deg. degree(s).

de·gauss (di·gous′) *v.t.* To neutralize, cancel, or destroy the magnetic field of. [<DE- + GAUSS]

de·gen·er·a·cy (di·jen′ər·ə·sē) *n.* 1 The state of being degenerate, or the process of degenerating. 2 Degenerate behavior.

de·gen·er·ate (di·jen′ə·rāt) *v.i.* **·at·ed, ·at·ing** 1 To become worse or inferior. 2 *Biol.* To revert to a lower type; deteriorate. —*adj.* (di·jen′ər·it) 1 Having become worse or inferior; deteriorated. 2 Morally depraved or perverted. —*n.* (-it) 1 A deteriorated or degraded animal or human. 2 A morally depraved or perverted person. [<L *de-* down, away + *generare* create] **—de·gen′er·ate·ly** *adv.* **—de·gen′er·a′tive** *adj.* **—de·gen′er·ate·ness** *n.*

de·gen·er·a·tion (di·jen′ə·rā′shən) *n.* 1 The process of degenerating. 2 A degenerate condition. 3 Progressive deterioration of an organ, tissue, or part.

de·grad·a·ble (di·grā′də·bəl) *adj. Chem.* Capable of being degraded, as a compound.

deg·ra·da·tion (deg′rə·dā′shən) *n.* 1 The act of degrading. 2 The state of being reduced in rank, honor, etc.

de·grade (di·grād′) *v.* **·grad·ed, ·grad·ing** *v.t.* 1 To reduce in rank, status, quality, etc. 2 To debase or lower in character, morals, etc. 3 To bring into contempt; dishonor. 4 *Geol.* To reduce the height of by erosion. 5 *Chem.* To break down (an organic compound) into simpler parts. —*v.i.* 6 To degenerate; become of a lower type. [<L *de-* down + *gradus* position, step]

de·grad·ing (di·grā′ding) *adj.* Debasing; humiliating.

de·gree (di·grē′) *n.* 1 One of a succession of steps, grades, or stages. 2 Relative rank, position, or dignity: an executive of high *degree.* 3 Relative extent, amount, or intensity: burns of the first *degree.* 4 Relative manner, condition, ability, etc. 5 *Gram.* One of the forms in which an adjective or adverb is compared: "Worst" is the superlative *degree* of "bad." 6 An academic rank or title conferred by an institution of learning. 7 One remove in the direct line of descent. 8 A subdivision or unit on a scale, as for temperature. 9 The 360th part of a circle. 10 *Math.* The power to which an algebraic quantity is raised. 11 *Music* a A line or space of a staff. b The interval between two such lines or spaces. 12 *Law* A grade of seriousness: murder in the first *degree.* **—by degrees** Little by little; gradually. **—to a degree** 1 Extremely. 2 Somewhat. [< L *de-* down + *gradus* a step]

de·hisce (di·his′) *v.i.* **·hisced, ·hisc·ing** *Biol.* To burst open, as a cocoon or a seed pod. [< L *de-* down + *hiscere* to gape, yawn] **—de·his′cence** *n.* **—de·his′cent** *adj.*

de·hu·man·ize (dē·^{h}yōō′mən·īz) *v.t.* **·ized, ·iz·ing** To divest or deprive of human qualities or attributes; make abstract or mechanical. **—de·hu′man·i·za′tion** *n.*

de·hu·mid·i·fi·er (dē′^{h}yōō·mid′ə·fī′ər) *n.* An apparatus for removing moisture from the air.

de·hu·mid·i·fy (dē′^{h}yōō·mid′ə·fī) *v.t.* **·fied, ·fy·ing** To render less humid; remove moisture from. **—de′hu·mid′i·fi·ca′tion** *n.*

de·hy·drate (dē·hī′drāt) *v.* **·drat·ed, ·drat·ing** *v.t.* 1 To deprive of water. 2 To remove water from. *—v.i.* 3 To suffer loss of water. **—de′hy·dra′tion, de·hy′dra·tor** *n.*

de-ice (dē·īs′) *v.t. & v.i.* **·iced, ·ic·ing** 1 To remove ice from. 2 To prevent ice forming on. **—de·ic′er** *n.*

de·i·fy (dē′ə·fī) *v.t.* **·fied, ·fy·ing** 1 To make a god of; rank as a deity. 2 To regard or worship as a god. [< L *deus* god + *facere* make] **—de·if′ic** (-if′ik) *adj.* **—de·i·fi·ca·tion** (dē′ə·fə·kā′shən), **de′i·fi′er** *n.*

deign (dān) *v.i.* 1 To think it befitting or suitable (to do something). *—v.t.* 2 To condescend to grant or allow. [< L *dignari* to deem worthy]

de·ism (dē′iz·əm) *n.* The belief, based on the testimony of reason, that God created the world and set it in motion, subject to natural laws, but takes no interest in it or in its inhabitants. [< L *deus* a god + -ISM] **—de′ist** *n.* **—de·is′tic** or **·ti·cal** *adj.* **—de·is′ti·cal·ly** *adv.*

de·i·ty (dē′ə·tē) *n. pl.* **·ties** 1 A god, goddess, or divine person. 2 Divine nature or status; godhead; divinity. **—the Deity** GOD. [< L *deus* a god]

dé·jà vu (dā·zhä vōō′, dā·zhȧ vü′) *Psychol.* A distortion of memory in which a new situation or experience is regarded as having happened before. [F, lit., already seen]

de·ject (di·jekt′) *v.t.* To depress in spirit; make unhappy. [< L *de-* down + *jacere* throw] **—de·jec′tion** *n.*

de·ject·ed (di·jek′tid) *adj.* In low spirits; depressed; disheartened. **—de·ject′ed·ly** *adv.* **—de·ject′ed·ness** *n.*

dé·jeu·ner (dā·zhœ·nā′) *n.* 1 A late breakfast. 2 A luncheon. [F, breakfast]

de ju·re (dē jŏŏr′ē) By right; rightfully or legally. [L]

deka- *combining form* DECA-. Also **dek-.**

Del. Delaware.

del. delegate; delete; deliver.

de·lay (di·lā′) *v.t.* 1 To put off to a later time; postpone; defer. 2 To cause to be late; detain. *—v.i.* 3 To linger; procrastinate. *—n.* 1 The act of delaying or the condition of being delayed. 2 The period of time during which a thing or person is delayed. [< L *de-* off + *laxare* to slacken] **—de·lay′er** *n.* **—Syn.** *n.* 1 deferment, postponement, stop, stay.

de·le (dē′lē) *v.t.* **de·led, de·le·ing** *Printing* To take out; delete. [< L *delere* erase]

de·lec·ta·ble (di·lek′tə·bəl) *adj.* Giving pleasure; delightful; charming. [< L *delectare* to please] **—de·lec′ta·bil′i·ty, de·lec′ta·ble·ness** *n.* **—de·lec′ta·bly** *adv.*

de·lec·ta·tion (dē′lek·tā′shən) *n.* 1 Delight; enjoyment. 2 Amusement; entertainment.

del·e·ga·cy (del′ə·gə·sē) *n. pl.* **·cies** 1 The act of delegating or the condition of being delegated. 2 The authority given a delegate. 3 A body of delegates.

del·e·gate (del′ə·gāt, -git) *n.* 1 A person empowered to act for others; deputy; representative. 2 *U.S.* A nonvoting participant representing a Territory in the House of Representatives. 3 A member of the House of Delegates. *—v.t.* (-gāt) **·gat·ed, ·gat·ing** 1 To send as a representative, with authority to act; depute. 2 To commit or entrust (powers, authority, etc.) to another. *—adj.* (-gāt, -git) Sent as a deputy. [< L *de-* down + *legare* send]

del·e·ga·tion (del′ə·gā′shən) *n.* 1 The act of delegating. 2 A group of delegates; also, delegates collectively.

de·lete (di·lēt′) *v.t.* **·let·ed, ·let·ing** To take out or otherwise cancel (written or printed matter). [< L *delere* erase, destroy] **—de·le′tion** *n.*

del·e·te·ri·ous (del′ə·tir′ē·əs) *adj.* Causing moral or physical injury. [< Gk. *dēlētērios* harmful] **—del′e·te′ri·ous·ly** *adv.* **—del′e·te′ri·ous·ness** *n.*

delft (delft) *n.* 1 A glazed earthenware, usu. blue and white, made first at Delft, Netherlands. 2 Any tableware resembling this. Also **delf** (delf), **delft′ware′** (-wâr′). [< *Delft*, a town in the Netherlands]

del·i (del′ē) *n. pl.* **·is** *Informal* DELICATESSEN.

de·lib·er·ate (di·lib′ə·rāt) *v.* **·at·ed, ·at·ing** *v.i.* 1 To consider carefully and at length. 2 To consider reasons or arguments so as to reach a decision. *—v.t.* 3 To think about or consider carefully; weigh. *—adj.* (di·lib′ər·it) 1 Acting with or characterized by deliberation; not hasty. 2 Done after deliberation; intentional. 3 Slow and careful, as in movement. [< L *de-* completely + *librare* weigh] **—de·lib′er·ate·ly** *adv.* **—de·lib′er·ate·ness** *n.* **—Syn.** *adj.* 1 careful, thoughtful. 2 studied. 3 measured, unhurried.

de·lib·er·a·tion (di·lib′ə·rā′shən) *n.* 1 The act of deliberating. 2 *Often pl.* Discussion or consideration of all sides of a problem or issue. 3 Thoughtfulness and care in deciding or acting.

de·lib·er·a·tive (di·lib′ə·rā′tiv, -ər·ə·tiv) *adj.* Of, resulting from, or involved in deliberation. **—de·lib′er·a′tive·ly** *adv.* **—de·lib′er·a′tive·ness** *n.*

del·i·ca·cy (del′ə·kə·sē) *n. pl.* **·cies** 1 The quality of being delicate. 2 Fragility or frailty, as of health. 3 Need for careful or subtle treatment: a question of great *delicacy.* 4 Refinement of feeling, appreciation, etc. 5 Sensitiveness of touch, response, performance, etc. 6 A fine consideration for others. 7 A choice bit of food.

del·i·cate (del′ə·kit) *adj.* 1 Nicely light, mild, subtle, etc., as in flavor or color. 2 Exceedingly fine in quality, construction, texture, etc. 3 Very subtle: a *delicate* distinction. 4 Frail; fragile. 5 Easily injured or disordered: a *delicate* stomach. 6 Requiring cautious or subtle handling or treatment. 7 Nicely sensitive in feeling, appreciating, discriminating, etc: a *delicate* ear for music. 8 Extremely accurate or sensitive, as an instrument. 9 Finely skillful in touch or technique. 10 Tactful and considerate of others. [< L *delicatus* pleasing] **—del′i·cate·ly** *adv.* **—del′i·cate·ness** *n.*

del·i·ca·tes·sen (del′ə·kə·tes′ən) *n.* A store that sells cooked or preserved foods, as cooked meats, salads, cheeses, pickles, etc. [< G *Delicatesse* dainty food]

de·li·cious (di·lish′əs) *adj.* Extremely pleasant or enjoyable, esp. to the taste. [< L *delicia* a delight] **—de·li′cious·ly** *adv.* **—de·li′cious·ness** *n.*

De·li·cious (di·lish′əs) *n.* A variety of sweet winter apple.

de·light (di·līt′) *n.* 1 Great pleasure; joyful satisfaction. 2 That which affords extreme enjoyment. 3 The quality of delighting; charm. *—v.i.* 1 To take great pleasure; rejoice: with *in* or the infinitive. 2 To give great enjoyment. *—v.t.* 3 To please or gratify highly. [< L *de-* away + *lacere* entice] **—de·light′ed** *adj.* **—de·light′ed·ly** *adv.*

de·light·ful (di·līt′fəl) *adj.* Affording delight; very pleasing; charming. **—de·light′ful·ly** *adv.* **—de·light′ful·ness** *n.*

De·li·lah (di·lī′lə) In the Bible, the mistress of Samson, who betrayed him to the Philistines. *Judges* 16:4-20.

de·lim·it (di·lim′it) *v.t.* To prescribe the limits of; bound. **—de·lim′i·ta′tion** *n.* **—de·lim′i·ta′tive** *adj.*

de·lin·e·ate (di·lin′ē·āt) *v.t.* **·at·ed, ·at·ing** 1 To draw in outline; trace out. 2 To portray pictorially. 3 To describe verbally. [< L *de-* completely + *linea* a line] **—de·lin′e·a′tion, de·lin′e·a′tor** *n.* **—de·lin′e·a′tive** *adj.*

de·lin·quen·cy (di·ling′kwən·sē) *n. pl.* **·cies** 1 Neglect of duty. 2 A fault; offense. 3 Illegal or antisocial behavior of a juvenile.

de·lin·quent (di·ling′kwənt) *adj.* 1 Neglectful of or failing in duty or obligation; faulty. 2 Due and unpaid, as taxes. —*n.* A person who is delinquent, esp. a young person who engages in illegal or antisocial behavior. [< L *de-* down, away + *linquere* leave] —**de·lin′quent·ly** *adv.*

del·i·quesce (del′ə·kwes′) *v.i.* **·quesced, ·quesc·ing** 1 To become liquid by absorption of moisture from the air, as certain salts. 2 To melt or pass away gradually. [< L *de-* completely + *liquescere* melt] —**del′i·ques′cence** *n.* —**del′i·ques′cent** *adj.*

de·lir·i·ous (di·lir′ē·əs) *adj.* 1 Suffering from delirium. 2 Pertaining to or caused by delirium. 3 Extremely excited. —**de·lir′i·ous·ly** *adv.* —**de·lir′i·ous·ness** *n.*

de·lir·i·um (di·lir′ē·əm) *n.* 1 A temporary mental disturbance associated with fever, intoxication, etc., and marked by agitation, hallucinations, and incoherence. 2 Intense excitement; frenzy. [< L *delirare* to deviate from a straight line]

delirium tre·mens (trē′mənz) Delirium caused by excessive use of alcoholic liquors. [NL, trembling delirium]

de·liv·er (di·liv′ər) *v.t.* 1 To hand over; transfer possession of. 2 To carry and distribute: to *deliver* mail. 3 To utter; say: to *deliver* a speech. 4 To assist (a female) in the birth of (a child). 5 To free from evil, danger, etc.; rescue. 6 To send forth; discharge; emit. 7 To give; strike, as a blow. 8 To throw or pitch, as a ball. 9 *Informal* To bring (votes, etc.) to the support of a political candidate. —*v.i.* 10 *Informal* To achieve good or proper results; perform well. [< L *de-* down, away + *liberare* set free] —**de·liv′er·a·ble** *adj.* —**de·liv′er·er** *n.*

de·liv·er·ance (di·liv′ər·əns) *n.* 1 The act of delivering or state of being delivered. 2 An opinion or judgment publicically uttered.

de·liv·er·y (di·liv′ər·ē) *n. pl.* **·er·ies** 1 The act of delivering. 2 Something delivered. 3 The act of releasing or setting free. 4 The act or manner of giving a speech, pitching a ball, etc. 5 Childbirth.

dell (del) *n.* A small, secluded valley, esp. a wooded one. [< OE]

de·louse (dē·lous′) *v.t.* **·loused, ·lous·ing** To remove lice from.

Del·phi (del′fī) *n.* An ancient city in Greece, famous for its oracle of Apollo. —**Del·phi·an** (del′fē·ən) *adj., n.* —**Del′·phic** *adj.*

del·phin·i·um (del·fin′ē·əm) *n.* Any of a genus of perennial plants having spikes of spurred flowers, usu. blue. [< Gk. *delphinion* larkspur]

del·ta (del′tə) *n.* 1 The fourth letter in the Greek alphabet. (Δ, δ). 2 An alluvial silt deposit, usu. triangular, at or in the mouth of a river. —**del·ta·ic** (del·tā′ik) *adj.*

del·toid (del′toid) *n.* The large shoulder muscle which contracts to move the arm sideways. —*adj.* 1 Triangular. 2 Of or pertaining to the deltoid. [< Gk. *delta* the letter Δ + *eidos* form]

de·lude (di·lo͞od′) *v.t.* **·lud·ed, ·lud·ing** To mislead the mind or judgment of; deceive. [< L *de-* down, away + *ludere* to play] —**de·lud′er** *n.*

del·uge (del′yo͞oj) *v.t.* **·uged, ·ug·ing** 1 To flood with water; inundate. 2 To overwhelm: He *deluged* her with compliments. —*n.* 1 A great flood; inundation. 2 Anything that comes like a flood. —**the Deluge** The flood in the time of Noah. *Gen.* 7. [< L *diluere* wash away]

de·lu·sion (di·lo͞o′zhən) *n.* 1 The act of deluding or the state of being deluded. 2 A false, irrational, and persistent belief. —**de·lu′sion·al** *adj.*

de·lu·sive (di·lo͞o′siv) *adj.* Tending to delude; misleading; deceptive. Also **de·lu·so·ry** (di·lo͞o′sər·ē) —**de·lu′sive·ly** *adv.* —**de·lu′sive·ness** *n.*

de luxe (di lo͝oks′, di luks′, di lo͞oks′) Luxurious; of superior quality. [F, lit., of luxury]

delve (delv) *v.* **delved, delv·ing** *v.i.* To make careful investigation for facts, knowledge, etc.: to *delve* into a crime. [< OE *delfan*] —**delv′er** *n.*

Dem. Democrat; Democratic.

de·mag·net·ize (dē·mag′nə·tīz) *v.t.* **·ized, ·iz·ing** To deprive of magnetism. —**de·mag′net·i·za′tion, de·mag′net·iz′er** *n.*

dem·a·gogue (dem′ə·gôg, -gog) *n.* One who attempts to gain power by arousing the prejudices and passions of the people. Also **dem′a·gog.** [< Gk. *dēmos* people + *agein* lead] —**dem′a·gog′ic** (-goj′ik) or **·i·cal** *adj.* —**dem′a·gog′i·cal·ly** *adv.* —**dem′a·gog′ism** (-gog′iz·əm) or **dem′a·gogu′ism, dem′·a·gogu′er·y** (-gog′ər·ē), **dem·a·go·gy** (dem′ə·gō′jē, -gôg′ē, -gog′ē) *n.*

de·mand (di·mand′, -mänd′) *v.t.* 1 To ask for boldly; insist upon. 2 To claim as due; ask for authoritatively. 3 To ask to know; inquire formally. 4 To have need for; require. 5 *Law* a To summon to court. b To make formal claim to (property). —*v.i.* 6 To make a demand. —*n.* 1 The act of demanding, or that which is demanded. 2 A requirement; claim; need. 3 *Econ.* a The desire to possess combined with the ability to purchase. b The amount of a given commodity people will buy at a certain price. —**in demand** Desired; sought after. —**on demand** On presentation: a note payable *on demand.* [< L *de-* down, away + *mandare* to command; order] —**de·mand′a·ble** *adj.* —**de·mand′er** *n.*

de·mand·ing (di·mand′ing, -mänd′) *adj.* Making many difficult demands on one's energy, time, patience, etc. —**de·mand′ing·ly** *adv.*

de·mar·cate (di·mär′kāt, dē′mär·kāt) *v.t.* **·cat·ed, ·cat·ing** 1 To mark the bounds or limits of; delimit. 2 To distinguish; separate. [Back formation < DEMARCATION]

de·mar·ca·tion (dē′mär·kā′shən) *n.* 1 The fixing of boundaries or limits. 2 The boundaries or limits fixed. 3 Limitation; discrimination. Also **de′mar·ka′tion.** [< Sp. *de-* down + *marcar* mark a boundary]

dé·marche (dā·märsh′) *n.* 1 A manner of approach or mode of procedure. 2 In diplomacy, a change in plan of action. [F]

de·mean[1] (di·mēn′) *v.t.* To behave or conduct (oneself). [< OF *de-* down + *mener* lead]

de·mean[2] (di·mēn′) *v.t.* To lower in character or reputation; degrade; debase. [< DE- + MEAN[2]]

de·mean·or (di·mē′nər) *n.* 1 Behavior; deportment 2 Appearance; mien.

de·ment·ed (di·men′tid) *adj.* Deprived of reason; insane. —**de·ment′ed·ly** *adv.* —**de·ment′ed·ness** *n.*

de·men·tia (di·men′shə, -shē·ə) *n.* Impairment or deterioration of mental capacity. [L, madness]

dementia pre·cox (prē′koks) *Obs.* SCHIZOPHRENIA. [NL, premature dementia] Also **dementia prae′cox.**

de·mer·it (di·mer′it) *n.* 1 In schools, etc., a mark for failure or misconduct. 2 Censurable conduct. [< L *demerere* deserve]

de·mesne (di·mān′, -mēn′) *n.* 1 *Law* Real estate held in one's own right. 2 A lord's manor house and adjoining lands. 3 Any landed estate. 4 A region or domain. [< OF *demaine* domain]

De·me·ter (di·mē′tər) *Gk. Myth.* The goddess of agriculture, marriage, and fertility.

demi- *prefix* 1 Half: *demisemiquaver.* 2 Inferior or less in size, quality, etc.; partial: *demigod.* [< L *dimidius* half]

dem·i·god (dem′ē·god′) *n.* 1 An inferior deity. 2 A man with the attributes of a god. —**dem′i·god′dess** *n. Fem.*

dem·i·john (dem′ē·jon′) *n.* A large, juglike glass or crockery vessel enclosed in wickerwork. [< F *dame-jeanne,* lit., Lady Jane]

de·mil·i·ta·rize (dē·mil′ə·tə·rīz′) *v.t.* **·rized, ·riz·ing** 1 To remove the military control of; free from militarism. 2 To remove military equipment and troops from and declare neutral, as an area or zone. —**de·mil′i·ta·ri·za′tion** *n.*

dem·i·mon·daine (dem′ē·mon·dān′) *n.* A woman of the demimonde. [F]

dem·i·monde (dem′ē·mond, dem′ē·mond′) *n.* 1 A class of women who are kept as the mistresses of wealthy patrons. 2 Prostitutes collectively. 3 Any class of people whose behavior or attainments are somewhat questionable. [F < *demi-* half, partial + *monde* world]

de·mise (di·mīz′) *n.* 1 Death. 2 *Law* A transfer or conveyance of rights or estate. —*v.* **·mised, ·mis·ing** *v.t.* 1 To bestow (sovereign power) by death or abdication. 2 *Law* To lease (an estate) for life or for a term of years. —*v.i.* 3 To pass by will or inheritance. [< OF *demettre* send away] —**de·mis′a·ble** *adj.*

dem·i·sem·i·qua·ver (dem′ē·sem′ē·kwā′vər) *n. Music* A thirty-second note.

dem·i·tasse (dem′ē·tas′, -täs′) *n.* 1 A small cup in which after-dinner coffee is served. 2 The coffee itself. [F]

de·mo·bil·ize (dē·mō′bəl·īz) *v.t.* **·ized, ·iz·ing 1** To disband (troops). **2** To discharge (a person) from military service. **—de·mo′bil·i·za′tion** *n.*

de·moc·ra·cy (di·mok′rə·sē) *n. pl.* **·cies 1** Government in which political control is shared by all the people, either directly or by representatives whom they elect. **2** A state so governed. **3** Political, legal, or social equality. [< Gk. *dēmos* people + *krateein* to rule]

dem·o·crat (dem′ə·krat) *n.* **1** One who favors a democracy. **2** One who believes in political and social equality.

Dem·o·crat (dem′ə·krat) *n.* A member of the Democratic party in the U.S.

dem·o·crat·ic (dem′ə·krat′ik) *adj.* **1** Of, pertaining to, or characterized by the principles of democracy. **2** Of, for, or appealing to all or most people. **3** Practicing social equality; not snobbish. **—dem′o·crat′i·cal·ly** *adv.*

Democratic Party One of the two major political parties in the U.S.

de·moc·ra·tize (di·mok′rə·tīz) *v.t. & v.i.* **·tized, ·tiz·ing** To make or become democratic. **—de·moc′ra·ti·za′tion** *n.*

dé·mo·dé (dā·mô·dā′) *adj.* Old-fashioned; outmoded; out of style. [F]

de·mod·u·late (dē·moj′ōō·lāt) *v.t.* **·lat·ed, ·lat·ing** To restore (a modulated radio signal) to intelligible form. **—de·mod′u·la′tion** *n.*

de·mod·u·la·tor (de·moj′ōō·lāt′ər) *n.* A device for receiving a modulated radio signal.

de·mog·ra·phy (di·mog′rə·fē) *n.* The science dealing with vital and social statistics. [< Gk. *dēmos* people + -GRAPHY] **—de·mog′ra·pher, de·mog′ra·phist** *n.* **—dem·o·graph·ic** (dem′ə·graf′ik) or **·i·cal** *adj.* **—dem′o·graph′i·cal·ly** *adv.*

de·mol·ish (di·mol′ish) *v.t.* **1** To tear down; raze, as a building. **2** To destroy utterly; ruin. [< L *de-* down + *moliri* build] **—de·mol′ish·er, de·mol′ish·ment** *n.*

dem·o·li·tion (dem′ə·lish′ən) *n.* The act or result of demolishing; destruction. **—dem′o·li′tion·ist** *n.*

demolition bomb A bomb with a high explosive charge used to demolish buildings.

de·mon (dē′mən) *n.* **1** An evil spirit; devil. **2** A wicked or cruel person. **3** A person of great energy, skill, etc. [< Gk. *daimōn*] **—de·mon·ic** (di·mon′ik) *adj.* **—de·mon′i·cal·ly** *adv.*

de·mon·e·tize (dē·mon′ə·tīz) *v.t.* **·tized, ·tiz·ing 1** To deprive (currency) of standard value. **2** To withdraw from use as currency. **—de·mon′e·ti·za′tion** *n.*

de·mo·ni·ac (di·mō′nē·ak) *adj.* **1** Of, like, or befitting a demon; devilish. **2** Possessed by or as by demons. **3** Mad; violent; frenzied. Also **de·mo·ni·a·cal** (dē′mə·nī′ə·kəl) **—***n.* One possessed of a demon. **—de′mo·ni′a·cal·ly** *adv.*

de·mon·ism (dē′mən·iz′əm) *n.* **1** Belief in demons. **2** DEMONOLATRY. **3** DEMONOLOGY. **—de′mon·ist** *n.*

de·mon·ol·a·try (dē′mən·ol′ə·trē) *n.* Worship of demons. [< DEMON + Gk. *latreia* worship] **—de′mon·ol′a·ter** *n.*

de·mon·ol·o·gy (dē′mən·ol′ə·jē) *n.* The study of demons. **—de′mon·ol′o·gist** *n.*

de·mon·stra·ble (di·mon′strə·bəl) *adj.* Capable of being proved or demonstrated. **—de·mon′stra·ble·ness, de·mon′·stra·bil′i·ty** *n.* **—de·mon′stra·bly** *adv.*

dem·on·strate (dem′ən·strāt) *v.* **·strat·ed, ·strat·ing** *v.t.* **1** To explain or describe by use of experiments, examples, etc. **2** To explain or show the operation or use of. **3** To prove or show by logic; make evident. **4** To exhibit; make clear, as emotions. **—***v.i.* **5** To take part in a public demonstration. **6** To make a show of military force. [< L *de-* completely + *monstrare* show, point out]

dem·on·stra·tion (dem′ən·strā′shən) *n.* **1** The act of making known. **2** Cogent proof by the use of facts, principles, and arguments. **3** A presentation of how something operates or is done. **4** An organized public exhibition of welcome, approval, or condemnation, as by a mass meeting or procession. **5** A show of military force or invincibility. **—Syn. 2** evidence, testimony, substantiation.

de·mon·stra·tive (di·mon′strə·tiv) *adj.* **1** Demonstrating or pointing out. **2** Convincing and conclusive. **3** Showing feelings openly or expressively. **4** *Gram.* Indicating the person or object referred to: *This* and *that* are *demonstrative* pronouns and adjectives. **—***n.* A demonstrative pronoun or adjective. **—de·mon′stra·tive·ly** *adv.* **—de·mon′·stra·tive·ness** *n.*

dem·on·stra·tor (dem′ən·strā′tər) *n.* **1** One who demonstrates, as a salesman offering a new product. **2** A participant in a mass demonstration. **3** Something, as a new product, used for demonstration.

de·mor·al·ize (di·môr′əl·īz, -mor′-, dē′-) *v.t.* **·ized, ·iz·ing 1** To undermine the morale of. **2** To throw into disorder. **—de·mor′al·i·za′tion, de·mor′al·iz′er** *n.*

de·mote (di·mōt′) *v.t.* **·mot·ed, ·mot·ing** To reduce to a lower grade or rank. [< DE- + (PRO)MOTE] **—de·mo′tion** *n.*

de·mul·cent (di·mul′sənt) *adj.* Soothing. **—***n.* A soothing medication. [< L *de-* down + *mulcere* soothe]

de·mur (di·mûr′) *v.i.* **·murred, ·mur·ring 1** To offer objections. **2** To delay; hesitate. **3** *Law* To interpose a demurrer. **—***n.* **1** A delay. **2** An objection. [< L *de-* completely + *morari* to delay]

de·mure (di·myŏŏr′) *adj.* **1** Sedate; modest. **2** Affecting modesty; coy. [< OF *demore*] **—de·mure′ly** *adv.* **—de·mure′·ness** *n.*

de·mur·rage (di·mûr′ij) *n.* **1** The delaying of a vessel, truck, etc., beyond the specified time for departure because of loading or unloading. **2** Compensation for such delay. [< OF *demourer* to delay]

de·mur·rer (di·mûr′ər) *n.* **1** *Law* A plea for the dismissal of a suit on the grounds that the facts presented by the opposition, although true, do not validly support the claim. **2** Any objection. **3** One who demurs.

de·my·thol·o·gize (dē·mə·thol′ə·gīz) *v.t.* **·gized, ·giz·ing 1** To strip away the myth from. **2** *Theol.* To reinterpret (the Bible, religious subjects, etc.) without mythology. **—de·my·thol′o·gi·za′tion** *n.*

den (den) *n.* **1** A cavern occupied by animals; a lair. **2** A squalid residence or gathering place. **3** A room where one can work, read, etc., in private . **—***v.i.* **denned, den·ning** To dwell in, or as in, a den. [< OE *denn*]

Den. Denmark.

de·nar·i·us (di·nâr′ē·əs) *n. pl.* **·nar·i·i** (-nâr′ē·ī) **1** A silver coin of ancient Rome; the penny of the New Testament. **2** A gold coin of ancient Rome. [< L *denarius* of ten; because it was worth ten asses]

de·na·tion·al·ize (dē·nash′ən·əl·īz′) *v.t.* **·ized, ·iz·ing** To deprive of national character, status, rights, etc. **—de·na′·tion·al·i·za′tion** *n.*

de·nat·u·ral·ize (dē·nach′ər·əl·īz′, -nach′rəl-) *v.t.* **·ized, ·iz·ing 1** To render unnatural. **2** To deprive of citizenship. **—de·nat′u·ral·i·za′tion** *n.*

de·na·ture (dē·nā′chər) *v.t.* **·tured, ·tur·ing 1** To alter the nature of. **2** To make (alcohol, fat, etc.) unfit for drinking or eating without destroying other useful properties. **—de·na′tur·ant, de·na′tur·a′tion** *n.*

den·drite (den′drīt) *n.* **1** Any mineral crystallizing in a branching, treelike form or having treelike markings. **2** *Physiol.* One of the branching processes of a nerve cell. **—den·drit′ic** (-drit′ik) or **·i·cal** *adj.* **—den·drit′i·cal·ly** *adv.* [< Gk. *dendron* tree]

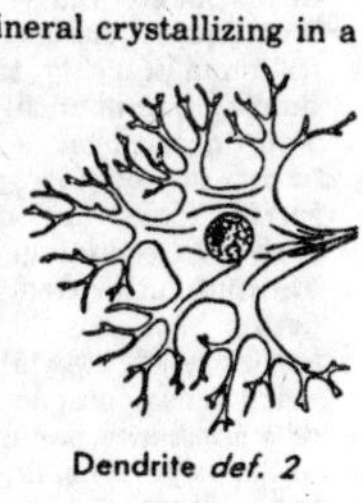

Dendrite *def. 2*

den·drol·o·gy (den·drol′ə·jē) *n.* The science of trees. [< Gk. *dendron* tree + -LOGY] **—den·drol′o·gist** *n.*

-dendron *combining form* Tree; treelike formation: *philodendron.* [< Gk. *dendron* tree]

den·gue (deng′gē, -gā) *n.* An infectious tropical disease transmitted by mosquitoes and characterized by fever, rash, and pain in the joints. [< Swahili]

de·ni·al (di·nī′əl) *n.* **1** A refusal to grant a request. **2** A declaration that a statement is untrue; contradiction. **3** A disowning or disavowal; rejection. **4** A refusal to agree with or believe in a doctrine, proposal, etc. **—Syn. 1** declining, rebuff. **3** repudiation, renunciation.

de·nic·o·tin·ize (dē·nik′ə·tin·īz′) *v.t.* **·ized, ·iz·ing** To remove nicotine from.

de·ni·er[1] (di·nī′ər) *n.* One who makes denial.
den·ier[2] (den′yər, də·nir′) *n.* A unit of weight for measuring the fineness of rayon, nylon, or silk thread. [< L *denarius* of ten]
den·i·grate (den′ə·grāt) *v.t.* **·grat·ed, ·grat·ing** To slander; defame. [< L *de-* completely + *nigrare* blacken] **—den′i·gra′tion, den′i·gra′tor** *n.* **—den·i·gra·to·ry** (den′ə·grə·tôr′ē, -tō′rē) *adj.*
den·im (den′əm) *n.* A sturdy twilled cotton used for overalls, uniforms, etc. [< F *(serge) de Nîmes* (serge) of Nîmes, where first made]
den·i·zen (den′ə·zən) *n.* **1** A resident; inhabitant. **2** A person who frequents a place. **3** A person, animal, or thing at home in a region, although not a native. —*v.t. Brit.* NATURALIZE. [< AF *deinz* inside] **—den′i·zen·a′tion** *n.*
Den·mark (den′märk) *n.* A kingdom in NW Europe, 16,619 sq. mi., cap. Copenhagen.

denom. denomination.
de·nom·i·nate (di·nom′ə·nāt) *v.t.* **·nat·ed, ·nat·ing** To give a name to; call. [< L *denominare*] **—de·nom′i·na·ble** (-ə·nə·bəl) *adj.*
de·nom·i·na·tion (di·nom′ə·nā′shən) *n.* **1** The act of naming. **2** The name or designation of a class of things. **3** A specific unit of value: coins of all *denominations.* **4** A religious sect or group having a specific name. **—de·nom′i·na′tion·al** *adj.* **—de·nom′i·na′tion·al·ism, de·nom′i·na′tion·al·ist** *n.* **—de·nom′i·na′tion·al·ly** *adv.*
de·nom·i·na·tive (di·nom′ə·nə·tiv, -nā′tiv) *adj.* **1** That gives or constitutes a name; appellative. **2** Derived from a noun or adjective. —*n.* A word, esp. a verb, derived from a noun or adjective, as *to garden.* **—de·nom′i·na·tive·ly** *adj.*
de·nom·i·na·tor (di·nom′ə·nā′tər) *n.* **1** One who or that which names. **2** That term of a fraction which expresses the number of equal parts into which the numerator is divided; divisor.
de·no·ta·tion (dē′nō·tā′shən) *n.* **1** The act of denoting. **2** The actual, explicit meaning or object denoted by a word. **3** That which indicates; a sign.
de·note (di·nōt′) *v.t.* **·not·ed, ·not·ing** **1** To mark; point out or make known. **2** To signify; indicate. **3** To designate; mean: said of words, symbols, etc. [< L *de-* down + *notare* to mark] **—de·not′a·ble, de·no·ta·tive** (di·nō′tə·tiv, dē′nō·tā′tiv) *adj.* **—de·no′ta·tive·ly** *adv.*
de·noue·ment (dā·nōō·mäṅ′) *n.* **1** The final unraveling or outcome of the plot of a play, novel, etc. **2** Any final solution. Also **dé·noue·ment′.** [< F *dénouement* < *dénouer* to untie]
de·nounce (di·nouns′) *v.t.* **·nounced, ·nouncing** **1** To condemn openly and vehemently; inveigh against. **2** To inform against; accuse. **3** To give formal notice of the termination of (a treaty, truce, etc.). [< L *de-* down + *nuntiare* proclaim, announce] **—de·nounce′ment, de·nounc′er** *n.* — **Syn. 1** decry, charge, attack, censure, curse.
de no·vo (dē nō′vō) Once again; anew. [L]
dense (dens) *adj.* **dens·er, dens·est** **1** Having its parts crowded closely together; compact; **2** Hard to penetrate. **3** Stupid; dull-witted. [< L *densus*] **—dense′ly** *adv.* **—dense′ness** *n.*
den·si·ty (den′sə·tē) *n. pl.* **·ties** **1** The state or quality of being dense; compactness. **2** Stupidity. **3** *Physics* The mass of a substance per unit of its volume. **4** The number of units, as persons, families, etc., per specified area.
dent (dent) *n.* A small depression made by striking or pressing; indentation. —*v.t.* To make a dent in. —*v.i.* To become dented. [Var. of DINT]
dent. dental; dentist; dentistry.
den·tal (den′təl) *adj.* **1** Of or pertaining to the teeth. **2** Of or pertaining to dentistry. **3** *Phonet.* Produced with the tip of the tongue against or near the upper front teeth. —*n. Phonet.* A dental consonant. [< L *dens, dentis* a tooth]
den·tate (den′tāt) *adj.* **1** Having teeth or toothlike processes; toothed. **2** *Bot.* Serrated, as certain leaves. **—den′tate·ly** *adv.* **—den·ta′tion** *n.*
den·ti·frice (den′tə·fris) *n.* A preparation for cleaning the teeth. [< L *dens, dentis* tooth + *fricare* rub]
den·tine (den′tēn, -tin) *n.* The bonelike substance forming the body of a tooth beneath the enamel. Also **den′tin** (-tin). **—den′tin·al** *adj.* • See TOOTH.
den·tist (den′tist) *n.* One who practices dentistry. [< F *dent* a tooth]
den·tist·ry (den′tis·trē) *n.* **1** The medical science concerned with preserving, treating, and repairing the teeth and their associated structures. **2** The work of a dentist.
den·ti·tion (den·tish′ən) *n.* **1** The process or period of teething. **2** The kind, number, and arrangement of the teeth in the mouth. [< L *dentire* cut teeth]
den·ture (den′chər) *n.* A block or set of teeth, esp. artificial ones. [< F *dent* tooth] **—den′tur·al** *adj.*
de·nu·date (di·nyōō′dāt, den′yōō·dāt) *adj.* Naked; stripped, as of foliage. —*v.t.* **·dat·ed, ·dat·ing** DENUDE.
de·nude (di·nyōōd′) *v.t.* **·nud·ed, ·nud·ing** **1** To strip the covering from. **2** *Geol.* To wear away and expose by erosion. [< L *de-* down, completely + *nudare* to strip] **—den·u·da·tion** (den′yōō·dā′shən, dē′nyōō-) *n.*
de·nun·ci·ate (di·nun′sē·āt) *v.t.* & *v.i.* **·at·ed, ·at·ing** DENOUNCE. [< L *denuntiare.* See DENOUNCE.] **—de·nun′ci·a′tor** *n.* **—de·nun·ci·a·to·ry** (di·nun′sē·ə·tôr′ē, -tō′rē) *adj.*
de·nun·ci·a·tion (di·nun′sē·ā′shən) *n.* **1** The act of denouncing, esp. a vehement and public condemnation. **—de·nun′ci·a′tive** *adj.* **—de·nun′ci·a′tive·ly** *adv.*
de·ny (di·nī′) *v.t.* **·nied, ·ny·ing** **1** To declare to be untrue; contradict. **2** To reject (a doctrine, etc.) as false or not real. **3** To refuse to give; withhold. **4** To refuse (someone) a request. **5** To refuse to acknowledge; disown; repudiate. **6** To refuse access to. **—deny oneself** To refuse oneself a gratification. [< L *de-* completely + *negare* refuse]
de·o·dar (dē′ə·där) *n.* **1** A large Himalayan cedar, prized for its fragrant wood. **2** This wood. [< Skt. *devadāru* divine tree]
de·o·dor·ant (dē·ō′dər·ənt) *adj.* Destroying, absorbing, or disguising bad odors. —*n.* A deodorant substance, as a cream, spray, etc. [< DE- + L *odorare* have an odor]
de·o·dor·ize (dē·ō′dər·īz) *v.t.* **·ized, ·iz·ing** To modify, destroy, or disguise the odor of. **—de·o′dor·i·za′tion, de·o′dor·iz′er** *n.*
de·ox·i·dize (dē·ok′sə·dīz) *v.t.* **·dized, ·diz·ing** To remove oxygen, esp. chemically combined oxygen, from. **—de·ox′i·di·za′tion, de·ox′i·diz′er** *n.*
de·ox·y·ri·bo·nu·cle·ic acid (dē·ok′sē·rī·bō·nyōō·klē′ik, -klā′ik) A complex compound present in the nucleus of every living cell, consisting of units whose sequence in a spiral configuration determines the unique genetic make-up of the organism.
dep. depart; department; departure; deponent; deposed; deposit; depot; deputy.
de·part (di·pärt′) *v.i.* **1** To go away; leave. **2** To deviate; differ; vary: with *from.* **3** To die. —*v.t.* **4** To leave: to *depart* this life. [< OF *de-* away + *partir* divide]
de·part·ment (di·pärt′mənt) *n.* **1** A separate and distinct part, division, or subdivision of a government, business, school, etc.: the accounting *department;* French *department.* **2** A special area of activity, skill, etc.: Cooking is my *department.* **3** In France, a government administrative district. [< OF *departir* divide] **—de·part·men·tal** (dē′pärt·men′təl) *adj.* **—de′part·men′tal·ly** *adv.* **—de′part·men′tal·ism** *n.*
department store A retail store where a wide variety of merchandise is sold in separate departments.
de·par·ture (di·pär′chər) *n.* **1** The act of departing or leaving. **2** The act of deviating from a method, set of ideas, etc.: with *from.* **3** A starting out, as on a new venture.
de·pend (di·pend′) *v.i.* **1** To trust; have full reliance: with *on* or *upon.* **2** To be determined by or contingent on something else: with *on* or *upon.* **3** To rely for maintenance, support, etc.: with *on* or *upon.* **4** To hang down: with *from.* [< L *de-* down + *pendere* hang]
de·pend·a·ble (di·pen′də·bəl) *adj.* That can be depended upon; trustworthy. **—de·pend′a·bil′i·ty, de·pend′a·ble·ness** *n.* **—de·pend′a·bly** *adv.*
de·pen·dence (di·pen′dəns) *n.* **1** The condition of being determined by or dependent on some one or something else. **2** Reliance on another person or thing. **3** Subordination. **4** Reciprocal reliance; trust. Also **de·pen′dance.**
de·pen·den·cy (di·pen′dən·sē) *n. pl.* **·cies** **1** DEPENDENCE.

2 Something subordinate. 3 A territory or state that is subject to another state.

de·pen·dent (di·pen′dənt) *adj.* 1 Depending or contingent upon something else: often with *on* or *upon.* 2 Needing support or aid from another: with *on.* 3 Subordinate. 4 Hanging down: with *from.* —*n.* One who looks to another for support, aid, etc. Also, esp. for noun, **de·pen′dant.**

de·per·son·al·ize (dē·pûr′sən·ə·līz′) *v.t.* **·ized, ·iz·ing** 1 To deprive of distinctive character or personality. 2 To make impersonal: to *depersonalize* history. **—de·per′son·al·i·za′tion** *n.*

de·pict (di·pikt′) *v.t.* 1 To portray or represent by drawing, sculpturing, painting, etc. 2 To describe verbally. [< L *depictus,* pp. of *depingere* to paint] **—de·pic′ter, de·pic′tion** *n.*

dep·i·late (dep′ə·lāt) *v.t.* **·lat·ed, ·lat·ing** To remove hair from. [< L *de-* away + *pilus* hair] **—dep′i·la′tion, dep′i·la′tor** *n.*

de·pil·a·to·ry (di·pil′ə·tôr′ē, -tō′rē) *adj.* Having the power to remove hair. —*n.* A preparation for removing hair, wool, etc., from skin or hides.

de·plane (di·plān′) *v.i.* **·planed, ·plan·ing** To disembark from an aircraft.

de·plete (di·plēt′) *v.t.* **·plet·ed, ·plet·ing** 1 To reduce or lessen, as by use, exhaustion, or waste. 2 To empty wholly or partially. [< L *de-* not + *plere* to fill] **—de·ple′tion** *n.* **—de·ple′tive** *adj.*

de·plor·a·ble (di·plôr′ə·bəl, -plō′rə-) *adj.* Lamentable; regrettable. **—de·plor′a·bil′i·ty** *n.* **—de·plor′a·bly** *adv.*

de·plore (di·plôr′, -plōr′) *v.t.* **·plored, ·plor·ing** To feel or express deep regret or concern for; lament. [< L *de-* completely + *plorare* bewail]

de·ploy (di·ploi′) *v.t.* 1 To spread out (troops, etc.) strategically or in a line of battle. 2 To use or arrange in a strategic manner. —*v.i.* 3 To be deployed. [< LL *displicare* scatter] **—de·ploy′ment** *n.*

de·po·lar·ize (dē·pō′lə·rīz) *v.t.* **·ized, ·iz·ing** 1 To break up or remove the polarization of. 2 To deprive of polarity. **—de·po′lar·i·za′tion, de·po′lar·iz′er** *n.*

de·po·lit·i·cize (dē·pə·lit′ə·sīz′) *v.t.* **·cized, ·ciz·ing** To make nonpolitical. Also **de·po·lit′i·cal·ize′** (-kəl·īz′).

de·po·nent (di·pō′nənt) *adj.* In Latin and Greek grammar, denoting a verb that has the form of the passive but is active in meaning. —*n.* 1 A deponent verb. 2 *Law* One who gives sworn testimony, esp. in writing. [< L *deponere* lay aside]

de·pop·u·late (dē·pop′yə·lāt) *v.t.* **·lat·ed, ·lat·ing** To remove the inhabitants from, by massacre, famine, etc. [< L *de-* away + *populus* people] **—de·pop′u·la′tion, de·pop′u·la′tor** *n.*

de·port (di·pôrt′, -pōrt′) *v.t.* 1 To banish or expel from a country. 2 To behave or conduct (oneself). [< L *de-* away + *portare* carry] **—de′por·ta′tion** *n.*

de·port·ment (di·pôrt′mənt, -pōrt′-) *n.* The manner in which one behaves or conducts oneself.

de·pose (di·pōz′) *v.* **·posed, ·pos·ing** *v.t.* 1 To deprive of official rank or office; oust, as a king. 2 To state on oath. —*v.i.* 3 To bear witness. [< OF *de-* down + *poser* put] **—de·pos′a·ble** *adj.* **—de·pos′al** *n.*

de·pos·it (di·poz′it) *v.t.* 1 To give in trust or for safekeeping. 2 To give as part payment or as security. 3 To set down; put. 4 To cause, as sediment, to form a layer. —*n.* 1 Money deposited, as in a bank. 2 Something, as money, given as security or first payment. 3 The act of depositing. 4 In Canada, money put up as evidence of good faith by a candidate for Parliament or a Legislature. 5 A depositary. 6 Something, as sediment, deposited. 7 An accumulated mass of iron, oil, salt, etc. **—on deposit** Placed for safekeeping. [< L *deponere* lay aside]

de·pos·i·tar·y (di·poz′ə·ter′ē) *n. pl.* **·tar·ies** 1 A person entrusted with anything for safekeeping; a trustee. 2 A place where things are stored; depository.

dep·o·si·tion (dep′ə·zish′ən, dē′pə-) *n.* 1 The act of depositing. 2 That which is deposited; esp. an accumulation. 3 The written testimony of a sworn witness. 4 Allegation; evidence. 5 The act of deposing, as from office.

de·pos·i·tor (di·poz′ə·tər) *n.* One who makes a deposit, esp. of money in a bank.

de·pos·i·to·ry (di·poz′ə·tôr′ē, -tō′rē) *n. pl.* **·ries** 1 A place where things are put for safekeeping. 2 A person to whom something is entrusted for safekeeping.

de·pot (dē′pō, *Mil. & Brit.* dep′ō) *n.* 1 A warehouse or storehouse. 2 A railroad or bus station. 3 *Mil.* A storehouse or collecting station for personnel or materiel. [< L *depositum* a pledge, deposit]

de·prave (di·prāv′) *v.t.* **·praved, ·prav·ing** To render bad or worse, esp. in morals; corrupt; pervert. [< L *de-* completely + *pravus* corrupt, wicked] **—de·praved′** *adj.* **—de·prav′er, dep·ra·va·tion** (dep′rə·vā′shən) *n.*

de·prav·i·ty (di·prav′ə·tē) *n. pl.* **·ties** 1 The state of being depraved; wickedness. 2 A depraved act or habit.

dep·re·cate (dep′rə·kāt) *v.t.* **·cat·ed, ·cat·ing** 1 To express disapproval of or regret for. 2 To belittle; depreciate. [< L *de-* away + *precari* pray] **—dep′re·cat′ing·ly** *adv.* **—dep′re·ca′tion, dep′re·ca′tor** *n.* • The use of *deprecate* as a synonym for *depreciate* is regarded as incorrect by many, but it is increasingly common: While not wishing to *deprecate* their motives, he did question their judgement.

dep·re·ca·to·ry (dep′rə·kə·tôr′ē, -tō′rē) *adj.* 1 Belittling; apologetic. 2 Tending to deprecate; disparaging. Also **dep′re·ca′tive** (-kā′tiv) *adj.*

de·pre·ci·a·ble (di·prē′shē·ə·bəl) *adj.* That can be depreciated in value.

de·pre·ci·ate (di·prē′shē·āt) *v.* **·at·ed, ·at·ing** *v.t.* 1 To lessen the worth of; lower the price or rate of. 2 To disparage; belittle. —*v.i.* 3 To become less in value, etc. [< L *de-* down + *pretium* price] **—de·pre′ci·a′tor** *n.* **—de·pre′ci·a·to′ry** *adj.* • See DEPRECATE.

de·pre·ci·a·tion (di·prē′shē·ā′shən) *n.* 1 A loss in value of equipment, etc., through usage or wear. 2 A loss in the purchasing power of money. 3 A belittling or disparagment of something.

dep·re·date (dep′rə·dāt) *v.t. & v.i.* **·dat·ed, ·dat·ing** To prey upon; pillage; plunder. [< L *de-* completely + *praeda* booty, prey] **—dep′re·da′tion, dep′re·da′tor** *n.*

de·press (di·pres′) *v.t.* 1 To lower the spirits of; sadden. 2 To lessen in vigor, force, or energy. 3 To lessen the price or value of. 4 To press or push down. [< L *de-* down + *primere* to press] **—de·press′ing** *adj.* **—de·press′ing·ly** *adv.* **—de·pres′sor** (-ər) *n.*

de·pres·sant (di·pres′ənt) *adj.* Lessening vital activity. —*n.* 1 A drug that reduces the rate or intensity of vital functions. 2 A sedative.

de·pressed (di·prest′) *adj.* 1 Sad; dejected. 2 Pressed down. 3 Flattened from above; sunk below the surface. 4 Reduced in amount, degree, value, etc. 5 *Biol.* Broader than high; flat. **—Syn.** 1 downcast, low, blue, downhearted, forlorn, desolate.

depressed area A region characterized by unemployment, a low standard of living, etc.

de·pres·sion (di·presh′ən) *n.* 1 The act of depressing, or the state of being depressed. 2 Low spirits or vitality. 3 A low or hollow place. 4 A period marked by a severe decline in business or trade, unemployment, etc. 5 Low atmospheric pressure; also, a region of low atmospheric pressure. 6 *Psychiatry* A profound, immobilizing dejection and despair. **—de·pres′sive** *adj.* **—de·pres′sive·ly** *adv.*

dep·ri·va·tion (dep′rə·vā′shən) *n.* 1 The act of depriving, or the state of being deprived. 2 Loss; want.

de·prive (di·prīv′) *v.t.* **·prived, ·priv·ing** 1 To take something away from; divest. 2 To keep from acquiring, using, or enjoying. [< L *de-* completely + *privare* strip, remove] **—de·priv′a·ble** *adj.*

de·pro·gram (dē·prō′gram) *v.t.* **·gramed** or **·grammed, ·gram·ing** or **·gram·ming** To try to convince (one) to forsake something learned well, esp. a religious belief.

dept. department; deponent; deputy.

depth (depth) *n.* 1 The state or quality of being deep. 2 Extent or distance downward, inward, or backward. 3 *Usu. pl.* The deepest part. 4 *Usu. pl.* The innermost part. 5 *Usu. pl.* The part of greatest intensity: the *depths* of despair. 6 Profundity of thought or feeling. 7 Intensity of color or shade. 8 Lowness of pitch. —**in depth** In a thorough and extensive manner. [ME *depthe*]

depth charge An explosive charge so engineered that it explodes at a certain depth under water. Also **depth bomb.**

dep·u·ta·tion (dep′yə·tā′shən) *n.* 1 A person or persons acting for another; a delegation. 2 The act of deputing, or the state of being deputed.

de·pute (di·pyōōt′) *v.t.* **·put·ed, ·put·ing** 1 To appoint as an agent, deputy, or delegation. 2 To transfer, as authority, to another. [<L *de-* away + *putare* think]

dep·u·tize (dep′yə·tīz) *v.* **·tized, ·tiz·ing** *v.t.* 1 To appoint as a deputy. —*v.i.* 2 To act as a deputy.

dep·u·ty (dep′yə·tē) *n. pl.* **·ties** 1 One appointed to act for another; representative agent. 2 A member of a legislative assembly in certain countries. [<OF *deputer* depute]

der., deriv. derivation; derivative; derived.

de·rail (dē·rāl′) *v.t.* 1 To cause to leave the rails, as a train. —*v.i.* 2 To leave the rails. —**de·rail′ment** *n.*

de·rail·leur (di·rā′lər) *n.* A spring-powered mechanism on a bicycle that allows the rider to change gears by transferring the drive chain from one to another size of sprocket wheels. [<F *dérailleur*]

de·range (di·rānj′) *v.t.* **·ranged, ·rang·ing** 1 To disturb the arrangement of; disorder. 2 To make insane. [<F *déranger*]

de·range·ment (di·rānj′mənt) *n.* 1 The act of deranging, or state of being deranged. 2 Any severe mental disorder.

der·by (dûr′bē) *n. pl.* **·bies** A stiff, felt hat with curved brim and round crown. [<DERBY]

Der·by (dûr′bē, *Brit.* där′bē) 1 An annual horse race for three-year-olds run, since 1780, at Epsom Downs in Surrey, England. 2 Any important horse race, esp. the Kentucky Derby. [Founded by the 12th Earl of *Derby*, d. 1834]

Derby

der·e·lict (der′ə·likt) *adj.* 1 Neglectful of obligation; remiss. 2 Deserted or abandoned. —*n.* 1 That which is deserted or abandoned, as a ship at sea. 2 A person considered as socially outcast; a vagrant. [<L *de-* completely + *relinquere* abandon]

der·e·lic·tion (der′ə·lik′shən) *n.* 1 Neglect or failure in duty. 2 Voluntary abandonment of something. 3 The state or fact of being abandoned.

de·ride (di·rīd′) *v.t.* **·rid·ed, ·rid·ing** To treat or laugh at with contempt; ridicule. [<L *de-* completely + *ridere* laugh, mock] —**de·rid′er** *n.* —**de·rid′ing·ly** *adv.*

de ri·gueur (də rē·gœr′) *French* 1 Necessary according to etiquette; required by good form. 2 Fashionable.

de·ri·sion (di·rizh′ən) *n.* 1 The act of deriding; ridicule; scorn. 2 An object of ridicule or scorn.

de·ri·sive (di·rī′siv) *adj.* Expressive of or characterized by derision. Also **de·ri·so·ry** (di·rī′sər·ē). —**de·ri′sive·ly** *adv.* —**de·ri′sive·ness** *n.*

der·i·va·tion (der′ə·vā′shən) *n.* 1 The act of deriving, or the condition of being derived. 2 Something derived; a derivative. 3 Origin; source. 4 The tracing of a word from its origins; also, a statement of this. 5 The formation of a word from another word, as by the addition of a prefix or suffix. —**der′i·va′tion·al** *adj.*

de·riv·a·tive (di·riv′ə·tiv) *adj.* Derived; not original or basic. —*n.* 1 That which is derived. 2 A word developed from a basic word, as by the addition of a prefix or suffix. 3 *Chem.* A compound formed or regarded as being formed from another. —**de·riv′a·tive·ly** *adv.* —**de·riv′a·tive·ness** *n.*

de·rive (di·rīv′) *v.* **·rived, ·riv·ing** *v.t.* 1 To draw or receive, as from a source, principle, or root; be descended from. 2 To deduce; draw, as a conclusion. 3 To trace the derivation of (a word). 4 *Chem.* To obtain (a compound) from another. —*v.i.* 5 To have derivation; originate. [<L *de-* from + *rivus* stream] —**de·riv′a·ble** *adj.* —**de·riv′er** *n.*

derm (dûrm) *n.* DERMIS. [<Gk. *derma* skin]

der·ma (dûr′mə) *n.* DERMIS. —**der′mal** *adj.*

der·ma·tol·o·gy (dûr′mə·tol′ə·jē) *n.* The branch of medical science that relates to the skin and its diseases. [<Gk. *derma, dermatos* skin + -LOGY] —**der·ma·to·log·i·cal** (dûr′·mə·tə·loj′i·kəl) *adj.* —**der′ma·tol′o·gist** *n.*

der·mis (dûr′mis) *n.* The layer of skin just below the epidermis; true skin. [<Gk. *derma* skin]

der·o·gate (der′ə·gāt) *v.* **·gat·ed, ·gat·ing** *v.i.* 1 To take away; detract, as from reputation: with *from.* 2 To do something that causes one to lose the esteem of others. [<L *de-* away + *rogare* ask, propose a law] —**der′o·ga′tion** *n.*

de·rog·a·tive (di·rog′ə·tiv) *adj.* Tending to derogate or detract; derogatory. —**de·rog′a·tive·ly** *adv.*

de·rog·a·to·ry (di·rog′ə·tôr′ē, -tō′rē) *adj.* Harmful to the reputation or esteem of a person or thing; disparaging. —**de·rog′a·to′ri·ly** *adv.*

der·rick (der′ik) *n.* 1 An apparatus with a hinged boom for hoisting heavy objects into place. 2 The framework over the mouth of an oil well or similar drill hole. [<*Derrick,* 17th c. London hangman]

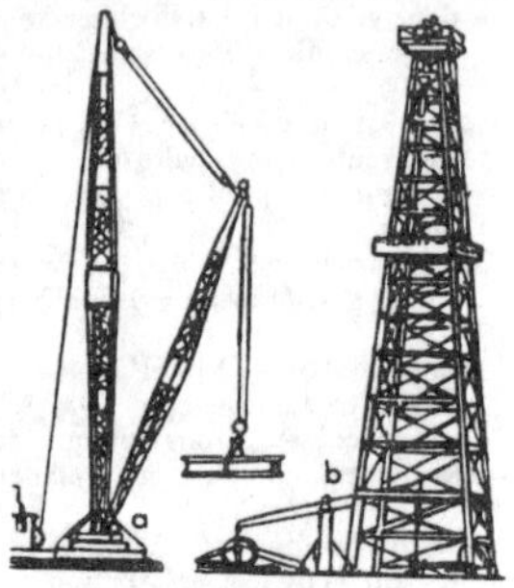

Derricks
a. hoisting. b. oil well.

der·ri·ere (der′ē·er′) *n.* The buttocks. Also **der·ri·ère.** [<F, lit., rear, back part]

der·ring-do (der′ing·dōō′) *n.* Daring deeds; reckless courage. [<ME *dorrying don* daring to do; mistaken for a noun phrase]

der·rin·ger (der′in·jər) *n.* A short-barreled pistol with a large bore. [<Henry *Derringer,* 19th c. U.S. gunsmith, who invented it]

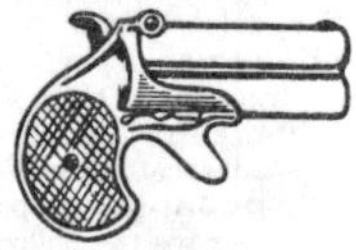

Derringer

der·vish (dûr′vish) *n.* A member of any of several Mohammedan religious orders, some of whom practice whirling as a religious exercise. [<Pers. *darvish*]

de·sal·i·nate (dē·sal′ə·nāt, -sāl′ə-) *v.t.* **·nat·ed, ·nat·ing** To remove salt from, esp. from sea water to make it drinkable. —**de·sal′i·na′tion** *n.*

de·salt (dē·sôlt′) *v.t.* To remove the salt from.

desc. descendant.

des·cant (des′kant) *n.* 1 A discourse or a series of remarks. 2 *Music* **a** A varied melody or song. **b** An ornamental variation of the main melody. **c** A counterpoint above the plain song. **d** The upper part in part music. —*v.t.* (des·kant′, dis-) 1 To discourse at length: with *on* or *upon.* 2 *Music* **a** To make a descant. **b** To sing. [<L *dis-* away + *cantus* a song]

de·scend (di·send′) *v.i.* 1 To move from a higher to a lower point. 2 To slope or incline downward. 3 To stoop; lower oneself. 4 To come down by inheritance; be inherited. 5 To be derived by heredity: with *from.* 6 To come overwhelmingly, as in an attack or visit: with *on* or *upon.* 7 To pass, as from the general to the particular. 8 *Astron.* To move southward or toward the horizon, as a star. —*v.t.* 9 To move from an upper to a lower part of; go down. [<L *de-* down + *scandere* climb] —**de·scend′er** *n.*

de·scen·dant (di·sen′dənt) *n.* 1 One who is an offspring of a particular ancestor, group, etc. 2 Anything derived from something earlier.

de·scen·dent (di·sen′dənt) *adj.* 1 Descending. 2 Issuing by descent, as from an ancestor.

de·scend·i·ble (di·sen′də·bəl) *adj.* 1 That can be descended. 2 That can pass by descent; inheritable. Also **de·scend′a·ble.**

de·scent (di·sent′) *n.* 1 The act of descending. 2 Decline; deterioration. 3 A declivity; slope. 4 Lineage; ancestry. 5 A genealogical generation. 6 A hostile raid or invasion. 7 The transmission of an estate by inheritance.

descr. descriptive.

de·scribe (di·skrīb′) *v.t.* **·scribed, ·scrib·ing** 1 To give an account of; represent with spoken or written words. 2 To draw the figure of; trace; outline. [<L *de-* down + *scribere* write] —**de·scrib′a·ble** *adj.* —**de·scrib′er** *n.* —**Syn.** 1 narrate, relate, recount, portray, characterize.

de·scrip·tion (di·skrip′shən) *n.* 1 The act of describing.

2 An account, statement, or report that describes. 3 A drawing or tracing. 4 Sort; kind; nature.

de·scrip·tive (di·skrip′tiv) *adj.* Characterized by or containing description; serving to describe. **—de·scrip′tive·ly** *adv.* **—de·scrip′tive·ness** *n.*

de·scry (di·skrī′) *v.t.* **·scried, ·scry·ing** 1 To discover with the eye; discern; detect. 2 To discover by observation. [< OF *des-* away + *crier* to cry] **—de·scri′er** *n.*

des·e·crate (des′ə·krāt) *v.t.* **·crat·ed, ·crat·ing** To divert from a sacred to a common use; profane. [< DE- + L *sacrare* make holy] **—des′e·crat′er** or **des′e·cra′tor, des′e·cra′tion** *n.*

de·seg·re·gate (dē·seg′rə·gāt) *v.t.* **·gat·ed, ·gat·ing** To eliminate racial segregation in. **—de′seg·re·ga′tion** *n.*

de·sen·si·tize (dē·sen′sə·tīz) *v.t.* **·tized, ·tiz·ing** To make less sensitive. **—de·sen′si·ti·za′tion, de·sen′si·tiz′er** *n.*

des·ert[1] (dez′ərt) *n.* 1 An arid, usu. sandy region abnormally deficient in rainfall or natural moisture. 2 Any uncultivated and desolate region. *—adj.* Of, from, or like a desert. [< LL *desertum* < L *deserere* abandon]

de·sert[2] (di·zûrt′) *n.* 1 The state of deserving reward or punishment. 2 *Often pl.* That which is deserved or merited. [< OF *deservir* deserve]

de·sert[3] (di·zûrt′) *v.t.* 1 To forsake or abandon. 2 To forsake in violation of one's oath or orders. *—v.i.* 3 To abandon one's post, duty, etc. [< L *deserere* abandon] **—de·sert′·er, de·ser′tion** *n.*

des·ert·i·fi·ca·tion (dez′ər·tə·fə·kā′shən) *n.* The process of becoming a desert.

de·serve (di·zûrv′) *v.* **·served, serv·ing** *v.t.* 1 To be entitled to or worthy of. *—v.i.* 2 To be worthy. [< L *de-* completely + *servire* serve] **—de·serv′er** *n.*

de·served (di·zûrvd′) *adj.* Earned; merited. **—de·serv·ed·ly** (di·zûr′vid·lē) *adv.* **—de·serv′ed·ness** *n.*

des·ha·bille (dez′ə·bēl′) *n.* DISHABILLE.

des·ic·cant (des′ə·kənt) *adj.* Producing dryness. *—n.* A desiccant agent or substance.

des·ic·cate (des′ə·kāt) *v.* **·cat·ed, ·cat·ing** *v.t.* 1 To remove the moisture from, as for preserving. 2 To dry thoroughly. *—v.i.* 3 To become dry. [< L *de-* completely + *siccare* dry out] **—des′ic·ca′tion, des′ic·ca′tor** *n.* **—des′ic·ca′tive** *adj., n.*

de·sid·er·a·tum (di·sid′ə·rä′təm, -zid′-, -rā′təm) *n. pl.* **·ta** (-tə) Something desirable. [< L *desiderare* to desire]

de·sign (di·zīn′) *v.t.* 1 To make, draw, or prepare preliminary plans or sketches of. 2 To plan and make with art or skill. 3 To form or make (plans, schemes, etc.) in the mind; invent. 4 To intend; purpose. *—v.i.* 5 To make drawings or plans; be a designer. 6 To plan mentally; conceive. *—n.* 1 A plan, sketch or pattern for making something. 2 A decorative or artistic arrangement of forms, colors, etc.: a floral *design.* 3 Any arrangement of parts, shapes, etc., that forms a complete and functioning unit: the new car *designs.* 4 The act or art of designing. 5 A purpose or pattern: to seek a *design* in the chaos of history. 6 *Often pl.* A plot, scheme, or intention, usu. secret or sinister: with *on, upon,* or *against.* 7 Any plan, undertaking, or objective: a *design* to achieve better living conditions. [< L *designare* designate] **—de·sign′a·ble** *adj.*

des·ig·nate (dez′ig·nāt) *v.t.* **·nat·ed, ·nat·ing** 1 To indicate by some mark, sign, or name. 2 To name; characterize. 3 To select or appoint for a specific purpose, duty, office, etc. *—adj.* (dez′ig·nit, -nāt) Designated; selected. [< L *de-* completely + *signare* to mark] **—des′ig·na′tor** *n.*

des·ig·na·tion (dez′ig·nā′shən) *n.* 1 An indicating or pointing out. 2 An appointment or nomination. 3 A distinguishing mark, name, or title.

de·sign·ed·ly (di·zī′nid·lē) *adv.* By design; purposely; intentionally.

de·sign·er (di·zī′nər) *n.* 1 One who creates useful, decorative, or artistic designs. 2 A contriver; schemer.

de·sign·ing (di·zī′ning) *n.* 1 The act or art of making designs or sketches. 2 The act of plotting or scheming. *—adj.* 1 Artful; scheming. 2 That makes designs, patterns, etc. **—de·sign′ing·ly** *adv.*

de·sir·a·ble (di·zīr′ə·bəl) *adj.* 1 Worth having or seeking; beneficial. 2 Arousing desire; attractive. **—de·sir′a·bil′i·ty, de·sir′a·ble·ness** *n.* **—de·sir′a·bly** *adv.*

de·sire (di·zīr′) *v.t.* **·sired, ·sir·ing** 1 To wish or long for; crave. 2 To ask for; request. *—n.* 1 A longing; craving; yearning. 2 A request; wish. 3 Something desired. 4 Sexual appetite; passion. [< L *desiderare*] **—de·sir′er** *n.* **—Syn.** *v.* 1 want, covet, thirst after, yearn for, aspire after.

de·sir·ous (di·zīr′əs) *adj.* Having or characterized by desire: often with *of.*

de·sist (di·zist′) *v.i.* To cease; stop: often with *from.* [< L *de-* from + *sistere* stop, cease] **—de·sis′tance** *n.*

desk (desk) *n.* 1 A table, usu. with drawers, etc., specially adapted for writing or studying. 2 A lectern. 3 A place in a public building, hotel, etc., which provides specific services: information *desk.* 4 A department in a newspaper office: the society *desk.* 5 A music stand in an orchestra; also, the musicians who use it. [< LL *discus* disk]

des·o·late (des′ə·lit) *adj.* 1 Uninhabited; deserted. 2 Laid waste; devastated. 3 Lonely; solitary. 4 Without friends; forlorn; sorrowful. *—v.t.* (des′ə·lāt) **·lat·ed, ·lat·ing** 1 To deprive of inhabitants. 2 To lay waste; devastate. 3 To make sorrowful or forlorn. 4 To abandon. [< L *de-* completely + *solus* alone] **—des′o·late·ly** *adv.* **—des′o·late·ness, des′o·lat′er, des′o·la′tor** *n.*

des·o·la·tion (des′ə·lā′shən)*n.* 1 Loneliness; dreariness. 2 Sadness; grief. 3 A laying waste; devastation. 4 A desolate condition or place.

de·spair (di·spâr′) *v.t.* To lose or abandon hope: with *of.* *—n.* 1 Utter hopelessness and discouragement. 2 That which causes despair or which is despaired of. [< L *de-* away + *sperare* to hope] **—de·spair′ing** *adj.* **—de·spair′ing·ly** *adv.*

des·patch (di·spach′) *v. & n.* DISPATCH.

des·per·a·do (des′pə·rä′dō, -rā′dō) *n. pl.* **·does** or **·dos** A desperate, dangerous outlaw or criminal.

des·per·ate (des′pər·it) *adj.* 1 Without care for danger; reckless, as from despair. 2 Resorted to in a last extremity; drastic. 3 In frantic need, desire, etc.: *desperate* for money. 4 Hopelessly bad or critical: in *desperate* circumstances. [< L *desperare.* See DESPAIR.] **—des′per·ate·ly** *adv.* **—des′·per·ate·ness** *n.* **—Syn.** 1 rash, foolhardy, imprudent, risky. 2 extreme, severe.

des·per·a·tion (des′pə·rā′shən) *n.* 1 The state of being desperate. 2 The recklessness of despair.

des·pi·ca·ble (des′pi·kə·bəl, di·spik′ə·bəl) *adj.* Despised; contemptible; mean; vile. [< L *despicari* despise] **—des′pi·ca·bil′i·ty, des′pi·ca·ble·ness** *n.* **—des′pi·ca·bly** *adv.*

de·spise (di·spīz′) *v.t.* **·spised, ·spis·ing** To regard as contemptible or worthless; scorn. [< L *de-* down + *specere* look at] **—de·spis′er** *n.*

de·spite (di·spīt′) *prep.* In spite of; notwithstanding. *—n.* 1 An act of defiance or contempt. 2 Extreme malice; hatred; spite. **—in despite of** Notwithstanding; in spite of. [< L *despectus* a looking down, contempt]

de·spoil (di·spoil′) *v.t.* To deprive of something by force; plunder. [< L *de-* completely + *spoliare* rob] **—de·spoil′er, de·spoil′ment, de·spo·li·a·tion** (di·spō′lē·ā′shən) *n.*

de·spond (di·spond′) *v.i.* To lose spirit, courage, or hope; be depressed. *—n. Archaic* DESPONDENCY. [< L *de-* away + *spondere* to promise] **—de·spond′ing·ly** *adv.*

de·spon·den·cy (di·spon′dən·sē) *n.* Loss of spirit, courage, or hope. Also **de·spon′dence.**

de·spon·dent (di·spon′dənt) *adj.* Dejected in spirit; disheartened. **—de·spon′dent·ly** *adv.*

des·pot (des′pət, -pot) *n.* 1 An absolute monarch; autocrat. 2 A hard master; tryant. [< Gk. *despotēs* a master]

des·pot·ic (de·spot′ik, di-) *adj.* Of or like a despot; tyrannical. **—des·pot′i·cal·ly** *adv.*

des·pot·ism (des′pə·tiz′əm) *n.* 1 Absolute power; autocracy. 2 Any tyrannical control.

des·sert (di·zûrt′) *n.* Something served at the close of a meal, as pastry, pudding, fruit, cheese, etc. [< F *desservir* clear a table]

des·ti·na·tion (des′tə·nā′shən) *n.* 1 The final place or point toward which a journey, letter, etc., is directed. 2 The ultimate purpose or goal of anything.

des·tine (des′tin) *v.t.* **·tined, ·tin·ing** 1 To design or set apart for a distinct purpose or end. 2 to determine the future of, as by destiny or fate. —**destined for** 1 Bound for; directed toward. 2 Fated or set apart for. [< L *destinare* make fast]

des·ti·ny (des′tə·nē) *n. pl.* **·nies** 1 That to which any person or thing is destined. 2 Inevitable necessity; fate.

des·ti·tute (des′tə·tyōōt) *adj.* 1 Entirely lacking: with *of.* 2 Being in want; extremely poor. [< L *destituere* abandon] —**des′ti·tu′tion** *n.*

de·stroy (di·stroi′) *v.t.* 1 To ruin utterly; consume. 2 To demolish; tear down. 3 To put an end to; do away with. 4 To kill. 5 To make ineffective; counteract. [< L *de-* down + *struere* build]

de·stroy·er (di·stroi′ər) *n.* 1 One who or that which destroys. 2 A small, speedy, heavily armed warship.

de·struct (di·strukt′) *n.* The act of deliberately destroying a defective missile, rocket, etc., after launch. —*v.i.* To undergo deliberate destruction.

de·struc·ti·ble (di·struk′tə·bəl) *adj.* Capable of being destroyed. —**de·struc′ti·bil′i·ty, de·struc′ti·ble·ness** *n.*

de·struc·tion (di·struk′shən) *n.* 1 The act of destroying, or state of being destroyed. 2 That which destroys. [< L *destruere* destroy]

de·struc·tive (di·struk′tiv) *adj.* 1 Causing destruction: with *of* or *to.* 2 Tending to negate, discourage, make ineffective, etc. —**de·struc′tive·ly** *adv.* —**de·struc′tive·ness** *n.*

des·ue·tude (des′wə·tyōōd) *n.* A condition of disuse. [< L *desuescere* put out of use]

des·ul·to·ry (des′əl·tôr′ē, -tō′rē) *adj.* 1 Aimless; changeable; unmethodical. 2 Not connected or relevant; random. [< L *de-* down + *salire* to leap, jump] —**des′ul·to′ri·ly** *adv.* —**des′ul·to′ri·ness** *n.*

det. detach; detachment; detail.

de·tach (di·tach′) *v.t.* 1 To unfasten and make separate; disconnect. 2 To send off for a special service, duty, etc., as a regiment or a ship. [< F *détacher*] —**de·tach′a·bil′i·ty** *n.* —**de·tach′a·ble** *adj.*

de·tached (di·tacht′) *adj.* 1 Separated; disconnected. 2 Not involved emotionally or intellectually; unbiased; disinterested. —**de·tach′ed·ly** (-tach′id·lē) *adv.* —**de·tach′ed·ness** *n.*

de·tach·ment (di·tach′mənt) *n.* 1 The act of detaching. 2 The condition of being detached; separation. 3 *Mil.* A unit of troops sent, organized, or trained for special duty. 4 A disinterestedness, aloofness, or impartiality.

de·tail (di·tāl′, dē′tāl) *n.* 1 A small part, item, or particular of a whole. 2 A dealing with or attending to such items or particulars: to go into too much *detail.* 3 *Mil.* a A small detachment assigned to some particular task. b The person or persons assigned. 4 In art and architecture, a minor but essential component of the finished work. —**in detail** Item by item. —*v.t.* (di·tāl′) 1 To report minutely; give the details of. 2 (*often* dē′tāl) To select for a special service, duty, etc. [< F *dé-* completely + *tailler* cut up]

de·tain (di·tān′) *v.t.* 1 To restrain from going; stop; delay. 2 To keep back; withhold. 3 To hold in custody. [< L *de-* away + *tenere* hold] —**de·tain′er, de·tain′ment** *n.*

de·tect (di·tekt′) *v.t.* 1 To discover. 2 To expose or uncover, as a crime, fault, or a criminal. 3 *Telecom.* DEMODULATE. [< L *de-* away + *tegere* to cover] —**de·tect′a·ble** or **·i·ble** *adj.* —**de·tect′er** *n.* —**Syn.** 1 perceive, find, discern. 2 reveal, disclose, unearth.

de·tec·tion (di·tek′shən) *n.* 1 The act of detecting or the condition of being detected. 2 *Telecom.* Any method of demodulation.

de·tec·tive (di·tek′tiv) *n.* A person, often a policeman, whose work is to investigate crimes, discover evidence, etc. —*adj.* 1 Of or pertaining to detectives or their work. 2 Of or for detection.

de·tec·tor (di·tek′tər) *n.* 1 One who or that which detects. 2 *Telecom.* DEMODULATOR.

dé·tente (dā·tänt′) *n.* An easing, as of discord between nations. [F]

de·ten·tion (di·ten′shən) *n.* 1 The act of detaining or keeping in custody. 2 The state of being detained. —**de·ten′tive** *adj.*

de·ter (di·tûr′) *v.t.* **·terred, ·ter·ring** To prevent or restrain (someone) from acting or proceeding, as by reminding of difficulties, dangers, etc. [< L *de-* away + *terrere* frighten] —**de·ter′ment** *n.*

de·terge (di·tûrj′) *v.t.* **·terged, ·terg·ing** 1 To cleanse, as a wound. 2 To wipe off. [< L *de-* away + *tergere* wipe]

de·ter·gent (di·tûr′jənt) *adj.* Having cleansing qualities. —*n.* A cleansing substance, esp. a synthetic substitute for soap. —**de·ter′gence, de·ter′gen·cy** *n.*

de·te·ri·o·rate (di·tir′ē·ə·rāt′) *v.t. & v.i.* **·rat·ed, ·rat·ing** To make or become worse; reduce in quality, value, etc. [< L *deterior* worse] —**de·te′ri·o·ra′tion** *n.* —**de·te′ri·o·ra′tive** *adj.* —**Syn.** decline, degenerate, ebb, fall off, wane.

de·ter·mi·nant (di·tûr′mə·nənt) *adj.* DETERMINATIVE. —*n.* Something that determines.

de·ter·mi·nate (di·tûr′mə·nit) *adj.* 1 Definitely limited or fixed; specific; distinct. 2 Settled; conclusive. 3 Resolute; decisive. —**de·ter′mi·nate·ly** *adv.* —**de·ter′mi·nate·ness** *n.*

de·ter·mi·na·tion (di·tûr′mə·nā′shən) *n.* 1 The act of determining or the condition of being determined. 2 A firm resolve or intention. 3 The quality of being firmly resolute. 4 The fixing of the size, quality, amount, etc., of anything; also, the result of this.

de·ter·mi·na·tive (di·tûr′mə·nā′tiv, -mə·nə·tiv) *adj.* Tending or having power to determine. —*n.* That which determines. —**de·ter′mi·na′tive·ly** *adv.* —**de·ter′mi·na′tive·ness** *n.*

de·ter·mine (di·tûr′min) *v.* **·mined, ·min·ing** *v.t.* 1 To settle or decide, as an argument or question. 2 To ascertain or fix, as after investigation or observation. 3 To cause to reach a decision. 4 To influence or affect: Demand *determines* supply. 5 To give purpose or direction to. 6 To set bounds to; limit. 7 *Law* To limit; terminate. —*v.i.* 8 To decide; resolve. 9 *Law* To come to an end. [< L *de-* completely + *terminare* to end] —**de·ter′min·er** *n.*

de·ter·mined (di·tûr′mind) *adj.* 1 Settled; resolved. 2 Of firm purpose; resolute. —**de·ter′mined·ly** *adv.* —**de·ter′·mined·ness** *n.*

de·ter·min·ism (di·tûr′mə·niz′əm) *n. Philos.* The doctrine that man's decisions and actions are determined not by free choice but by antecedent causes acting upon his character. —**de·ter′min·ist** *adj., n.* —**de·ter′min·is′tic** *adj.*

de·ter·rent (di·tûr′ənt) *adj.* Tending or serving to deter. —*n.* Something that deters. —**de·ter′rence** *n.*

de·test (di·test′) *v.t.* To hate; abhor. [< L *detestari* denounce] —**de·test′er** *n.* —**Syn.** despise, dislike, abominate.

de·test·a·ble (di·tes′tə·bəl) *adj.* Extremely hateful; abhorrent; odious. —**de·test′a·bil′i·ty, de·test′a·ble·ness** *n.* —**de·test′a·bly** *adv.*

de·tes·ta·tion (dē′tes·tā′shən) *n.* 1 Extreme hatred; abhorrence. 2 A person or thing detested.

de·throne (dē·thrōn′) *v.t.* **·throned, ·thron·ing** To remove from the throne; depose.

det·o·nate (det′ə·nāt) *v.t. & v.i.* **·nat·ed, ·nat·ing** To explode or cause to explode suddenly and with violence. [< L *de-* down + *tonare* to thunder] —**det′o·na′tion, det′o·na′·tor** *n.*

de·tour (dē′tōōr, di·tōōr′) *n.* 1 A roundabout way or deviation from a direct route or course of action. 2 A road substituted for part of a main road temporarily impassable. —*v.t. & v.i.* To go or cause to go by a detour. [< F *dé-* away + *tourner* to turn]

de·tract (di·trakt′) *v.t.* 1 To take away; withdraw. —*v.i.* 2 To take away a part, as from a reputation, enjoyment, etc.: with *from.* [< L *de-* away + *trahere* draw, pull] —**de·trac′tion, de·trac′tor** *n.* —**de·trac′tive** *adj.*

det·ri·ment (det′rə·mənt) *n.* 1 Something that impairs, injures, or causes loss. 2 Injury or loss. [< L *deterere* rub away] —**det′ri·men′tal** *adj.* —**det′ri·men′tal·ly** *adv.*

de·tri·tus (di·trī′təs) *n.* 1 *Geol.* Fragments or particles of rock resulting from erosion, glacial action, etc. 2 Any debris. [< L *deterere* rub away] —**de·tri′tal** *adj.*

deuce[1] (dyōōs) *n.* 1 Two; esp. a card or side of a die having two spots. 2 In tennis, a score tied at 40 or at five games each, requiring that either side win two successive points for the game or two successive games for the set. [< L *duo* two]

deuce[2] (dyōōs) *n. Informal* The devil; damn: a mild oath. [Prob. < LG *de duus* the deuce (lowest throw at dice)]

deu·ced (dyōō′sid, dyōōst) *adj.* Devilish; exceeding. —*adv.* Devilishly. —**deu′ced·ly** *adv.*

De·us (dā′ōōs, dē′əs) *n.* God [L].

Deut. Deuteronomy.

deu·te·ri·um (dyōō·tir′ē·əm) *n.* The isotope of hydrogen having twice the mass of ordinary hydrogen. [< Gk. *deuteros* second]

deuterium oxide HEAVY WATER.

deu·ter·on (dyōō′tər·on) *n.* The nucleus of a deuterium atom.

Deu·ter·on·o·my (dyōō′tər·on′ə·mē) *n.* The fifth book of the Old Testament. [< Gk. *deuteros* second + *nomos* law]

de·val·ue (dē·val′yōō) *v.t.* **·val·ued, ·val·u·ing** 1 To reduce or annul the value of. 2 To fix the value of (a currency) at a point below par. Also **de·val′u·ate** (-yōō·āt). —**de·val′u·a′tion** *n.*

dev·as·tate (dev′ə·stāt) *v.t.* **·tat·ed, ·tat·ing** 1 To lay waste, as by war, fire, etc. 2 To crush; overwhelm. [< L *de-* completely + *vastare* lay waste] —**dev′as·tat′ing·ly** *adv.* —**dev′·as·ta′tion, dev′as·ta′tor** *n.*

devel. development.

de·vel·op (di·vel′əp) *v.t.* 1 To expand or bring out the potentialities, capabilities, etc., of. 2 To expand; enlarge upon; work out, as a plot or idea. 3 To increase the strength, effectiveness, etc., of: to *develop* one's body. 4 To make more extensive or productive, as atomic power. 5 *Phot.* a To bring (a picture) to view by subjecting an exposed photographic film or plate to a developer. b To subject (a plate or film) to a developer. 6 *Music* To elaborate on (a theme). —*v.i.* 7 To increase in capabilities, maturity, etc. 8 To advance from a lower to a higher state; grow; evolve. 9 To disclose itself; become apparent: The plot of a novel *develops.* [< OF *de-* + *voluper* to fold] —**de·vel′op·a·ble** *adj.*

de·vel·op·er (di·vel′əp·ər) *n.* 1 One who or that which develops. 2 One who builds housing, shopping centers, etc., on a speculative basis. 3 *Phot.* A chemical solution for developing photographs.

de·vel·op·ment (di·vel′əp·mənt) *n.* 1 The act of developing or the state or condition of being developed. 2 Something that has been developed. 3 An event; happening; occurrence. —**de·vel·op·men·tal** (di·vel′əp·men′təl) *adj.* —**de·vel′op·men′tal·ly** *adv.*

de·vi·ate (dē′vē·āt) *v.* **·at·ed, ·at·ing** *v.i.* 1 To turn aside from a course or a norm; diverge. 2 To differ, as in thought or belief. —*v.t.* 3 To cause to turn aside. —*n.* (dē′vē·it) One who deviates, esp. in sexual behavior: also **de·vi·ant** (dē′vē·ənt). [< L *de-* from + *via* a road] —**de′vi·a′tion, de′vi·a′tor** *n.*

de·vice (di·vīs′) *n.* 1 Something invented and constructed for special use; contrivance. 2 A plan or scheme, esp. a sly or tricky one. 3 A means to obtain an artistic effect. 4 A fanciful design or pattern, as in ornamentation. 5 A motto or emblem, as on a shield. —**leave to one's own devices** To allow (a person) to follow his own wishes, without help, guidance, etc. [< OF *devis* intention, will]

dev·il (dev′əl) *n.* 1 *Sometimes cap.* In theology, the prince and ruler of the kingdom of evil; Satan. 2 Any subordinate evil spirit; a demon. 3 A wicked person. 4 A wretched fellow: poor *devil.* 5 A person of great energy, daring, or effrontery. 6 Any of various toothed machines, as for cutting or tearing up rags. 7 PRINTER'S DEVIL. 8 Something difficult to do, understand, solve, etc. —**between the devil and the deep blue sea** In a dilemma. —**give the devil his due** To acknowledge the virtues of even a bad or disliked person. —**the devil to pay** Trouble to be expected as a consequence. —*v.t.* **dev·iled** or **·illed, dev·il·ing** or **·il·ling** 1 To prepare (food) by seasoning highly. 2 To cut up, as cloth, in a devil. 3 To harass; tease; bedevil. [< Gk. *diabolos* slanderer]

dev·il·fish (dev′əl·fish′) *n. pl.* **·fish** or **·fish·es** Any of various large marine animals of grotesque appearance, as an octopus and certain large rays.

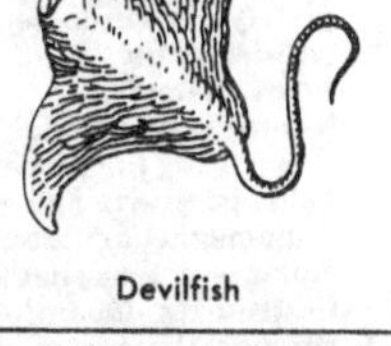
Devilfish

dev·il·ish (dev′əl·ish, dev′lish) *adj.* 1 Having the qualities of the devil; diabolical; malicious. 2 Challenging; complex. 3 Mischievous; impish. 4 *Informal* Excessive; extreme. —*adv.* Excessively; very. —**dev′il·ish·ly** *adv.* —**dev′il·ish·ness** *n.*

dev·il-may-care (dev′əl·mā·kâr′) *adj.* Careless; reckless; heedless of consequences.

dev·il·ment (dev′əl·mənt) *n.* 1 Mischief; impish action or tricks. 2 Wickedness; evil.

devil's advocate 1 A Roman Catholic official whose duty is to raise objections to a candidate for beatification or canonization. 2 One who takes an unpopular or indefensible side in an argument in order to provoke discussion or test the validity of accepted views.

dev·il's-food cake (dev′əlz·fōōd′) A rich chocolate cake.

dev·il·try (dev′əl·trē) *n. pl.* **·tries** 1 Wanton and malicious mischief. 2 Evil magic or art. Also **dev′il·ry** (-rē).

de·vi·ous (dē′vē·əs) *adj.* 1 Winding or deviating from a straight course; rambling. 2 Straying from the proper or usual way. 3 Not straightforward or honest. [< L *de-* from + *via* way] —**de′vi·ous·ly** *adv.* —**de′vi·ous·ness** *n.*

de·vise (di·vīz′) *v.* **·vised, ·vis·ing** *v.t.* 1 To form in the mind; invent; contrive. 2 *Law* To transmit (real estate) by will. —*v.i.* 3 To form a plan. —*n. Law* 1 A gift of lands by will. 2 The act of bequeathing lands. 3 A will, or a clause in a will, conveying real estate. [< OF *deviser* divide, distinguish, contrive] —**de·vis′a·ble** *adj.* —**de·vis′er** *n.* —**Syn.** *v.* 1 produce, plan, fashion, concoct.

de·vi·see (di·vī′zē′, dev′ə·zē′) *n. Law* The person to whom a devise is made.

de·vi·sor (di·vī′zər, -zôr) *n. Law* One who gives by will.

de·vi·tal·ize (dē·vī′təl·īz) *v.t.* **·ized, ·iz·ing** 1 To deprive of life; kill. 2 To weaken; enfeeble. —**de·vi′tal·i·za′tion** *n.*

de·void (di·void′) *adj.* Not possessing; destitute: with *of.* [< OF *devoidier* empty out]

de·voir (də·vwär′, dev′wär) *n.* 1 Duty. 2 *pl.* Respectful words of greeting or courtesy. [< L *debere* owe]

de·volve (di·volv′) *v.* **·volved, ·volv·ing** *v.t.* 1 To cause (powers, obligations, etc.) to pass to a successor or substitute. —*v.i.* 2 To pass from a possessor to a successor or substitute: with *to, on,* or *upon.* [< L *de-* down + *volvere* roll] —**de·volve′ment, dev·o·lu·tion** (dev′ə·lōō′shən) *n.*

De·vo·ni·an (di·vō′nē·ən) *adj. & n.* See GEOLOGY.

de·vote (di·vōt′) *v.t.* **·vot·ed, ·vot·ing** 1 To give or apply (attention, time, or oneself) completely to a purpose, activity, another person, etc. 2 To set apart; dedicate; consecrate. [< L *de-* away + *vovere* vow]

de·vot·ed (di·vō′tid) *adj.* 1 Feeling or showing devotion; ardent; devout. 2 Set apart, as by a vow; consecrated. —**de·vot′ed·ly** *adv.* —**de·vot′ed·ness** *n.*

dev·o·tee (dev′ə·tē′, -tā′, di·vō′tē′) *n.* 1 One intensely devoted to something or someone. 2 A religious zealot.

de·vo·tion (di·vō′shən) *n.* 1 The quality or condition of being devoted. 2 Strong attachment or affection. 3 *Usu. pl.* An act of worship; prayer. 4 Piety. 5 The act of devoting. —**de·vo′tion·al** *adj.* —**de·vo′tion·al·ly** *adv.*

de·vour (di·vour′) *v.t.* 1 To eat up greedily. 2 To destroy; lay waste to. 3 To take in greedily with the mind or senses: He *devoured* the book. 4 To engross the attention of. 5 To engulf; absorb. [< L *de-* down + *vorare* to gulp, swallow] —**de·vour′er** *n.*

de·vout (di·vout′) *adj.* 1 Earnestly religious; pious. 2 Heartfelt; sincere. 3 Containing or expressing devotion. [< L *devovere* devote] —**de·vout′ly** *adv.* —**de·vout′ness** *n.*

dew (dyōō) *n.* 1 Moisture condensed from the atmosphere in small drops upon cool surfaces. 2 Anything suggesting the freshness of dew: the *dew* of youth. 3 Moisture generally, esp. when in minute drops, as perspiration, tears, etc. —*v.t.* To wet with or as with dew; bedew. [< OE *dēaw*]

dew·ber·ry (dyōō′ber′ē, -bər·ē) *n. pl.* **·ries** Any of various low-growing blackberries.

dew·claw (dyōō′klô′) *n.* A rudimentary toe, claw, or hoof on the feet of certain animals, as dogs, hogs, deer, etc. —**dew′clawed′** *adj.*

dew·drop (dyōō′drop′) *n.* A drop of dew.

Dew·ey decimal system (dōō′ē) A numerical system for classifying books, used in libraries, etc. [< Melvil *Dewey,* 1851–1931, U.S. librarian]

dew·lap (d^y^o͞o′lap′) *n.* The pendulous skin under the throat of cattle and certain other animals. [ME *dewlappe*] **—dew′lapped′** *adj.*

Dewlap

DEW line (d^y^o͞o) A chain of radar stations in North America at about the 70th parallel, maintained by the U.S. in cooperation with Canada. [< *D(istant) E(arly) W(arning)*]

dew point The temperature at which the water vapor in the air condenses to a liquid.

dew·y (d^y^o͞o′ē) *adj.* **dew·i·er, dew·i·est 1** Moist, as with dew. **2** Of or like dew. **3** Refreshing. **—dew′i·ly** *adv.* **—dew′i·ness** *n.*

dex·ter (dek′stər) *adj.* **1** Of, pertaining to, or situated on the right side or hand. **2** *Her.* On the wearer's right, the spectator's left. [L]

dex·ter·i·ty (dek·ster′ə·tē) *n.* **1** Manual skill; adroitness. **2** Mental quickness or skill. [< L *dexteritas* skill < *dexter* on the right]

dex·ter·ous (dek′strəs, -stər·əs) *adj.* **1** Possessing dexterity; adroit. **2** Done with dexterity. Also **dex·trous** (dek′·strəs). **—dex′ter·ous·ly, dex′trous·ly** *adv.* **—dex′ter·ous·ness, dex′trous·ness** *n.*

dex·tral (dek′strəl) *adj.* **1** Of, pertaining to, or situated on the right side. **2** Right-handed. **—dex′tral·ly** *adv.* **—dex·tral·i·ty** (dek·stral′ə·tē) *n.*

dex·trin (dek′strin) *n.* A water-soluble carbohydrate formed by the partial breakdown of starch, used as an adhesive, filler, etc. Also **dex·trine** (dek′strin, -strēn). [< DEXTR(O)- + IN]

dextro- *combining form* Turned or turning to the right: used esp. in chemistry and physics: *dextrin, dextrose.* Also **dextr-.** [< L *dexter* right]

dex·trose (dek′strōs) *n.* The common isomeric form of glucose, occurring in animals and plants. [< DEXTR(O)- + (GLUC)OSE]

DF., D.F., Df direction finding.

DFC, D.F.C. Distinguished Flying Cross.

D.G. by the grace of God (L *Dei gratia*).

dg, dg. decigram(s).

DHQ Division Headquarters.

di- *prefix* **1** Twice; double. **2** *Chem.* Containing two atoms, molecules, etc.: *dioxide.* [< Gk. *dis* twice]

di., dia. diameter.

dia- *prefix* Through; across; between: *diagonal.* Also **di-.** [< Gk. *dia-* through]

di·a·be·tes (dī′ə·bē′tēz, -tis) *n.* **1** Any of several diseases characterized by thirst and excessive urinary secretion. **2** DIABETES MELLITUS. [< Gk. *dia-* through + *bainein* go] **—di·a·bet·ic** (dī′ə·bet′ik, -bē′tik) *adj., n.*

diabetes mel·li·tus (mə·lī′təs) A chronic form of diabetes in which glucose accumulates in the blood and is excreted in the urine. [NL, lit., honey diabetes < L *mel* honey]

di·a·bol·ic (dī′ə·bol′ik) *adj.* **1** Of, pertaining to, or coming from the devil; satanic. **2** Fiendishly wicked or cruel. Also **di′a·bol′i·cal.** [< Gk. *diabolos* devil] **—di′a·bol′i·cal·ly** *adv.* **—di·ab·o·lism** (dī·ab′ə·liz′əm) *n.* **—Syn. 2** malevolent, infernal, demoniacal.

di·ac·o·nate (dī·ak′ə·nit, -nāt) *n.* **1** The office, rank, or tenure of a deacon. **2** Deacons collectively. **—di·ac′o·nal** *adj.*

di·a·crit·ic (dī′ə·krit′ik) *n.* DIACRITICAL MARK. **—***adj.* DIACRITICAL. [< Gk. *dia-* between + *krinein* distinguish]

di·a·crit·i·cal (dī′ə·krit′i·kəl) *adj.* Marking a difference; distinguishing. **—di′a·crit′i·cal·ly** *adv.*

diacritical mark A mark, point, or sign attached to a letter to indicate its pronunciation.

di·a·dem (dī′ə·dem) *n.* **1** A crown worn as a symbol of royalty. **2** Regal power; sovereignty. [< Gk. *diadēma*]

di·aer·e·sis (dī·er′ə·sis) *n.* DIERESIS.

diag. diagram.

di·ag·nose (dī′əg·nōs′, -nōz′) *v.* **·nosed, ·nos·ing** *v.t.* To perceive or distinguish by diagnosis. **—***v.i.* To make a diagnosis.

di·ag·no·sis (dī′əg·nō′sis) *n.* **1** The art or act of identifying diseases, disorders, etc., by their characteristic symptoms. **2** An examination of the facts in any situation in order to understand its nature: a *diagnosis* of city traffic. **3** The conclusions reached by diagnosing. [< Gk. *diagignōskein* discern] **—di·ag·nos·tic** (dī′əg·nos′tik) *adj.* **—di′ag·nos′ti·cal·ly** *adv.*

di·ag·nos·ti·cian (dī′əg·nos·tish′ən) *n.* One who is versed in diagnosis.

di·ag·o·nal (dī·ag′ə·nəl) *adj.* **1** Crossing or moving obliquely; slanting. **2** Marked by oblique lines or the like. **3** *Geom.* **a** Joining two nonadjacent vertices of a figure. **b** Joining two nonadjacent edges of a solid. **—***n.* **1** *Geom.* A diagonal line or plane. **2** Anything running diagonally. [< L *dia-* across + *gonia* angle] **—di·ag′o·nal·ly** *adv.*

di·a·gram (dī′ə·gram) *n.* **1** A drawing, plan, or outline that illustrates or explains an object, area, concept, etc. **2** A figure drawn to demonstrate a geometrical proposition or relationship. **3** A graph or chart. **—***v.t.* **·gramed** or **·grammed, ·gram·ing** or **·gram·ming** To represent or illustrate by a diagram. [< Gk. *dia-* across + *graphein* write] **—di·a·gram·mat·ic** (dī′ə·grə·mat′ik) or **·i·cal** *adj.* **—di′a·gram·mat′i·cal·ly** *adv.*

di·al (dī′əl, dīl) *n.* **1** A graduated circular plate or face on which an amount, a direction, or degree are indicated by a moving pointer. **2** The face of a watch or clock. **3** A disk or knob used to indicate and change frequencies in a radio or television set. **4** A rotating disk, as on a telephone, used to indicate a number. **5** SUNDIAL. **—***v.t. & v.i.* **di·aled** or **di·alled, di·al·ing** or **di·al·ling 1** To measure or survey with a dial. **2** To indicate on a dial. **3** To telephone by means of a dial. **4** To adjust a radio or television set to (a station, program, etc.). [< Med. L *dialis* daily] **—di′al·er, di′al·ler** *n.*

dial. dialect; dialectic; dialectical.

di·a·lect (dī′ə·lekt) *n.* **1** The aggregate variations from standard language of the speech peculiar to a local region: the Southern *dialect* of American English. **2** Loosely, the speech adopted by a particular class, trade, or profession; jargon. **3** An imperfect use of the standard language by those to whom another language is native. **4** A language or group of languages with distinguishing characteristics but related in their origins: The Romance languages are *dialects* of Latin. **—***adj.* Of or in a dialect. [< Gk. *dialektos* discourse, way of speaking]

di·a·lec·tal (dī′ə·lek′təl) *adj.* Of or characterized by a dialect. **—di′a·lec′tal·ly** *adv.*

di·a·lec·tic (dī′ə·lek′tik) *n.* **1** *Usu. pl.* The art or practice of examining ideas logically, as by a method of question and answer. **2** Any method of logical argument. **3** *Often pl.* The philosophic mode of argumentation used by Hegel and adapted to socialist ideology by Marx. **—***adj.* **1** Pertaining to or using dialectic. **2** DIALECTAL. [< Gk. *dialektika (technē)* (art) of discourse]

di·a·lec·ti·cal (dī′ə·lek′ti·kəl) *adj.* **1** Of, pertaining to, or using dialectic. **2** DIALECTAL. **—di′a·lec′ti·cal·ly** *adv.*

di·a·lec·ti·cian (dī′ə·lek·tish′ən) *n.* **1** A logician. **2** One who specializes in dialects.

di·a·logue (dī′ə·lôg, -log) *n.* **1** A conversation. **2** A literary work in which the characters are represented as conversing. **3** An open exchange of different points of view for the purpose of mutual understanding. **4** Those sections of a play, story, etc., devoted to conversation. **—***v.* **·logued, ·logu·ing** *v.t.* **1** To express in dialogue form. **—***v.i.* **2** To carry on a dialogue. Also **di′a·log.** [< Gk. *dialegesthai* converse] **—di′a·log′ic** (dī′ə·loj′ik) or **·i·cal** *adj.* **—di·al·o·gist** (dī·al′ə·jist, dī′ə·lôg′ist, -log′-) *n.*

di·al·y·sis (dī·al′ə·sis) *n. pl.* **·ses** (-sēz) **1** *Chem.* The separation of dissolved substances from colloids in a liquid by their unequal permeation through a membrane. **2** *Med.* Removal by dialysis of toxic substances in the blood as a result of inadequate kidney function. [< Gk. *dia-* completely + *lyein* loosen] **—di·a·lyt·ic** (dī′ə·lit′ik) *adj.* **—di′a·lyt′i·cal·ly** *adv.*

diam. diameter.

di·a·mag·net·ic (dī′ə·mag·net′ik) *adj.* *Physics* Of or designating the property of forming an induced magnetic field opposite to and weaker than the inducing field. **—***n.* A diamagnetic substance. **—di′a·mag′net·ism** (-mag′nə·tiz′·əm) *n.* **—di′a·mag·net′i·cal·ly** *adv.*

di·am·e·ter (dī·am′ə·tər) *n.* **1** A straight line passing through the center of a circle, sphere, figure, etc., and reaching from one boundary to the other. **2** The length of such a line. 3 The width or thickness of an object as measured by such a line. [<Gk. *dia-* through + *metron* measure]

di·a·met·ri·cal (dī′ə·met′ri·kəl) *adj.* 1 Of or pertaining to a diameter. 2 Directly and totally opposite, different, contrary, etc.: also **di′a·met′ric.** —**di′a·met′ri·cal·ly** *adv.*

dia·mond (dī′mənd, dī′ə-) *n.* 1 A colorless, crystalline, extremely hard form of carbon, valued as a gem and as an abrasive or cutting tool. 2 *Geom.* A plane figure bounded by four equal straight lines, and having two of the angles acute and two obtuse; a lozenge or rhombus. 3 In card games: **a** A lozenge-shaped, red spot on a playing card. **b** A card having such a mark. **c** *pl.* A suit so marked. 4 The square enclosed by the lines between the bases on a baseball field; also, loosely, the field itself. —*adj.* Of or like diamonds. —*v.t.* To adorn with or as with diamonds. [<LL *daimas*]

diamond anniversary A 60th or 75th anniversary. Also **diamond jubilee.**

dia·mond·back (dī′mənd·bak′, dī′ə-) *n.* 1 An edible turtle inhabiting salt marshes of the S U.S., having diamond-shaped markings on the shell: also **diamondback terrapin.** 2 A large rattlesnake of the SE U.S., having a diamond pattern on the back: also **diamondback rattlesnake.**

Di·an·a (dī·an′ə) *Rom. Myth.* Goddess of the hunt, virginity, and the moon.

di·a·pa·son (dī′ə·pā′zən, -sən) *n.* 1 Either of two principal stops in a pipe organ, extending throughout the instrument's entire range and producing its characteristic tone quality. 2 The complete range of a musical instrument or voice. [<Gk. *dia pasōn (chordōn)* through all (the notes)]

di·a·per (dī′pər, dī′ə-) *n.* 1 A soft, absorbent cloth or other material, folded and placed between a baby's legs and fastened around the waist. 2 A repeated, usu. geometric design. —*v.t.* 1 To put a diaper on (an infant). 2 To decorate with a repeated design. [<Med. Gk. *dia-* completely + *aspros* white]

di·aph·a·nous (dī·af′ə·nəs) *adj.* 1 Transparent or translucent, as a sheer fabric. 2 Vague or insubstantial. [<Gk. *dia-* through + *phainein* show] —**di·aph′a·nous·ly** *adv.* —**di·aph′a·nous·ness** *n.*

di·a·pho·re·sis (dī′ə·fə·rē′sis) *n.* Copious perspiration. [<Gk. *dia-* across, through + *phorein* carry] —**di·a·pho·ret·ic** (dī′ə·fə·ret′ik) *adj., n.*

di·a·phragm (dī′ə·fram) *n.* 1 The muscular partition between the thoracic and abdominal cavities; the midriff. 2 Any dividing membrane or partition. 3 Something resembling a diaphragm in shape or elasticity, as the thin, vibrating disk of a telephone. 4 A perforated mechanism which regulates the amount of light entering the lens of a camera, telescope, etc. 5 A contraceptive device consisting of a flexible rubber cap inserted in the vagina to cover the uterine cervix. —*v.t.* To act upon or furnish with a diaphragm. [<Gk. *dia-* across + *phragma* a fence] —**di·a·phrag·mat·ic** (dī′ə·frag·mat′ik) *adj.* —**di′a·phrag·mat′i·cal·ly** *adv.*

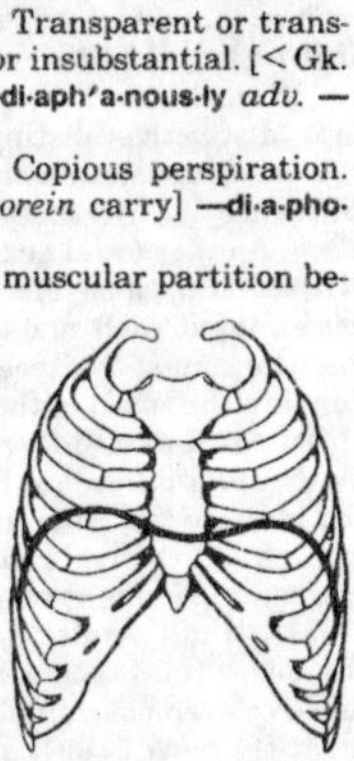

Diaphragm *def. 1*

di·a·rist (dī′ə·rist) *n.* One who keeps a diary.

di·ar·rhe·a (dī′ə·rē′ə) *n.* Abnormally frequent and fluid evacuation of the bowels. Also **di′ar·rhoe′a.** [<Gk. *dia-* through + *rheein* to flow] —**di′ar·rhe′al** or **·rhoe′al, di′ar·rhe′ic** or **·rhoe′ic, di′ar·rhet′ic** or **·rhoet′ic** (-ret′ik) *adj.*

di·a·ry (dī′ə·rē) *n. pl.* **·ries** 1 A written, daily record of the writer's experiences, feelings, activities, etc. 2 A book for keeping such a record. [<LL *diarium* <L *dies* a day]

di·as·po·ra (dī·as′pə·rə) *n.* 1 *Usu. cap.* **a** The dispersion of the Jews among the Gentiles after the Babylonian exile. **b** The Jews so dispersed. **c** Jews or Jewish communities outside Palestine or the state of Israel. 2 Any dispersion of a people having a common heritage.

di·a·stase (dī′ə·stās) *n.* A vegetable enzyme that converts starch into maltose and dextrose. [<Gk. *diastasis* a separation]

di·as·to·le (dī·as′tə·lē) *n.* 1 The rhythmic relaxation and dilation of the heart between contractions. 2 In classical prosody, the lengthening of a syllable naturally short. [<Gk. *diastolē* a separation, lengthening] —**di·as·tol·ic** (dī′ə·stol′ik) *adj.*

di·as·tro·phism (dī·as′trə·fiz′əm) *n.* The process by which the earth's crust is reshaped, producing continents and ocean beds, plateaus, mountains, valleys, etc. [<Gk. *dia-* across + *strephein* to turn] —**di·a·stroph·ic** (dī′ə·strof′ik) *adj.*

di·a·ther·my (dī′ə·thûr′mē) *n.* Medical treatment by means of heat generated in the body by high-frequency radiation. [<Gk. *dia-* through + *thermē* heat] —**di′a·ther′mic** *adj.*

di·a·tom (dī′ə·təm, -tom) *n.* Any of numerous species of microscopic green algae having siliceous walls. [<Gk. *dia-* through + *temnein* to cut] —**di·a·to·ma·ceous** (dī′ə·tə·mā′shəs) *adj.*

di·a·ton·ic (dī′ə·ton′ik) *adj. Music* Of or designating the regular tones of a major or minor scale. [<Gk. *dia-* throughout + *teinein* stretch]

di·a·tribe (dī′ə·trīb) *n.* An abusive denunciation; invective. [<Gk. *diatribē* a wearing away]

di·ba·sic (dī·bā′sik) *adj.* Containing two atoms of hydrogen replaceable by basic radicals or atoms to form a salt. —**di·ba·sic·i·ty** (dī′bā·sis′ə·tē) *n.*

dib·ble (dib′əl) *n.* A pointed tool for planting seeds, setting slips, etc. Also **dib·ber** (dib′ər). —*v.t.* **·bled ·bling** To make holes in (soil) with a dibble. [?]

dice (dīs) *n. pl. of* **die** 1 Small cubes of bone, ivory, plastic, etc., having the sides marked with spots from one to six. 2 A game of chance played with such cubes. 3 Any small cubes. —*v.* **diced, dic·ing** *v.t.* 1 To cut into small cubes. 2 To gamble away or win with dice. —*v.i.* 3 To play at dice. —**dic′er** *n.*

dic·ey (dī′sē) *adj.* **dic·i·er, dic·i·est** *Informal* Risky; chancy. [<DICE + -Y[1]]

di·chot·o·my (dī·kot′ə·mē) *n. pl.* **·mies** 1 Division into two, usu. opposing parts, viewpoints, etc. 2 *Logic* The division of a class into two mutually exclusive subclasses, as minerals into gold and not-gold. 3 *Biol.* A forking in pairs; successive bifurcation. [<Gk. *dicho-* in two + *temnein* to cut] —**di·chot′o·mous** *adj.* —**di·chot′o·mous·ly** *adv.*

di·chro·mat·ic (dī′krō·mat′ik) *adj.* 1 Having two colors. 2 *Zool.* Having two kinds of coloration not due to age or sex. 3 Colorblind; able to see only two of the three primary colors. —**di·chro·ma·tism** (dī·krō′mə·tiz′əm) *n.*

dick·ens (dik′ənz) *n. Informal* The devil: a euphemistic oath. [?]

dick·er (dik′ər) *v.t. & v.i.* To trade, haggle, or barter, esp. on a small scale. —*n.* The act of dickering. [ME *dyker*]

dick·ey (dik′ē) *n.* 1 A detachable shirt or blouse front. 2 A detachable collar. 3 A bib or pinafore. 4 A small bird: also **dickey bird.** 5 An outside seat on a carriage, as for the driver. Also **dick′y.** [<*Dicky,* dim. of the name *Richard*]

di·cot·y·le·don (dī′kot·ə·lēd′n, dī·kot′-) *n.* A flowering plant having seeds with two cotyledons. —**di′cot·y·le′do·nous** *adj.*

dict. dictation; dictator; dictionary.

dic·ta (dik′tə) *n.pl.* of DICTUM.

Dic·ta·phone (dik′tə·fōn) *n.* A type of instrument that records and reproduces spoken words, as for transcription by a stenographer: a trade name.

dic·tate (dik′tāt, dik·tāt′) *v.* **·tat·ed, ·tat·ing** *v.t.* 1 To utter or read aloud (something) to be recorded by another. 2 To prescribe authoritatively, as commands, terms, rules, etc. —*v.i.* 3 To utter aloud something to be recorded by another. 4 To give orders. —*n.* (dik′tāt) 1 An authoritative suggestion, rule, or command. 2 A precept or prompting. [<L *dictare,* freq. of *dicere* say, speak]

dic·ta·tion (dik·tā′shən) *n.* 1 The act of dictating. 2 The matter or material dictated. —**dic·ta′tion·al** *adj.*

dic·ta·tor (dik′tā·tər, dik·tā′tər) *n.* 1 A political ruler with absolute power. 2 One who orders, commands, or prescribes. 3 A person who dictates words. —**dic'ta·tor·ship'** *n.*

dic·ta·to·ri·al (dik'tə·tôr'ē·əl, -tō'rē-) *adj.* 1 Given to dictating; overbearing; autocratic. 2 Of or pertaining to a dictator or his rule. —**dic'ta·to'ri·al·ly** *adv.* —**Syn.** 1 dogmatic, arbitrary, despotic, opinionated, arrogant.

dic·tion (dik'shən) *n.* 1 The use, choice and arrangement of words and modes of expression. 2 The manner of enunciating words in speaking or singing. [<L *dicere* say]

dic·tion·ar·y (dik'shən·er'ē) *n. pl.* **·ar·ies** 1 A book containing the words of a language arranged alphabetically, usu. with their syllabication, pronunciation, definition, and etymology. 2 A similar work having definitions or equivalents in another language. 3 Any list of specialized words or terms arranged alphabetically and defined. [<Med. L *dictionarium* a collection of words and phrases]

dic·tum (dik'təm) *n. pl.* **dic·ta** (-tə) or **·tums** 1 An authoritative, dogmatic, or positive utterance; a pronouncement. 2 A popular saying; a maxim. [<L *dicere* say]

did (did) *p.t.* of DO[1].

di·dac·tic (dī·dak'tik, di-) *adj.* 1 Intended to instruct; expository. 2 Morally instructive; preceptive. 3 Overly inclined to teach; pedantic. Also **di·dac'ti·cal.** [<Gk. *didaskein* teach] —**di·dac'ti·cal·ly** *adv.* —**di·dac'ti·cism** *n.*

di·dac·tics (dī·dak'tiks, di-) *n. pl. (construed as sing.)* The science or art of instruction or education.

did·dle[1] (did'l) *v.* **·dled, ·dling** *Informal v.t.* 1 To cheat. —*v.i.* 2 To dawdle; pass time idly. [?] —**did'dler** *n.*

did·dle[2] (did'l) *v.i.* **·dled, ·dling** *Informal* To jerk up and down or back and forth; jiggle. [<ME *diddiren* quiver, shake, tremble]

did·n't (did'nt) Contraction of *did not.*

di·do (dī'dō) *n. pl.* **·dos** or **·does** *Informal* An extravagant caper; antic. [?]

Di·do (dī'dō) *Rom. Myth.* The founder and queen of Carthage. In the *Aeneid,* she falls in love with Aeneas and kills herself when he leaves her.

didst (didst) *Archaic* Second person singular past tense of DO[1]: used with *thou.*

die[1] (dī) *v.i.* **died, dy·ing** 1 To suffer death; expire. 2 To suffer the pains of death: The coward *dies* a thousand deaths. 3 To lose energy, force, importance, etc.: with *away, down,* or *out.* 4 To fade away: The smile *died* on his lips. 5 To become extinct: with *out* or *off.* 6 To become indifferent or insensible: with *to:* to *die* to the world. 7 *Informal* To desire exceedingly, as if to death: He's *dying* to meet her. 8 To stop functioning, as an engine. 9 To faint or swoon. [<ON *deyja*]

die[2] (dī) *n. pl.* **dice** *for defs. 1 and 2,* **dies** *for def. 3* 1 A small cube used in games. See DICE. 2 A cast, as in playing dice; stake; hazard. 3 Any of various tools, mechanisms, patterns, etc., for cutting, molding, shaping, or stamping. —**the die is cast** The irrevocable choice has been made. —*v.t.* To cut or stamp with or as with a die. [<L *datum* something given]

die-hard (dī'härd') *n.* 1 One who fights to the last. 2 One who obstinately refuses to modify his views; esp., a rigid conservative. —*adj.* Strongly resistent to change; unyielding. Also **die'hard'.**

di·e·lec·tric (dī'ə·lek'trik) *Electri. adj.* Nonconducting. Also **di'e·lec'tri·cal.** —*n.* A dielectric substance, medium, or material. —**di'e·lec'tri·cal·ly** *adv.*

di·er·e·sis (dī·er'ə·sis) *n. pl.* **·ses** (-sēz) Two dots (¨) placed over the second of two adjacent vowels that are to be pronounced separately; often replaced by a hyphen: *reëlect, re-elect.* [<Gk. *diairesis* a division] —**di·e·ret·ic** (dī'ə·ret'ik) *adj.*

die·sel engine (dē'zəl) An internal-combustion engine in which fuel oil is ignited by the heat resulting from the high compression of air in the cylinder. Also **Diesel engine.** [<R. *Diesel,* 1858–1913, German inventor]

Di·es I·rae (dē'ez, dē'as; ir'ā, ir'ē) A medieval Latin hymn about the Day of Judgment, often used in certain masses for the dead. [L, day of wrath]

di·e·sis (dī'ə·sis) *n. Printing* The double dagger (‡), a reference mark for the third in a series. [<L, semitone]

di·et[1] (dī'ət) *n.* 1 Limited or prescribed food and drink, as for losing weight, for controlling disease, etc. 2 One's daily or normal food and drink. —*v.t.* 1 To regulate or restrict the food and drink of. —*v.i.* 2 To take food and drink according to a regimen. [<Gk. *diaita* a way of living] —**di'et·er** *n.*

di·et[2] (dī'ət) *n.* 1 An official assembly. 2 *Usu. cap.* In certain countries, a legislative assembly. [<L *dies* a day]

di·e·tar·y (dī'ə·ter'ē) *n. pl.* **·tar·ies** 1 A system or regimen of dieting. 2 A daily or regulated allowance of food. —*adj.* Of or relating to diet: also **di·e·tet·ic** (dī'ə·tet'ik), **di'e·tet'i·cal.** —**di'e·tet'i·cal·ly** *adv.*

di·e·tet·ics (dī'ə·tet'iks) *n. pl. (construed as sing.)* The study of diet in relation to health.

di·e·ti·tian (dī'ə·tish'ən) *n.* One skilled in dietetics or in planning menus for large numbers of people. Also **di'e·ti'cian.**

diff. difference; different; differential.

dif·fer (dif'ər) *v.i.* 1 To be dissimilar; be distinct, as in kind or appearance: often with *from.* 2 To hold contrary or unlike views; disagree: often with *with.* [<L *dis-* apart + *ferre* carry] —**Syn.** 1 vary, contrast. 2 dissent, clash.

dif·fer·ence (dif'ər·əns, dif'rəns) *n.* 1 The state, quality, or an instance of being different. 2 The way in which persons or things are different. 3 A distinguishing characteristic. 4 A disagreement, controversy, or quarrel. 5 Distinction; discrimination. 6 *Math.* The result obtained by subtraction. —**make a difference** 1 To change or have an effect on something. 2 To distinguish or discriminate: with *between.* —*v.t.* **·enced, ·enc·ing** To make or mark as different; distinguish.

dif·fer·ent (dif'ər·ənt, dif'rənt) *adj.* 1 Not the same; distinct; other. 2 Not alike; dissimilar. 3 Not ordinary; unusual. 4 Various. [<L *differre* differ] —**dif'fer·ent·ly** *adv.* —**dif'fer·ent·ness** *n.* • In American usage, *from* is established as the idiomatic preposition to follow *different;* when, however, a clause follows the connective, *than* is gaining increasing acceptance: a result *different than* (=*from that which* or *from what*) had been expected.

dif·fer·en·tial (dif'ə·ren'shəl) *adj.* 1 Relating to, showing, or marked by a difference. 2 Being or making a difference; distinctive; distinguishing. 3 *Mech.* Characterized by a construction in which a movement is obtained by the difference in two motions in the same direction. —*n.* *Mech.* A differential gear. —**dif'fer·en'tial·ly** *adv.*

differential gear *Mech.* An arrangement of gears that has an input shaft and two output shafts and is set up so that the sum of the speeds of the output shafts is proportional to the speed of the input shaft.

dif·fer·en·ti·ate (dif'ə·ren'shē·āt) *v.* **·at·ed, ·at·ing** *v.t.* 1 To constitute a difference between; mark off. 2 To perceive and indicate the differences of or between. —*v.i.* 3 To discriminate; perceive a difference. 4 To acquire a distinct character; become specialized. —**dif'fer·en'ti·a'tion** *n.*

dif·fi·cult (dif'ə·kult, -kəlt) *adj.* 1 Hard to do or be done; arduous. 2 Hard to understand; perplexing. 3 Hard to persuade or overcome; stubborn. 4 Hard to please, deal with, or satisfy. —**dif'fi·cult·ly** *adv.* —**Syn.** 1 onerous, irksome, laborious. 2 troublesome, complicated. 4 trying, perverse.

dif·fi·cul·ty (dif'ə·kul'tē, -kəl-) *n. pl.* **·ties** 1 The state or quality of being difficult. 2 Something difficult, as a problem, obstacle, objection, or hindrance. 3 *Often pl.* A distressing or embarrassing state of affairs. 4 A quarrel. [<L *dis-* away, not + *facilis* easy]

dif·fi·dent (dif'ə·dənt) *adj.* Showing or characterized by a lack of self-confidence; timid; shy. [<L *dis-* away + *fidere* to trust] —**dif'fi·dence** *n.* —**dif'fi·dent·ly** *adv.*

dif·fract (di·frakt') *v.t.* 1 To separate into parts. 2 To subject to diffraction. [<L *dis-* away + *frangere* break] —**dif·frac'tive** *adj.* —**dif·frac'tive·ly** *adv.* —**dif·frac'tive·ness** *n.*

dif·frac·tion (di·frak'shən) *n. Physics* A change in the path of light or other wave motion, as sound, when passing near the edge of an obstacle, through slits, etc.

dif·fuse (di·fyōōz') *v.t. & v.i.* **·fused, ·fus·ing** 1 To pour or send out so as to spread in all directions; permeate. 2 To subject to or spread by diffusion. —*adj.* (di·fyōōs') 1 Excessively wordy. 2 Widely spread out. [<L *dis-* away, from + *fundere* pour] —**dif·fuse'ly** (-fyōōs'-) *adv.* —**dif·fuse'ness, dif·fus·er** or **dif·fus·or** (di·fyōō'zər) *n.* —**dif·fus'i·ble** *adj.*

dif·fu·sion (di·fyōō′zhən) *n.* 1 The act or process of diffusing, or the state of being diffused. 2 Wordiness; verbosity. 3 The scattering of light rays. 4 *Physics* The intermingling of the atoms or molecules of two substances initially unmixed but in contact.

dif·fu·sive (di·fyōō′siv) *adj.* 1 Tending to diffuse. 2 Characterized by diffusion. —**dif·fu′sive·ly** *adv.* —**dif·fu′sive·ness** *n.*

dig (dig) *v.* **dug** (*Archaic* **digged**), **dig·ging** *v.t.* 1 To break up, turn up, or remove (earth, etc.), as with a spade, claws, or the hands. 2 To make or form by or as by digging. 3 To obtain by digging: to *dig* clams. 4 To thrust into or against, as a tool, heel, or elbow. 5 To uncover by effort or study: often with *up* or *out:* to *dig* up evidence. 6 *Slang* To understand or like. —*v.i.* 7 To break or turn up earth, etc. 8 To force or make a way by or as by digging. 9 *Informal* To work hard and steadily; plod. —**dig in** 1 To dig trenches. 2 To entrench (oneself). 3 *Informal* To begin to work intensively. —*n. Informal* 1 A thrust; poke. 2 A sarcastic remark; slur. 3 An archeological excavation. 4 *pl.* Living quarters. [<OF *diguer* <Gmc.]

di·gest (di·jest′, dī-) *v.t.* 1 To convert (food) into forms that can be assimilated by the body. 2 To take in or assimilate mentally. 3 To arrange in systematic form, usu. by condensing. 4 To tolerate patiently; endure. 5 *Chem.* To soften or decompose by subjecting to heat or moisture. —*v.i.* 6 To be assimilated, as food. 7 To assimilate food. 8 To be subjected to heat, moisture, chemical agents, etc. —*n.* (dī′jest) A systematic, classified, and abridged collection of writings, as of news, scientific material, legal statutes, etc. [<L *dis-* away + *gerere* carry] —**di·gest′er** *n.*

di·gest·i·ble (di·jes′tə·bəl, dī-) *adj.* Capable of being digested or assimilated. —**di·gest′i·bil′i·ty** *n.*

di·ges·tion (di·jes′chən, dī-) *n.* 1 The process of digesting food. 2 The power to digest food. 3 The reception and assimilation of ideas.

di·ges·tive (di·jes′tive, dī-) *adj.* Pertaining or conducing to digestion. —*n.* Something to aid digestion.

dig·ger (dig′ər) *n.* 1 One who or that which digs. 2 Any implement or machine for digging.

dig·gings (dig′ingz) *n. pl.* 1 A mining or excavation site. 2 Materials dug out of such a site. 3 *Informal* Lodgings.

dig·it (dij′it) *n.* 1 A finger or toe. 2 Any one of the ten Arabic numeral symbols, 0 to 9. [<L *digitus* finger]

dig·i·tal (dij′ə·təl) *adj.* 1 Of, pertaining to, or like the fingers or digits. 2 DIGITATE. 3 Of, like, or pertaining to a digital computer. 4 Of or pertaining to a recording system in which sounds are transcribed as binary digits, to be replayed electronically with a very high degree of fidelity. —**dig′i·tal·ly** *adv.*

digital audio tape An audio tape recorded by means of digital recording, so that the sound is reproduced with little or no distortion.

digital computer An electronic computing machine which receives problems and processes the answers in numerical form.

dig·i·tal·is (dij′ə·tal′is, -tā′lis) *n.* 1 FOXGLOVE. 2 The dried leaves of foxglove. 3 A medicine obtained from these leaves, used as a heart stimulant. [<L, finger-shaped]

dig·i·tate (dij′ə·tāt) *adj.* 1 Having digits on the feet or hands. 2 Resembling a finger. 3 *Bot.* Having fingerlike leaflets. Also **dig′i·tat·ed** *adj.* —**dig′i·tate·ly** *adv.* • See LEAF.

dig·i·tize (dij′ə·tīz) *v.* **·tized, ·tiz·ing.** To represent musical sounds or factual data in digital form for computerized processing.

dig·ni·fied (dig′nə·fīd) *adj.* Having or characterized by dignity; stately. —**dig′ni·fied·ly** *adv.*

dig·ni·fy (dig′nə·fī) *v.t.* **·fied, ·fy·ing** 1 To impart or add dignity to. 2 To give a high-sounding name to. [<L *dignus* worthy + *facere* make]

dig·ni·tar·y (dig′nə·ter′ē) *n. pl.* **·tar·ies** One having an important position or office.

dig·ni·ty (dig′nə·tē) *n. pl.* **·ties** 1 A grave or lofty stateliness, as of manner or language. 2 High rank, title, or position. 3 The state or quality of being excellent, worthy, or honorable: the *dignity* of work. 4 Pride or self-respect: beneath one's *dignity.* [<L *dignus* worthy]

di·graph (dī′graf, -gräf) *n.* Two characters representing a single sound, as *oa* in *boat.* —**di·graph′ic** *adj.*

di·gress (di·gres′, dī-) *v.i.* To turn aside from the main subject in speaking or writing; ramble; wander. [<L *di-* away, apart + *gradi* go, step] —**di·gres′sion** *n.*

di·gres·sive (di·gres′iv, dī-) *adj.* Given to or marked by digression. —**di·gres′sive·ly** *adv.* —**di·gres′sive·ness** *n.*

di·he·dral (dī·hē′drəl) *adj.* Two-sided; formed by or having two plane faces. —*n.* 1 DIHEDRAL ANGLE. 2 The inclination of aircraft or bird wings. [<DI- + Gk. *hedra* base]

dihedral angle An angle formed by two intersecting planes.

dik-dik (dik′dik′) *n.* A small NE African antelope. [<native African name]

dike[1] (dīk) *n.* 1 An embankment to protect low land from being flooded. 2 A bank or dirt formed by the excavation of a ditch. 3 A protective obstruction; barrier. 4 A ditch. 5 A raised causeway. 6 *Brit.* A low wall for enclosing land. 7 *Geol.* A mass of igneous rock filling a fissure in other rocks. —*v.t.* **diked, dik·ing** 1 To furnish with a dike. 2 To drain by ditching. [<OE *dīc*] —**dik′er** *n.*

dike[2] (dīk) *n. Slang* LESBIAN. [?]

dil. dilute.

di·lap·i·date (di·lap′ə·dāt) *v.t. & v.i.* **·dat·ed, ·dat·ing** To fall or cause to fall into partial ruin or decay. [<L *dis-* away + *lapidare* throw stones] —**di·lap′i·da′tion** *n.*

di·lap·i·dat·ed (di·lap′ə·dāt′id) *adj.* Being in a state of partial ruin or decay; run-down.

di·la·ta·tion (dil′ə·tā′shən, dī′lə-) *n.* 1 DILATION. 2 *Med.* An excessive enlargement of an organ, orifice, or part.

di·late (dī·lāt, dī′-) *v.* **·lat·ed, ·lat·ing** *v.t.* 1 To make wider, larger or expanded. —*v.i.* 2 To expand; become larger or wider. 3 To speak or write diffusely; enlarge; expatiate: with *on* or *upon.* [<L *dis-* apart + *latus* wide] —**di·lat′a·bil′i·ty** *n.* —**di·lat′a·bly** *adv.* —**di·la′tive** *adj.*

di·la·tion (dī·lā′shən, di-) *n.* 1 The process of dilating or the state of being dilated. 2 That which is dilated.

dil·a·to·ry (dil′ə·tôr′ē, -tō′rē) *adj.* 1 Given to or characterized by delay; tardy; slow. 2 Causing delay. —**dil′a·to′ri·ly** *adv.* —**dil′a·to′ri·ness** *n.*

dil·do (dil′dō) *n. pl.* **·dos** A device used as an artificial penis for sexual stimulation. Also **dil′doe.** [?]

di·lem·ma (di·lem′ə) *n.* 1 A necessary choice between equally undesirable alternatives. 2 A situation requiring a choice but apparently lacking a satisfactory resolution. 3 *Logic* An argument presenting two (or more) alternatives, equally conclusive against the antagonist. —**the horns of a dilemma** The equally undesirable alternatives between which a choice must be made. [<Gk. *di-* two + *lēmma* a premise] —**dil·em·mat·ic** (dil′ə·mat′ik) *adj.* —**Syn.** 2 predicament, quandary.

dil·et·tan·te (dil′ə·tänt′, -tän′tē, -tan′tē, dil′ə·tänt′) *n. pl.* **·tantes, ·tan·ti** (-tän′tē, -tan′tē) 1 A person whose interest in a subject is merely superficial or for amusement. 2 A person who loves the arts. —*adj.* Pertaining to or like a dilettante. [<Ital. *dilettare* to delight] —**dil′et·tan′ish** *adj.* —**dil′et·tan′te·ism, dil′et·tan′tism** *n.*

dil·i·gence[1] (dil′ə·jəns) *n.* 1 Assiduous application; industry. 2 Meticulous care or attention.

dil·i·gence[2] (dil′ə·jəns, *Fr.* dē·lē·zhäns′) *n.* A public stagecoach used esp. in 18th-century France.

dil·i·gent (dil′ə·jənt) *adj.* 1 Having or showing careful and sustained effort or application; industrious; hardworking. 2 Done or pursued painstakingly: *diligent* search. [<L *diligens* attentive] —**dil′i·gent·ly** *adv.*

dill (dil) *n.* 1 Any of various plants related to parsley and having aromatic, pungent seeds and leaves used as a flavoring. 2 The seeds or leaves. [<OE *dile*]

dill pickle A dill-flavored, pickled cucumber.

dil·ly·dal·ly (dil′ē·dal′ē) *v.i.* **·dal·lied, ·dal·ly·ing** To waste time, esp. in indecision or vacillation. [Redupl. of DALLY]

di·lute (di·lōōt′, dī-) *v.t.* **·lut·ed, ·lut·ing** 1 To make weaker or less concentrated by admixture. 2 To reduce the intensity, strength, or purity of (a color, drug, etc.) by admixture. —*adj.* Weak; diluted. [<L *dis-* away + *luere* wash] —**di·lute′ness** *n.*

di·lu·tion (di·lōō′shən, dī-) *n.* 1 The act of diluting. 2 The state or degree of being diluted. 3 Something diluted.

di·lu·vi·al (di·lōō′vē·əl) *adj.* Of, produced by, or pertaining to a flood. Also **di·lu′vi·an.** [<L *diluere* wash away]

dim (dim) *adj.* **dim·mer, dim·mest** 1 Obscure or somewhat dark from faintness of light. 2 Not distinctly seen; shadowy. 3 Not clearly perceived or remembered; vague. 4 Not perceiving or understanding clearly; obtuse. 5 Faint, as a sound. 6 Lacking luster or brightness; dull. 7 Not encouraging or hopeful: *dim* prospects. —*v.t. & v.i.* **dimmed, dim·ming** To render or grow dim. [< OE *dim(m)*] —**dim′ly** *adv.* —**dim′ness** *n.*

dim. dimension; diminuendo; diminutive.

dime (dīm) *n.* A coin of the U.S. and Canada, equal to ten cents or one tenth of a dollar. [< L *decima* a tenth part]

di·men·sion (di·men′shən) *n.* 1 Any measurable extent or magnitude, as length, breadth, or thickness. 2 *pl.* Actual measurements, as of length or breadth. 3 *Often pl.* Scope; importance; magnitude. [< L *dimensio*] —**di·men′sion·al** *adj.* —**di·men′sion·al·ly** *adv.*

dimin. diminuendo; diminutive.

di·min·ish (di·min′ish) *v.t.* 1 To make smaller or less; decrease, as in size, rank, importance, etc. 2 *Music* To lessen (an interval) by a half-step. —*v.i.* 3 To become smaller or less; dwindle; decrease. [< OF *diminuer* < OF *menusier* make smaller] —**di·min′ish·a·ble** *adj.* —**di·min′ish·ment** *n.*

di·min·u·en·do (di·min′yōō·en′dō) *Music adj. & adv.* Gradually lessening in volume of sound: expressed by the sign >. —*n. pl.* **·dos** A diminuendo passage. [< L *diminuere* diminish]

dim·i·nu·tion (dim′ə·n^yōō′shən) *n.* The act of diminishing, or the condition of being diminished.

di·min·u·tive (di·min′yə·tiv) *adj.* 1 Of relatively small size; tiny; little. 2 Expressing diminished size: said of certain suffixes. —*n.* 1 A word formed from another to express diminished size, or familiarity, affection, etc., as: *Johnny, piglet, babykin.* 2 A very small variety or form of anything.

dim·i·ty (dim′ə·tē) *n. pl.* **·ties** A sheer cotton fabric, usu. with a figured weave, used for dresses, curtains, etc. [< Gk. *dimitos* having a double thread]

dim·mer (dim′ər) *n.* 1 Anything that dims. 2 A control for varying the brightness of one or more electric lights.

dim·out (dim′out′) *n.* A reduction of night lighting in a city or certain area.

dim·ple (dim′pəl) *n.* 1 A slight, natural depression on a surface of the body, as on the cheek or chin. 2 A similar depression on any smooth surface. —*v.t. & v.i.* **dim·pled, dim·pling** To mark with dimples; form dimples. [ME *dympull*] —**dim′ply** *adj.*

dim·wit (dim′wit′) *n. Slang* A stupid or simple-minded person. —**dim′wit′ted** *adj.* —**dim′wit′ted·ly** *adv.* —**dim′wit′ted·ness** *n.*

din (din) *n.* A loud continuous noise or clamor; a rattling or clattering sound. —*v.* **dinned, din·ning** *v.t.* 1 To assail with confusing noise. 2 To urge or press insistently. —*v.i.* 3 To make a din. [< OE *dyne*]

dine (dīn) *v.* **dined, din·ing** *v.i.* 1 To eat dinner. 2 To eat: with *on* or *upon.* —*v.t.* 3 To entertain at dinner. [< OF *disner*]

din·er (dī′nər) *n.* 1 One who dines. 2 A railroad dining car. 3 An informal restaurant usu. with booths and an eating counter and having a relatively long, narrow shape.

di·nette (dī·net′) *n.* A small dining area; dining alcove.

ding (ding) *v.t.* 1 To ring; sound, as a bell. 2 *Informal* To instill by constant repetition; din. —*v.i.* 3 To ring or sound. 4 *Informal* To speak with constant repetition. —*n.* The sound of a bell or a sound like it. [Imit.]

ding·dong (ding′dong′, -dông′) *n.* The repeated, ringing sound of a bell. —*adj. Informal* Energetically and closely contested, as a race. —*v.i.* To make the sound of ding-dong. [Imit.]

din·ghy (ding′gē, ding′ē) *n. pl.* **·ghies** 1 Any of various small rowing boats, as a small skiff, a ship's boat, etc. 2 An inflatable rubber life raft. Also **din′gey.** [< Hind. *dīngī* boat]

din·go (ding′gō) *n. pl.* **din·goes** The native wild dog of Australia. [< native Australian name]

din·gy (din′jē) *adj.* **din·gi·er, din·gi·est** 1 Of a drab color, as if soiled; dull. 2 Grimy; shabby. [?] —**din′gi·ly** *adv.* —**din′gi·ness** *n.*

dining car A railway car in which meals are served.

dining room A room in which meals are served.

dink·ey (ding′kē) *n. Informal* A small engine used for shunting freight. [< DINKY]

dink·y (ding′kē) *adj.* **dink·i·er, dink·i·est** *Informal* Tiny; insignificant. [?]

din·ner (din′ər) *n.* 1 The principal meal of the day. 2 A banquet in honor of a person or event. 3 A formal feast. [< OF *disner* dine]

dinner jacket A tuxedo jacket.

din·ner·ware (din′ər·wâr′) *n.* The dishes used in a household for serving food.

di·no·saur (dī′nə·sôr) *n.* Any of a group of four-limbed, in some species gigantic, reptiles that became extinct by the end of the Mesozoic period. [< Gk. *deinos* terrible + *sauros* lizard] —**di′no·sau′ri·an** *adj., n.*

dint (dint) *n.* 1 A dent. 2 Active force; effort: now chiefly in the phrase **by dint of.** —*v.t.* 1 To make a dent in. 2 To drive in forcibly. [< OE *dynt* blow]

dioc. diocesan; diocese.

di·o·cese (dī′ə·sēs, -sis) *n.* The territory or the churches under a bishop's jurisdiction. [< Gk. *dioikēsis,* orig. management of a house] —**di·oc·e·san** (dī·os′ə·sən, dī′ə·sē′sən) *adj.*

di·ode (dī′ōd) *n. Electronics* A circuit element which permits current to pass in one direction only; a rectifier. [< DI(A)- + Gk. *hodos* a road, way]

di·oe·cious (dī·ē′shəs) *adj. Bot.* Having separate male and female flowers. [< DI- + Gk. *oikia* house, dwelling] —**di·oe′cious·ly** *adv.* —**di·oe′cious·ness** *n.*

Di·o·ny·sus (dī′ə·nī′səs) *Gk. Myth.* The god of wine and fertility. Also **Di′o·ny′sos.** —**Di·o·nys·i·an** (dī′ə·nish′ən, -nis′ē·ən, -nī′sē·ən), **Di′o·nys′i·ac** (-nis′ē·ak) *adj.*

di·op·ter (dī·op′tər) *n. Optics* The unit for measuring the refractive power of a lens, mirror, etc., determined by the reciprocal of its focal length in meters. Also **di·op′tre.** [< Gk. *dioptra* an optical instrument] —**di·op′tric** or **·tri·cal** *adj.*

di·o·ra·ma (dī′ə·rä′mə, -ram′ə) *n.* 1 A miniature scene painted on cloth transparencies and so lit that changes in the scene are produced in view of the spectators. 2 A group of modeled figures, for exhibition, set in a naturalistic foreground against a painted background. [< Gk. *dia-* through + *horama* a sight] —**di·o·ram·ic** (dī′ə·ram′ik) *adj.*

di·ox·ide (dī·ok′sīd, -sid) *n.* An oxide containing two atoms of oxygen to the molecule.

dip (dip) *v.* **dipped, dip·ping** *v.t.* 1 To put or let down into a liquid momentarily. 2 To lift up and out by scooping, bailing, etc. 3 To lower and then raise, as a flag in salute. 4 To baptize by immersion. 5 To plunge (animals) into a disinfectant. 6 To dye by immersion. 7 *Chem.* To coat (a metallic surface) by immersion. 8 To make (candles) by repeatedly immersing wicks in wax or tallow. —*v.i.* 9 To plunge into and come out of water or other liquid, esp. quickly. 10. To plunge one's hand or a receptacle into water, etc., so as to take something out. 11 To withdraw or take part of something saved, etc.: with *into.* 12 To sink or go down suddenly. 13 To go down; decline. 14 To engage in or inquire into something slightly or superficially. —*n.* 1 The act of dipping. 2 A liquid or sauce into which something is to be dipped. 3 An amount removed by dipping. 4 An object used for dipping. 5 A brief swim. 6 A sloping downward or inclination; also, the amount of this. 7 A slight depression or hollow. 8 An abrupt downward movement; drop. 9 A candle made by dipping. 10 *Slang* A pickpocket. [< OE *dyppan*]

diph·the·ri·a (dif·thir′ē·ə, dip-) *n.* An acute contagious disease caused by a bacillus and characterized by the formation of a false membrane in the upper air passages. [< Gk. *diphthera* leather, membrane] —**diph·the·rit·ic** (dif′thə·rit′ik, dip′-), **diph·the′ri·al, diph·the′ric** *adj.*

diph·thong (dif′thông, -thong, dip′-) *n.* A combination of two vowel sounds in one syllable, as *oi* in *coil* and *ou* in *doubt,* or as *i* in *fine* and *a* in *name.* [< Gk. *di-* two + *phthongos* sound] —**diph·thon′gal** *adj.*

diph·thong·ize (dif′thông·īz, -thong-, dip′-) *v.* **·ized, ·iz·ing** *v.t.* 1 To pronounce as a diphthong. —*v.i.* 2 To become a diphthong. —**diph′thong·i·za′tion,** *n.*

dipl. diplomat; diplomatic.

di·plo·ma (di·plō′mə) *n.* 1 A certificate bestowed by a school, college, or university on those who have completed a course of study or have earned a degree. 2 A certificate bestowing some honor or privilege. [< Gk. *diplōma* paper folded double, a letter]

di·plo·ma·cy (di·plō′mə·sē) *n. pl.* **·cies** 1 The art, science, or practice of conducting negotiations between nations. 2 Tact or skill in dealing with people.

dip·lo·mat (dip′lə·mat) *n.* 1 A person who represents his country in its official relations with other countries. 2 A person who is skilled and tactful in dealing with others. Also **di·plo·ma·tist** (di·plō′mə·tist). [< L *diploma* a document]

dip·lo·mat·ic (dip′lə·mat′ik) *adj.* 1 Of or pertaining to diplomats or to diplomacy. 2 Skillful and tactful in dealing with people. **—dip′lo·mat′i·cal·ly** *adv.*

dip·per (dip′ər) *n.* 1 A person employed in dipping. 2 A long-handled, cup-shaped utensil for dipping liquids, etc. 3 Any of several American diving birds, esp. the water ouzel.

Dip·per (dip′ər) *n.* Either of two constellations, the Big Dipper or the Little Dipper.

dip·so·ma·ni·a (dip′sə·mā′nē·ə) *n.* An uncontrollable craving for alcoholic drink. [< Gk. *dipsa* thirst + -MANIA] **—dip′so·ma′ni·ac** (-ak) *n.* **—dip·so·ma·ni·a·cal** (dip′sə·mə·nī′ə·kəl) *adj.*

dip·ter·ous (dip′tər·əs) *adj.* 1 Of or pertaining to an order of insects having a single pair of membranous wings, including the flies, gnats, mosquitoes, etc. 2 *Bot.* Two-winged, as certain seeds and fruits. [< Gk. *dipteros* two-winged]

dip·tych (dip′tik) *n.* 1 A pair of writing tablets hinged together and used in ancient Greece and Rome. 2 A double picture or design on a pair of hinged panels. [< Gk. *diptycha* pair of tablets]

dir. director.

dire (dīr) *adj.* **dir·er, dir·est** 1 Extremely calamitous; dreadful; terrible. 2 Urgent; exigent: *dire* necessity. [< L *dirus* fearful] **—dire′ly** *adv.* **—dire′ness** *n.*

di·rect (di·rekt′, dī-) *v.t.* 1 To control or conduct the affairs of; manage; govern. 2 To order or instruct with authority; command. 3 *Music* To lead as a conductor. 4 To tell (someone) the way. 5 To cause to move, face, or go in a desired direction; aim: He *directed* his gaze toward her. 6 To indicate the destination of, as a letter. 7 To intend, as remarks to be heard by a person; address: Did you *direct* that remark at me? 8 **a** To supervise the filming or staging of (a play, motion picture, etc.). **b** To supervise the performance of (actors, etc.). *—v.i.* 9 To give commands or guidance. 10 To supervise the production of a play, motion picture, etc. *—adj.* 1 Having or being the straightest course; shortest; nearest. 2 Free from intervening agencies or conditions; immediate; first-hand. 3 Unbroken in the line of descent; lineal. 4 Complete; total: the *direct* opposite. 5 Straightforward; candid; plain. 6 *Electr.* Flowing in one direction only: *direct* current. *—adv.* In a direct manner; directly. [< L *dis-* apart + *regere* set straight] **—di·rect′ness** *n.* **—Syn.** 1 supervise, run, guide, oversee.

direct discourse Language quoted in the exact words of the speaker or writer.

di·rec·tion (di·rek′shən, dī-) *n.* 1 The act of directing; supervision. 2 *Usu. pl.* Information or instructions for doing something, going somewhere, etc. 3 An order or command. 4 The position or course of movement of a point or object in its spatial relationship to something else: to go in a northerly *direction.* 5 Trend, tendency, way, etc.: a new *direction* in medicine. 6 The art or act of directing actors, musicians, films, plays, etc.

di·rec·tion·al (di·rek′shən·əl, dī-) *adj.* 1 Of, pertaining to, or indicating a direction in space. 2 *Telecom.* Of or having a preferred direction or directions of radiation or reception, as an antenna.

direction finder *Telecom.* A device with which the direction of radio signals may be determined.

di·rec·tive (di·rek′tiv, dī-) *n.* An official order or regulation. *—adj.* That directs or points out, rules, or governs.

di·rect·ly (di·rekt′lē, dī-) *adv.* 1 In a direct line or manner. 2 Without medium, agent, or go-between. 3 Immediately; as soon as possible. 4 Exactly; precisely. *—conj. Brit.* As soon as.

direct mail Mail sent directly to individuals that promotes the sale of merchandise or services or solicits contributions. **—di·rect′-mail′** *adj.*

direct object The word or words that indicate the person or thing receiving the action of a transitive verb, as *ball* in *She threw him the ball.*

di·rec·tor (di·rek′tər, dī-) *n.* 1 One who or that which directs. 2 A member of a governing body, as of a club or corporation. 3 A conductor of an orchestra. 4 One who directs or stages a film, play, etc. **—di·rec′tor·ship′** *n.* **—di·rec′tress** *n. Fem.*

di·rec·tor·ate (di·rek′tər·it, dī-) *n.* 1 A body of directors. 2 The office of a director.

di·rec·to·ri·al (di·rek′tôr′ē·əl, -tō′rē-, dī-) *adj.* 1 That directs; directive. 2 Pertaining to a director or directorate.

di·rec·to·ry (di·rek′tər·ē, dī-) *n. pl.* **·ries** 1 An alphabetical or classified list, as of the names and addresses of the inhabitants of a city. 2 A book of rules. 3 A body of directors; directorate. *—adj.* Containing directions.

direct primary A primary election in which candidates for office are nominated directly by the voters and not by a body of delegates.

direct tax A tax, as on income or property, levied directly on the taxpayer.

dire·ful (dīr′fəl) *adj.* Most dire; dreadful; terrible. **—dire′·ful·ly** *adv.* **—dire′ful·ness** *n.*

dirge (dûrj) *n.* 1 A song or melody expressing grief and mourning. 2 A funeral hymn. [< L *dirige* direct (imperative), the first word of the antiphon (*Psalms* 5:8) of matins in the Latin burial office]

dir·i·gi·ble (dir′ə·jə·bəl) *n.* A lighter-than-air aircraft

Dirigible *(rigid type)*

equipped with means for propulsion and steering. *—adj.* That may be directed or controlled. [< L *dirigere* to direct + -IBLE]

dirk (dûrk) *n.* A dagger or poniard. *—v.t.* To stab with a dirk. [?]

dirn·dl (dûrn′dəl) *n.* 1 A dress with a full skirt gathered to a tight bodice. 2 Such a skirt without the bodice: also **dirndl skirt.** [< G *Dirne* girl]

dirt (dûrt) *n.* 1 Any foul or filthy substance, as mud, grime, etc.; filth. 2 Loose earth or soil. 3 Something mean or contemptible. 4 Obscenity in speech, writing, or pictures. 5 Obscene gossip. 6 In mining, washed-down soil, gravel, etc., containing precious metal. *—adj.* Made of earth. [< ON *drit*]

dirt-cheap (dûrt′chēp′) *adj. Informal* Very inexpensive. *—adv.* At a low cost.

dirt farmer *Informal* A farmer who does his own work.

dirt·y (dûr′tē) *adj.* **dirt·i·er, dirt·i·est** 1 Unclean; filthy. 2 Causing one to be covered with dirt: a *dirty* job. 3 Not clear; clouded; muddy: said of colors. 4 Obscene. 5 Despicable; base; contemptible. 6 Not sportsmanlike or fair. 7 Conveying anger or annoyance: a *dirty* look. 8 Producing excessive fallout: said of nuclear explosions. 9 Stormy; foul, as weather. *—v.t. & v.i.* **dirt·ied, dirt·y·ing** To make or become dirty or soiled. **—dirt′i·ly** *adv.* **—dirt′i·ness** *n.*

Dis (dis) *Rom. Myth.* 1 The god of the lower world. 2 The kingdom of the dead.

dis-[1] *prefix* 1 Apart; away from: *dismiss.* 2 The reverse of or the undoing of: *disarm.* 3 Deprivation of some quality, power, rank, etc.: *disable.* 4 Not: *distasteful.* 5 Completely; thoroughly (with a negative word): *disannul.* [< L]

dis-[2] *prefix* Var. of DI- [< Gk. *dis* twice]

dis. distance, distant.

dis·a·bil·i·ty (dis′ə·bil′ə·tē) *n. pl.* **·ties** 1 That which disables; an infirmity or handicap. 2 Lack of ability; inability. 3 Legal incapacity or inability to act.

dis·a·ble (dis·ā′bəl) *v.t.* **·a·bled, ·a·bling 1** To render incapable or unable; cripple. **2** To render legally incapable, as of inheriting property, etc. **—dis·a′ble·ment** *n.*

dis·a·buse (dis′ə·byōōz′) *v.t.* **·a·bused, ·a·bus·ing** To rid of a false notion or impression.

dis·ad·van·tage (dis′əd·van′tij, -vän′-) *n.* **1** An unfavorable condition, element, or circumstance; drawback; hindrance. **2** Loss; detriment. *—v.t.* **·taged, ·tag·ing** To injure the interest of; prejudice; hinder.

dis·ad·van·taged (dis′əd·van′təjd) *adj.* Having less than what is regarded as basic or minimal for decent living, as money, social equality, etc.; underprivileged.

dis·ad·van·ta·geous (dis·ad′vən·tā′jəs) *adj.* Attended with disadvantage; detrimental; inconvenient. **—dis·ad′·van·ta′geous·ly** *adv.*

dis·af·fect (dis′ə·fekt′) *v.t.* To destroy or weaken the affection or loyalty of; alienate. **—dis′af·fec′tion** *n.*

dis·af·fect·ed (dis′ə·fek′tid) *adj.* Alienated in feeling or loyalty; estranged. **—dis′af·fect′ed·ly** *adv.*

dis·a·gree (dis′ə·grē′) *v.i.* **·a·greed, ·a·gree·ing 1** To vary in opinion; differ; dissent. **2** To quarrel. **3** To fail to agree or harmonize, as facts. **4** To produce an unfavorable effect, as food or climate: with *with.*

dis·a·gree·a·ble (dis′ə·grē′ə·bəl) *adj.* **1** Repugnant to taste, sentiment, opinion, or the senses; displeasing. **2** Not pleasant or agreeable; bad-tempered. **—dis′a·gree′a·ble·ness, dis′a·gree′a·bil′i·ty** *n.* **—dis′a·gree′a·bly** *adv.*

dis·a·gree·ment (dis′ə·grē′mənt) *n.* **1** Failure to agree; disparity; variance. **2** A difference of opinion. **3** A quarrel; altercation.

dis·al·low (dis′ə·lou′) *v.t.* **1** To refuse to allow or permit. **2** To reject as untrue or invalid. **—dis′al·low′ance** *n.*

dis·ap·pear (dis′ə·pir′) *v.i.* **1** To pass from sight or view; fade away; vanish. **2** To cease to exist: His anger *disappeared.* **—dis′ap·pear′ance** *n.*

dis·ap·point (dis′ə·point′) *v.t.* **1** To fail to fulfill the expectation, hope, or desire of. **2** To prevent the fulfillment of (a hope or plan); frustrate. [< OF *des-* away + *appointer* arrange, appoint] **—dis′ap·point′ing·ly** *adv.*

dis·ap·point·ment (dis′ə·point′mənt) *n.* **1** The state, condition, or sense of being disappointed. **2** A person or thing that disappoints.

dis·ap·pro·ba·tion (dis·ap′rə·bā′shən) *n.* Disapproval; unfavorable judgment.

dis·ap·prove (dis′ə·prōōv′) *v.* **·proved, ·prov·ing** *v.t.* **1** To regard with disfavor or censure; condemn. **2** To refuse assent to; decline to approve. *—v.i.* **3** To have or express an unfavorable opinion: often with *of.* **—dis′ap·prov′al** *n.* **—dis′ap·prov′ing·ly** *adv.* **—Syn. 1** dislike, object to, frown upon, denounce, disparage.

dis·arm (dis·ärm′) *v.t.* **1** To deprive of weapons. **2** To render harmless. **3** To allay or reduce suspicion, aloofness, or hostility. *—v.i.* **4** To lay down arms. **5** To reduce or restrict the size of armed forces.

dis·ar·ma·ment (dis·är′mə·mənt) *n.* **1** The act of disarming. **2** The reduction or limitation of armed forces or of certain types of weapons.

dis·arm·ing (dis·är′ming) *adj.* Removing suspicion, aloofness, hostility, etc.: a *disarming smile.* **—dis·arm′ing·ly** *adv.*

dis·ar·range (dis′ə·rānj′) *v.t.* **·ranged, ·rang·ing** To disturb the arrangement of. **—dis′ar·range′ment** *n.*

dis·ar·ray (dis′ə·rā′) *n.* **1** Lack of order or tidiness; confusion. **2** Disordered or insufficient dress. *—v.t.* To throw into disorder, as an army.

dis·as·sem·ble (dis′ə·sem′bəl) *v.t.* **·bled, ·bling** To take apart. **—dis′as·sem′bly** *n.*

dis·as·so·ci·ate (dis′ə·sō′shē·āt) *v.t.* **·at·ed, ·at·ing** To separate from association: He wished to *disassociate* himself from the government's policy. **—dis′as·so′ci·a′tion** *n.*

dis·as·ter (di·zas′tər, -zäs′-) *n.* Any sudden event that causes great damage; a great misfortune or calamity. [< MF *des-* away + *astre* a star]

dis·as·trous (di·zas′trəs, -zäs′-) *adj.* Causing or accompanied by disaster; calamitous. **—dis·as′trous·ly** *adv.* **—dis·as′trous·ness** *n.*

dis·a·vow (dis′ə·vou′) *v.t.* To disclaim responsibility for or approval of; repudiate. **—dis′a·vow′al, dis′a·vow′er** *n.*

dis·band (dis·band′) *v.t.* **1** To break up (an organization, etc.). **2** To remove from military service. *—v.i.* **3** To cease to be an organization. **—dis·band′ment** *n.*

dis·bar (dis·bär′) *v.t.* **·barred, ·bar·ring** To deprive of the status of a lawyer; expel from the bar. **—dis·bar′ment** *n.*

dis·be·lief (dis′bi·lēf′) *n.* A lack of belief.

dis·be·lieve (dis′bi·lēv′) *v.t.* & *v.i.* **·lieved, ·liev·ing** To refuse to believe; deem false. **—dis′be·liev′er** *n.*

dis·bur·den (dis·bûr′dən) *v.t.* **1** To relieve (someone or something) of a burden; unload. **2** To get rid of (a burden). *—v.i.* **3** To put off a burden.

dis·burse (dis·bûrs′) *v.t.* **·bursed, ·burs·ing** To pay out; expend. [< OF *des-* away + *bourse* a purse] **—dis·burs′a·ble** *adj.* **—dis·burse′ment, dis·burs′er** *n.*

disc (disk) *n.* **1** A phonograph record. **2** DISK. [Var. of DISK]

disc. discount; discover; discovered.

dis·card (dis·kärd′) *v.t.* **1** To cast aside as useless or undesirable; reject. **2** In card games, to throw out (a card or cards) from one's hand; also, to play (a card, other than a trump, of a different suit from the suit led). *—v.i.* **3** In card games, to throw out a card or cards from one's hand. *—n.* (dis′kärd) **1** The act of discarding. **2** A card or cards discarded. **3** A person or thing cast off.

dis·cern (di·sûrn′, di·zûrn′) *v.t.* **1** To perceive, as with sight or mind; apprehend. **2** To discriminate mentally; recognize subtle differences. *—v.i.* **3** To distinguish; discriminate. [< L *dis-* apart + *cernere* to separate] **—dis·cern′er, dis·cern′ment** *n.* **—dis·cern′i·ble** *adj.* **—Syn. 1** recognize, detect, discover. **2** distinguish.

dis·cern·ing (di·sûr′ning, -zûr′-) *adj.* Quick to discern; discriminating; penetrating. **—dis·cern′ing·ly** *adv.*

dis·charge (dis·chärj′) *v.* **·charged, ·charg·ing** *v.t.* **1** To unload; remove the contents of: to *discharge* a ship. **2** To remove or send forth: to *discharge* passengers. **3** To send forth; emit (fluid). **4** To shoot or fire, as a gun, bow, shot, or arrow. **5** To dismiss from office; fire. **6** To release, as a prisoner, soldier, or patient. **7** To relieve of duty: to *discharge* a jury. **8** To perform or fulfill the functions and duties of (a trust, office, etc.). **9** To pay (a debt) or meet (an obligation or duty). **10** *Electr.* To free of an electrical charge. *—v.i.* **11** To get rid of a load, burden, etc. **12** To go off, as a cannon. **13** To give or send forth contents. **14** *Electr.* To lose a charge of electricity. *—n.* (*also* dis′chärj) **1** The act of discharging or the state or condition of being discharged. **2** That which discharges, as a certificate releasing one from military service. **3** That which is discharged, as blood from a wound. **4** *Electr.* **a** The equalization of potential between terminals of a charged capacitor when connected by a conductor. **b** A disruptive flow of current through a dielectric, esp. through a gas. **—dis·charge′a·ble** *adj.* **—dis·charg′er** *n.*

dis·ci·ple (di·sī′pəl) *n.* **1** A student or follower of a teacher or a doctrine. **2** One of the 12 chosen companions and apostles of Jesus. [< L *discipulus*] **—dis·ci′ple·ship** *n.*

dis·ci·pli·nar·i·an (dis′ə·plə·nâr′ē·ən) *n.* One who is strict in disciplining others.

dis·ci·pli·nar·y (dis′ə·plə·ner′ē) *adj.* **1** Of, relating to, or having the nature of discipline. **2** Used in discipline.

dis·ci·pline (dis′ə·plin) *n.* **1** Systematic and rigorous training of the mental, moral, and physical powers by instruction and exercise. **2** The result of this. **3** Self-control. **4** Control over others, as by enforcing obedience. **5** Orderly conduct, etc., resulting from such control. **6** Punishment; chastisement. **7** A specific branch of learning or knowledge. **8** A system of rules, as of a church. **9** A small, penitential whip or scourge. *—v.t.* **·plined, ·plin·ing 1** To train to obedience or subjection. **2** To drill; educate. **3** To punish or chastise. [< L *disciplina* instruction < *discipulus* disciple] **—dis′ci·plin·er** *n.*

disc jockey A person who conducts and announces a radio or television program that presents recorded music, usu. interspersed with comments and commercials.

dis·claim (dis·klām′) *v.t.* **1** To deny; repudiate; disavow. **2** To renounce a right or claim to.

dis·claim·er (dis·klā′mər) *n.* A disclaiming act, notice, or instrument.

dis·close (dis·klōz′) *v.t.* **·closed, ·clos·ing 1** To lay bare; uncover. **2** To make known; divulge. **—dis·clos′er** *n.*

dis·clo·sure (dis·klō′zhər) *n.* **1** The act or process of disclosing. **2** Anything disclosed.

dis·co (dis′kō) *n. pl.* ·cos *Informal* DISCOTHÈQUE.
dis·coid (dis′koid) *adj.* Pertaining to or like a disk or disks. —*n.* A disk or disklike object.
dis·col·or (dis·kul′ər) *v.t.* 1 To give an unnatural color to; stain. —*v.i.* 2 To become stained, faded, or of a changed color. —**dis·col′or·a′tion, dis·col′or·ment** *n.*
dis·com·fit (dis·kum′fit) *v.t.* 1 To defeat the plans or purposes of; frustrate. 2 To embarrass. 3 To vanquish. [< OF *des-* away + *confire* prepare] —**dis·com′fi·ture** *n.*
dis·com·fort (dis·kum′fərt) *n.* 1 The state of being uncomfortable; uneasiness. 2 That which causes an uncomfortable condition. —*v.t.* To make uneasy; trouble.
dis·com·mode (dis′kə·mōd′) *v.t.* ·mod·ed, ·mod·ing To cause inconvenience to. [< DIS + L *commodus* convenient] —**Syn.** bother, trouble, disturb.
dis·com·pose (dis′kəm·pōz′) *v.t.* ·posed, ·pos·ing 1 To disturb the composure of; make uneasy. 2 To disorder or disarrange.
dis·com·po·sure (dis′kəm·pō′zhər) *n.* The state of being discomposed.
dis·con·cert (dis′kən·sûrt′) *v.t.* 1 To cause to lose one's composure or confidence; confuse; upset. 2 To frustrate, as a plan. [< MF *dis-* apart + *concerter* agree] —**dis′con·cert′·ing** *adj.* —**dis′con·cert′ing·ly** *adv.*
dis·con·nect (dis′kə·nekt′) *v.t.* To undo or break the connection of; detach; separate.
dis·con·nect·ed (dis′kə·nek′tid) *adj.* 1 Not connected; disjointed. 2 Incoherent; rambling. —**dis′con·nect′ed·ly** *adv.* —**dis′con·nect′ed·ness** *n.*
dis·con·so·late (dis·kon′sə·lit) *adj.* 1 Without consolation; inconsolable; sad. 2 Gloomy; cheerless. [< L *dis-* not + *consolari* console] —**dis·con′so·late·ly** *adv.* —**dis·con′so·late·ness, dis·con′so·la′tion** *n.*
dis·con·tent (dis′kən·tent′) *n.* Lack of contentment; dissatisfaction: also **dis′con·tent′ment.** —*v.t.* To made discontented.
dis·con·tent·ed (dis′kən·tent′əd) *adj.* Dissatisfied; not content. —**dis′con·tent′ed·ly** *adv.* —**dis′con·tent′ed·ness** *n.*
dis·con·tin·ue (dis′kən·tin′yōō) *v.* ·tin·ued, ·tin·u·ing *v.t.* 1 To break off or cease from; stop. 2 To cease using, receiving, etc. —*v.i.* 3 To come to an end; stop. —**dis′con·tin′u·ance, dis′con·tin′u·a′tion** *n.*
dis·con·ti·nu·i·ty (dis′kon·tə·n^{y}ōō′ə·tē) *n.* 1 Lack of continuity. 2 A gap or interruption.
dis·con·tin·u·ous (dis′kən·tin′yōō·əs) *adj.* Not continuous; interrupted; broken. —**dis′con·tin′u·ous·ly** *adv.* —**dis′con·tin′u·ous·ness** *n.*
dis·cord (dis′kôrd) *n.* 1 Lack of agreement; contention; strife. 2 *Music* A dissonant combination of tones; dissonance. 3 Harsh or disagreeable noises. —*v.i.* To be out of accord or harmony; clash. [< L *dis-* away + *cor, cordis* heart]
dis·cor·dant (dis·kôr′dənt) *adj.* 1 Contradictory; inconsistent. 2 Quarrelsome. 3 Not harmonious; dissonant. —**dis·cor′dance, dis·cor′dan·cy,** *n.* —**dis·cor′dant·ly** *adv.*
dis·co·thèque (dis′kə·tek, dis·kə·tek′) *n.* A night club or other public place offering recorded music for dancing. [F, lit., record library]
dis·count (dis′kount) *n.* 1 An amount deducted from a sum to be paid. 2 In lending money, the interest deducted in advance. 3 The act of discounting. 4 The rate of discount. —**at a discount** At less than the face value or amount regularly charged. —*v.t.* (dis′kount, dis·kount′) 1 To deduct, as a portion of an amount owed. 2 To buy or sell (a bill or note) for face value less interest. 3 To fail to heed; disregard. 4 To believe only part of. 5 To take into account beforehand so as to lessen value, effect, enjoyment, etc. —*v.i.* 6 To lend money, deducting the interest beforehand. [< L *dis-* away + *computare* compute] —**dis′·count·a·ble** *adj.* —**dis′count·er** *n.*
dis·coun·te·nance (dis·koun′tə·nəns) *v.t.* ·nanced, ·nanc·ing 1 To look upon with disfavor. 2 To abash; disconcert. [< MF *des-* away + *contenancer* to favor]
dis·cour·age (dis·kûr′ij) *v.t.* ·aged, ·ag·ing 1 To deprive of courage; dispirit; dishearten. 2 To deter or dissuade: with *from.* 3 To obstruct; hinder. 4 To attempt to prevent by disapproval. —**dis·cour′age·ment, dis·cour′ag·er** *n.* —**dis·cour′ag·ing** *adj.* —**dis·cour′ag·ing·ly** *adv.*
dis·course (dis′kôrs, dis·kôrs′) *n.* 1 Familiar conversation; talk. 2 Formal expression of thought, oral or written. —*v.i.* (dis·kôrs′) ·coursed, ·cours·ing 1 To set forth one's thoughts and conclusions concerning a subject: with *on* or *upon.* 2 To converse; confer. [< L *dis-* apart + *cursus* a running] —**dis·cours′er** *n.*
dis·cour·te·ous (dis·kûr′tē·əs) *adj.* Showing discourtesy; rude. —**dis·cour′te·ous·ly** *adv.* —**dis·cour′te·ous·ness** *n.*
dis·cour·te·sy (dis·kûr′tə·sē) *n. pl.* ·sies 1 Rudeness; impoliteness. 2 An impolite act or remark.
dis·cov·er (dis·kuv′ər) *v.t.* To come upon, find out, make known, or realize, esp. for the first time. [< OF *des-* away + *covrir* to cover] —**dis·cov′er·a·ble** *adj.* —**dis·cov′er·er** *n.*
dis·cov·er·y (dis·kuv′ər·ē) *n. pl.* ·er·ies 1 The act of discovering. 2 Something discovered.
dis·cred·it (dis·kred′it) *v.t.* 1 To disbelieve. 2 To injure the credit or reputation of. 3 To show to be unworthy of belief or confidence. —*n.* 1 Distrust or disbelief. 2 Dishonor or disgrace. 3 Something that causes distrust or disgrace. —**dis·cred′it·a·ble** *adj.* —**dis·cred′it·a·bly** *adv.*
dis·creet (dis·krēt′) *adj.* Showing consideration of the privacy or trust of others, as by suppressing curious inquiry; prudent; circumspect. [< LL *discretus* pp. of *discernere* discern] —**dis·creet′ly** *adv.* —**dis·creet′ness** *n.*
dis·crep·an·cy (dis·krep′ən·sē) *n. pl.* ·cies 1 Disagreement or difference; inconsistency. 2 An example of this. [< L < *dis-* away + *crepare* creak] —**dis·crep′ant** *adj.* —**dis·crep′ant·ly** *adv.*
dis·crete (dis·krēt′) *adj.* 1 Distinct or separate. 2 Made up of distinct parts or separate units. [< LL *discretus.* See DISCREET.] —**dis·crete′ly** *adv.* —**dis·crete′ness** *n.*
dis·cre·tion (dis·kresh′ən) *n.* 1 The quality of being discreet; prudence; caution. 2 Liberty of action; freedom in the exercise of judgment. —**at one's discretion** According to one's own judgment.
dis·cre·tion·ar·y (dis·kresh′ə·ner′ē) *adj.* Left to one's own judgment. Also **dis·cre′tion·al.**
dis·crim·i·nate (dis·krim′ə·nāt) *v.* ·nat·ed ·nat·ing *v.i.* 1 To act with partiality. 2 To observe a difference. —*v.t.* 3 To discern the difference in or between. 4 To make or constitute a difference in or between. —*adj.* (-nit) Noting or involving differences. [< L *dis-* apart + *crimen* a judgment] —**dis·crim′i·nat′ing** *adj.* —**dis·crim′i·nat′ing·ly** *adv.* —**dis·crim′i·nat′or** *n.*
dis·crim·i·na·tion (dis·krim′ə·nā′shən) *n.* 1 The act of discriminating or the ability to discriminate. 2 Biased or unfair judgments or treatment.
dis·crim·i·na·tive (dis·krim′ə·nā′tiv) *adj.* Having or practicing discrimination. Also **dis·crim′i·na·to′ry** (-nə·tôr′ē, -tō′rē). —**dis·crim′i·na′tive·ly** *adv.*
dis·cur·sive (dis·kûr′siv) *adj.* Wandering from one subject or point to another; digressive. [< L *discursus* a running to and fro] —**dis·cur′sive·ly** *adv.* —**dis·cur′sive·ness** *n.*
dis·cus (dis′kəs) *n.* 1 A circular plate, usu. of metal, thrown for distance as a test of strength in athletic contests. 2 Such a contest. [< Gk. *diskos*]

Discus thrower

dis·cuss (dis·kus′) *v.t.* To treat of in conversation or in writing. [< L *discutere*] —**dis·cuss′er** *n.* —**dis·cuss′i·ble** *adj.* —**Syn.** argue, debate, deliberate, examine.
dis·cus·sion (dis·kush′ən) *n.* The act of discussing.
dis·dain (dis·dān′) *v.t.* To consider unworthy of one's regard or notice; scorn. —*n.* A feeling of superiority and dislike; proud contempt. [< OF *des-* away + *deignier* deign] —**dis·dain′ful** *adj.* —**dis·dain′ful·ly** *adv.*
dis·ease (di·zēz′) *n.* 1 Any disturbed or abnormal condition in the living organism. 2 A specific ailment or illness.

3 Any disturbed or harmful condition. —*v.t.* **-eased, -eas·ing** To cause disease in; disorder; derange. [<OF *des-* away + *aise* ease] —**dis·eased'** *adj.*

dis·em·bark (dis'im·bärk') *v.t. & v.i.* **1** To put or go ashore from a ship. **2** To get off or land: to *disembark* from an airplane at San Francisco. —**dis·em'bar·ka'tion, dis'em·bark'ment** *n.*

dis·em·bod·y (dis'im·bod'ē) *v.t.* **-bod·ied, -bod·y·ing** To free from the body or from physical existence. —**dis'em·bod'i·ment** *n.*

dis·em·bow·el (dis'im·bou'əl, -boul') *v.t.* **-bow·eled** or **-bow·elled, -bow·el·ing** or **-bow·el·ling 1** To take out the bowels of; eviscerate. **2** To remove the contents of.

dis·en·chant (dis'in·chant', -chänt') *v.t.* To free from enchantment or illusion. —**dis'en·chant'ment** *n.*

dis·en·cum·ber (dis'in·kum'bər) *v.t.* To free from encumbrance or burden.

dis·en·fran·chise (dis'in·fran'chīz) *v.t.* **chised, -chis·ing** DISFRANCHISE.

dis·en·gage (dis'in·gāj') *v.t. & v.i.* **-gaged, -gag·ing** To set free or be free, as from engagement, attachment, etc. —**dis'en·gage'ment** *n.*

dis·en·tan·gle (dis'in·tang'gəl) *v.t.* **-gled, -gling** To free or relieve of entanglement or complications. —**dis'en·tan'gle·ment** *n.*

dis·es·tab·lish (dis'ə·stab'lish) *v.t.* To deprive of established status or character, esp. to withdraw state patronage from a church.

dis·es·teem (dis'ə·stēm') *v.t.* To feel a lack of esteem for. —*n.* Lack of esteem.

dis·fa·vor (dis·fā'vər) *n.* **1** Lack of favor; disapproval; dislike. **2** The state of being disliked or opposed. **3** An unkind act. —*v.t.* To treat or regard without favor.

dis·fig·ure (dis·fig'yər) *v.t.* **-ured, -ur·ing** To mar or destroy the figure or beauty of; render unsightly; deform. —**dis·fig'ure·ment, dis·fig'u·ra'tion** *n.*

dis·fran·chise (dis·fran'chīz) *v.t.* **-chised, -chis·ing 1** To deprive of a privilege, right, or grant. **2** To deprive of a right of citizenship, esp. the right to vote. —**dis·fran'chis·er, dis·fran'chise·ment** *n.*

dis·gorge (dis·gôrj') *v.t. & v.i.* **-gorged, -gorg·ing 1** To throw out, as from the throat or stomach; eject; vomit. **2** To give up unwillingly. [<OF *des-* from + *gorge* throat]

dis·grace (dis·grās') *v.t.* **-graced, -grac·ing 1** To bring reproach or shame upon. **2** To put out of favor. —*n.* **1** The state of a person who has lost respect or favor. **2** Loss of respect or favor. **3** That which disgraces. [<Ital. < *dis-* away + *grazia* favor] —**dis·grac'er** *n.*

dis·grace·ful (dis·grās'fəl) *adj.* Characterized by or causing disgrace; shameful. —**dis·grace'ful·ly** *adv.* —**dis·grace'ful·ness** *n.* —**Syn.** infamous, scandalous, ignoble.

dis·grun·tle (dis·grun'təl) *v.t.* **-grun·tled, -grun·tling** To disappoint and make discontended.

dis·guise (dis·gīz') *v.t.* **-guised, -guis·ing 1** To hide or change the appearance of. **2** To misrepresent or cover up the actual nature or character of. —*n.* **1** The act of disguising, or the state of being disguised. **2** Something that disguises. [<OF *des-* down + *guise* guise] —**dis·guis'ed·ly** (-id·lē) *adv.* —**dis·guis'er** *n.*

dis·gust (dis·gust') *v.t.* **1** To offend the senses of. **2** To affect with loathing or aversion. —*n.* Strong aversion or repugnance. [<MF *des-* away + *gouster* to taste] —**dis·gust'ed** *adj.* —**dis·gust'ed·ly** *adv.*

dis·gust·ing (dis·gus'ting) *adj.* Provoking disgust; revolting. —**dis·gust'ing·ly** *adv.*

dish (dish) *n.* **1** A concave or hollow vessel for serving or holding food; also, anything of similar shape. **2** The amount of food served in a dish; also **dish'ful. 3** Prepared food: my favorite *dish.* —*v.t.* **1** To serve as food: often with *up* or *out.* **2** To make concave. —*v.i.* **3** To become concave; sink in. [<L *discus* disk]

dis·ha·bille (dis'ə·bēl') *n.* **1** A state of being partially or negligently dressed, as in night clothes. **2** The clothes worn in this state. [<F *des-* away + *habiller* to dress]

dis·har·mo·ny (dis·här'mə·nē) *n. pl.* **-nies** Lack of harmony; incongruity; discord. —**dis·har·mo·ni·ous** (dis'här·mō'nē·əs) *adj.*

dish·cloth (dish'klôth', -kloth') *n.* A cloth used in washing dishes. Also **dish'rag'** (-rag').

dis·heart·en (dis·här'ten) *v.t.* To weaken the spirit or courage of; discourage. —**dis·heart'en·ing** *adj.* —**dis·heart'en·ing·ly** *adv.* —**dis·heart'en·ment** *n.*

di·shev·el (di·shev'əl) *v.t.* **-eled** or **-elled, -el·ing** or **-el·ling 1** To disarrange, as hair or clothing. **2** To disarrange the hair, clothing, etc. of (a person). [<MF *des-* away + *chevel* hair]

di·shev·eled (di·shev'əld) *adj.* Disarranged or disorderly; untidy. Also **di·shev'elled.**

dis·hon·est (dis·on'ist) *adj.* **1** Lacking in honesty; untrustworthy. **2** Characterized by fraudulence. —**dis·hon'es·ty** *n.* —**dis·hon'est·ly** *adv.*

dis·hon·or (dis·on'ər) *v.t.* **1** To disgrace or insult. **2** To seduce. **3** To decline or fail to pay, as a note. —*n.* **1** Lack or loss of honor or respect. **2** Something that causes such a lack or loss. **3** Refusal or failure to pay a note, etc., when due. *Brit. sp.* **-our.**

dis·hon·or·a·ble (dis·on'ər·ə·bəl) *adj.* Characterized by or bringing dishonor or reproach. —**dis·hon'or·a·bly** *adv.*

dis·il·lu·sion (dis'i·lo͞o'zhən) *v.t.* To free from illusion or delusion. —*n.* The act of freeing or the state of being freed from illusion. Also **dis'il·lu'sion·ment.**

dis·in·cen·tive (dis'in·sen'tiv) *n.* Something tending to discourage a course of action; deterrent.

dis·in·cli·na·tion (dis·in'klə·nā'shən) *n.* Lack of disposition, as to do something; unwillingness.

dis·in·cline (dis'in·klīn') *v.t. & v.i.* **-clined, -clin·ing** To make or be unwilling or averse.

dis·in·fect (dis'in·fekt') *v.t.* **1** To free from infection, harmful bacteria, etc. **2** To clean with a disinfectant. —**dis'in·fec'tion** *n.*

dis·in·fec·tant (dis'in·fek'tənt) *adj.* Disinfecting. —*n.* A substance used to destroy harmful bacteria.

dis·in·for·ma·tion (dis·in'fər·mā'shən) *n.* False, misleading information deliberately disseminated.

dis·in·gen·u·ous (dis'in·jen'yo͞o·əs) *adj.* Not sincere or candid; artful; deceitful. —**dis'in·gen'u·ous·ly** *adv.*

dis·in·her·it (dis'in·her'it) *v.t.* To deprive of an inheritance or of a right or privilege. —**dis'in·her'i·tance** *n.*

dis·in·te·grate (dis·in'tə·grāt, di·zin'-) *v.t. & v.i.* **-grat·ed, -grat·ing** To reduce or become reduced into parts or particles. —**dis·in'te·gra·ble** (-grə·bəl) *adj.* —**dis·in'te·gra'tion** *n.*

dis·in·ter (dis'in·tûr') *v.t.* **-terred, -ter·ring 1** To dig up, as from a grave. **2** To bring to light. —**dis'in·ter'ment** *n.*

dis·in·ter·est (dis·in'tər·ist, -trist) *n.* **1** Lack of interest; indifference. **2** Freedom from bias; impartiality.

dis·in·ter·est·ed (dis·in'tər·is·tid, -tris·tid, -tə·res'-) *adj.* **1** Free from self-interest or bias. **2** Lacking interest; uninterested. —**dis·in'ter·est·ed·ly** *adv.* —**dis·in'ter·est·ed·ness** *n.* —**Syn. 1** unselfish, impartial, detached, **2** apathetic, unconcerned, indifferent. • **disinterested, uninterested** *Disinterested* and *uninterested* are widely used interchangeably, but in precise usage *disinterested* refers to a lack of special or personal interest (the arbiter's *disinterested* decision) and *uninterested* to a lack of any interest whatsoever (an *uninterested* spectator, nodding through the performance).

dis·join (dis·join') *v.t.* To separate; undo; part. —*v.i.* To become divided or separated.

dis·joint (dis·joint') *v.t.* **1** To put out of joint. **2** To take apart. **3** To destroy the coherence, connections, or sequence of. —*v.i.* **4** To break into parts. —**dis·joint'ed** *adj.* —**dis·joint'ed·ly** *adv.* —**dis·joint'ed·ness** *n.*

dis·junc·tion (dis·jungk'shən) *n.* A disjoining or separation. Also **dis·junc'ture** (-chər).

dis·junc·tive (dis·jungk'tiv) *adj.* **1** Helping or serving to disjoin. **2** *Gram.* Expressing separation or disjoining, as certain conjunctions, as *either/or, else, otherwise,* etc. —*n.* *Gram.* A disjunctive conjunction. [<L *disjungere* disjoin]

disk (disk) *n.* **1** A flat, more or less circular plate of any material. **2** Any surface that is flat and circular. **3** A quoit or discus. **4** A phonograph record. **5** A round, flat, magnetically-coated plate on which computer data and programs may be stored.

disk brake A brake in which a durable pad is pressed against a metal disk to provide a retarding force.

disk drive An electronic device that writes information from computer memory onto disks, and reads information from disks.

disk harrow A harrow consisting of a series of disks set on edge, used for plowing.

Disk harrow

disk jockey DISC JOCKEY.

dis·like (dis·līk′) *v.t.* **·liked, ·lik·ing** To regard with aversion or antipathy. —*n.* Distaste; repugnance; aversion. —**dis·lik′a·ble, dis·like′a·ble** *adj.* —**dis·lik′er** *n.*

dis·lo·cate (dis′lō·kāt, dis·lō′kāt) *v.t.* **·cat·ed, ·cat·ing** 1 To put out of joint, as a bone. 2 To put out of proper place or order. —**dis′lo·ca′tion** *n.*

dis·lodge (dis·loj′) *v.* **·lodged, ·lodg·ing** *v.t.* 1 To remove or drive out, as from an abode. —*v.i.* 2 To leave a place of abode; move. —**dis·lodg′ment,** *n.*

dis·loy·al (dis·loi′əl) *adj.* False to one's allegiance; faithless. —**dis·loy′al·ly** *adv.*

dis·loy·al·ty (dis·loi′əl·tē) *n. pl.* **·ties** 1 The state of being disloyal. 2 A disloyal act.

dis·mal (diz′məl) *adj.* 1 Gloomy; cheerless; mournful. 2 Calamitous; horrible. [< L *dies mali* evil or unpropitious days] —**dis′mal·ly** *adv.* —**dis′mal·ness** *n.*

dis·man·tle (dis·man′təl) *v.t.* **·tled, ·tling** 1 To strip of furniture, equipment, clothing, etc. 2 To take apart; reduce to pieces. [< ME *des-* away + *manteller* cover with a cloak] —**dis·man′tle·ment** *n.*

dis·may (dis·mā′) *v.t.* To put at a loss, as from surprise, fear, or disappointment; cause to lose spirit or confidence. —*n.* A state of being dismayed. [ME *dismayen*]

dis·mem·ber (dis·mem′bər) *v.t.* 1 To cut or pull limb from limb. 2 To separate into parts and distribute. [< L *dis-* apart + *membrum* a limb] —**dis·mem′ber·ment** *n.*

dis·miss (dis·mis′) *v.t.* 1 To put out of office or service; discharge. 2 To cause or allow to depart. 3 To put aside; reject. [< L *dis-* away + *mittere* send] —**dis·mis′sal** *n.* —**dis·miss′i·ble** *adj.*

dis·mount (dis·mount′) *v.i.* 1 To get off a horse, etc. —*v.t.* 2 To remove from a mounting, as a jewel. 3 To dismantle (a machine). 4 To cause to dismount; unseat. —*n.* The act or manner of dismounting.

dis·o·be·di·ent (dis′ə·bē′dē·ənt) *adj.* Neglecting or refusing to obey; refractory. —**dis′o·be′di·ence** *n.* —**dis′o·be′di·ent·ly** *adv.*

dis·o·bey (dis′ə·bā′) *v.t. & v.i.* To refuse or fail to obey. —**dis′o·bey′er** *n.*

dis·o·blige (dis′ə·blīj′) *v.t.* 1 To neglect or refuse to oblige. 2 To inconvenience. 3 To slight; affront.

dis·or·der (dis·ôr′dər) *n.* 1 The state of being disarranged. 2 Disregard or neglect of orderliness. 3 A disturbance of the peace; breach of public order. 4 A derangement of bodily or mental function; illness. —*v.t.* 1 To throw out of order; disarrange. 2 To disturb the natural functions of, as body or mind.

dis·or·der·ly (dis·ôr′dər·lē) *adj. & adv.* 1 Being in or causing disorder; not orderly. 2 Lawless; disreputable. —**dis·or′der·li·ness** *n.*

dis·o·ri·ent (dis·ôr′ē·ənt, -ō′rē-) *v.t.* 1 To cause to lose the sense of direction or location. 2 *Psychol.* To cause confusion in regard to spatial, temporal, or human relationships. —**dis·o′ri·en·ta′tion** *n.*

dis·own (dis·ōn′) *v.t.* To refuse to acknowledge responsibility for or ownership of; repudiate.

dis·par·age (dis·par′ij) *v.t.* **·aged, ·ag·ing** 1 To speak of slightingly; undervalue. 2 To bring discredit or dishonor upon. [< OF *des-* down, away + *parage* equality, rank] —**dis·par′age·ment, dis·par′ag·er** *n.* —**dis·par′ag·ing·ly** *adv.* —**Syn.** 1 belittle, depreciate, decry, discredit.

dis·pa·rate (dis·par′it, dis′pə·rit) *adj.* That cannot be compared; dissimilar. [< L *dis-* apart + *parare* make ready] —**dis′pa′rate·ly** *adv.* —**dis′pa′rate·ness** *n.*

dis·par·i·ty (dis·par′ə·tē) *n. pl.* **·ties** The state of being dissimilar; difference. [< L *dis-* apart + *paritas* equality]

dis·pas·sion (dis·pash′ən) *n.* Freedom from passion, emotion, or bias.

dis·pas·sion·ate (dis·pash′ən·it) *adj.* Free from passion, prejudice, or personal interest; detached. —**dis·pas′sion·ate·ly** *adv.* —**dis·pas′sion·ate·ness** *n.*

dis·patch (dis·pach′) *v.t.* 1 To send off, esp. on official business. 2 To transact with promptness. 3 To kill summarily. —*n.* 1 The act of dispatching. 2 A message, news story, etc., sent with haste. 3 Speed; promptness; expedition. 4 The act of killing. [< Ital. *dispacciare*]

dis·patch·er (dis·pach′ər) *n.* One who dispatches, esp., one who directs the movement of trains, trucks, etc.

dis·pel (dis·pel′) *v.t.* **·pelled, ·pel·ling** To scatter; drive away; disperse. [< L *dis-* away + *pellere* to drive]

dis·pen·sa·ble (dis·pen′sə·bəl) *adj.* 1 That can be dispensed with; unnecessary. 2 That can be distributed to others. —**dis·pen′sa·bil′i·ty, dis·pen′sa·ble·ness** *n.*

dis·pen·sa·ry (dis·pen′sər·ē) *n. pl.* **·ries** A place where medicines or medical treatment is dispensed.

dis·pen·sa·tion (dis′pən·sā′shən) *n.* 1 A dealing out; distribution. 2 Something dealt out or distributed. 3 Special exemption granted from the requirements of a law, rule, or obligation. 4 *Theol.* Any of the systems in which God has revealed his mind and will to man. —**dis′pen·sa′tion·al** *adj.* —**dis′pen·sa′tor** *n.*

dis·pen·sa·to·ry (dis·pen′sə·tôr′ē, -tō′rē) *n. pl.* **·ries** A manual describing medicinal preparations.

dis·pense (dis·pens′) *v.* **·pensed, ·pens·ing** *v.t.* 1 To give or deal out in portions; distribute. 2 To compound and give out (medicines). 3 To administer, as laws. 4 To relieve or excuse; absolve. —*v.i.* 5 To grant exemption or dispensation. —**dispense with** To do without; relinquish; forgo. [< L *dis-* away + *pendere* weigh] —**dis·pens′er** *n.*

dis·perse (dis·pûrs′) *v.* **·persed, ·pers·ing** *v.t.* 1 To cause to scatter and go off in various directions. 2 To dispel; dissipate: The sun *dispersed* the mists. 3 To separate (light) into its component spectral colors. —*v.i.* 4 To scatter and go off in various directions. [< L *dis-* away + *spargere* scatter] —**dis·per′sal, dis·pers′er** *n.* —**dis·pers′i·ble, dis·per′sive** *adj.*

dis·per·sion (dis·pûr′zhən, -shən) *n.* 1 The act of dispersing or the state of being dispersed. 2 The separation of light rays of different colors by the action of a prism or lens.

dis·pir·it (dis·pir′it) *v.t.* To cause to lose heart or hope; weaken the spirit of; depress. —**dis·pir′it·ed** *adj.* —**dis·pir′it·ed·ly** *adv.* —**dis·pir′it·ed·ness** *n.*

dis·place (dis·plās′) *v.t.* **·placed, ·plac·ing** 1 To move from the proper place. 2 To take the place of; supplant. 3 To remove from a position or office; discharge.

displaced person A person forced to flee his country or home.

dis·place·ment (dis·plās′mənt) *n.* 1 The act of displacing, or the state of being displaced. 2 The weight, volume, or mass of a fluid displaced by a body floating in it. 3 The difference between the original position of an object and its position at some later time.

dis·play (dis·plā′) *v.t.* 1 To show; make apparent to the eye or the mind. 2 To reveal, as ignorance. —*n.* 1 The act of displaying. 2 The thing or things displayed. 3 Ostentatious show. [< LL *displicare* scatter]

dis·please (dis·plēz′) *v.t. & v.i.* **·pleased, ·pleas·ing** To annoy, vex, or offend.

dis·pleas·ure (dis·plezh′ər) *n.* The state of being displeased. —**Syn.** dissatisfaction, vexation, annoyance.

dis·port (dis·pôrt′, -pōrt′) *v.i.* 1 To play; gambol. —*v.t.* 2 To amuse (oneself). [< L *dis-* away + *portare* carry]

dis·pos·a·ble (dis·pō′zə·bəl) *adj.* 1 Subject to disposal. 2 Easily discarded after use. —**dis·pos′a·bil′i·ty** *n.*

dis·po·sal (dis·pō′zəl) *n.* 1 Orderly arrangement or distribution. 2 A getting rid of, as by gift or sale. 3 Power of control, management, or distribution. 4 A settling of affairs. —**at one's disposal** Ready at one's convenience.

dis·pose (dis·pōz′) *v.* **·posed, ·pos·ing** *v.t.* 1 To put in order; arrange properly. 2 To incline or influence the mind of. 3 To put or set in a particular place or location. 4 To settle (affairs). —*v.i.* 5 To arrange or settle something. —**dis·pose of** 1 To settle; finish. 2 To throw away. 3 To get rid of by selling or giving. [< OF *dis-* apart + *poser* put, pose] —**dis·pos'er** *n.*

dis·po·si·tion (dis'pə·zish'ən) *n.* 1 The act of disposing; arrangement, as of troops. 2 Final settlement or management. 3 Control; power. 4 Natural tendency or temperament; bent; propensity. 5 A selling or giving away.

dis·pos·sess (dis'pə·zes') *v.t.* To deprive (someone) of possession, as of a house or land. —**dis'pos·ses'sion, dis'·pos·ses'sor** *n.*

dis·praise (dis·prāz') *v.t.* **·praised, ·prais·ing** To speak of with disapproval; disparage. —*n.* The expression of unfavorable opinion.

dis·proof (dis·prōōf') *n.* 1 The act or process of disproving. 2 A fact or evidence that disproves.

dis·pro·por·tion (dis'prə·pôr'shən, -pōr'-) *n.* Lack of proportion or symmetry. —*v.t.* To make disproportionate. —**dis'pro·por'tion·al** *adj.* —**dis'pro·por'tion·al·ly** *adv.*

dis·pro·por·tion·ate (dis'prə·pôr'shən·it, -pōr'-) *adj.* Out of proportion with regard to size, form, or value. —**dis'pro·por'tion·ate·ly,** *adv.* —**dis'pro·por'tion·ate·ness** *n.*

dis·prove (dis·prōōv') *v.t.* **·proved, ·prov·ing** To prove to be false or erroneous; refute. —**dis·prov'a·ble** *adj.*

dis·put·a·ble (dis·pyōō'tə·bəl, dis'pyōō·tə·bəl) *adj.* That can be disputed; controvertible. —**dis·put'a·bil'i·ty** *n.* —**dis·put'a·bly** *adv.*

dis·pu·tant (dis·pyōō'tənt, dis'pyōō·tənt) *adj.* Disputing. —*n.* One who disputes; a party to a dispute.

dis·pu·ta·tion (dis'pyōō·tā'shən) *n.* 1 The act of disputing; controversy; argumentation. 2 A controversy or debate, often a formal one.

dis·pu·ta·tious (dis'pyōō·tā'shəs) *adj.* Inclined to dispute. Also **dis·put·a·tive** (dis·pyōō'tə·tiv). —**dis'pu·ta'tious·ly** *adv.* —**dis'pu·ta'tious·ness** *n.*

dis·pute (dis·pyōōt') *v.* **·put·ed, ·put·ing** *v.t.* 1 To argue about; discuss. 2 To question the validity, genuineness, etc., of. 3 To strive for, as a prize. 4 To resist; oppose. —*v.i.* 5 To argue. 6 To quarrel; wrangle. —*n.* 1 A controversial discussion. 2 A wrangle; quarrel. [< L *dis-* away + *putare* think] —**dis·put'er** *n.*

dis·qual·i·fi·ca·tion (dis·kwol'ə·fə·kā'shən) *n.* 1 The state of being disqualified. 2 That which disqualifies.

dis·qual·i·fy (dis·kwol'ə·fī) *v.t.* **·fied, ·fy·ing** 1 To render unqualified or unfit; incapacitate; disable. 2 To pronounce unqualified or ineligible, esp. in sports.

dis·qui·et (dis·kwī'ət) *n.* Restlessness; uneasiness. Also **dis·qui'e·tude** (-kwī'ə·tyōōd). —*v.t.* To make anxious or uneasy.

dis·qui·si·tion (dis'kwi·zish'ən) *n.* A systematic treatise or discourse. [< L *dis-* from + *quaerere* seek, ask]

dis·re·gard (dis'ri·gärd') *v.t.* 1 To pay no attention to; ignore. 2 To treat without respect or attention; slight. —*n.* Want of regard; neglect; slight. —**dis're·gard'ful** *adj.*

dis·re·pair (dis'ri·pâr') *n.* The state of being out of repair.

dis·rep·u·ta·ble (dis·rep'yə·tə·bəl) *adj.* Being in or causing ill repute; disgraceful. —**dis·rep'u·ta·ble·ness** *n.* —**dis·rep'u·ta·bly** *adv.*

dis·re·pute (dis'ri·pyōōt') *n.* Lack or loss of reputation; ill repute.

dis·re·spect (dis'ri·spekt') *n.* Lack of respect; discourtesy. —*v.t.* To treat or regard with lack of respect. —**dis're·spect'ful** *adj.* —**dis're·spect'ful·ly** *adv.* —**dis're·spect'·ful·ness** *n.*

dis·robe (dis·rōb') *v.t.* & *v.i.* **·robed, ·rob·ing** To undress. —**dis·robe'ment** *n.*

dis·rupt (dis·rupt') *v.t.* & *v.i.* 1 To burst or break asunder. 2 To act to interrupt the normal or proper course of (a meeting, etc.). [< L *dis-* apart + *rumpere* burst] —**dis·rupt'er** or **dis·rup'tor, dis·rup'tion** *n.*

dis·rup·tive (dis·rup'tiv) *adj.* 1 Acting or tending to disrupt. 2 Marked by disruption. —**dis·rup'tive·ly** *adv.* —**dis·rup'tive·ness** *n.*

dis·sat·is·fac·tion (dis'sat·is·fak'shən) *n.* 1 A dissatisfied state or feeling; discontent. 2 Something that dissatisfies.

dis·sat·is·fac·to·ry (dis'sat·is·fak'tər·ē) *adj.* Creating dissatisfaction or discontent.

dis·sat·is·fy (dis·sat'is·fī) *v.t.* **·fied, ·fy·ing** To fail to satisfy; disappoint; displease.

dis·sect (di·sekt', dī-) *v.t.* 1 To separate the disparate tissues of (an organism.) 2 To analyze critically; examine. [< L < *dis-* apart + *secare* to cut] —**dis·sec'tion, dis·sec'tor** *n.*

dis·sect·ed (di·sek'tid) *adj.* 1 Cut in pieces. 2 Deeply cut into lobes or segments, as a leaf.

dis·sem·ble (di·sem'bəl) *v.* **·bled, ·bling** *v.t.* 1 To conceal the true nature of (intentions, feelings, etc.) so as to deceive. 2 To pretend to feel: to *dissemble* shock. —*v.i.* 3 To conceal one's true nature, intentions, etc.; act hypocritically. [< OF *dis-* not, away + *sembler* seem] —**dis·sem'·blance, dis·sem'bler** *n.*

dis·sem·i·nate (di·sem'ə·nāt) *v.t.* **·nat·ed, ·nat·ing** To spread about; scatter; promulgate. [< L *dis-* away + *seminare* to sow] —**dis·sem'i·na'tion, dis·sem'i·na'tor** *n.*

dis·sen·sion (di·sen'shən) *n.* Angry or violent difference of opinion. —**Syn.** discord, strife, conflict, disagreement.

dis·sent (di·sent') *v.i.* 1 To differ in thought or opinion; disagree. 2 To refuse adherence to an established church. —*n.* The act or state of dissenting. [< L *dis-* apart + *sentire* think, feel] —**dis·sent'er** *n.*

dis·sen·tient (di·sen'shənt) *adj.* Dissenting; disagreeing. —*n.* One who dissents.

dis·ser·ta·tion (dis'ər·tā'shən) *n.* An extended treatise or discourse; thesis. [< L *dissertare* examine, discuss]

dis·serv·ice (dis·sûr'vis) *n.* An ill turn; a slight or injury.

dis·sev·er (di·sev'ər) *v.t.* 1 To divide; separate. 2 To separate into parts. —*v.i.* 3 To separate; part. —**dis·sev'er·ance, dis·sev'er·ment** *n.*

dis·si·dence (dis'ə·dəns) *n.* Disagreement; dissent.

dis·si·dent (dis'ə·dənt) *adj.* Dissenting; differing. —*n.* One who dissents; dissenter. [< L *dis-* apart + *sedere* sit]

dis·sim·i·lar (di·sim'ə·lər) *adj.* Unlike; different. —**dis·sim'i·lar'i·ty** *n.* —**dis·sim'i·lar·ly** *adv.*

dis·sim·i·la·tion (di·sim'ə·lā'shən) *n.* The act or process of becoming dissimilar.

dis·si·mil·i·tude (dis'si·mil'ə·tyōōd) *n.* Lack of resemblance or likeness. [< L *dis-* not + *similis* alike]

dis·sim·u·late (di·sim'yə·lāt) *v.t.* & *v.i.* **·lat·ed, ·lat·ing** To conceal (intentions, feelings, etc.) by pretense; dissemble. [< L *dissimulare* to feign] —**dis·sim'u·la'tion, dis·sim'u·la'·tor** *n.*

dis·si·pate (dis'ə·pāt) *v.* **·pat·ed, ·pat·ing** *v.t.* 1 To disperse or drive away. 2 To disintegrate or dissolve utterly. 3 To squander: to *dissipate* a fortune. —*v.i.* 4 To become dispersed; scatter. 5 To engage in excessive or dissolute pleasures. [< L *dissipare*]

dis·si·pat·ed (dis'ə·pā'tid) *adj.* Given to or showing dissipation. —**dis'si·pat'ed·ly** *adv.* —**dis'si·pat'ed·ness** *n.*

dis·si·pa·tion (dis'ə·pā'shən) . *n.* 1 The act of dissipating or the state of being dissipated. 2 Excessive indulgence, esp. in pleasures. 3 Idle distraction or amusement.

dis·so·ci·ate (di·sō'shē·āt) *v.* **·at·ed, ·at·ing** *v.t.* 1 To separate from association or connection; detach. 2 *Chem.* To resolve by dissociation. —*v.i.* 3 To break an association. 4 *Chem.* To undergo dissociation. [< L *dis-* apart + *sociare* join together] —**dis·so'ci·a'tive** *adj.*

dis·so·ci·a·tion (di·sō'sē·ā'shən, -shē·ā'-) *n.* 1 The act of dissociating; state of separation. 2 *Chem.* The reversible separation of the constituents of a compound.

dis·sol·u·ble (di·sol'yə·bəl) *adj.* Capable of being dissolved. —**dis'sol·u·bil'i·ty, dis·sol'u·ble·ness** *n.*

dis·so·lute (dis'ə·lōōt) *adj.* Dissipated; immoral; profligate. [< L *dissolutus,* loose, pp. of *dissolvere* dissolve] —**dis'so·lute·ly** *adv.* —**dis'so·lute·ness** *n.*

dis·so·lu·tion (dis'ə·lōō'shən) *n.* 1 The act or state of dissolving or breaking up into parts; disintegration. 2 An ending or breaking up, as of an assembly, business, or partnership. 3 Death.

dis·solve (di·zolv') *v.t.* & *v.i.* **·solved, ·solv·ing** 1 To change or make change from a solid to a fluid condition. 2 To pass or cause to pass into or combine with a solution. 3 To end or conclude; terminate, as a meeting or marriage. 4 To fade or cause to fade into or out of view, as a motion-picture or television scene. 5 To vanish or make vanish. —*n.* In films and television, the slow emergence of one scene out of another. [< L *dis-* apart + *solvere* loosen] —**dis·solv'a·ble** *adj.* —**dis·sol'vent** *adj., n.* —**dis·solv'er** *n.*

dis·so·nance (dis′ə·nəns) *n.* 1 A discordant mingling of sounds. 2 *Music* A combination of tones that give a harsh or unpleasant effect when sounded together. 3 Harsh disagreement. Also **dis′so·nan·cy.**

dis·so·nant (dis′ə·nənt) *adj.* 1 Having the quality of dissonance. 2 Naturally hostile; incongruous. [< L *dis-* away + *sonare* to sound] **—dis′so·nant·ly** *adv.*

dis·suade (di·swād′) *v.t.* **·suad·ed, ·suad·ing** To change the plans of (a person) by persuasion or advice: with *from.* [< L *dis-* away + *suadere* persuade] **—dis·suad′er, dis·sua′sion** (-swā′zhən) *n.* **—dis·sua′sive** (-swā′siv) *adj.*

dis·syl·la·ble (di·sil′ə·bəl, dī-, dis′sil′ə·bəl, dī′-) *n.* A word of two syllables. Also **di·syl′la·ble.**

dist. distance; distant; distinguished; district.

dis·taff (dis′taf, -täf) *n.* 1 A staff that holds the flax or wool for use in spinning. 2 Woman; also, woman's work or domain. [< OE *dis* bundle of flax + *stæf* staff]

Distaff

distaff side The maternal branch of a family.

dis·tal (dis′təl) *adj.* Remote from the point of attachment; peripheral. [< DISTANT] **—dis′tal·ly** *adv.*

dis·tance (dis′təns) *n.* 1 The space or interval separating two objects, points, or places. 2 The length of a line segment connecting two points 3 The period between two points of time. 4 The state of being separated in space or time. 5 A distant place or point. 6 Reserve; haughtiness; coldness. 7 *Music* The interval between two tones. —*v.t.* **·tanced, ·tanc·ing** To leave behind, as in a race; outstrip; excel.

dis·tant (dis′tənt) *adj.* 1 Separated in space or time; far apart. 2 Not closely related in qualities, relationship, or in position; remote. 3 Reserved or unapproachable; formal. 4 Indistinct; faint. 5 Not obvious or plain; indirect. [< L *dis-* apart + *stare* to stand] **—dis′tant·ly** *adv.*

dis·taste (dis·tāst′) *n.* Aversion; dislike.

dis·taste·ful (dis·tāst′fəl) *adj.* Causing or denoting distaste. **—dis·taste′ful·ly** *adv.* **—dis·taste′ful·ness** *n.* **—Syn.** disagreeable, offensive, unpleasant, disgusting.

Dist. Atty. District Attorney.

dis·tem·per[1] (dis·tem′pər) *n.* 1 Any of several infectious diseases of animals. 2 Ill humor. 3 Civil disturbance. —*v.t.* 1 To disturb or derange the functions of; disorder. 2 To ruffle; disturb. [< Med. L < *dis-* away + *temperare* regulate, mix]

dis·tem·per[2] (dis·tem′pər) *n.* 1 A pigment mixed with yolk of eggs or glue, used chiefly for murals. 2 The art of painting with such materials, or a painting executed in them. —*v.t.* 1 To mix, as colors, for distemper painting. 2 To color or paint with distemper. —*adj.* Of or pertaining to decoration done with distemper. [< Med. L *dis-* apart + *temperare* mix, mingle, soak]

dis·tend (dis·tend′) *v.t. & v.i.* To expand; swell; dilate, as by pressure from within. [< L < *dis-* apart + *tendere* to stretch] **—dis·ten′si·ble** *adj.* **—dis·ten′sion, dis·ten′tion** *n.*

dis·tich (dis′tik) *n.* In prosody, a couplet. [< Gk. *di-* two + *stichos* row, line]

dis·till (dis·til′) *v.* **·tilled, ·til·ling** *v.t.* 1 To subject to or as to distillation. 2 To extract or produce by distillation: to *distill* whiskey. 3 To give forth —*v.i.* 4 To undergo distillation. 5 To exude in drops. Also **dis·til′.** [< L *de-* down + *stillare* to drop, trickle] **—dis·til′la·ble** *adj.*

dis·til·late (dis′tə·lit, -lāt) *n.* The condensed product separated by distillation.

dis·til·la·tion (dis′tə·lā′shən) *n.* 1 Separation of the volatile parts of a mixture by vaporizing and subsequently condensing. 2 The parts so separated and condensed; distillate. 3 The essential quality of anything.

dis·til·ler (dis·til′ər) *n.* 1 One who or that which distills. 2 A maker and seller of distilled liquors.

dis·til·ler·y (dis·til′ər·ē) *n. pl.* **·ler·ies** An establishment for distilling, esp. alcoholic liquors.

dis·tinct (dis·tingkt′) *adj.* 1 Clear to the senses or mind; plain; unmistakable; definite. 2 Clearly standing apart from other objects; unconnected; separate. 3 Decidedly different; not alike. [< L *distinctus,* pp. of *distinguere* distinguish] **—dis·tinct′ly** *adv.* **—dis·tinct′ness** *n.*

dis·tinc·tion (dis·tingk′shən) *n.* 1 A distinguishing mark or quality; a characteristic difference. 2 The act of distinguishing; discrimination. 3 Fame; eminent reputation. 4 Excellence; superiority. 5 A mark of honor or regard.

dis·tinc·tive (dis·tingk′tiv) *adj.* Characteristic; distinguishing. **—dis·tinc′tive·ly** *adv.* **—dis·tinc′tive·ness** *n.*

dis·tin·gué (dis′tang·gā′, *Fr.* dēs·taṅ·gā′) *adj.* Distinguished. [F] **—dis′tin·guée′** *adj. Fem.*

dis·tin·guish (di·sting′gwish) *v.t.* 1 To indicate or constitute the differences of or between. 2 To recognize as separate or distinct; discriminate. 3 To divide into classes; classify. 4 To bring fame or credit upon. 5 To perceive by one of the physical senses. —*v.i.* 6 To make or discern differences. [< L *distinguere* to separate] **—dis·tin′guish·a·ble** *adj.* **—dis·tin′guish·a·bly** *adv.*

dis·tin·guished (di·sting′gwisht) *adj.* 1 Famous; eminent. 2 Having an air of distinction; dignified.

dis·tort (dis·tôrt′) *v.t.* 1 To twist or bend out of shape. 2 To twist the meaning of; misrepresent. [< L *dis-* apart + *torquere* to twist] **—dis·tort′er, dis·tort′ed·ness** *n.* **—Syn. 2** misconstrue, mislead, falsify, misquote.

dis·tor·tion (dis·tôr′shən) *n.* 1 The act of distorting. 2 The quality of being distorted. 3 Something distorted. **—dis·tor′tion·al** *adj.*

distr. distribute; distribution; distributor.

dis·tract (dis·trakt′) *v.t.* 1 To divert (the mind, etc.) in a different direction. 2 To bewilder; confuse. 3 To make frantic; craze. [< L *dis-* away + *trahere* to draw] **—dis·tract′er** *n.* **—dis·tract′i·ble, dis·tract′ing, dis·trac′tive** *adj.*

dis·tract·ed (dis·trak′tid) *adj.* 1 Bewildered or harassed. 2 Mentally deranged; mad. **—dis·tract′ed·ly** *adv.*

dis·trac·tion (dis·trak′shən) *n.* 1 A drawing off or diversion of the mind. 2 Confusion; perplexity. 3 Strong agitation, distress, or grief. 4 Mental aberration; madness. 5 Anything that distracts or diverts.

dis·train (dis·trān′) *v.t. Law* 1 To take and detain (personal property) as security for a debt, claim, etc. 2 To subject (a person) to distress. —*v.i.* 3 To impose a distress. [< L *dis-* completely + *stringere* draw tight] **—dis·train′a·ble** *adj.* **—dis·train′er** or **dis·train′or** *n.*

dis·traint (dis·trānt′) *n. Law* The act or process of distraining.

dis·trait (dis·trā′) *adj.* Absent-minded. [F]

dis·traught (dis·trôt′) *adj.* 1 Distracted or bewildered, as by anxiety; upset. 2 Maddened; tormented. [< L *distrahere,* distract]

dis·tress (dis·tres′) *v.t.* 1 To cause to be anxious or worry. 2 To inflict suffering upon; subject to pain or agony. —*n.* 1 The state of being distressed; pain, trouble, worry, etc. 2 Anything causing such a condition. 3 A condition requiring immediate help: a ship in *distress.* 4 *Law* **a** DISTRAINT. **b** Goods taken by distraint. [< OF < L *distringere* draw asunder] **—dis·tress′ful** *adj.* **—dis·tress′ful·ly** *adv.* **—dis·tress′ful·ness** *n.*

dis·tressed (dis·trest′) *adj.* 1 Feeling distress; troubled, anxious, pained, etc. 2 Deliberately marred so as to look antique: a *distressed* commode.

dis·trib·ute (dis·trib′yōōt) *v.t.* **·ut·ed, ·ut·ing** 1 To divide and deal out in shares. 2 To classify; categorize. 3 To scatter, as in an area or over a surface. 4 To put or arrange into distinctive parts or places. [< L *dis-* away + *tribuere* give, allot] **—dis·trib′ut·a·ble** *adj.*

dis·tri·bu·tion (dis′trə·byōō′shən) *n.* 1 The act of distributing. 2 That which is distributed. 3 The arrangement in number and place of a set of things: the *distribution* of doctors throughout the U.S. 4 In commerce, all the steps involved in the delivery of goods from producer to consumer.

dis·trib·u·tive (dis·trib′yə·tiv) *adj.* 1 Serving or tending to distribute. 2 Pertaining to distribution. 3 *Gram.* Referring to the members of a group separately. —*n.* A distributive pronoun or adjective, as *each, every,* etc. —**dis·trib′u·tive·ly** *adv.* —**dis·trib′u·tive·ness** *n.*

dis·trib·u·tor (dis·trib′yə·tər) *n.* **1** One who or that which distributes. **2** A device that connects the spark plugs of an engine in turn to a high-voltage source.

dis·trict (dis′trikt) *n.* **1** A division of territory specially defined, as for judicial, political, educational, or other purposes. **2** Any region of space; a tract. —*v.t.* To divide into districts. [< Med. L *districtus* jurisdiction]

district attorney The elected or appointed prosecuting officer of a specific judicial district.

dis·trust (dis·trust′) *v.t.* To feel no trust for or confidence in. —*n.* A lack of trust or confidence. —**dis·trust′ful** *adj.* —**dis·trust′ful·ly** *adv.* —**Syn.** *v.* suspect, mistrust, doubt. *n.* doubt, suspicion, disbelief.

dis·turb (dis·tûrb′) *v.t.* **1** To interfere with or destroy the peace or quiet of. **2** To trouble mentally or emotionally; ruffle or annoy. **3** To upset the order or system of. **4** To interrupt. **5** To cause inconvenience to. [< L *dis-* completely + *turbare* to disorder] —**dis·turb′er** *n.*

dis·tur·bance (dis·tûr′bəns) *n.* **1** The act of disturbing or the condition of being disturbed. **2** That which disturbs. **3** A public commotion.

dis·u·nite (dis′yōō·nīt′) *v.* **·nit·ed, ·nit·ing** *v.t.* **1** To break the union of; separate. **2** To alienate; estrange, as friends. —*v.i.* **3** To come apart. —**dis·un′ion** (-yōōn′yən) *n.*

dis·use (dis·yōōs′) *n.* The state of no longer being used. —*v.t.* (dis·yōōz′) **·used, ·us·ing** To cease to use or practice.

ditch (dich) *n.* A narrow trench in the ground, as for drainage. —*v.t.* **1** To dig a ditch in. **2** To run or throw into a ditch; derail. **3** *Slang* To abandon; get rid of. —*v.i.* **4** To make a ditch. [< OE *dīc*] —**ditch′er** *n.*

dith·er (dith′ər) *n.* A state of nervousness or anxiety. [Var. of earlier *didder* tremble, shake] —**dith′er·y** *adj.*

dith·y·ramb (dith′ə·ram, -ramb) *n.* **1** In ancient Greece, a passionate hymn to Dionysus. **2** Any wild or vehement speech or writing. [< Gk. *dithyrambos*] —**dith′y·ram′bic** (-ram′bik) *adj.*

dit·to (dit′ō) *n. pl.* **·tos** The same thing repeated, often expressed by two inverted commas, called **ditto marks,** beneath the word intended to be duplicated. —*adv.* As before; likewise. —*v.t.* **·toed, ·to·ing** To copy; duplicate. [Ital. < L *dictum*]

dit·ty (dit′ē) *n. pl.* **·ties** A short, simple song; lay. [< L *dictatum* a thing said]

dit·ty-bag (dit′ē·bag′) *n.* A sailor's bag for needles, thread, personal belongings, etc. [?]

dit·ty-box (dit′ē·boks′) *n.* A small box used in place of a ditty-bag.

di·u·ret·ic (dī′yōō·ret′ik) *adj.* Stimulating the secretion of urine. —*n.* A diuretic medicine. [< Gk. *dia-* thoroughly + *ourēsis* urination]

di·ur·nal (dī·ûr′nəl) *adj.* **1** Happening every day; daily. **2** Done in or pertaining to the daytime. [< L *diurnus* daily] —**di·ur′nal·ly** *adv.*

Div. Divinity.

div. divided; dividend; division; divisor; divorced.

di·va (dē′və) *n. pl.* **·vas** or **·ve** (-vā) PRIMA DONNA (def. 1). [Ital. < *divo* divine]

di·va·lent (dī·vā′lənt) *adj.* BIVALENT.

di·van (di·van′, dī′van) *n.* A couch or sofa. [< Pers. *dēvān*]

dive (dīv) *v.* **dived** or **dove, dived, div·ing** *v.i.* **1** To plunge, usually headfirst, into water, etc. **2** To submerge, as a submarine. **3** To plunge the body, hand, or an object into something. **4** To enter suddenly or abruptly: He *dived* into the forest. **5** To descend at a steep angle and at high speed. **6** To become engrossed or deeply involved. —*v.t.* **7** To plunge (the body, hand, or an object) into something. **8** To cause (an airplane) to descend at a steep angle. —*n.* **1** A plunge head foremost into water. **2** A steep plunge, as of an airplane. **3** *Informal* A disreputable resort; den. [< OE *dūfan* dive and *dyfan* immerse]

dive bomber An airplane which dives toward its target to drop its bombs at close range.

div·er (dī′vər) *n.* **1** One whose work is to explore or gather objects under water. **2** A bird that dives.

di·verge (di·vûrj′, dī-) *v.i.* **·verged, ·verg·ing 1** To extend or lie in different directions from the same point. **2** To vary from a typical form; differ. **3** *Math.* To approach no finite limit. [< L *dis-* apart + *vergere* to incline] —**di·ver′gence, di·ver′gen·cy** *n.* —**di·ver′gent** *adj.* —**di·ver′gent·ly** *adv.*

di·vers (dī′vərz) *adj.* More than one, but not a great number. [< L *diversus* different] —**Syn.** several, sundry, various.

di·verse (di·vûrs′, dī-, dī′vûrs) *adj.* **1** Differing one from another; distinct. **2** Varied. [< L *diversus,* pp. of *divertere* divert] —**di·verse′ly** *adv.* —**di·verse′ness** *n.*

di·ver·si·fy (di·vûr′sə·fī, dī-) *v.t.* **·fied, ·fy·ing** To make diverse; impart variety to; vary. —**di·ver′si·fi·ca′tion** *n.*

di·ver·sion (di·vûr′zhən, -shən, dī-) *n.* **1** The act of diverting or turning aside. **2** *Mil.* An attack or feint intended to divert enemy troops from the point where a full scale attack is to be made. **3** That which diverts; amusement; recreation. —**di·ver′sion·ar·y** *adj.*

di·ver·si·ty (di·vûr′sə·tē, dī-) *n. pl.* **·ties 1** The state of being diverse; dissimilitude. **2** Variety: a *diversity* of interests.

di·vert (di·vûrt′, dī-) *v.t.* **1** To turn aside; deflect, as in direction, interest, or purpose. **2** To amuse; entertain. [< L *dis-* apart + *vertere* turn] —**di·vert′er** *n.* —**di·vert′ing** *adj.* —**di·vert′ing·ly** *adv.*

di·ver·tisse·ment (di·vûr′tis·mənt, *Fr.* dē·ver·tēs·mäṅ′) *n.* **1** A brief performance, often a ballet, between the acts of a play. **2** An amusement. [F, lit., diversion]

di·vest (di·vest′, dī-) *v.t.* **1** To strip, as of clothes. **2** To deprive, as of office, rights, or honors. [< L *dis-* apart + *vestire* clothe]

di·vest·i·ture (di·ves′tə·chər, dī-) *n.* The act of divesting, or the state of being divested. Also **di·vest′ment.**

di·vide (di·vīd′) *v.* **·vid·ed, ·vid·ing** *v.t.* **1** To cut or separate into parts. **2** To distribute in shares; portion out. **3** To separate into classes; categorize. **4** To separate; keep apart. **5** To form the boundary between. **6** To graduate with lines; calibrate. **7** *Math.* **a** To subject to division. **b** To be an exact divisor of. **8** To cause to disagree. —*v.i.* **9** To be or come apart; separate. **10** To disagree. **11** To vote in two groups, one for and one against a measure. **12** To share. —*n.* *Geol.* A ridge of land separating one drainage system from another. [< L *dividere* separate] —**di·vid′a·ble** *adj.* —**di·vid′er** *n.*

di·vid·ed (di·vī′did) *adj.* **1** Parted; disunited. **2** *Bot.* Having deep incisions.

div·i·dend (div′ə·dend) *n.* **1** *Math.* A number or quantity on which division is performed. **2** A sum of money to be distributed according to some fixed scheme, as profit on shares. [< L *dividendum* thing to be divided]

div·i·na·tion (div′ə·nā′shən) *n.* **1** The act of trying to foretell the future. **2** A forecast; augury. **3** A successful or clever guess. —**di·vin·a·to·ry** (di·vin′ə·tôr′ē, -tō′rē) *adj.*

di·vine (di·vīn′) *adj.* **1** Pertaining to, proceeding from, or of the nature of God or of a god; sacred. **2** Addressed or offered up to God. **3** Altogether excellent or admirable. —*n.* A theologian or clergyman. —*v.* **·vined, ·vin·ing** *v.t.* **1** To foretell or prophesy. **2** To surmise; guess. —*v.i.* **3** To practice divination. [< L *divinus*] —**di·vine′ly** *adv.* —**di·vine′·ness, di·vin′er** *n.*

diving bell A vessel, open below and supplied with air under pressure, in which divers can work under water.

diving board A springboard extending over water, as a swimming pool, used for performing dives.

diving suit A garment designed to protect a diver and supply him with air while under water.

divining rod A forked twig believed to bend downward when carried over underground water, mineral deposits, etc.

di·vin·i·ty (di·vin′ə·tē) *n. pl.* **·ties 1** The quality or character of being divine. **2** A divine being; deity. **3** Theology. **4** A divine attribute, virtue, or quality. —**the Divinity** The Deity; God.

di·vis·i·ble (di·viz′ə·bəl) *adj.* Capable of being divided, esp. with a zero remainder. —**di·vis′i·bil′i·ty** *n.* —**di·vis′i·bly** *adv.*

di·vi·sion (di·vizh′ən) *n.* **1** The act of dividing. **2** A part, section, or particular category. **3** A disagreement; discord. **4** That which separates, divides, or makes different. **5** The act of sharing; distribution. **6** *Math.* The operation of finding the factor by which a divisor must be multiplied to produce a given dividend. **7** *Mil.* A major tactical and administrative unit that can function independently, in the army commanded by a major general. **8** A separation into opposing groups of voters in a legislative body. **—di·vi′sion·al** *adj.*

di·vi·sive (di·vī′siv, di·vis′iv, -viz′-) *adj.* Provoking dissension, discord, or disunity. **—di·vi′sive·ly** *adv.* **—di·vi′sive·ness** *n.*

di·vi·sor (di·vī′zər) *n. Math.* A number by which another number or quantity is divided.

di·vorce (di·vôrs′, -vōrs′) *n.* **1** The legal dissolution of a marriage. **2** Severance; separation. **—***v.* **·vorced, ·vorc·ing** *v.t.* **1** To free legally from a marriage relationship. **2** To sunder; sever; separate. **3** To obtain a legal divorce from. **—***v.i.* **4** To get a divorce. [< L *divortium* < *divertere* separate, divert] **—di·vorce′ment** *n.*

di·vor·cee (di·vôr′sē′, -vōr′-) *n.* A divorced person.

di·vor·cée (di·vôr′sā′, -vōr′-, di·vôr′sā, -vōr′-) *n.* A divorced woman. **—di·vor′cé′** *n. Masc.* [F]

div·ot (div′ət) *n.* A piece of turf cut from the sod by the stroke of a golf club. [< Scot. *devat*]

di·vulge (di·vulj′, dī-) *v.t.* **·vulged, ·vulg·ing** To tell, as a secret; disclose; reveal. [< L *dis-* away + *vulgare* make public] **—di·vulge′ment, di·vul′gence** (-jəns), **di·vulg′er** *n.*

div·vy (div′ē) *Slang n. pl.* **·vies** A share; dividend. **—***v.t.* **·vied, ·vy·ing** To divide; often with *up.* [Short for DIVIDE]

Dix·ie (dik′sē) *n.* The southern United States: also **Dixie Land.**

Dix·ie·land (dik′sē·land′) *n.* A style of jazz originally played in New Orleans.

diz·zy (diz′ē) *adj.* **·zi·er, ·zi·est 1** Having a feeling of whirling and confusion; giddy. **2** Causing or caused by giddiness. **3** *Informal* Thoughtless; capricious; silly; stupid. **—** *v.t.* **·zied, ·zy·ing** To make giddy; confuse. [< OE *dysig* foolish] **—diz′zi·ly** *adv.* **—diz′zi·ness** *n.*

dkg, dkg. dekagram(s).

dkl, dkl. dekaliter(s).

dkm, dkm. dekameter(s).

dks, dks. dekastere(s).

D/L demand loan.

dl, dl. deciliter(s).

D.Lit., D.Litt. Doctor of Letters (Literature) (L *Doctor Lit(t)erarum*).

dlr. dealer.

D.L.S. Doctor of Library Science.

DM., Dm. Deutsche mark.

dm, dm. decameter(s); decimeter(s).

D.M.D. Doctor of Dental Medicine (L *Dentariae Medicinae Doctor*).

D.Mus. Doctor of Music.

DMZ demilitarized zone.

D.N. our Lord (L *Dominus noster*).

DNA deoxyribonucleic acid.

do[1] (do͞o) *v.* **did, done, do·ing, does** *v.t.* **1** To perform, as an action; execute, as a piece of work. **2** To finish; complete. **3** To deal with or take care of: to *do* chores. **4** To cause or produce; bring about: to *do* good. **5** To exert; put forth: He *did* his best. **6** To work at as one's occupation. **7** To translate. **8** To present (a play, etc.): to *do* Hamlet. **9** To play the part of: to *do* Ophelia. **10** To cover; travel: to *do* a mile in four minutes. **11** To visit: to *do* the Louvre. **12** To serve; be sufficient for: Five dollars will *do* me. **13** To extend; render: to *do* homage. **14** To solve; work out, as a problem. **15** To serve, as a term in prison. **16** *Informal* To cheat; swindle. **—***v.i.* **17** To exert oneself; strive: to *do* or die. **18** To conduct or behave oneself. **19** To fare; get along: I *did* badly in the race. **20** To suffice; serve the purpose. **—do away with 1** To throw away; discard. **2** To kill; destroy. **—do by** To act toward. **—do for 1** To provide for; care for. **2** *Informal* To ruin; kill. **—do in** *Slang* To kill. **—do over** To redecorate. **—do up 1** To tie up, as a parcel. **2** To roll up or arrange, as the hair. **3** To clean; repair. **4** To tire out. **—make do** To get along with whatever is available. **—** *auxiliary* As an auxiliary, *do* is used: **1** Without specific meaning in negative, interrogative, and inverted constructions: I *do* not want it; *Do* you want to leave?; Little *did* he know. **2** To add force to imperatives: *Do* hurry. **3** To express emphasis: I *do* believe you. **4** As a substitute for another verb: Did he come? Yes, he *did.* **—***n. pl.* **do's** or **dos** *Informal* A social gathering; festivity. [< OE *dōn*]

do[2] (dō) *n. Music* In solmization, the tone C or the first tone of a diatonic scale. [Ital. See GAMUT.]

D.O. Doctor of Osteopathy.

do. ditto.

D.O.A. dead on arrival.

do·a·ble (do͞o′ə·bəl) *adj.* Capable of being done.

dob·bin (dob′in) *n.* A horse, esp. a plodding or patient one. [Var. of *Robin* < *Robert*]

Do·ber·man pin·scher (dō′bər·mən pin′shər) One of a breed of large, short-haired dogs, usu. black with rusty brown markings. [< L. *Doberman,* 19th c. Ger. breeder]

Doberman pinscher

doc. document.

doc·ile (dos′əl, *Brit.* dō′sīl) *adj.* **1** Easy to train; teachable. **2** Easy to manage or handle. [< L *docilis* able to be taught] **—doc′ile·ly** *adv.* **—do·cil·i·ty** (do·sil′ə·tē, dō-) *n.* **—Syn. 2** tractable, complaint, obedient, pliant.

dock[1] (dok) *n.* **1** An artificial basin for ships. **2** The water between two adjoining piers. **3** A pier or wharf. **—***v.t.* **1** To bring (a ship or boat) into a dock. **—***v.i.* **2** To come into a dock. [< MDu. *docke*]

dock[2] (dok) *n.* **1** The solid part of an animal's tail. **2** An animal's tail when clipped or bobbed. **—***v.t.* **1** To cut off the end of (a tail, etc.); clip. **2** To clip short the tail of. **3** To take a part from (wages, etc.). **4** To take a part from the wages of. [ME *dok*]

dock[3] (dok) *n.* An enclosed space for prisoners on trial in court. [< Flemish *dok* cage]

dock[4] (dok) *n.* A large-leaved weed of the buckwheat family. [< OE *docce*]

dock·age[1] (dok′ij) *n.* **1** A charge for docking. **2** Provision for docking. **3** The act of docking.

dock·age[2] (dok′ij) *n.* **1** Curtailment, as of wages; reduction. **2** Waste matter in grain.

dock·et (dok′it) *n.* **1** A condensed statement of a document. **2** *Law.* A record of the principal steps taken in a case; also, the register of such records. **3** A calendar of the cases to be tried in a court. **4** Any calendar of business. **5** A tag or label attached to a parcel ready for delivery. **—** *v.t.* **1** To place on a docket. **2** To attach a docket or label to. [?]

dock·yard (dok′yärd′) *n.* **1** A place for building or repairing ships. **2** *Brit.* A navy yard.

doc·tor (dok′tər) *n.* **1** A qualified practitioner of medicine or surgery in any of its branches. **2** A person who has received the highest academic degree, as a Ph.D., or has had a high honorary degree conferred on him. **3** A medicine man, wizard, or conjurer. **—***v.t. Informal* **1** To prescribe for or treat medicinally. **2** To repair. **3** To alter; falsify, as evidence. **—***v.i. Informal* **4** To practice medicine. **5** To take medicine or undergo medicinal treatment. [L, a teacher] **—doc′tor·al** *adj.*

doc·tor·ate (dok′tər·it) *n.* The degree, status, or title of one who holds a doctor's degree.

doc·tri·naire (dok′trə·nâr′) *adj.* Theoretical; visionary. **—***n.* One whose views are derived from theories rather than from facts.

doc·trine (dok′trin) *n.* That which is set forth for acceptance or belief, esp., in religion, a belief or precept; dogma. [< L *doctrina* teaching]

doc·u·dra·ma (dok′yə·drä′mə, -dra′-) *n.* A television drama or series based on fact, presented in documentary style.

doc·u·ment (dok′yə·mənt) *n.* Written or printed matter conveying authoritative information, records, or evidence. **—***v.t.* **1** To prove by documentary evidence. **2** To supply with notes and references to authoritative material: to *document* a text. [< L *documentum* a lesson] **—doc′u·men·ta′tion** *n.*

doc·u·men·ta·ry (dok′yə·men′tər·ē) *adj.* **1** Of, pertaining to, supported by, or based upon documents: also

doc′u·men′tal. 2 Of, pertaining to, or of the nature of a presentation, as in a film, that purports to record with little or no fictionalization the action displayed. —*n. pl.* **·ries** A documentary film, television show, etc.

dod·der (dod′ər) *v.i.* To tremble or totter, as from age. [ME *dadiren*]

dodeca- *combining form* Twelve; of or having twelve: *dodecagon.* Also, **dodec-**. [< Gk. *dōdeka*]

do·dec·a·gon (dō·dek′ə·gon) *n. Geom.* A figure, esp. a plane figure, with twelve sides and twelve angles. [< Gk. *dōdekagōnon*]

do·dec·a·he·dron (dō′dek·ə·hē′drən) *n. pl.* **·drons** or **·dra** (-drə) A solid bounded by twelve plane faces. —**do′dec·a·he′dral** *adj.*

Dodecahedron

dodge (doj) *v.* **dodged, dodg·ing** *v.t.* 1 To avoid by a sudden turn or twist. 2 To evade by cunning or trickery. —*v.i.* 3 To move or change position suddenly, as to avoid a blow. 4 To practice trickery; be deceitful. —*n.* 1 An act of dodging. 2 A trick to deceive or cheat. [?]

dodg·er (doj′ər) *n.* 1 One who dodges. 2 A tricky fellow. 3 A small handbill. 4 A cooked cake of Indian meal.

do·do (dō′dō) *n. pl.* **·does** or **·dos** An extinct bird of Mauritius about the size of a turkey. [< Pg. *doudo* foolish]

Dodo

doe (dō) *n.* The female of the deer, antelope, hare, rabbit, or kangaroo. [< OE *dā*]

do·er (do͞o′ər) *n.* One who does something, esp., one who accomplishes a lot.

does (duz) Present tense, third person singular, of DO.

doe·skin (dō′skin′) *n.* 1 The skin of a doe. 2 A heavy, twilled, cotton fabric napped on one side; also, a woolen fabric resembling doeskin.

does·n't (duz′ənt) Contraction of *does not.*

doff (dof, dôf) *v.t.* 1 To take off, as clothing. 2 To take off (the hat) in salutation. 3 To discard. [Contraction of DO OFF]

dog (dôg, dog) *n.* 1 A carnivorous, domesticated mammal of worldwide distribution and many varieties, related to the wolf. 2 Any of a family (*Canidae*) of animals including the dog, wolf, jackal, etc. 3 The male of the dog and similar animals: a *dog* fox. 4 PRAIRIE DOG. 5 *Mech.* Any small device that holds or grips. 6 ANDIRON. 7 A fellow; man-about-town: a gay *dog.* 8 A scoundrel; rascal. 9 *Slang* HOT DOG. 10 *pl. Slang* Feet. —**go to the dogs** *Informal* To be ruined; degenerate. —**put on the dog.** *Slang* To make a pretentious display. —*adv.* Very; utterly: *dog-tired.* —*v.t.* **dogged, dog·ging** To follow persistently; hound; hunt. [< OE *dogga*]

dog biscuit A hard biscuit for feeding dogs.

dog-cart (dôg′kärt′, dog′-) *n.* 1 A one-horse vehicle with two seats set back to back. 2 A cart hauled by dogs.

dog days The hot, sultry season in July and August.

doge (dōj) *n.* The elective chief magistrate in the former republics of Venice and Genoa. [Ital.] —**doge′dom, doge′·ship** *n.*

dog-ear (dôg′ir′, dog′-) *n.* The corner of a page turned down to mark a place. —*v.t.* To turn or fold down the corner of (a page). —**dog′eared′** *adj.*

dog·fight (dôg′fīt′, dog′-) *n.* 1 A fight between or as between dogs. 2 *Mil.* Combat at close quarters between aircraft or tanks.

dog·fish (dôg′fish′, dog′-) *n. pl.* **·fish** or **·fish·es** One of various small sharks.

dog·ged (dôg′id, dog′-) *adj.* Persistent; stubborn. —**dog′·ged·ly** *adv.* —**dog′ged·ness** *n.*

dog·ger·el (dôg′ər·əl, dog′-) *n.* Trivial, awkwardly written verse. —*adj.* Of or composed of such verse. Also **dog′·grel.** [ME]

dog·gish (dôg′ish, dog′-) *adj.* 1 Like a dog; snappish. 2 *Informal* Stylish; chic. —**dog′gish·ly** *adv.* —**dog′gish·ness** *n.*

dog-gone (dôg′gôn′, dog′gon′) *v.t.* **-goned, -gon·ing** *Informal* DAMN. —*adj.* & *adv.* DAMN. [Euphemism for *God damn*]

dog·gy (dôg′ē, dog′-) *adj.* **·gi·er, ·gi·est** Of or pertaining to dogs: a *doggy* smell. —*n. pl.* **·gies** A pet dog. Also **dog′gie.**

dog house A shelter for a dog; kennel. —**in the dog house** *Slang* Out of favor.

do·gie (dō′gē) *n.* In the w U.S., a stray or motherless calf. [?]

dog·ma (dôg′mə, dog′-) *n. pl.* **·mas** or **·ma·ta** (-mə·tə) 1 *Theol.* A system of teachings of religious truth as maintained by the Christian church or any portion of it. 2 Any doctrine asserted and adopted on authority. 3 Any accepted principle, maxim, or tenet. [< Gk. *dogma* opinion]

dog·mat·ic (dôg·mat′ik, dog-) *adj.* 1 Stating opinions without evidence. 2 Overly positive or arrogant. 3 Of, like, or pertaining to dogma. Also **dog·mat′i·cal.** —**dog·mat′i·cal·ly** *adv.* —**dog·mat′i·cal·ness** *n.* —**Syn.** 2 opinionated, overbearing, dictatorial. 3 doctrinal.

dog·ma·tism (dôg′mə·tiz′əm, dog′-) *n.* Positive or arrogant assertion, as of belief, without proof.

dog·ma·tize (dôg′mə·tīz, dog′-) *v.* **·tized, ·tiz·ing** *v.i.* 1 To express oneself dogmatically. —*v.t.* 2 To declare or assert as a dogma. —**dog′ma·tist, dog′ma·ti·za′tion, dog′ma·tiz′er** *n.*

dog·nap (dôg′nap′) *v.t.* **·napped** or **·naped, ·nap·ping** or **·nap·ing** To steal (a dog), esp. for sale to a medical research laboratory. [< DOG + (KID)NAP] —**dog′nap′per, dog′nap′er** *n.*

do-good·er (do͞o′go͝od′ər) *n.* A well-meaning but naive reformer or social activist whose efforts are futile or foolish.

dog rose The wild brier of Europe, bearing pink flowers.

dog sled A sled drawn by dogs. Also **dog sledge.**

dog's life *Informal* A wretched existence.

Dog Star The star Sirius.

dog's-tooth violet (dôgz′to͞oth′, dogz′-) *n.* Any of various small, spring-flowering herbs of the lily family. Also **dog′tooth′ violet.**

dog tag 1 A small plate for a dog, usu. indicating ownership. 2 *Informal* A soldier's identification tag.

dog·tooth (dôg′to͞oth′, dog′-) *n.* A human canine tooth or eyetooth. Also **dog tooth.**

dog-trot (dôg′trot′, dog′-) *n.* A regular and easy trot.

dog-watch (dôg′woch′, -wôch′, dog′-) *n. Naut.* One of the two watches aboard ship, each of two hours, from 4 to 6 and 6 to 8 P.M.

dog·wood (dôg′wo͝od′, dog′-) *n.* Any of certain trees or shrubs, as the **flowering** or **Virginia dogwood,** with large decorative pinkish white flowers.

Dogwood blossoms

do·gy *n.* (dō′gē) *n.* DOGIE.

doi·ly (doi′lē) *n. pl.* **·lies** A matlike napkin, used under dishes, as a decoration, etc. [< *Doily* or *Doyley,* 17th c. English draper]

do·ings (do͞o′ingz) *n. pl.* Proceedings; acts; course of conduct.

do-it-your·self (do͞o′it·yər·self′) *adj.* Of, pertaining to, used in, or engaged in construction, repair, or other work that an amateur does without professional help.

dol. (*pl.* **dols.**) dollar.

dol·drums (dol′drəmz) *n. pl.* 1 Those parts of the ocean near the equator where calms or fitful winds prevail. 2 A dull, depressed, or bored condition of mind; the dumps. [?]

dole (dōl) *n.* 1 Something given to the needy, as food or money. 2 A sum of money officially paid to an unemployed person for sustenance. 3 Something given out in small portions. —*v.t.* **doled, dol·ing** To dispense in small quantities; distribute: usu. with *out.* [< OE *dāl*]

dole·ful (dōl′fəl) *adj.* Melancholy; mournful. Also **dole′·some** (-səm). [< LL *dolium* grief] —**Syn.** dismal, sad, sorrowful, woeful. —**dole′ful·ly** *adv.* —**dole′ful·ness** *n.*

dol·i·cho·ce·phal·ic (dol′i·kō·sə·fal′ik) *adj.* Having a long skull, the breadth less than one third of the length. Also **dol′i·cho·ceph′a·lous** (-sef′ə·ləs). [< Gk. *dolichos* long + *kephalē* head]

doll (dol) *n.* 1 A child's toy representing a person. 2 A pretty but superficial woman. 3 *Slang* Any girl or woman. 4 *Slang* Any person warmly regarded. —*v.t.* & *v.i. Slang* To dress elaborately: with *up.* [< *Doll,* a nickname for Dorothy]

dol·lar (dol′ər) *n.* 1 The basic monetary unit of the United States, having the legal value of 100 cents. 2 The basic monetary unit of various other countries, as Canada and Argentina. 3 A U.S. legal coin or paper greenback worth 100 cents. 4 A loose term for the peso, the Haitian gourde, and other coins. [< G *Taler*]
dollar diplomacy The policy of utilizing the financial power of a country to strengthen its foreign relations or to promote private commercial interests abroad.
dollar sign The sign ($) meaning dollar or dollars before a number. Also **dollar mark.**
dol·ly (dol′ē) *n. pl.* **·lies** 1 DOLL (def. 1). 2 A light hand truck, with wheels or rollers, used for moving heavy loads. 3 A low, wheeled platform on which a motion-picture or television camera is set. —*v.i.* **·lied, ly·ing** To move a television or motion-picture camera toward a scene or subject: with *in.* [< *Dolly,* a nickname for Dorothy]
dol·man (dol′mən) *n. pl.* **dol·mans** A woman's coat with dolman sleeves. [< Turkish *dōlāmān* long robe]
dolman sleeve A sleeve tapering from a wide opening at the armhole to a narrow one at the wrist.
dol·men (dol′men) *n.* A monument of large stones set on end and capped with a single huge stone or stones. [< Cornish *tolmen* hole of stone]
dol·o·mite (dol′ə·mīt) *n.* A brittle mineral form of calcium magnesium carbonate. [< D. de *Dolomieu,* 1750–1801, French geologist]
do·lor (dō′lər) *n.* Sorrow; anguish. [L]
do·lor·ous (dō′lər·əs, dol′ər-) *adj.* Expressing or causing sorrow or pain. **—do′lor·ous·ly** *adv.* **—do′lor·ous·ness** *n.*
dol·phin (dol′fin) *n.* 1 Any of various members of the whale family, having beaklike snouts. 2 *Naut.* A spar or buoy for mooring boats. [< Gk. *delphis*]

Dolphin

dolt (dōlt) *n.* A stupid person. [< ME *dold* stupid] **—dolt′·ish** *adj.*
-dom *suffix of nouns* 1 State or condition of being: *freedom.* 2 Domain of: *kingdom.* 3 All those having a certain rank, state, or condition: *Christendom.* [< OE *dōm* state]
dom. domestic; dominion.
do·main (dō·mān′) *n.* 1 A territory over which dominion is exercised. 2 A department, as of knowledge. 3 Land owned by one person; estate. [< L < *dominus* lord]
dome (dōm) *n.* 1 A vaulted, hemispherical roof; a cupola. 2 Any cuplike top or covering. —*v.* **domed, dom·ing** *v.t.* 1 To furnish or cover with a dome. 2 To shape like a dome. —*v.i.* 3 To rise or swell upward like a dome. [< Ital. *duomo* cupola]
do·mes·tic (də·mes′tik) *adj.* 1 Belonging to the family, house, or household. 2 Fond of family life, duties, or housekeeping. 3 Domesticated; tame. 4 Produced in one's own country. —*n.* A household servant. [< L *domus* house] **—do·mes′ti·cal·ly** *adv.*
do·mes·ti·cate (də·mes′tə·kāt) *v.* **·cat·ed, ·cat·ing** *v.t.* 1 To train for domestic use; tame. 2 To make domestic. —*v.i.* 3 To become domestic. **—do·mes′ti·ca′tion** *n.*
do·mes·tic·i·ty (dō′mes·tis′ə·tē) *n. pl.* **·ties** 1 Fondness of home and family. 2 A household.
domestic science HOME ECONOMICS.
dom·i·cile (dom′ə·səl, -sīl) *n.* A home, house, or dwelling. —*v.t.* & *v.i.* **·ciled, ·cil·ing** *v.t.* To settle in a domicile. Also **dom′i·cil.** [< L *domus* house]
dom·i·cil·i·ar·y (dom′ə·sil′ē·er′ē) *adj.* Pertaining to a fixed or a private residence.
dom·i·nance (dom′ə·nəns) *n.* The state or condition of being dominant. Also **dom′i·nan·cy.**
dom·i·nant (dom′ə·nənt) *adj.* 1 Ruling; governing; prevailing. 2 Having a masking effect on a contrasting or recessive factor in the genetic endowment of an organism. —*n. Music* The tone a perfect fifth above the tonic. **—dom′·i·nant·ly** *adv.*
dom·i·nate (dom′ə·nāt) *v.* **·nat·ed, ·nat·ing** *v.t.* 1 To control; govern. 2 To have supreme or masterful power or influence over. 3 To tower above; loom over: The city *dominates* the plain. —*v.i.* 4 To have control; hold sway. [< L *dominare* rule, dominate] **—dom′i·na′tion, dom′i·na′tor** *n.*
dom·i·neer (dom′ə·nir′) *v.t.* & *v.i.* 1 To tyrannize; bully. 2 To tower or loom (over or above). [< L *dominus* lord]
dom·i·neer·ing (dom′ə·nir′ing) *adj.* Overbearing; arrogant. **—dom′i·neer′ing·ly** *adv.* **—Syn.** authoritative, despotic, imperious, tyrannical.
Do·min·i·can (də·min′i·kən) *adj.* 1 Of or pertaining to St. Dominic or a monastic order following his rule. 2 Of or pertaining to the Dominican Republic or its people. —*n.* 1 A member of a Dominican order. 2 A citizen or native of the Dominican Republic.
Dominican Republic A republic on the E part of Hispaniola in the Caribbean, 18,700 sq. mi., cap. Santo Domingo.

dom·i·nie (dom′ə·nē) 1 In Scotland, a schoolmaster. 2 *Informal* Any minister. [< L *dominus* lord]
do·min·ion (də·min′yən) *n.* 1 Sovereign authority; sway. 2 A country under a particular government. 3 Formerly, a self-governing member of the Commonwealth of Nations. [< L *dominus* lord]
Dominion Day July 1, the anniversary of the federation of Canada into a dominion (July 1, 1867), a legal holiday in Canada.
dom·i·no[1] (dom′ə·nō) *n. pl.* **·noes** or **·nos** 1 A small mask for the eyes. 2 A loose robe, hood, and mask worn at masquerades. [< MF, a clerical garment] • See MASK.
dom·i·no[2] (dom′ə·nō) *n. pl.* **·noes** or **·nos** 1 A small oblong piece of wood, etc., divided on one side into halves left blank or marked with dots. 2 *pl. (construed as sing.)* A game played with such pieces. —*adj.* Describing the view or political theory that a series of events is unavoidably contingent on the occurrence of an initial event, as a row of dominoes collapses when the first is toppled.
don[1] (don) *n.* 1 A Spanish gentleman or nobleman. 2 An important personage. 3 *Informal* In English universities, a head, fellow, or tutor of a college. [Sp. < L *dominus* lord]
don[2] (don) *v.t.* **donned, don·ning** To put on, as a garment. [Contraction of *do on*]
Don (don) *n.* Mr.; sir: a title of respect in Spain and Spanish-speaking countries.
do·ña (dō′nyä) *n.* A Spanish lady. [Sp. < L *domina* lady]
Do·ña (dō′nyä) *n.* Lady; madam: a title of respect in Spain and Spanish-speaking countries.
do·nate (dō′nāt, dō·nāt′) *v.t.* **·nat·ed, ·nat·ing** To bestow as a gift, esp. to a cause; present; contribute. [< L *donare* give < *donum* a gift] **—do′na·tor** *n.*
do·na·tion (dō·nā′shən) *n.* 1 The act of donating. 2 That which is donated; a gift.
done (dun) *p.p.* of DO[1]. —*adj.* 1 Completed. 2 Cooked sufficiently. **—done for** 1 Without hope; destined to worsen, die, etc. 2 In a hopeless condition; ruined, defeated, etc.
do·nee (dō·nē′) *n.* One who receives a gift.
don·jon (dun′jən, don′-) *n.* The principal tower or keep of a medieval castle. [Var. of DUNGEON]
Don Juan (don ʰwän′, don jo͞o′ən, *Sp.* dôn hwän′) 1 A legendary Spanish nobleman and seducer of women. 2 Any seducer.
don·key (dong′kē, dung′-) *n.* 1 Any of a domesticated species of the ass. 2 A stupid or stubborn person. [?]
don·na (don′ə, *Ital.* dôn′nä) *n.* An Italian lady. [Ital. < L *domina* lady]
Don·na (don′ə, *Ital.* dôn′nä) *n.* Lady; madam: a title of respect, used in Italy and Italian-speaking countries.
don·nish (don′ish) *adj.* 1 Of or like an English don. 2 Formal; pedantic.
do·nor (dō′nər) *n.* 1 A giver; donator. 2 One from whom blood is taken for transfusion or from whom tissue, an organ, etc., is obtained for another. [< L *donare* give]
do-noth·ing (do͞o′nuth′ing) *n.* An idler.

Don Quix·ote (don kwik′sət, ki·hō′tē; *Sp.* dôn kē·hō′tā) The hero of Cervantes' romance of that name, a satire on chivalry. Also **Don Qui·jo′te.**

don't (dōnt) Contraction of *do not.* • The use of *don't* for *doesn't (She don't care)* is now nonstandard in speech and writing. However, it is still used informally in educated conversation in parts of the U.S.

doo·dad (do͞o′dad) *n. Informal* **1** DOOHICKEY. **2** A small ornament; bauble.

doo·dle (do͞od′l) *v.i. Informal* To draw pictures, symbols, etc., while the mind is otherwise occupied. —*n.* A drawing so made. [dial. E *doodle* be idle]

doo·dle·bug (do͞od′l·bug′) *n.* **1** The larva of the ant lion. **2** Loosely, any droning insect. [? < DOODLE + BUG]

doo·hick·ey (do͞o′hik′ē) *n. Informal* Any contrivance or device, the name of which is not known or immediately recalled; doodad.

doom (do͞om) *v.t.* **1** To pronounce judgment upon; condemn. **2** To destine to disaster. **3** To decree as a penalty. —*n.* **1** Death; ruin. **2** Destiny. **3** Judicial decision; condemnation; sentence. —**crack of doom** The signal for the Last Judgment. [< OE *dōm*] —**Syn.** *n.* **1** destruction, downfall, end. **2** fate, lot, portion.

dooms·day (do͞omz′dā′) *n.* The day of the Last Judgment, or of any final judgment.

door (dôr, dōr) *n.* **1** A hinged, sliding, or revolving frame used for closing or opening an entrance or exit. **2** DOORWAY. **3** Any means or avenue of exit or entrance. **4** The house or room to which a door is attached: three *doors* down the street. [< OE *duru* pair of doors and *dor*]

door·bell (dôr′bel′, dōr′-) *n.* A device at a door to sound a signal that someone wishes admittance.

door·jamb (dôr′jam′, dōr′-) *n.* The vertical piece at the side of a doorway.

door·keep·er (dôr′kē′pər, dōr′) *n.* A guardian or keeper of a door.

door·knob (dôr′nob′, dōr′-) *n.* The handle for turning the catch to open a door.

door·man (dôr′man′, dōr′-) *n. pl.* **·men** (-men′, -mən) An attendant at the door of a hotel, apartment house, etc., who assists persons entering and leaving the building.

door·mat (dôr′mat′, dōr′-) *n.* A mat placed at an entrance for wiping off the shoes.

door·nail (dôr′nāl′, dōr′-) *n.* A nail or stud with a large head formerly used to ornament doors. —**dead as a doornail** Quite dead.

door·sill (dôr′sil′, dōr′-) *n.* The sill or threshold of a door: also **door sill.**

door·step (dôr′step′, dōr′-) *n* A step or one of a series of steps leading to a door.

door·stop (dôr′stop′, dōr′-) *n.* A device to keep a door open.

door·way (dôr′wā′, dōr′-) *n.* **1** Any opening closed by a door. **2** Any access.

door·yard (dôr′yärd′, dōr′-) *n.* A yard around, or esp. in front of the door of, a house.

dope (dōp) *n.* **1** *Slang* Any drug used for inducing euphoria. **2** *Slang* A drug addict. **3** *Slang* Any information or forecast. **4** Any thick liquid or semifluid, as a lubricant, etc. **5** Any substance used in treating a cloth surface, as of an airplane wing, to increase strength or produce tautness. **6** *Slang* A stupid person. —*v.t.* **doped, dop·ing 1** To give dope to. **2** *Slang* To stupefy or exhilarate as by a drug: often with *up.* —**dope out** *Slang* **1** To plan. **2** To figure out; solve. [< Du. *doop* dipping sauce < *doopen* dip]

do·pey (dō′pē) *adj.* **·pi·er, ·pi·est** *Slang* **1** Stupefied from narcotics. **2** Stupid; dull. —**do′pi·ly** *adv.* —**do′pi·ness** *n.*

Dop·pler effect (dop′lər) *Physics* The change in the observed frequency of a wave due to the relative motion of the observer and the source. [< C. J. *Doppler,* 1803–1853, Austrian physicist and mathematician]

Dor·ic (dôr′ik, dor′-) *adj. Archit.* Of or constructed in the earliest and simplest of the three orders of Greek architecture, characterized by thick, fluted columns and plain capitals. [< Gk. *Dōris,* a district of ancient Greece] • See CAPITAL.

dorm (dôrm) *n. Informal* DORMITORY.

dor·mant (dôr′mənt) *adj.* **1** Sleeping. **2** Quiet; motionless. **3** Sleeping or resting, as certain animals and plants in winter. **4** Not erupting: said of a volcano. **5** Inactive; unused. [< L *dormire* to sleep] —**dor′man·cy** *n.*

Dormer

dor·mer (dôr′mər) *n. Archit.* **1** A vertical window in a small gable rising from a sloping roof: also **dormer window. 2** The gable in which this window is set. [< OF *dormeor* < *dormir* to sleep]

dor·mi·to·ry (dôr′mə·tôr′ē, -tō′·rē) *n. pl.* **·ries 1** A large room in which many persons sleep. **2** A building providing sleeping and living accommodations, esp. at a school or college. [< L *dormire* to sleep]

dor·mouse (dôr′mous′) *n. pl.* **·mice** One of various small, Old World, squirrel-like rodents. [? < OF *dormir* to sleep + MOUSE]

Dormouse

dor·sal (dôr′səl) *adj.* Of, pertaining to, on, or near the back. [< L *dorsum* back] —**dor′sal·ly** *adv.*

do·ry (dôr′ē, dō′rē) *n. pl.* **·ries** A deep, flat-bottomed rowboat with a sharp prow and flat stern, adapted for rough weather. [< native Honduran name]

dos·age (dō′sij) *n.* **1** The administering of medicine in prescribed quantity. **2** The total dose to be given, as medicine, X-rays, etc.

dose (dōs) *n.* **1** The quantity of medicine prescribed to be taken at one time; also, the degree of exposure to X-rays or other radiation in a certain period of time. **2** Anything disagreeable given as a prescription or infliction. —*v.* **dosed, dos·ing** *v.t.* **1** To give medicine to in a dose. **2** To give, as medicine or drugs, in doses. —*v.i.* **3** To take medicines. [< L *dosis* < Gk., orig., a giving] —**dos′er** *n.*

do·sim·e·ter (dō·sim′ə·tər) *n. Med.* An instrument for measuring exposure to X-rays or other radiation. [< DOSE + -METER]

dos·si·er (dos′ē·ā, dôs′-, dô·syā′) *n.* A collection of documents, etc., relating to a particular matter or person. [F]

dost (dust) Archaic second person singular, present tense of DO: used with *thou.*

dot[1] (dot) *n.* **1** A minute, round, or nearly round mark. **2** *Music* A point, written after a note or rest, which lengthens its value by half; also, a staccato mark. **3** A precise moment of time: on the *dot.* **4** A signal of shorter duration than the dash, used in the transmission of messages. —*v.* **dot·ted, dot·ting** *v.t.* **1** To mark with a dot or dots. **2** To spread or scatter like dots. **3** To cover with dots. —*v.i.* **4** To make a dot or dots. [< OE *dott* head of a boil] —**Syn.** *n.* **1** flake, fleck, speck, spot.

dot[2] (dot) *n.* A woman's marriage dowry. [< L *dos, dotis*] —**do·tal** (dōt′l) *adj.*

do·tage (dō′tij) *n.* **1** Feebleness of mind, as a result of old age; senility. **2** Foolish and extravagant affection. [< DOTE + -AGE]

do·tard (dō′tərd) *n.* A senile old person.

dote (dōt) *v.t.* **dot·ed, dot·ing 1** To lavish extreme fondness: with *on* or *upon.* **2** To be in one's dotage. [< MDu. *doten* be silly] —**dot′er** *n.* —**dot′ing·ly** *adv.*

doth (duth) Archaic third person singular, present tense of DO.

dot·ty (dot′ē) *adj.* **·ti·er, ·ti·est 1** Consisting of or marked with dots. **2** *Informal* Of unsteady or feeble gait. **3** *Brit. Informal* Slightly demented; odd; eccentric. —**dot′ti·ly** *adv.* —**dot′ti·ness** *n.*

Dou·ay Bible (do͞o·ā′) An English translation of the Latin Vulgate edition of the Bible for use in the Roman Catholic Church. Also **Douay Version.**

doub·le (dub′əl) *adj.* **1** Having two of a sort together; being in pairs; coupled. **2** Twice as large, much, strong, heavy, valuable, or many. **3** Consisting of two unlike parts: a *double* standard. **4** Ambiguous, deceitful, or two-faced. **5** Doubled; folded. **6** *Bot.* Having the petals increased in number. —*n.* **1** Something that is twice as much. **2** A fold or plait. **3** A person or thing that closely resembles another. 4 An apparition or wraith. 5 A turning about or shift in direction. 6 A stand-in for an actor. 7 *pl.* A tennis game between two pairs of players; also, two successive faults in tennis. 8 In baseball, a two-base hit. 9 In card playing, the act of doubling. See DOUBLE (*v.* def. 7). **—on** (or **at**) **the double** In double-time: a military command. —*v.* **doub·led, doub·ling** *v.t.* 1 To make twice as great in number, size, value, force, etc. 2 To fold or bend one part of upon another: usually with *over, up, back,* etc. 3 To do over again; repeat. 4 To be twice the quantity or number of. 5 To act or be the double of. 6 *Naut.* To sail around: to *double* a cape. 7 In bridge, to increase the value of (an opponent's bid) if the contract is fulfilled, or to increase the penalty if the contract is not fulfilled. —*v.i.* 8 To become double. 9 To turn and go back on a course: often with *back.* 10 To act or perform in two capacities. 11 In baseball, to hit a double. 12 In bridge, to double a bid. **—double up** 1 To bend over or cause to bend over, as from pain or laughter. 2 To share one's quarters, bed, etc., with another. 3 In baseball, to complete a double play upon. —*adv.* 1 Twice. 2 In twice the quantity. Also **doub'ly** (dub'lē) *adv.* [< L *duplus* double] **—doub'ler** *n.*

doub·le-bar·reled (dub'əl·bar'əld) *adj.* 1 Having two barrels, as a shotgun. 2 Doubly effective. 3 Ambiguous in meaning.

doub·le-bass (dub'əl·bās') *n.* The largest and deepest-toned of the stringed instruments played with a bow.

double bed A bed wide enough for two people.

double boiler A cooking utensil consisting of two pots, one fitting into the other.

doub·le-breast·ed (dub'əl·bres'tid) *adj.* Having two rows of buttons and a double thickness of cloth across the breast, as the jacket of a suit.

double chin A fat, fleshy fold under the chin.

doub·le-cross (dub'əl·krôs', -kros') *Slang v.t.* To betray by not acting as promised; cheat. —*n.* (-krôs', -kros') The act of or an instance of betrayal. **—doub'le-cross'er** *n.*

double dagger See DAGGER.

doub·le-date (dub'əl·dāt') *v.t.* & *v.i.* **-dat·ed, -dat·ing** To make or go out on a double date (with).

double date *Informal* A social appointment made by two couples.

doub·le-deal·ing (dub'əl·dē'ling) *adj.* Treacherous; deceitful. —*n.* Duplicity. **—doub'le-deal'er** *n.*

doub·le-deck·er (dub'əl·dek'ər) *n.* 1 Any structure, vehicle, or vessel having two decks or levels. 2 A sandwich made with three slices of bread and two layers of filling.

doub·le-edged (dub'əl·ejd') *adj.* 1 Having two cutting edges. 2 Applicable both for as well as against.

dou·ble-en·ten·dre (dōō·blän·tän'dr', dub'əl än·tän'·drə) *n.* A word or phrase of double meaning, the less obvious one often risqué. [F]

double entry A method of bookkeeping in which every transaction is made to appear as both a debit and a credit. **—doub'le-en'try** *adj.*

doub·le-faced (dub'əl·fāst') *adj.* 1 Having two faces. 2 Deceitful; hypocritical.

double feature A program of two full-length motion pictures.

doub·le-head·er (dub'əl·hed'ər) *n.* Two games, esp. of baseball, played in succession on the same day by the same two teams.

double indemnity A clause in a life insurance policy by which a payment of double the face value of the policy is made in the event of accidental death.

doub·le-joint·ed (dub'əl·join'tid) *adj.* Having a joint in which the bones have unusual freedom of movement.

doub·le-park (dub'əl·pärk') *v.t.* & *v.i.* To park (a motor vehicle) alongside another already parked along the curb. **—doub'le-park'ing** *n.*

double play In baseball, a play in which two base runners are put out.

double pneumonia Pneumonia in both lungs.

doub·le-quick (dub'əl·kwik') *n.* & *v.* DOUBLE-TIME.

doub·le-reed (dub'əl·rēd') *n. Music* A wind instrument with a reed of two segments joined at one end. —*adj.* Having such a reed.

double standard A code of conduct permitting more sexual liberty to men than to women.

doub·let (dub'lit) *n.* 1 One of a pair of like things. 2 A pair or couple. 3 A short, close-fitting, outer garment, worn by men in the 15th to 17th centuries. 4 One of a pair of words derived from the same source but entering a language through different routes, as *regal* and *royal.* [< OF, something folded]

Doublet *def. 3*

doub·le-take (dub'əl·tāk') *n.* The delayed reaction, with visible evidence of surprise, to a joke or situation, used as a comic device.

double talk 1 Speech in which meaningless syllable combinations are substituted for expected words. 2 Ambiguous talk meant to deceive.

doub·le-think (dub'əl·thingk') *n.* 1 The capacity to hold contradictory opinions in full knowledge of their contradiction. 2 Confused thought. Also **dou'ble·think'.**

doub·le-time (dub'əl·tīm') *n.* In the U.S. Army, a rate of march of 180 steps a minute. —*v.t.* & *v.i.* **-timed, -tim·ing** To march or cause to march at this pace.

doub·loon (du·blōōn') *n.* A former Spanish gold coin. [< Sp. *doblón*]

doubt (dout) *v.t.* 1 To hesitate to believe; question. 2 To hold as uncertain. —*v.i.* 3 To be uncertain or unconvinced. 4 To be mistrustful. —*n.* 1 Lack of certain knowledge; uncertainty. 2 A matter or case of indecision. 3 A question, objection, or difficulty. [< L *dubitare*] **—doubt'a·ble** *adj.* **—doubt'er** *n.* **—doubt'ing·ly** *adv.* **—Syn.** *v.* 1 distrust, mistrust, suspect. *n.* 1 hesitancy, misgiving.

doubt·ful (dout'fəl) *adj.* 1 Subject to doubt; not definite. 2 Uncertain; undecided. 3 Indistinct; ambiguous. 4 Questionable; dubious. **—doubt'ful·ly** *adv.* **—doubt'ful·ness** *n.*

doubt·less (dout'lis) *adv.* 1 Without doubt; unquestionably. 2 Probably. Also **doubt'less·ly.** —*adj.* Having no doubt.

douche (dōōsh) *n.* 1 A jet of water or vapor sprayed on or into the body for medicinal or hygienic reasons. 2 The instrument for administering it. 3 A bath using these facilities. —*v.t.* & *v.i.* **douched, douch·ing** To give or take a douche. [< Ital. *doccia* a water pipe]

dough (dō) *n.* 1 A soft mass of flour, liquid, and other ingredients mixed for baking into bread, cake, etc. 2 Any soft pasty mass. 3 *Slang* Money. [< OE *dāh*] **—dough'y** *adj.*

dough·boy (dō'boi') *n. Informal* Formerly, an infantry soldier.

dough·nut (dō'nut) *n.* A small, usu. ring-shaped cake, fried in deep fat.

dough·ty (dou'tē) *adj.* **·ti·er, ·ti·est** *Archaic* Brave; valiant: now chiefly in humorous use. [< OE *dohtig*] **—dough'ti·ly** *adv.* **—dough'ti·ness** *n.*

Douglas fir A large tree of the pine family, found in w U.S. Also **Douglas hemlock, Douglas pine, Douglas spruce.** [< David *Douglas,* 1798–1834, Scottish botanist]

dour (dour, dōōr) *adj.* 1 Gloomy; sullen. 2 Aloof; forbidding. 3 Unyielding. [< L *durus*] **—dour'ly** *adv.* **—dour'ness** *n.*

douse[1] (dous) *v.* **doused, dous·ing** *v.t.* 1 To plunge into liquid. 2 To drench with water or other liquid. 3 To put out quickly: to *douse* a light. —*v.i.* 4 To become drenched or immersed. —*n.* A ducking or drenching. [?]

douse[2] (dous) *v.* DOWSE[2].

dove[1] (duv) *n.* 1 A pigeon. 2 A symbol of the Holy Spirit. 3 A symbol of peace. 4 One who favors conciliation and negotiation rather than militancy, as in a dispute. 5 Any gentle creature. [ME] **—dov'ish** *adj.*

dove[2] (dōv) *p.t.* of DIVE.

dove·cote (duv'kōt', kot') *n.* A small house, often raised and divided into compartments, for domestic pigeons. Also **dove'cot'** (-kot').

dove·tail (duv′tāl′) *n.* 1 A manner of joining boards, timbers, etc., by interlocking wedge-shaped tenons and spaces. 2 The joint so made. —*v.t. & v.i.* 1 To join by means of a dovetail or dovetails. 2 To fit in closely or aptly.

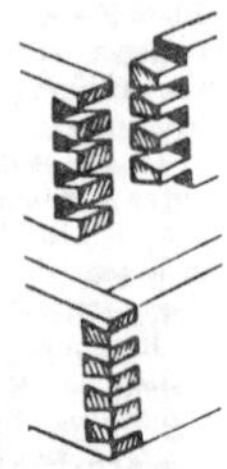

Dovetail joint

dow·a·ger (dou′ə·jər) *n.* 1 In English law, a widow holding property or title from her late husband. 2 Any elderly lady of dignified bearing. [< OF *douage* a dower]

dow·dy (dou′dē) *adj.* **·di·er, ·di·est** Not neat or fashionable; shabby. Also **dow′dy·ish.** —*n. pl.* **·dies** 1 A slatternly woman. 2 A fruit pie baked in a deep dish. [< ME *doude* a slut] —**dow′di·ly** *adv.* —**dow′di·ness** *n.*

dow·el (dou′əl) *n.* A pin or peg that fits into a corresponding hole, used for joining together two adjacent pieces. —*v.t.* **·eled** or **·elled, ·el·ing** or **·el·ling** To fasten with dowels. [< MLG *dovel* plug]

dow·er (dou′ər) *n.* 1 A widow's life portion of her husband's property. 2 The sum of one's natural gifts; endowment. —*v.t.* 1 To provide with a dower. 2 To endow, as with a talent. [< L *dos, dotis* a dowry]

down[1] (doun) *adv.* 1 From a higher to a lower place, level, position, etc. 2 In or into a lower place, position, etc. 3 On or to the ground. 4 To or toward the south. 5 From a former or earlier time or owner. 6 To a smaller bulk, diminished volume, greater density, etc.: to boil syrup *down.* 7 To or into a less active state. 8 To a lower rate, price, demand or amount. 9 Into or in an attitude of intensity, earnestness, etc.: to get *down* to work. 10 In or into ill health. 11 In or into subjection: His competitors kept him *down.* 12 Completely; entirely: loaded *down* with honors. 13 In cash, as at the time of purchase. 14 On or as on paper: Take *down* his words. —*adj.* 1 Going or facing toward a lower position or place: a *down* elevator. 2 In a lower place: The wires are *down.* 3 Gone, brought, or paid down. 4 Downcast; dejected. 5 Sick in bed. 6 In games, behind an opponent's score by (a number of) points, goals, etc. 7 In football, not in play. —**down and out** Disabled, destitute, or socially outcast. —**down on** Opposed to, as from anger, ill will, or enmity. —*v.t.* 1 To knock, throw, or put down; subdue. 2 To swallow: to *down* a beer. —*prep.* 1 In a descending direction along, upon, or in. 2 From an earlier to a later period in the duration of: —*n.* 1 A downward movement; a descent. 2 A reverse of fortune: the ups and *downs* of life. 3 In football, any of the four consecutive plays during which a team must advance the ball at least ten yards in order to maintain possession of it. [< OE *adūne* < *of dune* from the hill]

down[2] (doun) *n.* 1 The fine, soft feathers of birds. 2 Anything resembling soft fine hair or feathers. [< ON *dūnn*]

down[3] (doun) *n.* 1 A hill having a broad, treeless, grass-grown top. 2 *pl.* Turf-covered, undulating upland. 3 A dune. [< OE *dūn*]

down·cast (doun′kast′, -käst′) *adj.* 1 Directed downward. 2 Low in spirits; dejected; despondent.

down·er (doun′ər) *n. Slang* Any of various drugs that depress the central nervous system, as barbiturates.

down·fall (doun′fôl′) *n.* 1 A sudden, heavy fall of rain or snow. 2 A fall; disgrace. —**down′fall′en** *adj.*

down·grade (doun′grād′) *n.* A descending slope. —**on the downgrade** Declining in health, reputation, status, etc. —*adj. & adv.* DOWNHILL. —*v.t.* **·grad·ed, ·grad·ing** To reduce in status, salary, etc.

down·heart·ed (doun′här′tid) *adj.* Dejected; discouraged. —**down′heart′ed·ly** *adv.*

down·hill (doun′hil′, doun′hil′) *adj.* Descending; sloping. —*adv.* Toward the bottom of a hill. —**go downhill** To decline, as in success, health, etc.

down·play (doun′plā′) *v.t.* To play down; minimize.

down·pour (doun′pôr′, -pōr′) *n.* A heavy fall of rain.

down·right (doun′rīt′) *adj.* 1 Frank; plain; outspoken. 2 Thorough; utter; absolute. —*adv.* In the extreme; utterly.

Down's syndrome (dounz) Congenital mental and physical retardation due to a chromosomal anomaly, accompanied by variable signs including a flat face and pronounced epicanthic folds. [< J. L. H. *Down,* 1828–96, Eng. physician]

down·stairs (doun′stârz′) *adj.* On a lower floor or level. —*n.* The downstairs region of a building. —*adv.* 1 Down the stairs. 2 Toward a lower floor.

down·stream (doun′strēm′) *adj. & adv.* In the direction of the current; down the stream.

down·town (doun′toun′) *adj.* 1 Of or in the part of a city geographically lower than the other parts. 2 Of, in, or characteristic of the business section of a city. —*adv.* To, toward, or in the downtown part of a city. —*n.* The chief business section of a city.

down·trod·den (doun′trod′n) *adj.* 1 Trodden under foot. 2 Oppressed; subjugated. Also **down′trod′.**

down·turn (doun′tûrn′) *n.* A downward turn or decline, as in popularity or in a state's economy.

down·ward (doun′wərd) *adj. & adv.* 1 From a higher to a lower position. 2 From that which is more remote, as in place or time. Also **down′ward·ly, down′wards** *adv.*

down·y (doun′ē) *adj.* **down·i·er, down·i·est** 1 Of, like, or covered with down. 2 Soft; soothing. —**down′i·ness** *n.*

dow·ry (dou′rē) *n. pl.* **·ries** 1 The property a wife brings to her husband in marriage. 2 Any endowment or gift. [< L *dos, dotis*]

dowse[1] (dous) *v. & n.* DOUSE[1].

dowse[2] (douz) *v.i.* **dowsed, dows·ing** To search for water, minerals, etc., with a divining rod. [?] —**dows′er** *n.*

dowsing rod DIVINING ROD.

dox·ol·o·gy (dok·sol′ə·jē) *n. pl.* **·gies** A hymn of praise to God, esp. the one beginning "Praise God, from whom all blessings flow." —**greater doxology** The Gloria in Excelsis. —**lesser doxology** The Gloria Patri. [< Gk. *doxa* praise + *legein* speak]

doz, doz. dozen(s).

doze (dōz) *v.* **dozed, doz·ing** *v.i.* 1 To sleep lightly; nap. —*v.t.* 2 To spend (time) napping. —**doze off** To drift into a light sleep. —*n.* A light, unsound sleep. [< Scand.]

doz·en (duz′ən) *n. pl.* **doz·ens** or **doz·en** 1 A group or set of 12. 2 A large unspecific number: *dozens* of errands. [< L < *duo* two + *decem* ten] —**doz′enth** *adj.*

do·zy (dō′zē) *adj.* **·zi·er, ·zi·est** DROWSY. —**do′zi·ly** *adv.*

DP, D.P. displaced person.

dpt. department; deponent.

Dr. doctor; drive.

dr. debtor; dram(s).

drab[1] (drab) *adj.* 1 Dull; colorless. 2 Dull, yellowish gray. 3 Made of heavy, yellowish gray cloth. —*n.* 1 A yellowish gray color. 2 A heavy cloth so colored. [< OF *drap* cloth] —**drab′ly** *adv.* —**drab′ness** *n.*

drab[2] (drab) *n.* A slattern; a slut. [< Celtic]

drach·ma (drak′mə) *n. pl.* **·mas** or **·mae** (-mē) 1 The modern basic monetary unit of Greece. 2 An ancient Greek silver coin. [< Gk. *drachmē*]

Dra·co·ni·an (drā·kō′nē·ən) *adj.* Severe; merciless. [< *Draco,* 7th-cent. B.C. Athenian, reputed author of an inflexible code of laws] Also **dra·co′ni·an.**

draft (draft, dräft) *n.* 1 A current of air. 2 The act of drinking or inhaling; also, that which is so taken in, as water or air. 3 *Naut.* The depth to which a vessel sinks in the water. 4 The act of drawing a load, etc.; also, that which is drawn. 5 A plan, outline or sketch, as of a piece of writing, work to be done, etc. 6 A written order for money drawn by one person, bank, etc., and payable to another. 7 A device for controlling the airflow in a furnace, stove, etc. 8 A military or naval conscription; also, those so conscripted. 9 A drain or lessening: a *draft* on one's time. —**on draft** Ready to be drawn, as beer, etc., from a cask or the like. —*v.t.* 1 To outline in writing; sketch; delineate. 2 To select and draw off, as for military service; conscript. 3 To draw off or away. —*adj.* 1 Suitable or used for pulling heavy loads: a *draft* animal. 2 Drawn from a cask, as beer. [< OE *dragan* to draw] —**draft′er, draft′i·ness** *n.*

draft·ee (draf·tē′, dräf-) *n.* A person drafted for service in the armed forces.

drafts·man (drafts′mən, dräfts′-) *n. pl.* **·men** (-mən) 1 One who prepares drawings, plans, etc., as in architecture and engineering. 2 One who plans and draws up legal documents, speeches, etc. —**drafts′man·ship** *n.*

draft·y (draf′tē, dräf′-) *adj.* **draft·i·er, draft·i·est** Having or exposed to drafts. —**draft′i·ly** *adv.* —**draft′i·ness** *n.*

drag (drag) *v.* **dragged, drag·ging** *v.t.* 1 To pull along by main force. 2 To sweep or search the bottom of, as with a net; dredge. 3 To catch or recover, as with a net. 4 To pull along heavily and wearily. 5 To harrow (land). 6 To continue tediously: often with *on* or *out.* —*v.i.* 7 To be pulled along the ground. 8 To move heavily or slowly. 9 To pass slowly, as time. 10 To operate a dredge. —*n.* 1 The act of dragging. 2 That which drags or is dragged, as a grapple, a dredge, a dragnet. 3 A heavy four-wheeled carriage. 4 Something that impedes motion, as the brake on a wagon wheel. 5 A slow or difficult movement: to walk with a *drag.* 6 *Slang* Influence; pull. 7 *Slang* A puff of a cigarette. 8 *Slang* A dull, boring person or thing. 9 *Slang* Women's clothing worn by a man. [<OE *dragan*]

drag·gle (drag'əl) *v.* **·gled, ·gling** *v.t.* & *v.i.* To make or become soiled or wet by dragging in mud or over damp ground. [Freq. of DRAG]

drag·net (drag'net') *n.* 1 A net drawn along the bottom of the water or along the ground, for taking fish or small animals. 2 Organized measures for capturing criminals.

drag·o·man (drag'ə·mən) *n. pl.* **·mans** (-mənz) or **·men** (-mən) An interpreter for travelers in the Near East. [<LGk. *dragoumanos* <Ar. *tarjumān* translator]

drag·on (drag'ən) *n.* 1 A mythical, serpentlike, winged monster. 2 A fierce or overbearing person. [<Gk. *drakōn* serpent]

drag·on·fly (drag'ən·flī) *n. pl.* **·flies** Any of various large insects having a long, slender body and four narrow wings.

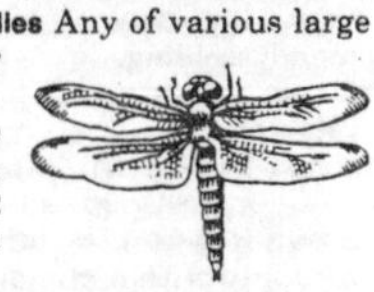

Dragonfly

dra·goon (drə·gōōn') *n.* In some European armies, a cavalryman. —*v.t.* 1 To harass by dragoons. 2 To coerce; browbeat. [<F *dragon* a firearm, dragon]

drag race An automobile race, esp. of hot rods, in which contestants strive for minimum elapsed time over a straight course.

drain (drān) *v.t.* 1 To draw off gradually, as a fluid. 2 To draw water or fluid from: to *drain* a swamp. 3 To empty. 4 To exhaust; use up. —*v.i.* 5 To flow off or leak away gradually. 6 To become empty. —*n.* 1 The act of draining. 2 Continuous strain, leak, or outflow. 3 A pipe, trench, tube, etc., for draining. [<OE *drēahnian* strain out] —**drain'er** *n.*

drain·age (drā'nij) *n.* 1 The act of draining. 2 A system of drains. 3 That which is drained off. 4 The area drained.

drain·pipe (drān'pīp') *n.* Pipe used for draining.

drake (drāk) *n.* A male duck. [ME]

dram (dram) *n.* 1 A unit of apothecaries' weight equal to one eighth of an ounce. Also **fluid dram.** 2 A unit of avoirdupois weight equal to one sixteenth of an ounce. 3 A drink of alcoholic liquor. 4 A small portion; a bit. [<L <Gk. *drachmē*]

dra·ma (drä'mə, dram'ə) *n.* 1 A literary composition to be performed upon the stage; a play. 2 The art or profession of writing, acting, or producing plays: often with *the.* 3 A series of striking actions or events like those in a play. [Gk., a deed, an action]

dra·mat·ic (drə·mat'ik) *adj.* 1 Of, connected with, or like the drama. 2 Vivid, intense, etc. —**dra·mat'i·cal·ly** *adv.*

dra·mat·ics (drə·mat'iks) *n.pl.* 1 A dramatic performance, esp. by amateurs. 2 *(construed as sing. or pl.)* The art of staging or acting plays.

dram·a·tis per·so·nae (dram'ə·tis pər·sō'nē) *Latin* The characters of a play.

dram·a·tist (dram'ə·tist) *n.* One who writes plays.

dra·ma·ti·za·tion (dram'ət·ə·za'shən, dräm-) *n.* 1 The act of dramatizing. 2 A dramatized version (of a novel). 3 A dramatized re-creation of an actual event.

dram·a·tize (dram'ə·tīz) *v.t.* **·tized, ·tiz·ing** 1 To convert for stage use. 2 To tell, represent, or interpret (events, one's personality, etc.) in a theatrical manner. *Brit. sp.* **·tise.** —**dram'a·ti·za'tion** (-ə·tə·zā'shən) *n.*

dram·a·tur·gy (dram'ə·tûr'jē) *n.* The art of making or producing dramas. [<G <Gk. <*drama* + *ergein* work] —**dram'a·tur'gic** or **·i·cal** *adj.* —**dram'a·turge** (-tûrj), **dram'a·tur'gist** *n.*

drank (drangk) *p.t.* of DRINK.

drape (drāp) *v.* **draped, drap·ing** *v.t.* 1 To cover or adorn in a graceful fashion, as with drapery or clothing. 2 To arrange in graceful folds. —*v.i.* 3 To hang in folds. —*n.* 1 *Usu. pl.* Drapery; curtain. 2 The way in which cloth hangs, as in clothing. [<OF *draper* to weave <*drap* cloth]

drap·er·y (drā'pər·ē) *n. pl.* **·er·ies** 1 Decorative fabric hung in loose folds, usu. in an artistic arrangement. 2 *pl.* Curtains.

dras·tic (dras'tik) *adj.* 1 Acting vigorously. 2 Extreme; severe. [<Gk. *drastikos* effective] —**dras'ti·cal·ly** *adv.*

drat(drat') *interj.* DAMN (interj.), a mild oath.

draught (draft, dräft) *n., v., & adj. Chiefly Brit.* DRAFT.

draughts (drafts, dräfts) *n.pl. Brit.* CHECKERS.

draughts·man (drafts'mən, dräfts'-) *n. pl.* **·men** (-mən) DRAFTSMAN. —**draughts'man·ship** *n.*

draw (drô) *v.* **drew, drawn, draw·ing** *v.t.* 1 To cause to move to or with the mover; pull; haul. 2 To acquire or obtain: to *draw* water. 3 To cause to flow forth: to *draw* blood. 4 To induce: to *draw* praise. 5 To take off, on, or out, as gloves or a sword. 6 To earn, as a salary or interest. 7 To remove, as money from a bank. 8 To deduce; formulate: to *draw* a conclusion. 9 To attract; allure. 10 To close, as curtains, a bag, etc. 11 To elicit; bring out, as truth. 12 To stretch out tightly; also, to manufacture by stretching or hammering, as wire. 13 DISEMBOWEL: to *draw* a chicken. 14 To take in; inhale, as breath. 15 To drain of contents, as a pond. 16 To win or obtain, as by chance. 17 *Naut.* To require (a specified depth) to float: said of vessels. 18 To depict or sketch; delineate, as with lines or words. 19 To write out as a check or deed: often with *up.* 20 To leave undecided, as a game or contest. —*v.i.* 21 To exert a pulling force. 22 To come or go: to *draw* near. 23 To exercise an attracting influence. 24 To pull out a weapon. 25 To shrink; become contracted, as a wound. 26 To cause pus or blood to gather in one spot, as a poultice. 27 To obtain money, supplies, etc., from some source. 28 To produce a current of air: The fire *draws* well. 29 To end a contest without decision; tie. 30 *Naut.* To fill or swell out with wind. 31 To sketch; delineate: he *draws* well. 32 To steep, as tea. —**draw down** To reduce or deplete by using; expend. —**draw on** 1 To rely upon: He *drew on* his reputation. 2 To lure or entice. 3 To approach its end. —**draw out** 1 To protract; prolong. 2 To cause (someone) to give information or express opinions. —**draw the line** To fix the limit. —**draw up** 1 To put in required legal form, as a will. 2 To bring or come to a halt. 3 To straighten (oneself); stiffen, as in anger. —*n.* 1 An act of drawing or state of being drawn; also, that which is drawn. 2 A tie game. 3 Anything that draws or attracts. 4 A drawn chance or ticket. [<OE *dragan*]

draw·back (drô'bak') *n.* 1 Anything that checks or hinders progress, success, etc. 2 REBATE.

draw·bridge (drô'brij') *n.* A bridge that can be raised, let down, or drawn aside.

Drawbridge

draw·ee (drô'ē') *n.* One on whom an order for the payment of money is drawn.

draw·er (drô'ər) *n.* 1 One who draws. 2 One who draws a bill of exchange, money order, etc. 3 (drôr) A sliding receptacle, as in a bureau, table, etc.

draw·ers (drôrz) *n. pl.* A trouserlike undergarment.

draw·ing (drô′ing) *n.* 1 The act of one who or that which draws. 2 A picture, sketch, delineation, or design. 3 The art of representing objects by lines. 4 A lottery.

draw·ing-card (drô′ing·kärd′) *n.* Any feature that attracts a crowd.

draw·ing-room (drô′ing·ro͞om′, -ro͝om′) *n.* 1 A room for reception of company. 2 The company assembled in such a room. 3 A small private room in a sleeping car on a train. [< WITHDRAWING ROOM]

draw·knife (drô′nīf′) *n. pl.* **·knives** (-nīvz′) A knife with a handle at each end, used for shaving off wood surfaces. Also **draw′ing knife.**

drawl (drôl) *v.t. & v.i.* To speak or pronounce slowly, esp. vowels. —*n.* The act of drawling. [?] **—drawl′er** *n.* **—drawl′·ing·ly** *adv.* **—drawl′y** *adj.*

drawn (drôn) *adj.* 1 Tied or undecided, as a game. 2 Eviscerated: a *drawn* fowl. 3 Haggard; showing strain: His face looked *drawn.*

drawn butter Butter melted and prepared as a sauce.

drawn work Ornamental openwork made by pulling out threads of fabric and embroidering or hemstitching the edges of the openings.

draw·string (drô′string′) *n.* A string or cord run through a hem, which pulls together or closes an opening.

dray (drā) *n.* A low, heavy vehicle for carrying heavy articles. —*v.t.* To transport by means of a dray. [< OE *dræge* dragnet]

dray·age (drā′ij) *n.* 1 The act of conveying in a dray. 2 The charge for draying.

dray·man (drā′mən) *n. pl.* **·men** (-mən) A man who drives a dray.

dread (dred) *v.t. & v.i.* To anticipate with great fear or anxiety. —*adj.* 1 Causing great fear; terrible. 2 Exciting awe. —*n.* 1 Unconquerable fright or terror. 2 Fear joined to awe. [< OE *drædan* to fear]

dread·ful (dred′fəl) *adj.* 1 Inspiring dread or awe; terrible. 2 *Informal* Disagreeable; very bad; revolting. **—dread′·ful·ly** *adv.* **—dread′ful·ness** *n.*

dread·nought (dred′nôt′) *n.* Any battleship of great size. Also **dread′naught′.**

dream (drēm) *n.* 1 A train of thoughts or images passing through the mind in sleep. 2 A mental condition similar to that of one sleeping; daydreaming. 3 A visionary idea or fancy. 4 Something so beautiful, pleasant, etc., as to seem possible only in a dream. —*v.* **dreamed** or **dreamt** (dremt), **dream·ing** *v.t.* 1 To see or imagine in a dream. 2 To imagine as in a dream. 3 To while away, as in idle reverie. —*v.i.* 4 To have a dream or dreams. 5 To have a vague idea or conception of something. **—dream up** *Informal.* To concoct or create. [< OE *drēam*] **—dream′er** *n.* **—dream′ful** *adj.* **—dream′ful·ly** *adv.* **—Syn.** *n.* 2 fancy, fantasy, reverie. *v.* 2 muse, meditate, reflect.

dream·y (drē′mē) *adj.* **dream·i·er, dream·i·est** 1 Given to dreams. 2 Appropriate to dreams; shadowy. 3 Soothing; soft: *dreamy* music. 4 Filled with dreams; visionary. — **dream′i·ly** *adv.* **—dream′i·ness** *n.*

drear (drir) *adj.* DREARY.

drear·y (drir′ē) *adj.* **drear·i·er, drear·i·est** 1 Gloomy; sad; dismal. 2 Monotonous; lifeless; dull. [< OE *drēorig* sad, bloody] **—drear′i·ly** *adv.* **—drear′i·ness** *n.* **—drear′i·some** *adj.*

dredge[1] (drej) *n.* A device for bringing up mud, silt, etc., from under water. —*v.* **dredged, dredg·ing** *v.t.* 1 To clear or widen by means of a dredge. 2 To remove, catch, or gather by a dredge. —*v.i.* 3 To use a dredge. [?] **—dredg′er** *n.*

dredge[2] (drej) *v.t.* 1 To sprinkle or dust with flour before cooking. 2 To sift; sprinkle. [?]

dreg·gy (dreg′ē) *adj.* **·gi·er, ·gi·est** Containing dregs; full of dregs; foul. **—dreg′gi·ness** *n.* **—dreg′gish** *adj.*

dregs (dregz) *n. pl.* 1 The sediment of liquids. 2 The worthless or coarse part: the *dregs* of society.

drench (drench) *v.t.* 1 To wet thoroughly; soak. 2 In veterinary science, to force (an animal) to swallow, as medicine. —*n.* 1 A liquid medicine, administered to an animal. 2 A water solution for soaking. 3 The act of drenching. [< OE *drencan* cause to drink] **—drench′er** *n.*

dress (dres) *v.t.* 1 To clothe; supply with clothing. 2 To trim or decorate; adorn. 3 To treat medicinally, as a wound. 4 To comb and arrange (hair). 5 To prepare (stone, timber, leather, etc.) for use or sale. 6 To clean (fowl, game, fish, etc.) for cooking. 7 To till, trim, or prune. 8 To put in proper alignment, as troops. 9 *Informal* To scold: usu. with *down.* —*v.i.* 10 To put on or wear clothing, esp. formal clothing. 11 To come into proper alignment. — **dress up** To put on or wear clothing more elaborate than that usually worn. —*n.* 1 Clothes; apparel. 2 A gown or frock of a woman or child. 3 Formal attire. 4 External appearance; guise. —*adj.* 1 Of, pertaining to, or suitable for making dresses: *dress* goods. 2 To be worn on formal occasions: a *dress* suit. [< OF *dresser* arrange]

dress circle Seats in a theater or concert hall, usu. the first gallery behind and above the orchestra, originally reserved for patrons in evening dress.

dress·er[1] (dres′ər) *n.* 1 One who dresses something, as shop windows, leather, etc. 2 One who assists another to dress. 3 One who dresses well: a fancy *dresser.*

dress·er[2] (dres′ər) *n.* 1 A chest of drawers for clothing supporting a swinging mirror. 2 A cupboard for dishes. [OF *dresseur* < *dresser* to dress]

dress goods Fabrics for dresses.

dress·ing (dres′ing) *n.* 1 The act of one who dresses. 2 That with which anything, as a wound, is dressed. 3 A seasoned sauce served with salads and vegetables. 4 A seasoned stuffing of bread, rice, etc., for fowl or meats.

dress·ing-down (dres′ing·doun′) *n. Informal* A reprimand; scolding.

dressing gown A loose gown worn while dressing or relaxing.

dress·ing-room (dres′ing·ro͞om′, -ro͝om′) *n.* A room used for dressing, as in a theater.

dress·ing-ta·ble (dres′ing·tā′bəl) *n.* A small table equipped with a mirror; a vanity.

dress·mak·er (dres′mā′kər) *n.* One who makes women's dresses, etc. —*adj.* Not severely tailored, but having soft, feminine lines. **—dress′ma′king** *adj., n.*

dress parade A formal military parade.

dress rehearsal The last rehearsal of a play before the public performance, in full costume.

dress suit A man's formal evening suit.

dress·y (dres′ē) *adj.* **dress·i·er, dress·i·est** *Informal* 1 Fond of dress. 2 Showy; elegant. **—dress′i·ness** *n.*

drew (dro͞o) *p.t.* of DRAW.

drib·ble (drib′əl) *v.t. & v.i.* **·bled, ·bling** 1 To fall or let fall in drops; drip. 2 To drool; slobber. 3 In certain games, to propel (the ball) by bouncing or kicking. —*n.* 1 A dripping or trickle of liquid. 2 In basketball and soccer, the act of dribbling. [Freq. of earlier *drib* < DRIP] **—drib′bler** *n.*

drib·let (drib′lit) *n.* A small amount. Also **drib′blet.**

dried (drīd) *p.t. & p.p.* of DRY.

dri·er[1] (drī′ər) *n.* 1 One who or that which dries. 2 An additive for paints, etc., used to speed drying. 3 A mechanical device for drying.

dri·er[2] (drī′ər) Comparative of DRY.

dri·est (drī′ist) Superlative of DRY.

drift (drift) *n.* 1 That which is carried onward by a current: a *drift* of clouds. 2 A heap of any matter piled up by wind or sea. 3 A tendency, trend, or meaning: the *drift* of a discourse. 4 A number of objects moving onward by one force, as logs in a river. 5 The distance a ship or airplane is driven from its course by wind, etc. 6 An ocean current. 7 *Geol.* Material transported by moving masses of ice or by running water. 8 *Mining* A horizontal passage in a mine. —*v.t.* 1 To carry along, as on a current. 2 To cause to pile up in heaps, as snow, or sand. —*v.i.* 3 To float or be carried along, as by a current. 4 To wander aimlessly. 5 To accumulate in heaps. [< OE *drīfan* to drive]

drift·age (drif′tij) *n.* 1 The act of drifting. 2 Anything that has drifted. 3 Deviation due to drifting.

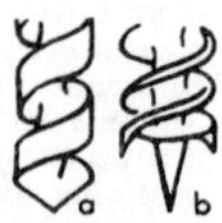

Drills
a. metal.
b. wood.

drift·er (drif′tər) *n. Informal* A person having no settled home or occupation.

drift·wood (drift′wo͝od′) *n.* Wood floated or drifted by water, esp. by the sea.

drill[1] (dril) *n.* 1 A tool for boring metal or other hard substance. 2 The art or action of training in military exercises. 3 Thorough and regular exercises in any branch of knowledge, activity, or industry. 4 A snail that feeds on oysters through holes it drills in their shells. —*v.t.* **1** To bore a hole in. **2** To bore (a hole). **3** To train or teach by methodical exercises. —*v.i.* **4** To use a drill. **5** To engage in an exercise or exercises. [Du. *dril* < *drillen* to bore] — **drill′er** *n.*

drill[2] (dril) *n.* **1** A machine for planting seeds in rows. **2** A small furrow in which seeds are sown. **3** A row of seeds so planted. —*v.t.* To plant in rows. [?]

drill[3] (dril) *n.* Heavy, twilled linen or cotton cloth. Also **drill′·ing.** [< G *Drilich* cloth with three threads]

drill·mas·ter (dril′mas′tər, -mäs′tər) *n.* A trainer in military or other exercises.

drill press An upright drilling machine.

dri·ly (drī′lē) *adv.* DRYLY.

drink (dringk) *v.* **drank** (*Archaic* **drunk**), **drunk** (*Archaic* **drunk·en**), **drink·ing** *v.t.* **1** To swallow, as water. **2** To absorb (a liquid or moisture). **3** To take in eagerly through the senses or the mind: with *in.* **4** To make a toast. **5** To swallow the contents of. —*v.i.* **6** To swallow a liquid. **7** To consume alcoholic liquors, esp. to excess. **8** To drink a toast: with *to.* —*n.* **1** Any beverage. **2** Alcoholic liquor. **3** The practice of drinking to excess. [< OE *drincan*] —**drink′a·ble** *adj.* —**drink′er** *n.*

drip (drip) *n.* **1** A falling in drops. **2** That which drips. **3** *Slang* A person regarded as socially inept. —*v.t.* & *v.i.* **dripped, drip·ping** To fall or let fall in drops. [< OE *dryppan* to drip]

drip-dry (drip′drī′) *v.i.* **-dried, -dry·ing** To dry after being hung while dripping wet, as fabrics requiring little or no ironing. —*adj.* Designed to be drip-dried, as a fabric or garment.

drip·ping (drip′ing) *n.* **1** That which falls in drops. **2** *Usu. pl.* Fat exuded from meat in cooking. **3** The act of falling in drops.

drive (drīv) *v.* **drove, driv·en, driv·ing** *v.t.* **1** To propel onward or forward. **2** To force to act or work. **3** To bring to a state or condition. **4** To cause to penetrate: often with *in:* to *drive* in a nail. **5** To form by penetrating or passing through: to *drive* a well. **6** To control the movements of: to *drive* an automobile. **7** To transport in a vehicle. **8** To carry on or complete (trade, a bargain, etc.) with energy. **9** In sports, to strike and propel (a ball) with force. **10** *Mech.* To provide power for. —*v.i.* **11** To move forward rapidly or with force. **12** To operate or travel in a vehicle. **13** To have an object or intention: with *at:* What are you *driving* at? **14** To aim a blow: with *at.* —**let drive at** To aim or discharge a blow, missile, etc. —*n.* **1** The act of driving. **2** A road for driving. **3** A journey in a vehicle. **4** A basic need, longing, or pressure. **5** Energy; vitality. **6** A hunt or round-up, as of cattle. **7** An organized campaign to achieve a certain goal. **8** A hard, swift stroke or thrust. **9** *Mech.* A system for transmitting mechanical power. **10** A mass of floating logs. [< OE *drīfan*] —**Syn.** *v.* **1** impel, push, press, thrust.

drive-in (drīv′in′) *n.* A restaurant, motion-picture theater, etc., serving patrons in their automobiles. —*adj.* So constructed as to be a drive-in.

driv·el (driv′əl) *v.* **driv·eled** or **driv·elled, driv·el·ing** or **driv·el·ling** *v.i.* **1** To let saliva flow from the mouth; slobber. **2** To flow like saliva. **3** To talk in a foolish manner. —*v.t.* **4** To let flow from the mouth. **5** To say in a foolish manner. —*n.* **1** A flow of saliva from the mouth. **2** Senseless talk. [< OE *dreflian*] —**driv′el·er** or **driv′el·ler** *n.*

driv·en (driv′ən) *p.p.* of DRIVE.

driv·er (drī′vər) *n.* **1** One who or that which drives, as the operator of any vehicle. **2** Any of various machine parts which transmit motion. **3** A wooden-headed golf club for driving from the tee. • See GOLF. **4** A demanding boss or overseer.

drive·way (drīv′wā′) *n.* A private road providing access to a building or house.

driz·zle (driz′əl) *v.t.* & *v.i.* **·zled, ·zling** To rain in fine drops. —*n.* A light rain. [?] —**driz′zly** *adj.*

drogue (drōg) *n.* A parachute or similar device used to slow or stabilize an aircraft or spacecraft. [? Related to DRAG]

droll (drōl) *adj.* Odd in a humorous or quaint way. —*n.* A droll person. [MF *drôle* jester] —**drol′ly** *adv.*

droll·er·y (drō′lər·ē) *n. pl.* **·er·ies** **1** Comical speech or manners. **2** The quality of being droll. **3** A facetious or amusing story.

-drome *combining form* Racecourse: *hippodrome.* [< Gk. *dromos* a running]

drom·e·dar·y (drom′ə·der′ē) *n. pl.* **·dar·ies** The one-humped Arabian camel trained for riding. [< LL < Gk. *dromas, dromad-* a dromedary, a running]

Dromedary

drone[1] (drōn) *v.* **droned, dron·ing** *v.i.* **1** To make a dull, humming sound; hum. **2** To speak in a slow, dull tone. —*v.t.* **3** To say in a slow, dull tone. —*n.* **1** A dull, humming sound, as of a bee. **2** One of the pipes of the bagpipe that plays a single tone. **3** BAGPIPE. [< ME *drone* a male bee]

drone[2] (drōn) *n.* **1** A stingless male bee that gathers no honey. **2** A loafer; idler. —*v.i.* **droned, dron·ing** To live in idleness. [< OE *drān*]

drool (dro͞ol) *v.t.* & *v.i.* **1** To drivel; slaver. **2** To speak foolishly. —*n.* **1** SPITTLE. **2** *Informal* Foolish talk. [Alter. of DRIVEL]

droop (dro͞op) *v.i.* **1** To sink down. **2** To lose vigor or vitality. **3** To become dejected. —*v.t.* **4** To allow to hang or sink down. —*n.* A hanging down. [< ON *drūpa*] —**droop′ing** *adj.* —**droop′ing·ly** *adv.*

droop·y (dro͞o′pē) *adj.* **droop·i·er, droop·i·est** Tending to droop. —**droop′i·ness** *n.*

drop (drop) *n.* **1** A globule of liquid. **2** A very small quantity of anything, as of a liquid. **3** Anything that resembles a drop of liquid. **4** A fall, or the distance fallen. **5** A sudden change of level. **6** Any of various contrivances that drop or hang, as a drop curtain in a theater. **7** A trap door. **8** *pl.* Any liquid medicine given by the drop. **9** A slot for letters. **10** A fall in prices. —*v.* **dropped, drop·ping** *v.t.* **1** To let fall in drops. **2** To let fall in any way. **3** To give birth to: said of animals. **4** To say in a casual way. **5** To write (a note, etc.) **6** To bring down or cause to fall. **7** To stop, have done with, or give up. **8** To leave at a specific place. **9** To omit (a syllable, letter, or word). **10** *Slang* To lose (money), as in gambling. **11** To discharge or dismiss. —*v.i.* **12** To fall in drops. **13** To fall rapidly; come down. **14** To fall down exhausted, injured, or dead. **15** To crouch, as a hunting dog at sight of game. **16** To come to an end; cease; stop. **17** To fall into some state or condition. **18** To fall behind: often with *behind* or *back.* —**drop in** To pay an unexpected call. —**drop out** To leave; withdraw from. [< OE *dropa*]

drop curtain A theater curtain lowered in front of the stage between the acts.

drop·forge (drop′fôrj′) *v.t.* **·forged, ·forg·ing** To forge (metal) between dies by using a drop hammer.

drop hammer A machine for forging, stamping, etc., in which a heavy weight sliding between vertical guides strikes the metal.

drop·kick (drop′kik′) *n.* In football, a kick given the ball just as it is rebounding after being dropped.

drop-kick (drop′kik′) *v.t.* & *v.i.* To kick (a football) in the manner of a dropkick.

drop·let (drop′lit) *n.* A little drop.

drop·out (drop′out′) *n.* **1** A student who leaves school or college before graduation. **2** One who abandons any undertaking before completing it.

drop·per (drop′ər) *n.* **1** One who or that which drops. **2** A glass tube with a suction bulb at one end for dispensing a liquid in drops.

drop·ping (drop′ing) *n.* **1** The act of falling or letting fall in drops. **2** *pl.* Animal dung.

drop·si·cal (drop′si·kəl) *adj.* Of or afflicted by dropsy.

drop·sy (drop′sē) *n.* An abnormal accumulation of watery fluid in body tissues or cavities. [ME *dropesie,* ult. < Gk. *hydōr* water] —**drop·si·cal** (drop′si·kəl), **drop′sied** *adj.*

drosh·ky (drosh′kē, drôsh′kē) *n. pl.* **·kies** A light, open, four-wheeled Russian carriage. Also **dros′ky.** [< Russ. *drozhki*]

dro·soph·i·la (drō·sof′ə·lə, drə-) *n. pl.* **·lae** (-lē) Any of a genus of fruit flies, used for research in genetics. [< Gk. *drosos* dew + *phileein* to love]

dross (drôs, dros) *n.* **1** Refuse or impurity in melted metal. **2** Waste matter; refuse. [< OE *drōs*] **—dross′i·ness** *n.* **—dross′y** *adj.* **—Syn. 2** debris, junk, remains, rubbish.

drought (drout) *n.* Long-continued dry weather; want of rain. Also **drouth** (drouth). [< OE *drūgoth*] **—drought′y** *adj.*

drove[1] (drōv) *p.t.* of DRIVE.

drove[2] (drōv) *n.* **1** A number of animals driven or herded for driving. **2** A moving crowd of human beings. *—v.t.* **·droved, drov·ing** To drive (cattle, etc.) for some distance. [< OE *drāf*] **—drov′er** *n.*

drown (droun) *v.t.* **1** To kill by suffocation in water or other liquid. **2** To flood; deluge. **3** To overwhelm; overpower; extinguish. *—v.i.* **4** To die by suffocation in water or other liquid. [< Scand.]

drowse (drouz) *v.* **drowsed, drows·ing** *v.i.* **1** To be sleepy; doze. *—v.t.* **2** To make sleepy. **3** To pass (time) in drowsing. *—n.* The state of being half asleep. [< OE *drūsian* become sluggish]

drow·sy (drou′zē) *adj.* **·si·er, ·si·est 1** Almost asleep; sleepy. **2** Lulling; soporific: *drowsy* music. **—drow′si·ly** *adv.* **—drow′si·ness** *n.*

drub (drub) *v.t.* **drubbed, drub·bing 1** To beat, as with a stick. **2** To vanquish; overcome. *—n.* A blow; thump. [< Ar. *darb* a beating] **—drub′ber** *n.*

drub·bing (drub′ing) *n.* A thorough beating or one-sided defeat.

drudge (druj) *v.i.* **drudged, drudg·ing** To toil; work hard at menial tasks. *—n.* One who toils at menial tasks. [ME *druggen*]

drudg·er·y (druj′ər·ē) *n. pl.* **·er·ies** Dull, wearisome, or menial work.

drug (drug) *n.* **1** Any substance used in or as a medicine. **2** Any narcotic. **3** An overabundant commodity: a *drug* on the market. *—v.t.* **drugged, drug·ging 1** To mix drugs with (food, drink, etc.). **2** To administer drugs to. **3** To stupefy or poison with or as with drugs. [< MF *drogue*]

drug addict One addicted to a habit-forming drug.

drug·gist (drug′ist) *n.* One who compounds prescriptions and sells drugs; a pharmacist.

drug·store (drug′stôr′, -stōr′) *n.* A place where prescriptions are compounded, and drugs and miscellaneous merchandise are sold.

dru·id (drōō′id) *n.* One of an order of priests in ancient Gaul, Britain, and Ireland. [< L *druidae, druides* < Celtic] **—dru·id′ic, dru·id′i·cal** *adj.* **—dru′id·ism** *n.*

drum (drum) *n.* **1** A percussion instrument consisting of a hollow, usu. cylindrical object with skin or vellum stretched over each end, played by beating with drumsticks or the hands. **2** The sound produced by beating this instrument. **3** Anything resembling a drum in shape, as a cylindrical receptacle. **4** Any mechanical device shaped like a drum. **5** TYMPANIC MEMBRANE *—v.* **drummed, drum·ming** *v.t.* **1** To perform on or as on a drum. **2** To expel in disgrace: usu. with *out.* **3** To summon by beating a drum. **4** To force upon the attention by constant repetition. *—v.i.* **5** To beat a drum. **6** To beat on anything continuously. **—drum up** To seek: to *drum up* trade. [Prob. < MDu. *tromme*]

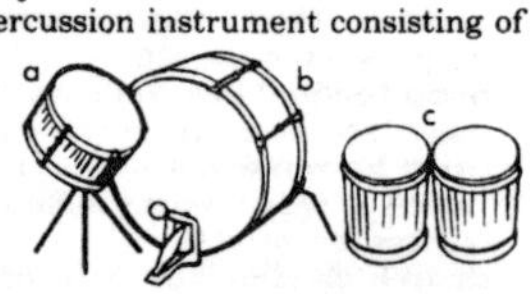

Drums
a. snare. b. bass. c. bongo.

drum·beat (drum′bēt′) *n.* The sound of a drum; also, the action of beating a drum.

drum·head (drum′hed′) *n.* **1** The membrane stretched over the end of a drum. **2** *Naut.* The top of a capstan.

drum ma·jor·ette (mā′jə·ret′) A woman who leads or precedes a marching band or accompanies such a band while twirling a baton. **—drum major** *Masc.*

drum·mer (drum′ər) *n.* **1** One who plays a drum. **2** *Informal* A traveling salesman.

drum·stick (drum′stik′) *n.* **1** A stick for beating a drum. **2** The lower segment of the leg of a cooked fowl.

drunk (drungk) *p.p.* of DRINK; former *p.t.*. *—adj.* **1** Being in a state of altered consciousness by the effect of alcoholic liquor, in which motor ability, mental acuity, and judgment are impaired; intoxicated. **2** Saturated; glutted: *drunk* with victory. **3** DRUNKEN (def. 3). *—n. Informal* **1** A drunk person. **2** A fit of drunkenness.

drunk·ard (drungk′ərd) *n.* One who habitually drinks to intoxication; a sot.

drunk·en (drungk′ən) *adj.* **1** DRUNK (def. 1). **2** Habitually drunk. **3** Resulting from or characterized by excessive drinking. **4** Occurring while intoxicated: *drunken* driving. **—drunk′en·ly** *adv.* **—drunk′en·ness** *n.*

drupe (drōōp) *n.* A soft, fleshy fruit enclosing a stone or seed, as the peach or cherry. [< Gk. *druppa* overripe olive] **—dru·pa·ceous** (drōō·pā′shəs) *adj.*

drupe·let (drōōp′lit) *n.* A little drupe, as the individual parts of a raspberry.

dry (drī) *adj.* **dri·er, dri·est 1** Lacking moisture; not wet or damp. **2** Not covered by water: *dry* land. **3** Not green, as wood. **4** Having little or no rain: the *dry* season. **5** Lacking lubrication, as bearings. **6** Thirsty. **7** Lacking interest; lifeless; dull. **8** Slyly shrewd, as wit. **9** Free from sweetness: said of wines. **10** Subject to or in favor of a prohibitory liquor law: a *dry* town. **11** Not giving milk: a *dry* cow. **12** Not liquid; solid: said of merchandise, etc. **13** Tearless: said of the eyes. **14** Characterized by absence of bloodshed. **15** Without butter: said of toast. **16** Wanting in cordiality; not genial. *—v.t. & v.i.* **dried, dry·ing** To make or become dry. **—dry up 1** To cease or cause to cease flowing. **2** *Informal* To stop talking. *—n. pl.* **dries** The state or condition of being dry. [< OE *dryge*] **dry′a·ble** *adj.* **—dry′ly, dri′ly** *adv.* **—dry′ness** *n.*

dry·ad (drī′əd, -ad) *Gk. Myth.* WOOD NYMPH. [< Gk. < *drys, dryos* an oak tree] **—dry·ad′ic** (drī·ad′ik) *adj.*

dry battery Two or more dry cells connected together.

dry cell A sealed primary electric cell with a moist paste as its electrolyte.

dry·clean (drī′klēn′) *v.t.* To clean (clothing, etc.) with solvents other than water, such as carbon tetrachloride, etc. **—dry′clean′er, dry′clean′ing** *n.*

dry·dock (drī′dok′) *n.* A dock constructed so that the water can be pumped out when building or repairing ships. *—v.t. & v.i.* To put in or go into drydock.

dry·er (drī′ər) *n.* DRIER[1] (def. 3).

dry-eyed (drī′īd′) *adj.* Not weeping.

dry farming In an arid country, the raising of crops without irrigation, mainly by reducing evaporation and by raising drought-resisting crops. **—dry farmer**

dry goods Textile fabrics, as distinguished from groceries, hardware, etc.

Dry Ice Solid carbon dioxide, used as a refrigerant: a trade name.

dry measure A system of units for measuring the volume of dry commodities, as fruits, grain, etc.

dry nurse A nurse who cares for an infant without suckling it. **—dry′-nurse′** *v.* **(-nursed, -nurs·ing)**

dry·point (drī′point′) *n.* **1** An etching needle used to cut lines in copperplate without the use of acid. **2** A work thus engraved or the method thus used.

dry rot 1 A fungous disease causing timber to crumble into powder. **2** A disease of vegetables, fruits, etc.

dry run 1 *Mil.* Practice in aiming and firing weapons without using live ammunition. **2** Any rehearsal or practice exercise.

d.t. delirium tremens: also **d.t.'s**; double-time.

Du. Dutch.

du·al (d[y]ōō′əl) *adj.* **1** Of or pertaining to two. **2** Composed of two. [< L *duo* two] **—du·al·i·ty** (d[y]ōō·al′ə·tē) *n.* **—du′al·ly** *adv.*

du·al·ism (d[y]ōō′əl·iz′əm) **1** The state of being dual. **2** Any of various theories which assert that there are two fundamental elements or principles in the nature of man, reality, the universe, etc., as the principles of good and evil or mind and matter. **—du′al·ist** *n.* **—du′al·is′tic** *adj.* **—du′al·is′ti·cal·ly** *adv.*

dub[1] (dub) *v.t.* **dubbed, dub·bing 1** To confer knighthood upon by tapping on the shoulder with a sword. **2** To call or honor by a title, description, epithet, etc. [< OE *dubbian*] **—Syn. 2** name, nickname, term, style.

dub[2] (dub) *Slang n.* A clumsy, second-rate player in any game. *—v.t.* **dubbed, dub·bing** To bungle (a golf stroke, etc.). [?]

dub[3] ((dub) *v.t.* **dubbed, dub·bing** To insert or blend (dialogue, music, etc.) into the sound track of a film, or into a radio or television broadcast. *—n.* That which is so inserted. [Short for DOUBLE] **—dub′bing** *n.*

du·bi·e·ty (dʸōō·bī′ə·tē) *n. pl.* **·ties 1** The quality of being doubtful. **2** Something doubtful. [< L *dubius* doubtful]

du·bi·ous (dʸōō′bē·əs) *adj.* **1** In a state of doubt; doubtful. **2** Causing doubt. **3** Of uncertain result. **4** Questionable; suspect: a *dubious* person. [< L *dubium* doubt] **—du′bi·ous·ly** *adv.* **—du′bi·ous·ness** *n.*

du·cal (dʸōō′kəl) *adj.* Of or pertaining to a duke or a duchy. [< LL *ducalis* of a leader] **—du′cal·ly** *adv.*

duc·at (duk′ət) *n.* **1** One of several European coins. **2** *Slang* A ticket. [< LL *ducatus,* orig., a duchy]

du·ce (dōō′chā) *n. Ital.* A leader; commander. **—il Duce** The title assumed by Benito Mussolini as leader of the Italian Fascists.

duch·ess (duch′is) *n.* **1** The wife or widow of a duke. **2** The female sovereign of a duchy. [< LL *ducissa*]

duch·y (duch′ē) *n. pl.* **duch·ies** The territory or dominion of a duke or duchess; a dukedom. [< LL *ducatus*]

duck[1] (duk) *n.* **1** A web-footed, short-legged, broad-billed water bird. **2** The female of this bird. **3** The flesh of this bird. **4** *Informal* A dear; darling. **5** *Slang* A person; a fellow. [< OE *dūce,* lit. diver]

Mallard duck

duck[2] (duk) *v.t. & v.i.* **1** To plunge briefly under water. **2** To lower quickly, as the head. **3** To dodge; evade (a blow or punishment). **4** To avoid (a duty, person, etc.). *—n.* The act of ducking. [ME *duken* to dive, ult. < Gmc.]

duck[3] (duk) *n.* **1** A strong, tightly woven fabric, as of linen or cotton. **2** *pl.* Trousers made of this fabric. [Du. *doek* cloth]

duck·bill (duk′bil′) *n.* PLATYPUS.

duck·pin (duk′pin′) *n.* A pin 9 inches high and 3½ inches in diameter at the body, used in **duckpins,** a game of tenpins.

duck·weed (duk′wēd′) *n.* Any of several small, floating aquatic plants common in streams and ponds.

duck·y (duk′ē) *adj. Slang* Delightful; darling.

duct (dukt) *n.* **1** Any tube or passage by which a fluid is conveyed. **2** *Anat.* A tubular passage for fluid: the bile *duct.* **3** *Electr.* A tubular channel for carrying wires or cables. [L *ductus* a leading < *ducere* to lead]

duc·tile (duk′til, -tīl′) *adj.* **1** Capable of being hammered thin or drawn out, as certain metals. **2** Easily led; tractable. [< L *ducere* lead] **—duc·til′i·ty, duc′tile·ness** *n.*

duct·less gland (dukt′lis) Any of several hormone-producing glands whose secretions are released directly into the blood or lymph.

dud (dud) *n.* **1** A shell or bomb that fails to explode. **2** *Informal* Any person or thing that fails. [Du. *dood* dead]

dude (dʸōōd) *n.* **1** A fop; dandy. **2** In the W U.S., a city person, esp. one from the E U.S. who is vacationing on a ranch. **3** *Slang* A man; fellow. [?] **—dud′ish** *adj.*

dude ranch A ranch operated for tourists.

dudg·eon (duj′ən) *n.* Sullen displeasure. [?]

duds (dudz) *n.pl. Informal* **1** Clothing. **2** Belongings in general. [ME *dudde* a cloak]

due (dʸōō) *adj.* **1** Owing and demandable; payable. **2** That should be given; appropriate. **3** Suitable; sufficient: *due* cause for alarm. **4** Appointed or expected to arrive. **5** Ascribable; owing: with *to:* The delay was *due* to rain. *—n.* **1** That which is due. **2** *pl.* Fee: club *dues.* *—adv.* Directly; exactly: *due* east. [< OF *deu,* pp. of *devoir* owe] • *Due to* as a preposition, though widely used, is still questioned by some, who would substitute for it *because of* or *on account of: Because of* (not *due to*) rain, we were delayed.

du·el (dʸōō′əl) *n.* **1** A prearranged combat between two persons, usu. fought with deadly weapons. **2** A struggle between two parties. *—v.t. & v.i.* **du·eled** or **·elled, du·el·ing** or **·el·ling** To fight or fight with, in a duel. [< L *duellum,* var. of *bellum* war] **—du′el·er** or **du′el·ler, du′el·ist** or **du′el·list** *n.*

du·en·na (dʸōō·en′ə) *n.* **1** An elderly woman who watches over a young woman in Spanish and Portuguese families. **2** A governess or chaperon. [Sp. < L *domina* lady]

du·et (dʸōō·et′) *n.* **1** A musical composition for two voices or instrumentalists. **2** The performance of such a composition; also, the two persons who perform. [< L *duo* two]

duff (duf) *n.* A thick flour pudding boiled in a bag. [Var. of DOUGH]

duf·fel bag (duf′əl) A sack, usu. of canvas or duck, used to carry clothing and personal possessions. [< *Duffel,* a town near Antwerp]

duf·fer (duf′ər) *n. Informal* One who performs in an incompetent manner. [?]

dug[1] (dug) *p.t. & p.p.* of DIG.

dug[2] (dug) *n.* A teat or udder. [?]

du·gong (dōō′gong) *n.* A whalelike, herbivorous sea mammal of the East Indies and Australia. [< Malay *duyong*]

dug·out (dug′out′) *n.* **1** A canoe formed of a hollowed log. **2** An underground shelter against bombs, tornadoes, etc. **3** In baseball, a low, boxlike structure to shelter the players when not at bat or in the field.

duke (dʸōōk) *n.* **1** An English peer of the highest rank, below a prince or an archbishop. **2** A Continental noble of corresponding rank. **3** A prince ruling over a duchy or a small state. [< L *dux* leader]

duke·dom (dʸōōk′dəm) *n.* DUCHY.

dukes (dʸōōks) *n. pl. Slang* The fists. [Short for *Duke of Yorks,* orig. rhyming slang for forks; later fingers, fists]

dul·cet (dul′sit) *adj.* Pleasant to the ear. [< L *dulcis* sweet] **—Syn.** sweet, soothing, agreeable, melodious.

dul·ci·mer (dul′sə·mər) *n.* A stringed musical instrument played with two padded hammers. [? < L *dulcis* sweet + *melos* a song]

dull (dul) *adj.* **1** Having a blunt edge or point. **2** Not acute or intense: *dull* pain. **3** Not quick, as in thought. **4** Lacking perception or sensibility. **5** Depressed; sad. **6** Boring: a *dull* affair. **7** Not brisk or active; sluggish. **8** Not bright or vivid, as colors. **9** Cloudy; overcast; a *dull* day. **10** Muffled; indistinct, as sounds. *—v.t. & v.i.* To make or become dull. [ME *dul* < MLG] **—dull′ish** *adj.* **—dul′ly** *adv.* **—dull′ness** or **dul′ness** *n.*

dull·ard (dul′ərd) *n.* A dull or stupid person.

dulse (duls) *n.* A reddish brown, edible seaweed. Also **dulce.** [< Ir. *duileasg*]

du·ly (dʸōō′lē) *adv.* **1** In accordance with what is due; fitly. **2** In due time or manner. **3** When due.

dumb (dum) *adj.* **1** Having no power of speech. **2** Not using words or sounds; silent. **3** *Informal* Stupid. [OE] **—dumb′ly** *adv.* **—dumb′ness** *n.*

dumb·bell (dum′bel′) *n.* **1** A gymnastic device consisting of a handle with a weighted ball at each end. **2** *Slang* A stupid person.

dumb·found (dum′found′) *v.t.* To strike dumb with amazement. Also **dum′found.** [Blend of DUMB and CONFOUND] **—Syn.** confuse, confound, amaze, astonish.

dumb show 1 Gestures without words. **2** In early English drama, part of a play done in pantomime.

dumb·wait·er (dum′wā′tər) *n.* **1** A movable serving table. **2** An elevator for carrying food, etc., between floors.

dum·my (dum′ē) *n. pl.* **dum·mies 1** *Informal* A stupid person. **2** A figure made to represent a human being: a ventriloquist's *dummy;* a *dummy* for displaying clothes. **3** A stuffed figure used in bayonet or tackling practice. **4** In certain card games, an exposed hand played by the opposite player; also, the player to whom that hand has been dealt. **5** A person who represents another in a transaction, but who poses as acting for himself. **6** *Printing* A model book, usu. blank, made up as a pattern. *—adj.* **1** Sham; counterfeit. **2** Supposedly acting for oneself while really acting for another. **3** Made to resemble some object, but having no real use; artificial: a *dummy* door. —*v.t.* **dum·mied, ·my·ing** To lay out (printed matter) as a guide for making up a column or page. [<DUMB]

dump (dump) *v.t.* **1** To drop or throw down abruptly. **2** To empty out, as from a container. **3** To empty (a container), as by overturning. **4** To throw (goods) on a market in quantity and at low prices. **5** To get rid of. —*v.i.* **6** To fall or drop. **7** To unload commodities. **8** To unload refuse. —*n.* **1** A dumping ground, as for refuse. **2** That which is dumped. **3** A place where ammunition, supplies, etc. are held for rapid distribution. **4** *Slang* A poor, ill-kept dwelling or place. [<Scand.] —**dump'er** *n.*

dump·ling (dump'ling) *n.* **1** A small piece of dough filled with fruit, meat, or vegetables, and cooked by baking, steaming, or frying. **2** A small mass of dough dropped into boiling soup or stew.

dumps (dumps) *n. pl.* A gloomy state of mind; melancholy. [?<MDu. *domp* mental haze]

Dump·ster (dump'stər) *n.* a large metal container for garbage, fitted with a lid and a mechanism for dumping into a garbage truck: a trade name.

dump truck A truck which unloads by tilting back the cargo bin and opening the tailgate.

dump·y[1] (dump'ē) *adj.* **dump·i·er, dump·i·est** Sullen or discontented; sulky; gloomy.

dump·y[2] (dump'ē) *adj.* **dump·i·er, dump·i·est** Short and thick; stocky. —**dump'i·ly** *adv.* —**dump'i·ness** *n.*

dun[1] (dun) *v.t. & v.i.* **dunned, dun·ning** To press (a debtor) for payment. —*n.* **1** One who duns. **2** A demand for payment. [?]

dun[2] (dun) *adj.* Grayish or reddish brown. —*n.* Dun color. —*v.t.* **dunned, dun·ning** To make dun-colored. [<OE *dunn*]

dunce (duns) *n.* A stupid or ignorant person. [<Johannes *Duns* Scotus, 13th-century theologian]

dunce cap A conical paper cap formerly placed on the head of a dull-witted pupil.

dune (dyōōn) *n.* A hill of loose sand heaped up by the wind. [<MDu. *dūne*]

dung (dung) *n.* **1** Animal excrement; manure. **2** Anything foul. —*v.t.* To cover or enrich with dung. [<OE]

dun·ga·ree (dung'gə·rē') *n.* **1** A coarse cotton cloth, used for working clothes, tents, sails, etc. **2** *pl.* Working clothes made of this fabric. [<Hind. *dungrī*]

dun·geon (dun'jən) *n.* **1** A dark underground prison. **2** DONJON. [<OF *donjon*]

dung·hill (dung'hil') *n.* **1** A heap of manure. **2** Figuratively, a vile abode or condition.

dunk (dungk) *v.t. & v.i.* To dip or sop (bread, doughnuts, etc.) into tea, coffee, soup, etc. [<OHG *dunkōn*]

dun·nage (dun'ij) *n.* **1** Loose packing used to protect cargo on board ship or goods in a container from damage. **2** BAGGAGE. [?]

du·o (dyōō'ō) *n. pl.* **du·os** DUET. [L, two]

duo- *combining form* Two. [<L *duo* two]

du·o·dec·i·mal (dyōō'ō·des'ə·məl) *adj.* Of, pertaining to, or based on twelve. —*n.* A twelfth. [<L *duodecim* twelve]

du·o·dec·i·mo (dyōō'ō·des'ə·mō) *n. pl.* **·mos** **1** The size of pages made from a printer's sheet folded into twelve leaves, approximately 5 × 7½ inches. **2** A book made up of pages of this size. —*adj.* Made up of pages of this size.

du·o·de·num (dyōō'ə·dē'nəm, dyōō·od'ə·nəm) *n. pl.* **·na** (-nə) or **·nums** That part of the small intestine next to the stomach. [<Med. L *duodenum (digitorum)* of twelve (fingers): with ref. to its length] —**du'o·de'nal** *adj.* • See INTESTINE.

dup. duplicate

dupe (dyōōp) *n.* A victim of deception. —*v.t.* **duped, dup·ing** To make a dupe of. [<L *upupa* a hoopoe (a bird thought to be stupid)] —**dup'a·ble** *adj.* —**dup'er·y** *n.* —**Syn.** *n.* gull, fool, ninny, victim. *v.* fool, deceive, trick, hoodwink.

du·ple (dyōō'pəl) *adj.* **1** Double. **2** *Music* Having two beats to a measure. [<L *duplus* double]

du·plex (dyōō'pleks) *adj.* Double; twofold. —*n.* A duplex house or apartment. [<L *duo* two + stem of *plicare* fold]

duplex apartment An apartment having rooms on two floors with an interior stairway.

duplex house A house having two one-family units.

du·pli·cate (dyōō'plə·kit) *adj.* **1** Made or done exactly like an original. **2** Double. **3** Designating a way of playing a card game in which, for purposes of comparing scores, the same hands are played by different players. —*n.* **1** An exact copy of an original. **2** A double or counterpart. **3** A duplicate game of cards. —*v.t.* (dyōō'plə·kāt) **·cat·ed, ·cat·ing** **1** To make an exact copy of. **2** To double; make twofold. **3** To repeat, as an effort. [<L *duplicare* to double] —**du'pli·cate·ly** *adv.* —**du'pli·ca'tion** *n.* —**du'pli·ca'tive** *adj.*

du·pli·ca·tor (dyōō'plə·kā'tər) *n.* A device for making duplicates, as of written or typewritten matter.

du·plic·i·ty (dyōō·plis'ə·tē) *n. pl.* **·ties** Deception in speech or conduct. [<L *duplex* twofold] —**Syn.** deceitfulness, double-dealing, dissimulation, hypocrisy.

du·ra·ble (dyōōr'ə·bəl) *adj.* Able to continue long in the same state. [<L *durus* hard] —**du'ra·bil'i·ty, du'ra·ble·ness** *n.* —**du'ra·bly** *adv.* —**Syn.** lasting, strong, enduring, stable.

du·ra ma·ter (dyōōr'ə mā'tər, mä'tər) The tough fibrous membrane enclosing the brain and spinal cord. [<L *dura* hard + *mater* mother] —**du'ral** *adj.*

du·ra·men (dyōō·rā'min) *n.* The heartwood of a tree trunk. [L, hardness]

dur·ance (dyōōr'əns) *n.* Confinement in prison. [<L *durare* last, endure]

du·ra·tion (dyōō·rā'shən) *n.* **1** The period of time during which anything lasts. **2** Continuance in time. [<L *durare* endure]

dur·bar (dûr'bär) *n.* **1** In India, a reception formerly given by a native ruler or high British officer. **2** The room in which this is held. [<Pers. *darbār* court]

du·ress (dyōō·res', dyōōr'is) *n.* **1** Compulsion by force or fear. **2** Restraint, as by confinement in prison. [<OF *duresse* hardness, constraint <L *durus* hard]

dur·ing (dyōōr'ing) *prep.* **1** Throughout the time, existence, or action of. **2** In the course of; at some period in. [<L *durare* endure]

durst (dûrst) Archaic *p.t.* of DARE.

du·rum (dyōōr'əm) *n.* A species of wheat widely grown for macaroni and spaghetti products. [<L *durus* hard]

dusk (dusk) *n.* **1** The dark period of twilight. **2** Partial darkness; semidarkness. —*adj.* Dusky. —*v.t. & v.i.* To make or grow dim. [<OE *dox* dark]

dusk·y (dus'kē) *adj.* **dusk·i·er, dusk·i·est** **1** Somewhat dark in color, esp. swarthy. **2** Shadowy; dim. **3** Gloomy. —**dusk'i·ly** *adv.* —**dusk'i·ness** *n.*

dust (dust) *n.* **1** Any substance, as earth, reduced to powder. **2** A cloud of this substance. **3** GOLD DUST. **4** A dead body; remains. **5** The earth. **6** Confusion; controversy. —**bite the dust** To fall wounded or dead. —*v.t.* **1** To wipe or brush dust from. **2** To sprinkle with powder, etc. **3** To soil with dust. —*v.i.* **4** To wipe dust from furniture, etc. [<OE *dūst*] —**dust'less** *adj.*

dust bowl A region where topsoil has been blown away by dust storms during periods of drought.

dust·er (dus'tər) *n.* **1** One who or that which dusts. **2** A cloth or brush for removing dust. **3** A garment or covering to protect from dust.

dust jacket A removable covering for a book, usu. of paper.

dust·pan (dust'pan') *n.* A shovellike implement into which rubbish from a floor is swept.

dust storm A windstorm carrying clouds of dust along with it.

dust·y (dus'tē) *adj.* **dust·i·er dust·i·est** **1** Covered with dust. **2** Dull or grayish. **3** Powdery. —**dust'i·ness** *n.*

Dutch (duch) *adj.* **1** Of or pertaining to the Netherlands, its people, or their language. **2** *Slang* German. —*n.* **1** The people of the Netherlands: with *the.* **2** *Slang* Germans: with *the.* **3** The language of the Netherlands. —**in Dutch** *Slang* In trouble or disfavor. —**go Dutch** *Informal* To have each participant pay his own expenses.

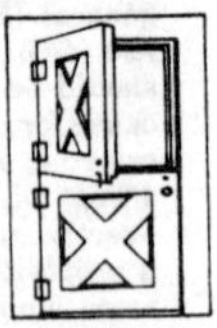

Dutch door

Dutch door A door divided horizontally in the middle, thus allowing either half to be opened separately.

Dutch·man (duch'mən) *n. pl.* **·men** (-mən) **1** A citizen or native of the Netherlands. **2** *Slang* A German.

Dutch oven 1 A brick oven that cooks after the source of fire is removed. 2 A heavy pot with a tight-fitting lid. 3 A metal oven used in front of an open fire.

Dutch treat *Informal* Entertainment at which each person pays his own bill.

Dutch uncle A very frank and severe critic.

du·te·ous (dʸōō'tē·əs) *adj.* Obedient; dutiful. —**du'te·ous·ly** *adv.* —**du'te·ous·ness** *n.*

du·ti·a·ble (dʸōō'tē·ə·bəl) *adj.* Subject to impost duty.

du·ti·ful (dʸōō'ti·fəl) *adj.* 1 Submissive; obedient. 2 Showing respect or a sense of duty; respectful. —**du'ti·ful·ly** *adv.* —**du'ti·ful·ness** *n.*

du·ty (dʸōō'tē) *n. pl.* **·ties** 1 Something which one is legally or morally bound to pay, do, or perform. 2 A specific obligatory service or function: to do sea *duty.* 3 A moral obligation; right action; also, a sense of this: *duty* calls. 4 Respectful or obedient conduct, as to one's parents. 5 A tax, as upon goods imported, exported, or consumed. [<OF *deu* DUE]

du·ty-free (dʸōō'tē·frē') *adj. & adv.* Free from customs duties.

du·vet (dʸōō·vē', dʸōō'-) *n.* COMFORTER (def. 2).

du·ve·tyn (dōō'və·tēn, duv'tēn') *n.* A fabric with a velvetlike surface. Also **du've·tine, du've·tyne.** [<F *duvet* down]

D.V., D.v. God willing (L *Deo volente*).

dwarf (dwôrf) *n.* A person, animal, or plant that is unusually small. —*v.t.* 1 To stunt development of. 2 To cause to appear small by comparison. —*v.i.* 3 To become stunted. —*adj.* Smaller than others of its kind; stunted. [<OE *dweorh*] —**dwarf'ish** *adj.* —**dwarf'ish·ly** *adv.* —**dwarf'ish·ness** *n.*

dwell (dwel) *v.i.* **dwelt or dwelled, dwell·ing** 1 To have a fixed abode; reside. 2 To linger, as on a subject: with *on* or *upon.* [<OE *dwellan* hinder, stay] —**dwell'er** *n.*

dwell·ing (dwel'ing) *n.* A place used for residence. —**Syn.** domicile, abode, habitation, house, home.

dwin·dle (dwin'dəl) *v.t. & v.i.* **·dled, ·dling** To make or become smaller or less; diminish; decline. [<OE *dwinan* waste away]

dwt. pennyweight.

DX, D.X. distance; distant.

Dy dysprosium.

dy·ad (dī'ad, -əd) *n.* A pair, as of things or persons.

dyb·buk (dib'ək) *n.* In Jewish folklore, a wandering soul believed to possess a living person's body.

dye (dī) *v.* **dyed, dye·ing** *v.t.* 1 To fix a color in (fabric, hair, etc.) by soaking in liquid coloring matter. 2 To stain; color; tint. —*v.i.* 3 To take or give color by dyeing. —*n.* A fluid or coloring matter used for dyeing; also, the color or hue produced by dyeing. [<OE *deag* dye, color] —**dy'er** *n.*

dyed-in-the-wool (dīd'in·thə·wŏŏl') *adj.* 1 Dyed before being woven. 2 Thoroughgoing; complete.

dye·ing (dī'ing) *n.* The act, process, or trade of fixing colors in cloth or the like.

dye·stuff (dī'stuf') *n.* Any material used for dyeing.

dy·ing (dī'ing) *adj.* 1 Near to death; expiring. 2 About to end or disappear. 3 Of, pertaining to, or at the time of death. —*n.* Death.

dyke[1] (dīk) *n. & v.* DIKE[1].

dyke[2] *n.* DIKE[2].

dy·nam·ic (dī·nam'ik) *adj.* 1 Of or pertaining to motion or unbalanced forces. 2 Of or pertaining to dynamics. 3 Mentally or spiritually energetic, forceful, or powerful: a *dynamic* leader. Also **dy·nam'i·cal.** [<Gk. *dynamis* power] —**dy·nam'i·cal·ly** *adv.*

dy·nam·ics (dī·nam'iks) *n. pl. (construed as sing. in defs. 1 and 3)* 1 The branch of physics that treats of the motion or equilibrium of bodies or of the forces that produce such motion or equilibrium. 2 The forces producing or governing activity or movement of any kind: spiritual *dynamics.* 3 *Music* The production of varying degrees of loudness; also, the words, symbols, etc., indicating this.

dy·na·mism (dī'nə·miz'əm) *n.* The quality of being dynamic, vital, or enthusiastic.

dy·na·mite (dī'nə·mīt) *n.* 1 An explosive composed of nitroglycerin held in an absorbent substance. 2 *Slang* Anything wonderful or spectacular. —*v.t.* **·mit·ed, ·mit·ing** To blow up or shatter with dynamite. [<Gk. *dynamis* power] —**dy'na·mit'er** *n.*

dy·na·mo (dī'nə·mō) *n. pl.* **·mos** 1 A machine for changing mechanical energy into electrical energy by electromagnetic induction. 2 A vital, energetic person. [Short for DYNAMOELECTRIC machine]

dynamo- *combining form* Force; power: *dynamometer.* [<Gk. *dynamis* power]

dy·na·mo·e·lec·tric (dī'nə·mō·i·lek'trik) *adj.* Pertaining to the relation between electricity and mechanical energy. Also **dy'na·mo·e·lec'tri·cal.**

dy·na·mom·e·ter (dī'nə·mom'ə·tər) *n.* An instrument for measuring force exerted or power expended. [DYNAMO- + -METER] —**dy·na·mo·met·ric** (dī'nə·mō·met'rik) or **·ri·cal** *adj.* —**dy'na·mom'e·try** *n.*

dy·nast (dī'nast, -nəst) *n.* A monarch; ruler. [<Gk. *dynasthai* be powerful]

dy·nas·ty (dī'nəs·tē, *esp. Brit.* din'ə·stē) *n. pl.* **·ties** 1 A succession of sovereigns in one line of family descent. 2 The length of time during which one family is in power. —**dy·nas·tic** (dī·nas'tik) or **·ti·cal** *adj.* —**dy·nas'ti·cal·ly** *adv.*

dyne (dīn) *n. Physics* A unit of force equal to 10^{-5} newton. [<Gk. *dynamis* power]

dys- *combining form* Bad; defective; difficult: *dyspepsia.* [Gk., bad, difficult]

dys·en·ter·y (dis'ən·ter'ē) *n.* A severe inflammation of the large intestine, marked by bloody evacuations. [<Gk. *dys-* bad + *enteron* intestine] —**dys'en·ter'ic** or **·i·cal** *adj.*

dys·func·tion (dis·fungk'shən) *n.* Deterioration of proper functioning, as of some bodily organ —**dys·func'tion·al** *adj.*

dys·lex·i·a (dis·lek'sēə) *n.* An impairment or loss of the ability to read. [<Gk. *dys-* bad + *lexis* speech]

dys·pep·sia (dis·pep'sha, -sē·ə) *n.* Difficult or painful digestion. [<Gk. *dys-* hard + *peptein* cook, digest]

dys·pep·tic (dis·pep'tik) *adj.* 1 Relating to or suffering from dyspepsia. 2 Gloomy; cross. Also **dys·pep'ti·cal.** —*n.* A dyspeptic person. —**dys·pep'ti·cal·ly** *adv.*

dys·pha·sia (dis·fā'zhə, -zhē·ə) *n.* Difficulty in understanding or using speech due to disease of or injury to the brain. [<Gk. *dys-* hard + *phasis* utterance]

dys·pro·si·um (dis·prō'sē·əm, -shē-) *n.* A highly magnetic element (symbol Dy) of the rare-earth series. [<Gk. *dys-* hard + *prosienai* to approach]

dys·to·pia (dis·tō'pē·ə) *n.* An imaginary place with an inhuman regime or intolerable conditions, the opposite of a utopia.

dys·tro·phy (dis'trə·fē) *n. pl.* **·phies** 1 Defective or faulty nutrition. 2 Any of various neurological or muscular disorders. [<Gk. *dys-* hard, defective + *trophē* nourishment]

dz. dozen.

E

E, e (ē) *n. pl.* **E's, e's, Es, es** (ēz) **1** The fifth letter of the English alphabet. **2** Any spoken sound representing the letter *E* or *e*. **3** *Music* The third tone in the diatonic scale of C major. **4** Something shaped like an E. **5** *Math.* The number used as the base of the natural logarithms, roughly 2.718. —*adj.* Shaped like an E.

E, E. English.

E, E., e, e. east; eastern.

E. earl; earth.

ea. each.

each (ēch) *adj.* Being one of two or more individuals somehow loosely associated: *Each* shoe was muddy. —*pron.* Every one of any number or group considered individually; each one. —*adv.* For or to each person, article, etc.; apiece: one dollar *each.* [< OE *ælc*]

each other Each of two or more in reciprocal relation or action; one another: We saw *each other* at the theater last night but didn't speak.

ea·ger (ē′gər) *adj.* Having or showing an intense desire for something. [< L *acer* sharp] **—ea′ger·ly** *adv.* **—ea′ger·ness** *n.* **—Syn.** avid, desirous, keen, zealous.

ea·gle (ē′gəl) *n.* **1** A large diurnal bird of prey with powerful wings and keen eyesight. **2** A former gold coin of the United States, value $10. **3** A picture or design of an eagle, used as an emblem on a seal, flag, etc. **4** In golf, two strokes less than par in playing a hole. [< L *aquila*]

ea·gle-eyed (ē′gəl·īd′) *adj.* Keen-sighted.

ea·glet (ē′glit) *n.* A young eagle.

ear[1] (ir) *n.* **1** The organ of hearing in man and other mammals. **2** The external part of this organ. **3** The sense of hearing. **4** A discriminating perception of sounds. **5** Attentive consideration; heed. **6** Anything like the external ear, as a projecting piece, handle, etc. **—be all ears** *Informal* To pay eager attention to. **—have** (or **keep**) **an ear to the ground** To be or keep aware of public opinion, current trends, etc. **—up to the ears** *Informal* Almost overwhelmed, as by work. [< OE *ēare*] **—eared** *adj.*

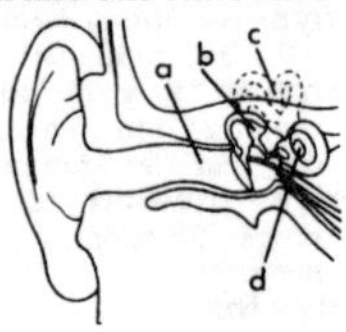

Ear
a. auditory canal.
b. middle ear.
c. semicircular canals.
d. cochlea.

ear[2] (ir) *n.* The grain-bearing part of a cereal plant. —*v.i.* To form ears, as grain. [< OE *ēar*]

ear·ache (ir′āk′) *n.* Pain inside the ear.

ear·drum (ir′drum′) *n.* TYMPANIC MEMBRANE.

eared (ird) *adj.* **1** Having an ear or ears: an *eared* cup. **2** Having a specified kind or number of ears: used in combination: *floppy-eared.*

earl (ûrl) *n.* A member of the British nobility ranking below a marquess and above a viscount. [< OE *eorl* nobleman] **—earl′dom, earl′ship** *n.*

ear·ly (ûr′lē) *adj.* **·li·er, ·li·est 1** Near the beginning of any stated period of time or of a movement, series, etc. **2** Ancient. **3** Being or occurring sooner than is usual or necessary. **4** About to be or happen. —*adv.* **1** At or near the beginning of a period of time or of a movement, series, etc. **2** Before the expected or ordinary time. **3** In ancient times. **—early on** Near the beginning. [< OE *ǣr* sooner + *-līce* -ly] **—ear′li·ness** *n.*

ear·mark (ir′märk′) *v.t.* **1** To make a mark of identification on. **2** To mark an animal's ear. **3** To set aside for special purposes, as money. —*n.* **1** An owner's mark on an animal's ear. **2** Any mark of identification.

ear·muff (ir′muf′) *n.* One of a pair of coverings for the ears, worn as a protection against cold.

earn (ûrn) *v.t.* **1** To receive, as salary or wages, for labor. **2** To merit as a result, reward, or punishment. **3** To bring in (interest, etc.) as gain or profit. [< OE *earnian*] **—earn′·er** *n.*

ear·nest[1] (ûr′nist) *adj.* **1** Intent and direct in purpose; zealous. **2** Marked by deep feeling or conviction; heartfelt. **3** Serious; important. —*n.* Seriousness. **—in earnest** With full and serious intent. [< OE *eorneste*] **—ear′nest·ly** *adv.* **—ear′nest·ness** *n.*

ear·nest[2] (ûr′nist) *n.* **1** Money paid in advance to bind a bargain. **2** A pledge. [< Heb. *'ērābōn*]

earn·ings (ûr′ningz) *n.pl.* **1** Wages; salary. **2** Profits.

ear·phone (ir′fōn′) *n.* A device for converting electrical energy, as from a radio or telephone, into audible sound.

ear·ring (ir′ring′) *n.* An ear ornament.

ear·shot (ir′shot′) *n.* The distance at which sounds may be heard.

earth (ûrth) *n.* **1** *Often cap.* The planet on which man lives; the planet of the solar system third in distance from the sun. • See PLANET. **2** The people who inhabit this planet. **3** The abode of man, considered as distinct from heaven and hell. **4** The dry land portion of the surface of the globe. **5** Soil; dirt; ground. **6** The hole of a burrowing animal. **7** Worldly interests and pursuits. **—down to earth** Realistic. **—run to earth** To hunt down and find, as a fox. —*v.t.* **1** To protect with earth. **2** To chase, as a fox, into a burrow or hole. —*v.i.* **3** To burrow or hide in the earth, as a fox. [< OE *eorthe*]

earth·en (ûr′thən) *adj.* **1** Made of earth or baked clay. **2** EARTHLY.

earth·en·ware (ûr′thən·wâr′) *n.* **1** A kind of slightly porous baked clay. **2** Ceramics made from such clay.

earth·ly (ûrth′lē) *adj.* **1** Of or pertaining to the earth. **2** Secular; worldly. **3** *Informal* Possible; imaginable. **—earth′li·ness** *n.*

earth·quake (ûrth′kwāk′) *n.* A tremor of a portion of the earth's crust, caused by volcanic or other disturbances below the earth's surface.

earth·shine (ûrth′shīn′) *n.* *Astron.* Sunlight reflected by earth that dimly illuminates parts of the moon not exposed to direct sunlight.

earth·ward (ûrth′wərd) *adv.* Toward the earth: also **earth′wards.** —*adj.* Moving toward the earth.

earth·work (ûrth′wûrk′) *n.* **1** *Mil.* A fortification made of earth. **2** *Engin.* An operation requiring the removal of or filling in with earth.

earth·worm (ûrth′wûrm′) *n.* A burrowing worm that lives in and enriches the soil.

earth·y (ûr′thē) *adj.* **earth·i·er, earth·i·est 1** Of or like earth or soil; made of earth. **2** Unrefined; coarse. **3** Simple; natural; robust; lusty. **—earth′i·ness** *n.*

ear·wax (ir′waks′) *n.* A waxy substance found in the passages of the external ear.

ear·wig (ir′wig′) *n.* A beetlelike insect erroneously believed to enter the human ear. —*v.t.* **·wigged, ·wig·ging** To influence by secret and stealthy counsel. [< OE *ēarwicga*]

ease (ēz) *n.* **1** Freedom from pain, agitation, or worry; comfort. **2** Freedom from or absence of apparent effort; facility. **3** Freedom from affectation, formality, etc.; naturalness. —*v.* **eased, eas·ing** *v.t.* **1** To relieve the mental or physical pain or oppression of; comfort. **2** To make less painful or oppressive. **3** To lessen the pressure, weight, tension, etc., of. **4** To move, lower, or put in place carefully. —*v.i.* **5** To diminish in severity, speed, etc.: often with *up* or *off.* [< OF *aise* < LL *adjacens, -entis* neighboring] **—ease′ful** *adj.* **—ease′ful·ly** *adv.* **—ease′ful·ness, eas′er** *n.* **—Syn.** *n.* **1** rest, luxury, repose, content. **2** expertness.

ea·sel (ē′zəl) *n.* A folding frame for supporting a picture, panel, etc. [< Du. *ezel* easel, orig., an ass]

ease·ment (ēz′mənt) *n.* **1** An easing or being eased. **2** Anything that gives ease or relief. **3** *Law* The privilege or right of making limited use of another's adjacent property.

eas·i·ly (ē′zə·lē) *adv.* **1** In an easy manner. **2** Without question: *easily* the winner. **3** Possibly.

eas·i·ness (ē′zi·nis) *n.* The state of being at ease, or of being easy to do or accomplish.

east (ēst) *n.* 1 The general direction in which the sun appears at sunrise. 2 The point of the compass at 90°, directly opposite west. 3 Any direction, region, or part of the horizon near that point. —**the East** 1 Asia, esp. China, Japan, and the other countries of E Asia. 2 In the U.S., the region east of the Allegheny Mountains and north of Maryland. —*adj.* 1 To, toward, facing, or in the east. 2 Coming from the east. —*adv.* In or toward the east; in an easterly direction. [< OE *ēast*]

east·bound (ēst′bound′) *adj.* Going eastward. Also **east′-bound′.**

East·er (ēs′tər) *n.* 1 A Christian festival commemorating the resurrection of Christ. 2 The day on which this festival is celebrated, the Sunday immediately after the first full moon that occurs on or after March 21: also **Easter Sunday.** [< OE *Eastre* goddess of spring]

east·er·ly (ēs′tər·lē) *adj.* 1 Of, in, or toward the east; eastward. 2 From the east: said of winds. —*adv.* Toward the east: also **east′ern·ly.** —*n.* A storm from the east.

east·ern (ēs′tərn) *adj.* 1 Of, pertaining to, from or situated in the east. 2 *Usu. cap.* Pertaining to the East. 3 Moving to or from the east; easterly.

Eastern Church 1 The Christian Church of the Byzantine Empire. 2 The Eastern Orthodox Church.

east·ern·er (ēs′tərn·ər) *n. Often cap.* One who dwells in the eastern part of the U.S.

Eastern Hemisphere See HEMISPHERE.

Eastern Orthodox Church Any of the modern Christian Churches employing the Byzantine rite and honoring the primacy of the patriarch of Constantinople, as the Russian and Greek Orthodox Churches.

Eastern (Roman) Empire The Byzantine Empire.

East·er·tide (ēs′tər·tīd′) *n.* The season of Easter; a period extending in various churches from Easter to Ascension Day, Whitsunday, or Trinity Sunday.

East Germany See GERMANY.

east·ward (ēst′wərd) *adj.* To, toward, or in the east. —*adv.* Toward the east: also **east′wards.** Also **east′ward·ly.**

eas·y (ē′zē) *adj.* **eas·i·er, eas·i·est** 1 Involving little effort, discomfort, or difficulty. 2 Causing no pain, anxiety, or distress. 3 Relaxed and unpretentious: an *easy* manner. 4 Not harsh or stern; lenient; indulgent. 5 Unresisting; tractable: *easy* prey. 6 Comfortable; pleasant: in *easy* circumstances. 7 Gentle; moderate: an *easy* pace. 8 Undemanding; reasonable: *easy* terms. 9 *Econ.* **a** In little demand: said of commodities. **b** Plentiful, therefore obtainable at low interest rates: said of money. —*adv. Informal* 1 Easily. 2 Slowly and cautiously. —**go easy on** *Informal* 1 To use cautiously. 2 To be lenient or indulgent toward. —**take it easy** *Informal* 1 To relax. 2 To stay calm. [< OE *aise* EASE] —**Syn.** *adj.* 1 effortless, simple. 3 natural.

eas·y·go·ing (ē′zē·gō′ing) *adj.* Not inclined to effort or worry; complacently unconcerned.

easy mark *Informal* A person easily fooled.

eat (ēt) *v.* **ate** (āt or *Brit.* et) or *Regional* **eat** (et), **eat·en, eat·ing** *v.t.* 1 To take (food) into the mouth and swallow. 2 To consume or destroy as if by eating: to *eat* away one's savings. 3 To wear into or away; corrode; rust. 4 To make (a way or hole) by or as by gnawing or chewing. —*v.i.* 5 To take in food; have a meal. —**eat one's words** To retract what one has said. [< OE *etan*] —**eat′a·ble** *n., adj.* —**eat′er** *n.*

eats (ēts) *n. pl. Informal* Food.

eau de Co·logne (ō′də kə·lōn′) *n. pl.* **eaux** (ō′-) A toilet water; cologne. [F, lit., water of Cologne]

eaves (ēvz) *n. pl.* The projecting edge of a roof. [< OE *efes* edge]

eaves·drop (ēvz′drop′) *v.i.* **·dropped, ·drop·ping** To listen secretly, as to a private conversation. [With ref. to one who listens while standing outside under dripping eaves] —**eaves′drop′per, eaves′drop′·ping** *n.*

Eaves

ebb (eb) *v.i.* 1 To recede, as the tide. 2 To decline; fail. —*n.* 1 The flowing away of tidewater to the ocean; low tide: also **ebb tide.** 2 A condition or period of decline. [< OE *ebbian*]

eb·on·ite (eb′ən·īt) *n.* Hard rubber; vulcanite. [< EBONY]

eb·on·y (eb′ən·ē) *n. pl.* **·on·ies** 1 A hard, heavy wood, usu. black, used for cabinetwork, etc. 2 A hardwood tree of Ceylon and S India. —*adj.* 1 Made of ebony. 2 Black. [< Gk. *ebenos* ebony < Egyptian *hebni*]

e·bul·lient (i·bul′yənt) *adj.* 1 Bubbling over with enthusiasm. 2 In a boiling condition. [< L *ex-* out + *bullire* boil] —**e·bul′lient·ly** *adv.* —**e·bul′lience, e·bul′lien·cy** *n.*

eb·ul·li·tion (eb′ə·lish′ən) *n.* 1 The bubbling of a liquid; boiling. 2 Any sudden or violent agitation.

ec·cen·tric (ek·sen′trik) *adj.* 1 Not having the same center: *eccentric* circles. 2 Not having the axis or support exactly in the center: an *eccentric* wheel. 3 Deviating from a circular form or path: *eccentric* orbit. 4 Erratic; odd; unconventional: *eccentric* behavior. —*n.* 1 A person characterized by unusual or erratic behavior. 2 *Mech.* A disk mounted out of center on a driving shaft in order to produce reciprocating motion. [< Gk. *ek-* out, away + *kentron* center] —**ec·cen′tri·cal·ly** *adv.* —**Syn.** *adj.* 4 peculiar, strange, bizarre, singular.

ec·cen·tric·i·ty (ek′sen·tris′ə·tē) *n. pl.* **·ties** 1 An odd or capricious act. 2 The state or quality of being eccentric.

Eccl., Eccles. Ecclesiastes.

eccl., eccles. ecclesiastical.

Ec·cle·si·as·tes (i·klē′zē·as′tēz) *n.* A book of the Old Testament. [< Gk. *ekklēsia* assembly]

ec·cle·si·as·tic (i·klē′zē·as′tik) *adj.* Ecclesiastical. —*n.* A cleric; churchman. [< Gk. *ekklēsia* assembly]

ec·cle·si·as·ti·cal (i·klē′zē·as′ti·kəl) *adj.* Of or pertaining to the church, esp. considered as an organized and governing power. —**ec·cle′si·as′ti·cal·ly** *adv.*

Ecclus. Ecclesiasticus.

ech·e·lon (esh′ə·lon) *n.* 1 A steplike troop, fleet, or airplane formation, in which each rank, ship, or airplane is behind and to the right or left of the one preceding. 2 A military unit described according to its position or function: rear *echelon;* command *echelon.* 3 A level of responsibility or power, as in an organization. 4 The persons at such a level. —*v.t. & v.i.* To form in echelon. [< F *échelle* ladder < L *scala*]

e·chid·na (i·kid′nə) *n.* An egg-laying mammal of Australia, etc.; a spiny anteater. [< Gk., viper, adder]

Echidna

e·chi·no·derm (i·kī′nə·dûrm) *n.* An invertebrate marine animal such as a starfish or sea urchin, characterized by a spiny exterior and radially arranged body parts. [< Gk. *echinos* hedgehog + *derma* skin] —**e·chi′no·der′ma·tous** (-dûr′mə·təs) *adj.*

ech·o (ek′ō) *n. pl.* **·oes** 1 The sound or repetition of sound produced by the reflection of sound waves from an opposing surface. 2 A close imitation of another's views or thoughts. 3 A response or reaction, esp. sympathetic. 4 A suggestion or trace; reminder: an *echo* of the past. —*v.t.* 1 To repeat or send back (sound) by echo. 2 To repeat the words, opinions, etc., of. 3 To repeat (words, opinions, etc.) in imitation of another. —*v.i.* 4 To resound or reverberate by or as by echo. [< Gk. *ēchō*] —**ech′o·er** *n.*

ech·o·lo·ca·tion (ek′ō·lō·kā′shən) *n.* Determination of the position and form of objects by means of sound waves reflected by them. [ECHO + LOCATION] —**ech′o·lo·cate′** *v.* **(·cat·ed, ·cat·ing)**

é·clair (ā·klâr′, i·klâr′) *n.* A small pastry filled with custard or whipped cream and usu. iced with chocolate. [F, lit., flash of lightning]

é·clat (ā·klä′, i·klä′) *n.* 1 Brilliant or ostentatious achievement. 2 Dazzling style; stunning effect. 3 Renown; celebrity; glory. [< F *éclater* burst out]

ec·lec·tic (ek·lek′tik, ik-) *adj.* 1 Selecting from various sources. 2 Composed of selections from various sources. —*n.* One who uses an eclectic method. [< Gk. *ek-* out +

legein select] **—ec·lec′ti·cal·ly** *adv.* **—ec·lec′ti·cism** (-tə·siz′·əm) *n.*

e·clipse (i·klips′) *n.* **1** *Astron.* The dimming or elimina-

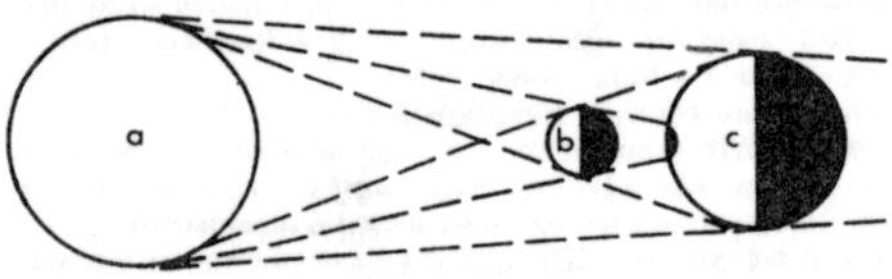

Solar eclipse
a. sun. b. moon. c. earth.

tion of light reaching an observer from a heavenly body. A **lunar eclipse** is caused by the passage of the moon through the earth's shadow; a **solar eclipse** by the passage of the moon between the sun and the observer. **2** Any dimming or passing into obscurity, as of fame. *—v.t.* **e·clipsed, e·clips·ing 1** To cause an eclipse of; darken. **2** To dim or obscure: Age *eclipsed* her beauty. **3** To outshine; surpass. [< Gk. *ek-* out + *leipein* leave] **—Syn.** *v.* **1** obscure, hide, conceal. **3** overshadow.

e·clip·tic (i·klip′tik, ē-) *n. Astron.* **1** That plane, passing through the center of the sun, which contains the orbit of the earth: also **plane of the ecliptic. 2** The great circle in which this plane intersects the celestial sphere. *—adj.* Pertaining to eclipses or to the ecliptic. **—e·clip′ti·cal** *adj.* **—e·clip′ti·cal·ly** *adv.* • See ZONE.

ec·logue (ek′lôg, -log) *n.* A poem containing discourses or dialogues, with shepherds as principal speakers. Also **ec′log.** [< Gk *eklogē* selection]

e·col·o·gy (i·kol′ə·jē) *n.* **1** That division of biology which treats of the relations between organisms and their environment. **2** The system of relationships between organisms and their environments. [< Gk. *oikos* home + -LOGY] **—ec′o·log′ic** (ek′ə·loj′ik) or **·i·cal** *adj.* **—ec′o·log′i·cal·ly** *adv.* **—e·col′o·gist** *n.*

econ. economic; economics; economy.

ec·o·nom·ic (ek′ə·nom′ik, ē′kə-) *adj.* **1** Of or relating to the production, distribution, or management of wealth. **2** Of or pertaining to the financial matters of a country, household, etc. **3** Of or pertaining to the science of economics. **4** Of practical utility: *economic* botany. [< Gk. *oikonomia.* See ECONOMY.]

ec·o·nom·i·cal (ek′ə·nom′i·kəl, ē′kə-) *adj.* **1** Careful in management; frugal; saving. **2** Not exaggerated or excessive: an *economical* style of writing. **3** ECONOMIC. **—ec′o·nom′i·cal·ly** *adv.*

ec·o·nom·ics (ek′ə·nom′iks, ē′kə-) *n. pl. (construed as sing.)* **1** The science that treats of the production, distribution, and consumption of wealth. **2** Financial matters.

e·con·o·mist (i·kon′ə·mist) *n.* **1** One who is proficient in economics. **2** A frugal person.

e·con·o·mize (i·kon′ə·mīz) *v.* **·mized, ·miz·ing** *v.t.* **1** To use thriftily. *—v.i.* **2** To be frugal. **—e·con′o·miz′er** *n.*

e·con·o·my (i·kon′ə·mē) *n. pl.* **·mies 1** The management of the financial and other resources of a country, community, etc. **2** Care and frugality in the use of money, time, resources, etc.; also, an instance of this. **3** A particular system of producing or managing material resources: an industrial *economy.* **4** Any practical organization of parts in a system. [< Gk. *oikonomia* < *oikos* house + *nemein* manage]

e·con·o·my-sized (i·kon′ə·mē·sīzd′) *adj.* Large-sized: a term used in consumer advertising. Also **e·con′o·my-size′** (-sīz′).

ec·o·sys·tem (ē′kō·sis′təm, ek′ō-) *n. Ecol.* A community of organisms and their nonliving environment. [< Gk. *oikos* habitat + SYSTEM]

ec·ru (ek′rōō, ā′krōō) *adj.* Light brown; tan; beige. [< OF *escru* < L *ex-* thoroughly + *crudus* raw]

ec·sta·sy (ek′stə·sē) *n. pl.* **·sies 1** The state of being beside oneself through overpowering emotion or mental exaltation. **2** Intense joy; rapture. **3** A state of trance. [< Gk. *ekstasis* distraction] **—Syn. 1** frenzy, transport. **2** bliss.

ec·stat·ic (ek·stat′ik) *adj.* Of, pertaining to, like, or in a state of ecstasy. *—n.* A person subject to ecstasies or trances. **—ec·stat′i·cal·ly** *adv.*

ecto- *combining form* Without; outside; external: *ectoderm.* [< Gk. *ektos* outside]

ec·to·derm (ek′tə·dûrm) *n.* The outer layer of the embryo, from which the epithelium and the nervous system develop. **—ec′to·der′mal, ec′to·der′mic** *adj.*

-ectomy *combining form* Removal of a part by cutting out: used in surgical terms to indicate certain kinds of operations: *appendectomy.* [< Gk. *ek-* out + *temnein* to cut]

ec·to·plasm (ek′tə·plaz′əm) *n.* The luminous substance alleged to emanate from the body of a spiritualist medium during a trance. **—ec′to·plas′mic** *adj.*

Ec·ua·dor (ek′wə·dôr) *n.* A republic in NW South America; 104,306 sq. mi., cap. Quito. **—Ec′·ua·do′re·an, Ec′ua·do′·ri·an** *adj., n.*

ec·u·men·i·cal (ek′·yōō·men′i·kəl) *adj.* **1** General; universal. **2** Of or pertaining to ecumenism. **3** Belonging to or accepted by the Christian church everywhere. [< Gk. *oikoumenē (gē)* the inhabited (world) < *oikein* dwell] **—ec′u·men′i·cal·ly** *adv.*

ec·u·men·ism (e·kyōō′mə·niz′əm, ek′yōō·men′iz·əm) *n.* The beliefs or practices of those who desire worldwide unity and cooperation among all Christian churches. Also **ec·u·men·i·cal·ism** (ek′yōō·men′ə·kəl·iz·əm).

ec·ze·ma (ek′sə·mə, eg′zə·mə, eg·zē′mə) *n.* An inflammatory skin disease often attended by itching, watery discharge, and lesions. [< Gk. *ek-* out + *zeein* to boil]

-ed[1] *suffix* Used to form the past tense of regular verbs: *walked, played.* [< OE *-ede, -ode, -ade*]

-ed[2] *suffix* Used to form the past participles of regular verbs: *clothed, washed.* [< OE *-ed, -ad, -od*]

-ed[3] *suffix* **1** Having; possessing; characterized by: *toothed, green-eyed.* **2** Like; resembling: *bigoted.* [< OE *-ede*]

ed. edited; edition; editor.

E·dam cheese (ē′dəm, ē′dam) A mild curd cheese, originally Dutch, made in round balls. [< *Edam,* a town in the NW Netherlands]

Ed·da (ed′ə) *n.* Either of two collections of Old Icelandic or Old Norse literature. [< ON] **—Ed·da·ic** (e·dā′ik), **Ed′dic** *adj.*

ed·dy (ed′ē) *n. pl.* **·dies** A circling current of water, air, or other fluid. *—v.t. & v.i.* **·died, ·dy·ing** To move, or cause to move, in or as in an eddy. [< ON *idha*]

e·del·weiss (ā′dəl·vīs) *n.* A small perennial alpine herb with white woolly leaves. [< G *edel* noble + *weiss* white]

e·de·ma (i·dē′mə) *n.* A morbid accumulation of fluid in various parts of the body. [< Gk. *oidēma* a tumor]

E·den (ēd′n) *n.* **1** In the Bible, the garden that was the first home of Adam and Eve. **2** Any delightful place.

e·den·tate (ē·den′tāt, i·den′-) *adj.* **1** Toothless. **2** Of or pertaining to an order of mammals some of which lack teeth, including sloths, anteaters, and armadillos. *—n.* A creature without teeth. [< L *ex-* without + *dens, dentis* tooth]

edge (ej) *n.* **1** The thin, sharp cutting part of a blade. **2** Sharpness; keenness: the *edge* of her wit. **3** An abrupt border or margin; verge; brink: the *edge* of a cliff; on the *edge* of tears. **4** A bounding or dividing line: the *edge* of a plain. **5** *Informal* Advantage. **—on edge 1** Nervous; irritable. **2** Keenly eager. *—v.* **edged, edg·ing** *v.t.* **1** To sharpen. **2** To put an edging or border on. **3** To move cautiously sidewise. **4** To move by degrees; inch. **5** *Informal* To defeat by a slight margin: often with *out.* *—v.i.* **6** To move sidewise. **7** To move by degrees. [< OE *ecg*]

edge·ways (ej′wāz′) *adv.* **1** With the edge forward. **2** On, by, with, along, or in the direction of the edge. Also **edge′wise** (-wīz′).

edg·ing (ej′ing) *n.* Anything serving as or attached to an edge; trimming.

edg·y (ej′ē) *adj.* **edg·i·er, edg·i·est 1** Having an edge or edges. **2** Irritable; on edge. **—edg′i·ness** *n.*

ed·i·ble (ed′ə·bəl) *adj.* Fit to eat. —*n. Usu. pl.* Something suitable for food. [< L *edere* eat] —**ed′i·bil′i·ty** *n.*

e·dict (ē′dikt) *n.* An official proclamation or decree. [< L < *ex-* out + *dicere* say]

ed·i·fice (ed′ə·fis) *n.* A building or other structure, esp. if large or imposing. [< L *aedes* building + *facere* make]

ed·i·fy (ed′ə·fī) *v.t.* **fied, fy·ing** To strengthen morally; enlighten. [< L *aedes* building + *facere* make] —**ed′i·fi·ca′tion, ed′i·fi′er** *n.* —**ed′i·fy′ing** *adj.* —**ed′i·fy′ing·ly** *adv.*

ed·it (ed′it) *v.t.* **1** To manage the preparation and publication of (a newspaper, etc.). **2** To compile, arrange and emend for publication. **3** To correct and prepare for publication. **4** To prepare (a film, recording tape, etc.) for showing or hearing by cutting, splicing, or rearranging. [< L *editus,* p.p. of *edere* publish, give out]

edit. edited; edition; editor.

e·di·tion (i·dish′ən) *n.* **1** A published form of a literary work, or a copy of the form so published. **2** The total number of copies of a book, magazine, etc., issued at one time.

ed·i·tor (ed′i·tər) *n.* **1** One who prepares manuscripts, copy, etc., for publication. **2** One who writes editorials. —**ed′i·tor·ship′** *n.*

ed·i·to·ri·al (ed′i·tôr′ē·əl, -tō′rē-) *adj.* **1** Of, pertaining to, or emanating from an editor. **2** Of, pertaining to, being, or like an editorial. —*n.* A magazine or newspaper article, radio or television commentary, etc., that expresses the opinions of the editors or publishers, or of management. —**ed′i·to′ri·al·ly** *adv.*

ed·i·to·ri·al·ize (ed′i·tôr′ē·əl·īz′, -tō′rē-) *v.i.* **·ized, ·iz·ing 1** To express opinions in editorial form. **2** To insert editorial opinions into the reporting of facts.

editor in chief *pl.* **editors in chief** The chief editor of a publication.

E.D.T., e.d.t. eastern daylight time.

ed·u·ca·ble (ej′ŏŏ·kə·bəl) *adj.* Capable of being educated. —**ed′u·ca·bil′i·ty** *n.*

ed·u·cate (ej′ŏŏ·kāt) *v.t.* **·cat·ed, ·cat·ing 1** To develop or train the mind, capabilities, and character of by or as by formal schooling or instruction; teach. **2** To train for some special purpose. **3** To develop and train (taste, special ability, etc.). **4** To provide schooling for. [< L *educare* bring up] —**ed′u·ca′tor** *n.*

ed·u·cat·ed (ej′ŏŏ·kā′tid) *adj.* **1** Developed and informed by education. **2** Having a cultivated mind, speech, manner, etc.

ed·u·ca·tion (ej′ŏŏ·kā′shən) *n.* **1** The development and training of one's mind, character, skills, etc., as by instruction, study, or example. **2** Instruction and training in an institution of learning. **3** The knowledge and skills resulting from such instruction and training. **4** Teaching as a system, science, or art; pedagogy. —**ed′u·ca′tion·al** *adj.* —**ed′u·ca′tion·al·ly** *adv.*

ed·u·ca·tive (ej′ŏŏ·kā′tiv) *adj.* **1** Tending or helping to educate; instructive. **2** Of or pertaining to education.

e·duce (i·dyōōs′) *v.t.* **e·duced, e·duc·ing 1** To call forth; draw out; evoke. **2** To develop or formulate, as from data. [< L *ex-* out + *ducere* to lead] —**e·duc′i·ble** *adj.* —**e·duc·tion** (i·duk′shən), **e·duc′tor** *n.*

-ee *suffix of nouns* **1** A person who undergoes the action or receives the benefit of the main element: *payee.* **2** A person who is described by the main element: *absentee.* [< L *-atus*]

E.E. Electrical Engineer.

E.E.C. European Economic Community.

eel (ēl) *n. pl.* **eels** or **eel** A fish having an elongated snakelike body without scales or pelvic fins. [< OE *ǣl*] —**eel′y** *adj.*

American eel

eel·grass (ēl′gras′, -gräs′) *n.* A plant of grasslike appearance that grows under water.

e'en (ēn) *adv.* Even. —*n. Regional* Evening.

e'er (âr) *adv.* Ever.

-eer *suffix* **1** One who is concerned with, works with, or produces the thing mentioned: *engineer.* **2** To be concerned with: *electioneer.* [< L *-arius*]

ee·rie (ē′rē, ir′ē) *adj.* **1** Inspiring fear or awe; weird. **2** Affected by fear; awed. Also **ee′ry.** [< OE *earg* timid] —**ee′ri·ly** *adv.* —**ee′ri·ness** *n.*

ef·face (i·fās′) *v.t.* **·faced, ·fac·ing 1** To rub out, as written characters; erase; cancel. **2** To obliterate or destroy. **3** To make (oneself) inconspicuous or insignificant. [< L *ex-* out + *facies* face] —**ef·face′a·ble** *adj.* —**ef·face′ment, ef·fac′er** *n.*

ef·fect (i·fekt′) *n.* **1** A result or consequence of some cause or agency. **2** The power or capacity to produce a result; efficacy. **3** The condition of being in actual operation: When does the ruling go into *effect?* **4** Actual meaning: usu. with *to:* They wrote to this *effect.* **5** An impression or reaction resulting from something seen, done, or experienced: the *effect* of a play. **6** Something causing a particular impression or reaction: many weird *effects.* **7** *pl.* Movable goods or property; belongings. —**in effect 1** In fact; actually. **2** In essence; virtually. **3** In operation or force. —**take effect** To begin to show results; become operative. —*v.t.* **1** To bring about; cause. **2** To achieve; accomplish. [< L *ex-* out + *facere* do, make] —**ef·fect′er** *n.* —**Syn.** *n.* **1** upshot, outcome, conclusion. • See AFFECT[1].

ef·fec·tive (i·fek′tiv) *adj.* **1** Producing a desired effect or result. **2** Impressive; striking. **3** In force, as a law. **4** Ready, as an army. —*n.* A soldier or military unit ready for active duty. —**ef·fec′tive·ly** *adv.* —**ef·fec′tive·ness** *n.*

ef·fec·tu·al (i·fek′chōō·əl) *adj.* **1** Possessing or exercising power to produce a desired effect. **2** In force; legal. —**ef·fec′tu·al′i·ty** (-al′ə·tē) *n.* —**ef·fec′tu·al·ly** *adv.*

ef·fec·tu·ate (i·fek′chōō·āt) *v.t.* **·at·ed, ·at·ing** To bring about; effect. —**ef·fec′tu·a′tion** *n.*

ef·fem·i·nate (i·fem′ə·nit) *adj.* **1** Having womanish traits or qualities inappropriate to a man; unmanly. **2** Characterized by weakness, a lack of dynamism, overrefinement, etc.: an *effeminate* culture. [< L *ex-* out + *femina* a woman] —**ef·fem′i·na·cy** (-nə·sē) *n.* —**ef·fem′i·nate·ly** *adv.*

ef·fer·ent (ef′ər·ənt) *adj.* Carrying or carried outward, as impulses from the central nervous system to muscles, etc. —*n.* An efferent part, as a nerve or blood vessel. [< L *ex-* out + *ferre* carry]

ef·fer·vesce (ef′ər·ves′) *v.i.* **·vesced, ·vesc·ing 1** To give off bubbles of gas, as carbonated water. **2** To issue forth in bubbles, as a gas. **3** To show exhilaration or lively spirits. [< L *ex-* out + *fervescere* to boil.] —**ef′fer·ves′cence, ef′fer·ves′cen·cy** *n.* —**ef′fer·ves′cent** *adj.* —**ef′fer·ves′cent·ly** *adv.*

ef·fete (i·fēt′) *adj.* **1** Incapable of further production; exhausted; barren. **2** Characterized by weakness, self-indulgence, decadence, etc. [< L *ex-* out + *fetus* a breeding] —**ef·fete′ness** *n.*

ef·fi·ca·cious (ef′ə·kā′shəs) *adj.* Producing or capable of producing an intended effect. [< L *efficere* to effect] —**ef′fi·ca′cious·ly** *adv.* —**ef′fi·ca′cious·ness** *n.*

ef·fi·ca·cy (ef′ə·kə·sē) *n. pl.* **·cies** Power to produce a desired result or effect.

ef·fi·cien·cy (i·fish′ən·sē) *n. pl.* **·cies 1** The character of being efficient; effectiveness. **2** The ratio of the output energy of an organism or machine to input energy.

ef·fi·cient (i·fish′ənt) *adj.* **1** Acting or operating effectively with little waste of energy, effort, or material. **2** Productive of effects or results; causative. [< L *efficere* to effect] —**ef·fi′cient·ly** *adv.* —**Syn. 1** skillful, competent. **2** operative, effectual.

ef·fi·gy (ef′ə·jē) *n. pl.* **·gies 1** A figure representing a person, as in sculpture or numismatics. **2** A representation of a despised person. —**burn** (or **hang**) **in effigy** To burn or hang publicly an image of a person who is hated. [< L *effigies* image]

ef·flo·resce (ef′lô·res′, -lō-) *v.i.* **·resced, ·resc·ing 1** *Bot.* To bear flowers. **2** *Chem.* To become powdery through loss of water of crystallization. [< L *ex-* thoroughly + *florescere* to bloom]

ef·flo·res·cence (ef′lô·res′əns, -lō-) *n.* **1** *Bot.* The time or act of flowering. **2** The process or result of efflorescing. —**ef′flo·res·cent** *adj.*

ef·flu·ent (ef′lōō·ənt) *adj.* Flowing out. —*n.* An outflow, as of water from a lake or stream. [< L < *ex-* out + *fluere* to flow] —**ef′flu·ence** *n.*

ef·flu·vi·um (i·flōō′vē·əm) *n. pl.* **·vi·a** (-vē·ə) or **·vi·ums 1** An invisible emanation. **2** A noxious or ill-smelling exhalation, as from decaying matter. [< L, a flowing out] —**ef·flu′vi·al, ef·flu′vi·ous** *adj.*

ef·fort (ef′ərt) *n.* **1** A voluntary exertion of mental or physical power in order to accomplish something. **2** An endeavor; attempt. **3** A result or display of power; an achievement. [< L *ex-* out + *fortis* strong] —**Syn. 1** strain, stress, exertion.

ef·fort·less (ef′ərt·lis) *adj.* Showing or making no effort; easy. —**ef′fort·less·ly** *adv.* —**ef′fort·less·ness** *n.*

ef·front·er·y (i·frun′tər·ē) *n. pl.* **·er·ies** Insolent assurance; audacity; impudence. [< L *ex-* out + *frons, frontis* forehead, face]

ef·ful·gence (i·ful′jəns) *n.* A shining forth brilliantly; beaming brightness; radiance. [< L *ex-* out + *fulgere* to shine] —**ef·ful′gent** *adj.* —**ef·ful′gent·ly** *adv.*

ef·fuse *v.* (i·fyōōz′) **·fused, ·fus·ing** *v.t.* **1** To pour forth; shed. —*v.i.* **2** To emanate; exude. —*adj.* (i·fyōōs′) **1** *Bot.* Spread loosely or flat. **2** *Zool.* Having the lips separated, as a shell. [< L *effusus*, pp. of *effundere* to pour out]

ef·fu·sion (i·fyōō′zhən) *n.* **1** The act or product of pouring forth. **2** An outpouring, as of fancy or sentiment. **3** *Pathol.* The escape of blood or other fluid, as into the cellular tissue.

ef·fu·sive (i·fyōō′siv) *adj.* **1** Overflowing with sentiment; overly demonstrative; gushing. **2** Pouring forth. —**ef·fu′sive·ly** *adv.* —**ef·fu′sive·ness** *n.*

Eg. Egypt; Egyptian.

e.g. for example (L *exempli gratia*).

e·gad (i·gad′, ē·gad′) *interj.* By God!: a mild oath. [Prob. alter. of *ah, God!*]

e·gal·i·tar·i·an (i·gal′ə·târ′ē·ən) *adj.* Of, believing in, or characterized by the doctrine of political and social equality. —*n.* A person who advocates this doctrine. [< F *égalité* equality] —**e·gal′i·tar′i·an·ism** *n.*

egg[1] (eg) *n.* **1** A reproductive body containing the germ and the food yolk of birds, insects, reptiles, or fishes, enclosed in a membranous or shell-like covering. **2** Such a body, esp. that of domestic fowl, used as food. **3** The female reproductive cell; an ovum. **4** Something like a hen's egg in shape. **5** *Slang* Person: a good *egg.* —*v.t.* **1** To mix or cover with eggs. **2** *Informal* To pelt with eggs. —**lay an egg** *Slang* To fail: said of a play, joke, etc. [< ON]

egg[2] *v.t.* To instigate or incite; urge: usu. with *on.* [< ON *eggja*]

egg·head (eg′hed′) *n. Slang* An intellectual; a highbrow: usu. slightly derisive.

egg·nog (eg′nog′) *n.* A drink made of eggs, milk, sugar, and nutmeg, and sometimes with alcoholic liquor.

egg·plant (eg′plant′, -plänt′) *n.* **1** A widely cultivated herb of the nightshade family, with large, egg-shaped, edible fruit. **2** The fruit, used as a vegetable.

egg·shell (eg′shel′) *n.* **1** The brittle outer envelope of a bird's egg. **2** A light ivory color. **3** A thin and delicate porcelain.

e·gis (ē′jis) *n.* AEGIS.

eg·lan·tine (eg′lən·tīn, -tēn) *n.* SWEETBRIER. [< OF *aiglent,* ult. < L *acus* needle]

e·go (ē′go, eg′ō) *n. pl.* **e·gos 1** The conscious self. **2** *Psychoanal.* The superficial conscious part of the psyche, developed in response to environment. **3** Self-centeredness; egotism; conceit. [L, I]

e·go·cen·tric (ē′gō·sen′trik, eg′ō-) *adj.* Caring excessively or only for one's self or personal interests; self-centered. —*n.* An egocentric person. —**e′go·cen·tric′i·ty** (-sen·tris′ə·tē) *n.*

e·go·ism (ē′gō·iz′əm, eg′ō-) *n.* **1** Excessive interest in or concern about one's self; self-centeredness; conceit. **2** The doctrine that the goal of human conduct is the perfection or happiness of the ego or self. —**e′go·ist** *n.* —**e·go·ist′ic** or **·i·cal** *adj.* —**e′go·is′ti·cal·ly** *adv.* • See EGOTISM.

e·go·ma·ni·a (ē′gō·mā′nē·ə, -mān′yə, eg′ō-) *n.* Abnormal or excessive egotism. —**e′go·ma′ni·ac** *n.* —**e′go·ma·ni′a·cal** (-mə·nī′ə·kəl) *adj.*

e·go·tism (ē′gə·tiz′əm, eg′ə-) *n.* **1** The excessive and habitual practice of talking only about oneself or one's concerns. **2** CONCEIT. **3** EGOISM. —**e′go·tist** *n.* —**e′go·tis′tic** or **·ti·cal** *adj.* —**e′go·tis′ti·cal·ly** *adv.* • *Egoism* and *egotism* are often used interchangeably. However, *egoism* is felt by many to manifest itself more in self-centered thought and inner concern, whereas *egotism* is outwardly revealed in speech and actions.

e·gre·gious (i·grē′jəs, -jē·əs) *adj.* Unusually or conspicuously bad; flagrant. [< L *ex-* out + *grex, gregis* the herd] —**e·gre′gious·ly** *adv.* —**e·gre′gious·ness** *n.*

e·gress (ē′gres) *n.* **1** A going out, as from a building. **2** A place of exit. **3** The right to exit. Also **e·gres′sion.** [< L *ex-* out + *gradi* go] —**Syn. 1** emergence, exit.

e·gret (ē′grit) *n.* A heron characterized, in the breeding season, by long and loose plumes drooping over the tail and, usu., white plumage. [< OF *aigrette*]

E·gypt (ē′jipt) *n.* A republic of NE Africa, 386,198 sq. mi., capital Cairo. • See also map at AFRICA.

Egypt. Egyptian.

E·gyp·tian (i·jip′·shən) *adj.* Of or pertaining to Egypt, its people, or their culture. —*n.* **1** One of the people of Egypt, ancient or modern. **2** The Hamitic language of the ancient Egyptians.

E·gyp·tol·o·gy (ē′jip·tol′ə·jē) *n.* The science or study of the antiquities of Egypt. —**E′gyp·tol′o·gist** *n.*

eh (ā, e) *interj.* What: used as an interrogative.

ei·der (ī′dər) *n.* A large sea duck of northern regions. Also **eider duck.** [< ON *æðhr*]

ei·der·down (ī′dər·doun′) *n.* **1** The down of the eider used for stuffing pillows and quilts. **2** A quilt so stuffed.

ei·det·ic (ī·det′ik) *adj. Psychol.* Of or pertaining to exceptionally clear and detailed visualization. [< Gk. *eidētikos* pertaining to images]

Eiffel Tower (ī′fəl) An iron tower in Paris, 984 feet high, designed for the Exposition of 1889. [< A. G. *Eiffel,* 1832–1923, French engineer]

eight (āt) *n.* **1** The sum of seven plus one; 8; VIII. **2** A set or group of eight members. [< OE *eahta*] —**eight** *adj., pron.*

eight·een (ā′tēn′) *n.* **1** The sum of 17 plus 1; 18; XVIII. **2** A set or group of 18 members. —**eight′een′** *adj., pron.*

eight·eenth (ā′tēnth′) *adj. & adv.* Next in order after the 17th. —*n.* **1** The element of an ordered set that corresponds to the number 18. **2** One of 18 equal parts.

eight·fold (āt′fōld′) *adv.* So as to be eight times as many or as great. —*adj.* **1** Consisting of eight parts. **2** Eight times as many or as great.

eighth (ātth, āth) *adj. & adv.* Next in order after the seventh. —*n.* **1** The element of an ordered set that corresponds to the number eight. **2** One of eight equal parts.

eighth note *Music* A note having one eighth of the time value of a whole note. • See NOTE.

eight·i·eth (ā′tē·ith) *adj. & adv.* Tenth in order after the 70th. —*n.* **1** The element of an ordered set that corresponds to the number 80. **2** One of 80 equal parts.

eight·y (ā′tē) *adj.* Consisting of ten more than 70. —*n. pl.* **·ties 1** The product of eight and ten; 80; LXXX. **2** A set or group of 80 members. **3** *pl.* The numbers, years, etc. between 80 and 90. —**eight′y** *adj., pron.*

ein·stein·i·um (īn·stīn′ē·əm) *n.* An artificially produced radioactive element (symbol Es). [< Albert *Einstein,* 1879–1955, German-born U.S. physicist]

ei·ther (ē′thər, ī′-) *adj.* **1** One or the other of two: Use *either* foot on the pedal. **2** Each of two; one and the other: on *either* side. —*pron.* One of two; one or the other. —*conj.* In one of two or more cases: used as a correlative introducing a first alternative, the second and any other being preceded by *or: Either* I shall go *or* he will come. —*adv.* Also; any more so: used as an intensifier after negative statements: He could not speak, and I could not *either.* [< OE *ǣgther*]

e·jac·u·late (i·jak′yə·lāt) *v.* **·lat·ed, ·lat·ing** *v.t.* 1 To utter suddenly. 2 To eject suddenly, as semen. —*v.i.* 3 To eject semen. [< L *ex-* out + *jaculari* to throw] —**e·jac′u·la′tion, e·jac′u·la′tor** *n.* —**e·jac′u·la·to′ry** *adj.*

e·ject (i·jekt′) *v.t.* 1 To throw or drive out by sudden force; expel. 2 EVICT. [< L *ex-* out + *jacere* to throw] —**e·jec′tion, e·ject′ment** *n.* —**e·jec′tive** *adj.* —**e·jec′tive·ly** *adv.* —**Syn.** 1 banish, oust, exile, deport.

eke (ēk) *v.t.* **eked, ek·ing** 1 To supplement; piece out: usu. with *out.* 2 To obtain or produce (a living) with difficulty: usu. with *out.* [< OE *ēcan*]

EKG electrocardiogram.

e·kis·tics (i·kis′tiks) *n. pl. (construed as sing.)* The study of human settlements, including area planning and the relationship between communities. [< Gk. *oikos* habitat + -ICS] —**e·kis′tic** *adj.*

el (el) *n. Informal* ELEVATED RAILROAD.

e·lab·o·rate (i·lab′ə·rāt) *v.* **·rat·ed, ·rat·ing** *v.t.* 1 To create and work out with care and in detail. 2 To produce by labor; make. —*v.i.* 3 To speak or write so as to embellish a matter, subject, etc., with additional details: with *on* or *upon.* —*adj.* (-ər·it) 1 Developed in detail and with care: an *elaborate* plan. 2 Ornate; complicated, as a design. 3 PAINSTAKING. [< L *ex-* out + *laborare* to work] —**e·lab′o·rate·ly** *adv.* —**e·lab′o·rate·ness, e·lab′o·ra′tion** *n.* —**e·lab′o·ra′tive** *adj.* —**Syn.** *v.* 1 develop, devise. 2 execute. —*adj.* 2 showy, extravagant, fancy.

é·lan (ā·län′) *n.* Verve; dash; vivacity. [F < *élancer* to dart, throw out]

e·land (ē′lənd) *n.* A large oxlike African antelope with twisted horns. [Du., elk]

Eland

e·lapse (i·laps′) *v.i.* **e·lapsed, e·laps·ing** To slip by; pass away: said of time. [< L *elapsus,* pp. of *elabi* glide away]

e·las·mo·branch (i·las′mō·brangk, i·laz′-) *n.* Any of a class of fishes having lamellar gills and cartilaginous skeletons, including sharks and rays. [< Gk. *elasmos* metal plate + *branchia* gill]

e·las·tic (i·las′tik) *adj.* 1 Spontaneously returning to a former size, shape, etc., after being altered from it. 2 Capable of quick recovery, as from misfortune. 3 Changing or adapting readily in response to new circumstances or demands. —*n.* 1 A stretchable fabric having rubber or rubberlike threads woven therein. 2 A garter, suspender, etc., made of this fabric. 3 RUBBER BAND. [< Gk. *elastikos* driving] —**e·las′ti·cal·ly** *adv.*

e·las·tic·i·ty (i·las′tis′ə·tē, ē′las-) *n.* The quality or condition of being elastic.

e·late (i·lāt′) *v.t.* **·lat·ed, ·lat·ing** To raise the spirits of; excite. —*adj.* Exalted or triumphant; exultant. [< L *elatus* lifted up] —**e·lat′ed** *adj.* —**e·lat′ed·ly** *adv.* —**e·lat′ed·ness** *n.*

e·la·tion (i·lā′shən) *n.* Exalted feeling, as from pride or joy; exultation.

el·bow (el′bō) *n.* 1 The joint at the bend of the arm between the upper and lower arm, esp. the knoblike outer projection of this joint. 2 A similar joint in the foreleg of a quadruped. 3 Anything resembling an elbow, as a short angular pipe fitting. —*v.t.* 1 To push or jostle with or as with the elbows. 2 To make (one's way) by such pushing. —*v.i.* 3 To move ahead in such a manner. [< OE *elnboga*]

el·bow·room (el′bō·ro͞om′, -ro͝om′) *n.* Room enough to move or function without hindrance.

el·der[1] (el′dər) *n.* 1 A shrub of the honeysuckle family, with white flowers and purple-black or red berries. 2 Any of various unrelated shrubs and trees, as the box elder. [OE *ellærn*]

eld·er[2] (el′dər) *adj.* 1 Having lived longer; earlier born; older. 2 Having superior or prior rank, position, validity, etc. 3 Earlier in time; former. —*n.* 1 An older or aged person. 2 ANCESTOR. 3 An older person having a certain position of authority, as in a community. 4 Any of various officers in certain Christian churches. [< OE *eldra*]

el·der·ber·ry (el′dər·ber′ē, -bər·ē) *n. pl.* **·ber·ries** The drupe of the common elder.

eld·er·ly (el′dər·lē) *adj.* Somewhat old; approaching old age. —**eld′er·li·ness** *n.*

eld·est (el′dist) *adj.* First-born; oldest.

El Do·ra·do (el də·rä′dō) 1 A legendary South American realm rich in gold and jewels. 2 Any region rich in gold or opportunity. Also **El′do·ra′do.**

elec., elect. electric; electrical; electricity.

e·lect (i·lekt′) *v.t.* 1 To choose for an office by vote. 2 To take by choice or selection. 3 *Theol.* To choose or set aside for eternal life. —*v.i.* 4 To make a choice. —*adj.* 1 Elected to office, but not yet in charge: used in compounds, as president-*elect.* 2 *Theol.* Chosen of God for salvation. 3 Selected; chosen; picked out. —*n.* An elect person. [< L *ex-* out + *legere* choose]

e·lec·tion (i·lek′shən) *n.* 1 The selecting of a person or persons for office, as by ballot. 2 Any choice or act of choosing. 3 In Calvinism, the predestination of some individuals to be saved by God.

e·lec·tion·eer (i·lek′shən·ir′) *v.i.* 1 To endeavor to win an election. 2 To canvass for votes.

e·lec·tive (i·lek′tiv) *adj.* 1 Of or pertaining to a choice by vote. 2 Obtained or resolved by election. 3 Exerting the privilege of choice. 4 Subject to choice; optional. —*n.* An optional study in a school or college curriculum. —**e·lec′tive·ly** *adv.* —**e·lec′tive·ness** *n.*

e·lec·tor (i·lek′tər) *n.* 1 One who elects; a qualified voter. 2 A member of the electoral college. 3 One of the German princes who had the right of electing the Holy Roman Emperor. —**e·lec′tor·al** *adj.*

electoral college The body of electors chosen by the voters of the states and the District of Columbia to elect formally the president and vice president of the U.S. Each elector is traditionally expected but not legally bound to reflect the popular vote of his state.

e·lec·tor·ate (i·lek′tər·it) *n.* 1 The entire body of qualified voters. 2 The rank or territory of an elector in the Holy Roman Empire.

E·lec·tra (i·lek′trə) *Gk. Myth.* The daughter of Agamemnon and Clytemnestra and sister of Orestes.

e·lec·tric (i·lek′trik) *adj.* 1 Relating to, derived from, produced, or operated by electricity. 2 Containing, producing, or carrying electricity. 3 Dynamic; exciting; electrifying; also, tense, as if electrified. —*n.* A street car, train, or other vehicle run by electricity. [< Gk. *ēlektron* amber: in ref. to static charge produced when amber is rubbed]

e·lec·tri·cal (i·lek′tri·kəl) *adj.* 1 ELECTRIC. 2 Of or skilled in the use or science of electricity. —**e·lec′tri·cal·ly** *adv.*

electrical energy Readily transportable energy produced industrially by transforming other forms of energy; electricity.

electric cell Any of various devices consisting of two dissimilar metals or materials immersed in an electrolyte, capable of generating electricity by chemical action.

electric chair 1 A chair used for electrocuting criminals. 2 The sentence of death by electrocution.

electric eel An eellike fish of tropical America, capable of delivering powerful electric shocks.

electric eye PHOTOELECTRIC CELL.

e·lec·tri·cian (i·lek′trish′ən, ē′lek-) *n.* One skilled in the installation and repair of electrical equipment.

e·lec·tric·i·ty (i·lek′tris′ə·tē, ē′lek-) *n.* 1 A property of matter associated with atomic particles that are capable of attracting and repelling each other over relatively long distances, and which can be made to perform work. 2 A flow of such particles, usu. electrons, used as a source of power or energy. 3 The science dealing with electricity.

electric ray A ray fish having an electric organ with which it stuns its prey.

e·lec·tri·fy (i·lek′trə·fī) *v.t.* **·fied, ·fy·ing** 1 To charge with, or subject to electricity. 2 To equip for the use of or operation by electricity. 3 To supply with electricity. 4 To arouse; startle; thrill. —**e·lec′tri·fi·ca′tion** *n.*

electro- *combining form* Electric; by, with, or of electricity: *electrocardiogram.*

e·lec·tro·car·di·o·gram (i·lek′trō·kär′dē·ə·gram′) *n.* A graph showing electrical activity of the heart.

e·lec·tro·car·di·o·graph (i·lek′trō·kär′dē·ə·graf′, -gräf′) *n.* An instrument for recording the electrical activity of the heart, used in the diagnosis of heart diseases. **—e·lec·tro·car·di·og·ra·phy** (i·lek′trō·kär′dē·og′rə·fē) *n.*

e·lec·tro·chem·is·try (i·lek′trō·kem′is·trē) *n.* The science of electrical and chemical interactions. **—e·lec′tro·chem′i·cal** *adj.* **—e·lec′tro·chem′i·cal·ly** *adv.*

e·lec·tro·cute (i·lek′trə·kyōōt) *v.t.* **·cut·ed, ·cut·ing** **1** To kill by electricity. **2** To execute in an electric chair. [<ELECTRO- + (EXE)CUTE] **—e·lec′tro·cu′tion** *n.*

e·lec·trode (i·lek′trōd) *n. Electr.* A conducting element through which an electric charge leaves or enters an electrolytic cell, vacuum tube, electric arc, furnace, etc.

e·lec·tro·dy·nam·ics (i·lek′trō·dī·nam′iks) *n. pl. (construed as sing.)* The branch of physics which deals with the interactions of magnetic fields and electric currents. **—e·lec′tro·dy·nam′ic** or **·i·cal** *adj.*

e·lec·tro·en·ceph·a·lo·gram (i·lek′trō·en·sef′ə·lə·gram′) *n.* A record of electric activity in the brain.

e·lec·tro·en·ceph·a·lo·graph (i·lek′trō·en·sef′ə·lə·graf′) *n.* A device for recording electric activity in the brain.

e·lec·trol·y·sis (i·lek′trol′ə·sis) *n.* **1** The decomposing of an electrolyte by an electric current. **2** The use of an electrified needle to destroy the roots of unwanted body hair.

e·lec·tro·lyte (i·lek′trə·līt) *n.* A substance composed of ions and capable of conducting electricity when dissolved or molten. [<ELECTRO- + Gk. *lytos* loosened] **—e·lec·tro·lyt·ic** (i·lek′trə·lit′ik) or **·i·cal** *adj.* **—e·lec′tro·lyt′i·cal·ly** *adv.*

e·lec·tro·lyze (i·lek′trə·līz) *v.t.* **·lyzed, ·lyz·ing** To decompose by electric current.

e·lec·tro·mag·net (i·lek′trō·mag′nit) *n.* A core of soft iron or the like, which temporarily becomes a magnet during the passage of an electric current through a coil of wire surrounding it.

electromagnetic spectrum The total range of electromagnetic waves comprising, in order of increasing wavelength, cosmic, gamma, and X-rays, ultraviolet, visible light, infrared, and radio waves.

electromagnetic wave A wave which is propagated through space by simultaneously alternating magnetic and electric fields.

e·lec·tro·mag·net·ism (i·lek′trō·mag′nə·tiz′əm) *n.* **1** Magnetism developed by electricity. **2** The branch of physics concerned with the relation between electricity and magnetism. **—e·lec′tro·mag·net′ic** (-mag·net′ik) or **·i·cal** *adj.* **—e·lec′tro·mag·net′i·cal·ly** *adv.*

e·lec·tro·mo·tive (i·lek′trə·mō′tiv) *adj.* Producing or tending to produce an electric current.

electromotive force That which tends to produce the flow of electricity from one point to another; voltage.

e·lec·tron (i·lek′tron) *n.* An atomic particle having a negative electric charge equal to 1.602×10^{-19} coulomb and a mass equal to 1/1837 that of a proton. [<Gk. *ēlektron* amber. See ELECTRIC.]

e·lec·tro·neg·a·tive (i·lek′trō·neg′ə·tiv) *adj.* **1** Bearing a charge like that of an electron; electrically negative. **2** Tending to form a chemical bond or bonds by attracting electrons.

e·lec·tron·ic (i·lek′tron′ik, ē′lek-) *adj.* **1** Of or pertaining to electrons or electronics. **2** Operating or produced by the movement of electrons or other carriers of electric charge, as in an electron tube or semiconductor device. **—e·lec′·tron′i·cal·ly** *adv.*

electronic mail **1** The transmission of text between computers, either by wire or by satellite transmission. **2** Text information sent by this system.

electronic music Music based on an arrangement of electronically produced, organized, or altered sounds, recorded on tape.

e·lec·tron·ics (i·lek′tron′iks, ē′lek-) *n. pl. (construed as sing.)* The study of the properties and behavior of electrons and other carriers of electric charge, esp. with reference to technical and industrial applications.

electron microscope A microscope which uses high-energy streams of electrons in order to magnify objects too small to reflect the relatively large wavelengths of visible light.

electron tube A sealed tube in which a flow of electrons from a cathode to an anode is controlled or influenced by the voltages on one or more grids through which it must pass.

electron volt A unit of energy equal to that acquired by an electron which passes through a potential difference of one volt, approximately 1.602×10^{-19} joule.

e·lec·tro·plate (i·lek′trə·plāt′) *v.t.* **—plat·ed, ·plat·ing** To coat with metal by electrolysis. *—n.* An electroplated article. **—e·lec′tro·plat′er** *n.*

e·lec·tro·pos·i·tive (i·lek′trō·poz′ə·tiv) *adj.* **1** Bearing a charge like that of a proton; electrically positive. **2** Tending to form a chemical bond or bonds by losing electrons.

e·lec·tro·scope (i·lek′trə·skōp) *n.* An instrument for detecting an electric charge by the attraction or repulsion of pith balls or strips of metal foil. **—e·lec′tro·scop′ic** (-skop′ik) *adj.*

e·lec·tro·stat·ic (i·lek′trō·stat′ik) *adj.* Of, pertaining to, produced by, or caused by electric charges at rest.

e·lec·tro·stat·ics (i·lek′trō·stat′iks) *n. pl. (construed as sing.)* The branch of physics that treats of electric charges at rest.

e·lec·tro·ther·a·py (i·lek′trō·ther′ə·pē) *n.* The treatment of disease by electricity. **—e·lec′tro·ther′a·pist** *n.*

e·lec·tro·type (i·lek′trō·tīp′) *n.* **1** A facsimile plate of any surface made by the electric deposition of metal on the surface, esp. such a plate made of a page of type for printing. **2** An impression made from such a plate. **3** The process of electrotyping. *—v.t.* **·typed, ·typ·ing** To make an electrotype of. **—e·lec′tro·typ′er** *n.*

el·ee·mos·y·nar·y (el′ə·mos′ə·ner′ē, el′ē·ə-) *adj.* **1** Of or pertaining to charity or alms. **2** Charitable; nonprofit: *eleemosynary* institutions. **3** Aided by or dependent upon charity. *—n. pl.* **·nar·ies** A recipient of charity. [<Med. L *eleemosyna* alms]

el·e·gance (el′ə·gəns) *n.* **1** The state or quality of being elegant or refined. **2** Anything elegant. Also **el′e·gan·cy.**

el·e·gant (el′ə·gənt) *adj.* **1** Characterized by a tasteful luxuriousness and grace of style, design, content, etc. **2** Possessing or exhibiting a refined taste and gracefulness of manner, dress, etc. **3** *Informal* Excellent; capital. **4** Marked by appropriateness and simplicity: an *elegant* solution. [<L *elegans* fastidious] **—el′e·gant·ly** *adv.* **—Syn. 2** refined, polished.

el·e·gi·ac (el′ə·jī′ək, i·lē′jē·ak) *adj.* **1** Pertaining to elegies. **2** Of the nature of an elegy; sad; plaintive. **3** In ancient prosody, written in couplets consisting of one hexameter and one pentameter line. Also **el′e·gi′a·cal.** *—n. pl.* Verse composed in the elegiac spirit or form.

el·e·gize (el′ə·jīz) *v.t. & v.i.* **·gized, ·giz·ing** To mourn or commemorate in elegaic form. **—el·eg·ist** (el′ə·jist) *n.*

el·e·gy (el′ə·jē) *n. pl.* **·gies** **1** A meditative poem with sorrowful theme. **2** A classical poem written in elegiac verse. **3** A musical composition of a sad or meditative character. [<Gk. *elegos* a song]

el·e·ment (el′ə·mənt) *n.* **1** A component or essential part, esp. of anything complex. **2** *pl.* First principles or fundamental ideas; rudiments. **3** One of the four substances (earth, air, fire, and water) anciently supposed to make up all things. **4** *pl.* Atmospheric conditions or powers, as rain, wind, etc. **5** An essential or determining factor. **6** A group or class having certain characteristics in common: the *rowdy* element in the crowd. **7** The natural or appropriate sphere or environment for a person or thing. **8** *Eccl.* The bread and wine of the Lord's Supper. **9** Any of a number of substances composed entirely of atoms having identical nuclear charges, as gold, carbon, sodium, etc. **10** One of the primary parts of an organism; a cell. **11** *Geom.* One of the forms or data which together compose a figure, as a line, a point, a plane, a space. **12 a** Any one of the members of a set. **b** A term in an algebraic expression. [<L *elementum* first principle]

el·e·men·tal (el′ə·men′təl) *adj.* **1** Of or pertaining to an element or elements. **2** Having to do with rudiments or first principles; basic. **3** Of or like the basic, powerful forces or drives in man or nature. **—el′e·men′tal·ly** *adv.*

el·e·men·ta·ry (el′ə·men′tər·ē) *adj.* **1** ELEMENTAL. **2** Rudi-

CHEMICAL ELEMENTS

Each weight in parentheses represents the mass number of the most stable isotope of the element so designated.

	Symbol	Atomic Number	Atomic Weight
actinium	Ac	89	(227)
aluminum	Al	13	26.9815
americium	Am	95	(243)
antimony	Sb	51	121.75
argon	Ar	18	39.948
arsenic	As	33	74.9216
astatine	At	85	(210)
barium	Ba	56	137.34
berkelium	Bk	97	(248)
beryllium	Be	4	9.0122
bismuth	Bi	83	208.980
boron	B	5	10.811
bromine	Br	35	79.904
cadmium	Cd	48	112.40
calcium	Ca	20	40.08
californium	Cf	98	(251)
carbon	C	6	12.01115
cerium	Ce	58	140.12
cesium	Cs	55	132.905
chlorine	Cl	17	35.453
chromium	Cr	24	51.996
cobalt	Co	27	58.9332
copper	Cu	29	63.546
curium	Cm	96	(247)
dysprosium	Dy	66	162.50
einsteinium	Es	99	(254)
erbium	Er	68	167.26
europium	Eu	63	151.96
fermium	Fm	100	(257)
fluorine	F	9	18.9984
francium	Fr	87	(223)
gadolinium	Gd	64	157.25
gallium	Ga	31	69.72
germanium	Ge	32	72.59
gold	Au	79	196.967
hafnium	Hf	72	178.49
helium	He	2	4.0026
holmium	Ho	67	164.930
hydrogen	H	1	1.00797
indium	In	49	114.82
iodine	I	53	126.9044
iridium	Ir	77	192.2
iron	Fe	26	55.847
krypton	Kr	36	83.80
lanthanum	La	57	138.91
lawrencium	Lr	103	(257)
lead	Pb	82	207.19
lithium	Li	3	6.939
lutetium	Lu	71	174.97
magnesium	Mg	12	24.312
manganese	Mn	25	54.9380
mendelevium	Md	101	(256)
mercury	Hg	80	200.59
molybdenum	Mo	42	95.94
neodymium	Nd	60	144.24
neon	Ne	10	20.183
neptunium	Np	93	(237)
nickel	Ni	28	58.71
niobium	Nb	41	92.906
nitrogen	N	7	14.0067
nobelium	No	102	(254)
osmium	Os	76	190.2
oxygen	O	8	15.9994
palladium	Pd	46	106.4
phosphorus	P	15	30.9738
platinum	Pt	78	195.09
plutonium	Pu	94	(244)
polonium	Po	84	(209)
potassium	K	19	39.102
praseodymium	Pr	59	140.907
promethium	Pm	61	(145)
protactinium	Pa	91	(231)
radium	Ra	88	(226)
radon	Rn	86	(222)
rhenium	Re	75	186.2
rhodium	Rh	45	102.905
rubidium	Rb	37	85.47
ruthenium	Ru	44	101.07
samarium	Sm	62	150.35
scandium	Sc	21	44.956
selenium	Se	34	78.96
silicon	Si	14	28.086
silver	Ag	47	107.868
sodium	Na	11	22.9898
strontium	Sr	38	87.62
sulfur	S	16	32.064
tantalum	Ta	73	180.948
technetium	Tc	43	(97)
tellurium	Te	52	127.60
terbium	Tb	65	158.924
thallium	Tl	81	204.37
thorium	Th	90	232.038
thulium	Tm	69	168.934
tin	Sn	50	118.69
titanium	Ti	22	47.90
tungsten	W	74	183.85
uranium	U	92	238.03
vanadium	V	23	50.942
xenon	Xe	54	131.30
ytterbium	Yb	70	173.04
yttrium	Y	39	88.905
zinc	Zn	30	65.37
zirconium	Zr	40	91.22

mentary; basic; fundamental. **3** Simple. **—el′e·men′ta·ri·ly** *adv.* **—el′e·men′ta·ri·ness** *n.*

elementary particle Any of the subatomic particles, as the electron, neutron, proton, etc., which are not a composite of other more fundamental entities.

elementary school A school giving a course of education in the first six or eight grades.

el·e·phant (el′ə·fənt) *n.* A massively built, almost hairless mammal of Asia or Africa having a flexible trunk and tusks valued as the chief source of ivory. [< Gk. *elephas*] **—el′e·phan′·tine** (-fan′tēn, -tin, -tīn) *adj.*

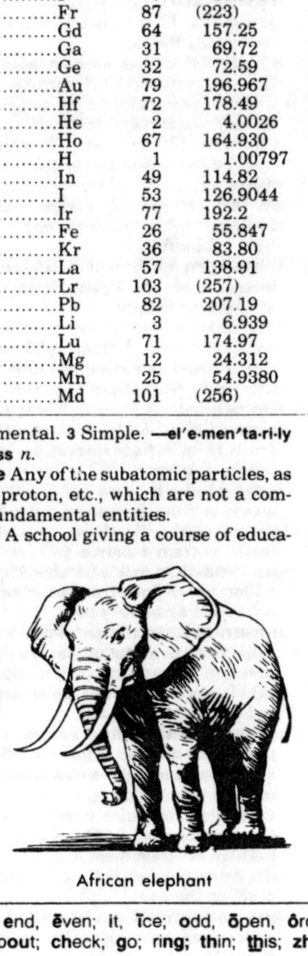
African elephant

el·e·phan·ti·a·sis (el′ə·fən·tī′ə·sis) *n.* A disease characterized by massive swelling due to obstruction of lymph vessels by a parasitic worm. [< ELEPHANT + -IASIS]

El·eu·sin·i·an (el′yo͞o·sin′ē·ən) *adj.* Of or pertaining to Eleusis or the Eleusinian mysteries.

Eleusinian mysteries The secret religious rites celebrated each spring in the ancient Greek city of Eleusis.

el·e·vate (el′ə·vāt) *v.t.* **·vat·ed, ·vat·ing 1** To raise; lift up. **2** To raise in rank, status, position, etc. **3** To raise the spirits of; inspire. **4** To raise the moral or intellectual level of. [< L *ex-* out, up + *levare* lighten] **—Syn. 1** heighten. **2** promote, advance. **3** exalt, cheer.

el·e·vat·ed (el′ə·vā′tid) *adj.* **1** Raised, esp. above the ground. **2** Exalted morally or intellectually. **—***n. Informal* ELEVATED RAILROAD.

elevated railroad A railroad that operates principally on an elevated framework so as to allow the passage of traffic and pedestrians below it. Also **elevated railway.**

el·e·va·tion (el′ə·vā′shən) *n.* **1** The act of elevating or the condition of being elevated. **2** An elevated place. **3** Height above sea level or the earth's surface. **4** *Astron.* The angular distance of a celestial body above the horizon. **5** In dancing, the ability to perform leaps. **6** *Eccl.* The raising of the eucharistic elements: also **elevation of the Host.**

el·e·va·tor (el′ə·vā′tər) *n.* 1 One who or that which elevates. 2 A hoisting mechanism for grain. 3 A warehouse where grain is elevated, stored, and distributed. 4 A movable platform or cage for carrying freight or passengers up or down, as in a building. 5 *Aeron.* A movable airfoil used to control an aircraft's ascent or descent. • See AIRPLANE.

e·lev·en (i·lev′ən) *n.* 1 The sum of ten plus one; 11; XI. 2 A set or group of 11 members. [< OE *endleofan*] **—e·lev′en** *adj., pron.*

e·lev·enth (i·lev′ənth) *adj. & adv.* Next in order after the tenth. *—n.* 1 The element of an ordered set that corresponds to the number 11. 2 One of eleven equal parts.

eleventh hour The last opportunity.

elf (elf) *n. pl.* **elves** (elvz) 1 A dwarfish, mischievous sprite. 2 A small person or child. [< OE *ælf*]

elf·in (el′fin) *adj.* Of or like an elf; esp. tiny, mischievous, etc. *—n.* ELF.

elf·ish (el′fish) *adj.* ELFIN. **—elf′ish·ly** *adv.* **—elf′ish·ness** *n.*

elf·lock (elf′lok′) *n. Usu. pl.* A lock of hair, matted as if by elves.

e·lic·it (i·lis′it) *v.t.* To draw out or forth, as by some attraction or inducement; bring to light. [< L *ex-* out + *lacere* entice] **—e·lic′i·ta′tion, e·lic′i·tor** *n.*

e·lide (i·līd′) *v.t.* **e·lid·ed, e·lid·ing** 1 To omit (a vowel or syllable) in writing or pronouncing a word. 2 To omit; ignore. [< L *ex-* out + *laedere* to strike] **—e·lid′i·ble** *adj.*

el·i·gi·ble (el′ə·jə·bəl) *adj.* 1 Capable of being chosen or elected. 2 Worthy of acceptance. *—n.* One who is eligible. [< L *eligere* to select, elect] **—el′i·gi·bil′i·ty** *n.* **—el′i·gi·bly** *adv.* **—Syn.** 1 qualified, fitted. 2 suitable, desirable.

e·lim·i·nate (i·lim′ə·nāt) *v.t.* **·nat·ed, ·nat·ing** 1 To get rid of. 2 To disregard as irrelevant or incorrect; ignore. 3 *Physiol.* To void; excrete. [< L *ex-* out + *limen* a threshold] **—e·lim′i·na′tion, e·lim′i·na′tor** *n.* **—e·lim′i·na′tive** *adj.*

e·li·sion (i·lizh′ən) *n.* The eliding or striking out of a part of a word, as in "o'er" for "over."

e·lite (i·lēt′) *n.* 1 The choicest part, as of a society. 2 A small but powerful group. 3 A size of typewriter type, equivalent to 10-point, with 12 characters to the inch. Also **é·lite′**. [< F < L *electa* choice]

e·lit·ism (i·lēt′iz·əm) *n.* Rule by an elite, or advocacy of such rule. **—e·li′tist** *adj., n.*

e·lix·ir (i·lik′sər) *n.* 1 A sweetened alcoholic medicinal preparation. 2 A substance which alchemists believed would change base metals to gold. 3 A cordial alleged to prolong youth. 4 The essential principle of something. 5 A cure-all; panacea. [< Ar. *al-iksīr* < Gk. *xērion* medicated powder]

E·liz·a·be·than (i·liz′ə·bē′thən, -beth′ən) *adj.* Relating to Elizabeth I of England, or to her era. *—n.* An Englishman who lived during the reign of Elizabeth I.

Elizabethan sonnet A sonnet which has the rhyme scheme *abab cdcd efef gg.*

elk (elk) *n. pl.* **elks** or **elk** 1 A large deer of N Europe and Asia, with broad antlers. 2 A large N. American deer; wapiti. [< ON *elgr*]

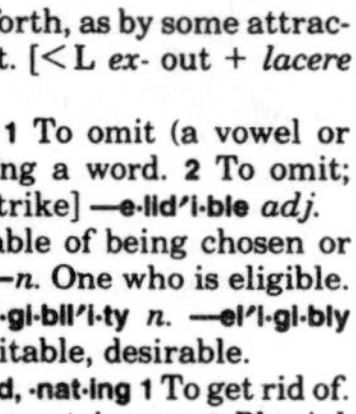

American elk

elk·hound (elk′hound′) *n.* A hunting dog of Norwegian origin, of medium size, with a short, robust body and thick gray coat. Also **Norwegian elkhound.**

ell (el) *n.* Anything shaped like the letter L, as an addition at right angles to one side of a house.

el·lipse (i·lips′) *n. Geom.* A plane curve such that the sum of the distances from any point of the curve to two fixed points is a constant. [< ELLIPSIS]

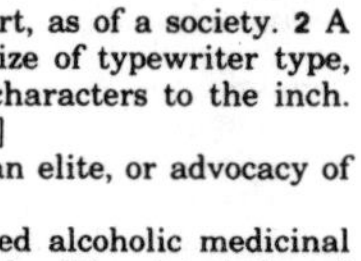

Ellipse
DE major axis
BC minor axis
FA + AF′ = FA′ + A′F′

el·lip·sis (i·lip′sis) *n. pl.* **·ses** (-sēz) 1 The omission of a word or words necessary to complete a sentence or expression. 2 A sudden jump from one thought or subject to another without the inclusion of logical connectives. 3 Marks indicating omission, as . . . or * * *. [< Gk. *elleipsis* a falling short]

el·lip·ti·cal (i·lip′ti·kəl) *adj.* 1 Of, pertaining to, or shaped like an ellipse. 2 Characterized by ellipsis; shortened by the omission of a word or words. Also **el·lip′tic.** **—el·lip′ti·cal·ly** *adv.*

elm (elm) *n.* 1 A tall, graceful, deciduous shade tree of America, Europe, and Asia. 2 Its wood. [< OE]

el·o·cu·tion (el′ə·kyōō′shən) *n.* 1 The art of speaking or reading in public. 2 Manner of utterance. [< L *ex-* out + *loqui* speak] **—el′o·cu′tion·ar′y** *adj.* **—el′o·cu′tion·ist** *n.*

E·lo·him (e·lō·him′, -lō′him) *n.* God: Hebrew name in the Old Testament. [< Heb. *'Elōhim,* pl. of *'Elōah* God]

e·lon·gate (i·lông′gāt, i·long′-) *v.t. & v.i.* **·gat·ed, ·gat·ing** To make or grow longer; lengthen. *—adj.* 1 Made longer; lengthened. 2 Long and slender. **—e′lon·ga′tion** *n.*

e·lope (i·lōp′) *v.i.* **e·loped, e·lop·ing** To run away, esp. to get married in secret. [< ME *alepen* run away] **—e·lope′ment, e·lop′er** *n.*

el·o·quence (el′ə·kwəns) *n.* 1 Graceful, articulate, and convincing expression; also, the art or forcefulness of such expression. 2 The quality of being forceful or persuasive.

el·o·quent (el′ə·kwənt) *adj.* 1 Having or exhibiting eloquence. 2 Expressive; affecting: an *eloquent* glance. [< L < *ex-* out + *loqui* speak] **—el′o·quent·ly** *adv.*

El Sal·va·dor (el sal′və·dôr, *Sp.* el säl′vä·thôr′) *n.* A republic of w Central America, 8,260 sq. mi., cap. San Salvador. • See map at CENTRAL AMERICA.

else (els) *adv.* 1 In a different place, time, or way. 2 If the case or facts were different; otherwise. *—adj.* 1 In addition. 2 Other: It was someone *else.* [< OE *elles*]

else·where (els′hwâr′) *adv.* In or to another place or places; somewhere or anywhere else.

e·lu·ci·date (i·lōō′sə·dāt) *v.t.* **·dat·ed, ·dat·ing** To clarify by explaining. [< L *ex-* out + *lucidus* clear] **—e·lu′ci·da′tion** *n.* **—e·lu′ci·da′tive** *adj.*

e·lude (i·lōōd′) *v.t.* **e·lud·ed, e·lud·ing** 1 To avoid or escape from by swiftness or cleverness. 2 To escape the notice or understanding of. [< L *ex-* out + *ludere* to play] **—e·lud′i·ble** *adj.* **—e·lu·sion** (i·lōō′zhən) *n.*

e·lu·sive (i·lōō′siv) *adj.* 1 Tending to elude. 2 Difficult to understand. **—e·lu′sive·ly** *adv.* **—e·lu′sive·ness** *n.*

elves (elvz) *n.pl.* of ELF.

elv·ish (el′vish) *adj.* ELFISH. **—elv′ish·ly** *adv.*

E·ly·sian (i·lizh′ən, -ē·ən) *adj.* 1 Of Elysium. 2 Supremely happy; blissful.

E·ly·si·um (i·lizh′ē·əm, i·liz′-) *Gk. Myth.* The abode of the blessed dead: also **Elysian Fields.** *—n.* A place or a condition of supreme delight.

em (em) *n.* 1 The thirteenth letter in the English alphabet, written M or m. 2 *Printing* The square of the body size of a type, used as a standard unit of measurement.

em- *prefix* Var. of EN-[1]: *embody.*

EM enlisted man (men); Electrician's Mate.

e·ma·ci·ate (i·mā′shē·āt) *v.t.* **·at·ed, ·at·ing** To make abnormally thin, as from starvation. [< L *emaciare* waste away] **—e·ma′ci·a′tion** *n.*

e·ma·ci·at·ed (i·mā′shē·ā′tid) *adj.* Very thin; wasted away, as from disease or starvation.

em·a·nate (em′ə·nāt) *v.i.* **·nat·ed, ·nat·ing** To come or flow forth, as from a source. [< L *ex-* out + *manare* to flow]

em·a·na·tion (em′ə·nā′shən) *n.* 1 The act of emanating. 2 That which flows from an origin or source. **—em′a·na′tive** *adj.* **—em′a·na′tive·ly** *adv.*

e·man·ci·pate (i·man′sə·pāt) *v.t.* **·pat·ed, ·pat·ing** 1 To release from bondage or slavery. 2 To release from any oppression or restraint. [< L *ex-* out + *manus* hand + *capere* take] **—e·man′ci·pa′tion, e·man′ci·pa′tor** *n.* **—e·man′ci·pa·to′·ry** (-pə·tôr′ē, -tō′rē) *adj.*

e·mas·cu·late (i·mas′kyə·lāt) *v.t.* **·lat·ed, ·lat·ing** 1 To castrate. 2 To deprive of force or effectiveness. [< L *ex-* away + *masculus* male] **—e·mas′cu·la′tion, e·mas′cu·la′tor** *n.*

em·balm (im·bäm′) *v.t.* 1 To treat (a dead body) so as to preserve from quick decay. 2 To perfume. 3 To preserve the memory of. [< OF < *em-* in + *basme* balm] **—em·balm′er, em·balm′ment** *n.*

em·bank (im·bangk′) *v.t.* To confine or protect by a bank, dike, or the like.

em·bank·ment (im·bangk′mənt) *n.* 1 A protecting or supporting bank of earth or stones. 2 The process of strengthening by a bank.

em·bar·go (im·bär′gō) *n. pl.* **·goes** 1 A prohibition by a government temporarily restraining vessels from leaving or entering its ports. 2 Authoritative stoppage of any commerce. 3 Any imposed impediment or hindrance. —*v.t.* **·goed, ·go·ing** To lay an embargo upon. [< Sp. *embargar* to restrain]

em·bark (im·bärk′) *v.i.* 1 To go aboard a ship, airplane, etc., as for a voyage. 2 To get started, as with a venture: usu. with *on* or *upon.* —*v.t.* 1 To put or take aboard a ship, airplane, etc. 2 To invest (money) or involve (a person) in a venture. [< LL *in-* in + *barca* boat] **—em′bar·ka′tion, em·bark′ment** *n.*

em·bar·rass (im·bar′əs) *v.t.* 1 To make ill at ease, self-conscious, and uncomfortable. 2 To involve in difficulties, esp. in business. 3 To hamper; encumber. 4 To render difficult; complicate. [< F *embarrasser*] **—em·bar′rass·ing** *adj.* **—em·bar′rass·ing·ly** *adv.* **—em·bar′rass·ment** *n.* **—Syn.** 1 abash, discomfit, disconcert, rattle.

em·bas·sy (em′bə·sē) *n. pl.* **·sies** 1 The mission or office of an envoy or ambassador. 2 The official residence of an ambassador and his staff. 3 An ambassador and his associates. [< Med. L *ambactia* service]

em·bat·tle (em·bat′l) *v.t.* **·tled, ·tling** 1 To prepare or equip for battle or conflict. 2 To fortify, as a town.

em·bat·tled (em·bat′ld) *adj.* Ready for battle or conflict: *embattled* politicians.

em·bed (im·bed′) *v.t.* **·bed·ded, ·bed·ding** 1 To set firmly in surrounding matter. 2 To keep in the mind, memory, etc. **—em·bed′ment** *n.*

em·bel·lish (im·bel′ish) *v.t.* 1 To add ornamental features to. 2 To heighten the interest of, as a story, by adding details that are often fictitious. [< OF *embellir* beautify] **—em·bel′lish·ment** *n.*

em·ber (em′bər) *n.* 1 A live coal or glowing brand. 2 *pl.* A dying fire. [< OE *ǣmerge*]

Ember days *Eccl.* A three-day period of fasting and prayer observed quarterly by Roman Catholics and some other denominations. [< OE *ymbrendæg* a recurring day]

em·bez·zle (im·bez′əl) *v.t.* **·zled, ·zling** To appropriate fraudulently for one's own use; steal. [< AF *embesiler*] **—em·bez′zle·ment, em·bez′zler** *n.*

em·bit·ter (im·bit′ər) *v.t.* To render bitter, unhappy, or resentful. **—em·bit′ter·ment** *n.*

em·bla·zon (em·blā′zən) *v.t.* 1 To adorn with or as with heraldic designs; decorate. 2 To set off in resplendent colors. **—em·bla′zon·er, em·bla′zon·ment, em·bla′zon·ry** (-rē) *n.*

em·blem (em′bləm) *n.* 1 A figurative representation or symbol of an idea, organization, or object. 2 A distinctive badge. [< L *emblema* inlaid work]

em·blem·at·ic (em′blə·mat′ik) *adj.* Of or serving as an emblem. Also **em′blem·at′i·cal. —em′blem·at′i·cal·ly** *adv.*

em·bod·i·ment (im·bod′i·mənt) *n.* 1 The act of embodying, or the state of being embodied. 2 Something that embodies or exemplifies; incarnation.

em·bod·y (im·bod′ē) *v.t.* **·bod·ied, ·bod·y·ing** 1 To invest with or as with a body. 2 To collect into one whole; incorporate. 3 To express concretely.

em·bold·en (im·bōl′dən) *v.t.* To give courage to.

em·bo·lism (em′bə·liz′əm) *n.* The stopping up of a blood vessel by an embolus. [< Gk. *embolismos* insertion] **—em·bo·lis′mic** *adj.*

em·bo·lus (em′bə·ləs) *n. pl.* **·li** (-lī) A body carried by the blood stream, as a clot or bubble, capable of obstructing blood flow. [< Gk. *embolos* something inserted]

em·bos·om (em·bŏŏz′əm, -bōō′zəm) *v.t.* 1 To take to the bosom; embrace. 2 To shelter.

em·boss (im·bôs′, -bos′) *v.t.* 1 To cover or adorn (a surface) with raised figures, designs, etc. 2 To raise or represent (designs, figures, etc.) from or upon a surface. 3 To decorate sumptuously. [< OF *embocer*] **—em·boss′er, em·boss′ment** *n.*

em·bou·chure (äm·bōō·shŏŏr′) *n.* 1 The point of discharge of a river or stream. 2 Position or adjustment of the lips, tongue, and associated organs in playing a wind instrument. 3 A mouthpiece, esp. of a wind instrument. [< OF *em-* in + *bouche* mouth]

em·bour·geoise·ment (äm·bŏŏr·zhwäz·môṅ′) *n.* The fact or process of becoming bourgeois. [F]

em·bow·er (em·bou′ər) *v.t.* To place in a shelter, as of foliage.

em·brace (im·brās′) *v.* **·braced, ·brac·ing** *v.t.* 1 To put one's arms around in greeting or affection. 2 To accept willingly; adopt. 3 To avail oneself of: to *embrace* an offer. 4 To encircle. 5 To include; contain. 6 To take in visually or mentally. —*v.i.* 7 To hug each other. —*n.* The act of embracing; a clasping in the arms. [< L *in-* in + *bracchia* arm] **—em·brace′a·ble** *adj.* **—em·brace′ment, em·brac′er** *n.* **—Syn.** 1 hug, caress, hold. 2 espouse, endorse.

em·bra·sure (em·brā′zhər) *n.* 1 An opening in a wall, as for a cannon. 2 *Archit.* The sloping of an opening in a wall, as of a window, so as to enlarge its interior profile. [F]

em·bro·cate (em′brō·kāt) *v.t.* **·cat·ed, ·cat·ing** To moisten and rub, as with liniment or oil. [< Med. L < *embrocha* an ointment] **—em·bro·ca′tion** *n.*

em·broi·der (im·broi′dər) *v.t.* 1 To ornament with designs in needlework. 2 To execute in needlework. 3 To exaggerate, as a narrative, with usu. fictitious details. —*v.i.* 4 To make embroidery. [< EN-[1] + obs. *broider* < MF *brouder* to stitch] **—em·broi′der·er** *n.*

em·broi·der·y (im·broi′dər·ē) *n. pl.* **·der·ies** 1 Ornamental needlework. 2 The art of producing such work. 3 Embellishing details, as of a story.

em·broil (em·broil′) *v.t.* 1 To involve in dissension or conflict. 2 To throw into uproar or confusion. [< OF *em-* in + *brouiller* confuse] **—em·broil′ment** *n.*

em·bry·o (em′brē·ō) *n. pl.* **·os** 1 An animal in the early stages of development of the fertilized ovum. 2 The fertilized human ovum during two months following implantation in the uterus. 3 A rudimentary plant within the seed. 4 Anything in process of developing its distinctive form. **—in embryo** In an undeveloped or incipient stage. —*adj.* Pertaining to an embryo; rudimentary: also **em′bry·al.** [< Gk. *en-* in + *bryein* to swell]

Seed showing embryo a. seed coat. b. embryo. c. endosperm.

em·bry·ol·o·gy (em′brē·ol′ə·jē) *n.* The science which deals with the origin, structure, and development of the embryo. **—em′bry·o·log′ic** (-ə·loj′ik) or **·i·cal** *adj.* **—em′bry·o·log′i·cal·ly** *adv.* **—em′bry·ol′o·gist** *n.*

em·bry·on·ic (em′brē·on′ik) *adj.* 1 Of, pertaining to, or like an embryo. 2 Undeveloped. Also **em·bry·o·nal** (em′brē·ə·nəl, em·brī′-).

em·cee (em′sē′) *Informal n.* Master of ceremonies. —*v.i.* & *v.t.* **em·ceed, em·cee·ing** To act or direct as master of ceremonies. [< *m(aster of) c(eremonies)*]

e·mend (i·mend′) *v.t.* To make corrections or changes in (a literary work, etc.). Also **e·men·date** (ē′men·dāt). [< L *ex-* out + *menda* a fault] **—e·mend′a·ble** *adj.*

e·men·da·tion (ē′men·dā′shən, em′ən-) *n.* 1 A correction or alteration. 2 The act of emending. **—e′men·da′tor** *n.* **—e·mend·a·to·ry** (i·men′də·tôr′ē, -tō′rē) *adj.*

em·er·ald (em′ər·əld, em′rəld) *n.* A bright green precious stone, a variety of beryl. —*adj.* 1 Of or like the emerald. 2 Of a rich green color. [< OF *emeraude, esmeraldus*]

e·merge (i·murj′) *v.i.* **e·merged, e·merg·ing** 1 To come forth into view or existence. 2 To become noticeable or apparent: The truth *emerged.* [< L *ex-* out + *mergere* to dip] **—e·mer·gent** (i·mûr′jənt) *adj.* **—e·mer′gence** *n.*

e·mer·gen·cy (i·mûr′jən·sē) *n. pl.* **·cies** A sudden, unexpected state of affairs calling for immediate action.

e·mer·i·tus (i·mer′ə·təs) *adj.* Retired from active service but retained in an honorary position. [< L *emereri* earn, deserve]

e·mer·sion (ē·mûr′zhən, -shən) *n.* The act or process of emerging.

em·er·y (em′ər·ē, em′rē) *n.* A very hard variety of corundum that occurs mixed with other minerals, used as an abrasive. [< Gk. *smuris* emery powder]

emery board A small, flat board covered with powdered emery, used in manicuring.

e·met·ic (i·met′ik) *adj.* Causing vomiting. —*n.* A medicine used to induce vomiting. [< Gk. *emeein* to vomit]

EMF, E.M.F., emf, e.m.f. electromotive force.

-emia *combining form* Blood; used in names of diseases: *leukemia.* [< Gk. *haima* blood]

em·i·grant (em′ə·grənt) *adj.* Leaving one country or region to settle in another. —*n.* One who emigrates.

em·i·grate (em′ə·grāt) *v.i.* **·grat·ed, ·grat·ing** To go from one country, or section of a country, to settle in another. [< L *ex-* out + *migrare* to move] **—em·i·gra′tion** *n.*

é·mi·gré (em′ə·grā, *Fr.* ā·mē·grā′) *n.* An emigrant; esp. a political refugee. Also **e·mi·gré.** [F]

em·i·nence (em′ə·nəns) *n.* **1** An outstanding rank or degree. **2** A lofty place, as a hill. **3** *Usu. cap.* A title of honor applied to cardinals of the Roman Catholic Church. Also **em′i·nen·cy.**

ém·i·nence grise (ā·mē·näṅs grēz′) One who secretly exercises great power. [F, lit., gray eminence]

em·i·nent (em′ə·nənt) *adj.* **1** Standing out from others by achievement or station; outstanding. **2** Rising above other things: an *eminent* tower. [< L *eminere* stand out, project] **—em′i·nent·ly** *adv.* **—Syn. 1** distinguished, prominent.

eminent domain *Law* The right of a state to take private property for public use, usu. giving compensation.

e·mir (ə·mir′) *n.* A prince or commander in certain Muslim lands, esp. Arabia. Also **e·meer′.** [< Ar. *amīr* ruler] — **e·mir′ate** *n.*

em·is·sar·y (em′ə·ser′ē) *n. pl.* **·sar·ies 1** A person sent on a special mission, often as a representative of a government. **2** A secret agent. [< L *emittere* send out]

e·mis·sion (i·mish′ən) *n.* **1** Something emitted. **2** The act of emitting. **3** *Electronics* The ejection of electrons from a surface. **—e·mis′sive** *adj.*

e·mit (i·mit′) *v.t.* **e·mit·ted, e·mit·ting 1** To send or give out; discharge. **2** To utter (cries, etc.). **3** To put into circulation, as money. [< L *ex-* out + *mittere* send] **—e·mit′ter** *n.*

Em·my (em′ē) *n. pl.* **Em·mys** or **Em·mies** A gold-plated statuette awarded annually for exceptional performances and productions on television.

e·mol·lient (i·mol′yənt, -ē·ənt) *adj.* Softening or soothing. —*n. Med.* A soothing preparation for the skin or mucous membranes. [< L *ex-* thoroughly + *mollis* soft]

e·mol·u·ment (i·mol′yə·mənt) *n.* The compensation, gain, or profit arising from an office or employment. [< L *ex-* out + *molere* to grind]

e·mote (i·mōt′) *v.i.* **e·mot·ed, e·mot·ing** *Informal* To exhibit an exaggerated emotion, as in acting a melodramatic role. [Back formation < EMOTION]

e·mo·tion (i·mō′shən) *n.* **1** Any feeling, esp. a strong or intense feeling, as of love, joy, fear, etc., often accompanied by complex physiological changes. **2** Such feelings collectively, or the power of experiencing them. [< L *ex-* out + *movere* to stir, move]

e·mo·tion·al (i·mō′shən·əl) *adj.* **1** Of or pertaining to emotion. **2** Marked by a disposition to express emotion: an *emotional* person. **3** Expressing emotion and often designed to arouse emotion in others: an *emotional* speech. **—e·mo′tion·al·ism, e·mo·tion·al·i·ty** (i·mō′shə·nal′ə·tē) *n.* — **e·mo′tion·al·ly** *adv.*

e·mo·tion·a·lize (i·mō′shən·əl·īz′) *v.t.* **·ized, ·iz·ing** To make emotional. **—e·mo′tion·al·i·za′tion** *n.*

e·mo·tive (i·mō′tiv) *adj.* Expressing or tending to excite emotion. **—e·mo′tive·ly** *adv.*

em·pan·el (im·pan′əl) *v.t.* **·eled** or **·elled, ·el·ing** or **·el·ling** IMPANEL.

em·pa·thize (em′pə·thīz) *v.t. & v.i.* **·thized, ·thiz·ing** To regard with or feel empathy.

em·pa·thy (em′pə·thē) *n.* The identification of oneself with another and the resulting capacity to feel or experience sensations, emotions, or thoughts similar to those being experienced by the other. [< Gk. *en-* in + *pathos* feeling] **—em·pa·thet·ic** (em′pə·thet′ik), **em·path·ic** (im·path′ik) *adj.*

em·per·or (em′pər·ər) *n.* The ruler of an empire. [< L *imperare* to order]

em·pha·sis (em′fə·sis) *n. pl.* **·ses** (-sēz) **1** Special attention, importance, or stress: to place *emphasis* on discipline. **2** Forceful expression. **3** A stress laid upon some spoken or written words. [< Gk. *en-* in + *phainein* to show]

em·pha·size (em′fə·sīz) *v.t.* **·sized, ·siz·ing** To make especially distinct or prominent.

em·phat·ic (im·fat′ik) *adj.* **1** Conveying or expressing emphasis. **2** Forceful and decisive. **—em·phat′i·cal·ly** *adv.*

em·phy·se·ma (em′fə·sē′mə, -zē′mə) *n.* An inflated condition of the lungs marked by breathlessness due to loss of elasticity of the air sacs. [< Gk. *emphysēma* an inflation] **—em′phy·sem′a·tous** *adj.*

em·pire (em′pīr) *n.* **1** A state, or union of states, governed by an emperor. **2** Any vast organization or enterprise under unified control. [< L *imperium* rule]

Em·pire (äm·pir′, em′pīr) *adj.* Of or designating a style, as of clothing, furniture, or architecture, characteristic of the first French Empire, 1804–1815, under Napoleon I.

Empire Day VICTORIA DAY.

em·pir·ic (em·pir′ik) *n.* **1** One who believes experience is the source of knowledge. **2** *Archaic* A quack or charlatan. —*adj.* Empirical. [< Gk. *empeiria* experience]

em·pir·i·cal (em·pir′i·kəl) *adj.* Relating to or based on experience and observation rather than on theory or principle. **—em·pir′i·cal·ly** *adv.*

em·pir·i·cism (em·pir′ə·siz′əm) *n.* **1** Empirical character, method, or practice. **2** Belief in experiment alone. **3** *Philos.* The doctrine that all knowledge is derived from experience through the senses. **—em·pir′i·cist** *n.*

em·place·ment (im·plās′mənt) *n.* **1** The position assigned to guns or other military equipment. **2** A setting in place. **3** Position; location.

em·plane (im·plān′) *v.i.* **·planed, ·plan·ing** To board an airplane.

em·ploy (im·ploi′) *v.t.* **1** To engage the services of; hire. **2** To provide work and livelihood for. **3** To make use of: to *employ* cunning. **4** To devote or apply: to *employ* all one's energies. —*n.* The state of being employed. [< L *implicare* involve, fold in]

em·ploy·a·ble (im·ploi′ə·bəl) *adj.* Capable of being employed. —*n.* An employable person. **—em′ploy·a·bil′i·ty** *n.*

em·ploy·ee (im·ploi′ē, em′ploi·ē′) *n.* One who works for another or for a private or public organization in return for salary or wages. Also **em·ploy′e.**

em·ploy·er (im·ploi′ər) *n.* **1** A person or business firm that employs people for salary or wages. **2** One who employs.

em·ploy·ment (im·ploi′mənt) *n.* **1** The act of employing, or the state of being employed. **2** The work or duties of an employee. **—Syn. 1** use. **2** occupation, trade, business, job, profession.

em·po·ri·um (em·pôr′ē·əm, -pō′rē-) *n. pl.* **·ri·ums** or **·ri·a** (-ē·ə) **1** A large store carrying a variety of merchandise. **2** A market place. [< Gk *emporion* a market]

em·pow·er (im·pou′ər) *v.t.* **1** To delegate authority to. **2** To enable or permit.

em·press (em′pris) *n.* **1** A woman who rules an empire. **2** The wife or widow of an emperor.

emp·ty (emp′tē) *adj.* **·ti·er, ·ti·est 1** Having nothing or no one within. **2** Without value or meaning; insincere: *empty* promises. **3** Senseless; frivolous; idle: *empty* talk. **4** *Informal* Hungry. —*v.* **emp·tied, emp·ty·ing** *v.t.* **1** To make empty. **2** To transfer the contents of: to *empty* a bucket. **3** To transfer or remove (the contents) of a container: to *empty* water. —*v.i.* **4** To become empty. **5** To discharge or pour out. —*n. pl.* **emp·ties** Something empty, as a bottle, freight car, etc. [< OE *æmetig*] **—emp′ti·ly** *adv.* **—emp′ti·ness** *n.* **—Syn. 1** vacant, void, unoccupied, bare. **2** vain.

emp·ty-hand·ed (emp′tē·han′did) *adj.* Having or carrying nothing.

emp·ty-head·ed (emp′tē·hed′·id) *adj.* Foolish.

em·pyr·e·al (em·pir′ē·əl, em′pə·rē′əl, -pī-) *adj.* Of the empyrean; heavenly. [< Gk. *empyros* in the fire]

em·py·re·an (em′pə·rē′ən, -pī-) *n.* **1** Among the ancients, the region of pure fire, the highest heaven. **2** The sky; firmament. —*adj.* EMPYREAL.

Emu

e·mu (ē′myōō) *n.* An Australian flightless bird, related to but somewhat smaller than the ostrich. [< Pg. *ema*]

E.M.U., emu, e.m.u. electromagnetic units.
em·u·late (em′yə·lāt) *v.t.* **·lat·ed, ·lat·ing 1** To try to equal or surpass, esp. by imitating or copying. **2** To rival with some success. [< L *aemulari* to rival < *aemulus* jealous] —**em′u·la′tion, em′u·la′tor** *n.* —**em′u·la′tive** *adj.*
em·u·lous (em′yə·ləs) *adj.* Eager or striving to equal or excel another. —**em′u·lous·ly** *adv.*
e·mul·si·fy (i·mul′sə·fī) *v.t.* **·fied, ·fy·ing** To make or convert into an emulsion. —**e·mul′si·fi·ca′tion, e·mul′si·fi′er** *n.*
e·mul·sion (i·mul′shən) *n.* **1** A liquid mixture in which a substance is suspended in minute globules, as butterfat in milk. **2** *Phot.* A substance sensitive to light, used to coat films. [< L *emulgere* to drain out] —**e·mul′sive** *adj.*
en (en) *n.* **1** The fourteenth letter in the English alphabet, written N or n. **2** *Printing* A space half the width of an em.
en-¹ *prefix* **1** To cover or surround with; to place into or upon: *encircle.* **2** To make; cause to be: *enable.* **3** *(used as an intensifier) encompass.* [< L *in* in, into]
en-² *prefix* In, into; on: *endemic.* [< Gk. *en* in, into]
-en¹ *suffix* **1** To cause to be or become: *harden.* **2** To cause to have; gain: *strengthen.* [< OE *-nian*]
-en² *suffix* Made of; resembling: *woolen.* [< OE]
-en³ *suffix (used in the past participles of many strong verbs): broken.* [< OE]
-en⁴ *suffix (used in the plural of certain nouns): oxen, children.* [< OE *-an,* pl. ending of the weak declension]
-en⁵ *suffix* Small; little: *kitten.* [< OE]
en·a·ble (in·ā′bəl, en-) *v.t.* **·bled, ·bling 1** To make able; give means or power to. **2** To make possible or more easy.
en·act (in·akt′, en-) *v.t.* **1** To make into a law. **2** To represent in or as in a play.
en·act·ment (in·akt′mənt, en-) *n.* **1** A law enacted; statute. **2** The act of establishing a law.
en·am·el (in·am′əl) *n.* **1** A vitreous material fused to metals, porcelain, and other materials for protection or decoration. **2** A work executed in such material. **3** A glossy lacquer or varnish used for leather, paper, etc. **4** Any hard, glossy coating. **5** The layer of hard, glossy material forming the exposed outer covering of the teeth. • See TOOTH. —*v.t.* **·eled** or **·elled, ·el·ing** or **·el·ling 1** To cover or inlay with enamel. **2** To surface with or as with enamel. **3** To adorn with different colors, as if with enamel. [< AF *en-* on + OF *esmail* enamel] —**en·am′el·er, en·am′el·ler, en·am′el·ist, en·am′el·list, e·nam′el·work** *n.*
en·am·el·ware (in·am′əl·wâr′) *n.* Enameled kitchen utensils.
en·am·or (in·am′ər, en-) *v.t.* To inspire with ardent love: usu. followed by *of* or *with:* He was much *enamored* of her. *Brit. sp.* **en·am′our.** [< L *in-* in + *amor* love]
en bloc (en blok′, *Fr.* äṅ blôk′) In one piece; as a whole. [F]
enc. enclosed, enclosure.
en·camp (in·kamp′, en-) *v.i.* To stay in or set up a camp. —*v.t.* To place in a camp. —**en·camp′ment** *n.*
en·cap·su·late (in·kap′sə·lāt′, -syə-, en-) *v.t.* **·lat·ed, ·lat·ing 1** To enclose in or as if in a capsule. **2** To summarize. Also **en·cap′sule** (-səl, -syəl). —**en·cap′su·la′tion** *n.*
en·case (in·kās′, en-) *v.t.* **·cased, ·cas·ing** To place or enclose in or as in a case. —**en·case′ment** *n.*
en·caus·tic (in·kôs′tik, en-) *adj.* **1** Painted in wax and having the hues fixed by heat. **2** Processed or fixed by heat: *encaustic* tile. —*n.* The art of encaustic painting. [< Gk. *enkaustikos*]
-ence *suffix* Action, quality, state, or condition: *prominence.* [< L *-entia,* suffix used to form nouns from present participles]
en·ceinte (äṅ·saṅt′) *adj. French* With child; pregnant.
en·ceph·a·li·tis (en′sef·ə·lī′tis, in·sef′-) *n.* Inflammation of the brain. —**en′ceph·a·lit′ic** (-lit′ik) *adj.*
encephalo- *combining form* Brain: *encephalitis.* Also **encephal-.** [< Gk. *enkephalos*]
en·ceph·a·lon (in·sef′ə·lon, en-) *n. pl.* **·la** (-lə) The brain. [< Gk. *enkephalos*] —**en·ceph′a·lous, en·ce·phal′ic** *adj.*
en·chain (in·chān′, en-) *v.t.* **1** To bind with or as with a chain. **2** To hold captive, as attention. —**en·chain′ment** *n.*
en·chant (in·chant′, -chänt′, en-) *v.t.* **1** To put a magic spell upon. **2** To delight or charm completely. [< L *in-* in + *cantare* sing] —**en·chant′er, en·chant′ment** *n.* —**en·chant′·ress** (-tris) *n. Fem.*
en·chant·ing (in·chant′ing, en-) *adj.* Fascinating; delightful; charming. —**en·chant′ing·ly** *adv.*
en·chi·la·da (en′chi·lä′də) *n.* A rolled tortilla stuffed with meat or cheese and flavored with chile. [Sp.]
en·ci·pher (in·sī′fər, en-) *v.t.* To convert (a message) from plain text into cipher.
en·cir·cle (in·sûr′kəl, en-) *v.t.* **·cled, ·cling 1** To form a circle around. **2** To go around; make a circuit of. —**en·cir′cle·ment** *n.*
encl. enclosed, enclosure
en·clave (en′klāv, än′-) *n.* **1** A part of a country surrounded by the territory of a foreign government. **2** Any area of distinct character enclosed within a larger area. [F < L *in-* in + *clavis* key]
en·close (in·klōz′, en-) *v.t.* **·closed, ·clos·ing 1** To surround or fence in. **2** To place in a cover, envelope, etc., often in addition to a letter or message. **3** To contain. [< OF *enclore* shut in] —**en·clos′er** *n.*
en·clo·sure (in·klō′zhər, en-) *n.* **1** Something enclosed, as in a letter or parcel. **2** An enclosed area. **3** That which encloses, as a fence. **4** The act of enclosing, or the state of being enclosed.
en·code (in·kōd′, en-) *v.t.* **·cod·ed, ·cod·ing** To transform (a message) from plain text into code. —**en·cod′er** *n.*
en·co·mi·ast (in·kō′mē·ast, en-) *n.* One who writes or speaks encomiums. —**en·co′mi·as′tic** or **·ti·cal** *adj.*
en·co·mi·um (in·kō′mē·əm, en-) *n. pl.* **·mi·ums** or **·mi·a** (-me·ə) A formal expression of praise; eulogy. [< Gk. *enkōmion* eulogy]
en·com·pass (in·kum′pəs, -kom′-, en-) *v.t.* **1** To form a circle around; encircle. **2** To surround; hem in. **3** To include; embrace. —**en·com′pass·ment** *n.*
en·core (äng′kôr, -kōr, än′-) *n.* **1** A request by an audience for the repetition of a performance, usu. indicated by sustained applause. **2** The performance given in response to the audience. —*v.t.* **·cored, ·cor·ing** To call for an encore by (a performer) or of (a performance). [< F, again]
en·coun·ter (in·koun′tər, en-) *n.* **1** A coming together, esp. when casual or unexpected. **2** A hostile meeting; contest. —*v.t.* **1** To meet accidentally; come upon. **2** To meet in conflict; face in battle. **3** To be faced with (opposition, difficulties, etc.). —*v.i.* **4** To meet accidentally or in battle. [< L *in-* in + *contra* against]
encounter group A relatively unstructured group of persons whose aim is to express their feelings as deeply and spontaneously as possible, using a variety of techniques such as unrestrained verbalization and physical contact.
en·cour·age (in·kûr′ij, en-) *v.t.* **·aged, ·ag·ing 1** To inspire with courage, hope, or confidence. **2** To help or be favorable toward. [< OF *en-* in + *corage* courage] —**en·cour′ag·er** *n.* —**Syn. 1** hearten, embolden, rally. **2** foster, abet.
en·cour·age·ment (in·kûr′ij·mənt, en-) *n.* **1** The act of encouraging, or the state of being encouraged. **2** A person or thing that encourages.
en·croach (in·krōch′, en-) *v.i.* **1** To intrude upon the possessions or rights of another, esp. by stealth: with *on* or *upon.* **2** To make inroads beyond the proper or usual limits. [< OF *encrochier* to seize with a hook] —**en·croach′·er, en·croach′ment** *n.*
en·crust (in·krust′, en-) *v.t.* **1** To cover with a crust or hard coat. **2** To decorate, as with jewels. [< OF < L < *in-* on + *crustare* form a crust] —**en′crus·ta′tion** *n.*
en·cum·ber (in·kum′bər, en-) *v.t.* **1** To obstruct or hinder in action or movement, as with a burden. **2** To make hard to use; block. **3** To weigh down or burden, as with duties. [< OF *encombrer*]
en·cum·brance (in·kum′brəns, en-) *n.* **1** That which encumbers. **2** *Law* Any lien or liability attached to real property.
-ency *suffix* Var. of -ENCE: *urgency.*
ency., encyc., encycl. encyclopedia.
en·cyc·li·cal (in·sik′li·kəl, -sī′kli-, en-) *adj.* Intended for

general circulation. Also **en·cyc′lic.** —*n. Eccl.* A circular letter addressed by the pope to all the bishops. [< Gk. *enkyklios* circular]

en·cy·clo·pe·di·a (in·sī′klə·pē′dē·ə, en-) *n.* A work containing information on all subjects, or exhaustive of one subject. Also **en·cy·clo·pae′di·a.** [< Gk. *enkyklios paideia* a general education] —**en·cy·clo·pe′dic, en·cy·clo·pae′dic** *adj.*

en·cyst (in·sist′, en-) *v.t. & v.i.* To envelop or become enclosed in a cyst, sac, etc. —**en′cys·ta·tion, en·cyst′ment** *n.*

end (end) *n.* **1** The terminal point or part of any object having length; extremity. **2** The point in time at which some process ceases. **3** The last part; conclusion; the *end* of the game. **4** The farthest limit of the space occupied by an object; edge or boundary. **5** A desired purpose; intention. **6** A result; consequence. **7** Death. **8** The extent or limit; the *end* of his strength. **9** In football, a player stationed at the end of a line. —**at loose ends** In an unsettled or confused state. —**in the end** At last. —**no end** *Informal* A great deal: *no end* of trouble. —*v.t.* **1** To bring to a finish or termination; conclude. **2** To be the end of. —*v.i.* **3** To come to an end. [< OE *ende*]

en·dan·ger (in·dān′jər, en-) *v.t.* To expose to danger; imperil. —**en·dan′ger·ment** *n.*

en·dear (in·dir′, en-) *v.t.* To make dear or beloved. —**en·dear′ing** *adj.* —**en·dear′ing·ly** *adv.*

en·dear·ment (in·dir′mənt, en-) *n.* **1** An act or utterance that expresses affection. **2** The act of endearing.

en·deav·or (in·dev′ər, en-) *n.* An earnest attempt or effort to do or accomplish a desired end. —*v.t.* **1** To make an effort to do or bring about; try: usu. used with an infinitive. —*v.i.* **2** To make an effort; strive. *Brit. sp.* **en·deav·our.** [ME *endeveren* to exert oneself] —**en·deav′or·er** *n.*

en·dem·ic (en·dem′ik) *adj.* Occurring or existing only in a particular country or area or among a certain group: an *endemic* plant or disease. Also **en·dem′i·cal.** [< Gk. *en-* in + *dēmos* people]

end·ing (en′ding) *n.* **1** The final or concluding part. **2** An end or extremity. **3** One or more letters or syllables added to the base of a word, esp. to indicate an inflection.

en·dive (en′dīv, än′dēv) *n.* **1** Any of various herbs related to chicory and commonly used as salad greens. **2** The blanched head of a young chicory plant, used in salads. [< L *entibus* endive]

Endive *def. 2*

end·less (end′lis) *adj.* **1** Having no end; boundless. **2** Lasting or seeming to last forever; interminable. **3** Forming a closed loop or circle. —**end′less·ly** *adv.* —**end′less·ness** *n.*

end·most (end′mōst′) *adj.* Placed or being at the extreme end; most remote.

endo- *combining form* Within; inside: *endocarp.* Also **end-.** [< Gk. *endon* within]

en·do·carp (en′dō·kärp) *n. Bot.* The inner layer of a pericarp, as the hard part of a cherry stone.

en·do·crine (en′dō·krin, -krīn, -krēn) *adj.* **1** Denoting an organ or gland that produces one or more hormones that pass directly into the blood. **2** Pertaining to a hormonal secretion. —*n.* The secretion of a ductless gland. [< ENDO- + Gk. *krinein* separate] —**en′do·cri′nal** (-krī′nəl) *adj.*

en·do·cri·nol·o·gy (en′dō·kri·nol′ə·jē, -krī-) *n.* The branch of medicine dealing with the structure and function of the endocrine glands and their hormones. —**en′do·cri·nol′o·gist** *n.*

en·dog·e·nous (en·doj′ə·nəs) *adj.* Originating or growing within something, as cells within the wall of the parent cell. —**en·dog′e·nous·ly** *adv.*

en·dor·phin (en·dôr′fin) *n.* Any of a group of substances made up of amino acids, produced by the brain, that suppress pain naturally. [< END(O)- + (M)ORPHIN(E)]

en·dorse (in·dôrs′, en-) *v.t.* **·dorsed, ·dors·ing 1** To write, esp. one's name, on the back of, as a check or other document. **2** To support: to *endorse* a policy or candidate. [< L *in-* on + *dorsum* back] —**en·dors′a·ble** *adj.*

en·dor·see (in·dôr·sē′, en-) *n.* One to whom an endorsed document or its value is transferred.

en·do·skel·e·ton (en′dō·skel′ə·tən) *n.* The internal supporting structure of an animal, characteristic of all vertebrates. —**en′do·skel′e·tal** *adj.*

en·do·sperm (en′dō·spûrm) *n. Bot.* The protein nutrient within the embryo of a seed. • See EMBRYO.

en·dow (in·dou′, en-) *v.t.* To provide with a permanent fund or income. **2** To furnish or equip, as with talents or natural gifts: usu. with *with.* [< OF *en-* in + *douer* to provide with a dowry]

en·dow·ment (in·dou′mənt, en-) *n.* **1** Money or property given to provide an institution or person with an income. **2** Any natural gift, as beauty. **3** The act of endowing.

end product The result or outcome.

end table A small table to be placed beside chairs, at the end of a sofa, etc.

en·due (in·dʸōō′, en-) *v.t.* **·dued, ·du·ing** To provide or endow: with *with.* [Fusion of OF *enduire* introduce and OF *enduire* clothe]

en·dur·ance (in·dʸŏŏr′əns, en-) *n.* **1** The capacity to bear pain, distress, or prolonged hardship. **2** The ability to continue or to carry on. **3** The act of enduring.

en·dure (in·dʸŏŏr′, en-) *v.* **·dured, ·dur·ing** *v.t.* **1** To bear or undergo, as pain, grief, or injury, esp. without yielding. **2** To tolerate; put up with. —*v.i.* **3** To last; continue to be. **4** To suffer without yielding; hold out. [< L *in-* in + *durare* harden] —**en·dur′a·ble** *adj.*

en·dur·ing (in·dʸŏŏr′ing, en-) *adj.* **1** Lasting; permanent. **2** Long-suffering. —**en·dur′ing·ly** *adv.* —**en·dur′ing·ness** *n.*

end·wise (end′wīz′) *adv.* **1** With the end foremost or uppermost. **2** On end. **3** Lengthwise. Also **end′ways′** (-wāz′).

-ene *suffix Chem.* Denoting an open-chain, unsaturated hydrocarbon having at least one double bond: *ethylene.*

ENE, E.N.E., ene, e.n.e. east-northeast.

en·e·ma (en′ə·mə) *n.* **1** A liquid injected into the rectum as a purgative or for diagnostic purposes. **2** Such an injection. [< Gk. *en-* in + *hienai* send]

en·e·my (en′ə·mē) *n. pl.* **·mies 1** One who hates or bears ill will toward another; foe. **2** One hostile to an organization, idea, etc. **3** A hostile nation or military force; also, a member of a hostile nation or force. —*adj.* Of a hostile army or power. [< L *in-* not + *amicus* friend]

en·er·get·ic (en′ər·jet′ik) *adj.* Having, acting with, or displaying energy; vigorous. [< Gk. *energein* be active] —**en′er·get′i·cal·ly** *adv.*

en·er·gize (en′ər·jīz) *v.* **·gized, ·giz·ing** *v.t.* To give energy or power to; activate. —**en′er·giz′er** *n.*

en·er·gy (en′ər·jē) *n. pl.* **·gies 1** The power by which anything acts effectively. **2** The power to be physically or mentally active, often without the normal attendant fatigue. **3** Force or power in activity: His singing lacks *energy.* **4** *Physics* The ability to do work. See also ATOMIC ENERGY, CHEMICAL ENERGY, ELECTRICAL ENERGY, GEOTHERMAL ENERGY, KINETIC ENERGY, MECHANICAL ENERGY, POTENTIAL ENERGY, SOLAR ENERGY. **5** The motive power essential to modern technology, derived from various natural sources. —*adj.* Of, for, caused by, or relating to energy or the lack of it: the *energy* crisis; *energy* needs. [< Gk. *en-* on, at + *ergon* work]

en·er·gy-in·ten·sive (en′ər·jē·in·ten′siv) *adj.* Representing a heavy investment of energy to produce or manufacture, as a material.

en·er·vate (en′ər·vāt) *v.t.* **·vat·ed, ·vat·ing** To deprive of energy or strength; weaken. —*adj.* (i·nûr′vit) Enervated. [< L *enervare* weaken] —**en·er·va′tion, en′er·va·tor** *n.*

en fa·mille (än fà·mē′y′) *French* Within the family; at home; informally.

en·fant ter·ri·ble (än·fän′te·rē′bl′) A person whose unconventional speech, behavior, attitudes, etc., causes embarrassment or controversy. [F, lit., terrible child]

en·fee·ble (in·fē′bəl, en-) *v.t.* **·bled, ·bling** To make feeble. —**en·fee′ble·ment, en·fee′bler** *n.*

en·fi·lade (en′fə·lād′, -läd′) *Mil. v.t.* **·lad·ed, ·lad·ing** To fire down the length of, as a column of troops. —*n.* **1** Gunfire that can rake lengthwise a line of troops, etc. **2** A position exposed to a raking fire. [F < *enfiler* to thread]

en·fold (in·fōld, en-) *v.t.* **1** To wrap in layers. **2** To clasp in the arms; embrace. —**en·fold′er** *n.*

en·force (in·fôrs′, -fōrs′, en-) *v.t.* **·forced, ·for·ing 1** To compel obedience to, as laws. **2** To compel (performance, obedience, etc.) by physical or moral force. **3** To make convincing, as an argument. [< L *in-* in + *fortis* strong] —**en·force′a·ble** *adj.* —**en·force′·ment, en·forc′er** *n.*

en·fran·chise (in·fran′chīz, en-) *v.t.* **·chised, ·chis·ing 1** To endow with a franchise, as the right to vote. **2** To set free, as from bondage. [< OF *en-* in + *franc* free] **—en·fran′chise·ment** *n.*

Eng. England; English.

eng. engine; engineer; engineering; engraved.

en·gage (in·gāj′, en-) *v.* **·gaged, ·gag·ing** *v.t.* **1** To bind by a promise, pledge, etc. **2** To promise to marry: usu. in the passive. **3** To hire, as a lawyer, or his services; secure the use of, as a room. **4** To hold the interest or attention of. **5** To hold (interest or attention); occupy. **6** To begin a battle with. **7** To mesh or interlock, as gears. —*v.i.* **8** To bind oneself by a promise, pledge, etc. **9** To devote or occupy oneself: to *engage* in research. **10** To begin a battle. **11** To mesh, as gears. [< OF *en-* in + *gager* to pledge]

en·gaged (in·gājd′, en-) *adj.* **1** Pledged to be married. **2** Occupied or busy. **3** Partially sunk or built into another structure, as columns. **4** Meshed or interlocked, as gears. **5** Involved in a contest or conflict.

en·gage·ment (in·gāj·mənt, en-) *n.* **1** Something that engages or binds, as an appointment, promise, or obligation. **2** The condition of being engaged; a betrothal. **3** The act of engaging. **4** An entering into battle; also, the battle itself. **5** *pl.* Pecuniary obligations. **6** A salaried position.

en·gag·ing (in·gā′jing, en-) *adj.* Attracting interest; charming; winning. **—en·gag′ing·ly** *adv.*

en garde (äṅ gärd′) On guard: a fencing term. [F]

en·gen·der (in·jen′dər, en-) *v.t.* To cause to exist; produce. [< L *ingenerare* to generate in]

engin. engineering.

en·gine (en′jin) *n.* **1** A machine that uses energy, esp. energy from a fuel, to perform work. **2** A railroad locomotive. **3** Any apparatus: the *engines* of war. [< L *ingenium* talent, skill]

en·gi·neer (en′jə·nir′) *n.* **1** One practicing any branch of engineering. **2** One who runs or manages an engine. **3** A manager; inventor; plotter. **4** A member of the division of an army which constructs bridges, clears and builds roads and airfields, etc. —*v.t.* **1** To put through or manage by contrivance: to *engineer* a scheme. **2** To plan and superintend as an engineer.

en·gi·neer·ing (en′jə·nir′ing) *n.* The application of scientific knowledge to the solution of practical problems, as in designing structures and apparatus.

Eng·land (ing′glənd) *n.* **1** The s part and largest political division of Great Britain, 50,237 sq. mi., cap. London. **2** Loosely, Great Britain, or the United Kingdom of Great Britain and Northern Ireland. • See map at UNITED KINGDOM.

Eng·lish (ing′glish) *adj.* Of, pertaining to, or derived from England, its people, or their language. —*n.* **1** The people of England: with *the.* **2** The Germanic language spoken by the people of the British Isles, most of the Commonwealth, and of the United States. **3** The English language as used in a particular region or time or by a specified group: American *English.* **4** In billiards, bowling, etc., a spin imparted to the ball by the manner of striking it or releasing it. —*v.t.* **1** To translate into English. **2** To Anglicize, as a foreign word.

English horn A woodwind instrument, with a pitch a fifth lower than an oboe.

Eng·lish·man (ing′glish·mən) *n. pl.* **·men** (-mən) A native or citizen of England. **—Eng·lish·wom·an** (-wŏŏm′ən) *n. Fem.* (*pl.* **·wom·en**) (-wim′in)

English muffin A round flat roll of unsweetened, raised dough baked on a griddle.

English setter One of a breed of dogs, usu. white marked with black or tan, trained to point to game.

English sparrow HOUSE SPARROW.

en·gorge (in·gôrj′, en-) *v.t.* **·gorged, ·gorg·ing 1** To congest (an organ) with blood or other fluid. **2** To devour or swallow greedily. [< F *engorger*] **—en·gorge′ment** *n.*

engr. engineer; engraved; engraver; engraving.

en·graft (in·graft′, -gräft′, en-) *v.t.* **1** To graft (a piece cut from a plant or tree) to another tree or plant for propagation. **2** To implant. **—en·graft′ment** *n.*

en·grave (in·grāv′, en-) *v.t.* **·graved, ·grav·ing 1** To carve or etch figures, letters, etc., into (a surface). **2** To impress deeply. **3** To cut (pictures, lettering, etc.) into metal, stone, or wood, for printing. **4** To print from plates made by such a process. [< EN-[1] + GRAVE[3]] **—en·grav′er** *n.*

en·grav·ing (in·grā′ving, en-) *n.* **1** The act or art of cutting designs on a plate. **2** An engraved design on a plate. **3** A picture or design printed from an engraved plate.

en·gross (in·grōs′, en-) *v.t.* **1** To occupy completely; absorb. **2** To copy in large writing; make a formal transcript of. **3** To monopolize, as the supply of a product. [< LL *ingrossare* write large] **—en·gross′er, en·gross′ment** *n.* **—en·gross′ing** *adj.*

en·gulf (in·gulf′, en-) *v.t.* To swallow up; bury or overwhelm.

en·hance (in·hans′, -häns′, en-) *v.t.* **·hanced, ·hanc·ing** To make higher or greater, as in reputation, cost, beauty, quality, etc. [< L *in-* in + *altus* high] **—en·hance′ment** *n.* **—Syn.** heighten, intensify, strengthen, improve.

e·nig·ma (i·nig′mə) *n.* **1** An obscure or ambiguous saying; a riddle. **2** A baffling or inexplicable circumstance, person, etc. [< Gk. *ainissesthai* speak in riddles]

en·ig·mat·ic (en′ig·mat′ik, ē′nig-) *adj.* Of or like an enigma; ambiguous; puzzling. Also **en′ig·mat′i·cal. —en′ig·mat′i·cal·ly** *adv.*

en·join (in·join′, en-) *v.t.* **1** To order authoritatively and emphatically. **2** To impose (a condition, course of action, etc.) on a person or group: to *enjoin* compliance. **3** To forbid or prohibit, esp. by judicial order. [< L *in-* + *jungere* join] **—en·join′er** *n.*

en·joy (in·joi′, en-) *v.t.* **1** To experience joy or pleasure in; receive pleasure from the possession or use of. **2** To have the use or benefit of. [< L *in-* + *gaudere* rejoice] **—en·joy′a·ble** *adj.* **—en·joy′a·ble·ness** *n.* **—en·joy′a·bly** *adv.*

en·joy·ment (in·joi′mənt, en-) *n.* **1** The act or state of enjoying; pleasure. **2** Something that gives joy or pleasure.

en·kin·dle (in·kin′dəl, en-) *v.t.* **·dled, ·dling 1** To set on fire; kindle. **2** To stir up; excite. **—en·kin′dler** *n.*

en·lace (in·lās′, en-) *v.t.* **·laced, ·lac·ing 1** To bind with or as with laces. **2** To intertwine; entangle. **—en·lace′ment** *n.*

en·large (in·lärj′, en-) *v.* **·larged, ·larg·ing** *v.t.* **1** To make greater or larger; increase the amount or extent of; expand. —*v.i.* **2** To become greater or larger; increase; widen. **3** To express oneself in greater detail: with *on* or *upon.* **—en·larg′er** *n.*

en·large·ment (in·lärj′mənt, en-) *n.* **1** The act of enlarging, or the state of being enlarged. **2** Something enlarged, as a photograph made larger than its original negative.

en·light·en (in·līt′n, en-) *v.t.* **1** To impart knowledge to; cause to know or understand; teach. **2** To convey information to; inform. **—en·light′en·er** *n.*

en·light·en·ment (in·līt′n·mənt, en-) *n.* The act of enlightening or the state of being enlightened. **—the Enlightenment** A philosophical movement of the 18th century characterized by a belief in the paramount value of reason as an instrument of progress and the use of the empirical method in scientific inquiry.

en·list (in·list′, en-) *v.t.* **1** To engage for service, as in the army or navy. **2** To gain the help or interest of (a person or his services). —*v.i.* **3** To enter military services voluntarily. **4** To join in some venture, cause, etc.

enlisted man A member of the armed forces ranking below a noncommissioned officer or petty officer.

en·list·ment (in·list′mənt, en-) *n.* **1** The act of enlisting, or the state of being enlisted. **2** The term for which one enlists.

en·li·ven (in·lī′vən, en-) *v.t.* **1** To make lively, cheerful, or sprightly. **2** To make active or vigorous; stimulate. **—en·li′ven·er, en·li′ven·ment** *n.*

en masse (än mas′, en) In a mass or body; all together. [F]

en·mesh (in·mesh′, en-) *v.t.* To ensnare or entangle in or as in a net.

en·mi·ty (en′mə·tē) *n. pl.* **·ties 1** The spirit of an enemy; hostility. **2** The state of being an enemy; a hostile condition. [< L *inimicus* hostile]

en·no·ble (i·nō′bəl, en-) *v.t.* **·bled, ·bling 1** To make honorable or noble in nature, quality, etc. **2** To confer a title of nobility upon. **—en·no′ble·ment, en·no′bler** *n.*

en·nui (än′wē, än·wē′) *n.* A feeling of listless weariness resulting from satiety, inactivity, etc.; lassitude. [F]

e·nor·mi·ty (i·nôr′mə·tē) *n. pl.* **·ties 1** The state of being outrageous or extremely wicked. **2** A flagrant instance of depravity; an atrocity. **3** Great size or extent; enormousness. • Traditionally, *enormity* refers to great wickedness, not to great size or extent, whereas *enormousness* means greatness in any sense. One speaks of the *enormity* of a crime but the *enormousness* of an Olympic stadium. However, *enormity* (def. 3) is now often used, esp. to express great extent, complexity, difficulty, etc.: The *enormity* of the task filled him with awe.

e·nor·mous (i·nôr′məs) *adj.* **1** Excessive or extraordinary in size, amount, or degree. **2** Wicked above measure; atrocious. [< L *enormis* immense] **—e·nor′mous·ly** *adv.* **—e·nor′mous·ness** *n.* • See ENORMITY.

e·nough (i·nuf′) *adj.* Adequate for demand or need; sufficient. *—n.* An ample supply. *—adv.* So as to be sufficient. *—interj.* It is enough; stop. [< OE *genoh, genog*]

en·plane (in·plān′, en-) *v.i.* **·planed, ·plan·ing** To board an airplane.

en·quire (in·kwīr′, en-) *v.* **·quired, ·quir·ing** INQUIRE.

en·quir·y (in·kwīr′ē, in′kwə·rē) *n. pl.* **·quir·ies** INQUIRY.

en·rage (in·rāj′, en-) *v.t.* **·raged, ·rag·ing** To throw into a rage; infuriate.

en rap·port (än ra·pôr′) In accord. [F]

en·rap·ture (in·rap′chər, en-) *v.t.* **·tured, ·tur·ing** To bring into a state of rapture; delight.

en·rich (in·rich′, en-) *v.t.* **1** To make rich; increase the wealth of. **2** To make fertile, as soil. **3** To increase or enhance the quality of. **4** To increase the food value of, as bread. **5** To adorn. [< OF *en-* in + *riche* rich] **—en·rich′er, en·rich′ment** *n.*

en·roll (in·rōl′, en-) *v.* **·rolled, ·roll·ing** *v.t.* **1** To write or record (a name) in a roll; register. **2** To enlist. **3** To place on record, as a document. **4** To roll up; wrap. *—v.i.* **5** To place one's name on a list. Also **en·rol′.** [< OF *enroller*]

en·roll·ment (en·rōl′mənt) *n.* **1** The act of enrolling. **2** An enrolled entry; a record. **3** The number enrolled. Also **en·rol′ment.**

en route (än ro͞ot′, en) On the way. [F]

Ens. Ensign.

en·sconce (in·skons′, en-) *v.t.* **·sconced, ·sconc·ing 1** To fix securely or comfortably in some place; settle snugly. **2** To shelter; hide.

en·sem·ble (än·säm′bəl) *n.* **1** The parts of a thing viewed as a whole; general effect. **2** A combination of clothing and accessories that match or harmonize. **3** *Music* **a** A group of performers. **b** Music for such a group. **c** Collective accuracy of balance and style by such a group. **4** Any group of actors or dancers who perform together, usu. excluding the star performers; also, the performance of such a group. [< L *in-* in + *simul* at the same time]

en·shrine (in·shrīn′, en-) *v.t.* **·shrined, ·shrin·ing 1** To place in or as in a shrine. **2** To cherish devoutly; hold sacred. **—en·shrine′ment** *n.*

en·shroud (en·shroud′) *v.t.* To cover with or as with a shroud; conceal.

en·sign (en′sən, -sīn) *n.* **1** A flag or banner, esp. a national standard or naval flag. **2** (en′sən) See GRADE. **3** In the British Army, until 1871, a commissioned officer who carried the flag of his regiment or company. **4** A badge or symbol, as of office. [< L *insignia* insignia]

en·si·lage (en′sə·lij) *n.* **1** The process of preserving succulent fodder in closed pits or silos. **2** The fodder thus preserved. *—v.t.* **·laged, ·lag·ing** ENSILE. [< F *en-* in + *silo* silo]

en·sile (in·sīl′, en-) *v.t.* **·siled, ·sil·ing** To store in a silo for preservation, as fodder.

en·slave (in·slāv′, en-) *v.t.* **·slaved, ·slav·ing** To make a slave of; dominate. **—en·slave′ment, en·slav′er** *n.*

en·snare (in·snâr′, en-) *v.t.* **·snared, ·snar·ing** To catch in a snare; trick.

en·sue (in·so͞o′, en-) *v.i.* **·sued, ·su·ing 1** To occur afterward or subsequently; follow. **2** To follow as a consequence; result. [< L *in-* on, in + *sequi* follow]

en·sure (in·sho͝or′, en-) *v.t.* **·sured, ·sur·ing 1** To make safe or secure; provide protection: with *against* or *from:* to *ensure* against tyranny. **2** To make sure or certain; guarantee: to *ensure* fairness. **3** INSURE (def. 1). [< ME *insuren, ensuren* to insure]

-ent *suffix* **1** Having the quality of (the main element): *potent.* **2** One who or that which performs the action of (the main element): *superintendent.* [< L *-ens,* suffix of present participle]

en·tab·la·ture (in·tab′lə·chər, en-) *n. Archit.* The uppermost part of a columnar system, consisting of the architrave, frieze, and cornice. [< Ital. *intavolatura*]

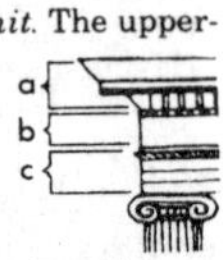

Entablature
a. cornice.
b. frieze.
c. architrave.

en·tail (in·tāl′, en-) *v.t.* **1** To impose or result in as a necessary consequence. **2** *Law* To restrict the inheritance of (real property) to an unalterable succession of heirs. *—n.* **1** Anything transmitted as an inalienable inheritance. **2** An estate limited to a particular class of heirs, as eldest sons. [ME *entailen*] **—en·tail′ment** *n.*

en·tan·gle (in·tang′gəl, en-) *v.t.* **·gled, ·gling 1** To catch in or as in a snare; hamper. **2** To make tangled; complicate. **3** To involve in difficulties. **—en·tang′le·ment, en·tang′ler** *n.*

en·tente (än·tänt′) *n.* **1** An understanding between two or more nations in regard to a cooperative policy or action. **2** The parties to such an understanding. [F]

entente cor·diale (kôr·dyal′) Friendliness between governments. [F, lit., cordial understanding]

en·ter (en′tər) *v.t.* **1** To come or go into: to *enter* a room; The thought never *entered* my head. **2** To set or insert in: to *enter* a nail. **3** To become a member or members of; join. **4** To begin: often with *upon:* to *enter* upon a new career. **5** To gain admission for. **6** To write or record, as in a list. **7** To report (goods, a vessel, etc.) to the customhouse. **8** *Law* To place on the records of a court, as evidence. *—v.i.* **9** To come or go inward. **10** To become a member or members; join. **—enter into 1** To begin; start. **2** To engage in. **3** To consider or discuss. [< L *intrare* < *intra* within]

en·ter·ic (en·ter′ik) *adj.* **1** Of or pertaining to the intestine. **2** Having an intestine. [< Gk. *enteron* intestine < *entos* within]

en·ter·i·tis (en′tə·rī′tis) *n.* Inflammation of the intestines, esp. of the small intestine.

entero- *combining form* Intestine. Also **enter-.** [< Gk. *enteron* intestine]

en·ter·prise (en′tər·prīz) *n.* **1** Any projected task or work; esp., a risky or bold undertaking. **2** Boldness, energy, and invention in practical affairs. [< F *entre-* between + *prendre* take]

en·ter·pris·ing (en′tər·prī′zing) *adj.* Energetic and adventuresome; showing initiative. **—en′ter·pris′ing·ly** *adv.*

en·ter·tain (en′tər·tān′) *v.t.* **1** To hold the attention of; amuse; divert. **2** To extend hospitality to; receive as a guest. **3** To take into consideration, as a proposal. **4** To keep or bear in mind: to *entertain* a grudge. *—v.i.* **5** To receive and care for guests. [< OF *entretenir* to hold between] **—en′ter·tain′er** *n.*

en·ter·tain·ing (en′tər·tā′ning) *adj.* Of a character to entertain; amusing; diverting. **—en′ter·tain′ing·ly** *adv.*

en·ter·tain·ment (en′tər·tān′mənt) *n.* **1** The state of being entertained; pleasure or amusement. **2** A source or means of amusement. **3** The act of entertaining.

en·thrall (in·thrôl′, en-) *v.t.* **·thralled, ·thral·ling 1** To keep spellbound; fascinate; charm. **2** ENSLAVE. Also **en·thral′.** **—en·thrall′ment, en·thral′ment** *n.*

en·throne (in·thrōn′, en-) *v.t.* **·throned, ·thron·ing 1** To put upon a throne; invest with power, as a king. **2** To seat or place in a position of authority. **3** To exalt; revere. **—en·throne′ment** *n.*

en·thuse (in·tho͞oz′, en-) *v.t. & v.i.* **·thused, ·thus·ing** *Informal* To make or become enthusiastic. [Back formation from ENTHUSIASM]

en·thu·si·asm (in·tho͞o′zē·az′əm, en-) *n.* **1** Earnest and intense feeling; zeal. **2** A source or cause of such feeling. [< Gk. *enthusiasmos* inspiration]

en·thu·si·ast (in·tho͞o′zē·ast, en-) *n.* **1** One moved by enthusiasm, as for a cause or activity. **2** A religious zealot.

en·thu·si·as·tic (in·tho͞o′zē·as′tik, en-) *adj.* Characterized by or showing enthusiasm; ardent; zealous. **—en·thu'·si·as'ti·cal·ly** *adv.*

en·tice (in·tīs', en-) *v.t.* **·ticed, ·tic·ing** To lead on or attract by arousing hope of pleasure, profit, etc. [< OF *enticier* arouse] **—en·tice'ment, en·tic'er** *n.* **—en·tic'ing·ly** *adv.*

en·tire (in·tīr', en-) *adj.* **1** Complete in all its parts; whole. **2** Consisting of only one piece; not broken or divided. **3** Pure; unalloyed. **4** Uncastrated: an *entire* horse. **5** *Bot.* Having a smooth margin, as a leaf. [< L *integer* whole, intact] **—en·tire'ly** *adv.* **—en·tire'ness** *n.* **—Syn. 2** intact, of a piece, undivided.

en·tire·ty (in·tī'rət·ē, en-) *n. pl.* **·ties 1** The state of being entire; completeness; wholeness. **2** That which is entire.

en·ti·tle (in·tīt'l, en-) *v.t.* **·tled, ·tling 1** To give a right or legal authority to; authorize or qualify. **2** To give a name or designation to. **3** To give (a person) a title.

en·ti·ty (en'tə·tē) *n. pl.* **·ties 1** Anything that exists or may be supposed to exist. **2** Being; existence, esp. when complete or self-contained. [< L *entitas* < *ens,* pr.p. of *esse* be]

en·tomb (in·tōōm', en-) *v.t.* **1** To place in or as in a tomb; bury. **2** To serve as a tomb for. **—en·tomb'er, en·tomb·ment** *n.*

en·to·mol·o·gy (en'tə·mol'ə·jē) *n.* The branch of zoology dealing with insects. [< Gk. *entomon* insect] **—en·to·mo·log·i·cal** (en'tə·mə·loj'i·kəl) or **·log'ic** *adj.* **—en'to·mo·log'i·cal·ly** *adv.* **—en·to·mol'o·gist** *n.*

en·tou·rage (än'tōō·räzh') *n.* **1** Associates, companions, or attendants. **2** Environment. [< OF *entourer* surround]

en·tr'acte (än·trakt', *Fr.* äṅ·trakt') *n.* **1** The time between any two acts of a play or opera. **2** A musical interlude, dance, or the like, performed between acts. [F]

en·trails (en'trālz, -trəlz) *n. pl.* The internal parts, esp. the intestines, of an animal. [< LL *intralia*]

en·train (in·trān', en-) *v.t.* & *v.i.* To put or go aboard a railway train.

en·trance[1] (en'trəns) *n.* **1** The act of entering. **2** A passage into a house or other enclosed space. **3** The right or power of entering; entrée. [< OF *entrer* enter]

en·trance[2] (in·trans', -träns', en-) *v.t.* **·tranced, ·tranc·ing 1** To fill with rapture or wonder; delight; charm. **2** To put into a trance. **—en·trance'ment** *n.* **—en·tranc'ing** *adj.* **—en·tranc'ing·ly** *adv.*

en·trant (en'trənt) *n.* One who enters, esp. one who enters a contest or competition.

en·trap (in·trap', en-) *v.t.* **·trapped, ·trap·ping 1** To catch in or as in a trap. **2** To trick into danger or difficulty; deceive; ensnare. **—en·trap'ment** *n.*

en·treat (in·trēt', en-) *v.t.* & *v.i.* To ask earnestly or abjectly; beseech; implore. [< OF *entraiter* to deal with, treat] **—en·treat'ment** *n.*

en·treat·y (in·trē'tē, en-) *n. pl.* **·treat·ies** An earnest request; supplication.

en·trée (än'trā, än·trā') *n.* **1** The act or privilege of entering; access. **2** The principal course at a dinner or luncheon. Also **en·tree'.** [F]

en·trench (in·trench', en-) *v.t.* **1** To fortify or protect with or as with a trench. **2** To establish firmly: The idea was *entrenched* in his mind. *—v.i.* **3** To encroach or trespass: with *on* or *upon.* **—en·trench'ment** *n.*

en·tre nous (än'tr' nōō') *French* Between ourselves; confidentially.

en·tre·pre·neur (än'trə·prə·nûr') *n.* One who undertakes to start and conduct an enterprise or business, assuming full control and risk. [F < *entreprendre* to undertake] **—en'tre·pre·neur'i·al** (-ē·əl) *adj.*

en·tro·py (en'trə·pē) *n.* **1** *Physics* A measure of the degree to which the energy of a system is unavailable for work. **2** In information theory, an analogous measure reflecting uncertainty of knowledge. [< Gk. *entropē* a turning]

en·trust (in·trust', en-) *v.t.* **1** To place something, as a duty or responsibility, in the care or trust of. **2** To give over for care, safekeeping, or performance.

en·try (en'trē) *n. pl.* **·tries 1** The act of coming or going in; entrance. **2** A place of entrance; a small hallway. **3** The act of entering an item in a register or list. **4** An item entered in such a list. **5** The reporting at a customhouse of a ship's arrival and the nature of her cargo. **6** *Law* The act of assuming actual possession of property by entering upon it. **7** A contestant entered in a race or competition. [< F *entrer* to enter]

en·twine (in·twīn', en-) *v.t.* & *v.i.* **·twined, ·twin·ing** To twine around; twine or twist together.

e·nu·mer·ate (i·nʸōō'mə·rāt) *v.t.* **·at·ed, ·at·ing 1** To name one by one; list. **2** To count or ascertain the number of. [< L *ex-* out + *numerare* count] **—e·nu'mer·a'tion, e·nu'·mer·a'tor** *n.* **—e·nu'mer·a'tive** *adj.*

e·nun·ci·ate (i·nun'sē·āt, -shē-) *v.* **·at·ed, ·at·ing** *v.t.* **1** To pronounce or articulate (words), esp. clearly and distinctly. **2** To state with exactness, as a theory. **3** To announce or proclaim. *—v.i.* **4** To utter or pronounce words. [< L *ex-* out + *nunciare* announce] **—e·nun'ci·a'tion, e·nun'·ci·a'tor** *n.* **—e·nun'ci·a'tive** *adj.*

en·u·re·sis (en'yə·rē'sis) *n. Pathol.* Involuntary urination, esp. during sleep. [< Gk. *en-* in + *oureein* urinate]

env. envelope.

en·vel·op (in·vel'əp) *v.t.* **·oped, ·op·ing 1** To wrap or enclose completely. **2** To hide or obscure, as by enclosing: to *envelop* in fog. **3** To surround. [< OF *en-* in + *voluper* to wrap, fold] **—en·vel'op·er, en·vel'op·ment** *n.*

en·ve·lope (en'və·lōp, än'-) *n.* **1** A folded wrapper of paper, usu. with gummed edges, for enclosing a letter or the like. **2** Anything that encloses completely or wraps around. [< OF *enveloper* to envelop]

en·ven·om (in·ven'əm) *v.t.* **1** To impregnate with venom; poison. **2** To make vindictive; embitter. [< OF < *en-* in + *venim* venom]

en·vi·a·ble (en'vē·ə·bəl) *adj.* Of a nature to cause envy or admiration. **—en'vi·a·ble·ness** *n.* **—en'vi·a·bly** *adv.*

en·vi·ous (en'vē·əs) *adj.* Having, showing, or caused by envy. **—en'vi·ous·ly** *adv.* **—en'vi·ous·ness** *n.*

en·vi·ron (in·vī'rən, en-) *v.t.* To be or extend around; encircle; surround. [< OF, around, about]

en·vi·ron·ment (in·vī'rən·mənt, -ərn-, en-) *n.* **1** The aggregate of all conditions affecting the existence, growth, and welfare of an organism or group of organisms. **2** Surroundings or external circumstances. **—en·vi'ron·men'tal** *adj.* **—en·vi'ron·men'tal·ly** *adv.*

en·vi·ron·ment·al·ist (in·vī'rən·men'təl·ist, -ərn-) *n.* **1** One who advocates preservation of the environment, as from commercial exploitation. **2** One who attaches more importance to environment than to heredity as a determinant in the development of a person or a group. **—en·vi'ron·ment'al·ism** *n.*

en·vi·rons (in·vī'rəns, en-) *n. pl.* The surrounding region; outskirts; suburbs.

en·vis·age (in·viz'ij, en-) *v.t.* **·aged, ·ag·ing 1** To form a mental image of; visualize. **2** To form an idea about; conceptualize. **—en·vis'age·ment** *n.*

en·vi·sion (in·vizh'ən, en-) *v.t.* To see or foresee in the imagination: to *envision* the future.

en·voy (en'voi, än'-) *n.* **1** A diplomatic agent of a government, ranking next below an ambassador. **2** One sent on a mission. [< F < OF *envoier* to send on the way]

en·vy (en'vē) *n.* **1** A feeling of resentment and jealousy over the possessions, achievements, etc., of another. **2** Desire for something belonging to another. **3** An object of envy. *—v.t.* **·vied, ·vy·ing 1** To regard with envy. **2** To feel envy because of. [< L *invidia*] **—en'vi·er** *n.* **—en'vy·ing·ly** *adv.* **—Syn.** *n.* **2** greed, covetousness, cupidity.

en·wrap (in·rap', en-) *v.t.* **·wrapped, ·wrap·ping** To wrap or envelop. **—en·wrap'ment** *n.*

en·zyme (en'zīm, -zim) *n.* A proteinlike substance produced by cells and having the power to initiate or accelerate specific biochemical reactions in an organism. [< Gk. < *en-* in + *zymē* leaven] **—en·zy·mat·ic** (en'zī·mat'ik, -zi-) *adj.*

E·o·cene (ē'ə·sēn) *n.* & *adj.* See GEOLOGY. [< Gk. *ēōs* dawn + *kainos* new]

e·o·li·an (ē·ō'lē·ən) *adj.* Pertaining to or caused by the winds; wind-borne. [< L *Aeolus,* god of the winds]

E·o·lith·ic (ē'ə·lith'ik) *adj. Anthropol.* Of or pertaining to a period of primitive human culture, known by crude tools of bone and chipped stone. [< Gk. *ēōs* dawn + *lithos* stone]

e·on (ē′on) *n.* **1** An incalculable period of time; an eternity. **2** *Geol.* A time interval including two or more eras. [< Gk. *aiōn* age] —**e·o·ni·an** (ē·ō′nē·ən) *adj.*

E·os (ē′əs) *Gk. Myth.* The goddess of the dawn.

-eous *suffix* Of the nature of: *gaseous.* [< L *-eus*]

ep·au·let (ep′ə·let) *n.* A shoulder ornament, as on uniforms. Also **ep′au·lette.** [F, dim. of *épaule* shoulder]

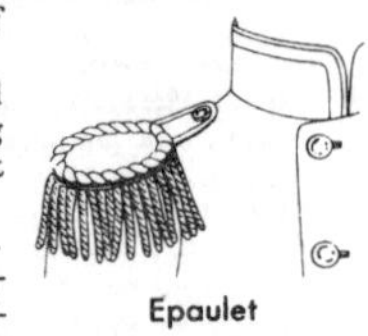

Epaulet

é·pée (ā·pā′) *n.* A sharp-pointed dueling sword with no cutting edge. [F < L *spatha* a broad, flat blade] —**é·pée′ist** *n.*

Eph, Eph., Ephes. Ephesians.

e·phed·rine (e·fed′rin) *n.* An alkaloid having various physiological effects, used mainly to reduce nasal congestion and relieve asthma. Also **e·phed′rin.** [< NL *Ephedra,* a genus of plants + -INE]

e·phem·er·al (i·fem′ər·əl) *adj.* **1** Living one day only, as certain insects. **2** Short-lived; transitory. —*n.* Anything lasting for a very short time. [Gk. *ephēmeros* < *epi-* on + *hēmera* day] —**e·phem′er·al·ly** *adv.* —**e·phem′er·al·ness** *n.* —**Syn.** *adj.* **2** transient, passing, temporal, temporary.

e·phem·er·id (i·fem′ər·id) *n.* Any of an order of insects characterized by a short-lived, fragile, adult phase, as the mayfly. [< NL < Gk. *ephēmeros* EPHEMERAL.]

E·phe·sian (i·fē′zhən) *adj.* Of or pertaining to Ephesus. —*n.* A citizen of Ephesus.

E·phe·sians (i·fē′zhənz) *n. pl. (construed as sing.)* The New Testament epistle to the church at Ephesus.

Eph·e·sus (ef′ə·səs) *n.* An ancient Greek city in w Asia Minor.

eph·or (ef′ôr, -ər) *n. pl.* **·ors** or **·o·ri** (-ə·rī) In ancient Sparta, one of a body of elected, supervising magistrates. [< Gk. *ephoran* to oversee]

E·phra·im (ē′frē·əm, ē′frəm) **1** In the Old Testament, Joseph's second son. **2** The tribe descended from him.

E·phra·im·ite (ē′frē·əm·īt) *n.* A descendant of Ephraim or a member of his tribe.

epi- *prefix* **1** Upon; above; among; outside: *epidermis.* **2** Besides; over; in addition to: *epilogue.* **3** Near; close to; beside. [< Gk. *epi* upon, on]

ep·ic (ep′ik) *n.* **1** A long, narrative poem celebrating in stately, formal verse heroic or grandiose events or achievements. **2** Any novel, play, historical event, etc., having a heroic or grandiose quality or theme. —*adj.* **1** Of, pertaining to, or like an epic. **2** Grand, noble, legendary, or heroic: also **ep′i·cal.** [< Gk. < *epos* song, word]

ep·i·ca·lyx (ep′ə·kā′liks, -kal′iks) *n. pl.* **·ca·lyx·es** or **·ca·ly·ces** (-kā′lə·sēz) *Bot.* A ring of bracts resembling the calyx of a flower, located near the true calyx.

ep·i·can·thic fold (ep′ə·kan′thik) A vertical fold of skin at the inner corner of the eyelid, found chiefly in certain Asian peoples. Also **ep′i·can′thus.** [< Gk. *epi-* upon + *kanthos* corner of the eye]

ep·i·carp (ep′ə·kärp) *n. Bot.* The outer layer of a pericarp.

ep·i·cene (ep′ə·sēn) *adj.* Belonging to or partaking of the characteristics of both sexes. —*n.* An epicene person. [< Gk. *epi-* upon + *koinos* common] —**ep′i·cen′ism** *n.*

ep·i·cen·ter (ep′ə·sen′tər) *n. Geol.* **1** The point on the earth's surface above the point of origin of an earthquake. **2** A focus or central point. —**ep′i·cen′tral** *adj.*

ep·i·cure (ep′ə·kyŏŏr) *n.* A person who enjoys and is knowledgeable about good food and drink; gourmet. [< *Epicurus,* 342?–370 B.C., Greek philosopher] —**ep′i·cu·re′an** (-kyŏŏ·rē′ən) *adj., n.* —**ep′i·cu·re′an·ism, ep′i·cur·ism** *n.*

Ep·i·cu·re·an (ep′ə·kyŏŏ·rē′ən) *adj.* Pertaining to the Greek philosopher Epicurus or to his doctrine that the chief goods of life are freedom from pain and peace of mind. —*n.* A follower of Epicurus. —**Ep′i·cu·re′an·ism′** *n.*

ep·i·dem·ic (ep′ə·dem′ik) *adj.* Affecting many in a large area or community at once: also **ep′i·dem′i·cal.** —*n.* **1** A disease temporarily prevalent in a community or throughout a large area. **2** A circumstance that suddenly becomes widespread: an *epidemic* of business failures. [< Gk. *epi-* upon + *dēmos* people] —**ep′i·dem′i·cal·ly** *adv.*

ep·i·der·mis (ep′ə·dûr′mis) *n.* The outer covering of the skin; the cuticle. [< Gk. *epi-* upon + *derma* skin] —**ep′i·der′mal, ep′i·der′mic** *adj.*

ep·i·glot·tis (ep′ə·glot′is) *n.* The leaf-shaped piece of cartilage, at the base of the tongue, that closes the trachea, or windpipe, during the act of swallowing. [< NL < Gk. *epi-* upon + *glōtta* tongue] —**ep′i·glot′tal** *adj.*

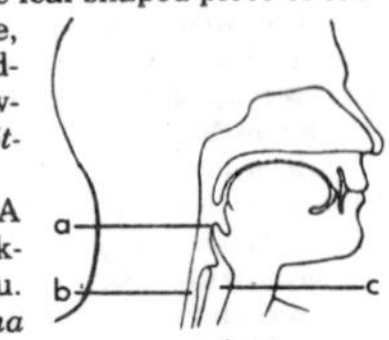

a. epiglottis.
b. esophagus.
c. trachea.

ep·i·gram (ep′ə·gram) *n.* **1** A pithy, caustic, or thought-provoking saying. **2** A short, witty, usu. satiric poem. [< Gk. *epigramma* an inscription] —**ep′i·gram·mat′ic** or **·i·cal** *adj.* —**ep′i·gram·mat′i·cal·ly** *adv.* —**ep′i·gram′ma·tist** *n.*

ep·i·graph (ep′ə·graf, -gräf) *n.* **1** A carved inscription on a monument, tomb, etc. **2** A quotation prefixed to a book, chapter, etc. [< Gk. < *epi-* upon + *graphein* write] —**ep′i·graph′ic** or **·i·cal** *adj.* —**ep′i·graph′i·cal·ly** *adv.*

e·pig·ra·phy (i·pig′rə·fē) *n.* **1** Inscriptions collectively. **2** The deciphering, study, interpretation, etc., of inscriptions. —**e·pig′ra·pher, e·pig′ra·phist** *n.*

ep·i·lep·sy (ep′ə·lep′sē) *n. Pathol.* A chronic nervous affection characterized by sudden interruption of consciousness, sometimes accompanied by convulsions. Also **ep′i·lep′si·a.** [< Gk. *epi-* upon + *lambanein* seize]

ep·i·lep·tic (ep′ə·lep′tik) *adj.* Pertaining to or affected with epilepsy. —*n.* One who has epilepsy. —**ep′i·lep′ti·cal·ly** *adv.*

ep·i·logue (ep′ə·lôg, -log) *n.* **1** A concluding section, as of a novel or play, that rounds out or comments on the work. **2** A short speech to the audience delivered by an actor after the conclusion of a play. **3** The actor who delivers such a speech. Also **ep′i·log.** [< Gk. *epi-* upon, in addition + *legein* say]

ep·i·neph·rine (ep′ə·nef′rin, -rēn) *n.* An adrenal hormone, used to raise blood pressure and as a heart stimulant, etc. Also **ep′i·neph′rin** (-rin). [< EPI- + Gk. *nēphros* kidney]

e·piph·a·ny (i·pif′ə·nē) *n. pl.* **·nies** A sudden recognition of or insight into the meaning, reality, or significance of something. [< Gk. *epiphainein* to manifest]

E·piph·a·ny (i·pif′ə·nē) *n.* January 6, a festival commemorating the manifestation of Christ to the Gentiles, represented by the Magi.

ep·i·phyte (ep′ə·fīt) *n. Bot.* A plant growing nonparasitically upon another. [< EPI- + Gk. *phyton* plant] —**ep′i·phyt′ic** (-fit′ik) or **·i·cal** *adj.* —**ep′i·phyt′i·cal·ly** *adv.*

Epis., Episc. Episcopal; Episcopalian.

Epis., Epist. Epistle.

e·pis·co·pa·cy (i·pis′kə·pə·sē) *n. pl.* **·cies** **1** Government of a church by bishops. **2** A bishop's state or office. **3** A body of bishops collectively. [< LL *episcopus* bishop]

e·pis·co·pal (i·pis′kə·pəl) *adj.* **1** Of or pertaining to bishops. **2** Having a government vested in bishops. [< LL < *episcopus* bishop] —**e·pis′co·pal·ly** *adv.*

E·pis·co·pal (i·pis′kə·pəl) *adj.* Belonging or pertaining to the Protestant Episcopal Church, or to any church in the Anglican communion.

Episcopal Church PROTESTANT EPISCOPAL CHURCH.

e·pis·co·pa·li·an (i·pis′kə·pā′lē·ən, -pāl′yən) *n.* An advocate of episcopacy. —*adj.* Pertaining to or favoring episcopal government.

E·pis·co·pa·li·an (i·pis′kə·pā′lē·ən, i·pāl′yən) *n.* A member of the Protestant Episcopal Church. —*adj.* EPISCOPAL. —**E·pis′co·pa′li·an·ism** *n.*

e·pis·co·pate (i·pis′kə·pit, -pāt) *n.* **1** The office, dignity, or term of office of a bishop. **2** A bishop's see. **3** Bishops collectively.

ep·i·sode (ep′ə·sōd) *n.* **1** An incident or story in a literary work, separable from, yet related to it. **2** A notable incident or action occurring as a break in the regular course of events. **3** An installment of a serial. [< Gk. *epi-* upon + *eisodos* entrance] —**ep′i·sod′ic** (-sod′ik) or **·i·cal, ep′i·so′dal** or **·di·al** *adj.* —**ep′i·sod′i·cal·ly** *adv.*

e·pis·te·mol·o·gy (i·pis′tə·mol′ə·jē) *n. pl.* **·gies** That department of philosophy which investigates critically the nature, methods, limits, and validity, of human knowledge. [< Gk. *epistēmē* knowledge + -LOGY] **—e·pis·te·mo·log·i·cal** (i·pis′tə·mə·loj′i·kəl) *adj.* **—e·pis′te·mo·log′i·cal·ly** *adv.* **—e·pis′te·mol′o·gist** *n.*

e·pis·tle (i·pis′əl) *n.* 1 A letter; esp., a long, formal letter that instructs. 2 *Usu. cap.* One of the letters of an apostle. 3 *Usu. cap.* A selection from an apostle's letter, read in certain church services. [< Gk. *epi-* on + *stellein* send]

e·pis·to·lar·y (i·pis′tə·ler′ē) *adj.* 1 Belonging or suitable to a letter or correspondence by letter. 2 Included in or maintained by letters. Also **ep·is·tol·ic** (ep′is·tol′ik), **ep′is·tol′i·cal.**

ep·i·taph (ep′ə·taf, -täf) *n.* An inscription on a tomb or monument in honor or in memory of the dead. [< Gk. *epi-* upon, at + *taphos* a tomb] **—ep′i·taph′ic** (-taf′ik) *adj.*

ep·i·the·li·um (ep′ə·thē′lē·əm) *n. pl.* **·li·ums** or **·li·a** (-lē·ə) The membranous tissue covering the inner and outer surfaces of the body [< EPI- + Gk. *thēlē* nipple]

ep·i·thet (ep′ə·thet) *n.* A word or phrase, often disparaging, used to describe or to substitute for the name of a person or thing. [< L < Gk. < *epi-* upon + *tithenai* place] **—ep′i·thet′ic** or **·i·cal** *adj.*

e·pit·o·me (i·pit′ə·mē) *n.* 1 A typical example; essence; embodiment: the *epitome* of arrogance. 2 A concise summary; abridgement. [< Gk. *epitomē*] **—ep·i·tom·ic** (ep′ə·tom′ik) or **·i·cal** *adj.* **—e·pit′o·mist, e·pit′o·miz′er** *n.*

e·pit·o·mize (i·pit′ə·mīz) *v.t.* **·mized, ·miz·ing** 1 To abridge. 2 To be an epitome of.

ep·i·zo·ot·ic (ep′ə·zō·ot′ik) *adj.* Common to or affecting many animals at one time. —*n.* An epizootic disease: also **ep′i·zo′o·ty** (-zō′ə·tē). [< EPI- + Gk. *zōion* animal]

e plu·ri·bus u·num (ē plŏŏr′ə·bəs yōō′nəm) *Latin* One out of many: a motto of the U.S.

ep·och (ep′ək, *Brit.* ē′pok) *n.* 1 A point in time which marks the beginning of some new development, condition, discovery, etc. 2 An interval of time regarded in terms of extraordinary events and far-reaching results. 3 *Geol.* A time interval shorter than a period. 4 *Astron.* An arbitrarily chosen moment of time, used as a reference point. [< Gk. *epochē* a stoppage, point of time] **—ep′och·al** *adj.*

ep·ode (ep′ōd) *n.* 1 That part of a Greek ode following the strophe and antistrophe. 2 A species of lyric poem, in which a longer line is followed by a shorter one. [< Gk. *epi-* in addition + *aidein* sing]

ep·o·nym (ep′ə·nim) *n.* 1 A person from whose name the name of a nation, epoch, etc., is derived or supposedly derived. 2 A person whose name is identified with some epoch, movement, etc. [< Gk. *epi-* upon + *onyma* name] **—ep′o·nym′ic** (-nim′ik), **e·pon·y·mous** (i·pon′ə·məs) *adj.*

e·pox·y (i·pok′sē) *adj.* Designating an oxygen-carbon bond characteristic of certain durable resins used for varnishes and adhesives. [< EP(I) + OXY-]

ep·si·lon (ep′sə·lon) *n.* The fifth letter of the Greek alphabet (Ε, ϵ).

Epsom salts A bitter, white salt, magnesium sulfate, used as a cathartic. Also **Epsom salt.** [< *Epsom*, England]

eq. equal; equation; equivalent.

eq·ua·ble (ek′wə·bəl, ē′kwə-) *adj.* 1 Of uniform condition or movement; steady; even. 2 Not readily disturbed. [< L *aequare* make equal] **—eq′ua·bil′i·ty** (-bil′ə·tē) *n.* **—eq′ua·bly** *adv.*

e·qual (ē′kwəl) *adj.* 1 Of the same size, quantity, intensity, value, etc. 2 Having the same rank, rights, importance, etc. 3 Fair; impartial; just: *equal* laws. 4 Having the strength, ability, requirements, etc., that are needed: with *to.* 5 Balanced; level; even. —*v.t.* **e·qualed** or **e·qualled, e·qual·ing** or **e·qual·ling** 1 To be or become equal to. 2 To do or produce something equal to. —*n.* A person or thing equal to another. [< L *aequus* even] **—e′qual·ly** *adv.* **—e′qual·ness** *n.*

e·qual·i·tar·i·an (i·kwol′ə·târ′ē·ən) *adj.* & *n.* EGALITARIAN.

e·qual·i·ty (i·kwol′ə·tē) *n. pl.* **·ties** 1 The state or an instance of being equal. 2 An equation.

e·qual·ize (ē′kwəl·īz) *v.t.* **·ized, ·iz·ing** 1 To make equal. 2 To render uniform. *Brit. sp.* **e′qual·ise. —e′qual·i·za′tion, e′qual·iz′er** *n.*

e·qua·nim·i·ty (ē′kwə·nim′ə·tē, ek′wə-) *n.* Evenness of mind or temper; composure; calmness. [< L *aequus* even + *animus* mind] **—Syn.** repose, serenity, self-possession, poise, tranquility.

e·quate (i·kwāt′) *v.t.* **e·quat·ed, e·quat·ing** 1 To make equal. 2 To treat, consider, or express as equivalent. 3 *Math.* To indicate the equality of.

e·qua·tion (i·kwā′zhən, -shən) *n.* 1 The process or act of making equal. 2 The state of being equal. 3 A complex of interrelated and variable elements or factors: the human *equation.* 4 A mathematical statement expressing the equality of two quantities. 5 *Chem.* A quantitative, symbolic representation of a chemical reaction. **—e·qua′tion·al** *adj.* **—e·qua′tion·al·ly** *adv.*

e·qua·tor (i·kwā′tər) *n.* 1 A circle around the earth, at right angles to its axis and equidistant from the poles. 2 Any similar circle, as of the sun, a planet, etc. 3 CELESTIAL EQUATOR. [< LL *(circulus) aequator* equalizer (circle)]

e·qua·to·ri·al (ē′kwə·tôr′ē·əl, -tō′rē-) *adj.* 1 Of, pertaining to, or near an equator. 2 Pertaining to conditions at or near the earth's equator.

Equatorial Guinea (gin′ē) *n.* A republic in w Africa, 9,828 sq. mi., cap. Santa Isabel. • See map at AFRICA.

eq·uer·ry (ek′wə·rē) *n. pl.* **·ries** 1 An officer having charge of the horses of a prince or nobleman. 2 An attendant upon a member of a royal household, as in England. Also **eq′uer·y.** [< OF *escuier* riding master]

e·ques·tri·an (i·kwes′trē·ən) *adj.* 1 Pertaining to horses or horsemanship. 2 On horseback. —*n.* One skilled in horsemanship. [< L *equus* a horse] **—e·ques′tri·enne′** (-en′) *n. Fem.*

equi- *combining form* Equal; equally: *equidistant.* [< L *aequus* equal]

e·qui·an·gu·lar (ē′kwē·ang′gyə·lər) *adj.* Having angles that are all equal.

e·qui·dis·tant (ē′kwə·dis′tənt) *adj.* Equally distant. **—e′qui·dis′tance** *n.*

e·qui·lat·er·al (ē′kwə·lat′ər·əl) *adj.* Having all the sides equal. **—e′qui·lat′er·al·ly** *adv.*

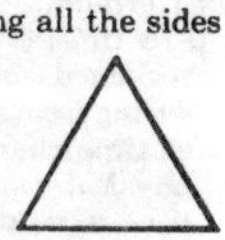

Equilateral triangle

e·qui·li·brate (ē′kwə·lī′brāt, i·kwil′ə-) *v.t.* & *v.i.* **·brat·ed, ·brat·ing** 1 To bring into or be in a state of equilibrium. 2 To balance or counterbalance. [< L *aequus* equal + *libratus* level] **—e′qui·li·bra′tion, e′qui·li′·bra·tor** *n.*

e·qui·lib·ri·um (ē′kwə·lib′rē·əm) *n.* 1 A state of balance produced by the counteraction of two or more forces or influences in a system. 2 Bodily balance. 3 Mental or emotional balance or poise. Also **e′qui·lib′ri·ty.** [< L *aequus* equal + *libra* a balance]

e·quine (ē′kwīn, ek′win) *adj.* Of, pertaining to, or like a horse. —*n.* A horse. [< L *equus* horse]

e·qui·noc·tial (ē′kwə·nok′shəl) *adj.* 1 Of, occurring at, or pertaining to either equinox.

e·qui·nox (ē′kwə·noks) *n.* 1 One of the two times in each year when the sun crosses the celestial equator, making day and night of equal length all over the earth. The **vernal** or **spring equinox** takes place about Mar. 21, the **autumnal equinox** about Sept. 21. 2 Either of two opposite points at which the sun crosses the celestial equator on these dates. [< L *aequus* equal + *nox* night]

e·quip (i·kwip′) *v.t.* **e·quipped, e·quip·ping** 1 To furnish or prepare with whatever is needed for any purpose or undertaking. 2 To dress or attire; array. [< OF *equiper*]

eq·ui·page (ek′wə·pij) *n.* 1 The equipment for a camp, army, etc. 2 A carriage, with its horses, attendants, etc.

e·quip·ment (i·kwip′mənt) *n.* 1 The act or process of equipping. 2 The state of being equipped or furnished. 3 Those things with which a person, group, or thing is equipped for some special purpose or service.

e·qui·poise (ē′kwə·poiz, ek′wə-) *n.* 1 Equality or equal distribution, as of weight and power; equilibrium. 2 COUNTERPOISE.

eq·ui·ta·ble (ek′wə·tə·bəl) *adj.* 1 Characterized by equity, or fairness and just dealing, impartial. 2 *Law* Of, pertaining to, or valid in equity, as distinguished from common law or statute law. —**eq′ui·ta·ble·ness** *n.* —**eq′ui·ta·bly** *adv.*

eq·ui·ty (ek′wə·tē) *n. pl.* **·ties** **1** Fairness or impartiality; justness. **2** Something that is fair or equitable. **3** *Law* **a** Justice based on natural reason or ethical judgment. **b** That field of jurisprudence superseding statute law and common law when these are considered inadequate or inflexible for the purposes of justice. **4** The value of property in excess of mortgage or other liens. [< L *aequus* equal]

e·quiv·a·lence (i·kwiv′ə·ləns) *n.* The state of being equivalent. Also **e·quiv′a·len·cy.**

e·quiv·a·lent (i·kwiv′ə·lənt) *adj.* **1** Equal in value, force, meaning, etc. **2** *Chem.* Having the same valence or the same combining weight. —*n.* **1** That which is equivalent; something equal in value, power, effect, etc. **2** *Chem.* The weight of an element which combines with or displaces eight grams of oxygen or one gram of hydrogen. [< L *aequus* equal + *valere* be worth] —**e·quiv′a·lent·ly** *adv.* —**Syn.** *adj.* **1** alike, analogous, reciprocal, tantamount, same.

e·quiv·o·cal (i·kwiv′ə·kəl) *adj.* **1** Having two or more meanings or interpretations. **2** Uncertain; doubtful. **3** Suspicious; questionable; dubious. [< L *aequus* equal + *vox* voice] —**e·quiv′o·cal·ly** *adv.* —**e·quiv′o·cal·ness** *n.*

e·quiv·o·cate (i·kwiv′ə·kāt) *v.i.* **·cat·ed, ·cat·ing** To use ambiguous language with intent to deceive. —**e·quiv′o·ca′tion, e·quiv′o·ca′tor** *n.*

-er[1] *suffix* **1** A person or thing that performs the action of the root verb: *checker.* **2** A person concerned with or practicing a trade or profession: *glover.* **3** One who lives in or comes from: *New Yorker.* **4** A person, thing, or action related to or characterized by: *three-decker.* [< OE *-ere, -are*]

-er[2] *suffix* More: used in the comparative degree of adjectives and adverbs: *harder, later.* [< OE *-ra, -or*]

-er[3] *suffix* Repeatedly: used in frequentative verbs: *stutter.* [< OE *-rian*]

Er erbium.

e·ra (ir′ə, ē′rə) *n.* **1** A system of chronological notation reckoned from some fixed point of time. **2** A period of time dating from an important date, occurrence, etc. **3** A period of time characterized by certain social, intellectual, or physical conditions, etc. **4** A date or event from which time is reckoned: the Christian *era.* **5** Any of the major divisions of geological time. [< L *aera* counters for reckoning]

e·rad·i·cate (i·rad′ə·kāt) *v.t.* **·cat·ed, ·cat·ing** **1** To pull up by the roots; root out. **2** To destroy utterly. [< L *e-* out + *radix* a root] —**e·rad′i·ca·ble** (-ə·kə·bəl) *adj.* —**e·rad′i·ca′tion, e·rad′i·ca′tor** *n.* —**Syn. 2** abolish, extirpate, blot out, erase, eliminate. —**e·rad′i·ca′tive** *adj.*

e·rase (i·rās′) *v.t.* **e·rased, e·ras·ing** **1** To remove or wipe out. **2** To remove all signs or traces of; obliterate. **3** To remove (recorded matter) from (a tape). **4** *Slang* To kill. [< L *e-* out + *radere* scrape] —**e·ras′a·ble** *adj.*

e·ras·er (i·rā′sər) *n.* Something that erases, as a piece of rubber, felt, etc.

e·ra·sure (i·rā′shər, -zhər) *n.* **1** The act of erasing or the state of being erased. **2** Anything erased. **3** The place where something has been erased.

Er·a·to (er′ə·tō) *Gk. Myth.* The Muse of lyric and love poetry.

er·bi·um (ûr′bē·əm) *n.* A soft metallic element (symbol Er) of the rare-earth series. [< *(Ytt)erby,* town in Sweden where first found]

ere (âr) *prep. Archaic* Prior to; before in time. —*conj.* **1** Earlier than; before. **2** Sooner than; rather than. [< OE *ǣr*]

Er·e·bus (er′ə·bəs) *Gk. Myth.* A dark region under the earth through which the dead pass on their way to Hades.

e·rect (i·rekt′) *v.t.* **1** To construct, as a house; build. **2** To assemble the parts of; set up. **3** To set upright; lift up: to *erect* a flagpole. **4** To construct or formulate, as a theory. **5** To establish or cause to exist. —*adj.* **1** Upright in position, form, or posture; vertical. **2** Sticking upward or outward; bristling. [< L *e-* out + *regere* make straight] —**e·rect′ly** *adv.* —**e·rect′ness** *n.*

e·rec·tile (i·rek′təl, -tīl) *adj.* Capable of becoming erect. —**e′rec·til′i·ty** *n.*

e·rec·tion (i·rek′shən) *n.* **1** Something erected, as a building. **2** The act of erecting or the state of being erected. **3** The raising up or stiffening of a body part, as the penis, through the accumulation of blood in erectile tissue; also, the state of being so raised and stiffened.

e·rec·tor (i·rek′tər) *n.* **1** One who or that which erects. **2** *Anat.* Any of various muscles which stiffen or hold up a part of the body.

ere·long (âr′lông′, -long′) *adv.* Before much time has passed; soon.

er·e·mite (er′ə·mīt) *n.* HERMIT. [< Gk. *erēmitēs*] —**er·e·mit·ic** (er′ə·mit′ik) or **·i·cal,** *adj.*

erg (ûrg) *n. Physics* A unit of work or energy equal to 10^{-7} joule. [< Gk. *ergon* work]

er·go (ûr′gō) *conj. & adv.* Hence; therefore. [L]

er·gos·ter·ol (ûr·gos′tə·rōl) *n.* A sterol, first obtained from ergot, which is converted by ultraviolet light into vitamin D. [< ERGO(T) + STEROL]

er·got (ûr′gət) *n.* **1** A parasitic fungus that infects rye and other grasses and which yields several biologically potent alkaloids. **2** The disease caused by this fungus. [< OF *argot* spur of a cock] —**er·got·ic** (ər·got′ik), **er′got·ed** *adj.*

E·rie (ir′ē) *n. pl.* **E·rie** or **E·ries** A member of a tribe of North American Indians of Iroquoian stock, formerly inhabiting the S shores of Lake Erie.

Er·in (âr′in, ir′in) *n.* Ireland.

erl·king (ûrl′king′) *n.* In Germanic folklore, the king of the elves, malicious toward children.

er·mine (ûr′min) *n.* **1** A weasel of the N hemisphere, having brown fur that in winter turns white with a black tip on the tail. **2** Its fur, used in Europe for the facings of official robes, as of judges. **3** The position, rank, or functions of a judge. [< OF *ermine*] —**er′mined** *adj.*

Ermine

erne (ûrn) *n.* SEA EAGLE. [< OE *earn*]

e·rode (i·rōd′) *v.* **e·rod·ed, e·rod·ing** *v.t.* **1** To eat or wear into or away. **2** *Geol.* To wear down by the action of wind, water, etc. **3** To form, as a canyon, by such action. —*v.i.* **4** To become eroded. [< L *e-* off + *rodere* gnaw]

e·rog·e·nous (i·roj′ə·nəs) *adj.* Producing erotic feeling; exciting sexual desire. Also **er·o·gen·ic** (er′ə·jen′ik). [< Gk. *erōs* love + -GENOUS]

Er·os (ir′os, er′os) *Gk. Myth.* The god of love, son of Aphrodite.

e·ro·sion (i·rō′zhən) *n.* The act of eroding, or the state of being eroded.

e·rot·ic (i·rot′ik) *adj.* **1** Of, pertaining to, or tending to arouse sexual love or desire. **2** Easily aroused sexually. —*n.* An erotic person. [< Gk. *erōs* love] —**e·rot′i·cal·ly** *adv.* —**e·rot′i·cism** *n.*

e·rot·i·ca (i·rot′i·kə) *n. pl. (often construed as sing.)* Erotic pictures, books, etc. [< Gk. *erōtikos* < *erōs* love]

err (ûr) *v.i.* **erred, err·ing** **1** To make a mistake; be wrong. **2** To go astray morally; sin. [< L *errare* wander]

er·rand (er′ənd) *n.* **1** A trip made to carry a message, to purchase something, to attend to personal business, etc. **2** The reason for such a trip. [< OE *ǣrende* message, news]

er·rant (er′ənt) *adj.* **1** Roving or wandering. **2** Straying from a course that is considered proper, moral, etc. [< L *iter* a journey] —**er′rant·ly** *adv.*

er·rant·ry (er′ənt·rē) *n.* The vocation, conduct, or career of a knight errant.

er·rat·ic (i·rat′ik) *adj.* **1** Not conforming to rules or standards; queer; eccentric. **2** Irregular, as in course or direction; wandering; straying. —*n.* An erratic person or thing. Also **er·rat′i·cal.** [< L *errare* wander] —**er·rat′i·cal·ly** *adv.* —**Syn. 1** odd, peculiar, capricious, abnormal, unpredictable, whimsical, changeable.

er·ra·tum (i·rā′təm, e·rä′-) *n. pl.* **·ra·ta** (-rā′tə, -rä′tə) An error, as in writing or printing. [L]

er·ro·ne·ous (ə·rō′nē·əs, e·rō′-) *adj.* Marked by error; incorrect; mistaken. —**er·ro′ne·ous·ly** *adv.* —**er·ro′ne·ous·ness** *n.*

er·ror (er′ər) *n.* **1** The condition of being incorrect, esp. in matters of opinion or belief. **2** Something done, said, or believed wrongly; inaccuracy; mistake. **3** Any misplay in baseball which prolongs the batter's time at bat or permits a base runner to make one or more bases. 4 A wrongdoing; transgression; sin. [< L < *errare* wander]

er·satz (er·zäts′) *n.* A substitute or replacement, usu. inferior to the original. —*adj.* Substitute. [< G *ersetzen* replace]

Erse (ûrs) *n.* 1 SCOTTISH GAELIC. 2 IRISH GAELIC. [< ME *Erisch* Irish]

erst (ûrst) *Archaic adv.* 1 Formerly; long ago; once. 2 In the beginnning. —*adj.* First. [< OE *ǣrest*]

erst·while (ûrst′hwīl′) *adj.* Former. —*adv. Archaic* Formerly.

e·ruct (i·rukt′) *v.t. & v.i.* BELCH. Also **e·ruc′tate.** [< L *e-* out + *ructare* belch] —**e·ruc′ta′tion** *n.*

er·u·dite (er′yōō·dīt) *adj.* Very learned; scholarly. [< L *erudire* instruct] —**er′u·dite·ly** *adv.* —**er′u·dite·ness** *n.*

er·u·di·tion (er′yōō·dish′ən) *n.* Extensive knowledge or learning.

e·rupt (i·rupt′) *v.i.* 1 To cast forth smoke, lava, etc., suddenly and with violence: The volcano *erupted.* 2 To burst forth: Steam is *erupting* from the volcano. 3 To break through a gum, as a tooth. 4 To become covered with a rash or pimples. —*v.t.* 5 To cause to burst forth. [< L *e-* out + *rumpere* burst]

e·rup·tion (i·rup′shən) *n.* 1 The act or process, or an instance, of erupting. 2 That which erupts, as lava from a volcano. 3 A breaking out, as in a rash. 4 Any sudden outbreak or outburst.

e·rup·tive (i·rup′tiv) or *adj.* Of, pertaining to, or formed by eruption. —**e·rup′tive·ly** *adv.* —**e·rup′tive·ness** *n.*

-ery *suffix of nouns* 1 A business, place of business, or place where something is done: *brewery.* 2 A place or residence for: *nunnery.* 3 A collection of goods, wares, etc.: *pottery.* 4 The qualities or practices of: *snobbery.* 5 An art, trade, or profession: *cookery.* 6 A state of being: *slavery.* [< OF *-ier*]

er·y·sip·e·las (er′ə·sip′ə·ləs, ir′ə-) *n.* An acute infectious disease of the skin, accompanied by inflammation and fever. [< Gk. *erysis* a reddening + *pella* skin]

e·ryth·ro·cyte (i·rith′rō·sīt) *n.* A red blood corpuscle, formed in bone marrow and containing hemoglobin, and serving to carry oxygen to body tissues. [< Gk. *erythros* red + -CYTE] —**e·ryth′ro·cyt′ic** (-sit′ik) *adj.*

-es[1] An inflectional ending used to form the plural of nouns ending in a sibilant *(glasses, fuses, fishes)* or an affricate *(witches, judges).* [< OE *-as*]

-es[2] An inflectional ending used to form the third person singular present indicative of verbs ending in a sibilant, affricate, or vowel: *kisses, poaches, goes.* [ME *-es*]

Es einsteinium.

E·sau (ē′sô) In the Bible, the elder son of Isaac and Rebecca, who sold his birthright to his brother Jacob.

es·ca·drille (es′kə·dril′) *n.* 1 A unit of a European air command; esp., in France, a squadron of six airplanes. 2 A squadron of naval vessels. [F < Sp. *escuadra* a squadron]

es·ca·lade (es′kə·lād′) *v.t.* **·lad·ed, ·lad·ing** To scale (a wall, etc.) or enter (a fortress, etc.) by using ladders. —*n.* An attack by escalading. [< Sp. *escalar* to climb < L *scala* a ladder]

es·ca·late (es′kə·lāt) *v.t. & v.i.* **·lat·ed, ·lat·ing** 1 To increase or be increased: to *escalate* a war. 2 To ascend or carry up, as on an escalator. [Back formation from ESCALATOR] —**es′·ca·la′tion** *n.*

es·ca·la·tor (es′kə·lā′tər) *n.* A moving stairway, built on an endless loop of chain. [< *Escalator,* a trade name]

escalator clause A clause in a contract stipulating an increase or decrease in wages, prices, etc., under certain specified conditions.

es·cal·lop (e·skol′əp, -skal′-) *n. & v.* SCALLOP. Also **es·cal′op.**

es·ca·pade (es′kə·pād) *n.* 1 A reckless adventure or mischievous prank. 2 An escape from restraint. [< Sp. *escapar* to escape]

es·cape (ə·skāp′, e·skāp′) *v.* **es·caped, es·cap·ing** *v.t.* 1 To get away from; flee from, as guards or prison. 2 To avoid, as harm or evil. 3 To slip or come from involuntarily: No cry *escaped* him. 4 To slip away from or elude (notice or recollection). —*v.i.* 5 To get free from or avoid arrest, custody, danger, etc. 6 To fade or slip away; disappear; vanish. 7 To come forth; emerge; leak: Gas is *escaping* from the stove. —*n.* 1 The act of escaping. 2 The fact or state of having escaped. 3 A means of escape. 4 Mental relief from monotony, anxiety, etc.: literature of *escape.* 5 Flow, as of a fluid; leakage. [< L *ex-* out + *cappa* a cloak] —**es·cap′·a·ble** *adj.* —**es·cap′er** *n.*

es·cape·ment (ə·skāp′mənt, e·skāp′-) *n.* 1 A device used in timepieces for regulating movement, consisting of an escape wheel and a detent or lock, through which periodic impulses are sent to the balance wheel. 2 A mechanism controlling the horizontal movement of a typewriter carriage.

escape velocity The minimum velocity at which a body has energy to escape from a gravitational field, as from that of the earth.

escape wheel A toothed wheel in an escapement.

es·cap·ism (ə·skā′piz·əm) *n.* A diversion of the mind from those realities of life which are unpleasant or monotonous, esp. by entertainment, daydreaming, etc. —**es·cap′ist** *adj., n.*

es·ca·role (es′kə·rōl) *n.* A variety of endive, used in salads.

es·carp·ment (es·kärp′mənt) *n.* 1 A precipitous artificial slope about a fortification or position. 2 A steep slope or cliff. [< Ital. *scarpa* a slope]

-esce *suffix* To become or grow; begin to be or do: *phosphoresce.* [< L *-escere,* suffix of inceptive verbs]

-escence *suffix* State or quality: *effervescence.* [< L *-escentia*]

-escent *suffix* Beginning to be, have, or do: *effervescent.* [< L *-escens,* suffix of pr.p. of inceptive verbs]

es·cheat (es·chēt′) *Law v.t. & v.i.* To revert, or cause to revert, to the state or crown. —*n.* 1 The reversion of property to the state in the U.S., or to the crown in England, when there are no legal heirs. 2 Property so reverted. [< OF *es-* out + *cheoir* fall] —**es·cheat′a·ble** *adj.* —**es·cheat′age** *n.*

es·chew (es·chōō′) *v.t.* To shun, as something unworthy or injurious. [< OF *eschiver*] —**es·chew′al** *n.*

es·cort (es·kôrt′) *v.t.* To accompany; go with, as from courtesy or to protect. —*n.* (es′kôrt) 1 One or more persons accompanying another person or persons, an object, etc., for protection or as a mark of respect. 2 One or more ships, planes, etc. accompanying another to furnish protection, guidance, etc. 3 A male who accompanies a woman on a date. [< Ital. *scorgere* lead]

es·cri·toire (es′kri·twär′) *n.* A writing desk. [< OF < L *scribere* write]

es·crow (es′krō, es·krō′) *n. Law* A deed, bond, piece of property, or money put in the custody of a third person until certain conditions are fulfilled. [< OF *escroe* a scroll]

es·cu·do (es·kōō′dō) *n. pl.* **·dos** 1 The monetary unit of Portugal and Portuguese territories. 2 An obsolete silver or gold coin of the Hispanic countries. [< L *scutum* shield]

es·cu·lent (es′kyə·lənt) *adj.* Suitable for food; edible. —*n.* Anything suitable for food. [< L *esca* food]

es·cutch·eon (i·skuch′ən) *n. Her.* The surface, usu. shield-shaped, upon which armorial bearings are displayed; a heraldic shield. [< L *scutum* shield]

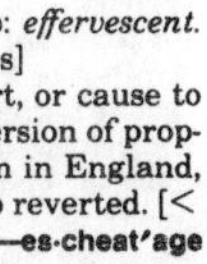

Escutcheon

Es·dras (ez′drəs) In the Douay Bible, the name for Ezra.

-ese *suffix* 1 A native or inhabitant of: *Milanese.* 2 The language or dialect of: *Chinese.* 3 Originating in; denoting the inhabitants or language of: *Tirolese.* 4 In the manner or style of: *journalese.* [< L *-ensis*]

ESE, E.S.E., ese, e.s.e. east southeast.

Es·ki·mo (es′kə·mō) *n. pl.* **·mos** 1 A member of a Mongoloid people indigenous to the Arctic coasts of North America, Greenland, and NE Siberia. 2 The language of the Eskimos. —**Es′ki·mo′an** *adj.*

Eskimo dog One of a breed of large, sturdy, broad-chested dogs used by the Eskimos to pull sleds.

e·soph·a·gus (i·sof′ə·gəs) *n. pl.* **·gi** (-gī, -jī) The tube through which food passes from the mouth to the stomach; gullet. [< Gk. *oisophagos*] **—e·so·phag·e·al** (ē′sō·faj′ē·əl, i·sof′ə·jē′əl), **e·soph′a·gal** (-ə·gəl) *adj.* • See LIVER.

es·o·ter·ic (es′ə·ter′ik) *adj.* **1** Confined to a select circle; confidential. **2** Designed for or understood by an initiated and enlightened few; abstruse; profound. [< Gk. *esōterikos* inner] **—es′o·ter′i·cal·ly** *adv.*

ESP extrasensory perception.

esp., espec. especially.

es·pal·ier (es·pal′yər) *n.* **1** A trellis on which small trees, shrubs, etc., are trained to grow in flat patterns. **2** A tree or row of plants so trained. —*v.t.* To train on or furnish with an espalier. [F]

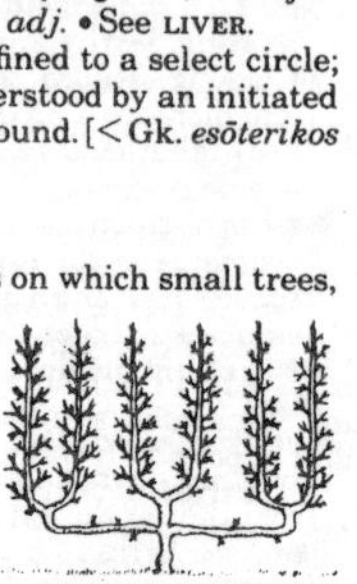

Espaliered tree

es·pe·cial (es·pesh′əl) *adj.* Exceptional; outstanding; special. [< OF, special] **—es·pe′cial·ly** *adv.*

Es·pe·ran·to (es′pə·rän′tō) *n.* An artificial language with a vocabulary based on words common to important European languages. [< Dr. *Esperanto*, pen name of L. L. Zamenhof, 1859–1917, Russ. scholar] **—Es′pe·ran′tism, Es′pe·ran′tist** *n.*

es·pi·al (es·pī′əl) *n.* **1** The act of spying or observing. **2** Discovery or notice.

es·pi·o·nage (es′pē·ə·näzh, -naj, -nij) *n.* **1** The practice of spying. **2** The employment and activities of spies and secret agents, esp. in time of war. [< F < *espier* espy]

es·pla·nade (es′plə·nād′, -näd′) *n.* A level open space, as before a fortress or along a waterside, for promenading, driving, etc. [F < L *ex* out + *planus* level]

es·pou·sal (es·pou′zəl) *adj.* Of or pertaining to a betrothal or marriage. —*n.* **1** Betrothal. **2** Marriage. **3** The act of taking up or supporting, as a cause or principle.

es·pouse (es·pouz′) *v.t.* **·poused, ·pous·ing 1** To take as a spouse; marry. **2** To take up or support, as a cause or doctrine. [< L *spondere* promise] **—es·pous′er** *n.*

es·pres·so (es·pres′ō) *n. pl.* **·sos** Coffee made from dark, roasted beans, usu. by an infusion of steam under pressure. [Ital. < *esprimere* to press out]

es·prit (es·prē′) *n.* Spirit; wit. [F < L *spiritus*]

esprit de corps (də kôr) A feeling of pride in and devotion to the common goals of some group. [F, lit., spirit of a body]

es·py (es·pī′) *v.t.* **es·pied, es·py·ing** To catch sight of; see. [< OF *espier* to look, spy]

Esq., Esqr. Esquire.

-esque *suffix* Like; in the manner or style of: *picturesque, arabesque.* [F < Ital. *-esco*]

Es·qui·mau (es′kə·mō) *n. pl.* **·mau** or **·maux** (mōz) ESKIMO.

es·quire (es′kwīr, es·kwīr′) *n.* **1** *Usu. cap.* A title of courtesy, usu. abbreviated after a man's surname. **2** In England, a member of the gentry ranking next below a knight. **3** A candidate for knighthood serving as an attendant to a knight. [< LL *scutarius* shield-bearer]

-ess *suffix* Female: *goddess, lioness.* [< OF < LL *-issa*]

es·say (e·sā′) *v.t.* To try to do or accomplish; attempt. —*n.* **1** (es′ā) A literary composition, esp. one dealing with a single subject from a personal point of view. **2** (e·sā′) An endeavor; effort. [< OF *essai* a trial] **—es·say′er** *n.*

es·say·ist (es′ā·ist) *n.* A writer of essays.

es·sence (es′əns) *n.* **1** The intrinsic nature or characteristic quality of anything; that which makes a thing what it is. **2** Something that is; an existent being or entity. **3** A substance considered to have, in concentrated form, the special qualities (as flavor, scent, etc.) of the plant, food, drug, etc. from which it was taken. **4** An alcoholic solution of such a substance. **5** Perfume; scent. [< L *esse* be] **—Syn. 1** substance, gist, quintessence, reality, kernel, pith, core.

es·sen·tial (ə·sen′shəl) *adj.* **1** Of or pertaining to the essence or intrinsic nature of anything; substantial; basic. **2** Indispensable, necessary, or highly important. —*n.* That which is fundamental, basic, or indispensable. **—es·sen′ti·al′i·ty** (-shē·al′ə·tē) *n.* **—es·sen′tial·ly** *adv.*

essential oil Any of a group of volatile oils which give to plants their characteristic odor and taste.

-est[1] *suffix* Most: used in the superlative degree of adjectives and adverbs: *hardest, latest.* [< OE *-ast, -est, -ost*]

-est[2] An archaic inflectional ending used in the second person singular present and past indicative, with *thou: eatest, walkest.* [< OE]

EST, E.S.T., e.s.t. eastern standard time.

es·tab·lish (es·tab′lish) *v.t.* **1** To settle or fix firmly; make stable or permanent. **2** To set up; found, as an institution or business. **3** To set up; install (oneself or someone else) in business, a position, etc. **4** To cause to be recognized or accepted. **5** To put into effect permanently; ordain, as laws. **6** To gain acceptance for; prove, as a theory or argument. **7** To appoint (a church) as a national institution. [< L *stabilire* to make firm or stable] **—es·tab′lish·er** *n.*

established church A church maintained by a nation and receiving financial support out of public funds.

es·tab·lish·ment (es·tab′lish·mənt) *n.* **1** The act of establishing. **2** The state of being established. **3** Anything established, as a place of business. **—the Establishment** Those collectively who occupy positions of influence and status in a society.

es·tate (es·tāt′) *n.* **1** One's entire property, possessions, and wealth. **2** Landed property, esp. a large tract of land with an elaborate residence, etc. **3** Condition or state: man's *estate.* **4** A class or order of persons in a state. **5** *Law* The degree, nature, and amount of one's lawful interest in any property. [< L *status* state]

estate car *Brit.* STATION WAGON.

es·teem (es·tēm′) *n.* Favorable opinion or estimation; respect; regard. —*v.t.* **1** To value highly. **2** To think to be; deem; consider: to *esteem* one fortunate. [< L *aestimare* to value]

es·ter (es′tər) *n. Chem.* Any of numerous organic compounds comparable to inorganic salts, formed by the reaction of an acid with an alcohol. [< G *Essigäther* vinegar ether]

Es·ther (es′tər) **1** In the Bible, the Jewish wife of a Persian king. **2** The Old Testament book that tells her story.

es·thete (es′thēt) *n.* AESTHETE.

es·thet·ic (es·thet′ik) *adj.* AESTHETIC.

es·thet·ics (es·thet′iks) *n.* AESTHETICS.

es·ti·ma·ble (es′tə·mə·bəl) *adj.* **1** Deserving of esteem. **2** That may be estimated or calculated. **—es′ti·ma·ble·ness** *n.* **—es′ti·ma·bly** *adv.*

es·ti·mate (es′tə·māt) *v.* **·mat·ed, ·mat·ing** *v.t.* **1** To form an approximate opinion of (size, amount, number, etc.); calculate roughly. **2** To form an opinion about; judge, as character. —*v.i.* **3** To make or submit an estimate. —*n.* (es′tə·mit) **1** A rough calculation. **2** A statement, as by a builder, in regard to the cost of certain work. **3** A judgment; opinion; evaluation. [< L *aestimare* to value] **—es′ti·ma′tive** *adj.* **—es′ti·ma′tor** *n.*

es·ti·ma·tion (es′tə·mā′shən) *n.* **1** The act of estimating. **2** Opinion; estimate. **3** Esteem; regard.

Es·to·ni·an (es·tō′nē·ən) *adj.* Of or pertaining to Estonia, its people, or their language. —*n.* **1** A native or citizen of Estonia. **2** The Finno-Ugric language of the Estonians.

es·top (es·top′) *v.t.* **·topped, ·top·ping** To stop or prevent, esp. by estoppel. [< LL *stuppare* to stop up]

es·top·pel (es·top′əl) *n. Law* A legal impediment by which one is forbidden to contradict or deny one's own previous statement or act.

es·trange (es·trānj′) *v.t.* **·tranged, ·trang·ing 1** To make (someone previously friendly or affectionate) indifferent or hostile; alienate. **2** To remove or dissociate (oneself, etc.): to *estrange* oneself from society. [< L *extraneus* foreign] **—es·trange′ment** *n.*

es·tro·gen (es′trə·jən) *n.* Any of several hormones exercising a critical influence on the female sexual cycle. [< ESTRUS + -GEN] **—es′tro·gen′ic** *adj.*

es·trus (es′trəs, ēs′-) *n. Zool.* The peak of the sexual cycle in animals, culminating in ovulation; heat or rut, esp. in female mammals. [< Gk. *oistros* a gadfly] **—es′tru·al** *adj.*

es·tu·ar·y (es′chōō·er′ē) *n. pl.* **·ar·ies 1** The wide mouth of a river where it is met by and mixes with the sea. **2** An arm or inlet of a sea. [< L *aestus* tide]

-et *suffix* Small; little: *islet.* [< OF < LL *-itus, -ita*]

e·ta (ā′tə, ē′-) *n.* The seventh letter of the Greek alphabet (H, η).

et al. and others (L *et alii*); and elsewhere (L *et alibi*).

etc. et cetera.

et cet·er·a (et set′ər·ə, set′rə) And other things; and the rest; and so forth. Also **et caet′er·a.** [L]

etch (ech) *v.t.* 1 To produce (a design, drawing, etc.) on glass, metal, etc. by the corrosive action of an acid. 2 To engrave (metal, glass, etc.) in this manner. 3 To impress deeply and clearly. —*v.i.* 4 To make etchings. [< G *ätzen*] **—etch′er** *n.*

etch·ing (ech′ing) *n.* 1 The act, art, or process of making designs on metal, glass, etc., by the corrosive action of acid. 2 A figure or design formed by etching. 3 An impression or print made from an etched plate.

e·ter·nal (i·tûr′nəl) *adj.* 1 Having neither beginning nor end of existence; infinite in duration. 2 Having no end; everlasting. 3 Continued without interruption; perpetual. 4 Independent of time or its conditions; timeless; unchangeable; immutable. 5 Of or pertaining to eternity. 6 Appearing interminable; incessant: Vaughn and his *eternal* jokes. —**the Eternal** God. [< L *aeternus*] **—e·ter′nal·ly** *adv.* **—e·ter′nal·ness** *n.*

Eternal City Rome.

e·ter·ni·ty (i·tûr′nə·tē) *n. pl.* **·ties** 1 The fact, state, or quality of being eternal. 2 Infinite duration or existence. 3 A seemingly endless or limitless time. 4 Immortality.

e·ter·nize (i·tûr′nīz) *v.t.* **·nized, ·niz·ing** 1 To make eternal. 2 To perpetuate the fame of; immortalize. *Brit. sp.* **e·ter′·nise. —e·ter′ni·za′tion** *n.*

-eth[1] An archaic inflectional ending used in the third person singular present indicative of some verbs: *eateth, drinketh.* [< OE *-ath, -eth, -oth*]

-eth[2] *suffix* Var. of -TH[2].

Eth. Ethiopia; Ethiopian; Ethiopic.

eth·ane (eth′ān) *n.* A colorless, odorless gas, of the paraffin series, contained in natural gas and illuminating gas. [< ETHYL]

eth·a·nol (eth′ə·nôl) *n.* ALCOHOL (def. 1).

e·ther (ē′thər) *n.* 1 *Chem* **a** A colorless, flammable, volatile, liquid organic compound, used as an anesthetic and solvent. **b** Any of a group of organic compounds in which an oxygen atom is joined with two organic radicals. 2 A perfectly elastic medium formerly assumed to pervade all of space. 3 The upper air. [< L *aether* sky]

e·the·re·al (i·thir′ē·əl) *adj.* 1 Having the nature of ether or air. 2 Light; airy; fine; subtle; exquisite. 3 Existing in or belonging to the ether or upper air; aerial; heavenly. 4 Of or pertaining to ether. **—e·the′re·al′i·ty, e·the′re·al·ness** *n.* **—e·the′re·al·ly** *adv.*

e·the·re·al·ize (i·thir′ē·əl·īz) *v.t. & v.i.* **·ized, ·iz·ing** To make or become ethereal. **—e·the′re·al·i·za′tion** *n.*

e·ther·ize (ē′thə·rīz) *v.t.* **·ized, ·iz·ing** 1 To subject to the influence of ether; anesthetize. 2 To change into ether. — **e′ther·i·za′tion, e′ther·iz′er** *n.*

eth·ic (eth′ik) *adj.* Ethical; moral. —*n.* 1 The philosophy or a system of morals; ethics. 2 A single principle of a system of ethics. [< Gk. *ēthos* character, custom]

eth·i·cal (eth′i·kəl) *adj.* 1 Pertaining or relating to ethics. 2 Treating of morals. 3 In accordance with right principles, as defined by a given system of ethics or professional conduct. **—eth′i·cal′i·ty, eth′i·cal·ness** *n.* **—eth′i·cal·ly** *adv.* — **Syn.** 3 moral, just, righteous, virtuous.

eth·ics (eth′iks) *n.pl.* (*construed as sing. in defs.* 1 & 3) 1 The study and philosophy of human conduct, with emphasis on the determination of right and wrong. 2 The basic principles of right action, esp. with reference to a particular person, profession, etc. 3 A work or treatise on morals.

E·thi·o·pi·a (ē′thē·ō′pē·ə) *n.* A constitutional monarchy in E Africa, 350,000 sq. mi., cap. Addis Ababa. **—E′thi·o′pi·an** *adj., n.* • See map at AFRICA.

eth·nic (eth′nik) *adj.* 1 Of, pertaining to, or belonging to groups of mankind who are of the same race or nationality and who share a common language, culture, etc. 2 Pertaining to peoples neither Jewish nor Christian. —*n.* *Informal* A member of a minority ethnic group, esp., in the U.S., a nonblack minority. Also **eth′ni·cal.** [< Gk. *ethnos* nation] **—eth′ni·cal·ly** *adv.* **—eth·nic·i·ty** (eth·nis′ə·te) *n.*

ethno- *combining form* Race, nation; peoples: *ethnography.* Also **ethn-.**

eth·nog·ra·phy (eth·nog′rə·fē) *n.* 1 The branch of anthropology that is concerned with the classification and description of particular, esp. primitive, human cultures. 2 Loosely, ethnology.

eth·nol·o·gy (eth·nol′ə·jē) *n.* The science of the subdivisions and families of men, their origins, characteristics, distribution, and physical and linguistic classification. — **eth·no·log·i·cal** (eth′nō·loj′i·kəl) or **eth′no·log′ic** *adj.* **—eth′·no·log′i·cal·ly** *adv.*

e·thol·o·gy (i·thol′e·jē) *n.* The science of animal behavior. [< Gk. *ēthos* character + -LOGY] **—e·tho·log·ic** (ē′thə·loj′ik) or **·i·cal** *adj.* **—e·thol′o·gist** *n.*

eth·yl (eth′il) *n. Chem.* The hydrocarbon radical of the paraffin series, present in numerous widely used compounds. [ETH(ER) + -YL] **—eth·yl′ic** *adj.*

ethyl alcohol ALCOHOL (def. 1).

eth·y·lene (eth′ə·lēn) *n. Chem.* A colorless, flammable, unsaturated hydrocarbon contained in coal gas.

e·ti·ol·o·gy (ē′tē·ol′ə·jē) *n.* 1 The science or branch of knowledge which deals with causes or origins. 2 That branch of medicine that treats of the causes of disease. 3 The causes or origin of a particular disease. [< Gk. *aitia* cause + -LOGY] **—e·ti·o·log·i·cal** (ē′tē·ə·loj′i·kəl) *adj.* — **e′ti·o·log′i·cal·ly** *adv.* **—e′ti·ol′o·gist** *n.*

et·i·quette (et′ə·ket, -kət) *n.* The rules and customs for polite social or professional behavior. [< OF *estiquette* routine, ticket]

Et·na (et′nə) *n.* A volcano in NE Sicily; 10,902 feet. **—Et·ne·an** (et·nē′ən) *adj.*

Eton jacket A short black jacket cut off square at the hips and worn open, usu. with a white, overlapping collar, the **Eton collar.** [< *Eton* College, British public school]

E·tru·ri·a (i·trŏŏr′ē·ə) *n.* An ancient country of W. CEN. Italy. **—E·tru′ri·an** *adj., n.*

E·trus·can (i·trus′kən) *adj.* Of or relating to ancient Etruria, its people, language, or culture. —*n.* 1 One of the ancient people of Etruria. 2 The extinct language of the Etruscans.

et. seq. and the following (L *et sequens*); and those that follow (L *et sequentes* or *et sequentia*).

-ette *suffix* 1 Little, small: *kitchenette.* 2 Resembling; like; imitating: *leatherette.* 3 Feminine: *farmerette.* [F]

é·tude (ā′tyōōd) *n. Music* A composition designed to illustrate and develop some phase of technique, but often played as well for its artistic merit. [F, study]

et·y·mol·o·gy (et′ə·mol′ə·jē) *n. pl.* **·gies** 1 The history of a word, prefix, suffix, etc., tracing it back to its earliest known form or root. 2 The branch of linguistics dealing with the origin and development of words, prefixes, etc. [< Gk. *etymon* original meaning + -LOGY]

eu- *prefix* Good; well: *euphony.* [< Gk. *eus* good]

Eu europium.

eu·ca·lyp·tus (yōō′kə·lip′təs) *n. pl.* **·lyp·tus·es** or **·lyp·ti** (-tī) Any of a genus of large, chiefly Australian evergreen trees of the myrtle family, widely used as timber and in the preparation of drugs, esp. the volatile, pungent, essential **oil of eucalyptus.** [< Gk. *eu-* well + *kalyptos* covered]

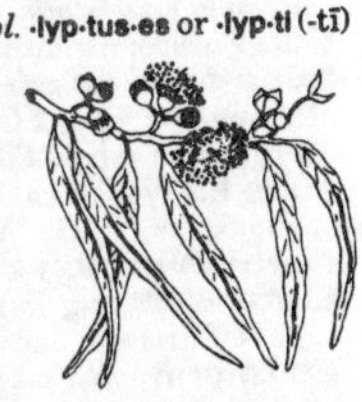

Eucalyptus branch

Eu·char·ist (yōō′kə·rist) *n.* 1 A Christian sacrament in which bread and wine are consecrated, distributed, and consumed in commemoration of the passion and death of Christ. 2 The consecrated bread and wine of this sacrament.[< Gk. *eu-* well + *charizesthai* give thanks] **—eu′cha·ris′tic** or **·ti·cal** *adj.*

eu·chre (yōō′kər) *n.* 1 A card game for two to four players, played with 32 cards. 2 An instance of euchring an opponent or of being euchred. —*v.t.* **eu·chred** (-kərd), **eu·chring** 1 In the game of euchre, to prevent (an opponent) from taking three tricks. 2 *Informal* To outwit or defeat.

Eu·clid·e·an (yōō·klid′ē·ən) *adj.* Of or pertaining to Euclid, his geometry, or a geometry based on similar principles. Also **Eu·clid′i·an.**

eu·gen·ic (yo͞o·jen′ik) *adj.* Relating to or fitted for the development and improvement of the race. Also **eu·gen′·i·cal.** [<Gk. *eugenēs* well-born] **—eu·gen′i·cal·ly** *adv.*

eu·gen·i·cist (yo͞o·jen′ə·sist) *n.* A student or advocate of eugenics. Also **eu·ge·nist** (yo͞o′jə·nist, yo͞o·jen′ist).

eu·gen·ics (yo͞o·jen′iks) *n. pl. (construed as sing.)* The science and art of improving a race or breed by mating individuals with desired characteristics.

eu·lo·gist (yo͞o′lə·jist) *n.* One who eulogizes.

eu·lo·gize (yo͞o′lə·jīz) *v.t.* **·gized, ·giz·ing** **1** To speak or write a eulogy about. **2** To praise highly. *Brit. sp.* **eu′lo·gise. —eu·lo·gis·tic** (yo͞o′lə·jis′tik) or **·ti·cal** *adj.* **—eu′lo·gis′ti·cal·ly** *adv.* **Meu′lo·giz′er** *n.* **—Syn. 2** laud, extol, glorify.

eu·lo·gy (yo͞o′lə·jē) *n. pl.* **·gies** **1** A spoken or written composition in praise of a person's life or character. **2** High praise. Also **eu′lo·gism, eu·lo·gi·um** (yo͞o·lō′jē·əm). [<Gk. *eu-* well + *legein* speak] **—eu·log·ic** (yo͞o·loj′ik) *adj.*

Eu·men·i·des (yo͞o·men′ə·dēz) *Gk. Myth.* FURIES.

eu·nuch (yo͞o′nək) *n.* A castrated man, esp. one formerly employed as a harem attendant or an Oriental palace official. [<Gk. *eunouchos* chamber attendant]

eu·phe·mism (yo͞o′fə·miz′əm) *n.* **1** A mild or agreeable expression substituted for a realistic description of something disagreeable. **2** The use of such an expression. [<Gk. *euphemizein* to euphemize] **—eu′phe·mist** *n.* **—eu′phe·mis′tic** or **·ti·cal** *adj.* **—eu′phe·mis′ti·cal·ly** *adv.*

eu·phe·mize (yo͞o′fə·mīz) *v.t. & v.i.* **·mized, ·miz·ing** To say or write in euphemistic form. **—eu′phe·miz′er** *n.*

eu·phon·ic (yo͞o·fon′ik) *adj.* **1** Agreeable in sound; euphonious. **2** Of or pertaining to euphony.

eu·pho·ni·ous (yo͞o·fō′nē·əs) *adj.* Pleasant in sound, as a word; characterized by euphony. **—eu·pho′ni·ous·ly** *adv.* **—eu·pho′ni·ous·ness** *n.*

eu·pho·ni·um (yo͞o·fō′nē·əm) *n. Music* A type of small tuba, often used in bands. [<Gk. *euphōnos* euphonious]

eu·pho·ny (yo͞o′fə·nē) *n. pl.* **·nies** **1** Agreeableness of sound. **2** Pleasant-sounding combination or arrangement of words. [<Gk. *eu-* good + *phonē* sound]

eu·phor·bi·a (yo͞o·fôr′bē·ə) *n.* Any plant of a large and widely distributed genus of herbs, characterized by their milky juice and various medicinal properties [<*Euphorbos,* a Greek physician of the first century A.D.]

eu·pho·ri·a (yo͞o·fôr′ē·ə, -fō′rē-) *n.* **1** A sense of great well-being and joy. **2** *Psychol.* Exaggerated and usu. unfounded high spirits. [<Gk. *eupherein* be well] **—eu·phor·ic** (yo͞o·fôr′ik, -for′-) *adj.*

eu·phu·ism (yo͞o′fyo͞o·iz′əm) *n.* **1** An artificial, elegant style of speech or writing characterized by the excessive use of alliteration, antithesis, balance, etc. **2** An instance of such a style. **3** Affected elegance in language [<*Euphues,* character created by John Lyly, English writer, 1554?–1606] **—eu′phu·ist** *n.* **—eu′phu·is′tic** or **·ti·cal** *adj.* **—eu′phu·is′ti·cal·ly** *adv.*

Eur. Europe; European.

Eur·a·sian (yo͞o·rā′zhən, -shən) *adj.* **1** Pertaining to both Europe and Asia. **2** Of European and Asian descent. —*n.* A person of mixed European and Asian parentage.

eu·re·ka (yo͞o·rē′kə) *interj.* I have found (it): a triumphal exclamation. [<Gk. *heurēka*]

eu·rhyth·mics (yo͞o·rith′miks) *n.* EURYTHMICS.

Euro- *combining form* **1** Europe. **2** European. **3** Europe and. **4** European and. Also **Eur-.**

Eu·ro·crat (yo͞or′ō·krat) *n.* A member of the administrative staff of the European Economic Community. [<EURO- + -CRAT, a pun on BUREAUCRAT]

Eu·ro·dol·lar (yo͞or′ō·dol′ər) *n.* A U.S. dollar on deposit outside the U.S., esp. in one of the western European countries. [<EURO- + DOLLAR]

Eu·ro·pa (yo͞o·rō′pə) *Gk. Myth.* A Phoenician princess abducted to Crete by Zeus in the guise of a bull.

Eu·rope (yo͞or′əp) *n.* A continent comprising the W part of the Eurasian land mass, between the Atlantic Ocean and Asia, about 3,800,000 square miles. **—Eu·ro·pe·an** (yo͞or′ə·pē′ən) *adj., n.*

European Economic Community The official name of the Common Market, an economic association originally established in 1958 by France, Italy, West Germany, and the Benelux nations.

Eu·ro·pe·an·ize (yo͞or′ə·pē′ən·īz) *v.t.* **·ized, ·iz·ing** To make European in characteristics, views, culture, etc. **—Eu′ro·pe′an·i·za′tion** *n.*

European plan The system of hotel-keeping by which lodging and service are charged for separately from meals.

eu·ro·pi·um (yo͞o·rō′pē·əm) *n.* A soft metallic element (symbol Eu) of the rare earth series. [<L *Europa* Europe]

Eu·ryd·i·ce (yo͞o·rid′ə·sē) *Gk. Myth.* The wife of Orpheus.

eu·ryth·mics (yo͞o·rith′miks) *n. pl. (construed as sing.)* The art of performing rhythmical bodily movement, usu. in interpretation of music. [<Gk. *eurythmia* harmony]

Eu·sta·chi·an tube (yo͞o·stā′shē·ən, -shən) A passage between the pharynx and the inner ear, serving to equalize air pressure on both sides of the eardrum. [<Bartolommeo *Eustachio,* Italian anatomist, died 1574.]

Eu·ter·pe (yo͞o·tûr′pē) *Gk. Myth.* The Muse of lyric song and music. **—Eu·ter′pe·an** *adj.*

eu·tha·na·si·a (yo͞o′thə·nā′zhē·ə, -zhə) *n.* **1** Painless, peaceful death. **2** The deliberate putting to death of a person suffering from a painful and incurable disease; mercy killing. [<Gk. *eu-* good + *thanatos* death]

eu·tha·nize (yo͞o′thə·nīz) *v.t.* **·nized, ·niz·ing** To put to death painlessly.

eu·then·ics (yo͞o·then′iks) *n. pl. (construed as sing.)* The science of improving the human race by the control of environmental factors. [<Gk. *euthenia* prosperity, welfare] **—eu′the·nist** *n.*

eu·troph·ic (yo͞o·trof′ik, -trō′fik) *adj. Ecol.* Of lakes and other bodies of water, enriched in nutrients resulting in luxurious organic growth and depletion of dissolved oxygen. **—eu·troph′i·ca′tion** *n.*

e·vac·u·ant (i·vak′yo͞o·ənt) *adj. Med.* Producing evacuation; cathartic, diuretic, or emetic.

e·vac·u·ate (i·vak′yo͞o·āt) *v.* **·at·ed, ·at·ing** *v.t.* **1** *Mil.* **a** To give up or abandon possession of; withdraw from, as a fortress or city. **b** To withdraw (troops, inhabitants, etc.) from a threatened area or place. **2** To depart from; vacate. **3** To produce a near vacuum in. **4** *Physiol.* To discharge or eject, as from the bowels. —*v.i.* **5** To withdraw, as from a threatened area or place. [<L<*e-* out + *vacuare* make empty] **—e·vac′u·a′tion** *n.* **—e·vac′u·a′tive** *adj.*

e·vac·u·ee (i·vak′yo͞o·ē′) *n.* One who has been removed from or has abandoned his home.

e·vade (i·vād′) *v.* **e·vad·ed, e·vad·ing** *v.t.* **1** To escape or get away from by tricks or cleverness. **2** To avoid or get out of. —*v.i.* **3** To avoid doing something by clever or deceitful means. [<L *e-* out + *vadere* go] **—e·vad′a·ble** *adj.* **—e·vad′·er** *n.* **—Syn. 1** elude. **2** dodge, neglect, foil, shun.

e·val·u·ate (i·val′yo͞o·āt) *v.t.* **·at·ed, ·at·ing** To find or determine the amount, worth, value, etc., of; appraise. [<OF *e-* out + *valu* value] **—e·val′u·a′tion** *n.* **—Syn.** assess, estimate, adjudge.

ev·a·nesce (ev′ə·nes′) *v.t.* **·nesced, ·nesc·ing** To disappear by degrees; vanish. [<L *e-* out + *vanescere* vanish]

Europe

ev·a·nes·cent (ev′ə·nes′ənt) *adj.* Passing away, or liable to pass away, gradually or imperceptibly. **—ev′a·nes′·cence** *n.* **—ev′a·nes′cent·ly** *adv.*

e·van·gel[1] (i·van′jəl) *n.* **1** The Christian gospel. **2** *Usu. cap.* One of the four Gospels of the New Testament. **3** Any good news or glad tidings. [< Gk. *euangelion* good news]

e·van·gel[2] (i·van′jəl) *n.* EVANGELIST.

e·van·gel·i·cal (ē′van·jel′i·kəl, ev′ən-) *adj.* **1** In or agreeing with the four Gospels or the teachings of the New Testament. **2** Of, pertaining to, or believing in the authority of Scripture and salvation through Christ. **3** EVANGELISTIC. **—***n.* A member of an evangelical church, or of an evangelical party within a church. Also **e′van·gel′ic.** **—e′van·gel′i·cal·ism, e′van·gel′i·cism** *n.* **—e′van·gel′i·cal·ly** *adv.*

e·van·gel·ism (i·van′jə·liz′əm) *n.* The zealous preaching or spreading of the gospel.

e·van·gel·ist (i·van′jə·list) *n.* **1** *Usu. cap.* One of the four writers of the New Testament Gospels; Matthew, Mark, Luke, or John. **2** An itinerant or missionary preacher; a revivalist.

e·van·gel·is·tic (i·van′jə·lis′tik) *adj.* **1** Of or pertaining to evangelism or an evangelist. **2** EVANGELICAL. **3** Zealous or missionary in character. **—e·van′gel·is′ti·cal·ly** *adv.*

e·van·gel·ize (i·van′jəl·īz) *v.* **·ized, ·iz·ing** *v.t.* **1** To preach the gospel to. **2** To convert to Christianity. **—***v.i.* **3** To preach the gospel. **—e·van′gel·i·za′tion, e·van′gel·iz′er** *n.*

e·vap·o·rate (i·vap′ə·rāt) *v.* **·rat·ed, ·rat·ing** *v.t.* **1** To convert into vapor. **2** To remove moisture from. **—***v.i.* **3** To become vapor. **4** To yield vapor. **5** To vanish; disappear. [< L *e-* out, away + *vapor* vapor] **—e·vap′o·ra′tive** *adj.* **—e·vap′o·ra′tion, e·vap′o·ra·tor** *n.*

evaporated milk Unsweetened milk with much of its water content removed.

e·va·sion (i·vā′zhən) *n.* **1** The act of evading. **2** A means or an instance of doing this; subterfuge.

e·va·sive (i·vā′siv) *adj.* **1** Not direct, open or straightforward: an *evasive* answer. **2** Tending to elude; elusive. **—e·va′sive·ly** *adv.* **—e·va′sive·ness** *n.*

eve (ēv) *n.* **1** EVENING. **2** The evening before some special day. **3** The time immediately preceding some event. [Var. of EVEN[2]]

Eve (ēv) In the Bible, the first woman, Adam's wife.

e·ven[1] (ē′vən) *adj.* **1** Flat; smooth; level: *even* surfaces. **2** Steady; unchanging; constant: to keep an *even* tempo. **3** The same, as in number or quantity. **4** Being on the same line or level: horses *even* in the stretch. **5** Not easily disturbed; calm; tranquil: an *even* disposition. **6** Owing nothing and being owed nothing. **7** Exact; precise: an *even* pint. **8** Exactly divisible by 2. **9** Fair; equitable. **10** Balanced. **—get even** To get revenge: retaliate. **—***adv.* **1** Indeed; truly: to feel sad, *even* disconsolate. **2** Exactly; precisely: Do *even* as you are told. **3** Still, yet: an *even* better idea. **4** At the same time; while: It happened *even* as you spoke. **5** However unlikely it seems: *Even* I can understand the difficulties involved. **—***v.t. & v.i.* To make or become even. [< OE *efen* level] **—e′ven·ly** *adv.* **—e′ven·ness** *n.* **—Syn. 2** regular, unvarying. **5** easy, serene, stable.

e·ven[2] (ē′vən) *n. Archaic* Evening. [< OE *ǣfen*]

e·ven·fall (ē′vən·fôl′) *n.* Early evening; dusk.

e·ven·hand·ed (ē′vən·han′did) *adj.* Treating all alike; impartial. **—e′ven·hand′ed·ly** *adv.* **—e′ven·hand′ed·ness** *n.*

eve·ning (ēv′ning) *n.* **1** The closing part of the day and beginning of the night. **2** The period, roughly, from after dinner until bedtime; also, this period spent in some specific activity, entertainment, etc. **3** A closing or declining part of any state or period: the *evening* of life. [< OE *ǣfen*]

evening dress Clothing worn on formal occasions in the evening. Also **evening clothes.**

evening primrose A biennial herb with conspicuous yellow flowers that open in the evening.

evening star A bright planet, as Venus, seen in the western sky just after sunset.

e·ven·song (ē′vən·sông′, -song′) *n.* **1** VESPERS. **2** In the Anglican Church, a service held in the evening. [< OE *ǣfensang*]

e·vent (i·vent′) *n.* **1** Anything that happens or comes to pass. **2** The result or outcome of any action. **3** One of the items making up a program of sports. [< L *e-* out + *venire* come] **—Syn. 1** occurrence, happening, episode, incident.

e·vent·ful (i·vent′fəl) *adj.* **1** Attended or characterized by important events. **2** MOMENTOUS. **—e·vent′ful·ly** *adv.* **—e·vent′ful·ness** *n.*

e·ven·tide (ē′vən·tīd′) *n.* Evening time.

e·ven·tu·al (i·ven′cho͞o·əl) *adj.* Taking place after a period of time or as a result of a succession of events; subsequent. [< EVENT] **—e·ven′tu·al·ly** *adv.*

e·ven·tu·al·i·ty (i·ven′cho͞o·al′ə·tē) *n. pl.* **·ties** A possible occurrence; possibility.

e·ven·tu·ate (i·ven′cho͞o·āt) *v.i.* **·at·ed, ·at·ing** To result finally. **—e·ven′tu·a′tion** *n.*

ev·er (ev′ər) *adv.* **1** At any time: Did you *ever* get there? **2** In any way: How can I *ever* repay you? **3** At all times; always: I shall be *ever* grateful. [< OE *ǣfre*]

ev·er·glade (ev′ər·glād) *n.* A tract of low swampy land covered with tall grass. **—the Everglades** A swampy subtropical region of southern Florida.

ev·er·green (ev′ər·grēn′) *adj.* Having leaves throughout the year. **—***n.* **1** An evergreen tree or plant. **2** *pl.* Evergreen twigs and branches, used for decoration.

ev·er·last·ing (ev′ər·las′ting, -läs′-) *adj.* **1** Lasting forever; eternal. **2** Interminable; incessant. **—***n.* **1** ETERNITY. **2** A plant, the flowers of which retain their form and color when dried. **—the Everlasting** God. **—ev′er·last′ing·ly** *adv.* **—ev′er·last′ing·ness** *n.*

ev·er·more (ev′ər·môr′, -mōr′) *adv.* Always.

e·ver·sion (i·vûr′zhən) *n.* **1** The act of everting. **2** The state of being everted.

e·vert (i·vûrt′) *v.t.* To turn inside out; turn outward. [< L *e-* out + *vertere* to turn]

eve·ry (ev′rē, ev′ər·ē) *adj.* **1** All taken one by one. **2** All possible; very great: Show him *every* consideration. **3** Each: *every* third man. [< OE *ǣre* ever + *ǣlc* each]

eve·ry·bod·y (ev′rē·bod′ē, -bud′ē) *pron.* Every person; everyone.

eve·ry·day (ev′rē·dā′, -dā′) *adj.* **1** Suitable for every day. **2** Happening every day. **3** Common; usual; ordinary.

eve·ry·one (ev′rē·wun′, -wən) *pron.* All people in general; everybody.

every one Each individual person or thing out of a specific group or number: *Every one* of my front windows was broken.

eve·ry·thing (ev′rē·thing′) *pron.* **1** All things that exist. **2** All things that relate to a specific subject, circumstance, etc.: I have *everything* I need for the trip. **—***n.* That which is of the highest importance: Money is *everything* to some people.

eve·ry·where (ev′rē·hwâr′) *adv.* At or in every place.

e·vict (i·vikt′) *v.t.* To expel (a tenant) by legal process; dispossess; put out. [< L *e-* out + *vincere* conquer] **—e·vic′·tion, e·vic′tor** *n.*

ev·i·dence (ev′ə·dəns) *n.* **1** That which makes evident or clear; an outward sign or indication. **2** That which serves to prove. **3** *Law* That which is submitted to a court to establish the truth or falsehood of something alleged or presumed. **4** *Law* A witness. **—in evidence** In plain view; visible. **—***v.t.* **·denced, ·denc·ing 1** To make evident; show clearly; display. **2** To support by one's testimony; attest.

ev·i·dent (ev′ə·dənt) *adj.* Plain, manifest, or clear, as to the mind or the senses; obvious. [< L *e-* out + *videre* see] **—ev′i·dent·ly** *adv.*

ev·i·den·tial (ev′ə·den′shəl) *adj.* Being, pertaining to, or furnishing evidence. **—ev′i·den′tial·ly** *adv.*

e·vil (ē′vəl) *adj.* **1** Morally bad; wicked; sinful or depraved. **2** Injurious; unwholesome; harmful. **3** Causing or threatening misfortune; unlucky. **4** Arising from real or reputed immorality: an *evil* name. **—***n.* **1** Wicked conduct or disposition; sinfulness; moral depravity. **2** Something that harms or hurts. [< OE *yfel*] **—e′vil·ly** *adv.* **—e′vil·ness** *n.*

e·vil·do·er (ē′vəl·do͞o′ər) *n.* A wicked person. **—e′vil·do′·ing** *n.*

evil eye In folklore, a look or stare having the power to harm anyone toward whom it is directed. **—e'vil-eyed'** *adj.*

e·vil-mind·ed (ē'vəl·mīn'did) *adj.* Evil in thought or disposition. **—e'vil-mind'ed·ly** *adv.* **—e'vil-mind'ed·ness** *n.*

e·vince (i·vins') *v.t.* **e·vinced, e·vinc·ing** To show plainly or certainly; make evident; display. [< L *evincere* to conquer] **—e·vin'ci·ble** *adj.* **—e·vin'ci·bly** *adv.*

e·vis·cer·ate (i·vis'ə·rāt) *v.t.* **·at·ed, ·at·ing 1** DISEMBOWEL. **2** To remove the essential or vital parts of (anything). [< L *e-* out + *viscera* entrails] **—e·vis'cer·a'tion** *n.*

e·voke (i·vōk') *v.t.* **e·voked, e·vok·ing 1** To call or summon forth; elicit, as an emotion or reply. **2** To summon up (spirits) by or as by spells. [< L *e-* out + *vocare* call] **—ev·o·ca·ble** (ev'ə·kə·bəl, i·vok'ə-) **ev·o·ca·tive** (i·vok'ə·tiv) *adj.* **—ev·o·ca·tion** (ev'ə·kā'shən, ē'vō-) *n.*

ev·o·lu·tion (ev'ə·lōō'shən, ēv'ə-) *n.* **1** The process of unfolding; development or growth. **2** Anything evolved. **3** *Biol.* **a** The theory that all forms of life originated by descent, with gradual or abrupt modifications, from preexisting forms which themselves trace backward in a continuing series to the most rudimentary organisms. **b** The series of changes by which a given type of organism has acquired the physiological and structural characteristics differentiating it from other types. **4** *Math.* The operation of extracting a root. **5** A move or maneuver, as of troops. **6** A movement forming one of a series of complex motions. **7** The emission or setting free, as of gas, energy, etc. [< L *evolvere* to evolve] **—ev'o·lu'tion·al, ev'o·lu'tion·ar·y,** *adj.* **—ev'o·lu'tion·al·ly** *adv.* **—ev'o·lu'tion·ism** *n.* **—ev'o·lu'tion·ist** *n., adj.*

e·volve (i·volv') *v.* **e·volved, e·volv·ing** *v.t.* **1** To work out or develop gradually: to *evolve* a plan. **2** *Biol.* To develop, as by a differentiation of parts or functions, to a more highly organized condition. **3** To give or throw off (vapor, heat, etc.); emit. *—v.i.* **4** To undergo the process of evolution. **5** To open out; develop. [< L *evolvere* < *e-* out + *volvere* roll] **—e·volv'a·ble** *adj.* **—e·volv'ent** *adj., n.* **—e·volve'ment** *n.*

ewe (yōō, *Regional* yō) *n.* A female sheep. [< OE *eowu*]

ew·er (yōō'ər) *n.* A wide-mouthed pitcher, sometimes with a lid. [< OF *evier*]

Ewer

ex[1] (eks) *prep.* **1** In finance, without the right to have or to participate in; excluding: *ex* bonus, *ex* dividend. **2** In commerce, free out of; not subject to charge until taken out of: *ex* elevator, *ex* ship, *ex* store. [L, out]

ex[2] (eks) *n. pl.* **ex·es** The letter X or x.

ex-[1] *prefix* **1** Out; out of: *exit, exhale.* **2** Remove from; free from: *exonerate.* **3** Thoroughly: *exasperate.* **4** Once; former: used with a hyphen: *ex-president.* [< L *ex* from, out of]

ex-[2] *prefix* Out of; from; forth: *exodus.* [< Gk. *ex* out]

Ex, Ex. Exodus.

ex. examined; example; exception.

ex·ac·er·bate (ig·zas'ər·bāt) *v.t.* **·bat·ed, ·bat·ing** To make more intense or severe. [< L *ex-* completely + *acerbus* bitter, harsh] **—ex·ac'er·ba'tion** *n.*

ex·act (ig·zakt') *adj.* **1** Clear and complete; definite; precise: *exact* instructions. **2** Absolutely accurate: *exact* answers. **3** Specified or required: an *exact* amount. **4** Rigorous; demanding; strict: an *exact* teacher. *—v.t.* **1** To compel the yielding or payment of; extort. **2** To demand; insist upon as a right. **3** To require; call for: The task will *exact* great effort. [< L *exigere* determine] **—ex·act'a·ble** *adj.* **—ex·act'er, ex·ac'tor** *n.*

ex·act·ing (ig·zak'ting) *adj.* **1** Strict and demanding: an *exacting* boss. **2** Requiring attention, patience, effort, etc.: an *exacting* task. **—ex·act'ing·ly** *adv.* **—ex·act'ing·ness** *n.*

ex·ac·tion (ig·zak'shən) *n.* **1** The act of exacting; extortion. **2** Something exacted, as a compulsory levy.

ex·act·ly (ig·zakt'lē) *adv.* **1** In an exact manner. **2** Yes indeed; quite so.

ex·act·ness (ig·zakt'nis) *n.* The condition or quality of being accurate and precise. Also **ex·act'i·tude** (-tōōd).

ex·ag·ger·ate (ig·zaj'ə·rāt) *v.* **·at·ed, ·at·ing** *v.t.* **1** To describe or think about as greater than is actually the case. **2** To increase or enlarge beyond what is normal or expected. *—v.i.* **3** To describe or think about something in exaggerated terms. [< L *ex-* out + *agger* mound, heap] **—ex·ag'ger·at'ed·ly, ex·ag'ger·at'ing·ly** *adv.* **—ex·ag'ger·a'tion, ex·ag'ger·a'tor** *n.*

ex·alt (ig·zôlt') *v.t.* **1** To raise high; lift up; elevate. **2** To raise in rank, character, honor, etc. **3** To glorify or praise; pay honor to. **4** To fill with delight, pride, etc. **5** To increase the force or intensity of, as colors. [< L *ex-* out + *altus* high] **—ex·alt'er** *n.*

ex·al·ta·tion (eg'zôl·tā'shən) *n.* **1** The act of exalting. **2** The state of being exalted. **3** An extreme or sometimes exaggerated sense of well-being, importance, or power.

ex·am (ig·zam') *n. Informal* An examination.

ex·am·i·na·tion (ig·zam'ə·nā'shən) *n.* **1** The act or process of examining or the state of being examined. **2** A testing of knowledge, progress, skill, qualifications, etc.; also, the questions used in such testing. **3** *Law* A formal interrogation. **—ex·am'i·na'tion·al** *adj.*

ex·am·ine (ig·zam'in) *v.t.* **·ined, ·in·ing 1** To inspect or scrutinize with care; investigate critically. **2** To test as to knowledge, qualifications, physical fitness, etc. **3** To interrogate formally. [< L *examen* a testing] **—ex·am'in·a·ble** *adj.* **—ex·am'i·nee', ex·am'in·er** *n.*

ex·am·ple (ig·zam'pəl, -zäm'-) *n.* **1** Something that belongs to and typifies a group of things, and that is singled out as a sample of the group. **2** A thing or person suitable to be used as a model. **3** A case serving or designed to serve as a warning. **4** A problem or exercise, as in mathematics, that is worked out or designed to be worked out to illustrate a method or principle. *—v.t.* **·pled, ·pling** To exemplify: now used only in the passive. [< L *exemplum* something taken out]

ex·as·per·ate (ig·zas'pə·rāt) *v.t.* **·at·ed, ·at·ing 1** To irritate or annoy exceedingly; infuriate. **2** To make worse; intensify; inflame. [< L *exasperare* make rough] **—ex·as'per·at'er, ex·as'per·a'tion** *n.* **—ex·as'per·at'ing** *adj.* **—ex·as'per·at'ing·ly** *adv.*

Exc. Excellency.

Ex·cal·i·bur (eks·kal'ə·bər) *n.* In Arthurian legend, the sword of King Arthur.

ex ca·the·dra (eks kə·thē'drə, kath'i-) Officially; with authority: used esp. in certain papal pronouncements. [L, lit. from the chair]

ex·ca·vate (eks'kə·vāt) *v.t.* **·vat·ed, ·vat·ing 1** To make a hole or cavity in. **2** To form or make (a tunnel, etc.) by digging out or scooping. **3** To remove by digging or scooping out, as soil. **4** To uncover by digging, as ruins. [< L *ex-* out + *cavus* hollow] **—ex'ca·va'tion, ex'ca·va'tor** *n.*

ex·ceed (ik·sēd') *v.t.* **1** To surpass, as in quantity, quality, measure, or value. **2** To go beyond the limit or extent of: to *exceed* one's income. *—v.i.* **3** To be superior; surpass others. [< L *ex-* out, beyond + *cedere* go]

ex·ceed·ing (ik·sē'ding) *adj.* Greater than usual; surpassing; extraordinary. **—ex·ceed'ing·ly** *adv.*

ex·cel (ik·sel') *v.t. & v.i.* **·celled, ·cel·ling** To go beyond or above; outdo; surpass (another or others). [< L *excellere* rise]

ex·cel·lence (ek'sə·ləns) *n.* **1** The state or quality of excelling; superiority. **2** That in which a person or thing excels or is superior. Also **ex'cel·len·cy.**

Ex·cel·len·cy (ek'sə·lən·sē) *n. pl.* **·cies** An honorary title of various high officials, as a governor, ambassador, foreign president, etc.: usu. preceded by *His, Her, Your,* etc.

ex·cel·lent (ek'sə·lənt) *adj.* Having good qualities in a high degree; superior in worth, value, etc. [< L *excellere* rise] **—ex'cel·lent·ly** *adv.* **—Syn.** admirable, capital, choice, fine, first-class.

ex·cel·si·or (ik·sel'sē·ər) *n.* A packing material composed of long, fine, wood shavings. [< *Excelsior,* a trade name]

ex·cept (ik·sept') *v.t.* **1** To leave or take out; exclude; omit. *—v.i.* **2** To object; take exception; with *to.* *—prep.* With the exception of; save; but: Tell no one *except* me. *—conj.* **1** *Informal* But for the fact that; only: I'd go *except* I don't have time. **2** *Archaic* Unless. [< L *ex-* out + *capere* take]

ex·cept·ing (ik·sep'ting) *prep.* Except.

ex·cep·tion (ik·sep'shən) n. **1** The act of excepting or the condition of being excepted. **2** A person or thing different from or not conforming to a general rule, principle, class, etc. **3** An objection, complaint, or quibble. **4** *Law* A formal objection to the decision of a court during trial. —**take exception** To take offense, disagree, or object.

ex·cep·tion·a·ble (ik·sep′shən·ə·bəl) *adj.* Open to exception or objection. —**ex·cep′tion·a·bly** *adv.*

ex·cep·tion·al (ik·sep′shən·əl) *adj.* Unusual or uncommon, esp. in a superior way. —**ex·cep′tion·al·ly** *adv.*

ex·cerpt (ek′sûrpt) *n.* An extract from written or printed matter. —*v.t.* (ik·sûrpt′) To take out, as a passage or quotation; extract. [< L *ex-* out + *carpere* pluck, seize]

ex·cess (ik·ses′) *n.* **1** The condition of exceeding what is ordinary, reasonable, or required. **2** An amount greater than is necessary; overabundance. **3** The amount by which one thing is greater than another; surplus. **4** Overindulgence; intemperance. —**to excess** To an unnecessary or extreme degree or extent. —*adj.* (*also* ek′ses) Being above a stipulated amount; extra. [< L *excedere* go beyond]

ex·ces·sive (ik·ses′iv) *adj.* Being in, tending to, marked by excess; immoderate; extreme. —**ex·ces′sive·ly** *adv.* —**ex·ces′sive·ness** *n.*

excess profits Net profits beyond the normal average for a period of years.

exch. exchange; exchequer.

ex·change (iks·chānj′) *n.* **1** The act of giving or receiving one thing as an equivalent for another; bartering. **2** Interchange: an *exchange* of wit, remarks, etc. **3** A substituting of one thing for another. **4** Something given or substituted for another. **5** A place where merchants, brokers, etc., buy, sell, or trade: a stock *exchange.* **6** A central telephone office. **7** A system of paying debts without transfer of actual money but by means of credits, drafts, etc.; also, the fee charged for this. **8** BILL OF EXCHANGE. **9** The value of one currency in terms of another currency. **10** The difference in value between two currencies. **11** *pl.* Checks, drafts, etc., presented to a clearing-house for settlement. —*v.* **·changed, ·chang·ing 1** To give or part with for something regarded as of equal value, etc.: to *exchange* francs for dollars. **2** To give and receive in turn; reciprocate. **3** To replace by or give up for something else: to *exchange* poverty for wealth. —*v.i.* **4** To be given or taken in exchange. **5** To make an exchange. [< L *ex-* out + *cambiare* exchange] —**ex·change′a·bil′i·ty** *n.* —**ex·change′a·ble** *adj.* —**ex·change′a·bly** *adv.*

ex·cheq·uer (iks·chek′ər, eks′chek·ər) *n.* **1** The treasury, as of an organization or state. **2** *Informal* One's personal financial resources. [< OF *eschequier* counting table, chessboard]

Ex·cheq·uer (iks·chek′ər, eks′chek·ər) *n.* The administrative department of the British government having the management of the public revenue.

ex·cise[1] (ek′sīz, ek′sīs) *n.* **1** An indirect tax on commodities manufactured, produced, sold, used, or transported within a country. **2** A license fee for various sports, trades, or occupations. —*v.t.* **·cised, ·cis·ing** To levy an excise upon. [< L *ad-* to + *census* a tax]

ex·cise[2] (ik·sīz′) *v.t.* **·cised, ·cis·ing** To cut out or cut off, as in a surgical operation: to *excise* a cyst. [< L *ex-* out + *caedere* cut] —**ex·ci·sion** (ik·sizh′ən) *n.*

ex·cit·a·ble (ik·sī′tə·bəl) *adj.* **1** Easily excited; high-strung. **2** Susceptible to stimuli. —**ex·cit′a·bil′i·ty, ex·cit′a·ble·ness** *n.* —**ex·cit′a·bly** *adv.*

ex·ci·ta·tion (ek′sī·tā′shən) *n.* The act of exciting or the state of being excited.

ex·cite (ik·sīt′) *v.t.* **·cit·ed, ·cit·ing 1** To arouse (a feeling, interest, etc.) into being or activity; evoke. **2** To arouse feeling in; stimulate the emotions of. **3** To cause action in; stir to activity or motion. **4** To bring about; stir up: to *excite* a riot. **5** *Physics* To give increased energy to. [< L *ex-* out + *ciere* arouse, stir up] —**ex·cit′ed** *adj.* —**ex·cit′ed·ly** *adv.* —**ex·cit′er** *n.* —**Syn. 1, 2, 3** awaken, stir, inspire, provoke, kindle, evoke. **4** foment, incite.

ex·cite·ment (ik·sīt′mənt) *n.* **1** The act of exciting or the state of being excited. **2** That which excites.

ex·cit·ing (ik·sī′ting) *adj.* Causing or full of excitement; stirring; rousing. —**ex·cit′ing·ly** *adv.*

ex·claim (iks·klām′) *v.t.* & *v.i.* To say or cry out abruptly, as in surprise or anger. [< L *ex-* out + *clamare* cry] —**ex·claim′er** *n.*

ex·cla·ma·tion (eks′klə·mā′shən) *n.* **1** The act of exclaiming. **2** An abrupt or emphatic expression, outcry, etc. —**ex·clam·a·to·ry** (iks·klam′ə·tôr′ē, -tō′rē) *adj.*

exclamation mark A mark (!) placed after an interjection or exclamation to indicate its character. Also **exclamation point.**

ex·clude (iks·klōōd′) *v.t.* **·clud·ed, ·clud·ing 1** To keep from entering; shut out; bar. **2** To refuse to notice or consider. **3** To put out; eject. [< L *ex-* out + *claudere* close] —**ex·clud′a·ble** *adj.* —**ex·clud′er, ex·clu′sion** *n.*

ex·clu·sive (iks·klōō′siv) *adj.* **1** Intended for or possessed by a single group or individual; not shared: *exclusive* fishing rights. **2** Found, known, printed, etc., by only one person or source: an *exclusive* news item. **3** Regarded as totally incompatible, different, unrelated, etc.: mutually *exclusive* theories. **4** Restricting membership, admittance, etc.; reluctant to accept outsiders. **5** Expensive to frequent or patronize: an *exclusive* restaurant. **6** Complete; undivided: his *exclusive* attention to music. **7** Not including; not comprising: usu. followed by *of: exclusive* of fees. —*n.* Something exclusive, esp. an exclusive news item or story. —**ex·clu′sive·ly** *adv.* —**ex·clu′sive·ness** *n.*

ex·com·mu·ni·cate (eks′kə·myōō′nə·kāt) *v.t.* **·cat·ed, ·cat·ing 1** To punish by an ecclesiastical sentence of exclusion from the sacraments and communion of the church. **2** To expel in disgrace from any organization. —*adj.* Excommunicated. —*n.* An excommunicated person [< LL *excommunicare* to put out of the community] —**ex′com·mu′ni·ca′tion, ex′com·mu′ni·ca′tor** *n.*

ex·co·ri·ate (ik·skôr′ē·āt, -skō′rē-) *v.t.* **·at·ed, ·at·ing 1** To scratch or abrade the skin of. **2** To denounce scathingly. [< L *ex-* out, off + *corium* skin] —**ex·co′ri·a′tion** *n.*

ex·cre·ment (eks′krə·mənt) *n.* Refuse matter discharged from an animal body; feces. —**ex′cre·men′tal** *adj.*

ex·cres·cence (iks·kres′əns) *n.* **1** An unnatural or disfiguring outgrowth, as a wart. **2** Any unnatural addition or development. **3** A natural outgrowth, as hair. [< L *ex-* out + *crescere* grow] —**ex·cres′cent** *adj.*

ex·cre·ta (iks·krē′tə) *n. pl.* Waste matter, as urine, sweat, etc., eliminated from the bodily system. —**ex·cre′tal** *adj.*

ex·crete (iks·krēt′) *v.t.* **·cret·ed, ·cret·ing** To eliminate, as waste matter, by normal discharge. [< L *excretus*, pp. of *excernere* separate out] —**ex·cre′tion** *n.* —**ex·cre′tive, ex′cre·to′ry** *adj.*

ex·cru·ci·ate (iks·krōō′shē·āt) *v.t.* **·at·ed, ·at·ing** To inflict extreme mental or physical pain upon. [< L *ex-* completely + *cruciare* torture] —**ex·cru′ci·a′tion** *n.*

ex·cru·ci·at·ing (iks·krōō′shē·āt·ing) *adj.* **1** Causing great physical or mental pain. **2** Extreme; intense. —**ex·cru′ci·at′ing·ly** *adv.*

ex·cul·pate (eks′kəl·pāt, ik·skul′-) *v.t.* **·pat·ed, ·pat·ing** To declare free from blame; prove innocent. [< EX-[1] + L *culpare* blame. —**ex′cul·pa′tion** *n.* —**ex·cul′pa·to′ry** *adj.*

ex·cur·sion (ik·skûr′zhən, -shən) *n.* **1** A short journey, usu. for pleasure. **2** A boat or train trip at reduced rates, accommodating passengers in groups. **3** Such passengers collectively. **4** A digression; deviation. **5** *Physics* Half the amplitude of a vibration or oscillation. [< L *excursio* < *excurrere* to run out] —**ex·cur′sion·ist** *n.*

ex·cur·sive (ik·skûr′siv) *adj.* Digressive; rambling; wandering; desultory. —**ex·cur′sive·ly** *adv.* —**ex·cur′sive·ness** *n.*

ex·cuse (ik·skyōōz′) *v.t.* **·cused, ·cus·ing 1** To pardon and overlook (a fault, offense, etc.). **2** To try to free (someone) from blame; seek to remove blame from. **3** To offer a reason or apology for (an error, fault, etc.); try to obtain pardon for or minimize. **4** To serve as a reason for; justify. **5** To release or dismiss, as from attendance. **6** To refrain from exacting or enforcing, as a demand or claim. —*n.* (ik·skyōōs′) **1** A plea or reason given to justify an offense, neglect, failure, etc. **2** Something that excuses, as from attendance. **3** One who or that which is a bad or inferior example: a poor *excuse* for a statesman. [< L *ex-* out, away + *causa* charge, accusation] —**ex·cus′a·ble** *adj.* —**ex·cus′a·bly** *adv.* —**ex·cus′er** *n.*

exec. executive; executor.

ex·e·cra·ble (ek′sə·krə·bəl) *adj.* 1 Abominable; accursed. 2 Appallingly bad. —**ex′e·cra·bly** *adv.*

ex·e·crate (ek′sə·krāt) *v.* **·crat·ed, ·crat·ing** *v.t.* 1 To curse, or call down evil upon. 2 To detest; abhor. —*v.i.* 3 To utter curses. [< L *execrari* to curse] —**ex′e·cra′tion, ex′e·cra′tor** *n.* —**ex′e·cra′tive** *adj.*

ex·ec·u·tant (ig·zek′yə·tənt) *n.* 1 One who does or carries out something. 2 A performer, as of music.

ex·e·cute (ek′sə·kyo͞ot) *v.t.* **·cut·ed, ·cut·ing** 1 To do or carry out fully. 2 To put in force; administer, as a law. 3 To put to death by legal sentence. 4 *Law* To make (a will, deed, etc.) legal or valid. 5 To perform, as a maneuver or a musical work. 6 To produce or create. [< L *ex-* out + *sequi* follow] —**ex′e·cut′a·ble** *adj.* —**ex′e·cut′er** *n.* —**Syn.** 1 perform, fulfill, effect. 2 enforce.

ex·e·cu·tion (ek′sə·kyo͞o′shən) *n.* 1 The act of doing, putting into force, etc. 2 A putting to death, as by legal decree. 3 The manner, style, or skill with which something is done. 4 *Law* A judicial writ, as for the seizure of goods, etc.

ex·e·cu·tion·er (ek′sə·kyo͞o′shən·ər) *n.* One who executes a death sentence.

ex·ec·u·tive (ig·zek′yə·tiv) *adj.* 1 Having the function or skill of executing or performing. 2 Having ability or aptitude for directing or controlling. 3 Of or pertaining to direction or control; administrative, as distinguished from *judicial* and *legislative.* —*n.* 1 An official or body of officials charged with the administration of the laws and affairs of a nation or state. 2 A person or group having administrative control, as of a business or other organization.

Executive Mansion 1 The official residence of the president of the U.S. 2 The residence of the governor of a State.

ex·ec·u·tor (ig·zek′yə·tər) *n.* 1 *Law* A person nominated by the will of another to execute the will. 2 One who executes, in any sense. —**ex·ec·u·trix** (ig·zek′yə·triks) *n. Fem.* (*pl.* **·trix′es** or **ex·ec′u·tri′ces**) (-trī′sēz)

ex·e·ge·sis (ek′sə·jē′sis) *n. pl.* **·ses** (-sēz) Explanation of the language and thought of a literary work; esp. Biblical interpretation. [< Gk. *ēgeisthai* to lead the way] —**ex′e·get′ic** (-jet′ik) *adj.* —**ex′e·get′i·cal·ly** *adv.*

ex·em·plar (ig·zem′plər, -plär) *n.* 1 A model, pattern, or original, to be copied or imitated. 2 A typical example; archetype. [< L *exemplum* example]

ex·em·pla·ry (ig·zem′plər·ē) *adj.* 1 Serving as a model or example worthy of imitation; commendable. 2 Serving as a warning example: *exemplary* damages. 3 Serving to exemplify; illustrative. —**ex·em′pla·ri·ly** *adv.* —**ex·em′pla·ri·ness** *n.*

ex·em·pli·fy (ig·zem′plə·fī) *v.t.* **·fied, ·fy·ing** 1 To show by example; illustrate. 2 *Law* To make an authenticated transcript from, as a public record. [L *exemplum* example + *facere* make] —**ex·em′pli·fi·ca′tion** *n.* —**ex·em′pli·fi·ca′tive** *adj.*

ex·empt (ig·zempt′) *v.t.* To free or excuse from some obligation to which others are subject; grant immunity to. —*adj.* Free, clear, or excused, as from some duty. —*n.* A person who is exempted, as from military service. [< L *ex-* out + *emere* buy, take] —**ex·empt′i·ble** *adj.* —**ex·emp′tion** *n.* —**Syn.** *v.* release, remit, discharge, let off, spare.

ex·er·cise (ek′sər·sīz) *v.* **·cised, ·cis·ing** *v.t.* 1 To subject to drills, systematic movements, etc., so as to train or develop (troops, muscles, the mind, etc.). 2 To make use of; employ. 3 To perform or execute, as duties. 4 To wield; exert, as influence or authority. 5 To make a habit of: used reflexively or in the passive: to be *exercised* in good works. 6 To occupy the mind of; esp. to make anxious. —*v.i.* 7 To take exercise. 8 To undergo training. —*n.* 1 A putting into use or practice. 2 A specific bodily activity or movement for developing strength, agility, etc. 3 Something played or practiced to develop a specific skill or technique: a violin *exercise.* 4 A problem or lesson to be worked out. 5 *pl.* A program or ceremony: graduation *exercises.* [< L *exercere* to practice] —**ex′er·cis′a·ble** *adj.*

ex·er·cised (ek′sər·sīzd) *adj.* Harassed; agitated.

ex·er·cis·er (ek′sər·sī′zər) n. 1 One who exercises. 2 An apparatus for body exercise.

ex·ert (ig·zûrt′) *v.t.* To put forth or put in action, as strength, force, or faculty; bring into strong or vigorous action. —**exert oneself** To put forth effort. [< L *exertus* < *exserere* thrust out] —**ex·er′tive** *adj.*

ex·er·tion (ig·zûr′shən) *n.* 1 The act of exerting some power, faculty, etc. 2 Vigorous action or effort.

ex·e·unt (ek′sē·ənt, -o͝ont) They go out: a stage direction. [L]

ex·fo·li·ate (eks·fō′lē·āt) *v.t.* & *v.i.* **·at·ed, ·at·ing** 1 To remove scales or splinters (from). 2 To peel off in thin flakes, as the bark of a tree. [< L *ex-* off + *folium* a leaf] —**ex·fo′li·a′tion** *n.* —**ex·fo′li·a·tive** *adj.*

ex·hale (eks·hāl′, ig·zāl′) *v.* **·haled, ·hal·ing** *v.i.* 1 To expel air or vapor; breathe out. 2 To pass off or rise as a vapor; evaporate. —*v.t.* 3 To breathe forth or give off. 4 To draw off; cause to evaporate. [< L *ex-* out + *halare* breathe] —**ex·hal′a·ble** *adj.* —**ex·ha·la·tion** (eks′hə·lā′shən, eg′zə-) *n.*

ex·haust (ig·zôst′) *v.t.* 1 To make tired; wear out completely. 2 To drain of resources, strength, etc.; use up. 3 To draw off, as gas, steam, etc., from or as from a container. 4 To empty (a container) or contents; drain. 5 To study, treat of, or develop thoroughly and completely: to *exhaust* a subject. —*v.i.* 6 To pass out as the exhaust: The steam *exhausts* from the pipe. —*n.* 1 **a** Waste gases or vapor discharged from an engine. **b** The system by which these are vented. 2 The discharge of any waste gas, as by a fan. [< L *ex-* out + *haurire* draw] —**ex·haust′er, ex·haust′i·bil′i·ty** *n.* —**ex·haust′i·ble** *adj.*

ex·haust·ed (ig·zôs′tid) *adj.* 1 Used up; consumed; spent. 2 Extremely tired or weak. —**ex·haust′ed·ly** *adv.*

ex·haust·ing (ig·zôs′ting) *adj.* Producing or tending to produce exhaustion; wearying.

ex·haus·tion (ig·zôs′chən) *n.* 1 Extreme fatigue or weakness. 2 The condition of being entirely used up or spent.

ex·haus·tive (ig·zôs′tiv) *adj.* 1 Having the effect or tendency to exhaust. 2 Complete and totally comprehensive: an *exhaustive* study. —**ex·haus′tive·ly** *adv.* —**ex·haus′tive·ness** *n.*

ex·hib·it (ig·zib′it) *v.t.* 1 To present to view; display. 2 To show or reveal. 3 To present for public inspection or entertainment. —*v.i.* 4 To place something on display. —*n.* 1 A public showing or display. 2 Any object or objects exhibited. 3 *Law* A document or object marked for use as evidence. [< L *ex-* out + *habere* hold, have] —**ex·hib′i·tive, ex·hib′i·to′ry** *adj.* —**ex·hib′i·tor, ex·hib′it·er** *n.*

ex·hi·bi·tion (ek′sə·bish′ən) *n.* 1 The act of exhibiting; display. 2 Anything exhibited. 3 A public showing, as of works of art, etc.

ex·hi·bi·tion·ism (ek′sə·bish′ən·iz′əm) *n.* 1 The tendency to display one's personal qualities in a manner that will attract attention. 2 A perversion characterized by a tendency to expose publicly a part of the body, as the genitals, for sexual pleasure. —**ex′hi·bi′tion·ist** *n.*

ex·hil·a·rate (ig·zil′ə·rāt) *v.t.* **·rat·ed, ·rat·ing** To induce a lively or enlivening feeling in; enliven; cheer; stimulate. [< L *ex-* completely + *hilaris* glad] —**ex·hil′a·ra′tion** *n.* —**Syn.** elate, exalt, animate, gladden, invigorate.

ex·hort (ig·zôrt′) *v.t.* To urge by earnest appeal or argument; advise or caution strongly. [< L *ex-* completely + *hortari* urge] —**ex·hor·ta·tion** (eg′zôr·tā′shən, ek′sər-), **ex·hort′er** *n.*

ex·hume (ig·zyo͞om′, iks·hyo͞om′) *v.t.* **·humed, ·hum·ing** 1 To dig out of the earth, as a dead body. 2 To disclose; reveal. [< L *ex-* out + *humus* ground] —**ex·hu·ma·tion** (eks′hyo͞o·mā′shən) *n.*

ex·i·gen·cy (ek′sə·jən·sē, ig·zij′ən-) *n. pl.* **·cies** 1 The state of being urgent or exigent. 2 A condition requiring immediate attention. 3 *Usu. pl.* Urgent needs or demands. Also **ex′i·gence.**

ex·i·gent (ek′sə·jənt) *adj.* 1 Urgent; pressing. 2 Very demanding or exacting. [< L *exigere* to demand]

ex·ig·u·ous (ig·zig′yo͞o·əs, ik·sig′-) *adj.* Scanty; meager. [< L *exiguus* scanty] —**ex·i·gu·i·ty** (ek′sə·gyo͞o′ə·tē), **ex·ig′u·ous·ness** *n.*

ex·ile (eg′zīl, ek′sīl) *n.* 1 Separation, either enforced or by choice, from one's home or native land. 2 One separated from his native country or home; an expatriate. —*v.t.* **ex·iled, ex·il·ing** To expel from and forbid to return to a native land or home; banish. [< L *exsilium*]

ex·ist (ig·zist′) *v.i.* 1 To have actual being or reality; be.

2 To continue to live or be. 3 To be present; occur. [< L *existere*] —**ex·is′tent** *adj.*

ex·is·tence (ig·zis′təns) *n.* 1 The state or fact of being or existing. 2 Possession or continuance of being; life. 3 A manner of being or existing. 4 Anything that exists; a being; entity.

ex·is·ten·tial (eg′zis·ten′shəl) *adj.* 1 Of, or pertaining to, or stating the fact of existence. 2 Of or pertaining to existentialism. —**ex′is·ten′tial·ly** *adv.*

ex·is·ten·tial·ism (eg′zis·ten′shəl·iz′əm) *n.* A philosophical doctrine holding that existence takes precedence over essence, and that man, being totally free in an indifferent and purposeless universe, is responsible only to himself for the actions he takes in the development of his self. —**ex′is·ten′tial·ist** *adj., n.*

ex·it (eg′zit, ek′sit) *n.* 1 A way or passage out; egress. 2 The departure of an actor from the stage. 3 Any departure. —*v.i.* To go out. [< L *exitus* < *exire* go out]

ex li·bris (eks li′bris, lē′-) 1 From the books (of): used as an inscription or label on a book. 2 BOOKPLATE. [L]

exo- *combining form* Out; outside; external: *exogamy.* Also, **ex-**. [< Gk. *exō* outside]

ex·o·bi·ol·o·gy (ek′sō·bī·ol′ə·jē) *n.* The science dealing with the search for and study of forms of life native to parts of the universe other than the earth. —**ex′o·bi′o·log′i·cal** *adj.* —**ex′o·bi·ol′o·gist** *n.*

Exod. Exodus.

ex·o·dus (ek′sə·dəs) *n.* A going forth, or departure. —**the Exodus** The departure of the Israelites from Egypt under the guidance of Moses, described in **Exodus**, the second book of the Old Testament. [< Gk. *ex-* out + *hodos* way]

ex of·fi·ci·o (eks ə·fish′ē·ō) By virtue of or because of office or position. [L]

ex·og·a·my (eks·og′ə·mē) *n.* The custom that dictates marrying outside one's own tribe or clan. —**ex·og′a·mous, ex·o·gam·ic** (ek′sō·gam′ik) *adj.*

ex·og·e·nous (eks·oj′ə·nəs) *adj.* 1 *Bot.* Growing by the addition of concentric rings under the surface and outside previous growth. 2 Originating from without. [< F *exogène* having additional layers] —**ex·og′e·nous·ly** *adv.*

ex·on·er·ate (ig·zon′ə·rāt) *v.t.* **·at·ed, ·at·ing** 1 To free from accusation or blame; acquit. 2 To relieve or free from a responsibility. [< L *ex-* out, away + *onus, oneris* burden] —**ex·on′er·a′tion** *n.* —**ex·on′er·a′tive** *adj.*

ex·oph·thal·mic (ek′sof·thal′mik) *adj.* Pertaining to or accompanied by abnormal protrusion of the eyeballs. [< Gk. *ex-* out + *ophthalmos* eye] —**ex·oph·thal′mia, ex′oph·thal′mos** *n.*

ex·or·bi·tant (ig·zôr′bə·tənt) *adj.* Going beyond usual and proper limits; excessive; extravagant. [< LL *exorbitare* go astray] —**ex·or′bi·tance, ex·or′bi·tan·cy** *n.* —**ex·or′bi·tant·ly** *adv.*

ex·or·cise (ek′sôr·sīz) *v.t.* **·cised, ·cis·ing** 1 To cast out (an evil spirit) by prayers or incantations. 2 To free of an evil spirit. Also **ex′or·cize.** [< Gk. *exorkizein*] —**ex′or·cism′, ex′or·cist** *n.*

ex·or·di·um (ig·zôr′dē·əm, ik·sôr′-) *n. pl.* **·di·ums** or **·di·a** (-dē·ə) The introductory part, as of a discourse; a prelude. [< L *exordiri* begin] —**ex·or′di·al** *adj.*

ex·ot·ic (ig·zot′ik) *adj.* 1 Belonging by nature or origin to another part of the world; foreign. 2 Unusually strange or different; fascinating. —*n.* Something exotic. [< Gk. *exōtikos* foreign < *exō* outside] —**ex·ot′i·cal·ly** *adv.* —**ex·ot′i·cism** *n.*

ex·pand (ik·spand′) *v.t.* 1 To increase the range, scope, volume, size, etc., of. 2 To spread out by unfolding or extending; open. 3 To write or develop in full the details or form of. —*v.i.* 4 To grow larger, wider, etc.; unfold; increase. [< L *ex-* out + *pandere* spread] —**ex·pand′er** *n.*

ex·panse (ik·spans′) *n.* 1 A vast continuous area or stretch. 2 Expansion.

ex·pan·si·ble (ik·span′sə·bəl) *adj.* Capable of being expanded. —**ex·pan′si·bil′i·ty** *n.*

ex·pan·sion (ik·span′shən) *n.* 1 The act of expanding or the state of being expanded. 2 The amount of increase in size, scope, volume, etc. 3 That which is expanded.

ex·pan·sive (ik·span′siv) *adj.* 1 Able or tending to expand. 2 Characterized by expansion; broad; extensive; comprehensive. 3 Amiable and effusive; outgoing. —**ex·pan′sive·ly** *adv.* —**ex·pan′sive·ness** *n.*

ex·pa·ti·ate (ik·spā′shē·āt) *v.i.* **·at·ed, ·at·ing** To speak or write in a lengthy manner; elaborate: with *on* or *upon.* [< L *ex(s)patiari* to spread out] —**ex·pa′ti·a′tion, ex·pa′ti·a′tor** *n.* —**ex·pa′ti·a·to′ry** (-tôr′ē, -tō′rē) *adj.*

ex·pa·tri·ate (eks·pā′trē·āt) *v.t.* **·at·ed, ·at·ing** 1 To exile; banish. 2 To withdraw (oneself) from one's native land. —*n.* (-it, -āt) An expatriated person. —*adj.* Banished; exiled. [< L *ex-* out + *patria* native land] —**ex·pa′tri·a′tion** *n.*

ex·pect (ik·spekt′) *v.t.* 1 To look forward to as certain or probable; anticipate in thought. 2 To look for as right, proper, or necessary; require. 3 *Informal* To presume; suppose. [< L *ex-* out + *spectare* look at] —**ex·pect′a·ble** *adj.*

ex·pec·tan·cy (ik·spek′tən·sē) *n. pl.* **·cies** 1 The act or state of expecting; expectation. 2 An object of expectation. Also **ex·pec′tance.**

ex·pec·tant (ik·spek′tənt) *adj.* 1 Waiting or looking forward in expectation. 2 Awaiting the birth of a child. —*n.* One who is expecting something. —**ex·pec′tant·ly** *adv.*

ex·pec·ta·tion (ek′spek·tā′shən) *n.* 1 The act of expecting something; also, the mental attitude of one who expects something. 2 *Often pl.* A prospect or hope of good to come. 3 Something expected.

ex·pect·ing (ik·spek′ting) *adj.* Pregnant; also, due to give birth.

ex·pec·to·rant (ik·spek′tər·ənt) *adj.* Relating to or promotive of the discharge of mucus from the respiratory tract. —*n.* An expectorant medicine.

ex·pec·to·rate (ik·spek′tə·rāt) *v.t. & v.i.* **·rat·ed, ·rat·ing** 1 To discharge, as mucus, by coughing up and spitting. 2 To spit. [< L *ex-* out + *pectus, -oris* breast] —**ex·pec′to·ra′tion** *n.*

ex·pe·di·en·cy (ik·spē′dē·ən·sē) *n. pl.* **·cies** 1 The state or quality of being expedient. 2 That which is expedient. 3 The doing of what is politic or advantageous, regardless of justice or right. Also **ex·pe′di·ence.**

ex·pe·di·ent (ik·spē′dē·ənt) *adj.* 1 Serving to promote a desired end; suitable; useful; advisable. 2 Pertaining to or based on utility or advantage rather than what is just or right. —*n.* 1 That which furthers or promotes an end. 2 A device; shift. [< L *expedire* make ready] —**ex·pe′di·ent·ly** *adv.*

ex·pe·dite (ek′spə·dīt) *v.t.* **·dit·ed, ·dit·ing** 1 To speed up the process or progress of; facilitate. 2 To do quickly. [< L *expedire* make ready] —**ex′pe·dit′er** *n.*

ex·pe·di·tion (ek′spə·dish′ən) *n.* 1 A journey, march or voyage for a definite purpose. 2 The body of persons engaged in such a journey, together with their equipment. 3 Speed; dispatch. [< L *expedire* make ready, extricate]

ex·pe·di·tion·ar·y (ek′spə·dish′ən·er′ē) *adj.* Of, like, or constituting an expedition.

ex·pe·di·tious (ek′spə·dish′əs) *adj.* Quick; speedy. —**ex′pe·di′tious·ly** *adv.* —**ex′pe·di′tious·ness** *n.*

ex·pel (ik·spel′) *v.t.* **·pelled, ·pel·ling** 1 To drive out by force or authority; force out. 2 To dismiss, as a pupil from a school; eject. [< L *ex-* out + *pellere* drive, thrust] —**ex·pel′la·ble** *adj.* —**Syn.** 1 remove, dispel, evict, oust, banish, exile.

ex·pend (ik·spend′) *v.t.* To pay out or spend; use up. [< L *ex-* out + *pendere* weigh]

ex·pend·a·ble (ik·spen′də·bəl) *adj.* 1 That may be expended. 2 Capable of being consumed, used, or sacrificed, as men and materiel in warfare.

ex·pen·di·ture (ik·spen′də·chər) *n.* 1 The act of expending; outlay. 2 That which is expended; expense.

ex·pense (ik·spens′) *n.* 1 *pl.* **a** Costs or charges of something: the *expenses* of a trip. **b** Money to pay for such costs or charges. 2 Anything requiring the outlay of money: A boat is an *expense.* 3 Any cost, sacrifice, or loss: at the *expense* of his health.

ex·pen·sive (ik·spen′siv) *adj.* Causing or involving much expense; costly. —**ex·pen′sive·ly** *adv.* —**ex·pen′sive·ness** *n.*

ex·pe·ri·ence (ik·spir′ē·əns) *n.* 1 The act of undergoing or being involved in an event, situation, etc. 2 Something lived through or undergone: an amazing *experience.* 3 The sum total of one's knowledge, observations, perceptions, etc.: It is outside my *experience.* 4 The duration of one's involvement with a particular activity, occupation, etc. 5 The skill or knowledge acquired from such involvement. —*v.t.* **·enced, ·enc·ing** To undergo or be involved in personally. [< L *experiri* try out] —**Syn.** *v.* know, understand, feel, realize, have, apprehend.

ex·pe·ri·en·tial (ik·spir'ē·en'shəl) *adj.* Pertaining to or acquired by experience; empirical. —**ex·pe'ri·en'tial·ly** *adv.*

ex·per·i·ment (ik·sper'ə·mənt) *n.* 1 A procedure or test meant to yield or illustrate a principle, effect, or fact. 2 The conducting of such procedures or tests. —*v.i.* (-ment) To make experiments. [< L *experimentum* < *experiri* try out] —**ex·per'i·ment'er** *n.*

ex·per·i·men·tal (ik·sper'ə·men'təl) *adj.* 1 Of, derived from, or known by experiment or experience. 2 Still in development: *experimental* aircraft. —**ex·per'i·men'tal·ism, ex·per'i·men'tal·ist** *n.* —**ex·per'i·men'tal·ly** *adv.*

ex·per·i·men·ta·tion (ik·sper'ə·mən·tā'shən, -men'-) *n.* The act or practice of experimenting.

ex·pert (ek'spûrt) *n.* One who has special skill or knowledge; a specialist. —*adj.* (*also* ik·spûrt') 1 Skillful as the result of practice; dexterous. 2 Of or from an expert. [< L *expertus,* pp. of *experiri* try out] —**ex·pert'ly** *adv.* —**ex·pert'·ness** *n.*

ex·per·tise (ek'spər·tēz') *n.* The skill, knowledge, or experience of an expert. [F]

ex·pi·ate (ek'spē·āt) *v.t.* **·at·ed, ·at·ing** To atone for; make amends for. [< L *ex-* completely + *piare* appease] —**ex'pi·a'tion, ex'pi·a'tor** *n.* —**ex'pi·a·to'ry** *adj.*

ex·pi·ra·tion (ek'spə·rā'shən) *n.* 1 The natural termination of anything, as of a lease. 2 The act of breathing out, as air from the lungs. 3 That which is breathed out. 4 Death. —**ex·pir·a·to·ry** (ik·spī'rə·tôr'ē, -tō'rē) *adj.*

ex·pire (ik·spīr') *v.* **·pired, ·pir·ing** *v.i.* 1 To exhale one's last breath; die. 2 To breathe out. 3 To die out, as embers. 4 To come to an end; terminate. —*v.t.* 5 To breathe out. [< L *ex-* out + *spirare* breathe] —**ex·pir'er** *n.*

ex·plain (ik·splān') *v.t.* 1 To make plain or clear; make understandable. 2 To give a meaning to; interpret. 3 To give reasons for; state the cause or purpose of. —*v.i.* 4 To give an explanation. [< L *ex-* out + *planare* make level] —**ex·plain'a·ble** *adj.*

ex·pla·na·tion (ek'splə·nā'shən) *n.* 1 The act of explaining. 2 Something, as a statement, that explains. 3 Meaning; significance; sense.

ex·plan·a·to·ry (ik·splan'ə·tôr'ē, -tō'rē) *adj.* Serving or tending to explain. Also **ex·plan'a·tive.** —**ex·plan'a·to'ri·ly** *adv.*

ex·ple·tive (eks'plə·tiv) *n.* 1 An exclamation, often profane. 2 A word or syllable employed to fill out a sentence, complete a rhythmical pattern, etc. —*adj.* Added to fill out a sentence, etc.: also **ex'ple·to'ry** (-tôr'ē, -tō'rē). [< L *ex-* completely + *plere* fill]

ex·pli·ca·ble (eks'pli·kə·bəl, iks·plik'ə·bəl) *adj.* Capable of explanation.

ex·pli·cate (eks'plə·kāt) *v.t.* **·cat·ed, ·cat·ing** To clear from obscurity; explain. [< L *ex-* out + *plicare* fold] —**ex'pli·ca'·tion, ex'pli·ca'tor** *n.* —**ex'pli·ca'tive** *adj.*

ex·plic·it (ik·splis'it) *adj.* 1 Plainly stated; clearly expressed. 2 Having no disguised meaning or reservation; definite; open. [< L *explicare* unfold, explicate. See EXPLICATE.] —**ex·plic'it·ly** *adv.* —**ex·plic'it·ness** *n.*

ex·plode (ik·splōd') *v.* **·plod·ed, ·plod·ing** *v.t.* 1 To cause to expand violently or pass suddenly from a solid to a gaseous state. 2 To cause to burst or blow up violently and with noise. 3 To disprove utterly; refute. —*v.i.* 4 To be exploded or blow up. 5 To burst forth noisily or violently: to *explode* with laughter. 6 To become greater very quickly. [< L *explodere,* orig., drive off the stage, hiss < *ex-* out + *plaudere* clap] —**ex·plod'er** *n.*

ex·ploit (eks'ploit, ik·sploit') *n.* A deed or act, esp. one marked by heroism, daring, skill, or brilliancy. —*v.t.* (ik·sploit') 1 To use for one's own advantage; take advantage of. 2 To put to use; make use of. [< OF] —**ex·ploit'a·ble** *adj.* —**ex'ploi·ta'tion, ex·ploi'ter** *n.*

ex·plore (ik·splôr', -splōr') *v.* **·plored, ·plor·ing** *v.t.* 1 To search through or travel in or over, as new lands, for discovery. 2 To look into or examine carefully; scrutinize. —*v.i.* 3 To make explorations. [< L *explorare* investigate < *ex-* out + *plorare* cry out] —**ex'plo·ra'tion, ex·plor'er** *n.* —**ex·plor·a·to·ry** (ik·splôr'ə·tôr'ē), **ex·plor'a·tive** *adj.*

ex·plo·sion (ik·splō'zhən) *n.* 1 The act of exploding; rapid release of energy, usu. causing a loud noise. 2 A sudden and violent outbreak, as of physical or emotional forces. 3 A sudden and large increase.

ex·plo·sive (ik·splō'siv) *adj.* 1 Pertaining to or characterized by explosion. 2 Liable to explode, become violent, or cause turmoil: *explosive* news. —*n.* A material that can explode or cause an explosion. —**ex·plo'sive·ly** *adv.* —**ex·plo'sive·ness** *n.*

ex·po·nent (ik·spō'nənt) *n.* 1 One who explains or expounds. 2 *Math.* A number or symbol placed as a superscript to the right of a quantity to indicate a power, reciprocal, or root. 3 Any person or thing that symbolizes or exemplifies something. [< L *exponere* indicate] —**ex·po·nen·tial** (ek'spə·nen'shəl) *adj.* —**ex'po·nen'tial·ly** *adv.*

ex·port (ik·spôrt', -spōrt', eks'pôrt, -pōrt) *v.t.* To carry or send, as goods or raw materials, to other countries for sale or trade. —*n.* (eks'pôrt, -pōrt) 1 The act of exporting; exportation. 2 That which is exported; esp. merchandise. —*adj.* (eks'pôrt, -pōrt) Of or pertaining to exports or exportation. [< L *ex-* out + *portare* carry] —**ex·port'a·ble** *adj.* —**ex'por·ta'tion, ex·port'er** *n.*

ex·pose (ik·spōz') *v.t.* **·posed, ·pos·ing** 1 To lay open, as to harm, ridicule, etc. 2 To leave open to the action of a force or influence. 3 To present to view; show; display. 4 To cause to be known; make public, as a crime. 5 To lay open or make known the crimes, faults, etc., of (a person). 6 To abandon so as to cause the death of: to *expose* an unwanted child. 7 *Phot.* To admit light to (a sensitized film or plate). [< MF *exposer* < L *exponere*] —**ex·pos'er** *n.*

ex·po·sé (ek'spō·zā') *n.* A disclosure or exposure of something corrupt, evil, etc. [F]

ex·po·si·tion (eks'pə·zish'ən) *n.* 1 A large, comprehensive, public exhibition, as a world's fair. 2 A detailed explanation or commentary. 3 Any detailed presentation of a topic, either written or oral. 4 The part of a play that tells something about the characters, what has happened before, etc. [< L *expositio* < *exponere* to expose] —**ex·pos'·i·tor** *n.* —**ex·pos'i·to'ry** *adj.*

ex post fac·to (eks pōst fak'tō) Arising or done after the fact but having a retroactive effect. [L]

ex·pos·tu·late (ik·spos'chə·lāt) *v.i.* **·lat·ed, ·lat·ing** To reason earnestly with a person, against some action: usu. with *with.* [< L *ex-* out + *postulare* demand] —**ex·pos'tu·la'tion** *n.* —**ex·pos'tu·la'tive, ex·pos'tu·la·to'ry** *adj.*

ex·po·sure (ik·spō'zhər) *n.* 1 The act or process of exposing, or the state of being exposed in any sense. 2 Situation in relation to the sun, elements, or points of the compass: The house had a southern *exposure.* 3 *Phot.* a The act of subjecting a sensitized film or plate to light rays or other radiation. b The time necessary for this. c An amount of film necessary for one picture.

ex·pound (ik·spound') *v.t.* 1 To set forth in detail; state, as a doctrine or theory. 2 To explain the meaning or significance of; interpret. [< L *exponere* to put forth, expose] —**ex·pound'er** *n.*

ex·press (ik·spres') *v.t.* 1 To put (thought or opinion) into spoken or written words. 2 To make apparent; reveal. 3 To represent in symbols, as in art or mathematics. 4 To send by express. 5 To press out; squeeze out, as juice or moisture. 6 To force out by or as by pressure. —**express oneself** To make known one's thoughts, feelings, or creative impulses. —*adj.* 1 Set forth distinctly; explicit; direct. 2 Specially prepared; adapted to a specific purpose. 3 Traveling at high speeds. 4 Designed for fast driving. 5 Making few stops: an *express* elevator. 6 Exact: an *express* likeness. —*adv.* By fast delivery. —*n.* 1 A system of transporting goods rapidly. 2 The goods so sent. 3 A message, money, etc. sent with speed. 4 Any means of rapid transmission. 5 An express train, elevator, etc. [< L *ex-* out + *pressare* to press] —**ex·press'er** *n.* —**ex·press'i·ble** *adj.*

ex·press·age (ik·spres'ij) *n.* 1 The transportation of goods by special system. 2 Amount charged for this.

ex·pres·sion (ik·spresh'ən) *n.* 1 The act of representing or expressing something by using words, gestures, art, music, etc. **2** Any means by which some truth or idea is conveyed: the *expression* of pleasure. **3** The manner of expressing or doing something, esp. an effective or eloquent manner. **4** A phrase or saying. **5** A gesture, tone, facial aspect, etc., that conveys a thought or feeling. **6** A pressing out, as of juice. **7** *Math.* A meaningful group of characters, numbers, etc.

ex·pres·sion·ism (ik·spresh′ən·iz′əm) *n.* An early 20th-century movement in the arts, characterized by the use of distortion, abstraction, exaggeration, and symbolism to depict subjective experience rather than objective reality. **—ex·pres′sion·ist** *n., adj.* **—ex·pres′sion·is′tic** *adj.*

ex·pres·sive (ik·spres′iv) *adj.* **1** Of or characterized by expression. **2** Expressing or indicating: a look *expressive* of hate. **3** Meaningful; significant: an *expressive* glance. **—ex·pres′sive·ly** *adv.* **—ex·pres′sive·ness** *n.*

ex·press·ly (ik·spres′lē) *adv.* With definitely stated intent or application; exactly and unmistakably; in direct terms.

ex·press·way (ik·spres′wā′) *n.* A highway designed for rapid travel.

ex·pro·pri·ate (eks·prō′prē·āt) *v.t.* **·at·ed, ·at·ing 1** To take from the owner, esp. for public use. **2** To deprive of ownership or property. [< LL *ex-* out + *proprium* property] **—ex·pro′pri·a′tion, ex·pro′pri·a′tor** *n.*

ex·pul·sion (ik·spul′shən) *n.* **1** The act of expelling; forcible ejection. **2** The state of being expelled. **—ex·pul′sive** *adj.*

ex·punge (ik·spunj′) *v.t.* **·punged, ·pung·ing** To blot or scratch out, as from a record or list; obliterate. [< L *ex-* out + *pungere* prick] **—ex·pung′er** *n.*

ex·pur·gate (eks′pər·gāt) *v.t.* **·gat·ed, ·gat·ing** To remove from (a book, etc.) whatever is considered objectionable, immoral, etc. [< L *ex-* out + *purgare* cleanse] **—ex′pur·ga′tion, ex′pur·ga′tor** *n.* **—ex·pur·ga·to·ry** (ik·spûr′gə·tôr′ē, -tō′rē) *adj.*

ex·qui·site (eks′kwi·zit, ik·skwiz′it) *adj.* **1** Skillfully and delicately made or designed: an *exquisite* silk fan. **2** Delicately beautiful: an *exquisite* child. **3** Unusually refined and sensitive, as in perception or judgment: *exquisite* taste. **4** Extremely fine; consummate: an *exquisite* interpretation. **5** Intense; extreme: *exquisite* pain or pleasure. *—n.* One overly sensitive or fastidiously elegant in taste, manners, perceptions, etc. [< L *ex-* out + *quarere* seek] **—ex′qui·site·ly** *adv.* **—ex′qui·site·ness** *n.*

ext. extension; external; extinct; extra; extract.

ex·tant (ek′stənt, ik·stant′) *adj.* Still existing and known; not lost or extinct. [< L *ex-* out + *stare* stand]

ex·tem·po·ra·ne·ous (ik·stem′pə·rā′nē·əs) *adj.* **1** Done or made with no preparation; unpremeditated. **2** Somewhat prepared but not memorized, rehearsed, etc., as a speech. **3** Made with what is at hand; improvised. [< L *ex-* out + *tempus, temporis* time] **—ex·tem′po·ra′ne·ous·ly** *adv.* **—ex·tem′po·ra′ne·ous·ness** *n.*

ex·tem·po·rar·y (ik·stem′pə·rer′ē) *adj.* EXTEMPORANEOUS. **—ex·tem′po·rar′i·ly** *adv.* **—ex·tem′po·rar′i·ness** *n.*

ex·tem·po·re (ik·stem′pər·ē) *adj.* Extemporaneous; unstudied; offhand. *—adv.* Without special preparation; extemporaneously. [< L *ex tempore* out of the time]

ex·tem·po·rize (ik·stem′pə·rīz) *v.t. & v.i.* **·rized, ·riz·ing** To do, make, or compose without preparation; improvise. **—ex·tem′po·ri·za′tion, ex·tem′po·riz′er** *n.*

ex·tend (ik·stend′) *v.t.* **1** To open or stretch to full length. **2** To make longer. **3** To cause to last or continue until or for a specified time. **4** To widen or enlarge the range, scope, meaning, etc., of: to *extend* the duties of an office. **5** To hold out or put forth, as the hand. **6** To give or offer to give: to *extend* hospitality. **7** To straighten, as a leg or arm. *—v.i.* **8** To be extended; stretch. **9** To reach, as in a specified direction: This road *extends* west. **—extend oneself** To put forth great effort. [< L *ex-* out + *tendere* stretch] **—ex·tend′i·bil′i·ty** *n.* **—ex·tend′i·ble** *adj.*

ex·ten·si·ble (ik·sten′sə·bəl) *adj.* That may be extended. **—ex·ten′si·bil′i·ty, ex·ten′si·ble·ness** *n.*

ex·ten·sion (ik·sten′shən) *n.* **1** The act of extending or the condition of being extended. **2** Something extended or additional, as an annex to a building, a second telephone in a home, a branch of a school or university, an extended time limit for a debt, etc. **3** The straightening of a flexed limb. *—adj.* Capable of extending or being extended. **—ex·ten′sion·al** *adj.*

ex·ten·sive (ik·sten′siv) *adj.* **1** Great in area. **2** Broad or wide in scope, range, influence, etc. **3** Large in amount, extent, etc.; considerable: *extensive* damage. **—ex·ten′sive·ly** *adv.* **—ex·ten′sive·ness** *n.*

ex·ten·sor (ik·sten′sər, -sôr) *n.* A muscle that contracts to produce extension.

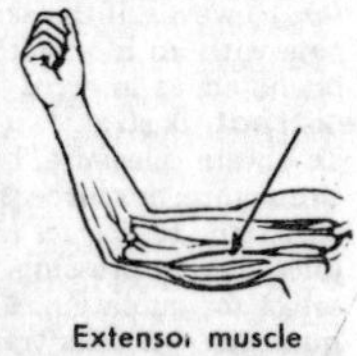

Extensor muscle

ex·tent (ik·stent′) *n.* **1** The dimension, amount, or degree to which anything is extended; reach; size. **2** Range, scope, or limits of something: the *extent* of his power. **3** A large area or space: an *extent* of pastureland.

ex·ten·u·ate (ik·sten′yōō·āt) *v.t.* **·at·ed, ·at·ing 1** To represent as less blameworthy; make excuses for. **2** To cause to seem less serious or blameworthy: *extenuating* circumstances. [< L *extenuare* weaken < *ex-* out + *tenuis* thin] **—ex·ten′u·a′tion, ex·ten′u·a′tor** *n.*

ex·te·ri·or (ik·stir′ē·ər) *adj.* **1** Of, on, or for the outside. **2** Acting or coming from outside. *—n.* **1** Something located outside; an outside part or surface. **2** External features or qualities. [< L compar. of *exterus* outside] **—ex·te′ri·or·ly** *adv.*

ex·ter·mi·nate (ik·stûr′mə·nāt) *v.t.* **·nat·ed, ·nat·ing** To destroy entirely; annihilate. [< L *exterminare* to drive out] **—ex·ter′min·a′tion** *n.* **—ex·ter′mi·na′tive, ex·ter′mi·na·to′ry** (-tôr′ē, -tō′rē) *adj.* **—Syn.** demolish, eradicate, remove, root out, abolish.

ex·ter·mi·na·tor (ik·stûr′mə·nā′tər) *n.* One who or that which exterminates; esp., one whose business is the elimination of rodents, insects, etc.

ex·ter·nal (ik·stûr′nəl) *adj.* **1** Of, pertaining to, or situated on the outside; exterior. **2** On, of, or for the outside of the body: an *external* medicine. **3** Visible from the outside. **4** Having existence separate from one's perceptions. **5** Coming or acting from outside. **6** Merely for outward appearance; superficial: *external* show. *—n.* **1** An exterior or outer part. **2** *Usu. pl.* Outward and often superficial appearances, circumstances, etc. [< L *externus* outer < *exterus* outside] **—ex′ter·nal′i·ty** *n.* **—ex·ter′nal·ly** *adv.*

ex·ter·nal·ize (ik·stûr′nəl·īz) *v.t.* **·ized, ·iz·ing 1** To give shape to; embody. **2** To make outwardly real. **—ex·ter′nal·i·za′tion** *n.*

ex·tinct (ik·stingkt′) *adj.* **1** No longer active or burning: an *extinct* volcano. **2** No longer existing: an *extinct* animal. **3** Void; lapsed: an *extinct* title. [< L *ex(s)tinguere* extinguish]

ex·tinc·tion (ik·stingk′shən) *n.* **1** The act of extinguishing, or the state of being extinguished; extinguishment. **2** A dying out or becoming extinct. **3** The act of destroying, or the state of being destroyed.

ex·tin·guish (ik·sting′gwish) *v.t.* **1** To put out; quench, as a fire. **2** To make extinct; wipe out. **3** To obscure or throw into the shade; eclipse. [< L *ex-* completely + *stinguere* quench] **—ex·tin′guish·a·ble** *adj.* **—ex·tin′guish·er, ex·tin′guish·ment** *n.*

ex·tir·pate (ek′stər·pāt) *v.t.* **·pat·ed, ·pat·ing** To root out or up; eradicate; destroy wholly. [< L *ex-* out + *stirps* stem, root] **—ex′tir·pa′tion** *n.* **—ex′tir·pa′tive** *adj.*

ex·tol (ik·stōl′) *v.t.* **·tolled, ·tol·ling** To praise in the highest terms; magnify. Also **ex·toll′**. [< L *ex-* out, up + *tollere* raise] **—ex·tol′ler, ex·tol′ment** or **ex·toll′ment** *n.*

ex·tort (ik·stôrt′) *v.t.* To obtain from a person by violence, threat, oppression, or abuse of authority; wring; wrest. [< L *ex-* out + *torquere* twist] **—ex·tort′er** *n.* **—ex·tor′tive** *adj.*

ex·tor·tion (ik·stôr′shən) *n.* **1** The act or practice of extorting. **2** The exacting of an excessively high price for something. **3** That which has been extorted. **—ex·tor′tion·ar′y, ex·tor′tion·ate** *adj.* **—ex·tor′tion·er** or **·ist** *n.*

ex·tra (eks′trə) *adj.* **1** Being more, better, larger, etc., than what is required or expected. **2** Additional: an *extra* charge. —*n.* **1** An extra person or thing. **2** Something additional or special, often at an additional cost. **3** A copy or an edition of a newspaper issued for some special purpose, or at a special time. **4** An actor hired for a special scene, as a mob scene. —*adv.* Unusually; exceptionally. [Prob. short for EXTRAORDINARY]

extra- *prefix* Beyond or outside the scope, range, limits, etc., of. [L < *exter* on the outside] • *Adjectives* formed with the prefix *extra-* are usu. written solid, as in *extracurricular.* However, if the second element of the compound begins with an *a* or with a capital letter, the word is hyphenated, as in *extra-atmospheric.*

ex·tract (ik·strakt′) *v.t.* **1** To draw or pull out by force. **2** To obtain (pleasure, benefit, etc.) from some action, circumstance, or source. **3** To obtain by force, extortion, pressure, etc.: to *extract* money. **4** To obtain (a concentrate, juice, etc.) by pressing, chemical action, etc. **5** To copy out; select for quotation. **6** *Math.* To calculate (the root of a number). —*n.* (eks′trakt) Something extracted or drawn out, as: **a** A concentrate or essence of a food, flavoring, etc.: vanilla *extract.* **b** A selection or passage from written or spoken matter. [< L *ex-* out + *trahere* draw, pull] —**ex·tract′a·ble** or **ex·tract′i·ble** *adj.* —**ex·trac′tive** *adj., n.* —**ex·tract′or** *n.*

ex·trac·tion (ik·strak′shən) *n.* **1** The act of extracting, as a tooth. **2** That which is extracted. **3** Lineage; descent.

ex·tra·cur·ric·u·lar (eks′trə·kə·rik′yə·lər) *adj.* Of or pertaining to activities outside a school's regular curriculum, as clubs, school publications, etc.

ex·tra·dite (eks′trə·dīt) *v.t.* **·dit·ed, ·dit·ing** **1** To deliver up (an accused person, prisoner, etc.) as to another state or nation. **2** To obtain the extradition of. —**ex′tra·dit′a·ble** *adj.*

ex·tra·di·tion (eks′trə·dish′ən) *n.* The surrender of an accused person, prisoner, etc., by one government or state to another. [< L *ex-* out + *traditio* a surrender]

ex·tra·ne·ous (ik·strā′nē·əs) *adj.* Not intrinsic, relevant, or essential to matter under consideration. [< L *extraneus* foreign] —**ex·tra′ne·ous·ly** *adv.* —**ex·tra′ne·ous·ness** *n.*

ex·traor·di·nar·y (ik·strôr′də·ner′ē; *esp. for def. 3,* eks′·trə·ôr′də·ner′ē) *adj.* **1** Beyond or out of the common order, course, or method. **2** Exceeding the ordinary or usual; exceptional; remarkable. **3** Employed for a special purpose or occasion; special: an envoy *extraordinary.* —**ex·traor′di·nar′i·ly** *adv.* —**Syn. 1,2** amazing, marvelous, uncommon, unusual, unprecedented, odd, rare.

ex·trap·o·late (ik·strap′ə·lāt) *v.t. & v.i.* **·lat·ed, ·lat·ing** **1** *Math.* To estimate (a function) beyond the range of known values. **2** To infer (a possibility) beyond the strict evidence of a series of facts, events, observations, etc. [< EXTRA- + (INTER)POLATE] —**ex·trap′o·la′tion** *n.*

ex·tra·sen·so·ry (eks′trə·sen′sər·ē) *adj.* Outside of or beyond normal sensory perception.

ex·tra·ter·res·tri·al (ek′trə·tə·res′trē·əl) *adj.* Being or from outside the earth or its atmosphere.

ex·tra·ter·ri·to·ri·al (eks′trə·ter′ə·tôr′ē·əl, -tō′rē-) *adj.* **1** Exempt from territorial jurisdiction; not subject to the laws of one's abode: the *extraterritorial* rights of an ambassador. **2** Beyond the national territory: *extraterritorial* possessions. —**ex′tra·ter′ri·to′ri·al′i·ty** (-al′ə·tē) *n.* —**ex′tra·ter′ri·to′ri·al·ly** *adv.*

ex·trav·a·gance (ik·strav′ə·gəns) *n.* **1** Excessive expenditure of money. **2** Exaggerated or unreasonable conduct or speech. **3** An instance of excessive or immoderate conduct, speech, or spending. Also **ex·trav′a·gan·cy.**

ex·trav·a·gant (ik·strav′ə·gənt) *adj.* **1** Excessively free or lavish in expenditure. **2** Immoderate; fantastic; unrestrained: *extravagant* behavior. **3** Unusually ornate or fanciful: an *extravagant* costume. **4** Exorbitant. [< L *extra-* outside + *vagari* wander] —**ex·trav′a·gant·ly** *adv.* —**ex·trav′a·gant·ness** *n.*

ex·trav·a·gan·za (ik·strav′ə·gan′zə) *n.* **1** A lavish or fantastic composition in literature, music, or the drama. **2** Any lavish and spectacular entertainment or show.

ex·treme (ik·strēm′) *adj.* **1** At or to the farthest limit or point; outermost. **2** In the utmost degree; very great: *extreme* joy. **3** Far from the normal, average, or usual. **4** Immoderate; radical; *extreme* opinions. **5** Drastic: *extreme* measures. **6** Last; final: *extreme* unction. —*n.* **1** The utmost or highest degree, limit, etc.: the *extreme* of cruelty. **2** Either of the two ends or limits of a series, range, etc.: *extremes* of temperature. **3** An act or condition that is extreme or drastic. —**go to extremes** To be excessive or immoderate in action, thought, etc. [< L *extremus,* superl. of *exterus* outside] —**ex·treme′ly** *adv.* —**ex·treme′ness** *n.*

extreme unction In the Roman Catholic Church, the rite of anointing those sick or injured who are in danger of death.

ex·trem·ist (ik·strē′mist) *n.* One who supports or advocates extreme measures or holds extreme views. —*adj.* Of or pertaining to extremists. —**ex·trem′ism** *n.*

ex·trem·i·ty (ik·strem′ə·tē) *n. pl.* **·ties** **1** The utmost or farthest point; termination, end, or edge. **2** The greatest degree. **3** Desperate distress or need. **4** *pl.* Extreme measures. **5** *Usu. pl.* The end part of a limb or appendage.

ex·tri·cate (eks′trə·kāt) *v.t.* **·cat·ed, ·cat·ing** To free from hindrance, difficulties, etc.; disentangle. [< L *ex-* out + *tricae* troubles] —**ex·tri·ca·ble** (eks′tri·kə·bəl) *adj.* —**ex′tri·ca·bly** *adv.* —**ex·tri·ca′tion** *n.*

ex·trin·sic (ek·strin′sik) *adj.* **1** Not belonging to the essential nature or makeup of something; not inherent. **2** Originating from the outside; extraneous. [< L *extrinsecus* outwardly < *exter* outside + *secus* besides] —**ex·trin′si·cal·ly** *adv.* —**ex·trin′si·cal·ness** *n.*

ex·tro·vert (eks′trō·vûrt) *n.* One whose attention and interest are directed chiefly towards other people and the external world rather than towards himself. [< EXTRA- + L *vertere* turn] —**ex′tro·ver′sion** *n.*

ex·trude (ik·strōōd′) *v.* **·trud·ed, ·trud·ing** *v.t.* **1** To force, thrust, or push out; expel, as through a small opening. —*v.i.* **2** To protrude. [< L *ex-* out + *trudere* thrust] —**ex·tru′sion** *n.* —**ex·tru′sive** *adj.*

ex·u·ber·ance (ig·zōō′bər·əns) *n.* **1** The state or quality of being exuberant. **2** An instance of this. Also **ex·u′ber·an·cy.**

ex·u·ber·ant (ig·zōō′bər·ənt) *adj.* **1** Characterized by high spirits, enthusiasm, and vitality. **2** Effusive; overflowing; lavish. **3** Marked by plentifulness; producing copiously. [< L *ex-* completely + *uberare* be fruitful] —**ex·u′ber·ant·ly** *adv.*

ex·ude (ig·zōōd′, ik·sōōd′) *v.* **·ud·ed, ·ud·ing** —*v.i.* **1** To ooze or trickle forth, as sweat. —*v.t.* **2** To ooze or give off gradually. **3** To seem to possess; manifest: to *exude* hope. [< L *ex-* out + *sudare* sweat] —**ex·u·da·tion** (eks′yōō·dā′shən) *n.*

ex·ult (ig·zult′) *v.i.* To rejoice in or as in triumph; take great delight. [< L *ex-* out + *salire* leap] —**ex·ul·ta·tion** (ig′·zul·tā′shən, ek′sul-) *n.* —**ex·ult′ing·ly** *adv.*

ex·ul·tant (ig·zul′tənt) *adj.* **1** Rejoicing triumphantly. **2** Denoting great joy. —**ex·ul′tant·ly** *adv.*

ex·ur·ban·ite (eks·ûr′bən·īt) *n.* One living outside a city in a residential area beyond the suburbs, who commutes to work in the city, and who is sometimes considered above a suburbanite in economic and social status. [< EX(TRA-) + (SUB)URBANITE]

ex·ur·bi·a (eks·ûr′bē·ə) *n.* A residential area outside a city, usu. beyond the suburbs; also, such areas collectively. [< EX- + L *urbs* city]

ex·u·vi·ate (ig·zōō′vē·āt, ik·sōō′-) *v.t. & v.i.* **·at·ed, ·at·ing** To cast off or shed (skin, shell, etc.); molt. [< L *exuviae* parts cast off]

eye (ī) *n.* **1** Any organ of sight in animals. **2** Either of two balls of tissue set into the front of the vertebrate skull and consisting of specialized parts such as cornea, iris, lens, retina, optic nerve, and associated muscles, together with surrounding facial tissues, as eyelids, etc. **3** *Often pl.* The power to see; sight. **4** A glance; look. **5** Attentive observation. **6** A capacity for discerning, judging, appreciating, etc.: an *eye* for color. **7** *Often pl.* Judgment; estimation. **8** Anything that resembles the human eye in shape, function, place, etc.: the *eye* of a needle, the *eye* of

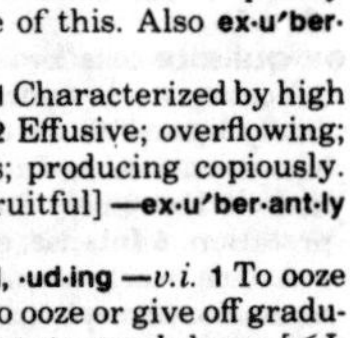

Human eye
a. retina. **b.** lens. **c.** pupil. **d.** cornea. **e.** iris. **f.** optic nerve.

a potato, etc. 9 *Meteorol.* The calm central area of a hurricane or cyclone. **—keep an eye out** or **peeled** To watch for; keep alert. **—lay** (or **set**) **eyes on** To see. **—see eye to eye** To share a common view; agree. **—with an eye to** Looking forward to; planning for; considering. —*v.t.* **eyed, ey·ing** or **eye·ing** 1 To look at carefully; scrutinize. 2 To make a hole in. [< OE *ēage*]

eye·ball (ī′bôl′) *n.* The globe or ball of the eye. —*v.t. Slang* To look at in an intent way; stare at.

eye·brow (ī′brou′) *n.* 1 The bony arch over the eye. 2 Its covering, esp. the hairs.

eye·cup (ī′kup′) *n.* A small cup with rim curved to hold medicated or cleansing liquid against the eyeball.

eyed (īd) *adj.* 1 Having a specified kind or number of eyes: *blue-eyed.* 2 Having eyelike spots.

eye·drop·per *n.* DROPPER (def. 2)

eye·ful (ī′fo͝ol′) *n.* 1 An amount of something in the eye. 2 A full or complete look. 3 *Slang* A person or thing of striking or unusual appearance.

eye·glass (ī′glas′, ī′gläs′) *n.* 1 Any lens used to assist vision, as a monocle, loupe, etc. 2 *pl.* A pair of corrective lenses mounted in a supporting frame. 3 An eyecup.

eye·hole (ī′hōl′) *n.* 1 A round opening through which to pass a pin, hook, rope, or the like. 2 A peephole. 3 The eye's socket.

eye·lash (ī′lash′) *n.* One of the stiff curved hairs growing from the edge of the eyelids.

eye·less (ī′lis) *adj.* Lacking eyes; sightless.

eye·let (ī′lit) *n.* 1 A small hole or opening. 2 A hole made in canvas, leather, etc., and lined with metal. 3 A metal ring for such a hole. 4 In embroidery, a small hole with an edging of decorative stitches. —*v.t.* To make eyelets in.

eye·lid (ī′lid′) *n.* One of the folds of skin that sweep over and cover the eye.

eye-o·pen·er (ī′ō′pən·ər) *n.* 1 Anything startling or unusual. 2 *Informal* A drink of liquor, esp. one taken early in the morning.

eye·piece (ī′pēs′) *n.* The lens or system of lenses nearest the eye in an optical instrument.

eye shadow A cosmetic preparation, tinted blue, green, black, etc., applied to the eyelids to enhance the eyes.

eye·shot (ī′shot′) *n.* Range of vision.

eye·sight (ī′sīt′) *n.* 1 The power or sense of sight. 2 Extent of vision; view.

eye·sore (ī′sôr′, ī′sōr′) *n.* Anything that offends the sight.

eye·strain (ī′strān′) *n.* Fatigue of the eyes due to overuse or faulty focusing.

eye·tooth (ī′to͞oth′) *n. pl.* **eye·teeth** One of the upper canine teeth.

eye·wash (ī′wosh′, ī′wôsh′) *n.* 1 A medicinal wash for the eyes. 2 *Slang* Nonsense; bunk.

eye·wit·ness (ī′wit′nis) *n.* One who has seen a thing or an occurrence with his own eyes and hence can give testimony about it.

ey·ry, ey·rie (âr′ē, ir′ē) *n.* AERIE.

F

F, f (ef) *n. pl.* **F's, f's, Fs, fs** (efs) *n.* 1 The sixth letter of the English alphabet. 2 Any spoken sound representing the letter *F* or *f.* 3 Something shaped like an F. 4 *Music* The fourth tone in the diatonic scale of C major. 5 In education, a grade meaning failure. —*adj.* Shaped like an F.

F Fahrenheit; farad; fluorine.

F. Fahrenheit; farad; February; Fellow; France; French; Friday.

f. farad; fathom; feminine; fluid; folio; following; *Music* forte; franc.

fa (fä) *n. Music* In solmization, the fourth tone of a diatonic scale. [< Ital.]

Fa·bi·an (fā′bē·ən) *adj.* Designating a policy of delay and caution. —*n.* A member of the Fabian Society. [< *Fabius,* Roman general who defeated Hannibal] **—Fa′bi·an·ism** *n.* **—Fa′bi·an·ist** *n., adj.*

Fabian Society An English association, formed in 1884, with the aim of achieving socialism by easy stages.

fa·ble (fā′bəl) *n.* 1 A brief story embodying a moral, often with animals as the characters. 2 A myth or legend. 3 A falsehood; lie. —*v.t. & v.i.* **fa·bled, fa·bling** To invent or tell (fables, lies, etc.). [< L *fabula* < *fari* say, speak]

fab·ric (fab′rik) *n.* 1 Any woven, felted, or knitted cloth. 2 Something that has been fabricated, constructed, or put together. 3 The manner of construction; workmanship. [< L *fabrica* a workshop]

fab·ri·cate (fab′rə·kāt) *v.t.* **·cat·ed, ·cat·ing** 1 To make, assemble, or manufacture. 2 To invent, as lies or reasons; concoct. [< L *fabricare* to construct] **—fab′ri·ca′tion, fab′ri·ca′tor** *n.*

fab·u·list (fab′yə·list) *n.* 1 A composer of fables. 2 One who falsifies or fabricates.

fab·u·lous (fab′yə·ləs) *adj.* 1 Fictitious; mythical. 2 Unbelievable; incredible. [< L *fabula* FABLE] **—fab′u·lous·ly** *adv.* **—fab′u·lous·ness** *n.*

fa·cade (fə·säd′, fa-) *n.* 1 *Archit.* The front or chief face of a building. • See ROMANESQUE. 2 A false or deceptive look or manner. [< L *facies* a face]

face (fās) *n.* 1 The front portion of the head. 2 The front or most important surface: the *face* of a clock; the *face* of a playing card. 3 A side or surface of a solid. 4 The outward appearance, effect, or impression: to put on a bold *face.* 5 *Informal* Effrontery; audacity. 6 A grimace: to make a *face.* 7 *Printing* **a** The impression surface of type or of a printing plate. **b** The size or style of the type. 8 The value printed on a bond, paper money, etc. **—face to face** 1 In one another's presence. 2 Confronting: with *with.* **—in the face of** 1 In the presence of; confronting. 2 In opposition to; in defiance of **—lose face** To lose standing or reputation. **—save face** To protect one's dignity in the opinion of others. —*v.* **faced, fac·ing** *v.t.* 1 To bear or turn the face toward; front upon: The house *faces* the street. 2 To cause to turn in a given direction, as soldiers. 3 To meet face to face; confront: to *face* great odds. 4 To realize or be aware of: to *face* facts. 5 To cover with a layer or surface of another material. 6 To make smooth the surface of; dress: to *face* stone. 7 To turn face upward, as a playing card. —*v.i.* 8 To be turned or placed with the face in a given direction: The house *faces* west. 9 To turn in a given direction: *Face* right. **—face down** To disconcert by a bold stare or manner. **—face the music** *Slang* To accept the consequences. **—face up to** 1 To meet with courage; confront. 2 To realize; become aware of. [< L *facies*] **—face′a·ble** *adj.*

face card A playing card bearing the picture of a king, queen, or jack.

face-lift·ing (fās′lif′ting) *n.* Cosmetic surgery that tightens sagging tissues and removes facial wrinkles.

fac·et (fas′it) *n.* 1 Any of the flat surfaces on a gem or similar object. 2 One side or aspect of a person's mind or character. —*v.t.* **fac·et·ed** or **·et·ted, fac·et·ing** or **·et·ting** To cut or work facets upon. [< F *facette,* lit., small face]

fa·ce·tious (fə·sē′shəs) *adj.* Indulging in or marked by wit or humor; jocular. [< L *facetia* wit + -OUS] **—fa·ce′tious·ly** *adv.* **—fa·ce′tious·ness** *n.* **—Syn.** clever, droll, funny, pungent, waggish.

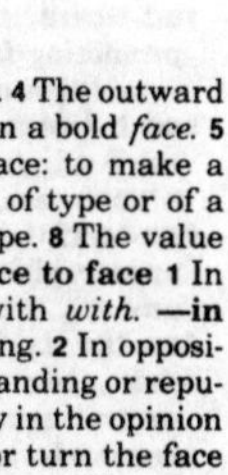

Facets

face value 1 The value printed on paper money, coins, etc. 2 The apparent or seeming value; at *face value.*

fa·cial (fā′shəl) *adj.* Of, near, or affecting the face. —*n.* A massage or other treatment for the face. **—fa′cial·ly** *adv.*

fac·ile (fas′il) *adj.* 1 Easy to do or master. 2 Easily moved or persuaded; pliant. 3 Ready or quick in performance; dexterous. [< L *facilis* easy to do < *facere* do] **—fac′ile·ly** *adv.* **—fac′ile·ness** *n.* • *Facile* means *easy* but implies that little effort is expended and that the result is not worth much. A *facile* style of violin playing is superficial and lacking in depth. An *easy* style is relaxed but has both depth and precision.

fa·cil·i·tate (fə·sil′ə·tāt) *v.t.* **·tat·ed, ·tat·ing** To make easier or more convenient.

fa·cil·i·ty (fə·sil′ə·tē) *n. pl.* **·ties** 1 Ease or readiness in doing; dexterity. 2 Readiness of compliance; pliancy. 3 *Often pl.* Any means, aid, or convenience; dining *facilities.* 4 A place or office equipped to fulfill a special function: a government *facility.* [< L *facilitas* ability < *facere* do]

fac·ing (fā′sing) *n.* 1 The lining on the edge of a garment, as on the lapel of a coat or a hem. 2 A protective or decorative covering or layer. 3 A material used in facing.

fac·sim·i·le (fak·sim′ə·lē) *n.* 1 An exact copy or reproduction. 2 *Telecom.* A method of transmitting graphic information, as an electrical signal. —*adj.* Of or like a facsimile. [< L *fac simile* make like]

fact (fakt) *n.* 1 Anything that is done or happens. 2 Anything actually existent. 3 Any statement strictly true; truth; reality. [< L *factum* < *facere* do]

fac·tion (fak′shən) *n.* 1 A number of persons combined for a common purpose, esp. a dissenting group within a larger group; clique. 2 Violent opposition, as to a government; dissension. [< L *factio* < *facere* do.] **—fac′tion·al** *adj.* **—fac′tion·al·ism** *n.*

fac·tious (fak′shəs) *adj.* Given to, characterized by, or promoting faction; turbulent; partisan. **—fac′tious·ly** *adv.* **—fac′tious·ness** *n.*

fac·ti·tious (fak·tish′əs) *adj.* Artificial; affected; unnatural. [< L *factitus* < *facere* do] **—fac·ti′tious·ly** *adv.* **—fac·ti′tious·ness** *n.*

fac·toid (fak′toid′) *n.* Someone or something contrived to appear plausible or factual. [< FACT + -OID] **—fac′toid′al** *adj.*

fac·tor (fak′tər) *n.* 1 *Math.* One of two or more quantities that when multiplied make a given product. 2 One of several elements or causes that produce a result. 3 An agent who transacts business for another, usu. on commission. 4 *Biol.* A gene. —*v.t. Math.* To express as a product of factors. [< L, maker < *facere* make]

fac·to·ry (fak′tər·ē) *n. pl.* **·ries** A building or buildings used for manufacturing. [< L *factor* < *facere* make]

fac·to·tum (fak·tō′təm) *n.* An employee hired to do all kinds of work. [< L *facere* do + *totum* everything]

fac·tu·al (fak′chōō·əl) *adj.* Pertaining to, containing, or consisting of facts; literal and exact. **—fac′tu·al·ly** *adv.*

fac·ul·ty (fak′əl·tē) *n. pl.* **·ties** 1 Any natural endowment or acquired power: the *faculty* of seeing, feeling, reasoning. 2 Any special skill or unusual ability; knack. 3 The members of any one of the learned professions, collectively. 4 The body of instructors in a school, university, or college. 5 A department of learning or instruction: the history *faculty.* [< L *facultas*]

fad (fad) *n.* A passing fancy or fashion. [?] **—fad′dish, fad′·dy** *adj.* **—fad′dist** *n.*

fade (fād) *v.* **fad·ed, fad·ing** *v.i.* 1 To lose brightness or clearness; become indistinct. 2 To lose freshness, vigor, youth, etc. —*v.t.* 3 To cause to fade. **—fade in** In motion pictures, etc., to come into view gradually. **—fade out** In motion pictures, etc., to disappear gradually. [< OF *fade* pale, insipid] **—Syn.** 1 dim, pale. 2 age, decline, wane, wither.

fae·ces (fē′sēz) *n. pl.* FECES.

fa·er·ie (fā′ə·rē, fâr′ē) *n.* 1 Fairyland. 2 *Archaic* A fairy. —*adj. Archaic* Of or pertaining to fairies.

fag (fag) *v.* **fagged, fag·ging** *v.i.* 1 To weary oneself by working. 2 To work as a fag. —*v.t.* 3 To tire out by hard work. —*n.* 1 In an English public school, a boy who does menial tasks for an older boy. 2 A piece of drudgery. 3 *Slang* A cigarette. [?]

fag end 1 The frayed end, as of a rope. 2 A remnant or last part. 3 *Informal* The worse part of a bargain or similar arrangement. 4 The butt of a cigar or cigarette. [< ME *fagge* flap + END]

fag·ot (fag′ət) *n.* 1 A bundle of sticks or branches, as used for fuel. 2 Pieces of wrought iron or steel to be worked into bars. —*v.t.* 1 To make a fagot of. 2 To ornament by fagoting. [< OF] Also **fag′got.**

fag·ot·ing (fag′ət·ing) *n.* 1 Embroidery in which a number of threads of a material are drawn out and the cross-threads tied together in the middle. 2 Criss-cross hemstitching. Also **fag′got·ing.**

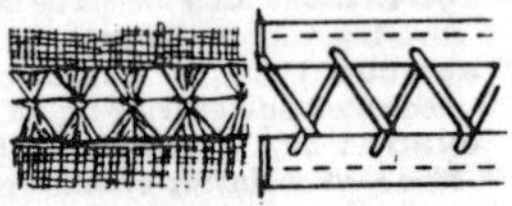
Fagoting *defs. 1 & 2*

Fahr·en·heit (far′ən·hīt) *adj.* Of, for, or designating a temperature scale in which the freezing point of water is 32° and the boiling point 212° at standard atmospheric pressure. [< G. D. *Fahrenheit,* 1686–1736, German physicist]

fail (fāl) *v.i.* 1 To be unsuccessful. 2 To be deficient or wanting, as in ability, faithfulness, etc. 3 To give out, break, or stop working. 4 To fade away; disappear. The light *failed* rapidly. 5 To weaken gradually, as in illness or death. 6 To go bankrupt. 7 To receive a failing grade. —*v.t.* 8 To prove to be inadequate or of no help to. 9 To leave undone or unfulfilled; neglect: He *failed* to carry out orders. 10 In education: a To receive a failing grade in. b To assign a failing grade to (a pupil). —*n.* Failure: now only in the phrase **without fail.** [< L *fallere* to deceive]

fail·ing (fā′ling) *n.* A minor fault; foible. —*adj.* 1 Characterized by failure. 2 Diminishing; weakening. **—fail′ing·ly** *adv.*

faille (fāl, fīl) *n.* An untwilled silk dress fabric having a light grain or cord. [F]

fail-safe (fāl′sāf′) *adj.* 1 Of or indicating a system that makes automatic adjustments for safety in case of failure. 2 *Mil.* Describing a system designed to prevent erroneous or unauthorized attacks.

fail·ure (fāl′yər) *n.* 1 The act of failing: *failure of sight.* 2 One who or that which fails. 3 A proving unsuccessful in business, etc. 4 Neglect or non-performance of a duty.

fain (fān) *adj. Archaic* 1 Reluctantly willing. 2 Glad; rejoiced. 3 Eager; desirous. —*adv.* Gladly: with *would.* [< *OE fægen*]

faint (fānt) *v.i.* To lose consciousness temporarily; swoon. —*adj.* 1 Lacking in purpose or courage; timid. 2 Ready to faint; weak. 3 Weak and feeble, as in effort. 4 Indistinct; dim. —*n.* A swoon: also **faint′ing.** [< OF *faindre* to feign] **—faint′ly** *adv.* **—faint′ness** *n.*

faint-heart·ed (fānt′här′tid) *adj.* Timid; cowardly. **—faint′-heart′ed·ly** *adv.* **—faint′-heart′ed·ness** *n.*

fair[1] (fâr) *adj.* 1 Free from clouds; sunny; clear. 2 Open; distinct. 3 Free from spot or blemish. 4 Just; upright; honest. 5 Having light color or hue: *fair* hair. 6 Pleasing to the eye; beautiful. 7 Moderately satisfactory or excellent; passably good or large: a *fair* crop. 8 Easily legible. 9 In games and sports, according to rule: a *fair* tackle. 10 In a favorable direction: *fair* wind. 11 Properly open to attack: He is *fair* game. —*adv.* 1 Justly; honestly: deal *fair* with me. 2 In clear view; squarely; distinctly. **—for fair** For sure. [< OE *fæger*] **—fair′ish** *adj.* **—fair′ness** *n.*

fair[2] (fâr) *n.* 1 An exhibit and sale of things, often for charity. 2 An exhibit of agricultural products, manufactures, or other articles of value or interest: a county *fair,* an industrial *fair.* 3 A regular gathering of buyers and sellers. [< L *feria* a holiday]

fair-and-square (fâr′ən·skwâr′) *adj.* Thoroughly fair-dealing and honest. —*adv.* In a straightforward way; honestly.

fair·ground (fâr′ground′) *n.* The ground or enclosure in which a fair is held.

fair-haired (fâr′hârd′) *adj.* 1 Flaxen-haired. 2 *Informal* Favorite.

fair·ly (fâr′lē) *adv.* 1 In a just manner; equitably. 2 Moderately; tolerably: a *fairly* tall building. 3 Positively; completely: The crowd *fairly* roared. 4 Clearly; distinctly.

fair-mind·ed (fâr′mīn′did) *adj.* Free from bias or bigotry; open to reason. **—fair′mind′ed·ly** *adv.* **—fair′mind′ed·ness** *n.*

fair shake *Slang* A fair chance or treatment.

fair-spo·ken (fâr′spō′kən) *adj.* Having grace of speech; pleasant; polite.

fair-trade (fâr′trād′) *v.t.* **-trad·ed, -trad·ing** To charge a price no less than the minimum price set by the manufacturer. —*adj.* Of or pertaining to such a price.

fair·way (fâr′wā′) *n.* **1** The proper course through a channel or harbor. **2** That part of a golf course on which the grass is short.

fair-weath·er (fâr′weth′ər) *adj.* **1** Suitable for fair weather. **2** Useful or dependable only in favorable circumstances: *fair-weather* friends.

fair·y (fâr′ē) *n. pl.* **fair·ies 1** An imaginary being of small and graceful human form. **2** *Slang* A male homosexual. —*adj.* **1** Of or pertaining to fairies. **2** Like a fairy; dainty; graceful. [< OF *faerie* enchantment]

fair·y·land (fâr′ē·land′) *n.* The fancied abode of the fairies.

fairy tale 1 A tale about fairies; an imaginative story. **2** An incredible statement.

fait ac·com·pli (fā′tə·kôṅ·plē′, *Fr.* fe·tȧ-) *French* A thing done beyond recall or opposition.

faith (fāth) *n.* **1** Belief without evidence. **2** Confidence; trust. **3** Belief in God, the Bible, etc. **4** A specific religion. **5** Anything given adherence or credence: a man's political *faith.* **6** Allegiance; faithfulness. **—bad faith** Deceit; dishonesty. **—in faith** Indeed; truly. **—in good faith** Honestly.

faith·ful (fāth′fəl) *adj.* **1** True, trustworthy, or loyal: a *faithful* servant; *faithful* to one's agreement. **2** True; accurate; exact. **3** Worthy of belief or confidence. **4** Full of faith. **—the faithful 1** Those who truly believe in a religion. **2** The devoted members of a group or organization. **—faith′ful·ly** *adv.* **—faith′ful·ness** *n.*

faith·less (fāth′lis) *adj.* **1** Not faithful; disloyal. **2** Deceptive and unreliable. **3** Lacking faith. **—faith′less·ly** *adv.* **—faith′less·ness** *n.* **—Syn. 1** deceitful, false, perfidious, treacherous.

fake (fāk) *n. Informal* Anything or any person not genuine; a fraud. —*adj.* Spurious. —*v.* **faked, fak·ing** *v.t.* **1** To attempt to pass off as genuine. **2** To feign. —*v.i.* **3** To practice faking. [?] **—fak′er, fak′er·y** *n.*

fa·kir (fə·kir′, fā′kər) *n.* **1** A Muslim ascetic or religious mendicant. **2** Loosely, a Hindu Yogi. [< Ar. *faqīr* poor]

Fa·lange (fā′lanj, fə·lanj′) *n.* The official fascist party of Spain since 1939. [Sp., a phalanx] **—Fa·lan′gist** *n.*

fal·cate (fal′kāt) *adj.* Sickle- or scythe-shaped. [< L *falx* sickle]

fal·con (fal′kən, fô′-, fôl′-) *n.* **1** Any of various fast-flying birds of prey, having a large head and long tail. **2** Any of various hawks used in sport, esp. the peregrine falcon, with long, pointed wings. [< LL *falco*]

Falcon *def. 2*

fal·con·ry (fal′kən·rē, fô′-, fôl′-) *n.* The training or using of falcons for sport. **—fal′con·er** *n.*

fal·de·ral (fäl′də·räl, fal′də·ral) *n.* **1** Any trifling ornament. **2** Nonsense. **3** A meaningless refrain in old songs.

fall (fôl) *v.* **fell, fall·en, fall·ing** *v.i.* **1** To drop by force of gravity from a higher to a lower place or position. **2** To drop from an erect position: He *fell* to his knees. **3** To collapse: The bridge *fell.* **4** To become less in measure, number, etc. **5** To descend or become less in rank, estimation, importance, etc. **6** To be wounded or slain, as in battle. **7** To be overthrown, as a government. **8** To be taken or captured: The fort *fell.* **9** To yield to temptation; sin. **10** To hit; land: The bombs *fell* short. **11** To slope downward. **12** To hang down; droop. **13** To begin and continue: Night *fell.* **14** To pass into a state or condition: to *fall* asleep. **15** To experience or show dejection: His face *fell.* **16** To come or happen by chance: Suspicion *fell* on him. **17** To happen; occur: Hallowe'en *falls* on Tuesday. **18** To be directed: His glance *fell* on me. **19** To happen or come at a specific place: The accent *falls* on the last syllable. **20** To be classified or divided: with *into.* **—fall away 1** To become lean or emaciated. **2** To die; decline. **—fall away from** To renounce allegiance to. **—fall back** To recede; retreat. **—fall back on** (or **upon**) **1** *Mil.* To retreat to. **2** To resort to; have recourse to. **—fall flat** To fail to produce the intended effect or result. **—fall for** *Informal* **1** To be deceived by. **2** To fall in love with. **—fall in with 1** To meet and accompany. **2** To agree with; conform to. **—fall off 1** To drop. **2** To become less. **—fall on** (or **upon**) **1** To attack; assail. **2** To find; discover. **—fall out 1** To quarrel. **2** To happen; result. **—fall short 1** To be inadequate. **2** To fail to reach something, as a target, goal, or standard. **—fall through** To come to nothing; fail. —*adj. Often cap.* **1** Of, for, or pertaining to autumn. **2** *Slang* Easily duped: a *fall* guy. —*n.* **1** The act, process, or result of falling. **2** *Usu. pl.* A waterfall; cascade. **3** That which falls or is caused to fall; also, the amount of descent. **4** *Often cap.* Autumn. **5** In wrestling, the throwing of an opponent, so that his back hits the floor. **—the Fall** The disobedience of Adam and Eve. [< OE *feallan*]

fal·la·cious (fə·lā′shəs) *adj.* Of, pertaining to, or involving a fallacy. **—fal·la′cious·ly** *adv.* **—fal·la′cious·ness** *n.* **—Syn.** deceptive, erroneous, illusory, misleading.

fal·la·cy (fal′ə·sē) *n. pl.* **·cies 1** Something false or deceptive, as an idea or opinion. **2** The quality of being false or misleading. **3** Any reasoning, argument, etc., that contains an error of logic. [< L *fallere* deceive]

fall·en (fô′lən) *adj.* **1** Having come down by falling. **2** Overthrown; disgraced; ruined. **3** Dead.

fall guy *Slang* A dupe; gullible person.

fal·li·ble (fal′ə·bəl) *adj.* **1** Liable to error or mistake. **2** Liable to be erroneous or false. [< L *fallere* deceive] **—fal′li·bly** *adv.* **—fal′li·bil′i·ty, fal′li·ble·ness** *n.*

falling star METEOR.

Fal·lo·pi·an tube (fə·lō′pē·ən) One of a pair of slender ducts that carry the ovum from the ovary to the uterus. [< G. *Fallopio,* 16th c. Ital. anatomist] • See OVARY.

fall·out (fôl′out′) *n.* **1** The descent of minute particles of radioactive material resulting from a nuclear explosion. **2** The particles themselves. **3** Any incidental result; unplanned or unpredictable consequences. Also **fall′-out′.**

fal·low[1] (fal′ō) *adj.* Left unseeded after being plowed. —*n.* **1** Land left unseeded after plowing. **2** The act of plowing land and leaving unseeded. —*v.t. & v.i.* To make, keep, or become fallow. [< OE *fealga* fallow land] **—fal′low·ness** *n.*

fal·low[2] (fal′ō) *adj.* Pale yellow or pale red. [< OE *fealu* tawny]

fallow deer A fallow-colored, European deer about three feet high and spotted white in the summer.

Fallow deer

false (fôls) *adj.* **1** Contrary to truth or fact. **2** Not real or genuine; artificial. **3** Added only for decoration, deception, etc.: a *false* door. **4** Lying; dishonest. **5** Faithless; treacherous. **6** Out of tune. **7** Not correctly named: *false* foxglove. [< L *falsus,* pp. of *fallere* deceive] **—false′ly —false′ness** *n.*

false·hood (fôls′ho͝od) *n.* **1** Lack of accord to fact or truth; untruthfulness. **2** An intentional untruth; a lie. **3** The act of lying. **4** An untrue belief.

false ribs The lower five pairs of ribs that in human beings do not unite directly with the sternum.

false step 1 A stumble. **2** An error or blunder.

fal·set·to (fôl·set′ō) *n. pl.* **·tos** The higher, less colorful register of a voice. —*adj.* Of, for, or singing in falsetto. —*adv.* In falsetto. [Ital., dim. of *falso* false]

fal·si·fy (fôl′sə·fī) *v.* **·fied, ·fy·ing** *v.t.* **1** To misrepresent; tell lies about. **2** To prove to be false; disprove. **3** To tamper fraudulently with, as a document. —*v.i.* 4 To tell falsehoods; lie. —**fal′si·fi·ca′tion, fal′si·fi′er** *n.*

fal·si·ty (fôl′sə·tē) *n. pl.* **·ties** 1 The quality of being false. 2 A false statement, thing, or appearance. 3 Deceitfulness; dishonesty.

fal·ter (fôl′tər) *v.i.* 1 To be hesitant or uncertain; waver. 2 To move unsteadily; stumble. 3 To speak haltingly; stammer. —*v.t.* 4 To utter haltingly. —*n.* A faltering. [ME *falteren*] —**fal′ter·er** *n.* —**fal′ter·ing·ly** *adv.*

fame (fām) *n.* 1 Public reputation, esp. when favorable. 2 Great renown. [< L *fama* report, reputation]

famed (fāmd) *adj.* Well-known; renowned; celebrated.

fa·mil·ial (fə·mil′yəl, -mil′ē·əl) *adj.* Of, pertaining to, or associated with the family.

fa·mil·iar (fə·mil′yər) *adj.* 1 Well acquainted; thoroughly versed: followed by *with.* 2 Intimate; close, as in friendship. 3 Informal: *familiar* verse. 4 Exercising undue intimacy; forward; bold. 5 Well known; common; frequent; customary. —*n.* 1 An intimate friend. 2 A spirit supposed to attend a witch or sorcerer. [< L *familia* family] —**fa·mil′iar·ly** *adv.*

fa·mil·i·ar·i·ty (fə·mil′ē·ar′ə·tē, -mil′yar′-) *n. pl.* **·ties** 1 The state or condition of being familiar. 2 Intimate knowledge, as of a subject. 3 Conduct implying familiar intimacy. 4 *Often pl.* Offensively familiar conduct.

fa·mil·iar·ize (fə·mil′yə·rīz) *v.t.* **·ized, ·iz·ing** 1 To make (oneself or someone) accustomed or familiar. 2 To cause to be well known or familiar. —**fa·mil′iar·i·za′tion** *n.*

fam·i·ly (fam′ə·lē, fam′lē) *n. pl.* **·lies** 1 A group of persons, consisting of parents and their children. 2 The children as distinguished from the parents. 3 A group of persons forming a household. 4 A succession of persons connected by blood, name, etc. 5 Distinguished or ancient lineage. 6 *Biol.* A taxonomic category higher than a genus. 7 Any class of like or related things, as a group of languages. —*adj.* Of, belonging to, or suitable for a family. [< L *familia* < *famulus* servant]

Family Allowance In Canada, a monthly allowance paid by the government to mothers for each child under the age of 16.

family name SURNAME.

family planning Control by means of contraceptive measures of the timing and number of births in a family.

family tree 1 A diagram of a family showing its ancestors and various branches of descendants. 2 The ancestors themselves.

fam·ine (fam′in) *n.* 1 A widespread scarcity of food. 2 A great scarcity of anything. 3 Starvation. [< L *fames* hunger]

fam·ish (fam′ish) *v.t. & v.i.* 1 To starve or cause to starve. 2 To have or cause to have great hunger.

fa·mous (fā′məs) *adj.* 1 Having fame or celebrity; renowned. 2 *Informal* Admirable, excellent. —**fa′mous·ly** *adv.* —**fa′mous·ness** *n.*

fan[1] (fan) *n.* 1 A wedge-shaped or circular device held in the hand and used for agitating the air, as for cooling or ventilation. 2 Any of various machines for producing currents of air. 3 Something shaped like a fan. —*v.* **fanned, fan·ning** *v.t.* 1 To move or stir (air) with or as with a fan. 2 To direct air upon, with or as with a fan. 3 To move or stir to action; excite. 4 To spread like a fan. 5 In baseball, to cause (a batter) to strike out. —*v.i.* 6 To spread out like a fan. 7 In baseball, to strike out. [< L *vannus* winnowing fan] —**fan′ner** *n.*

fan[2] (fan) *n.* An enthusiastic devotee or admirer, as of a sport, entertainment, performer, etc. [< FANATIC]

fa·nat·ic (fə·nat′ik) *adj.* Inordinately and unreasonably enthusiastic: also **fa·nat′i·cal.** —*n.* One who is fanatic about something. [< L *fanum* a temple] —**fa·nat′i·cal·ly** *adv.* —**fa·nat·i·cism** (fə·nat′ə·siz′əm) *n.* —**Syn.** *n.* enthusiast, monomaniac, zealot. *adj.* extreme, irrational, zealous.

fan·ci·er (fan′sē·ər) *n.* One having a taste for or knowledge about something: a bird *fancier.*

fan·ci·ful (fan′si·fəl) *adj.* 1 Proceeding from or produced by fancy; not real. 2 Imaginative. 3 Odd; curious. —**fan′ci·ful·ly** *adv.* —**fan′ci·ful·ness** *n.*

fan·cy (fan′sē) *n. pl.* **·cies** 1 Imagination, esp., if whimsical or odd. 2 Any imaginary notion, representation, or image. 3 A notion or whim. 4 A liking or fondness, resulting from caprice. 5 A pet pursuit; hobby; fad. 6 Taste exhibited in artistic invention or design. —*adj.* **·ci·er, ·ci·est** 1 Ornamental; decorative; elaborate: *fancy* embroidery. 2 Evolved from the fancy; imaginary. 3 Capricious; whimsical. 4 In commerce, of higher grade than the average: *fancy* fruits. 5 Extravagant; exorbitant: *fancy* prices. 6 Selectively bred to a type, as an animal. 7 Performed with grace and skill: the *fancy* bowing of a violinist. —*v.t.* **·cied, ·cy·ing** 1 To imagine; picture. 2 To take a fancy to; like. 3 To believe without proof or conviction; suppose. [Short for FANTASY]

fan·cy·work (fan′sē·wûrk′) *n.* Embroidery, tatting, crocheting, lacework, etc.

fan·dan·go (fan·dang′gō) *n. pl.* **·gos** 1 A Spanish dance in triple time. 2 The music for this dance. [Sp.]

fan·fare (fan′fâr′) *n.* 1 A flourish, as of trumpets. 2 A noisy demonstration. [F]

fang (fang) *n.* 1 A long pointed tooth or tusk by which an animal seizes or tears its prey. 2 One of the long, curved, hollow or grooved teeth with which a serpent injects its poison into its victim. 3 Any of various pointed objects, organs, or devices. [< OE] —**fanged** (fangd) *adj.*

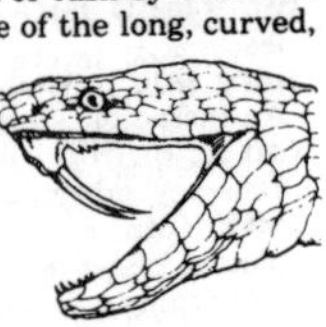

Fangs *def. 2*

fan·light (fan′līt′) *n.* A semicircular window, usu. over a door, with bars radiating from the middle of its base.

fan mail Complimentary letters to public performers, as actors, musicians, etc.

fan·tail (fan′tāl′) *n.* 1 A variety of domestic pigeon having fanlike tail feathers. 2 Any end or tail shaped like a fan. —**fan·tailed** (fan′tāld′) *adj.*

fan-tan (fan′tan′) *n.* 1 A Chinese gambling game. 2 A game of cards. [< Chinese *fan t'an* repeated divisions]

fan·ta·si·a (fan·tā′zē·ə, -zhə, fan′tə·zē′ə) *n. Music* A composition in a very free form. [Ital., lit., a fancy]

fan·ta·size (fan′tə·sīz) *v.* **·sized, ·siz·ing** *v.i.* 1 To imagine or daydream about fantastic events. —*v.t.* 2 To create in fantasy, as in daydreaming. —**fan′ta·sist** *n.*

fan·tasm (fan′taz·əm) *n.* PHANTASM.

fan·tas·ma·go·ri·a (fan·taz′mə·gôr′ē·ə, -gō′rē·ə) *n.* PHANTASMAGORIA.

fan·tas·tic (fan·tas′tik) *adj.* 1 Of an odd appearance; grotesque. 2 Capricious; whimsical: a *fantastic* imagination. 3 Unreal; fanciful; illusory. 4 Unbelievably good; incredible. —*n.* One who is fantastic in conduct or appearance. Also **fan·tas′ti·cal.** [< Gk. *phantazein* to present to the mind] —**fan·tas′ti·cal·ly** *adv.* —**fan·tas′ti·cal′i·ty** (-kal′ə·tē), **fan·tas′ti·cal·ness** *n.*

fan·ta·sy (fan′tə·sē, -zē) *n. pl.* **·sies** 1 Imagination; fancy. 2 A fantastic notion or mental image. 3 A sequence of mental images serving to fulfill a need. 4 *Music* FANTASIA. 5 An imaginative creative work, as a poem. [< Gk. *phantasia* appearance < *phainein* to show]

far (fär) *adj.* **far·ther** or **fur·ther, far·thest** or **fur·thest** 1 Very distant in space or time. 2 Extending widely or at great length. 3 Being the more distant of the two: the *far* end. —*adv.* 1 At a distant point or place. 2 To or from a great distance in space or time. 3 To a great degree; much: *far* wiser. —**by far** In a great degree; by much. —**far and away** By a great deal. —**far and wide** In every place; everywhere: also **far and near.** —**far out** FAR-OUT. [< OE *feor*] —**far′ness** *n.*

far·ad (far′əd, -ad) *n. Electr.* A unit equal to the measure of a capacitor that stores one coulomb per volt of impressed potential difference. [< Michael *Faraday,* 1791–1867, English scientist]

far·a·way (fär′ə·wā′) *adj.* 1 Distant: a *faraway* town. 2 Absent-minded; abstracted: a *faraway* look.

farce (färs) *n.* 1 A short comedy with exaggerated effects and incidents. 2 A ridiculous proceeding; an absurd failure. —*v.t.* **farced, farc·ing** To fill out with witticisms, jibes, etc., as a play. [< L *farcire* to stuff] —**far·cial** (fär′shəl) *adj.*

far·ci·cal (fär′si·kəl) *adj.* Of, pertaining to, or of the nature of a farce; absurd. —**far′ci·cal·ly** *adv.* —**far′ci·cal·ness, far′ci·cal′i·ty** *n.* —**Syn.** comical, laughable, ludicrous, ridiculous.

fare (fâr) *v.i.* **fared, far·ing** 1 To be in a specified state; get on. 2 To turn out; happen. 3 To eat; be supplied with food. —*n.* 1 Money or its equivalent paid for transportation of a passenger. 2 A passenger carried for hire. 3 Food and drink. [< OE *faran* go, travel]

Far East The countries of E Asia, as China, Japan, Korea, etc. —**Far Eastern**

fare·well (fâr′wel′) *n.* 1 A parting salutation; a good-by. 2 The act of parting. —*interj.* (fâr′wel′) May you fare well. —*adj.* Parting; closing. [Earlier *fare well*]

far-fetched (fär′fecht′) *adj.* Neither natural nor obvious; improbable.

far-flung (fär′flung′) *adj.* Having great range; extending over great distances.

fa·ri·na (fə·rē′nə) *n.* A meal or flour made from cereals, nuts, potatoes, etc. and used as a breakfast food. [< L *far* spelt]

far·i·na·ceous (far′ə·nā′shəs) *adj.* 1 Containing or yielding starch. 2 Like meal; mealy.

farm (färm) *n.* 1 A tract of land forming a single property and devoted to the cultivation of crops, the raising of livestock, the production of dairy products, etc. 2 A tract of water used for the cultivation of marine life: an oyster *farm.* 3 In baseball, a minor-league club used for training recruits. —*v.t.* 1 To cultivate (land). 2 To let out the services of (a person) for hire. 3 To arrange for (work) to be performed by persons not in the main organization; subcontract: with *out.* 4 In baseball, to place (a player) with a minor-league team for training: with *out.* —*v.i.* 5 To practice farming; be a farmer. [< L *firmare* fix, settle < *firmus* firm]

farm·er (färm·ər) *n.* A person whose occupation is farming land, raising livestock, producing dairy products, etc.; esp., the owner, operator, or manager of a farm.

farm·hand (färm′hand′) *n.* One who works for wages on a farm. Also **farm laborer.**

farm·house (färm′hous′) *n.* The main home on a farm, occupied by the farmer's family.

farm·ing (fär′ming) *n.* 1 The act of one who farms. 2 The management of or labor on a farm. —*adj.* Engaged in or used for agriculture: a *farming* region.

farm·stead (färm′sted) *n.* A farm and the buildings on it.

farm·yard (fârm′yârd′) *n.* A space surrounded or enclosed by farm buildings.

far·o (fâr′ō) *n.* A game of cards in which the players bet as to the order in which certain cards will appear. [?< *Pharaoh*]

far-off (fâr′ôf′, -of′) *adj.* Situated at a great distance; remote.

far-out (fär′out′) *adj.* **far·ther-out, far·thest-out** *Informal* 1 Far removed from the ordinary; unconventional; avant-garde. 2 Highly theoretical; far from common experience; abstruse. 3 Inspired; transported; wildly enthusiastic. 4 Far removed or very distant in space.

far-out·er (fär′out′ər) *n.* An unconventional person.

far·ra·go (fə·rā′gō, -rä′-) *n. pl.* **·goes** A confused mixture; medley: a *farrago* of nonsense. [L, salad, mixture]

far-reach·ing (fä′rē′ching) *adj.* 1 Producing effects that extend far: a *far-reaching* decision. 2 Reaching far either in time or in space.

far·row (far′ō) *n.* A litter of pigs. —*v.t. & v.i.* To give birth to (young): said of swine. [< OE *fearh* young pig]

far·see·ing (fär′sē′ing) *adj.* 1 Seeing afar. 2 Having foresight.

far·sight·ed (fär′sī′tid) *adj.* 1 Able to see things at a distance more clearly than things near at hand. 2 Farseeing. —**far′sight′ed·ly** *adv.* —**far′sight′ed·ness** *n.*

far·ther (fär′t͟hər) Comparative of FAR. —*adj.* More distant in space; more advanced. —*adv.* 1 To or at a more distant point in space. 2 More fully or completely.

far·ther·most (fär′t͟hər·mōst′) *adj.* Farthest.

far·thest (fär′t͟hist) Superlative of FAR. —*adj. & adv.* 1 Most distant or advanced in space. 2 To the greatest degree or extent.

far·thing (fär′t͟hing) *n.* 1 Formerly, one fourth of an English penny. 2 A small trifle. [< OE *feortha* a fourth]

far·thin·gale (fär′t͟hing·gāl) *n.* A woman's hoop skirt of the 16th and 17th centuries. [< Sp. *verdugo* a rod, hoop]

Farthingale

fas·ces (fas′ēz) *n. pl.* In ancient Rome, a bundle of rods enclosing an ax, borne as a symbol of power. [L]

fas·ci·a (fash′ē·ə) *n. pl.* **·ci·ae** (-i·ē) 1 *Anat.* Connective tissue forming sheets or layers. 2 Something that binds together; a band. [L, a band] —**fas′ci·al** *adj.*

fas·ci·cle (fas′i·kəl) *n.* 1 A bundle or cluster, as of fibers in the body. 2 A number of sheets of printed work bound together. [< L *fascia* a bundle]

fas·cic·u·late (fə·sik′yə·lit) *adj.* Composed of or growing in bundles. Also **fas′ci·cled, fas·cic′u·lar, fas·cic′u·lat′ed.**

fas·ci·nate (fas′ə·nāt) *v.* **·nat·ed, ·nat·ing** *v.t.* 1 To attract irresistibly, as by beauty or other qualities; captivate. 2 To hold spellbound, as by terror. —*v.i.* 3 To be fascinating. [< L *fascinare* to charm] —**fas′ci·nat′ing·ly** *adv.* —**fas′ci·na′tor** *n.*

fas·ci·na·tion (fas′ə·nā′shən) *n.* 1 The act of fascinating. 2 The state of being fascinated. 3 Enchantment; charm.

fas·cism (fash′iz·əm) *n.* Any authoritarian system of government characterized by state economic control, militaristic nationalism, propaganda, and the crushing of opposition. [< L *fascis* a bundle, group] —**fas·cis′tic** *adj.* —**fas·cis′ti·cal·ly** *adv.* —**fas′cist** *n.*

Fas·cism (fash′iz·əm) *n.* The system of one-party government developed by the Fascisti in Italy. —**Fas′cist** *n.*

Fa·scis·ti (fə·shis′tē, *Ital.* fä·shē′stē) *n. pl. of* **Fa·scis′ta** The members of a totalitarian society formed in Italy under Benito Mussolini and in control of the government, 1922–43.

fash·ion (fash′ən) *n.* 1 The prevailing style or mode, esp. in dress. 2 A manner of doing a thing; method; way. 3 The make or shape of a thing. 4 Common practice or custom; usage. 5 Something fashionable. —*v.t.* 1 To give shape or form to. 2 To conform; accommodate; fit. [< L *facere* to make] —**fash′ion·er** *n.*

fash·ion·a·ble (fash′ən·ə·bəl) *adj.* 1 Conforming to fashion; stylish. 2 Of, pertaining to, or like persons of fashion. —**fash′ion·a·bly** *adv.* —**fash′ion·a·ble·ness** *n.*

fash′ion·mon·ger (fash′ən·mung′gər, -mong′-) *n.* One who follows or initiates fashions.

fashion plate One whose attire is perfect, according to the current fashion.

fast[1] (fast, fäst) *adj.* 1 Firm in place; not easily moved. 2 Firmly secured or bound. 3 Constant; steadfast. 4 Not subject to fading: said of colors. 5 Resistant: *acid-fast.* 6 Sound or deep, as sleep. 7 Acting or moving quickly; swift. 8 Performed quickly: *fast* work. 9 Suitable for quick movement: a *fast* track. 10 Requiring rapidity of action or motion: a *fast* schedule. 11 Indicating a time in advance of the true time: The clock is *fast.* 12 Given to dissipation or moral laxity: *fast* living. 13 *Phot.* Usable for short exposure, as a quick-moving shutter or a sensitive film. —*adv.* 1 Firmly; fixedly; securely. 2 Soundly: *fast* asleep. 3 Quickly; rapidly; swiftly. 4 Dissipatedly; recklessly: to live *fast.* 5 *Archaic* Near: *fast* by. [< OE *fæst*]

fast[2] (fast, fäst) *v.i.* To go without food, wholly or in part, as in observance of a religious duty. —*n.* 1 Abstinence from food, partial or total. 2 A period prescribed for fasting. [< OE *fæstan*]

fast·back (fast′bak′, fäst′-) *n.* 1 An automobile's continuous, downward-sloping roof from windshield to rear bumper. 2 An automobile having such a design.

fast day A day set apart for religious fasting.

fast·en (fas′ən, fäs′-) *v.t.* 1 To attach or secure; connect. 2 To make fast; secure: to *fasten* a door. 3 To direct, as attention or the eyes, steadily. 4 To cause to be attributed: to *fasten* blame. —*v.i.* 5 To take fast hold; cling: usually with *on.* **6** To become firm or attached. [< OE *fæst* fixed] **—fast′en·er** *n.*

fast·en·ing (fas′ən·ing, fäs′-) *n.* **1** The act of making fast. **2** That which fastens, as a bolt, hook, clasp, etc.

fas·tid·i·ous (fas·tid′ē·əs) *adj.* **1** Hard to please. **2** Overly delicate or sensitive; squeamish. [< L *fastidium* disgust] **—fas·tid′i·ous·ly** *adv.* **—fas·tid′i·ous·ness** *n.*

fast·ness (fast′nis, fäst′-) *n.* **1** A fortress; stronghold. **2** The state or quality of being fast.

fat (fat) *adj.* **fat·ter, fat·test 1** Having much or superfluous flesh; corpulent; obese. **2** Containing much oil, grease, etc. **3** Broad; thick: a *fat* book. **4** Stupid; dull. **5** Prosperous; thriving; flourishing. **6** Rich in products or in profits; rewarding: a *fat* office. **7** Well-filled: a *fat* larder. **—***n.* **1** A greasy, soft or semisolid substance produced by animals and plants and having essential functions in vital processes. **2** An obese condition; corpulence. **3** The richest or most desirable part of anything: the *fat* of the land. **4** Any of various compounds of carbon, oxygen, and hydrogen which are glycerol esters of certain acids. **—***v.t.* & *v.i.* **fat·ted, fat·ting** FATTEN. [< OE *fætt*] **—fat′ly** *adv.* **—fat′ness** *n.*

fa·tal (fāt′l) *adj.* **1** Causing death. **2** Bringing ruin; destructive. **3** Portentous; ominous. **4** Determining fate or destiny; fateful. [< L *fatum* fate] **—fa′tal·ly** *adv.*

fa·tal·ism (fā′təl·iz′əm) *n.* **1** *Philos.* The doctrine that every event is predetermined by fate and inevitable. **2** A disposition to accept every event as preordained. **—fa′tal·is′tic** *adj.* **—fa′tal·is′ti·cal·ly** *adv.* **—fa′tal·ist** *n.*

fa·tal·i·ty (fā·tal′ə·tē, fə-) *n. pl.* **·ties 1** Destiny; a decree of fate. **2** A disastrous or fatal event. **3** A death resulting from a disastrous event; also, one who suffers such a death. **4** Liability to danger or disaster.

fate (fāt) *n.* **1** That power which is thought to determine one's future, success or failure, etc. **2** Destiny; fortune; lot. **3** Evil destiny; doom. **4** Outcome; final result. **—***v.t.* **fat·ed, fat·ing** To predestine: obsolete except in passive: They were *fated* to meet again. [< L *fatum* < *fari* speak]

fat·ed (fā′tid) *adj.* Determined by fate; destined.

fate·ful (fāt′fəl) *adj.* **1** Full of a significance or meaning that can be understood only after the fact; prophetic. **2** Important; critical: a *fateful* decision. **3** Controlled by fate. **—fate′ful·ly** *adv.* **—fate′ful·ness** *n.*

Fates (fāts) *Gk. Myth.* The three goddesses who control human destiny.

fa·ther (fä′thər) *n.* **1** A man who has begotten a child. **2** A man fulfilling the role of father, as by adoption of a child. **3** STEPFATHER. **4** Any male ancestor; forefather. **5** An originator or founder of something. **6** A priest. **7** *Eccl.* Any one of the early historical or doctrinal writers of the Christian Church. **8** *pl.* The chiefs of a city or assembly. **—***v.t.* **1** To beget as a father. **2** To found, create, or make. **3** To act as a father to. [< OE *fæder*] **—fa′ther·hood** *n.* **—fa′ther·less** *adj.*

Fa·ther (fä′thər) *n.* The Deity; God.

father confessor 1 A priest to whom one may confess. **2** Any one in whom one confides.

fa·ther-in-law (fä′thər·in·lô′) *n. pl.* **fa·thers-in-law** The father of one's husband or wife.

fa·ther·land (fä′thər·land′) *n.* The land of one's birth or the land where one's ancestors were born.

fa·ther·ly (fä′thər·lē) *adj.* **1** Of, pertaining to, or like a father. **2** Manifesting the affection of a father; paternal. **—fa′ther·li·ness** *n.*

Father's Day A memorial day observed in honor of fathers on the third Sunday in June.

fath·om (fath′əm) *n. pl.* **·oms** or **·om** A measure equal to six feet, used mainly for depths. **—***v.t.* **1** To find the depth of; sound. **2** To get to the bottom of; understand; interpret. [< OE *fæthm* the span of two arms outstretched] **—fath′om·a·ble** *adj.* **—fath′om·less** *adj.*

fa·tigue (fə·tēg′) *n.* **1** Exhaustion of physical or mental strength. **2** *Metall.* The failure of metals under prolonged or repeated stress. **3** FATIGUE DUTY. **4** *pl.* Clothes worn on fatigue duty. **—***v.t.* & *v.i.* **·tigued, ·ti·guing** To make or become weak or weary from physical or mental effort; tire out. [< L *fatigare*] **—fa·ti′guing·ly** *adv.*

fatigue duty Common labor done by soldiers.

fat·ling (fat′ling) *adj.* Fat; plump. **—***n.* A young animal fattened for slaughter.

fat·ten (fat′n) *v.t.* & *v.i.* To make or become fat. **—fat′ten·er** *n.*

fat·tish (fat′ish) *adj.* Somewhat fat.

fat·ty (fat′ē) *adj.* **fat·ti·er, fat·ti·est 1** Containing fat. **2** Greasy. **—fat′ti·ly** *adv.* **—fat′ti·ness** *n.*

fatty acid Any of a series of organic acids which react with glycerol to form fats and with metallic bases to form soaps.

fa·tu·i·ty (fə·tyōō′ə·tē) *n. pl.* **·ties 1** Something idiotic or stupid. **2** Imbecility; idiocy. [< L *fatuus* foolish]

fat·u·ous (fach′ōō·əs) *adj.* Stubbornly or complacently stupid. [< L *fatuus* foolish] **—fat′u·ous·ly** *adv.* **—fat′u·ous·ness** *n.*

fau·ces (fô′sēz) *n. pl.* The passage between the back of the mouth and the pharynx. [L] **—fau′cal** (-kəl), **fau′cial** (-shəl) *adj.*

fau·cet (fô′sit) *n.* A spout fitted with a valve, for drawing liquids through a pipe. [< OF *fausser* break into, damage]

fault (fôlt) *n.* **1** A slight offense; misdeed. **2** Whatever impairs excellence; an imperfection or defect. **3** Responsibility for an error or misdeed. **4** *Geol.* A fracture in a rock formation that causes strata to shift along the line of fracture. **5** In tennis, etc., an error in serving. **—at fault 1** In the wrong. **2** Worthy of blame. **—to a fault** Exceedingly; excessively: generous *to a fault.* **—***v.t.* **1** To find fault with; blame. **2** *Geol.* To cause a fault in. **—***v.i.* **3** *Geol.* To fracture so as to produce a fault. [< L *fallere* deceive] **—fault′ful·ly** *adv.* **—fault′ful·ness** *n.*

Fault *def. 4*

fault·find·er (fôlt′fīnd′dər) *n.* A person given to finding fault. **—fault′find′ing** *adj., n.*

fault·less (fôlt′lis) *adj.* Without fault; flawless. **—fault′less·ly** *adv.* **—fault′less·ness** *n.*

fault·y (fôl′tē) *adj.* **fault·i·er, fault·i·est 1** Having faults or blemishes. **2** Characterized by faults of conduct. **—fault′i·ly** *adv.* **—fault′i·ness** *n.*

faun (fôn) *n. Rom. Myth.* A half-human deity with pointed ears and goat's feet. [< L]

fau·na (fô′nə) *n. pl.* **fau·nas** or **fau·nae** (-nē) Animals collectively, esp. those species represented in a given area or period. [< L *Fauna,* a rural goddess]

Faust (foust) In medieval legend, an old philosopher who sells his soul to the devil, Mephistopheles, for wisdom, power, and youth.

faux pas (fō pä′) *pl.* **faux pas** (fō päz′) A social error; a breach of tact or manners. [F, lit., false step]

Faun

fa·vor (fā′vər) *n.* **1** A kind or helpful act. **2** The state or condition of being approved. **3** Favoritism; bias; partiality. **4** Something given as a small gift or souvenir. **—in favor of 1** On the side of. **2** To the benefit of; payable to. **—***v.t.* **1** To look upon with favor or kindness; like. **2** To treat with partiality. **3** To make easier; facilitate. **4** To be in favor of; support; help. **5** To do a favor for; oblige. **6** To use carefully; spare, as an injured foot. **7** *Informal* To resemble. *Brit. sp.* **fa′vour.** [< L *favere* to favor] **—fa′vor·er** *n.*

fa·vor·a·ble (fā′vər·ə·bəl) *adj.* **1** Advantageous: to obtain a loan on *favorable* terms. **2** Disposed to favor; approving. **3** Promising: a *favorable* outlook. **—fa′vor·a·ble·ness** *n.* **—fa′vor·a·bly** *adv.* **—Syn. 1** beneficial, convenient, helpful. **3** auspicious, propitious.

fa·vored (fā′vərd) *adj.* **1** Having a specific aspect or appearance: *ill-favored.* **2** Aided; privileged.

fa·vor·ite (fā′vər·it) *adj.* Regarded with special favor; preferred. **—***n.* **1** A person or animal considered to have the best chance in a contest. **2** A person or thing particularly liked or favored.

fa·vor·it·ism (fā′vər·ə·tiz′əm) *n.* 1 A disposition to favor unfairly or unreasonably. 2 The state or condition of being a favorite.

fawn[1] (fôn) *v.i.* 1 To show cringing fondess, as a dog: often with *on* or *upon.* 2 To seek favor by or as by cringing. [<OE *fægnian* rejoice] **—fawn′er** *n.* **—fawn′ing·ly** *adv.*

fawn[2] (fôn) *n.* 1 A young deer in its first year. 2 Light yellowish brown. *—adj.* Having this color. [<L *fetus* offspring]

fax (faks) *n.* A facsimile (def. 2). *—v.t.* To send a facsimile electronically, as of a document over telephone lines.

faze (fāz) *v.t.* **fazed, faz·ing** *Informal* To worry; disturb; disconcert. [<OE *fēsian* frighten]

Fawn

FBI, F.B.I. Federal Bureau of Investigation.

fcap., fcp. foolscap.

FCC, F.C.C. Federal Communications Commission.

F clef See CLEF.

FDA, F.D.A. Food and Drug Administration.

Fe iron (L *ferrum*)

fe·al·ty (fē′əl·tē) *n. pl.* **·ties** Fidelity, as of a vassal to his lord. [<L *fidelitas* fidelity]

fear (fir) *n.* 1 An emotion excited by danger, evil, or pain; apprehension; dread. 2 Uneasiness about a thing; anxiety. 3 That which causes fear. 4 Reverence or awe. *—v.t.* 1 To be afraid of; be fearful of. 2 To look upon with awe or reverence. 3 To be anxious about; be apprehensive about. *—v.i.* 4 To be afraid; feel fear. 5 To be anxious or doubtful. [<OE *fǣr* peril, sudden attack] **—fear′less** *adj.* **—fear′less·ly** *adv.* **—fear′less·ness** *n.*

fear·ful (fir′fəl) *adj.* 1 Experiencing fear; afraid. 2 Inspiring fear; terrible. 3 Caused by fear: *fearful* tremblings. 4 *Informal* Very bad, large, etc.: a *fearful* mistake. **—fear′ful·ly** *adv.* **—fear′ful·ness** *n.*

fear·some (fir′səm) *adj.* 1 Causing fear; alarming. 2 Timid; frightened. **—fear′some·ly** *adv.* **—fear′some·ness** *n.*

fea·si·ble (fē′zə·bəl) *adj.* 1 That may be done; practicable. 2 Capable of being successfully used. 3 Reasonable;probable. [<OF *faisable* <*faire* do] **—fea′si·bil′i·ty, fea′si·ble·ness** *n.* **—fea′si·bly** *adv.*

feast (fēst) *n.* 1 A sumptuous meal. 2 Anything affording great pleasure or enjoyment. 3 A festival. *—v.t.* 1 To give a feast for; entertain lavishly. 2 To delight; gratify: He *feasted* his eyes on her beauty. *—v.i.* 3 To partake of a feast. [<L *festus* joyful] **—feast′er** *n.*

feat (fēt) *n.* A notable act or performance, as one displaying skill, endurance, or daring. [<L *factum* a deed]

feath·er (fe*th*′ər) *n.* 1 One of the elongated structures which cover the body and wings of a bird. 2 Something resembling a feather. 3 Kind; class or species: birds of a *feather.* 4 In rowing, the act of feathering. 5 *pl.* Plumage. 6 Dress or attire. **—a feather in one's cap** An achievement to be proud of. *—v.t.* 1 To fit with a feather, as an arrow. 2 To cover or adorn with feathers. 3 To join by a tongue and groove. 4 In rowing, to turn (the oar blade) horizontally as it comes from the water, thereby lessening resistance. 5 *Aeron.* To turn one edge of (a propeller blade) windward to cut drag. *—v.i.* 6 To grow or become covered with feathers. 7 To move, spread, or expand like feathers. **—feather one's nest** To provide well for one's future. [<OE *fether*] **—feath′ered** *adj.*

feath·er·bed (fe*th*′ər·bed′) *v.i.* **·bed·ded, ·bed·ding** To have unnecessary workmen or slow down production so as to reduce unemployment: said of labor unions.

feath·er·weight (fe*th*′ər·wāt′) *n.* 1 A boxer or wrestler weighing from 118 to 126 pounds. 2 A person weighing very little. 3 An insignificant person or thing. *—adj.* 1 Of little weight. 2 Insignificant.

feath·er·y (fe*th*′ər·ē) *adj.* 1 Covered with or resembling feathers. 2 Light, soft, or fluffy. **—feath′er·i·ness** *n.*

fea·ture (fē′chər) *n.* 1 Any part of the human face. 2 *pl.* The whole face. 3 A distinguishing part or characteristic; salient point. 4 A magazine or newspaper article or story on a special subject. 5 A full-length motion picture. 6 Something or someone outstanding or special. *—v.t.* **fea·tured, fea·tur·ing** 1 To make a feature of, as in a newspaper story. 2 To be a feature of. 3 To portray or outline the features of. 4 *Slang* To imagine; fancy. [<L *factura* a making <*facere* do] **—fea′ture·less** *adj.*

fea·tured (fē′chərd) *adj.* 1 Having a particular kind of facial features: *fine-featured.* 2 Given special prominence.

Feb. February.

feb·ri·fuge (feb′rə·fyōōj) *n.* A medicine for reducing fever. [<L *febris* fever + *fugere* flee] **—fe·brif·u·gal** (fə·brif′yə·gəl) *adj.*

fe·brile (fē′brəl, feb′rəl) *adj.* 1 Pertaining to fever. 2 Caused by or indicating fever. [<L *febris* fever]

Feb·ru·ar·y (feb′rōō·er′ē) *n. pl.* **·ar·ies** or **·ar·ys** The second month of the year, having twenty-eight or, in leap years, twenty-nine days. [<L *februa,* a Roman purificatory festival, celebrated on Feb. 15]

fe·ces (fē′sēz) *n. pl.* Human or animal excrement. [<L *faex* sediment] **—fe·cal** (fē′kəl) *adj.*

feck·less (fek′lis) *adj.* 1 Feeble; helpless. 2 Futile; useless. [<Scot. *feck* vigor + -LESS] **—feck′less·ly** *adv.* **—feck′less·ness** *n.*

fe·cund (fē′kund, fek′und) *adj.* Fruitful, fertile. [<L *fecundus*] **—fe·cun·di·ty** (fi·kun′də·tē) *n.* **—Syn.** productive, prolific, rich, teeming.

fe·cun·date (fē′kən·dāt, fek′ən-) *v.t.* **·dat·ed, ·dat·ing** To impregnate; fertilize. **—fe′cun·da′tion** *n.*

fed[1] (fed) *p.t. & p.p.* of FEED.

fed[2] (fed) *n. Often cap. Slang* A Federal agent. **—the Feds** The Federal Reserve Board.

fed. federal; federated; federation.

fed·er·al (fed′ər·əl, -rəl) *adj.* 1 Of or pertaining to a form of government in which each state agrees to grant control of common affairs to a central authority. 2 Of or pertaining to a government so established. *—n.* An advocate of federalism. [<L *foedus* a league] **—fed′er·al·ly** *adv.*

Fed·er·al (fed′ər·əl, -rəl) *adj.* 1 Of, pertaining to, or representing the United States. 2 Supporting the Union cause in the American Civil War. *—n.* One who favored or fought for the Union cause in the American Civil War.

Federal Bureau of Investigation A branch of the Department of Justice which investigates all violations of Federal laws other than those specifically assigned to other agencies.

fed·er·al·ism (fed′ər·əl·iz′əm, fed′rəl-) *n.* The doctrine of federal union in government.

Fed·er·al·ism (fed′ər·əl·iz′əm, fed′rəl-) *n.* The principles of the Federal Party.

fed·er·al·ist (fed′ər·əl·ist, fed′rəl-) *n.* An advocate of federalism. **—fed′er·al·is′tic** *adj.*

Fed·er·al·ist (fed′ər·əl·ist, fed′rəl-) *n.* One who supported the Federal Party.

fed·er·al·ize (fed′ər·əl·īz, fed′rəl-) *v.t.* **·ized, ·iz·ing** To bring together under federal government. **—fed′er·al·i·za′tion** *n.*

Federal Party A political party (1787–1830) which advocated the adoption of the United States Constitution and the formation of a strong national government. Also **Federalist Party.**

fed·er·ate (fed′ə·rāt) *v.t. & v.i.* **·at·ed, ·at·ing** To unite in a federation. *—adj.* United in a federation. [<L *foedus* a league]

fed·er·a·tion (fed′ə·rā′shən) *n.* 1 The act of uniting under a federal government or under a central authority. 2 A federated body; league. **—fed′er·a·tive** *adj.*

fe·do·ra (fə·dôr′ə, -dō′rə) *n.* A low hat, usu. of soft felt, with the crown creased lengthwise. [<*Fédora,* a play by V. Sardou, 1831–1908, French playwright]

fee (fē) *n.* 1 A payment, as for professional service. 2 A charge for a privilege, as a license, membership, etc. 3 A gratuity; tip. 4 *Law* An estate of inheritance in land. 5 In feudal law, a fief. [<OF *fé, fief* fief, property money]

fee·ble (fē′bəl) *adj.* **fee·bler, fee·blest** 1 Lacking muscular strength; weak; frail. 2 Lacking force or effectiveness; inadequate: a *feeble* argument. [<L *flebilis* tearful] **—fee′ble·ness** *n.* **—fee′bly** *adv.*

add, āce, câre, pälm; end, ēven; it, īce; odd, ōpen, ôrder; tŏŏk, pōōl; up, bûrn; ə = *a* in *above, u* in *focus;* yōō = *u* in *fuse;* oil; pout; check; go; ring; thin; *th*is; zh, *vision.* < derived from; ? origin uncertain or unknown.

fee·ble-mind·ed (fē′bəl·mīn′did) *adj.* Mentally deficient. **—fee′ble-mind′ed·ly** *adv.* **—fee′ble-mind′ed·ness** *n.*

feed (fēd) *n.* 1 Food; esp. food for domestic animals; fodder. 2 The amount of fodder given at one time. 3 The motion that carries material into a machine. 4 The machinery supplying this motion. 5 The material supplied to a machine. 6 *Informal* A meal. —*v.* **fed, feed·ing** *v.t.* 1 To give food to; supply with food. 2 To give as food. 3 To furnish with what is necessary for the continuance, growth, or operation of: to *feed* a furnace; to *feed* steel to a factory. 4 To enlarge; increase: Compliments *feed* his vanity. —*v.i.* 5 To take food; eat: said of animals. 6 To subsist; depend: usu. with *on:* to *feed* on hopes. [< OE *fēdan*] **—feed′er** *n.*

feed·back (fēd′bak′) *n.* 1 The transfer of energy from the output of an electronic or other system to the input, usu. causing major changes in the system characteristics. 2 A process whereby the results of action serve continually to modify further action.

feed·stock (fēd′stok′) *n.* Any raw material supplied to a machine or factory that processes it into products.

feel (fēl) *v.* **felt, feel·ing** *v.t.* 1 To examine by touching. 2 To perceive by the senses: to *feel* pain. 3 To experience emotionally: to *feel* joy. 4 To be affected by: to *feel* a snub. 5 To be convinced of: to *feel* the need for reform. —*v.i.* 6 To seem; appear. The air *feels* humid. 7 To have a sensation of: to *feel* cold. 8 To have the emotions or opinions stirred: to *feel* strongly about something. 9 To have compassion for: to *feel* for a sick friend. 10 To be in a specific frame of mind: to *feel* scared. 11 To examine by touching; grope: to *feel* around a wall. **—feel like** *Informal* To have a desire or inclination for. **—feel out** 1 To examine the possibilities of (a situation). 2 To talk to (a person) so as to determine opinions, ideas, etc. **—feel up to** To feel able to do. —*n.* 1 The act of feeling. 2 The sense of touch. 3 A sensation: a *feel* of spring in the air. 4 The quality of a thing perceived by touch: Fur has a soft *feel.* [< OE *fēlan*]

feel·er (fē′lər) *n.* 1 One who or that which feels. 2 An organ of touch; an antenna; tentacle. 3 Something asked or proposed in order to ascertain another's viewpoint.

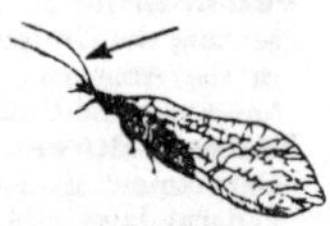

Feelers

feel·ing (fē′ling) *n.* 1 The sense of touch. 2 A particular physical sensation: a *feeling* of cold. 3 A state of consciousness: a rested *feeling,* etc. 4 An emotion: a hostile *feeling.* 5 *Often pl.* Sensitivity; sensibility: to hurt one's *feelings.* 6 Pity; sympathy. 7 Presentiment; foreboding. 8 Opinion; conviction: my *feeling* on the matter. 9 The ability to express or portray emotion: to perform with great *feeling* —*adj.* Having warm sensibilities; sympathetic. **—feel′ing·ly** *adv.*

feet (fēt) *n.pl.* of FOOT.

feign (fān) *v.t.* 1 To simulate; pretend. 2 To invent deceptively, as excuses. 3 To make up or imagine, as stories. —*v.i.* 4 To pretend. [< L *fingere* to shape] **—feign·ed·ly** (fā′·nid·lē), **feign′ing·ly** *adv.* **—feign′er** *n.*

feint (fānt) *n.* 1 A ruse or pretense. 2 In boxing, fencing, war, etc., an apparent or pretended blow or attack meant to divert an opponent's attention. —*v.i.* To make a feint. [< F *feindre* to feign]

feis·ty (fīs′tē) *adj.* **feis·ti·er, feis·ti·est** *Informal* 1 Lively or flamboyant in manner or appearance. 2 Spirited to the point of being challenging; spunky. **—feis′ti·ness** *n.*

feld·spar (feld′spär, fel′-) *n.* Any one of a group of crystalline minerals consisting of silicates of aluminum with potassium, sodium, or calcium. [< G *Feld* field + SPAR]

fe·lic·i·tate (fə·lis′ə·tāt) *v.t.* **·tat·ed, ·tat·ing** To wish joy or happiness to; congratulate. [< L *felix* happy] **—fe·lic′i·ta′·tion** *n.*

fe·lic·i·tous (fə·lis′ə·təs) *adj.* 1 Marked by or producing felicity. 2 Appropriate; apt. **—fe·lic′i·tous·ly** *adv.*

fe·lic·i·ty (fə·lis′ə·tē) *n. pl.* **·ties** 1 Happiness, comfort, and content. 2 Something causing happiness. 3 A pleasing faculty for expression, as in art, writing, etc. 4 A clever or apt expression. [< L *felix* happy]

fe·line (fē′līn) *adj.* 1 Of or pertaining to cats or catlike animals. 2 Catlike; sly. —*n.* One of the cat family. [< L *felis* cats] **—fe′line·ly** *adv.* **—fe·lin·i·ty** (fə·lin′ə·tē) *n.*

fell[1] (fel) *v.t.* 1 to cause to fall: to *fell* a tree. 2 In sewing, to finish with a flat seam. —*n.* 1 A seam made by joining edges, folding them under, and stitching flat. 2 The timber cut down during one season. [< OE *fellan*] **—fell′a·ble** *adj.*

fell[2] (fel) *p.t.* of FALL.

fell[3] (fel) *adj.* 1 Fierce; cruel; barbarous. 2 Hideous. [< OF *felon* felon]

fell[4] (fel) *n.* A hide or pelt. [< OE, hide]

fel·lah (fel′ə) *n. pl.* **fel·lahs** or **fel·la·heen** or **·hin** (fel′ə·hēn′) A peasant; laborer, as in Egypt. [Ar. *fellāh*]

fel·la·ti·o (fə·lā′shē·ō, -lät′ē-) *n.* Oral contact with the penis. [< L *fellare* to suck]

fel·low (fel′ō) *n.* 1 A man; boy. 2 A person or individual. 3 A companion. 4 An equal. 5 One of a pair; mate. 6 A trustee in some educational institutions. 7 A member of a scholarly society. 8 A graduate student of a university holding a fellowship or stipend. 9 *Informal* A girl's beau. —*adj.* Joined or associated in some way: a *fellow* student. [< OE *fēolaga* business partner]

fel·low·ship (fel′ō·ship) *n.* 1 Association; companionship. 2 The condition of being sharers or partakers, as in some activity. 3 A body of persons having similar tastes, views, or interests. 4 A foundation, as in a college or university, the income of which is given to aid a student; also, the income so given. 5 Membership in a scholarly society.

fel·on[1] (fel′ən) *n.* One who has committed a felony. —*adj.* Wicked; criminal; treacherous. [< Med. L *fello*]

fel·on[2] (fel′ən) *n.* Inflammation of the tissue near the nail of a finger or toe. [< OF *feloun*]

fe·lo·ni·ous (fə·lō′nē·əs) *adj.* 1 Malicious; villainous. 2 Like or involving legal felony. **—fe·lo′ni·ous·ly** *adv.* **—fe·lo′ni·ous·ness** *n.* **—Syn.** 2 criminal, illegal, unlawful.

fel·o·ny (fel′ə·nē) *Law n. pl.* **·nies** One of the gravest of crimes, as treason, murder, rape, etc., and punishable by imprisonment or death.

felt[1] (felt) *p.t. & p.p.* of FEEL.

felt[2] (felt) *n.* 1 A fabric made by compacting wool, fur, or hair, by pressure, chemical action, moisture, and heat. 2 An article made of felt. —*adj.* Made of felt. —*v.t.* 1 To make into felt. 2 To overlay with felt. [< OE]

fe·luc·ca (fə·luk′ə, fe-) *n.* A small, swift Mediterranean vessel propelled by lateen-rigged sails and by oars. [< Ar. *falūkah*]

fem. female; feminine.

fe·male (fē′māl) *adj.* 1 Of or pertaining to the sex that brings forth young or produces ova. 2 Of, pertaining to, or like this sex; feminine. 3 Designating a plant or flower which has a pistil but no stamen. 4 *Mech.* Denoting a part having a hollow or bore into which a matching part fits. —*n.* A female person, animal, or plant. [< L *femina* woman] **—fe′male·ness** *n.*

fem·i·nine (fem′ə·nin) *adj.* 1 Of or pertaining to the female sex. 2 Belonging to or characteristic of womankind; womanly. 3 Lacking in manly qualities; effeminate. 4 *Gram.* Applicable to females only or to objects classified as female. —*n. Gram.* A word belonging to the feminine gender. [< L *femina* a woman] **—fem′i·nine·ly** *adv.* **—fem′i·nine·ness, fem·i·nin·i·ty** (fem′ə·nin′ə·tē) *n.*

feminine rhyme Rhyme in which the primary accent falls on the first syllable of a two- or three-syllable word, as *never, ever* or *laziness, craziness.*

fem·i·nism (fem′ə·niz′əm) *n.* 1 The doctrine which declares that social, political, and economic rights for women be the same as those for men. 2 A movement advocating this doctrine. **—fem′i·nist** *n.* **—fem′i·nis′tic** *adj.*

fem·i·nize (fem′ə·nīz) *v.t. & v.i.* **·nized, ·niz·ing** To make or become effeminate or feminine. **—fem′i·ni·za′tion** *n.*

femme (fám) *n. French* A woman; wife.

fe·mur (fē′mər) *n. pl.* **fe·murs** or **fem·o·ra** (fem′ər·ə) *Anat.* The long bone that forms the chief support of the thigh; thighbone. [< L, thigh] **—fem·o·ral** (fem′ər·əl) *adj.*

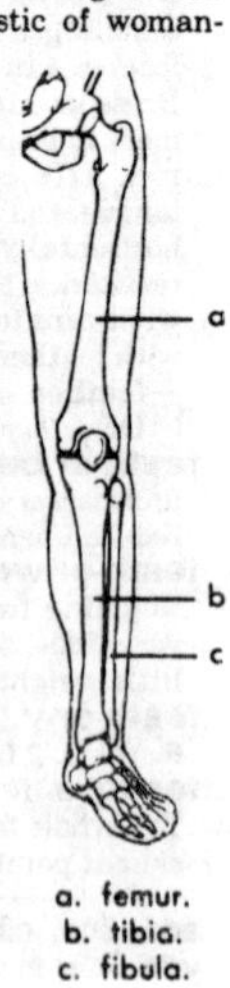

a. femur.
b. tibia.
c. fibula.

fen (fen) *n.* A marsh; bog. [< OE *fenn*]

fence (fens) *n.* 1 An enclosing structure or barrier of rails, pickets, wires, or the like. 2 The art of fencing. 3 Skill in repartee or debate. 4 A receiver of stolen goods, or the place where such goods are received. **—on the fence** Undecided or noncommittal. *—v.* **fenced, fenc·ing** *v.t.* 1 To enclose with or as with a fence. 2 To separate with or as with a fence. *—v.i.* 3 To engage in the art of fencing. 4 To avoid giving direct answers; parry. 5 To deal in stolen goods. [Var. of DEFENSE] **—fenc'er** *n.*

fenc·ing (fen'sing) *n.* 1 The art of using a foil, sword, or other similar weapon. 2 Skillful parrying of prying questions. 3 Material for fences; also, fences collectively.

fend (fend) *v.t.* 1 To ward off; parry: usu. with *off.* *—v.i.* 2 To offer resistance; parry. 3 To provide or get along: with *for:* to *fend* for oneself. [Short for DEFEND]

fend·er (fen'dər) *n.* 1 One who or that which fends or wards off. 2 The part of a frame of a motor vehicle that covers each wheel. 3 A metal guard before an open fire. 4 A device at the front of a locomotive or streetcar, used to push aside objects on the tracks.

Fe·ni·an (fē'nē·ən, fēn'yən) *n.* A member of an Irish society formed in New York in the mid-19th century to seek independence for Ireland. *—adj.* Of the Fenians. [< Ir. *Fiann,* a legendary Irish warrior] **—Fe'ni·an·ism** *n.*

fen·nel (fen'əl) *n.* An edible herb of the parsley family, with yellow flowers and aromatic seeds.

feoff (fef, fēf) *v.t.* **feoffed, feoff·ing** To give or grant a fief to. *—n.* FIEF. [< OF *fief* FIEF] **—feof'fer, feoff'ment** *n.*

FEPC, F.E.P.C. Fair Employment Practices Committee.

-fer *combining form* One who or that which bears: *conifer.* [< L *ferre* bear]

fe·ral (fir'əl) *adj.* 1 Undomesticated; existing in a wild state. 2 Pertaining to or characteristic of the wild state; savage. [< L *ferus* wild]

fer-de-lance (fâr'də·läns') *n.* A venomous snake of tropical South America. [F, lit., iron head of a lance]

fer·ment (fər·ment') *v.t.* 1 To produce fermentation in. 2 To stir with anger; agitate. *—v.i.* 3 To undergo fermentation; work. 4 To be agitated, as by emotion. *—n.* (fûr'ment) 1 A substance productive of fermentation, as yeast. 2 FERMENTATION. 3 Excitement or agitation. [< L *fermentum* < *fervere* to boil] **—fer·ment'a·ble** or **·i·ble** *adj.* **—fer·ment'a·bil'i·ty** *n.*

fer·men·ta·tion (fûr'mən·tā'shən) *n.* 1 The decomposition of organic compounds by the action of enzymes. 2 Commotion, agitation, or excitement.

fer·mi·um (fer'mē·əm, fûr'-) *n.* An artificially produced radioactive element (symbol Fm). [< E. *Fermi,* 1901–54, Italian physicist]

fern (fûrn) *n.* Any of a widely distributed class of flowerless, seedless plants, having leaves (fronds) which carry the reproductive spores. [< OE *fearn*] **—fern'y** *adj.*

fern·er·y (fûr'nər·ē) *n. pl.* **·er·ies** A place in which ferns are grown.

fe·ro·cious (fə·rō'shəs) *adj.* 1 Savage; bloodthirsty; rapacious. 2 *Informal* Very great: *ferocious* heat. [< L *ferus* wild] **—fe·ro'cious·ly** *adv.* **—fe·ro'cious·ness** *n.*

fe·roc·i·ty (fə·ros'ə·tē) *n. pl.* **·ties** The state or quality of being ferocious. **—Syn.** savagery, cruelty, brutality.

-ferous *combining form* Bearing or producing: *coniferous.* [< L *ferre* to bear]

fer·ret (fer'it) *n.* A small weasel sometimes trained to hunt rodents. *—v.t.* 1 To search out by careful investigation: with *out.* 2 To drive out of hiding with a ferret. 3 To hunt with ferrets. *—v.i.* 4 To hunt by means of ferrets. 5 To search. [< L *fur* a thief] **—fer'ret·er** *n.*

Ferret

fer·ric (fer'ik) *adj.* Pertaining to iron, esp. in the trivalent state. [< L *ferrum* iron + IC]

Fer·ris wheel (fer'is) A giant, vertical, power-driven wheel that revolves on a stationary axle and bears swinging observation cars for passengers. [< G. W. G. *Ferris,* 1859–96, U.S. engineer]

fer·rite (fer'īt) *n.* Any of various ferromagnetic, nonmetallic substances composed of ferric oxide and other metallic oxides.

ferro- *combining form* 1 Derived from, containing, or alloyed with iron: *ferromagnetic.* 2 Containing ferrous iron. [< L *ferrum* iron]

fer·ro·con·crete (fer'ō·kon'krēt, -kon·krēt') *n.* Concrete reinforced with steel rods, bars, cables, etc.

fer·ro·mag·net·ic (fer'ō·mag·net'ik) *adj. Physics* Having magnetic properties similar to those of iron. **—fer'ro·mag'ne·tism** *n.*

fer·rous (fer'əs) *adj.* 1 *Chem.* Of or pertaining to bivalent iron. 2 Having or deriving from iron. [< L *ferrum* iron + -OUS]

fer·ru·gi·nous (fə·rōō'jə·nəs) *adj.* 1 Of or like iron. 2 Rust-colored. [< L *ferrum* iron]

fer·rule (fer'əl, -ōōl, -ōōl) *n.* 1 A metal ring or cap, as on the end of a cane. 2 A bushing or thimble. 3 FERULE. *—v.t.* **·ruled, ·rul·ing** To furnish with a ferrule. [< L *viriae* bracelets]

fer·ry (fer'ē) *v.* **fer·ried, fer·ry·ing** *v.t.* 1 To carry across a relatively narrow body of water in a boat. 2 To cross (a river, bay, etc.) in a boat. 3 To bring or take (an airplane or vehicle) to a point of delivery. *—v.i.* 4 To cross a body of water in a boat or by ferry. *—n. pl.* **·ries** 1 FERRYBOAT. 2 The place of crossing a river, bay, or the like, by boat. 3 The legal right to operate a service that transports people or goods across waterways. [< OE *ferian* carry]

fer·ry·boat (fer'ē·bōt') *n.* A boat used to transport passengers, vehicles, goods, etc., across a river, bay, etc.

fer·ry·man (fer'ē·mən) *n. pl.* **·men** (-mən) One who has charge of or works on a ferry.

fer·tile (fûr'təl) *adj.* 1 Producing or capable of producing abundantly. 2 Reproducing or capable of reproducing. 3 Capable of growth or development; said of seeds or eggs. 4 Productive; prolific; inventive: a *fertile* imagination. [< L *fertilis* < *ferre* to bear] **—fer'tile·ly** *adv.* **—fer'tile·ness** *n.*

fer·til·i·ty (fər·til'ə·tē) *n.* The state or quality of being fertile.

fer·til·ize (fûr'təl·īz) *v.t.* **·ized, ·iz·ing** 1 To render fertile or fruitful. 2 To render (an ovum) capable of growth, usu. by fusion with a male gamete. 3 To enrich, as soil. **—fer'til·iz'a·ble** *adj.* **—fer'til·i·za'tion** *n.*

fer·til·i·zer (fûr'təl·īz'ər) *n.* 1 One who or that which fertilizes. 2 A fertilizing material applied to soil, as guano, manure, etc.

fer·ule (fer'əl, -ōōl) *n.* A flat stick or ruler sometimes used for punishing children. *—v.t.* **fer·uled, fer·ul·ing** To punish with a ferule. [< L *ferula* giant fennel, rod]

fer·vent (fûr'vənt) *adj.* 1 Having or showing great emotional warmth, devotion, or enthusiasm; ardent; fervid. 2 Burning, or very hot. [< L *fervere* be hot] **—fer'ven·cy, fer'vent·ness** *n.* **—fer'vent·ly** *adv.*

fer·vid (fûr'vid) *adj.* 1 Fervent; zealous. 2 Hot; glowing; fiery. [< L *fervere* be hot] **—fer·vid'i·ty, fer'vid·ness** *n.* **—fer'vid·ly** *adv.*

fer·vor (fûr'vər) *n.* 1 Great intensity of feeling; ardor; zeal. 2 Heat; warmth. *Brit. sp.* **fer'vour.** [< L *fervere* be hot] **—Syn.** 1 enthusiasm, passion, intenseness, gusto, zest.

fes·cue (fes'kyōō) *n.* A tough grass, valuable for pasturage. [< L *festuca* a stalk, straw]

fess (fes) *n. Her.* A horizontal band across the middle of the shield, having a breadth equal to one third of the field. Also **fesse.** [< L *fascia* band]

fes·tal (fes'təl) *adj.* Pertaining to a festival, feast, or holiday; festive. [< L *festum* a feast] **—fes'tal·ly** *adv.*

fes·ter (fes'tər) *v.i.* 1 To generate pus. 2 To become embittered; rankle. 3 To decay; rot. *—v.t.* 4 To cause to fester or rankle. *—n.* An ulcerous sore. [< L *fistula* ulcer]

fes·ti·val (fes'tə·vəl) *n.* 1 A period of feasting or celebration. 2 A season devoted periodically to some form of entertainment. 3 A series of performances, art exhibits, etc.: a jazz *festival.* *—adj.* FESTIVE. [< L *festivus* festive]

fes·tive (fes'tiv) *adj.* Pertaining or suited to a feast or festival; gay; joyful. [< L *festum* feast] **—fes'tive·ly** *adv.* **—fes'tive·ness** *n.*

fes·tiv·i·ty (fes·tiv′ə·tē) *n. pl.* **·ties 1** FESTIVAL (def. 1). **2** Gaiety; merrymaking. **3** A social activity or celebration.

fes·toon (fes·to͞on′) *n.* **1** A decorative garland hanging in a curve between two points. **2** An ornamental carving resembling such a garland. —*v.t.* **1** To decorate with festoons. **2** To fashion into festoons. **3** To link together by festoons. [< F < Ital. *festa* a feast] —**fes·toon′ery** *n.*

fe·tal (fēt′l) *adj.* Of, pertaining to, or characteristic of a fetus: the *fetal* position.

fetch (fech) *v.t.* **1** To go after and bring back. **2** To draw forth; bring, as a reply. **3** To bring as a price. **4** *Informal* To captivate; charm. **5** *Naut.* To reach or arrive at. **6** *Informal* To strike or deliver, as a blow. —*v.i.* **7** To go after and bring things back. **8** *Naut.* To take a course. —*n.* The act of fetching. [< OE *feccan*] —**fetch′er** *n.*

fetch·ing (fech′ing) *adj. Informal* Most attractive; taking; fascinating. —**fetch′ing·ly** *adv.*

fete (fāt) *n.* A festival; holiday. —*v.t.* **fet·ed, fet·ing** To honor with festivities. Also **fête.** [F < OF *feste* feast]

fet·id (fet′id, fē′tid) *adj.* Emitting an offensive odor. [< L *fetere* stink] —**fet′id·ly** *adv.* —**fet′id·ness** *n.*

fet·ish (fet′ish, fē′tish) *n.* **1** A natural object believed to be endowed with magical powers. **2** Any object of excessive devotion. **3** *Psychiatry* An object, usu. nonsexual in nature, that arouses sexual feelings. Also **fet′ich.** [< Pg. *feitiço* a charm < L *factitius* artificial]

fet·ish·ism (fet′ish·iz′əm, fē′tish-) *n.* **1** The belief in or worship of fetishes. **2** *Psychiatry* Sexual pleasure or excitement derived from an object not normally associated with sex. Also **fet′ich·ism.** —**fet′ish·ist** *n.* —**fet′ish·is′tic** *adj.*

fet·lock (fet′lok′) *n.* **1** The tuft of hair above and behind a horse's hoof. **2** The joint at this place. [ME *fitlok, fetlak*] • See HORSE.

fet·ter (fet′ər) *n.* **1** A shackle for the ankles. **2** Anything that restricts or confines. —*v.t.* **1** To fasten fetters upon; shackle. **2** To prevent the activity of; restrain. [< OE *feter, fetor*]

fet·tle (fet′l) *v.t.* **fet·tled, fet·tling** *Regional* To put in good order; arrange. —*n.* State or condition, as of spirits: in fine *fettle.* [ME *fetlen* prepare < OE *fetel* a belt]

fe·tus (fē′təs) *n. pl.* **fe·tus·es** The young in the womb of animals, esp. in the later stages of development. [L]

feud[1] (fyo͞od) *n.* **1** Vindictive strife or hostility between families or clans, often hereditary. **2** Any quarrel or conflict. —*v.i.* To engage in a feud; quarrel bitterly. [< OHG *fehida* hatred, revenge] —**feud′er, feud′ist** *n.*

feud[2] (fyo͞od) *n.* In feudalism, a fief. [< Med. L *feudum*]

feu·dal (fyo͞o′dəl) *adj.* **1** Of, pertaining to, or like feudalism. **2** Relating to a fief. [< Med. L *feudum* feud[2]] —**feu′dal·ly** *adv.*

feu·dal·ism (fyo͞o′dəl·iz′əm) *n.* The medieval European system of a vassal's holding land from a lord on condition of military aid and other services. Also **feudal system.** —**feu′dal·ist** *n.* —**feu′dal·is′tic** *adj.*

feu·dal·ize (fyo͞o′dəl·īz) *v.t.* **·ized, ·iz·ing** To bring under the feudal system; render feudal. —**feu′dal·i·za′tion** *n.*

feu·da·to·ry (fyo͞o′də·tôr′ē, -tō′rē) *adj.* Holding or held by feudal tenure. —*n. pl.* **·ries 1** A feud or fief. **2** A vassal.

fe·ver (fē′vər) *n.* **1** Body temperature above the normal. **2** A disorder or illness marked by high temperature. **3** Emotional excitement or enthusiasm. —*v.t.* To affect with fever. [< L *febris*]

fever blister COLD SORE. Also **fever sore.**

fe·ver·few (fē′vər·fyo͞o′) *n.* An erect bushy herb bearing white-rayed, composite flowers. [< L *febris* fever + *fugare* put to flight]

fe·ver·ish (fē′vər·ish) *adj.* **1** Affected with fever. **2** Causing a fever. **3** Very excited, eager, or impatient. —**fe′ver·ish·ly** *adv.* —**fe′ver·ish·ness** *n.*

fe·ver·ous (fē′vər·əs) *adj.* FEVERISH. —**fe′ver·ous·ly** *adv.*

fe·ver·wort (fē′vər·wûrt′) *n.* A perennial weedy herb of the honeysuckle family having a root sometimes used as a purgative and emetic. Also **fe′ver·root′** (-ro͞ot′, -ro͝ot′).

few (fyo͞o) *adj.* Limited in number; not many. —*n. & pron.* A small number; some. —**quite a few** An appreciable number. —**the few** The minority. [< OE *fēawe*] —**few′·ness** *n.*

fey (fā) *adj.* Acting in an eccentric, somewhat whimsical, or otherworldly manner. [< F *féer* enchant]

fez (fez) *n. pl.* **fez·zes** A brimless, tapering, felt hat, usu. red with a black tassel, worn esp. by men in Egypt and elsewhere. [< Turkish *fes,* after *Fez,* a city in Morocco]

Fez

ff. folios; following; fortissimo.

FHA Federal Housing Authority.

fi·an·cé (fē′än·sā′, fē·än′sā) *n.* A man engaged to be married. [F < OF < *fier* to trust]

fi·an·cée (fē′än·sā′, fē·än′sā) *n.* A woman engaged to be married. [F < OF < *fier* to trust]

fi·as·co (fē·as′kō) *n. pl.* **·cos** or **·coes** A complete or humiliating failure. [Ital.]

fi·at (fē′at, -ət) *n.* An authoritative command that something be done; an order or decree. [L, let it be done]

fiat money Paper money made legal tender but not backed by gold or silver and usu. not redeemable into coin.

fib (fib) *n.* A petty falsehood. —*v.i.* **fibbed, fib·bing** To tell a fib. [?] —**fib′ber** *n.*

fi·ber (fī′bər) *n.* **1** A fine filament. **2** A threadlike component of a substance, as of wood, cotton, spun glass, etc. **3** A material composed of filaments. **4** The texture of anything. **5** Character; nature; make-up: a woman of strong *fiber.* Also **fi′bre.** [< L *fibra* fiber] —**fi′bered, fi′ber·less** *adj.*

fi·ber·board (fī′bər·bôrd′, -bōrd′) *n.* A tough, stiff material made of cellulose fibers compressed and rolled into sheets.

Fi·ber·glas (fī′bər·glas′, -gläs′) *n.* FIBERGLASS: a trade name.

fi·ber·glass (fī′bər·glas′, -gläs′) *n.* A flexible, nonflammable material made of glass spun into filaments, used for textiles, insulators, etc. Also **fiber glass.**

fi·bril (fī′brəl) *n.* **1** A minute fiber. **2** *Bot.* ROOT HAIR. [< NL *fibrilla,* dim. of L *fibra* fiber] —**fi′bril·lar** *adj.*

fi·bril·late (fib′rə·lāt, fī′brə-) *v.i.* **·lat·ed, ·lat·ing** To undergo fibrillation.

fi·bril·la·tion (fib′rə·lā′shən, fī′brə-) *n.* Rapid, irregular, uncoordinated contractions of the muscle fibers of the heart.

fi·brin (fī′brin) *n.* An insoluble protein formed in and aiding the clotting of blood. [< L *fibra* fiber]

fi·broid (fī′broid) *adj.* Of the nature of fiber; fibrous: a *fibroid* tumor.

fi·bro·sis (fī·brō′sis) *n.* Increase of fibrous tissue due to disease; fibroid degeneration.

fi·brous (fī′brəs) *adj.* Composed of or having the character of fibers.

fib·u·la (fib′yo͞o·lə) *n. pl.* **·las** or **·lae** (-lē) The smaller of the two bones between the human knee and ankle or its counterpart in animals. [L, a clasp] —**fib′u·lar** *adj.* • See FEMUR.

-fic *suffix* Making; causing: *beatific.* [< L *facere* make]

-fication *suffix* The making, rendering, or causing to be of a certain character: *beatification.* [< L *facere* make]

fiche (fēsh) *n.* MICROFICHE.

fi·chu (fish′o͞o) *n.* A triangular piece of light material worn about the neck. [F < *ficher* put on hastily]

Fichu

fick·le (fik′əl) *adj.* Inconstant in feeling or purpose; capricious. [< OE *ficol* crafty] —**fick′le·ness** *n.* —**Syn.** changeable, unsteady, erratic, irresolute, mercurial.

fic·tion (fik′shən) *n.* **1** Literature made up of imaginary events and characters, as novels, short stories, plays, etc.; also, such works collectively. **2** The act of feigning or imagining that which does not exist or is not actual. **3** That which is feigned or imagined. [< L *fictio* < *fingere* to form] —**fic′·tion·al** *adj.* —**fic′tion·al·ly** *adv.* —**fic′tive** (fik′tiv) *adj.*

fic·ti·tious (fik·tish′əs) *adj.* **1** Of or like fiction; imaginary. **2** Not real; counterfeit; false: a *fictitious* name. —**fic·ti′tious·ly** *adv.* —**fic·ti′tious·ness** *n.*

fid (fid) *n. Naut.* **1** A supporting bar to hold a topmast in place. **2** A large tapering wooden pin used for opening ropes when splicing, etc. [?]

-fid *combining form* Divided into; split: *bifid.* [< L *findere* to split]

fid·dle (fid′l) *n.* **1** VIOLIN. **2** *Naut.* A rack or frame used at table on board ship in rough weather to keep the dishes in place. —**fit as a fiddle** In fine health and spirits. —**play second fiddle** To perform in a subordinate role. —*v.* **fid·dled, fid·dling** *v.i.* 1 *Informal* To play on a fiddle. 2 To toy or tinker nervously with an object. —*v.t.* 3 *Informal* To play (an air, tune, etc.) on a fiddle. 4 To trifle; fritter: to *fiddle* time away. [< OE *fithele*] —**fid′dler** *n.*

fiddler crab A small burrowing crab the male of which has one much enlarged claw.

fid·dle·stick (fid′l·stik′) *n.* 1 *Informal* A violin bow. 2 A trifling or absurd thing.

fid·dle·sticks (fid′l·stiks′) *interj.* Nonsense!

fi·del·i·ty (fə·del′ə·tē, fī-) *n. pl.* **·ties** 1 Faithfulness in honoring an obligation, vow, duty, etc. 2 Strict adherence to truth or fact. 3 Exactness in the reproduction of something. 4 *Electronics* The accuracy with which an amplifier or other system reproduces the important characteristics of its input signal at the output. [< L *fides* faith] —**Syn.** 1 constancy, loyalty, allegiance. 2 honesty, integrity.

fidg·et (fij′it) *v.i.* 1 To move about restlessly. 2 To toy with something nervously. —*v.t.* 3 To make restless. —*n.* 1 *Often pl.* Nervous restlessness: to have the *fidgets.* 2 A restless person; one who fidgets. [< obs. *fidge* move about] —**fidg′et·y** *adj.* **(·i·er, ·i·est)** —**fidg′et·i·ness** *n.*

fi·du·ci·ar·y (fi·d^{y}o͞o′shē·er′ē, -shə·rē) *adj.* 1 Of or pertaining to a trustee or guardian. 2 Relying on the confidence of the public, as for paper currency or value. 3 Held in trust. —*n. pl.* **·ar·ies** *Law* A person who holds a thing in trust. [< L *fiducia* trust]

fie (fī) *interj.* An expression of impatience or disapproval. [< L *fi* an expression of disgust]

fief (fēf) *n.* A landed estate held under feudal tenure. [< Med. L *feudum* feud[2]]

field (fēld) *n.* 1 A relatively large area of open land. 2 A piece of cleared land set apart and enclosed for tillage or pasture. 3 A region of the countryside considered as yielding some natural product: a coal *field.* 4 Any wide or open expanse: an ice *field.* 5 An airport. 6 *Mil.* An area of action or operations. 7 In sports or contests: **a** The area on which the game is played. **b** An area usu. enclosed by a running track where contests in hurling, throwing, and leaping are held in track-and-field meets. **c** In baseball, the outfield. **d** The contestants, as in a race or other contest. **e** The players actually playing on a field. 8 A sphere or area of study, knowledge, or practice: the *field* of physics. 9 In business or research, an area of work away from the main office, laboratory, etc. 10 *Physics* A region of space throughout which a physical effect, as gravitational force, can be detected. 11 The background area of a painting, coin, flag, heraldic shield, etc. 12 *Optics* The space or apparent surface within which objects are seen in an optical instrument. —**play the field** *Informal* To be interested or active in all or many aspects of something. —**take** (or **leave**) **the field** To begin (or cease) an activity, military contest, etc. —*adj.* 1 Of, pertaining to, or found in the fields. 2 Used in, or for use in, the fields. 3 Played on a field. —*v.t.* 1 To catch and return (a ball in play), as in baseball. 2 To put (a player or team) on the field. —*v.i.* 3 In baseball, cricket, etc., to play as a fielder. [< OE *feld*]

field artillery Light or heavy artillery so mounted as to be freely movable.

field day 1 A day when troops are taken to the field for maneuvers. 2 A school holiday devoted to athletic sports. 3 Any day of display, excitement, or celebration.

field·er (fēl′dər) *n.* In baseball, cricket, etc., a player stationed in the field.

field glasses A small, portable telescope for binocular use. Also **field glass.**

field goal 1 In football, a goal scored from the field by means of a kick. 2 In basketball, a goal scored with the ball in active play.

field hand An agricultural laborer.

field hockey HOCKEY (def. 2).

field hospital A hospital established on or near a field of battle.

field marshal An officer of the highest rank in the armies of several European nations.

field officer An army major, lieutenant colonel, or colonel.

field of force *Physics* FIELD (def. 10).

field·stone (fēld′stōn′) *n.* Loose stone found naturally in fields, often used in building.

field trip A trip outside the classroom for purposes of first-hand observation and study.

field·work (fēld′wûrk′) *n.* A temporary fortification thrown up in the field.

field work Observations or performance in the field, as by scientists, surveyors, etc.

fiend (fēnd) *n.* 1 An evil spirit; a devil; demon. 2 An intensely malicious or wicked person. 3 *Informal* One exceptionally interested or skilled in a certain subject or activity. 4 *Informal* One addicted to some harmful habit. —**the Fiend** Satan; the devil. [< OE *fēond* devil]

fiend·ish (fēn′dish) *adj.* Of, pertaining to, or resembling a fiend; diabolical. —**fiend′ish·ly** *adv.* —**fiend′ish·ness** *n.*

fierce (firs) *adj.* **fierc·er, fierc·est** 1 Having a violent and cruel nature or temper; savage; ferocious. 2 Violent in action; furious. 3 Vehement; passionate; extreme. 4 *Informal* Very bad, difficult, disagreeable, etc. [< L *ferus* wild] —**fierce′ly** *adv.* —**fierce′ness** *n.*

fier·y (fī′ər·ē, fīr′ē) *adj.* **fier·i·er, fier·i·est** 1 Of, like, or containing fire. 2 Blazing; glowing. 3 Passionate; spirited; ardent. 4 Easily aroused, as to anger. 5 Inflamed, as a sore. —**fier′i·ly** *adv.* —**fier′i·ness** *n.*

fi·es·ta (fē·es′tə) *n.* 1 A religious festival. 2 Any celebration or holiday. [Sp. < L *festa* feast]

fife (fīf) *n.* A small, shrill-toned, flutelike wind instrument. —*v.t.* & *v.i.* **fifed, fif·ing** To play on a fife. [< OHG *pfifa,* ult. < L *pipare* to peep, chirp] —**fif′er** *n.*

Fife

fif·teen (fif′tēn′) *n.* 1 The sum of 14 plus 1; 15; XV. 2 A set or group of 15 members. [< OE *fiftēne*] —**fif′teen** *adj., pron.*

fif·teenth (fif′tēnth′) *adj.* & *adv.* Next in order after the 14th. —*n.* 1 The element of an ordered set corresponding to the number 15. 2 One of fifteen equal parts.

fifth (fifth) *adj.* & *adv.* Next in order after the fourth. —*n.* 1 The element of an ordered set corresponding to the number 5. 2 One of five equal parts. 3 *Music* The interval between a tone and another tone four steps away in a diatonic scale. 4 One fifth of a U.S. gallon used as a measure of spirituous liquors. [< OE *fifta*]

fifth column A group, within a city or country, of civilian sympathizers with an enemy. —**fifth columnist**

fifth wheel A superfluous thing or person.

fif·ti·eth (fif′tē·ith) *adj.* & *adv.* Tenth in order after the 40th. —*n.* 1 The element of an ordered set that corresponds to the number 50. 2 One of 50 equal parts.

fif·ty (fif′tē) *n. pl.* **fif·ties** 1 The product of five and ten; 50; L. 2 A set or group of 50 members. 3 The numbers, years, etc., between 50 and 60. [< OE *fiftig*] —**fif′ty** *adj., pron.*

fif·ty-fif·ty (fif′tē·fif′tē) *adj. Informal* Sharing equally, as benefits. —*adv. Informal* Equally.

fig (fig) *n.* 1 A small, sweet, many-seeded fruit, usu. marketed in dried, processed form. 2 The tree that bears this fruit. [< L *ficus*]

Figs

fig. figurative(ly); figure(s).

fig·eat·er (fig′ē′tər) *n.* A large beetle common in the s U.S. that eats ripe fruits.

fight (fīt) *v.* **fought, fight·ing** *v.t.* 1 To struggle against in battle or physical combat. 2 To box with in a boxing match. 3 To struggle against in any manner. 4 To carry on or engage in (a battle, duel, court action, etc.). 5 To make (one's way) by struggling. 6 To cause to fight, as dogs or gamecocks. —*v.i.* 7 To take part in battle or physical combat. 8 To box, esp. professionally. 9 To struggle in any manner. —**fight shy of** To avoid meeting or facing. —*n.* 1 Conflict or struggle between adversaries. 2 An effort to attain an object in spite of opposition. 3 Power or disposition to fight; pugnacity. [< OE *feohtan*]

fight·er (fī′tər) *n.* 1 One who fights. 2 A pugnacious or spirited person. 3 *Mil.* A fast, highly maneuverable airplane: also **fighter plane.**

fig·ment (fig′mənt) *n.* Something imagined or feigned; a fiction. [< L *figmentum* anything made < *fingere* to form]

fig·ur·a·tion (fig′yə·rā′shən) *n.* 1 The act of shaping something. 2 External form or shape. 3 Representation using figures. 4 *Music* Ornamentation or variation.

fig·ur·a·tive (fig′yər·ə·tiv) *adj.* 1 Of, using, or like a figure or figures of speech; not literal; metaphorical. 2 Of or pertaining to the representation of form or figure. 3 Representing by means of a form or figure; emblematic. —**fig′ur·a·tive·ly** *adv.* —**fig′ur·a·tive·ness** *n.*

fig·ure (fig′yər, *Brit.* fig′ər) *n.* 1 The visible form or outline of something. 2 The human form. 3 A person, esp. if active or prominent in some specific way: a *figure* in world affairs. 4 A representation or likeness of a person or thing. 5 The impression made by a person's appearance or conduct: a sorry *figure.* 6 An illustration, diagram, or drawing. 7 A pattern or design, as in a fabric. 8 a A number or the numeral that represents it. b An amount represented by a number. c *pl.* Mathematical calculations: a head for *figures.* 9 In dancing or skating, a movement or pattern of movements. 10 *Geom.* A surface or space enclosed by lines or planes. 11 *Music* Any short succession of tones or chords that produces a single, complete impression. —*v.* **fig·ured, fig·ur·ing** *v.t.* 1 To make an image, picture, or other representation of; depict. 2 To form an idea or mental image of; imagine. 3 To ornament or mark with a design. 4 To compute numerically; calculate. 5 To express metaphorically; symbolize. 6 *Informal* To think; believe; predict. 7 *Music* To embellish; ornament —*v.i.* 8 To be conspicuous; appear prominently. 9 To make computations; do arithmetic. —**figure in** To include or add in. —**figure on** (or **upon**) 1 To think over; consider. 2 To plan; expect. —**figure out** 1 To reckon; to ascertain. 2 To solve; understand. —**figure up** To total. [< L *figura* form < *fingere* to form] —**fig′ur·er** *n.*

fig·ured (fig′yərd) *adj.* 1 Adorned or marked with designs: *figured* cottons. 2 Represented by figures; pictured.

fig·ure·head (fig′yər·hed′) *n.* 1 A carved or ornamental figure on a prow of a vessel. 2 A person having nominal leadership but no real power.

Figurehead

figure of speech An expression, as a metaphor or simile, that uses words not in their usual or literal sense but to produce a fanciful or vivid impression.

fig·u·rine (fig′yə·rēn′) *n.* A small, ornamental figure made of porcelain, wood, ivory, etc.; a statuette.

fig·wort (fig′wûrt′) *n.* 1 A plant with small, dark-colored flowers, formerly supposed to cure scrofula. 2 Any plant of the figwort family.

Fi·ji (fē′jē) *n.* 1 A group of islands, a member of the Commonwealth of Nations, in the sw Pacific, 7,057 sq. mi., cap. Suva. 2 A native or citizen of Fiji. —**Fi′ji·an** *adj., n.*

fil·a·gree (fil′ə·grē) *n., adj., v.* FILIGREE.

fil·a·ment (fil′ə·mənt) *n.* 1 A fine thread or fiber. 2 Any threadlike structure or appendage. 3 *Bot.* The part of the stamen supporting the anther. • See STAMEN. 4 *Electr.* The slender wire in a lamp bulb that is heated to incandescence by an electric current. • See INCANDESCENT. [< LL *filare* spin < L *filum* a thread] —**fil·a·men·ta·ry** (fil′ə·men′tə·rē), **fil′a·men′tous** *adj.*

fi·lar·i·a (fi·lâr′ē·ə) *n. pl.* **·i·ae** (-i·ē) Any of various parasitic threadworms infecting man and other animals. [< L *filum* a thread] —**fi·lar′i·al, fi·lar′i·an** *adj.*

fil·bert (fil′bərt) *n.* The edible nut of various cultivated hazel trees; hazelnut. [< St. *Philibert,* near whose feast (Aug. 22) these nuts ripen]

filch (filch) *v.t.* To steal slyly and in small amounts; pilfer. [?] —**filch′er** *n.*

file[1] (fīl) *n.* 1 Any device to keep papers in order for reference. 2 A collection of papers, documents, or data arranged for reference. 3 Any orderly succession or line of men or things. —**on file** In or as in a file for reference. —*v.* **filed, fil·ing** *v.t.* 1 To put on file for reference. 2 To send (a news item or story) to a newspaper. 3 To submit (a job application, etc.) for consideration. 4 To institute (a legal action, divorce proceeding, etc.). —*v.i.* 5 To march in file, as soldiers. 6 To make an application, as for a job. [< L *filum* a thread] —**fil′er** *n.*

file[2] (fīl) *n.* 1 A hard steel tool with ridged faces for smoothing or abrading surfaces. 2 Anything used to abrade, smooth, or polish. —*v.t.* **filed, fil·ing** 1 To cut, smooth, or sharpen with a file. 2 To remove with a file: with *away* or *off:* to *file* away rust. [< OE *fīl*] —**fil′er** *n.*

file·fish *n. pl.* **·fish** or **·fish·es** Any of certain fish with prickly scales.

fi·let (fi·lā′, fil′ā) *n.* 1 Net lace having a square mesh. 2 FILLET (def. 2). [< L *filum* thread]

fi·let mi·gnon (fi·lā′ min·yon′, *Fr.* fē·le′ mē·nyôn′) *n. pl.* **fi·lets mi·gnons** A small, choice fillet of beef tenderloin. [F]

fil·i·al (fil′ē·əl, fil′yəl) *adj.* 1 Of, pertaining to, or befitting a son or daughter. 2 *Genetics* Pertaining to a generation following the parental. [< L *filius* a son] —**fil′i·al·ly** *adv.*

fil·i·bus·ter (fil′ə·bus′tər) *n.* 1 A member of a legislative body who attempts to obstruct legislation by prolonged speaking to consume time. 2 An instance of such prolonged speaking. 3 An adventurer who takes part in an unlawful military expedition into a foreign country. —*v.i.* 1 To obstruct legislation by long speeches. 2 To act as a freebooter or adventurer. —*v.t.* 3 To block passage of (legislation) by constant delay. [< Du. *vrijbuiter* freebooter] —**fil′i·bus′ter·er** *n.*

fil·i·gree (fil′ə·grē) *n.* 1 Delicate ornamental work formed of intertwisted gold or silver wire. 2 Anything fanciful and delicate, but purely ornate. —*adj.* Made of or adorned with filigree. —*v.t.* **·greed, ·gree·ing** To adorn with filigree. Also **fil′la·gree.** [< L *filum* thread + *granum* a grain]

fil·ing (fī′ling) *n.* 1 The act of using a file. 2 *Usu. pl.* A particle removed by a file.

Fil·i·pi·no (fil′ə·pē′nō) *n. pl.* **·nos** A native or citizen of the Philippines. —*adj.* Of or pertaining to the Philippines.

fill (fil) *v.t.* 1 To make full; put as much in as possible. 2 To occupy or be diffused through the whole of. 3 To abound in. 4 To stop up or plug: to *fill* a tooth. 5 To supply with what is necessary or ordered: to *fill* a prescription. 6 To occupy (an office or position). 7 To put someone into (an office or position). 8 To feed to fullness. 9 To build up or make full, as an embankment or a ravine, by adding fill. —*v.i.* 10 To become full. —**fill in** 1 To fill completely, as an excavation. 2 To insert (something), as into a blank space. 3 To insert something into (a blank space). 4 To be a substitute. —**fill (someone) in on** *Informal* To bring (someone) up to date on additional details or facts. —**fill out** 1 To become fuller or more rounded. 2 To make complete, as an application. —**fill the bill** *Informal* To do or be what is wanted or needed. —*n.* 1 That which fills or is sufficient to fill or satisfy: to have one's *fill* of adventure. 2 An embankment built up by filling in with stone, gravel, etc. 3 Something, as stone, gravel, etc., used to fill in a hole, depression, etc. [< OE *fyllan* fill]

fill·er (fil′ər) *n.* 1 One who or that which fills. 2 Any substance used for filling, as: a A substance used to add weight or bulk. b A composition for filling pores or holes in wood. c Tobacco used for the inside of cigars. d Paper for a loose-leaf notebook. 3 A brief piece of writing, used to fill space in a newspaper or magazine.

fil·let (fil·lit) *n.* 1 A narrow band or ribbon for binding the hair. 2 (*usu.* fi·lā′, fil′ā) A strip of boneless meat or fish. 3 A thin band or strip of anything. —*v.t.* 1 To bind or adorn with a fillet or band. 2 (*usu.* fil′ā, fi·lā′) To bone and slice into fillets. [< L *filum*]

fill-in (fil′in′) *n.* 1 A person or thing included to fill a gap or omission. 2 *Informal* A summary of facts.

fill·ing (fil′ing) *n.* 1 The act of making or becoming full. 2 Something used to fill a cavity or vacant space. 3 In weaving, the weft or woof. 4 A food mixture used between slices of bread, layers of cake, etc.

filling station SERVICE STATION (def. 1).

fil·lip (fil′əp) *n.* 1 A quick snap or blow with the end of a finger. 2 Anything which serves to stimulate or incite. —*v.t.* 1 To strike or project by or as by a fillip. 2 To stimulate or incite by a fillip. —*v.i.* 3 To make a fillip. [Var. of FLIP]

fil·ly (fil′ē) *n. pl.* **fil·lies** 1 A young mare. 2 *Informal* A sprightly girl. [< ON *fylja*]

film (film) *n.* 1 A thin coating, layer, or membrane. 2 A haze or blur. 3 A flexible roll or sheet of cellulose material coated with light-sensitive emulsion, used for making photographs. 4 **a** A sequence of pictures, each slightly different from the last, photographed on a single strip of film (def. 3) for projection on a screen, giving the optical illusion of continuous, ordered movement. **b** Such films, collectively; the movies. **c** The art of making such films. —*v.t.* 1 To cover or obscure by or as by a film. 2 To photograph, esp. with a motion-picture camera. 3 To record on motion-picture film, as a story or event. —*v.i.* 4 To become covered or obscured by a film. 5 To take motion-picture films. [< OE *filmen* membrane]

film·ic (fil′mik) *adj.* 1 Produced or represented in a motion-picture film. 2 Of, relating to, or suitable for films or filmmaking.

film·mak·ing (film′mā′king, fil′-) *n.* The art or industry of making motion-picture films. —**film′mak′er** *n.*

film·strip (film′strip′) *n.* A length of film containing frames of still pictures projected on a screen, usu. as a visual aid in lectures.

film·y (fil′mē) *adj.* **film·i·er, film·i·est** 1 Of or like a film. 2 Covered with a film; hazy. —**film′i·ly** *adv.* —**film′i·ness** *n.*

fil·ter (fil′tər) *n.* 1 Any device used to strain solid particles or remove impurities from a liquid, air, etc. 2 Any of various devices that on the basis of frequency selectivity block part of a flow of energy, as light, electricity, sound, etc. —*v.t.* 1 To pass (liquids, air, etc.) through a filter. 2 To separate (solid matter, impurities, etc.) from a liquid, air, etc., by a filter. 3 To act as a filter for. —*v.i.* 4 To pass through or as if through a filter. 5 To leak out, as news. [< Med. L *filtrum*] —**fil′ter·er** *n.*

fil·ter·a·ble (fil′tər·ə·bəl) *adj.* 1 That can be separated by filtering. 2 Capable of passing through a filter: *filterable* virus. Also **fil·tra·ble** (fil′trə·bəl). —**fil′ter·a·bil′i·ty** *n.*

filth (filth) *n.* 1 Anything that soils or makes foul. 2 A foul or dirty condition. 3 Moral defilement; obscenity. [< OE *fylth*]

filth·y (fil′thē) *adj.* **filth·i·er, filth·i·est** 1 Of the nature of or containing filth. 2 Obscene. 3 Morally foul. —**filth′i·ly** *adv.* —**filth′i·ness** *n.*

fil·trate (fil′trāt) *v.t.* **·trat·ed, ·trat·ing** FILTER. —*n.* The liquid or other substance that has passed through a filter. [< Med. L *filtrum* a filter] —**fil·tra′tion** *n.*

fin (fin) *n.* 1 A membranous extension from the body of a fish or other aquatic animal, serving to propel, balance, or steer it. 2 Any finlike or projecting part, appendage, or attachment. 3 FLIPPER (def. 2). 4 *Slang* The hand. —*v.* **finned, fin·ning** *v.t.* 1 To cut up or trim off the fins of (a fish). —*v.i.* 2 To beat the water with the fins, as a whale when dying. [< OE *finn*]

fin. finance; financial; finish.

fi·na·gle (fi·nā′gəl) *v.* **·gled, ·gling** *Informal* 1 To get (something) by trickery or deceit. 2 To cheat or trick (someone). —*v.i.* 3 To use trickery or deceit; be sly. 4 In card games, to renege. [?] —**fi·na′gler** *n.*

fi·nal (fī′nəl) *adj.* 1 Being, pertaining to, or coming at the end; ultimate; last. 2 Making further action or controversy unnecessary; conclusive. 3 Relating to or consisting in the end or purpose aimed at: a *final* cause. —*n.* 1 Something that is terminal or last. 2 *Usu. pl.* The last match in a series of games. 3 The last examination of a term in a school or college. [< L *finis* end] —**fi′nal·ly** *adv.*

fi·na·le (fi·nä′lē, -nal′ē) *n.* The last part, as the final scene of a theatrical presentation or the last movement in a musical composition. [Ital., final]

fi·nal·ist (fī′nəl·ist) *n.* A contestant who takes part in the final round of competition.

fi·nal·i·ty (fī·nal′ə·tē) *n. pl.* **·ties** 1 The state or quality of being final. 2 A final, conclusive, or decisive act, determination, offer, etc.

fi·nal·ize (fī′nəl·īz) *v.t.* **·ized, ·iz·ing** To bring to a state of completion. • *Finalize* was formed by the traditional pattern of conversion from adjective to verb that is apparent in such words as *brutalize* and *fertilize.* Although it is considered by some discriminating writers and speakers as an example of bureaucratic jargon, *finalize* has had wide acceptance in both American and British English.

fi·nance (fi·nans′, fī′nans) *n.* 1 The management or science of monetary affairs. 2 *pl.* The monetary resources, as of a country, business, or individual. —*v.t.* **·nanced, ·nanc·ing** 1 To manage the finances of. 2 To supply the money for. [< OF *finer* settle < *fin* end]

fi·nan·cial (fi·nan′shəl, fī-) *adj.* 1 Of or pertaining to finance; monetary. 2 Of or pertaining to those dealing professionally with money and credit. —**fi·nan′cial·ly** *adv.*

fin·an·cier (fin′ən·sir′) *n.* One skilled in or occupied with financial affairs. —*v.i.* To manage financial operations, esp. unscrupulously.

fin·back (fin′bak′) *n.* RORQUAL. Also **finback whale.**

finch (finch) *n.* A small, seed-eating bird, as a bullfinch, goldfinch, or wild canary. [< OE *finc*]

Finch

find (fīnd) *v.* **found, find·ing** *v.t.* 1 To come upon unexpectedly. 2 To perceive or discover, as by search, experience, or examination. 3 To recover (something lost). 4 To reach; arrive at. 5 To give a judicial decision upon. 6 To gain or recover the use of. 7 To consider or think: I *found* the play a bore. —*v.i.* 8 To arrive at and express a judicial decision: to *find* for the plaintiff. —**find oneself** To become aware of one's special ability or vocation. —**find out** To detect or discover. —**find out about** To learn the truth concerning. —*n.* A thing found or discovered. [< OE *findan*]

find·er (fīn′dər) *n.* 1 One who or that which finds. 2 An optical viewer used to aim or focus a camera or large telescope.

fin de siè·cle (faṅ də sye′kl′) *French* The close of the 19th century, viewed as a period of transition in social and moral values.

find·ing (fīn′ding) *n.* 1 The act of one who finds. 2 A discovery or conclusion.

fine[1] (fīn) *adj.* **fin·er, fin·est** 1 Excellent in quality; admirable; superior. 2 Enjoyable; pleasant. 3 Light and delicate, as in texture, etc. 4 Made up of very small particles: *fine* dirt. 5 Thin or narrow: *fine* wire. 6 Very small: *fine* print. 7 Very sharp: a *fine* cutting edge. 8 Cloudless; sunny: *fine* weather. 9 Subtle; acute: a *fine* point. 10 Elegant; cultivated; polished. 11 Overly elegant; pretentious; showy. 12 Refined; pure, as syrup. 13 Containing a specified proportion of pure metal: said of gold or silver. —*adv. Informal* Very much; well. —*v.t. & v.i.* **fined, fin·ing** To make or become fine or finer. [< L *finire* to complete < *finis* end] —**fine′ly** *adv.* —**fine′ness** *n.*

fine[2] (fīn) *n.* An amount of money forfeited as a penalty. —**in fine** Finally. —*v.t.* **fined, fin·ing** To exact a fine from. [< OF *fin* settlement, end]

fine arts The arts of drawing, painting, and sculpture, and often including music, literature, drama, dance, and architecture.

fine-drawn (fīn′drôn′) *adj.* 1 Drawn out finely. 2 Developed very subtly or too subtly.

fine-grained (fīn′grānd′) *adj.* Having a close, fine grain, as some leathers and woods.

fin·er·y (fī′nər·ē) *n. pl.* **·er·ies** Elegant or showy clothes, accessories, decorations, etc.

fines herbes (fēn ârb) *French* A mixture of herbs used to season soups, stews, etc.

fine-spun (fīn′spun′) *adj.* 1 Drawn or spun out to an extreme degree of fineness. 2 Subtle.

fi·nesse (fi·nes′) *n.* 1 Subtle skill or style, as in a performance. 2 Adroit and tactful handling of a situation or person. 3 A stratagem or artifice. 4 In bridge, an attempt to take a trick with a lower card when one holds a higher card, in the hope that the opposing hand yet to play will not hold a taking card of intermediate value. —*v.* **fi·nessed, fi·ness·ing** *v.t.* 1 To change or bring about by finesse. 2 In bridge, to play as a finesse. —*v.i.* 3 To use finesse. 4 In bridge, to make a finesse. [< F *fin* fine[1]]

fine-toothed comb (fīn′tōōtht′) A comb with fine teeth very close together. Also **fine′-tooth′ comb.** —**go over with a fine-toothed comb** To leave no part unsearched or unexamined.

fin·ger (fing′gər) *n.* 1 One of the digits of the hand, esp. excluding the thumb. 2 That part of a glove which covers a finger. 3 Any small projecting piece or part, like a finger. 4 A unit of measure, roughly equal to either the width of a finger or the length of the middle finger. —**burn one's fingers** To suffer the consequences of meddling or interfering. —**have a finger in the pie** 1 To take part in some matter. 2 To meddle. —**have at one's finger tips** To have ready and available knowledge of or access to. —**put one's finger on** To identify or indicate correctly. —**put the finger on** *Slang* 1 To betray to the police. 2 To indicate (the victim) of a planned crime. —**twist around one's (little) finger** To be able to influence or manage with ease. —*v.t.* 1 To touch or handle with the fingers; toy with. 2 To steal; purloin. 3 *Music* a To play (an instrument) with the fingers. b To mark the notes of (music) showing which fingers are to be used. 4 *Slang* To betray. —*v.i.* 5 To touch or feel anything with the fingers. [< OE] —**fin′ger·er** *n.*

fin·ger·board (fing′gər·bôrd′, -bōrd′) *n. Music* The strip of wood upon which the strings are pressed by the fingers of the player of a stringed instrument.

fin·ger·bowl (fing′gər·bōl′) *n.* A bowl containing water for cleansing the fingers at the table after eating.

fin·gered (fing′gərd) *adj.* 1 Having fingers; digitate. 2 *Music* Having notations to mark the fingering.

fin·ger·ing (fing′gər·ing) *n.* 1 The act of touching or feeling with the fingers. 2 *Music* a The act or manner of using the fingers in playing an instrument. b The notation indicating what fingers are to be used.

fin·ger·ling (fing′gər·ling) *n.* A small or young fish, esp. a salmon or trout.

fin·ger·nail (fing′gər·nāl′) *n.* The horny plate at the end of a finger.

fin·ger·print (fing′gər·print′) *n.* An impression of the skin pattern on the inner surface of a finger tip, used for identification. —*v.t.* To take the fingerprints of.

fin·i·al (fin′ē·əl) *n. Archit.* An ornament at the apex of a spire, pinnacle, or the like. [< L *finis* end]

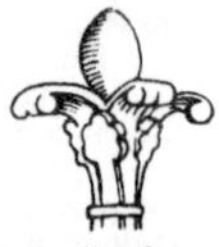
Finial

fin·i·cal (fin′i·kəl) *adj.* FINICKY [< FINE[1]] —**fin′i·cal·ly** *adv.* —**fin′i·cal′i·ty** (-kal′ə·tē), **fin′i·cal·ness** *n.*

fin·ick·ing (fin′i·king) *adj.* FINICKY.

fin·ick·y (fin′i·kē) *adj.* **·ick·i·er, ·ick·i·est** Overly fastidious, precise, or fussy. —**fin′ick·i·ness** *n.*

fi·nis (fin′is, fī′nis) *n. pl.* **fi·nis·es** The end. —**write finis to** To end. [L]

fin·ish (fin′ish) *v.t.* 1 To complete or bring to an end. 2 To come to or reach the end of: to *finish* a trip. 3 To use up entirely. 4 To kill or destroy. 5 To defeat; make powerless. 6 To bring the surface of (wood, leather, etc.) to a desired condition. —*v.i.* 7 To reach or come to an end; stop. —*n.* 1 The conclusion or last stage of anything. 2 Something that finishes or completes. 3 Completeness; perfection. 4 Refinement and poise in manners, speech, etc. 5 The surface quality or texture, as on wood, cloth, etc. 6 A material used to finish a surface, as wax, varnish, etc. 7 Downfall or defeat; also, the cause. [< L *finire* < *finis* end] —**fin′ish·er** *n.* —**Syn.** *v.* 1, 2 terminate, conclude, close. —*n.* 1 end, close, termination, cessation, completion.

fin·ished (fin′isht) *adj.* 1 Carried to a high degree of perfection; polished. 2 Ended; concluded. 3 Very accomplished. 4 Ruined; undone.

finishing school A school in which girls are taught various social graces.

fi·nite (fī′nīt) *adj.* 1 Having boundaries or limits; not infinite. 2 Subject to natural limitations: man's *finite* powers. 3 *Gram.* Limited by number, person, tense, and mood: said of verb forms that can serve as predicates in sentences. —*n.* Finite things collectively, or that which is finite: usu. with *the.* [< L *finitus* limited, pp. of *finire* to end] —**fi′nite·ly** *adv.* —**fi′nite·ness** *n.*

fin·i·tude (fin′ə·tyōōd, fī′nə-) *n.* The quality or condition of being finite.

fink (fingk) *n. Slang* 1 An unpleasant or obnoxious person. 2 A strikebreaker.

Fin·land (fin′lənd) *n.* A republic of N Europe, 117,913 sq. mi., cap. Helsinki.

Finn (fin) *n.* A native or citizen of Finland.

fin·nan had·die (fin′ən had′ē) Smoked haddock. [< *Findhorn*, a Scottish town where originally prepared]

Finn·ish (fin′ish) *adj.* Of or pertaining to Finland, its people, or their language. —*n.* The Finno-Ugric language of Finland.

Fin·no-U·gric (fin′ō·yōō′grik) *n.* A subfamily of the Uralic languages, including Finnish, Estonian, Lapp, Magyar, etc. Also **Fin′no-U′gri·an.**

fin·ny (fin′ē) *adj.* 1 Having fins. 2 Of or like a fish. 3 Abounding in fish.

fiord (fyôrd, fyōrd) *n.* A long, narrow inlet of the sea, with high rocky banks. [Norw.]

fir (fûr) *n.* 1 An evergreen tree of the pine family, cone-bearing and resinous. 2 Its wood. [< OE *fyrh*]

fire (fīr) *n.* 1 The state or form of combustion that is manifested in light, flame, and heat. 2 Something burning: the *fire* in the furnace. 3 A destructive burning: a brush *fire.* 4 Something resembling fire in its brilliance, heat, etc. 5 Intense feeling or enthusiasm; ardor. 6 An intense suffering, severe trial, or ordeal. 7 Torture or death by fire. 8 Vividness, as of imagination. 9 Fever. 10 A discharge of firearms. 11 Any rapid burst or volley: a *fire* of questions. —**between two fires** Exposed to attack, criticism, etc., from both sides. —**catch (on) fire** To ignite. —**hang fire** 1 To fail or delay to discharge. 2 To be delayed, as a decision. —**miss fire** 1 To fail to discharge. 2 To be ineffective; fail. —**on fire** 1 Burning; ablaze. 2 Ardent; zealous. —**open fire** 1 To begin to shoot. 2 To begin; commence. —**set on fire** or **set fire to** 1 To ignite. 2 To excite, as passions. —**take fire** 1 To begin to burn. 2 To begin to respond or be excited. —**under fire** 1 Exposed to gunshot or artillery fire. 2 Exposed to critical or other attack. —*v.* **fired, fir·ing** *v.t.* 1 To set on fire. 2 To tend the fire of: to *fire* a furnace. 3 To bake or expose to heat. 4 To cause to glow or shine. 5 To inflame the emotions or passions of; excite. 6 To discharge, as a gun or bullet. 7 To hurl, as with force: to *fire* questions. 8 To discharge from employment. —*v.i.* 9 To become ignited. 10 To discharge firearms. 11 To discharge a missile. 12 To become inflamed or excited. 13 To tend a fire. —**fire away** To begin, esp. in asking questions. [< OE *fȳr*] —**fir′er** *n.*

fire alarm 1 An alarm calling attention to a fire or its whereabouts. 2 An apparatus for giving an alarm of fire.

fire·arm (fīr′ärm′) *n.* Any weapon, esp. a rifle or pistol, from which a missile, as a bullet, is hurled by an explosive.

fire·ball (fīr′bôl′) *n.* 1 The cloud of intensely hot and glowing material at the center of a nuclear explosion. 2 A very bright meteor. 3 Ball-shaped lightning. 4 *Slang* An aggressive, energetic person.

fire boat A boat equipped to fight fires.

fire·bomb (fīr′bom′) *n.* A bomb designed to cause a fire, usu. on impact. —*v.t.* To attack with a firebomb. —**fire′·bomb′er** *n.*

fire·box (fīr′boks′) *n.* The combustion chamber of a furnace, locomotive, etc.

fire·brand (fīr′brand′) *n.* 1 A burning or glowing piece of wood. 2 A person who causes trouble or dissension.

fire·break (fīr′brāk′) *n.* A strip of plowed or cleared land made to prevent the spread of fire in woods or on a prairie.

fire·brick (fīr′brik′) *n.* A heat-resistant brick, used for lining furnaces.

fire·bug (fīr′bug′) *n. Informal* A person who deliberately sets property on fire; a pyromaniac.

fire·clay (fīr′klā′) *n.* A heat-resistant clay.
fire·crack·er (fīr′krak′ər) *n.* A small paper cylinder charged with gunpowder, designed to explode with a loud noise.
fire·damp (fīr′damp′) *n.* **1** A flammable gas, esp. methane, found in coal mines. **2** An explosive mixture of this gas and air.
fire drill The drilling of persons to accustom them to proper action in case of fire.
fire·eat·er (fīr′ē′tər) *n.* **1** A performer who pretends to eat fire. **2** A hot-headed person eager to fight or quarrel.
fire engine A truck that carries personnel and equipment for fighting fires.
fire escape A means for escaping from a burning building, as a metal stairway or ladder, affixed to an outer wall.
fire extinguisher A portable fire-fighting apparatus containing certain chemicals that are ejected by pressure through a short hose.
fire·fly (fīr′flī′) *n. pl.* **·flies** Any of various luminescent, night-flying beetles.
fire·house (fīr′hous′) *n.* A building for the housing of fire-fighting equipment and personnel.
fire hydrant A hydrant for furnishing water in case of fire.
fire·light (fīr′līt′) *n.* The light from a fire.
fire·man (fīr′mən) *n. pl.* **·men** (-mən) **1** One trained or employed to extinguish fires. **2** One who tends a fire or furnace.
fire·place (fīr′plās′) *n.* A recess or structure built to contain a fire; esp., the part of a chimney that opens into a room.
fire·plug (fīr′plug′) *n.* FIRE HYDRANT.
fire·pow·er (fīr′pou′ər) *n. Mil.* **1** Capacity for delivering fire, as from the guns of a ship. **2** The total amount of fire delivered by a given weapon or unit.
fire·proof (fīr′pro͞of′) *adj.* Resistant to fire; not easily burned. —*v.t.* To make resistant to fire.
fire sale A sale of goods damaged by fire.
fire·side (fīr′sīd′) *n.* **1** The hearth or space about the fireplace. **2** Home. **3** Family life.
fire station FIREHOUSE.
fire·storm (fīr′stôrm′) *n.* A violent, widespread fire, as one caused by a nuclear explosion.
fire·trap (fīr′trap′) *n.* A building in which the danger from fire is great.
fire·wall (fīr′wôl′) *n.* A fireproof wall designed to block the progress of a fire.
fire·wa·ter (fīr′wô′tər, -wot′ər) *n.* Strong liquor: a term first used by North American Indians.
fire·wood (fīr′wo͝od′) *n.* Wood used as fuel.
fire·works (fīr′wûrks′) *n.pl.* **1** Any of various explosive or combustible devices that when ignited produce a brilliant or colored light display and usu. a loud noise. **2** An exhibition of or as of fireworks.
firing line 1 The line of active engagement in battle. **2** The troops within effective rifle range of the enemy. **3** The foremost position in any activity.
firing squad A group of military riflemen assigned to execute a death sentence.
fir·kin (fûr′kən) *n.* A wooden vessel for lard, etc. [< MDu. *vierdelkijn* little fourth]
firm[1] (fûrm) *adj.* **1** Not yielding readily to touch or pressure; solidly composed; compact. **2** Difficult to move; stable. **3** Enduring; steadfast; constant: a *firm* loyalty. **4** Having or showing strength, determination, etc.: a *firm* voice. **5** Not fluctuating widely, as prices. —*v.t. & v.i.* To make or become firm, solid, or compact. —*adv.* Solidly; resolutely; fixedly. [< L *firmus*] **—firm′ly** *adv.* **—firm′ness** *n.* —**Syn.** *adj.* **3** resolute, steady, immovable, true, stout.
firm[2] (fûrm) *n.* **1** A commercial, industrial, or financial partnership. **2** Any business organization. [< L *firmare* to confirm < *firmus* firm]
fir·ma·ment (fûr′mə·mənt) *n.* The expanse of the heavens; sky. [< L *firmamentum* a support] **—fir′ma·men′tal** *adj.*
first (fûrst) *adj.* **1** Preceding all others in the order of numbering. **2** Prior to all others in time; earliest. **3** Nearest or foremost in place from a given point. **4** Highest or foremost in character, rank, etc.; chief. **5** *Music* Of or designating the principal or highest part, voice, or instrument. —**in the first place** To start with. —*n.* **1** One who or that which is first in position, rank, time, etc. **2** The element of an ordered set that corresponds to the number one. **3** The beginning. **4** A winning position in a contest. **5** *Music* The principal or highest part, voice, or instrument. **6** In English universities, the highest rank in examinations for honors; also, one taking the highest rank. **7** *pl.* The best grade of certain commercial products. —**at first** (or **from the first**) At the beginning or origin. —*adv.* **1** Before all others in order, time, place, rank, etc. **2** Preferably; sooner. **3** For the first time. [< OE *fyrst*]
first aid Treatment given in any emergency while awaiting expert medical attention. **—first′-aid′** *adj.*
first base In baseball, the base first reached by the runner, at the right-hand angle of the infield.
first-born (fûrst′bôrn′) *adj.* First brought forth; eldest. —*n.* The child first born.
first-class (fûrst′klas′, -kläs′) *adj.* **1** Belonging to the highest rank or the best quality. **2** Of or designating a class of mail consisting of letters, post cards, or other matter sealed against inspection. **3** Of or using the most expensive accommodations. —*adv.* By first-class accommodations or mail.
first finger The finger next to the thumb; forefinger.
first·hand (fûrst′hand′) *adj. & adv.* Direct from the original source.
first lady The wife of the President of the U.S.
first lieutenant See GRADE.
first·ling (fûrst′ling) *n.* The first of anything.
first·ly (fûrst′lē) *adv.* In the first place; first.
first mortgage A mortgage having priority over all other liens.
first person 1 That form of a pronoun or verb that refers to the speaker or writer, as *I* (or *we*) *understand.* **2** A style of narrative writing in which the writer is or acts as the narrator of the story.
first-rate (fûrst′rāt′) *adj.* Of the finest class, quality, or character. —*adv.* Excellently.
first sergeant See GRADE.
first water 1 The finest quality and purest luster: said of gems. **2** The utmost excellence of anything.
firth (fûrth) *n.* An arm of the sea; estuary.
fis·cal (fis′kəl) *adj.* **1** Of or pertaining to the treasury or finances of a government. **2** Financial. [< L *fiscus* a purse]
fiscal year Any twelve-month period at the end of which financial accounts are balanced.
fish (fish) *n. pl.* **fish** or (with reference to different species) **fish·es 1** A vertebrate, cold-blooded, aquatic animal with gills, usu. scales, and fins. **2** Loosely, any animal habitually living in the water. **3** The flesh of a fish used as food. —*adj.* Of, pertaining to, like, or made from, fish. —*v.t.* **1** To catch or try to catch fish in (a body of water). **2** To catch or try to catch (fish, eels, etc.). **3** To search or grope for and bring out: usu. with *up* or *out.* —*v.i.* **4** To catch or try to catch fish. **5** To try to get something in an artful or indirect manner: usu. with *for:* to *fish* for compliments. [< OE *fisc*] **—fish′a·ble** *adj.*
fish and chips *Brit.* Fish fillets fried in deep fat, and French fried potatoes.
fish bowl (fish′bōl′) *n.* A bowl, usu. glass, serving as a small aquarium for fish.
fish·er (fish′ər) *n.* **1** FISHERMAN. **2** A dark brown, forest-dwelling, weasel-like carnivore of N North America.
fish·er·man (fish′ər·mən) *n. pl.* **·men** (-mən) **1** One who fishes for sport or as an occupation. **2** A fishing boat.
fish·er·y (fish′ər·ē) *n. pl.* **·er·ies 1** The fishing industry. **2** A place for fishing. **3** FISH HATCHERY.
Fishes *n.pl.* PISCES.

Fisher

add, **āce**, **câre**, **pälm**; **end**, **ēven**; **it**, **īce**; **odd**, **ōpen**, **ôrder**; **to͝ok**, **po͞ol**; **up**, **bûrn**; **ə** = *a* in *above*, *u* in *focus;* **yo͞o** = *u* in *fuse;* **oil**; **pout**; **check**; **go**; **ring**; **thin**; **this**; **zh**, *vision.* < derived from; ? origin uncertain or unknown.

fish hatchery A place designed for the propagation, hatching, and nurture of fish.

fish hawk OSPREY.

fish hook A hook, usu. barbed, for catching fish.

fishing tackle The equipment used for fishing, as rod, reel, line, hooks, etc.

fish·meal (fish′mēl′) *n.* Ground dried fish, used as fertilizer or animal food.

fish·mon·ger (fish′mung′gər, -mong′-) *n.* A dealer in fish.

fish story *Informal* An extravagant or incredible narrative.

fish·wife (fish′wīf′) *n. pl.* **·wives** (-wīvz′) **1** A woman who sells fish. **2** A shrill-mouthed, abusive woman.

fish·y (fish′ē) *adj.* **fish·i·er, fish·i·est 1** Of or like fish. **2** Abounding in fish. **3** *Informal* Questionable; improbable. **4** Vacant of expression; dull. **—fish′i·ly** *adv.* **—fish′i·ness** *n.*

fis·sile (fis′əl) *adj.* **1** Capable of being split or undergoing fission. **2** Tending to split. [< L *fissilis* < *findere* to split] **—fis·sil·i·ty** (fi·sil′ə·tē) *n.*

fis·sion (fish′ən) *n.* **1** The act of splitting or breaking apart. **2** *Biol.* The splitting of a unicellular organism into two daughter cells as a mode of asexual reproduction. **3** *Physics* The splitting of an atomic nucleus into particles and smaller nuclei with the release of energy. [< L *fissus,* pp. of *findere* to split] **—fis′sion·a·ble** *adj.*

fis·sure (fish′ər) *n.* **1** A narrow opening, cleft, or crevice. **2** A splitting apart or break; cleavage. *—v.t. & v.i.* **fis·sured, fis·sur·ing** To crack; split; cleave. [< L *fissus,* pp. of *findere* to split]

fist (fist) *n.* **1** The hand closed tightly, as for striking. **2** *Informal* **a** The hand. **b** Handwriting. **3** *Printing* An index mark (☞). *—v.t.* To strike with the fist. [< OE *fyst*]

fist·ful (fist′fŏŏl′) *n. pl.* **·fuls** A handful.

fist·ic (fis′tik) *adj.* Of or pertaining to boxing; pugilistic.

fist·i·cuffs (fis′ti·kufs) *n.pl.* A fight with the fists. [< FIST + *cuff* a blow]

fis·tu·la (fis′chŏŏ·lə) *n. pl.* **·las** or **·lae** (-lē) *Pathol.* An abnormal channel leading from a hollow organ or cavity to the outside or another part of the body. [< L, a pipe] **—fis′tu·lar, fis′tu·lous** *adj.*

fit[1] (fit) *adj.* **fit·ter, fit·test 1** Adapted or suited to an end, purpose, situation, etc. **2** Proper; suitable; appropriate. **3** *Informal* Ready: *fit* to be tied. **4** In good physical condition. *—v.* **fit·ted** or **fit, fit·ting** *v.t.* **1** To be suitable for. **2** To be of the right size and shape for. **3** To make or alter to the proper size: to *fit* a suit. **4** To provide with what is suitable or necessary. **5** To put in place carefully or exactly. *—v.i.* **6** To be suitable or proper. **7** To be of the proper size, shape, etc. *—n.* **1** The condition or manner of fitting. **2** The act of fitting. **3** Something that fits. [ME] **—fit′ness, fit′ter** *n.* **—Syn.** *adj.* **1** apt, pertinent, applicable, relevant, germane, apropos. **2** meet, becoming.

fit[2] (fit) *n.* **1** A sudden onset of a disorder or symptom: a coughing *fit.* **2** Convulsions. **3** A sudden overmastering emotion or feeling: a *fit* of rage. **4** An impulsive or irregular action: a *fit* of industry. **—by fits** (or **by fits and starts**) Spasmodically; irregularly. [< OE *fitt* struggle]

fitch·ew (fich′ōō) *n.* **1** POLECAT (def. 1). **2** The fur of this animal. Also **fitch** (fich). [< MDu. *fisse, vitsche*]

fit·ful (fit′fəl) *adj.* Occurring in or characterized by irregular or uneasy movements, phases, etc.; spasmodic. **—fit′ful·ly** *adv.* **—fit′ful·ness** *n.*

fit·ly (fit′lē) *adv.* In a fit manner or time; properly.

fit·ting (fit′ing) *adj.* Fit or suitable for the intended purpose. *—n.* **1** The act of adjusting, measuring, etc., for a proper fit. **2** A mechanical fixture or part. **3** *pl.* Furnishings or accessories for a house, boat, etc. **—fit′ting·ly** *adv.* **—fit′ting·ness** *n.*

five (fīv) *n.* **1** The sum of four plus one; 5; V. **2** A set or group of five members. [< OE *fīf*] **—five** *adj., pron.*

five-and-ten-cent store (fīv′ən·ten′sent′) A store selling miscellaneous, inexpensive articles. Also **five-and-dime** (fīv′ən·dīm′).

five·fold (fīv′fōld′) *adj.* **1** Made up of five. **2** Five times as much or as great. *—adv.* In a fivefold manner or degree.

Five Nations Five confederated tribes of Iroquois Indians in the NE U.S. and Canada, namely, Mohawks, Oneidas, Onondagas, Cayugas, and Senecas.

fiv·er (fī′vər) *n. Informal* A five-dollar bill or a five-pound note.

fix (fiks) *v.t.* **1** To make firm or secure; attach securely. **2** To set or direct (attention, gaze, etc.) steadily. **3** To look at steadily or piercingly: He *fixed* her with his eyes. **4** To attract and hold, as attention or regard. **5** To decide definitely; settle. **6** To decide or agree on; determine: We *fixed* a date. **7** To place firmly in the mind. **8** To lay, as blame or responsibility, on. **9** To repair, mend, tend to, heal, etc. **10** To arrange or put in order; adjust, as hair. **11** To make ready and cook (food or a meal). **12** *Informal* To arrange or influence the outcome, decision, etc., of (a race, game, jury, etc.) by bribery or collusion. **13** *Informal* To chastise or get even with. **14** To prepare (specimens) for microscopic study. **15** *Chem.* To cause to form a stable compound. **16** *Phot.* To bathe (exposed film) in chemicals which prevent further reaction to light. **17** To regulate or stabilize (wages, prices, etc.). *—v.i.* **18** To become firm or fixed. **19** *Informal* To intend or prepare: I'm *fixing* to go. **—fix on** (or **upon**) To decide upon; choose. **—fix up** *Informal* **1** To repair. **2** To arrange or put in order. **3** To supply the needs of. *—n.* **1** *Informal* A position of embarrassment; dilemma. **2** An observed or calculated position of a ship, aircraft, etc. **3** *Slang* A contest, decision, etc., that has been influenced by bribery or corruption. **4** *Slang* A single shot of an addictive drug. [< L *fixus,* pp. of *figere* fasten] **—fix′a·ble** *adj.* **—fix′er** *n.*

fix·a·tion (fik·sā′shən) *n.* **1** The act of fixing, or the state of being fixed. **2** An obsession. **3** *Psychoanal.* An early-occurring and excessive concentration of the libido on a particular object or person.

fix·a·tive (fik′sə·tiv) *adj.* Serving to render permanent. *—n.* A fixative substance, as a mordant or varnish.

fixed (fikst) *adj.* **1** Firmly attached; stable. **2** Established; unchanging. **3** Resolute; firm. **4** Keeping nearly the same relative position. **5** Equipped: all *fixed* for camp. **6** *Informal* Bribed: a *fixed* jury. **7** *Informal* Provided with money, possessions, etc.: He's well *fixed.* **—fix·ed·ly** (fik′sid·lē) *adv.* **—fix′ed·ness** *n.*

fix·ings (fik′singz) *n. pl. Informal* Accessories; trimmings: a dinner and all the *fixings.*

fix·i·ty (fik′sə·tē) *n. pl.* **·ties 1** The state or quality of being fixed; stability. **2** Anything fixed.

fix·ture (fiks′chər) *n.* **1** Anything fixed firmly in its place. **2** Any permanently attached device or apparatus in a house, store, etc.: a light *fixture.* **3** One so long associated with something as to be considered permanently fixed.

fizz (fiz) *v.i.* To make a hissing noise. *—n.* **1** A hissing noise. **2** An effervescing beverage. [Imit.] **—fizz′y** *adj.*

fiz·zle (fiz′əl) *v.i.* **fiz·zled, fiz·zling 1** To make a hissing noise. **2** *Informal* To fail, esp. after a good start. **—fizzle out** *Informal* To become a failure. *—n.* **1** A spluttering; fizzing. **2** *Informal* A failure. [?]

fjord (fyôrd) *n.* FIORD.

FL Florida (P.O. abbr.).

fl. floor; florin(s); fluid.

Fla. Florida.

flab (flab) *n.* Flabby body tissue. [Back formation < FLABBY]

flab·ber·gast (flab′ər·gast) *v.t. Informal* To astound; confound; amaze.

flab·by (flab′ē) *adj.* **·bi·er, ·bi·est 1** Lacking muscle tone; flaccid. **2** Lacking vigor; feeble. [< FLAP] **—flab′bi·ness** *n.*

flac·cid (flak′sid) *adj.* Lacking firmness or elasticity; flabby. [< L *flaccidus* < *flaccus* limp] **—flac′cid·ly** *adv.* **—flac·cid′i·ty, flac′cid·ness** *n.*

flack (flak) *n. Slang* PRESS AGENT. [?] **—flack′er·y** *n.*

fla·con (fla·kôn′) *n.* A stoppered bottle or flask. [F < Med. L *flasco*]

flag[1] (flag) *n.* **1** A piece of cloth commonly bearing a device or colors and used as a standard, symbol, or signal. **2** The bushy part of the tail of a dog, as that of a setter. **3** The tail of a deer. **4** *pl. Ornithol.* The long feathers on the leg of a hawk or other bird of prey. **5** *Music* Any of the flag-shaped lines extending from the stem of certain notes to indicate their value. *—v.t.* **flagged, flag·ging 1** To mark out or adorn with flags. **2** To signal with a flag. **—flag down** To cause to stop, as a train, by signaling. [?] **—flag′ger** *n.*

flag[2] (flag) *n.* **1** Any of various plants having sword-shaped leaves and growing in moist places; iris. 2 The leaf of a flag. —*v.t.* **flagged, flag·ging** To calk the seams of (a cask) with flags or rushes. [ME *flagge*]

flag[3] (flag) *v.i.* **flagged, flag·ging 1** To become tired or weak. **2** To become limp. [?]

flag[4] (flag) *n.* Split stone for paving; a flagstone. —*v.t.* **flagged, flag·ging** To pave with flagstones. [< ON *flaga* slab of stone] **—flag′ger** *n.*

Flag Day June 14, a holiday commemorating the adoption of the official U.S. flag on June 14, 1777.

flag·el·lant (flaj′ə·lənt, flə·jel′ənt) *n.* A person given to whipping himself or being whipped, to secure pardon from sin or to excite himself sexually. Also **flag′el·la′tor.** [< L *flagellum* a whip]

flag·el·late (flaj′ə·lāt) *v.t.* **·lat·ed, ·lat·ing** To whip; scourge. —*n. Biol.* A protozoan having one or more whiplike processes. —*adj. Biol.* Having or resembling a flagellum: also **flag′el·lat′ed. —flag′el·la′tion** *n.*

fla·gel·lum (flə·jel′əm) *n. pl.* **·la** (-ə) **1** *Biol.* A lashlike appendage, as the mobile process of certain protozoa. **2** *Bot.* RUNNER (def. 5). **3** A whip. [L, whip]

flag·eo·let (flaj′ə·let′) *n.* A flute blown at the end instead of at the side. [F, dim. of OF *flageol*]

Flageolet

flag·ging[1] (flag′ing) *adj.* Growing weak; becoming languid or exhausted: *flagging* spirits.

flag·ging[2] (flag′ing) *n.* **1** A pavement of flagstones; also, flagstones collectively. **2** The act of paving with flagstones.

fla·gi·tious (flə·jish′əs) *adj.* Flagrantly wicked; atrocious; heinous. [< L *flagitium* disgraceful act] **—fla·gi′tious·ly** *adv.* **—fla·gi′tious·ness** *n.*

flag officer Any naval officer above the rank of captain who is entitled to fly the flag of his command.

flag·on (flag′ən) *n.* A vessel with a handle, spout, and lid, used to serve liquors. [< Med. L *flasco* < Gmc.]

flag·pole (flag′pōl′) *n.* A pole on which a flag is displayed. Also **flag′staff′** (-staf′, -stäf′)

fla·grant (flā′grənt) *adj.* Openly scandalous; notorious. [< L *flagrare* to blaze, burn] **—fla′grance, fla′gran·cy** *n.* **—fla′grant·ly** *adv.* **—Syn.** glaring, outrageous, shocking.

flag·ship (flag′ship′) *n.* The ship in a naval formation that carries a flag officer and displays his flag.

flag·stone (flag′stōn′) *n.* A broad, flat stone suitable for pavements.

flail (flāl) *n.* An implement consisting of a wooden bar (the swingle) hinged or tied to a handle, for separating grain by beating. —*v.t. & v.i.* To beat with or as with a flail. [< L *flagellum* a whip]

flair (flâr) *n.* **1** Talent; aptitude. **2** Discernment; taste. **3** *Informal* A dashing style or quality. [< L *fragrare* to give off a smell]

flak (flak) *n.* **1** Anti-aircraft fire. **2** *Informal* Criticism: political *flak.* [G < *Fl(ieger)* aircraft + *A(bwehr)* defense + *K(anonen)* guns]

flake[1] (flāk) *n.* **1** A thin piece of anything; scale; fleck. **2** A small flat mass: a *flake* of snow. —*v.t. & v.i.* **flaked, flak·ing 1** To peel off in flakes. **2** To form into flakes. **3** To spot or become spotted with flakes. [< Scand.]

flake[2] (flāk) *v.* **flaked, flak·ing** *Slang v.i.* **1** To retire or go to sleep, as from exhaustion: usu. with *out.* —*v.t.* **2** To fatigue; exhaust: usu. with *out.*

flak·y (flā′kē) *adj.* **flak·i·er, flak·i·est 1** Resembling or consisting of flakes. **2** Easily separable into flakes. **—flak′i·ly** *adv.* **—flak′i·ness** *n.*

flam·beau (flam′bō) *n. pl.* **·beaux** (-bōz) A burning torch. [F< OF *flamme* flame]

flam·boy·ant (flam·boi′ənt) *adj.* **1** Characterized by extravagance; showy; bombastic. **2** Ornate. **3** Having a wavy edge, as of flame. [F< OF *flambe* flame] **—flam·boy′ance, flam·boy′an·cy** *n.* **—flam·boy′ant·ly** *adv.*

flamboyant architecture A highly florid style of French Gothic architecture.

flame (flām) *n.* **1** The burning, luminous gas of a fire; blaze. **2** A state of luminous burning. **3** Excitement or passion. **4** *Slang* A sweetheart. —*v.* **flamed, flam·ing** *v.i.* **1** To give out flame; blaze; burn. **2** To light up or burn as if on fire; flash. **3** To become enraged or excited. **—flame up** To erupt in or as in flames. [< L *flamma*] **—flam′er** *n.* **—flam′ing·ly** *adv.*

fla·men·co (flə·meng′kō, -men′-, flä-) *n.* A style of singing and dancing practiced by the gypsies of Andalusia. [Sp., Flemish, because the gypsies were thought to be from Flanders]

flame·out (flām′out′) *n.* The sudden loss of the flame in a jet engine.

flame-throw·er (flām′thrō′ər) *n. Mil.* A weapon that throws a stream of burning fuel.

fla·min·go (flə·ming′gō) *n. pl.* **·gos** or **·goes** A long-necked bird of a pink or red color, having very long legs. [< Pg. *flamingo* or Sp. *flamenco*]

Flamingo

flam·ma·ble (flam′ə·bəl) *adj.* Easily set on fire and likely to burn rapidly; highly combustible. **—flam′ma·bil′i·ty** *n.*

flange (flanj) *n.* A projecting rim or edge, as on a car wheel, etc., used for guidance, strength, or attachment to another object. —*v.* **flanged, flang·ing** *v.t.* To supply with a flange. [?< OF *flangir* to bend]

flank (flangk) *n.* **1** The hind part of an animal's side, between the ribs and the hip. • See HORSE. **2** A cut of meat from this part. **3** The side of anything. **4** The side, right or left, of a military force or marching column. —*v.t.* **1** To be on one or both sides of. **2** *Mil.* **a** To get around and in back of (an enemy position or unit). **b** To attack the flank of. —*adj.* Of, on, or from the flank or side. [< OF *flanc*] **—flank′er** *n.*

flan·nel (flan′əl) *n.* **1** A loosely-woven, soft fabric of wool, or of cotton and wool. **2** *pl.* Clothing made of flannel, esp. heavy underwear. [?< Welsh *gwlān* wool] **—flan′nel·ly** *adj.*

flan·nel·et (flan′əl·et′) *n.* A cotton fabric similar to flannel. Also **flan′nel·ette′.**

flap (flap) *n.* **1** A broad, thin, and loosely hanging part or attachment. **2** The motion of such a part. **3** A movable control surface along the rear edge of a wing of an airplane. **4** *Slang* An agitated or tempestuous reaction. —*v.* **flapped, flap·ping** *v.t.* **1** To move by beating: to *flap* the wings. **2** To move with a flapping sound. **3** To strike with something flat and flexible. —*v.i.* **4** To move by beating the wings. **5** To move as if blown by the wind. **6** *Slang* To lose one's composure. [Imit.]

flap·jack (flap′jak′) *n.* A griddle cake or pancake.

flap·per (flap′ər) *n.* **1** One who or that which flaps. **2** *Informal* A young girl, esp. in the 1920's, given to exaggerated styles and to sophisticated conduct.

flare (flâr) *v.* **flared, flar·ing** *v.i.* **1** To blaze or burn with a brilliant, wavering light. **2** To break out in sudden emotion: often with *up* or *out.* **3** To open or spread outward. —*v.t.* **4** To cause to flare. —*n.* **1** A large, bright, but unsteady light. **2** A signaling device that makes a clear, bright flame. **3** A widening or spreading outward, as of the sides of a funnel; also, the part that widens or spreads out. [?] **—flar′ing·ly** *adv.* **—Syn.** *v.* **1,** *n.* **1** flash, flicker, glare, shine.

flare-up (flâr′up′) *n.* **1** A sudden outburst of flame or light. **2** A sudden outbreak of anger.

flash (flash) *v.i.* **1** To break forth with light or fire suddenly and briefly. **2** To gleam; glisten. **3** To move very quickly. **4** To be known or perceived in an instant. —*v.t.* **5** To send forth (fire, light, etc.) in brief flashes. **6** To send or communicate with great speed. **7** *Informal* To display briefly or ostentatiously: to *flash* a badge. —*n.* **1** A sudden gleam of light. **2** A sudden outburst, as of anger. **3** A moment; instant. **4** Display; esp., a vulgar, showy display. **5** A brief news dispatch. —*adj.* **1** Obtained by flashlight, as a photograph. **2** Flashy; smart; sporty. [ME *flaschen*] **—flash′er** *n.,* **flash′ing·ly** *adv.*

flash·back (flash′bak′) *n.* **1** In fiction, motion pictures, etc., a break in continuity made by the presentation of a scene or event occurring earlier. **2** Such a scene or event.

flash bulb An electric bulb that makes a short, bright flash, used in photography.

flash burn A severe burn produced by exposure to intense heat, esp. that of a nuclear explosion.

flash·cube (flash′kyōōb′) *n.* A small, rotatable cube containing four flash bulbs for use with a camera.

flash flood A sudden, brief flood.

flash gun A device that holds a flashbulb and supplies electricity to trigger it.

flash·ing (flash′ing) *n.* **1** The act of one who or that which flashes. **2** A metal joint or flange used to keep a roof watertight. —*adj.* Emitting flashes. —**flash′ing·ly** *adv.*

flash lamp A lamp for taking flash photographs.

flash·light (flash′līt′) *n.* **1** A small, portable electric light powered by batteries. **2** A light, as in a lighthouse, shown only at regular intervals. **3** A brief and brilliant light for taking photographs.

flash·y (flash′ē) *adj.* **flash·i·er, flash·i·est** **1** Pretentious and cheap; showy; tawdry. **2** Flashing or bright for a moment. —**flash′i·ly** *adv.* —**flash′i·ness** *n.*

flask (flask, fläsk) *n.* **1** Any of variously shaped receptacles, usu. of glass, used in laboratory work. **2** A small container, often of metal, for carrying liquids or liquor on the person. [< Med. L *flasco*]

flat[1] (flat) *adj.* **flat·ter, flat·test** **1** Having a plane, usu. horizontal surface. **2** Broad, level, and thin: a *flat* board. **3** Having full contact with another surface. **4** Lying prone upon the ground; prostrate. **5** Positive; absolute: a *flat* refusal. **6** Having little flavor or sparkle: a *flat* drink. **7** Without air: a *flat* tire. **8** Having little activity; slow: a *flat* market. **9** Not varying; uniform: a *flat* rate. **10** *Music* **a** Below the true or right pitch. **b** Lowered by a semitone. **c** Having flats in the signature. **11** Without gloss, as a painted surface. **12** In painting: **a** Uniform in tint. **b** Lacking contrast and perspective: *flat* figures. —*adv.* **1** In a flat state or position. **2** In a flat manner. **3** *Music* Below the true pitch. **4** Exactly; precisely: It weighed ten pounds *flat*. —**flat out** *Informal* **1** With maximum effort; all-out. **2** Openly: to say *flat out* that he's a liar. —*n.* **1** A flat surface. **2** A strip of level land, esp. low meadowland over which the tide flows. **3** *Usu. pl.* Shoal. **4** Anything that is flat. **5** *Music* **a** A tone a half step lower than a tone from which it is named, identified by the character ♭. **b** The character ♭. **6** A wooden frame covered with canvas, used as stage scenery. **7** A deflated pneumatic tire. **8** A shallow, earth-filled tray for seed germination. —*v.t. & v.i.* **flat·ted, flat·ting** To make or become flat. [< ON *flatr*] —**flat′tish** *adj.* —**flat′ly** *adv.* —**flat′ness** *n.*

flat[2] (flat) *n.* A set of rooms on one floor; apartment. [< OE *flet* floor]

flat·boat (flat′bōt′) *n.* A large boat with a flat bottom, for freighting merchandise.

flat-bot·tomed (flat′bot′əmd) *adj.* Having the bottom flat: usu. said of boats.

flat·car (flat′kär′) *n.* A railroad freight car, usu. without sides or covering.

flat·fish (flat′fish′) *n. pl.* **·fish** or **·fish·es** Any of various marine fishes having a compressed body and both eyes on one side, as the flounder, halibut, sole, etc.

flat·foot (flat′fo͝ot′) *n.* **1** An abnormal foot condition in which the entire sole touches the ground. **2** *Slang* A policeman.

flat-foot·ed (flat′fo͝ot′id) *adj.* **1** Having flat feet. **2** Uncompromising; resolute; positive. —**flat′-foot′ed·ly** *adv.*

flat·i·ron (flat′ī′ərn) *n.* An iron without a built-in heat source, used for pressing cloth.

flat silver Silver spoons, knives, forks, etc.

flat·ten (flat′n) *v.t. & v.i.* **1** To make or become flat or flatter. **2** To make or become prostrate. —**flat′ten·er** *n.*

flat·ter (flat′ər) *v.t.* **1** To praise unduly or insincerely. **2** To try to win over by flattery. **3** To please or gratify. **4** To represent too favorably: The picture *flatters* her. **5** To display to advantage. —*v.i.* **6** To use flattery. —**flatter oneself** To believe: I *flatter* myself that my gifts are acceptable. [< OF *flater* fawn, caress] —**flat′ter·er** *n.* —**flat′ter·ing·ly** *adv.*

flat·ter·y (flat′ər·ē) *n. pl.* **·ter·ies** **1** The act of flattering. **2** Undue or insincere praise. —**Syn.** **2** adulation, acclamation, compliments, plaudits.

flat·top (flat′top′) *n. Slang* **1** An aircraft carrier. **2** A crew cut.

flat·u·lence (flach′ə·ləns, -yo͞o-) *n.* **1** Gas in the stomach or intestines. **2** Pompousness; vanity. Also **flat′u·len·cy.** [< L *flatus* a blowing < *flare* to blow] —**flat′u·lent, flat′u·ous** *adj.* —**flat′u·lent·ly** *adv.*

flat·ware (flat′wâr′) *n.* **1** Dishes that are more or less flat. **2** Knives, forks, and spoons.

flat·worm (flat′wûrm′) *n.* Any of a large group of unsegmented, flat-bodied worms, often parasitic, as the tapeworm.

flaunt (flônt) *v.i.* **1** To make an ostentatious display. **2** To wave or flutter freely. —*v.t.* **3** To display in an ostentatious or impudent manner. —*n.* **1** The act of flaunting. **2** A boast; vaunt. [?< Scand.] —**flaunt′y** *adj.* **(·i·er, ·i·est)** —**flaunt′ing·ly** *adv.* —**flaunt′er** *n.* • *Flaunt* and *flout* should not be confused. To *flaunt* is to wave or make an ostentatious display. To *flout* is to regard with contempt: to *flout* convention.

flau·tist (flô′tist) *n.* FLUTIST.

fla·vin (flā′vən) *n.* **1** Any of a group of natural yellow pigments, as riboflavin, etc. **2** A yellow dye derived from coal tar. Also **fla·vine** (flā′vēn). [< L *flavus* yellow + -IN]

fla·vor (flā′vər) *n.* **1** The quality of a thing that affects the sense of taste. **2** Odor; scent. **3** Distinctive quality. **4** Flavoring. —*v.t.* To give flavor or any distinguishing quality to. *Brit. sp.,* **fla′vour.** [< OF *flaor*] —**fla′vor·less, fla′vor·ous, fla′vor·y** *adj.*

fla·vor·ing (flā′vər·ing) *n.* A substance, as an essence or extract, for giving flavor.

flaw (flô) *n.* **1** An inherent defect, as in construction. **2** A crack; fissure. **3** A fault or error. —*v.t. & v.i.* To make or become defective or faulty. [< ON *flaga* slab of stone] —**flaw′less** *adj.* —**flaw′less·ly** *adv.* —**flaw′less·ness** *n.*

flax (flaks) *n.* **1** A plant with blue flowers, having a seed, called *flaxseed* or *linseed,* and a fibrous stem. **2** The soft fiber of the flax plant, used in the manufacture of linen. [< OE *fleax*] —**flax′y** *adj.* **(·i·er, ·i·est)**

flax·en (flak′sən) *adj.* **1** Of, pertaining to, or like flax. **2** Of a light golden color.

flax·seed (flaks′sēd′, flak′-) *n.* The seed of the flax plant; linseed.

flay (flā) *v.t.* **1** To strip off the skin from. **2** To attack with scathing criticism. **3** To pillage; rob. [< OE *flēan*] —**flay′er** *n.*

flea (flē) *n.* A jumping, wingless insect that feeds upon the blood of mammals or birds. [< OE *flēa*]

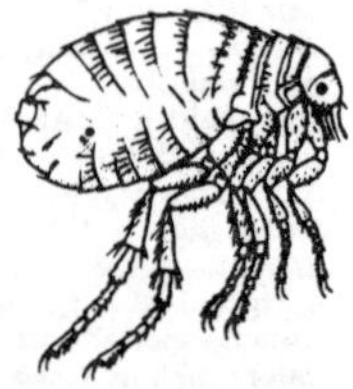

Flea

flea·bane (flē′bān′) *n.* Any of various plants supposed to repel fleas.

flea-bit·ten (flē′bit′n) *adj.* **1** Bitten by or swarming with fleas. **2** Squalid; shabby.

fleck (flek) *n.* **1** A dot or speck. **2** A particle; flake. —*v.t.* To mark with flecks. [? ON *flekkr* spot]

flec·tion (flek′shən) *n.* **1** The act of bending. **2** A curved or bent part. [< L *flectere* to bend] —**flec′tion·al** *adj.*

fled (fled) *p.t. & p.p.* of FLEE.

fledge (flej) *v.* **fledged, fledg·ing** *v.t.* **1** To furnish with feathers, as an arrow. **2** To bring up (a young bird) until ready for flight. —*v.i.* **3** To grow enough feathers for flight. [< OE *-flycge* feathered in *unflycge* not ready to fly]

fledg·ling (flej′ling) *n.* **1** A young bird just fledged. **2** A tyro; an inexperienced person. Also **fledge′ling.**

flee (flē) *v.* **fled, flee·ing** *v.i.* **1** To run away, as from danger. **2** To move away quickly; disappear. **3** To leave abruptly. —*v.t.* **4** To run away from. [< OE *flēon*] —**fle′er** *n.* —**Syn.** **3** decamp, depart, escape, fly.

fleece (flēs) *n.* **1** The wool coat of a sheep. **2** The wool sheared from a sheep at one time. **3** Anything like fleece. **4** A textile fabric with a soft, silky pile. —*v.t.* **fleeced, fleec·ing** **1** To shear the fleece from. **2** To defraud; cheat. [< OE *flēos*] —**fleec′er** *n.*

fleec·y (flē′sē) *adj.* **fleec·i·er, fleec·i·est** Pertaining to, like, or covered with a fleece. **—fleec′i·ly** *adv.* **—fleec′i·ness** *n.*

fleer (flir) *v.t.* **1** To jeer at. *—v.i.* **2** To sneer. *—n.* **1** Derision or scorn. **2** A leer. [< Scand.] **—fleer′ing·ly** *adv.*

fleet[1] (flēt) *adj.* Moving swiftly; rapid. *—v.i.* To move swiftly. [< OE *flēotan* to float] **—fleet′ly** *adv.* **—fleet′ness** *n.*

fleet[2] (flēt) *n.* **1** A number of vessels under one command. **2** The entire number of vessels belonging to one government; a navy. **3** A number of vessels, aircraft, or vehicles engaged in the same activity: a fishing *fleet;* a *fleet* of trucks. [< OE *flēot* ship]

fleet·ing (flē′ting) *adj.* Passing quickly; transitory. **—fleet′ing·ly** *adv.* **—fleet′ing·ness** *n.*

Flem·ish (flem′ish) *adj.* Of or pertaining to Flanders, its people, or language. *—n.* **1** The people of Flanders. **2** The Low German language of Flanders.

flesh (flesh) *n.* **1** The soft tissues of a human or animal body, esp. the muscular portions. **2** Meat, esp. that of mammals. **3** The human body as opposed to the spirit. **4** Mankind. **5** All creatures. **6** The sensual side of human nature. **7** The color of a white person's skin. **8** The soft, edible parts of fruits and vegetables. **—in the flesh 1** In person. **2** Alive. **—own flesh and blood** One's family; relatives. *—v.t.* **1** To initiate, as troops, in a first battle experience. **2** To incite, as hawks, for hunting by feeding with meat. **3** To make fat. **—flesh out** To give substance to: to *flesh out* an idea. [< OE *flæsc*] **—flesh′less** *adj.*

flesh-col·ored (flesh′kul′ərd) *adj.* Having the color of the skin of a white person.

flesh·ly (flesh′lē) *adj.* **·li·er, ·li·est 1** Pertaining to the body; corporeal. **2** Sensual; carnal. **3** Fleshy; fat; plump. *—adv.* In a fleshly manner. **—flesh′li·ness** *n.*

flesh·pot (flesh′pot′) *n.* **1** A pot to cook meat in. **2** *pl.* Any form of indulgence; luxury.

flesh·y (flesh′ē) *adj.* **flesh·i·er, flesh·i·est 1** Having much flesh; plump; fat. **2** Of, pertaining to, or like flesh. **3** Consisting of firm pulp; succulent, as a peach or an apple. **—flesh′i·ness** *n.*

fleur-de-lis (flœr′də·lē′, -lēs′) *n. pl.* **fleurs-de-lis** (-də·lēz′) **1** IRIS (defs. 2 & 3). **2** An ornament or heraldic device having the shape of an iris. Also **fleur′-de-lys′.** [F, flower of lily]

Fleur-de-lis

flew (flōō) *p.t.* of FLY[1].

flex (fleks) *v.t.* & *v.i.* **1** To bend. **2** To contract, as a muscle. *—n. Brit.* A pliant insulated electric cord. [< L *flexus,* pp. of *flectere* bend] **—flex·ion** (flek′shən) *n.*

flex·i·ble (flek′sə·bəl) *adj.* **1** Capable of being bent without breaking; pliant. **2** Tractable; yielding; compliant. Also **flex·ile** (flek′sil). **—flex′i·bil′i·ty, flex′i·ble·ness** *n.* **—flex′i·bly** *adv.*

flex·or (flek′sər) *n.* A muscle that contracts to bend a joint.

flex·time (fleks′tīm′) *n.* The system of allowing workers to arrange their own convenient working hours.

flex·u·ous (flek′shōō·əs) *adj.* **1** Winding or turning about. **2** Unsteady; wavering. [< L *flexus.* See FLEX.] **—flex·u·os·i·ty** (flek′shōō·os′ə·tē) *n.*

flex·ure (flek′shər) *n.* **1** The state of being bent or flexed. **2** A bent part; turn; curve.

flib·ber·ti·gib·bet (flib′ər·tē·jib′it) *n.* An impulsive, flighty, or gossipy person. Also **flib′ber·di·gib′bit, flib′ber·ty·gib′bet.** [Imit.]

flick[1] (flik) *v.t.* **1** To strike with a quick, light stroke, as with a whip. **2** To remove with such a motion: to *flick* dust. **3** To cause to snap, as a whip. *—v.i.* **4** To move in a quick, darting manner. **5** To flutter. *—n.* **1** A quick, light stroke, as with a whip. **2** The sound of such a stroke. **3** A streak or splash. [Imit.]

flick[2] (flik) *n. Slang* A movie. [Short for FLICKER[1]]

flick·er[1] (flik′ər) *v.i.* **1** To burn or shine with an unsteady light. **2** To move jerkily, as lightning. **3** To flutter the wings. *—v.t.* **4** To cause to flicker. *—n.* **1** A waving light. **2** A flickering or fluttering motion. [< OE *flicorian* move the wings] **—flick′er·ing·ly** *adv.* **—flick′er·y** *adj.* **—Syn.** *n.* **1,** *v.* **1** flare, glimmer, sparkle, twinkle.

flick·er[2] (flik′ər) *n.* Any of several species of woodpecker. [Imit.]

Flicker

flied (flīd) *p.t.* & *p.p.* of FLY[1] (def. 7).

fli·er (flī′ər) *n.* **1** That which flies. **2** A pilot of an aircraft. **3** A printed handbill. **4** *Informal* A venture, as in the stock market.

flight (flīt) *n.* **1** The act, process, or power of flying. **2** The distance flown. **3** A group or flock flying through the air together. **4** A single trip of an airplane. **5** In the U.S. Air Force, a tactical unit of two or more aircraft. **6** A soaring and sustained effort or utterance. **7** A continuous series of stairs or steps. **8** The act of fleeing. **—put to flight** To cause to flee or run; rout. [< OE *flyht*] **—flight′less** *adj.*

flight·y (flī′tē) *adj.* **flight·i·er, flight·i·est 1** Silly; capricious; frivolous. **2** Easily excited or confused; unstable. **—flight′i·ly** *adv.* **—flight′i·ness** *n.*

flim·sy (flim′zē) *adj.* **·si·er, ·si·est 1** Not substantial or solid: a *flimsy* chair. **2** Ineffective; trivial: a *flimsy* reason. *—n. pl.* **flim·sies** A thin paper used for carbon copies. [? < FILM] **—flim′si·ly** *adv.* **—flim′si·ness** *n.*

flinch (flinch) *v.i.* To shrink back, as from pain or danger; wince. *—n.* Any act of flinching. [< OF *flenchir, flechier* to bend] **—flinch′er** *n.* **—flinch′ing·ly** *adv.*

fling (fling) *v.* **flung, fling·ing** *v.t.* **1** To throw with violence; hurl. **2** To cast off. **3** To put abruptly or violently. **4** To hurl (oneself) into something completely. **5** To overthrow, as in wrestling. **6** To emit, as a fragrance. *—v.i.* **7** To move or rush, as with anger. *—n.* **1** The act of flinging. **2** A try; attempt. **3** A time of lively action or indulgence. **4** A lively Scottish dance. [< Scand.] **—fling′er** *n.*

flint (flint) *n.* **1** A very hard, dull-colored variety of quartz which produces a spark when struck with steel. **2** A piece of material from which sparks are easily struck. **3** Anything very hard or cruel. [< OE]

flint glass A soft, lead-oxide glass, used esp. for lenses.

flint·lock (flint′lok′) *n.* **1** A gunlock in which a flint was used to ignite the powder in the pan. **2** A firearm equipped with such a gunlock.

Flintlock

flint·y (flin′tē) *adj.* **flint·i·er, flint·i·est 1** Made of, containing, or resembling flint. **2** Hard; obdurate. **—flint′i·ly** *adv.* **—flint′i·ness** *n.*

flip[1] (flip) *v.* **flipped, flip·ping** *v.t.* **1** To throw or put in motion with a jerk; flick. **2** To toss, as a coin. *—v.i.* **3** To move with a jerk. **4** To strike lightly and quickly. **5** *Slang* To lose one's sanity or self-control, as from joy, anger, wonder, etc.: often with *out.* *—n.* A quick movement; flick. [?]

flip[2] (flip) *adj. Informal* Casual to the point of impudence; flippant. [Short for FLIPPANT]

flip-flop (flip′flop′) *n.* A somersault or handspring.

flip·pant (flip′ənt) *adj.* Marked by a lack of concern or respect; impertinent; disrespectful. [< FLIP[1]] **—flip′pan·cy, flip′pant·ness** *n.* **—flip′pant·ly** *adv.*

flip·per (flip′ər) *n.* **1** A flattened limb used in swimming, as by seals, etc. **2** A rubber shoe having a long, paddlelike piece, used by skin divers and other swimmers. **3** *Slang* The hand.

flirt (flûrt) *v.i.* **1** To play at courtship by trying to attract attention or admiration. **2** To trifle; toy: to *flirt* with danger. **3** To move with sudden jerk motions. *—v.t.* **4** To toss or throw with a jerk. *—n.* **1** A person who flirts. **2** A flirting motion; fling. [?] **—flir·ta′tion, flirt′er** *n.* **—flirt′y** *adj.*

flir·ta·tious (flər·tā′shəs) *n.* Inclined to flirt. **—flir·ta′tious·ly** *adv.* **—flir·ta′tious·ness** *n.*

flit (flit) *v.* **flit·ted, flit·ting** *v.i.* **1** To move or pass rapidly and lightly. **2** To pass away, as time. *—n.* A flitting motion. [< ON *flytja* remove, move] **—flit′ter** *n.*

flitch (flich) *n.* A side of a hog salted and cured; side of bacon. *—v.t.* To cut into flitches. [< OE *flicce*]

flit·ter (flit′ər) *v.t.* & *v.i.* To flutter; flit. [Freq. of FLIT]

fliv·ver (fliv′ər) *n.* A cheap automobile. [?]

float (flōt) *v.i.* **1** To rest on the surface of a liquid. **2** To drift on the surface of a liquid, in air, etc. 3 To move or drift without purpose. 4 To hover; stay vaguely: The image *floated* in his mind. —*v.t.* 5 To cause to rest on the surface of a liquid. 6 To put in circulation; place on sale: to *float* a loan. 7 To irrigate; flood. —*n.* 1 An object that floats, as a cork on a bait line or a hollow ball in a tank. 2 A truck or wheeled platform, decorated for display in a pageant. [<OE *flotian* float] —**float'a·ble** *adj.*

float·a·tion (flō·tā'shən) *n.* FLOTATION.

float·er (flō'tər) *n.* 1 *Informal* A voter who votes fraudulently elsewhere than in his own district. 2 A vagrant.

float·ing (flō'ting) *adj.* 1 Buoyed up by a liquid or gas. 2 Not settled or attached; moving about. 3 Not in the normal position: a *floating* kidney. 4 Not funded: said of short-term debts. 5 Not invested permanently: said of capital. —*n.* The act of floating. —**float'ing·ly** *adv.*

floating ribs The two lowest pairs of ribs in a human being, attached to the vertebrae but not to the sternum or to the other ribs.

floc·cu·late (flok'yə·lāt) *v.t. & v.i.* **·lat·ed, ·lat·ing** To gather or be joined together in loose masses, as soil, clouds, etc. [<L *floccus* lock of wool] —**floc'cu·la'tion** *n.*

floc·cu·lent (flok'yə·lənt) *adj.* 1 Resembling wool; woolly; fluffy. 2 Covered with a soft, waxy secretion. 3 Coalescing in flakes. [<L *floccus* lock of wool]

flock[1] (flok) *n.* 1 A company or collection of animals, as sheep, goats, or birds. 2 The members of a church. 3 A company of persons; a crowd. —*v.i.* To assemble or go in flocks, crowds, etc.; congregate. [<OE *flocc*] —**Syn.** *n.* 1 bevy, drove, flock, herd.

flock[2] (flok) *n.* 1 A tuft of wool or the like. 2 Short refuse wool or cotton, used as stuffing and in upholstery. [Prob. < L *floccus* lock of wool]

floe (flō) *n.* A massive, flat sheet of floating ice; also, a broken piece of such ice floating freely. [?<ON *flo* a layer]

flog (flog, flôg) *v.t.* **flogged, flog·ging** 1 To beat with a whip, rod, etc. 2 To work to a punishing degree: to *flog* one's memory. 3 *Brit. Informal* To sell, esp. fraudulently or illegally. [?<L *flagellare*] —**flog'ger** *n.*

flood (flud) *n.* 1 An unusually large overflow of water onto land. 2 The coming in of the tide. 3 A copious flow or stream, as of sunlight, lava, etc. 4 A stage light that throws a broad beam. —*v.t.* 1 To cover with a flood; deluge. 2 To fill or overwhelm as with a flood. —*v.i.* 3 To overflow. 4 To flow in a flood; gush. [<OE *flōd*] —**flood'er** *n.*

flood·gate (flud'gāt') *n.* 1 A gate for regulating the flow of water. 2 Any free vent for an outpouring, as of tears.

flood·light (flud'līt') *n.* 1 Artificial illumination of great brilliancy and broad beams. 2 A lighting unit for providing such illumination. —*v.t.* To illuminate with a floodlight.

flood tide 1 The rising tide. 2 The high point of anything.

floor (flôr, flōr) *n.* 1 The surface in a room upon which one walks. 2 A level of a building; story. 3 Any similar bottom surface: the *floor* of a bridge. 4 In any parliamentary body, the part of the hall occupied by its members. 5 The right to address an assembly: to have the *floor*. 6 The main business hall of an exchange. 7 The lowest price charged for a given thing. —*v.t.* 1 To cover or provide with a floor. 2 To throw down. 3 *Informal* To defeat. 4 *Informal* To baffle. [<OE *flōr*] —**floor'er** *n.*

floor·board (flôr'bôrd', -bōrd') *n.* 1 One of the boards of a floor. 2 The floor in an automobile.

floor·ing (flôr'ing, flō'ring) *n.* 1 Material for the making of a floor. 2 A floor or floors.

floor leader A legislative leader chosen by his own party and having charge of party organization and activities on the floor.

floor show Entertainment in a night club or cabaret.

floor·walk·er (flôr'wô'kər, flōr'-) *n.* In a retail store, one who oversees the employees on a floor, directs customers, etc.

flop (flop) *v.* **flopped, flop·ping** *v.i.* 1 To move or beat about with thuds. 2 To fall loosely and heavily. 3 *Informal* To fail. —*v.t.* 4 To cause to strike, slap, or drop with a thud. —*n.* 1 The sound or act of flopping. 2 *Informal* An utter failure. [Var. of FLAP] —**flop'pi·ly** *adv.* —**flop'pi·ness** *n.* —**flop'py** *adj.* **(·i·er, ·i·est)**

flop·house (flop'hous') *n.* A cheap hotel

floppy disk A flexible computer disk.

flo·ra (flôr'ə, flō'rə) *n. pl.* **·ras** or **·rae** (-ē) Plants collectively, esp. the species respresented in a given area or period. [<L *Flora* < *flos, floris* flower]

Flo·ra (flôr'ə, flō'rə) *Rom. Myth.* The goddess of flowers.

flo·ral (flôr'əl, flō'rəl) *adj.* Of, like, or pertaining to flowers.

Flor·en·tine (flôr'ən·tēn, -tīn, flor'-) *adj.* Of or pertaining to the city of Florence, Italy. —*n.* An inhabitant or native of Florence.

flo·res·cence (flô·res'əns, flō-) *n. Bot.* The state of being in blossom. [<L *florere* to bloom] —**flo·res'cent** *adj.*

flo·ret (flôr'it, flō'rit) *n.* 1 A little flower. 2 *Bot.* One of the small flowers that make up a head of a composite flower, as in sunflowers, dandelions, etc. [<L *flos, floris* flower]

flo·ri·cul·ture (flôr'ə·kul'chər, flō'rə-) *n.* The cultivation of flowers. —**flo'ri·cul'tur·al** *adj.* —**flo'ri·cul'tur·al·ly** *adv.* —**flo'ri·cul'tur·ist** *n.*

flor·id (flôr'id, flor'-) *adj.* 1 Having a lively reddish hue. 2 Extremely ornate. [<L *flos, floris* a flower) —**flo·rid·i·ty** (flə·rid'ə·te), **flor'id·ness** *n.* —**flor'id·ly** *adv.* —**Syn.** 1 rosy, rubicund, ruddy. 2 gaudy, ornate.

flor·in (flôr'in, flor'in) *n.* 1 A British coin, equal to two shillings. 2 GUILDER. [<Ital. *fiore* a flower; from the lily stamped on the old coins]

flo·rist (flôr'ist, flō'rist, flor'ist) *n.* A grower of or dealer in flowers. [<L *flos, floris* flower]

floss (flôs, flos) *n.* 1 FLOSS SILK. 2 The silk of some plants, as corn. 3 The stray silk on silkworm cocoons. 4 A flossy surface, fluff. [?<OF *flosche*]

floss silk Soft silk thread used in embroidery.

floss·y (flôs'ē, flos'ē) *adj.* **floss·i·er, floss·i·est** 1 Like floss; light; silky. 2 *Informal* Ornate; frilly.

flo·ta·tion (flō·tā'shən) *n.* 1 The act or state of floating. 2 The act of floating or financing, as of an issue of bonds, etc., by bankers. 3 *Metall.* A method of separating pulverized ores by placing them in a froth of oils and chemicals to which they selectively adhere.

flo·til·la (flō·til'ə) *n.* 1 A small fleet. 2 In the U.S. Navy, an organized group of destroyers. [<Sp. *flota* a fleet]

flot·sam (flot'səm) *n.* 1 *Law* Goods cast or swept from a vessel into the sea and found floating. 2 Any worthless objects. 3 Vagrants or unattached persons. [<AF *floteson* <*floter* float]

flounce[1] (flouns) *n.* A gathered or plaited strip, as on a skirt. —*v.t.* **flounced, flounc·ing** To furnish with flounces. [<ME *frouncen* to curl]

flounce[2] (flouns) *v.i.* **flounced, flounc·ing** 1 To move with exaggerated tosses of the body, as in anger or petulance. 2 To plunge; founder: said of animals. —*n.* The act of flouncing. [?]

floun·der[1] (floun'dər) *v.i.* 1 To struggle clumsily as if mired or injured. 2 To speak or act in a clumsy or confused manner. —*n.* A stumbling or struggling motion. [? Blend of FLOUNCE[2] and FOUNDER] —**floun'der·ing·ly** *adv.*

floun·der[2] (floun'dər) *n.* Any of certain species of flatfish, valued as food. [?<Scand.]

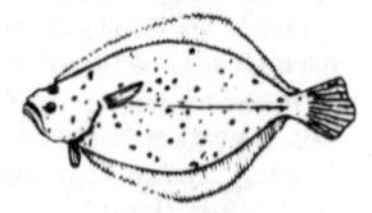

Flounder

flour (flour) *n.* 1 The ground and bolted substance of wheat. 2 The finely ground particles of any cereal. 3 Any finely powdered substance. —*v.t.* 1 To make into flour. 2 To cover with flour. [Var. of FLOWER] —**flour'y** *adj.*

flour·ish (flûr'ish) *v.i.* 1 To grow or fare well; thrive. 2 To be at the peak of success or development. 3 To move with sweeping motions. 4 To write with ornamental strokes.—*v.t.* 5 To brandish; wave. —*n.* 1 An ornamental mark or design, as in writing. 2 Anything done for display alone. 3 The act of brandishing or waving. 4 *Music* A short, elaborate passage; fanfare. [<L *florere* to bloom] —**flour'ish·er** *n.* —**flour'ish·ing·ly** *adv.*

flout (flout) *v.t.* To show contempt for; scoff at. —*v.i.* To mock; jeer. —*n.* A gibe; scoff. [?<ME *flouten* play the flute] —**flout'er** *n.* —**flout'ing·ly** *adv.* • See FLAUNT.

flow (flō) *v.i.* 1 To move along in a stream, as a liquid or gas. 2 To move like water. 3 To stream forth; proceed from a source. 4 To move with continuity and pleasing rhythm, as music. 5 To fall in waves, as garments or hair. 6 To be full or too full; abound. 7 To come in or rise, as the tide. —*v.t.* 8 To flood; inundate. —*n.* 1 The act of flowing. 2 That which flows; something flowing. 3 The incoming of the tide. 4 The quantity or rate of flow. [< OE *flōwan*]

flow chart A diagram showing the succession of steps in a process.

flow·er (flou′ər, flour) *n.* 1 *Bot.* The organ of reproduction in a plant; blossom. 2 A blooming plant. 3 The brightest, choicest part, period, or specimen of anything. 4 *pl. Chem.* A fine powder obtained by sublimation: *flowers* of sulfur. —*v.i.* 1 To put forth blossoms; bloom. 2 To come to full development. —*v.t.* 3 To decorate with flowers or a floral pattern. [< OF *flour, flor* < L *flos, floris* a flower] —**flow′·er·y** *adj.* (**·i·er, ·i·est**) —**flow′er·i·ly** *adv.* —**flow′er·i·ness** *n.*

flow·er·et (flou′ər·it, flou′rit) *n.* FLORET.

flow·er·pot (flou′ər·pot′, flour′-) *n.* A container, often of earthenware, for growing plants.

flown (flōn) *p.p.* of FLY[1].

fl. oz. fluid ounce(s).

flu (flo͞o) *n. Informal* Influenza.

flub (flub) *Informal v.t. & v.i.* **flubbed, flub·bing** To do or manage (something) badly; botch or bungle: to *flub* one's chance. —*n.* A blunder; failure. [?]

fluc·tu·ate (fluk′cho͞o·āt) *v.* **·at·ed, ·at·ing** *v.i.* 1 To change or vary often and in an irregular manner. 2 To move with successive rise and fall; undulate. —*v.t.* 3 To cause to fluctuate. [< L *fluctus* a wave] —**fluc′tu·ant** *adj.* —**fluc′tu·a′tion** *n.* —**Syn.** 1 alternate, vacillate, waver, oscillate.

flue[1] (flo͞o) *n.* 1 A channel or passage for smoke, air, or gases, as in a chimney. 2 An air channel in a wind instrument. [?]

flue[2] (flo͞o) *n.* Lint; down; fluff. [< Flemish *vluwe* down]

flu·ent (flo͞o′ənt) *adj.* 1 Smooth and effortless, as in speaking or writing; facile. 2 Flowing freely and easily; smooth. [< L *fluere* to flow] —**flu′en·cy** (-sē) *n.* —**flu′ent·ly** *adv.*

fluff (fluf) *n.* 1 Nap or down. 2 Anything downy or fluffy. 3 *Informal* An error, esp. in reading or speaking lines. —*v.t.* 1 To shake (hair, etc.) so as to make soft and loose. 2 *Informal* To make an error, as in reading lines. —*v.i.* 3 To become fluffy. [? Blend of FLUE[2] + PUFF]

fluff·y (fluf′ē) *adj.* **fluff·i·er, fluff·i·est** 1 Downy; feathery. 2 Light and airy. —**fluff′i·ly** *adv.* —**fluff′i·ness** *n.*

flu·id (flo͞o′id) *adj.* 1 Capable of flowing, as a liquid or gas. 2 Of or pertaining to liquid. 3 Capable of changing; not fixed: a *fluid* policy. 4 Smooth: a *fluid* style. —*n.* A substance that flows, as a liquid or gas. [< L *fluere* to flow] —**flu·id·ic** (flo͞o·id′ik) *adj.* —**flu·id′i·ty, flu′id·ness** *n.* —**flu′id·ly** *adv.*

fluid dram A unit equal to 0.125 or ⅛ fluid ounce.

fluid ounce A unit of volume used for liquids, equal to 1/16 pint or 1.804 cubic inches.

fluke[1] (flo͝ok) *n.* 1 A pointed part of an anchor that holds to the ground. 2 One of the lobes of the tail of a whale. 3 A barb on a harpoon, arrow, etc. [? < FLUKE[2]]

fluke[2] (flo͝ok) *n.* 1 Any of several parasitic worms infesting sheep, etc. 2 A flatfish or flounder. [< OE *flōc*]

fluke[3] (flo͝ok) *n.* 1 A lucky stroke, as in pool. 2 Any lucky stroke. [?] —**fluk′ey** or **fluk′y,** (**·i·er, ·i·est**) *adj.*

flume (flo͞om) *n.* 1 A chute or conduit with water flowing through, as for transporting logs. 2 A narrow passage through which a torrent passes. —*v.t.* **flumed, flum·ing** To move or transport, as logs, by means of a flume. [< L *flumen* river < *fluere* to flow]

flum·mer·y (flum′er·ē) *n. pl.* **·mer·ies** 1 Any of several light, easily digested foods, as a kind of custard. 2 Empty talk; humbug. [< Welsh *llymru*]

flung (flung) *p.t. & p.p.* of FLING.

flunk (flungk) *Informal v.t.* 1 To fail in, as an examination. 2 To give a failing grade to. —*v.i.* 3 To fail, as in an examination. 4 To give up. —**flunk out** To leave or cause to leave a school because of failure in studies. —*n.* A complete failure. [?]

flunk·y (flung′kē) *n. pl.* **flunk·ies** 1 An obsequious or servile person. 2 An assistant assigned to do humble tasks. 3 A male servant in livery. Also **flunk′ey.** [?]

flu·or (flo͞o′ər, -ôr) *n.* FLUORITE. [< L, a flowing]

flu·o·resce (flo͞o′ə·res′) *v.i.* **·resced, ·resc·ing** To become fluorescent; exhibit fluorescence.

flu·o·res·cence (flo͞o′ə·res′əns) *n. Physics* 1 The property by which certain substances absorb radiation and emit light of a different, usu. longer wavelength. 2 The light so produced. [< FLUOR + -ESCENCE] —**flu′o·res′cent** *adj.*

fluorescent lamp A lamp, usu. tubular, containing a vapor that radiates on the passing of an electric current and energizes a fluorescent coating in the tube.

fluor·i·date (flo͝or′ə·dāt, flo͞o′ə·ri·dāt) *v.t.* **·dat·ed, ·dat·ing** To add a fluoride to (drinking water), esp. as a means of preventing tooth decay. —**fluor′i·da′tion** *n.*

flu·o·ride (flo͞o′ə·rīd, -rid) *n. Chem.* A binary compound of fluorine and another element.

flu·o·rine (flo͞o′ə·rēn, -rin) *n.* An intensely reactive, normally gaseous element (symbol F) belonging to the halogen group.

flu·o·rite (flo͞o′ə·rīt) *n.* A variously colored mineral composed of calcium and fluorine, used in metallurgy.

fluoro- *combining form* 1 *Chem.* Indicating the presence of fluorine in a compound: *fluorite.* 2 Fluorescence: *fluoroscope.* Also **fluor-.**

fluor·o·scope (flo͝or′ə·skōp, flo͞o′ər·ə-) *n.* A device for observing objects enclosed in media opaque to ordinary light, but transparent to X-rays. —**fluor′o·scop′ic** (-skop′·ik) *adj.* —**fluor·os′co·py** (flo͝or·os′kə·pē, flo͞o′ə·ros′-) *n.*

flu·or·spar (flo͞o′ôr·spär′, flo͞o′ər-) *n.* FLUORITE.

flur·ry (flûr′ē) *v.t.* **·ried, ·ry·ing** To bewilder or confuse. —*n. pl.* **flur·ries** 1 A light snowfall or rain. 2 A light gust of wind. 3 A sudden commotion or agitation. 4 A sudden spell of activity or movement, as in stock-market prices or in trading. 5 *Informal* Any sudden outburst: a *flurry* of base hits. [Blend of FLUTTER and HURRY]

flush[1] (flush) *v.i.* 1 To become red in the face; blush. 2 To flow suddenly; rush. 3 To be washed out or cleansed by a sudden flow of water. 4 To glow. 5 To rise from cover, as game birds. —*v.t.* 6 To cause to blush. 7 To encourage; excite: *flushed* with victory. 8 To wash out by a flow of water. 9 To startle (birds) from cover. 10 To make level or straight. —*n.* 1 A warm glow; blush. 2 Sudden elation or excitement. 3 A sudden growth; bloom: the first *flush* of manhood. 4 A sudden gush of water. 5 A sudden sensation of heat. —*adj.* 1 Full of life; vigorous. 2 Powerful and direct, as a blow. 3 Having the surfaces in the same plane; level. 4 Full; copious. 5 Well supplied with money. —*adv.* 1 So as to be level, straight, or even. 2 In a direct manner; squarely: a punch *flush* in the jaw. [ME *flusschen*] —**flush′er** *n.*

flush[2] (flush) *n.* In some card games, a hand of cards all of one color, esp., in poker, of one suit.

flus·ter (flus′tər) *v.t. & v.i.* To make or become confused, agitated, or befuddled. —*n.* Confusion of mind. [? < Scand.]

flute (flo͞ot) *n.* 1 A tubular wind instrument of small diameter with holes and usu. keys along the side and a mouthpiece on the side near one end. 2 A groove, usu. semicircular, as in a column or drill. 3 A groovelike pleat in fabric. —*v.* **flut·ed, flut·ing** *v.i.* 1 To play on a flute. 2 To produce a high, clear sound. —*v.t.* 3 To sing or utter like a flute. 4 To make flutes in, as a column. [< OF *flaute*] —**flute′like′, flut′y** *adj.*

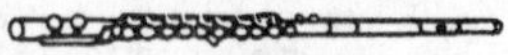

Flute

flut·ing (flo͞o′ting) *n.* Adornment with flutes or grooves.

flut·ist (flo͞o′tist) *n.* A flute player.

flut·ter (flut′ər) *v.i.* 1 To wave rapidly and irregularly, as in the wind. 2 To flap the wings rapidly. 3 To move or proceed with irregular motion. 4 To move about lightly and quickly; flit. 5 To be excited or nervous. —*v.t.* 6 To cause to flutter. 7 To excite; fluster. —*n.* 1 The act of fluttering. 2 Agitation or confusion. 3 A rapid, unwanted vibration in a device. [< OE *flotorian*] —**flut′ter·er** *n.* —**flut′·ter·y** *adj.* —**Syn.** *v.* 1 agitate flap, oscillate, vibrate.

flu·vi·al (flo͞o′vē·əl) *adj.* Of, found in, or formed by a river. [< L *fluvius* river]

flux (fluks) *n.* 1 A flowing; esp., the flowing in of the tide. 2 A constant changing; fluctuation. 3 An abnormal discharge of body fluids. 4 *Metall.* A substance that promotes the fusing of minerals or metals, as borax. 5 *Physics* The rate of flow of water, heat, electricity, etc., over a surface. —**bloody flux** DYSENTERY. —*v.t.* 1 To make fluid; melt; fuse. 2 To treat, as metal, with a flux. [< L *fluxus* < *fluere* to flow] —**flux·a'tion** *n.*

flux·ion (fluk'shən) *n.* 1 The act of flowing or melting. 2 Continuous change. 3 *Pathol.* An abnormal discharge of body fluids. —**flux'ion·al** *adj.* —**flux'ion·al·ly** *adv.*

fly[1] (flī) *v.* **flew** or **flied** (def. 7), **flown, fly·ing** *v.i.* 1 To move through the air by using wings, as a bird. 2 To travel by aircraft; also, to operate an aircraft. 3 To move through the air with speed, as an arrow or bullet. 4 To wave or move in the air, as a flag. 5 To pass swiftly: The years *flew* by. 6 To move swiftly. 7 In baseball, to bat a ball high into the air. 8 To flee. —*v.t.* 9 To cause to wave or float in the air. 10 To operate (an aircraft). 11 To pass over in an aircraft: to *fly* the Atlantic. 12 To transport by aircraft. 13 To flee from. —**fly at** To attack. —**fly in the face of** To defy openly. —*n. pl.* **flies** 1 A strip on a garment to cover buttons, zippers, etc. 2 The flap at the entrance of a tent. 3 The length of an extended flag. 4 A baseball batted high into the air. 5 A light passenger carriage. 6 *pl.* In a theater, the space above the stage and behind the proscenium. —**on the fly** 1 While flying. 2 *Informal* While in great haste. [< OE *flēogan*]

fly[2] (flī) *n. pl.* **flies** 1 One of various small dipterous insects, esp. the common housefly. 2 Any of various other flying insects. 3 A fish hook concealed by feathers, etc., to resemble an insect. [< OE *flyge*]

fly·blown (flī'blōn') *adj.* Tainted or spoiled, as with fly eggs or larvae.

fly-by (flī'bī') *n. pl.* **-bys** The passage of a spacecraft relatively near a body in space.

fly-by-night (flī'bī·nīt') *adj.* Financially irresponsible. —*n.* One who is financially untrustworthy.

fly·catch·er (flī'kach'ər) *n.* Any of a large order of birds that feed upon insects while in flight.

Flycatcher

fly·er (flī'ər) *n.* FLIER.

fly-fish (flī'fish') *v.i.* To fish with artificial flies as bait. —**fly'-fish'ing** *n.*

fly·ing (flī'ing) *adj.* 1 Intended or adapted for motion through the air. 2 Moving rapidly. 3 Floating or suspended: a *flying* banner. 4 Hasty; hurried: a *flying* trip. —*n.* The act of flight.

flying buttress *Archit.* An arch extending from the wall of a building to a supporting abutment and serving to resist the outward thrust of the wall.

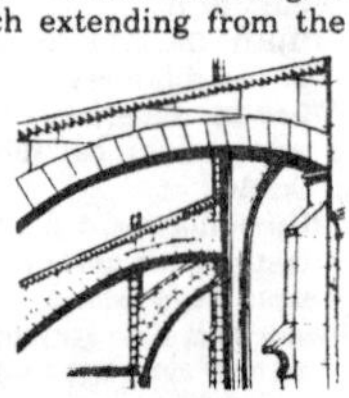

Flying buttresses

flying colors Victory or success.

flying fish A fish of warm seas, with large pectoral fins that enable it to glide through the air for short distances.

flying jib A small sail set beyond the jib.

flying saucer UFO.

fly·leaf (flī'lēf') *n. pl.* **·leaves** A blank leaf at the beginning or end of a book, pamphlet, etc.

fly·pa·per (flī'pā'pər) *n.* An adhesive paper, or one impregnated with poison, for catching or killing flies.

fly·speck (flī'spek') *n.* 1 The dot made by the excrement of a fly. 2 Any slight speck. —*v.t.* To mark with flyspecks.

fly·weight (flī'wāt') *n.* A boxer weighing 112 pounds or less, the lightest weight class.

fly·wheel (flī'hwēl') *n.* A heavy wheel that resists sudden changes of speed, thus securing uniform rotation in a machine.

FM frequency modulation.

Fm fermium.

F-num·ber (ef'num'bər) *n. Phot.* The ratio of the focal length of a lens to its effective diameter.

foal (fōl) *n.* The young of a horse, mule, etc. —*v.t.* & *v.i.* To give birth to (a foal). [< OE *fola*]

foam (fōm) *n.* 1 A collection of minute bubbles forming a frothy mass. 2 Frothy saliva or sweat. 3 The white crest of a breaking wave. —*v.i.* 1 To gather or form foam; froth. —*v.t.* 2 To cause to foam. [< OE *fām*] —**foam'less** *adj.*

foam rubber Rubber having a porous structure due to incorporation of air bubbles prior to vulcanizing.

foam·y (fō'mē) *adj.* **foam·i·er, foam·i·est** 1 Covered with or full of foam. 2 Like foam. —**foam'i·ly** *adv.* —**foam'i·ness** *n.*

fob[1] (fob) *n.* 1 A watch pocket in the waistband of trousers. 2 A chain or ribbon connected to a watch and hanging out of a watch pocket. 3 An ornament on a watch chain or ribbon. [?]

fob[2] (fob) *v.t.* **fobbed, fob·bing** *Archaic* To cheat; trick. —**fob off** 1 To dispose of or palm off by craft or deceit: to *fob off* worthless stock. 2 To put off; attempt to placate, as with promises. [ME *fobben*]

F.O.B., f.o.b. free on board.

fo·cal (fō'kəl) *adj.* Pertaining to, at, or limited to a certain point or focus. —**fo'cal·ly** *adv.*

fo·cal·ize (fō'kəl·īz) *v.t.* & *v.i.* **·ized, ·iz·ing** To adjust or come to a focus; focus. —**fo'cal·i·za'tion** *n.*

focal length *Optics* The distance from the surface of a lens or mirror to its focus. Also **focal distance.**

fo'c's'le (fōk'səl) *n.* FORECASTLE.

fo·cus (fō'kəs) *n. pl.* **·cus·es** or **·ci** (-sī) 1 *Optics* **a** The point where light rays converge after passage through a lens or after reflection from a mirror. **b** The point from which such rays appear to diverge. 2 **a** Adjustment so as to form a clear image: to be out of *focus.* **b** The relative clarity of an image. 3 *Physics* The meeting point of any system of rays, beams, or waves. 4 Any central point of activity, attraction, etc.: the *focus* of an earthquake. —*v.t.* **fo·cused** or **fo·cussed, fo·cus·ing** or **fo·cus·sing** 1 To adjust the focus of. 2 To bring to a focus. 3 To concentrate. —*v.i.* 4 To come to a focus. [L, hearth] —**fo'cus·er** *n.*

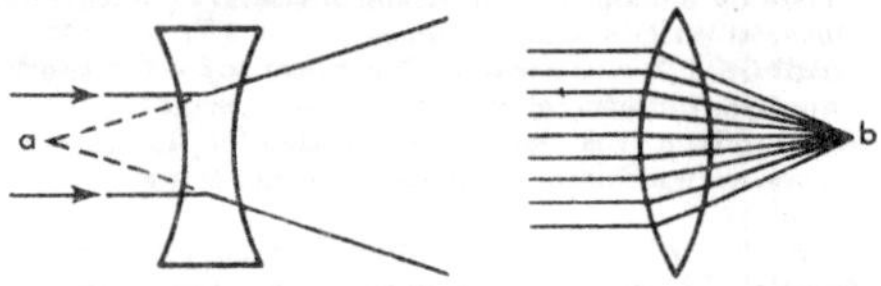

Foci

Refracted light rays of concave lens at left diverge, forming the virtual focus at a. Refracted rays of convex lens at right converge to focus at b.

fod·der (fod'ər) *n.* Coarse feed, for horses, cattle, etc., as hay or straw. —*v.t.* To supply with fodder. [< OE *fōdor*]

foe (fō) *n.* An enemy; adversary. [Fusion of OE *fāh* hostile and *gefāh* an enemy] —**Syn.** antagonist, competitor, opponent, rival.

foe·man (fō'mən) *n. pl.* **·men** (-mən) *Archaic* A foe.

foe·tus (fē'təs) *n.* FETUS. —**foe'tal** *adj.*

fog (fog, fôg) *n.* 1 Condensed water vapor suspended in the atmosphere at or near the earth's surface. 2 Any hazy condition of the atmosphere, or the material causing it. 3 Bewilderment; confusion. 4 A blur obscuring a developed photographic image. —*v.* **fogged, fog·ging** *v.t.* 1 To surround with or as with fog. 2 To confuse; bewilder. 3 *Phot.* To cloud with a fog. —*v.i.* 4 To become foggy. [? < Scand.]

fog bank A mass of fog.

fog·bound (fog'bound', fôg-) *adj.* 1 Covered with fog: the *fogbound* eastern states. 2 Unable to depart, as a ship or airplane, because of fog.

fog·gy (fog'ē, fôg'ē) *adj.* **fog·gi·er, fog·gi·est** 1 Full of fog. 2 Indistinct; blurred. 3 Mentally confused. —**fog'gi·ly** *adv.* —**fog'gi·ness** *n.*

fog·horn (fog'hôrn', fôg'-) *n.* 1 A horn for sounding a warning to ships during a fog. 2 A powerful, harsh voice.

fo·gy (fō'gē) *n. pl.* **fo·gies** A person having old-fashioned notions: now usu. in the phrase **old fogy.** —*adj.* Old-fashioned; out-of-date. Also **fo'gey, fo'gie.** [?] —**fo'gy·ish** *adj.* —**fo'gy·ism** *n.*

foi·ble (foi'bəl) *n.* A slight fault or weakness in one's character. [< F < *faible* feeble]

foil[1] (foil) *v.t.* To prevent the success of; frustrate. [< OF *fouler, fuler* crush, trample down]

foil[2] (foil) *n.* **1** Metal in very thin sheets. **2** A leaf of bright metal placed beneath an inferior gem to heighten the color or luster. **3** A person or thing serving to set off by contrast something different. **4** The reflecting coating on the back of a mirror. **5** A leaflike, Gothic ornamentation, as in windows, etc. —*v.t.* **1** To apply foil to; cover with foil. **2** To set off by contrast. **3** To adorn, as windows, with foils. [< L *folium* leaf]

Foils *def. 5*

foil[3] (foil) *n.* A long, flexible fencing sword having a protective button on the point. [?]

foist (foist) *v.t.* **1** To put in or introduce slyly. **2** To pass off (something spurious) as genuine. [? < dial. Du. *vuisten* hold in the hand]

fold[1] (fōld) *v.t.* **1** To turn back (something) upon itself one or more times. **2** To close; collapse: to *fold* an umbrella. **3** To place together and interlock: to *fold* one's hands. **4** To wrap up; enclose. **5** To embrace; enfold. —*v.i.* **6** To come together in folds. **7** *Slang* To fail; close: often with *up.* —*n.* **1** The act of folding. **2** Something folded. **3** The crease made by folding. **4** *Geol.* A smooth bend or flexure in a layer of rock. [< OE *fealdan*]

fold[2] (fōld) *n.* **1** A pen, as for sheep. **2** A flock of sheep. **3** Any group, as the congregation of a church. —*v.t.* To shut up in a fold, as sheep. [< OE *fald*]

-fold *suffix* **1** Having (a specified number of) parts: a *three-fold* blessing. **2** (A specified number of) times as great, or as much: to reward *tenfold.* [< OE *fealdan* fold]

fold·er (fōl′dər) *n.* **1** One who or that which folds. **2** A folded sheet of light cardboard for holding loose papers, as for storage in a file. **3** Any similar item used to hold papers, as a large envelope. **4** A timetable or other printed paper that may be readily folded.

fol·de·rol (fol′də·rol) *n.* FALDERAL.

fo·li·a·ceous (fō′lē·ā′shəs) *adj.* **1** Of the nature or form of a leaf. **2** Having leaves; foliate. [< L *folium* a leaf]

fo·li·age (fō′lē·ij) *n.* **1** Leaves collectively. **2** A representation of leaves, flowers, and branches, used in architectural ornamentation. [< F < L *folium* a leaf] —**fo′li·aged** *adj.*

fo·li·ate (fō′lē·āt, -it) *adj.* Having leaves. —*v.* **·at·ed, ·at·ing** *v.t.* **1** To beat into a thin plate, as gold. —*v.i.* **2** To split into leaves or laminae. **3** To put forth leaves. [< L *folium* a leaf]

fo·li·a·tion (fō′lē·ā′shən) *n.* **1** The process by which leaves are developed; growth and development into a leaf. **2** The act of beating a metal into a thin sheet or foil. **3** *Archit.* Decoration with leaflike shapes or tracery; also, one of such ornaments. **4** The numbering of the leaves of a book, etc.

fo·lic acid (fō′lik) A constituent of the vitamin-B complex, found in green leaves, etc. [< L *folium* leaf]

fo·li·o (fō′lē·ō, fōl′yō) *n. pl.* **·li·os** **1** A sheet of paper folded once, thereby forming two leaves or four pages of a book, etc. **2** A book of the largest size, usu. more than 11 inches high, composed of such sheets. **3** A page of a book with a number on one side only. **4** The number of a page. —*adj.* Consisting of a sheet or sheets folded once. —*v.t.* To number the pages of (a book or manuscript) consecutively. [< L *folium* a leaf]

folk (fōk) *n. pl.* **folk** or **folks** **1** A people; nation; race. **2** *Usu. pl.* People of a particular group or class: old *folks.* **3** *pl. Informal* People in general. **4** *pl. Informal* One's family. —*adj.* **1** Of, pertaining to, originating among, or characteristic of the common people of a district or country. **2** Of, pertaining to, or being music written by or characteristic of such common people, and handed down by them. **3** Of, pertaining to, or being music written in imitation of genuine folk music. [< OE *folc*]

Folk, in the adjectival use, may appear as the first element in two-word phrases; as in:

folk art	**folk literature**	**folk song**
folk custom	**folk music**	**folk tale**
folk dance	**folk singer**	**folk tune**

folk·lore (fōk′lôr′, -lōr′) *n.* **1** The traditions, beliefs, customs, sayings, stories, etc., preserved among the common people. **2** The study of folk cultures. —**folk′lor′ist** *n.*

folk·sy (fōk′sē) *adj.* **·si·er, ·si·est** *Informal* Friendly; sociable; unpretentious.

folk·ways (fōk′wāz′) *n. pl.* The traditional habits, customs, and behavior of a given group, tribe, or nation.

fol·li·cle (fol′i·kəl) *n.* **1** *Anat.* A small cavity or saclike structure: a hair *follicle.* **2** *Bot.* A dry seed vessel of one carpel. [< L *follis* bag] —**fol·lic·u·lar** (fə·lik′yə·lər) *adj.*

fol·low (fol′ō) *v.t.* **1** To go or come after. **2** To seek to overtake. **3** To accompany; attend. **4** To hold to the course of: to *follow* a path. **5** To conform to. **6** To be under the leadership of. **7** To work at as a livelihood. **8** To come after as a result. **9** To take as a model; imitate. **10** To watch or observe closely: to *follow* sports. **11** To understand the meaning of. —*v.i.* **12** To happen or come after something in time, sequence, or motion. **13** To understand. **14** To come after as a result. —**follow out** To carry out, as instructions. —**follow through** To perform fully; complete, as a stroke or action. —**follow up** **1** To pursue closely. **2** To achieve more by acting upon what has already been done. —*n.* The act of following. [< OE *folgian*] —**Syn.** **2** chase, pursue. **11** comprehend, grasp, see.

fol·low·er (fol′ō·ər) *n.* **1** An imitator or disciple. **2** An attendant or servant.

fol·low·ing (fol′ō·ing) *adj.* Next in order; succeeding or ensuing. —*n.* A body of adherents, attendants, or disciples.

fol·low-through (fol′ō·thrōō′) *n.* **1** In some sports, the continuing of a motion, as the swing of a racket or bat, after contact with the ball. **2** Any continuing, as of an effort, to completion.

fol·low-up (fol′ō·up′) *adj.* Of or pertaining to a repeated or following action or thing; reinforcing; supplementary. —*n.* A supplementary action or thing that follows, reinforces, or expands upon an initial effort.

fol·ly (fol′ē) *n. pl.* **·lies** **1** The condition of being foolish or deficient in understanding. **2** Any foolish act, idea, or undertaking. **3** Immoral conduct. [< F *fol* fool]

fo·ment (fō·ment′) *v.t.* **1** To stir up or incite, as rebellion or discord. **2** To treat with warm water or medicated lotions. [< L *fomentum* a poultice] —**fo′men·ta′tion, fo·ment′·er** *n.*

fond (fond) *adj.* **1** Liking: with *of: fond* of music. **2** Cherished: *fond* hopes. **3** Loving or affectionate; devoted: a *fond* glance. **4** *Archaic* Silly. [< ME *fon* be foolish] —**fond′ly** *adv.* —**fond′ness** *n.*

fon·dant (fon′dənt) *n.* A soft, molded confection. [F < *fondre* melt]

fon·dle (fon′dəl) *v.* **·dled, ·dling** *v.t.* To handle lovingly; caress. [< FOND] —**fon′dler** *n.*

fon·due (fon·dōō′) *n.* A dish made of grated cheese with eggs, butter, etc. [F < *fondre* melt]

font[1] (font) *n.* **1** A receptacle for the water used in baptizing. **2** A receptacle for holy water. **3** A fountain. **4** Origin; source. [< L *fons, fontis* a fountain]

font[2] (font) *n.* A full assortment of printing type of a particular face and size. [< F *fondre* melt]

food (fōōd) *n.* **1** That which is taken in and absorbed for the growth and repair of organisms. **2** Solid as opposed to liquid nourishment. **3** That which increases, keeps active, or sustains. [< OE *fōda*] —**Syn.** **1** aliment, fare, nutriment, victuals.

food chain *Ecol.* The relationship of organisms considered as food sources or consumers or both.

food poisoning Illness caused by toxins present in food either naturally or as a result of bacterial spoilage.

food·stuff (fōōd′stuf′) *n.* Anything used as or made into food.

fool (fōōl) *n.* **1** A person lacking in understanding, judgment, or common sense. **2** A jester, formerly kept at court and in great households. **3** A dupe; butt. —*v.i.* **1** To act like a fool. —*v.t.* **2** To make a fool of; deceive. —**fool around** *Informal* **1** To waste time on trifles. **2** To hang about idly. —**fool away** *Informal* To spend foolishly; squander. —

fool with 1 To meddle with. 2 To joke with. 3 To play with. [<L *follis* a bellows; later, a windbag]

fool·er·y (fo͞o′lə·rē) *n. pl.* **·er·ies** Foolish conduct; anything foolish.

fool·har·dy (fo͞ol′här′dē) *adj.* Bold without judgment; reckless; rash. **—fool′har′di·ly** *adv.* **—fool′har′di·ness** *n.*

fool·ish (fo͞o′lish) *adj.* 1 Showing or resulting from folly or stupidity; unwise. 2 Ridiculous; absurd. **—fool′ish·ly** *adv.* **—fool′ish·ness** *n.*

fool·proof (fo͞ol′pro͞of′) *adj.* 1 So simple as to be understood by anyone. 2 So constructed as to operate always smoothly and safely.

fools·cap (fo͞olz′kap′) *n.* A size of writing paper about 13 by 16 inches or 13½ by 17 inches.

fool's gold PYRITE.

foot (fo͝ot) *n. pl.* **feet** 1 The terminal part of the leg, upon which a person or animal stands or moves. 2 Anything corresponding to the foot: the *foot* of a chair; the *foot* of a stocking. 3 The lowest part; bottom: the *foot* of a ladder. 4 The part or end opposite the head: the *foot* of a bed. 5 A unit of length equal to 12 inches or 0.3048 meter. 6 A unit of poetic meter consisting of a fixed group of stressed and unstressed syllables. 7 *Brit.* Infantry. **—on foot** 1 Walking. 2 Happening; going on. **—put one's foot down** To be decisive. **—put one's foot in it** To get into an embarrassing scrape. **—under foot** 1 In the way. 2 On the ground. **—***v.i.* 1 To walk. 2 To dance. **—***v.t.* 3 To move on or through by walking or dancing. 4 To furnish with a foot, as a stocking. 5 To add, as a column of figures. 6 *Informal* To pay, as a bill. **—foot it** To walk, run, or dance. [<OE *fōt*]

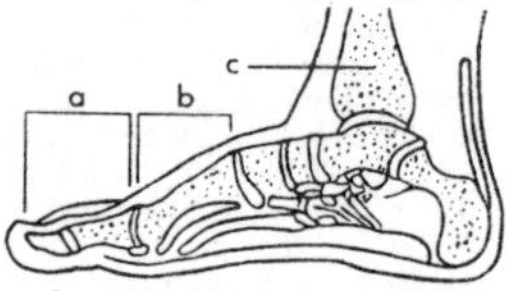

Structure of the human foot
a. phalanges. b. metatarsal.
c. tibia.

foot·age (fo͝ot′ij) *n.* Length in feet.

foot-and-mouth disease (fo͝ot′ən·mouth′) An acute viral disease of domestic animals, esp. cattle, in which blisters form about the mouth and hoofs.

foot·ball (fo͝ot′bôl′) *n.* 1 A game played between two teams on a field with goals at each end, points being scored by running or passing an oval ball across the opponent's goal line, or kicking it between the goal posts. 2 The ball itself. 3 *Brit.* **a** Soccer. **b** Rugby.

foot·ball·er (fo͝ot′bôl′ər) *n.* A football player, esp., *Brit.*, a soccer player.

foot·board (fo͝ot′bôrd′, -bōrd′) *n.* 1 Something to rest the feet upon. 2 An upright piece at the foot of a bedstead.

foot·bridge (fo͝ot′brij′) *n.* A bridge for persons on foot.

foot-can·dle (fo͝ot′kan′dəl) *n.* A unit for measuring intensity of illumination, equal to one lumen per square foot.

foot·drag·ging (fo͝ot′drag′ing) *n.* Willful delay; reluctance to act. **—foot′drag′ger** *n.*

foot·ed (fo͝ot′id) *adj.* Having a specified kind or number of feet: used in combination: *four-footed; splayfooted.*

foot·er (fo͝ot′ər) *n.* A person or thing having a specified number of feet in height or length: used in combination: a *six-footer.*

foot·fall (fo͝ot′fôl′) *n.* The sound of a footstep; also, a footstep.

foot·hill (fo͝ot′hil′) *n.* A low hill near the base of a mountain.

foot·hold (fo͝ot′hōld′) *n.* 1 A support for the foot. 2 Established position.

foot·ing (fo͝ot′ing) *n.* 1 A place to stand or walk on, esp. with regard to its physical condition: insecure *footing.* 2 A foothold: to have a firm *footing.* 3 A secure, established position. 4 A basis for relationship: to be on a good *footing* with someone.

foot·lights (fo͝ot′līts′) *n. pl.* 1 Lights in a row near the front of a stage. 2 The profession of acting.

foot·loose (fo͝ot′lo͞os′) *adj.* Not bound to any person or duty; unattached.

foot·man (fo͝ot′mən) *n. pl.* **·men** (-mən) A male servant who answers the door, waits at table, etc.

foot·note (fo͝ot′nōt′) *n.* A note of reference or explanation at the foot of a page.

foot·pad (fo͝ot′pad′) *n.* A robber on foot.

foot·path (fo͝ot′path′, -päth′) *n.* A path for persons on foot. Also **foot′way′** (-wā′).

foot-pound (fo͝ot′pound′) *n.* The work done in moving a body one foot against a force of one pound.

foot·print (fo͝ot′print′) *n.* An impression left by a foot. Also **foot′mark′** (-märk′). **—Syn.** spoor, trace, track.

foot·race (fo͝ot′rās′) *n.* A race among runners on foot. **—foot′rac′er, foot′rac′ing** *n.*

foot·rest (fo͝ot′rest′) *n.* A stool, chair extension, etc., for supporting the feet.

foot soldier A soldier who fights while on foot; infantryman.

foot·sore (fo͝ot′sôr′, -sōr′) *adj.* Having sore feet, as from excessive walking.

foot·step (fo͝ot′step′) *n.* 1 The action of or the distance covered by a foot in stepping. 2 The sound of a step. 3 FOOTPRINT. 4 A step for going up or down.

foot·stool (fo͝ot′sto͞ol′) *n.* A low stool for the feet of someone sitting.

foot·wear (fo͝ot′wâr′) *n.* Covering for the feet, as boots, shoes, socks, stockings.

foot·work (fo͝ot′wûrk′) *n.* Use or control of the feet, as in boxing or tennis.

fop (fop) *n.* A man affectedly fastidious in dress or deportment; a dandy. [ME] **—fop′pish** *adj.* **—fop′pish·ly** *adv.* **—fop′per·y, fop′pish·ness** *n.*

for (fôr, *unstressed* fər) *prep.* 1 To the extent of: a desert *for* miles. 2 Through the duration of: good *for* a week. 3 To the number or amount of: a check *for* six dollars. 4 At the price of: a hat *for* ten dollars. 5 On account of: He is respected *for* his ability. 6 In honor of: named *for* his grandfather. 7 Appropriate to: a time *for* work. 8 In place or instead of: using a book *for* a desk. 9 In favor of: a vote *for* peace. 10 In the interest of: Who speaks *for* me? 11 Tending toward, as with longing or desire: a passion *for* jewelry. 12 As affecting: good *for* your health. 13 Belonging, given, attributed, or assigned to: a package *for* you; the reason *for* going. 14 In proportion to: big *for* his age. 15 As the equivalent of: blow *for* blow. 16 In spite of: *for* all that. 17 In order to reach: He left *for* his office. 18 In order to become, find, keep, or obtain: looking *for* a job. 19 At (a particular time or occasion): We agreed to meet *for* lunch. 20 As being or supposed to be: We took him *for* an honest man. **—***conj.* Owing to the fact that; because: He could not leave, *for* he was expecting a visitor. [<OE]

for- *prefix* 1 Away; off; past: *forget, forgo.* 2 Very; extremely: *forlorn.* [<OE *for-*]

for·age (fôr′ij, for′-) *n.* 1 Any food suitable for horses or cattle. 2 The act of seeking food. **—***v.* **for·aged, for·ag·ing** *v.t.* 1 To search through for food or supplies. 2 To provide with forage. 3 To obtain by foraging. **—***v.i.* 4 To search for food or supplies. 5 To search: usu. with *about* or *for.* 6 To make a foray. [<OF *feurre* fodder] **—for′ag·er** *n.*

fo·ra·men (fō·rā′mən) *n. pl.* **·ram·i·na** (-ram′ə·nə) *Anat.* A natural aperture or passage, as in a bone, etc. [<L *forare* bore]

for·a·min·i·fer (fôr′ə·min′ə·fər, for′-) *n.* One of an order of tiny, unicellular marine animals, having a shell perforated by many holes. **—fo·ram·i·nif·e·ral** (fə·ram′ə·nif′ə·rəl), **fo·ram′i·nif′e·rous** *adj.* [<L *foramen* a hole + *ferre* to bear]

for·as·much as (fôr′əz·much′) Since; because. Also **for as much as.**

for·ay (fôr′ā, for′ā) *v.i.* 1 To venture out, as to raid or explore. **—***v.t.* 2 *Archaic* To pillage. **—***n.* 1 A raid, esp. on a military mission: a *foray* behind enemy lines. 2 A venturing out, as into unfamiliar surroundings. [<OF *feurre* forage] **—for′ay·er** *n.*

for·bade, for·bad (fər·bad′, fôr-) *p.t.* of FORBID.

for·bear[1] (fôr·bâr′, fər-) *v.* **·bore, ·borne, ·bear·ing** *v.t.* 1 To refrain from (an action) voluntarily. **—***v.i.* 2 To abstain or refrain. 3 To be patient or act patiently. [<OE *forberan*] **—for·bear′ing·ly** *adv.* **—for·bear′er** *n.*

for·bear[2] (fôr′bâr′) *n.* FOREBEAR.

for·bear·ance (fôr·bâr′əns, fər-) *n.* 1 The act of forbearing; the patient endurance of offenses. 2 A refraining from retaliation or retribution.

for·bid (fər·bid′, fôr-) *v.t.* **for·bade** or **for·bad, for·bid·den** or **for·bid, for·bid·ding 1** To command not to do, use, enter, etc. **2** To prohibit the use or doing of. **3** To make impossible. [< OE *forbēodan*] **—for·bid′dance, for·bid′der** *n.*

for·bid·ding (fər·bid′ing, fôr-) *adj.* Such as to repel; frightening; repulsive. **—for·bid′ding·ly** *adv.*

force (fôrs, fōrs) *n.* **1** Power and energy, esp. when used to constrain or coerce. **2** *Physics* That which is capable of accelerating a body that has mass. **3** The capacity to convince or move. **4** Binding effect; efficacy: a rule still in *force.* **5** An organized body of individuals engaged in some activity: a police *force.* **6** A military or naval unit. **7** The total military power, as of a nation. **8** A person or group wielding power effectively. —*v.t.* **forced, forc·ing 1** To compel to do something by or as by force. **2** To get or obtain by or as by force: to *force* an answer. **3** To bring forth by or as by effort: to *force* a smile. **4** To break open, as a door or lock. **5** To make, as a passage or way, by force. **6** To press or impose upon someone as by force. **7** To strain, as the voice. **8** To hasten the growth of, as plants in a hothouse. **9** To rape. **10** In baseball: **a** To put out (a base runner) who has been compelled by another base runner to leave one base for the next. **b** To allow (a run) in such a manner when the bases are full. **11** In card games: **a** To compel (a player) to play a trump card. **b** To compel a player to play (a particular card). **12** To stimulate the growth of artificially, as plants in a hothouse. [< L *fortis* brave, strong] **—force′a·ble** *adj.* **—forc′er** *n.*

forced (fôrst, fōrst) *adj.* **1** Compelled; compulsory. **2** Strained; affected: *forced* gaiety. **3** Speeded up, with few or no pauses: a *forced* march.

force·ful (fôrs′fəl, fōrs′-) *adj.* Acting with or full of force; strong; effective. **—force′ful·ly** *adv.* **—force′ful·ness** *n.* **—Syn.** efficient, impressive, powerful, vigorous.

force·meat (fôrs′mēt′, fōrs′-) *n.* Finely chopped, seasoned meat served separately or used as stuffing. [< L *farcire* to stuff + MEAT]

for·ceps (fôr′səps) *n.* A two-bladed instrument for grasping and compressing or pulling, used by watchmakers, surgeons, dentists, etc. [L, pincers]

for·ci·ble (fôr′sə·bəl) *adj.* Accomplished by or having force. **—for′ci·ble·ness** *n.* **—for′ci·bly** *adv.*

ford (fôrd, fōrd) *n.* A place in a stream that can be crossed in a vehicle or by wading. —*v.t.* **1** To go across (a stream, river, etc.) at a ford. **2** To drive across a river or stream at a ford, as cattle, etc. [< OE] **—ford′a·ble** *adj.*

for·done (fôr·dun′) *adj. Archaic* Weary; exhausted.

fore (fôr, fōr) *adj.* **1** Preceding in place or time; antecedent; prior. **2** Situated at or toward the front. —*n.* The foremost part or place. **—to the fore 1** To or at the front. **2** At hand; available. —*adv.* **1** *Naut.* At or toward the bow of a ship. **2** In front; forward. —*interj.* In golf, a warning to any person who stands in the way of the ball. [< OE]

fore- *prefix* **1** Prior in time, place, or rank, as in *foreknow, foreman,* etc. **2** In or at the front; front, as in *forecastle, forefoot,* etc. [< OE *fore-, for-* before]

fore-and-aft (fôr′ən·aft′, fōr′-) *adj. Naut.* Lying or going in the direction of the ship's length: *fore-and-aft* sails.

fore and aft *Naut.* **1** From the bow to the stern. **2** In, at, or toward both bow and stern.

fore·arm[1] (fôr·ärm′, fōr-) *v.t.* **1** To arm beforehand. **2** To prepare in advance.

fore·arm[2] (fôr′ärm′, fōr′-) *n.* The part of the arm between the elbow and the wrist.

fore·bear (fôr′bâr′, fōr′-) *n.* An ancestor. [Earlier *fore-be-er,* one who has existed formerly]

fore·bode (fôr·bōd′, fōr-) *v.t. & v.i.* **·bod·ed, ·bod·ing 1** To have a premonition of (evil or harm). **2** To portend; predict. [< FORE- + BODE] **—fore·bod′er** *n.*

fore·bod·ing (fôr·bōd′ing, fōr-) *n.* Apprehension of coming misfortune. **—fore·bod′ing·ly** *adv.*

fore·brain (fôr′brān′, fōr′-) *n.* The largest part of the brain in vertebrates, including the cerebral hemispheres, thalamus, etc.

fore·cast (fôr′kast′, -käst′, fōr′-) *v.t.* **·cast, ·cast·ing 1** To calculate or plan beforehand. **2** To predict; foresee. **3** To foreshadow. —*n.* **1** *Meteorol.* A prediction of weather conditions on the basis of charted data. **2** A prophecy or prediction. **—fore′cast·er** *n.* **—Syn.** *v.* **2** augur, foretell, prophesy, prognosticate. *n.* **2** foresight, foreknowledge.

fore·cas·tle (fōk′səl, fôr′kas′əl, -käs′-, fōr′-) *n. Naut.* **1** The forward part of a ship. **2** In a merchant vessel, the forward compartment with living quarters for sailors.

fore·close (fôr·klōz′, fōr-) *v.* **·closed, ·clos·ing** *v.t.* **1** *Law* **a** To deprive (a mortgager in default) of the right to redeem mortgaged property. **b** To take away the power to redeem (a mortgage or pledge). **2** To shut out; exclude. —*v.i.* **3** To foreclose a mortgage. [< OF *for-* outside + *clore* to close] **—fore·clos′a·ble** *adj.* **—fore·clo′sure** (-klō′zhər) *n.*

fore·fa·ther (fôr′fä′thər, fōr′-) *n.* An ancestor.

fore·fin·ger (fôr′fing′gər, fōr′-) *n.* The finger next to the thumb; index finger.

fore·foot (fôr′fŏŏt′, fōr′-) *n. pl.* **·feet** A front foot of a four-footed animal.

fore·front (fôr′frunt′, fōr′-) *n.* The front part or position, esp. with regard to rank, importance, etc.

fore·gath·er (fôr·gath′ər, fōr-) *v.* FORGATHER.

fore·go[1] (fôr·gō′, fōr-) *v.* FORGO.

fore·go[2] (fôr·gō′, fōr-) *v.t. & v.i.* **fore·went, fore·gone, fore·go·ing** To go before or precede in time, place, etc.

fore·go·ing (fôr·gō′ing, fōr-) *adj.* Occurring previously.

fore·gone (fôr′gôn′, -gon′, fōr′-) *adj.* **1** Determined already; previous. **2** Inevitable: a *foregone* conclusion.

fore·ground (fôr′ground′, fōr′-) *n.* **1** That part of a landscape or picture nearest the spectator. **2** Any prominent position.

fore·hand (fôr′hand′, fōr′-) *adj.* **1** Front. **2** Of or pertaining to a tennis stroke in which the palm of the racket hand faces forward in the direction of the stroke. —*n.* **1** Superiority; advantage. **2** A forehand tennis stroke.

fore·hand·ed (fôr′han′did, fōr′-) *adj.* **1** Done in good time; early. **2** Having money saved; thrifty. **—fore′hand′·ed·ness** *n.*

fore·head (fôr′id, for′-, -hed) *n.* **1** The part of the face above the eyes. **2** The front part of a thing.

for·eign (fôr′in, for′-) *adj.* **1** Situated outside one's own country or locale. **2** Belonging to, characteristic of, or derived from another country; not native. **3** Not usual or characteristic of: something *foreign* to one's nature. **4** Occurring where not normally found: a *foreign* object in the eye. **5** Not pertinent; irrelevant. [< LL *forānus* located on the outside] **—for′eign·ness** *n.*

foreign affairs International affairs in relation to the home government.

for·eign-born (fôr′in·bôrn′, for′-) *adj.* Born in another country; not native.

for·eign·er (fôr′in·ər, for′-) *n.* A native or citizen of a foreign country.

foreign office A department of a government in charge of foreign affairs.

fore·know (fôr·nō′, fōr-) *v.t.* **·knew, ·known, ·know·ing** To know beforehand. **—fore·knowl·edge** (fôr′nol′ij, fōr′-) *n.*

fore·leg (fôr′leg′, fōr′-) *n.* A front leg of a four-footed animal.

fore·lock (fôr′lok′, fōr′-) *n.* A lock of hair growing over the forehead.

fore·man (fôr′mən, fōr′-) *n. pl.* **·men** (-mən) **1** The overseer of a body of workers, as in a factory. **2** The spokesman of a jury. **—fore′man·ship** *n.*

fore·mast (fôr′mast′, -mäst′, -məst, fōr′-) *n.* The mast nearest a ship's bow.

fore·most (fôr′mōst, -məst, fōr′-) *adj.* First in place, time, rank, or importance. —*adv.* In the first place; first. [< OE *formest,* superl. of *forma* first]

fore·named (fôr′nāmd′, fōr′-) *adj.* Named before; mentioned previously.

fore·noon (fôr′nōōn′, fōr′-, fôr·nōōn′, fōr-) *n.* That part of the day from sunrise to noon; the morning.

fo·ren·sic (fə·ren′sik) *adj.* **1** Of, pertaining to, or appropriate for courts of justice or public debate. **2** Argumentative; rhetorical. [< L *forum* market place, forum] **—fo·ren′si·cal·ly** *adv.*

fore·or·dain (fôr′ôr·dān′, fōr′-) *v.t.* To ordain beforehand; predestinate.

fore·paw (fôr′pô′, fōr′-) *n.* A front paw.

fore·quar·ter (fôr′kwôr′tər, fōr′-) *n.* The front portion of a side of beef, etc., including the leg and adjacent parts.

fore·run (fôr·run′, fōr-) *v.t.* **·ran, ·run, ·run·ning** 1 To foreshadow; herald. 2 To run in advance of; precede. 3 To forestall.

fore·run·ner (fôr′run′ər, fōr′-) *n.* 1 A person sent before to give news, a warning, etc. 2 A sign or portent of something to come. 3 A predecessor; ancestor.

fore·sail (fôr′sāl′, -səl, fōr′-) *n. Naut.* 1 A square sail on the foremast of a square-rigged vessel. 2 The fore-and-aft sail on a schooner's foremast.

fore·see (fôr·sē′, fōr-) *v.t.* **fore·saw, fore·seen, fore·see·ing** To know beforehand; anticipate. —**fore·see′a·ble** *adj.* —**fore·se′er** *n.*

fore·shad·ow (fôr·shad′ō, fōr-) *v.t.* To suggest or indicate beforehand; prefigure. —**fore·shad′ow·er** *n.*

fore·sheet (fôr′shēt′, fōr′-) *n. Naut.* 1 A rope used to trim a foresail. 2 *pl.* The forward space in a boat.

fore·shore (fôr′shôr′, fōr′shōr′) *n.* That part of a shore uncovered at low tide.

fore·short·en (fôr·shôr′tən, fōr-) *v.t.* In drawing, to shorten the lines of (an object) so as to create the illusion of depth and distance.

fore·show (fôr·shō′, fōr-) *v.t.* **·showed, ·shown, ·show·ing** To show or indicate beforehand.

fore·side (fôr′sīd′, fōr′-) *n.* 1 The front. 2 Land along the shore.

fore·sight (fôr′sīt′, fōr′-) *n.* 1 Thoughtful care for the future. 2 The act or capacity of foreseeing. —**fore′sight′ed** *adj.* —**fore′sight′ed·ness** *n.*

fore·skin (fôr′skin′, fōr′-) *n.* The loose skin that covers the end of the penis; prepuce.

for·est (fôr′ist, for′-) *n.* 1 A large tract of land covered with trees and underbrush. 2 Such trees. —*adj.* Of or inhabiting a forest. —*v.t.* To plant with trees; make a forest of. [< Med. L *(silva) foresta* an unenclosed (wood)]

fore·stall (fôr·stôl′, fōr-) *v.t.* 1 To prevent by taking prior measures. 2 To realize or prepare for beforehand; anticipate. [< OE *foresteall* an ambush] —**fore·stall′er** *n.* —**Syn.** 1 avert, deter, prohibit, ward off.

for·est·a·tion (fôr′is·tā′shən, for′-) *n.* The planting or conservation of forests.

fore·stay (fôr′stā′, fōr′-) *n. Naut.* A cable from the head of the foremast to the stem.

for·est·er (fôr′is·tər, for′-) *n.* 1 One in charge of a forest, its timber, or its game.. 2 Any forest dweller.

for·est·ry (fôr′is·trē, for′-) *n.* The science of planting, developing, and managing forests.

fore·taste (fôr·tāst′, fōr-) *v.t.* **·tast·ed, ·tast·ing** To have some experience or taste of beforehand. —*n.* (fôr′tāst′, fōr′-) A taste or brief experience beforehand. —**fore·tast′er** *n.*

fore·tell (fôr·tel′, fōr-) *v.t. & v.i.* **·told, ·tell·ing** To tell or declare in advance; predict; prophesy. —**fore·tell′er** *n.*

fore·thought (fôr′thôt′, fōr′-) *n.* 1 Consideration or planning beforehand. 2 Prudent care for the future.

fore·to·ken (fôr·tō′kən, fōr-) *v.t.* To foreshow or presage; foreshadow. —*n.* (fôr′tō′kən, fōr′-) A token in advance.

fore·top (fôr′top′, fōr′-) *n. Naut.* A platform at the head of the lower section of a foremast.

fore·top·gal·lant (fôr′top·gal′ənt, -tə-, fōr′-) *adj. Naut.* Of, pertaining to, or designating the mast, sail, yard, etc., immediately above the foretopmast.

fore·top·mast (fôr·top′mast′, -mäst′, -məst, fōr-) *n. Naut.* The section of a mast above the foretop.

fore·top·sail (fôr·top′sāl′, -səl, fōr-) *n.* The sail set on the foretopmast.

for·ev·er (fôr·ev′ər, fər-) *adv.* 1 To the end of time. 2 At all times; incessantly.

for·ev·er·more (fôr·ev′ər·môr, -mōr, fər-) *adv.* For all time and eternity; forever.

fore·warn (fôr·wôrn′, fōr-) *v.t.* To caution beforehand. —**fore·warn′er** *n.*

fore·word (fôr′wûrd′, fōr′-) *n.* An introductory note or statement at the beginning of a publication; preface.

for·feit (fôr′fit) *v.t.* To incur the loss of through some fault, omission, error, or offense. —*adj.* Lost by way of a penalty. —*n.* 1 A thing lost by way of penalty for some default. 2 FORFEITURE. [< OF *forfait* a misdeed < L *foris* outside + *factum* deed] —**for′feit·a·ble** *adj.* —**for′feit·er** *n.*

for·fei·ture (fôr′fi·chər) *n.* 1 The act of forfeiting. 2 That which is forfeited.

for·gath·er (fôr·gath′ər) *v.i.* 1 To meet or assemble. 2 To meet by chance. 3 To associate socially.

for·gave (fôr·gāv′, fər-) *p.t.* of FORGIVE.

forge[1] (fôrj, fōrj) *n.* 1 A furnace for heating metal ready for hammering or shaping. 2 A shop or factory having such a furnace. 3 A place where metal is refined, as in producing wrought iron. —*v.* **forged, forg·ing** *v.t.* 1 To shape (metal) by heating and hammering. 2 To fashion or form in any way. 3 To make, alter, or imitate with intent to defraud. —*v.i.* 4 To commit forgery. 5 To work as a smith. [< OF, ult. < L *fabrica* smithy] —**forg′er** *n.*

forge[2] (fôrj, fōrj) *v.i.* **forged, forg·ing** 1 To move slowly forward, as in overcoming resistance. 2 To move suddenly with a spurt: to *forge* ahead into the lead. [? Alter. of FORCE]

for·ger·y (fôr′jər·ē, fōr′-) *n. pl.* **·ger·ies** 1 The illegal act of falsely making or altering something, as money, a signature, etc. 2 Anything forged.

for·get (fər·get′, fôr-) *v.* **for·got, for·got·ten** or **for·got, for·get·ting** *v.t.* 1 To be unable to recall (something previously known) to the mind. 2 To fail (to do something) unintentionally; neglect. 3 To lose interest in or regard for: I will never *forget* you. —*v.i.* 4 To lose remembrance of something. —**forget oneself** 1 To be unselfish. 2 To act in an unbecoming manner. [< OE *forgietan*] —**for·get′ter** *n.*

for·get·ful (fər·get′fəl, fôr-) *adj.* 1 Having little power to retain or recall. 2 Neglectful; careless. —**for·get′ful·ly** *adv.* —**for·get′ful·ness** *n.*

for·get-me-not (fər·get′mē·not′) *n.* An herb of the borage family, with blue or white flowers.

for·get·ta·ble (fər·get′ə·bəl, fôr-) *adj.* That may be forgotten. Also **for·get′a·ble.**

for·give (fər·giv′, fôr-) *v.* **for·gave, for·giv·en, for·giv·ing** *v.t.* 1 To grant pardon for or remission of (something). 2 To cease to blame or feel resentment against. 3 To remit, as a debt. —*v.i.* 4 To show forgiveness. [< OE *forgiefan*] —**for·giv′a·ble** *adj.* —**for·giv′er** *n.* —**Syn.** 1 absolve, exculpate, excuse, exonerate.

for·give·ness (fər·giv′nis, fôr-) *n.* 1 The act of forgiving. 2 A disposition to forgive.

for·giv·ing (fər·giv′ing, fôr-) *adj.* Disposed to forgive; merciful. —**for·giv′ing·ly** *adv.* —**for·giv′ing·ness** *n.*

for·go (fôr·gō′) *v.t.* **for·went, for·gone, for·go·ing** 1 To refrain from. 2 To give up; go without. [< OE *forgān* to pass over] —**for·go′er** *n.*

for·got (fər·got′, fôr-) *p.t.* and alternative *p.p.* of FORGET.

for·got·ten (fər·got′n, fôr-) *p.p.* of FORGET.

fork (fôrk) *n.* 1 An implement having a handle and two or more tines or prongs, used for handling food. 2 A pronged agricultural or mechanical implement: a *pitchfork.* 3 The point at which a road, stream, tree trunk, or bough branches off. 4 Each of the branches so formed. —*v.t.* 1 To make fork-shaped. 2 To pierce, pitch, or dig with a fork. —*v.i.* 3 To branch; bifurcate: The trail *forked.* —**fork out** (or **over** or **up**) *Slang* To pay or hand over. [< OE *forca* < L *furca*]

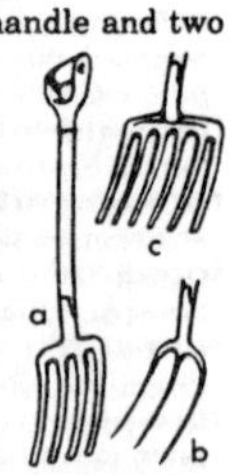

Forks *def. 2*
a. spading.
b. hay.
c. ensilage.

forked (fôrkt, fôr′kid) *adj.* 1 Having a fork, or shaped like a fork. 2 Diverging into two branches: *forked* lightning. —**fork′ed·ly** *adv.* —**fork′ed·ness** *n.*

for·lorn (fər·lôrn′, fôr-) *adj.* 1 Left in distress; deserted. 2 Miserable; pitiable. 3 All but hopeless, as an effort. [< OE *forlēosan* lose, abandon] —**for·lorn′ly** *adv.* —**for·lorn′ness** *n.*

form (fôrm) *n.* 1 The outward or visible shape of a body as distinguished from its substance or color. 2 A body or figure of a living being. 3 A mold or frame for shaping. 4 A specific structure, condition, or appearance: carbon in the *form* of diamonds. 5 A specific type or species: democracy as a *form* of government. 6 Style, manner, and procedure, as opposed to content. 7 Behavior or conduct according to custom, ceremony, or decorum. 8 Manner or fashion of doing something. 9 Condition of body or mind: to be in good *form.* 10 A formula or draft used as a guide. 11 A document with spaces left for the insertion of information. 12 A long bench without a back. 13 *Brit.* A grade or class in a school. 14 *Printing* The body of type and cuts secured in a frame. 15 *Gram.* Any of the various shapes assumed by a word in a particular context, as *talk, talks, talked, talking.* —*v.t.* 1 To give shape to; mold; fashion. 2 To construct in the mind; devise. 3 To combine or organize into. 4 To develop; acquire, as a habit. 5 To go to make up; be an element of. 6 To shape by discipline or training. 7 *Gram.* To construct (a word) by adding or combining elements. —*v.i.* 8 To take shape; assume a specific form or arrangement. 9 To begin to exist. [< L *forma*] —**form'er** *n.*

-form *combining form* Like; in the shape of: *fusiform.* [< L *forma* form]

for·mal (fôr'məl) *adj.* 1 Of, pertaining to, made, or based on established forms, methods, rules, etc. 2 Marked by or demanding elaborate dress, ceremony, etc.: a *formal* banquet. 3 Correct for elaborate or ceremonious occasions: *formal* attire. 4 Regular or symmetrical in form, design, etc.: a *formal* garden. 5 Stiff; punctilious: a *formal* manner. 6 Made or done in accordance with social customs and etiquette: a *formal* invitation. 7 Of or pertaining to external appearance or form: the *formal* elements of a painting. 8 Of or designating language of a more elaborate vocabulary and construction than that of everyday speech or writing. 9 Of or pertaining to the characteristic composition of anything. —**for'mal·ly** *adv.* —**for'mal·ness** *n.*

for·mal·de·hyde (fôr·mal'də·hīd) *n.* A colorless pungent gas, used in solution as a preservative and disinfectant. [< FORM(IC) + ALDEHYDE]

for·mal·ism (fôr'məl·iz'əm) *n.* Scrupulous observance of prescribed forms, esp. in religious worship, social life, art, etc. —**for'mal·ist** *n.* —**for'mal·is'tic** *adj.*

for·mal·i·ty (fôr·mal'ə·tē) *n. pl.* **·ties** 1 The state or character of being formal. 2 Adherence to standards and rules. 3 A proper order of procedure. 4 A formal act, method, or ceremony.

for·mal·ize (fôr'məl·īz) *v.t.* **·ized, ·iz·ing** 1 To make official or binding. 2 To make formal. 3 To give form to. —**for'mal·i·za'tion, for'mal·iz'er** *n.*

for·mat (fôr'mat) *n.* 1 The form, size, typeface, and general style of a book or other publication. 2 Any plan or arrangement. [< L *formare* to form]

for·ma·tion (fôr·mā'shən) *n.* 1 The act or process of forming or developing. 2 Manner in which anything is shaped or composed; structure. 3 Anything that is formed. 4 The disposition of military troops, ships, persons, etc., as in a column, line, or square. 5 *Geol.* A series of associated rocks, having similar conditions of origin.

form·a·tive (fôr'mə·tiv) *adj.* 1 Serving to shape, develop, or form. 2 Pertaining to formation or development. 3 *Gram.* Serving to form words. —*n. Gram.* 1 An element, as a prefix or suffix, added to the root of a word to give it a new grammatical form. 2 A word formed in this way. —**form'a·tive·ly** *adv.* —**form'a·tive·ness** *n.*

for·mer (fôr'mər) *adj.* Going before in time; previously mentioned; preceding. —**the former** The first of two mentioned persons or things. [< OE *forma* first]

for·mer·ly (fôr'mər·lē) *adv.* In or at a past time.

for·mic (fôr'mik) *adj.* 1 Pertaining to ants. 2 Designating an organic acid found in ants, spiders, nettles, etc.

For·mi·ca (fôr·mī'kə, fər-) *n.* A plastic used in sheets as table tops, paneling, etc.: a trade name.

for·mi·da·ble (fôr'mi·də·bəl, fôr·mid'ə-) *adj.* 1 Exciting fear or awe; impressive. 2 Difficult to accomplish. [< L *formidare* to fear] —**for'mi·da·ble·ness** *n.* —**for'mi·da·bly** *adv.* —**Syn.** 1 dire, dreadful, fearful, redoubtable. 2 insurmountable, overwhelming.

form·less (fôrm'lis) *adj.* Without form; shapeless. —**form'less·ly** *adv.* —**form'less·ness** *n.*

for·mu·la (fôr'myə·lə) *n. pl.* **·las** or **·lae** (-lē) 1 A fixed form of words, esp. a conventional expression or statement. 2 Any set method for doing something. 3 A medical prescription. 4 A prescription for a baby's liquid food. 5 Any recipe. 6 *Math.* A rule or combination expressed in algebraic or symbolic form. 7 *Chem.* A symbolic representation of the composition and structure of a chemical compound. [L, dim. of *forma* form]

for·mu·lar·ize (fôr'myə·lə·rīz) *v.t.* **·ized, ·iz·ing** FORMULATE.

for·mu·lar·y (fôr'myə·ler'ē) *n. pl.* **·lar·ies** 1 A collection of forms, formulas, etc.: a *formulary* of drugs. 2 A church ritual. 3 A formula.

for·mu·late (fôr'myə·lāt) *v.t.* **·lat·ed, ·lat·ing** 1 To express in a formula, or as a formula. 2 To put or state in exact, concise form. —**for'mu·la'tion, for'mu·la'tor** *n.*

for·mu·lize (fôr'myə·līz) *v.t.* **·lized, ·liz·ing** FORMULATE (def. 1). —**for'mu·li'zer** *n.*

for·myl (fôr'mil) *n.* The univalent radical of formic acid. [< FORM(IC) + -YL]

for·ni·cate (fôr'nə·kāt) *v.i.* **·cat·ed, ·cat·ing** To commit fornication. [< L *fornix* brothel, vault] —**for'ni·ca'tor** *n.*

for·ni·ca·tion (fôr'nə·kā'shən) *n.* Sexual intercourse between unmarried persons.

for·sake (fər·sāk', fôr-) *v.t.* **for·sook** (-sŏŏk'), **for·sak·en** (-sā'kən), **for·sak·ing** 1 To give up; renounce. 2 To abandon; desert. [< OE *forsacan*]

for·sooth (fər·sōōth', fôr-) *adv.* In truth; certainly: chiefly ironical. [< OE *forsōth*]

for·swear (fôr·swâr') *v.* **·swore, ·sworn, ·swear·ing** *v.t.* 1 To renounce seriously or upon oath. 2 To deny upon oath. —*v.i.* 3 To swear falsely; commit perjury. —**forswear oneself** To perjure oneself. [< OE *forswerian* swear falsely]

for·syth·i·a (fôr·sith'ē·ə, -sī'thē·ə, fər-) *n.* An early-blooming shrub having yellow flowers. [< William *Forsyth,* 1737–1804, Brit. botanist]

fort (fôrt, fōrt) *n.* A military enclosure armed and equipped against enemy attack; fortification. [< L *fortis* strong]

forte[1] (fôrt) *n.* That which one does most readily or excellently: Dancing is her *forte.* [< OF *fort* strong]

for·te[2] (fôr'tā, -tē) *Music n.* A musical chord or passage to be performed loudly. —*adj. & adv.* Loud. [< Ital. < L *fortis* strong]

forth (fôrth, fōrth) *adv.* 1 Forward in place, time, or order. 2 Outward, as from seclusion. —**and so forth** And so on; and the like: equivalent to *etc.* [< OE]

forth·com·ing (fôrth'kum'ing, fōrth'-) *adj.* 1 Ready or about to appear. 2 Available when expected or needed: Aid was not *forthcoming.* —*n.* A coming forth.

forth·right (fôrth'rīt', fōrth'-) *adj.* Straightforward; direct. —*adv.* 1 Straightforwardly; with directness or frankness. 2 At once. —**Syn.** candid, blunt, open, honest.

forth·with (fôrth'with', -wi*th*', fōrth'-) *adv.* Without delay; immediately.

for·ti·eth (fôr'tē·ith) *adj. & adv.* Tenth in order after the 30th. —*n.* 1 The element of an ordered set that corresponds to the number 40. 2 One of 40 equal parts.

for·ti·fi·ca·tion (fôr'tə·fə·kā'shən) *n.* 1 A fortified structure or place, as a fort. 2 A strengthening or enriching. 3 The act or science of fortifying.

for·ti·fy (fôr'tə·fī) *v.* **·fied, ·fy·ing** *v.t.* 1 To provide with defensive works against attack. 2 To confirm; corroborate. 3 To strengthen the structure of; reinforce. 4 To give physical or moral strength to. 5 To strengthen, as wine, by adding brandy. 6 To enrich (food) by adding minerals, vitamins, etc. —*v.i.* 7 To raise defensive works. [< L *fortis* strong + *facere* make] —**for'ti·fi'a·ble** *adj.* —**for'ti·fi'er** *n.*

for·tis·si·mo (fôr·tis'ə·mō, *Ital.* fōr·tēs'sē·mō) *adj. & adv. Music* Very loud. [Ital., superl. of *forte* strong]

for·ti·tude (fôr'tə·t(y)ōōd) *n.* Patient and constant courage to endure pain, adversity, or peril. [< L *fortis* strong]

fort·night (fôrt'nīt', -nit') *n.* A period of two weeks; fourteen days. [< OE *fēowertēne* fourteen + *niht* night]

fort·night·ly (fôrt'nīt'lē) *adj.* Occurring, coming, or issued every fortnight. —*adv.* Once a fortnight.

for·tress (fôr'tris) *n.* A large permanent fort; a stronghold. —*v.t.* To furnish or strengthen with a fortress. [< L *fortis* strong]

for·tu·i·tous (fôr·tyo͞o′ə·təs) *adj.* **1** Occurring by chance; accidental: a *fortuitous* circumstance. **2** Fortunate; lucky. [< L *fortuitus* < *fors* chance] **—for·tu′i·tous·ly** *adv.* **—for·tu′i·tous·ness** *n.* • Although traditionally the use of *fortuitous* in the sense of fortunate has been deplored, such use is now widespread in all but the most formal written contexts.

for·tu·i·ty (fôr·tyo͞o′ə·tē) *n. pl.* **·ties** A chance occurrence.

for·tu·nate (fôr′chə·nit) *adj.* **1** Happening by a favorable chance; lucky. **2** Having good fortune. **—for′tu·nate·ly** *adv.* **—for′tu·nate·ness** *n.* • See FORTUITOUS.

for·tune (fôr′chən) *n.* **1** Chance or luck as the cause of good or bad in human affairs: often personified. **2** That which befalls one as his lot, whether good or bad. **3** Future destiny: to tell *fortunes.* **4** Good luck; success. **5** A large amount of money or possessions; wealth. [< L *fortuna* < *fors* chance]

fortune hunter One who seeks to obtain wealth by marriage.

for·tune·tell·er (fôr′chən·tel′ər) *n.* One who claims to foretell a person's future. **—for′tune·tell′ing** *adj., n.*

for·ty (fôr′tē) *n. pl.* **·ties** **1** The product of four and ten; 40; XL. **2** A set or group of 40 members. **3** *pl.* The numbers, years, etc., between 40 and 50. [< OE *fēowertig*] **—for′ty** *adj., pron.*

for·ty-nin·er (fôr′tē·nī′nər) *n.* An adventurer or pioneer who went to California in 1849, the year of the gold rush.

fo·rum (fôr′əm, fō′rəm) *n. pl.* **·rums** or **·ra** (-rə) **1** The public market place of an ancient Roman city, where most legal and political business was transacted. **2** A tribunal; a court. **3** An assembly for discussion of public affairs. [L]

for·ward (fôr′wərd) *adj.* **1** At, of, or toward the front. **2** For deferred delivery: a *forward* purchase. **3** Advanced toward maturity or completion; esp., precocious. **4** Bold; brash. **5** Advanced; progressive; also, extreme: *forward* in opinion. **6** Ready; eager. *—adv.* **1** Toward the future. **2** Toward the front; ahead; onward. **3** To a prominent position; into view: to come *forward.* **—forward of** In advance of. *—n.* A player who leads the attack and plays in the forward line of his team, as in basketball or hockey. *—v.i.* **1** To promote. **2** To send; transmit; esp. to send (mail) on to a new address. [< OE *foreweard*] **—for′ward·ly** *adv.* **—for′ward·er, for′ward·ness** *n.*

forward pass In football, a pass made toward the opponent's goal.

for·wards (fôr′wərdz) *adv.* FORWARD.

fos·sa (fôs′ə, fos′ə) *n. pl.* **fos·sae** (-ē) *Anat.* A shallow depression or trench. [L, ditch]

fosse (fôs, fos) *n.* Ditch; moat. Also **foss.** [F < L *fossa* ditch]

fos·sil (fos′əl, fôs′-) *n.* **1** A remnant or trace of an organism of a past geological age, preserved in the earth's crust. **2** *Informal* A person or thing that is behind the times, or out of date. *—adj.* **1** Dug out of the earth; petrified. **2** Of or like a fossil. **3** Outworn; antiquated. [< L *fossilis* dug up]

Fossil fern

fos·sil·if·er·ous (fos′əl·if′ər·əs) *adj.* Containing fossils.

fos·sil·ize (fos′əl·īz) *v.* **·ized, ·iz·ing** *v.t.* **1** To change into a fossil; petrify. **2** To make antiquated or out of date. *—v.i.* **3** To become a fossil. **—fos′sil·i·za′tion** *n.*

fos·ter (fôs′tər, fos′-) *v.t.* **1** To rear; bring up, as a child. **2** To promote the growth of; forward; help: to *foster* genius. **3** To keep; cherish; nurse: to *foster* a grudge. *—adj.* Having the relation of being a specific family member, but unrelated by blood: a *foster* child. [< OE *fōstrian* nourish]

fought (fôt) *p.t. & p.p.* of FIGHT.

foul (foul) *adj.* **1** Offensive or disgusting to the senses. **2** Dirty; filthy. **3** Clogged or choked with foreign matter: a *foul* pipe line. **4** Spoiled, as food. **5** Entangled; encumbered: a *foul* anchor. **6** Stormy or unpleasant: *foul* weather. **7** Obscene; profane: *foul* language. **8** Wicked; detestable. **9** Not according to justice or rule; unfair. **10** In baseball, of or pertaining to a foul ball or foul line. *—n.* **1** An act of fouling, colliding, or becoming entangled. **2** A breach of rule in various sports and games. **3** In baseball, a foul ball. *—v.t.* **1** To make foul or dirty. **2** To clog or choke, as a drain. **3** To entangle; snarl, as a rope in a pulley. **4** *Naut.* To cover or encumber (a ship's bottom) with barnacles, seaweed, etc. **5** To collide with. **6** To dishonor; disgrace. **7** In sports, to commit a foul against. **8** In baseball, to bat (the ball) outside of the foul lines. *—v.i.* **9** To be or become foul or fouled. **10** In sports, to violate a rule. **11** In baseball: **a** To bat a foul ball. **b** To be retired by batting a foul ball which is caught before it strikes the ground: usually with *out.* **—foul up** *Slang* To bungle: make a mess (of). [< OE *fūl*] **—foul′ly** *adv.* **—foul′ness** *n.*

fou·lard (fo͞o·lärd′) *n.* A lightweight silk, cotton, or rayon fabric, usu. printed, used for dresses, ties, etc. [F]

foul ball In baseball, a ball batted so that it falls outside the foul lines.

foul line In baseball, a line drawn from home plate through first or third base to the limits of the field.

foul play **1** In games and sports, a violation of rule. **2** Any treacherous act, often with the implication of murder.

found[1] (found) *v.t.* To give origin to; establish: to *found* a college. **—found on** **1** To form and base one's opinion. **2** To rest as on a foundation. [< L *fundus* base, bottom] **—found′er** *n.*

found[2] (found) *v.t.* **1** To cast, as iron, by melting and pouring into a mold. **2** To make by casting molten metal. [< L *fundere* pour] **—found′er** *n.*

found[3] (found) *p.t. & p.p.* of FIND.

foun·da·tion (foun·dā′shən) *n.* **1** The act of founding or establishing. **2** That on which anything is founded; basis. **3** A fund or endowment for the permanent maintenance of an institution. **4** An endowed institution. **5** A base or supporting structure upon which a building, wall, machine, etc., is erected. **6** A cosmetic application underlying other makeup. **—foun·da′tion·al** *adj.*

foundation garment A girdle or corset.

foun·der (foun′dər) *v.i.* **1** *Naut.* To fill with water and sink. **2** To collapse; cave in; fail. **3** To stumble; go lame, as a horse. *—v.t.* **4** To cause to founder. [< OF *fondrer* to sink < L *fundus* bottom]

found·ling (found′ling) *n.* A deserted infant of unknown parentage. [< ME *founden,* pp. of *finden* find]

foun·dry (foun′drē) *n. pl.* **·dries** **1** A place in which articles are cast from metal. **2** The operation of founding. Also **foun′der·y** (-dər·ē).

fount[1] (fount) *n.* **1** FOUNTAIN. **2** Any source; wellspring.

fount[2] (fount) *n.* FONT[2].

foun·tain (foun′tən) *n.* **1** A spring or jet of water issuing from the earth. **2** The origin or source of anything. **3** An artificial jet or spray of water, as for drinking, cooling the air, or display. **4** A structure designed for such a jet to rise and fall in. **5** A container for holding oil, ink, etc. **6** SODA FOUNTAIN. [< L *fons, fontis*]

foun·tain·head (foun′tən·hed′) *n.* **1** The source of a stream. **2** Any main source. **—Syn. 2** beginning, fount, origin, wellspring.

four (fôr, fōr) *n.* **1** The sum of three plus one; 4; IV. **2** A set or group of four members. [< OE *fēower*] **—four** *adj., pron.*

four-flush (fôr′flush′, fōr′-) *v.i.* **1** To bluff by betting on a hand containing four cards of one suit but lacking the fifth. **2** *Slang* To bluff. **—four′flush′er** *n.*

four·fold (fôr′fōld′, fōr′-) *adj.* **1** Made up of four. **2** Being four times as great or as much. *—adv.* Four times as great or as much.

four-foot·ed (fôr′fo͝ot′id, fōr′-) *adj.* Having four feet.

Four Hundred The most exclusive social group of a place: with *the.*

four-in-hand (fôr′in·hand′, fōr′-) *n.* **1** A four-horse team driven by one person; also, a vehicle drawn by four horses. **2** A necktie tied in a slipknot with the ends hanging vertically. *—adj.* Of or designating a four-in-hand.

four-let·ter word (fôr′let′ər, fōr′-) Any of various obscene or offensive words, typically of few letters and usu. having a sexual or scatological meaning.

four·pence (fôr′pəns, fōr′-) *n.* The sum of four English pennies; also, a former British silver coin of that value.

four-post·er (fôr′pōs′tər, fōr′-) *n.* A bedstead with four tall posts at the corners.

four·score (fôr′skôr′, fōr′skōr′) *adj. & n.* Four times twenty; eighty.

four·some (fôr′səm, fōr′-) *n.* 1 A game, esp. of golf, in which four players take part, two on each side; also, the players. 2 Any group of four.

four·square (fôr′skwâr′, fōr′-) *adj.* 1 Square. 2 Firm; solid. 3 Sincere; without guile. —*n.* A square.

four·teen (fôr′tēn′, fōr′-) *n.* 1 The sum of 13 plus 1; 14; XIV. 2 A set or group of 14 members. [< OE *fēowertēne*] —**four′teen′** *adj., pron.*

four·teenth (fôr′tēnth′, fōr′-) *adj. & adv.* Next in order after the 13th. —*n.* 1 The element of an ordered set corresponding to the number 14. 2 One of 14 equal parts.

fourth (fôrth, fōrth) *adj. & adv.* Next in order after the third. —*n.* 1 The element of a numbered set that corresponds to the number four. 2 One of four equal parts; a quarter. 3 *Music* The interval between a tone and another three steps away in a diatonic scale.

fourth dimension The temporal coordinate of a point in space-time.

fourth·ly (fôrth′lē, fōrth′-) *adv.* In the fourth place.

Fourth of July INDEPENDENCE DAY.

fowl (foul) *n. pl.* **fowl** or **fowls** 1 Any of the common domestic birds used as food, as the chicken, turkey, duck, etc. 2 The flesh of fowls. 3 Poultry in general. 4 Birds collectively: *wildfowl.* —*v.i.* To catch or hunt wildfowl. [< OE *fugol*] —**fowl′er** *n.*

fowl·ing-piece (fou′ling·pēs′) *n.* A light gun for bird-shooting.

fox (foks) *n.* 1 A wild, carnivorous animal of the dog family, having a pointed muzzle and long bushy tail, commonly reddish brown in color, noted for its cunning. 2 The fur of the fox. 3 A sly, crafty person. —*v.t.* 1 To trick; outwit. 2 To stain, as paper or timber, with a reddish color. —*v.i.* 3 To become reddish in color. [< OE]

Fox

fox·fire (foks′fīr′) *n.* The phosphorescent light emitted by certain fungi in rotted wood.

fox·glove (foks′gluv′) *n.* Any plant of a genus of the figwort family, esp. one that is a source of digitalis.

fox·hole (foks′hōl′) *n.* A shallow pit dug by a soldier as cover against enemy fire.

fox·hound (foks′hound′) *n.* A large, strong, very swift dog trained to hunt foxes.

fox·tail (foks′tāl′) *n.* 1 The tail of a fox. 2 Any of various species of grass bearing a dense spike of flowers.

fox terrier A small, wire- or smooth-haired terrier, formerly trained to drive out foxes from their lairs.

fox·trot (foks′trot′) *n.* 1 A pace between a trot and a walk: used of horses. 2 A ballroom dance in 2/4 or 4/4 time, having a variety of steps. Also **fox trot.** —*v.i.* **·trot·ted, ·trot·ting** To do a foxtrot.

fox·y (fok′sē) *adj.* **fox·i·er, fox·i·est** 1 Of or like a fox; crafty. 2 Discolored; foxed. 3 Denoting a wild flavor found in wine made from some American grapes. —**fox′i·ness** *n.*

foy·er (foi′ər, -ā) *n.* 1 A public room or lobby, as in a theater or hotel. 2 An entrance room in a house. [F < L, hearth]

F.P., fp, f.p. footpound(s).

fp, fp., f.p. freezing point.

fps, f.p.s. feet per second; foot-pound-second (system).

Fr francium.

fr. fragment; franc; from.

Fra (frä) *n.* Brother: a friar's title. [Ital. < L *frater* brother]

fra·cas (frā′kəs) *n.* A noisy fight; brawl. [< Ital. *fracassare* shatter]

frac·tion (frak′shən) *n.* 1 A disconnected part; fragment. 2 A tiny bit. 3 *Math.* A number expressed as a quotient of two other numbers, esp. a pair of integers with the divisor greater than the dividend, as 7/10. 4 *Chem.* A component separated from a mixture by crystallization, distillation, etc. —*v.t.* To separate into fractions. [< L *fractus,* pp. of *frangere* to break] —**frac′tion·al** *adj.* —**frac′tion·al·ly** *adv.*

frac·tious (frak′shəs) *adj.* 1 Disposed to rebel; unruly. 2 Peevish; cross. —**frac′tious·ly** *adv.* —**frac′tious·ness** *n.*

frac·ture (frak′chər) *n.* 1 The act of breaking, or the state of being broken. 2 A break or crack. 3 A break in a bone or cartilage. —*v.t. & v.i.* **·tured, ·tur·ing** To break or be broken; crack. [< L *fractus,* pp. of *frangere* to break] —**frac′·tur·al** *adj.*

frag (frag) *v.t.* **fragged, frag·ging** *Mil. Slang* To destroy or attempt to destroy with a grenade, as a superior officer or military property. [< *fragmentation bomb,* a type of grenade] —**frag′ging** *n.*

frag·ile (fraj′əl, -īl) *adj.* Easily broken; frail; delicate. [< L *frangere* to break] —**frag′ile·ly** *adv.* —**fra·gil·i·ty** (frə·jil′ə·tē), **frag′ile·ness** *n.*

frag·ment (frag′mənt) *n.* 1 A part broken off; a detached portion. 2 An unfinished or incomplete part: *fragments* of a novel. [< L *fragmentum*]

frag·men·tar·y (frag′mən·ter′ē) *adj.* Composed of fragments; broken; incomplete: also **frag·men′tal.** —**frag′men·tar′i·ly** *adv.* —**frag′men·tar′i·ness** *n.*

frag·men·ta·tion (frag′mən·tā′shən) *n.* The breaking up into fragments.

fra·grance (frā′grəns) *n.* The state or quality of being fragrant; a sweet odor. Also **fra′gran·cy.**

fra·grant (frā′grənt) *adj.* Having an agreeable or sweet smell. [< L *fragrare* smell sweet] —**fra′grant·ly** *adv.*

frail (frāl) *adj.* 1 Easily broken or destroyed. 2 Slender; delicate. 3 Easily tempted; liable to be led astray. [< L *fragilis* fragile] —**frail′ly** *adv.* —**frail′ness** *n.*

frail·ty (frāl′tē) *n. pl.* **·ties** 1 The state of being frail. 2 A fault or moral weakness.

frame (frām) *v.* **framed, fram·ing** *v.t.* 1 To surround with or put in a frame. 2 To put together; build, as a house. 3 To put in words; utter: to *frame* a reply. 4 To draw up: to *frame* a law. 5 To think out; conceive, as a plan. 6 *Informal* To incriminate (an innocent person) by false charges. —*n.* 1 Something composed or constructed of parts united to one another in a system; a framework. 2 The general arrangement or constitution of a thing. 3 Structure or build, as of a person. 4 A machine characterized by a wooden framework or structure: a silk *frame.* 5 A case or border made to enclose or surround a thing, as a window, door, picture, etc. 6 A mental state or condition; mood. 7 In tenpins and bowling, a division of the game during which a player bowls at one setting of the pins. 8 The triangular rack in which the balls in a pool game are bunched ready for the break. 9 One of the individual exposures in a roll of motion-picture film. 10 In television, a single complete scanning of the field of view. [< OE *framian* to benefit] —**fram′er** *n.*

frame house A house built on a wooden framework covered by siding, boards, stucco, etc.

frame of reference 1 A preexisting body of circumstances, facts, or ideas that shape perception, thought, opinion, etc.; orientation. 2 *Physics* A set of orthogonal axes specifying position or motion.

frame-up (frām′up′) *n. Informal* 1 Anything deceitfully prearranged. 2 A conspiracy to convict a person on a false charge.

frame·work (frām′wûrk′) *n.* 1 A skeleton structure for supporting or enclosing something. 2 Any structure or arrangement; plan.

franc (frangk) *n.* 1 A French coin and the basic monetary unit of France. 2 The corresponding basic monetary unit of Belgium, Switzerland, etc. [< OF *Franc (orum rex)* king of the Franks, the motto on the first of these coins]

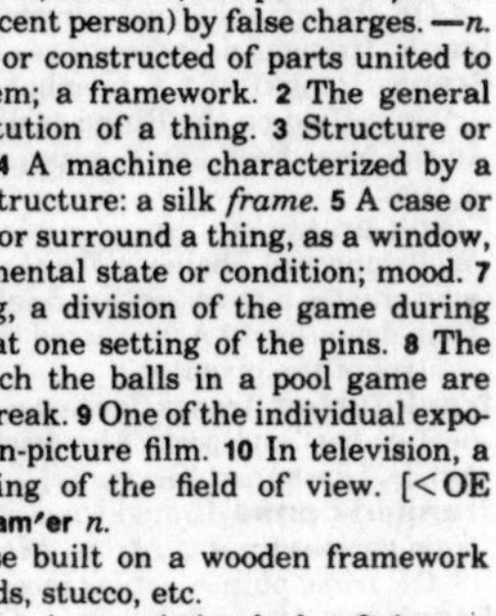

France (frans, fräns) *n.* A republic of w Europe, 212,974 sq. mi., cap. Paris.

fran·chise (fran′-

chīz) *n.* 1 A political or constitutional right reserved to or vested in the people, as the right of suffrage. 2 *Law* A right to do something, as run a railroad, a bus line, etc. 3 The territory or boundary of a special privilege or immunity. 4 Authorization granted by a manufacturer to sell his products. [< OF *franc, franche* free] **—fran′chised** *adj.* **—fran′chise·ment** *n.*

Fran·cis·can (fran·sis′kən) *n.* A member of the mendicant order founded in 1209 by St. Francis of Assisi. *—adj.* 1 Of or pertaining to St. Francis. 2 Of or pertaining to the religious order of Franciscans.

fran·ci·um (fran′sē·əm) *n.* A radioactive element (symbol Fr), isolated from actinium. [< FRANCE]

Franco- *combining form* French: *Franco-Prussian.* [< LL *Francus* a Frank]

Fran·co·phile (frang′kə·fīl) *n.* A non-French admirer of France, its people, customs, etc. *—adj.* Kindly disposed toward France.

Fran·co·phobe (frang′kə·fōb) *n.* A person who fears or dislikes France or French things. *—adj.* Fearful of France.

fran·gi·ble (fran′jə·bəl) *adj.* Easily broken; fragile. [< L *frangere* to break] **—fran′gi·bil′i·ty, fran′gi·ble·ness** *n.* **—Syn.** breakable, brittle, delicate, frail.

fran·gi·pan·i (fran′ji·pan′ē, -pä′nē) *n.* 1 A perfume derived from the West Indian red jasmine. 2 The plant. Also **fran′gi·pane** (-pān). [< Marquis *Frangipani,* 16th c. Roman nobleman, who created a perfume.]

frank[1] (frangk) *adj.* 1 Candid and open; honest. 2 Not concealed or disguised; evident. *—v.t.* 1 To mark, as a letter or package, so as to be sent free of charge. 2 To send, as a letter, free of charge. *—n.* 1 The right to send mail free. 2 The mail so sent. 3 The signature that authenticates it. [< OF *franc* frank, free] **—frank′ly** *adv.* **—frank′ness** *n.*

frank[2] (frangk) *n. Informal* FRANKFURTER.

Frank (frangk) *n.* 1 A member of one of the Germanic tribes settled on the Rhine early in the Christian era. 2 In the Near East, any European. [< LL *Francus* a Frank < Gmc.]

Frank·en·stein (frangk′ən·stīn) *n.* 1 The hero of Mary Wollstonecraft Shelley's *Frankenstein,* a medical student who creates a monster that finally slays him. 2 Frankenstein's monster. 3 Any created thing that gets beyond the control of the inventor.

frank·furt·er (frangk′fər·tər) *n.* A smoked sausage, as of beef or beef and pork. Also **frank′fort, frank′fort·er, frank·furt.** [< *Frankfurt,* Germany]

frank·in·cense (frangk′in·sens) *n.* An aromatic resin from various trees of Africa, Arabia, etc., used as incense. [< OF *franc* pure + *encens* incense]

Frank·ish (frang′kish) *adj.* Of or pertaining to the Franks. *—n.* The Germanic language of the Franks.

frank·lin (frangk′lin) *n.* In late medieval England, a free landholder not of noble birth, ranking below the gentry. [< Med. L *francus* free]

fran·tic (fran′tik) *adj.* Excessively excited by fear, worry, grief, etc.; frenzied. [< OF *frenetique* frenetic] **—fran′ti·cal·ly, fran′tic·ly** *adv.* **—fran′tic·ness** *n.*

frap·pé (fra·pā′) *adj.* Iced; chilled. *—n.* 1 A fruit juice frozen to a mush. 2 A liqueur or other beverage poured over shaved ice. [F, pp. of *frapper* to chill]

fra·ter·nal (frə·tûr′nəl) *adj.* 1 Of or befitting a brother; brotherly. 2 Of or pertaining to a fraternal order or association. 3 Derived from separately fertilized ova: said of twins who are not identical.[< L *frater* brother] **—fra·ter′·nal·ism** *n.* **—fra·ter′nal·ly** *adv.*

fraternal society An organization, often secret, for fellowship and the attainment of some mutual benefit. Also **fraternal association, fraternal order.**

fra·ter·ni·ty (frə·tûr′nə·tē) *n. pl.* **·ties** 1 The condition or relation of brotherhood; brotherliness. 2 A social or service organization, usu. having Greek letter names, and consisting of men students of American colleges. 3 A group of men of the same profession, interests, etc.: the medical *fraternity.*

frat·er·nize (frat′ər·nīz) *v.* **·nized, ·niz·ing** *v.i.* 1 To be friendly or fraternal. 2 To be friendly with the enemy or with the people of an occupied or conquered territory. **—frat′er·ni·za′tion, frat′er·niz′er** *n.*

frat·ri·cide (frat′rə·sīd) *n.* 1 One who kills his brother or sister. 2 The killing of a brother or sister. [< L *frater* brother + -CIDE] **—frat′ri·ci′dal** *adj.*

Frau (frou) *n. pl.* **Frau·en** (-ən) *German* A married woman: as a title, the German equivalent of *Mrs.*

fraud (frôd) *n.* 1 Deception; trickery; guile. 2 *Law* Any artifice or deception practiced to cause one to surrender something of value or a legal right. 3 One who acts fraudulently; a cheat. 4 A deceptive or spurious thing. [< L *fraus, fraudis* deceit]

fraud·u·lent (frô′jə·lənt) *adj.* Proceeding from, characterized by, or practicing fraud. **—fraud′u·lence, fraud′u·len·cy** *n.* **—fraud′u·lent·ly** *adv.*

fraught (frôt) *adj.* Involving; full of: *fraught* with meaning. [< MDu. *vrachten* to load]

Fräu·lein (froi′līn) *n. German* An unmarried woman: as a title, the German equivalent of *Miss.*

fray[1] (frā) *n.* A fight; brawl. [Var. of AFFRAY]

fray[2] (frā) *v.t. & v.i.* To wear, rub, or become worn, as by friction; ravel. [< L *fricare* to rub]

fraz·zle (fraz′əl) *Informal v.t. & v.i.* **·zled, ·zling** 1 To fray or become frayed; fret or tatter. 2 To tire out; weary. 3 To be or cause to be nervous or worried. *—n.* The condition of being frazzled. [? Blend of FRAY[2] + obs. *fasel* ravel]

FRB, F.R.B. Federal Reserve Bank; Federal Reserve Board.

freak (frēk) *n.* 1 A sudden change of mind; a whim. 2 One who or that which is malformed or abnormal; monstrosity. 3 *Slang* One who is given to the use of drugs, esp. illegal drugs. 4 *Slang* One who is very unconventional by society's standards. 5 *Slang* One who is very interested in or enthusiastic about something: an opera *freak. —adj.* Very different; strange; abnormal. **—freak out** *Slang* 1 To experience, often in an unpleasant way, the effects of certain drugs, esp. psychedelic drugs. 2 To behave, without the use of such drugs, in ways similar to those of persons who do use them: to *freak out* over a rock concert.[?] **—freak′ish, freak′y (·i·er, ·i·est)** *adj.* **—freak′ish·ly** *adv.* **—freak′ish·ness** *n.*

freak-out (frēk′out′) *n. Slang* 1 The experience of freaking out. 2 One who freaks out; also, a gathering of such people. [?]

freck·le (frek′əl) *n.* A small mark on the skin produced by exposure to the sun. *—v.* **freck·led, freck·ling** *v.t.* 1 To mark with freckles. *—v.i.* 2 To become marked with freckles. [< ON *freknur* freckles]

free (frē) *adj.* **fre·er, fre·est** 1 Having liberty of action or thought; independent. 2 Not confined, imprisoned, or enslaved. 3 Not subject to despotic or arbitrary rule. 4 Not subject to certain regulations or impositions: *free* trade. 5 Not encumbered or burdened: *free* from debt. 6 Without charge or cost: *free* samples. 7 Available to all; open: a *free* port. 8 Acquitted, as from a legal charge. 9 Not occupied or busy: I am *free* all day. 10 Not limited by strict rules or conventions: *free* verse. 11 Not literal or precise: a *free* translation. 12 Not formal or conventional. 13 Frank; candid. 14 Impertinent; forward. 15 Not constrained; easy. 16 Not attached or fixed: the *free* end of a rope. 17 Not combined chemically: *free* oxygen. 18 Unobstructed; open: a *free* road. 19 Generous; liberal. **—set free** To let go; release. **—make free with** To use freely. *—adv.* 1 Without cost or charge. 2 In a free manner. *—v.t.* **freed, free·ing** 1 To make free; release from bondage, obligation, worry, etc. 2 To clear or rid of obstruction. [< OE *frēo*] **—free′ly** *adv.* **—free′ness** *n.*

-free *combining form* Free of; devoid of: *carefree.*

free·bie (frē′bē) *n. Slang* Anything, as a ticket to a sports event, that is given free.

free·board (frē′bôrd′, -bōrd′) *n.* The side of a vessel between the water line and the main deck.

free·born (frē′bôrn′) *adj.* Not born in servitude.

free city A city having an independent government.

freed·man (frēd′mən) *n. pl.* **·men** (-mən) An emancipated slave.

free·dom (frē′dəm) *n.* 1 The condition or quality of being free. 2 Exemption from political restraint or autocratic control; independence. 3 Liberty of choice or action. 4 Exemption; immunity: *freedom* from want; *freedom* from arrest. 5 Exemption or release from obligations, ties, etc.

6 Ease; facility. 7 Frankness; candor. 8 A bold or excessive familiarity. 9 Unrestricted use: He had *freedom* of the library. [< OE *frēodōm*]

free enterprise An economic system based upon private ownership and operation of business with a minimum of government control.

free-for-all (frē′fə·rôl′) *n.* A fight, game, or competition, open to all comers.

free·hand (frē′hand′) *adj.* Drawn by hand without aid of measurements or instruments: a *freehand* drawing.

free hand Authority to act on one's own.

free-hand·ed (frē′han′did) *adj.* Generous.

free·hold (frē′hōld′) *n.* 1 An estate in lands. 2 Land held for life without limitations or conditions. **—free′hold′er** *n.*

free-lance (frē′lans′, -läns′) *v.i.* **-lanced, -lanc·ing** To serve or work as a free lance. *—adj.* Working or acting as a free lance. **—free′-lanc′er** *n.*

free lance 1 A writer, performer, etc., who does not work exclusively for any one employer. 2 A medieval soldier who sold his services to any state or cause. 3 One who supports a cause independently.

free·man (frē′mən) *n. pl.* **·men** (-mən) 1 One not a slave or serf. 2 One having full political rights and privileges.

Free·ma·son (frē′mā′sən) *n.* A member of an extensive secret order dating from the Middle Ages, the members denoting themselves **Free and Accepted Masons.**

free·ma·son·ry (frē′mā′sən·rē) *n.* Sympathy or community of interests in general.

free on board Put on board a train, ship, or other carrier, without charge.

free·si·a (frē′zhē·ə, -sē·ə, -zhə) *n.* A South African plant of the iris family, having fragrant flowers. [< F.H.T. *Freese,* died 1876, German physician]

free silver The free and unlimited coinage of silver, particularly at a fixed ratio to gold.

Free-soil (frē′soil′) *adj.* Of or pertaining to the Free-soil party, organized in the U.S. in 1848 to oppose the extension of slavery.

free-spo·ken (frē′spō′kən) *adj.* Unreserved or frank in speech; blunt; forthright. **—free′-spo′ken·ly** *adv.*

free·stone (frē′stōn′) 1 Any stone, as sandstone or limestone, easily cut without splitting. 2 A peach or plum whose ripened pulp is easily freed from its pit. *—adj.* Having a pit from which the pulp is easily freed.

free-style (frē′stīl′) *adj.* In competitive swimming, using or marked by the freedom to use whichever stroke the swimmer chooses. *—n.* Free-style swimming.

free·think·er (frē′thing′kər) *n.* An independent thinker; esp., one who forms his own religious beliefs without regard to church authority. **—free′think′ing** *adj., n.*

free trade Commerce between countries free from restrictions such as tariffs, customs duties, etc.

free verse Verse marked by the absence or irregularity of rhyme and by the use of irregular rhythms.

free·way (frē′wā′) *n.* A multiple-lane road designed for high speeds.

free-will (frē′wil′) *adj.* Made of one's own free choice.

free will The power of self-determination; the capacity to choose freely between alternatives.

freeze (frēz) *v.* **froze, fro·zen, freez·ing** *v.i.* 1 To become converted from a fluid to a solid state by loss of heat. 2 To become stiff or hard with cold, as wet clothes. 3 To be very cold: It's *freezing* in here! 4 To become covered or obstructed with ice. 5 To adhere by freezing. 6 To be damaged or killed by freezing or frost. 7 To become motionless, as if frozen, through fear, awe, etc. 8 To become formal or unyielding in manner. *—v.t.* 9 To change into ice. 10 To make stiff or hard by freezing the moisture of. 11 To cover or obstruct with ice. 12 To damage or kill by freezing or frost. 13 To make or hold motionless or in position, through fear, awe, etc. 14 To fix or stabilize (prices, stocks, wages, etc.) so as to prevent change, as by government order. **—freeze out** *Informal* To exclude or drive away, as by unfriendliness or severe competition. *—n.* 1 The act of freezing or the state of being frozen. 2 A spell of freezing weather. 3 The fixing of prices, labor, etc. [< OE *frēosan*]

freeze-dry (frēz′drī′) *v.t.* **-dried, -dry·ing** To freeze (foods, bone tissue, etc.) and remove their water content in a near-vacuum.

freez·er (frē′zər) *n.* 1 A refrigerator for freezing foods or keeping frozen foods. 2 An apparatus for making ice-cream.

freez·ing (frēz′ing) *n.* The freezing point of water: temperatures below *freezing.*

freezing point *Physics* The temperature at which a liquid passes into the solid state under given pressure.

freight (frāt) *n.* 1 a The service of transporting commodities by land, air, or water. b The commodities so transported. 2 The price paid for the transportation of commodities. 3 FREIGHT TRAIN. *—v.t.* 1 To load with commodities for transportation. 2 To load; burden: a sentence *freighted* with adjectives. 3 To send or transport as or by freight. [< MDu. *vracht* a load]

freight·age (frā′tij) *n.* 1 A cargo. 2 The price charged for carrying goods. 3 The transportation of merchandise.

freight car A railway car for carrying freight.

freight·er (frā′tər) *n.* A ship for transporting freight.

freight train A railroad train comprised of freight cars.

French (french) *adj.* Of or pertaining to France, its people, or their language. *—n.* 1 The language of France. 2 The people of France: used with *the.*

French Canadian 1 A descendant of French settlers in Canada. 2 The language of the French Canadians. **—French′-Ca·na′di·an** *adj.*

French chalk A soft chalk for making lines on fabric or for removing grease stains.

French Community A political association comprising France and six of her former colonies, now the states of Chad, Central African Republic, Congo (Brazzaville), Gabon, Malagasy, and Senegal.

French cuff A cuff of a sleeve turned back and secured to itself with a link.

French doors A pair of adjoining doors, often set with glass panes, hinged to opposite door jambs and opening in the middle.

French dressing A salad dressing consisting of olive oil, spices, vinegar, salt, etc.

French fried Cooked by frying crisp in deep fat: said esp. of potatoes (**French fries**).

French horn A keyed, brass wind instrument with a long, coiled tube which ends in a widely flaring bell.

French horn

French·i·fy (fren′chə·fī) *v.t.* **·fied, ·fy·ing** To make French in form or character.

French kiss A kiss with lips apart and tongues touching.

French leave An informal, unauthorized, or hurried departure.

French·man (french′mən) *n. pl.* **·men** (-mən) A native or citizen of France. **—French·wom·an** (french′wŏŏm′ən) *n. Fem.* (*pl.* **·wom·en**) (-wim′ən)

French Revolution The revolution in France against the monarchy, beginning in 1789 and ending in 1799 when Napoleon assumed power.

French toast Bread dipped in a batter of beaten eggs and milk, and fried in shallow fat.

French windows A pair of casement windows attached to opposite window jambs and opening in the middle.

fre·net·ic (frə·net′ik) *adj.* Frenzied; frantic. Also **fre·net′i·cal.** [< Gk. *phrenitis* insanity] **—fre·net′i·cal·ly** *adv.* **—Syn.** distracted, distraught, maniacal, raving, wild.

fren·zy (fren′zē) *n. pl.* **·zies** 1 Violent agitation or action. 2 A brief madness or delirium. *—v.t.* **·zied, ·zy·ing** To throw into frenzy; make frantic. [< Gk. *phrenitis* delirium < *phrēn* mind]

freq. frequency; frequently; frequentative.

fre·quen·cy (frē′kwən·sē) *n. pl.* **·cies** 1 Repeated or frequent occurrence. 2 *Physics* The number of occurrences of a periodic event, as a cycle of a wave, vibration, or oscillation, per unit of time. 3 *Stat.* The number of times a given case, value, or score occurs in a set of data. 4 *Ecol.* The relative number of plant and animal species in a given region. Also **fre′quence.**

frequency modulation *Telecom.* A system in which the modulation signal causes the carrier to vary in frequency.

fre·quent (frē′kwənt) *adj.* **1** Occurring or appearing often. **2** Habitual; persistent. —*v.t.* (*usu.* fri·kwent′) **1** To visit often. **2** To be in or at often or habitually. [< L *frequens, -entis* crowded] —**fre′quen·ta′tion, fre·quent′er** *n.* —**fre′quent·ly** *adv.*

fre·quen·ta·tive (fri·kwen′tə·tiv) *Gram. adj.* Denoting repeated or habitual action: a *frequentative* verb. —*n.* An iterative or frequentative verb.

fres·co (fres′kō) *n. pl.* **·coes** or **·cos 1** The art of painting on a surface of plaster, esp. while the plaster is still moist. **2** A picture so painted. —*v.t.* **fres·coed, fres·co·ing** To paint in fresco. [Ital., fresh] —**fres′co·er, fres′co·ist** *n.*

fresh[1] (fresh) *adj.* **1** Newly made, obtained, received, etc.: *fresh* coffee; *fresh* footprints. **2** Additional; further: *fresh* supplies. **3** Not salted, pickled, smoked, etc. **4** Not spoiled, stale, musty, etc. **5** Not faded, worn, etc.: *fresh* colors. **6** Not salt: *fresh* water. **7** Pure; refreshing: *fresh* air. **8** Appearing healthy or youthful. **9** Not fatigued; active. **10** Inexperienced; unsophisticated. **11** *Meteorol.* Moderately rapid and strong: a *fresh* breeze. **12** Having a renewed supply of milk: said of a cow that has recently calved. [< OF *freis* < Gmc.] —**fresh′ly** *adv.* —**fresh′ness** *n.*

fresh[2] (fresh) *adj. Slang* Flippant; impertinent. [< G *frech* impudent]

fresh·en (fresh′ən) *v.t.* & *v.i.* To make or become fresh. —**fresh′en·er** *n.*

fresh·et (fresh′it) *n.* **1** A sudden flood in a stream. **2** A fresh-water stream flowing into the sea.

fresh·man (fresh′mən) *n. pl.* **·men** (-mən) **1** A first-year student in a college, high school, etc. **2** A beginner; novice. —*adj.* Of or for a freshman.

fresh·wa·ter (fresh′wô′tər, -wot′ər) *adj.* **1** Pertaining to or living in fresh water. **2** Experienced in sailing on fresh water only. **3** Of no experience; untrained. **4** Not well known; somewhat provincial.

fret[1] (fret) *v.* **fret·ted, fret·ting** *v.t.* **1** To irritate; worry; annoy. **2** To wear or eat away, as by rubbing or gnawing. **3** To form by wearing away. **4** To make rough; agitate. —*v.i.* **5** To be angry, troubled, or irritated. **6** To be worn or eaten away. **7** To become rough or agitated. —*n.* **1** The act of fretting. **2** A worn spot. **3** A state of irritation, ill temper, or vexation. [< OE *fretan* devour]

fret[2] (fret) *n.* One of a series of ridges on the fingerboard of a musical instrument, as a guitar. —*v.t.* **fret·ted, fret·ting** To provide with frets, as of a stringed instrument. [?]

fret[3] (fret) *n.* Ornamental work or an ornament, usu. characterized by angular interlocked or interlacing lines. —*v.t.* **fret·ted, fret·ting** To ornament with fretwork. [< OF *frette* a lattice, trellis]

Frets[3]

fret·ful (fret′fəl) *adj.* Inclined to fret; peevish. —**fret′ful·ly** *adv.* —**fret′ful·ness** *n.*

fret·work (fret′wûrk′) *n.* **1** Interlaced ornamental work composed of frets. **2** Perforated ornamental work.

Freu·di·an (froi′dē·ən) *adj.* Pertaining or conforming to the teachings of Sigmund Freud. —*n.* One who upholds the psychoanalytic theories of Freud. —**Freu′di·an·ism** *n.*

Fri. Friday.

fri·a·ble (frī′ə·bəl) *adj.* Easily crumbled or pulverized. [< L *friare* crumble] —**fri′a·bil′i·ty, fri′a·ble·ness** *n.*

fri·ar (frī′ər) *n.* A member of one of the mendicant religious orders, as the Dominicans or Franciscans. [< L *frater* brother]

fri·ar·y (frī′ər·ē) *n. pl.* **·ar·ies 1** A monastery. **2** The institution of friars.

fric·as·see (frik′ə·sē′, frik′ə·sē′) *n.* A dish of meat cut small, stewed, and served with gravy. —*v.t.* **·seed, ·see·ing** To make into a fricassee. [< F *fricasser* sauté]

fric·a·tive (frik′ə·tiv) *Phonet. adj.* Describing those consonants produced by the forced escape and friction of the breath through a narrow aperture, as (f), (v), (th). —*n.* A consonant so produced. [< L *fricare* rub]

fric·tion (frik′shən) *n.* **1** The rubbing of one thing against another. **2** The force that opposes relative motion of two surfaces in contact. **3** Lack of harmony; conflict. [< L *fricare* rub] —**fric′tion·al** *adj.* —**fric′tion·al·ly** *adv.* —**Syn. 1** abrasion, chafing, wearing. **3** disagreement, discord, dissent.

Fri·day (frī′dē, -dā) *n.* **1** The sixth day of the week. **2** The faithful servant of Robinson Crusoe. **3** Any loyal helper. [< OE *Frīgedæg* day of the Norse goddess *Frigga,* wife of Odin]

fried (frīd) *p.t.* & *p.p.* of FRY.

fried cake A cruller or doughnut fried in fat.

friend (frend) *n.* **1** A person whom one knows well and cherishes. **2** An acquaintance. **3** A person who promotes or favors something: a *friend* of wildlife. **4** A person of the same nation or group as oneself; ally. [< OE *frēond*]

Friend (frend) *n.* A member of the Society of Friends; a Quaker. —**Friend′ly** *adj.*

friend·less (frend′lis) *adj.* Having no friends. —**friend′·less·ness** *n.*

friend·ly (frend′lē) *adj.* **·li·er, ·li·est 1** Pertaining to, befitting, or like a friend or friendship; amicable. **2** Not hostile. **3** Helpful; favorable. —*adv.* In a friendly manner. —**friend′li·ly** *adv.* —**friend′li·ness** *n.*

friend·ship (frend′ship) *n.* **1** The state or fact of being friends. **2** Mutual affection or regard.

fri·er (frī′ər) *n.* FRYER.

Frie·sian (frē′zhən) *n.* FRISIAN.

frieze[1] (frēz) *n. Archit.* **1** The horizontal band, either plain or elaborately sculptured, running between the cornice and architrave of an entablature. **2** Any ornamented horizontal band or strip, as around a building, wall, etc. [< Med. L *frisium* fringe]

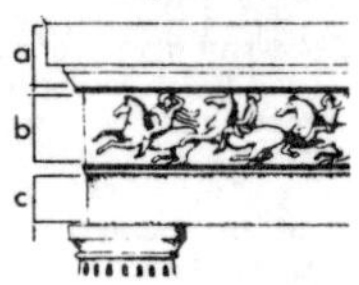

a. cornice. b. frieze. c. architrave.

frieze[2] (frēz) *n.* A coarse woolen cloth with shaggy nap. [< MF *frise*]

frig·ate (frig′it) *n.* A square-rigged war vessel in use up until the early 19th century. [< Ital. *fregata*]

frigate bird Either of two species of large, long-winged, tropical sea birds noted for their rapacity.

fright (frīt) *n.* **1** Sudden and violent alarm or fear. **2** *Informal* Anything ugly, ridiculous, or shocking in appearance. —*v.t.* FRIGHTEN. [< OE *fryhto*]

Frigate

fright·en (frīt′n) *v.t.* **1** To throw into a state of fear or fright; terrify; scare. **2** To drive by scaring: with *away* or *off.* —*v.i.* **3** To become frightened. —**fright′en·ing·ly** *adv.*

fright·ful (frīt′fəl) *adj.* **1** Causing fear or terror. **2** Shocking; repulsive. **3** *Informal* Fearfully bad or unpleasant: a *frightful* toothache. **4** *Informal* Great; extreme: a *frightful* gossip. —**fright′ful·ly** *adv.* —**fright′ful·ness** *n.*

frig·id (frij′id) *adj.* **1** Very cold. **2** Lacking in warmth of feeling; stiff. **3** Lacking in sexual feeling or response: said of women. [< L *frigere* be cold] —**frig′id·ly** *adv.* —**fri·gid·i·ty** (frə·jid′ə·tē), **frig′id·ness** *n.* —**Syn. 1** bitter, freezing, glacial, icy. **2** distant, stuffy, remote, reserved.

frigid zone The areas within the Arctic or the Antarctic Circle. • See ZONE.

fri·jole (frē′hōl; *Sp.* frē·hō′lā) *n. pl.* **·joles** (-hōlz, *Sp.* -hō′·lās) A bean used as food by Latin-American peoples. Also **fri′jol.** [Sp.]

frill (fril) *n.* **1** An ornamental ruffle. **2** *pl.* Affected airs or manners. **3** Any unnecessary ornament or decoration. **4** *Zool.* A ruff of feathers, hair, or membrane on certain birds or animals. —*v.t.* **1** To make into a frill. **2** To put frills on. [?] —**frill′er** *n.* —**frill′y** *adj.* **(·i·er, ·i·est).**

fringe (frinj) *n.* **1** An ornamental border or trimming of hanging threads or tassels. **2** Any outer edge or margin. —*v.t.* **fringed, fring·ing 1** To ornament with a fringe. **2** To serve as a fringe or border for. [< L *fimbria* a fringe]

fringe benefit Any of various benefits received from an employer apart from salary, as insurance, pension, vacation, etc.

frip·per·y (frip′ər·ē) *n. pl.* **·per·ies** 1 Showy or gaudy clothes. 2 Showy affectation in dress, manner, etc. [<OF *freperie*]

Fris·bee (friz′bē) *n.* A light plastic disk used in play by being tossed with a spin from person to person: a trade name. Also **fris′bee.**

fri·sé (fri·zā′) *n.* An upholstery or rug fabric having a thick pile of uncut loops or of cut and uncut loops in a design. [F < *friser* to curl]

Fris·ian (frizh′ən, -ē·ən) *adj.* Of or pertaining to the Dutch province of Friesland, its people, or their language. —*n.* 1 A native or inhabitant of Friesland. 2 The West Germanic language of the Frisians.

frisk (frisk) *v.t.* 1 To move briskly or playfully. 2 *Slang* To search (someone) for weapons, smuggled goods, etc., by running the hand rapidly over his clothing. 3 *Slang* To steal from in this way. —*v.i.* 4 To leap about playfully; frolic. —*n.* 1 A playful skipping about. 2 *Slang* A frisking. [<OF *frisque* lively] **—frisk′er** *n.*

frisk·y (fris′kē) *adj.* **frisk·i·er, frisk·i·est** Lively or playful. **—frisk′i·ly** *adv.* **—frisk′i·ness** *n.*

frit·il·lar·y (frit′ə·ler′ē) *n. pl.* **·lar·ies** 1 A plant of the lily family with checkered flowers. 2 One of various butterflies having brown wings with black spots. [<L *fritillus* a dice box; with ref. to the spots on dice]

frit·ter[1] (frit′ər) *v.t.* 1 To waste (time, money, etc.) little by little: usu. with *away.* 2 To break or tear into small pieces. —*n.* A small piece or fragment: a shred. [?]

frit·ter[2] (frit′ər) *n.* A small fried cake, often containing corn, fruit, or pieces of meat. [<L *frigere* fry]

fri·vol·i·ty (fri·vol′ə·tē) *n. pl.* **·ties** 1 The quality of being frivolous. 2 A frivolous act, thing, or practice.

friv·o·lous (friv′ə·ləs) *adj.* 1 Petty; trivial; unimportant. 2 Lacking seriousness, sense, or reverence; trifling; silly. [<L *frivolus* silly] **—friv′o·lous·ly** *adv.* **—friv′o·lous·ness** *n.*

frizz (friz) *v.t. & v.i.* **frizzed, frizz·ing** 1 To form into tight, crisp curls, as the hair. 2 To form into small, tight tufts, as the nap of cloth. —*n.* That which is frizzed, as hair. Also **friz.** [<F *friser*] **—frizz′i·ly** *adv.* **—frizz′i·ness** *n.*

friz·zle[1] (friz′əl) *v.t. & v.i.* **friz·zled, friz·zling** 1 To fry or cook with a sizzling noise. 2 To make or become curled or crisp, as by frying. [Blend of FRY and SIZZLE]

friz·zle[2] (friz′əl) *v.t. & v.i.* **friz·zled, friz·zling** To frizz hair. [?]

fro (frō) *adv.* Away from; back: used in the phrase *to-and-fro.* —*prep. Scot.* From. [<ON *frā* from]

frock (frok) *n.* 1 A dress. 2 A monk's robe. 3 FROCK COAT. —*v.t.* 1 To clothe in a frock. 2 To invest with ecclesiastic office. [<OF *froc*]

frock coat A coat for men's wear, usu. double-breasted, having knee-length skirts.

frog (frog, frôg) *n.* 1 One of various small, tailless, web-footed amphibians. 2 The triangular, horny pad in the sole of a horse's foot. 3 A section of a railway track where rails cross or join. 4 An ornamental fastening on a cloak or a coat. **—a frog in one's throat** A slight hoarseness. [<OE *frogga*]

Frog

frog·gy (frog′ē, frôg′ē) *adj.* **·gi·er, ·gi·est** Of, like, or abounding in frogs. **—frog′gi·ness** *n.*

frog·man (frog′mən, -man′, frôg′-) *n. pl.* **·men** (-mən, -men′) A swimmer or diver equipped for underwater work, as with a wet suit, flippers, and a breathing apparatus, used esp. for wartime demolition.

frol·ic (frol′ik) *n.* 1 A scene of gaiety. 2 A gay act; a prank. 3 A party. —*v.i.* **frol·icked, frol·ick·ing** To play merrily; gambol. —*adj.* Full of mirth or playfulness; merry. [<MDu. *vro* glad] **—frol′ick·er** *n.*

frol·ic·some (frol′ik·səm) *adj.* Full of frolic; playful: also **frol′ick·y. —Syn.** blithe, gleeful, lighthearted, merry.

from (frum, from; *unstressed* frəm) *prep.* 1 Starting at (a particular place or time): the plane *from* Chicago. 2 Out of: She drew a pistol *from* her purse. 3 Not near to or in contact with: We kept him *from* her. 4 Out of the control or authority of: released *from* custody. 5 Out of the totality of: six cigarettes *from* the pack. 6 As being other or another than: He couldn't tell me *from* my brother. 7 Outside or beyond the possibility of: We kept them *from* leaving. 8 Because of: Skill comes *from* practice. 9 With (some person, place, or thing) as the instrument, maker, or source: a note *from* your mother. [<OE *fram, from*]

frond (frond) *n. Bot.* 1 A leaflike expansion, as the so-called leaf of ferns and seaweeds. 2 The leaf of a palm. [L *frons, frondis* leaf]

front (frunt) *n.* 1 The forward part or surface of anything. 2 The position directly ahead or before a person or thing: the steps in *front* of the church. 3 A face of a building; usu. the face on the entrance side. 4 The line of contact of opposing armies; also, a battle zone. 5 Land facing a road, body of water, etc.; frontage. 6 A coalition of diverse forces working for a common aim: a labor *front.* 7 The forehead or face. 8 Bearing or demeanor, esp. in facing a problem. 9 Outward behavior contrasted with inner feelings: a bold *front.* 10 *Informal* An outward semblance of wealth or position. 11 A person chosen for his prestige to serve as an official of an organization; a figurehead. 12 A person, group, or business serving as a cover for underhanded activities. 13 A starched shirt front, worn by men with formal clothes. 14 In hotels, the bellhop first in line. 15 *Meteorol.* The boundary between masses of cold and warm air. —*adj.* 1 Of, pertaining to or viewed from the front. 2 Situated on, at, or in the front. 3 *Phonet.* Describing those vowels produced with the front of the tongue raised toward the hard palate, as (ē) in *feed.* —*v.t.* 1 To have the front opposite to; face. 2 CONFRONT. 3 To furnish with a front. 4 To serve as a front for. —*v.i.* 5 To face in a specific direction. 6 To be or serve as a front. [<L *frons, frontis* forehead]

front·age (frun′tij) *n.* 1 The front part of a building. 2 The land between a building and the street. 3 The length of something that fronts. 4 The fact or action of facing in a certain direction.

fron·tal (frun′təl) *adj.* 1 Of, pertaining to, on, or at the front. 2 Of or relating to the forehead. **—fron′tal·ly** *adv.*

fron·tier (frun·tir′) *n.* 1 The part of a nation's territory that borders on another country. 2 That portion of a country bordering on the wilderness, newly or thinly settled by pioneer settlers. 3 Any region of thought or knowledge not yet explored: a *frontier* of science. —*adj.* Of, from, inhabiting, or characteristic of a frontier. [<OF *front* front]

fron·tiers·man (frun·tirz′mən) *n. pl.* **·men** (-mən) One who lives on the frontier.

fron·tis·piece (frun′tis·pēs′, fron′-) *n.* 1 An illustration or picture facing the title page of a book. 2 An ornamental front; a façade. [<L *frons,* forehead + *specere* look at]

front-page (frunt′pāj′) *adj.* Of great significance or importance, meriting placement on the front page of a publication.

frost (frôst, frost) *n.* 1 Frozen water vapor or dew. 2 The action of freezing. 3 A temperature below the freezing point. 4 Coldness and austerity of manner. 5 *Slang* A failure. —*v.t.* 1 To cover with frost. 2 To damage or kill by frost. 3 To apply frosting to. [<OE] **—frost′less** *adj.*

frost·bite (frôst′bīt′, frost′-) *n.* The condition of having some part of the body partially frozen. —*v.t.* **·bit, ·bit·ten, ·bit·ing** To injure by partial freezing.

frost·ing (frôs′ting, fros′-) *n.* 1 A mixture of sugar, eggs, butter, etc., used to cover a cake. 2 The rough surface produced on metal, glass, etc., in imitation of frost.

frost·y (frôs′tē, fros′-) *adj.* **frost·i·er, frost·i·est** 1 Attended with frost; freezing. 2 Covered with or as with frost; hoary. 3 Cold and distant in manner. **—frost′i·ly** *adv.* **—frost′i·ness** *n.*

froth (frôth, froth) *n.* 1 A mass of bubbles; foam. 2 Something trivial or frivolous. —*v.t.* (frôth, froth) 1 To cause to foam. 2 To cover with froth. 3 To give forth in the form of foam. —*v.i.* 4 To form or give off froth; foam. [< ON *frodha*]

froth·y (frô′thē, -t͟hē, froth′ē, frot͟h′-) *adj.* froth·i·er, froth·i·est 1 Consisting of, covered with, or full of froth. 2 Frivolous; trivial. —**froth′i·ly** *adv.* —**froth′i·ness** *n.*

frou·frou (frōō′frōō′) *n.* 1 A rustling, as of silk. 2 *Informal* Affected elegance; fanciness. [F]

fro·ward (frō′ərd, -wərd) *adj.* Disobedient; perverse. [< FRO + -WARD] —**fro′ward·ly** *adv.* —**fro′ward·ness** *n.*

frown (froun) *v.i.* 1 To contract the brow, as in displeasure or concentration; scowl. 2 To show one's displeasure or disapproval: with *on* or *upon.* —*v.t.* 3 To make known (one's displeasure, disgust, etc.) by contracting one' s brow. 4 To silence, rebuke, etc., by or as by a frown. —*n.* 1 A wrinkling of the brow, as in anger; a scowl. 2 Any manifestation of displeasure. [< OF *froigner*] —**frown′er** *n.* —**frown′ing·ly** *adv.*

frow·zled (frou′zəld) *adj.* Unkempt; disheveled.

frow·zy (frou′zē) *adj.* **·zi·er, ·zi·est** Slovenly in appearance; unkempt; untidy. Also **frow′sy.** [?] —**frow′zi·ness** *n.*

froze (frōz) *p.t.* of FREEZE.

fro·zen (frô′zən) *p.p.* of FREEZE. —*adj.* 1 Having become ice or covered over with ice. 2 Killed or damaged by freezing. 3 Preserved by freezing. 4 Subject to extreme cold, as a climate or region. 5 Made motionless, as by fear. 6 Unfriendly; cold. 7 Not readily converted into cash: *frozen* assets. 8 Arbitrarily maintained at a given level: said of prices, wages, etc.

frozen custard A smooth-textured frozen dairy product, consisting of skim milk, sweetener, and flavoring, usu. served in an ice-cream cone; ice milk.

FRS Federal Reserve System.

F.R.S. Fellow of the Royal Society.

frt. freight.

fruc·ti·fy (fruk′tə·fī) *v.* **·fied, ·fy·ing** *v.t.* 1 To make fruitful; fertilize. —*v.i.* 2 To bear fruit. [< L *fructus* fruit + *facere* do, make] —**fruc·tif′er·ous** *adj.* —**fruc′ti·fi·ca′tion** *n.*

fruc·tose (fruk′tōs) *n.* A simple sugar occurring in sweet fruit, honey, etc.

frug (frōōg) *n.* An energetic dance characterized by rhythmic twisting movements of the body. —*v.i.* **frugged, frug·ging** To perform this dance. [?] —**frug·ger** *n.*

fru·gal (frōō′gəl) *adj.* 1 Exercising economy; saving; sparing. 2 Meager or inexpensive. [< L *frugalis*] —**fru·gal′i·ty** *n.* —**fru′gal·ly** *adv.* —**Syn.** 1 parsimonious, provident, thrifty, stinting. 2 mean, scanty.

fruit (frōōt) *n. pl.* **fruits** or, collectively, **fruit** 1 The seed-bearing part of a plant. 2 An edible, usu. seed-bearing plant product, esp. a sweet and succulent one. 3 *Usu. pl.* Any natural product of value to man: the *fruits* of the earth. 4 Offspring; issue. 5 A consequence, outcome, or result; the *fruits* of labor. —*v.t. & v.i.* To bear or make bear fruit. [< OF < L *fructus*]

fruit·age (frōō′tij) *n.* 1 Fruit collectively. 2 The state, process, or time of producing fruit. 3 Any result or effect of action.

fruit·er (frōō′tər) *n.* 1 A vessel that carries fruit. 2 A fruit-bearing tree.

fruit·er·er (frōō′tər·ər) *n. Chiefly Brit.* A dealer in fruits.

fruit fly Any of various flies whose larvae feed on fruit, esp. drosophila, a small fly used in genetic research.

fruit·ful (frōōt′fəl) *adj.* 1 Bearing fruit or offspring abundantly; prolific. 2 Producing results; productive. —**fruit′ful·ly** *adv.* —**fruit′ful·ness** *n.*

fru·i·tion (frōō·ish′ən) *n.* 1 The bearing of fruit. 2 The yielding of natural or expected results; fulfillment. 3 Enjoyment. [< L < *frui* enjoy]

fruit·less (frōōt′lis) *adj.* 1 Yielding no fruit; barren. 2 Yielding no results; useless; vain. —**fruit′less·ly** *adv.* —**fruit′less·ness** *n.*

fruit sugar FRUCTOSE.

fruit·y (frōō′tē) *adj.* **fruit·i·er, fruit·i·est** 1 Like fruit in taste, flavor, etc. 2 Full of interest; intriguing. 3 Rich or sweet in tone or manner, often considered flusome. 4 *Slang* Odd; queer; crazy. —**fruit′i·ness** *n.*

frump (frump) *n.* A dowdily dressed, usu. unattractive woman. [? < MDu. *verrompelen* wrinkle] —**frump′ish, frump′y** *adj.* **(·i·er, ·i·est)** —**frump′ish·ly, frump′i·ly** *adv.* —**frump′ish·ness, frump′i·ness** *n.*

frus·trate (frus′trāt) *v.t.* **·trat·ed, ·trat·ing** 1 To keep (someone) from doing or achieving something; defeat the efforts or hopes of. 2 To keep, as plans or schemes, from being fulfilled; thwart. [< L *frustrari* disappoint] —**Syn.** 2 defeat, foil, balk, nullify.

frus·tra·tion (frus·trā′shən) *n.* 1 The act of frustrating or the state of being frustrated. 2 An instance of being frustrated. 3 Something that frustrates.

fry[1] (frī) *v.t. & v. i.* **fried, fry·ing** To cook or be cooked in hot fat, usu. over direct heat. —*n. pl.* **fries** 1 A dish of anything fried. 2 A social occasion, usu. a picnic, at which foods are fried and eaten: a fish *fry.* [< L *frigere*]

fry[2] (frī) *n. pl.* **fry** 1 Young fish. 2 Small adult fish, esp. in large numbers. 3 Young offspring. [? < OF *frier* spawn]

fry·er (frī′ər) *n.* 1 One who or that which fries. 2 A young chicken, suitable for frying.

frying pan A metal pan, usu. shallow and with a long handle, for frying foods. Also **fry pan.**

ft. feet; foot; fort.

FTC, F.T.C. Federal Trade Commission.

fth, fthm. fathom.

ft.-lb. foot-pound.

fuch·sia (fyōō′shə, -shē·ə) *n.* 1 A plant related to the evening primrose, having red, pink, white, or purple drooping flowers. 2 A bright bluish red. —*adj.* Bright bluish red. [< L. *Fuchs,* 1501–66, German botanist.]

fud·dle (fud′l) *v.* **·dled, ·dling** *v. t.* To confuse or make stupid with drink. —*v.i.* To tipple. [?]

fud·dy-dud·dy (fud′ē·dud′ē) *n. pl.* **·dud·dies** *Informal* 1 An old-fashioned person. 2 A faultfinding, fussy person. [?]

fudge (fuj) *n.* 1 A soft confection made of butter, sugar, chocolate, etc. 2 Humbug; nonsense. —*v.i.* **fudged, fudg·ing** 1 To violate or ignore a rule or customary practice. 2 To fail to take a stand; equivocate; hedge. —*v.t.* 3 To make, adjust, or fit together in a clumsy or dishonest manner. 4 To fail to make clear or be decisive about. [?]

fu·el (fyōō′əl) *n.* 1 Combustible matter burned as a source of energy. 2 An element, as plutonium, used in a nuclear reaction to provide energy. 3 Whatever feeds or sustains any expenditure, outlay, passion, or excitement. —*v.t. & v.i.* **fu·eled** or **fu·elled, fu·el·ing** or **fu·el·ling** To supply with or take in fuel. [< OF *fouaille* ult. < L *focus* hearth] —**fu·el·er, fu′el·ler** *n.*

fu·gi·tive (fyōō′jə·tiv) *adj.* 1 Fleeing or having fled, as from pursuit, danger, arrest, etc. 2 Not fixed or lasting; transient. 3 Wandering; shifting. 4 Treating of subjects of passing interest; occasional. —*n.* One who or that which flees; a runaway or deserter. [< L *fugere* flee] —**fu′gi·tive·ly** *adv.* —**fu′gi·tive·ness** *n.*

fugue (fyōōg) *n.* 1 *Music* A form or composition in polyphonic style based upon one, two, or more themes that are introduced by several voices or instruments in turn and are treated contrapuntally. 2 *Psychiatry* A period during which a patient suffers loss of memory, and, after recovery, recalls nothing of the amnesic period. [< F < Ital. *fuga* < L, flight]

Führ·er (fyōōr′ər, *Ger.* fü′rər) *German* Leader: a title applied to Adolf Hitler. Also **Fuehr′er.**

-ful *suffix* 1 Full of; characterized by: *joyful.* 2 Able to; tending to: *helpful.* 3 Having the character of: *manful.* 4 The quantity or number that will fill: *cupful.* [< OE < *full* full] • Nouns ending in *-ful* form the plural by adding *-s,* as in *cupfuls, spoonfuls.*

ful·crum (fōōl′krəm) *n. pl.* **·crums** or **·cra** (-krə) 1 The support on or against which a lever rests. 2 Any prop or support

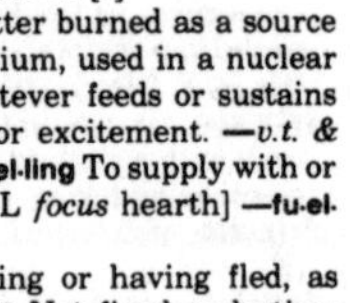

Fulcrum

ful·fill (fōō·fil′) *v.t.* 1 To perform, as a duty or command. 2 To bring into effect or to consummation. 3 To finish; come to the end of. 4 To fill the requirements of; satisfy, as the conditions of a contract. Also **ful·fil′ (·filled, ·fill·ing).** [< OE *fulfyllan*] —**ful·fill′er** *n.* —**ful·fill′ment, ful·fil′ment** *n.*

ful·gent (ful′jənt) *adj.* Beaming or shining brightly radiant. [< L *fulgere* to gleam] **—ful′gen·cy** *n.* **—ful′gent·ly** *adv.*

full[1] (fo͝ol) *adj.* 1 Containing or holding all that is possible or usual; filled. 2 Complete; whole; entire: to charge the *full* price. 3 Total; absolute: a *full* stop. 4 Having many or abounding in: with *of*: *full* of errors. 5 Maximum in size, intensity, extent, degree, etc.: *full* speed. 6 Containing much information, detail, etc.: a *full* report. 7 Filled or satisfied, as with food or drink. 8 Having resonance, depth, and volume: a *full* tone. 9 Having the face wholly illuminated: said of the moon. • See MOON. 10 Having risen to its highest level: said of the tide. 11 Plump or rounded out: a *full* face. 12 Having ample, loose folds: a *full* skirt. 13 Engrossed in or affected by: *full* of ideas; *full* of fear. 14 Filled with emotion: My heart is *full*. —*n.* The maximum degree, extent, size, etc. —*adv.* 1 To the utmost degree or extent; completely. 2 Directly. —*v.t.* 1 To make full; gather, as a sleeve. —*v.i.* 2 To become full. [< OE *ful*]

full[2] (fo͝ol) *v.t. & v.i.* To make or become thicker and more compact, by shrinking: said of wool cloth. [Back formation < FULLER, *n.*]

full·back (fo͝ol′bak′) *n.* In American football, one of the backfield, traditionally the player farthest from the line of scrimmage.

full-blood·ed (fo͝ol′blud′id) *adj.* 1 Of pure or unmixed blood; thoroughbred: also **full′-blood′**. 2 Vigorous.

full-blown (fo͝ol′blōn′) *adj.* 1 Fully unfolded from the bud; in full bloom. 2 Completely developed.

full-dress (fo͝ol′dres′) *adj.* 1 Characterized by or requiring full dress: a *full-dress* dinner. 2 Complete and thorough.

full dress Formal day or evening clothes.

full·er (fo͝ol′ər) *n.* One who fulls and cleanses cloth. [< OE *fullere* < L *fullo*]

fuller's earth (fo͝ol′ərz) An absorbent clay used as a filter and in removing grease from wool.

full-fledged (fo͝ol′flejd′) *adj.* 1 Having grown feathers sufficient for flying. 2 Completely developed, trained, experienced, etc. 3 Of full rank.

full-grown (fo͝ol′grōn′) *adj.* Completely grown.

full moon 1 The moon when it shows its whole disk illuminated. 2 The time when this occurs.

full·ness (fo͝ol′nis) *n.* The state or quality of being full. Also **ful′ness.**

full-scale (fo͝ol′skāl′) *adj.* 1 Unreduced; scaled to actual size: a *full-scale* drawing. 2 All-out: a *full-scale* attack.

full stop A period ending a sentence.

full-time (fo͝ol′tīm′) *adj.* Working or involving full time: a *full-time* student.

full time The amount of time thought of as being equal to all of a person's normal or regular working hours: to go to school *full time.*

ful·ly (fo͝ol′ē) *adv.* 1 Completely; entirely. 2 Sufficiently. 3 At least: *fully* a hundred people.

ful·mi·nate (ful′mə·nāt) *v.* **·nat·ed, ·nat·ing** *v.i.* 1 To explode or detonate violently. 2 To shout accusations, threats, etc.; denounce. —*v.t.* 3 To cause to explode violently. 4 To shout (accusations, threats, etc.). —*n. Chem.* An explosively unstable compound. [< L *fulmen, fulminis* lightning] **—ful′mi·na′tion, ful′mi·na′tor** *n.* **—ful′mi·na·to′ry** (-tôr′ē, -tō′rē) *adj.*

ful·some (fo͝ol′səm, ful′-) *adj.* Offensive and distasteful because excessive: *fulsome* praise. [< FULL, *adj.* + -SOME] **—ful′some·ly** *adv.* **—ful′some·ness** *n.*

fum·ble (fum′bəl) *v.* **fum·bled, fum·bling** *v.i.* 1 To search for something blindly or clumsily; grope: with *for* or *after.* 2 To do something clumsily or nervously. 3 To handle or touch something nervously or awkwardly. 4 In sports, to fail to catch or hold the ball. —*v.t.* 5 To handle clumsily or awkwardly. 6 To do (something) badly or awkwardly; bungle. 7 To make (one's way) unsteadily. 8 In sports, to fumble (the ball). —*n.* The act or an instance of fumbling. [Prob. < Scand.] **—fum′bler** *n.*

fume (fyo͞om) *n.* 1 Any poisonous, irritating, or odorous smoke or vapor. 2 Furious anger. —*v.* **fumed, fum·ing** *v.i.* 1 To give off fumes. 2 To pass off in a mist or vapor. 3 To express or show anger, irritation, etc. —*v.t.* 4 To expose to fumes. [< L *fumus* smoke] **—fum′er** *n.*

fu·mi·gant (fyo͞o′mə·gənt) *n.* Any gaseous disinfectant or insecticide.

fu·mi·gate (fyo͞o′mə·gāt) *v.t.* **·gat·ed, ·gat·ing** To subject to smoke or fumes, as for killing vermin. [< L *fumus* smoke + *agere* to drive] **—fu′mi·ga′tion, fu′mi·ga′tor** *n.*

fun (fun) *n.* 1 Amusement; mirth; enjoyment. 2 One who or that which provides such amusement or enjoyment. 3 Playful, amusing activity. —*adj. Informal* Providing amusement or enjoyment. —*v.i.* **funned, fun·ning** *Informal* To indulge in fun; make sport; jest. [?< ME *fonne* a fool]

func·tion (fungk′shən) *n.* 1 The specific, natural, or proper action or activity of something. 2 One's appropriate or assigned duties or activities. 3 The normal action of any organ or set of organs: the respiratory *function.* 4 A public or official ceremony or entertainment. 5 *Math.* A variable whose value depends on the value of another variable. —*v.i.* 1 To perform as expected or required; operate properly. 2 To perform the role of something else. [< L *fungi* perform]

func·tion·al (fungk′shən·əl) *adj.* 1 Of or belonging to a function or functions. 2 Designed for or suited to a particular operation or use: *functional* architecture. 3 *Med.* Affecting performance only; not traceable to a physical cause. **—func′tion·al·ly** *adv.*

func·tion·ar·y (funk′shən·er′ē) *n. pl.* **·ar·ies** A person who serves in a particular capacity, esp. one who works in a governmental or political position.

fund (fund) *n.* 1 A sum of money or stock of convertible wealth employed in, set aside for, or available for a business enterprise or other purpose. 2 *pl.* Money in general: out of *funds.* 3 A reserve store; an ample stock: a *fund* of humor. —*v.t.* 1 To convert into a more or less permanent debt bearing a fixed rate of interest. 2 To furnish a fund for. 3 To amass. [< L *fundus* bottom] **—fund′a·ble** *adj.*

fun·da·ment (fun′də·mənt) *n.* The buttocks; also, the anus. [< L *fundus* bottom, land]

fun·da·men·tal (fun′də·men′təl) *adj.* 1 Basic; indispensable; essential: *fundamental* principles. 2 Primary; chief: his *fundamental* error. 3 *Physics* Designating that component of a periodic oscillation that has the lowest frequency. —*n.* 1 Anything that serves as the foundation or basis of a system, as a truth, law, or principle. 2 *Music* The root of a chord. 3 *Physics* The fundamental component of a periodic oscillation. **—fun′da·men′tal·ly** *adv.*

fun·da·men·tal·ism (fun′də·men′təl·iz′əm) *n.* 1 *Often cap.* The belief that all statements made in the Bible are literally true. 2 *Often cap. U.S.* A movement among Protestants holding that such belief is essential to Christian faith. 3 Strict adherence to or observance of basic precepts. **—fun′da·men′tal·ist** *n.*

fu·ner·al (fyo͞o′nər·əl) *n.* 1 The rites and ceremonies preceding and accompanying burial; obsequies. 2 A gathering or procession of persons on the occasion of a burial. —*adj.* Pertaining to, suitable for, or used at a funeral. [< L *funus, funeris*]

funeral home A business establishment equipped to prepare the dead for burial or cremation, and often having facilities for funeral services. Also **funeral parlor.**

fu·ne·re·al (fyo͞o·nir′ē·əl) *adj.* 1 Pertaining to or suitable for a funeral. 2 Mournful; gloomy. **—fu·ne′re·al·ly** *adv.*

fun·gi·cide (fun′jə·sīd, fung′gə-) *n.* A compound that kills fungi or destroys their spores. **—fun′gi·ci′dal** *adj.*

fun·goid (fung′goid) *adj.* Resembling a mushroom or fungus. —*n.* A fungus.

fun·gous (fung′gəs) *adj.* Of, pertaining to, or like a fungus. Also **fun·gal.**

fun·gus (fung′gəs) *n. pl.* **fun·gus·es** or **fun·gi** (fun′jī, fung′·gī) 1 Any of a group of plants that reproduce by spores and have no stems, leaves, roots, or chlorophyll, comprising the mushrooms, puffballs, molds, smuts, etc. 2 Anything that springs up rapidly like a fungus. —*adj.* Fungous. [< L, a mushroom]

fu·nic·u·lar (fyo͞o·nik′yə·lər) *adj.* Pulled by a cable. —*n.*

A railway on which cars are pulled up or lowered by a cable. Also **funicular railway.** [< L *funiculus* small cord]

funk[1] (fungk) *n. Informal* 1 Cowardly fright; panic. 2 Low spirits; depression. —*v.t.* 1 To shrink from; be afraid of. 2 To frighten; scare. —*v.i.* 3 To shrink through fear or aversion; try to back out. [? < Flemish *fonck* fear]

funk[2] (fungk) *n. Slang* Jazz music that has an earthy, blues quality.

funk·y (fungk′ē) *adj.* **funk·i·er, funk·i·est** 1 Having a foul odor; malodorous. 2 *Slang* **a** Having a quality expressive of jazz blues; soulful; earthy. **b** Earthily sensual. **c** Conspicuously individual; expressively idiosyncratic, as in dress.

fun·nel (fun′əl) *n.* 1 A wide-mouthed conical vessel, terminating in a tube, for filtering, decanting, etc. 2 A smoke pipe, chimney, or flue. 3 A smokestack on a steamship. 4 Any funnellike part or process. —*v.t. & v.i.* **·neled** or **·nelled, ·nel·ing** or **·nel·ling** To pass or move through or as through a funnel. [< L *infundibulum* < *in-* into + *fundere* pour]

Funnels

fun·ny (fun′ē) *adj.* **·ni·er, ·ni·est** 1 Affording fun; comical; ludicrous; laughable. 2 *Informal* Puzzling; strange; unusual. —*n. pl.* **·nies** *Informal* 1 Something funny. 2 *pl.* A comic strip. —**fun′ni·ly** *adv.* —**fun′ni·ness** *n.* —**Syn.** *adj.* 1 amusing, humorous, droll, farcical, jolly, jovial.

funny bone A sensitive spot at the elbow where the ulnar nerve is near the surface.

fur (fûr) *n.* 1 The soft, fine, hairy coat covering the skin of many mammals. 2 The skin and hair of fur-bearing animals, esp. when prepared for use in making garments rugs, etc. 3 *Often pl.* Apparel made of such skins. 4 Any fuzzy covering, as coating on the tongue. —*v.* **furred, fur·ring** *v.t.* 1 To cover, line, trim or clothe with fur. 2 To apply furring to, as for lathing. —*v.i.* 3 To become coated, as the tongue. [< OF *forrer* line with fur < Gmc.]

fur·be·low (fûr′bə·lō) *n.* 1 A plaited flounce or ruffle. 2 Any showy ornament. —*v.t.* To decorate elaborately or fussily. [< F *falbala* fringe, flounce]

fur·bish (fûr′bish) *v.t.* 1 To make bright by rubbing; burnish. 2 To restore to brightness or beauty; renovate: often with *up.* [< OF *forbir*] —**fur′bish·er** *n.*

fur·cate (fûr′kāt) *v.i.* **·cat·ed, ·cat·ing** To separate into diverging parts; fork. —*adj.* Forked: also **fur′cat·ed.** [< L *furca* fork] —**fur′cate·ly** *adv.* —**fur·ca′tion** *n.*

Fu·ries (fyo͝or′ēz) *Gk. Myth.* The three goddesses who took vengeance on unpunished criminals.

fu·ri·ous (fyo͝or′ē·əs) *adj.* 1 Full of anger; raging. 2 Violent; fierce. 3 Very great; excessive. —**fu′ri·ous·ly** *adv.* —**fu′ri·ous·ness** *n.* —**Syn.** 1 irate, fuming, angry, wrathful, boiling. 2 wild, vehement, turbulent, frenzied, frantic, stormy.

furl (fûrl) *v.t.* 1 To roll up and make secure, as a sail to a spar. —*v.i.* 2 To become furled. —*n.* 1 The act of furling. 2 Something furled. [< OF *fermlier* < *ferm* close + *lier* bind]

fur·long (fûr′lông, -long) *n.* A measure of length, one-eighth of a mile or 220 yards. [< OE *furh* furrow + *lang* long]

fur·lough (fûr′lō) *n.* An authorized leave of absence, esp. one granted to a person in the armed forces. —*v.t.* To grant a furlough to. [< Du. *verlof*]

fur·nace (fûr′nis) *n.* 1 A chamber for heating, fusing, hardening, etc., usu. by heat derived from burning a fuel. 2 A chamber in which fuel is burned to heat a building. [< L *fornax*]

fur·nish (fûr′nish) *v.t.* 1 To equip, or fit out, as with fittings or furniture. 2 To supply; provide. [< OF *furnir*] —**fur′nish·er** *n.*

fur·nish·ings (fûr′nish·ingz) *n. pl.* 1 Articles of clothing and accessories. 2 Furniture, carpets, etc., as for a home or office.

fur·ni·ture (fûr′nə·chər) *n.* 1 Movable household articles, such as chairs, tables, bureaus, beds, etc. 2 Necessary equipment, as for a ship, shop, etc. [< F *fourniture* < *fournir* furnish]

fu·ror (fyo͝or′ôr) *n.* 1 Fury. 2 Great excitement or enthusiasm. 3 An object of enthusiasm; a fad; a craze. [< L *furere* to rage]

furred (fûrd) *adj.* 1 Having fur. 2 Made, trimmed, or lined with fur. 3 Wearing fur. 4 Coated, as the tongue.

fur·ri·er (fûr′ē·ər, -yər) *n.* 1 A person who makes, sells, repairs, or stores fur garments. 2 A person who processes fur, as for garments.

fur·ring (fûr′ing) *n.* 1 Fur linings or trimmings. 2 Trimming or lining with fur. 3 A coating, as on the tongue. 4 The act of applying strips of wood or metal to create a level surface or air spaces. 5 The strips of wood or metal so used.

fur·row (fûr′ō) *n.* 1 A trench made in the earth by a plow. 2 One of the grooves in the face of a millstone. 3 Any groove or wrinkle. —*v.t.* 1 To make furrows in; plow. 2 To make wrinkles in, as the brow. —*v.i.* 3 To become wrinkled. [< OE *furh*] —**fur′row·er** *n.*

fur·ry (fûr′ē) *adj.* **fur·ri·er, fur·ri·est** 1 Of or like fur. 2 Covered with or clad in fur. —**fur′ri·ness** *n.*

fur·ther (fûr′thər) Comparative of FAR. —*adv.* 1 At or to a more distant or remote point in space or time. 2 To a greater degree; more. 3 In addition; besides; also. —*adj.* 1 More distant or advanced in time or degree. 2 Wider or fuller; additional. 3 More distant in space; farther. —*v.t.* To help forward; promote. [< OE *furthra*] —**fur′ther·er** *n.*

fur·ther·ance (fûr′thər·əns) *n.* 1 The act of furthering; advancement. 2 That which furthers.

fur·ther·more (fûr′thər·môr′, -mōr′) *adv.* In addition; moreover.

fur·ther·most (fûr′thər·mōst′) *adj.* Furthest or most remote.

fur·thest (fûr′thist) Superlative of FAR. —*adv.* 1 At or to the most distant or remote point in space or time. 2 To the greatest degree. —*adj.* 1 Most distant, remote, or advanced in time or degree. 2 Most distant in space.

fur·tive (fûr′tiv) *adj.* 1 Done on the sly; secret; stealthy. 2 Not direct; evasive. [< F < L *fur* a thief] —**fur′tive·ly** *adv.* —**fur′tive·ness** *n.*

fu·ry (fyo͝or′ē) *n. pl.* **·ries** 1 A state or fit of violent anger or rage. 2 Violent action or agitation; fierceness; frenzy. 3 A person of violent temper, esp. a woman. [< L *furere* rave]

furze (fûrz) *n.* A spiny evergreen leguminous shrub having yellow flowers. [< OE *fyrs*] —**furz′y** *adj.*

fuse[1] (fyo͞oz) *n.* 1 A treated cord, ribbon, etc., used to carry fire to explosives. 2 FUZE. [< L *fusus* a spindle]

fuse[2] (fyo͞oz) *v.t. & v.i.* **fused, fus·ing** 1 To liquefy by heat; melt. 2 To join or cause to join as if by melting together. —*n. Electr.* An enclosed length of fusible metal set in a circuit to melt and open the circuit in case of an overload. [< L *fusus,* pp. of *fundere* pour]

fu·see (fyo͞o·zē′) *n.* 1 A wooden match not extinguishable by wind. 2 A flare used as a signal on a railroad, by truck drivers, etc. [< L *fusus* spindle]

fu·se·lage (fyo͞o′sə·läzh, -zə-) *n. Aeron.* The part of an airplane that accomodates the crew, passengers, etc., and to which the lifting and control surfaces are fastened. [F < L *fusus* a spindle] • See AIRPLANE.

fu·sel oil (fyo͞o′zəl, -səl) A volatile, poisonous liquid, consisting of a mixture of complex alcohols, produced in small amounts in the production of ethyl alcohol by fermentation. Also **fu′sel.** [< G *Fusel* inferior spirits]

fu·si·ble (fyo͞o′zə·bəl) *adj.* Capable of being fused or melted by heat. —**fu′si·bil′i·ty, fu′si·ble·ness** *n.* —**fu′si·bly** *adv.*

fu·si·form (fyo͞o′zə·fôrm) *adj.* Shaped like a spindle. [< L *fusus* spindle + -FORM]

fu·sil (fyo͞o′zəl) *n.* A flintlock musket. [< OF *foisil* a steel for striking sparks, ult. < L *focus* a hearth]

fu·si·lier (fyo͞o′zə·lir′) *n.* 1 A soldier armed with a fusil. 2 A title of certain British regiments whose soldiers formerly carried fusils. Also **fu′si·leer′.** [F]

fu·sil·lade (fyo͞o′zə·lād′, -sə-, -läd′) *n.* 1 A simultaneous discharge of firearms. 2 Any rapid volley, as of questions. —*v.t.* **·lad·ed, ·lad·ing** To attack or kill by a fusillade. Also **fu′si·lade′** [< F *fusil* fusil]

fu·sion (fyo͞o′zhən) *n.* 1 The act of blending, or the state of being blended throughout. 2 The coalescing of two political parties, or the state of coalescence: often used attributively: a *fusion* ticket. 3 The act or process of changing from a solid into a liquid by the agency of heat;

melting. 4 *Physics* A nuclear reaction in which light nuclei fuse into those of a heavier element, with the release of great energy. [<L *fusus,* pp. of *fundere* pour]

fu·sion·ism (fyōō′zhən·iz′əm) *n.* The doctrine, advocacy, or practice of fusion in politics. —**fu′sion·ist** *n.*

fuss (fus) *n.* 1 Nervous agitation or excitement, esp. over trivial matters; bustle; ado. 2 A quarrel. 3 An excessive praising of something. 4 An objection or protest. —*v.i.* 1 To make a fuss. 2 To fret or fidget, as a baby. —*v.t.* 3 *Informal* To bother or perplex with trifles. [?] —**fuss′er** *n.*

fuss·budg·et (fus′buj′it) *n. Informal* One who is fussy or too particular.

fuss·y (fus′ē) *adj.* **fuss·i·er, fuss·i·est** 1 Inclined to fuss; fidgety; fretful. 2 Troublesome to do or make. 3 Overly ornate or detailed. —**fuss′i·ly** *adv.* —**fuss′i·ness** *n.*

fus·tian (fus′chən) *n.* 1 Formerly, a kind of stout cloth made of cotton and flax; now, a coarse, twilled cotton fabric, such as corduroy or velveteen. 2 Pretentious verbiage; bombast. —*adj.* 1 Made of fustian. 2 Pompous; bombastic. [<Med. L]

fust·y (fus′tē) *adj.* **fust·i·er, fust·i·est** 1 Musty; moldy; rank. 2 Old-fashioned; fogeyish. [<OF *fuste,* barrel odor] —**fust′i·ly** *adv.* —**fust′i·ness** *n.*

fu·tile (fyōō′təl, -til; *esp. Brit.* -tīl) *adj.* 1 Of no avail; done in vain; useless. 2 Frivolous; trivial: *futile* chatter. [<L *futilis* pouring out easily, useless] —**fu′tile·ly** *adv.* —**fu′tile·ness, fu·til′i·ty** *n.*

fu·ton (fōō′ton) *n.* A tightly stuffed mat, used for sleeping directly on the floor. [<Jap.]

fu·ture (fyōō′chər) *n.* 1 The time yet to come. 2 That which will be or happen in time to come. 3 The condition, rank, status, etc., of a person or thing in time to come, esp. a condition of success or achievement: a business with a *future.* 4 *Usu. pl.* Any security sold or bought upon an agreement for future delivery. 5 *Gram.* a A verb tense denoting action that will take place at some time to come. b A verb in this tense. —*adj.* 1 Such as will or may be in time to come. 2 Pertaining to or expressing time to come. [<L *futurus*]

fu·tur·is·tic (fyōō′chər·is′tik) *adj.* Of or pertaining to the future. —**fu′tur·is′ti·cal·ly** *adv.*

fu·tu·ri·ty (fyōō·tʸōōr′ə·tē) *n. pl.* **·ties** 1 The future. 2 The state or quality of being future. 3 The people of the future. 4 A future possibility.

fuze (fyōōz) *n.* 1 A mechanical or electrical device that fires the explosive charge of a shell, bomb, grenade, etc. 2 FUSE[1]. [Var. of FUSE[1]]

fu·zee (fyōō·zē′) *n.* FUSEE.

fuzz[1] (fuz) *n.* Fine particles of down, wool, vegetable fiber, etc. —*v.t. & v.i.* To cover or become covered with fuzz. [?]

fuzz[2] (fuz) *n. Slang* Police. [?]

fuzz·y (fuz′ē) *adj.* **fuzz·i·er, fuzz·i·est** 1 Covered with fuzz. 2 Lacking clarity: *fuzzy* thinking; a *fuzzy* image. —**fuzz′i·ly** *adv.* —**fuzz′i·ness** *n.*

fwd. forward.

-fy *suffix of verbs* 1 Make; form into: *deify.* 2 Cause to be; become: *liquefy.* [<L *facere* do, make]

G

G, g (jē) *n. pl.* **G's, g's** or **Gs, gs, gees** (jēz) 1 The seventh letter of the English alphabet. 2 Any spoken sound representing the letter *G* or *g.* 3 *Music* The fifth tone in the diatonic scale of C major. 4 *Physics* The acceleration of a body due to gravity: written in lower case. 5 *Slang Usu. cap.* One thousand dollars; a grand. 6 Something shaped like a G. —*adj.* Shaped like a G.

G. German; (specific) gravity.

G., g. gauge; grain(s); gram(s); guinea(s); gulf.

g general intelligence; goalkeeper; (specific) gravity.

GA Georgia (P.O. abbr.).

G.A. General Agent; General Assembly.

G.A., G/a, g.a. general average.

Ga gallium.

Ga. Georgia.

gab (gab) *n. Informal* Idle talk; loquacity. —*v.i.* **gabbed, gab·bing** To talk much or idly; chatter. [?<ON *gabba* mock]

gab·ar·dine (gab′ər·dēn, gab′ər·dēn′) *n.* 1 A diagonally woven, twilled, worsted fabric, used for coats, suits, etc. 2 A similar, softer fabric of mercerized cotton. 3 GABERDINE (def. 1). [Var. of GABERDINE]

gab·ble (gab′əl) *v.* **·bled, ·bling** *v.i.* 1 To talk rapidly and incoherently; babble. 2 To utter rapid, cackling sounds, as geese. —*v.t.* 3 To utter rapidly and incoherently. —*n.* 1 Noisy and incoherent or foolish talk. 2 Cackling, as of geese. [? Freq. of GAB] —**gab′bler** *n.*

gab·by (gab′ē) *adj. Informal* **·bi·er, ·bi·est** Given to talk; loquacious. —**gab′bi·ness** *n.*

gab·er·dine (gab′ər·dēn, gab′ər·dēn′) 1 A long, loose, coarse cloak worn by Jews in medieval times. 2 *Chiefly Brit.* GABARDINE. [<MF *gaverdine*]

ga·ble (gā′bəl) *n. Archit.* 1 The upper usu. triangular part of an end wall enclosed by the sloping ends of a ridged roof. 2 The entire end wall of a building, the upper section of which is a gable. —*v.t. & v.i.* **ga·bled, ga·bling** To build or be built with gables. [Prob.<ON *gafl*] —**ga′·bled** *adj.*

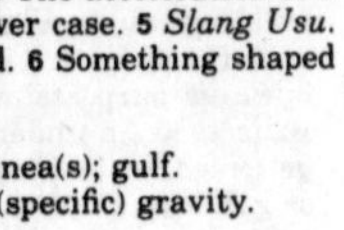

Gable

gable roof A ridge roof terminating in a gable at each end.

Ga·bon (gȧ·bôn′) *n.* A republic of w Africa, 102,290 sq. mi., cap. Libreville. —**Ga·bon·ese** (gab·ə·nēz′) *adj., n.* • See map at AFRICA.

Ga·bri·el (gā′brē·əl) In the Bible, an archangel, appearing as the messenger of God.

gad[1] (gad) *v.i.* **gad·ded, gad·ding** To roam abroad idly; ramble; stray. —*n.* The act of gadding. [Back formation from obs. *gadling* vagabond] —**gad′der** *n.*

gad[2] (gad) *n.* 1 A pointed tool for breaking up ore or rock. 2 A goad (def. 1). —*v.t.* **gad·ded, gad·ding** 1 To break up with a gad. 2 To use a gad or rod upon. [<ON *gaddr*]

Gad (gad) *interj. & n. Archaic* God: a variant form used euphemistically in oaths.

gad·a·bout (gad′ə·bout′) *n.* One who roams or strays habitually. —*adj.* Fond of gadding.

gad·fly (gad′flī′) *n. pl.* **·flies** 1 A large fly that torments cattle and horses. 2 A person who annoys or pesters by criticizing, often constructively. [<GAD[2] + FLY]

gadg·et (gaj′it) *n.* Any small, usu. mechanical or electronic device or contrivance. [?] —**gadg′et·ry** *n.*

gad·o·lin·i·um (gad′ə·lin′ē·əm) *n.* A metallic element (symbol Gd) of the rare-earth series. [<J. *Gadolin,* 1760–1852, Finnish chemist]

Gael (gāl) *n.* One of the Celts of Ireland, the Scottish Highlands, and the Isle of Man.

Gael·ic (gā′lik) *adj.* Of or relating to the Gaels, or to their languages. —*n.* The languages of the Gaels.

gaff (gaf) *n.* 1 A sharp iron hook at the end of a pole, for landing a large fish. 2 *Naut.* A spar for extending the upper edge of a fore-and-aft sail. 3 A gamecock's steel spur. 4 *Slang* Loud or abusive talk. —*v.t.* To strike or land with a gaff. [<OF *gaffe*]

gaffe (gaf) *n.* A clumsy mistake; a blunder; faux pas. [F]

gaf·fer (gaf′ər) *n.* An old man. [Alter. of GODFATHER]

gag (gag) *n.* 1 Something placed in or across the mouth to prevent speech or crying out. 2 Any restraint on free speech or discussion. **3** An instrument for holding open the jaws during a dental operation. **4** A humorous remark or action interpolated by an actor in a play or the like. **5** A practical joke. —*v.* **gagged, gag·ging** *v.t.* **1** To keep from speaking or crying out by means of a gag. **2** To keep from speaking or discussing freely, as by force or authority. **3** To cause nausea in; cause to retch. **4** *Slang* To introduce one's own words or improvise actions into (a theatrical role): often with *up.* —*v.i.* **5** To heave with nausea; retch. **6** *Slang* To make jokes or actions of an improvised nature. [ME *gaggen;* prob. imit.] —**gag′ger** *n.*

gage[1] (gāj) *n., v.* **gaged, gag·ing** GAUGE.

gage[2] (gāj) *n.* **1** Something given as security for some act; a pledge. **2** Something, as a gauntlet, thrown down as a challenge. [< OF *gage* a pledge]

gag·gle (gag′əl) *v.i.* **gag·gled, gag·gling** To cackle; gabble. —*n.* **1** A flock of geese. **2** A group, as of talkative women. [Imit.]

gag·man (gag′man′) *n. pl.* **·men** (-men′) A person hired to write humorous material for comedians, etc.

gai·e·ty (gā′ə·tē) *n. pl.* **·ties 1** Merrymaking; fun. **2** A gay, merry manner. **3** Bright and showy finery.

gai·ly (gā′lē) *adv.* **1** Joyously; merrily. **2** Brightly; showily.

gain (gān) *v.t.* **1** To obtain by or as by effort; earn. **2** To get in competition; win. **3** To reach; arrive at. **4** To get or undergo as an increase, profit, addition, etc.: to *gain* interest or weight. —*v.i.* **5** To increase in weight or speed. **6** To make progress; increase; improve. **7** To draw nearer or farther away: He *gained* on me steadily. —*n.* **1** *Often pl.* An increase or profit, as in money. **2** An increase in size, weight, speed, etc. **3** An improvement or advantage. **4** *Electronics* The ratio of output signal power to input signal power. [< OF *gaaignier* < Gmc.] —**Syn.** *v.* **1** achieve, acquire, attain, get, master, realize, reap.

gain·er (gā′nər) *n.* **1** One who or that which gains. **2** A fancy dive, consisting of a back somersault from a forward facing takeoff.

gain·ful (gān′fəl) *adj.* Yielding profit; lucrative. —**gain′ful·ly** *adv.* —**gain′ful·ness** *n.*

gain·say (gān′sā′) *v.t.* **gain·said, gain·say·ing 1** To deny. **2** To contradict. **3** To speak or act against; oppose. [< OE *gegn-* against + SAY] —**gain′say′er** *n.*

'gainst (genst) *prep.* Against.

gait (gāt) *n.* **1** The manner of walking or stepping. **2** Any of various movements of a horse's feet, as the canter, pace, trot, run, etc. —*v.t.* To train (a horse) to a particular gait. [< ON *gata* way]

gait·ed (gā′tid) *adj.* Having a (particular) gait.

gai·ter (gā′tər) *n.* **1** A covering for the lower leg or ankle, as a legging or spat. **2** A shoe covering the ankle and having no opening in front and usu. elastic sides. **3** An overshoe with a cloth top. [< F *guêtre*]

Gaiter *def. 1*

Gal. Galatians.

gal. gallon(s).

ga·la (gā′lə, gal′ə, gä′lə) *n.* A festive celebration. —*adj.* Festive or appropriate for a festive occasion. [< MF *gale*]

ga·lac·tic (gə·lak′tik) *adj.* **1** *Astron.* Of or pertaining to a galaxy or to the Milky Way. **2** Relating to or obtained from milk. [< Gk. *galaktikos* milky]

Gal·a·had (gal′ə·had), **Sir** In Arthurian romance, the purest and noblest knight of the Round Table, son of Lancelot.

gal·an·tine (gal′ən·tēn) *n.* A cold preparation of boned, stuffed, and seasoned chicken, veal, etc., served in its own jelly. [F]

gal·ax·y (gal′ək·sē) *n. pl.* **·ax·ies 1** *Astron.* Any of the very large systems of stars, nebulae, and other celestial bodies, comparable with the Milky Way. **2** *Usu. cap.* MILKY WAY. **3** Any brilliant group, as of persons. [< L *galaxias* the Milky Way < Gk. *gala* milk]

gale[1] (gāl) *n.* **1** A strong wind, esp. one between 32 and 63 miles per hour. **2** An outburst: *gales* of merriment. [?]

gale[2] (gāl) *n.* A branching, sweet-smelling marsh shrub of the E U.S. [< OE *gagel*]

ga·le·na (gə·lē′nə) *n.* A mineral form of lead sulfide, an important ore of lead. Also **ga·le·nite** (gə·lē′nīt). [L, lead ore]

Gal·i·le·an (gal′ə·lē′ən) *adj.* Of or pertaining to Galileo.

Gal·i·lee (gal′ə·lē) *n.* A hill region of N Israel. —**Gal′i·le′an** *adj., n.*

gall[1] (gôl) *n.* **1** The bitter fluid secreted by the liver; bile. **2** Bitter feeling; rancor. **3** Something bitter. **4** *Slang* Cool impudence; effrontery. [< OE *gealla*]

gall[2] (gôl) *n.* **1** An abrasion or irritation produced by friction. **2** Irritation; annoyance. **3** A person or thing that irritates or annoys. —*v.t.* **1** To make sore by friction; chafe. **2** To vex or irritate. —*v.i.* **3** To be or become chafed or irritated. [Prob. < GALL[3]]

gall[3] (gôl) *n.* **1** An excrescence on plants, caused by various parasitic organisms. **2** A similar excrescence on animals. [< L *galla* the gallnut]

gal·lant (gal′ənt) *adj.* **1** Brave; daring; chivalrous. **2** Stately; imposing; noble. **3** Showy; gay, as in attire. **4** (ga·lant′, -länt′, gal′ənt) Polite and attentive to women; courteous. —*n.* (ga·lant′, -länt′, gal′ənt) **1** A brave and high-spirited man. **2** A man who is attentive to women; also, a man of fashion. [< OF *galer* rejoice] —**gal′lant·ly** *adv.* —**Syn.** *adj.* **1** courageous, fearless, valiant, bold. **4** mannerly, civil, gracious, cordial, affable.

gal·lant·ry (gal′ən·trē) *n. pl.* **·ries 1** Courage; heroism; chivalrousness. **2** Polite or showy attention to women. **3** A gallant act.

gall bladder A small, pear-shaped, muscular pouch situated beneath the liver in man and serving as a reservoir for bile. • See LIVER.

gal·le·on (gal′ē·ən) *n.* A sailing vessel of the 15th to 17th centuries, usu. armed and having three or four decks. [< Med. L. *galea* galley]

gal·ler·y (gal′ər·ē) *n. pl.* **·ler·ies 1** A long, narrow, usu. roofed balcony or other passage projecting from the inner or outer wall of a building. **2** *U.S.* In the South, a veranda. **3** A platform with seats which projects from the rear or side walls of a theater, legislative chamber, church, etc., out over the main floor; specifically, in a theater, the highest of such platforms, containing the cheapest seats. **4** The audience occupying the gallery seats; also, the spectators at a sporting event, etc. **5** The general public and its tastes. **6** A long, narrow room or corridor. **7** A room or building used for the display of works of art. **8** A collection of works of art. **9** A room suggestive of a gallery, used for business purposes: a shooting *gallery;* a photographer's *gallery.* **10** An underground passage, as in a mine. —*v.t.* **gal·ler·ied, gal·ler·y·ing** To furnish or adorn with a gallery or galleries. [< Med. L *galeria*]

gal·ley (gal′ē) *n. pl.* **·leys 1** A long, low vessel used in ancient and medieval times, propelled by oars and sails or by oars alone. **2** A large rowboat. **3** The kitchen of a ship. **4** *Printing* **a** A long tray, for holding composed type. **b** GALLEY PROOF. [< Med. L *galea*]

galley proof *Printing* Proof printed from composed type, used to correct errors or make changes before page composition.

gall·fly (gôl′flī′) *n. pl.* **·flies** Any of various insects whose larvae promote the growth of galls on plants.

Gal·lic (gal′ik) *adj.* Of or pertaining to ancient Gaul or modern France.

gal·lic acid (gal′ik) A crystalline organic acid prepared from certain nutgalls and from tannin and used in the making of inks, dyestuffs, etc.

Gal·li·cism (gal′ə·siz′əm) *n.* A French idiom, as used in any other language.

Gal·li·cize (gal′ə·sīz) *v.t. & v.i.* **·cized, ·ciz·ing** To make or become French in character, language, etc.; Frenchify.

gal·li·na·ceous (gal′ə·nā′shəs) *adj.* Of or pertaining to an order of birds, including chickens, turkeys, partridges, etc. [< L *gallina* hen] —**gal′li·na′cean** *n.*

gall·ing (gô′ling) *adj.* Chafing; irritating; vexing. —**gall′·ing·ly** *adv.*

gal·li·pot (gal′i·pot) *n.* A small earthen jar, used esp. by pharmacists for medicines. [? < GALLEY + POT]

gal·li·um (gal′ē·əm) *n.* A rare metallic element (symbol Ga), used in high-temperature thermometers, semiconductor devices, etc. [< L *gallus* a cock, trans. of *Lecoq* de Boisbaudran, 1838–1912, French chemist]

gal·li·vant (gal′ə·vant) *v.i.* To go about, esp. in search of fun and pleasure. [? Alter. of GALLANT]

gall·nut (gôl′nut′) *n.* An excrescence on a plant, resembling a nut in form.
Gallo- *combining form* French; pertaining to the French or to France. [<L *Gallus* a Gaul]
gal·lon (gal′ən) *n.* 1 A unit of volume equal to 4 quarts. 2 A dry measure; one eighth of a bushel. [<OF]
gal·lop (gal′əp) *n.* 1 A fast, natural gait of a horse or other quadruped. 2 The act of riding, or a ride at a gallop. 3 Any speedy action. —*v.i.* 1 To ride at a gallop. 2 To go, run, or move very fast. —*v.t.* 3 To cause to run at a gallop. [<OF *galop* <Gmc.] **—gal′lop·er** *n.*
gal·lows (gal′ōz) *n. pl.* **·lows** or **·lows·es** A framework consisting of two or more uprights supporting a crossbeam, used for execution by hanging. Also **gallows tree.** [<OE *galga*]
gall·stone (gôl′stōn′) *n.* A concretion found in the gall bladder or bile duct.
gal·op (gal′əp) *n.* 1 A lively dance in double measure. 2 The music for such a dance. [F, a gallop]
ga·lore (gə·lôr′, -lōr′) *adj.* In abundance; in great numbers: refreshments *galore.* [<Irish *go leór,* enough]
ga·losh (gə·losh′) *n. Usu. pl.* An overshoe reaching above the ankle and worn in stormy weather. Also **ga·loshe′.** [< OF *galoche*]
gal·van·ic (gal·van′ik) *adj.* 1 Pertaining to galvanism. 2 Resembling or pertaining to a physiological response to an electric current; spasmodic. Also **gal·van′i·cal.** **—gal·van′i·cal·ly** *adv.*
gal·va·nism (gal′və·niz′əm) *n.* 1 Electricity, esp. when produced by chemical action. 2 The therapeutic application of electric current. [<L. *Galvani,* 1737–98, Italian physiologist]
gal·va·nize (gal′və·nīz) *v.t.* **·nized, ·niz·ing** 1 To stimulate to muscular action by electricity. 2 To rouse to action; startle; excite. 3 To protect (iron or steel) from rust with a coating of zinc. **—gal′va·ni·za′tion** *n.*
galvanized iron Iron coated with zinc.
gal·va·nom·e·ter (gal′və·nom′ə·tər) *n.* An apparatus for measuring electric current. **—gal·va·no·met·ric** (gal′və·nō·met′rik, gal·van′ō-) or **·ri·cal** *adj.*
gam (gam) *n. Slang* A leg, esp. a shapely leg of a woman. [<OF *gambe*]
Gam·bi·a (gam′bē·ə) *n.* A republic in w Africa, 4,003 sq. mi., cap. Bathurst. Also **the Gambia. —Gam′bi·an** *adj., n.* • See map at AFRICA.
gam·bit (gam′bit) *n.* 1 One of various openings in chess, in which a pawn or piece is risked to obtain an advantage. 2 Any opening move or strategy. [<Ital. *gambetto* a tripping up]
gam·ble (gam′bəl) *v.* **gam·bled, gam·bling** *v.i.* 1 To risk or bet something of value on the outcome of an event, a game of chance, etc. 2 To take a risk to obtain a desired result. —*v.t.* 3 To wager or bet (something of value). 4 To lose or squander by gaming: usu. with *away.* —*n.* 1 Any risky or uncertain venture. 2 A gambling transaction. [<OE *gamenian* sport, play] **—gam′bler** *n.*
gam·bol (gam′bəl) *v.i.* **·boled** or **·bolled, ·bol·ing** or **·bol·ling** To skip or leap about in play; frolic. —*n.* A skipping about in sport. [<Ital. *gamba* leg]
gam·brel (gam′brəl) *n.* 1 The hock of an animal. 2 *Archit.* A roof having its slope broken by an obtuse angle: also **gambrel roof.** [<LL *gamba* leg]

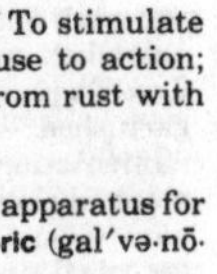
Gambrel roof

game[1] (gām) *n.* 1 Any physical or mental contest, played according to rules, and depending on strength, skill, or luck to win. 2 A definite portion or division of such a contest. 3 The number of points required to win: *Game* is 100 points. 4 Success; victory: The *game* is ours. 5 Equipment used in certain games: to buy a *game.* 6 Manner or art of competitive playing. 7 Amusement; fun; sport; play: to make a *game* of cooking. 8 Something thought of as competitive, requiring skill, etc.: the *game* of politics. 9 A strategy; scheme; plan: What is your *game?* 10 Wild animals or birds pursued or caught for sport or profit; also their flesh. 11 Any object of pursuit or attack: They were fair *game* for ridicule. 12 *Slang* A business; vocation; esp. one involving risk. —*v.i.* **gamed, gam·ing** To gamble at cards, dice, etc., for money or other stakes. —*adj.* 1 Of or pertaining to hunted wild birds or animals or their flesh. 2 Plucky; spirited; intrepid. 3 Ready; willing. [<OE *gamen*]
game[2] (gām) *adj. Informal* Lame or hurt: a *game* leg. [?]
game bird Any bird commonly hunted as game, as pheasant, wild duck, or partridge.
game·cock (gām′kok′) *n.* A rooster bred and trained for fighting. Also **game cock.**
game·keep·er (gām′kē′pər) *n.* A person having the care of game, as in a preserve or park.
game·ly (gām′lē) *adv.* In a game manner; pluckily. Also **gam′i·ly.**
game·ness (gām′nis) *n.* Pluck; bravery.
game·ster (gām′stər) *n.* One who gambles; gambler.
gam·ete (gam′ēt, gə·mēt′) *n.* Either of two mature reproductive cells, an ovum or sperm, which in uniting produce a zygote. [<Gk. *gametē* wife, or *gametēs* husband] **—ga·met·ic** (gə·met′ik) *adj.* **—ga·met′i·cal·ly** *adv.*
game theory In games and conflicts, the mathematical analysis of various strategies in order to determine the specific strategy having maximum potential.
ga·me·to·phyte (gə·mē′tə·fīt) *n.* That phase or generation of a plant which produces gametes. **—gam·e·to·phyt·ic** (gam′ə·tō·fit′ik) *adj.*
gam·in (gam′in; *Fr.* gȧ·maṅ′) *n.* 1 A neglected boy of city streets. 2 A girl with elfin charm. [F]
gam·ing (gā′ming) *n.* The act or practice of gambling.
gam·ma (gam′ə) *n.* 1 The third letter in the Greek alphabet (Γ, γ). 2 The third in a series or group.
gamma globulin A component of blood serum which contains various antibodies.
gamma rays Electromagnetic waves having higher frequencies and energies than X-rays and, thus, greater penetrating power.
gam·mer (gam′ər) *n. Brit. Regional* An old woman; grandmother. [Alter. of GODMOTHER]
gam·mon[1] (gam′ən) *n.* In backgammon, a defeat in which the winner throws all his men before the loser throws off any. —*v.t.* To obtain a gammon over. [? ME *gamen* a game]
gam·mon[2] (gam′ən) *Brit. Informal n.* Deceitful nonsense or trickery. [?]
gam·mon[3] (gam′ən) *n.* 1 A cured ham. 2 The bottom end of a side of bacon. [<LL *gamba* leg]
-gamous *combining form* Pertaining to marriage or union for reproduction: *polygamous.* [<Gk. *gamos* marriage + -OUS]
gam·ut (gam′ət) *n.* 1 The entire range of musical tones. 2 The whole range of anything: the *gamut* of emotions. [<Med. L *gamma ut* < *gamma,* the first note of the early musical scale + *ut* (later, *do*); the names of the notes of the scale were taken from a medieval Latin hymn: *Ut* queant laxis *Re*sonare fibris, *Mi*ra gestorum *Fa*muli tuorum, *Sol*ve polluti *La*bii reatum, *S*ancte *I*ohannes]
gam·y (gā′mē) *adj.* **gam·i·er, gam·i·est** 1 Having the flavor of game, esp. when somewhat tainted. 2 Full of pluck; disposed to fight. 3 Risqué.
-gamy *combining form* Marriage or union for reproduction: *polygamy.* [<Gk. *gamos* marriage]
gan·der (gan′dər) *n.* 1 A male goose. 2 A dunce. 3 *Slang* A look; glance. [<OE *gandra*]
gang[1] (gang) *n.* 1 A group of persons acting or operating together: a *gang* of workers. 2 A group of criminals operating together as a unit. 3 A neighborhood group, usu. of young people, often engaged in antisocial behavior. 4 A group of friends. 5 A set of similar tools, etc. —*v.t.* 1 To unite into or as into a gang. 2 *Informal* To attack as a group. —*v.i.* 3 To come together as a gang; form a gang. [<OE *gangan* go]
gang·land (gang′land′) *n.* Criminal gangs collectively.
gan·gling (gang′gling) *adj.* Awkwardly tall and loosely built. Also **gan′gly.** [<Regional *gangrel* wanderer < OE *gangan* go]

gan·gli·on (gang′glē·ən) *n. pl.* **·gli·ons** or **·gli·a** (glē·ə) **1** A nexus or center of nerve cells. **2** Any center of energy, activity, or strength. [< Gk., tumor] **—gan·gli·on·ic** (gang′glē·on′ik) *adj.*

gang·plank (gang′plangk′) *n.* A temporary passageway between a vessel and a wharf. [< obs. *gang* way, going + PLANK]

gang-rape (gang′rāp′) *n.* Rape committed successively by the individuals in a group. —*v.t.* **-raped, -rap·ing** To subject to gang-rape.

gan·grene (gang′grēn, gang·grēn′) *n.* Death and decay of tissue due to inadequate blood supply, injury, etc. —*v.t. & v.i.* **gan·grened, gan·gren·ing** To cause gangrene in or become affected by gangrene. [< Gk. *gangraina*] **—gan′gre·nous** (-grə·nəs) *adj.*

gang·ster (gang′stər) *n.* A member of a gang of criminals. **—gang′ster·ism** *n.*

gang·way (gang′wā′) *n.* **1** A passageway through, into, or out of any enclosure; esp. a temporary passageway made of planks. **2** GANGPLANK. —*interj.* Get out of the way! Stand aside! [< Obs. *gang* way, going + WAY]

gan·net (gan′it) *n.* Any of several large sea birds related to the pelicans. [< OE *ganot*]

gan·oid (gan′oid) *adj.* Of or pertaining to a large division of fishes, including sturgeons, bowfins, etc., having rows of hard, shiny scales or plates. —*n.* A ganoid fish. [< Gk. *ganos* brightness + -OID]

gant·let[1] (gônt′lit, gant′-) *n.* **1** GAUNTLET[1]. **2** GAUNTLET[2].

gan·try (gan′trē) *n. pl.* **·tries** **1** A raised, horizontal framework for supporting a traveling crane, railway signals, etc. **2** A movable tower used in servicing or assembling rockets. **3** A frame to hold a barrel horizontally. [< OF *chantier* < L *cantherius* framework]

gaol (jāl) *n. Brit.* JAIL. [Var. of JAIL] **—gaol′er** *n.*

gap (gap) *n.* **1** An opening or parting in anything; aperture; breach; chasm. **2** A deep cleft in a mountain ridge. **3** A break in continuity; an interruption. **4** A difference, as between opinions. —*v.t. & v.i.* **gapped, gap·ping** To make or have a gap or opening in (something). [< ON, gap, abyss]

gape (gāp, gap) *v.i.* **gaped, gap·ing** **1** To stare openmouthed, as in awe or surprise. **2** To open the mouth wide, as in yawning. **3** To be or become open wide; present a wide opening. —*n.* **1** The act of gaping. **2** A gap. [< ON *gapa*] **—gap′er** *n.*

gar (gär) *n. pl.* **gars** or **gar** Any of several fishes having a spearlike snout. [< GARFISH]

G.A.R. Grand Army of the Republic.

ga·rage (gə·räzh′, -räj′, *Brit.* gar′ij) *n.* A building in which motor vehicles are parked, serviced, or repaired. —*v.t.* **ga·raged, ga·rag·ing** To put or keep in a garage. [< OF *garer* protect < Gmc.]

garb (gärb) *n.* **1** Clothes, esp. as characteristic of some office, rank, etc. **2** External appearance or manner. —*v.t.* To clothe; dress. [< MF *garbe* gracefulness]

gar·bage (gär′bij) *n.* **1** Refuse matter, as waste food, empty bottles, paper, etc. **2** Anything worthless or disgusting. [Prob. < AF]

gar·ble (gär′bəl) *v.t.* **gar·bled, gar·bling** **1** To mix up or confuse; make incomprehensible: to *garble* a message. **2** To change the meaning of (a document, report, etc.) with intent to mislead or misrepresent. [< Ital. *garbellare* < Ar. *gharbala* sift]

gar·çon (gár·sôn′) *n. pl.* **·çons** (-sôn′) A waiter. [F, boy]

gar·den (gär′dən) *n.* **1** A place for the cultivation of flowers, vegetables, or small plants. **2** Any fertile or highly cultivated territory. **3** A piece of ground, commonly with ornamental plants or trees, used as a public park. —*adj.* **1** Of, for, used, or grown in a garden. **2** Ordinary; common. **3** Like a garden; ornamental: *garden* spot of the world. —*v.t.* **1** To cultivate as a garden. —*v.i.* **2** To till or work in a garden. [< AF *gardin*] **—gar′den·er** *n.*

gar·de·ni·a (gär·dēn′yə, -dē′nē·ə) *n.* **1** Any of a genus of mainly tropical evergreen shrubs or trees with fragrant yellow or white flowers. **2** The flower itself. [< A. *Garden,* 1730–91, Scottish naturalist]

gar·fish (gär′fish′) *n. pl.* **·fish** or **·fish·es** A fish with a spearlike snout; a gar. [< OE *gār* spear + FISH]

gar·gan·tu·an (gär·gan′chōō·ən) *adj. Often cap.* Huge; gigantic; prodigious. [< *Gargantua,* the peace-loving giant in Rabelais' satire *Gargantua and Pantagruel*]

gar·gle (gär′gəl) *v.* **gar·gled, gar·gling** *v.t.* **1** To rinse (the throat) with a liquid agitated by air from the windpipe. —*v.i.* **2** To use a gargle. **3** To make a sound as if gargling. —*n.* A liquid for gargling. [< OF *gargouille* throat]

gar·goyle (gär′goil) *n.* A waterspout, usu. carved in a grotesque human or animal figure, projecting from the gutter of a building. [< OF *gargouille* throat] **—gar′goyled** *adj.*

Gargoyle

gar·ish (gâr′ish) *adj.* Bright and showy, esp. in a gaudy or vulgar manner. [< ME *gauren* to stare] **—gar′ish·ly** *adv.* **—gar′ish·ness** *n.* **—Syn.** flashy, ornate, tawdry, cheap, ostentatious.

gar·land (gär′lənd) *n.* **1** A wreath of leaves, flowers, etc., as a token of victory, joy, or honor. **2** An anthology of short literary selections. —*v.t.* To deck with or as with a garland. [< OF *garlande*]

gar·lic (gär′lik) *n.* **1** A hardy bulbous perennial of the same genus as the onion. **2** Its pungent bulb, used in cooking. [< OE *gār* spear + *lēac* leek] **—gar′lick·y** *adj.*

gar·ment (gär′mənt) *n.* **1** An article of clothing. **2** *pl.* Clothes. **3** Any covering. —*v.t.* To clothe. [< OF *garnir* garnish]

gar·ner (gär′nər) *v.t.* To gather or store; collect. —*n.* **1** GRANARY. **2** Any storage place. [< L *granarium* a granary]

gar·net (gär′nit) *n.* **1** One of various glassy silicate minerals, used as abrasives and sometimes as gems. **2** Its usual color, a deep red. [< Med. L *granatum* a pomegranate]

gar·nish (gär′nish) *v.t.* **1** To decorate, as with ornaments; embellish. **2** In cookery, to decorate (food) for the table. **3** *Law* To give warning to (someone) to answer to an action; garnishee. —*n.* **1** Something placed around food for ornamentation or a relish. **2** Anything added as an ornament; embellishment. **—gar′nish·er** *n.* [< OF *garnir* prepare < Gmc.]

gar·nish·ee (gär′nish·ē′) *v.t.* **·eed, ·ee·ing** *Law* **1** To secure by garnishment (any debt or property, in the hands of a third person, which is due or belonging to the defendant in attachment). **2** To warn (a person) by garnishment. —*n. Law* A person warned not to pay or deliver money or effects to a defendant, pending a judgment of a court.

gar·nish·ment (gär′nish·mənt) *n.* **1** The act of garnishing. **2** That which garnishes; embellishment; ornament. **3** *Law* A warning or summons; specifically, a notice not to pay or deliver money or effects to a defendant, but to appear and answer the plaintiff's suit.

gar·ni·ture (gär′ni·chər) *n.* Anything used to garnish; embellishment.

gar·pike (gär′pīk′) *n. pl.* **·pike** or **·pikes** A freshwater gar.

gar·ret (gar′it) *n.* A space, room, or rooms directly under a roof. [< OF *garite* a watchtower]

gar·ri·son (gar′ə·sən) *n.* **1** The military force defending a fort, town, etc. **2** The place where such a force is stationed. —*v.t.* **1** To place troops in (a fort, town, etc.) for its defense. **2** To station (troops) in a fort, town, etc. **3** To be the garrison of. [< OF *garir* defend < Gmc.]

gar·rote (gə·rot′, -rōt′) *n.* **1** An iron collar tightened by a screw for strangling, formerly used as a means of capital punishment, esp. in Spain. **2** This method of punishment. **3** Any similar method of strangulation, as with a rope or wire. —*v.t.* **gar·rot·ed, gar·rot·ing** **1** To execute with a garrote. **2** To throttle, esp. in order to rob. Also **ga·rote′, ga·rotte′, gar·rotte′.** [Sp. *garotte* a stick, cudgel] **—gar·rot′er, gar·rot′ter** *n.*

gar·ru·lous (gar′yə·ləs) *adj.* Given to continual and tedious talking. [< L *garrulus* talkative] **—gar′ru·lous·ly** *adv.* **—gar·ru·li·ty** (gə·rōō′lə·tē), **gar′ru·lous·ness** *n.* **—Syn.** talkative, loquacious, verbose, effusive, long-winded.

gar·ter (gär′tər) *n.* An elastic band or fastening device used to hold a stocking in place. —*v.t.* To support or fasten with a garter. [< OF *garet* bend of the knee]

garter snake Any of a genus of small, harmless, viviparous, striped snakes.

gas (gas) *n.* **1** *Physics* That fluid form of matter which is compressible within limits, and which diffuses readily and is capable of indefinite expansion in all directions. 2 Any gas or vapor other than air: tear *gas*, fuel *gas*. 3 Flatulence. 4 *Informal* a Gasoline. b The accelerator of an automobile. 5 *Slang* Empty boasting. 6 *Slang* A person or thing that is fun, exciting, etc. —*v.* **gassed, gas·sing** *v.t.* 1 To overcome, affect, or kill by gas or gas fumes. 2 To treat or saturate with gas. 3 To supply with gas or gasoline. 4 *Slang* To provide fun, excitement, etc., for. —*v.i* 5 To give off gas. 6 *Slant* To boast. [Coined by J. B. van Helmont, 1577–1644, Belgian chemist]

gas chamber A chamber in which executions are performed by means of poison gas.

gas·e·ous (gas′ē·əs, -yəs) *adj.* 1 Having the nature or form of gas. 2 Unsubstantial.

gas fitter One who installs and repairs gas fixtures.

gash (gash) *v.t.* To make a long, deep cut in. —*n.* a long, deep cut or flesh wound. [< OF *garser* scratch]

gas·i·fy (gas′ə·fī) *v.t.* & *v.i.* **·fied, ·fy·ing** To convert into or become gas: to *gasify* coal. **—gas′i·fi·ca′tion, gas′i·fi′er** *n.*

gas jet 1 A burner or nozzle on a gas fixture. 2 The jet of flame on a gas burner.

gas·ket (gas′kit) *n.* 1 *Mech.* A ring, disk, or plate of packing used to seal a joint against leaks. 2 *Naut.* A rope or cord used to confine furled sails to the yard or boom. Also **gas′kin** (-kin), **gas′king** (-king). [?]

gas·light (gas′līt′) *n.* 1 Light from burning illuminating gas. 2 A lamp fueled by gas. **—gas′light′ing** *n.*

gas mask A covering for the nose, mouth, and eyes, equipped with a respirator and worn as protection against toxic or irritant gases.

gas·o·hol (gas′ə·hôl, -hol) *n.* A mixture of 90 percent gasoline and 10 percent alcohol, used as a fuel.

gas·o·line (gas′ə·lēn, gas′ə·lēn′) *n.* A volatile, flammable liquid hydrocarbon derived from petroleum and used as a fuel and solvent. Also **gas′o·lene.** [< GAS + -OL + -INE]

gas·om·e·ter (gas·om′ə·tər) *n.* 1 An apparatus for measuring gases. 2 A reservoir for storing gas.

gasp (gasp, gäsp) *v.i.* 1 To take in the breath suddenly and sharply; breathe convulsively, as from fear or exhaustion. —*v.t.* 2 To say or utter with gasps. —*n.* An act of gasping. [< ON *geispa*]

gas station SERVICE STATION (def. 1).

gas·sy (gas′ē) *adj.* **gas·si·er, gas·si·est** 1 Of, like, or containing gas. 2 Flatulent. 3 *Slang* Addicted to idle chatter or boastful talk. **—gas′si·ness** *n.*

gas·tight (gas′tīt′) *adj.* Not permitting the passage of gas.

gas·tric (gas′trik) *adj.* Of, pertaining to, in, or near the stomach.

gastric juice A thin, acid digestive fluid secreted by glands in the lining of the stomach.

gas·tri·tis (gas·trī′tis) *n*, Inflammation of the stomach. **—gas·trit·ic** (gas·trit′ik) *adj.*

gastro- *combining form* Stomach or stomach and: *gastrointestinal.* [< Gk. *gastēr* stomach]

gas·tro·in·tes·ti·nal (gas′trō·in·tes′tə·nəl) *adj.* Of or pertaining to the stomach and the intestines.

gas·tron·o·my (gas·tron′ə·mē) *n.* The art or science of good eating; epicurism. [< GASTRO- + Gk. *nomos* law] **—gas·tron′o·mer, gas·tro·nome** (gas′trə·nōm), **gas·tron′o·mist** *n.* **—gas′tro·mon′ic** or **·i·cal** *adj.*

gas·tro·pod (gas′trə·pod) *n.* One of a large class of mollusks, usu. having a spiral one-piece shell and a creeping organ, including the snails, slugs, limpets, etc., —*adj.* Of or like a gastropod. **—gas·trop·o·dan** (gas·trop′ə·dən) *adj.*

gas·tru·la (gas′trŏŏ·lə) *n. pl.* **·lae** (-lē), **·las** An embryo at the stage after the blastula, consisting of two layers of tissue enfolding a central cavity with an opening to the outside. [< Gk. *gastēr* stomach] **—gas′tru·lar** *adj.*

gas·works (gas′wûrks′) *n. pl. (construed as sing.)* A factory where illuminating or fuel gas is prepared.

gat (gat) *n. Slang* A pistol. [Short for GATLING GUN]

gate (gāt) *n.* 1 A movable barrier, commonly swinging on hinges and usu. used as an entrance or exit through a fence or wall. 2 An opening or passageway, as in a barrier, fence, wall, or enclosure. 3 Any entrance, exit, or means of access. 4 A barrier that swings up or down, as at a railroad crossing. 5 A valve or structure controlling a flow of liquid or gas. • See VALVE. 6 The total paid admissions or total attendance, as at a sports event. 7 *Electronics* a Any of various circuits having several inputs and a single output whose state depends on the state of the inputs, used in computers. b A terminal of a semiconductor device that controls the flow of current through the device. —*v.t.* **gat·ed, gat·ing** *Electronics* To control (a current or voltage) by means of a gate. [< OE *geat* opening]

gate-crash (gāt′krash′) *v.t. Informal* To gain admittance to, as a party or other function, without invitation or without paying. **—gate′crash′er** *n.*

gate·leg table (gāt′leg′) A table with swinging legs which support drop leaves and fold back when the leaves are let down.

gate·post (gāt′pōst′) *n.* Either of two posts between which a gate swings.

gate·way (gāt′wā′) *n.* 1 An entrance that is or may be closed with a gate. 2 Any means of entrance or access.

gath·er (ga<u>th</u>′ər) *v.t.* 1 To bring together in one place or group. 2 To bring together from various places, sources, etc. 3 To bring closer to oneself: to *gather* one's skirts. 4 To pick, harvest, or collect. 5 To collect or summon up, as one's energies. 6 To increase in amount or degree: The storm *gathered* force. 7 To clasp or enfold: to *gather* someone into one's arms. 8 To conclude or infer. 9 To draw (cloth) into folds or pleats. 10 To wrinkle (the brow). —*v.i.* 11 To come together. 12 To increase. 13 To wrinkle up, as the brow. 14 To come to a head, as a boil. —*n.* A pleat. [< OE *gadrian*] **—gath′er·a·ble** *adj.* **—gath′er·er** *n.*

gath·er·ing (ga<u>th</u>′ər ·ing) *n.* 1 The action of one who or that which gathers. 2 That which is gathered, as an assemblage of people. 3 A series of pleats. 4 An abcess or boil.

Gat·ling gun (gat′ling) An early machine gun having a rotating cluster of barrels. [< R. J. *Gatling.* 1818–1903, U.S. inventor]

GATT General Agreement on Tariffs and Trade.

gauche (gōsh) *adj.* Socially awkward or clumsy; boorish. [F, left]

gauche·rie (gōsh·rē′) *n.* 1 A gauche action or remark. 2 Clumsiness; tactlessness.

Gau·cho (gou′chō) *n. pl.* **·chos** A cowboy of the South American pampas. [Sp.]

gaud·y (gô′dē) *adj.* **gaud·i·er, gaud·i·est** Obtrusively brilliant in color: garish; flashy. **—gaud′i·ly** *adv.* **—gaud′i·ness** *n.*

gauge (gāj) *n.* 1 An instrument for measuring, indicating, or regulating quantity, dimension, capacity, etc. 2 A standard or system of measurement or comparison. 3 The measure of something as expressed by means of such a system or standard: the *gauge* of a shotgun bore. 4 The distance between rails of a railroad track or a pair of wheels on an axis. —*v.t.* **gauged, gaug·ing** 1 To measure or regulate with or as with a gauge. 2 To estimate, appraise, or judge. 3 To bring into conformity with a standard. [< OF, a measure] **—gauge′a·ble** *adj.* **—gaug′er** *n.*

Gaul (gôl) *n.* 1 An ancient name for what is, roughly, the area of modern France and Belgium. 2 A native of ancient Gaul. 3 A Frenchman.

Gaul·ish (gô′lish) *adj.* Of ancient Gaul, its people, or their Celtic language. —*n.* The extinct Celtic language of Gaul.

Gaull·ism (gôl′iz′əm) *n.* The policies or philosophy of Charles de Gaulle and his followers. **—Gaull′ist** *adj., n.*

gaunt (gônt) *adj.* 1. Emaciated, as from lack of food; lank; lean; meager; thin. 2 Grim; desolate. [ME] **—gaunt′ly** *adv.*

gaunt·let[1] (gônt′lit, gänt′-) *n.* 1 In medieval armor, a leather glove covered with metal plates. 2 Any glove with a long, flaring extension over the wrist; also, the extension. [< OF *gant* glove] **—gaunt′let·ed** *adj.*

gaunt·let[2] (gônt′lit, gänt′-) *n.* 1 A punishment wherein the victim runs between two rows of men who strike him with clubs or switches as he passes. 2 A series of difficulties or unpleasant events. **—run the gauntlet** (or **gant-**

let) To be exposed to a series of hostile attacks or unpleasant incidents. [< Sw. *gatlopp* a running down a lane]

gauss (gous) *n. pl.* **gauss** *Physics* A unit of magnetic induction, equal to 10^4 webers per square meter. [< K. F. *Gauss,* 1777–1855, German mathematician]

gauze (gôz) *n.* **1** A light, loosely woven fabric. **2** Any thin open-woven material: wire *gauze.* **3** A mist. —*adj.* Resembling or made of gauze. [< MF *gaze*] —**gauz′i·ly** *adv.* —**gauz′i·ness** *n.* —**gauz·y (·i·er, ·i·est)** *adj.*

gave (gāv) *p.t.* of GIVE.

gav·el (gav′əl) *n.* A mallet used by a presiding officer to call for order or attention. [?]

ga·vi·al (gā′vē·əl) *n.* A large crocodile of s Asia, having long, slender jaws. [< Hind. *ghariyāl*]

ga·votte (gə·vot′) *n.* **1** A lively French dance, resembling the minuet. **2** Music for such a dance. [< Provençal *gavoto* Alpine dance]

G.A.W. guaranteed annual wage.

gawk (gôk) *v.i. Informal* To stare or behave awkwardly and stupidly. —*n.* An awkward, stupid fellow. [?]

gawk·y (gô′kē) *adj.* **gawk·i·er, gawk·i·est** Awkward and dull; clumsy. —**gawk′i·ly** *adv.* —**gawk′i·ness** *n.*

gay (gā) *adj.* **1** Joyous; light-spirited; merry. **2** Brilliant; showy: *gay* colors. **3** Loving or given to pleasure and amusement. **4** *Informal* HOMOSEXUAL. [< OF *gai*] —**gay′·ness** *n.* —**gay′some** *adj.* —**Syn. 1** cheerful, happy, merry, vivacious, lively, sunny, blithe. **2** sparkling, bright, vivid, shiny.

gay·e·ty (gā′ə·tē) *n.* GAIETY.

gay·ly *adv.* GAILY.

Gay Nine·ties (nīn′tēz) The decade from 1890 to 1900.

gaz. gazette; gazetteer.

gaze (gāz) *v.i.* **gazed, gaz·ing** To look earnestly and steadily, as in scrutiny, admiration, or concern. —*n.* A continued or intense look. [< Scand.] —**gaz′er** *n.*

ga·ze·bo (gə·zē′bō, -zā-) *n. pl.* **·bos** or **·boes** A small, open structure, as in a garden, and often commanding a wide view. [? < GAZE]

ga·zelle (gə·zel′) *n.* Any of various small antelopes with long necks and large, gentle eyes. [< Ar. *ghazāl* gazelle]

Gazelle

ga·zette (gə·zet′) *n.* **1** A newspaper. **2** *Brit.* Any official government journal announcing appointments, promotions, etc. —*v.t. Brit.* **ga·zet·ted, ga·zet·ting** To publish or announce in a gazette. [< dial. Ital. (Venetian) *gazeta* a coin, orig. the price of the paper]

gaz·et·teer (gaz′ə·tir′) *n.* **1** A dictionary or alphabetical list of geographical names. **2** A writer for a gazette.

gaz·pa·cho (gäz·pä′chō) *n. pl.* **·chos** A cold soup made with tomatoes and other ingredients, as olive oil, garlic, peppers, bread crumbs, and spices. [Sp.]

G.B. Great Britain.

GCT, G.C.T., G.c.t. Greenwich civil time.

Gd gadolinium.

gds. goods.

Ge germanium.

gear (gir) *n.* **1** *Mech.* **a** A set of moving parts that transmit motion, often changing its rate or direction. **b** One of several possible arrangements of such a set of parts: low *gear.* **c** A wheel with teeth around its edge, designed to engage a part with similar teeth and transmit motion; cogwheel. **d** Any group of parts performing a specific function: the steering *gear.* **2** Any equipment, tools, etc., for some specific task or purpose, as the rigging of a ship, a repairman's tools, etc. **3** Clothes, esp. for a specific purpose: a skier's *gear.* **4** Harmonious and effective action: out of *gear.* —*v.t.* **1 a** To equip with gears. **b** To connect by means of gears. **2** To regulate so as to match or suit something else: to *gear* production to demand. **3** To put gear on; harness; dress. —*v.i.* **4** To come into or be in gear; mesh. [< ON *gervi* equipment]

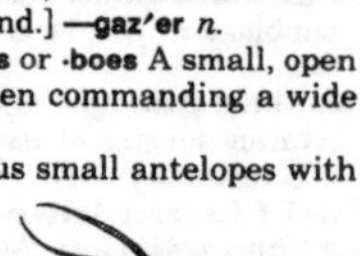

Gears *def. 1c*

gear·box (gir′boks′) *n.* The transmission of an automobile, truck, bus, etc.

gear·ing (gir′ing) *n.* Gears or related parts that transmit mechanical power.

gear·shift (gir′shift′) *n.* A device for engaging or disengaging gears.

gear·wheel (gīr′hwēl′) *n.* COGWHEEL.

geck·o (gek′ō) *n. pl.* **geck·os** or **geck·oes** Any of a family of small lizards having toes with adhesive disks; wall lizard. [< Malay *gēkoq,* imit. of its cry]

Gecko

gee[1] (jē) *v.t. & v.i.* To turn to the right. —*interj.* Turn to the right! a call in driving animals without reins. [?]

gee[2] (jē) *interj. Informal* An exclamation of surprise, awe, etc. Also **gee whiz.** [Euphemistic contr. of JESUS]

geek (gēk) *n.* A carnival performer who publicly bites off the head of a live animal, as a chicken, as a sensational spectacle. [Prob. var. of Brit. dial. *geck* fool]

geese (gēs) *n. pl.* of GOOSE[1].

gee·zer (gē′zər) *n. Slang* An old, usu. eccentric man. [Var. of earlier *guiser* one in disguise < GUISE]

ge·fil·te fish (gə·fil′tə) Ground fish mixed with eggs, seasonings, bread crumbs, etc., made into balls or cakes and simmered in broth. Also **ge·fül′te.** [Yiddish, lit., filled]

Ge·hen·na (gi·hen′ə) *n.* **1** The valley of Hinnom near Jerusalem, where offal was thrown and fires kept burning to purify the air. **2** A place of torment. **3** In the New Testament, hell. [< Hebrew *ge- hinnom* valley of *Hinnom*]

Gei·ger counter (gī′gər) An electronic instrument for detecting and counting ionizing particles and rays, used to measure radioactivity. [< Hans *Geiger,* 1882–1945, German physicist]

gei·sha (gā′shə) *n. pl.* **·sha** or **·shas** A Japanese girl trained to entertain men by singing, dancing, etc.

gel (jel) *n.* A colloidal dispersion of a liquid in a solid, usu. forming a semisolid of jellylike consistency. —*v.i.* **gelled, gel·ling** To change into a gel; jellify. [Short for GELATIN]

gel·a·tin (jel′ə·tin) *n.* **1** A brittle, tasteless protein produced from animal tissues, which forms a gel with water. **2** A gel made usu. with gelatin and used as a base for desserts, aspics, etc. Also **gel′a·tine.** [< L *gelare* freeze]

ge·lat·i·nize (ji·lat′ə·nīz) *v.* **·nized, ·niz·ing** *v.t.* **1** To turn into or treat with gelatin. —*v.i.* **2** To be changed into gelatin or jelly. —**ge·lat′i·ni·za′tion** *n.*

ge·lat·i·nous (ji·lat′ə·nəs) *adj.* **1** Of the nature of gelatin. **2** Of or containing gelatin. —**ge·lat′i·nous·ly** *adv.* —**ge·lat′·i·nous·ness** *n.*

geld (geld) *v.t.* **geld·ed** or **gelt, geld·ing** To castrate, esp. a horse. [< ON *gelda*]

geld·ing (gel′ding) *n.* A castrated animal, esp. a horse.

gel·id (jel′id) *adj.* Very cold; icy; frozen. [< L *gelidus*] —**ge·lid′i·ty** *n.* —**gel′id·ly** *adv.*

gelt (gelt) *n. Slang* Money. [< G & Du. *geld* & Yiddish *gelt*]

gem (jem) *n.* **1** A precious or semiprecious stone, esp. when cut and polished; jewel. **2** Anything rare, delicate, and perfect, as a work of literature or art. **3** A light, muffinlike cake. —*v.t.* **gemmed, gem·ming** To adorn with or as with gems. [< L *gemma* jewel]

gem·i·nate (jem′ə·nāt) *v.t. & v.i.* **·nat·ed, ·nat·ing** To make or become double; pair. —*adj.* (-nit) *Bot.* Occurring in pairs, as leaves. [< L *geminus* a twin] —**gem′i·na′tion** *n.*

Gem·i·ni (jem′ə·nī) *n.* A constellation and the third sign of the zodiac; the Twins. • See ZODIAC.

gem·ma (jem′ə) *n. pl.* **·mae** (-ē) *Bot.* **1** A bud. **2** A budlike growth that becomes a new organism. [L]

gem·mate (jem′āt) *adj. Bot.* **1** Bearing buds. **2** Reproducing by buds. —**gem·ma′tion** *n.*

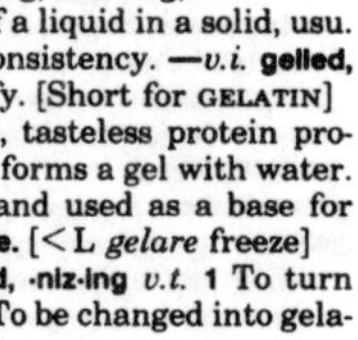

Gemsbok

gems·bok (gemz′bok) *n. pl.* **·bok** or **·boks** A South African antelope having long, sharp, nearly straight horns and a tufted tail. [< G *Gemse* chamois + *Bock* a buck]

ge·müt·lich·keit (gə·müt′likh·kīt) *n. Often cap.* Good feeling, geniality, and comfort. [G]

-gen *suffix of nouns* **1** That which produces: *oxygen.* **2** That which is produced: *antigen.* [< Gk. *-genēs* born]

Gen. General; Genesis; Geneva.

gen. gender; genera; general; generally; generator; genetic; genitive; genus.

gen·darme (zhän′därm; *Fr.* zhäṅ·dȧrm′) *n. pl.* **·darmes** (-därmz; *Fr.* -dȧrm′) One of a corps of armed police, esp. in France. [F< *gens d'armes* men of arms]

gen·der (jen′dər) *n.* **1** *Gram.* In many languages, a grammatical designation of nouns and pronouns governing the form assumed by the words which modify or refer to them. **2** Any one of these designations, esp. masculine, feminine, or neuter. **3** *Informal* Sex. [< L *genus, -eris* kind]

gene (jēn) *n.* A unit occupying a distinct position on a chromosome and having a crucial function in the transmission of a specific characteristic from parent to offspring. [< G *Gen,* ult.< -GEN]

geneal. genealogical; genealogy.

ge·ne·al·o·gy (jē′nē·ol′ə·jē, -nē·al′-, jen′ē-) *n. pl.* **·gies 1** A record of descent from some ancestor; a list of ancestors and their descendants. **2** Descent in a direct line; pedigree. **3** The science that treats of pedigrees. [< Gk. *genea* race + -LOGY] **—ge·ne·a·log·i·cal** (jē′nē·ə·loj′i·kəl, jen′ē-) *adj.* **—ge′ne·a·log′i·cal·ly** *adv.* **—ge·ne·al′o·gist** *n.*

gen·e·ra (jen′ər·ə) *n.pl.* of GENUS.

gen·er·al (jen′ər·əl, -rəl) *adj.* **1** Pertaining to, including, or affecting all or the whole; not local or particular: a *general* election. **2** Common to or current among the majority; prevalent: the *general* opinion. **3** Not restricted in application: a *general* principle. **4** Not limited to or dealing with a particular class; unspecialized: a *general* store; a *general* practitioner. **5** Not detailed or precise: a *general* idea. **6** Usual or customary: one's *general* habit. **7** Superior in rank: attorney *general.* *—n.* **1** See GRADE. **2** The chief of a religious order. **3** A general statement, fact, or principle. [< L *generalis* of a race or kind < *genus* kind]

General Assembly 1 The principal deliberative body of the United Nations in which every member nation is represented. **2** *U.S.* The legislature in some states.

gen·er·al·cy (jen′ər·əl·sē, -rəl-) *n. pl.* **·cies** Rank, authority, or tenure of office of a general.

general delivery 1 A post-office department in which mail is kept for the addressee until called for. **2** Mail so addressed.

general election 1 An election to choose from among previously nominated candidates. **2** An election in which all qualified voters participate.

gen·er·al·is·si·mo (jen′ər·əl·is′i·mō, -rəl-) *n. pl.* **·mos** In certain countries, the supreme commander of all the armed forces. [Ital.]

gen·er·al·ist (jen′ər·əl·ist, -rəl-) *n.* One who has a general knowledge of or background in several different fields, as distinguished from a specialist.

gen·er·al·i·ty (jen′ə·ral′ə·tē) *n. pl.* **·ties 1** The main part; majority. **2** Anything general or not specific; esp. a vague statement. **3** The state of being general or generalized.

gen·er·al·ize (jen′ər·əl·īz′, -rəl-) *v.* **·ized, ·iz·ing** *v.t.* **1** To treat as having general or wide application. **2** To cause to be used or understood generally or widely; popularize. **3** To draw or frame (a general rule or principle) from particular evidence, facts, etc. **4** To draw or frame a general rule or principle from (particular evidence, facts, etc.). *—v.i.* **5** To talk in unspecific terms; be vague. **6** To draw general ideas or inferences from particulars. **—gen′er·al·i·za′tion** *n.*

gen·er·al·ly (jen′ər·əl·ē, -rəl-) *adv.* **1** For the most part; ordinarily; in most but not all cases. **2** Without going into particulars. **3** So as to include or apply to all.

gen·er·al·ship (jen′ər·əl·ship, -rəl-) *n.* **1** The rank, authority, or tenure of a general. **2** A general's military skill. **3** Management or leadership.

general staff A body of officers who assist a commander in military policy and strategy.

gen·er·ate (jen′ə·rāt) *v.t.* **·at·ed, ·at·ing 1** To produce or cause to be; bring into being. **2** To beget as a parent; procreate. [< L *generare* < *genus* kind]

gen·er·a·tion (jen′ə·rā′shən) *n.* **1** The process of begetting or procreating. **2** Production or origination by any process; creation: the *generation* of electricity. **3** A step or degree in natural descent. **4** The average time elapsing between the birth of parent and offspring, and usu. estimated for humans at 30 years. **5** A body of persons existing at the same time or having common interests, characteristics, or outlooks.

gen·er·a·tive (jen′ə·rə·tiv, -rā′tiv) *adj.* **1** Of or relating to generation. **2** Having the power to generate.

gen·er·a·tor (jen′ə·rā′tər) *n.* **1** One who or that which generates or originates. **2** An apparatus in which the generation of a gas is effected. **3** A machine that changes heat or mechanical energy into electricity.

ge·ner·ic (ji·ner′ik) *adj.* **1** Of or pertaining to a whole group or class; general. **2** Not having proprietary status: said esp. of names for drugs. **3** *Biol.* Of or like a genus. [< L *genus, generis* race, kind + -IC] **—ge·ner′i·cal·ly** *adv.*

gen·er·os·i·ty (jen′ə·ros′ə·tē) *n. pl.* **·ties 1** The quality of being generous. **2** A generous act.

gen·er·ous (jen′ər·əs, -rəs) *adj.* **1** Giving or bestowing liberally; munificent. **2** Having noble qualities; honorable; high-minded: a *generous* nature. **3** Abundant; plentiful: a *generous* gift. **4** Full-flavored. [< L *generosus* of noble birth < *genus* kind] **—gen′er·ous·ly** *adv.* **—gen′er·ous·ness** *n.* **—Syn. 1** bountiful, liberal, lavish, bounteous, prodigal. **2** magnanimous, humane, beneficent, benevolent.

gen·e·sis (jen′ə·sis) *n. pl.* **·ses** (-sēz) **1** The act or mode of originating; creation. **2** Origin; beginning. [< Gk. *genēsis* origin]

Gen·e·sis (jen′ə·sis) *n.* The first book of the Pentateuch in the Old Testament.

-genesis *combining form* Development; genesis; evolution: *parthenogenesis.*

gen·et[1] (jen′it, jə·net′) *n.* **1** Any of certain small carnivores related to the civets. **2** The fur of the genet. Also **ge·nette′.** [< Ar. *jarnait* genet]

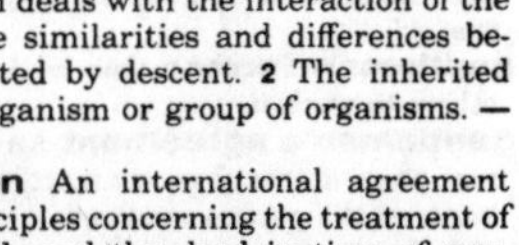

Genet

gen·et[2] (jen′it) *n.* JENNET.

ge·net·ic (jə·net′ik) *adj.* **1** Of or pertaining to the origin of something. **2** Of or relating to genetics. Also **ge·net′i·cal. —ge·net′i·cal·ly** *adv.*

ge·net·ics (jə·net′iks) *n. pl. (construed as sing.)* **1** That branch of biology which deals with the interaction of the genes in producing the similarities and differences between individuals related by descent. **2** The inherited characteristics of an organism or group of organisms. **—ge·net′i·cist** *n.*

Geneva Convention An international agreement that set up certain principles concerning the treatment of prisoners, the wounded, and the dead in time of war, signed at Geneva, Switzerland in 1864.

gen·ial (jēn′yəl, jē′nē·əl) *adj.* **1** Kindly in disposition; cordial and pleasant in manner. **2** Imparting warmth, comfort, or life: a *genial* climate. [< L *genialis* of birth, pleasant] **—ge·ni·al·i·ty** (jē′nē·al′ə·tē) *n.* **—ge′nial·ly** *adv.* **—Syn. 1** affable, friendly, cheerful, blithe, sunny, light-hearted, warm, good-natured.

-genic *combining form* **1** Forming or producing. **2** Formed or produced by. **3** Suitable to. [< -GEN + -IC]

ge·nie (jē′nē) *n.* JINNI.

gen·i·tal (jen′ə·təl) *adj.* Of or pertaining to the reproductive organs, or to the process of generation. [< L *genitalis* of birth]

gen·i·ta·li·a (jen′ə·tā′lē·ə, -tāl′yə) *n. pl.* GENITALS.

gen·i·tals (jen′ə·təlz) *n. pl.* The external organs of generation; sexual organs.

gen·i·tive (jen′ə·tiv) *Gram. adj.* **1** Indicating source, origin, possession, or the like. **2** Pertaining to a case in Latin, Greek, etc., corresponding in part to the English possessive. *—n.* **1** The genitive case. **2** A word in this case. [< L *genitivus* of origin <*gignere* beget] —**gen·i·ti·val** (jen′ə·tī′·vəl) *adj.* —**gen′i·ti′val·ly** *adv.*

gen·ius (jēn′yəs) *n. pl.* **gen·ius·es**; *for def. 6* **ge·ni·i** (jē′·nē·ī). **1** Extraordinary intellectual or creative gifts. **2** Remarkable aptitude, talent, or capacity: a *genius* for oratory. **3** A person having such gifts or abilities. **4** The dominant nature or essential character of a nation, era, place, etc. **5** A representative type; embodiment. **6** In Roman antiquity: **a** A beneficient spirit or evil demon supposed to accompany one through life. **b** A guardian or tutelary spirit of a person or place. **7** A person having strong influence over another. [L, tutelary spirit]

gen·o·cide (jen′ə·sīd) *n.* The systematic extermination of a racial or national group. [<Gk. *genos* race + -CIDE]

gen·re (zhän′rə) *n.* A type or category, as of art, literature, etc. [F<L *genus, -eris* race, kind]

genre painting Painting that portrays everyday life.

gens (jenz) *n. pl.* **gen·tes** (jen′tēz) In Roman antiquity, a clan of descendants of a common male ancestor. [L]

gent (jent) *n. Slang* A gentleman.

gen·teel (jen·tēl′) *adj.* **1** Having or characterized by refinement, good taste, elegance, etc.: now used in a somewhat derogatory or humorous sense. **2** Artificially polite, refined, or elegant. [<MF *gentil* gentle] —**gen·teel′ly** *adv.*

gen·tian (jen′shən) *n.* **1** Any of a large genus of plants with flowers of various colors and usu. a tubular or bell-shaped corolla. **2** The root of the yellow gentian, having tonic properties. [<L *gentiana*]

gen·tile (jen′tīl) *n.* **1** *Often cap.* Any person not a Jew, esp. a Christian. **2** Formerly, among Christians, a pagan. **3** *Often cap.* Among Mormons, a non-Mormon. —*adj. Often cap.* Of, being, or relating to a gentile. [<L *gentilis* of a gens, foreign]

gen·til·i·ty (jen·til′ə·tē) *n. pl.* **·ties 1** The quality of being genteel; refinement: now often used ironically. **2** The condition of being well-born. **3** Well-born persons collectively.

gen·tle (jen′təl) *adj.* **1** Mild and serene in nature or disposition. **2** Not harsh or rough; soft: a *gentle* touch. **3** Tame; docile: a *gentle* horse. **4** Not steep or abrupt: a *gentle* slope. **5** Of good birth; upper-class. **6** Refined; polite. —*v.t.* **gen·tled, gen·tling 1** To tame, as a horse. **2** To soothe. [<L *gentilis* of good birth<*gens, gentis* race, clan] —**gen′tly** *adv.* —**gen′tle·ness** *n.*

gen·tle·folk (jen′təl·fōk′) *n. pl.* Persons of good family and good breeding. Also **gen′tle·folks′**.

gen·tle·man (jen′təl·mən) *n. pl.* **·men** (-mən) **1** A man who is considerate, courteous, and socially correct. **2** A man of good birth and social position. **3** Any man: in the plural, used as a form of address. —**gen′tle·man·ly, gen′tle·man·like′** *adj.*

gentleman farmer One who owns a farm, but hires others to work it.

gentleman's agreement An agreement, usu. less formal than a treaty or contract, guaranteed only by the honor of the parties involved.

gen·tle·wom·an (jen′təl·wŏŏm′ən) *n. pl.* **·wom·en** (-wim′in) **1** A woman of good birth and social position. **2** A considerate, gracious, well-mannered woman.

gen·tri·fi·ca·tion (jen′tri·fi·kā′shən) *n.* The rebuilding of older residential sections of a city for people able to pay for such improvements.

gen·try (jen′trē) *n.* **1** People of good position or birth; in England, the upper class exclusive of the nobility. **2** Any specified class or group of people. [<OF *gentil* gentle]

gen·u·flect (jen′yə·flekt) *v.i.* To bend the knee, as in worship. [<L *genu* knee + *flectere* to bend] —**gen·u·flec′tion** *n.*

gen·u·ine (jen′yŏŏ·in) *adj.* **1** Of the original stock; purebred. **2** Not spurious, false, or counterfeit; real; authentic. **3** Not affected or hypocritical; frank; sincere; true. [<L *genuinus* innate] —**gen′u·ine·ly** *adv.* —**gen′u·ine·ness** *n.*

ge·nus (jē′nəs) *n. pl.* **gen·e·ra** (jen′ər·ə) **1** A biological category ranking below the family or subfamily and consisting of one or more species. **2** A kind; class. [L, race, kind]

geo- *combining form* Earth; ground: *geocentric.*

ge·o·cen·tric (jē′ō·sen′trik) *adj.* **1** Having or pertaining to the earth as center. **2** Measured from the earth or the earth's center. —**ge′o·cen′tri·cal** *adj.*

ge·ode (jē′ōd) *n. Geol.* A stone having a cavity lined with crystals. [<Gk. *geōdēs* earth] —**ge·od·ic** (jē·od′ik) *adj.*

geodesic dome An approximately hemispherical structure formed of straight elements that make up a network of rigid polygons.

ge·od·e·sy (jē·od′ə·sē) *n.* The study and measurement of the size and shape of the earth. [<Gk. *geodaisia* earth division] —**ge·o·des·ic** (jē′ə·des′ik, -dē′sik) *adj.* —**ge·od′e·sist** *n.*

ge·o·det·ic (jē′ə·det′ik) *adj.* Of, pertaining to, determined, or effected by geodesy. Also **ge′o·det′i·cal.** —**ge′o·det′i·cal·ly** *adv.*

geog. geographer; geographic; geography.

geographical mile NAUTICAL MILE.

ge·og·ra·phy (jē·og′rə·fē) *n. pl.* **·phies 1** The science that describes the surface of the earth and its associated physical, biological, economic, political, and demographic characteristics. **2** The physical aspect, features, etc., of a place or area. [<GEO- + Gk. *graphein* write, describe] —**ge·og′·ra·pher** *n.* —**ge′o·graph′ic** or **·i·cal** *adj.* —**ge′o·graph′i·cal·ly** *adv.*

geol. geologic; geological; geologist; geology.

ge·ol·o·gy (jē·ol′ə·jē) *n. pl.* **·gies 1** The science that studies the origin, history, constitution, and structure of the earth. **2** The structure of a particular part of the earth. —**ge·o·log·ic** (jē′ə·loj′ik) or **·i·cal** *adj.* —**ge′o·log′i·cal·ly** *adv.* —**ge·ol′o·gist** *n.* • See GEOLOGICAL TIME SCALE, next page.

geom. geometer; geometric; geometrical; geometry.

ge·om·e·ter (jē·om′ət·ər) *n.* One who is expert in geometry. Also **ge·om·e·tri·cian** (jē·om′ə·trish′ən).

ge·o·met·ric (jē′ə·met′rik) *adj.* **1** Pertaining to or according to the rules and principles of geometry. **2** Of or characterized by straight lines, regular curves, and angles: a *geometric* design. Also **ge′o·met′ri·cal.** —**ge′o·met′·ri·cal·ly** *adv.*

geometric progression *Math.* A sequence of terms in which each term except the first is a constant multiple of its predecessor, as 2, 4, 8, 16, 32, 64.

ge·om·e·try (jē·om′ə·trē) *n. pl.* **·tries** The branch of mathematics that deals with the properties, relations, and measurement of points, lines, angles, surfaces, and solids. [<GEO- + Gk. *metrein* measure]

ge·o·phys·ics (jē′ə·fiz′iks) *n. pl. (construed as sing.)* The science that investigates the physical forces, influences, and phenomena associated with the earth. —**ge′o·phys′i·cal** *adj.* —**ge′o·phys′i·cist** *n.*

ge·o·pol·i·tics (jē′ō·pol′ə·tiks) *n. pl. (construed as sing.)* The study of the interrelationship of geography, climate, etc., and politics. —**ge′o·po·lit′i·cal** *adj.* —**ge′o·po·lit′i·cal·ly** *adv.* —**ge′o·pol′i·ti′cian** *n.*

geor·gette (jôr·jet′) *n.* A sheer, lightly crinkled, silk or silklike fabric, used for blouses, gowns, etc. Also **georgette crepe.** [<*Georgette,* a trade name]

Geor·gian (jôr′jən) *adj.* **1** Of or pertaining to the reigns or period of the four Georges in England, 1714–1830, or of George V, 1910–36. **2** Of or pertaining to Georgia in the U.S.S.R., to the Georgians, or to their language. —*n.* **1** A native or citizen of the Georgian S.S.R. **2** The language of the Georgians.

ge·o·ther·mal (jē′ə·thûr′məl) *adj.* Of or pertaining to the earth's internal heat. [<GEO- + THERMAL]

geothermal energy Subterranean heat generated in vast quantities by natural radioactivity, utilized chiefly as steam and hot water from hot springs.

ge·ot·ro·pism (jē·ot′rə·piz′əm) *n.* A biological response to gravity, as the downward growth of the roots of a plant. —**ge·o·trop·ic** (jē′ə·trop′ik) *adj.* —**ge′o·trop′i·cal·ly** *adv.*

Ger. German; Germany.

ger. gerund.

ge·ra·ni·um (ji·rā′nē·əm) *n.* **1** Any of a large genus of plants with showy pink or purple flowers. **2** A cultivated plant with usu. scented leaves and red, pink, or white flowers in showy cymes. [<Gk. *geranion,* lit., little crane]

ger·bil (jûr′bil) *n.* A mouselike rodent with a long tail and long hind legs adapted for leaping, native to Africa and Asia. [<NL *gerboa* jerboa]

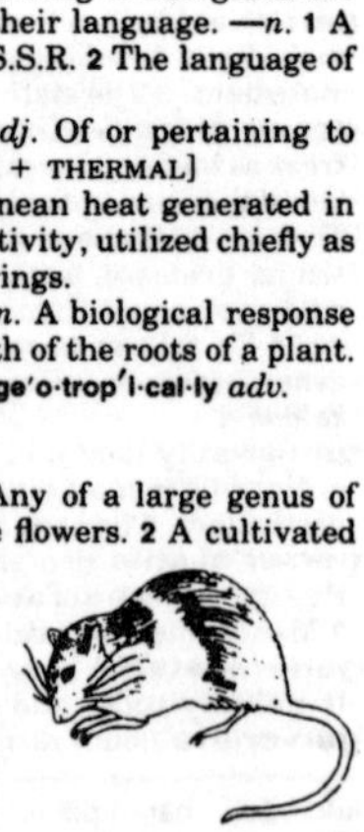

Gerbil

GEOLOGICAL TIME SCALE

This table defines the geological eras, time periods, and epochs listed in the first three columns. Each of these terms may be used as both a noun (e.g., *the Mesozoic, the Jurassic, the Pleistocene*) and as an adjective with the meaning: Of, pertaining to, or characteristic of that specific era, period, or epoch (e.g., the *Mesozoic* era, *Mesozoic* evolution, *Jurassic* reptiles, *Pleistocene* climate variation, etc.).

Read from bottom to top.

Eras	*Time Periods Rock Systems*	*Time Epochs Rock Series*	*Approx. Duration Million Years*	*Approx. Percent Total Age*	*Life Forms*
Cenozoic	Quaternary	Recent Pleistocene	1	2	Rise and dominance of man.
	Upper Tertiary	Pliocene Miocene	65		Modern animals and plants.
	Lower Tertiary	Oligocene Eocene Paleocene			Rapid development of modern mammals, insects, and plants.
Mesozoic	Upper Cretaceous		75	5	Primitive mammals; last dinosaurs; last ammonites.
	Lower Cretaceous				Rise of flowering plants.
	Jurassic		45		First birds, first mammals. Diversification of reptiles; climax of ammonites; coniferous trees.
	Triassic		45		Rise of dinosaurs; bony fishes.
Paleozoic	Permian		45	9	Rise of reptiles. Modern insects. Last of many plant and animal groups.
	Pennsylvanian } Carboniferous		75		First reptiles. Amphibians; primitive insects; seed ferns; primitive conifers.
	Mississippian				Climax of shell-crushing sharks. Primitive ammonites.
	Devonian		50		First amphibians, first land snails. Primitive land plants. Climax of brachiopods.
	Silurian		20		First traces of land life. Scorpions. First lungfishes. Widespread coral reefs.
	Ordovician		70		First fish. Climax of trilobites. First appearance of many marine invertebrates.
	Cambrian		50		First marine invertebrates, including trilobites.
Proterozoic Archeozoic	Pre-Cambrian		About 3,000	84	First signs of life. Algae.

Age of oldest dated rocks: about 3,500,000,000 years.

ger·fal·con (jûr′fal′kən, -fôl′-, -fô′-) *n.* GYRFALCON.

ger·i·at·rics (jer′ē·at′riks) *n. pl. (construed as sing.)* The branch of medicine which deals with the diseases and physiological changes associated with aging and old people. [< Gk. *gēras* old age + *iatros* physician] **—ger·i·at·ric** *adj.*

ger·kin (gûr′kin) *n.* GHERKIN.

germ (jûrm) *n.* **1** Any rudimentary living substance that can develop into an organism. **2** A microorganism that causes disease; microbe. **3** The primary source from which something may be developed. [< L *germen* offshoot]

ger·man¹ (jûr′mən) *n.* **1** The cotillion, a dance. **2** A party at which it is the chief feature. [Short for *German cotillion*]

ger·man² (jûr′mən) *adj.* Having the same parents or grandparents: used after the noun: cousins *german*, brothers *german*. [< L *germanus* closely related]

Ger·man (jûr′mən) *adj.* Of, pertaining to, or characteristic of Germany, its people, or their language. *—n.* **1** A native or citizen of Germany. **2** The West Germanic language used throughout most of Germany and in parts of Switzerland and Austria: also **New High German.**

German cockroach A small, brownish, winged cockroach, a common household pest in urban buildings.

ger·man·der (jər·man′dər) *n.* **1** An herb of the mint family, with purple flowers. **2** A variety of speedwell. [< OF < Med. L < Gk. < *chamai* on the ground + *drys* an oak]

ger·mane (jər·mān′) *adj.* **1** In close relationship; relevant; pertinent. **2** Akin; german. [See GERMAN²]

Ger·man·ic (jər·man′ik) *adj.* **1** GERMAN. **2** Of, relating to, or characteristic of any of the Germanic languages or of the people who speak or spoke them. *—n.* **1** A subfamily of the Indo-European family of languages, divided into the branches **East Germanic,** including Gothic (extinct); **North Germanic** or Scandinavian, including Norwegian, Swedish, Danish, Icelandic, and Faroese; and **West Germanic,** including all the High and Low German languages and dialects, among which are German, Dutch, Flemish, Frisian, English, Yiddish, Plattdeutsch, etc. **2** The prehistoric parent of these languages: called **Primitive Germanic, Pro′to-Germanic** (prō′tō-).

ger·ma·ni·um (jər·mā′nē·əm) *n.* A gray, brittle, metallic element (symbol Ge) used as a semiconductor, esp. in transistors. [< L *Germania* Germany]

German shepherd dog

Ger·man·ize (jûr′mən·īz) *v.t. & v.i.* **·ized, ·iz·ing** To make or become German in speech, customs, etc. **—Ger′man·i·za′tion** *n.*

German measles RUBELLA.

German shepherd A breed of dog with muscular body,

often trained as Seeing Eye dogs or as guard dogs. Also **German shepherd dog** or **German police dog**.

German silver NICKEL SILVER.

Ger·ma·ny (jûr′mə·nē) *n. pl.* **·ma·nys** A republic of CEN. EUROPE, 137,214 SQ. MI., CAP. BERLIN; DIVIDED 1945-1990 into the **German Democratic Republic** or East Germany, cap. Berlin, a Soviet ally, and the **German Federal Republic** or West Germany, cap. Bonn, a member of NATO.

germ cell A cell specialized for reproduction.

ger·mi·cide (jûr′mə·sīd) *n.* Any agent used todestroy pathogenic microorganisms. [< GERM + -CIDE] **—ger′mi·ci′dal** *adj.*

ger·mi·nal (jûr′mə·nəl) *adj.* **1** Pertaining to or constituting a germ. **2** Being in the first stage of development.

ger·mi·nant (jûr′mə·nənt) *adj.* That germinates or sprouts.

ger·mi·nate (jûr′mə·nāt) *v.* **·nat·ed, ·nat·ing** *v.i.* **1** To begin to grow or develop; sprout. *—v.t.* **2** To cause to sprout. [<L *germinare*] **—ger′mi·na′tion, ger′mi·na′tor** *n.* **—ger′mi·na′tive** *adj.*

germ plasm *Biol.* Reproductive cells, esp. the part which contains the genes.

ger·on·tol·o·gy (jer′ən·tol′ə·jē) *n.* The scientific study of the phenomena of aging. [<Gk. *gerōn, gerontos* old man + -LOGY] **—ger′on·tol′o·gist** *n.*

ger·ry·man·der (jer′i·man′dər, ger′-) *v.t.* To alter, as the shape of voting districts of a state or region, to the contrived advantage of a political party or other group. *—n.* A contrived or unfair redistricting of a state or region. [<E. *Gerry,* 1744–1814, + (SALA)MANDER; from the shape of a district formed in Massachusetts while Gerry was governor]

ger·und (jer′ənd) *n.* A verbal noun ending in *-ing,* functioning as a noun, but capable of taking objects and adverbial modifiers. Example: *Writing* poetry well is an art. [<L *gerundum* acting, doing] **—ge·run·di·al** (jə·run′dē·əl) *adj.*

ge·run·dive (jə·run′div) *adj.* Like, pertaining to, or having the nature of the gerund. *—n.* **1** In Latin, a verbal adjective having the gerund stem and used as future passive participle, expressing obligation, fitness, or necessity. **2** A similar verbal adjective in any language.

gest (jest) *n.* **1** *Archaic* A deed; exploit. **2** A tale of adventure, esp. one in verse. Also **geste.** [<L *gesta* deeds]

ge·stalt (gə·shtält′) *n. pl.* **ge·stalt·en** (-shtält′ən) or **ge·stalts** *Often cap.* An arrangement of elements comprising an entity having properties not to be found in its constituent parts. [<G, form]

Gestalt psychology A school of psychology which interprets biological and psychic processes in terms of closely integrated patterns that are different from the sums of their parts.

Ge·sta·po (gə·stä′pō) *n.* The secret police of Nazi Germany. [G *Ge(heime) Sta(ats)po(lizei)* Secret State Police]

ges·tate (jes′tāt) *v.t.* **·tat·ed, ·tat·ing 1** To carry in the womb during pregnancy. **2** To form in the mind. [Back formation from GESTATION]

ges·ta·tion (jes·tā′shən) *n.* **1** Pregnancy, esp. the period of carrying a fetus in the womb. **2** The formation or period of development of an idea or program. [<L *gestare* carry young] **—ges·ta′tion·al** *adj.*

ges·tic·u·late (jes·tik′yə·lāt) *v.* **·lat·ed, ·lat·ing** *v.i.* **1** To make motions with the hands or arms, as in speaking. *—v.t.* **2** To express by gestures. [<L *gestus* bearing, gesture] **—ges·tic′u·la′tion** *n.* **—ges·tic′u·la′tive** *adj.*

ges·ture (jes′chər) *n.* **1** An expressive motion of the body and esp. of the hand or hands, used for emphasis or to express some idea or emotion. **2** Something said or done for mere effect or as a concession to manners, courtesy, etc. *—v.* **·tured, ·tur·ing** *v.i.* **1** To make gestures. *—v.t.* **2** To express by gestures. [<L *gestus,* pp. of *gerere* carry on, do] **—ges′tur·er** *n.*

get (get) *v.* **got** or *Archaic* **gat, got** or *U.S.* **got·ten, get·ting** *v.t.* **1** To come into possession of; obtain. **2** To go for and bring back: to *get* one's hat. **3** To cause to come, go, move, etc.: We *got* him to talk; I can't *get* the window up. **4** To take; carry away: *Get* your things out of this house. **5** To prepare: to *get* breakfast. **6** To bring to a state or condition: to *get* the work done. **7** To find out or obtain by calculation, experiment, etc.: to *get* the range of a gun. **8** To communicate with; contact: We can't *get* them on the phone. **9** To receive as a reward, punishment, etc.: to *get* ten years in jail. **10** To obtain, receive, or earn: to *get* permission. **11** To capture; catch. **12** To learn or master: to *get* a lesson. **13** To become sick with. **14** To board; catch, as a train. **15** To beget: said chiefly of animals. **16** *Informal* To come to an understanding of; comprehend: I *get* the idea. **17** *Informal* To possess: with *have* or *has:* He has *got* quite a temper. **18** To square accounts with: I'll *get* you yet. **19** *Informal* To be obliged or forced to do: with *have* or *has:* I have *got* to go home. **20** *Informal* To make helpless or ineffective: Drink finally *got* him. **21** *Informal* To strike; hit: That shot *got* him in the arm. **22** *Slang* To puzzle; baffle. **23** *Slang* To cause irritation or pleasure to: His impudence *gets* me. **24** *Slang* To notice: *Get* that dress she's wearing. *—v.i.* **25** To arrive: When does the train *get* there? **26** To come or go: *Get* in here! **27** To board; enter: to *get* on a train. **28** To become: to *get* drunk. **—get across 1** To make or be convincing or clear. **2** To be successful, as in projecting one's personality. **—get ahead** To succeed; prosper. **—get along 1** To leave; go. **2** To be successful or fairly successful, as in business. **3** To be friendly. **4** To proceed. **5** To grow old or older. **—get around 1** To become known. **2** To move about. **3** To avoid; circumvent. **4** To flatter, cajole, etc., so as to obtain the favor of. **—get at 1** To reach; arrive at: to *get at* the truth. **2** To intend; mean: I don't see what you're *getting at.* **3** To apply oneself to: to *get* at a problem. **—get away 1** To escape. **2** To leave; go. **3** To start. **—get away with** *Slang* To do (something) without discovery, criticism, or punishment. **—get back at** *Slang* To revenge oneself on. **—get by 1** To pass: This *got by* the censor. **2** *Informal* To manage to survive. **—get in 1** To arrive. **2** To interject effectively, as a remark. **—get lost 1** To lose one's way. **2** *Slang* Go away! **—get off 1** To descend from; dismount. **2** To leave; depart. **3** To be relieved, as of duty. **4** To be released without punishment; escape penalty. **5** To utter: to *get off* a joke. **6** To take off: *Get off* your wet clothes. **—get on 1** To mount, as a horse. **2** To get along. **—get out 1** To depart. **2** To escape. **3** To become known, as a secret. **4** To publish; issue. **—get over 1** To recover from, as illness or surprise. **2** To get across. **—get through 1** To finish. **2** To survive. **—get to 1** To start or begin. **2** To succeed, as in reaching or making clear to: also **get through to. —get together 1** To collect, as facts. **2** To meet; assemble. **3** *Informal* To come to an agreement. **—get up 1** To rise, as from sleep. **2** To prepare and arrange; devise. **3** *Informal* To dress up. [<ON *geta*] **—get′ta·ble, get′a·ble** *adj.* **—get′ter** *n.* • See GOT and GOTTEN.

get·a·way (get′ə·wā′) *n.* **1** An escape. **2** The start, as of a race.

Geth·sem·a·ne (geth·sem′ə·nē) *n.* A garden outside Jerusalem, the scene of the agony, betrayal, and arrest of Jesus. *Matt.* 26:36.

get-to·geth·er (get′tə·geth′ər) *n.* An informal gathering.

get-up (get′up′) *n.* *Informal* **1** The general appearance or make-up of something. **2** Costume; dress.

gew-gaw (gʸōō′gô) *adj.* Showy; gaudy. *—n.* A flashy trinket; bauble. [?]

gey·ser (gī′zər) *n.* A spring from which intermittent jets of steam, hot water, or mud are ejected. [<ON *geysa* gush]

Gha·na (gä′nə) *n.* A republic of the Commonwealth of Nations in W Africa, 92,100 sq. mi., cap. Accra. **—Gha′na·ian** (-nē·ən) *adj., n.* • See map at AFRICA.

ghast·ly (gast′lē, gäst′-) *adj.* **·li·er, ·li·est 1** Having a haggard, deathlike appearance. **2** Terrifying or shocking. **3**

Informal Very bad: a *ghastly* blunder. —*adv.* In a ghastly manner. [< OE *gāstlīc* ghostly] —**ghast′li·ness** *n.*

ghat (gôt) *n.* **1** In India, a stairway on a river bank, usu. leading to a temple. **2** In India, a mountain pass. Also **ghaut.** [< Hind. *ghāt*]

ghee (gē) *n.* In India, clarified butter, usu. made from milk of the water buffalo. Also **ghi.** [< Hind. *ghī*]

gher·kin (gûr′kin) *n.* **1** A small prickly cucumber used for pickles. **2** Any small, immature cucumber used for pickling. [< LGk. *angourion* cucumber]

ghet·to (get′ō) *n. pl.* **·tos** **1** In Europe, a part of a city in which Jews were formerly required to live. **2** A section of a city, often rundown or overcrowded, inhabited chiefly by a minority group. **3** Any community or group separated physically or culturally from the rest of society. [Ital.]

ghet·to·ize (get′ō·īz) *v.t.* **·ized, ·iz·ing** To make into a ghetto. —**ghet′to·iz·a′tion** *n.*

ghost (gōst) *n.* **1** A disembodied spirit, esp. of a dead person and supposedly able to manifest itself to the living in various ways. **2** The soul or spirit: now only in the phrase **give up the ghost,** to die. **3** A shadow or semblance; slight trace. **4** A false, secondary image produced in an optical instrument or on a television screen. **5** *Informal* A ghost writer. —*v.t. & v.i.* **1** To haunt as a ghost. **2** *Informal* To write as a ghost writer. [< OE *gāst* spirit] —**ghost′like′** *adj.*

ghost·ly (gōst′lē) *adj.* **·li·er, ·li·est** **1** Of, pertaining to, or like a ghost; spectral. **2** Spiritual. —**ghost′li·ness** *n.*

ghost town A deserted town.

ghost-write (gōst′rīt′) *v.i. & v.t.* **-wrote, -writ·ten, -writ·ing** To do literary work credited to another. —**ghost writer**

ghoul (gōōl) *n.* **1** In Oriental legend, an evil spirit supposed to prey on corpses. **2** A person who robs dead bodies. **3** One who delights in revolting things. [< Ar. *ghūl*] —**ghoul′ish** *adj.* —**ghoul′ish·ly** *adv.* —**ghoul′ish·ness** *n.*

GHQ General Headquarters.

GI (jē′ī′) *n. pl.* **GI's, GIs** *Informal* A soldier, esp. an enlisted man, in the U.S. Army. —*adj.* **1** Of, pertaining to, or issued by the government to U.S. military forces. **2** *Informal* Conforming to U.S. military regulations. Also **G.I.** [< *G(overnment) I(ssue)*]

G.I., g.i. gastrointestinal.

gi. gill².

gi·ant (jī′ənt) *n.* **1** Any imaginary person of gigantic size. **2** Any person or thing of great size, either physically, mentally, or figuratively. —*adj.* Gigantic. [< Gk. *gigas, gigantos*] —**gi′ant·ess** *n. Fem.*

gi·ant·ism (jī′ənt·iz′əm) *n.* GIGANTISM.

giant panda PANDA (def. 2).

giaour (jour) *n.* An unbeliever: a term of opprobrium applied by Muslims. [< Pers. *gaur*]

gib·ber (jib′ər, gib′-) *v.i.* To talk rapidly and incoherently; jabber. —*n.* Unintelligible talk; gibberish. [Imit.]

gib·ber·ish (jib′ər·ish, gib′-) *n.* **1** Incoherent or unintelligible talk. **2** Pretentiously difficult or obscure language. —**Syn. 1** babble, gabble, double talk, gobbledygook.

gib·bet (jib′it) *n.* **1** An upright timber with a crosspiece projecting at right angles from its upper end, upon which criminals were formerly hanged. **2** GALLOWS. —*v.t.* **·bet·ed** or **·bet·ted, ·bet·ing** or **·bet·ting** **1** To execute by hanging. **2** To hang and expose on a gibbet. **3** To hold up to public contempt. [< OF *gibe* a staff]

Gibbon

gib·bon (gib′ən) *n.* A slender, long-armed arboreal ape of s Asia. [F]

gib·bous (gib′əs, jib′-) *adj.* **1** Irregularly rounded; convex, as the moon when less than full and yet more than half full. **2** Humpbacked. Also **gib·bose** (gib′ōs, gi·bōs′). [< L *gibbus* a hump] —**gib′bous·ly** *adv.* —**gib′bous·ness** *n.* • See MOON.

gibe (jīb) *v.t. & v.i.* **gibed, gib·ing** To mock; sneer; scoff. —*n.* An expression of sarcasm and ridicule. [? < OF *giber* treat roughly in play] —**gib′er** *n.* —**Syn.** *v.* deride, taunt, scorn, ridicule.

gib·let (jib′lit, gib′-) *n.* One of the edible visceral parts of a fowl, as the gizzard, heart, or liver. [< OF *gibelet*]

gid·dy (gid′ē) *adj.* **·di·er, ·di·est** **1** Dizzy. **2** Causing dizziness. **3** Foolish; silly; frivolous. —*v.t. & v.i.* **gid·died, gid·dy·ing** To make or become giddy. [< OE *gydig* insane] —**gid′·di·ly** *adv.* —**gid′di·ness** *n.*

gift (gift) *n.* **1** That which is given; a donation; present. **2** The act, right, or power of giving. **3** A natural endowment; aptitude; talent. —*v.t.* **1** To give as a present to. **2** To make a gift of. [< OE < *gifan* give]

gift·ed (gif′tid) *adj.* Having unusual ability or talent: a *gifted* child. —**gift′ed·ly** *adv.* —**gift′ed·ness** *n.*

gig¹ (gig) *n.* **1** A light, two-wheeled vehicle drawn by one horse. **2** A long, light ship's boat; also, a speedy, light rowboat. —*v.* **gigged, gig·ging** *v.i.* To ride in a gig. [?]

gig² (gig) *n. Slang* **1** A demerit, as in the army. **2** A job or engagement, esp. as a musician or singer. [?]

giga- *prefix* One billion or 10^9 (times a given unit). [< Gk. *gigas* giant]

gi·gan·tic (jī·gan′tik) *adj.* **1** Like a giant; colossal; huge. **2** Tremendous; extraordinary. [See GIANT.]

gi·gan·tism (jī·gan′tiz·əm) *n.* Excessive growth of the body due to disturbances in the pituitary gland.

gig·gle (gig′əl) *v.i.* **gig·gled, gig·gling** To laugh in a high-pitched, nervous manner; titter. —*n.* Such a laugh; titter. [Imit.] —**gig′gler** *n.* —**gig′gly** *adj.*

gig·o·lo (jig′ə·lō, zhig′-) *n. pl.* **·los** **1** A woman's paid dancing partner or escort. **2** A man supported by a woman as her lover. [F, prob. < *gigolette* a prostitute]

gig·ot (jig′ət, *Fr.* zhē·gō′) *n.* **1** A leg of lamb or mutton. **2** A sleeve having the shape of a leg of mutton. [F]

gigue (zhēg) *n.* A lively dance, often the final movement in a suite of dances. [F]

Gi·la monster (hē′lə) A large, poisonous lizard with a stout orange and black body, found in the sw U.S. [< *Gila* River in New Mexico and Arizona]

Gila monster

gild¹ (gild) *v.t.* **gild·ed** or **gilt, gild·ing** **1** To coat with or as with gold or gold leaf. **2** To give a pleasing or attractive appearance to; gloss over. [< OE *gyldan*] —**gild′er** *n.*

gild² (gild) *n.* GUILD.

gill¹ (gil) *n.* **1** A respiratory organ that absorbs dissolved oxygen from water circulating through it, as in fishes, mollusks, etc. • See OYSTER. **2** A flap of tissue at the side of the head or neck, as the wattle of a fowl. **3** One of the thin radial plates inside the cap of a mushroom. [< Scand.]

gill² (jil) *n.* A liquid measure, one fourth of a pint. [< OF *gelle* measure for wine]

gil·li·flow·er (jil′ē·flou′ər) *n.* Any of various plants having clove-scented flowers, esp. the carnation. Also **gil′ly·flow′er.** [< Gk. *karyophyllon* clove]

gilt¹ (gilt) A *p.t. & p.p.* of GILD. —*adj.* Gilded; yellow like gold. —*n.* The gold or goldlike material used in gilding.

gilt² (gilt) *n.* A young female pig. [< ON *gyltr*]

gilt-edge (gilt′ej′) *adj.* **1** Having the edges gilded: said of paper. **2** Of the best quality or highest price: said of bonds, securities, etc. Also **gilt′-edged′.**

gim·bals (gim′bəlz, jim′-) *n. pl. (construed as sing.)* A device for allowing a suspended object, as a ship's compass, to rotate freely on two axes 90° apart. [< L *gemellus,* dim. of *geminus* twin]

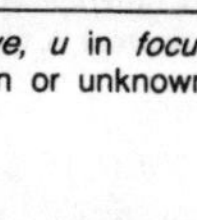

Gimbals

gim·crack (jim′krak) *n.* A useless trinket; bauble. —*adj.* Cheap and showy. [?] —**gim′crack·er·y** *n.*

gim·let (gim′lit) *n.* A small boring tool with a cross handle and a spiral point. —*v.t.* To make a hole in with a gimlet. [< OF *guimbelet*]

gim·mick (gim′ik) *n. Informal* **1** Something new or ingenious, as a gadget, scheme, stunt, etc., usu. devised to win publicity or make something more attractive. **2** A secret or surprising element; twist. **3** Any object whose name cannot be recalled. **4** A secret device for controlling the movements of a prize wheel. **—***v.t. Slang* To add gimmicks to: often with *up*. [?] **—gim′mick·y** *adj.*

gim·mick·ry (gim′ik·rē) *n. Informal* **1** The use of gimmicks, esp. if indiscriminate. **2** Gimmicks. Also **gim′mick·e·ry** (-ə·rē).

gimp[1] (gimp) *n.* A narrow, flat, ornamental trimming, used for dresses, furniture, etc. [?]

gimp[2] (gimp) *n. Informal* **1** A lame or crippled person. **2** A limp. **—***v.i.* To limp. [?] **—gimp′y** *adj.* **(·i·er, ·i·est)**

gin[1] (jin) *n.* **1** An alcoholic liquor distilled from various grains and flavored with juniper berries. **2** Such a liquor with other flavoring. [Short for Du. *jenever* juniper]

gin[2] (gin) *v.t. & v.i.* **gan, gin·ning** *Archaic* To begin.

gin[3] (jin) *n.* **1** A machine for separating cotton fibers from the seeds. **2** A snare or trap. **—***v.t.* **ginned, gin·ning 1** To catch in a trap. **2** To remove the seeds from (cotton) in a gin. [Short for ME *engin* engine]

gin[4] (jin) *n.* GIN RUMMY.

gin·ger (jin′jər) *n.* **1** The pungent, spicy rootstock of a tropical plant, used in medicine and cookery. **2** The plant itself. **3** *Informal* Liveliness; spunk. [< Gk. *zingiberis*]

ginger ale A carbonated soft drink flavored with ginger.

ginger beer A soft drink similar to ginger ale.

gin·ger·bread (jin′jər·bred′) *n.* **1** A light sweet cake flavored with ginger. **2** Gaudy or unnecessary ornament. [Alter. of OF *gingebras* preserved ginger < LL]

gin·ger·ly (jin′jər·lē) *adj.* Cautious or careful. **—***adv.* Cautiously; carefully. [?]

gin·ger·snap (jin′jər·snap′) *n.* A flat, brittle cooky flavored with ginger and molasses.

ging·ham (ging′əm) *n.* A plain-weave cotton fabric, usu. in checks or stripes. [< Malay *ginggang*]

gin·gi·vi·tis (jin′jə·vī′tis) *n.* Inflammation of the gums. [< L *gingiva* gum]

gink (gingk) *n. Slang* An odd fellow; guy. [?]

Ginkgo branch

gink·go (ging′kō) *n. pl.* **·goes** A hardy, widely cultivated deciduous tree native in China, having fanlike foliage. Also **ging′·ko.** [Jap.]

gin·mill (jin′mil′) *n. Slang* A saloon.

gin rummy A variety of rummy, a card game.

gin·seng (jin′seng) *n.* **1** Either of two related herbs native in North America and China, having an aromatic root used medicinally. **2** The root, or a preparation made from it. [< Chin. *jen shen*]

gip (jip) *n., v.* **gipped, gip·ping** GYP.

Gip·sy (jip′sē) *n. pl.* **·sies** GYPSY.

gipsy moth GYPSY MOTH.

gi·raffe (jə·raf′, -räf′) *n. pl.* **·raffes** or **·raffe** A large spotted African ruminant, having a very long neck and limbs; the tallest of the quadrupeds. [< Ar. *zarāfah*]

Giraffe

gird (gûrd) *v.t.* **gird·ed** or **girt, gird·ing 1** To surround with a belt or girdle. **2** To encircle; hem in. **3** To prepare (oneself) for action. **4** To clothe; equip. [< OE *gyrdan*]

gird·er (gûr′dər) *n.* A principal horizontal beam of a structure, receiving a vertical load.

gir·dle (gûr′dəl) *n.* **1** A belt, cord, or sash worn around the waist. **2** A woman's corsetlike, usu. elastic undergarment, reaching from the waist to below the hips. **3** Anything that encircles. **4** The edge of a cut gem. **5** An encircling cut through the bark of a branch or tree. **—***v.t.* **gir·dled, gir·dling 1** To fasten a girdle or belt around. **2** To encircle; encompass. **3** To make an encircling cut through the bark of (a branch or tree). [< OE *gyrdel*] **—gir′dler** *n.*

girl (gûrl) *n.* **1** A female child. **2** A young unmarried woman. **3** A female servant. **4** *Informal* A sweetheart. **5** *Informal* A woman of any age. [< ME *gurle*] **—girl′ish** *adj.* **—girl′ish·ly** *adv.* **—girl′ish·ness** *n.*

girl Friday A female office worker who performs a variety of tasks. [< GIRL + (MAN) FRIDAY]

girl friend *Informal* **1** A boy's or man's sweetheart, favorite female companion, etc. **2** A female friend.

girl·hood (gûrl′ho͝od) *n.* The state or time of being a girl.

girl·ie (gûr′lē) *adj. Informal* Featuring nude or nearly nude women or pictures of them: a *girlie* magazine.

girl scout A member of an organization, **Girl Scouts of America,** formed in 1912.

girt[1] (gûrt) *v.t.* **1** To gird; girdle. **2** To fasten with a girth, strap, etc. [< GIRD]

girt[2] (gûrt) *p.t. & p.p.* of GIRD.

girth (gûrth) *n.* **1** A band or strap for fastening a pack or saddle to a horse's back. **2** A girdle. **3** The circumference of a person's waist, a tree, etc. **—***v.t.* **1** To bind with a girth. **2** To encircle. **3** To find the girth of. [< ON *gjordh*]

gist (jist) *n.* The substance, point, or main idea. [< OF *giste* place of rest < *gesir* to lie] **—Syn.** heart, core, essence.

give (giv) *v.* **gave, giv·en, giv·ing** *v.t.* **1** To turn over to another without receiving anything in exchange. **2** To transfer to the possession or control of another for a price or equal value. **3** To hand over for safekeeping, delivery, etc. **4** To offer, esp. as entertainment: to *give* a play, toast, etc. **5** To be the cause or source of: The sun *gives* light. **6** To provide or furnish; impart: to *give* the news on TV. **7** To express by word or gesture. **8** To be the agent of transfer of, as a disease. **9** To grant: to *give* permission. **10** To impose, as a punishment. **11** To emit or show, as a movement, shout, etc. **12** To administer, as medicine. **13** To deal; inflict, as a blow. **14** To concede or yield: to *give* ground. **15** To devote or sacrifice: to *give* one's life. **16** To confer, as a title. **—***v.i.* **17** To make gifts. **18** To yield, as from pressure, melting, or thawing; collapse. **19** To be springy or resilient; bend. **—give away 1** To bestow as a gift. **2** To bestow (the bride) upon the bridegroom. **3** To reveal or disclose. **—give back** To return. **—give in 1** To yield. **2** To collapse, as under stress. **—give off** (or **forth**) To send forth; emit, as odors. **—give out 1** To send forth; emit. **2** To distribute. **3** To make known; publish. **4** To become worn out, exhausted, etc. **—give rise to** To cause or result in. **—give up 1** To surrender; cede; hand over. **2** To stop; cease. **3** To desist from as hopeless. **4** To lose all hope for. **5** To devote wholly. **—***n.* The quality of being yielding; elasticity. [< OE *giefan*] **—giv′er** *n.*

give-and-take (giv′ən·tāk′) *n.* **1** Fair exchange; equal compromise. **2** An exchange of ideas or wit.

give·a·way (giv′ə·wā′) *n.* A betrayal or revelation, often unintentional. **—***adj.* Featuring awards of money or prizes, as a television show.

giv·en (giv′ən) *adj.* **1** Habitually inclined: with *to.* **2** Specified; stated. **3** Donated; presented. **4** Admitted as a fact or a premise. **—***n.* A datum; premise.

given name One's first name, as distinguished from one's family name.

give-up (giv′up′) *n.* The practice of splitting a stockbroker's commission with another broker at the direction of the customer.

giz·mo (giz′mō) *n. pl.* **·mos** *Informal* Any gadget. [?]

giz·zard (giz′ərd) *n.* **1** The second stomach of birds, in which the food is ground. **2** *Slang* The stomach. [< L *gigeria* cooked entrails of poultry]

Gk. Greek.

gla·brous (glā′brəs) *adj. Biol.* Without hair or down. [< L *glaber* bald, smooth]

gla·cé (gla·sā′; *Fr.* glà·sā′) *adj.* **1** Iced; frozen. **2** Having a glossy surface resembling ice. **3** Covered with an icing or glaze, as certain candies. **—***v.t.* **·céed, ·cé·ing 1** To cover with icing. **2** To render smooth and glossy. [F < *glace* ice]

gla·cial (glā′shəl) *adj.* **1** Of, pertaining to, or caused by glaciers. **2** Of or pertaining to a glacial epoch. **3** Very cold or icy. **4** Cold in manner, appearance, etc.: a *glacial* look. [< L *glacies* ice] **—gla′cial·ly** *adv.*

glacial epoch Any portion of geological time in which glaciers covered much of the earth's surface.

gla·ci·ate (glā′shē·āt) *v.t.* **·at·ed, ·at·ing 1** To cover with glacial ice. **2** To affect or change by glacial action. **3** To convert into ice. **—gla′ci·a′tion** *n.*

gla·cier (glā'shər) *n.* A field of ice which moves slowly downward over slopes or through valleys until it either melts or breaks off to form icebergs. [<L *glacies* ice]

glad (glad) *adj.* **glad·der, glad·dest 1** Happy; joyful. **2** Causing joy or happiness. **3** Most willing: She is *glad* to do it. **4** Bright; cheerful. [<OE *glæd* shining, glad] **—glad'ly** *adv.* **—glad'ness** *n.* **—Syn. 1** pleased, contented, gay, merry, cheery, buoyant.

glad·den (glad'n) *v.t.* & *v.i.* To make or become glad.

glade (glād) *n.* **1** An open space in a wood. **2** An everglade. [Prob. akin to *glad* in obs. sense "sunny"]

glad hand *Slang* A hearty welcome.

glad·i·a·tor (glad'ē·ā'tər) *n.* **1** A man who fought with deadly weapons, as in the ancient Roman amphitheater, for popular amusement. **2** One who engages in any kind of fight or controversy. [<L *gladius* sword] **—glad·i·a·to·ri·al** (glad'ē·ə·tôr'ē·əl, -tō'rē-) *adj.*

glad·i·o·lus (glad'ē·ō'ləs) *n. pl.* **·lus·es** or **·li** (-lī) A plant of the iris family with fleshy bulbs, sword-shaped leaves, and spikes of colored flowers. Also **glad·i·o·la** (glad'ē·ō'lə), **glad'i·ole** (-ōl). [<L *gladius* sword]

glad·some (glad'səm) *adj.* **1** Joyous; pleasing. **2** Cheerful. **—glad'some·ly** *adv.* **—glad'some·ness** *n.*

Glad·stone (glad'stōn, -stən) *n.* A suitcase hinged in the middle lengthwise so that it may open into halves: also **Gladstone bag.** [<W. E. *Gladstone,* 1809–98, English statesman]

glair (glâr) *n.* The white of eggs mixed with vinegar, used as a size in gilding, etc. **2** Anything slimy or sticky, as egg whites. *—v.t.* To treat with glair. Also **glaire.** [<OF *glaire*] **—glair'y** *adj.*

glam·or·ize (glam'ər·īz) *v.t.* **·rized, ·riz·ing** To make glamorous. **—glam'or·i·za'tion** *n.*

glam·or·ous (glam'ər·əs) *adj.* Radiating glamour; alluring. Also **glam'our·ous.** **—glam'or·ous·ly, glam'our·ous·ly** *adv.*

glam·our (glam'ər) *n.* **1** Alluring charm, fascination, or attraction. **2** Originally, a delusion caused by a magic spell. Also **glam'or.** [Scot., var. of GRAMMAR]

glance (glans, gläns) *v.* **glanced, glanc·ing** *v.i.* **1** To strike something at an angle and bounce off. **2** To look quickly or hurriedly. **3** To glint; flash. **4** To make passing reference; allude. *—v.t.* **5** To cause to strike something at an angle and bounce off. *—n.* **1** A quick look. **2** A momentary gleam. **3** A glancing movement or rebound. [<OF *glacier* to slip]

gland (gland) *n.* **1** Any of various tissues or organs that secrete substances essential to the body or for the elimination of waste products: salivary *glands;* endocrine *glands.* **2** A node of nonsecreting tissue: lymph *gland.* [<L *glandula,* dim. of *glans, glandis* acorn]

glan·ders (glan'dərz) *n. pl. (construed as sing.)* A contagious disease of horses, mules, etc., characterized by nasal discharges and fever. [<OF *glandre* a gland] **—glan'dered, glan'der·ous** *adj.*

glan·du·lar (glan'jə·lər) *adj.* Of, bearing, or like glands.

glans (glanz) *n. pl.* **glan·des** (-dēz) The rounded tip of the penis or clitoris. [L, lit., an acorn]

glare[1] (glâr) *v.* **glared, glar·ing** *v.i.* **1** To shine with great and dazzling intensity. **2** To gaze or stare fiercely. **3** To be conspicuous or ostentatious. *—v.t.* **4** To express with a glare. *—n.* **1** A dazzling light. **2** An intense, usu. hostile look or gaze. **3** Gaudiness. [<ME *glaren*]

glare[2] (glâr) *n.* A glassy, smooth surface, as of ice. *—adj.* Having a glassy, smooth surface. [? <GLARE[1]]

glar·ing (glâr'ing) *adj.* **1** Looking or staring fixedly or hostilely. **2** Emitting an excessively brilliant light. **3** Plainly conspicuous: a *glaring* mistake. **—glar'ing·ly** *adv.*

glar·y (glâr'ē) *adj.* **glar·i·er, glar·i·est** Dazzling; glaring.

glas·nost (glas'nost) *n.* An official policy of greater openness in governmental policymaking. [<Russ.]

glass (glas, gläs) *n.* **1** A hard, amorphous, brittle, usu. translucent substance of varying composition, usu. made y fusing sand with various oxides chosen according to the properties desired. **2** Any substance resembling glass. **3** An article made of glass, as a window pane, a goblet or tumbler, a mirror, telescope, barometer, etc. **4** *pl.* EYEGLASSES. **5** *pl.* BINOCULARS. **6** The amount of something contained in a drinking glass. **7** GLASSWARE. *—v.t.* **1** To enclose with glass. **2** To reflect; mirror. **3** To give a glazed surface to. *—adj.* Made of, relating to, or like glass. [<OE *glæs*]

glass·blow·ing (glas'blō'ing, gläs'-) *n.* The process of blowing air through a tube into molten glass to form a desired shape. **—glass'blow'er** *n.*

glass·ful (glas'fŏŏl, gläs'-) *n. pl.* **·fuls** As much as can be contained in a drinking glass.

glass snake A legless lizard of the southern U.S., having a very brittle tail.

glass·ware (glas'wâr', gläs'-) *n.* Articles made of glass.

glass wool A mass of fibers of spun glass used for filtration, insulation, etc.

glass·y (glas'ē, gläs'ē) *adj.* **glass·i·er, glass·i·est 1** Composed of or like glass. **2** Fixed, blank, and uncomprehending: a *glassy* stare. **—glass'i·ly** *adv.* **—glass'i·ness** *n.*

glau·co·ma (glou·kō'mə, glô-) *n.* A disease of the eye characterized by increased pressure within the eyeball and partial or total loss of vision. [<Gk. *glaukos* bluish gray] **—glau·com'a·tous** (-kom'ə·təs) *adj.*

glau·cous (glô'kəs) *adj.* **1** Having a yellowish green color. **2** *Bot.* Having a powdery, bluish white bloom, as grapes, blueberries, etc. [<Gk. *glaukos* bluish gray]

glaze (glāz) *v.* **glazed, glaz·ing** *v.t.* **1** To fit, as a window, with glass panes. **2** To provide (a building, etc.) with windows. **3** To coat, as pottery, with a glasslike surface applied by fusing. **4** To cover with a glaze, as meat or biscuits. **5** To make glossy, as by polishing. *—v.i.* **6** To become glassy; take on a glaze. *—n.* **1** A smooth, shining, transparent surface. **2** A substance used to produce it, as on pottery. **3** An icy surface. **4** Transparent stock or icing applied to the surface of meat, fish, vegetables, etc. [ME *glasen*<*glas* glass] **—glaz'er, glaz'i·ness** *n.* **—glaz'y** *adj.*

gla·zier (glā'zhər) *n.* **1** One who fits panes of glass. **2** One who applies glaze to pottery. **—gla'zier·y** *n.*

glaz·ing (glā'zing) *n.* **1** A glaze. **2** The act or art of applying glaze. **3** Window panes, collectively. **4** The act or art of setting glass.

gleam (glēm) *n.* **1** A glimmer or flash of light. **2** A small, faint light. **3** Something likened to a flash of light: a *gleam* of wit. *—v.i.* **1** To shine with a gleam. **2** To appear clearly and briefly, as a signal fire. *—v.t.* **3** To show with a gleam. [<OE *glǣm*] **—gleam'y** *adj.* **—Syn.** *v.* **1** flash, sparkle, glitter, glare, dazzle.

glean (glēn) *v.t.* & *v.i.* **1** To collect (information, facts, etc.) by patient effort. **2** To gather (the leavings) from a field after the crop has been reaped. **3** To gather the leavings from (a field, etc.). [<LL *glenare*] **—glean'er** *n.*

glebe (glēb) *n.* **1** Land attached to an ecclesiastical benefice as part of its endowment. **2** *Archaic* Any field. [<L *gleba* lump of earth]

glee (glē) *n.* **1** Joy; gaiety; merriment. **2** A part song for three or more unaccompanied, usu. male voices. [<OE *glēo*] **—glee'some** (-səm) *adj.* **—Syn. 1** mirth, exuberance, delight, hilarity, fun.

glee club A group organized to sing light choral music.

glee·ful (glē'fəl) *adj.* Feeling or exhibiting glee; joyous. **—glee'ful·ly** *adv.* **—glee'ful·ness** *n.*

glen (glen) *n.* A small, secluded valley. [Scot. Gael. *glenn*]

Glen·gar·ry (glen·gar'ē) *n.* A woolen Scottish cap for men, having a lengthwise crease along the top and short streamers in back. Also **Glengarry bonnet.** [<*Glengarry,* a valley in Scotland]

glib (glib) *adj.* **glib·ber, glib·best 1** Speaking or writing with smooth fluency. **2** More facile than sincere; superficial: a *glib* compliment. **3** Characterized by easiness or informality. [Prob.<MLG *glibberich* slippery] **—glib'ly** *adv.* **—glib'ness** *n.*

glide (glīd) *v.* **glid·ed, glid·ing** *v.i.* **1** To move, slip, or flow smoothly or easily. **2** To pass unnoticed, as time. **3** *Aeron.* To descend gradually and without power; also, to operate a glider. **4** *Music & Phonet.* To produce a glide. *—v.t.* **5** To cause to glide. —*n.* 1 The act of gliding; a gliding motion. 2 *Music* An unbroken passage from tone to tone. 3 *Phonet.* A transitional sound made in passing from the position of one speech sound to that of another. [< OE *glīdan*]

glid·er (glī′dər) *n.* 1 One who or that which glides. 2 An

Glider *def. 2*

aircraft similar to an airplane but without an engine, supported by currents of air. 3 A couch hung in a metal frame so as to glide back and forth.

glim·mer (glim′ər) *v.i.* 1 To shine with a faint, unsteady light; flicker. 2 To appear fitfully or faintly. —*n.* 1 A faint, unsteady light. 2 A momentary apprehension; glimpse: a *glimmer* of the truth. [Prob. < Scand.] —**glim′mer·ing** *n.*

glimpse (glimps) *n.* 1 A momentary view or look. 2 A glimmer; inkling. —*v.* **glimpsed, glimps·ing** *v.t.* 1 To see for an instant. —*v.i.* 2 To look for an instant. [< Gmc.]

glint (glint) *v.i.* To gleam; glitter. —*n.* A gleam. [< Scand.] —**Syn.** *v.* sparkle, flash, glimmer, shine.

glis·sade (gli·säd′, -sād′) *v.i.* **·sad·ed, ·sad·ing** To slide or glide. —*n.* 1 The act of gliding down a slope, as of ice or snow. 2 A sliding step in dancing. [< F *glisser* slip]

glis·san·do (gli·sän′dō) *n. pl.* **·di** (-dē) or **·dos** *Music* A rapid, gliding passage from tone to tone. [< GLISSADE]

glis·ten (glis′ən) *v.i.* To sparkle; shine; gleam. —*n.* A shining. [< OE *glisnian* shine] —**glis′ten·ing·ly** *adv.*

glis·ter (glis′tər) *Archaic v.i.* GLISTEN. —*n.* GLITTER. [< MDu. *glisteren*]

glitch (glich) *n. pl. Slang* 1 A malfunction or mishap. 2 A sudden shift from normal function, as in electric power. 3 A false signal. [Prob. < G *glitschen* to slide, slip]

glit·ter (glit′ər) *v.i.* 1 To sparkle with a gleaming light. 2 To be bright or colorful. —*n.* Sparkle; brilliancy. [< ON *glitra*] —**glit′ter·ing, glit′ter·y** *adj.*

gloam·ing (glō′ming) *n.* The twilight; dusk. [< OE *glōmung*]

gloat (glōt) *v.i.* 1 To look with cruel or triumphant satisfaction. 2 To think about something with exultation or avarice. [?]

glob·al (glō′bəl) *adj.* 1 Of or involving the world in its entirety: *global* war. 2 Spherical.

globe (glōb) *n.* 1 Something perfectly round; sphere. 2 The earth. 3 A spherical map of the earth or of the heavens. [< L *globus*]

globe·fish (glōb′fish′) *n. pl.* **·fish** or **·fish·es** A fish of tropical seas, covered with spines and able, when disturbed, to inflate its body into a globular form.

globe-trot·ter (glōb′trot′ər) *n.* One who travels all over the world. —**globe′-trot′ting** *n., adj.*

glo·bose (glō′bōs) *adj.* Spherical. Also **glo′bous** (-bəs). [< L *globus* ball] —**glo′bose·ly** *adv.* —**glo·bos·i·ty** (glō·bos′ə·tē) *n.*

glob·u·lar (glob′yə·lər) *adj.* 1 Spherical. 2 Formed of globules. 3 Worldwide.

glob·ule (glob′yo͞ol) *n.* A small globe or spherical particle. [< L < *globus* ball]

glock·en·spiel (glok′ən·spēl, -shpēl) *n.* A musical instrument consisting of a chromatic series of metal bars played by striking with hammers. [< G *Glocken* bells + *Spiel* play]

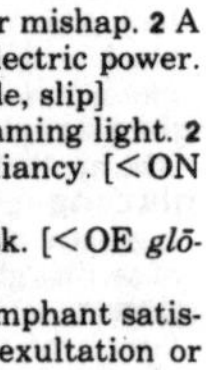

Glockenspiel

glom·er·ate (glom′ər·it) *adj.* Clustered compactly. [< L < *glomus, glomeris* a mass] —**glom′er·a′tion** (-ā′shən) *n.*

gloom (glo͞om) *n.* 1 Depression of the mind or spirits; melancholy. 2 Partial or total darkness. 3 A dark or gloomy place. —*v.i.* 1 To look sullen or dejected. 2 To be or become dark or threatening. —*v.t.* 3 To make dark, sad, or sullen. [< ME *glom(b)en* look sad]

gloom·y (glo͞o′mē) *adj.* **gloom·i·er, gloom·i·est** 1 Melancholy; morose. 2 Causing gloom or melancholy. 3 Dark; dismal; obscure. —**gloom′i·ly** *adv.* —**gloom′i·ness** *n.* —**Syn.** 1 Sad, downcast, despondent, somber, sorrowful.

Glo·ri·a (glôr′ē·ə, glō′rē·ə) *n. pl.* **·ri·as** 1 Any of several Christian doxologies sung in Latin and named for the opening phrase, as **Gloria in ex·cel·sis** (eks·chel′səs, ek·shel′-) (Glory to God in the highest) or **Gloria Pa·tri** (pä′trē) (Glory to the Father). 2 A musical setting for a Gloria. [L, glory]

glo·ri·fy (glôr′ə·fī, glō′rə-) *v.t.* **·fied, ·fy·ing** 1 To honor or worship: to *glorify* God. 2 To make exalted or blessed. 3 To praise; extol. 4 To represent as better or finer than the facts warrant. [< L *gloria* glory + -FY] —**glo′ri·fi′er** *n.*

glo·ri·ous (glôr′ē·əs, glō′rē-) *adj.* 1 Full of glory. 2 Bestowing glory. 3 Deserving glory. 4 Extremely delightful; splendid: a *glorious* time. —**glo′ri·ous·ly** *adv.* —**glo′ri·ous·ness** *n.*

glo·ry (glôr′ē, glō′rē) *n. pl.* **·ries** 1 Distinguished honor, praise, or renown. 2 Something that brings or deserves honor, praise, or renown. 3 Adoration; worshipful praise. 4 Splendor; magnificence. 5 The bliss of heaven. 6 A state of exaltation, well-being, prosperity, etc.: He was in his *glory.* 7 Radiance; brilliancy. 8 A nimbus; halo. —*v.i.* **glo·ried, glo·ry·ing** To rejoice proudly or triumphantly; exult: with *in.* [< L *gloria*]

gloss[1] (glôs, glos) *n.* 1 The brightness or sheen of a polished surface. 2 A deceptive or superficial appearance or show. —*v.t.* 1 To make smooth or lustrous, as by polishing. 2 To attempt to hide (errors, defects, etc.) by falsehood or equivocation: with *over.* —*v.i.* 3 To become shiny. [< Scand.] —**gloss′er** *n.*

gloss[2] (glôs, glos) *n.* 1 An explanatory note; esp. a marginal or interlinear note or translation. 2 A glossary. —*v.t.* 1 To write glosses for. 2 To excuse or change by false or superficial explanations: usu. with *over.* —*v.i.* 3 To make glosses. [< Gk. *glōssa* a foreign word, language] —**gloss′er** *n.*

glos·sa·ry (glos′ə·rē, glôs′-) *n. pl.* **·ries** An explanatory list of the difficult, technical, or foreign words used in a particular work or area of knowledge. [< L *glossa* gloss[2]] —**glos·sar·i·al** (glo·sâr′ē·əl, glô-) *adj.* —**glos·sar′i·al·ly** *adv.* —**glos′sa·rist** *n.*

gloss·y (glôs′ē, glos′ē) *adj.* **gloss·i·er, gloss·i·est** 1 Having a bright or polished surface. 2 Outwardly or speciously attractive. —**gloss′i·ly** *adv.* —**gloss′i·ness** *n.*

glot·tal (glot′l) *adj.* Of, pertaining to, or articulated in the glottis.

glot·tis (glot′is) *n. pl.* **glot·tis·es** or **glot·ti·des** (-ə·dēz) The passage between the vocal folds at the upper opening of the larynx. [< Gk. *glōtta* tongue]

glove (gluv) *n.* 1 A covering for the hand, having a separate sheath for each finger. 2 A padded, leather mitt for catching a baseball. 3 BOXING GLOVE. —*v.t.* **gloved, glov·ing** 1 To put gloves on. 2 To cover with or as with a glove. 3 To serve as a glove for. [< OE *glōf*]

glov·er (gluv′ər) *n.* A maker or seller of gloves.

glow (glō) *v.i.* 1 To give off light, with or without heat or flame. 2 To be bright or red, as with animation. 3 To be animated with strong emotion. 4 To be excessively hot; burn. —*n.* 1 Brightness or incandescence, as of a heated substance. 2 Bright color; ruddiness. 3 Strong emotion or enthusiasm. 4 Bodily warmth, as caused by exercise, etc. [< OE *glōwan*] —**glow′ing** *adj.* —**glow′ing·ly** *adv.*

glow·er (glou′ər) *v.i.* To stare with an angry frown; scowl sullenly. —*n.* A fierce or sullen stare. [? < Scand.] —**glow′er·ing·ly** *adv.*

glow·fly (glō′flī′) *n.* A firefly.

glow·worm (glō′wûrm′) *n.* 1 A European beetle, the larva and wingless female of which display bioluminescence. 2 The luminous larva of American fireflies.

glox·in·i·a (glok·sin′ē·ə) *n.* A plant having large bell-shaped spotted flowers. [< B. P. *Gloxin,* 18th-century German physician]

gloze (glōz) *v.t.* **glozed, gloz·ing** GLOSS[2] (def. 1). [< OF *gloser* explain, gloss[2]]

glu·cose (glo͞o′kōs) *n.* 1 A simple sugar, widely distributed in plants and animals and playing a key part in the storage and release of vital energy; dextrose. 2 A viscous, yellowish solution of various sugars obtained by incomplete hydrolysis of starch; corn syrup. [< Gk. *gleykys* sweet wine + -OSE] —**glu·cos′ic** (-kos′ik) *adj.*

glue (glo͞o) *n.* 1 A viscid cement or adhesive used to stick things together, derived from boiling animal skin, bones, and cartilage. 2 Any of a number of adhesive substances. —*v.t.* **glued, glu·ing** To stick together with or as with glue. [< LL *glus, glutis*] **—glue'y** *adj.*

glum (glum) *adj.* **glum·mer, glum·mest** Moody and silent; sullen. [Akin to GLOOM] **—glum'ly** *adv.* **—glum'ness** *n.*

glume (glo͞om) *n.* One of the chafflike bracts enclosing the flowers of grasses and sedges. [< L *gluma* husk]

glut (glut) *v.* **glut·ted, glut·ting** *v.t.* 1 To fill or supply to excess; satiate; gorge. 2 To furnish (the market) with an excessive quantity of goods so that supply exceeds demand. —*v.i.* 3 To eat gluttonously. —*n.* 1 An excessive supply; plethora. 2 The act of glutting, or the condition of being glutted. [< L *glutire* swallow]

glu·ten (glo͞ot'n) *n.* A tough, sticky, nutritious protein substance found in wheat and other grain. [L, glue] —**glu'te·nous** *adj.*

glu·te·us (glo͞ot'ē·əs, glo͞o·tē'əs) *n. pl.* **·te·i** (-tē·ī) Any of the three muscles that form each buttock. [< Gk. *gloutos* rump] **—glu'te·al** *adj.*

glu·ti·nous (glo͞o'tə·nəs) *adj.* Gummy; sticky. **—glu'ti·nous·ly** *adv.* **—glu'ti·nous·ness** *n.*

glut·ton[1] (glut'n) *n.* 1 An excessive eater. 2 One who has an excessive appetite for anything. [< L *gluto* a glutton] **—glut'ton·ous** *adj.* **—glut'ton·ous·ly** *adv.*

glut·ton[2] (glut'n) *n.* A wolverine, esp. of Europe. [Trans. of G *Vielfrass* great eater]

glut·ton·y (glut'ən·ē) *n. pl.* **·ton·ies** The act or habit of eating to excess.

glyc·er·in (glis'ər·in) *n.* GLYCEROL. Also **glyc'er·ine.**

glyc·er·ol (glis'ər·ōl, -ol) *n.* A sweet, oily, colorless alcohol formed by hydrolysis of fats. [< Gk. *glykeros* sweet + -OL]

gly·co·gen (glī'kə·jən) *n.* A complex carbohydrate formed in animal tissues, principally the liver, and readily convertible to glucose as needed. [< Gk. *glykys* sweet + -GEN] **—gly'co·gen'ic** (-jen'ik) *adj.*

gly·col (glī'kōl, -kol) *n.* 1 A colorless, viscid compound derived from ethylene and used as an antifreeze and solvent. 2 Any of a series of alcohols having two hydroxyl radicals. [< GLYC(ERIN) + -OL]

gm, gm. gram(s).

G-man (jē'man') *n. pl.* **-men** (-men') *Informal* An agent of the Federal Bureau of Investigation. [< G(OVERNMENT) MAN]

gnarl (närl) *n.* A hard protuberance or knot on a tree. —*v.t.* To make twisted or deformed. [Back formation from GNARLED]

gnarled (närld) *adj.* 1 Having gnarls; knotty. 2 Rough, weatherbeaten, and usu. bent: *gnarled* hands. Also **gnarl'y.** [Prob. < ME *knorre* a knot]

gnash (nash) *v.t.* 1 To grind (the teeth) together, as in rage or pain. 2 To bite with grinding teeth. —*v.i.* 3 To grind the teeth together. [< Scand.]

gnat (nat) *n.* Any of various small, usu. biting, two-winged flies. [< OE *gnæt*]

gnaw (nô) *v.* **gnawed, gnawed** or **gnawn** (nôn), **gnaw·ing** *v.t.* 1 To bite or eat away little by little. 2 To make by gnawing. 3 To bite on repeatedly. 4 To wear away; erode. 5 To torment or oppress with fear, pain, etc. —*v.i.* 6 To bite or chew, or corrode persistently. 7 To cause constant worry, pain, etc. [< OE *gnagan*] **—gnaw'er** *n.* **—gnaw'ing** *adj., n.* **—gnaw'ing·ly** *adv.*

gneiss (nīs) *n.* A coarse-grained, granitelike rock in which there is a distinctly layered arrangement of the components. [< G *Gneis*] **—gneiss'ic** *adj.*

gnome (nōm) *n.* In folklore, one of a race of dwarfs believed to live underground as guardians of treasure. [< NL *gnomus*] **—gnom'ish** *adj.*

gno·mic (nō'mik, nom'ik) *adj.* Of, like, or using maxims; aphoristic. Also **gno'mi·cal.** [< Gk. *gnōmē* thought, maxim]

gno·mon (nō'mon) *n.* The upright piece whose shadow points out the time of day on a sundial; also, anything, as a pillar, used for a similar purpose. [< Gk. *gnōmōn* an indicator]

gnos·tic (nos'tik) *adj.* Of or possessing knowledge. Also **gnos'ti·cal.** [< Gk. *gnōsis* knowledge.] **—gnos'ti·cal·ly** *adv.*

Gnos·tic (nos'tik) *adj.* Of or pertaining to the Gnostics or Gnosticism. —*n.* An adherent of Gnosticism.

Gnos·ti·cism (nos'tə·siz'əm) *n.* A philosophical and religious system (first to sixth century) teaching that knowledge rather than faith was the key to salvation.

GNP, G.N.P. gross national product.

gnu (nyo͞o) *n. pl.* **gnus** or **gnu** A South African antelope having an oxlike head with curved horns, a mane, and a long tail; a wildebeest. [< Kaffir *nqu*]

Gnu

go[1] (gō) *v.* **went, gone, go·ing** *v.i.* 1 To proceed or pass along; move. 2 To move from a place; leave; depart. 3 To pass away; disappear; end. 4 To be free or freed. 5 To be in motion or operation; work properly: The watch is *going* now. 6 To extend or reach: The pipe *goes* to the basement; a road *going* to Baltimore. 7 To be, continue, or appear in a specified state or condition: to *go* unpunished. 8 To be valid, accepted, etc.: Anything *goes.* 9 To pass into a state or condition; become: to *go* insane. 10 To proceed or end in a specified manner: The party *went* well. 11 To be suitable; fit: The music *goes* with these words. 12 To have a proper or specific place; belong: The towels *go* on top. 13 To be phrased, expressed, sung, etc.: The song *goes* like this. 14 To emit or produce a specified sound or signal. 15 To engage oneself in an activity or occupation: to *go* to sea; to *go* fishing. 16 To pass: said of time. 17 To be awarded, given, or applied: This *goes* toward canceling the debt. 18 To have recourse; resort: to *go* to court. 19 To be known: What name does she *go* by? 20 To be sold or bid for. 21 To help; tend: This *goes* to prove my argument. 22 To serve as a part; contribute: the talent and dedication that *go* to make an artist. 23 To be abolished or surrendered. 24 To collapse; fail: The walls *went* last in the fire. 25 To subject oneself: He *went* to great pains to do it. 26 To die. 27 To be about to do or act: They were *going* to protest. 28 *Informal* To use a toilet: said of children: Does he have to *go?* —*v.t.* 29 To furnish; put up: to *go* bail. 30 To contribute; share: to *go* halves. 31 *Informal* To bet; wager. 32 *Informal* To put up with; tolerate. **—go about** 1 To be occupied or busy with. 2 *Naut.* To change to the other tack. **—go along** 1 To accompany. 2 To agree. **—go around** 1 To move about or circulate. 2 To be enough to furnish even shares. **—go at** 1 To attack. 2 To work at. **—go back on** 1 To forsake; be untrue to. 2 To fail to fulfill or abide by. **—go by** 1 To pass. 2 To conform to or be guided by: to *go by* the rules. **—go for** 1 To try to get: He *went for* his gun. 2 To attack. 3 *Informal* To be strongly attracted by. **—go in for** *Informal* 1 To strive for or advocate. 2 To have a liking for. **—go into** 1 To investigate. 2 To take up, as an occupation. 3 To be contained in. **—go off** 1 To explode or be discharged, as a gun. 2 *Informal* To happen; result. **—go on** 1 To act; behave. 2 To happen: What's *going on* here? **—go out** 1 To cease or be extinguished, as a light. 2 To be drawn forth in sympathy. 3 To strike. 4 To become obsolete. **—go over** 1 To turn on its side. 2 To rehearse; repeat. 3 To examine carefully. 4 *Informal* To succeed. **—go through** 1 To search thoroughly. 2 To experience; undergo. 3 To use up; exhaust. **—go through with** To undertake to finish. **—go under** 1 To be overwhelmed or conquered. 2 To fail, as a business. **—go up** To increase, as prices or values. **—go with** 1 To harmonize with. 2 *Informal* To keep company with. **—go without** To do or be without. **—let go of** 1 To release one's hold of. 2 To abandon one's interest or share in. —*n.* 1 The act of going. 2 *Informal* Energy; vigor. 3 *Informal* A try; attempt. 4 *Informal* A success. 5 *Informal* The fashion; mode: with *the.* 6 *Informal* A proceeding; turn of affairs. **—no go** *Informal* Useless; hopeless. **—on the go** *Informal* Busy; in constant motion. —*adj.* Operating or proceeding as planned: All systems are *go.* [< OE *gān*] **—go'er** *n.*

go[2] (gō) *n.* A Japanese game played with counters or stones on the intersections of lines on a board. [Jap.]

GO general orders.

goad (gōd) *n.* 1 A pointed stick for driving oxen. 2 Something that spurs or incites. —*v.t.* To urge or drive with or as with a goad. [< OE *gād*] —**Syn.** *v.* incite, spur, prick, urge.

go·a·head (gō′ə·hed′) *adj.* 1 Giving permission to proceed: a *go-ahead* signal. 2 Energetic. —*n.* Permission to proceed: usu. with *the.*

goal (gōl) *n.* 1 A point, end, or place that one is striving to reach: the *goal* of a race; a *goal* in life. 2 In certain games, the area or object that a ball, puck, etc., must reach to score; also, the act of making such a score or the score so made. [ME *gol*]

goal·ie (gō′lē) *n.* A goalkeeper.

goal·keep·er (gōl′kē′pər) *n.* In certain games, as hockey, soccer, etc., a player stationed at the goal to prevent a score from being made. Also **goal′tend′er** (-ten′dər).

goat (gōt) *n.* 1 Any of various agile, bearded, hollow-horned mammals related to the sheep and including wild and domesticated forms. 2 A lecherous man. 3 *Slang* SCAPEGOAT. —**get one's goat** *Slang* To anger or annoy by teasing, tormenting, etc. [< OE *gāt*] —**goat′ish** *adj.* —**goat′ish·ly** *adv.* —**goat′ish·ness** *n.*

Goat *n.* CAPRICORN.

goat·ee (gō·tē′) *n.* A small, pointed beard on a man's chin.

Goatee

goat·herd (gōt′hûrd′) *n.* One who tends goats.

goat·skin (gōt′skin′) *n.* 1 The hide of a goat. 2 Leather made from it.

goat·suck·er (gōt′suk′ər) *n.* Any of numerous nocturnal, insectivorous birds with wide mouths, as the whippoorwill or nighthawk.

gob[1] (gob) *n.* A small piece, mass, or chunk. [< OF *gobe* mouthful, lump]

gob[2] (gob) *n.* *Slang* A sailor. [?]

gob·bet (gob′it) *n.* 1 A piece or fragment, esp. of meat. 2 A chunk; lump. [< OF *gobe* lump]

gob·ble[1] (gob′əl) *v.* **gob·bled, gob·bling** *v.t.* 1 To swallow (food) greedily. 2 *Slang* To seize or acquire greedily. —*v.i.* 3 To eat greedily. [< ME *gobben*] —**gob′bler** *n.*

gob·ble[2] (gob′əl) *n.* The sound made by the male turkey. —*v.i.* **gob·bled, gob·bling** To utter a gobble. [Var. of GABBLE]

gob·ble·dy·gook (gob′əl·dē·go͝ok′) *n.* *Informal* Involved, pedantic, and pompous talk or writing. Also **gob′·ble·de·gook′.** • *Gobbledygook* usually refers to wordiness, the unnecessary use of long words, and a stuffy style often encountered in bureaucratic memoranda. "The writer is disposed to regard as contrary to efficient office procedure the utilization of government communications apparatus to conduct nongovernment business," for example, means "Don't use our phones to conduct your personal business."

gob·bler (gob′lər) *n.* A male turkey.

go-be·tween (gō′bə·twēn′) *n.* An agent or mediator between other persons.

gob·let (gob′lit) *n.* A drinking glass with a stem, base, and no handle. [< OF *gobel* a drinking cup]

gob·lin (gob′lin) *n.* A supernatural, grotesque creature regarded as malicious or mischievous. [< OF *gobelin*]

go·by (gō′bē) *n. pl.* **·by** or **·bies** Any of various small, spiny-finned, chiefly marine fishes, usu. having ventral fins united to form a suction disk. [< Gk. *kōbios,* small fish]

go-by (gō′bī′) *n. pl.* **-bys** *Informal* An intended slight.

go·cart (gō′kärt′) *n.* 1 STROLLER (def. 1). 2 A light carriage.

god (god) *n.* 1 A male being regarded as immortal and as possessing supernatural powers that control nature, man, or some aspect of life; deity. 2 An image or symbol of such a being; idol. 3 Any person or thing made an object of supreme or excessive devotion. [< OE] —**god′ship** *n.*

God (god) *n.* The Supreme Being, creator and ruler of the universe, conceived of as eternal, omniscient, good, and almighty.

god·child (god′chīld′) *n. pl.* **·chil·dren** (-chil′drən) A child for whom a person becomes sponsor at baptism.

god·daugh·ter (god′dô′tər) *n.* A female godchild.

god·dess (god′is) *n.* 1 A female being regarded as immortal and as possessing supernatural powers that control nature, man, or some aspect of life. 2 A surpassingly beautiful or beloved woman.

god·fa·ther (god′fä′t͟hər) *n.* A man who becomes sponsor for a child at its baptism.

God-fear·ing (god′fir′ing) *adj.* Pious; devout.

God-giv·en (god′giv′ən) *adj.* 1 Given by God. 2 Fortunate; welcome.

god·head (god′hed′) *n.* Godhood; divinity.

God·head (god′hed′) *n.* God; the Deity.

god·hood (god′ho͝od) *n.* The state or quality of being a god.

Go·di·va (gə·dī′və) An 11th-century noblewoman who, according to English legend, rode naked through Coventry as the condition of the removal of her husband's oppressive taxes.

god·less (god′lis) *adj.* 1 Not believing in God or a god; atheistic. 2 Wicked. —**god′less·ly** *adv.* —**god′less·ness** *n.*

god·like (god′līk′) *adj.* Similar to or suited for God or a god.

god·ly (god′lē) *adj.* **·li·er, ·li·est** Filled with love for God; pious. —**god′li·ness** *n.*

god·moth·er (god′mut͟h′ər) *n.* A woman who becomes sponsor for a child at baptism.

god·par·ent (god′pâr′ənt) *n.* A godfather or godmother.

God's acre A cemetery.

god·send (god′send′) *n.* A thing much needed or desired that comes unexpectedly at the opportune time, as if sent by God.

god·son (god′sun′) *n.* A male godchild.

God·speed (god′spēd′) *n.* God speed you: a wish for a safe journey or for success.

god·wit (god′wit) *n.* Any of various shore birds with long legs and a long, upturned bill. [?]

go-get·ter (gō′get′ər) *n.* *Informal* A hustling, energetic, aggressive person.

gog·gle (gog′əl) *n.* 1 A rolling or staring of the eyes. 2 *pl.* Large eyeglasses used as protection against strong light, wind, dust, etc. —*adj.* Prominent; staring. —*v.* **gog·gled, gog·gling** *v.i.* 1 To stare with bulging eyes. 2 To roll sidewise: said of the eyes. —*v.t.* 3 To roll (the eyes). [< ME *gogelen* look aside] —**gog′gle-eyed′** (-īd′) *adj.*

go-go (gō′gō′) *adj.* *Slang* 1 Of or describing discothèques, the usu. unrestrained, erotic dances performed there, or the dancers, typically young women, who entertain with such dances. 2 Lively, modern, glamorous, etc. [< F *à gogo* joyfully]

Goi·del·ic (goi·del′ik) *n.* A branch of the Celtic languages including Irish, the Gaelic of the Scottish Highlands, and Manx; Gaelic. —*adj.* Of or pertaining to the Gaels or their languages. Also **Goi·dhel′ic.** [< OIrish *Gōidel* a Gael]

go·ing (gō′ing) *n.* 1 The act of departing or moving; leaving. 2 The condition of the ground or roads with reference to ease of walking, riding, etc. 3 Progress or circumstances affecting it. —**goings on** *Informal* Behavior; conduct; actions. —*adj.* 1 Continuing to function: a *going* concern. 2 Moving; working. 3 In existence: available: the best bargain *going.* 4 Departing; leaving. —**going on** *Informal* Approaching (a particular age or time).

goi·ter (goi′tər) *n.* A chronic enlargement of the thyroid gland, often visible as a swelling on the front part of the neck. Also **goi′tre.** [< L *guttur* throat] —**goi′trous** *adj.*

go-kart (gō′kärt′) *n.* KART. [< *Go Kart,* a trade name]

gold (gōld) *n.* 1 A precious metallic element (symbol Au) of yellow color; it is very heavy, ductile, and malleable, and occurs in nature uncombined with other elements. 2 A coin of gold. 3 Money; wealth. 4 The deep yellow color of gold. 5 Something likened to gold, as in worth or value. —*adj.* Of, like, or made of gold. [< OE]

gold·brick (gōld′brik′) *n.* 1 *Informal* A worthless thing deceitfully sold or given as something valuable: also **gold brick.** 2 *Slang* A person who shirks or tries to shirk work: also **gold′brick′er.** —*v.i.* *Slang* 1 To shirk (work or duty). 2 To cheat.

gold digger *Informal* A woman who uses her personal relations with men to get money and gifts from them.

gold dust Gold in fine particles.

gold·en (gōl′dən) *adj.* 1 Made of or consisting of gold. 2 Having the color or luster of gold; bright yellow. 3 Unusually valuable or excellent. 4 Of great excellence or achievement: a *golden* age. **—gold′en·ly** *adv.* **—gold′en·ness** *n.*

Golden Fleece *Gk. Myth.* A fleece of gold guarded by a dragon and stolen by Jason with the aid of Medea.

gold·en·glow (gōl′dən·glō′) *n.* A tall, flowering herb with showy composite heads of yellow-rayed flowers.

golden mean The avoidance of extremes; wise moderation.

gold·en·rod (gōl′dən·rod′) *n.* A North American herb of the composite family, with erect stalks carrying clusters of small, yellow flowers in late summer.

golden rule The rule of life given in *Matt.* 7:12: "Whatsoever ye would that men should do to you, do ye even so to them."

golden wedding Fiftieth wedding anniversary.

gold-filled (gōld′fild′) *adj.* Made of a base metal covered with gold.

gold·finch (gōld′finch′) *n.* **1** A European finch having a yellow patch on the wings. **2** An American finch of which the male has a yellow body with a black tail.

American goldfinches

gold·fish (gōld′fish′) *n. pl.* **·fish** or **·fish·es** A small carp of golden color originally of China, now cultivated in many varieties.

gold leaf A very thin foil of gold. **—gold-leaf** (gōld′lēf′) *adj.*

gold·mine (gōld′mīn′) *n.* **1** A place where gold is mined. **2** *Informal* A very productive or profitable source: A dictionary is a *goldmine* of information.

gold rush A mass movement of people to an area where gold has been discovered.

gold·smith (gold′smith′) *n.* One who makes objects of gold. **—gold′smith′ing** *n.*

gold standard A monetary system based on a specified weight of gold as the unit of value.

golf (gôlf, golf, gôf, gof) *n.* An outdoor game played on a large course with a small hard ball and a set of clubs, the object being to direct the ball into a series of holes in as few strokes as possible. —*v.i.* To play golf. [ME] **—golf′·er** *n.*

Golf clubs
a. driver. b. No. 6 iron. c. No. 9 iron. d. putter.

golf course The course over which a game of golf is played. Also **golf links.**

Gol·go·tha (gol′gə·thə) *n.* A place near Jerusalem where Jesus was crucified.

Go·li·ath (gə·lī′əth) In the Bible, a Philistine giant, slain by David.

gol·ly (gol′ē) *interj.* An exclamation of surprise, awe, etc. [Euphemism for GOD]

go·losh (gə·losh′) *n.* GALOSH.

Go·mor·rah (gə·môr′ə, -mor′ə) *n.* In the Bible, a city on the shore of the Dead Sea. Also **Go·mor′rha.** See SODOM.

-gon *combining form* Having (a certain number of) angles: *pentagon.* [< Gk. *gonia* an angle]

gon·ad (gō′nad) *n.* An organ in which reproductive cells develop; an ovary or testis. [< Gk. *gonos* seed] **—go·nad′al** *adj.*

gon·do·la (gon′də·lə) *n.* **1** A long, narrow, flat-bottomed boat, high-peaked at the ends, used in Venice on the canals. **2** A large flat-bottomed river boat of light build. **3** A long, shallow, open freight car. **4** *Aeron.* The car attached below a dirigible or balloon. **5** A small car suspended from a moving cable, as on a ski lift. [< Ital. *gondolar* to rock]

Gondola *def. 1*

gon·do·lier (gon′də·lir′) *n.* One who poles or rows a gondola.

gone (gôn, gon) *p.p.* of GO. —*adj.* **1** Departed. **2** Ruined; lost. **3** Past. **4** Dead. **5** Faint; weak. **6** Finished; consumed. **7** *Slang* First-rate. **—far gone 1** Exhausted. **2** Almost dead. **3** Absorbed; involved: *far gone* in reverie.

gon·er (gôn′ər, gon′-) *n. Informal* A person or thing that is ruined or beyond saving.

gon·fa·lon (gon′fə·lon′, -lən) *n.* A flag or ensign fixed to a revolving frame or a crossyard, generally with streamers. [< Ital. *gonfalone* < Gmc.]

gong (gông, gong) *n.* **1** A metal percussion instrument shaped like a shallow dish. **2** A bell shaped like a saucer. [Malay]

gon·or·rhe·a (gon′ə·rē′ə) *n.* A venereal disease affecting the mucous membrane of the genital organs, usu. characterized by inflammation and a purulent discharge. Also **gon′or·rhoe′a.** [< Gk. *gonos* seed + *rheein* flow] **—gon′or·rhe′al, gon′or·rhoe′al** *adj.*

goo (go͞o) *n. Informal* **1** Any sticky fluid. **2** Sentimentality; mawkishness. [?]

goo·ber (go͞o′bər) *n. U.S.* A peanut. Also **goober pea.** [< Bantu *nguba*]

good (go͝od) *adj.* **bet·ter, best 1** Satisfactory in quality or kind: *good* food; *good* eyes. **2** Striking in appearance: a *good* figure. **3** Morally excellent; virtuous; worthy. **4** Kind; benevolent. **5** Well-behaved. **6** Proper; desirable: *good* manners. **7** Pleasing; agreeable: *good* news. **8** Beneficial; salutary: *good* for business. **9** Favorable; approving: a *good* opinion. **10** Skillful; proficient: a *good* swimmer. **11** Orthodox; conforming: a *good* Democrat. **12** Reliable; dependable: a *good* investment. **13** Considerable: a *good* supply: a *good* while. **14** Full: a *good* two miles off. **15** Valid; sound: *good* money. **—as good as** Practically; virtually: It is *as good as* done. **—good and** *Informal* **1** Very: He's *good and* hungry. **2** Completely: when I'm *good and* ready. **—good for 1** *Informal* Able or likely to give, produce, etc.: *good for* ten dollars; *good for* a laugh. **2** Likely to continue or last: *good for* a week. **—hold good for** To apply: That *holds good for* everyone. **—make good 1** To compensate for; replace. **2** To carry out; accomplish. **3** To prove. **4** To be successful. —*n.* **1** That which is good. **2** Benefit; profit; advantage: for the *good* of mankind. See also GOODS. **—for good (and all)** Finally; for the last time **—to the good** To one's profit, advantage, etc. —*interj.* An exclamation of satisfaction or assent. —*adv. Informal* Well. [< OE *gōd*]

Good Book The Bible: with *the.*

good-by (go͝od′bī′) *adj., n. & interj. pl.* **-bys** (-bīz′) Farewell. Also **good-bye.** [Contraction of *God be with you*]

good-for-noth·ing (go͝od′fər·nuth′ing) *n.* A worthless person. —*adj.* Useless.

Good Friday The Friday before Easter, a day commemorating the crucifixion of Jesus.

good-heart·ed (go͝od′här′tid) *adj.* Kind. **—good′heart′·ed·ly** *adv.* **—good′heart′ed·ness** *n.*

good humor A pleasant, cheerful mood or temper. **—good′-hu′mored** *adj.* **—good′hu′mored·ly** *adv.*

good·ies (go͝od′ēz) *n.pl.* of GOODY.

good·ish (go͝od′ish) *adj.* **1** Somewhat good; not bad. **2** Rather large; considerable.

good-look·ing (go͝od′lo͝ok′ing) *adj.* Attractive; handsome. **—Syn.** beautiful, comely, becoming, fair, lovely.

good·ly (go͝od′lē) *adj.* **·li·er, ·li·est 1** Comely; attractive. **2** Large; sizable. **—good′li·ness** *n.*

good·man (go͝od′mən) *n. pl.* **·men** (-mən) *Archaic* **1** Master; Mr.: a title for a man below the rank of gentleman. **2** A husband; head of a family.

good-na·tured (go͝od′nā′chərd) *adj.* Having a pleasant disposition; not easily provoked. **—good′na′tured·ly** *adv.* **—good′na′tured·ness** *n.*

good·ness (go͝od′nis) *n.* **1** The state or quality of being good. **2** Excellence. **3** Virtue. **4** Kindness. —*interj.* An exclamation of surprise, awe, etc.

goods (go͝odz) *n. pl.* **1** Merchandise. **2** Property, esp. personal property. **3** A fabric: linen *goods.* **4** *Brit.* Freight.

Good Samaritan A person who helps one in trouble.

Good Shepherd Jesus.

good-sized (go͝od′sīzed′) *adj.* Fairly large.

good-tem·pered (go͝od′tem′pərd) *adj.* Of a good disposition. **—good′tem′pered·ly** *adv.*

good·wife (gŏŏd′wīf′) *n. pl.* **·wives** (-wīvz′) *Archaic* **1** Mrs. **2** The mistress of the house.

good will **1** A desire for the well-being of others. **2** Cheerful willingness or consent. **3** Prestige and friendly relations built up by a business or member of a profession. Also **good·will** (gŏŏd′wil′).

good·y[1] (gŏŏd′ē) *n. pl.* **good·ies** *Archaic* A term of civility to women of humble station. [< GOODWIFE]

good·y[2] (gŏŏd′ē) *n. pl.* **good·ies** *Informal* **1** *Usu. pl.* Anything coveted, considered attractive, or highly valued. **2** *Usu. pl.* Something good to eat. **3** A prissy or sanctimonious person: also **good′y-good′y.** —*adj. Informal* Mawkishly good or pious: also **good′y-good′y.** —*interj.* A childish exclamation of joy: also **good′y-good′y.**

goo·ey (gōō′ē) *adj.* **goo·i·er, goo·i·est** *Informal* Like goo; sticky. **2** Sentimental; mawkish. —**goo′i·ness** *n.*

goof (gōōf) *Slang n.* **1** A stupid, foolish person. **2** A blunder. —*v.i. & v.t.* **1** To blunder; botch. **2** To waste time: usu. with *off* or *around.* [?] —**goof′y** *adj.* **(·i·er, ·i·est)** —**goof′i·ly** *adv.* —**goof′i·ness** *n.*

goof·ball (gōōf′bôl′) *n. Slang* A barbiturate, as a sleeping pill, or an amphetamine, or a mixture of them.

goo·gol (gōō′gol) *n.* **1** *Math.* The number 10 raised to the hundredth power (10^{100}) or 1 followed by 100 zeros. **2** Any enormous number. [Adopted by E. Kasner, 1878–1955, U.S. mathematician, from a child's word]

gook (gōōk) *n. Slang* A gummy or sticky substance or mixture. —**gook′y** *adj.* **(·i·er, ·i·est)**

goon (gōōn) *n. Slang* **1** A roughneck; thug; esp. one employed during a labor strike. **2** A stupid person. [< a character created by E. C. Segar, 1894–1938, U.S. cartoonist]

goose[1] (gōōs) *n. pl.* **geese** **1** One of a subfamily of wild or domesticated web-footed birds larger than ducks and smaller than swans. **2** The female of the goose: distinguished from *gander.* **3** *pl.* **goos·es** A tailor's heavy pressing iron, having a curved handle. **4** A silly creature; ninny. —**cook one's goose** *Informal* To spoil one's chances. [< OE *gōs*]

Blue goose

goose[2] (gōōs) *Slang v.t.* **goosed, goos·ing** **1** To prod or poke unexpectedly in the backside. **2** To accelerate an engine in irregular spurts. —*n. pl.* **goos·es** A sudden or unexpected prod or poke in the backside. [? Special use of GOOSE[1]]

goose·ber·ry (gōōs′ber′ē, -bər·ē, gōōz′-) *n. pl.* **·ries** **1** The tart fruit of a spiny shrub. **2** This shrub. [? GOOSE[1] + BERRY]

goose·flesh (gōōs′flesh′) *n.* A roughened condition of the skin produced by cold, fear, etc. Also **goose bumps, goose pimples.**

goose·neck (gōōs′nek′) *n.* Any of various mechanical devices curved or able to bend like a goose's neck.

goose-step (gōōs′step′) *n.* A marching step in some armies in which the legs are alternately lifted and held straight out. —*v.i.* To march in this manner.

G.O.P. Grand Old Party (Republican Party of the U.S.).

go·pher (gō′fər) *n.* **1** A burrowing North American rodent, esp. one with large cheek pouches. **2** One of various western North American ground squirrels. **3** A large, burrowing land tortoise of the s U.S. [?]

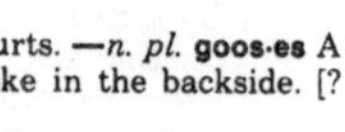

Gopher *def. 1*

Gor·di·an knot (gôr′dē·ən) **1** The intricate knot tied by Gordius, an ancient Phrygian king. The knot was incapable of being untied except by a future ruler of Asia, and it remained tied until Alexander the Great cut through it with his sword. **2** A difficulty that can be overcome only by the application of unusual or bold measures.

gore[1] (gôr, gōr) *v.t.* **gored, gor·ing** To pierce, as with a tusk or a horn. [< OE *gar*] —**gor′er** *n.*

gore[2] (gôr, gōr) *n.* A triangular piece of cloth sewn into a garment, sail, etc., for greater fullness. —*v.t.* **gored, gor·ing** To shape into or furnish with a gore. [< OE *gāra* triangular piece of land]

gore[3] (gôr, gōr) *n.* Blood after having been shed, esp. when clotted or dried. [< OE *gor* dirt, filth]

gorge (gôrj) *n.* **1** A deep, narrow ravine or passage. **2** A jam: an ice *gorge.* **3** The throat or gullet. **4** The act of gorging. **5** That which is gorged, as a full meal. **6** Anger, disgust, etc.: to make one's *gorge* rise. —*v.* **gorged, gorg·ing** *v.t.* **1** To stuff with food; glut. **2** To swallow gluttonously; gulp down. —*v.i.* **3** To stuff oneself with food. [< L *gurges* a whirlpool] —**gor′ger** *n.*

gor·geous (gôr′jəs) *adj.* **1** Resplendently beautiful, esp. as to color: a *gorgeous* sunset. **2** *Informal* Very pretty, delightful, amusing, etc. [< OF *gorgias* elegant] —**gor′·geous·ly** *adv.* —**gor′geous·ness** *n.*

Gor·gon (gôr′gən) *Gk. Myth.* One of three sisters with serpents for hair, so hideous that they turned the beholder to stone.

Gor·gon·zo·la (gôr′gən·zō′lə) *n.* A soft, blue-veined Italian cheese, somewhat like Roquefort. [< *Gorgonzola,* a town in Italy]

go·ril·la (gə·ril′ə) *n.* **1** An African anthropoid ape about five and a half feet tall with a massive body and limbs, long arms, and tusklike canine teeth. **2** *Slang* A tough person, esp. a gangster. [< Gk. *Gorillai,* an African tribe]

Gorilla

gor·mand (gôr′mənd) *n.* GOURMAND.

gor·mand·ize (gôr′mən·dīz) *v.t. & v.i.* **·ized, ·iz·ing** To eat voraciously or gluttonously. —**gor′·mand·iz′er** *n.*

gorse (gôrs) *n.* FURZE. [< OE *gors(t)*] —**gors′y** *adj.*

go·ry (gôr′ē, gō′rē) *adj.* **·ri·er, ·ri·est** Bloody. —**gor′i·ly** *adv.* —**go′ri·ness** *n.*

gosh (gosh) *interj.* A mild oath. [Euphemistic var. of GOD]

gos·hawk (gos′hôk′, gôs′-) *n.* A powerfully built, short-winged hawk formerly used in falconry. [< OE *gōs* goose + *hafoc* a hawk]

Go·shen (gō′shən) *n.* **1** In the Bible, the district in Egypt occupied by the Israelites. **2** A land of plenty.

gos·ling (goz′ling) *n.* A young goose.

gos·pel (gos′pəl) *n.* **1** *Often cap.* The teaching of the Christian Church, esp. the message of salvation preached by Jesus Christ and the apostles. **2** Any doctrine considered worthy of devoted or unquestioning support. **3** Anything regarded as absolutely true: also **gospel truth.** —*adj.* **1** *Often cap.* Of or relating to the gospel; evangelical. **2** Of, pertaining to, or being a type of religious music originally associated with evangelism, and combining elements of the spiritual, folk music, blues, and jazz. [< OE *godspell* good news]

Gos·pel (gos′pəl) *n.* Any of the first four books of the New Testament.

gos·sa·mer (gos′ə·mər) *n.* **1** A fine thread of spider's silk, usu. floating in the air. **2** A fine, transparent fabric. **3** Something fine and filmy, as gossamer. —*adj.* Thin and light as gauze; flimsy: also **gos′sa·mer·y.** [ME, Indian summer]

gos·sip (gos′əp) *n.* **1** Mischievous or idle talk, usu. about the affairs of others. **2** One who tattles or talks idly: also **gos′sip·er.** —*v.i.* To talk idly, usu. about the affairs of others. [< OE *god sibb* a godparent] —**gos′sip·y** *adj.*

got (got) *p.t. & p.p.* of GET. • **have** (or **has**) **got** In the sense of must, *have* or *has got* is in wide informal use to add emphasis: I *have* (or *I've*) *got* to leave. In the sense of possess, *have* or *has got* is still more common in informal speech: *He has got plenty of money.* This usage has long been challenged on the grounds (1) that *have got* properly means "have acquired," and (2) that *got* is superfluous, since *have* alone would convey the same meaning. However, since *have* is so much used as an auxiliary that it has lost much of its primary sense of "possess," *got* serves to restore and emphasize this meaning.

Goth (goth, gôth) *n.* **1** A member of an ancient East Germanic people that overran the Roman Empire in the third and fourth centuries. **2** A rude or uncivilized person.

Goth. Gothic; gothic.

goth·ic (goth′ik) *adj. Often cap.* **1** Medieval. **2** Barbaric; uncivilized. **3** Of or in a literary genre characterized by an atmosphere of mystery and gloom, violence, bizarre characters and happenings, etc. [< GOTH] **—goth′i·cal·ly** *adv.*

Goth·ic (goth′ik) *adj.* **1** Of the Goths or their language. **2** Of or like a style of architecture developed in w Europe from the 12th to 16th centuries and characterized by high steep roofs, pointed arches and vaulting, flying buttresses, and the use of large, stained-glass windows. —*n.* **1** The language of the Goths. **2** The Gothic style in architecture.

gothic type *U.S.* A type face having all the strokes of uniform width and without serifs.

got·ten (got′n) *p.p.* of GET. • *Gotten,* obsolete in British, is current in American English in the sense of "obtained": We have *gotten* the necessary funds. *Gotten* is also used in the sense of "become": He has *gotten* fat.

gouache (gwäsh) *n.* **1** A method of water-color painting with opaque colors mixed with water and gum. **2** A painting executed by this method. [< Ital. *guazzo* a spray]

Gou·da cheese (gou′də, go͞o′-) A mild, yellow cheese, often coated with a red waxy rind. [< *Gouda,* a town in the Netherlands]

gouge (gouj) *n.* **1** A chisel having a curved, hollow blade, used for making grooves, etc. **2** A groove made, or as if made, by it. **3** *Informal* Stealing or cheating. —*v.t.* **gouged, goug·ing 1** To cut or scoop out with or as with a gouge. **2** To scoop, force, or tear out. **3** *Informal* To cheat; also, to charge exorbitant prices to. [< LL *gulbia*] **—goug′er** *n.*

gou·lash (go͞o′läsh, -lash) *n.* A stew made with beef or veal and vegetables, seasoned with paprika, etc. [< Hung. *gulyas (hus)* shepherd's (meat)]

gourd (gôrd, gōrd, go͝ord) n. **1** The fruit with a hard rind, as pumpkin or squash, of various trailing plants or vines. **2** The plant producing such fruit. **3** Any of various items made from the rinds of such fruit, as dippers, bowls, rattles, etc. [< L *cucurbita*]

Gourd *def. 1*

gour·mand (go͝or′mənd; *Fr.* go͞or·mäṅ′) *n.* A person who takes great pleasure in eating and drinking, but without the knowledge or discrimination of a gourmet. [< OF, a glutton]

gour·met (go͞or·mā′; *Fr.* go͞or·me′) *n.* A person who has a considerable knowledge and appreciation of fine foods and wines. [F < OF, a winetaster]

gout (gout) *n.* **1** A disease characterized by painful inflammation of a joint, as of the great toe, and an excess of uric acid in the blood. **2** A drop; clot. [< L *gutta* a drop]

gout·y (gou′tē) *adj.* **gout·i·er, gout·i·est 1** Affected with gout. **2** Of or pertaining to gout. **3** Swollen. **—gout′i·ly** *adv.* **—gout′i·ness** *n.*

Gov. Governor.

gov., govt. government.

gov·ern (guv′ərn) *v.t.* **1** To rule or control by right or authority. **2** To control or influence morally or physically. **3** To serve as a rule or regulation for; determine: This decision *governed* the case. **4** To discipline or curb. —*v.i.* **5** To exercise authority. [< L *gubernare* to steer] **—gov′ern·a·ble** *adj.* **—gov′ern·ance** (-ər·nəns) *n.*

gov·ern·ess (guv′ər·nis) *n.* A woman employed in a private home to train and instruct children.

gov·ern·ment (guv′ərn·mənt, -ər-) *n.* **1** The authoritative direction and administration of the affairs of men in a nation, state, city, etc.; rule. **2** The governing body of a nation, state, city, etc. **3** A particular form of ruling or governing: democratic *government.* **4** A governed territory. **5** Management; control. **—gov′ern·men′tal** *adj.* **—gov′ern·men′tal·ly** *adv.*

Government House In British colonies, the official residence of a governor.

gov·er·nor (guv′ər·nər) *n.* **1** One who governs; esp. the chief executive of a state or colony. **2** A feedback controller, as for regulating the speed of a machine.

governor general *pl.* **governors general** or **governor generals** A high-ranking governor, esp. one who has deputy governors under him, as in the British Commonwealth. *Brit. sp.* **gov′er·nor-gen′er·al** *n. pl.* **gov′er·nors-gen′er·al**

gov·er·nor·ship (guv′ər·nər·ship) *n.* **1** The office of a governor. **2** A governor's term of office.

gown (goun) *n.* **1** A woman's dress, esp. when elegant or costly. **2** A long and loose outer robe worn as a distinctive or official habit, as by judges, clergymen, etc. **3** Any loose usu. long outer garment. **4** Those people associated administratively or educationally with a college or university in a town: town and *gown.* —*v.t. & v.i.* To dress in a gown. [< Med. L *gunna* a loose robe]

goy (goi) *n. pl.* **goy·im** (goi′im) or **goys** (goiz) A non-Jew; a Gentile. [Yiddish]

G.P. general paresis; general practitioner.

g.p.m. gallons per minute.

GPO, G.P.O. General Post Office; Government Printing Office.

g.p.s. gallons per second.

GQ, G.Q., g.q. general quarters.

Gr. Grecian; Greece; Greek.

gr. grade; grain(s); gram(s); grammar; gravity; great; gross; group.

Graaf·i·an follicle (gräf′ē·ən, graf′-) *Anat.* Any of the small sacs in the ovary of a mammal that contain a developing ovum. [< Regnier de *Graaf,* 1641–73, Du. anatomist]

grab (grab) *v.* **grabbed, grab·bing** *v.t.* **1** To grasp or seize forcibly or suddenly. **2** To take possession of violently or dishonestly. —*v.i.* **3** To make a sudden grasp. **4** *Slang* To involve or hold emotionally; affect. —*n.* **1** The act of grabbing, or that which is grabbed. **2** An apparatus for grappling. **—up for grabs** *Slang* Available to anyone with the means or money. [< MDu. *grabben*] **—grab′ber** *n.*

grab bag 1 A bag or box filled with miscellaneous articles, from which one draws something unseen on payment of a price for each grab or draw. **2** Any miscellaneous collection.

grab·by (grab′ē) *adj.* **grab·bi·er, grab·bi·est** *Informal* Offensively acquisitive or pushy; grasping. **—grab′bi·ness** *n.*

grace (grās) *n.* **1** Beauty or harmony of form, movement, manner, mode of expression, etc. **2** Any attractive characteristic, quality, etc. **3** Social aptness or thoughtfulness. **4** An extension of time granted, as in the payment of a debt. **5** *Theol.* **a** The love of God toward mankind. **b** A state of mind or spirit that is pleasing to God. **c** A power coming from God that enables one to achieve such a state. **d** Any divine favor. **6** A short prayer before or after meals. **7** Good will; favor. **8** *Music* An ornament, as a trill or turn. —*v.t.* **graced, grac·ing 1** To add grace and beauty to; adorn. **2** To dignify; honor. **3** *Music* To ornament with grace notes or other embellishments. [< L *gratia* favor]

grace·ful (grās′fəl) *adj.* Having or characterized by grace of form, movement, manner, etc. **—grace′ful·ly** *adv.* **—grace′ful·ness** *n.*

grace·less (grās′lis) *adj.* Lacking grace, charm, etc. **—grace′less·ly** *adv.* **—grace′less·ness** *n.*

grace note *Music* An ornamental, melodic note foreign to the harmony, esp. a short note on or just before the beat.

gra·cious (grā′shəs) *adj.* **1** Kind, courteous, and affable. **2** Compassionate; lenient. **3** Pleasantly luxurious and comfortable: *gracious* living. **—gra′cious·ly** *adv.* **—gra′cious·ness** *n.* **—Syn. 1** polite, cordial, amiable. **2** benevolent, considerate, sympathetic.

grack·le (grak′əl) *n.* Any of several large North American blackbirds. [< L *graculus* a jackdaw]

grad (grad) *n. Informal* A graduate.

grad. graduate; graduated.

gra·date (grā′dāt) *v.t. & v.i.* **·dat·ed, ·dat·ing 1** To pass or cause to pass imperceptibly from one shade or degree of intensity to another, as colors. **2** To arrange or group, as to size, quality, etc.

gra·da·tion (grā·dā′shən) *n.* **1** Orderly or continuous change by steps or degrees from one size, quality, state, etc., to another. **2** A step, degree, rank, or relative position in a graded series. **3** The act or process of arranging in grades or stages. [< L *gradatio* a going by steps < *gradus* a step] **—gra·da′tion·al** *adj.* **—gra·da′tion·al·ly** *adv.*

---

add, āce, câre, pälm; end, ēven; it, īce; odd, ōpen, ôrder; to͝ok, po͞ol; up, bûrn; ə = *a* in *above, u* in *focus;* **yo͞o** = *u* in *fuse;* **oil; pout; check; go; ring; thin; this; zh,** *vision.* < derived from; ? origin uncertain or unknown.

COMPARATIVE GRADES IN THE UNITED STATES ARMED SERVICES

Army	*Air Force*	*Marine Corps*	*Navy*
General	General	General	Admiral
Lieutenant General	Lieutenant General	Lieutenant General	Vice Admiral
Major General	Major General	Major General	Rear Admiral (upper half)
Brigadier General	Brigadier General	Brigadier General	Rear Admiral (lower half)
Colonel	Colonel	Colonel	Captain
Lieutenant Colonel	Lieutenant Colonel	Lieutenant Colonel	Commander
Major	Major	Major	Lieutenant Commander
Captain	Captain	Captain	Lieutenant
1st Lieutenant	1st Lieutenant	1st Lieutenant	Lieutenant Junior Grade
2nd Lieutenant	2nd Lieutenant	2nd Lieutenant	Ensign
Chief Warrant Officer W-4 Chief Warrant Officer W-3 Chief Warrant Officer W-2 Warrant Officer W-1	Same	Same	Same
Sergeant Major or Specialist 9	Chief Master Sergeant	Master Gunnery Sergeant or Sergeant Major	Master Chief Petty Officer
Master Sergeant, First Sergeant, or Specialist 8	Senior Master Sergeant	Master Sergeant or First Sergeant	Senior Chief Petty Officer
Sergeant First Class, Platoon Sergeant, or Specialist 7	Master Sergeant	Gunnery Sergeant	Chief Petty Officer
Staff Sergeant or Specialist 6	Technical Sergeant	Staff Sergeant	Petty Officer First Class
Sergeant or Specialist 5	Staff Sergeant	Sergeant	Petty Officer Second Class
Corporal or Specialist 4	Sergeant	Corporal	Petty Officer Third Class
Private First Class	Airman First Class	Lance Corporal	Seaman
Private E-2	Airman	Private First Class	Seaman Apprentice
Private E-1	Airman Basic	Private	Seaman Recruit

grade (grād) *n.* **1** A degree or step in any scale, as of quality, ability, dignity, etc. **2** A group of persons of the same rank or station. **3** A rank in the U.S. armed forces. **4** A class of things of the same quality or value: a high *grade* of wool. **5 a** One of the divisions of an elementary or secondary school, usu. covering a year of work. **b** The pupils in such a division. **6** *pl.* GRADE SCHOOL: with *the.* **7** A scholastic rating or mark on an examination or in a course. **8** The degree of inclination of the surface of a road or the like; also, the part of a road, etc., that slopes. —*v.* **grad·ed, grad·ing** *v.t.* **1** To arrange or classify by grades or degrees, according to size, quality, etc. **2** To assign a grade to. **3** To make level or properly inclined. —*v.i.* **4** To be of a specific rank, degree, or grade. [< L *gradus* step] — **grad'er** *n.*

-grade *combining form* Manner of moving or walking: *plantigrade.* [< L *gradi* walk]

grade crossing A place where a road and a railroad or two railroads cross on the same level.

grade school ELEMENTARY SCHOOL.

gra·di·ent (grā'dē·ənt) *adj.* Rising or descending gently or by degrees. —*n.* **1** A slope or grade. **2** The degree of inclination of such a slope. **3** *Physics* The maximum rate of change of a variable, as pressure, temperature, etc., with respect to position. [< L *gradi* to walk]

grad·u·al (graj'o͞o·əl) *adj.* Moving, changing, developing, etc., slowly and by degrees. [< L *gradus* a step] **—grad'u·al·ly** *adv.* **—grad'u·al·ness** *n.*

grad·u·ate (graj'o͞o·āt) *v.* **·at·ed, ·at·ing** *v.t.* **1** To grant a diploma or degree to. **2** To mark in units or degrees, as a thermometer scale; calibrate. **3** To arrange into grades or divisions, as according to size or quality. —*v.i.* **4** To receive a diploma or degree indicating completion of a course of study. **5** To change by degrees. —*n.* (graj'o͞o·it) **1** One who has completed any academic or professional course. **2** A graduated vessel used in measuring liquids, etc. —*adj.* (graj'o͞o·it) **1** Having a degree or diploma from a college, school, etc. **2** Designed for or pertaining to students working towards a degree beyond the bachelor's. [< L *gradus* step, degree] **—grad'u·a'tor** *n.*

grad·u·a·tion (graj'o͞o·ā'shən) *n.* **1** The act of graduating, as a scale, or state of being graduated, as a series of colors. **2** An equal division or dividing line in a graduated scale. **3** In education: **a** A graduating or being graduated. **b** The ceremony marking this; commencement.

graf·fi·to (grə·fē'tō) *n. pl.* **·ti** (-tē) **1** Any design, or scribbled motto, etc., drawn on a wall or other exposed surface. **2** *Archeol.* A pictograph scratched on a wall or other surface. [< Ital. *graffio* a scratch, ult. < Gk. *graphein* write]

graft[1] (graft, gräft) *n.* **1** A piece of living plant or animal tissue excised and inserted in a new site in the same or a different organism. **2** The juncture between such a graft and the place where it is inserted. **3** A union resembling a graft. —*v.t.* **1** To implant (tissue) in a new site in a living organism. —*v.i.* **2** To insert grafts. **3** To be or become grafted. [< LL *graphium* stylus < Gk. *graphein* write] — **graft'age** (-ij), **graft'er** *n.*

graft[2] (graft, gräft) *n.* **1** The attainment of personal advantage or profit by dishonest or unfair means, esp. through one's political connections. **2** Anything thus gained. —*v.t.* **1** To obtain by graft. —*v.i.* **2** To practice graft. [?] **—graft'er** *n.*

gra·ham (grā'əm) *adj.* Made from unrefined wheat flour. [< S. *Graham,* 1794–1851, U.S. dietary reformer.]

Grail (grāl) *n.* In medieval legend, the cup or platter used by Jesus at the Last Supper. [< Med. L *gradalis*]

grain (grān) *n.* **1** A seed or kernel, as of wheat, corn, rice, etc. **2** Any of the common cereal plants, as wheat, oats, rye, barley, etc. **3** Any minute, hard particle, as of sugar or sand. **4** Any very small amount: a *grain* of sense. **5** The arrangement or direction of particles or fibers, as of wood, stone, leather, etc. **6** The patterns produced on a surface by such arrangements or directions. **7** The smallest unit used in the systems of weights of the U.S. and Great Britain. **8** The innate quality or character of a thing. **9** Natural disposition or nature. —*v.t.* **1** To form into grains; granulate. **2** To paint or stain in imitation of the grain of wood, marble, etc. —*v.i.* **3** To form grains. [< L *granum* a seed]

grain alcohol ETHYL ALCOHOL.

grain elevator A warehouse for the storage of grain.

grain·y (grā'nē) *adj.* **grain·i·er, ·grain·i·est 1** Composed of grains or kernels; granular. **2** Having the patterns of grains, as the surface of wood. **—grain'i·ness** *n.*

gram (gram) *n.* A metric unit of mass or weight, equal to 10^{-3} (0.0001) kilogram, or about 0.035 ounce. [< Gk. *gramma* letter, small thing]

-gram[1] *combining form* Something written or drawn: *telegram.* [< Gk. *gramma* a letter]

-gram[2] *combining form* Gram: *kilogram.* [< GRAM]

gram. grammar; grammarian; grammatical.

gram calorie See CALORIE.

gram·mar (gram'ər) *n.* **1** The systematic analysis of the classes and structure of words (morphology) and of their arrangements and interrelationships in larger constructions (syntax). 2 A system of morphological and syntactical rules and principles for speaking and writing a given language. 3 A treatise or book dealing with such rules. 4 Speech or writing considered with regard to current standards of correctness. 5 The elements of any science or art, or a book or treatise dealing with them. [< Gk. *grammatikē (technē)* literary (art)]

gram·mar·i·an (grə·mâr′ē·ən) *n.* A specialist in grammar.

grammar school 1 ELEMENTARY SCHOOL. 2 *Brit.* SECONDARY SCHOOL.

gram·mat·i·cal (grə·mat′i·kəl) *adj.* 1 Conforming to the principles of standard speech or writing. 2 Of or pertaining to grammar. **—gram·mat′i·cal·ly** *adv.* **—gram·mat′i·cal·ness** *n.*

gram molecule MOLE⁴. Also **gram-mo·lec·u·lar weight** (gram′mə·lek′yoo·lər).

gram·o·phone (gram′ə·fōn) *n.* PHONOGRAPH. [< *Gramophone,* a trade name]

gram·pus (gram′pəs) *n. pl.* **·pus·es** 1 A large dolphinlike cetacean of northern waters. 2 KILLER WHALE. [< L *crassus piscis* fat fish]

gran·a·ry (grā′nər·ē, gran′ər-) *n. pl. pl.* **·ries** 1 A storehouse for grain. 2 A country or region where grain grows in abundance. [< L *granum* grain]

grand (grand) *adj.* 1 Of imposing character or aspect; magnificent, as in size, beauty, etc. 2 Main; principal: the *grand* hall. 3 Preeminent; noble, distinguished. 4 Highest in rank or order: a *grand* duke. 5 Pretentiously haughty or arrogant. 6 Lofty; exalted: a *grand* style. 7 Complete; overall: the *grand* total. 8 *Informal* Very good, excellent, etc.: We had a *grand* time. **—***n.* 1 A grand piano. 2 *Slang* One thousand dollars. [< L *grandis*] **—grand′ly** *adv.* **—grand′ness** *n.* **—Syn.** 1 great, mighty, impressive, sublime. 5 ostentatious, showy, pompous. 6 elevated, eloquent, sublime.

gran·dam (gran′dam, -dəm) *n. Archaic* 1 GRANDMOTHER. 2 An old woman. Also **gran′dame** (-dām, -dəm). [< AF *graund dame*]

Grand Army of the Republic An organization of Union veterans of the Civil War, organized in 1866.

grand·aunt (grand′ant′, -änt′) *n.* GREAT-AUNT.

grand·child (grand′child′) *n. pl.* **·chil·dren** A child of one's son or daughter.

grand·dad (gran′dad′) *n. Informal* Grandfather.

grand·daugh·ter (gran′dô′tər, grand′-) *n.* A daughter of one's son or daughter.

grand duchess 1 The wife or widow of a grand duke. 2 A woman holding sovereign rights over a grand duchy. 3 In czarist Russia, a daughter of a czar.

grand duchy The domain of a grand duke or grand duchess.

grand duke 1 A sovereign who rules over a grand duchy and ranks just below a king. 2 In czarist Russia, any brother, son, uncle, or nephew of a czar.

grande dame (gränd däm) A woman of great dignity or notable achievements. [F, lit., great lady]

gran·dee (gran·dē′) *n.* A Spanish or Portuguese nobleman of the highest rank. [< Sp. *grande* great]

gran·deur (gran′jər, -jŏŏr) *n.* The quality of being grand; magnificence; sublimity.

grand·fa·ther (grand′fä′thər) *n.* The father of one's father or mother. **—grand′fa′ther·ly** *adj.*

grand gui·gnol (grän gē·nyôl′) *Often cap.* A dramatic presentation of a sensationally gruesome or horrifying character. [< *Le Grand Guignol,* former theater in Paris featuring such dramas]

gran·dil·o·quent (gran·dil′ə·kwənt) *adj.* Speaking in or characterized by a pompous or bombastic style. [< L < *grandis* great + *loqui* speak] **—gran·dil′o·quence** *n.*

gran·di·ose (gran′dē·ōs) *adj.* 1 Having an imposing style; impressive. 2 Affecting grandeur; pompous, bombastic. [< L *grandis* great] **—gran′di·ose·ly** *adv.* **—gran·di·os·i·ty** (gran′dē·os′ə·tē) *n.*

grand jury A jury of 12 or more persons impaneled to evaluate accusations against a suspect and bring an indictment if there is enough evidence to merit a regular trial.

grand·ma (grand′mä′, gran′mä′, gram′mä) *n. Informal* Grandmother. Also **grand′ma·ma′** (-ma·ma′, -mä′mə).

grand mal (grän mäl′) An epileptic seizure characterized by severe convulsions followed by coma: distinguished from *petit mal.* [F, lit., great sickness]

grand·moth·er (grand′muth′ər) *n.* The mother of one's father or mother. **—grand′moth′er·ly** *adj.*

grand·neph·ew (grand′nef′yōō, -nev′-, gran′-) *n.* A son of one's nephew or niece.

grand·niece (grand′nēs′, gran′-) *n.* A daughter of one's nephew or niece.

Grand Old Party In U.S. politics, the Republican party.

grand opera An opera in which the entire text is sung.

grand·pa (grand′pä′, gram′pä′) *n. Informal* Grandfather. Also **grand′pa·pa′** (-pə·pä′, -pä′pə).

grand·par·ent (grand′pâr′ənt, gran′-) *n.* The parent of one's parent.

grand piano A piano in which the strings are placed horizontally in a curved frame.

Grand piano

grand·sire (grand′sīr′) *n. Archaic* 1 GRANDFATHER. 2 Any male ancestor preceding a father. 3 Any venerable man.

grand slam 1 In bridge, the winning of all 13 tricks in a round of play. 2 In baseball, a home run with all the bases loaded. 3 In certain sports, as golf, the winning of all major or specified contests in a season, on a tour, etc.

grand·son (grand′sun′, gran′-) *n.* A son of one's son or daughter.

grand·stand (grand′stand′, gran′-) *n.* The principal structure for spectators at any public spectacle or sports event. **—***v.i. Informal* To show off in an attempt to win applause.

grand·un·cle (grand′ung′kəl) *n.* GREAT-UNCLE.

grange (grānj) *n. Brit.* A farm, with its dwelling house, barns, etc. [< L *granum* grain]

Grange (grānj) *n.* 1 The order of Patrons of Husbandry, a nation-wide association of U.S. farmers, founded in 1867. 2 One of the local lodges of the Patrons of Husbandry. **—Grang′er** *n.*

gran·ite (gran′it) *n.* 1 A hard, coarse-grained, igneous rock composed principally of quartz, feldspar, and mica. 2 Great strength, endurance, etc. [< Ital. *granire* make grainy] **—gra·nit·ic** (grə·nit′ik) or **·i·cal** *adj.*

gran·ite·ware (gran′it·wâr′) *n.* 1 A variety of ironware coated with hard enamel. 2 A variety of fine, hard pottery.

gran·ny (gran′ē) *n. pl.* **·nies** *Informal* 1 Grandmother. 2 An old woman. 3 An excessively fussy person. 4 GRANNY KNOT. Also **gran′nie.**

granny knot An incorrectly tied square knot. Also **granny's knot, granny's bend.**

gra·no·la (grə·nō′lə) *n.* A mixture of dry cereals, nuts, and raisins, chopped fine and marketed as a health food.

grant (grant, gränt) *v.t.* 1 To give or accord, as permission, a request, etc. 2 To confer or bestow, as a privilege, charter, favor, etc. 3 To admit as true, esp. something not proved, as for the sake of argument; concede. 4 To transfer (property), esp. by deed. **—***n.* 1 The act of granting. 2 Something granted, as property, funds for a specific purpose, etc. [< AF *granter,* ult. < L *credere* believe] **—grant′a·ble** *adj.* **—grant′er,** *Law* **grant′or** *n.*

grant·ee (gran·tē′, grän-) *n.* One who receives a grant.

gran·u·lar (gran′yə·lər) *adj.* 1 Composed of, like, or containing grains or granules. 2 Having a grainy surface. Also **gran′u·lose** (-lōs). **—gran′u·lar′i·ty** (-lar′ə·tē) *n.*

gran·u·late (gran′yə·lāt) *v.t. & v.i.* **·lat·ed, ·lat·ing** 1 To make or become granular; form into grains. 2 To become or cause to become rough on the surface by the formation of granules. **—gran′u·la′tion** *n.* **—gran′u·la′tive** *adj.*

gran·ule (gran′yōōl) *n.* A small grain or particle.

grape (grāp) *n.* 1 The smooth-skinned, edible, juicy, berrylike fruit of various species of the grapevine, from which most wines are made. 2 Any grapevine yielding this fruit. 3 Figuratively, wine. 4 A dark blue color with a slight reddish tint. [<OF, bunch of grapes, hook < Gmc.]

grape·fruit (grāp′fro͞ot′) *n.* A large, round, pale yellow citrus fruit.

grape·shot (grāp′shot′) *n.* A cluster of cast-iron shot to be discharged from a cannon.

grape sugar DEXTROSE.

grape·vine (grāp′vīn) *n.* 1 Any of a genus of woody, climbing plants characterized by profuse clusters of berrylike juicy fruit. 2 *Informal* Any secret or unofficial means by which information, rumors, etc., are circulated.

graph (graf, gräf) *n.* 1 A diagram indicating any sort of relationship between two or more things by means of a system of dots, curves, bars, or lines. 2 *Math.* A set of points drawn on a coordinate system so that each point satisfies a given function. —*v.t.* To represent in the form of a graph. [Short for *graphic formula*]

-graph *combining form* 1 That which writes or records: *telegraph.* 2 A writing or record: *monograph.* [<Gk. *graphein* write]

graph·ic (graf′ik) *adj.* 1 Vividly effective and detailed. 2 Of, like, or represented by graphs. 3 Of, pertaining to, or expressed in handwriting. 4 Written or expressed by means of signs, symbols, etc. 5 Of or pertaining to the graphic arts. Also **graph′i·cal.** [<Gk. *graphein* write] —**graph′i·cal·ly, graph′ic·ly** *adv.*

graphic arts 1 Loosely, any of the visual arts, as painting, drawing, photography, etc. 2 Those arts which involve impressions printed from blocks, screens, etc., as printing, lithography, etching, wood-engraving, etc.

graph·ics (graf′iks) 1 *(n. pl., construed as singular)* The art or science of drawing. 2 *(n. pl.)* Illustrations created by a computer.

graph·ite (graf′īt) *n.* A soft, black, chemically inert, crystalline form of carbon with a metallic luster and oily feel, used as a lubricant and in the making of lead pencils. [<Gk. *graphein* write] —**gra·phit·ic** (grə·fit′ik) *adj.*

graph·ol·o·gy (graf·ol′ə·jē) *n.* The analysis of handwriting, esp. to interpret character and personality. [<Gk. *graphein* write + -LOGY] —**graph·o·log·i·cal** (graf′ə·loj′i·kəl) *adj.* —**graph·ol′o·gist** *n.*

-graphy *combining form* A written description of: *geography.* [<Gk. *graphein* write]

grap·nel (grap′nəl) *n.* 1 A metal bar with hooks or claws at one end, used for grasping objects. 2 *Naut.* A boat's anchor with many flukes. [<OF *grapin* a hook]

grap·ple (grap′əl) *v.* **grap·pled, grap·pling** *v.t.* 1 To take hold of; grasp firmly. —*v.i.* 2 To use a grapnel. 3 To seize or come to grips with another, as in wrestling. 4 To deal or contend: with *with.* —*n.* 1 A close hold, as in wrestling. 2 GRAPNEL (def. 1). [<OF *grappil* grapnel] —**grap′pler** *n.*

grap·pling iron (grap′ling) GRAPNEL (def. 1).

grasp (grasp, gräsp) *v.t.* 1 To lay hold of with or as with the hand; grip. 2 To seize greedily or eagerly; snatch. 3 To take hold of with the mind; understand. —*v.i.* 4 To make grasping motions. —**grasp at** 1 To try to seize. 2 To accept eagerly or desperately. —*n.* 1 The act of seizing or grasping. 2 The ability to seize and hold. 3 Power of comprehension; understanding. [ME *graspen*] —**grasp′er** *n.*

grasp·ing (gras′ping, gräs′-) *adj.* Greedy; avaricious.

grass (gras, gräs) *n.* 1 The vegetation typically forming a green carpet over the ground of lawns, pastures, etc. 2 Any of a large family of monocotyledons, as wheat, oats, sugar cane, bamboo, and various forage plants. 3 Ground covered with grass; lawn or pasture. 4 Any plants resembling the true grasses, as the sedges, the rushes, etc. 5 *Slang* MARIHUANA. —*v.t.* 1 To cover with grass or turf. 2 To feed with grass; pasture. —*v.i.* 3 To graze on grass. 4 To produce grass; become covered with grass. [<OE *græs*]

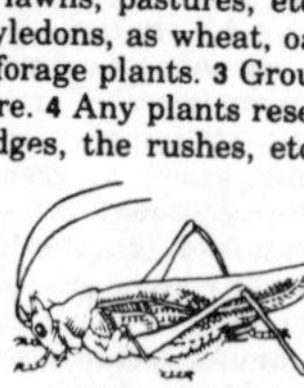

Grasshopper

grass·hop·per (gras′hop′ər, gräs′-) *n.* Any of several insects, including the locust and katydid, having powerful hind legs adapted for leaping.

grass·land (gras′land′, gräs′-) *n.* 1 Land reserved for pasturage or mowing. 2 Land in which grasses predominate.

grass roots 1 Ordinary people, esp. those apart from the centers of political power or influence. 2 The primary source or foundation. —**grass′roots′** *adj.*

grass widow A woman separated from her husband by causes other than death.

grass·y (gras′ē, gräs′ē) *adj.* **grass·i·er, grass·i·est** Abounding in, covered with, consisting of, or resembling grass. —**grass′i·ly** *adv.* —**grass′i·ness** *n.*

grate[1] (grāt) *v.* **grat·ed, grat·ing,** *v.t.* 1 To reduce to small particles by rubbing against a rough surface. 2 To rub or grind so as to produce a harsh, scraping sound. 3 To annoy; irritate; to *grate* the nerves. —*v.i.* 4 To sound harshly, from or as from scraping or grinding; creak. 5 To have an irritating effect: with *on* or *upon.* [<OF *grater* < Gmc.] —**grat′er** *n.*

grate[2] (grāt) *n.* 1 A framework of bars to hold fuel in burning. 2 A similar framework used to prohibit entry through a window or other opening. 3 A fireplace. —*v.t.* **grat·ed, grat·ing** To fit with a grate or grates. [<L *cratis* a lattice]

grate·ful (grāt′fəl) *adj.* 1 Having or expressing gratitude; thankful. 2 Affording gratification; pleasurable; agreeable. [<L *gratus* pleasing + -FUL] —**grate′ful·ly** *adv.* —**grate′ful·ness** *n.* —*Syn.* 1 obliged, beholden, indebted to, under obligation.

grat·i·fi·ca·tion (grat′ə·fə·kā′shən) *n.* 1 The act of gratifying or the state of being gratified. 2 Something that gratifies.

grat·i·fy (grat′ə·fī) *v.t.* **·fied, ·fy·ing** 1 To give pleasure or satisfaction to. 2 To satisfy or indulge, as a desire or need. [<L *gratus* pleasing + -FY] —**grat′i·fi′er** *n.* —**grat′i·fy′ing** *adj.*, —**grat′i·fy′ing·ly** *adv.*

grat·ing[1] (grā′ting) *n.* 1 GRATE[2] (def. 2). 2 *Physics* A series of fine grooves cut in a smooth surface, used to disperse light and produce spectra.

grat·ing[2] (grā′ting) *adj.* 1 Harsh in sound; rasping. 2 Annoying; irritating. —**grat′ing·ly** *adv.*

gra·tis (grat′is, grā′tis) *adv.* Without recompense; freely. —*adj.* Given free of charge. [<L *gratia* favor]

grat·i·tude (grat′ə·tʸo͞od) *n.* A feeling of thankfulness.

gra·tu·i·tous (grə·tʸo͞o′ə·təs) *adj.* Given freely without charge or conditions. 2 Without cause; uncalled for; unnecessary. [<L *gratuitus* given as a favor] —**gra·tu′i·tous·ly** *adv.* —**gra·tu′i·tous·ness** *n.*

gra·tu·i·ty (grə·tʸo͞o′ə·tē) *n. pl.* **·ties** 1 A present. 2 Money given in return for service, etc.; a tip.

gra·va·men (grə·vā′men) *n. pl.* **·va·mens** or **·vam·i·na** (-vam′ə·nə) The essence of a charge or grievance; the burden of a complaint. [<L < *gravis* heavy]

grave[1] (grāv) *adj.* **grav·er, grav·est** 1 Of momentous import; weighty; important. 2 Severely dangerous; critical. 3 Serious; dignified; sedate, as in manner or speech. 4 Somber in color or fashion. 5 Low in tone or pitch. —*n.* (grāv, gräv) A mark (\`) used in French to indicate the open quality of *e* or in English to indicate a falling inflection or the pronunciation of a final *ed,* as in *preparèd:* also **grave accent.** [<L *gravis* heavy] —**grave′ly** *adv.* —**grave′ness** *n.*

grave[2] (grāv) *n.* 1 A place for the burial of a dead body, usu. an excavation in the ground. 2 A tomb. —**the grave** Death. [<OE *græf*]

grave[3] (grāv) *v.t.* **graved, grav·en, grav·ing** 1 To engrave; carve with a chisel. 2 To sculpture. 3 To impress deeply, as on the memory. [<OE *grafan* dig]

grave·dig·ger (grāv′dig′ər) *n.* One who digs graves.

grav·el (grav′əl) *n.* 1 A mixture of small, usu. rounded, pebbles or stones. 2 *Pathol.* The formation in the kidneys of numerous granular concretions. —*v.t.* **grav·eled** or **grav·elled, grav·el·ing** or **grav·el·ling** 1 To cover or fill with gravel. 2 To bring up short, as in embarrassment or confusion. 3 *Informal* To irritate; annoy. [<OF *grave* sand] —**grav′el·ly, grav′el·y** *adj.*

grav·en (grā′vən) *adj.* Carved or cut.

graven image A carved or graven idol.

grave·stone (grāv′stōn′) *n.* A memorial stone, placed at a grave.

grave·yard (grāv′yärd′) *n.* A burial place; a cemetery.

graveyard shift *Informal* A work shift during the late night, usu. from midnight to eight in the morning.

grav·i·tate (grav′ə·tāt) *v.i.* **·tat·ed, ·tat·ing 1** To be attracted by force of gravity. **2** To move or be attracted as though drawn by a powerful force: with *to* or *toward.* **3** To sink or fall to the lowest level. **—grav′i·tat′er** *n.* **—grav′i·ta′tive** *adj.*

grav·i·ta·tion (grav′ə·tā′shən) *n.* **1** *Physics* The force whereby any two bodies attract each other in proportion to the product of their masses and inversely as the square of the distance between them. **2** The act or process of gravitating. **—grav′i·ta′tion·al** *adj.* **—grav′i·ta′tion·al·ly** *adv.*

grav·i·ty (grav′ə·tē) *n. pl.* **·ties 1** The force that attracts bodies toward the center of the earth. **2** A similar force exerted on other bodies by any object in space. **3** Weight. **4** Gravitation. **5** Extreme importance; seriousness. **6** Danger; peril: the *gravity* of their plight. **7** Dignified reserve; sedateness. **—***adj.* Employing gravity; worked by gravity. [< L *gravis* heavy]

gra·vure (grə·vyŏŏr′) *n.* **1** A process of printing using etched plates, used esp. in photogravure. **2** A print made by such a process. [< F *graver* engrave]

gra·vy (grā′vē) *n. pl.* **·vies 1** The juice that exudes from meat being cooked. **2** A sauce made from these juices. **3** *Slang* Any added, easily acquired payment or income. [ME *gravey*]

gravy boat A boat-shaped dish in which gravy is served.

gray (grā) *adj.* **1** Of a color intermediate between black and white and lacking hue. **2** Having gray hair; hoary. **3** Old; aged. **—***n.* **1** A color between black and white with no hue. **2** Something gray, esp. a gray animal. **—***v.t. & v.i.* To make or become gray. [< OE *græg*] **—gray′ly** *adv.* **—gray′·ness** *n.*

gray·beard (grā′bird′) *n.* An old man.

gray·ish (grā′ish) *adj.* Somewhat gray.

gray·ling (grā′ling) *n. pl.* **·ling** or **·lings** A freshwater, troutlike fish of N waters.

gray matter 1 The grayish substance of the brain, composed of nerve cell bodies and few fibers. **2** *Informal* Intelligence.

graze[1] (grāz) *v.* **grazed, graz·ing** *v.i.* **1** To feed upon growing grass or herbage. **—***v.i.* **2** To put (cattle, etc.) to feed on growing grass or herbage. **—***n.* The act of cropping or feeding upon growing grass or the like. [< OE *grasian* < *græs* grass] **—graz′er** *n.*

graze[2] (grāz) *v.* **grazed, graz·ing** *v.t.* **1** To touch or rub against lightly in passing. **2** To scrape or cut slightly in passing. **—***v.i.* **3** To touch lightly in passing. **4** To scrape slightly. **—***n.* **1** A light or passing touch. **2** A scrape or abrasion. [?] **—graz′er** *n.* **—graz′ing·ly** *adv.*

graz·ing (grā′zing) *n.* A pasture.

Gr.Br., Gr.Brit. Great Britain.

grease (grēs) *n.* **1** Animal fat, esp. when soft or melted. **2** A thick, oily substance derived from petroleum and used as a lubricant. **—***v.t.* (grēs, grēz) **greased, greas·ing 1** To apply grease to. **2** *Slang* To influence by gifts or bribes. [< L *crassus* fat] **—greas′er** *n.*

grease·paint (grēs′pānt′) *n.* A paste, with a grease base, used in theatrical make-up.

grease·wood (grēs′wŏŏd′) *n.* Any of various stunted, prickly shrubs of the w U.S. Also **grease′bush′** (-bŏŏsh′).

greas·y (grē′sē, -zē) *adj.* **greas·i·er, greas·i·est 1** Smeared or spotted with grease. **2** Containing much grease or fat: oily. **3** Resembling grease; smooth; unctuous. **—greas′i·ly** *adv.* **—greas′i·ness** *n.*

great (grāt) *adj.* **1** Very large in size, expanse, etc.; immense; vast. **2** Large in number, quantity, etc.: a *great* assembly. **3** Long in extent or time: a *great* distance; a *great* while. **4** Of very considerable degree, intensity, etc.: a *great* sorrow. **5** Unusually important, impressive, or remarkable: a *great* achievement. **6** Of unusual excellence; superior; eminent: a *great* dancer. **7** Noble and elevated, as in character, action, feeling, etc.: a *great* humanitarian. **8** Most important of its kind; chief; main: the *great* prize. **9** *Informal* Adept; skilled: usu. with *at: great* at sports. **10** *Informal* Excellent; first-rate: to have a *great* time. **11** More remote by a single generation than the relationship indicated: used in combination with a hyphen: *great*-uncle, *great*-grandson. **—***adv. Informal* Very well. **—***n. Usu. pl.* A person who is great, noble, distinguished, etc.: with *the:* one of the *greats.* [< OE *grēat*] **—great′ly** *adv.* **—great′ness** *n.*

great-aunt (grāt′ant′, -änt′) *n.* The aunt of either of one's parents; grandaunt.

Great Bear The constellation Ursa Major. • See Ursa Major.

Great Brit·ain (brit′n) The principal part of the United Kingdom of Great Britain and Northern Ireland, located on an island west of Europe and comprising England, Scotland, and Wales.

great calorie See calorie.

great circle *Geom.* A circle formed on the surface of a sphere by a plane which passes through the center of the sphere.

great·coat (grāt′kōt′) *n.* A heavy overcoat.

Great Dane One of a breed of short-haired dogs of large size and great strength.

Great Dane

great-grand·child (grāt′·grand′chīld′) *n.* A child of a grandchild.

great-grand·par·ent (grāt′·grand′pâr′ənt) *n.* The parent of a grandparent.

great-heart·ed (grāt′här′tid) *adj.* **1** Courageous; valorous. **2** Having a generous or noble nature; magnanimous.

Great Lakes A chain of five freshwater lakes on the Canada-United States border: Lakes Superior, Michigan, Huron, Erie, and Ontario.

great seal The chief seal of a government, used to authenticate important documents.

great-un·cle (grāt′·ung′kəl) *n.* The uncle of either of one's parents; granduncle.

greave (grēv) *n.* Armor to protect the leg from knee to ankle. [< OF *greve*]

grebe (grēb) *n.* Any of a family of swimming and diving birds related to the loons. [F *grèbe*]

Gre·cian (grē′shən) *adj.* Greek. **—***n.* **1** A Greek. **2** A scholar of Greek.

Greco- *combining form* Greek: *Greco-Roman.*

Gre·co-Ro·man (grē′kō·rō′mən) *adj.* Of or pertaining to Greece and Rome together: *Greco-Roman* art.

Greece (grēs) *n.* A republic of SE Europe, 50,547 sq. mi., cap. Athens.

greed (grēd) *n.* Eager and selfish desire for something. [Back formation < greedy]

greed·y (grē′dē) *adj.* **greed·i·er, greed·i·est 1** Eager to obtain; covetous; grasping. **2** Having an excessive appetite for food or drink. [< OE *grǣdig*] **—greed′i·ly** *adv.* **—greed′i·ness** *n.*

Greek (grēk) *n.* **1** A native or citizen of Greece. **2** The language of ancient or modern Greece. **—***adj.* **1** Of or pertaining to Greece, its people, or their language. **2** Of or pertaining to the Greek Orthodox Church.

Greek Catholic 1 A member of an Eastern Orthodox Church. **2** uniate.

Greek Orthodox Church 1 The established church of Greece, an autonomous branch of the Eastern Orthodox Church. 2 Loosely, the Eastern Orthodox Church. Also **Greek Church.**

green (grēn) *adj.* 1 Having the spectrum color between blue and yellow, the characteristic color of lawn grass. 2 Covered with grass, green plants or foliage: the *green* hills. 3 Not yet ripe. 4 Consisting of edible leaves and vegetables: a *green* salad. 5 Immature or unskilled; inexperienced. 6 Naive; gullible. 7 Not seasoned or ready for use: *green* wood. 8 Sickly pale; wan. 9 *Informal* Jealous. —*n.* 1 The color of the spectrum between blue and yellow, the characteristic color of lawn grass. 2 A green pigment or dye. 3 A level, grassy piece of land: the village *green.* 4 In golf: a The area of smooth, closely cropped turf surrounding the hole. b The entire course. 5 *pl.* The leaves and stems of certain plants, as lettuce, spinach, etc., used as food. 6 *pl.* Green leaves or branches, often used as decorations, etc. —*v.t. & v.i.* To become or cause to become green. [<OE *grēne*] —**green′ish** *adj.* —**green′ly** *adv.*

green·back (grēn′bak′) *n.* Any piece of legal U.S. paper money printed in green on the back.

green bean A string bean.

green·bri·er (grēn′brī′ər) *n.* A species of smilax having woody stems with thorns and blue-black berries.

green·er·y (grē′nər·ē) *n. pl.* **·er·ies** 1 A place where plants are grown. 2 A mass of green plants; verdure.

green·gage (grēn′gāj′) *n.* A green-skinned variety of plum. [<GREEN + *gage* a plum]

green·horn (grēn′hôrn′) *n. Informal* An inexperienced person. [<GREEN + HORN; with ref. to the horns of an immature animal]

green·house (grēn′hous′) *n.* A building constructed mainly of glass, for the growing or protection of plants.

green·ing (grē′ning) *n.* One of several varieties of apples having a greenish yellow skin when ripe.

green light 1 A green signal used to indicate that traffic may proceed. 2 *Informal* Approval or authorization of an intended action, program, etc.

green onion A young onion having a long white bulb and green tubular leaves; scallion.

green pepper The unripe fruit of the red pepper, eaten as a vegetable.

green·room (grēn′ro͞om′, -ro͝om′) *n.* The common waiting room for performers in a theater when they are off stage.

green·sward (grēn′swôrd′) *n.* Turf green with grass.

green tea Tea leaves withered and rolled but not allowed to undergo fermentation.

green thumb Success or skill in growing plants.

Green·wich time (gren′ich; *chiefly Brit.* gren′ij) The mean solar time at the meridian at Greenwich, England, used as a reference in determining standard time throughout most of the world.

green·wood (grēn′wo͝od′) *n.* A forest in leaf.

greet (grēt) *v.t.* 1 To address words of friendliness, courtesy, respect, etc., to, as in speaking or writing. 2 To receive or meet in a specified manner. 3 To come into the sight or awareness of: The sea *greeted* their eyes. [<OE *grētan*] —**greet′er** *n.*

greet·ing (grē′ting) *n.* 1 The act or words of one who greets. 2 *Often pl.* A message of welcome or regards.

greeting card A card sent to express sentiments in acknowledgment of an event, as a birthday; esp., such a card printed and illustrated and sold commercially.

gre·gar·i·ous (gri·gâr′ē·əs) *adj.* 1 Habitually living in flocks, herds, or companies. 2 Of or pertaining to a flock or herd. 3 Socially outgoing and affable. [<L *grex, gregis* a flock] —**gre·gar′i·ous·ly** *adv.* —**gre·gar′i·ous·ness** *n.*

Gre·go·ri·an calendar (grə·gôr′ē·ən′) The calendar used now by most countries of the world and devised by Pope Gregory XIII in 1582 as a correction of the Julian calendar.

Gregorian chant The system of monodic plainsong used in the liturgy of the Roman Catholic and other churches, established during the reign of Gregory I.

grem·lin (grem′lin) *n.* 1 A mischievous, invisible imp said to ride airplanes and cause mechanical trouble. 2 Any unidentified source of trouble. [?]

gre·nade (gri·nād′) *n.* 1 A small bomb designed to be thrown by hand or fired from a rifle or launching device. 2 A glass bottle containing a flammable mixture, tear gas, etc., that is ignited or dispersed when the bottle is broken. [F, a pomegranate]

gren·a·dier (gren′ə·dir′) *n.* 1 Formerly, a soldier assigned to throw grenades. 2 A member of a specially constituted corps or regiment, as the British Grenadier Guards.

gren·a·dine[1] (gren′ə·dēn′, gren′ə·dēn) *n.* A loosely woven silk, cotton, woolen, or rayon fabric. [F]

gren·a·dine[2] (gren′ə·dēn′, gren′ə·dēn) *n.* A beverage syrup made from currants or pomegranates. [<F *grenade* a pomegranate]

grew (gro͞o) *p.t.* of GROW.

grew·some (gro͞o′səm) *adj.* GRUESOME.

grey (grā) *adj. Chiefly Brit.* GRAY.

grey·hound (grā′hound′) *n.* One of a breed of tall, slender dogs with a long narrow head and smooth short coat, used for hunting and racing. [<OE *grīghund*]

Greyhound

grid (grid) *n.* 1 A grating of parallel bars; gridiron. 2 A system of parallel lines superimposed horizontally and vertically upon a map, chart, etc. 3 A metal bar or plate in an electric storage cell or battery. 4 *Electronics* An electrode mounted between the cathode and anode of an electron tube, used to control the flow of electrons. [Short for GRIDIRON]

grid·dle (grid′l) *n.* A shallow pan for baking or frying pancakes. —*v.t.* **grid·dled, grid·dling** To cook on a griddle. [<L *cratis* wickerwork]

grid·dle·cake (grid′l·kāk′) *n.* A thin, flat batter cake baked on a griddle; pancake.

grid·i·ron (grid′ī′ərn) *n.* 1 A framework of metal bars for broiling or cooking foods. 2 Any object resembling a cooking gridiron. 3 A football field. [ME *gredire*]

grid·lock (grid′lok′) *n.* A total stoppage of traffic, esp. when all cross traffic is blocked at intersections.

grief (grēf) *n.* 1 Intense sorrow or mental suffering resulting from loss, affliction, regret, etc. 2 A cause of such sorrow. [<OF *grever* grieve] —**Syn. 1** affliction, agony, distress, sadness, tribulation, trouble, woe.

grief-strick·en (grēf′strik′ən) *adj.* Overwhelmed by grief.

griev·ance (grē′vəns) *n.* 1 Something that annoys, causes resentment, etc. 2 A written or vocal complaint against a wrong suffered.

grieve (grēv) *v.* **grieved, griev·ing** *v.t.* 1 To cause great sorrow or grief to; make sad. —*v.i.* 2 To feel sorrow or grief; mourn; lament. [<L *gravis* heavy] —**griev′er** *n.* —**griev′ing** *adj.* —**griev′ing·ly** *adv.*

griev·ous (grē′vəs) *adj.* 1 Causing grief or sorrow. 2 Expressive of grief or distress: a *grievous* complaint. 3 Severe: a *grievous* pain or illness. 4 Atrocious; heinous: *grievous* sin. —**griev′ous·ly** *adv.* —**griev′ous·ness** *n.*

grif·fin (grif′ən) *n. Gk. Myth.* A creature with the head and wings of an eagle and the body of a lion. Also **grif′fon.** [<Gk. *gryps*]

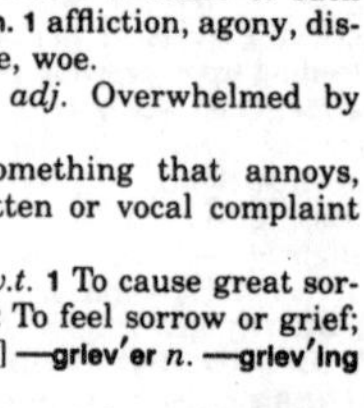

Griffin

grill (gril) *v.t.* 1 To cook on a gridiron; broil. 2 To torture with heat. 3 To cross-examine persistently and searchingly. —*v.i.* 4 To be cooked on a gridiron. —*n.* 1 A gridiron. 2 That which is broiled on a gridiron. 3 A grillroom. 4 A grille. [<OF *greil*]

grille (gril) *n.* A grating or screen, esp. one of wrought metal for an open door or window. Also **grill.** [F, var. of *gril* grill]

grilled (grild) *adj.* 1 Having a grille. 2 Broiled.

grill·room (gril′ro͞om′, -ro͝om′) *n.* A restaurant or eating place specializing in grilled food.

grill·work (gril′wûrk′) *n.* 1 A grille. 2 The design or structure of a grille.

grilse (grils) *n. pl.* **grilse** or **grils·es** A young salmon after its first return to fresh water. [?]

grim (grim) *adj.* **grim·mer, grim·mest** 1 Stern and forbidding in aspect or nature. 2 Fierce; ferocious: a *grim* attack. 3 Unyielding; resolute: *grim* courage. 4 Unpleasant; repellent: the *grim* job of counting bodies. [< OE] —**grim′ly** *adv.* —**grim′ness** *n.*

gri·mace (grim′əs, gri·mās′) *n.* A distortion of the face, usu. occasioned by annoyance, disgust, contempt, etc.; a wry face. —*v.i.* **·maced, ·mac·ing** To make grimaces. [< MF < Gmc.] —**gri′mac·er** *n.*

gri·mal·kin (gri·mal′kin, -môl′-) *n.* 1 A cat, esp. an old female cat. 2 A malevolent old woman. [< GRAY + dial. *malkin* hussy]

grime (grīm) *n.* Dirt or soot, esp. when rubbed into a surface. —*v.t.* **grimed, grim·ing** To make dirty; begrime. [< MDu. *grīme*]

grim·y (grī′mē) *adj.* **grim·i·er, grim·i·est** Full of or covered with grime; dirty. —**grim′i′ly** *adv.* —**grim′i·ness** *n.*

grin (grin) *v.* **grinned, grin·ning** *v.i.* 1 To smile broadly. 2 To draw back the lips so as to show the teeth, as in pain, rage, etc. —*n.* The act or facial look of grinning. [< OE *grennian*] —**grin′ner** *n.* —**grin′ning·ly** *adv.*

grind (grīnd) *v.* **ground, grind·ing** *v.t.* 1 To sharpen, polish, or shape by friction. 2 To reduce to fine particles, as by crushing or friction. 3 To rub or press gratingly or harshly: to *grind* one's teeth. 4 To oppress; harass cruelly. 5 To operate by turning a crank, as a coffee mill. 6 To produce by or as by grinding. 7 *Informal* To teach laboriously. —*v.i.* 8 To perform the operation of grinding. 9 To undergo grinding. 10 To rub; grate. 11 *Informal* To study or work hard and steadily. —*n.* 1 The act of grinding. 2 A degree of fineness obtained by grinding. 3 *Informal* Difficult, tedious work or study. 4 *Informal* A hard-working student. [< OE *grindan*] —**grind′ing** *adj., n.* —**grind′ing·ly** *adv.*

grind·er (grīn′dər) *n.* 1 One who or that which grinds, as a knife sharpener, coffee mill, etc. 2 A molar tooth.

grind·stone (grīnd′stōn′) *n.* 1 An abrasive wheel spun on its axis and used for shaping metal, sharpening tools, etc. 2 A millstone.

grin·go (gring′gō) *n. pl.* **·gos** In Latin America, a foreigner, particularly an American or Englishman: a contemptuous term. [Sp., gibberish]

grip (grip) *n.* 1 The act of grasping firmly or holding fast, as with the hands, teeth, etc. 2 The manner of doing this. 3 The power or strength to do this: He lost his *grip.* 4 Ability to understand mentally. 5 Self-control; mastery. 6 Control; power: in the *grip* of circumstances. 7 A valise; gripsack. 8 That part of a thing by which it is grasped. 9 One of various mechanical grasping devices. 10 *Slang* A stagehand; a scene-shifter. —*v.* **gripped** or **gript, grip·ping** *v.t.* 1 To take firm hold of with or as with the hand; hold onto tightly. 2 To join or attach securely with a grip. 3 To seize or capture, as the mind or imagination of. —*v.i.* 4 To take firm hold. 5 To take hold of the attention, imagination, etc. [< OE *gripe* < *gripan* seize] —**grip′per** *n.* —**grip′·ping** *adj.* —**grip′ping·ly** *adv.*

gripe (grīp) *v.* **griped, grip·ing** *v.t.* 1 To cause pain in the bowels of. 2 *Slang* To vex; annoy. —*v.i.* 3 *Informal* To grumble; complain. 4 To suffer pains in the bowels. —*n.* 1 *pl.* Intermittent pains in the bowels. 2 *Slang* A complaint. [< OE *grīpan*] —**grip′er** *n.* —**grip′y** *adj.*

grippe (grip) *n.* INFLUENZA. [F < *gripper* seize] —**grip′py** *adj.*

grip·sack (grip′sak′) *n.* A traveling bag.

gris·ly (griz′lē) *adj.* **·li·er, ·li·est** Terrifying; horrible. [< OE *grislīc*] —**gris′li·ness** *n.*

grist (grist) *n.* 1 A portion of grain to be ground. 2 Ground grain. —**grist for** (or **to**) **one's mill** Anything that one can use to advantage. [< OE *grist*]

gris·tle (gris′əl) *n.* Cartilage, esp. in meat. [< OE] —**gris′·tly** *adj.* —**gris′tli·ness** *n.*

grist·mill (grist′mil′) *n.* A mill for grinding grain.

grit (grit) *n.* 1 Rough, hard particles, as of sand or fine gravel. 2 A coarse compact sandstone adapted for grindstones. 3 Resolute courage; pluck. —*v.* **grit·ted, grit·ting** *v.t.* 1 To grind or press (the teeth) together, as in anger or determination. —*v.i.* 2 To give forth a grating sound. [< OE *grēot*]

Grit (grit) *Can. n.* A member of the Liberal Party. —*adj.* Of or pertaining to the Liberal Party.

grits (grits) *n. pl.* Coarsely ground grain, esp. corn.

grit·ty (grit′ē) *adj.* **·ti·er, ·ti·est** 1 Of, containing, or like grit. 2 Full of pluck. —**grit′ti·ly** *adv.* —**grit′ti·ness** *n.*

griz·zle (griz′əl) *v.t. & v.i.* **griz·zled, griz·zling** To become or cause to become gray. —*n.* Gray. [< OF *gris* gray] —**griz′·zled** *adj.*

griz·zly (griz′lē) *adj.* **·zli·er, ·zli·est** Grayish. —*n. pl.* **·zlies** GRIZZLY BEAR.

griz·zly bear A large, powerful, grayish bear of w North America.

Grizzly bear

gro. gross.

groan (grōn) *v.i.* 1 To utter a low, prolonged sound of or as of pain, sorrow, etc. 2 To be oppressed or overburdened. —*v.t.* 3 To utter or express with groans. —*n.* A low moaning sound uttered in anguish, distress, or derision. [< OE *grānian*] —**groan′er** *n.* —**groan′ing** *adj., n.* —**groan′ing·ly** *adv.*

groat (grōt) *n.* A former English silver coin of the 14th–17th centuries. [< MDu. *groot*]

groats (grōts) *n. pl.* Hulled and crushed oats or wheat. [< OE *grotan*]

gro·cer (grō′sər) *n.* A retail dealer in food supplies and other household articles. [< OF *grossier,* lit., one who trades in grosses]

gro·cer·y (grō′sər·ē, grōs′rē) *n. pl.* **·cer·ies** 1 A grocer's store. 2 *pl.* Supplies sold by a grocer.

grog (grog) *n.* 1 A mixture of liquor, esp. rum, and water. 2 Any liquor. [< *Old Grog,* nickname of Admiral E. Vernon, 1684–1757, who first rationed it to English sailors]

grog·gy (grog′ē) *adj.* **·gi·er, ·gi·est** 1 Dazed, as from weakness or exhaustion. 2 Drunk. [< GROG] —**grog′gi·ly** *adv.* —**grog′gi·ness** *n.*

grog·ram (grog′rəm) *n.* A rough-textured fabric of silk, silk and mohair, or silk and wool. [< F *gros grain* grosgrain]

grog·shop (grog′shop′) *n. Brit.* A barroom; saloon.

groin (groin) *n.* 1 The fleshy hollow where the thigh joins the abdomen. 2 *Archit.* The line of intersection of two vaults. • See VAULT. —*v.t.* To build with or form into groins. [? < OE *grynde* abyss, hollow]

grom·met (grom′it) *n.* 1 *Naut.* A ring of rope, as on the peak of a sail. 2 A metallic eyelet, as for a mailbag. [< OF *gromette*]

groom (groom, grŏŏm) *n.* 1 A person who cares for horses in the stable. 2 BRIDEGROOM. —*v.t.* 1 To take care of; esp. to clean, curry, and brush (a horse). 2 To make neat, clean, and smart. 3 To prepare by training and developing, as for political or other service. [ME *grom*]

grooms·man (groomz′mən, grŏŏmz′-) *n. pl.* **·men** (-mən) The best man at a wedding.

groove (groov) *n.* 1 A furrow, channel, or long hollow, esp. one cut by a tool for something to fit into or work in. 2 A fixed routine in the affairs of life. —*v.t.* **grooved, groov·ing** 1 To form a groove in. 2 To fix in a groove. 3 *Slang* To take satisfaction or delight in; dig. —*v.i.* 4 *Slang* To find satisfaction or delight. [< MDu. *groeve*] —**groov′er** *n.*

groov·y (groo′vē) *adj.* **groov·i·er, groov·i·est** *Slang* Satisfying; delightful; great.

grope (grōp) *v.* **groped, grop·ing** *v.i.* To feel about with or as with the hands, as in the dark; feel one's way. —*v.t.* To seek out or find by or as by groping. [< OE *grāpian.*] —**grop′er** *n.* —**grop′ing** *adj.*

gros·beak (grōs′bēk′) *n.* Any of various small birds allied to the finches and having a short stout beak. [F *gros* large + BEAK]

gros·grain (grō′grān) *n.* A closely woven, corded silk or rayon fabric, used for ribbons, etc. [F, large grain]

gross (grōs) *adj.* 1 Conspicuously bad; glaring; flagrant:

add, āce, câre, päIm; end, ēven; it, īce; odd, ōpen, ôrder; tŏŏk, pōōl; up, bûrn; ə = *a* in *above, u* in *focus;* yōō = *u* in *fuse;* oil; pout; check; go; ring; thin; this; zh, *vision.* < derived from; ? origin uncertain or unknown.

a *gross* lie or error. 2 Excessively or repulsively large and coarse. 3 Vulgar; obscene; indelicate. 4 Lacking in perception or feeling; dull; insensitive. 5 Coarse in texture or composition. 6 Dense; thick. 7 Undiminished by deductions; total; entire: *gross* earnings. —*n.* 1 *pl.* **gross** Twelve dozen, as a unit. 2 *pl.* **gross·es** The total or entire amount. —**in the gross** 1 In bulk; all together. 2 Wholesale: also **by the gross.** —*v.t.* & *v.i.* To make or earn (total profit) before deduction of expenses, taxes, etc. [<LL *grossus* thick] —**gross'ly** *adv.* —**gross'ness** *n.* —**Syn.** *adj.* 1 dreadful, deplorable, awful shocking, heinous. 2 lumpish, hulking, bulky. 3 improper, unseemly, coarse.

gross national product The total market value of a nation's goods and services before any deductions.

gross ton A unit of weight equal to 2,240 pounds.

gro·tesque (grō·tesk') *adj.* 1 Bizarre or extravagantly odd in shape, look, design, composition, etc. 2 Absurdly odd or eccentric; fantastically strange: *grotesque* behavior. —*n.* Something grotesque. [<Ital. *grotta* a grotto, excavation] —**gro·tesque'ly** *adv.* —**gro·tesque'ness** *n.*

grot·to (grot'ō) *n. pl.* **·toes** or **·tos** 1 A small cave. 2 An artificial cavelike structure. [<L *crypta* crypt]

grouch (grouch) *v.i.* To grumble; be surly or discontented. —*n.* 1 A discontented, grumbling person. 2 A grumbling, sulky mood. 3 A complaint. [<OF *groucher* murmur] —**grouch'i·ly** *adv.* —**grouch'i·ness** *n.* —**grouch'y** *adj.* **(·i·er, ·i·est)**

ground[1] (ground) *n.* 1 The firm, solid portion of the earth at or near the surface. 2 Soil; earth; dirt. 3 Any tract or portion of land, esp. one put to special use: a parade *ground.* 4 *Often pl.* Private land, esp. the lawns, gardens, etc., surrounding a home or estate. 5 A topic, discussion or subject, or any part thereof: to cover the same old *ground.* 6 *Often pl.* A sufficient cause; good reason; basis: *grounds* for divorce. 7 *Often pl.* A basic proposition or premise; foundation: *grounds* for an argument. 8 The background or main surface, as of a painting. 9 *pl.* The particles that settle at the bottom of a liquid; dregs. 10 **a** A point in an electric circuit considered to have zero potential and used as a reference for other voltages. **b** A point of this kind actually connected to the earth. —**cover ground** 1 To proceed rapidly or a certain distance. 2 To accomplish quickly and efficiently. —**from the ground up** In a detailed manner; thoroughly. —**gain ground** 1 To make progress. 2 To gain favor, popularity, power, etc. —**get off the ground** To get underway; develop. —**give ground** To concede; yield. —**hold** (or **stand**) **one's ground** To maintain one's position, opinions, etc. —**lose ground** 1 To slip backward; drop behind. 2 To lose in favor, popularity, power, etc. —**on home** (or **one's own**) **ground** 1 At home. 2 On a familiar topic, subject, etc. —*adj.* 1 Being on the ground or on a level with it. 2 Growing or living on or in the ground. 3 Fundamental. —*v.t.* 1 To put, place, or set on the ground. 2 To fix firmly on a basis; found; establish. 3 To train (someone) in first principles or elements. 4 To cause (an airplane or pilot) to stay on the ground. 5 *Naut.* To cause to run aground, as a ship. 6 To furnish (a surface) with a ground or background for painting, etc. 7 To connect (an electric circuit or device) to a ground. —*v.i.* 8 To come or fall to the ground. 9 In baseball: **a** To hit a grounder. **b** To be retired on a grounder: usu. with *out.* 10 *Naut.* To run aground. [<OE *grund*]

ground[2] (ground) *p.t.* & *p.p.* of GRIND.

ground bass *Music* A bass part repeated continually against varied melody and harmony in the other parts.

ground crew The crew required for the servicing, repairing, and maintenance of aircraft.

ground·er (groun'dər) *n.* In baseball, a batted ball that rolls or bounces along the ground. Also **ground ball.**

ground floor The floor of a building level or almost level with the ground.

ground·hog (ground'hôg', -häg) *n.* WOODCHUCK.

ground·less (ground'lis) *adj.* Without foundation, reason, or cause. —**ground'less·ly** *adv.* —**ground'less·ness** *n.*

ground·ling (ground'ling) *n.* 1 An animal that burrows in the ground. 2 A plant that grows close to the ground. 3 A fish that keeps to the bottom. 4 A person of unrefined tastes.

ground·nut (ground'nut') *n.* 1 Any of several plants having edible tubers attached to the roots, as the peanut. 2 The edible tuber of such a plant.

ground pine An evergreen, generally creeping plant.

ground plan 1 The plan of the ground floor of a building. 2 Any preliminary plan or outline.

ground rule 1 In sports, any of the rules applying to conditions peculiar to a particular playing field. 2 *pl.* The basic rules of operation in any activity.

ground·sel (ground'səl) *n.* 1 A common composite herb, having yellow flower heads without rays. 2 GROUNDSILL. [<OE *gundæswelgæ*, lit., that swallows pus]

ground·sill (ground'sil') *n.* The lowest horizontal timber in a frame building.

ground squirrel Any of various burrowing rodents related to the squirrels, as the chipmunk and gopher.

ground·swell (ground'swel') *n.* 1 A broad, deep swell or heaving of the sea caused by prolonged storms or earthquakes. 2 Any upsurge or wave of public sentiment, opinion, etc. Also **ground swell.**

ground water Water that collects beneath the surface of the earth.

ground·work (ground'wûrk') *n.* 1 Foundation; basis. 2 Preparation.

ground zero The point on the ground directly beneath or above the detonation of a nuclear bomb.

group (grōōp) *n.* 1 A number of closely placed or associated persons or things regarded as a unit. 2 A number of individuals classed together because of common characteristics, interests, etc. 3 Figures or objects forming a harmonious unit of design. 4 *Chem.* **a** A number of connected atoms constituting part of a molecule. **b** A set of elements having similar properties. 5 In the U.S. Air Force, a unit constituting a subdivision of a wing. 6 In the U.S. Army or Marine Corps, a tactical unit consisting of two or more battalions. —*v.t.* 1 To place or classify in a group or groups. —*v.i.* 2 To form a group or groups. [<Ital. *groppo* knot, lump <Gmc.]

group·er (grōō'pər) *n.* A large food fish of warm seas, related to the sea bass. [<Pg. *garupa*]

group·ie (grōō'pē) *n. Slang* A fan or supporter, esp. a young woman who follows a performer in a rock group on tour.

grouse[1] (grous) *n. pl.* **grouse** Any of a family of plump-bodied game birds having mottled plumage.

grouse[2] (grous) *v.i.* **groused, grous·ing** To grumble; complain. —*n.* A complaint; grievance. [?] —**grous'er** *n.*

Grouse

grove (grōv) *n.* A small wood or group of trees, esp. without underbrush. [<OE grāf]

grov·el (gruv'əl, grov'-) *v.i.* **grov·eled** or **grov·elled, grov·el·ing** or **grov·el·ling** 1 To crawl face downward or lie prostrate, as in servility or fear. 2 To act with abject humility. 3 To take pleasure in what is base or sensual. [Back formation <earlier *groveling,* prone <ON *ā grūfū* face down] —**grov'el·er** or **grov'el·ler** *n.*

grow (grō) *v.* **grew, grown, grow·ing** *v.i.* 1 To increase in size by assimilation of nourishment or a natural process. 2 To progress toward maturity. 3 To sprout and develop. 4 To flourish; thrive. 5 To increase in size, quantity, intensity, etc. 6 To become. 7 To come to be; develop. 8 To become fixed or attached by or as by growth. —*v.t.* 9 To cause to grow; raise by cultivation. 10 To produce or develop by a natural process. 11 To cover with a growth: used in the passive. —**grow on** To become gradually more pleasing or important to. —**grow up** To become an adult. [<OE *grōwan*] —**grow'er** *n.*

growl (groul) *n.* 1 A low, guttural sound, as that made by an angry animal. 2 A sound similar to this. —*v.i.* 1 To utter a growl. 2 To speak in a gruff, surly manner. 3 To rumble, as distant thunder. —*v.t.* 4 To express by growling. [ME *groulen* to rumble] —**growl'er** *n.*

grown (grōn) *p.p.* of GROW. —*adj.* Mature; fully developed.

grown-up (grōn'up') *n.* A mature person; adult: also **grown'up'.** —*adj.* 1 Adult. 2 Of, for, or typical of adults.

growth (grōth) *n.* 1 The process of growing. 2 A stage of development or maturity reached in growing. 3 An increase in size, number, etc. 4 Something produced by or in the process of growing. 5 An abnormal formation, as a wart, tumor, etc.

grub (grub) *v.* **grubbed, grub·bing** *v.i.* 1 To dig in the ground. 2 To drudge; toil. 3 To make careful or plodding search; rummage. —*v.t.* 4 To dig up; root out. 5 To clear (ground) of roots, stumps, etc. 6 *Slang* To get by begging; mooch. —*n.* 1 A fat, wormlike larva, as of beetles and some other insects. 2 DRUDGE. 3 *Slang* Food. [ME *grubben*] —**grub'ber** *n.*

grub·by (grub'ē) *adj.* **·bi·er, ·bi·est** 1 Dirty; messy. 2 Full of grubs. —**grub'bi·ly** *adv.* —**grub'bi·ness** *n.* —**Syn.** 1 slovenly, sloppy, untidy, unkempt.

grub·stake (grub'stāk') *n.* Money, supplies, etc., provided, as to a mining prospector, on condition of receiving a share of his findings. —*v.t.* **·staked, ·stak·ing** To supply with a grubstake.

grudge (gruj) *v.t.* **grudged, grudg·ing** 1 To envy the possessions or good fortunes of (another). 2 To give or allow unwillingly and resentfully; begrudge. —*n.* Ill will or resentment, as for some remembered wrong. [< OF *groucher*] —**grudg'er** *n.* —**grudg'ing·ly** *adv.*

gru·el (grōō'əl) *n.* A semiliquid food made by boiling meal in water or milk. —*v.t.* **gru·eled** or **gru·elled, gru·el·ing** or **gru·el·ling** To work, wear down, or exhaust by hard work, punishment, etc. [< OF, meal]

gru·el·ing (grōō'əl·ing) *adj.* Severely trying; exhausting. Also **gru'el·ling.**

grue·some (grōō'səm) *adj.* Inspiring horror and loathing; grisly. [? < MDu. *gruwen* to shudder + -SOME] —**grue'·some·ly** *adv.* —**grue'some·ness** *n.*

gruff (gruf) *adj.* 1 Rough or brusque in manner. 2 Hoarse; harsh. [< Du. *grof* rough] —**gruff'ly** *adv.* —**gruff'ness** *n.*

grum·ble (grum'bəl) *v.* **grum·bled, grum·bling** *v.i.* 1 To complain in a surly manner; mutter discontentedly. 2 To make growling sounds in the throat. 3 To rumble, as thunder. —*v.t.* 4 To say with a grumble. —*n.* 1 A surly complaint; discontented muttering. 2 A rumble. [? < MDu. *grommen* to growl] —**grum'bler** *n.* —**grum'bling·ly** *adv.* —**grum'bly** *adj.*

grump·y (grum'pē) *adj.* **grump·i·er, grump·i·est** Ill-tempered; grouchy; cranky. [? Blend of GRUNT and DUMP] —**grump'i·ly** *adv.* —**grump'i·ness** *n.*

grun·ion (grun'yən) *n.* A small fish common on the coast of California, noted for the regularity of its inshore spawning activities at the time of a nearly full moon.

grunt (grunt) *v.i.* 1 To make a short, guttural sound typical of a hog. 2 To make a similar sound, as in annoyance, assent, effort, etc. —*v.t.* 3 To express by grunting. —*n.* 1 A short, guttural sound, as of a hog. 2 A chiefly tropical marine fish that makes grunting sounds. 3 *Mil. Slang* A U.S. infantryman. [< OE *grunnettan*] —**grunt'er** *n.*

Gru·yère (grē·yâr', grōō-; *Fr.* grü·yâr') *n.* A light yellow Swiss cheese, usu. without holes. [< *Gruyère,* a town in Switzerland]

gr. wt. gross weight.

gry·phon (grif'ən) *n.* GRIFFIN.

G.S. General Secretary; General Staff.

G.S.A. Girl Scouts of America.

G-string (jē'string') *n.* 1 A narrow loincloth. 2 A similar cloth, often gaudily ornamented, worn esp. by stripteasers. [?]

gt. great.

gtd. guaranteed.

GU, g.u. genitourinary.

gua·no (gwä'nō) *n. pl.* **·nos** 1 The accumulated excrement of sea birds, found esp. on islands off the Peruvian coast and used as fertilizer. 2 A manufactured nitrogenous fertilizer resembling this. [< Quechua *huanu* dung]

guar. guaranteed.

guar·an·tee (gar'ən·tē') *n.* 1 A pledge or formal assurance that something will meet stated specifications or that a specified act will be performed. 2 Something given as security. 3 GUARANTOR. 4 Something that assures a certain outcome. —*v.t.* **·teed, ·tee·ing** 1 To give a guarantee for; certify or vouch for. 2 To assume responsibility for. 3 To secure against loss or damage. 4 To give assurance of; promise. [Var. of GUARANTY]

guar·an·tor (gar'ən·tər, -tôr') *n.* One who guarantees or makes a guaranty.

guar·an·ty (gar'ən·tē) *n. pl.* **·ties** 1 A pledge to assume responsibility in case of default for debts or obligations incurred by another. 2 A deposit, etc., made or held as security. 3 GUARANTOR. —*v.t.* **·tied, ·ty·ing** To guarantee. [< OF *guarantie* < *guarant* a warrant < Gmc]

guard (gärd) *v.t.* 1 To keep protective watch over, as to shield or defend from harm or loss. 2 To maintain supervisory watch over, as to prevent escape. 3 To keep in check; control. —*v.i.* 4 To take precautions: with *against.* —*n.* 1 One who guards, as a sentry, prison employee, etc. 2 Watchful care or supervision. 3 Protection; defense. 4 A device that protects, shields, etc. 5 A posture or attitude of defense. 6 A person or body of persons providing protection, ceremonial escort, etc. 7 In football, either of two offensive line players whose position is next to the center. 8 In basketball, either of two players covering the rear of the court. —**off (one's) guard** Unprepared for defense, protection, etc. —**on (one's) guard** On the alert; vigilant. —**stand guard** 1 To act as sentry. 2 To keep careful watch. [< OF *garder* < Gmc.] —**guard'er** *n.* —**Syn.** *v.* 1 protect, safeguard, preserve.

guard·ed (gär'did) *adj.* Cautious; restrained: *guarded* comments. —**guard'ed·ly** *adv.* —**guard'ed·ness** *n.*

guard·house (gärd'hous') *n.* 1 Quarters for military guards. 2 A military jail for minor offenders.

guard·i·an (gär'dē·ən) *n.* 1 *Law* One who guards or has protective care. 2 One legally empowered to care for the person or property of another, esp. an infant or minor. —**guard'i·an·ship** *n.*

guard·rail (gärd'rāl') *n.* 1 A protective railing, as at the edge of a balcony or between opposing lanes of traffic. 2 A rail placed next to a main rail of a track to prevent trains from derailing.

guard·room (gärd'rōōm', -rŏŏm') *n.* A room used by a military guard while on duty.

guards·man (gärdz'mən) *n. pl.* **·men** (-mən) A member of certain military bodies, as the U.S. National Guard or the British royal household troops.

Gua·te·ma·la gwä'tə·mä'lä) *n.* A republic of N Central America, 42,042 sq. mi., cap. Guatemala (also Guatemala City). —**Gua'te·ma'lan** *adj., n.* • See map at CENTRAL AMERICA.

gua·va (gwä'və) *n.* 1 A tropical American tree or shrub bearing sweet, yellow-skinned fruit. 2 Its fruit, used esp. for making jelly. [Sp. *guayaba* < S. Am.Ind.]

gua·yu·le (gwä·yōō'lā) *n.* 1 A woody composite plant of sw North America. 2 The resinous latex of this plant, yielding a natural rubber: also **guayule rubber.** [Sp. < Nah.]

gu·ber·na·to·ri·al (gʸōō'bər·nə·tôr'ē·əl, -tō'rē) *adj.* Of or pertaining to a governor or the office of governor. [< L *gubernare* govern]

gudg·eon (guj'ən) *n.* 1 A small Old World freshwater fish. 2 A person easily duped. 3 Anything swallowed credulously. —*v.t.* To cheat; dupe. [< L *gobio* goby]

guer·don (gûr'dən) *n.* A reward; recompense. [< Med. L *widerdonum*]

Guern·sey (gûrn'zē) *n. pl.* **·seys** One of a breed of dairy cattle originally from the island of Guernsey, Channel Islands.

guer·ril·la (gə·ril'ə) *n.* One of an irregular, independent band of partisan soldiers often harassing opposing troops. Also **gue·ril'la.** [< Sp. *guerra* a war] —*adj.* Of or carried on by guerrillas.

guess (ges) *v.t. & v.i.* 1 To form a judgment or opinion (of something) on uncertain or incomplete knowledge. 2 To judge or estimate correctly. 3 To believe; think. —*n.* 1 An opinion or conclusion reached by guessing. 2 The act of guessing. [Prob. < Scand.] —**guess'er** *n.*

guess·timate (ges'tə·mit) *n. Slang* A prediction based in part on guesswork. [< GUESS + (ES)TIMATE]

guess·work (ges'wûrk') *n.* The process or result of guessing.
guest (gest) *n.* **1** A person received or entertained by another as a visitor or recipient of hospitality. **2** One paying for lodging and services at a hotel, etc. **3** A visiting performer or participant in a program. [<ON *gestr*]
guff (guf) *n. Slang* Foolish or uncalled-for talk; nonsense. [Imit.]
guf·faw (gə·fô') *n.* A burst of loud, boisterous laughter. —*v.i.* To utter such laughter. [Imit.]
gui·dance (gīd'ns) *n.* **1** The act, process, or result of guiding. **2** Advice; counseling. **3** Leadership; direction.
guide (gīd) *v.* **guid·ed, guid·ing** *v.t.* **1** To lead, accompany, direct, show the way, etc. **2** To direct the motion or action of, as a vehicle, tool, etc. **3** To lead or direct the affairs, standards, opinions, etc., of. —*v.i.* **4** To act as a guide. —*n.* **1** One who shows the way by accompanying or going in advance, as in conducting travelers, sightseers, etc. **2** One who or that which provides direction, inspiration, etc. **3** Something that guides or informs, as a book, sign, or set of instructions. **4** A device acting as an indicator or serving to restrict motion of a part. [<OF *guider*] —**guid'er** *n.*
guide·book (gīd'bŏŏk') *n.* A handbook for travelers or tourists, containing descriptions of places, routes, etc.
guided missile An unmanned missile whose course can be altered after launch.
guide·line (gīd'līn') *n.* A statement, policy, etc. indicating the limits or scope of an undertaking.
guide·post (gīd'pōst') *n.* A signpost giving directions to travelers.
gui·don (gīd'ən) *n.* A small flag carried by a military unit as an emblem. [<Ital. *guidone* <*guida* guide]
gui·gnol (gē·nyôl') *n. Often cap.* GRAND GUIGNOL.
guild (gild) *n.* **1** In medieval times, an association of craftsmen or merchants. **2** An association of persons with kindred pursuits, interests, or aims. [<ON *gildi* payment] —**guilds'man** *n.* (*pl.* **·men**)
guil·der (gil'dər) *n.* The basic monetary unit of the Netherlands. [Alter. of Du. *gulden* gulden]
guild·hall (gild'hôl') *n.* **1** The hall where a guild meets. **2** TOWN HALL.
guile (gīl) *n.* Deceitful slyness; duplicity. [<OF <Gmc.]
guile·ful (gīl'fəl) *adj.* Full of guile; slyly deceitful. —**guile'ful·ly** *adv.* —**guile'ful·ness** *n.*
guile·less (gīl'lis) *adj.* Free from guile; artless; ingenuous. —**guile'less·ly** *adv.* —**guile'less·ness** *n.*
guil·le·mot (gil'ə·mot) *n.* Any of several narrow-billed diving birds of N latitudes. [<F *Guillaume* William]
guil·lo·tine (gil'ə·tēn, gē'ə-, gē·ə·tēn') *n.* An instrument for beheading, consisting of a weighted knife dropped between two slotted uprights. —*v.t.* **·tined, ·tin·ing** To behead with the guillotine. [<Dr. J. I. *Guillotin,* 1738–1814, Fr. physician]

Guillotine

guilt (gilt) *n.* **1** The state or fact of having committed a crime, legal offense, or wrongdoing. **2** Responsibility for having committed a crime or wrong; culpability. **3** A feeling of blameworthiness for having committed a crime or wrong. [<OE *gylt*]
guilt·less (gilt'lis) *adj.* **1** Free from guilt; innocent; blameless. **2** Without experience or knowledge: with *of.* —**guilt'less·ly** *adv.* —**guilt'less·ness** *n.*
guilt·y (gil'tē) *adj.* **guilt·i·er, guilt·i·est** **1** Responsible for having committed a crime, offense, or wrongdoing. **2** Involving, expressing, feeling, or characterized by guilt. —**guilt'i·ly** *adv.* —**guilt'i·ness** *n.* —**Syn.** culpable, blameworthy.
guimpe (gamp, gimp) *n.* A blouse worn under a jumper or pinafore. [F]
guin·ea (gin'ē) *n.* **1** An amount or unit of British money equal to one pound and one shilling. **2** A former British gold coin equal to this amount. [<*Guinea,* Africa, orig. source of gold for the coin]
Guin·ea (gin'ē) *n.* **1** A republic of w Africa, 94,925 sq. mi., cap. Conakry. **2** Formerly, a coastal region of w Africa. • See map at AFRICA.
guinea fowl A domestic fowl of African origin, having dark gray plumage with white spots. Also **guinea hen.**
guinea pig **1** A domesticated rodent with short ears and no visible tail, used in biological and medical experiments. **2** Any subject of experimentation or research.
Guin·e·vere (gwin'ə·vir) In Arthurian legend, Arthur's queen and mistress of Lancelot. Also **Guin'e·ver** (-vər).
guise (gīz) *n.* **1** Outward appearance; aspect. **2** False appearance or assumed manner; pretense. **3** Garb; costume. [<OF <Gmc.]
gui·tar (gi·tär') *n.* A musical instrument having a fretted fingerboard and usu. six strings, played by plucking. [<Gk. *kithara* lyre] —**gui·tar'ist** *n.*

Guitar

Gu·lag (gōō'läg) *n.* A Soviet labor camp. [<Russ.]
gulch (gulch) *n.* A narrow, steep-sided ravine.
gul·den (gŏŏl'dən) *n. pl.* **·dens** or **·den** GUILDER. [Du. and G, lit., golden]
gules (gyōōlz) *n. Her.* The color red. [<OF *gueules* red-dyed ermine fur]
gulf (gulf) *n.* **1** A considerable area of marine water partly enclosed by an indentation of a coastline. **2** An abyss; chasm. **3** A wide separation or gap not easily bridged. —*v.t.* ENGULF. [<Gk. *kolpos* a bay]
Gulf States States bordering on the Gulf of Mexico: Alabama, Florida, Louisiana, Mississippi, and Texas.
gull[1] (gul) *n.* Any of various usu. gray and white aquatic birds with long wings, webbed feet, and a hooked bill. [ME]
gull[2] (gul) *v.t* To trick; deceive; dupe. —*n.* One who is easily tricked or deceived; a dupe. [?]
Gul·lah (gul'ə) *n.* **1** One of a group of Negroes dwelling on a narrow coastal strip and outlying islands of South Carolina, Georgia, and NE Florida. **2** The language or dialect spoken by these people.
gul·let (gul'it) *n.* **1** The passage from the mouth to the stomach; esophagus. **2** The throat. [<L *gula* throat]
gul·li·ble (gul'ə·bəl) *adj.* Easily duped or deceived; credulous. [<GULL[2]] —**gul'li·bil'i·ty** *n.* —**gul'li·bly** *adv.*
gul·ly (gul'ē) *n. pl.* **·lies** A channel, ravine, etc., cut in the earth by running water, as after a rainfall. —*v.t.* **·lied, ·ly·ing** To cut or wear a gully in. [Var. of GULLET]
gulp (gulp) *v.t.* **1** To swallow avidly or in large amounts. **2** To keep back as if by swallowing. —*v.i.* **3** To swallow, gasp, or choke, as in nervousness or astonishment. —*n.* **1** The act of gulping. **2** An amount swallowed in gulping. [<MDu. *gulpen*] —**gulp'er** *n.* —**gulp'ing·ly** *adv.*
gum[1] (gum) *n.* **1** A sticky, colloidal substance exuded by various plants and forming on drying an amorphous, brittle mass. **2** A similar plant exudate, as resin, rubber, etc. **3** Any of various viscous, sticky, or adhesive substances. **4** CHEWING GUM. **5** Any of various trees that yield gum, as an eucalyptus, sweet gum, tupelo, etc.: also **gum tree.** —*v.* **gummed, gum·ming** *v.t.* **1** To smear, stiffen, or attach with gum. —*v.i.* **2** To exude or form gum. **3** To become sticky, clogged, etc., as with gum. —**gum up** *Slang* To bungle; ruin. [<Gk. *kommi*]
gum[2] (gum) *n. Often pl.* The fleshy tissue that surrounds the base of the teeth and the area of the jaws inside the mouth. —*v.t.* **gummed, gum·ming** To chew with the gums. [<OE *gōma* inside of mouth]
gum arabic The gum obtained from several species of acacia trees, and widely used as an emulsifier.
gum·bo (gum'bō) *n. pl.* **·bos** **1** The okra or its pods. **2** A soup or stew containing okra. **3** A fine soil of the North American plains that forms a very sticky mud. [<Bantu]
gum·boil (gum'boil') *n.* A small boil or abscess formed on the gum.
gum·drop (gum'drop') *n.* A chewy, sugar-coated candy usu. made with gum arabic or gelatin.
gum·my (gum'ē) *adj.* **·mi·er, ·mi·est** **1** Consisting of, containing, or resembling gum. **2** Covered with gum. **3** Sticky; viscous. —**gum'mi·ness** *n.*

gump·tion (gump′shən) *n. Informal* Initiative; enterprise; spirit. [?]

gum resin A mixture of gum and resin that exudes as a milky juice from certain plants and gradually hardens in the air.

gum·shoe (gum′shōō′) *n.* 1 *Slang* DETECTIVE. 2 *pl.* SNEAKERS. 3 A rubber shoe or overshoe. —*v.i.* **·shoed, ·shoe·ing** *Slang* To go stealthily and noiselessly; sneak.

gun (gun) *n.* 1 A piece of ordnance fixed in a mount, whose essential element is a metal tube from which a projectile is launched at high velocity, usu. in a fairly flat trajectory. 2 A portable firearm, as a pistol or rifle. 3 The firing of a large gun. 4 Any device resembling a gun in form or function. 5 The throttle of an engine. —**stick to one's guns** To persist in an opinion, course of action, etc. —*v.* **gunned, gun·ning** *v.i.* 1 To go hunting with a gun. —*v.t.* 2 To shoot with a gun: often with *down.* 3 To open the throttle of (an engine) so as to accelerate. —**gun for** 1 To seek with intent to harm, thwart, or kill. 2 To seek eagerly. [ME *gunne*]

gun·boat (gun′bōt′) *n.* A small, armed vessel used to patrol rivers and coastal waters.

gun·cot·ton (gun′kot′n) *n.* A highly explosive nitrocellulose.

gun·fire (gun′fīr′) *n.* The firing of a gun or guns.

gung-ho (gung′hō′) *adj. Slang* Irrepressibly or excessively enthusiastic. [< Chin., lit., work together]

gun·lock (gun′lok′) *n.* The mechanism of a gun by which the charge is exploded.

gun·man (gun′mən) *n. pl.* **·men** (-mən) A man armed with a gun, esp. a criminal or killer.

gun·met·al (gun′met′l) *n.* 1 A bronze alloy formerly used for making small cannon. 2 Any of various metals or alloys made to resemble this metal or used in making guns. 3 A dark gray: also **gunmetal gray.** —*adj.* Dark gray.

gun moll *Slang* A female associate of a gangster.

gun·nel[1] (gun′əl) *n.* GUNWALE.

gun·nel[2] (gun′əl) *n.* Any of several long-bodied fishes of N marine waters. [?]

gun·ner (gun′ər) *n.* 1 A soldier, sailor, or member of an aircraft crew who operates a gun. 2 See GRADE. 3 One who hunts with a gun.

gun·ner·y (gun′ər·ē) *n.* The science and techniques of making and using guns.

gun·ny (gun′ē) *n. pl.* **·nies** A coarse fabric of jute or hemp, used for making sacks. [< Hind. *gonī*]

gun·ny·sack (gun′ē·sak′) *n.* A sack made of gunny.

gun·pow·der (gun′pou′dər) *n.* An explosive mixture of potassium nitrate, charcoal, and sulfur.

gun·run·ner (gun′run′ər) *n.* One who smuggles or carries on illegal traffic in firearms and ammunition. —**gun′·run′ning** *n.*

gun·shot (gun′shot′) *n.* 1 The shooting of a gun. 2 Shot fired from a gun. 3 The range of a gun.

gun-shy (gun′shī′) *adj.* Afraid of the sound of gunfire.

gun·smith (gun′smith′) *n.* One who makes or repairs firearms.

gun·stock (gun′·stok′) *n.* The wooden part of a firearm, holding the lock and barrel.

Gunstock

gun·wale (gun′əl) *n.* The upper edge of the side of a boat or ship. [< GUN + WALE (plank)]

gup·py (gup′ē) *n. pl.* **·pies** A small, colorful, tropical freshwater fish popular as an aquarium fish. [R. J. L. *Guppy,* early 20th c. naturalist of Trinidad]

gur·gle (gûr′gəl) *v.* **gur·gled, gur·gling** *v.i.* 1 To flow with a bubbling, liquid sound. 2 To make such a sound. —*v.t.* 3 To utter with a gurgling sound. —*n.* The act or sound of gurgling. [Var. of GARGLE] —**gur′gling·ly** *adv.*

gur·nard (gûr′nərd) *n. pl.* **·nards** or **·nard** A spiny-finned marine fish with winglike pectoral fins. [< F *grognard* grumbler]

gur·ney (gûr′nē) *n. pl.* **·neys** A stretcher mounted on wheels. [?]

gu·ru (gōō′rōō) *n. pl.* **·rus** 1 One who provides instruction or spiritual leadership in Hindu mysticism. 2 A teacher or leader regarded as having special knowledge, powers, etc. [< Hind.]

gush (gush) *v.i.* 1 To flow out suddenly and in volume. 2 To produce a sudden outflow. 3 To express oneself with exaggerated sentiment or enthusiasm. —*v.t.* 4 To pour forth (blood, tears, etc.). —*n.* 1 A sudden outpouring. 2 *Informal* An exaggerated display of sentiment. [Prob. < Scand.] —**gush′ing·ly** *adv.* —**Syn.** spurt, spout, jet.

gush·er (gush′ər) *n.* 1 One who or that which gushes. 2 A free-flowing oil well.

gush·y (gush′ē) *adj.* **gush·i·er, gush·i·est** Overly effusive or sentimental. —**gush′i·ly** *adv.* —**gush′i·ness** *n.*

gus·set (gus′it) *n.* A triangular piece of cloth fitted into a garment to give added strength or more room. —*v.t.* To furnish with a gusset. [< OF *gousse* a pod, shell]

gust (gust) *n.* 1 A sudden, strong blast of wind. 2 A sudden outburst of strong emotion. —*v.i.* To blow in gusts.

gus·ta·to·ry (gus′tə·tôr′ē, -tō′rē) *adj.* Of or relating to the sense of taste. [< L *gustus* taste]

gus·to (gus′tō) *n.* 1 Keen enjoyment; relish; zest. 2 Great vigor or fervor. [< L *gustus* taste]

gust·y (gus′tē) *adj.* **gust·i·er, gust·i·est** 1 Characterized by or blowing in gusts. 2 Bursting forth in or as in a gust. —**gust′i·ly** *adv.* —**gust′i·ness** *n.*

gut (gut) *n.* 1 The alimentary canal, esp. the intestine. 2 *Usu. pl.* The bowels. 3 CATGUT. 4 *pl. Slang* Stamina; courage; grit. —*v.t.* **gut·ted, gut·ting** 1 To take out the intestines of; eviscerate. 2 To destroy the interior or contents of. —*adj. Slang* 1 Central; basic; fundamental: *gut* issues. 2 Deeply felt, as though physically experienced: a *gut* conviction. [< OE *guttas* viscera]

gut·less (gut′lis) *adj. Slang* Lacking courage or spirit. —**gut′less·ly** *adv.* —**gut′less·ness** *n.*

gut·sy (gut′sē) *adj.* **gut·si·er, gut·si·est** *Slang* Courageous; dauntless; gritty. —**gut′si·ness** *n.*

gut·ta-per·cha (gut′ə·pûr′chə) *n.* A rubberlike substance obtained from the sap of various Malayan trees, used as an electrical insulator, a dental plastic, etc. [< Malay *getah* gum + *percha* gum tree]

gut·ter (gut′ər) *n.* 1 A trough or channel along the eaves of a house to carry off rainwater. 2 A waterway for carrying off surface water at the side of a road or street. 3 A groove, trench, or trough as on either side of a bowling alley. 4 A place or living condition characterized by great squalor, poverty, etc. —*v.t.* 1 To form gutters, channels, or grooves in. —*v.i.* 2 To flow in channels or streams. 3 To melt rapidly or flicker markedly, as a lighted candle. [< L *gutta* a drop]

gut·ter·snipe (gut′ər·snīp′) *n.* 1 A neglected child who roams the streets. 2 Anyone of a lowly and despised class or condition.

gut·tur·al (gut′ər·əl) *adj.* 1 Pertaining to the throat. 2 Produced or formed in the throat. 3 Hoarse; harsh; rasping. 4 *Phonet.* VELAR. —*n. Phonet.* A velar sound. [< L *guttur* throat] —**gut·tur·al·i·ty** (gut′ə·ral′ə·tē), **gut′tur·al·ness** *n.* —**gut′tur·al·ly** *adv.*

gut·ty (gut′ē) *adj.* **gut·ti·er, gut·ti·est** *Slang* Courageous; strong; plucky.

guy[1] (gī) *n.* A rope, cable, etc., that steadies or secures something, as a mast. —*v.t.* To secure with a guy. [?]

guy[2] (gī) *n.* 1 *Informal* A fellow; man. 2 *Brit.* A person of grotesque appearance. —*v.t.* To ridicule; make fun of. [< *Guy* Fawkes, 1570–1606, English conspirator]

Guy·a·na (gī·an′ə) *n.* A member of the Commonwealth of Nations in NE South America, 83,000 sq. mi., cap. Georgetown. • See map at BRAZIL.

guz·zle (guz′əl) *v.t. & v.i.* **·zled, ·zling** To drink greedily or immoderately. [? < OF *gosier* throat] —**guz′zler** *n.*

gym (jim) *n. Informal* 1 GYMNASIUM. 2 A course or class in physical training.

gym·na·si·um (jim·nā′zē·əm) *n. pl.* **·si·ums** or **·si·a** (-zē·ə) 1 A building or room containing equipment for physical education activities and sports. 2 (gim·nä′zē·ōōm) *Sometimes cap.* In Germany and some other European countries, a secondary school that prepares students for universities. [L < Gk. *gymnazein* exercise, train naked]

gym·nast (jim′nast, -nəst) *n.* One expert in gymnastics.
gym·nas·tic (jim·nas′tik) *adj.* Relating to gymnastics. —**gym·nas′ti·cal·ly** *adv.*
gym·nas·tics (jim·nas′tiks) *n. pl. (construed as sing.)* Exercises for the development of bodily strength and agility, often performed in a gymnasium with special equipment.
gym·no·sperm (jim′nə·spûrm′) *n.* One of a class of plants having ovules not enclosed in an ovary, as conifers, ginkgoes, etc. [< Gk. *gymnos* naked + SPERM] —**gym′no·sper′mous** *adj.*
gyn., gynecol. gynecology.
gy·ne·col·o·gy (gī′nə·kol′ə·jē, jī′nə-, jin′ə-) *n.* The branch of medicine dealing with the reproductive functions and diseases of women. [< Gk. *gynē, gynaikos* woman + -LOGY] —**gy′ne·co·log′i·cal** *adj.* —**gy′ne·col′o·gist** *n.*
gyp (jip) *Informal v.t. & v.i.* **gypped, gyp·ping** To cheat or swindle. —*n.* **1** An instance of gypping. **2** One who gyps. [< GYPSY]
gyp·sum (jip′səm) *n.* A mineral hydrous sulfate of lime, used in making plaster of Paris, fertilizers, etc. [< Gk. *gypsos* chalk]
gyp·sy (jip′sē) *n. pl.* **·sies** One who resembles or leads the wandering life of a Gypsy. —*v.i.* **·sied, sy·ing** To wander from place to place in the manner of the Gypsies.
Gyp·sy (jip′sē) *n. pl.* **·sies 1** A member of a wandering people that migrated to Europe from India in the 15th century and now live in many parts of the world. **2** The language of these people; Romany. [Short for EGYPTIAN]
gypsy moth A small moth whose larvae feed on foliage and are highly destructive to trees.
gy·rate (jī′rāt) *v.i.* **·rat·ed, ·rat·ing 1** To rotate or revolve. **2** To move in a spiral or circle. —*adj.* Convoluted; coiled. [< Gk. *gyrus* a circle] —**gy·ra′tion, gy′ra·tor** *n.* —**gy·ra·to·ry** (jī′rə·tôr·ē, -tō′rē) *adj.*
gyr·fal·con (jûr′fal′kən, -fôl′-, -fô′-) *n.* A large falcon of Arctic regions. [< OF < OHG *Gir* vulture + OF *faucon* falcon]
gy·ro (jī′rō) *n.* GYROSCOPE.
gyro- *combining form* Circle, ring, or spiral: *gyroscope.* [< Gk. *gyros* circle]
gy·ro·com·pass (jī′rō·kum′pəs, -kom′-) *n.* A compass that uses a gyroscope rather than the magnetic poles to maintain its reference direction.
gyro pilot AUTOMATIC PILOT.
gy·ro·plane (jī′rə·plān′) *n.* An airplane whose lift is obtained from rotation of airfoils about a nearly vertical axis.
gy·ro·scope (jī′rə·skōp) *n.* An instrument consisting of a rotating mass whose axis remains fixed in space unless it is subjected to external torque. —**gy′ro·scop′ic** (-skop′ik) *adj.*

Gyroscope

gyro stabilizer A device that uses a gyroscope as a reference in maintaining something in a stable position.
gyve (jīv) *n. Usu. pl.* A shackle, esp. for the leg. —*v.t.* **gyved, gyv·ing** To shackle. [ME]

H

H, h (āch) *n. pl.* **H's, h's, Hs, hs** (ā′chiz) **1** The eighth letter of the English alphabet. **2** Any spoken sound representing the letter *H* or *h.* **3** Something shaped like an H. —*adj.* Shaped like an H.
H hydrogen
h., h harbor; hardness; height; hit(s).
ha (hä) *interj.* An exclamation expressing surprise, triumph, laughter, etc.
ha hectare(s).
ha·be·as cor·pus (hā′bē·əs kôr′pəs) *Law* A writ commanding a person having another in custody to produce the detained person before a court. [L, you shall have the body]
hab·er·dash·er (hab′ər·dash′ər) *n.* **1** A dealer in men's furnishings, such as, shirts, socks, ties, etc. **2** *Brit.* A dealer in ribbons. trimmings, thread, needles, and other small wares. [< AF *hapertas* kind of fabric]
hab·er·dash·er·y (hab′ər·dash′ər·ē) *n. pl.* **·er·ies 1** The goods sold by haberdashers. **2** A haberdasher's shop.
hab·er·geon (hab′ər·jən) *n.* A coat of mail for the breast and neck, shorter than a hauberk. [< OF *hauberc* hauberk]
ha·bil·i·ment (hə·bil′ə·mənt) *n.* **1** An article of clothing. **2** *pl.* Clothes; garb. [< OF *habiller* dress, make fit]
hab·it (hab′it) *n.* **1** A tendency toward an action or condition, which by repetition has become involuntary. **2** An action so induced. **3** Habitual condition, appearance, or temperament; physical or mental make-up. **4** *Biol.* A characteristic mode of growth or aspect of a plant or animal. **5** An outer garment or garments; esp., a woman's costume for horseback riding. **6** The distinctive garment of a religious order. —*v.t.* To furnish with a habit; clothe; dress. [< L *habitus* condition, dress < *habere* have] —**Syn.** *n.* **1** custom, practice, routine, rule, wont.
hab·it·a·ble (hab′it·ə·bəl) *adj.* Suitable to be lived in. [< L *habitare* inhabit] —**hab·it·a·bil·i·ty** (hab′it·ə·bil′ə·tē), **hab′it·a·ble·ness** *n.* —**hab′it·a·bly** *adv.*
hab·i·tant (hab′ə·tənt) *n.* **1** INHABITANT. **2** (hab′ə·tänt) In Canada, a farmer who is a French settler or a descendant of a French settler.
hab·i·tat (hab′ə·tat) *n.* The region where a species or individual naturally or usu. lives or is found. [L, it dwells]
hab·i·ta·tion (hab′ə·tā′shən) *n.* **1** A place of residence; home. **2** The act or state of inhabiting.
ha·bit·u·al (hə·bich′o͞o·əl) *adj.* **1** Of, pertaining to, or constituting a habit. **2** Resulting from habit or repeated use; inveterate: a *habitual* liar. **3** Frequently seen, done, etc.; usual; inevitable: the *habitual* roar of city traffic. —**ha·bit′u·al·ly** *adv.* —**ha·bit′u·al·ness** *n.*
ha·bit·u·ate (hə·bich′o͞o·āt) *v.t.* **·at·ed, ·at·ing 1** To make familiar by repetition or use; accustom. **2** *Informal* To go to habitually; frequent. —**ha·bit′u·a′tion** *n.*
hab·i·tude (hab′ə·t(y)o͞od) *n.* **1** Habitual method, character, constitution, or tendency; habit. **2** Customary relation or association.
ha·bit·u·é (hə·bich′o͞o·ā′) *n.* A habitual visitor or frequenter of a place, such as a restaurant. [F < *habituer* accustom]
Habs·burg (haps′bûrg; *Ger.* häps′bo͝orkh) *n.* HAPSBURG.
ha·ci·en·da (hä′sē·en′də) *n.* In Spanish America, a landed estate; a country house. [Sp. < L *facienda* things to be done]
hack[1] (hak) *v.t.* **1** To cut or chop crudely or irregularly. **2** To break up, as clods of earth. —*v.i.* **3** To make cuts or notches with heavy, crude blows. **4** To emit short, dry coughs. —**hack it** *Slang* To cope with it; do it. —*n.* **1** A gash, cut, or nick. **2** An ax or other tool for hacking. **3** A short, dry cough. [< OE *haccian* to cut] —**hack′er** *n.*
hack[2] (hak) *n.* **1** A horse for hire. **2** A horse used for work or for ordinary riding. **3** An old, worn-out horse. **4** A coach for hire. **5** TAXICAB. **6** A writer who hires himself out for any kind of writing jobs; a literary drudge. —*v.t.* **1** To let out for hire, as a horse. —*v.i.* **2** To ride a horse, as for recreation. **3** *Informal* To drive a taxicab. —*adj.* **1** Of or designated for a taxicab: a *hack* stand. **2** For hire for drudging work: a *hack* writer. **3** Done merely for pay: a *hack* job. [< HACKNEY]
hack·a·more (hak′ə·môr, -mōr) *n.* A rawhide halter or rope used for training colts. [< Sp. *jaquima* halter]
hack·ber·ry (hak′ber′ē, -bər·ē) *n. pl.* **·ries 1** An American tree related to the elm and having cherrylike edible fruit. **2** The fruit or wood of this tree. [< ON *heggr* hedge + BERRY]
hack·le[1] (hak′əl) *n.* **1** One of the ruff feathers of a cock or

other bird. 2 An artificial fly made of a hackle feather, used as an angler's lure: also **hackle fly.** 3 *pl.* The erectile hairs on the neck and back of a dog. **—get one's hackles up** To arouse one's anger; put one out of temper. *—v.t.* **hack·led, hack·ling** To furnish (a fly) with a hackle. [ME *hechele*] **—hack′ler** *n.*

hack·le[2] (hak′əl) *v.t. & v.i.* **hack·led, hack·ling** To cut or chop roughly or crudely; mangle; hack. [Freq. of HACK[1]]

hack·ney (hak′nē) *n. pl.* **·neys** 1 One of a breed of driving and saddle horses. 2 A horse kept for hire. 3 A coach for hire: also **hackney coach.** *—v.t.* 1 To make trite by constant use. 2 To let out or use as a hackney. *—adj.* Let out for hire. [ME *hakeney*]

hack·neyed (hak′nēd) *adj.* Made commonplace by too frequent use; trite.

hack·saw (hak′sô′) *n.* A saw made up of a fine-toothed blade set in a frame, used for cutting metal.

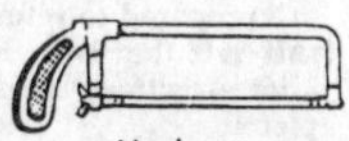

Hacksaw

had (had) *p.t. & p.p.* of HAVE.

had·dock (had′ək) *n. pl.* **·dock** or **·docks** A food fish of the North Atlantic, related to the cod. [ME]

Ha·des (hā′dēz) *Gk. Myth.* 1 The god of the underworld; Pluto. 2 The kingdom over which Hades rules, the abode of the dead. *—n. Informal* Hell.

hadj (haj) *n.* The pilgrimage to Mecca required of every Muslim at least once in his life. [Ar. *hajj* pilgrimage]

hadj·i (haj′ē) *n.* A Muslim who has made the pilgrimage to Mecca. Also **hadj·ee.** [Ar. *ḥājjī* pilgrim]

had·n't (had′nt) Contraction of *had not.*

haem·or·rhoid (hem′ə·roid) *n.* HEMORRHOID.

haf·ni·um (haf′nē·əm) *n.* A metallic element (symbol Hf) occurring with and resembling zirconium. [< L *Hafnia* Copenhagen]

haft (haft, häft) *n.* A handle, esp. the handle of a cutting weapon. *—v.t.* To supply with or set in a haft or handle. [< OE *hæft*]

hag (hag) *n.* 1 An ugly, forbidding, malicious old woman. 2 A witch; sorceress. [< OE *hægtes* witch] **—hag′gish** *adj.* **—Syn.** 1 beldam, crone, granny.

Ha·gar (hā′gər) In the Bible, Abraham's concubine, mother of Ishmael.

hag·fish (hag′fish′) *n. pl.* **·fish** or **·fish·es** A primitive eel-like marine fish with a circular, jawless mouth and horny teeth, parasitic on other fish.

Hag·ga·dah (hə·gä′də, *Hebrew* hä·gô′dô) *n. pl.* **·doth** (-dōth) 1 An anecdote or parable in the Talmud, used to clarify a point of law. 2 The ritual, including the story of the Exodus, read during the Seder on Passover. Also **Hag·ga′da.** [Heb.] **—hag·gad·ic** (hə·gad′ik, -gäd′-) *adj.* **—hag·ga·dist** (hə·gä′dist) *n.*

hag·gard (hag′ərd) *adj.* Worn and gaunt in appearance. [< OF *hagard* wild hawk] **—hag′gard·ly** *adv.* **—hag′gard·ness** *n.* **—Syn.** careworn, emaciated, exhausted, wan.

hag·gis (hag′is) *n.* A Scottish dish made of a sheep's heart and liver with onions and suet, mixed with oatmeal and boiled in a sheep's stomach. [ME *hagas*]

hag·gle (hag′əl) *v.* **hag·gled, hag·gling** *v.t.* 1 To cut unskillfully; mangle. *—v.i.* 2 To argue about price or terms. *—n.* The act of haggling. [< ON *höggva* to cut] **—hag′gler** *n.*

hag·i·og·ra·phy (hag′ē·og′rə·fē, hā′jē-) *n. pl.* **·phies** 1 The writing or study of saints' lives. 2 A collection of biographies of saints. **—hag′i·og′ra·pher** *n.* **—hag′i·o·graph′·ic** or **·i·cal** *adj.*

hag·i·ol·o·gy (hag′ē·ol′ə·jē, hā′jē-) *n. pl.* **·gies** 1 A list of saints. 2 A treatise on saints' lives; sacred writings. [< Gk. *hagios* sacred + -LOGY] **—hag·i·o·log·ic** (hag′ē·ə·loj′ik, hā′·jē-) *adj.* **—hag′i·ol′o·gist** *n.*

hag-rid·den (hag′rid′n) *adj.* Tormented or distressed, as by nightmares or painful thoughts.

hah (hä) *interj. & n.* HA.

hai·ku (hī·koo) *n. pl.* **·ku** A Japanese verse form, consisting of three lines of five, seven, and five syllables respectively.

hail[1] (hāl) *n.* 1 Pellets of ice, sometimes fairly large, that often fall during thunderstorms. 2 Anything falling thickly and with violence: a *hail* of blows. *—v.i.* 1 To pour down hail. *—v.t.* 2 To hurl or pour down like hail. [< OE *hægel*]

hail[2] (hāl) *v.t.* 1 To call loudly to in greeting; salute. 2 To call to so as to attract attention. 3 To name as; designate. *—v.i.* 4 To call out or signal so as to attract attention. **—hail from** To come from; have as one's original home. *—n.* 1 A call to attract attention; greeting. 2 The distance a shout can be heard: within *hail.* *—interj.* Salutations! [< ON *heill* whole, hale] **—hail′er** *n.*

hail·stone (hāl′stōn′) *n.* A pellet of hail.

hail·storm (hāl′stôrm′) *n.* A storm in which hail falls.

hair (hâr) *n.* 1 One of the filaments of modified epidermal tissue growing from the skin of people and animals. 2 Any mass of such filaments. 3 *Bot.* A threadlike outgrowth on plants. 4 An exceedingly minute space, degree, etc.: to escape by a *hair.* *—adj.* Like, made of, or for hair. **—let one's hair down** To drop one's reserve; relax. **—not turn a hair** To remain calm and unruffled. **—split hairs** To quibble; make petty distinctions. [< OE *hǣr*]

hair·breadth (hâr′bredth′) *n.* An extremely small space or distance. *—adj.* Having only the breadth of a hair; very narrow. Also **hairs′-breadth′, hair's′-breadth′.**

hair·cloth (hâr′klôth′, -kloth′) *n.* A fabric containing horsehair, used chiefly in upholstering.

hair·cut (hâr′kut′) *n.* The act of cutting the hair or the style in which it is cut. **—hair′cut′ter** *n.*

hair-do (hâr′doo′) *n.* A style of dressing the hair; coiffure.

hair·dress·er (hâr′dres′ər) *n.* One who arranges and cuts hair. **—hair′dress′ing** *n.*

hair·less (hâr′lis) *adj.* 1 Being without hair. 2 Having lost the hair; bald. **—hair′less·ness** *n.*

hair·line (hâr′līn′) *n.* 1 A narrow stripe in textile fabrics. 2 The outline of hair on the head.

hair·pin (hâr′pin′) *n.* A U-shaped pin made of wire, bone, plastic, etc., for keeping the hair in place. • See PIN.

hair-rais·ing (hâr′rā′zing) *adj.* Causing fright or shock. **—hair′-rais′er** *n.* **—Syn.** bloodcurdling, frightful, horrifying.

hair shirt A rough garment of haircloth worn for religious penance.

hair-split·ting (hâr′split′ing) *n.* Insistence upon minute or trivial distinctions. *—adj.* Drawing excessively nice distinctions. **—hair′-split′ter** *n.*

hair·spring (hâr′spring′) *n.* The fine spring attached to the balance wheel of a watch or clock.

hair-trig·ger (hâr′trig′ər) *n.* A trigger, as of a firearm, actuated by a very small force. *—adj.* Set in operation by the slightest provocation.

hair·y (hâr′ē) *adj.* **hair·i·er, hair·i·est** 1 Covered with, made of, or like hair. 2 *Slang* **a** Troublesome; difficult. **b** Dangerous; harrowing. **—hair′i·ness** *n.*

Hai·ti (hā′tē) *n.* A republic occupying the w part of Hispaniola in the Caribbean, 10,714 sq. mi., cap. Port-au-Prince. • See map at DOMINICAN REPUBLIC.

Hai·ti·an (hā′shən, -tē·ən) *n.* 1 A citizen or native of Haiti. 2 The dialect of French spoken in Haiti. *—adj.* Of or pertaining to Haiti, its people, or their dialect.

hake (hāk) *n. pl.* **hake** or **hakes** Any of various food fishes related to the cod. [ME]

ha·kim (hä·kēm′) *n.* In Muslim countries, a governor; also, a judge or physician. Also **ha·keem′, ha·kem′.** [Ar., wise, learned]

hal·berd (hal′bərd) *n.* A weapon in the form of a battle-ax and pike at the end of a long staff. Also **hal′bard, hal′bert** (-bərt). [< MHG < *helm* handle + *barte* broad-ax]

hal·ber·dier (hal′bər·dir′) *n.* A solder armed with a halberd.

hal·cy·on (hal′sē·ən) *n.* 1 A mythical bird, identified with the kingfisher, said to have calmed the sea at the time of the winter solstice. 2 Any kingfisher of Australasia. *—adj.* Calm; peaceful: the *halcyon* days of youth. [< Gk. *halkyōn* kingfisher]

hale[1] (hāl) *v.t.* **haled, hal·ing** 1 To drag by force; haul; pull. 2 To compel to go. [< MLG *halen*] **—hal′er** *n.*

hale[2] (hāl) *adj.* Of sound and vigorous health. [< OE *hāl.*] **—hale′ly** *adv.* **—hale′ness** *n.* **—Syn.** bouncing, robust, strong, well.

half (haf, häf) *n. pl.* **halves** (havz, hävz) One of two equal parts or a quantity equal to such a part. —**by halves** 1 Incompletely. 2 With little enthusiasm. —**go halves** To share in equal parts. —*adj.* 1 Being one of two equal parts of a thing. 2 Partial; approximately one half of, in amount or value. —*adv.* To the degree or extent of a half; partially. [< OE *hælf*]

half-and-half (haf′ən·haf′, häf′ən·häf′) *adj.* 1 *U.S.* A mixture of milk and cream in equal quantities. 2 *Brit.* A mixture of beer and stout, porter and ale, etc., in equal quantities. —*adv.* In two equal divisions; equally.

half·back (haf′bak′, häf′-) *n.* In American football, either of two players in the backfield, originally stationed halfway between the line and the fullback.

half-baked (haf′bākt′, häf′-) *adj.* 1 Baked on one side or not baked through; doughy. 2 *Informal* Imperfectly planned or conceived. 3 *Informal* Immature; unseasoned.

half-blood (haf′blud′) *n.* 1 A person having only one parent of a specified stock; a half-breed. 2 An animal, as a cow, sheep, etc., of crossed inferior and superior stock. —*adj.* Being half-blood or half-breed. Also **half′-blood′ed.**

half blood The relationship between persons who have one parent only in common.

half-breed (haf′brēd′, häf′-) *n.* One having parents of different racial origin. —*adj.* Half of one breed and half of another; coming of mixed stock: also **half′-bred′** (-bred′).

half brother A brother related through only one parent.

half-caste (haf′kast′, häf′käst′) *n.* One born of mixed European and Asian blood; also, any half-breed. —*adj.* Of mixed European and other blood.

half cock (haf′kok′, häf′-) The position of the hammer of a firearm when partly raised, but not releasable by the trigger. —**go off half-cocked** or **at half cock** 1 To be discharged prematurely. 2 To act or speak hastily or without deliberation. —**half′-cocked′** *adj.*

half crown A British silver coin of the value of two shillings and sixpence.

half-dol·lar (haf′dol′ər, häf′-) *n.* A U.S. silver coin worth fifty cents.

half eagle A former gold coin of the U.S. having a value of five dollars.

half·heart·ed (haf′här′tid, häf′-) *adj.* Showing little interest or enthusiasm. —**half′heart′ed·ly** *adv.* —**half′heart′·ed·ness** *n.*

half hitch A knot made by passing the end of a rope around itself once and then through the loop so formed.

half hour 1 A period of thirty minutes. 2 The point midway between the hours. —**half′-hour′ly** *adv.*

half-life (haf′līf′, häf′-) *n. Physics* The time taken for half the nuclei in a sample of a radioactive isotope to disintegrate. Also **half-life period.**

half-mast (haf′mast′, häf′mäst′) *n.* The position of a flag halfway up the staff, as in respect to the dead. —*v.t.* To put, as a flag, at half-mast.

half-moon (haf′mo͞on′, häf′-) *n.* 1 The moon when half its disk is illuminated. 2 Something similar in shape to a half-moon. • See MOON.

half nel·son (nel′sən) A wrestling hold in which one arm is passed below the opponent's armpit and the hand is pressed against the back of his neck.

half note *Music* A note whose duration is half that of a whole note. • See NOTE.

half·pen·ny (hā′pən·ē, hāp′nē) *n. pl.* **half·pence** (hā′pəns) or **half·pen·nies** (hā′pən·ēz, hāp′nēz) A British coin equivalent to one half of a penny. —*adj.* 1 Worth a halfpenny. 2 Trifling in cost or value.

half pint 1 A measure of capacity equal to one half of a pint. 2 *Slang* A small person.

half sister A sister related through only one parent.

half-sole (haf′sōl′, häf′-) *v.t.* **-soled, -sol·ing** To repair by affixing a half sole.

half sole The sole of a shoe, boot, etc., extending from the shank to the toe.

half-staff (haf′staf′, häf′stäf′) *n.* & *v.* HALF-MAST.

half step 1 *Music* A semitone. 2 *Mil.* A step of 15 inches at quick time; in double time, one of 18 inches.

half-tim·bered (haf′tim′bərd, häf′-) *adj.* Built of heavy timbers, with the spaces between filled with masonry or plaster.

half-time (haf′tīm′, häf′-) *n.* An interval of suspended play between the halves of sports contests.

half·tone (haf′tōn′, häf′-) *n.* 1 An illustration obtained by photographing an original through a finely ruled glass screen, the lights and shadows appearing when printed as minute lines or dots. 2 *Music* A semitone. —*adj.* Of, pertaining to, using, or made by the halftone process.

half-track (haf′trak′, häf′-) *adj.* Designating a type of military vehicle propelled by endless tracks, but steered by a pair of wheels in front. —*n.* A half-track vehicle.

half·way (haf′wā′, häf′-) *adv.* At or to half the distance. —*adj.* 1 Midway between two points. 2 Partial; inadequate.

halfway house 1 A place to stop halfway through a journey. 2 A residence where people who have been withdrawn from society, as former drug addicts or prisoners, are prepared to return to an active life.

half-wit (haf′wit′, häf′) *n.* A stupid or foolish person; idiot. —**half′-wit′ted** *adj.* —**Syn.** dolt, imbecile, nitwit, simpleton.

hal·i·but (hal′ə·bət, hol′-) *n. pl.* **·but** or **·buts** Any of various large, edible flatfish of N seas. [< ME *haly* holy + *butte* fish]

Halibut

hal·ide (hal′īd, -id, hā′līd, -lid) *n. Chem.* Any compound of a halogen with an element or radical, as a bromide, chloride, etc. —*adj.* Resembling a halide. Also **hal·id** (hal′id, hā′lid).

hal·i·dom (hal′ə·dəm) *n. Archaic* 1 Holiness. 2 A holy relic. 3 A holy place; sanctuary. [< OE *halig* holy + -DOM]

hal·ite (hal′īt, hā′līt) *n.* Unrefined sodium chloride; rock salt. [< Gk. *hals* salt + -ITE]

hal·i·to·sis (hal′ə·tō′sis) *n.* Malodorous breath. [< L *halitus* breath + -OSIS]

hall (hôl) *n.* 1 A passage or corridor in a building. 2 A small room or enclosure at the entry of a house; a vestibule; lobby. 3 A building or room for public business, entertainments, meetings, etc. 4 In a school, university, or college, a building used as a dormitory, classroom building, laboratory, etc. 5 The meeting place or headquarters of an organization or society; also, the organization itself. 6 *Brit.* A college dining room. 7 The large main room of a castle or other great house. 8 The country residence of a baron, squire, etc. [< OE *heall*]

hal·le·lu·jah (hal′ə·lo͞o′yə) *interj.* Praise ye the Lord! —*n.* A musical composition whose principal theme is found in the word *hallelujah.* Also **hal′le·lu′iah.** [< Heb. *hallēlū* praise + *yāh* Jehovah]

hal·liard (hal′yərd) *n.* HALYARD.

hall·mark (hôl′märk′) *n.* 1 An official mark stamped on gold and silver articles in England to guarantee their purity. 2 Any mark or proof of genuineness. —*v.t.* To stamp with a hallmark. [< Goldsmiths' *Hall,* London, where the assaying and stamping were done + MARK]

hal·loo (hə·lo͞o′) *interj.* 1 An exclamation to attract attention, express surprise, etc. 2 A shout to incite hounds to the chase. —*n.* A cry of "halloo." —*v.i.* 1 To shout "halloo"; cry out. —*v.t.* 2 To incite or encourage with shouts. 3 To shout to; hail. 4 To shout (something). Also **hal·lo, hal·loa** (hə·lō). [< OF *halloer* pursue noisily]

hal·low (hal′ō) *v.t.* 1 To make holy; consecrate. 2 To look upon as holy; reverence. [< OE *halig* holy]

hal·lowed (hal′ōd; *in liturgical use, usu.* hal′ō·id) *adj.* 1 Sacred; holy. 2 Revered as sacred. —**hal′lowed·ness** *n.*

Hal·low·e'en (hal′ō·ēn′) *n.* The evening of Oct. 31, vigil of All Saints' Day, now popularly observed esp. by children by masquerading and playful solicitations for sweets, etc. [< *(All-)hallow(s) e(v)en*]

Hal·low·mass (hal′ō·məs) *n. Archaic* ALL SAINTS' DAY. Also **Hal′low·mas.** [< *(All-)hallow-mass*]

hal·lu·ci·nate (hə·lo͞o′sə·nāt) *v.i.* **·nat·ed, ·nat·ing** 1 To have hallucinations. —*v.t.* 2 To envision or perceive as a hallucination. [< L *hallucinari* wander mentally]

hal·lu·ci·na·tion (hə·lo͞o′sə·nā′shən) *n.* 1 An apparent perception without any corresponding external stimulus. 2 A sense object perceived but not present in reality. —**hal·lu·ci·na·to·ry** (hə·lo͞o′sə·nə·tôr′ē, -tō′rē) *adj.*

hal·lu·ci·no·gen (hə·lo͞o′sin·ə·jən) *n.* Any substance capable of inducing hallucinations. **—hal·lu′ci·no·gen′ic** *adj.*

ha·lo (hā′lō) *n. pl.* **·los** or **·loes 1** A luminous circle around the sun or the moon. **2** A radiance encircling the head in portrayals of sacred personages. **3** The splendor with which imagination surrounds an object of affection or esteem. **—***v.* **·loed, ·lo·ing** *v.t.* **1** To enclose in a halo. **—***v.i.* **2** To form a halo. [< Gk. *halōs*]

hal·o·gen (hal′ə·jən) *n. Chem.* Any of a group of chemically similar elements comprising fluorine, chlorine, bromine, iodine, and astatine. [< Gk. *hals* sea, salt + -GEN] — **ha·log·e·nous** (hə·loj′ə·nəs) *adj.*

hal·oid (hal′oid, hā′loid) *adj.* **1** Resembling sea salt. **2** Pertaining to or derived from a halogen. **—***n.* A haloid salt.

halt[1] (hôlt) *n.* A complete stop of progress, operation, etc. **—call a halt** To put a stop to. **—***v.t. & v.i.* To stop; bring or come to a halt. [< OHG *halten* to stop] **—Syn.** *v.* cease, pause, rest, stay.

halt[2] (hôlt) *v.i.* **1** To be imperfect; proceed lamely. **2** To be in doubt; waver. **3** *Archaic* To walk with a limp. **—***adj. Archaic* Crippled; limping in gait. **—***n. Archaic* Lameness. **—the halt** Those who are crippled. [< OE *healt* lame] — **halt′ing·ly** *adv.* **—halt′ing·ness** *n.*

hal·ter (hôl′tər) *n.* **1** A strap or rope by which to hold or lead a horse or other animal. **2** A hangman's rope. **3** Execution by hanging. **4** A woman's blouse designed for exposing the back and arms to the sun, fastened around the neck and waist. **—***v.t.* To secure with a halter. [< OE *hælftre*]

halve (hav, häv) *v.t.* **halved, halv·ing 1** To divide into two equal parts; share equally. **2** To take away half of. **3** In golf, to play (a match or hole) in the same number of strokes as one's opponent. [< HALF]

halves (havz, hävz) *n.pl.* of HALF.

hal·yard (hal′yərd) *n. Naut.* A rope for hoisting or lowering a sail, a flag, etc. [< HALE[1]]

ham (ham) *n.* **1** The thigh of a hog, smoked, salted, etc., for food. **2** *pl.* The buttocks. **3** The space or region behind the knee joint; the hock of quadrupeds. **4** *Slang* A performer who overacts. **5** An amateur radio operator. **—***v.t.* **hammed, ham·ming** *Slang* To overact; use exaggerated speech and gestures: often in the expression **ham it up.** [< OE *hamm*] **—ham′my** *adj.* **(·i·er, ·i·est)**

Ham (ham) In the Bible, the youngest son of Noah.

ham·a·dry·ad (ham′ə·drī′əd, -ad) *n. pl.* **·ads** or **·a·des** (-ə·dēz) *Gk. Myth.* A wood nymph whose life was connected with that of the tree she inhabited. [< Gk. *hama* together with + *drys* oak tree]

ham·burg (ham′bûrg) *n.* Hamburger. Also **hamburg steak.**

ham·burg·er (ham′bûr′gər) *n.* **1** Finely ground beef. **2** Such meat fried or broiled in the form of a patty. Also **hamburger steak. 3** A sandwich consisting of such meat placed in a bun. [< *Hamburg,* Germany]

Ham·ite (ham′īt) *n.* **1** One alleged to be a descendant of Ham. **2** A member of the Caucasoid ethnic stock originating in NE Africa and the Canary Islands.

Ha·mit·ic (ha·mit′ik) *adj.* Of or pertaining to Ham, or the Hamites, or their languages. **—***n.* A North African group of languages including ancient Egyptian, extinct Libyan, and the modern Berber dialects and the Cushitic languages of Ethiopia and Somaliland.

ham·let (ham′lit) *n.* A little village; a cluster of houses in the country. [< OF *hamelet*]

Ham·let (ham′lit) *n.* **1** One of Shakespeare's best-known tragedies. **2** The hero of this play.

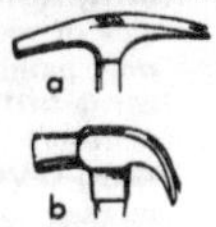

Hammers
a. tack.
b. claw.

ham·mer (ham′ər) *n.* **1** A hand tool with a head at right angles to the handle, used for driving nails, pounding, etc. **2** A machine or part of a machine performing functions similar to those of a heavy hand hammer. **3** That part of a gunlock which strikes the cap or cartridge. • See REVOLVER. **4** A padded piece that strikes the string of a piano. **5** An auctioneer's mallet. **6** *Anat.* The malleus of the middle ear. **—under the hammer** For sale at auction. **—***v.t.* **1** To strike with or as with a hammer; drive, as a nail. **2** To shape or fasten with a hammer. **3** To form or force as if with hammer blows. **—***v.i.* **4** To strike blows with or as with a hammer. [< OE *hamer*] **—ham′mer·er** *n.* **—Syn** *v.* **1** bang, beat, pound, whack.

ham·mer·head (ham′ər·hed′) *n.* A voracious shark of warm seas, having a transversely elongated head like that of a hammer with the eyes at each end.

ham·mer·lock (ham′ər·lok′) *n.* A wrestling grip in which the arm is twisted behind the back and upwards.

ham·mock (ham′ək) *n.* A couch of canvas or netting, swung from supports at both ends. [Sp. *hamaca*]

ham·per[1] (ham′pər) *v.t.* To hinder the movements of: restrain. [ME *hampren*]

ham·per[2] (ham′pər) *n.* A large covered basket, as for food, laundry, etc. [< OF *hanapier*]

ham·ster (ham′stər) *n.* A small burrowing rodent often kept as a pet or for laboratory experiments. [< OHG *hamustro*]

ham·string (ham′string′) *n.* A tendon at the back of the human knee or at the back of the hock of a quadruped. **—***v.t.* **·strung, ·string·ing 1** To cut the hamstring of; cripple. **2** To make ineffective or helpless.

hand (hand) *n.* **1** The part of the human forelimb that is attached to the forearm below the wrist, used for holding and grasping. **2** The corresponding segment of a limb in apes, etc. **3** Side or direction: She sat at his right *hand.* **4** A role in doing something: They all had a *hand* in it. **5** *pl.* Possession; control: It is in your *hands* now. **6** Aid; assistance: to lend a *hand.* **7** A pledge of betrothal, or a giving in marriage. **8** A manual laborer. **9** A person as the performer of an action: a book written by many *hands.* **10** A person with reference to his ability: a good *hand* with children. **11** Skill; ability; touch. **12** A specified remove from a source: a story heard at second *hand.* **13** *pl.* The members of a group. **14** The cards held by a player at one deal; also, the player. **15** The playing of the cards at one deal. **16** Clapping of hands; applause. **17** Handwriting. **18** A person's signature. **19** The pointer of a clock or watch. **20** Four inches, the approximate width of the hand, used as a measure for the height of horses, etc. **—a great hand at** or **for** A person specially fond of or clever at. **—at first hand** At the source. **—at hand** Within reach; convenient. **—at the hand of** From the hand of; by the operation of. **—by hand** With the hands only: a dress made *by hand.* **—have one's hands full** To have all or more than one can do. **—in hand 1** In one's possession. **2** In process of being done. **3** Entirely under control. **—off one's hands** Out of one's care or control. **—on hand 1** In present or rightful possession. **2** In place; present. **—on one's hands** In one's care; under one's responsibility **—on the other hand** Looking at the opposed point of view. **—out of hand 1** Unruly; lawless. **2** Immediately; without delay. — **wash one's hands of** To dismiss from consideration. — *v.t.* **1** To give, pass, or deliver with or as with the hand. **2** To lead or help with the hand. **—hand down 1** To transmit, as to one's successors. **2** To deliver, as the decision of a court. **—hand it to** *Slang* To acknowledge the abilities, success, etc., of. **—hand on** To pass on; transmit. **—hand out** To mete out; distribute. **—hand over** To give up possession of; surrender. [< OE]

hand·bag (hand′bag′) *n.* **1** A bag or purse for personal articles, as a wallet, cosmetics, etc., carried by women. **2** A small suitcase.

hand·ball (hand′bôl′) *n.* **1** A game in which a ball is struck with the hand and kept bounding against a wall. **2** The rubber ball used in this game.

hand·bar·row (hand′bar′ō) *n.* **1** A litter or stretcher, carried by two handles at each end. **2** A wheelbarrow.

hand·bill (hand′bil′) *n.* A small advertising sheet or notice, usu. distributed by hand.

hand·book (hand′bo͝ok′) *n.* A guidebook or reference manual of a size small enough to be carried about.

hand·breadth (hand′bredth′) *n.* The breadth of the hand; a palm. Also **hand's′-breadth′** (handz′-).

---

hand cart A cart pushed by hand.
hand·clasp (hand′klasp′, -kläsp′) *n.* A clasping of a person's hand in greeting, agreement, farewell, etc.
hand·cuff (hand′kuf′) *n.* One of two manacles connected by a chain, and designed to be locked around the wrists. —*v.t.* To put handcuffs on; manacle.

Handcuffs

hand·ed (han′did) *adj.* 1 Having hands. 2 Having a specific type or number of hands: used in combination: *right-handed.*
hand·ful (hand′fo͝ol) *n. pl.* **hand·fuls** 1 As much as a hand can hold at once. 2 A small quantity. 3 *Informal* Something or someone hard to handle.
hand·gun (hand′gun′) *n.* A firearm held and fired in one hand, as a pistol.
hand·i·cap (han′dē·kap′) *n.* 1 A condition imposed to equalize the chances of competitors in a contest. 2 A race or contest in which such conditions are imposed. 3 A disadvantage or hindrance. —*v.t.* **·capped, ·cap·ping** 1 To impose a handicap on. 2 To be a handicap to. [<*hand in cap,* a lottery game in which winners were penalized] —**hand′i·cap′per** *n.* —**Syn.** *n.* 3 burden, encumbrance, impediment, shortcoming.
hand·i·craft (han′dē·kraft′, -kräft′) *n.* 1 Skill and expertness in working with the hands. 2 A trade or craft calling for such skill. [<HAND + CRAFT]
hand·i·work (han′dē·wûrk′) *n.* 1 Work done by the hands. 2 Work done by one's self. 3 The outcome of one's undertakings.
hand·ker·chief (hang′kər·chif) *n.* 1 A small, square piece of soft cloth for wiping the face or nose. 2 A neckerchief.
han·dle (han′dəl) *v.* **han·dled, han·dling** *v.t.* 1 To touch, feel, etc., with the hands. 2 To manage or use with the hands. 3 To manage or direct; control. 4 To deal with: to *handle* a disagreement. 5 To trade or deal in: to *handle* cotton. 6 To act toward; treat. —*v.i.* 7 To respond to handling. —*n.* That part of an object intended to be grasped with the hand. —**fly off the handle** To be suddenly and unreasonably angry. [<OE *handlian*]
han·dle·bar (han′dəl·bär′) *n.* 1 A bent bar with grips on both ends, used in steering a bicycle, motorcycle, etc. 2 *pl. Informal* A long curved mustache.
han·dler (hand′lər) *n.* 1 One who or that which handles, esp. one who trains certain animals. 2 The trainer of a boxer, wrestler, etc.
hand-made (hand′mād′) *adj.* Made by hand or by hand tools.
hand·maid (hand′mād′) *n.* A female servant or attendant. Also **hand′maid′en.**
hand-me-down (hand′mē·doun′) *Informal adj.* Passed on to another after use; secondhand. —*n.* A hand-me-down garment.
hand organ A device that produces music when a hand crank is turned.
hand-out (hand′out′) *n. Informal* 1 Anything given to a beggar. 2 Anything given with little or no expectation of return. 3 A printed press release distributed to reporters.
hand-picked (hand′pikt′) *adj.* Picked or selected with special care.
hand·rail (hand′rāl′) *n.* A rail that can be grasped by the hand, as at the edge of a balcony or stairway.
hand·saw (hand′sô′) *n.* A saw wielded with one hand.
hand·sel (hand′səl, han′-) *n.* 1 A gift as a token of good will or to secure good luck. 2 Money given as a gift at New Year's. —*v.t.* **·seled** or **·selled, ·sel·ing** or **·sel·ling** To give handsel to. [<ON *hand* hand + *sal* gift]
hand·set (hand′set′) *n.* A telephone mouthpiece and receiver placed at opposite ends of a single unit.
hand·shake (hand′shāk′) *n.* A clasping and shaking of a person's hand, as in greeting.
hand·some (han′səm) *adj.* 1 Agreeable to the eye or to good taste; of pleasing aspect. 2 Of liberal dimensions or proportions. 3 Marked by generosity or liberality. [<HAND + -SOME, orig. with sense "easy to handle"] —**hand′some·ly** *adv.* —**hand′some·ness** *n.*
hands-on (handz′on′, -ôn′) *adj.* Designating an action that requires active participation: *hands-on* techniques.
hand·spike (hand′spīk′) *n.* A bar used as a lever.
hand·spring (hand′spring′) *n.* A stunt in which the performer flips forward or backward from an upright position, landing first on the hands and then on the feet.
hand-to-hand (han′tə·hand′) *adj.* At close quarters: a *hand-to-hand* fight.
hand-to-mouth (han′tə·mouth′) *adj.* Being at or below the subsistence level, with nothing to spare: a *hand-to-mouth* existence.
hand·work (hand′wûrk′) *n.* Work done by hand.
hand·writ·ing (hand′rī′ting) *n.* 1 The form of writing peculiar to a given person. 2 Penmanship. 3 Matter written by hand with a pencil, pen, etc.
hand·y (han′dē) *adj.* **hand·i·er, hand·i·est** 1 Ready at hand or convenient for use; nearby. 2 Skillful with the hands. 3 Easy to handle: said of a ship or a tool. —**hand′i·ly** *adv.* —**hand′i·ness** *n.*
han·dy·man (han′dē·man′) *n. pl.* **·men** (-mən) One good at odd jobs
hang (hang) *v.* **hung** or *(esp. for v. defs. 3 & 9)* **hanged, hang·ing** *v.t.* 1 To fasten to something above; suspend. 2 To attach, so as to allow some motion. 3 To execute on a gallows. 4 To cover or furnish by something suspended. 5 To fasten in position or at the correct angle. 6 To cause a deadlock, as in a jury's vote. —*v.i.* 7 To be suspended; dangle. 8 To be suspended without visible support; float. 9 To be put to death on the gallows. 10 To project out; overhang. 11 To droop; incline downward. 12 To be imminent or impending. 13 To be dependent or contingent. 14 To be uncertain or in doubt. 15 To attend closely: to *hang* on someone's words. 16 To be or remain in deadlock, as a jury. —**hang around** (or **about**) 1 To linger or loiter. 2 To group around. —**hang back** To be reluctant. —**hang fire** 1 To fail to fire promptly, as a firearm. 2 To be delayed. —**hang in** *Slang* To stay; persevere; hold on. —**hang out** 1 To lean out. 2 To suspend out in the open. 3 *Slang* To reside or spend one's time: usu. with *at* or *in.* —**hang together** 1 To stay together. 2 To be coherent or consistent. —**hang up** 1 To place on hooks or hangers. 2 To end a telephone call by replacing the receiver. 3 To become caught or jammed, as a machine part. 4 To delay or suspend. —*n.* 1 The way a thing hangs. 2 *Informal* Familiar knowledge; knack. 3 A bit: I don't care a *hang.* —**get the hang of** *Informal* To come to understand or be able to do. [<OE *hangian* hang down and *hon* suspend and ON *hanga*] • *Hanged* and *hung* are the two past tenses and past participles of *hang,* and each has a distinct meaning. Criminals are *hanged.* Pictures, curtains, etc., are *hung.*
han·gar (hang′ər, -gär) *n.* A shelter or shed, esp. for aircraft. [F]
hang·dog (hang′dôg′, -dog′) *adj.* Of mean, sneaking, or abject appearance. —*n.* A skulking person; sneak.
hang·er (hang′ər) *n.* 1 One who hangs things. 2 A device on which something is hung. 3 A shaped frame on which a garment is suspended or draped.
hang·er-on (hang′ər·on′) *n. pl.* **hang·ers-on** A self-attached dependent; parasite.
hang·ing (hang′ing) *adj.* 1 Suspended from something; dangling. 2 Involving death on the gallows. 3 Lying on a slope: a *hanging* garden. 4 Drooping and dejected. 5 Held in abeyance. —*n.* 1 The act of suspending. 2 Execution on the gallows. 3 Drapery, tapestry, etc., hung from a wall.
hang·man (hang′mən) *n. pl.* **·men** (-mən) A public executioner.
hang·nail (hang′nāl′) *n.* Skin partially torn loose at the side or root of a fingernail. [Var. of earlier *agnail* <OE *ang-* painful + *nægl* NAIL]
hang·out (hang′out′) *n. Slang* A habitual meeting place or resort.
hang·o·ver (hang′ō′vər) *n. Informal* 1 A person, thing, or idea surviving from the past. 2 The aftereffects from overindulgence in alcohol.
hang-up (hang′up′) *n. Slang* 1 A psychological difficulty; esp., a neurotic obsession. 2 Anything blocking a natural or normal process.
hank (hangk) *n.* 1 A measure of yarn, varying for different materials. 2 A rope, string, coil, or tie. [<Scand.]
han·ker (hang′kər) *v.i.* To yearn; want greatly. [<Du. *hankeren* long for] —**han′ker·er** *n.*

han·ky-pan·ky (hang′kē-pang′kē) *n. Slang* Underhanded activity; deception.

Han·sard (han′sərd) *n.* The printed record of the proceedings of the British and Canadian Parliaments. [<Luke *Hansard,* 1752–1828, Brit. printer]

hanse (hans) *n.* **1** A guild of medieval merchants. **2** An entrance fee; esp., one paid by merchants not members of a guild. **—the Hanse** HANSEATIC LEAGUE. [<OHG *hansa* band]

Han·se·at·ic League (han′sē·at′ic) A league of about 85 towns and cities in northern Germany and neighboring countries, called **Hanse towns,** which banded together in the Middle Ages for protection and trade.

han·sel (han′səl) *n. & v.* HANDSEL.

Han·sen's disease (han′sənz) LEPROSY.

han·som (han′səm) *n.* A low, two-wheeled, one-horse cab, with the driver mounted back of the top. Also **hansom cab.** [<J. A. *Hansom,* 1803–82, English architect]

Hansom

Ha·nuk·kah (khä′·nōō·kə) *n.* A Jewish festival occurring in early December, in memory of the rededication of the temple at Jerusalem under the Maccabees in 164 B.C. Also **Ha′nu·kah** [<Heb., dedication]

hap·haz·ard (hap′haz′ərd) *adj.* Accidental; happening by chance. *—adv.* By chance; at random. *—n.* Mere chance; hazard. [<HAP + HAZARD] **—hap′haz′ard·ly** *adv.* **—hap′haz′ard·ness** *n.*

hap·less (hap′lis) *adj.* Unfortunate; unlucky. **—hap′·less·ly** *adv.* **—hap′less·ness** *n.*

hap·pen (hap′ən) *v.i.* **1** To take place or occur. **2** To come about or occur by chance. **3** To chance; have the fortune. **4** To come by chance: to *happen* upon the answer. **5** To come or go by chance: with *in, along, by,* etc. **—happen to 1** To befall. **2** To become of. [<HAP]

hap·pen·ing (hap′ən·ing) *n.* **1** Something that happens; an event. **2** A staged but usu. partly improvised event, often bizarre, intended to elicit a response.

hap·pen·stance (hap′ən·stans, -stəns) *n. Informal* A chance occurrence. [<HAPPEN + (CIRCUM)STANCE]

hap·py (hap′ē) *adj.* **·pi·er, ·pi·est 1** Enjoying, giving, or indicating pleasure; joyous; blessed. **2** Fortunately effective; opportune; felicitous. **3** Yielding or marked by great pleasure. [<HAP] **—hap′pi·ly** *adv.* **—hap′pi·ness** *n.*

hap·py-go-luck·y (hap′ē·gō·luk′ē) *adj.* Trusting easily to luck; improvident; haphazard. *—adv.* As one pleases; anyhow; at will.

Haps·burg (haps′bûrg; *Ger.* häps′bōōrkh) *n.* A German family whose princes ruled over various parts of Europe from the Middle Ages to 1918. Also **House of Hapsburg.**

ha·ra-ki·ri (hä′rä·kē′rē) *n.* Ritual suicide by disembowelment, practiced by high-ranking Japanese when disgraced or in lieu of execution. Also **ha′ra-ka′ri** (-kä′rē). [<Jap. *hara* belly + *kiri* cut]

ha·rangue (hə·rang′) *n.* An oration; esp., a loud and vehement speech. *—v.* **·rangued, ·rangu·ing** *v.t.* To address in a harangue. *—v.i.* To deliver a harangue. [<OF] **—ha·rangu′er** *n.*

har·ass (har′əs, hə·ras′) *v.t.* **1** To trouble or worry persistently. **2** *Mil.* To worry (an enemy) by repeated raids and small attacks. [<OF *harer* set dogs on] **—har′ass·er, har′ass·ment** *n.* **—Syn. 1** annoy, bother, disturb, plague, torment.

har·bin·ger (här′bin·jər) *n.* A forerunner and announcer of something to come. *—v.t.* To act as a harbinger to; presage [<OF **herbergeor** provider of shelter]

har·bor (här′bər) *n.* **1** A port or haven that provides shelter for ships. **2** Any place of refuge or rest. *—v.t.* **1** To give refuge to; shelter; protect. **2** To entertain in the mind; cherish. *—v.i.* **3** To take shelter in a habor. *Brit. sp.* **har′bour.** [<OE *here* army + *beorg* refuge] **—har′bor·er** *n.*

har·bor·age (här′bər′ij) *n.* **1** A port or place of shelter for ships. **2** Any shelter or refuge.

har·bor·mas·ter (här′bər·mas′tər, -mäs′-) *n.* **1** An officer who inspects vessels in harbor. **2** The chief of the harbor police.

hard (härd) *adj.* **1** Solid and firm; not easily dented. **2** Capable of endurance; hardy. **3** Difficult to accomplish or solve. **4** Unyielding; hardhearted. **5** Harsh or cruel: *hard* words. **6** Shrewd and obstinate. **7** Oppressive; difficult to endure. **8** Rigorous in terms: a *hard* bargain. **9** Persistent or energetic: a *hard* worker. **10** Harsh or unpleasant: a *hard* face. **11** Stormy; inclement: a *hard* winter. **12** Indisputable; definite: *hard* facts. **13** Strictly factual: *hard* news. **14** Having mineral salts in solution that interfere with the action of soap: *hard* water. **15** Containing much alcohol: *hard* liquor. **16** Addictive: said of drugs. **17** *Phonet.* Denoting *c* or *g* when pronounced explosively, as in *cod* or *god,* rather than as a fricative or an affricate. **—be hard on 1** To treat with severity. **2** To be burdensome or difficult for. **—hard of hearing** Deaf or partially deaf. **—hard up** Completely lacking in something, esp. money. *—adv.* **1** With great energy; vigorously. **2** Intently; earnestly. **3** Harshly or severely. **4** With effort or difficulty. **5** Securely; tightly. **6** So as to become hard: It was frozen *hard.* **7** In close proximity: We live *hard* by the church. [<OE *heard*] **—hard′ness** *n.*

hard-and-fast (härd′ən·fast′, -fäst′) *adj.* Absolutely binding: a *hard-and-fast* rule.

hard·back (härd′bak′) *adj* HARD-COVER. *—n.* A hard-cover book.

hard-bit·ten (härd′bit′n) *adj.* Tough; unyielding.

hard·board (härd′bôrd′, -bōrd′) *n.* A material composed of fibers from wood chips pressed into sheets.

hard-boiled (härd′boild′) *adj.* **1** Boiled until solidified: said of an egg. **2** *Informal* Hardened or unyielding in character; tough.

hard cash Actual money as distinguished from debts or claims to be collected or settled.

hard coal ANTHRACITE.

hard-core (härd′kôr′) *adj.* **1** Thoroughly dedicated, determined, loyal, etc., to a cause or movement: *hard-core* radicals. **2** Extremely explicit: *hard-core* pornography. **3** Of or pertaining to the hard core.

hard core 1 The basic, central, or most important part; nucleus. **2** Unemployed or underemployed people not trained for any job.

hard-cov·er (hard′kuv′ər) *adj.* Designating a book bound in a rigid material. Also **hard′bound′.**

hard disk A nonflexible computer disk, capable of more information storage and faster read-write capability than a floppy disk.

hard·en (här′dən) *v.t.* **1** To make hard or harder; make solid. **2** To make unyielding, pitiless, or indifferent. **3** To strengthen or make firm in character, disposition, etc. **4** To make tough, strong, or hardy; inure. *—v.i.* **5** To become hard. **6** In commerce: **a** To become higher, as prices. **b** To become stable. **—hard′en·er** *n.*

hard·fist·ed (härd′fis′tid) *adj.* Avaricious or miserly; stingy. **—hard′fist′ed·ly** *adv.* **—hard′fist′ed·ness** *n.*

hard-hat (härd′hat′) *Informal n.* A construction worker. *—adj.* Having to do with construction work and workers.

hard hat Any of various helmets worn for protection, as by construction workers, motorcyclists, etc. • See HELMET.

hard·head·ed (härd′hed′id) *adj.* **1** Shrewd and practical. **2** Inclined to obstinacy; stubborn. **—hard′head′ed·ly** *adv.* **—hard′head′ed·ness** *n.*

hard·heart·ed (härd′här′tid) *adj.* Lacking pity or sympathy; unfeeling. **—hard′heart′ed·ly** *adv.* **—hard′heart′ed·ness** *n.*

har·di·hood (här′dē·hŏŏd) *n.* **1** Sturdy courage. **2** Boldness; effrontery.

hard line An unyielding position, as in negotiation. **—hard′-line′** *adj.* **—hard′-lin′er** *n.*

hard·ly (härd′lē) *adv.* **1** Scarcely; not quite or only just: He'd *hardly* arrived before we left. **2** With difficulty or great pains. 3 Not likely; not at all: Are you new on the job? *Hardly!* 4 Rigorously; harshly; severely.

hard-nosed (härd′nōzd′) *adj.* *Slang* Hard-bitten, unyielding, or firmly businesslike.

hard palate The hard front portion of the roof of the mouth. • See MOUTH.

hard·pan (härd′pan′) *n.* 1 Hard clay or soil under soft soil. 2 A firm foundation; solid basis.

hard sauce A creamed mixture of butter, sugar, and flavorings, used as a sauce with puddings, etc.

hard sell *Informal* The use of aggressive methods of salesmanship.

hard·shell (härd′shel′) *adj.* 1 Having a hard shell, as a lobster or crab, previous to shedding the carapace. 2 Stubbornly devoted to one's principles; uncompromising.

hard·ship (härd′ship) *n.* 1 A difficult condition in life. 2 Anything hard to endure.

hard·tack (härd′tak′) *n.* Large, unleavened biscuit used as army and navy rations. [< HARD + earlier *tack* food]

hard·top (härd′top′) *adj.* Describing an automobile with the body design of a convertible, but with a rigid top. —*n.* Such a car.

hard·ware (härd′wâr′) *n.* 1 Manufactured articles, esp. of metal, as machines, utensils, tools, weapons, etc. 2 The machines and equipment needed for a task or function, esp. in data processing, as distinct from personnel, plans, programs, etc. 3 *Informal* Weapons: military *hardware.*

hard·wood (härd′wo͝od′) *n.* 1 Wood of broad-leaved trees as distinguished from that of coniferous trees. 2 Any tough, heavy wood. 3 A tree yielding hardwood.

hard-working (härd′wôrk′ing, härd′wôrk′-) *adj.* Accustomed to working hard; industrious.

har·dy (här′dē) *adj.* **·di·er, ·di·est** 1 Inured to hardship; robust. 2 Showing hardihood; bold; audacious; strenuous. 3 Able to survive cold weather without protection: said of plants. 4 Rigid; strong; durable. [< OF *hardir* embolden] —**har′di·ly** *adv.* —**har′di·ness** *n.*

hare (hâr) *n. pl.* **hares** or **hare** Any of various long-eared, herbivorous mammals closely related to rabbits, but larger and swifter. [< OE *hara*]

Hare

hare·bell (hâr′bel′) *n.* A hardy, widely distributed species of campanula; bluebell. [ME *harebelle*]

hare·brained (hâr′brānd′) *adj.* Foolish; flighty.

hare·lip (hâr′lip′) *n.* A congenital fissure of the upper lip. —**hare′lipped′** *adj.*

har·em (hâr′əm, har′-) *n.* 1 The apartments of a Muslim household reserved for females. 2 The wives, concubines, etc., occupying the harem. Also **ha·reem** (hä·rēm′). [Ar. *harīm* something forbidden or sacred]

har·i·cot (har′ə·kō) *n.* 1 A stew of meat, esp. mutton. 2 The seeds or pods of edible beans; also, the kidney bean. [F]

ha·ri-ka·ri (hä′rē·kä′rē) *n.* HARA-KIRI.

hark (härk) *v.i.* To listen: usu. in the imperative. —**hark back** To return to some previous place or point. [ME *herkien*]

hark·en (här′kən) *v.* HEARKEN. —**hark′en·er** *n.*

har·le·quin (här′lə·kwin, -kin) *n.* A buffoon. —*adj.* 1 Comic; buffoonlike. 2 Many-colored, usu. in a diamond pattern. [< OF *Herlequin*]

Har·le·quin (här′lə·kwin, -kin) *n.* A traditional comic character in pantomime, dressed in many-colored tights, wearing a mask, and carrying a wooden sword.

har·lot (här′lət) *n.* A whore; prostitute. [< OF *herlot* fellow, rogue]

har·lot·ry (här′lət·rē) *n.* 1 The trade of a prostitute. 2 Prostitutes collectively.

harm (härm) *n.* 1 That which inflicts injury or loss. 2 The injury inflicted; hurt. 3 Offense against morality; wrong. —*v.t.* To damage; hurt. [< OE *hearm* insult] —**harm′er** *n.* —**Syn.** *n.* 1 blemish, detriment, impairment, abuse.

harm·ful (härm′fəl) *adj.* Able to injure; detrimental. —**harm′ful·ly** *adv.* —**harm′ful·ness** *n.*

harm·less (härm′lis) *adj.* 1 Not harmful; innocuous. 2 Without hurt, loss, or liability. —**harm′less·ly** *adv.* —**harm′less·ness** *n.*

har·mon·ic (här·mon′ik) *adj.* 1 Producing, characterized by, or pertaining to harmony; consonant. 2 *Music* Pertaining to harmony, as distinguished from melody or rhythm. 3 *Physics* Of or pertaining to a component of a periodic quantity whose frequency is an integral multiple of that of the periodic quantity. —*n.* 1 *Physics* **a** Any component of a periodic oscillation whose frequency is an integral multiple of the fundamental frequency. **b** A component of a complex tone having such a frequency. 2 *Music* An overtone, usu. with a harmonic frequency, sounded alone, as by lightly stopping a string. Also **har·mon′i·cal.** [< Gk. *harmonia* harmony] —**har·mon′i·cal·ly** *adv.*

har·mon·i·ca (här·mon′i·kə) *n.* 1 A musical instrument played by blowing through slots containing small metal reeds; a mouth organ. 2 An instrument composed of a series of hemispherical glasses, glass bowls or tubes, etc., played by rubbing the moistened rims with a finger. [< L *harmonicus* harmonic]

Harmonica

harmonic distortion A form of distortion, as in an amplifier, loudspeaker, etc., in which extraneous harmonics are added to the signal.

har·mo·ni·ous (här·mō′nē·əs) *adj.* 1 Characterized by harmony or agreement; in accord. 2 Having the parts pleasingly related; symmetrical, congruous. 3 Pleasing to the ear. —**har·mo′ni·ous·ly** *adv.* —**har·mo′ni·ous·ness** *n.*

har·mo·nist (här′mə·nist) *n.* A master of musical harmony.

har·mo·ni·um (här·mō′nē·əm) *n.* REED ORGAN. [< L *harmonia* harmony]

har·mo·nize (här′mə·nīz) *v.t.* & *v.i.* **·nized, ·niz·ing** 1 To make or become harmonious or suitable. 2 To arrange or sing in musical harmony. *Brit. sp.* **har′mo·nise.** —**har′mo·ni·za′tion, har′mo·niz′er** *n.*

har·mo·ny (här′mə·nē) *n. pl.* **·nies** 1 Accord or agreement in feeling, manner, or action. 2 A state of order, agreement, or completeness in the relations of parts of a whole to each other. 3 Pleasing sounds; music. 4 *Music* **a** Any agreeable combination of simultaneous tones. **b** The constitution and succession of groups of tones that sound simultaneously in music. [< Gk. *harmonia* < *harmos* joint]

har·ness (här′nis) *n.* 1 The combination of traces, straps, etc., forming the gear of a draft animal and used to attach it to a vehicle or plow. 2 *Archaic* The defensive armor of a soldier or of his horse. 3 Any similar apparatus or gear. —**in harness** Engaged in one's daily work. —*v.t.* 1 To put harness on, as a horse. 2 To make use of the power of: to *harness* a waterfall. [< OF *harneis*]

harp (harp) *n.* 1 A musical instrument consisting of a roughly triangular frame fitted with strings of graded lengths and played by plucking. 2 Something resembling a harp. —*v.i.* 1 To play on a harp. 2 To speak or write persistently; dwell tediously: with *on* or *upon.* [< OE *hearpe*] —**harp′er, harp′ist** *n.*

Harp

har·poon (här·po͞on′) *n.* A barbed missile weapon, carrying a long cord, for catching whales or large fish. —*v.t.* To strike with a harpoon. [< OF *harpe* claw] —**har·poon′er, har·poon·eer′** (-ir′) *n.*

harp·si·chord (härp′sə·kôrd) *n.* A keyboard instrument similar to a piano, but having the strings plucked by quills or leather points instead of being struck by felt-covered hammers. [< LL *harpa* harp + L *chorda* string] —**harp′si·chord·ist** *n.*

har·py (här′pē) *n. pl.* **·pies** A rapacious person; a plunderer. [< HARPY]

Har·py (här′pē) *n. pl.* **·pies** *Gk. Myth.* One of three winged monsters with the head of a woman and the legs and talons of a bird. [< Gk. *Harpyia*, lit., seizers]

har·que·bus (här′kwə·bəs) *n.* An ancient hand firearm, the predecessor of the musket. [< MDu. *hakebusse* hook-gun] **—har′que·bus·ier′** (-ir′) *n.*

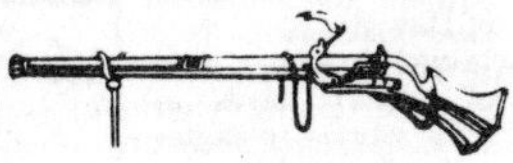

Harquebus

har·ri·dan (har′ə·dən) *n.* A vixenish old woman; a hag. [< OF *haridelle* a worn-out horse]

har·ri·er[1] (har′ē·ər) *n.* **1** One who or that which harries. **2** Any of various hawks, esp. the marsh hawk.

har·ri·er[2] (har′ē·ər) *n.* **1** A small hound used for hunting hares. **2** A team runner in a cross-country race. [< HARE]

har·row (har′ō) *n.* A farm implement, commonly a frame set with spikes or vertical disks, for leveling plowed ground or breaking clods. *—v.t.* **1** To draw a harrow over. **2** To disturb the mind or feelings of painfully; distress. *—v.i.* **3** To undergo harrowing. [ME *harwe*] **—har′row·er** *n.* **—Syn.** *v.* **2** oppress, torment, worry. • See DISK HARROW.

har·row·ing (har′ō·ing) *adj.* Lacerating or tormenting to the feelings. **—har′row·ing·ly** *adv.*

har·ry (har′ē) *v.* **har·ried, har·ry·ing** *v.t.* **1** To lay waste; pillage; sack. **2** To harass. *—v.i.* **3** To make raids for plunder. [< OE *hergian* ravage]

harsh (härsh) *adj.* **1** Grating or rough to the senses; discordant; rasping. **2** Rigorous; severe; unfeeling: a *harsh* judge. **3** Bleak in appearance: a *harsh* landscape. [ME *harsk*] **—harsh′ly** *adv.* **—harsh′ness** *n.*

hart (härt) *n.* **1** The male of the European red deer, esp. after it has passed its fifth year. **2** A stag. [< OE *heort*]

harte·beest (härt′bēst′, här′tə-) *n. pl.* **·beests** or **·beest** A large antelope of Africa with long, backward-curving horns. Also **hart′beest.** [< Du. *hert* hart + *beest* beast]

harts·horn (härts′hôrn′) *n.* **1** Sal volatile, formerly obtained from deer horns. **2** The antler of a hart.

har·um-scar·um (hâr′əm·skâr′əm) *adj.* Reckless; irresponsible. *—adv.* In a reckless manner. *—n.* A reckless or thoughtless person. [< obs. *hare* frighten + SCARE]

har·vest (här′vist) *n.* **1** A crop, as of grain, vegetables, fruits, etc., ready for gathering. **2** The time or season of gathering. **3** The act of gathering in a crop. **4** The product of any toil or effort. *—v.t.* **1** To gather (a crop). **2** To gather the crop of (a field, etc.). **3** To achieve as a result of preparation and effort. *—v.i.* **4** To gather a crop. [< OE *hærfest*]

har·vest·er (här′vis·tər) *n.* **1** One who harvests. **2** A reaping machine.

har·vest·man (här′vist·mən) *n. pl.* **·men** (-mən) **1** One who labors in the harvest. **2** DADDY-LONGLEGS.

harvest moon The full moon closest to the autumnal equinox.

has (haz) Present indicative, third person sing. of HAVE.

has-been (haz′bin′) *n. Informal* A person or thing no longer popular or effective.

hash (hash) *n.* **1** A dish of chopped and cooked meat and vegetables, usu. fried. **2** A mess; jumble. **3** Any mixture. **4** *Slang* Hashish. **—make a hash of** *Informal* To bungle; spoil. **—settle (one's) hash** *Informal* To silence, finish off, or put down (a person). *—v.t.* To cut or chop into small pieces; mince. **—hash over** *Informal* To talk or think about carefully; mull. [< OF *hacher* to chop]

hash house *Slang* A cheap restaurant.

hash·ish (häsh′ēsh, -ish) *n.* The extracted resin of the Indian hemp plant, chewed or smoked for its intoxicating effects. Also **hash′eesh.** [< Ar. *hashīsh* hemp]

Has·i·dim (khä·sē′dim) *n. pl.* of **Has·id** (khä′sid) CHASSIDIM.

has·n't (haz′ənt) Contraction of *has not.*

hasp (hasp, häsp) *n.* A fastening for a door, box, etc., passing over a staple and secured usu. by a padlock. *—v.t.* To shut or fasten with a hasp. [< OE *hæpse*]

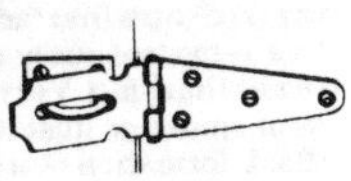

Hasp

has·sle (has′əl) *Slang n.* A quarrel; squabble. *—v.i.* **·sled, ·sling 1** To argue. *—v.t.* **2** To annoy; harass. [? < HAGGLE + TUSSLE]

has·sock (has′ək) *n.* **1** An upholstered footstool. **2** A rank tuft of coarse or boggy grass. [< OE *hassuc* coarse grass]

hast (hast) Archaic second person singular, present tense, of HAVE.

haste (hāst) *n.* **1** Speed of movement or action; dispatch. **2** Necessity for speed; urgency. **3** Hurry; precipitancy. **—in haste 1** Quickly. **2** Thoughtlessly; rashly. **—make haste** To hurry; rush. *—v.t. & v.i.* **hast·ed, hast·ing** *Archaic* To hasten. [< OF < Gmc.]

hast·en (hā′sən) *v.t.* To cause to hurry or move quickly; expedite. *—v.i.* To be quick; hurry. **—hast′en·er** *n.*

hast·y (hās′tē) *adj.* **hast·i·er, hast·i·est 1** Acting or done with haste. **2** Acting or done impetuously; rash. **3** Quick-tempered; irascible. **—hast′i·ly** *adv.* **—hast′i·ness** *n.*

hasty pudding Pudding made of cereal, seasoning, and boiling water or milk.

hat (hat) *n.* A covering for the head, often with a crown and brim. **—pass the hat** To take up a collection. **—talk through one's hat** *Informal* To talk nonsense; also, to bluff. **—under one's hat** *Informal* Secret; private. *—v.t.* **hat·ted, hat·ting** To cover or supply with a hat. [< OE *hæt*]

hat·band (hat′band′) *n.* A ribbon or other band surrounding a hat above the brim.

hatch[1] (hach) *n.* **1** *Naut.* **a** An opening in the deck of a vessel affording passage to the hold. **b** The cover over a hatch. **2** Any similar opening in the floor or roof of a building. **3** The lid or cover for such an opening. [< OE *hæcc* grating]

hatch[2] (hach) *v.t.* **1** To bring forth (young) from the egg by incubation. **2** To bring forth young from (the egg). **3** To devise, as a plan. **4** To contrive secretly; plot. *—v.i.* **5** To emerge from the egg. **6** To produce young: said of eggs. *—n.* **1** The act of hatching. **2** The brood hatched at one time. [ME *hacchen*] **—hatch′er** *n.*

hatch[3] (hach) *v.t.* To mark with hatchings. *—n.* A shade line in drawing or engraving. [< OF *hache* an ax]

hatch·back (hach′bak′) *n.* An automobile with a hatch that opens upward from the rear of the vehicle.

hatch·er·y (hach′ər·ē) *n. pl.* **·er·ies** A place where the eggs of poultry or fish are hatched in large quantities.

hatch·et (hach′it) *n.* A small short-handled ax, for use with one hand. **—bury the hatchet** To cease from hostilities; make peace. [< OF *hache* an ax]

Hatchets

hatch·ing (hach′ing) *n.* **1** In drawing or engraving, the marking with fine parallel lines for shading. **2** Such lines or shading.

hatch·ment (hach′mənt) *n. Her.* The armorial bearings of a dead person, usu. blazoned on a lozenge-shaped panel, as over a tomb. [Alter. of ACHIEVEMENT]

hatch·way (hach′wā′) *n.* HATCH[1].

hate (hāt) *v.* **hat·ed, hat·ing** *v.t.* **1** To regard with extreme aversion; detest. **2** To be unwilling; dislike. *—v.i.* **3** To feel hatred. *—n.* **1** Intense aversion; animosity. **2** A person or thing detested. [< OE *hatian*] **—hat′er** *n.*

hate·ful (hāt′fəl) *adj.* **1** Exciting strong aversion; odious. **2** Feeling or showing hatred. **—hate′ful·ly** *adv.*

hath (hath) Archaic third person singular, present tense, of HAVE.

ha·tred (hā′trid) *n.* Bitter dislike or aversion; antipathy; animosity. **—Syn.** abhorrence, detestation, enmity, hate, hostility.

hat·ter (hat′ər) *n.* One who makes or deals in hats.

hau·berk (hô′bûrk) *n.* A coat of chain mail. [< OF *hauberc*]

haugh·ty (hô′tē) *adj.* **·ti·er, ·ti·est 1** Proud and disdainful; arrogant. **2** *Archaic* Lofty; exalted. [< OF *haut* high] **—haugh′ti·ly** *adv.* **—haugh′ti·ness** *n.*

haul (hôl) *v.t.* **1** To pull or draw with force; drag. **2** To transport as if by pulling. **3** *Naut.* To shift the course of (a ship) *—v.i.* **4** To drag or pull. **5** To shift in direction: said of the wind. **6** *Naut.* To change course, esp. so as to sail nearer the wind. **—haul off 1** To draw back the arm so as to deliver a blow. **2** *Naut.* To change course so as to move farther away from an object. —**haul up** 1 To come to a stop. 2 *Naut.* To sail nearer the wind. —*n.* 1 A pulling with force. 2 That which is obtained by hauling. 3 The drawing of a fish net. 4 The amount caught in, or as in, one pull of a net. 5 The distance over which anything is hauled. [< OF *haler* < Gmc.] —**haul′er** *n.*

haul·age (hô′lij) *n.* 1 The act of hauling. 2 The force used in hauling. 3 The charge made for hauling.

haunch (hônch, hänch) *n.* 1 The fleshy part of the hip, the buttock, and the upper thigh. 2 The combined loin and leg of an animal. [< OF *hanche* < Gmc.] —**haunched** *adj.*

haunt (hônt, hänt) *v.t.* 1 To visit frequently or customarily. 2 To appear to as a disembodied spirit. 3 To recur persistently to the mind or memory of. 4 To visit often; frequent, as a saloon. —*v.i.* 5 To make ghostly appearances. —*n.* 1 A place often visited. 2 *Regional* A ghost. [< OF *hanter* < Gmc.] —**haunt′er** *n.*

haunt·ed (hôn′tid, hän′-) *adj.* Frequently visited, esp. by ghosts or apparitions.

haunt·ing (hôn′ting, hän′-) *adj.* Difficult to forget; frequently occurring to memory. —**haunt′ing·ly** *adv.*

haut·boy (hō′boi, ō′-) *n.* OBOE. [< F *haut* high (in tone) + *bois* wood]

haute cou·ture (ōt kōō·tür′) High fashion, represented esp. by the leading designers of stylish apparel. [F, lit., high sewing]

haute cui·sine (ōt kwi·zēn′, *Fr.* ōt kwē·zēn′) An elaborate or elegant cuisine. [F, lit., high cooking]

hau·teur (hō·tûr′; *Fr.* ō·tœr′) *n.* Haughty manner or spirit; haughtiness. [F]

haut monde (ō mōnd) *French* High society.

have (hav) *v.t.* Present indicative: I, you, we, they **have** (*Archaic* **thou hast**), he, she, it **has** (*Archaic* **hath**); past indicative **had** (*Archaic* **thou hadst**); present subjunctive **have**; past subjunctive **had**; *p.p.* **had**; *pr.p.* **hav·ing** 1 To hold as a possession; own. 2 To possess as a characteristic, attribute, etc. 3 To receive; get: I *had* a letter today. 4 To entertain, as an opinion or doubt. 5 To manifest or exercise: *Have* patience! 6 To experience; undergo. 7 To be affected with. 8 To carry on; engage in. 9 To cause to be: *Have* him here at 9 o'clock. 10 To allow or tolerate: I will *have* no interference. 11 To possess a certain relation to: to *have* the wind at one's back. 12 To be in relationship to or association with: to *have* three children. 13 To bring forth or beget (young). 14 To maintain or declare: so rumor *has* it. 15 *Informal* To baffle: He *had* me there. 16 *Informal* To trick; cheat: I've been *had!* 17 *Informal* To engage in sexual relations with. —*auxiliary* As an auxiliary *have* is used: a With past participles to express completed action: I *have* gone. b With the infinitive to express obligation: I *have* to go. —**have at** To attack. —**have done** To stop; desist. —**have it in for** *Informal* To hold a grudge against. —**have it out** To continue a fight or discussion to a final settlement. —**have on** To be clothed in. [< OE *habban*]

ha·ven (hā′vən) *n.* 1 An anchorage for ships; harbor; port. 2 A refuge; shelter. —*v.t.* To shelter (a vessel, etc.). [< OE *hæfen*] —**Syn.** *n.* 2 asylum, retreat, sanctuary.

have-not (hav′not′) *n.* A person or country lacking in resources and wealth.

have·n't (hav′ənt) Contraction of *have not.*

hav·er·sack (hav′ər·sak) *n.* A bag, slung from the shoulder, for a soldier's or a hiker's rations. [< G *Habersack* oat sack]

hav·oc (hav′ək) *n.* 1 General carnage or destruction; ruin. 2 Tumultuous disorder, confusion, or uproar. —**cry havoc** To give a signal for pillage and destruction. —**play havoc with** To bring to confusion; destroy; ruin. —*v.t.* **hav·ocked, hav·ock·ing** *Archaic* To lay waste; destroy. [< OF *havot* plunder < Gmc.] —**hav′ock·er** *n.*

haw[1] (hô) *n. & interj.* A sound used in hesitating speech. —*v.i.* To hesitate in speaking: to hem and *haw.*

haw[2] (hô) *n.* The fruit of the hawthorn. [< OE *haga*]

haw[3] (hô) *n. & interj.* An order to turn to the left, given to a yoked team. —*v.t. & v.i.* To turn to the left. [?]

Ha·wai·ian (hə·wī′yən) *adj.* Of or pertaining to the Hawaiian Islands, their people, or their language. —*n.* 1 A native or citizen of the Hawaiian Islands. 2 The Polynesian language of the aboriginal Hawaiians.

Hawaiian Islands A group of islands in the N Pacific constituting the state of Hawaii.

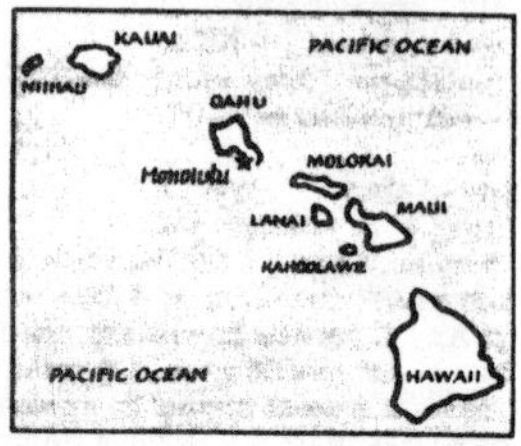

Hawaiian Islands

hawk[1] (hôk) *n.* 1 Any of various birds of prey related to eagles and kites, with relatively short rounded wings, a hooked beak, and strong claws. 2 One who favors militancy rather than conciliation and negotiation, as in a dispute. —*v.i.* 1 To hunt game with trained hawks. —*v.t.* 2 To hunt or catch in flight, as a hawk does. [< OE *hafoc, hafuc*] —**hawk′er** *n.* —**hawk′ish** *adj.*

hawk[2] (hôk) *v.t. & v.i.* To cry (goods) for sale in the streets or in public places; peddle. [Back formation < HAWKER]

hawk[3] (hôk) *v.t.* 1 To cough up (phlegm). —*v.i.* 2 To clear the throat with a coughing sound. —*n.* The sound of a forcible effort to raise phlegm from the throat. [Imit.]

hawk·er (hô′kər) *n.* One who cries goods for sale; a street peddler. [< MLG *hoker* a peddler, huckster]

hawk-eyed (hôk′īd′) *adj.* Having keen eyesight.

hawk moth Any of a family of stout-bodied moths having a long mouthpiece for sucking the nectar from flowers.

hawks·bill (hôks′bil′) A tropical sea turtle with a carapace of overlapping scales valued as tortoise shell. Also **hawk′bill, hawk's-bill.**

hawse·hole (hôz′hōl′) *n. Naut.* A hole in the bow of a vessel for the passage of a hawser.

haw·ser (hô′zər) *n. Naut.* A large rope or cable used in mooring, towing, etc. [< OF *haucier* to lift]

haw·thorn (hô′thôrn) *n.* Any of various thorny, spring-flowering shrubs or small trees of the rose family with white or pink flowers and small applelike fruits. [< OE *haguthorn*]

hay (hā) *n.* Grass, clover, etc., cut and dried for fodder. —*v.t.* 1 To plant (land) with hay. —*v.i.* 2 To process grass, etc.; make hay. [< OE *hēg*]

hay·cock (hā′kok′) *n.* A dome-shaped pile of hay in a field.

hay fever An allergic reaction to pollen or other antigens characterized by sneezing and inflammation of the eyes and air passages.

hay·loft (hā′lôft′, -loft′) *n.* A loft in a barn or stable for storing hay.

hay·mak·er (hā′mā′kər) *n.* 1 One who makes hay. 2 *Slang* A powerful, swinging blow of the fist.

hay·mow (hā′mou′) *n.* 1 A mass of hay stored in a hayloft. 2 A hayloft.

hay·ride (hā′rīd′) *n.* A pleasure ride in a wagon partly filled with hay.

hay·seed (hā′sēd′) *n. Slang* A country person; yokel.

hay·stack (hā′stak′) *n.* A pile of hay. Also **hay·rick** (hā′·rik′).

hay·wire (hā′wīr′) *n.* Wire for baling hay. —*adj. Slang* 1 Confused; mixed up. 2 Crazy: to go *haywire.* [Slang sense < loggers' term for poor or broken equipment mended with haywire]

haz·ard (haz′ərd) *n.* 1 Exposure to loss or injury; risk; peril. 2 A chance result or occurrence. 3 A gambling game played with dice. 4 An obstacle on a golf course, as a bunker or sand trap. —*v.t.* 1 To expose to danger; imperil. 2 To risk; venture. [< OF *hasard*] —**Syn.** *n.* 1 danger, jeopardy. 2 gamble, risk, speculation.

haz·ard·ous (haz′ər·dəs) *adj.* Involving danger of risk or loss. —**haz′ard·ous·ly** *adv.* —**haz′ard·ous·ness** *n.*

haze[1] (hāz) *n.* 1 Very fine suspended particles in the air, as of smoke or dust. 2 A vague or muddled mental state. [Back formation < HAZY]

haze[2] (hāz) *v.t.* **hazed, haz·ing** To subject (new students, members, etc.) to humiliating horseplay or pointless harassment. [?] —**haz′er** *n.*

ha·zel (hā′zəl) *n.* 1 A bushy shrub or small tree of the birch family yielding a hard-shelled edible nut. 2 A yellowish brown. —*adj.* Of the color hazel. [< OE *hæsel*]

ha·zel·nut (hā′zəl·nut′) *n.* The nut of the hazel.
haz·y (hā′zē) *adj.* **haz·i·er, haz·i·est 1** Misty, smoky, etc. **2** Confused; obscure. [?] **—haz′i·ly** *adv.* **—haz′i·ness** *n.*
H-bomb (āch′bom′) *n.* HYDROGEN BOMB.
he (hē) *pron.* **1** The male person or being previously mentioned or understood, in the nominative case. **2** Anyone: *He* who hesitates is lost. **—***n. pl.* **hes** A male. [< OE]
He helium.
head (hed) *n.* **1** The part of the body of man and most animals that contains the brain and the ears, eyes, mouth, and nose. **2** An analogous part in other organisms. **3** A representation of a head, as in art. **4** Mind; intelligence: Use your *head.* **5** Mental aptitude: a good *head* for figures. **6** Mental poise; self-possession: He kept his *head.* **7** A person: learned *heads.* **8** (*pl.* **head**) An individual considered as a unit of counting: six *head* of cattle. **9** A part or end that has a shape, position, or relationship resembling or analogous to that of a head: the *head* of a bed. **10** The source, as of a river. **11** The fore or forward part: the *head* of a column of troops. **12** A headland; cape. **13** A leader, chief; director. **14** One having topmost rank: the *head* of one's profession. **15** The top or uppermost part: the *head* of the stairs. **16** A heading, headline, etc. **17** A division of a subject, discourse, etc.: He had little to say on that *head.* **18** Culmination; climax: to come to a *head.* **19** The maturated part of a boil or abscess before breaking. **20** Advance in the face of opposition: to make *head* against the storm. **21** A compact cluster of leaves, flowers, or seeds, as of cabbage, clover, or grain. **22** The foam that rises to the surface of beer, ale, etc. **23** The measure of stored-up force or capacity, as of steam. **24** The height of a column or body of fluid above a certain point, considered as causing pressure: a *head* of water driving a turbine. **25** The striking, holding, or pushing part, as of a club, hammer, pin, etc. **26** The obverse of a coin. **27** *Naut.* A toilet. **28** The membrane stretched over a drum or tambourine. **29** The active part of a tool or device: a cutting *head;* a recording *head.* **30** HEADMASTER. **31** *Slang* One who habitually uses a drug that distorts perception, as LSD or marihuana: an acid *head;* a *pothead.* **—go to one's head 1** To make intoxicated or lightheaded. **2** To cause to become conceited. **—out of** (or **off**) **one's head** Crazy; delirious. **—over one's head 1** Beyond one's ability to understand. **2** To someone of higher authority. **—turn one's head** To make vain or conceited. **—***v.t.* **1** To be first or foremost in or on: to *head* the list. **2** To be chief or leader of; command. **3** To turn or direct the course of: to *head* a vessel toward shore. **4** To furnish with a head. **5** To remove the head or top of, as a tree. **6** In soccer, to hit (the ball) with the head. **—***v.i.* **7** To move in a specified direction or toward a specified point. **8** To come to or form a head. **—head off** To intercept the course of: We'll *head* him *off* at the pass. **—head up** *Informal* To be in charge. **—***adj.* **1** Principal; chief. **2** Situated at the top or front. **3** Directed against the front: a *head* wind. [< OE *hēafod*]
head·ache (hed′āk′) *n.* **1** A pain in the head. **2** *Informal* A source of vexation or trouble. **—head′a′chy** (-ā′kē) *adj.*
head·board (hed′bôrd′, -bōrd′) *n.* A board at the head, as of a bed.
head·cheese (hed′chēz′) *n.* A pressed, jellied loaf made of small pieces of the head and feet of a hog or calf.
head·dress (hed′dres′) *n.* **1** A covering or ornament for the head. **2** A hair style; coiffure.
head·ed (hed′id) *adj.* **1** Furnished with a head or heading. **2** Formed or grown into a head. **3** Having a specified kind or number of heads: used in combination: *flat-headed, two-headed.*
head·er (hed′ər) *n.* **1** *Informal* A headlong fall or plunge. **2** A device for putting on the heads of nails, pins, etc. **3** A machine for removing the heads of grain.
head·first (hed′fûrst′) *adv.* **1** With the head leading or foremost. **2** Impetuously; precipitately. Also **head′fore′·most′** (-fôr′mōst′, -məst, -fōr′-).
head·gear (hed′gir′) *n.* **1** A headdress or the like. **2** The parts of a harness fitted around the head.
head-hunt·ing (hed′hun′ting) *n.* Among certain primitive peoples, the custom of decapitating slain enemies and preserving the heads as trophies. **—head′-hunt′er** *n.*
head·ing (hed′ing) *n.* **1** Something at the head or top part. **2** A title, caption, or the like at the top or beginning of a page, chapter, division, etc.
head·land (hed′lənd) A cliff or point of land projecting into a body of water.
head·less (hed′lis) *adj.* **1** Without a head. **2** Without a leader. **3** Stupid.
head·light (hed′līt′) *n.* A powerful front light, as of a vehicle.
head·line (hed′līn′) *n.* **1** An attention-getting word or words set in large type at the head of a newspaper column or news story. **2** A line at the head of a page, containing title, page number, etc. **—***v.t.* **·lined, ·lin·ing 1** To provide with a headline. **2** To be the headliner of (a show, etc.).
head·lin·er (hed′lī′nər) *n.* The main performer or act, as of a variety show.
head·lock (hed′lok′) *n.* A wrestling grip in which an adversary's head is held between one's arm and body.
head·long (hed′lông′, -long′) *adv.* **1** Headfirst. **2** Impetuously; rashly. **3** With unbridled speed or force. **—***adj.* **1** Done with the head leading: a *headlong* plunge. **2** Impetuous; rash. **3** Rapid and forceful.
head·man (hed′mən, -man′) *n. pl.* **·men** (mən) **1** A leader or person of authority. **2** A workman in charge of other workers; foreman; overseer.
head·mas·ter (hed′mas′tər, -mäs′-) *n.* The man in charge of a usu. private school. Also **head master.**
head·mis·tress (hed′mis′tris) *n.* The woman in charge of a usu. private school. Also **head mistress.**
head·most (hed′mōst′) *adj.* Most advanced; foremost.
head-on (hed′on′, -ôn′) *adj.* Front end to front end; a *head-on* collision. **—***adv.* **1** With the front ends meeting: to collide *head-on.* **2** Directly: to meet adversity *head-on.*
head·phone (hed′fōn′) *n.* A device for changing electric signals to sound, held to the ear by a band passing over the head.
head·piece (hed′pēs′) *n.* **1** A protective covering for the head. **2** Intelligence.
head·quar·ters (hed′kwôr′tərz) *n.pl. (often construed as sing.)* **1** The operating base of one in command, as of an army unit or police force. **2** Any center of operations.
head·set (hed′set′) *n.* **1** A pair of headphones. **2** A device for holding an earphone and a transmitter at one's head.
head·ship (hed′ship) *n.* The office or position of one having chief authority.
heads·man (hedz′mən) *n. pl.* **·men** (-mən) One who executes those condemned to be beheaded.
head·stall (hed′stôl′) *n.* The part of a bridle that fits over the horse's head.
head·stand (hed′stand′) *n.* The act of holding one's body upside-down in a vertical position.
head start An advance start or advantage, as in a race or comparable situation.
head·stock (hed′stok′) *n. Mech.* A device supporting the end or head of a part.
head·stone (hed′stōn′) *n.* A stone marking the head of a grave.
head·strong (hed′strông′, -strong′) *adj.* **1** Stubbornly bent on having one's own way; willfully obstinate. **2** Characterized by such obstinacy. **—head′strong′ness** *n.*
heads-up (hedz′up′) *adj. Slang* Smart or alert: used esp. of sports competition: a *heads-up* play.
head·wait·er (hed′wā′tər) *n.* In a restaurant, one who supervises the seating of guests, the activities of waiters, etc.
head·wa·ters (hed′wô′tərz, -wot′ərz) *n. pl.* The waters at or near the source of a river or stream.
head·way (hed′wā′) *n.* **1** Forward motion; progress. **2** The interval of time between scheduled vehicles. **3** Overhead clearance, as under an arch.
head wind A wind blowing directly opposite to the course of a ship, airplane, etc.
head·work (hed′wûrk′) *n.* Mental labor.
head·y (hed′ē) *adj.* **head·i·er, head·i·est 1** Tending to affect

the mind or senses; intoxicating. 2 Headstrong. **—head′i·ly** *adv.* **—head′i·ness** *n.*

heal (hēl) *v.t.* 1 To restore to health or soundness; make well again. 2 To cause the cure or recovery of (a wound, injury, etc.). 3 To smooth over or resolve (a breach, quarrel, etc.). 4 To free from grief, worry, etc. *—v.i.* 5 To become well or sound. 6 To perform a cure or cures. [< OE *hǣlan*] **—heal′a·ble** *adj.* **—heal′er** *n.*

health (helth) *n.* 1 Soundness of body or mind; well-being. 2 General condition of body or mind: poor *health.* 3 General well-being, as of a nation. 4 A toast wishing good health. [< OE *hǣlth*]

health·ful (helth′fəl) *adj.* 1 Promoting good health; wholesome. 2 Healthy. **—health′ful·ly** *adv.* **—health′ful·ness** *n.*

health·y (hel′thē) *adj.* **health·i·er, health·i·est** 1 Having good health. 2 Indicative or characteristic of sound health: a *healthy* complexion. 3 Conducive to health or well-being. 4 *Informal.* Hearty; big: a *healthy* shove. **—health′i·ly** *adv.* **—health′i·ness** *n.* **—Syn.** 1 healthful, well, sound, hardy, hale. 2 vigorous, strong, robust.

heap (hēp) *n.* 1 A collection of things piled up; a pile. 2 *Often pl. Informal* A large number; lot. *—v.t.* 1 To pile into a heap. 2 To fill or pile into or onto to an excessive degree. 3 To give or bestow in great quantities: to *heap* insults on someone. *—v.i.* 4 To form or rise in a heap. [< OE *hēap* a crowd]

hear (hir) *v.* **heard** (hûrd), **hear·ing** *v.t.* 1 To perceive (sound) by means of the ear. 2 To listen to. 3 To give heed to. 4 To learn or be informed of: I *hear* you are leaving town. 5 To listen to and review in an official capacity: to *hear* a case in court. 6 To respond to and grant: *Hear* our prayers! *—v.i.* 7 To perceive or be capable of perceiving sound by means of the ear. 8 To be informed or made aware. [< OE *hēran*] **—hear′er** *n.*

hear·ing (hir′ing) *n.* 1 The capacity to hear. 2 The sense by which sounds are perceived. 3 An opportunity to be heard. 4 The range within which sound may be heard. 5 A judicial examination, as of an accused person.

heark·en (här′kən) *v.i.* To pay attention; listen attentively. [< OE *heorcnian*]

hear·say (hir′sā′) *n.* Information received indirectly, as through common talk; rumor.

hearse (hûrs) *n.* A vehicle used in a funeral for carrying a dead person to the cemetery. [ME *herse* a harrow, frame]

heart (härt) *n.* 1 A hollow muscular structure which maintains the circulation of the blood by alternate contraction and dilation. 2 Feeling, as compassion, earnest desire, or deep emotion, regarded as emanating from the heart. 3 Love; affection: to win her *heart.* 4 Mood; spirit: a heavy *heart.* 5 Courage; resolution: to lose *heart.* 6 A person, esp. one regarded with love or affection: many brave *hearts.* 7 Innermost part; core or center. 8 Essential part; gist: the *heart* of the matter. 9 A conventionalized representation of the heart. 10 **a** A playing card marked with this symbol. **b** *pl.* The suit of cards bearing this symbol. 11 *pl.* A card game in which one tries to win none or all of the hearts. [< OE *heorte*]

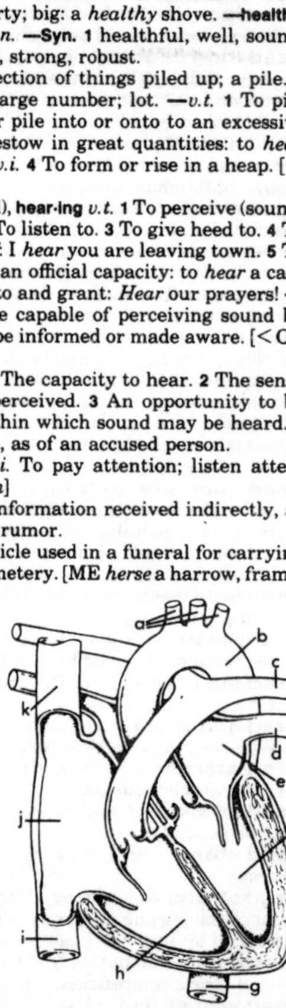

Heart
a. arteries to head and arms. b. aorta. c. pulmonary artery. d. pulmonary vein. e. left atrium. f. left ventricle. g. aorta carries blood to abdomen and legs. h. right ventricle. i. inferior vena cava. j. right atrium. k. superior vena cava.

heart·ache (härt′āk′) *n.* Deep mental anguish; grief; sorrow.

heart·beat (härt′bēt′) *n.* One complete cycle of dilation and contraction of the heart.

heart·break (härt′brāk′) *n.* Deep grief; overwhelming sorrow. **—heart′break′ing** *adj.* **—heart′break′ing·ly** *adv.*

heart·bro·ken (härt′brō′kən) *adj.* Overwhelmingly grieved.

heart·burn (härt′bûrn′) *n.* A burning sensation in the esophagus, due to regurgitation of acid from the stomach.

heart·ed (här′tid) *adj.* Having a specified kind of heart: used in combination: *kindhearted.*

heart·en (här′tən) *v.t.* To give courage to.

heart·felt (härt′felt′) *adj.* Deeply felt; most sincere.

hearth (härth) *n.* 1 The floor of a fireplace, furnace, etc. 2 The fireside; home. 3 In a blast furnace, the lowest part, through which the melted metal flows. [< OE *heorth*]

hearth·stone (härth′stōn′) *n.* 1 A stone forming a hearth. 2 A fireside; home.

heart·i·ly (här′tə·lē) *adv.* 1 Sincerely or cordially. 2 Earnestly; enthusiastically. 3 Abundantly and with good appetite. 4 Completely; thoroughly.

heart·less (härt′lis) *adj.* Without sympathy or compassion; pitiless. **—heart′less·ly** *adv.* **—heart′less·ness** *n.*

heart-rend·ing (härt′ren′ding) *adj.* Causing great anguish or distress. **—heart′-rend′ing·ly** *adv.*

heart·sick (härt′sik′) *adj.* Deeply disappointed or despondent. Also **heart′sore′** (-sôr′, -sōr′).

heart-strick·en (härt′strik′ən) *adj.* Overwhelmed with grief or fear.

heart·strings (härt′stringz′) *n.pl.* The strongest feelings or affections.

heart-to-heart (härt′tə·härt′) *adj.* Frank, intimate, and sincere: a *heart-to-heart* talk.

heart·wood (härt′wŏŏd′) *n.* The hard older wood at the central part of a tree trunk or woody stem.

heart·y (här′tē) *adj.* **heart·i·er, heart·i·est** 1 Cordial; genial: a *hearty* welcome. 2 Strongly felt; vigorous: a *hearty* dislike. 3 Healthy; robust. 4 Plentiful and satisfying: a *hearty* meal. *—n. pl.* **heart·ies** *Archaic* A fellow or comrade, esp. a sailor. **—heart′i·ness** *n.*

heat (hēt) *n.* 1 The condition or sensation of being hot. 2 Comparatively high temperature or degree of warmth. 3 Energy associated with and proportional to the random motions of the molecules of a substance or body. 4 The condition or process of maintaining a warm temperature, as in a home. 5 Hot weather or climate. 6 Intensity, as of feeling, excitement, or activity. 7 A time or instance of such activity or feeling: the *heat* of battle. 8 A recurring state of sexual activity in female mammals. 9 In sports: **a** A single bout or round. **b** A preliminary race to determine the finalists. *—v.t. & v.i.* 1 To make or become hot or warm. 2 To excite or become excited. [< OE *hǣtu*]

heat·ed (hē′tid) *adj.* Marked by aroused feelings, esp. anger: a *heated* debate. **—heat′ed·ly** *adv.*

heat·er (hē′tər) *n.* A device or apparatus designed to generate or transmit heat.

heath (hēth) *n.* 1 *Chiefly Brit.* An area of open land covered with heather or similar dense, low-growing, shrubby growth. 2 Heather or a similar plant. [< OE *hǣth*]

hea·then (hē′*th*ən) *n. pl.* **·thens** or **·then** 1 One who does not worship the God of Judaism, Christianity, or Islam; a pagan. 2 Any irreligious or primitively ignorant person. *—adj.* Of or typical of a heathen or heathens; pagan. **—hea′then·dom** *n.* **—hea′then·ish** *adj.* [< OE *hǣthen*]

heath·er (he*th*′ər) *n.* Any of several low-growing evergreen shrubs with minute leaves and small, densely clustered pinkish-lavender flowers. [< ME *hadder?* < HEATH] **—heath′er·y** *adj.*

heat lightning Sporadic lightning without thunder, usu. seen near the horizon at the close of a hot day.

heat wave A prolonged period of hot weather.

heave (hēv) *v.* **heaved** or *chiefly Naut.* **hove, heav·ing** *v.t.* 1 To raise with effort. 2 To throw with effort or force. 3 To cause to swell, rise, or move up and down. 4 To emit with a deep breath, as a sigh. 5 *Naut.* **a** To raise, haul up, or pull on (an anchor, cable, etc.). **b** To cause (a ship) to move by or as by hauling on cables or ropes. *—v.i.* 6 To rise, swell up, or move up and down repeatedly. 7 To breathe with effort; gasp. 8 To vomit or retch. 9 *Naut.* **a** To move or proceed: said of ships. **b** To haul, pull, or push. *—n.* The action, effort, or result of heaving. [< OE *hebban*] **—heav′·er** *n.*

heav·en (hev′ən) *n.* **1** In Christian theology, the abode of God, the angels, and of deserving souls after death. **2** A similar state or concept in other religions. **3** A place or condition of supreme happiness. **4** *Often pl.* Divine providence. **5** *Usu. pl.* The region above and surrounding the earth; the sky. [< OE *heofon*] **—heav′en·ward** *adj., adv.* **—heav′en·wards** *adv.*

Heav·en (hev′ən) *n.* God; Providence.

heav·en·ly (hev′ən·lē) *adj.* **1** Of or belonging to the heaven of God or theology. **2** Of the sky or extraterrestrial universe: *heavenly* bodies. **3** Characterized by great happiness or beauty. **—heav′en·li·ness** *n.*

heaves (hēvz) *n.pl. (construed as sing. or pl.)* A respiratory disease of horses resulting in quick, labored breathing, heaving of the flanks, and coughing.

Heav·i·side layer (hev′ē·sīd) A layer of the ionosphere which begins about 65 miles above the earth and reflects certain radio waves. [< O. *Heaviside,* d. 1925, English physicist]

heav·y (hev′ē) *adj.* **heav·i·er, heav·i·est 1** Of great or considerable weight; hard to lift or carry. **2** Of relatively great weight in relation to volume: a *heavy* metal. **3** Of more than the usual weight, thickness, etc.: a *heavy* fabric. **4** Laden or as if laden or weighted: air *heavy* with moisture. **5** Of or involving a great amount, volume, etc.: *heavy* trading. **6** Forceful; powerful: a *heavy* blow. **7** Concentrated; intense: *heavy* gunfire. **8** Thick, broad, and massive: *heavy* features. **9** Pervasive and often oppressive: a *heavy* odor. **10** Hard to do: *heavy* work. **11** Hard to bear; oppressive: *heavy* taxes. **12** Sorrowful; despondent: a *heavy* heart. **13** Serious; grave: a *heavy* offense. **14** Dull; ponderous: a *heavy* prose style. **15** Lacking lightness, grace, etc.: a *heavy* tread. **16** Having a dense, doughy texture. **17** Not easily digested. **18** Using or consuming something in great amounts: a *heavy* eater. **19** Of a theatrical role, intensely dramatic. **20** Pregnant: *heavy* with child. **21** Producing on a large or massive scale: *heavy* industry. **22** *Mil.* **a** Of great size, weight, etc.: *heavy* artillery. **b** Armed with such equipment: *heavy* infantry. **—*adv.*** Heavily. **—*n. pl.*** **heav·ies 1** A heavy, dramatic theatrical role, as that of a villain; also, one who plays such a role. **2** Something heavy. [< OE *hefig*] **—heav′i·ly** *adv.* **—heav′i·ness** *n.*

heav·y-dut·y (hev′ē·dyōō′tē) *adj.* Made so as to bear up under long wear, strain, or use.

heav·y-hand·ed (hev′ē·han′did) *adj.* **1** Lacking adroitness; clumsy. **2** Oppressive; overbearing. **—heav′y-hand′ed·ly** *adv.* **—heav′y-hand′ed·ness** *n.* **—Syn. 1** bungling, awkward, unhandy. **2** inconsiderate, insensitive, thoughtless.

heav·y-heart·ed (hev′ē·här′tid) *adj.* Sad; despondent. **—heav′y-heart′ed·ly** *adv.* **—heav′y-heart′ed·ness** *n.*

heavy hydrogen DEUTERIUM.

heavy spar BARITE.

heavy water Water composed of oxygen and deuterium.

heav·y·weight (hev′ē·wāt′) *n.* **1** One of more than average weight. **2** A boxer or wrestler over 175 pounds in weight. **3** *Informal* A person of considerable importance, influence, etc.

He·be (hē′bē) *Gk. Myth.* The goddess of youth and the cupbearer of the gods.

He·bra·ic (hi·brā′ik) *adj.* Relating to or characteristic of the Hebrew people, culture, language, etc. Also **He·bra′i·cal.** [< Gk. *Hebraios* Hebrew] **—He·bra′i·cal·ly** *adv.*

He·bra·ism (hē′brā·iz′əm, -brə-) *n.* **1** A distinctive characteristic of Hebrew culture, thought, etc. **2** A Hebrew idiom. **3** Judaism. **—He′bra·is′tic** or **·ti·cal** *adj.*

He·bra·ist (hē′brā·ist, -brə-) *n.* One learned in Hebrew or having a scholarly knowledge of Hebraic thought and traditions.

He·brew (hē′brōō) *n.* **1** A member of one of the Semitic peoples claiming descent from Abraham; an Israelite. **2** The Semitic language of these people, used in the Old Testament and by Jews as a scholarly and religious language. **3** A modern form of this language, used esp. in Israel. **—Epistle to the Hebrews** A New Testament book addressed to Hebrew Christians: also **Hebrews.** **—*adj.*** Of or relating to the Hebrews.

Hebrew calendar JEWISH CALENDAR.

Hec·a·te (hek′ə·tē) *Gk. Myth.* A goddess of the earth, moon, and underworld.

heck (hek) *interj. Slang* A euphemism for hell.

heck·le (hek′əl) *v.t.* **heck·led, heck·ling** To harass (a speaker) with taunts, annoying questions, etc. [< ME *hechele* a comb for flax] **—heck′ler** *n.*

hec·tare (hek′târ) *n.* A metric unit of area equal to 10,000 square meters, or 2.471 acres. [F < Gk. *hekaton* a hundred + F *are* ARE[2]]

hec·tic (hek′tik) *adj.* **1** Characterized by intense excitement, chaotic confusion, etc. **2** Characterized by the flushed, feverish, or wasted condition associated with certain diseases, as tuberculosis. [< Gk. *hektikos* consumptive] **—hec′ti·cal·ly** *adv.*

hec·to·graph (hek′tə·graf, -gräf) *n.* A duplicating device having a gelatin pad for making multiple copies of a writing or drawing. **—*v.t.*** To copy by hectograph. [< Gk. *hekaton* a hundred + -GRAPH] **—hec′to·graph′ic** *adj.*

hec·tor (hek′tər) *v.t. & v.i.* **1** To bully; badger. **2** To tease; torment. **—*n.*** A bully. [< HECTOR]

Hec·tor (hek′tər) *Gk. Myth.* A Trojan hero, son of Priam and Hecuba, killed by Achilles.

Hec·u·ba (hek′yōō·bə) *Gk. Myth.* The wife of Priam.

he'd (hēd) Contraction of *he had* or *he would.*

hedge (hej) *n.* **1** A fence or barrier formed by bushes set close together. **2** The act or an instance of hedging. **—*v.*** **hedged, hedg·ing** *v.t.* **1** To surround or border with a hedge. **2** To guard or hem in with or as with barriers: usu. with *in.* **3** To try to compensate for possible loss from (a bet, investment, etc.) by making offsetting bets or investments. **—*v.i.*** **4** To make offsetting bets, investments, etc. **5** To avoid definite statement or involvement; refuse to commit oneself. [< OE *hegg*] **—hedg′er** *n.*

hedge·hog (hej′hôg′, -hog′) *n.* **1** A small, nocturnal, insectivorous mammal of the Old World having the back and sides covered with stout spines. **2** The porcupine.

hedge·hop (hej′hop′) *v.i.* **·hopped, ·hop·ping** To fly close to the ground in an airplane. **—hedge′hop′per** *n.*

hedge·row (hej′rō′) *n.* A hedge formed by a row of shrubs or trees growing close together.

he·don·ism (hē′dən·iz′əm) *n.* **1** Devotion to or pursuit of pleasure; self-indulgence. **2** The ethical doctrine that the seeking of pleasure is the primary good. [< Gk. *hēdonē* pleasure] **—he′don·ist** *n.* **—he′don·is′tic** *adj.* **—he′don·is′ti·cal·ly** *adv.*

-hedral *combining form* Having a (specified) number of sides or surfaces: *octahedral.*

-hedron *combining form* A figure or crystal having a (specified) number of sides or surfaces: *octahedron.* [< Gk. *hedra* side, surface]

heed (hēd) *v.t.* To take special notice of; pay attention to. **—*v.i.*** To pay attention. **—*n.*** Careful attention or consideration. [< OE *hēdan*] **—heed′er** *n.*

heed·ful (hēd′fəl) *adj.* Attentive. **—heed′ful·ly** *adv.* **—heed′ful·ness** *n.*

heed·less (hēd′lis) *adj.* Not taking heed; inattentive or careless. **—heed′less·ly** *adv.* **—heed′less·ness** *n.*

hee-haw (hē′hô′) *n.* **1** The bray of a donkey. **2** Loud laughter resembling this. **—*v.i.*** **1** To bray. **2** To guffaw. [Imit.]

heel[1] (hēl) *n.* **1** In man, the rounded posterior part of the foot. **2** A similar or corresponding part, as of the foot of an animal or the palm of the hand where it joins the wrist. **3** The part of a sock, shoe, etc., that covers the heel. **4** The supporting part of a shoe, boot, etc., attached to the sole beneath the heel. • See SHOE. **5** Something resembling or placed like a heel, as an end of a loaf of bread. **6** *Slang* A contemptible, treacherous fellow; a cad. **—*v.t.*** **1** To supply with a heel. **2** To follow or pursue closely. [< OE *hēla*] **—heel′less** *adj.*

heel[2] (hēl) *v.t. & v.i. Naut.* To lean or cause to lean to one side, as a ship. **—*n.*** The act of heeling; a list. [< OE *hieldan*]

heeled (hēld) *adj.* 1 Having heels, as shoes. 2 *Slang* a Supplied with money. b Armed, as with a gun.

heel·er (hē′lər) *n.* 1 *Informal* WARD HEELER. 2 One who heels shoes.

heft (heft) *v.t. Informal* 1 To test the weight of by lifting. 2 To lift up; heave. —*v.i.* 3 To weigh. —*n.* Heaviness; weight. [< HEAVE]

heft·y (hef′tē) *adj.* **heft·i·er, heft·i·est** *Informal* 1 Heavy; weighty. 2 Big and powerful; muscular. —**heft′i·ly** *adv.* —**heft′i·ness** *n.*

he·gem·o·ny (hi·jem′ə·nē, hi·gem′-, hej′ə·mō′nē) *n. pl.* **·nies** Dominance or influence, as of one state over others. [< Gk. *hēgemonia* < *hēgeesthai* lead] —**heg·e·mon·ic** (hej′ə·mon′ik) *adj.*

He·gi·ra (hi·jī′rə, hej′ə·rə) *n.* The flight of Mohammed from Mecca to Medina in 622, regarded as the beginning of the Mohammedan era. [< Ar. *hijrah* departure]

heif·er (hef′ər) *n.* A young cow, esp. one that has not borne a calf. [< OE *hēahfore*]

heigh (hā, hī) *interj.* An exclamation to attract attention, give encouragement, etc.

heigh-ho (hī′hō′, hā′-) *interj.* An exclamation of weariness, disappointment, surprise, etc.

height (hīt) *n.* 1 Measure or distance from the lowest part or level to the top or uppermost extent; altitude, elevation, or stature. 2 The condition of being high or tall. 3 The highest or uppermost part or point. 4 Something high; an eminence. 5 The greatest or most intense degree: the *height* of stupidity. [< OE *hīehtho*]

height·en (hīt′n) *v.t. & v.i.* 1 To make or become high or higher. 2 To make or become greater in degree, amount, etc.; intensify. —**height′en·er** *n.*

hei·nous (hā′nəs) *adj.* Extremely wicked; atrocious; hateful. [< OF *haine* hatred] —**hei′nous·ly** *adv.* —**hei′nous·ness** *n.*

heir (âr) *n.* 1 One who inherits or is legally entitled to inherit the property, title, or rank of another. 2 One who acquires a position, distinctive quality, etc., from a predecessor as if by inheritance. [< L *heres*] —**heir′dom, heir′·ship** *n.*

heir apparent *pl.* **heirs apparent** One who according to law becomes the heir if he survives his ancestor.

heir·ess (âr′is) *n.* A woman or girl who is an heir, esp. one of considerable wealth.

heir·loom (âr′lōōm) *n.* 1 Something, as a valued possession, that has been handed down within a family for generations. 2 *Law* A piece of personal property inherited by an heir. [< HEIR + obs. *loom* tool]

heir presumptive *pl.* **heirs presumptive** One who is at present heir to another but whose claims may become void by birth of a nearer relative.

heist (hīst) *Slang v.t.* To steal. —*n.* A robbery; theft. [Var. of HOIST]

He·ji·ra (hə·jī′rə, hej′ə·rə) *n.* HEGIRA.

Hek·a·te (hek′ə·tē) HECATE.

held (held) *p.t. & p.p.* of HOLD.

Hel·en of Troy (hel′ən) *Gk. Myth.* A beautiful woman who was the wife of Menelaus and whose elopement with Paris caused the Trojan War.

hel·i·cal (hel′i·kəl) *adj.* Of or shaped like a helix; spiral. —**hel′i·cal·ly** *adv.*

hel·i·ces (hel′ə·sēz) *n.pl.* of HELIX.

hel·i·cop·ter (hel′ə·kop′tər, hē′lə-) *n.* A type of aircraft whose lift is obtained from airfoils rotating on a vertical axis and which is capable of rising and descending vertically. [< Gk. *helix, -ikos* a spiral + *pteron* a wing]

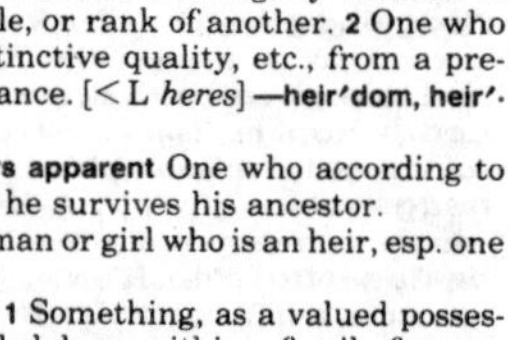

Four-passenger helicopter

helio- *combining form* Sun; of the sun: *heliotropic.* [< Gk. *hēlios* the sun]

he·li·o·cen·tric (hē′lē·ə·sen′trik) *adj.* Having or considering the sun as a center. Also **he′li·o·cen′tri·cal.** —**he′li·o·cen′tri·cal·ly** *adv.*

he·li·o·graph (hē′lē·ə·graf′, -gräf′) *n.* 1 An instrument for taking photographs of the sun. 2 A photograph taken by sunlight. 3 A mirror for signaling by flashes of light. —*v.t. & v.i.* To signal with a heliograph. —**he·li·og·ra·pher** (hē′lē·og′rə·fər), **he′li·og′ra·phy** *n.* —**he′li·o·graph′ic** *adj.*

He·li·os (hē′lē·os) *Gk. Myth.* The sun god.

he·li·o·trope (hē′lē·ə·trōp′, hēl′yə-) *n.* 1 Any of a genus of herbs with small white or purplish fragrant flowers. 2 Any of various plants which turn toward the sun. 3 The common valerian. 4 BLOODSTONE. 5 A pinkish purple. [< Gk. *hēlios* sun + *trepein* to turn]

he·li·ot·ro·pism (hē′lē·ot′rə·piz′əm) *n.* The tendency of certain organisms, esp. plants, to grow or move toward or away from the source of light. Also **he′li·ot′ro·py.** —**he·li·o·trop·ic** (hē′lē·ə·trop′ik, -trō′pik, hēl′yə-) *adj.* —**he′li·o·trop′i·cal·ly** *adv.*

hel·i·port (hel′ə·pôrt′, -pōrt′, hē′lə-) *n.* An airport for helicopters.

he·li·um (hē′lē·əm) *n.* An inert, odorless, nonflammable, gaseous element (symbol He), abundant on the sun and other stars. [NL < Gk. *hēlios* sun]

he·lix (hē′liks) *n. pl.* **he·lix·es** or **hel·i·ces** (hel′ə·sēz) 1 *Geom.* A curve lying on the surface of a cone or cylinder and cutting each element at a constant angle greater than 0° and less than 90°. 2 Any spiral. 3 *Anat.* The spiral cartilage of the external ear. 4 *Archit.* A small volute. [L < Gk., a spiral]

Helix

hell (hel) *n.* 1 *Sometimes cap.* a In Christianity and other religions, the abode of evil spirits after death, considered a place of eternal torment. b In certain ancient religions, the dwelling place of the spirits of the dead. 2 The powers of evil. 3 Any place, condition, or cause of extreme suffering, evil, etc. —*interj. Slang* An exclamation of anger, annoyance, disappointment, etc. —*v.i. Slang* To behave in an unrestrained or riotous manner: with *around.* [< OE *hel*]

he'll (hēl) Contraction of *he will* or *he shall.*

Hel·las (hel′əs) *n.* Greece.

hell·bend·er (hel′ben′dər) *n.* A large aquatic salamander of SE North America.

hell-bent (hel′bent′) *adj. Slang* Recklessly determined, directed, or eager: *hell-bent* for trouble.

hel·le·bore (hel′ə·bôr, -bōr) *n.* 1 A perennial herb related to the buttercup, having rhizomes that contain a toxic alkaloid with cathartic and stimulating properties. 2 Any of certain herbs of the lily family having rhizomes containing a similar toxic substance. [< Gk. *helleboros*]

Hel·lene (hel′ēn) *n.* A Greek. Also **Hel·le′ni·an.**

Hel·len·ic (he·len′ik, -lē′nik) *adj.* 1 Of or pertaining to the Hellenes; Greek. 2 Of or pertaining to the language and culture of ancient Greece. —*n.* The Greek language, including its ancient and modern forms.

Hel·le·nism (hel′ə·niz′əm) *n.* 1 Ancient Greek character, ideals, or civilization. 2 A characteristic Greek idiom or phrase. 3 Adoption of Greek speech, manners, and culture. —**Hel′le·nist** *n.*

Hel·le·nis·tic (hel′ə·nis′tik) *adj.* 1 Of or pertaining to Greek culture, influence, or language, esp. when widespread following the conquests of Alexander the Great.

Hel·le·nize (hel′ə·nīz) *v.t. & v.i.* **·nized, ·niz·ing** To make or become Greek or Hellenic; adopt or imbue with Greek language or customs. —**Hel·le·ni·za·tion** (hel′ə·nə·zā′shən, -nī·zā′-) *n.* —**Hel′le·niz′er** *n.*

hell·fire (hel′fīr′) *n.* The flames or torment of hell.

hel·lion (hel′yən) *n. Informal* A mischievous person given to wild and unpredictable actions. [?]

hell·ish (hel′ish) *adj.* 1 Of or like hell; diabolical. 2 *Informal* Extremely bad or unpleasant; horrible. —**hell′ish·ly** *adv.* —**hell′ish·ness** *n.*

hel·lo (hə·lō′) *interj.* 1 An exclamation used as a greeting or in answering the telephone. 2 An exclamation of surprise or to gain attention. —*n. pl.* **hel·loes** The greeting or calling of "hello." —*v.t. & v.i.* **·loed, ·lo·ing** To call "hello" to.

helm (helm) *n.* 1 *Naut.* The steering apparatus of a vessel, as the tiller or wheel. 2 A position of control, responsibility, or leadership. —*v.t.* To manage the helm of; steer; direct. [< OE *helma* rudder]

hel·met (hel′mit) *n.* **1** A protective covering for the head, used in ancient and modern warfare. **2** A protective head covering, as of leather or plastic, worn by athletes, firemen, motorcyclists, etc. **3** Something resembling a helmet. [< OF, dim. of *helme* < Gmc.] **—hel′met·ed** *adj.*

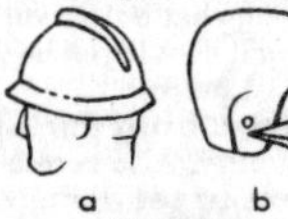
a b
Helmets
a. construction.
b. football.

hel·minth (hel′minth) *n.* A worm, esp. a parasitic intestinal worm. [< Gk. *helmins* a worm]
helms·man (helmz′mən) *n. pl.* **·men** (-mən) One who steers a vessel by taking the helm.
hel·ot (hel′ət, hē′lət) *n.* **1** *Usu. cap.* A serf of ancient Sparta. **2** Any slave. [< Gk. *heilōs*]
help (help) *v.t.* **1** To give assistance to; aid. **2** To assist in some action, motion, etc.: with *on, into, out of, up, down,* etc. **3** To give support to; contribute to: to *help* a good cause. **4** To give relief to; ease: to *help* a cold. **5** To be responsible for: He can't *help* his infirmities. **6** To refrain from: I couldn't *help* giggling. **7** To serve, as with food. **8** To wait on, as a sales clerk. *—v.i.* **9** To give assistance. **10** To be useful or effective: Nothing seems to *help.* **—cannot help but** To be compelled to; must. *—n.* **1** Aid; assistance. **2** Support; comfort. **3** Remedy; relief. **4 a** A worker hired to help. **b** Such workers collectively. [< OE *helpan*] **—help′er** *n.* **—Syn.** *v.* **1** succor, assist. **4** benefit, improve.
help·ful (help′fəl) *adj.* Providing help; beneficial. **—help′·ful·ly** *adv.* **—help′ful·ness** *n.*
help·ing (hel′ping) *n.* A serving of food for one person.
help·less (help′lis) *adj.* **1** Unable to help oneself; feeble. **2** Incompetent; incapable. **3** Incapable of helping; powerless. **—help′less·ly** *adv.* **—help′less·ness** *n.*
help·mate (help′māt) *n.* A helper and partner, esp. a wife or husband. Also **help·meet** (help′mēt).
hel·ter-skel·ter (hel′tər·skel′tər) *adv.* In a hurried and confused manner. *—adj.* Hurried and confused. *—n.* Disorderly hurry or confusion. [?]
helve (helv) *n.* A handle, as of an ax. [< OE *helfe*]
hem[1] (hem) *n.* **1** A finished border on fabric, made by folding one edge over and sewing it down. **2** A comparable border or edge. *—v.t.* **hemmed, hem·ming 1** To make a hem on. **2** To border; edge. **3** To shut in; enclose; restrict: with *in, about,* etc. [< OE] **—hem′mer** *n.*
hem[2] (hem) *n. & interj.* A sound, as of clearing the throat. *—v.i.* **hemmed, hem·ming 1** To make the sound "hem." **2** To hesitate in speaking. [Imit.]
he-man (hē′man′) *n. pl.* **·men** (-men′) *Informal* A virile, muscular man.
hem·a·tite (hem′ə·tīt, hē′mə-) *n.* A red mineral form of iron oxide, one of the important ores of iron. [< Gk. *haima* blood] **—hem·a·tit·ic** (hem′ə·tit′ik, hē′mə-) *adj.*
hemato- *combining form* Blood: *hematology.* Also before vowels, **hemat-.** [< Gk. *haima, haimatos* blood]
he·ma·tol·o·gy (hē′mə·tol′ə·jē, hem′ə-) *n.* The study of the blood and its diseases. **—he′ma·tol′o·gist** *n.*
he·ma·to·ma (hē′mə·tō′mə, hem′ə-) *n. pl.* **·to·ma·ta** (-tō′·mə·tə) or **·to·mas** *Pathol.* A swelling containing a mass of effused blood.
hemi- *prefix* Half: *hemisphere.* [< Gk. *hēmi-* half]
hem·i·dem·i·sem·i·qua·ver (hem′ē·dem′ē·sem′ē·kwā′·vər) *n. Music Chiefly Brit.* A sixty-fourth note.
he·mip·ter·ous (hi·mip′tər·əs) *adj.* Pertaining to an order of insects having usu. suctorial mouth parts and four wings, including true bugs, crickets, etc. Also **he·mip′ter·al.** [< Gk. *hēmi-* half + *pteron* wing]
hem·i·sphere (hem′ə·sfir) *n.* **1** Half of a sphere. **2 a** A half of the terrestrial or celestial globe, esp. one of the halves of the earth, including the **Northern** and **Southern Hemispheres,** divided at the equator, and the **Eastern** and **Western Hemispheres,** divided at a meridian. The Eastern Hemisphere includes Europe, Asia, Africa, and Australia; the Western Hemisphere includes North and South America. **b** A map or projection of one of these. **—hem·i·spher·ic** (hem′ə·sfer′ik) or **·i·cal** *adj.*
hem·i·stich (hem′i·stik) *n.* **1** Half of a line of poetic verse. **2** A short or incomplete line of verse. [< Gk. *hēmi-* half + *stichos* a row, line of poetry]
hem·line (hem′līn′) *n.* The line formed by the lower edge of a garment, as a dress.
hem·lock (hem′lok) *n.* **1** Any evergreen tree of a genus of coniferous evergreen trees of North America and Asia. **2** The wood of this tree. **3** A large poisonous plant related to parsley: also **poison hemlock. 4** A poison made from this. [< OE *hymlice*]

Hemlock branch

hemo- *combining form* Blood: *hemoglobin.* [< Gk. *haima* blood]
he·mo·glo·bin (hē′mə·glō′bin, hem′ə-) *n.* The pigment in red blood corpuscles which readily forms unstable compounds with oxygen and carbon dioxide and thus transports these gases throughout the body.
he·mo·phil·i·a (hē′mə·fil′ē·ə, -fil′yə, hem′ə-) *n.* A sex-linked, hereditary disorder characterized by deficient clotting of the blood and profuse bleeding. [< Gk. *haima* blood + *philia* fondness] **—he·mo·phil·i·ac** (hē′mə·fil′ē·ak, hem′ə-) *n.* **—he·mo·phil·ic** (hē′mə·fil′ik, hem′ə-) *adj.*
hem·or·rhage (hem′ər·ij, hem′rij) *n.* Discharge of blood from a ruptured blood vessel. *—v.i.* **·rhaged, ·rhag·ing** To bleed copiously. [< Gk. *haima* blood + *rhēgnynai* burst] **—hem·or·rhag·ic** (hem′ə·raj′ik) *adj.*
hem·or·rhoid (hem′ə·roid) *n.* A varicose vein in the region of the anus. [< Gk. *haima* blood + *rheein* flow] **—hem′or·rhoi′dal** *adj.*
he·mo·stat (hē′mə·stat, hem′ə-) *n.* Any device or drug that checks bleeding.
hemp (hemp) *n.* **1** A tall, annual herb with small green flowers and fibrous stems. **2** The tough, strong fiber from this plant, used to make rope, cloth, etc. **3** Any similar fiber or plant. **4** A hallucinogenic drug prepared from the plant, as hashish. [< OE *henep*]
hemp·en (hem′pən) *adj.* Of hemp.
hem·stitch (hem′stich′) *n.* An ornamental openwork stitch made by pulling out a number of parallel threads and gathering the remaining cross threads in regularly spaced groups. *—v.t.* To sew or ornament with such stitches. **—hem′stitch′er** *n.*
hen (hen) *n.* A female bird, esp. the mature female of the common domestic fowl. [< OE *henn*]
hen·bane (hen′bān′) *n.* A poisonous plant related to belladonna and yielding a medicinal alkaloid.
hence (hens) *adv.* **1** Therefore; consequently. **2** From this time; from now: a month *hence.* **3** From this place; away. *—interj. Archaic* Depart; begone. [< OE *heonan* from here]
hence·forth (hens′fôrth′, -fōrth′, hens′fôrth′, -fōrth′) *adv.* From this time on. Also **hence′for′ward** (-fôr′wərd).
hench·man (hench′mən) *n. pl.* **·men** (-mən) **1** A faithful follower or retainer. **2** A subservient supporter of a powerful, often disreputable person. [< OE *hengst* horse + MAN]
hen·e·quen (hen′ə·kin) *n.* **1** A coarse, sisal-like plant fiber. **2** A tropical American agave yielding this fiber. Also **hen′e·quin.** [Sp. < Taino]
hen·na (hen′ə) *n.* **1** An Oriental shrub with lance-shaped leaves and fragrant flowers. **2** A reddish cosmetic dye made from the leaves of this plant. **3** A bright reddish brown. *—v.t.* **·naed, ·na·ing** To color with henna. [< Ar. *henna*]
hen·peck (hen′pek′) *v.t.* To domineer over or nag persistently at (one's husband). **—hen′pecked** *adj.*
hen·ry (hen′rē) *n. pl.* **·ries** or **·rys** *Electr.* A unit of inductance equal to that of a circuit in which a change in current of one ampere per second induces an electromotive force of one volt. [< J. *Henry,* 1797–1878, U.S. physicist]
hep (hep) *adj. Slang* Knowledgeable; hip. [?]
he·pat·ic (hi·pat′ik) *adj.* **1** Of, pertaining to, or resembling the liver. **2** Affecting the liver. *—n.* A drug acting on the liver. [< Gk. *hēpar* the liver]

he·pat·i·ca (hi·pat′ə·kə) *n.* Any of several small perennial herbs related to buttercups with three-lobed leaves and variously colored flowers. [< L *hepaticus* of the liver]

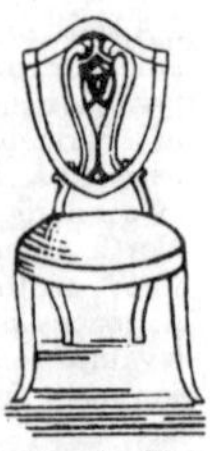

Hepplewhite chair

hep·a·ti·tis (hep′ə·tī′tis) *n.* Inflammation of the liver, usu. due to viral infection.

Hep·ple·white (hep′əl·ʰwīt) *adj.* Denoting an 18th-century English style of furniture characterized by graceful curves and light, slender woodwork. [< G. *Hepplewhite,* d. 1786, the designer]

hepta- *combining form* Seven: *heptagon.* Also, before vowels, **hept-**. [< Gk. *hepta* seven]

hep·ta·gon (hep′tə·gon) *n.* A polygon having seven sides and seven angles. —**hep·tag·o·nal** (hep·tag′ə·nəl) *adj.*

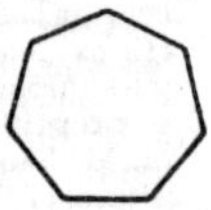

Heptagon

hep·tam·e·ter (hep·tam′ə·tər) *n.* A line of verse having seven metrical feet.

her (hûr) *pron.* The objective case of *she.* —*pronominal adj.* Of, belonging to, made or used by her: *her* garden; *her* style. [< OE *hire*]

Her·a·cles (her′ə·klēz) *Gk. & Rom. Myth.* HERCULES. Also **Her′a·kles.** —**Her′a·cle′an** *adj.*

her·ald (her′əld) *n.* **1** The bearer of significant news, an important message, etc. **2** A forerunner or portent of something to come; harbinger. **3** *Brit.* An official who traces and records genealogies, assigns heraldic arms, etc. —*v.t.* **1** To announce; proclaim. **2** To foretell the coming of. [< Gmc.] —**he·ral·dic** (hi·ral′dik) *adj.*

her·ald·ry (her′əl·drē) *n. pl.* **·ries 1** The art or occupation of establishing and devising coats of arms, tracing and recording genealogies, etc. **2** Coats of arms or similar heraldic bearings collectively. **3** Pomp or ceremony suggestive of heraldry.

herb (ûrb, hûrb) *n.* **1** A seed plant devoid of persistent woody tissue. **2** A plant used in medicine or for flavoring food. [< L *herba* grass, herbage]

her·ba·ceous (hûr·bā′shəs) *adj.* Of, pertaining to, or typical of herbs.

herb·age (ûr′bij, hûr′-) *n.* **1** Herbs or grass, esp. used as pasturage. **2** The succulent leaves, stems, etc., of herbaceous plants.

herb·al (hûr′bəl, ûr′-) *adj.* Of or pertaining to herbs. —*n.* A learned work on plants, esp. medicinal herbs.

herb·al·ist (hûr′bəl·ist, ûr′-) *n.* A dealer in or expert on herbs, esp. medicinal herbs.

her·bar·i·um (hûr·bâr′ē·əm) *n. pl.* **·bar·i·ums** or **·bar·i·a** (-bâr′ē·ə) **1** A collection of dried plants scientifically arranged. **2** A room or building containing such a collection.

her·bi·cide (hûr′bə·sīd) *n.* A substance used to kill plants, esp. weeds. —**her′bi·ci′dal** *adj.*

her·bi·vore (hûr′bə·vôr, -vōr) *n.* A herbivorous animal.

her·biv·o·rous (hûr·biv′ər·əs) *adj.* Feeding on plants or vegetable matter. [< L *herba* grass + *vorare* devour]

her·cu·le·an (hûr·kyōō′lē·ən, hûr′kyə·lē′ən) *adj.* **1** Having great physical strength. **2** Requiring great strength or endurance: *a herculean task.*

Her·cu·le·an (hûr·kyōō′lē·ən, hûr′kyə·lē′ən) *adj.* Of or pertaining to Hercules.

Her·cu·les (hûr′kyə·lēz) *Gk. & Rom. Myth.* A son of Zeus, renowned for his strength and endurance. —*n.* Any man of great size and strength.

herd[1] (hûrd) *n.* **1** A group of animals, as cattle or sheep, that stay or are kept together. **2** A large, often unthinking or easily led crowd. —*v.t. & v.i.* To bring or keep together in or as in a herd. [< OE *heord*] —**herd′er** *n.*

herd[2] (hûrd) *n.* A herdsman: used chiefly in combination: *cowherd.* —*v.t.* To care for or drive (sheep, cattle, etc.). [< OE *hirde* herdsman]

herds·man (hûrdz′mən) *n. pl.* **·men** (-mən) One who tends a herd.

here (hir) *adv.* **1** In, at, or to this place: Come *here.* **2** At this point or stage: *Here* he gave up. **3** As indicated: often used for emphasis after a noun: these books *here.* **4** In this present life. —*n.* This point or stage: from *here* on. —*interj.* An exclamation used to answer a roll call, etc. [< OE *hēr*] • *Here,* as an adverb, is correctly used after a noun: The people *here* need help. Although such use may appear somewhat adjectival in function, *here* is not an adjective, and it should not be used before a noun: These *here* people need help.

here·a·bout (hir′ə·bout′) *adv.* About this place; in this vicinity. Also **here′a·bouts′.**

here·af·ter (hir·af′tər, -äf′-) *adv.* **1** At some future time. **2** From this time forth. **3** In the state of life after death. —*n.* A future existence, esp. after death.

here·at (hir·at′) *adv.* **1** At this time or point. **2** Because of this.

here·by (hir·bī′) *adv.* By means of this.

he·red·i·ta·ble (hə·red′i·tə·bəl) *adj.* HERITABLE. —**he·red′·i·ta·bil′i·ty** *n.* —**he·red′i·ta·bly** *adv.*

he·red·i·tar·y (hə·red′ə·ter′ē) *adj.* **1 a** Inherited or capable of being inherited legally. **b** Having title or right through legal inheritance: *hereditary* ruler. **2** Transmitted by biological heredity from one's parents or ancestors. **3** Passed on by or as by one's forebears: *hereditary* rights. —**he·red′i·tar′i·ly** *adv.* —**he·red′i·tar′i·ness** *n.*

he·red·i·ty (hə·red′ə·tē) *n. pl.* **·ties 1** Transmission of characteristics from parents to offspring by a code embodied in the genes in the chromosomes. **2** The tendency of an organism to develop in the likeness of its progenitors because of such transmission. **3** The sum total of an individual's genetic inheritance.

Her·e·ford (her′ə·fərd) *n.* One of a breed of reddish cattle with white markings. [< *Hereford,* England]

here·in (hir·in′) *adv.* **1** In this; in this place or thing. **2** In this instance, circumstance, etc.

here·in·af·ter (hir′in·af′tər, -äf′-) *adv.* In a subsequent part of this (document, statement, text, etc.).

here·in·be·fore (hir′in·bi·fôr′, -fōr′) *adv.* In a preceding part of this (document, statement, text, etc.).

here·of (hir·uv′) *adv.* Of this; about this.

here·on (hir·on′, -ôn′) *adv.* On this: hereupon.

her·e·sy (her′ə·sē) *n. pl.* **·sies 1** A religious or doctrinal belief contrary to those of an established body or authority. **2** Any similar unorthodox or controversial belief. **3** Adherence to such beliefs. [< Gk. *hairesis* a sect]

her·e·tic (her′ə·tik) *n.* **1** One who maintains a heresy, esp. a religious heresy. **2** One whose views are unorthodox and controversial.

he·ret·i·cal (hə·ret′i·kəl) *adj.* Of, involving, or typical of heresy or heretics. —**he·ret′i·cal·ly** *adv.*

here·to (hir·tōō′) *adv.* To this thing, instance, etc.

here·to·fore (hir′tə·fôr′, -fōr′) *adv.* Previously; hitherto.

here·un·to (hir·un′tōō, -un·tōō′) *adv.* To this; hereto.

here·up·on (hir′ə·pon′, -pôn′, hir′ə·pon′, -pôn′) *adv.* Upon this; following immediately after this.

here·with (hir·with′, -wiṯẖ′) *adv.* **1** Along with this. **2** By this means; thus.

her·i·ta·ble (her′ə·tə·bəl) *adj.* **1** Capable of being inherited. **2** Capable of inheriting. [< OF *heriter* inherit] —**her′i·ta·bil′i·ty** *n.* —**her′i·ta·bly** *adv.*

her·i·tage (her′ə·tij) *n.* **1** Something that is or can be inherited. **2** Tradition, culture, rights, etc., transmitted from generation to generation. [< OF < *heriter* inherit]

her·maph·ro·dite (hûr·maf′rə·dīt) *n.* **1** A person or animal having both male and female sexual characteristics. **2** A single plant having both stamens and pistils. —*adj.* Of or like a hermaphrodite. [< Gk. *Hermaphroditos* son of Hermes and Aphrodite] —**her·maph′ro·dit′ic** (-dit′ik) *adj.* —**her·maph′ro·dit′i·cal·ly** *adv.* —**her·maph′ro·dit·ism, her·maph′ro·dism** *n.*

hermaphrodite brig A sailing vessel with a square-rigged foremast and a fore-and-aft rigged mainmast.

Her·mes (hûr′mēz) *Gk. Myth.* The messenger of the gods, and god of cunning, travelers, and commerce.

her·met·ic (hûr·met′ik) *adj.* Impervious to liquids or gases. Also **her·met′i·cal.** [< Gk. *Hermes (Trismegistus),* god of alchemy] —**her·met′i·cal·ly** *adv.*

her·mit (hûr′mit) *n.* **1** A person who abandons society and lives alone, often for religious contemplation. **2** A spicy molasses cooky. [< Gk. *erēmos* solitary] —**her·mit′ic** or **·i·cal** *adj.* —**her·mit′i·cal·ly** *adv.*

her·mit·age (hûr′mə·tij) *n.* **1** The dwelling place of a hermit. **2** A secluded dwelling; retreat.

hermit crab Any of a family of soft-bodied crabs that live in discarded shells of snails or other mollusks.

her·ni·a (hûr′nē·ə) *n.* Protrusion of an intestine or other organ through a barrier that normally holds it. [L] —**her′ni·al** *adj.*

he·ro (hir′ō) *n. pl.* **·roes** 1 A person of great courage, spirit, etc., esp. one who has undergone great danger or difficulty. 2 Any admirable or highly regarded man. 3 The main male character in a fictional or dramatic work. 4 In classical mythology, a man of both mortal and divine parentage, noted for outstanding courage, fortitude, etc. 5 A sandwich made from a loaf of bread or large roll split lengthwise. [< Gk. *hērōs*]

he·ro·ic (hi·rō′ik) *adj.* 1 Of or typical of a hero. 2 Characterized by or requiring great daring, strength, etc.: a *heroic* attempt. 3 Describing or in a style befitting the deeds of heroes: *heroic* poetry. 4 Larger than life size, as a statue. Also **he·ro′i·cal.** —*n.* 1 *pl.* Melodramatic behavior intended to display one's bravery, prowess, etc. 2 *pl.* HEROIC VERSE. —**he·ro′i·cal·ly** *adv.*

heroic couplet An English verse form consisting of two rhyming lines of iambic pentameter.

heroic verse A verse form, as the heroic couplet or blank verse, used esp. in epic and dramatic poetry.

her·o·in (her′ō·in) *n.* A white, odorless, habit-forming narcotic derived from morphine. [< *Heroin,* a trade name]

her·o·ine (her′ō·in) *n.* 1 A girl or woman of heroic character. 2 The chief female character in a fictional or dramatic work.

her·o·ism (her′ō·iz′əm) *n.* Qualities or behavior of or befitting a hero or heroine.

her·on (her′ən) *n.* One of a family of long-necked and long-legged wading birds. [< OF *hairon* < Gmc.]

Great blue heron

he·ro-wor·ship (hir′ō·wûr′·ship) *n.* Extravagant admiration for one regarded as a hero.

her·pes (hûr′pēz) *n.* Any of several acute viral diseases characterized by eruption of small blisters on the skin or mucous membrane. [< Gk. *herpein* to creep]

herpes zos·ter (zos′tər) SHINGLES.

her·pe·tol·o·gy (hûr′pə·tol′ə·jē) *n.* The branch of zoology that treats of reptiles and amphibians. [< Gk. *herpeton* a reptile + -LOGY] —**her·pe·to·log·i·cal** (hûr′pə·tə·loj′i·kəl) *adj.* —**her′pe·tol′o·gist** *n.*

Herr (her) *n. pl.* **Her·ren** (her′ən) *German* A title of address, equivalent to the English *Mr.*

her·ring (her′ing) *n. pl.* **·rings** or **·ring** Any of various marine fishes, esp. a small, silvery, food fish of the North Atlantic. [< OE *hæring*]

her·ring·bone (her′ing·bōn′) *n.* 1 A pattern, as of a fabric, consisting of parallel rows of short, slanting lines arranged at opposing angles. 2 Something having or forming such a pattern. —*adj.* Having or forming such a pattern. —*v.t.* & *v.i.* **·boned, ·bon·ing** To form or mark with such a pattern.

hers (hûrz) *pron.* 1 Belonging or pertaining to her: the form of the possessive case of the pronoun *she* when used in predicative position, without a following noun, or after *of:* That book is *hers;* those eyes of *hers.* 2 The things or persons belonging to or relating to her; *Hers* is the best.

her·self (hər·self′) *pron.* 1 The reflexive form of *her:* She blamed *herself.* 2 The emphatic or intensive form of *she:* She *herself* called me. 3 Her normal or true self: She is not *herself* lately.

hertz (hûrts) *n. pl.* **hertz** or **hertz·es** *Physics* A unit of frequency, as of waves, equal to one cycle per second. [< H. *Hertz,* 1857–94, German physicist]

he's (hēz) Contraction of *he is* or *he has.*

hes·i·tan·cy (hez′ə·tən·sē) *n. pl.* **·cies** The act or condition of hesitating. Also **hes′i·tance.**

hes·i·tant (hez′ə·tənt) *adj.* Hesitating or tending to hesitate; faltering, indecisive, or uncertain. —**hes′i·tant·ly** *adv.* —**Syn.** irresolute, undecided, unsure, doubtful.

hes·i·tate (hez′ə·tāt) *v.i.* **·tat·ed, ·tat·ing** 1 To delay doubtfully or irresolutely; pause uncertainly; waver. 2 To be unwilling; have qualms. 3 To pause or falter in speaking. [< L *haesitare,* freq. of *haerere* to stick] —**hes′i·tat′er** *n.* —**hes′i·tat′ing·ly** *adv.*

hes·i·ta·tion (hez′ə·tā′shən) *n.* 1 The act of hesitating. 2 A state of uncertainty or doubt. 3 A pause or faltering in speech. —**hes′i·ta′tive** *adj.* —**hes′i·ta′tive·ly** *adv.*

Hes·per·i·des (hes·per′ə·dēz) *Gk. Myth.* 1 The daughters of Atlas who guarded the golden apples later stolen by Hercules. 2 The garden where these apples grew. [< Gk. *hesperis* western]

Hes·pe·rus (hes′pər·əs) *n.* The evening star, esp. Venus. Also **Hes′per.** [< Gk. *Hesperos*]

Hes·sian (hesh′ən) *n.* 1 A native or inhabitant of Hesse. 2 A soldier from Hesse hired by the British to fight in the American Revolution. —*adj.* Of or from Hesse.

Hessian fly A small fly whose larva is very destructive to wheat.

he·tae·ra (hi·tir′ə) *n. pl.* **·tae·rae** (-tir′ē) or **·ras** In ancient Greece, an often educated or cultured courtesan or concubine. Also **he·tai·ra** (hi·tī′rə).

hetero- *combining form* Other; different: *heterogeneous.* Also, before vowels, **heter-.** [< Gk. *heteros* other]

het·er·o·dox (het′ər·ə·doks′) *adj.* At variance with an established or generally accepted doctrine or belief, esp. in religion; unorthodox. [< Gk. *hetero-* other + *doxa* opinion] —**het′er·o·dox′y** *n.*

het·er·o·dyne (het′ər·ə·dīn′) *adj. Telecom.* Describing a technique in which alternating currents of different frequencies are mixed so that they modulate each other and produce in the output components with frequencies equal to the sum and difference of the original frequencies. —*v.t.* **·dyned, ·dyn·ing** To cause such mixing and modulation of (electric signals).

het·er·o·ge·ne·ous (het′ər·ə·jē′nē·əs) *adj.* 1 Consisting of dissimilar elements or ingredients. 2 At variance; unlike; differing. [< Gk. *hetero-* other + *genos* kind] —**het·er·o·ge·ne·i·ty** (het′ər·ə·jə·nē′ə·tē), **het′er·o·ge′ne·ous·ness** *n.* —**het′er·o·ge′ne·ous·ly** *adv.*

het·er·o·nym (het′ər·ə·nim′) *n.* A word spelled like another, but having a different sound and meaning, as *bass* (a male voice) and *bass* (a fish). [< HETER(O)- + Gk. *onyma* name] —**het·er·on·y·mous** (het′ə·ron′ə·məs) *adj.*

het·er·o·sex·u·al (het′ər·ə·sek′shōō·əl) *adj.* 1 Of or characterized by sexual desire for members of the opposite sex. 2 *Biol.* Of or involving different sexes. —*n.* A heterosexual person. —**het′er·o·sex′u·al′i·ty** (-sek′shōō·al′ə·tē) *n.* —**het′er·o·sex′u·al·ly** *adv.*

heu·ris·tic (ʰyōō·ris′tik) *adj.* Guiding or stimulating to learn or make discoveries, as in education. [< Gk. *heuriskein* find out] —**heu·ris′ti·cal·ly** *adv.*

hew (ʰyōō) *v.* **hewed, hewn** or **hewed, hew·ing** *v.t.* 1 To make or shape with or as with blows of an ax. 2 To hack or chop with an ax, sword, etc. 3 To fell with or as with blows of an ax. —*v.i.* 4 To make repeated cutting blows, as with an ax. 5 To keep steadfastly. [< OE *hēawan*] —**hew′er** *n.*

hex (heks) *v.t. Informal* To cause bad luck to; jinx. —*n.* 1 An evil spell. 2 A persistent tendency to bad luck. [< G *Hexe* witch]

hexa- *combining form* Six: *hexagon.* Also, before vowels, **hex-.** [< Gk. *hex* six]

hex·a·chlo·ro·phene (hek′sə·klôr′ə·fēn′) *n.* An antibacterial agent used in some soaps.

hex·a·gon (hek′sə·gon) *n.* A polygon with six sides and six angles. [< HEXA- + Gk. *gonia* angle] —**hex·ag·o·nal** (hek·sag′ə·nəl) *adj.* —**hex·ag′·on·al·ly** *adv.*

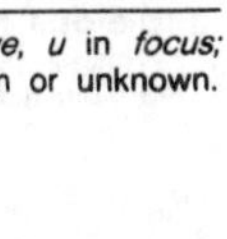

Hexagon

hex·a·gram (hek′sə·gram) *n.* A figure formed by constructing exterior equilateral triangles on the sides of a regular hexagon.

hex·a·he·dron (hek′sə·hē′drən) *n. pl.*

-drons or **-dra** (-drə) A polyhedron bounded by six plane faces. —**hex′a·he′dral** *adj.*

hex·am·e·ter (hek·sam′ə·tər) *n.* **1** A line of verse having six metrical feet. **2** Verse consisting of such lines. —**hex·a·met·ric** (hek′sə·met′rik), **hex′a·met′ri·cal** *adj.*

hex·a·pod (hek′sə·pod) *adj.* Having six legs. —*n.* INSECT (def. 1). —**hex·ap·o·dous** (hek·sap′ə·dəs) *adj.*

hey (hā) *interj.* An exclamation expressing surprise, calling for attention, etc.

hey·day (hā′dā′) *n.* The time of greatest vitality, vigor, influence, etc. [?]

HF, h.f., h-f. high frequency.

Hf hafnium.

hf. half.

HG, H.G. High German.

Hg mercury (L *hydrargyrum*).

hg. hectogram(s); heliogram.

hgt. height.

H.H. His (or Her) Highness; His Holiness.

hhd. hogshead.

H-hour (āch′our′) *n.* The hour appointed for a military operation to begin.

hi (hī) *interj. Informal* An exclamation of greeting.

HI Hawaii (P.O. abbr.).

hi·a·tus (hī·ā′təs) *n. pl.* **-tus·es** or **-tus** **1** A gap or break, with a part missing, as in a manuscript; lacuna. **2** Any interruption or break. **3** In pronunciation, a pause due to the concurrence of two separate vowels without an intervening consonant, as in *pre-eminent.* [L]

hi·ba·chi (hi·bä′chē) *n. pl.* **-chis** A charcoal-burning brazier, used for cooking food, etc. [< Jap. *hi* fire + *bachi* bowl]

hi·ber·nal (hī·bûr′nəl) *adj.* Pertaining to winter; wintry. [< L *hibernus* wintry]

hi·ber·nate (hī′bər·nāt) *v.t.* **-nat·ed, -nat·ing** **1** To pass the winter, esp. in a torpid state, as certain animals. **2** To pass the time in seclusion or inactivity. [< L *hibernare*] —**hi′·ber·na′tion** *n.*

Hi·ber·ni·a (hī·bûr′nē·ə) *n.* The Latin and poetic name for Ireland. —**Hi·ber′ni·an** *adj., n.*

hi·bis·cus (hī·bis′kəs, hi-) *n.* Any of a genus of usu. tropical plants with showy, variously colored flowers. [< Gk. *hibiskos* mallow]

hic·cup (hik′əp) *n.* A spasmodic contraction of the diaphragm accompanied by an involuntary sound. —*v.i.* **-cuped** or **-cupped, -cup·ing** or **-cup·ping** To have the hiccups; make a hiccup. Also **hic·cough** (hik′əp). [Imit.]

hic ja·cet (hik jā′set) Here lies: often inscribed on tombstones. [L]

hick (hik) *n. Informal* A person, usu. from rural areas, of unsophisticated manners, speech, dress, etc. [< RICHARD]

hick·o·ry (hik′ər·ē) *n. pl.* **-ries** **1** Any of various North American trees of the walnut family, yielding an edible nut and having hard, tough, heavy wood. **2** Something made of this wood, as a switch. [< Amer. Ind.]

hid (hid) *p.t. & a p.p.* of HIDE[1].

hi·dal·go (hi·dal′gō; *Sp.* ē·thäl′gō) *n. pl.* **-gos** (-gōz; *Sp.* -gōs) *Spanish* A Spanish nobleman of the lower rank. —**hi·dal′ga** (-gä) *n. Fem.*

hid·den (hid′n) *p.p.* of HIDE[1]. —*adj.* **1** Unseen; out of sight. **2** Not known or revealed.

hide[1] (hīd) *v.* **hid, hid·den** or **hid, hid·ing** *v.t.* **1** To put or keep out of sight; conceal. **2** To keep secret; withhold from knowledge: to *hide* one's fears. **3** To block or obstruct the sight of. —*v.i.* **4** To keep oneself out of sight; remain concealed. [< OE *hȳdan*] —**hid′er** *n.* —**Syn.** **1** secrete, cover, screen, bury. **2** cover up, cloak, mask, disguise, camouflage, veil, suppress.

hide[2] (hīd) *n.* **1** An animal skin, esp. as material for leather. **2** *Informal* The human skin. —*v.t.* **hid·ed, hid·ing** **1** To whip; flog severely. **2** To remove the hide from. [< OE *hȳd*]

hide·a·way (hīd′ə·wā′) *n.* A place of seclusion or retreat.

hide·bound (hīd′bound′) *adj.* **1** Obstinately fixed in opinion; narrow-minded. **2** Having the skin tight over the skeletal structure: said of animals.

hid·e·ous (hid′ē·əs) *adj.* Shocking or dreadful; ghastly; revolting. [< OF *hisde, hide* fright] —**hid′e·ous·ly** *adv.* —**hid′e·ous·ness** *n.*

hide-out (hīd′out′) *n.* A place of concealment and safety; hiding place.

hid·ing[1] (hī′ding) *n.* **1** The act of one who hides. **2** The condition of being hidden.

hid·ing[2] (hī′ding) *n. Informal* A flogging.

hie (hī) *v.t. & v.i.* **hied, hie·ing** or **hy·ing** To hasten; hurry: often reflexive. [< OE *hīgian*]

hi·er·ar·chy (hī′ər·är′kē) *n. pl.* **-chies** **1** A system of church government by ecclesiastics graded and empowered according to rank. **2** A body of ruling clergymen. **3** A group of things, people, ideas, etc., arranged in order of importance. [< Gk. *hieros* sacred + *archos* ruler] —**hi′er·ar′chic, hi′er·ar′chi·cal, hi′er·ar′chal** *adj.*

hi·er·at·ic (hī′ə·rat′ik) *adj.* **1** Of or used by priests; sacerdotal; consecrated. **2** Of or pertaining to a cursive form of ancient Egyptian hieroglyphs. Also **hi′er·at′i·cal.** [< Gk. *hieratikos* of a priest's office]

hi·er·o·glyph·ic (hī′ər·ə·glif′ik, hī′rə·glif′ik) *n.* **1** *Usu. pl.* Picture writing, esp. of the ancient Egyptians. **2** A character or symbol used in such writing. **3** A symbol, word, etc., difficult to understand. **4** *pl.* Illegible handwriting. Also **hi·er·o·glyph** (hī′ər·ə·glif′, hī′rə·glif′). —*adj.* Of, like, pertaining to, or written in hieroglyphics: also **hi·er·o·glyph** (hī′ər·ə·glif′, hī′rə·glif′). [< Gk. *hieros* sacred + *glyphein* carve] —**hi′er·o·glyph′i·cal·ly** *adv.*

Hieroglyphics

hi-fi (hī′fī′) *adj.* Of or having high fidelity. —*n. pl.* **-fis** A sound-reproducing system, esp. one with high fidelity.

hig·gle (hig′əl) *v.i.* **hig·gled, hig·gling** To dispute about terms; haggle; chaffer. [Var. of HAGGLE] —**hig′gler** *n.*

hig·gle·dy-pig·gle·dy (hig′əl·dē·pig′əl·dē) *adj.* In a disordered state; jumbled; muddled. —*adv.* In a confused manner. [?]

high (hī) *adj.* **1** Having great or considerable height; lofty; tall. **2** Having a (specified) height: an inch *high.* **3** Located a considerable distance above the ground, street, etc. **4** Extending to or performed from a height: a *high* dive. **5** Of relatively great importance, influence, etc.: a *high* official. **6** Of relatively great force, measure, degree, etc.: *high* voltage. **7** Of superior quality, character, etc.: *high* art. **8** Advanced, well developed, or complex: usu. in the comparative degree: *higher* mathematics. **9** Most important; chief: a *high* priest. **10** Fully advanced or culminated: *high* noon. **11** Grave; serious: *high* treason. **12** Expensive; costly: Rent is *high.* **13** Luxurious: *high* living. **14** Strict or formal, as in doctrine, ceremony, etc. **15** Elated; merry: *high* spirits. **16** Far from the equator: *high* latitudes. **17** **a** Having a frequency of relatively great measure, as a tone. **b** Producing such tones: a *high* voice. **18** Of or indicating an arrangement of gears for producing the highest ratio of output speed to input speed. **19** Slightly tainted: said esp. of game meat. **20** *Informal* Feeling the effects of liquor or drugs. —*adv.* **1** To or at a high level, position, degree, etc. **2** In a high manner. **3** At a high pitch. —*n.* **1** A high level, position, etc. **2** *Meteorol.* A region of relatively high atmospheric pressure. **3** An arrangement of gears that produces the greatest ratio of output speed to input speed. **4** *Slang* The euphoria produced by drugs. [< OE *hēah*]

high and dry **1** Above the reach of water. **2** Stranded; helpless.

high and low Everywhere.

high and mighty Haughty; imperious.

high·ball[1] (hī′bôl′) *n.* An alcoholic drink, usu. whiskey to which is added water or a carbonated beverage, served with ice. [?]

high·ball[2] (hī′bôl) *n.* A railroad signal meaning to go ahead. —*v.i.* *Slang* To go at great speed. [< a ball that could be raised or lowered, once used as a signal]

high·born (hī′bôrn′) *adj.* Of noble birth.

Highboy

high·boy (hī′boi′) *n.* A tall chest of drawers usu. in two sections, with the upper section recessed, set upon legs.

high·bred (hī′bred′) *adj.* 1 Of a fine pedigree. 2 Characterized by fine manners or good breeding.

high·brow (hī′brou′) *Informal n.* A person of cultivated or intellectual tastes: sometimes a term of derision. *—adj.* Of or suitable for such a person.

high·chair (hī′châr′) *n.* A baby's chair having an eating tray and tall legs.

High Church The group in the Anglican Church that exalts the authority of the church and emphasizes the value of ritual. **—High′-Church′man** *n.*

high-class (hī′klas′, -kläs′) *adj.* Superior, as in quality, rank, etc.

high comedy Comedy presenting the world of polite society and relying chiefly on witty, sophisticated dialogue and situations.

high·er-up (hī′ər·up′) *n. Informal* A person of superior rank or position.

high·fa·lu·tin (hī′fə·lo͞ot′n) *adj. Informal* Excessively pompous or grand. Also **high′fa·lu′ting.** [?]

high fidelity The electronic processing of a signal without adding significant distortion. **—high′-fi·del′i·ty** *adj.*

high-flown (hī′flōn′) *adj.* 1 Pretentious. 2 Extravagant in style.

high·fly·ing (hī′flī′ing) *adj.* 1 Flying at a considerable height. 2 Having extravagant ideas or opinions, a lavish style of living, etc. **—high′fli′er, high′fly′er** *n.*

high frequency A wave frequency between 3 and 30 megahertz.

High German 1 The standard German language. 2 German as used in S Germany.

high-grade (hī′grād′) *adj.* Of superior quality.

high·hand·ed (hī′han′did) *adj.* Officious; overbearing. **—high′hand′ed·ly** *adv.* **—high′hand′ed·ness** *n.*

high-hat (hī′hat′) *Informal n.* A snob. *—adj.* Aristocratic; snobbish. *—v.t.* **-hat·ted, -hat·ting** To snub; treat snobbishly.

high hat A top hat.

high·jack (hī′jak′) *v. Informal* HIJACK. **—high′jack′er** *n.*

high jump An athletic event in which the contestants jump for height over a horizontal bar.

high·land (hī′lənd) *n.* An elevation of land, usu. mountainous in character. **—the Highlands** The mountainous part of N Scotland. *—adj.* Of or pertaining to a highland.

high·land·er (hī′lən·dər) *n.* An inhabitant of a highland; mountaineer.

High·land·er (hī′lən·dər) *n.* A native of the Scottish Highlands; a Gael.

Highland fling A lively Scottish dance.

high-lev·el language (hī′lev′əl) A computer programming language that uses plain English words or simple mathematical expressions.

high·light (hī′līt′) *n.* 1 *pl.* The bright spots in a photograph or picture. 2 A part or detail of special importance or vividness. *—v.t.* 1 *pl.* To give a highlight to. 2 To give special emphasis to; feature. 3 To be the highlight of.

high·ly (hī′lē) *adv.* 1 In a high rank or position. 2 Very much; extremely. 3 With much approval; favorably. 4 At a high price or rate.

High Mass In the Roman Catholic Church, a Mass that is sung and accompanied by full ceremony.

high-mind·ed (hī′mīn′did) *adj.* Having lofty ideals or feelings. **—high′-mind′ed·ly** *adv.* **—high′-mind′ed·ness** *n.*

high·ness (hī′nis) *n.* The quality or condition of being high.

High·ness (hī′nis) *n.* A title of honor belonging to persons of royal rank: with *His, Her,* or *Your.*

high-pitched (hī′picht′) *adj.* 1 High in pitch. 2 Having a steep slope: said of roofs.

high-pres·sure (hī′presh′ər) *adj.* 1 Having, withstanding, or using a high pressure. 2 Exerting vigorous, persuasive tactics: *high-pressure* salesmanship. *—v.t.* **·sured, ·sur·ing** To persuade or influence by such methods.

high-rise (hī′rīz′) *adj.* Describing a relatively tall building or structure. *—n.* A tall building, as a many-storied apartment house: also **high rise.**

high school A secondary school, typically comprising grades 10, 11, and 12, and sometimes grade 9. **—high′-school′** *adj.* **—high′-school′er** *n.*

high seas The unenclosed waters of the ocean or sea, esp. those beyond the territorial jurisdiction of any one country or nation.

high-sound·ing (hī′soun′ding) *adj.* Ostentatious or imposing in sound or meaning.

high-spir·it·ed (hī′spir′ə·tid) *adj.* 1 Full of energy and courage. 2 Fun-loving; vivacious.

high-strung (hī′strung′) *adj.* Highly sensitive and nervous; excitable.

hight (hīt) *adj. Archaic* Called or named. [<OE *hātan* to call]

high-ten·sion (hī′ten′shən) *adj.* Of, for, at, or using a relatively high voltage.

high-test (hī′test′) *adj.* 1 Meeting difficult tests or requirements. 2 Denoting a very volatile gasoline with a high octane number.

high tide 1 The maximum tidal elevation of the water at any point; also, the time of its occurrence. 2 Any culminating point in a series of events.

high time 1 About time; not a moment too soon. 2 *Slang* An occasion of great fun and revelry: also **high old time.**

high-toned (hī′tōnd′) *adj.* 1 *Informal* Fashionable; swank. 2 Noble, lofty, and honorable. 3 High in pitch.

high treason Treason against the sovereign or state.

high-wa·ter mark (hī′wô′tər, -wot′ər) 1 The highest point reached by a body of water. 2 Any highest point, as of achievement.

high·way (hī′wā) *n.* 1 A public road, usu. a main road. 2 A way to some goal or objective.

high·way·man (hī′wā′mən) *n. pl.* **·men** (-mən) Formerly, one who practiced robbery on the highway.

H.I.H. His (or Her) Imperial Highness.

hi·jack (hī′jak′) *v.t. Informal* 1 To steal a shipment of (goods, bootleg liquor, etc.) by force. 2 To rob or steal (a truck, etc., carrying such goods). 3 To seize control of (an aircraft) while in flight by the threat or use of force and redirect it to a different destination; skyjack. 4 To rob, swindle, etc., by force or coercion. [?] **—hi′jack′er** *n.*

hi·jinks (hī′jingks′) *n. pl. Informal* Rough and often mischievous play; horseplay. [?]

hike (hīk) *v.* **hiked, hik·ing** *v.i.* 1 To go on foot, as for pleasure or on a military march; tramp. *—v.t.* 2 To increase, raise, or lift: usu. with *up.* *—n.* 1 A journey on foot; a long walk. 2 *Informal.* An increase: a price *hike.* [?]

hi·lar·i·ous (hi·lâr′ē·əs, -lar′-, hī-) *adj.* Boisterously funny and gay. **—hi·lar′i·ous·ly** *adv.* **—hi·lar′i·ous·ness** *n.*

hi·lar·i·ty (hi′lâr′ə·tē, -lar′-, hī-) *n. pl.* **·ties** Boisterous fun and gaiety. [<Gk. *hilaros* cheerful]

hill (hil) *n.* 1 A natural elevation rising above the earth's surface and smaller than a mountain. 2 A heap or pile: a *molehill.* 3 A small mound of earth placed over or around certain plants and tubers. 4 The plants and tubers so surrounded. **—the Hill** CAPITOL HILL. *—v.t.* 1 To surround or cover with hills, as potatoes. 2 To form a hill or heap of. [<OE *hyll*]

hill·bil·ly (hil′bil′ē) *n. pl.* **·lies** *Informal* A person from the mountains or a backwoods area, esp. of the S U.S.

hill·ock (hil′ək) *n.* A small hill; a mound. **—hill′ock·y** *adj.*

hill·side (hil′sīd′) *n.* The side of a hill.

hill·top (hil′top′) *n.* The summit of a hill.

hill·y (hil′ē) *adj.* **hill·i·er, hill·i·est** 1 Full of hills. 2 Like a hill; steep. **—hill′i·ness** *n.*

hilt (hilt) *n.* The handle and guard of a sword or dagger. *—v.t.* To provide with a hilt. [<OE]

hi·lum (hī′ləm) *n. pl.* **·la** (-lə) The scar on a seed at its former point of attachment. Also **hi′lus** (-ləs). [<L, a trifle]

him (him) *pron.* The objective case of the pronoun *he.* [<OE]

H.I.M. His (or Her) Imperial Majesty.

him·self (him·self′) *pron.* 1 The emphatic or intensive form of the pronouns *he* or *him:* He *himself* told me. 2 The reflexive form of *him:* He asked *himself.* 3 His true or usual self or condition: He's not *himself* today.

hind[1] (hīnd) *adj.* **hind·er, hind·most** or **hind·er·most** Rear; posterior. [< OE *hindan* behind]

hind[2] (hīnd) *n.* The female of the red deer, esp. when fully mature.

hind[3] (hīnd) *n. Archaic* A farm laborer; also, a peasant. [< OE *hīwan* domestics]

Hind. Hindi; Hindu; Hindustan; Hindustani.

hind·brain (hīnd′brān′, hīn′-) *n.* The posterior part of the brain which includes the cerebellum and medulla oblongata.

hin·der[1] (hin′dər) *v.t.* **1** To keep back or delay; check. **2** To prevent; obstruct. —*v.i.* **3** To be an obstruction or obstacle. [< OE *hinder* behind] —**hin′der·er** *n.* —**Syn. 1** impede, stop, stay, halt, bar, block. **2** encumber, foil, frustrate.

hind·er[2] (hīn′dər) *adj.* Pertaining to or situated at the rear. [< OE]

Hin·di (hin′dē) *n.* The official language of India.

hind·most (hīnd′mōst′, hīn′-) *adj.* Closest to the rear. Also **hind′er·most′** (hīn′dər-).

Hin·doo (hin′dōō) *n.* HINDU.

Hin·doo·ism (hin′dōō·iz′əm) *n.* HINDUISM.

hind·quar·ter (hīnd′kwôr′tər, hīn′-) *n.* **1** One of the two back parts of a carcass of beef, veal, lamb, etc., including a hind leg. **2** *pl.* The posterior part of any quadruped.

hin·drance (hin′drəns) *n.* **1** The act of hindering. **2** A person or thing that hinders or obstructs.

hind·sight (hīnd′sīt′, hīn′-) *n.* **1** Insight into the nature and difficulties of a situation after the event. **2** The rear sight of a gun or rifle.

Hin·du (hin′dōō) *n.* **1** A person who professes Hinduism. **2** Loosely, a native of India. —*adj.* Of Hindus, their language, religion, etc.

Hin·du·ism (hin′dōō·iz′əm) *n.* The religion and social system of the Hindus, derived from Brahmanism, and influenced by Buddhism.

Hin·du·sta·ni (hin′dōō·stä′nē, -stan′ē) *n.* The principal dialect of Hindi. —*adj.* Of or pertaining to Hindustan, its people, or to Hindustani.

hinge (hinj) *n.* **1** A device allowing one part to turn upon another, esp. the hook or joint on which a door or shutter swings or turns. **2** A device consisting of two metal plates joined by a rod, used as to connect a lid to a box. **3** A natural joint, as in the shell of an oyster. **4** A pivotal point on which anything depends for its effect or course. —*v.* **hinged, hing·ing** *v.i.* **1** To have one's course determined by an action or eventuality; be dependent: with *on* or *upon.* —*v.t.* **2** To attach by or equip with hinges. [ME *hengen*]

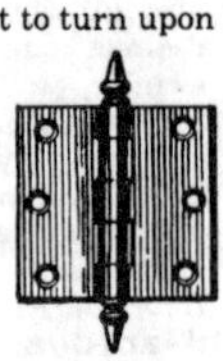

Hinge

hin·ny (hin′ē) *n. pl.* **·nies** The offspring of a stallion and a female donkey. [< Gk. *ginnos*]

hint (hint) *n.* **1** An indirect suggestion or implication. **2** A small amount or part: a *hint* of rain. —*v.t.* **1** To suggest indirectly; imply. —*v.i.* **2** To make hints: often with *at.* [< OF *hentan* seize, grasp] —**hint′er** *n.* —**Syn.** *n.* **1** reminder, tip, prompting, innuendo, insinuation. —*v.* **1** allude to, insinuate, remind, prompt.

hin·ter·land (hin′tər·land′, -lənd) *n.* **1** The region lying behind the district along a seacoast or riverside. **2** The region remote from urban areas; the back country. [G]

hip[1] (hip) *n.* **1** The lateral part of the body between the brim of the pelvis and the free part of the thigh. **2** The joint between the thigh bone and the pelvis: also **hip joint.** **3** *Archit.* The external angle in which adjacent roof slopes meet each other. —*v.t.* **hipped, hip·ping** *Archit.* To build with a hip or hips, as a roof. [< OE *hype*]

hip[2] (hip) *n.* The fruit of a rose. [< OE *hēope*]

hip[3] (hip) *adj. Slang* Aware; informed: often followed by *to.* [?]

hip·bone (hip′bōn′) *n.* The innominate bone.

hipped[1] (hipt) *adj.* Having hips of a specified kind: used in combination: *heavy-hipped.*

hipped[2] (hipt) *adj.* **1** *Slang* Unduly interested or engrossed by something; obsessed: *hipped* on socialism. **2** *Brit.* Affected with hypochondria or depression.

hip·pie (hip′ē) *n.* One of a group of young people whose alienation from conventional society is expressed by informal and eccentric clothing, a preoccupation with drugs and mysticism, and an interest in communal living. [Var. of HIPSTER]

hip·po (hip′ō) *n. Informal* A hippopotamus.

Hip·po·cratic oath (hip′ə·krat′ik) An oath credited to Hippocrates, and detailing the ethical code of the medical profession, still administered to those entering the practice of medicine.

hip·po·drome (hip′ə·drōm) *n.* **1** An arena, stadium, or large structure for horse shows, circuses, etc. **2** In ancient Greece and Rome, a course or track for horse races and chariot races. [< Gk. *hippos* horse + *dromos* running]

hip·po·pot·a·mus (hip′ə·pot′ə·məs) *n. pl.* **·mus·es** or **·mi** (-mī) A massive, herbivorous, short-legged, thick-skinned African mammal. [< Gk. *hippos* horse + *potamos* river]

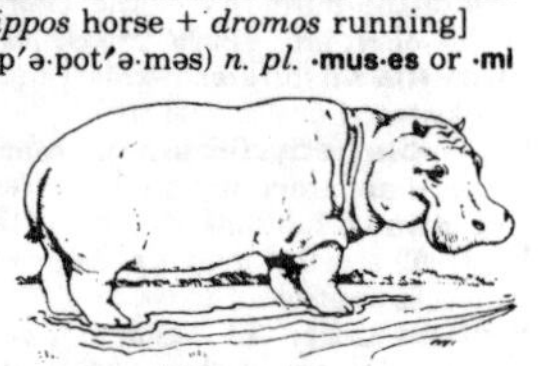

Hippopotamus

hip·ster (hip′stər) *n. Slang* One who is hip, as one versed in jazz. [< HIP[3] + -STER]

hire (hīr) *v.t.* **hired, hir·ing 1** To obtain the services of (a person) or the use of (a thing) in exchange for payment; employ; rent: to *hire* a new plant manager; to *hire* a tuxedo for a formal dinner. **2** To grant the use of (a thing) or the services of (a person) for a fee; let: often with *out.* —*n.* **1** Compensation for labor, services, etc. **2** The act of hiring or the condition of being hired. [< OE *hȳran*] —**hir′a·ble, hire′a·ble** *adj.* —**hir′er** *n.*

hire·ling (hīr′ling) *n.* One who serves for hire, esp. such a one whose motives are primarily mercenary.

hir·sute (hûr′sōōt, hir′-, hûr·sōōt′, hir-) *adj.* Hairy. [< L *hirsutus* rough] —**hir′sute·ness** *n.*

his (hiz) *pron.* **1** Belonging or pertaining to him: the possessive case of the pronoun *he,* used predicatively or after *of:* This room is *his;* that laugh of *his.* **2** The things, persons, etc., belonging or pertaining to him: Her book is better than *his;* He protects himself and *his.* —*pronominal adj.* The possessive case of the pronoun *he,* used attributively: *his* book. [< OE]

His·pa·ni·a (his·pā′nē·ə, -nyə, -pä′-) *n.* The Latin name for what is now Spain and Portugal.

His·pan·ic (his·pan′ik) *adj.* Of or pertaining to the countries or people of Spain, Portugal, and Latin America, or to their languages, customs, or culture. —*n. U.S.* A native or inhabitant of Spanish America; Spanish American.

hiss (his) *n.* **1** The prolonged sound of *s,* as that made by escaping air. **2** Such a sound made to express disapproval, hatred, etc. —*v.i.* **1** To make or emit a hiss or hisses. **2** To express disapproval or hatred by hissing. —*v.t.* **3** To express disapproval or hatred of by hissing. **4** To express by means of a hiss or hisses. **5** To pursue, drive off, silence, etc., by hissing: usu. with *off, down,* etc. [< OE *hyscan* jeer at] —**hiss′er** *n.*

hist (hist) *interj.* An exclamation to attract attention, command silence, etc. [Imit.]

hist. histology; historian; historical; history.

his·ta·mine (his′tə·mēn, -min) *n.* A product of protein metabolism found in all organisms and released profusely in allergic reactions. [< Gk. *histion* tissue + AMINE]

his·tol·o·gy (his·tol′ə·jē) *n.* The branch of anatomy concerned with the microscopic structure of tissues. [< Gk. *histion* tissue + -LOGY] —**his·to·log·i·cal** (his′tə·loj′i·kəl) *adj.* —**his·tol′o·gist** *n.*

his·to·ri·an (his·tôr′ē·ən, -tō′rē-) *n.* **1** One who writes a history. **2** One versed in history.

his·tor·ic (his·tôr′ik, -tor′-) *adj.* **1** Celebrated in history; notable; memorable; outstanding: the *historic* ascent of Mt. Everest. **2** HISTORICAL. • Current usage favors *historic* (def. 1) rather than *historical* to describe any outstanding or memorable event or achievement.

his·tor·i·cal (his·tôr′i·kəl, -tor′-) *adj.* **1** Of or relating to history. **2** Serving as a record or as evidence of past events, etc.: a *historical* letter. **3** Dealing with past events, etc.: a *historical* novel. **4** Factually true or real. **5** HISTORIC (def. 1). —**his·tor′i·cal·ly** *adv.* —**his·tor′i·cal·ness** *n.* • See HISTORIC.

historical present *Gram.* The present tense used to narrate a past event.

his·to·ri·og·ra·pher (his·tôr′ē·og′rə·fər, -tō′rē-) *n.* A historian, esp. one hired to write an official history of an institution, etc. —**his·to′ri·og′ra·phy** *n.*

his·to·ry (his′tə·rē, his′trē) *n. pl.* **·ries** 1 A recorded narrative of past events, esp. those concerning a particular period, nation, individual, etc. 2 The branch of knowledge dealing with the events and people of the past. 3 The aggregate of events concerning a given subject, object, etc.: the *history* of their marriage. 4 Past events in general: in the course of *history.* 5 A past worthy of notice. 6 Something in the past: This is all *history* now. 7 A drama, story, etc., of past events, whether real or imaginary. [< Gk. *historia* knowledge, narrative]

his·tri·on·ic (his′trē·on′ik) *adj.* 1 Of or pertaining to actors, acting, or to the stage. 2 Theatrical in manner, esp. if excessively so. [< L *histrio* actor] —**his′tri·on′i·cal·ly** *adv.*

his·tri·on·ics (his′trē·on′iks) *n.pl.* 1 *(construed as sing.)* The art of dramatic representation. 2 *(construed as pl.)* Excessive or artificial display of emotion.

hit (hit) *v.* **hit, hit·ting** *v.t.* 1 To come against or in contact with, usu. with impact or force. 2 To inflict (a blow, etc.). 3 To strike with a blow. 4 To cause to strike or come against with force: with *on, against,* etc.: I *hit* my leg on the door. 5 To strike with or as with a missile: He *hit* the robber in the leg. 6 To move or propel by striking: He *hit* the ball over the fence. 7 To reach, arrive at, or achieve: to *hit* a new low; to *hit* upon the solution. 8 To suit: The idea *hit* her fancy. 9 To affect adversely: His death *hit* her hard. 10 *Informal* To go at vigorously or to excess: to *hit* the bottle. 11 *Slang* To ask or demand of: with *for:* He *hit* me for a loan. 12 *Slang* To arrive at: We *hit* the city late. 13 In baseball, to make a (specified base) hit: to *hit* a triple. —*v.i.* 14 To deliver a blow or blows: often with *out.* 15 To strike with force; bump: often with *against.* —*n.* 1 A stroke, blow, shot, etc., that reaches its mark. 2 COLLISION. 3 A success: The play was a *hit.* 4 A piece of wit or sarcasm. 5 BASE HIT. [< ON *hitta* come upon] —**hit′ter** *n.*

hit-and-run (hit′ən·run′) *adj.* Designating or involving an automobile operator who hits a pedestrian or another vehicle and drives away without stopping.

hitch (hich) *n.* 1 A stop or sudden halt. 2 A hindrance or obstacle, as to an enterprise. 3 The act of catching or fastening, as by a rope, hook, etc.; also, a connection so made. 4 *Naut.* Any of various knots made with rope, rigging, etc. 5 A limp; hobble. 6 *Slang* A ride given in hitchhiking. 7 *Slang* A period of time spent in military service, prison, etc. —*v.t.* 1 To fasten or tie, esp. temporarily, with a knot, rope, strap, etc. 2 To secure to a vehicle: often with *up:* to *hitch* up a trailer to a car. 3 To move or shift with a jerk or jerks: He *hitched* himself around in his chair. 4 *Informal* To marry: usu. in the passive. 5 *Slang* To obtain (a ride) by hitchhiking. —*v.i.* 6 To move with jerks: to *hitch* forward. 7 To become caught or entangled. 8 *Slang* To travel by hitchhiking. [ME *hicchen*]

Hitches *def. 4*
a. half. b. clove. c. rolling.

hitch·hike (hich′hīk′) *Informal v.i.* 1 To travel by signalling for rides from passing vehicles. —*v.t.* 2 To obtain (a ride) by this method. —**hitch′hik′er** *n.*

hith·er (hith′ər) *adv.* In this direction; toward this place. —*adj.* Nearer. [< OE *hider*]

hith·er·most (hith′ər·mōst′) *adj.* Nearest in this direction or to this place.

hith·er·to (hith′ər·to͞o′, hith′ər·to͞o′) *adv.* Up to this time; until now.

hith·er·ward (hith′ər·wərd) *adv.* HITHER. Also **hith′er·wards.**

hit-or-miss (hit′ər·mis′) *adj.* Heedless; haphazard. —*adv.* In a hit-or-miss way; haphazardly.

Hit·tite (hit′īt) *n.* 1 One of an ancient people who established a powerful empire in Asia Minor and N Syria about 2000–1200 B.C. 2 The language of the Hittites. —*adj.* Of the Hittites, their culture, or language.

hive (hīv) *n.* 1 A structure in which bees may dwell. 2 A colony of bees. 3 A place full of activity. 4 A teeming crowd of people. —*v.* **hived, hiv·ing** *v.t.* 1 To cause (bees) to enter a hive. 2 To store (honey) in a hive. 3 To store (anything) for future use. —*v.i.* 4 To enter or dwell in or as in a hive. [< OE *hȳf*]

hives (hīvz) *n.* Any of various skin diseases characterized by wheals, itching, etc., esp. urticaria. [?]

H.J. here lies (L *hic jacet*).

H.L. House of Lords.

hl, hl. hectoliter(s).

H.M. His (or Her) Majesty.

hm, hm. hectometer(s).

H.M.S. His (or Her) Majesty's Service (or Ship, Steamer).

ho (hō) *interj.* 1 A call to excite attention. 2 An exclamation expressing surprise, pleasure, derision, etc. 3 An exclamation directing attention to some distant point: Land *ho!* Westward *ho!* Also **hoa.** [Imit.]

Ho holmium.

hoa·gie (hō′gē) *n.* HERO (def. 5). Also **hoa′gy** *n.* (*pl.* **·gies**). [?]

hoar (hôr, hōr) *adj.* 1 White or gray with age; hoary. 2 White or grayish white in color. 3 Ancient. —*n.* 1 HOARFROST. 2 The condition of being white with age or frost; hoariness. [< OE *hār* gray-haired]

hoard (hôrd, hōrd) *n.* An accumulation of something put away for safeguarding or for future use. —*v.t.* 1 To gather and store away or hide for future use. —*v.i.* 2 To gather and store away food, money, etc. [< OE *hord* treasure] —**hoard′er** *n.*

hoar·frost (hôr′frôst′, -frost′, hōr′-) *n.* A white coating of frost on a surface.

hoar·hound (hôr′hound′, hōr′-) *n.* HOREHOUND.

hoarse (hôrs, hōrs) *adj.* **hoars·er, hoars·est** 1 Harsh and rough in sound. 2 Having the voice harsh and rough. [< OE *hā(r)s*] —**hoarse′ly** *adv.* —**hoarse′ness** *n.*

hoars·en (hôr′sən, hōr′-) *v.t. & v.i.* To make or become hoarse or harsh.

hoar·y (hôr′ē, hō′rē) *adj.* **hoar·i·er, hoar·i·est** 1 White or grayish white, as from age. 2 Ancient. —**hoar′i·ness** *n.*

hoax (hōks) *n.* A deception or fraud, usu. practiced as a joke. —*v.t.* To deceive with a hoax. [< HOCUS(-POCUS)] —**hoax′er** *n.*

hob[1] (hob) *n.* 1 A shelflike projection at the back or on the side of a fireplace, used as a warming place. 2 A steel mandrel for cutting screw threads. [?]

hob[2] (hob) *n.* A fairy; hobgoblin; elf. —**play hob with** To throw into confusion; upset; ruin. [Orig., a nickname for ROBERT]

hob·ble (hob′əl) *v.* **hob·bled, hob·bling** *v.i.* 1 To walk with or as with a limp. 2 To move or proceed in an irregular or clumsy manner. —*v.t.* 3 To hamper the free movement of (a horse, etc.), as by tying the legs together. 4 To cause to move lamely or awkwardly. —*n.* 1 A limping gait. 2 A rope, strap, etc., used to fetter the forelegs of an animal. [ME *hoppeln* hobble] —**hob′bler** *n.*

hob·ble·de·hoy (hob′əl·dē·hoi′) *n.* 1 An awkward youth. 2 An adolescent boy. Also **hob′be·de·hoy′** (hob′ə·dē-). [?]

hob·by (hob′ē) *n. pl.* **·bies** A subject or activity pursued for pleasure rather than for payment. [< *Robin,* a personal name] —**hob′by·ist** *n.*

hob·by·horse (hob′ē·hôrs′) *n.* 1 ROCKING HORSE. 2 A toy consisting of a stick with a wooden horse's head attached.

hob·gob·lin (hob′gob′lin) *n.* 1 An imp or goblin. 2 An imaginary cause of fear or terror. [< HOB[2] + GOBLIN]

hob·nail (hob′nāl′) *n.* 1 A nail for studding the soles of heavy shoes. 2 Any of a series of ornamental knobs, as on glassware. —**hob′nailed** *adj.*

hob·nob (hob′nob) *v.i.* **·nobbed, ·nob·bing** 1 To drink together familiarly and convivially. 2 To be on familiar terms. [< OE *habban* have + *nabban* have not]

ho·bo (hō′bō) *n. pl.* **·boes** or **·bos** 1 TRAMP. 2 A migratory, unskilled workman. [?] —**ho′bo·ism** *n.*

Hob·son's choice (hob′sənz) An apparent choice in which there is no real freedom to choose or in which the alternatives are equally unsatisfactory. [<T. Hobson, 1544-1631, English liveryman, who required his customers to take the horse nearest the door]

hock[1] (hok) *n.* The backward-projecting joint of the hind leg of the horse, ox, pig, etc., corresponding to the ankle in man. —*v.t.* To disable by cutting the tendons of the hock; hamstring. [<OE *hōh* heel] • See HORSE.

hock[2] (hok) *n.* Any white Rhine wine. [<*Hochheim,* a German town where it was first produced]

hock[3] (hok) *Informal v.t.* PAWN. —*n.* The state of being in pawn. —**in hock** *Informal* **1** In pawn. **2** In debt. **3** In prison. [<Du. *hok* prison, debt]

hock·ey (hok′ē) *n.* **1** A game played on ice by opposing players on skates who try to drive a puck into their opponent's goal with a hockey stick; ice hockey. **2** A game similar to this but played on foot on a turfed field, using a small ball instead of a puck; field hockey. [?]

hockey stick **1** A hooked stick used in ice hockey. **2** A curved stick used in field hockey.

hock·shop (hok′shop′) *n. Slang* PAWNSHOP.

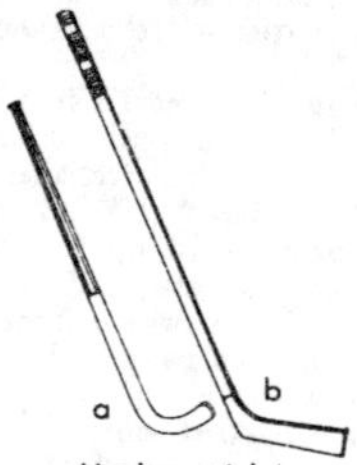

Hockey sticks
a. field. b. ice.

ho·cus (hō′kəs) *v.t.* **·cused** or **·cussed, ·cus·ing** or **·cus·sing** **1** To deceive by a trick. **2** To drug; dope. **3** To add drugs to, as a drink. [Abbreviation of HOCUS-POCUS]

ho·cus-po·cus (hō′kəs·pō′kəs) *n.* **1** A verbal formula used in conjuring. **2** A magician's trick. **3** Any trick or deception. —*v.t. & v.i.* **·cused** or **·cussed, ·cus·ing** or **·cus·sing** *Informal* To cheat; trick. [A sham Latin phrase]

hod (hod) *n.* **1** A long-handled receptacle for holding bricks and mortar. **2** A coal scuttle. [<OF *hotte*]

hodge-podge (hoj′poj′) *n.* A jumbled mixture; conglomeration. [ME *hochepot*]

Hodg·kin's disease (hoj′kinz) A progressive disease marked by enlargement of the lymph nodes, lymphoid tissue, and spleen. [<Dr. T. *Hodgkin,* 1798–1866, English physician]

hoe (hō) *n.* A tool for digging, scraping, and tilling, having a flat, thin blade set nearly at a right angle to a long handle. —*v.t. & v.i.* **hoed, hoe·ing** To dig, scrape, or till with a hoe. [<OF *houe*] —**ho′er** *n.*

Hoes
a. garden. b. weeding.

hoe·cake (hō′kāk′) *n.* A thin cake of Indian meal, originally baked on a hoe.

hoe·down (hō′doun′) *n.* **1** A square dance. **2** A social occasion where hoedowns are danced. [?]

hog (hôg, hog) *n.* **1** A pig, esp. one that is full-grown. **2** An animal related to the pig, as the peccary. **3** *Informal* A filthy or gluttonous person. —*v.t.* **hogged, hog·ging** *Slang* To take more than one's share of; grab selfishly. [<OE *hogg*]

hog·gish (hôg′ish, hog′-) *adj.* **1** Of or like a hog. **2** Greedy, selfish, dirty, etc. —**hog′gish·ly** *adv.* —**hog′gish·ness** *n.*

hog·nose (hôg′nōz′, hog′-) *n.* A harmless North American snake with a flattened head and prominent snout.

hogs·head (hôgz′hed′, hogz′-) *n.* **1** A large cask. **2** Any of various liquid measures, esp., in the U.S., a unit equal to 63 gallons.

hog·tie (hôg′tī′, hog′-) *v.t.* **·tied, ·ty·ing** or **·tie·ing** **1** To tie all four feet or the hands and feet of. **2** *Informal* To keep from taking effective action.

hog·wash (hôg′wosh′, -wôsh′, hog′-) *n.* **1** Kitchen refuse, swill, etc., fed to hogs. **2** *Informal* Ridiculous speech or writing; nonsense.

hoi pol·loi (hoi′ pə·loi′) The common people; the masses: with *the:* usu. used contemptuously. [Gk., the many]

hoist (hoist) *v.t.* To raise to a higher position; lift or heave up, esp. by some mechanical means. —*n.* **1** A machine for hoisting; lift. **2** The act of hoisting; a boost. **3** *Naut.* The length of a sail between the boom and the peak or the jaws of the gaff. [?] —**hoist′er** *n.*

hoi·ty-toi·ty (hoi′tē·toi′tē) *adj.* **1** Self-important; putting on airs. **2** Flighty; giddy. **3** Petulant; huffy. [Reduplication of obs. *hoit* to romp]

hoke (hōk) *Slang v.t.* **hoked, hok·ing** To make more intense, dramatic, spectacular, etc., by obvious or artificial means: usu. with *up.* —*n.* HOKUM. [<HOKUM]

ho·kum (hō′kəm) *n. Slang* **1** Obvious and contrived comic or sentimental devices or effects in a play, novel, movie, etc. **2** Nonsense; bunk. [Alter. of HOCUS]

hold[1] (hōld) *v.* **held, held** or *in legal use* **hold·en, hold·ing** *v.t.* **1** To take and keep in the hand, arms, etc.; grasp. **2** To prevent the movement or escape of: *Hold* the bus! **3** To restrain from acting or speaking: *Hold* your tongue! **4** To keep in a specified place, position, or state: to *hold* one's arm up. **5** To regard in a specified manner; consider: to *hold* someone dear. **6** To require to fulfill, as the conditions of a contract; obligate. **7** To support or keep in position: Ropes *held* the tower in position. **8** To be capable of enclosing or containing: The barrel *holds* ten gallons. **9** To maintain in the mind; believe: to *hold* an opinion. **10** To conduct or engage in; carry on: to *hold* court or services. **11** To have and retain ownership or control of; keep as one's own; occupy: to *hold* the position of chairman. **12** To get and retain possession or control of: to *hold* an enemy town; to *hold* one's attention. **13** To keep for later use, delivery, etc.: to *hold* a hotel room. **14** *Music* To prolong or sustain (a note or rest). —*v.i.* **15** To maintain a grip or grasp. **16** To remain firm or unbroken: if the rope *holds;* He *held* to his purpose. **17** To continue unchanged: The breeze *held* all day. **18** To be or remain true, valid, etc.: This decision *holds.* **19** To check or restrain oneself; forbear: usu. used in the imperative. —**hold down** **1** To suppress; keep under control. **2** *Informal* To occupy (a job, etc.) successfully. —**hold forth** To harangue; preach or speak at length. —**hold off** **1** To keep at a distance. **2** To refrain. —**hold on** **1** To maintain a grip or hold. **2** To persist; continue. **3** *Informal* To stop or wait: used in the imperative. —**hold one's own** To maintain one's position, as in a contest; lose no ground. —**hold out** **1** To stretch forth; offer. **2** To last to the end: Our supplies *held out.* **3** To continue resistance; endure; persist. **4** *U.S. Slang* To keep back part or all of (something). —**hold out for** *Informal* To insist upon as a condition of an agreement: He *held out for* a higher salary. —**hold up** **1** To support; prop. **2** To exhibit to view. **3** *Informal* To last; endure. **4** To delay; stop. **5** *Informal* To rob. —*n.* **1** The act or manner of holding, as with the hands. **2** In wrestling, a specific grip on an opponent. **3** A controlling force or influence. **4** A place to grasp. **5** A place of confinement. [<OE *haldan*]

hold[2] (hōld) *n. Naut.* The space below the decks of a vessel where cargo is stowed. [<HOLE]

hold·er (hōl′dər) *n.* **1** One who or that which holds. **2** An owner; possessor. **3** *Law* One who holds a check, promissory note, etc., for which he is entitled to receive payment.

hold·ing (hōl′ding) *n.* **1** The act of one who or that which holds. **2** A tenure or right of possession. **3** *Often pl.* Property held by legal right, esp. stocks or bonds.

holding company A company that holds stock in one or more companies for investment or operating purposes, or both.

hold·o·ver (hōld′ō′vər) *n.* **1** One who or that which remains from a previous time, engagement, or situation. **2** One who continues in office after his term has expired.

hold-up (hōld′up′) *n.* **1** Stoppage, delay, or obstruction of some activity. **2** A forcible stoppage to commit robbery, esp. of a traveler, a train, etc.

hole (hōl) *n.* **1** A cavity extending into a solid body, as a pit, cave, etc. **2** An opening or aperture in anything: a *hole* in a dress. **3** A deep place in a stream or creek. **4** An animal's burrow or den. **5** A small, dingy room, dwelling, etc. **6** A prison cell. **7** A fault or defect: the *holes* in his argument. **8** *Informal* A dilemma or predicament. **9** In golf: **a** A small sunken cup into which the ball must be hit. **b** Any of the 9 or 18 sections of a course, from the tee to the cup inclusive. **10** *Electronics* An empty electron energy state in a crystal, acting as a positive charge carrier with the magnitude of an electron. —**in the hole** *Informal* In debt. —*v.* **holed, hol·ing** *v.t.* **1** To make a hole or holes in; perforate. **2** To drive or put into a hole, as in billiards or golf. 3 To dig (a shaft, tunnel, etc.). *—v.i.* 4 To make a hole or holes. **—hole up** 1 To hibernate, as in a hole. 2 To take refuge in hiding. [< OE *hol*]

hol·i·day (hol′ə·dā) *n.* 1 A day appointed by law or custom for the suspension of general business, usu. in commemoration of some person or event. 2 Any day of rest. 3 *Often pl.* A period of festivity or leisure; a vacation. *—adj.* Suitable for a holiday; festive. *—v.i.* To vacation. [< OE *hālig dæg* holy day]

hol·i·day·mak·er (hol′ə·dā·mā′kər) *n. Brit.* One who is on vacation.

ho·li·ly (hō′lə·lē) *adv.* In a holy manner; piously; sacredly.

ho·li·ness (hō′lē·nis) *n.* The state or quality of being holy. **—His** (or **Your**) **Holiness** A title of the Pope.

hol·land (hol′ənd) *n.* Unbleached linen, glazed or unglazed. [< HOLLAND, where first made]

Hol·land (hol′ənd) *n.* NETHERLANDS.

hol·lan·daise sauce (hol′ən·dāz′, hol′ən·dez′) A creamy sauce made of butter, yolks of eggs, lemon juice or vinegar, and seasoning. [< F *hollandais* of Holland]

hol·ler (hol′ər) *v.t. & v.i. Informal* To call out loudly; shout; yell. *—n.* A loud shout; yell. [Imit.]

hol·low (hol′ō) *adj.* 1 Having empty space or a cavity within; not solid: a *hollow* tree. 2 Sunken: *hollow* cheeks. 3 Depressed or sunk below the surface; concave. 4 Empty; vacant; insincere: *hollow* praise. 5 Muffled; dully reverberating: a *hollow* sound. 6 Hungry. *—n.* 1 Any depression in a body; a cavity. 2 A small valley. *—v.t. & v.i.* To make or become hollow. [< OE *holh*] **—hol′low·ly** *adv.* **—hol′low·ness** *n.*

hol·ly (hol′ē) *n. pl.* **·lies** 1 Any of various trees and shrubs with glossy, sharp-pointed leaves and red berries, often used as Christmas ornaments. 2 The holm. [< OE *holen*]

hol·ly·hock (hol′ē·hok) *n.* A plant with hairy leaves and tall spikes of large flowers of numerous shades. [< ME *holi* holy + *hoc* mallow]

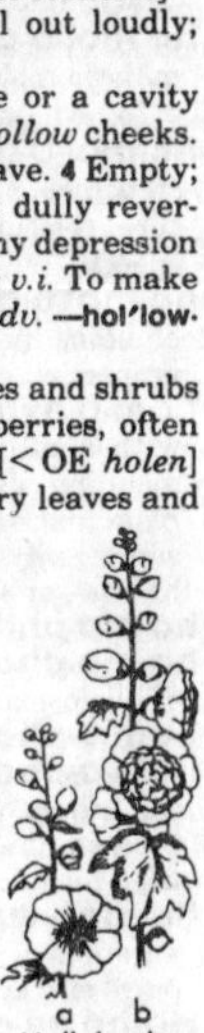
a b
Hollyhocks
a. single.
b. double.

hol·mi·um (hōl′mē·əm) *n.* A metallic element (symbol Ho) of the rare-earth group. [< *Holmia,* Latinized name of Stockholm]

holo- *combining form* Whole; wholly: *holograph.* [< Gk. *holos* whole]

hol·o·caust (hol′ə·kôst) *n.* 1 A sacrifice wholly consumed by fire. 2 Wholesale destruction or loss of life by fire, war, etc. [< Gk. *holos* whole + *kaustos* burnt] **—hol′o·caus′tal, hol′o·caus′tic** *adj.*

Hol·o·cene (hol′ə·sēn) *adj. & n.* See GEOLOGY. [< HOLO- + Gk. *kainos* recent]

hol·o·gram (hol′ə·gram) *n.* An image on film of the interference pattern made by holography. [< HOLO- + GRAM[1]]

hol·o·graph (hol′ə·graf, -gräf) *n.* 1 A document wholly in the handwriting of the person whose signature it bears. 2 HOLOGRAM. [< HOLO- + Gk. *graphein* write] **—hol′o·graph′ic** or **·i·cal** *adj.*

ho·log·ra·phy (hə·log′rə·fē) *n.* A process in which light reflected by a laser-illuminated object interferes with a reference beam and forms on film a pattern containing all the information needed to project a three-dimensional image of the object. [< HOLO- + -GRAPHY]

Hol·stein (hōl′stīn, -stēn) *n.* One of a breed of black-and-white cattle bred for both beef and milk: also **Hol′stein-Frie′sian** (-frē′zhən). [< *Holstein,* a former Danish duchy, now part of Schleswig-Holstein]

hol·ster (hōl′stər) *n.* A pistol case. [< Du.]

ho·ly (hō′lē) *adj.* **·li·er, ·li·est** 1 Devoted to religious or sacred use; consecrated; hallowed. 2 Of highest spiritual purity; saintly. 3 Evoking or worthy of veneration, awe, respect, etc. 4 Religious: a *holy* war. *—n. pl.* **ho·lies** A holy thing or place. [< OE *hālig*] **—Syn.** *adj.* 1 sanctified, sacred, sacrosanct. 2 godly, pure, angelic, righteous.

Holy City A city considered sacred by the believers in a religion, as Jerusalem or Mecca.

Holy Communion The Eucharist or Lord's Supper.

holy day A sacred day, as the Sabbath, or one set apart for religious uses.

Holy Father A title of the Pope.

Holy Ghost The third person of the Trinity. Also **Holy Spirit.**

Holy Grail GRAIL.

Holy Land PALESTINE.

Holy Mother VIRGIN MARY.

holy of holies The innermost and most sacred shrine of the Jewish tabernacle.

holy orders The state of being ordained to the ministry of a church: a term used chiefly in the Anglican, Eastern, and Roman Catholic churches.

Holy Roman Empire An empire in CEN. and w Europe, established in 962 and lasting until 1806, regarded as an extension of the Western Roman Empire.

Holy Saturday The Saturday before Easter.

Holy See The court, position, or authority of the Pope.

ho·ly·stone (hō′lē·stōn′) *n.* A flat piece of soft sandstone used for cleaning the wood decks of a vessel. *—v.t.* **·stoned, ·ston·ing** To scrub with a holystone. [?]

Holy Synod The supreme governing body in any of the Eastern Orthodox churches.

Holy Week The week before Easter.

Holy Writ BIBLE.

hom·age (hom′ij, om′-) *n.* 1 Deep regard, honor, respect, or veneration, esp. as shown by some action. 2 In feudal law, formal acknowledgment of tenure by a tenant to his lord. [< LL *homo* vassal, client, man]

hom·bre (ôm′brā, om′brē) *n. Slang* A man. [Sp.]

hom·burg (hom′bûrg) *n.* A man's felt hat with slightly rolled-up brim and crown dented lengthwise. [< *Homburg,* Germany]

Homburg

home (hōm) *n.* 1 One's dwelling place or residence. 2 The country, state, city, etc., where one lives or was reared. 3 A family thought of as a unit: a happy *home.* 4 A place regarded as a home: She found a *home* in the convent. 5 The seat or habitat of something; the place of origin: New Orleans is the *home* of jazz. 6 An establishment for the shelter and care of the needy or infirm. 7 In some games, the goal that must be reached in order to win or score. **—at home** 1 In one's own house, place, or country. 2 At ease, as if in familiar surroundings. 3 Prepared to receive callers. *—adj.* 1 Of or pertaining to one's home or country. 2 At the place regarded as the base of operations: the *home* office; a *home* game. 3 Going to the point; effective: a *home* thrust. *—adv.* 1 To, at, or in the direction of home. 2 To the place or point intended: to thrust the dagger *home.* 3 Deeply and intimately; to the heart: Her words struck *home.* *—v.* **homed, hom·ing** *v.t.* 1 To carry or send to a home. 2 To furnish with a home. *—v.i.* 3 To go to a home; fly home, as homing pigeons. 4 To have residence. **—home in on** To direct toward, seek, or find a destination, target, etc., esp. by radio or radar. [< OE *hām*]

home·bod·y (hōm′bod′ē) *n. pl.* **·bod·ies** A person who takes an interest in a home or who likes to stay at home.

home·bred (hōm′bred′) *adj.* 1 Bred at home; native; domestic. 2 Uncultivated; crude.

home·brew (hōm′brōō′) *n.* An alcoholic beverage distilled or brewed at home.

home·com·ing (hōm′kum′ing) *n.* 1 A return home. 2 In many American colleges and universities, an annual celebration for visiting alumni.

home economics The sciences and arts having practical application to domestic functions, including nutrition, cooking, child care, etc.

home-grown (hōm′grōn′) *adj.* Grown at home, as fruits and vegetables.

home·land (hōm′land′) *n.* The country of one's birth or allegiance.

home·less (hōm′lis) *adj.* Having no home. **—home′less·ness** *n.*

home·like (hōm′līk′) *adj.* Comfortable, pleasant, cozy, etc., as in a home.
home·ly (hōm′lē) *adj.* **·li·er, ·li·est 1** Having a familiar everyday character; unpretentious. **2** Having plain features; not good-looking. **3** Domestic. **—home′li·ness** *n.*
home·made (hōm′mād′) *adj.* **1** Made at home. **2** Simple; unpretentious; crude.
ho·me·op·a·thist (hō′mē·op′ə·thist, hom′ē-) *n.* One who advocates or practices homeopathy. Also **ho·me·o·path** (hō′mē·ə·path′, hom′ē-).
ho·me·op·a·thy (hō′mē·op′ə·thē, hom′ē-) *n.* A system of medicine that prescribes minute doses of such medicines as would produce in a healthy person the symptoms of the disease treated. [<Gk. *homoios* similar + -PATHY] **—ho·me·o·path·ic** (hō′mē·ə·path′ik, hom′ē-) *adj.*
home plate In baseball, the base at which the batter stands when batting and to which he must return to score.
hom·er (hō′mər) *n. Informal* HOME RUN.
Ho·mer·ic (hō·mer′ik) *adj.* Of or pertaining to Homer or his age or writings. Also **Ho·me·ri·an** (hō·mir′ē·ən), **Ho·mer′i·cal.**
home rule Self-government in local affairs.
home run In baseball, a base hit in which the ball is driven far enough to allow the batter to touch all bases and score a run.
home·sick (hōm′sik′) *adj.* Sad through longing for home; nostalgic. **—home′sick′ness** *n.*
home·spun (hōm′spun′) *n.* **1** Fabric woven at home. **2** A loose, rough fabric having the appearance of tweed. *—adj.* **1** Made at home. **2** Made of homespun. **3** Plain and simple; unpretentious.
home·stead (hōm′sted) *n.* **1** A home, together with subsidiary buildings and adjacent land. **2** A tract of land occupied by a settler under the Homestead Act (1862) or its revisions. *—v.i. U.S.* To become a settler on a homestead under the Homestead Act. *—v.t. U.S.* To settle on land under the Homestead Act. **—home′stead′er** *n.*
Homestead Act A Congressional enactment of 1862 which granted 160 acres of land to a settler to develop and later own.
home·stretch (hōm′strech′) *n.* **1** The last part of a racecourse before the winning post is reached. **2** The last part of any journey or endeavor.
home·ward (hōm′wərd) *adj., adv.* Toward home. Also **home′wards.**
home·work (hōm′wûrk′) *n.* **1** Lessons assigned to students to be done outside the classroom. **2** Work, esp. piecework, done for wages at home. **3** Preparatory work or research, as for a meeting.
home·y (hō′mē) *adj.* **hom·i·er, hom·i·est** *Informal* Simple, pleasant, comfortable, etc.; homelike. **—home′y·ness** or **hom′i·ness** *n.*
hom·i·cide (hom′ə·sīd, hō′mə-) *n.* **1** The killing of one human being by another. **2** A person who has killed another. [<L *homo* man + -CIDE] **—hom′i·ci′dal** *adj.* **—hom′i·ci′dal·ly** *adv.*
hom·i·let·ics (hom′ə·let′iks) *n. pl. (construed as sing.)* The branch of theology that treats of the composition and delivery of sermons. [<Gk. *homilētikos* sociable] **—hom′i·let′ic** or **·i·cal** *adj.* **—hom′i·let′i·cal·ly** *adv.* **—hom′i·list** *n.*
hom·i·ly (hom′ə·lē) *n. pl.* **·lies 1** A sermon, esp. one based on the Bible. **2** A lecture on morals or conduct. [<Gk. *homilia* <*homilos* assembly] **—hom′i·let′ic** or **·i·cal** *adj.*
hom·ing (hō′ming) *adj.* **1** Heading homeward. **2** Pertaining to methods and devices for directing an aircraft or missile to a given point.
homing pigeon A pigeon capable of finding its way home from great distances, used for conveying messages.
hom·i·nid (hom′ə·nid, hō′mə-) *n.* A member of a family of the primate order, now represented only by modern man. *—adj.* Of or pertaining to this group. [<L *homo, hominis* man]
hom·i·noid (hom′ə·noid, hō′mə-) *n.* Any of a superfamily of the primate order, including the large manlike apes and modern and prehistoric man. *—adj.* Of this superfamily. [<L *homo, hominis* man]
hom·i·ny (hom′ə·nē) *n.* Hulled dried corn (maize), coarsely ground and boiled for food. Also **hominy grits.** [<Algonquian *rockahominie* parched corn]
ho·mo[1] (hō′mō) *n* Any of a genus of errect, large-brained primates, now represented only by modern man. [L]
ho·mo[2] (hō′mō) *n. pl* **·mos** *Slang* HOMOSEXUAL.
homo- *combining form* Same; similar; equal: *homogeneous.* [<Gk. *homos* same]
ho·mo·ge·ne·ous (hō′mə·jē′nē·əs, hom′ə-) *adj.* **1** Of the same composition or character throughout. **2** Of the same kind, nature, etc., as another; similar. [<Gk. *homos* the same + *genos* race] **—ho′mo·ge′ne·ous·ly** *adv.* **—ho·mo·ge·ne·i·ty** (hō′mə·jə·nē′ə·tē, hom′ə-), **ho′mo·ge′ne·ous·ness** *n.*
ho·mog·en·ize (hə·moj′ə·nīz) *v.t.* **·ized, ·iz·ing 1** To render homogeneous. **2 a** To distribute throughout a fluid, as tiny particles. **b** To make (milk) more uniform by emulsification of its butterfat. **—ho·mog′en·ized** *adj.* **—ho·mog′en·i·za′tion, ho·mog′en·iz′er** *n.*
hom·o·graph (hom′ə·graf, -gräf, hō′mə-) *n.* A word identical with another in spelling, but differing from it in origin and meaning, and sometimes in pronunciation, as *bass,* a fish, and *bass,* a male voice.
ho·mol·o·gize (hō·mol′ə·jīz) *v.* **·gized, ·giz·ing** *v.t.* **1** To make homologous. **2** To demonstrate the homologies of. *—v.i.* **3** To be homologous; correspond in structure or value.
ho·mol·o·gous (hō·mol′ə·gəs) *adj.* **1** Having a similar structure, proportion, value, or position. **2** Identical in nature, relation, or the like. [<Gk. *homos* the same + *logos* speech]
ho·mol·o·gy (hō·mol′ə·jē) *n. pl.* **·gies** The state or quality of being homologous; correspondence in structure and properties. [HOMO- + -LOGY]
hom·o·nym (hom′ə·nim, hō′mə-) *n.* **1** A word identical with another in pronunciation, but differing from it in meaning, origin, and usu. in spelling, as *fair* and *fare, read* and *reed.* **2** Loosely, a homograph. [<Gk. *homos* same + *onyma* name] **—hom·o·nym·ic** (hom′ə·nim′ik, hō′mə-) or **·i·cal** *adj.*
ho·mo·phile (hō′mō·fīl) *n.* A homosexual.
ho·mo·pho·bi·a (hō′mō·fō′bē·ə) *n.* Hatred or fear either of homosexuals or of homosexuality.
hom·o·phone (hom′ə·fōn, hō′mə-) *n.* HOMONYM (def.1).
hom·o·phon·ic (hom′ə·fon′ik, hō′mə-) *adj.* **1** Of, pertaining to, or having the same sound. **2** *Music* Having one predominant part carrying the melody, with other parts used for harmony. **—ho·moph·o·ny** (hō·mof′ə·nē) *n.*
ho·mop·ter·ous (hō·mop′tər·əs) *adj.* Of or pertaining to an order of insects having sucking mouth parts and two pairs of membranous wings of uniform thickness.
Homo sa·pi·ens (sā′pē·enz) The scientific term for the human race. [<HOMO + L *sapiēns* <*sapere* to have taste, be wise]
ho·mo·sex·u·al (hō′mə·sek′shōō·əl, hom′ə-) *adj.* Pertaining to or characterized by homosexuality. *—n.* A homosexual person.
ho·mo·sex·u·al·i·ty (hō′mə·sek′shōō·al′ə·tē, hom′ə-) *n.* **1** Sexual attraction toward a person of the same sex. **2** Sexual relations between persons of the same sex.
ho·mun·cu·lus (hō·mung′kyə·ləs) *n. pl.* **·li** (-lī) An undersized man; dwarf. [L, dim. of *homo* man] **—ho·mun′cu·lar** *adj.*
Hon. Honorable.
hon. honorably; honorary.
Hond. Honduras.
Hon·du·ras (hon·dʸōōr′əs) A republic of NE Central America, 43,227 sq. mi., cap. Tegucigalpa. **—Hon·du′ran** *adj., n.* • See map at CENTRAL AMERICA.
hone (hōn) *n.* A block of fine compact stone for sharpening edged tools, razors, etc. *—v.t.* **honed, hon·ing** To sharpen, as a razor, on a hone. [<OE *hān* stone] **—hon′er** *n.*
hon·est (on′ist) *adj.* **1** Not given to lies, theft, cheating, etc. **2** Not false or misleading; true: an *honest* answer. **3** Free from fraud; fair; equitable: an *honest* test. **4** Earned or acquired in a just and fair manner: an *honest* living. **5** Frank; open; sincere: an *honest* face. [<L *honos* honor] **—hon′est·ly** *adv.* **—Syn. 1** trustworthy, reliable, fair, honorable, upright. **2** frank, candid, straightforward, artless, forthright. **3** just, impartial, unbiased.
hon·es·ty (on′is·tē) *n.* The quality of being honest.
hon·ey (hun′ē) *n.* **1** A sweet food made by bees from the nectar of flowers. **2** Sweetness or lusciousness in general. **3** Darling; dear: a term of endearment. **4** *Informal* Some-

thing considered as an excellent example of its kind: a *honey* of a boat. —*v.* **hon·eyed** or **hon·ied, hon·ey·ing** —*v.t.* **1** To talk in an endearing or flattering manner to. **2** To sweeten. —*v.i.* **3** To talk fondly or in a coaxing manner. —*adj.* Honeylike; sweet. [< OE *hunig*]

hon·ey·bee (hun′ē·bē′) *n.* A bee that makes honey, esp. the common hive bee.

hon·ey·comb (hun′ē·kōm′) *n.* **1** A structure of close-packed, hexagonal cells with walls of wax, made by bees to contain their honey, eggs, etc. **2** Anything resembling a honeycomb. —*v.t.* **1** To fill with small holes or passages. **2** To pervade; corrupt. —*v.i.* **3** To become full of holes or passages. [< OE *hunigcamb*] —**hon′ey·combed′** *adj.*

Honeybee

hon·ey·dew (hun′ē·dyōō′) *n.* **1** A sweet secretion of certain plants and insects. **2** HONEYDEW MELON.

honeydew melon A greenish white melon with a smooth skin and sweet flesh.

hon·eyed (hun′ēd) *adj.* **1** Covered with or full of honey. **2** Sweetly flattering; soothing; agreeable.

honey locust A large, thorny North American tree with feathery foliage, bearing long pods with a sweet pulp between the seeds.

hon·ey·moon (hun′ē·mōōn) *n.* **1** A wedding trip. **2** A period of agreement or concord immediately after a marriage. **3** Any brief period of agreement or concord.

hon·ey·suck·le (hun′ē·suk′əl) *n.* **1** Any of a genus of ornamental shrubs having small, usu. fragrant tubular crimson flowers. **2** A plant resembling honeysuckle, as certain azaleas and columbines.

hon·ied (hun′ēd) *adj.* HONEYED.

honk (hôngk, hongk) *n.* The cry of a wild goose or a sound imitating it, as that of an automobile horn. —*v.i.* To utter or make a honk or honks. —*v.t.* To cause to emit a honk or honks, as an automobile horn. [Imit.]

hon·ky-tonk (hông′kē·tôngk′, hong′kē·tongk′) *n. Slang* A noisy, disreputable barroom or night club. —*adj.* Describing a type of tinkling, ragtime piano playing or music. [Prob. imit.]

hon·or (on′ər) *n.* **1** High regard or respect. **2** Fame; renown; glory. **3** A cause of pride or esteem: an *honor* to be chosen. **4** A sense of what is right and just; integrity: to act with *honor.* **5** A reputation for being just, good, fair, etc.: a man of *honor.* **6** High rank or dignity: the *honor* of the office. **7** *Often pl.* An outward token or sign of respect or regard, as a decoration, ceremony, etc. **8** *pl.* **a** Recognition given to students for outstanding scholarship, etc. **b** Academic courses for advanced or exceptional students, usu. in addition to regular courses. **9** Privilege: May I have the *honor* of this dance? **10** In bridge, one of the five highest cards of any suit. **11** In golf, the privilege of playing first from the tee. —**do the honors** To act as host or hostess. —*v.t.* **1** To regard with honor or respect. **2** To treat with courtesy or respect. **3** To do or bestow something in honor of. **4** To accept or pay, as a check or draft. —*adj.* Of or showing honor or respect: an *honor* guard. *Brit. sp.* **-our.** [< L] —**hon′or·er** *n.*

Hon·or (on′ər) *n.* A title or form of address for a judge, mayor, etc.: preceded by *Your, His,* or *Her.*

hon·or·a·ble (on′ər·ə·bəl) *adj.* **1** Worthy of honor. **2** Conferring honor. **3** Consistent with or acting in accordance with principles of honor; conforming to a code of honor. **4** Accompanied by marks or testimonials of honor. **5** Entitled to honor: formal title of respect prefixed to the names of persons holding important offices. *Brit. sp.* **-our·a·ble.** —**hon′or·a·ble·ness** *n.* —**hon′or·a·bly** *adv.*

hon·o·rar·i·um (on′ə·râr′ē·əm) *n. pl.* **-i·ums** or **-i·a** A gratuity given for services rendered when law, custom, or propriety forbids a set fee. [< L *honorarium (donum)* honorary (gift)]

hon·or·ar·y (on′ə·rer′ē) *adj.* **1** Done, conferred, or held merely as an honor. **2** Designating an office or title bestowed as a sign of honor, without emoluments or without powers or duties. **3** Depending solely on one's honor: said of a debt or other obligation not legally binding.

hon·or·if·ic (on′ə·rif′ik) *adj.* Conferring or implying honor or respect. —*n.* Any honorific title, word, phrase, etc. —**hon′or·if′i·cal·ly** *adv.*

honor system A system whereby work, school examinations, etc., are undertaken without supervision.

hooch[1] (hōōch) *n. Slang* Intoxicating liquor. [< *Hutanuwu,* Alaskan Indian tribe that made liquor]

hooch[2] (hōōch) *Slang* **1** A thatched hut. **2** Any dwelling. [< Japanese *uchi* house]

hood[1] (hŏŏd) *n.* **1** A soft or flexible covering for the head and the back of the neck, often attached to a garment. **2** Anything of similar form or character, as a monk's cowl or an ornamental fold attached to the back of an academic gown. **3** In falconry, a cover for the entire head of a hawk. **4** A projecting cover to a hearth, ventilator, etc. **5** A movable cover, as of the engine of an automobile, etc. —*v.t.* To cover or furnish with or as with a hood. [< OE *hōd*]

hood[2] (hŏŏd) *n. Slang* A hoodlum.

-hood *suffix of nouns* **1** Condition of; state of being: *babyhood, falsehood.* **2** Class or totality of those having a certain character: *priesthood.* [< OE *-hād* state, condition]

hood·lum (hōōd′ləm, hŏŏd′-) *n.* **1** A rowdy or thug. **2** A criminal. [?] —**hood′lum·ism** *n.*

hoo·doo (hōō′dōō) *n.* **1** VOODOO. **2** *Informal* A person or thing that brings bad luck; a jinx. —*v.t. Informal* To bring bad luck to; bewitch. [Var. of VOODOO] —**hoo′doo·ism** *n.*

hood·wink (hŏŏd′wingk′) *v.t.* To deceive as if by blinding; dupe; delude. [< HOOD[1] + WINK] —**hood′wink′er** *n.*

hoo·ey (hōō′ē) *n. & interj. Slang.* Nonsense.

hoof (hŏŏf, hōōf) *n. pl.* **hoofs** or **hooves** **1** The horny sheath encasing the ends of the foot in the horse, swine, ox, etc. **2** An animal with hoofs. —**on the hoof** Alive; not butchered: said of cattle. —*v.t. & v.i.* **1** To trample with the hoofs. **2** *Informal* To walk or dance: usu. with *it.* [< OE *hōf*] —**hoofed** (hŏŏft, hōōft) *adj.*

hoof-and-mouth disease (hŏŏf′ən·mouth′) FOOT-AND-MOUTH DISEASE.

hoof·er (hŏŏf′ər, hōōf′-) *n. Slang* A professional dancer, esp. a tap dancer.

hook (hŏŏk) *n.* **1** A curved or bent piece serving to catch or hold another object. **2** A fishhook. **3** A cutting tool having a curved blade, as a sickle. **4** A trap or snare. **5** Something shaped like a hook as: **a** A sharply curved organ of an animal or plant. **b** A bend in a river. **c** A curved point of land or a cape. **d** A hook-shaped written character. **6** In golf, a ball that curves to the left of a right-handed player or vice versa. **7** In baseball, a curve. **8** In boxing, a short blow delivered crosswise and with the elbow bent and rigid. —*v.t.* **1** To fasten, attach, or take hold of with or as with a hook. **2** To catch on a hook, as fish. **3** *Informal* To trick; take in: I've been *hooked.* **4** To make or bend in the shape of a hook; crook. **5** To catch on or toss with the horns, as a bull. **6** To make, as a rug, by looping thread, yarn, etc., through canvas or burlap with a hook. **7** *Slang* To steal; pilfer. **8** In baseball, to throw (a ball) with a hook. **9** In boxing, to strike with a hook. **10** In golf, to drive (the ball) in a hook. —*v.i.* **11** To curve like a hook; bend. **12** To be fastened with a hook. [< OE *hōc*]

hook·ah (hŏŏk′ə) *n.* A form of tobacco pipe by which the smoke is drawn through water; a narghile. Also **hook′a.** [< Ar. *huqqah*]

hooked (hŏŏkt) *adj.* **1** Curved like a hook. **2** Supplied with a hook. **3** Made with a hook. **4** *Slang* **a** Addicted, as to a narcotic: often with *on.* **b** Excessively enthusiastic or obsessed with a person or thing: often with *on.* **5** *Slang* Married.

hook·er[1] (hŏŏk′ər) *n.* A fishing boat used on the English and Irish coasts. [< Du. *hoek* hook]

hook·er[2] (hŏŏk′ər) *n. Slang* A drink, esp. an alcoholic one. [< HOOK, prob. with ref. to the bend of the arm in drinking]

hook·er[3] (hŏŏk′ər) *n. Slang* A prostitute. [< Corlears *Hook,* formerly a notorious waterfront district in Manhattan]

hook·up (ho͝ok′up′) *n.* **1** **a** An assembly of electronic parts, circuits, etc. **b** A diagram of such an assembly. **2** A mechanical connection, as of gas or water lines. **3** *Informal* An alliance or pact between governments, organizations, etc.

hook·worm (ho͝ok′wûrm′) *n.* **1** Any of various parasitic nematode worms infesting the intestines of man and several animals, such as sheep, dogs, cattle, etc. **2** Infestation with hookworms: also **hookworm disease.**

hook·y (ho͝ok′ē) *n.* *Informal* Truant: used only in the phrase **to play hooky.** [< HOOK in sense of "to escape"]

hoo·li·gan (ho͞o′lə·gən) *n.* A hoodlum; rowdy; ruffian. [< *Hooligan,* name of an Irish family in London] **—hoo′li·gan·ism** *n.*

hoop (ho͞op, ho͝op) *n.* **1** A circular band of metal, wood, etc., esp. one used to confine the staves of a barrel, cask, etc. **2** A child's toy in the shape of a large ring. **3** A framework made of rings of whalebone, steel, etc., used for expanding a woman's skirt. **4** The band of a finger ring. **—***v.t.* **1** To surround or fasten with hoops. **2** To encircle. [< OE *hōp*]

hoop·la (ho͞op′lä) *n.* *Slang* Excitement; fervor. [Orig., a coach driver's exclamation]

hoo·poe (ho͞o′po͞o, -pō) *n.* A vividly colored European bird with an erectile crest and a long bill. [< L *upupa*]

hoop skirt A full skirt shaped over a structure of hoops.

Hoop skirt

hoo·ray (ho͞o·rā′, hə-, ho͞o-) *interj. n.* & *v.* HURRAH.

hoose·gow (ho͞os′gou) *n.* *Slang* Jail or prison. [< Sp. *juzgado* tribunal]

hoot (ho͞ot) *v.i.* **1** To jeer or call out, as in contempt or disapproval. **2** To utter the low, hollow cry of an owl. **—***v.t.* **3** To jeer at or mock with hooting cries. **4** To drive off with shouts of contempt, disapproval, etc. **5** To express by hooting. **—***n.* **1** A cry uttered in derision. **2** The cry of an owl. **3** *Slang* A whit: not worth a *hoot.* [Imit.]

hootch (ho͞och) *n.* HOOCH[2].

hoot·en·an·ny (ho͞ot′n·an′ē) *n. pl.* **·nies** **1** A gathering of folk singers. **2** A gadget; thingamajig. [?]

hooves (ho͞ovz, ho͝ovz) A *pl.* of HOOF.

hop[1] (hop) *v.* **hopped, hop·ping** *v.i.* **1** To move in short leaps with one foot off the ground. **2** To jump about by raising both or all feet simultaneously, as a frog. **3** *Informal* To take a trip, esp. a brief one: with *up, down,* or *over.* **—***v.t.* **4** To jump over, as a fence. **5** *Informal* To board or catch; get on: to *hop* a train. **—***n.* **1** The act or result of hopping. **2** *Informal* A dance or dancing party. **3** *Informal* A short flight in an airplane. [< OE *hoppian*]

hop[2] (hop) *n.* **1** A climbing herb related to hemp with female flowers borne in small green cones. **2** *pl.* The dried multiple fruit of this plant: used to flavor beer and in medicine. [< MDu. *hoppe*]

hope (hōp) *v.* **hoped, hop·ing** *v.t.* **1** To desire with expectation of fulfilment. **2** To wish; want. **—***v.i* **3** To have desire or expectation: usu. with *for:* to *hope* for the best. **—***n.* **1** Desire accompanied by expectation. **2** The reason or cause of such desire. **3** The thing hoped for. **4** A person or thing about which one can be hopeful. [< OE *hopian*]

hope chest A box or chest used by young women to hold linen, clothing, etc., in anticipation of marriage.

hope·ful (hōp′fəl) *adj.* **1** Full of hope; promising. **2** Having qualities that excite hope. **—***n.* A person who seems likely to succeed. **—hope′ful·ness** *n.*

hope·ful·ly (hōp′fə·lē) *adv.* **1** In a hopeful manner. **2** It is hoped; one hopes: *Hopefully,* a strike can be averted. • *Hopefully* (def. 2), considered by some a questionable usage, is current in formal as well as informal contexts. It modifies the entire clause that follows it (in the example above, *a strike can be averted*), not the verb only. It is thus analogous to *incidentally* (def. 2), and is hardly a grammatical anomaly.

hope·less (hōp′lis) *adj.* **1** Without hope; despairing. **2** Affording no ground for hope. **—hope′less·ly** *adv.* **—hope′less·ness** *n.*

Ho·pi (hō′pē) *n.* **1** One of a group of North American Pueblo Indians of Shoshonean linguistic stock, now on a reservation in NE Arizona. **2** Their Shoshonean lauguage.

hopped-up (hopt′up′) *adj.* *Slang* **1** Stimulated by a narcotic drug. **2** Excited; exhilarated. **3** Modified for high speed, as an engine. [? < HOP[2]]

hop·per (hop′ər) *n.* **1** One who or that which hops. **2** A hopping insect. **3** A box, tank, or funnel-shaped container whose contents can be emptied by opening its bottom.

hop·scotch (hop′skoch′) *n.* A child's game in which the player hops on one foot over a diagram marked (scotched) on the ground to recover the block, pebble, etc., previously tossed into successive sections of the diagram.

hor. horizon; horizontal.

horde (hôrd, hōrd) *n.* **1** A multitude, pack, or swarm, as of men, animals, or insects. **2** A clan or tribe of Mongolian nomads. **3** Any nomadic group. **—***v.i* **hord·ed, hord·ing** To gather in a horde. [< Turk. *ordū* camp]

hore·hound (hôr′hound′, hōr′-) *n.* **1** A whitish plant related to mint. **2** A bitter extract of this plant. **3** A candy flavored with horehound. [< OE *hārhūne*]

ho·ri·zon (hə·rī′zən) *n.* **1** The line of the apparent meeting of the sky with the earth or sea. **2** The plane passing through a position on the earth's surface at right angles to the line of gravity. **3** *Usu. pl.* The limits of one's knowledge, interests, experience, etc. [< Gk *horos* limit, bound] • See PERSPECTIVE.

hor·i·zon·tal (hôr′ə·zon′təl, hor′-) *adj.* **1** Parallel to the horizon; level. **2** In the plane of the horizon. **3** Of, on, or close to the horizon. **4** Equal and uniform: a *horizontal* tariff. **5** Made up of similar units; a *horizontal* trust. **—***n.* A line or plane assumed to be parallel with the horizon. **—hor′i·zon′tal·ly** *adv.*

hor·mone (hôr′mōn) *n.* **1** An internal secretion released in minute amounts into the blood stream by a specific gland or other tissue and stimulating a specific physiological activity. **2** A similar substance in plants. [< Gk. *hormaein* excite] **—hor·mo·nal** (hôr·mō′nəl), **hor·mon·ic** (hôr·mon′ik) *adj.*

horn (hôrn) *n.* **1** A permanent bonelike growth projecting from the head of various hoofed animals, as oxen, sheep, etc.; also, the antler of a deer, shed annually. **2** Any natural growth that protrudes from an animal's head, as a feeler, antenna, tentacle, etc. **3** The substance of which animal horns are made. **4** A somewhat similar substance made synthetically. **5** An object formed from or shaped like a horn: a powder *horn.* **6** A wind instrument made of brass, esp. the French horn. **7** *Slang* A trumpet or other brass or wind instrument. **8** Any pointed or tapering projection. **9** One of the extremities of a crescent moon. **10** A cape or peninsula. **11** The pommel of a saddle. **12** The point of an anvil. **13** A flaring tube used to collect or project sound, as in some loudspeakers. **14** A device for sounding warning signals; an automobile *horn.* **—on the horns of a dilemma** Forced to choose between two painful alternatives. **—***adj.* Of horn or horns. **—***v.t* **1** To provide with horns. **2** To shape like a horn. **3** To attack with the horns; gore. **—horn in** *Slang* To enter without invitation. [< OE] **—horned** *adj.*

horn·bill (hôrn′bil′) *n.* A large tropical bird having a large bill surmounted by a hornlike extension.

horn·blende (hôrn′blend) *n.* A common, greenish black, silicate mineral containing iron, magnesium, calcium, and aluminum.

horned toad A harmless, flat-bodied, spiny lizard with a very short tail and toadlike appearance.

horned viper A venomous African snake with a horny projection over each eye.

hor·net (hôr′nit) *n.* Any of various social wasps capable of inflicting a severe sting. [< OE *hyrnet*]

horn of plenty CORNUCOPIA.

horn·pipe (hôrn′pīp′) *n.* **1** A lively English country dance. **2** The music of such a dance. **3** An obsolete musical instrument resembling the clarinet.

horn·swog·gle (hôrn′swog′əl) *v.t.* **·gled, ·gling** *Slang* To deceive; bamboozle; cheat.

horn·y (hôr′nē) *adj.* **horn·i·er, horn·i·est** **1** Of or like horn. **2** Having horns. **3** Hard and calloused. **4** Translucent; semiopaque. **—horn′i·ness** *n.*

hor·o·loge (hôr′ə·lōj, hor′-) *n.* **1** A timepiece, as a clock, sundial, etc. 2 A clock tower. [< Gk. *hōra* time + *legein* tell]

ho·rol·o·ger (hô·rol′ə·jər, hō-) *n.* One skilled in horology. Also **ho·rol′o·gist.**

ho·rol·o·gy (hô·rol′ə·jē, hō-) *n.* The science of measuring time or building timepieces. **—hor·o·log·ic** (hôr′ə·loj′ik, hor′-) or **·i·cal** *adj.*

hor·o·scope (hôr′ə·skōp, hor′-) *n.* 1 In astrology, the aspect of the heavens, with special reference to the positions of the planets at any instant. 2 A figure or statement showing such aspect, from which astrologers profess to foretell the future of an individual, country, etc. [< Gk. < *hōra* hour + *skopeein* to watch]

hor·ren·dous (hô·ren′dəs, ho-) *adj.* Frightful; dreadful. [< L *horrere* to bristle] **—hor·ren′dous·ly** *adv.* **—hor·ren′·dous·ness** *n.*

hor·ri·ble (hôr′ə·bəl, hor′-) *adj.* 1 Arousing horror. 2 Very unpleasant or offensive. [< L *horrere* to bristle] **—hor′ri·ble·ness** *n.* **—hor′ri·bly** *adv.* **—Syn.** frightful, terrible, dreadful, hideous, ghastly.

hor·rid (hôr′id, hor′-) *adj.* 1 Causing horror or repugnance: dreadful. 2 Very unpleasant, obnoxious, etc. [< L *horrere* to bristle] **—hor′rid·ly** *adv.* **—hor′rid·ness** *n.*

hor·rif·ic (hô·rif′ik, ho-) *adj.* Causing horror.

hor·ri·fy (hôr′ə·fī, hor′-) *v.t.* **·fied, ·fy·ing** 1 To affect or fill with horror. 2 To shock; appall. **—hor′ri·fi·ca′tion** *n.*

hor·ror (hôr′ər, hor′-) *n.* 1 A strong feeling of fear, repugnance, terrified alarm, etc. 2 A quality, experience, etc., that arouses such feeling. 3 Intense dislike; aversion. 4 *Informal* Something very unpleasant, ugly, etc. [< L]

hors de com·bat (ôr də kôn·bä′) Out of combat; out of action. [F]

hors d'oeuvre (ôr dûrv′; *Fr.* ôr dœ′vr′) *pl.* **hors d'oeuvres** (-dûrvz′) or **hors d'oeuvre** An appetizer served usu. before a meal. [F]

horse (hôrs) *n.* 1 A large, hoofed mammal with a long mane and tail, used since early times for riding, pulling and carrying loads, etc. 2 The adult male of this animal, as distinguished from a mare. 3 Soldiers mounted on horses; cavalry. 4 A framelike, usu. four-legged device for supporting something. 5 A padded device used for gymnastic exercises such as vaulting. —*v.* **horsed, hors·ing** *v.t.* 1 To furnish with a horse or horses; mount. —*v.i.* 2 *Informal* To engage in horseplay: usu. with *around.* —*adj.* Coarse or large for its kind: *horse* chestnut. [< OE *hors*]

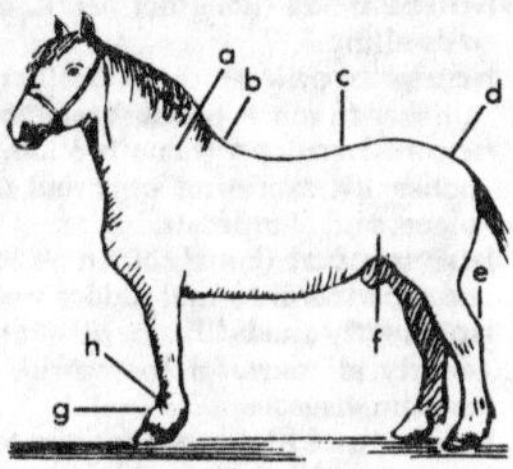

Horse
a. shoulder. b. withers. c. loins. d. croup. e. hock. f. flank. g. pastern. h. fetlock.

horse·back (hôrs′bak′) *n.* A horse's back. —*adv.* On a horse's back.

horse car 1 A streetcar drawn by horses. 2 A car for transporting horses.

horse chestnut 1 A large ornamental tree having palmate compound leaves, clusters of white flowers, and glossy seeds in burs. 2 The seed of this tree.

Horse chestnut fruit, leaves, and flower

horse·flesh (hôrs′flesh′) *n.* 1 HORSEMEAT. 2 Horses collectively, esp. racehorses or riding horses.

horse·fly (hôrs′flī′) *n. pl.* **·flies** A large fly, the female of which sucks the blood of horses and other mammals.

horse·hair (hôrs′hâr′) *n.* 1 The hair of a horse, esp. from the mane or tail. 2 Cloth made from such horse's hair.

horse·hide (hôrs′hīd′) *n.* 1 The hide of a horse. 2 Leather made from a horse's hide.

horse latitudes The regions around 35° north or south latitude, characterized by calms and light variable winds.

horse·laugh (hôrs′laf′, -läf′) *n.* A loud, boisterous laugh.

horse·man (hôrs′mən) *n. pl.* **·men** (-mən) 1 A man who rides a horse. 2 A man who is skilled in riding or managing horses.

horse·man·ship (hôrs′mən·ship) *n.* Equestrian skill.

horse·meat (hôrs′mēt′) *n.* The flesh of a horse used for pet food and sometimes human food.

horse opera *Slang* A motion picture or television show about cowboys, ranch life, etc., in the w U.S.

horse·play (hôrs′plā′) *n.* Rough, boisterous play.

horse·pow·er (hôrs′pou′ər) *n.* A unit of power equal to 550 foot-pounds per second, or about 746 watts.

horse·rad·ish (hôrs′rad′ish) *n.* 1 A coarse plant with a large, pungent root. 2 A condiment made from this root.

horse sense *Informal* Common sense.

horse·shoe (hôr′shōō′, hôrs′-) *n.* 1 A U-shaped piece of metal nailed to the bottom of a horse's hoof for protection. 2 Something shaped like this. 3 *pl. (construed as sing.)* A game in which players toss horseshoes at a stake. —*v.t.* **·shoed, ·shoe·ing** To equip with horseshoes.

horseshoe crab A large, marine arthropod with a carapace shaped like a horseshoe and a long, sharp tail.

horse·tail (hôrs′tāl′) *n.* Any of several nonflowering plants having hollow, jointed stems and reproducing by means of spores.

horse·whip (hôrs′hwip′) *n.* A whip for driving or managing horses. —*v.t.* **·whipped, ·whip·ping** To thrash with a horsewhip.

horse·wom·an (hôrs′wŏŏm′ən) *n. pl.* **·wom·en** (-wim′in) A woman who is skilled in riding or managing horses.

hors·y (hôr′sē) adj. **hors·i·er, hors·i·est** 1 Pertaining to or suggestive of horses. 2 Devoted to horses or horse racing. Also **hors′ey (·i·er, ·i·est).** **—hors′i·ly** *adv.* **—hors′i·ness** *n.*

hort. horticultural; horticulture.

hor·ta·to·ry (hôr′tə·tôr′ē, -tō′rē) *adj.* Giving or expressing exhortation, encouragement, etc. Also **hor′ta·tive.** [< L *hortari* to urge]

hor·ti·cul·ture (hôr′tə·kul′chər) *n.* The art and science of growing vegetables, fruits, flowers, etc. [< L *hortus* garden + *cultura* cultivation] **—hor′ti·cul′tur·al** *adj.* **—hor′ti·cul′tur·al·ly** *adv.* **—hor′ti·cul′tur·ist** *n.*

Hos. Hosea.

ho·san·na (hō·zan′ə) *interj. & n.* An exclamation or cry of praise to God. [< Heb. *hōshī′āhnnā* save, I pray]

hose (hōz) *n. pl.* **hose** *for defs. 1 & 2,* **hos·es** *for def. 3* 1 *pl.* Stockings or socks. 2 *Usu. pl.* A tight-fitting, trouser-like garment formerly worn by men. 3 A flexible tube or pipe for conveying water or other fluids. —*v.t.* **hosed, hos·ing** To water, wash, or douse with a hose. [< OE *hosa*]

Ho·se·a (hō·zē′ə, -zā′ə) *n.* 1 A Hebrew minor prophet of the eighth century B.C. 2 The book of the Old Testament bearing his name.

ho·sier·y (hō′zhər·ē) *n.* Stockings and socks collectively.

hosp. hospital.

hos·pice (hos′pis) *n.* A place of lodging or shelter, as one maintained by a monastic order. [< L *hospes* host, guest]

hos·pi·ta·ble (hos′pi·tə·bəl, hos·pit′ə·bəl) adj. 1 Welcoming and entertaining guests with generous kindness. 2 Characterized by hospitality. 3 Open-minded; receptive. [< L *hospitare* entertain] **—hos′pi·ta·ble·ness** *n.* **—hos′pi·ta·bly** *adv.*

hos·pi·tal (hos′pi·təl) *n.* An institution for the reception, care, and treatment of the sick or injured. [< L *hospes* guest]

hos·pi·tal·i·ty (hos′pə·tal′ə·tē) *n. pl.* **·ties** The spirit, practice, or act of being hospitable.

hos·pi·tal·ize (hos′pi·təl·īz′) *v.t.* **·ized, ·iz·ing** To put in a hospital for treatment. **—hos′pi·tal·i·za′tion** *n.*

host[1] (hōst) *n.* 1 One who entertains or receives guests. 2 An innkeeper. 3 A person who introduces and interviews guests, as on certain television or radio shows. 4 An organism that supports a parasite. —*v.t.* *Informal* To conduct or entertain in the role of a host. [< L *hospes* guest, host]

host[2] (hōst) *n.* 1 A large number; a multitude. 2 An army. [< L *hostis* enemy]

host[3] (hōst) *n. Often cap.* The bread or wafer of the Eucharist. [< L *hostia* sacrificial victim]

hos·tage (hos′tij) *n.* A person held as a pledge or prisoner until the terms of a stipulation are met. [< OF]

hos·tel (hos′təl) *n.* A lodging place, esp. one for young people while hiking or traveling. [< L *hospes* guest]

hos·tel·ry (hos′təl·rē) *n. pl.* **·ries** An inn, hotel, etc.

host·ess (hōs′tis) *n.* 1 A woman who acts as a host. 2 A woman employed to greet or be of service to customers, as at a restaurant, resort, etc.

hos·tile (hos′təl, *esp. Brit.* hos′tīl) *adj.* 1 Of or pertaining to an enemy. 2 Feeling, showing, or characterized by enmity, antagonism, etc. 3 Unfavorable or forbidding. [< L *hostilis*] **—hos′tile·ly** *adv.* **—Syn.** 2 unfriendly, antagonistic, malicious, unsociable. 3 adverse, untoward, opposing, contrary.

hos·til·i·ty (hos·til′ə·tē) *n. pl.* **·ties** 1 The state of being hostile. 2 *pl.* Warlike activities; warfare.

hos·tler (hos′lər, os′-) *n.* A stableman; groom. [< OF *hostelier* innkeeper]

hot (hot) *adj.* **hot·ter, hot·test** 1 At or having a high or relatively high temperature. 2 Producing a burning or biting sensation to the taste or touch. 3 Marked by passion, zeal, or intensity. 4 Fiery; angry; wrathful. 5 Violent; raging: a *hot* battle. 6 *Informal* So new as not to have lost its freshness, excitement, etc.: a *hot* tip; a *hot* bulletin. 7 *Slang* Recently stolen or smuggled: *hot* goods. 8 *Music Slang* Characterized by rapid tempo, driving rhythm, and daring harmony, as some jazz. 9 Following very closely: in *hot* pursuit. 10 *Slang* Excellent; very good. 11 *Informal* Extremely controversial: a *hot* issue. 12 *Informal* Very popular: a *hot* new singer. 13 In hunting, distinct: said of a scent. 14 Energized with electricity: a *hot* wire. 15 Dangerously radioactive. *—adv.* In a hot manner. [< OE *hāt*] **—hot′ly** *adv.* **—hot′ness** *n.*

hot air *Slang* Empty or pretentious talk.

hot·bed (hot′bed′) *n.* 1 A bed of earth warmed by fermentation and usu. protected by glass, used for promoting rapid growth of plants. 2 A place or condition favoring rapid growth or activity, esp. of a kind to be deplored.

hot-blood·ed (hot′blud′id) *adj.* Excitable; passionate.

hot cake A pancake.

hotch·potch (hoch′poch) *n.* HODGEPODGE.

hot cross bun A bun marked with a cross of frosting, eaten esp. during Lent.

hot dog *Informal* A frankfurter, usu. served in a split roll.

ho·tel (hō·tel′) *n.* An establishment or building providing lodging, food, etc., for paying customers. [< OF *hostel* inn]

hot·foot (hot′fo͝ot′) *v.t. Informal* To hurry; go hastily. *—adv. Informal* Hurriedly; hastily. *—n. pl.* **·foots** The prank of furtively wedging a match between the upper and sole of someone's shoe and lighting it.

hot·head (hot′hed′) *n.* A hotheaded person.

hot·head·ed (hot′hed′id) *adj.* 1 Quick-tempered. 2 Impetuous; rash. **—hot′head′ed·ly** *adv.* **—hot′head′ed·ness** *n.*

hot·house (hot′hous′) *n.* A greenhouse heated artificially for the cultivation of certain plants.

hot line A direct means of communication, esp. a telephone line kept available for emergency use.

hot plate A small, portable, gas or electric stove, having one or two burners.

hot rod *Slang* An automobile modified for increased power and speed.

hot·shot (hot′shot) *n. Slang* One with great skill or expertise; a whiz.

Hot·ten·tot (hot′ən·tot) *n.* 1 A member of a people of s Africa believed to be related to the Bantus and Bushmen. 2 The language of these people.

hou·dah (hou′də) *n.* HOWDAH.

hound (hound) *n.* 1 Any of various breeds of usu. short-haired, long-eared hunting dogs. 2 *Informal* A devotee; enthusiast. *—v.t.* 1 To hunt or pursue persistently. 2 To nag persistently. [< OE *hund*]

hounds·tooth check (houndz′to͞oth′) A textile pattern of broken checks. Also **hound's-tooth check.**

hour (our) *n.* 1 A unit of time equal to one twenty-fourth of a day; sixty minutes. 2 The point of time indicated by a chronometer, watch, or clock; the time of day. 3 A set, appointed, or definite time. 4 *pl.* Prayers to be repeated at stated times of the day. [< Gk. *hōra* time, period]

hour·glass (our′glas′, -gläs′) *n.* A glass vessel having two parts connected by a narrow neck, used for measuring time by the running of sand from the upper to the lower part.

Hourglass

hou·ri (ho͞o′rē) *n.* 1 In Muslim belief, one of the beautiful virgins awaiting the faithful in Paradise. 2 Any sensually beautiful woman. [< Ar. *hūrīyah* black-eyed woman]

hour·ly (our′lē) *adj.* 1 Of, happening, done, etc., every hour. 2 Constant or frequent. *—adv.* 1 At or during each or any hour. 2 Constantly; frequently.

house (hous) *n.* 1 A building intended for human habitation. 2 A household; family. 3 A building used for any purpose: a coffee *house.* 4 The abode of a fraternity, order, etc.: a sorority *house.* 5 A dormitory or residence hall in a college or university. 6 A legislative body; also, the chamber it occupies. 7 A place of business. 8 A business firm: the *house* of Morgan. 9 The management of a business, gambling establishment, etc. 10 A theater; also, the audience in a theater. 11 *Often cap.* A line of ancestors and descendants regarded as forming a single family: the *House* of Tudor. 12 In astrology, one of the twelve divisions of the heavens, each division having special significance in casting horoscopes. *—v.* (houz) **housed, hous·ing** *v.t.* 1 To take or put into a house. 2 To store in a house or building. 3 To fit into a mortise, joint, etc. *—v.i.* 4 To take shelter or lodgings; dwell. [< OE *hūs*] **—house′ful** *n.*

house arrest Detention in one's own house, often under guard, instead of in prison.

house·boat (hous′bōt′) *n.* A boat or barge fitted out as a dwelling.

house·break·er (hous′brā′kər) *n.* One who breaks into a house to rob. **—house′break′ing** *n.*

house·bro·ken (hous′brō′kən) *adj.* Trained to live in a house by excreting only out-of-doors or in a specified place: said of animals.

house·coat (hous′kōt′) *n.* A long, loose-skirted garment designed for informal indoor wear.

house·fly (hous′flī′) *n. pl.* **·flies** The common fly found in nearly all parts of the world, an agent in transmitting certain diseases.

house guest A guest invited to stay one or more nights.

house·hold (hous′hōld) *n.* 1 A number of persons dwelling under the same roof. 2 The home and all the things pertaining to it. *—adj.* Domestic.

house·hold·er (hous′hōl′dər) *n.* 1 The head of a family. 2 One who owns or rents a home.

house·keep·er (hous′kē′pər) *n.* A woman who does or directs others to do the domestic work in a home. **—house′keep′ing** *n.*

house·maid (hous′mād′) *n.* A woman employed to do housework.

housemaid's knee A chronic inflammation of the bursa in front of the knee.

House of Commons The lower house of the British and Canadian Parliaments.

house of correction An institution for lesser criminals; reform school.

House of Lords The upper house of the British Parliament.

House of Representatives 1 The lower branch of the legislature of the U.S. and of many of its state legislative bodies. 2 A similar legislative body in certain other countries.

house organ A publication issued regularly by a business for its employees, affiliates, etc.

house party An entertaining of guests for several days, usu. in a country house or a college fraternity.

house physician A physician resident by appointment in a hospital, hotel, etc.

house sparrow A small brown and gray bird of European origin, now common in the U.S.

house·top (hous′top′) *n.* The top or roof of a house. — **from the housetops** Publicly; for all to hear.

house·wife (hous′wīf′) *n. pl.* **·wives** (-wīvz′) **1** A married woman who performs the domestic duties of a household as her principal occupation. **2** (usu. huz′if) A small sewing kit. —**house′wife′ly** *adj., adv.*

house·wife·ry (hous′wīf′rē) *n.* The work of a housewife.

house·work (hous′wûrk′) *n.* The work of keeping house, as cleaning, cooking, laundering, etc.

hous·ing[1] (hou′zing) *n.* **1** The act of providing with a house or shelter. **2** A house or lodging: *housing* for the flood victims. **3** Houses, apartments, etc., provided or built for many people. **4** Something that shelters or covers. **5** *Mech.* A recess, enclosure, bracket, etc., in one part for holding or covering another part.

hous·ing[2] (hou′zing) *n.* **1** An ornamental covering for a horse. **2** *pl.* TRAPPINGS (def. 3). [< OF *houce*]

hove (hōv) A *p.t.* of HEAVE.

hov·el (huv′əl, hov′-) *n.* **1** A wretched dwelling; hut. **2** An open shed for sheltering animals, tools, etc. —*v.t.* **·eled** or **·elled, ·el·ing** or **·el·ling** To shelter in a hovel. [?]

hov·er (huv′ər, hov′-) *v.i.* **1** To remain suspended in or near one place in the air. **2** To linger; be nearby, as if waiting or watching: with *around, near,* etc. **3** To remain in an uncertain or irresolute state: with *between.* —*n.* The act of hovering. [< obs. *hove* to float] —**hov′er·er** *n.*

Hov·er·craft (huv′ər·kraft′, hov′-, -kräft′) *n.* A vehicle traveling over ground or water on a cushion of air produced by fans directed downward: a trade name. Also **hov′er·craft′.**

how (hou) *adv.* **1** In what way or manner; by what means. **2** To what degree, extent, amount, etc. **3** In what state or condition. **4** For what reason or purpose. **5** For what price. **6** By what name or designation. **7** To what effect; with what meaning. **8** *Informal* What: *How* is that again? —*n.* Way of doing or becoming; method. [< OE *hū*]

how·be·it (hou·bē′it) *adv. Archaic* Be that as it may.

how·dah (hou′də) *n.* A seat on the back of an elephant. [< Hind. *haudah*]

Howdah

how·dy (hou′dē) *interj. Informal* Hello; hi!

how·ev·er (hou·ev′ər) *adv.* **1** In whatever manner; by whatever means. **2** To whatever degree or extent. **3** How; in what manner: *However* did it happen? —*conj.* Notwithstanding; still; but: *However,* he arrived late.

how·it·zer (hou′it·sər) *n.* An artillery piece with a barrel longer than that of a mortar, and firing in a high trajectory with medium muzzle velocity. [< Czech *houfnice* catapult]

howl (houl) *v.i.* **1** To utter the loud, mournful wail of a wolf or dog. **2** To utter such a cry in rage, grief, etc. **3** To make a similar sound. **4** To laugh loudly. —*v.t.* **5** To utter or express with a howl or howls. **6** To drive or effect with a howl or howls. —*n.* **1** The cry of a wolf or dog. **2** Any sound suggesting this, esp. a cry of grief or rage. **3** *Informal* Something considered hilariously funny. [Imit.]

howl·er (hou′lər) *n.* **1** One who or that which howls. **2** *Informal* An absurd mistake or blunder.

howl·ing (hou′ling) *adj.* **1** That howls. **2** Dismal; mournful. **3** *Slang* Prodigious; tremendous: a *howling* success.

how·so·ev·er (hou′sō·ev′ər) *adv.* **1** In whatever manner. **2** To whatever extent.

hoy·den (hoid′n) *n.* A romping, boisterous girl; tomboy. —*adj.* Rude or unseemly; bold. —*v.i.* To romp rudely or indecently. [?] —**hoy′den·ish** *adj.*

Hoyle (hoil) *n.* A book of rules for indoor games, esp. for card games. [< E. *Hoyle,* 1672–1769, English writer]

HP, H.P., hp, h.p. high pressure; horsepower.

HQ, H.Q., hq, h.q. headquarters.

H.R. Home Rule; House of Representatives.

hr, h.r. home run(s).

hr. hour(s).

H.R.H. His (or Her) Royal Highness.

H.S. High School.

ht. heat; height.

hub (hub) *n.* **1** The central part of a wheel. **2** Any center of activity, interest, etc. [? < HOB]

hub·bub (hub′ub) *n.* Tumult; uproar.

hu·bris (hyōō′bris) *n.* Overweening pride and insolence, often bringing about retribution. [Gk.]

huck·a·back (huk′ə·bak) *n.* A coarse, durable linen or cotton cloth used for towels. Also **huck, huck′a·buck** (-buk). [?]

huck·le·ber·ry (huk′əl·ber′ē) *n. pl.* **·ries** **1** The edible berry of a species of heath often confused with the blueberry. **2** The shrub producing this berry. [?]

huck·ster (huk′stər) *n.* **1** A glib and aggressive salesman, esp. one having a flamboyant manner. **2** Any peddler or hawker of small wares. **3** *Informal* A producer or writer of advertising commercials, as on radio or television. —*v.t.* **1** To peddle. **2** To promote by showy or aggressive means. [< MDu. *hoekster*] —**huck′ster·ism** *n.*

HUD, H.U.D. Housing and Urban Development.

hud·dle (hud′l) *v.* **hud·dled, hud·dling** *v.i.* **1** To crowd closely together. **2** To draw or hunch oneself together, as from cold. **3** To come together for a conference or huddle. —*v.t.* **4** To bring together in a group. **5** To hunch (oneself) together. —*n.* **1** A confused crowd or collection of persons or things. **2** In football, the grouping of a team before each play, in which signals and instructions are given. **3** Any small, intimate conference. [?]

Hud·son seal (hud′sən) Muskrat fur dyed and trimmed to resemble sealskin. [< *Hudson* Bay in N Canada]

hue[1] (hyōō) *n.* **1** The particular shade or tint of a color. **2** The distinguishing attribute of a chromatic color, as red, green, blue, etc. **3** Color. [< OE *hēow* appearance]

hue[2] (hyōō) *n.* A vociferous cry; shouting. [< OF *hu* cry]

huff (huf) *n.* A feeling of anger and resentment. —*v.t.* **1** To offend; make angry. **2** To treat insolently or arrogantly. —*v.i.* **3** To be offended. **4** To puff; blow. [Imit.] —**huff′ish** *adj.* —**huff′ish·ly** *adv.* —**huff′ish·ness** *n.*

huff·y (huf′ē) *adj.* **huff·i·er, huff·i·est** **1** Easily offended. **2** Angry. —**huff′i·ly** *adv.* —**huff′i·ness** *n.*

hug (hug) *v.* **hugged, hug·ging** *v.t.* **1** To clasp tightly within the arms, as from affection. **2** To keep fondly in the mind; cherish, as a belief or opinion. **3** To keep close to, as a shore. —*v.i.* **4** To lie close; nestle. —*n.* A close embrace. [< Scand.]

huge (ʰyōōj) *adj.* Very large in size, degree, or extent. [< OF *ahuge* high] —**huge′ly** *adv.* —**huge′ness** *n.*

hug·ger-mug·ger (hug′ər·mug′ər) *n.* Confusion and disorder. —*adj.* **1** Confused; jumbled. **2** Secret; sly. [?]

huh (hu) *interj.* An exclamation of inquiry, surprise, contempt, etc.

hu·la (hōō′lə) *n.* A native Hawaiian dance that tells a story in pantomime. Also **hu′la-hu′la.** [< Hawaiian]

hulk (hulk) *n.* **1** The body of a ship, esp. of one that is old or wrecked. **2** A heavy, clumsy ship. **3** An abandoned wreck or shell. **4** A bulky or unwieldy object or person. —*v.i.* To rise or loom bulkily: usu. with *up.* [< Gk. *holkas* towed vessel]

hulk·ing (hul′king) *adj.* Bulky; unwieldy. Also **hulk′y.**

hull (hul) *n.* **1** An outer covering, as a husk of grain or a nutshell. **2** The calyx attached to a strawberry, tomato, etc. **3** *Naut.* The body of a ship, exclusive of the masts and rigging. **4** The outermost structures of a spacecraft, missile, etc. —*v.t.* To shell; free from the hull. [< OE *hulu* a covering] —**hull′er** *n.*

hul·la·ba·loo (hul′ə·bə·lōō′) *n.* A loud and confused noise; uproar; tumult.

hum (hum) *v.* **hummed, hum·ming** *v.i.* **1** To make a low, continuous, buzzing sound, as a bee. **2** To sing with the lips closed. **3** To give forth a confused, indistinct sound, as of mingled voices. **4** *Informal* To be busily active. —*v.t.* **5** To sing, as a tune, with the lips closed. **6** To put into a specified state by humming: to *hum* someone to sleep. —*n.* A dull, low, continuous sound. [Imit.] —**hum′mer** *n.*

hu·man (ʰyōō′mən) adj. **1** Of, pertaining to, or like man

add, āce, câre, pälm; end, ēven; it, īce; odd, ōpen, ôrder; tŏŏk, pōōl; up, bûrn; ə = *a* in *above, u* in *focus;* yōō = *u* in *fuse;* oil; pout; check; go; ring; thin; this; zh, *vision.* < derived from; ? origin uncertain or unknown.

or mankind. 2 Created by or belonging to man or mankind: *human* problems. 3 Characterized by or exemplifying the strengths, weaknesses, emotions, struggles, etc., typical of man and mankind: a very *human* situation. —*n.* A human being. [< L *humanus*] **—hu′man·ness** *n.*

hu·mane (ʰyōō·mān′) *adj.* 1 Having or showing kindness, tenderness, compassion, etc. 2 Tending to refine or make civilized. **—hu·mane′ly** *adv.* **—hu·mane′ness** *n.* **—Syn. 1** charitable, merciful, sympathetic, benevolent, clement.

hu·man·ism (ʰyōō′mən·iz′əm) *n.* 1 The quality or condition of being human. 2 A humane concern for man and his welfare. 3 A philosophy in which man, his interests, and development are made central and dominant, tending to exalt the cultural and rational elements of man rather than the supernatural or speculative. 4 A devotion to the humanities. **—hu′man·ist** *n.* **—hu′man·is′tic** *adj.* **—hu′man·is′ti·cal·ly** *adv.*

Hu·man·ism (ʰyōō′mən·iz′əm) *n.* The intellectual and literary movement of the 14th to 16th centuries which exalted Greek and Roman culture. **—Hu′man·ist** *n.*

hu·man·i·tar·i·an (ʰyōō·man′ə·târ′ē·ən) *n.* One who seeks to promote the welfare of mankind; a philanthropist. —*adj.* 1 That aids others. 2 Of humanitarianism. **—hu·man′i·tar′i·an·ism** *n.*

hu·man·i·ty (ʰyōō·man′ə·tē) *n. pl.* **·ties** 1 Mankind collectively. 2 Human nature. 3 The state or quality of being human. 4 The state or quality of being humane. **—the humanities** The branches of learning including literature, language, philosophy, fine arts, etc., as distinguished from the sciences.

hu·man·ize (ʰyōō′mən·īz) *v.t. & v.i.* **·ized, ·iz·ing** To make or become humane or human. **—hu′man·i·za′tion** *n.*

hu·man·kind (ʰyōō′mən·kīnd′) *n.* Mankind.

hu·man·ly (ʰyōō′mən·lē) *adv.* 1 In accordance with man's nature or experience. 2 Within human power or knowledge. 3 Humanely.

hu·ma·noid (ʰyōō′me·noid) *adj.* Resembling a human being. —*n.* A creature resembling a human being.

hum·ble (hum′bəl) *adj.* **·bler, ·blest** 1 Having or expressing a sense of selflessness, meekness, modesty, etc. 2 Lowly in condition, rank, etc.; unpretending. —*v.t.* **hum·bled, hum·bling** 1 To reduce the pride of; humiliate. 2 To lower in rank or dignity; abase. [< L *humus* ground] **—hum′ble·ness, hum′bler** *n.* **—hum′bly** *adv.* **—Syn.** *adj.* 1 modest, meek, selfless, unassuming, submissive.

humble pie A pie made of the edible entrails **(humbles)** of a deer, formerly served to servants at hunting feasts. **—eat humble pie** To be forced to admit one's mistakes and apologize.

hum·bug (hum′bug) *n.* 1 A deception; sham. 2 Foolish talk; nonsense. 3 An impostor. —*v.t.* **·bugged, ·bug·ging** To deceive. —*interj.* Nonsense! [?] **—hum′bug·ger, hum′bug·ger·y** *n.*

hum·ding·er (hum′ding′ər) *n. Slang* One who or that which excels. [?]

hum·drum (hum′drum′) *adj.* Without interest; tedious. —*n.* Something humdrum. [< HUM + DRUM]

hu·mer·us (hyōō′mər·əs) *n. pl.* **·mer·i** (-mər·ī) The bone of the upper arm or forelimb. [L, shoulder] **—hu·mer·al** (ʰyōō′mər·əl) *adj.*

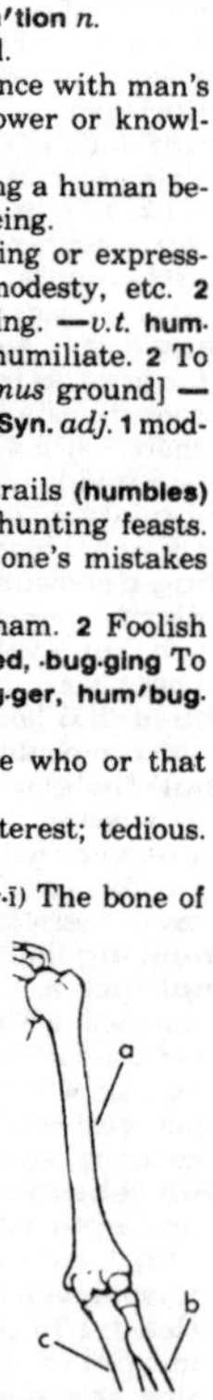

a. humerus.
b. radius.
c. ulna.

hu·mid (ʰyōō′mid) *adj.* Containing moisture; damp. [< L *humere* be moist] **—hu′·mid·ly** *adv.*

hu·mid·i·fy (ʰyōō·mid′ə·fī) *v.t.* **·fied, ·fy·ing** To make moist or humid, as the atmosphere of a room. **—hu·mid′i·fi·ca′tion, hu·mid′i·fi′er** *n.*

hu·mid·i·ty (ʰyōō·mid′ə·tē) *n.* 1 Moisture; dampness, esp. of the atmosphere. 2 The measure of the water vapor in the air. • See RELATIVE HUMIDITY. Also **hu′mid·ness.**

hu·mi·dor (ʰyōō′mə·dôr) *n.* A place or container for storing cigars or tobacco so that moisture is retained.

hu·mil·i·ate (ʰyōō·mil′ē·āt) *v.t.* **·at·ed, ·at·ing** To lower or offend the pride or self-respect of; mortify; humble. [< L *humilis* lowly] **—hu·mil′i·a′tion** *n.*

hu·mil·i·ty (ʰyōō·mil′ə·tē) *n. pl.* **·ties** The state or quality of being humble. **—Syn.** modesty, meekness, unpretentiousness, docility, humbleness.

hum·ming·bird (hum′ing·bûrd′) *n.* Any of a family of tiny, nectar-feeding birds with brilliant plumage, long, needle-like bills, and having very rapid wing motion.

Hummingbird

hum·mock (hum′ək) *n.* 1 A small hill or knoll. 2 A pile or ridge of ice on an ice field. [?] **—hum′mock·y** *adj.*

hu·mor (ʰyōō′mər) *n.* 1 A person's disposition, mood, or state of mind. 2 The quality of being amusing, comical, ludicrous, etc. 3 The capacity to perceive, appreciate, or give expression to what is amusing, comical, ludicrous, etc. 4 A sudden whim or caprice. 5 A fluid or fluidlike substance of the body. In medieval times the humors, consisting of blood, phlegm, yellow bile, and black bile, were supposed to give rise to the sanguine, phlegmatic, choleric, and melancholic temperaments, respectively. **—out of humor** Irritated; annoyed. —*v.t.* 1 To comply with the moods or caprices of. 2 To accommodate or adapt oneself to. *Brit. sp.* **hu′mour.** [L, liquid]

hu·mor·esque (ʰyōō′mə·resk′) *n.* A lively or fanciful musical composition.

hu·mor·ist (ʰyōō′mər·ist) *n.* 1 A writer or entertainer who specializes in the narration of humorous stories or jokes. 2 A wag or joker.

hu·mor·ous (ʰyōō′mər·əs) *adj.* 1 Full of humor; amusing. 2 Having or able to express humor. **—hu′mor·ous·ly** *adv.* **—hu′mor·ous·ness** *n.* **—Syn.** comic, funny, witty, farcical, droll.

hump (hump) *n.* 1 A rounded protuberance, esp. one formed by a curved spine or by a fleshy growth on the back. 2 A mound. 3 *Slang* A fit of ill humor or gloominess. **—over the hump** Beyond the point where force or effort is needed. —*v.t.* 1 To bend or round (the back) in a hump; hunch. —*v.i.* 2 *Slang* **a** To put forth extra effort; go all-out. **b** To move fast. [?] **—hump′y** *adj.* **(·i·er, ·i·est)**

hump·back (hump′bak′) *n.* 1 A back with a hump. 2 A hunchback. 3 A large whale with a low humplike dorsal Dfin. **—hump′backed′** *adj.*

humph (humf) *interj.* An exclamation of doubt or dissatisfaction.

hu·mus (ʰyōō′məs) *n.* The organic matter of the soil, as leaf mold and other decomposing materials. [L, ground]

Hun (hun) *n.* 1 One of a barbarous nomadic Asian people who invaded Europe in the fourth and fifth centuries. 2 Any barbarous or destructive person.

hunch (hunch) *n.* 1 A hump. 2 A lump or hunk. 3 A sudden shove. 4 *Informal* A premonition. —*v.t.* 1 To bend, as the back, so as to form a hump; arch. —*v.i.* 2 To move or thrust oneself forward. 3 To stand or sit with the body bent or crooked. [?]

hunch·back (hunch′bak′) *n.* A person having a deformed back. **—hunch′backed′** *adj.*

hun·dred (hun′drid) *adj.* Being 10 more than 90. —*n.* The sum of 90 plus 10; 100; C. [< OE]

hun·dred·fold (hun′drid·fōld′) *n.* An amount a hundred times as great as a given unit. —*adj.* Indicating a hundred times as much or as many. —*adv.* By a hundred: with *a* or (Brit.) *an.*

hun·dredth (hun′dridth) *n.* 1 The element of an ordered set that corresponds to the number 100. 2 One of a hundred equal parts. —*adj.* Being tenth in order after the ninetieth.

hun·dred·weight (hun′drid·wāt′) *n.* 1 In the U.S., a weight of 100 pounds. 2 In Great Britain, a weight of 112 pounds.

hung (hung) *p.t. & p.p.* of HANG. • See HANG.

Hung. Hungarian; Hungary.

Hun·gar·i·an (hung·gâr′ē·ən) *adj.* Of or pertaining to Hungary, its people, or their language. —*n.* 1 A native or citizen of Hungary. 2 The Finno-Ugric language of the Hungarians; Magyar.

Hun·ga·ry (hung′gə·rē) A republic of CEN. Europe, 35,912 sq. mi., cap. Budapest.

hun·ger (hung′gər) *n.* **1** A need or craving for food. **2** The discomfort or physical debility caused by lack of food. **3** Any strong desire. —*v.i.* **1** To feel hunger. **2** To have a craving or desire: with *for* or *after:* to *hunger* for a chance to return to one's homeland. [< OE]

hunger strike A refusal to eat until certain demands are met.

hung over *Slang* Suffering from a hangover.

hun·gry (hung′grē) *adj.* **·gri·er, ·gri·est 1** Having or feeling hunger. **2** Indicating hunger. **3** Eagerly desiring; craving. **4** Barren: said of land. **—hun′gri·ly** *adv.* **—hun′gri·ness** *n.*

hung up *Slang* **1** Delayed. **2** Preoccupied or obsessed. **3** Sidetracked or impeded: *hung up* on legal technicalities.

hunk (hungk) *n. Informal* A large piece; chunk. [?]

hun·ky-do·ry (hung′kē·dôr′ē, -dō′rē) *adj. Informal* OK; satisfactory. [< slang *hunky* safe, satisfactory]

hunt (hunt) *v.t.* **1** To pursue (game) for the purpose of killing or catching. **2 a** To search (a region) for game. **b** To search (a place): to *hunt* a room. **3** To search for diligently; look for. **4** To use (hounds or horses) in hunting. **5** To chase; pursue. **6** To persecute; harass. —*v.i.* **7** To pursue game or other wild animals; follow the chase. **8** To make a search; seek. —*n.* **1** The act of hunting. **2** A search. **3** The participants in a hunt. **4** A district hunted over. [< OE *huntian*]

hunt·er (hun′tər) *n.* **1** A person who hunts. **2** A horse or dog used in hunting.

hunt·ing (hun′ting) *n.* The act of a person or animal that hunts.

hunt·ress (hun′tris) *n.* A woman who hunts.

hunts·man (hunts′mən) *n. pl.* **·men** (-mən) **1** One who hunts. **2** The attendant who has charge of the hounds in a hunt.

hur·dle (hûr′dəl) *n.* **1** In racing, a framework to be leaped over by horses or runners. **2** *pl.* A type of race in which this occurs: usu. with *the.* **3** Any obstacle or difficulty. —*v.* **·dled, ·dling** *v.t.* **1** To leap over, as an obstacle in a race. **2** To surmount (a difficulty, etc.). —*v.i.* **3** To leap over hurdles, obstacles, etc. [< OE *hyrdel*] **—hur′dler** *n.*

hur·dy-gur·dy (hûr′dē·gûr′dē) *n. pl.* **·dies** A hand or barrel organ. [?]

hurl (hûrl) *v.t.* **1** To throw with violence; fling. **2** To throw down; overthrow. **3** To utter with vehemence. —*v.i.* **4** To throw something. **5** To move or rush violently. —*n.* The act of throwing. [ME *hurlen*] **—hurl′er** *n.*

hur·ly-bur·ly (hûr′lē·bûr′lē) *n. pl.* **·lies** Tumult; uproar. [?]

Hu·ron (ʰyŏŏr′on) *n.* **1** A member of any one of four confederated tribes of North American Indians of Iroquoian stock. **2** The Iroquoian language of these tribes.

hur·rah (hŏŏ·rô′, hə·rä′) *interj.* An exclamation expressing triumph or joy. —*n.* A shout of "hurrah." —*v.i.* To shout a hurrah or hurrahs. [Imit.]

hur·ri·cane (hûr′ə·kān′) *n.* A tropical cyclone having winds moving at about 75 miles per hour or more, usu. originating in the West Indies. [< Cariban]

hurricane deck The upper deck of a passenger ship, esp. of a river steamer.

hur·ried (hûr′ēd) *adj.* **1** In haste; rushed. **2** Done in haste; hasty. **—hur′ried·ly** *adv.* **—hur′ried·ness** *n.*

hur·ry (hûr′ē) *v.* **hur·ried, hur·ry·ing** *v.i.* **1** To act or move rapidly or in haste; hasten. —*v.t.* **2** To cause or urge to act or move more rapidly. **3** To hasten the progress, completion, etc., of, often unduly: to *hurry* a decision. —*n. pl.* **hur·ries 1** The act of hurrying. **2** Eager haste; precipitation. [?]

hur·ry-scur·ry (hûr′ē·skûr′ē) *v.i.* **·ried, ·ry·ing** To act hurriedly. —*adj.* Hurried; confused. —*n. pl.* **·ries** Bustling, confused haste. —*adv.* With disorderly haste; pell-mell.

hurt (hûrt) *v.* **hurt, hurt·ing** *v.t.* **1** To cause physical harm or suffering to; injure. **2** To harm or damage: to *hurt* one's reputation. **3** To cause mental or emotional suffering to; wound; offend. —*v.i.* **4** To be painful or sore: My feet *hurt.* **5** To cause damage, hurt, etc. —*n.* **1** An injury or wound. **2** Damage. **3** An injury to the feelings. [< OF *hurter* to hit] **—hurt′er** *n.*

hurt·ful (hûrt′fəl) *adj.* Causing hurt. **—hurt′ful·ly** *adv.* **—hurt′ful·ness** *n.*

hur·tle (hûr′təl) *v.* **hur·tled, hur·tling** *v.i.* **1** To crash violently: with *against* or *together.* **2** To move or rush swiftly and with force. —*v.t.* **3** To drive, shoot, or throw violently. [Freq. of ME *hurten* to hit, hurt]

hus·band (huz′bənd) *n.* A married man; man with a wife. —*v.t.* **1** To use or spend wisely; conserve. **2** *Archaic* To be a husband to; marry. **3** *Archaic* To till; cultivate. [< OE < *hūs* house + *bonda* freeholder]

hus·band·man (huz′bənd·mən) *n. pl.* **·men** (-mən) A farmer.

hus·band·ry (huz′bən·drē) *n.* **1** Farming. **2** Thrifty management.

hush (hush) *v.t.* **1** To make silent or quiet. **2** To soothe; allay, as fears. —*v.i.* **3** To be or become silent or still. —**hush up 1** To make quiet. **2** To keep from becoming known. —*n.* Deep silence; stillness; quiet. —*interj.* Be still. [ME *hussht* quiet]

hush·a·by (hush′ə·bī) *interj.* An expression used to lull a child to sleep.

hush-hush (hush′hush′) *adj. Informal* Secret.

hush money A bribe to secure secrecy.

hush·pup·py (hush′pup′ē) *n. pl.* **·pies** In the S U.S., a fried ball of cornmeal dough. [< its use as dog food]

husk (husk) *n.* **1** The outer covering of certain fruits or seeds. **2** Any covering, esp. when comparatively worthless. —*v.t.* To remove the husk of. [ME *huske*] **—husk′er** *n.*

husk·y[1] (hus′kē) *adj.* **husk·i·er, husk·i·est 1** Abounding in husks; like husks. **2** Somewhat hoarse: said of the voice. **—husk′i·ly** *adv.* **—husk′i·ness** *n.*

husk·y[2] (hus′kē) *adj.* **husk·i·er, husk·i·est** Strong; muscular. —*n. pl.* **husk·ies** A strong or powerfully built person. [with ref. to toughness of husks] **—husk′i·ness** *n.*

husk·y[3] (hus′kē) *n. pl.* **husk·ies** *Often cap.* A strong, thick-furred dog, used to pull sleds in the Arctic. [? Alter. of ESKIMO]

hus·sar (hŏŏ·zär′) *n.* A member of any light-armed cavalry regiment in European armies, usu. with brilliant dress uniforms. [< Ital. *corsaro* corsair]

hus·sy (huz′ē, hus′ē) *n. pl.* **·sies** A saucy or forward girl: used in reproach or playfully. [Alter. of HOUSEWIFE]

hust·ings (hus′tingz) *n.pl. (usu. construed as sing.)* **1** A place where political speeches are made. **2** The proceedings at an election. **3** A political campaign. [< ON *hūs* house + *thing* assembly]

hus·tle (hus′əl) *v.* **hus·tled, hus·tling** *v.t.* **1** To push or knock about roughly; jostle. **2** To force or push roughly and hurriedly. **3** *Informal* To cause to be done or proceed rapidly. **4** *Slang* To sell or obtain in an aggressive, often underhanded manner. —*v.i.* **5** To push one's way; shove; elbow. **6** *Informal* To act or work with energy and speed. **7** *Slang* **a** To obtain money in an aggressive, usu. underhanded manner. **b** To be a prostitute. —*n.* **1** The act of hustling. **2** *Informal* Energetic activity; push. [MDu. *hutselen* shake, toss] **—hus′tler** *n.*

hut (hut) *n.* A small, crude cabin or shack. —*v.t. & v.i.* **hut·ted, hut·ting** To shelter or live in a hut. [< OHG *hutta*]

hutch (huch) *n.* **1** A box, chest, etc., for storage. **2** A low cupboard, as for china, with open shelves on top. **3** A coop or pen for rabbits, etc. **4** A hut. [< LL *hutica*]

huz·za (hə·zä′) *n. & interj.* Hurrah: a shout of joy. Also **huz·zah′, huz·zay′** (-zā).

H.V., hv, h.v. high voltage.

hwy. highway.

hy·a·cinth (hī′ə·sinth) *n.* **1** A plant related to the lily with a spike of small, fragrant flowers. **2** The bulb or flower of this plant. **3** A gem, a brownish, reddish, or orange zircon. [< L < Gk. *hyakinthos*] **—hy′a·cin′thine** (-thin, -thīn) *adj.*

Hyacinth

hy·ae·na (hī·ē′nə) *n.* HYENA.

hy·a·line (hī'ə·lin, -līn) *adj.* Resembling glass; transparent. —*n.* Something transparent or glassy. [< Gk. *hyalos* glass]

hy·brid (hī'brid) *n.* **1** An offspring of two animals or plants of different species, varieties, breeds, etc. **2** Anything of mixed origin or unlike parts. **3** *Ling.* A word composed of elements from more than one language. —*adj.* Of, pertaining to, or like a hybrid. [< L *hybrida*] —**hy'brid·ism** *n.*

hy·brid·ize (hī'brid·īz) *v.t. & v.i.* **·ized, ·iz·ing** To produce or cause to produce hybrids. —**hy·brid·i·za·tion** (hī'brid·ə·zā'shən, -ī·zā'-) *n.*

hy·dra (hī'drə) *n. pl.* **·dras** or **·drae** (-drē) **1** A freshwater polyp. **2** Any persistent evil. [< L *Hydra* < Gk.]

Hy·dra (hī'drə) *Gk. Myth.* The many-headed serpent that grew two heads for each one that was cut off.

hy·dran·ge·a (hī·drān'jē·ə, -jə) *n.* An ornamental shrub with opposite leaves and clusters of large, showy flowers. [< HYDR(O)- + Gk. *angeion* vessel]

hy·drant (hī'drənt) *n.* A large, upright street pipe from which water may be obtained from a water main for fighting fires, cleaning streets, etc. [< HYDR(O)- + -ANT]

hy·drate (hī'drāt) *n.* A compound formed by the union of molecules of water with other molecules or atoms. —*v.t.* **·drat·ed, ·drat·ing** To combine with water or its elements to form a hydrate. [< HYDR(O)- + -ATE] —**hy'drat·ed** *adj.* —**hy·dra·tion** (hī·drā'shən) *n.*

hy·drau·lic (hī·drô'lik) *adj.* **1** Of or involving the moving of water, or force exerted by water. **2** Denoting a machine or device operated by liquid under pressure. **3** Hardening under water: *hydraulic* cement. [< Gk. *hydraulos* water organ] —**hy·drau'li·cal·ly** *adv.*

hy·drau·lics (hī·drô'liks) *n.pl. (construed as sing.)* The science and technology dealing with or based on the mechanical behavior of liquids.

hy·dride (hī'drīd, -drid) *n.* A compound of hydrogen with another element or a radical. Also **hy'drid** (-drid).

hy·dro (hī'drō) *n. pl.* **·dros** *Can.* **1** Hydroelectric power. **2** A hydroelectric power plant.

hydro- *combining form* **1** Water; of, related to, or resembling water: *hydroelectric.* **2** *Chem.* Denoting a compound of hydrogen: *hydrochloric.* Also, before vowels, **hydr-**. [< Gk. *hydōr* water]

hy·dro·car·bon (hī'drə·kär'bən) *n.* A compound of hydrogen and carbon only, as methane, benzene, acetylene, etc.

hy·dro·ceph·a·lus (hī'drə·sef'ə·ləs) *n.* An abnormal, usu. congenital condition marked by an enlarged head and brain damage due to an accumulation of fluid within the cranium. [< HYDRO- + Gk. *kephalē* head] —**hy'dro·ceph'a·loid** (-loid), **hy'dro·ceph'a·lous** *adj.*

hy·dro·chlo·ric (hī'drə·klôr'ik, -klō'rik) *adj.* Pertaining to or designating a colorless, corrosive, gaseous compound of hydrogen and chlorine which forms a strong acid (**hydrochloric acid**) in aqueous solution.

hy·dro·cy·an·ic (hī'drō·sī·an'ik) *adj.* Of, pertaining to, or designating an unstable, volatile, colorless, and extremely poisonous compound of hydrogen, carbon, and nitrogen which forms a weak acid in aqueous solution.

hy·dro·dy·nam·ics (hī'drō·dī·nam'iks) *n.pl. (construed as sing.)* The branch of physics that deals with the dynamics of liquids.

hy·dro·e·lec·tric (hī'drō·i·lek'trik) *adj.* Of or pertaining to electricity developed from water power. —**hy·dro·e·lec·tric·i·ty** (hī'drō·i·lek·tris'ə·tē) *n.*

hy·dro·flu·or·ic (hī'drō·floo͞'ər·ik) *adj.* Pertaining to or designating a volatile, colorless compound of hydrogen and fluorine which forms a corrosive acid in aqueous solution.

hy·dro·foil (hī'drə·foil) *n.* **1** One of a set of fins attached to a vessel to provide a reaction force with the water at high speeds and lift the hull from the water. **2** A vessel equipped with hydrofoils.

hy·dro·gen (hī'drə·jən) *n.* The lighest and most abundant element (symbol H) in the universe, on earth found mainly in combination with oxygen as water. [< Gk. *hydōr* water + *-genēs* born] —**hy·drog·e·nous** (hī·droj'ə·nəs) *adj.*

hy·dro·gen·ate (hī·droj'ə·nāt', hī'drə·jə·nāt') *v.t.* **·at·ed, ·at·ing** To treat with, expose to, or cause to combine with hydrogen. —**hy'dro·gen·a'tion** *n.*

hydrogen bomb An extremely powerful thermonuclear bomb based on the fusion of light nuclei, as of deuterium and lithium.

hydrogen ion The positively charged atom of hydrogen present in all acids.

hydrogen peroxide A very unstable compound that decomposes to form water and oxygen.

hydrogen sulfide A colorless, gaseous, poisonous compound of hydrogen and sulfur, having a characteristic odor of rotten eggs.

hy·drog·ra·phy (hī·drog'rə·fē) *n.* The scientific investigation and study of navigable waters, rivers, coasts, etc. —**hy·drog'ra·pher** *n.* —**hy'dro·graph'ic** or **·i·cal** *adj.*

hy·droid (hī'droid) *adj.* Of or pertaining to a class of mostly marine organisms including the hydra. —*n.* A hydra or polyp.

hy·drol·y·sis (hī·drol'ə·sis) *n.* A chemical reaction by which an aqueous solution of a neutral salt exhibits properties of a weak acid or a weak base or both. [< HYDRO- + -LYSIS] —**hy·dro·lyt·ic** (hī'drə·lit'ik) *adj.*

hy·dro·lyte (hī'drə·līt) *n.* Any substance capable of undergoing hydrolysis.

hy·dro·lyze (hī'drə·līz) *v.t. & v.i.* **·lyzed, ·lyz·ing** To undergo or cause to undergo hydrolysis. —**hy'dro·lyz'a·ble** *adj.* —**hy·dro·ly·za·tion** (hī'drə·lə·zā'shən, -lī·zā'-) *n.*

hy·drom·e·ter (hī·drom'ə·tər) *n.* An instrument for measuring the specific gravity of a liquid or solution. —**hy·dro·met·ric** (hī'drə·met'rik) or **·ri·cal** *adj.* —**hy·drom'e·try** *n.*

hy·drop·a·thy (hī·drop'ə·thē) *n.* A method of treating ailments of any kind by the use of water. —**hy·dro·path·ic** (hī'drə·path'ik) or **·i·cal** *adj.* —**hy·drop'a·thist** *n.*

hy·dro·pho·bi·a (hī'drə·fō'bē·ə) *n.* **1** RABIES. **2** Any morbid dread of water. —**hy'dro·pho'bic** *adj.*

hy·dro·phyte (hī'drə·fīt) *n.* Any plant living only in water or wet ground. —**hy·dro·phyt·ic** (hī'drə·fit'ik) *adj.*

hy·dro·plane (hī'drə·plān) *n.* **1** A seaplane. **2** A small motorboat designed so that its hull skims over the water at high speeds. **3** A hydrofoil. —*v.i.* **·planed, ·plan·ing** **1** To operate or travel in a hydroplane. **2** To skim over the surface of water.

hy·dro·pon·ics (hī'drə·pon'iks) *n.pl. (construed as sing.)* The cultivation of plants without earth in tanks of nutrient solutions. [< HYDRO- + Gk. *ponos* labor] —**hy'dro·pon'ic** *adj.*

hy·dro·sphere (hī'drə·sfir) *n.* The total water of the earth.

hy·dro·stat (hī'drə·stat) *n.* A device that controls the level of liquid in a container. —**hy'dro·stat'ic** or **·i·cal** *adj.*

hy·dro·stat·ics (hī'drə·stat'iks) *n. pl. (construed as sing.)* The scientific study of the mechanical behavior of stationary liquids.

hy·dro·ther·a·peu·tics (hī'drō·ther'ə·pyoo͞'tiks) *n.pl. (construed as sing.)* Therapy involving the use of water. Also **hy'dro·ther'a·py** (-ther'ə·pē). —**hy'dro·ther'a·peu'tic** *adj.*

hy·drot·ro·pism (hī·drot'rə·piz'əm) *n.* The orientation of a plant or plant part in response to moisture. —**hy·dro·trop·ic** (hī'drə·trop'ik) *adj.*

hy·drous (hī'drəs) *adj.* Pertaining to or designating a hydrate.

hy·drox·ide (hī·drok'sīd) *n.* A compound containing hydroxyl.

hy·drox·yl (hī·drok'sil) *n.* The univalent radical consisting of one atom of oxygen and one of hydrogen. [< HYDR(O) + OX(YGEN) + -YL]

hy·dro·zo·an (hī'drə·zō'ən) *adj.* Of or pertaining to a class of coelenterates, mostly marine, including hydroids, medusas, etc. —*n.* A hydrozoan animal.

Hyena

hy·e·na (hī·ē'nə) *n.* A wolflike carnivorous mammal of Africa and Asia, with very strong, large teeth, striped or spotted body, and a piercing cry. [< Gk. *hyaina* < *hys* pig]

Hy·ge·ia (hī·jē'ə) *Gk. Myth.* The goddess of health.

hy·giene (hī′jēn, -ji·ēn) *n.* 1 The science and preservation of health. 2 Practices and conditions that promote good health. [< Gk. *hygienios* healthful]

hy·gi·en·ic (hī′jē·en′ik, hī·jē′nik, -jen′ik-) *adj.* 1 Of or pertaining to hygiene. 2 Sanitary; clean. **—hy′gi·en′i·cal·ly** *adv.*

hy·gi·en·ics (hī′jē·en′iks, hī·jē′niks) *n. pl. (construed as sing.)* The science of preserving and promoting health.

hy·gi·en·ist (hī′jē·ən·ist) *n.* One who studies or is versed in the principles of hygiene.

hygro- *combining form* Moisture; humidity: *hygroscope.* [< Gk. *hygros* wet]

hy·grom·e·ter (hī·grom′ə·tər) *n.* An instrument that measures humidity in the atmosphere. **—hy·gro·met·ric** (hī′grə·met′rik) *adj.*

hy·gro·scope (hī′grə·skōp) *n.* A device for estimating the humidity of the air.

hy·gro·scop·ic (hī′grə·skop′ik) *adj.* 1 Pertaining to the hygroscope. 2 Absorbing moisture from the atmosphere.

hy·la (hī′lə) *n.* Any of various species of tree frog. [< Gk. *hyle* wood]

hy·men (hī′mən) *n.* A thin membrane partially covering the entrance of the vagina of a virgin; maidenhead. [< Gk. *hymēn* membrane]

Hy·men (hī′mən) *Gk. Myth.* The god of marriage.

hy·me·ne·al (hī′mə·nē′əl) *adj.* Of marriage. **—*n.*** A wedding song.

hy·men·op·ter·an (hī′mən·op′tər·ən) *adj.* Of or pertaining to an order of insects typically living in colonies and, when winged, having four membranous wings: also **hy′men·op′ter·ous.** **—*n.*** An insect of this order, as a bee, wasp, ant, etc. [< Gk. *hymen* membrane + *pteron* a wing]

hymn (him) *n.* 1 A song of praise to God. 2 Any religious song. 3 A poem of praise. **—*v.*** **hymned, hymn·ing** *v.t.* 1 To express or praise in hymns. **—*v.i.*** 2 To sing hymns or praises. [< Gk. *hymnos* a song, ode] **—hym′nic** (-nik) *adj.* **—hym′nist** *n.*

hym·nal (him′nəl) *n.* A book of hymns: also **hymn book.** **—*adj.*** Of a hymn or hymns.

hym·nol·o·gy (him·nol′ə·jē) *n.* 1 The study of hymns, including their history, use, etc. 2 Hymns collectively.

hy·oid (hī′oid) *n.* A U-shaped bone at the base of the tongue. **—*adj.*** Of or pertaining to the hyoid. [< Gk. *υ* the letter upsilon + *eidos* form]

hype (hīp) *Slang v.t.* **hyped, hyp·ing** 1 To deceive; fool. 2 To stimulate with or as with drugs: with *up.* **—*n.*** 1 A deception; fraud. 2 A promotional talk or message.

hyper- *prefix* Over; above; excessive: *hypertension.* [< Gk. *hyper* above]

hy·per·ac·id (hī′pər·as′id) *adj.* Excessively acid. **—hy′per·a·cid′i·ty** (-ə·sid′ə·tē) *n.*

hy·per·bar·ic (hī′pər·bar′ik) *adj.* Of, having, or using pressures in excess of the usual pressure of the atmosphere.

hy·per·bo·la (hī·pûr′bə·lə) *n. Math.* A curve formed by the set of points having the property that the difference of their distances from two fixed points is a constant. [< Gk. *hyperbolē* a throwing beyond, excess]

hy·per·bo·le (hī·pûr′bə·lē) *n.* Deliberate exaggeration in writing or speaking, used to create an effect, as in *He was as tall as a mountain.* [< Gk. *hyperbolē* excess]

hy·per·bol·ic (hī′pər·bol′ik) *adj.* 1 Of or containing hyperbole; exaggerating. 2 Of, pertaining to, or shaped like a hyperbola. Also **hy′per·bol′i·cal.** **—hy′per·bol′i·cal·ly** *adv.*

hy·per·bo·lize (hī·pûr′bə·līz) *v.t. & v.i.* **·lized, ·liz·ing** To express in or use hyperbole.

hy·per·bo·re·an (hī′pər·bôr′ē·ən, -bō′rē-) *adj.* Of the far north; arctic; frigid.

Hy·per·bo·re·an (hī′pər·bôr′ē·ən, -bō′rē-) *n. Gk. Myth.* One of a people supposed to dwell in a blessed land beyond the north wind. [< Gk. *hyper-* beyond + *Boreas* north wind]

hy·per·crit·i·cal (hī′pər·krit′i·kəl) *adj.* Excessively critical or fussy. **—hy′per·crit′i·cal·ly** *adv.*

hy·per·gol·ic (hī′pər·gol′ik) *adj.* Indicating a combination of rocket fuel and oxidizer that ignites spontaneously. [< HYP(ER)- + Gk. *ergon* work]

hy·per·me·tro·pi·a (hī′pər·mə·trō′pē·ə) *n.* A focusing defect of the eye in which distant objects are more distinct than those near at hand; far-sightedness. Also **hy′per·met′ro·py** (-met′rə·pē), **hy′per·o′pi·a** (-ō′pē·ə). [< Gk. *hypermetros* excessive + *ōps* eye] **—hy′per·me·trop′ic** (-mə·trop′ik, -trō′pik) *adj.*

hy·per·son·ic (hī·pər·son′ik) *adj.* Of, at, or pertaining to speeds of mach 5 or greater.

hy·per·ten·sion (hī′pər·ten′shən) *n.* Excessively high arterial blood pressure. **—hy′per·ten′sive** *adj., n.*

hy·per·thy·roid·ism (hī′pər·thī′roid·iz′əm) *n.* 1 Excessive activity of the thyroid gland. 2 Any disorder caused by such activity. **—hy′per·thy′roid** *adj.*

hy·per·tro·phy (hī·pûr′trə·fē) *n.* The excessive development of an organ or tissue. **—*v.i.*** **·phied, ·phy·ing** To grow excessively. **—hy·per·troph·ic** (hī′pər·trof′ik, -trō′fik) or **·i·cal** *adj.*

hy·phen (hī′fən) *n.* A mark (- or ‒ or :) used to connect the elements of certain compound words, to show division of a word at the end of a line, and to indicate a unit modifier: a *hit-and-run* driver. [< Gk. *hypo-* under + *hen* one]

hy·phen·ate (hī′fən·āt) *v.t.* **·at·ed, ·at·ing** 1 To connect by a hyphen. 2 To write with a hyphen. **—hy′phen·a′tion** *n.*

hyp·no·sis (hip·nō′sis) *n.pl.* **·ses** (-sēz) A change in consciousness, sometimes induced in one person by another, that makes an individual highly receptive to suggestion. [< Gk. *hypnos* sleep]

hyp·not·ic (hip·not′ik) *adj.* 1 Of or producing hypnosis. 2 Tending to produce sleep. 3 Spellbinding; entrancing. **—*n.*** 1 An agent efficacious in producing sleep. 2 A hypnotized person. **—hyp·not′i·cal·ly** *adv.*

hyp·no·tism (hip′nə·tiz′əm) *n.* 1 The act, practice, or technique of inducing hypnosis. 2 The theory of hypnosis. **—hyp′no·tist** *n.*

hyp·no·tize (hip′nə·tīz) *v.t.* **·tized, ·tiz·ing** 1 To produce hypnosis in. 2 To fascinate; entrance. *Brit. sp.* **hyp′no·tise.** **—hyp′no·tiz′a·ble** *adj.* **—hyp′no·ti·za′tion** (-tə·zā′shən, -tī·zā′-), **hyp′no·tiz′er** *n.*

hy·po[1] (hī′pō) *n.* SODIUM THIOSULFATE.

hy·po[2] (hī′pō) *n. Informal* 1 A hypodermic syringe or injection. 2 A hypochondriac.

hypo- *prefix* 1 Under; beneath; less than: *hypodermic.* 2 *Chem.* Indicating the lowest degree of oxidation: *hypophosphate.* 3 *Med.* Denoting a lack of or deficiency in: *hypothyroidism.* [< Gk. *hypo* under]

hy·po·al·ler·gen·ic (hī′pō·al′ər·jen′ik) *adj.* Not likely to produce an allergic reaction.

hy·po·chlo·rite (hī′pə·klôr′īt, -klō′rīt) *n.* A salt of hypochlorous acid.

hy·po·chlo·rous (hī′pə·klôr′əs, -klō′rəs) *adj.* Denoting an unstable acid formed by the solution of chlorine in water, used as an oxidizing and bleaching agent.

hy·po·chon·dri·a (hī′pə·kon′drē·ə) *n.* Excessive anxiety about one's health or minor ailments, often accompanied by imagined symptoms of illness. Also **hy·po·chon·dri·a·sis** (hī′pō·kən·drī′ə·sis). [< HYPO- + Gk. *chondros* cartilage]

hy·po·chon·dri·ac (hī′pə·kon′drē·ak, hip′ə-) *adj.* 1 Pertaining to or affected by hypochondria. 2 Of, pertaining to, or situated in the hypochondrium. Also **hy·po·chon·dri·a·cal** (hī′pō·kən·drī′ə·kəl). **—*n.*** A person subject to hypochondria. **—hy′po·chon·dri′a·cal·ly** *adv.*

hy·po·chon·dri·um (hī′pə·kon′drē·əm, hip′ə-) *n. pl.* **·dri·a** (-drē·ə) The abdomen on either side just under the ribs. [< HYPO- + Gk. *chondros* cartilage]

hy·poc·ri·sy (hi·pok′rə·sē) *n. pl.* **·sies** A pretending to be what one is not; extreme insincerity; dissimulation. [< Gk. *hypokrisis* acting a part, feigning] **—Syn.** pretense, dissembling, affectation, sham, fakery.

hyp·o·crite (hip′ə·krit) *n.* One who pretends to have virtues, feelings, qualities, etc., that he does not possess. [< Gk. *hypokritēs* an actor.] **—hyp′o·crit′i·cal** *adj.* **—hyp′o·crit′i·cal·ly** *adv.* **—Syn.** deceiver, dissembler, pretender, cheat.

hy·po·der·mic (hī′pə·dûr′mik) *adj.* 1 Of or pertaining to the tissue just under the skin. 2 Of or pertaining to a hypodermic injection. —*n.* A hypodermic injection or syringe.

hypodermic injection An injection under the skin.

hypodermic syringe A syringe having a sharp, hollow needle for injection of a drug or medicine into the hypodermis.

hy·po·der·mis (hī'pə·dûr'məs) *n.* The tissue just under the skin.

hy·po·gas·tri·um (hī'pə·gas'trē·əm) *n. pl.* **·tri·a** (-trē·ə) *Anat.* The lower middle part of the abdomen. [<HYPO- + Gk. *gastēr* belly] —**hy'po·gas'tric** *adj.*

hy·po·gly·ce·mi·a (hī'pō·gli·sē'mē·ə) *n. Med.* A subnormal amount of blood sugar, usually caused by the presence of too much insulin. [<HYPO- + Gk. *glykys* sweet + -EMIA] —**hy'po·gly·ce'mic** *adj.*

hy·po·phos·phate (hī'pə·fos'fāt) *n.* A salt of hypophosphoric acid.

hy·po·phos·phite (hī'pə·fos'fīt) *n.* A salt of hypophosphorous acid.

hy·po·phos·phor·ic (hī'pō·fos·fôr'ik, -for'ik) *adj.* Denoting a crystalline acid formed from moist phosphorus by oxidation.

hy·po·phos·pho·rous (hī'pə·fos'fər·əs) *adj.* Denoting an acid composed of hydrogen, oxygen, and phosphorus, and having a powerful reducing action.

hy·po·sul·fite (hī'pō·sul'fīt) *n.* 1 SODIUM THIOSULFATE. 2 A salt of hyposulfurous acid.

hy·po·sul·fu·rous (hī'pō·sul·fyŏŏr'əs, hī'pə·sul'fər·əs) *adj.* Pertaining to or designating an unstable acid of strong reducing and bleaching properties.

hy·pot·e·nuse (hī·pot'ə·n^{y}ōōs, hi-) *n. Geom.* The side of a right triangle opposite the right angle. Also **hy·poth'e·nuse** (-poth'-). [<Gk. *hypo-* under + *teinein* to stretch]

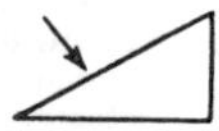
Hypotenuse

hy·po·thal·a·mus (hī'pə·thal'ə·məs) *n.* A region at the base of the brain that controls temperature and various visceral activities. —**hy·po·tha·lam·ic** (hī'pə·thə·lam'ik) *adj.*

hy·poth·e·cate (hī·poth'ə·kāt, hi-) *v.t.* **·cat·ed, ·cat·ing** To give (personal property) in pledge as security for debt. [<LL *hypotheca* pledge] —**hy·poth'e·ca'tion, hy·poth'e·ca'tor** *n.*

hy·poth·e·sis (hī·poth'ə·sis, hi-) *n. pl.* **·ses** (-sēz) 1 A set of assumptions provisionally accepted as a basis of reasoning, experiment, or investigation. 2 An unsupported or ill-supported theory. [<Gk. *hypotithenai* put under]

hy·poth·e·size (hī·poth'ə·sīz, hi-) *v.* **·sized, ·siz·ing** *v.t.* To make a hypothesis of. —*v.i.* To conceive or suggest hypotheses.

hy·po·thet·i·cal (hī'pə·thet'i·kəl) *adj.* 1 Having the nature of or based on hypothesis; assumed conditionally or tentatively as a basis for argument or investigation. 2 Given to using hypotheses. Also **hy'po·thet'ic.** —**hy'po·thet'i·cal·ly** *adv.*

hy·po·thy·roid·ism (hī'pō·thī'roid·iz'əm) *n.* 1 Deficient production of thyroid hormone. 2 The resulting syndrome, including lethargy, obesity, etc. —**hy'po·thy'roid** *adj. & n.*

hy·son (hī'sən) *n.* A grade of green tea from China. [<Chin. *hsi-ch'un,* lit., blooming spring]

hys·sop (his'əp) *n.* 1 A bushy, medicinal herb of the mint family, with small clusters of blue flowers. 2 A plant furnishing the twigs used in certain Mosaic rites. [<Gk. *hyssōpos* <Heb. *ēzōb*]

hys·ter·ec·to·my (his'tə·rek'tə·mē) *n. pl.* **·mies** Removal of all or part of the uterus by surgery. [<Gk. *hystera* womb + *ek-* out + *tomē* a cutting]

hys·te·ri·a (his·tir'ē·ə, -ter'-) *n.* 1 A psychoneurotic condition characterized by symptons of organic disorders, as blindness, deafness, etc. 2 Uncontrollable emotional excitement. Also **hys·ter·ics** (his·ter'iks). [<Gk. *hystera* the womb, thought to be the source of such symptoms]

Hz hertz.

I

I, i (ī) *n. pl.* **I's, i's, Is, is** 1 The ninth letter of the English alphabet. 2 Any spoken sound representing the letter *I* or *i.* 3 In Roman notation, the symbol for one. 4 Something shaped like an I. —*adj.* Shaped like an I.

I (ī) *pron.* The first person singular pronoun in the nominative case, used to denote the person speaking or writing. —*n, pl.* **I's** The self; the ego. [<OE *ic*]

I iodine.

I. Island(s); Isle(s).

i. interest; intransitive; island.

IA Iowa (P.O. abbr.).

Ia. Iowa.

IAAF International Amateur Athletic Federation.

IAEA International Atomic Energy Agency (of the United Nations).

i·amb (ī'amb) *n.* In prosody, a metrical foot of two syllables, an unaccented one followed by an accented one. [<Gk. *iambos*]

i·am·bic (ī·am'bik) *adj.* Of, using, or like iambs. —*n.* 1 An iamb. 2 A verse of iambic feet.

i·am·bus (ī·am'bəs) *n. pl.* **·bus·es** or **·bi** (-bī) IAMB.

-iasis *suffix Med.* Denoting a disease or abnormal condition: *psoriasis.* [<Gk., suffix of action]

-iatrics *combining form* Denoting treatment of disease: *pediatrics.* [<Gk. *iatros* healer]

i·at·ro·gen·ic (ī·at'rə·jen'ik) *adj. Med.* Caused unintentionally by the physician or by the manner of treatment: said of disorders. [<Gk. *iatros* healer + -GENIC] —**i·at'ro·gen'i·cal·ly** *adv.*

-iatry *combining form* Medical or curative treatment: *psychiatry.* [<Gk. *iatreia* healing]

ib., ibid. ibidem.

I·be·ri·an (i·bir'ē·ən) *adj.* Of or pertaining to Iberia, its people, or its dead language. —*n.* 1 A native or citizen of Iberia. 2 The language of the ancient Iberians. [<L *Iberus* <Gk.]

i·bex (ī'beks) *n. pl.* **i·bex·es** or **i·bi·ces** (ī'bə·sēz, ib'ə-) One of various wild goats of Europe and Asia, with long, recurved horns. [L]

Ibex

i·bi·dem (ib'ə·dem', i·bī'dem) *adv. Latin* In the same place: used to refer to the same work, chapter, etc., just mentioned.

i·bis (ī'bis) *n. pl.* **i·bis·es** or **i·bis** A wading bird related to the heron, with a long bill curved downward. [<Gk. <Egypt. *hab*]

-ible *suffix* -ABLE.

-ic *suffix* (for forming adjectives with the following meanings) 1 Of or pertaining to: *volcanic.* 2 Like; resembling; characteristic of: *angelic.* 3 Consisting of; containing: *alcoholic.* 4 Produced by or in the manner of: *Homeric.* 5 Related to; connected with: *domestic.* 6 *Chem.* Having a higher valence than that indicated by *-ous*: said of elements in compounds: *cupric.* [<Gk. *-ikos*]

-ical *suffix* 1 Forming adjectives from nouns ending in *-ic* or *-ics: ethical, musical.* 2 Forming adjectives from adjectives ending in *-ic,* often parallel in meaning: *comic, comical,* but sometimes with extended or special meaning: *economic, economical.* [<-IC + -AL]

Ic·a·rus (ik'ə·rəs, ī'kə-) *Gk. Myth.* The son of Daedalus, who, escaping from Crete, flew too near the sun so that the wax that fastened his artificial wings melted and he fell into the sea. —**I·car·i·an** (i·kâr'ē·ən, ī-) *adj.*

ICBM Intercontinental Ballistic Missile.

ICC, I.C.C. Interstate Commerce Commission.

ice (īs) *n.* 1 The solid state of water, assumed at or below 32° F. or O° C. 2 Something resembling ice. 3 A frozen dessert made without cream, as sherbet. 4 Icing for cake.

5 *Slang* A diamond or diamonds. **—break the ice** 1 To break through reserve or formality. 2 To make a start. —**on ice** *Slang* 1 Set aside for future action. 2 Sure; already determined. **—on thin ice** *Informal* In a difficult or dangerous situation. —*v.* **iced, ic·ing** *v.t.* 1 To cause to congeal into ice. 2 To cover with ice. 3 To chill with or as with ice. 4 To frost, as cake, with icing. 5 In ice hockey, to shoot (the puck) from one's own end of the rink past the opponent's goal line. 6 *Slang* To clinch victory in (a contest). —*v.i.* 7 To freeze. [< OE *īs*]

Ice., Icel. Iceland; Icelandic.

ice age GLACIAL EPOCH.

ice·berg (īs′bûrg′) *n.* 1 A thick mass of floating ice that has separated from a glacier. 2 *Informal* A cold, unemotional person. [< Du. *ijsberg* ice mountain]

ice·boat (īs′bōt′) *n.* 1 A boatlike framework with runners and sails for sailing over ice. 2 ICEBREAKER.

ice·bound (īs′bound′) *adj.* Surrounded or obstructed by ice: an *icebound* ship or harbor.

ice·box (īs′boks′) *n.* REFRIGERATOR.

ice·break·er (īs′brā′kər) *n.* A ship having a strong prow and powerful engines, used to break up ice in icebound waters.

ice cap An extensive mass of ice permanently covering a tract of land and moving in all directions from a center.

ice cream A mixture of cream or butterfat, flavoring, sweetening, and often eggs, beaten to a uniform consistency and frozen. **—ice′-cream′** *adj.*

iced (īst) *adj.* 1 Coated or covered with ice. 2 Made cold with ice. 3 Covered with icing, as cake.

ice field A large field of floating ice. Also **ice floe.**

ice hockey HOCKEY (def. 1).

Ice·land (īs′lənd) *n.* A republic on an island in the North Atlantic, 39,758 sq. mi., cap. Reykjavik.

Ice·land·er (īs′lan′dər) *n.* A native or citizen of Iceland.

Ice·land·ic (īs·lan′dik) *adj.* Of or pertaining to Iceland, its people, or their language. —*n.* The language of Iceland.

ice·man (īs′man′, -mən) *n. pl.* **·men** (-men′, -mən) One who makes or delivers ice.

ice milk A sweet, smooth frozen food, like ice cream, made of skim milk.

ice pack 1 A large tract of floating ice cakes frozen together. 2 A container for cracked ice, used medically to relieve pain, reduce swelling, etc.

ice pick A sharp pointed tool for breaking ice into small pieces.

ice sheet A large continental glacier.

ice-skate (īs′skāt′) *v.i.* **-skat·ed, -skat·ing** To skate on ice. **—ice skater**

ice skate SKATE (defs. 1 & 2).

ich·neu·mon (ik·nyōō′mən) *n.* 1 MONGOOSE. 2 ICHNEUMON FLY. [< Gk. *ichneumōn*, lit., tracker]

ichneumon fly A hymenopterous insect the larvae of which feed upon other larvae or insects. • See OVIPOSITOR.

i·chor (ī′kôr, ī′kər) *Gk. Myth.* An ethereal fluid supposed to flow in the veins of the gods. —*n.* A watery discharge from a sore. [< Gk. *ichōr*] **—i·chor·ous** (ī′kər·es) *adj.*

ichthyo- *combining form* Fish: *ichthyology.* [< Gk. *ichthys* fish]

ich·thy·ol·o·gy (ik′thē·ol′ə·jē) *n.* The branch of zoology that treats of fishes. **—ich·thy·o·log·ic** (ik′thē·ə·loj′ik), **ich′·thy·o·log′i·cal** *adj.* **—ich′thy·ol′o·gist** *n.*

ich·thy·o·sau·rus (ik′thē·ə·sôr′əs) *n. pl.* **·sau·ri** (-sôr′ī) Any of an order of extinct marine reptiles having a porpoiselike form with four paddlelike limbs. Also **ich′thy·o·saur′.** [< ICHTHYO- + Gk. *sauros* lizard]

-ician *suffix of nouns* One skilled in, or engaged in, the field of: *logician, mathematician.* [< F *-icien*]

i·ci·cle (ī′si·kəl) *n.* A hanging mass of ice formed by dripping water. [< OE *īs* ice + *gicel* piece of ice, icicle] **—i′ci·cled** *adj.*

i·ci·ly (ī′sə·lē) *adv.* In an icy manner.

ic·ing (ī′sing) *n.* A coating for cakes and pastry, usu. made of sugar and water, flavoring, egg whites, cream, butter, etc.; frosting.

ick·y (ik′ē) *adj.* **ick·i·er, ick·i·est** *Slang* Distasteful; repulsive. [Alter. of STICKY] **—ick′i·ness** *n.*

i·con (ī′kon) *n. pl.* **i·cons** or **i·con·es** (ī′kə·nēz) 1 In the Eastern Orthodox Church, a holy picture or mosaic of Jesus, Mary, etc. 2 An image or likeness. [< Gk. *eikon* image] **—i·con′ic, i·con′i·cal** *adj.*

icono- *combining form* Image; of or related to images: *iconoscope.* [< Gk. *eikōn* image]

i·con·o·clast (ī·kon′ə·klast) *n.* 1 One who destroys religious images. 2 One who attacks traditional beliefs or institutions. [< Gk. *eikōn* image + *-klastēs* breaker] **—i·con′·o·clasm** *n.* **—i·con′o·clas′tic** *adj.* **—i·con′o·clas′ti·cal·ly** *adv.*

i·con·o·scope (ī·kon′ə·skōp) *n.* An electron tube used in television to convert an optical image to an electric signal, containing a photosensitive surface scanned by an electron beam.

-ics *suffix of nouns* 1 Art, science, or field of study of: *mathematics.* 2 Methods, practices, or activities of: *athletics.* [See -IC.] • Nouns ending in *-ics* are construed as singular when they strictly denote an art, science, or system *(Mathematics is difficult).* They are construed as plural if they denote personal attributes *(His mathematics are poor),* inherent qualities *(The acoustics are bad),* or specific activities *(Athletics are compulsory).*

ic·tus (ik′təs) *n. pl.* **·tus·es** or **·tus** 1 A sudden attack or fit. 2 A metrical stress or accent. [L, pp. of *icere* to strike]

i·cy (ī′sē) *adj.* **i·ci·er, i·ci·est** 1 Made of or covered with ice. 2 Extremely cold or slippery, like ice. 3 Resembling ice. 4 Unfriendly; cold: an *icy* stare. **—i′ci·ness,** *n.* **Syn. 4** chilly, hostile, inimical, uncordial.

id (id) *n. Psychoanal.* The part of the psyche that is impelled towards fulfilling instinctual needs; the reservoir of libido. [< L *id* it]

I'd (īd) Contraction of *I would, I had,* or *I should.*

ID Idaho (P.O. abbr.).

I.D. identification; Infantry Division; Intelligence Department.

Id., Ida. Idaho.

id. the same (L *idem*).

-idae *suffix Zool.* Used to form the names of families of animals: *Canidae,* the dog family. [< Gk. *-idai* plural patronymic suffix]

-ide *suffix Chem.* 1 Denoting a binary compound: sodium *chloride.* 2 Used to form name of groups or series of related substances: *lanthanide* series. Also **-id.** [< L *-idus*]

i·de·a (ī·dē′ə) *n.* 1 A thought, concept, or image present in the mind. 2 A definitely formulated thought; belief; opinion. 3 A plan or project. 4 A vague thought or supposition: I had an *idea* you'd come. 5 *Informal* Meaning; aim: What's the *idea?* 6 In Platonic philosophy, the archetype or model of which all existing things are imperfect representations. [< Gk. < *ideein* see]

i·de·al (ī·dē′əl, ī·dēl′) *adj.* 1 Of, relating to, or existing in ideas, images, or concepts of the mind. 2 Existing only in imagination or notion as regards perfection, etc.; imaginary. 3 Supremely excellent or desirable; perfect: the *ideal* job. 4 In philosophy, existing as an archetypal idea or model. —*n.* 1 That which is taken as a standard of perfection, excellence, or beauty; model; type. 2 An ultimate aim or goal. 3 That which exists only in imagination. [< L *idealis*]

i·de·al·ism (ī·dē′əl·iz′əm) *n.* 1 The practice or habit of conceiving of things as ideal or as they should be rather than as they actually are. 2 The forming of and striving after ideals. 3 In art and literature, the treatment of persons or things according to an imaginative or preconceived idea of perfection instead of adhering strictly to facts. 4 In philosophy, any theory which holds that reality is essentially spiritual or mental and that there is no world of objects apart from a reacting mind or consciousness.

i·de·al·ist (ī·dē′əl·ist) *n.* 1 One who idealizes. 2 A visionary or a romantic. 3 An exponent of idealism in art, philosophy, or literature. —**i·de'al·is'tic** or **·ti·cal** *adj.* —**i·de'al·is'ti·cal·ly** *adv.*

i·de·al·ize (ī·dē'əl·īz) *v.* **·ized, ·iz·ing** *v.t.* To represent or think of (a person, thing, etc.) as conforming to some standard, usu. unattainable, of perfection or beauty; make ideal; exalt. —*v.i.* To form an ideal or ideals. —**i·de·al·i·za·tion** (ī·dē'əl·ə·zā'shən, -ī·zā'-), **i·de'al·iz'er** *n.*

i·de·al·ly (ī·dē'əl·ē) *adv.* **1** In an ideal manner; perfectly. **2** In imagination or theory.

i·de·ate (ī·dē'āt) *v.* **·at·ed, ·at·ing** *v.t.* To form an idea of; conceive. —*v.i.* To form ideas; think. —**i'de·a'tion** *n.* —**i'de·a'tion·al** *adj.*

i·dée fixe (ē·dā' fēks') *pl.* **i·dées fixes** (ē·dā' fēks') *French* A fixed idea; obsession.

i·dem (ī'dem, ē'-, id'em) *n. & adj. Latin* The same: often as referring to what was previously mentioned.

i·den·ti·cal (ī·den'ti·kəl) *adj.* **1** The very same. **2** Alike in all respects. [< L IDEM] —**i·den'ti·cal·ly** *adv.* —**i·den'ti·cal·ness** *n.*

identical twins Twins having the same genetic makeup, derived from a single fertilized ovum.

i·den·ti·fi·ca·tion (ī·den'tə·fə·kā'shən) *n.* **1** The act of identifying or the state of being identified. **2** Anything by which the identity of a person or thing can be established.

i·den·ti·fy (ī·den'tə·fī) *v.t.* **·fied, ·fy·ing 1** To determine as a particular person or thing. **2** To consider or treat as the same: He *identifies* money with happiness. **3** To serve as a means of identification of. **4** To join or associate in interest, action, etc.: usu. with *with.* **5** *Psychoanal.* To unconsciously incorporate (in one's self) the identity of someone else. [< LL *identitas* identity + -FY] —**i·den'ti·fi'a·ble** *adj.* —**i·den'ti·fi'er** *n.*

i·den·ti·ty (ī·den'tə·tē) *n. pl.* **·ties 1** The state of being identical. **2** The state of being exactly that which has been claimed, asserted, or described. **3** The distinctive character belonging to an individual; individuality. **4** A mathematical equation that is satisfied by all values of its variables for which the expressions involved have meaning. [< LL *identitas* < IDEM]

ideo- *combining form* Idea; of or pertaining to ideas: *ideograph.* [< Gk. *idea* a form, idea]

i·de·o·graph (ī'dē·ə·graf', -gräf, id'ē-) *n.* **1** A graphic symbol or sign of an object or idea but without representation of the actual word for the object or idea, as in Egyptian hieroglyphics. **2** A symbol, as +, =, ¶, $, etc. Also **i'de·o·gram'** (-gram'). —**i'de·o·graph'ic** or **·i·cal** *adj.* —**i'de·o·graph'i·cal·ly** *adv.*

i·de·o·logue (ī'dē·ə·lôg, -log, id'ē-) *n.* One who is committed to an ideology. [F]

i·de·ol·o·gy (ī'dē·ol'ə·jē, id'ē-) *n. pl.* **·gies 1** The ideas, doctrines, or way of thinking characteristic of a political or economic theory or system. **2** The science that treats of the nature and evolution of ideas. **3** Visionary or impractical thinking. [IDEO- + -LOGY] —**i·de·o·log·ic** (ī'dē·ə·loj'ik, id'ē-) or **·i·cal** *adj.* —**i'de·o·log'i·cal·ly** *adv.* —**i'de·ol'o·gist** *n.*

ides (īdz) *n.pl.* In the ancient Roman calendar, the 15th of March, May, July, and October, and the 13th of the other months. [< L *idus*]

id est (id est) *Latin* That is.

id·i·o·cy (id'ē·ə·sē) *n. pl.* **·cies 1** An extreme degree of congenital mental deficiency. **2** A foolish utterance or act.

id·i·om (id'ē·əm) *n.* **1** An expression not readily analyzable from its grammatical construction or from the meaning of its component parts, as *to put up with* (tolerate, endure). **2** The dialect or language characteristic of a certain group, class, trade, region, etc.: legal *idiom.* **3** The distinctive form or construction of a particular language. **4** Specific character, form, or style, as in art, literature, music, etc. [< Gk. *idiōma* peculiarity, property]

id·i·o·mat·ic (id'ē·ə·mat'ik) *adj.* **1** Using many idioms. **2** Of or like idioms. **3** Characteristic of a certain language or dialect. Also **id'i·o·mat'i·cal.** —**id'i·o·mat'i·cal·ly.** *adv.*

id·i·o·syn·cra·sy (id'ē·ə·sing'krə·sē) *n. pl.* **·sies 1** Any distinctive quality, characteristic, habit, etc. peculiar to an individual; quirk. **2** The physical and mental constitution unique to an individual or group. [< Gk. *idios* peculiar + *synkrasis* a mixing together] —**id'i·o·syn·crat'ic** (-sin·krat'ik) *adj.* —**id'i·o·syn·crat'i·cal·ly** *adv.*

id·i·ot (id'ē·ət) *n.* **1** A person having an extreme degree of congenital mental deficiency. **2** Any foolish or stupid person. [< Gk. *idiōtēs* private person]

id·i·ot·ic (id'ē·ot'ik) *adj.* **1** Of, like, or characteristic of an idiot. **2** Senseless; stupid. —**id'i·ot'i·cal·ly** *adv.*

i·dle (īd'l) *adj.* **1** Not occupied; doing nothing. **2** Not being used: *idle* factories. **3** Averse to labor; lazy. **4** Used for leisure. **5** Without effect; useless: *idle* talk. —*v.* **i·dled, i·dling** *v.i.* **1** To spend time in idleness. **2** To saunter or move idly. **3** To operate without a load, as an engine or motor. —*v.t.* **4** To pass in idleness; waste, as a day. **5** To cause to be idle, as a person or an industry. [< OE *īdel* empty, useless] —**i'dle·ness, i'dler** *n.* —**i'dly** *adv.* —**Syn.** *adj.* **3** inactive, indolent, laggard, slothful. *v.* **1** dally, laze, loaf, lounge.

i·dol (īd'l) *n.* **1** An image of a god, esp. a heathen god, to which worship is offered. **2** In the Bible, a false god. **3** Any object of extreme or passionate devotion. **4** A source of error; a fallacy. [< Gk. *eidōlon* image, phantom]

i·dol·a·ter (ī·dol'ə·tər) *n.* **1** An adorer of images. **2** One who is inordinately fond of some person or thing. [< Gk. *eidōlon* an idol + *latreuein* worship] —**i·dol'a·tress** (-tris) *n. Fem.*

i·dol·a·trous (ī·dol'ə·trəs) *adj.* **1** Of or like idolatry. **2** Extravagant in admiration. —**i·dol'a·trous·ly** *adv.* —**i·dol'a·trous·ness** *n.*

i·dol·a·try (ī·dol'ə·trē) *n. pl.* **·tries 1** The worship of idols. **2** Excessive admiration or devotion.

i·dol·ize (ī'dəl·īz) *v.* **·ized, ·iz·ing** *v.t.* **1** To have inordinate love for; adore. **2** To worship as an idol. —*v.i.* **3** To worship idols. —**i'dol·i·za'tion, i'dol·iz'er** *n.*

i·dyll (īd'l) *n.* **1** A short poem or prose piece depicting simple scenes of pastoral life. **2** Any event or scene suitable for such a work. **3** A romantic episode. Also **i'dyl.** [< Gk. *eidos* form] —**i'dyl·list, i'dyl·ist** *n.*

i·dyl·lic (ī·dil'ik) *adj.* **1** Of or like an idyll. **2** Charmingly romantic or picturesque. —**i·dyl'li·cal·ly** *adv.*

-ie *suffix* Little; dear: *birdie:* often used in nicknames or affectionately, as in *Annie.* [Var. of -Y]

IE, I.E. Indo-European.

i.e. that is (L *id est*).

-ier *suffix of nouns* One who is concerned with or works with: *cashier.* Also **-yer:** *lawyer.* [< OF < L *-ārius*]

if (if) *conj.* **1** On the supposition or condition that: We'll go by plane *if* the weather permits. **2** Allowing that; although: *If* he was there, I didn't see him. **3** Whether: I am not sure *if* he is at home. —*n.* **1** A supposition. **2** A condition. [< OE *gif*]

if·fy (if'ē) *adj.* **if·fi·er, if·fi·est** *Informal* Uncertain or doubtful because dependent on unknown or chancy conditions: an *iffy* proposition. [< IF] —**if'fi·ness** *n.*

ig·loo (ig'lo͞o) *n. pl.* **·loos** An Eskimo house, dome-shaped and usu. built of blocks of packed snow. Also **ig'lu.** [< Eskimo *igdlu*]

ig·ne·ous (ig'nē·əs) *adj.* **1** Of or like fire. **2** *Geol.* Pertaining to the heat inside the earth: said esp. of rocks formed from molten magma. [< L *ignis* fire]

ig·nis fat·u·us (ig'nis fach'o͞o·əs) *pl.* **ig·nes fat·u·i** (ig'nēz fach'o͞o·ī) **1** An evanescent light seen in the air over marshy places; will-o'-the-wisp. **2** A deceptive goal or ambition; a delusion. [Med. L, lit., foolish fire]

ig·nite (ig·nīt') *v.* **ig·nit·ed, ig·nit·ing** *v.t.* **1** To set on fire; cause to burn. **2** To cause to glow with intense heat. **3** To excite. —*v.i.* **4** To start burning. [< L *ignire* set on fire] —**ig·nit'a·ble, ig·nit'i·ble** *adj.* —**ig·nit'a·bil'i·ty, ig·nit'i·bil'i·ty, ig·nit'er, ig·nit'or** (-ər) *n.*

ig·ni·tion (ig·nish'ən) *n.* **1** The act of igniting. **2** The explosion of the fuel mixture in the cylinder of an internal-combustion engine. **3** The electrical system that does this.

ig·no·ble (ig·nō'bəl) *adj.* Unworthy or degraded in character or quality. [< L *ignobilis* < IN-[1] + *nobilis* noble] —**ig·nob'ly** *adv.* —**ig'no·bil'i·ty, ig·no'ble·ness** *n.* —**Syn.** base, contemptible, despicable, low, mean.

ig·no·min·i·ous (ig'nə·min'ē·əs) *adj.* **1** Marked by or implying dishonor or disgrace. **2** Deserving ignominy; despicable. **3** Abasing; humiliating. —**ig'no·min'i·ous·ly** *adv.* —**ig'no·min'i·ous·ness** *n.*

ig·no·min·y (ig'nə·min'ē) *n. pl.* **·min·ies 1** Disgrace or dishonor. **2** That which causes disgrace. [< L *in-* not + *nomen* name, reputation]

ig·no·ra·mus (ig′nə·rā′məs, -ram′əs) *n. pl.* **·mus·es** An ignorant person. [< L, we do not know]

ig·no·rance (ig′nər·əns) *n.* The state or quality of being ignorant.

ig·no·rant (ig′nər·ənt) *adj.* **1** Lacking education or knowledge. **2** Lacking awareness: with *of.* **3** Not informed or experienced: with *in.* **4** Manifesting or caused by ignorance. [< L *ignorare* not to know] **—ig′no·rant·ly** *adv.*

ig·nore (ig·nôr′, -nōr′) *v.t.* **·nored, ·nor·ing** To refuse to notice or recognize; disregard intentionally. [< L *ignorare* not to know] **—ig·nor′er** *n.*

I·go·rot (ē′gə·rōt′, ig′ə-) *n. pl.* **·rot** or **·rots** **1** One belonging to a group of Malay tribes living in northern Luzon, Philippines. **2** The Indonesian language of these tribes. Also **I·gor·ro·te** (ē′gôr·rō′tā).

i·gua·na (i·gwä′nə) *n.* Any of a family of large, harmless lizards of tropical America. [< Cariban]

Iguana

IHS, ihs A monogram of the name Jesus, derived from the Greek ΙΗ(ΣΟΥ)Σ, Jesus.

i·kon (ī′kon) *n.* ICON.

IL Illinois (P.O. abbr.).

-ile *suffix* Of, like, pertaining to; capable of; suited to: *docile, mobile.* Also **-il,** as in *civil, fossil.* [< L *-ilis*]

il·e·um (il′ē·əm) *n.* The last section of the small intestine, following the jejunum and leading to the large intestine. [L] **—il·e·ac** (il′ē·ak) *adj.*

i·lex (ī′leks) *n.* **1** A tree or shrub of the holly family. **2** The holm oak. [L, holm oak]

I.L.G.W.U. International Ladies' Garment Workers' Union.

Il·i·ad (il′ē·əd) *n.* An ancient Greek epic poem on the siege of Ilium (Troy), ascribed to Homer.

il·i·um (il′ē·əm) *n. pl.* **·i·a** (-ē·ə) *Anat.* The flat upper portion of the hipbone. [L, flank] **—il′i·ac** *adj.* • See PELVIS.

Il·i·um (il′ē·əm) TROY. Also **Il′i·on** (-ən).

ilk (ilk) *adj. & n. Obs.* Same. **—of that ilk** Of that race, class, or kind. [< OE *ilka* the same]

ill (il) *adj.* **1** Not well; sick. **2** Evil; bad: *ill* repute. **3** Hostile; unfriendly: *ill* will. **4** Not favorable; dangerous: *ill* wind. **5** Of inferior quality; imperfect. **—***n.* Anything that brings about misfortune, harm, sickness, evil, etc. **—***adv.* **1** Not well; badly. **2** With difficulty; hardly. **3** Unfavorably; unkindly: to speak *ill* of someone. **—ill at ease** Uneasy; uncomfortable. [< ON *illr*]

I'll (īl) **1** I will. **2** I shall.

Ill. Illinois.

ill., illus., illust. illustrated; illustration; illustrator.

ill-ad·vised (il′əd·vīzd′) *adj.* Acting or resulting from improper advice or deliberation; unwise. **—ill′-ad·vis′ed·ly** (-vīz′id·lē) *adv.*

ill-bred (il′bred′) *adj.* Badly taught, reared, or trained; rude. **—Syn.** boorish, discourteous, impolite, unmannerly.

ill breeding Bad manners.

ill-con·sid·ered (il′kən·sid′ərd) *adj.* Unwise.

ill-dis·posed (il′dis·pōzd′) *adj.* **1** Unfriendly. **2** Not willing or agreeable; averse.

il·le·gal (i·lē′gəl) *adj.* Contrary to the law; not legal. **—il·le·gal·i·ty** (il′ē·gal′ə·tē) *n.* (*pl.* **·ties**) **—il·le′gal·ly** *adv.*

il·leg·i·ble (i·lej′ə·bəl) *adj.* Not legible; undecipherable. **—il·leg′i·bly** *adv.* **—il·leg′i·bil′i·ty, il·leg′i·ble·ness** *n.*

il·le·git·i·mate (il′i·jit′ə·mit) *adj.* **1** Born out of wedlock. **2** Illogical; unsound. **3** Contrary to rule or proper procedure; irregular. **—il′le·git′i·mate·ly** *adv.* **—il′le·git′i·ma·cy** (-ə·mə·sē) *n.* (*pl.* **·cies**)

ill-fat·ed (il′fāt′id) *adj.* **1** Certain to end badly. **2** Unlucky.

ill-fa·vored (il′fā′vərd) *adj.* **1** Repulsive; ugly. **2** Objectionable.

ill-found·ed (il′foun′did) *adj.* Based on insufficient or faulty reasons or facts.

ill-got·ten (il′got′n) *adj.* Obtained dishonestly.

ill-hu·mor (il′ʰyōō′mər) *n.* A morose or disagreeable state of mind. **—ill′-hu′mored** *adj.*

il·lib·er·al (i·lib′ər·əl) *adj.* **1** Not generous; stingy. **2** Narrow-minded. **3** Lacking culture; vulgar. **—il·lib′er·al·ly** *adv.* **—il·lib′er·al·ism** (-iz′əm) *n.* **—il·lib′er·al′i·ty** (-al′ə·tē) *n.*

il·lic·it (i·lis′it) *adj.* Not permitted; unlawful. [< L *in-* not + *licitus* licit] **—il·lic′it·ly** *adv.* **—il·lic′it·ness** *n.*

il·lim·it·a·ble (i·lim′i·tə·bəl) *adj.* That cannot be limited; boundless; endless. **—il·lim′it·a·bly** *adv.* **—il·lim′it·a·bil′i·ty, il·lim′it·a·ble·ness** *n.*

Il·li·nois (il′ə·noi′, -noiz′) *n. pl.* **·nois** A North American Indian belonging to any one of the Algonquian tribes of Illinois.

illit. illiterate.

il·lit·er·a·cy (i·lit′ər·ə·sē) *n. pl.* **·cies** **1** The state of being illiterate. **2** A mistake in speaking or writing, usu. resulting from a lack of education.

il·lit·er·ate (i·lit′ər·it) *adj.* **1** Unable to read or write. **2** Having or showing little or no education. **—***n.* An illiterate person, esp. one who cannot read or write. [< L *in-* not + *literatus* literate] **—il·lit′er·ate·ly** *adv.* **—il·lit′er·ate·ness** *n.*

ill-man·nered (il′man′ərd) *adj.* Having bad manners; discourteous; rude.

ill nature Peevishness; surliness; sullenness. **—ill′-na′tured** *adj.* **—ill′-na′tured·ly** *adv.* **—ill′-na′tured·ness** *n.*

ill·ness (il′nis) *n.* **1** The state of being in poor health. **2** An ailment; sickness.

il·log·i·cal (i·loj′i·kəl) *adj.* Not logical or reasonable. **—il·log′i·cal′i·ty, il·log′i·cal·ness** *n.* **—il·log′i·cal·ly** *adv.*

ill-spent (il′spent′) *adj.* Unwisely wasted.

ill-starred (il′stärd′) *adj.* Unfortunate; unlucky, as if under an evil star.

ill-suit·ed (il′sōōt′əd) *adj.* Not well matched or suited.

ill temper A cross, irritable disposition. **—ill′-tem′pered** *adj.* **—ill′-tem′pered·ly** *adv.* **—ill′-tem′pered·ness** *n.*

ill-timed (il′tīmd′) *adj.* Inappropriate; not suitable.

ill-treat (il′trēt′) *v.t.* To treat badly; maltreat; abuse. **—ill′-treat′ment** *n.*

il·lu·mi·nant (i·lōō′mə·nənt) *adj.* Giving light; illuminating. **—***n.* Any material used for illuminating.

il·lu·mi·nate (i·lōō′mə·nāt) *v.* **·nat·ed, ·nat·ing** *v.t.* **1** To give light to; light up. **2** To explain; make clear. **3** To enlighten, as the mind. **4** To make illustrious. **5** To decorate with lights. **6** To decorate (a manuscript, letter, etc.) with ornamental borders, figures, etc., of gold or other colors. **—***v.i.* **7** To light up. [< L *in-* thoroughly + *luminare* to light] **—il·lu′mi·na′tive** *adj.* **—il·lu′mi·na′ting·ly** *adv.* **—il·lu′mi·na′tor** *n.*

il·lu·mi·na·tion (i·lōō′mə·nā′shən) *n.* **1** The act of illuminating or the state of being illuminated. **2** Decoration by lighting. **3** An amount of or the intensity of light. **4** Mental or spiritual enlightenment. **5** Embellishment of manuscript, with colors and gold, or a particular figure or design in such ornamentation.

il·lu·mine (i·lōō′min) *v.t. & v.i.* **·mined, ·min·ing** To illuminate or be illuminated. **—il·lu′mi·na·ble** *adj.*

ill-use (il′yōōz′) *v.t.* **·used, ·us·ing** To treat roughly, cruelly, or unjustly; abuse. **—***n.* (-yōōs′) Bad treatment; misuse. **—ill′-us′age** (-yōō′sij, -yōō′zij) *n.*

il·lu·sion (i·lōō′zhən) *n.* **1** An unreal image or appearance. **2** A sensory impression which misrepresents the true character of the object perceived: an optical *illusion.* **3** A false or misleading idea or concept; delusion: the *illusions* of youth. **4** A thin material resembling tulle. [< L *illusio* mocking < *illudere* make sport of] **—il·lu′sion·al, il·lu′sion·ar·y** (-er·ē) *adj.*

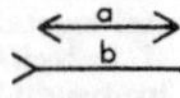

Illusion *def. 2*
Lines *a* and *b* are the same length, but *b* looks longer.

il·lu·so·ry (i·lōō′sər·ē, -zər-) *adj.* Misleading; deceptive; unreal. Also **il·lu′sive** (-siv). **—il·lu′so·ri·ly** *adv.* **—il·lu′so·ri·ness** *n.*

il·lus·trate (il′əs·trāt, i·lus′trāt) *v.t.* **·trat·ed, ·trat·ing** **1** To explain or make clear by means of figures, examples, etc. **2** To furnish with drawings, pictures, etc., as a book or article. [< L *in-* thoroughly + *lustrare* illuminate] **—il′lus·tra′tor** *n.*

il·lus·tra·tion (il′əs·trā′shən) *n.* **1** That which illustrates, as an example, comparison, anecdote, etc. **2** A print, drawing, or picture inserted in written or printed text. **3** The act or art of illustrating.

il·lus·tra·tive (i·lus′trə·tiv, il′əs·trā′tiv) *adj.* Serving to illustrate or exemplify. **—il·lus′tra·tive·ly** *adv.*

il·lus·tri·ous (i·lus′trē·əs) *adj.* Very famous; celebrated; renowned. [< L *in-* in + *lustrum* light) **—il·lus′tri·ous·ly** *adv.* **—il·lus′tri·ous·ness** *n.*

ill will Enmity; hostility; hate. **—Syn.** animosity, antipathy, dislike, hatred.

il·ly (il′lē) *adv.* Badly; ill. • While *illy* is regularly formed from the adjective *ill,* discriminating writers prefer to use *ill* as the adverb as well.

Il·lyr·i·a (i·lir′ē·ə) *n.* An ancient country along the E coast of the Adriatic. **—Il·lyr·i·an** *adj., n.*

I'm (īm) Contraction of *I am.*

im- *prefix* 1 EM-. 2 IN-.

im·age (im′ij) *n.* 1 A representation of a person or thing, as a statue, picture, idol, etc. 2 The picture or counterpart of an object produced by a lens, mirror, etc. 3 A natural resemblance; likeness; counterpart. 4 A mental picture, impression, or idea. 5 The way in which a person or thing is popularly perceived or regarded: a politician striving to improve his *image.* 6 A metaphor or a simile. 7 A symbol; embodiment; type. *—v.t.* **·aged, ·ag·ing** 1 To form a mental picture of; imagine. 2 To make a visible representation of; portray; delineate. 3 To mirror; reflect. 4 To describe vividly in speech or writing. 5 To symbolize. [< L *imago*]

im·age·ry (im′ij·rē, -ə·rē) *n. pl.* **·ries** 1 The act of making images. 2 Mental images. 3 Decorative images, esp. statues. 4 Figurative description in speech or writing.

im·ag·i·na·ble (i·maj′ə·nə·bəl) *adj.* That can be imagined. **—im·ag′i·na·bly** *adv.*

im·ag·i·nar·y (i·maj′ə·ner′ē) *adj.* 1 Existing only in imagination; unreal. 2 *Math.* Having a negative square, as $\sqrt{-1}$. **—im·ag′i·nar′i·ly** *adv.*

im·ag·i·na·tion (i·maj′ə·nā′shən) *n.* 1 The act or power of producing images in the mind of things not actually present to the senses. 2 The creative act or faculty of producing mental images and concepts that are or seem to be totally new and original. 3 That which is imagined, as a mental image or fantasy. 4 An irrational notion or belief. **—im·ag′i·na′tion·al** *adj.*

im·ag·i·na·tive (i·maj′ə·nə·tiv, -nā′tiv) *adj.* 1 Having a capacity for or given to imagining. 2 Characterized by or proceeding from imagination. **—im·ag′i·na·tive·ly** *adv.* **—im·ag′i·na·tive·ness** *n.*

im·ag·ine (i·maj′in) *v.* **·ined, ·in·ing** *v.t.* 1 To form a mental image of; conceive or create in the mind. 2 To suppose or conjecture. *—v.i.* 3 To use the imagination. 4 To make conjectures; suppose. [< L *imago* image]

im·a·gism (im′ə·jiz′əm) *n.* A movement in modern poetry characterized by the use of precise, concrete images and free verse. **—im′a·gist** (-jist) *n.* **—im′a·gis′tic** *adj.*

i·ma·go (i·mā′gō) *n. pl.* **i·ma·goes** or **i·mag·i·nes** (i·maj′ə·nēz) An insect in the reproductive phase following metamorphosis. [L, image]

im·bal·ance (im·bal′əns) *n.* A lack of proper equilibrium, proportion, functioning, etc.

im·be·cile (im′bə·sil) *adj.* 1 Mentally deficient. 2 Stupid; foolish. *—n.* 1 A person with a marked degree of congenital mental deficiency. 2 Any foolish or stupid person. [< L *imbecillus* weak]

im·be·cil·i·ty (im′bə·sil′ə·tē) *n. pl.* **·ties** 1 The condition or quality of being imbecile. 2 Foolishness or stupidity, as of action, speech, etc.

im·bibe (im·bīb′) *v.* **·bibed, ·bib·ing** *v.t.* 1 To drink in; drink. 2 To take in (moisture); absorb. 3 To receive into the mind or character. *—v.i.* 4 To drink. [< L *in-* in + *bibere* to drink] **—im·bib′er** *n.*

im·bri·cate (im′brə·kāt) *v.* **·cat·ed, ·cat·ing** *v.t.* 1 To lay so as to overlap, as tiles on a roof. *—v.i.* 2 To overlap. *—adj.* (-brə·kit) 1 Overlapping one another, as tiles, bird feathers, etc. 2 Decorated as with overlapping tiles: also **im′bri·cat′ed, im′bri·ca′tive.** [< L *imbricare* cover with tiles] **—im′·bri·ca′tion** *n.* **—im′bri·ca′tive·ly** *adv.*

im·bro·glio (im·brōl′yō) *n. pl.* **·glios** 1 A confused or troublesome misunderstanding; an entanglement. 2 Any confused situation. [Ital.]

im·brue (im·brōō′) *v.t.* **·brued, ·bru·ing** To stain or wet, esp. with blood. [< OF *embreuver*]

im·bue (im·byōō′) *v.t.* **·bued, ·bu·ing** 1 To wet thoroughly; saturate. 2 To impregnate with color; dye. 3 To fill, as the mind, with emotions, principles, etc. [< L *imbuere* wet]

IMF International Monetary Fund.

imit. imitation; imitative.

im·i·tate (im′ə·tāt) *v.t.* **·tat·ed, ·tat·ing** 1 To try to be the same as. 2 To mimic. 3 To make a copy of; duplicate. 4 To assume the appearance of; look like. [< L *imitari* imitate] **—im·i·ta·ble** (im′ə·tə·bəl) *adj.* **—im′i·ta·bil′i·ty, im′i·ta′tor** *n.*

im·i·ta·tion (im′ə·tā′shən) *n.* 1 The act of imitating. 2 That which results from imitating; likeness; copy. *—adj.* Imitating something genuine or superior: *imitation* diamonds.

im·i·ta·tive (im′ə·tā′tiv) *adj.* 1 Given to or characterized by imitation. 2 Formed after a copy or model. 3 Fictitious; counterfeit. 4 *Ling.* Designating a word that approximates a natural sound, as *buzz, clink, swish.* **—im′i·ta′·tive·ly** *adv.* **—im′i·ta′tive·ness** *n.*

im·mac·u·late (i·mak′yə·lit) *adj.* 1 Without spot or blemish; totally clean. 2 Without evil or sin; pure. 3 Faultless; flawless. [< L *in-* not + *maculatus* spotted] **—im·mac′u·late·ly** *adv.* **—im·mac′u·late·ness** *n.* **—Syn.** 1 impeccable, spotless, unsullied. 2 innocent, irreproachable, sinless.

Immaculate Conception In the Roman Catholic Church, the doctrine that the Virgin Mary was conceived in her mother's womb free from original sin.

im·ma·nence (im′ə·nəns) *n.* The condition or fact of being immanent. Also **im′ma·nen·cy.**

im·ma·nent (im′ə·nənt) *adj.* Remaining or operating within; inherent. [< L *in-* in + *manere* stay] **—im′ma·nent·ly** *adv.*

Im·man·u·el (i·man′yōō·əl) *n.* A name of the Messiah.

im·ma·te·ri·al (im′ə·tir′ē·əl) *adj.* 1 Not made of matter; incorporeal. 2 Unimportant. **—im′ma·te′ri·al·ly** *adv.* **—im′·ma·te′ri·al·ness** *n.*

im·ma·ture (im′ə·chŏŏr′, -tyŏŏr′) *adj.* 1 Not mature or ripe; not full-grown. 2 Not complete or perfected. **—im′ma·ture′ly** *adv.* **—im′ma·tur′i·ty** *n.*

im·meas·ur·a·ble (i·mezh′ər·ə·bəl) *adj.* Not capable of being measured; vast; boundless. **—im·meas′ur·a·bil′i·ty** *n.* **—im·meas′ur·a·bly** *adv.*

im·me·di·a·cy (i·mē′dē·ə·sē) *n.* The condition or quality of being immediate.

im·me·di·ate (i·mē′dē·it) *adj.* 1 Without anything intervening: the *immediate* cause of his death. 2 Not appreciably separated in space or time; closest; nearest: the *immediate* past. 3 Next or closest in rank, relationship, etc.: his *immediate* successor. 4 Present; current: our *immediate* problem. 5 Without delay; instant: his *immediate* reaction. [< Med. L *immediatus*] **—im·me′di·ate·ness** *n.*

im·me·di·ate·ly (i·mē′dē·it·lē) *adv.* 1 In an immediate manner. 2 Instantly; at once. 3 Without the intervention of anything; directly. *—conj.* As soon as.

im·me·mo·ri·al (im′ə·môr′ē·əl, -mō′rē-) *adj.* Reaching back beyond memory. **—im′me·mo′ri·al·ly** *adv.*

im·mense (i·mens′) *adj.* 1 Very great in degree or size; vast; huge. 2 *Informal* Very good; excellent. [< L *in-* not + *mensus,* pp. of *metiri* to measure] **—im·mense′ly** *adj.*

im·men·si·ty (i·men′sə·tē) *n. pl.* **·ties** 1 The state or quality of being immense; vastness. 2 Boundless space.

im·merge (i·mûrj′) *v.* **·merged, ·merg·ing** *v.t.* 1 To immerse. *—v.i.* 2 To plunge, as into a liquid; sink. [< L *in-* in + *mergere* dip] **—im·mer′gence** *n.*

im·merse (i·mûrs′) *v.t.* **·mersed, ·mers·ing** 1 To plunge or dip entirely in water or other fluid. 2 To involve deeply; engross: He *immersed* himself in study. 3 To baptize by submerging in water. [< L *immergere* dip] **—im·mer′sion** *n.*

im·mi·grant (im′ə·grənt) *n.* A person who immigrates. *—adj.* Immigrating.

im·mi·grate (im′ə·grāt) *v.* **·grat·ed, ·grat·ing** *v.i.* 1 To come into a new country or region for the purpose of settling there. *—v.t.* 2 To bring in as an immigrant or settler. [< L *in-* in + *migrare* migrate] **—im′mi·gra′tion** *n.* **—im′mi·gra·to′ry** (-tôr′ē, -tō′rē) *adj.*

im·mi·nence (im′ə·nəns) *n.* 1 The state of being imminent. 2 Something imminent, esp. impending evil. Also **im′mi·nen·cy.**

im·mi·nent (im′ə·nənt) *adj.* About to happen; impending: said esp. of danger or misfortune. [< L *imminere* lean over, impend] **—im′mi·nent·ly** *adv.*

im·mis·ci·ble (i·mis′ə·bəl) *adj.* Not capable of mixing, as oil and water. [< L *in-* not + *miscere* to mix] —**im·mis′ci·bly** *adv.* —**im·mis′ci·bil′i·ty** *n.*

im·mo·bile (i·mō′bəl, -bēl) *adj.* 1 Unmovable; stable. 2 Not moving; motionless. —**im·mo·bil·i·ty** (i′mō·bil′ə·tē) *n.*

im·mo·bi·lize (i·mō′bə·līz) *v.t.* **·lized, ·liz·ing** 1 To make immovable; fix in place, as a limb. 2 To make unable to move or mobilize, as troops. 3 To withdraw (specie) from circulation and hold as security for banknotes. —**im·mo′bi·li·za′·tion** (-lə·zā′shən, -lī·zā′-) *n.*

im·mod·er·ate (i·mod′ər·it) *adj.* Not moderate; excessive. —**im·mod′er·ate·ly** *adv.* —**im·mod′er·ate·ness, im·mod′·er·a′tion** *n.*

im·mod·est (i·mod′ist) *adj.* 1 Wanting in modesty; indelicate or indecent. 2 Impudent; bold. —**im·mod′est·ly** *adv.* —**im·mod′es·ty** *n.*

im·mo·late (im′ə·lāt) *v.t.* **·lat·ed, ·lat·ing** To sacrifice, esp. to kill as a sacrifice. [< L *immolare* sprinkle with sacrificial meal] —**im′mo·la′tion, im′mo·la′tor** *n.*

im·mor·al (i·môr′əl, i·mor′-) *adj.* 1 Contrary to moral principles; not right or good. 2 Impure; lewd; licentious. —**im·mor′al·ly** *adv.* • See UNMORAL.

im·mo·ral·i·ty (im′ə·ral′ə·tē) *n. pl.* **·ties** 1 The quality or condition of being immoral. 2 An immoral act.

im·mor·tal (i·môr′təl) *adj.* 1 Having unending existence; deathless. 2 Lasting or enduring forever. —*n.* 1 A person considered worthy of immortality. 2 In mythology, a god. —**im·mor′tal·ly** *adv.* —**Syn** *adj.* 1 deathless, imperishable, undying. 2 endless, infinite, permanent, perpetual.

im·mor·tal·i·ty (im′ôr·tal′ə·tē) *n.* 1 Exemption from death; eternal life. 2 Eternal fame.

im·mor·tal·ize (i·môr′təl·īz) *v.t.* **·ized, ·iz·ing** To make immortal, as in fame or life.

im·mor·telle (im′ôr·tel′) *n.* Any of various xerophytic plants having usu. composite flowers that do not wilt. [F]

im·mov·a·ble (i·mōō′və·bəl) *adj.* 1 That cannot be moved or stirred from its place; fixed. 2 Motionless. 3 Steadfast; unchangeable. 4 Not having the feelings easily roused; impassive. —*n. Law* Any piece of land, together with trees, buildings, etc., that is considered not movable. —**im·mov′a·bil′i·ty, im·mov′a·ble·ness** *n.* —**im·mov′a·bly** *adv.*

im·mune (i·myōōn′) *adj.* 1 Exempt, as from a penalty, burden, duty, or taxation. 2 Protected from a communicable or allergic disease by the presence of antibodies in the blood. 3 Pertaining to immunity or immunization. [< L *in-* not + *munus* service, duty] —**im·mu·ni·ty** (i·myōō′nə·tē) *n.* (*pl.* **·ties**)

im·mu·nize (im′yə·nīz) *v.t.* **·nized, ·niz·ing** To make immune, as by inoculation. —**im·mu·ni·za·tion** (im′yə·nə·zā′·shən, -nī·zā′-) *n.*

immuno- *combining form* Immune; immunity: *immunology.* [< IMMUNE]

im·mu·nol·o·gy (im′yə·nol′ə·jē) *n.* The science which treats of the reactions of animal tissues against foreign proteins, as in viruses, allergens, tissue transplants, etc. [< IMMUNO- + -LOGY] —**im·mu·no·log·ic** (i·myōō′nə·loj′ik), **im·mu′no·log′i·cal** *adj.* —**im′mu·nol′o·gist** *n.*

im·mu·no·sup·pres·sive (im·yōō′nō·sə·pres′iv) *adj. Med.* Acting to suppress natural immune responses, as to foreign tissue in an organ transplant. —**im·mu′no·su·pres′·sion** *n.*

im·mure (i·myŏŏr′) *v.t.* **·mured ·mur·ing** To shut up within or as within walls. [< L *in-* in + *muris* wall] —**im·mure′·ment** *n.*

im·mu·ta·ble (i·myōō′tə·bəl) *adj.* Not changing or altering; unchangeable. [< L *immutabilis*] —**im·mu′ta·bil′i·ty, im·mu′ta·ble·ness** *n.* —**im·mu′ta·bly** *adv.*

imp (imp) *n.* 1 A small devil or demon. 2 A mischievous person, esp. a child. [< LL *impotus* a shoot]

imp. imperative; imperfect; imperial; impersonal; import; important; importer; imprimatur; improper.

im·pact (im·pakt′) *v.t.* To press firmly together; pack; wedge. —*n.* (im′pakt) 1 The act of striking; collision. 2 The forcible contact of a moving body with another. 3 A powerful influence: the *impact* of science on culture. [< L *impingere* to thrust against] —**im·pac′tion** *n.*

im·pact·ed (im·pak′tid) *adj.* 1 Packed firmly. 2 Denoting a tooth wedged between the jawbone and another tooth in such a way as to prevent its emergence through the gums.

im·pair (im·pâr′) *v.t.* To diminish in quality, strength, or value; injure; damage. [< LL *in-* thoroughly + *pejorare* make worse] —**im·pair′er, im·pair′ment** *n.*

im·pa·la (im·pä′lə) *n.* An African antelope with spreading horns in the male. [< native African name]

im·pale (im·pāl′) *v.t.* **·paled, ·pal·ing** 1 To fix upon a pale or sharp stake. 2 To torture or put to death by thrusting a sharp stake through the body. 3 To make helpless: to *impale* someone with a glance. [< L *in-* in + *palus* a stake] —**im·pale′ment** *n.*

im·pal·pa·ble (im·pal′pə·bəl) *adj.* 1 Imperceptible to the touch. 2 Not easily grasped or discerned by the mind. —**im·pal′pa·bil′i·ty** *n.* —**im·pal′pa·bly** *adv.*

im·pan·el (im·pan′əl) *v.t.* **·eled** or **·elled, ·el·ing** or **·el·ling** 1 To enroll upon a panel or list, as for jury duty. 2 To draw from such a list, as a jury. —**im·pan′el·ment** *n.*

im·part (im·pärt′) *v.t.* 1 To make known; tell; communicate. 2 To give a portion of; give. —*v.i.* 3 To give a part; share. [< L *in-* on + *partire* to share] —**im·par·ta′tion, im·part′er** *n.*

im·par·tial (im·pär′shəl) *adj.* Not partial; unbiased; just. —**im·par′tial·ly** *adv.* —**im·par′tial·ness** *n.*

im·par·ti·al·i·ty (im′pär·shē·al′ə·tē, im·pär′-) *n.* The quality or character of being impartial.

im·pass·a·ble (im·pas′ə·bəl, -päs′-) *adj.* Not capable of being traveled over or through. —**im·pass′a·bly** *adv.* —**im·pass′a·bil′i·ty, im·pass′a·ble·ness** *n.*

im·passe (im′pas, im·pas′) *n.* 1 A blind passage open only at one end; blind alley. 2 Any serious and insurmountable obstacle or problem. [F]

im·pas·si·ble (im·pas′ə·bəl) *adj.* 1 Incapable of suffering pain or injury. 2 Not easily aroused emotionally; apathetic. [< L *in-* not + *passibilis* suffering] —**im·pas′si·bly** *adv.* —**im·pas′si·bil′i·ty, im·pas′si·ble·ness** *n.*

im·pas·sion (im·pash′ən) *v.t.* To affect with passion; inflame.

im·pas·sioned (im·pash′ənd) *adj.* Fervent; passionate; ardent. —**im·pas′sioned·ly** *adv.*

im·pas·sive (im·pas′iv) *adj.* 1 Insensible to suffering or pain. 2 Unmoved by or not exhibiting feeling; calm. —**im·pas′sive·ly** *adv.* —**im·pas′sive·ness, im·pas·siv·i·ty** (im′pa·siv′ə·tē) *n.*

im·pa·tience (im·pā′shəns) *n.* 1 Lack of patience, esp. when faced with delay, opposition, etc. 2 A restless longing or eagerness.

im·pa·ti·ens (im·pā′shē·enz) *n.* Any of a genus of plants whose ripe seed vessels suddenly snap open when touched. [L]

im·pa·tient (im·pā′shənt) *adj.* 1 Not possessed of patience; disturbed by or intolerant of delay, pain, opposition, etc. 2 Exhibiting or expressing impatience. —**im·pa′·tient·ly** *adv.* —**im·pa′tient·ness** *n.*

im·peach (im·pēch′) *v.t.* 1 To bring discredit upon; challenge: to *impeach* one's honesty. 2 To charge with crime or misdemeanor, esp. to arraign (a public official) before a competent tribunal on such a charge. [< LL *impedicare* entangle] —**im·peach′a·bil′i·ty, im·peach′ment** *n.* —**im·peach′a·ble** *adj.*

im·pec·ca·ble (im·pek′ə·bəl) *adj.* 1 Not liable to commit sin or wrong. 2 Without fault or error; flawless. [< L *in-* not + *peccare* to sin] —**im·pec′ca·bil′i·ty** *n.* —**im·pec′ca·bly** *adv.*

im·pe·cu·ni·ous (im′pə·kyōō′nē·əs) *adj.* Having no money; poor. [< L *in-* not + *pecunia* money] —**im′pe·cu′ni·ous·ly** *adv.* —**im′pe·cu′ni·os′i·ty** (-kyōō′nē·os′ə·tē), **im′pe·cu′·ni·ous·ness** *n.*

im·pe·dance (im·pēd′ns) *n.* 1 The ratio of voltage to current in an alternating-current circuit, in general a complex number combining resistance and reactance. 2 Any analogous ratio, as in acoustics or mechanics.

impede (im·pēd′) *v.t.* **·ped·ed, ·ped·ing** To retard or hinder in progress or action; obstruct. [L *impedire,* lit., shackle the feet] —**im·ped′er** *n.*

im·ped·i·ment (im·ped′ə·mənt) *n.* **1** That which hinders or impedes; an obstruction. **2** A speech defect, as a stammer. **3** *Law* Anything that prevents the contraction of a valid marriage. **—im·ped′i·men′tal, im·ped′i·men′ta·ry** *adj.* **—Syn. 1** barrier, encumbrance, hindrance, obstacle.

im·ped·i·men·ta (im·ped′ə·men′tə) *n.pl.* Things that impede or burden, as baggage or supplies when traveling.

im·pel (im·pel′) *v.t.* **·pelled, ·pel·ling 1** To drive or push (something) forward or onward. **2** To urge or force (someone) to an action, course, etc.; incite; compel. [< L *in-* on + *pellere* to drive] **—im·pel′lent** *adj., n.* **—im·pel′ler** *n.*

im·pend (im·pend′) *v.i.* **1** To be imminent; threaten, as something evil or destructive. **2** To be suspended; hang: with *over.* [< L *in-* on + *pendere* to hang] **—im·pen′dence, im·pen′den·cy** *n.*

im·pend·ing (im·pen′ding) *adj.* **1** About to happen; threatening; imminent. **2** Hanging over.

im·pen·e·tra·ble (im·pen′ə·trə·bəl) *adj.* **1** That cannot be penetrated or pierced. **2** That cannot be comprehended or solved: an *impenetrable* mystery. **3** Not to be affected or influenced: an *impenetrable* conscience. **—im·pen′e·tra·bil′i·ty, im·pen′e·tra·ble·ness** *n.* **—im·pen′e·tra·bly** *adv.*

im·pen·i·tent (im·pen′ə·tənt) *adj.* Not penitent; hardened. **—im·pen′i·tence, im·pen′i·ten·cy** *n.* **—im·pen′i·tent·ly** *adv.*

imper. imperative.

im·per·a·tive (im·per′ə·tiv) *adj.* **1** Expressive of positive command; authoritative. **2** *Gram.* Designating that mood of the verb which expresses command, entreaty, or exhortation. **3** Not to be evaded or avoided; obligatory. **—***n.* **1** Something imperative, as a command, rule, duty, etc. **2** *Gram.* The imperative mood; also, a verb in this mood. [< L *imperare* to command] **—im·per′a·tive·ly** *adv.* **—im·per′a·tive·ness** *n.*

im·pe·ra·tor (im′pə·rā′tər, -tôr) *n.* The official designation of the Roman emperors. [L< *imperare* to command] **—im·per′a·to′ri·al** *adj.*

im·per·cep·ti·ble (im′pər·sep′tə·bəl) *adj.* That cannot easily be perceived by the senses or mind, as by reason of smallness, slowness, etc. **—im′per·cep′ti·ble·ness, im′per·cep′ti·bil′i·ty** *n.* **—im′per·cep′ti·bly** *adv.* **—im′per·cep′tive** *adj.*

imperf. imperfect; imperforate.

im·per·fect (im·pûr′fikt) *adj.* **1** Not perfect; defective. **2** Not complete; unfinished. **3** *Gram.* Pertaining to or of a tense of a verb that indicates past action as uncompleted, continuous, or synchronous with some other action. **—***n.* *Gram.* The imperfect tense, or a verb expressing this tense. **—im·per′fect·ly** *adv.* **—im·per′fect·ness** *n.*

im·per·fec·tion (im′pər·fek′shən) *n.* **1** Lack of perfection: also **im·per′fect·ness. 2** A defect; fault.

im·per·fo·ra·ble (im·pûr′fər·ə·bəl) *adj.* That cannot be perforated.

im·per·fo·rate (im·pûr′fər·it) *adj.* **1** Without perforations; not perforated. **2** Not separated by a line of perforations, as stamps. **3** *Med.* Lacking a normal opening. Also **im·per′fo·rat′ed** (-rā′tid). **—***n.* An unperforated stamp. **—im·per′fo·ra′tion** *n.*

im·pe·ri·al (im·pir′ē·əl) *adj.* **1** Of or pertaining to an empire, or to an emperor or an empress. **2** Designating the legal weights and measures of the United Kingdom. **3** Of or pertaining to a country having control over colonies or the like. **4** Majestic; regal. **5** Superior in size or quality. **—** *n.* **1** A pointed tuft of hair on the chin. **2** Anything of more than usual size or excellence. **3** A size of paper, 23 in. X 31 in. [< L *imperium* rule] **—im·pe′ri·al·ly** *adv.*

imperial gallon The British gallon, equal to 277.42 cu. in.

im·pe·ri·al·ism (im·pir′ē·əl·iz′əm) *n.* **1** A policy that aims at creating, maintaining, or extending an empire comprising other nations, territories, etc., all controlled by a central government. **2** The development or exploitation of the economic resources of another country without necessarily assuming direct political control. **3** Imperial character, authority, or spirit. **—im·pe′ri·al·ist** *adj., n.* **—im·pe′ri·al·is′tic** *adj.* **—im·pe′ri·al·is′ti·cal·ly** *adv.*

im·per·il (im·per′il) *v.t.* **·iled** or **·illed, ·il·ing** or **·il·ling** To place in peril; endanger.

im·pe·ri·ous (im·pir′ē·əs) *adj.* **1** Domineering; overbearing; arrogant. **2** Urgent; imperative. [< L *imperium* rule] **—im·pe′ri·ous·ly** *adv.* **—im·pe′ri·ous·ness** *n.*

im·per·ish·a·ble (im·per′ish·ə·bəl) *adj.* Not perishable or subject to decay; enduring; indestructible. **—im·per′ish·a·bil′i·ty, im·per′ish·a·ble·ness** *n.* **—im·per′ish·a·bly** *adv.*

im·per·ma·nent (im·pûr′mə·nənt) *adj.* Not permanent or lasting. **—im·per′ma·nence, im·per′ma·nen·cy** *n.* **—im·per′ma·nent·ly** *adv.*

im·per·me·a·ble (im·pûr′mē·ə·bəl) *adj.* Not permitting passage, esp. of fluids, moisture, etc. **—im·per′me·a·bil′i·ty** *n.* **—im·per′me·a·bly** *adv.*

impers. impersonal.

im·per·son·al (im·pûr′sən·əl) *adj.* **1** Not personal: an *impersonal* deity. **2** Not relating to a particular person or thing: an *impersonal* statement. **3** Unsympathetic; cold: an *impersonal* attitude. **4** *Gram.* Having or containing an intermediate subject: said esp. of verbs. In English the subject of an impersonal verb is usu. the pronoun *it.* **—***n.* An impersonal verb. **—im·per′son·al′i·ty** (-al′ə·tē) *n.* **—im·per′son·al·ly** *adv.*

im·per·son·ate (im·pûr′sən·āt) *v.t.* **·at·ed, ·at·ing 1** To mimic the appearance, mannerisms, etc., of. **2** To act or play the part of. **3** To represent in human form; personify: He *impersonates* the quality of virtue. **—***adj.* (-it) Embodied in a person; personified. **—im·per′son·a′tion, im·per′son·a′tor** *n.*

im·per·ti·nence (im·pûr′tə·nəns) *n.* **1** The state or quality of being impertinent. **2** Insolence; rudeness. **3** Unfitness; irrelevancy. **4** An impertinent act. Also **im·per′ti·nen·cy.**

im·per·ti·nent (im·pûr′tə·nənt) *adj.* **1** Rude; impudent. **2** Irrelevant; not to the point. **3** Not suitable or fitting. **—im·per′ti·nent·ly** *adv.*

im·per·turb·a·ble (im′pər·tûr′bə·bəl) *adj.* Incapable of being agitated or perturbed; calm; impassive. **—im′per·turb′a·bil′i·ty, im′per·turb′a·ble·ness** *n.* **—im′per·turb′a·bly** *adv.*

im·per·vi·ous (im·pûr′vē·əs) *adj.* **1** Permitting no passage of fluids, light rays, etc.; impenetrable. **2** Not influenced or affected by. [< L *in-* not + *per-* through + *via* way, road] **—im·per′vi·ous·ly** *adv.* **—im·per′vi·ous·ness** *n.*

im·pe·ti·go (im′pə·tī′gō) *n.* A contagious bacterial skin infection characterized by blisters that break and form yellow encrusted sores. [L, an attack]

im·pet·u·ous (im·pech′ōō·əs) *adj.* **1** Characterized by energy or violent force: *impetuous* haste. **2** Spontaneous; impulsive. [< L *impetuosus*] **—im·pet′u·os′i·ty** (-os′ə·tē), **im·pet′u·ous·ness** *n.* **—im·pet′u·ous·ly** *adv.*

im·pe·tus (im′pə·təs) *n.* **1** The energy or momentum of a moving body. **2** Any force that begins or sets in motion; incentive. [L< *impetere* rush upon]

impf. imperfect.

im·pi·e·ty (im·pī′ə·tē) *n. pl.* **·ties 1** Lack of piety; irreverence. **2** An impious act. **3** Disrespect, as toward parents.

im·pinge (im·pinj′) *v.i.* **·pinged, ·ping·ing 1** To strike; collide: with *on, upon,* or *against.* **2** To encroach; infringe: with *on* or *upon.* [< L *in-* against + *pangere* to strike] **—im·pinge′ment, im·ping′er** *n.*

im·pi·ous (im′pē·əs, im′pī′əs) *adj.* Not pious; lacking reverence, as toward God or one's parents. **—im′pi·ous·ly** *adv.* **—im′pi·ous·ness** *n.*

imp·ish (im′pish) *adj.* **1** Of or like an imp. **2** Mischievous. **—imp′ish·ly** *adv.* **—imp·ish·ness** *n.*

im·pla·ca·ble (im·plak′ə·bəl, -plā′kə-) *adj.* **1** That cannot be placated or appeased. **2** Unalterable; inexorable. **—im·pla′ca·bil′i·ty, im·pla′ca·ble·ness** *n.* **—im·pla′ca·bly** *adv.*

im·plant (im·plant′, -plänt′) *v.t.* **1** To insert or graft in or onto living tissue. **2** To instill, as principles. **3** To plant, as seeds. **—***n.* (im′plant′, -plänt′) *Med.* Something implanted in the body, as a tissue graft or therapeutic device. **—im′plan·ta′tion, im·plant′er** *n.*

im·plau·si·ble (im·plô′zə·bəl) *adj.* Not plausible. **—im·plau′si·bly** *adv.*

im·ple·ment (im′plə·mənt) *n.* A thing used in work; a utensil; tool. **—***v.t.* (-ment) **1** To fulfill; accomplish. **2** To provide what is needed for; supplement. **3** To furnish with implements. [< L *implementum* a filling up] **—im′ple·men′tal** *adj.* **—im′ple·men·ta′tion** *n.*

im·pli·cate (im′plə·kāt) *v.t.* **·cat·ed, ·cat·ing 1** To show to be involved, as in a plot or crime. 2 To imply. 3 To fold or twist together; entangle. [< L *in-* in + *plicare* to fold] —**im′pli·ca′tive, im·pli·ca·to·ry** (im′pli·kə·tôr′ē, -tō′rē) *adj.*

im·pli·ca·tion (im′plə·kā′shən) *n.* 1 The act of implicating or the state of being implicated. 2 The act of implying. 3 Something implied, esp. so as to lead to a deduction.

im·plic·it (im·plis′it) *adj.* 1 Implied or to be understood, but not specifically stated. 2 Absolute; unquestioning: *implicit* trust. 3 Virtually contained or involved in, though not immediately apparent or stated; inherent. [< L *implicare* involve] —**im·plic′it·ly** *adv.* —**im·plic′it·ness** *n.*

im·plied (im·plīd′) *adj.* Contained, understood, or indicated, but not directly stated. —**im·pli·ed·ly** (im·plī′id·lē) *adv.*

im·plode (im·plōd′) *v.t. & v.i.* **·plod·ed, ·plod·ing** To burst inward, esp. forcibly. [< IN-[2] + (EX)PLODE]

im·plore (im·plôr′, -plōr′) *v.* **·plored, ·plor·ing** *v.t.* 1 To beseech; entreat. 2 To beg for urgently; pray for. —*v.i.* 3 To make urgent supplication. [< L *in-* thoroughly + *plorare* cry out] —**im·plor′er** *n.* —**im·plor′ing·ly** *adv.*

im·plo·sion (im·plō′zhən) *n.* An act or instance of imploding. —**im·plo′sive** (-siv) *adj.*

im·ply (im·plī′) *v.t.* **·plied, ·ply·ing** 1 To involve necessarily as a circumstance, condition, effect, etc.: An action *implies* an agent. 2 To indicate (a meaning not expressed); hint at; intimate. [< L *implicare* involve] • See INFER.

im·po·lite (im′pə·līt′) *adj.* Not polite; rude. —**im′po·lite′ly** *adv.* —**im′po·lite′ness** *n.*

im·pol·i·tic (im·pol′ə·tik) *adj.* Not politic; imprudent; injudicious. —**im′po·lit′i·cal·ly, im·pol′i·tic·ly** *adv.*

im·pon·der·a·ble (im·pon′dər·ə·bəl) *adj.* 1 Without weight. 2 Impossible to evaluate or foresee. —*n.* Anything imponderable. —**im·pon′der·a·bil′i·ty, im·pon′der·a·ble·ness** *n.* —**im·pon′der·a·bly** *adv.*

im·port (im·pôrt′, -pōrt′, im′pôrt, -pōrt) *v.t.* 1 To bring (goods) into one country from a foreign country in commerce. 2 To bring in; introduce. 3 To mean; signify. —*v.i.* 4 To be of importance or significance; matter. —*n.* (im′pôrt, -pōrt) 1 Importation. 2 That which is imported. 3 Meaning; significance. 4 Importance. [< L *in-* in + *portare* carry] —**im·port′a·ble** *adj.*

im·por·tance (im·pôr′təns) *n.* The condition or quality of being important.

im·por·tant (im·pôr′tənt) *adj.* 1 Of great import, consequence, prominence, or value. 2 Pompous; pretentious. [< L *importare* bring in] —**im·por′tant·ly** *adv.* —**Syn.** 1 momentous, serious, significant, weighty.

im·por·ta·tion (im′pôr·tā′shən, -pōr-) *n.* 1 The act of importing merchandise, etc. 2 That which is imported.

im·port·er (im·pôr′tər, -pōr′-) *n.* One who imports goods from a foreign country.

im·por·tu·nate (im·pôr′chə·nit) *adj.* Urgent in requesting or demanding; insistent; pertinacious. —**im·por′tu·nate·ly** *adv.* —**im·por′tu·nate·ness** *n.*

im·por·tune (im′pôr·t*y*ōōn′, im·pôr′chən) *v.* **·tuned, ·tun·ing** *v.t.* 1 To annoy or trouble with persistent requests or demands. —*v.i.* 2 To make persistent requests or demands. [< L *importunus* having no access, vexatious] —**im′por·tun′er** *n.*

im·por·tu·ni·ty (im′pôr·t*y*ōō′nə·tē) *n. pl.* **·ties** 1 The act of importuning. 2 The state of being importunate. 3 *pl.* Importunate demands.

im·pose (im·pōz′) *v.t.* **·posed, ·pos·ing** 1 To place or lay by authority: to *impose* a tax. 2 To place by or as by force: to *impose* opinions on another. 3 To force (oneself, one's presence, etc.) upon others. 4 To palm off (something) as true or genuine; foist. 5 *Printing* To arrange in a form, as pages of type. —**impose on** (or **upon**) 1 To take advantage of; presume. 2 To cheat or deceive by trickery. [< L *imponere* put in] —**im·pos′a·ble** *adj.* —**im·pos′er** *n.*

im·pos·ing (im·pō′zing) *adj.* Very impressive because of manner, appearance, size, etc. —**im·pos′ing·ly** *adv.* —**im·pos′ing·ness** *n.*

im·po·si·tion (im′pə·zish′ən) *n.* 1 The act of imposing. 2 A severe or unjust demand, requirement, duty, etc. 3 A deception; imposture. 4 A tax, toll, or duty.

im·pos·si·bil·i·ty (im·pos′ə·bil′ə·tē) *n. pl.* **·ties** 1 The fact or state of being impossible. 2 That which is impossible.

im·pos·si·ble (im·pos′ə·bəl) *adj.* 1 Not capable of existing or occurring. 2 Hopelessly difficult to do or accomplish. 3 Utterly objectionable or intolerable. —**im·pos′si·bly** *adv.*

im·post (im′pōst) *n.* Something imposed, esp. a customs duty. —*v.t.* To classify (imported goods) so as to determine the customs duty. [< L *in-* on + *ponere* lay, place]

im·pos·tor (im·pos′tər) *n.* One who deceives, esp. one who goes under an assumed name or identity. [< L *imponere* lay on, impose]

im·pos·ture (im·pos′chər) *n.* Deception by means of false pretenses.

im·po·tence (im′pə·təns) *n.* The state or quality of being impotent. Also **im′po·ten·cy.**

im·po·tent (im′pə·tənt) *adj.* 1 Lacking in physical power; week; feeble. 2 Unable to have sexual intercourse: said of the male. 3 Powerless, defenseless, or ineffectual. —**im′po·tent·ly** *adv.*

im·pound (im·pound′) *v.t.* 1 To shut up in a pound, as a stray dog. 2 To place in legal custody. 3 To collect (water) in a reservoir, etc., as for irrigation. —**im·pound′age, im·pound′er** *n.*

im·pov·er·ish (im·pov′ər·ish) *v.t.* 1 To reduce to poverty. 2 To exhaust the fertility or quality of, as soil. [< OF *em-* thoroughly + *povre* poor] —**im·pov′er·ish·er, im·pov′er·ish·ment** *n.*

im·prac·ti·ca·ble (im·prak′ti·kə·bəl) *adj.* Impossible or unreasonably difficult to do or to use. —**im·prac′ti·ca·bil′i·ty, im·prac′ti·ca·ble·ness** *n.* —**im·prac′ti·ca·bly** *adv.*

im·prac·ti·cal (im·prak′ti·kəl) *adj.* Not practical. —**im·prac′ti·cal′i·ty** (-kal′ə·tē) *n.*

im·pre·cate (im′prə·kāt) *v.t.* **·cat·ed, ·cat·ing** To invoke, as a judgment, calamity, or curse. [< L *in-* on + *precari* pray] —**im′pre·ca·to′ry** (-kə·tôr′ē, -tō′rē) *adj.* —**im′pre·ca′tion, im′pre·ca′tor** *n.*

im·preg·na·ble (im·preg′nə·bəl) *adj.* 1 Incapable of being taken by attack. 2 Unyielding; unassailable. [< L *in-* not + *prehendere* to take] —**im·preg′na·bil′i·ty** *n.* —**im·preg′na·bly** *adv.*

im·preg·nate (im·preg′nāt) *v.t.* **·nat·ed, ·nat·ing** 1 To make pregnant. 2 To fertilize. 3 To saturate or permeate. 4 To fill or imbue with emotion, ideas, principles, etc. —*adj.* Made pregnant. —**im·preg′na·ble** (-nə·bəl) *adj.* —**im′preg·na′tion, im·preg′na·tor** *n.*

im·pre·sa·ri·o (im′prə·sä′rē·ō) *n. pl.* **·sa·ri·os** One who organizes or manages an opera or ballet company, concerts, etc. [Ital. < *impresa* undertaking]

im·pre·scrip·ti·ble (im′pri·skrip′tə·bəl) *adj.* Incapable of being taken away; inalienable: *imprescriptible* rights. [< F] —**im′pre·scrip′ti·bil′i·ty** *n.* —**im′pre·scrip′ti·bly** *adv.*

im·press[1] (im·pres′) *v.t.* 1 To produce a marked effect upon, as the mind; influence. 2 To fix firmly in the mind. 3 To form or make (an imprint or mark) by pressure; stamp. 4 To form or make an imprint or mark upon. 5 To press: to *impress* one's hand into the mud. —*n.* (im′pres) 1 The act of impressing. 2 A mark or seal produced by pressure. 3 A stamp. 4 An impression or effect made on the mind. [< L *in-* on + *premere* to press] —**im·press′er** *n.*

im·press[2] (im·pres′) *v.t.* 1 To compel to enter public service by force: to *impress* seamen. 2 To seize (property) for public use. [< *in-* in + PRESS[1]] —**im·press′er, im·press′ment** *n.*

im·press·i·ble (im·pres′ə·bəl) *adj.* Capable of being impressed or of receiving an impression; susceptible. —**im·press′i·bil′i·ty, im·press′i·ble·ness** *n.* —**im·press′i·bly** *adv.*

im·pres·sion (im·presh′ən) *n.* 1 The act of impressing. 2 A stamp, mark, figure, etc. made by pressure. 3 An effect produced on the senses, the mind, or the feelings. 4 An effect or change: Our hard work made little *impression* on the lawn. 5 A vague or indistinct remembrance; a notion. 6 *Printing* **a** The imprint of type, illustrations, etc., on a page or sheet. **b** All the copies of a book, etc., printed at one time. **c** One copy of a book, engraving, etching, etc. —**im·pres′sion·al** *adj.*

im·pres·sion·a·ble (im·presh′ən·ə·bəl) *adj.* Sensitive to impressions; easily molded or influenced. **—im·pres′sion·a·bil′i·ty, im·pres′sion·a·ble·ness** *n.*

im·pres·sion·ism (im·presh′ən·iz′əm) *n* 1 A theory and school of art, developed in the 19th century, which attempted to produce, mainly by the vivid simulation of light, the immediate impressions made by the subject on the artist. 2 In literature, the presenting of the most immediate and arresting aspects of character, emotion, etc., without using explicit realistic detail. 3 *Music* A style of composition, developed by Debussy and Ravel, striving to create impressions, moods, etc., by the use of new tonal effects. **—im·pres′sion·ist** *adj., n.* **—im·pres′sion·is′tic** *adj.*

im·pres·sive (im·pres′iv) *adj.* Producing or tending to produce a strong impression on the mind, emotions, etc., esp. one of awe or admiration. **—im·pres′sive·ly** *adv.* **—im·pres′sive·ness** *n.*

im·pri·ma·tur (im′pri·mä′tər, -mā′-, im·prim′ə·tyŏŏr) *n.* 1 An official license to print or publish a book or pamphlet. 2 Approval in general; sanction. [L, let it be printed]

im·print (im·print′) *v.t.* 1 To produce or reproduce (a figure, mark, etc.) by pressure: to *imprint* a design on wax. 2 To mark (something), as with a stamp or seal. 3 To fix firmly in the memory. —*n.* (im′print) 1 A mark or character made by imprinting. 2 An effect or impression, as on the mind or memory. 3 A publisher's or printer's name, place of publication, date, etc., printed in a book or other publication. [<L *in-* in + *premere* to press]

im·pris·on (im·priz′ən) *v.t.* 1 To put into or keep in a prison. 2 To confine or restrain in any way. **—im·pris′on·ment** *n.* **—Syn.** 1 immure, incarcerate, jail. 2 constrain.

im·prob·a·ble (im·prob′ə·bəl) *adj.* Not likely to happen or to be true. **—im·prob·a·bil·i·ty** (im′prob·ə·bil′ə·tē, im·prob′-), **im·prob′a·ble·ness** *n.* **—im·prob′a·bly** *adv.*

im·promp·tu (im·promp′tyŏŏ) *adj.* Made, done, or uttered on the spur of the moment; extempore; offhand. —*n.* Anything impromptu. —*adv.* Without preparation. [F <L *in promptu* in readiness]

im·prop·er (im·prop′ər) *adj.* 1 Not fit or appropriate; unsuitable. 2 Contrary to accepted standards of taste, conduct, speech, etc. 3 Not true or correct. **—im·prop′er·ly** *adv.* **—im·prop′er·ness** *n.*

improper fraction A fraction in which the numerator is greater than or equal to the denominator, as 9/5 or 3/3.

im·pro·pri·e·ty (im′prə·prī′ə·tē) *n. pl.* **·ties** 1 The state or quality of being improper. 2 Anything that is improper. 3 A violation of good usage in speech or writing.

im·prove (im·prōōv′) *v.* **·proved, ·prov·ing** *v.t.* 1 To make better the quality, condition, etc., of. 2 To use to good advantage; utilize. 3 To increase the value of, as land by cultivation. —*v.i.* 4 To become better. 5 To make improvements: with *on* or *upon.* [<OF *en-* into + *prou* profit] **—im·prov′a·bil′i·ty, im·prov′a·ble·ness, im·prov′er** *n.* **—im·prov′a·ble** *adj.* **—im·prov′a·bly** *adv.*

im·prove·ment (im·prōōv′mənt) *n.* 1 The act of improving. 2 An improved condition. 3 A person or thing that is better than its predecessors. 4 Anything that increases the value, excellence, etc., of something.

im·prov·i·dent (im·prov′ə·dənt) *adj.* Taking no thought for future needs; thriftless. **—im·prov′i·dence** *n.* **—im·prov′i·dent·ly** *adv.*

im·pro·vise (im′prə·vīz) *v.t. & v.i.* **·vised, ·vis·ing** 1 To compose, recite, sing, etc., without previous preparation; extemporize. 2 To make or devise from what is at hand. [<L *in-* not + *provisus* foreseen] **—im·pro′vi·sa′tion·al** *adj.* **—im·prov·i·sa·tion** (im·prov′ə·zā′shən, im′prə·vī·zā′shən), **im′pro·vis′er** *n.*

im·pru·dent (im·prōō′dənt) *adj.* Not prudent; lacking discretion. **—im·pru′dence** *n.* **—im·pru′dent·ly** *adv.*

im·pu·dence (im′pyə·dəns) *n.* 1 The quality of being impudent. 2 Impudent language or behavior. Also **im′pu·den·cy.**

im·pu·dent (im′pyə·dənt) *adj.* Offensively bold; insolent. [<L *in-* not + *pudens* modest] **—im′pu·dent·ly** *adv.*

im·pugn (im·pyōōn′) *v.t.* 1 To attack by words or arguments. 2 To challenge or oppose as false. [<L *in-* against + *pugnare* to fight] **—im·pugn′a·ble** *adj.* **—im·pug·na·tion** (im′pəg·nā′shən), **im·pugn′er, im·pugn′ment** *n.*

im·pulse (im′puls) *n.* 1 A force, esp. one that acts for a short time and produces motion. 2 The change in momentum produced by such a force. 3 A sudden mental urge to act, caused by the feelings or by some external stimulus. 4 Any natural, unreasoned tendency or propensity: a kind *impulse.* 5 *Physiol.* The propagation of a stimulus through nerve or muscle tissue. [<L *impulsus,* pp. of *impellere.* See IMPEL.]

im·pul·sion (im·pul′shən) *n.* 1 The act of impelling. 2 The state of being impelled. 3 That which impels, whether a force, tendency, or motive.

im·pul·sive (im·pul′siv) *adj.* 1 Acting on impulse: an *impulsive* child. 2 Resulting from impulse; unpremeditated: an *impulsive* act. 3 Having the power to impel or drive. **—im·pul′sive·ly** *adv.* **—im·pul′sive·ness** *n.*

im·pu·ni·ty (im·pyōō′nə·tē) *n. pl.* **·ties** Freedom from punishment or from injurious consequences. [<L *in-* not + *poena* punishment]

im·pure (im·pyŏŏr′) *adj.* 1 Containing something dirty; unclean. 2 Obscene; unchaste. 3 Containing idiomatic or grammatical faults. 4 Unfit for religious use; unhallowed. 5 Mixed with foreign matter; adulterated. 6 Not consistent in style, form, color, etc.; mixed. **—im·pure′ly** *adv.* **—im·pure′ness** *n.*

im·pu·ri·ty (im·pyŏŏr′ə·tē) *n. pl.* **·ties** 1 The state of being impure. 2 Something impure.

im·pu·ta·tion (im′pyōō·tā′shən) *n.* 1 The act of imputing. 2 Something imputed, as an accusation or insinuation. **—im·pu·ta·tive** (im·pyōō′tə·tiv) *adj.* **—im·pu′ta·tive·ly** *adv.*

im·pute (im·pyōōt′) *v.t.* **·put·ed, ·put·ing** To attribute, as a fault or crime, to a person; ascribe. [<L *in-* in + *putare* reckon, think) **—im·put′a·bil′i·ty, im·put′er** *n.* **—im·put′a·ble** *adj.* **—im·put′a·bly** *adv.*

in (in) *prep.* 1 Contained or included within: six rooms *in* the house. 2 Amidst; surrounded by: *in* the rain. 3 Within the class or group of: a man *in* real estate. 4 Occupied or concerned with: *in* search of truth. 5 Wearing, decorated with, etc.: that girl *in* blue. 6 Made out of: This watch is *in* gold. 7 So as to form or constitute: arranged *in* a spiral. 8 Into: sinking *in* the mud. 9 As a part or function of; belonging to: We knew you had it *in* you. 10 According to or within the scope or range of: *in* my opinion; to come *in* hearing. 11 During the course of: a concert given *in* the evening. 12 At or before the end of: due *in* three days. 13 With regard or respect to: Students vary *in* talent. 14 Affected by; under the influence of: *in* doubt. 15 By means of; using: speaking *in* whispers. 16 For the purpose of: to run *in* pursuit. 17 By reason or as a result of: to run *in* fear. —*adv.* 1 To or toward the inside from the outside: Please come *in.* 2 Inside; indoors: to stay *in* all day. 3 So as to be part of, contained by, or included with: to join *in;* to stir *in* flour. 4 So as to be in a certain position, place, or condition: Pull *in* the net. **—all in** *Informal* Exhausted. **—be in for** *Informal* To have the certain expectation of receiving (usu. something unpleasant). **—have it in for** *Informal* To resent; bear ill will toward. **—in that** Because; since: *In that* you're here already, you might as well stay. **—in with** In association or friendship with. —*adj.* 1 Having control, success, or authority. 2 On the inside; inner. 3 Leading or going in: the *in* train. 4 *Informal* a Privileged in status. b Much publicized and often admired. 5 *Informal* Understandable only to a select few: *in* jokes. —*n.* 1 A member of a party in office or power, a team at bat, etc. 2 *Informal* Favored position or influence: an *in* with the boss. **—ins and outs** The full complexities, details, etc.: to know the *ins and outs* of a business. [<OE] • See INTO.

in-[1] *prefix* Not; without; un-; non-: *inactive.* Also **il-** (as in *illiterate*), **im-** (as in *imbalance*), **ir-** (as in *irregular*). [L] Following is a list of words beginning with this prefix.

inaffable	**incompassionate**	**inconsumable**
inauthentic	**incompliance**	**incoordinate**
incircumspect	**incompliant**	**incoordination**
incoercible	**incomposite**	**indeciduous**
incohesive	**incomprehensive**	**indecorum**
incommunicative	**incomputable**	**indeficiency**
incommutability	**incondensable**	**indefinitive**
incommutable	**inconducive**	**indemonstrability**
incompact	**incongruent**	**indemonstrable**

indetectable	ineloquent	inobservance
indetectible	inequable	inobtrusive
indevotion	ineradicable	inoppressive
indevout	inerasable	inopulent
indiscipline	inevident	inquietude
indiscoverable	inexcitable	insalubrious
indisposable	inexecution	insatiety
indistinction	inexertion	insubmissive
indistinctive	inexistence	insuppressible
individable	inexistent	intransferable
indivinity	inexplainable	intransformable
indivision	inexplicit	intransfusible
indocile	inexplosive	intransmissible
indocility	inextensible	intransmutable
inductile	inextension	intransparent
inductility	infeasible	inutilitarian
indurable	infecund	inveracity
inefficacious	infecundity	inverisimilitude
inefficacy	infrugal	invirile
ineffulgent	inhomogeneity	invirility
inelaborate	inhomogeneous	inviscid
ineloquence	inhumanitarian	invital

in-[2] *prefix* In; into; on; within; toward: *include.* Also used intensively, as in *inflame.* Also **il-, im-, ir-.** [Fusion of IN, *prep. & adv.* + L *in-*]

-in *suffix Chem.* Used generally to denote neutral compounds, as fats, proteins, and glycerides: *stearin.* [Var. of -INE[2]]

IN Indiana (P.O. abbr.).

In indium.

in. inch(es).

in·a·bil·i·ty (in′ə·bil′ə·tē) *n.* The state of being unable; lack of necessary power, ability, etc. —**Syn.** impotence, incapability, incapacity, incompetence.

in ab·sen·ti·a (in ab·sen′shē·ə, -shə) *Latin* In absence (of the person concerned).

in·ac·ces·si·ble (in′ak·ses′ə·bəl) *adj.* Not accessible; incapable of being reached, seen, obtained, etc. —**in′ac·ces′·si·bil′i·ty, in′ac·ces′i·ble·ness** *n.* —**in′ac·ces′si·bly** *adv.*

in·ac·cu·ra·cy (in·ak′yər·ə·sē) *n. pl.* **·cies** 1 The state or condition of being inaccurate. 2 Something which is inaccurate.

in·ac·cu·rate (in·ak′yər·it) *adj.* Not accurate, correct, or exact. —**in·ac′cu·rate·ly** *adv.* —**in·ac′cu·rate·ness** *n.*

in·ac·tion (in·ak′shən) *n.* Absence of action, activity, or motion; idleness.

in·ac·ti·vate (in·ak′tə·vāt) *v.t.* **·vat·ed, ·vat·ing** To make inactive. —**in·ac′ti·va′tion** *n.*

in·ac·tive (in·ak′tiv) *adj.* 1 Characterized by inaction; inert. 2 Marked by absence of effort or action; indolent. 3 *Mil.* Not engaged in military duty. —**in·ac′tive·ly** *adv.* —**in·ac·tiv′i·ty, in·ac′tive·ness** *n.*

in·ad·e·quate (in·ad′ə·kwit) *adj.* Not adequate; insufficient. —**in·ad′e·qua·cy, in·ad′e·quate·ness** *n.* —**in·ad′e·quate·ly** *adv.*

in·ad·mis·si·ble (in′əd·mis′ə·bəl) *adj.* Not allowed, approved, or to be admitted. —**in′ad·mis′i·bil′i·ty** *n.*

in·ad·ver·tence (in′əd·vûr′təns) *n.* 1 The quality of being inadvertent. 2 Something inadvertent, as an error or oversight. Also **in′ad·ver′ten·cy.**

in·ad·ver·tent (in′əd·vûr′tənt) *adj.* 1 Not careful or attentive; negligent. 2 Unintentional; not deliberate: an *inadvertent* omission of the translator's name. [< L *in-* not + *advertere* to turn toward] —**in′ad·ver′tent·ly** *adv.*

in·ad·vis·a·ble (in′əd·vī′zə·bəl) *adj.* Not advisable. —**in′·ad·vis′a·bil′i·ty** *n.* —**in′ad·vis′a·bly** *adv.*

in·al·ien·a·ble (in·āl′yən·ə·bəl) *adj.* Not transferable; that cannot be rightfully taken away. —**in·al′ien·a·bil′i·ty** *n.* —**in·al′ien·a·bly** *adv.*

in·am·o·ra·ta (in·am′ə·rä′tə, in′am-) *n.* A woman whom one loves; a fiancée or mistress. [Ital. < *in-* in + *amore* love] —**in·am′o·ra′to** (-tō) *n. Masc.*

in·ane (in·ān′) *adj.* 1 Lacking sense or significance; pointless; silly: an *inane* remark. 2 Empty; vapid. [< L *inanis* empty] —**in·ane′ly** *adv.*

in·an·i·mate (in·an′ə·mit) *adj.* 1 Without life; not animate. 2 Not lively; dull; torpid. —**in·an′i·mate·ly** *adv.* —**in·an′i·mate·ness** *n.*

in·a·ni·tion (in′ə·nish′ən) *n.* 1 The state of being empty. 2 Exhaustion from lack of nourishment. [< L *inanis* empty]

in·an·i·ty (in·an′ə·tē) *n. pl.* **·ties** 1 The condition of being inane. 2 A frivolous or silly act, remark, etc.

in·ap·pli·ca·ble (in·ap′lə·kə·bəl, in′ə·plik′ə·bəl) *adj.* 1 Not applicable. 2 Not suitable or fitting. —**in·ap′pli·ca·bil′i·ty, in·ap′pli·ca·ble·ness** *n.* —**in·ap′pli·ca·bly** *adv.*

in·ap·po·site (in·ap′ə·zit) *adj.* Not apposite; not pertinent. —**in·ap′po·site·ly** *adv.*

in·ap·pre·ci·a·ble (in′ə·prē′shē·ə·bəl, -shə·bəl) *adj.* So slight as to escape notice; negligible. —**in′ap·pre′ci·a·bly** *adv.*

in·ap·pro·pri·ate (in′ə·prō′prē·it) *adj.* Not appropriate; unsuitable. —**in′ap·pro′pri·ate·ly** *adv.* —**in′ap·pro′pri·ate·ness** *n.*

in·apt (in·apt′) *adj.* 1 Not apt; inappropriate. 2 Not skillful; clumsy. —**in·apt′ly** *adv.* —**in·apt′ness** *n.*

in·ap·ti·tude (in·ap′tə·tyōōd) *n.* 1 Unsuitability. 2 Lack of aptitude; incapacity.

in·ar·tic·u·late (in′är·tik′yə·lit) *adj.* 1 Unintelligible; indistinct: an *inarticulate* howl. 2 Incapable of speech; dumb. 3 Unable to speak coherently or to express oneself fully. 4 *Zool.* Lacking joints or segments. —**in′ar·tic′u·late·ly** *adv.* —**in′ar·tic′u·late·ness** *n.*

in·ar·tis·tic (in′är·tis′tik) *adj.* Not artistic; devoid of good taste. —**in′ar·tis′ti·cal·ly** *adv.*

in·as·much as (in′əz·much′ az′) 1 Since; because; seeing that. 2 To the degree that.

in·at·ten·tion (in′ə·ten′shən) *n.* Lack of or failure to give attention; heedlessness.

in·at·ten·tive (in′ə·ten′tiv) *adj.* Failing to pay attention; not attentive. —**in′at·ten′tive·ly** *adv.* —**in′at·ten′tive·ness** *n.*

in·au·di·ble (in·ô′də·bəl) *adj.* That cannot be heard. —**in·au′di·bil′i·ty** *n.* —**in·au′di·bly** *adv.*

in·au·gu·ral (in·ô′gyə·rəl) *adj.* 1 Of or pertaining to an inauguration. 2 Being the first of a series; introducing. —*n.* 1 An inaugural speech. 2 INAUGURATION.

in·au·gu·rate (in·ô′gyə·rāt) *v.t.* **·rat·ed, ·rat·ing** 1 To induct into office with formal ceremony. 2 To begin or commence upon formally. 3 To celebrate the public opening or first use of. [< L *inaugurare* take omens, consecrate, install] —**in·au′gu·ra′tor** *n.*

in·au·gu·ra·tion (in·ô′gyə·rā′shən) *n.* The act of inaugurating; esp., a ceremony of induction into office.

in·aus·pi·cious (in′ô·spish′əs) *adj.* Not auspicious; unlucky. —**in′aus·pi′cious·ly** *adv.* —**in′aus·pi′cious·ness** *n.*

inbd. inboard.

in·board (in′bôrd′, -bōrd′) *adj. & adv.* 1 *Naut.* Inside the hull or bulwarks of a ship. 2 Near the fuselage of an airplane. 3 Mounted within the chassis of an automobile or other vehicle rather than on the wheels: *inboard* brakes.

in·born (in′bôrn′) *adj.* Present at birth; innate. —**Syn.** congenital, inbred, ingrained, inherent, intrinsic.

in·bound (in′bound′) *adj.* Bound inward; incoming: an *inbound* ship.

in·bred (in′bred′) *adj.* 1 Inborn; innate. 2 Bred from closely related parents.

in·breed (in′brēd′, in′brēd′) *v.t.* **·bred, ·breed·ing** 1 To develop within. 2 To breed by continual mating of closely related stock.

Inc. Incorporated.

inc. inclosure; including; inclusive; income; incorporated; increase.

In·ca (ing′kə) *n.* One of the native Quechuan Indians dominant in Peru at the time of the Spanish conquest. —**In′can** *adj., n.*

in·cal·cu·la·ble (in·kal′kyə·lə·bəl) *adj.* 1 That cannot be counted or calculated. 2 Uncertain; unpredictable. —**in·cal′cu·la·bil′i·ty** *n.* —**in·cal′cu·la·bly** *adv.*

in·can·desce (in′kən·des′) *v.t. & v.i.* **·desced, ·desc·ing** To be or cause to be incandescent. —**in′can·des′cence, in′can·des′cen·cy** *n.*

in·can·des·cent (in′kən·des′ənt) *adj.* 1 Made luminous or glowing with heat. 2 Extremely bright or brilliant. [<

L *in-* in + *candescere* to become hot] **—in'can·des'cent·ly** *adv.*

incandescent lamp An electric lamp whose filament is heated and made incandescent by an electric current.

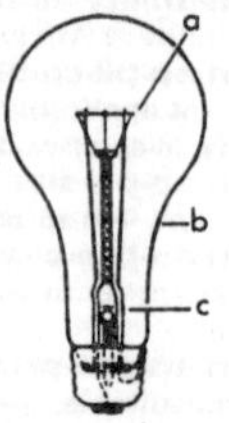

Incandescent lamp
a. filament.
b. glass bulb.
c. lead-in wires.

in·can·ta·tion (in'kan·tā'shən) 1 The utterance of magical words for enchantment or exorcism. 2 The formula so used. [< L *incantare* make an incantation] **—in·can·ta·to·ry** (in·kan'tə·tôr'ē, -tō'rē) *adj.*

in·ca·pa·ble (in·kā'pə·bəl) *adj.* 1 Not capable; lacking power, capacity or ability: with *of.* 2 Without legal qualifications or eligibility. **—in·ca'pa·bil'i·ty, in·ca'pa·ble·ness** *n.* **—in·ca'pa·bly** *adv.*

in·ca·pac·i·tate (in'kə·pas'ə·tāt) *v.t.* **·tat·ed, ·tat·ing** 1 To make incapable or unfit; disable. 2 *Law* To disqualify. **—in'ca·pac'i·ta'tion** *n.*

in·ca·pac·i·ty (in'kə·pas'ə·tē) *n. pl.* **·ties** 1 Lack of capacity; incapability. 2 *Law* Want of competency.

in·car·cer·ate (in·kär'sər·āt) *v.t.* **·at·ed, ·at·ing** 1 To imprison; put in jail. 2 To confine. [< L *in-* in + *carcer* jail] **—in·car'cer·a'tion, in·car'cer·a'tor** *n.*

in·car·na·dine (in·kär'nə·dīn, -din) *v.t.* **·dined, ·din·ing** To dye or stain red or flesh-colored. *—adj.* 1 Flesh-colored. 2 Blood-red. [F < Ital. *incarnato* flesh-colored]

in·car·nate (in·kär'nāt) *v.t.* **·nat·ed, ·nat·ing** 1 To give bodily form to. 2 To give concrete shape or form to; actualize. 3 To be the embodiment of; typify. *—adj.* (-nit) 1 Invested with flesh. 2 Embodied; personified: a fiend *incarnate.* 3 Flesh-colored. [< LL *incarnare* embody in flesh]

in·car·na·tion (in'kär·nā'shən) *n.* 1 The condition of being incarnate, esp. the embodiment of a god or spirit in human form, as an avatar. 2 *Often cap.* The assumption of human nature by Jesus Christ. 3 The embodiment of a quality, idea, principle, etc.

in·case (in·kās') *v.t.* **·cased, ·cas·ing** ENCASE. **—in·case'·ment** *n.*

in·cau·tion (in·kô'shən) *n.* A lack of care or caution.

in·cau·tious (in·kô'shəs) *adj.* Not cautious or careful; rash. **—in·cau'tious·ly** *adv.* **—in·cau'tious·ness** *n.*

in·cen·di·ar·y (in·sen'dē·er'ē) *adj.* 1 Of, pertaining to, or involving a malicious setting on fire of property. 2 Generating intense heat so as to cause fire: an *incendiary* bomb. 3 Inciting riot, disturbance, etc. *—n. pl.* **·ries** 1 One who maliciously sets property on fire. 2 One who incites riots, quarrels, etc. 3 An incendiary bomb or substance. [< L *incendere* set on fire] **—in·cen'di·a·rism** (-ə·riz'əm) *n.*

in·cense[1] (in·sens') *v.t.* **·censed, ·cens·ing** To inflame to anger; enrage. [< L *incendere* set on fire] **—in·cense'ment, in·cen'sor** *n.*

in·cense[2] (in'sens) *n.* 1 An aromatic substance that emits perfume during burning. 2 The odor or fumes from such a substance. 3 Any agreeable odor. *—v.* **·censed, ·cens·ing** *v.t.* 1 To perfume with incense. 2 To burn incense to as an act of worship. *—v.i.* 3 To burn incense. [< L *incendere* set on fire]

in·cen·tive (in·sen'tiv) *adj.* Encouraging or motivating action. *—n.* That which incites, or tends to incite, to action; motive; stimulus. [< L *incinere* set the tune] **—in·cen'tive·ly** *adv.*

in·cep·tion (in·sep'shən) *n.* A beginning or initial period; start. [< L *incipere* begin]

in·cep·tive (in·sep'tiv) *adj.* 1 Beginning; initial. 2 *Gram.* Denoting the commencement of an action. *—n. Gram.* An inceptive word. [< L *incipere* begin] **—in·cep'tive·ly** *adv.*

in·cer·ti·tude (in·sûr'tə·t(y)ōōd) *n.* The state of being uncertain; doubt.

in·ces·sant (in·ses'ənt) *adj.* Continued or repeated without cessation. [< L *in-* not + *cessare* cease] **—in·ces'san·cy** (-ən·sē) *n.* **—in·ces'sant·ly** *adv.* **—Syn.** ceaseless, constant, perpetual, unremitting, unending, persistent, continuous, unceasing.

in·cest (in'sest) *n.* Sexual intercourse between persons too closely related for legal marriage. [< L *in-* not + *castus* chaste]

in·ces·tu·ous (in·ses'chōō·əs) *adj.* 1 Guilty of incest. 2 Of the nature of incest. **—in·ces'tu·ous·ly** *adv.* **—in·ces'tu·ous·ness** *n.*

inch (inch) *n.* 1 A unit of length, equal to 1/12 of a foot or 25.4 millimeters. 2 An exceedingly small amount, distance, degree, etc. **—by inches** (or **inch by inch**) Gradually; very slowly. *—v.t. & v.i.* To move by inches or small degrees. [< L *uncia* the twelfth part]

inch·meal (inch'mēl') *adv.* Inch by inch; piecemeal. Also **by inchmeal.**

in·cho·ate (in·kō'it, in'kō·āt) *adj.* Only begun or entered upon; incipient. [< L *incohare* begin] **—in·cho'ate·ly** *adv.* **—in'cho·a'tion, in·cho'ate·ness** *n.*

in·cho·a·tive (in·kō'ə·tiv) *adj. Gram.* Inceptive. *—n.* An inceptive verb.

inch·worm (inch'wûrm') *n.* MEASURING WORM.

in·ci·dence (in'sə·dəns) *n.* 1 A falling upon, or the direction or manner of falling upon or affecting. 2 ANGLE OF INCIDENCE. 3 The degree of occurrence or effect of something: a high *incidence* of typhus.

in·ci·dent (in'sə·dənt) *n.* 1 Anything that takes place; event; occurrence. 2 A subordinate or minor event or act. *—adj.* 1 Falling or striking upon: *incident* rays. 2 Likely to occur in connection with: the discomfort *incident* to surgery. [< L *incidere* fall upon]

in·ci·den·tal (in'sə·den'təl) *adj.* 1 Occurring in the course of something else; contingent. 2 Happening without regularity or design; casual. *—n.* 1 Something that is incidental. 2 *Usu. pl.* Minor expenses or items.

in·ci·den·tal·ly (in'sə·den'təl·ē; *for def. 2 usu.* -dent'lē) *adv.* 1 In an incidental manner. 2 By the way: *Incidentally,* I forgot to jot down her name.

in·cin·er·ate (in·sin'ər·āt) *v.t.* **·at·ed, ·at·ing** To consume with fire; reduce to ashes; cremate. [< L *in-* in + *cinis, cineris* ashes] **—in·cin'er·a'tion** *n.*

in·cin·er·a·tor (in·sin'ə·rā'tər) *n.* A furnace for reducing refuse, etc., to ashes.

in·cip·i·ent (in·sip'ē·ənt) *adj.* Just beginning; in the first stages. [< L *incipere* begin] **—in·cip'i·ence, in·cip'i·en·cy** *n.* **—in·cip'i·ent·ly** *adv.*

in·cise (in·sīz') *v.t.* **·cised, ·cis·ing** 1 To cut into with a sharp instrument. 2 To engrave. [< L *incidere* cut into]

in·ci·sion (in·sizh'ən) *n.* 1 The act of incising. 2 A cut; gash. 3 A slit or opening made with a cutting instrument, as in an operation. 4 Incisiveness; keenness.

in·ci·sive (in·sī'siv) *adj.* 1 Cutting; incising. 2 Acute; penetrating; sharp: *incisive* wit. **—in·ci'sive·ly** *adv.* **—in·ci'sive·ness** *n.*

in·ci·sor (in·sī'zər) *n.* A front or cutting tooth; in man, one of eight such teeth, four in each jaw. • See TOOTH.

in·ci·ta·tion (in'sī·tā'shən) *n.* 1 An act or inciting. 2 An incentive; stimulus.

in·cite (in·sīt') *v.t.* **·cit·ed, ·cit·ing** To urge to action; instigate; stir up. [< L *in-* thoroughly + *citare* rouse] **—in·cite'·ment, in·cit'er** *n.*

in·ci·vil·i·ty (in'sə·vil'ə·tē) *n. pl.* **·ties** 1 The state or quality of being uncivil. 2 An uncivil or rude act.

incl. inclosure; including.

in·clem·ent (in·klem'ənt) *adj.* 1 Rough; stormy: *inclement* weather. 2 Merciless; harsh. [< L *in-* not + *clemens* clement] **—in·clem'en·cy** *n.* **—in·clem'ent·ly** *adv.*

in·cli·na·tion (in'klə·nā'shən) *n.* 1 Deviation or the degree of deviation from the vertical or horizontal; slant. 2 A slope. 3 A tendency; predilection. **—in'cli·na'tion·al** *adj.*

in·cline (in·klīn') *v.* **·clined, ·clin·ing** *v.i.* 1 To slant; slope. 2 To have a tendency. 3 To tend in some quality or degree: purple *inclining* toward blue. 4 To bow or bend the head or body, as in courtesy. *—v.t.* 5 To cause to bend, lean, or slope. 6 To influence. 7 To bow, as the head. **—incline one's ear** To hear with favor; heed. *—n.* (in'klīn) That which inclines from the horizontal; a gradient; slope. [< L *in-* on + *clinare* to lean] **—in·clin'a·ble** *adj.*

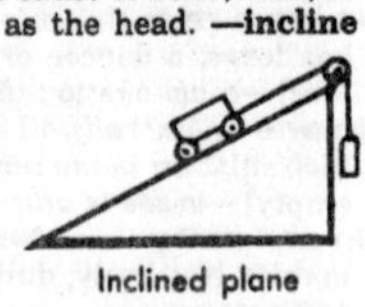
Inclined plane

in·clined (in·klīnd') *adj.* 1 Slanted; sloping. 2 Disposed; apt: *inclined* to be lazy.

inclined plane A plane inclined to the horizontal, esp. a simple machine along which a body can be moved and lifted by a force smaller than its weight.

in·close (in·klōz′) *v.t.* **·closed, ·clos·ing** ENCLOSE.
in·clude (in·klōōd′) *v.t.* **·clud·ed, clud·ing** 1 To have as a component part; contain. 2 To place in a general category, aggregate, etc. 3 To enclose within; confine. [<L *in-* in + *claudere* to shut] **—in·clud′a·ble, in·clud′i·ble** *adj.*
in·clu·sion (in·klōō′zhən) *n.* 1 The act of including. 2 That which is included.
in·clu·sive (in·klōō′siv) *adj.* 1 Including the things, limits, or extremes mentioned: from A to Z *inclusive.* 2 Including or taking into account everything pertinent or applicable: an *inclusive* list of purchases. **—in·clu′sive·ly** *adv.* **—in·clu′sive·ness** *n.*
incog. incognito.
in·cog·ni·to (in·kog′nə·tō, in′kəg·nē′tō) *adj. & adv.* With one's true name or identity not revealed. *—n. pl.* **·tos** (-tōz) 1 The state or disguise of being incognito. 2 One who lives, travels, etc., incognito. [<L *in-* not + *cognoscere* know]
in·co·her·ence (in′kō·hir′əns) *n.* 1 Want of coherence. 2 Something incoherent. Also **in′co·her′en·cy.**
in·co·her·ent (in′kō·hir′ənt) *adj.* 1 Without logical order or progression; disconnected. 2 Not clear; confused; muddled, as in speech or thought. 3 Without physical coherence of parts. **—in′co·her′ent·ly** *adv.*
in·com·bus·ti·ble (in·kəm·bus′tə·bəl) *adj.* Incapable of being burned. *—n.* An incombustible substance. **—in·com·bus′ti·bil′i·ty, in′com·bus′ti·ble·ness** *n.*
in·come (in′kum) *n.* Money, or other benefit, periodically received, as from one's labor, investments, etc. [ME, a coming in]
income tax A tax levied on the income or profits of individuals and of corporations.
in·com·ing (in′kum′ing) *adj.* Coming in or about to come in: *incoming* profits.
in·com·men·su·ra·ble (in′kə·men′shər·ə·bəl, -sər·ə-) *adj.* 1 Lacking a common measure or standard of comparison. 2 *Math.* Not expressible in terms of a common measure or unit: *incommensurable* numbers. *—n.* That which is incommensurable. **—in′com·men′su·ra·bil′i·ty, in′com·men′su·ra·ble·ness** *n.* **—in′com·men′su·ra·bly** *adv.*
in·com·men·su·rate (in′kə·men′shər·it) *adj.* 1 Incommensurable. 2 Inadequate; disproportionate. **—in′com·men′su·rate·ly** *adv.* **—in′com·men′su·rate·ness** *n.*
in·com·mode (in′kə·mōd′) *v.t.* **·mod·ed, ·mod·ing** To cause inconvenience to; disturb. [<L *in-* not + *commodus* convenient] **—Syn.** annoy, bother, put out, trouble.
in·com·mo·di·ous (in′kə·mō′dē·əs) *adj.* 1 Not spacious or roomy. 2 Inconvenient. **—in′com·mo′di·ous·ly** *adv.* **—in′com·mo′di·ous·ness, in′com·mod′i·ty** (-mod′ə·tē) *n.*
in·com·mu·ni·ca·ble (in′kə·myōō′nə·kə·bəl) *adj.* 1 Not capable of being communicated or told. 2 Not communicative. **—in′com·mu′ni·ca·bly** *adv.* **—in′com·mu′ni·ca·bil′i·ty** *n.*
in·com·mu·ni·ca·do (in′kə·myōō′nə·kä′dō) *adj. & adv.* Confined without the opportunity to communicate, as a prisoner. [Sp.]
in·com·pa·ra·ble (in·kom′pər·ə·bəl) *adj.* 1 Not admitting of comparison, because of being so superior; matchless. 2 Unsuitable for comparison. **—in·com′pa·ra·bil′i·ty, in·com′pa·ra·ble·ness** *n.* **—in·com′pa·ra·bly** *adv.*
in·com·pat·i·ble (in′kəm·pat′ə·bəl) *adj.* 1 Incapable of living or acting together in agreement or harmony. 2 Incapable of being used in combination; mutually discordant or antagonistic. 3 In disagreement; contradictory. *—n. Usu. pl.* Incompatible persons or things. **—in′com·pat′i·bil′i·ty** *n.* **—in′com·pat′i·bly** *adv.*
in·com·pe·tent (in·kom′pə·tənt) *adj.* 1 Not competent; unable to do what is required. 2 Not legally qualified. *—n.* An incompetent person. **—in·com′pe·tence, in·com′pe·ten·cy** *n.* **—in·com′pe·tent·ly** *adv.*
in·com·plete (in′kəm·plēt′) *adj.* 1 Not complete or finished. 2 Lacking in certain parts. 3 Imperfect. **—in′com·plete′ly** *adv.* **—in′com·plete′ness, in′com·ple′tion** *n.*
in·com·pre·hen·si·ble (in′kom·pri·hen′sə·bəl, in·kom′-) *adj.* 1 Not comprehensible; not understandable. 2 *Archaic* That cannot be included or confined within limits. **—in·com′pre·hen·si·bil′i·ty, in·com′pre·hen′si·ble·ness** *n.* **—in·com′pre·hen′si·bly** *adv.*
in·com·pre·hen·sion (in′kom·pri·hen′shən) *n.* Lack of comprehension or understanding.
in·com·press·i·ble (in′kəm·pres′ə·bəl) *adj.* Incapable of being pressed together or into a smaller space. **—in′com·press′i·bil′i·ty** *n.*
in·con·ceiv·a·ble (in′kən·sē′və·bəl) *adj.* That cannot be conceived, believed, imagined, etc. **—in′con·ceiv′a·ble·ness, in′con·ceiv′a·bil′i·ty** *n.* **—in′con·ceiv′a·bly** *adv.*
in·con·clu·sive (in′kən·klōō′siv) *adj.* 1 Not leading to an ultimate conclusion; indecisive. 2 Not achieving a definite result; ineffective. **—in′con·clu′sive·ly** *adv.* **—in′con·clu′sive·ness** *n.*
in·con·gru·i·ty (in′kən·grōō′ə·tē) *n. pl.* **·ties** 1 The state or quality of being incongruous. 2 That which is incongruous.
in·con·gru·ous (in·kong′grōō·əs) *adj.* 1 Not harmonious or compatible. 2 Not fit or suitable. 3 Not consistent or corresponding; disagreeing. [<L *in-* not + *congruus* harmonious] **—in·con′gru·ous·ly** *adv.* **—in·con′gru·ous·ness** *n.*
in·con·se·quent (in·kon′sə·kwənt) *adj.* 1 Not following logically. 2 Irrelevant; inconsequential. 3 Not according to proper sequence. **—in·con′se·quence** *n.* **—in·con′se·quent·ly** *adv.*
in·con·se·quen·tial (in′kon·sə·kwen′shəl, in·kon′-) *adj.* 1 Of little consequence; trivial. 2 Illogical. **—in·con′se·quen′ti·al′i·ty** (-kwen′shē·al′ə·tē) *n.* **—in·con′se·quen′tial·ly** *adv.*
in·con·sid·er·a·ble (in′kən·sid′ər·ə·bəl) *adj.* Very small in amount or extent; trivial. **—in′con·sid′er·a·ble·ness** *n.* **—in′con·sid′er·a·bly** *adv.*
in·con·sid·er·ate (in′kən·sid′ər·it) *adj.* 1 Not considerate; thoughtless. 2 Lacking sufficient consideration. **—in′con·sid′er·ate·ly** *adv.* **—in′con·sid′er·ate·ness, in′con·sid′er·a′tion** *n.*
in·con·sis·ten·cy (in′kən·sis′tən·sē) *n. pl.* **·cies** 1 The state or quality of being inconsistent. 2 That which is inconsistent. Also **in′con·sis′tence.**
in·con·sis·tent (in′kən·sis′tənt) *adj.* 1 Not in agreement or compatible with other assertions, facts, etc. 2 Self-contradictory. 3 Changeable; erratic; capricious, as in thought or behavior. **—in′con·sis′tent·ly** *adv.*
in·con·sol·a·ble (in′kən·sōl′ə·bəl) *adj.* Not to be consoled or soothed. **—in′con·sol′a·bil′i·ty, in′con·sol′a·ble·ness** *n.* **—in′con·sol′a·bly** *adv.*
in·con·so·nant (in·kon′sə·nənt) *adj.* Not consonant; inharmonious. **—in·con′so·nant·ly** *adv.* **—in·con′so·nance** *n.*
in·con·spic·u·ous (in′kən·spik′yōō·əs) *adj.* Not conspicuous; not attracting attention. **—in′con·spic′u·ous·ly** *adv.* **—in′con·spic′u·ous·ness** *n.*
in·con·stant (in·kon′stənt) *adj.* Not constant; fickle; variable. **—in·con′stan·cy** *n.* **—in·con′stant·ly** *adv.*
in·con·test·a·ble (in′kən·tes′tə·bəl) *adj.* Not admitting of controversy. **—in′con·test′a·bly** *adv.*
in·con·ti·nent (in·kon′tə·nənt) *adj.* 1 Having no self-control, esp. in sexual matters. 2 Unable to hold back bodily discharges or evacuations. **—in·con′ti·nence, in·con′ti·nen·cy** *n.* **—in·con′ti·nent·ly** *adv.*
in·con·tro·vert·i·ble (in′kon·trə·vûr′tə·bəl) *adj.* Not admitting of dispute or controversy; undeniable. **—in′con·tro·vert′i·bil′i·ty, in′con·tro·vert′i·ble·ness** *n.* **—in′con·tro·vert′i·bly** *adv.*
in·con·ven·ience (in′kən·vēn′yəns) *n.* 1 The state or quality of being inconvenient. 2 Something inconvenient. *—v.t.* **·ienced, ·ienc·ing** To cause inconvenience to; trouble.
in·con·ven·ient (in′kən·vēn′yənt) *adj.* Not convenient; causing difficulty or bother; troublesome. **—in′con·ven′ient·ly** *adv.*
in·con·vert·i·ble (in′kən·vûr′tə·bəl) *adj.* Not interchangeable, as paper money into specie. **—in′con·vert′i·bil′i·ty, in′con·vert′i·ble·ness** *n.* **—in′con·vert′i·bly** *adv.*
in·cor·po·rate (in·kôr′pə·rāt) *v.* **·rat·ed, ·rat·ing** *v.t.* 1 To take into or include as part of a whole. 2 To form into a legal corporation. 3 To combine or unite into one body or whole; blend; mix. *—v.i.* 4 To become combined or united as one body or whole. 5 To form a legal corporation. *—adj.* (-pər·it) 1 Joined or combined into one. 2 Incorporated

legally. [< LL *incorporare* embody] —**in·cor′po·ra′tive** *adj.* —**in·cor′po·ra′tor** *n.*

in·cor·po·rat·ed (in·kôr′pə·rā′tid) *adj.* 1 Constituting a legal corporation. 2 Combined.

in·cor·po·ra·tion (in·kôr′pə·rā′shən) *n.* 1 The act of incorporating. 2 A corporation.

in·cor·po·re·al (in′kôr·pôr′ē·əl, -pō′rē-) *adj.* 1 Not consisting of matter; immaterial; spiritual. 2 *Law* Having no material existence, but regarded as existing by the law; *incorporeal* rights. —**in′cor·po′re·al·ly** *adv.*

in·cor·rect (in′kə·rekt′) *adj.* 1 Inaccurate or untrue. 2 Not proper; unsuitable. 3 Erroneous; faulty. —**in′cor·rect′·ly** *adv.* —**in′cor·rect′ness** *n.*

in·cor·ri·gi·ble (in·kôr′ə·jə·bəl, -kor′-) *adj.* That cannot be corrected, changed, or reformed: an *incorrigible* liar. —*n.* An incorrigible person. [< L *in-* not + *corrigere* to correct] —**in·cor′ri·gi·ble·ness, in·cor′ri·gi·bil′i·ty** *n.* —**in·cor′ri·gi·bly** *adv.*

in·cor·rupt (in′kə·rupt′) *adj.* 1 Not morally corrupt. 2 Not spoiled or decayed; uncontaminated; pure. 3 Free from errors, changes, or alterations, as a text. Also **in′cor·rupt′ed.** —**in′cor·rupt′ly** *adv.* —**in′cor·rupt′ness** *n.*

in·cor·rupt·i·ble (in′kə·rup′tə·bəl) *adj.* Incapable of corruption; esp. not accessible to bribery. —**in′cor·rupt′i·bil′i·ty, in′cor·rupt′i·ble·ness** *n.* —**in′cor·rupt′i·bly** *adv.* —**Syn.** conscientious, honest, loyal, trustworthy.

incr. increased; increasing.

in·crease (in·krēs′) *v.* **·creased, ·creas·ing** *v.i.* 1 To become greater, as in amount, size, degree, etc.; grow. 2 To grow in numbers, esp. by reproduction. —*v.t.* 3 To make greater, as in amount, size, degree, etc.; augment; enlarge. —*n.* (in′krēs) 1 The act or process of increasing. 2 The result or amount of increasing. [< L *in-* in + *crescere* grow] —**in·creas′a·ble** *adj.* —**in·creas′ing·ly** *adv.*

in·cred·i·ble (in·kred′ə·bəl) *adj.* Seeming too far-fetched or extraordinary to be believed or possible. —**in·cred′i·bil′·i·ty, in·cred′i·ble·ness** *n.* —**in·cred′i·bly** *adv.*

in·cre·du·li·ty (in′krə·dyōō′lə·tē) *n.* Indisposition or refusal to believe. Also **in·cred·u·lous·ness** (in·krej′ə·ləs·nis).

in·cred·u·lous (in·krej′ə·ləs) *adj.* 1 Refusing belief; skeptical. 2 Caused by or showing doubt or disbelief. [< L *in-* not + *credulus* gullible] —**in·cred′u·lous·ly** *adv.*

in·cre·ment (in′krə·mənt) *n.* 1 The act of increasing; enlargement. 2 That which is added; increase. [< L *increscere.* See INCREASE] —**in′cre·men′tal** (-men′təl) *adj.*

in·crim·i·nate (in·krim′ə·nāt) *v.t.* **·nat·ed, ·nat·ing** To charge with or involve in a crime or fault. [< L *in-* in + *criminare* accuse one of a crime] —**in·crim′i·na′tion, in·crim′i·na′tor** *n.* —**in·crim′i·na·to′ry** (-nə·tôr′ē, -tō′rē) *adj.*

in·crust (in·krust′) *v.t.* ENCRUST.

in·cu·bate (in′kyə·bāt, ing′-) *v.* **·bat·ed, ·bat·ing** *v.t.* 1 To sit upon (eggs) in order to hatch; brood. 2 To hatch (eggs) in this manner or by artificial heat. 3 To maintain under conditions favoring optimum growth or development, as bacterial cultures. —*v.i.* 4 To sit on eggs; brood. 5 To undergo incubation. [< L *in-* on + *cubare* to lie] —**in′cu·ba′tive** *adj.*

in·cu·ba·tion (in′kyə·bā′shən, ing′-) *n.* 1 The act of incubating or the condition of being incubated. 2 The period between exposure to an infectious disease and the appearance of symptoms.

in·cu·ba·tor (in′kyə·bā′tər, ing′-) *n.* Any of various enclosures kept at a stable temperature, as for incubating eggs or bacterial cultures, or nurturing a premature infant.

in·cu·bus (in′kyə·bəs, ing′-) *n. pl.* **·bus·es** or **·bi** (-bī) 1 Anything that tends to weigh down or discourage. 2 A nightmare. 3 A male demon supposed to have sexual intercourse with sleeping women. [< LL, nightmare]

in·cul·cate (in·kul′kāt, in′kul-) *v.t.* **·cat·ed, ·cat·ing** To impress upon the mind by frequent and emphatic repetition; instill. [< L *inculcare* tread on] —**in·cul·ca·tion** (in′kul·kā′shən), **in′cul·ca′tor** *n.*

in·cul·pate (in·kul′pāt, in′kul-) *v.t.* **·pat·ed, ·pat·ing** To incriminate. [< L *in-* in + *culpa* fault] —**in′cul·pa′tion** *n.* —**in·cul′pa·to·ry** (-pə·tôr′ē, -tō′rē) *adj.*

in·cum·ben·cy (in·kum′bən·sē) *n. pl.* **·cies** 1 The state of being incumbent. 2 That which is incumbent. 3 The holding of an office or the period during which it is held.

in·cum·bent (in·kum′bənt) *adj.* 1 Resting upon one as a duty or moral obligation; obligatory. 2 Resting, leaning, or weighing wholly or partly upon something. —*n.* One who holds an office. [< L *incumbere* recline]

in·cum·ber *v.* ENCUMBER.

in·cu·nab·u·la (in′kyōō·nab′yə·lə) *n. pl. of* **in·cu·nab·u·lum** (-ləm) 1 The beginnings of anything. 2 Specimens of printing and block engraving that appeared before A.D. 1500. [< L *in-* in + *cunabula,* dim. pl. of *cunae* a cradle] —**in′cu·nab′u·lar** *adj.*

in·cur (in·kûr′) *v.t.* **·curred, ·cur·ring** To meet with or become subject to, as unpleasant consequences, esp. through one's own action; bring upon oneself. [< L *incurrere* run into]

in·cur·a·ble (in·kyōōr′ə·bəl) *adj.* Not able to be cured or remedied. —*n.* One having an incurable disease. —**in·cur′·a·bil′i·ty, in·cur′a·ble·ness** *n.* —**in·cur′a·bly** *adv.*

in·cu·ri·ous (in·kyōōr′ē·əs) *adj.* Lacking curiosity; not interested. —**in·cu·ri·os·i·ty** (in′kyōōr·ē·os′ə·tē), **in·cu′ri·ous·ness** *n.* —**in·cu′ri·ous·ly** *adv.*

in·cur·sion (in·kûr′zhən, -shən) *n.* A hostile invasion; raid. [< L *incurrere* run into] —**in·cur′sive** *adj.*

in·curve (in·kûrv′) *v.t. & v.i.* To curve inward. —*n.* (in′·kûrv′) In baseball, a pitched ball that curves inward toward the batter.

in·cus (ing′kəs) *n. pl.* **in·cu·des** (in·kyōō′dēz) *Anat.* The central one of three small bones in the middle ear; anvil. [L, anvil]

Ind. India; Indian; Indiana; Indies.

ind. independence; independent; index; indicated; indicative; indigo; indirect; industrial.

in·debt·ed (in·det′id) *adj.* 1 Having contracted a debt. 2 Owing gratitude; beholden.

in·debt·ed·ness (in·det′id·nis) *n.* 1 The state of being indebted. 2 The amount of one's debts.

in·de·cen·cy (in·dē′sən·sē) *n. pl.* **·cies** 1 The quality of being indecent; offensiveness. 2 An indecent act, word, etc.

in·de·cent (in·dē′sənt) *adj.* 1 Offensive to decency or propriety; immodest; obscene. 2 Contrary to what is fit and proper. —**in·de′cent·ly** *adv.*

in·de·ci·pher·a·ble (in′di·sī′fər·ə·bəl) *adj.* Impossible to decipher or read; illegible. —**in′de·ci′pher·a·bil′i·ty** *n.*

in·de·ci·sive (in′də·sī′siv) *adj.* 1 Not decisive. 2 Hesitant; irresolute. —**in·de·ci·sion** (in′di·sizh′ən) *n.* —**in′de·ci′sive·ly** *adv.*

in·de·clin·a·ble (in′di·klīn′ə·bəl) *adj. Gram.* Not having any inflected forms indicating case, number, or gender. —**in′de·clin′a·bly** *adv.*

in·dec·or·ous (in·dek′ə·res, in′di·kôr′əs, -kō′rəs) *adj.* Not decorous or proper; unsuitable. —**in·dec′or·ous·ly** *adv.* —**in·dec′or·ous·ness** *n.*

in·deed (in·dēd′) *adv.* Admittedly; truly; undeniably. —*interj.* An exclamation of surprise, irony, incredulity, etc. [< IN + DEED]

indef. indefinite.

in·de·fat·i·ga·ble (in′də·fat′ə·gə·bəl) *adj.* Not yielding readily to fatigue; tireless. [< L *in-* not + *defatigare* to tire out] —**in′de·fat′i·ga·bil′i·ty, in′de·fat′i·ga·ble·ness** *n.* —**in′de·fat′i·ga·bly** *adv.* —**Syn.** persevering, unfaltering, unflagging, untiring.

in·de·fea·si·ble (in′də·fē′zə·bəl) *adj.* Incapable of being annulled, set aside, or made void. —**in′de·fea′si·bil′i·ty** *n.* —**in′de·fea′si·bly** *adv.*

in·de·fen·si·ble (in′di·fen′sə·bəl) *adj.* 1 Incapable of being justified, excused, etc. 2 Incapable of being defended. —**in′de·fen′si·bil′i·ty, in′de·fen′si·ble·ness** *n.* —**in·de·fen′si·bly** *adv.*

in·de·fin·a·ble (in′di·fī′nə·bəl) *adj.* That cannot be defined or described; vague; subtle. —**in′de·fin′a·ble·ness** *n.* —**in′de·fin′a·bly** *adv.*

in·def·i·nite (in·def′ə·nit) *adj.* 1 Not definite or precise; uncertain; vague. 2 Without fixed boundaries or limits. 3 *Gram.* Not defining or determining, as the *indefinite* articles *a* and *an.* —**in·def′i·nite·ly** *adv.* —**in·def′i·nite·ness** *n.*

in·de·his·cent (in′də·his′ənt) *adj. Bot.* Not opening when ripe: said of certain grains and fruits. —**in′de·his′·cence** *n.*

in·del·i·ble (in·del′ə·bəl) *adj.* 1 That cannot be removed, erased, etc. 2 Making indelible marks: an *indelible* pen. [< L *in-* not + *delibilis* perishable] **—in·del′i·bil′i·ty** *n.* **—in·del′i·bly** *adv.*

in·del·i·ca·cy (in·del′ə·kə·sē) *n. pl.* **·cies** 1 The quality of being indelicate. 2 An indelicate act, word, etc., offensive to propriety or refined feeling.

in·del·i·cate (in·del′ə·kit) *adj.* 1 Offensive to propriety; immodest. 2 Unfeeling; tactless. **—in·del′i·cate·ly** *adv.*

in·dem·ni·fy (in·dem′nə·fī) *v.t.* **·fied, ·fy·ing** 1 To compensate for loss or damage sustained. 2 To make good (a loss). 3 To give security against future loss or damage to. [< L *indemnis* unhurt + -FY] **—in·dem′ni·fi·ca′tion, in·dem′ni·fi′er** *n.*

in·dem·ni·ty (in·dem′nə·tē) *n. pl.* **·ties** 1 That which is given as compensation for a loss or for damage. 2 An agreement to remunerate another for loss or to protect him against liability. 3 Exemption from penalties or liabilities incurred. [< L *indemnis* unhurt]

inden., indent. indention (printing).

indent[1] (in·dent′) *v.t.* 1 To set, as the first line of a paragraph, in from the margin. 2 To cut or mark the edge of with toothlike notches; serrate. 3 To indenture, as an apprentice. —*v.i.* 4 To be notched or cut. 5 To set a line, etc., in from the margin. —*n.* (in′dent, in·dent′) 1 A cut or notch in the edge of anything. 2 An indenture. 3 An indented line or paragraph. [< L *in-* in + *dens, dentis* tooth]

in·dent[2] (in·dent′; *n. also* in′dent) *v.t.* 1 To make a dent in. 2 To press inward so as to form a mark, hollow, etc. —*n.* A dent.

in·den·ta·tion (in′den·tā′shən) *n.* 1 The act of indenting. 2 A cut or notch in an edge or border. 3 An indention, as of a line or paragraph. 4 A dent.

in·den·tion (in·den′shən) *n.* 1 A dent. 2 *Printing* **a** The setting in of a line or body of type at the left side. **b** The space thus left blank.

in·den·ture (in·den′chər) *n.* 1 *Law* A contract in duplicate between parties. 2 *Often pl.* A legal instrument for binding an apprentice or a servant to his master. 3 The act of indenting, or the state of being indented. —*v.t.* **·tured, ·tur·ing** 1 To bind by indenture, as an apprentice. 2 To indent.

in·de·pen·dence (in′di·pen′dəns) *n.* 1 The quality or condition of being independent, esp. freedom from dependence upon or control by others. 2 An income large enough to live on without being employed.

Independence Day July 4, a U.S. holiday, marking the adoption of the Declaration of Independence on July 4, 1776.

in·de·pen·den·cy (in′di·pen′dən·sē) *n. pl.* **·cies** 1 Independence. 2 An independent state.

in·de·pen·dent (in′di·pen′dənt) *adj.* 1 Not under the control or rule of others; self-governing. 2 Not part of or connected to another group, etc.; separate: an *independent* merchant. 3 Not identified with any political party or faction. 4 Not under the influence or guidance of others; self-reliant. 5 Of, possessing, or indicating an income that permits one to live without labor or dependence on others. —*n.* 1 One who is independent. 2 *Often cap.* One who is not an adherent of any political party. **—in′de·pen′dent·ly** *adv.*

independent clause *Gram.* A clause that constitutes or is capable of constituting a sentence.

in-depth (in′depth′) *adj.* Extensive and thorough; not superficial; penetrating: an *in-depth* opinion survey.

in·de·scrib·a·ble (in′di·skrīb′ə·bəl) *adj.* Impossible to describe; beyond description. **—in′de·scrib′a·bil′i·ty, in′de·scrib′a·ble·ness** *n.* **—in′de·scrib′a·bly** *adv.*

in·de·struct·i·ble (in′di·struk′tə·bəl) *adj.* Impossible to destroy; proof against damage or harm. **—in′de·struct′i·bil′i·ty, in′de·struct′i·ble·ness** *n.* **—in′de·struct′i·bly** *adv.*

in·de·ter·mi·na·ble (in′di·tûr′mi·nə·bəl) *adj.* 1 Not capable of exact determination or measurement. 2 Not capable of being clearly decided or established. **—in′de·ter′mi·na·ble·ness** *n.* **—in′de·ter′mi·na·bly** *adv.*

in·de·ter·mi·nate (in′di·tûr′mə·nit) *adj.* 1 Not definite in extent, amount, or nature. 2 Not clear or precise; vague; undefined. **—in′de·ter′mi·nate·ly** *adv.* **—in′de·ter′mi·na·cy** (-nə·sē), **in′de·ter′mi·nate·ness** *n.*

in·de·ter·mi·na·tion (in′di·tûr′mə·nā′shən) *n.* 1 Lack of determination. 2 The state of being indeterminate.

in·dex (in′deks) *n. pl.* **·dex·es** or **·di·ces** (-də·sēz) 1 Anything used to indicate, point out, or guide, as the hand of a clock, a pointer, etc. 2 Anything that manifests or denotes: an *index* of character. 3 An alphabetical list, usu. found at the back of a book or other publication, of the names and topics included in the work and the page numbers on which they can be found. 4 A descriptive list or catalogue: an *index* of paintings. 5 *Math.* **a** An exponent. **b** A number placed near a radical sign to indicate the order of the root. **c** A subscript or superscript indicating position, order, etc. 6 A number that is a function of and which represents a set of data: the air-pollution *index.* 7 A mark [☞] employed to direct attention. —*v.t.* 1 To provide with an index. 2 To enter in an index. 3 To indicate; mark. [L]

In·dex (in′deks) *n.* In the Roman Catholic Church, a list of books that cannot be read without special permission.

in·dex·a·tion (in′dek·sā′shən) *n.* The adjustment of income, prices, taxes, interest payments, etc. according to a rise or fall in the cost-of-living index.

index finger The forefinger: so called from its universal use as a pointer or indicator.

In·di·a (in′dē·ə) *n.* A republic of the Commonwealth of Nations located on a subcontinent of s Asia, 1,259,797 sq. mi., cap. New Delhi.

India ink 1 A black pigment composed of a mixture of lampblack with gelatin and water, used in drawing and printing. 2 A liquid ink made from this pigment.

In·di·a·man (in′dē·ə·mən) *n. pl.* **·men** (-mən) A large merchant ship formerly used in trade with India.

In·di·an (in′dē·ən) *n.* 1 A member of any of the aboriginal races of North America (**American Indians**), South America, and the West Indies. 2 A citizen or native of India. 3 A citizen or native of the East Indies. —*adj.* 1 Of or pertaining to the aboriginal races of North America, South America, or the West Indies, or any of their languages. 2 Of or pertaining to India, its peoples, or any of their languages, esp. Hindi. 3 Of or pertaining to the East Indies, its peoples, or any of their languages.

Indian club A bottle-shaped wooden club used in gymnastic exercises.

Indian corn CORN (defs. 1 & 2).

Indian file SINGLE FILE.

Indian giver *Informal* One who gives a present and then wants it back.

Indian meal CORNMEAL.

Indian pipe A saprophytic forest plant lacking leaves and chlorophyll, having a single flower on an unbranched stem.

Indian pudding A pudding made with cornmeal, milk, and molasses.

Indian summer A period of mild weather, usu. occurring after the first frosts in late autumn.

Indian tobacco An annual weedy plant with hairy leaves and small, pale-blue flowers.

India paper 1 A thin, yellowish, absorbent printing paper, used in taking the prints from engraved plates. 2 A thin, tough, and opaque printing paper, used for Bibles, etc.

India rubber Unvulcanized rubber derived from latex.

In·dic (in′dik) *adj.* Pertaining to India, its peoples, languages, and culture; Indian. —*n.* A branch of the Indo-Iranian subfamily of Indo-European languages, including Sanskrit, Hindi, Romany, etc.

in·di·cate (in′də·kāt) *v.t.* **·cat·ed, ·cat·ing** 1 To be or give a sign of: Those clouds *indicate* rain. 2 To point out; direct attention to: to *indicate* the correct page. 3 To express or make known, esp. briefly or indirectly. 4 To show or suggest the need for. [< L *in-* in + *dicare* point out, proclaim] —**in′di·ca·to′ry** (-kə·tôr′ē, -tō′rē) *adj.* —**Syn.** 1 betoken, mean, signify. 2 designate. 3 imply.

in·di·ca·tion (in′də·kā′shən) *n.* 1 The act of indicating. 2 That which indicates. 3 A degree or reading as shown on an indicator.

in·dic·a·tive (in·dik′ə·tiv) *adj.* 1 Serving to indicate or signify. 2 *Gram.* Of or pertaining to a mood in which an act or condition is stated or questioned as an actual fact, rather than as a potentiality or an unrealized condition. —*n. Gram.* The indicative mood, or a verb in this mood. —**in·dic′a·tive·ly** *adv.*

in·di·ca·tor (in′də·kā′tər) *n.* 1 One who or that which indicates or points out. 2 Any device or apparatus that indicates the amount, condition, or position of something. 3 *Chem.* A substance that reveals states of acidity, oxidation, etc. by changing color under known conditions.

in·di·ces (in′də·sēz) *n.pl.* of INDEX.

in·dict (in·dīt′) *v.t.* 1 *Law* To prefer an indictment against. 2 To charge with a crime. [< AF *enditer* make known, inform] —**in·dict′a·ble** *adj.* —**indict′er, in·dict′or** *n.*

in·dict·ment (in·dīt′mənt) *n.* 1 The act of indicting, or the state of being indicted. 2 A formal written charge of crime, presented by a grand jury on oath to a court.

in·dif·fer·ence (in·dif′ər·əns, -rəns) *n.* The state or quality of being indifferent.

in·dif·fer·ent (in·dif′ər·ənt, -rənt) *adj.* 1 Having no inclination, concern, or interest; apathetic. 2 Only average or ordinary in size, excellence, etc.; without distinction. 3 Without any preference; neutral. 4 Having little or no importance or value. [< L *indifferens* making no difference] —**in·dif′fer·ent·ly** *adv.*

in·dig·e·nous (in·dij′ə·nəs) *adj.* 1 Originating naturally in a (specified) place or country; native. 2 Innate; inherent. [< L *indigena* native] —**in·dig′e·nous·ly** *adv.* —**in·dig′e·nous·ness** *n.*

in·di·gent (in′də·jənt) *adj.* Needy; poor. [< L *indigere* to lack, want] —**in′di·gence, in′di·gen·cy** *n.* —**in′di·gent·ly** *adv.*

in·di·gest·i·ble (in′dī·jes′tə·bəl) *adj.* Not digestible; difficult to digest. —**in′di·gest′i·bil′i·ty, in′di·gest′i·ble·ness** *n.* —**in′di·gest′i·bly** *adv.*

in·di·ges·tion (in′dī·jes′chən) *n.* 1 Difficult or defective digestion of food. 2 An instance of indigestion.

in·dig·nant (in·dig′nənt) *adj.* Having or showing indignation. —**in·dig′nant·ly** *adv.*

in·dig·na·tion (in′dig·nā′shən) *n.* Anger, esp. at something unjust, mean, or base. [< L *indignari* think unworthy]

in·dig·ni·ty (in·dig′nə·tē) *n. pl.* **·ties** Something that tends to degrade or mortify; an insult; affront.

in·di·go (in′di·gō) *n.* 1 A blue dye obtained from certain plants or synthetically produced. 2 A deep violet blue. Also **indigo blue.** 3 A plant yielding indigo. —*adj.* Deep violet blue: also **in′di·go-blue′** (-blo͞o′). [< Gk. *Indikon (pharmakon)* Indian (dye)]

indigo bunting A North American finch, the male of indigo-blue color. Also **indigo bird.**

in·di·rect (in′də·rekt′) *adj.* 1 Not straight or direct: an *indirect* route. 2 Not open, honest, or straightforward: an *indirect* answer to a question. 3 Not directly intended or related; secondary: an *indirect* result. 4 Not in the exact words of the speaker or source. —**in′di·rect′ly** *adv.* —**in′di·rect′ness** *n.*

indirect discourse *Gram.* Language reported or quoted but with changes made in person or tense, as in *He said he would go.*

in·di·rec·tion (in′də·rek′shən) *n.* 1 Indirect course, action, practice, or method. 2 Dishonest means; deceit.

indirect lighting Lighting that is reflected or diffused to give a minimum of glare and shadow.

indirect object *Gram.* The person or thing that receives the secondary or indirect action of the verb, as *him* in *She gave him the pie.*

indirect tax A tax paid for by one person, as an importer, but ultimately paid for by the consumer in the form of a higher market price.

in·dis·cern·i·ble (in′di·sûr′nə·bəl, -zûr-) *adj.* Not able to be discerned; not easily perceived. —**in′dis·cern′i·bly** *adv.*

in·dis·creet (in′dis·krēt′) *adj.* Lacking discretion; imprudent. —**in′dis·creet′ly** *adv.* —**in′dis·creet′ness** *n.* —**Syn.** tactless, undiplomatic, blunt.

in·dis·crete (in′dis·krēt′) *adj.* Not discrete.

in·dis·cre·tion (in′dis·kresh′ən) *n.* 1 The state of being indiscreet. 2 An indiscreet act, word, etc.

in·dis·crim·i·nate (in′dis·krim′ə·nit) *adj.* 1 Showing no discrimination; careless, casual, or promiscuous: an *indiscriminate* collector of bric-à-brac. 2 Mingled in confusion; random. —**in′dis·crim′i·nate·ly** *adv.* —**in′dis·crim′i·nat′ing** *adj.* —**in′dis·crim′i·na′tion** *n.*

in·dis·pen·sa·ble (in′dis·pen′sə·bəl) *adj.* Not to be dispensed with; absolutely necessary. —*n.* An indispensable person or thing. —**in′dis·pen′sa·bil′i·ty, in′dis·pen′sa·ble·ness** *n.* —**in′dis·pen′sa·bly** *adv.*

in·dis·pose (in′dis·pōz′) *v.t.* **·posed, ·pos·ing** 1 To make unwilling or averse; disincline. 2 To make unfit; disqualify. 3 To make ill or ailing.

in·dis·posed (in′dis·pōzd′) *adj.* 1 Ill; unwell. 2 Disinclined; unwilling. —**in′dis·posed′ness** (-pōzd′-, -pō′zid-) *n.*

in·dis·po·si·tion (in′dis·pə·zish′ən) *n.* 1 Slight illness. 2 Unwillingness; disinclination.

in·dis·put·a·ble (in′dis·pyo͞o′tə·bəl, in·dis′pyo͞o·tə·bəl) *adj.* Incapable of being disputed; unquestionable. —**in′dis·put′a·bil′i·ty, in′dis·put′a·ble·ness** *n.* —**in′dis·put′a·bly** *adv.*

in·dis·sol·u·ble (in′di·sol′yə·bəl) *adj.* 1 That cannot be dissolved, destroyed, or disintegrated. 2 Perpetually binding. —**in′dis·sol′u·bil′i·ty, in′dis·sol′u·ble·ness** *n.* —**in′dis·sol′u·bly** *adv.*

in·dis·tinct (in′dis·tingkt′) *adj.* 1 Not clearly distinguishable or separable by the senses; dim; vague. 2 Not well-defined or clear to the intellect; obscure; uncertain. —**in′dis·tinct′ly** *adv.* —**in′dis·tinct′ness** *n.* —**Syn.** 1 cloudy, faint, unclear, blurry, bleary. 2 abstruse, confused, undefined, vague.

in·dis·tin·guish·a·ble (in′dis·ting′gwish·ə·bəl) *adj.* 1 Not capable of being distinguished, as in size or appearance, from something else. 2 Not distinct; difficult to perceive clearly. —**in′dis·tin·guish·a·bil′i·ty, in′dis·tin′guish·a·ble·ness** *n.* —**in′dis·tin′guish·a·bly** *adv.*

in·dite (in·dīt′) *v.t.* **·dit·ed, ·dit·ing** To put into words or writing; write; compose. [< L *in-* in + *dictare* declare] —**in·dite′ment, in·dit′er** *n.*

in·di·um (in′dē·əm) *n.* A rare metallic element (symbol In), found mainly in zinc ores. [< NL *indicum* indigo]

in·di·vid·u·al (in′də·vij′o͞o·əl) *adj.* 1 Existing as an entity; single; particular. 2 Designed or intended for a single person or thing. 3 Pertaining, belonging, or peculiar to one particular person or thing. 4 Having peculiar or distinctive characteristics: an *individual* style. —*n.* A single being or thing; esp., a particular human being. [< L in- not + *dividuus* divisible] • The use of *individual* as a noun to refer to one human being should be avoided except when a person is to be distinguished from others in a group: *Two individuals stepped forward to volunteer.* Even in such a context, *people* may be preferred as being less pretentious.

in·di·vid·u·al·ism (in′də·vij′o͞o·əl·iz′əm) *n.* 1 The quality of being individual or separate. 2 Personal independence in action, character, or interest. 3 A personal peculiarity; idiosyncrasy. 4 A theory or doctrine in ethics and politics that stresses the supreme importance of the individual. 5 Egoism. —**in′di·vid′u·al·ist** *n.* —**in′di·vid′u·al·is′tic** *adj.*

in·di·vid·u·al·i·ty (in′də·vij′o͞o·al′ə·tē) *n. pl.* **·ties** 1 Something that distinguishes one person or thing from others. 2 Distinctive character or personality. 3 The quality or state of existing separately. 4 An individual.

in·di·vid·u·al·ize (in′də·vij′o͞o·əl·īz′) *v.t.* **·ized, ·iz·ing** 1 To make individual; distinguish. 2 To treat, mention, or consider individually. —**in′di·vid′u·al·i·za′tion** (-ə·zā′shən, -ī·zā′-) *n.*

in·di·vid·u·al·ly (in′də·vij′o͞o·əl·ē) *adv.* 1 As a single person or thing; separately: to greet each guest *individually; individually* wrapped candies. 2 Having individual characteristics; distinctively.

in·di·vis·i·ble (in′də·viz′ə·bəl) *adj.* Not divisible; incapable of being divided. —**in′di·vis′i·bil′i·ty** *n.* —**in′di·vis′i·bly** *adv.*

In·do·chi·na (in′dō·chī′nə) *n.* **1** The SE peninsula of Asia,

Indochina

including Burma, Khmer Republic (Cambodia), Laos, Malaysia, Thailand, North Vietnam, and South Vietnam. **2** The E part of the peninsula, formerly under French domination, including Khmer Republic, Laos, North Vietnam, and South Vietnam.

In·do-Chi·nese (in′dō·chī·nēz′, -nēs′) *n. pl.* **·nese 1** A native or citizen of Indochina. **2** A member of the Mongoloid peoples living in Indochina. *—adj.* Of or pertaining to Indochina, its peoples, or their languages.

in·doc·tri·nate (in·dok′trə·nāt) *v.t.* **·nat·ed, ·nat·ing 1** To instruct in doctrines, principles, etc. **2** To instruct; teach. [< LL *in-* into + *doctrinare* teach] **—in·doc′tri·na′tion, in·doc′tri·na′tor** *n.*

In·do-Eu·ro·pe·an (in′dō·yŏŏr′ə·pē′ən) *n.* A very extensive family of languages comprising most of the languages of Europe and many of India and SW Asia. The principal subfamilies are Hellenic, Italic, Celtic, Germanic, Indo-Iranian, Armenian, Albanian, and Balto-Slavic. *—adj.* Of or pertaining to the Indo-European family of languages, or to the peoples speaking them.

In·do-Ger·man·ic (in′dō·jər·man′ik) *n., adj.* Indo-European: the German term.

in·do·lent (in′də·lənt) *adj.* Averse to exertion; habitually inactive or idle. [< L *in-* not + *dolere* feel pain] **—in′do·lence** *n.* **—in′do·lent·ly** *adv.*

in·dom·i·ta·ble (in·dom′i·tə·bəl) *adj.* Not easily subdued or disheartened; unconquerable. [< L *in-* not + *domitus* tamed] **—in·dom′i·ta·ble·ness** *n.* **—in·dom′i·ta·bly** *adv.*

In·do·ne·sia (in′dō·nē′zhə, -shə) *n.* A republic of SE Asia, comprising several large and numerous small islands, 735,268 sq. mi., cap. Djakarta.

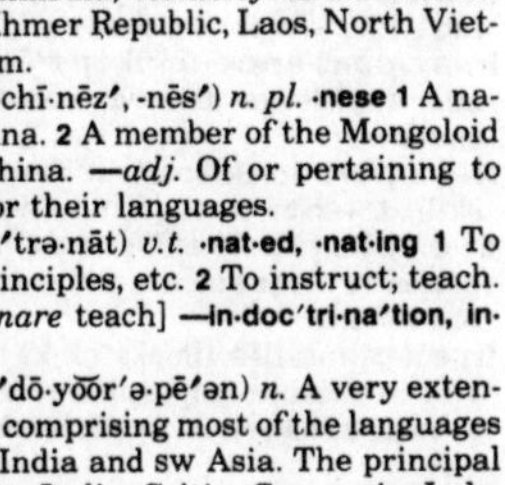

In·do·ne·sian (in′dō·nē′zhən, -shən) *n.* **1** A native or citizen of Indonesia. **2** The language of Indonesia, officially named **Ba·ha·sa Indonesia** (bä·hä′sə), based on Malay. *—adj.* Of or pertaining to Indonesia, its peoples, or their languages.

in·door (in′dôr′, -dōr′) *adj.* **1** Being, living, done, etc., inside a building or house. **2** Of or pertaining to the inside of a building or house.

in·doors (in′dôrz′, -dōrz′) *adv.* In or toward the inside of a building or house.

in·dorse (in·dôrs′) *v.t.* **·dorsed, ·dors·ing** ENDORSE. **—in·dorse′ment** *n.*

In·dra (in′drə) In early Hindu mythology, the god of the firmament and of rain.

in·du·bi·ta·ble (in·dyōō′bə·tə·bəl) *adj.* Not open to doubt; unquestionable; certain. [< L *in-* not + *dubitare* to doubt] **—in·du′bi·ta·ble·ness** *n.* **—in·du′bi·ta·bly** *adv.* **—Syn.** indisputable, manifest, sure, undeniable.

in·duce (in·dyōōs′) *v.t.* **·duced, ·duc·ing 1** To lead on to a specific action, belief, etc.; persuade. **2** To bring on; cause: a sickness *induced* by fatigue. **3** *Electr.* To produce by a process of induction. **4** To reach as a conclusion by an inductive process of reasoning. [< L *in-* in + *ducere* to lead] **—in·duc′er** *n.* **—in·duc′i·ble** *adj.*

in·duce·ment (in·dyōōs′mənt) *n.* **1** An incentive; motive. **2** The act of inducing.

in·duct (in·dukt′) *v.t.* **1** To install formally in an office, benefice, etc. **2** To introduce; initiate. **3** To bring into a military service. [< L *inducere* lead in]

in·duc·tance (in·duk′təns) *n.* **1** The property of an electric device or circuit whereby a changing current in itself or a circuit nearby produces a voltage in itself. **2** The measure of this property. **3** An ideal device whose only property is inductance.

in·duc·tee (in′duk·tē′) *n.* One inducted into military service.

in·duc·tion (in·duk′shən) *n.* **1** The act or process of inducting or the state of being inducted; initiation; installation. **2** The process of arriving at a general conclusion from observation of particular facts; also, the conclusion so arrived at. **3** The bringing forward of separate facts as evidence in order to prove a general statement. **4** *Electr.* The production of magnetization or electrification in a body by the mere proximity of a magnetic field or electric charge, or of an electric current in a conductor by the variation of the magnetic field in its vicinity. **—in·duc′tion·al** *adj.*

induction coil *Electr.* A transformer in which pulses of direct current fed into the primary winding induce a high alternating voltage in the secondary, used in automotive ignition systems.

in·duc·tive (in·duk′tiv) *adj.* **1** Persuasive; inducing. **2** Of, using, or produced by logical induction. **3** Introductory. **4** Of or produced by electrical or magnetic induction. **—in·duc′tive·ly** *adv.* **—in·duc′tive·ness** *n.*

in·duc·tor (in·duk′tər) *n.* **1** One who or that which inducts. **2** *Electr.* Any device whose principal property is its inductance

in·due (in·dyōō′) *v.t.* **·dued, ·du·ing** ENDUE.

in·dulge (in·dulj′) *v.* **·dulged, ·dulg·ing** *v.t.* **1** To gratify, as desires or whims. **2** To gratify the desires, whims, etc., of. *—v.i.* **3** To yield to or gratify one's desires; indulge oneself; with *in.* [< L *indulgere* be kind to, concede] **—in·dulg′er** *n.* **—in·dulg′ing·ly** *adv.*

in·dul·gence (in·dul′jəns) *n.* **1** The act of indulging or of being indulgent. **2** That which is indulged in. **3** A privilege or favor. **4** Permission to defer payment, as of a note. **5** In the Roman Catholic Church, remission of the temporal punishment still due to sin after sacramental absolution. Also **in·dul′gen·cy.**

in·dul·gent (in·dul′jənt) *adj.* Prone to indulge; lenient. **—in·dul′gent·ly** *adv.*

in·du·rate (in′dyōō·rāt) *v.t. & v.i.* **·rat·ed, ·rat·ing 1** To make or become hard. **2** To make or become callous or unsympathetic; harden. *—adj.* (-rit) Hard or hardened: also **in′du·rat′ed.** [< L *indurare* make hard] **—in′du·ra′tion** *n.* **—in′du·ra′tive** *adj.*

in·dus·tri·al (in·dus′trē·əl) *adj.* **1** Of, like, or resulting from industry. **2** Engaged in industry. **3** Used specifically in industry. **4** Of or for workers in industry. *—n.* **1** One engaged in industry. **2** A stock or security issued by an established industry. **—in·dus′tri·al·ly** *adv.*

industrial arts The technical skills used in industry, esp. as subjects of study in schools.

in·dus·tri·al·ism (in·dus′trē·əl·iz′əm) *n.* A social or economic system that results from and is dominated by large-scale industries. —**in·dus′tri·al·ist** *adj., n.*

in·dus·tri·al·ize (in·dus′trē·əl·īz′) *v.t.* **·ized, ·iz·ing** **1** To make industrial: to *industrialize* a village. **2** To make or organize into an industry. —**in·dus′tri·al·i·za′tion** (-ə·zā′·shən, -ī·zā′-) *n.*

industrial relations The relationships between employers and employees.

industrial union A labor union in which membership is open to all workers in a particular industry.

in·dus·tri·ous (in·dus′trē·əs) *adj.* Hard-working; diligent. —**in·dus′tri·ous·ly** *adv.* —**in·dus′tri·ous·ness** *n.* —**Syn.** assiduous, busy, occupied, persevering, sedulous.

in·dus·try (in′dəs·trē) *n. pl.* **·tries** **1** Diligent or constant application to work or business. **2** Any branch of productive work or manufacture; also, the capital or workers employed in it: the steel *industry;* the farming *industry.* **3** The business or the activities of manufacturing as a whole. [< L *industrius* diligent]

in·dwell (in′dwel′) *v.* **·dwelt, ·dwel·ling** *v.t.* To dwell in; inhabit. —*v.i.* To dwell; abide: with *in.* —**in′dwell′er** *n.*

-ine[1] *suffix of adjectives* Like; pertaining to; of the nature of: *marine, canine.* [< L *-inus,* adj. suffix]

-ine[2] *suffix* **1** *Chem.* **a** Used in the names of halogens: *bromine, fluorine.* **b** Used to indicate an alkaloid or nitrogen base: *morphine, amine.* **c** Var. of -IN. **2** Used in names of commercial products: *gasoline.* [Special use of -INE[1]]

-ine[3] *suffix* Like; resembling: *crystalline.* [L < Gk. *-inos*]

in·e·bri·ate (in·ē′brē·āt) *v.t.* **·at·ed, ·at·ing** **1** To make drunk; intoxicate. **2** To exhilarate; excite. —*n.* (-it, -āt) A habitual drunkard. —*adj.* (-it, -āt) Intoxicated: also **in·e′·bri·at′ed.** [< L *in-* thoroughly + *ebriare* make drunk] —**in·e′·bri·a′tion** *n.*

in·e·bri·e·ty (in′ē·brī′ə·tē) *n.* Drunkenness.

in·ed·i·ble (in·ed′ə·bəl) *adj.* Not edible; not fit to eat. —**in·ed′i·bil′i·ty** *n.*

in·ef·fa·ble (in·ef′ə·bəl) *adj.* **1** Too overwhelming for expression in words; indescribable. **2** Too lofty or sacred to be spoken. [< L *in-* not + *effabilis* utterable] —**in·ef′fa·bil′i·ty** *n.* —**in·ef′fa·bly** *adv.*

in·ef·fec·tive (in′i·fek′tiv) *adj.* **1** Not effective. **2** Incompetent. —**in′ef·fec′tive·ly** *adv.* —**in′ef·fec′tive·ness** *n.*

in·ef·fec·tu·al (in′i·fek′cho͞o·əl) *adj.* **1** Not effectual. **2** Unsuccessful; fruitless. —**in′ef·fec′tu·al′i·ty, in′ef·fec′tu·al·ness** *n.* —**in′ef·fec′tu·al·ly** *adv.*

in·ef·fi·cient (in′i·fish′ənt) *adj.* **1** Not efficient or productive as regards expenditure of time, energy, etc. **2** Not capable; incompetent. —**in′ef·fi′cien·cy** *n.* —**in′ef·fi′cient·ly** *adv.*

in·e·las·tic (in′i·las′tik) *adj.* Not elastic; inflexible; unyielding; unadaptable. —**in·e·las·tic·i·ty** (in′i·las′tis′ə·tē) *n.*

in·el·e·gant (in·el′ə·gənt) *adj.* **1** Not elegant; lacking in beauty, polish, grace, refinement, good taste, or the like. **2** Coarse; crude. —**in·el′e·gance, in·el′e·gan·cy** *n.* —**in·el′e·gant·ly** *adv.*

in·el·i·gi·ble (in·el′ə·jə·bəl) *adj.* Not eligible; disqualified; unsuitable. —*n.* An ineligible person. —**in·el′i·gi·bil′i·ty** *n.* —**in·el′i·gi·bly** *adv.*

in·e·luc·ta·ble (in′i·luk′tə·bəl) *adj.* Not to be escaped or avoided; inevitable. [< L *in-* not + *eluctabilis* surmountable] —**in′e·luc′ta·bil′i·ty** *n.* —**in·e·luc′ta·bly** *adv.*

in·ept (in·ept′) *adj.* **1** Not suitable or fit. **2** Absurd; foolish. **3** Clumsy; awkward. [< L *in-* not + *aptus* fit] —**in·ep′ti·tude, in·ept′ness** *n.* —**in·ept′ly** *adv.*

in·e·qual·i·ty (in′i·kwol′ə·tē) *n. pl.* **·ties** **1** The condition of being unequal; also, an instance of this. **2** Disparity in social position, opportunity, etc. **3** Lack of evenness or proportion, variableness: *inequalities* of surface. **4** *Math.* A statement indicating that two quantities are not equal, or esp. that one is greater than the other.

in·eq·ui·ta·ble (in·ek′wə·tə·bəl) *adj.* Not fair or just. —**in·eq′ui·ta·bly** *adv.*

in·eq·ui·ty (in·ek′wə·tē) *n. pl.* **·ties** **1** Want of equity; injustice. **2** An instance of injustice.

in·ert (in·ûrt′) *adj.* **1** Without any inherent power to move. **2** Very slow; sluggish. **3** Devoid of reactive properties: *inert* gas. [< L *iners*] —**in·ert′ly** *adv.* —**in·ert′ness** *n.*

in·er·tia (in·ûr′shə) *n.* **1** The state of being inert; sluggishness. **2** *Physics* The tendency of any material body to maintain its velocity indefinitely unless accelerated or decelerated by some force. [L, idleness] —**in·er′tial** *adj.*

in·es·cap·a·ble (in′ə·skā′pə·bəl) *adj.* Inevitable; unavoidable. —**in′es·cap′a·bly** *adv.*

in·es·sen·tial (in′ə·sen′shəl) *adj.* Not essential; unnecessary. —*n.* Something not essential.

in·es·ti·ma·ble (in·es′tə·mə·bəl) *adj.* That cannot be measured or estimated because of value, greatness, etc. —**in·es′ti·ma·bly** *adv.*

in·ev·i·ta·ble (in·ev′ə·tə·bəl) *adj.* **1** That cannot be prevented; unavoidable. **2** Customary; usual. [< L *in-* not + *evitare* avoid] —**in·ev′i·ta·bil′i·ty, in·ev′i·ta·ble·ness** *n.* —**in·ev′i·ta·bly** *adv.*

in·ex·act (in′ig·zakt′) *adj.* Not exact, accurate, or true. —**in′ex·act′i·tude, in′ex·act′ness** *n.* —**in′ex·act′ly** *adv.*

in·ex·cus·a·ble (in′ik·skyo͞o′zə·bəl) *adj.* Impossible to excuse or justify. —**in′ex·cus′a·bil′i·ty** *n.* —**in′ex·cus′a·bly** *adv.*

in·ex·haust·i·ble (in′ig·zôs′tə·bəl) *adj.* **1** Incapable of being exhausted or used up. **2** Incapable of fatigue; tireless. —**in′ex·haust′i·bil′i·ty,** *n.* —**in′ex·haust′i·bly** *adv.*

in·ex·o·ra·ble (in·ek′sər·ə·bəl) *adj.* Not to be moved by entreaty; unyielding. [< L *in-* not + *exorare* move by entreaty] —**in·ex′o·ra·bil′i·ty, in·ex′o·ra·ble·ness** *n.* —**in·ex′o·ra·bly** *adv.*

in·ex·pe·di·ent (in′ik·spē′dē·ənt) *adj.* Not expedient or suitable; impracticable. —**in′ex·pe′di·ence, in′ex·pe′di·en·cy** (*pl.* **·en·cies**) *n.* —**in′ex·pe′di·ent·ly** *adv.*

in·ex·pen·sive (in′ik·spen′siv) *adj.* Not expensive; costing little. —**in′ex·pen′sive·ly** *adv.* —**in′ex·pen′sive·ness** *n.*

in·ex·pe·ri·ence (in′ik·spir′ē·əns) *n.* Lack of the skill and knowledge derived from experience. —**in′ex·pe′ri·enced** *adj.*

in·ex·pert (in·ek′spərt, in′ik·spûrt′) *adj.* Not expert; not skilled. —**in·ex′pert·ly** *adv.* —**in·ex′pert·ness** *n.*

in·ex·pi·a·ble (in·ek′spē·ə·bəl) *adj.* That may not be expiated or made amends for. —**in·ex′pi·a·ble·ness** *n.* —**in·ex′·pi·a·bly** *adv.*

in·ex·plic·a·ble (in·eks′pli·kə·bəl, in′iks·plik′ə·bəl) *adj.* Not explicable; impossible to explain or understand. —**in′ex·pli·ca·bil′i·ty, in′ex·plic′a·ble·ness** *n.* —**in·ex′pli·ca·bly** *adv.*

in·ex·press·i·ble (in′iks·pres′ə·bəl) *adj.* Incapable of being expressed; unutterable. —**in′ex·press′i·bil′i·ty, in′ex·press′i·ble·ness** *n.* —**in′ex·press′i·bly** *adv.*

in·ex·press·ive (in′ik·spres′iv) *adj.* Not expressive; conveying little meaning or expression. —**in′ex·press′ive·ly** *adv.* —**in′ex·press′ive·ness** *n.*

in ex·ten·so (in ik·sten′sō) *Latin* At full length.

in·ex·tin·guish·a·ble (in′ik·sting′gwish·ə·bəl) *adj.* Not to be extinguished or put out. —**in′ex·tin·guish·a·bly** *adv.*

in ex·tre·mis (in iks·trē′mis) *Latin* At the point of death.

in·ex·tri·ca·ble (in·eks′tri·kə·bəl) *adj.* **1** So involved that extrication is impossible. **2** That cannot be disentangled or undone. **3** Impossible to solve. —**in·ex′tri·ca·bil′i·ty, in·ex′tri·ca·ble·ness** *n.* —**in·ex′tri·ca·bly** *adv.*

Inf. Infantry.

inf. below (L *infra*); inferior; infinitive; information.

in·fal·li·ble (in·fal′ə·bəl) *adj.* **1** Incapable of fallacy or error. **2** Not apt to fail; reliable; certain: an *infallible* cure. **3** In Roman Catholic theology, incapable of error in matters relating to faith and morals: said of the Pope speaking *ex cathedra.* —*n.* One who or that which is infallible. —**in·fal′li·bil′i·ty, in·fal′li·ble·ness** *n.* —**in·fal′li·bly** *adv.*

in·fa·mous (in′fə·məs) *adj.* **1** Having an odious reputation; notorious. **2** Involving or deserving infamy. [< L *in-* not + *fama* fame] —**in′fa·mous·ly** *adv.* —**in′fa·mous·ness** *n.*

in·fa·my (in′fə·mē) *n. pl.* **·mies** **1** Total lack of honor or reputation. **2** The state of being infamous. **3** An infamous act.

in·fan·cy (in′fən·sē) *n. pl.* **·cies** **1** The state of being an infant. **2** *Law* The years during which one is a minor. **3** The earliest period in the development of something.

in·fant (in′fənt) *n.* **1** A baby. **2** *Law* A minor; in most states of the U.S., a person under 21 years of age. —*adj.* **1** Of, for, or like infants or infancy. **2** In the earliest state. [< L *in-* not + *fans,* pr.p. of *fari* to talk]

in·fan·ta (in·fan′tə) *n.* 1 A daughter of a Spanish or Portuguese king. 2 The wife of an infante. [Sp., infant]

in·fan·te (in·fan′tā) *n.* A son, except the eldest, of a Spanish or Portuguese king. [Sp., infant]

in·fan·ti·cide (in·fan′tə·sīd) *n.* 1 The murder of a baby. 2 One who murders a baby.

in·fan·tile (in′fən·tīl, -til) *adj.* 1 Of, pertaining to, or characteristic of infants or infancy. 2 In the earliest period of development. Also **in′fan·tine** (-tīn, -tin).

infantile paralysis POLIOMYELITIS.

in·fan·til·ism (in′fən·təl·iz′əm) *n.* Abnormal persistence of infantile mental and physical qualities into adult life.

in·fan·try (in′fən·trē) *n. pl.* **·tries** Soldiers or units of an army that are trained and equipped to fight on foot. [< Ital. *infante* boy, page, foot soldier]

in·fan·try·man (in′fən·trē·mən) *n. pl.* **·men** (-mən) A foot soldier.

in·farc·tion (in·färk′shən) *n.* Death of tissue due to deprivation of blood caused by an obstruction, as in a heart attack. [< L *in-* in + *farcire* to stuff]

in·fat·u·ate (in·fach′o͞o·āt) *v.t.* **·at·ed, ·at·ing** 1 To make foolish or fatuous. 2 To inspire with foolish passion. [< L *in-* very + *fatuus* foolish] **—in·fat′u·a′tion** *n.*

in·fect (in·fekt′) *v.t.* 1 To contaminate with disease-producing organisms. 2 To communicate disease to, as a person, etc. 3 To affect or influence, as with emotion, beliefs, etc., esp. harmfully; taint. [< L *inficere* dip into, stain] **—in·fect′er, in·fec′tor** *n.* **—Syn.** 3 corrupt, debauch, deprave, lead astray, pollute.

in·fec·tion (in·fek′shən) *n.* 1 The act of infecting, esp. the producing of a disease or harmful condition by entrance of disease-producing germs into an organism. 2 Any diseased condition so produced. 3 The communication of a quality, emotion, belief, etc., as by example. 4 That which infects.

in·fec·tious (in·fek′shəs) *adj.* 1 That may be communicated by infection. 2 Capable of causing infection. 3 Tending to spread from one to another: *infectious* laughter. **—in·fec′tious·ly** *adv.* **—in·fec′tious·ness** *n.*

in·fec·tive (in·fek′tiv) *adj.* Causing or capable of causing infection; infectious.

in·fe·lic·i·tous (in′fə·lis′ə·təs) *adj.* Not felicitous, happy, or suitable in application, condition, or result. **—in′fe·lic′i·tous·ly** *adv.* **—in′fe·lic′i·tous·ness** *n.*

in·fe·lic·i·ty (in′fə·lis′ə·tē) *n. pl.* **·ties** 1 The state of being infelicitous; unhappiness. 2 That which is infelicitous, as an inappropriate remark, act, etc.

in·fer (in·fûr′) *v.* **·ferred, ·fer·ring** *v.t.* 1 To conclude by reasoning from evidence or premises; deduce. 2 To involve or imply as a conclusion; give evidence of. 3 To suggest; hint. *—v.i.* 4 To draw inferences. [< L *in-* in + *ferre* carry] **—in·fer′a·ble, in·fer′ri·ble** *adj.* **—in·fer′rer** *n.* • **infer, imply** To *infer* is to make a rational or logical conclusion based on evidence: *I inferred from the absence of cutting teeth that the animal was herbivorous. Imply* may refer to the drawing of a necessary conclusion, and in this sense it is interchangeable with *infer: The possibility of life on other planets implies* (or *infers*) *the presence of amino acids.* But more often *imply* means simply to suggest or hint, and in this sense the use of *infer* (def. 3) should be avoided because it is ambiguous. *She implied that he was scared* is clear, but *She inferred* . . . might mean that she concluded privately that he was scared because of his manner or appearance.

in·fer·ence (in′fər·əns) *n.* 1 The act of inferring. 2 That which is inferred, as a deduction.

in·fer·en·tial (in′fə·ren′shəl) *adj.* Of or deduced by inference. **—in′fer·en′tial·ly** *adv.*

in·fe·ri·or (in·fir′ē·ər) *adj.* 1 Poor or mediocre in quality: an *inferior* meal. 2 Lower in merit, importance, or rank. 3 Situated or placed lower, as certain parts of the body. 4 *Astron.* Between the earth and the sun: an *inferior* planet. *—n.* One who or that which is inferior. [< L *inferus* low]

in·fe·ri·or·i·ty (in·fir′ē·ôr′ə·tē, -or′-) *n.* The state or quality of being inferior.

inferiority complex An exaggerated sense of one's own limitations and incapacities, sometimes compensated for by aggressive behavior.

in·fer·nal (in·fûr′nəl) *adj.* 1 In mythology, of the world of the dead. 2 Of hell. 3 Hellish; diabolical. 4 *Informal* Damned; outrageous. [< L *infernus* situated below] **—in·fer′nal·ly** *adv.*

infernal machine A device maliciously contrived to destroy life or property by explosion.

in·fer·no (in·fûr′nō) *n. pl.* **·nos** 1 The infernal regions; hell. 2 Any place comparable to hell. [Ital.]

in·fer·tile (in·fûr′til) *adj.* Not fertile or productive; sterile; barren. **—in′fer·til′i·ty** *n.*

in·fest (in·fest′) *v.t.* To overrun or spread in large numbers so as to be unpleasant or unsafe. [< L *infestus* hostile] **—in′fes·ta′tion, in·fest′er** *n.*

in·fi·del (in′fi·dəl) *n.* 1 One who does not believe in a particular or the prevailing religion. 2 One who does not believe in any religion. 3 One who does not accept a particular theory, belief, etc. *—adj.* 1 That is an infidel. 2 Of infidels or unbelief. [< L *in-* not + *fidelis* faithful]

in·fi·del·i·ty (in′fi·del′ə·tē) *n. pl.* **·ties** 1 Lack of fidelity, esp. violation of the marriage vow by adultery. 2 Any disloyal act. 3 The state of being an infidel.

in·field (in′fēld′) *n.* 1 The space enclosed within the four base lines of a baseball field. 2 The infielders collectively.

in·field·er (in′fēl′dər) *n.* In baseball, the first, second, and third basemen, the shortstop, and, when fielding the ball, the pitcher and catcher.

in·fight·ing (in′fīt′ing) *n.* 1 Fighting or boxing at close range. 2 Bitter dissension or struggle, esp. between rivals within an organization: political *infighting.* **—in′fight′er** *n.*

in·fil·trate (in·fil′trāt; *esp. for v. defs. 2, 3* in′fil·trāt) *v.* **·trat·ed, ·trat·ing** *v.t.* 1 To cause (a liquid or gas) to pass into or through something. 2 To pass through or into; permeate. 3 *Mil.* To pass through, as enemy lines. *—v.i.* 4 To pass into or through. *—n.* That which infiltrates or has infiltrated. **—in′fil·tra′tion** *n.* **—in·fil′tra·tive** *adj.*

in·fi·nite (in′fə·nit) *adj.* 1 So great as to be immeasurable and unbounded; limitless. 2 All-embracing; absolute: *infinite* love. 3 Very great, numerous, etc.: to take *infinite* pains. 4 *Math.* a Larger than any given number or value; arbitrarily large. b Capable of being arranged in a one-to-one correspondence with a proper subset of itself, as the set of natural numbers. *—n.* That which is infinite. **—the Infinite** God. [< L *in-* not + *finitus* finite] **—in′fi·nite·ly** *adv.* **—in′fi·nite·ness** *n.*

in·fin·i·tes·i·mal (in′fin·ə·tes′ə·məl) *adj.* 1 Too small to be measured or calculated. 2 *Math.* Arbitrarily close to zero in value. *—n.* An infinitesimal quantity. [< L *infinitus* infinite + *-esimus* (after *centesimus* hundredth)] **—in′fin·i·tes′i·mal·ly** *adv.*

in·fin·i·tive (in·fin′ə·tiv) *Gram. adj.* Of, pertaining to, or using the infinitive. *—n.* A verb form expressing action or condition without reference to person, tense, or number, as *to run.* In English, its sign *to* is omitted after most auxiliaries, as in "He should *go* now," but is retained when the infinitive functions as a noun, as in "*To ride* horses was his favorite sport." [< LL *infinitivus* unlimited]

in·fin·i·tude (in·fin′ə·t(y)o͞od) *n.* 1 The quality of being infinite. 2 An infinite quantity.

in·fin·i·ty (in·fin′ə·tē) *n. pl.* **·ties** 1 The quality of being infinite. 2 Something, as space or time, regarded as boundless or endless. 3 *Math.* An infinite number or set. [< L *infinitus* infinite]

in·firm (in·fûrm′) *adj.* 1 Feeble or weak, as from age. 2 Lacking purpose or determination of mind. 3 Not legally secure. [< L *in-* not + *firmus* strong] **—in·firm′ly** *adv.* **—in·firm′ness** *n.* **—Syn.** 1 ailing, fragile, frail, ill, sickly.

in·fir·ma·ry (in·fûr′mər·ē) *n. pl.* **·ries** 1 A place for the treatment of the sick or injured, as in a school, factory, etc.; dispensary. 2 A small hospital.

in·fir·mi·ty (in·fûr′mə·tē) *n. pl.* **·ties** 1 A physical weakness or disability. 2 A defect of personality or character. 3 An infirm condition; feebleness.

in·fix (in·fiks′) *v.t.* 1 To fix or drive in, as by thrusting. 2

To instill; inculcate. 3 *Gram.* To insert (an infix) within a word. —*n.* (in′fiks) *Gram.* A modifying addition inserted in the body of a word. —**in·fix′ion** *n.*

infl. influence; influenced.

in·flame (in·flām′) *v.* **·flamed, ·flam·ing** *v.t.* 1 To set on fire. 2 To excite to violent emotion or activity. 3 To excite or make more intense, as anger or lust. 4 To cause inflammation in; heat morbidly. —*v.i.* 5 To catch fire. 6 To become excited or aroused. 7 To become inflamed by infection, etc. [< L *in-* in + *flammare* to flame] —**in·flam′er** *n.*

in·flam·ma·ble (in·flam′ə·bəl) *adj.* 1 Readily set on fire; combustible; flammable. 2 Easily excited or roused to passion. —*n.* A combustible substance. —**in·flam′ma·bil′i·ty, in·flam′ma·ble·ness** *n.* —**in·flam′ma·bly** *adv.*

in·flam·ma·tion (in′flə·mā′shən) *n.* 1 *Pathol.* A localized reaction to infection, injury, etc., characterized by heat, redness, swelling, and pain. 2 The act of inflaming.

in·flam·ma·to·ry (in·flam′ə·tôr′ē, -tō′rē) *adj.* 1 Calculated to arouse passions, riot, violence, etc.; seditious. 2 Inducing or provoking inflammation.

in·flate (in·flāt′) *v.* **·flat·ed, ·flat·ing** *v.t.* 1 To fill with gas or air so as to distend or expand; blow up. 2 To increase or puff up: to *inflate* one's pride. 3 To increase unduly, esp. so that the nominal value exceeds the real: to *inflate* currency or prices. —*v.i.* 4 To become inflated. [< L *in-* in + *flare* blow] —**in·fla′ta·ble** *adj.* —**in·fla′ter, in·fla′tor** *n.*

in·fla·tion (in·flā′shən) *n.* 1 The act of inflating, or the state of being inflated. 2 An increase of currency in circulation or an overissue of credit, resulting in a rise of price levels when or if demand for goods exceeds supply. 3 The resulting rise in price levels. —**in·fla′tion·ar′y** *adj.*

in·flect (in·flekt′) *v.t.* 1 *Gram.* To give the inflections of (a word); conjugate or decline. 2 To vary the pitch of (the voice); modulate. 3 To turn inward or aside; deflect; curve. [< L *in-* in + *flectere* to bend]

in·flec·tion (in·flek′shən) *n.* 1 A bending or bend; curvature; angle. 2 *Gram.* **a** A pattern of change undergone by words to express grammatical and syntactical relations, as of case, number, gender, person, tense, etc. **b** An inflectional element. **c** An inflected form. 3 A change in pitch or intensity in the voice. *Brit. sp.* **in·flex′ion.**

in·flec·tion·al (in·flek′shən·əl) *adj.* Of, having, relating to, or showing grammatical inflection. *Brit. sp.* **in·flex′ion·al.** —**in·flec′tion·al·ly** *adv.*

in·flex·i·ble (in·flek′sə·bəl) *adj.* 1 Unyielding; firm; stubborn. 2 Incapable of being physically bent; rigid. 3 That cannot be altered or varied: the *inflexible* laws of nature. —**in·flex′i·bil′i·ty, in·flex′i·ble·ness** *n.* —**in·flex′i·bly** *adv.* —**Syn.** 1 dogged, obstinate, steadfast. 2 stiff. 3 fixed, unalterable.

in·flict (in·flikt′) *v.t.* 1 To cause (pain, wounds, etc.), as with a blow. 2 To impose, as punishment. 3 To impose as if by force: to *inflict* one's views on the public. [< L *in-* on + *fligere* to strike] —**in·flict′er, in·flic′tor** *n.* —**in·flic′tive** *adj.*

in·flic·tion (in·flik′shən) *n.* 1 The act or process of inflicting. 2 That which is inflicted.

in·flo·res·cence (in′flə·res′əns) *n.* 1 The act of flowering. 2 The arrangement of flowers on a plant stem. 3 A single flower; also, flowers collectively. [< LL *inflorescere* come into flower] —**in′flo·res′cent** *adj.*

in·flow (in′flō′) *n.* The act of flowing in, or that which flows in.

in·flu·ence (in′flo͞o·əns) *n.* 1 The power of a person or thing to produce an effect upon others, often indirectly or intangibly. 2 The effect of such power. 3 Power arising from social, financial, moral, or similar authority. 4 A person or thing that has or exerts influence. —*v.t.* **·enced, ·enc·ing** To have or exert influence on. [< L *in-* in + *fluere* to flow] —**in′flu·enc′er** *n.*

in·flu·en·tial (in′flo͞o·en′shəl) *adj.* Having or exercising great influence or power; effective. —**in′flu·en′tial·ly** *adv.*

in·flu·en·za (in′flo͞o·en′zə) *n.* An acute, sometimes epidemic, infectious disease of varying severity caused by a virus and characterized by inflammation of the air passages, fever, and nervous and muscular prostration. [< L *influere* flow in] —**in′flu·en′zal** *adj.*

in·flux (in′fluks′) *n.* 1 A continuous flowing or pouring in. 2 The mouth of a river. [< L *influere* flow in]

in·fold (in·fōld′) *v.t.* ENFOLD.

in·form (in·fôrm′) *v.t.* 1 To give (someone) facts or information; make something known to. 2 To give character to; animate. —*v.i.* 3 To give information, esp. to accuse or charge others, usu. for gain: with *on* or *against.* [< L *informare* give form to, describe.] —**Syn.** 1 advise, apprise, acquaint, notify.

in·for·mal (in·fôr′məl) *adj.* 1 Not in the usual or prescribed form; unofficial. 2 Without ceremony or formality; casual. 3 Not requiring formal clothes. 4 Describing a manner of speech or writing characteristic of familiar conversation. —**in·for′mal·ly** *adv.*

in·for·mal·i·ty (in′fôr·mal′ə·tē) *n. pl.* **·ties** 1 Absence of regular or official form. 2 An informal act or proceeding.

in·form·ant (in·fôr′mənt) *n.* 1 One who imparts information. 2 A native speaker of a language whose speech is used by linguists in recording and studying linguistic forms, sounds, etc.

in·for·ma·tion (in′fər·mā′shən) *n.* 1 Knowledge acquired or derived. 2 Timely or specific knowledge. 3 In computer science: **a** Anything that reduces uncertainty. **b** A numerical measure of the degree to which uncertainty is reduced. **c** Coded material fed to a computer or communications system. —**in′for·ma′tion·al** *adj.*

information retrieval The methods by which recorded and stored information, as that in a computer, may be retrieved and made use of when required. —**in′for·ma′tion-re·triev′al** *adj.*

in·form·a·tive (in·fôr′mə·tiv) *adj.* Instructive; affording information. Also **in·form′a·to′ry.**

in·form·er (in·fôr′mər) *n.* 1 One who makes a complaint or accusations against others, usu. for gain. 2 One who imparts information.

infra- *prefix* Below; beneath; on the lower part: *infrastructure.* [L *infra*]

in·frac·tion (in·frak′shən) *n.* The act of breaking or violating a rule, law, agreement, etc. [< L *infringere* destroy]

in·fran·gi·ble (in·fran′jə·bəl) *adj.* 1 Not breakable or capable of being broken into parts. 2 Not to be infringed or violated. [< L *in-* not + *frangere* to break] —**in·fran′gi·bil′i·ty, in·fran′gi·ble·ness** *n.* —**in·fran′gi·bly** *adv.*

in·fra·red (in′frə·red′) *adj.* Designating electromagnetic waves having wavelengths exceeding those of visible red light but shorter than those of radio waves.

in·fra·struc·ture (in′frə·struk′chər) *n.* The essential elements of a structure, system, plan of operations, etc.

in·fre·quent (in·frē′kwənt) *adj.* Occurring at widely separate intervals; uncommon. —**in·fre′quence, in·fre′quen·cy** *n.* —**in·fre′quent·ly** *adv.*

in·fringe (in·frinj′) *v.t.* **·fringed, ·fring·ing** To break or disregard the terms or requirements of, as an oath or law; violate. —**infringe on** (or **upon**) To transgress or trespass on rights or privileges. [< L *in-* in + *frangere* to break] —**in·fringe′ment, in·fring′er** *n.*

in·fu·ri·ate (in·fyo͝or′ē·āt) *v.t.* **·at·ed, ·at·ing** To make furious. —*adj.* (-it) Infuriated; enraged. [< L *in-* in + *furia* rage] —**in·fu′ri·ate·ly, in·fu′ri·at′ing·ly** *adv.* —**in·fu′ri·a′tion** *n.*

in·fuse (in·fyo͞oz′) *v.t.* **·fused, ·fus·ing** 1 To instill or inculcate, as principles or qualities. 2 To inspire; imbue; with *with.* 3 To pour in or upon. 4 To steep or soak so as to make an extract: to *infuse* tea leaves. [< L *in-* in + *fundere* pour] —**in·fus′er** *n.*

in·fus·i·ble (in·fyo͞o′zə·bəl) *adj.* Incapable of or resisting fusion or melting. —**in·fus′i·bil′i·ty, in·fus′i·ble·ness** *n.*

in·fu·sion (in·fyo͞o′zhən) *n.* 1 The act of infusing, imbuing, or pouring in. 2 That which is infused. 3 The process of steeping or soaking any substance in a liquid to extract its properties without boiling. 4 The liquid extract so obtained.

in·fu·so·ri·an (in′fyo͞o·sô′rē·ən, -sō′rē-) *n.* Any of various aquatic protozoans found in infusions of decaying matter, that move by vibrating cilia. —*adj.* Of or pertaining to such protozoans.

-ing[1] *suffix* 1 The act or art of doing the action expressed in the root verb: *hunting.* 2 The product or result of an action: a *painting.* 3 Material for: *flooring.* 4 That which performs the action of the root verb: a *covering.* [< OE *-ung, -ing*]

-ing[2] *suffix* Used in the present participle of verbs and in participial adjectives: He is *talking;* an *eating* apple. [< OE *-ende*]

in·gen·ious (in·jēn′yəs) *adj.* 1 Possessed of skill in making or inventing. 2 Cleverly conceived or made. [< L *ingenium* natural ability] —**in·gen′ious·ly** *adv.* —**in·gen′ious·ness** *n.* —**Syn.** 1 adroit, clever, creative, resourceful.

in·gé·nue (an′zhə·nōō′, än′-, -jə-; *Fr.* aṅ·zhā·nü′) *n. pl.* **·nues** (-nōōz′; *Fr.* -nü′) 1 A young woman or girl who is artless, ingenuous, or innocent. 2 In the theater, the role of such a person. 3 An actress who fills such a role. Also **in′ge·nue.** [< L *ingenuus* natural]

in·ge·nu·i·ty (in′jə·nʸōō′ə·tē) *n.* 1 Cleverness in making or originating. 2 Originality of execution or design.

in·gen·u·ous (in·jen′yōō·əs) *adj.* 1 Free from dissimulation; frank. 2 Innocent; artless. [< L *ingenuus* inborn, natural, frank] —**in·gen′u·ous·ly** *adv.* —**in·gen′u·ous·ness** *n.*

in·gest (in·jest′) *v.t.* To swallow or absorb, as a food, poison, etc. [< L *in-* in + *gerere* carry] —**in·ges′tion** *n.* —**in·ges′tive** *adj.*

in·gle·nook (ing′gəl·nŏŏk′) *n.* A corner by the fireplace. [Scot.]

in·glo·ri·ous (in·glôr′ē·əs, -glō′rē-) *adj.* 1 Characterized by failure or disgrace. 2 Without glory; obscure. —**in·glo′ri·ous·ly** *adv.* —**in·glo′ri·ous·ness** *n.*

in·go·ing (in′gō′ing) *adj.* Entering; going in.

in·got (ing′gət) *n.* A mass of cast metal from the crucible, as a bar of gold. [< IN-² + OE *geoton* pour]

in·graft (in·graft′, -gräft′) *v.t.* ENGRAFT.

in·grain (in·grān′) *v.t.* To fix deeply; impress indelibly upon the mind or character.

in·grained (in·grānd′) *adj.* 1 Deeply rooted; firmly fixed. 2 Thorough; inveterate.

in·grate (in′grāt) *n.* One who is ungrateful. [< L *in-* not + *gratus* pleasing]

in·gra·ti·ate (in·grā′shē·āt) *v.t.* **·at·ed, ·at·ing** To bring (oneself) into the favor or confidence of others. —**in·gra′ti·at′ing·ly** *adv.* —**in·gra′ti·a′tion** *n.* —**in·gra′ti·a·to′ry** (-ə·tôr′ē, -tō′rē) *adj.* [< L *in gratiam* in favor]

in·grat·i·tude (in·grat′ə·tʸōōd) *n.* Lack of gratitude; thanklessness.

in·gre·di·ent (in·grē′dē·ənt) *n.* 1 Any of the things that enter into the composition of a mixture. 2 A component part of anything. [< L *in-* in + *gradi* to walk]

in·gress (in′gres) *n.* 1 The right of entrance. 2 A place of entrance. 3 The act of entering. [< L *ingredi* enter] —**in·gres′sion, in·gres′sive·ness** *n.* —**in·gres′sive** *adj.*

in-group (in′grōōp′) *n.* Any group, usu. with common interests and goals, considered by its members to have a certain exclusiveness.

in·grown (in′grōn′) *adj.* 1 Grown into the flesh, as a toenail. 2 Growing inward or within. —**in′grow′ing** *adj.*

in·gui·nal (ing′gwə·nəl) *adj.* Of, pertaining to, or near the groin: an *inguinal* hernia. [< L *inguen* groin]

in·gulf (in·gulf′) *v.t.* ENGULF. —**in·gulf′ment** *n.*

in·hab·it (in·hab′it) *v.t.* To live or dwell in (a specified region, house, etc.); occupy as a home. [< L *in-* in + *habitare* dwell] —**in·hab′it·a·bil′i·ty, in·hab′i·ta′tion, in·hab′i·ter** *n.* —**in·hab′it·a·ble** *adj.*

in·hab·i·tant (in·hab′ə·tənt) *n.* One making his home in a specified region, house, etc.; a resident.

in·ha·lant (in·hā′lənt) *adj.* Used for inhaling. —*n.* A medicine, etc., to be inhaled in vapor form.

in·hale (in·hāl′) *v.* **·haled, ·hal·ing** *v.t.* To draw into the lungs, as breath or fumes; breathe in. —*v.i.* To draw breath, fumes, etc., into the lungs. [< L *in-* in + *halare* breathe] —**in·ha·la′tion** (in′hə·lā′shən) *n.*

in·hal·er (in·hā′lər) *n.* 1 One who inhales. 2 A device for administering a medicinal vapor, oxygen, etc.: also **in·ha·la·tor** (in′hə·lā′tər)

in·har·mon·ic (in′här·mon′ik) *adj.* Not harmonic; harsh in sound: also **in′har·mon′i·cal.**

in·har·mo·ni·ous (in′här·mō′nē·əs) *adj.* Lacking in harmony or agreement; in conflict. —**in′har·mo′ni·ous·ly** *adv.* —**in′har·mo′ni·ous·ness** *n.*

in·here (in·hir′) *v.i.* **·hered, ·her·ing** To be a permanent or essential part: with *in.* [< L *in-* in + *haerere* to stick]

in·her·ent (in·hir′ənt, -her′-) *adj.* Naturally and inseparably associated with a person or thing; innate. —**in·her′ence, in·her′en·cy** (*pl.* **·cies**) *n.* —**in·her′ent·ly** *adv.* —**Syn.** essential, natural, characteristic, instinctual, native.

in·her·it (in·her′it) *v.t.* 1 To receive, as property or a title, by succession or will; fall heir to. 2 To receive (traits, qualities, etc.) by or as if by heredity: She *inherits* her mother's good looks. —*v.i.* 3 To come into or possess an inheritance. [< L *in-* in + *heres* heir] —**in·her′i·tor** *n.*

in·her·it·a·ble (in·her′ə·tə·bəl) *adj.* 1 Capable of being passed on to heirs or descendants. 2 Qualified to take by inheritance. [< AF *enheritable*] —**in·her′it·a·bil′i·ty, in·her′it·a·ble·ness** *n.* —**in·her′it·a·bly** *adv.*

in·her·i·tance (in·her′ə·təns) *n.* 1 Anything acquired by succession: legacy. 2 The act of inheriting. 3 The right to inherit. 4 Physical, mental, or cultural characteristics derived from one's ancestry.

inheritance tax A tax imposed on an inherited estate.

in·hib·it (in·hib′it) *v.t.* 1 To keep from happening or from acting; block or prevent the action of. 2 To keep from spontaneous activity, feeling, etc.; restrain. 3 To forbid or prohibit. —*v.i.* 4 To cause inhibition. [< L *in-* in + *habere* have, hold] —**in·hib′it·a·ble, in·hib′i·tive, in·hib′i·to′ry** *adj.* —**in·hib′i·tor** or **in·hib′i·ter** *n.*

in·hi·bi·tion (in′hi·bish′ən, in′i-) *n.* 1 The act of inhibiting or the state of being inhibited. 2 The repression of an impulse, as by a mental process. 3 The process by which an impulse is repressed.

in·hos·pi·ta·ble (in·hos′pi·tə·bəl, in′hos·pit′ə·bəl) *adj.* 1 Not hospitable. 2 Affording no shelter or subsistence; barren. —**in·hos′pi·ta·ble·ness, in·hos′pi·tal′i·ty** (-tal′ə·tē) *n.* —**in·hos′pi·ta·bly** *adv.*

in·hu·man (in·ʰyōō′mən) *adj.* Not being or acting in accordance with the nobler qualities of human beings; brutal or savage. —**in·hu′man·ly** *adv.* —**in·hu′man·ness** *n.*

in·hu·mane (in′ʰyōō·mān′) *adj.* Not humane; having no compassion for others. —**in′hu·mane′ly** *adv.*

in·hu·man·i·ty (in′ʰyōō·man′ə·tē) *n. pl.* **·ties** 1 The state of lacking human or humane qualities; cruelty. 2 A cruel act.

in·im·i·cal (in·im′i·kəl) *adj.* 1 Like an enemy; unfriendly. 2 Tending to hurt; adverse: *inimical* to the public welfare. [< L *in-* not + *amicus* friend] —**in·im′i·cal′i·ty** (-kal′ə·tē) *n.* —**in·im′i·cal·ly** *adv.* —**Syn.** 1 antagonistic, hostile, alien. 2 contrary, disadvantageous.

in·im·i·ta·ble (in·im′ə·tə·bəl) *adj.* That cannot be imitated; matchless. —**in·im′i·ta·bil′i·ty, in·im′i·ta·ble·ness** *n.* —**in·im′i·ta·bly** *adv.*

in·iq·ui·tous (in·ik′wə·təs) *adj.* Wicked; unjust. —**in·iq′ui·tous·ly** *adv.* —**in·iq′ui·tous·ness** *n.*

in·iq·ui·ty (in·ik′wə·tē) *n. pl* **·ties** 1 Deviation from right; wickedness. 2 A wrongful or unjust act. [< L *iniquus* unequal]

init. initial; in the beginning (L *initio*).

in·i·tial (in·ish′əl) *adj.* Having to do with or standing at the beginning; first. —*n.* The first letter of a word, esp. a name. —*v.t.* **·tialed** or **·tialled, ·tial·ing** or **·tial·ling** To mark or sign with initials. [< L *initium* beginning]

in·i·tial·ly (in·ish′ə·lē) *adv.* At first; at the beginning.

Initial Teaching Alphabet An alphabet of 43 characters representing the sounds of English, used in teaching children to read.

in·i·ti·ate (in·ish′ē·āt) *v.t.* **·at·ed, ·at·ing** 1 To begin; originate. 2 To introduce, as into a club, usu. with ceremony. 3 To instruct in fundamentals or principles. —*adj.* (-it, -āt) Initiated. —*n.* (-it, -āt) 1 One who is being or has been newly initiated. 2 One who is learned in some special field. [< L *initium* beginning] —**in·i′ti·a′tor** *n.* —**Syn.** 1 start, commence, inaugurate, invent, create.

in·i·ti·a·tion (in·ish′ē·ā′shən) *n.* 1 The act of initiating. 2 Ceremonial admission, as into a society.

in·i·ti·a·tive (in·ish′ē·ə·tiv) *n.* 1 A first move. 2 The ability for original conception and independent action. 3 The process by which the electorate initiates or enacts legislation. 4 The process by which a group of citizens may propose by petition a legislative measure to the voters. —*adj.*

Pertaining to initiation; preliminary. —**in·i'ti·a·tive·ly** *adv.*

in·i·ti·a·to·ry (in·ish'ē·ə·tôr'ē, -tō'rē) *adj.* **1** Introductory. **2** Serving to initiate.

in·ject (in·jekt') *v.t.* **1** To force in (a fluid) under pressure. **2** To introduce a fluid into by means of a syringe or hypodermic needle. **3** To introduce (something new or lacking): with *into:* to *inject* life into a party. **4** To throw in, as a remark, usu. by way of interruption. [<L *in-* in + *jacere* to throw] —**in·jec'tion, in·jec'tor** *n.*

in·ju·di·cious (in'jōō·dish'əs) *adj.* Not judicious or wise; wanting in judgment. —**in'ju·di'cious·ly** *adv.* —**in'ju·di'cious·ness** *n.*

in·junc·tion (in·jungk'shən) *n.* **1** The act of enjoining; a command. **2** *Law* A judicial order requiring the party enjoined to take or, usu., to refrain from some specified action. [<L *injungere* join to, enjoin]

in·jure (in'jər) *v.t.* **·jured, ·jur·ing 1** To do harm or hurt to. **2** To do wrong to; treat with injustice. [<L *injuria* injury] —**in'jur·er** *n.*

in·ju·ri·ous (in·jŏŏr'ē·əs) *adj.* **1** Hurtful or harmful. **2** Offensive; insulting; abusive. —**in·ju'ri·ous·ly** *adv.* —**in·ju'ri·ous·ness** *n.*

in·ju·ry (in'jər·ē) *n. pl.* **·ries 1** Harm or damage, esp. to the body. **2** A wrong or injustice done to another. [<L *injurius* unjust]

in·jus·tice (in·jus'tis) *n.* **1** The violation or denial of justice. **2** An unjust act; a wrong.

ink (ingk) *n.* **1** A colored liquid or viscous substance, used in writing, printing, etc. **2** The dark fluid ejected by a cuttlefish, octopus, etc. —*v.t.* To spread ink upon; mark or color with ink. [<LL *encaustum* purple ink] —**ink'er** *n.*

ink·horn (ingk'hôrn') *n.* A small vessel made of horn, formerly used to hold ink.

ink·ling (ingk'ling) *n.* A slight intimation; a faint notion; hint. [ME *inkle* hint]

ink·stand (ingk'stand') *n.* A rack for holding pens and an inkwell.

ink·well (ingk'wel') *n.* A small container for ink.

ink·y (ing'kē) *adj.* **ink·i·er, ink·i·est 1** Consisting of, stained with, like, or containing ink. **2** Black. —**ink'i·ness** *n.*

in·laid (in'lād', in·lād') *adj.* **1** Inserted into a surface so as to form a decorative design. **2** Having a surface decorated in such a way.

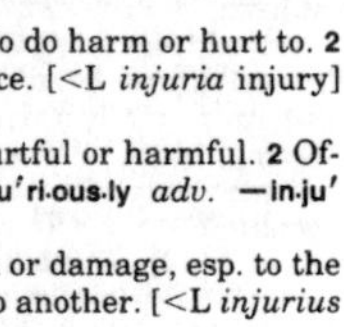

Inlaid decoration

in·land (in'lənd) *adj.* **1** Remote from the sea. **2** Located in or limited to the interior of a country. **3** Not foreign; domestic. —*n.* (in'lənd, -land') The interior of a country. —*adv.* (in'lənd, -land') Toward the interior of a land.

in-law (in'lô') *n. Informal* A relative by marriage.

in·lay (in·lā', in'lā') *v.t.* **in·laid, in·lay·ing 1** To set decorative patterns or designs of (ivory, gold, etc.) into the surface of an object. **2** To decorate by inserting such patterns or designs. —*n.* (in'lā) **1** That which is inlaid. **2** A pattern or design so produced. **3** A filling made to fit into a tooth cavity and then cemented in place. —**in'lay'er** *n.*

in·let (in'let) *n.* **1** A small body of water connected to a larger one. **2** An entrance, as to a culvert.

in loc. cit. in the place cited (L *in loco citato*).

in lo·co pa·ren·tis (in lō'kō pə·ren'tis) *Latin* In the place of a parent.

in·ly (in'lē) *adv.* **1** In the inner parts; inwardly. **2** Thoroughly.

in·mate (in'māt) *n.* **1** One who is kept or confined in an institution, hospital, prison, etc. **2** One who lives in a place with others. [?]

in me·di·as res (in mē'dē·əs rāz', rēz') *Latin* In the midst of things; into the heart of the matter.

in me·mo·ri·am (in mə·môr'ē·əm, -mō'rē-) *Latin* In memory (of); as a memorial (to).

in·most (in'mōst') *adj.* **1** Farthest from the exterior. **2** Most secret or most intimate.

inn (in) *n.* **1** A place providing lodging and meals for travelers; hotel. **2** A restaurant or tavern. [<OE <*inn* in]

in·nards (in'ərdz) *n. pl. Informal* Inner or interior parts or organs; the insides.

in·nate (i·nāt', in'āt) *adj.* Native to or original with the individual; inborn. [<L *in-* in + *nasci* be born] —**in·nate'ly** *adv.* —**in·nate'ness** *n.* —**Syn.** congenital, inherent, natural.

in·ner (in'ər) *adj.* **1** At a point farther in or inward; interior. **2** Of or pertaining to the mind or spirit. **3** Private or secret: *inner* feelings. —**in'ner·ly** *adv.* —**in'ner·ness** *n.*

inner city A central part of a large city, usu. characterized by poverty and often populated by minority groups. —**in'ner-cit'y** *adj.*

inner ear The innermost part of the ear, the essential organ of hearing, containing the cochlea, the auditory nerve, and the semicircular canals that govern equilibrium.

in·ner·most (in'ər·mōst') *adj.* Inmost; farthest within. —*n.* The inmost part, thing, or place.

inner tube A flexible, inflatable tube, used to hold the air in some tires.

in·ning (in'ing) *n.* **1** In baseball, the period in which one team is at bat, completed by three outs. **2** *Often pl.* The period during which a party or person is in power. [<OE *innung,* gerund of *innian* put in]

inn·keep·er (in'kē'pər) *n.* The proprietor of an inn.

in·no·cence (in'ə·səns) *n.* **1** The condition of being free from evil or guile. **2** Childlike simplicity. **3** Freedom from guilt, as for some specific crime or charge. Also **in'no·cen·cy** (*pl.* **·cies**).

in·no·cent (in'ə·sənt) *adj.* **1** Free from evil, guile, or wrongdoing. **2** Free from the guilt of a specific crime or charge. **3** Free from qualities that can harm: *innocent* pastimes. **4** Not maliciously intended: an *innocent* remark. —*n.* One ignorant of evil, as a young child. [<L *in-* not + *nocere* to harm] —**in'no·cent·ly** *adv.*

in·noc·u·ous (i·nok'yōō·əs) *adj.* **1** Having no harmful qualities. **2** Not stimulating or controversial; banal, inoffensive, etc. [<L *in-* not + *nocuus* harmful] —**in·noc'u·ous·ly** *adv.* —**in·noc'u·ous·ness** *n.*

in·nom·i·nate bone (i·nom'ə·nit) The large, irregular bone, consisting of the ilium, ischium, and pubis, which in the adult grow together; the hipbone. [<LL *innominatus* without specific name]

in·no·vate (in'ō·vāt, in'ə-) *v.* **·vat·ed, ·vat·ing** *v.i.* To make changes or alterations in; bring in new ideas, methods, etc. [<L *in-* in + *novare* make new] —**in'no·va'tive** *adj.* —**in'no·va'tor** *n.*

in·no·va·tion (in'ō·vā'shən, in'ə-) *n.* **1** The act of innovating. **2** Something new; a change or novelty.

in·nox·ious (i·nok'shəs) *adj.* Free from harmful qualities. [<L *in-* not + *noxius* noxious]

in·nu·en·do (in'yōō·en'dō) *n. pl.* **·dos** or **·does** An indirect suggestion, remark, etc., usu. disparaging; insinuation. [L, by nodding at, intimating]

in·nu·mer·a·ble (i·n^{y}ōō'mər·ə·bəl) *adj.* Too numerous to be counted; myriad. —**in·nu'mer·a·bil'i·ty, in·nu'mer·a·ble·ness** *n.* —**in·nu'mer·a·bly** *adv.*

in·nu·mer·a·cy (in·n^{y}ōō'mər·ə·sē) *n.* The state of being innumerate.

in·nu·mer·ate (in·n^{y}ōō'mər·it) *adj.* Unable to understand the basic concepts of mathematics.

in·oc·u·late (in·ok'yə·lāt) *v.t.* **·lat·ed, ·lat·ing 1** To immunize (a person or animal) by administering a serum or vaccine to. **2** To introduce microorganisms into (a culture medium, soil, an animal or plant, etc.). **3** To implant ideas, opinions, etc., in the mind of. [<L *inoculare* engraft an eye or bud] —**in·oc'u·la·ble, in·oc'u·la·tive** *adj.* —**in·oc'u·la'tion, in·oc'u·la'tor** *n.*

in·of·fen·sive (in'ə·fen'siv) *adj.* Giving no offense; causing nothing displeasing or harmful. —**in'of·fen'sive·ly** *adv.* —**in'of·fen'sive·ness** *n.*

in·op·er·a·ble (in·op'ər·ə·bəl) *adj.* **1** Not suitable for surgical procedures. **2** Not practicable.

in·op·er·a·tive (in·op'ər·ə·tiv) *adj.* Having no effect or result; ineffectual. —**in·op'er·a·tive·ness** *n.*

in·op·por·tune (in·op'ər·t^{y}ōōn') *adj.* Untimely, inappropriate, or inconvenient. —**in·op'por·tune'ly** *adv.* —**in·op'por·tune'ness** *n.*

in·or·di·nate (in·ôr'də·nit) *adj.* Not restrained by prescribed rules or bounds; immoderate. —**in·or'di·na·cy** (-nə·sē), **in·or'di·nate·ness** *n.* —**in·or'di·nate·ly** *adv.* —**Syn.** excessive, exorbitant, extravagant, unreasonable.

in·or·gan·ic (in'ôr·gan'ik) *adj.* **1** Devoid of organized vital structure; not being animal or vegetable. **2** Not the result of living or organic processes. **—in′or·gan′i·cal·ly** *adv.*

inorganic chemistry The branch of chemistry that treats of substances lacking carbon but includes the carbonates and cyanides.

in per·pet·u·um (in pər·pech′o͞o·əm) *Latin* Forever; perpetually.

in·put (in′po͝ot′) *n.* **1** Something put into a system or device, as energy into a machine, food into the body, data into a computer, or a signal into an electronic device. **2** A place or point of introduction, as of data into a computer. **3** An effect or influence resulting from contributing opinions, information, suggestions, etc.: The staff had real *input* in the directive.

in·quest (in′kwest) *n.* A judicial inquiry, aided by a jury, into a matter, esp. a death possibly resulting from a crime. [< L *inquisita (res)* (thing) inquired (into)]

in·qui·et (in·kwī′ət) *adj.* Restless; uneasy. **—in·qui′e·tude** (-ə·to͞od′) *n.*

in·quire (in·kwīr′) *v.* **·quired, ·quir·ing** *v.t.* **1** To seek information about. *—v.i.* **2** To ask questions; make inquiries. **3** To make investigation; search into carefully: with *into.* **—inquire after** To ask about the well-being of. [< L *in-* into + *quaerere* seek] **—in·quir′er** *n.* **—in·quir′ing·ly** *adv.*

in·quir·y (in·kwīr′ē, in′kwə·rē) *n. pl.* **·quir·ies 1** The act of inquiring. **2** Investigation; research. **3** A query.

in·qui·si·tion (in′kwə·zish′ən) *n.* **1** An investigation. **2** The proceedings and findings of a jury of inquest. **3** Any searching examination or questioning. [< L *inquisitio*] **—in′qui·si′tion·al** *adj.* **—in′qui·si′tion·al·ly** *adv.*

In·qui·si·tion (in′kwə·zish′ən) *n.* **1** A former tribunal of the Roman Catholic Church appointed to examine and punish heretics. **2** The activities of this tribunal.

in·quis·i·tive (in·kwiz′ə·tiv) *adj.* **1** Given to questioning, esp. to satisfy curiosity. **2** Inclined to the pursuit of knowledge. **—in·quis′i·tive·ly** *adv.* **—in·quis′i·tive·ness** *n.*

in·quis·i·tor (in·kwiz′ə·ter) *n.* **1** One who makes an official investigation. **2** *Often cap.* An official of the Inquisition.

in·quis·i·to·ri·al (in·kwiz′ə·tôr′ē·əl, -tō′rē-, in′kwiz-) *adj.* **1** After the manner of an inquisitor; disposed to ask searching questions. **2** Pertaining to a court of inquisition or to an inquisitor. **—in·quis′i·to′ri·al·ly** *adv.*

in re (in rē′) *Latin Law* In the case or matter of; concerning: *in re* Smith vs. Jones.

I.N.R.I. Jesus of Nazareth, King of the Jews (L *Iesus Nazarenus Rex Iudaeorum*).

in·road (in′rōd′) *n.* **1** A hostile entrance into a country or territory; a raid. **2** Any detrimental encroachment: *inroads* upon one's health.

in·rush (in′rush′) *n.* A sudden rushing in. **—in·rush·ing** *adj.*

ins. inches; inspector; insurance.

in·sane (in·sān′) *adj.* **1** Foolish, extravagant, or impractical. **2** Mentally ill; deranged. **3** Too mentally disturbed to be legally responsible. **—in·sane′ly** *adv.* **—in·sane′ness** *n.*

in·san·i·tar·y (in·san′ə·ter′ē) *adj.* Not clean; unhealthful. **—in·san′i·tar′i·ness, in·san′i·ta′tion** *n.*

in·san·i·ty (in·san′ə·tē) *n. pl.* **·ties 1** Irrationality; extreme folly. **2** Mental illness; derangement. **3** *Law* Mental unsoundness to the degree of being not responsible in various legally defined respects. • *Insanity* and *insane* are no longer scientific terms in medicine and psychiatry and have been replaced by more specific terms describing various states of mental illness. However, both words are still acceptable in legal parlance.

in·sa·tia·ble (in·sā′shə·bəl, -shē·ə·bəl) *adj.* Not to be sated or satisfied; unappeasable. Also **in·sa′ti·ate** (-it). **—in·sa′ti·a·bil′i·ty, in·sa′tia·ble·ness** *n.* **—in·sa′tia·bly** *adv.*

in·scribe (in·skrīb′) *v.t.* **·scribed, ·scrib·ing 1** To write or engrave (signs, words, names, etc.). **2** To mark the surface of with engraved or written characters. **3** To dedicate, as a book. **4** To enter the name of on a list. **5** *Geom.* To enclose (a figure) with another so that a particular subset of the points in one figure coincides with points in the other. [< L *in-* on, in + *scribere* write] **—in·scrib′er** *n.*

in·scrip·tion (in·skrip′shən) *n.* **1** The act of inscribing, or that which is inscribed. **2** Incised or relief lettering on a durable object. **3** An entry in a list, roll, etc. **4** A dedication written in a book or the like. **—in·scrip′tion·al, in·scrip′tive** *adj.*

in·scru·ta·ble (in·skro͞o′tə·bəl) *adj.* That cannot be searched into; incomprehensible. [< L *in-* not + *scrutare* look at] **—in·scru′ta·bil′i·ty, in·scru′ta·ble·ness** *n.* **—in·scru′ta·bly** *adv.* **—Syn.** enigmatic, impenetrable, mysterious.

in·sect (in′sekt) *n.* **1** Any of a large class of arthropods having three distinct body segments, three pairs of legs, one pair of antennae, and usu. two pairs of wings. **2** Loosely, any small invertebrate resembling an insect, as spiders, centipedes, ticks, etc. [< L *(animal) insectum* (animal) notched] **—in·sec′te·an** (-sek′tē·ən) *adj.*

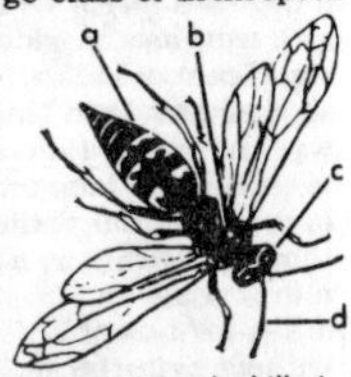

Insect (cicada killer) a. abdomen. b. thorax. c. head. d. antenna.

in·sec·ti·cide (in·sek′tə·sīd) *n.* Any substance that kills insects.

in·sec·ti·vore (in·sek′tə·vôr, -vōr) *n.* **1** Any of an order of insect-eating mammals, as shrews, moles, and hedgehogs. **2** Any animal or plant that feeds on insects. **—in·sec·tiv·o·rous** (in′sek·tiv′ər·əs) *adj.*

in·se·cure (in′sə·kyo͝or′) *adj.* **1** Not secure or safe: *insecure* footing. **2** In danger of breaking or failing; not firm or stable. **3** Not confident; anxious; uncertain. **—in′se·cure′ly** *adv.* **—in′se·cure′ness, in·se·cu·ri·ty** (in′sə·kyo͝or′ə·tē) *n.*

in·sem·i·nate (in·sem′ə·nāt) *v.t.* **·nat·ed, ·nat·ing 1** To impregnate by injecting semen. **2** To implant ideas in. **3** To sow seeds in, as soil. [< L *in-* in + *seminare* to sow] **—in·sem′i·na′tion** *n.*

in·sen·sate (in·sen′sāt, -sit) *adj.* **1** Showing a lack of sense or reason. **2** Hard-hearted; cruel. **3** Inanimate. **—in·sen′sate·ly** *adv.* **—in·sen′sate·ness** *n.*

in·sen·si·ble (in·sen′sə·bəl) *adj.* **1** Not capable of or deprived of perception or feeling. **2** Unconscious. **3** Indifferent, unaware, or apathetic. **4** Inanimate. **5** Imperceptible. **—in·sen′si·bil′i·ty, in·sen′si·ble·ness** *n.* **—in·sen′si·bly** *adv.*

in·sen·si·tive (in·sen′sə·tiv) *adj.* **1** Not sensitive to impressions. **2** Unresponsive to the feelings of others. **—in·sen′si·tive·ly** *adv.* **—in·sen′si·tive·ness, in·sen′si·tiv′i·ty** *n.*

in·sen·ti·ent (in·sen′shē·ənt, -shənt) *adj.* Inanimate. **—in·sen′ti·ence, in·sen′ti·en·cy** *n.*

in·sep·a·ra·ble (in·sep′ər·ə·bəl) *adj.* Incapable of being separated or disjoined: *inseparable* friends. **—in·sep′a·ra·ble·ness** *n.* **—in·sep′a·ra·bly** *adv.*

in·sert (in·sûrt′) *v.t.* **1** To put or place into something else. **2** To put between or among other things. *—n.* (in′sûrt) **1** That which is inserted. **2** A circular or the like placed within a newspaper or book for mailing. [< L *in-* in + *serere* place, join] **—in·sert′er** *n.*

in·ser·tion (in·sûr′shən) *n.* **1** The act of inserting, or the state of being inserted. **2** That which is inserted, as lace or embroidery placed between pieces of plain fabric. **3** Additional or explanatory material inserted in a written or printed page.

in·set (in·set′) *v.t.* To set in; implant. *—n.* (in′set′) **1** A leaf or leaves inserted, as in a book or newspaper. **2** Influx, as of the tide.

in·shore (in′shôr′, -shōr′, in′shôr′, -shōr′) *adj.* **1** Being or occurring near the shore. **2** Coming toward the shore. *—adv.* Toward the shore.

in·side (in′sīd′, -sīd′) *n.* **1** The side, surface, or part that is within. **2** That which is contained; contents. **3** Inner thoughts or feelings. **4** *pl. Informal* Inner organs; entrails. *—adj.* **1** Situated or occurring on or in the inside. **2** Suited for or pertaining to the inside. **3** For use indoors: *inside* paint. **4** Private; confidential: *inside* reports. *—adv.* (in′·sīd′) **1** In or into the interior. **2** Indoors. **—inside out 1** Reversed so that the inside is exposed. **2** Thoroughly; completely. *—prep.* (in′sīd′) In or into the interior of; within. **—inside of** *Informal* Within the time or distance of.

in·sid·er (in′sī′dər) *n.* 1 One who is a member of a special group. 2 One who has special information or advantages.

in·sid·i·ous (in·sid′ē·əs) *adj.* 1 Designed to entrap; full of wiles. 2 Doing or contriving harm. 3 Awaiting a chance to harm. 4 Causing harm by stealthy, usu. imperceptible means: an *insidious* disease. [< L *insidere* sit in, lie in wait] **—in·sid′i·ous·ly** *adv.* **—in·sid′i·ous·ness** *n.*

in·sight (in′sīt′) *n.* 1 Intellectual discernment. 2 A perception of the inner nature of a thing; intuition.

in·sig·ni·a (in·sig′nē·ə) *n. sing. or pl.* 1 A badge, emblem, etc., used as a mark of office or distinction. 2 Something significant or indicative of a calling. [< L *in-* in + *signum* sign, emblem] • In Latin and formerly in English, *insignia* was the plural form of **in·sig·ne** (in·sig′nē). Now, however, *insignia* has virtually replaced *insigne* in the singular. The plural form *insignias* is well established, although *insignia* is still sometimes used in its original plural sense.

in·sig·nif·i·cant (in′sig·nif′ə·kənt) *adj.* 1 Not significant; without importance. 2 Meaningless. 3 Without dignity; not imposing: an*insignificant* person. **—in′sig·nif′i·cance, in′sig·nif′i·can·cy** *n.* **—in′sig·nif′i·cant·ly** *adv.* **—Syn.** 1 petty, trifling, trivial. 2 immaterial, irrelevant.

in·sin·cere (in′sin·sir′) *adj.* Not sincere, honest, or genuine; hypocritical. **—in′sin·cere′ly** *adv.*

in·sin·cer·i·ty (in′sin·ser′ə·tē) *n. pl.* **·ties** 1 Lack of sincerity. 2 An insincere act, remark, etc.

in·sin·u·ate (in·sin′yōō·āt) *v.t.* **·at·ed, ·at·ing** 1 To indicate slyly or deviously. 2 To infuse or instill gradually or subtly into the mind. 3 To introduce gradually, artfully, or stealthily: to *insinuate* oneself into an enviable position. [< L *insinuare* to curve] **—in·sin′u·a′ting·ly** *adv.* **—in·sin′u·a′tive** *adj.* **—in·sin′u·a′tor** *n.*

in·sin·u·a·tion (in·sin′yōō·ā′shən) 1 The act of insinuating. 2 An injurious suggestion or implication. 3 A subtly ingratiating act, remark, etc.

in·sip·id (in·sip′id) *adj.* 1 Without flavor; tasteless. 2 Unexciting; dull. [< L *in-* not + *sapidus* savory] **—in·sip′id·ly** *adv.* **—in·sip′id·ness** *n.*

in·si·pid·i·ty (in′si·pid′ə·tē) *n. pl.* **·ties** 1 The quality of being insipid. 2 An insipid person or thing.

in·sist (in·sist′) *v.i.* 1 To make emphatic or repeated assertion, demand, or request: often with *on* or *upon* —*v.t.* 2 To state or demand emphatically: He *insisted* that he was right. [< L *in-* on + *sistere* to stand] **—in·sis′tence, in·sis′ten·cy** *n.*

in·sis·tent (in·sis′tənt) *adj.* 1 Emphatic; urgent. 2 Standing out prominently; conspicuous: *insistent* colors. **—in·sist′ence, in·sist′en·cy** *n.* (*pl.* **·cies**) **—in·sis′tent·ly** *adv.*

in si·tu (in sī′tyōō, si′-) *Latin* In its original site or position.

in·snare (in·snâr′) *v.t.* **·snared, ·snar·ing** ENSNARE.

in·so·bri·e·ty (in′sə·brī′ə·tē) *n.* Lack of moderation, esp. in drinking.

in·so·far (in′sō·fär′) *adv.* To such extent: usu. with *as.*

in·sole (in′sōl′) *n.* 1 The fixed inner sole of a boot or shoe. 2 A removable inner sole used to improve the fit of a shoe.

in·so·lence (in′sə·ləns) *n.* The quality of being insolent; offensive impertinence.

in·so·lent (in′sə·lənt) *adj.* 1 Defiantly offensive in language or manner. 2 Grossly disrespectful. [< L *insolens* unusual, haughty] **—in′so·lent·ly** *adv.*

in·sol·u·ble (in·sol′yə·bəl) *adj.* 1 Not capable of being dissolved, as in a liquid; not soluble. 2 That cannot be explained or solved. **—in·sol′u·bil′i·ty, in·sol′u·ble·ness** *n.* **—in·sol′u·bly** *adv.*

in·solv·a·ble (in·sol′və·bəl) *adj.* Not able to be explained or solved; insoluble. **—in·sol′va·bly** *adv.*

in·sol·vent (in·sol′vənt) *adj.* 1 Unable to meet the claims of creditors; bankrupt. 2 Inadequate for the payment of debts. 3 Of or pertaining to bankrupts. —*n.* A bankrupt person. **—in·sol′ven·cy** *n.* (*pl.* **·cies**)

in·som·ni·a (in·som′nē·ə) *n.* Chronic inability to sleep. [< L *insomnis* sleepless] **—in·som′ni·ac′** (-nē·ak′) *n.*

in·so·much (in′sō·much′) *adv.* 1 To such a degree or extent: used with *that* or *as.* 2 Since: used with *as.*

in·sou·ci·ance (in·sōō′sē·əns; *Fr.* aṅ·sōō·syäṅs′) *n.* Carefree unconcern; heedlessness. [F]

in·sou·ci·ant (in·sōō′sē·ənt; *Fr.* aṅ·sōō·syäṅ′) *adj.* Without concern or care; carefree. [F< *in-* not + *souciant,* pr. p. of *soucier* to care] **—in·sou′ci·ant·ly** *adv.*

insp. inspected; inspector.

in·spect (in·spekt′) *v.t.* 1 To look at or examine carefully. 2 To examine or review officially, as troops. [< L *in-* into + *specere* to look] **—Syn.** 1 investigate, scan, scrutinize.

in·spec·tion (in·spek′shən) *n.* 1 A critical viewing or investigation. 2 An official examination. **—in·spec′tion·al** *adj.*

in·spec·tor (in·spek′tər) *n.* 1 One who inspects. 2 An officer of the police usu. ranking next below the superintendent. **—in·spec′tor·al, in′spec·to′ri·al** (-tôr′ē·əl, -tō′rē-) *adj.* **—in·spec′tor·ship′** *n.*

in·spi·ra·tion (in′spə·rā′shən) *n.* 1 The infusion of an idea, an emotion, or mental influence. 2 That which is so infused. 3 A stimulus to creativity in thought or action. 4 The state or quality of being inspired. 5 Divine or supernatural influence. 6 A person or thing that inspires. 7 The act of drawing air into the lungs. **—in′spi·ra′tion·al** *adj.* **—in′spi·ra′tion·al·ly** *adv.*

in·spire (in·spīr′) *v.* **·spired, ·spir·ing** *v.t.* 1 To stir or affect by some mental or spiritual influence: stimulate. 2 To imbue with a specified idea or feeling: to *inspire* survivors with hope. 3 To give rise to: Fear *inspires* hatred. 4 To motivate or cause by supernatural influence. 5 To draw into the lungs; inhale. 6 To prompt the saying or writing of indirectly: This rumor was *inspired* by my enemies. —*v.i.* 7 To draw in breath; inhale. 8 To give or provide inspiration. [< L *inspirare* breathe into] **—in·spir′a·ble** *adj.* **—in·spir′er** *n.* **—in·spir′ing·ly** *adv.*

in·spir·it (in·spir′it) *v.t.* To fill with spirit or life; exhilarate. **—in·spir′it·ing·ly** *adv.*

in·spis·sate (in·spis′āt) *v.t. & v.i.* **·sat·ed, ·sat·ing** To thicken, as by evaporation; condense. —*adj.* Thickened; condensed. [< L *in-* thoroughly + *spissare* thicken] **—in·spis·sa·tion** (in′spi·sā′shən) **in′spis·sa′tor** *n.*

Inst. Institute; Institution.

inst. instant; instantaneous; instrument.

in·sta·bil·i·ty (in′stə·bil′ə·tē) *n. pl.* **·ties** 1 Lack of stability or firmness. 2 Inconstancy; changeableness. 3 Flimsiness of construction.

in·sta·ble (in·stā′bəl) *adj.* UNSTABLE.

in·stall (in·stôl′) *v.t.* 1 To place in office, etc., with formal ceremony. 2 To establish in a place or position. 3 To place in position for service or use. [< Med. L *in-* in + *stallare* to seat] **—in·stal·la·tion** (in′stə·lā′shən), **in·stall′er** *n.*

in·stall·ment[1] (in·stôl′mənt) *n.* 1 A partial payment of a price due, made at regular intervals. 2 One of several parts of anything furnished at different times, as written material appearing serially in a magazine, newspaper, etc. Also **in·stal′ment.** [< obs. *estall* arrange payments < OF *estaler* stop, fix]

in·stall·ment[2] (in·stôl′mənt) *n.* The act of installing or the state of being installed. Also **in·stal′ment.**

installment plan The paying for goods or services by means of installments.

in·stance (in′stəns) *n.* 1 Something offered or occurring as an example; a case. 2 The act of suggesting or urging; a request. 3 A step in proceeding: in the first *instance.* —**for instance** For example. —*v.t.* **·stanced, ·stanc·ing** 1 To refer to an illustration or example. 2 To serve as an example of; exemplify. [< L *instantia* a standing near]

in·stant (in′stənt) *adj.* 1 Immediately impending; imminent. 2 Of the current month. 3 Direct; immediate: an *instant* result. 4 Urgent: an *instant* need for help. 5 Available in premixed or soluble form for quick preparation, as pudding, coffee, etc. —*n.* 1 A particular point of time. 2 A very brief portion of time; moment. —**the instant** As soon as. [< OF < L *in-* upon + *stare* to stand]

in·stan·ta·ne·ous (in′stən·tā′nē·əs) *adj.* 1 Acting or done instantly. 2 Of or at a particular instant. **—in′stan·ta′ne·ous·ly** *adv.* **—in′stan·ta′ne·ous·ness** *n.*

in·stan·ter (in·stan′tər) *adv.* Without an instant of delay. [< L]

in·stant·ly (in′stənt·lē) *adv.* Immediately; at once.

in·state (in·stāt′) *v.t.* **·stat·ed, ·stat·ing** To establish in a certain office or rank; induct.

in·stead (in·sted′) *adv.* In one's or its stead or place: Give me that *instead.* —**instead of** In place of.

in·step (in′step′) *n.* **1** The upper part of the human foot from the toes to the ankle. **2** That part of a shoe, stocking, etc., that covers the instep.

in·sti·gate (in′stə·gāt) *v.t.* **·gat·ed, ·gat·ing 1** To bring about by inciting; foment. **2** To urge or incite to an action or course. [< L *instigare*] **—in′sti·ga′tion, in′sti·ga′tor** *n.* **—in′·sti·ga′tive** *adj.*

in·still (in·stil′) *v.t.* **·stilled, ·still·ing 1** To put into the mind gradually, as if drop by drop. **2** To pour in by drops. Also **in·stil′.** [< L *instillare* to drop, drip] **—in′stil·la′tion** (in′stə·lā′shən), **in·stil′ler, in·still′ment** or **in·stil′ment** *n.*

in·stinct (in′stingkt) *n.* **1** The innate ability of animals to perform functions peculiar to each species without training. **2** A natural aptitude. *—adj.* (in·stingkt′) Imbued or filled with: a picture *instinct* with life. [< L *instinguere* impel]

in·stinc·tive (in·stingk′tiv) *adj.* Of the nature of, or prompted by, instinct; innate: also **in·stinc′tu·al** (-chōō·əl). **—in·stinc′tive·ly** *adv.*

in·sti·tute (in′stə·tyōōt′) *v.t.* **·tut·ed, ·tut·ing 1** To establish; found. **2** To set in operation; initiate. **3** To appoint to an office, position, etc. *—n.* **1** An established organization or society pledged to some special purpose and work. **2** The building occupied by such an organization. **3** An established principle, rule, or order. [< L *in-* in, on + *statuere* set up, stand] **—in′sti·tut′er, in′sti·tu′tor** *n.* **—Syn.** *v.* **1** erect, install, set up. **2** begin, commence, start.

in·sti·tu·tion (in′stə·tyōō′shən) *n.* **1** An established principle, law, or usage. **2** A corporate body or establishment organized for an educational, medical, charitable, or similar purpose. **3** The building occupied by such an establishment. **4** The act of instituting or establishing: the *institution* of an investigation. **5** *Informal* A well-known person or thing.

in·sti·tu·tion·al (in′stə·tyōō′shən·əl) *adj.* **1** Of, like, or pertaining to an institution. **2** Designating a form of advertising intended to promote good will and prestige, rather than to get immediate sales. **—in′sti·tu′tion·al·ly** *adv.*

in·sti·tu·tion·al·ize (in′stə·tyōō′shən·əl·īz) *v.t.* **·ized, ·iz·ing 1** To make institutional. **2** To turn into or regard as an institution. **3** *Informal* To put (someone) in an institution.

in·struct (in·strukt′) *v.t.* **1** To impart knowledge or skill to, esp. by systematic method. **2** To give specific orders or directions to. **3** To give information or explanation to; inform. [< L *in-* in + *struere* build]

in·struc·tion (in·struk′shən) *n.* **1** The act of instructing; teaching. **2** Imparted knowledge. **3** The act of giving specific directions or commands. **4** *pl.* The directions given. **—in·struc′tion·al** *adj.*

in·struc·tive (in·struk′tiv) *adj.* Serving to instruct; conveying knowledge; informative. **—in·struc′tive·ly** *adv.* **—in·struc′tive·ness** *n.*

in·struc·tor (in·struk′tər) *n.* **1** One who instructs; a teacher. **2** In the U.S., a college teacher of lower rank than the lowest professorial grade. **—in·struc′tor·ship** *n.*

in·stru·ment (in′strə·mənt) *n.* **1** A means by which work is done; an implement or tool. **2** A device for making measurements, records, etc. **3** Any means of accomplishment. **4** A device for the production of musical sounds. **5** A person doing the will of another. **6** *Law* A formal document, as a contract, deed, etc. [< L *instrumentum* < *instruere* fit out]

in·stru·men·tal (in′strə·men′təl) *adj.* **1** Serving as a means or instrument; serviceable. **2** For or produced by musical instruments. **3** Done by or pertaining to a mechanical instrument or a tool. **—in·stru·men′tal·ly** *adv.*

in·stru·men·tal·ist (in′strə·men′təl·ist) *n.* One who plays a musical instrument.

in·stru·men·tal·i·ty (in′strə·men·tal′ə·tē) *n. pl.* **·ties 1** The condition of being instrumental. **2** That which is instrumental; means.

in·stru·men·ta·tion (in′strə·men·tā′shən) *n.* **1** *Music* The arranging of compositions for performance by instruments. **2** The technique of using precision instruments.

instrument panel The panel containing the indicators of performance in an automobile, airplane, or other apparatus. Also **instrument board.**

in·sub·or·di·nate (in′sə·bôr′də·nit) *adj.* Not obedient; not submitting to authority. *—n.* A disobedient person.

in·sub·or·di·na·tion (in′sə·bôr′də·nā′shən) *n.* An act of being disobedient to constituted authorities.

in·sub·stan·tial (in′səb·stan′shəl) *adj.* **1** Not substantial; flimsy. **2** Not material; unreal. **—in′sub·stan′ti·al′i·ty** (-shē·al′ə·tē) *n.*

in·suf·fer·a·ble (in·suf′ər·ə·bəl, -rə·bəl) *adj.* Not to be endured; intolerable. **—in·suf′fer·a·ble·ness** *n.* **—in·suf′fer·a·bly** *adv.*

in·suf·fi·cien·cy (in′sə·fish′ən·sē) *n. pl.* **·cies** Lack of sufficiency; inadequacy in amount, power, etc.; deficiency.

in·suf·fi·cient (in′sə·fish′ənt) *adj.* Inadequate for some need, purpose, or use. **—in′suf·fi′cient·ly** *adv.*

in·su·lar (in′syə·lər) *adj.* **1** Of or pertaining to an island or its inhabitants. **2** Standing alone; isolated. **3** Not broad, liberal, or cosmopolitan: *insular* ideas. [< L *insula* island] **—in′su·lar·ism, in·su·lar·i·ty** (in′syə·lar′ə·tē) *n.*

in·su·late (in′sə·lāt) *v.t.* **·lat·ed, ·lat·ing 1** To place in a detached state or situation; isolate. **2** To apply (to walls, electric wiring, etc.) a nonconducting substance or device. **3** To prevent or slow the passage of heat, electricity, sound, or other energy to or from. [< L *insula* island]

in·su·la·tion (in′sə·lā′shən) *n.* **1** The act of insulating. **2** Any nonconducting material used in insulating.

in·su·la·tor (in′sə·lā′tər) *n.* **1** One who or that which insulates. **2** A nonconducting substance or device used to insulate.

in·su·lin (in′sə·lin) *n.* **1** A hormone essential for carbohydrate metabolism, secreted by island cells in the pancreas. **2** A preparation of this hormone made from animal pancreas and used to control diabetes. [< NL *insula* island]

in·sult (in·sult′) *v.t.* To treat with insolence, contempt, or rudeness. *—n.* (in′sult) Something offensive said or done; an indignity. [< L *insultare* leap at, insult] **—in·sult′er** *n.* **—in·sult′ing·ly** *adv.* **—Syn.** *v.* abuse, affront, hurt, offend.

in·su·per·a·ble (in·sōō′pər·ə·bəl) *adj.* That cannot be overcome; insurmountable. [< L *in-* not + *superare* overcome] **—in·su′per·a·bil′i·ty, in·su′per·a·ble·ness** *n.* **—in·su′per·a·bly** *adv.*

in·sup·port·a·ble (in′sə·pôr′tə·bəl, -pōr′-) *adj.* **1** Intolerable; insufferable. **2** Without grounds; unjustifiable. **—in′·sup·port′a·ble·ness** *n.* **—in′sup·port′a·bly** *adv.*

in·sur·ance (in·shŏŏr′əns) *n.* **1** The act of insuring. **2** Something that provides protection or security. **3** A system by which pecuniary indemnity is guaranteed by one party to another in certain contingencies, as death, accident, damage, etc. **4** A contract (**insurance policy**) made under such a system. **5** The consideration paid for insuring; premium. **6** The sum that the insurer has agreed to pay in case the specified contingency occurs.

in·sure (in·shŏŏr′) *v.* **·sured, ·sur·ing** *v.t.* **1** To contract to pay or be paid an indemnity in the event of harm to or the loss or death of. **2** ENSURE (def. 1). **3** ENSURE (def. 2). *—v.i.* **4** To issue or take out a policy of insurance. [< OF *enseurer* make sure < *en-* in + *seur* sure] **—in·sur′a·bil′i·ty** *n.* **—in·sur′a·ble** *adj.*

in·sured (in·shŏŏrd′) *n.* A person who carries insurance against loss of life, damage to property, etc.

in·sur·er (in·shŏŏr′ər) *n.* A person or company that provides insurance against damage or loss.

in·sur·gence (in·sûr′jəns) *n.* The act of rising in revolt; uprising. **—in·sur′gen·cy** *n.* (*pl.* **·cies**)

in·sur·gent (in·sur′jənt) *adj.* Rising in rebellion against an existing government. *—n.* One who takes part in active opposition to constituted authorities. [< L *in-* against + *surgere* to rise]

in·sur·mount·a·ble (in′sər·moun′tə·bəl) *adj.* That cannot be surmounted, passed over, or overcome. **—in′·sur·mount′a·bil′i·ty** *n.* **—in′sur·mount′a·bly** *adv.*

in·sur·rec·tion (in′sə·rek′shən) *n.* An organized resistance to established government. [< L *insurgere* rise up against] **—in′sur·rec′tion·al** *adj.* **—in′sur·rec′tion·ar′y** *adj.*, *n.* **—in′sur·rec′tion·ism, in′sur·rec′tion·ist** *n.*

in·sus·cep·ti·ble (in′sə·sep′tə·bəl) *adj.* Not susceptible; incapable of being moved or impressed. —**in′sus·cep′ti·bil′i·ty** *n.* —**in′sus·cep′ti·bly** *adv.*

in·tact (in·takt′) *adj.* Left complete or unimpaired. [<L *intactus* untouched] —**in·tact′ness** *n.*

in·ta·glio (in·tal′yō, -tä′lyō) *n. pl.* **·glios** or **·gli** (-lyē) **1** A sunken design engraved into a surface. **2** The art of making such designs. **3** A work, esp. a gem, with such carving. —*v.t.* **1** To engrave with a sunken design. **2** To represent in intaglio. [<Ital. *in-* in + *tagliare* to cut]

in·take (in′tāk′) *n.* **1** That which is taken in. **2** The amount or substance taken in. **3** The point at which a fluid is taken into a channel or container.

in·tan·gi·ble (in·tan′jə·bəl) *adj.* **1** Not capable of being touched; impalpable. **2** Not directly perceivable or readily grasped. —*n.* Something intangible but often noteworthy or influential nevertheless. —**in·tan′gi·bil′i·ty, in·tan′gi·ble·ness** *n.* —**in·tan′gi·bly** *adv.*

in·te·ger (in′tə·jər) *n.* **1** Any member of the set [. . . −3, −2, −1, 0, 1, 2, 3, . . .]; a whole number. **2** A whole. [<L, whole]

in·te·gral (in′tə·grəl) *adj.* **1** Constituting a completed whole. **2** Constituting an essential part of a whole. **3** *Math.* Of or being an integer or integers. —*n.* An entire thing; a whole. —**in′te·gral·ly** *adv.* —**in′te·gral′i·ty** (-gral′ə·tē) *n.*

in·te·grate (in′tə·grāt) *v.* **·grat·ed, ·grat·ing** *v.t.* **1** To make or form into a whole; unify. **2** To combine (parts) into a whole. **3** *U.S.* **a** To make (schools, housing, public facilities, etc.) available to people of all races and ethnic groups on an equal basis. **b** To remove any barriers imposing segregation upon (religious, racial, or other groups). —*v.i.* **4** To become integrated. [<L *integer* whole, intact] —**in·te·gra·tion** (in′tə·grā′shən), **in′te·gra′tion·ist** (*esp. for def.* 3), **in′te·gra′tor** *n.* —**in′te·gra′tive** *adj.*

in·te·gra·ted cir·cuit (in′tə·gra′tid) A tiny electronic circuit and its connections fabricated on a chip, or slice, of a semiconductor made of silicon or gallium; chip.

in·teg·ri·ty (in·teg′rə·tē) *n.* **1** Uprightness of character; honesty. **2** Unimpaired state; soundness. **3** Undivided or unbroken state; completeness. [<L *integer* whole]

in·teg·u·ment (in·teg′yə·mənt) *n.* An outer covering or envelope, as the skin of an animal, coat of a seed, etc. [<L *integere* to cover] —**in·teg′u·men′ta·ry** *adj.*

in·tel·lect (in′tə·lekt) *n.* **1** The power to perceive, interpret, know, and understand. **2** Great and keen intelligence. **3** A person having such intelligence.

in·tel·lec·tu·al (in′tə·lek′cho͞o·əl) *adj.* **1** Of or pertaining to the intellect: *intellectual* ability. **2** Possessing or showing a high degree of intelligence and knowledge. **3** Requiring intelligence or study: *intellectual* pursuits. —*n.* A person of trained intelligence, or one whose work requires exercise of the intellect. [<L *intellectualis*] —**in′tel·lec′tu·al′i·ty, in′tel·lec′tu·al·ness** *n.* —**in′tel·lec′tu·al·ly** *adv.*

in·tel·lec·tu·al·ism (in′tə·lək′cho͞o·əl·iz′əm) *n.* Devotion to use of the intellect or to intellectual occupations.

in·tel·li·gence (in·tel′ə·jəns) *n.* **1** The ability to exercise mental functions. **2** The ability to grasp the significant factors of a complex problem or new situation. **3** Information acquired or communicated; news. **4** The gathering of secret information, esp. of a political or military nature. **5** A group of persons assigned to gather such secret information. **6** An intelligent being.

intelligence quotient A score obtained on any of various intelligence tests that are standardized to give an average score of 100 to the total population tested.

intelligence test Any test designed to measure the mental capacity of a person.

in·tel·li·gent (in·tel′ə·jənt) *adj.* **1** Learning easily; of active mind. **2** Showing intelligence: an *intelligent* reply. **3** Endowed with intellect; reasoning: Man is an *intelligent* animal. [<L *intelligere* understand, perceive] —**in·tel′li·gent·ly** *adv.* —**Syn. 2** astute, bright, clever, discerning.

in·tel·li·gent·si·a (in·tel′ə·jent′sē·ə, -gent′-) *n. pl.* Those considered as, or considering themselves as, the enlightened, educated class of a country; intellectual people collectively. [<Russ. *intelligentsiya.*]

in·tel·li·gi·ble (in·tel′ə·jə·bəl) *adj.* Capable of being understood; clear. —**in·tel′li·gi·bil′i·ty, in·tel′li·gi·ble·ness** *n.* —**in·tel′li·gi·bly** *adv.*

in·tem·per·ance (in·tem′pər·əns) *n.* **1** Lack of moderation or due restraint. **2** Excessive use of alcohol.

in·tem·per·ate (in·temp′pər·it) *adj.* **1** Characterized by lack of moderation. **2** Given to excessive use of alcoholic liquors. **3** Stormy; inclement: *intemperate* weather. —**in·tem′per·ate·ly** *adv.* —**in·tem′per·ate·ness** *n.*

in·tend (in·tend′) *v.t.* **1** To have in mind to accomplish or do. **2** To make or destine for a purpose, use, etc.: a game *intended* for adults. **3** To mean: She *intended* nothing by the remark. [<L *intendere* stretch out (for)] —**in·tend′er** *n.*

in·ten·dant (in·ten′dənt) *n.* A supervisor or director, esp. a colonial or provincial administrative official serving under a French, Spanish, or Portuguese monarchy.

in·tend·ed (in·ten′did) *adj.* **1** Meant or planned; intentional. **2** Looking to the future; prospective. —*n. Informal* One's future wife or husband.

in·tense (in·tens′) *adj.* **·tens·er, ·tens·est 1** Strained or exerted to a high degree; fervid: *intense* study. **2** Extreme in degree, concentration, or measure: *intense* light. **3** Putting forth strenuous effort. **4** Susceptible to or exhibiting strong emotions. [<L *intendere* stretch out (for)] —**in·tense′ly** *adv.* —**in·tense′ness** *n.*

in·ten·si·fy (in·ten′sə·fī) *v.t. & v.i.* **·fied, ·fy·ing** To make or become intense or more intense; increase in degree. —**in·ten′si·fi·ca′tion, in·ten′si·fi′er** *n.*

in·ten·si·ty (in·ten′sə·tē) *n. pl.* **·ties 1** The state or quality of being intense. **2** Extreme depth or violence of feeling, activity, etc. **3** The measure of how intense a force, flow of energy, etc., is.

in·ten·sive (in·ten′siv) *adj.* **1** Increasing in force or degree. **2** Characterized by intensity and thoroughness: *intensive* research. **3** Characterized by a relatively heavy investment in (something specified) as compared with other factors: used in combination: a *labor-intensive* industry. **4** *Gram.* Adding emphasis or force, as the pronoun *myself* in "I myself did it." —*n.* **1** That which intensifies. **2** *Gram.* An intensive word, prefix, etc. —**in·ten′sive·ly** *adv.* —**in·ten′sive·ness** *n.*

in·tent (in·tent′) *adj.* **1** Having the mind fixed; earnest: *intent* on winning. **2** Firmly or constantly directed: an *intent* gaze. —*n.* **1** The meaning expressed by an act or words. **2** An aim or purpose. —**to all intents and purposes** In practically every aspect. [<L *intendere* stretch out (for)] **in·tent′ly** *adv.* —**in·tent′ness** *n.*

in·ten·tion (in·ten′shən) *n.* **1** A settled plan for doing a certain thing. **2** That upon which the mind is set; purpose. **3** *pl. Informal* Purpose with respect to a proposal of marriage.

in·ten·tion·al (in·ten′shən·əl) *adj.* Done purposely or with intention. [Med. L *intentionalis*] —**in·ten′tion·al·ly** *adv.*

in·ter (in·tûr) *v.t.* **·terred, ·ter·ring** To place in a grave or tomb; bury. [<L *in-* in + *terra* earth]

inter- *prefix* **1** With each other; together: *interact.* **2** Mutual; mutually: *intercommunion.* **3** Between (the units signified): *international.* **4** Occurring or situated between: *intercostal.* [<L *inter* between]

in·ter·act (in′tər·akt′) *v.i.* To act on each other. —**in′ter·ac′·tion** *n.* —**in′ter·ac′tive** *adj.*

in·ter·breed (in′tər·brēd′) *v.* **·bred, ·breed·ing** *v.t.* **1** To breed (animals or plants) by uniting different varieties, etc. —*v.i.* **2** To be mated with another variety.

in·ter·ca·lar·y (in·tûr′kə·ler′ē) *adj.* Inserted into the calendar: said of a month, day, etc., such as February 29 in leap year. [<L *intercalarius*]

in·ter·ca·late (in·tûr′kə·lāt) *v.t.* **·lat·ed, ·lat·ing 1** To insert or interpolate. **2** To insert, as an additional day or month, into the calendar. [<L *inter-* between + *calare* proclaim, call] —**in·ter′ca·la′tion** *n.*

in·ter·cede (in′tər·sēd′) *v.i.* **·ced·ed, ·ced·ing 1** To plead in behalf of another. **2** To act as a mediator in order to resolve disagreements between or among others. [<L *inter-* between + *cedere* pass, go] —**in′ter′ced′er** *n.* —**Syn. 2** arbitrate, intervene, moderate, referee.

in·ter·cel·lu·lar (in′tər·sel′yə·lər) *adj. Biol.* Situated between or among cells.

in·ter·cept (in′tər·sept′) *v.t.* **1** To seize or stop on the way to a destination: to *intercept* contraband; to *intercept* a pass. **2** To stop, interrupt, or prevent. **3** To cut off from connection, sight, etc. 4 *Math.* To contain or include, as between two points of a curve. —*v.i.* 5 In various sports, to intercept a pass intended for an opponent. —*n.* (in′·tər·sept) *Math.* A point in which a figure intersects an axis of a coordinate system. [< L *inter-* between + *capere* seize] —**in′ter·cep′tion** *n.* —**in′ter·cep′tive** *adj.*

in·ter·cep·tor (in′tər·sep′tər) *n.* 1 One who or that which intercepts. 2 A fast plane adapted to the pursuit and interception of enemy aircraft. Also **in′ter·cep′ter.**

in·ter·ces·sion (in′tər·sesh′ən) *n.* The act of interceding between persons; entreaty in behalf of others. —**in′ter·ces′sion·al, in′ter·ces′so·ry** (-ses′ə·rē) *adj.* —**in′ter·ces′sor** *n.*

in·ter·change (in′tər·chānj′) *v.* **·changed, ·chang·ing** *v.t.* 1 To put each of (two things) in the place of the other. 2 To give and receive in return, as gifts; exchange. 3 To alternate: to *interchange* work and rest. —*v.i.* 4 To make an interchange. —*n.* (in′·tər·chānj′) 1 The act, process, or an instance of interchanging. 2 A system of roadways and ramps that allow traffic to pass between intersecting highways, expressways, etc. —**in′ter·chang′er** *n.*

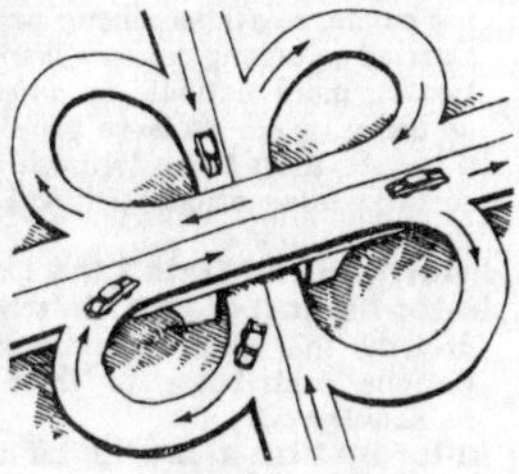

Cloverleaf interchange

in·ter·change·a·ble (in′tər·chān′jə·bəl) *adj.* Capable of being interchanged or substituted one for the other. [OF *entrechangeable*] —**in′ter·change′a·bil′i·ty, in′ter·change′a·ble·ness** *n.* —**in′ter·change′a·bly** *adv.*

in·ter·col·le·giate (in′tər·kə·lē′jit, -jē·it) *adj.* Existing, representing, or conducted between colleges and universities: *intercollegiate* sports.

in·ter·com (in′tər·kom) *n. Informal* A system that enables voice communication between persons in different parts of a building, ship, airplane, etc.

in·ter·com·mu·ni·cate (in′tər·kə·myōō′nə·kāt) *v.t.* **·cat·ed, ·cat·ing** To communicate mutually, as between individuals, rooms, different units of a factory, etc. —**in′ter·com·mu′ni·ca′tive** *adj.* —**in′ter·com·mu′ni·ca′tion** *n.*

in·ter·con·nect (in′tər·kə·nekt′) *v.t. & v.i.* To connect with one another. —**in′ter·con·nec′tion** *n.*

in·ter·con·ti·nen·tal (in′tər·kon′tə·nen′təl) *adj.* 1 Existing, extending, or carried on between or among continents. 2 Able to travel between or among continents: *intercontinental* ballistic missiles.

in·ter·cos·tal (in′tər·kos′təl) *adj.* Between the ribs. [< L *inter-* between + *costa* rib] —**in′ter·cos′tal·ly** *adv.*

in·ter·course (in′tər·kôrs, -kōrs) *n.* 1 Mutual exchange or communication. 2 The interchange of ideas. 3 SEXUAL INTERCOURSE. [< L *inter-* between + *currere* to run]

in·ter·de·nom·i·na·tion·al (in′tər·di·nom′ə·nā′shən·əl) *adj.* Carried on by or involving different religious denominations.

in·ter·de·pend·ence (in′tər·di·pen′dəns) *n.* Dependence on one another; mutual dependence. Also **in′ter·de·pend′en·cy** (-dən′sē). —**in′ter·de·pend′ent** *adj.* —**in′ter·de·pend′ent·ly** *adv.*

in·ter·dict (in′tər·dikt′) *v.t.* 1 To prohibit or restrain authoritatively. 2 In the Roman Catholic Church, to exclude from religious privileges. —*n.* 1 A prohibitive order; ban. 2 In the Roman Catholic Church, a ban excluding a person, parish, etc. from religious privileges. [< L *interdicere* forbid] —**in′ter·dic′tion, in′ter·dic′tor** *n.* —**in′ter·dic′tive, in′·ter·dic′to·ry** *adj.* —**in′ter·dic′tive·ly** *adv.*

in·ter·dis·ci·pli·nar·y (in′tər·dis′ə·plə·ner′ē) *adj.* Involving two or more disciplines: an *interdisciplinary* approach to the study of American history.

in·ter·est (in′tər·ist, -trist) *n.* 1 A feeling of attraction or curiosity about something. 2 The power to excite or hold such a feeling. 3 Something bringing about this feeling: a man of many *interests.* 4 *Often pl.* That which is of advantage or profit. 5 Payment made for the use of money; also, the money so paid, usu. a percentage of the amount borrowed. 6 Something added in repaying: to return a blow with *interest.* 7 A right or share in something, esp. a business enterprise. 8 The persons involved in an industry, cause, etc.: the oil *interest.* 9 Importance: a story of little *interest.* 10 Power to procure favor or regard; influence. —**in the interest of** In behalf of; for. —*v.t.* (*also* in′tə·rest) 1 To excite or hold the curiosity or attention of. 2 To cause to have a share or interest in; induce to participate. [< L *interesse* lie between, be important]

in·ter·est·ed (in′tər·is·tid, -tris-, -təres′-) *adj.* 1 Having the attention attracted or the feelings engaged. 2 Biased; not impartial. 3 Being a part owner. —**in′ter·est·ed·ly** *adv.* —**in′ter·est·ed·ness** *n.*

in·ter·est·ing (in′tər·is·ting, -tris-, -tə·res′-) *adj.* Possessing or exciting interest. —**in′ter·est·ing·ly** *adv.* —**in′ter·est·ing·ness** *n.* —**Syn.** appealing, engaging, enthralling, fascinating.

in·ter·face (in′tər·fās′) *n.* 1 A surface common to two parts or bodies. 2 A stage or point at which separate things interact: the man-machine *interface.* —*v.* **·faced, ·fac·ing** —*v.i.* 1 To act as an interface. —*v.t.* 2 To provide with an interface.

in·ter·fere (in′tər·fir′) *v.i.* **·fered, ·fer·ing** 1 To come into conflict or opposition; clash. 2 To take part unasked in the concerns of others; meddle. 3 To intervene for a specific purpose. 4 *Physics* To act in opposition, as waves of light, sound, or electricity. 5 In sports, to obstruct the actions of an opponent in an illegal manner. —**interfere with** To thwart; hinder. [< L *inter-* between + *ferire* to strike] —**in′ter·fer′er** *n.* —**in′ter·fer′ing·ly** *adv.*

in·ter·fer·ence (in′tər·fir′əns) *n.* 1 The act of interfering; conflict; collision. 2 *Physics* The action of wave trains, as of light, sound, or electricity, that on meeting tend to cancel each other. 3 In sports, obstruction of the actions of an opponent in an illegal manner.

in·ter·fold (in′tər·fōld′) *v.t. & v.i.* To fold together or one within the other.

in·ter·fuse (in′tər·fyōōz′) *v.* **·fused, ·fus·ing** *v.t.* 1 To cause to blend. 2 To cause to permeate. —*v.i.* 3 To blend; fuse. —**in′ter·fu′sion** *n.*

in·ter·im (in′tər·im) *n.* An intervening period of time; meantime. —*adj.* For or during an intervening period of time. [< L, meanwhile]

in·te·ri·or (in·tir′ē·ər) *adj.* 1 Existing, pertaining to, or occurring within something; internal. 2 Inland or far from the borders. 3 Of a private or confidential nature. —*n.* 1 The internal part; inside. 2 The inland or central region of a country. 3 The domestic affairs of a country. 4 Inner nature; basic character. [< L, compar. of *inter* within] —**in·te′ri·or′i·ty** (-ôr′ə·tē, -or′-) *n.* —**in·te′ri·or·ly** *adv.*

interior decorator One whose work is the furnishing and decorating of interiors of houses, offices, etc. —**interior decorating**

interj. interjection.

in·ter·ject (in′tər·jekt′) *v.t.* To throw between other things: introduce abruptly; interpose. [< L *inter-* between + *jacere* to throw]

in·ter·jec·tion (in′tər·jek′shən) *n.* 1 *Gram.* A word expressing emotion or simple exclamation, as *oh! alas! look!* 2 A sudden interposition or interruption. —**in′ter·jec′tion·al** *adj.* —**in′ter·jec′tion·al·ly** *adv.*

in·ter·lace (in′tər·lās′) *v.* **·laced, ·lac·ing** *v.t.* 1 To pass over and under one another; weave. 2 To unite intricately. —*v.i.* 3 To pass over and under one another: *interlacing* branches. —**in′ter·lace′ment** *n.*

in·ter·lard (in′tər·lärd′) *v.t.* To scatter throughout with something different, as for variety. —**in′ter·lard′ment** *n.*

in·ter·lay (in′tər·lā′) *v.t.* **·laid, ·lay·ing** 1 To lay between or among. 2 To decorate or diversify with something laid between.

in·ter·leaf (in′tər·lēf′) *n. pl.* **·leaves** (-lēvz′) A blank leaf inserted or bound between others in a book, etc.

in·ter·leave (in′tər·lēv′) *v.t.* **·leaved. ·leav·ing** To insert an interleaf or interleaves into (a book).

in·ter·line[1] (in'tər·līn') *v.t.* **·lined, ·lin·ing** 1 To write or print between the lines of. 2 To insert between lines. —**in'ter·lin'er** *n.*

in·ter·line[2] (in'tər·līn') *v.t.* **·lined, ·lin·ing** To put a lining between the usual lining and the outer fabric of a garment.

in·ter·lin·e·ar (in'tər·lin'ē·ər) *adj.* 1 Situated on or occurring between lines. 2 Having translations or glosses inserted between the lines, as in a text. Also **in'ter·lin'e·al** (-ē·əl).

in·ter·lin·ing (in'tər·lī'ning) *n.* 1 A lining between the usual lining and the outer fabric of a garment. 2 The material of which it is made.

in·ter·lock (in'tər·lok') *v.t. & v.i.* To join together; link with one another. —**in'ter·lock'er** *n.*

in·ter·loc·u·tor (in'tər·lok'yə·tər) *n.* 1 One who takes part in a conversation. 2 The center man in a minstrel troupe. [<L *interloqui* speak between, converse]

in·ter·loc·u·to·ry (in'tər·lok'yə·tôr'ē, -tō'rē) *adj.* 1 Consisting of or pertaining to dialogue; conversational. 2 *Law* Done during the progress of a lawsuit, but not final.

in·ter·lop·er (in'tər·lō'pər) *n.* One who thrusts himself into a place without right. [<INTER- + Du. *loopen* to run] —**Syn.** interposer, intruder, meddler, trespasser.

in·ter·lude (in'tər·lo͞od) *n.* 1 An intervening time or space. 2 An independent performance, usu. light or humorous, introduced between the acts of a play or the parts of a performance. 3 A passage of music that forms a transition. [<L *inter-* between + *ludus* a game, play]

in·ter·mar·ry (in'tər·mar'ē) *v.i.* **·ried, ·ry·ing** 1 To become connected by marriage: said of different races, religions, clans, families, etc. 2 To marry each other: said of members of the same clan, family, etc. —**in'ter·mar'riage** (-rij) *n.*

in·ter·med·dle (in'tər·med'l) *v.i.* **·dled, ·dling** To interfere unduly in the affairs of others. —**in'ter·med'dler** *n.*

in·ter·me·di·ar·y (in'tər·mē'dē·er'ē) *adj.* 1 Situated, acting, or coming between. 2 Acting as a mediator. —*n. pl.* **·ies** An agent or mediator.

in·ter·me·di·ate (in'tər·mē'dē·it) *adj.* Being or occurring in a middle place or degree. —*n.* 1 Something intermediate. 2 INTERMEDIARY. —*v.i.* (-āt) **·at·ed, ·at·ing** To act as an intermediary; mediate. [<L *intermedius* middle] —**in'ter·me'di·ate·ly** *adv.* —**in'ter·me'di·ate·ness** *n.*

in·ter·ment (in·tûr'mənt) *n.* The act of interring; burial.

in·ter·mez·zo (in'tər·met'sō, -med'zō) *n. pl.* **·zos** or **·zi** (-sē, -zē) 1 A song, chorus, or short ballet given between the acts of a play or opera. 2 A short movement connecting large divisions of a musical composition. 3 A short instrumental piece composed as if between larger movements. [Ital. <L *intermedius* intermediate]

in·ter·mi·na·ble (in·tûr'mə·nə·bəl) *adj.* Continuing, or seeming to continue, for a very long time; endless. —**in·ter'mi·na·bly** *adv.*

in·ter·min·gle (in'tər·ming'gəl) *v.t. & v.i.* **·gled, ·gling** To mingle together; mix.

in·ter·mis·sion (in'tər·mish'ən) *n.* 1 Temporary cessation. 2 An interval, as between acts in the theater. [<L *intermittere* send between] —**in'ter·mis'sive** *adj.*

in·ter·mit (in'tər·mit') *v.t. & v.i.* **·mit·ted, ·mit·ting** To stop temporarily or at intervals. [<L *inter-* between + *mittere* send, put] —**in'ter·mit'tence** *n.*

in·ter·mit·tent (in'tər·mit'ənt) *adj.* Alternately ceasing and beginning; not continuous. —**in'ter·mit'tent·ly** *adv.*

in·ter·mix (in'tər·miks') *v.t. & v.i.* To mix together; intermingle. —**in'ter·mix'ture** *n.*

in·ter·mod·u·la·tion distortion (in'tər·moj'o͞o·lā'shən) *Electronics* A form of distortion produced when a flaw in an amplifier or other device causes signals of different frequencies that are present simultaneously to modulate each other.

in·tern[1] (in·tûrn') *v.t.* To confine within the limits of a country or area, as enemy aliens or prisoners of war. [<L *internus* internal] —**in·tern'ment** *n.*

in·tern[2] (in'tûrn) *n.* A medical doctor undergoing resident training in a hospital. —*v.i.* To serve as an intern in a hospital. [See INTERN[1].] —**in'tern·ship** *n.*

in·ter·nal (in·tûr'nəl) *adj.* 1 Situated in or applicable to the inside; interior. 2 Pertaining to or derived from the inside. 3 Pertaining to the inner self or the mind; subjective. 4 Pertaining to the domestic affairs of a country. —*n.* 1 *pl.* The internal bodily organs; entrails. 2 The essential quality of anything. [<L *internus* <*in* in] —**in·ter'nal·ly** *adv.*

in·ter·nal-com·bus·tion (in·tûr'nəl·kəm·bus'chən) *adj.* Denoting a type of engine in which the fuel is burned in the engine itself rather than in an external device.

internal medicine The branch of medicine concerned with diagnosis and nonsurgical treatment of internal diseases.

internal revenue Income accruing to a government from a variety of taxes.

in·ter·na·lize (in·tûr'nə·līz) *v.t.* **·ized, ·iz·ing** To incorporate into one's own self the habits, beliefs, etc., of another or others. —**in·ter'na·li·za'tion** *n.*

in·ter·na·tion·al (in'tər·nash'ən·əl) *adj.* 1 Of or pertaining to the relations among nations: *international* law. 2 Carried on among nations: *international* trade. 3 Between two or more nations: an *international* treaty. —**in'ter·na'tion·al'i·ty** *n.* —**in'ter·na'tion·al·ly** *adv.*

In·ter·na·tion·al (in'tər·nash'ən·əl) *n.* Any of three consecutive international political organizations of socialists and communists.

International Date Line DATE LINE.

in·ter·na·tion·al·ism (in'tər·nash'ən·əl·iz'əm) *n.* The doctrine that political and economic cooperation among nations contributes to their common good. —**in'ter·na'tion·al·ist** *adj., n.*

in·ter·na·tion·al·ize (in'tər·nash'ən·əl·īz') *v.t.* **·ized, ·iz·ing** To make international, as in character or administration. —**in'ter·na'tion·al·i·za'tion** *n.*

in·terne (in'tûrn) *n.* INTERN[2].

in·ter·ne·cine (in'tər·nē'sin, -ne'-, -sīn, in·tər'nə·sēn, -sən) *adj.* 1 Involving great slaughter to both sides. 2 Ruinous; deadly. [<L *inter-* among + *necare* to kill]

in·tern·ee (in'tûr·nē') *n.* A person detained as an enemy alien, prisoner of war, etc.

in·ter·nist (in·tûr'nist) *n.* A physician specializing in internal medicine.

in·ter·pel·late (in'tər·pel'āt, -pə·lāt') *v.t.* **·lat·ed, ·lat·ing** To ask (a member of a government) for an official explanation of an action or a policy. [<L *inter-* between + *pellere* to drive] —**in'ter·pel'lant** *adj., n.* —**in·ter·pel·la·tion** (in'tər·pə·lā'shən, in·tûr'-) *n.*

in·ter·pen·e·trate (in'tər·pen'ə·trāt) *v.* **·trat·ed, ·trat·ing** *v.t.* 1 To penetrate thoroughly; permeate. 2 To penetrate mutually. —*v.i.* 3 To penetrate each other. 4 To penetrate between or among parts or things. —**in'ter·pen'e·tra'tion** *n.*

in·ter·per·son·al (in'tər·pûr'sən·əl) *adj.* Existing between people: *interpersonal* relations.

in·ter·phone (in'tər·fōn') *n.* A system providing telephone communication within a building, office, ship, etc.

in·ter·plan·e·tar·y (in'tər·plan'ə·ter'ē) *adj.* Between or among planets.

in·ter·play (in'tər·plā') *n.* Mutual or reciprocal action or influence; interaction.

in·ter·po·late (in·tûr'pə·lāt) *v.* **·lat·ed, ·lat·ing** *v.t.* 1 To alter, as a manuscript, by the insertion of new or unauthorized matter. 2 To insert (such matter). 3 *Math.* To estimate a value of (a function) between known values. —*v.i.* 4 To make interpolations. [<L *inter-* between + *polire* to polish] —**in·ter'po·la'ter, in·ter'po·la'tion, in·ter'po·la'tor** *n.* —**in·ter'po·la'tive** *adj.*

in·ter·pose (in'tər·pōz') *v.* **·posed, ·pos·ing** *v.t.* 1 To place between other things; insert. 2 To introduce by way of intervention: He *interposed* his authority. 3 To inject, as a remark, into a conversation, argument, etc. —*v.i.* 4 To come between; intervene. 5 To put in a remark; interrupt. [<L *inter-* between + *ponere* put] —**in'ter·pos'er, in·ter·po·si·tion** (in·tər·pə·zish'ən) *n.* —**in'ter·pos'ing·ly** *adv.*

in·ter·pret (in·tûr'prit) *v.t.* 1 To give the meaning of; make clear. 2 To derive a particular understanding of; construe. 3 To bring out the meaning of by artistic representation or performance. 4 To translate. —*v.i.* 5 To act as interpreter. 6 To explain [<L *interpres* agent, interpreter] —**in·ter'pret·a·bil'i·ty** *n.* —**in·ter'pret·a·ble** *adj.* —**Syn.** 1 clarify, elucidate, explain, illuminate.

in·ter·pre·ta·tion (in·tûr'prə·tā'shən) *n.* 1 The act or result of interpreting. 2 The performance or representation of a work of art so as to reveal one's conception of it. [F] —**in·ter'pre·ta'tion·al** *adj.*

in·ter·pret·er (in·tûr′prit·ər) *n.* **1** One who interprets. **2** One who serves as translator between people speaking different languages.

in·ter·pre·tive (in·tûr′prə·tiv) *adj.* **1** Designed or fitted to interpret; explanatory: *interpretive* reporting. **2** Containing an interpretation; embodying ideas or facts. **3** Admitting of interpretation; constructive. Also **in·ter′pre·ta′tive** (-tā′tiv). —**in·ter′pre·tive·ly** *adv.*

in·ter·ra·cial (in′tər·rā′shəl) *adj.* Of, between, or for persons of different races. —**in′ter·ra′ci·al·ly** *adv.*

in·ter·reg·num (in′tər·reg′nəm) *n. pl.* **·nums** or **·na** **1** The time during which a high executive office is vacant. **2** A suspension of executive authority through a change of government. **3** Any period of temporary suspension. [<L *inter-* between + *regnum* reign]

in·ter·re·late (in′tər·ri·lāt′) *v.t. & v.i.* **·lat·ed** **·lat·ing** To bring or come into reciprocal relation. —**in′ter·re·la′tion, in′ter·re·la′tion·ship** *n.*

interrog. interrogative

in·ter·ro·gate (in·ter′ə·gāt) *v.* **·gat·ed, ·gat·ing** *v.t.* To put questions to; question. —*v.i.* To ask questions. [<L *inter-* between + *rogare* ask] —**in·ter′ro·ga′tor** *n.*

in·ter·ro·ga·tion (in·ter′ə·gā′shən) *n.* **1** The act of interrogating. **2** A question; query. **3** A formal or official questioning, as of a prisoner or witness. —**in·ter′ro·ga′tion·al** *adj.*

interrogation point QUESTION MARK. Also **interrogation mark.**

in·ter·rog·a·tive (in′tə·rog′ə·tiv) *adj.* Denoting inquiry; questioning. —*n. Gram.* A word, phrase, or sentence used to ask a question, as *Who is there?* —**in′ter·rog′a·tive·ly** *adv.*

in·ter·rog·a·to·ry (in′tə·rog′ə·tôr′ē, -tō′rē) *adj.* Pertaining to, expressing, or implying a question. —*n. pl.* **·to·ries** A question; interrogation. —**in′ter·rog′a·to′ri·ly** *adv.*

in·ter·rupt (in′tə·rupt′) *v.t.* **1** To cause a delay or break in: to *interrupt* service. **2** To break the continuity, course, or sameness of. **3** To break in on (someone) talking, working, etc. —*v.i.* **4** To break in upon an action or speech. [<L *inter-* between + *rumpere* to break] —**in′ter·rupt′er** *n.* —**in′ter·rup′tive** *adj.*

in·ter·rup·tion (in′tə·rup′shən) *n.* **1** The act of interrupting. **2** A break in continuity; an interval. **3** Obstruction caused by breaking in upon any course, progress, or motion.

in·ter·scho·las·tic (in′tər·skə·las′tik) *adj.* Between or among schools: *interscholastic* basketball.

in·ter·sect (in′tər·sekt′) *v.t.* **1** To pass across; cut through or into so as to divide. —*v.i.* **2** To cross each other. [<L *inter-* between + *secare* to cut]

in·ter·sec·tion (in′tər·sek′shən) *n.* **1** The act of intersecting. **2** The point or line of contact between two lines, planes, etc. **3** The area where two streets cross. —**in′ter·sec′tion·al** *adj.*

in·ter·sperse (in′tər·spûrs′) *v.t.* **·spersed, ·spers·ing** **1** To scatter among other things; set here and there. **2** To diversify or adorn with other things scattered here and there. [<L *inter-* among + *spargere* scatter] —**in′ter·spers′ed·ly** *adv.* —**in′ter·sper′sion** (-spûr′zhən) *n.*

in·ter·state (in′tər·stāt′) *adj.* Between different states, as of the U.S.: *interstate* commerce.

in·ter·stel·lar (in′tər·stel′ər) *adj.* Situated or occurring among the stars.

in·ter·stice (in·tûr′stis) *n. pl.* **·stic·es** (-stə·sēz), -stis·iz) **1** A narrow space betweeen adjoining parts or things. **2** A crack; crevice. [<L *inter-* between + *sistere* cause to stand] —**in·ter·sti·tial** (in′tər·stish′əl) *adj.* —**in′ter·sti′tial·ly** *adv.*

in·ter·twine (in′tər·twīn′) *v.t. & v.i.* **·twined, ·twin·ing** To unite by twisting or interlacing.

in·ter·twist (in′tər·twist′) *v.t. & v.i.* To twist together; intertwine.

in·ter·ur·ban (in′tər·ûr′bən) *adj.* Between cities or towns. —*n.* A railroad connecting cities or towns.

in·ter·val (in′tər·vəl) *n.* **1** The time that intervenes between two events or periods. **2** An open space between two objects; distance between points. **3** *Music* **a** The difference in pitch between two tones. **b** A sound composed of two tones sounded simultaneously. —**at intervals** **1** From time to time. **2** At a series of points with spaces between. [<L *inter-* between + *vallum* rampart] —**Syn.** **1** interim, interlude, intermission, pause.

in·ter·vene (in′tər·vēn′) *v.i.* **·vened, ·ven·ing** **1** To come between by action or authority; interfere or mediate. **2** To occur, as something irrelevant or unexpected: I will come if nothing *intervenes.* **3** To be located between. **4** To take place between other events or times. [<L *inter-* between + *venire* come] —**in′ter·ven′er** *n.* —**in′ter·ven′ient** (-vēn′yənt) *adj., n.*

in·ter·ven·tion (in′tər·ven′shən) *n.* **1** The act of coming between. **2** Interference with the acts of others. **3** Interference in the affairs of one country by another. **4** An intervening time, event, or thing. —**in′ter·ven′tion·al** *adj.* —**in·ter·ven·tion·ist** (in′tər·ven′shən·ist) *adj., n.*

in·ter·view (in′tər·vyōō) *n.* **1** A meeting between two or more people, as to evaluate qualifications or consider for employment. **2** A meeting for soliciting views or opinions, as by reporters or investigators. **3** The report of such a meeting. —*v.t.* To have an interview with. [<L *inter-* between + *videre* see] —**in′ter·view′er** *n.*

in·ter·weave (in′tər·wēv′) *v.t. & v.i.* **·wove** or **·weaved, ·wo·ven, ·weav·ing** To weave together; intermingle or connect closely.

in·tes·tate (in·tes′tāt) *adj.* **1** Not having made a will. **2** Not legally devised or disposed of by will. —*n.* A person who dies intestate. [<L *in-* not + *testari* make a will] —**in·tes·ta·cy** (in·tes′tə·sē) *n.*

in·tes·tine (in·tes′tin) *n. Usu. pl.* The part of the alimentary canal between the stomach and the anus, consisting of the long **small intestine** and the shorter, wider **large intestine** including the colon and rectum. —*adj.* Internal with regard to state or community; domestic. [<L *intestinus* internal] —**in·tes′ti·nal** *adj.* —**in·tes′ti·nal·ly** *adv.*

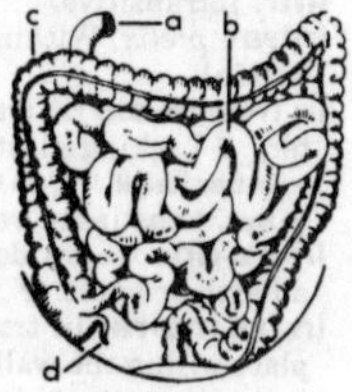

Human intestines
a. duodenum. **b.** small intestine. **c.** colon. **d.** vermiform appendix.

in·thrall (in·thrôl′) *v.* ENTHRALL.

in·throne (in·thrōn′) *v.* **·throned, ·thron·ing** ENTHRONE.

in·ti·fa·da (in′ti·fä′dä) *n. Arabic* Open rebellion.

in·ti·ma·cy (in′tə·mə·sē) *n. pl.* **·cies** **1** Close or confidential friendship. **2** An intimate act. **3** Illicit sexual connection: a euphemism.

in·ti·mate[1] (in′tə·mit) *adj.* **1** Closely connected by friendship or association; personal; confidential. **2** Pertaining to the inmost being; innermost. **3** Adhering closely; close. **4** Proceeding from within; internal. **5** Having illicit sexual relations (with): a euphemism. —*n.* A close or confidential friend. [<L *intimus,* superl. of *intus* within] —**in′ti·mate·ly** *adv.*

in·ti·mate[2] (in′tə·māt) *v.t.* **·mat·ed, ·mat·ing** **1** To make known without direct statement; hint; imply. **2** To make known formally; declare. [<L *intimare* announce] —**in′ti·ma′ter** *n.*

in·ti·ma·tion (in′tə·mā′shən) *n.* **1** Information communicated indirectly; a hint. **2** A declaration or notification.

in·tim·i·date (in·tim′ə·dāt) *v.t.* **·dat·ed, ·dat·ing** **1** To make timid; cause fear in. **2** To force or restrain by threats or violence. [<L *in-* very + *timidus* afraid] —**in·tim′i·da′tion, in·tim′i·da′tor** *n.*

in·ti·tle (in·tīt′l) *v.t.* **·tled, ·tling** ENTITLE.

in·to (in′tōō) *prep.* **1** To or toward the inside of. **2** Extending within (a period of time). **3** In the direction of. **4** To the condition or form of: grew from a tadpole *into* a frog. **5** To the practice or study of: to go *into* medicine. **6** *Slang* Actively engaged or involved with, as an interest: He's *into* mysticism. [<OE] • *In, into, in to* all have different meanings. *In* shows presence or location: *She is in the office. Into* always implies motion: *She went into the office.* Confusion may arise if *in* and *into* are used interchangeably: *They walked into the water* means something quite different from *They walked in the water.* The phrase *in to* is

made up of the adverb *in* and the preposition *to: They went into the conference room,* but *They went in to the meeting.*

in·tol·er·a·ble (in·tol′ər·ə·bəl) *adj.* Not tolerable; insufferable. **—in·tol′er·a·bil′i·ty, in·tol′er·a·ble·ness** *n.* **—in·tol′er·a·bly** *adv.*

in·tol·er·ance (in·tol′ər·əns) *n.* 1 Refusal to tolerate opposing beliefs; bigotry. 2 Incapacity or unwillingness to bear or endure. Also **in·tol′er·an·cy.**

in·tol·er·ant (in·tol′ər·ənt) *adj.* 1 Not disposed to tolerate contrary beliefs or opinions; bigoted. 2 Unable or unwilling to bear or endure: with *of: intolerant* of opposition. **—in·tol′er·ant·ly** *adv.*

in·tomb (in·to͞om′) *v.t.* ENTOMB.

in·to·na·tion (in′tō′nā′shən, in′tə-) *n.* 1 The modulation of the voice in speaking. 2 The act of intoning, as of the church service by a priest. 3 *Music* Production of tones, as by the voice, esp. in regard to precision of pitch.

in·tone (in·tōn′) *v.* **·toned ·ton·ing** *v.t.* 1 To utter or recite in a musical monotone; chant. 2 To give particular tones or intonation to. *—v.i.* 3 To utter a musical monotone; chant. [<L *in-* in + *tonus* tone] **—in·ton′er** *n.*

in to·to (in tō′tō) *Latin* Entirely.

in·tox·i·cate (in·tok′sə·kāt) *v.t.* **·cat·ed, ·cat·ing** 1 To make drunk; inebriate. 2 To elate or excite to a degree of frenzy. 3 To poison, as by toxins, drugs, etc. [<L *in-* in + *toxicum* poison] **—in·tox′i·cant** *adj., n.* **—in·tox′i·ca′tion** *n.* **—in·tox′i·ca′tive** *adj.*

intr. intransitive.

intra- *prefix* Within; inside of: *intramural.* [<L *intra* within]

in·trac·ta·ble (in·trak′tə·bəl) *adj.* 1 Not tractable; refractory. 2 Lacking plastic quality; difficult to treat or work. **—in·trac′ta·bil′i·ty, in·trac′ta·ble·ness** *n.* **—in·trac′ta·bly** *adv.* **—Syn.** 1 obstinate, rebellious, stubborn.

in·tra·dos (in·trā′dos) *n.* The interior or lower surface of an arch or vault. [F <L *intra-* within + *dorsum* back]

in·tra·mu·ral in′trə·myo͝or′əl) *adj.* 1 Situated or taking place within the walls or confines of a city, an educational institution, etc. 2 *Anat.* Situated or occurring within the substance of the walls of a bodily organ. [<INTRA- + L *murus* wall]

in·tra·mus·cu·lar (in′trə·mus′kyə·lər) *adj.* Situated or injected within a muscle or muscular tissue.

in·tran·si·gent (in·tran′sə·jənt) *adj.* Refusing to agree or compromise; irreconcilable. *—n.* One who is intransigent; a radical or revolutionary. [<L *in-* not + *transigere* agree] **—in·tran′si·gence, in·tran′si·gen·cy** (-jən·sē) *n.*

in·tran·si·tive (in·tran′sə·tiv) *Gram. adj.* 1 Not taking or requiring an object, as certain verbs. 2 Of or pertaining to such verbs. *—n.* An intransitive verb. **—in·tran′si·tive·ly** *adv.*

in·tra·state (in′trə·stāt′) *adj.* Confined within or pertaining to a single state, usu. of the U.S.

in·tra·u·ter·ine device (in′trə·yo͞o′tər·ən, -ēn) A contraceptive device consisting usu. of a plastic coil, spiral, or loop that is inserted and left within the uterus for as long as contraception is desired. Also **intrauterine contraceptive device.**

in·tra·ve·nous (in′trə·vē′nəs) *adj.* Injected into or situated within a vein. **—in′tra·ve′nous·ly** *adv.*

in·trench (in·trench′) *v.t. & v.i.* ENTRENCH.

in·trep·id (in·trep′id) *adj.* Unshaken in the presence of danger; dauntless. [<L *in-* not + *trepidus* agitated] **—in·tre·pid·i·ty** (in′trə·pid′ə·tē) *n.* **—in·trep′id·ly** *adv.*

in·tri·ca·cy (in′tri·kə·sē) *n. pl.* **·cies** 1 The quality of being complicated or entangled. 2 A complication; complexity.

in·tri·cate (in′tri·kit) *adj.* 1 Exceedingly entangled, complicated, or involved. 2 Difficult to follow or understand. [<L *in-* in + *tricae* difficulties] **—in′tri·cate·ly** *adv.* **—in′tri·cate·ness** *n.*

in·trigue (in·trēg′, in′trēg) *n.* 1 The working for an end by secret or underhand means; a plot or scheme. 2 An illicit love affair; liaison. *—v.* **·trigued, ·tri·guing** *v.t.* 1 To arouse and hold the interest or curiosity of; beguile. 2 To plot for; bring on or get by secret or underhand means. *—v.i.* 3 The use secret or underhand means; make plots. 4 To carry on a secret or illicit love affair. [<L *in-* in + *tricae* difficulties] **—in·tri′guer** *n.*

in·trin·sic (in·trin′sik, -zik) *adj.* 1 Belonging to the nature of a thing or person; inherent; essential. 2 Contained or being within. [<L *intrinsecus* internally] **—in·trin′si·cal·ly** *adv.*

introd. introduction; introductory.

in·tro·duce (in′trə·dʸo͞os′) *v.t.* **·duced, ·duc·ing** 1 To bring (someone) to acquaintance with another. 2 To present formally. 3 To bring (someone) to acquaintance with or knowledge of something: with *to.* 4 To bring into notice, use, or practice. 5 To bring or put into; insert. 6 To bring forward for consideration: to *introduce* a resolution. 7 To begin; start: to *introduce* a new line of questioning. [<L *intro-* in + *ducere* to lead] **—in′tro·duc′er** *n.* **—in′tro·duc′i·ble** *adj.*

in·tro·duc·tion (in′trə·duk′shən) *n.* 1 The act of introducing. 2 The means of introducing one person to another, as by letter, card, etc. 3 A preface by an author or speaker in explanation of the subject or design of his writing or discourse. 4 An elementary treatise: an *introduction* to chemistry. 5 *Music* A short opening passage or movement.

in·tro·duc·to·ry (in′trə·duk′tər·ē) *adj.* Serving as an introduction; preliminary. Also **in′tro·duc′tive.** **—in′tro·duc′to·ri·ly** *adv.*

in·tro·it (in·trō′it) *n.* 1 In the Roman Catholic Church, an antiphon said or chanted at the beginning of the Eucharist: also **Entrance Antiphon.** 2 In the Anglican Church, an anthem or hymm sung at the beginning of a Communion service. [<L *intro-* in + *ire* go]

in·tro·spec·tion (in′trə·spek′shən) *n.* 1 The act of looking within. 2 The examination of one's own mental and emotional processes. [<L *intro-* within + *specere* to look] **—in′tro·spec′tive** *adj.* **—in′tro·spec′tive·ly** *adv.*

in·tro·ver·sion (in′trə·vûr′zhən, -shən, in′trə·vûr′zhən) *n.* 1 The act or process of introverting. 2 The condition of or tendency toward being an introvert. **—in′tro·ver′sive** (-vûr′siv) *adj.*

in·tro·vert (in′trə·vûrt) *n.* One whose attention and interest are primarily directed inwardly towards himself rather than towards other people or the external world. *—v.t.* To turn within; cause to take an inward direction. *—adj.* Characterized by or tending to introversion. [<L *intro-* within + *vertere* to turn]

in·trude (in·tro͞od′) *v.* **·trud·ed, ·trud·ing** *v.t.* 1 To thrust or force in without leave or excuse. *—v.i.* 2 To come in without leave or invitation; thrust oneself in. 3 *Geol.* To enter by intrusion. [<L *in-* in + *trudere* to thrust] **—in·trud′er** *n.*

in·tru·sion (in·tro͞o′zhən) *n.* 1 The act of intruding; encroachment. 2 *Geol.* **a** The thrusting of molten rock into an earlier formation. **b** A rock thus formed within an earlier formation.

in·tru·sive (in·tro͞o′siv) *adj.* 1 Coming without warrant; intruding; obtrusive; prone to intrude. 2 *Geol.* Formed by intrusion, as certain igneous rocks. [See INTRUDE.] **—in·tru′sive·ly** *adv.* **—in·tru′sive·ness** *n.*

in·trust (in·trust′) *v.t.* ENTRUST.

in·tu·i·tion (in′tʸo͞o·ish′ən) *n.* 1 Quick perception of truth or knowledge without conscious attention or reasoning. 2 That which is perceived or known intuitively. [<L *intueri* look upon] **—in′tu·i′tion·al** *adj.* **—in′tu·i′tion·al·ly** *adv.*

in·tu·i·tive (in·tʸo͞o′ə·tiv) *adj.* 1 Perceived by the mind without rigorous logic or analysis. 2 Discovering truth or reaching a just conclusion without resort to the powers of reason. **—in·tu′i·tive·ly** *adv.* **—in·tu′i·tive·ness** *n.*

In·u·it (in′o͞o·wit) *n.* 1 One of a Mongoloid people indigenous to the Arctic coasts of North America, Greenland, and NE Siberia. 2 The language of the Inuit, belonging to the Eskimo-Aleut family. [<Eskimo *inuit* people, men]

in·un·date (in′ən·dāt) *v.t.* **·dat·ed, ·dat·ing** To cover or fill by overflowing. [<L *in-* in + *undare* overflow] **—in′un·da′tion, in′un·da′tor** *n.* **—Syn.** deluge, drown, flood, overwhelm.

in·ure (in·yo͝or′) *v.* **·ured, ·ur·ing** *v.t.* 1 To harden or toughen; habituate. *—v.t.* 2 To have or take effect; be applied. [<OF *en-* (causative) + *euvre* work, use] **—in·ure′ment** *n.*

in u·te·ro (in yo͞o′tər·ō) *Latin* In the uterus; prior to birth.

inv. invented; invention; inventor; invoice.

in·vade (in·vād′) *v.* **·vad·ed, ·vad·ing** *v.t.* 1 To enter with hostile intent, as for conquering. 2 To encroach upon; trespass on. 3 To spread over or penetrate injuriously: Disease *invaded* the lungs. *—v.i.* 4 To make an invasion. [<L *in-* in + *vadere* go] **—in·vad′er** *n.*

in·va·lid[1] (in′və·lid) *n.* A sickly person, or one disabled, as by wounds, disease, etc. —*adj.* 1 Enfeebled by ill health. 2 Pertaining to or for the use of sick persons. —*v.t.* 1 To cause to become invalid; disable. 2 To release (a soldier, sailor, etc.) from active service because of injury or illness. [< F < L *invalidus* not strong] —**in′va·lid·ism** *n.*

in·val·id[2] (in·val′id) *adj.* Without force, weight, or cogency; void. [< L *invalidus*] —**in·va·lid·i·ty** (in′və·lid′ə·tē) *n.* —**in·val′id·ly** *adv.*

in·val·i·date (in·val′ə·dāt) *v.t.* **·dat·ed, ·dat·ing** To weaken or destroy the force or validity of; annul. —**in·val′i·da′tion, in·val′i·da′tor** *n.*

in·val·u·a·ble (in·val′yōō·ə·bəl, -yōō·bəl) *adj.* Of a value beyond estimation; very precious. —**in·val′u·a·ble·ness** *n.* —**in·val′u·a·bly** *adv.*

in·var·i·a·ble (in·vâr′ē·ə·bəl) *adj.* That does not or cannot vary or be varied; always uniform. —**in·var′i·a·bil′i·ty, in·var′i·a·ble·ness** *n.* —**in·var′i·a·bly** *adv.*

in·var·i·ant (in·vâr′ē·ənt) *adj.* Constant or unchanged, esp. with respect to a mathematical operation. —*n.* An invariant quantity. —**in·var′i·ance** *n.*

in·va·sion (in·vā′zhən) *n.* 1 The act of invading; a military incursion for conquest, reconquest, or plunder. 2 Any attack with harmful intent or result. 3 Encroachment, as by an act of intrusion or trespass. —**in·va·sive** (in·vā′siv) *adj.*

in·vec·tive (in·vek′tiv) *n.* Violent, verbal denunciation or accusation; vituperation. —*adj.* Using or characterized by harsh words of abuse. [< L *invectus,* p.p. of *invehere.* See INVEIGH.] —**in·vec′tive·ly** *adv.* —**in·vec′tive·ness** *n.*

in·veigh (in·vā′) *v.i.* To utter vehement censure or invective: with *against.* [< L *in-* into + *vehere* carry] —**in·veigh′er** *n.*

in·vei·gle (in·vā′gəl, -vē′-) *v.t.* **·gled, ·gling** 1 To lead on, as by trickery or flattery; draw; entice. 2 To win over or seduce; captivate. [< OF *aveugle* blind] —**in·vei′gle·ment, in·vei′gler** *n.*

in·vent (in·vent′) *v.t.* 1 To create the idea, form, or existence of by original thought or effort; devise. 2 To make up, as something untrue or contrary to fact. [< L *invenire* come upon, discover] —**in·vent′i·ble** *adj.*

in·ven·tion (in·ven′shən) *n.* 1 The act or process of inventing (something new). 2 That which is invented. 3 Skill or ingenuity in contriving. 4 A fabrication; falsehood.

in·ven·tive (in·ven′tiv) *adj.* 1 Skillful at inventing; ingenious. 2 Of or having to do with invention. —**in·ven′tive·ly** *adv.* —**in·ven′tive·ness** *n.*

in·ven·tor (in·ven′tər) *n.* One who invents; esp., the originator of some method, process, or device.

in·ven·to·ry (in′vən·tôr′ē, -tō′rē) *n. pl.* **·ries** 1 An itemized list of articles, with the number and value of each. 2 The items so listed or to be listed, as the stock of goods of a business. —*v.t.* **·ried, ·ry·ing** 1 To make an inventory of; to list in detail. 2 To list in an inventory. [< L *invenire* come upon, find out] —**in′ven·to′ri·al** (-tôr′ē·əl, -tō′rē-) *adj.* —**in′ven·to′ri·al·ly** *adv.*

in·ver·ness (in′vər·nes′) *n.* A long coat with a wide, usu. removable, cape. Also **Inverness cape.** [< *Inverness,* Scotland]

in·verse (in·vûrs′, in′vûrs) *adj.* Opposite in order or effect; inverted. —*n.* That which is inverted. —*v.t.* **·versed, ·vers·ing** To invert. —**in·verse′ly** *adv.*

in·ver·sion (in·vûr′zhən, -shən) *n.* 1 The act of inverting. 2 The state of being inverted. 3 a A change in the order of a set of things. b That which results from such a change. 4 In rhetoric or grammar, a reversal of the natural order of words in a phrase or sentence. 5 *Meteorol.* A condition in which atmospheric temperature increases with increasing altitude, often trapping pollutants near the ground. —**in·ver′sive** *adj.*

in·vert (in·vûrt′) *v.t.* 1 To turn upside down or inside out. 2 To reverse the position, order, or sequence of. 3 To change to the opposite. 4 *Music* To interchange the tones or parts of. —*v.i.* 5 To undergo inversion. —*n.* (in′vûrt) 1 One who or that which is inverted. 2 HOMOSEXUAL. [< L *in-* in + *vertere* to turn] —**in·vert′i·ble** *adj.* —**in·ver′tor** *n.*

in·ver·te·brate (in·vûr′tə·brit, -brāt) *adj.* Lacking a backbone; not vertebrate. —*n.* Any animal having no backbone. —**in·ver′te·bra·cy** (-brə·sē), **in·ver′te·brate·ness** *n.*

in·vest (in·vest′) *v.t.* 1 To use (money or capital) for the purchase of property, stocks, securities, etc., with the expectation of profit or income. 2 To spend (money, time, effort, etc.) in hopes of a return. 3 To place in office formally; install. 4 To give power, authority, or rank to. 5 To cover or surround as if with a garment: Mystery *invested* the whole affair. 6 To surround or hem in; lay siege to. —*v.i.* 7 To make an investment or investments. [< L *in-* on + *vestire* clothe] —**in·ves′tor** *n.*

in·ves·ti·gate (in·ves′tə·gāt) *v.* **·gat·ed, ·gat·ing** *v.t.* 1 To search or inquire into; examine in detail. —*v.i.* 2 To make an investigation. [< L *in-* in + *vestigare* to track, trace] —**in·ves′ti·ga·ble** (-tə·gə·bəl), **in·ves′ti·ga′tive** *adj.* —**in·ves′ti·ga′tor** *n.* —**Syn.** explore, inspect, review, scrutinize, study.

in·ves·ti·ga·tion (in·ves′tə·gā′shən) *n.* 1 The act of investigating; careful inquiry or research. 2 An inquiry by authority, as by a legislative committee, into certain facts. 3 A systematic examination of some scientific question.

in·ves·ti·ture (in·ves′tə·chər) *n.* 1 The act or ceremony of investing (a person) with power, rank, or authority. 2 That which invests, clothes, or covers.

in·vest·ment (in·vest′mənt) *n.* 1 The placing of money, capital, or other resources to gain a profit, as in interest. 2 That which is invested. 3 That in which one invests. 4 INVESTITURE (def. 1). 5 *Mil.* The surrounding of a fort or town by an enemy force to create a state of siege; a blockade.

in·vet·er·ate (in·vet′ər·it) *adj.* 1 Firmly established by long continuance; deep-rooted. 2 Confirmed in a particular character or habit. [< L *inveterare* make old] —**in·vet′er·a·cy** (*pl.* **·cies**), **in·vet′er·ate·ness** *n.* —**in·vet′er·ate·ly** *adv.*

in·vid·i·ous (in·vid′ē·əs) *adj.* 1 Expressing, prompted by, or provoking envy or ill will. 2 Unjustly discriminating. [< L *invidia* envy] —**in·vid′i·ous·ly** *adv.* —**in·vid′i·ous·ness** *n.*

in·vig·or·ate (in·vig′ər·āt) *v.t.* **·at·ed, ·at·ing** To give energy to; animate. [< L *in-* in + *vigor* vigor + -ATE[2]] —**in·vig′or·at′ing·ly** *adv.* —**in·vig′or·a′tion** *n.*

in·vin·ci·ble (in·vin′sə·bəl) *adj.* Not to be overcome; unconquerable. [< L *invincibilis*] —**in·vin′ci·bil′i·ty, in·vin′ci·ble·ness** *n.* —**in·vin′ci·bly** *adv.*

in·vi·o·la·ble (in·vī′ə·lə·bəl) *adj.* That must not or cannot be violated: an *inviolable* agreement. —**in·vi′o·la·bil′i·ty, in·vi′o·la·ble·ness** *n.* —**in·vi′o·la·bly** *adv.*

in·vi·o·late (in·vī′ə·lit) *adj.* Not violated or profaned; unbroken. —**in·vi′o·late·ly** *adv.* —**in·vi′o·la·cy** (-ə·lə·sē), **in·vi′o·late·ness** *n.*

in·vis·i·ble (in·viz′ə·bəl) *adj.* 1 Not visible; not capable of being seen. 2 Not in sight; concealed. 3 Referring to resources or reserves that do not appear in regular processes or in financial statements. —*n.* One who or that which is invisible. —**the Invisible** 1 God. 2 The spiritual world. —**in·vis′i·bil′i·ty, in·vis′i·ble·ness** *n.* —**in·vis′i·bly** *adv.*

in·vi·ta·tion (in′və·tā′shən) *n.* 1 The act of inviting. 2 A means of inviting: a written *invitation.* 3 An act of alluring or encouraging; inducement: The unlocked door was an *invitation* to burglary.

in·vite (in·vīt′) *v.* **·vit·ed, ·vit·ing** *v.t.* 1 To ask (someone) politely to be present in some place or to perform some action. 2 To make formal or polite request for: to *invite* suggestions. 3 To present inducement for: The situation *invites* criticism. 4 To tempt; entice. —*n.* (in′vīt) *Slang* An invitation. [< L *invitare* entertain] —**in·vit′er** *n.*

in·vit·ing (in·vī′ting) *adj.* That invites or allures. —**in·vit′ing·ly** *adv.* —**in·vit′ing·ness** *n.*

in·vo·ca·tion (in′və·kā′shən) *n.* 1 The act of invoking. 2 An opening prayer in a church service. 3 The act of conjuring an evil spirit. 4 The formula or incantation thus used. —**in·voc·a·to·ry** (in·vok′ə·tôr′ē, -tō′rē) *adj.*

in·voice (in′vois) *n.* A list of goods sent to a purchaser, etc., containing prices and charges for shipping. —*v.t.* **·voiced, ·voic·ing** To itemize; make an invoice of. [< F *envoyer* send]

in·voke (in·vōk′) *v.t.* **·voked, ·vok·ing** 1 To call on for aid, protection, etc.; address, as in prayer. 2 To call for, as in supplication. 3 To summon or conjure by incantation, as evil spirits. [< L *in-* on + *vocare* to call] **—in·vok′er** *n.*

in·vo·lu·cre (in′və·lo͞o′kər) *n. Bot.* A ring of bracts surrounding the base of a flower, flower cluster, or fruit. [< L *involucrum* covering] **—in′vo·lu′cral** *adj.*

Involucre of thistle

in·vol·un·tar·y (in·vol′ən·ter′ə) *adj.* 1 Contrary to one's will or wish. 2 Unintentional. 3 Independent of conscious control: *involuntary* muscles. **—in′vol′un·tar′i·ly** *adv.* **—in·vol′un·tar′i·ness** *n.*

in·vo·lute (in′və·lo͞ot) *adj.* 1 Complicated; not straightforward. 2 *Bot.* Having the edges rolled inward, as a leaf. 3 *Zool.* Coiled in a close spiral, as a shell. Also **in′vo·lut′ed.** [< L *involutus* involved]

in·vo·lu·tion (in′və·lo͞o′shən) *n.* 1 The act of involving or the state of being involved; complication. 2 Something involved, rolled up, or entangled. 3 *Math.* The raising of a number or quantity to a power.

in·volve (in·volv′) *v.t.* **·volved, ·volv·ing** 1 To have as a necessary circumstance, condition, or outcome; entail: The study of medicine *involves* hard work. 2 To affect: The collision *involved* four cars. 3 To commit (oneself); engage, as in a productive effort: usu. in p.p.: to want to feel *involved.* 4 To draw into entanglement, trouble, etc.; implicate. 5 To make intricate or difficult; complicate. 6 To hold the attention of; engross. 7 To wrap up or conceal; envelop. 8 To wind in spirals or curves; coil. [< L *involvere* roll into or up] **—in·volve′ment** *n.*

in·vul·ner·a·ble (in·vul′nər·ə·bəl) *adj.* Not capable of being wounded; having no weak point. **—in·vul′ner·a·bil′i·ty, in·vul′ner·a·ble·ness** *n.* **—in·vul′ner·a·bly** *adv.* **—Syn.** indomitable, invincible, inviolable, unassailable.

in·ward (in′wərd) *adv.* 1 Toward the inside, center, or interior. 2 Into the spirit or mind. Also **in′wards.** ***—adj.*** 1 Situated within, esp. with reference to the body; inner. 2 Pertaining to the mind or spirit. 3 Proceeding toward the inside. 4 Inland. **—*n. pl.*** (in′ərdz) The internal organs; entrails. [< OE *inweard*]

in·ward·ly (in′wərd·lē) *adv.* 1 In an inward manner; esp., in one's thoughts and feelings; secretly. 2 Within. 3 Toward the center or interior; inward.

in·ward·ness (in′wərd·nis) *n.* 1 The inner quality or meaning. 2 The state of being inward or internal, mentally or physically.

in·weave (in·wēv′) *v.t.* **·wove** or **·weaved, ·wov·en, ·weav·ing** To weave in or together.

in·wrap (in·rap′) *v.t.* **·wrapped, ·wrap·ping** ENWRAP.

in·wreathe (in·rēth′) *v.t.* **·wreathed, ·wreath·ing** ENWREATHE.

in·wrought (in·rôt′) *adj.* Worked into, as a fabric or metalwork, so as to form part of it.

I·o (ī′ō) *Gk. Myth.* A maiden loved by Zeus and changed by him into a heifer to escape the jealous wrath of Hera.

i·o·dide (ī′ə·dīd) *n.* A compound of iodine with another element or radical.

i·o·dine (ī′ə·dīn, -din, -dēn) *n.* 1 A grayish black crystalline element (symbol I) of the halogen group, having a metallic luster and yielding violet-colored fumes when heated. 2 An antiseptic solution **(tincture of iodine)** of iodine in alcohol. Also **i′o·din.** [< Gk. *iōdēs* violetlike]

i·o·dize (ī′ə·dīz) *v.t.* **·dized, ·diz·ing** To treat with an iodide or iodine. **—i′o·diz′er, i′o·di·za′tion** *n.*

i·o·do·form (ī·ō′də·fôrm′) *n.* A yellow, crystalline compound of iodine, used as an antiseptic. [< IODINE + FORM(YL)]

i·on (ī′ən, ī′on) *n.* An atom or connected group of atoms that has an excess or deficiency of electrons and is, hence, electrically charged. [< Gk. *iōn,* p.p. of *ienai* go]

-ion *suffix* 1 Action or process of: *communion.* 2 Condition or state of being: *union.* 3 Result of: *opinion.* [< L *-io, -ionis*]

i·on·ic (ī·on′ik) *adj.* Of, pertaining to, or composed of ions.

I·on·ic (ī·on′ik) *adj. Archit.* Of or pertaining to an order of Greek architecture characterized by decorative scrolls on the capitals of the columns. • See CAPITAL.

i·on·ize (ī′ən·īz) *v.t.* **·ized, ·iz·ing** To convert, totally or in part, into ions. **—i′on·iz′a·ble** *adj.* **—i′on·i·za′tion, i′on·iz′er** *n.*

i·on·o·sphere (ī·on′ə·sfir) *n.* A layer of the earth's atmosphere extending from about 30 miles to over 250 miles above the surface, consisting of partially ionized gases. [< ION + SPHERE]

i·o·ta (ī·ō′tə) *n.* 1 The ninth letter and fourth vowel in the Greek alphabet (Ι,ι): corresponding to English I,i. 2 A small or insignificant mark or part. **—Syn.** 2 jot, particle, shred, speck, whit.

I O U 1 I owe you. 2 A paper having on it these letters followed by a named sum of indebtedness and the borrower's signature. Also **I.O.U.**

i.p. in passing (chess).

IPA, I.P.A. International Phonetic Alphabet; International Phonetic Association.

ip·e·cac (ip′ə·kak) *n.* 1 A South American plant related to madder. 2 The dried roots of this plant. 3 An extract of the root of this plant, used to induce vomiting. Also **ip·e·cac·u·an·ha** (ip′ə·kak′yo͞o·ä′nə). [< Tupian *ipe* little + *kaa* tree, herb + *guéne* causing sickness]

Iph·i·ge·ni·a (if′ə·jə·nī′ə) *Gk. Myth.* The daughter of Agamemnon, sacrificed by her father to Artemis, who rescued her and made her a priestess.

ip·se dix·it (ip′sē dik′sit) *Latin* A dogmatic assertion; dictum: lit., he himself has said.

ip·so fac·to (ip′sō fak′tō) By the fact itself; in and by the very fact or act. [L]

IQ, I.Q. intelligence quotient.

Ir iridium.

Ir. Ireland; Irish.

I.R.A. Irish Republican Army.

I·ran (i·ran′, ē·rän′) *n.* A constitutional monarchy in sw Asia, 630,000 sq. mi., cap. Teheran. **—I·ra·ni·an** (ī·rā′nē·ən) *adj., n.*

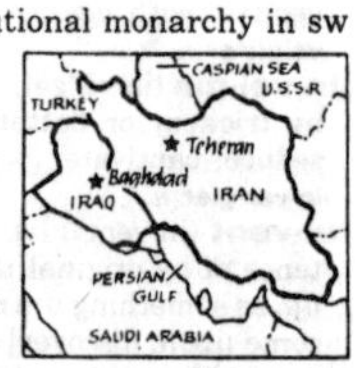

Iran and Iraq

I·raq (i·rak′, ē·räk′) *n.* A republic of sw Asia, 171,599 sq. mi., cap. Baghdad. Also **I·rak′.**

I·ra·qi (ē·rä′kē) *n. pl.* **·qi** or **·qis** A citizen or native of Iraq. ***—adj.*** Of or pertaining to Iraq or its people.

i·ras·ci·ble (i·ras′ə·bəl, ī-) *adj.* 1 Easily angered; irritable. 2 Caused by anger. [< L *irasci* be angry.] **—i·ras′ci·bil′i·ty, i·ras′ci·ble·ness** *n.* **—i·ras′ci·bly** *adv.*

i·rate (ī·rāt′, ī′rāt) *adj.* Moved to anger; wrathful. [< L *ira* anger] **—i·rate′ly** *adv.* **—i·rate′ness** *n.*

IRBM intermediate range ballistic missile.

ire (īr) *n.* Strong resentment; anger. [< L *ira* anger] **—ire′·ful** (-fəl) *adj.* **—ire′ful·ly** *adv.* **—ire′ful·ness** *n.*

Ire. Ireland.

Ire·land (īr′lənd) *n.* A republic occupying most of the island Ireland, 26,260 sq. mi., cap. Dublin.

ir·i·des·cence (ir′ə·des′əns) *n.* The rainbowlike appearance shown by various bodies, as oil films, mother-of-pearl, etc., when they reflect light. [< Gk. *iris, iridos* rainbow + -ESCENCE] **—ir′i·des′cent** *adj.* **—ir′i·des′cent·ly** *adv.*

i·rid·i·um (i·rid′ē·əm, ī-) *n.* A brittle, silver-gray, metallic element (symbol Ir) of extreme hardness, used in certain alloys for penpoints, jewelry, etc. [< Gk. *iris, iridis* rainbow + -IUM]

i·ris (ī′ris) *n. pl.* **i·ris·es** or **ir·i·des** (ir′ə·dēz, ī′rə-) 1 The colored muscular membrane that surrounds the pupil of the eye. • See EYE. 2 Any of a genus of plants with sword-shaped leaves and large flowers. 3 The flower itself, having three upright petals and three drooping sepals. 4 A rainbow. [< Gk. *iris* rainbow]

Bearded iris

I·ris (ī′ris) *Gk. Myth.* The goddess of the rainbow.

I·rish (ī′rish) *n.* 1 The people of Ireland: used with *the.* 2 People of Irish parentage, collectively. 3 The Celtic language used in Ireland. ***—adj.*** Of or pertaining to Ireland, its people, or their language.

Irish Gaelic IRISH (def. 3).

I·rish·man (ī′rish·mən) *n. pl.* **·men** (-mən) 1 A citizen or native of Ireland. 2 A person of Irish descent. **—I′rish·wom′an** (*pl.* **·wom·en**) *n. Fem.*

Irish potato The common or white potato.

Irish setter A large long-haired hunting dog with a silky, red-brown coat.
Irish stew A stew usu. made with mutton, potatoes, and onions.
Irish terrier A small dog with a wiry reddish or golden brown coat.
Irish wolfhound A large, powerful hunting dog.
irk (ûrk) *v.t.* To annoy or weary; irritate. [ME *irken*]
irk·some (ûrk′səm) *adj.* Troublesome or tiresome. **—irk′some·ly** *adv.* **—irk′some·ness** *n.* **—Syn.** annoying, tedious, vexing, wearisome.
i·ron (ī′ərn) *n.* **1** A tough, abundant, malleable, ductile, and strongly magnetic metallic element (symbol Fe) essential to animal and plant life, used in a wide range of alloys essential to industry. **2** A tool, weapon, utensil, etc., made of iron. **3** *pl.* Fetters, esp. for the feet. **4** A golf club having a metal head. • See GOLF. **5** A device with a smooth, flat surface that is heated and used to press wrinkles out of cloth. **6** A preparation of iron used as a medicine. **—in irons** Fettered or in chains. **—***adj.* **1** Made of iron. **2** Resembling iron in hardness, firmness, etc.: an *iron* constitution. **—***v.t.* **1** To smooth or press (cloth) with an iron. **2** To fetter. **3** To furnish or arm with iron. **—***v.i.* **4** To smooth or press cloth, clothing, etc. with an iron. **—iron out** To eliminate, as difficulties. [< OE *īren*] **—i′ron·er** *n.*
Iron Age The last and most advanced of the three prehistoric stages of human technology, preceded by the Stone Age and Bronze Age.
i·ron·bound (ī′ərn·bound′) *adj.* **1** Bound with iron. **2** Faced or surrounded with rocks; rugged. **3** Hard to change; unyielding.
i·ron·clad (i′ərn·klad′) *adj.* **1** Protected by iron or steel. **2** Inflexible: an *ironclad* contract. **3** Strong. **—***n.* A former type of warship sheathed with armor.
iron curtain An impenetrable barrier of secrecy and censorship, originally used to describe the dividing line between w Europe and the Soviet Union's sphere of influence.
iron hand Severe and rigorous control; despotism. **—i′ron-hand′ed** *adj.*
i·ron·ic (ī·ron′ik) *adj.* **1** Conveying a meaning that contradicts the literal sense of the words used. **2** Being the reverse of what was expected. **3** Of the nature of or given to the use of irony. Also **i·ron′i·cal.** **—i·ron′i·cal·ly** *adv.* **—i·ron′i·cal·ness** *n.*
i·ron·ing board (ī′ərn·ing) A board, usu. on legs, covered with smooth material and used for ironing clothes, etc.
iron lung An apparatus used to maintain artificial respiration in a person enclosed in it from the neck down.
i·ron·mon·ger (ī′ərn·mung′gər, -mong′-) *n. Chiefly Brit.* A dealer in iron articles and hardware. **—i·ron·mon·ger·y** (ī′ərn·mung′gər·ē, -mong′-) *n.*
iron pyrites PYRITE.
i·ron·side (ī′ərn·sīd′) *n.* **1** A person or thing of tremendous strength or endurance. **2** *pl. (construed as sing.)* An ironclad vessel.
i·ron·ware (ī′ərn·wâr′) *n.* Iron utensils, tools, ornaments, etc.; hardware.
i·ron·weed (ī′ərn·wēd′) *n.* Any of a genus of weedy plants with hard stems and heads of tubular purple flowers.
i·ron·wood (ī′ərn·wŏŏd′) *n.* **1** Any of various trees of unusually hard, heavy, or strong wood. **2** The wood itself.
i·ron·work (ī′ərn·wûrk′) *n.* Anything made of iron, as parts of a building. **—i′ron·work′er** *n.*
i·ron·works (ī′ərn·wûrks′) *n. sing. & pl.* An establishment for the manufacture of iron or of heavy ironwork.
i·ro·ny (ī′rə·nē) *n. pl.* **·nies** **1** The use of words to signify the opposite of what they usu. express, as: "When he lost his wallet, he said, 'This is my lucky day.' " **2** A condition of affairs or events exactly the reverse of what was expected or hoped for. [< Gk. *eirōneia* affected ignorance, pretense]
Ir·o·quoi·an (ir′ə·kwoi′ən) *n.* **1** A large North American Indian linguistic stock including the confederacy of the Five Nations and certain other tribes. **2** A member of any of the Iroquoian tribes. **—***adj.* Of or pertaining to the Iroquois Indians, or to any of their languages.
Ir·o·quois (ir′ə·kwoi, -kwoiz) *n. pl.* **·quois** A member of any of the North American Indian tribes formerly living in New York State, comprising the confederacy of the Five Nations.
ir·ra·di·ate (i·rā′dē·āt) *v.* **·at·ed, ·at·ing** *v.t.* **1** To expose to or treat with light or other radiant energy. **2** To make clear or understandable; enlighten. **3** To send forth in or as in rays of light; radiate. **—***v.i.* **4** To emit rays; shine. **5** To become radiant. [< L *in-* thoroughly + *radiare* to shine] **—ir·ra′di·ance, ir·ra′di·a′tion, ir·ra′di·a′tor** *n.* **—ir·ra′di·ant, ir·ra′di·a′tive** *adj.*
ir·ra·tion·al (i·rash′ən·əl) *adj.* **1** Not possessed of or not exercising reasoning powers. **2** *Math.* Not expressible as an integer or a quotient of integers, as $\sqrt{3}$. **3** Contrary to reason; absurd. **—ir·ra′tion·al′i·ty, ir·ra′tion·al·ness** *n.* **—ir·ra′tion·al·ly** *adv.*
ir·re·claim·a·ble (ir′i·klā′mə·bəl) *adj.* That cannot be reclaimed or redeemed. **—ir′re·claim′a·bil′i·ty, ir′re·claim′a·ble·ness** *n.* **—ir′re·claim′a·bly** *adv.*
ir·rec·on·cil·a·ble (i·rek′ən·sī′lə·bəl, i·rek′ən·sī′lə·bəl) *adj.* That cannot be reconciled. **—***n.* One who will not agree or become reconciled. **—ir·rec′on·cil′a·bil′i·ty, ir·rec′on·cil′a·ble·ness** *n.* **—ir·rec′on·cil′a·bly** *adv.*
ir·re·cov·er·a·ble (ir′i·kuv′er·ə·bəl) *adj.* That cannot be recovered or regained; lost beyond recall. **—ir′re·cov′er·a·bil′i·ty** *n.* **—ir′re·cov′er·a·bly** *adv.*
ir·re·deem·a·ble (ir′i·dē′mə·bəl) *adj.* **1** Not to be redeemed or replaced by an equivalent. **2** That cannot be changed or corrected. **3** Not to be redeemed in coin: said of certain types of paper money. **—ir′re·deem′a·bly** *adv.*
Ir·re·den·tist (ir′i·den′tist) *n.* Any member of a political party, esp. one established in Italy in 1878, that advocates the reunion with the "mother country" of a separated national group or region. [< Ital. *(Italia) irredenta* unredeemed (Italy)] **—Ir′re·den′tism** *n.*
ir·re·duc·i·ble (ir′i·dyōō′sə·bəl) *adj.* Not reducible. **—ir′re·duc′i·bil′i·ty, ir′re·duc′i·ble·ness** *n.* **—ir′re·duc′i·bly** *adv.*
ir·ref·ra·ga·ble (i·ref′rə·gə·bəl, ir′i·frag′ə·bəl) *adj.* That cannot be refuted or disproved. [< L *in-* not + *refragari* oppose] **—ir·ref′ra·ga·bil′i·ty, ir·ref′ra·ga·ble·ness** *n.* **—ir·ref′ra·ga·bly** *adv.*
ir·ref·u·ta·ble (i·ref′yə·tə·bəl, ir′i·fyōō′tə·bəl) *adj.* Not refutable; that cannot be disproved. **—ir·ref′u·ta·bil′i·ty** *n.* **—ir·ref′u·ta·bly** *adv.*
irreg. irregular; irregularly.
ir·re·gard·less (ir′i·gärd′lis) *adj. & adv. Nonstand.* Regardless.
ir·reg·u·lar (i·reg′yə·lər) *adj.* **1** Not regular; departing from the usual or accepted state of things: an *irregular* heartbeat. **2** Not symmetrical or even: *irregular* features. **3** Not conforming in action or character to rule, duty, discipline, etc.: *irregular* habits. **4** Not belonging to a regular military force. **5** *Gram.* Not inflected or conjugated according to the most prevalent pattern: *irregular* verbs. **6** Not according to rule; not complying with legal formalities. **—***n.* An irregular person or thing. **—ir·reg′u·lar·ly** *adv.* **—Syn. 1** abnormal, erratic. **2** asymmetrical, uneven. **3** lawless, uncontrolled.
ir·reg·u·lar·i·ty (i·reg′yə·lar′ə·tē) *n. pl.* **·ties** **1** The condition of being irregular; an aberration, inconsistency, etc. **2** Something in an irregular state or condition.
ir·rel·e·vant (i·rel′ə·vənt) *adj.* Not relevant or pertinent. **—ir·rel′e·vance, ir·rel′e·van·cy** *(pl.* **·cies)** *n.* **—ir·rel′e·vant·ly** *adv.*
ir·re·li·gion (ir′i·lij′ən) *n.* The state of being without or opposed to religion; unbelief. **—ir′re·lig′ion·ist** *n.*
ir·re·li·gious (ir′i·lij′əs) *adj.* **1** Not religious; indifferent or opposed to religion. **2** Not in accordance with religious practices; profane. **—ir′re·lig′ious·ly** *adv.* **—ir′re·lig′ious·ness** *n.*
ir·re·me·di·a·ble (ir′i·mē′dē·ə·bəl) *adj.* Not to be remedied; irreparable. **—ir′re·me′di·a·ble·ness** *n.* **—ir′re·me′di·a·bly** *adv.*
ir·re·mis·si·ble (ir′ə·mis′ə·bəl) *adj.* Impossible to forgive

or pardon; not remissible. —**ir′re·mis′si·bil′i·ty, ir′re·mis′si·ble·ness** *n.* —**ir′re·mis′si·bly** *adv.*

ir·re·mov·a·ble (ir′i·mōō′və·bəl) *adj.* Not removable; permanent. —**ir′re·mov′a·bil′i·ty** *n.* —**ir′re·mov′a·bly** *adv.*

ir·rep·a·ra·ble (i·rep′ər·ə·bəl) *adj.* That cannot be repaired, rectified, or made amends for. —**ir·rep′a·ra·bil′i·ty, ir·rep′a·ra·ble·ness** *n.* —**ir·rep′a·ra·bly** *adv.*

ir·re·place·a·ble (ir′i·plā′sə·bəl) *adj.* Not capable of being replaced by another.

ir·re·pres·si·ble (ir′i·pres′ə·bəl) *adj.* Not repressible; that cannot be restrained. —**ir′re·pres′si·bil′i·ty, ir′re·pres′si·ble·ness** *n.* —**ir′re·pres′si·bly** *adv.*

ir·re·proach·a·ble (ir′i·prō′chə·bəl) *adj.* Not reproachable; blameless. [< F *irréprochable*] —**ir′re·proach′a·bil′i·ty, ir′re·proach′a·ble·ness** *n.* —**ir′re·proach′a·bly** *adv.*

ir·re·sis·ti·ble (ir′i·zis′tə·bəl) *adj.* Not resistible; too urgent, inviting, etc., to be withstood —**ir′re·sis′ti·bil′i·ty, ir′re·sis′ti·ble·ness** *n.* —**ir′re·sis′ti·bly** *adv.*

ir·res·o·lute (i·rez′ə·lōōt) *adj.* Wanting in firmness of purpose; wavering. —**ir·res′o·lute′ly** *adv.* —**ir·res′o·lute′·ness, ir·res′o·lu′tion** *n.*

ir·re·spec·tive (ir′i·spek′tiv) *adj.* Regardless: with *of.* —**ir′re·spec′tive·ly** *adv.*

ir·re·spon·si·ble (ir′i·spon′sə·bəl) *adj.* **1** Not responsible or sober in action; careless in heeding responsibilities. **2** Not responsible for one's actions; not accountable, as because of age or mental illness. —*n.* A person who is irresponsible. —**ir′re·spon′si·bil′i·ty, ir′re·spon′si·ble·ness** *n.* —**ir′re·spon′si·bly** *adv.*

ir·re·spon·sive (ir′i·spon′siv) *adj.* Giving no response. —**ir′re·spon′sive·ness** *n.*

ir·re·triev·a·ble (ir′i·trē′və·bəl) *adj.* Not retrievable; irreparable. —**ir′re·triev′a·bil′i·ty, ir′re·triev′a·ble·ness** *n.* —**ir′·re·triev′a·bly** *adv.*

ir·rev·er·ence (i·rev′ər·əns) *n.* **1** The quality or condition of being irreverent. **2** An irreverent act or remark.

ir·rev·er·ent (i·rev′ər·ənt) *adj.* Lacking in proper reverence; without respect. —**ir·rev′er·ent·ly** *adv.*

ir·re·vers·i·ble (ir′i·vûr′sə·bəl) *adj.* That cannot be reversed, repealed, or annulled. —**ir′re·vers′i·bil′i·ty, ir′re·vers′i·ble·ness** *n.* —**ir′re·vers′i·bly** *adv.*

ir·rev·o·ca·ble (i·rev′ə·kə·bəl) *adj.* Incapable of being revoked; unalterable. —**ir·rev′o·ca·bil′i·ty, ir·rev′o·ca·ble·ness** *n.* —**ir·rev′o·ca·bly** *adv.*

ir·ri·gate (ir′ə·gāt) *v.t.* **·gat·ed, ·gat·ing 1** To supply (land) with water by means of ditches or other artificial channels. **2** *Med.* To wash out (a wound, body cavity, etc.) with water or other fluid. [< L *irrigare* bring water to] —**ir′ri·ga·ble** (ir′ə·gə·bəl) *adj.* —**ir′ri·ga′tion, ir′ri·ga′tor** *n.*

ir·ri·ta·ble (ir′ə·tə·bəl) *adj.* **1** Showing impatience or ill temper on little provocation; irascible. **2** Responsive to stimuli. **3** *Pathol.* Abnormally sensitive. [< L *irritare* irritate] —**ir′ri·ta·bil′i·ty, ir′ri·ta·ble·ness** *n.* —**ir′ri·ta·bly** *adv.*

ir·ri·tant (ir′ə·tənt) *adj.* Causing irritation. —*n.* **1** An agent of inflammation, pain, etc. **2** A provocation; spur. —**ir′ri·tan·cy** *n.*

ir·ri·tate (ir′ə·tāt) *v.t.* **·tat·ed, ·tat·ing 1** To excite ill temper or impatience in; exasperate. **2** To make sore or inflamed. **3** *Biol.* To excite, as organic tissue, to a characteristic reaction. [< L *irritare* irritate] —**ir′ri·tat′ing·ly** *adv.* —**ir′ri·ta′tive** *adj.* —**ir′ri·ta′tor** *n.*

ir·ri·ta·tion (ir′ə·tā′shən) *n.* **1** The act of irritating. **2** The state of being irritated. **3** A person or thing that irritates.

ir·rup·tion (i·rup′shən) *n.* **1** A breaking or rushing in. **2** A violent incursion. [< L *irruptus,* pp. of *irrumpere* burst in] —**ir·rup′tive** *adj.*

IRS Internal Revenue Service.

is (iz) Present tense, third person singular of BE. [< OE]

Is, Is., Isa. Isaiah.

is. island(s); isle(s).

I·saac (ī′zək) In the Bible, the son of Abraham and Sarah, and father of Esau and Jacob.

i·sa·go·ge (ī′sə·gō′jē) *n.* An introduction, as to a work of scholarship. [< Gk. *eisagein* introduce] —**i′sa·gog′ic** (-goj′·ik) *adj.*

I·sa·iah (ī·zā′ə, ī·zī′ə) A major Hebrew prophet of the eighth century B.C. —*n.* A book of the Old Testament attributed wholly or in part to him. Also **I·sai′as** (-əs). —**I·sa′ian** *adj.*

Is·car·i·ot (is·kar′ē·ət) JUDAS ISCARIOT.

is·che·mi·a (is·kē′mē·ə) *n.* Inadequate blood circulation in an organ or tissue. Also **is·chae′mi·a.** [< Gk. *ischein* to hold, check + *haima* blood] —**is·che′mic** *adj.*

is·chi·um (is′kē·əm) *n. pl.* **·chi·a** (-kē·ə) The posterior part of the hipbone. Also **is·chi·on** (is′kē·ən). [< Gk. *ischion* hip, hip joint] —**is′chi·al** (-əl) *adj.* • See PELVIS.

-ise *Chiefly Brit.* -IZE.

-ish *suffix* **1** Of or belonging to (a national group): *Danish.* **2** Of the nature of; like: *clownish.* **3** Verging toward the character of: *bookish.* **4** Somewhat; rather: *tallish.* **5** *Informal* Approximately: *fiftyish.* [< OE *-isc*]

Ish·ma·el (ish′mā·əl) In the Bible, the son of Abraham and Hagar, exiled with the latter. —*n.* An outcast.

Ish·ma·el·ite (ish′mē·əl·īt′) *n.* **1** A traditional descendant of Ishmael. *Gen.* 21: 9–21. **2** Any wanderer; outcast. —**Ish·ma·el·it′ish** (-ī′tish) *adj.*

Ish·tar (ish′tär) In Babylonian and Assyrian mythology, the wife of Tammuz and goddess of love and fertility.

i·sin·glass (ī′zing·glas, ī′zən-, -gläs) *n.* **1** A preparation of gelatin made from fish bladders. **2** Mica, esp. in thin, translucent sheets. [< MDu. *huysenblas* sturgeon bladder]

I·sis (ī′sis) In Egyptian mythology, the goddess of fertility, sister and wife of Osiris.

isl. island(s).

Is·lam (is′ləm, iz′-, is·läm′) *n.* **1** The religion of the Muslims, which maintains that there is but one God, Allah, and that Mohammed is his prophet. **2** The body of Muslim believers, their culture, and the countries they inhabit. —**Is·lam′ic** *adj.* —**Is′lam·ism, Is′lam·ite** *n.*

Is·lam·ize (is′ləm·īz, iz′-) *v.t. & v.i.* **·ized, ·iz·ing** To convert or conform to Islam.

is·land (ī′lənd) *n.* **1** A land mass, usu. of moderate size, surrounded by water. **2** Anything isolated or like an island. **3** A raised safety area in the middle of a wide street or at a crossing. **4** *Anat.* A group of cells differing from the surrounding tissue. —*v.t.* To make into an island or islands; insulate. [< OE *īgland,* lit., island land]

is·land·er (ī′lən·dər) *n.* An inhabitant of an island.

isle (īl) *n.* A small island. —*v.* **isled, isl·ing** *v.t.* To make into an isle. [< L *insula* island]

is·let (ī′lit) *n.* A little island. • See ATOLL.

ism (iz′əm) *n.* A doctrine or system: often applied satirically or disparagingly. [< -ISM]

-ism *suffix of nouns* **1** The act, process, or result of: *ostracism.* **2** The condition of being: *skepticism.* **3** The characteristic action or behavior of: *heroism.* **4** The beliefs, teachings, or system of: *Calvinism.* **5** Devotion to; adherence to the teachings of: *nationalism.* **6** A characteristic or peculiarity of: said of language or idiom: *Americanism.* **7** *Med.* An abnormal condition: *alcoholism.* [< Gk. *-ismos*]

is·n't (iz′ənt) Contraction of *is not.*

iso- *combining form* Equal; the same; identical: *isobar.* Also **is-.** [< Gk. *isos* equal]

i·so·bar (ī′sə·bär) *n.* **1** *Meteorol.* A line, as on a weather map, composed of points having identical barometric pressure. **2** *Physics* Any of several nuclei of different elements that have the same mass number. [< ISO- + Gk. *baros* weight] —**i′so·bar′ic** (-bar′ik) *adj.*

i·soch·ro·nal (i·sok′rə·nəl) *adj.* Of or characterized by equal intervals of time. Also **i·so·chron·ic** (ī′sə·kron′ik), **i·soch′ro·nous.** [< ISO- + Gk. *chronos* time] —**i·soch′ro·nous·ly** *adv.*

i·so·cline (ī′sə·klīn) *n. Geol.* A rock fold in which the strata are so closely pressed that they are parallel. [< ISO- + Gk. *klinein* to bend] —**i·so·cli·nal** (ī′sə·klī′nəl), **i′so·clin′ic** (-klin′ik) *adj.*

i·so·gon·ic (ī′sə·gon′ik) *adj.* **1** Having equal angles. **2** Denoting a line composed of points on the earth having identical magnetic declination. Also **i·sog·o·nal** (ī·sog′ə·nəl). —*n.* An isogonic line. [< ISO- + Gk. *gōnia* angle]

i·so·late (ī′sə·lāt, is′ə-) *v.t.* **·lat·ed, ·lat·ing 1** To place in a detached or separate situation; set apart. **2** *Electr.* To insulate. **3** *Chem.* To obtain in a pure form, as an element or compound. **4** *Med.* To set apart from others, as a person with a communicable disease. **5** *Bacteriol.* To obtain a pure culture of (a specified virus or bacterium). —*n.* A unit or group that is set apart. [< Ital. *isolare* isolate <

isola island < L *insula* island] **—i·so·la'tion, i'so·la'tor** *n.* — **Syn.** *v.* **1** banish, seclude, segregate. **4** quarantine.

i·so·la·tion·ism (ī'sə·lā'shən·iz'əm) *n.* The advocacy of national self-sufficiency and freedom from foreign political and economic alliances. **—i'so·la'tion·ist** *adj., n.* **—i'so·la'tion·is'tic** *adj.*

i·so·mer (ī'sə·mər) *n.* Any of two or more compounds having the same molecular formula but with a different arrangement of the atoms in a molecule. [< ISO- + Gk. *meros* part] **—i'so·mer'ic** (-mer'ik) *adj.* **—i·som·er·ism** (ī·som'ər·iz'əm) *n.*

i·som·er·ous (ī·som'ər·əs) *adj.* Equal in number, as the members of the successive whorls of a flower.

i·so·met·ric (ī'sō·met'rik) *adj.* **1** Having equal measures. **2** Having a constant measure. Also **i'so·met'ri·cal.** [< ISO- + Gk. *metron* measure] **—i'so·met'ri·cal·ly** *adv.*

isometric exercises A means of strengthening muscles by forcefully contracting them against immovable resistance. Also **i'so·met'rics.**

i·so·morph (ī'sə·môrf) *n.* An organism or crystal superficially like another morphologically. [< ISO- + Gk. *morphē* form] **—i'so·mor'phism** *n.*

i·so·mor·phic (ī'sə·môr'fik) *adj.* **1** Of or denoting an isomorph. **2** *Math.* Exhibiting a one-to-one correspondence between elements and analogy between the operations performed on those elements, as two sets.

i·sos·ce·les (ī·sos'ə·lēz) *adj. Geom.* Having two sides of equal length, as a triangle. [< Gk. *isoskelēs* equal-legged]

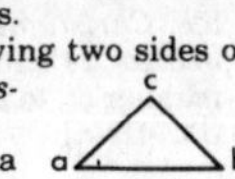

Isosceles triangle
(ac = bc)

i·so·therm (ī'sə·thûrm) *n.* A line, as on a weather map, composed of points that have the same temperature. [< ISO- + Gk. *thermē* heat]

i·so·ther·mal (ī'sə·thûr'məl) *adj.* Having a constant or uniform temperature. —*n.* ISOTHERM. **—i'so·ther'mal·ly** *adv.*

i·so·ton·ic (ī'sə·ton'ik) *adj.* **1** Having the same tension. **2** *Physiol.* Exerting the same osmotic pressure, as blood or other specified fluid. **3** *Music* Pertaining to, characterized by, or having equal tones. [< ISO- + Gk. *tonos* accent, tone] **—i·so·to·nic·i·ty** (ī'sə·tō·nis'ə·tē) *n.*

i·so·tope (ī'sə·tōp) *n.* Any of two or more forms of an element having the same atomic number and similar chemical properties but differing in atomic weight. [< ISO- + Gk. *topos* place] **—i·so·top·ic** (ī'sə·top'ik, -tō'pik) *adj.* — **i·sot·o·py** (ī·sot'ə·pē) *n.*

i·so·trop·ic (ī'sə·trop'ik, -trō'pik) *adj. Physics* Exhibiting the same physical properties in every direction. Also **i'so·trope, i·sot·ro·pous** (ī·sot'rə·pəs). [< ISO- + Gk. *tropos* a turn]

Is·ra·el (iz'rē·əl) *n.* **1** A republic at the E end of the Mediterranean, 7,993 sq. mi., cap. Jerusalem. • See map at JORDAN. **2** The Jewish people, traditionally regarded as descended from Israel (Jacob). **3** The kingdom in the northern part of ancient Palestine. **4** The name bestowed upon Jacob after he had wrestled with the angel. *Gen.* 32:28.

Is·rae·li (iz·rā'lē) *n. pl.* **·lis** or **·li** A citizen or native of modern Israel. —*adj.* Of or pertaining to modern Israel or its people.

Is·ra·el·ite (iz'rē·əl·īt') *n.* Any of the people of ancient Israel or their descendants; a Hebrew; a Jew. —*adj.* Of or pertaining to ancient Israel or the Israelites. **—Is'ra·el·it'·ish** (-ī'tish), **Is'ra·el·it'ic** (-it'ik) *adj.*

is·su·ance (ish'yōō·əns) *n.* The act of putting, sending, or giving out; distribution. **—is'su·ant** *adj.*

is·sue (ish'yōō) *v.* **·sued, ·su·ing** *v.t.* **1** To give out or deliver in a public or official manner: to *issue* a magazine. **2** To deal out or distribute: to *issue* ammunition. **3** To send forth; let out. —*v.i.* **4** To come forth or flow out; emerge. **5** To come as a result or consequence; proceed. **6** To be given out or published; appear. **7** To come as profit or revenue; accrue: with *out of.* —*n.* **1** A subject of discussion or interest; the matter at hand. **2** Result; outcome; upshot. **3** The action of giving out or supplying officially or publicly. **4** An item or amount which is issued. **5** Offspring; progeny. **6** Profits; proceeds. **7** The act of going out; outflow. **8** A place or way of egress. **9** *Law* The point in question between parties to an action. [< L *ex-* out of + *ire* go] **—at issue** Under dispute; in question. **—take issue** To disagree. **—is'su·er** *n.* **—Syn.** *v.* **1** print, publish. **2** allot, dispense. **3** discharge, emit.

-ist *suffix* **1** One who or that which does or has to do with: *catechist.* **2** One whose profession is: *pharmacist.* **3** A student or devotee of: *genealogist.* **4** One who advocates or adheres to: *socialist.* [< Gk. *-istēs*]

isth·mi·an (is'mē·ən) *adj.* Of or pertaining to an isthmus. —*n.* An inhabitant of an isthmus.

isth·mus (is'məs) *n. pl.* **·mus·es** or **·mi** (-mī) A narrow body of land connecting two larger bodies. **—the Isthmus** The Isthmus of Panama. [< Gk. *isthmos* narrow passage]

is·tle (ist'lē) *n.* A fiber derived from various tropical American plants, used for carpets, cordage, etc. [< Nahuatl *ichtli*]

it (it) *pron.* The neuter pronoun, nominative and objective of the third person singular, used: **1** As a substitute for things or for infants and animals when the sex is unspecified. **2** As the subject of an impersonal verb: *It* rained. **3** As the subject or object of a clause regarding a general condition or state of affairs: *It* was warm. **4** As the subject or predicate nominative of a verb whose logical subject is anticipated: Who was *it? It* was John. **5** As the indefinite subject of a verb introducing a clause or phrase: *It* seems that he knew. **6** *Informal* As the indefinite object after certain verbs in idiomatic expressions: to lord *it* over; to face *it.* —*n.* In certain children's games, the player required to perform some specified act. [< OE *hit*]

It., Ital. Italian; Italy.

it., ital. italic; italics.

I.T.A., i/t/a Initial Teaching Alphabet.

I·tal·ian (i·tal'yən) *n.* **1** A native or citizen of Italy. **2** A person of Italian parentage. **3** The language of Italy. —*adj.* Of or pertaining to Italy, its people, or their language.

i·tal·ic (i·tal'ik) *Printing n.* A style of type in which the letters slope, as *these:* also **i·tal'ics.** —*adj.* Designating, or printed in, italic.

I·tal·ic (i·tal'ik) *adj.* Relating to any of the peoples of ancient Italy. —*n.* A subfamily of the Indo-European languages.

i·tal·i·cize (i·tal'ə·sīz) *v.t. & v.i.* **·cized, ·ciz·ing** **1** To print in italics. **2** To underscore (written words or phrases) with a single line to indicate italics. *Brit. sp.* **·cise.**

It·a·ly (it'ə·lē) *n.* A republic of s Europe, 116,286 sq. mi., cap. Rome.

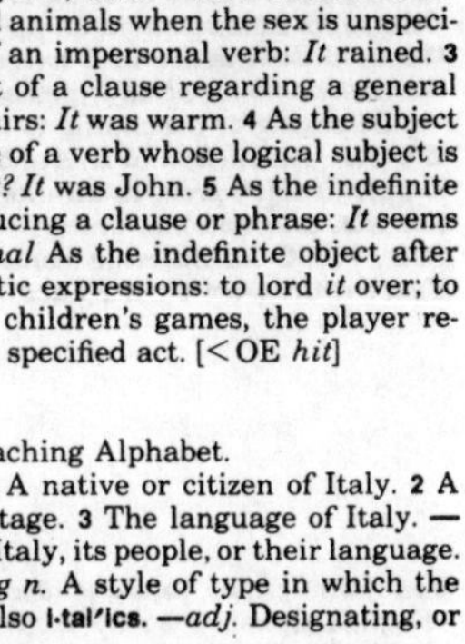

itch (ich) *v.i.* **1** To feel a peculiar irritation of the skin which inclines one to scratch the part affected. **2** To have a desire or longing; crave. —*n.* **1** SCABIES. **2** An itching of the skin. **3** A restless desire or yearning. [< OE *giccan*] **—itch'i·ness** *n.* **—itch'y** *adj.*

-ite[1] *suffix of nouns* **1** A native of: *Brooklynite.* **2** An adherent of: *Darwinite.* **3** A descendant of: *Israelite.* **4** *Mineral.* A rock or mineral: *graphite.* **5** *Zool.* A part of the body or of an organ: *somite.* **6** *Paleontol.* A fossil: *ammonite.* **7** Like; resembling; related to: often used in the names of commercial products: *dynamite.* [< Gk. *-itēs*]

-ite[2] *suffix* A salt or ester of an acid whose name ends in *-ous: sulfite.* [< F *-ite*]

i·tem (ī'təm) *n.* **1** A separate article or entry in an account, etc. **2** A newspaper paragraph. —*v.t.* To set down by items. —*adv.* Likewise. [L, likewise]

i·tem·ize (ī′təm·īz) *v.t.* **·ized, ·iz·ing** To set down or specify by items. —**i′tem·i·za′tion, i′tem·iz′er** *n.*

it·er·ate (it′ə·rāt) *v.t.* **·at·ed, ·at·ing** To utter or do again. [< L *iterum* again] —**it′er·a·ble** (it′ər·ə·bəl) *adj.* —**it′er·ance, it′er·a′tion** *n.*

it·er·a·tive (it′ə·rā′tiv, it′ər·ə·tiv) *adj.* Characterized by repetition; repetitious.

i·tin·er·an·cy (ī·tin′ə·rən·sē, i·tin′-) *n.* A passing from place to place in circuit. Also **i·tin′er·a·cy.**

i·tin·er·ant (ī·tin′ər·ənt, i·tin′-) *adj.* Going from place to place. —*n.* One who travels from place to place. [< L *iter, itineris* journey] —**i·tin′er·ant·ly** *adv.* —**Syn.** *adj.* nomadic, peripatetic, wandering, wayfaring.

i·tin·er·ar·y (ī·tin′ə·rer′ē, i·tin′-) *n. pl.* **·ar·ies** 1 A detailed account or diary of a journey. 2 A plan of a proposed tour. 3 A route pursued in traveling. 4 A guidebook. —*adj.* 1 Pertaining to or done on a journey. 2 ITINERANT. [< L *iter, itineris* journey, route]

i·tin·er·ate (ī·tin′ər·āt, i·tin′-) *v.i.* **·at·ed, ·at·ing** To journey from place to place in or on circuit. —**i·tin′er·a′tion** *n.*

-itis *suffix* Inflammation of: *laryngitis.* [< Gk.]

it'll (it′l) Contraction of *it will* and *it shall.*

its (its) *pronominal adj.* (possessive case of the pronoun *it*) Belonging or pertaining to it: *its* color.

it's (its) Contraction of *it is* and *it has.*

it·self (it·self′) *pron.* It: an intensive or reflexive use.

IU, I.U. international unit(s).

IUD, IUCD intrauterine (contraceptive) device.

I've (īv) Contraction of *I have.*

-ive *suffix of adjectives* 1 Having a tendency or predisposition to: *disruptive.* 2 Having the nature, character, or quality of: *massive.* [< L *-ivus*]

i·vied (ī′vēd) *adj.* Overgrown with ivy.

i·vo·ry (ī′vər·ē) *n. pl.* **·ries** 1 The hard, creamy-white dentine that forms the tusks of the elephant, walrus, etc. 2 Any ivorylike substance. 3 *pl.* Things made of or similar to ivory; esp. in slang use, the teeth, dice, keys of a piano, etc. 4 The color of ivory. —*adj.* Made of or resembling ivory. [< L *ebur* ivory]

Ivory Coast A republic of w Africa, 128,364 sq. mi., cap. Abidjan. • See map at AFRICA.

ivory nut The hard, ivorylike seed of a South American palm, used for small carvings, buttons, etc.

ivory tower A retreat from reality and action to the world of dreams and ideals.

i·vy (ī′vē) *n. pl.* **i·vies** 1 Any of a genus of woody climbing plants with glossy, trilobate, evergreen leaves. 2 Any of various climbing or creeping plants, as poison ivy, Virginia creeper, etc. [< OE *īfig*]

Ivy League An association of colleges and universities in the NE U.S., regarded as high in scholastic and social distinction.

IWW, I.W.W. Industrial Workers of the World.

-ize *suffix of verbs* 1 To make; cause to become or resemble: *Christianize.* 2 Subject to the action of; affect with: *oxidize.* 3 Change into; become: *mineralize.* 4 To act in the manner of; to practice: *sympathize. Brit. sp., often* **-ise.** [< Gk. *-izein*]

J

J, j (jā) *n. pl.* **J's, j's, Js, js** (jāz) 1 The tenth letter of the English alphabet. 2 Any spoken sound representing the letter *J* or *j.* 3 Something shaped like a J, as a bolt or hook. —*adj.* Shaped like a J.

J joule.

J. Judge; Justice.

JA, J.A. Joint Account; Judge Advocate.

jab (jab) *v.t. & v.i.* **jabbed, jab·bing** 1 To poke or thrust sharply. 2 To punch or strike with sharp blows. —*n.* A sharp thrust or poke: punch. [ME *jobben*]

jab·ber (jab′ər) *v.t. & v.i.* To speak rapidly or unintelligibly; chatter. —*n.* Rapid or unintelligible talk. [Imit.]

ja·bot (zha·bō′, jab′ō; *Fr.* zhȧ·bō′) *n. pl.* **·bots** (-bōz′; *Fr.* -bō′) A frill, as of lace, worn down the front of a woman's blouse or, formerly, on a man's shirt. [F]

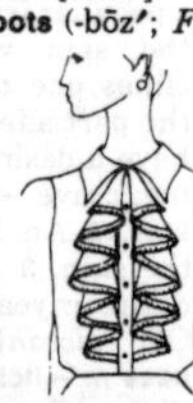

Jabot

ja·cinth (jā′sinth, jas′inth) *n.* 1 HYACINTH. 2 A reddish orange color. [< L *hyacinthus* hyacinth]

jack (jak) *n.* 1 *Mech.* **a** One of various machines or devices used to replace a human worker: often used in combination: *bootjack.* **b** Any of various devices using the principle of a lever, screw, etc., placed under or against a load and used to lift or move it. 2 A man or boy. 3 A manual laborer: often used in combination: *lumberjack.* 4 *Often cap.* A sailor. 5 A male donkey; jackass. 6 JACK RABBIT. 7 Any of various birds, as a jackdaw. 8 *Electr.* A socket equipped with a spring clip for holding a plug to make a connection. 9 A playing card with a young man's picture on it; knave. 10 One of the small, pronged metal pieces used in the game of jacks; a jackstone. 11 A ship's flag showing its nationality; union jack. 12 *Slang* Money. —*v.t.* 1 To raise or lift with or as with a jack. 2 *Informal* To advance, as a price or charge: often with *up.* [< *Jack,* a personal name]

jack·al (jak′əl, -ôl) *n.* 1 Any of various wild dogs of Africa and Asia, usu. yellowish gray in color. 2 One who does base or menial work for another. [< Pers. *shaghal*]

jack-a-napes (jak′ə·nāps) *n.* An impertinent fellow; an upstart. [< *Jack Napes,* nickname of William de la Pole, 15th c. Duke of Suffolk]

jack·ass (jak′as′) *n.* 1 The male ass. 2 A stupid person; fool.

jack·boot (jak′bōōt′) *n.* A heavy boot reaching above the knee.

jack·daw (jak′dô′) *n.* A small, black bird of Europe, related to the crow.

jack·et (jak′it) *n.* 1 A short coat, usu. not extending below the hips. 2 A close-fitting outer covering, as the paper cover for a bound book, a paper or cardboard cover for a phonograph record, the skin of a potato, the casing of a bullet, an open envelope or folder for filing letters, documents, etc. —*v.t.* To cover with or put into a jacket. [< OF *jaque* a coat] —**jack′et·ed** *adj.*

Jack Frost Wintry or frosty weather personified.

jack-in-the-box (jak′in·t͟hə·boks′) *n. pl.* **-box·es** A toy consisting of a grotesque figure in a box, springing up when the lid is unfastened. Also **jack′-in-a-box′.**

jack-in-the-pul·pit (jak′in·t͟hə·pōōl′pit) *n. pl.* **·pits** A small woodland plant of the arum family, with flowers on a spadix enclosed in a greenish purple spathe.

Jack-in-the-pulpit Fruit and flower

jack·knife (jak′nīf′) *n. pl.* **·knives** (-nīvz) 1 A large pocket knife with recessed handle into which the blade is folded. 2 A dive during which the body is doubled from the hips with the hands touching the ankles, and then straightened before entering the water. —*v.t. & v.i.* **·knifed, ·knif·ing** To fold or double up, as a jacknife.

jack-of-all-trades (jak′əv·ôl′trādz′) *n.* One who is able to do many kinds of work.

jack-o'-lan·tern (jak′ə·lan′tərn) *n.* 1 IGNIS FATUUS (def. 1). 2 A lantern made of a pumpkin carved into a face.

jack·pot (jak′pot′)*n.* 1 In poker, a pot that must accumulate till one of the players gets a pair of jacks or cards of higher value on the deal. 2 Any prize or stakes in which winnings or contributions accumulate. —**hit the jackpot** *Informal* To win the biggest possible prize; to achieve a major success.

jack rabbit One of a genus of large American hares with strong hind legs and long ears.

jacks (jaks) *n. pl. (construed as sing.)* A children's game in which small, pronged pieces of metal are picked up in a certain sequence while bouncing a ball.

jack·stone (jak'stōn') *n.* **1** JACK (def. 10). **2** *pl. (construed as sing.)* JACKS.

jack·straw (jak'strô') *n.* **1** A straw effigy. **2** One of a set of straws or thin strips of wood used in playing a child's game (**jackstraws**).

Ja·cob (jā'kəb) In the Bible, a Hebrew patriarch, son of Isaac and father of the founders of the twelve tribes of Israel.

Jac·o·be·an (jak'ə·bē'ən) *adj.* Of or pertaining to the time of James I of England and sometimes of James II. —*n.* A Jacobean writer or politician. [< LL *Jacobus* James]

Jac·o·bin (jak'ə·bin) *n.* **1** A member of a French revolutionary society that inaugurated the Reign of Terror, 1793. **2** An extreme revolutionist. [< LL *Jacobus* James; with ref. to the church of St. James, in Paris, where the society met]

Jac·o·bite (jak'ə·bīt) *n.* An adherent of James II of England after his abdication in 1688, or of his royal line. —*adj.* Of the Jacobites: also **Jac·o·bit·ic** (jak'ə·bit'ik) or **·i·cal.**

Jacob's ladder **1** A ladder from earth to heaven that Jacob saw in a dream. *Gen.* 28:12. **2** *Naut.* A rope ladder, often with wooden steps.

jade[1] (jād) *n.* **1** A tough, hard, silicate mineral, usu. green or white, used for making jewelry. **2** The color of green jade. [< Sp. *(piedra de) ijada* (stone for) colic]

jade[2] (jād) *n.* **1** An old, worn-out horse. **2** A flirtatious or disreputable girl or woman. —*v.t. & v.i.* **jad·ed, jad·ing** To weary or become weary by hard service. [?]

jad·ed (jā'did) *adj.* **1** Worn-out; exhausted. **2** Bored or indifferent, as from overindulgence or too much experience. —**jad'ed·ly** *adv.* —**jad'ed·ness** *n.*

jae·ger (yā'gər, *also* jā'gər *for def.* 1) *n.* **1** A sea bird that pursues and robs smaller birds of their prey. **2** A huntsman or hunting attendant. [< OHG *jagōn* to hunt]

jag[1] (jag) *n.* A projecting point; notch; tooth. —*v.t.* **jagged, jag·ging** **1** To cut notches or jags in. **2** To cut unevenly or with slashing strokes, as a garment. [ME *jagge*]

jag[2] (jag) *n. Slang* A spree or fit: a crying *jag.* —**have a jag on** *Slang* To be intoxicated, as on liquor or drugs. [?]

jag·ged (jag'id) *adj.* Having jags or notches. —**jag'ged·ly** *adv.* —**jag'ged·ness** *n.*

jag·uar (jag'wär, jag'yōō·är) *n.* A large, tawny, spotted cat of tropical America. [< Tupian *jaguara*]

Jah·veh (yä've) YAHWEH. Also **Jah'we.**

jai a·lai (hī'lī', hī'ə·lī') A Latin-American game, similar to handball, in which players wear a long curved basket attached to one arm. [< Basque, jolly festival]

Jaguar

jail (jāl) *n.* **1** A prison. **2** A building used to confine persons awaiting trial or those guilty of minor offenses. —*v.t.* To put or hold in jail. [< OF *jaiole*]

jail·bird (jāl'bûrd') *n. Informal* A prisoner, esp. one often confined to prison.

jail·er (jā'lər) *n.* The officer in charge of a jail. Also **jail'or.**

Jain (jīn) *n.* An adherent of Jainism. Also **Jai·na** (jī'nə). [< Hind. *Jaina* < *jina* victorious]

Jain·ism (jī'niz·əm) *n.* A religion of India founded in the sixth century B.C. and marked by asceticism and belief in the transmigration of the soul.

jal·ap (jal'əp) *n.* **1** The dried root of any of several Mexican plants related to the morning glory. **2** A purgative drug obtained from this root. [< Sp. *(purga de) Jalapa* (medicine from) Jalapa] —**ja·lap·ic** (jə·lap'ik) *adj.*

ja·lop·y (jə·lop'ē) *n. pl.* **·lop·ies** *Informal* A decrepit automobile. [?]

ja·lou·sie (jal'ōō·sē, zhal'ōō·zē') *n.* A blind, window, shutter, or door having adjustable horizontal slats, as of metal or glass, for regulating the passage of light and air. [< F, lit., jealousy]

jam[1] (jam) *v.* **jammed, jam·ming** *v.t.* **1** To press or force into a tight place or position; wedge or squeeze in. **2** To fill and block up by crowding. **3** To bruise or crush by violent pressure. **4** To cause (a machine, part, etc.) to become wedged or stuck fast so that it cannot work. **5** To transmit signals designed to block reception of (a radio broadcast, station, etc.). —*v.i.* **6** To become wedged; stick fast. **7** To press or wedge; push. **8** In jazz music, to take part in a jam session. —*n.* **1** A jamming or being jammed. **2** A number of people or objects closely crowded together. **3** *Informal* A predicament. —*adv.* Completely: *jam* full. [?]

jam[2] (jam) *n.* A pulpy conserve of fruit boiled with sugar. [?< JAM[1], *v.*]

Jam. Jamaica.

Ja·mai·ca (jə·mā'kə) *n.* An independent member of the Commonwealth of Nations, located on an island in the Caribbean, 4,411 sq. mi., cap. Kingston. —**Ja·mai'can** *adj., n.* • See map at CUBA.

jamb (jam) *n.* A side post or side of a doorway, window, etc. [< OF *jambe* leg, support]

jam·bo·ree (jam'bə·rē') *n.* **1** *Informal* A boisterous frolic or spree. **2** A large, esp. international, assembly of Boy Scouts. [?]

jam session An informal gathering of jazz musicians performing improvisations.

Jan, Jan. January

jan·gle (jang'gəl) *v.* **·gled, ·gling** *v.i.* **1** To make harsh, annoying sounds. **2** To quarrel or bicker. —*v.t.* **3** To cause to make harsh, annoying sounds. —*n.* **1** Discordant sound. **2** Quarreling. [< OF *jangler*] —**jan'gler** *n.*

jan·i·tor (jan'i·tər) *n.* One who has the care of a building, offices, etc. [< L< *janua* door]

jan·i·zar·y (jan'ə·zer'ē) *n. pl.* **·zar·ies** *Often cap.* **1** A soldier in a corps of Turkish troops, established in the 14th century and abolished in 1826. **2** A loyal or submissive supporter. Also **jan'i·sar·y, jan'is·sar·y.**

Jan·u·ar·y (jan'yōō·er'ē) *n. pl.* **·ar·ies** or **·ar·ys** The first month of the year, containing 31 days. [< JANUS]

Ja·nus (jā'nəs) *Rom. Myth.* The god of portals and beginnings, having two faces, one in front, one in back of his head.

Ja·nus-faced (jā'nəs·fāst') *adj.* Deceitful; two-faced.

Jap. Japan; Japanese.

ja·pan (jə·pan') *n.* **1** Any of various lacquers or varnishes having a hard glossy finish. **2** Objects decorated or lacquered in the Japanese manner. **3** A varnish used as a drier for pigments. —*v.t.* **·panned, ·pan·ning** To varnish or lacquer with or as with japan. [< JAPAN]

Ja·pan (jə·pan') *n.* A constitutional monarchy of E Asia, located on a group of islands, 142,720 sq. mi., cap. Tokyo.

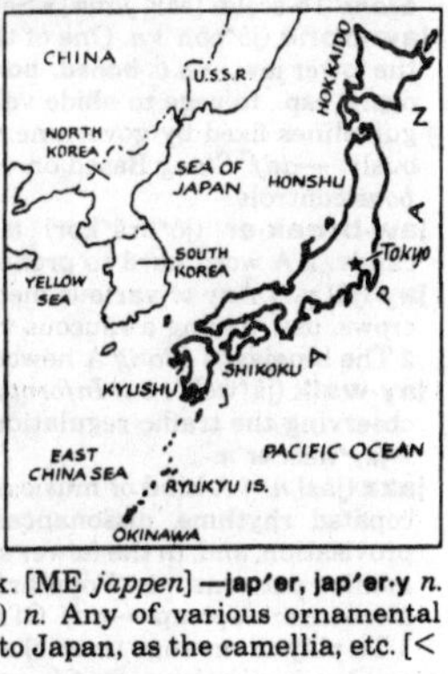

Jap·a·nese (jap'ə·nēz', -nēs') *adj.* Of or pertaining to Japan, its people, or their language. —*n.* **1** A native or citizen of Japan. **2** The language of Japan.

Japanese beetle A lustrous green and brown beetle that feeds on grasses, leaves, and fruits.

jape (jāp) *v.i.* **japed, jap·ing** To joke; make jests. —*n.* A joke or trick. [ME *jappen*] —**jap'er, jap'er·y** *n.*

ja·pon·i·ca (jə·pon'i·kə) *n.* Any of various ornamental flowering shrubs native to Japan, as the camellia, etc. [< NL, Japanese]

jar[1] (jär) *n.* **1** A deep, wide-mouthed vessel, as of glass. **2** The quantity a jar contains: also **jar'ful'.** [< Ar. *jarrah*]

jar[2] (jär) *v.* **jarred, jar·ring** *v.i.* **1** To shake or rattle, as from a shock or blow. **2** To make a harsh, discordant sound. **3** To have an unpleasant or painful effect: with *on* or *upon.* **4** To disagree or conflict; clash. —*v.t.* **5** To cause to shake or rattle, as by a shock or blow. **6** To affect unpleasantly or painfully; shock. 7 To cause to make a harsh, noisy sound. —*n.* 1 A jolting or shaking, as from a sudden shock. 2 A noisy, harsh sound. 3 Discord; strife. [Imit.]

jar·di·nière (jär′də·nir′; *Fr.* zhȧr·dē·nyâr′) *n.* An ornamental pot or stand for flowers or plants. [F]

jar·gon (jär′gən) *n.* 1 Unintelligible speech; gibberish. 2 Any language thought to be meaningless or excessively confused. 3 The technical or specialized language of a particular profession, group, etc. 4 A mixture of two or more dissimilar languages; pidgin. —*v.i.* To talk in jargon; gabble. [< OF]

jas·mine (jas′min, jaz′-) *n.* 1 An ornamental shrub related to the olive, with fragrant flowers used in scented tea and in making perfume. 2 Any of various similar plants. [< Per. *yāsmin*]

Ja·son (jā′sən) *Gk. Myth.* The prince who led the Argonauts in search of the Golden Fleece.

jas·per (jas′pər) *n.* An opaque, usu. red, brown, or yellow variety of quartz, used for vases and other articles. Also **jas′per·ite.** [< Gk. *jaspis*]

jaun·dice (jôn′dis, jän′-) *n.* 1 Abnormal yellowness of the skin, eyeballs, etc., due to bile pigments in the blood. 2 A hostile or resentful state of mind, as that caused by prejudice, envy, etc. —*v.t.* **·diced, ·dic·ing** 1 To affect with jaundice. 2 To affect with prejudice, envy, etc. [< L *galbinus* yellowish]

jaunt (jônt, jänt) *n.* A short journey; pleasure trip; excursion. —*v.i.* To make such a trip. [?]

jaunt·y (jôn′tē, jän′-) *adj.* **jaunt·i·er, jaunt·i·est** Sprightly; lively. [< F *gentil* elegant] **—jaunt′i·ly** *adv.* **—jaunt′i·ness** *n.*

ja·va (jä′və, jav′ə) *n. Sometimes cap. Slang* Coffee.

Ja·va (jä′və, jav′ə) *n.* 1 A type of coffee. 2 A domestic fowl. [< *Java*, where first grown]

Java man An extinct species of man identified with bone fragments found in Java.

Jav·a·nese (jav′ə·nēz′, -nēs′) *adj.* Of or pertaining to Java, its language, or its people. —*n. pl.* **·nese** 1 A native or citizen of Java. 2 The Indonesian language of central Java, closely related to Malay.

jave·lin (jav′lin, jav′ə·lin) *n.* 1 A short, light spear. 2 A long spear with wooden shaft, thrown for distance in an athletic contest. [< MF]

jaw (jô) *n.* 1 One of the two bony structures forming the framework of the mouth; a maxilla or a mandible. 2 The mouth. 3 Anything like or suggesting a jaw, as one of the gripping parts of a vise. 4 *Slang* Needless talk; scolding; abuse. —*v.i. Slang* 1 To talk; jabber. 2 To scold. —*v.t.* 3 *Slang* To scold. [ME *jawe*] • See TOOTH.

jaw·bone (jô′bōn′) *n.* One of the bones of the jaw, esp. of the lower jaw. —*v.t.* **·boned, ·bon·ing** *Slang* 1 To urge vigorously; esp., to urge to abide voluntarily by price or wage guidelines fixed by government. —*v.i.* 2 To argue vigorously. —*adj. Slang* Based on voluntary compliance: *jawbone* controls.

jaw·break·er (jô′brā′kər) *n. Informal* 1 Very hard candy. 2 A word hard to pronounce.

jay (jā) *n.* 1 Any of various medium-sized birds related to crows, usu. having a raucous voice and striking coloring. 2 The bluejay. 3 *Slang* A newcomer; greenhorn. [< OF]

jay·walk (jā′wôk′) *v.i. Informal* To cross a street without observing the traffic regulations. [< JAY (def. 3) + WALK] **—jay′walk′er** *n.*

jazz (jaz) *n.* 1 A kind of music achieving its effects by syncopated rhythms, dissonances, solo and ensemble improvisation, and, in the newer styles, by sophisticated harmonic patterns. 2 Popular dance music. 3 *Slang* Nonsense; claptrap. —*adj.* Of or pertaining to jazz. —*v.t.* 1 To play or arrange (music) as jazz. —*v.i.* 2 To dance to or play jazz. —**jazz up** *Slang* To make exciting or more exciting. [?]

jazz·y (jaz′ē) *adj.* **jazz·i·er, jazz·i·est** 1 Resembling or characteristic of jazz. 2 *Slang* **a** Showy or loud, as clothes. **b** Lively or swinging. **—jazz′i·ly** *adv.* **—jazz′i·ness** *n.*

J.C. Jesus Christ; Julius Caesar.

J.C.D. Doctor of Canon Law (L *Juris Canonici Doctor*); Doctor of Civil Law (L *Juris Civilis Doctor*).

jct., jctn. junction.

JD juvenile delinquent (or delinquency).

J.D. Doctor of Laws (L *Jurum Doctor*).

Je, Je. June.

jeal·ous (jel′əs) *adj.* 1 Suspicious and resentful of a rival or of rivalry in general. 2 Hostile or envious over the advantages, good fortune, etc., of others. 3 Earnestly vigilant in guarding or keeping something: *jealous* of our freedoms. 4 Resulting from or showing such feelings: a *jealous* rage. [< Gk. *zēlos* zeal] **—jeal′ous·ly** *adv.* **—jeal′ous·ness** *n.*

jeal·ous·y (jel′əs·ē) *n. pl.* **·ous·ies** The state or quality of being jealous in any sense.

jean (jēn) *n.* 1 A sturdy, twilled cotton cloth, used esp. in work clothes or for casual wear. 2 *pl.* Trousers made of this fabric. 3 *pl. Informal* Trousers. [< ME *Jene, Gene* Genoa, where it was made]

jeep (jēp) *n.* A small, sturdy motor vehicle with four-wheel drive and a load capacity of one quarter of a ton. [Alter. of *G.P.*, for General Purpose (Vehicle), its military designation]

Jeep

jeer (jir) *v.i.* 1 To speak or shout in a derisive, mocking manner; scoff. —*v.t.* 2 To treat with derision or mockery; scoff at. —*n.* A derisive or taunting sound or word. [?] **—jeer′er** *n.* **—jeer′ing·ly** *adv.*

Je·ho·vah (ji·hō′və) God. [< Heb. *YHWH*, used as a symbol for the name of God, which is never spoken]

Jehovah's Witnesses A Christian sect strongly opposed to war, firmly believing in a literal interpretation of the Bible and in the imminence of the Last Judgment.

je·june (jə·jōōn′) *adj.* 1 Lifeless; dry; dull. 2 Wanting in substance; barren. 3 Not mature; puerile; childish. [< L *jejunus* hungry] **—je·june′ly** *adv.* **—je·june′ness** *n.*

je·ju·num (jə·jōō′nəm) *n. pl.* **·na** (-nə) The part of the small intestine between the duodenum and the ileum. [< L *jejunus* hungry, empty]

jell (jel) *v.i.* & *v.t.* 1 To jelly; congeal. 2 To assume or cause to assume definite form. [< JELLY]

jel·li·fy (jel′ə·fī) *v.t.* & *v.i.* **·fied, ·fy·ing** To make or turn into jelly. **—jel′li·fi·ca′tion** *n.*

jel·lo (jel′ō) *n.* A fruit-flavored gelatin dessert. [< *Jell-O*, a trade name]

jel·ly (jel′ē) *n. pl.* **·lies** 1 A semisolid gelatinous food product, as fruit juice boiled with sugar or meat juice boiled down. 2 Any substance having the consistency of jelly. —*v.t.* & *v.i.* **·lied, ·ly·ing** To bring or turn to jelly. [< L *gelare* freeze]

jel·ly·bean (jel′ē·bēn′) *n.* A bean-shaped candy with a glazed outer coating.

jel·ly·fish (jel′ē·fish′) *n. pl.* **·fish** or **·fish·es** 1 Any of a class of marine coelenterates having transparent and usu. umbrella-shaped bodies with stinging tentacles. 2 *Informal* A person with a weak will.

jen·net (jen′it) *n.* 1 A small Spanish horse. 2 A female donkey. [< Sp. *jinete* a light horseman]

jen·ny (jen′ē) *n. pl.* **·nies** 1 SPINNING JENNY. 2 The female of certain birds and animals: *jenny* wren, *jenny* ass. [< *Jenny*, a personal name]

jeop·ard·ize (jep′ər·dīz) *v.t.* **·ized, ·iz·ing** To put in jeopardy; expose to loss or injury; imperil. Also **jeop′ard.**

jeop·ard·y (jep′ər·dē) *n. pl.* **·ard·ies** 1 Exposure to death, loss, or injury; danger; peril. 2 The peril in which a defendant is put when placed on trial for a crime. [< OF *jeu parti* even chance]

Jer, Jer. Jeremiah.

jer·bo·a (jər·bō′ə) *n.* Any of various small nocturnal rodents with the long hind legs adapted for jumping. [< Ar. *yarbu'*]

Jerboa

jer·e·mi·ad (jər′ə·mī′ad) *n.* A lament; tale of woe. [< F *Jérémie* Jeremiah]

Jer·e·mi·ah (jer′ə·mī′ə) A major Hebrew prophet who flourished in the seventh century B.C. —*n.* An Old Testament book containing his prophecies. Also **Jer′e·mi′as.**

jerk[1] (jûrk) *v.t.* 1 To give a sharp, sudden pull or twist to. 2 To throw or move with a sharp, suddenly arrested motion. 3 To utter in broken or abrupt manner. —*v.i.* 4 To give a jerk or jerks. 5 To move with sharp, sudden motions; twitch. —*n.* 1 A short, sharp pull, twitch, or fling. 2 An involuntary muscular spasm. 3 *Slang* A stupid or unsophisticated person. [?] —**jerk'i·ly** *adv.* —**jerk'i·ness** *n.* —**jerk'y** *adj.* (**·i·er, ·i·est**)

jerk[2] (jûrk) *v.t.* To cure (meat) by cutting into strips and drying. —*n.* Jerked meat: also **jerk'y.** [< Sp. *charquear*]

jer·kin (jûr'kin) *n.* A sleeveless, close-fitting jacket. [?]

jerk·wa·ter (jûrk'wô'tər, -wot'ər) *adj. Informal* Insignificant; small: a *jerkwater* college. —*n.* A train serving a branch line. [< JERK[1], *v.* + WATER]

jer·ry·build (jer'ē·bild') *v.t.* **·built, ·build·ing** To build flimsily and of inferior materials. [?] —**jer'ry·built'** *adj.*

jer·sey (jûr'zē) *n. pl.* **·seys** 1 A plain-knitted, elastic, ribbed fabric of wool, cotton, etc. 2 Any close-fitting, pullover, upper garment, as those worn by athletes, sailors, etc. —*adj.* Made of jersey.

Jer·sey (jûr'zē) *n.* One of a breed of fawn-colored cattle, originating in the island of Jersey and noted for milk rich in butterfat.

Je·ru·sa·lem artichoke (ji·rōō'sə·ləm, -lem) 1 A tall sunflower having an edible tuber. 2 Its potatolike tuber. [Alter. of Ital. *girasole* sunflower + ARTICHOKE]

jess (jes) *n.* A short strap fastened to the leg of a hawk, used in falconry. [< L *jactus* a throw] —**jessed** *adj.*

jes·sa·mine (jes'ə·min) *n.* JASMINE.

jest (jest) *n.* 1 Something said or done as a joke, prank, witticism, etc. 2 A mood of frivolity or fun: said in *jest.* 3 An object of laughter or raillery; a laughingstock. —*v.i.* 1 To speak or act in a playful or trifling manner. 2 To scoff; jeer. —*v.t.* 3 To scoff at; ridicule. [< L *gesta* deeds]

jest·er (jes'tər) *n.* 1 One who jests. 2 A medieval court fool.

Je·su (jē'zōō, -sōō, jā'-) Jesus.

Jes·u·it (jezh'ōō·it, jez'yōō-) *n.* 1 A member of the Society of Jesus, a religious order founded in 1534 by Ignatius Loyola. 2 A crafty or scheming person. —**Jes'u·it'ic** or **·i·cal** *adj.* —**Jes'u·it'i·cal·ly** *adv.*

Je·sus (jē'zəs) The founder of Christianity, probably living from about 6 B.C. to A.D. 29 or 30, revered as the Christ or Messiah. Also **Jesus Christ, Jesus of Nazareth.** See CHRIST.

jet[1] (jet) *n.* 1 A rich black variety of hard coal, used, when highly polished, for beads, etc. 2 A deep, glossy black. —*adj.* Made of or resembling jet. [< Gk. *gagatēs*]

jet[2] (jet) *n.* 1 A flow or gush, as of gas or liquid, coming from a narrow orifice. 2 A spout or nozzle. 3 JET AIRPLANE. 4 JET ENGINE. —*v.t. & v.i.* **jet·ted, jet·ting** 1 To spurt forth or emit in a stream; spout. 2 To travel or send by jet airplane. [< F *jeter* to throw]

jet airplane A jet-propelled airplane. Also **jet aircraft.**

jet-black (jet'blak') *adj. & n.* Deep, glossy black.

jet engine An engine that develops thrust by ejecting a fluid to the rear, esp. gases and heated air.

jet lag A disruption of the body's accustomed rhythms of sleep, hunger, etc., owing to the change of time zones when traveling long distances by jet aircraft.

jet·lin·er (jet'lī'nər) *n.* A large, commercial jet aircraft.

jet·port (jet'pôrt', -pōrt') *n.* An airport designed to accommodate jet aircraft.

jet-pro·pelled (jet'prə·peld') *adj.* Driven by jet propulsion.

jet propulsion 1 Propulsion by means of a jet of gas or other fluid. 2 *Aeron.* Aircraft propulsion by means of jet engines. —**jet'-pro·pul'sion** *adj.*

jet·sam (jet'səm) *n.* 1 Discarded cargo, equipment, etc., which is thrown overboard from a ship in peril and which either sinks or is washed ashore. 2 Any discarded objects. [< JETTISON]

jet set A group of wealthy, international celebrities who frequently travel long distances, as by jet aircraft, for vacations, social events, etc. —**jet-set·ter** (jet'set'ər) *n.*

jet stream 1 The exhaust gas or fluid expelled from a jet engine, rocket motor, etc. 2 *Meteorol.* A high-velocity, usu. westerly wind circulating near the base of the stratosphere.

jet·ti·son (jet'ə·sən) *v.t.* 1 To eject, drop, throw, etc., as from a ship, airplane, or spacecraft. 2 To discard or abandon (an impediment). —*n.* 1 The act of ejecting fuel, cargo, etc. 2 Jetsam. [< L *jactatio*]

jet·ty (jet'ē) *n. pl.* **·ties** 1 A wall-like structure in a body of water serving to control or divert a current, protect a harbor, etc. 2 A wharf or pier. [< OF < *jeter* to throw]

Jew (jōō) *n.* 1 A member or descendant of the Hebrew people. 2 Any person professing Judaism. —**Jew·ess** (jōō'·is) *n. Fem. (sometimes considered disparaging)*

jew·el (jōō'əl) *n.* 1 A precious stone; gem. 2 A pin, ring, etc., usu. made of precious metals set with gems, etc. 3 Any person or thing of rare excellence. 4 A bit of precious stone, crystal, or glass used as a bearing in a watch. —*v.t.* **·eled** or **·elled, ·el·ing** or **·el·ling** To adorn with or as with jewels. [< L *jocus* a game, joke]

jew·el·er (jōō'əl·ər) *n.* A dealer in or maker of jewelry. Also **jew'el·ler.**

jew·el·ry (jōō'əl·rē) *n.* Jewels collectively. *Brit. sp.* **jew·el·ler·y.**

jew·fish (jōō'fish') *n. pl.* **·fish** or **·fish·es** Any of various large fish of American waters, as the giant sea bass found off California or the grouper found off Florida.

Jew·ish (jōō'ish) *adj.* Of or having to do with the Jews or Judaism. —*n. Informal* YIDDISH. —**Jew'ish·ness** *n.*

JEWISH CALENDAR

Months correspond approximately to those in parentheses. The civil year begins with Tishri, the ecclesiastical year with Nisan.

Name of month	*Number of days*
Tishri (September–October)	30
Heshvan (October–November)	29
in some years	30
Kislev (November–December)	29
in some years	30
Tebet (December–January)	29
Shebat (January–February)	30
Adar * (February–March)	29
in leap year	30
Nisan (March–April)	30
Iyar (April–May)	29
Sivan (May–June)	30
Tammuz (June–July)	29
Av (July–August)	30
Elul (August–September)	29

* Adar is followed in leap year by the intercalary month Veadar, or Adar Sheni, having 29 days.

Jew·ry (jōō'rē) *n. pl.* **·ries** Jewish people collectively.

jew's-harp (jōōz'härp') *n.* A small musical instrument with a lyre-shaped metal frame held between the teeth, and played by plucking a free and flexible strip of metal.

Jez·e·bel (jez'ə·bel) In the Bible, the wife of Ahab, notorious for her evil life. —*n.* A bold, shameless, or wicked woman.

jg, j.g. junior grade.

jib[1] (jib) *n. Naut.* A triangular sail extending from the foretopmast to the jib boom or the bowsprit. —*Informal* **cut of one's jib** One's appearance. —*v.t. & v.i.* **jibbed, jib·bing** *Naut.* To shift or swing; jibe. Also **jibb.** [?]

jib[2] (jib) *v.i.* **jibbed, jib·bing** 1 To move restively sidewise or backward; refuse to go forward, as a horse. 2 To refuse to do something; balk. —*n.* A horse that jibs: also **jib'ber.** [?]

jib boom *Naut.* A spar forming a continuation of the bowsprit.

jibe[1] (jīb) *v.* **jibed, jib·ing** *v.i.* 1 *Naut.* To swing from one side of a vessel to the other: said of a sail or its boom. 2 To change course so that the sails shift in this manner. —*v.t.* 3 To cause to swing from one side of a vessel to the other. [< Du. *gijben*]

jibe[2] (jīb) *n. & v.* **jibed, jib·ing** GIBE.

jibe[3] (jīb) *v.i.* **jibed, jib·ing** To agree; be in accordance. [?]

jif·fy (jif'ē) *n. pl.* **·fies** *Informal* An instant; moment. Also **jiff.** [?]

jig (jig) *n.* 1 A rapid, gay dance or the music for it, usu. in triple time. 2 *Mech.* A tool or fixture used to guide cutting tools.

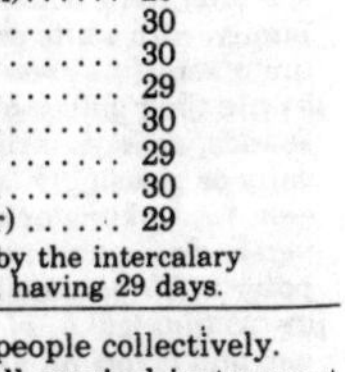

a. drill jig.
b. matter to be drilled.
c. support block.

3 A fish hook that is jiggled up and down or drawn through the water. 4 A wire sieve or system of sieves used in separating ore by vibration. —*v.* **jigged, jig·ging** *v.i.* 1 To dance or play a jig. 2 To move with quick, jerky motions. 3 To fish with a jig. 4 To use a jig. —*v.t.* 5 To jerk up and down or to and fro. 6 To catch (fish) with a jig. 7 To hold, produce, etc., with a jig. [?]

jig·ger[1] (jig′ər) *n.* 1 One who or that which jigs. 2 A small glass or cup for measuring liquor, usu. holding 1½ fluid ounces; also, the amount of liquor so measured. 3 *Naut.* a Any of several small sails. b JIGGERMAST. 4 Any of various mechanical devices having a jolting movement. 5 An unidentified gadget.

jig·ger[2] (jig′ər) *n.* CHIGGER.

jig·ger·mast (jig′ər·mast′, -mäst′) *n. Naut.* The aftermast in a yawl or a four-masted vessel.

jig·gle (jig′əl) *v.t. & v.i.* **·gled, ·gling** To move with slight, quick jerks. —*n.* A jiggling movement. [Freq. of JIG] —**jig·gly** *adj.*

jig·saw (jig′sô′) *n.* A fine, narrow saw, often power-operated, capable of cutting intricate curves.

jigsaw puzzle A puzzle, the object of which is to reassemble a mounted picture or design which has been cut into interlocking pieces.

jilt (jilt) *v.t.* To cast off (a previously favored lover or sweetheart). —*n.* One who capriciously discards a lover. [?] —**jilt′er** *n.*

jim crow (jim′krō′) Segregation of or discrimination against Negroes. Also **Jim Crow.** [< a Negro character in an old minstrel song] —**jim′-crow′** *adj.* —**jim′-crow′ism** *n.*

jim·my (jim′ē) *n. pl.* **·mies** A short crowbar, often used by burglars. —*v.t.* **·mied, ·my·ing** To break or pry open with a jimmy. [< *Jimmy,* dim. of *James.*]

jim·son·weed (jim′sən·wēd′) *n.* A tall, coarse, evil-smelling, very poisonous annual weed of the nightshade family, with white and purple flowers. Also **jimp·son weed** (jimp′sən). [< *Jamestown,* Va., where first observed.]

jin·gle (jing′gəl) *v.* **·gled, ·gling** *v.i.* 1 To make light, ringing sounds, as keys striking together. 2 To sound rhythmically or pleasingly on the ear. —*v.t.* 3 To cause to jingle. —*n.* 1 A tinkling or clinking sound. 2 A light, rhythmical verse; also, a short song using such verse: She is a composer of TV *jingles.* [Imit.] —**jin′gly** *adj.*

jin·go (jing′gō) *n. pl.* **·goes** One who boasts of his patriotism and favors an aggressive foreign policy. —*adj.* Of or like jingoes. [?] —**jin′go·ism, jin′go·ist** *n.* —**jin′go·is′tic** *adj.*

jin·ni (ji·nē′, jin′ē) *n. pl.* **jinn** *Muslim Myth.* A supernatural being able to assume animal or human form, and often called upon to serve men. Also **jin·nee′.** [< Ar. *jinnī*]

jin·rik·sha (jin·rik′shô) *n.* A small, two-wheeled passenger carriage drawn by one man. Also **jin·rick′sha, jin·rik′i·sha.** [< Jap. *jin* man + *riki* power + *sha* carriage]

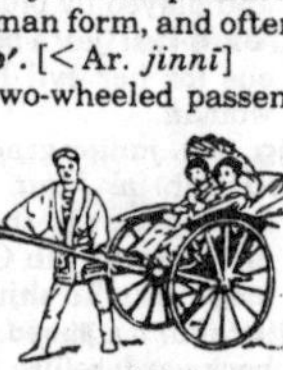
Jinriksha

jinx (jingks) *n.* A person or thing supposed to bring bad luck; a hoodoo. —*v.t.* To bring bad luck to. [< Gk. *iynx* the wryneck (a bird used in witchcraft)]

jit·ney (jit′nē) *n. pl.* **·neys** A motor vehicle that carries passengers for a small fare. [?]

jit·ter (jit′ər) *v.i. Informal* To talk or act nervously. —**the jitters** *Informal* Nervousness and anxiety. [?] —**jit′ter·y** *adj.* —**jit′ter·i·ness** *n.*

jit·ter·bug (jit′ər·bug′) *n.* 1 A person who dances energetically to swing or jazz music. 2 A fast, energetic dance performed to such music. —*v.i.* **·bugged, ·bug·ging** To dance energetically to swing or jazz music.

jiu·jit·su, jiu·jut·su (jo͞o·jit′so͞o) *n.* JUJITSU.

jive (jīv) *n. Slang* 1 The jargon of jazz music and its enthusiasts. 2 Jazz music. 3 Misleading or nonsensical talk; bull. —*v.* **jived, jiv·ing** *v.t.* 1 To talk to nonsensically or misleadingly. —*v.i.* 2 To talk to someone nonsensically or misleadingly. 3 To play or dance to jive. [?]

Jl July.

job (job) *n.* 1 A piece of work of a definite extent or character done for a set fee. 2 A specific duty, chore, or task. 3 A position of employment; situation. 4 An object or the material being worked on. 5 The act or result of working on something: That was a bad *job.* 6 *Informal* An illegal or criminal act, as a robbery. 7 *Informal* Any affair, circumstance, happening, etc.: to make the best of a bad *job.* 8 *Informal* A difficult task. —*v.* **jobbed, job·bing** *v.i.* 1 To work by the job or piece. 2 To be a jobber. —*v.t.* 3 To buy in bulk and resell in lots to dealers. 4 To sublet (work) among separate contractors. —*adj.* Of or pertaining to a job. [?]

Job (jōb) A Biblical character who suffered many afflictions as a test of his faith. —*n.* The book of the Old Testament recounting his story.

job·ber (job′ər) *n.* 1 One who buys goods in bulk from the manufacturer or importer and sells to the retailer. 2 One who works by the job, or on small jobs.

job·less (job′lis) *adj.* 1 Without a job. 2 Of or pertaining to those without a job. —**job′less·ness** *n.*

job lot A collection of miscellaneous goods sold as a lot.

Jo·cas·ta (jō·kas′tə) *Gk. Myth.* The queen of Thebes who unwittingly married her own son Oedipus.

jock[1] (jok) *n.* 1 *Informal* JOCKSTRAP. 2 *Slang* An athlete. [< JOCK(STRAP)]

jock[2] (jok) *n. Informal* 1 JOCKEY. 2 DISC JOCKEY.

jock·ey (jok′ē) *n. pl.* **·eys** One employed to ride horses in races. —*v.* **·eyed, ·ey·ing** *v.i.* 1 To maneuver for an advantage. 2 To be tricky; cheat. 3 To ride as a jockey. —*v.t.* 4 To maneuver or guide by skillful handling or control. 5 To trick; cheat. 6 To ride (a horse) in a race. [Dim. of *Jock,* a nickname for *John*]

jock·strap (jok′strap′) *n.* An elastic support for the male genitals, as of athletes. [Slang *jock* the male genitals + STRAP]

jo·cose (jō·kōs′) *adj.* Humorous; funny. [< L *jocus* joke] —**jo·cose′ly** *adv.* —**jo·cose′ness, jo·cos·i·ty** (jō·kos′ə·tē) *n.* —**Syn.** droll, facetious, jocular, merry.

joc·u·lar (jok′yə·lər) *adj.* 1 Humorous; joking. 2 Intended as a joke. [< L *jocus* a joke] —**joc′u·lar′i·ty** (-lar′ə·tē) *n.* —**joc′u·lar·ly** *adv.*

joc·und (jok′ənd, jō′kənd) *adj.* Cheerful; gay; jovial. [< L *jucundus* pleasant] —**jo·cun·di·ty** (jō·kun′də·tē) *n.* (*pl.* **·ties**). —**joc′und·ly** *adv.*

jodh·pur (jod′pər) *n.* 1 A riding shoe that ends just above the ankle, buckled on the side. 2 *pl.* Wide riding breeches, close-fitting from knee to ankle. [< *Jodhpur,* India]

Jodhpurs *def. 2*

jog (jog) *v.* **jogged, jog·ging** *v.t.* 1 To push or touch with a slight jar; shake. 2 To nudge. 3 To stimulate (one's memory). —*v.i.* 4 To move with a slow, steady pace. 5 To proceed slowly or monotonously: with *on* or *along.* —*n.* 1 A slight push or nudge. 2 A slow steady motion or pace. [?] —**jog′ger** *n.*

jog·gle[1] (jog′əl) *v.t. & v.i.* **·gled, ·gling** To shake slightly; jolt. —*n.* A slight shake; jolt. [Freq. of JOG]

jog·gle[2] (jog′əl) *n.* 1 A joint created by making a projection in one surface that will fit into a notch made in another. 2 DOWEL. —*v.t.* **·gled, ·gling** To put together with joggles. [?]

jog trot 1 A slow, easy trot. 2 A humdrum or unhurried routine.

john (jon) *n. Slang* A toilet.

John (jon) One of the twelve apostles, reputed author of the fourth Gospel, three Epistles, and the Book of Revelation: also **Saint John.** —*n.* The Gospel or one of the three Epistles credited to him.

John Bull The personification of England or of an Englishman.

John Doe (dō) 1 In a legal action or document, a name given to someone whose real name is unknown. 2 An average man.

John Han·cock (han′kok′) *Informal* A person's autograph. [< *John Hancock,* first signer of the Declaration of Independence]

john·ny·cake (jon′ē·kāk′) *n.* A kind of bread made with cornmeal.

john·ny-jump-up (jon′ē·jump′up′) *n.* 1 A naturalized, wild variety of pansy. 2 Any of various violets.

joie de vi·vre (zhwä də vēv′r′) Zest for life. [F, lit., joy of living]

join (join) *v.t.* 1 To set or bring together; connect. 2 To come to a junction with; become part of. 3 To become a member of, as a club. 4 To unite in act or purpose: to *join* forces. 5 To come to as a companion or participant: When will you *join* us? 6 To unite in marriage. 7 To engage in (battle. etc.). 8 *Informal* To adjoin. —*v.i.* 9 To come together; connect; unite. 10 To enter into association or agreement. 11 To take part: usu. with *in*. —*n.* A place of joining; joint. [< L *jungere*]

join·er (joi′nər) 1 One who or that which joins. 2 An artisan who finishes woodwork in houses. 3 *Informal* One who becomes a member of many organizations, clubs, etc.

join·er·y (joi′nər·ē) *n.* 1 The art or work of a joiner. 2 The articles constructed by a joiner.

joint (joint) *n.* 1 The place, point, or line where two or more things are joined together. 2 The manner in which two things are joined together: a tight *joint.* 3 One of the components of an articulated whole. 4 *Anat.* A place of union of two bones; an articulation. 5 One of the large pieces into which a carcass is divided by a butcher. 6 *Slang* A marihuana cigarette. 7 *Slang* A somewhat disreputable bar, nightclub, etc. 8 *Slang* Any place of dwelling or gathering. —**out of joint** 1 Not fitted at the joint; dislocated. 2 Disordered; disorganized. —*adj.* 1 Produced by combined action. 2 Shared by two or more. 3 Participated in or used by two or more. —*v.t.* 1 To fasten by means of a joint or joints. 2 To form or shape into a joint or joints, as a board. 3 To separate into joints, as meat. [< L *junctus* joined]

joint account A bank account in the name of two or more persons, each of whom may deposit and withdraw funds.

joint committee A committee made up of members from both houses of a bicameral legislature.

joint·ed (join′tid) *adj.* Having joints.

joint·ly (joint′lē) *adv.* In a joint manner.

joint return A single income tax return in which the incomes of a husband and wife are combined.

joint-stock company (joint′stok′) A business company whose capital is divided into shares owned by each of the members in the form of transferable stocks.

join·ture (join′chər) *n. Law* 1 A settlement, as of land, made to a wife by her husband to be used by her after his death. 2 The property so settled. [< L *jungere* join]

joist (joist) *n.* A horizontal timber supporting a floor or ceiling. —*v.t.* To furnish with joists. [< L *jacere* to lie down]

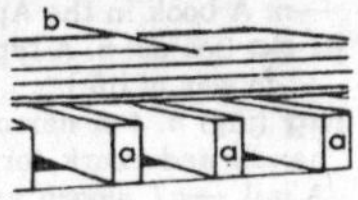

a. joists. b. floor boards.

joke (jōk) *n.* 1 Something said or done to cause amusement, esp. a brief, comic story. 2 A person or thing that causes laughter, ridicule, etc. 3 Something said or done in fun or to tease. —*v.* **joked, jok·ing** *v.t.* 1 To tease; kid. —*v.i.* 2 To make jokes; jest. [< L *jocus*] —**jok′ing·ly** *adv.* —**Syn.** *n.* 1 jest, witticism, gag, crack, wisecrack, quip.

jok·er (jō′kər) *n.* 1 One who jokes. 2 In a deck of cards, an extra card to be used in certain games. 3 *U.S.* A concealed provision in a legislative bill to render it ineffectual or to undermine its original purpose. 4 Any hidden ruse or difficulty.

jol·li·fy (jol′ə·fī) *v.t. & v.i.* **·fied, ·fy·ing** *Informal* To be or cause to be merry or jolly. —**jol·li·fi·ca·tion** (jol′ə·fə·kā′shən) *n.*

jol·ly (jol′ē) *adj.* **·li·er, ·li·est** Full of life and mirth; gay; merry. —*adv. Brit. Informal* Extremely; very: a *jolly* good time. —*v.t.* **·lied, ·ly·ing** *Informal* 1 To attempt to put in good humor by flattery or coaxing: often with *along* or *up.* 2 To make fun of. [< OF *joli*] —**jol′li·ly** *adv.* —**jol′li·ness, jol·li·ty** (jol′ə·tē) *n.* —**Syn.** *adj.* joyful, gleeful, jovial, joyous.

jol·ly·boat (jol′ē·bōt′) *n.* A small boat belonging to a ship. [< Dan. *jolle* yawl + BOAT]

Jolly Roger A black flag bearing a white skull and crossbones; a pirate flag.

jolt (jōlt) *v.t.* 1 To strike or shake about, as with a blow. 2 To surprise or stun. —*v.i.* 3 To move with jolts or bumps, as over a rough road. —*n.* 1 A sudden bump or jerk. 2 A surprise or shock. [?] —**jolt′er** *n.* —**jolt′y** *adj.*

Jo·nah (jō′nə) In the Bible, a Hebrew prophet of the eighth or ninth century B.C., who was thrown overboard and swallowed by a large fish, but three days later was cast upon shore alive. —*n.* 1 The book of the Old Testament telling his story. 2 Any person or thing regarded as bringing bad luck. Also **Jo·nas** (jō′nəs).

Jon·a·than (jon′ə·thən) In the Bible, the son of Saul and close friend of David. —*n.* A variety of late autumn apple.

jon·gleur (jong′glər; *Fr.* zhôn·glœr′) *n.* A medieval minstrel; also, later, a storyteller or buffoon. [< OF]

jon·quil (jon′kwil, jong′-) *n.* A species of narcissus having short-crowned yellow or white flowers. [< L *juncus* a rush]

Jor·dan (jôr′dən) *n.* A constitutional monarchy of W Asia, 37,000 sq. mi., cap. Amman. —**Jor·da·ni·an** (jôr·dā′nē·ən) *adj., n.*

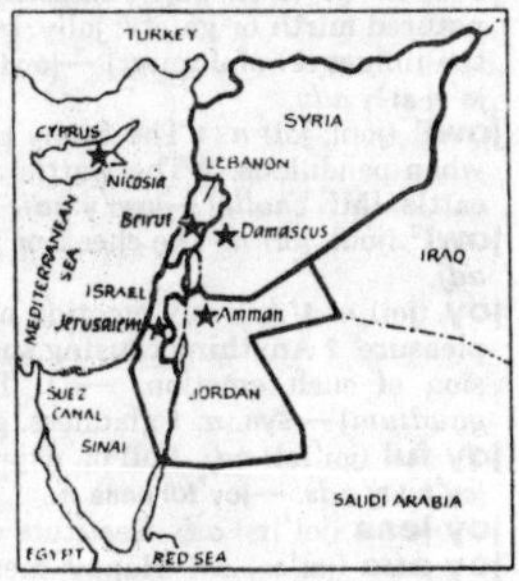

Jordan, Syria, and Israel

Jordan almond 1 A large Spanish almond. 2 A candy-coated almond. [< OF *jardin* garden + ALMOND]

Jos. Joseph.

Jo·seph (jō′zəf, -səf) In the Bible: 1 A Hebrew patriarch, son of Jacob and Rachel, sold into slavery in Egypt by his brothers. 2 Husband of Mary the mother of Jesus.

josh (josh) *Slang v.t. & v.i.* To tease (someone) good-humoredly. —*n.* A good-natured joke. [? Blend of JOKE and BOSH] —**josh′er** *n.*

Josh. Joshua.

Josh·u·a (josh′ōō·ə) In the Bible, the successor of Moses as leader of the Israelites. —*n.* The book of the Old Testament ascribed to him.

Joshua tree A tall, treelike desert plant with branches that end in a cluster of leaves.

joss (jos) *n.* A statue or idol of a Chinese god. [Pidgin English < Pg. *deos* God]

joss house A Chinese temple.

joss stick A stick of perfumed paste burned by the Chinese as incense.

jos·tle (jos′əl) *v.t. & v.i.* **·tled, ·tling** To push or crowd; elbow; hustle; bump. —*n.* A collision, bumping against, or slight shaking. [Freq. of JOUST] —**jos′tler** *n.*

jot (jot) *v.t.* **jot·ted, jot·ting** To make a hasty note of: usu. with *down.* —*n.* The least bit; an iota. [< IOTA]

jot·ting (jot′ing) *n.* A brief note.

joule (joul, jōōl) *n. Physics* A unit of work or energy equal to one watt acting for one second. [< James Prescott *Joule,* 1818–89, English physicist]

jounce (jouns) *v.t. & v.i.* **jounced, jounc·ing** To shake or bounce; jolt. —*n.* A shake; a bump. [?]

jour. journal; journalist; journeyman.

jour·nal (jûr′nəl) *n.* 1 A record of daily occurrences, as a diary. 2 A record of the proceedings of a legislature, club, etc. 3 A daily newspaper. 4 Any periodical or magazine. 5 *Naut.* A logbook. 6 In bookkeeping: **a** DAYBOOK. **b** In double entry, a book in which transactions of the day are entered in systematic form in order to facilitate later posting in the ledger. 7 *Mech.* The part of a shaft or axle which is held by a bearing. [< L *diurnus* daily]

journal box *Mech.* The box or bearing for a rotating axle or shaft.

jour·nal·ese (jûr′nəl·ēz′, -ēs′) *n.* A style of writing supposedly characteristic of newspapers, magazines, etc.

jour·nal·ism (jûr′nəl·iz′əm) *n.* 1 The gathering, writing, editing, or publishing of news, as for a newspaper, magazine, radio, or television. 2 Newspapers and magazines collectively.

jour·nal·ist (jûr′nəl·ist) *n.* One whose occupation is journalism. —**jour′nal·is′tic** *adj.* —**jour′nal·is′ti·cal·ly** *adv.*

jour·ney (jûr′nē) *n.* **1** Travel from one place to another; a trip. **2** Something that suggests such travel: one's *journey* through life. —*v.i.* To travel; go on a journey. [<OF *journee* a day's travel] —**jour′ney·er** *n.* —**Syn.** *n.* **1** excursion, tour, voyage, cruise, expedition.

jour·ney·man (jûr′nē·mən) *n. pl.* **·men** (-mən) **1** A craftsman who has finished his apprenticeship and is employed by another. **2** Any ordinary, competent, but not exceptional worker, craftsman, etc.

joust (joust, just, jo͞ost) *n.* A match with lances between mounted knights. —*v.i.* To engage in a joust. [<LL *juxtare* to approach] —**joust′er** *n.*

Jove (jōv) JUPITER. —**by Jove!** An exclamation expressing surprise, emphasis, etc. —**Jo·vi·an** (jō′vē·ən) *adj.*

jo·vi·al (jō′vē·əl) *adj.* Possessing or expressive of good-natured mirth or gaiety; jolly. [<LL *Jovialis* (born under the influence) of Jupiter] —**jo·vi·al·i·ty** (jō′vē·al′ə·tē) *n.* —**jo′vi·al·ly** *adv.*

jowl[1] (joul, jōl) *n.* **1** The fleshy part of the lower jaw, esp. when pendulous. **2** The wattle of fowls. **3** The dewlap of cattle. [ME *cholle*] —**jowl′y** *adj.*

jowl[2] (joul, jōl) *n.* The cheek or jaw. [<OE *ceafl*] —**jowled** *adj.*

joy (joi) *n.* **1** A lively emotion of happiness, delight, and pleasure. **2** Anything causing such emotion. **3** The expression of such emotion. —*v.i.* To be glad; rejoice. [<L *gaudium*] —**Syn.** *n.* **1** gladness, glee, cheerfulness, gaiety.

joy·ful (joi′fəl) *adj.* Full of, expressing, or causing joy. —**joy′ful·ly** *adv.* —**joy′ful·ness** *n.*

joy·less (joi′lis) *adj.* Destitute of joy. —**joy′less·ly** *adv.*

joy·ous (joi′əs) *adj.* Happy; merry; gay. —**joy′ous·ly** *adv.*

joy·ride (joi′rīd′) *n. Informal* A ride taken exclusively for pleasure, esp. in a stolen car or other vehicle and often operated recklessly. —**joy′rid′er** *n.* —**joy′rid′ing** *n.*

joy·stick (joi′stik′) *n.* A hand-operated, upright, tiltable electronic device used in playing computer and video games.

J.P. Justice of the Peace.

Jr., jr. junior.

ju·bi·lant (jo͞o′bə·lənt) *adj.* Filled with or showing great joy or triumph. [<L *jubilare* exult] —**ju′bi·lance** *n.* —**ju′bi·lant·ly** *adv.* —**Syn.** overjoyed, rapturous, elated, exultant, triumphant.

ju·bi·late (jo͞o′bə·lāt) *v.t. & v.i.* **·lat·ed, ·lat·ing** To rejoice; exult. [<L *jubilare*] —**ju′bi·la′tion** *n.*

ju·bi·lee (jo͞o′bə·lē′, jo͞o′bə·lē′) *n.* **1** A special anniversary of an event, as the 50th; also, the celebration of this. **2** Any time or season of rejoicing; a commemoration or festivity. [LL<Heb. *yōbēl* ram's horn, trumpet]

Ju·dah (jo͞o′də) In the Bible, the fourth son of Jacob and Leah, or the tribe descended from him. —*n.* The kingdom of ancient Palestine, comprising the tribes of Judah and Benjamin.

Ju·da·ic (jo͞o·dā′ik) *adj.* Of the Jews or Judaism; Jewish. Also **Ju·da′i·cal.** —**Ju·da′i·cal·ly** *adv.*

Ju·da·ism (jo͞o′dē·iz′əm) *n.* **1** The religion of the Jews, comprising a belief in and worship of one God only, with doctrines based on ancient Hebrew Scripture, the Talmud, and rabbinical tradition. **2** The culture, traditions, ceremonies, practices, etc., of the Jews. **3** Jews collectively. —**Ju′da·ist** *n.* —**Ju′da·is′tic** *adj.*

Ju·das (jo͞o′dəs) In the Bible, the disciple of Jesus who betrayed him: also **Judas Is·car·i·ot** (is·kar′ē·ət). —*n.* One who betrays another under the guise of friendship.

Judas tree A leguminous tree having profuse reddish purple flowers. [From a tradition that Judas hanged himself from such a tree]

Ju·de·a (jo͞o·dē′ə) The southern part of ancient Palestine under the Roman Empire. —**Ju·de′an** *adj., n.*

judge (juj) *n.* **1** An official, elected or appointed, invested with authority to administer legal justice. **2** In contests, controversies, etc., one who selects the winner, evaluates the merits of contestants, etc. **3** One qualified to have opinions on the worth or value of something: a good *judge* of wines. **4** In Jewish history, one of the rulers of the Israelites from the death of Joshua to the anointing of Saul. —*v.* **judged, judg·ing** *v.t.* **1** To hear and decide in an official capacity the merits of (a case) or the guilt of (a person); try. **2** To select the winner of (a contest). **3** To settle (a controversy). **4** To appraise or evaluate: to *judge* a painting. **5** To estimate: to *judge* a distance. **6** To consider; think: We *judged* it improper. **7** To censure; criticize: *Judge* her not. —*v.i.* **8** To act as a judge; sit in judgment. **9** To form a judgment or estimate. **10** To make a decision. [<L *judex*] —**judg′er** *n.*

judge advocate *pl.* **judge advocates** *Mil.* A legal officer of the U.S. Army, esp. the prosecutor at a court-martial.

Judg·es (juj′iz) *n. pl. (construed as sing.)* The seventh book of the Old Testament.

judge·ship (juj′ship) *n.* The office, duties, or period in office of a judge.

judg·ment (juj′mənt) *n.* **1** The act of judging. **2** The result or outcome of judging; as: **a** A legal decision, order, or sentence. **b** An obligation or debt resulting from a court decision. **c** A record of such a decision. **d** Any decision or opinion. **e** An evaluation or estimation. **f** Censure; criticism. **3** An ability to make decisions or evaluations that are wise, reasonable, and valid. **4** A disaster or affliction regarded as inflicted by God. Also **judge′ment.** —**judg·men′tal** *adj.*

Judgment Day *Theol.* The day or time of the Last Judgment.

ju·di·ca·to·ry (jo͞o′də·kə·tôr′ē, -tō′rē) *adj.* Pertaining to the administration of justice. —*n. pl.* **·ries** **1** A court of law; also, such courts collectively. **2** Any system of administering justice. [<L *judicare* to judge]

ju·di·ca·ture (jo͞o′də·kə·cho͝or) *n.* **1** The action of administering justice. **2** The right or power to administer justice; jurisdiction. **3** A court of justice. **4** Judges collectively.

ju·di·cial (jo͞o·dish′əl) *adj.* **1** Of, pertaining to, or resulting from the administration of justice. **2** Of, pertaining to, or connected with a court or judge. **3** Discriminating; unbiased; impartial. [<L *judex* a judge] —**ju·di′cial·ly** *adv.*

ju·di·ci·ar·y (jo͞o·dish′ē·er′ē, -dish′ə·rē) *adj.* Of or pertaining to courts of justice, judges, or their duties. —*n. pl.* **·ar·ies** **1** That department of government which administers the law. **2** A system of legal courts. **3** Judges collectively.

ju·di·cious (jo͞o·dish′əs) *adj.* Having, acting on, or resulting from sound judgment: wise; prudent. [<L *judicium* a judgment] —**ju·di′cious·ly** *adv.* —**ju·di′cious·ness** *n.*

Ju·dith (jo͞o′dith) A Jewish woman who rescued her countrymen by slaying the Assyrian general Holofernes. —*n.* A book in the Apocrypha relating her story.

ju·do (jo͞o′dō) *n.* A type of jujitsu. [<Jap. *ju* gentle, pliant + *do* way of life]

jug (jug) *n.* **1** A narrow-necked, stout vessel, usu. with a handle and a cork, for keeping or carrying liquids. **2** *Slang* A jail. —*v.t.* **jugged, jug·ging** **1** To put into a jug. **2** To stew (meat, esp. hare) in an earthenware pot. **3** *Slang* To imprison. [<*Jug*, a nickname for *Joan*]

jug·ger·naut (jug′ər·nôt) *n.* A massive force that destroys whatever resists it. [<JUGGERNAUT]

Jug·ger·naut (jug′ər·nôt) An incarnation of the Hindu deity Vishnu whose idol was drawn on a heavy car under the wheels of which devotees were said to have thrown themselves to be crushed. [<Hind. *jagannāth* lord of the universe]

jug·gle (jug′əl) *v.* **·gled, ·gling** *v.t.* **1** To toss (balls, plates, etc.) into the air, keeping them in continuous motion by successively catching and tossing them up again. **2** hold or catch (a ball, etc.) awkwardly or precariously. **3** To manipulate in order to deceive. —*v.i.* **4** To perform as a juggler. **5** To practice deception or trickery. —*n.* **1** A feat of juggling. **2** A trick or deception. [<L *joculari* to jest] —**jug′gler** *n.*

jug·gler·y (jug′lər·ē) *n. pl.* **·gler·ies** **1** The art of a juggler. **2** Deception; trickery.

jug·u·lar (jug′yə·lər, jo͞o′gyə-) *adj. Anat.* Pertaining to the throat or neck. —*n.* One of the large veins on either side of the neck that returns blood from the head to the heart. Also **jugular vein.** [<L *jugulum* a collar bone]

juice (jo͞os) *n.* **1** The watery matter in fruits, plants, and vegetables. **2** *Usu. pl.* The fluids of the body. **3** The essence of anything. **4** *Slang* **a** Electric current. **b** Any liquid fuel. **5** *Informal* Vital energy. [<L *jus*]

juic·er (jo͞o′sər) *n.* A device for extracting juice from fruits or vegetables.

juic·y (jo͞o′sē) *adj.* **juic·i·er, juic·i·est 1** Abounding with juice; moist. **2** *Informal* Full of interest; colorful; spicy. **3** *Informal* Financially profitable; lucrative. —**juic′i·ly** *adv.* —**juic′i·ness** *n.*

ju·jit·su (jo͞o·jit′so͞o) *n.* A Japanese system of unarmed self-defense in which the strength and weight of one's opponent are used to one's own advantage. Also **ju·jut·su** (jo͞o·jit′so͞o, -jo͝ot′-). [< Jap. *ju* soft + *jitsu* art]

ju·jube (jo͞o′jo͞ob) *n.* **1** Any of several trees or shrubs related to the buckthorn. **2** Its edible fruit. **3** (*often* jo͞o′·jo͞o′bē′) A gelatinous candy lozenge. [< Gk. *zizyphon*]

juke·box (jo͞ok′boks′) *n.* A large automatic phonograph, usu. coin-operated and permitting selection of the records to be played. Also **juke box.** [< Gullah *juke,* orig. a brothel (of west African origin) + BOX[1]]

Jul, Jul. July.

ju·lep (jo͞o′lip) *n.* A drink made of brandy or whisky, sugar, cracked ice, and flavored with fresh green mint. Also **mint julep.** [< Pers. *gūlāb* rose water]

Jul·ian (jo͞ol′yən) *adj.* Of, pertaining to, or named after Julius Caesar.

…ndar The calendar introduced by Julius … having each year divided into 12 months … every fourth year containing 366 …

…) *n.* A clear meat soup containing … or cut into thin strips. —*adj.* Cut into …*nne* potatoes. [< F *Julienne,* a personal …

…o͞o′lē·et, jo͞ol′yit) The heroine of Shakespeare's …*d Juliet.*

…jo͞o·lī′, jo͞o-) *n. pl.* **Ju·lies** or **·lys** The seventh month …e calendar year, having 31 days. [< L *(mensis) Julius* (month) of Julius Caesar]

jum·ble (jum′bəl) *v.* **·bled, ·bling** *v.t.* **1** To mix in a confused mass; put or throw together without order. **2** To confuse in the … **3** To meet or unite confusedly. —*n.* A confus… [?]

jum·bo … *n. pl.* **·bos** A very large person, animal, or thing. —… Larger than usual. [< *Jumbo,* an elephant exhibited by P. T. Barnum]

jump (jump) *v.i.* **1** To spring from the ground, floor, etc., by the action of the muscles of the feet and legs. **2** To move abruptly or with jerks. **3** To leap off or from something, esp. from an airplane when using a parachute. **4** To pass abruptly from one thing or subject to another. **5** To rise abruptly, as prices. **6** *Slang* To be full of noisy activity. **7** In bridge, to make a jump bid. **8** In checkers, to capture an opponent's piece by passing over it to a vacant square beyond. —*v.t.* **9** To leap over. **10** To cause to rise, as prices. **12** To pass over; leave out; skip. **13** To leave or move from abruptly: to *jump* the track. **14** *Informal* To get on or off (a train, etc.) by or as by jumping. **15** *Informal* To assault; attack. **16** *Slang* To leave or quit abruptly or secretly: to *jump* town. **17** *Informal* To respond to before the proper time: to *jump* a traffic light. **18** In checkers, to capture (an opponent's piece). **19** In bridge, to raise (the bid) by making a jump bid. —**jump at 1** To accept quickly or eagerly. **2** To reach (a conclusion) hastily and illogically. —*n.* **1** The act of jumping; a leap. **2** The length or height of a leap. **3** That which is jumped over. **4** An athletic contest to determine skill in jumping. **5** An abrupt rise or increase: a *jump* in prices. **6** *Informal* A head start; advantage. **7** An involuntary movement, as when startled. **8** A short trip. **9** In checkers, the capture of another's piece. [?]

jump bid In bridge, a bid higher than needed to beat or raise a previous declaration.

jump·er[1] (jum′pər) *n.* **1** One who or that which jumps. **2** *Electr.* A short length of connecting wire, esp. one used temporarily.

jum·per[2] (jum′pər) *n.* **1** A one-piece, sleeveless dress worn over a blouse or sweater. **2** *pl.* ROMPERS. **3** A loose outer jacket worn over or instead of other clothes. [< OF *juppe* a jacket]

jumping bean The seed of certain Mexican plants which rolls or jerks about owing to the movements of the larva of a small moth inside.

jumping jack A toy figure of a man, whose jointed limbs are moved by strings.

jump·ing-off place (jum′ping·ôf′, -of′) **1** A very remote or deserted place. **2** The beginning of a venture or enterprise.

jump seat An extra seat that folds up, as in the rear of a limousine or taxi.

jump shot In basketball, a shot attempted at the height of a leap.

jump suit 1 A one-piece garment consisting of pants with a blouse or shirt attached. **2** A kind of coverall worn by parachutists, mechanics, etc.

jump·y (jum′pē) *adj.* **jump·i·er, jump·i·est 1** Subject to sudden changes; fluctuating. **2** Nervous; apprehensive. —**jump′i·ness** *n.*

Jun, Jun. June.

Jun., jun. junior.

junc., junct. junction.

jun·co (jung′kō) *n. pl.* **·cos** Any of various sparrowlike birds having white underparts. [< Sp., a rush]

junc·tion (jungk′shən) *n.* **1** The act of joining, or condition of being joined. **2** A place of union or meeting, as of railroads. [< L *jungere* join] —**junc′tion·al** *adj.*

junc·ture (jungk′chər) *n.* **1** An act of joining; junction. **2** A point or line of joining. **3** A point in time. **4** A crisis; exigency. **5** *Ling.* A significant manner of transition between consecutive speech sounds.

June (jo͞on) *n.* The sixth month of the calendar year, having 30 days. [< L *(mensis) Junius* (month) of the Junii, a Roman gens]

June bug A large, brightly colored beetle that appears in May or early June. Also **June beetle.**

jun·gle (jung′gəl) *n.* **1** Land, usu. in tropical regions, covered with trees and a dense thicket of high grass, vines, brush, etc. **2** Any similar tangled mass. **3** *Slang* A camp for hoboes. **4** *Slang* A place or circumstance of fierce competition for survival, success, etc. [< Skt. *jangala* dry, desert]

jun·ior (jo͞on′yər) *adj.* **1** Younger in years or lower in rank. **2** Denoting the younger of two, and distinguishing a father from a son, usu. abbreviated *Jr.* **3** Belonging to youth or earlier life. **4** Later in date. **5** Pertaining to a junior or juniors in a high school or college. —*n.* **1** The younger of two. **2** One later or lower in service or rank. **3** A third-year student in a high school or college. [< L comp. of *juvenis* young]

junior college A college offering only two years of study after high school.

junior high school The school that is attended between elementary school and senior high school, usu. comprising grades 7, 8, and 9.

ju·ni·per (jo͞o′nə·pər) *n.* Any of a genus of evergreen shrubs and trees having scalelike leaves and aromatic, berrylike cones. [< L *juniperus*]

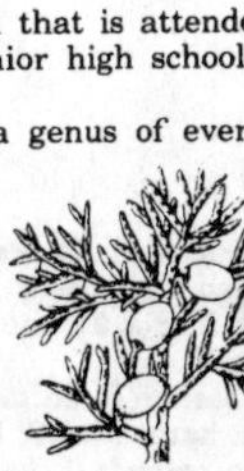

Juniper branch

junk[1] (jungk) *n.* **1** Castoff materials, as metal, glass, paper etc. **2** Anything of little value or importance. **3** *Slang* A narcotic, esp. heroin. —*v.t.* To scrap, demolish, or cast aside. [< L *juncus* rush] —**junk′y** *adj.* **(·i·er, ·i·est)**

junk[2] (jungk) *n.* A large Chinese vessel with high poop, prominent stem, full stern and lugsails. [< Malay *djong* a ship]

Jun·ker (yo͝ong′kər) *n.* A member of the landowning Prussian aristocracy. [< G *jung* young + *Herr* master]

jun·ket (jung′kit) *n.* **1** A feast or picnic. **2** A pleasure trip. **3** A trip taken with all expenses paid by a government, company, etc. **4** A dessert made of milk and rennet. —*v.i.* To go on a junket. [< AF *jonquette* rush basket]

junk·ie (jung′kē) *n. Slang* One addicted to narcotic drugs, esp. to heroin. Also **junk·y** (*pl.* **·ies**).

junk·man (jungk′man′) *n. pl.* **·men** (-men′) One who purchases, collects, and sells junk.
junk·yard (jungk′yärd′) *n.* A place where junk is thrown or collected.
Ju·no (jōō′nō) *Rom. Myth.* The wife of Jupiter, queen of the gods and goddess of marriage.
Ju·no·esque (jōō′nō·esk′) *adj.* Resembling the stately beauty of Juno.
jun·ta (hōōn′tə, jun′-) *n.* **1** A Central or South American legislative council. **2** A group of people, often military leaders, who exercise control over a government, esp. following a coup d'état. Also **jun′to** (-tō). [< L *juncta* joined]
Ju·pi·ter (jōō′pə·tər) *Rom. Myth.* The god ruling over all the other gods and all men. —*n.* The planet of the solar system fifth in distance from the sun. See PLANET.
Ju·ras·sic (jōō·ras′ik) *adj., n.* See GEOLOGY. [< the *Jura* mountain range in E France and W Switzerland]
ju·rid·i·cal (jōō·rid′i·kəl) *adj.* Relating to law and judicial proceedings. Also **ju·rid′ic.** [< L *jus, juris* law + *dicere* declare] **—ju·rid′i·cal·ly** *adv.*
ju·ris·dic·tion (jŏŏr′is·dik′shən) *n.* **1** Lawful right to exercise official authority. **2** The range or scope of such authority. **3** A court, or series of courts, of justice. **4** Power, authority, or control. [< L *jus, juris* law + *dicere* declare] **—ju′ris·dic′tion·al** *adj.* **—ju′ris·dic′tion·al·ly** *adv.*
ju·ris·pru·dence (jŏŏr′is·prōōd′ns) *n.* **1** The philosophy or science of law. **2** A particular system or division of law: medical *jurisprudence.* [< L *jus, juris* law + *prudentia* knowledge]
ju·ris·pru·dent (jŏŏr′is·prōōd′nt) *adj.* Skilled in jurisprudence. —*n.* A person learned in the law. **—ju′ris·pru·den′·tial** (-prōō·den′shəl) *adj.*
ju·rist (jŏŏr′ist) *n.* **1** One versed in the science of laws. **2** A judge. [< L *jus, juris* law]
ju·ris·tic (jōō·ris′tik) *adj.* Of a jurist or the law. Also **ju·ris′·ti·cal.** **—ju·ris′ti·cal·ly** *adv.*
ju·ror (jŏŏr′ər, -ôr) *n.* One who serves on a jury or is sworn in for jury duty.
ju·ry[1] (jŏŏr′ē) *n. pl.* **·ries** **1** A body of persons (usu. twelve) sworn to hear evidence in a legal proceeding and to arrive at an unprejudiced verdict on the basis of the facts as presented. **2** A committee to decide the winner or winners in a competition. [< L *jurare* swear < *jus, juris* law]
ju·ry[2] (jŏŏr′ē) *adj. Naut.* Rigged up temporarily: a *jury* mast. [?]
just (just) *adj.* **1** Upright; honest. **2** Fair; impartial: a *just* trial. **3** Merited; deserved: a *just* tribute. **4** Correct; accurate. **5** Valid; legitimate: a *just* complaint. **6** Righteous. —*adv.* **1** To the exact point, instant, or degree; precisely. **2** But now; this moment or time: He is *just* beginning. **3** A moment ago: He has *just* left. **4** By very little; barely: *just* missed. **5** Only: *just* an amateur. **6** *Informal* Simply; positively: That gift is *just* wonderful. **—just about** Almost; nearly. [< L *justus* < *jus* law] **—just′ly** *adv.* **—just′ness** *n.*
jus·tice (jus′tis) *n.* **1** The quality of being just, fair, or impartial; evenhandedness. **2** Adherence to truth or fact; validity; correctness. **3** The rendering of what is due or merited; also, that which is due or merited; just deserts. **4** Conformity to right principles; honesty; integrity. **5** A judge. **6** JUSTICE OF THE PEACE. **7** The administration of law. **—do justice to 1** To deal with adequately. **2** To enjoy or appreciate fully. **—do oneself justice 1** To be fair to oneself. **2** To do the best of which one is capable. [< L *justus* < *jus* law]
justice of the peace A magistrate elected or appointed within a county or township, to punish minor offenses against the law, commit cases to a higher court, perform marriages, etc.
jus·ti·fi·a·ble (jus′tə·fī′ə·bəl, jus′tə·fī′-) *adj.* Capable of being justified. **—jus′ti·fi′a·bil′i·ty** *n.* **—jus′ti·fi′a·bly** *adv.*
jus·ti·fi·ca·tion (jus′tə·fə·kā′shən) *n.* **1** The act of justifying or the state of being justified. **2** The grounds of justifying; that which justifies. **—jus′ti·fi·ca′tive** *adj.*
jus·ti·fy (jus′tə·fī) *v.* **·fied, ·fy·ing** *v.t.* **1** To show to be just, right, or proper. **2** To declare or prove guiltless or blameless. **3** To show sufficient reason for (something done). **4** *Printing* To adjust (lines) to the proper length by spacing. —*v.i.* **5** *Law* **a** To show sufficient reason for something done. **b** To qualify as a bondsman. **6** *Printing* To be properly spaced. [< L *justus* just + *facere* make] **—jus′ti·fi′er** *n.*
jut (jut) *v.i.* **jut·ted, jut·ting** To extend beyond the main portion; project: often with *out.* —*n.* Anything that juts; a projection. [Var. of JET[2]]
jute (jōōt) *n.* **1** Either of two Asian plants cultivated for the strong fibers in the stem. **2** The fiber of this plant, used for bags, cordage, etc. [< Skt. *jūta* a braid of hair]
Jute (jōōt) *n.* A member of a Germanic tribe that invaded Britain in the fifth century.
ju·ve·nile (jōō′və·nīl, -nəl) *adj.* **1** Characteristic of youth; young. **2** Adapted to or suitable for youth. —*n.* **1** A young person; child. **2** An actor who interprets youthful roles. **3** A book for children. [< L *juvenis* young]
juvenile court A law court in which cases involving children under a specified age are heard.
jux·ta·pose (juks′tə·pōz′) *v.t.* **·posed, ·pos·ing** To place close together; put side by side. [< L *juxta* near + POSE]
jux·ta·po·si·tion (juks′tə·pə·zish′ən) *n.* A placing close together or side by side; contiguity.

K

K, k (kā) *n. pl.* **K's, k's, Ks, ks** (kāz) **1** The 11th letter of the English alphabet. **2** Any spoken sound representing the letter *K* or *k.* **3** Something shaped like a K. —*adj.* Shaped like a K.
K potassium (L *kalium*); Kelvin.
K., k. karat (carat); kilogram; king; knight; knot *(naut.)*; kopec; calends (L *kalendae*).
KA Kansas (P.O. abbr.).
Ka·a·ba (kä′ə·bə, kä′bə) *n.* The Muslim shrine at Mecca enclosing a sacred black stone, supposedly given to Abraham by the angel Gabriel.
kab·a·la (kab′ə·lə, kə·bä′lə) *n.* CABALA.
ka·bu·ki (kä·bōō′kē, kə-) *n.* A form of Japanese drama based on popular themes and employing elaborate costume, stylized gesture, music, and dancing. [Jap.]
kad·dish (kä′dish) *n. Often cap.* In Judaism, a daily prayer recited in the synagogue service, in one form used by mourners. [< Aramaic *qaddīsh* holy]
kaf·fee·klatsch (kôf′ē·klach′, -kläch′, kof′-) *n.* A social gathering for conversation while coffee is served. [G, lit., coffee + gossip]
kaf·fir (kaf′ər) *n.* A variety of sorghum grown in dry regions as a grain and forage plant. Also **kaf′ir, kafir corn, kaffir corn.**
Kaf·fir (kaf′ər) *n.* **1** A member of a group of South African Bantu tribes. **2** The language of these tribes. Also **Kaf′ir.**
Kaf·ka·esque (käf′kə·esk′) *adj.* Characteristic of the novels of Franz Kafka; esp., bizarre or absurd, and often marked by the ineffectuality of the individual: made helpless by the *Kafkaesque* turn of events.
kaf·tan (kaf′tən, käf·tän′) *n.* CAFTAN.
kai·ak (kī′ak) *n.* KAYAK.
kai·ser (kī′zər) *n.* **1** Emperor. **2** *Usu. cap.* The title designating the rulers of the Holy Roman Empire (962–1806), of Austria (1804–1918), and of Germany (1871–1918). [G < L *Caesar* Caesar]
kale (kāl) *n.* **1** A variety of headless cabbage yielding curled leaves. **2** *Slang* Money. [Var. of COLE]
ka·lei·do·scope (kə·lī′də·skōp) *n.* **1** A device consisting of a tube that contains mirrors and a hole for viewing, capable of producing symmetrical patterns by reflection of an image, often the image of small bits of material contained within. **2** A rapidly changing series of scenes, events, patterns, etc. [< Gk. *kalos* beautiful + *eidos* form

+ -SCOPE] —**ka·lei·do·scop·ic** (kə·lī′də·skop′ik), **ka·lei′do·scop′i·cal** *adj.* —**ka·lei′do·scop′i·cal·ly** *adv.*

kal·ends (kal′əndz) *n.pl.* CALENDS.

Ka·le·va·la (kä′lə·vä′lä) *n.* The national epic of Finland.

ka·lif (kā′lif, kal′if) *n.* CALIPH.

kal·mi·a (kal′mē·ə) *n.* Any of several North American evergreen shrubs with clusters of rose, purple, or white flowers. [< Peter *Kalm,* 1716–79, Swedish botanist]

Kal·muck (kal′muk) *n.* **1** A member of one of the Mongol tribes extending from western China to the valley of the Volga river. **2** The language of these tribes. Also **Kal′muk.**

kal·so·mine (kal′sə·mīn) *n.* CALCIMINE.

ka·mi·ka·ze (kä′mi·kä′zē) *n.* In World War II, a Japanese pilot pledged to die by crashing his bomb-laden plane against a target. [< Jap. *kami* a god + *kaze* the wind]

Kan., Kans., Kas. Kansas.

Ka·nak·a (kə·nak′ə, kan′ə·kə) *n.* **1** A native of Hawaii. **2** Any South Sea Islander.

kan·ga·roo (kang′gə·rōō′) *n. pl.* **·roos** Any of a large family of leaping herbivorous marsupials of the Australian region, having short forelimbs, strong hind limbs, and a long, tapering tail. [native Australian name]

Kangaroo

kangaroo court An unofficial court in which the law is disregarded or willfully misinterpreted or misapplied.

kangaroo rat Any of various hopping, mouselike rodents of the sw U.S. and Mexico.

ka·o·lin (kā′ə·lin) *n.* A pure, white clay used in making porcelain. Also **ka′o·line.** [< Chin. *Kao Ling* High Ridge, a mountain where first mined]

ka·pok (kā′pok) *n.* A cottonlike fiber covering the seeds of a tropical tree, used for stuffing mattresses, etc. [< Malay *kāpoq*]

kap·pa (kap′ə) *n.* The tenth letter in the Greek alphabet (Κ, κ).

ka·put (kä·pōōt′, kə-) *adj. Slang.* Ruined; done for. [G]

kar·a·kul (kar′ə·kəl) *n.* **1** A breed of sheep of central Asia. **2** The curly, lustrous fur of newborn karakul lambs. [< *Kara Kul,* lake in central Siberia]

kar·at (kar′ət) *n.* A measure used to express the percentage of gold in an alloy on a scale from 0 to 24; for example, 18-karat gold is 75% pure. [Var. of CARAT]

ka·ra·te (kə·rä′tē) *n.* An Oriental style of self-defense using sudden forceful blows with the side of the hand. [Jap., lit., empty-handed]

kar·ma (kär′mə, kûr′-) *n.* The law of cause and effect regulating one's future life; inevitable retribution, a concept developed by the Buddhists. [Skt., action]

kart (kärt) *n.* A small, low, motorized vehicle for one person, used esp. in racing. [Var. of CART] —**kart′ing** *n.*

karyo- *combining form Biol.* Nucleus: *karyotype.* [< Gk. *karyon* a nut]

kar·y·o·tin (kar′ē·ō′tin) *n.* CHROMATIN. [< KARYO- + (CHROMA)TIN]

kar·y·o·type (kar′ē·ə·tīp′) *n.* The complete array of somatic chromosomes characteristic of any given species, type, or strain of organism.

ka·sher (kä′shər) *adj., n., v.* KOSHER.

kata- *prefix* CATA-.

ka·ty·did (kā′tē·did) *n.* Any of several large, arboreal, green insects related to grasshoppers and crickets. [Imit. of its sound]

kau·ri (kou′rē) *n.* **1** A tall, coniferous, evergreen tree of New Zealand. **2** The wood of this tree. **3** KAURI GUM. Also **kau′ry.** [< Maori]

kauri gum A fresh or fossil resinous exudation of the kauri tree, used in varnishes, etc. Also **kauri copal, kauri resin.**

kay·ak (kī′ak) *n.* A hunting canoe of arctic America, made of sealskins stretched over a pointed frame, leaving a hole amidships where the navigator sits. [< Eskimo]

Kayak

kay·o (kā′ō) *Slang v.t.* **kay·oed, kay·o·ing** In boxing, to knock out. —*n.* A knockout. [< *k(nock) o(ut)*]

ka·zoo (kə·zōō′) *n. pl.* **·zoos** A toy musical instrument, a tube to which is attached a membrane which vibrates when the player hums into the tube. [?]

K.C. King's Counsel; Knights of Columbus.

kc, kc. kilocycle(s).

ke·a (kā′ə, kē′ə) *n.* A large, green New Zealand parrot. [Maori]

kedge (kej) *Naut. n.* A light anchor used in warping, to free a vessel from shoals, etc. Also **kedge anchor.** —*v.* **kedged, kedg·ing** *v.i.* **1** To move a vessel by hauling up to a kedge anchor placed at a distance. **2** To be moved in this way. —*v.t.* **3** To move (a vessel) in this way. [? < ME *caggen* to tie]

keel (kēl) *n.* **1** *Naut.* The lowest lengthwise member of the framework of a vessel, serving to give it stability. **2** Figuratively, a ship. **3** Anything suggesting a keel in shape or function. —**on an even keel 1** In a level position. **2** Steady. —*v.t.* **1** To provide with a keel. **2** To upset (a vessel). —*v.i.* **3** To roll over. —**keel over 1** To turn bottom up; capsize. **2** To fall over or be felled unexpectedly. **3** *Informal* To faint. [< ON *kjölr*]

keel·haul (kēl′hôl′) *v.t.* **1** *Naut.* To haul (a man) under a ship from one side to the other or from stem to stern, a former punishment. **2** To reprove severely.

keel·son (kēl′sən) *n. Naut.* A beam running lengthwise above the keel of a ship. [< LG *kielswīn,* lit., keel timber]

keen[1] (kēn) *adj.* **1** Very sharp, as a knife. **2** Cutting; piercing, as wit. **3** Vivid; pungent. **4** Having or exhibiting sharpness or penetration. **5** Acute: *keen* sight. **6** Exceptionally intelligent. **7** Characterized by intensity: a *keen* appetite. **8** *Informal* Impatient; eager: *keen* to be off. [< OE *cēne*] —**keen′ly** *adv.* —**keen′ness** *n.* —**Syn. 2** acute, sharp. **6** brilliant, penetrating.

keen[2] (kēn) *n.* A wailing cry; dirge. —*v.i.* To wail loudly over the dead. [< Irish *caoinim* I wail] —**keen′er** *n.*

keep (kēp) *v.* **kept, keep·ing** *v.t.* **1** To have and retain possession or control of; hold. **2** To withhold knowledge of, as a secret. **3** To manage or conduct: to *keep* a shop. **4** To guard or defend from harm: May God *keep* you. **5** To be faithful to the conditions of: *keep* a promise. **6** To maintain by action or conduct: to *keep* silence. **7** To preserve unchanged: *Keep* the home fires burning. **8** To make regular entries in: to *keep* a diary. **9** To maintain a written record of: to *keep* accounts. **10** To have regularly for sale: to *keep* groceries. **11** To have in one's employ. **12** To celebrate or observe, as a holiday. **13** To conduct, as a meeting. **14** To detain or restrain; prevent: What *kept* you? **15** To hold prisoner; confine. **16** To remain; hold to: *Keep* your present course. **17** To hold or maintain in the same position or state as before: *Keep* your seat. —*v.i.* **18** To continue in a condition, place, or action: They *kept* firing. **19** To remain; stay: often with *up, down, in, out, off, away,* etc. **20** To remain sound, fresh, etc. **21** *Informal* To be in session: School *keeps* till three o'clock. —**keep back 1** To restrain. **2** To withhold. —**keep in with** *Informal* To remain in the good graces of. —**keep on** To continue; persist. —**keep time 1** To indicate time correctly, as a clock. **2** To count or observe rhythmic accents. —**keep to oneself 1** To refrain from revealing. **2** To be solitary. —**keep track of** (or **tabs on**) To continue to be informed about. —**keep up 1** To keep pace with; not fall behind. **2** To maintain in good condition or repair. **3** To cause to stay awake. —*n.* **1** Means of subsistence; livelihood. **2** A medieval castle or fortress. **3** That in which something is kept. —**for keeps** *Informal* For permanent keeping; for ever. [< OE *cēpan* observe]

keep·er (kē′pər) *n.* **1** An overseer, guard, or guardian. **2** One who observes or obeys: a *keeper* of promises.

keep·ing (kē′ping) *n.* **1** Custody, charge, or possession. **2** Maintenance; support. **3** Observance: the *keeping* of Christmas. **4** Preservation for the future. —**in keeping with** In accord with.

keep·sake (kēp′sāk′) *n.* Anything kept, or given to be kept; a memento.

kef (kēf, kāf), *n.* 1 A voluptuous, dreamy condition. 2 Indian hemp, smoked to produce this condition. [<Ar. *kaif* good humor]

keg (keg) *n.* 1 A small, strong barrel, usu. of 5- to 10-gallon capacity. 2 One hundred pounds of nails. [<ON *kaggi*]

keg·ler (keg′lər) *n. Informal* One who bowls; a bowler. [G *Kegel* ninepin]

kelp (kelp) *n.* 1 Any of various large, brown, coarse seaweeds. 2 The ashes of seaweed, used as a source of iodine.

Kel·vin scale (kel′vin) The absolute scale of temperature, having zero equal to about −273°C or −459.4°F. [<Lord *Kelvin,* 1824–1907, British physicist]

ken (ken) *v.t.* **kenned** or **kent, ken·ning** *Scot.* To know; have knowledge of —*n.* Reach of sight or knowledge; cognizance. [<OE *cennan* make known]

Ken. Kentucky.

ken·nel (Kən′əl) *n.* 1 A house for a dog or for a pack of hounds. 2 A pack of hounds. 3 *pl.* A professional establishment where dogs are bred, raised, boarded, trained, etc. —*v.* **·neled** or **·nelled, ·nel·ing** or **·nel·ling** *v.t.* 1 To keep or confine in a kennel. —*v.i.* 2 To take shelter in a kennel. [<L *canis* a dog]

ke·no (kē′nō) *n.* A game of chance resembling lotto.

Kenya (kēn′yə, ken′-) *n.* An independent member of the Commonwealth of Nations in E Africa, 224,960 sq. mi., cap. Nairobi. —**Kenyan** *adj., n.* • See map at AFRICA.

kep·i (kep′ē) *n. pl.* **kep·is** A military cap with a flat crown and a visor. [<G *Kappe* a cap]

kept (kept) *p.t. & p.p.* of KEEP.

ker·a·tin (ker′ə·tin) *n.* A tough, insoluble protein that forms the main ingredient of hair, horns, nails, etc. [<Gk. *keras, keratos* horn] —**ke·rat·i·nous** (kə·rat′ə·nəs) *adj.*

kerb (kûrb) *n. Brit.* The curb of a pavement.

ker·chief (kûr′chif) *n.* 1 A square of linen, silk, or other fabric used to cover the head or neck. 2 A handkerchief. [<OF *couvrir* to cover + *chef* head] —**ker′chiefed** *adj.*

kerf (kûrf) *n.* 1 The cut made by a saw, ax, etc. 2 A piece cut off. [<OE *cyrf* a cutting]

ker·mes (kûr′mēz) *n.* 1 The dried bodies of a species of scale insect. 2 A red dye made from these bodies. 3 A small oak tree of the Mediterranean area on which the insects are found: also **kermes oak.** [<Ar. *qirmiz*]

ker·mess (kûr′mis) *n.* 1 In Belgium and the Netherlands, a carnival or outdoor festival. 2 Any similar festival, usu. to raise funds for charity. Also **ker′mis.** [<Du. *kerk misse* church mass]

kern (kûrn) *n. Printing* That part of a type which overhangs the shaft or shank, as of an italic *f.* —*v.t.* To make (type) with a kern. [<F *carne* projecting angle]

ker·nel (kûr′nəl) *n.* 1 A grain or seed, as of corn or other cereal. 2 The inner, fleshy part of a nut or fruit stone. 3 The central part of anything; —*v.i.* To envelop as a kernel. [<OE *cyrnel,* dim. of *corn* a seed]

ker·o·sene (ker′ə·sēn, kar′-, ker·ə·sēn′, kar-) *n.* A liquid mixture of hydrocarbons, derived from petroleum and used as fuel. [<Gk. *kēros* wax + -ENE]

ker·sey (kûr′zē) *n. pl.* **·seys** A lightweight, ribbed woolen cloth. [<*Kersey,* village in England]

kes·trel (kes′trəl) *n.* A European falcon noted for its ability to hover in the air against the wind. [<OF *cresserelle*]

ketch (kech) *n.* A fore-and-aft rigged, two-masted vessel having the jigger mast forward of the rudder post and aft of the mainmast. [ME *cache*]

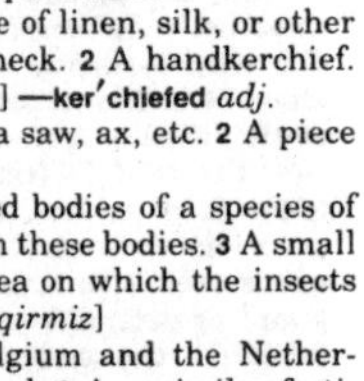

Ketch

ketch·up (kech′əp) *n.* A condiment of the consistency of a thick purée, made of tomatoes, onions, and various spices. [<Chin. *ke-tsiap* brine of pickled fish]

ke·tone (kē′tōn) *n.* Any of a series of organic compounds composed of two hydrocarbon radicals and a single bivalent group containing an atom of carbon bonded to an atom of oxygen. [<F *acétone* acetone] —**ke·ton·ic** (kē·ton′ik) *adj.*

ket·tle (ket′l) *n.* 1 A metallic vessel for stewing or boiling. 2 TEAKETTLE. [<ON *ketill*] —**kettle of fish** A troublesome situation.

ket·tle·drum (ket′l·drum′) *n.* A drum having a brass shell and tunable parchment head.

key[1] (kē) *n.* 1 A device for turning the catch or bolt of a lock in order to lock or unlock something. 2 An instrument for turning a bolt, etc., as in winding a clock. 3 Anything serving to explain or solve something: the *key* to a mystery. 4 Any one of the finger levers used to operate typewriters, typesetting machines, a telegraph sending apparatus, etc. 5 *Music* **a** A lever to be pressed by a finger in playing an instrument. **b** A set of associated tones forming a diatonic scale and all related to one principal tone, the tonic. 6 The tone or pitch of the voice. 7 Tone or style of expression. 8 *Archit.* KEYSTONE. —*v.t.* 1 To fasten with or as with a key. 2 To wedge tightly or support firmly with a key, wedge, etc. 3 To complete (an arch) by adding the keystone. —**key up** 1 to raise the pitch of. 2 To cause excitement, anticipation, etc., in. —*adj.* Of chief or decisive importance: a *key* position. [<OE *cæg*]

key[2] (kē) *n.* A low island, esp. one of coral, along a coast. [<Sp. *cayo*]

key·board (kē′bôrd′, -bōrd′) *n.* 1 A row of keys as in a piano or typewriter. 2 A set of keys or buttons for entering information into a computer.

keyed (kēd) *adj.* 1 Having keys: said of musical instruments, etc. 2 Pitched in a specific key. 3 Secured by a keystone.

key·hole (kē′hōl′) *n.* A hole for a key, as in a door or lock.

key·note (kē′nōt′) *n.* 1 *Music* The tonic of a key: also **key tone.** 2 A basic idea, fact, principle, or sentiment. —*v.t.* **·not·ed, ·not·ing** 1 To sound the keynote of. 2 To give the essential points of, as a political platform.

keynote speech A speech, as at a political convention, presenting the primary issues of interest. Also **keynote address.**

key·pad (kē′pad′) *n.* A set of keys, like those on a typewriter keyboard, used to insert sets of numbers into a computer.

key·punch (kē′punch′) *n.* A machine with a keyboard, used to record information on punch cards or tapes by punching patterns of holes thereon.

key signature *Music* The sharps or flats following the clef at the beginning of each staff, to indicate the key.

key·stone (kē′stōn′) *n.* 1 *Archit.* The uppermost and last-set stone of an arch, which locks its members together. 2 The fundamental element, as of a science or doctrine.

Keystone

kg, kg. kilogram(s); keg(s).

khak·i (kak′ē, kä′kē) *adj.* Having a tannish brown or olive-drab color. —*n. pl.* **khak·is** 1 A tannish brown or olive-drab color. 2 A cloth of this color, used esp. for military uniforms. 3 *Usu. pl.* Trousers or a uniform of this cloth. [<Hind. *khākī* dusty]

khan[1] (kän, kan) *n.* An Oriental inn surrounding a courtyard. [<Ar. *khān* an inn]

khan[2] (kän, kan) *n.* 1 In various Oriental countries during the Middle Ages, a ruler or chief. 2 A title of respect for any of various dignitaries in Iran, India, Afghanistan, etc. [<Pers. *khān* prince]

khe·dive (kə·dēv′) *n.* The title of the Turkish viceroys of Egypt from 1867 to 1914.

Khmer Republic (kmer) A country of SW Indochina, 69,844 sq. mi., cap. Pnompenh. • See map at INDOCHINA.

kHz kilohertz.

kib·butz (ki·bo͝ots′) *n. pl.* **kib·butz·im** (-bo͝ot·sēm′) A collective farming settlement in Israel. [<Heb. *qibbūṣ*]

kib·itz (kib′its) *v.i. Informal* To act as a kibitzer.

kib·itz·er (kib′it·sər) *n. Informal* One who observes other persons' affairs, esp. someone who watches and offers gratuitous advice to a player or players in a card game. [Yiddish]

ki·bosh (kī′bosh) *n. Slang* Nonsense or humbug. —**put the kibosh on** To put a stop to; quash. [?]

kick (kik) *v.i.* 1 To strike out with the foot or feet; give a blow with the foot. 2 To strike out with the foot habitually; this horse *kicks.* 3 To recoil, as a firearm. 4 *Informal* To object; complain. —*v.t.* 5 To strike with the foot. 6 To drive or impel by striking with the foot. 7 To strike in recoiling. 8 In football, to score (a goal) by a kick. 9 *Slang* To rid oneself of (a habit, esp. a drug habit]. **—kick about** (or **around**) 1 To abuse; neglect. 2 *Informal* To roam from place to place. 3 *Informal* To give thought or consideration to; discuss. **—kick back** 1 To recoil violently or unexpectedly, as a gun. 2 *Informal* To pay (part of a commission, salary, etc.) to someone in a position to grant privileges. **—kick in** 1 *Informal* To contribute or participate by contributing. 2 *Slang* To die. **—kick off** 1 In football, to put the ball in play. 2 *Slang* To die. **—kick oneself** To have remorse or regret. **—kick out** *Informal* To eject violently, as with a kick. **—kick the bucket** *Slang* To die. **—kick up** *Slang* To make or stir up (trouble, confusion, etc.). **—kick upstairs** To give an apparent promotion to (someone) in order to remove from a position of actual power. *—n.* 1 A blow with the foot. 2 The recoil of a firearm. 3 In football, one who kicks. 4 *Slang* An act of violent opposition or objection. 5 Something that excites, as the alcoholic content of drink. 6 Effective action or power. 7 *Often pl. Slang* Stimulation; pleasure: to do something for *kicks.* **—on a kick** *Slang* Intensely but often temporarily interested in a subject or activity. [ME *kiken*]

kick·back (kik′bak′) *n.* 1 A recoil; repercussion. 2 Money comprising part of a commission, fee, etc., returned by prior agreement or coercion, often illegal or unethical.

kick·er (kik′ər) *n.* 1 One who or that which kicks. 2 *Slang* A surprising element or turn of events.

kick·off (kik′ôf′, -of′) *n.* 1 In football, the kick with which a game or half is begun. 2 Any beginning.

kick·shaw (kik′shô) *n.* 1 Something fantastic or trifling. 2 Any fancy or unrecognizable dish of food. Also **kick′·shaws.** [< F *quelque chose* something]

kick·y (kik′ē) *adj.* **kick·i·er, kick·i·est** *Slang* Stimulating; exciting. **—kick′i·ness** *n.*

kid (kid) *n.* 1 A young goat. 2 Leather made from the skin of young goats, esp. as used in gloves, shoes, etc. 3 The meat of a young goat. 4 *Informal* A child or infant. *—adj.* 1 Made of kidskin. 2 *Informal* Younger: my *kid* brother. *—v.t. & v.i.* **kid·ded, kid·ding** 1 To give birth to (young): said of goats. 2 *Slang* To tease jokingly. 3 *Slang* To deceive or try to deceive (someone). [< ON *kidh*] **—kid′der** *n.*

kid·dy (kid′ē) *n. pl.* **kid·dies** *Informal* A small child. Also **kid′die.**

kid glove A glove made of kidskin or similar material. **—handle with kid gloves** To treat in a tactful or gingerly manner.

kid·nap (kid′nap) *v.t.* **·naped** or **·napped, ·nap·ing** or **·nap·ping** 1 To seize and carry off (someone) by force or fraud, usu. followed by a demand for ransom. 2 To steal (a child). [< KID + *nap,* dial. var. of NAB] **—kid′nap′er, kid′nap·per** *n.*

kid·ney (kid′nē) *n. pl.* **·neys** 1 One of a pair of organs at the back of the abdominal cavity in vertebrates. They regulate the volume, acidity, and composition of body fluids by filtering the blood and excreting waste products as urine. 2 This organ of a slaughtered animal, used as food. 3 Temperament; disposition. 4 Type or kind. [?]

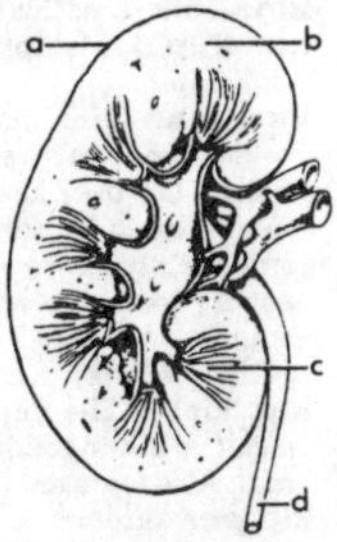

Human kidney
a. cortex. b. medulla.
c. renal pyramid.
d. ureter.

kidney bean The kidney-shaped seed of a plant of the bean family, cultivated for food.

kidney stone Any calculus occurring in the kidney or urinary passages.

kid·skin (kid′skin′) *n.* Leather from the skin of a young goat, used for gloves, shoes, etc.

kif (kēf) *n.* KEF.

Ki·ku·yu (kē·kōō′yōō) *n. pl.* **·yu** or **·yus** 1 A member of one of the main Negro tribes of Kenya. 2 The Bantu language of this tribe.

kill¹ (kil) *v.t.* 1 To deprive of life; slay. 2 To slaughter for food; butcher. 3 To destroy; put an end to. 4 To destroy the active qualities of; neutralize: to *kill* lye. 5 To spoil the effect of; offset, as a color. 6 To cancel; cross out: to *kill* a paragraph. 7 To stop (an engine, electric current, etc.). 8 To pass (time) aimlessly. 9 *Informal* To overwhelm with strong emotion, laughter, etc. *—v.i.* 10 To slay or murder. 11 To suffer or undergo death; die: These plants *kill* easily. *—n.* 1 An animal killed as prey. 2 The act of killing, esp. in hunting. **—in at the kill** Present at the climax of a chase or other undertaking. [ME *killen*] **—Syn.** *v.* 1 assassinate, execute, murder, slaughter.

kill² (kil) *n.* A creek, stream, or channel. [< Du. *kil*]

kill·deer (kil′dir) *n. pl.* **·deers** or **·deer** A small North American plover marked with two black bands at the breast. Also **kill′dee** (-dē). [Imit. of its cry]

kill·er (kil′ər) *n.* 1 A destroyer of life; a slayer. 2 A murderer or an assassin.

killer whale Any of various small predaceous whales, as the grampus, etc.

Killer whale (grampus)

kill·ing (kil′ing) *n.* 1 The act of taking life. 2 *Informal* A phenomenal profit resulting from bold financial speculation. *—adj.* 1 Lethal; destructive. 2 Very tiring: a *killing* day. 3 *Slang* Very amusing.

kill·joy (kil′joi′) *n.* One who dampens the enthusiasm or pleasure of others.

kiln (kil, kiln) *n.* An oven or furnace for baking, burning, or drying various products, as bricks, lime, enamel, pottery, etc. [< L *culina* kitchen]

kiln-dry (kil′drī′, kiln′-) *v.t.* **·dried, ·dry·ing** To dry in a kiln.

kil·o (kil′ō, kē′lō) *n. pl.* **kil·os** 1 KILOGRAM. 2 KILOMETER.

kilo- *prefix* One thousand (times a given unit): used chiefly in the metric system of weights and measures: *kilogram.* [< Gk. *chilioi* a thousand]

kil·o·cal·o·rie (kil′ə·kal′ə·rē) *n.* A great calorie: equal to 1,000 calories.

kil·o·cy·cle (kil′ə·sī′kəl) *n.* 1 One thousand cycles. 2 KILOHERTZ.

kil·o·gram (kil′ə·gram) *n.* 1 The basic metric unit of mass and weight, equal to the mass of a prototype kept in Sèvres, France, and equal to approximately 2.2 pounds. 2 The weight of a one-kilogram mass at the surface of the earth. Also **kil′o·gramme.**

kilogram calorie See CALORIE.

kil·o·hertz (kil′ə·hûrts′) *n. pl.* **·hertz, hertz·es** A unit of frequency equal to 1,000 cycles per second. [< KILO- + HERTZ]

kil·o·me·ter (ki·lom′ə·tər, kil′ə·mē′tər) *n.* A metric unit of length equal to 1,000 meters or about ⅝ mile. Also **kil′o·me′tre.**

kil·o·ton (kil′ə·tun) *n.* 1 A thousand tons. 2 A unit equivalent to the explosive power of 1,000 tons of TNT: used in expressing the energy of nuclear weapons.

kil·o·watt (kil′ə·wät) *n.* One thousand watts.

kil·o·watt-hour (kil′ə·wät·our′) *n.* The work done or the energy released by one kilowatt acting for one hour.

kilt (kilt) *n.* 1 A short pleated skirt worn by Scottish Highland men. 2 A girl's or woman's skirt resembling a kilt. *—v.t.* 1 To pleat. 2 To furnish with a kilt. [Prob. < Scand.]

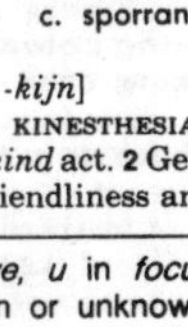

a. plaid.
b. kilt.
c. sporran.

kil·ter (kil′tər) *n.* *Informal* Proper or working order: My radio is out of *kilter.* *Brit.* sp. **kel′ter.** [?]

ki·mo·no (kə·mō′nə, ki·mō′nō) *n. pl.* **·nos** 1 A Japanese loose robe fastened with a sash. 2 A woman's dressing gown.

kin (kin) *n.* 1 Relationship; consanguinity. 2 Collectively, relatives by blood. *—adj.* Of the same blood or ancestry. [< OE *cyn*] **—Syn.** *n.* 1 blood, descent, family, stock.

-kin *suffix* Little; small: *lambkin.* [< MDu. *-kijn*]

kin·aes·the·sia (kin′is·thē′zhə, -zhē·ə), *n.* KINESTHESIA.

kind¹ (kīnd) *adj.* 1 Friendly and helpful: a *kind* act. 2 Gentle: *kind* to children. 3 Characterized by friendliness and gentleness: a *kind* remark. [< OE *gecynde*] **—Syn. 1** charitable, generous, good, good-hearted. **2** humane, kindly.

kind[2] (kīnd) *n.* **1** Variety; sort. **2** Basic nature; essence. **3** A number of persons or things of the same character; a class. **4** A modification of a given sort of thing; a species. **—in kind** With something of the same sort: to repay a blow *in kind.* **—kind of** *Informal* Rather; somewhat. **—of a kind 1** Of the same sort or variety. **2** Of imperfect quality: poetry *of a kind.* [< OE *cynd*]

kin·der·gar·ten (kin′dər·gär′tən) *n.* A school for children, usu. five or six years of age, to encourage socialization by group play and readiness for first-grade skills. [< G < *Kinder* children + *Garten* garden]

kin·der·gart·ner (kin′dər·gärt′nər) *n.* **1** A kindergarten teacher. **2** A kindergarten pupil.

kind·heart·ed (kīnd′här′tid) *adj.* Having a kind and sympathetic nature. **—kind′heart′·ed·ly** *adv.*

kin·dle (kin′dəl) *v.* **·dled, ·dling** *v.t.* **1** To cause (a flame, fire, etc.) to burn; light. **2** To set fire to; ignite. **3** To excite or inflame, as the feelings. **4** To make bright or glowing. —*v.i.* **5** To start burning. **6** To become excited. **7** To become bright or glowing. [< ON *kynda*] **—kin′dler** *n.*

kin·dling (kind′ling) *n.* Small sticks of wood and other inflammable material with which a fire is kindled.

kind·ly (kīnd′lē) *adj.* **·li·er, ·li·est 1** Having or manifesting kindness; sympathetic. **2** Having a favorable or grateful effect; beneficial. —*adv.* In a kind manner or spirit; good-naturedly. **—kind′li·ness** *n.*

kind·ness (kīnd′nəs) *n.* **1** The quality of being kind; good will. **2** A kind act; a favor. **3** A kindly feeling.

kin·dred (kin′drəd) *adj.* **1** Of the same family. **2** Of a like nature or character; congenial. —*n.* **1** Relationship; consanguinity. **2** Relatives by blood. **3** Affinity. [< OE *cyn* family + *rǣden* condition, state]

kine (kīn) *n. Archaic* Cattle; plural of cow[1].

kin·e·mat·ics (kin′ə·mat′iks) *n.pl. (construed as sing.)* The branch of mechanics dealing with motion without reference to forces. [< Gk. *kineein* to move] **—kin′e·mat′ic** or **·i·cal** *adj.* **—kin′e·mat′i·cal·ly** *adv.*

kin·e·scope (kin′ə·skōp) *n.* **1** A cathode-ray tube on which a television picture is displayed. **2** A film record of a television program. [KINE(TIC) + -SCOPE]

ki·ne·sics (ki·nē′siks) *n.* The study of the nonverbal part of language, esp. gestures and body language, as part of overall communication. [< Gk. *kinesis* motion + -ICS]

kin·es·the·si·a (kin′əs·thē′zhə, -zhē·ə) *n.* The sensation of muscular movement, bodily position, etc. Also **kin′es·the′sis** (-thē′sis). [< Gk. *kineein* to move + *aisthēsis* perception] **—kin′es·thet′ic** (-thet′ik) *adj.*

ki·net·ic (ki·net′ik) *adj.* **1** Producing motion; motor. **2** Consisting in or depending upon motion: *kinetic* energy. [< Gk. *kineein* to move]

kinetic energy Energy in motion, as in electric currents, waterfalls, burning fuel, etc.

ki·net·ics (ki·net′iks) *n.pl. (construed as sing.)* The branch of mechanics that deals with the dynamics of material bodies.

kin·folk (kin′fōk′) *n. pl.* Relatives collectively; kin. Also **kin′folks.**

king (king) *n.* **1** The sovereign male ruler of a kingdom. **2** A person or thing of great importance, position, or power: a *king* of finance. **3** A playing card bearing the semblance of a king. **4** In chess, the principal piece. **5** In checkers, a piece that has reached the adversary's king row. —*adj.* Great, as in size or importance: often in combination: *kingbolt, king* cobra. [< OE *cyng*]

king·bird (king′bûrd′) *n.* Any of various aggressive American flycatchers.

king·bolt (king′bōlt′) *n.* A vertical bolt attaching the body of a vehicle to the front axle and serving as a pivot in turning.

king cobra A large, poisonous snake found in India.

king crab 1 HORSESHOE CRAB. **2** Any of several very large edible crabs, esp. a variety found in Alaska.

king·dom (king′dəm) *n.* **1** The territory, people, state, or realm ruled by a king or a queen; a monarchy. **2** Any field of independent authority, action, or influence; sphere. **3** One of the three divisions of the natural world, known as the *animal, vegetable,* and *mineral kingdoms.*

king·fish (king′fish′) *n. pl.* **·fish** or **·fish·es 1** One of various American food fishes common in N Atlantic coastal waters. **2** *Informal* An uncontested leader in a local government, legislative body, etc.

king·fish·er (king′fish′ər) *n.* Any of several brightly colored birds, usu. crested, which feed on fish.

King James Version The Authorized Version, an English translation of the Bible published in 1611 under the auspices of James I, still used by English-speaking Protestants.

king·let (king′lit) *n.* **1** A little or unimportant king. **2** Any of several small birds resembling the warblers.

king·ly (king′lē) *adj.* **·li·er, ·li·est** Pertaining to or worthy of a king; regal. —*adv.* In a regal or kingly way. **—king′li·ness** *n.*

Kingfisher

king·pin (king′pin′) *n.* **1** KINGBOLT. **2** In tenpins, the foremost pin of a set. **3** In ninepins, the center pin. **4** *Slang* A person of first importance.

king post In carpentry, a single vertical strut supporting the apex of a triangular truss and resting on a crossbeam.

king row In checkers, the row of squares nearest to either of the players.

Kings (kingz) *n.pl. (construed as sing.)* **1** Either of two books of the Old Testament, I and II Kings. **2** In the Douay Bible, four books including I and II Kings and I and II Samuel.

King's English A style of English considered as standard. Also **Queen's English.**

king's evil Scrofula: once supposed to be curable by a monarch's touch.

king·ship (king′ship) *n.* **1** Royal state; kinghood **2** Government by a king. **3** The person of a king.

king-size (king′sīz′) *adj. Informal* Larger or longer than normal. Also **king′-sized′.**

king snake A large harmless snake of the S U.S. that feeds largely on rats, mice, and other snakes.

king's ransom A very large amount of money.

kink (kingk) *n.* **1** An abrupt bend, twist, or tangle, as in a wire or rope. **2** A tightly twisted curl, as in hair or wool. **3** A mental quirk or prejudice. **4** A hindrance, obstruction, or difficulty. **5** A crick; cramp. —*v.t. & v.i.* To form or cause to form a kink or kinks. [Du., twist, curl]

kink·a·jou (king′kə·jōō) *n.* A nocturnal, arboreal carnivore of South and Central America, having large eyes and a prehensile tail. [< F *quincajou*]

kink·y (kingk′ē) *adj.* **kink·i·er, kink·i·est 1** Having many kinks: *kinky* hair. **2** *Slang* Odd, eccentric, or zany: *kinky* sexuality. **—kink′i·ness** *n.*

kins·folk (kinz′fōk′) *n.pl.* KINFOLK.

kin·ship (kin′ship) *n.* **1** Family relationship. **2** Close relationship.

kins·man (kinz′mən) *n. pl.* **·men** (-mən) A blood relation. **—kins′wom′an** (-woom′ən) (*pl.* **·wom·en**) *n. Fem.*

ki·osk (kē′osk, kē·osk′) *n.* **1** An open ornamental summerhouse in Turkey. **2** A similar, smaller structure made to serve as a booth, newsstand, bandstand, or the like. [< Turk. *köshk* < *Pers. kūshk*]

Kiosk *def. 2*

kip (kip) *n.* The untanned skin of a calf or other young or small animal. Also **kip′skin′** (-skin′) [?]

kip·per (kip′ər) *n.* **1** A salmon, herring, or other food fish cured by kippering. **2** The male salmon during the spawning season. —*v.t.* To cure by drying or smoking. [< OE *cypera* spawning salmon]

Kir·ghiz (kir·gēz′) *n. pl.* **·ghiz** or **·ghiz·es 1** One of a Turkic people of the Mongoloid race, largely nomadic, dwelling in central Asia. **2** The Turkic language of the Kirghiz.

kirk (kûrk) *n. Scot.* A church. **—the Kirk** The established Presbyterian Church of Scotland.

kir·mess (kûr′mis) *n.* KERMESS.

kir·tle (kûrt′l) *n.* A garment with a skirt; a frock or mantle. [< OE *crytel*] **—kir′tled** *adj.*

kis·met (kiz′met, kis′-) *n.* Appointed lot; fate. [Turk. < Ar. *qisma* < *qasama* divide]

kiss (kis) *n.* 1 A caress with the lips. 2 A gentle touch. 3 Any of various forms of candy. —*v.t. & v.i.* 1 To touch with the lips, as in greeting or love. 2 To touch slightly. [< OE *cyssan* to kiss] —**kiss′a·ble** *adj.*

kit (kit) *n.* 1 A container, as a box or a knapsack, in which to pack belongings. 2 A small pail. 3 A collection of articles and appliances for any special purpose: a tool *kit.* 4 A set of parts for assembly, esp. by the consumer. —**the whole kit and caboodle** The whole collection of persons or things. [< MDu. *kitte* jug]

kitch·en (kich′ən) *n.* 1 A room set apart for cooking food. 2 A culinary department; cuisine. [< L *coquina*]

kitch·en·ette (kich′ən·et′) *n.* A small kitchen.

kitchen garden A garden in which vegetables and fruits are grown for home use.

kitchen police *Mil.* 1 Enlisted men detailed to perform kitchen chores. 2 These chores.

kitch·en·ware (kich′ən·wâr′) *n.* Kitchen utensils.

kite (kīt) 1 Any of certain birds of prey of the hawk family, having long, pointed wings and a forked tail. 2 A light frame, usu. of wood, covered with paper or light fabric, to be flown in the air at the end of a long string. 3 Any of several light sails for use in a very light wind. 4 In commerce: **a** Any negotiable paper not representing a genuine transaction but so employed as to obtain money. **b** A bank check drawn with insufficient funds on deposit to secure the advantage of the time period prior to collection. —*v.* **kit·ed, kit·ing** *v.i.* 1 *Informal* To soar or fly like a kite. 2 In commerce, to obtain money by the use of kites. —*v.t.* 3 In commerce, to issue as a kite. [< OE *cȳta*]

kith and kin (kith) Friends and relatives. [< OE *cȳth* acquaintance]

kitsch (kich) *n.* Art or literary works, etc., having broad popular appeal and little aesthetic merit. [G]

kit·ten (kit′n) *n.* A young cat or other feline animal. [< OF *chitoun*]

kit·ten·ish (kit′ən·ish) *adj.* Playfully coy. —**kit′ten·ish·ly** *adv.* —**kit′ten·ish·ness** *n.*

kit·ti·wake (kit′ē·wāk) *n.* A gull of northern seas having the hind toe rudimentary.

kit·ty[1] (kit′ē) *n. pl.* **·ties** 1 In certain card games, the pool to which each player contributes a percentage of his winnings. 2 Money pooled or set aside for any specific purpose. [< KIT]

kit·ty[2] (kit′ē) *n. pl.* **·ties** 1 A kitten. 2 A pet name for a cat.

kit·ty-cor·nered (kit′ē·kôr′nərd) *adj.* CATERCORNERED.

ki·wi (kē′wē) *n. pl.* **·wis** A flightless bird of New Zealand, having a long bill. [Maori; imit. of its cry]

KKK, K.K.K. Ku Klux Klan.

kl, kl. kiloliter(s).

Klan (klan) *n.* KU KLUX KLAN.

Klans·man (klanz′mən) *n. pl.* **·men** (-mən) A member of the Ku Klux Klan.

Kleen·ex (klē′neks) *n.* A soft, paper tissue, used as a handkerchief: a trade name.

klep·to·ma·ni·a (klep′tə·mā′nē·ə) *n.* An uncontrollable, abnormal propensity to steal. [< Gk. *kleptein* to steal + -MANIA] —**klep′to·ma′ni·ac** (-mā′nē·ak) *n.*

klieg light (klēg) A powerful arc light used while making motion pictures. [< A. *Kliegl,* 1872–1927, and his brother John, 1869–1959, U.S. stage-lighting pioneers.]

klutz (klutz) *n. Slang* A clumsy or inept person; oaf. [< G *Klotz* block of wood, lout] —**klutz′y** *adj.* **(·i·er, ·i·est)**

km, km. kilometer(s).

knack (nak) *n.* 1 The trick of doing a thing readily and well. 2 Cleverness; adroitness. 3 A clever device. [ME, a sharp blow] —**Syn.** 2 aptitude, dexterity, facility.

knack·wurst (näk′wûrst) *n.* A short, thick sausage, usu. highly seasoned. [G < *knacken* sputter + *Wurst* sausage]

knap·sack (nap′sak) *n.* A bag of leather or canvas worn across the shoulders, for carrying clothing, supplies, etc. [< Du. *knappen* to bite + *zak* a sack]

knave (nāv) *n.* 1 A dishonest person; rogue. 2 A playing card, the jack. [< OE *cnafa* servant]

knav·er·y (nā′vər·ē) *n. pl.* **·er·ies** 1 Deceitfulness; trickery. 2 An instance of deceitful action or behavior.

knav·ish (nā′vish) *adj.* Of, pertaining to, or characteristic of a knave. —**knav′ish·ly** *adv.* —**knav′ish·ness** *n.*

knead (nēd) *v.t.* 1 To mix and work, as dough or clay, into a uniform mass, usu. by pressing, turning, etc., with the hands. 2 To work upon with the hands; massage. 3 To make by or as by kneading. [< OE *cnedan*] —**knead′er** *n.*

knee (nē) *n.* 1 The joint of the human leg midway between the hip and the ankle. 2 A joint in the foreleg of various animals corresponding to the knee. 3 Anything like or suggesting a bent knee. 4 The part of a stocking or garment covering the knee. —**bring to one's knees** To cause to surrender. —*v.t.* To touch or strike with the knee. [< OE *cnēow*]

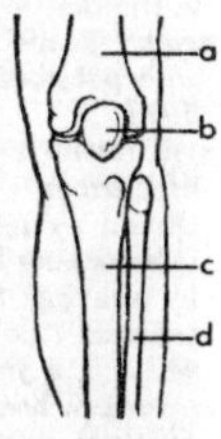

Knee
a. femur.
b. patella.
c. tibia.
d. fibula.

knee·cap (nē′kap′) *n.* 1 PATELLA: also **knee′pan′.** 2 A protective covering or padding for the knee: also **knee′pad′.**

knee-deep (nē′dēp′) *adj.* 1 Up to the knees. 2 Sunk to the knee.

knee·hole (nē′hōl′) *n.* A recess for the knees, as in a desk. —*adj.* Having such a recess.

knee-jerk (nē′jûrk′) *adj. Informal* Acting in a way that displays unthinking acceptance of preconceived ideas or stereotypes: *knee-jerk* liberals.

knee jerk A reflex action of the lower leg caused by a tapping of the tendon just below the kneecap.

kneel (nēl) *v.i.* **knelt** or **kneeled, kneel·ing** To fall or rest on the bent knee or knees. [< OE *cnēowlian*] —**kneel′er** *n.*

knell (nel) *n.* 1 The tolling of a bell, as in announcing a death. 2 An omen of death, failure, etc. —*v.i.* 1 To sound a knell; toll. 2 To give a sad or warning sound. —*v.t.* 3 To proclaim or announce by a knell. [< OE *cnyllan* knock]

knelt (nelt) *p.t. & p.p.* of KNEEL.

knew (nyōō) *p.t.* of KNOW.

Knick·er·bock·er (nik′ər·bok′ər) *n.* 1 A descendant of one of the early Dutch settlers in New York State. 2 A New Yorker. [< Diedrich *Knickerbocker,* fictitious author of Washington Irving's *History of New York* (1809)]

knick·er·bock·ers (nik′ər·bok′ərz) *n. pl.* Wide short breeches gathered below the knee.

knick·ers (nik′ərz) *n. pl.* 1 KNICKERBOCKERS. 2 Formerly, a woman's undergarment, similar to bloomers.

knick·knack (nik′nak) *n.* A trifling article; trinket; trifle. [Reduplication of KNACK]

knife (nīf) *n. pl.* **knives** (nīvz) 1 A cutting instrument consisting of a sharp single-edged or double-edged blade, commonly set in a handle. 2 An edged blade forming a part of an implement or machine. 3 A weapon such as a cutlass or sword. —**go under the knife** *Informal* To undergo a surgical operation. —*v.t.* **knifed, knif·ing** 1 To stab or cut with a knife. 2 *Slang* To work against with underhand methods. —**knife in the back** *Informal* To undermine the reputation, position, etc., of. [< OE *cnīf*]

knight (nīt) *n.* 1 In medieval times, a gentleman admitted with special ceremonies to honorable military rank. 2 *Brit.* The holder of an honorary, nonhereditary rank next below that of baronet, giving him the title of *Sir.* 3 A champion or devoted follower, as of a cause, principle, or woman. 4 A member of any society in which the official title of knight obtains. 5 A chessman bearing a horse's head. —*v.t.* To make (someone) a knight. [< OE *cniht* boy, servant]

knight-er·rant (nīt′er′ənt) *pl.* **knights-er·rant** A medieval knight who went forth to redress wrongs or seek adventures.

knight-er·rant·ry (nīt′er′ən·trē) *n. pl.* **·ries** 1 The customs and practices of the knights-errant. 2 Quixotic behavior or action.

knight·hood (nīt′hŏŏd) *n.* 1 The character, dignity, rank, or vocation of a knight. 2 Knights collectively. 3 CHIVALRY.

knight·ly (nīt′lē) *adj.* **1** Pertaining to a knight; chivalrous. **2** Composed of knights: a *knightly* order. **—knight′li·ness** *n.*

Knights of Columbus A fraternal society of Roman Catholic men.

Knight Templar *pl.* **Knights Templars** *for def. 1;* **Knights Templar** *for def. 2* **1** A member of a great military order founded in 1119 for the protection of pilgrims in Jerusalem; also **Templar.** **2** A member of a certain Masonic order in the U.S.

knish (kə-nish′) *n.* A small square or round of dough filled with potatoes, meat, kasha, etc., and baked or fried. [Yiddish]

knit (nit) *v.* **knit** or **knit·ted, knit·ting** *v.i.* **1** To form (a fabric or garment) by interlocking loops of a single yarn or thread by means of needles. **2** To make into fabric by interlocking loops of thread, as on a machine, instead of by weaving. **3** To fasten or unite closely and firmly. **4** To contract (the brows). **—***v.i.* **5** To make a fabric by interweaving a yarn or thread. **6** To grow together firmly, as a broken bone. **—***n.* A knitted garment or fabric. [< OE *cnyttan*] **—knit′ter** *n.*

knit·ting (nit′ing) *n.* **1** The act of one who or that which knits. **2** The fabric or garment thus produced.

knitting needle A straight, slender rod, pointed at one or both ends, used in sets of two or more for hand knitting.

knives (nīvz) *n.pl.* of KNIFE.

knob (nob) *n.* **1** A rounded protuberance. **2** A rounded handle, as of a door. **3** A rounded mountain; knoll. [< MLG *knobbe.*] **—knobbed** (nobd) *adj.*

knob·by (nob′ē) *adj.* **·bi·er, ·bi·est** **1** Shaped like a knob: *knobby* knees. **2** Full of knobs. **—knob′bi·ness** *n.*

knock (nok) *v.t.* **1** To give a heavy blow to; hit. **2** To strike (one thing) against another; bring into collision. **3** To drive or impel by striking: to *knock* a ball over a fence. **4** To make or cause by striking: to *knock* a hole in a wall. **5** *Slang* To find fault with; carp. at. **—***v.i.* **6** To strike a blow or blows, as with the fist or a club. **7** To come into collision; bump. **8** To make a pounding noise: to *knock* on a door. **9** *Slang* to find fault; carp. **—knock about** (or **around**) **1** To strike repeatedly; hit from side to side. **2** To wander from place to place. **3** To treat neglectfully; abuse. **—knock down** **1** To take apart for convenience in shipping or storing. **2** In auctions, to sell to the highest bidder. **—knock off** **1** To leave off; stop, as work, talking, etc. **2** To deduct. **3** To do or make quickly or easily. **4** *Slang* To kill or defeat. **—knock out** **1** In boxing, to defeat (an opponent) by striking him to the ground. **2** To render unconscious or exhausted. **—knock together** To build or make roughly or hurriedly. **—knock up** **1** *Brit.* To rouse, as by knocking on the door. **2** *Brit. Informal* To tire out; exhaust. **—***n.* **1** A sharp blow; a rap; also, a knocking. **2** *Mech.* A sharp noise indicating some malfunction, as badly timed combustion in an engine. **3** *Informal* Hostile criticism. [< OE *cnocian*] **—Syn.** *v.* **1** bang, punch, smack, smite, strike, pat, smash, clobber, rap, hammer, hit, pound, thrash, wallop.

knock·a·bout (nok′ə-bout′) *adj.* **1** Characterized by noisiness or roughness. **2** Adapted for any kind of rough use. **—***n.* **1** *Naut.* A small, partially, decked yacht, carrying a mainsail and jib rigged fore-and-aft. **2** Something fit for knockabout use.

knock·down (nok′doun′) *adj.* **1** Having sufficient force to fell or overthrow. **2** Constructed so as to be easily taken apart. **—***n.* **1** A blow that fells. **2** Any unassembled, prefabricated article.

knock·er (nok′ər) *n.* **1** One who knocks. **2** A hinged metal hammer fastened to a door as a means of signaling for admittance.

knock·knee (nok′nē′) *n.* An inward curvature of the legs that causes the knees to touch in walking. **—knock′-kneed′** *adj.*

knock·out (nok′out′) *adj.* Rendering insensible; overpowering. **—***n.* **1** A knockout blow. **2** *Slang* An overwhelmingly attractive person or thing.

knockout drops Drops of a powerful drug put into a drink to produce unconsciousness.

knock·wurst (näk′wûrst) *n.* KNACKWURST.

knoll (nōl) *n.* A small hill; mound. [< OE *cnoll* hill]

knot (not) *n.* **1** A fastening made by tightly intertwining one or more ropes, cords, etc. **2** A lump formed of hard tangles in a string, cord, etc. **3** An ornamental bow of silk, lace, etc. **4** A hard, gnarled portion of the trunk of a tree where a branch grows out. **5** *Bot.* A node or joint in a stem. **6** A cluster or group, as of persons. **7** *Naut.* **a** A division of a log line used to determine the rate of a ship's motion. **b** A speed of one nautical mile per hour. **c** One nautical mile. **8** A knob. **9** A bond or union. **10** A hard lump resembling a knot: a *knot* of muscle. **11** An intricate or complex difficulty; problem. **12** A state of being drawn taut, as from nervous tension: a stomach in *knots.* **—***v.* **knot·ted, knot·ting** *v.t.* **1** To tie in a knot; form a knot or knots in. **2** To secure or fasten by a knot. **3** To form knobs, bosses, etc., in. **—***v.i.* **4** To form a knot or knots. **5** To tie knots for fringe. [< OE *cnotta*]

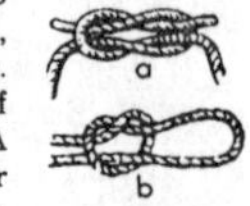

Knots
a. square or reef. b. single bowknot.

knot·grass (not′gras′, -gräs′) *n.* A widely distributed weed related to buckwheat, with jointed stems. Also **knot′weed.**

knot·hole (not′hōl′) *n.* A hole, as in a plank, left by the falling out of a knot.

knot·ted (not′əd) *adj.* **1** Tied with a knot or into knots. **2** Having knots; knotty. **3** Ornamented with knots. **4** KNOTTY (def. 2).

knot·ter (not′ər) *n.* **1** A person or machine employed for removing knots. **2** One who or that which knots.

knot·ty (not′ē) *adj.* **·ti·er, ·ti·est** **1** Having, full of, or tied in knots. **2** Difficult; intricate. **—knot·ti·ness** *n.*

knout (nout) *n.* A whip or scourge used formerly in Russia to inflict punishment. **—***v.t.* To flog with the knout. [< Russ. *knut*]

know (nō) *v.* **knew, known, know·ing** *v.t.* **1** To perceive or understand clearly or with certainty: to *know* the truth. **2** To have information about: to *know* their plans. **3** To have experience of or familiarity with. **4** To distinguish between: to *know* peas from beans. **5** To have securely in the mind or memory: to *know* historical facts. **6** To have practical skill in or knowledge of: often with *how.* **—***v.i.* **7** To have knowledge: often with *of.* **8** To be or become aware or cognizant. **—***n.* The fact or condition of knowing; knowledge. **—in the know** *Informal* Having full or privileged information. [< OE *cnāwan*] **—know′a·ble** *adj.* **—know′er** *n.* **—Syn.** *v.* **1** apprehend, comprehend, discern, perceive.

know-how (nō′hou′)*n.* *Informal* Knowledge of how to perform a complicated procedure; technical skill.

know·ing (nō′ing) *adj.* **1** Perceptive; astute. **2** Possessing sly or secret knowledge. **3** Conscious; intentional. **4** Having knowledge or information. **—know′ing·ly** *adv.* **—know′ing·ness** *n.* **—Syn.** **1** acute, clever, discerning, keen, shrewd.

knowl·edge (nol′ij) *n.* **1** Information or understanding acquired through experience. **2** Information acquired through study. **3** The act, fact, or state of knowing. **4** The accumulated body of facts concerning a specified field of study. **5** Everything that has been learned, discovered, or perceived. **—to the best of one's knowledge** As far as one can determine. [< OE *cnawan* know]

knowl·edge·a·ble (nol′ij-ə-bəl) *adj.* *Informal* Having knowledge or intelligence.

known (nōn) *p.p.* of KNOW.

know-noth·ing (nō′nuth′ing) *n.* An uneducated person; an ignoramus.

Know-Noth·ing (nō′nuth′ing) *n.* A member of a party in U.S. politics (1853–56), which aimed at excluding foreign-born persons from the government.

knuck·le (nuk′əl) *n.* **1** One of the joints of the fingers, esp. one connecting the fingers to the rest of the hand. **2** The knee or ankle joint of certain animals, used as food. **3** *pl.* A device of metal, fitting over the knuckles, used as a weapon. **—***v.i.* **knuck·led, knuck·ling** To hold the knuckles on the ground in shooting a marble. **—knuckle down** To apply oneself seriously and assiduously. **—knuckle under** To give in; yield. [< MLG *knökel*]

knurl (nûrl) *n.* **1** A protuberance; knot. **2** One of a series of small ridges on the edge of a thumbscrew or coin. **—***v.t.* To produce a series of knurls on. [?] **—knurl′y** *adj.*

KO, K.O., k.o. knockout.

ko·a·la (kō·ä′lə) *n.* An arboreal marsupial of Australia having thick gray fur, large hairy ears, and sharp claws. [< native Australian name]

Koalas

Ko·di·ak bear (kō′dē·ak) A very large brown bear found along the coast of Alaska. [< *Kodiak* Island, Alaska]

Koh·i·nor (kō′i·no͝or′) *n.* A very large diamond, one of the British crown jewels since 1849. Also **Koh′i·noor′**, **Koh′i·nur′**. [< Pers. *kōhinūr* mountain of light]

kohl·ra·bi (kōl·rä′bē, kōl′rä-) *n. pl.* **·bies** A vegetable related to cabbage, having a bulbous edible stem. [< Ital. *cavolo* cabbage + *rapa* turnip]

ko·la (kō′lə) *n.* COLA.

kola nut The seed of the cola, bitter in taste and containing caffeine. Also **cola nut.**

ko·lin·sky (kə·lin′skē, kō-) *n. pl.* **·skies 1** Any of several minks of northern China and Russia. **2** The fur of any of these. [< Russ. *kolinski* of Kola, a Russian peninsula]

ko·mat·ik (kō·mad′ik) *n. Can.* An Eskimo sled. [< Eskimo]

koo·doo (ko͞o′do͞o) *n.* KUDU.

kook (ko͝ok) *n. Slang* An unconventional, eccentric, or unbalanced person [? < CUCKOO]

kook·y (ko͞o′kē) *adj.* **kook·i·er, kook·i·est** *Slang* Of or characteristic of a kook. Also **kook′ie.** **—kook′i·ness** *n.*

kop (kop) *n.* In South Africa, a hill; headland. [< Du., a head]

ko·peck (kō′pek) *n.* A monetary unit and small copper or bronze coin of Russia; one one-hundredth of a ruble.

Ko·ran (kō·rän′, -ran′) *n.* The Muslims' sacred scripture, accepted by them as the revelations of Allah (God) to Mohammed.

Ko·re·a (kô·rē′ə, kō-) *n.* A former country located on a peninsula of E Asia, divided into the **Democratic People's Republic of Korea,** a republic on the N part of the peninsula, 46,812 sq. mi., cap. Pyongyang: also **North Korea;** and the **Republic of Korea,** a republic on the S part of the peninsula, 38,542 sq. mi., cap. Seoul: also **South Korea. —Ko·re′an** *adj., n.*

ko·ru·na (kô·ro͞o′nä) *n.* The basic monetary unit of Czechoslovakia.

ko·sher (kō′shər) *adj.* **1** Permitted by the Jewish ceremonial law; clean: said usu. of food. **2** Dealing in kosher food. **3** *Slang* All right; legitimate. **—*n.*** A shop selling kosher food; also the food sold there. **—*v.t.*** (kosh′ər) To make kosher. [< Heb. *kāshēr* fit, proper]

kou·miss (ko͞o′mis) *n.* KUMISS.

kow·tow (lou′tou′) *n.* Formerly, a Chinese form of obeisance in which one knelt and touched the forehead to the ground before a superior. **—*v.i.* 1** To make such obeisance. **2** To act in an obsequious or servile manner. [< Chin. *k'o-t'ou,* lit., knock the head] **—kow′tow′er** *n.*

KP, K.P. kitchen police.

Kr krypton.

kraal (kräl) *n.* **1** A village or group of native huts in S Africa, usu. surrounded by a stockade. **2** The social unit such a community represents. **3** An enclosure for cattle. [Afrikaans]

krait (krīt) *n.* Any of several very venomous snakes of S Asia. [< Hind. *karait*]

K-ra·tion (kā′rash′ən, -rā′shən) *n.* An emergency ration for soldiers of the U.S. Armed Forces in World War II.

krem·lin (krem′lin) *n.* The citadel of a Russian town. [< Russ. *kreml′* citadel]

Krem·lin (krem′lin) **1** The citadel of Moscow, enclosing the former palace of the Czar. **2** The government of the U.S.S.R.

Krem·lin·ol·o·gist (krem′lin·ol′ə·jist) *n.* A political analyst of the operation, policies, etc., of the government of the U.S.S.R. **—Krem′lin·ol′o·gy** *n.*

kreu·zer (kroit′sər) *n.* Any of several former small silver or copper coins of Austria and Germany. Also **kreut′zer.**

krill (kril) *n.* Tiny crustaceans, the chief food of antarctic whales and other marine animals. [< Norw. *kril* the young of fish]

krim·mer (krim′ər) *n.* A fur resembling Persian lamb prepared from skins of Crimean lambs. [< G *Krim* Crimea]

kris (krēs) *n.* A dagger with a wavy blade used in Malaysia. [< Malay]

Kris with sheath

Krish·na (krish′nə) *n.* A celebrated Hindu deity, an incarnation of Vishnu. **—Krish′na·ism** *n.*

Kriss Krin·gle (kris kring′gəl) St. Nicholas; Santa Claus. [< G *Christkindl* Christ child]

kro·na (krō′nə; *Sw.* kro͞o′nə) *n. pl.* **kro·nor** (krō′nôr) The basic monetary unit of Sweden.

kro·ne (krō′nə) *n.* **1** *pl.* **kro·ner** (krō′nər) A gold coin, the basic monetary unit of Norway and Denmark. **2** *pl.* **kro·nen** (krō′nən) Any of several former European gold coins.

kryp·ton (krip′ton) *n.* A colorless, inert, gaseous element (symbol Kr) present in minute amounts in the atmosphere. [< Gk. *kryptos* hidden]

KS Kansas (P.O. abbr.)

kt. karat.

ku·chen (ko͞o′khən) *n.* A yeast dough coffee cake. [G]

ku·dos (kyo͞o′dos) *n.* Glory, credit, or acclaim because of achievement. [< Gk. *kydos* glory] • *Kudos* is sometimes mistakenly assumed to be the plural of "*kudo.*"

ku·du (ko͞o′do͞o) *n.* A large striped African antelope, having long, spiraling horns in the male. [< native African name]

Kudu

Ku Klux·er (kyo͞o′kluk′sər) A member of the Ku Klux Klan

Ku Klux Klan (kyo͞o′kluks′ klan′) **1** A secret society in the S U.S. after the Civil War, aiming to prevent Negro ascendancy. **2** A modern secret society, founded in 1915 at Atlanta, Ga., aiming at arbitrary regulation of life by white Protestants. [< Gk. *kyklos* a circle + CLAN]

ku·lak (kyo͞o′lak, kyo͞o·lak′) *n.* A well-to-do Russian peasant who exploited poorer peasants and opposed Soviet collectivization of the land. [Russ., lit., fist]

ku·miss (ko͞o′mis) *n.* Fermented mare's milk, used by the Tatar tribes of CEN Asia. Also **ku′mys.** [< Russ. *kumys*]

kum·mel (kim′əl; *Ger.* kü′mal) *n.* A German or Russian liqueur flavored with aniseed, cumin, or caraway. [< L *cuminum* cumin]

kum·quat (kum′kwot) *n.* **1** A small orange-colored citrus fruit having a sweet rind and sour pulp. **2** The small tree bearing this fruit. [< Chin. *chin-chü,* lit., golden orange]

Kuo·min·tang (kwō′min′tang′) *n.* The nationalist party of China, founded in 1911 by Sun Yat-sen and led after 1927 by Chiang Kai-shek.

Kurd (kûrd, ko͝ord) *n.* One of a Muslin people dwelling chiefly in Kurdistan.

Kurd·ish (kûr′dish, ko͝or′-) *adj.* Of or pertaining to the Kurds, their language, etc. **—*n.*** The Iranian language of the Kurds.

Ku·wait (ko͞o·wāt′) *n.* A Shiekdom of NE Arabia, 5,000 sq. mi. cap. Kuwait. • See map at SAUDI ARABIA.

kw, kw. kilowatt(s).

kwash·i·or·kor (kwäsh′ē·ôr′kôr) *n.* A disease produced in children by prolonged lack of protein in the diet and characterized by potbelly, edema, and permanently impaired development. [< native African name]

K.W.H., kw-h, kw.-hr., kw-hr kilowatt-hour(s).

KY Kentucky (P.O. abbr.).

Ky. Kentucky.

L

L, l (el) *n. pl.* **L's, l's, Ls, ls** (elz) **1** The 12th letter of the English alphabet. **2** Any spoken sound representing the letter *L* or *l.* **3** In Roman notation, the symbol for 50. **4** Something shaped like an L. —*adj.* Shaped like an L.

L Latin; length; longitude; Linnaeus.

L., l. lake; latitude; law; leaf; league; left; length; line; link; lira; lire; low; pound (L *libra*).

l, l. liter(s).

la[1] (lä) *n. Music* In solmization, the sixth tone of a diatonic scale. [< Med. L. See GAMUT.]

la[2] (lä, lô) *interj.* Look! O!: an exclamation expressing surprise, emphasis, etc.

LA Louisiana (P.O. abbr.)

L.A. (el'ā') *Informal* Los Angeles.

La lanthanum.

La. Louisiana.

lab (lab) *n. Informal* A laboratory.

lab. laboratory.

la·bel (lā'bəl) *n.* **1** A slip, as of paper, affixed to something to indicate its character, ownership, destination, etc. **2** A brief, descriptive, written or spoken phrase designating certain characteristics of a person or group. —*v.t.* **·beled** or **·belled, ·bel·ing** or **·bel·ling 1** To mark with a label; attach a label to. **2** To classify; designate. [< OF, a ribbon] —**la'bel·er** or **la'bel·ler** *n.*

la·bi·a (lā'bē·ə) *n.pl.* of LABIUM.

la·bi·al (lā'bē·əl) *adj.* **1** Of or pertaining to the lips. **2** *Phonet.* Formed, articulated, or modified by the lips. —*n. Phonet.* A labial sound, as *b, p, m.* [< L *labium* a lip] —**la'bi·al·ly** *adv.*

la·bi·ate (lā'bē·āt, -it) *adj.* Having lips or liplike parts. Also **la'bi·at'ed.** [< L *labium* a lip]

la·bile (lā'bīl, -bil) *adj.* Prone to undergo change; unstable. [< L *labi* to slip, fall] —**la·bil'i·ty** *n.*

la·bi·o·den·tal (lā'bē·ō·den'təl) *adj. Phonet.* Formed with the lower lip and the upper front teeth, as *f* and *v* in English. —*n.* A sound so formed. [< Latin *labium* lip + *dens* tooth]

la·bi·um (lā'bē·əm) *n. pl.* **·bi·a** (-bē·ə) **1** A lip or liplike organ or part. **2** *pl.* The folds of skin and of mucous membrane of the vulva. [L, a lip]

la·bor (lā'bər) *n.* **1** Hard and exhausting physical or mental exertion. **2** That which requires exertion or effort; a task. **3** Wage earners collectively. **4** Workers who engage in manual work. **5** Work done by workers as a group. **6** The process of giving birth. —*v.i.* **1** To do work; toil. **2** To move with difficulty or painful exertion. **3** To be in the process of giving birth. —*v.t.* **4** To develop in too minute detail: to *labor* a point. —**labor under** To be hindered or troubled by: to *labor under* a misapprehension. *Brit. sp.* **la'bour.** [< L, toil, distress] —**la'bor·ing·ly** *adv.*

lab·o·ra·to·ry (lab'rə·tôr'ē, -tō'rē; *Brit.* lə·bor'ə·trē) *n. pl.* **·ries 1** A place adapted to conducting scientific experiments, analyses, etc. **2** A department, as in a factory, for research, testing, etc. —*adj.* Pertaining to or performed in a laboratory. [< L *laborare* to labor]

Labor Day In the U.S. and Canada, the first Monday in September, set aside as a legal holiday in honor of labor.

la·bored (lā'bərd) *adj.* Performed laboriously; strained: a *labored* joke. *Brit. sp.* **la'boured.**

la·bor·er (lā'bər·ər) *n.* One who performs physical or manual work, esp. if unskilled. *Brit. sp.* **la'bour·er.**

la·bo·ri·ous (lə·bôr'ē·əs, -bō'rē-) *adj.* **1** Requiring much labor; toilsome. **2** Diligent; industrious. **3** Strained; labored. *Brit. sp.* **la·bour'ious.** —**la·bo'ri·ous·ly** *adv.* —**la·bo'ri·ous·ness** *n.* —**Syn. 1** arduous, difficult, onerous. **2** assiduous; persevering.

la·bor·ite (lā'bər·īt) *n.* One who supports labor interests, esp. in politics. *Brit. sp.* **la'bour·ite.**

la·bor-sav·ing (lā'bər·sā'ving) *adj.* Doing away with, or lessening the need for, manual work.

labor union An association of working men and women organized to protect and promote their common interests, esp. in negotiations with management with regard to wages, hours, working conditions, etc.; a trade union.

Labour Party In Great Britain, a political party drawing its chief support from the working class and committed to socialistic reform. —**La·bour·ite** (lā'bər·īt) *n.*

la·bur·num (lə·bûr'nəm) *n.* Any of a genus of leguminous shrubs or trees having pendulous yellow flowers and poisonous seeds. [L]

lab·y·rinth (lab'ə·rinth) *n.* **1** A confusing, winding network of passages or paths; a maze. **2** Any perplexing combination or condition. **3** *Anat.* The winding passages of the inner ear. —**lab'y·rin'thine** (-thin, -thēn) or **·thi·an** or **·thic** or **·thi·cal** *adj.* —**lab'y·rin'thi·cal·ly** *adv.*

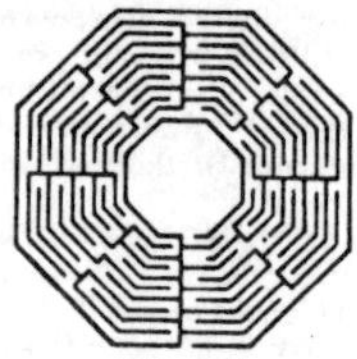

Labyrinth

Lab·y·rinth (lab'ə·rinth) *n. Gk. Myth.* The maze used to confine the Minotaur, constructed by Daedalus for Minos of Crete. [< Gk. *labyrinthos*]

lac[1] (lak) *n.* A resinous substance exuded by a s Asian scale insect and used in making varnishes, etc.

lac[2] (lak) *n.* LAKH.

lace (lās) *n.* **1** A cord or string for fastening together the parts of a shoe, a corset, etc. **2** A delicate network of threads of linen, silk, cotton, etc., arranged in figures or patterns. **3** A dash of spirits, as in tea or coffee. —*v.* **laced, lac·ing** *v.t.* **1** To draw together by tying the lace or laces of. **2** To pass (a cord or string) through hooks, eyelets, etc., as a lace. **3** To trim with or as with lace. **4** To compress the waist of (a person) by tightening laces, as of a corset. **5** To intertwine or interlace. **6** To streak, as with color. **7** To add a dash of spirits to. **8** *Informal* To beat; thrash. —*v.i.* **9** To be fastened by means of a lace. —**lace into 1** To attack. **2** To scold. [< L *laqueus* a noose, trap]

lac·er·ate (las'ər·āt) *v.t.* **·at·ed, ·at·ing 1** To tear raggedly, as the flesh. **2** To hurt; injure, as the feelings. —*adj.* Jagged; torn. [< L *lacer* mangled] —**lac'er·a·ble, lac'er·a'tive** *adj.* —**lac'er·a'tion** *n.* —**Syn.** *v.* **1** rend, rip, rupture, split, sunder.

lace·wing (lās'wing') *n.* Any of certain insects having four lacy wings, including species that destroy insect pests.

Adult lacewing

lace·work (lās'wûrk') *n.* **1** Lace. **2** Any openwork resembling lace.

lach·es (lach'iz) *n. Law* Inexcusable delay in asserting a right. [< L *laxus* lax]

lach·ry·mal (lak'rə·məl) *adj.* **1** Of or pertaining to tears. **2** Pertaining to tear-producing glands. —*n. pl.* The glands that secrete tears. Also **lac'ri·mal.** [< L *lacrima* a tear]

lach·ry·ma·to·ry (lak'rə·mə·tôr'ē, -tō·rē) *n. pl.* **·ries** A small, narrow-necked bottle found in ancient tombs, used to contain the tears of mourners. —*adj.* **1** Producing tears. **2** Containing tears. Also **lac'ri·ma·to'ry.**

lach·ry·mose (lak'rə·mōs') *adj.* **1** Shedding tears; tearful. **2** Causing sadness; mournful. Also **lac'ri·mose.** —**lach'ry·mose·ly** *adv.*

lac·ing (lā'sing) *n.* **1** The act of fastening, as with a lace. **2** Lace. **3** A connecting or strengthening member; crosspiece. **4** *Informal.* A thrashing. **5** Any ornamental braid, as of gold or silver.

lack (lak) *v.t.* **1** To be without; have none or too little of. **2** To be short by; require: It *lacks* two months till summer. —*v.i.* **3** To be wanting or deficient; be missing. —*n.* **1** The state of being needy or without something. **2** Want; deficiency. **3** That which is needed. [ME *lac*]

lack·a·dai·si·cal (lak′ə·dā′zi·kəl) *adj.* Languishing; listless; apathetic. **—lack′a·dai′si·cal·ly** *adv.* **—lack′a·dai′si·cal·ness** *n.*

lack·ey (lak′ē) *n. pl.* **·eys 1** A male servant. **2** Any servile attendant or follower. *—v.t. & v.i.* To attend or act as a lackey. Also **lac′quey.** [< OF *laquay*]

lack·lus·ter (lak′lus′tər) *adj.* **1** Wanting luster; dull, as hair. **2** Lacking spirit or liveliness; dull or perfunctory: a *lackluster* performance. *—n.* A lack of luster; dullness. *Brit. sp.* **·lus·tre.**

La·co·ni·a (lə·kō′nē·ə) *n.* A region and ancient country in the SE Peloponnesus, Greece, of which Sparta was the capital. **—La·co′ni·an** *adj., n.*

la·con·ic (lə·kon′ik) *adj.* Using or consisting of few words; short and forceful. Also **la·con′i·cal.** [< Gk. *Lakōn* a Spartan, with ref. to the habitual terseness of Spartan speech]

lac·quer (lak′ər) *n.* **1** A quick-drying varnish made from resin, nitrocellulose, and sometimes a pigment, dissolved in a volatile solvent. **2** A varnish yielding a high polish made from the resin of a tree of SE Asia. **3** Objects coated with such varnish: also **lac′quer·work′.** *—v.t.* To coat or varnish with lacquer. Also **lack′er.** [< Pg. *lacré* sealing wax]

la·crosse (lə·krôs′,-kros′) *n.* A field sport played with a ball and long-handled, netted rackets in which two teams of ten players each try to send the ball between the opponents' goal posts. [< F *la crosse* hooked stick]

lac·tate (lak′tāt) *v.i.* **·tat·ed, ·tat·ing** To form or secrete milk. *—n.* A salt or ester of lactic acid. [< L *lac, lactis* milk] **—lac·ta′tion** *n.*

lac·te·al (lak′tē·əl) *adj.* Pertaining to or like milk; conveying a milklike fluid. Also **lac′te·an, lac′te·ous.** *—n.* One of the lymphatic vessels that take up chyle from the small intestine. [< *lac, lactis* milk]

lac·tic (lak′tik) *adj.* Of or derived from milk.

lactic acid A bitter, syrupy acid contained in sour milk and produced by the fermentation of lactose.

lac·to·fla·vin (lak′tō·flā′vin) *n.* RIBOFLAVIN.

lac·tose (lak′tōs) *n.* A white crystalline sugar present in milk.

la·cu·na (lə·kyōō′nə) *n. pl.* **·nas** or **·nae** (-nē) **1** A space from which something has been omitted; gap. **2** A minute cavity in bone or tissue. Also **la·cune′** (-kyōōn′). [L, a hole, pool] **—la·cu′nal** (-nəl), **la·cu′nar** (-nər) *adj.*

lac·y (lā′sē) *adj.* **lac·i·er, lac·i·est 1** Having an open design or pattern like lace. **2** Of lace. **—lac′i·ly** *adv.* **—lac′i·ness** *n.*

lad (lad) *n.* A boy or youth. Also **lad′die.** [ME *ladde*]

lad·der (lad′ər) *n.* **1** A device of wood, metal, etc., for climbing up and down that consists of two vertical side pieces connected by horizontal pieces. **2** A means of raising one's status or position by stages. [< OE *hlæder*]

lade (lād) *v.* **lad·ed, lad·ed** or **lad·en, lad·ing** *v.t.* **1** To load with a burden or cargo. **2** To weight down; burden. **3** To dip or lift (a liquid) in or out with a ladle or dipper. *—v.i.* **4** To receive cargo. **5** To dip or lift a liquid. [< OE *hladan* to load]

lad·en (lād′n) A *p.p.* of LADE. *—adj.* Burdened: *laden* with care.

lad·ing (lā′ding) *n.* **1** The act of loading. **2** A load or cargo.

la·dle (lād′l) *n.* **1** A cup-shaped utensil, with a long handle, for dipping out or conveying liquids. **2** A device like this in form or function. *—v.t.* **·dled, ·dling** To dip up and carry in a ladle. [< OE *hladan* lade] **—la′dler** *n.*

la·dy (lā′dē) *n. pl.* **·dies 1** A refined and well-bred woman. **2** A woman of good family and recognized social standing. **3** Any woman: in the plural, used as a form of address. **4** A woman who is at the head of a household: the *lady* of the house. **5** A sweetheart or wife. **6** In Great Britain: **a** A marchioness, countess, viscountess, or baroness. **b** A title given by courtesy to a daughter of a duke, marquis, or earl, or to the wife of a baronet or knight or one having the courtesy title of *Lord.* *—adj.* **1** Of, like or becoming to a lady. **2** Female: a *lady* carpenter. [< OE *hlæfdige,* lit., bread-kneader] • In modern usage, *lady* in the sense of any woman is considered to be either falsely genteel or old-fashioned. Terms such as *saleslady, cleaning lady, lady doctor,* etc., are to be avoided. *Woman* is the more appropriate term for any adult female human being as well as for female persons in various occupations: a *woman* doctor, a *saleswoman,* a cleaning *woman.*

La·dy (lā′dē) *n. pl.* **·dies 1** The Virgin Mary: usu. with *Our.* **2** In Great Britain, a title of honor or nobility.

la·dy·bug (lā′dē·bug′) *n.* A small, roundish, spotted, usu. brightly colored beetle that feeds on aphids and other insect pests. Also **lady beetle, la′dy·bird′** (-burd′).

Ladybug

Lady Day March 25, the feast of the Annunciation, observed in honor of the Virgin Mary.

la·dy·fin·ger (lā′dē·fing′gər) *n.* A small sponge cake; so called from its shape.

la·dy-in-wait·ing (lā′dē·in·wā′ting) *n. pl.* **la·dies-in-wait·ing** A lady of a royal household in attendance at court upon a queen or princess.

la·dy-kill·er (lā′dē·kil′ər) *n. Informal* A man supposed to be peculiarly fascinating to women. **—la′dy-kill′ing** *adj., n.*

la·dy·like (lā′dē·līk) *adv.* Like or suitable to a lady; refined.

la·dy·ship (lā′dē·ship) *n.* **1** The rank or condition of a lady. **2** *Often cap.* The term used in speaking to or of a woman having the title of *Lady:* with *her* or *your.*

la·dy-slip·per (lā′dē·slip′ər) *n.* Any of a genus of wild orchids having flowers with pouchlike petals resembling a slipper. Also **la′dy′s-slip′per.**

lag (lag) *v.i.* **lagged, lag·ging** To stay or fall behind. *—n.* **1** The act of lagging; retardation of motion, development, etc. **2** The amount of such retardation. [?] **—Syn.** *v.* dawdle, drag, linger, loiter, retard.

la·ger (lä′gər) *n.* Beer that has been aged for several months before use. Also **lager beer.** [< G *Lagerbier,* lit., storehouse beer]

lag·gard (lag′ərd) *n.* One who lags; a loiterer. *—adj.* Falling behind; slow. **—lag′gard·ly** *adv.* **—lag′gard·ness** *n.*

la·gniappe (lan·yap′, lan′yap) *n.* A small present given to the purchaser of an article by a storekeeper; a gratuity. Also **la·gnappe′.** [< Amer. Sp. *la* the + *ñapa* lagniappe]

la·goon (lə·gōōn′) *n.* **1** A shallow body of salt water separated from but connecting with the sea, esp. one within an atoll. • See ATOLL. **2** A shallow body of fresh water usu. connecting with a river or lake. [< L *lacuna* hole, pond]

la·ic (lā′ik) *adj.* Pertaining to the laity; secular or nonprofessional. Also **la′i·cal.** *—n.* A layman. [< Gk. *laos* the people] **—la′i·cal·ly** *adv.*

laid (lād) *p.t. & p.p.* of LAY[1]. **—laid up 1** Injured or sick. **2** Out of service, as a dismantled ship. **3** Stored or put away for future use.

laid-back (lād′bak′) *adj. Slang.* Relaxed; not uptight.

laid paper Paper covered with close, parallel, watermarked lines.

lain (lān) *p.p.* of LIE[1].

lair (lâr) *n.* The resting place or den of a wild animal. [< OE *leger* bed]

laird (lârd) *n. Scot.* A lord; also, the proprietor of a landed estate. **—laird′ly** *adj.* **—laird′ship** *n.*

lais·sez faire (les′ā fâr′) **1** The principle of permitting industrial and commercial competition without government control. **2** Noninterference in any undertaking. Also **lais′ser faire′.** [F, lit., let do] **—lais′sez-faire′** *adj.*

la·i·ty (lā′ə·tē) *n. pl.* **·ties 1** People who are not members of the clergy. **2** Those outside any specified profession. [< LAY[2]]

lake[1] (lāk) *n.* **1** A sizable inland body of water, usu. fresh. **2** A pond formed by the widening of a river or stream. **3** A pool of any liquid: a *lake* of asphalt. [< L *lacus*]

lake[2] (lāk) *n.* **1** A red pigment made by combining a dye, as cochineal, with a metallic oxide. **2** Any insoluble pigment fixed within the fibers of a fabric by the interaction of mordant and dye. [Var. of LAC[1]]

lake dwelling A prehistoric dwelling erected on piles over the waters of a lake. **—lake dweller**

lake trout Any of various freshwater trout and salmon, esp. a large game trout of N North America. Also **lake salmon.**

lakh (lak) *n.* In India and Pakistan: **1** The amount 100,000: said esp. of rupees. **2** Any very large number or amount. [< Skt. *lākshā* mark]

lam[1] (lam) *v.t.* **lammed, lam·ming** *Slang* To beat; thrash; punish. [?]

lam[2] (lam) *Slang v.i.* **lammed, lam·ming** To run away; flee hastily. —*n.* Sudden flight. —**on the lam** In flight; fleeing. —**take it on the lam** To flee hastily; run away. [?]

Lam, Lam. Lamentations.

la·ma (lä′mə) *n.* **1** A priest or monk of Lamaism ranking high in the hierarchy. **2** A title of courtesy given to all monks of Lamaism. [< Tibetan *blama*]

La·ma·ism (lä′mə·iz′əm) *n.* The religious system of Tibet and Mongolia, a variety of Buddhism, introduced into Tibet in the 7th century. —**La′ma·ist** *n.* —**La′ma·is′tic** *adj.*

la·ma·ser·y (lä′mə·ser′ē) *n. pl.* **·ser·ies** A Buddhist monastery of Tibet or Mongolia. [< F *lama* a lama]

lamb (lam) *n.* **1** A young sheep. **2** Its flesh consumed as food. **3** Any gentle or innocent person. **4** An unsophisticated person; simpleton. —**like a lamb 1** Mildly; very gently. **2** Unsuspicious; easily misled. —*v.i.* To give birth: said of sheep. [< OE]

lam·baste (lam·bāst′) *v.t.* **·bast·ed, ·bast·ing** *Slang* **1** To beat or thrash. **2** To scold; castigate. [?]

lamb·da (lam′də) *n.* The 11th letter of the Greek alphabet (Λ, λ).

lam·bent (lam′bənt) *adj.* **1** Playing with a soft, undulatory movement; gliding. **2** Softly radiant. **3** Touching lightly but brilliantly: *lambent* wit. —**lam′bent·ly** *adv.* [< L *lambere* to lick] —**lam′ben·cy, lam′bent·ness** *n.* —**Syn. 1** dancing, flickering, licking, wavering. **2** glistening, lustrous, refulgent.

lamb·kin (lam′kin) *n.* **1** A little lamb. **2** Figuratively, a cherished child. Also **lamb′ie.**

Lamb of God Christ.

lam·bre·quin (lam′bər·kin, -brə-) *n.* **1** A draped strip, as of cloth or leather, hanging from the casing above a window, doorway, etc. **2** An ornamental covering for a helmet. [< Du. *lamperkin*]

lamb·skin (lam′skin′) *n.* **1** A lamb's skin, esp. with the wool preserved. **2** Leather or parchment made from the pelt of a lamb.

lame (lām) *adj.* **1** Crippled or disabled, esp. in the legs. **2** Poor; halting: a *lame* apology. **3** Sore; painful: a *lame* back. —*v.t.* **lamed, lam·ing** To make lame; cripple. [< OE *lama*] —**lame′ly** *adv.* —**lame′ness** *n.*

la·mé (la·mā′) *n.* A fabric woven of flat gold or silver thread, sometimes mixed with silk or other fiber. [< F *lamer* laminate]

lame duck *Informal* **1** A helpless or disabled person. **2** An elected government official whose term continues some time after his defeat for reelection.

la·mel·la (lə·mel′ə) *n. pl.* **·lae** (-ē) *Biol.* A thin plate or lamina, as the gills of a bivalve, the radial plates on the underside of a mushroom cap, etc. [< L, dim. of *lamina* lamina] —**lam·el·lar** (lə·mel′ər, lam′ə·lər), **lam·el·late** (lam′ə·lāt, lə·mel′āt) *adj.*

la·mel·li·branch (lə·mel′i·brangk) *n.* One of a class of bivalve mollusks, having platelike gills and a compressed body, as clams, mussels, and oysters. —*adj.* Of or pertaining to this class. [< L *lamella* lamella + Gk. *branchia* gills —**la·mel′li·bran′chi·ate** (-brang′kē·āt, -it) *adj., n.*

la·ment (lə·ment′) *v.t.* **1** To feel or express sorrow for. —*v.i.* **2** To feel or express sorrow; mourn. —*n.* **1** The expression of grief; lamentation. **2** A plaintive song or melody. [< L *lamentum* a wailing, weeping] —**la·ment′er** *n.*

lam·en·ta·ble (lam′ən·tə·bəl, lə·men′-) *adj.* **1** Expressing sorrow; mournful. **2** Exciting regret or dissatisfaction: a *lamentable* failure. —**lam′en·ta·bly** *adv.*

lam·en·ta·tion (lam′ən·tā′shən) *n.* **1** The act of lamenting or bewailing. **2** An utterance of profound regret or grief.

Lam·en·ta·tions (lam′ən·tā′shəns) *n. pl. (construed as sing.)* A lyrical poetic book of the Old Testament, attributed to Jeremiah.

lam·i·na (lam′ə·nə) *n. pl.* **·nae** (-nē) or **·nas 1** A thin scale, sheet, or layer. **2** *Bot.* The flat expanded portion of a leaf. [L] —**lam′i·nal, lam′i·nar** *adj.*

lam·i·nate (lam′ə·nāt) *v.* **·nat·ed, ·nat·ing** *v.t.* **1** To beat, roll, or press, as metal, into thin sheets. **2** To cut or separate into thin sheets. **3** To make, as plastic materials or plywood, of layers joined together. **4** To cover with thin sheets. —*v.i.* **5** To become separated into sheets or laminae. —*adj.* Consisting of or disposed in laminae. [< L *lamina* a leaf] —**lam′i·na′tion** *n.*

lamp (lamp) *n.* **1** A device used to produce light artificially, as from electricity or burning fuel. **2** A similar device for producing therapeutic heat or light. **3** Something that holds such a device. —*v.t. Slang* To look at. [< Gk. *lampein* to shine]

lamp·black (lamp′blak′) *n.* Fine carbon deposited from smoke, used as a pigment in printer's ink, etc.

lam·poon (lam·po͞on′) *n.* A written satire designed to bring a person into ridicule or contempt. —*v.t.* To abuse or satirize in a lampoon. [< MF *lampons* let's drink] —**lam·poon′er** or **lam·poon′ist, lam·poon′er·y** *n.* —**Syn.** *v.* deride, mock, ridicule.

lamp·post (lamp′pōst′) *n.* A post supporting a lamp in a street, park, etc.

lam·prey (lam′prē) *n.* An eel-like, parasitic, jawless fish, having a circular suctorial mouth and rasping teeth. Also **lam′per eel, lamprey eel.** [< L *lambere* to lick + *petra* rock]

lance (lans, läns) *n.* **1** A long shaft with a spearhead, used as a thrusting weapon. **2** A lancet. **3** A thrust with a lance or lancet. **4** One who uses a lance; lancer. —*v.t.* **lanced, lanc·ing 1** To pierce with a lance. **2** To cut or open with a lancet. [< L *lancea* a light spear]

lance corporal In the British army, a private serving as corporal, but not receiving extra pay.

lance·let (lans′lit, läns′-) *n.* Any of several small, fish-like, invertebrate sea animals having some vertebrate characteristics.

Lan·ce·lot (lan′sə·lot, län′-) In Arthurian romance, the bravest of the knights of the Round Table, lover of Guinevere.

lan·ce·o·late (lan′sē·ə·lit, -lāt) *adj.* Shaped like the head of a lance or spear, as some leaves. Also **lan′ce·o·lar** (-lər), **lan′ce·o·lat′ed.** [< L *lanceola* a small lance] • See LEAF.

lanc·er (lan′sər, län′-) A cavalry soldier armed with a lance.

lance sergeant In the British army, a corporal assigned the duties of a sergeant without additional pay.

lan·cet (lan′sit, län′-) *n.* **1** A surgeon's small, pointed knife, usu. two-edged. **2** *Archit.* **a** A lancet-shaped or sharply pointed window: also **lancet window. b** A sharply pointed arch: also **lancet arch. 3** A small lance. [< F *lancette,* dim. of *lance*]

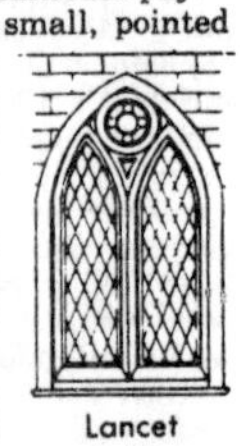

Lancet windows

lance·wood (lans′wo͝od′, läns′-) *n.* **1** A tough, elastic wood used for fishing rods, billiard cues, etc. **2** Any of various tropical trees yielding this wood.

land (land) *n.* **1** The solid part of the earth, esp. where not covered by water. **2** Ground or soil: fertile *land.* **3** A nation or country; also its people. **4** Ground held as property; real estate. **5** Rural or farming regions: to return to the *land.* **6** In economics, natural resources. —*v.t.* **1** To transfer from a vessel to the shore. **2** To bring to rest on land or water: He *landed* the plane at Washington. **3** To bring to some point, condition, or state: His words *landed* him in trouble. **4** In fishing, to bring (a fish) from the water or into a net, boat, etc. **5** *Informal* To obtain or win: to *land* a job. **6** *Informal* To deliver, as a blow. —*v.i.* **7** To go or come ashore, as from a boat. **8** To touch at a port: said of ships. **9** To descend and come to rest, as after flight. **10** To come to some place, condition, or state: to *land* in jail. [< OE]

lan·dau (lan′dô, -dou) *n.* **1** A type of closed automobile body the rear top of which may be raised or lowered. **2** A four-wheeled covered carriage with a double top that can be folded back. [< *Landau,* a German city where it was first made]

Landau *def. 2*

land bank A bank taking mortgages on real estate.

land·ed (lan′did) *adj.* 1 Having an estate in land. 2 Consisting of land: *landed* holdings.

landed immigrant *Can.* A person who has been admitted to Canada as a potential citizen.

land·fall (land′fôl′) *n.* 1 A sighting of or coming to land from the air or sea. 2 The land so sighted.

land·fill (land′fil′) *n.* 1 The disposal of garbage, trash, excavated earth, etc., by depositing in a site, often used to build up swampy or shoreline areas. 2 Materials so used. 3 A site where such deposits are made.

land·form (land′fôrm′) *n.* A physical feature of the earth's surface, as a plateau, cape, or mountain.

land grant Governmental land granted to a railroad, state educational institution, etc. **—land′-grant′** *adj.*

land·hold·er (land′hōl′dər) *n.* A person who owns or occupies land. **—land′hold′ing** *adj., n.*

land·ing (lan′ding) *n.* 1 The act of going or placing ashore. 2 The act of coming to earth, as after flying, falling, etc. 3 The place where a ship or boat docks to take on or discharge cargo or passengers; pier. 4 The place at the head of a staircase, or a platform interrupting a flight of stairs.

landing craft One of several types of military vessels esp. designed for the landing of men and material upon a hostile shore.

landing field A tract of ground properly surfaced for the landing and take-off of aircraft.

landing gear The structure under an aircraft designed to support it when on land or water.

landing strip A narrow, surfaced runway for the landing and takeoff of aircraft.

land·la·dy (land′lā′dē) *n. pl.* **·dies** 1 A woman who owns and lets real estate to others. 2 A woman who keeps an inn, hotel, boarding house, etc.

land·less (land′lis) *adj.* Owning no land.

land·locked (land′lokt′) *adj.* 1 Surrounded, or almost surrounded, by land, as a bay. 2 Living in or confined to fresh instead of sea water: *landlocked* salmon.

land·lord (land′lôrd′) *n.* 1 An owner of land, buildings, etc., that are leased or let to others. 2 A person who keeps an inn, hotel, boarding house, etc.

land·lub·ber (land′lub′ər) *n.* An awkward or inexperienced person on board a ship.

land·mark (land′märk′) *n.* 1 A fixed object serving as a boundary mark to a tract of land. 2 A prominent or memorable object in the landscape, serving as a guide. 3 A distinguishing fact, event, etc., of a period. 4 A historic or architecturally important building, site, etc., preserved by law for posterity.

land mine An explosive weapon hidden on or just under the surface of the ground.

land office A U.S. government office of the Department of the Interior for the transaction of business pertaining to public lands.

land-office business (land′ô′fis, -of′is) *Informal* A flourishing business conducted at a rapid pace.

land·own·er (land′ō′nər) *n.* One who owns real estate.

land·scape (land′skāp) *n.* 1 A stretch of country as seen from a single point. 2 A picture representing natural scenery. *—v.* **·scaped, ·scap·ing** *v.t.* 1 To improve or change the natural features or appearance of, as a park or garden. *—v.i.* 2 To be a landscape gardener. [<Du. *land* land + *-schap* -ship] **—land′scap·er** *n.*

landscape architecture The art of converting a given area of land into a unified ornamental development. **—landscape architect.**

landscape gardening The art of improving the appearance of a plot of ground by planting trees, lawns, flower beds, etc. **—landscape gardener.**

land·scap·ist (land′skā·pist) *n.* A painter of landscapes.

land·slide (land′slīd′) *n.* 1 The slipping of a mass of earth from a higher to a lower level. 2 The mass that has slipped down. 3 *Informal* An overwhelming plurality of votes for one political party or candidate in an election.

lands·man (landz′mən) *n. pl.* **·men** (-men) 1 One who lives on the land. 2 An inexperienced sailor.

land·ward (land′wərd) *adv.* Being or going toward the land. Also **land′wards.** *—adj.* Facing the land.

lane (lān) *n.* 1 A narrow way or path, confined between fences, walls, hedges, or similar boundaries. 2 Any prescribed route or passage to avoid collisions, as for vehicles on a highway or for airplanes and ships. [<OE *lanu* lane]

lang·syne (lang′sīn′, -zīn′) *Scot. adv.* Long since; long ago. *—n.* The past; old times. Also **lang syne.**

lan·guage (lang′gwij) *n.* 1 The expression and communication of emotions or ideas between human beings by means of speech, either written or spoken. 2 The vocal sounds or their written symbol used in such expression and communication. 3 The means of communication among members of a single nation or group; tongue: the French *language.* 4 Transmission of emotions or ideas between any living creatures by any means. 5 The vocabulary or technical expressions used in a specific business, science, etc.; jargon. 6 One's characteristic manner of expression or use of speech. 7 The study of a language or languages. [<L *lingua* tongue, language]

lan·guid (lang′gwid) *adj.* 1 Indisposed to physical exertion; affected by weakness. 2 Wanting in interest or animation. 3 Lacking in force or quickness of movement. [<*languere* languish] **—lan′guid·ly** *adv.* **—lan′guid·ness** *n.* **—Syn.** 1 drooping, fatigued, languorous, listless, weary.

lan·guish (lang′gwish) *v.i.* 1 To grow faint or listless. 2 To live or be in wretched circumstances: to *languish* in a dungeon. 3 To affect a look of sentimental longing or melancholy. 4 To pine with love or desire. [<L *languere* languish] **—lan′guish·er, lan′guish·ment** *n.*

lan·guis·ing (lang′gwish·ing) *adj.* 1 Lacking interest or force. 2 Sentimentally pensive. 3 Becoming weak or listless. **—lan′guish·ing·ly** *adv.*

lan·guor (lang′gər) *n.* 1 Lassitude of body or depression of mind. 2 Amorous dreaminess. 3 The absence of activity: dullness. [<L *languere* languish] **—lan′guor·ous** *adj.* **—lan′guor·ous·ly** *adv.* **—lan′guor·ous·ness** *n.*

lan·gur (läng·gyŏŏr′) *n.* Any of various agile, long-tailed Asian monkeys. [<Skt. *lāngūlin,* lit., having a tail]

lan·iard (lan′yərd) *n.* LANYARD.

lank (langk) *adj.* 1 Long and lean. 2 Long, straight, and thin: *lank* hair. [<OE *hlanc* flexible] **—lank′ly** *adv.* **—lank′ness** *n.*

lank·y (lang′kē) *adj.* **lank·i·er, lank·i·est** Tall and thin in an ungainly way. **—lank′i·ly** *adv.* **—lank′i·ness** *n.*

lan·o·lin (lan′ə·lin) *n.* A fatty substance obtained from the wool of sheep, used as an ingredient in cosmetics. Also **lan′o·line** (-lin, -lēn). [<L *lan(a)* wool + *ol(eum)* oil + -IN]

lan·tern (lan′tərn) *n.* 1 A case with transparent sides, as on a lamppost or of portable character, for enclosing and protecting a light. 2 *Archit.* A glassed-in or open structure on a roof or tower, open below and admitting light and air. 3 The chamber at the top of a lighthouse housing the light. 4 MAGIC LANTERN. [<Gk. *lamptēr*]

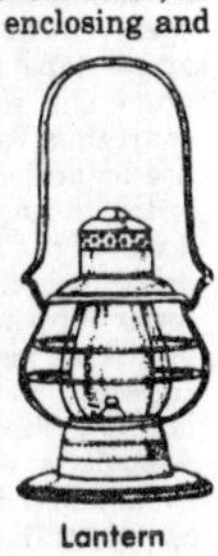

Lantern

lantern jaws Long, thin jaws, giving the cheeks a hollow appearance. **—lan′tern-jawed′** (-jôd′) *adj.*

lan·tha·nide (lan′thə·nīd) *n.* Any of a series of elements beginning with lanthanum and ending with lutetium in the periodic table and having almost identical chemical properties. • See PERIODIC TABLE OF ELEMENTS. [<LANTHAN(UM)]

lan·tha·num (lan′thə·nəm) *n.* A soft, silvery metallic element (symbol La) of the lanthanide series. [NL <Gk. *lanthanein* lie concealed]

lan·yard (lan′yərd) *n.* 1 *Naut.* A short, thick rope used on a ship, esp. for setting up riggings. 2 A cord used in firing certain kinds of cannon. 3 A stout cord worn around the neck by sailors for attaching a knife. [<OF *lasniere* a thong]

Lao (lou) *adj., n. pl.* **Lao** or **Laos** LAOTIAN.

La·oc·o·on (lā·ok′ə·won, -ō·won) *Gk. Myth.* A priest of

Apollo who warned the Trojans against the wooden horse of the Greeks, and was destroyed with his two sons by two serpents.

La·os (la'os, lä'ōs) *n.* A republic in NW Indochina, 91,428 sq. mi., cap. Vientiane. • See map at INDOCHINA.

La·o·tian (lā·ō'shən, lou'-) *adj.* Of or pertaining to Laos, its people, or their language. —*n.* **1** A native or citizen of Laos. **2** The language of these people.

lap[1] (lap) *n.* **1** The upper and front surface of the thighs and knees when one is seated. **2** The part of the clothing that covers the front of the thighs when one sits down. **3** A place for supporting or fostering: fortune's *lap.* **4** A loose fold or flap of a garment. **5** That part of a thing that extends over another thing: the *lap* of a shingle. **6** One course around a race track. —*v.* **lapped, lap·ping** *v.t.* **1** To fold and wrap around something. **2** To lay (one thing) partly over or beyond another. **3** To reach or extend partly over or beyond; overlap. **4** To surround with love, care, etc.: *lapped* in luxury. **5** To get one or more laps ahead of (an opponent) in a race. —*v.i.* **6** To be folded. **7** To lie partly upon or beside something else; overlap. [<OE *lappa* a fold or hanging part of a garment] —**lap'per** *n.*

lap[2] (lap) *v.t. & v.i.* **lapped, lap·ping 1** To scoop up (a liquid) into the mouth with the tongue: said usu. of animals. **2** To wash against (the shore, etc.) with a slight, rippling sound: said of water. —**lap up 1** To scoop up (a liquid) with the tongue. **2** *Informal* To accept eagerly: to *lap up* praise. —*n.* **1** The act of lapping; a lick. **2** The sound of lapping. [<OE *lapian*] —**lap'per** *n.*

lap·a·ro·scope (lap'ə·rə·skōp) *n.* A narrow, cylindrical optical instrument used for examination of abdominal organs. —**lap·a·ros·co·py** (lap'ə·ros'kə·pē) *n.*

lap dog A very small pet dog.

la·pel (lə·pel') *n.* One of the parts of the front of a coat that is attached to the collar and is folded back. [Dim. of LAP[1]]

lap·i·dar·y (lap'ə·der'ē) *adj.* Of the art of working in precious stones. —*n. pl.* **·dar·ies** One who cuts, engraves, and sets precious stones. [<L *lapis, lapidis* stone]

lap·is laz·u·li (lap'is laz'yoo·lē) **1** A rich blue semiprecious stone. **2** The color of this stone. [<L *lapis* a stone + Med. L *lazulus* azure]

Lapp (lap) *n.* **1** One of a Mongoloid people of short stature inhabiting Lapland: also **lap'land'er.** **2** The Finno-Ugric language of the Lapps: also **Lap'pish** (-pish).

lap·pet (lap'it) *n.* **1** A small lap or flap for ornamenting a garment, etc. **2** A hanging, fleshy process, as a bird's wattle, an ear lobe, etc.

lap robe A heavy blanket used to keep the lap and lower limbs warm, as while sitting in a wheelchair, riding in an open vehicle, or watching outdoor sports.

lapse (laps) *v.i.* **lapsed, laps·ing 1** To pass slowly or by degrees; slip: to *lapse* into a coma. **2** To deviate from virtue or truth. **3** To pass, as time. **4** To become void, usu. by disuse or neglect: The agreement *lapsed.* **5** *Law* To be forfeited to another because of the negligence, failure, or death of the holder. —*n.* **1** A gradual slipping or passing away, as of time. **2** A minor fault or mistake. **3** A fall to a lower form or state. **4** A deviation from what is right, proper, or just: a *lapse* in conduct. **5** *Law* The defeat of a right or privilege through fault, failure, or neglect. [<L *lapsus* a slip <*labi* glide, slip] —**laps'a·ble, laps'i·ble** *adj.* —**laps'er** *n.* —**Syn.** *v.* **1** fall, sink. **2** err, stray. **3** elapse, slip by. *n.* **2** blunder, error.

lap·wing (lap'wing') *n.* A plover like, crested bird of the Old World, having an unsteady flight and shrill cry. [<OE *hlēapwince*]

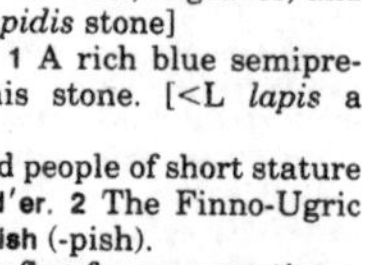

Lapwing

lar·board (lä'bərd, -bōrd', -bōrd') *adj. & adv. Naut.* Being on the left, or port, side of a ship as one faces the bow. —*n.* The left, or port, side of a ship. [ME *laddebord*]

lar·ce·nist (lär'sə·nist) *n.* A thief; one who commmits larceny. Also **lar'ce·ner** (-nər).

lar·ce·ny (lär'sə·nē) *n. pl.* **·nies** *Law* The taking, without claim of right or without permission, of the personal goods of another; theft. [<L *latrocinari* rob] —**lar'ce·nous** *adj.* —**lar'ce·nous·ly** *adv.* • The distinction between **grand larceny** (more than a specified amount) and **petty** (or **petit**) **lar·ceny** (less than such an amount) has been dropped in many parts of the U.S.

larch (lärch) *n.* **1** Any of several cone-bearing deciduous trees. **2** The strong, durable wood of this tree. [<L *larix*]

lard (lärd) *n.* The semisolid oil of hog's fat after rendering. —*v.t.* **1** To prepare (meat or poultry) for cooking by covering with or inserting something, as strips of fat. **2** To cover or smear with grease. **3** To mix with something so as to enrich or improve. [<L *lardum*] —**lard'y** *adj.*

lar·der (lär'dər) *n.* **1** A room where the provisions of a household are kept. **2** Provisions. [<L *lardum* lard]

lar·es and pe·na·tes (lâr'ēz; lā'rēz; pə·nā'tēz) **1** *Usu. cap.* The household gods of ancient Rome. **2** The cherished belongings of a household.

large (lärj) *adj.* **larg·er, larg·est 1** Absolutely or relatively big as regards size, dimensions, quantity, range, etc. **2** Having unusual breadth or scope: *large* ideas. **3** Extensive in operation: a *large* car dealer. —*n.* Liberty: now used only in the phrase **at large 1** To the fullest extent; in full. **2** Free or unrestrained in movement; at liberty. **3** Not included within particular limitations: in general. **4** Elected from a state as a whole rather than from a particular district: a congressman *at large.* [<L *largus* abundant] —**large'ness** *n.* **Syn. 1** ample, colossal, enormous, huge, vast, great.

large calorie See CALORIE.

large·ly (lärj'lē) *adv.* **1** In a large quantity. **2** To a great extent; generally.

large-scale (lärj'skāl') *adj.* Of large size or scope.

lar·gess (lär·jes', -zhes', lär'jəs) *n.* **1** A gift, gratuity. **2** Liberality; bounty. Also **lar·gesse'.** [<L *largus* abundant]

lar·ghet·to (lär·get'ō) *Music adj. & adv.* Slow, in a time not quite so slow as *largo.* —*n. pl.* **·tos** A larghetto movement or section. [Ital. <*largo* largo]

larg·ish (lär'jish) *adj.* Somewhat large.

lar·go (lär'gō) *Music adj. & adv.* Slow; stately. —*n. pl.* **·gos** A largo movement. [Ital. <L *largus* abundant]

lar·i·at (lar'ē·ət) *n.* **1** A rope, esp. of horsehair, for tethering animals. **2** LASSO. —*v.t.* To fasten or catch with a lariat. [<Sp. *la* the + *reata* rope]

lark[1] (lärk) *n.* **1** Any of a large family of small songbirds, as the European skylark. **2** Any of various similar birds, as the meadowlark, etc. [<OE *lāferce*]

lark[2] (lärk) *n. Informal* A hilarious time; humorous adventure. —*v.t.* **1** To make fun of; tease. —*v.i.* **2** To play pranks; frolic. [<ON *leika* to leap] —**lark'er** *n.* —**lark'some, lark'y** *adj.* **(·i·er, ·i·est)**

lark·spur (lärk'spûr) *n.* DELPHINIUM.

lar·ri·gan (lar'ə·gən) *n. Can.* A moccasin made of prepared oiled leather, used chiefly by lumbermen. [?]

lar·ri·kin (lar'ə·kin) *n. Chiefly Austral.* A rough, disorderly fellow; rowdy. [?]

lar·rup (lar'əp) *Informal v.t.* **·ruped, ·rup·ing** To beat; thrash. —*n.* A blow. [?] —**lar'rup·er** *n.*

lar·va (lär'və) *n. pl.* **·vae** (·vē) or **·vas** An early, immature form of an animal that is structurally unlike the adult, as the first stage of an insect after leaving the egg, the tadpole of a frog, etc. [L, a ghost, a mask] —**lar'val** *adj.*

la·ryn·ge·al (lə·rin'je·əl, -jəl) *adj.* **1** Of, pertaining to, or near the larynx: also **la·ryn'ge·an.** **2** Used for treating the larynx, as an instrument.

lar·yn·gi·tis (lar'ən·jī'tis) *n.* Inflammation of the larynx —**lar'yn·git'ic** (-jit'ik) *adj.*

laryngo- *combining form.* The larynx; pertaining to the larynx: *laryngoscope.*

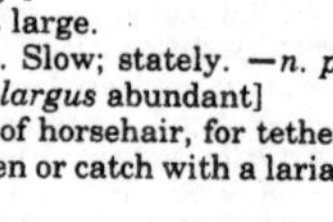

Larynx

la·ryn·go·scope (lə·ring'gə·skōp, ·rin'jə·) *n.* An instrument for inspecting the larynx. —**lar·yn'go·scop'ic** (-skop'ik) *adj.* —**lar·yn·gos·co·py** (la'ring·gos'kə·pē) *n.*

lar·ynx (lar'ingks) *n. pl.* **la·ryn·ges** (lə·rin'jēz) or **lar·ynx·es 1** The human organ of voice, consisting of a structure of cartilage and muscle in the upper trachea, and containing the vocal cords whose vibrations produce sound. 2 A similar structure in most vertebrates. [<Gk. *larynx*]

las·car (las′kər) *n.* An East Indian native, serving as a sailor. [<Ar. *al-askar* the army]

las·civ·i·ous (lə·siv′ē·əs) *adj.* 1 Having wanton desires; lustful; lewd. 2 Producing sensual desires. [<L *lascivus* wanton, lustful] **—las·civ′i·ous·ly** *adv.* **—las·civ′i·ous·ness** *n.*

la·ser (lā′zər) *n.* A device in which energy supplied to an atomic or molecular system is released as a narrow beam of coherent light whose wavelength depends on the energy transitions of the atoms or molecules. [<*l(ight) a(mplification by) s(timulated) e(mission of) r(adiation)*]

lash (lash) *n.* 1 A thong on a whip handle; a whip. 2 A stroke with or as with a whip. 3 A sharp, sarcastic remark. 4 An eyelash. 5 Any heavy blow, as of waves beating the shore. *—v.t.* 1 To strike or urge forward with or as with a whip. 2 To throw or move quickly or suddenly, as from side to side: to *lash* the tail. 3 To beat or dash against with force or violence: The waves *lashed* the pier. 4 To attack or criticize severely. 5 To arouse the emotions of, as with words. 6 To bind or tie with or as with a lashing. *—v.i.* 7 To move quickly or violently; dash. **—lash out** 1 To strike out violently or wildly. 2 To break into angry or vehement speech. [ME *lashe*] **—Syn.** *v.* 1 beat, flog, hit, thrash, whip. 4 berate, scold, upbraid.

lash·ing (lash′ing) *n.* 1 A fastening made by passing a rope, cord, or the like, around two or more objects. 2 The rope used to do this. 3 A whipping. 4 A severe scolding.

lass (las) *n.* A young woman; girl. [<Scand.]

las·sie (las′ē) *n.* A little girl; a lass.

las·si·tude (las′ə·tʸōōd) *n.* A feeling of languor; weariness. [<L *lassus* faint]

las·so (las′ō, las·ōō′) *n. pl.* **·sos** or **·soes** A long rope or leather thong, with a running noose, for catching horses and cattle. *—v.t.* To catch with a lasso. [<L *laqueus* a snare] **—las′so·er** *n.*

last[1] (last, läst) *adj.* 1 Having no successor; final. 2 Next before the present; most recent. 3 Least fit or likely; most remote. 4 Beyond or above all others; utmost. 5 Beneath all others. *—adv.* 1 After all others in time or order. 2 At a time next preceding the present: He was *last* seen heading west. 3 In conclusion. *—n.* 1 The end: a rebel to the *last.* 2 The final appearance, experience, or mention. 3 The element of an ordered set that has no successor. **—at last** Finally. **—at long last** Finally. **—breathe one's last** To die. **—see the last of** Never to see again. [<OE *latost*] **—last′ly** *adv.*

last[2] (last, läst) *v.i.* 1 To remain in existence; endure. 2 To continue unchanged or unaltered; persevere. 3 To be as much as or more than needed; hold out: Will our supplies *last?* [<OE *læsten* follow a track] **—last′er** *n.*

last[3] (last, läst) *n.* A shaped form, usu. of wood, on which to make a boot or shoe. *—v.t.* To fit to or form on a last. **—stick to one's last** to attend to one's own business or work. [<OE *læst* a boot] **—last′er** *n.*

last·ing (las′ting, läs′-) *adj.* Continuing, durable, or permanent: a *lasting* sorrow. *—n.* Endurance; continuance. **—last′ing·ly** *adv.* **—last′ing·ness** *n.*

Last Judgment The final judgment of mankind to be rendered by God at the end of the world.

last straw The final element in a series of trying situations that results in loss of patience, etc.

Last Supper The last meal of Jesus with his disciples before the Crucifixion.

last word 1 The final say, as in a dispute. 2 *Informal* Something considered not capable of being improved. 3 *Informal* The latest or most modern fashion, style, advancement, etc.

Lat. Latin; Latvia.

lat. latitude.

latch (lach) *n.* A catch for fastening a door, lid, shutter, etc. *—v.t. & v.i.* To fasten by means of a latch; close. **—latch on to** *Slang* 1 To fasten (oneself) 2 To obtain; get. [<OE *læccan* seize]

latch·key (lach′kē′) *n.* A key for releasing a latch, esp. on an outside or front door.

latchkey child A child who comes home after school to an empty house, the parents or guardians being still at work.

latch·string (lach′string′) *n.* A string for lifting a latch, passing through a hole above it to the outside.

late (lāt) *adj.* **lat·er** or **lat·ter, lat·est** or **last** 1 Coming after the appointed time; tardy. 2 Far advanced toward the end or close. 3 Recent or comparatively recent. 4 Deceased, esp. recently deceased. *—adv.* **lat·er, lat·est** or **last** 1 After or beyond the usual proper or appointed time. 2 Not long ago; recently. 3 After a while; in course of time. **—of late** In time not long past; recently. [<OE *læt* late, slow] **—late′ness** *n.*

la·teen (la·tēn′) *adj. Naut.* 1 Designating a rig common in the Mediterranean, having a triangular sail (**lateen sail**) suspended from a long yard set obliquely to the mast. 2 Equipped with such a sail. *—n.* A craft equipped with a lateen sail. [<F *(voile) latine* Latin (sail)]

Lateen sail

Late Greek The Greek language from about A.D. 200 to 600.

Late Latin the Latin language from about A.D. 200 to 700.

late·ly (lāt′lē) *adv.* Not long ago; recently.

la·tent (lā′tənt) *adj.* Not visible or apparent; dormant. [<L *latere* be hidden] **—la′ten·cy** *n.* **—la′tent·ly** *adv.*

lat·er (lā′tər) Comparative of LATE. **—later on** Subsequently.

lat·er·al (lat′ər·əl) *adj.* Pertaining to, proceeding from, or directed toward the side. *—n.* 1 A lateral protuberance or outgrowth. 2 LATERAL PASS. [<L *latus, lateris* a side] **—lat′er·al·ly** *adv.*

lateral pass In football, a pass thrown parallel to the line of scrimmage or toward one's own goal.

lat·est (lā′tist) A superlative of LATE. **—at the latest** No later than (a particular time). **—the latest** *Informal* 1 The newest, most fashionable style, trend, etc. 2 The most recent news or development.

la·tex (lā′teks) *n. pl.* **lat·i·ces** (lat′ə·sēz) or **la·tex·es** 1 The viscid, milky emulsion secreted by certain plants, as the milkweed, rubber tree, etc. 2 A watery emulsion of rubber or synthetic plastic, used in making adhesives, paint, etc. [L, a liquid]

lath (lath, la<u>th</u>) *n.* 1 One of a number of strips of wood or metal serving to support plaster, shingles, slates, etc. 2 Any building material of similar use. 3 Lathing. *—v.t.* To cover or line with laths. [<OE *lætt*] **—lath′er** *n.*

lathe (lā<u>th</u>) *n.* A machine for shaping articles on which an object is mounted and rotated, while a cutting tool is thrust against it. *—v.t.* **lathed, lath·ing** To form or shape on a lathe. [?]

lath·er (la<u>th</u>′ər) *n.* 1 Foam or froth of soapsuds. 2 Foam of profuse sweating, as of a horse. **—in a lather** *Informal* In a state of intense excitement or agitation. *—v.t.* 1 To cover with lather. 2 *Informal* To flog; thrash. *—v.i.* 3 To become covered with lather. 4 To form lather. [<OE *lēathor* washing soda] **—lath′er·y** *adj.* **—lath′er·er** *n.*

lath·ing (lath′ing, la<u>th</u>′-) *n.* 1 The act or process of covering with laths. 2 The foundation of laths on which plaster may be laid. 3 Any work with laths or like material. Also **lath·work** (-wûrk′)

Lat·in (lat′n) *adj.* 1 Pertaining to ancient Latium or its inhabitants. 2 Pertaining to or denoting the peoples or countries, as France, Italy, Spain, Portugal, Rumania, etc., whose languages are derived from that of ancient Rome. *—n.* 1 One of the people of ancient Latium. 2 A member of any of the modern Latin peoples. 3 The Indo-European, Italic language of ancient Latium and Rome. **—La·ti·nic** (lə·tin′ik) *adj.*

Latin America Those countries of the Western Hemisphere s of the U.S. in which the languages spoken, Spanish, Portuguese, and French, are derived from Latin. **—Lat′in-A·mer′i·can** *adj*

Latin American A native or inhabitant of Latin America.

Lat·in·ate (lat′ən·āt) *adj.* Resembling or derived from Latin.

Latin Church That part of the Catholic Church which accepts the pope as supreme authority on earth; Roman Catholic Church.

Lat·in·ism (lat′ən·iz′əm) *n.* An idiom peculiar to or imitating Latin. **—Lat′in·is′tic** *adj.*

Lat·in·ist (lat′ən·ist) *n.* A scholar versed in Latin.

Lat·in·ize (lat′ən·īz) *v.* **·ized, ·iz·ing** *v.t.* **1** To translate into Latin. **2** To give Latin characteristics to. *—v.i.* **3** To use Latin words, forms, etc. **—Lat′in·i·za′tion, Lat′in·iz′er** *n.*

la·ti·no (la·tē′nō) *n. pl.* **·nos** *Often cap.* A Latin American. [Am. Sp. < Sp., Latin]

lat·ish (lā′tish) *adj.* Rather late.

lat·i·tude (lat′ə·to͞od) *n.* **1** *Geog.* Distance on the earth's surface toward or away from the equator expressed as an arc of a meridian. **2** A region or place with reference to its distance north or south of the equator: warm *latitudes.* **3** Freedom from restrictions, as in action or thought. **4** Range or scope. [< L *latus* broad] **—lat′i·tu′di·nal** *adj.*

lat·i·tu·di·nar·i·an (lat′ə·to͞o′də·nâr′ē·ən) *adj.* Broad, tolerant, or lax, esp. in religious principles. *—n.* One who is extremely tolerant; a freethinker. [< L *latitudo* latitude] **—lat′i·tu′di·nar′i·an·ism** *n.*

La·ti·um (lā′shē·əm) *n.* A region and ancient country in CEN. Italy, original home of the Latins.

la·trine (lə·trēn′) *n.* A toilet, esp. in a camp, barracks, etc. [< L *latrina* a bath]

lat·ter (lat′ər) A comparative of LATE. *—adj.* **1** Of, relating to, or nearer the end. **2** Recent or more recent; later. **—the latter** The second of two mentioned persons or things. [< OE *lætra*] **—lat′ter·ly** *adv.*

lat·ter-day (lat′ər·dā′) *adj.* Belonging to the present; modern. **—Syn.** contemporary, current, recent, up-to-date.

Latter-Day Saint MORMON.

lat·tice (lat′is) *n.* **1** Openwork of metal or wood, formed by crossing or interlacing strips or bars. **2** Anything made of such work, as a window, a blind, or a screen. **3** *Physics* An arrangement consisting of a module periodically repeated throughout a region or space. *—v.t.* **lat·ticed, lat·tic·ing 1** To furnish or enclose with a lattice. **2** To arrange or interlace like latticework. [< OF *latte* a lath]

Lattice

lat·tice·work (lat′is·wûrk′) *n.* **1** A lattice. **2** In embroidery, stitching in an outline resembling a lattice.

Lat·vi·an (lat′vē·ən) *adj.* Of or pertaining to Latvia, its people, or their language. *—n.* **1** A native or citizen of Latvia. **2** The language of the Latvians.

laud (lôd) *n.* **1** Praise or commendation. **2** A song or hymn of praise or honor. **3** *pl.* In the Roman Catholic Church, a morning service consisting of the psalms, immediately following matins, and constituting with the latter the first of the seven canonical hours: also **Lauds.** *—v.t.* To praise; extol. [< L *laus, laudis* praise] **—laud′er** *n.*

laud·a·ble (lô′də·bəl) *adj.* Worthy of approval; praiseworthy. **—laud′a·bil′i·ty, laud′a·ble·ness** *n.* **—laud′a·bly** *adv.*

lau·da·num (lô′də·nəm) *n.* **1** Tincture of opium. **2** Formerly, any preparation of opium. [< L *ladanum* a resinous juice]

lau·da·tion (lô·dā′shən) *n.* The act of praising; praise.

laud·a·to·ry (lô′də·tôr′ē, -tō′rē) *adj.* Eulogizing; praising. Also **laud′a·tive.** [< L *laudare* praise, celebrate]

laugh (laf, läf) *v.i.* **1** To show amusement, hilarity, derision, etc., by expressions of the face and by a series of explosive sounds made in the chest and throat. **2** To be or appear gay or lively. *—v.t.* **3** To express by laughter. **4** To move or influence by laughter or ridicule: He *laughed* himself out of his worries. **—laugh at 1** To express amusement concerning. **2** To make light of; belittle **—laugh off** To dismiss or reject lightly or scornfully. *—n.* **1** The act or sound of laughter. **2** *Informal* Anything producing laughter. **—have the last laugh** To triumph after apparent defeat. [< OE *hlæhhan*] **—laugh′er** *n.*

laugh·a·ble (laf′ə·bəl, läf′-) *adj.* Ridiculous; exciting laughter. **—laugh′a·ble·ness** *n.* **—laugh′a·bly** *adv.*

laugh·ing (laf′ing, läf′-) *adj.* **1** Expressing amusement, etc., by laughing: a *laughing* child. **2** Seeming to laugh: a *laughing* hyena. **—no laughing matter** A very serious matter. *—n.* LAUGHTER. **—laugh′ing·ly** *adv.*

laughing gas Nitrous oxide used as an anesthetic, sometimes with exhilarating effect.

laugh·ing·stock (laf′ing·stok′, läf′-) *n.* A butt for ridicule.

laugh·ter (laf′tər, läf′-) *n.* **1** The sound or action of laughing. **2** Any exclamation or expression indicating merriment or derision.

launch[1] (lônch, länch) *v.t.* **1** To cause to move into water for the first time, as a newly built ship. **2** To set afloat, as a boat or log. **3** To make a beginning of: to *launch* an enterprise. **4** To start (someone) on a career, course, etc. **5** To give a start to the flight or course of, as a rocket, torpedo, or airplane. *—v.i.* **6** To put or go to sea: usu. with *out* or *forth.* **7** To start on a career, course, etc. **8** To begin something with vehemence or urgency. He *launched* into an argument. **—launch out** To start; commence, esp. something new. *—n.* **1** The act of launching. **2** The process of being launched. [< OF *lance* lance] **—launch′er** *n.*

launch[2] (lônch, länch) *n.* **1** The largest of the boats carried by a warship. **2** A large, open boat, propelled by steam or electricity, and used as a pleasure craft. [< Pg. *lancha*]

launching pad The platform from which a rocket or spacecraft is launched.

laun·der (lôn′dər, län′-) *v.t.* **1** To wash, or wash and iron, as clothing. **2** To cleanse or purify. **3** *Slang* To conceal the original source of (funds). *—v.i.* **4** To wash or wash and iron laundry. [< OF *lavendier* a washerwoman] **—laun′der·er** *n.* **—laun′dress** (-dris) *n. Fem.*

laun·dro·mat (lôn′drə·mat, län-) *n.* An establishment, usu. self-service, where the customer brings laundry to be washed and dried in coin-operated machines. [< *Laundromat,* a trade name]

laun·dry (lôn′drē, län′-) *n. pl.* **·dries 1** A room or building for laundering clothes. **2** Articles to be washed. [< OF *lavendier*] **—laun′dry·man** (-mən) *n.*

lau·re·ate (lô′rē·it) *adj.* **1** Crowned or decked with laurel, as an honor. **2** Deserving of distinction; preeminent, esp. as a poet. *—n.* **1** A person honored for achievement, as in an art or science. **2** POET LAUREATE. [< L *laurus* laurel] **—lau′re·ate·ship′** *n.*

lau·rel (lôr′əl, lor′-) *n.* **1** An evergreen shrub of the Mediterranean area, with aromatic, lance-shaped leaves. **2** The leaves of this shrub. **3** Any of various similar shrubs, as the mountain laurel. **4** *pl.* A crown or wreath of laurel, indicating honor or high merit. **—rest on one's laurels** To be content with what one has already achieved. *—v.t.* **·reled** or **·relled, ·rel·ing** or **·rel·ling 1** To wreathe or crown with laurel. **2** To honor. [< L *laurus*]

laus De·o (lôs dē′ō, dā′ō) *Latin* Praise be to God.

la·va (lä′və, lav′ə) *n.* **1** Melted rock, issuing from a volcanic crater or a fissure in the earth's surface. **2** Such rock when solidified. [< Ital., orig., a stream of rain]

lav·a·liere (lav′ə·lir′) *n.* A piece of jewelry, consisting of a necklace and pendant. Also **lav′a·lier′.** [< F < Louise de *La Vallière,* 1644–1710, mistress of Louis XIV]

lav·a·to·ry (lav′ə·tôr′ē, -tō′rē) *n. pl.* **·ries 1** A room in a public or semipublic place, as in a school or hotel, provided with appliances for washing, usu. toilets, and sometimes urinals. **2** Any bathroom. **3** A basin to wash in. [< L *lavare* to wash]

lave (lāv) *v.t. & v.i.* **laved, lav·ing 1** To wash; bathe. **2** To flow along or against as if washing. [< L *lavare* to wash]

lav·en·der (lav′ən·dər) *n.* **1** A plant of the mint family yielding a fragrant oil **(oil of lavender). 2** The dried flowers and leaves of this plant, used to scent linens, etc. **3** The color of lavender flowers, a pale purple. *—adj.* Of, pertaining to, or like lavender. *—v.t.* To scent with lavender. [< Med. L *lavendula*]

Spike lavender

lav·ish (lav′ish) *adj.* **1** Bestowed, expended, or existing in profusion: *lavish* gifts. **2** Spending extravagantly; prodigal. **3** Exaggerated; unrestrained: *lavish* compliments. *—v.t.* To give or bestow profusely or generously.

[< OF *lavache* a downpour of rain] **—lav′ish·er, lav′ish·ness** *n.* **—lav′ish·ly** *adv.* **—Syn.** *adj.* **1** abundant, bountiful, copious, generous. *v.* indulge with, heap upon.

law (lô) *n.* **1** A custom or rule of conduct which a community, state, etc., considers binding upon its members, and which is enforced by compelling authority or legislation. **2** A body of such rules. **3** The condition of society when such rules are observed: to establish *law* and order. **4** The body of rules related to a specified subject: criminal *law.* **5** Statute and common law, as opposed to equity. **6** An enactment of a legislature, as opposed to a constitution. **7** The system of courts administering remedial justice: to resort to the *law.* **8** The branch of knowledge concerned with jurisprudence: to study *law.* **9** The vocation of an attorney, solicitor, etc.: to practice *law.* **10** The legal profession as a whole. **11** A rule of conduct having divine origin. **12** An imperative rule or command: His word is *law.* **13** Any rule of conduct or procedure: the *laws* of hospitality. **14** In science, a statement of the manner or order in which a defined group of natural phenomena occur under certain conditions. **15** *Math.* A rule or formula governing a function or the performance of an operation. **16** The police, personifying legal force: preceded by *the.* [< OE *lagu*] **—go to law** To take a case or complaint to court to be settled. **—lay down the law 1** To scold thoroughly. **2** To give firm orders. **—read law** To study for a legal degree. **—the Law 1** The first five books of the Old Testament, containing the Mosaic law. **2** The Old Testament.

law-a·bid·ing (lô′ə·bī′ding) *adj.* Obedient to or abiding by the law.

law-break·er (lô′brā′kər) *n.* One who violates the law. **—law′-break′ing** *n., adj.*

law court A court where trials or hearings are held and justice under the law is administered.

law·ful (lô′fəl) *adj.* **1** Permitted by law; legitimate: *lawful* acts. **2** Enforceable at law: *lawful* claims. **3** Valid, or regarded as valid: said of a marriage. **—law′ful·ly** *adv.* **—law′ful·ness** *n.*

law·giv·er (lô′giv′ər) *n.* One who makes or enacts a law or laws; a legislator. **—law′giv′ing** *adj., n.*

law·less (lô′lis) *adj.* **1** Not subject or obedient to law of any sort. **2** Without the sanction or authority of law. **3** Without the protection of law: a *lawless* fugitive. **4** Uncontrollable; unbridled. **—law′less·ly** *adv.* **—law′less·ness** *n.*

law·mak·ing (lô′mā′king) *n.* The enacting of laws; legislation. **—law′mak′er** *n.*

lawn[1] (lôn) *n.* A piece of ground, esp. around a home, with grass kept closely mown. [< OF *launde*] **—lawn′y** *adv.*

lawn[2] (lôn) *n.* Fine thin linen or cotton fabric. [ME < *Laon,* France, where it was formerly made]

lawn mower A machine for clipping the grass of lawns, either power-driven or propelled by hand.

lawn tennis Tennis played outdoors on a clay or grass-covered court.

Law of Moses The Pentateuch; the Mosaic law.

law·ren·ci·um (lô·ren′sē·əm) *n.* An artificially produced radioactive element (symbol Lr). [< E. O. *Lawrence,* 1901–58, U.S. physicist]

law·suit (lô′sōōt′) *n.* A proceeding in a court of law for redress of wrongs.

law·yer (lô′yər) *n.* One who practices law and represents clients in lawsuits or gives legal advice.

lax (laks) *adj.* **1** Lacking tenseness or firmness; yielding. **2** Not stringent or energetic. **3** Wanting exactness of meaning or application. [< L *laxus* loose] **—lax′i·ty, lax′ness** *n.* **—lax′ly** *adv.*

lax·a·tive (lak′sə·tiv) *n.* A substance that has the power to loosen the bowels, as milk of magnesia. *—adj.* Tending to loosen the bowels and relieve constipation. [< L *laxatus,* p.p. of *laxare* relax]

lay[1] (lā) *v.* **laid, lay·ing** *v.t.* **1** To cause to lie. **2** To put or place; *Lay* the book on the table. **3** To strike or beat down; overthrow. **4** To cause to settle or subside, as dust, a storm, etc. **5** To calm or allay, as doubts. **6** To place in regular order or proper position: to *lay* title. **7** To think out; devise: to *lay* plans. **8** To attribute or ascribe: to *lay* blame. **9** To give importance to. **10** To bring forward; advance, as a claim. **11** To bring forth from the body and deposit, as an egg. **12** To construct; build, as a foundation. **13** To make (a table) ready for a meal. **14** To bury; inter. **15** To impose, as taxes, punishment, etc. **16** To spread over a surface: to *lay* a fixative. **17** To strike with or apply, as in punishment. **18** To locate: The scene is *laid* in the boudoir. **19** To set or prepare, as a trap. **20** To place as a wager or bet: He *laid* twenty dollars on the favorite. *—v.i.* **21** To bring forth and deposit eggs. **22** To place a bet or bets. **23** To lie; recline: an incorrect use. **—lay aside** (or **by**) To store up; save. **—lay away 1** To store up; save. **2** To bury. **—lay before** To put forward or present, as a report. **—lay down 1** To give up (one's life). **2** To state or proclaim: to *lay down* the law. **3** To bet. **—lay for** *Informal* To wait to attack or harm. **—lay hold of** To seize or grasp. **—lay in** To procure and store. **—lay into** *Informal* To attack vigorously. **—lay it on** *Informal* To be extravagant or exorbitant, as in praise or demands. **—lay off 1** To take off and put aside, as clothes. **2** To survey; mark off. **3** To dismiss (a worker) from a job, usu. temporarily. **4** *Informal* To take a rest; stop working. **5** *Slang* To stop annoying, teasing, etc. **—lay on 1** To put on; apply, as color. **2** To beat or strike; attack. **—lay out 1** To spend. **2** To prepare for burial. **3** *Slang* To strike prostrate or unconscious. **4** To set forth, as a plan. **—lay over** To stop, as for a rest on a journey. **—lay siege to** To besiege. **—lay up 1** To make a store of. **2** To confine, as by illness or injury. *—n.* **1** The manner in which something lies or is placed; relative arrangement: the *lay* of the land. **2** *Whaling* A share in the profits. [< OE lecgan] • **lay, lie** Educated speaking and writing require a careful distinction between these two related verbs. *Lay (laid, laying),* meaning to place or put, takes an object: *He lays his briefcase on the desk. Lie (lay, lain, lying),* meaning to rest, recline, or be situated, does not take an object: *The dog lies on the rug.* The confusion occurs because the present tense of *lay* is identical with the past tense of *lie: Lay your coat over that chair; Yesterday he lay on the couch for two hours.*

lay[2] (lā) *adj.* Pertaining to the laity; nonprofessional; inexperienced. [< Gk. *laos* the people]

lay[3] (lā) *p.t.* of LIE[1].

lay[4] (lā) *n.* A song, ballad, or narrative poem. [< OF *lai.*]

lay·a·bout (lā′ə·bout′) *n. Chiefly Brit.* A lazy, idle person; a good-for-nothing.

lay·a·way (lā′ə·wā′) *n.* An agreement to make a series of payments to buy merchandise that is delivered when fully paid for. Also **layaway plan.**

lay-by (lā′bī′) *n. pl.* **-bys** *Brit.* A roadside area where vehicles may turn off, as for repairs or parking.

lay·er (lā′ər) *n.* **1** One who or that which lays. **2** A single horizontal thickness, as a stratum or lamina. **3** *Bot.* A shoot or twig bent into the ground to take root without being detached from the parent plant. *—v.t. Bot.* To propagate (a plant) by means of a layer. **—lay′er·ing** *n.*

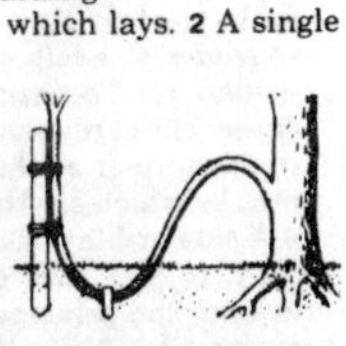

Layer *def. 3*

layer cake A cake of two or more layers separated by a sweetened filling or icing and usu. frosted.

lay·ette (lā·et′) *n.* A full equipment of clothes, bedding, etc., for a newly born child. [< MDu. *lade* a chest, trunk]

lay figure 1 A jointed model of the human body that can be arranged in various positions and used by artists as a model. **2** A mere puppet; a tool of the interests of others.

lay·man (lā′mən) *n. pl.* **·men** (-mən) A man not belonging to the clergy or other profession or body of experts.

lay·off (lā′ôf′, -of′) *n.* **1** The act of discharging or firing workmen or employees, esp. temporarily. **2** A period of discontinuance of work.

lay-out (lā′out′) *n.* **1** That which is laid out; a set of articles set out or provided. **2** A laying out or planning, as of a piece of work, a campaign, etc. **3** The make-up of a book, magazine, etc. Also **lay′out.**

lay-o·ver (lā′ō′vər) *n.* STOPOVER.

lay-up (lā′up′) *n.* In basketball, a shot taken close to the basket and usu. bounced off the backboard.

la·zar (la′zər, lāz′ər) *n.* A diseased beggar, esp. a leper. [< LAZARUS]

laz·a·ret·to (laz′ə·ret′ō) *n. pl.* **·tos** 1 A hospital for people with contagious diseases, esp. leprosy. 2 A ship or building used for quarantine. 3 In certain ships, a storeroom near the stern. Also **laz′a·ret′, laz′a·rette′.** [< Ital.]

Laz·a·rus (laz′ə·rəs) In the Bible: **a** A brother of Martha and Mary, raised from the dead by Jesus. **b** A sick beggar described in a parable as being rewarded after death, while a rich man was punished in hell. *Luke* 16:19–31.

laze (lāz) *v.* **lazed, laz·ing** *v.i.* 1 To be lazy; loaf. —*v.t.* 2 To pass (time) in idleness. —*n.* Idleness; laziness.

la·zy (lā′zē) *adj.* **·zi·er, ·zi·est** 1 Indisposed to exertion; indolent. 2 Moving or acting slowly or heavily. [?] —**la′zi·ly** *adv.* —**la′zi·ness** *n.* —**Syn.** 1 idle, inactive, slothful, sluggish.

la·zy·bones (lā′zē·bōnz′) *n. Informal* A lazy person.

lb. pound (L *libra*).

lbs. pounds.

L.C. Library of Congress.

L/C, l/c letter of credit; lower case.

lc. left center; lower case (printing); in the place cited (L *loco citato*).

LD, L.D. Low Dutch.

ldg. landing; leading; loading.

lea (lē) *n.* A grassy field or plain. [< OE *lēah*]

lea. league; leather; leave.

leach (lēch) *v.t.* 1 To run a liquid through (ashes, etc.) so as to remove the soluble portions. 2 To remove (soluble portions) by passing a liquid through them. —*v.i.* 3 To lose soluble matter by percolating. 4 To be removed by percolating. —*n.* 1 The process of leaching. 2 The solution obtained by leaching. [< OE *leccan* wet, irrigate] —**leach′·er** *n.*

lead[1] (lēd) *v.* **led, lead·ing** *v.t.* 1 To go with or ahead of so as to show the way; guide. 2 To guide by or as by pulling: to *lead* a person by the hand. 3 To serve as a direction or route for: The path *led* them to a valley. 4 To cause to go in a certain direction, as wire, water, etc. 5 To direct the affairs, actions, etc., of: to *lead* an army. 6 To have the first or foremost place among: He *led* the field. 7 To influence or control the opinions, thoughts, actions, etc., of. 8 To live or experience; pass: to *lead* a happy life. 9 To begin or open: to *lead* a discussion. 10 In card games, to begin a round of play with: He *led* the ace. —*v.i.* 11 To act as guide; conduct. 12 To have leadership or command; be in control. 13 To submit to being guided: The horse *leads* easily. 14 To be first or in advance. 15 To afford a way or passage: The road *led* into a swamp. 16 In card games, to make the first play. 17 In boxing, to strike at an opponent: to *lead* with a left. —**lead off** To make a beginning; start. —**lead on** To entice or tempt. —**lead to** To result in; cause: His carelessness *led to* his downfall. —*n.* 1 Position in advance or at the head; priority. 2 The distance, time, etc., by which anything precedes. 3 Leadership; guidance. 4 A clue or hint: Have you any *leads?* 5 In cards, etc., the right to play first or the card or suit played first. 6 In drama, the principal part or the actor who performs in such a part. 7 *Electr.* A wire that joins to a circuit device. 8 In baseball, the distance from base of a runner ready to run to the next base. 9 A leash for leading a dog. 10 In journalism, the opening paragraph of a news story. —*adj.* Acting as leader: the *lead* dog. [< OE *lǣden* cause to go] —**Syn.** *v.* 1 conduct, direct, escort. 7 induce, persuade.

lead[2] (led) *n.* 1 A soft, heavy, gray metallic element (symbol Pb) forming many technologically useful alloys and compounds. 2 Any one of various articles made of lead or its alloys. 3 *Printing* A thin strip of type metal used to separate lines of type. 4 *Naut.* A weight of lead used in sounding at sea. 5 A thin rod of graphite, used in pencils. 6 WHITE LEAD. 7 Bullets. —*v.t.* 1 To cover, weight, fasten, line, or fill with lead. 2 *Printing* To separate (lines of type) with leads. —*v.i.* 3 To become filled or clogged with lead. [< OE *lēad*] —**lead′y** *adj.*

lead·en (led′n) *adj.* 1 Made of lead. 2 Of a dull gray color. 3 Heavy. 4 Dull or sluggish. 5 Depressed; sad. —**lead′en·ly** *adv.* —**lead′en·ness** *n.*

lead·er (lē′dər) *n.* 1 One who leads or commands. 2 One who has the ability to lead. 3 That which leads, as the foremost horse of a team. 4 *Music* **a** A conductor of an orchestra, band, etc. **b** A principal musician or vocalist. 5 In journalism, the chief editorial or article of a newspaper. 6 An article of merchandise offered at a special price to attract customers. 7 *Printing pl.* Dots, dashes, etc., printed in rows and used to guide the eye from one side of a page to the other. 8 In fishing, a short line of gut, nylon, etc., attaching the hook or lure to the line. 9 A pipe to carry water, as from a roof.

lead·er·ship (lē′dər·ship) *n.* 1 The office or position of a leader. 2 Ability to lead. 3 Leaders as a group.

lead-in (lēd′in′) *n.* 1 A wire connecting an antenna to a transmitter or receiver. 2 Anything that introduces something.

lead·ing[1] (lē′ding) *adj.* 1 First or most prominent; foremost. 2 That guides, directs, or influences: a *leading* question. 3 Situated at the head or front. —*n.* A directing or guiding. —**lead′ing·ly** *adv.*

lead·ing[2] (led′ing) *n.* 1 The act of covering or separating with lead. 2 Sheets or strips of lead.

lead-off (lēd′ôf′, -of′) *n.* 1 A beginning. 2 The opening movement in any of various games. 3 The player who leads off.

lead pencil (led) A pencil of graphite encased in wood, etc.

lead poisoning (led) Poisoning due to cumulative absorption of small amounts of lead into the body.

lead time (lēd) The time required to put into effect a plan or program, as to manufacture a commercial product or a military weapon.

leaf (lēf) *n. pl.* **leaves** (lēvz) 1 A photosynthetic, lateral outgrowth from the stem of a plant, commonly broad, flat, thin, and green. 2 Leaves collectively; leafage. 3 Loosely, a petal. 4 A single sheet of paper, as in a book, on each side of which is a page. 5 A hinged, folding, sliding, or removable part or section, as of a table, gate, screen, or folding door. 6 A very thin sheet of metal: gold *leaf.* —**turn over a new leaf** To change one's ways or conduct for the better. —*v.i.* 1 To put forth or produce leaves. —*v.t.* 2 To turn or run through the pages of a book: often with *through.* [< OE *lēaf*]

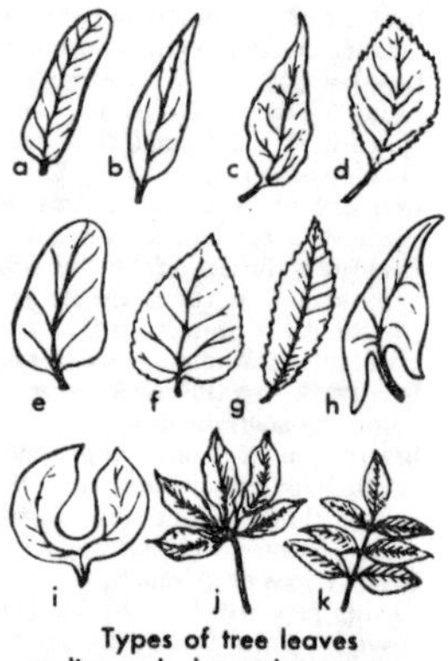

Types of tree leaves
a. linear. b. lanceolate. c. acuminate. d. acute. e. obtuse. f. ovate. g. serrate. h. sagittate. i. binate. j. digitate. k. compound.

leaf·age (lē′fij) *n.* FOLIAGE.

leaf bud A bud that develops into a leaf or a branch.

leaf·less (lēf′lis) *adj.* Having or bearing no leaves. —**leaf′less·ness** *n.*

leaf·let (lēf′lit) *n.* 1 A little leaf or leaflike part. 2 *Bot.* One of the separate divisions of a compound leaf. 3 A small printed sheet (or sheets) of printed matter, often folded but left unstitched.

leaf·stalk (lēf′stôk′) *n.* PETIOLE.

leaf·y (lē′fē) *adj.* **leaf·i·er, leaf·i·est** 1 Having or full of leaves. 2 Producing broad leaves. 3 Like a leaf or leaves. —**leaf′i·ness** *n.*

league[1] (lēg) *n.* A measure of distance, varying from about 2.42 to 4.6 statute miles. [< LL *leuga, leuca*]

league[2] (lēg) *n.* 1 An alliance of persons or states for mutual support in a common cause. 2 In sports, an association of ball teams that play among themselves. —*v.t. & v.i.* **leagued, lea·guing** To join in a league; combine. [< Ital. < *legare* to bind] —**lea·guer** (lē′gər) *n.*

League of Nations An international organization

(1920–1946) established primarily for the preservation of peace.

Le·ah (lē′ə) In the Bible, one of Jacob's wives.

leak (lēk) *n.* 1 An opening that permits the unintended entrance or escape of something. 2 Anything which permits the transmission, loss, or escape of something: a *leak* in the espionage system. 3 Leakage. —*v.i.* 1 To let a liquid, etc., enter or escape undesignedly, as through a hole or crack. 2 To pass in or out accidentally: often with *in* or *out.* 3 To become known despite efforts at secrecy: usu. with *out.* —*v.t.* 4 To let (a liquid, etc.) enter or escape undesignedly. 5 To disclose (privileged information) with or without authorization. [< ON *leka* to drip] —**leak′i·ness** *n.* —**leak′y** *adj.* **(·i·er, ·i·est)**

leak·age (lē′kij) *n.* 1 The act of leaking. 2 Something that leaks. 3 The quantity that leaks.

lean¹ (lēn) *v.* **leaned** or **leant** (lent), **lean·ing** *v.i.* 1 To incline from an erect position. 2 To incline against or rest on something for support. 3 To depend or rely: with *on* or *upon:* to *lean* on friendship. 4 To have a mental inclination: to *lean* toward an opinion. —*v.t.* 5 To cause to incline from an erect position. 6 To place (one thing) against another for support. —*n.* A leaning; inclination. [< OE *hleonian*]

lean² (lēn) *adj.* 1 Not fat or stout; thin. 2 With little or no fat: *lean* meat. 3 Lacking in richness, productiveness, etc.: a *lean* harvest. —*n.* Meat with little or no fat. [< OE *hlæne* thin] —**lean′ly** *adv.* —**lean′ness** *n.*

Le·an·der (lē·an′dər) *Gk. Myth.* The lover of Hero. [Gk., lion man]

lean·ing (lē′ning) *n.* 1 The act of one who or that which leans. 2 An inclination; tendency.

lean-to (lēn′tōō′) *n. pl.* **-tos** (-tōōz′) 1 A building having a single-sloping roof with its apex against an adjoining wall. 2 A rude shelter of branches or planks which slope from a crossbar to the ground.

leap (lēp) *v.* **leaped** or **leapt** (lēpt or lept), **leap·ing** *v.i.* 1 To jump with the feet in the air; spring. 2 To move suddenly by or as by jumping. —*v.t.* 3 To clear by jumping over. 4 To cause to leap: to *leap* a horse. —*n.* 1 The act of leaping. 2 A place to leap from or over. 3 The space passed over in leaping. 4 A sudden change or transition. [< OE *hlēapan*] —**leap′er** *n.*

leap·frog (lēp′frôg′, -frog′) *n.* A game in which one player puts his hands on the bent back of another and leaps over him. —*v.* **·frogged, ·frog·ging** *v.t.* 1 To jump over as in the game of leapfrog. 2 To move ahead of by turns or stages. —*v.i.* 3 To jump as in the game of leapfrog.

leap year A year of 366 days, an additional day being added to February. Every year exactly divisible by four, or, in century years, by 400, is a leap year.

learn (lûrn) *v.* **learned** or **learnt, learn·ing** *v.t.* 1 To acquire knowledge of or skill in by observation, study, instruction, etc. 2 To find out; ascertain: to *learn* the facts. 3 To memorize. 4 To acquire by or as by practice: to *learn* good habits. —*v.i.* 5 To gain knowledge; acquire skill. 6 To be informed; hear. [< OE *leornian*] —**learn′er** *n.*

learn·ed (lûr′nid) *adj.* 1 Having extensive learning or knowledge. 2 Characterized by or demanding extensive study or scholarship. —**learn′ed·ly** *adv.* —**learn′ed·ness** *n.*

learn·ing (lûr′ning) *n.* 1 The act of acquiring knowledge or skill. 2 The knowledge or skill thus acquired.

lease (lēs) *v.t.* **leased, leas·ing** 1 To grant the temporary possession and profits of, as lands, buildings, etc., usu. for a specified rent; let. 2 To hold under a lease. —*n.* 1 A contract for leasing land, buildings, etc. 2 The duration of such leasing. [< L *laxare* loosen] —**leas′a·ble** *adj.*

leash (lēsh) *n.* A line or thong, as for holding in check a dog, etc. —*v.t.* To hold or restrain by or as by a leash. [< L *laxus* loose]

least (lēst) *adj.* Smallest in size, value, etc. —*n.* That which is least. —**at least** 1 By the lowest estimate. 2 At any rate. —**not in the least** Not in any degree; not at all. —*adv.* In the smallest degree. [< OE *læssa* less]

least·wise (lēst′wīz′) *adv. Informal* At least; at any rate. Also **least′ways′** (-wāz′).

leath·er (leth′ər) *n.* 1 The skin or hide of an animal, when tanned or dressed for use. 2 Something made of leather. —*v.t.* 1 To cover or furnish with leather. 2 *Informal* To beat with or as with a leather strap. [< OE *lether*] —**leath′er·y** *adj.* —**leath′er·i·ness** *n.*

leath·ern (leth′ərn) *adj.* Made of leather.

leath·er·neck (leth′ər·nek′) *n. Slang* A member of the U.S. Marine Corps.

leave¹ (lēv) *v.* **left, leav·ing** *v.t.* 1 To go or depart from; quit. 2 To allow to remain behind: to *leave* a plow in a field. 3 To place or deposit so as to cause to remain behind: to *leave* word. 4 To cause to remain after departure, cessation, healing, etc.: The war *left* its mark. 5 To allow to continue or be as specified: *Leave* the light on. 6 To refer or entrust to another for doing, deciding, etc.: I *leave* the matter to you. 7 To terminate connection, employment, etc., with: to *leave* a job. 8 To have as a remainder: Three minus two *leaves* one. 9 To have remaining after death: to *leave* a large family. 10 To bequeath. —*v.i.* 11 To depart or go away. —**leave off** To cease. —**leave out** 1 To omit from consideration. 2 To fail to include. [< OE *læfan,* lit., let remain] —**leav′er** *n.* —**Syn.** 2 abandon, desert, forsake, relinquish. 11 withdraw, flee, set out. • The use of *leave* as a synonym for *let* in the sense of refraining from disturbing, bothering, etc., is only acceptable when *leave* is followed by a noun or pronoun and also by the word "alone." Thus, *Leave your little brother alone* may be substituted for *Let your little brother alone.* However, such a substitution can result in ambiguity since *leave alone,* in this context, may be interpreted to mean that the little brother is to be left by himself.

leave² (lēv) *n.* 1 Permission to do something. 2 Permission to be absent from duty or the period when such permission is effective: also **leave of absence.** —**take leave** 1 To depart; go away. 2 To abandon; quit: with *of:* He *took leave* of his senses. [< OE *lēaf* permission]

leave³ (lēv) *v.i.* **leaved, leav·ing** To put forth leaves.

leaved (lēvd) *adj.* 1 Having leaves. 2 Having a certain number or kind of leaves.

leav·en (lev′ən) *n.* 1 An agent that lightens baked goods by forming gas bubbles in it, as yeast or baking powder. 2 A piece of yeasty dough; sourdough. 3 Any influence or addition that causes general change of the whole. —*v.t.* 1 To add a leaven to; make light. 2 To affect in character; imbue. [< L *levare* raise] —**leav′en·ing** *n.*

leaves (lēvz) *n. pl.* of LEAF.

leave-tak·ing (lēv′tā′king) *n.* A taking leave; a farewell.

leav·ing (lē′ving) *n.* 1 The act of departure. 2 *pl.* Things left; scraps. 3 *pl.* Refuse; offal.

Leb·a·nese (leb′ə·nēz′, -nēs′) *n.* A citizen or native of Lebanon. —*adj.* Of or pertaining to Lebanon or its people.

Leb·a·non (leb′ə·nən) *n.* A republic of sw Asia, 3,400 sq. mi., cap. Beirut. • See map at JORDAN.

Le·bens·raum (lā′bəns·roum) *n. German* Territory into which a nation claims it must expand to fulfill its economic needs; literally, space for living.

lech·er (lech′ər) *n.* A habitually lewd or excessively sensual man. [< OHG *leccōn* lick]

lech·er·ous (lech′ər·əs) *adj.* Given to or characterized by lewdness or lust. —**lech′er·ous·ly** *adv.* —**lech′er·ous·ness** *n.*

lech·er·y (lech′ər·ē) *n.* Free indulgence in lust; gross sensuality.

lec·i·thin (les′ə·thin) *n.* A complex ester containing phosphorus and nitrogen, an essential constituent of plant and animal cells, esp. abundant in nerve tissue, egg yolk, semen, etc. [< Gk. *lekithos* an egg's yolk + -IN]

lect. lecture; lecturer.

lec·tern (lek′tərn) *n.* A reading desk, esp. one in a church, from which parts of the service are read. [< L *lectus,* pp. of *legere* read]

lec·ture (lek′chər) *n.* 1 A talk delivered aloud for instruction or entertainment. 2 A lengthy reprimand. —*v.* **·tured, ·tur·ing** *v.t.* 1 To deliver lectures to; instruct by lecturing. 2 To rebuke authoritatively or at length. —*v.i.* 3 To give a lecture. [< L *lectura* an act of reading] —**lec′tur·er, lec′ture·ship** *n.* —**Syn.** *n.* 1 address, discourse, oration, speech.

led (led) *p.t. & p.p.* of LEAD[1].
Le·da (lē′də) *Gk. Myth.* The mother of Clytemnestra, of Helen of Troy, and of Castor and Pollux.
ledge (lej) *n.* **1** A shelf. **2** Something resembling a shelf, as a ridge of rock or a projection from a building. **3** A lode or vein. [ME *legge*] —**ledg′y** *adj.*
ledg·er (lej′ər) *n.* The principal book of accounts of a business establishment, in which all transactions are entered to show the debits and credits of each account. [ME *legger*]
ledger line *Music* A short line added above or below a staff for notes too high or too low to be written on the staff.
lee (lē) *n.* **1** The direction opposite that from which the wind comes. **2** The side, as of a ship, that is sheltered from the wind. **3** Any shelter or protection. —*adj.* Pertaining to the side opposite to that from which the wind comes: a *lee* shore. [< OE *hlēo* a shelter]
leech[1] (lēch) *n.* **1** Any of various segmented, bloodsucking worms living in water or damp ground; esp. one formerly used in medicine for drawing blood. **2** One who clings to another in order to gain something. **3** *Archaic* A physician. —*v.t.* To bleed with leeches. [< OE *lǣce,* orig., a physician] —**leech′er** *n.*
leech[2] (lēch) *n. Naut.* **1** Either of the vertical edges of a square sail. **2** The after edge of a fore-and-aft sail. [ME *lich*]
leek (lēk) *n.* An edible plant of the lily family, closely allied to the onion. [< OE *lēac*]
leer (lir) *n.* A sly look or glance expressing lust, malicious intent, etc. —*v.i.* To look with a leer. [< OE *hlēor* a cheek, face] —**leer′ing·ly** *adv.*
leer·y (lir′ē) *adj.* **leer·i·er, leer·i·est** *Informal* Suspicious; wary. —**leer′i·ness** *n.*
lees (lēz) *n. pl.* Sediment, esp. of wine, dregs. [< OF *lie*]
lee·ward (lē′wərd, *Naut.* lo͞o′ərd) *adj. Naut.* Of or toward the direction in which the wind blows: opposed to *windward.* —*n.* The lee side or direction. —*adv.* Toward the lee; also **lee′ward·ly.**
lee·way (lē′wā) *n.* **1** The leeward drift of a vessel or aircraft. **2** Something, as extra time, space, or money, that provides for greater freedom of action; margin.
left[1] (left) *p.t. & p.p.* of LEAVE[1].
left[2] (left) *adj.* **1** Of, designating, for, or on that side of the body which is toward the north when one faces the rising sun. **2** Situated closer to the left hand of an observer than to his right: the *left* fork of a road. **3** Designating that side or bank of a river which is on the left when the observer faces downstream. —*n.* **1** The left side. **2** Anything on, toward, or for the left side. **3** *Often cap.* In politics, a liberal, socialistic, or radical position, or a party or group advocating such a position, so designated because of the views of the party occupying seats on the left side of the presiding officer in certain European legislative bodies: used with *the.* **4** In boxing, the left hand or a blow with the left hand. [< OE *lyft*]
left-hand (left′hand′) *adj.* **1** Of, for, or located on the left side or hand. **2** Turning, opening, or swinging to the left.
left-hand·ed (left′han′did) *adj.* **1** Having a tendency to use the left hand or arm more than the right. **2** Done with the left hand. **3** Adapted for use by the left hand, as a tool. **4** Clumsy; awkward. **5** Without sincerity; indirect: a *left-handed* compliment. **6** Turning or moving from right to left;counterclockwise. —**left′hand′ed·ly** *adv.* —**left′hand′ed·ness** *n.*
left·ist (lef′tist) *n.* In politics, one who is a member of or sympathetic to the left. —*adj.* Liberal or radical.
left·o·ver (left′ō′vər) *n.* A part not used or consumed. —*adj.* Remaining unconsumed.
left wing That part of any group advocating leftist policies. —**left′-wing′** *adj.* —**left′-wing′er** *n.*
left·y (lef′tē) *n. pl.* **·ties** *Slang* A left-handed person.
leg (leg) *n.* **1** One of the limbs of man or an animal used for supporting the body and for walking. **2** Something that resembles a leg or gives support: the *leg* of a table. **3** That portion of a garment or stocking which covers the leg. **4** *Naut.* The distance run by a vessel on one tack. **5** Any appreciable section of a journey. **6** *Geom.* Any side of a triangle except its base or hypotenuse. —**have not a leg to stand on** To have no valid excuse, argument, etc. —**on one's last legs** On the verge of failure, death, or collapse. —**pull one's leg** *Slang* To fool or make fun of someone. —**shake a leg** *Slang* To make haste; hurry. —*v.i.* **legged, leg·ging** *Informal* To walk; run: often with *it.* [< ON *leggr*]
leg. legal; legate; legato; legislation.
leg·a·cy (leg′ə·sē) *n. pl.* **·cies** **1** Something left by will; a bequest. **2** Something handed down or derived from an ancestor or earlier time. [< L *legare* bequeath]
le·gal (lē′gəl) *adj.* **1** Created or permitted by law. **2** Of, pertaining to, or connected with law. **3** Capable of being remedied by a resort to statute law rather than to equity. **4** Of or suitable for lawyers: a *legal* approach. [< L *lex, legis* law] —**le′gal·ly** *adv.*
le·gal·ese (lē′gə·lēz′, -lēs′) *n.* A style of writing characteristic of members of the legal profession.
le·gal·ism (lē′gəl·iz′əm) *n.* A too strict or literal interpretation of or adherence to a law or code. —**le′gal·is′tic** *adj.* —**le′gal·ist** *n.*
le·gal·i·ty (li·gal′ə·tē) *n. pl.* **·ties** **1** The condition or quality of being legal. **2** Something legal, as a law.
le·gal·ize (lē′gəl·iz) *v.t.* **·ized, ·iz·ing** To make legal; sanction. *Brit. sp.* **·ise.** —**le′gal·i·za′tion** (-ə·zā′shən, -ī·zā′-) *n.*
legal tender Money that may not be legally refused by a creditor.
leg·ate (leg′it) *n.* **1** An official envoy or emissary. **2** A representative of the pope in various functions. [< L *legare* send as a deputy, bequeath] —**leg′ate·ship** *n.*
leg·a·tee (leg′ə·tē′) *n.* The recipient of a legacy.
le·ga·tion (li·gā′shən) *n.* **1** A diplomatic mission sent to a foreign country; also, those persons composing it. **2** The official residence or place of business of such a diplomatic mission, usu. ranking below an embassy.
le·ga·to (li·gä′tō) *adj. & adv. Music* In a smooth, connected manner. [< Ital. *legare* to bind]
leg·end (lej′ənd) *n.* **1** An unauthenticated story from early times, preserved by tradition and popularly thought to have a basis in fact. **2** Such stories, collectively. **3** An unusually famous or notable person, thing, or event. **4** An inscription or motto on a coin or monument. **5** A key to a map or chart. **6** A title, brief explanation, etc., accompanying an illustration. [< L *legere* read]
leg·en·dar·y (lej′ən·der′ē) *adj.* **1** Of, based on, or known from legends. **2** Traditional.
leg·er·de·main (lej′ər·də·mān′) *n.* **1** Sleight of hand. **2** Any artful trick or deception. [< F *léger de main,* lit., light of hand] —**leg′er·de·main′ist** *n.*
leg·ged (leg′id, legd) *adj.* Having a specified kind or number of legs: used in combination: *two-legged.*
leg·ging (leg′ing) *n. Usu. pl.* A warm or protective covering for the leg.
leg·gy (leg′ē) *adj.* **·gi·er, ·gi·est** **1** Having disproportionately long legs. **2** Having shapely legs: said of women.
leg·horn (leg′ərn, -hôrn) *n.* **1** A fine plaiting of wheat straw. **2** A bonnet or hat made of this plaiting. **3** *Often cap.* One of a breed of small, hardy, domestic fowls. [< *Leghorn,* a port in NW Italy]
leg·i·ble (lej′ə·bəl) *adj.* Capable of being deciphered or read with ease. [< L *legere* to read] —**leg′i·bil′i·ty, leg′i·ble·ness** *n.* —**leg′i·bly** *adv.*
le·gion (lē′jen) *n.* **1** A division of the ancient Roman army, comprising between 4,200 and 6,000 men. **2** *Usu. pl.* A large military force. **3** A great number; multitude. [< L *legere* choose, levy an army]
le·gion·ar·y (lē′jən·er′ē) *adj.* Of pertaining to, or being a legion. —*n. pl.* **·ar·ies** A soldier of a legion.
le·gion·naire (lē′jən·âr′) *n.* A member of a legion.
legis. legislation, legislative; legislature.
leg·is·late (lej′is·lāt) *v.* **·lat·ed, ·lat·ing** *v.i.* **1** To make a law or laws. —*v.t.* **2** To bring about or effect by legislation.
leg·is·la·tion (lej′is·lā′shən) *n.* **1** The making of a law or laws. **2** The law or laws made by a legislative power. [< L *lex, legis* a law + *latus* carried]
leg·is·la·tive (lej′is·lā′tiv) *adj.* **1** Having the power to make or enact laws. **2** Of, pertaining to, or suitable to legislation. **3** Of or pertaining to a legislature. **4** Created or enforced by legislation. —*n.* LEGISLATURE.
leg·is·la·tor (lej′is·lā′tər) *n.* A member of a legislature.
leg·is·la·ture (lej′is·lā′chər) *n.* A body of persons empowered to make laws for a country or state.

le·git (lə·jit′) *Slang n.* The legitimate theater. —*adj.* Legitimate.

le·git·i·mate (lə·jit′ē·mit) *adj.* **1** Having the sanction of law, lawful. **2** Born in wedlock. **3** Genuine; valid. **4** Logically correct; reasonable. **5** Based on or resulting from strict hereditary rights: a *legitimate* heir to the throne. **6** In the theater, designating or of plays or musicals produced live on a stage, as distinguished from motion pictures, etc. —*v.t.* (lə·jit′ə·māt) **·mat·ed, ·mat·ing 1** To make legitimate. **2** To justify. [< L *legitimus* lawful] —**le·git′i·ma·cy, le·git′i·mate·ness** *n.* —**le·git′i·mate·ly** *adv.* —**Syn. 1** legal, licit, rightful. **3** authentic, bona fide, real.

le·git·i·mist (lə·jit′ə·mist) *n.* One who supports legitimate authority or supports a person having a legitimate claim to a throne. Also **le·git′i·ma·tist.** —**le·git′i·mism** *n.* —**le·git′i·mis′tic** *adj.*

le·git·i·mize (lə·jit′ə·mīz) *v.t.* **·mized, ·miz·ing 1** To make legitimate. **2** To make acceptable or tolerable: to assert that some TV programs *legitimize* violence. Also **le·git′i·ma·tize** (-mə·tīz). —**le·git′i·mi·za′tion** *n.*

leg-of-mut·ton (leg′ə·mut′n) *adj.* Being full at one end and tapering at the other, as a leg of mutton: a *leg-of-mutton* sleeve or sail.

leg·ume (leg′yōōm, lə·gyōōm′) *n.* **1** The fruit of a leguminous plant, a pod splitting open along two sutures, as a bean pod. **2** Any leguminous plant. [< L *legumen,* lit., a gatherable thing]

le·gu·mi·nous (lə·gyōō′mə·nəs) adj. **1** Of or pertaining to legumes. **2** Belonging to the group of plants bearing fruit in a pod and usu. having compound leaves.

leg·work (leg′wûrk′) *n. Informal* The physical activity incidental to doing research.

lei (lā, lā′ē) *n. pl.* **leis** In Hawaii, a garland or wreath of flowers and leaves, usu. worn around the neck. [< Hawaiian]

lei·sure (lē′zhər, lezh′ər) *n.* Time during which one is free from the demands of work or duty. —**at leisure 1** Free from work or duties. **2** Not employed. —**at one's leisure** When it is convenient or easy. —*adj.* **1** Free or unoccupied: *leisure* time. **2** Having leisure: the *leisure* class. [< L *licere* be permitted]

lei·sure·ly (lē′zhər·lē, lezh′ər-) *adj.* Without hurry; deliberate; slow: also **lei′sured** (-zhərd) —*adv.* In a leisurely manner. —**lei′sure·li·ness** *n.*

leit·mo·tif (līt′mō·tēf′) *n.* **1** *Music* A recurring theme used to indicate a certain person, attribute, or idea, as in an opera. **2** Something recurring like a musical theme. Also **leit′mo·tiv′.** [< G *Leitmotiv* leading motif]

LEM (lem) lunar excursion module.

lem·an (lem′ən, lē′mən) *n. Archaic* A lover; esp., a mistress. [< OE *lēof* beloved + *mann* a man]

lem·ming (lem′ing) *n.* Any of several small, mouselike, arctic rodents with a short tail and furry feet. [Norw.]

lem·on (lem′ən) *n.* **1** A citrus fruit with a yellow rind and very acid pulp and juice. **2** The tree that produces this fruit. **3** A bright yellow. **4** *Slang* Something or someone disappointing or unpleasant. —*adj.* **1** Flavored with or containing lemon. **2** Bright yellow. [< Pers. *līmūn*]

lem·on·ade (lem′ən·ād′) *n.* A drink made of lemon juice, water, and sugar.

le·mur (lē′mər) *n.* A small, mostly nocturnal mammal related to the monkeys, with fox-like face and soft fur, found chiefly in Madagascar. [< L *lemures* ghosts]

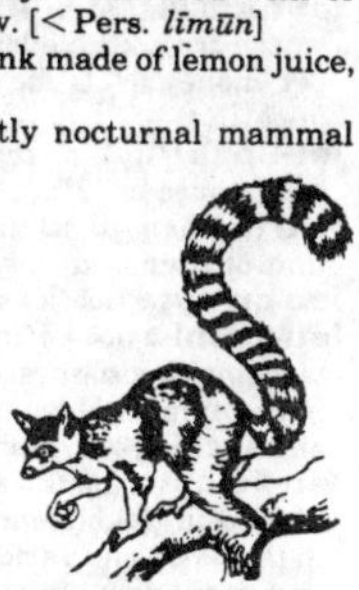

Ring-tailed lemur

lend (lend) *v.* **lent, lend·ing** *v.t.* **1** To grant the temporary use of. **2** To grant the use of (money) at interest. **3** To impart; furnish. **4** To accommodate (oneself or itself): The statement *lends* itself to misinterpretation. —*v.i.* **5** To make a loan or loans. [< OE *lænan*] —**lend′er** *n.*

lend-lease (lend′lēs′) *n.* In World War II, the furnishing of goods and services to any country whose defense was deemed vital to the defense of the U.S.

length (lengkth) *n.* **1** Linear extension from end to end, usu. the greatest dimension of a surface or body. **2** The state or quality of being long. **3** Duration in time. **4** Distance in space. **5** A long expanse. **6** A piece or section of something: a *length* of rope. **7** The linear extent of something specified or understood, used as a unit of measure: an arm's *length.* —**at length 1** Finally; at last. **2** In full. —**go to great lengths** (or **any length**) To do everything that is needed. [< OE *lengthu* < *lang* long]

length·en (lengk′thən) *v.t. & v.i.* To make or become longer. —**Syn.** elongate, expand, extend, stretch.

length·wise (lengkth′wīz′) *adj. & adv.* In the direction of the length. Also **length′ways′** (-wāz′).

length·y (lengk′thē) *adj.* **length·i·er, length·i·est** Long, esp. unduly long. —**length′i·ly** *adv.* —**length′i·ness** *n.*

le·ni·en·cy (lē′nē·ən·sē, lēn′yən-) *n. pl.* **·cies 1** The quality of being lenient; mercifulness. **2** A lenient act. Also **le′ni·ence.**

le·ni·ent (lē′nē·ənt, lēn′yənt) *adj.* Not exacting full retribution; merciful or mild. [< L *lenis* soft, mild] —**le′ni·ent·ly** *adv.*

Len·in·ism (len′in·iz′əm) *n.* The social and political doctrines based upon the teachings of Lenin. —**Len′in·ist, Len′in·ite** *n., adj.*

len·i·tive (len′ə·tiv) *adj.* Soothing; mitigating. —*n.* That which soothes or mitigates. [< L *lenire* soothe]

len·i·ty (len′ə·tē) *n.* The state or quality of being lenient. [< L *lenitas* softness]

lens (lenz) *n.* **1** A piece of glass or other transparent substance, having one surface curved and the other plane, or both curved, by which rays of light may be made to converge or to diverge. **2** Two or more lenses used in combination. **3** Any device for concentrating or dispersing radiation. **4** A biconvex transparent body, whose function is to focus light rays upon the retina. [< L *lens* a lentil; so called from the similarity in form] • See EYE.

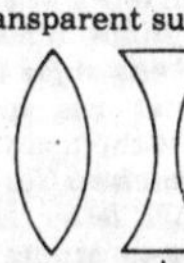

Lenses
a. biconvex.
b. biconcave.

lent (lent) *p.t. & p.p.* of LEND.

Lent (lent) *n. Eccl.* A period of forty days (excluding Sundays), observed in Christian churches from Ash Wednesday to Easter as a season of penitence and self-denial. [< OE *lengten* the spring]

Lent·en (len′tən) *adj.* **1** Of or suitable for Lent. **2** Plain; meager. Also **lent′en.**

len·til (len′təl) *n.* **1** A leguminous plant with small, lens-like, edible seeds. **2** The seed itself. [< L *lens, lentis* a lentil]

len·to (len′tō) *adj. & adv. Music* Slow; slowly. [Ital. < L *lentus*]

l'en·voi (len′voi; *Fr.* läṅ·vwȧ′) *n.* A postscript to or the closing stanza of certain poems. Also **l'en′voy.**

Le·o (lē′ō) *n.* A constellation and the fifth sign of the zodiac; the Lion. [L, a lion] • See ZODIAC.

Le·o·nid (lē′ə·nid) *n.* One of the meteors that form a shower about November 14. [< LEO, whence they appear to radiate]

le·o·nine (lē′ə·nīn) *adj.* Of, pertaining to, or like a lion. [< L *leo, leonis* a lion]

leop·ard (lep′ərd) *n.* **1** A ferocious mammal of the cat family of Asia and Africa, having a fawn, dark-spotted coat. **2** The jaguar. [< Gk. *leōn* a lion + *pardos* a panther]

Leopard *def. 1*

le·o·tard (lē′ə·tärd) *n. Often pl.* A closefitting garment, usu. with long sleeves and legs, worn as practice clothes by dancers, acrobats, etc. [< J. *Léotard,* 19th c. French aerialist]

lep·er (lep′ər) *n.* One afflicted with leprosy. [< Gk. *lepros* scaly]

lep·i·dop·ter·ous (lep′ə·dop′tər·əs) *adj.* Of or pertaining to an order of insects, the butterflies and moths, having four wings covered with minute scales. Also **lep′i·dop′ter·al.** [< Gk. *lepis, lepidos* scale + *pteron* wing] **—lep′i·dop′ter·an** *n., adj.*

lep·re·chaun (lep′rə·kôn) *n.* In Irish folklore, a fairy cobbler who, if caught and held, must reveal the location of treasure. [< O Irish *lu* little + *corpān,* dim. of *corp* body]

lep·ro·sy (lep′rə·sē) *n.* A chronic, bacterial disease characterized by skin lesions, nerve paralysis, and physical mutilation. [< L *lepra* leper]

lep·rous (lep′rəs) *adj.* 1 Having leprosy. 2 Of or like leprosy. Also **lep′er·ous** (-ər·əs). **—lep′rous·ly** *adv.* **—lep′rous·ness** *n.*

-lepsy *combining form* Seizure; attack: *catalepsy.* Also **-lepsia.**

les·bi·an (lez′bē·ən) *Often cap. n.* A homosexual woman. *—adj.* Of or pertaining to lesbians. [< *Lesbos,* the home of Sappho, reputed to have been homosexual]

les·bi·an·ism (lez′bē·ən·iz′əm) *n. Often cap.* Homosexuality among women.

lese-maj·es·ty (lēz′maj′is·tē) *n.* An offense against the sovereign power; treason. Also *Fr.* **lèse-ma·jes·té** (lez′ma·zhes·tā′) [< L *laedere* injure + *majestas* majesty]

le·sion (lē′zhən) *n.* 1 A hurt; injury. 2 Any abnormal or injurious change in an organ or tissue. [< L *laedere* injure]

Le·so·tho (le·sō′tō) *n.* An independent member of the Commonwealth of Nations in s Africa, 11,716 sq. mi., cap. Maseru. • See map at AFRICA.

less (les) Comparative of LITTLE. *—adj.* 1 Not as large or great in size, quantity, or degree. 2 Inferior in rank, importance, etc. *—n.* A smaller part or amount. *—adv.* To an inferior or smaller degree or extent; not so much. *—prep.* Minus: nine *less* six. [< OE *lǣssa*]

-less *suffix* 1 Deprived of; without: *motherless.* 2 That does not or is not: *harmless.* 3 Beyond the range of (the action of the main element): *countless.* [< OE *lēas* free from]

les·see (les·ē′) *n.* One holding property under a lease. [< OF *lesser, laissier* let, leave]

less·en (les′ən) *v.t.* 1 To make less; decrease. 2 To make little of; disparage. *—v.i.* 3 To become less. **—less′en·er** *n.* **—less′en·ing** *adj., n.* **—Syn.** 1 abate, diminish, dwindle, shrink, wane. 2 belittle, depreciate.

less·er (les′ər) *adj.* Less; smaller; inferior.

Lesser Bear The constellation Ursa Minor.

les·son (les′ən) *n.* 1 A specific assignment or division in a course of instruction. 2 *pl.* A course of instruction: painting *lessons.* 3 Knowledge gained by experience. 4 A portion of the Bible read or appointed to be read in divine service. 5 A reprimand. [< L *lectio* a reading]

les·sor (les′ôr, les·ôr′) *n.* One who grants a lease.

lest (lest) *conj.* 1 For fear that: We hid it *lest* he should see it. 2 That: following expressions indicating alarm or anxiety: We were worried *lest* the money run out. [< OE *(thy) lǣs the* (by the) less that]

let[1] (let) *v.* **let, let·ting** *v.t.* 1 To allow; permit. 2 To allow to go, come, or pass: They would not *let* us on board. 3 To cause; make: She *let* him know the truth. 4 To cause to escape or be released: to *let* blood. 5 To rent (a room, house, etc.). 6 To assign, as a contract, esp. after bidding. 7 As an auxiliary verb, *let* is used to express command, suggestion, or acquiescence: *Let* it pour!; *Let* Bonnie play the lead. *—v.i.* 8 To be rented or leased. **—let alone** 1 To refrain from disturbing, bothering, etc. 2 To say nothing of; not to mention: He can't float, *let alone* swim. **—let be** 1 To leave alone. 2 To stop; cease. **—let down** 1 To lower. 2 To reduce effort or concentration. 3 To disappoint. **—let off** 1 To discharge or reduce, as pressure. 2 To excuse from an engagement, duty, or penalty; dismiss. **—let on** *Informal* 1 To pretend. 2 To reveal; allow to be known. **—let out** 1 To release. 2 To reveal; divulge. 3 To make (a garment) larger by releasing a part. 4 To rent or lease. 5 *Informal* To dismiss or be dismissed, as a school. **—let up** To slacken; abate. **—let up on** *Informal* To cease applying pressure or harsh measures to. [< OE *lǣtan*] • See LEAVE.

let[2] (let) *n.* 1 Anything that obstructs or hinders. 2 In tennis or other racket games, a stroke or point that does not count and must be played over. **—without let or hindrance** With no hindrance or obstruction. *—v.t. Archaic* **let** or **let·ted, let·ting** To hinder or impede; obstruct. [< OE *lettan* hinder]

-let *suffix of nouns* 1 Small; little: *kinglet.* 2 A band or small article for (a specific part of the body): *wristlet.* [< OF]

let·down (let′doun′) *n.* 1 Decrease, as of speed or energy. 2 *Informal* Disillusionment; disappointment.

le·thal (lē′thəl) *adj.* 1 Causing death; fatal. 2 Pertaining to death. [< L *lethum, letum* death] **—le′thal·ly** *adv.*

le·thar·gic (li·thär′jik) *adj.* Affected by lethargy. Also **le·thar′gi·cal.** **—le·thar′gi·cal·ly** *adv.*

leth·ar·gize (leth′ər·jīz) *v.t.* **·gized, ·giz·ing** To make lethargic.

leth·ar·gy (leth′ər·jē) *n. pl.* **·gies** 1 A state of abnormal drowsiness or prolonged sleep. 2 Great indifference; apathy. [< Gk. *lēthē* oblivion] **—Syn.** 1 coma, stupor. 2 inactivity, sluggishness.

Le·the (lē′thē) *Gk. Myth.* The river of forgetfulness, one of the five rivers surrounding Hades. *—n.* Oblivion; forgetfulness. **—Le·the·an** (lē′thē·ən, li·thē′-) *adj.*

let's (lets) Contraction of *let us.*

Lett (let) *n.* 1 A native or inhabitant of Latvia and adjacent Baltic regions. 2 LETTISH.

let·ter (let′ər) *n.* 1 A mark or character used to represent a speech sound and usu. part of an alphabet. 2 A written or printed communication, usu. sent by mail. 3 A document granting authority, right, privilege, or the like. 4 Literal or exact meaning. 5 *pl.* Literary knowledge or erudition; also, literature in general: the domain of *letters.* 6 An emblem given in schools to athletes, etc., usu. in the form of the initial letter of the school. *—v.t.* 1 To write with letters. 2 To mark with letters. [< L *littera* a letter of the alphabet, in pl., an epistle] **—let′ter·er** *n.*

letter carrier A person whose work is to deliver mail.

let·tered (let′ərd) *adj.* 1 Able to read and write; literate. 2 Having literary learning. 3 Inscribed with letters.

let·ter·head (let′ər·hed′) *n.* 1 A printed heading, usu. a name and address, at the top of a sheet of letter paper. 2 A sheet of paper with such a heading.

let·ter·ing (let′ər·ing) *n.* 1 The act of drawing letters or of marking or stamping with letters. 2 Letters so drawn, marked, or stamped.

letter of credit A letter issued by a bank authorizing the bearer to draw money up to a certain amount from other banks.

let·ter-per·fect (let′ər·pûr′fikt) *adj.* 1 Perfectly memorized, as a speech, dramatic role, etc. 2 Correct in every detail.

let·ter·press (let′ər·pres′) *n.* 1 Letters and words printed, as distinguished from illustrations. 2 Printing made from type or plates with a raised surface.

letters of marque A governmental document licensing an individual to arm a vessel and prey upon enemy merchant shipping.

letters patent An open document, under seal of the government, granting some special right, authority, privilege, or property.

Let·tish (let′ish) *adj.* Of or pertaining to the Letts or their language. *—n.* The Baltic language of the Letts.

let·tuce (let′is) *n.* 1 A garden plant of several varieties whose crisp, edible leaves are used for salad. 2 *Slang* Paper money. [< L *lac, lactis* milk; with ref. to its milky juice]

let·up (let′up′) *n. Informal* 1 A stopping; cessation. 2 A brief pause or lull.

le·u (le′o͞o) *n. pl.* **lei** (lā) A silver coin, the basic monetary unit of Rumania. Also **ley.**

leu·co·cyte (lo͞o′kə·sīt′) *n.* LEUKOCYTE.

leu·ke·mi·a (lo͞o·kē′mē·ə) *n.* Any of various diseases of the bloodmaking tissues, characterized by a marked increase in the number of leukocytes, usu. accompanied by anemia and swelling of lymph nodes, spleen, etc. **—leu·ke′mic** *adj.*

leu·ko·cyte (lo͞o′kə·sīt) *n.* Any of various colorless cells formed in the bone marrow and lymph nodes and found in the blood and various tissues, where they constitute an important agent against infection. [< Gk. *leukos* white + -CYTE]

Lev, Lev., Levit. Leviticus.

le·vant (lə·vant′) *n.* A morocco leather having a somewhat irregular grain. Also **Levant morocco.** [< the LEVANT]

Le·vant (lə·vant′) *n.* The regions on the E Mediterranean, from w Greece to w Egypt: with *the.* —**Le·van·tine** (lə·van′tin, lev′ən·tīn, -tēn) *adj., n.*

le·va·tor (lə·vā′tər) *n.* pl. **le·va·to·res** (lev′ə·tôr′ēz, -tō′rēz) or **le·va·tors** *Anat.* A muscle that raises an organ or part. [< L *levare* to raise]

lev·ee[1] (lev′ē) *n.* **1** An embankment built beside a river to prevent overflow. **2** A steep natural bank. —*v.t.* To furnish with a levee or levees. [< L *levare* to raise]

lev·ee[2] (lev′ē, lə·vē′) *n.* A morning reception or assembly at the house of a sovereign or great personage. [< L *levare* to raise]

lev·el (lev′əl) *adj.* **1** Having a flat and even surface without any variations in height. **2** Conforming to a horizontal plane; not sloping. **3** Having the same height as or being in the same plane with something else. **4** Equal to something or someone in importance, development, rank, etc. **5** Calm; sensible; well-balanced. **6** Even or steady in tone, color, etc. —**one's level best** *Informal* One's very best. —*n.* **1** A horizontal line, surface, plane, or position. **2** A horizontal or flat area of land, etc. **3** The condition of being horizontal: Water seeks its own *level.* **4** Height or altitude. **5** A device for determining a horizontal line or plane; also, a measuring of variations in height by using such a device. **6** Rank or position in any scale of values. —**on the level** *Informal* Honest; fair. —*v.* **lev·eled** or **lev·elled, lev·el·ing** or **lev·el·ling** *v.t.* **1** To give a flat or horizontal surface to: often with *off.* **2** To reduce to the ground: to *level* a building. **3** To bring to a common condition, state, etc. **4** To knock down. **5** To aim or direct, as a rifle, the eyes, etc. —*v.i.* **6** To aim a weapon directly at a mark or target. **7** To bring persons or things to a common state or condition. **8** *Informal* To be honest: Let me *level* with you. —**level off** To fly a plane parallel with the ground. —*adv.* In or on a level line. [< L *libella,* dim. of *libra* balance] —**lev′el·ly** *adv.* —**lev′el·er, lev′el·ler, lev′el·ness** *n.* —**Syn.** *adj.* **1** horizontal, plane, smooth. *v.* **1** smooth. **2** demolish, raze.

lev·el-head·ed (lev′əl·hed′id) *adj.* Having sound common sense; not impulsive. —**lev′el-head′ed·ness** *n.*

lev·er (lev′ər, lē′vər) *n.* **1** A device consisting of a rigid structure, often a straight bar, turning freely on a fixed point (the fulcrum). A force applied at one point of the rigid structure does work at another with a mechanical advantage equal to the ratio of the distances of the points from the fulcrum. **2** Any one of various tools used for prying, as a crowbar. **3** Any means of exerting effective power. —*v.t. & v.i.* To move with or use a lever. [< L *levare* to raise]

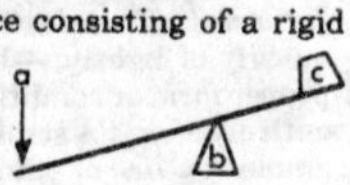

Lever
a. force. b. fulcrum. c. weight.

lev·er·age (lev′ər·ij, lē′vər-) *n.* **1** The action of a lever. **2** The mechanical advantage of a lever. **3** Increased power or advantage.

lev·er·et (lev′ər·it) *n.* A hare less than a year old. [< L *lepus* a hare]

Le·vi (lē′vī) In the Bible: **1** The third son of Jacob. **2** The tribe descended from him.

le·vi·a·than (lə·vī′ə·thən) *n.* **1** A large aquatic but unidentified animal mentioned in the Bible. **2** Anything colossal in size of its kind. [< Heb. *liwyāthān*]

Le·vis (lē′vīz) *n. pl.* Tight-fitting, heavy denim trousers, with rivets inserted at points of greatest strain: a trade name. Also **le′vis.** [< *Levi* Strauss, U.S. manufacturer]

lev·i·tate (lev′ə·tāt) *v.i. & v.t.* **·tat·ed, ·tat·ing** To rise or cause to rise and float in the air. [L *levis* light, on analogy with *gravitate*] —**lev′i·ta′tor** *n.*

lev·i·ta·tion (lev′ə·tā′shən) *n.* **1** The act of levitating or the state of being levitated. **2** The illusion of suspending heavy objects or the human body in the air without support.

Le·vite (lē′vīt) *n.* One of the tribe or family of Levi, acting as assistant to the priests of the tribe.

Le·vit·i·cal (lə·vit′i·kəl) *adj.* Of the Levites, the book of Leviticus, or its laws.

Le·vit·i·cus (lə·vit′i·kəs) *n.* The third book of the Old Testament, containing ceremonial laws.

lev·i·ty (lev′ə·tē) *n. pl.* **·ties** **1** Lightness or humor; lack of gravity in mood, character, or behavior. **2** Fickleness. [< L *levis* light]

lev·u·lose (lev′yə·lōs) *n.* FRUCTOSE. [< L *laevus* left + -UL(E) + -OSE[2]]

lev·y (lev′ē) *v.* **lev·ied, lev·y·ing** *v.t.* **1** To impose (a tax, fine, etc.). **2** To enlist or call up (troops, etc.) for military service. **3** To prepare for or wage (war). —*v.i.* **4** To make a levy. **5** *Law* To seize property in order to fulfill a judgment: usu. with *on.* —*n. pl.* **lev·ies** **1** The act of levying (a tax, troops, etc.). **2** Something levied. [< L *levare* to raise] —**lev′i·er** *n.*

lewd (lo͞od) *adj.* **1** Characterized by lust; lascivious. **2** Obscene; bawdy. [< OE *lǣwede* lay, unlearned] —**lewd′ly** *adv.* —**lewd′ness** *n.* —**Syn.** **1** carnal, lecherous, licentious, lustful. **2** indecent.

lew·is·ite (lo͞o′is·īt) *n.* An organic compound containing arsenic, prepared as a blister-producing poison gas. [< W. L. *Lewis,* 1878–1943, U.S. chemist]

lex (leks) *n. pl.* **le·ges** (lē′jēz) Law. [L]

lex. lexicon.

lexicog. lexicographer; lexicography.

lex·i·cog·ra·phy (lek′sə·kog′rə·fē) *n.* The act, business, or principles of writing or compiling a dictionary. [< Gk. *lexikon* lexicon + *graphein* write] —**lex′i·cog′ra·pher** *n.* —**lex′i·co·graph′ic** (-kō·graf′ik) or **·i·cal** *adj.* —**lex′i·co·graph′i·cal·ly** *adv.*

lex·i·con (lek′sə·kon) *n.* **1** A word list or vocabulary pertaining to a specific subject, field, author, etc. **2** DICTIONARY. [< Gk. *lexikos* pertaining to words]

Ley·den jar (lī′dən) *Electr.* A condenser for static electricity, consisting of a glass jar coated inside and out with metal foil and with a conducting rod passing through the stopper and connected to the inner coating. [< *Leyden,* Netherlands]

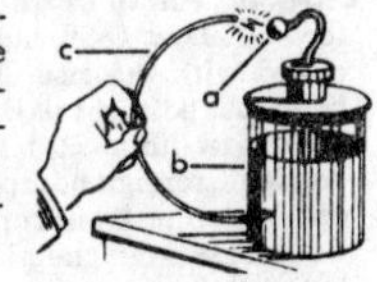

Leyden jar
a. brass rod and ball. b. metal foil. c. discharging wire.

LF, L.F., l.f., l-f. low frequency.

LG, LG., L.G. Low German.

lg. lge. large.

LGk. Late Greek.

lgth. length.

LH, L.H., l.h. left hand.

L.I. Long Island.

Li lithium.

li·a·bil·i·ty (lī′ə·bil′ə·tē) *n. pl.* **·ties** **1** The state of being liable. **2** That for which one is liable. **3** *pl.* Debts or financial obligations. **4** Any drawback or obstacle.

li·a·ble (lī′ə·bəl) *adj.* **1** Justly or legally responsible, as for payment. **2** Inclined to get or have; subject to: *liable* to headaches. **3** Likely; apt: I am *liable* to see them. **4** Undesirably likely: *liable* to lose his money. [< L *ligare* to bind]

li·aise (lē·āz′) *v.i.* **·aised, ·ais·ing** *Chiefly Brit. Informal* To act as an agent or intermediary; communicate. [Back formation < LIAISON]

li·ai·son (lē′ə·zon, lē·ā′zon; *Fr.* lē·ā·zôn′) *n.* **1** A bond or close relationship; union. **2** An illicit sexual relationship. **3** Any form of intercommunication, as between military units, etc. **4** In cookery, a thickening agent. **5** In speaking French, the carrying over of a final consonant to a succeeding word beginning with a vowel or silent *h.* —*adj.* Of, bringing about, or involved in a liaison. [< L *ligare* to bind]

li·an·a (lē·an′ə, -ä′nə) *n.* A twining or climbing plant of tropical forests, with ropelike, woody stems. Also **li·ane** (lē·än′). [< F *liane*]

li·ar (lī′ər) *n.* One who tells lies.

lib (lib) *n. Slang* LIBERATION (def. 2). —**lib′ber** *n.*

Lib. Liberal; Liberia.

lib. book (L *liber*); librarian; library.

li·ba·tion (lī·bā′shən) *n.* **1** The act of pouring out liquid, as in honor of a deity. **2** The liquid poured out. **3** Humorously, a drink. [< L *libare* pour out (as an offering)]

li·bel (lī′bəl) *n. Law* **1** Anything written, drawn, etc., esp. if published or publicly circulated, that tends to damage a person's reputation. **2** The act or crime of publishing or circulating such libel. —*v.t.* **·beled** or **·belled, ·bel·ing** or **·bel·ling** 1 To publish or circulate a libel concerning. 2 To defame or disparage in any way. [< L *libellus,* dim. of *liber* book] —**li′bel·er, li′bel·ler** *n.* • See SLANDER.

li·bel·ous (lī′bəl·əs) *adj.* 1 Containing that which defames or libels. 2 Given to uttering libels. Also **li′bel·lous.** —**li′bel·ous·ly, li′bel·lous·ly** *adv.*

lib·er·al (lib′ər·əl, lib′rəl) *adj.* 1 Generous in giving; bounteous. 2 Abundant; lavish: a *liberal* reward. 3 Of or based on the liberal arts: a *liberal* education. 4 Characterized by or favoring policies of reform and progress and generally opposing conservatism or reaction. 5 Not bigoted or prejudiced; broad-minded. 6 Not restricted to the literal meaning: a *liberal* interpretation of a rule. —*n.* One favoring liberal policies or doctrines, as in politics, religion, etc. Also **lib′er·al·ist.** [< L *liber* free] —**lib′er·al·is′tic** *adj.* —**lib′er·al·ly** *adv.*

Lib·er·al (lib′ər·əl, lib′rəl) *adj.* Of or pertaining to any of various political parties, esp. the Liberal Party of Great Britain or of Canada. —*n.* A member of such a party.

liberal arts The course of study that includes literature, philosophy, languages, history, etc., as distinguished from purely scientific or technical subjects; the humanities.

lib·er·al·ism (lib′ər·əl·iz′əm, -rəl-) *n.* 1 Liberal beliefs or principles, as in politics, religion, etc. 2 The quality or condition of being liberal.

lib·er·al·i·ty (lib′ə·ral′ə·tē) *n. pl.* **·ties** 1 The quality of being liberal. 2 Generosity. 3 Broad-mindedness. 4 A gift; donation.

lib·er·al·ize (lib′ər·əl·īz′) *v.t. & v.i.* **·ized, ·iz·ing** To make or become liberal. —**lib′er·al·i·za′tion** (lib′ər·əl·ə·zā′shən, -ī·zā′-, lib′rəl-), **lib′er·al·iz′er** *n.*

Liberal Party 1 In Great Britain, a political party formed about 1832, but whose power, since 1918, has declined with the rise of the Labour Party. 2 One of the principal political parties of Canada.

lib·er·ate (lib′ə·rāt) *v.t.* **·at·ed, ·at·ing** 1 To set free, as from bondage, foreign occupation, etc. 2 *Informal* To free from oppression or from conventions considered oppressive. 3 To release from chemical combination. [< L *liber* free] —**lib′er·a′tor** *n.*

lib·er·a·tion (lib′ər·ā′shən) *n.* 1 The act of liberating, or the state of being liberated. 2 A political and social movement formed to promote the interests of a group regarded as the object of unfair discrimination or bias: women's *liberation.* —**lib′er·a′tion·ist** *n.*

Li·be·ri·a (lī·bir′ē·ə) *n.* A republic of w Africa, 43,000 sq. mi., cap. Monrovia. —**Li·ber′i·an** *adj., n.* • See map at AFRICA.

lib·er·tine (lib′ər·tēn) *n.* One who does not restrain his desires or appetites; a debauchee. —*adj.* Dissolute; licentious. [< L *liber* free] —**lib′er·tin·ism** *n.*

lib·er·ty (lib′ər·tē) *n. pl.* **·ties** 1 The state of being free in action or thought from the domination of others or from restricting circumstances; freedom. 2 The possession and exercise of the right of self-government. 3 A particular permission, right, or privilege. 4 In the U.S. Navy, permission to be absent from one's ship or station, usu. for less than 48 hours. 5 *Often pl.* Unusual or undue freedom or familiarity. —**at liberty** 1 Free; unconfined. 2 Having permission to do something. 3 Not in use. 4 Unemployed. [< L *libertas* < *liber* free] —**Syn.** 1 emancipation, independence, liberation, self-determination.

Liberty Bell The bell in Independence Hall, Philadelphia, rung July 4, 1776, when the Declaration of Independence was adopted.

Liberty Ship A U.S. merchant ship of about 10,000 tons displacement and built in large numbers during World War II.

li·bid·i·nous (li·bid′ə·nəs) *adj.* Lustful; lewd. [< L *libido* lust] —**li·bid′i·nous·ly** *adv.* —**li·bid′i·nous·ness** *n.*

li·bi·do (li·bē′dō, -bī′-) *n.* 1 *Psychoanal.* The instinctual craving or drive behind all human activities. 2 Sexual desire or instinct. [L, lust] —**li·bid′i·nal** (-bid′ə·nəl) *adj.*

Li·bra (lī′brə, lē′-) *n.* A constellation and the seventh sign of the zodiac; the Scales. [L, a balance] • See ZODIAC.

li·brar·i·an (lī′brâr′ē·ən) *n.* 1 A person in charge of a library. 2 A person qualified by training for library service.

li·brar·y (lī′brer·ē, -brə·rē) *n. pl.* **·brar·ies** 1 A collection of books, pamphlets, computer programs, etc., esp. one arranged for easy location of desired material. 2 A building, room, etc., containing such a collection. [< L *liber* book]

li·bret·tist (li·bret′ist) *n.* A writer of librettos.

li·bret·to (li·bret′ō) *n. pl.* **·tos** or **·ti** (-ē) 1 The words of an opera, oratorio, etc. 2 A book containing these words. [Ital. < L *liber* book]

Lib·ya (lib′ē·ə) *n.* A republic of N Africa, 679,358 sq. mi., caps. Tripoli and Benghazi. —**Lib′y·an** *adj., n.* • See map at AFRICA.

lice (līs) *n.pl.* of LOUSE.

li·cense (lī′səns) *n.* 1 A legal permit to do something. 2 A written or printed certificate of a legal permit. 3 Unrestrained liberty of action; disregard of propriety. 4 Allowable deviation from an established rule, form, or standard: poetic *license.* —*v.t.* **·censed, ·cens·ing** To grant a license to or for; authorize. Also **li′cence.** —**li′cens·a·ble** *adj.* —**li′cens·er, li′cenc·er** *n.*

li·cen·see (lī′sən·sē′) *n.* One to whom a license is granted. Also **li′cen·cee′.**

li·cen·ti·ate (lī·sen′shē·it, -āt) *n.* 1 A person licensed to practice a certain profession: a *licentiate* in dental surgery. 2 In some Continental universities, a person holding a degree intermediate between bachelor and doctor.

li·cen·tious (lī·sen′shəs) *adj.* Morally or sexually unrestrained; wanton; lewd. [< L *licentia* freedom] —**li·cen′tious·ly** *adv.* —**li·cen′tious·ness** *n.*

li·chee (lē′chē) *n.* LITCHI.

li·chen (lī′kən) *n.* Any of numerous low-growing plants composed of an alga and a fungus growing symbiotically, usu. on surfaces inhospitable to higher plants, as bare rock. —*v.t.* To cover with lichens. [< Gk. *leichēn,* lit., licker] —**li′chen·ous** *adj.*

lic·it (lis′it) *adj.* Lawful; permitted. [< L *licere* be allowed] —**lic′it·ly** *adv.*

lick (lik) *v.t.* 1 To pass the tongue over the surface of. 2 To bring to a specified condition by passing the tongue over: to *lick* a surface clean. 3 To take in by the tongue. 4 To move or pass lightly over: The waves *licked* the shore. 5 *Informal* a To defeat. b To thrash; beat. —*v.i.* 6 To move quickly or lightly. —**lick into shape** *Informal* To put in proper form or condition. —**lick up** To consume or devour entirely. —*n.* 1 A stroke of the tongue in licking. 2 A small amount: a *lick* of paint. 3 SALT LICK. 4 *Informal* A blow or whack. 5 *Usu. pl. Informal* An opportunity or turn: to get in one's *licks.* 6 *Informal* A stroke: Not a *lick* of work was done. [< OE *liccian* to lick] —**lick′er** *n.*

lick·er·ish (lik′ə·rish) *adj.* 1 Eager to taste or enjoy. 2 Lustful. [Var. of LECHEROUS] —**lick′er·ish·ly** *adv.* —**lick′er·ish·ness** *n.*

lick·e·ty-split (lik′ə·tē·split′) *adv. Slang* At full speed.

lick·spit·tle (lik′spit′l) *n.* A servile flatterer.

lic·o·rice (lik′ə·rish, -ris) *n.* 1 A perennial plant of the pea family. 2 Its root or a flavoring agent made from it. 3 A usu. black candy having this flavor. [< Gk. *glycyrrhiza* sweet root]

lic·tor (lik′tər) *n.* In ancient Rome, one of the officers or guards attending the chief Roman magistrates and bearing the fasces as a symbol of office. [L]

Lictor

lid (lid) *n.* 1 A movable cover for putting on top of a pan, box, or other receptacle. 2 An eyelid. 3 *Slang* A hat. [< OE *hlid*] —**lid′ded** *adj.*

lie[1] (lī) *v.i.* **lay, lain, ly·ing** 1 To be or place oneself in a horizontal position, as on a bed: often with *down.* 2 To be on or rest against a usu. horizontal surface: The book is *lying* on the shelf. 3 To be or continue in a specified condition or position: to *lie* in ambush. 4 To be situated: Rome *lies* in a plain. 5 To extend in some direction: Our route *lies* northward. 6 To have source or cause; exist: usu. with *in:* His trouble *lies* in his carelessness. 7 To be buried. —**lie (or lay) down on the job** *Informal* To do less than one's best. —**lie in wait (for)** To wait in ambush (for). —**lie low** *Slang* To go into hiding or remain inactive so as to conceal one's motives, plans, etc. —**lie over** To wait for attention, etc., until a later time. —*n.* The position or arrangement in which a thing lies; manner of lying; lay. [OE *licgan*] • See LAY[1].

lie[2] (lī) *n.* 1 An untrue statement intended to deceive; falsehood. 2 Anything that deceives or creates a false impression. —**give the lie to** 1 To accuse of lying. 2 To expose as false. —*v.* **lied, ly·ing** *v.i.* 1 To make untrue statements knowingly, esp. with intent to deceive. 2 To give an erroneous or misleading impression: Figures do not *lie.* —*v.t.* 3 To obtain by lying: He *lied* his way out of trouble. [< OE *licgan*] —**Syn.** *n.* 1 fabrication, falsification, fib, untruth.

Liech·ten·stein (lik′ten·stīn; *Ger.* lēkh′tən·shtīn) *n.* A principality of CEN. Europe, 61 sq. mi., cap. Vaduz.

lied (lēd; *Ger.* lēt) *n. pl.* **lied·er** (lē′dər) *German* A lyric poem or ballad set to music.

Lie·der·kranz (lē′dər·kränts) *n.* A soft cheese with a strong flavor and odor: a trade name.

lie detector A polygraph for recording variations in the pulse, rate of respiration, electrical resistance of the skin, etc., that occur while responding to questions, interpretable as evidence of lying.

lief (lēf) *adv.* Willingly; freely: now only in the phrase **would** (or **had**) **as lief.** [< OE *lēof* dear]

liege (lēj) *adj.* 1 In feudal law: **a** Bound in vassalage to a lord. **b** Having the right to the allegiance of a vassal. 2 Faithful; loyal. —*n.* In feudal law: 1 A vassal; also, a citizen. 2 A lord. [< Med. L *laeticus* free]

lien (lēn, lē′ən) *n.* A legal claim on property, as security for a debt. [< L *ligare* to tie]

lieu (lo͞o) *n.* Place; stead: now only in the phrase **in lieu of.** [< L *locus*]

Lieut. Lieutenant.

lieu·ten·ant (lo͞o·ten′ənt, *Brit.* lef·ten′ənt) *n.* 1 See GRADE. 2 A person who fills the place of a superior, as during his absence. [< F *lieu* place + *tenant,* pr.p. of *tenir* hold] —**lieu·ten′an·cy** *n.*

lieutenant colonel See GRADE.

lieutenant commander See GRADE.

lieutenant general See GRADE.

lieutenant governor 1 An officer authorized to perform the duties of a governor in case of his absence, disability, or death. 2 In Canada, the official head of the government of a province, appointed by the governor general. —**lieu·ten′ant-gov′er·nor·ship′** *n.*

life (līf) *n. pl.* **lives** (līvz) 1 That state in which animals and plants exist which distinguishes them from inorganic substances and is characterized by metabolism, growth, and reproduction. 2 That vital state, the loss of which means death: to give one's *life.* 3 The period of animate existence from birth until death, or a part or specific aspect of it. 4 Any conscious and intelligent existence: *life* after death. 5 Energy and animation; spirit; to put *life* into an enterprise. 6 A source of liveliness, animation, etc.: to be the *life* of the party. 7 A vital property, principle, or essence of something: Rhythm is the *life* of jazz. 8 A living being; a person: Many *lives* were lost. 9 Living things in the aggregate: plant *life.* 10 Human existence or affairs: daily *life* in the city. 11 A certain manner or way of living: the *life* of a recluse. 12 A biography. 13 The duration of efficiency, usefulness, popularity, etc., of anything: the *life* of a machine. 14 In art, the form or shape of something that actually exists: to paint from *life.* —**for dear life** with great urgency or intensity. —**for life** 1 For the remainder of one's existence. 2 To save one's life. —**take life** To kill. —**take one's own life** To kill oneself. —*adj.* 1 Lasting from a given point until death: a *life* sentence. 2 In art, studying from a living model: a *life* class. [< OE *līf*]

life belt A life preserver in the form of a belt.

life·blood (līf′blud′) *n.* 1 The blood necessary to life; vital blood. 2 The essence or vital principle of something.

life·boat (līf′bōt′) *n.* A strong, buoyant boat used in rescuing shipwrecked or drowning persons; esp., one of such boats carried on a ship.

life buoy A life preserver, usu. in the shape of a ring.

life expectancy The statistically probable length of life of a person.

life·guard (līf′gärd′) *n.* An expert swimmer hired by a bathing resort, pool, etc., to protect the safety of bathers.

life insurance 1 Insurance in which a specified sum is paid to the beneficiary or beneficiaries after the death of the insured. 2 Insurance paid to the insured upon reaching a certain age. Also **life assurance.**

life jacket A life preserver in the form of a jacket.

Life jacket

life·less (līf′lis) *adj.* 1 Dead. 2 Inanimate: *lifeless* stone. 3 Wanting in energy, power, vigor, or spirit; dull. 4 Uninhabited by living things. —**life′less·ly** *adv.* —**life′less·ness** *n.* —**Syn.** 1 deceased, defunct. 2 inert. 3 listless, spiritless, torpid.

life·like (līf′līk′) *adj.* Resembling something living; true to life. —**life′like′ness** *n.*

life line 1 Any rope or line used, grasped by, or attached to persons in dangerous situations. 2 Any route for transporting vital supplies, rescuing persons, etc.

life·long (līf′lông′, -long′) *adj.* Lasting or continuing throughout one's life: a *lifelong* handicap.

life preserver A buoyant device, often inflatable, in the form of a belt, jacket, ring, etc., used to keep a person afloat in water.

lif·er (lī′fər) *n. Slang* One serving a prison sentence for life.

life·sav·er (līf′sā′vər) *n.* 1 One who or that which saves drowning persons. 2 *Informal* One who or that which aids a person in need, distress, etc. —**life′sav′ing** *n.*

life-size (līf′sīz′) *adj.* Of natural size; of the size of the object portrayed. Also **life′-sized′.**

life style A person's typical mode of conduct or behavior; a way of living.

life·time (līf′tīm′) *n.* The whole period of one's life. —*adj.* Lasting for the duration of one's life: a *lifetime* job.

life·work (līf′wûrk′) *n.* The work to which one devotes his entire working life.

lift (lift) *v.t.* 1 To raise to a higher position or place; hoist. 2 To hold up or support in the air. 3 To raise to a higher degree or condition; exalt. 4 To make clearly audible; shout: to *lift* a cry. 5 To subject (the face) to plastic surgery, so as to restore an appearance of youth. 6 *Informal* To take surreptitiously; steal; also, to plagiarize. 7 To pay off, as a mortgage. —*v.i.* 8 To put forth effort in order to raise something: All together now, *lift!* 9 To yield to upward pressure; rise. 10 To rise or disperse; dissipate: The fog *lifted.* —*n.* 1 The act or an instance of lifting or rising. 2 The distance through which something rises or is raised. 3 The amount lifted. 4 A machine or device for lifting. 5 A stimulation of the mind or feelings. 6 A rise in condition; promotion. 7 Elevated carriage or position: the *lift* of her chin. 8 Any assistance. 9 A ride in a vehicle offered to a pedestrian. 10 *Brit.* An elevator. 11 A slight rise in the ground. 12 In shoemaking, any layer of material forming the heel. 13 *Aeron.* The vertical component of the aerodynamic force on an aircraft. [< ON *lypta* raise in the air] —**lift′er** *n.*

lift·off (lift′ôf′, -of′) *n.* The vertical ascent of a rocket or spacecraft.

lig·a·ment (lig′ə·mənt) *n.* 1 A band of tough tissue binding together bones, etc., or holding organs in place. 2 A bond or connecting tie. [< L *ligare* to bind] —**lig′a·men′tal, lig′a·men′ta·ry, lig′a·men′tous** *adj.*

li·gate (lī′gāt, lī·gāt′) *v.t.* **·gat·ed, ·gat·ing** To tie with a ligature. —**li·ga′tion** *n.*

lig·a·ture (lig′ə·chər) *n.* 1 The act of tying, binding, or constricting. 2 Something used for this, esp. a thread or wire used in surgery. 3 *Printing* Two or more connected letters, as *fi, ffi, œ.* 4 *Music* A slur or the notes joined by a slur. —*v.t.* **·tured, ·tur·ing** LIGATE. [< L *ligare* to bind]

light[1] (līt) *n.* 1 *Physics* **a** The form of electromagnetic radiation that stimulates the organs of sight, having wavelengths between about 3,900 and 7,700 angstroms. **b** Ultraviolet or infrared light radiation. 2 The natural condition that permits vision; luminosity. 3 The sensation produced by exciting the organs of vision and visual centers of the brain. 4 A source of light, as the sun, a lamp, beacon, etc. **5** That which admits light, as a window. **6** Daylight; dawn. **7** A point of view; aspect; to see things in a new *light.* **8** A flame to kindle something. **9** A traffic signal. **10** A noteworthy or eminent person. **11** In art, the representation of light. **12** A particular expression on the face or in the eyes: a *light* of recognition. —**according to one's lights** In accord with one's principles, abilities, etc. —**come to light** To be exposed or revealed. —**in the light of** In view of; considering —**see the light (of day) 1** To be born or to begin. **2** To comprehend; become enlightened. **3** To come into public knowledge. —**shed light on** To make plain or clear. —*adj.* **1** Full of light; not dark; bright. **2** Giving off light. **3** Of a faint or pale color. —*v.* **light·ed** or **lit, light·ing** *v.t.* **1** To set burning; ignite; kindle. **2** To illuminate or cause to be illuminated: to *light* a lamp. **3** To brighten or animate. **4** To guide or conduct with light: The fires *lighted* him home. —*v.i.* **5** To take fire; start burning. **6** To become bright or luminous; usu. with *up.* [<OE *lēoht*] —**light'er** *n.* —**light'less** *adj.*

light² (līt) *adj.* **1** Having little weight; not heavy. **2** Not heavy in relation to size, bulk, etc.: a *light* car. **3** Below the proper or usual weight: a *light* coin. **4** Having little force: a *light* blow. **5** Not clumsy or heavy in appearance or construction: a *light* building. **6** Less than normal or usual in amount: a *light* snowfall. **7** Easy to digest: a *light* dessert. **8** Well leavened; not coarse: *light* bread. **9** Low in alcoholic content: a *light* wine. **10** Not long or loud: *light* applause. **11** Soft and clear, as a sound or voice. **12** Loose or porous: *light* soil. **13** Easy to do, bear, handle, etc.: a *light* task. **14** Not important or serious: *light* party chatter. **15** Gay; cheerful: a *light* mood. **16** Flighty; giddy: *light* in the head. **17** Loose in morals. **18** Easy; nimble: *light* on one's feet. **19** Meant primarily for entertainment: *light* reading. **20** Easily awakened: a *light* sleeper. **21** Not heavily armed: *light* troops. **22** *Meteorol.* Designating a breeze moving from 4 to 7 miles an hour. —**make light of** To treat or consider as trifling. —*v.i.* **light·ed** or **lit, light·ing 1** To descend and settle down after flight, as a bird; land. **2** To happen or come, as by chance: with *on* or *upon.* **3** To get down, as from a horse; dismount. **4** To fall; strike, as a blow. —**light into** *Slang* **1** To attack. **2** To scold. —**light out** *Slang* To depart in haste. —*adv.* Lightly. [<OE *lēoht, līht*] —**Syn.** *adj.* **4** soft, weak. **6,10** mild, moderate. **15** happy, airy, carefree.

light-armed (līt'ärmd') *adj.* Carrying light weapons.

light·en¹ (līt'n) *v.t.* **1** To illuminate. **2** To make light or more light, as a color. —*v.i.* **3** To become light or more light. **4** To flash or shine. **5** To flash lightning.

light·en² (līt'n) *v.t.* **1** To make less heavy. **2** To reduce the load of: to *lighten* ship. **3** To make less burdensome or oppressive. **4** To relieve from distress; gladden. —*v.i.* **5** To become less heavy. —**Syn. 3** alleviate, lessen, reduce. **4** cheer, encourage, enliven.

light·er¹ (lī'tər) *n.* One who or that which lights something, esp. a device for lighting a cigarette, cigar, or pipe.

light·er² (lī'tər) *n.* A bargelike vessel used in loading or unloading ships lying offshore. —*v.t. & v.i.* To transport (goods) by lighter. [<Du. *lichten* make light, unload]

Lighter

light·er·age (lī'tər·ij) *n.* **1** The price for unloading a ship by lighters. **2** The removal or conveying of a cargo by lighters.

light·face (lī'fās') *n. Printing* Type having light, thin lines. —**light'faced'** *adj.*

light-fin·gered (līt'fing'gərd) *adj.* Skilled at petty theft, esp. at picking pockets.

light-foot·ed (līt'fo͝ot'id) *adj.* Nimble or swift in running or dancing. —**light'-foot'ed·ly** *adv.* —**light'-foot'ed·ness** *n.*

light-head·ed (līt'hed'id) *adj.* **1** Silly; frivolous. **2** Dizzy; delirious. —**light'-head'ed·ly** *adv.* —**light'-head'ed·ness** *n.*

light·heart·ed (līt'här'tid) *adj.* Free from care; gay. —**light'heart'ed·ly** *adv.* —**light'heart'ed·ness** *n.*

light heavyweight A boxer or wrestler weighing between 161 and 175 pounds.

light·house (līt'hous') *n.* A tower equipped with high-power lamps, for guiding ships at night.

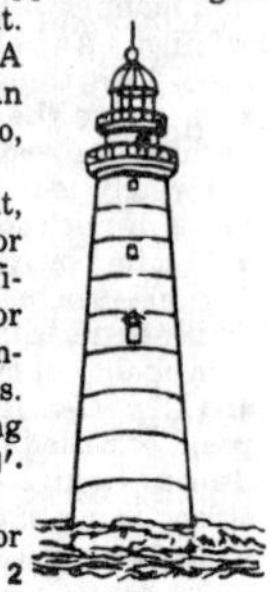
Lighthouse

light·ing (lī'ting) *n.* **1** Illumination. **2** A distribution of light, as in a picture. **3** An arrangement of lights, esp. on a stage; also, the devices providing such light.

light·ly (līt'lē) *adv.* **1** With little weight, force, or pressure. **2** In a slight degree or amount. **3** Gaily; cheerily. **4** With no difficulty; easily. **5** With a light or swift step or motion. **6** Carelessly; heedlessly. **7** Wantonly; irreverently. **8** For slight reasons.

light-mind·ed (līt'mīn'did) *adj.* Lacking seriousness; frivolous; silly. —**light'-mind'ed·ly** *adv.* —**light'-mind'ed·ness** *n.*

light·ness¹ (līt'nis) *n.* **1** The state or quality of being bright or illuminated. **2** Paleness, as of a color.

light·ness² (līt'nis) *n.* **1** The state or quality of having little weight. **2** Cheerfulness. **3** Lack of seriousness; levity. **4** Nimbleness or grace. **5** Lack of severity or hardness.

light·ning (līt'ning) *n.* **1** A sudden discharge of electricity between clouds or between a cloud and the earth. **2** The flash made by this. —*adj.* Fast; rapid: a *lightning* movement. [<ME *lighten* to flash]

lightning bug FIREFLY.

lightning rod A sharp-pointed, grounded metallic conductor used to protect buildings from lightning. Also **lightning conductor.**

light opera OPERETTA.

light pen A pen-shaped electronic device used to generate graphics by drawing with it on a computer screen.

light·ship (līt'ship') *n.* A vessel, having warning lights, signals, etc., moored in dangerous waters as a guide to ships.

light·some (līt'səm) *adj.* **1** Lighthearted. **2** Nimble. **3** Frivolous. —**light'some·ly** *adv.* —**light'some·ness** *n.*

light·weight (līt'wāt') *n.* **1** A boxer or wrestler weighing between 127 and 135 pounds. **2** *Slang* An unimportant, incompetent, or stupid person. —*adj.* **1** Having little weight. **2** Of or pertaining to lightweights. **3** Trivial.

light-year (līt'yir') *n.* The distance that light travels in one year, 5.878 trillion miles: used as a unit of astronomical distance.

lig·ne·ous (lig'nē·əs) *adj.* Composed of or like wood; woody. [<L *lignum* wood]

lig·nite (lig'nīt) *n.* A brownish coal, often retaining the original woody texture, and intermediate between peat and true coal. [<L *lignum* wood] —**lig·nit'ic** (-nit'ik) *adj.*

lig·num vi·tae (lig'nəm vī'tē) *n.* **1** A small tropical American tree. **2** Its greenish brown, hard, heavy wood. [L, lit., wood of life]

like¹ (līk) *v.* **liked, lik·ing** *v.t.* **1** To take pleasure in; enjoy. **2** To have affection or kindly feeling for. **3** To wish; prefer: He would *like* us to do it. —*v.i.* **4** To feel inclined; choose: Do as you *like!* —*n. Usu. pl.* Preference; inclination: one's *likes* and dislikes. [<OE *līcian*] —**lik'a·ble, like'a·ble** *adj.* —**lik'a·ble·ness, like'a·ble·ness, lik'er** *n.* —**Syn.** *v.* **1** appreciate, relish, savor. **2** care for, fancy, love.

like² (līk) *adj.* **1** Similar in qualities, appearance, etc. **2** Identical or nearly identical; equal: Take a *like* amount of plaster. **3** *Regional:* Likely or about to; expected: I am *like* to cry. —**like . . . , like . . .** As the one is, so the other will be: *like* father, *like* son. —*adv.* **1** In the manner of; as if: To run *like* mad. **2** *Informal* Likely: *Like* as not we'll meet again. **3** *Slang* To a certain extent; somewhat: he was fat, *like.* **4** *Slang* Approximately; about: We had *like* two weeks to get ready. **5** *Slang* The point is; you must understand that: modifying a whole clause: *Like,* he had nowhere to go. —*prep.* **1** Similar to; resembling: you look *like* your father. **2** Characteristic of: That's just *like* him! **3** In the mood or frame of mind for: to feel *like* sleeping. **4** So as to indicate, promise, or presage: to look *like* rain. **5** Such as: furs *like* beaver. —**like anything** (or **blazes, the devil,** etc.) *Informal* With great speed, force, violence, etc. —*n.* That which is similar to equivalent to, or of the same nature as, something else. —**the like** (or **likes**) **of** *Informal* Any thing or person like. —*v.i. Regional* To come near: He *liked* (or *had liked*) to have died. —*conj.* 1 *Informal* As; in the manner that: It all happened *like* you said. 2 *Informal* As if: It looks *like* he's going to fall. [< OE *gelīc*] • **like, as** *Like* is nonstandard as a conjunction at the formal level of writing, where clauses being compared are related by *as: He entertained us with great charm, as we knew he would.* At the informal level, because *like* signals a coming comparison more strongly than *as, like* is in widespread use. Moreover, *like* is well accepted informally when it serves to complete a linking verb with the sense of *as if: It sounds like a train's coming; It looks like we're in for trouble.*

-like *suffix of adjectives* Resembling or similar to: *childlike, wavelike, shell-like.*

like·li·hood (līk′lē·ho͝od) *n.* Probability: In all *likelihood,* he will be late.

like·ly (līk′lē) *adj.* **·li·er, ·li·est** 1 Apparently true or real; probable. 2 Reasonably to be expected; liable. 3 Apt to please; promising. 4 Suitable: a *likely* place to swim. —*adv.* Probably.

like-mind·ed (līk′mīn′did) *adj.* Similar in opinions, tastes, etc.

lik·en (lī′kən) *v.t.* To represent as similar; compare.

like·ness (līk′nis) *n.* 1 The state or quality of being like; a resemblance. 2 A copy, picture, or representation. 3 Form; guise: to appear in the *likeness* of an eagle.

like·wise (līk′wīz′) *adv.* 1 In like manner. 2 Also; moreover.

lik·ing (lī′king) *n.* 1 Fondness. 2 Taste; preference.

li·lac (lī′lak, -lək, -lok) *n.* 1 An ornamental shrub having clusters of small, fragrant, usu. purplish flowers. 2 The flower. 3 A light purple color, like that of a lilac. —*adj.* Of a light purple color. [< Pers. *līlak* bluish]

lil·i·a·ceous (lil′ē·ā′shəs) *adj.* Of or pertaining to lilies or plants of the lily family, as onions, hyacinths, etc.

Lil·li·put (lil′i·put, -pət) In Swift's *Gulliver's Travels,* a country inhabited by tiny people.

Lil·li·pu·tian (lil′i·pyo͞o′shən) *adj.* 1 Of Lilliput or its inhabitants. 2 Very small. —*n.* 1 An inhabitant of Lilliput. 2 A very small person.

lilt (lilt) *n.* 1 A brisk, merry song. 2 Rhythmic movement, swing, or flow. —*v.t. & v.i.* To sing or speak in a light, rhythmic manner. [ME *lulte*]

lil·y (lil′ē) *n. pl* **lil·ies** 1 Any of a large genus of bulbous plants having showy, usu. trumpetlike flowers. 2 The flower of these plants. 3 Any of numerous plants resembling the true lilies: *waterlily.* 4 The heraldic fleur-de-lis. —*adj.* Like a white lily; pure and delicate. [< L *lilium*]

Tiger lily

lil·y-liv·ered (lil′ē·liv′ərd) *adj.* Cowardly.

lily of the valley A low liliaceous plant with two leaves and a raceme of white, fragrant, cup-shaped flowers.

lil·y-white (lil′ē·hwīt′) *adj.* 1 White as a lily. 2 Pure; unsullied: often used ironically. 3 Composed of or admitting white people only: a *lily-white* college.

li·ma bean (lī′mə) 1 A common cultivated bean with broad pods. 2 Its large flat edible seed. Also **Li′ma bean.** [< *Lima,* Peru]

limb[1] (lim) *n.* 1 A leg, arm, or wing. 2 A large, major branch of a tree. 3 A person or thing forming a part, branch, or extension of something else. —**out on a limb** *Informal* In a risky position or situation. —*v.t.* To dismember. [< OE *lim*]

limb[2] (lim) *n.* An edge, as of a disk; esp. the edge of the disk of the moon or other heavenly body. [< L *limbus* edge]

limbed (limd) *adj.* Having a specified number or kind of limbs: used in combination: *strong-limbed, four-limbed.*

lim·ber[1] (lim′bər) *adj.* 1 Easily bent; flexible. 2 Lithe and agile; supple. —*v.t. & v.i.* To make or become limber: often with *up.* [?] —**lim′ber·ly** *adv.* —**lim′ber·ness** *n.* —**Syn.** *adj.* 1 elastic, pliable, pliant. 2 lissom, nimble.

lim·ber[2] (lim′bər) *n.* A two-wheeled, detachable vehicle at the forepart of a gun carriage. —*v.t. & v.i.* To attach a limber. [?]

lim·bo (lim′bō) *n.* 1 *Often cap. Theol.* A region on the edge of hell to which are consigned the souls of the righteous who died before the coming of Jesus and the souls of infants who died before baptism. 2 A place of neglect or oblivion for unwanted persons or things. [< L *limbus* border]

Lim·burg·er cheese (lim′bûr·gər) A soft, white cheese with a strong odor. Also **Lim′burg cheese.** [< *Limburg,* Belgium]

lime[1] (līm) *n.* Calcium oxide in either its dry state (**quicklime**) or combined with water (**slaked lime**), used in mortar, cement, and as a conditioner for acid soil. —*v.t.* **limed, lim·ing** To treat or mix with lime. [< OE *līm*]

lime[2] (līm) *n.* 1 A small, acid, citrus fruit with a green rind. 2 The small, semitropical tree bearing this fruit. [< Ar. *limah*]

lime[3] (līm) *n.* LINDEN. [< OE *lind* linden]

lime·kiln (līm′kil′, -kiln′) *n.* A kiln for burning limestone, seashells, etc., to produce lime.

lime·light (līm′līt′) *n.* 1 A powerful light produced by burning lime, originally used in the theatre as a spotlight. 2 A position of prominence or notoriety.

lim·er·ick (lim′ər·ik) *n.* A humorous verse of five anapestic lines. [< *Limerick,* a county in Ireland]

lime·stone (līm′stōn′) *n.* A rock composed wholly or in part of calcium carbonate.

lime·wa·ter (līm′wô′tər, -wot′ər) *n.* A saturated solution of lime in water, used as an antacid.

lime·y (lī′mē) *n. Slang* 1 A British sailor: from the former practice of averting scurvy on long voyages by eating limes. 2 Any Englishman.

lim·it (lim′it) *n.* 1 A boundary enclosing a specified area. 2 *pl.* An area near or enclosed by a boundary: city *limits.* 3 The utmost point, degree, or extent beyond which something no longer functions, avails, etc.: to reach the *limit* of one's patience. 4 The maximum amount permitted: a *limit* of two cans per person. 5 *Math.* A number such that the difference between it and the final term of a sequence of numbers becomes arbitrarily small as the sequence is made arbitrarily long. —**off limits** Forbidden to military personnel except on official business. —**the limit** *Slang* One who or that which is considered intolerable, exasperating, etc. —*v.t.* To keep within a limit; restrict. [< L *limes, limites*] —**lim′it·a·ble, lim·i·ta·tive** (lim′ə·tā′tiv) *adj.* —**lim′it·er** *n.* —**Syn.** *v.* check, circumscribe, restrain, restrict.

lim·i·ta·tion (lim′ə·tā′shən) *n.* 1 The act of limiting or the condition of being limited. 2 Something that limits; restriction. 3 *Law* A period of time fixed by law within which certain acts are to be performed to render them valid.

lim·it·ed (lim′it·id) *adj.* 1 Having or confined to certain limits; restricted. 2 Held in check by law or or a constitution, as a government, monarchy, etc. 3 Making only a few specific stops or carrying only a certain number of passengers, as a train. 4 *Brit. & Can.* Restricted in liability to the amount invested in stock of a business: a *limited* company. —*n.* A limited train, bus, etc. —**lim′i·ted·ly** *adv.* —**lim′i·ted·ness** *n.*

lim·it·ing (lim′it·ing) *adj. Gram.* Designating adjectives that limit or specify rather that describe, as *several, this, two,* etc.

lim·it·less (lim′it·lis) *adj.* Without limits; infinite; boundless.

limn (lim) *v.t.* 1 To draw or paint. 2 To describe in words. [< L *lumen* light] —**lim·ner** (lim′ər, -nər) *n.*

Li·moges ware (lē·mōzh′; *Fr.* lē·môzh′) A type of fine porcelain manufactured at Limoges, France.

lim·ou·sine (lim′ə·zēn′, lim′ə·zēn) *n.* 1 A large automobile, originally with a closed compartment for passengers, and a roof projecting over the driver's open seat. 2 Any large, luxurious automobile. [< *Limousin,* France]

limp[1] (limp) *v.i.* 1 To walk with a halting or irregular gait. 2 To proceed in a defective or irregular manner: His logic *limps.* —*n.* The step of a lame person [?] —**limp′er** *n.*

limp[2] (limp) *adj.* 1 Lacking stiffness; flaccid. 2 Not positive, firm, or vigorous. [?] —**limp'ly** *adv.* —**limp'ness** *n.*

lim·pet (lim'pit) *n.* Any of several usu. marine gastropods with a small conical shell, that clings to underwater plants, rocks, etc. [<LL *lampreda* lamprey]

lim·pid (lim'pid) *adj.* 1 Characterized by liquid clearness; transparent. 2 Clear and intelligible; lucid: a *limpid* style. [<L *limpidus* clear] —**lim·pid·i·ty** (lim·pid'ə·tē), **lim'pid·ness** *n.* —**lim'pid·ly** *adv.*

lim·y (lī'mē) *adj.* **lim·i·er lim·i·est** 1 Containing or covered with lime or birdlime. 2 Resembling lime.

lin. lineal; linear.

lin·age (lī'nij) *n.* 1 The number of lines of printed or written matter. 2 Payment based on lines written.

linch·pin (linch'pin') *n.* A pin through that part of an axle outside the wheel, to keep a wheel in place. [<OE *lynis* linchpin + PIN]

lin·den (lin'dən) *n.* Any of a genus of trees with heart-shaped leaves and usu. fragrant, cream-colored flowers. [<OE *lind* linden, lime tree]

line[1] (līn) *n.* 1 A string, rope, or cord, as used for hanging clothes, fishing, measuring, etc. 2 A pipe, wire, cable, etc., for conveying electricity, gas, oil, etc. 3 In a telephone or telegraph system: **a** A wire or cable conducting communication signals between two stations. **b** The system as a whole. **c** A connection in such a system. 4 Any slender mark or stroke, as drawn with a pen, pencil, tool, etc. 5 Something resembling this, as a band or strip. 6 A furrow or wrinkle on the face or hands. 7 In art, a mark or stroke used to represent a form or forms, as distinguished from shading or color. 8 *Music* One of the parallel horizontal strokes that form a musical staff. 9 A boundary or border: the Mason-Dixon *line.* 10 Contour; outline: the shore *line.* 11 *Geog.* **a** The equator. **b** Any circle, arc, or boundary used to plot the earth's surface: the date *line.* 12 *Math.* A set of points, straight or curved, conceived of as having length without breadth or thickness. 13 A row of persons or things. 14 A row of printed or written words bounded by the margins of a page or column. 15 A single row of words forming a verse of poetry. 16 A short letter; note. 17 *pl.* The words of a play or of an actor's part. 18 Alignment. 19 Agreement; conformity: Bring him into *line.* 20 A division or demarcation between contrasting qualities, classes, etc. 21 A course of action, thought, procedure, etc.: a *line* of argument. 22 A course of movement; route: the *line* of march. 23 General plan, concept, or construction: a novel on heroic *lines.* 24 One's business, vocation, or branch of activity. 25 Extent or scope of one's talent, ability, etc.: Comedy is not in his *line.* 26 Merchandise of a particular type or quality: the cheap *line.* 27 A series of persons or things connected chronologically: the *line* of senators from Ohio. 28 Lineage; ancestry. 29 A railroad track or roadbed. 30 Any system of public transportation. 31 *Mil.* **a** A series of fortifications presenting an extended front. **b** A trench or rampart. **c** An arrangement or disposition of troops: the front *line.* **d** Combat forces, as distinguished from the staff, special services, etc. 32 In football: **a** The linemen collectively. **b** LINE OF SCRIMMAGE. 33 *Informal* **a** A glib manner of speech. **b** The words spoken in this manner, intended to sway or influence —**draw the (a) line** To establish a limit. —**get a line on** *Informal* To get information about. —**hold the line** 1 To stand firm. 2 To prevent others from advancing. —**in line for** Next in succession for. —**toe the line** To obey; behave. —*v.* **lined, lin·ing** *v.t.* 1 To mark with lines. 2 To place in a line; bring into alignment or conformity: often with *up.* 3 To form a line along: Police *lined* the side of the road. 4 To place something in a line along: to *line* a wall with archers. 5 In baseball, to bat (the ball) in a line drive. —*v.i.* 6 To form a line: usu. with *up.* —**line out** In baseball, to be retired by batting a line drive to a fielder. —**line up** 1 To form a line. 2 To bring into alignment. 3 To organize for or against some activity, issue, etc. [<L *linea* linen thread]

line[2] (līn) *v.t.* **lined, lin·ing** 1 To apply a covering or layer to the inside surface of. 2 To serve as a covering or surface for: Paintings *lined* the wall. 3 To fill or supply: to *line* one's pockets with candy. [<OE *līn* flax]

lin·e·age[1] (lin'ē·ij) *n.* 1 Direct descent from a progenitor. 2 Ancestry; family. [<L *linea* line]

line·age[2] (lī'nij) *n.* LINAGE.

lin·e·al (lin'ē·əl) *adj.* 1 Of or being in a direct line of descent. 2 Based upon or derived from ancestors; hereditary. 3 Made of lines; linear. —**lin'e·al·ly** *adv.*

lin·e·a·ment (lin'ē·ə·mənt) *n.* 1 An outline or contour, esp. of the face. 2 A distinguishing feature of the face.

lin·e·ar (lin'ē·ər) *adj.* 1 Pertaining to or composed of lines. 2 Very narrow and long: a *linear* leaf. • See LEAF. 3 Denoting a measurement in one dimension.

linear measure 1 Measurement by length. 2 A unit or system of units for measuring length.

line·back·er (līn'bak'ər) *n.* In football, a defensive player whose normal position is just behind the line of scrimmage. —**line'back'ing** *n.*

line drive In baseball, a ball batted with such force as to travel almost parallel to the ground.

line·man (līn'mən) *n. pl.* **·men** (-mən) 1 In surveying, a man who holds the tape, line, or chain. 2 A man who installs or repairs lines, as for electricity, telephones, etc. 3 A man who inspects railroad tracks. 4 In football, one of the players making up the line, which includes the center, two guards, two tackles and two ends.

lin·en (lin'in) *n.* 1 A thread or fabric spun or woven from the fibers of flax. 2 Articles made of linen but now often of cotton: bed *linen,* table *linen.* —*adj.* Made of linen. [<OE *līn* flax]

line of force *Physics* A line in a field of force tangent to the direction of the force at each of its points.

line of scrimmage In football, the imaginary line, parallel to the goal lines, on which the ball rests and along which the opposing linemen take position at the start of play.

lin·er[1] (lī'nər) *n.* 1 A ship, aircraft, etc., operated commercially by a specific line. 2 One who or that which marks or traces lines. 3 In baseball, a line drive.

lin·er[2] (lī'nər) *n.* 1 One who makes linings. 2 A lining, or a piece used in forming a lining.

lines·man (līnz'mən) *n. pl.* **·men** (-mən) 1 In tennis, the official watching the lines of the court for faults. 2 In football, the official marking the distances gained or lost in each play. 3 LINEMAN.

line·up (līn'up') *n.* 1 In football, basketball, etc.: **a** The arrangement of players when drawn up for action. **b** Those players who are going to start in the game. 2 Suspects in crime lined up for identification and questioning. 3 An array of people united by some common aim or purpose. Also **line'-up'.**

ling[1] (ling) *n.* 1 A codlike food fish of the North Atlantic. 2 BURBOT. [ME *leng*]

ling[2] (ling) *n.* HEATHER. [<ON *lyng*]

-ling *suffix of nouns:* 1 Little; young; *duckling.* 2 A person or thing related to or characterized by: *worldling.* [<OE]

lin·ger (ling'gər) *v.i.* 1 To stay on as if reluctant to leave. 2 To move slowly; saunter: to *linger* on the way. 3 To delay or be slow: often with *over:* to *linger* over a meal. 4 To continue in life —*v.t.* 5 To pass (time) slowly or idly: with *away* or *out.* [<OE *lengen* to delay] —**lin'ger·er** *n.* —**Syn.** 1 dawdle, delay. 2 hang back, lag, loiter.

lin·ge·rie (län'zhə·rē) *n.* Women's underwear. [<F *linge* linen]

lin·go (ling'gō) *n. pl.* **lin·goes** 1 Language, esp. if strange or unintelligible. 2 The specialized vocabulary and idiom of a profession, class, etc.: medical *lingo.* [<L *lingua* tongue]

lin·gua fran·ca (ling'gwə frang'kə) 1 A mixture of French, Spanish, Italian, Greek, and Arabic, spoken in the Mediterranean ports. 2 Any mixed jargon used as a commercial or trade language, such as pidgin English. [Ital., lit., language of the Franks]

lin·gual (ling'gwəl) *adj.* 1 Pertaining to the tongue. 2 Pertaining to the use of the tongue in utterance. —*n. Phonet.* A sound pronounced chiefly with the tongue, as (t), (d), and (l). [<L *lingua* the tongue]

lin·guist (ling'gwist) *n.* 1 One who knows many languages. 2 An authority in linguistics. [<L *lingua* the tongue + -IST]

lin·guis·tic (ling·gwis'tik) *adj.* Of or pertaining to language or to linguistics. Also **lin·guis'ti·cal.** —**lin·guis'ti·cal·ly** *adv.*

lin·guis·tics (ling·gwis′tiks) *n. pl. (Construed as singular)* The science of language, its origin, structure, modifications, etc., including phonetics, phonemics, morphology, syntax, and semantics.

lin·i·ment (lin′ə·mənt) *n.* A medicated liquid used externally to soothe sprains, muscular soreness, etc. [<L *linire* anoint]

lin·ing (lī′ning) *n.* Material used to line something, often by being attached: the *lining* of a skirt.

link[1] (lingk) *n.* **1** One of the loops or rings of which a chain is made. **2** Something which connects separate things; a tie: a *link* with the past. **3** A single part or element in a whole: the weak *link* in his story. **4** A section of a chain of sausages. **5** A measure equal to 7.92 inches, used in surveying. **6** *Chem.* BOND. —*v.t. & v.i.* To connect by or as by links; unite. [<Scand.] —**Syn.** *v.* attach, combine, fuse, join.

link[2] (lingk) *n.* A torch. [?]

link·age (ling′kij) *n.* **1** The act of linking, or the state of being linked. **2** A series or system of links.

linking verb A verb that merely connects the subject and the predicate complement of a sentence without asserting action, as the verbs *be, appear, become, feel,* etc.

links (lingks) *n. pl.* GOLF COURSE. [<OE *hlic* slope]

link·up (lingk′up′) *n.* **1** A linking together; contact: the *linkup* of space vehicles. **2** A pooling or combining, as of resources or efforts.

lin·net (lin′it) *n.* Any of various small, Old World songbirds related to finches. [<L *linum* flax; from its feeding on flax seeds]

lino. linotype.

li·no·le·um (li·nō′lē·əm) *n.* A floor covering with a smooth, washable surface, made of oxidized linseed oil, ground cork, pigments, etc., pressed into a flat sheet. [<L *linum* flax + *oleum* oil]

Li·no·type (lī′nə·tīp) *n.* A typesetting machine, operated by a keyboard, which casts a complete line of type on a single metal bar: a trade name. Also **li·no·type.** —**li′no·typ′er, li′no·typ′ist** *n.*

lin·seed (lin′sēd′) *n.* FLAXSEED. [<OE *līn* flax + SEED]

linseed oil An oil made from flaxseed, used in oil paints, linoleum, etc.

lin·sey-wool·sey (lin′zē·wŏŏl′zē) *n. pl.* —**wool·seys** A cloth made of linen and wool or cotton and wool mixed. [ME *lynsy-wolsye*]

lint (lint) *n.* **1** The soft down of raveled or scraped linen. **2** Fuzzy bits of thread, cloth, etc. [<L *linum* flax] —**lint′y** *adj.* (**·i·er, ·i·est**)

lin·tel (lin′təl) *n.* horizontal top piece, as over a doorway or window opening. [<L *limes, limites* limit]

lint·ers (lin′tərz) *n. pl.* Cotton fuzz and fibers left behind on a cotton gin, used as batting, for stuffing upholstery, etc.

li·on (lī′ən) *n.* **1** A large, tawny carnivore of the cat family, native to Africa and Asia, the adult male having a long mane. **2** An animal resembling the lion, as the cougar. **3** A person of great courage, strength, etc. **4** A prominent or notable person. [<Gk. *leōn*]

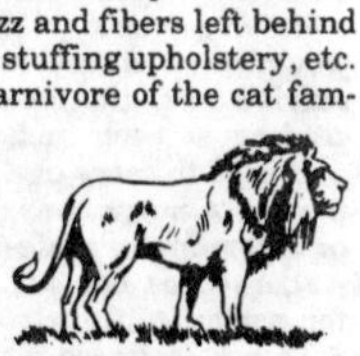

Lion

Li·on (lī′ən) *n.* LEO.

li·on·ess (lī′ən·is) *n.* A female lion.

li·on·heart·ed (lī′ən·härt′tid) *adj.* Brave; courageous.

li·on·ize (lī′ən·īz) *v.t.* **·ized, ·iz·ing** To treat or regard as a celebrity. —**li′on·i·za′tion** *n.*

lip (lip) *n.* **1** One of the two folds of flesh that cover the mouth. **2** Something resembling a lip, as the edge of a wound. **3** Any edge or rim of a cavity or something hollow. **4** A projecting or flared edge, as on a bell, pitcher, spout, etc. **5** EMBOUCHURE. **6** *Slang* Impertinent speech; sass. **7** *Anat.* LABIUM. **8** *Bot.* Any liplike structure, as the lower petal of an orchid. —**bite one's lips** To refrain from showing anger, annoyance, etc. —**hang on (someone's) lips** To listen to with great attention. —**keep a stiff upper lip** To keep up one's courage; be stoical. —*v.t.* **lipped, lip·ping** To touch with the lips; esp., to kiss. —*adj.* **1** Of, formed by, or applied to the lips. **2** Superficial; insincere: *lip* service. [<OE *lippa*]

lip·oid (lip′oid) *adj.* Of or like fat. [<Gk. *lipos* fat + -OID]

lip·o·suc·tion (lip′ō·suk′shən) *n.* The surgical removal of fat cells from bodily tissue by vacuum suction.

lipped (lipt) *adj.* Having a lip or lips: used in combination: *tight-lipped.*

lip-read (lip′rēd) *v.t. & v.i.* **-read, -read·ing** To interpret (speech) by lip reading.

lip reading Interpretation of speech by watching the position of the lips and mouth of the speaker, practiced esp. by the deaf. —**lip reader**

lip·stick (lip′stik′) *n.* A small, colored cosmetic stick of creamy texture, used to tint lips.

lip-sync (lip′singk) *v.t. & v.i.* To synchronize movements of the lips and mouth with sound recorded earlier, esp. a singer's voice.

liq. liquid; liquor.

liq·ue·fac·tion (lik′wə·fak′shən) *n.* The process of liquefying or the state of being liquefied.

liq·ue·fy (lik′wə·fī) *v.t. & v.i.* **·fied, ·fy·ing** To convert into or become liquid. [<L *liquere* be liquid + *facere* make]

li·ques·cent (li·kwes′ənt) *adj.* Being or having a tendency to become liquid. —**li·ques′cence, li·ques′cen·cy** *n.*

li·queur (li·kûr′) *n.* A strong alcoholic beverage, usu. sweet and having various flavorings; a cordial. [<OF *licur* liquor]

liq·uid (lik′wid) *adj.* **1** Flowing or capable of flowing. **2** *Physics* Composed of molecules having free movement among themselves, but without a tendency to expand indefinitely like a gas. **3** Limpid; clear. **4** Smooth and flowing, as movements or sounds. **5** *Phonet.* Vowellike in production, as the consonants (l) and (r). **6** Easily converted into cash: *liquid* assets. —*n.* **1** A liquid substance. **2** *Phonet.* The consonants (l) and (r). [<L *liquere* be liquid] —**li·quid·i·ty** (li·kwid′ə·tē), **liq′uid·ness** *n.* —**liq′uid·ly** *adv.*

liq·ui·date (lik′wə·dāt) *v.* **·dat·ed, ·dat·ing** *v.t.* **1** To determine and settle the liabilities of (an estate, firm, etc.) and apportion the assets. **2** To determine and settle the amount of, as indebtedness or damages. **3** To pay, as a debt. **4** To convert into cash. **5** To do away with, esp. to murder. —*v.t.* **6** To settle one's debts. [<Med. L *liquidare* make liquid or clear] —**liq′ui·da′tor** *n.*

liq·ui·da·tion (lik′wə·dā′shən) *n.* The act of liquidating or the state of being liquidated. —**go into liquidation** To cease from transacting business and gather in assets, settle debts, and divide surpluses, if any.

liquid measure A unit or system of units for measuring liquids. • See MEASURE.

liq·uor (lik′ər) *n.* **1** Any alcoholic drink, esp. one that is distilled. **2** A liquid, as broth, milk, etc. —*v.t.* **1** *Slang* To ply with alcoholic liquor: often with *up.* —*v.i.* **2** *Slang* To drink alcoholic liquor, esp. in quantity: usu. with *up.* [<L *liquor*]

liq·uo·rice (lik′ə·ris, -rish) *n.* LICORICE.

li·ra (lir′ə; *Ital.* lē′rä) *n. pl.* **li·re** (lir′ə; *Ital.* lē′rā) **1** A small coin and the basic monetary unit of Italy. **2** The Turkish pound, the basic monetary unit of Turkey. **3** *pl.* **lir·oth** or **lir·ot** The Israeli pound, the basic monetary unit of Israel.

lisle (līl) *n.* A fine, strong, twisted cotton thread, used in knitting stockings, etc. [<*Lisle,* now Lille, France]

lisp (lisp) *n.* **1** A speech defect or affectation in which the sibilants (s) and (z) are pronounced like (th) in *thank* and (th) in *this.* **2** The act or habit of speaking with a lisp. **3** The sound of a lisp. —*v.t. & v.i.* **1** To pronounce or speak with a lisp. **2** To speak imperfectly or in a childlike manner. [<OE *wlispian*] —**lisp′er** *n.*

lis·some (lis′əm) *adj.* **1** Flexible; lithe. **2** Nimble; agile. Also **lis′som.** [Alter. of LITHESOME] —**lis′some·ly** *adv.*

list[1] (list) *n.* A series of words, numbers, names, etc.; a roll or catalogue. —*v.t.* To place on or in a list or catalogue, esp. in alphabetical or numerical order. [<OF *liste*]

list[2] (list) *n.* **1** The selvage or edge of a woven textile fabric. **2** A strip of fabric, wood, etc. **3** A colored stripe. —*adj.* Made of list. —*v.t.* **1** To edge with lists of cloth. **2** To sew or arrange in strips or stripes. [<OE *līste*]

list[3] (list) *v.t. & v.i.* To lean or incline to one side, as a ship. —*n.* A leaning or inclination to one side. [< OE *lystan* please]

list[4] (list) *v.t. & v.i. Archaic* To listen to or listen. [< OE *hlyst* hearing]

lis·ten (lis′ən) *v.i.* **1** To make an effort to hear; give ear. **2** To pay attention, as to warning or advice. —**listen in 1** To overhear others talking, esp. on a telephone. **2** To hear a radio program. —*n.* The act of listening. [< OE *hlysnan*] —**lis′ten·er** *n.* —**Syn.** *v.* **1** attend, hearken. **2** heed.

list·er (lis′tər) *n. Agric.* A plow having a double moldboard for throwing up ridges on both sides of the furrow.

list·ing (lis′ting) *n.* **1** LIST[1]. **2** A place or item in a list. **3** The act of including an item in a list or of compiling a list.

list·less (list′lis) *adj.* Inattentive or indifferent, as from lack of energy or spirit; languid. [< OE *lust* desire + -LESS] —**list′less·ly** *adv.* —**list′less·ness** *n.*

list price The price of goods as published in price lists or catalogues.

lists (lists) *n. pl.* **1** A jousting field or the barriers surrounding it. **2** A jousting tournament. **3** Any area of combat. —**enter the lists** To accept a challenge; enter combat. [< OF *liste* border]

lit (lit) A *p.t. & p.p.* of LIGHT[1] and LIGHT[2].

lit. liter; literal; literally; literary; literature.

lit·a·ny (lit′ə·nē) *n. pl.* **·nies 1** A form of prayer, consisting of a series of supplications said by the clergy, to which the choir or people repeat the same response. **2** Any repetitive listing or dreary account. [< Gk. *litaneuein* pray]

li·tchi (lē′chē) *n.* **1** A Chinese evergreen tree of the soapberry family, producing small, thin-shelled, edible fruits called, when dried, **litchi nuts**. **2** The fruit of this tree. [< Chin. *li-chih*]

-lite *combining form Mineral.* Stone; stonelike: *cryolite*. [< Gk. *lithos* stone]

li·ter (lē′tər) *n.* The basic metric unit of volume or capacity, equal to the volume of one kilogram of water at 4°C and 760 mm. atmospheric pressure; 10^{-3} (0.001) cubic meter or about 1.06 liquid quarts. [< Gk. *litra* pound]

lit·er·a·cy (lit′ər·ə·sē) *n.* The state of being literate.

lit·er·al (lit′ər·əl) *adj.* **1** Strictly based on the exact, standard meanings of the words or expressions: a *literal* interpretation of the Bible. **2** Following the exact words or construction of the original: a *literal* translation. **3** Matter-of-fact; unimaginative: a *literal* person. **4** Exact as to fact or detail; not exaggerated. [< L *littera* letter] —**lit′er·al′i·ty, lit′er·al·ness** *n.*

lit·er·al·ism (lit′ər·əl·iz′əm) *n.* **1** Close adherence to the exact word or sense. **2** REALISM (def. 2). —**lit′er·al·ist** *n.*

lit·er·al·ly (lit′ər·ə·lē) *adv.* **1** In a literal manner. **2** *Informal* In a manner of speaking; figuratively: used for emphasis: He was *literally* green with envy.

lit·er·ar·y (lit′ə·rer′ē) *adj.* **1** Of, pertaining to, or used in literature. **2** Versed in or devoted to literature. **3** Engaged or occupied in the field of literature: a *literary* man. —**lit′er·ar′i·ly** *adv.* —**lit′er·ar′i·ness** *n.*

lit·er·ate (lit′ər·it) *adj.* **1** Able to read and write. **2** Educated; well-read. **3** LITERARY (def. 2). **4** Clear; lucid. —*n.* A literate person. [< L *littera* letter]

lit·e·ra·ti (lit′ə·rä′tē) *n. pl.* Educated, cultured, or literary people collectively.

lit·e·ra·tim (lit′ə·rä′tim, -rā′-) *adv.* Letter for letter; with exact literalness; literally. [L]

lit·er·a·ture (lit′ər·ə·cho͝or, lit′rə·chər) *n.* **1** Written or printed works collectively, esp. those works characterized by creativeness and imagination, as poetry, fiction, essays, etc. **2** The writings that pertain to a particular epoch, country, language, or branch of learning: French *literature*. **3** The act or occupation of producing literary works. **4** *Music* The total number of compositions for a particular instrument or ensemble. **5** Any printed matter: campaign *literature*. [< L *littera* letter]

-lith *combining form* Stone; rock: *monolith*. [< Gk. *lithos* a stone]

Lith. Lithuania; Lithuanian.

lith., litho., lithog. lithograph; lithography.

lith·arge (lith′ärj, li·thärj′) *n.* A yellow or red oxide of lead used in glassmaking, storage batteries, etc. [< Gk. *lithos* stone + *argyros* silver]

lithe (līth) *adj.* Bending easily; limber. [< OE *lithe*] —**lithe′ly** *adv.* —**lithe′ness** *n.*

lithe·some (līth′səm) *adj.* Lithe; nimble.

lith·i·a (lith′ē·ə) *n.* A white, alkaline compound of lithium and oxygen. [< Gk. *lithos* stone]

-lithic *combining form* Pertaining to a (specified) stage in the use of stone: *neolithic*.

lith·i·um (lith′ē·əm) *n.* A very light, soft metallic element (symbol Li) having properties similar to sodium. [< Gk. *lithos* stone]

litho- *combining form* Stone; related to stone. [< Gk. *lithos* stone]

lith·o·graph (lith′ə·graf, -gräf) *v.t.* To produce or reproduce by lithography. —*n.* A lithographic print. [LITHO- + -GRAPH] —**li·thog·ra·pher** (li·thog′rə·fər) *n.* —**lith′o·graph′·ic** or **·i·cal** *adj.* —**lith′o·graph′i·cal·ly** *adv.*

li·thog·ra·phy (li·thog′rə·fē) *n.* The art of producing printed matter from a stone or metal plate on which the design or matter to be printed consists of a material that accepts ink, the other parts being ink-repellent.

lith·o·sphere (lith′ə·sfir) *n.* The crust of the earth.

li·thot·o·my (li·thot′ə·mē) *n. pl.* **·mies** A surgical operation to remove a stone from the bladder. [< Gk. *lithos* stone + *temnein* to cut] —**lith·o·tom·ic** (lith′ə·tom′ik) or **·i·cal** *adj.*

Lith·u·a·ni·an (lith′o͞o·ā′nē·ən) *adj.* Of or pertaining to Lithuania, its people, or their language. —*n.* **1** A native or citizen of Lithuania. **2** The Balto-Slavic language of the Lithuanians.

lit·i·gant (lit′ə·gənt) *adj.* Engaged in litigation. —*n.* A party to a lawsuit.

lit·i·gate (lit′ə·gāt) *v.* **·gat·ed, ·gat·ing** *v.t.* **1** To bring before a court of law. —*v.i.* **2** To carry on a lawsuit. [< L < *lis, litis* lawsuit + *agere* do, act] —**lit′i·ga·ble** (-gə·bəl) *adj.* —**lit′i·ga′tor** *n.*

lit·i·ga·tion (lit′ə·gā′shən) *n.* **1** The act of litigating. **2** A lawsuit.

li·tig·ious (li·tij′əs) *adj.* **1** Inclined to carry on litigations. **2** Subject to litigation. **3** Of or pertaining to litigation. —**li·tig′ious·ly** *adv.* —**li·tig′ious·ness** *n.*

lit·mus (lit′məs) *n.* A dyestuff made from various lichens which turns red in an acid and blue in a basic medium. [< ON *litr* color + *mosi* moss]

litmus paper An acid and alkali indicator made of paper colored with litmus.

li·tre (lē′tər) *n.* LITER.

lit·ter (lit′ər) *n.* **1** The offspring borne at one time by a cat, dog, or other multiparous animal. **2** A stretcher used for conveying sick or wounded. **3** A couch carried on shafts protruding at each end, and used to carry one person. **4** Straw, hay, or other similar material, used as bedding for horses, cattle, etc. **5** Things scattered about in disorder. **6** Discarded trash scattered about, as in a public park or street. —*v.t.* **1** To bring forth young: said of animals. **2** To furnish, as cattle, with litter. **3** To cover or strew with or as with litter. **4** To throw or spread about carelessly. —*v.i.* **5** To give birth to a litter of young. **6** To strew trash, garbage, etc., about. [< L *lectus* bed] —**lit′ter·y** *adj.*

Litter *def. 3*

lit·té·ra·teur (lit′ər·ə·tûr′) *n.* A professional literary man, esp. a writer. Also **lit′ter·a·teur′**. [F]

lit·ter·bug (lit′ər·bug′) *n. Informal* A person who litters sidewalks, parks, and other public places.

lit·tle (lit′l) *adj.* **less** or **lit·tler, least** or **lit·tlest 1** Small or comparatively small in size: a *little* car. **2** Small or smaller than is usual in amount, degree, or scope: a *little* talent. **3** Being in the early years of life: when I was *little*. **4** Below the normal distance or time; brief. **5** Insignificant; trivial: a *little* quarrel. **6** Narrow-minded; mean: a *little* nature. **7** Lacking effectiveness, force, intensity, etc.: *little* perseverance. —*n.* A small quantity, space, time, degree, etc. —**little by little** By small degrees or amounts; gradually.

—**make little of** To treat as unimportant. —**think little of 1** To regard as unimportant or trivial. **2** To have no hesitation or reluctance about. —*adv.* **less, least 1** In a small degree; slightly. **2** Not at all: used before a verb: She *little* knows how much I care. [<OE *lytel*] —**lit'tle·ness** *n.*

Little Bear URSA MINOR.

Little Dipper A group of stars, somewhat dipper-shaped; Ursa Minor. • See URSA MINOR.

little magazine A usu. noncommercial magazine that publishes new or experimental writing and art work.

little slam In bridge, the winning of 12 tricks in one round of play.

little theater 1 A theater primarily for the production of low-cost or experimental drama. **2** The drama produced in these theaters.

lit·to·ral (lit'ər·əl) *n.* A shore and the country contiguous to it. —*adj.* Of or on the shore. [<L *litus, litoris* seashore]

li·tur·gi·cal (li·tûr'ji·kəl) *adj.* Of, pertaining to, or used in liturgies. Also **li·tur'gic.** —**li·tur'gi·cal·ly** *adv.*

lit·ur·gy (lit'ər·jē) *n. pl.* **·gies 1** A collection of prescribed forms for public worship. **2** The Eucharistic rite. [<Gk. *leitourgia* public duty]

liv·a·ble (liv'ə·bəl) *adj.* **1** Agreeable or fit for living in or with. **2** Endurable. Also **live'a·ble.** —**liv'a·ble·ness, live'a·ble·ness** *n.*

live[1] (liv) *v.* **lived, liv·ing** *v.i.* **1** To be alive; have life. **2** To continue in life. **3** To endure or persist; last: This day will *live* in infamy. **4** To maintain life; subsist: to *live* on a pittance. **5** To depend for food; feed: with *on* or *upon:* to *live* on carrion. **6** To dwell; abide. **7** To conduct or pass one's life in a specified manner: to *live* frugally. **8** To enjoy a varied and active life. —*v.t.* **9** To pass: to *live* the life of a saint. **10** To practice in one's life: to *live* a lie. —**live down** To live in such a manner as to expiate or erase the memory of (a crime, error, shame, etc.). —**live high** To live luxuriously. —**live in** To reside, as a domestic, at one's place of employment. —**live through** To have experience of and survive. —**live up to** To fulfill the hopes, terms, or character of. [<OE *lifian* live]

live[2] (līv) *adj.* **1** Possessing life; living; alive. **2** Of or pertaining to life or living beings. **3** Burning or glowing: a *live coal.* **4** Of present interest and importance; vital: a *live* topic. **5** Possessing liveliness; energetic. **6** In television, radio, etc., transmitted directly to audiences at the time of performance rather than being filmed or recorded. **7** In records, tapes, etc., performed and recorded before an audience. **8** Unexploded: a *live* shell. **9** Carrying an electrical current: a *live* wire. **10** Ready for printing: *live* type; also, ready for typecasting: *live* copy. **11** Swarming with living creatures. **12** Pure; vivid: *live* color. **13** In mechanics, having ability to impart motion or force. **14** In sports, being in play: a *live* ball. [Short for ALIVE]

-lived *combining form* Having a (specified kind of) life or life span or (a given number of) lives: *long-lived, nine-lived.* [<LIFE] • Having been formed from *life, -lived* is properly pronounced (līvd). The prounounciation (livd) is based on the mistaken assumption that the verb *live* is the source of *-lived.*

live-in (liv'in') *adj.* Living at the home or other place where one works: a *live-in* housekeeper.

live·li·hood (līv'lē·hŏŏd) *n.* Means of maintaining life: subsistence. [<ME <OE *līf* life + *lād* way]

live·long (liv'lông', -long') *adj.* Whole; entire: the *livelong* day. [ME *lefe longe*]

live·ly (līv'lē) *adj.* **·li·er, ·li·est 1** Full of energy or motion: a *lively* child. **2** Filled with activity or incident: a *lively* party. **3** Intensely active or alive, as in the mind: a *lively* wit. **4** Joyful; gay: a *lively* song. **5** Vivid; bright: *lively* colors. **6** Brisk: a *lively* wind. **7** Responsive to impact; resilient: a *lively* ball. —*adv.* In a lively manner. [<OE *līflīce*] —**live'li·ly** *adv.* —**live'li·ness** *n.* —**Syn.** *adj.* **1** active, bouncy, energetic, vivacious.

li·ven (lī'vən) *v.t. & v.i.* To make or become lively or cheerful: often with *up.*

live oak 1 Any of several species of evergreen oak trees. **2** Its hard, durable wood.

liv·er[1] (liv'ər) *n.* **1** The largest glandular organ of vertebrates, having many vital functions, as storing vitamins and nutrients, purifying the blood, producing bile, etc. **2** A digestive gland in invertebrates. **3** The liver of certain animals, used as food. [<OE *lifer*]

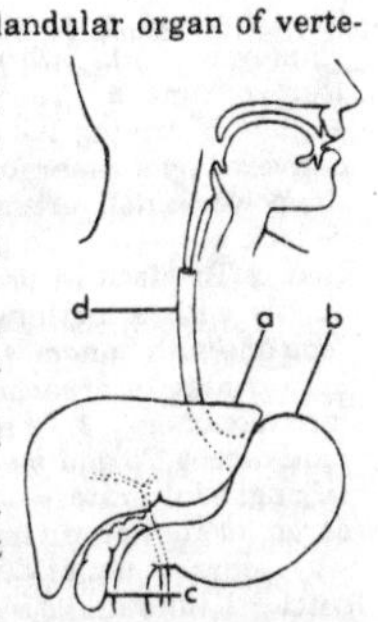

a. liver. b. stomach. c. gall bladder. d. esophagus.

liv·er[2] (liv'ər) *n.* **1** One who lives, esp. in a specified way: a high *liver.* **2** A dweller; resident.

liv·er·ied (liv'ər·ēd) *adj.* Dressed in livery.

liv·er·ish (liv'ər·ish) *adj.* **1** Having a liver disorder; bilious. **2** Out of sorts; peevish.

liv·er·wort (liv'ər·wûrt') *n.* **1** Any of a class of primitive, nonvascular plants related to mosses. **2** HEPATICA.

liv·er·wurst (liv'ər·wûrst') *n.* A sausage containing ground liver. [<G *Leberwurst*]

liv·er·y (liv'ər·ē) *n. pl.* **·er·ies 1** A particular dress or uniform worn by servants. **2** The distinguishing dress of any association or organization. **3** Any characteristic covering or outward appearance. **4** The stabling and care of horses for compensation. **5** A livery stable. [<L *liber* free]

liv·er·y·man (liv'ər·ē·mən) *n. pl.* **·men** (-mən) A man who keeps a livery stable.

livery stable A stable where horses are boarded for a fee and horses and vehicles are kept for hire.

lives (līvz) *n.pl.* of LIFE.

live·stock (līv'stok') *n.* Domestic animals kept for farm purposes, sale, or profit.

live wire 1 A wire carrying an electric current. **2** *Informal* An energetic person.

liv·id (liv'id) *adj.* **1** Black-and-blue, as bruised flesh. **2** Ashy-pale; pallid. **3** Very angry; furious. [<L *livere* be livid] —**li·vid·i·ty** (li·vid'ə·tē), **liv'id·ness** *n.* —**liv'id·ly** *adv.*

liv·ing (liv'ing) *adj.* **1** Having life; live. **2** Of or suitable for life or its sustenance: *living* conditions. **3** Enough to sustain life or live on: a *living* wage. **4** Still operating, functioning, or in use: a *living* language. **5** True to life: lifelike: a *living* image. **6** Involving persons still alive. —*n.* **b** The condition of being alive. **2** Means of supporting life; livelihood. **3** Manner of life. —**the living** Those who are alive.

living death A painful, wretched existence.

living room A room designed for the general occupancy of a family and entertainment of guests.

liz·ard (liz'ərd) *n.* **1** Any of a large group of reptiles having an elongate, scaly body, a long tail, and usu. four legs, as the chameleon, iguana, gecko, etc. **2** Leather made from the skin of a lizard. [<L *lacerta*]

LL, L.L. Late Latin; Legal Latin; Low Latin.

ll. leaves; lines.

lla·ma (lä'mə) *n.* A south American wooly-haired, humpless animal related to the camel, used in the Andes as a beast of burden and as a source of wool and milk. [<Quechua]

Llama

lla·no (lä'nō; *Sp.* lyä'nō) *n. pl.* **·nos** A flat, grassy plain, as those of N South America. [<L *planus* plain, flat]

LL.D. Doctor of Laws (L *Legum Doctor*).

LM (lem) lunar module.

lo (lō) *interj.* Look! observe! [<OE *lā*]

loach (lōch) *n.* Any of various small, freshwater, Old World fishes having barbels at the mouth. [<OF *loche*]

load (lōd) *n.* **1** That which is laid upon or put into anything for conveyance. **2** A quantity carried or conveyed at one time: often used in combination: a *busload.* **3** The weight supported by a structure. **4** Something carried or borne with difficulty, esp. a grievous mental burden. **5** A charge for a firearm. 6 An amount of work expected from an employee. 7 *pl. Informal* A great amount; abundance: *loads* of time. 8 *Mech.* The resistance met by a motor or engine in driving its machinery. 9 *Electr.* **a** The power delivered by a generator or circuit. **b** The device to which the power is delivered. **—get a load of** *Slang* To listen to or look at. —*v.t.* 1 To put something on or into to be carried. 2 To place in or on a carrier: to *load* wood. 3 To supply with something excessively or in abundance: to *load* one with honors. 4 To weigh down or oppress: burden. 5 To charge (a firearm) with ammunition. 6 To put film into (a camera). 7 To make heavy on one side or end: to *load* dice. 8 To add a substance to for the purpose of falsifying; adulterate. —*v.i.* 9 To take on or put on a load or cargo. 10 To charge a firearm with ammunition. [< OE *lād* way, journey, act of carrying goods] **—load′er** *n.*

load·ed (lō′did) *adj. Slang* 1 Having a great deal of money. 2 Drunk.

load·star (lōd′stär) *n.* LODESTAR.

load·stone (lōd′stōn′) *n.* LODESTONE.

loaf[1] (lōf) *v.i.* 1 To spend time lazily or aimlessly. 2 To neglect one's work. —*v.t.* 3 To spend (time) idly: with *away.* [Back formation < LOAFER]

loaf[2] (lōf) *n. pl.* **loaves** (lōvz) 1 A shaped mass of bread. 2 Any mass of food having a somewhat rectangular shape. [< OE *hlāf* bread]

loaf·er (lō′fər) *n.* 1 One who loafs; an idler. 2 A casual shoe resembling a moccasin. [? < G *Landläufer* an idler]

loam (lōm) *n.* A rich soil of sand and clay, containing organic matter. —*v.t.* To cover or fill with loam. [< OE *lām*] **—loam′y (·i·er, ·i·est)** *adj.*

loan (lōn) *n.* 1 Something lent, esp. a sum of money lent at interest. 2 The act of lending. —*v.t. & v.i.* To lend. [< OE *lān*]

loan shark *Informal* One who lends money at extremely high or illegal rates of interest.

loan word A word adopted from another language and naturalized, as the English word *chauffeur,* taken from the French.

loath (lōth, lō<u>th</u>) *adj.* Strongly disinclined; averse: often with *to.* **—nothing loath** 1 Willing. 2 Willingly. [< OE *lāth* hateful]

loathe (lō<u>th</u>) *v.t.* **loathed, loath·ing** To feel great hatred or disgust for; abhor; detest. [< OE *lāthian* be hateful] **—loath′er** *n.*

loath·ing (lō′<u>th</u>ing) *n.* Extreme dislike or disgust; aversion; abhorrence.

loath·ly[1] (lō<u>th</u>′lē) *adj.* Loathsome; repulsive.

loath·ly[2] (lōth′lē) *adv.* Not willingly.

loath·some (lō<u>th</u>′səm) *adj.* Causing loathing. **—loath′·some·ly** *adv.* **—loath′some·ness** *n.*

loaves (lōvz) *n.pl.* of LOAF.

lob (lob) *v.* **lobbed, lob·bing** *v.t.* 1 To pitch or strike (a ball, etc.) in a high, arching curve. —*v.i.* 2 To move clumsily or heavily. 3 To lob a ball. —*n.* 1 In tennis, a stroke that sends the ball high into the air. 2 In cricket, a slow, underhand ball. [?] **—lob′ber** *n.*

lo·bate (lō′bāt) *adj.* 1 Composed of or having lobes. 2 Lobelike. Also **lo′bat·ed.** **—lo′bate·ly** *adv.*

lo·ba·tion (lō·bā′shən) *n.* 1 A lobate structure. 2 LOBE.

lob·by (lob′ē) *n. pl.* **·bies** 1 A hall, vestibule, or foyer on the main floor of a theater, hotel, etc. 2 The persons or groups of persons who lobby in the interest of a special group, industry, etc. —*v.* **·bied, ·by·ing** *v.i.* 1 To attempt to influence a legislator or legislators. —*v.t.* 2 To attempt to obtain passage or defeat of (a bill, etc.) by such means. [Med. L *lobia* porch] **—lob′by·er** *n.* **—Syn.** 1 entrance hall, lounge, waiting room.

lob·by·ist (lob′ē·ist) *n.* One who engages in the practice of lobbying. **—lob′by·ism** *n.*

lobe (lōb) *n.* 1 A rounded projecting part, as of a body organ, leaf, etc. 2 The soft lower extension of the external ear. [< Gk. *lobos*] **—lo′bar, lobed** *adj.*

lo·be·li·a (lō·bē′lē·ə, -bēl′yə) *n.* Any of a large genus of plants with showy flowers, usu. borne in racemes. [< Matthias de *Lobel,* 1538–1616, Flemish botanist]

lob·lol·ly (lob′lol·ē) *n. pl.* **·lies** 1 A pine of the s U.S., having a scaly bark. 2 The wood of this tree. Also **loblolly pine.** [< dial. E *lob* bubble + *lolly* broth]

lo·bo (lō′bō) *n. pl.* **·bos** TIMBER WOLF. [Sp., wolf]

lob·ster (lob′stər) *n.* 1 Any of numerous edible marine crustaceans having five pairs of legs, the first pair forming claws, and compound eyes. 2 One of various similar crustaceans. 3 The flesh of these crustaceans, used as food. [< L *locusta* lobster, locust]

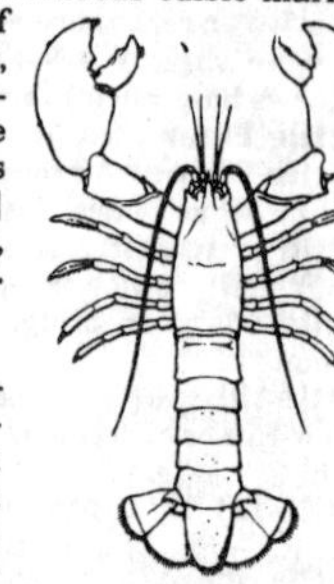

Lobster

lob·ule (lob′yōōl) *n.* A small lobe, or a subdivision of a lobe. **—lob′·u·lar, lob′u·late** (-lit, -lāt) *adj.*

loc. local; location.

lo·cal (lō′kəl) *adj.* 1 Of, pertaining to, or characteristic of a particular place or a limited portion of space. 2 Pertaining to place in general. 3 Not broad or universal: *local* customs. 4 Relating to or affecting a specific part of the body. 5 Making every stop on its run: a *local* train. —*n.* 1 A local subway, bus, or train. 2 A local branch of a trade union or fraternal organization. 3 An item of local interest in a newspaper. [< L *locus* place] **—lo′cal·ly** *adv.*

local color In literature and art, the presentation of the characteristic manners, speech, dress, scenery, etc., of a certain period or region so as to achieve a sense of realism.

lo·cale (lō·kal′, -käl′) *n.* Locality, esp. with reference to events or features associated with it. [F]

lo·cal·ism (lō′kəl·iz′əm) *n.* 1 A local custom or idiom. 2 A word, meaning, pronunciation, etc., peculiar to a locality. 3 Fondness for a particular place or locality.

lo·cal·i·ty (lō·kal′ə·tē) *n. pl.* **·ties** 1 A definite place, location, or position. 2 The condition of having a location.

lo·cal·ize (lō′kəl·īz) *v.t.* **·ized, ·iz·ing** 1 To limit or assign to a specific area or locality. 2 To determine the place of origin of. **—lo′cal·i·za′tion** *n.*

local option The right of a county, town, etc., to determine by vote whether something, as the sale of liquor, shall be permitted within its limits.

lo·cate (lō′kāt, lō·kāt′) *v.* **·cat·ed, ·cat·ing** *v.t.* 1 To discover the position or source of; find. 2 To assign place or locality to: to *locate* a scene in a valley. 3 To establish in a place; situate: My office is *located* in Portland. 4 To designate the site of, as a mining claim. —*v.i.* 5 *Informal* To establish oneself or take up residence; settle. [< L *locare* < *locus* place] **—lo′ca·tor** *n.*

lo·ca·tion (lō·kā′shən) *n.* 1 The act of locating, or the state of being located. 2 A place, position, or site. 3 A plot of ground used or to be used for a special purpose. 4 A site, away from a studio, selected for filming scenes in a motion picture.

loc·a·tive (lok′ə·tiv) *adj. Gram.* In Latin, Greek, Sanskrit, etc., designating the case of the noun denoting place where or at which. —*n.* 1 The locative case. 2 A word in this case. [< L *locare* locate]

loc. cit. in the place cited (L *loco citato*).

loch (lokh, lok) *n. Scot.* 1 A lake. 2 A bay, or arm of the sea.

lo·ci (lō′sī, -kī, -kē) *n.pl.* of LOCUS.

lock[1] (lok) *n.* 1 A device to secure a door, drawer, etc., operated by a special key or combination. 2 Any of various mechanical devices used to fix something in place, prevent something from working, etc. 3 A spring mechanism for exploding the charge of a firearm. 4 A section of a canal, etc., enclosed by gates at either end, within which the water level may be varied to raise or lower vessels from one level to another. 5 An interlocking or fastening together. 6 Any of various holds in wrestling. **—lock, stock, and barrel** *Informal* Totally; completely. —*v.t.* 1 To secure or fasten by means of a lock. 2 To shut, confine, or exclude by means of a lock: with *in, up,* or *out.* 3 To join or unite; link: to *lock* arms. 4 To embrace closely. 5 To make immovable, as by jamming or by a lock. 6 To move (a ship) by means of locks. —*v.i.* 7 To become locked or fastened. 8 To become joined or linked. **—lock out** To subject (workers) to a lockout. **—lock up** 1 To fasten the doors of by locking. 2 To put in jail. 3 To make sure that (something specified) will turn out the way one wants it to: enough backing to *lock up* the nomination. [<OE *loc* fastening, enclosure] **—Syn.** *n.* 1 bolt, catch, fastening, latch.

lock[2] (lok) *n.* 1 A tuft of hair; tress. 2 *pl.* A head of hair. 3 A small quantity of hay, wool, etc. [<OE *locc*]

lock·er (lok′ər) *n.* 1 One who or that which locks. 2 A closet, cabinet, chest, etc., usu. having a lock, and used for personal belongings. 3 A refrigerated cabinet for frozen foods.

locker room A room equipped with lockers.

lock·et (lok′it) *n.* A small, hinged case suspended on a necklace or chain, often holding a portrait. [<OF *loc* latch]

lock·jaw (lok′jô′) *n.* 1 TETANUS. 2 Abnormal muscular contraction causing the jaws to clench.

lock·out (lok′out′) *n.* The closing of a place of business to force workers to accept the employer's terms.

lock·smith (lok′smith′) *n.* A maker or repairer of locks.

lock step A marching step in which each marcher follows as closely as possible the one ahead.

lock·up (lok′up′) *n.* 1 The act of locking up or the state of being locked up. 2 A jail.

lo·co (lō′kō) *n.* 1 LOCOWEED. 2 LOCO DISEASE. **—*adj.*** *Slang* Crazy; insane. [Sp., insane]

lo·co ci·ta·to (lō′kō sī·tā′tō) *Latin* In the place cited.

loco disease An ailment affecting the nervous system of livestock that have eaten locoweed. Also **lo·co·ism** (lō′·kō·iz′əm).

lo·co·mo·tion (lō′kə·mō′shən) *n.* The act or power of moving from one place to another. [<L *loco* from a place + *motio* movement]

lo·co·mo·tive (lō′kə·mō′tiv) *adj.* 1 Pertaining to locomotion. 2 Moving or able to move from one place to another. 3 Self-propelling: said of machines. **—*n.*** A self-propelling electric, diesel, or steam engine on wheels, esp. one for use on a railway.

lo·co·mo·tor (lō′kə·mō′tər) *adj.* Of or pertaining to locomotion. **—*n.*** One who or that which has the power of locomotion.

locomotor ataxia A chronic disease of the spinal cord, usu. caused by syphilis and characterized by lack of muscular coordination and loss of reflexes.

lo·co·weed (lō′kō·wēd′) *n.* Any of several leguminous plants of w U.S., often poisonous to livestock.

lo·cus (lō′kəs) *n.* *pl.* **·ci** (-sī, -kī, kē) 1 A place; locality. 2 *Math.* A set containing those points and only those points that satisfy a given set of conditions. [L]

lo·cust (lo′kəst) *n.* 1 Any of various large grasshoppers, esp. those moving in swarms and destructive of vegetation. 2 A cicada. 3 Any of various leguminous North American trees and shrubs having compound leaves and drooping racemes of flowers. 4 The hard, durable wood of certain of these trees. 5 Any of various other trees, esp. the honey locust. [<L *locusta*]

lo·cu·tion (lō·kyōō′shən) *n.* 1 A manner of speech. 2 A verbal idiom or phrase. [<L *loqui* speak]

lode (lōd) *n.* 1 A mineral-bearing vein filling a fissure in rock. 2 A deposit of ore between definite boundaries of associated rock. [<OE *lād* way, journey]

lode·star (lōd′stär′) *n.* 1 A guiding star, esp. the North Star. 2 Any guiding principle or ideal.

lode·stone (lōd′stōn′) *n.* 1 A magnetically polarized piece of magnetite. 2 Anything that has magnetic or magneticlike attraction.

lodge (loj) *v.* **lodged, lodg·ing** *v.t.* 1 To furnish with temporary living quarters; house. 2 To rent a room or rooms to. 3 To serve as a shelter or dwelling for. 4 To deposit for safekeeping or storage. 5 To place or implant, as by throwing, thrusting, etc. 6 To place (a complaint, information, etc.) before proper authority. 7 To confer or invest (power, etc.). **—*v.i.*** 8 To take temporary shelter or quarters. 9 To live in a rented room or rooms. 10 To become fixed in some place or position. **—*n.*** 1 A small house, hut, or cabin. 2 A small dwelling on an estate. 3 The lair of a wild animal, esp. of beavers. 4 A local chapter of a secret or fraternal society, or its meeting place. 5 A small hut or tepee of American Indians; also, its inhabitants. [<Med. L *lobia, laubia* porch, gallery]

lodg·er (loj′ər) *n.* One who lodges; esp. one who rents a room or rooms in the house of another.

lodg·ing (loj′ing) *n.* 1 A place of temporary abode. 2 *pl.* A room or rooms hired as a place of residence in the house of another.

lodging house A house other than a hotel where lodgings are let.

lodg·ment (loj′mənt) *n.* 1 The act of lodging or the state of being lodged. 2 LODGINGS. 3 Accumulated material left by deposit. Also **lodge′ment.**

loess (lō′is, lœs) *n.* *Geol.* A powdery, yellowish brown loam found widely in North America, Europe, and Asia, believed to have been chiefly deposited by the wind. [<G *lösen* pour, dissolve]

loft (lôft, loft) *n.* 1 A low space or attic directly under a roof. 2 A large, unpartitioned storeroom on an upper floor of a warehouse, etc. 3 An elevated gallery, as in a church. 4 HAYLOFT. 5 A backward slope on the face of a golf club; also, a stroke with such a club which lifts the ball high in the air. 6 A place for keeping pigeons. **—*v.t.*** 1 To keep or house in a loft. 2 In sports, to strike (a ball) so that it rises or travels in a high arc. **—*v.i.*** 3 To strike a ball so that it rises in a high arc. [<ON, upper room, air, sky]

loft·y (lôf′tē, lof′-) *adj.* **loft·i·er, loft·i·est** 1 Very high. 2 Exalted or elevated in character, language, etc. 3 Haughty; arrogant. **—loft′i·ly** *adv.* **—loft′i·ness** *n.* **—Syn.** 1 tall. 2 grand, majestic, sublime. 3 disdainful.

log[1] (lôg, log) *n.* 1 A bulky piece or length of timber cut down and cleared of branches. 2 *Naut.* **a** A device for showing the speed of a vessel. **b** A record of the daily speed and progress of a vessel. 3 Any of various records of performance, progress, etc. **—*v.*** **logged, log·ging** *v.t.* 1 To cut (trees) into logs. 2 To cut down the trees of (a region) for timber. 3 *Naut. & Aeron.* **a** To enter in a logbook. **b** To travel (a specified distance) as shown by a log. **c** To travel at (a specified speed). **—*v.i.*** 4 To cut down trees and transport logs for sawing into lumber. [? <Scand.]

log[2] (lôg, log) *n.* LOGARITHM.

lo·gan·ber·ry (lō′gən·ber′ē) *n.* *pl.* **·ries** 1 A hybrid shrub obtained by crossing the red raspberry with the blackberry. 2 The edible fruit of this shrub. [<J. H. *Logan*, 1841–1928, of California, the originator]

log·a·rithm (lôg′ə·rith′əm, log′-) *n.* *Math.* The exponent showing the power to which a constant, called the base, must be raised in order to produce a given number. [<Gk. *logos* word, ratio + *arithmos* number] **—log′a·rith′mic** or **·mi·cal** *adj.* **—log′a·rith′mi·cal·ly** *adv.*

log·book (lôg′bŏŏk′, log′-) *n.* The book in which the official record of a ship, aircraft, etc., is entered. Also **log book.**

loge (lōzh) *n.* A box in a theater; stall. [<OF]

log·ger (lôg′ər, log′-) *n.* 1 A person engaged in logging; a lumberjack. 2 A machine used for loading logs.

log·ger·head (lôg′ər·hed′, log′-) *n.* 1 A blockhead; fool. 2 A large sea turtle of tropical Atlantic waters: also **loggerhead turtle.** **—at loggerheads** Engaged in a quarrel. [<regional E *logger* log tied to a horse's leg + HEAD]

log·gi·a (loj′ē·ə, lô′jə; *Ital.* lôd′jä) *n.* A roofed, open gallery, attached to the side, or sides, of a building and having a colonnade on one or more sides. [<OF *loge*]

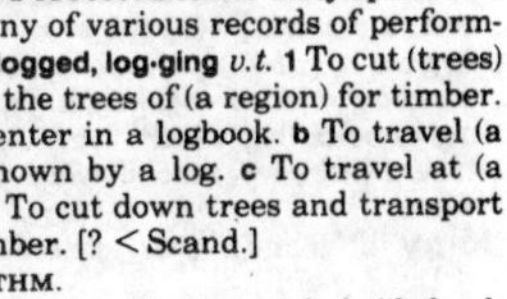

Loggia

log·ging (lôg′ing, log′-) *n.* The occupation of felling timber and transporting logs to a mill or market.

log·ic (loj′ik) *n.* 1 The science which investigates the principles of valid reasoning and correct inference. 2 The basic principles of reasoning applicable to any field of knowledge: the *logic* of science. 3 Reasoning or argumentation in general, esp. when relevant or effective: The *logic* of his answer was unassailable. 4 The connection or interrelation of facts, events, etc., esp. when viewed as inevitable. [< Gk. *logos* word, speech, thought]

log·i·cal (loj′i·kəl) *adj.* 1 Relating to or of the nature of logic. 2 Conforming to the laws of logic. 3 Capable of or characterized by clear reasoning. —**log′i·cal′i·ty** (-kal′ə·tē), **log′i·cal·ness** *n.* —**log′i·cal·ly** *adv.*

-logical *combining form* Of or related to a (specified) science or study: *biological.* Also **-logic.** [< -LOG(Y)]

logic circuit Any of various circuits used in computers and electronic control systems, having several inputs and an output that is on or off, depending on the condition of the inputs; a gate.

lo·gi·cian (lō·jish′ən) *n.* One versed in logic.

lo·gis·tics (lō·jis′tiks) *n. pl. (construed as singular)* The branch of military science concerned with procurement, equipment, maintenance, and transportation, as of personnel, facilities, and materiel. [< Gk. *logistēs* calculator] —**lo·gis′tic, lo·gis′ti·cal** *adj.*

log·o (lôg′ō, log′ō) *n. pl.* **log·os** LOGOTYPE (def. 2).

Lo·gos (lō′gos, -gōs, log′os) *n.* 1 In classical Greek philosophy, reason, thought of as the controlling principle of the universe. 2 In Christian theology, the creative and sustaining spirit of divine wisdom, esp. as made manifest in the second person of the Trinity, Jesus Christ.

log·o·type (lôg′ə·tīp, log′-) *n.* 1 *Printing* A type bearing a syllable or word. 2 A distinctively styled representation of a company name, trademark, etc.

log·roll (lôg′rōl′, log′-) *v.t.* 1 To obtain passage of (a bill) by logrolling. —*v.i.* 2 To engage in logrolling.

log·roll·ing (lôg′rō′ling, log′-) *n.* 1 Handling and removing of logs, as in clearing land. 2 A trading of votes among politicians for mutual assistance on their separate projects. 3 BIRLING. —**log′roll′er** *n.*

-logue *combining form* Speech; recitation; discourse: *monologue.* Also **-log.** [< Gk. *logos* word, speech]

log·wood (lôg′wŏŏd′, log′-) *n.* 1 A Central American tree. 2 Its heavy, reddish wood. 3 A dye obtained from this wood.

lo·gy (lō′gē) *adj.* **·gi·er, ·gi·est** *Informal* Dull; lethargic. [? < Du. *log* dull]

-logy *combining form* 1 The science or study of: *biology.* 2 Speech; discourse. [< Gk. *logos* word, study]

Lo·hen·grin (lō′ən·grin) In German medieval legend, son of Parsifal and a knight of the Holy Grail.

loin (loin) *n.* 1 The part of the body of a human being or quadruped between the lower ribs and hip bone. 2 *pl.* Loosely, the hips, thighs, and the genital region. 3 The forepart of the hindquarters of beef, lamb, veal, etc., with the flank removed. —**gird up one's loins** To prepare for action. [< L *lumbus*] • See HORSE.

loin·cloth (loin′klôth′, -kloth′) *n.* A piece or strip of cloth worn about the loins.

loi·ter (loi′tər) *v.i.* 1 To pass time idly or aimlessly; loaf. 2 To linger on the way; dawdle. —*v.t.* 3 To pass (time) idly: with *away.* [ME *loyteren*] —**loi′ter·er** *n.* —**loi′ter·ing·ly** *adv.* —**Syn.** 1 laze. 2 delay, lag, procrastinate, tarry.

Lo·ki (lō′kē) In Norse mythology, a god who created disorder and mischief.

loll (lol) *v.i.* 1 To lie or lean in a relaxed or languid manner. 2 To hang loosely; droop. —*v.t.* 3 To permit to droop or hang, as the tongue. —*n.* The act of lolling. [ME *lollen*] —**loll′er** *n.*

Lol·lard (lol′ərd) *n.* One of a sect of religious and political reformers in England in the 14th and 15th centuries, followers of John Wyclif. [< MDu. *lollaerd,* lit., grumbler, mumbler (of prayers)]

lol·li·pop (lol′ē·pop) *n.* A lump or piece of hard candy attached to the end of a stick. Also **lol′ly·pop.** [?< dial. E *lolly* tongue + POP¹]

lol·ly (lol′ē) *n. pl.* **·lies** *Brit.* 1 A piece of candy, esp. hard candy. 2 *Informal* Ice cream, flavored ices, etc., frozen on a stick. 3 *Slang* Money. [Short for LOLLIPOP]

Lom·bard (lom′bərd, -bärd, lum′-) *n.* 1 One of a Germanic tribe that established a kingdom in northern Italy, 568–774. 2 A native or citizen of Lombardy. —**Lom·bar′dic** *adj.*

lone (lōn) *adj.* 1 Standing by itself; isolated. 2 Unaccompanied; solitary. 3 Unmarried or widowed. 4 Lonesome. [Var. of ALONE] —**lone′ness** *n.*

lone·ly (lōn′lē) *adj.* **·li·er, ·li·est** 1 Deserted or unfrequented by human beings. 2 Solitary or isolated. 3 Sad from being alone. 4 Producing such sadness: a *lonely* melody. —**lone′li·ly** *adv.* —**lone′li·ness** *n.*

lo·ner (lō′nər) *n. Informal* One who keeps away from other people.

lone·some (lōn′səm) *adj.* 1 Depressed or sad because of loneliness. 2 Producing a feeling of loneliness. 3 Deserted; secluded. —**lone′some·ly** *adv.* —**lone′some·ness** *n.*

long¹ (lông, long) *adj.* 1 Having relatively great linear extension; not short. 2 Having relatively great extension in time; prolonged. 3 Extended either in space or time to a specified degree: an hour *long,* a foot *long.* 4 Of relatively great distance: a *long* trip. 5 In excess of the usual or standard duration, quantity, extent, etc.: a *long* five minutes; a *long* movie. 6 Retentive: a *long* memory. 7 Having many items or units: a *long* list. 8 Extending into the future or beyond present considerations: to take a *long* look at a problem. 9 Slow; tedious. 10 Great in risk: a *long* chance. 11 In finance, holding stocks, securities, etc., in anticipation of a rise in prices. 12 *Phonet.* Indicating the sounds of *a, e, i, o, u* as they are pronounced in *mate, scene, nice, dote, fuse.* 13 In English prosody, accented. —*n.* Something long, as a garment, vowel, syllable, etc. —**the long and (the) short of** The entire story of; gist. —*adv.* 1 For or during a long time or period: I can't stay *long.* 2 For a (specified) length of time: How *long* did the play run? 3 Through the whole extent or duration. 4 At a point of duration far distant: *long* before or after. —**as** (or **so**) **long as** 1 During the time that. 2 Under condition that; since. —**before long** Soon. —**for long** For a long time. [< OE *lang, long*]

long² (lông, long) *v.i.* To have a strong or yearning wish: with *for.* [< OE *langian*] —**Syn.** covet, crave, desire, hanker, pine.

long. longitude.

long·boat (lông′bōt′, long′-) *n. Naut.* The largest boat carried on a sailing vessel.

long·bow (lông′bō′, long′-) *n.* A wooden bow, often six feet long, drawn by hand.

long-dis·tance (lông′dis′təns, long′-) *adj.* 1 To or from a distant place. 2 Of or relating to long distances: a *long-distance* runner. —*adv.* By long-distance telephone.

long distance The telephone exchange or operator dealing with long-distance calls.

long division Arithmetical division involving numbers whose numerals have several digits and showing each step of the process.

long-drawn (lông′drôn′, long′-) *adj.* Prolonged. Also **long′-drawn′-out′** (-out′).

lon·gev·i·ty (lon·jev′ə·tē) *n.* 1 Great age or length of life. 2 The tendency to live long. [< L *longus* long + *aevum* age]

long face An expression indicating sadness. —**long-faced** (lông′fāst′, long′-) *adj.*

long green *Slang* Paper money.

long·hair (lông′hâr′, long′-) *n. Slang* 1 A person having intellectual interests or tastes, esp. for classical music. 2 A man or boy with long hair, esp. a hippie. —**long′hair′, long′haired′** *adj.*

long·hand (lông′hand′, long′-) *n.* Ordinary handwriting with the words spelled in full.

long·head·ed (lông′hed′id, long′-) *adj.* 1 DOLICHOCEPHALIC. 2 *Informal* Shrewd; foresighted. Also **long′-head′·ed.** —**long′head′ed·ly** *adv.* —**long′head′ed·ness** *n.*

long·horn (lông′hôrn′, long′-) *n.* One of a breed of domestic cattle with long horns: also **Texas longhorn.**

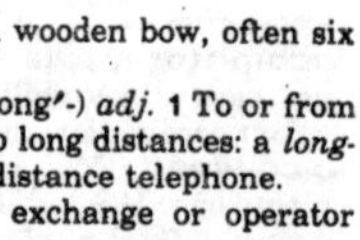

Longhorn

long·ing (lông′ing, long′-) *n.* A strong, eager craving. —*adj.* Having or showing such a craving. —**long′ing·ly** *adv.*

lon·gi·tude (lon′ji·to͞od) *n.* 1 *Geog.* Distance east or west on the earth measured by the angle which the meridian through a specific place makes as it intersects with some standard meridian, as that of Greenwich, England. 2 *Astron.* The angular distance from the vernal equinox to the great circle passing through a point on the celestial sphere. [< L *longus* long]

lon·gi·tu·di·nal (lon′ji·to͞o′də·nəl) *adj.* **1** Of or pertaining to longitude or length. **2** Running lengthwise. —**lon′gi·tu′·di·nal·ly** *adv.*

long-lived (lông′līvd′, -livd′, long′-) *adj.* Existing or living for an unusually long time. —**long′-lived′ness** *n.*

long-play·ing (lông′plā′ing, long′-) *adj.* Designating a phonograph record with microgrooves, played at 33⅓ revolutions per minute.

long-range (lông′rānj′, long′-) *adj.* **1** Designed to shoot or move over distances: a *long-range* projectile. **2** Taking account of, or extending over, a long span of future time.

long·shore·man (lông′shôr′mən, -shōr′-, long′-) *n. pl.* **·men** (-mən) A person whose occupation is loading and unloading ships.

long shot *Informal* **1** A bet made with little chance of winning and hence carrying great odds. **2** Something backed at great odds, as a horse. —**not by a long shot** Decidedly not.

long·sight·ed (lông′sī′tid, long′-) *adj.* **1** Having or showing foresight; sagacious. **2** Farsighted. —**long′sight′ed·ness** *n.*

long-stand·ing (lông′stan′ding, long′-) *adj.* Having existed for a long time.

long-suf·fer·ing (lông′suf′ər·ing, long′-) *adj.* Patiently enduring trouble, misfortune, etc., for a long time. —*n.* Patient endurance of injuries or offense: also **long′suf′fer·ance.**

long-term (lông′tûrm′, long′-) *adj.* Active or valid for a relatively long time: a *long-term* lease.

long·time (lông′tīm′, long′-) *adj.* For a long time.

long ton 2,240 pounds avoirdupois.

long-wind·ed (lông′win′did, long′-) *adj.* **1** Not losing one's breath easily. **2** Speaking or writing in a tedious, overlong manner. —**long′-wind′ed·ly** *adv.* —**long′-wind′ed·ness** *n.*

long·wise (lông′wīz′, long′-) *adv.* LENGTHWISE. Also **long′·ways′** (-wāz′)

loo[1] (lo͞o) *n.* **1** An old card game. **2** A pool of forfeits used in loo. [<F *lanturelu*]

loo[2] (lo͞o) *n. Brit. Informal* Toilet. [? <F *lieux (d'aisances)* public convenience, toilets]

look (lo͝ok) *v.i.* **1** To direct the eyes toward something in order to see. **2** To direct one's attention or consideration. **3** To make examination or inquiry: to *look* through a desk. **4** To appear to be; seem. **5** To face in a specified direction; front. **6** To expect: with an infinitive. —*v.t.* **7** To direct the eyes upon: He *looked* her up and down. **8** To express by looks: to *look* one's hatred. **9** To give the appearance of being (a specified age). **10** To influence by looks: to *look* someone into silence. —**look after** To take care of. —**look down on** To regard condescendingly or contemptuously. —**look for 1** To search for. **2** To expect. —**look forward to** To anticipate pleasurably. —**look in** (or **in on**) To make a short visit to. —**look into** To examine; make inquiry. —**look like 1** To resemble. **2** To indicate the probability of: It *looks like* rain. —**look on 1** To be a spectator. **2** To consider; regard. —**look oneself** To seem to be in good health, good spirits, etc. —**look out** To be on the watch; take care. —**look over** To examine; scrutinize. —**look to 1** To attend to. **2** To turn to, as for help, advice, etc. —**look up 1** To search for and find, as in a file, dictionary, etc. **2** *Informal* To discover the whereabouts of. **3** *Informal* To improve; become better. —**look up to** To have respect for. —*n.* **1** The act of looking or seeing. **2** Aspect or expression: a fiendish *look.* **3** *Usu. pl. Informal* Personal appearance, esp. when attractive. **4** Appearance in general: I do not like the *look* of the thing. [<OE *lōcian*] —**Syn.** *v.* **1** gaze, glance, regard. **3** search. **6** anticipate.

look-a·like (lo͝ok′ə·līk′) *n. Informal* One of two or more that are alike in appearance; a double.

look·er (lo͝ok′ər) *n.* **1** One who looks or watches. **2** *Slang* A handsome or good-looking person.

look·er-on (lo͝ok′ər·on′) *n. pl.* **look·ers-on** A spectator; onlooker.

look·ing-glass (lo͝ok′ing·glas′, -gläs′) *n.* A mirror.

look-out (lo͝ok′out′) *n.* **1** Careful or alert watchfulness. **2** An elevated place for observation. **3** A person or group engaged in keeping watch. **4** *Informal* Concern; care: It's your own *look-out.*

loom[1] (lo͞om) *v.i.* **1** To appear or come into view indistinctly, esp. so as to seem large or ominous. **2** To appear to the mind as threatening or portentous. [?]

loom[2] (lo͞om) *n.* A machine in which yarn or thread is woven into a fabric. [<OE *gelōma* tool]

loon[1] (lo͞on) *n.* Any of several diving, fish-eating waterfowl, having a distinctive cry. [< ON *lomr*]

Loon

loon[2] (lo͞on) *n.* A crazy or stupid person. [ME *loun*]

loon·y (lo͞o′nē) *Slang. adj.* **loon·i·er, loon·i·est 1** Lunatic or demented. **2** Foolish; erratic. —*n. pl.* **loon·ies** A demented or crazy person.

loop (lo͞op) *n.* **1** The more or less oval-shaped bend that is created when a string, rope, etc., is crossed over on itself. **2** Something shaped like a loop, as certain ornamental fastenings. **3** A complete, vertical, circular turn made by an airplane in flight. **4** *Electr.* A closed path in an electric circuit. **5** Any of several types of intrauterine contraceptive devices. —**loop the loop** To make a vertical, circular turn, as an airplane in flight. —*v.t.* **1** To form a loop or loops in or of. **2** To fasten, connect, or encircle by means of a loop or loops. **3** To fly (an aircraft) in a loop or loops. —*v.i.* **4** To make a loop or loops. **5** To move by forming loops, as a measuring worm. [ME *loupe*]

looped (lo͞opt) *adj. Slang* Drunk.

loop·hole (lo͞op′hōl′) *n.* **1** A narrow opening, as in a wall, through which small arms are fired. **2** A means of escaping or evading something disagreeable.

loose (lo͞os) *adj.* **loos·er, loos·est 1** Not fastened or confined; unattached. **2** Not tightly stretched; slack. **3** Not tight, as a garment. **4** Not firmly fastened or secured: a *loose* bolt. **5** Not bundled, tied, or fastened together. **6** Not dense or compact: *loose* soil. **7** Not in individual packages or containers: *loose* sugar. **8 a** Not constricted: a *loose* cough. **b** Moving freely or too often: *loose* bowels. **9** Free from confinement, restraint, etc. **10** Not controlled or restrained: a *loose* tongue. **11** Not chaste; lewd. **12** Not precise or exact: a *loose* translation. **13** Free and relaxed: a *loose* walk. —**on the loose 1** Unconfined; at large. **2** *Informal* Free and unrestrained in behavior. —*adv.* **1** In a loose manner. **2** So as to become loose: The dog broke *loose.* —*v.* **loosed, loos·ing** *v.t.* **1** To set free, as from bondage, penalty, etc. **2** To untie or undo. **3** To loosen; slacken. **4** To make less strict or rigid. **5** To let fly; shoot, as arrows. —*v.i.* **6** To become loose. **7** To loose something. [<ON *lauss*] —**loose′ly** *adv.* —**loose′ness** *n.*

loose-joint·ed (lo͞os′join′tid) *adj.* **1** Having joints not tightly articulated. **2** Limber.

loose-leaf (lo͞os′lēf′) *adj.* Designed for the easy insertion and removal of pages.

loos·en (lo͞o′sən) *v.t.* **1** To untie or undo, as bonds. **2** To set free; release. **3** To make less tight, firm, or compact. **4** To relax the strictness of, as discipline. —*v.i.* **5** To become loose or looser. —**loos′en·er** *n.*

loot (lo͞ot) *v.t.* & *v.i.* To plunder. —*n.* **1** Goods taken as spoils by an enemy during war. **2** Anything unlawfully taken. **3** *Slang* Money. [<Hind. *lūt*] —**loot′er** *n.*

lop[1] (lop) *v.t.* **lopped, lop·ping 1** To trim the branches, twigs, etc., from, as a tree. **2** To cut off, as branches, twigs, etc. —*n.* Something lopped off. [?] —**lop′per** *n.*

lop[2] (lop) *v.* **lopped, lop·ping** *v.i.* **1** To droop or hang down. **2** To move about in an awkward manner. —*v.t.* **3** To permit to droop or hang down. —*adj.* Drooping. [?]

lope (lōp) *v.t.* & *v.i.* **loped, lop·ing** To run or cause to run with a steady, swinging stride. —*n.* A slow, easy stride. [<ON *hlaupa* to leap, run] —**lop′er** *n.*

lop-eared (lop′ird′) *adj.* Having drooping ears.

lop-sid·ed (lop′sī′did) *adj.* **1** Heavy or hanging down on one side. **2** Lacking in symmetry or balance. —**lop′-sid′ed·ly** *adv.* —**lop′-sid′ed·ness** *n.*

loq. he (or she, or it) speaks (L *loquitur*).

lo·qua·cious (lō·kwā′shəs) *adj.* Given to continual talking. [< L *loqui* to talk] **—lo·qua′cious·ly** *adv.* **—lo·qua′cious·ness, lo·quac·i·ty** (lō·kwas′ə·tē) *n.* **—Syn.** chattering, garrulous, talkative, verbose, vociferous.

lo·ran (lôr′an, lō′ran) *n.* A navigation system by which a ship or an aircraft may determine its position from radio signals transmitted by fixed stations. [< *lo(ng-)ra(nge) n(avigation)*]

lord (lôrd) *n.* **1** One possessing supreme power and authority; a ruler. **2** In feudal law, the owner of a manor under grant from the crown. **3** In Great Britain: **a** Any nobleman **(lord temporal)** holding the title of marquis, earl, viscount, or baron and having a seat in the House of Lords. **b** An archbishop or bishop **(lord spiritual)** who is a member of the House of Lords. **—the Lords** The House of Lords. **—***v.t.* To invest with the title of lord. **—lord it (over)** To act in a domineering or arrogant manner (toward). [< OE *hlāford,* lit., bread-keeper]

Lord (lôrd) *n.* **1** God. **2** Jesus. **3** In Great Britain, a title of honor or nobility.

Lord Chancellor The highest British officer of state, presiding officer of the House of Lords. Also **Lord High Chancellor.**

lord·ly (lôrd′lē) *adj.* **·li·er, ·li·est 1** Of, pertaining to, or befitting a lord. **2** Lofty; noble. **3** Haughty; insolent. **—***adv.* In a lordly manner. **—lord′li·ness** *n.*

lor·do·sis (lôr·dō′sis) *n.* Inward curvature of the spine. [< Gk. *lordos* bent backward] **—lor·dot′ic** (-dot′ik) *adj.*

Lord's Day Sunday.

lord·ship (lôrd′ship) *n.* **1** The dominion, power, or authority of a lord. **2** Sovereignty in general. **3** *Often cap.* The title by which noblemen (excluding dukes), bishops, and judges in England are addressed: preceded by *Your* or *His.*

Lord's Prayer The prayer taught by Jesus to his disciples. *Matt.* 6: 9–13.

Lord's Supper *Eccl.* **1** The Eucharist; the Holy Communion. **2** The Last Supper.

lore (lôr, lōr) *n.* **1** The body of traditional, popular, often anecdotal knowledge about a particular subject. **2** Learning or erudition. [< OE *lār*]

Lo·re·lei (lôr′ə·lī; *Ger.* lō′rə·lī) In German folklore, a siren on a rock in the Rhine, who lured boatmen to shipwreck by her singing.

lor·gnette (lôr·nyet′) *n.* A pair of eyeglasses or opera glasses with a handle. [< F *lorgner* to spy, peer]

lorn (lôrn) *adj. Archaic* **1** Without kindred or friends; forlorn. **2** Lost. [< OE *loren,* p.p. of *lēosan* lose]

lor·ry (lôr′ē, lor′ē) *n. pl.* **·ries 1** A low, four-wheeled wagon without sides. **2** *Brit.* A motor truck. [?]

lo·ry (lō′rē, lôr′ē) *n. pl.* **·ries** Any of certain parrots of Australia and neighboring islands. [Malay *lūrī*]

lose (lōōz) v. **lost, los·ing** *v.t.* **1** To be unable to find; mislay. **2** To fail to keep, control, or maintain: to *lose* one's footing. **3** To suffer or undergo the loss of, as by accident, death, removal, etc. **4** To fail to gain or win. **5** To fail to utilize or take advantage of; miss: to *lose* a chance. **6** To fail to see or hear: I *lost* not a word of the speech. **7** To fail to keep in sight, memory, etc. **8** To cease to have: to *lose* one's sense of duty. **9** To squander; waste, as time. **10** To wander from so as to be unable to find: to *lose* the path. **11** To outdistance or elude. **12** To cause the loss of: His rashness *lost* him his opportunity. **13** To bring to destruction or ruin: All hands were *lost.* **—***v.i.* **14** To suffer loss. **15** To be defeated. **—lose oneself 1** To lose one's way. **2** To disappear or hide. **3** To become engrossed. **—lose out** *Informal* To fail or be defeated. [< OE *lōsian* be lost] **—los′er** *n.*

los·ing (lōō′zing) *n.* **1** The act of one who or that which loses. **2** *pl.* Money lost, esp. in gambling. **—***adj.* **1** That incurs loss: a *losing* business. **2** Not winning; defeated: the *losing* team.

loss (lôs, los) *n.* **1** The act of losing or the state of being lost. **2** One who or that which is lost. **3** The harm, privation, etc., caused by losing someone or something. **4** *pl.* Soldiers killed, wounded, or captured in battle. **5** In insurance, the amount owed to the insured by the insurer because of death, property damage, theft, etc. **6** *Physics* Any part of the energy of a system that cannot be made to do useful work. **—at a loss 1** At so low a price as to result in a loss. **2** In confusion or doubt. [< OE *los*]

loss leader An item in a store sold at a reduced price or below cost to bring in customers.

lost (lôst, lost) *adj.* **1** Not to be found or recovered; missing. **2** No longer seen, enjoyed, etc.: *lost* friends. **3** Not won or gained: a *lost* cause. **4** Having wandered from the way. **5** Helpless. **6** Ruined physically or morally. **7** Wasted; squandered: a *lost* opportunity. **8** Abstracted; rapt: *lost* in thought. **9** Bewildered; perplexed. **10** No longer known or used: a *lost* art. **—be lost to 1** To belong to no longer. **2** To be insensible or hardened to. **3** To be unavailable to. **—be lost upon** (or **on**) To have no effect upon (a person). **—Syn. 1** mislaid, misplaced. **4** astray. **9** confused, dazed.

lot (lot) *n.* **1** Anything, as dice or a piece of paper, used in determining something by chance. **2** The act or the result of deciding something in this manner. **3** The share that comes to one as the result of drawing lots. **4** The part in life that comes to one without his planning; chance; fate. **5** A number of persons or things considered as a group. **6** A parcel or quantity of land. **7** *Informal* A certain kind of person: he is a bad *lot.* **8** *Often pl. Informal* A great quantity or amount: a *lot* of money, *lots* of trouble. **9** A motion-picture studio and the adjacent area. **—the lot** The entire amount or quantity. **—throw** (or **cast**) **in one's lot with** To share the fortunes of. **—***adv.* Very much: a *lot* worse. **—***v.* **lot·ted, lot·ting** *v.t.* **1** To divide, as land, into lots. **2** To apportion by lots; allot. **—***v.i.* **3** To cast lots. [< OE *hlot*]

• lots, lots of These words, meaning "a great deal" or "many," are common and unobjectionable in informal speech and writing: *She is lots cleverer than I; They make lots of complaints.* They should be avoided, however, in formal contexts.

Lot (lot) In the Bible, a nephew of Abraham who was permitted to escape the destruction of Sodom. Lot's wife, disobeying a warning, looked back at the city and was turned into a pillar of salt.

loth (lōth) *adj.* LOATH.

Lo·thar·i·o (lō·thâr′ē·ō) *n. pl.* **·os** A seducer; libertine. [< *Lothario,* a rake in Nicholas Rowe's play *The Fair Penitent,* 1703]

lo·tion (lō′shən) *n.* A cosmetic or medicinal liquid preparation for external use. [< L *lotio* washing]

lot·ter·y (lot′ər·ē) *n. pl.* **·ter·ies 1** A method of awarding prizes involving numbered chances, the winning numbers being selected by drawing lots. **2** Any chance disposition of any matter. [< Ital. *lotto* lottery, lot]

lot·to (lot′ō) *n.* A game of chance played with numbered cards and disks. [Ital., lot, lottery]

lo·tus (lō′təs) *n.* **1** One of various tropical waterlilies with large floating leaves and showy flowers; esp. the **white** and **blue lotuses** of the Nile and the **sacred lotus** of India. **2** Any of a genus of leguminous herbs or shrubs. **3** *Archit.* A representation or conventionalization of the lotus flower, bud, or leaves. Also **lo′tos.** [< Gk. *lōtos*]

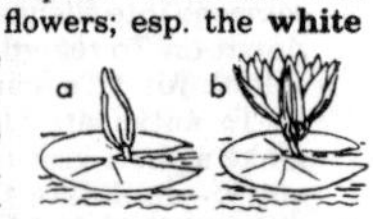

Lotus. a. bud and leaf. b. blossom and leaf.

lo·tus-eat·er (lō′təs·ē′tər) *n.* **1** In the *Odyssey,* one who lives in irresponsible enjoyment from eating the fruit of a certain unidentified plant. **2** Any indolent or irresponsible person.

loud (loud) *adj.* **1** Having great volume or intensity of sound. **2** Making a great sound or noise: a *loud* engine. **3** Pressing or urgent; clamorous: a *loud* demand. **4** *Informal* Very showy: a *loud* tie. **5** *Informal* Offensively noisy and talkative: a *loud* boor. **—***adv.* With loudness; loudly. [< OE *hlūd*] **—loud′ly** *adv.* **—loud′ness** *n.*

loud·ish (loud′ish) *adj.* Somewhat loud.

loud·mouthed (loud′mouthd′, -moutht′) *adj.* Possessed of a loud voice; offensively clamorous or talkative.

loud·speak·er (loud′spē′kər) *n.* A device for converting electrical energy to sound.

lou·is (lōō′ē) *n.* LOUIS D'OR.

lou·is d'or (lōō′ē dôr) **1** A French gold coin worth twenty francs. **2** An old French gold coin not issued after the Revolution.

lounge (lounj) *v.* **lounged, loung·ing** *v.i.* **1** To lie, lean, move, etc., in an idle or lazy manner. 2 To pass time indolently. —*v.t.* 3 To spend or pass indolently, as time. —*n.* 1 The act of lounging. 2 A room in a hotel, club, etc., for lounging. 3 A couch or sofa. **—loung′er** *n.* [?]

loupe (lo͞op) *n.* A small magnifying glass held in the eye, used esp. by jewelers. [F]

lour (lour) *v.* LOWER².

louse (lous) *n. pl.* **lice** (līs) 1 Any of various small, wingless, parasitic insects that suck blood and inhabit the hair, fur, or feathers of the host animal. 2 Any of various insects or arthropods externally parasitic on various animals. 3 An aphid **(plant louse).** 4 *Slang pl.* **lous·es** A contemptible person. —*v.t. & v.i. Slang* To ruin; bungle: with *up.* [< OE *lūs*]

lous·y (lou′zē) *adj.* **lous·i·er, lous·i·est** 1 Infested with lice. 2 *Slang* Dirty. 3 *Slang* Contemptible; mean. 4 *Slang* Inferior; poor. 5 *Slang* Having plenty (of): usu. with *with: lousy* with money.

lout (lout) *n.* An awkward, stupid fellow; boor. [? < ON *lutr* bent, stooped] **—lout′ish** *adj.* **—lout′ish·ly** *adv.* **—lout′·ish·ness** *n.*

lou·ver (lo͞o′vər) *n.* 1 A window or other opening designed for ventilation and having slats **(louver boards)** sloped to keep out the rain while admitting light and air. 2 A slat in such an opening. 3 Any of several narrow openings used for ventilation. [< OF *lover*]

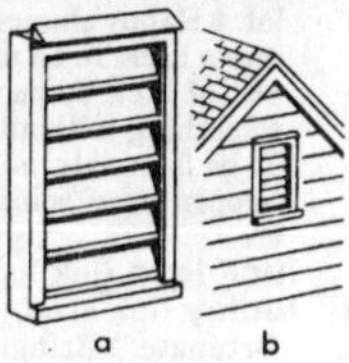

Louver
a. detail. b. installed.

lov·a·ble (luv′ə·bəl) *adj.* Worthy of love; amiable; also, inspiring love. Also **love′a·ble.** **—lov′a·bly** *adv.* **—lov′a·bil′i·ty, lov′a·ble·ness** *n.*

love (luv) *n.* 1 A strong tender affection; deep devotion, as to one's child, parent, etc. 2 The affection felt by two persons who are sexually attracted to one another. 3 A person who is the object of another's affection. 4 A very great interest or fondness: *love* of learning. 5 *Often cap.* A god of love, as Cupid or Eros. 6 In tennis, a score of nothing. **—fall in love** To begin feeling affection and passionate interest. **—for the love of** For the sake of. **—in love** Experiencing love; enamored. **—make love** 1 To have sexual intercourse. 2 To embrace; kiss. —*v.* **loved, lov·ing** *v.t.* 1 To feel love or affection for. 2 To take pleasure or delight in; like very much. 3 To caress. —*v.i.* 4 To feel love, esp. for one of the opposite sex; be in love. [< OE *lufu*] **—Syn.** *n.* 1 attachment, fondness.

love apple TOMATO.

love·bird (luv′bûrd′) *n.* Any of several small parrots that appear to show great affection for their mates.

love knot A knot tied in pledge of love and constancy; also, a representation of it, as in jewelry.

love·less (luv′lis) *adj.* 1 Unloving. 2 Unloved. **—love′less·ly** *adv.* **—love′less·ness** *n.*

love-lies-bleed·ing (luv′līz′blē′ding) *n.* A species of amaranth with drooping spikes of red flowers.

love·lorn (luv′lôrn) *adj.* Forsaken by or pining for a lover.

love·ly (luv′lē) *adj.* **·li·er, ·li·est** 1 Possessing mental or physical qualities that inspire admiration or love. 2 Beautiful. 3 *Informal* Enjoyable; pleasing: a *lovely* visit. [< OE *luflic*] **—love′li·ness** *n.*

love potion A magic drink designed to arouse love toward a certain person in the drinker.

lov·er (luv′ər) *n.* 1 One who loves. 2 One who is in love; specifically, a paramour: said esp. of a man. 3 *pl.* A couple who are in love with each other. 4 One who enjoys or is strongly attracted by some object or diversion. **—lov′er·ly** *adj., adv.*

love seat A small sofa for two persons.

love·sick (luv′sik′) *adj.* 1 Languishing with love. 2 Indicating or expressing such a condition: a *lovesick* serenade. **—love′sick′ness** *n.*

lov·ing (luv′ing) *adj.* 1 Feeling love. 2 Expressing love. **—lov′ing·ly** *adv.* **—lov′ing·ness** *n.*

loving cup 1 A drinking cup, usu. with two or more handles, formerly passed from hand to hand around a circle of friends. 2 A cup like this, given as a trophy.

lov·ing-kind·ness (luv′ing·kīnd′nis) *n.* Kindness that comes from or expresses love.

low¹ (lō) *adj.* 1 Not high or tall. 2 Near the horizon: a *low* moon. 3 Situated below a recognized level: a *low* marsh. 4 Having less than the normal or regular height or depth: The river is *low.* 5 Cut so as to expose the shoulders, back, or neck. 6 Having depth of pitch; deep. 7 Having little volume or strength; soft. 8 Being little in degree, number, amount, etc. 9 Below standard quality: a *low* grade of beef. 10 Dead; prostrate: He lies *low.* 11 Deep, as a bow. 12 Depressed or melancholy. 13 Humble, as in rank or position. 14 Not refined; coarse; vulgar. 15 Not favorable; poor: a *low* opinion of oneself. 16 Relatively recent: a *low* date. 17 Not well provided with: *low* on supplies. 18 *Phonet.* Pronounced with the tongue low and flat; open: said of vowels. 19 Little advanced in structure, complexity, function, etc.: a *low* form of plant life. 20 Lacking in vigor. 21 *Mech.* Giving the greatest force and the least speed: *low* gear. 22 *Geog.* Pertaining to latitudes near the equator. —*adv.* 1 In a low way. 2 In or to a low position. 3 At a low price; cheap. 4 In a humble rank or degraded condition. 5 Softly. 6 At a low pitch. 7 Near the equator or the horizon. **—lie low** 1 To be or remain in hiding. 2 To hold one's tongue till the proper moment; wait. —*n.* 1 A low level, degree, etc. 2 An arrangement of gears in a motor vehicle, etc., providing the greatest force or torque and the lowest speed. [< ON *lāgr*] **—low′ness** *n.*

low² (lō) *n.* The moo or bellow of cattle: also **low′ing.** —*v.i.* 1 To bellow, as cattle; moo. —*v.t.* 2 To utter by lowing. [< OE *hlōwan*]

low-born (lō′bôrn′) *adj.* Of humble birth.

low·boy (lō′boi′) *n.* A short-legged dressing table, with drawers.

low-bred (lō′bred′) *adj.* Vulgar; ill-bred.

low·brow (lō′brou′) *Informal n.* A person of uncultivated tastes; a nonintellectual. —*adj.* Of or suitable for such a person: also **low′browed′.** **—low′brow′ism** *n.*

Low Church A group in the Anglican Church that stresses evangelical doctrine and attaches little importance to ritual, church authority, and the sacraments. —**Low′-Church′** *adj.* **—Low-Church·man** (lō′chûrch′mən) *n.*

low comedy Comedy characterized by slapstick and lively physical action rather than by witty dialogue.

Low Countries The Netherlands, Belgium, and Luxembourg.

low-down¹ (lō′doun′) *n. Slang* Inside or secret information; the truth of a matter.

low-down² (lō′doun′) *adj. Informal* Degraded; mean.

low·er¹ (lō′ər) Comparative of LOW. —*adj.* 1 Inferior in position, value, rank, etc. 2 *Geol.* Older; designating strata normally beneath the newer (and upper) rock formations. —*n.* That which is beneath something above; esp., a lower berth. —*v.t.* 1 To bring to a lower position or level; let down, as a window. 2 To reduce in degree, quality, amount, etc.: to *lower* prices. 3 To bring down in estimation, rank, etc.; humble or degrade. 4 To weaken or undermine. 5 To change, as a sound, to a lower pitch or volume. —*v.i.* 6 To become lower; sink. **—Syn.** *v.* 2 decrease, diminish, lessen. 3 abase, debase. 6 fall.

low·er² (lou′ər) *v.i.* 1 To look angry or sullen; scowl. 2 To appear dark and threatening, as the weather. —*n.* A scowl; a gloomy aspect. [ME *louren*]

low·er-case (lō′ər·kās′) *adj. Printing* Of, in, or describing lower case. —*v.t.* **-cased, -cas·ing** To set as or change to lower-case letters.

lower case *Printing* The small letters of a font of type, distinguished from capital letters.

low·er-class·man (lō′ər·klas′mən, -kläs′-) *n. pl.* **·men** (-mən) A freshman or a sophomore.

Lower House In a legislature having two branches, the more representative and, usu., larger branch; in the U.S., the House of Representatives; in Great Britain and Canada, the House of Commons.

low·er·ing (lou′ər·ing) *adj.* 1 Overcast with clouds; threatening. 2 Frowning or sullen. —**low′er·ing·ly** *adv.* —**low′er·ing·ness** *n.*

low·er·most (lō′ər·mōst′) *adj.* Lowest.

lower world 1 The abode of the dead; hell; Hades: also **lower regions.** 2 The earth.

Low German 1 The collective languages of the Low Countries, including Dutch, Flemish, and Frisian, and of the N lowlands of Germany (Plattdeutsch). 2 That division of the Germanic languages which includes Dutch, Flemish, Frisian, English, etc.

low-key (lō′kē′) *adj.* Having a low degree of intensity; understated. Also **low-keyed** (lō′kēd′).

low·land (lō′lənd) *adj.* Pertaining to or characteristic of a low or level country. —*n.* (*also* lō′land′) *Usu. pl.* Land lower than the adjacent country; level land. —**the Lowlands** The less elevated districts lying in the south and east of Scotland. —**Low′land′er** *n.*

Low Latin The Latin language of any period after the classical, esp. of the Middle Ages.

low·ly (lō′lē) *adj.* **·li·er, ·li·est** 1 Low, as in position, rank, etc. 2 Meek, modest, or humble. —*adv.* 1 In a low position, manner, etc. 2 Meekly, modestly, or humbly. —**low′li·ness** *n.*

low mass A mass without music celebrated by one priest, usu. assisted by an altar boy.

low-mind·ed (lō′mīn′did) *adj.* Having low, mean, or vulgar thoughts, sentiments, or motives.

low-pitched (lō′picht′) *adj.* Low in tone, key, or range of tone, as a voice.

low-pres·sure (lō′presh′ər) *adj.* Requiring or having a low degree of pressure.

low-rise (lō′rīz′) *adj.* Describing a relatively low building or structure. —*n.* A building having no more than a few stories and usu. not having an elevator: also **low rise.**

low-spir·it·ed (lō′spir′it·id) *adj.* Lacking spirit or animation; despondent. —**low′-spir′it·ed·ly** *adv.* —**low′-spir′it·ed·ness** *n.*

low tide 1 The lowest stage of an ebb tide. 2 The time when this stage occurs.

low water 1 The lowest level of the water, as in a lake or river. 2 Low tide.

lox[1] (loks) *n.* Smoked salmon. [<G *lachs* salmon]

lox[2] (loks) *n.* Liquid oxygen. [<*l(iquid) ox(ygen)*]

loy·al (loi′əl) *adj.* 1 Constant and faithful in any relationship implying trust or confidence. 2 Unswerving in allegiance to constituted authority, as one's country or sovereign. 3 Characterized by or showing loyalty. [<L *legalis* legal] —**loy′al·ism** *n.* —**loy′al·ly** *adv.* —**Syn.** 1 devoted, steadfast, true, trustworthy.

loy·al·ist (loi′əl·ist) *n.* One who adheres to and defends his sovereign or state.

Loy·al·ist (loi′əl·ist) *n.* 1 One who was loyal to the British crown during the American Revolution. 2 One who was loyal to the Republic during the Spanish Civil War.

loy·al·ty (loi′əl·tē) *n. pl.* **·ties** The state, quality, or an instance of being loyal; allegiance; fidelity.

loz·enge (loz′inj) *n.* A small medicated or sweetened tablet. [<OF *losenge*]

LP (el′pē′) *adj.* Designating a phonograph record with fine grooves, played at 33⅓ revolutions per minute. —*n.* An LP record: a trade name. [<L(ONG)-P(LAYING)]

Lr lawrencium.

l.s.c. in the place cited above (L *loco supra citato*).

LSD (el′es′dē′) *n.* A drug that produces states similar to those of schizophrenia, used illicitly as a hallucinogen. [< *l(y)s(ergic acid) d(iethylamide)*]

£.s.d. pounds, shillings, pence (Brit.).

Lt. Lieutenant.

l.t., l.tn. long ton.

Ltd., ltd. limited.

Lu lutetium.

lub·ber (lub′ər) *n.* 1 An awkward, ungainly fellow. 2 LANDLUBBER. [?] —**lub′ber·ly** *adj., adv.* —**lub′ber·li·ness** *n.*

lu·bri·cant (lōō′brə·kənt) *adj.* Lubricating. —*n.* A substance, as grease or oil, used to coat parts that move against each other, to make them work easily and to reduce friction.

lu·bri·cate (lōō′brə·kāt) *v.t.* **·cat·ed, ·cat·ing** 1 To apply grease, oil, or other lubricant to so as to reduce friction and wear. 2 To make slippery or smooth. [<L *lubricus* slippery] —**lu′bri·ca′tive** *adj.* —**lu′bri·ca′tion, lu′bri·ca′tor** *n.*

lu·bric·i·ty (lōō·bris′ə·tē) *n.* 1 Smoothness; slipperiness. 2 Shiftiness; trickiness. 3 Lewdness. —**lu·bri·cous** (lōō′brə·kəs), **lu·bri·cious** (lōō·brish′əs) *adj.* [<L *lubricus* slippery]

lu·cent (lōō′sənt) *adj.* 1 Giving off light; shining; luminous. 2 Clear or translucent. [<L *lucere* to shine]

lu·cerne (lōō·sûrn′) *n. Chiefly Brit.* ALFALFA. Also **lu·cern′.**

lu·cid (lōō′sid) *adj.* 1 Easily understood; clear. 2 Mentally sound; rational. 3 Giving forth light; shining. 4 Translucent. [<L *lucere* to shine] —**lu·cid·i·ty** (lōō·sid′ə·tē), **lu′cid·ness** *n.* —**lu′cid·ly** *adv.*

lu·ci·fer (lōō′sə·fər) *n.* A match that ignites by friction. [<*Lucifer*]

Lu·ci·fer (lōō′sə·fər) *n.* 1 The planet Venus when it is the morning star. 2 Satan, esp. as the leader of the revolt of the angels before his fall from heaven. [<L *lux, lucis* light + *ferre* to bear] —**Lu·cif·er·ous** (lōō·sif′ər·əs) *adj.*

Lu·cite (lōō′sīt) *n.* A thermoplastic transparent plastic: a trade name.

luck (luk) *n.* 1 That which happens by chance; fortune or lot. 2 Happy chance; good fortune; success. —**be down on one's luck** To be unlucky. —**be in luck** To be lucky. —**be out of luck** To be unlucky. —**try one's luck** To try to do something without certainty of success. —*v.i. Informal* 1 To be fortunate; succeed through good luck: with *out.* 2 To happen upon something by good luck: with *in, on, onto,* etc.

luck·less (luk′lis) *adj.* Unlucky. —**luck′less·ly** *adv.*

luck·y (luk′ē) *adj.* **luck·i·er, luck·i·est** 1 Favored by fortune; fortunate. 2 Bringing or resulting in good luck. 3 Thought to bring good luck. —**luck′i·ly** *adv.* —**luck′i·ness** *n.* —**Syn.** 1 blessed, happy, successful. 2 auspicious, propitious.

lu·cra·tive (lōō′krə·tiv) *adj.* Productive of wealth; profitable. [<L *lucrum* wealth] —**lu′cra·tive·ly** *adv.*

lu·cre (lōō′kər) *n.* Money or riches: now chiefly in the phrase **filthy lucre,** usu. used humorously. [<L *lucrum* gain]

lu·cu·brate (lōō′kyōō·brāt) *v.i.* **·brat·ed, ·brat·ing** 1 To study or write laboriously, esp. at night. 2 To write in a learned manner. [<L *lucubrare* to work by candlelight]

lu·cu·bra·tion (lōō′kyōō·brā′shən) *n.* 1 Close and earnest meditation or study. 2 The product of such study; esp., a pedantic or overelaborated work. 3 *Often pl.* Any literary work. —**lu′cu·bra·to′ry** (-brə·tôr′ē, -tō′rē) *adj.*

lu·di·crous (lōō′də·krəs) *adj.* Exciting laughter because absurd, incongruous, ridiculous, etc. [<L *ludere* to play] —**lu′di·crous·ly** *adv.* —**lu′di·crous·ness** *n.*

luff (luf) *n. Naut.* 1 The sailing of a ship close to the wind. 2 The foremost edge of a fore-and-aft sail. —*v.i. Naut.* To bring the bow of a vessel toward the wind; sail near the wind. [<OF *lof*]

Luft·waf·fe (lōōft′väf′ə) *n. German* The German air force in World War II.

lug[1] (lug) *n.* 1 A projection for carrying or supporting something. 2 *Slang* A clumsy or stupid fellow. [?]

lug[2] (lug) *v.t. & v.i.* **lugged, lug·ging** To carry or pull with effort; drag. —*n.* LUGSAIL. [Prob.<Scand.]

lug[3] (lug) *n.* LUGWORM.[?]

luge (lōōzh) *n.* A specially designed, streamlined sled for racing. —*v.i.* **luged, lug·ing, luge·ing** To race using a luge.

lug·gage (lug′ij) *n.* Suitcases, valises, etc., used by a traveler; baggage. [<LUG[2]]

lug·ger (lug′ər) *n.* A small boat with lugsails.

lug·sail (lug′səl, -sāl′) *n.* A four-cornered sail, hung from a yard that slants across the mast. [<LUG[2]]

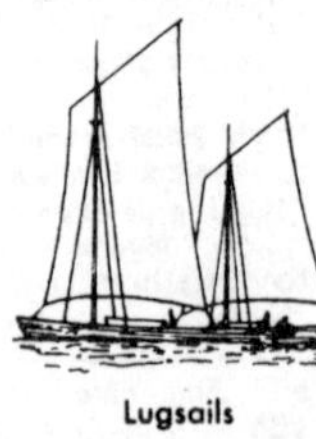

Lugsails

lu·gu·bri·ous (lōō·gyōō′brē·əs) *adj.* Sad, mournful, or dismal, esp. in a ludicrous way. [<L *lugere* mourn] —**lu·gu′bri·ous·ly** *adv.* —**lu·gu′bri·ous·ness** *n.*

lug·worm (lug′wûrm′) *n.* An annelid worm with bristles on the back, found along seashores.

Luke (lōōk) The evangelist and reputed author of the third Gospel and the Acts of the Apostles: also **Saint Luke.** —*n.* The third Gospel.

luke·warm (lo͞ok′wôrm′) *adj.* 1 Moderately warm; tepid. 2 Without conviction, warmth, or enthusiasm; indifferent. [Prob.< OE *hlēow* warm + WARM] —**luke′warm′ly** *adv.* —**luke′warm′ness** *n.*

lull (lul) *v.t.* 1 To soothe to sleep. 2 To calm; allay, as suspicions. —*v.i.* 3 To become calm. —*n.* An interval of calm, quiet, or diminishing activity. [ME *lullen*] —**Syn.** *v.* 1 hush, pacify, quiet, tranquilize. 2 alleviate, mitigate.

lull·a·by (lul′ə·bī) *n. pl.* **·bies** A song to lull a child to sleep. —*v.t.* **·bied, ·by·ing** To soothe with or as with a lullaby.

lu·lu[1] (lo͞o′lo͞o′) *n. Slang* Anything exceptional or remarkable, as a difficult examination, a beautiful person, etc. [Prob. < *Lulu,* formed from *Louise*]

lu·lu[2] (lo͞o′lo͞o′) *n. Slang* A sum of money paid to legislators for expenses. [< in *lieu* of (itemized accounting of expenses)]

lum·ba·go (lum·bā′gō) *n.* Pain in the lower part of the back. [< L *lumbus* loin]

lum·bar (lum′bər, -bär) *adj.* Pertaining to or situated near the loins. [< L *lumbus* loin]

lum·ber[1] (lum′bər) *n.* 1 Timber sawed into boards, planks, etc. 2 Disused articles, as household furniture, that take up room or are stored away. —*v.t.* 1 To cut down (timber). 2 To fill or obstruct with useless articles. —*v.i.* 3 To cut down or saw timber for marketing. [? var. of *Lombard* in obs. sense of "money-lender, pawnshop"; hence, stored articles] —**lum′ber·er** *n.*

lum·ber[2] (lum′bər) *v.i.* 1 To move or proceed in a heavy or awkward manner. 2 To move with a rumbling noise. —*n.* A rumbling noise. [ME *lomeren*] —**lum′ber·ing·ly** *adv.* —**lum′ber·ing·ness** *n.*

lum·ber·jack (lum′bər·jak) *n.* A person whose occupation is felling trees, cutting them into logs, and transporting the logs to a sawmill.

lum·ber·man (lum′bər·mən) *n. pl.* **·men** (-mən) 1 LUMBERJACK. 2 One who deals in lumber.

lum·ber·yard (lum′bər·yärd′) *n.* A yard for the storage or sale of lumber.

lu·men (lo͞o′mən) *n. pl.* **·mens** or **·mi·na** (-mə·nə) *Physics* A unit for measuring luminous flux, equal to the light emitted in a unit solid angle by a uniform point source of one candela. [L, light]

lu·mi·nar·y (lo͞o′mə·ner′ē) *n. pl.* **·nar·ies** 1 Any body that gives light, as the sun or moon. 2 One who has achieved great fame. [< L *lumen* light]

lu·mi·nesce (lo͞o′mə·nes′) *v.i.* **·nesced, ·nesc·ing** To exhibit luminescence.

lu·mi·nes·cence (lo͞o′mə·nes′əns) *n.* An emission of light, as fluorescence, not directly attributable to the heat which produces incandescence. [< L *lumen* light + -ESCENCE] —**lu′mi·nes′cent** *adj.*

lu·mi·nif·er·ous (lo͞o′mə·nif′ər·əs) *adj.* Producing or conveying light. [< L *lumen* light + -FEROUS]

lu·mi·nous (lo͞o′mə·nəs) *adj.* 1 Giving or emitting light; shining. 2 Full of light; well lighted; bright. 3 Easily understood; clear. [< L *lumen* light] —**lu′mi·nous·ly** *adj.* —**lu·mi·nos·i·ty** (lo͞o′mə·nos′ə·tē), **lu′mi·nous·ness** *n.*

lum·mox (lum′əks) *n. Informal* A heavy, clumsy, usu. stupid person. [?]

lump[1] (lump) *n.* 1 A shapeless mass. 2 A mass of things thrown together. 3 A protuberance; swelling. 4 A heavy, ungainly person, esp., one who is stupid. —**in a** (or **the**) **lump** All together; with no distinction. —*v.t.* 1 To put together in one mass, group, etc. 2 To consider or treat collectively: to *lump* facts. 3 To make lumps in or on. —*v.i.* 4 To become lumpy. [Prob. < Scand.]

lump[2] (lump) *v.t. Informal.* To put up with (something disagreeable): Like it or *lump* it. [?]

lump·ish (lum′pish) *adj.* 1 Like a lump. 2 Stupid; dull. 3 Clumsy; heavy. —**lump′ish·ly** *adv.* —**lump′ish·ness** *n.*

lump sum An entire amount paid at one time.

lump·y (lum′pē) *adj.* **lump·i·er, lump·i·est** 1 Full of or covered with lumps. 2 Lumpish or gross. 3 Rough: a *lumpy* sea. —**lump′i·ly** *adv.* —**lump′i·ness** *n.*

Lu·na (lo͞o′nə) *Rom. Myth.* The goddess of the moon. —*n.* The moon.

lu·na·cy (lo͞o′nə·sē) *n. pl.* **·cies** 1 Insanity. 2 Wild foolishness; senseless conduct. [< LUNATIC]

luna moth A large North American moth having light green wings with long tails. Also **Luna moth.** [< L *luna* moon; from the crescent-shaped spots on its wings]

Luna moth

lu·nar (lo͞o′nər) *adj.* 1 Of or pertaining to the moon. 2 Round or shaped like a crescent. 3 Measured by revolutions of the moon. [< L *luna* the moon]

lunar module *Aerospace* A part of a space vehicle designed to land astronauts on the moon and lift them off to link up with the command module. Also **lunar excursion module.**

lunar month The interval between two new moons.

lunar year Twelve lunar months.

lu·nate (lo͞o′nāt) *adj.* Crescent-shaped. Also **lu′nat·ed.** [< L *luna* the moon]

lu·na·tic (lo͞o′nə·tik) *adj.* 1 Insane. 2 Of, pertaining to, or for the insane. 3 Irrational; wildly foolish. Also **lu·nat·i·cal** (lo͞o·nat′i·kəl). —*n.* 1 An insane person. 2 A very foolish person. [< L *luna* the moon] —**Syn.** *adj.* 1 demented, deranged, mad, unbalanced. 3 foolhardy, rash.

lunch (lunch) *n.* 1 A light meal, esp. the one between breakfast and dinner. 2 Food provided for a lunch. —*v.i.* 1 To eat lunch. —*v.t.* 2 To furnish lunch for. [?] —**lunch′er** *n.*

lunch·eon (lun′chən) *n.* A lunch, esp. one taken with others.

lunch·eon·ette (lun′chən·et′) *n.* A restaurant where light lunches can be obtained.

lunch·room (lunch′ro͞om′, -ro͝om′) *n.* 1 A room, as in a school, where lunches may be eaten and sometimes where food may be obtained. 2 LUNCHEONETTE.

lung (lung) *n.* Either of the two porous organs of respiration in the thorax of vertebrates, having the function of absorbing oxygen and discharging carbon dioxide. [< OE *lungen*]

lunge (lunj) *n.* 1 A sudden pass or thrust, as with a sword or a bayonet. 2 A sudden forward lurch; plunge. —*v.* **lunged, lung·ing** —*v.i.* 1 To make a lunge or pass; thrust. 2 To move with a lunge. —*v.t.* 3 To thrust with or as with a lunge. [< F *allonger* prolong < L *ad* to + *longus* long] —**lung′er** *n.*

lung·fish (lung′fish′) *n. pl.* **·fish** or **·fish·es** Any of various fishes having both lungs and gills.

lung·wort (lung′wûrt′) *n.* Any of various herbs related to borage, having spotted leaves and bluish flowers.

Lu·per·ca·li·a (lo͞o′pər·kā′lē·ə, -kāl′yə) *n.* An ancient Roman fertility festival celebrated on February 15. Also **Lu′per·cal** (-kal). —**Lu′per·ca′li·an** *adj.*

lu·pine[1] (lo͞o′pīn) *adj.* Of, pertaining to, or like a wolf; wolfish. [< L *lupus* wolf]

lu·pine[2] (lo͞o′pin) *n.* Any of a genus of leguminous plants bearing flowers in long racemes, used for forage. [< L *lupinus* wolflike]

lu·pus (lo͞o′pəs) *n.* Any of various diseases affecting the skin, esp. **lupus vul·ga·ris** (vul·gar′is) or tuberculosis of the skin. [L, wolf]

lurch[1] (lûrch) *v.i.* 1 To roll suddenly to one side, as a ship at sea. 2 To move unsteadily; stagger. —*n.* A lurching or unsteady movement. [?]

lurch[2] (lurch) *n.* A specified defeat in cribbage. —**leave in the lurch** To leave in an embarrassing or difficult position. [< F *lourche,* name of a game]

lure (lo͝or) *n.* 1 A feathered device resembling a bird, sometimes baited with food and fastened to a falconer's wrist to recall the hawk. 2 In angling, an artificial bait; also, a decoy for animals. 3 Anything that invites by the prospect of advantage or pleasure. —*v.t.* **lured, lur·ing** 1 To attract or entice.

Lures *def. 2*

2 To recall (a hawk) with a lure. [<OF *leurre* bait] —**lur′er** *n.* —**Syn.** *v.* 1 allure, draw, inveigle, invite, tempt.

lu·rid (lŏŏr′id) *adj.* 1 Violent; terrible; sensational: a *lurid* crime. 2 Shining or suffused with a red glow, as of flames seen through smoke or clouds. 3 Pale; sallow. [<L *luridus* sallow] —**lu′rid·ly** *adv.* —**lu′rid·ness** *n.*

lurk (lûrk) *v.i.* 1 To lie hidden, as in ambush. 2 To exist unnoticed or unsuspected. 3 To move secretly or furtively; slink. [ME *lurken*] —**lurk′er** *n.* —**lurk′ing·ly** *adv.*

lus·cious (lush′əs) *adj.* 1 Very pleasant to taste and smell; delicious. 2 Appealing to any of the senses. 3 Too sweet; cloying. [? Blend of LUSH and DELICIOUS] —**lus′cious·ly** *adv.* —**lus′cious·ness** *n.*

lush[1] (lush) *adj.* 1 Full of juice or succulence; fresh and tender. 2 Of or characterized by abundant growth. 3 Elaborate, extravagant, or ornate. [? <L *laxus* loose] —**lush′ly** *adv.* —**lush′ness** *n.*

lush[2] (lush) *Slang n.* 1 A drunkard; sot: also **lush′er.** 2 Strong or intoxicating liquor. —*v.t. & v.i. Slang* To drink (alcoholic liquor). [?]

lust (lust) *n.* 1 A very strong craving or desire. 2 An intense sexual appetite. —*v.i.* To have an intense desire, esp. sexual desire. [<OE, pleasure]

lus·ter (lus′tər) *n.* 1 Sheen; gloss. 2 Radiance; brightness. 3 Brilliance or splendor, as of beauty, character, or achievement. 4 The glossy look given to certain pottery by glazing. 5 A glossy fabric of wool and cotton. —*v.* **·tered** or **·tred, ·ter·ing** or **·tring** *v.t.* 1 To give a luster or gloss to. —*v.i.* 2 To be or become lustrous. Also **lus′tre.** [<L *lustrum* purification]

lus·ter·ware (lus′tər·wâr′) *n.* Pottery given an irridescent look by the application of metallic compounds to the glaze.

lust·ful (lust′fəl) *adj.* Characterized or motivated by lust. —**lust′ful·ly** *adv.* —**lust′ful·ness** *n.*

lus·trate (lus′trāt) *v.t.* **·trat·ed, ·trat·ing** To make pure by ceremony. [<L *lustrum* purification] —**lus·tra′tion** *n.* —**lus′tra·tive** (-trə·tiv) *adj.*

lus·trous (lus′trəs) *adj.* Having luster. —**lus′trous·ly** *adv.* —**lus′trous·ness** *n.* —**Syn.** bright, burnished, effulgent, luminous.

lus·trum (lus′trəm) *n.* 1 The solemn ceremony of purification of the ancient Roman people, made every five years. 2 A period of five years. [L]

lust·y (lus′tē) *adj.* **lust·i·er, lust·i·est** Full of vigor and health; robust. —**lust′i·ly** *adv.* —**lust′i·ness** *n.*

lu·ta·nist (lōō′tə·nist) *n.* One who plays the lute. Also **lu′te·nist.**

lute[1] (lōōt) *n.* A stringed musical instrument having a large, pear-shaped body, played by plucking the strings with the fingers. [<Ar. *al′ūd* the piece of wood]

Lute

lute[2] (lōōt) *n.* A cementlike composition used to exclude air, as around pipe joints. —*v.t.* **lut·ed, lut·ing** To seal with lute. [<L *lutum* mud] —**lu·ta′tion** *n.*

lu·te·tium (lōō·tē′shəm) *n.* A metallic element (symbol Lu) of the lanthanide series. [< *Lutetia,* ancient name for Paris]

Lu·ther·an (lōō′thər·ən) *n.* A member of a Protestant sect (**Lutheran Church**) founded by Martin Luther in the 16th century. —*adj.* Pertaining to or devoted to the Lutheran Church or its doctrines. —**Lu′ther·an·ism** *n.*

lux (luks) *n. pl.* **lux·es** or **lu·ces** (lōō′sēz) *Physics* A unit of illumination equivalent to one lumen per square meter of surface. [L, light]

Lux. Luxembourg.

Lux·em·bourg (luk′səm·bûrg) *n.* A constitutional monarchy of N Europe, 998 sq. mi., cap. Luxembourg. Also **Lux′em·burg.** • See map at BELGIUM.

lux·u·ri·ance (lug·zhŏŏr′ē·əns, luk·shŏŏr′-) *n.* The quality or state of being luxuriant. Also **lux·u′ri·an·cy.**

lux·u·ri·ant (lug·zhŏŏr′ē·ənt, luk·shŏŏr′-) *adj.* 1 Exhibiting or characterized by vigor and abundance in growth. 2 Rich in nature, form, or content; extravagant, ornate, or abundant. 3 LUXURIOUS. —**lux·u′ri·ant·ly** *adv.*

lux·u·ri·ate (lug·zhŏŏr′ē·āt, luk·shŏŏr′-) *v.i.* **·at·ed, ·at·ing** 1 To take great pleasure; indulge oneself fully. 2 To live sumptuously. 3 To grow profusely. [<L *luxuria* luxury] —**lux·u′ri·a′tion** *n.*

lux·u·ri·ous (lug·zhŏŏr′ē·əs, luk·shŏŏr′-) *adj.* 1 Loving or indulging in luxury. 2 Characterized by or providing luxury. —**lux·u′ri·ous·ly** *adv.* —**lux·u′ri·ous·ness** *n.*

lux·u·ry (luk′shər·ē, lug′zhər·ē) *n. pl.* **·ries** 1 A way of life characterized by great comfort or pleasure. 2 Anything that contributes to comfort or pleasure but is not necessary to life, health, subsistence, etc. [<L *luxus* extravagance]

lv. leave(s).

-ly[1] *suffix of adjectives* 1 Like; characteristic of; pertaining to: *manly.* 2 Occurring every (specified interval): *weekly, daily.* [<OE *-lic*]

-ly[2] *suffix of adverbs* 1 In a (specified) manner: used to form adverbs from adjectives: *busily.* 2 Occurring every (specified interval): *yearly.* [<OE *-lice* <*-lic* -LY[1]] • In cases where an adjective already ends in *-ly,* the forms of the adjective and the adverb are often identical: a *kindly* smile; to speak *kindly.* Occasionally *-ly* is added to *-ly* (which then becomes *-li*), as in *surlily,* an awkward word to pronounce.

ly·cée (lē·sā′) *n. French* A public secondary school in France qualifying its students for a university. [<L *Lyceum* Lyceum]

ly·ce·um (lī·sē′əm) *n. pl.* **·ce·ums** or **·ce·a** (-sē′ə) 1 An organization providing popular instruction by lectures, debates, concerts, etc. 2 A public hall, as for lectures, discussions, etc. [<LYCEUM]

Ly·ce·um (lī·sē′əm) *n.* A grove near Athens in which Aristotle taught. [<Gk. *lykeios,* epithet of Apollo]

lyd·dite (lid′īt) *n.* A high explosive composed mainly of picric acid. [<*Lydd,* England]

lye (lī) *n.* 1 A solution leached from wood ashes, used in making soap. 2 Any strong alkali. [<OE *lēah*]

ly·ing[1] (lī′ing) *n.* The practice of telling lies; untruthfulness. —*adj.* Addicted to, conveying, or constituting falsehood. —**ly′ing·ly** *adv.* —**Syn.** *n.* deceit, deception, fabrication, prevarication. *adj.* false, mendacious.

ly·ing[2] (lī′ing) *pr. p.* of LIE[1].

ly·ing-in (lī′ing·in′) *n.* The confinement of women during childbirth. —*adj.* Of, for, or pertaining to childbirth: a *lying-in* hospital.

Lyme disease (līm) A tick-borne disease first marked by a rash, subsequently by arthritis and cardiac damage.

lymph (limf) *n.* A colorless fluid resembling plasma and containing white blood corpuscles, which moves in the lymph vessels of vertebrates and merges with the blood through certain veins. [<L *limpa* water]

lym·phat·ic (lim·fat′ik) *adj.* 1 Pertaining to, containing, or conveying lymph. 2 Without energy; listless. —*n.* A vessel that conveys lymph.

lymph node Any of the nodular bodies of spongy tissue found in the system of lymphatic vessels. Also **lymph gland.**

lympho- *combining form* Lymph; of or pertaining to lymph or the lymphatic system: *lymphocyte.*

lym·pho·cyte (lim′fə·sīt) *n.* A variety of leukocyte arising in the lymphatic system.

lym·phoid (lim′foid) *adj.* Of, pertaining to, or resembling lymph or a lymph node.

lynch (linch) *v.t.* To kill by mob action without legal sanction. [<LYNCH LAW] —**lynch′er, lynch′ing** *n.*

lynch law The practice of administering punishment by lynching. [<Capt. Wm. *Lynch,* 1742–1820, Virginia magistrate]

lynx (lingks) *n.* Any of several wildcats of Europe and North America, with a short tail, tufted ears, and long limbs. [<Gk. *lynx*]

lynx-eyed (lingks′īd′) *adj.* Having acute sight.

ly·on·naise (lī′ə·nāz′) *adj.* Made with finely sliced onions: *lyonnaise* potatoes. [<F *lyonnais* of Lyon]

Ly·ra (lī′rə) *n.* A northern constellation containing the star Vega. [Gk., lyre]

ly·rate (lī′rāt) *adj.* Resembling or suggesting the shape of a lyre. Also **ly′rat·ed.** —**ly′rate·ly** *adv.*

lyre (līr) *n.* A harplike stringed instrument, used by the ancient Greeks to accompany song and poetry. [<Gk.]

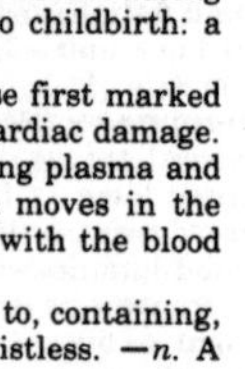
Lyre

lyre·bird (līr′bûrd′) *n.* An Australian bird distinguished in the male by tail feathers which resemble a lyre when spread.

lyr·ic (lir′ik) *adj.* **1** Of poetry, expressing the poet's personal emotions. **2** Of, pertaining to, or having written such poetry. **3** Musical; singing or meant to be sung. **4** Having or suitable for a relatively light, flexible vocal quality: a *lyric* tenor; a *lyric* aria. Also **lyr′i·cal.** —*n.* **1** A lyric poem. **2** *Usu. pl.* The words of a song, esp. as distinguished from the music. [<Gk. *lyra* a lyre] —**lyr′i·cal·ly** *adv.*

lyr·i·cist (lir′ə·sist) *n.* **1** One who writes the words of a song or the lyrics for a musical play. **2** A lyric poet.

ly·ser·gic acid (lī·sûr′jik) A toxic substance derived from ergot and forming the base of **lysergic acid di·eth·yl·am·ide** (dī′eth·əl·am′id), or LSD. [<Gk. *lusis* a loosening + ERG(OT) + -IC]

ly·sin (lī′sin) *n.* An antibody capable of destroying bacteria, blood corpuscles, etc. [See LYSIS]

ly·sis (lī′sis) *n.* **1** The process of cell destruction brought about by a lysin. **2** The gradual disappearing of a disease. [<Gk. *lyein* loose]

-lysis *combining form* A loosing, dissolving, etc.: *paralysis.* [<Gk. *loosening*]

-lyte[1] *combining form* A substance decomposed by a (specified) process: *electrolyte.* [<Gk. *lytos* dissolved]

-lyte[2] *combining form* -LITE.

-lytic *combining form* Loosing; dissolving: *paralytic.* [<Gk. *lysis* a loosening]

M

M, m (em) *n. pl.* **M's, m's, Ms, ms** (emz) **1** The 13th letter of the English alphabet. **2** Any spoken sound representing the letter *M* or *m.* **3** Something shaped like an M. **4** In Roman notation, the symbol for 1,000. **5** *Printing* EM. —*adj.* Shaped like an M.

M. Medieval; Monday; Monsieur.

M., m. male; married; masculine; medium; meridian, noon (L *meridies*).

m meter.

ma (mä, mô) *n.* Mama; mother. [Short for MAMA]

MA Massachusetts (P.O. abbr.).

M.A. Master of Arts (L *Magister Artium*); mental age.

ma'am (mam, mäm, məm) *n.* Madam.

ma·ca·bre (mə·kä′brə, -bər) *adj.* Grim; gruesome. Also **ma·ca′ber.** [<F *(danse) macabre* (dance) of death]

mac·ad·am (mə·kad′əm) *n.* **1** Small, broken stones for macadamizing a road. **2** A macadamized road. [<John L. *McAdam,* 1756–1836, British engineer]

mac·ad·am·ize (mə·kad′ə·mīz) *v.t.* **·ized, ·iz·ing** To make or finish (a road) with small broken stones, often with a tar or asphalt binder. —**mac·ad′am·i·za′tion** *n.*

ma·caque (mə·käk′) *n.* Any of a group of monkeys from Africa, Asia, and the East Indies. [<Pg. *macaco*]

mac·a·ro·ni (mak′ə·rō′nē) *n. pl.* **·nis** or **·nies** **1** An edible paste of wheat flour made into short tubes. **2** An English dandy of the 18th century. Also **mac′ca·ro′ni.** [<Ital. *macherone*]

mac·a·roon (mak′ə·rōōn′) *n.* A small cooky of ground almonds or coconut, white of egg, and sugar. [<Ital. *macherone* macaroni]

ma·caw (mə·kô′) *n.* A tropical American parrot with a long tail, harsh voice, and brilliant plumage. [<Pg. *macao*]

Mac·beth (mək·beth′) A king of Scotland, died 1057; hero of Shakespeare's tragedy of the same name.

Mac·ca·bees (mak′ə·bēz) A family of Jewish patriots who led a successful revolt against Syrian religious oppression. —*n. pl. (construed as sing.)* Two books of the Old Testament Apocrypha describing this revolt.

mace[1] (mās) *n.* **1** A club-shaped staff representing authority or an office. **2** A medieval steel war club, often with spiked metal head, for use against armor. [<OF *masse, mace*]

mace[2] (mās) *n.* An aromatic spice made from the covering of nutmeg seed. [<Gk. *makir* a spicy bark from India]

Mace (mās) *n.* A chemical solution that temporarily blinds or incapacitates one when sprayed in the face, used as a weapon. —*v.t.* **Maced, Mac·ing** To spray with Mace. [<Chemical *Mace,* a trade name]

Mac·e·do·ni·a (mas′ə·dō′nē·ə) *n.* The ancient Greek kingdom of **Mac·e·don** (mas′ə·don), a leading world power under Alexander the Great. —**Mac′e·do′ni·an** *adj., n.*

mac·er·ate (mas′ə·rāt) *v.* **·at·ed, ·at·ing** *v.t.* **1 a** To reduce to a soft mass by soaking. **b** To separate the soft parts of by soaking; digest. **2** To make thin; emaciate. —*v.i.* **3** To undergo maceration. [<L *macerare* make soft, knead]

mach., machin. machine; machinery; machinist.

ma·chet·e (mə·shet′ē, mə·shet′) *n.* A heavy knife used both as an implement and as a weapon in tropical America. [<L *marcus* a hammer]

Mach·i·a·vel·li·an (mak′ē·ə·vel′ē·ən) *adj.* Of or pertaining to Machiavelli, or to the unscrupulous doctrines of political opportunism associated with his name. —*n.* A follower of Machiavelli. Also **Mach′i·a·vel′i·an.** —**Mach′i·a·vel′li·an·ism′** *n.*

ma·chic·o·late (mə·chik′ə·lāt) *v.t.* **·lat·ed, ·lat·ing** To furnish with machicolations. [<Med. L *machicolare*]

ma·chic·o·la·tion (mə·chik′ə·lā′shən) *n. Archit.* An opening between a wall and a parapet, on a roof over an entrance, etc., to permit the dropping of missiles or boiling liquids on an enemy.

mach·i·nate (mak′ə·nāt) *v.t.* & *v.i.* **·nat·ed, ·nat·ing** To scheme, esp. with evil intent. [<L *machinari* contrive]

mach·i·na·tion (mak′ə·nā′shən) *n.* **1** The act of contriving a secret or hostile plan. **2** Such a plan or plot. —**mach′i·na′tor** *n.*

ma·chine (mə·shēn′) *n.* **1** Any combination of parts for utilizing, modifying, applying, or transmitting energy, performing a specific function, etc. **2** An automobile or other vehicle, as a bicycle, airplane, etc. **3** One who acts in a mechanical manner; a robot. **4** The organization of the powers of any complex body: the *machine* of government. **5** An organization within a political party, controlled by politicians chiefly by the use of patronage. —*adj.* **1** Of, for, or produced by a machine or machinery. **2** Mechanical; stereotyped. —*v.t.* **·chined, ·chin·ing** To shape, make, etc., by machinery. [<L *machina* contrivance]

ma·chine-gun (mə·shēn′gun′) *v.t.* **·gunned, ·gun·ning** To fire at or shoot with a machine gun.

machine gun An automatic gun that discharges small-arms ammunition in a rapid sequence.

machine language A language for programming a computer, written solely in binary digits (0, 1).

ma·chine-read·a·ble (mə·shēn′rē′də·bəl) *adj.* Being in a form that can be detected automatically for use by a computer: *machine-readable* numbers on a check.

ma·chin·er·y (mə·shē′nər·ē) *n. pl.* **·er·ies** **1** The parts of a machine, or a number of machines collectively. **2** Any combination of means working together to achieve a specific action or result: the *machinery* of elections.

machine shop A workshop for making or repairing machines.

machine tool A power-driven tool, esp. one designed for use on metals.

ma·chine-wash·a·ble (mə·shēn′wash′ə·bəl, -wôsh′-) *adj.* Capable of being washed in a washing machine without damage to color or fabric and without excessive shrinkage: said of garments, etc.

ma·chin·ist (mə·shē′nist) *n.* **1** One skilled in the use of machine tools. **2** A maker or repairer of machines.

ma·chis·mo (mä·chēz′mō, -chiz′-) *n.* Maleness or masculinity, esp. when associated with strong or exaggerated pride in or a conspicuous display of the qualities, attitudes, etc., considered characteristically masculine. [Sp. < *macho* male]

mach number (mak, mäk) The ratio of the speed of an object in a fluid medium to the speed of sound in the same medium. [< Ernst *Mach,* 1838–1916, Austrian physicist]

ma·cho (mä′chō) *n. pl.* **·chos** (-chōs) A virile man, esp. one who takes excessive pride in his virility. —*adj.* Of or characteristic of a macho. [Sp., male]

mack·er·el (mak′ər·əl) *n.* An Atlantic food fish, steel-blue above with blackish bars, and silvery beneath. [< OF *makerel*]

mackerel sky A high cloud formation resembling the markings on a mackerel's back.

mack·i·naw (mak′ə·nô) *n.* A short, double-breasted, outdoor coat, usu. made of heavy wool with a plaid pattern. Also **Mack′i·naw coat.** [< *Mackinac* Island, Michigan]

mack·in·tosh (mak′ən·tosh) *n.* **1** A raincoat. **2** A lightweight, waterproof fabric, originally rubber-coated. Also **mac′in·tosh.** [< Charles *Macintosh,* 1766–1843, Scottish chemist, inventor of the cloth]

mac·ra·mé (mak′rə·mā) *n.* **1** A fringe, lace, wall hanging, etc., made of coarsely knotted thread or cord. **2** The technique of making such items. [< Ar. *miqramah* a veil]

macro- *combining form* Large or long in size or duration: *macrocephaly.* Also **macr-.** [< Gk. *makros* large]

mac·ro·bi·ot·ics (mak′rō·bī·ot′iks) *n. pl. (construed as sing.)* A dietetic regimen advocating the use of whole-grain cereals, the avoidance of meat, etc. [< MACRO- + -BIOTIC] —**mac′ro·bi·ot′ic** *adj.* —**mac′ro·bi·ot′ic·al·ly** *adv.*

mac·ro·ceph·a·ly (mak′rō·sef′ə·lē) *n.* Excessive size of the head. [< MACRO- + Gk. *kephalē* head] —**mac′ro·ce·phal′ic** (-sə·fal′ik) *adj., n.* —**mac′ro·ceph′a·lous** *adj.*

mac·ro·cosm (mak′rə·koz′əm) *n.* **1** The great world; the universe. **2** Any large, multifaceted totality. [< MACRO- + Gk. *kosmos* world] —**mac′ro·cos′mic** *adj.*

ma·cron (mā′krən, -kron) *n.* A straight line (¯) over a vowel to show that it represents a long sound, as the ā in *day.* [< Gk. *makron,* neut. of *makros* long]

mac·u·la (mak′yə·lə) *n. pl.* **·lae** (-lē) **1** A spot, as of color on the skin. **2** *Astron.* A dark spot on the sun's surface. [L]

mad (mad) *adj.* **mad·der, mad·dest 1** Mentally deranged; insane. **2** Overpowered by strong emotion: *mad* with grief. **3** Foolish; reckless; unwise: a *mad* plan. **4** Wildly enthusiastic or fond of: *mad* about jazz. **5** Hilariously amusing or entertaining: a *mad* farce. **6** Angry; furious. **7** Having rabies. [< OE *gemǣd* insane] —**mad′ly** *adv.* —**mad′ness** *n.* —**Syn. 1** crazy, demented. **2** frantic, frenzied, wild, distracted, overwrought. **4** wild, crazy. **6** raging, fuming, infuriated, angered, wrathful.

mad·am (mad′əm) *n. pl.* **mes·dames** (mā·däm′, *Fr.* mā·dȧm′) *for def. 1,* **mad·ams** (mad′əmz) *for def. 2* **1** My lady; mistress: a respectful or polite term of address. **2** A woman in charge of a brothel. [< OF *ma* my + *dame* lady]

mad·ame (mad′əm, *Fr.* mȧ·dȧm′) *n. pl.* **mes·dames** (mā·däm′, *Fr.* mā·dȧm′) The French title of courtesy for a married woman, equivalent to *Mrs.:* abbreviated *Mme.* [F]

mad·cap (mad′kap′) *adj.* Wild; rattle-brained. —*n.* One who acts wildly or rashly.

mad·den (mad′n) *v.t. & v.i.* **1** To make or become mad or wild. **2** To inflame with anger; enrage. —**mad′den·ing** *adj.* —**mad′den·ing·ly** *adv.*

mad·der[1] (mad′ər) Comparative of MAD.

mad·der[2] (mad′ər) *n.* **1** Any of various shrubby, perennial hairy plants, esp. a vine with small, yellow flowers and a red, fleshy root. **2** A brilliant red dye formerly made from the madder root. [< OE *mædere*]

mad·ding (mad′ing) *adj.* Being or growing mad; delirious; raging.

made (mād) *p.t. & p.p.* of MAKE. —*adj.* **1** Put together; constructed: a badly *made* house. **2** Produced, esp. artificially. **3** Assured of success. —**have it made** *Slang* To be certain to succeed.

Ma·dei·ra (mə·dir′ə) *n.* A fortified wine made in the Madeira islands.

mad·e·moi·selle (mad′ə·mə·zel′, *Fr.* mȧd·mwȧ·zel′) *n. pl.* **mad·e·moi·selles,** *Fr.* **mes·de·moi·selles** (mād·mwȧ·zel′) **1** The French title of courtesy for unmarried women, equivalent to *Miss:* abbreviated *Mlle.* **2** A French nurse or governess. [F < *ma* my + *demoiselle* young lady]

made-to-or·der (mād′tə·ôr′dər) *adj.* **1** Made to specific measurements or for specific requirements. **2** Absolutely right or suitable.

made-up (mād′up′) *adj.* **1** Artificial; fictitious. **2** Complete; finished. **3** With make-up or cosmetics applied.

mad·house (mad′hous′) *n.* **1** A lunatic asylum. **2** A place of confusion, turmoil, and uproar.

mad·man (mad′man′, -mən) *n. pl.* **·men** (-men′, -mən) A lunatic; maniac. —**mad′wom′an** (-wŏŏm′ən) *n. Fem.*

Ma·don·na (mə·don′ə) *n.* **1** Mary, mother of Jesus. **2** A painting or statue of her. [Ital.< *ma* my + *donna* lady]

ma·dras (mə·dras′, -dräs′, mad′rəs) *n.* **1** A cotton cloth, usu. of several colors woven in various designs, esp. a plaid design. **2** A cotton or rayon fabric for curtains or draperies. **3** A large, brightly colored kerchief. [< *Madras,* India]

mad·re·pore (mad′rə·pôr, -pōr) *n.* Any of various corals that build reefs. [< Ital. *madrepora,* lit., mother stone] —**mad′re·por′ic** (-pôr′ik, -por′ik) *adj.*

mad·ri·gal (mad′rə·gəl) *n.* **1** A short lyric poem, usu. dealing with a pastoral or amatory subject. **2** A musical setting for such a poem, esp. a part song. **3** Any part song. [< LL *matricale* original, chief < L *matrix* womb]

mael·strom (māl′strəm) *n.* **1** A powerful, dangerous whirlpool. **2** Any violent, irresistible influence, emotion, etc. [< MDu. *malen* grind + *stroom* a stream]

mae·nad (mē′nad) *n.* **1** A priestess of Dionysus; a bacchante. **2** Any woman beside herself with frenzy or excitement. [< Gk. *mainas* frenzied] —**mae·nad′ic** *adj.*

ma·es·to·so (mä′es·tō′sō) *adj. & adv. Music* With majesty; stately. [Ital.]

ma·es·tro (mä·es′trō, mī′strō) *n.* A master in any art, esp. in music. [Ital]

Ma·fi·a (mä′fē·ä, maf′ē·ə) *n.* **1** In Sicily, a secret society, characterized by hostility to and deliberate flouting of the law. **2** A similar, criminal organization believed to exist in other countries. Also **Maf′fi·a.** [< Ital. *maffia*]

ma·fi·o·so (mäf′ē·ō′sō, -zō, maf′-) *n. pl.* **·si** (-sē, -zē) *Sometimes cap.* A member of the Mafia. [Ital. < MAFIA]

mag. magazine; magnet; magnetism; magnitude.

mag·a·zine (mag′ə·zēn′, mag′ə·zēn) *n.* **1** A periodical publication containing sketches, stories, essays, etc. **2** A depot, warehouse, etc., for storage, esp. for storage of explosives, ammunition, etc. **3** A chamber in a repeating firearm which holds the supply of reserve cartridges. **4** A supply chamber in a battery, camera, or the like. [< Ar. *makhzan* a storehouse]

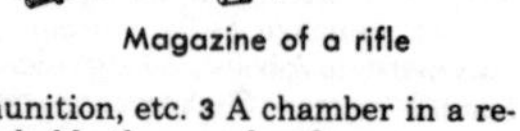

Magazine of a rifle

mag·da·len (mag′də·lin) *n.* A reformed prostitute. Also **mag′da·lene** (-lēn). [< Mary *Magdalene*]

Mag·el·lan·ic cloud (maj′ə·lan′ik) *Astron.* Either of two galaxies near the south pole of the heavens, looking like detached fragments of the Milky Way. [< F. *Magellan,* 1480–1521, Portuguese navigator]

ma·gen·ta (mə·jen′tə) *n.* **1** A red dyestuff derived from aniline. **2** A strong, purplish red. —*adj.* Purplish red. [< *Magenta,* Italy, where first discovered]

mag·got (mag′ət) *n.* A wormlike insect larva; a grub. [ME *maddock, mathek*] —**mag′got·y** *adj.*

Ma·gi (mā′jī) *n. pl.* of **Ma·gus** (mā′gəs) **1** The priestly caste of the Medes and Persians. **2** The three "wise men" who came "from the east" to Bethlehem to pay homage to the infant Jesus. [< Pers. *magu* priest, magician]

mag·ic (maj′ik) *n.* **1** Any supernatural power or control over natural laws or the forces of nature, esp. by the use of charms, etc. **2** The theatrical art of performing tricks and illusions by sleight of hand, mechanical devices, etc. **3** Any mysterious or spellbinding power or enchantment: the *magic* of her voice. —*adj.* **1** Of, used in, or produced by magic. **2** Bringing forth unusual results, as if by magic. • See MAGICAL. [< Gk. *magikos* of the Magi]

mag·i·cal (maj′i·kəl) *adj.* Magic. • The adjective *magic* is applied more commonly to the powers, influences, or practices, while *magical* is more frequently used of the effects of magic: *magic* arts, a *magic* wand, but a *magical* evening, a *magical* solution. —**mag′i·cal·ly** *adv.*

ma·gi·cian (mə·jish′ən) *n.* **1** An expert in magic arts. **2** Any person of unusual abilities.

magic lantern A device formerly used for projecting transparencies on a screen.

mag·is·te·ri·al (maj′is·tir′ē·əl) *adj.* **1** Of a magistrate, his duties, etc. **2** Like or befitting a master; commanding; authoritative. **3** Domineering; pompous. —**mag′is·te′ri·al·ly** *adv.*

mag·is·tra·cy (maj′is·trə·sē) *n. pl.* **·cies 1** The office or dignity of a magistrate. **2** The district under a magistrate's jurisdiction. **3** Magistrates collectively.

mag·is·trate (maj′is·trāt, -trit) *n.* **1** One clothed with public civil authority; an executive or judicial officer. **2** A minor public official, as a justice of the peace. [< L *magister* a master]

mag·ma (mag′mə) *n.* The molten mass within the earth from which igneous rocks are formed. [< Gk.] —**mag·mat·ic** (mag·mat′ik) *adj.*

Mag·na Car·ta (mag′nə kär′tə) **1** The Great Charter of English liberties, delivered June 19, 1215, by King John, at Runnymede, on the demand of the English barons. **2** Any fundamental constitution that secures personal liberty and civil rights. Also **Mag′na Char′ta.** [Med. L, lit., Great Charter]

mag·na cum lau·de (mag′nə kum lô′dē, mäg′nä ko͝om lou′də) With high honors: to be graduated *magna cum laude.* [L]

mag·na·nim·i·ty (mag′nə·nim′ə·tē) *n. pl.* **·ties 1** The quality or condition of being magnanimous. **2** A magnanimous deed.

mag·nan·i·mous (mag·nan′ə·məs) *adj.* Noble and generous; not petty, mean, or selfish. [< L *magnus* great + *animus* mind, soul] —**mag·nan′i·mous·ly** *adv.* —**mag·nan′i·mous·ness** *n.*

mag·nate (mag′nāt, -nit) *n.* A person of rank, power, or importance in any sphere. [< L *magnus* great]

mag·ne·sia (mag·nē′zhə, -shə, -zē·ə) *n.* The oxide of magnesium, used in medicine, glassmaking, etc. [< Gk. *Magnēsia (lithos)* (stone) of Magnesia] —**mag·ne′sian, mag·ne′sic** *adj.*

mag·ne·si·um (mag·nē′zē·əm, -zhəm) *n.* A light, malleable, ductile, metallic element (symbol Mg), used in structural alloys and in incendiary and photographic flash powders. [NL, magnesia]

mag·net (mag′nit) *n.* **1** Any mass of material capable of attracting bodies that are magnetized or capable of being magnetized. **2** A person or thing exercising a strong attraction. [< Gk. *Magnēs (lithos)* Magnesian (stone)]

mag·net·ic (mag·net′ik) *adj.* **1** Of, pertaining to, or caused or operated by a magnet or magnetism. **2** Capable of being magnetized. **3** Of the earth's magnetism. **4** Fascinatingly attractive or dynamic: a *magnetic* personality. —**mag·net′i·cal·ly** *adv.*

magnetic field That region in the neighborhood of a magnet or electric current in which magnetic effects are observable.

magnetic head A device for recording and playback by which magnetized particles on a moving tape are impressed with a pattern analogous to that of incident sound waves.

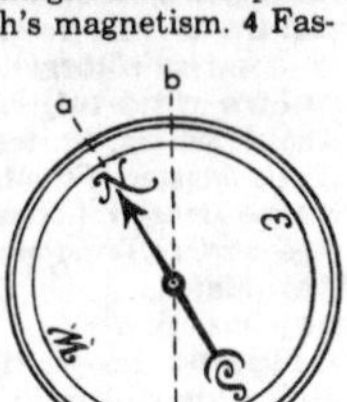

Magnetic needle
a. magnetic north.
b. true north.

magnetic needle A freely movable, needle-shaped bar of magnetized material which tends to align with an external magnetic field.

magnetic north The direction toward the magnetic pole of the earth that is closest to the North Pole.

magnetic pickup A phonograph pickup in which the movements of the stylus cause relative motion between a coil and a magnetic field and induce an electrical signal. Also **magnetic cartridge.**

magnetic pole 1 Either of the points of a magnet, usu. occurring in pairs of opposite polarity, at which the magnetic field is most intense. **2** Either of the earth's magnetic poles, called the **North** (or **South**) **Magnetic Pole.** These slowly change position and do not coincide with the geographical poles.

magnetic recording The process or the product of storing sound, TV programs, and other data in the form of ordered patterns of magnetized particles on tape which can be played back in the original form.

magnetic tape A thin ribbon coated with magnetized particles, usu. wound on a reel and used to preserve magnetic recordings.

mag·net·ism (mag′nə·tiz′əm) *n.* **1** The specific properties of a magnet, produced by the alignments of certain atoms and the movements of their electrons. **2** The science that studies magnetic phenomena. **3** The measure of the force of a magnetic field. **4** The sympathetic personal quality that attracts or interests.

mag·net·ite (mag′nə·tīt) *n.* A black, magnetic form of iron oxide; lodestone. [< MAGNET] —**mag′net·it′ic** (-tit′ik) *adj.*

mag·net·ize (mag′nə·tīz) *v.* **·ized, ·iz·ing** *v.t.* **1** To produce magnetic properties in. **2** To attract by strong personal influence; captivate. —*v.i.* **3** To become magnetic. —**mag′·net·iz′a·ble** *adj.* —**mag′net·i·za′tion, mag′net·iz′er** *n.*

mag·ne·to (mag·nē′tō) *n. pl.* **·tos** An electric alternator using a field produced by permanent magnets, sometimes used in ignition systems of internal-combustion engines.

mag·ne·tom·e·ter (mag′nə·tom′ə·tər) *n.* An instrument for measuring the intensity and direction of magnetic forces. —**mag′ne·tom′e·try** *n.*

Mag·nif·i·cat (mag·nif′ə·kat) *n.* The hymn or canticle of the Virgin Mary, beginning with the word *Magnificat* in the Latin version. *Luke* 1:46–55. [L, it magnifies]

mag·nif·i·cence (mag·nif′ə·səns) *n.* The state or quality of being magnificent.

mag·nif·i·cent (mag·nif′ə·sənt) *adj.* **1** Grandly imposing or beautiful: a *magnificent* ruin. **2** Sublime; exalted: *magnificent* prose. **3** Lavish; sumptuous: a *magnificent* banquet. **4** Exceptionally fine; excellent: a *magnificent* physique. [< L *magnus* great + *facere* make] —**mag·nif′i·cent·ly** *adv.*

mag·nif·i·co (mag·nif′ə·kō) *n. pl.* **·coes** A lordly personage. [Ital., magnificent]

mag·ni·fy (mag′nə·fī) *v.t.* **·fied, ·fy·ing 1** To increase the apparent size of, as with an optical instrument. **2** To increase the size of; enlarge. **3** To cause to seem greater; intensify. **4** To exaggerate. **5** *Archaic* To extol; exalt. [< L *magnus* great + *facere* make] —**mag′ni·fi′a·ble** *adj.* —**mag′·ni·fi·ca′tion, mag′ni·fi′er** *n.*

mag·nil·o·quent (mag·nil′ə·kwənt) *adj.* Characterized by a pompous or high-flown style or manner. [< L *magnus* great + *loqui* speak] —**mag·nil′o·quence** *n.* —**mag·nil′o·quent·ly** *adv.*

mag·ni·tude (mag′nə·tyo͞od) *n.* **1** Great size or extent. **2** Great importance or significance. **3** *Math.* **a** Any of the numbers associated with individual elements of a set and by which they can be compared. **b** That which is measurable. **4** *Astron.* A logarithmic measure of the relative or absolute brightness of stars, with lower numbers denoting greater brightness. [< L *magnus* large]

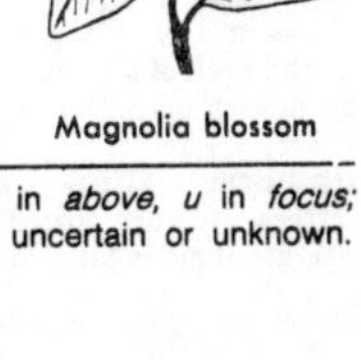
Magnolia blossom

mag·no·li·a (mag·nō′lē·ə, -nōl′·

y·ə) *n.* 1 Any of a genus of trees or shrubs with large, fragrant flowers. 2 The flower. [<Pierre *Magnol,* 1638–1715, French botanist]

mag·num (mag′nəm) *n.* A wine bottle of twice the ordinary size, holding about two quarts. [<L *magnus* great]

magnum o·pus (ō′pəs) The chief or most important work of an artist, writer, composer, etc. [L]

mag·pie (mag′pī) *n.* 1 Any of a genus of birds related to jays, having black and white plumage and a long tail. 2 A chatterbox; a garrulous gossip. [<*Mag,* dim. of *Margaret,* a personal name + PIE[2]]

mag·uey (mə·gā′, mag′wā) *n.* 1 Any of various Mexican agave plants including species yielding fiber or potable juice. 2 The fiber of certain of these plants. [<Taino]

Mag·yar (mag′yär, *Hungarian* mud′yär) *n.* 1 One of a people who invaded and conquered Hungary at the end of the ninth century; a Hungarian. 2 The Finno-Ugric language of Hungary. *—adj.* Of or pertaining to the Magyars or their language.

ma·ha·ra·ja (mä′hə·rä′jə) *n.* A Hindu prince; the title of some native rulers. Also **ma′ha·ra′jah.** [<Skt. *maha* great + *rājā* a king]

ma·ha·ra·ni (mä′hə·rä′nē) *n.* 1 A sovereign Hindu princess. 2 The wife of a maharaja. Also **ma′ha·ra′nee.** [<Skt. *maha* great + *rānī* a queen]

ma·hat·ma (mə·hat′mə, -hät′-) *n.* A great spiritual leader; a sage: a title of respect. [<Skt. *maha* great + *ātman* soul] **—ma·hat′ma·ism** *n.*

Ma·hi·can (mə·hē′kən) *n.* One of a tribe of Algonquian Indians formerly occupying the upper Hudson River valley. *—adj.* Of this tribe. [<Algonquian, lit., a wolf]

mah jong (mä′jong′, jông′) A game of Chinese origin, usu. for four persons, played with 144 marked tiles. Also **mah jongg.** [<dial. Chin. < Chin. *ma ch'iao,* lit., a house sparrow; from the design on one of the titles]

ma·hog·a·ny (mə·hog′ə·nē) *n.* 1 A large tropical American tree, with fine-grained, hard, reddish wood much used for cabinet work. 2 The wood itself. 3 Any of various shades of reddish brown. *—adj.* 1 Of mahogany. 2 Reddish brown. [?]

Ma·hom·e·tan (mə·hom′ə·tən) *adj., n.* MOHAMMEDAN.

ma·hout (mə·hout′) *n.* The keeper and driver of an elephant. [<Skt. *mahāmātra,* lit., great in measure]

maid (mād) *n.* 1 An unmarried woman or young girl. 2 A virgin. 3 A female servant. [Short for MAIDEN]

maid·en (mād′n) *n.* 1 An unmarried woman. 2 A young girl. 3 A virgin. 4 A race horse that has never won an event. *—adj.* 1 Of or for a maiden. 2 Virgin. 3 Unmarried. 4 First; initiatory: a *maiden* voyage. [<OE *mægden*] **—maid′en·li·ness** *n.* **—maid′en·ly** *adj., adv.*

maid·en·hair (mād′n·hâr′) *n.* A delicate and graceful fern with an erect black stem. Also **maidenhair fern.**

maid·en·head (mād′n·hed′) *n.* HYMEN.

maid·en·hood (mād′n·hŏŏd) *n.* The state of being a maiden. Also **maid′hood.**

maiden name A woman's surname before marriage.

maid of honor 1 An unmarried lady, usu. of noble birth, attendant upon a queen or princess. 2 An unmarried woman serving as the chief attendant of a bride at a wedding ceremony.

maid·ser·vant (mād′sûr′vənt) *n.* A female servant.

mail[1] (māl) *n.* 1 The governmental system for handling letters, etc., by post. 2 Letters, magazines, parcels, etc., sent from place to place by the post office. 3 The collection or delivery of postal matter. 4 A conveyance, as a train, plane, etc., for carrying postal matter. *—adj.* Pertaining to or used in handling mail. *—v.t.* To send by mail; post. [<OHG *malha* a pouch] **—mail′a·ble** *adj.*

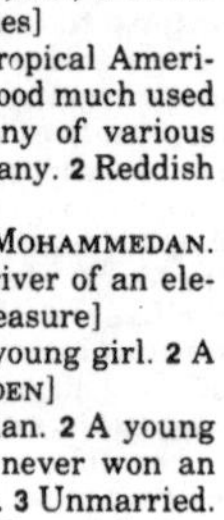

Chain mail armor

mail[2] (māl) *n.* 1 Armor of chains, rings, or scales. 2 Any strong covering or defense, as the shell of a turtle. *—v.t.* To cover with or as with mail. [<L *macula* spot, mesh of a net]

mail·box (māl′boks′) *n.* 1 A box in which letters, etc., are posted for collection. 2 A box into which private mail is put when delivered. Also **mail box.**

mail·gram (māl′gram′) *n. U.S.* A telegram, the message of which is usu. first telephoned to the receiver, then converted to written form and delivered in the next scheduled distribution of mail. [<MAIL + (TELE)GRAM]

mail·man (māl′man′, -mən) *n. pl.* **·men** (-men′, -mən) A man whose work is to deliver mail; postman.

mail order An order for goods, sent and filled by mail. **—mail′-or′der** *adj.*

maim (mām) *v.t.* To deprive of the use of a bodily part; mutilate; disable. [<OF *mahaigner*] **—maim′er** *n.*

main (mān) *n.* 1 A chief conduit or conductor, as for gas, water, or electricity. 2 The ocean. 3 Violent effort; strength: chiefly in the phrase **with might and main.** 4 The chief part; the most important point. **—in the main** On the whole; mostly. *—adj.* 1 First or chief in size, rank, importance, etc.; principal; chief; leading. 2 *Naut.* Near or connected with the mainsail or mainmast. **—by main force** (or **strength**) By sheer, undivided force or strength. [<OE *mægen*] **—main′ly** *adv.*

main drag *Slang* The principal street or section of a city.

main·frame (mān′frām′) *n.* The main part of a computer, or central processing unit, without the attached peripherals.

main·land (mān′land′, -lənd) *n.* A principal body of land; a continent, or part of a continent, as distinguished from an island. **—main′land′er** *n.*

main·line (mān′līn′) *n.* A main road, railroad line, etc. *—v.t. & v.i.* **·lined, ·lin·ing** *Slang* To inject (a narcotic drug, esp. heroin) directly into a vein. **—main′li′ner** *n.*

main·mast (mān′məst, -mast′) *n. Naut.* The principal mast of a vessel, usu. the second mast from the bow.

main·sail (mān′səl, -sāl′) *n. Naut.* A sail carried on the mainmast.

main·sheet (mān′shēt′) *n. Naut.* The sheet, or rope, by which the mainsail is trimmed and set.

main·spring (mān′spring′) *n.* 1 The principal spring of a mechanism, as of a watch. 2 The most important cause or motive.

main·stay (mān′stā′) *n.* 1 *Naut.* The supporting rope that extends forward from the mainmast. 2 A chief support.

Main Street 1 The principal business street of a small town. 2 The typically provincial customs, ways of thinking, etc., of a small town.

main·street·ing (mān′strēt′ing) *n. Can.* The practice of walking on the main streets of a town, esp. by a politician wishing to greet potential supporters.

main·tain (mān·tān′) *v.t.* 1 To carry on or continue; engage in, as a correspondence. 2 To keep unimpaired or in proper condition: to *maintain* roads. 3 To supply with food or livelihood; support; pay for. 4 To uphold; claim to be true. 5 To assert or state; affirm. 6 To hold or defend, as against attack. [<L *manu tenere,* lit., hold in one's hand] **—main·tain′a·ble** *adj.* **—main·tain′er** *n.*

main·te·nance (mān′tə·nəns) *n.* 1 The act of maintaining or the state of being maintained. 2 Means of support.

main·top (mān′top′) *n. Naut.* A platform at the head of the lower section of the mainmast.

main·top·mast (mān′top′məst) *n. Naut.* The mast next above the mainmast.

main yard *Naut.* The lower yard on the mainmast.

maî·tre d' (mā′trə dē′) *pl.* **maître d's** (dēz′) HEADWAITER. [F < MAÎTRE D'HÔTEL]

maî·tre d'hô·tel (mā′trə dō·tel′; *Fr.* me′tr′) *pl.* **maîtres d'hôtel** (mā′trə; *Fr.* me′tr′) 1 MAJORDOMO. 2 HEADWAITER. [F, lit. master of the house]

maize (māz) *n.* 1 CORN (defs. 1 & 2). 2 The yellow color of ripe corn. [<Taino *mahiz*]

Maj. Major.

maj. majority.

ma·jes·tic (mə·jes′tik) *adj.* Having or exhibiting majesty; stately; dignified. Also **ma·jes′ti·cal.** **—ma·jes′ti·cal·ly** *adv.* **—ma·jes′ti·cal·ness** *n.* **—Syn.** grand, impressive, awesome, grandiose, magnificent.

maj·es·ty (maj′is·tē) *n. pl.* **·ties** 1 Exalted dignity; stateliness; grandeur. 2 Sovereign power: the *majesty* of the law. [<L *majestas* greatness]

Maj·es·ty (maj′is·tē) *n. pl.* **·ties** A title or form of address for a sovereign; preceded by *His, Her, Your,* etc.

Maj. Gen. Major General.

ma·jol·i·ca (mə·jol′i·kə, -yol′-) *n.* A kind of Italian pottery, glazed and decorated, usu. in rich colors and Renaissance designs. [< Ital. *Majolica,* early name of *Majorca,* Spain]

ma·jor (mā′jər) *adj.* **1** Greater in number, quantity, or extent. **2** Greater in dignity, rank, or importance; principal; leading. **3** Considerable in extent, degree, etc.: a *major* repair. **4** Serious; grave: a *major* illness. **5** In education, of or designating the specific field of study specialized in by a candidate for a degree. **6** *Music* Of or characteristic of the tone successions or chords of a major scale, esp. the triad built on the tonic. **7** *Law* Being of legal age. —*n.* **1** See GRADE. **2** *Law* One who is of legal age. **3** *Music* A major key, chord, or interval. **4** In education: **a** A major subject or field of study. **b** A student who follows a (specified) course of study: an English *major.* —*v.i.* To pursue a definite field of study: with *in:* to *major* in history. [L, greater]

ma·jor·do·mo (mā′jər·dō′mō) *n. pl.* **·mos** **1** The chief steward of a royal or great household. **2** A butler. [< L *major* an elder + *domus* a house]

major general *pl.* **major generals** See GRADE.

ma·jor·i·ty (mə·jôr′ə·tē, -jor′-) *n. pl.* **·ties** **1** More than half of a given number or group; the greater part. **2** The amount or number by which one group of things exceeds another group; excess. **3** The age at which a person becomes legally responsible. **4** The rank or commission of a major. **5** In U.S. politics, the number of votes cast for a candidate over and above the number cast for his nearest opponent; a plurality. **6** The party having the most power in a legislature. [< L *major* greater]

major key *Music* A key based on the tones of a major scale.

major league **1** In baseball, either of the two main groups of professional teams in the U.S. **2** Any principal league in a professional sport. —**ma′jor-league′** *adj.*

major scale *Music* A diatonic scale with half steps after the third and seventh tones.

major suit In bridge, the suit of spades or of hearts.

make (māk) *v.* **made, mak·ing** *v.t.* **1** To bring about the existence of by the shaping or combining of materials; produce; build; construct; fashion. **2** To bring about; cause: Don't *make* trouble. **3** To bring to some state or condition; cause to be: The wind *made* him cold. **4** To appoint or assign; elect: They *made* him captain. **5** To form or create in the mind, as a plan. **6** To compose or create, as a poem or piece of music. **7** To understand or infer to be the meaning or significance: with *of:* What do you *make* of it? **8** To put forward; advance: to *make* an offer. **9** To utter or express: to *make* a declaration. **10** To obtain for oneself; earn; accumulate. **11** To add up to: Four quarts *make* a gallon. **12** To bring the total to: That *makes* five attempts. **13** To develop into; become: He *made* a good soldier. **14** To accomplish; effect or form: to *make* an agreement. **15** To estimate to be; reckon. **16** To induce or force; compel: He *made* me do it! **17** To draw up, enact, or frame, as laws, testaments, etc. **18** To prepare for use, as a bed. **19** To afford or provide: This brandy *makes* good drinking. **20** To be the essential element or determinant of: Stone walls do not a prison *make.* **21** To cause the success of: His speech *made* him politically. **22** To traverse; cover: to *make* fifty miles before noon. **23** To travel at the rate of: to *make* fifty miles per hour. **24** To arrive at; reach: to *make* Boston. **25** To board before departure: to *make* a train. **26** To earn so as to count on a score: to *make* a touchdown. **27** *Electr.* To complete (a circuit). **28** *Informal* To win a place on: to *make* the team. **29** In bridge, to win (a bid). **30** *Slang* To seduce. —*v.i.* **31** To cause something to assume a specified condition: to *make* fast. **32** To act in a certain manner: to *make* merry. **33** To start: They *made* to go. **34** To go or extend in some direction: with *to* or *toward.* **35** To flow, as the tide; rise, as water. —**make believe** To pretend, as in play. —**make do** To get along with what is available, esp. with an inferior substitute. —**make for** **1** To go toward. **2** To attack; assail. **3** To have effect on; contribute to. —**make it** *Informal* To do or achieve something; succeed. —**make off** To run away. —**make off with** To carry away; filch; purloin. —**make out** **1** To see; discern. **2** To comprehend; understand. **3** To try to prove or imply to be: They *made* us *out* criminals. **4** To fill out, as a printed form. **5** To succeed; manage. **6** *Slang* **a** To neck. **b** To have sexual intercourse. —**make over** **1** To renovate. **2** To transfer title or possession of. —**make up** **1** To compose; compound, as a prescription. **2** To be the parts of; comprise. **3** To settle differences: to kiss and *make up.* **4** To devise; invent: to *make up* an answer. **5** To supply what is lacking in. **6** To compensate for; atone for. **7** To settle; decide: to *make up* one's mind. **8** *Printing* To arrange, as lines, into columns or pages. **9** To put cosmetics on. —**make up to** *Informal* To make a show of friendliness and affection toward. —*n.* **1** The manner in which something is constructed. **2** Brand: a new *make* of automobile. **3** The act of making or producing. **4** The amount produced; yield. **5** The physical or mental qualities of a person. **6** The closing or completion of an electrical circuit. —**on the make** *Informal* **1** Greedy for profit, success, etc. **2** Eager for amorous conquest. [< OE *macian*]

make-be·lieve (māk′bi·lēv′) *adj.* Pretended; unreal. —*n.* A mere pretense; sham. —**Syn.** *adj.* false, sham, counterfeit, spurious, specious, fake.

mak·er (mā′kər) *n.* **1** One who or that which makes. **2** *Law* One who signs a promissory note.

Mak·er (mā′kər) *n.* God.

make·shift (māk′shift′) *adj.* Being a temporary substitute. —*n.* A temporary substitute in any emergency.

make·up (māk′up′) *n.* **1** The arrangement or manner in which the parts of anything are put together. **2** Mental or physical constitution or disposition. **3** *Printing* The arrangement of composed type in pages, columns, or forms. **4** The costumes, wigs, cosmetics, etc., used to assume a theatrical role; also, the art of applying or assuming them. **5** Cosmetics in general.

mak·ing (mā′king) *n.* **1** The act or process of causing, doing, forming, or constructing. **2** That which contributes to improvement or success. **3** A quantity of anything made at one time; batch. **4** *Often pl.* The necessary materials or qualities.

mal- *prefix* **1** Bad; ill; not: *maladjusted.* **2** Wrong(ly); defective(ly): *malformation; malformed.* [< L *malus* bad]

Mal, Mal. Malachi; Malay; Malayan.

Ma·lac·ca cane (mə·lak′ə) A walking stick made of rattan. [< *Malacca,* Malaya]

mal·a·chite (mal′ə·kīt) *n.* A green mineral carbonate of copper, used as an ore. [< Gk. *malachē* mallow; so called because resembling mallow leaves in color]

mal·ad·just·ed (mal′ə·jus′tid) *adj.* Poorly adjusted, as to the circumstances of one's life. —**mal′ad·just′ment** *n.*

mal·ad·min·is·ter (mal′əd·min′is·tər) *v.t.* To administer badly or dishonestly. —**mal′ad·min′is·tra′tion** *n.*

mal·a·droit (mal′ə·droit′) *adj.* Clumsy or blundering. [< MAL- + F *adroit* clever] —**mal′a·droit′ly** *adv.* —**mal′a·droit′·ness** *n.*

mal·a·dy (mal′ə·dē) *n. pl.* **·dies** **1** A disease; illness. **2** Any disordered condition. [< LL *male habitus,* lit., ill kept]

Mal·a·ga (mal′ə·gə) *n.* **1** A sweet white wine made originally in Málaga, Spain. **2** A variety of large, white grape.

Mal·a·gas·y (mal′ə·gas′ē) *n.* **1** A citizen or native of the Malagasy Republic. **2** The language of the Malagasy Republic. —*adj.* Of or pertaining to the Malagasy Republic, its people, or their language.

Malagasy Republic A republic comprising Madagascar and nearby islands, 228,000 sq. mi., cap. Tananarive. • See map at AFRICA.

mal·aise (mal·āz′, ma·lez′) *n.* **1** A feeling of uneasiness or discontent. **2** A physical feeling of weakness or languor. [F < *mal* ill + *aise* ease]

ma·la·mute (mä′lə·myo͞ot, mal′ə-) *n.* A large, thick-coated sled dog of Alaska. [< *Malemute,* an Alaskan tribe]

mal·a·prop (mal′ə·prop) *n.* MALAPROPISM. —*adj.* Using or marked by malapropisms: also **mal·a·prop·i·an** (mal′ə·prop′ē·ən). [< Mrs. *Malaprop.* a character in Sheridan's play, *The Rivals,* who absurdly misuses words]

mal·a·prop·ism (mal′ə·prop·iz′əm) *n.* 1 An absurd misuse of words that sound somewhat alike. 2 An example of this, as *Measles is highly contiguous* (instead of *contagious*). [< Mrs. *Malaprop.* See MALAPROP.]

mal·ap·ro·pos (mal′ap·rə·pō′) *adj.* Out of place; not appropriate. [< F *mal à propos* not to the point]

ma·lar·i·a (mə·lâr′ē·ə) *n.* 1 An infectious disease caused by a protozoan transmitted by infected anopheles mosquitoes, and resulting in intermittent chills and fever. 2 Any foul or unwholesome air; miasma. [< Ital. *mal' aria,* lit., bad air] **—ma·lar′i·al, ma·lar′i·an, ma·lar′i·ous** *adj.*

ma·lar·ky (mə·lär′kē) *n. Slang* Insincere or senseless talk; bunk. Also **ma·lar′key.** [?]

Ma·la·wi (mä′lä·wē) *n.* An independent member of the Commonwealth of Nations in SE Africa, 49,177 sq. mi., cap. Zomba. • See map at AFRICA.

Ma·lay (mā′lā, mə·lā′) *n.* 1 A member of the dominant race in Malaysia; a Malayan. 2 The Indonesian language spoken on the Malay Peninsula. *—adj.* Of or pertaining to Malaya or Malaysia.

Ma·lay·a (mə·lā′ə) *n.* A former federation of eleven states in the Commonwealth of Nations, now incorporated in Malaysia.

Mal·a·ya·lam (mal′ə·yä′ləm) *n.* The Dravidian language of the Malabar coast, India, related to Tamil.

Ma·lay·an (mə·lā′ən) *adj.* 1 MALAY. 2 INDONESIAN. *—n.* 1 MALAY (def. 1). 2 MALAY (def. 2). 3 INDONESIAN.

Ma·lay·o-Pol·y·ne·sian (mə·lā′ō·pol′ə·nē′zhən, -shən) *adj. & n.* AUSTRONESIAN.

Ma·lay·sia (mə·lā′zhə, -shə) *n.* An independent member

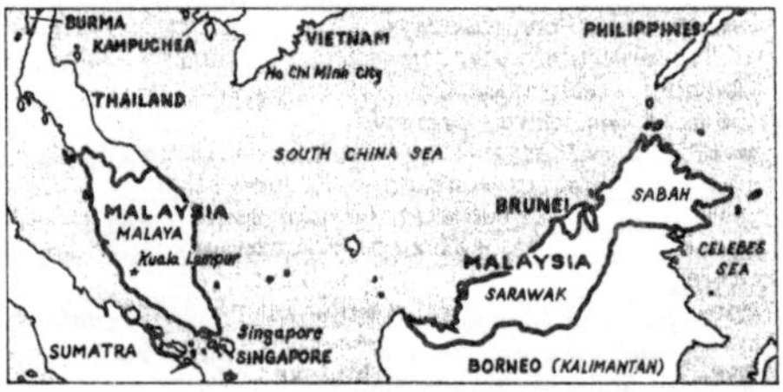

Malaysia

of the Commonwealth of Nations in SE Asia, 127,344 sq. mi., cap. Kuala Lumpur. **—Ma·lay′sian** *adj., n.*

mal·con·tent (mal′kən·tent, mal′kən·tent′) *adj.* Discontented or dissatisfied, esp. with a government or economic system. *—n.* A discontented person, esp. one rebellious against authority.

mal de mer (mal də mâr′) SEASICKNESS. [F]

Mal·dive Islands (mal′dīv, -dēv) A republic located on an island group SW of Sri Lanka, 115 sq. mi., cap. Malé. **—Mal·div·i·an** (mal·div′ē·ən) *adj., n.*

male (māl) *adj.* 1 Of or pertaining to the sex that begets young. 2 Masculine. 3 Made up of men or boys. 4 *Bot.* Having stamens, but no pistil; also, adapted to fertilize, but not to produce fruit, as stamens. 5 Denoting a tool or object which fits into a corresponding hollow part. *—n.* A male person, animal, or plant. [< L *masculus*]

mal·e·dic·tion (mal′ə·dik′shən) *n.* 1 An invocation of evil; a curse. 2 Slander. [< L *male* ill + *dicere* speak] **—mal′e·dic′to·ry** *adj.*

mal·e·fac·tor (mal′ə·fak′tər) *n.* One who commits a crime. [< L *male* ill + *facere* do] **—mal′e·fac′tion** *n.*

ma·lef·i·cent (mə·lef′ə·sənt) *adj.* Causing or doing evil or mischief; harmful. [< L *male* ill + *facere* do]

ma·lev·o·lent (mə·lev′ə·lənt) *adj.* Wishing evil toward others; malicious. [< L *male* ill + *volens* wishing] **—ma·lev′o·lence** *n.* **—ma·lev′o·lent·ly** *adv.*

mal·fea·sance (mal·fē′zəns) *n. Law* The performance of an unlawful or wrongful act, esp. by a public official. [< OF *mal* ill + *faire* do] **—mal·fea′sant** *adj., n.*

mal·for·ma·tion (mal′fôr·mā′shən) *n.* Any irregularity or deformation in the structure of an organism.

mal·formed (mal·fôrmd′) *adj.* Badly formed or made; deformed.

mal·func·tion (mal·fungk′shən) *n.* Impairment or disturbance of proper functioning. *—v.i.* To function incorrectly.

Ma·li (mä′lē) *n.* A republic of w Africa, 464,872 sq. mi., cap. Bamako. • See map at AFRICA.

mal·ic (mal′ik, mā′lik) *adj.* 1 Of, pertaining to, or obtained from apples. 2 Pertaining to or designating an acid contained in apples and other fruits. [< L *malum* apple]

mal·ice (mal′is) *n.* 1 A disposition to injure another; spite; ill will. 2 *Law* A willfully formed design to do another an injury: also **malice aforethought.** [< L *malus* bad]

ma·li·cious (mə·lish′əs) *adj.* Harboring or resulting from malice, ill will, or enmity; spiteful. **—ma·li′cious·ly** *adv.* **—ma·li′cious·ness** *n.* **—Syn.** hostile, malevolent, hateful, harmful, treacherous, invidious.

ma·lign (mə·līn′) *v.t.* To speak slander of. *—adj.* 1 Having an evil disposition toward others; ill-disposed; malevolent. 2 Tending to injure; pernicious. [< L *malignare* contrive maliciously] **—ma·lign′er** *n.* **—ma·lign′ly** *adv.* **—Syn.** *v.* slur, vilify, defame, depreciate, discredit, belittle, disparage.

ma·lig·nant (mə·lig′nənt) *adj.* 1 Having or manifesting extreme malevolence or enmity. 2 Evil in nature, or tending to do great harm. 3 *Pathol.* Tending to grow progressively worse. **—ma·lig′nance, ma·lig′nan·cy** *n.* **—ma·lig′nant·ly** *adv.*

ma·lig·ni·ty (mə·lig′nə·tē) *n. pl.* **·ties** 1 The state or quality of being malign; violent animosity. 2 Destructive tendency; virulence. 3 *Often pl.* An evil thing or event.

ma·lin·ger (mə·ling′gər) *v.i.* To feign sickness or incapacity, so as to avoid work. [< F *malingre* sickly] **—ma·lin′ger·er** *n.*

mall[1] (môl, mal) *n., v.* MAUL.

mall[2] (môl, mal) *n.* 1 A shaded, public promenade. 2 A large, often completely enclosed complex of shops and stores, usu. grouped around a central plaza or promenade and closed to motor vehicles. 3 A median strip between highways. [Short for *Pall-Mall,* a street in London]

mal·lard (mal′ərd) *n.* The common wild duck, closely related to domesticated ducks. [< OF *malart*] • See DUCK.

mal·le·a·ble (mal′ē·ə·bəl) *adj.* 1 Capable of being shaped by hammering, rolling, pressure, etc. 2 Capable of being disciplined, trained, changed, etc. [< L *malleus* hammer] **—mal′le·a·bil′i·ty, mal′le·a·ble·ness** *n.* **—mal′le·a·bly** *adv.*

mal·let (mal′it) *n.* 1 A wooden hammer or light maul. 2 A long-handled, hammerlike implement used to strike the ball in croquet or polo. 3 A light hammer with a round, usu. felt-covered head, for playing the vibraphone, etc. [< L *malleus* hammer]

Mallet *def. 1*

mal·le·us (mal′ē·əs) *n. pl.* **·le·i** (-lē·ī) *Anat.* The outermost of the three small bones of the middle ear. [L, a hammer]

mal·low (mal′ō) *n.* Any of a family of plants, including the hollyhock and marsh mallow, with lobed leaves and showy flowers. [< L *malva*]

malm·sey (mäm′zē) *n.* A rich sweet wine made in the Canary Islands, Madeira, Spain, and Greece. [< Gk. *Monembasia* Monemvasia, Greece]

mal·nu·tri·tion (mal′nyoo·trish′ən) *n.* Faulty or inadequate nutrition.

mal·oc·clu·sion (mal′ə·kloo′zhən) *n.* Faulty closure of the upper and lower teeth. [< MAL- + OCCLUSION]

mal·o·dor·ous (mal·ō′dər·əs) *adj.* Having a disagreeable smell. **—mal·o′dor·ous·ly** *adv.* **—mal·o′dor·ous·ness** *n.*

mal·prac·tice (mal·prak′tis) *n.* 1 Improper or illegal practice, as in medicine or law. 2 Improper or immoral conduct. **—mal·prac·ti·tion·er** (mal′prak·tish′ən·ər) *n.*

malt (môlt) *n.* 1 Grain, usu. barley, germinated and dried, used in brewing and as a nutrient. 2 Malt liquor; beer or ale. *—v.t.* 1 To cause (grain) to germinate and become malt. 2 To treat with malt, or extract of malt. *—v.i.* 3 To be changed into or become malt: said of grain. 4 To convert grain into malt. [< OE *mealt*] **—malt′y** *adj.* **(·i·er, ·i·est)**

Mal·ta (môl′tə) *n.* An independent member of the Commonwealth of Nations, an island in the CEN. Mediterranean, 122 sq. mi., cap. Valletta.

malted milk 1 A powder made of dehydrated milk and malted cereals, soluble in milk or water. 2 The beverage made with this powder.

Mal·tese (môl·tēz′, -tēs′) *adj.* Of or pertaining to Malta, its inhabitants, or their language. —*n. pl.* ·tese 1 A citizen or native of Malta. 2 The language of Malta. 3 MALTESE CAT.

Maltese cat A breed of domestic cat with long bluish gray hair.

Maltese cross A cross in the shape of four inward-pointing arrowheads meeting at the center. • See CROSS.

Mal·thu·si·an (mal·thōō′zē·ən, -zhən) *adj.* Pertaining to the theory of Thomas R. Malthus that population increases faster than food supplies and is restricted only by famine, disease, and war. —*n.* A believer in the theories of Malthus. [< Thomas R. *Malthus,* 1766–1834, English economist] —**Mal·thu′si·an·ism** *n.*

malt·ose (môl′tōs) *n.* A sweet, white, crystalline carbohydrate formed by the action of amylase on starch. Also **malt sugar.** [< MALT]

mal·treat (mal·trēt′) *v.t.* To treat badly or maliciously; abuse. —**mal·treat′ment** *n.*

mam·bo (mäm′bō) *n. pl.* ·bos 1 A rhumbalike ballroom dance. 2 The music for this dance. —*v.i.* To dance the mambo.

mam·ma[1] (mam′ə) *n. pl.* ·mae (-ē) The milk-secreting organ of a mammal; a breast, udder, or bag. [L, breast]

mam·ma[2] (mä′mə, mə·mä′) *n.* Mother. Also **ma′ma.** [< L *mamma* breast, ult. < baby talk]

mam·mal (mam′əl) *n.* Any of a class of vertebrate animals, including man, whose female suckles its young. [< L *mamma* breast]

mam·ma·ry (mam′ər·ē) *adj.* Of, pertaining to, or of the nature of the mammae or breasts.

mam·mog·ra·phy (ma·mog′rə·fē) *n.* X-ray examination of the breast or breasts. [< L *mamma* breast]

mam·mon (mam′ən) *n. Often cap.* Riches; wealth, esp. as a source of corruption. [< Aramaic *māmōnā* riches]

mam·moth (mam′əth) *n.* Any of a genus of extinct elephants with coarse hair and enormous upward-curving tusks. —*adj.* Huge; colossal. [< Russ. *mammot*]

Woolly mammoth

mam·my (mam′ē) *n. pl.* ·mies 1 Mother; mamma. 2 A Negro nurse of white children, esp. formerly in the s U.S. [Dim. of MAMMA]

man (man) *n. pl.* **men** (men) 1 A human being, specifically the most highly developed of the primates, differing from other animals in having erect posture, extraordinary development of the brain, and the power of articulate speech. 2 The human race. 3 An adult male of the human kind. 4 The male part of the race collectively. 5 A male person who is manly; also, manhood. 6 An adult male servant, member of a team, employee, etc. 7 A piece used in playing certain games, as chess or checkers. 8 A ship or vessel: used in composition: a *man-of-war.* 9 A husband; lover: *man* and wife; Her *man* is dead. 10 *Slang* Fellow: used in direct address: Hey, *man,* look at this! —**the Man** *Slang* A white man regarded as an agent of power. —*v.t.* **manned, man·ning** 1 To supply with men. 2 To take stations at, on, or in for work, defense, etc.: *Man* the pumps! —*adj.* Male. [< OE *mann*]

Man. Manila paper; Manitoba.

man. manual.

man·a·cle (man′ə·kəl) *n.* 1 *Usu. pl.* One of a connected pair of metallic instruments for confining or restraining the hands; a handcuff. 2 Anything that constrains or fetters. —*v.t.* ·cled, ·cling 1 To put manacles on. 2 To hamper; constrain. [< OF < L, dim. of *manus* hand]

man·age (man′ij) *v.,* ·aged, ·ag·ing *v.t.* 1 To direct or conduct the affairs or interests of. 2 To control the direction, operation, etc., of, as a machine. 3 To cause to do one's bidding; handle; manipulate. 4 To bring about or contrive: He always *manages* to win. 5 To handle or wield, as a weapon or implement. —*v.i.* 6 To carry on or conduct business or affairs. 7 To contrive to get along: I'll *manage.* [< L *manus* a hand]

man·age·a·ble (man′ij·ə·bəl) *adj.* Capable of being managed; tractable; docile. —**man′age·a·bil′i·ty, man′age·a·ble·ness** *n.* —**man′age·a·bly** *adv.*

man·age·ment (man′ij·mənt) *n.* 1 The act, art, or manner of managing, controlling, or conducting. 2 The skillful use of means to accomplish a purpose. 3 Managers or directors collectively.

man·ag·er (man′ij·ər) *n.* 1 One who manages; esp. one who has the control of a business. 2 One who directs or oversees the affairs of a household, athletic team, etc. 3 An adroit schemer; intriguer. —**man′ag·er·ship** *n.*

man·a·ge·ri·al (man′ə·jir′ē·əl) *adj.* Of, pertaining to, or characteristic of a manager or management.

ma·ña·na (mä·nyä′nä) *n. & adv. Spanish* Tomorrow.

man-at-arms (man′ət·ärmz′) *n. pl.* **men-at-arms** (men′-) A soldier; esp. a heavily armed soldier of medieval times.

man·a·tee (man′ə·tē′) *n.* A large, aquatic mammal of tropical Atlantic shores. [< Cariban *manattoui*]

Man·chu (man·chōō′, man′chōō) *n.* 1 One of a Mongoloid people that conquered China in 1643 and established the dynasty overthrown in 1912. 2 The language of this people. —*adj.* Of or pertaining to Manchuria, its people, or their language. —**Man·chu′ri·an** (-chŏŏr′ē·ən) *adj., n.*

-mancy *combining form* Divining, foretelling, or discovering by means of: *necromancy.* [< Gk. *manteia* power of divination]

man·da·mus (man·dā′məs) *n. Law* A writ issued by a higher court to a subordinate court, city, business, etc., commanding it to do something. [L, we command]

man·da·rin (man′də·rin) *n.* 1 A high official of the former Chinese Empire, either civil or military. 2 A distinguished, influential, usu. elderly person, esp. one of literary or intellectual attainment. 3 MANDARIN ORANGE. 4 A reddish orange color. —*adj.* 1 Of a mandarin. 2 Complex and ornate, as a literary style. [< Skt. *mantra* counsel]

Man·da·rin (man′də·rin) *n.* The Chinese language of N China, in the Peking dialect now the official language of the country.

mandarin orange Any of several sweet, loose-skinned oranges, as the tangerine.

man·da·tar·y (man′də·ter′ē) *n. pl.* ·tar·ies One to whom a mandate is given.

man·date (man′dāt, -dit) *n.* 1 An authoritative command or order. 2 A charge given to a nation by a congress or league of nations to develop and administer a conquered territory; also, the territory itself. 3 A judicial command from a higher court to a subordinate court or court officer. 4 An order from an electorate to the legislative body, or its representative, to follow a certain course of action. —*v.t.* (-dāt) ·dat·ed, ·dat·ing To assign (a territory) to a specific nation under a mandate. [< L *mandare* to command]

man·da·to·ry (man′də·tôr′ē, -tō′rē) *adj.* 1 Of, containing, or having received a mandate. 2 Positively required; obligatory. —*n. pl.* ·ries 1 MANDATARY. 2 MANDATE.

man·di·ble (man′də·bəl) *n.* 1 The lower jaw. 2 Either part of the beak of a bird. 3 One of a pair of biting jaws in an insect. [< L *mandere* chew] —**man·dib·u·lar** (man·dib′yə·lər), **man·dib′u·late** (-lit, -lāt) *adj., n.*

man·do·lin (man′də·lin, man′də·lin′) *n.* A stringed musical instrument related to the lute, having five pairs of strings. [< Ital. *mandolino* < L *pandura* a kind of lute] —**man′do·lin′ist** *n.*

man·drake (man′drāk) *n.* 1 A poisonous Old World plant of the nightshade family. 2 Its fleshy roots. 3 The May apple. Also **man·drag·o·ra** (man·drag′ə·rə). [< Gk. *mandragoras*]

man·drel (man′drəl) *n. Mech.* 1 A shaft on which an object or tool may be fixed for rotation. 2 A core about which wire may be coiled or metal or glass forged. Also **man′·dril.** [< F *mandrin* a lathe]

man·drill (man′dril) *n.* A large, ferocious w African baboon, hav-

Mandrill

ing cheeks and rump colored blue and scarlet. [< MAN + *drill,* a native African name]

mane (mān) *n.* **1** The long hair growing on and about the neck of some animals, as the horse, lion, etc. **2** Long human hair. [< OE *manu*] **—maned** (mānd) *adj.*

man-eat·er (man′ē′tər) *n.* **1** A cannibal. **2** An animal that devours or is supposed to devour human flesh, as a tiger, shark, etc.

ma·nège (ma·nezh′) *n.* **1** The art of training and riding horses. **2** A school of horsemanship; riding school. **3** The style and movements of a trained horse. Also **ma·nege′.** [F < Ital. *maneggiare* manage]

ma·neu·ver (mə·n^{y}o͞o′vər) *n.* **1 a** An extensive, planned movement of troops, warships, aircraft, etc. **b** *Often pl.* Such movements used in training or practice. **2** Any physically adroit movement or skill. **3** A controlled change in the flight path of an aircraft or spacecraft. **4** A skillful or cunning action to gain some specific end or object, often involving trickery. *—v.t.* **1** To put through a maneuver or maneuvers. **2** To put, bring, make, etc., by a maneuver or maneuvers. **3** To manipulate; conduct adroitly. *—v.i.* **4** To perform a maneuver or maneuvers. **5** To use tricks or stratagems; manage adroitly. [< L *manu operari* work with the hand] **—ma·neu′ver·a·bil′i·ty, ma·neu′ver·er** *n.* **—ma·neu′ver·a·ble** *adj.*

man Friday A person who devotedly serves another, like Robinson Crusoe's servant of that name; a factotum.

man·ful (man′fəl) *adj.* Having courage, strength, determination, etc. **—man′ful·ly** *adv.* **—man′ful·ness** *n.*

man·ga·nese (mang′gə·nēs, -nēz) *n.* A hard, brittle, metallic element (symbol Mn), used mainly in alloys. [< Med. L *magnesia* magnesia]

mange (mānj) *n.* A skin disease of domestic animals, caused by various burrowing mites and marked by itching and loss of hair. [< OF *manjue* an itch, eating]

man·ger (mān′jər) *n.* A trough or box for feeding horses or cattle. [< L *manducare* chew]

man·gle[1] (mang′gəl) *v.t.* **·gled, ·gling 1** To disfigure or mutilate, as by cutting, bruising, or crushing; lacerate. **2** To mar or ruin; spoil. [< AF *mangler*] **—man′gler** *n.*

man·gle[2] (mang′gəl) *n.* A machine for smoothing fabrics by pressing them between rollers. *—v.t.* **·gled, ·gling** To smooth with a mangle. [< Gk. *manganon* a pulley, a war machine]

man·go (mang′gō) *n. pl.* **·goes** or **·gos 1** The edible, fleshy fruit of a tropical evergreen tree. **2** The tree producing the fruit. [< Tamil *mān* a mango tree + *kāy* a fruit]

man·grove (mang′grōv, man′-) *n.* A tropical tree having branches that take root, forming dense thickets. [< Taino *mangle*]

man·gy (mān′jē) *adj.* **·gi·er, ·gi·est 1** Affected with the mange. **2** Shabby; threadbare. **—man′gi·ly** *adv.* **—man′gi·ness** *n.*

man·han·dle (man′han′dəl) *v.t.* **·dled, ·dling** To handle roughly, as in anger.

man·hat·tan (mən·hat′ən, man-) *n. Often cap.* A cocktail made of whisky and vermouth, often with a dash of bitters and a cherry. [< *Manhattan,* borough of New York City]

man·hole (man′hōl′) *n.* An opening through which one may enter a boiler, conduit, sewer, etc., for making repairs.

man·hood (man′ho͝od) *n.* **1** The state or time of being an adult male. **2** The state of being human. **3** Manly qualities, as courage, strength, etc. **4** Adult males collectively; men.

man-hour (man′our′) *n.* A unit equal to the average amount of work that can be done by one person in one hour.

ma·ni·a (mā′nē·ə, mān′yə) *n.* **1** A psychotic state characterized by an exaggerated sense of well-being, accompanied by excessive mental and physical activity. **2** A strong, ungovernable desire; a craze. [< Gk., madness]

-mania *combining form* A persistent or irrational preoccupation with: *nymphomania.*

ma·ni·ac (mā′nē·ak) *adj.* Having a mania; raving. *—n.* A person wildly or violently insane; a madman. **—ma·ni·a·cal** (mə·nī′ə·kəl) *adj.* **—ma·ni′a·cal·ly** *adv.*

man·ic (man′ik, mā′nik) *adj.* Pertaining to, like, or affected by mania.

man·ic-de·pres·sive (man′ik·di·pres′iv) *adj.* Denoting a mental disorder characterized by alternating depression and mania. *—n.* One who suffers from this disorder.

man·i·cure (man′ə·kyo͝or′) *n.* The care or treatment of the hands and fingernails. *—v.t. & v.i.* **·cured, ·cur·ing** To take care of or treat (the hands and nails). [< L *manus* hand + *cura* care] **—man′i·cur′ist** *n.*

man·i·fest (man′ə·fest′) *adj.* Clearly apparent to the understanding or the senses; palpable; obvious. *—v.t.* **1** To make plain to sight or understanding; reveal; display. **2** To prove; be evidence of. *—v.i.* **3** To appear or become evident; reveal itself. *—n.* A detailed listing of the cargo of a ship or plane for customs inspection. [< L *manifestus* evident, lit., struck by the hand] **—man′i·fest′ly** *adv.*

man·i·fes·ta·tion (man′ə·fə·stā′shən, -fes-) *n.* **1** The act of manifesting or the state of being manifested. **2** Something that manifests or reveals. **3** A public demonstration, as by a government or party, to display its power or special views. **—man′i·fes′tant** *n.*

man·i·fes·to (man′ə·fes′tō) *n. pl.* **·toes** An official declaration by an organized group or government body of intentions, motives, or principles of action. [< L *manifestus* manifest]

man·i·fold (man′ə·fōld) *adj.* **1** Of great variety; numerous. **2** Manifested in many ways, or including many acts or elements; complex. **3** Existing in great abundance. *—v.t.* To make more than one copy of at once, as with carbon paper on a typewriter. *—n.* **1** A copy made by manifolding. **2** A tube or pipe with several inlets or outlets. [< OE *manigfeald* varied, numerous] **—man′i·fold·ly** *adv.* **—man′·i·fold·ness** *n.*

man·i·kin (man′ə·kin) *n.* **1** A model of the human body. **2** A little man; dwarf. **3** MANNEQUIN. [< Du. *manneken,* dim. of *man* man]

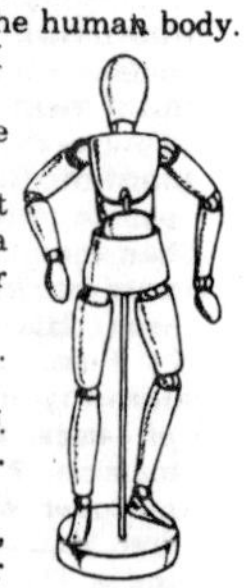

Manikin *def. 1*

ma·nil·a (mə·nil′ə) *n.* The fiber of the abaca. Also **Manila hemp, ma·nil′la.**

Ma·nil·a paper (mə·nil′ə) A heavy, light brown paper originally made of Manila hemp, now made of various fibers, used for wrapping, etc.

man·i·oc (man′ē·ok, mā′nē-) *n.* CASSAVA. [< Tupian *mandioca*]

ma·nip·u·la·ble (mə·nip′yə·lə·bəl) *adj.* Capable of being manipulated. Also **ma·nip′u·lat′a·ble. —ma·nip′u·la·bil′i·ty** *n.*

ma·nip·u·late (mə·nip′yə·lāt) *v.t.* **·lat·ed, ·lat·ing 1** To handle, operate, or use with or as with the hands, esp. with skill. **2** To influence or control artfully or deceptively. **3** To change or alter (figures, accounts, etc.), usu. fraudulently. [< L *manipulus* a handful] **—ma·nip′u·la′tion, ma·nip′u·la′tor** *n.* **—ma·nip′u·la′tive** *adj.*

man·kind (man′kīnd′, man′kīnd′) *n. (construed as sing. or pl.)* **1** The whole human species. **2** (man′kīnd′) Men collectively as distinguished from women.

man·ly (man′lē) *adj.* **·li·er, ·li·est 1** Possessing the qualities thought characteristic of or desirable in a man, as courage, strength, determination, etc. **2** Suitable to a man: the *manly* art of boxing. **—man′li·ly** *adv.* **—man′li·ness** *n.*

man·na (man′ə) *n.* **1** The miraculously supplied food on which the Israelites subsisted in the wilderness. *Exodus* 16:14–36. **2** Anything pleasant or rewarding that comes as a surprise. **3** A sweetish juice extracted from the stems of the European ash and used as a mild laxative. [< Aramaic *mannā*]

man·ne·quin (man′ə·kin) *n.* **1** A woman who models new clothes for display to potential customers. **2** A figure of the human body used by fashion designers, tailors, and display artists. [< Du. *manneken,* dim. of *man* man]

man·ner (man′ər) *n.* **1** The way in which something is done or takes place. **2** The demeanor, bearing, or behavior peculiar to a person; also, a distinguished air or bearing. **3** *pl.* General modes of life or conduct; esp., social behavior. **4** *pl.* Polite, civil, or well-bred behavior. **5** A characteristic style in art, literature, music, etc. **6** Sort or kind. **7** Character; guise. **—in a manner of speaking** In one way of describing; in a sense: She was, *in a manner of speaking,* a hard-nosed negotiator. [< L *manuarius* of the hand]

man·nered (man′ərd) *adj.* **1** Having a (specified) manner or manners: *ill-mannered.* **2** Affected; stilted; artificial.

man·ner·ism (man′ər·iz′əm) *n.* **1** An action, way of behaving, speech pattern, etc., that is characteristic of a particular person. **2** An artificial or affected manner or style. **—man′ner·ist** *n.* **—man′ner·is′tic** *adj.*

man·ner·ly (man′ər·lē) *adj.* Well-behaved; polite. *—adv.* With good manners; politely. **—man′ner·li·ness** *n.*

man·ni·kin (man′ə·kin) *n.* MANIKIN.

man·nish (man′ish) *adj.* **1** Resembling or characteristic of men, as in appearance, attitudes, etc.: said of a woman. **2** Suggesting that of a man: her *mannish* suit. **—man′nish·ly** *adv.* **—man′nish·ness** *n.*

ma·noeu·vre (mə·nʸōō′vər) *n., v. Chiefly Brit.* MANEUVER.

man-of-war (man′əv·wôr′, man′ə-) *n. pl.* **men-of-war** (men′-) A naval vessel armed for active hostilities.

man-of-war bird FRIGATE BIRD.

ma·nom·e·ter (mə·nom′ə·tər) *n.* An instrument for measuring pressure of a fluid. [< Gk. *manos* thin, rare + -METER] **—man·o·met·ric** (man′ə·met′rik) or **·ri·cal** *adj.*

man·or (man′ər) *n.* **1** *Brit.* A nobleman's or gentleman's landed estate. **2** In feudal England, a tract of land granted by the king to one as lord, with authority to exercise jurisdiction over it. **3** In colonial America, a tract of land originally granted as a manor and let by the proprietor to tenants. **4** A mansion, esp. one on an estate. [< L *manere* stay, remain] **—ma·no·ri·al** (mə·nôr′ē·əl, -nō′rē-) *adj.*

manor house The residence of the lord of a manor.

man·pow·er (man′pou′ər) *n.* **1** Power supplied by human physical effort: also **man power. 2** The number of persons available for any specific service, as for military duty or for industrial work.

man·qué (mäṅ·kā′) *adj.* That has failed in or fallen short of one's ambitions or aspirations: a painter *manqué.* [F, pp. of *manquer* to fail]

man·sard (man′särd) *n.* A roof with a double slope or pitch on all sides. Also **mansard roof.** [< F. *Mansard,* 1598–1666, French architect]

Mansard roof

manse (mans) *n.* A clergyman's house. esp. a Presbyterian minister's house. [< Med. L *mansa, mansus.* See MANSION.]

man·ser·vant (man′sûr′vənt) *n.* An adult male servant.

man·sion (man′shən) *n.* A large, imposing house. [< L < *mansus,* pp. of *manere* remain, dwell]

man·slaugh·ter (man′slô′tər) *n. Law* The unlawful killing of a person by another person but without malice.

man·tel (man′təl) *n.* The facing about a fireplace, including the shelf above it; also, the shelf. [< L *mantellum* cloak]

Mantel

man·tel·et (man′təl·et, mant′lit) *n.* **1** A small mantle or short cloak. **2** A protective screen or shelter.

man·tel·piece (man′təl·pēs′) *n.* A mantel shelf.

man·til·la (man·til′ə, man·tē′ʸə) *n.* **1** A woman's light scarf or head covering of lace, as worn in Spain, Mexico, Italy, etc. **2** Any short mantle. [Sp.]

man·tis (man′tis) *n. pl.* **·tis·es** or **·tes** (-tēz) *n.* PRAYING MANTIS [< Gk., a prophet, also a kind of insect]

man·tis·sa (man·tis′ə) *n. Math.* The decimal or fractional part of a logarithm. [< L, a trifling addition ? < Etruscan]

man·tle (man′təl) *n.* **1** A loose cloak, usu. without sleeves, worn over other garments, often thought of figuratively as a symbol of authority, greatness, etc. **2** Anything that covers, envelops, or conceals. **3** *Zool.* A membranous flap or fold in the body wall of a mollusk. • See OYSTER. **4** A mesh supporting certain salts, used to enclose a flame and produce light when heated. **5** The layer of the earth beneath the crust and outside the core. **6** MANTEL. *—v.* **·tled, ·tling** *v.t.* **1** To cover with or as with a mantle; conceal. *—v.i.* **2** To overspread or cover the surface of something. **3** To be or become covered, overspread, or suffused. [< L *mantellum,* a cloak, towel]

man·tra (man′trə) *n.* In Hinduism, a sacred word or phrase chanted repeatedly and used as an aid in meditation or in the attainment of psychic states. [Skt.]

man·u·al (man′yōō·əl) *adj.* **1** Of or involving the hands. **2** Done or operated by hand. **3** Involving or using physical strength or dexterity: *manual* labor. *—n.* **1** A compact handbook of instruction or directions. **2** A keyboard, as of an organ. **3** A systematic exercise in the handling of some military weapon. [< L *manus* hand] **—man′u·al·ly** *adv.*

manual training The training of pupils in carpentry, woodworking, etc.

manuf., manufac. manufacture; manufactured; manufacturer.

man·u·fac·to·ry (man′yə·fak′tər·ē) *n. pl.* **·ries** A factory.

man·u·fac·ture (man′yə·fak′chər) *v.t.* **·tured, ·tur·ing 1** To make or fashion by hand or machinery, esp. in large quantities. **2** To work into useful form, as wool or steel. **3** To invent (evidence, testimony, etc.) falsely; concoct. **4** To produce in a mechanical way, as art, poetry, etc. *—n.* **1** The production of goods by hand or by industrial processes. **2** Anything made by industrial art or processes; manufactured articles collectively. **3** The making or contriving of anything. [< L *manus* hand + *factura* a making] **—man′u·fac′tur·er** *n.* **—man′u·fac′tur·ing** *adj., n.*

man·u·mit (man′yə·mit′) *v.t.* **·mit·ted, ·mit·ting** To free from bondage, as a slave; emancipate; liberate. [< L *manu emittere,* lit., send forth from one's hand] **—man′u·mis′sion** (-mish′ən) *n.*

ma·nure (mə·nʸōōr′) *n.* Any substance, as dung, decaying animal or vegetable matter, or certain minerals, applied to fertilize soil. *—v.t.* **·nured, ·nur·ing** To apply manure or other fertilizer to, as soil. [< AF *maynoverer* work with the hands] **—ma·nur′er** *n.*

man·u·script (man′yə·skript) *n.* **1** A piece of writing, either written or typewritten, as distinguished from printed matter; esp., an author's copy of a work to be considered for publication. **2** Matter written by hand. *—adj.* Written by hand or typed. [< L *manus* hand + *scriptus* written]

Manx (mangks) *adj.* Pertaining to the Isle of Man, its people, or their language. *—n.* **1** The people of the Isle of Man collectively: with *the.* **2** The Gaelic language of the Manx, virtually extinct.

Manx cat (mangks) A variety of domestic cat having no tail.

Manx cat

man·y (men′ē) *adj.* **more, most** Constituting a large number; numerous. *—n.* **1** A large number. **2** The masses; crowd; multitude: with *the. —pron.* A large number of persons or things. [< OE *manig*] • *Many* followed by *a, an,* or *another* indicates a great number thought of singly: *Many a man has had to find this out for himself.* The phrase *a great many* is idiomatic; it resembles a collective noun, but takes only a plural verb: *A great many are involved.*

Ma·o·ri (mä′ō·rē, mou′rē) *n. pl.* **·ris** or **·ri 1** One of an aboriginal, light brown people of New Zealand, chiefly Polynesian, mixed somewhat with Melanesian. **2** The Polynesian language of these people. *—adj.* Of or pertaining to the Maoris or their language.

map (map) *n.* **1** A representation, esp. on a flat surface, of any region or part of the earth or sky. **2** Any maplike delineation. **3** *Slang* The face. *—v.t.* **mapped, map·ping 1** To make a map of. **2** To plan in detail: often with *out.* [< L, cloth, napkin] **—map′per** *n.*

ma·ple (mā′pəl) *n.* **1** Any of a large genus of deciduous trees of the north temperate zone, with opposite leaves and a two-winged fruit. **2** Its fine-grained, hard wood. **3** The amber-yellow color of the finished wood. **4** The flavor of maple sugar. [< OE *mapel(trēow)* maple (tree)]

maple sugar A brown, crystalline sugar obtained from maple syrup.

maple syrup The boiled, condensed sap of certain maple trees.

ma·quis (mä·kē′) *n.* **1** A zone of shrubby, mostly evergreen plants in the Mediterranean region, known as cover for game or bandits. **2** *pl.* **·quis** *Often cap.* A member of the French underground in World War II. [< Ital. *macchia* a thicket, orig., a spot]

mar (mär) *v.t.* **marred, mar·ring 1** To do harm to; impair or ruin. **2** To deface; disfigure. —*n.* A disfiguring mark; blemish; injury. [< OE *merran* injure] **—mar′rer** *n.*

Mar, Mar. March.

mar. marine; maritime; married.

mar·a·bou (mar′ə·bo͞o) *n.* **1** Any of various large storks, esp. the **African marabou,** whose soft, white, lower tail and wing feathers are used in millinery. **2** A plume from the marabou. Also **mar′a·bout** (-bo͞ot). [F]

Marabou

ma·ra·ca (mə·rä′kə) *n.* A percussion instrument made of a gourd or gourd-shaped rattle with beans or beads inside it. [< Tupian]

mar·a·schi·no (mar′ə·skē′nō, -shē′-) *n.* A cordial distilled from the fermented juice of a wild cherry. [Ital. < *marasca* a wild cherry]

maraschino cherry A cherry preserved in maraschino-flavored syrup or an imitation of it.

mar·a·thon (mar′ə·thon) *n.* **1** A footrace of 26 miles, 385 yards: so called from a messenger's legendary run from Marathon to Athens to announce the Athenian victory over the Persians, 490 B.C. **2** Any endurance contest. [< *Marathon,* a plain in Greece]

ma·raud (mə·rôd′) *v.i.* **1** To rove in search of booty. —*v.t.* **2** To invade for plunder; raid. —*n.* A foray. [< F *maraud* a rogue] **—ma·raud′er** *n.* **—Syn.** *v.t.* despoil, loot, pillage, ransack, ravage.

mar·ble (mär′bəl) *n.* **1** A compact, partly crystallized, variously colored limestone, used for building or ornaments. **2** A sculptured or inscribed piece of this stone. **3** A small ball made of this stone, or of baked clay, glass, or porcelain. **4** *pl.* A game played with such balls. —*v.t.* **·bled, ·bling** To color or vein in imitation of marble. —*adj.* **1** Made of or like marble. **2** Without feeling; cold. [< Gk. *marmaros,* lit., sparkling stone] **—mar′bly** *adj.*

marble cake A cake made of light and dark batter mixed to give a marblelike appearance.

mar·ble·ize (mär′bəl·īz) *v.t.* **·ized, ·iz·ing** To streak or grain in imitation of marble.

mar·cel (mär·sel′) *n.* A style of dressing the hair in even, continuous waves by means of special irons. Also **marcel wave.** —*v.t.* **·celled, ·cel·ling** To dress (the hair) in such a style. [< *Marcel* Grateau, d.1936, French hairdresser]

march[1] (märch) *n.* **1** Movement together on foot and in time, as of soldiers. **2** A movement, as of soldiers, from one stopping place to another. **3** The distance thus passed over. **4** Onward progress. **5** A piece of music for setting a marching tempo. —*v.i.* **1** To move with measured steps. **2** To walk in a solemn or dignified manner. **3** To proceed steadily; advance. —*v.t.* **4** To cause to march. [< MF *marcher* to walk, trample] **—march′er** *n.*

march[2] (märch) *n.* A region or district lying along a boundary line; frontier. [< OF *marche* < Gmc.]

March (märch) *n.* The third month of the year, having 31 days. [< L *Martius (mensis)* (month) of Mars]

March hare A hare in the breeding season, regarded as a symbol of madness.

mar·chion·ess (mär′shən·is) *n.* **1** The wife or widow of a marquis. **2** A woman having the rank corresponding to that of a marquis. [< Med. L *marchio, -onis* a captain of the marches]

march·pane (märch′pān) *n.* MARZIPAN.

Mar·di gras (mär′dē grä′) Shrove Tuesday; last day before Lent: celebrated as a carnival in certain cities. [F., lit., fat Tuesday]

mare[1] (mâr) *n.* The female of the horse and other equine animals. [< OE *mēre*]

mar·e[2] (mâr′ē) *n. pl.* **mar·i·a** (mâr′ē·ə) Any of the dark, seemingly flat areas of the moon. [L, sea]

mare's nest (mârz) *n.* **1** A seemingly important discovery that proves to be a fraud. **2** A chaotic or disorderly condition.

mar·ga·rine (mär′jə·rin, -rēn) *n.* A blend of hydrogenated vegetable oils resembling butter: also **mar′ga·rin** (-jə·rin). [F]

marge[1] (märj) *n. Archaic* A margin; border.

marge[2] (märj) *n. Brit. Informal* Margarine.

mar·gin (mär′jin) *n.* **1** A bounding line; border. **2** An allowance or reservation for contingencies or changes, as of time or money. **3** Range or scope; provision for increase or progress. **4** A sum of money deposited with a broker to protect him against loss in contracts undertaken for a buyer or seller of stocks, etc. **5** The difference between selling price and cost of production: profit *margin.* **6** The blank parts of a page that surround the printed or written text. —*v.t.* **1** To furnish with a margin; border. **2** In commerce, to deposit a margin upon. [< L *margo* edge] **—Syn.** *n.* **1** boundary, brink, edge, verge.

mar·gi·nal (mär′jə·nəl) *adj.* **1** Of or constituting a margin. **2** Written, printed, or placed on the margin. **3** *Econ.* Operating or furnishing goods at a rate barely meeting the costs of production. **4** Of a nature that barely qualifies as useful, productive, or necessary. **—mar′gi·nal·ly** *adv.*

mar·gi·nate (mär′jə·nāt) *v.t.* **·nat·ed, ·nat·ing** To provide with a margin or margins. —*adj.* Having a margin: also **mar′gi·nat′ed.** **—mar′gi·na′tion** *n.*

mar·grave (mär′grāv) *n.* **1** A hereditary title of certain German princes. **2** Formerly, the governor of a German border province. [< MHG *mark* a march[2] + *graf* a count]

mar·gue·rite (mär′gə·rēt′) *n.* **1** A daisy. **2** A cultivated chrysanthemum with single flowers. [F]

ma·ri·a·chi (mär·ē·ä′chē) *n.* **1** A wandering band of Mexican street musicians. **2** The musicians, usu. made up of singers and guitarists. **3** The music they play. [Mex. Sp.]

mar·i·gold (mar′ə·gōld) *n.* Any of various composite plants having yellow, orange, or red flowers. [< MARY, prob. with ref. to the Virgin Mary + GOLD]

Marihuana plant

mar·i·hua·na (mar′ə·hwä′nə, mär′-) *n.* **1** The hemp plant. **2** Its dried leaves and flower tops which when smoked in cigarettes or otherwise ingested can produce distorted perception and other hallucinogenic effects. Also **ma′ri·jua′na.** [Am. Sp.]

ma·rim·ba (mə·rim′bə) *n.* A form of xylophone having resonators. [< Bantu *marimba*]

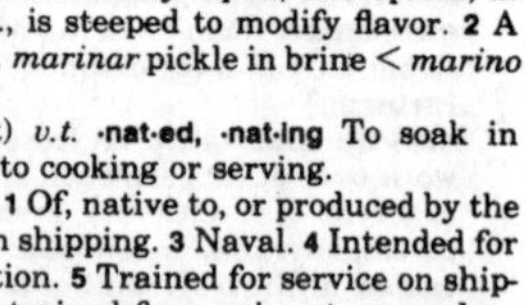
Marimba

ma·ri·na (mə·rē′nə) *n.* A basin or safe anchorage for small vessels, esp. one at which supplies, etc., may be obtained. [< L *marinus* of the sea]

mar·i·nade (mar′ə·nād′) *n.* **1** Any liquid, usu. spiced, in which meat, salad, etc., is steeped to modify flavor. **2** A dish so prepared. [< Sp. *marinar* pickle in brine < *marino* marine]

mar·i·nate (mar′ə·nāt) *v.t.* **·nat·ed, ·nat·ing** To soak in marinade preparatory to cooking or serving.

ma·rine (mə·rēn′) *adj.* **1** Of, native to, or produced by the sea. **2** Having to do with shipping. **3** Naval. **4** Intended for use at sea or in navigation. **5** Trained for service on shipboard. —*n.* **1** A soldier trained for service at sea and on land, esp. a member of the U.S. Marine Corps: also **Marine.** **2** Shipping, or shipping interests generally: the merchant *marine.* **3** A picture of the sea. [< L *marinus* < *mare* sea]

mar·i·ner (mar′ə·nər) *n.* A sailor. [< L *marinus* marine]

mar·i·o·nette (mar′ē·ə·net′) *n.* A jointed puppet moved by strings. [F]

Ma·ri·po·sa lily (mar′ə·pō′zə) A plant of the lily family, with showy, tulip-shaped flowers, growing in California and Mexico. Also **Mariposa tulip.** [< Sp. *mariposa* butterfly]

mar·i·tal (mar′ə·təl) *adj.* 1 Of or pertaining to marriage. 2 Of or pertaining to a husband. [< L *maritus* a husband] —**mar′i·tal·ly** *adv.*

mar·i·time (mar′ə·tīm) *adj.* 1 Situated on or near the sea: a *maritime* region. 2 Living on the borders of the sea: a *maritime* people. 3 Pertaining to the sea or matters connected with the sea. [< L < *mare* sea]

Maritime Provinces The provinces of New Brunswick, Nova Scotia, and Prince Edward Island on the Atlantic seaboard of E Canada.

mar·jo·ram (mär′jər·əm) *n.* Any of several perennial herbs related to mint, esp. **sweet marjoram** and **wild marjoram** (oregano) both used for seasoning in cookery. [< Med. L *majorana*]

mark[1] (märk) *n.* 1 A visible impression or sign produced or left on any substance by another. 2 A line, scratch, dot, scar, stain, or blemish. 3 TRADEMARK. 4 A cross made instead of a signature by one who cannot write. 5 A letter of the alphabet, number, or character by which quality is registered, as on a student's paper or record. 6 A symbol, written or printed: a punctuation *mark.* 7 An object serving to guide, direct, or point out, as a boundary, a place in a book, etc. 8 That which indicates the presence of something; a characteristic or symptom. 9 That which is aimed at, or toward which effort is directed; goal. 10 A proper bound or limit; standard. 11 A person easily duped: an easy *mark.* 12 An observing or noting; heed. —**make one's mark** To succeed. —**of mark** Famous; influential. —**up to the mark** Up to standard; in good health or condition, etc. —**wide of** (or **beside**) **the mark** Pointless. —*v.t.* 1 To make a mark or marks on. 2 To trace the boundaries of; limit. 3 To indicate by a mark or sign. 4 To make or produce by writing, drawing, etc. 5 To be a characteristic of; typify. 6 To destine: He was *marked* for fame. 7 To pay attention to; notice. 8 To make known; manifest. 9 To apply a price, identification, etc., to. 10 To give marks or grades to; grade. —*v.i.* 11 To take notice; pay attention. 12 To keep score or count. 13 To make a mark or marks. —**mark down** 1 To note down; record. 2 To put a lower price on, as for a sale. —**mark time** 1 To keep time by moving the feet but not advancing. 2 To pause in action. —**mark up** 1 To make marks on; deface. 2 To increase the price of. [< OE *mearc* boundary mark] —**mark′er** *n.*

mark[2] (märk) *n.* The former basic monetary unit of Germany, superseded in 1924 by the **reichs·mark** (rīkhs′·märk′) and, after World War II, by the **deut·sche·mark** (doi′chə·märk′) in West Germany and the **ost·mark** (ôst′märk′) in East Germany. [< MHG *marke*]

Mark (märk) 1 The evangelist and reputed author of the second Gospel: also **Saint Mark.** 2 The second Gospel.

marked (märkt) *adj.* Brought prominently to notice; prominent. —**mark·ed·ly** (mär′kid·lē) *adv.* —**mark′ed·ness** *n.*

mar·ket (mär′kit) *n.* 1 An open space or large building where merchandise, esp. produce, is displayed for sale: also **market place.** 2 A private store for the sale of provisions: a meat *market.* 3 The state of trade in goods, stocks, etc.; traffic: a brisk *market.* 4 A locality or country where anything can be bought or sold: the South American *markets.* 5 A gathering of people for selling and buying, esp. of a particular commodity: the wheat *market.* 6 Demand for commercial products or services. —**be in the market for** To be looking for an opportunity to buy. —**be on the market** To be for sale. —**play the market** To speculate in stocks, bonds, etc. —*v.t.* 1 To take or send to market for sale; sell. —*v.i.* 2 To deal in a market; sell or buy. 3 To buy food. [< L *merx, mercis* merchandise] —**mar′ket·a·bil′i·ty, mar′ket·er** *n.* —**mar′ket·a·ble** *adj.*

market price The current price.

market value The price which may be expected for a given commodity, security, or service under the conditions of a given market.

mark·ing (mär′king) *n.* 1 A distinctive mark or an arrangement of marks, as on an animal's coat: the zebra's *markings.* 2 The act of making a mark.

mark·ka (märk′kä) *n.* The basic monetary unit of Finland.

marks·man (märks′mən) *n. pl.* **·men** (-mən) One skilled in hitting the mark, as with a rifle or other weapon. —**marks′man·ship** *n.* —**marks′wom′an** (-wo͝om′ən) *n. Fem.*

mark-up (märk′up′) *n.* 1 A raising in the price of anything. 2 The difference between the wholesale cost price and the retail selling price.

marl (märl) *n.* A soil containing lime, clay, and sand, used as fertilizer. —*v.t.* To fertilize or spread with marl. [< LL *marga*] —**marl′y** *adj.* (**·i·er, ·i·est**)

mar·lin (mär′lin) *n.* Any of various deep-sea game fishes having the upper jaw protruding like a spike. [< MARLINE(SPIKE); because of the shape of its snout]

mar·line (mär′lin) *n. Naut.* A small rope used for winding around the ends of larger ropes to prevent raveling. Also **mar′ling** (-ling). [< MDu. *marren* to tie + *lijn* a line]

mar·line·spike (mär′lin·spīk′) *n. Naut.* A sharp-pointed iron pin used in splicing ropes. Also **mar′lin·spike′, mar′ling·spike′** (-ling-).

mar·ma·lade (mär′mə·lād) *n.* A preserve made in part with the rind of fruits, esp. citrus fruits. [< Gk. *melimēlon,* lit., honey apple]

mar·mo·set (mär′mə·set, -zet) *n.* A small Central and South American monkey with soft, woolly hair and a long tail. [< OF *marmouset* a grotesque figure]

Marmoset

mar·mot (mär′mət) *n.* Any of various small, stout, short-tailed, burrowing rodents with coarse fur, as the woodchuck. [< L *mus, muris* a mouse + *mons, montis* a mountain]

ma·roon[1] (mə·ro͞on′) *v.t.* 1 To put ashore and abandon on a desolate island or coast. 2 To abandon; leave helpless. —*n.* 1 In the West Indies and Dutch Guiana, formerly a fugitive Negro slave. 2 One of the descendants of these slaves. [< Sp. *cimarrón* wild]

ma·roon[2] (mə·ro͞on′) *n. & adj.* Dull, dark red. [< F *marron* a chestnut]

mar·plot (mär′plot′) *n.* One who, by meddling, mars or frustrates a design or plan.

marque (märk) *n.* A license of reprisal upon an enemy, as at sea in wartime. [F, mark, imprint]

mar·quee (mär·kē′) *n.* 1 An awning or rooflike structure over the entrance to a hotel, theater, etc. 2 A large field tent, esp. one used at lawn entertainments. [< F *marquise* a canopy]

Mar·que·san (mär·kā′sən) *adj.* Of the Marquesas Islands, their inhabitants, or their language. —*n.* 1 A native of the Marquesas Islands. 2 The Polynesian language spoken there.

mar·quess (mär′kwis) *n.* MARQUIS.

mar·que·try (mär′kə·trē) *n.* Inlaid work of wood, stones, ivory, etc., used to decorate furniture and floors. Also **mar′·que·te·rie.** [< MF *marque* a mark]

mar·quis (mär′kwis, *Fr.* mȧr·kē′) *n.* The title of a nobleman next in rank below a duke. [< OF *marche* boundary, a march[2]]

mar·quise (mär·kēz′) *n.* 1 The wife or widow of a marquis. 2 A woman who has a rank equal to that of a marquis.

mar·qui·sette (mär′ki·zet′, -kwi-) *n.* A sheer, lightweight, open-mesh fabric, used esp. for curtains. [F, dim. of *marquise* a canopy]

mar·riage (mar′ij) *n.* 1 The act of marrying, or the state of being married; wedlock. 2 A wedding. 3 Any close union. [< L *maritus* a husband]

mar·riage·a·ble (mar′ij·ə·bəl) *adj.* Fitted by age, physical condition, etc., for marriage. —**mar′riage·a·bil′i·ty, mar′·riage·a·ble·ness** *n.*

mar·ried (mar′ēd) *adj.* 1 Pertaining to marriage. 2 Having a spouse; wedded. —*n. Usu. pl. Informal* A married person. —**Syn.** 1 conjugal, connubial, hymeneal, matrimonial, nuptial.

mar·row (mar′ō) *n.* **1** A soft vascular tissue found in the central cavities of most bones. **2** The interior substance of anything; essence. [< OE *mearg*] **—mar′row·y** *adj.*

mar·row·bone (mar′ō·bōn′) *n.* **1** A bone containing marrow: also **marrow bone. 2** *pl.* One's knees.

mar·row·fat (mar′ō·fat′) *n.* A variety of large, rich pea. Also **marrow pea, marrowfat pea.**

mar·ry (mar′ē) *v.* **·ried, ·ry·ing** *v.t.* **1** To join as husband and wife in marriage. **2** To take in marriage. **3** To give in marriage: usu. with *off.* **4** To unite closely. *—v.i.* **5** To take a husband or wife. [< L *maritus* a husband, married] **—mar′ri·er** *n.*

Mars (märz) *Rom. Myth.* The god of war. *—n.* The planet of the solar system fourth distant from the sun. • See PLANET.

Mar·sa·la (mär·sä′lä) *n.* A light, sweet white wine originally made in Marsala, Sicily.

Mar·seil·laise (mär′sə·lāz′, *Fr.* mär·sā·yez′) *n.* The national anthem of the French Republic, written in 1792 by Rouget de Lisle. [F < *Marseille*]

mar·seille (mär·sāl′) *n.* A thick cotton fabric having a raised weave, similar to piqué. Also **mar·seilles** (mär·sālz′). [< *Marseille,* France]

marsh (märsh) *n.* A tract of low, wet land; swamp. [< OE *mersc*] **—marsh′i·ness** *n.* **—marsh′y** *adj.* **(·i·er, ·i·est)**

mar·shal (mär′shəl) *n.* **1** An officer authorized to regulate ceremonies, processions, etc. **2** A U.S. federal official appointed to a judicial district and having functions similar to those of a sheriff. **3** The head of the police force or fire department in some cities. **4** In some European countries, a military officer of high rank. *—v.t.* **·shaled** or **·shalled, ·shal·ing** or **·shal·ling 1** To arrange or dispose in order, as facts. **2** To array or draw up, as troops for battle. **3** To lead; usher. [< OHG *marah* a horse + *scalh* a servant] **—mar′·shal·cy** (-sē), **mar′shal·ship** *n.*

marsh gas METHANE.

marsh hawk An American hawk that nests on the ground in fields and marshes.

marsh·mal·low (marsh′mal′ō, -mel′ō) *n.* A soft, spongy confection made of syrup and gelatin.

marsh mallow A marsh plant with showy pink flowers.

marsh marigold A showy swamp plant related to the buttercup, having bright yellow flowers.

mar·su·pi·al (mär·soo͞′pē·əl) *n.* Any of an order of mammals lacking a placenta and carrying their young in a marsupium, as the kangaroo, opossum, etc. *—adj.* **1** Having a marsupium. **2** Pertaining to or like a marsupium or pouch.

mar·su·pi·um (mär·soo͞′pē·əm) *n. pl.* **·pi·a** (-pē·ə) A pouchlike fold, as on the abdomen of female marsupials, in which the young are carried. [L, a pouch, purse]

mart (märt) *n.* A market. [< L *mercatus* market]

mar·ten (mär′tən) *n.* **1** Any of a genus of weasellike, furbearing carnivorous mammals. **2** The valuable fur of the marten. [< OF *martre*]

Marten

Mar·tha (mär′thə) In the Bible, a friend of Jesus and sister of Lazarus and Mary.

mar·tial (mär′shəl) *adj.* **1** Pertaining to war or military life: court *martial.* **2** Suitable for war: *martial* music. **3** Fond of war; brave. [< L *Martialis* pertaining to Mars] **—mar′tial·ly** *adv.*

martial law Military jurisdiction exercised by a government temporarily over the population of a locality during war or an emergency.

Mar·tian (mär′shən) *adj.* Pertaining to the planet Mars. *—n.* One of the supposed inhabitants of Mars.

mar·tin (mär′tən) *n.* Any of certain short-beaked birds of the swallow family, as the **purple martin,** the **sand martin,** and the **house martin.** [ME]

mar·ti·net (mär′tə·net′) *n.* An overly strict disciplinarian, esp. military or naval. [< General *Martinet,* 17th c. French drillmaster]

mar·tin·gale (mär′tən·gāl) *n.* **1** A forked strap for holding down a horse's head by connecting the head gear with the bellyband. **2** *Naut.* A vertical spar under the bowsprit used in guying the stays. Also **mar′tin·gal** (-gal). [F]

mar·ti·ni (mär·tē′nē) *n. pl.* **·nis** A cocktail made of gin or vodka and dry vermouth, usu. served with a green olive or a twist of lemon peel. [?< *Martini* and Rossi, a company making vermouth]

mar·tyr (mär′tər) *n.* **1** One who submits to death rather than forswear his faith. **2** One who dies or suffers for principles, or sacrifices all for a cause. **3** One who suffers much or long, as from ill health or misfortune. *—v.t.* **1** To put to death as a martyr. **2** To torture; persecute. [< Gk. *martyr* a witness] **—mar′tyr·dom** *n.*

mar·tyr·ize (mär′tər·īz) *v.* **·ized, ·iz·ing** *v.t.* **1** To make a martyr of. *—v.i.* **2** To become a martyr. **—mar′tyr·i·za′tion** *n.*

mar·vel (mär′vəl) *v.* **·veled** or **·velled, ·vel·ing** or **·vel·ling** *v.i.* **1** To be filled with wonder, surprise, etc. *—v.t.* **2** To wonder at or about: with a clause as object. *—n.* **1** That which excites wonder; a prodigy. **2** A miracle. [< L *mirari* wonder at]

mar·vel·ous (mär′vəl·əs) *adj.* **1** Provoking astonishment or wonder; remarkable. **2** Supernatural; miraculous. **3** *Informal* Splendid; extraordinarily good. Also **mar′vel·lous. —mar′vel·ous·ly** *adv.* **—mar′vel·ous·ness** *n.* **—Syn. 1** amazing, extraordinary, prodigious, wonderful, singular.

Marx·ism (märk′siz·əm) *n.* The body of doctrine formulated by Karl Marx and Friedrich Engels which formed the foundations of socialism and communism. **—Marx′i·an** (-ē·ən) *adj.* **—Marx′ist** *adj., n.*

Marx·ism-Len·in·ism (märk′siz·əm·len′in·iz′əm) *n.* The philosophy of history and politics based upon the works of Marx and Lenin. **—Marx′ist-Len′in·ist** *n.*

Mar·y (mâr′ē) In the Bible: **1** The mother of Jesus. **2** The sister of Lazarus and Martha.

Mary Jane (jān) **1** A low-heeled, usu. patent-leather slipper with an ankle strap, worn esp. by young girls **2** *Slang* MARIHUANA.

Mary Mag·da·lene (mag′də·lēn, -lin) **1** The woman out of whom Jesus cast seven devils. **2** The penitent sinner whom Jesus forgave. Also **Mary Mag′da·len.**

mar·zi·pan (mär′zə·pan) *n.* A confection of grated almonds, sugar, and white of eggs, usu. made into a paste and molded into various shapes. [< Ital. *marzapane,* orig. a small box, a dry measure, a weight]

mas., masc. masculine.

mas·car·a (mas·kar′ə) *n.* A cosmetic used to darken the eyelashes. [< Sp. *máscara* a mask]

mas·con (mas′kon, mäs-) *n.* Any of various areas on the moon where increased gravitational forces cause deviations in the course of orbiting spacecraft. [< MAS(S) + CON(CENTRATION)]

mas·cot (mas′kot, -kət) *n.* A person, animal, or thing thought to bring good luck by its presence. [< Provençal *masco* a sorcerer]

mas·cu·line (mas′kyə·lin) *adj.* **1** Having the distinguishing qualities of the male sex. **2** Of, pertaining to, or suitable for males; manly. **3** *Gram.* Being of the male gender. *—n. Gram.* The masculine gender or a word of this gender. [< L *masculus* male] **—mas′cu·line·ly** *adv.* **—mas′cu·lin′i·ty** *n.*

ma·ser (mā′zər) *n. Physics* A device similar to a laser that operates with microwaves. [< *m(icrowave) a(mplification by) s(timulated) e(mission of) r(adiation)*]

mash (mash) *n.* **1** A pulpy mass. **2** A mixture of meal, bran, etc., and water, fed to cattle. **3** Crushed or ground grain or malt, infused in hot water to produce wort. **4** In wine-making, the crushed grapes before fermentation. *—v.t.* **1** To crush or beat into a mash. **2** To convert into mash, as malt or grain, by infusing in hot water. [< OE *māsc*]

mash·er (mash′ər) *n.* **1** One who or that which mashes. **2** *Slang* A man who persistently makes overtures to women unacquainted with him.

mash·ie (mash′ē) *n.* An iron golf club with a deep, short blade and much loft. Also **mash′y.** [?]

mask (mask, mäsk) *n.* **1** A cover or disguise for the features. **2** A protective appliance for the face

Masks
a. Greek tragedy.
b. Greek comedy.
c. domino.

or head: a gas *mask.* **3** Anything used to disguise or dissimilate; subterfuge. **4** A likeness of a face cast in plaster, clay, etc. **5** An elaborate dramatic presentation with music, fanciful costumes, etc., and actors masked as allegorical or mythological subjects; also, the text or music for it. **6** MASQUERADE. **7** An artistic covering for the face, used esp. by Greek and Roman actors. —*v.t.* **1** To cover, shield, or protect with or as with a mask. **2** To hide or conceal with or as with a mask; disguise. —*v.i.* **3** To put on a mask; assume a disguise. [< Ar. *maskharah* a buffoon] —**mask′er** *n.*

mask·ing tape An adhesive tape used to protect those parts of a surface not to be painted, sprayed, or otherwise treated.

mas·o·chism (mas′ə·kiz′əm) *n.* The obtaining of pleasure, esp. sexual gratification, by submitting to physical or mental cruelty. [< Leopold von Sacher-*Masoch,* 1835–95, Austrian writer] —**mas′o·chist** *n.* —**mas′o·chis′tic** *adj.* —**mas′och·is′ti·cal·ly** *adv.*

ma·son (mā′sən) *n.* One who lays brick and stone in building; also, a stonecutter. [< Med. L *macio*]

Ma·son (mā′sən) *n.* A member of the order of Freemasons.

Ma·son-Dix·on line (mā′sən·dik′sən) The boundary between Pennsylvania and Maryland, regarded as dividing the North and the South. Also **Mason and Dixon's line.**

Ma·son·ic (mə·son′ik) *adj.* Of or pertaining to Freemasons or Freemasonry. Also **ma·son′ic.**

Ma·son·ite (mā′sən·īt) *n.* A tough, dense fiberboard used as a building and construction material: a trade name.

ma·son·ry (mā′sən·rē) *n. pl.* **·ries 1** The art or work of building with brick or stone. **2** That which is built by masons or of materials which masons use.

masque (mask, mäsk), *n.* **1** MASK (def. 5). **2** MASQUERADE.

mas·quer·ade (mas′kə·rād′, mäs′-) *n.* **1** A party attended by persons masked and costumed. **2** The costumes and disguises worn on such an occasion. **3** A false show or disguise. —*v.i.* **·ad·ed, ·ad·ing 1** To take part in a masquerade. **2** To wear a mask or disguise. **3** To disguise one's true character; assume a false appearance. [< Sp. *máscara* a mask] —**mas′quer·ad′er** *n.*

mass (mas, mäs) *n.* **1** An assemblage of things that collectively make one quantity. **2** A body of matter; a lump. **3** The principal part of anything. **4** Extent of volume: bulk. **5** *Physics* The measure of the degree to which a body resists acceleration by a force, used also as a measure of the matter contained in the body. —**the masses** The common people. —*adj.* **1** Of, for, or consisting of the public in general. **2** Done on a large scale: *mass* production. —*v.t. & v.i.* To form into a mass; assemble. [< Gk. *maza* barley cake, lump] —**Syn.** *n.* **1** accumulation, aggregate, heap, collection, pile, group. *v.* accumulate, amass, gather, collect, pile up.

Mass (mas, mäs) *n. Eccl.* **1** The eucharistic liturgy in the Roman Catholic and some Anglican churches. **2** A celebration of this. **3** A musical setting for the fixed portions of this liturgy. Also **mass.** [< OE *mæsse*]

Mass. Massachusetts.

mas·sa·cre (mas′ə·kər) *n.* The indiscriminate, ruthless killing of human beings or animals; slaughter. —*v.t.* **·cred** (-kərd), **·cring** To kill indiscriminately or in great numbers. [< OF *maçacre* < *mache-col* butcher] —**mas′sa·crer** (-kə·rər, -krər) *n.*

mas·sage (mə·säzh′) *n.* A remedial treatment of kneading, rubbing, and otherwise manipulating a part or the whole of the body. —*v.t.* **·saged, ·sag·ing** To treat by massage. [< F *masser* to massage] —**mas·sag′er, mas·sag′ist** *n.*

mass·cult (mas′kult′) *n.* Someone or something having immense popularity and considered as an expression of popular culture: often used attributively. [< MASS + CULT(URE)]

mas·sé (ma·sā′) *n.* In billiards, a stroke with a cue held perpendicularly, causing the cue ball to return in a straight line or to describe a curve. Also **mas·sé′ shot.** [< F *masse* billiard cue, a mace]

mas·seur (mȧ·sûr′, *Fr.* mȧ·sœr′) *n.* A man whose work is giving massages. [F] —**mas·seuse** (ma·so͞oz′, -so͞os′; *Fr.* mȧ·sœz′) *n. Fem.*

mas·sive (mas′iv) *adj.* **1** Constituting a large mass; ponderous. **2** Belonging to the total mass of anything. **3** Without definite form, as a mineral; amorphous. **4** Imposing in scope or degree; having considerable magnitude. —**mas′·sive·ly** *adv.* —**mas′sive·ness** *n.* —**Syn. 1** ample, broad, capacious, extensive, spacious.

mass media Newspapers, magazines, paperbacks, radio, television, and motion pictures, considered as means of reaching a very wide public audience.

mass meeting A large public gathering for the discussion or promotion of some topic or cause, usu. political.

mass number *Physics* The number of protons and neutrons in an atom.

mass-pro·duce (mas′prə·dʸo͞os′) *v.t.* **·duced, ·duc·ing** To manufacture or produce by machinery (goods or articles) in great numbers or quantities. —**mass production**

mass·y (mas′ē) *adj.* **mass·i·er, mass·i·est** Massive; bulky. —**mass′i·ness** *n.*

mast[1] (mast, mäst) *n.* **1** *Naut.* A pole or spar, as of round timber or tubular metal, set upright in a sailing vessel to sustain the yards, sails, etc. **2** The upright pole of a derrick. **3** Any large, upright pole. —**before the mast** Serving as a common sailor. —*v.t.* To furnish with a mast or masts. [< OE *mæst*]

mast[2] (mast, mäst) *n.* The fruit of the oak, beech, and other trees; acorns, etc. [< OE *mæst*]

mas·ta·ba (mas′tə·bə) *n.* In ancient Egypt, an oblong, slope-sided building used as a mortuary chapel and place of offerings. Also **mas′ta·bah.** [< Ar. *maṣṭabah* bench]

Mastabas

mas·tec·to·my (mas·tek′tə·mē) *n. pl.* **·mies** The surgical removal of the breast. [< Gk. *mastos* breast + -ECTOMY]

mas·ter (mas′tər, mäs′-) *n.* **1** One who has authority over others, as the principal of a school, an employer, the head of a household, the owner of a domestic animal, etc. **2** One who has control of something; an owner. **3** In the U.S. merchant marine, the captain of a vessel. **4** One who is highly skilled; esp., an expert craftsman. **5** An artist of the first rank. **6** An original or a copy made from an original, as of a phonograph record, tape recording, or film, used as a source of making usu. numerous copies, as for commercial distribution. **7** A master key, switch, or other device. **8** *Chiefly Brit.* A male schoolteacher. **9** A title of respect for a young boy: *Master* Wilson. **10** An officer of the court who assists the judges. **11** One who has disciples or followers, esp. a religious leader. **12** One who gains the victory; a victor. —**the** (or **our**) **Master** Jesus. —*v.t.* **1** To overcome or subdue. **2** To become expert in: to *master* Greek. **3** To control or govern. —*adj.* **1** Being a master; being in control; chief. **2** Being an acknowledged expert: a *master* tactician. **3** Being a master from which others are duplicated. **4** Being a device that controls or can function in place of other mechanisms or that serves as a standard: a *master* key or switch. [< L *magister* greater] —**mas′ter·dom** *n.*

master builder 1 A contractor who employs men to build. **2** Formerly, an architect.

mas·ter·ful (mas′tər·fəl, mäs′-) *adj.* **1** Having the characteristics of a master; domineering. **2** Showing mastery, as of an art, situation, etc. —**mas′ter·ful·ly** *adv.* —**mas′ter·ful·ness** *n.*

mas·ter·ly (mas′tər·lē, mäs′-) *adj.* Characteristic of a master; befitting a master. —*adv.* In a masterly manner. —**mas′ter·li·ness** *n.*

mas·ter·mind (mas′tər·mīnd′, mäs′-) *n.* A person of great intelligence and executive ability. —*v.t.* To plan and direct (a project) skillfully.

Master of Arts 1 A degree conferred by an institution of higher learning for the completion of a prescribed course of graduate study. 2 A person who has received this degree.

master of ceremonies A person presiding over an entertainment or dinner and introducing the performers or speakers.

mas·ter·piece (mas′tər·pēs′, mäs′-) *n.* An artistic work done with consummate skill.

master sergeant See GRADE.

mas·ter·ship (mas′tər·ship, mäs′-) *n.* 1 The state, personality, or character of a master; also, mastery. 2 Masterly skill; preeminence.

master stroke A masterly or decisive action or achievement.

mas·ter·y (mas′tər·ē, mäs′-) *n.* 1 The condition of having power and control. 2 Great knowledge or skill. 3 Superiority in a contest; victory. —**Syn.** 1 command, dominion, sway. 2 expertness. 3 triumph.

mast·head (mast′hed′, mäst′-) *n.* 1 *Naut.* The top of a lower mast. 2 That part of a newspaper or magazine listing the ownership, publishers, editors, etc. —*v.t.* To raise to or display at the masthead, as a flag.

mas·tic (mas′tik) *n.* 1 A resin obtained from a small Mediterranean tree, used in varnish and as a styptic. 2 The tree: also **mastic tree.** 3 Any of various quick-drying adhesive pastes. [<Gk. *mastichē*]

mas·ti·cate (mas′tə·kāt) *v.t.* **·cat·ed, ·cat·ing** 1 To crush or grind (food) for swallowing; chew. 2 To reduce, as rubber, to a pulp by crushing or kneading. [<Gk. *mastichaein* gnash the teeth] —**mas′ti·ca′tion, mas′ti·ca′tor** *n.*

mas·ti·ca·to·ry (mas′tə·kə·tôr′ē, -tō′rē) *adj.* 1 Of, pertaining to, or used in mastication. 2 Adapted for chewing. —*n. pl.* **·ries** A substance chewed to increase the secretion of saliva.

mas·tiff (mas′tif, mäs′-) *n.* One of an English breed of large hunting dogs, with a heavy body and broad skull. [<OF *mastin*]

mas·to·don (mas′tə·don) *n.* Any of various extinct elephantlike mammals distinguished from mammoths chiefly by their molar teeth. [< Gk. *mastos* breast + *odous, odontos* tooth; from the nipple-shaped projections on its teeth]

Mastodon

mas·toid (mas′toid) *adj.* 1 Designating or pertaining to a process of the temporal bone behind the ear. 2 Nipplelike; breastlike. —*n.* 1 The mastoid process. 2 MASTOIDITIS. [<Gk. *mastos* breast + *eidos* form] • See SKULL.

mas·toid·i·tis (mas′toid·ī′tis) *n.* Inflammation of the mastoid process.

mas·tur·bate (mas′tər·bāt) *v.* **·bat·ed, ·bat·ing** *v.i.* 1 To excite one's genitals, as by contact, for sexual pleasure, usu. inducing orgasm. —*v.t.* 2 To induce orgasm in (another) by exciting the genitals without having sexual intercourse. [<L *masturbari*] —**mas′tur·ba′tion, mas′tur·ba′tor** *n.* —**mas′tur·ba·to′ry** (-bə·tôr′ē, -tō′rē) *adj.*

mat[1] (mat) *n.* 1 A flat article, woven or plaited, or made of a thick, sturdy material, to be laid on a floor and used to wipe one's feet. 2 Any flat piece of straw, plastic, etc., used as a floor covering, table protection, ornament, etc. 3 A thick, mattresslike pad used in a gymnasium for wrestling, acrobatics, etc. 4 Any twisted growth, as of hair or rushes. —*v.* **mat·ted, mat·ting** *v.t.* 1 To cover with or as with mats. 2 To knot or entangle into a mat. —*v.i.* 3 To become knotted or entangled. [<LL *matta*]

mat[2] (mat) *n.* 1 MATTE. 2 *Printing* MATRIX. 3 A border of cardboard, serving as the frame, or part of the frame, of a picture. —*v.t.* **mat·ted, mat·ting** 1 To produce a dull surface on, as metal or glass. 2 To provide (a picture) with a border of cardboard. —*adj.* MATTE. [<OF, dull]

mat·a·dor (mat′ə·dôr) *n.* A bullfighter who kills the bull with a thrust of a sword. [<Sp., *matar* to slay]

match[1] (mach) *n.* 1 A person or thing equal to another. 2 Two or more persons or things that harmonize or are alike. 3 A contest of skill, strength, etc.: a tennis *match.* 4 A marriage or an agreement to marry. 5 A person considered as a future husband or wife. —*v.t.* 1 To be similar to or in accord with in quality, degree, etc.: His looks *match* his mood. 2 To make or select as equals or as suitable for one another: to *match* pearls. 3 To marry. 4 To adapt: *Match* your efforts to your strength. 5 To compare so as to decide superiority; test: to *match* wits. 6 To set (equal opponents) in opposition: to *match* boxers. 7 To equal: No one could *match* him. —*v.i.* 8 To be equal, similar, or corresponding; suit. 9 To get married. —**match coins** To flip or reveal coins to make a decision. [<OE *gemæcca* companion] —**match′a·ble** *adj.* —**match′er** *n.*

match[2] (mach) *n.* 1 A splinter of soft wood or a piece of cardboard with a combustible tip that ignites by friction. 2 Formerly, a fuse of cotton wicking prepared to burn quickly or slowly, and used for firing cannon. [<Gk. *myxa* wick of a candle]

match·book (mach′bo͝ok′) *n.* A folder enclosing and usu. stapled to a set of cardboard matches.

match·less (mach′lis) *adj.* That cannot be matched or equaled; peerless. —**match′less·ly** *adv.* —**match′less·ness** *n.* —**Syn.** incomparable, unequaled, unparalleled, unrivaled.

match·lock (mach′lok′) *n.* 1 An old type of musket fired by placing a lighted match against the powder in the pan. 2 The gunlock on such a musket.

match·mak·er (mach′mā′kər) *n.* 1 One who plans or schemes to bring about marriages for others. 2 One who arranges games or contests. —**match′mak′ing** *adj., n.*

match play In golf, a form of play in which the score is computed by totaling the number of holes won or lost by each side.

mate[1] (māt) *n.* 1 An associate; comrade. 2 One that is paired with another, as in matrimony; also, an animal paired for propagation. 3 An equal in a contest; a match. 4 An officer of a merchant vessel, ranking next below the captain. 5 *Nav.* A petty officer. —*v.* **mat·ed, mat·ing** *v.t.* 1 To join as mates; marry. 2 To pair for breeding, as animals. 3 To associate; couple. —*v.i.* 4 To match; marry. 5 To pair. 6 To consort; associate. [<MLG *gemate*]

mate[2] (māt) *v.t.* **mat·ed, mat·ing** 1 In chess, to checkmate. 2 To defeat or confound. —*n.* A checkmate. —*interj.* Checkmate. [<CHECKMATE]

ma·té (mä′tā, mat′ā) *n.* 1 A beverage made by steeping the leaves of a Brazilian holly. 2 The plant or its dried leaves. [<Quechua]

ma·ter (mā′tər, mä′-) *n. Latin* Mother

ma·te·ri·al (mə·tir′ē·əl) *n.* 1 That of which anything is composed or may be constructed. 2 Collected facts, impressions, ideas, etc., for use in completing a creative endeavor. 3 The tools, instruments, articles, etc., for doing something. 4 A cloth or fabric. —*adj.* 1 Pertaining to anything having a physical existence. 2 Of or pertaining to the body or the appetites. 3 More interested in worldly things than in spiritual ones. 4 Important; significant: It makes no *material* difference to me. 5 Pertaining to matter as opposed to form. [<L *materia* matter]

ma·te·ri·al·ism (mə·tir′ē·əl·iz′əm) *n.* 1 The doctrine that the facts of experience are all to be explained by reference to the reality and laws of physical or material substance. 2 Undue regard for material and worldly rather than spiritual matters. —**ma·te′ri·al·ist** *adj., n.* —**ma·te′ri·al·is′tic** *adj.* —**ma·te′ri·al·is′ti·cal·ly** *adv.*

ma·te·ri·al·ize (mə·tir′ē·əl·īz′) *v.* **·ized, ·iz·ing** *v.t.* 1 To give material or actual form to; represent as material. 2 To cause (a spirit, etc.) to appear in visible form. —*v.i.* 3 To assume material or visible form; appear. 4 To take form or shape; be realized: Our plans never *materialized.* —**ma·te′ri·al·i·za′tion, ma·te′ri·al·iz′er** *n.*

ma·te·ri·al·ly (mə·tir′ē·əl·ē) *adv.* 1 In a material and important manner. 2 In essence or substance. 3 From a physical point of view.

ma·te·ri·a med·i·ca (mə·tir′ē·ə med′i·kə) *Med.* 1 The science that deals with medicinal substances, their nature, uses, effects, etc. 2 The substances employed as remedial agents. [<L *materia* matter + *medicus* medical]

ma·te·ri·el (mə·tir′ē·el′) *n.* Materials and equipment required for some purpose; esp., in an army, material things, as distinguished from personnel. Also **ma·té′ri·el′.** [<F]

ma·ter·nal (mə·tûr′nəl) *adj.* **1** Pertaining to a mother; motherly. **2** Connected with or inherited from one's mother. [< L *mater* a mother] **—ma·ter′nal·ly** *adv.*

ma·ter·ni·ty (mə·tûr′nə·tē) *n. pl.* **·ties 1** The condition of being a mother. **2** The qualities of a mother; motherliness. *—adj.* Pertaining to pregnancy or childbirth: *maternity* dress; *maternity* hospital.

math (math) *n. Informal* Mathematics.

math. mathematical; mathematician; mathematics.

math·e·mat·i·cal (math′ə·mat′i·kəl) *adj.* **1** Pertaining to or of the nature of mathematics. **2** Rigidly exact or precise. Also **math′e·mat′ic.** [< Gk. < *mathēma* learning] — **math′e·mat′i·cal·ly** *adv.*

math·e·ma·ti·cian (math′ə·mə·tish′ən) *n.* One skilled or trained in mathematics.

math·e·mat·ics (math′ə·mat′iks) *n.pl. (construed as sing.)* **1** The logical study of quantity, form, arrangement, and magnitude; esp., the methods for disclosing, by the use of rigorously defined concepts and symbols, the properties of quantities and relations. **2** A particular application or use of mathematics.

mat·in (mat′in) *n.* **1** *pl. Eccl.* The first of the canonical hours, usu. said at midnight. **2** *pl.* In the Anglican Church, the order for public worship in the morning. *—adj.* Of or belonging to the morning: also **mat′in·al.** [< OF *matin* early]

mat·i·née (mat′ə·nā′) *n.* An entertainment or reception held in the daytime; esp. a theatrical or cinematic performance given in the afternoon. Also **mat′i·nee′.** [F< *matin* morning]

matri- *combining form* Mother: *matricide.* [< L *mater, matris* mother]

ma·tri·arch (mā′trē·ärk) *n.* A woman who rules in her family or tribe. [< MATRI- + Gk. *archos* ruler] **—ma′tri·ar′·chal** *adj.* **—ma′tri·ar′chy** *n.*

mat·ri·cide (mat′rə·sīd, mā′trə-) *n.* **1** The killing of one's mother. **2** One who kills his or her mother. [< MATRI- + -CIDE] **—mat′ri·ci′dal** *adj.*

ma·tric·u·late (mə·trik′yə·lāt) *v.t. & v.i.* **·lat·ed, ·lat·ing 1** To enroll, esp. in a college or university as a candidate for a degree. **2** *Can.* To pass final high-school examinations. *—n.* A candidate for a college or university degree. [< Med. L. *matrix* womb, origin, public roll] **—ma·tric′u·lant, ma·tric′u·la′tion, ma·tric′u·la′tor** *n.*

mat·ri·mo·ny (mat′rə·mō′nē) *n. pl.* **·nies 1** The union of a man and a woman in marriage; wedlock. **2** The state of being married. [< L *matrimonium*] **—mat′ri·mo′ni·al** *adj.* — **mat′ri·mo′ni·al·ly** *adv.*

ma·trix (mā′triks) *n. pl.* **ma·tri·ces** (mā′trə·sēz, mat′rə-) or **ma·trix·es 1** That which contains and gives shape or form to anything. **2** A mold in which anything is cast or shaped. **3** *Printing* A papier-mâché, plaster, or other impression of a form, from which a plate for printing may be made. [L, womb, breeding animal]

ma·tron (mā′trən) *n.* **1** A married woman. **2** A woman of established age and dignity. **3** A housekeeper, or a female superintendent, as of an institution. [< L *mater* mother] **—ma′tron·al, ma′tron·ly** *adj.* **—ma′tron·li·ness** *n.*

matron of honor A married woman acting as chief attendant to a bride at her wedding.

Matt. Matthew.

matte (mat) *n.* A lusterless, dull, or roughened surface. — *adj.* Presenting a lusterless surface. Also **matt** (mat). [< OF, dull]

mat·ted (mat′id) *adj.* **1** Covered with mats or matting. **2** Clustered into a dense, tangled mass. **—mat′ted·ly** *adv.* — **mat′ted·ness** *n.*

mat·ter (mat′ər) *n.* **1** That which makes up the substance of anything; material. **2** *Physics* That which occupies space, is reciprocally convertible with energy, and from which all physical objects are made. **3** A specific substance: inorganic *matter.* **4** Importance: It's of no *matter.* **5** That which is actually stated or written, as contrasted with style or form. **6** A subject or thing: a family *matter.* **7** A subject for discussion or feeling. **8** A condition of affairs, esp. if unpleasant or unfortunate: What's the *matter?* **9** Pus. **10** Written or printed documents sent by mail. **11** Amount: a *matter* of a few dollars. **—as a matter of fact** Actually; in fact. **—for that matter** As far as that is concerned. *—v.i.* To be of concern or importance. [< L *materia* stuff]

matter of course That which is naturally and logically expected. **—mat·ter-of-course** (mat′ər·əv·kôrs′, -kōrs′) *adj.*

mat·ter-of-fact (mat′ər·əv·fakt′) *adj.* Closely adhering to facts; straightforward.

mat·ter-of-fact·ly (mat′ər·əv·fakt′lē) *adv.* In a matter-of-fact manner; straightforwardly. **—mat′ter-of-fact′ness** *n.*

Mat·thew (math′yōō) One of the twelve apostles, reputed author of the first Gospel. Also **Saint Matthew.** *—n.* The first Gospel.

mat·ting (mat′ing) *n.* **1** A woven fabric of fiber, straw, etc., used as a floor covering, etc. **2** The act or process of making mats. **3** A dull, flat surface effect.

mat·tock (mat′ək) *n.* A tool for digging and grubbing, resembling a pickax but having blades instead of points. [< OE *mattuc*]

Mattock

mat·tress (mat′rəs) *n.* A casing of ticking or other strong fabric filled with hair, cotton, foam rubber, etc., and used on or as a bed. [< Ar. *matrah* place where something is thrown]

mat·u·rate (mach′ōō·rāt, mat′yōō-) *v.i.* **·rat·ed, ·rat·ing 1** To ripen or mature. **2** To suppurate; form pus. [< L *maturare* ripen] **—mat′u·ra′tion** *n.* **—mat·u·ra·tive** (mach′ōō·rā′tiv, mə·chŏŏr′ə·tiv) *adj.*

ma·ture (mə·chŏŏr′, -tyŏŏr′) *adj.* **1** Completely developed; full-grown. **2** Fully developed in character and powers. **3** Highly developed; complete in detail: a *mature* scheme. **4** Due and payable, having reached its time limit: a *mature* bond. *—v.* **·tured, ·tur·ing** *v.t.* **1** To cause to ripen or come to maturity. **2** To perfect; complete. *—v.i.* **3** To come to maturity or full development; ripen. **4** To become due, as a note. [< L *maturus* of full age] **—ma·ture′ly** *adv.* **—ma·ture′ness** *n.* **—Syn.** *adj.* **1** adult, grown, grown-up, ripe.

ma·tur·i·ty (mə·chŏŏr′ə·tē, -tyŏŏr′-) *n.* **1** The state or condition of being mature. **2** Full development, as of the body. **3** The time at which a thing matures: a note payable at *maturity.*

ma·tu·ti·nal (mə·tyōō′tə·nəl) *adj.* Pertaining to morning; early. [< L *matutinus* early in the morning < *Matuta,* goddess of morning] **—ma·tu′ti·nal·ly** *adv.*

mat·zo (mät′sə, -sō) *n. pl.* **mat·zoth** (mät′sōth, -sōs) or **mat·zos** (-səs, -səz) Wafers of unleavened bread. [< Heb. *matstsāh* unleavened]

maud·lin (môd′lin) *adj.* **1** Foolishly and tearfully sentimental. **2** Made foolish from drinking too much alcoholic liquor. [< OF *Maudelene,* (Mary) Magdalen, who was often depicted with eyes swollen from weeping]

mau·gre (mô′gər) *prep. Archaic* In spite of. Also **mau′ger.** [< OF]

maul (môl) *n.* A heavy mallet for driving wedges, piles, etc. *—v.t.* **1** To beat and bruise; batter. **2** To handle roughly; abuse. [< L *malleus* hammer] **—maul′er** *n.*

maun·der (môn′dər) *v.i.* **1** To talk in a wandering or incoherent manner. **2** To move dreamily or idly. [?] **—maun′der·er** *n.*

Maun·dy Thursday (môn′dē) The day before Good Friday, commemorating the Last Supper of Jesus with his disciples. [< L *mandatum* command + THURSDAY]

Mau·ri·ta·ni·a (môr′ə·tā′nē·ə) *n.* A republic of w Africa, 419,229 sq. mi., cap. Nouakchott. **—Mau′ri·ta′ni·an** *adj., n.* • See map at AFRICA.

Mau·ri·ti·us (mô·rish′ē·əs) *n.* An independent member of the Commonwealth of Nations on an island in the Indian Ocean, 804 sq. mi., cap. Port Louis. **—Mau·ri′ti·an** *adj., n.*

mau·so·le·um (mô′sə·lē′əm) *n. pl.* **·le·ums** or **·le·a** (-lē′ə) A large, stately tomb. [< Gk. *Mausōleion* tomb of King

Mausolus, erected at Halicarnassus about 350 B.C.] — **mau'so·le'an** *adj.*

mauve (mōv, môv) *n.* Any of various pale purple shades of color. —*adj.* Of any of these shades. [< L *malva* mallow]

mav·en (mā'vən) *n.* An experienced person in some field. [< Yiddish]

mav·er·ick (mav'ər·ik) *n.* 1 An unbranded or orphaned animal, esp. a calf. 2 A person characterized by independence or nonconformity in relation to a group with which he is affiliated, as a political party. [< S. A. *Maverick,* 1803–70, Texas lawyer, who did not brand his cattle]

ma·vis (mā'vis) *n.* The European song thrush. [< OF *mauvis*]

ma·vour·neen (ma·vo͝or'nēn, -vôr'-) *n. Irish* My darling. Also **ma·vour'nin.** [< Irish *mo muirnīn*]

maw (mô) *n.* 1 The gullet, jaws, or mouth of a voracious animal. 2 Anything that swallows up or consumes. 3 The stomach. 4 The craw of a bird. [< OE *maga* stomach]

mawk·ish (mô'kish) *adj.* 1 Characterized by false or feeble sentimentality. 2 Provoking disgust; sickening. [< obs. *mawk* a maggot] —**mawk'ish·ly** *adv.* —**mawk'ish·ness** *n.*

max. maximum.

max·i (maks'ē) *n. pl.* **max·is** A long skirt or coat, usu. reaching to the ankle.

maxi- *combining form* 1 Very long. 2 Very great.

max·il·la (mak·sil'ə) *n. pl.* **·lae** (-ē) 1 The upper jawbone in vertebrates. 2 One of the pair or pairs of mouth parts behind the mandibles of an insect, crab, etc. [L, jaw] — **max·il·lar·y** (mak'sə·ler'ē, mak·sil'ər·ē) *adj., n.* (*pl.* **·lar·ies**).

max·im (mak'sim) *n.* A brief statement of a practical principle or proposition; a saying. [< L *maxima (propositio)* greatest (premise)] —**Syn.** adage, aphorism, epigram, motto, proverb.

max·i·mal (mak'sə·məl) *adj.* Greatest; highest possible.

max·i·mize (mak'sə·mīz) *v.t.* **·mized, ·miz·ing** To make as great as possible. —**max'i·mi·za'tion** *n.*

max·i·mum (mak'sə·məm) *n. pl.* **·mums** or **·ma** (-mə) The greatest quantity, amount, degree, or magnitude that is possible. —*adj.* 1 As large or great as possible. 2 Pertaining to or setting a maximum: *maximum* weight. [< L *maximus* greatest]

may (mā) *v., present* **may,** *past* **might** A verb now used only as an auxiliary followed by the infinitive without *to,* to express: 1 Permission or allowance: *May* I go? You *may.* 2 Desire or wish: *May* your tribe increase! 3 Contingency, esp. in clauses of result, concession, purpose, etc.: He died that we *might* live. 4 Possibility: You *may* be right. 5 *Law* Obligation or duty: the equivalent of *must* or *shall.* [< OE *mæg*] • See CAN[1].

May (mā) *n.* The fifth month of the year, containing 31 days. [< L *Maia,* goddess of growth]

Ma·ya (mä'yə) *n.* 1 A member of a tribe of Central American Indians, of Yucatán, N Guatemala, and British Honduras. 2 The language of the Mayas. —**Ma'yan** *adj., n.*

May apple 1 The oblong, yellowish fruit of a North American plant. 2 The plant itself.

may·be (mā'bē) *adv.* Perhaps; possibly.

May·day (mā'dā') *n.* An international radiotelephone signal of distress. [< F *m'aider* help me]

May Day 1 May 1, sometimes celebrated as a spring festival by crowning a May Queen, dancing around a Maypole, etc. 2 In some countries, an international labor holiday, observed with parades, rallies, etc.

may·flow·er (mā'flou'ər) *n.* Any of various plants that bloom in the spring, as the trailing arbutus, the hawthorn of Britain, etc.

Mayflower The ship on which the Pilgrims came to American in 1620.

may·fly (mā'flī') *n.* An insect with gauzy wings, which has a very brief life span in the adult phase.

may·hap (mā'hap) *adv. Archaic* It may happen; perhaps.

may·hem (mā'hem) *n.* 1 *Law* The offense of depriving a person by violence of any limb, member, or organ, or causing any mutilation of the body. 2 Egregious disorder or damage. [< OF *mahaigner* maim]

may·n't (mā'ənt, mānt) Contraction of *may not.*

may·on·naise (mā'ə·nāz', mā'ə·nāz') *n.* A sauce or dressing made by beating together raw egg yolk, olive oil, lemon juice or vinegar, and condiments. [F]

may·or (mā'ər, mâr) *n.* The chief magistrate of a city, borough or municipal corporation. [< L *major* greater] — **may'or·al** *adj.*

may·or·al·ty (mā'ər·əl·tē, mâr'əl-) *n. pl.* **·ties** The office or term of a mayor. [< OF *mairalté*]

May·pole (mā'pōl') *n.* A pole decorated with flowers and ribbons, around which dancing takes place on May Day.

May Queen A young girl crowned with flowers in May Day festivities.

mayst (mā'ist, māst) Archaic second person singular, present tense, of MAY. Also **may'est.**

May·time (mā'tīm') *n.* The month of May. Also **May'tide'** (-tīd').

maze (māz) *n.* 1 An intricate network of paths or passages; a labyrinth. 2 Uncertainty; perplexity. [< AMAZE] — **maz'i·ly** *adv.* —**maz'i·ness** *n.* —**maz'y** (**i·er, i·est**) *adj.*

ma·zur·ka (mə·zûr'kə, -zoor'-) *n.* 1 A lively Polish dance resembling the polka. 2 The music for such a dance. Also **ma·zour'ka.** [Polish, woman from Mazovia, a Polish province]

M.C. Maritime Commission; Master of Ceremonies; Medical Corps; Member of Congress.

Mc·Car·thy·ism (mə·kär'thē·iz'əm) *n.* The practice of making public and sensational accusations of disloyalty or corruption, usu. with doubtful evidence, ostensibly to expose pro-Communist activity. [< Joseph *McCarthy,* 1909–1957, U.S. Senator]

Mc·Coy (mə·koi'), *Slang* The authentic person or thing: used with *the.* Also **the real McCoy.** [? < Kid *McCoy,* 1873–1940, U.S. boxer]

Mc·In·tosh (mak'ən·tosh) *n.* A variety of apple. [< J. *McIntosh,* 18th c. fruit grower of Ontario, Canada]

MD 1 Maryland (P.O. abbr.) 2 muscular dystrophy.

M.D. Doctor of Medicine (L *Medicinae Doctor*); Medical Department; mentally deficient.

Md mendelevium.

Md. Maryland.

M-Day (em'dā') *n. Mil.* Mobilization day; the day a department of defense orders mobilization for war.

mdse. merchandise.

me (mē) *pron.* The objective case of *I.* [< OE *mē*] • **It's me, It's him, It's us, etc.** Anyone who answers the question "Who's there?" by saying "It's me" is using acceptable informal idiom. Here *It is I* would seem stilted, although at the formal level of writing it is expected: *They have warned me that it is I, and not he, who will have to bear the brunt of the criticism.*

ME Maine (P.O. abbr.).

Me, Me., M.E. Middle English.

Me methyl.

Me. Maine.

mead[1] (mēd) *n.* A alcoholic liquor of fermented honey and water to which malt, yeast, and spices are added. [< OE *meodu*]

mead[2] (mēd) *n. Archaic* A meadow. [< OE *mæd*]

mead·ow (med'ō) *n.* A tract of low or level grassland, esp. one producing grass for hay. [< OE *mædwe* < *mæd* mead] —**mead'ow·y** *adj.*

mead·ow·lark (med'ō·lärk') *n.* Any of a genus of North American songbirds related to the orioles.

Meadowlark

mea·ger (mē'gər) *adj.* 1 Deficient in quantity or quality; scanty. 2 Scantily supplied with fertility, strength, or richness. 3 Wanting in flesh; thin. Also **mea'·gre.** [< L *macer* lean] —**mea'ger·ly** *adv.* —**mea'ger·ness** *n.* —**Syn.** 1 inadequate, sparse, paltry, slight, exiguous. 3 emaciated, gaunt, skinny, spare.

meal[1] (mēl) *n.* 1 Comparatively coarsely ground and unbolted grain. 2 Any powder produced by grinding. [< OE *melu*]

meal[2] (mēl) *n.* 1 The food taken at one time; a repast. 2 Its occasion or time. [< OE *mæl* measure, time, meal]

meal·ie (mē'lē) *n.* In South Africa: a An ear of maize, b *pl.* Maize; Indian corn. [< Afrikaans *milje* < Pg. *milho* millet]

meal·time (mēl′tīm′) *n.* The habitual time for eating a meal.

meal·y (mē′lē) *adj.* **meal·i·er, meal·i·est** 1 Resembling meal; powdery. 2 Consisting of or containing meal. 3 Pale; wan. **—meal′i·ness** *n.*

meal·y-mouthed (mē′lē·moutht′, -mouth͟d′) *adj.* Unwilling to express adverse opinions plainly; insincere.

mean[1] (mēn) *v.* **meant, mean·ing** *v.t.* 1 To have in mind as a purpose or intent: I *meant* to visit him. 2 To intend or design for some purpose, destination, etc.: Was that remark *meant* for me? 3 To denote: The Latin word "vir" *means* "man." 4 To portend: Those clouds *mean* rain. —*v.i.* 5 To be disposed: He *means* well. 6 To be of specified importance or influence: Her beauty *means* everything to her. [< OE *mænan* tell, wish, intend]

mean[2] (mēn) *adj.* 1 Poor in quality; low in grade. 2 Of humble antecedents; lowly. 3 Having little value or importance. 4 Shabby, as in appearance. 5 Unkind or selfish. 6 *Informal* Ashamed; guilty: to feel *mean* about something. 7 Stingy; miserly. 8 *Informal* Sick or irritable: He feels *mean* in the morning. 9 *Slang* Excellent; skillful: to play a *mean* game of chess. 10 Ill-tempered; unmanageable: said of animals: a *mean* dog. [< OE *(ge)mæne,* common, ordinary] **—mean′ly** *adv.* **—mean′ness** *n.* **—Syn.** 1 inferior. 2 common, ordinary, plebeian. 5 base, contemptible, ignoble.

mean[3] (mēn) *n.* 1 The middle state between two extremes; moderation. 2 *Math.* An average, often an arithmetic mean. 3 *pl. (often construed as sing.)* The medium through which anything is done: a *means* to an end. 4 *pl.* Money or property; wealth. **—by all means** Without hesitation; certainly. **—by any means** In any manner possible; somehow. **—by means of** By the help or use of; through. **—by no means** Most certainly not. —*adj.* 1 Intermediate as to position between extremes. 2 Intermediate as to size, degree, or quality; average. 3 Of or indicating an average: the *mean* distance covered daily. [< L *medius* middle]

me·an·der (mē·an′dər) *v.i.* 1 To wind and turn in a course. 2 To wander aimlessly. —*n.* 1 A tortuous or winding course. 2 An aimless wandering. [< Gk. *Maiandros* a river known for its winding course] **—me·an′der·er** *n.*

mean·ie (mē′nē) *n. Informal* A mean or disagreeable person. Also **mean′y.**

mean·ing (mē′ning) *n.* 1 That which is intended to be conveyed or understood; the object or aim of an effort or expression. 2 That which is conveyed or understood; sense; significance. —*adj.* Having purpose or intention: usu. in combination: *well-meaning.* **—mean′ing·ful** *adj.* **—mean′ing·ful·ly, mean′ing·ly** *adv.*

mean·ing·less (mē′ning·lis) *adj.* Without meaning or significance. **—mean′ing·less·ly** *adv.* **—mean′ing·less·ness** *n.*

mean sun *Astron.* A fictitious sun considered to be moving uniformly with respect to the equator, a concept used to facilitate the computation of time.

meant (ment) *p.t. & p.p.* of MEAN[1].

mean·time (mēn′tīm′) *n.* Intervening time or occasion. —*adv.* MEANWHILE.

mean time Time reckoned on the motion of the mean sun. Also **mean solar time.**

mean·while (mēn′hwīl′) *adv.* In or during the intervening time. —*n.* MEANTIME.

meas. measure; measurable.

mea·sles (mē′zəlz) *n.* Either of two distinct, contagious viral diseases characterized by small red skin eruptions: a RUBEOLA. b RUBELLA, or German measles. [ME *masel* a blister]

mea·sly (mēz′lē) *adj.* **·sli·er, ·sli·est** 1 Affected with measles. 2 *Slang* So skimpy or paltry as to be beneath contempt.

meas·ur·a·ble (mezh′ər·ə·bəl) *adj.* 1 Capable of being measured or computed. 2 Limited; moderate. **—meas′ur·a·bil′i·ty, meas′ur·a·ble·ness** *n.* **—meas′ur·a·bly** *adv.*

meas·ure (mezh′ər) *n.* 1 The extent or dimensions of anything. 2 A standard or unit of measurement. 3 A system of measurements. • **See pp. 448–449 for tables of** MEASURES AND WEIGHTS **for metric and U.S. systems.** 4 An instrument or utensil used in measurement. 5 The act of measuring. 6 A quantity measured. 7 Reasonable limits; moderation: reward beyond *measure.* 8 A certain proportion; relative extent. 9 *Often pl.* A specific act or course: to take drastic *measures.* 10 A legislative bill. 11 That which makes up a total. 12 Any quantity regarded as a unit and standard of comparison with other quantities. 13 *Music* a The division of time by which melody and rhythm are regulated. b The portion of music contained between two bar lines; bar. 14 In prosody, meter. 15 A slow and stately dance or dance movement. **—in a measure** Somewhat; partly. **—take one's measure** To estimate one's character. —*v.* **·ured, ·ur·ing** *v.t.* 1 To take or ascertain the dimensions, quantity, capacity, etc., of, esp. by means of a measure. 2 To set apart, mark off, etc., by measuring: often with *off* or *out.* 3 To estimate by comparison; judge; weigh. 4 To serve as the measure of. 5 To bring into competition or comparison. 6 To traverse as if measuring; travel over. 7 To adjust; regulate. 8 To appraise or observe carefully with the eyes: She *measured* him up and down before replying. —*v.i.* 9 To make or take measurements. 10 To yield a specified measurement: The table *measures* six by four feet. 11 To admit of measurement. **—measure one's length** To fall prostrate at full length. **—measure out** To distribute or allot by measure. **—measure up** To fulfill, as expectations: often with *to.* [< L *metiri* to measure] **—meas′ur·er** *n.*

Two measures of music

meas·ured (mezh′ərd) *adj.* 1 Ascertained, adjusted, or proportioned by rule. 2 Slow and stately. 3 Deliberate. 4 Rhythmical. 5 Restrained. **—meas′ured·ly** *adv.* **—meas′ured·ness** *n.*

meas·ure·less (mezh′ər·lis) *adj.* Incapable of measurement; unlimited; immense.

meas·ure·ment (mezh′ər·mənt) *n.* 1 The process or result of measuring anything; mensuration. 2 The amount or extent determined by measuring. 3 A system of measuring units.

measuring worm A caterpillar larva of a moth that assumes the shape of a loop when in motion by alternately moving up the rear and forward parts of its body.

meat (mēt) *n.* 1 The flesh of animals used as food: sometimes excluding fish and fowl. 2 Anything eaten for nourishment; victuals: *meat* and drink. 3 The edible part of anything. 4 The essence, gist, or pith: the *meat* of an essay. 5 *Slang* Anything one likes very much or does with special ease. [< OE *mete*] **—meat′less** *adj.*

meat·ball (mēt′bôl) *n.* 1 Ground or chopped meat shaped into a ball and cooked in various ways, usu. served in a sauce. 2 *Slang* A dull or stupid person.

me·a·tus (mē·ā′təs) *n. pl.* **·tus** or **·tus·es** *Anat.* A passage or canal, esp. its external opening. [L, a passage]

meat·y (mē′tē) *adj.* **meat·i·er, meat·i·est** 1 Full of or resembling meat. 2 Full of genuine insight or significance; stimulating to the intellect. **—meat′i·ness** *n.*

mec·ca (mek′ə) *n.* 1 A place visited by many people; any attraction. 2 The object of one's aspiration, yearning, or effort. [< *Mecca,* Saudi Arabia, holy city of Islam]

mech., mechan. mechanical; mechanics; mechanism.

me·chan·ic (mə·kan′ik) *n.* One engaged in mechanical employment, esp. in making, using, or repairing machines or tools. —*adj.* 1 Pertaining to mechanics; mechanical. 2 Involving manual labor or skill. [< Gk. *mēchanē* a machine]

me·chan·i·cal (mə·kan′i·kəl) *adj.* 1 Of or pertaining to mechanics or the laws of mechanics. 2 Produced by a machine. 3 Operated by mechanism. 4 Operating as if by a machine or machinery. 5 Doing or done by mere force of habit. 6 Lifeless; expressionless: a *mechanical* recitation. 7 Skilled in the use of tools and mechanisms. 8 Having to do with certain physical skills or techniques: the *mechanical* aspects of singing. **—me·chan′i·cal·ly** *adv.* **—me·chan′i·cal·ness** *n.*

MEASURES AND WEIGHTS

Metric System

LENGTH

Unit	Equivalent in Meters	U.S. Equivalent
millimeter (mm)	0.001	0.03937 inch
centimeter (cm) = 10 millimeters	0.01	0.3937 inch
decimeter (dm) = 10 centimeters	0.1	3.937 inches
meter (m) = 10 decimeters or 100 centimeters or 1,000 millimeters	1	39.37 inches or 3.28 feet or 1.09 yards
decameter (dkm) = 10 meters	10	32.81 feet or 10.93 yards
hectometer (hm) = 10 decameters	100	328.08 feet or 109.36 yards
kilometer (km) = 10 hectometers	1,000	0.6214 mile or 1,093.6 yards or 3,280.8 feet

AREA

Unit	Equivalent in Square Meters	U.S. Equivalent
square millimeter (sq mm, mm^2)	0.000001	0.00155 square inch
square centimeter (sq cm, cm^2) = 100 square millimeters	0.0001	0.155 square inch
square decimeter (sq dm, dm^2) = 100 square centimeters	0.01	15.5 square inches
square meter (sq m, m^2) or **centare (ca)** = 100 square decimeters or 10,000 square centimeters or 1,000,000 square millimeters	1	10.76 square feet or 1.196 square yards
square decameter (sq dkm, dkm^2) or **are (a)** = 100 centares	100	119.60 square yards or 0.0247 acre
square hectometer (sq hm, hm^2) or **hectare (ha)** = 100 ares	10,000	2.47 acres
square kilometer (sq km, km^2) = 100 hectares	1,000,000	0.386 square mile or 247.105 acres

VOLUME (LIQUID MEASURE)

Unit	Equivalent in Liters	U.S. Equivalent
milliliter (ml)	0.001	0.034 fluid ounce
centiliter (cl) = 10 milliliters	0.01	0.338 fluid ounce
deciliter (dl) = 10 centiliters	0.1	3.38 fluid ounces
liter (l) = 10 deciliters or 100 centiliters or 1,000 milliliters	1	1.05 liquid quarts or 33.814 fluid ounces or 0.908 dry quart
decaliter (dkl) = 10 liters	10	2.64 gallons or 0.284 bushel
hectoliter (hl) = 10 decaliters	100	26.418 gallons or 2.838 bushels
kiloliter (kl) = 10 hectoliters	1,000	264.18 gallons

CUBIC MEASURE

Unit	Equivalent in Cubic Meters	U.S. Equivalent
cubic centimeter (cc, cu cm, cm^3) = 1,000 cubic millimeters	0.000001	0.061 cubic inch
cubic decimeter (cu dm, dm^3) = 1,000 cubic centimeters	0.001	61.023 cubic inches
decistere (ds)	0.1	3.53 cubic feet
cubic meter or stere (s) = 1,000 cubic decimeters or 1,000,000 cubic centimeters	1	1.308 cubic yards
decastere (dks)	10	13.1 cubic yards

MASS OR WEIGHT

Unit	Equivalent in Grams	U.S. Equivalent in Avoirdupois Weight
milligram (mg)	0.001	0.0154 grain
centigram (cg) = 10 milligrams	0.01	0.1543 grain
decigram (dg) = 10 centigrams	0.1	1.543 grains
gram (g) = 10 decigrams or 100 centigrams or 1,000 milligrams	1	15.43 grains or 0.03527 ounce
decagram (dkg) = 10 grams	10	0.3527 ounce
hectogram (hg) = 10 decagrams	100	3.527 ounces
kilogram (kg) = 10 hectograms	1,000	2.2046 pounds
quintal (q) = 100 kilograms	100,000	220.46 pounds
metric ton (t or MT) = 10 quintals or 1,000 kilograms	1,000,000	1.1 tons or 2,204.6 pounds

A metric carat (car.) (used in weighing gems) = 200 milligrams or 3.086 grains avoirdupois.

Other metric prefixes occasionally used are: micro- (one-millionth of), myria- (10,000 times), mega- (1,000,000 times) (a unit).

SYMBOLS

t	10^{12} times (a unit); tera-	c	10^{-2} times (a unit); centi-
g	10^{9} times (a unit); giga-	m	10^{-3} times (a unit); milli-
m	10^{6} times (a unit); mega-	μ	10^{-6} times (a unit); micro-
k	10^{3} times (a unit); kilo-	n	10^{-9} times (a unit); nano-
h	10^{2} times (a unit); hecto-	p *or* μμ	10^{-12} times (a unit); pico- *or* micromicro-
dk	10 times (a unit); deka-	Å, λ	Angstrom unit
d	10^{-1} times (a unit); deci-	μμ	micromicron
		μ	micron

mechanical advantage The ratio of the output force of a mechanism performing useful work to the input force.

mechanical energy The energy manifested in the motion of material bodies, as in the global motions of the winds and tides or in the release of a coiled spring.

me·chan·ics (mə·kan′iks) *n.* (*construed as sing.* defs. 1, 2; *usu. construed as pl.* def. 3) **1** The branch of physics that deals with the phenomena caused by the action of forces on material bodies. **2** The science and technology of machinery. **3** The mechanical or technical aspects of anything.

mech·a·nism (mek′ə·niz′əm) *n.* **1** The parts of a machine collectively. **2** The action or operation of a machine or a mechanical device. **3** Something similar to a machine in the arrangement and working of its parts, as the human body. **4** A process by which a given result is achieved: the *mechanisms* of heredity. **5** Technique; mechanical execution or action. **6** The philosophical doctrine that physical and chemical agencies alone are sufficient to explain all phenomena, including life. **—mech′a·nist** *n.* **—mech′a·nis′tic** *adj.* **—mech′a·nis′ti·cal·ly** *adv.*

mech·a·nize (mek′ə·nīz) *v.t.* **·nized, ·niz·ing 1** To make mechanical. **2** To convert (an industry, etc.) to machine pro-

MEASURES AND WEIGHTS

U.S. System

LENGTH

Unit	Metric Equivalent
inch (in.)	2.54 centimeters
foot (ft.) = 12 inches	30.48 centimeters or 0.3048 meter
yard (yd.) = 3 feet or 36 inches	0.9144 meter
rod (rd.) = 5.5 yards or 16.5 feet	5.0292 meters
furlong = 220 yards or 40 rods or ⅛ mile	201.168 meters
mile (mi.) = 5,280 feet or 1,760 yards or 8 furlongs	1.6093 kilometers

AREA

Unit	Metric Equivalent
square inch (sq. in.)	6.452 square centimeters
square foot (sq. ft.) = 144 square inches	0.093 square meter or 929.03 square centimeters
square yard (sq. yd.) = 9 square feet	0.836 square meter
square rod (sq. rd.) = 30.25 square yards	25.293 square meters
acre (A.) = 160 square rods or 4,840 square yards or 43,560 square feet	0.4047 hectare or 4,047 square meters
square mile (sq. mi.) = 640 acres	259.00 hectares or 2.590 square kilometers

LIQUID MEASURE

Unit	U.S. Equivalent in Cubic Inches	Metric Equivalent
gill (gi.) = 4 fluid ounces	7.219	0.118 liter
pint (pt.) = 4 gills	28.875	0.473 liter
quart (qt.) = 2 pints	57.75	0.946 liter
gallon (gal.) = 4 quarts	231	3.785 liters

The British imperial gallon (4 imperial quarts) = 4.546 liters or 277.42 cubic inches. The U.S. gallon is approximately ⅚ of the British imperial gallon.

APOTHECARIES' FLUID MEASURE

Unit	U.S. Equivalent in Cubic Inches	Metric Equivalent
minim (min.)	0.0038	0.0616 milliliter
fluid dram (fl. dr.) = 60 minims	0.225	3.697 milliliters
fluid ounce (fl. oz.) = 8 fluid drams	1.805	29.573 milliliters
pint (pt.) = 16 fluid ounces	28.875	0.473 liter

DRY MEASURE

Unit	U.S. Equivalent in Cubic Inches	Metric Equivalent
pint (pt.)	33.600	0.551 liter
quart (qt.) = 2 pints	67.200	1.101 liters
peck (pk.) = 8 quarts	537.605	8.810 liters
bushel (bu.) = 4 pecks	2,150.42	35.239 liters

CUBIC MEASURE

Unit	Metric Equivalent
cubic inch (cu. in.)	16.387 cubic centimeters
cubic foot (cu. ft.) = 1,728 cubic inches	0.028 cubic meter
cubic yard (cu. yd.) = 27 cubic feet	0.765 cubic meter
cord (cd.) (for cordwood) = 128 cubic feet	3.625 cubic meters

AVOIRDUPOIS WEIGHT

Unit	Metric Equivalent
grain (gr.)	0.0648 gram
dram (dr.) = 27.34 grains	1.772 grams
ounce (oz.) = 16 drams or 437.5 grains	28.349 grams
pound (lb.) = 16 ounces or 7,000 grains	453.59 grams or 0.453 kilograms
hundredweight (cwt.) = 100 pounds	45.36 kilograms
ton = 2,000 pounds	0.907 metric ton or 907.18 kilograms

TROY WEIGHT

Unit	Metric Equivalent
grain (gr.)	0.0648 gram
pennyweight (dwt.) = 24 grains	1.555 grams
ounce (oz. t.) = 20 pennyweight or 480 grains	31.103 grams
pound (lb. t.) = 12 ounces or 240 pennyweight or 5,760 grains	373.24 grams or 0.373 kilogram

APOTHECARIES' WEIGHT

Unit	Metric Equivalent
grain (gr.)	0.0648 gram
scruple (s.) = 20 grains	1.296 grams
dram (dr.) = 3 scruples or 60 grains	3.888 grams
ounce (oz.) = 8 drams or 480 grains	31.103 grams
pound (lb.) = 12 ounces or 5,760 grains	373.24 grams or 0.373 kilogram

SYMBOLS

\# pound(s)
′ foot, feet
″ inch(es)

Apothecaries' Measure

℔ pound(s)
ʒ dram(s)
℥ ounce(s)
℈ scruple(s)
♏, ♏, ♏ minim

duction. **3** *Mil.* To equip with tanks, trucks, etc. **—mech′a·ni·za′tion** *n.*

mech·a·no·ther·a·py (mek′ə·nō·ther′ə·pē) *n.* The treatment of disease with mechanical appliances of any kind. **—mech′a·no·ther′a·pist** *n.*

med. medical; medicine; medieval; medium.

med·al (med′l) *n.* A small piece of metal, bearing a device, usu. commemorative of some event or deed of bravery, scientific research, etc. —*v.t.* **·aled** or **·alled, ·al·ing** or **·al·ling** To confer a medal upon. [< L *metallum* metal] **—me·dal·lic** (mə·dal′ik) *adj.*

med·al·ist (med′l·ist) *n.* **1** A collector, engraver, or designer of medals. **2** The recipient of a medal awarded for services or merit. **3** In golf, the winner at medal play. Also **med′al·list.**

me·dal·lion (mə·dal′yən) *n.* **1** A large medal. **2** A decorative element, as of fabrics, shaped like a large medal.

medal play In golf, competition in which the score is based on the total number of strokes taken.

med·dle (med′l) *v.i.* **·dled, ·dling** To take part in or concern oneself with something that is not one's proper business; interefere: often with *in* or *with.* [< OF *medler, mesdler*] **—med·dler** (med′lər) *n.*

med·dle·some (med′l·səm) *adj.* Given to meddling or interfering. **—med′dle·some·ly** *adv.* **—med′dle·some·ness** *n.* **—Syn.** intrusive, obtrusive, officious.

Mede (mēd) *n.* One of an ancient Asiatic people who flourished in sw Asia.

Me·de·a (mə·dē′ə) *Gk. Myth.* A sorceress who helped Jason to obtain the Golden Fleece, and, when deserted by him, killed their children.

med·e·vac (med′ə·vak′) *n.* The evacuation of the wounded, as from battle sites, usu. by helicopter. [< *med(ical) evac(uation)*]

Med. Gk. Medieval Greek.

me·di·a (mē′dē·ə) *n. pl. of* **med·i·um 1** Means of disseminating information, entertainment, etc., such as books, newspapers, radio, television, motion pictures, and magazines.

2 In advertising, all means of communication that carry advertisements.

me·di·ae·val (mē′dē·ē′vəl, med′ē-, mid′-, mē·dē′vəl) *adj.* MEDIEVAL.

me·di·al (mē′dē·əl) *adj.* 1 Of or pertaining to the middle, in position or character or in calculation. 2 Ordinary; average. [< L *medius* middle] **—me′di·al·ly** *adv.*

me·di·an (mē′dē·ən) *n.* 1 *Geom.* A line that extends from a vertex of a triangle to the midpoint of the opposite side. 2 *Stat.* Of or designating a number *x* in a set of data such that if the data is divided into equal subsets *A* and *B*, every number in *A* is greater than or equal to *x* and every number in *B* is less than or equal to *x*. *—adj.* Of, being, or pertaining to a median or to the middle. **—me′di·an·ly** *adv.*

me·di·ate (mē′dē·āt) *v.* **·at·ed, ·at·ing** *v.t.* 1 To settle or reconcile by mediation, as differences. 2 To bring about or effect by mediation. 3 To serve as the medium for effecting (a result) or conveying (an object, information, etc.). *—v.i.* 4 To act between disputing parties in order to bring about a settlement, compromise, etc. 5 To occur or be in an intermediate relation or position. *—adj.* (-it) 1 Acting as an intervening agency; indirect. 2 Occurring or effected as a result of indirect or median agency. 3 Intermediate. [< L *mediare* stand between] **—me′di·ate·ly** *adv.* **—me′di·a′tive** *adj.* **—me′di·a′tor** *n.*

me·di·a·tion (mē′dē·ā′shən) *n.* 1 The act of mediating; intercession; interposition. 2 A friendly intervention in the disputes of others, with their consent, for the purpose of adjusting differences.

med·ic[1] (med′ik) *n.* Any of several cloverlike forage plants, esp. alfalfa. [< Gk. *Mēdikē (poa)* Median (grass) < *Mēdos* a Mede]

med·ic[2] (med′ik) *n. Informal* 1 A doctor, physician, or intern. 2 A medical aide or corpsman.

med·i·ca·ble (med′ə·kə·bəl) *adj.* Capable of relief by medicine; curable.

Med·i·caid (med′i·kād′) *n.* In the U.S., a tax-supported health insurance program for low-income people.

med·i·cal (med′i·kəl) *adj.* 1 Pertaining to medicine or its practice. 2 Having curative properties. [< L *medicus* a physician] **—med′i·cal·ly** *adv.*

med·i·ca·ment (med′ə·kə·mənt, mə·dik′ə-) *n.* Any substance used for the alleviation of disease or wounds. [< L *medicare* to heal]

Med·i·care (med′i·kâr′) *n.* In the U.S., a health insurance program supported in part by government funds, serving esp. the aged.

med·i·cate (med′ə·kāt) *v.t.* **·cat·ed, ·cat·ing** 1 To treat with a drug or other substance. 2 To tincture or impregnate with medicine. [< L *medicus* a physician] **—med′i·ca′tive, med′i·ca·to′ry** (-kə·tôr′ē, -tō′rē) *adj.*

med·i·ca·tion (med′ə·kā′shən) *n.* 1 Any substance used to treat disease, heal wounds, etc.; a medicine. 2 The act or process of medicating.

me·dic·i·nal (mə·dis′ə·nəl) *adj.* Adapted to cure or mitigate disease. **—me·dic′i·nal·ly** *adv.*

med·i·cine (med′ə·sin) *n.* 1 A substance used to treat disease, as a drug. 2 The science of preserving health and treating disease. 3 This science exclusive of surgery or obstetrics. 4 Among North American Indians, any agent or rite, as a **medicine dance, medicine song,** etc., used to invoke supernatural aid in health or disease. **—take one's medicine** To endure deserved or necessary hardship. *—v.t.* **·cined, ·cin·ing** To treat with medicine. [< L *medicus* physician]

medicine ball A large, heavy, leather-covered ball, thrown and caught for physical exercise.

medicine man Among North American Indians, one professing supernatural powers of healing and of invoking the spirits; a shaman.

med·i·co (med′ə·kō) *n. pl.* **·cos** *Informal* A doctor or a medical student.

me·di·e·val (mē′dē·ē′vəl, med′ē-, mid′-, mē·dē′vəl) *adj.* Belonging to or descriptive or characteristic of the Middle Ages. [< L *medius* middle + *aevum* age] **—me′di·e′val·ly** *adv.*

Medieval Greek The Greek language used from about 600 to 1500.

me·di·e·val·ism (mē′dē·ē′vəl·iz′əm, med′ē-, mid′-, mē·dē′vəl-) *n.* 1 The spirit or practices of the Middle Ages; the general tone of medieval life. 2 Devotion to the institutions, ideas, or traits of the Middle Ages. 3 A custom, idea, etc., of the Middle Ages. **—me′di·e′val·ist** *n.*

Medieval Latin The Latin language used from about 600 to 1500.

me·di·o·cre (mē′dē·ō′kər, mē′dē·ō′kər) *adj.* Of only middle quality; ordinary; commonplace. [< L *medius* middle]

me·di·oc·ri·ty (mē′dē·ok′rə·tē) *n. pl.* **·ties** 1 The condition of being mediocre. 2 Commonplace ability. 3 A commonplace person.

Medit. Mediterranean.

med·i·tate (med′ə·tāt) *v.* **·tat·ed, ·tat·ing** *v.i.* 1 To engage in contemplative thought. *—v.t.* 2 To think about; consider. 3 To think about doing; intend: to *meditate* mischief. [< L *meditari* muse, ponder] **—med′i·ta′tive** *adj.* **—med′i·ta′tive·ly** *adv.* **—med′i·ta′tor** *n.* **—Syn.** 1 contemplate, muse, reflect, ponder, consider, weigh.

med·i·ta·tion (med′ə·tā′shən) *n.* The act of meditating; deep, deliberate thought; contemplation.

Med·i·ter·ra·ne·an (med′ə·tə·rā′nē·ən) *n.* 1 The Mediterranean Sea or the regions surrounding it. 2 One who lives on or near the Mediterranean Sea. *—adj.* Of, pertaining to, or dwelling near the Mediterranean Sea.

me·di·um (mē′dē·əm) *n. pl.* **·di·ums** or **me·di·a** (-dē·ə) 1 An intermediate quality, degree, or condition; mean. 2 A surrounding or enveloping element; environment. 3 Any substance, as air, through or in which something may move or an effect be produced. 4 (*pl., usu.* **me·di·a**) An intermediate means or agency; instrument; esp., a means of communication that includes advertising: the mass *media;* Radio is the best *medium* to reach motorists. 5 (*pl.* **me·di·ums**) A person believed to be in communication with the spirits of the dead. 6 In painting, a liquid which gives fluency to the pigment. 7 Any nutritive substance adapted to the development of bacteria, viruses, and other microorganisms: also **culture medium.** *—adj.* Intermediate in quantity, quality, position, size, or degree; middle. [< L *medius* middle]

Med. L Medieval Latin.

med·lar (med′lər) *n.* 1 A small tree related to the apple. 2 Its hard, bitter fruit, edible when it begins to decay. [< Gk. *mespilē*]

med·ley (med′lē) *n.* 1 A mingled and confused mass of ingredients, usu. incongruous; jumble. 2 A composition of different songs or parts of songs arranged to run as a continuous whole. *—adj.* Composed of parts that are not alike; mixed. [< OF *medlee*]

me·dul·la (mə·dul′ə) *n. pl.* **·las** or **·lae** (-ē) 1 The inner portion of an organ or part. • See KIDNEY. 2 The marrow of long bones. 3 MEDULLA OBLONGATA. [< L *medius* middle] **—me·dul′lar, med·ul·lar·y** (med′ə·ler′ē, mi·dul′ər·ē) *adj.*

medulla ob·lon·ga·ta (ob′lông·gä′tə) The part of the brain next to the spinal cord. [L, oblong medulla]

me·du·sa (mə·d^{y}ōō′sə, -zə) *n. pl.* **·sas** or **·sae** (-sē, -zē) A jellyfish. **—me·du′san** *adj., n.* **—me·du′soid** *adj.*

Me·du·sa (mə·d^{y}ōō′sə, -zə) *Gk. Myth.* One of the three Gorgons killed by Perseus, who gave her head to Athena.

meed (mēd) *n. Archaic* A well-deserved reward; recompense. [< OE *mēd*]

meek (mēk) *adj.* 1 Of gentle and long-suffering disposition. 2 Submissive; compliant. 3 Humble; lowly. *—adv.* In a meek manner. [< ON *miukr* gentle, soft] **—meek′ly** *adv.* **—meek′ness** *n.*

meer·schaum (mir′shəm, -shôm, -shoum) *n.* 1 A soft, light, heat-resistant magnesium silicate mineral used for tobacco pipes, cigar holders, etc. 2 A pipe made from this material. [< G *Meer* sea + *Schaum* foam]

meet[1] (mēt) *v.* **met, meet·ing** *v.t.* 1 To come upon; encounter. 2 To make the acquaintance of. 3 To be at the place of arrival of: We *met* him at the station. 4 To come into contact or intersection with: where the path *meets* the road. 5 To keep an appointment with. 6 To come into the view, hearing, etc., of: A ghastly sight *met* our eyes. 7 To experience; undergo: to *meet* bad weather. 8 To oppose in battle; fight with. 9 To face or counter: to *meet* a blow with a blow. 10 To deal with; refute: to *meet* an accusation. 11 To comply with; act or result in conformity with, as expectations or wishes. **12** To pay, as a bill. —*v.i.* **13** To come together, as from different directions. **14** To come together in contact, conjunction, or intersection; join. **15** To assemble. **16** To make acquaintance or be introduced. **17** To come together in conflict or opposition; contend. **18** To agree. —**meet with 1** To come upon; encounter. **2** To deal or confer with. **3** To experience. —*n.* A meeting or assembly for some specific activity, esp. for an athletic contest. [< OE *mētan*]

meet² (mēt) *adj.* Suitable; appropriate; fit. [< OE *gemæte*] —**meet′ly** *adv.* —**meet′ness** *n.*

meet·ing (mē′ting) *n.* **1** A coming together. **2** An assembly of persons for some specific purpose. **3** A permanent group or unit of worshipers in the Society of Friends; also, their meeting house.

meeting house 1 A house used for public meetings of any kind. **2** A place of worship used by the Society of Friends.

meg. megacycle.

mega- *combining form* **1** Great; large; powerful: *megaphone.* **2** In the metric system, electricity, etc., a million, or a million times (a specific unit): *megahertz.* [< Gk. *megas* large]

meg·a·cy·cle (meg′ə·sī′kəl) *n.* **1** A million cycles. **2** MEGAHERTZ.

meg·a·death (meg′ə·deth) *n.* The death of one million persons: a term used in reference to nuclear warfare. [< MEGA- + DEATH]

meg·a·hertz (meg′ə·hûrtz′) *n.* A unit of frequency equal to one million cycles per second.

megalo- *combining form* Big; indicating excessive or abnormal size: *megalomania.* [< Gk. *megas, megalou* big]

meg·a·lo·ceph·a·ly (meg′ə·lō·sef′ə·lē) *n.* Unusual largeness of the head. Also **meg′a·lo·ce·pha′li·a** (-sə·fā′lē·ə). [< MEGALO- + Gk. *kephalē* head] —**meg′a·lo·ce·phal′ic** (-sə·fal′ik), **meg′a·lo·ceph′a·lous** *adj.*

meg·a·lo·ma·ni·a (meg′ə·lō·mā′nē·ə, -mān′yə) *n.* A mental disorder in which the subject thinks himself great or exalted. —**meg′a·lo·ma′ni·ac** *adj., n.*

meg·a·lop·o·lis (meg′ə·lop′ə·lis) *n.* A densely populated urban area, usu. including one or more major cities. [< MEGALO- + Gk. *polis* city] —**meg·a·lo·pol·i·tan** (meg′ə·lō·pol′ə·tən) *adj., n.*

meg·a·phone (meg′ə·fōn) *n.* A funnel-shaped device for projecting or directing sound. —*v.t. & v.i.* **·phoned, ·phon·ing** To address or speak through a megaphone.

Megaphone

meg·a·ton (meg′ə·tun′) *n.* A unit of nuclear explosive power equivalent to one million tons of TNT.

me·grim (mē′grim) *n.* **1** MIGRAINE. **2** *pl.* Dullness; depression of spirits. **3** A whim or fad. [< OF *migraine*]

mei·o·sis (mī·ō′sis) *n.* The process of cell division that gives rise to reproductive cells containing half the number of chromosomes normally present in the somatic cells of the organism. [< Gk. *meiōsis* lessening] —**mei·ot′ic** (-ot′ik) *adj.*

Meis·ter·sing·er (mīs′tər·sing′ər, *Ger.* mīs′tər·zing′ər) *n. pl.* **·sing·er** A member of any of various guilds of Germany, from the 14th to 16th centuries, who were devoted to the promotion of music and poetry. [G, master singer]

mel·an·cho·li·a (mel′ən·kō′lē·ə) *n.* A mental disorder characterized by apathy and depression of spirits. —**mel′an·cho′li·ac** *adj., n.*

mel·an·chol·y (mel′ən·kol′ē) *adj.* **1** Gloomy; sad. **2** Causing sadness or dejection. **3** Pensive. —*n.* **1** Low spirits; depression. **2** Pensive or sober reflection. [< Gk. *melas* black + *cholē* bile] —**mel′an·chol′ic** *adj., n.* —**mel′an·chol′i·cal·ly** *adv.* —**Syn.** *adj.* **1** dejected, depressed, downcast. *n.* **1** dejection, despondency, sadness.

Mel·a·ne·sian (mel′ə·nē′zhən, -shən) *n.* **1** One of the native people of Melanesia, having dark skins and thick, kinky hair. **2** A branch of the Austronesian family of languages spoken in Melanesia. —*adj.* Of or pertaining to Melanesia, its native inhabitants, or their languages.

mé·lange (mā·länzh′, -länj) *n.* A mixture or medley; miscellany. [F]

mel·a·nin (mel′ə·nin) *n.* The brownish black animal pigment contained in skin, hair, and other tissues. [< Gk. *melas* black]

Mel·ba toast (mel′bə) Thinly sliced bread toasted until brown and crisp. [< Nellie *Melba,* 1861–1931, Australian soprano]

meld¹ (meld) *v.t. & v.i.* In pinochle and other card games, to announce or declare (a combination of cards in the hand), for inclusion in one's total score. —*n.* A group of cards to be declared, or the act of declaring them. [< G *melden* announce]

meld² (meld) *v.t. & v.i.* To merge or blend. [Blend of MELT and WELD] —**meld′er** *n.*

me·lee (mā′lā, mā·lā′) *n.* A disorganized hand-to-hand fight involving a number of people; a brawl. Also *Fr.* **mê·lée** (me·lā′). [< OF *medlee* medley]

mel·io·rate (mēl′yə·rāt) *v.t. & v.i.* **·rat·ed, ·rat·ing** To improve, as in quality or condition; ameliorate. [< L *melior* better] —**mel′io·ra·ble, mel′io·ra′tive** *adj.* —**mel′io·ra′tion, mel′io·ra′tor** *n.* —**Syn. 1** amend, better, mend, promote.

mel·lif·er·ous (mə·lif′ər·əs) *adj.* Producing or bearing honey. Also **mel·lif′ic.** [< L *mel* honey + *ferre* bear]

mel·lif·lu·ent (mə·lif′lōō·ənt) *adj.* Mellifluous. —**mel·lif′lu·ence** *n.* —**mel·lif′lu·ent·ly** *adv.*

mel·lif·lu·ous (mə·lif′lōō·əs) *adj.* Sweetly or smoothly flowing; dulcet: a *mellifluous* voice. [< L *mel* honey + *fluere* flow] —**mel·lif′lu·ous·ly** *adv.* —**mel·lif′lu·ous·ness** *n.*

mel·low (mel′ō) *adj.* **1** Soft and sweet because of ripeness: *mellow* fruit. **2** Well-matured, as wines. **3** Full and rich; not harsh or strident: the *mellow* tones of a cello. **4** Gentle and understanding, as from age or experience. **5** Happy and relaxed, as from liquor. **6** Soft and friable, as soil. —*v.t. & v.i.* To make or become mellow. [ME *melwe*] —**mel′low·ly** *adv.* —**mel′low·ness** *n.*

me·lo·de·on (mə·lō′dē·ən) *n.* A small reed organ; harmonium. [< Gk. *melōdia* melody]

me·lod·ic (mə·lod′ik) *adj.* **1** Of or containing melody. **2** Melodious.

me·lo·di·ous (mə·lō′dē·əs) *adj.* **1** Producing or characterized by melody; tuneful. **2** Pleasant to hear. —**me·lo′di·ous·ly** *adv.* —**me·lo′di·ous·ness** *n.*

mel·o·dra·ma (mel′ə·drä′mə, -dram′ə) *n.* **1** Originally, a drama with a romantic story or plot, sensational incidents, and usu. including some music and song. **2** Any sensational and emotional drama, usu. having a happy ending. **3** Excessively dramatic or emotional behavior or language. [< Gk. *melos* song + *drama* drama]

mel·o·dra·mat·ic (mel′ə·drə·mat′ik) *adj.* Of, pertaining to, or like melodrama; sensational. —**mel′o·dra·mat′i·cal·ly** *adv.*

mel·o·dra·mat·ics (mel′ə·drə·mat′iks) *n.pl.* Melodramatic behavior.

mel·o·dy (mel′ə·dē) *n. pl.* **·dies 1** Pleasing sounds or an agreeable arrangement of such sounds. **2** *Music* **a** A succession of tones constituting, in combination, a whole. **b** The chief part or voice in a composition; the air. [< Gk. *melos* song + *aoidos* singer]

mel·on (mel′ən) *n.* **1** Any of various trailing plants of the gourd family bearing large, many-seeded fruits with a thick rind and sweet, pulpy flesh. **2** The fruit of any of these plants, as the watermelon, cantaloupe, etc. —**cut a (or the) melon** *Slang* To divide surplus profits, as among stockholders. [< Gk. *mēlopepōn* apple-shaped melon]

Melons

Mel·pom·e·ne (mel·pom′ə·nē) *Gk. Myth.* The Muse of tragedy.

melt (melt) *v.t. & v.i.* **melt·ed, melt·ed** (*Archaic* **mol·ten**), **melt·ing 1** To reduce or change from a solid to a liquid state by heat. **2** To dissolve, as in water.

3 To disappear or cause to disappear; dissipate: often with *away*. 4 To blend by imperceptible degrees; merge: often with *into*. 5 To make or become softened in feeling or attitude. —*n.* 1 Something melted. 2 A single operation of melting. 3 The amount melted in such an operation. [<OE *meltan*] —**melt'a·ble** *adj.* —**melt'er** *n.* —**Syn.** *v.* 1 fuse, liquefy. 5 appease, mollify, pacify.

melt·down (melt'doun') *n.* An overheating and eventual melting of radioactive nuclear fuel through its protective insulation, because of a malfunctioning cooling system in a nuclear reactor.

melting point The temperature at which a specified solid substance becomes liquid.

melting pot 1 A vessel in which things are melted; crucible. 2 A country, city, or region in which immigrants of various racial and cultural backgrounds are assimilated.

mel·ton (mel'tən) *n.* A heavy woolen cloth with a short nap, used for overcoats. [<*Melton* Mowbray, England]

mem·ber (mem'bər) *n.* 1 A person belonging to an incorporated or organized body, society, etc.: *a member* of a club. 2 A limb or other functional organ of an animal body or plant. 3 A part or element of a structural or composite whole. 4 *Math.* a The expression on one side or the other of an equation. b An element contained in a set. [<L *membrum* limb]

mem·ber·ship (mem'bər·ship) *n.* 1 The state of being a member. 2 The members of an organization, collectively. 3 The number of members.

mem·brane (mem'brān) *n.* A thin, pliable sheet of material, esp. animal or vegetable tissue serving as a cover, connection, or lining. [<L *membrana*, lit., limb coating]

me·men·to (mə·men'tō) *n. pl.* **·toes** or **·tos** A hint or reminder to awaken memory, esp. a souvenir. [<L *meminisse* remember]

memento mo·ri (môr'ī) *Latin* An emblem or reminder of death, as a skull, etc.: lit., remember that you must die.

mem·o (mem'ō) *n. pl.* **mem·os** *Informal* A memorandum.

mem·oir (mem'wär) *n.* 1 *pl.* A written account of a person's experiences, reminiscences, etc.; an autobiography. 2 A biography. 3 A monograph or report. [F <L *memoria* memory] —**mem'oir·ist** *n.*

mem·o·ra·bil·i·a (mem'ə·rə·bil'ē·ə) *n.pl.* Things worthy of remembrance, or an account of them. [<L *memorabilis* memorable]

mem·o·ra·ble (mem'ər·ə·bəl) *adj.* Worthy to be remembered; noteworthy. —**mem'o·ra·bil'i·ty, mem'o·ra·ble·ness** *n.*

mem·o·ran·dum (mem'ə·ran'dəm) *n. pl.* **·dums** or **·da** (-də) 1 A brief note of a thing or things to be remembered. 2 An informal note or letter, usu. sent from on person to another in an office. 3 *Law* A brief written outline of the terms of a transaction. 4 A statement of goods sent from a consignor to a consignee. [L, a thing to be remembered]

me·mo·ri·al (mə·môr'əl, -mō'rē-) *adj.* Commemorating the memory of a deceased person or of any event. —*n.* 1 Something designed to keep in remembrance a person, event, etc. 2 A presentation of facts made to a government or an official, and usu. accompanies by a petition. [<L *memorialis*]

Memorial Day The last Monday in May, a day set apart to honor the dead of any U.S. war, formerly celebrated May 30.

me·mo·ri·al·ize (mə·môr'ē·əl·īz', -mō'rē-) *v.t.* **·ized, ·iz·ing** 1 To commemorate. 2 To present a memorial to; petition.

mem·o·rize (mem'ə·rīz) *v.t.* **·rized, ·riz·ing** To commit to memory. —**mem'o·ri·za'tion, mem'o·riz'er** *n.*

mem·o·ry (mem'ər·ē, mem'rē) *n. pl.* **·ries** 1 The act, faculty, or capacity of remembering something that is past. 2 Everything that one can remember. 3 A specific act, event, person, or thing remembered. 4 The period of time covered by the faculty of remembrance: beyond the *memory* of man. 5 The state of being remembered. 6 Commemoration or remembrance: in *memory* of her parents. 7 The information storage unit of a computer. [<L *memor* mindful] —**Syn.** 1 recollection, remembrance, reminiscence.

mem·sah·ib (mem'sä·ib) *n. Anglo-Indian* A European lady: a name used by servants. [<MA'AM + Ar. *sāhib* master]

men (men) *n. pl.* of MAN.

men·ace (men'is) *v.* **·aced, ·ac·ing** *v.t.* 1 To threaten with evil or harm. —*v.i.* 2 To make threats; appear threatening. —*n.* 1 A threat. 2 A person or thing that is troublesome or dangerous. [<L *minari* threaten] —**men'ac·ing·ly** *adv.*

me·nad (mē'nad) *n.* MAENAD.

me·nage (mā·näzh'; *Fr.* mā·nȧzh') *n.* 1 The persons of a household, collectively. 2 Household management. Also **me·nage'**. [<L *mansio* house]

me·nag·er·ie (mə·naj'ər·ē) *n.* 1 A collection of wild animals kept for exhibition. 2 The enclosure in which they are kept. [<F]

mend (mend) *v.t.* 1 To make sound or seviceable again by repairing. 2 To correct errors or faults in; reform: *Mend* your ways. 3 To correct (some defect). —*v.i.* 4 To become better, as in health. 5 To heal. 6 To improve, as conditions. —*n.* 1 The act of repairing or patching. 2 A mended portion of a garment. —**on the mend** Recovering health; recuperating. [Var. of AMEND] —**mend'a·ble** *adj.* —**mend'er** *n.* —**Syn.** *v.* 1 patch, repair, restore, fix, overhaul. 2 better, improve, rectify.

men·da·cious (men·dā'shəs) *adj.* 1 Addicted to lying; deceiful. 2 Untrue; false. [<L *mendax* lying] —**men·da'cious·ly** *adv.* —**men·da'cious·ness, men·dac·i·ty** (men ·das'ə·tē) *n.*

men·de·le·vi·um (men'də·lē'vē·əm) *n.* A man-made radioactive element (symbol Md). [<D. I. *Mendeleyev*, 1834–1907, Russ. chemist]

Men·de·li·an (men·dē'lē·ən, -del'yen) *adj.* Of or pertaining to the principles of heredity discovered and set forth by Gregor Mendel. —**Men·de'li·an·ism, Men'del·ism** *n.*

men·di·cant (men'də·kənt) *adj.* 1 Depending on alms for a living; begging. 2 Pertaining to or like a beggar. —*n.* 1 A beggar. 2 A begging friar. [<L *mendicus* needy]

Men·e·la·us (men'ə·lā'əs) *Gk. Myth.* King of Sparta, a brother of Agamemnon and the husband of Helen of Troy.

men·ha·den (men·hād'n) *n.* A herringlike fish found along the N Atlantic coast, used as bait and as a source of oil and fertilizer. [Alter. of Algonquian *munnawhat* fertilizer]

me·ni·al (mē'nē·əl, mēn'yəl) *adj.* 1 Pertaining or appropriate to servants. 2 Servile; base. 3 Low; humble; esp., marked by low prestige or tedious routine: a *menial* job; *menial* tasks. —*n.* 1 A domestic servant. 2 A person of low or servile nature. [<L *mansio* house] —**me'ni·al·ly** *adv.*

me·nin·ges (mə·nin'jez) *n. pl.* of **me·ninx** (mē'ningks) The thin membranes enveloping the brain and spinal cord. [<Gk. *mēninx* membrane] —**me·nin'ge·al** *adj.*

men·in·gi·tis (men'ən·jī'tis) *n.* Inflammation of the meninges, often caused by infection. —**men'in·git'ic** (-jit'ik) *adj.*

me·nis·cus (mə·nis'kəs) *n. pl.* **·nis·cus·es** or **·nis·ci** (-nis'ī) 1 Any crescent-shaped body. 2 A lens convex on one side and concave on the other. 3 *Physics* The surface of a liquid column in a container, made convex or concave by capillarity. [<Gk. *mēniskos* crescent, dim. of *mēnē* the moon]

Meniscus lenses

Men·non·ite (men'ən·īt) *n.* A member of a Protestant sect characterized by simplicity in life and dress and opposed to the taking of oaths, the holding of public office, and military service. [<*Menno* Simons, 1492–1559, a leader of the sect in the Netherlands]

me·no (mā'nō) *adv. Music* Less. [<L *minus*]

men·o·pause (men'ə·pôz) *n.* Final cessation of menstruation; change of life. [<Gk. *mēn* month + PAUSE]

mensch (mensh) *n. pl.* **men·schen** *Colloq.* A genuine, respected, or honored person. [<Yiddish <G, person]

men·ses (men'sēz) *n. pl.* MENSTRUATION. [L, pl. of *mensis* month]

Men·she·vik (men'shə·vik) *n. pl.* **·vi·ki** (-vē'kē) or **·viks** A member of the conservative element in the Russian Social Democratic Party. Also **Men'she·vist**. [Russ. <*menshe* smaller, minority] —**Men'she·vism** *n.*

men·stru·al (men'strōō·əl) *adj.* 1 Of or pertaining to menstruation. 2 Monthly. Also **men'stru·ous**.

men·stru·ate (men'strōō·āt) *v.i.* **·at·ed, ·at·ing** To undergo menstruation. [<L *mensis* month]

men·stru·a·tion (men'strōō·ā'shən) *n.* A bloody flow from the uterus, resulting when an ovum is not fertilized and occurring in women at about monthly intervals.

men·stru·um (men′strōō·əm) *n. pl.* **·stru·ums** or **·stru·a** (-strōō·ə) The medium in which a substance is dissolved; solvent. [Med. L, solvent, menstrual blood]

men·su·ra·ble (men′shər·ə·bəl) *adj.* That can be measured. [<L *mensurare* to measure] **—men′su·ra·bil′i·ty** *n.*

men·su·ra·tion (men′shə·rā′shən) *n.* **1** The act, art, or process of measuring. **2** The mathematics of measurement.

-ment *suffix of nouns* **1** The product or result of: *achievement.* **2** The instrument or means of: *atonement.* **3** The process or action of: *government.* **4** The quality, condition, or state of being: *astonishment.* [<L *-mentum*]

men·tal (men′təl) *adj.* **1** Of or pertaining to the mind. **2** Done by or occurring in the mind, esp. without the aid of written symbols: *mental* arithmetic. **3** Affected by a disorder of the mind: a *mental* patient. **4** Psychiatric: a *mental* hospital. [<L *mens, mentis* mind] **—men′tal·ly** *adv.*

men·tal·i·ty (men·tal′ə·tē) *n. pl.* **·ties 1** Mental power, capacity, or activity. **2** A characteristic way of thinking; pattern of thought: a criminal *mentality.*

mental retardation *Psychol.* A failure in mental development that is severe enough to prevent normal participation in ordinary life; feeble-mindedness. Also **mental deficiency.**

men·thol (men′thôl, -thōl, -thol) *n.* A white, waxy, pungent organic compound used in medicines, cigarettes, etc. [<L *mentha* mint + -OL[1]] **—men·thol·at·ed** (men′thə·lā′tid) *adj.*

men·tion (men′shən) *v.t.* **1** To speak of incidentally, briefly, or in passing. **2** To cite, as for achievement. *—n.* **1** A brief or casual reference or notice. **2** A citing, as for achievement. [<L *mens, mentis* mind] **—men′tion·a·ble** *adj.* **—men′tion·er** *n.*

men·tor (men′tər, -tôr) *n.* A wise and trusted teacher, guide, and friend. [<*Mentor,* the wise guardian of Telemachus in the Odyssey.]

men·u (men′yōō, mān′-) *n. pl.* **men·us 1** A list of various dishes that are available at a restaurant or that comprise a specific meal. **2** The dishes themselves. **3** A list of options or functions that enable a computer user to make choices. [<L *minutus* small, detailed]

me·ow (mē·ou′, myou) *n.* The plaintive cry of a cat. *—v.i.* To make this sound. [Imit.]

Meph·is·toph·e·les (mef′is·tof′ə·lēz) In medieval legend, a devil to whom Faust sold his soul for wisdom and power. *—n.* A diabolical person. Also **Me·phis·to** (mə·fis′tō). **—Meph·is·to·phe·le·an** (mə·fis′tə·fē′lē·ən), **Me·phis′to·phe′li·an** *adj.*

me·phit·ic (mə·fit′ik) *adj.* **1** Poisonous; foul. **2** Foul-smelling. Also **me·phit′i·cal.** [<L *mephitis* noxious odor]

mer. meridian; meridional.

merc. mercantile; mercurial; mercury.

mer·can·tile (mûr′kən·til, -tīl) *adj.* **1** Of, pertaining to, or characteristic of merchants. **2** Of or like mercantilism. [<Ital. *mercante* merchant]

mer·can·til·ism (mûr′kən·til·iz′əm) *n.* A theory in political economy which states that the well-being of a country consists of a favorable balance of trade, an accumulation of bullion, and the development of agriculture and industry, all of which are to be regulated by the government. Also **mercantile system. —mer′can·til·ist** *adj., n.*

Mer·ca·tor projection (mər·kā′tər) A system of making maps in which the meridians form parallel straight lines, and the parallels of latitude (running perpendicular to the meridians) are increasingly further apart as they reach the poles, causing a corresponding distortion in areas and distances. [<G. *Mercator,* 1512–94, Flemish cartographer] • See map, next column.

mer·ce·nar·y (mûr′sə·ner′ē) *adj.* **1** Influenced by desire for gain or reward; greedy. **2** Serving in a foreign army for pay or profit; hired: *mercenary* soldiers. *—n. pl.* **·nar·ies 1** A mercenary soldier. **2** Any hireling. [<L *merces* reward, pay] **—mer′ce·nar′i·ly** *adv.* **—mer′ce·nar′i·ness** *n.*

mer·cer (mûr′sər) *n. Brit.* A dealer in cloth. [<L *merx, mercis* wares]

mer·cer·ize (mûr′sə·rīz) *v.t.* **·ized, ·iz·ing** To treat (cotton fabrics) with caustic soda so as to increase strength and color-absorbing qualities and impart a silky gloss. [<J. *Mercer,* 1791–1866, English inventor] **—mer′cer·i·za′tion** *n.*

mer·chan·dise (mûr′chən·dīz, -dīs) *n.* Anything bought and sold for profit; wares. *—v.t. & v.i.* (-dīz) **·dised, ·dis·ing 1** To buy and sell. **2** To promote the sale of (an article) through advertising, etc. Also **mer′chan·dize.** [See MERCHANT.] **—mer′chan·dis′er** *n.*

mer·chant (mûr′chənt) *n.* **1** A person who buys and sells commodities as a business or for profit. **2** A storekeeper. *—adj.* **1** Of or pertaining to merchants or merchandise. **2** Of the merchant marine. [<L *mercari* to traffic, buy <*merx* wares] **—Syn.** *n.* **1** businessman, trader, bourgeois. **2** dealer, shopkeeper, tradesman.

mer·chant·a·ble (mûr′chən·tə·bəl) *adj.* That can be bought or sold.

mer·chant·man (mûr′chənt·mən) *n. pl.* **·men** (-mən) A trading or merchant vessel.

merchant marine 1 All the vessels of a nation that are engaged in commerce and trade. **2** The officers and men employed on these vessels.

mer·ci (mer·sē′) *interj. French* Thank you.

Mer·ci·a (mûr′shē·ə, -shə) *n.* An ancient Anglo-Saxon kingdom of central England. **—Mer′ci·an** *adj., n.*

mer·ci beau·coup (mer·sē′ bō·kōō′) *French* Thank (you) very much.

mer·ci·ful (mûr′sə·fəl) *adj.* **1** Full of mercy; compassionate. **2** Characterized by or showing mercy. **—mer′ci·ful·ly** *adv.* **—mer′ci·ful·ness** *n.*

mer·ci·less (mûr′sə·lis) *adj.* Having or showing no mercy; pitiless. **—mer′ci·less·ly** *adv.* **—mer′ci·less·ness** *n.*

mer·cu·ri·al (mər·kyōōr′ē·əl) *adj.* **1** Apt to change moods abruptly and with little cause; volatile. **2** Suggestive of the qualities associated with the god Mercury; lively, quick, and ingenious: a *mercurial* wit. **3** Of, containing, or caused by the element mercury. *—n.* A preparation containing mercury. **—mer·cu′ri·al·ly** *adv.* **—mer·cu′ri·al·ness** *n.*

mer·cu·ri·al·ism (mər·kyōōr′ē·əl·iz′əm) *n.* Mercury poisoning.

mer·cu·ric (mər·kyōōr′ik) *adj.* Of or containing bivalent mercury.

mercuric chloride A white, crystalline, poisonous compound, used in photography and as a disinfectant. Also **mercury bichloride.**

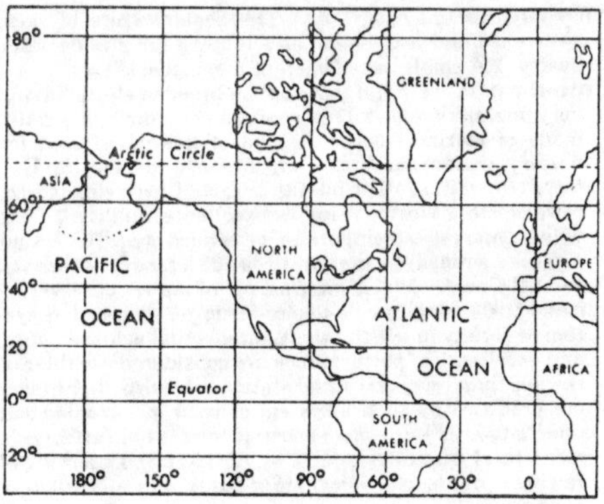

Mercator projection

Mer·cu·ro·chrome (mər·kyōōr′ə·krōm) *n.* An aqueous solution of an organic dye containing mercury and bromine, used as a local antiseptic: a trade name.

mer·cu·rous (mər·kyōōr′əs) *adj.* Of or containing monovalent mercury.

mer·cu·ry (mûr′kyə·rē) *n. pl.* **·ries 1** A heavy, silver-white metallic element (symbol Hg), liquid at ordinary temperatures; quicksilver. **2** The calibrated column of mercury in a thermometer or barometer. [<MERCURY]

Mer·cu·ry (mûr′kyə·rē) *Rom. Myth.* The herald and messenger of the gods, god of commerce, eloquence, and skill. —*n.* The planet of the solar system nearest the sun. • See PLANET. —**Mer·cur·i·al** (mər·kyŏŏr′ē·əl) *adj.*

mer·cy (mûr′sē) *n. pl.* **·cies** 1 Kind or compassionate behavior shown to an enemy, offender, etc., who is in one's power. 2 Compassion or kindness towards others, esp. those in distress. 3 The power to show clemency or forgiveness. 4 A fortunate happening or circumstance. —**at the mercy of** Wholly in the power of. [< L *merces* hire, payment, reward] —**Syn.** 1 benevolence, compassion, forbearance, leniency.

mere[1] (mir) *adj.* **mer·est** *(superl.)* Being no more or less than; nothing but: a *mere* child. [< L *merus* unmixed, bare]

mere[2] (mir) *n.* A pond; pool. [< OE *mere*]

mere·ly (mir′lē) *adv.* Nothing more than; only.

mer·e·tri·cious (mer′ə·trish′əs) *adj.* Deceitfully or artificially attractive; tawdry. [< L *meretrix* prostitute] —**mer′e·tri′cious·ly** *adv.* —**mer′e·tri′cious·ness** *n.*

mer·gan·ser (mər·gan′sər) *n.* Any of various fish-eating ducks, having long, saw-toothed bills and crested heads. [< L *mergere* to plunge + *anser* goose]

merge (mûrj) *v.t. & v.i.* **merged, merg·ing** To combine or be combined so as to lose separate identity; blend. [< L *mergere* dip, immerse]

merg·er (mûr′jər) *n.* 1 The act of merging. 2 A combination of two or more commercial interests or companies into one.

me·rid·i·an (mə·rid′ē·ən) *n.* 1 *Astron.* A great circle passing through the poles of the celestial sphere. 2 *Geog.* **a** A great circle of the earth, passing through both poles. **b** Either half of such a great circle, extending from one pole to the other. 3 The highest or culminating point of anything; the zenith. 4 In acupuncture, a pathway beneath the skin through which energy is believed to flow and along which specific acupuncture points are located. —*adj.* 1 Of or pertaining to noon. 2 Of or at the highest or culminating point. 3 Of or pertaining to a meridian. [< L *meridies* noon, south]

Meridians *def. 2*

me·ringue (mə·rang′) *n.* 1 The beaten white of eggs, sweetened and usu. baked as a topping for pies or other pastry. 2 A small baked shell of meringue. [F]

me·ri·no (mə·rē′nō) *n. pl.* **·nos** 1 A breed of sheep having very fine, silky wool. 2 This wool. 3 A soft fabric, originally made of merino wool. 4 A kind of fine yarn, used for hosiery, underwear, etc. —*adj.* Made of merino. [Sp.]

mer·it (mer′it) *n.* 1 The quality or fact of deserving praise, reward, etc. 2 Worth, value, or excellence; quality. 3 That which deserves esteem, praise, or reward. 4 *pl.* The actual rights or wrongs of a matter: to decide a case on its *merits.* —*v.t.* To deserve. [< L *meritus,* pp. of *merere* deserve]

mer·i·toc·ra·cy (mer′ə·tok′rə·sē) *n. pl.* **·ra·cies** 1 A system or society in which talent, intellectual achievements, and excellence of performance are considered worthier of reward than race, sex, social status, or wealth. 2 The leaders produced by such a system or society. —**mer·i·to·crat** (mer′ə·tə·krat′) *n.* —**mer·i·to·crat·ic** (mer′ə·tə·krat′ik) *adj.*

mer·i·to·ri·ous (mer′ə·tôr′ē·əs, -tō′rē-) *adj.* Deserving of reward, praise, etc. —**mer′i·to′ri·ous·ly** *adv.* —**mer′i·to′ri·ous·ness** *n.*

merit system A system in the civil service whereby appointments and promotions are made on the basis of merit, ascertained through qualifying examinations.

merle (mûrl) *n.* A European thrush. Also **merl.** [< L *merula* blackbird]

Mer·lin (mûr′lin) In medieval legends, a magician and prophet who aided King Arthur.

mer·maid (mûr′mād′) *n.* A legendary sea creature having the head and body of a woman and the tail of a fish. Also **mer′maid′en** (-mād′n). [< MERE[2] + MAID]

Mer·o·vin·gi·an (mer′ə·vin′jē·ən, -jən) *adj.* Of or pertaining to the first Frankish dynasty, founded by Clovis I in 486, and lasting until 751. —*n.* A member of this dynasty.

mer·ri·ment (mer′i·mənt) *n.* Gaiety; mirth.

mer·ry (mer′ē) *adj.* **·ri·er, ·ri·est** 1 Given to mirth and laughter. 2 Marked by cheerfulness and gay spirits. —**make merry** To be in high spirits. [< OE *myrige* pleasant] —**mer′ri·ly** *adv.* —**mer′ri·ness** *n.* —**Syn.** 1 blithe, frolicsome, gleeful, light-hearted.

mer·ry-an·drew (mer′ē·an′drōō) *n.* A clown.

mer·ry-go-round (mer′ē·gō·round′, mer′i-) *n.* 1 A revolving platform fitted with wooden horses, seats, etc., on which people ride for amusement; a carousel. 2 A whirl, as of pleasure.

mer·ry·mak·ing (mer′ē·mā′king) *n.* Festivity; gaiety. —**mer′ry·mak′er** *n.*

me·sa (mā′sə) *n.* A high, broad plateau with sharp, usu. rocky, slopes. [Sp. < L *mensa* table]

mé·sal·li·ance (mā·zal′ē·əns, *Fr.* mā·zà·lyäṅs′) *n.* A marriage with one of inferior social position. [F]

mes·cal (mes·kal′) *n.* 1 A spineless cactus of the sw U.S. and N Mexico, whose tops, **mescal buttons,** contain a hallucinogen. 2 An intoxicating liquor distilled from certain species of agave. [< Nahuatl *mexcalli*]

mes·ca·line (mes′kə·lēn, -lin) *n.* A white, crystalline alkaloid with hallucinogenic properties, extracted from mescal buttons.

mes·dames (mā·däm′, *Fr.* mā·dȧm′) *n.pl.* of MADAME.

mes·de·moi·selles (mād·mwȧ·zel′) *n.pl.* of MADEMOISELLE.

me·seems (mē·sēmz′) *v.* **me·seemed** *impersonal Archaic* It seems to me.

mes·en·ter·y (mes′ən·ter′ē) *n. pl.* **·ter·ies** A supporting membrane, esp. one that holds an intestine to the abdominal wall. [< Gk. *mesos* middle + *enteron* intestine] —**mes′·en·ter′ic** *adj.*

mesh (mesh) *n.* 1 One of the open spaces in a net, screen, sieve, etc. 2 *pl.* The cords or wires that form such open spaces. 3 A net or network. 4 Anything that entangles or involves. 5 *Mech.* The engagement of gear teeth. —*v.t. & v.i.* 1 To make or become entangled, as in a net. 2 To make or become engaged, as gear teeth. [< MDu. *maesche*]

mesh·work (mesh′wûrk′) *n.* Meshes; network.

mes·mer·ism (mes′mə·riz′əm, mez′-) *n.* HYPNOTISM. [< F. A. *Mesmer,* 1734–1815, German physician] —**mes·mer·ic** (mes·mer′ik, mez-), **mes·mer′i·cal** *adj.* —**mes·mer′i·cal·ly** *adv.* —**mes′mer·ist** *n.*

mes·mer·ize (mes′mə·rīz, mez′-) *v.t.* **·ized, ·iz·ing** 1 HYPNOTIZE. 2 To fascinate as if hypnotized. —**mes′mer·i·za′tion, mes′mer·iz′er** *n.*

meso- *combining form* 1 Situated in the middle: *mesocarp.* 2 Intermediate; between: *Mesolithic.* [< Gk. *mesos* middle]

mes·o·blast (mes′ə·blast, mē′sə-) *n.* The middle layer of cells of the embryo. [< MESO- + Gk. *blastos* sprout] —**mes′·o·blas′tic** *adj.*

mes·o·carp (mes′ə·kärp, mē′sə-) *n.* The middle layer of a mature fruit, as the flesh of a peach.

mes·o·derm (mes′ə·dûrm, mē′sə-) *n.* The mesoblast or tissues developed from it. —**mes′o·der′mal, ·der′mic** *adj.*

Mes·o·lith·ic (mes′ə·lith′ik, mē′sə-) *adj. Anthropol.* Pertaining to or describing the period of human culture following the Paleolithic, characterized by small, delicately worked stone artifacts and an economy transitional between food gathering and a settled agriculture. [< MESO- + Gk. *lithos* stone]

mes·on (mes′on, mē′son) *n. Physics* Any of a group of short-lived particles having a mass intermediate between that of the electron and the proton. [< Gk. *mesos* middle]

Mes·o·po·ta·mi·a (mes′ə·pə·tā′mē·ə) *n.* An ancient country of sw Asia between the Tigris and the lower Euphrates rivers, included in modern Iraq. [< Gk. < *mesos* middle + *potamos* river] —**Mes′o·po·ta′mi·an** *n., adj.*

Mes·o·zo·ic (mes′ə·zō′ik, mē′sə-) *adj. & n.* See GEOLOGY. [< MESO- + Gk. *zōion* animal]

mes·quite (mes·kēt′, mes′kēt) *n.* A spiny, deep-rooted shrub or small tree of the pea family, found from sw U.S. to Peru, having sweet pods used as fodder: also **mes·quit′.** [< Nahuatl *mizquitl*]

mess (mes) *n.* 1 A state of disorder, confusion, or untidiness. 2 A confusing, troublesome, or embarrassing situation. 3 A quantity of food sufficient for one meal or for a dish. 4 A portion of soft, partly liquid food, as porridge. 5 A number of persons who habitually take their meals together, as in military units; also, a meal taken by them. 6 MESS HALL. 7 Unpleasant or unclean food. —*v.i.* 1 To make a mess: often with *up.* 2 To eat with a mess (def. 5). —*v.t.* 3 To make a mess of; muddle: often with *up.* 4 To make dirty; befoul: often with *up.* 5 To provide meals for. —**mess around** (or **about**) To busy oneself; dabble. [< L *missus* course at a meal]

mes·sage (mes′ij) *n.* 1 A communication sent in any way. 2 A formal communication, as from a chief executive to a legislative body. 3 A communication embodying a truth, principle, or advice. 4 The carrying out of a mission; errand. 5 A television or radio commercial. [< L *missus,* pp. of *mittere*]

mes·sa·line (mes′ə·lēn′, mes′ə·lēn) *n.* A lightweight, lustrous, twilled silk fabric. [F]

mes·sen·ger (mes′ən·jər) *n.* 1 One sent with a message or on an errand of any kind. 2 A forerunner; herald.

mess hall A building or room where meals are regularly eaten, as by a military group.

Mes·si·ah (mə·sī′ə) *n.* 1 In Judaism, the name for the promised deliverer of the Hebrews. 2 In Christianity, Jesus. 3 Any long-awaited liberator. [< Hebrew *māshīah* anointed] —**Mes·si·an·ic** (mes′ē·an′ik) *adj.*

mes·sieurs (mes′ərz, *Fr.* mā·syœ′) *n. pl.* of MONSIEUR.

mess jacket A man's short, tailored jacket terminating at the waistline, worn by waiters, etc.

mess kit A small, compactly arranged unit containing cooking and eating utensils, used by soldiers and campers.

mess·mate (mes′māt′) *n.* A person with whom one eats at a mess, as in the army.

Messrs. (mes′ərz) *n.pl.* Messieurs: now used in English as the plural of *Mr.*

mes·sy (mes′ē) *adj.* **mes·si·er, mes·si·est** In or causing a mess. —**mess′i·ly** *adv.* —**mess′i·ness** *n.*

mes·ti·zo (mes·tē′zō) *n. pl.* **·zos** or **·zoes** Any one of mixed blood, esp. in Mexico and the w U.S., a person of Spanish and Indian blood. [Sp., lit., mixed] —**mes·ti′za** (-zə) *n. Fem.*

met (met) *p.t. & p.p.* of MEET[1].

meta- *prefix* 1 Changed in place or form; altered: *metamorphosis.* 2 *Anat. & Zool.* Behind; after; on the farther side of; later: *metacarpus.* 3 With; alongside. 4 Beyond; over; transcending: *metaphysics.* 5 *Chem.* a A modification of. b A derivative of. [< Gk. *meta* after, beside, with]

met·a·bol·ic (met′ə·bol′ik) *adj.* Of, pertaining to, or exhibiting metabolism.

me·tab·o·lism (mə·tab′ə·liz′əm) *n.* The aggregate of physical and chemical processes by which a living organism converts assimilated materials into living tissue, energy, and waste. [< Gk. *meta-* beyond + *ballein* throw]

me·tab·o·lize (mə·tab′ə·līz) *v.t. & v.i.* **·lized, ·liz·ing** To change by metabolism.

met·a·car·pus (met′ə·kär′pəs) *n.* 1 The five bones of the hand between the wrist and finger bones. 2 The corresponding bones in the forelimb of land vertebrates. [< Gk. *meta-* beyond + *karpos* wrist] —**met′a·car′pal** *adj., n.*

met·al (met′l) *n.* 1 Any of the elements that tend to lose electrons and form positive ions in chemical reactions, form bases in combination with hydroxyl groups and are usu. lustrous, malleable, ductile, and good conductors of heat and electricity. 2 A combination of such elements; an alloy. 3 Molten glass. 4 *Printing* Type metal; also, composed type. 5 The essential quality or substance of a person or thing. —*adj.* Of, like, or consisting of metal. —*v.t.* **·aled** or **·alled, ·al·ing** or **·al·ling** To furnish or cover with metal. [< L *metallum* mine, metal]

metal., metall. metallurgy.

me·tal·lic (mə·tal′ik) *adj.* 1 Made of, containing, or being a metal. 2 Yielding or producing metal. 3 Like or suggesting a metal: a *metallic* luster. 4 Hard; harsh: a *metallic* voice. —**me·tal′li·cal·ly** *adv.*

met·al·lif·er·ous (met′ə·lif′ər·əs) *adj.* Yielding or containing metal.

met·al·lur·gy (met′ə·lûr′jē) *n.* The technology of extracting metals from ores and producing alloys with desired properties. [< Gk. < *metallon* metal + *-ergos* working] —**met′al·lur′gic** or **·gi·cal** *adj.* —**met′al·lur′gist** *n.*

met·al·work (met′l·wûrk′) *n.* 1 Articles made of metal. 2 The making of such articles: also **met′al·work′ing.** —**met′al·work′er** *n.*

met·a·mor·phic (met′ə·môr′fik) *adj.* 1 Of or pertaining to metamorphosis. 2 *Geol.* Of, producing, or caused by metamorphism. Also **met′a·mor′phous.**

met·a·mor·phism (met′ə·môr′fiz·əm) *n.* 1 *Geol.* The changes in the composition and texture of rocks caused by heat, pressure, moisture, etc. 2 METAMORPHOSIS.

met·a·mor·phose (met′ə·môr′fōz) *v.* **·phosed, ·phos·ing** *v.t.* 1 To change the form of. —*v.i.* 2 To undergo metamorphism or metamorphosis.

met·a·mor·pho·sis (met′ə·môr′fə·sis) *n.pl.* **·pho·ses** (-fə·sēz) 1 A passing from one form or shape into another, esp. by means of sorcery, etc. 2 Complete transformation of character, purpose, circumstances, etc. 3 A person or thing metamorphosed. 4 *Biol.* A developmental change in form, structure, or function in an organism, esp. after leaving the egg and before attaining sexual maturity. [< Gk. *meta-* beyond + *morphē* form]

met·a·phor (met′ə·fôr, -fər) *n.* A figure of speech in which one object is likened to another by speaking of it as if it were that other, as in *The sun was a chariot of fire.* [< Gk. *meta-* beyond, over + *pherein* to carry] —**met′a·phor′ic** (-fôr′ik, -for′ik) or **·i·cal** *adj.* —**met′a·phor′i·cal·ly** *adv.* • *Metaphors* and *similes* both make comparisons, but the metaphor is distinguished from the simile by the omission of an introductory word such as "like" or "as." For example, *The moon is a silver coin* is a metaphor; *The moon is like a silver coin* is a simile.

met·a·phys·i·cal (met′ə·fiz′i·kəl) *adj.* 1 Of, pertaining to, or like metaphysics. 2 Very abstract or abstruse. 3 Designating certain poets of the 17th century whose verses were characterized by complex, intellectualized imagery. —**met′a·phys′i·cal·ly** *adv.*

met·a·phys·ics (met′ə·fiz′iks) *n.pl. (construed as sing.)* 1 The branch of philosophy that deals with the first principles of being and knowledge and with the essential nature of reality. 2 All speculative philosophy. [< Med. Gk. *ta meta ta physika* the (works) after the physics; in ref. to Aristotle's *Physics*] —**met′a·phy·si′cian** *n.*

me·tas·ta·sis (mə·tas′tə·sis) *n. pl.* **·ses** (-sēz) The transfer of a disease or its manifestations, as the cells of a malignant tumor, from one part of the body to another. [< Gk. *meta-* after + *histanai* to place] —**met′a·stat′ic** (-stat′ik) *adj.* —**met′a·stat′i·cal·ly** *adv.*

me·tas·ta·size (mə·tas′tə·sīz) *v.i.* **·sized, ·siz·ing** To spread by metastasis.

met·a·tar·sus (met′ə·tär′səs) *n. pl.* **·si** (-sī) 1 In human beings, the five bones between the ankle and the toes. 2 The corresponding part of the hind limb in land vertebrates. [< META- + TARSUS] —**met′a·tar′sal** *adj., n.*

Metatarsus

me·tath·e·sis (mə·tath′ə·sis) *n. pl.* **·ses** (-sēz) 1 The transposition of letters, syllables, or sounds in a word. 2 Any change or reversal. [< Gk. *meta-* over + *tithenai* to place] —**met·a·thet·ic** (met′ə·thet′ik) or **·i·cal** *adj.*

met·a·zo·an (met′ə·zō′ən) *n.* Any of a primary division of animals that develop from a single cell into a multicellular system of distinct tissues and organs: also **met′a·zo′on.** —*adj.* Of the metazoans: also **met′a·zo′ic.** [< META- + Gk. *zōion* animal]

mete[1] (mēt) *v.t.* **met·ed, met·ing** To distribute by measure; apportion: usu. with *out.* [< OE *metan* to measure] —**Syn.** allot, dispense, dole, parcel.

mete[2] (mēt) *n.* A boundary, usu. in the phrase **metes and bounds.** [< L *meta*]

me·tem·psy·cho·sis (mə·temp′sə·kō′sis, met′əm·sī-) *n. pl.* **·ses** Transmigration of souls. [< Gk. *meta-* over + *empsychoein* to animate]

me·te·or (mē′tē·ər, -ôr) *n. Astron.* A brief light produced by a small piece of matter from space which enters the earth's atmosphere with great velocity and is disintegrated by heat. [<Gk. *meteōros* high in the air]

meteor., meteorol. meteorological; meteorology.

me·te·or·ic (mē′tē·ôr′ik, -or′ik) *adj.* 1 Of or pertaining to meteors. 2 Pertaining to atmospheric phenomena; meteorological. 3 Like a meteor in brilliance or swiftness: a *meteoric* career. —**me′te·or′i·cal·ly** *adv.*

me·te·or·ite (mē′tē·ə·rīt′) *n.* 1 A solid mass that has fallen to the earth from space. 2 METEOROID. —**me′te·or·it′ic** (-ə·rit′ik) *adj.*

me·te·or·oid (mē′tē·ə·roid) *n. Astron.* One of innumerable small particles of matter moving through space.

me·te·or·ol·o·gy (mē′tē·ə·rol′ə·jē) *n.* The science that deals with atmospheric pheneomena, esp. those that relate to weather. [<Gk. *meteōros* high in the air + -LOGY] —**me′te·or′o·log′i·cal** (-ôr′ə·loj′ə·kəl) or **·log′ic** *adj.* —**me′te·or′o·log′i·cal·ly** *adv.* —**me′te·or·ol′o·gist** *n.*

me·ter[1] (mē′tər) *n.* An instrument for measuring and recording something. —*v.t.* To measure or test by means of a meter. [<METE[1]]

me·ter[2] (mē′tər) *n.* 1 The basic unit of length in the metric system, defined as equal to 1,650,763.73 wavelengths, in a vacuum, of the orange-red radiation of krypton 86, equal to about 39.37 inches. 2 A measured verbal rhythm, having, in verse, a definite arrangement of groups of accented and unaccented syllables in a line; also, a specific arrangement or pattern of such syllables. 3 *Music* The character of a composition as being divisible into measures equal in duration and similar in rhythmic construction. [<Gk. *metron* a measure]

-meter *combining form* 1 An instrument by which a thing is measured: *calorimeter.* 2 (A specified number of) units or meters: *kilometer.* 3 Containing (a specified number) of metrical feet: *hexameter.*

Meth. Methodist.

meth·a·done (meth′ə·dōn) *n.* A synthetic opiate used as an analgesic and experimentally as a substitute for heroin in the treatment of addicts. Also **meth′a·don** (-don). [<*(di)meth(yl)a(mino) d(iphenylheptan)one*]

meth·a·qua·lone (meth′ə·kwä′lon) *n.* An addictive drug used as a sedative; QUAALUDE.

meth·am·phet·a·mine (meth′am·fet′ə·mēn, - min) *n.* A chemical compound that allays hunger and stimulates the central nervous system. [<*meth(yl)* + AMPHETAMINE]

meth·ane (meth′ān) *n.* A colorless, flammable gas composed of one atom of carbon and four of hydrogen and forming the main constituent of natural gas. [<METH(YL) + -ANE]

methane series A series of saturated hydrocarbons in which the carbon atoms are linked in progressively longer chains.

meth·a·nol (meth′ə·nōl, -nol) *n.* A colorless, volatile, flammable, and highly toxic alcohol widely used in industry. [<METHAN(E) + -OL[1]]

Meth·e·drine (meth′ə·drēn) *n.* METHAMPHETAMINE: a trade name.

me·thinks (mē·thingks′) *v.* **me·thought** *impersonal Archaic* It seems to me; I think. [<OE *me* me + *thyncan* seem]

meth·od (meth′əd) *n.* 1 A systematic, established, or orderly procedure or way of doing anthing. 2 System, order, or regularity in general. 3 The disciplines and techniques used in any field of knowledge, creativity, etc.: the Renaissance *methods* of painting. 4 Orderly and systematic arrangement, as of ideas and topics, etc. [<Gk. *meta-* after + *hodos* way]

me·thod·i·cal (mə·thod′i·kəl) *adj.* 1 Characterized by or performed with method and order. 2 Orderly; systematic: a *methodical* worker. Also **me·thod′ic.** —**me·thod′i·cal·ly** *adv.* —**me·thod′i·cal·ness** *n.*

Meth·od·ist (meth′əd·ist) *n.* A member of any one of the Protestant churches that have grown out of the religious movement begun by John and Charles Wesley in England during the first half of the 18th century. —*adj.* Pertaining to or typical of methodists or Methodism. [<METHOD] —**Meth′od·ism** *n.* —**Meth′od·is′tic** or **·ti·cal** *adj.*

meth·od·ize (meth′əd·īz) *v.t.* **·ized, ·iz·ing** To subject to method; systematize. —**meth′od·i·za′tion** *n.*

meth·od·ol·o·gy (meth′ə·dol′ə·jē) *n. pl.* **·gies** 1 The science of methodical, systematic thinking, procedure, arrangement, etc. 2 The methods or procedures used in a particular field or discipline.

Me·thu·se·lah (mə·thōō′zə·lə) In the Bible, a Hebrew patriarch reputed to have lived 969 years. —*n.* Any very old man.

meth·yl (meth′əl) *n.* A univalent hydrocarbon radical having a single carbon atom. [<Gk. *methy* wine + *hylē* wood] —**me·thyl·ic** (mə·thil′ik) *adj.*

methyl alcohol METHANOL.

meth·yl·ate (meth′əl·āt) *v.t.* **·at·ed, ·at·ing** 1 To mix methanol into, as ethanol, esp. to make unfit to drink. 2 To introduce a methyl radical into. —**meth′yl·a′tion** *n.*

me·tic·u·lous (mə·tik′yə·ləs) *adj.* Extremely or excessively careful about details; finical. [<L *meticolosus* fearful] —**me·tic′u·los′i·ty** (-los′ə·tē) *n.* —**me·tic′u·lous·ly** *adv.* —**Syn.** exacting, fastidious, finicky, particular, punctilious.

mé·tier (mā·tyā′) *n.* 1 Trade; profession. 2 Activity or work in which one is an expert. [F]

mé·tis (mā·tē′) *n. pl.* **mé·tis** (-tē′, -tēs) A person of mixed American Indian and European, esp. French, ancestry. [F, lit., mixed]

me·ton·y·my (mə·ton′ə·mē) *n.* **·mies** A figure of speech that employs an associated or closely connected word rather than the word itself, as "the crown prefers" for "the king prefers." [<Gk. *meta-* altered + *onyma* name] —**met·o·nym·ic** (met′ə·nim′ik), **met′o·nym′i·cal** *adj.* —**met′o·nym′i·cal·ly** *adv.*

me-too·ism (mē′tōō′iz′əm) *n.* The practice of representing as one's own the popular or successful policies of another, esp. a political rival. —**me′-too′er** *n.*

Met·ra·zol (met′rə·zōl, -zol) *n.* A synthetic drug used as a heart and central nervous system stimulant: a trade name.

me·tre (mē′tər) *n. Chiefly Brit.* METER[2].

met·ric (met′rik) *adj.* 1 Of or pertaining to the metric system. 2 METRICAL (def. 1).

met·ri·cal (met′ri·kəl) *adj.* 1 Of, relating to, or composed in poetic meter. 2 Of, pertaining to, or used in measurement. —**met′ri·cal·ly** *adv.*

metric system A decimal system of weights and measures. • See MEASURE.

met·ri·fi·ca·tion (met′rə·fə·kā′shən) *n.* The adoption of the metric system or the conversion to metric units from those of another system. Also *Brit.* **met·ri·ca·tion** (met′rə·kā′shən). —**met·ri·fy** (met′rə·fī) *v.t.* & *v.i.* **(·fied, ·fy·ing).**

metro- *combining form* Measure: *metronome.* [<Gk. *metron* measure]

met·ro·nome (met′rə·nōm) *n.* An instrument for indicating tempo in music, consisting of a mechanical or electronic oscillator producing pulses at a fixed, controllable rate. [<METRO- + Gk. *nomos* law] —**met′ro·nom′ic** (-nom′ik) *adj.*

me·trop·o·lis (mə·trop′ə·lis) *n.* 1 The capital or the largest or most important city of a state or country. 2 Any large city that is the center of some activity. 3 The seat of a metopolitan bishop. [<Gk. *mētēr* mother + *polis* city]

met·ro·pol·i·tan (met′rə·pol′ə·tən) *adj.* 1 Of, like, or constituting a metropolis (defs. 1 & 2). 2 Of or designating a metropolitan or his province. —*n.* 1 An archbishop who has authority over the bishops of his ecclesiastical province. 2 One who lives in a metropolis or has the manners and customs of a metropolis.

-metry *combining form* The process, science, or art of measuring: *geometry.* [<Gk. *metron* a measure]

met·tle (met′l) *n.* 1 Inherent quality of character. 2 Courage; spirit. —**on one's mettle** Aroused to one's best efforts. [Var. of METAL] —**met′tled** *adj.*

met·tle·some (met′l·səm) *adj.* Having courage or spirit; ardent; fiery.

mew[1] (myōō) *n.* 1 A cage for molting hawks. 2 Any hiding place. 3 *pl. Chiefly Brit.* a A stable, usu. on an inner court or alley. b A narrow back street or alley. —*v.t.* To confine in or as in a cage: often with *up.* [<L *mutare* to change]

mew[2] (myōō) *n.* & *v.* MEOW.

mew[3] (myōō) *n.* A European sea gull. Also **mew gull.** [<OE *mæw*]

mewl (myōōl) *v.i.* To cry, as an infant. —*n.* An infant's cry or crying. [Imit.]

Mex. Mexican; Mexico.

Mex·i·can (mek′sə·kən) *n.* A citizen or native of Mexico. —*adj.* Of or pertaining to Mexico or its people.

Mexican War A war between the U.S. and Mexico (1846–48).

Mex·i·co (mek′sə·kō) *n.* A republic of s North America, 760,373 sq. mi., cap. Mexico (also Mexico City).

mez·za·nine (mez′ə·nēn, mez·ə·nēn′) *n.* **1** A low-ceilinged story or long, inner balcony between two main stories. Also **mezzanine floor, mezzanine story. 2** In a theater, the first balcony or the front rows of the first balcony. [<Ital. *mezzano* middle]

mez·zo (met′sō, med′zō, mez′ō) *adj.* Half; medium; moderate. —*adv. Music* Moderately: *mezzo* forte. [<L *medius* middle]

mez·zo-so·pran·o (met′sō·sə·pran′ō, -prän′ō, med′zō-, mez′ō) *n.* **1** A voice lower than a soprano and higher than a contralto. **2** A person possessing, or a part written for, such a voice.

mez·zo·tint (met′sō·tint′, med′zō-, mez′ō-) *n.* **1** A method of engraving on copper or steel by scraping or polishing those roughened parts of the plate where light and shadow are desired. **2** An impression so produced. —*v.t.* To engrave in or represent by mezzotint. [<Ital. *mezzo* middle + *tinto* tint] —**mez′zo·tint′er** *n.*

MF, MF. Middle French.

mfg. manufacturing.

mfr. manufacture; manufacturer.

Mg magnesium.

mg, mg., mgm milligram(s).

mgt. management.

MHG, MHG., M.H.G. Middle High German.

mi (mē) *n. Music* In solmization, the third tone of a diatonic scale. [Ital. See GAMUT.]

MI Michigan (P.O. abbr.).

mi, mi. mile(s).

mi·aou, mi·aow (mē·ou′) *n.* & *v.* MEOW.

mi·as·ma (mī·az′mə, mē-) *n. pl.* **·mas** or **·ma·ta** (-mə·tə) **1** The poisonous effluvium once supposed to rise from putrid matter, swamps, etc. **2** Any unwholesome influence or atmosphere. [<Gk., pollution] —**mi·as′mal, mi·as·mat·ic** (mī′az·mat′ik), **mi·as′mic** *adj.*

mi·ca (mī′kə) *n.* Any of a class of silicate minerals that readily separate into thin, tough sheets. [<L, crumb] —**mi·ca·ceous** (mī·kā′shəs) *adj.*

mice (mīs) *n. pl.* of MOUSE.

Mich. Michigan.

Mi·chael (mī′kəl) One of the archangels, conqueror of Lucifer. Also **Saint Michael.**

Mich·ael·mas (mik′əl·məs) *n.* September 29, the feast of St. Michael. Also **Michaelmas Day.**

mick·ey finn (mik′ē fin′) *Slang* A drugged, usu. alcoholic drink. Also **mick′ey, Mick′ey Finn.** [?]

Mic·mac (mik′mak) *n. pl.* **·mac** or **·macs** One of a tribe of Algonquian Indians of Nova Scotia, New Brunswick, and Newfoundland.

micro- *combining form* **1** Very small; minute: *microfilm, microgroove.* **2** Known or seen only by microscopic examination: *microorganism.* **3** In the sciences, using, requiring, or involved in microscopy: *microbiology.* **4** Enlarging or increasing in size or volume: *microscope.* **5** In systems of measurement, the one-millionth part of (the specified unit) (symbol μ): *microgram, microwatt.* Also **micr-.** [<Gk. *mikros* small]

mi·cro·bar (mī′krō·bär) *n.* A unit of pressure equal to 1.458×10^{-5} (0.00001458) pound per square inch.

mi·crobe (mī′krōb) *n.* A microscopic organism, esp. a disease-producing bacterium. [<Gk. *mikro-* small + *bios* life] —**mi·cro′bi·al, mi·cro′bi·an, mi·cro′bic** *adj.*

mi·cro·bi·ol·o·gy (mī′krō·bī·ol′ə·jē) *n.* The branch of biology that deals with microorganisms. —**mi′cro·bi′o·log′i·cal** *adj.* —**mi′cro·bi·ol′o·gist** *n.*

mi·cro·ceph·a·ly (mī′krō·sef′ə·lē) *n.* Abnormal smallness of the head or cranium. [<MICRO- + Gk. *kephalē* head] —**mi′cro·ce·phal′ic** (-sə·fal′ik), **mi′cro·ceph′a·lous** *adj.*

mi·cro·chem·is·try (mī′krō·kem′is·trē) *n.* The investigation of chemical reactions using minute quantities of substances. —**mi′cro·chem′i·cal** *adj.* —**mi′cro·chem′i·cal·ly** *adv.* —**mi′cro·chem′ist** *n.*

mi·cro·chip (mi′krō·chip′) *n.* A chip (def. 8).

mi·cro·com·put·er (mī′krō·kəm·pyōō′tər) *n.* A very small electronic computer.

mi·cro·cop·y (mī′krō·kop′ē) *n. pl.* **·cop·ies** A reduced photographic copy, as of a letter, manuscript, etc.

mi·cro·cosm (mī′krə·koz′əm) *n.* **1** A little world; esp., a community or environment regarded as a small-scale version or example of the universe or of a much larger entity. **2** Man seen as the epitome of the universe. Also **mi′cro·cos′mos** (-koz′məs). [<Gk. *mikros kosmos,* lit., little world]

mi·cro·fiche (mī′krō·fēsh′) *n.* A sheet of microfilm. [F <MICRO- + *fiche* card, slip of paper]

mi·cro·film (mī′krə·film) *n.* A film on which is a photographic reproduction of a printed page, document, or other object, highly reduced for ease in transmission and storage, and capable of reenlargement. —*v.t.* & *v.i.* To reproduce on microfilm.

mi·cro·form (mī′krō·fôrm′) *n.* A method of reproducing images greatly reduced in size, as on microfilm.

mi·cro·gram (mī′krə·gram) *n.* One millionth of a gram (symbol μg). Also **mi′cro·gramme.**

mi·cro·groove (mī′krə·grōōv) *n.* A very fine groove cut in the surface of a long-playing phonograph record.

mi·crom·e·ter (mī·krom′ə·tər) *n.* **1** An instrument for measuring very small distances or dimensions as used on a microscope or telescope. **2** MICROMETER CALIPER.

Micrometer

micrometer caliper A caliper or gauge having a micrometer screw.

micrometer screw A screw with finely cut threads and a circular, graduated head, which shows the position of the screw.

mi·crom·e·try (mī·krom′ə·trē) *n.* Measurement with a micrometer. —**mi·cro·met·ric** (mī′krō·met′rik) or **·ri·cal** *adj.* —**mi′cro·met′ri·cal·ly** *adv.*

mi·cron (mī′kron) *n.* The one-millionth part of a meter (symbol μ). [<Gk. *mikros* small]

Mi·cro·ne·sian (mī′krə·nē′zhən, -shən) *n.* **1** A native of Micronesia. **2** A group of Austronesian languages spoken in Micronesia. —*adj.* Of or pertaining to Micronesia, its people, or their languages.

mi·cro·or·gan·ism (mī′krō·ôr′gən·iz′əm) *n.* An organism visible only in an optical or electron microscope, as a bacterium, protozoan, or virus. Also **mi′cro·or′gan·ism.**

mi·cro·phone (mī′krə·fōn) *n.* A device for changing sound waves into corresponding electric signals.

mi·cro·pho·to·graph (mī′krō·fō′tə·graf, -gräf) *n.* **1** A very small or microscopic photograph, usu. magnified for viewing. **2** PHOTOMICROGRAPH. —**mi′cro·pho′to·graph′ic** *adj.* —**mi′cro·pho·tog′ra·phy** (-fə·tog′rə·fē) *n.*

mi·cro·print (mī′krə·print) *n.* A microphotograph examined only by means of a magnifying device.

mi·cro·proc·es·sor (mī′krō·pros′es·ər) *n.* An electronic computer contained on a single chip.

mi·cro·scope (mī′krə·skōp) *n.* Any of various instruments for magnifying objects too small to be seen or clearly observed by the naked eye. [<MICRO- + -SCOPE]

mi·cro·scop·ic (mī′krə·skop′ik) *adj.* **1** So small as to be visible only with the aid of a microscope. **2** Exceedingly small or minute. **3** Of, relating to, or done with a microscope or microscopy. **4** Resembling a microscope. Also **mi′cro·scop′i·cal.** —**mi′cro·scop′i·cal·ly** *adv.*

mi·cros·co·py (mī·kros′kə·pē, mī′krə·skō′pē) *n.* **1** The technique of using a microscope. **2** Investigation with a microscope. —**mi·cros′co·pist** *n.*

mi·cro·wave (mī′krə·wāv) *n.* An electromagnetic wave having a wavelength in the range longer than red light and shorter than radio waves.

mic·tu·rate (mik′chə·rāt) *v.i.* **·rat·ed, ·rat·ing** To urinate. [< L *micturire* desire to urinate] **—mic′tu·ri′tion** (-rish′ən) *n.*

mid[1] (mid) *adj.* Being in the middle. [< OE *midd*]

mid[2] (mid) *prep.* Amid; among. Also **'mid.**

mid- *combining form* **1** Being the middle point or part of: *mid-April, midmorning.* **2** In a middle or central position: *midpoint, midrib.*

mid. middle; midshipman.

Mi·das (mī′dəs) *Gk. Myth.* A king of Phrygia who had the power of turning whatever he touched into gold.

mid·brain (mid′brān′) *n.* The middle division of the brain.

mid·channel (mid′chan′əl) *n.* The middle part of a channel.

mid·day (mid′dā′) *n.* The middle part of the day; noon. *—adj.* Of or at midday.

mid·dle (mid′l) *adj.* **1** Equally distant from the extremes of place, position, time, etc.; central. **2** Being in neither the one nor the other extreme; intermediate. **3** *Often cap.* Designating a language midway in development between an earlier (Old) and later (Modern) form. *—n.* **1** The part or point equally distant from the extremes of place, position, time, etc. **2** Something that is intermediate. **3** The middle part of the body; waist. *—v.t.* **·dled, ·dling** To place in the middle. [< OE *middel*] **Syn.** *adj.* **1** median, mid, moderate. *n.* **1** midway, center.

middle age The time of life between youth and old age, commonly between 40 and 60. **—mid′dle-aged′** (-ājd′) *adj.*

Middle Ages The period in European history between classical antiquity and the Renaissance, usu. regarded as extending from the downfall of Rome, in 476, to about 1450.

mid·dle·brow (mid′l·brou′) *n.* A person who has conventional or middle-class tastes, interests, opinions, etc.

middle C *Music* The note written on the first ledger line above the bass staff and the first ledger line below the treble staff; also, the corresponding tone or key.

middle class The class of a society that occupies a position between the laboring class and the very wealthy or the nobility. **—mid′dle-class′** *adj.*

middle ear The part of the ear between the eardrum and the inner ear, including the tympanum and the ossicles (hammer, anvil, and stirrup). • See EAR.

Middle East The region usu. thought of as including Egypt and the countries of sw Asia west of India.

Middle English English as written and spoken from about 1100 to 1500.

Middle French French as written and spoken from the 14th to the 16th century.

Middle High German High German as written and spoken from about 1050 to 1450.

Middle Latin MEDIEVAL LATIN.

Middle Low German Low German as written and spoken from about 1100 to 1500.

mid·dle·man (mid′l·man′) *n. pl.* **·men** (-men′) **1** One who acts as an agent or go-between; intermediary. **2** One who buys in bulk from producers and sells to retailers or directly to consumers.

mid·dle·most (mid′l·mōst′) *adj.* MIDMOST.

mid·dle-of-the-road (mid′l·əv·t͟hə·rōd′) *adj.* Tending toward neither side or extreme; moderate, esp. in politics. **—mid′dle-of-the-road′er** *n.*

mid·dle·weight (mid′l·wāt′) *n.* A boxer or wrestler weighing between 147 and 160 pounds. *—adj.* Of middleweights.

Middle West That section of the U.S. between the Rocky Mountains and the eastern border of Ohio and north of the Ohio River and the southern borders of Kansas and Missouri. Also **middle west. —Middle Western —Middle Westerner**

mid·dling (mid′ling) *adj.* **1** Of middle rank, condition, size, or quality. **2** *Informal* In fair health. *—adv. Informal* Moderately; somewhat. *—n.* **1** Any of various products of medium size, quality, etc. **2** *pl.* The coarser part of ground wheat.

mid·dy (mid′ē) *n. pl.* **·dies** **1** *Informal* A midshipman. **2** MIDDY BLOUSE.

middy blouse A loosely fitting blouse having a wide sailor collar, worn by women and children.

Middy blouse

midge (mij) *n.* **1** A gnat or small fly. **2** A small person. [< OE *mycge*]

midg·et (mij′it) *n.* **1** An abnormally small person. **2** Anything very small of its kind. *—adj.* Small; diminutive. [Dim. of MIDGE]

mid·i (mid′ē) *n. pl.* **mid·is** A skirt, dress, or coat with a hemline at mid-calf. [< MIDDLE]

Mid·i·an·ite (mid′ē·ən·īt′) *n.* One of an ancient nomadic tribe of NW Arabia.

mid·i·ron (mid′ī′ərn) *n.* A golf club having a metal head and a medium loft.

mid·land (mid′lənd) *n.* The interior of a country or region. *—adj.* Of or located in the central part of a country or region.

Mid·land (mid′lənd) *n.* The dialect of Middle English spoken in London and the midland counties of England; esp. **East Midland,** the branch of Midland that is the direct predecessor of Modern English.

mid·most (mid′mōst′) *adj.* **1** Situated exactly in the middle. **2** Very intimate. *—adv.* In the midst or middle.

mid·night (mid′nīt′) *n.* The middle of the night; twelve o'clock at night. *—adj.* **1** Of or at midnight. **2** Like midnight in darkness, etc.

midnight sun The sun visible at midnight during the arctic and the antarctic summer.

mid·rib (mid′rib′) *n.* The central vein of a leaf.

mid·riff (mid′rif) *n.* **1** The diaphragm. **2** The part of the body between the chest and the abdomen. [< OE *midd* mid + *hrif* belly]

mid·ship (mid′ship′) *adj. Naut.* At or pertaining to the middle of a vessel's hull.

mid·ship·man (mid′ship′mən, mid·ship′-) *n. pl.* **·men** (-mən) **1** A student training to be a naval officer, esp. at the U.S. Naval Academy in Annapolis. **2** A British naval officer ranking between a naval cadet and the lowest commissioned officer. [< *amidshipman;* so called from being amidships when on duty]

mid·ships (mid′ships) *adv. Naut.* AMIDSHIPS.

midst (midst) *n.* The central part; middle: usu. in the phrase **in the midst of. —in our (your** or **their) midst** Among us (you, or them). *—prep.* Amidst. [< OE *midd* mid] **—Syn.** *n.* center, hub. *prep.* amid, among.

mid·stream (mid′strēm′) *n.* The middle of a stream.

mid·sum·mer (mid′sum′ər) *n.* **1** The middle of summer. **2** The time of the summer solstice, about June 21. *—adj.* Of, in, or like midsummer.

mid·term (mid′tûrm′) *adj. & adv.* In the middle of the term. *—n.* **1** The middle of the term. **2** *Informal* A midterm examination.

mid-Vic·to·ri·an (mid′vik·tôr′ē·ən, -tō′rē-) *adj.* **1** Of or characteristic of the middle period of Queen Victoria's reign in England, approximately 1850–80. **2** Outwardly strict in morals, manners, etc.; prudish. *—n.* **1** A person living in this era. **2** A person of Victorian ideas or tastes.

mid·way (mid′wā′, -wā′) *adj.* Being in the middle of the way or distance. *—adv.* Halfway. *—n.* (mid′wā′) At a fair, exposition, etc., the area where various amusements and sideshows are located.

mid·week (mid′wēk′) *n.* The middle of the week. *—adj.* In the middle of the week. **—mid′week′ly** *adj., adv.*

Mid·west (mid′west′) *n.* MIDDLE WEST. **—Mid′west′ern** *adj.*

mid·wife (mid′wīf′) *n. pl.* **·wives** (-wīvz′) A woman who assists women in childbirth. [< OE *mid* with + *wīf* wife]

mid·wife·ry (mid′wī′fər·ē, -wīf′rē) *n.* The act or skill of assisting women in childbirth.

mid·win·ter (mid′win′tər) *n.* **1** The middle of winter. **2** The winter solstice, about Dec. 21. *—adj.* Of, like, or in midwinter.

mid·year (mid′yir′) *n.* **1** The middle of the year. **2** An examination given in the middle of a school year.

mien (mēn) *n.* The bearing, demeanor, or expression of a person. [< DEMEAN]
miff (mif) *Informal v.t. & v.i.* To be or cause to be irritated or offended. —*n.* A huff. [?]
Mig (mig) *n.* A type of jet fighter plane of the Soviet air force. [< *Mi(koyan)* and *G(urevich)*, Soviet aircraft designers] Also **MIG.**
might[1] (mīt) *p.t.* of MAY[1].
might[2] (mīt) *n.* **1** Physical strength. **2** Great power, ability, or resources of any kind. —**with might and main** With one's whole strength. [< OE *meaht, miht*] —**Syn. 1** force, potency, puissance, vigor, power.
might·y (mī′tē) *adj.* **might·i·er, might·i·est 1** Possessed of might; powerful; strong. **2** Of unusual size, consequence, etc. —*adv. Informal* Very; exceedingly. —**might′i·ly** *adv.* —**might′i·ness** *n.*
mi·gnon·ette (min′yən·et′) *n.* A small plant having racemes of greenish, fragrant flowers. [F]
mi·graine (mī′grān) *n.* A recurrent, severe form of headache, temporarily disabling, usu. affecting one side of the head and often accompanied by nausea, dizziness, and sensitivity to light. [< Gk. *hēmi* half + *kranion* skull]
mi·grant (mī′grənt) *adj.* Migratory. —*n.* **1** A person or animal that migrates. **2** A worker who moves from place to place to find employment, esp. in harvesting crops: also **migrant worker.**
mi·grate (mī′grāt) *v.i.* **·grat·ed, ·grat·ing 1** To move, as from one place, region, etc., to another. **2** To move periodically from one region or climate to another, as birds or fish. [< L *migrare* roam, wander] —**mi′gra·tor** *n.*
mi·gra·tion (mī·grā′shən) *n.* **1** The act of migrating. **2** The totality of persons or animals migrating at one time. **3** *Chem.* The shifting of one or more atoms from one position in the molecule to another. **4** *Physics* The drift or movement of ions due to the effect of an electric field. —**mi·gra′tion·al** *adj.* —**mi·gra′tion·ist** *n.*
mi·gra·to·ry (mī′grə·tôr′ē, -tō′rē) *adj.* **1** Of or pertaining to migration. **2** Given to migrating. **3** Roving; nomadic.
mi·ka·do (mi·kä′dō) *n. pl.* **·dos** An emperor of Japan.
mike (mīk) *n. Informal* A microphone.
mil (mil) *n.* **1** A unit of length equal to .001 inch. **2** *Mil.* A unit of angular measure equal to 1/6400 of a circle, or about 0.0560 degree. [< L *millesimus* thousandth]
mil. mileage; military; militia; million.
mi·la·dy (mi·lā′dē) *n. pl.* **·dies** An English noblewoman or gentlewoman. [< *my lady*]
Mil·an·ese (mil′ən·ēz′, -ēs′) *adj.* Of or pertaining to Milan or its people. —*n. pl.* **·ese** A citizen or inhabitant of Milan.
milch (milch) *adj.* Giving milk, as a cow. [< OE *-milce*]
mild (mīld) *adj.* **1** Gentle in nature or disposition. **2** Moderate; temperate: a *mild* winter. **3** Not harsh or strong, as in flavor. [< OE *milde*] —**mild′ly** *adv.* —**mild′ness** *n.*
mil·dew (mil′d^{y}o͞o) *n.* **1** Any of various fungi that form a spotty coating on damp surfaces, as plant leaves, clothing, leather, etc. **2** Any of various plant diseases due to these fungi. —*v.t. & v.i.* To affect or be affected with mildew. [< OE *mildēaw* honeydew] —**mil′dew·y** *adj.*
mile (mīl) *n.* **1** A unit of length equal to 5,280 feet or 1.609 kilometers: also **statute mile. 2** NAUTICAL MILE. **3** AIR MILE. [< L *mille* thousand]

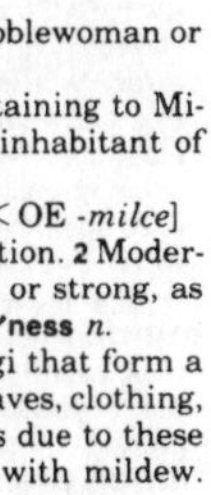

Milestone

mile·age (mī′lij) *n.* **1** Length or distance as measured in miles. **2** An allowance for expenses while traveling, reckoned at so much per mile. **3** Length of service, quality of performance, etc.; usefulness; advantage. Also **mil′age.**
mile·post (mīl′pōst′) *n.* A signpost indicating the distance in miles to or from a specified place.
mil·er (mī′lər) *n.* A person or animal who competes in a mile race.
mile·stone (mīl′stōn′) *n.* **1** A post, pillar, or stone set up to indicate distance in miles to or from a specified place. **2** An important event or turning point.
mi·lieu (mēl·yo͞o′; *Fr.* mē·lyœ′) *n.* Surroundings; environment. [F < OF *mi* middle + *lieu* place]
mil·i·tant (mil′ə·tənt) *adj.* **1** Actively engaged in war; fighting. **2** Aggressive or combative, esp. in support of a cause. —*n.* A militant person. [< L *militare* be a soldier] —**mil′i·tan·cy** *n.* —**mil′i·tant·ly** *adv.*
mil·i·ta·rism (mil′ə·tə·riz′əm) *n.* A policy or system emphasizing and exalting the military spirit and stressing the need of constant preparation for war. —**mil′i·ta·rist** *n.* —**mil′i·ta·ris′tic** *adj.* —**mil′i·ta·ris′ti·cal·ly** *adv.*
mil·i·ta·rize (mil′ə·tə·rīz′) *v.t.* **·rized, ·riz·ing 1** To imbue with militarism. **2** To prepare for war. —**mil′i·ta·ri·za′tion** *n.*
mil·i·tar·y (mil′ə·ter′ē) *adj.* **1** Of or relating to soldiers or to the army. **2** Made, performed, or supported by soldiers or the army. —*n.* **1** Armed forces; army: with *the.* **2** Army officials or officers: with *the.* [< L *miles, militis* soldier] —**mil′i·tar′i·ly** *adv.*
military attaché An army officer attached to his country's embassy or legation in a foreign country.
military intelligence 1 Information that is of military value to a country. **2** The branch of a government engaged in obtaining and interpreting such information.
military police A body of soldiers charged with police duties among troops.
mil·i·tate (mil′ə·tāt) *v.i.* **·tat·ed, ·tat·ing** To have influence: usu. with *against.* [< L *militare* be a soldier]
mi·li·tia (mə·lish′ə) *n.* An organized body of citizens, as the National Guard, drilled and equipped as soldiers but called to active service only in emergencies. —**mi·li′tia·man** (-mən) (*pl.* **·men**) [L, military service]
milk (milk) *n.* **1** The whitish emulsion secreted by the mammary glands of female mammals for the nourishment of their young, esp. cow's milk. **2** A liquid resembling milk, as coconut milk, latex, etc. —*v.t.* **1** To draw milk from the teats of (a female mammal). **2** To draw off as if by milking; extract: to *milk* sap from a tree. **3** To draw or extract something from: to *milk* someone of information. **4** To exploit; take advantage of. —*v.i.* **5** To milk a cow, etc. **6** To yield milk. [< OE *meolc, milc*]
milk-and-wa·ter (milk′ən·wô′tər, -wot′ər) *adj.* Weak and vacillating; namby-pamby.
milk leg A form of phlebitis sometimes affecting one or both legs of a woman after childbirth.
milk·maid (milk′mād′) *n.* DAIRYMAID.
milk·man (milk′man′) *n. pl.* **·men** (-men′) A man who sells or delivers milk.
milk of magnesia A white, aqueous suspension of hydroxide of magnesium, used as a laxative and antacid.
milk·shake (milk′shāk′) *n.* A drink made of chilled, flavored milk, and sometimes ice cream, mixed until frothy.
milk snake A small constrictor snake of North America having varying coloration in different areas. Also **milk adder.**
milk·sop (milk′sop′) *n.* A timid or unaggressive man.
milk sugar Lactose, the natural sugar in milk.
milk tooth Any of the first, temporary set of teeth in children and other young mammals.
milk·weed (milk′wēd′) *n.* Any of various plants having a milky juice.
milk·y (mil′kē) *adj.* **milk·i·er, milk·i·est 1** Containing or yielding milk. **2** Like milk, as in color. **3** Very mild or timid; spiritless. —**milk′i·ly** *adv.* —**milk′i·ness** *n.*
Milky Way *Astron.* A luminous band seen across the sky at night and composed of the aggregation of stars that contains the solar system; the Galaxy.
mill[1] (mil) *n.* **1** A machine for grinding grain into flour; also, the building in which this is done. **2** A machine for grinding or crushing hard substances of any kind: a pepper *mill.* **3** Any of various machines that by cutting, shaping, rolling, etc., treat or process raw material; usu. in combination: *sawmill.* **4** A factory. **5** Anything, as an agency or institution, that turns out products quickly and mechanically: a propaganda *mill.* **6** A difficult or painful experience: used chiefly in the phrase **through the mill.** —*v.t.* **1** To grind, shape, polish, roll, etc., in or with a mill.

2 To raise and ridge or corrugate the edge of (a coin). —*v.i.* 3 To undergo a milling process. 4 To move in a circular motion, as cattle: usu. with *about.* [<L *mola* millstone]

mill[2] (mil) *n.* The tenth part of a cent. [<L *millisimus* thousandth]

mill·dam (mil'dam') *n.* A dam built across a watercourse to raise its level sufficiently to turn a millwheel.

mil·len·ni·um (mi·len'ē·əm) *n. pl.* **·ni·a** (-ē·ə) or **·ums** 1 A period of a thousand years. 2 The thousand years during which Christ is to establish his kingdom on earth. *Rev.* 20:1–5. 3 Any period of happiness, peace, etc. [<L *mille* thousand + *annus* year] —**mil·len'ni·al** *adj.*

mil·le·pede (mil'ə·pēd) *n.* MILLIPEDE.

mil·le·pore (mil'ə·pôr, -pōr) *n.* Any of various reef-building corals forming massive concretions with numerous perforations. [<F *mille* thousand + *pore* pore]

mill·er (mil'ər) *n.* 1 One who keeps or tends a mill, esp. a flour mill. 2 A milling machine. 3 Any of various moths with scales forming a fine powder on their wings.

miller's thumb Any of various small, freshwater sculpins.

mil·let (mil'it) *n.* Any of various small-seeded cereal grasses cultivated for forage and as a cereal. [<L *milium*]

milli- *combining form* 1 The thousandth part of (a specified unit): *millimeter.* 2 A thousand: *millipede.* [<L *mille* a thousand]

mil·liard (mil'yərd, -yärd) *n.* & *adj.* See NUMBER. [<OF *milion* million]

mil·li·gram (mil'ə·gram) *n.* A metric unit of mass or weight equal to 10^{-6} (one millionth) kilogram or one thousandth of a gram. *Chiefly Brit. sp.* **mil'li·gramme.**

mil·li·li·ter (mil'ə·lē'tər) *n.* A metric unit of volume, equal to 10^{-3} (0.001) liter, or about 0.034 fluid ounce. *Chiefly Brit. sp.* **mil'li·li'tre.**

mil·li·me·ter (mil'ə·mē'tər) *n.* A metric unit of length equal to 10^{-3} (0.001) meter, or about 0.04 inch. *Chiefly Brit. sp.* **mil'li·me'ter.**

mil·li·ner (mil'ə·nər) *n.* A person who makes, trims, or sells women's hats. [<*Milaner* a man from Milan, Italy, who imported silks, etc.]

mil·li·ner·y (mil'ə·ner'ē, -nər·ē) *n.* 1 Women's hats. 2 The business of a milliner.

mil·lion (mil'yən) *n.* & *adj.* 1 See NUMBER. 2 An indefinitely great number. —*adj.* 1 Being a million. 2 Very many. [<Ital. *milione,* aug. of *mille* thousand]

mil·lion·aire (mil'yən·âr', mil'yən·âr') *n.* One whose wealth is valued at a million or more, as of dollars, pounds, etc.: also **mil'lion·naire'.**

mil·li·pede (mil'ə·pēd) *n.* Any of various arthropods having a cylindrical body marked by numerous segments bearing two pairs of walking legs. Also **mil'li·ped** (-ped). [<MILLI- + L *pes, pedis* foot]

mil·li·rem (mil'ə·rem') *n.* The thousandth part of a rem, the unit of absorbed radiation. [<MILLI- + rem]

mill·pond (mil'pond') *n.* A body of water dammed up to run a mill.

mill·race (mil'ra's') *n.* The sluice through which the water runs to turn a millwheel.

mill·stone (mil'stōn') *n.* 1 One of a pair of thick, heavy, stone disks for grinding something, as grain. 2 That which grinds or pulverizes. 3 A heavy burden. —**Syn.** 3 encumbrance, hindrance, onus, weight.

mill·wheel (mil'ʰwēl') *n.* The waterwheel that drives a mill.

mill·wright (mil'rīt') *n.* One who plans, builds, or installs machinery in a mill.

mi·lord (mi·lôrd') *n.* An English nobleman or gentleman. [<*my lord*]

milque·toast (milk'tōst) *n.* Any timid or excessively apologetic person. [<Caspar *Milquetoast,* a character created by H. T. Webster, 1885–1952, U.S. cartoonist]

mil·reis (mil'rās) *n.* 1 A former Brazilian monetary unit. 2 A former Portuguese monetary unit. [Pg., lit., a thousand reis]

milt (milt) *n.* 1 The sperm of a fish. 2 The reproductive organs of a male fish when filled with seminal fluid. —*v.t.* To impregnate (fish roe) with milt. [<OE *milte*]

mime (mīm) *n.* 1 The art or technique of portraying character or of narration by the use of body movement and without words. 2 A performer who practices this art; pantomimist. 3 In ancient Greece and Rome, a comedy or farce representing real persons or events. 4 An actor in such a mime. —*v.t.* & *v.i.* **mimed, mim·ing** To play (a part) using body movement only, without words. [<Gk. *mimos*] —**mim'er** *n.*

mim·e·o·graph (mim'ē·ə·graf', -gräf') *n.* An apparatus for reproducing copies of written or typewritten matter by means of a stencil. —*v.t.* To reproduce by means of a mimeograph. [<*Mimeograph,* a trade name]

mi·met·ic (mi·met'ik, mī-) *adj.* 1 Imitative. 2 Of, relating to, or exhibiting mimicry. [<Gk. *mimēsis* imitation] —**mi·met'i·cal·ly** *adv.*

mim·ic (mim'ik) *v.t.* **·icked, ·ick·ing** 1 To imitate the speech or actions of. 2 To copy closely; ape. 3 To have or assume the color, shape, etc., of. —*n.* One who or that which mimics. —*adj.* 1 Of the nature of mimicry. 2 Imitative. 3 Copying the real; simulated; mock: a *mimic* court. [<Gk. *mimos* mime] —**mim'i·cal** *adj.* —**mim'ick·er** *n.*

mim·ic·ry (mim'ik·rē) *n. pl.* **·ries** 1 The act or art of mimicking or imitating. 2 *Biol.* A superficial resemblance of one organism to another or to its environment, resulting in concealment or protection. —**Syn.** 1 imitation, parody, burlesque, take off.

mi·mo·sa (mi·mō'sə, -zə) *n.* Any of a genus of leguminous tropical herbs, shrubs, or trees, with feathery foliage and clusters of small flowers. [<L *mimus* mime; from its supposed mimicry of animal life]

min. mineralogy; minim(s); minimum; mining; minor; minute(s).

mi·na (mī'nə) *n.* MYNA. Also **mi'nah.**

min·a·ret (min'ə·ret') *n.* A high, slender tower attached to a Muslim mosque and surrounded by balconies, from which the summons to prayer is called by a muezzin. [<Ar. *manārah* lamp, lighthouse]

Minaret

min·a·to·ry (min'ə·tôr'ē, -tō'rē) *adj.* Threatening. Also **min'a·to'ri·al.** [<L *minari* threaten] —**min'a·to'ri·al·ly, min'a·to'ri·ly** *adv.*

mince (mins) *v.* **minced, minc·ing** *v.t.* 1 To cut or chop into small bits, as meat. 2 To subdivide minutely. 3 To diminish the force or strength of; moderate: He didn't *mince* words with her. 4 To do or express with affected primness or elegance. —*v.i.* 5 To walk with short steps or affected daintiness 6 To speak or behave with affected primness. —*n.* MINCEMEAT. [<L *minuere* lessen, make smaller] —**minc'er** *n.* —**minc'ing·ly** *adv.*

mince·meat (mins'mēt') *n.* A mixture of chopped apples, raisins, spices, etc., usu. without meat, used in mince pie. —**make mincement of** To destroy or defeat completely.

mince pie A pie made of mincement.

mind (mīnd) *n.* 1 The aggregate of all conscious and unconscious processes originating in and associated with the brain. 2 Memory: to bear in *mind.* 3 Opinion: to change one's *mind.* 4 Desire; inclination: to have a *mind* to leave. 5 Mental disposition, character, or temper: a cheerful *mind.* 6 Intellectual power or capacity: He has a fine *mind.* 7 An extremely intelligent person: She is one of the great *minds* of our time. 8 Sanity; reason: to lose one's *mind.* 9 Attention; concentration: to let one's *mind* wander. —**a piece of one's mind** An opinion, criticism, or rebuke very frankly or bluntly expressed. —**on one's mind** Occupying one's thoughts. —**out of one's mind** 1 Insane. 2 Deeply agitated; frantic. —**take one's mind off** To turn one's thoughts from. —*v.t.* 1 To pay attention to. 2 To be careful concerning: *Mind* your step. 3 To obey. 4 To care for; tend. 5 To object to; dislike: Do you *mind* the noise? 6 *Regional* To notice; perceive. 7 *Regional* To remember. —*v.i.* 8 To pay attention; take notice. 9 To be obedient. 10 To be concerned; care: I don't *mind.* 11 To be careful. [<OE *gemynd*] —**mind'er** *n.*

mind·ed (mīn'did) *adj.* 1 Having a specified kind of mind: *evil-minded.* 2 Inclined; disposed: usu. with *to.* 3 Keeping in mind; concerned about: *conservation-minded.*

mind·ful (mīnd′fəl) *adj.* Keeping in mind; heeding; aware. —**mind′ful·ly** *adv.* —**mind′ful·ness** *n.*

mind·less (mīnd′lis) *adj.* **1** Devoid of intelligence. **2** Not giving heed or attention; careless. —**mind′less·ly** *adv.*

mind reader One who claims to be able to know another person's thoughts. —**mind reading**

mine[1] (mīn) *n.* **1** An excavation in the earth for the extraction of coal, ore, precious stones, etc. **2** Any deposit of such material suitable for extraction. **3** *Mil.* **a** An underground tunnel dug beneath an enemy's fortifications. **b** A case of explosive material buried in the earth, or floating on or beneath the surface of water. **4** Any source of supply: a *mine* of ideas. —*v.* **mined, min·ing** *v.t.* **1** To dig (coal, ores, etc.) from the earth. **2** To dig into (the earth, etc.) for coal, ores, etc. **3** To make by digging, as a tunnel. **4** To obtain information, ideas, etc., from **5** UNDERMINE. **6** To place an explosive mine or mines in or under. —*v.i.* **7** To dig in a mine for coal, ores, etc. **8** To make a tunnel, etc., by digging **9** To place explosive mines. [<OF] —**min′er** *n.*

mine[2] (mīn) *pron.* **1** The possessive case of *I*, used predicatively: That book is *mine.* **2** The things of persons belonging or pertaining to me: His work is better than *mine.* —**of mine** Belonging or relating to me; my. —*pronominal adj. Archaic* My: *mine* eyes. [<OE *mīn*]

mine detector An instrument for locating explosive mines.

mine field An area in water or on land systematically planted with explosive mines.

mine layer A naval vessel provided with special equipment for the laying of mines.

min·er·al (min′ər·əl) *n.* **1** A naturally occurring substance obtained from the earth by mining, as ore, coal, granite, etc. **2** Any of certain elements essential to life and usu. having special physiological functions, as iron, calcium, iodine, etc. **3** Any substance that is neither animal nor vegetable. —*adj.* **1** Pertaining to, consisting of, or resembling minerals. **2** Impregnated with mineral constituents. [<L *minera* a mine]

min·er·al·ize (min′ər·əl·īz′) *v.t.* **·ized, ·iz·ing 1** To convert from a metal to a mineral, as iron to rust. **2** To convert to a mineral substance; petrify. **3** To impregnate with minerals or other inorganic substances.

min·er·al·o·gy (min′ə·ral′ə·jē, -räl′-) *n.* The science that deals with minerals. —**min′er·al′o·gist** *n.*

mineral oil 1 Any oil obtained from underground deposits, as petroleum. **2** A colorless, tasteless oil deprived from petroleum, used as a laxative.

mineral water Any water naturally or artificially impregnated with mineral salts or gases.

Mi·ner·va (mi·nûr′və) *Rom. Myth.* The goddess of wisdom, invention, and technical dexterity.

min·e·stro·ne (min′ə·strō′nē) *n.* A thick vegetable soup containing vermicelli, barley, etc., in a meat broth. [Ital.]

mine sweeper A ship equipped for the detection, destruction, and removal of marine mines.

Ming (ming) *n.* A Chinese dynasty (1368–1644), noted for its scholarship and artistic works, as porcelains.

min·gle (ming′gəl) *v.* **min·gled, min·gling** *v.t.* **1** To mix or unite together; blend. **2** To make or concoct by mixing. —*v.i.* **3** To be or become mixed, united, or closely joined. **4** To enter into company; mix or associate, as with a crowd. [<OE *mengan* to mix] —**min′gler** *n.*

min·i (min′ē) *n. pl.* **min·is 1** MINISKIRT. **2** *Informal* Anything smaller or shorter than others of its class. —*adj.* **·i·er, ·i·est** *Informal* Very small or miniaturized. [<MINI-]

mini- *combining form* Small; tiny; *miniskirt.* [<L *minimus* least, smallest]

min·i·a·ture (min′ē·ə·chər, min′ə·chər) *n.* **1** A portrait or painting of very small dimensions and delicate workmanship. **2** The art of painting such pictures. **3** A portrayal or copy of anything on a small scale. **4** Reduced scale, dimensions, or extent. —*adj.* Being or done on a small scale. [<L *miniare* paint red]

min·i·a·tur·ize (min′ē·ə·chər·īz, min′ə·chər·īz′) *v.t.* **·ized, ·iz·ing** To reduce the size of, as the parts of an instrument or machine. —**min′i·a·tur′i·za′tion** *n.*

min·i·bike (min′ē·bīk′) *n.* A small motorcycle with one seat.

min·i·cam (min′ə·kam) *n.* A small portable camera, usually one using 35-mm. film.

min·i·com·put·er (min′ē·kəm·pyōō′tər) *n.* A computer intermediate in size between a mainframe and a microcomputer.

min·im (min′im) *n.* **1** An apothecaries' measure, equal to 1/60 of a fluid dram, or about one drop. **2** *Music Brit.* A half note. **3** Something extremely small. —*adj.* Smallest. [<L *minimus* least, smallest]

min·i·mal (min′ə·məl) *adj.* Being or pertaining to a minimum; least; smallest. —**min′i·mal·ly** *adv.*

min·i·mize (min′ə·mīz) *v.t.* **·mized, ·miz·ing 1** To reduce to the smallest possible amount or degree. **2** To regard or represent as having the least possible importance, value, etc.

min·i·mum (min′ə·məm) *n. pl.* **·mums** or **·ma** (-mə) **1** The least possible quantity, amount, or degree. **2** The lowest degree, variation, etc., reached or recorded. —*adj.* Of, relating to, or being a minimum. [<L *minimus* smallest]

minimum wage A wage fixed by law or agreement as the smallest amount an employer may offer an employee in a specific group.

min·ing (mī′ning) *n.* The act, process, or business of extracting coal, ores, etc., from mines.

min·ion (min′yən) *n.* A servile favorite or follower: a term of contempt. [<F *mignon* darling]

min·i·scule (min′əs·kyōōl) *adj.* MINUSCULE.

min·i·ser·ies (min′ē·sir′ēz) *n.* A single program shown as a series over a sequence of several days.

min·i·skirt (min′i·skûrt′) *n.* A short skirt worn by women with the hemline well above the knee. [<MINI- + SKIRT]

min·is·ter (min′is·tər) *n.* **1** One who is authorized to preach, administer the sacraments, etc. in a church; clergyman. **2** The chief of a department of a government. **3** One commissioned to represent his government in diplomatic relations with another government, esp. one ranking next below an ambassador. **4** An agent of someone or something. —*v.i.* **1** To provide for the wants or needs of someone. **2** To be conductive; contribute. —*v.t.* **3** To administer or apply (a sacrament, aid, etc.) [<L, an attendant]

min·is·te·ri·al (min′is·tir′ē·əl) *adj.* **1** Of or pertaining to a minister or the ministry. **2** Pertaining to an administrative act performed on the basis of legal authority and not on the initiative of the agent. **3** Instrumental; causative.

min·is·trant (min′is·trənt) *adj.* Ministering.

min·is·tra·tion (min′is·trā′shən) *n.* **1** The act of serving as a minister. **2** Help; aid. —**min′is·tra′tive** *adj.*

min·is·try (min′is·trē) *n. pl.* **·tries 1** The clergy. **2** The office or duties of a minister of religion. **3** *Govt.* **a** Ministers collectively. **b** The office or duties of a minister; also, the building where his work is conducted. **c** A department presided over by a minister. **4** Ministration; service.

min·i·ver (min′ə·vər) *n.* A white fur, esp. such fur used in the Middle Ages for trimming. [<OF *menu vair,* lit., little spotted (fur)]

mink (mingk) *n.* **1** A small, semiaquatic, carnivorous mammal, related to the weasel and valued for its soft, thick, usu. brown fur. **2** The fur of this mammal. [<Scand.]

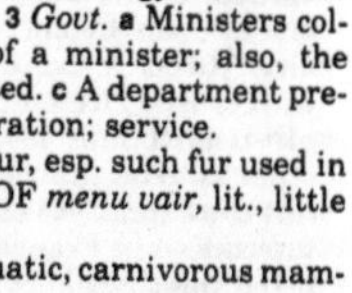

Mink

Minn. Minnesota.

min·ne·sing·er (min′ə·sing′ər) *n.* A lyric poet and singer of medieval Germany. [G<*Minne* love + *Singer* singer]

min·now (min′ō) *n.* **1** Any of various small cyprinoid fishes, often used as bait. **2** Any very small fish. Also **min′nie** (-nē). [<OE *myne* small fish]

Mi·no·an (mi·nō′ən) *adj.* Of or pertaining to an advanced Bronze Age civilization that flourished in Crete from about 3000 to 1100 B.C.

mi·nor (mī′nər) *adj.* **1** Less in number, quantity, or extent. **2** Of secondary importance or consideration. **3** Not yet of legal age. **4** In education, of or designating a course of study requiring fewer hours in class than a major field of study. **5** *Music* **a** Smaller than the corresponding major interval by a semitone. **b** Characterized by minor intervals, scales, or tones. **c** In a minor key. —*n.* **1** One not yet of legal age. **2** In education, a minor course of study. **3** *Music* A minor key, interval, etc. —*v.i.* In education, to study as a minor subject: with *in:* to *minor* in art. [L, less]

mi·nor·i·ty (mə·nôr′ə·tē, -nor′-, mī-) *n. pl.* **·ties 1** The smaller in number of two parts or parties. **2** The state or period of being under legal age. **3** MINORITY GROUP.

minority group A group comprising less than half of a population and differing from the others and esp. from a larger predominant group, as in race, religion, political affiliation, etc.

minor key *Music* A key or mode containing a minor third, characterized usu. by numerous chromatic tones.

minor league Any professional sports league not having the standing of a major league. —**mi′nor-league′** *adj.* —**mi′nor-lea′guer** *n.*

minor scale *Music* A scale, either diatonic or with various chromatic tones, containing a minor third.

minor suit In bridge, diamonds or clubs.

Mi·nos (mī′nəs, -nos) *Gk. Myth.* A king of Crete who became a judge of the lower world after his death.

Min·o·taur (min′ə·tôr) *Gk. Myth.* A monster, half man and half bull, who was confined in the Labyrinth where it was annually fed human flesh until killed by Theseus. [< Gk. *Minōs* Minos + *tauros* bull]

min·ster (min′stər) *n.* **1** A monastery church. **2** Any large church or cathedral. [< OE *mynster*]

min·strel (min′strəl) *n.* **1** In the Middle Ages, a wandering musician and poet, esp. one who composed and sang his own songs. **2** A performer in a minstrel show. **3** A poet; singer; musician. [< LL *ministerialis* servant, jester]

minstrel show A comic variety show of songs, dances, jokes, etc., given by a company of performers in blackface.

min·strel·sy (min′strəl·sē) *n. pl.* **·sies 1** The art of a minstrel. **2** Ballads or lyrics. **3** A troupe of minstrels.

mint[1] (mint) *n.* **1** A place where the coin of a country is manufactured. **2** A large sum or amount. **3** The source of a fabrication or invention. —*v.t.* **1** To make (money) by stamping; coin. **2** To invent or fabricate, as a word. —*adj.* Unused; in original condition: a *mint* stamp. [< L *Moneta* epithet of Juno, whose temple at Rome was used as a mint] —**mint′er** *n.*

mint[2] (mint) *n.* **1** Any of several aromatic herbs, esp. spearmint and peppermint. **2** A mint-flavored candy. [< Gk. *mintha*]

mint·age (min′tij) *n.* **1** The act of minting. **2** The coins so minted. **3** The duty paid for coining. **4** The impression placed upon a coin.

mint julep A drink made of bourbon or brandy mixed with crushed ice and sugar and flavored with fresh mint.

min·u·end (min′yo͞o·end) *n.* The number from which another is to be subtracted. [< L *minuere* lessen]

min·u·et (min′yo͞o·et′) *n.* **1** A stately dance for couples, introduced in France in the 17th century. **2** Music for or using the rhythm of this dance. [< L *minutus* small]

mi·nus (mī′nəs) *prep.* **1** Lessened by; less: 10 *minus* 5. **2** *Informal* Deprived of; lacking: *minus* a hat. —*adj.* **1** Of or used in subtraction. **2** Negative: a *minus* quantity. **3** Less than in quantity or quality: a B *minus.* —*n.* **1** MINUS SIGN. **2** A negative quantity. **3** A defect; drawback. [L, neut. of *minor* less]

min·us·cule (min′əs·kyo͞ol, mi·nus′kyo͞ol) *n.* **1** A small, cursive script used in the Middle Ages. **2** A letter in this script. **3** Any lower-case letter. —*adj.* **1** Of, like, or composed of minuscules. **2** Very small; miniature. [< L *minusculus,* dim. of *minor* less] • The spelling *miniscule,* often used in the sense of adj., def. 2, is apparently based on the erroneous assumption that the word is formed with the popular combining form *mini-,* meaning small.

minus sign A sign (−) denoting subtraction or a negative quantity.

min·ute[1] (min′it) *n.* **1** The 60th part of an hour; 60 seconds. **2** Any short period of time; moment. **3** The 60th part of a degree, indicated by the sign (′). **4** A memorandum. **5** *pl.* The official record of the proceedings of a meeting. —**up to the minute** In or having the latest style, equipment, etc. —*v.t.* **·ut·ed, ·ut·ing** To make a brief note of; record. [< L *minutus* small]

mi·nute[2] (mī·nyo͞ot′, mi-) *adj.* **1** Exceedingly small. **2** Unimportant; trifling. **3** Marked by exact, careful attention to details. [< L *minutus* small] —**mi·nute′ly** *adv.* —**mi·nute′ness** *n.* —**Syn. 1** infinitesimal, imperceptible, diminutive. **2** insignificant, inconsequential.

min·ute hand (min′it) The long hand of a timepiece that marks the minutes.

min·ute·man (min′it·man′) *n. pl.* **·men** (-men′) In the American Revolution, an armed citizen pledged to be ready for service at a minute's notice.

min·ute steak (min′it) A small, thin piece of beefsteak that can be cooked quickly.

mi·nu·ti·ae (mi·nyo͞o′shi·ē) *n.pl. of* **mi·nu′ti·a** (-shē·ə, -shə) Small or unimportant details. [L]

minx (mingks) *n.* A saucy, pert, or bold girl. [Prob. < LG *minsk* impudent woman]

Mi·o·cene (mī′ə·sēn) *adj. & n.* See GEOLOGY. [< Gk. *meiōn* less + *kainos* recent]

MIr. Middle Irish.

mir·a·cle (mir′ə·kəl) *n.* **1** An act or event that seems to transcend or contradict all known natural or scientific laws and is usu. thought to be supernatural in origin. **2** Any wonderful or amazing thing, fact, or event; a wonder. [< L *mirus* wonderful]

miracle play A medieval dramatic representation of the lives of the saints and their miracles.

mi·rac·u·lous (mi·rak′yə·ləs) *adj.* **1** Of the nature of a miracle; supernatural. **2** Surpassingly strange; wonderful. **3** Possessing the power to work miracles. —**mi·rac′u·lous·ly** *adv.* —**mi·rac′u·lous·ness** *n.*

mi·rage (mi·räzh′) *n.* **1** An optical illusion, as of an oasis in the desert or ships seen inverted in the air, that occurs when light rays from these usu. distant objects are refracted through layers of the atmosphere having different densities. **2** Anything that appears to be real or attainable but is not. [< L *mirari* wonder at]

mire (mīr) *n.* **1** Wet, swampy ground. **2** Deep mud or slush. —*v.* **mired, mir·ing** *v.t.* **1** To cause to sink or become stuck in mire. **2** To defile or soil with mud. **3** To entrap or involve. —*v.i.* **4** To sink in mire; bog down. [< ON *mȳrr*]

mirk (mûrk) *adj. & n.* MURK.

mir·ror (mir′ər) *n.* **1** Any of various reflecting surfaces, esp. glass when backed with a silver or aluminum coating. **2** Whatever reflects or clearly represents. **3** An exemplar; model. —*v.t.* To reflect or show an image of, as in a mirror. [< L *mirari* wonder at, admire]

mirth (mûrth) *n.* Gaiety of spirits; merriment; jollity. [< OE *myrig* pleasant, merry] —**mirth′ful** *adj.* —**mirth′ful·ly** *adv.* —**mirth′ful·ness** *n.*

MIRV multiple independently targeted reentry vehicle.

mir·y (mīr′ē) *adj.* **·i·er, ·i·est 1** Muddy; swampy. **2** Dirty. —**mir′i·ness** *n.*

mis- *prefix* Bad; badly; wrongly; unfavorably; dishonestly: *misdeed, misjudge.* [< OE *mis-* wrong]

mis·ad·ven·ture (mis′əd·ven′chər) *n.* An unlucky happening; misfortune. [< OF *mesaventure*]

mis·ad·vise (mis′əd·vīz′) *v.t.* **·vised, ·vis·ing** To advise wrongly or badly.

mis·al·li·ance (mis′ə·lī′əns) *n.* An undesirable alliance, esp. an unsuitable marriage.

mis·an·thrope (mis′ən·thrōp, miz′-) *n.* One who hates or distrusts his fellow men. Also **mis·an·thro·pist** (mis·an′thrə·pist). [< Gk. *misein* hate + *anthrōpos* a man] —**mis′an·throp′ic** (-throp′ik) or **·i·cal** *adj.* —**mis′an·throp′i·cal·ly** *adv.*

mis·an·thro·py (mis·an′thrə·pē) *n.* Hatred or distrust of mankind.

mis·ap·ply (mis′ə·plī′) *v.t.* **·plied, ·ply·ing** To use or apply incorrectly or dishonestly.

mis·ap·pre·hend (mis′ap·ri·hend′) *v.t.* To apprehend or understand wrongly.

mis·ap·pro·pri·ate (mis′ə·prō′prē·āt) *v.t.* **·at·ed, ·at·ing** To use or take improperly or dishonestly; misapply. —**mis′ap·pro′pri·a′tion** *n.*

mis·be·come (mis′bi·kum′) *v.t.* **·came, ·come, ·com·ing** To be unbecoming or not befitting to.

mis·be·got·ten (mis′bi·got′n) *adj.* Begotten unlawfully; illegitimate. Also **mis′be·got′.**

mis·be·have (mis′bi·hāv′) *v.i.* To behave badly. —**mis′·be·hav′ior** (-hāv′yər) *n.*

mis·be·lief (mis′bi·lēf′) *n.* A wrong or false belief.

mis·be·lieve (mis′bi·lēv′) *v.i.* **·lieved, ·liev·ing** To hold a false or unorthodox belief. **—mis′be·liev′er** *n.*

misc. miscellaneous; miscellany.

mis·cal·cu·late (mis·kal′kyə·lāt) *v.t. & v.i.* **·lat·ed, ·lat·ing** To calculate wrongly. **—mis′cal·cu·la′tion** *n.*

mis·call (mis·kôl′) *v.t.* To call by a wrong name.

mis·car·riage (mis·kar′ij) *n.* **1** *Med.* A premature delivery of a nonviable fetus; abortion. **2** Failure to reach a proper or just conclusion. **3** Failure to reach an expected destination.

mis·car·ry (mis·kar′ē) *v.i.* **·ried, ·ry·ing 1** To fail; go wrong. **2** To bring forth a fetus prematurely. **3** To fail to reach an expected destination, as mail.

mis·ce·ge·na·tion (mis′i·jə·nā′shən, mi·sej′ə-) *n.* Intermarriage or interbreeding between different races. [< L *miscere* mix + *genus* race] **—mis′ce·ge·net′ic** (-jə·net′ik) *adj.*

mis·cel·la·ne·ous (mis′ə·lā′nē·əs) *adj.* **1** Consisting of various things or types; varied; mixed. **2** Having various qualities, interests, or capabilities. [< L *miscellus* mixed] **—mis′cel·la′ne·ous·ly** *adv.* **—mis′cel·la′ne·ous·ness** *n.*

mis·cel·la·ny (mis′ə·lā′nē) *n. pl.* **·nies 1** *Often pl.* A collection of literary compositions on various subjects. **2** Any miscellaneous collection.

mis·chance (mis·chans′, -chäns′) *n.* An instance of bad luck; a mishap.

mis·chief (mis′chif) *n.* **1** Action or conduct, often playful in intent, that annoys or vexes. **2** A disposition to tease or annoy. **3** Damage, harm, or trouble. **4** A person or thing that causes harm, annoyance, etc. [< OF *meschever* come to grief]

mis·chie·vous (mis′chi·vəs) *adj.* **1** Inclined to tease, play pranks, annoy, etc. **2** Causing harm, injury, or damage. **3** Annoying; troublesome. **—mis′chie·vous·ly** *adv.* **—mis′chie·vous·ness** *n.*

mis·ci·ble (mis′i·bəl) *adj.* Capable of being mixed. [< L *miscere* mix] **—mis′ci·bil′i·ty** *n.*

mis·con·ceive (mis′kən·sēv′) *v.t. & v.i.* **·ceived, ·ceiv·ing** To conceive wrongly; misunderstand. **—mis′con·ceiv′er, mis′con·cep′tion** (-sep′shən) *n.*

mis·con·duct (mis′kən·dukt′) *v.t.* **1** To behave (oneself) improperly. **2** To mismanage. **—***n.* (mis·kon′dukt) **1** Improper conduct, esp. adultery. **2** Unlawful conduct. **3** Mismanagement, esp. if dishonest.

mis·con·strue (mis′kən·strōō′) *v.t.* **·strued, ·stru·ing** To interpret erroneously; misunderstand. **—mis′con·struc′tion** (-struk′shən) *n.*

mis·count (mis·kount′) *v.t. & v.i.* To count incorrectly. **—***n.* (mis′kount′) An incorrect count.

mis·cre·ant (mis′krē·ənt) *n.* **1** One who does evil. **2** *Archaic* An unbeliever. **—***adj.* **1** Villainous; evil. **2** *Archaic* Unbelieving. [< OF *mescreant* unbelieving]

mis·cue (mis·kyōō′) *n.* **1** In billiards, a stroke spoiled by a slipping of the cue. **2** *Informal* A mistake; slip. **—***v.i.* **·cued, ·cu·ing 1** To make a miscue. **2** In the theater, to miss one's cue or to answer another's cue.

mis·deal (mis·dēl)′) *v.t. & v.i.* **·dealt** (-delt′), **·deal·ing** In card games, to deal incorrectly. **—***n.* An incorrect deal.

mis·deed (mis·dēd′) *n.* A wrong or improper act. **—Syn.** offense, sin, transgression, violation.

mis·de·mean·or (mis′di·mē′nər) *n.* *Law* Any offense less serious than a felony.

mis·di·rect (mis′di·rekt′, -dī·rekt′) *v.t.* To direct or send wrongly. **—mis′di·rec′tion** *n.*

mis·do (mis·dōō′) *v.t. & v.i.* **·did, ·done, ·do·ing** To do wrongly; bungle. **—mis·do′er** *n.* **—mis·do′ing** *n.*

mis·em·ploy (mis′im·ploi′) *v.t.* To use wrongly or improperly. **—mis′em·ploy′ment** *n.*

mi·ser (mī′zər) *n.* Any stingy, grasping person, esp. one who hoards money avariciously. [< L *miser* wretched]

mis·er·a·ble (miz′ər·ə·bəl, miz′rə-) *adj.* **1** Wretchedly poor or unhappy. **2** Causing misery, discomfort, or unhappiness: a *miserable* cold. **3** Proceeding from or exhibiting misery: a bare, *miserable* room. **4** Of bad quality; inferior; worthless. **5** Pitiable; sorry. **6** Shameful; disgraceful. [< L *miserari* to pity] **—mis′er·a·ble·ness** *n.* **—mis′er·a·bly** *adv.* **—Syn. 4** unsatisfactory, shoddy, second-rate.

Mis·e·re·re (miz′ə·râr′ē, -rir′ē) *n.* **1** The 51st Psalm (the 50th in the Vulgate or Douay versions). **2** A musical setting of this psalm. [< L *misereri* have mercy]

mi·ser·ly (mī′zər·lē) *adj.* Of or like a miser; grasping; stingy. **—mi′ser·li·ness** *n.*

mis·er·y (miz′ər·ē) *n. pl.* **·er·ies 1** Extreme distress or suffering, esp. as a result of poverty, physical or mental pain, etc. **2** A cause of such distress or suffering. [< L *miser* wretched]

mis·fea·sance (mis·fē′zəns) *n.* *Law* The performance of a lawful act in an unlawful or culpably negligent manner. [< OF *mes-* mis- + *faire* do] **—mis·fea′sor** *n.*

mis·fire (mis·fīr′) *v.i.* **·fired, ·fir·ing 1** To fail to explode, fire, or become properly ignited, as a gun or engine. **2** To miss the desired or proper effect. **—***n.* An act or instance of misfiring.

mis·fit (mis·fit′) *v.t. & v.i.* **·fit·ted, ·fit·ting** To fail to fit or make fit. **—***n.* (mis′fit′, mis′fit′) **1** Something that fits badly. **2** (mis′fit′) A person who does not adjust well to his surroundings. **3** The act or condition of fitting badly.

mis·for·tune (mis·fôr′chən) *n.* **1** Bad luck; trouble; adversity. **2** An unlucky occurrence; calamity.

mis·give (mis·giv′) *v.* **·gave, ·giv·ing** *v.t.* **1** To make fearful, suspicious, or doubtful: My heart *misgives* me. **—***v.i.* **2** To be apprehensive.

mis·giv·ing (mis·giv′ing) *n.* A feeling of doubt, premonition, or apprehension.

mis·gov·ern (mis·guv′ərn) *v.t.* To govern or administer badly. **—mis·gov′ern·ment** *n.*

mis·guide (mis·gīd′) *v.t.* **·guid·ed, ·guid·ing** To guide wrongly in action or thought; mislead: *misguided* confidence. **—mis·guid′ance, mis·guid′er** *n.*

mis·han·dle (mis·han′dəl) *v.t.* **·dled, ·dling 1** To handle or treat roughly. **2** To manage badly.

mis·hap (mis′hap, mis·hap′) *n.* An unfortunate accident.

mish·mash (mish′mash′, -mosh′) *n.* A hodge-podge; jumble. Also **mish′-mash′**. [Reduplication of MASH]

mis·in·form (mis′in·fôrm′) *v.t.* To give false or erroneous information to. **—mis′in·form′ant, mis′in·for·ma′tion, mis′in·form′er** *n.*

mis·in·ter·pret (mis′in·tûr′prit) *v.t.* To interpret wrongly. **—mis′in·ter′pre·ta′tion, mis′in·ter′pret·er** *n.* **—Syn.** misunderstand, misconstrue, mistake, confuse.

mis·judge (mis·juj′) *v.t. & v.i.* To judge wrongly or unfairly. **—mis·judg′ment, mis·judge′ment** *n.*

mis·lay (mis·lā′) *v.t.* **·laid, ·lay·ing 1** To lay in a place not remembered; misplace. **2** To put down incorrectly: to *mislay* a carpet. **—mis·lay′er** *n.*

mis·lead (mis·lēd′) *v.t.* **·led** (-led′), **·lead·ing 1** To direct wrongly. **2** To lead astray or into error. **—mis·lead′er** *n.* **—mis·lead′ing** *adj.* **—mis·lead′ing·ly** *adv.*

mis·like (mis·līk′) *v.t.* **1** To dislike. **2** To displease. **—***n.* Dislike; disapproval.

mis·man·age (mis·man′ij) *v.t. & v.i.* **·aged, ·ag·ing** To manage badly or improperly. **—mis·man′age·ment, mis·man′ag·er** *n.*

mis·match (mis·mach′) *v.t.* To match badly or unsuitably. **—***n.* (mis′mach′) A bad or unsuitable match.

mis·mate (mis·māt′) *v.t. & v.i.* **·mated, ·mat·ing** To mate badly or inappropriately.

mis·name (mis·nām′) *v.t.* **·named, ·nam·ing** To call by a wrong name.

mis·no·mer (mis·nō′mər) *n.* **1** A name wrongly applied. **2** The giving of a wrong name to a person in a legal document. [< OF *mes-* wrongly + *nomer* name]

miso- *combining form* Hating; hatred: *misogynist.* [< Gk. *misein* hate]

mis·og·a·my (mis·og′ə·mē) *n.* Hatred of marriage. [< MISO- + -GAMY] **—mis·og′a·mist** *n.*

mis·og·y·ny (mis·oj′ə·nē) *n.* Hatred of women. [< MISO- + Gk. *gynē* woman] **—mis·og′y·nist** *n.* **—mis·og′y·nous** *adj.*

mis·place (mis·plās′) *v.t.* **·placed, ·plac·ing 1** To put in a wrong place. **2** To put in a place not remembered. **3** To give (trust, confidence, affection, etc.) unwisely.

mis·play (mis·plā′; *for n. also* mis′plā′) *v.t. & v.i.* In games, to play incorrectly or unskillfully. —*n.* A wrong play or move.

mis·print (mis·print′; *for n. also* mis′print′) *v.t.* To print incorrectly. —*n.* An error in printing.

mis·pri·sion (mis·prizh′ən) *n.* **1** *Law* Concealment of a crime, esp. of treason or felony. **2** Misconduct or neglect of duty by a public official. [< OF < *mes-* wrong + *prendre* take]

mis·prize (mis·prīz′) *v.t.* **prized, ·priz·ing** To undervalue the worth of; despise.

mis·pro·nounce (mis′prə·nouns′) *v.t. & v.i.* **·nounced, ·nounc·ing** To pronounce incorrectly or in a nonstandard way. —**mis′pro·nun′ci·a′tion** (-nun′sē·ā′shən) *n.*

mis·quote (mis·kwōt′) *v.t. & v.i.* **·quoted, ·quot·ing** To quote incorrectly. —**mis′quo·ta′tion** *n.*

mis·read (mis·rēd′) *v.t. & v.i.* **·read** (-red′), **·read·ing** (-rē′·ding) **1** To read incorrectly. **2** To misinterpret in or as if in reading.

mis·rep·re·sent (mis′rep·ri·zent′) *v.t.* **1** To give an incorrect or false representation of. **2** To represent (a client, constituent, etc.) badly. —**mis′rep·re·sen·ta′tion** *n.* —**mis′·rep·re·sen′ta·tive** *adj., n.*

mis·rule (mis·rōōl′) *v.t.* **·ruled, ·rul·ing** To rule unwisely or unjustly. —*n.* **1** Bad rule or government. **2** Disorder or riot.

miss[1] (mis) *n.* **1** A young girl: chiefly informal or in trade use: clothing for *misses.* **2** *Often cap.* A title used in speaking to an unmarried woman or girl: used without the name. See also Miss. [Contraction of MISTRESS]

miss[2] (mis) *v.t.* **1** To fail to hit or strike. **2** To fail to meet, catch, obtain, accomplish, see, hear, perceive, etc.: to *miss* the point. **3** To fail to attend, keep, perform, etc.: to *miss* church. **4** To overlook or fail to take advantage of, as an opportunity. **5** To discover or feel the loss or absence of. **6** To escape; avoid: He just *missed* being wounded. —*v.i.* **7** To fail to hit; strike wide of the mark. **8** To be unsuccessful; fail. —*n.* A failure to hit, find, attain, succeed, etc. [< OE *missan*]

Miss (mis) *n.* A title of address used with the name of a girl or an unmarried woman.

Miss. Mississippi.

mis·sal (mis′əl) *n.* The book containing all the prayers, lessons, etc., for the celebration of mass throughout the year. [< Med. L. *missalis (liber)* mass (book)]

mis·shape (mis·shāp′, mish·shāp′) *v.t.* **·shaped, ·shaped** or **·shap·en, ·shap·ing** To shape badly; deform. —**mis·shap′·en** *adj.*

mis·sile (mis′əl, *chiefly Brit.* mis′īl) *n.* **1** Any object, esp. a weapon, intended to be thrown or discharged, as a spear, bullet, arrow, etc. **2** GUIDED MISSILE. [< L *missus,* pp. of *mittere* send]

mis·sile·ry (mis′əl·rē) *n.* The science and technology of designing, building, and launching missiles, esp. guided missiles. Also **mis′sil·ry.**

miss·ing (mis′ing) *adj.* **1** Absent; lost; gone. **2** *Mil.* Absent: said of soldiers after combat whose fate has not been definitely ascertained.

missing link **1** Something lacking to complete a series. **2** A hypothetical creature assumed to be intermediate in development between man and the anthropoid ape.

mis·sion (mish′ən) *n.* **1** Any group of people delegated or sent to perform some specific task, business, or service. **2** The specific business, task, or service any person or group is sent or authorized to accomplish. **3** A group authorized by its government to conduct diplomatic, business, or political negotiations in a foreign country. **4** The foreign embassy or legation of an ambassador or envoy. **5** A group of missionaries authorized by a church to convert, teach, or aid the people of a foreign country or region. **6** The headquarters used or the specific region served by such a group of missionaries. **7** *pl.* The organized work of such missionaries. **8** A special series of religious services designed to convert people to or stimulate their faith in Christianity or another religion. **9** An educational, religious, or welfare center for the underprivileged. **10** That goal or task which one is or feels destined to accomplish in life. **11** *Mil.* A definite task assigned to an individual or unit, esp. a flight operation of a single aircraft or formation. —*adj.* Pertaining or belonging to a mission. —*v.t.* **1** To send on a mission. **2** To establish a mission in. [< L *missus,* pp. of *mittere* send] —**mis′sion·er** *n.*

mis·sion·ar·y (mish′ən·er′ē) *n. pl.* **·ar·ies** **1** A person sent to propagate religion or to do educational or charitable work, esp. in some foreign country or region. **2** One who spreads any new system or doctrine. —*adj.* Of, pertaining to, or like missions or missionaries.

Mis·sis·sip·pi·an (mis′ə·sip′ē·ən) *adj.* **1** Of or pertaining to the Mississippi River. **2** See GEOLOGY. —*n.* See GEOLOGY.

mis·sive (mis′iv) *n.* A letter or written message. [< L *missus,* pp. of *mittere* send]

mis·speak (mis·spēk′) *v.t. & v.i.* **·spoke, ·speak·ing** To speak or say incorrectly.

mis·spell (mis·spel′) *v.t. & v.i.* **·spelled** or **·spelt, ·spell·ing** To spell incorrectly.

mis·spell·ing (mis·spel′ing) *n.* An incorrect spelling.

mis·spend (mis·spend′) *v.t.* **·spent, ·spend·ing** To spend wastefully or wrongly.

mis·state (mis·stāt′) *v.t.* **·stat·ed, ·stat·ing** To state wrongly or falsely. —**mis·state′ment** *n.*

mis·step (mis·step′) *n.* **1** A false or wrong step. **2** An error in conduct; blunder.

mis·sus (mis′əz) *n. Informal* Wife: used with *the.* Also **mis′sis.** [Alter. of MISTRESS]

mist (mist) *n.* **1** An aggregation of fine drops of water in the atmosphere, similar to but less dense than fog. **2** Any suspension or cloud of small particles, as of dust. **3** Anything that dims or obscures, esp. a watery film before one's eyes. —*v.i.* **1** To be or become dim or misty; blur. **2** To rain in very fine drops. —*v.t.* **3** To make dim or misty; blur. [< OE]

mis·tak·a·ble (mis·tāk′ə·bəl) *adj.* Capable of being misunderstood or mistaken. —**mis·tak′a·bly** *adv.*

mis·take (mis·tāk′) *n.* An error in action, judgment, perception, impression, etc. —*v.* **·took, ·tak·en, ·tak·ing** *v.t.* **1** To understand wrongly; misinterpret. **2** To take (a person or thing) to be another. —*v.i.* **3** To make a mistake. [< ON *mis-* wrongly + *taka* take]

mis·tak·en (mis·tā′kən) *adj.* **1** Incorrect; wrong; erroneous: a *mistaken* idea. **2** Wrong in opinion, judgment, understanding, etc.: You are *mistaken.* —**mis·tak′en·ly** *adv.*

mis·ter (mis′tər) *n. Informal* Sir: used without the name. [Var. of MASTER]

Mis·ter (mis′tər) *n.* Master: a title of address prefixed to the name and to some official titles of a man: commonly written *Mr.*: *Mr.* Darwin; *Mr.* Chairman.

mis·tle·toe (mis′əl·tō) *n.* **1** An evergreen shrub with yellowish green leaves and poisonous white berries, parasitic on various trees. **2** A sprig of this hung as a Christmas decoration. [< OE *misteltān* mistletoe twig]

Mistletoe

mis·took (mis·tŏŏk′) *p.t.* of MISTAKE.

mis·tral (mis′trəl, *Fr.* mēs·trȧl′) *n.* A cold, dry, and violent NW wind blowing mostly through the S provinces of France. [F, lit., master (wind)]

mis·treat (mis·trēt′) *v.t.* To treat badly or unkindly; abuse. —**mis·treat′ment** *n.*

mis·tress (mis′tris) *n.* **1** A woman in authority or control, as: **a** The head of a household, institution, or estate. **b** An employer or supervisor of servants. **c** An animal owner. **2** *Chiefly Brit.* A female schoolteacher. **3** A woman with whom a man has an unlawful but usu. a long-lasting sexual relationship. **4** *Often cap.* Something having supremacy or power and personified as feminine. **5** A woman who is well skilled in or has mastered anything. [< OF *maistre* master]

Mis·tress (mis′tris) *n.* A title of address formerly applied to women, now generally supplanted by *Mrs.* or *Miss.*

mis·tri·al (mis·trī′əl) *n. Law* A trial that is void because of legal errors or because the jury cannot agree on a verdict.

mis·trust (mis·trust′) *n.* Lack of trust or confidence. —*v.t. & v.i.* To regard (someone or something) with suspicion or doubt. —**mis·trust′ful** *adj.* —**mis·trust′ful·ly** *adv.* —**mis·trust′·ful·ness** *n.* —**Syn.** *v.* distrust, suspect, doubt, disbelieve.

mist·y (mis′tē) *adj.* **mist·i·er, mist·i·est** 1 Containing, characterized by, or like mist. 2 Dimmed or obscured by or as by mist. 3 Lacking clarity; indistinct; vague. —**mist′i·ly** *adv.* —**mist′i·ness** *n.*

mis·un·der·stand (mis′un·dər·stand′, mis·un′-) *v.t.* & *v.i.* **·stood, ·stand·ing** To understand wrongly; misinterpret.

mis·un·der·stand·ing (mis′un·dər·stan′ding, mis·un′-) *n.* 1 A mistake as to meaning or motive. 2 A quarrel; disagreement.

mis·un·der·stood (mis′un·dər·stŏŏd′, mis·un′-) *adj.* 1 Wrongly understood or interpreted. 2 Not appreciated at true worth.

mis·us·age (mis·yōō′sij, -zij) *n.* 1 Wrong or improper use, as of a word. 2 Ill-treatment; abuse.

mis·use (mis·yōōs′) *n.* 1 Wrong or improper use; misapplication. 2 Ill-treatment; abuse. —*v.t.* (mis·yōōz′) **·used, ·us·ing** 1 To use or apply wrongly or improperly. 2 To abuse; maltreat. —**mis·us′er** *n.*

mis·val·ue (mis·val′yōō) *v.t.* **·ued, ·u·ing** To value wrongly.

mite[1] (mīt) *n.* Any of various minute arachnids including forms that are parasitic on man or on specific animals or plants. [<OE *mīte*] —**mit′y** *adj.*

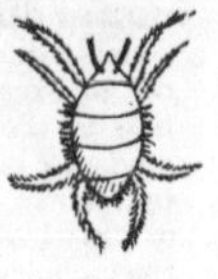

Mite

mite[2] (mīt) *n.* 1 Any very small amount, particle, or creature. 2 Any very small coin or sum of money. [<MDu. *mīte*]

mi·ter (mī′tər) *n.* 1 A tall, ornamental headdress terminating in two peaks, worn by popes, archbishops, bishops, and abbots. 2 The office or rank of a bishop. 3 MITER JOINT. 4 Either of the two beveled angles forming a miter joint. —*v.t.* 1 To confer a miter upon; raise to the rank of bishop. 2 To make or join with a miter joint. [<Gk. *mitra* belt, turban] —**mi′ter·er** *n.*

Miter *def. 1*

miter joint A joint made by the joining together of two pieces of material beveled at angles, as at the corner of a picture frame.

mit·i·gate (mit′ə·gāt) *v.t.* & *v.i.* **·gat·ed, ·gat·ing** To make or become milder or less severe; moderate. [<L *mitis* mild + *agere* do, drive] —**mit′i·ga′tion, mit′i·ga′tor** *n.* —**mit′i·ga′tive, mit′i·ga·to′ry** (-gə·tôr′ē, -tō′rē) *adj.*

mi·to·sis (mī·tō′sis) *n.* The type of cell division occurring in somatic cells, in which the chromosomes duplicate themselves longitudinally and then separate, so that each daughter cell has the same number and kind of chromosomes as the original cell. [<Gk. *mitos* thread + -OSIS] —**mi·tot·ic** (mī·tot′ik) *adj.* —**mi·tot′i·cal·ly** *adv.*

mi·tral (mī′trəl) *adj.* 1 Pertaining to or like a miter. 2 Of or pertaining to the mitral valve.

mitral valve *Anat.* A membranous valve between the left atrium and the left ventricle of the heart that functions to prevent the backflow of blood into the atrium.

mi·tre (mī′tər) *n.* & *v.* **·tred, ·tring** MITER.

mitt (mit) *n.* 1 A woman's glove that does not extend over the fingers. 2 In baseball, a padded glove used by the catcher and the first baseman. 3 MITTEN (def. 1). 4 *pl. Slang* The hands. 5 *Slang* A boxing glove.

mit·ten (mit′n) *n.* 1 A covering for the hand, encasing the four fingers together and the thumb separately. 2 MITT (def. 1). [<MF *mitaine*]

mix (miks) *v.* **mixed** or **mixt, mix·ing** *v.t.* 1 To put together in one mass or composite; blend. 2 To make by combining ingredients: to *mix* dough. 3 To combine or join: to *mix* business with pleasure. 4 To cause to associate or mingle: to *mix* social classes together. 5 HYBRIDIZE. —*v.i.* 6 To be mixed or blended. 7 To associate; get along. 8 To take part; become involved. —**mix up** 1 To blend thoroughly. 2 To confuse. 3 To implicate or involve. —*n.* 1 The act of mixing. 2 A mixture, esp. a commercial mixture of prepared ingredients: a cake *mix.* 3 A beverage, as soda or ginger ale, used in mixed drinks. 4 *Telecom.* The correct blending of two or more input signals into a composite signal. 5 A proportion, as of things that make up a mixture: evaluating the *mix* of black and white students in the city schools. 6 A combination of various elements; mixture: a movie providing a heady *mix* of violence, sex, and glamour. [<L *mixtus,* pp. of *miscere* mix]

mixed (mikst) *adj.* 1 Mingled or blended in a single mass. 2 Made up of different or incongruous elements, races, religions, qualities, etc. 3 Containing persons of both sexes: a *mixed* foursome.

mixed bag A mixture or assortment of miscellaneous elements.

mixed marriage Marriage between persons of different religions or races.

mixed number A number, as 3½, which is the sum of an integer and a fraction.

mixed-up (mikst′up′) *adj.* Confused or disordered.

mix·er (mik′sər) *n.* 1 One who or that which mixes. 2 *Informal* A person with reference to his ability to get along well in various groups. 3 *Informal* A party for getting acquainted with others.

mix·ture (miks′chər) *n.* 1 The act of mixing or the condition of being mixed. 2 Anything made or resulting from mixing things of different qualities, kinds, or types: a tea *mixture.* 3 *Chem.* A substance containing in variable proportions two or more ingredients which retain their individual properties and which may be separated without chemical change.

mix-up (miks′up′) *n.* 1 A confusion; muddle. 2 *Informal* A fight.

miz·zen (miz′ən) *n. Naut.* 1 MIZZENMAST. 2 A triangular sail set on the mizzenmast. —*adj.* Of or pertaining to the mizzenmast. Also **miz′en.** [<Ital. *mezzano* middle]

miz·zen·mast (miz′ən·məst, -mast′, -mäst′) *n. Naut.* 1 The mast aft or next aft of the mainmast. 2 The shorter of the two masts of a ketch or yawl.

mks, m.k.s., M.K.S. meter-kilogram-second (system).

mkt. market.

ML, ML., M.L. Medieval (or Middle) Latin.

ml, ml. milliliter(s).

MLG, MLG., M.L.G. Middle Low German.

Mlle, Mlle. Mademoiselle.

Mlles, Mlles. Mesdemoiselles.

MM. Messieurs.

mm, mm. millimeter(s).

Mme, Mme. Madame.

Mmes, Mmes. Mesdames.

MN Minnesota (P.O. abbr.).

Mn manganese.

mne·mon·ic (ni·mon′ik) *adj.* Pertaining to, aiding, or designed to aid the memory. Also **mne·mon′i·cal.** [<Gk. *mnēmōn* mindful]

mne·mon·ics (ni·mon′iks) *n. pl. (construed as sing.)* The science of or the techniques used in memory improvement.

-mo *suffix Printing* Folded into a (specified) number of leaves: said of a sheet of paper: 12*mo* or *duodecimo.* [L]

MO Missouri (P.O. abbr.).

M.O. mail order; Medical Officer; money order.

Mo molybdenum.

Mo. Missouri; Monday.

mo. month(s); monthly.

mo·a (mō′ə) *n.* Any of various extinct, ostrichlike birds of New Zealand. [<native name]

Mo·ab (mō′ab) *n.* An ancient country in the upland area east of the Dead Sea. —**Mo·ab·ite** (mō′əb·īt) *adj., n.*

moan (mōn) *n.* 1 A low mournful sound indicative of grief or pain. 2 A similar sound. —*v.i.* 1 To utter moans of grief or pain. 2 To make a low, mournful sound, as wind in trees. —*v.t.* 3 To lament; bewail. 4 To say with a moan. [ME *mone*]

moat (mōt) *n.* A deep, broad ditch, usu. filled with water, at the outside base of a fortress wall or castle. —*v.t.* To surround with or as with a moat. [<OF *mote* embankment]

mob (mob) *n.* 1 A disorderly or lawless crowd. 2 Any large crowd. 3 The lowest class of people; the masses; populace. 4 *Slang* A gang, as of criminals. —*v.t.* **mobbed, mob·bing 1** To attack in a mob. 2 To crowd around and annoy. 3 To crowd into, as a hall. [<L *mobile (vulgus)* movable (crowd)] — **mob′ber** *n.* —**mob′bish** *adj.* —**mob′bish·ly** *adv.*

mo·bile (mō′bəl, -bēl) *adj.* 1 Characterized by freedom of movement; movable. 2 Flowing freely. 3 Changing easily or quickly, as in expression, mood, etc. 4 Easily adaptable; versatile: a *mobile* intelligence. 5 Having or permitting movement or change in social status: a *mobile* society. 6 Designating a mobile. —*n.* (mō′bēl) A form of sculpture having freely moving parts, usu. suspended from rods, wires, etc. [<L *mobilis* movable] —**mo·bil·i·ty** (mō·bil′ə·tē) *n.*

mobile home *U.S.* A movable living unit, originally conceived of as a trailer but now designed more like a ranch house, which can be connected to utilities and is often put on a foundation as a permanent dwelling.

mo·bi·lize (mō′bə·līz) *v.* **-lized, -liz·ing** *v.t.* 1 To make ready for war, as an army, industry, etc. 2 To assemble for use; organize. 3 To put into circulation, movement, or use. —*v.i.* 4 To undergo mobilization. *Brit. sp.* **mo′bi·lise.** —**mo′·bi·li·za′tion** (-lə·zā′shən, -lī·zā′-) *n.*

mob·ster (mob′stər) *n. Slang* A gangster.

moc·ca·sin (mok′ə·sin) *n.* 1 A heelless foot covering made of soft leather or buckskin, formerly worn by North American Indians. 2 A shoe or slipper somewhat like a moccasin. 3 COTTONMOUTH. [<Algon.]

moccasin flower LADYSLIPPER.

mo·cha (mō′kə) *n.* 1 Any choice coffee, esp. one originally grown in Mocha, Arabia. 2 A coffee or coffee and chocolate flavoring. 3 A fine sheepskin leather used for making gloves.

mock (mok) *v.t.* 1 To treat or address scornfully or derisively; hold up to ridicule. 2 To ridicule by imitation; mimic derisively. 3 To deceive; delude. 4 To defy; make futile. 5 To imitate; counterfeit. —*v.i.* 6 To express or show ridicule, scorn, or contempt; scoff. —*adj.* Imitation; sham. —*n.* 1 An act of mocking; a jeer. 2 One who or that which is mocked. 3 An imitation; counterfeit. [<OF *mocquer*] — **mock′er** *n.* —**mock′ing·ly** *adv.*

mock·er·y (mok′ər·ē) *n. pl.* **-er·ies** 1 Derisive or contemptuous action or speech. 2 A person or thing laughed at or derided. 3 A deceitful or contemptible imitation: a *mockery* of justice. 4 Something ridiculously inappropriate or inadequate.

mock-he·ro·ic (mok′hi·rō′ik) *adj.* Imitating or satirizing the heroic manner, style, attitude, or character.

mock·ing·bird (mok′ing·bûrd′) *n.* A long-tailed, gray songbird common in the SE U.S., noted for imitating the songs of other birds.

Mockingbird

mock orange Any of a genus of hardy, deciduous shrubs with fragrant white flowers resembling orange blossoms.

mock-tur·tle soup (mok′tûr′·təl) Soup prepared from calf's head or other meat, and flavored to resemble green turtle soup.

mock·up (mok′up′) *n.* A model, usu. full-scale, as of a structure, machine, or apparatus, for purposes of study, testing, etc.

mod (mod) *adj.* Bold, flamboyant, and unconventional, as in dress or behavior. —*n. Sometimes cap.* One who dresses or behaves in a flamboyant or unconventional manner. [<MODERN]

mod. moderate; moderato; modern.

mo·dal (mōd′l) *adj.* Of or denoting a mode, esp. a mode of grammar, a mode in music, or a statistical mode. — **mo·dal′i·ty** (-dal′ə·tē) *n.* —**mo′dal·ly** *adv.*

modal auxiliary An auxiliary verb used with and indicating the mood of a principal verb. Modal auxiliaries are *may, might, must, can, would,* and *should.*

mode (mōd) *n.* 1 Manner, way, or method of acting, being, doing, etc. 2 Prevailing style or fashion of dress, behavior, etc. 3 *Gram.* MOOD. 4 *Music* Any of the seven possible permutations of the tones of a major scale in which the original order is preserved. 5 *Stat.* That value, magnitude, or score which occurs the greatest number of times in a given series of observations; norm. [<L *modus* measure, manner]

mod·el (mod′l) *n.* 1 An object, usu. in miniature, representing accurately something already existing, or something to be made or tested. 2 One who or that which serves as an example or pattern of excellence. 3 A person who poses for painters, sculptors, etc. 4 A person employed to wear articles of clothing to display them. 5 A type, style, or design. 6 An analogue or analogy: a mathematical *model* of an atom. —*v.* **-eled** or **-elled, -el·ing** or **-el·ling** *v.t.* 1 To plan or fashion after a model or pattern. 2 To make a model of. 3 To fashion; make. 4 To display by wearing, as an article of clothing. —*v.i.* 5 To make a model or models. 6 To pose or serve as a model (defs. 3 and 4). 7 To assume the appearance of natural form. —*adj.* 1 Serving or used as a model. 2 Worthy or suitable to be used as a model. [<L *modus* measure, manner] —**mod′el·er, mod′el·ler** *n.*

mo·dem (mō′dem) *n.* An electronic device that converts computer digital signals to analog form, and vice versa, so that information can be sent and received by telephone.

mod·er·ate (mod′ər·it) *adj.* 1 Keeping or kept within reasonable limits; not extreme. 2 Not strongly partisan, radical, or excessive: said of political, social, or religious beliefs or those holding such beliefs. 3 Mild; temperate: a *moderate* climate. 4 Medium or average, as in quality, extent, effect, etc. —*n.* A person of moderate views, opinions, or practices. —*v.* (mod′ə·rāt) **-at·ed, -at·ing** *v.t.* 1 To reduce the violence, severity, etc., of; make less extreme; restrain. 2 To preside over. —*v.i.* 3 To become less intense or violent; abate. 4 To act as moderator. [<L *moderare* regulate] — **mod′er·ate·ly** *adv.* —**mod′er·ate·ness** *n.*

mod·er·a·tion (mod′ə·rā′shən) *n.* 1 The quality or state of being moderate. 2 The act of moderating. —**in moderation** Within reasonable limits.

mod·e·ra·to (mod′ə·rä′tō) *adj. & adv. Music* In moderate time; moderately. [Ital.]

mod·er·a·tor (mod′ə·rā′tər) *n.* 1 One who or that which moderates. 2 One who presides over a meeting, debate, etc. 3 *Physics* A substance, as heavy water or graphite, that slows down neutrons in a nuclear reactor.

mod·ern (mod′ərn) *adj.* 1 Of, pertaining to, or characteristic of the present or most recent past; contemporary. 2 *Usu. cap.* Of, pertaining to, or characteristic of the present or most recent development of a language: *Modern* English. 3 Up-to-date: the most *modern* equipment. —*n.* 1 A person living in modern times or having modern views, characteristics, etc. 2 *Printing* A style of typeface characterized by contrasting heavy downstrokes and thin cross-strokes. [<LL *modernus* recent <L *modo* just now]

Modern English The English language after 1500.

Modern Greek The language of Greece since 1500.

mod·ern·ism (mod′ərn·iz′əm) *n.* 1 A practice, idiom, thought or behavior pattern, art form, etc., characteristic of modern times. 2 *Often cap.* The tendency in religious thought to reinterpret certain theological beliefs and teachings so as to be consistent with new scientific and philosophical learning. —**mod′ern·ist** *adj., n.* —**mod′ern·is′tic** *adj.* —**mod′ern·is′ti·cal·ly** *adv.*

mo·der·ni·ty (mə·dûr′nə·tē) *n. pl.* **-ties** 1 The quality or condition of being modern. 2 Something modern.

mod·ern·ize (mod′ərn·īz) *v.t. & v.i.* **-ized, -iz·ing** To make or become modern in ideas, standards, methods, etc. — **mod′ern·i·za′tion, mod′ern·iz′er** *n.*

mod·est (mod′ist) *adj.* 1 Having a moderate or unpretentious opinion of one's worth, ability, etc. 2 Characterized by reserve, propriety, or purity in dress, actions, speech, etc. 3 Not excessive; moderate; limited: a *modest* income. [<L *modestus* moderate] —**mod′est·ly** *adv.*

mod·es·ty (mod′is·tē) *n.* 1 Freedom from vanity. 2 Propriety and decorum, as in dress or behavior. 3 Moderation.

mod·i·cum (mod′i·kəm) *n. pl.* **-cums** or **-ca** (-kə) A moderate or small amount. [<L *modus* measure] —**Syn.** bit, little, minimum, smidgen.

mod·i·fi·ca·tion (mod′ə·fə·kā′shən) *n.* 1 The act of modifying, or the state of being modified. 2 A qualification, as in meaning. 3 A slight change or improvement, as in form or function. 4 A reduction or moderation.

mod·i·fi·er (mod′ə·fī′ər) *n.* 1 One who or that which modifies. 2 *Gram.* A word, phrase, or clause that modifies another word or group of words.

mod·i·fy (mod′ə·fī) *v.* **·fied, ·fy·ing** *v.t.* 1 To make somewhat different in form, character, etc.; vary. 2 To reduce in degree or extent; moderate. 3 *Gram.* To qualify the meaning of; restrict; limit. —*v.i.* 4 To be or become modified; change. [< L *modus* measure + *facere* make]

mod·ish (mō′dish) *adj.* In the current mode or style. —**mod′ish·ly** *adv.* —**mod′ish·ness** *n.* —**Syn.** fashionable, stylish, à la mode.

mo·diste (mō·dēst′) *n.* A woman who makes or deals in fashionable women's clothing. [F]

Mod. L. Modern Latin.

mod·u·late (moj′ōō·lāt) *v.* **·lat·ed, ·lat·ing** *v.t.* 1 To vary the tone, inflection, or pitch of. 2 To regulate or adjust. 3 *Music* To change or cause to change to a different key. 4 To intone or sing. 5 *Electronics* To vary a parameter, as frequency or amplitude of (a carrier wave). —*v.i.* 6 *Electronics* To alter a parameter of a carrier wave. 7 *Music* To make a transition from one key to another. [< L *modulari* regulate] —**mod′u·la·to′ry** (-lə·tôr′ē, -tō′rē) *adj.*

mod·u·la·tion (moj′ōō·lā′shən) *n.* 1 The act of modulating, or the state of being modulated. 2 A change in pitch or stress in the voice. 3 *Music* A transition from one key to another. 4 *Telecom.* **a** The changing of one or more of the parameters of a carrier wave. **b** The information transmitted by the carrier wave as a result of this.

mod·u·la·tor (moj′ōō·lā′tər) *n.* One who or that which modulates.

mod·ule (moj′ōōl) *n.* 1 A standard or unit of measurement. 2 *Archit.* A unit of measure, usu. the size of a single part of a construction, by which the proportions of the whole are determined. 3 A standard structural component repeatedly used, as in a building, computer, etc.: cubic *modules* used in the design of a table. 4 A preassembled, self-contained unit, usu. a component or subassembly of a larger structure: a housing *module;* a lunar *module.* [< L *modulus* < *modus* measure] —**mod′u·lar** *adj.*

mo·dus op·er·an·di (mō′dəs op′ə·ran′dē, -dī) A manner of operation or procedure. [L]

modus vi·ven·di (vi·ven′dē, -dī) 1 A manner of living. 2 A temporary arrangement pending a final settlement. [L]

mo·gul (mō′gul, mō·gul′) *n.* Any great or pretentious personage. —**Syn.** magnate, bigwig, big wheel, personage.

Mo·gul (mō′gul, mō·gul′) *n.* A Mongol; Mongolian; esp. one of the Mongol conquerors of Hindustan. Also **Mo·ghul′.**

mo·hair (mō′hâr) *n.* 1 The hair of the Angora goat. 2 A fabric made of mohair pile with a cotton or wool backing. [< Ar. *mukhayyar*]

Mo·ham·me·dan (mō·ham′ə·dən) *adj.* Of or pertaining to Mohammed or to his religion and institutions. —*n.* A follower of Mohammed or believer in Islam; a Muslim.

Mo·ham·me·dan·ism (mō·ham′ə·dən·iz′əm) *n.* The religion founded by Mohammed; Islam.

Mo·ha·ve (mō·hä′vē) *n.* A member of a tribe of North American Indians formerly living along the Colorado River. —*adj.* Of or pertaining to this tribe.

Mo·hawk (mō′hôk) *n.* 1 One of a tribe of North American Indians of Iroquoian stock, formerly ranging from the Mohawk River to the St. Lawrence. 2 The Iroquoian language of this tribe.

Mo·he·gan (mō·hē′gən) *n.* 1 One of a tribe of North American Indians of Algonquian linguistic stock, formerly living in Connecticut. 2 MAHICAN.

Mo·hi·can (mō·hē′kən) *n.* MAHICAN.

moi·dore (moi′dôr, -dōr) *n.* A former Portuguese or Brazilian gold coin.

moi·e·ty (moi′ə·tē) *n. pl.* **·ties** 1 A half. 2 An indefinite portion. [< L *medius* half]

moil (moil) *v.i.* To work hard; toil; drudge. —*n.* 1 Confusion; trouble. 2 Toil; drudgery. [< L *mollis* soft] —**moil′er** *n.* —**moil′ing·ly** *adv.*

moi·ré (mwä·rā′) *adj.* Having a wavelike or watered appearance, as certain fabrics. —*n.* 1 A fabric, as silk or rayon, having a wavy or watered pattern produced by engraved cylinders: also **moire** (mwär). 2 The wavy pattern. [F]

moist (moist) *adj.* 1 Having slight wetness; damp. 2 Tearful: *moist* eyes. [< OF *moiste*] —**moist′ly** *adv.* —**moist′ness** *n.*

mois·ten (mois′ən) *v.t. & v.i.* To make or become moist. —**mois′ten·er** *n.*

mois·ture (mois′chər) *n.* A small amount of liquid exuding from, diffused through, or resting on a substance; dampness. —**mois′tur·ize** *v.t.* (**·ized, ·iz·ing**)

mol (mōl) *n.* MOLE[4].

mo·lar (mō′lər) *n.* A grinding tooth with flattened crown, situated behind the canine and incisor teeth. —*adj.* 1 Grinding, or adapted for grinding. 2 Pertaining to a molar. [< L *mola* mill] • See TOOTH.

mo·las·ses (mə·las′iz) *n.* A thick, dark-colored syrup drained from raw sugar during the refining process. [< L *mellaceus* honeylike]

mold[1] (mōld) *n.* 1 A hollow form or matrix for shaping anything that is in a fluid or plastic condition. 2 A frame on or around which something is made or shaped. 3 That which is made or shaped in or on a mold. 4 The form or shape given by a mold. 5 General form or shape. 6 Distinctive character or type. —*v.t.* 1 To work into a particular shape or form; model. 2 To shape or cast in, as in, or on a mold. 3 To influence or direct: to *mold* another's opinions. 4 In founding, to form a mold of or from. 5 To ornament with molding. [< L *modulus,* dim. of *modus* measure, limit] —**mold′er** *n.*

mold[2] (mōld) *n.* 1 Any of various fungous growths usu. forming a furry coating on decaying food or in moist, warm places. 2 Any fungus producing such growths. —*v.t. & v.i.* To become or cause to become moldy. [Prob. < Scand.]

mold[3] (mōld) *n.* Earth that is fine and soft, and rich in organic matter. —*v.t.* To cover with mold. [< OE *molde* earth]

mold·board (mōld′bôrd′, -bōrd′) *n.* The curved metal plate of a plow, by which the earth is turned over and pulverized. [< MOLD[3] + BOARD]

mold·er (mōl′dər) *v.i.* To decay gradually and turn to dust. [Prob. < Scand.]

mold·ing (mōl′ding) *n.* 1 The act of shaping with or as with a mold. 2 Anything molded. 3 *Archit.* **a** A more or less ornamental strip, as around doors, windows, ceilings, etc. **b** A cornice or other projecting decorative member on a surface or angle of any part of a building.

mold·y (mōl′dē) *adj.* **mold·i·er, mold·i·est** 1 Covered with mold. 2 Musty, as from age, neglect, etc. —**mold′i·ness** *n.*

mole[1] (mōl) *n.* A small permanent spot on the skin, usu. elevated slightly and pigmented. [< OE *māl*]

mole[2] (mōl) *n.* Any of a family of small, insectivorous mammals with velvety fur, tiny eyes, and broad forefeet adapted for tunneling underground. [< MLG *molle*]

Mole

mole[3] (mōl) *n.* A jetty or breakwater partially enclosing an anchorage or harbor. [< L *moles* great mass]

mole[4] (mōl) *n.* That number of grams of a substance that is equal to its molecular weight; a gram molecule. [Short for MOLECULAR WEIGHT.]

Mo·lech (mō′lek) MOLOCH.

mo·lec·u·lar (mə·lek′yə·lər) *adj.* Of, effected by, or consisting of molecules.

molecular weight The sum of the atomic weights of all the constituent atoms of a molecule.

mol·e·cule (mol′ə·kyōōl) *n.* 1 The smallest particle of an element or compound having all the properties of the element or compound. 2 Any small particle. [< NL *molecula,* dim. of L *moles* mass]

mole·hill (mōl′hil′) *n.* A small heap or ridge of earth raised by a burrowing mole.

add, āce, câre, pälm; end, ēven; it, īce; odd, ōpen, ôrder; tŏŏk, pōōl; up, bûrn; ə = *a* in *above, u* in *focus;* yōō = *u* in *fuse;* oil; pout; check; go; ring; thin; this; zh, *vision.* < derived from; ? origin uncertain or unknown.

mole·skin (mōl'skin') *n.* 1 The soft skin of a mole, used as fur. 2 A heavy, twill fabric, usu. cotton, having a thick, soft nap on one side. 3 *Usu. pl.* Garments made of this fabric.

mo·lest (mə·lest') *v.t.* 1 To annoy or disturb. 2 To accost or interfere with sexually. [<L *molestus* troublesome] —**mo·les·ta·tion** (mō'les·tā'shən, mol'es-), **mo·lest'er** *n.*

moll (mol) *n. Slang* 1 A gangster's girl friend. 2 A prostitute. [<*Molly*, dim. of *Mary*]

mol·li·fy (mol'ə·fī) *v.t.* **·fied, ·fy·ing** 1 To make less angry. 2 To reduce the violence or intensity of. [<L *mollis* soft + *facere* make] —**mol'li·fi·ca'tion, mol'li·fi'er** *n.* —**mol'li·fy'·ing·ly** *adv.* —**Syn.** 1 soothe, pacify, appease, conciliate. 2 mitigate, ease, temper, allay.

mol·lusk (mol'əsk) *n.* Any of a large phylum of unsegmented, soft-bodied invertebrates, usu. having gills and a mantle which secretes a calcareous shell, and including snails, oysters, cuttlefish, slugs, octopuses, etc. Also **mol'·lusc.** [<L *molluscus (nux)* soft, thin-shelled (nut)]

mol·ly·cod·dle (mol'ē·kod'l) *n.* 1 Any excessively pampered or protected person. 2 An effeminate man or body. —*v.t.* **·dled, ·dling** To pamper; coddle. [<*Molly*, dim. of *Mary* + CODDLE] —**mol'ly·cod'dler** *n.*

Mo·loch (mō'lok) In the Bible, a god of the Ammonites and Phoenicians to whom human sacrifices were offered. —*n.* Any system or principle involving merciless sacrifice.

molt (mōlt) *v.t. & v.i.* to cast off or shed (feathers, horns, outer skin, etc.) in preparation for replacement by new growth. —*n.* 1 The molting process or season. 2 That which is molted. [<L *mutare* to change] —**molt'er** *n.*

mol·ten (mōl'tən) *Archaic p.p.* of MELT. —*adj.* 1 Reduced to fluid by heat; melted. 2 Made by being melted and then cast in a mold.

mol·to (môl'tō) *adv. Music* Much; very: *molto* adagio. [Ital. <L *multum* much]

mo·lyb·de·num (mə·lib'də·nəm) *n.* A hard, heavy, silver-white, metallic element (symbol Mo) having properties similar to tungsten, used in electrical equipment and hard steel alloys. [<Gk. *molybdos* lead]

mom (mom) *n. Informal* Mother.

mo·ment (mō'mənt) *n.* 1 A very short period of time; an instant. 2 A definite point in time, esp. the present time. 3 Consequence or importance: something of little *moment.* 4 A time of excellence, accomplishment, enjoyment, etc.: She has her *moments.* 5 *Physics* a The product of a quantity and its distance to some significant related point: *moment* of inertia. b The measure of a force about a given point or axis; torque. [<L *momentum* movement]

mo·men·tar·i·ly (mō'mən·ter'ə·lē) *adv.* 1 For a moment. 2 From moment to moment. 3 At any moment.

mo·men·tar·y (mō'mən·ter'ē) *adj.* Lasting but a moment. —**mo'men·tar'i·ness** *n.*

mo·men·tous (mō·men'təs) *adj.* Of great importance. —**mo·men'tous·ly** *adv.* —**mo·men'tous·ness** *n.* —**Syn.** weighty, serious, outstanding, memorable.

mo·men·tum (mō·men'təm) *n. pl.* **·ta** (-tə) or **·tums** 1 *Physics* a The quantity of motion in a body as measured by the product of its mass and velocity. b A similar quantity defined with respect to angular motion. 2 Any forward or ongoing motion; impetus. [L, movement]

Mon. Monday; Monseigneur.

Mon·a·co (mon'ə·kō, mə·nä'kō) *n.* An independent principality on the SE coast of France, 368 acres.

mon·ad (mon'ad, mō'nad) *n.* 1 An indestructible unit. 2 *Biol.* Any single-celled organism. 3 *Chem.* A univalent atom, radical, or element. —*adj.* Of, pertaining to, or consisting of a monad. [<Gk. *monas* a unit]

mon·arch (mon'ərk) *n.* 1 A hereditary constitutional sovereign, as a king, queen, etc. 2 One who or that which surpasses others of the same kind. 3 A large butterfly with orange-brown, black-veined wings whose larvae feed on milkweed. [<Gk. *monos* alone + *archein* rule] —**mo·nar·chal** (mə·när'kəl) *adj.* —**mo·nar'chal·ly** *adv.*

mo·nar·chi·cal (mə·när'ki·kəl) *adj.* Pertaining to, governed by, or favoring a monarch or monarchy. Also **mo·nar'chi·al, mo·nar'chic.** —**mo·nar'chi·cal·ly** *adv.*

mon·arch·ism (mon'ərk·iz'əm) *n.* 1 The government or principles of a monarchy. 2 The advocacy of a monarchy. —**mon'arch·ist** *adj., n.* —**mon'arch·is'tic** *adj.*

mon·ar·chy (mon'ər·kē) *n. pl.* **·chies** 1 Government by a monarch; sovereign control. 2 A government or territory ruled by a monarch.

mon·as·ter·y (mon'əs·ter'ē) *n. pl.* **·ter·ies** 1 A dwelling place occupied by monks, living under religious vows. 2 The monks living in such a place. [<Gk. *monastēs* a monk <*monazein* be alone]

mo·nas·tic (mə·nas'tik) *adj.* 1 Of, pertaining to, or like a monastery or the people who live there. 2 Ascetic. Also **mon·as·te·ri·al** (mon'əs·tir'ē·əl), **mo·nas'ti·cal.** —*n.* A monk or other religious recluse. —**mo·nas'ti·cal·ly** *adv.*

mo·nas·ti·cism (mə·nas'tə·siz'əm) *n.* 1 The monastic life or system. 2 Asceticism.

mon·a·tom·ic (mon'ə·tom'ik) *adj. Chem.* 1 Consisting of a single atom, as the molecules of certain elements. 2 Containing one replaceable or reactive atom. 3 UNIVALENT.

mon·au·ral (män·ôr'əl) *adj.* 1 Pertaining to the perception of sound by one ear only. 2 Designating the transmission or reproduction of sound through a single channel. [<MON(O)- + AURAL]

Mon·day (mun'dē, -dā) *n.* The second day of the week. [<OE *mōnandæg* day of the moon]

monde (mônd) *n. French* The world; society.

mo·ne·cious (mə·nē'shəs, mō-) *adj.* MONOECIOUS.

Mo·nel metal (mō·nel') A corrosion-resistant alloy of nickel, copper, and iron: a trade name.

mo·ner·an (mə·nir'ən) *n.* A living organism of the kingdom *Monera*, lacking a cell nucleus, including bacteria and some forms of algae. [<Gk. *monos* alone]

mon·e·tar·y (mon'ə·ter'ē, mun'-) *adj.* 1 Of or pertaining to currency or coinage. 2 Of or pertaining to money. [<L *moneta* mint] —**mon'e·tar'i·ly** *adv.*

mon·e·tize (mon'ə·tīz, mun'-) *v.t.* **·tized, ·tiz·ing** 1 To legalize as money. 2 To coin into money. [<L *moneta* mint, money] —**mon'e·ti·za'tion** *n.*

mon·ey (mun'ē) *n. pl.* **mon·eys** or **mon·ies** 1 Anything that serves as a common medium of exchange, a measure of value, or as a means for the payment of debts or services rendered, esp. coins and paper currency officially issued by a government. 2 A specific form or denomination of coin or paper currency. 3 MONEY OF ACCOUNT. 4 Assets having monetary value. 5 Profit or pecuniary gain: to make *money.* 6 Wealth: That town has *money.* [<L *moneta* money, mint]

mon·ey·bag (mun'ē·bag') *n.* 1 A bag for holding money. 2 *pl. Slang* A rich person; also, wealth.

mon·ey·chang·er (mun'ē·chān'jər) *n.* 1 A person who exchanges different kinds or denominations of money at a prescribed rate. 2 A device for holding and dispensing coins.

mon·eyed (mun'ēd) *adj.* 1 Possessed of money. 2 Consisting of or representing money: *moneyed* interests. —**Syn.** 1 wealthy, well-off, well-to-do, flush.

mon·ey-mak·ing (mun'ē·mā'king) *adj.* Likely to bring in money; profitable. —*n.* The acquisition of money or wealth. —**mon'ey-mak'er** *n.*

money of account A monetary denomination used in keeping accounts, but usu. not represented by a coin, as the mill.

money order An order for the payment of a specified sum of money, esp. such an order issued at a post office, bank, or telegraph office and payable at another.

mon·ger (mung'gər, mong'-) *n.* 1 A dealer or trader: chiefly in combination: *fishmonger.* 2 One who engages in or endorses discreditable practices: *scandalmonger; warmonger.* [<OE *mangian* to traffic]

Mon·gol (mong'gəl, -gol, -gōl) *n.* 1 A member of any of the Mongoloid peoples of Mongolia. 2 The Mongolian language of any of these peoples. 3 Any member of the Mongoloid ethnic group. —*adj.* 1 MONGOLIAN (def. 1) 2 MONGOLOID (def. 1).

Mon·go·li·an (mong·gō'lē·ən, -gōl'yən, mon-) —*adj.* 1 Of or pertaining to Mongolia or the Mongolian People's Republic. 2 MONGOLOID (def. 1). —*n.* 1A native or citizen of the Mongolian People's Republic. 2 Any one of a group of related languages used in Mongolia or the Mongolian People's Republic. 3 MONGOLOID.

Mongolian People's Republic A republic of CEN.

Asia, 590,966 sq. mi., cap. Ulan Bator. • See map at CHINA.
Mon·gol·ism (mong′gəl·iz′əm) *n.* DOWN'S SYNDROME.
Mon·go·loid (mong′gə·loid) *adj.* 1 Of or pertaining to one of the major racial groups of mankind, including most of the peoples of N and E Asia, the Eskimos, Malaysians, and some American Indians. 2 Resembling a Mongol or a Mongolian. 3 Of or afflicted with Down's syndrome or Mongolism. —*n.* A member of this racial group.
mon·goose (mong′go͞os, mung′-) *n. pl.* **·goos·es** A small, ferretlike, Old World mammal valued as a predator of rats and snakes, including venomous snakes. [<Marathi (an Indic language) *mangūs*]
mon·grel (mong′grəl, mung′-) *n.* 1 A plant or animal resulting from interbreeding different types or varieties; esp., a dog of mixed breed. 2 Any incongruous mixture. —*adj.* Of mixed breed, origin, character, etc. [<OE *gemang* mixture]
mon·i·ker (mon′ə·kər) *n. Slang* A name, signature, or mark of identification. Also **mon′ick·er.** [?]
mo·nism (mō′niz·əm, mon′iz·əm) *n. Philos.* The doctrine that only one ultimate substance or principle is responsible for the phenomena of the universe. [<Gk. *monos* single + -ISM] —**mo′nist** *n.* —**mo·nis′tic** or **·ti·cal** *adj.* —**mo·nis′ti·cal·ly** *adv.*
mo·ni·tion (mō·nish′ən) *n.* 1 A warning or admonition. 2 A legal or official notice or summons. [<L *monitus,* p.p. of *monere* warn]
mon·i·tor (mon′ə·tər) *n.* 1 A student selected to assist a teacher in various tasks. 2 One who advises or cautions. 3 Something that warns or advises. 4 Formerly, an iron-clad vessel having a low, flat deck with one or more turrets carrying heavy guns. 5 Any of several large carnivorous lizards of Australia, Africa and Asia. 6 *Telecom.* **a** A high-fidelity loudspeaker in the control room of a sound studio, used to check fidelity of reproduction. **b** A receiver for checking the quality of a station's broadcasts. 7 A computer screen; cathode-ray tube; video-display terminal. —*v.t.* 1 *Telecom.* To check (a station, broadcast, etc.) with or as with a monitor. 2 To assist or have charge of (a person or group) as a monitor (def. 1). 3 To keep watch over or check as a means of control: to *monitor* tax returns. [<L *monere* warn] —**mon′i·to′ri·al** *adj.*
mon·i·to·ry (mon′ə·tôr′ē, -tō′rē) *adj.* Conveying a warning; admonitory.
monk (mungk) *n.* 1 A man who is a member of a monastic order and is usu. vowed to poverty, chastity, and obedience. 2 Formerly, a religious hermit. [<Gk. *monos* alone]
mon·key (mung′kē) *n. pl.* **·keys** 1 Any of the primates except lemurs, anthropoid apes, and man, as marmosets, baboons, etc. 2 A person likened to a monkey, as a mischievous child. —*v.i. Informal* To play or trifle; meddle: often with *with* or *around with.* [?<MLG *Moneke,* name of an ape in a medieval epic]
monkey business *Slang* Foolish tricks; deceitful or mischievous behavior.

Monkey wrench

mon·key·shines (mung′kē·shīnz′) *n. pl. Slang* Frolicsome tricks or pranks.
monkey wrench A type of adjustable wrench
monks·hood (mungks′ho͝od′) *n.* Any of several species of aconite having usu. purple flowers with the upper sepal arched like a hood.
mon·o (mon′ō) *adj.* MONOPHONIC (def. 1) —*n.* MONONUCLEOSIS.
mono- *combining form* Single; one: *monobasic.* Also, before vowels, **mon-.** [<Gk. *monos* single]
mon·o·ba·sic (mon′ə·bā′sik) *adj. Chem.* Possessing a single hydrogen atom replaceable by a metal or positive radical: applied to acids.
mon·o·chro·mat·ic (mon′ə·krō·mat′ik) *adj.* Of a single color or different shades of a single color. —**mon′o·chro·mat′i·cal·ly** *adv.*
mon·o·chrome (mon′ə·krōm) *n.* A painting or drawing in a single color, or different shades of a single color. —*adj.* MONOCHROMATIC. —**mon′o·chro′mic** or **·mi·cal** *adj.*
mon·o·cle (mon′ə·kəl) *n.* An eyeglass for one eye. [<MONO- + L *oculus* eye] —**mon′o·cled** *adj.*
mon·o·cli·nal (mon′ə·klī′nəl) *adj. Geol.* Having an inclination in only one direction, or composed of rock strata so inclined. —**mon′o·cli′nal·ly** *adv.*
mon·o·cline (mon′ə·klīn) *n. Geol.* A stratum or fold of rocks inclined in only one direction. [<MONO- + Gk. *klinein* incline]
mon·o·cli·nous (mon′ə·klī′nəs) *adj. Bot.* Having both stamens and pistils in the same flower. [<MONO- + Gk. *klinē* bed, couch]
mon·o·cot·y·le·don (mon′ə·kot′ə·lēd′n) *n.* Any of a large class of flowering plants having only one cotyledon in the seed, no cambium, and usu. parallel-veined leaves, as grasses, lilies, etc. Also **mon′o·cot.** —**mon′o·cot′yle′·do·nous** *adj.*
mon·o·dy (mon′ə·dē) *n pl.* **·dies** 1 An elegy or dirge, esp. a poem on the death of a friend. 2 In Greek tragedy, an ode sung by one voice. 3 *Music* **a** A style in which one vocal part predominates. **b** A composition or passage in such a style. [<Gk. *monos* alone + *aedein* sing] —**mo·nod·ic** (mə·nod′ik), **mo·nod′i·cal** *adj.* —**mo·nod′i·cal·ly** *adv.* —**mon′o·dist** *n.*
mo·noe·cious (mə·nē′shəs) *adj.* Having stamens and pistils in separate blossoms on the same plant. [<MON(O)- + Gk. *oikos* house]
mo·nog·a·my (mə·nog′ə·mē) *n.* 1 The principle or practice of marriage with but one person at a time. 2 *Zool.* The habit of having but one mate. [<Gk. *monos* single + *gamos* marriage] —**mo·nog′a·mous** *adj.* —**mo·nog′a·mist** *n.*
mon·o·gram (mon′ə·gram) *n.* Two or more letters interwoven into one, as the initials of one's name. —*v.t.* **·grammed, ·gram·ming** To mark with a monogram. [<Gk. *monos* single + *gramma* letter] —**mon′o·gram·mat′ic** (-grə·mat′ik) *adj.*
mon·o·graph (mon′ə·graf, -gräf) *n.* A book, paper, or treatise written about a single topic, usu. in great detail. —**mo·nog·ra·pher** (mə·nog′rə·fər) *n.* —**mon′o·graph′ic** *adj.*
mon·o·lith (mon′ə·lith) *n.* 1 A single, usu. very large piece or block of stone, often in the shape of an obelisk. 2 Something like a monolith, as in size, structure, aspect, or quality.
mon·o·lith·ic (mon′ə·lith′ik) *adj.* 1 Of or resembling a monolith. 2 Single in character, as a political movement or ideology; marked by uniformity.
mon·o·logue (mon′ə·lôg, -log) *n.* 1 A story or drama told or performed by one person. 2 A lengthy speech by one person, occurring in conversation. 3 A literary composition, or a poem, written as a soliloquy. Also **mon′o·log.** [<Gk. *monos* alone + *logos* discourse] —**mon′o·logu′ist, mo·nol·o·gist** (mə·nol′ə·jist) *n.*
mon·o·ma·ni·a (mon′ə·mā′nē·ə, -mān′yə) *n.* 1 A mental disorder characterized by obsession with one idea or subject. 2 An unreasonable interest in or pursuit of something; craze. —**mon′o·ma′ni·ac** *n.*
mon·o·met·al·ism (mon′ō·met′l·iz′əm) *n.* The theory or system of a single metallic standard in coinage. Also **mon′o·met′al·ism.** —**mon′o·me·tal′lic** (-mə·tal′ik) *adj.*
mo·no·mi·al (mə·nō′mē·əl) *adj.* Consisting of a single term: a *monomial* expression. —*n. Math.* An expression consisting of a single term. [<MONO- + *-nomial,* as in *binomial*]
mon·o·nu·cle·o·sis (mon′ō·nʸo͞o′klē·ō′sis) *n.* A disease in which the blood contains an abnormal number of leukocytes with a single nucleus. Also **infectious mononucleosis.** [<MONO- + NUCLE(US) + -OSIS]
mon·o·phon·ic (mon′ə·fon′ik) *adj.* 1 Of, pertaining to, or functioning in the reproduction of sound through a single channel: a *monophonic* recording. 2 *Music* Consisting of a single unaccompanied melody.
mon·o·plane (mon′ə·plān) *n.* An airplane with only one wing on either side of the fuselage.
mo·nop·o·lize (mə·nop′ə·līz) *v.t.* **·lized, ·liz·ing** 1 To obtain or exercise a monopoly of. 2 To assume exclusive possession or control of. *Brit. sp.* **mo·nop′o·lise.** —**mo·nop′o·li·za′·tion, mo·nop′o·liz′er** *n.*

mo·nop·o·ly (mə·nop′ə·lē) *n. pl.* **·lies** 1 The exclusive ownership or control of a specific commodity or service. 2 A person, company, etc. having a monopoly. 3 Exclusive possession or control of anything. 4 The commodity or service under the control of a monopoly. 5 *Law* An exclusive license from the government for buying, selling, making, or using anything. [< Gk. *monos* alone + *pōlein* sell] **—mo·nop′o·lism** *n.* **—mo·nop′o·list** *adj., n.* **—mo·nop′o·lis′tic** *adj.*

mon·o·rail (mon′ō·rāl) *n.* 1 A single rail serving as a track for railway cars. 2 A railway using such a track.

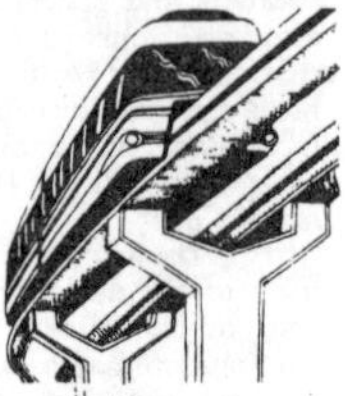

Monorail

mon·o·so·di·um glu·ta·mate (mon′ə·sōd′ē·əm glōō′tə·māt) A white salt obtained from various vegetable sources and having the property of intensifying the sensation of taste.

mon·o·syl·lab·ic (mon′ə·si·lab′·ik) *adj.* 1 Having only one syllable. 2 Using or speaking in monosyllables. 3 Very brief; terse, as in replying. **—mon′o·syl·lab′i·cal·ly** *adv.*

mon·o·syl·la·ble (mon′ə·sil′ə·bəl, mon′ə·sil′-) *n.* A word of one syllable.

mon·o·the·ism (mon′ə·thē·iz′əm) *n.* The doctrine that there is but one God. [< MONO- + Gk. *theos* god + -ISM] **—mon′o·the′ist** *n.* **—mon′o·the·is′tic** or **·ti·cal** *adj.* **—mon′o·the·is′ti·cal·ly** *adv.*

mon·o·tone (mon′ə·tōn) *n.* 1 Speech that does not vary in tone, pitch, or stress. 2 A sameness or monotony, as in style, color, etc. 3 A single musical tone unvaried in pitch; also, a chant in such a tone.

mo·not·o·nous (mə·not′ə·nəs) *adj.* 1 Tiresomely uniform or repetitious. 2 Not varied in inflection, cadence, or pitch. [< Gk. *monotonos* having a single tone] **—mo·not′o·nous·ly** *adv.* **—mo·not′o·nous·ness** *n.* **—Syn.** 1 tedious, dull, dreary.

mo·not·o·ny (mə·not′ə·nē) *n.* 1 A tiresome or tedious uniformity. 2 Sameness of tone or sound.

mon·o·treme (mon′ə·trēm) *n.* Any of an order of primitive, egg-laying mammals, including only duckbills and echidnas. [< MONO- + Gk. *trēma* hole] **—mon′o·trem′a·tous** (-trem′ə·təs) *adj.*

mon·o·type (mon′ə·tīp) *n.* 1 *Biol.* A unique member of a taxonomic group, as a single species in a genus. 2 *Printing* A print from a metal plate on which a design, painting, etc., has been made. **—mon·o·typ·ic** (mon′ə·tip′ik) *adj.*

Mon·o·type (mon′ə·tīp) *n. Printing* A machine which casts and sets type in single characters or units: a trade name.

mon·o·va·lent (mon′ə·vā′lənt) *adj. Chem.* UNIVALENT. **—mon′o·va′lence, mon′o·va′len·cy** *n.*

mon·ox·ide (mon·ok′sīd, mə·nok′-) *n.* An oxide with a single atom of oxygen per molecule.

Mon·roe Doctrine (mən·rō′) The doctrine, essentially formulated by President James Monroe, that any attempt by European powers to interfere in the affairs of the American countries or to acquire territory on the American continents would be regarded by the U.S. as an unfriendly act.

Mon·sei·gneur (mon·sēn′yər; *Fr.* môṅ·se·nyœr′) *n. pl.* **Mes·sei·gneurs** (me·se·nyœr′) 1 My lord: a French title given to princes of the church and formerly to the higher nobility. 2 One having this title. [< F *mon* my + *seigneur* lord]

mon·sieur (mə·syûr′, *Fr.* mə·syœ′) *n. pl.* **mes·sieurs** (mes′ərz, *Fr.* me·syœ′) The French title of courtesy for men, equivalent to *Mr.* and *sir:* abbreviated *M.* [< F *mon* + *sieur,* short for *seigneur* lord]

Mon·si·gnor (mon·sēn′yər, *Ital.* môn′sē·nyōr′) *n. pl.* **·gnors** or *Ital.* **·gno·ri** (-nyō′rē) A title of honor of certain prelates and Roman Catholic officials. Also **Mon·si·gno·re** (môn′sē·nyō′rā). [< F *monseigneur*]

mon·soon (mon·sōōn′) *n. Meteorol.* 1 A wind that blows along the Asiatic coast of the Pacific and from the Indian Ocean, in winter from the NE **(dry monsoon),** in summer from the SW **(wet monsoon).** 2 The rainy season of the summer monsoon. [< Ar. *mausim* season]

mon·ster (mon′stər) *n.* 1 Any plant or animal of markedly abnormal structure and appearance. 2 A person or thing that is abhorred because of its ugliness, cruelty, wickedness, etc. 3 An abnormally huge person, animal, or thing. 4 An imaginary animal of huge or hideous form. — *adj.* Enormous; huge. [< L *monstrum* divine omen]

mon·strance (mon′strəns) *n.* In Roman Catholic ritual, a sacred vessel in which the consecrated Host is exposed for adoration. [< L *monstrare* to show]

mon·stros·i·ty (mon·stros′ə·tē) *n. pl.* **·ties** 1 Anything unnaturally huge, malformed, or distorted. 2 The character or condition of being monstrous.

mon·strous (mon′strəs) *adj.* 1 Deviating greatly from the natural or normal. 2 Of extraordinary size; huge. 3 Hateful; hideous; intolerable. 4 Incredible; absurd. 5 Like an imaginary monster. **—mon′strous·ly** *adv.* **—mon′strous·ness** *n.*

mon·tage (mon·täzh′) *n.* 1 A composite picture made by superimposing several different pictures on one another. 2 In films or television, a swiftly run sequence of images or pictures illustrating a group of associated ideas. 3 A similar technique used in writing. [F, lit., a mounting]

month (munth) *n.* 1 One of the 12 parts into which the calendar year is divided, called a **calendar month.** 2 Loosely, thirty days or four weeks. 3 The twelfth part of a solar year, called a **solar month.** 4 The time during which the moon makes one revolution, equal on the average to 29.53 days, called a **lunar month.** [< OE *mōnath*]

month·ly (munth′lē) *adj.* 1 Continuing a month. 2 Payable, done, or happening once a month. —*adv.* Once a month. —*n. pl.* **·lies** 1 A periodical published once a month. 2 *pl. Informal* A menstrual period.

mon·u·ment (mon′yə·mənt) *n.* 1 Something, as a statue, building, plaque, etc., erected to perpetuate the memory of a person or of an event. 2 A notable work of art, heroic deed, scholarly production, etc., thought of as having enduring significance. 3 A stone boundary marker. 4 A tomb. [< L *monere* remind]

mon·u·men·tal (mon′yə·men′təl) *adj.* 1 Of, like, or serving as a monument. 2 Massive; impressive; enduring. 3 Outstanding; significant. 4 Very great: a *monumental* fraud. **—mon′u·men′tal·ly** *adv.*

moo (mōō) *v.i.* To make the low, mournful sound of a cow; low. —*n. pl.* **moos** This sound. [Imit.]

mooch (mōōch) *Slang v.t.* 1 To obtain without paying; beg. 2 To steal. —*v.i.* 3 To loiter about; skulk; sneak. [< OF *muchier* hide, skulk] **—mooch′er** *n.*

mood[1] (mōōd) *n.* 1 A particular, usu. temporary state of mind; humor; disposition. 2 *pl.* Fits of morose or sullen behavior. [< OE *mōd*]

mood[2] (mōōd) *n. Gram.* The form or forms of a verb which indicate that the speaker regards what he is saying as either a fact (indicative mood), a possibility, desire, etc. (subjunctive mood), or a command (imperative mood). [Var. of MODE]

mood·y (mōō′dē) *adj.* **mood·i·er, mood·i·est** 1 Given to petulant, sullen, or melancholy moods. 2 Expressive of such moods. **—mood′i·ly** *adv.* **—mood′i·ness** *n.*

moon (mōōn) *n.* 1 A body that orbits the earth from west

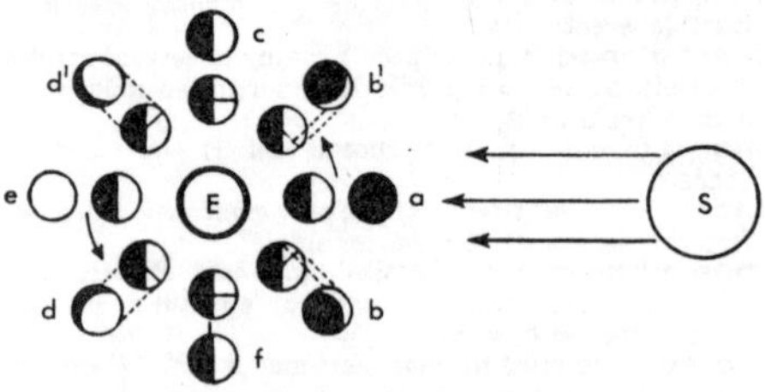

Phases of the moon

E. earth. S. sun. The outer circle represents views of the moon as seen from earth. a. new. b, b′. crescent. c. 1st quarter. d, d′. gibbous. e. full. f. 3rd quarter.

to east in 29.53 days. The moon has a mean diameter of 2,160 miles and a mean distance from the earth of 238,900 miles. 2 A particular phase of the moon: full *moon.* 3 A satellite revolving about any planet. 4 A month, esp. a lunar month. 5 Something resembling a moon or crescent. 6 Moonlight. —*v.i.* 1 To stare or wander about in an abstracted or listless manner. —*v.i.* 2 To pass (time) thus. [< OE *mōna*]

moon·beam (mo͞on′bēm′) *n.* A ray of moonlight.

moon·calf (mo͞on′kaf′, -käf′) *n.* 1 A stupid person; idiot. 2 A deformed person. [With ref. to the supposed bad influence of the moon]

moon·craft (mo͞on′kraft′, -kräft′) *n.* A spacecraft designed to travel to the moon.

moon·light (mo͞on′līt′) *n.* The light of the moon. —*adj.* Pertaining to or illuminated or done by moonlight. —*v.i. Informal* To work at a job in addition to one's regular job. —**moon′light′er, moon′light′ing** *n.*

moon·lit (mo͞on′lit′) *adj.* Lighted by the moon.

moon·quake (mo͞on′kwāk′) *n.* A trembling or shaking of the moon's surface analogous to an earthquake.

moon·scape (mo͞on′skāp′) *n.* 1 The moon's surface or a view of it. 2 Any barren or bleak terrain or site.

moon·shine (mo͞on′shīn′) *n.* 1 Moonlight. 2 Foolish talk; nonsense. 3 *Informal* Smuggled or illicitly distilled liquor.

moon·shin·er (mo͞on′shī′nər) *n. Informal* A person who makes liquor illegally.

moon·stone (mo͞on′stōn′) *n.* A whitish, cloudy feldspar, valued as a gem.

moon·struck (mo͞on′struk′) *adj.* 1 Lunatic; deranged. 2 Sentimentally romantic. Also **moon′strick′en** (-strik′ən).

moon·y (mo͞o′nē) *adj.* **moon·i·er, moon·i·est** 1 MOONSTRUCK. 2 Absent-minded.

moor[1] (mo͝or) *v.t.* 1 To secure (a ship, etc.) in one place by means of cables attached to shore, anchors, etc. 2 To secure in place; fix. —*v.i.* 3 To secure a ship in position; anchor. 4 To be secured by chains or cables. [< MDu. *maren* to fasten]

moor[2] (mo͝or) *n.* 1 A tract of often elevated, rolling wasteland sometimes covered with heath. 2 A marshy area often abounding in peat. [< OE *mōr*]

Moor (mo͝or) *n.* 1 A person of mixed Berber and Arab blood, inhabiting Morocco and the s Mediterranean coast. 2 Any of the Muslim people who invaded Spain in the 8th century. —**Moor′ish** *adj.*

moor·cock (mo͝or′kok′) *n.* The male moorfowl.

moor·fowl (mo͝or′foul′) *n.* A ptarmigan of the British Isles having reddish brown plumage throughout the year.

moor·hen (mo͝or′hen′) *n.* The female moorfowl.

moor·ing (mo͝or′ing) *n. Chiefly pl.* 1 The place where a vessel is moored. 2 Anything by which an object is fastened.

moose (mo͞os) *n. pl.* **moose** A very large deer of N North America having huge, palmate antlers in the male. 2 A large Old World elk. [< Algon.]

Moose

moot (mo͞ot) *adj.* 1 Still open to discussion; debatable: a *moot* point. 2 Altogether academic; having no practical significance. —*n.* 1 Discussion or argument. 2 In Anglo-Saxon times, a meeting of freemen for the discussion of local affairs. —*v.t.* 1 To debate; discuss. 2 To argue (a case) in a moot court. [< OE *mōt* assembly]

moot court A court for the trial of a fictitious suit by law students.

mop[1] (mop) *n.* 1 A bundle or mass of absorbent fabric, a sponge, or the like, attached to a handle, used for cleaning floors. 2 Any loosely tangled bunch or mass, as of hair. —*v.t.* **mopped, mop·ping** To rub or wipe with or as with a mop. [? < L *mappa* napkin]

mop[2] (mop) *n.* A grimace. —*v.i.* To make a wry face; grimace. [?]

mope (mōp) *v.i.* **moped, mop·ing** To be gloomy, listless, or dispirited. —*n.* 1 One who mopes. 2 *pl.* Dejection; depression. [Prob. < Scand.] —**mop′er** *n.* —**mop′ey** *adj.* (**-i·er, -i·est**).

mop·pet (mop′it) *n.* A child; youngster. [Dim. of ME *moppe* rag doll]

mo·raine (mə·rān′, mō-) *n. Geol.* A ridge or heap of earth, stones, etc., carried and deposited by a glacier. [F] —**mo·rain′al, mo·rain′ic** *adj.*

mor·al (môr′əl, mor′-) *adj.* 1 Of or pertaining to character and behavior from the point of view of right and wrong. 2 Good and virtuous in behavior, character, etc.; esp., sexually virtuous. 3 Concerned with the principles of right and wrong; ethical: *moral* values. 4 Capable of understanding the difference between right and wrong: a *moral* agent. 5 Coming from a sense of duty or one's conscience: a *moral* obligation. 6 Arising from one's sympathies or sense of justice but without overt action: *moral* support. 7 Probable but not yet proven objectively: a *moral* certainty. —*n.* 1 The moral point or lesson made by a story, action, etc. 2 *pl.* Conduct or behavior from the point of view of right and wrong, esp. sexual conduct. 3 A maxim. [< L *mos, moris* custom; in the pl., manners, morals] —**mor′al·ly** *adv.* • **moral, morale** *Moral,* with the stress on the first syllable, is both an adjective (meaning virtuous or ethical) and a noun (meaning a moral point or lesson): *It took moral courage to admit she was wrong; The moral is, "The weed of crime bears bitter fruit." Morale,* with the stress on the second syllable, is a noun only, and refers to a feeling of confidence or spirit, esp. within a group: *When the pay raise was canceled, morale fell sharply.*

mo·rale (mə·ral′, -räl′, mô-) *n.* State of mind with reference to confidence, courage, hope, etc. [< F *moral,* moral] • See MORAL.

mor·al·ist (môr′əl·ist, mor′-) *n.* 1 A teacher of morals. 2 One who leads a virtuous life. —**mor′al·is′tic** *adj.*

mo·ral·i·ty (mə·ral′ə·tē, mô-) *n. pl.* **·ties** 1 A doctrine or system of moral principles or conduct: Victorian *morality.* 2 Moral conduct; virtue. 3 The quality or condition of being morally right or wrong. 4 A moral lesson. 5 MORALITY PLAY.

morality play A form of allegorical drama of the 15th and 16th centuries in which the characters were personified virtues, vices, mental attributes, etc.

mor·al·ize (môr′əl·īz, mor′-) *v.* **·ized, ·iz·ing** *v.i.* 1 To make moral reflections; talk about morality. —*v.t.* 2 To explain in a moral sense; derive a moral from. 3 To improve the morals of. *Brit. sp.* **·ise.** —**mor′al·i·za′tion, mor′al·iz′er** *n.*

mo·rass (mə·ras′, mô-, mō-) *n.* 1 A tract of low-lying, soft, wet ground; marsh. 2 Anything that impedes or creates difficulties. [< OF *maresc*]

mor·a·to·ri·um (môr′ə·tôr′ē·əm, -tō′rē-, mor′-) *n. pl.* **·ri·ums** or **·ri·a** (-ē·ə) 1 A legal act authorizing a debtor or bank to suspend payments for a given period; also, the period during which it is in force. 2 Any authorized suspension of an activity. [< L *morari* to delay]

Mo·ra·vi·an (mô·rā′vē·ən, mō-) *adj.* Of or pertaining to Moravia or the Moravians. —*n.* 1 A native of Moravia. 2 One of a Christian sect founded in the 15th century by disciples of John Huss in Moravia.

mo·ray (môr′ā, mō·rā′) *n.* A brightly colored, voracious eel inhabiting tropical and subtropical waters, esp. among coral reefs. Also **moray eel.** [< L *muraena*]

mor·bid (môr′bid) *adj.* 1 Of, caused by, or having a disease. 2 Abnormally intrigued by the gruesome or unwholesome. 3 Grisly; gruesome: a *morbid* story. [< L *morbus* disease] —**mor·bid′i·ty, mor′bid·ness** *n.* —**mor′bid·ly** *adv.*

mor·dant (môr′dənt) *adj.* 1 Biting; pungent; sarcastic: *mordant* wit. 2 Acting to fix colors in dyeing. —*n.* 1 A substance that serves to fix a dye in a fabric, etc. 2 A corrosive substance used in etching lines on a metal plate. —*v.t.* To treat or imbue with a mordant. [< OF *mordre* to bite] —**mor′dan·cy** *n.* —**mor′dant·ly** *adv.*

more (môr, mōr) *adj. superlative* **most** 1 Greater in amount, extent, or number: comparative of *much* and *many.* 2 Additional; extra: *More* champagne, please. —*n.* 1 A greater or additional quantity, amount, degree, etc. 2 Something that exceeds something else. —*adv.* 1 In or to a greater extent or degree. 2 In addition; further. —**more or less** 1 Somewhat. 2 Approximately. [< OE *māra*]

add, āce, câre, pälm; end, ēven; it, īce; odd, ōpen, ôrder; to͝ok, po͞ol; up, bûrn; ə = *a* in *above, u* in *focus;* **yo͞o** = *u* in *fuse;* **oil; pout; check; go; ring; thin; this; zh,** *vision.* < derived from; ? origin uncertain or unknown.

more·o·ver (môr·ō′vər, mōr-) *adv.* Beyond what has been said; further; besides; likewise.

mo·res (môr′ēz, mō′rēz) *n.pl.* Established, traditional customs regarded as having the force of law. [L, pl. of *mos, moris* custom]

mor·ga·nat·ic (môr′gə·nat′ik) *adj.* Of or designating a legitimate marriage between a member of certain royal or noble families of Europe and a person of inferior rank, in which the titles and estates are not shared by the offspring or the inferior parent. [< OHG *morgen(geba)* morning (gift) (in lieu of a share in the estate)] **—mor′ga·nat′i·cal·ly** *adv.*

morgue (môrg) *n.* **1** A place where cadavers are kept awaiting identification or determination of cause of death. **2** The department of a newspaper or other periodical where reference material, back issues, etc., are filed. [F]

mor·i·bund (môr′ə·bund, -bənd, mor′-) *adj.* Dying; at the point of death. [< L *mori* die] **—mor′i·bun′di·ty** *n.*

mo·ri·on (môr′ē·on, mō′rē-) *n.* A crested helmet without visor worn by men in the 16th and 17th centuries. [< Sp. *morra* crown of the head]

Mo·ris·co (mə·ris′kō) *adj.* Moorish. **—***n. pl.* **·cos** or **·coes** A Moor, esp. a Spanish Moor.

Mor·mon (môr′mən) *n.* **1** A member of a religious sect officially called *The Church of Jesus Christ of Latter-Day Saints,* founded in the U.S. by Joseph Smith in 1830. **2** In Mormon belief, a prophet of the fourth century A.D. who wrote the **Book of Mormon,** a history of an early American people. **—Mor′mon·ism** *n.*

morn (môrn) *n.* **1** DAWN. **2** MORNING. [< OE *morgen*]

morn·ing (môr′ning) *n.* **1** The time from midnight to noon, or from sunrise to noon. **2** The first or early stage of anything. **—***adj.* Pertaining to or occurring in the morning. [< MORN, by analogy with EVENING]

morn·ing-glo·ry (môr′ning·glôr′ē, -glō′rē) *n. pl.* **·ries** Any of various twining vines having funnel-shaped flowers of various colors.

Morning-glories

morning sickness Nausea and vomiting experienced by some pregnant women in the morning hours, esp. in early pregnancy.

morning star Any of the planets, esp. Venus, when rising in the E sky shortly before the sun.

Mo·ro (môr′ō, mō′rō) *n. pl.* **·ros** **1** A member of one of the Muslim tribes of the s Philippines. **2** The Indonesian language of the Moros.

mo·roc·co (mə·rok′ō) *n.* A fine leather made from goatskin tanned with sumac. Also **morocco leather.**

Mo·roc·co (mə·rok′ō) *n.* A constitutional monarchy of NW Africa, 160,000 sq. mi., cap. Rabat. **—Mo·roc′can** *adj., n.* • See map at AFRICA.

mo·ron (môr′on, mō′ron) *n.* A person with a mild degree of mental retardation. [< Gk. *mōros* dull, sluggish] **—mo·ron·ic** (mô·ron′ik, mō-) *adj.* **—mo·ron′i·cal·ly** *adv.* **—mo′ron·ism, mo·ron′i·ty** *n.*

mo·rose (mə·rōs′) *adj.* Sullen; gloomy. [< L *mos, moris* manner, habit] **—mo·rose′ly** *adv.* **—mo·rose′ness** *n.* **—Syn.** sad, melancholy, surly, ill-tempered.

-morph *combining form* Having a (specified) form or shape. [< Gk. *morphē* form]

mor·pheme (môr′fēm) *n. Ling.* The smallest meaningful unit of a language, as a word, root, affix, or inflectional ending. *Man, run, pro-, -ess, -ing,* etc., are morphemes. [< Gk. *morphē* form]

Mor·phe·us (môr′fē·əs, -fyo͞os) *Gk. Myth.* The god of dreams. **—Mor′phe·an** *adj.*

-morphic *combining form* Having the form or shape of: *anthropomorphic.* [< Gk. *morphē* form]

mor·phine (môr′fēn) *n.* A bitter, white, crystalline alkaloid derived from opium, used in medicine to allay pain. Also **mor′phi·a** (-fē·ə). [F < MORPHEUS]

mor·phin·ism (môr′fin·iz′əm) *n.* Addiction to morphine.

mor·phol·o·gy (môr·fol′ə·jē) *n.* **1** The branch of biology that deals with the form and structure of plants and animals. **2** The branch of linguistics that deals with the arrangement, composition, and inflection of the morphemes of a language. [< Gk. *morphē* form + -LOGY] **—mor·pho·log·ic** (môr′fə·loj′ik) or **·i·cal** *adj.* **—mor′pho·log′i·cal·ly** *adv.* **—mor·phol′o·gist** *n.*

mor·ris (môr′is, mor′-) *n.* An old English folk dance. [Earlier *morys* Moorish]

Mor·ris chair (môr′is, mor′-) A large armchair with an adjustable back. Also **morris chair.** [< William *Morris,* 1834–96, English poet, artist, and craftsman]

mor·row (môr′ō, mor′ō) *n.* **1** The first day after the present or after a specified day or event. **2** *Archaic* Morning: good *morrow.* [< OE *morgen* morning]

Morse code A system of telegraphic signals used in transmitting messages composed of dots and dashes or short and long flashes representing the letters of the alphabet, numerals, etc. [< Samuel F. B. *Morse,* 1791–1872, U.S. inventor]

mor·sel (môr′səl) *n.* **1** A bit of food; bite. **2** A small piece of anything. [< OF, dim. of *mors* bite]

mor·tal (môr′təl) *adj.* **1** Subject to death. **2** Causing death; fatal. **3** Of or connected with death: *mortal* agony. **4** Deadly and unrelenting: a *mortal* foe. **5** Human: *mortal* desires. **6** Very great; extreme: a *mortal* fright. **7** Very long and tedious. **8** *Theol.* Incurring eternal death unless repented of: said of grave sins. **9** *Informal* Conceivable: every *mortal* reason for not going. **—***n.* A human being. **—***adv. Regional* Very; exceedingly: *mortal* tired. [< L *mors, mortis* death] **—mor′tal·ly** *adv.*

mor·tal·i·ty (môr·tal′ə·tē) *n.* **1** The quality of being mortal. **2** Death, esp. of large numbers of people. **3** The number of deaths in a population during a specified time. **4** Humanity; mankind.

mor·tar[1] (môr′tər) *n.* **1** A strong bowllike vessel in which substances are crushed or pounded with a pestle. **2** *Mil.* A muzzle-loading cannon for firing heavy shells at low muzzle velocity and great angles of elevation. [< L *mortarium*]

Mortar and pestle

mor·tar[2] (môr′tər) *n.* A mixture of lime, cement, etc., with sand and water, used in masonry, plastering, etc. **—***v.t.* To plaster or join with mortar. [< L *mortarium*]

mor·tar·board (môr′tər·bôrd′, -bōrd′) *n.* **1** A square board with a handle, on which a mason holds mortar. **2** An academic cap having a square, flat top and tassel.

mort·gage (môr′gij) *n. Law* **1** A transfer of ownership of property to a creditor as security for a loan or debt. **2** The contract effecting such a transfer. **—***v.t.* **·gaged, ·gag·ing** **1** To make over or pledge (property) by mortgage. **2** To pledge. [< OF, lit., dead pledge]

mort·ga·gee (môr′gi·jē′) *n.* The person to whom property is mortgaged.

mort·ga·gor (môr′gi·jər) *n.* A person who mortgages his property. Also **mort′gag·er.**

mor·ti·cian (môr·tish′ən) *n.* A funeral director; undertaker. [< L *mors, mortis* death + -ICIAN]

mor·ti·fi·ca·tion (môr′tə·fə·kā′shən) *n.* **1** Shame or humiliation caused by a loss of self-esteem or wounded pride. **2** The cause of such humiliation or shame. **3** Necrosis; gangrene. **4** In religion, the act of subduing the passions and appetites by fasting, penance, etc.

mor·ti·fy (môr′tə·fī) *v.* **·fied, ·fy·ing** *v.t.* **1** To humiliate. **2** To discipline or punish (the body, passions, etc.) by fasting or other ascetic practices. **3** To cause (a part of the body) to become gangrenous. **—***v.i.* **4** To practice ascetic self-discipline. **5** To become gangrenous. [< L *mors, mortis* death + *facere* make] **—mor′ti·fi′er** *n.* **—mor′ti·fy′ing·ly** *adv.*

mor·tise (môr′tis) *n.* A space hollowed out, as in a piece of wood, to receive a tenon or other projecting part. **—***v.t.* **·tised, ·tis·ing** **1** To cut or make a mortise in. **2** To join by a tenon and mortise. [< OF *mortaise*]

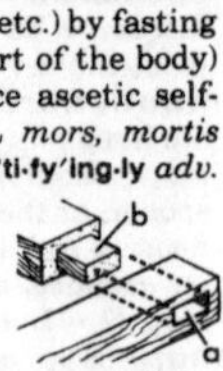

a. mortise.
b. tenon.

mort·main (môrt′mān) *n. Law* The perpetual and untransferable ownership of property, as by a religious or other corporation. [< Med. L *mortua manus* dead hand]

mor·tu·ar·y (môr′cho͞o·er′ē) *n. pl.* **·ar·ies** A place for the temporary reception of the dead before burial, esp. a fu neral home. —*adj.* 1 Of or pertaining to the burial of the dead. 2 Of death or the dead. [< L *mortuarius* belonging to the dead]

mos. months.

mo·sa·ic (mō·zā′ik) *n.* 1 Inlaid work composed of bits of stone, glass, etc., forming a pattern or picture. 2 The art or process of making a mosaic. 3 Anything resembling a mosaic. —*adj.* Of, pertaining to, or resembling mosaic. —*v.t.* **·icked, ·ick·ing** 1 To make by or as if by combining in a mosaic. 2 To decorate with mosaic. [< Gk. *mouseios* of the Muses, artistic] **—mo·sa·i·cist** (mō·zā′ə·sist) *n.*

Mo·sa·ic (mō·zā′ik) *adj.* Of or pertaining to Moses or his laws. Also **Mo·sa′i·cal.**

Mo·ses (mō′ziz) In the Bible, the leader who led the Israelites out of Egypt into the Promised Land and received the Ten Commandments from God.

mo·sey (mō′zē) *v.i. Slang* 1 To saunter, or stroll. 2 To go away. [?]

Mos·lem (moz′ləm, mos′-) *n. pl.* **·lems** or **·lem** MUSLIM. —*adj.* MUSLIM. **—Mos′lem·ism** *n.*

mosque (mosk) *n.* A Muslim temple of worship. [< Ar. *masjid*]

mos·qui·to (məs·kē′tō) *n. pl.* **·toes** or **·tos** Any of a family of small, dipterous insects having in the female mouth parts that puncture the skin of animals and suck their blood. [< Sp. *mosca* fly] **—mos·qui′tal** *adj.*

Mosquito

mosquito boat A patrol torpedo boat.

mosquito net A fine netting or gauze **(mosquito netting)** placed over beds, etc., to keep out mosquitoes.

moss (môs, mos) *n.* 1 Any of a large class of widespread, primitive, small plants having leaves and rootlike and stemlike parts, and reproducing by spores. 2 Any of several similar plants, as certain lichens. —*v.t.* To cover with moss. [< OE *mos*] **—moss′y** *adj.* **(·i·er, ·i·est) —moss′i·ness** *n.*

moss·back (môs′bak′, mos′-) *n.* An extremely conservative or reactionary person.

moss rose A cultivated variety of rose with a rough, mosslike calyx and flower stem.

most (mōst) *adj.* 1 Consisting of the greatest number: superlative of *many.* 2 Consisting of the greatest amount or degree: superlative of *much.* 3 In the majority of instances: *Most* dogs are friendly. **—for the most part** Generally; usually. —*n.* 1 The greater number; the larger part: the *most* of my belongings. 2 The greatest amount, quantity, or degree. **—at (the) most** Not more than; at the utmost extreme. **—make the most of** To take the utmost advantage of. —*adv.* 1 In or to the greatest or highest degree, quantity, or extent: used with adjectives and adverbs to form the superlative degree. 2 Very. 3 *Informal* Almost; nearly. [< OE *mæst*]

-most *suffix* Most: added to form superlatives: *hindmost.* [< OE *-mest*]

most·ly (mōst′lē) *adv.* For the most part; principally.

mot (mō) *n.* A witty remark. [F, word]

mote (mōt) *n.* A minute particle or speck, as of dust. [< OE *mot*]

mo·tel (mō·tel′) *n.* A hotel for motorists, usu. comprising cabins or rooms directly accessible from parking areas. [< MO(TOR) + (HO)TEL]

mo·tet (mō·tet′) *n. Music* A polyphonic song of a sacred nature, usu. unaccompanied. [< OF, dim. of *mot* word]

moth (môth, moth) *n. pl.* **moths** (môthz, môths, mothz, moths) Any of various, usu. nocturnal, lepidopterous insects distinguished from butterflies by their featherlike antennae and wings that fold flat over the abdomen. [< OE *moththe*]

moth·ball (môth′bôl′, moth′-) *n.* A ball of naphthalene, camphor, or other substance whose fumes repel moths that destroy woolen fabrics. —*adj.* In protective storage or in reserve: a *mothball* fleet. —*v.t.* To put in protective storage or reserve.

moth-eat·en (môth′ēt′n, moth′-) *adj.* 1 Eaten by the larvae of moths. 2 Worn out. 3 Old-fashioned.

moth·er[1] (muth′ər) *n.* 1 A woman who has borne a child. 2 A woman fulfilling the role of mother, as by adoption of a child. 3 STEPMOTHER. 4 The source or origin of anything. 5 An abbess or other nun of rank or dignity. 6 An elderly woman. —*v.t.* 1 To care for as a mother. 2 To bring forth as a mother; produce. 3 To admit or claim parentage, authorship, etc., of. —*adj.* 1 Native: *mother* tongue. 2 Of or characteristic of a mother: *mother* love. 3 Holding a maternal relation. [< OE *mōdor*] **—moth′er·less** *adj.*

moth·er[2] (muth′ər) *n.* A ropy, jellylike mass of bacteria that forms in vinegar and other fermenting liquids, used to start new batches. Also **mother of vinegar.** [Special use of MOTHER[1]]

Mother Car·ey's chicken (kâr′ēz) The petrel; esp., the storm petrel. [?]

Mother Goose 1 The imaginary narrator of a volume of folk tales, compiled in French by Charles Perrault in 1697. 2 The imaginary compiler of a collection of English nursery rhymes published in London about 1760 by John Newbery.

moth·er·hood (muth′ər·ho͝od) *n.* 1 The state of being or the qualities characteristic of a mother. 2 Mothers collectively.

Mother Hub·bard (hub′ard) 1 The main character in an old nursery rhyme. 2 A woman's loose, flowing gown.

moth·er-in-law (muth′ər·in·lô′) *n. pl.* **moth·ers-in-law** The mother of one's spouse.

moth·er·land (muth′ər·land′) *n.* 1 The country of one's birth. 2 The land of one's ancestors.

mother lode Any principal or rich vein of ore in a mine.

moth·er·ly (muth′ər·lē) *adj.* Of, resembling, or befitting a mother. —*adv.* In the manner of a mother. **—moth′er·li·ness** *n.*

moth·er-of-pearl (muth′ər·əv·pûrl′) *n.* The hard, iridescent lining of certain mollusk shells; nacre. —*adj.* Made of or ornamented with mother-of-pearl.

Mother's Day A day observed in honor of mothers, on the second Sunday in May.

mother tongue 1 One's native language. 2 A language from which another language has developed.

mother wit Natural or native intelligence; common sense.

moth·y (môth′ē, moth′ē) *adj.* **moth·i·er, moth·i·est** 1 Moth-eaten. 2 Full of moths.

mo·tif (mō·tēf′) *n.* 1 The main idea or central theme of a literary, musical, or artistic work. 2 In the decorative arts, a distinctive element of design. 3 The shortest fragment of a musical theme in which structure is evident. [F]

mo·tile (mō′tīl) *adj. Biol.* Having the power of or exhibiting spontaneous motion. [< L *motus,* p.p. of *movere* move] **—mo·til′i·ty** *n.*

mo·tion (mō′shən) *n.* 1 Any physical movement or spatial change in position or place. 2 A formal proposition in a deliberative assembly. 3 *Law* An application to a court to obtain an order, ruling, or direction. 4 A mental impulse or inclination. —*v.i.* 1 To make a gesture of direction or intent, as with the hand. —*v.t.* 2 To direct or guide by a gesture. [< L *motus,* p.p. of *movere* move] **—mo′tion·al, mo′tion·less** *adj.* **—mo′tion·less·ly** *adv.* **—mo′tion·less·ness** *n.* **—Syn.** *n.* 1 action, passage, transit.

motion picture 1 A sequence of filmed pictures giving the illusion of continuous movement; film (def. 4). 2 A story, drama, etc., adapted for and photographed as a motion picture. **—mo′tion-pic′ture** *adj.*

motion sickness Nausea and sometimes vomiting caused by the effect of certain movements on the inner ear, typically experienced in a moving vehicle, ship, or airplane.

mo·ti·vate (mō′tə·vāt) *v.t.* **·vat·ed, ·vat·ing** To provide with a motive; instigate; induce. **—mo′ti·va′tion** *n.* **—mo′ti·va′tion·al** *adj.*

mo·tive (mō′tiv) *n.* 1 Something, as a need or desire, that impels or incites a person to a certain course of action or behavior. 2 MOTIF. —*adj.* 1 Causing motion. 2 Relating to a motive or motives. —*v.t.* **·tived, ·tiv·ing** MOTIVATE. [< L *motus,* p.p. of *movere* move]

mot·ley (mot'lē) *adj.* 1 Composed of many different elements or types. 2 Variegated in color. —*n.* 1 A garment of various colors, such as was formerly worn by court jesters. 2 A many-colored, woolen fabric. 3 An incongruous mixture. [ME *motteley*]

mo·to·cross (mō'tō·kros', -krôs') *n.* A motorcycle race operated on a cross-country ski run or other trail, rather than on a paved surface.

mo·tor (mōtər) *n.* 1 A machine that converts electric energy into mechanical power. 2 An internal-combustion engine. 3 Anything that produces motion. 4 AUTOMOBILE. —*adj.* 1 Causing, producing, or imparting motion. 2 Driven or operated by a motor. 3 Of, pertaining to, or for vehicles operated by a motor. 4 Transmitting impulses from the nerve centers to the muscles. 5 Of or involving muscular movement. —*v.i.* To travel or ride in an automobile. [<L *motus*, p.p. of *movere*]

mo·tor·bike (mō'tər·bīk') *n. Informal* 1 A bicycle driven by a motor. 2 A lightweight motorcycle.

mo·tor·boat (mō'tər·bōt') *n.* A boat propelled by a motor.

mo·tor·bus (mō'tər·bus') *n. pl.* **·bus·es** or **·buss·es** A passenger bus. Also **motor coach**.

mo·tor·cade (mō'tər·kād) *n.* A procession of automobiles.

mo·tor·car (mō'tər·kär') *n.* AUTOMOBILE.

motor court MOTEL. Also **motor hotel, inn, lodge**.

mo·tor·cy·cle (mō'tər·sī'kəl) *n.* A two-wheeled vehicle propelled by an internal-combustion engine. —*v.i.* **·cled, ·cling** To travel or ride on a motorcycle. —**mo'tor·cy'clist** *n.*

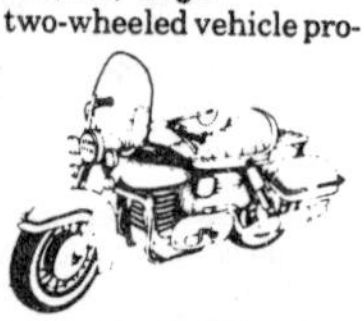
Motorcycle

motor home *U.S.* An automotive vehicle equipped with living accommodations and resembling a trailer but built on a single chassis.

mo·tor·ist (mō'tər·ist) *n.* One who drives an automobile or travels by automobile.

mo·tor·ize (mō'tər·īz) *v.t.* **·ized, ·iz·ing** To equip with a motor or motors or with motor-propelled vehicles.

mo·tor·man (mō·tər·mən) *n. pl.* **·men** (-mən) One who operates a passenger vehicle that is drawn by an electric motor, as a streetcar or subway.

motor pool A group of motor vehicles owned by a governmental or military agency for use by its personnel.

motor scooter A two- or three-wheeled vehicle having a floorboard for the feet, and a driver's seat, and propelled by an internal-combustion engine.

motor vehicle Any of various motor-driven vehicles that do not run on rails or tracks.

mot·tle (mot'l) *v.t.* **·tled ·tling** To mark with spots or streaks of different colors or shades. —*n.* 1 A spotted, blotched, or variegated appearance. 2 A spot or blotch. [<MOTLEY]

mot·tled (mot'ld) *adj.* Marked with spots of different colors or shades; variegated.

mot·to (mot'ō) *n. pl.* **·toes** or **·tos** 1 A word or phrase expressing a guiding principle or rule of conduct. 2 A phrase inscribed on something as being indicative of its qualities or uses. [Ital., word]

mou·jik (mōō·zhēk') *n.* MUZHIK.

mould (mōld) *n. & v. Brit.* MOLD.

moult (mōlt) *v. Brit.* MOLT.

mound (mound) *n.* 1 A heap or pile of earth, stones, etc., either natural or artificial. 2 A small hill or knoll. 3 In baseball, the slightly raised ground from which the pitcher pitches the ball. —*v.t.* 1 To fortify or enclose with a mound. 2 To heap up in a mound. [?]

Mound Builder One of the prehistoric Indians who built the burial mounds and fortifications found in the Mississippi basin and adjoining regions.

mount[1] (mount) *v.t.* 1 To ascend by climbing; go up, as stairs. 2 To climb or get up upon: to *mount* a horse. 3 To put on horseback. 4 To furnish with a horse. 5 To set or place in an elevated position: to *mount* a plaque on a wall. 6 To place or fix in or on a support, frame, slide, etc., as for exhibition, examination, etc.: to *mount* a photograph, to *mount* a butterfly. 7 To furnish, as a play, with scenery, costumes, etc. 8 To copulate with a female: said of a male animal. 9 *Mil.* a To place in position for use, as a cannon. b To stand or post (guard). c To prepare for and begin: to *mount* an offensive. —*v.i.* 10 To rise or ascend; to up. 11 To increase. 12 To get up on or on top of something. —*n.* 1 Anything, as a support, frame, jewel setting, etc., on or in which something is mounted. 2 Something which one mounts and rides, as a horse, bicycle, etc. 3 The act or manner of mounting or riding a horse, etc. [<L *mons, montis* mountain] —**mount'er** *n.*

mount[2] (mount) *n.* A mountain or hill: often used as part of a proper name: *Mount* Washington. [<L *mons, montis* mountain]

moun·tain (moun'tən) 1 A natural elevation of the earth's surface, higher than a hill and rising more or less steeply to a small summit area. 2 A large number or amount. 3 Something of great size. —*adj.* 1 Of, pertaining to, or like a mountain. 2 Living, growing, or located on a mountain. [<L *mons, montis* mountain]

mountain ash Any of various small trees and shrubs having compound leaves, dense clusters of white flowers, and vivid red fruit.

moun·tain·eer (moun'tən·ir') *n.* 1 An inhabitant of a mountainous district. 2 One who climbs mountains. —*v.i.* To climb mountains.

mountain goat A goatlike antelope of mountainous regions of W North America.

mountain laurel An evergreen shrub of E North America, having poisonous, shiny leaves and white or pink flowers.

mountain lion A large, tawny, unspotted wild cat of North and South America.

moun·tain·ous (moun'tən·əs) *adj.* 1 Full of mountains. 2 Huge. —**moun'tain·ous·ly** *adv.*

mountain sheep 1 BIGHORN. 2 Any wild sheep of mountainous regions.

Mountain Standard Time See STANDARD TIME.

moun·te·bank (moun'tə·bangk) *n.* 1 A vendor of quack medicines at fairs. 2 Any charlatan. [<Ital. *montare* to mount + *in* on + *banco* bench]

mount·ed (moun'tid) *adj.* 1 Seated on a horse. 2 Equipped with horses: *mounted* police. 3 Fitted or positioned for use or display.

Moun·tie (moun'tē) *n. Informal* A member of the Royal Canadian Mounted Police. Also **Mount'y**.

mount·ing (moun'ting) *n.* A frame, support, or setting for something.

mourn (môrn, mōrn) *v.i.* 1 To feel or express grief or sorrow, esp. for the dead. —*v.t.* 2 To grieve or sorrow for (someone dead). 3 To grieve over or lament (misfortune, failure, etc.). [<OE *murnan*] —**mourn'er** *n.*

mourner's bench *U.S.* At revival meetings, a bench near the preacher reserved for penitents.

mourn·ful (mōrn'fəl, mōrn'-) *adj.* 1 Indicating or expressing grief. 2 Oppressed with grief. 3 Causing sorrow. —**mourn'ful·ly** *adv.* —**mourn'ful·ness** *n.* —**Syn.** 2 sorrowful, rueful, disconsolate, grief-stricken.

mourn·ing (môr'ning, môr'-) *n.* 1 The act of sorrowing or expressing grief, esp. for the dead. 2 The outward manifestations of such grief, as the use of black clothes, half-masting of flags, etc. 3 The period during which one mourns.

mourning dove A wild dove of North America having gray plumage and a long, pointed, white-edged tail: so called for its plaintive call.

mouse (mous) *n. pl.* **mice** (mīs) 1 Any of numerous small rodents found throughout the world, esp. the common **house mouse**, which frequents human habitations. 2 *Informal* A timid person. 3 *Slang* A black eye. 4 A small, hand-held electronic device, used to control a cursor, or point to commands on a menu, instead of typing commands via the computer keyboard. —*v.* (mouz) **moused, mous·ing** *v.i.* 1 To hunt or catch mice. 2 To hunt for something cautiously and softly; prowl. [<OE *mūs*]

mous·er (mou'zər) *n.* A cat, dog, etc., that catches mice.

mousse (mōōs) *n.* 1 A light, frozen dessert made of whipped cream, white of egg, sugar, flavoring, etc. 2 A similar dish made with meat, fish, or vegatables: lobster *mousse*. [F]

mous·tache (məs·tash', mus'tash) *n.* MUSTACHE.

mous·y (mou'sē, -zē) *adj.* **mous·i·er, mous·i·est** 1 Infested with mice. 2 Of or like a mouse. 3 Quiet and timid. Also **mous′ey.**

mouth (mouth) *n. pl.* **mouths** (mouthz) 1 The opening at which food is taken into the body; also, the cavity between the lips and throat. 2 The human mouth thought of in terms of eating and speaking: Shut your *mouth; mouths* to feed. 3 An opening or entrance that can be likened to a mouth: as **a** That part of a stream where its waters are discharged into a river, lake, etc. **b** The entrance to a harbor. **c** The entrance or opening into a mine or cave. **d** The opening of a jar or similar container. —**down in** (or **at) the mouth** Disconsolate; dejected. —*v.t.* (mou*th*) 1 To utter in a forced or affected manner; declaim. 2 To seize or take in the mouth. 3 To repeat mechanically and without understanding. 4 To form (words) as if speaking but without sound. —*v.i.* 5 To speak in a forced or affected manner. [<OE *mūth*] —**mouth′er** (mou′*th*ər) *n.*

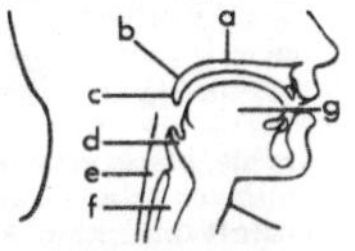

Human mouth
a. hard palate. b. soft palate. c. uvula. d. epiglottis. e. esophagus. f. trachea. g. tongue.

mouthed (mou*th*d, moutht) *adj.* Having a (specified kind of) mouth: used in combination: *loudmouthed.*

mouth·ful (mouth′fo͝ol′) *n. pl.* **·fuls** (-fo͝olz′) 1 As much as can be or is usually put into the mouth at one time. 2 A small quantity. 3 *Slang* A meaningful remark, usu. in the phrase **say a mouthful.**

mouth organ HARMONICA.

mouth·piece (mouth′pēs′) *n.* 1 Something that forms a mouth. 2 That part of any musical instrument, sports equipment, telephone, etc., that is used in or near the mouth. 3 One who speaks for others. 4 *Slang* A criminal lawyer.

mouth-to-mouth (mouth′tə·mouth′) *adj.* Of or describing a form of artificial respiration in which the rescuer places his mouth over the victim's mouth and breathes rhythmically and forcefully to inflate the victim's lungs and start respiration: *mouth-to-mouth* resuscitation.

mouth·wash (mouth′wash, -wôsh) *n.* A flavored solution, often antiseptic, used for cleansing the mouth or teeth, or for gargling.

mouth·y (mou′*th*ē, -thē) *adj.* **mouth·i·er, mouth·i·est** Very talkative; garrulous. —**mouth′i·ly** *adv.* —**mouth′i·ness** *n.*

mou·ton (mo͞o′ton) *n.* Processed sheepskin dyed and cut to resemble beaver or seal. [F, sheep]

mov·a·ble (mo͞o′və·bəl) *adj.* 1 Capable of being moved. 2 Changing in date from year to year: *movable* holidays. —*n.* 1 Anything that can be moved. 2 *Usu. pl. Law* Personal property, as distinguished from real or fixed property. Also **move′a·ble.** —**mov′a·ble·ness, mov′a·bil′i·ty** *n.* —**mov′a·bly** *adv.*

move (mo͞ov) *v.* **moved, mov·ing** *v.i.* 1 To change place or position, esp. to go from one place to another. 2 To change one's residence. 3 To make progress; advance. 4 To live or associate; be active: to *move* in cultivated circles. 5 To operate or revolve; work: said of machines, etc. 6 To take action; begin to act. 7 To be disposed of by sale. 8 To make an application, appeal, or proposal: to *move* for adjournment. 9 To evacuate: said of the bowels. 10 In chess, checkers, etc., to change the position of a piece. 11 *Informal* To go or depart rapidly. —*v.t.* 12 To change the place or position of. 13 To set or keep in motion. 14 To rouse, influence, or urge to some action. 15 To affect with passion, sympathy, etc.; stir; excite. 16 To propose for consideration, action, etc. 17 To cause (the bowels) to evacuate. —*n.* 1 The act of moving; movement. 2 A purposeful act or maneuver in the carrying out of a plan. 3 In chess, checkers, etc., the act of moving a piece; also, one's turn to move. 4 A change of residence. —**on the move** 1 Moving about from place to place. 2 Making progress. [<L *movere*]

move·ment (mo͞ov′mənt) *n.* 1 The act of changing place or position or of moving in any way. 2 A particular instance, technique, or manner of moving. 3 A series of actions, plans, etc., tending toward some goal or objective; also, the people so involved. 4 A trend or inclination. 5 *Mech.* A particular arrangement of related parts that produces a definite motion. 6 *Mil.* A maneuver. 7 *Music* One of the sections of a larger work, as of a symphony. 8 In art or literature, a quality that suggests motion or action. 9 In prosody, rhythmic flow; cadence. 10 An emptying of the bowels, or the matter so emptied.

mov·er (mo͞o′vər) *n.* One who or that which moves; esp., one engaged in the business of moving household goods.

mov·ie (mo͞o′vē) *n.* 1 A motion-picture film. 2 A motion-picture theater. 3 *pl.* A showing of films. 4 *pl.* The film industry. —*adj.* Of, in, or for movies. [Contraction of *moving picture*]

mov·ing (mo͞o′ving) *adj.* 1 Capable of or exhibiting movement. 2 Causing or producing motion or action. 3 Exciting or arousing the feelings or passions. —**mov′ing·ly** *adv.* —**mov′ing·ness** *n.* —**Syn.** 3 touching, affecting, stirring.

moving picture MOTION PICTURE.

moving staircase ESCALATOR.

mow[1] (mō) *v.* **mowed, mowed** or **mown, mowing** *v.t.* 1 To cut down (grain, grass, etc.) with a scythe or machine. 2 To cut the grain or grass of (a lawn, field, etc.). 3 To cut down or kill rapidly or indiscriminately: with *down.* —*v.i.* 4 To cut down grass or grain. [<OE *māwan*] —**mow′er** *n.*

mow[2] (mou) *n.* Hay or grain stored in a barn; also, the place of storage. —*v.t.* To store in a mow. [<OE *mūga*]

moz·za·rel·la (mot′sə·rel′ə) *n.* A soft, white, mild Italian cheese, used mainly in cooking. [Ital.]

MP, M.P. Member of Parliament; Military Police.

M.P., mp, m.p. melting point.

mp moderately soft (It. *mezzo piano*).

MPH, mph, m.p.h. miles per hour.

Mr. (mis′tər) *n. pl.* **Messrs.** (mes′ərz) A title prefixed to the name of a man. [Contraction of MISTER]

Mrs. (mis′iz) *n. pl.* **Mmes.** (mā·däm′) A title prefixed to the name of a married woman. [Contraction of MISTRESS]

Ms. (miz) *n. pl.* **Ms.'s** (miz′əz) A title prefixed to the name of a woman without specifying marital status. [Contraction of MISTRESS]

MS Mississippi (P.O. abbr.); multiple sclerosis.

MS, MS., ms, ms. (*pl.* **MSS, MSS., mss, mss.**) manuscript.

M.S., M.Sc. Master of Science (L *Magister Scientiae*).

MSG monosodium glutamate.

Msgr. Monsignor.

M.Sgt., M/Sgt Master Sergeant.

MST, M.S.T., m.s.t. Mountain Standard Time.

MT Montana (P.O. abbr.).

mt. (*pl.* **mts.**) mount; mountain.

m.t. mean time; metric ton; mountain time.

mtg. meeting; mortgage.

mtn. mountain.

Mt. Rev. Most Reverend.

mu (myo͞o) *n.* 1 The 12th letter in the Greek alphabet (M, μ), equivalent to *m.* 2 MICRON.

much (much) *adj.* **more, most** Great in quantity, amount, degree, etc. —*n.* 1 A great quantity, amount, degree, etc. 2 Something remarkable, important, or extensive. —**make much of** To treat or think of as of great importance. —*adv.* 1 To a great degree or extent. 2 For the most part; approximately. [<OE *mycel*] —**much′ness** *n.*

mu·ci·lage (myo͞o′sə·lij) *n.* 1 An aqueous solution of vegetable gum or similar substance, used as an adhesive. 2 Any of various gummy or gelatinous substances obtained from certain plants. [<LL *mucilago*] —**mu·ci·lag·i·nous** (myo͞o′si·laj′ə·nəs) *adj.* —**mu′ci·lag′i·nous·ness** *n.*

muck (muk) *n.* 1 Any moist dirt or filth, esp. mud. 2 Moist manure. 3 Dark soil consisting largely of decaying organic matter. 4 Something, as writings, that defames or injures. —*v.t.* 1 To fertilize with manure. 2 *Informal* To make dirty; pollute. 3 To remove muck from. [<ON *mykr*] —**muck′y** *adj.* **(·i·er, ·i·est)**

muck·rake (muk′rāk) *v.i.* **·raked, ·rak·ing** To search for or expose real or alleged corruption on the part of political officials, businessmen, etc. [<obs. *muckrake* a rake for dung] —**muck′rak′er** *n.*

mu·cous (myo͞o′kəs) *adj.* 1 Secreting mucus. 2 Pertaining to or resembling mucus; slimy. Also **mu'cold** (-koid). —**mu·cos'i·ty** (-kos'ə·tē) *n.*

mucous membrane The soft, smooth, moist tissue that lines the passages and cavities inside the body.

mu·cus (myōō'kəs) *n.* A viscid secretion of mucous membrane, serving as a lubricant.

mud (mud) *n.* **1** Wet and sticky earth; mire. **2** *Informal* Slanderous or malicious abuse. —*v.t.* **mud·ded, mud·ding** To soil or cover with mud. [?]

mud·dle (mud'l) *v.* **·dled, ·dling** *v.t.* **1** To mix in confusion; jumble. **2** To confuse mentally; bewilder. **3** To make muddy or turbid; roil. **4** To make a mess of; bungle. —*v.i.* **5** To act or think in a confused or ineffective manner. —*n.* A mixed or confused condition, as of the mind; a mess. [? < MUD]

mud·dle-head·ed (mud'l·hed'id) *adj.* Mentally confused.

mud·dler (mud'lər) *n.* **1** A stick for stirring liquids, esp. drinks. **2** One who muddles.

mud·dy (mud'ē) *adj.* **·di·er, ·di·est 1** Spattered or filled with mud. **2** Unclear; cloudy, as a color. **3** Confused or muddled in thought, meaning, etc. —*v.t.* & *v.i.* **·died, ·dy·ing** To become or cause to become muddy. —**mud'di·ly** *adv.* —**mud'di·ness** *n.*

mud·guard (mud'gärd') *n.* A guard over the wheel of a vehicle to protect from splashing mud.

mud·pup·py (mud'pup'ē) *n. pl.* **·pies** A salamander with four limbs and external, feathery gills, often found in muddy or stagnant water.

mud·sling·ing (mud'sling'ing) *n.* The practice of casting malicious slurs at an opponent, esp. in a political campaign. —**mud'sling'er** *n.*

mud turtle Any of various small turtles inhabiting muddy or brackish water.

mu·ez·zin (myōō·ez'in) *n.* In Muslim countries, a crier who calls the faithful to prayer, usu. from a minaret. Also **mu·ed'din** (-ed'in). [< Ar. *mu'adhdhin*]

muff[1] (muf) *v.t.* & *v.i.* **1** To perform (some act) clumsily; blunder. **2** In baseball, to fail to hold (the ball) in attempting a catch. —*n.* A bungling action. [?]

muff[2] (muf) *n.* A covering of fur or cloth, usu. cylindrical, into which the hands are thrust from opposite ends to keep them warm. [< F *moufle*]

muf·fin (muf'in) *n.* **1** A light, quick bread, baked in small cup-shaped tins. **2** ENGLISH MUFFIN. [?]

muf·fle (muf'əl) *v.t.* **·fled, ·fling 1** To wrap up in a blanket, scarf, etc., as for warmth or concealment. **2** To prevent from seeing, hearing, or speaking by wrapping the head. **3** To deaden the sound of by or as by wrapping. **4** To deaden (a sound). **5** To stifle; suppress. —*n.* Something used for muffling. [< OF *moufle* heavy mitten]

muf·fler (muf'lər) *n.* **1** A heavy scarf worn about the neck. **2** A device to reduce noise, as from the exhaust of an internal-combustion engine. **3** Anything used for muffling.

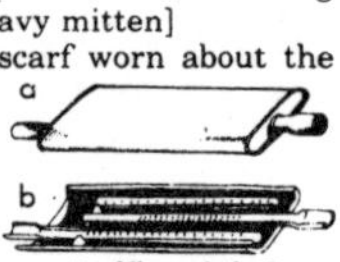

Muffler *def. 2*
a. assembled.
b. cross section.

muf·ti[1] (muf'tē) *n.* In Muslim countries, an expounder of religious law. [Ar.]

muf·ti[2] (muf'tē) *n.* Civilian dress; plain clothes, esp. when worn by one who normally wears a uniform. [< MUFTI[1]]

mug (mug) *n.* **1** A large drinking cup with a handle. **2** *Slang* The human face or mouth. **3** *Slang* A photograph of the face of a suspect: also **mug shot**. **4** *Slang* A criminal. —*v.* **mugged, mug·ging** *Slang v.t.* **1** To assault, usu. with the intent to rob. **2** To photograph (someone), esp. for official purposes. —*v.i.* **3** To make faces; grimace exaggeratedly. [?]

mug·ger (mug'ər) *n.* One who assaults another, often by surprise and in a public place or apartment house, usu. in order to rob. —**mug'ging** *n.*

mug·gy (mug'ē) *adj.* **·gi·er, ·gi·est** Warm, humid, and close. [< ON *mugga* drizzle] —**mug'gi·ness** *n.*

mug·wump (mug'wump) *n. U.S.* An independent, esp. in politics. [< Algon.] —**mug'wump·er·y, mug'wump·ism** *n.*

Mu·ham·mad·an (mōō·ham'ə·dən) *n.* MOHAMMEDAN. —**Mu·ham'mad·an·ism** *n.*

mu·jik (mōō·zhēk', mōō'zhik) *n.* MUZHIK.

mu·lat·to (mə·lat'ō, myōō-, -lä'tō) *n. pl.* **·toes 1** A person having one white and one Negro parent. **2** Anyone having mixed white and Negro ancestry. —*adj.* Of a light brown color. [< Sp. *mulato* of mixed breed < *mulo* mule]

mul·ber·ry (mul'ber'ē, -bər·ē) *n. pl.* **·ries 1** Any of various trees whose leaves are valued for silkworm culture. **2** The edible, blackberrylike fruit of a mulberry. **3** A deep purplish red color. [< L *morum* mulberry + OE *berie* a berry]

mulch (mulch) *n.* Any covering, as straw, compost, etc., placed on the ground around plants to protect their roots, as from frost or drying. —*v.t.* To cover with mulch. [ME *molsh*]

mulct (mulkt) *v.t.* **1** To punish by a fine. **2** To deprive (a person) of something fraudulently; cheat. —*n.* A fine or similar penalty. [< L *mulcta, multa* a fine]

mule[1] (myōōl) *n.* **1** A hybrid bred of the ass and horse, esp. a jackass and a mare. **2** A spinning machine that draws, stretches, and twists at one operation. **3** *Informal* A stubborn person. [< L *mulus*]

mule[2] (myōōl) *n.* A backless lounging slipper. [< L *mulleus* red slipper]

mule deer A deer of the w U.S., having long ears.

mule-skin·ner (myōōl'skin'ər) *n. Informal* A muledriver.

mu·le·teer (myōō'lə·tir') *n.* A mule-driver.

mul·ish (myōōl'ish) *adj.* Stubborn; recalcitrant. —**mul'ish·ly** *adv.* —**mul'ish·ness** *n.*

mull[1] (mul) *v.t.* To heat and spice, as wine or beer. [?]

mull[2] (mul) *v.t.* To ponder; cogitate: usu. with *over.* [< obs. *mull* grind < ME *mul* dust]

mul·lah (mul'ə, mōōl'ə) *n.* A Muslim trained in Islamic religious law and doctrine. Also **Mul'la.** [< Ar. *mawlā* master, sir]

mul·lein (mul'ən) *n.* Any of various tall, usu. hairy plants of the figwort family. Also **mul'len.** [< L *mollis* soft]

mul·let (mul'it) *n. pl.* **·lets** or **·let** Any of various marine and freshwater food fish, as the **gray mullet** and the **red mullet.** [< L *mullus* red mullet]

mul·li·gan (mul'i·gən) *n.* **1** A stew, originally made by tramps, composed of odds and ends of meat, vegetables, etc. Also **mulligan stew. 2** In golf, an extra shot, esp. a tee shot, after an inept first shot. [< *Mulligan,* Irish surname]

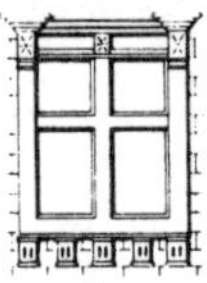

Mullions

mul·li·ga·taw·ny (mul'i·gə·tô'nē) *n.* An East Indian soup of meat and curry. [< Tamil *milagu-tannīr* pepper water]

mul·lion (mul'yən) *n.* A vertical dividing piece between lights or panels of windows, doors, etc. —*v.t.* To furnish with mullions. [? Var. of earlier *monial*]

multi- *combining form* **1** Much; many; consisting of many; as in:

multiangular	**multifaced**	**multinational**
multicellular	**multifaceted**	**multipointed**
multicolored	**multihued**	**multipurpose**
multidenominational	**multilevel**	**multiracial**
multidimensional	**multilingual**	**multistoried**
multidirectional	**multimillion**	**multisyllable**
multidisciplinary	**multimolecular**	**multivoiced**
multiethnic	**multination**	**multivolume**

2 Having more than two (or sometimes, more than one), as in **multicylinder, multiengine. 3** Many times over: *multimillionare.* Also **mult-.** [< L *multus* much]

mul·ti·far·i·ous (mul'tə·fâr'ē·əs) *adj.* Having great diversity or variety. [< L *multifarius*] —**mul'ti·far'i·ous·ly** *adv.* —**mul'ti·far'i·ous·ness** *n.*

mul·ti·fold (mul'tə·fōld) *adj.* Many times doubled.

mul·ti·form (mul'tə·fôrm) *adj.* Having many forms, shapes, or appearances. —**mul'ti·form'i·ty** *n.*

mul·ti·lat·er·al (mul'ti·lat'ər·əl) *adj.* **1** Having many sides. **2** Involving more than two nations, states, or parties.

mul·ti·me·di·a (mul'ti·mē'dē·ə) *adj.* Relating to or using two or more media, esp. a combination apprehended by different senses, as sight and hearing.

mul·ti·mil·lion·aire (mul'ti·mil'yən·âr', -mil'yən·âr', mul'tī-) *n.* A person having a fortune of many millions.

mul·tip·a·rous (mul·tip′ə·rəs) *adj.* 1 Having borne more than one child. 2 *Zool.* Giving birth to many at one time. [< MULTI- + *parere* give birth to]

mul·ti·par·tite (mul′ti·pär′tīt) *adj.* 1 Divided into many parts. 2 MULTILATERAL (def. 2).

mul·ti·ple (mul′tə·pəl) *adj.* 1 Containing or consisting of more than one part, element, characteristic, etc.; manifold. 2 Shared by or involving many. 3 *Electr.* Of or being a circuit having two or more conductors connected in parallel. —*n.* The product of a given number and another factor. [< LL *multiplus* manifold]

multiple myeloma A malignant tumor of the bone marrow occurring at numerous sites.

multiple sclerosis A chronic disease of the nervous system in which hard patches develop in the brain and spinal cord.

mul·ti·plex (mul′tə·pleks) *adj.* 1 Multiple; manifold. 2 *Telecom.* Designating a system for the simultaneous transmission of two or more messages or signals over the same channel.

mul·ti·pli·cand (mul′tə·plə·kand′) *n.* A number multiplied, or to be multiplied, by another. [< L *multiplicandus* to be multiplied]

mul·ti·pli·ca·tion (mul′tə·plə·kā′shən) *n.* 1 The process of multiplying. 2 The process of finding the sum (the *product*) of a number (the *multiplicand*) repeated a given number of times (the *multiplier*).

mul·ti·plic·i·ty (mul′tə·plis′ə·tē) *n.* 1 The condition of being manifold or various. 2 A large number.

mul·ti·pli·er (mul′tə·plī′ər) *n.* 1 One who or that which multiplies or causes multiplication. 2 The number by which a second number is multiplied.

mul·ti·ply (mul′tə·plī) *v.* **·plied, ·ply·ing** *v.t.* 1 To increase the quantity, amount, or degree of. 2 To perform the operation of multiplication upon. —*v.i.* 3 To become more in number, amount, or degree; increase. 4 To perform multiplication. [< L *multiplex* manifold] —**Syn.** 3 grow, enlarge, proliferate, expand.

mul·ti·stage (mul′tə·stāj) *adj.* 1 Having or characterized by stages in the completion of a process. 2 *Aerospace* Having several sections, as a rocket, each of which fulfills a given task.

mul·ti·tude (mul′tə·tyōōd) *n.* 1 A large crowd or gathering. 2 A great number. 3 The condition of being many. [< L *multus* much, many]

mul·ti·tu·di·nous (mul′tə·tyōō′də·nəs) *adj.* 1 Consisting of a vast number; numerous. 2 Having many elements, parts, aspects, etc. —**mul′ti·tu′di·nous·ly** *adv.* —**mul′ti·tu′di·nous·ness** *n.*

mul·ti·va·lent (mul′ti·vā′lənt) *adj. Chem.* Having three or more valences. —**mul′ti·va′lence** *n.*

mul·ti·ver·si·ty (mul′ti·vûr′sə·tē) *n. pl.* **·ties** A very large university with a student enrollment of many thousands, offering instruction and graduate study in many fields and often on a number of campuses. [< MULTI- + (UNI) VERSITY]

mum[1] (mum) *adj.* Silent; saying nothing. —*interj.* Hush! Be quiet! —**mum's the word** Say nothing.

mum[2] (mum) *v.i.* **mummed, mum·ming** To play or act in a mask, as at Christmas; be a mummer. [< OF *momer*]

mum[3] (mum) *n. Informal* A chrysanthemum.

mum·ble (mum′bəl) *v.t. & v.i.* **·bled, ·bling** To speak or utter in low, indistinct tones; mutter. —*n.* A low, mumbling speech; mutter. [ME *momelen*] —**mum′bler** *n.*

mum·ble·ty-peg (mum′bəl·tē·peg′) *n.* A game played with a jackknife, which is tossed and flipped in various ways so as to stick into the ground. Also **mum·ble-the-peg** (mum′bəl·thə·peg′).

mum·bo jum·bo (mum′bō jum′bō) 1 Any meaningless, usu. elaborate ritual or incantation. 2 Anything overly complicated or involved. [< *Mumbo Jumbo,* a village god of certain African tribes]

mum·mer (mum′ər) *n.* 1 One who wears a mask or disguise, as for certain festivals. 2 An actor, esp. one in a pantomime.

mum·mer·y (mum′ər·ē) *n. pl.* **·mer·ies** 1 A performance by mummers. 2 Any hypocritical or pretentious ceremony or performance.

mum·mi·fy (mum′ə·fī) *v.* **·fied, ·fy·ing** *v.t.* 1 To make a mummy of; preserve by drying. —*v.i.* 2 To dry up; shrivel. —**mum′mi·fi·ca′tion** *n.*

mum·my (mum′ē) *n. pl.* **·mies** 1 A body embalmed in the ancient Egyptian manner. 2 Any dead body which is very well preserved. 3 A person or thing that is dried up and withered. —*v.t. & v.i.* **·mied, ·my·ing** MUMMIFY. [< Pers. *mūm* wax]

Mummy and case

mumps (mumps) *n.pl. (construed as singular)* An acute, contagious, febrile disease of viral origin, characterized by swelling of the salivary glands. [pl. of obs. *mump* grimace]

munch (munch) *v.t. & v.i.* To chew with a crunching sound. [ME *monchen, manchen*] —**munch′er** *n.*

mun·dane (mun·dān′, mun′dān) *adj.* 1 Characterized by being ordinary, practical, and everyday. 2 Of or pertaining to the world. [< L *mundus* world] —**mun·dane′ly** *adv.* —**mun·dane′ness** *n.*

mu·nic·i·pal (myōō·nis′ə·pəl) *adj.* 1 Of or pertaining to a town or city or its government. 2 Having local self-government. [< L *municeps* free citizen] —**mu·nic′i·pal·ly** *adv.*

mu·nic·i·pal·i·ty (myōō·nis′ə·pal′ə·tē) *n. pl.* **·ties** An incorporated borough, town, or city.

mu·nic·i·pal·ize (myōō·nis′ə·pəl·īz) *v.t.* **·ized, ·iz·ing** To place under municipal authority or transfer to municipal ownership. —**mu·nic′i·pal′i·za′tion** *n.*

mu·nif·i·cent (myōō·nif′ə·sənt) *adj.* Extraordinarily generous or bountiful; liberal. [< L *munus* gift + *facere* to make] —**mu·nif′i·cence** *n.* —**mu·nif′i·cent·ly** *adv.*

mu·ni·tion (myōō·nish′ən) *n. Usu. pl.* Ammunition and all necessary war materiel. —*v.t.* To furnish with munitions. [< L *munire* fortify]

mu·ral (myŏŏr′əl) *n.* A painting or decoration on a wall. —*adj.* 1 Executed on or applied to a wall. 2 Of, pertaining to, or like a wall. [< L *murus* wall] —**mu′ral·ist** *n.*

mur·der (mûr′dər) *v.t.* 1 To kill (a human being) with premeditated malice. 2 To kill in a barbarous or inhuman manner; slaughter. 3 *Informal* To spoil by bad performance, etc.; mangle; butcher. —*v.i.* 4 To commit murder. —*n.* 1 The unlawful and intentional killing of one human being by another; homicide. 2 *Informal* Something very difficult, unpleasant, or dangerous. [Fusion of OE *morthor* + OF *murdre*] —**mur′der·er** *n.* —**mur′der·ess** *n. Fem.*

mur·der·ous (mûr′dər·əs) *adj.* 1 Of, pertaining to, or causing murder. 2 Capable of or plotting murder. 3 Violently hostile; menacing: a *murderous* look. 4 *Informal* Very difficult, unpleasant, or dangerous. —**mur′der·ous·ly** *adv.* —**mur′der·ous·ness** *n.*

mu·ri·at·ic acid (myŏŏr′ē·at′ik) HYDROCHLORIC ACID. [< L *muria* brine]

murk (mûrk) *n.* Darkness; gloom. [ME *mirke*]

murk·y (mûr′kē) *adj.* **murk·i·er, murk·i·est** 1 Dark; obscure. 2 Hazy; misty, as with fog. 3 Lacking in clarity; confused or ambiguous. —**murk′i·ly** *adv.* —**murk′i·ness** *n.*

mur·mur (mûr′mər) *n.* 1 A low sound continually repeated. 2 A complaint uttered in a low, indistinct voice. 3 An abnormal sound heard in some region of the body during auscultation: a heart *murmur.* —*v.i.* 1 To make a murmur. 2 To complain in a low tone. —*v.t.* 3 To utter in a low tone. [< L] —**mur′mur·er** *n.* —**mur′mur·ous** *adj.*

mur·rain (mûr′in) *n.* Any of various infectious diseases of domestic animals. [< L *mori* to die]

mus. museum; music.

mus·ca·dine (mus′kə·din, -dīn) *n.* A species of grape with a tough skin and musky flavor, grown in the s U.S. [< Prov. *muscat* muscat]

mus·cat (mus′kat, -kət) *n.* 1 A variety of sweet European grape used in making wine and raisins. 2 MUSCATEL. [< LL *muscus* musk]

---

add, āce, câre, pälm; end, ēven; it, īce; odd, ōpen, ôrder; tŏŏk, pōōl; up, bûrn; ə = *a* in *above, u* in *focus;* yōō = *u* in *fuse;* oil; pout; check; go; ring; thin; this; zh, *vision.* < derived from; ? origin uncertain or unknown.

mus·ca·tel (mus′kə·tel′) *n.* 1 A rich, sweet wine made from the muscat grape. 2 The muscat grape. Also **mus′ca·del′** (-del′).

mus·cle (mus′əl) *n.* 1 Any of the organs, composed of bundles of fibers, by whose contraction all bodily motion is effected. 2 The fibrous, elastic tissue of these organs. 3 Muscular strength. 4 *Informal* Power; force: a law with *muscle.* —*v.i.* **·cled, ·cling** *Informal* To push in or ahead by sheer physical strength. [< L *musculus,* lit., little mouse] —**mus′cled** *adj.*

mus·cle-bound (mus′əl·bound′) *adj.* Having enlarged, inelastic muscles, as from excessive exercise.

Mus·co·vite (mus′kə·vīt) *n.* 1 A native or inhabitant of Muscovy or of Moscow. 2 A Russian. —*adj.* Of or pertaining to Muscovy or to Russia.

Mus·co·vy (mus′kə·vē) *n.* Ancient Russia.

mus·cu·lar (mus′kyə·lər) *adj.* 1 Of, pertaining to, or accomplished by muscles. 2 Possessing strong muscles; powerful. —**mus′cu·lar′i·ty** (-lar′ə·tē) *n.* —**mus′cu·lar·ly** *adv.*

muscular dystrophy Any of various chronic diseases of undetermined cause, characterized by wasting away of muscles.

mus·cu·la·ture (mus′kyə·lə·chŏŏr′) *n.* 1 The disposition or arrangement of muscles in a part or organ. 2 The muscle system as a whole.

muse[1] (myōōz) *n.* A source of inspiration for artists, poets, etc. [< MUSE]

muse[2] (myōōz) *v.t.* & *v.i.* **mused, mus·ing** To consider thoughtfully or at length; ponder; meditate. —*n.* The state of musing; reverie. [< OF *muser* reflect] —**mus′er** *n.* —**Syn.** *v.* reflect, deliberate, dream, meditate.

Muse (myōōz) *Gk. Myth.* Any of the nine goddesses presiding over poetry, the arts, and the sciences.

mu·se·um (myōō·zē′əm) *n.* A building or place preserving and exhibiting works of nature, art, curiosities, etc.; also, any collection of such objects. [< Gk. *mouseion* temple of the Muses]

mush[1] (mush) *n.* 1 Thick porridge, made by boiling cornmeal in water or milk. 2 Anything soft and pulpy. 3 *Informal* Sentimentality. [Var. of MASH] —**mush′y** *adj.* **(-i·er, -i·est)**

mush[2] (mush) *v.i.* In Alaska and N Canada, to travel on foot, esp. over snow with a dog sled. —*interj.* Get along! a call of the drivers of a dog team. [? < F (Canadian) *marchons,* the cry of trappers to their dogs]

mush·room (mush′rōōm, -rŏŏm) *n.* 1 The fleshy, spore-bearing body of any of an order of fungi, consisting of an erect stalk and a caplike expansion. 2 Any nonpoisonous mushroom used as food, esp. the **field mushroom.** —*v.i.* 1 To grow or spread rapidly. 2 To expand into a mushroomlike shape. —*adj.* 1 Pertaining to or made of mushrooms. 2 Like a mushroom in shape or rapid growth. [< OF *mouscheron*]

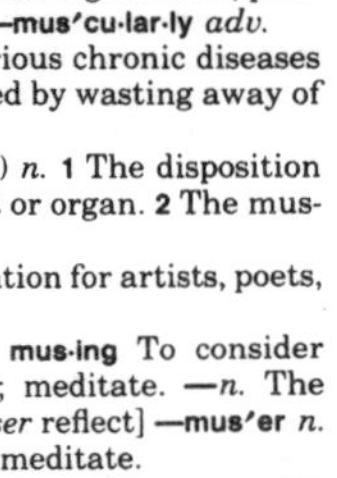

Agaric mushrooms

mu·sic (myōō′zik) *n.* 1 The art of organizing tones, esp. with respect to time, to form an aesthetic whole. 2 A composition, or mass of compositions: contemporary *music.* 3 Any pleasing succession or combination of sounds. —**face the music** To accept the consequences or punishment for one's actions. [< Gk. *mousikē (technē)* (art) of the Muses]

mu·si·cal (myōō′zi·kəl) *adj.* 1 Of, pertaining to, or characteristic of music. 2 Talented in or appreciative of music. 3 Set to music. —*n.* A theatrical or film production that tells a story by means of dialogue interspersed with music, songs, and dancing in a more or less popular idiom: also **musical comedy, musical play.** —**mu′si·cal·ly** *adv.* —**mu′·si·cal′i·ty** (-kal′ə·tē), **mu′si·cal·ness** *n.*

mu·si·cale (myōō′zə·kal′) *n.* An informal concert or private recital, often held in a home. [F]

music box A case containing a mechanism that reproduces melodies.

music hall 1 A public building devoted to musical entertainments. 2 *Brit.* A vaudeville house.

mu·si·cian (myōō·zish′ən) *n.* One skilled in music, esp. a professional performer or composer. —**mu·si′cian·ly** *adj.* —**mu·si′cian·ship** *n.*

mu·si·col·o·gy (myōō′zə·kol′ə·jē) *n.* The scientific and historical study of music. —**mu′si·col′o·gist** *n.*

mus·ing (myōō′zing) *adj.* Thoughtful; meditative. —*n.* The act of one who muses. —**mus′ing·ly** *adv.*

musk (musk) *n.* 1 A substance having a penetrating odor, obtained from a sac **(musk bag)** on the abdomen of the male musk deer. 2 A similar substance from certain other animals. 3 This substance, or a synthetic substitute, used to make perfumes. [< Pers. *mushk*]

musk deer A small hornless deer of CEN. and E Asia, of which the male has a musk-secreting gland.

mus·kel·lunge (mus′kə·lunj) *n. pl.* **·lunge** *n.* A large North American pike valued as a game fish. Also **mus′kal·lunge, mus′kie** (-kē). [< Algon.]

mus·ket (mus′kit) *n.* A large, long-barreled shoulder firearm, used esp. by soldiers on foot until superseded by the rifle. [< L *musca* fly]

mus·ket·eer (mus′kə·tir′) *n.* Formerly, a soldier armed with a musket.

mus·ket·ry (mus′kit·rē) *n.* 1 Muskets collectively. 2 The technique of operating small arms.

Mus·kho·ge·an (mus·kō′gē·ən, mus′kō·gē′ən) *n.* One of the principal North American Indian linguistic stocks, formerly inhabiting the SE U.S. Also **Mus·ko′gi·an.**

musk·mel·on (musk′mel′ən) *n.* Any of various melons having a pronounced aroma, esp. the cantaloupe.

musk ox A shaggy, horned ruminant of Greenland and North America, emitting a strong odor of musk.

musk·rat (musk′rat′) *n. pl.* **·rats** or **·rat** 1 A North American aquatic rodent yielding a valuable, glossy, dark brown fur and secreting a substance with a musky odor. 2 Its fur.

musk·y (mus′kē) *adj.* **musk·i·er, musk·i·est** Like or smelling of musk. —**musk′i·ly** *adv.* —**musk′i·ness** *n.*

Mus·lim (muz′ləm, mōōz′-, mōōs′-) *n. pl.* **·lims** or **·lim** A believer in Islam; Mohammedan. —*adj.* Of or pertaining to Islam or the Muslims. Also **Mus′lem.** —**Mus′lim·ism** *n.*

mus·lin (muz′lin) *n.* Any of several varieties of plain-weave cotton cloth ranging in texture from fine to heavy. [< F < Ital. *Mussolo* Mosul, city in Iraq where made]

muss (mus) *v.t. Informal* To make messy or untidy; rumple; often with *up.* —*n. Informal* 1 A state of disorder; mess. 2 A squabble. [Alter. of MESS]

mus·sel (mus′əl) *n.* 1 Any of various bivalve marine mollusks, esp. the common edible mussel. 2 Any of several freshwater mollusks, including species with bivalve shells yielding commercial mother-of-pearl. [< L *musculus,* dim. of *mus* mouse]

Mus·sul·man (mus′əl·mən) *n. pl.* **·mans** (-mənz) or **·men** (-mən) MUSLIM.

muss·y (mus′ē) *adj. Informal* **muss·i·er, muss·i·est** Disarranged; rumpled. —**muss′i·ly** *adv.* —**muss′i·ness** *n.*

must[1] (must) *v.* An auxiliary verb expressing: 1 Obligation or compulsion: *Must* you go? 2 Requirement: You *must* be healthy to be accepted. 3 Probability or supposition: You *must* be tired. 4 Conviction or certainty: War *must* follow. —*n. Informal* Something that ought to be done, required, seen, enjoyed, etc. —*adj. Informal* Important and essential: a *must* book. [< OE *mōste,* p.t. of *mōtan* may]

must[2] (must) *n.* Mustiness; mold. [Back formation < MUSTY]

must[3] (must) *n.* Unfermented juice pressed from the grape or other fruit. [< L *mustum (vinum)* new wine]

mus·tache (mus′tash, məs·tash′) *n.* 1 The growth of hair on the upper lip. 2 The hair or bristles growing near the mouth of an animal. Also **mus·ta′chio** (-tä′shō). [< Gk. *mystax* upper lip]

mus·tang (mus′tang) *n.* The wild horse of the American plains. [< Sp. *mesteño* wild animal]

mus·tard (mus′tərd) *n.* 1 Any of various plants related to cabbage, having yellow flowers and pods of round seeds. 2 The pungent seed of certain kinds of mustard, crushed for use as a condiment. 3 A strong, dark yellow color. [< OF *moustarde*]

mustard gas A synthetic organic sulfide, having a pungent odor and disabling effects, developed as a poison gas for military use.

mustard plaster A paste made of powdered mustard for use as a poultice.

mus·ter (mus′tər) *v.t.* **1** To summon or assemble (troops, etc.), as for service, review, or roll call. **2** To collect or summon: often with *up*: to *muster* up courage. —*v.i.* **3** To come together or assemble, as troops. —**muster in** (or **out**) To enlist in (or discharge from) military service. —*n.* **1** An assembling or an assemblage, esp. of troops for parade or review. **2** An official list of officers and men in a military troop or a ship's crew: also **muster roll.** **3** A specimen; pattern; sample. —**pass muster 1** To pass inspection. **2** To be acceptable or accepted. [< L *monstrare* to show]

must·y (mus′tē) *adj.* **must·i·er, must·i·est 1** Having a moldy, stale odor or taste. **2** Not original; trite; stale. **3** Dull; lifeless. [? Alter. of earlier *moisty* < MOIST] —**must′i·ly** *adv.* —**must′i·ness** *n.*

mu·ta·ble (myōō′tə·bəl) *adj.* **1** Capable of or liable to change. **2** Fickle; unstable. [< *mutare* to change] —**mu′·ta·ble·ness, mu·′ta·bil′i·ty** *n.* —**mu′ta·bly** *adv.*

mu·tant (myōō′tənt) *n.* A plant or animal showing a mutation.

mu·tate (myōō′tāt) *v.t.* & *v.i.* **·tat·ed, ·tat·ing** To undergo or subject to mutation.

mu·ta·tion (myōō·tā′shən) *n.* **1** The act or process of change; alteration. **2** A change or modification in form, function, etc. **3** *Biol.* A heritable characteristic not inherited from forebears but due to an alteration in a gene or genes in a germ cell. [< L *mutare* to change] —**mu·ta′tion·al, mu·ta·tive** (myōōt′ə·tiv) *adj.*

mute (myōōt) *adj.* **1** Uttering no word or sound; silent. **2** Lacking the power of speech; dumb. **3** Expressed without speech or sound: a *mute* refusal. **4** *Law* Refusing to plead upon arraignment. **5** *Phonet.* Not pronounced, as the *e* in *house.* —*n.* **1** One who refuses or is unable to speak. **2** *Music* A device to soften or muffle the tone of an instrument. **3** *Phonet.* A stop consonant. —*v.t.* **mut·ed, mut·ing** To soften or muffle the sound of (a musical instrument). [< L *mutus* dumb] —**mute′ly** *adv.* —**mute′ness** *n.*

mu·ti·late (myōō′tə·lāt) *v.t.* **·lat·ed, ·lat·ing 1** To deprive (a person, animal, etc.) of a limb or essential part; maim. **2** To damage or injure by the removal of an important part or parts: to *mutilate* a speech. [< L *mutilare* maim] —**mu′ti·la′tion, mu′ti·la′tor** *n.* —**mu′ti·la′tive** *adj.*

mu·ti·neer (myōō′tə·nir′) *n.* or One who takes part in mutiny. —*v.i.* To mutiny.

mu·ti·nous (myōō′tə·nəs) *adj.* **1** Disposed to or engaged in mutiny. **2** Characteristic of, relating to, or constituting mutiny. **3** Rebellious; unruly. —**mu′ti·nous·ly** *adv.* —**mu′ti·nous·ness** *n.*

mu·ti·ny (myōō′tə·nē) *n. pl.* **·nies** Rebellion against constituted authority; esp., a revolt of soldiers or sailors against their officers or commander. —*v.i.* **·nied, ·ny·ing** To take part in a mutiny. [< OF *mutin* riotous]

mutt (mut) *n. Slang* **1** A cur; mongrel dog. **2** A stupid person; blockhead. [< earlier *muttonhead* a stupid person]

mut·ter (mut′ər) *v.i.* **1** To speak in a low, indistinct tone. **2** To complain; grumble. **3** To make a low, rumbling sound. —*v.t.* **4** To say in a low, indistinct tone. —*n.* A low, indistinct utterance. [ME *muteren*] —**mut′ter·er** *n.* —**Syn. 1** mumble, murmur, whisper.

mut·ton (mut′n) *n.* The flesh of mature sheep as food. [< OF *moton* ram] —**mut′ton·y** *adj.*

mut·ton·chops (mut′n·chops′) *n. pl.* Side whiskers that are narrow at the temples and become broader at the cheeks.

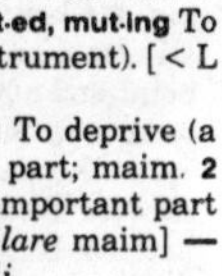

Muttonchops

mu·tu·al (myōō′chōō·əl) *adj.* **1** Shared, felt, received, etc., by each of two or more; reciprocal: *mutual* trust. **2** Having similar feelings each for the other or others: *mutual* enemies. **3** Possessed in common. [< L *mutuus* lent, exchanged, mutual] —**mu′tu·al′i·ty** *n.* —**mu′tu·al·ly** *adv.*

muu·muu (mōō′mōō′) *n.* A long, loose gown for women, originally worn in Hawaii.

Mu·zak (myōō′zak′) *n.* Unobtrusive popular recorded music played as background music, as in restaurants, shops, offices, etc.; also, the system for transmitting such music: a trade name.

mu·zhik (mōō·zhēk′, mōō′zhēk) *n.* A Russian peasant in Czarist times. Also **mu·zjik′.**

muz·zle (muz′əl) *n.* **1** The projecting jaws and nose of an animal. **2** A guard or covering for an animal's snout. **3** The discharging end of a firearm. —*v.t.* **·zled, ·zling 1** To put a muzzle on. **2** To restrain from speaking, expressing opinions, etc. [< LL *musus* snout] —**muz′zler** *n.*

Muzzle *def. 2*

muz·zle·load·er (muz′əl·lō′dər) *n.* A firearm loaded through the muzzle. —**muz·zle·load′ing** *adj.*

m.v. softly (It. *mezzo voce*).

my (mī) *pronominal adj.* **1** The possessive case of the pronoun *I* employed attributively. **2** An adjective used in certain forms of address: *my* lord. —*interj.* An exclamation of surprise: oh *my!* [< OE *mīn*]

my·ce·li·um (mī·sē′lē·əm) *n. pl.* **·li·a** (·lē·ə) The network of fine hyphae that makes up the main plant body of certain fungi, as mushrooms and molds. [< MYC(o) - + Gk. *hēlos* nail] —**my·ce′li·al, my·ce′li·an, my·ce′li·oid, my·ce·loid** (mī′·sə·loid) *adj.*

My·ce·nae (mī·sē′nē) *n.* An ancient city in NE Peloponnesus, Greece. —**My′ce·nae′an** *adj., n.*

myco- *combining form* Fungus: *mycology.* Also **myc-.** [< Gk. *mykēs* fungus]

my·col·o·gy (mī·kol′ə·jē) *n.* The branch of botany dealing with fungi. [< MYCO- + -LOGY] —**my·co·log·ic** (mī′kə·loj′ik) or **·i·cal** *adj.* —**my·col′o·gist** *n.*

my·co·sis (mī·kō′sis) *n. pl.* **·ses** (·sēz) **1** A parasitic fungous growth. **2** A disease caused by a parasitic fungus, as ringworm. [< MYC(o) - + -OSIS] —**my·cot′ic** (-kot′ik) *adj.*

my·e·li·tis (mī′ə·lī′tis) *n.* Inflammation of the spinal cord or of the bone marrow. [< Gk. *myelos* marrow + -ITIS]

my·na (mī′nə) *n.* One of various Asian, starlinglike birds often tamed and taught to mimic speech. Also **my′nah.** [< Hind. *mainā*]

Myn·heer (mīn·hâr′, ·hir′) *n.* Sir; Mr.: a Dutch title of address. [< Du. *mijn heer,* lit., my lord]

my·o·car·di·um (mī′ō·kär′dē·əm) *n.* The muscular tissue forming the heart. [< Gk. *mys* muscle + *kardia* heart] —**my′o·car′di·al** *adj.*

my·o·pi·a (mī·ō′pē·ə) *n.* **1** A defect in vision in which objects can be seen distinctly only when very near the eye; nearsightedness. **2** Lack of insight or good judgment. [< Gk. *myein* to close + *ōps* eye] —**my·op′ic** (-op′ik) *adj.*

myr·i·ad (mir′ē·əd) *adj.* Multitudinous; innumerable. —*n.* **1** A vast indefinite number. **2** Ten thousand. [< Gk. *myrios* numberless]

myr·i·a·pod (mir′ē·ə·pod) *n.* An arthropod having an elongated, segmented body bearing many pairs of appendages, a centipede or a millipede. [< Gk. *myrios* numberless + *pous, podos* foot]

myr·mi·don (mûr′mə·don, -dən) *n.* A faithful, obedient follower. [< MYRMIDON]

Myr·mi·don (mûr′mə′·don, -dən) *Gk. Myth.* One of a warlike people of Thessaly, followers of Achilles in the Trojan War.

myrrh (mûr) *n.* **1** An aromatic gum resin that exudes from several trees or shrubs of Arabia and E Africa, used in perfumes, incense, etc. **2** Any shrub or tree that yields this gum. [< L < Gk. *myrrha* < Ar. *myrr*]

myr·tle (mûr′təl) *n.* **1** An evergreen shrub with dense, glossy leaves that are fragrant when crushed, white or pink flowers, and black berries. **2** One of various other plants, as the periwinkle. [< Gk. *myrtos*]

my·self (mī·self′) *pron.* A form of the first person singular pronoun, used: **1** As a reflexive: I hurt *myself.* **2** As an intensive: I *myself* will see to it. **3** Informally as a compound object of a verb: She invited Helen, Jeff, and *myself.* **4** As a designation of one's normal or usual state: I haven't been *myself* lately.

mys·te·ri·ous (mis·tir′ē·əs) *adj.* **1** Of, implying, or characterized by mystery. **2** Unexplained; baffling. —**mys·te′ri·**

ous·ly *adv.* —**mys·te'ri·ous·ness** *n.* —**Syn.** 1 mystical, occult, secret, deep. 2 enigmatic, inexplicable, inscrutable, puzzling, perplexing.

mys·ter·y (mis'tər·ē) *n. pl.* **·ter·ies** 1 Something that cannot be explained or comprehended. 2 Any action, affair, or event so obscure or concealed as to arouse suspense, curiosity, or fear. 3 A story, play, film, etc. dealing with such actions or affairs. 4 Secrecy or obscurity: an event wrapped in *mystery*. 5 *Theol.* A truth known only through faith or revelation and incomprehensible to human reason. 6 *Eccl.* A sacrament, esp. the Eucharist. 7 *Usu. pl.* Secret rites or practices. 8 MYSTERY PLAY. [<Gk. *mystērion* secret worship, secret thing]

mystery play A medieval dramatic representation based on Biblical events or characters.

mys·tic (mis'tik) *adj.* 1 Of or pertaining to mystics or mysticism. 2 Of or designating an occult or esoteric rite, practice, belief, etc. 3 Mysterious; enigmatic. —*n.* One who practices mysticism or has mystical experiences. [<Gk. *mystikos* pertaining to secret rites]

mys·ti·cal (mis'ti·kəl) *adj.* 1 Characteristic of, relating to, or involving mysticism or mystics. 2 Believing in or practicing mysticism. 3 Inscrutable; inexplicable.

mys·ti·cism (mis'tə·siz'əm) *n.* 1 Any of various disciplines, usu. involving meditation and asceticism, by which one can supposedly attain intuitive knowledge of or direct union with God or some ultimate reality. 2 The experience of such knowledge or union. 3 Any theory or belief which states that it is possible to have immediate, intuitive experience of realities beyond man's senses or rational faculties. 4 Vague or obscure thinking.

mys·ti·fy (mis'tə·fī) *v.t.* **·fied, ·fy·ing** 1 To confuse or perplex, esp. deliberately. 2 To make obscure or mysterious. [<L *mysterium* mystery] —**mys'ti·fi·ca'tion, mys'ti·fi'er** *n.*

mys·tique (mis·tēk') *n.* A kind of legendary or superhuman quality or aura with which certain persons, things, or occupations are invested, making them objects of awe, curiosity, or veneration: the *mystique* of de Gaulle. [F]

myth (mith) *n.* 1 A traditional story, presented as historical, often purporting to explain some natural phenomenon, as the creation of life, and expressive of the character of a people, their gods, culture, heroes, religious beliefs, etc. 2 Any real or imaginary story, theme, or character that excites the interest or imagination of a people. 3 Myths collectively. 4 Any imaginary person or thing. 5 A false belief or opinion. [<Gk. *mythos* word, speech, story]

myth., mythol. mythology; mythological.

myth·i·cal (mith'i·kəl) *adj.* 1 Of or like a myth. 2 Existing only in a myth. 3 Imaginary; fictitious. Also **myth'ic.**

my·thol·o·gize (mi·thol'ə·jīz) *v.t.* **·gized, ·giz·ing** To make into a myth; glorify. [<F *mythologiser*]

my·thol·o·gy (mi·thol'ə·jē) *n. pl.* **·gies** 1 A collection of myths of a people, person, thing, event, etc. 2 The scientific collection and study of myths. —**myth·o·log·i·cal** (mith'ə·loj'i·kəl), **myth'o·log'ic** *adj.* —**myth'o·log'i·cal·ly** *adv.* —**my·thol'o·gist** *n.*

N

N, n (en) *n. pl.* **N's, n's, Ns, ns** (enz) 1 The 14th letter of the English alphabet. 2 Any spoken sound representing the letter *N* or *n*. 3 *Printing* EN. 4 *Math.* An indefinite number. 5 Something shaped like an N. —*adj.* Shaped like an N.

N nitrogen; knight (chess).

N, N., n. north; northern.

N. Navy; Norse; November.

n neutron.

n. name; net; neuter; noon; note; noun; number; born (L *natus*); our (L *noster*).

N.A. North America.

Na sodium (L *natrium*).

NAACP, N.A.A.C.P. National Association for the Advancement of Colored People.

nab (nab) *v.t.* **nabbed, nab·bing** *Informal* 1 To catch or arrest, as a criminal. 2 To seize suddenly. [? <Scand.]

na·bob (nā'bob) *n.* 1 A native governor in India under the Mogul empire. 2 A very rich and prominent man. [<Ar. *nuwwab*] —**na'bob·er·y, na'bob·ism** *n.* —**na'bob·ish** *adj.*

na·celle (nə·sel') *n. Aeron.* An enclosure for the cargo or power plant and sometimes the personnel of an airplane. [F, lit., small boat]

na·cho (nä'chō) *n. pl.* **·chos** A tortilla chip baked with a covering of beans, cheese, and peppers. [<Sp.]

na·cre (nā'kər) *n.* MOTHER-OF-PEARL. [F] —**na·cre·ous** (nā'krē·əs) *adj.*

na·dir (nā'dər, -dir) *n.* 1 The point of the celestial sphere intersected by a diameter extending from the zenith. 2 The lowest possible point. [<Ar. *nadir (es-semt)* opposite (the zenith)]

nag[1] (nag) *v.* **nagged, nag·ging** *v.t.* To torment with constant faultfinding, scolding, and urging. —*v.t.* To scold, find fault, or urge continually. —*n.* One who nags, esp. a woman. [Scand.] —**nag'ger** *n.* —**nag'ging·ly** *adv.* —**Syn.** *v.* berate, carp, harp, henpeck.

nag[2] (nag) *n.* 1 A pony or small horse. 2 An old or inferior horse. [ME *nagge*]

Na·hua·tl (nä'wät'l) *n.* The Uto-Aztecan language of the Aztecs and other Mexican and Central American Indian tribes. —*adj.* Designating or pertaining to this language.

nai·ad (nā'ad, nī'-) *n. pl.* **·ads** or **·a·des** (-ə·dēz) *Gk. & Rom. Myth.* One of the nymphs believed to dwell in and preside over watery sites.

na·if (nä·ēf') *adj.* NAIVE. Also **na·ïf'.** [F]

nail (nāl) *n.* 1 A thin, horny plate on the end of a finger or toe. 2 Claw, talon, or hoof. 3 A slender piece of metal having a point and a head, driven through or into wood, etc., as a fastener. —**hit the nail on the head** 1 To express something aptly. 2 To perform correctly. —**on the nail** *Informal* 1 Right away; immediately. 2 At the exact spot or moment. —*v.t.* 1 To fasten or fix in place with a nail or nails. 2 To close up or shut in by means of nails. 3 To secure by prompt action: to *nail* a contract. 4 To fix firmly or immovably: Terror *nailed* him to the spot. 5 To succeed in hitting or striking. 6 *Informal* To catch; intercept. 7 *Informal* To detect and expose, as a lie or liar. [<OE *nægel*] —**nail'er** *n.*

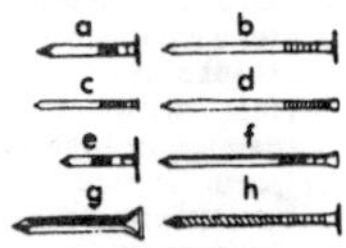

Nails *def. 3*
a, b. common. c. fiberboard. d. finishing. e. roofing. f. flooring. g. masonry.

nail·brush (nāl'brush') *n.* A brush with stiff bristles, used for cleaning the hands and fingernails.

nail file A fine, flat file used for smoothing and shaping the tips of the fingernails.

nain·sook (nān'sŏŏk) *n.* A soft, lightweight cotton fabric. [<Hind. *nainsukh* pleasure of the eye]

na·ive (nä·ēv') *adj.* 1 Simple and without affectation or sophistication. 2 Not consciously logical; uncritical. Also **na·ïve'.** [<F <L *nativus* natural, native] —**na·ive'ly** *adj.* —**na·ive'ness** *n.* —**Syn.** 1 artless, candid, open, unaffected, ingenuous.

na·ive·té (nä·ēv'tā', nä·ēv'tā) *n.* The state or quality of being naive. Also **na·ïve'té', na·ive·ty** (nä·ēv'tē, -ē'və·tē).

na·ked (nā'kid) *adj.* 1 Having no clothes or garments on. 2 Having no covering, as an unsheathed sword. 3 Having no defense or protection; exposed. 4 Being without concealment or excuse. [<OE *nacod*] —**na'ked·ly** *adv.* —**na'ked·ness** *n.*

naked eye The eye unaided by optical instruments.

N.A.M. National Association of Manufacturers.

N. Am. North American.

nam·ay·cush (nam'ə·kush, -ā-) *n.* The great lake trout of North America. Also **nay'ma·cush.** [<Algon. (Cree) *namekus* trout]

nam·by-pam·by (nam′bē·pam′bē) *adj.* Weakly sentimental or insipid. —*n. pl.* **-pam·bies 1** Namby-pamby talk, action, etc. **2** A person given to such talk or action. [<satirical name for Ambrose Philips, 1671–1749, Eng. poet]

name (nām) *n.* **1** The distinctive appellation by which a person or thing is known. **2** A descriptive designation; title. **3** General reputation. **4** An abusive appellation. **5** A memorable person, character, or thing: great *names* in music. —**by the name of** Named. —**call names** To insult by using uncomplimentary terms. —**in the name of** In behalf of. —**to one's name** Belonging to one: not a cent *to her name.* —*v.t.* **named, nam·ing 1** To give a name to. **2** To mention or refer to by name; cite. **3** To designate for some particular purpose or office; nominate. **4** To give the name of: *Name* the capital of Peru. **5** To set or specify, as a price or requirement. [<OE *nama*] —**nam′er** *n.*

name·less (nām′lis) *adj.* **1** Having no name; unnamed. **2** Having no fame or reputation. **3** Not suitable or fit to be spoken of. **4** Not to be named; inexpressible. **5** Illegitimate. —**name′less·ly** *adv.* —**name′less·ness** *n.*

name·ly (nām′lē) *adv.* That is to say; to wit.

name·plate (nām′plāt′) *n.* A piece of wood, metal, or plastic with a name inscribed on it, as on a door or desk.

name·sake (nām′sāk′) *n.* One who is named after or has the same name as another.

nan·a (nan′ə, nä′nä) *n.* Grandmother.

nan·keen (nan·kēn′) *n.* **1** A buff-colored Chinese cotton fabric. **2** *pl.* Clothes made of nankeen. Also **nan·kin′** [<*Nanking*, where originally made]

nan·ny (nan′ē) *n. pl.* **·nies** *Informal* **1** A female goat: also **nanny goat. 2** *Brit.* A child's nurse. [<*Nanny*, dim. of Ann]

nan·o·gram (nan′ə·gram) *n.* One billionth of a gram.

nan·o·me·ter (nan′ə·mē′tər) *n.* One billionth of a meter.

Na·o·mi (nā·ō′mē) In the Bible, the mother-in-law of Ruth.

nap[1] (nap) *n.* A short sleep; doze. —*v.i.* **napped, nap·ping** To take a nap; doze. —**be caught napping** To be caught unprepared or off guard. [<OE *hnappian* doze] —**nap′per** *n.*

nap[2] (nap) *n.* The short fibers on the surface of certain fabrics. —*v.t.* **napped, nap·ping** To raise a nap on. [<MDu. *noppe*] —**napped** *adj.*

na·palm (nā′päm) *n.* A jellied incendiary mixture based on gasoline. —*v.t.* & *v.i.* To attack or burn with napalm. [<NA(PHTHA) + *palm(itic) acid*, a fatty acid]

nape (nāp) *n.* The back of the neck. [ME]

na·per·y (nā′pər·ē) *n. pl.* **·per·ies** Household linen, as napkins, tablecloths, etc. [<OF *nape*]

naph·tha (naf′thə, nap′-) *n.* **1** A volatile, flammable mixture of hydrocarbons obtained by distilling petroleum, wood, etc. **2** Petroleum. [<Gk.]

naph·tha·lene (naf′thə·lēn, nap′-) *n.* A white, solid, volatile hydrocarbon, obtained from coal tar, used as a moth repellent and in making dyestuffs. Also **naph′tha·line** (-lēn, -lin), **naph′tha·lin.**

nap·kin (nap′kin) *n.* **1** A small cloth or piece of paper used during eating to wipe the mouth and hands and to protect the clothing. **2** *Brit.* A diaper. [<L *mappa* a cloth]

na·po·le·on (nə·pō′lē·ən, -pōl′yən) *n.* **1** A former French gold coin, equivalent to 20 francs. **2** A pastry composed of layers of puff paste filled with cream or custard. [<*Napoleon* Bonaparte, 1769–1821, Fr. emperor]

nap·py[1] (nap′ē) *adj.* **·pi·er, ·pi·est 1** Having or covered with nap. **2** Resembling nap. —**nap′pi·ness** *n.*

nap·py[2] (nap′ē) *n. pl.* **·pies** *Brit. Informal* A diaper.

nar·cis·sism (när′sə·siz′əm) *n.* Excessive interest in or admiration for oneself; self-love. Also **nar·cism** (när′siz·əm). [<NARCISSUS] —**nar′cis·sist** *n.* —**nar′cis·sis′tic** *adj.*

nar·cis·sus (när·sis′əs) *n. pl.* **·cis·sus·es, ·cis·si** (-sis′ē) **1** Any of a genus of bulbous plants having straplike leaves and flowers with a central, tubular crown, as the daffodil and jonquil. [<Gk. *narkissos*]

Nar·cis·sus (när·sis′əs) *Gk. Myth.* A youth who died for love of his own image in a pool, and was changed into a narcissus.

nar·co·sis (när·kō′sis) *n.* **·ses** (sēz) Stupor or unconsciousness produced by a narcotic drug. [<Gk.]

nar·co·syn·the·sis (när′kō·sin′thə·sis) *n.* Psychiatric treatment involving the use of certain drugs to encourage a patient to talk freely about himself.

nar·cot·ic (när·kot′ik) *n.* **1** Any of various drugs, as opium and its derivatives, that induce sleep and relieve pain, and are usu. addictive when used repeatedly. **2** Anything that serves to soothe, calm, or make drowsy. —*adj.* **1** Causing narcosis or stupor. **2** Pertaining to addiction to drugs or to persons addicted. **3** Causing drowsiness or dullness. [<Gk. *narkē* torpor] —**nar·cot′i·cal·ly** *adv.*

nar·co·tism (när′kə·tiz′əm) *n.* **1** NARCOSIS. **2** Addiction to narcotic drugs.

nar·co·tize (när′kə·tīz) *v.t.* **·tized, ·tiz·ing** To bring under the influence of a narcotic; stupefy. **nar′co·ti·za′tion** *n.*

nard (närd) *n.* SPIKENARD.

nar·es (nâr′ēz) *n. pl. of* **nar·is** (nâr′is) The nostrils or nasal passages. [L, nostrils]

nar·ghi·le (när′gə·li) *n.* HOOKAH. Also **nar′gi·le, nar′gi·leh.** [<Pers. *nārgīl* a coconut]

nark (närk) *n. Slang* A police undercover agent concerned with the detection of traffic in illegal drugs. Also **narc.** [? <NARC(OTIC AGENT)]

nar·rate (nar′āt, na·rāt′) *v.t.* **·rat·ed, ·rat·ing** To tell or relate as a story; give an account of. [<L *narrare* relate] —**nar′ra·tor, nar′rat·er** *n.*

nar·ra·tion (na·rā′shən) *n.* **1** The act of narrating the particulars of an event or series of events. **2** That which is narrated; narrative.

nar·ra·tive (nar′ə·tiv) *n.* **1** An orderly, continuous account of an event or series of events. **2** The act or art of narrating. —*adj.* Pertaining to narration. —**nar′ra·tive·ly** *adv.* —**Syn. 1** anecdote, report, story, tale.

nar·row (nar′ō) *adj.* **1** Having comparatively little distance from side to side. **2** Limited in extent or duration; circumscribed. **3** Illiberal; bigoted. **4** Limited in means or resources. **5** Niggardly; parsimonious. **6** Barely accomplished or sufficient: a *narrow* escape. **7** Scrutinizing closely: a *narrow* gaze. —*v.t.* & *v.i.* To make or become narrower, as in width or scope. —*n. Usu. pl.* A narrow strait or similar passage. [<OE *nearu*] —**nar′row·ly** *adv.* —**nar′row·ness** *n.*

narrow gauge 1 A width between railway tracks of less than 56.5 inches. **2** A railroad having narrow-gauge track. Also **narrow gage.** —**nar′row-gauge′, nar′row-gage′** *adj.*

nar·row-mind·ed (nar′ō·mīn′did) *adj.* **1** Having limited interests. **2** Prejudiced or bigoted. —**nar′row-mind′ed·ly** *adv.* —**nar′row-mind′ed·ness** *n.*

nar·whal (när′hwəl) *n.* An arctic cetacean having in the male a long, straight, spiraled tusk. Also **nar′wal, nar′whale′.** [<Dan. or Norw. *narhval*]

Narwhal

nar·y (nâr′ē) *adj. Regional* Never a; not one: with *a* or *an:* *nary* a cent. [<*ne'er a* never a]

NASA (nas′ə) National Aeronautics and Space Administration.

na·sal (nā′zəl) *adj.* **1** Of or pertaining to the nose. **2** *Phonet.* Pronounced with the voiced breath passing through the nose, as in (m), (n) and (ng). —*n. Phonet.* A nasal sound. [<L *nasus* the nose] —**na·sal·i·ty** (nā·zal′ə·tē) *n.* —**na′sal·ly** *adv.*

na·sal·ize (nā′zəl·īz) *v.* **·ized, ·iz·ing** *v.t.* **1** To give a nasal sound to. —*v.i.* **2** To pronounce oral sounds in the manner of nasals; talk through the nose. —**na′sal·i·za′tion** *n.*

nas·cent (nas′ənt, nā′sənt) *adj.* Beginning to exist or develop. [<L *nasci* be born] —**nas′cence, nas′cen·cy** *n.*

nascent state *Chem.* The condition of an atom or radical at the moment it is set free from a compound and ready to enter into combination with some other atom or radical. Also **nascent condition.**

na·stur·tium (na·stûr′shəm) *n.* **1** A common garden plant having spurred flowers of varying colors and rounded leaves with a cresslike taste. **2** The flower. [L]

nas·ty (nas′tē) *adj.* **·ti·er, ·ti·est 1** Filthy or offensively dirty. **2** Morally objectionable; indecent. **3** Difficult to handle or deal with: a *nasty* turn of events. **4** Painful; bad: a *nasty* cut. **5** Ill-natured; mean. [ME] —**nas′ti·ly** *adv.* —**nas′ti·ness** *n.*

na·tal (nāt′l) *adj.* Pertaining to one's birth; dating from birth. [< L *natus,* pp. of *nasci* be born]
na·tant (nā′tənt) *adj.* Floating on or swimming in water. [< L *natare* to swim]
na·ta·to·ri·al (nā′tə·tôr′ē·əl, -tō′rē-) *adj.* Swimming, or adapted for swimming. Also **na′ta·to′ry.**
na·ta·to·ri·um (nā′tə·tôr′ē·əm, -tō′rē-) *n. pl.* **·to·ri·ums** or **·to·ri·a** (-tôr′ē·ə, -tō′rē·ə) A swimming pool.
nathe·less (nāth′lis, nath′-) *adv. Archaic* Nevertheless. Also **nath·less** (nath′lis).
na·tion (nā′shən) *n.* **1** A people as an organized body politic, usu. associated with a particular territory and possessing a distinctive language and way of life. **2** A race or tribe having the same ancestry, history, language, etc.; a people. [< L *natio* breed, race]
na·tion·al (nash′ən·əl) *adj.* **1** Belonging to a nation as a whole. **2** Of, pertaining to, or characteristic of a specified nation. —*n.* One who is a member of a nation. **—na′tion·al·ly** *adv.*
national bank **1** A bank associated with and controlling the finances of a national government. **2** *U.S.* A bank chartered and supervised by the federal government.
National Guard The militia of each state of the U.S., supported in part by the federal government and subject to federal service in times of national emergency.
na·tion·al·ism (nash′ən·əl·iz′əm) *n.* **1** Devotion to the nation as a whole; patriotism. **2** A system demanding national ownership and control of all industries. **3** A demand for national independence. **—na′tion·al·ist** *adj., n.* **—na′tion·al·is′tic** *adj.* **—na′tion·al·is′ti·cal·ly** *adv.*
na·tion·al·i·ty (nash′ən·al′ə·tē) *n. pl* **·ties** **1** The condition of being national; national character. **2** A nation. **3** The condition of being a member of a specific nation by birth or citizenship.
na·tion·al·ize (nash′ən·əl·īz) *v.t.* **·ized, ·iz·ing** **1** To place under the control or ownership of a national government. **2** To give a national character to. **3** To make into a nation. *Brit. sp.* **·ise. —na′tion·al·i·za′tion, na′tion·al·iz′er** *n.*
na·tion-wide (nā′shən·wīd′) *adj.* Throughout the entire nation.
na·tive (nā′tiv) *adj.* **1** Born or produced in a region or country in which one lives; indigenous. **2** Of or pertaining to one's birth or to its place or circumstances. **3** Natural rather than acquired; inborn. **4** Of or pertaining to original inhabitants: usu. applied to non-European peoples. **5** Natural to any one or any thing. **6** Plain or simple; untouched by art. **7** Occurring in nature as a free element: *native* copper. —*n.* **1** One born in, or any product of, a given country or place. **2** Plants or animals common to a country or region. [< L *natus,* pp. of *nasci* be born.] **—na′tive·ly** *adv.* **—na′tive·ness** *n.* **—Syn.** *adj.* **3** innate, inherent.
na·tive-born (nā′tiv·bôrn′) *adj.* Born in the region or country specified.
na·tiv·i·ty (nā·tiv′ə·tē, nə-) *n. pl.* **·ties** **1** The coming into life or the world; birth. **2** A horoscope. **3** The condition of being a native. **—the Nativity** **1** The birth of Jesus. **2** Christmas Day.
Natl. national.
NATO (nā′tō) North Atlantic Treaty Organization.
nat·ty (nat′ē) *adj.* **·ti·er, ·ti·est** Smart; spruce; tidy: a *natty* dresser. [?] **—nat′ti·ly** *adv.* **—nat′ti·ness** *n.*
nat·u·ral (nach′ər·əl, -rəl) *adj.* **1** Of or pertaining to one's nature or constitution; inborn. **2** Of or pertaining to nature: *natural* history. **3** Of or pertaining to the existing order of things: *natural* law. **4** Coming within common experience: a *natural* result. **5** Not forced or artificial. **6** Without affectation. **7** Produced by nature: a *natural* bridge. **8** Connected by ties of consanguinity; being such by birth: a *natural* brother. **9** Born out of wedlock; illegitimate. **10** *Music* Neither sharped nor flatted: G *natural.* —*n.* **1** *Music* **a** A note on a line or a space that is affected by neither a sharp nor a flat. **b** A character (♮) which cancels the effect of an earlier flat or sharp: also **natural sign. 2** In keyboard musical instruments, a white key. **3** One lacking powers of reason or understanding; idiot. **4** *Informal* A person or thing admirably suited for some purpose or obviously destined for success. [< L *natura* nature] **—nat′u·ral·ness** *n.*
natural childbirth Childbirth regarded as a natural and relatively painless function in which the prospective mother is encouraged to participate consciously.
natural foods Foods processed minimally, although not necessarily organically grown.
natural gas A mixture of gaseous hydrocarbons, chiefly methane, generated naturally in petroleum deposits, used as a fuel.
natural history The observation and study, often not technical, of animals, plants, minerals, etc.
nat·u·ral·ism (nach′ər·əl·iz′əm, -rəl-) *n.* **1** Action or thought derived from or identified with exclusively natural desires and instincts. **2** In literature, art, etc., literal and unidealized representation of life and nature. **3** *Philos.* The doctrine that phenomena are derived from natural causes and can be explained by scientific laws.
nat·u·ral·ist (nach′ər·əl·ist, -rəl-) *n.* **1** One versed in natural sciences, as a zoologist or botanist. **2** An adherent of naturalism.
nat·u·ral·is·tic (nach′ər·əl·is′tik, -rəl-) *adj.* **1** In accordance with nature; not conventional or ideal. **2** According to the doctrines of naturalism. **3** Pertaining to naturalists.
nat·u·ral·ize (nach′ər·əl·īz, -rəl-) *v.* **·ized, ·iz·ing** *v.t.* **1** To confer the rights and privileges of citizenship upon, as an alien. **2** To adopt (a foreign word, custom, etc.) into the common use of a country or area. **3** To adapt (a foreign plant, animal, etc.) to the environment of a country or area. **4** To make natural; free from conventionality. —*v.i.* **5** To become as if native; adapt. *Brit. sp.* **·ise. —nat′u·ral·i·za′tion, nat′u·ral·iz′er** *n.*
nat·u·ral·ly (nach′ər·əl·ē, -rəl-) *adv.* **1** Without effort; spontaneously. **2** Without affectation or exaggeration. **3** As might have been expected; of course.
natural numbers The set of numbers (1, 2, 3, 4, . . .); the positive integers.
natural philosophy **1** NATURAL HISTORY. **2** PHYSICAL SCIENCES.
natural resource Any resource provided by nature, as soil, forests, minerals, water supply, and wild game.
natural sciences The sciences dealing with the physical universe.
natural selection *Biol.* The process whereby individual variations of advantage in a certain environment tend to become perpetuated in the race.
na·ture (nā′chər) *n.* **1** The qualities or essential traits of anything; essence. **2** General type or kind; behavior of a questionable *nature.* **3** The entire physical universe and its phenomena. **4** *Often cap.* The force that supposedly controls these. **5** The inherited or habitual condition and tendencies of a person; also, a specified cast of character: a gentle *nature.* **6** Man in a natural state; also, a simplified way of life resembling this state. **7** Natural scenery or the open spaces. [< L *natus,* pp. of *nasci* be born] **—Syn. 1** substance. **2** class, sort. **3** cosmos. **5** disposition, temperament.
naught (nôt) *n.* **1** Not anything; nothing. **2** A cipher; zero; the character 0. —*adj.* Of no value or account. —*adv.* Not in the least. [< OE *nā* not + *wiht* thing]
naugh·ty (nô′tē) *adj.* **·ti·er, ·ti·est** Perverse and disobedient; wayward. [< NAUGHT] **—naugh′ti·ly** *adv.* **—naugh′ti·ness** *n.*
nau·sea (nô′zhə, -zē·ə, -shə, -sē·ə) *n.* **1** A disagreeable sensation accompanied by an impulse to vomit. **2** A feeling of loathing. [< Gk. *nausia* seasickness < *naus* ship]
nau·se·ate (nô′zhē·āt, -zē-, -shē-, -sē-) *v.t. & v.i.* **·at·ed, ·at·ing** To affect with nausea or disgust. **—nau′se·a′tion** *n.*
nau·seous (nô′zhəs, -shəs) *adj.* **1** Nauseating; disgusting. **2** *Informal* Affected with nausea; queasy. **—nau′seous·ly** *adv.* **—nau′seous·ness** *n.* **—Syn. 1** offensive, repulsive, revolting, sickening. • *Nauseous* means provoking nausea or disgust: *a nauseous display of sentimentality. Nauseated* means affected with nausea or disgust: *nauseated during a boat ride; nauseated at political corruption. Nauseous* is widely used to mean *nauseated,* but especially in formal usage the distinction is observed.
naut. nautical.
nautch (nôch) *n.* In India, an entertainment featuring dancing girls **(nautch girls).** [< Hind. *nāch* dance]
nau·ti·cal (nô′ti·kəl) *adj.* Pertaining to ships, seamen, or navigation. [< Gk. *naus* ship] **—nau′ti·cal·ly** *adv.*
nautical mile A measure of distance equal to 1,852

meters or about 6,076 feet, used in sea and air navigation.

nau·ti·lus (nô′tə·ləs) *n. pl.* **·lus·es** or **·li** (-lī) A mollusk of southern seas, having a spiral shell with chambers lined with mother-of-pearl, esp. the **chambered** or **pearly nautilus.** [< Gk. *nautilos* sailor]

Chambered nautilus

nav. naval; navigation.

Nav·a·ho (nav′ə·hō) *n. pl.* **·hos** or **·hoes** One of a tribe of North American Indians now living on reservations in Arizona, New Mexico, and Utah. Also **Nav′a·jo.**

na·val (nā′vəl) *adj.* **1** Pertaining to ships and a navy. **2** Having a navy: a *naval* power. [< L *navis* ship]

nave (nāv) *n. Archit.* The main body of a cruciform church, between the side aisles. [< L *navis* ship]

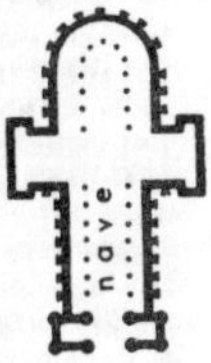

na·vel (nā′vəl) *n.* **1** The depression on the abdomen where the umbilical cord was attached. **2** A central part or point. [< OE *nafela*]

navel orange An orange, usu. seedless, having a small secondary fruit at the apex.

nav·i·cert (nav′ə·sûrt) *n. Brit.* A safe-conduct document authorizing a merchant vessel of a friendly or neutral nation to pass through a blockade. [< L *navis* ship + CERT(IFICATE)]

navig. navigation; navigator.

nav·i·ga·ble (nav′ə·gə·bəl) *adj.* **1** Capable of being traveled over by boats and ships: a *navigable* river. **2** Capable of being steered or directed: a *navigable* glider. **3** In condition for sailing. **—nav′i·ga·bly** *adv.* **—nav′i·ga·bil′i·ty, nav′i·ga·ble·ness** *n.*

nav·i·gate (nav′ə·gāt) *v.* **·gat·ed, ·gat·ing** *v.t.* **1** To travel over, across, or on by ship or aircraft. **2** To steer; direct the course of. *—v.i.* **3** To travel by means of ship or aircraft. **4** To steer or manage a ship or aircraft. **5** To plot a course for a ship or aircraft. [< L *navis* a boat + *agere* to drive]

nav·i·ga·tion (nav′ə·gā′shən) *n.* **1** The act of navigating. **2** The art of directing the course of vessels at sea or of aircraft in flight. **—nav′i·ga′tion·al** *adj.*

nav·i·ga·tor (nav′ə·gā′tər) *n.* **1** One who navigates, or directs the course of a ship, aircraft, etc. **2** A person skilled in navigation.

nav·vy (nav′ē) *n. pl.* **·vies** *Brit.* A laborer on canals, railways, etc.

na·vy (nā′vē) *n. pl.* **·vies 1** The marine military force of a country, under the control of a government department. **2** The entire shipping of a country engaged in trade and commerce; the merchant marine. **3** A fleet of ships.

navy bean The common small, dried, white bean.

navy blue Any of various shades of dark blue. Also **navy.**

navy yard A dockyard for the construction, repair, equipment, or care of warships.

na·wab (nə·wôb′) *n.* NABOB (def. 1). Also **na·wob′** [< Hind. *nawwāb* nabob]

nay (nā) *adv.* **1** No. **2** Not only so, but also: He is a good, *nay,* an excellent man. *—n.* **1** A negative vote or voter. **2** A negative; denial. [< ON *ne* not + *ei* ever]

Naz·a·rene (naz′ə·rēn) *n.* **1** An inhabitant of Nazareth. **2** A member of a group of early Christians. **—the Nazarene** Jesus. *—adj.* Of or pertaining to Nazareth or the Nazarenes. Also **Naz′a·re′an** (-rē′ən).

Naz·a·rite (naz′ə·rīt) *n.* A member of an ancient Hebrew sect who assumed certain vows, including abstaining from wine. Also **Naz′i·rite.** [< Heb. *nāzar* abstain] **—Naz′a·rit′ic** (-rit′ik), **Naz′i·rit′ic** *adj.*

Na·zi (nä′tsē, nat′sē, na′zē) *n.* A member of the National Socialist German Workers' Party, founded in 1919 and dominant from 1933 to 1945 in Germany under Hitler. *—adj.* Of or pertaining to the Nazis or their party. [G, short for *Nationalsozialistische (Partei)*]

Na·zi·fy (nä′tsə·fī, nat′sə-) *v.t.* **·fied, ·fy·ing** To subject to Nazi influence or control. **—Na′zi·fi·ca′tion** *n.*

Na·zism (nä′tsiz·əm, nat′siz-) *n.* The doctrines or practices of the Nazi party. Also **Na·zi·ism** (nä′tsē·iz′əm, nat′sē-).

N.B. New Brunswick.

N.B., n.b. note well (L *nota bene*).

Nb niobium.

NC North Carolina (P.O. abbr.).

N.C., N. Car. North Carolina.

NCO, N.C.O., n.c.o. noncommissioned officer.

ND North Dakota (P.O. abbr.).

N.D., n.d. no date.

N.D., N. Dak. North Dakota.

Nd neodymium.

NE Nebraska (P.O. abbr.).

NE, N.E., ne, n.e. northeast; northeastern.

N.E. New England.

Ne neon.

Ne·an·der·thal (nē·an′dər·täl, -thôl, -thol) *adj.* **1** Pertaining to a primitive, extinct form of man represented by various Old World fossils. **2** Uncouth; brutish. [< *Neanderthal,* a valley in w Germany]

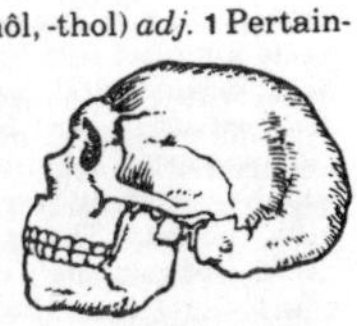

Neanderthal skull

Ne·a·pol·i·tan (nē′ə·pol′ə·tən) *adj.* Of or pertaining to Naples. *—n.* A citizen or resident of Naples.

neap tide (nēp) A tide having the lowest difference between high and low water levels and occurring at the first and third quarters of the moon. [< OE *nēp-* in *nēpflod* low tide]

near (nir) *adj.* **1** Not distant in place, time, or degree. **2** Closely related by blood or affection; familiar. **3** Closely touching one's interests. **4** In riding or driving, placed on the left. **5** Following or imitating closely; literal; a *near* copy. **6** Resembling or substituted for: *near* beer. **7** Avoiding by a narrow margin: a *near* escape **—near at hand 1** Close by. **2** In the immediate future. *—adv.* **1** At little distance: Don't come *near.* **2** *Informal* Nearly; approximately. **3** In a close relation. *—v.t. & v.i.* To come or draw near (to); approach. *—prep.* Close by or to. [< OE *nēar,* comp. of *nēah* nigh] **—near′ness** *n.*

near·by (nir′bī′) *adj. & adv.* Close at hand; adjacent.

near·ly (nir′lē) *adv.* **1** Almost: *nearly* asleep. **2** At no great distance; closely.

near·sight·ed (nir′sī′tid) *adj.* Able to see distinctly at short distances only; myopic. **—near′sight′ed·ly** *adv.* **—near′sight′ed·ness** *n.*

neat[1] (nēt) *adj.* **1** Characterized by strict order and cleanliness. **2** Well-proportioned; shapely. **3** Clever; adroit: a *neat* move. **4** Clear of extraneous matter; undiluted. **5** Remaining after every deduction; net. [< OF *net* < L *nitidus* shining] **—neat′ly** *adv.* **—neat′ness** *n.* **—Syn. 1** orderly, spruce, tidy, trig, trim. **3** deft.

neat[2] (nēt) *n. Archaic* **1** Bovine cattle. **2** A single bovine animal. *—adj.* Of bovine animals. [< OE *nēat*]

neath (nēth) *prep. Regional* BENEATH. Also **'neath.**

neat's-foot oil (nēts′fo͝ot′) An oil obtained by boiling the feet of cattle, used to dress leather.

neb (neb) *n.* **1** The beak or bill, as of a bird. **2** The tip end of a thing; nib, as of a pen. [< OE *nebb*]

Neb., Nebr. Nebraska.

neb·bish (neb′ish) *n.* A timid, weak, unaggressive person. [< Yiddish *nebach, nebech* poor thing]

neb·u·la (neb′yə·lə) *n. pl.* **·lae** (-lē) or **·las** *Astron.* A rarified, luminous or nonluminous mass of interstellar gas or dust. [L, vapor, mist] **—neb′u·lar** *adj.*

nebular hypothesis In astronomy, a hypothesis that the solar system existed originally in the form of a nebula.

neb·u·los·i·ty (neb′yə·los′ə·tē) *n. pl.* **·ties 1** NEBULA. **2** A misty or nebulous appearance.

neb·u·lous (neb′yə·ləs) *adj.* **1** Having its parts confused or mixed; indistinct: a *nebulous* idea. **2** Like a nebula. **—neb′u·lous·ly** *adv.* **—neb′u·lous·ness** *n.*

nec·es·sar·i·ly (nes′ə·ser′ə·lē) *adv.* **1** Inevitably; unavoidably. **2** Through necessity.

nec·es·sar·y (nes′ə·ser′ē) *adj.* 1 Being such in its nature that it must exist, occur, or be true; inevitable. 2 Absolutely needed to accomplish a desired result. —*n. pl.* **·sar·ies** That which is indispensable: usu. in the plural: the *necessaries* of life. [< L *necessarius*]

ne·ces·si·tate (nə·ses′ə·tāt) *v.t.* **·tat·ed, ·tat·ing** 1 To make necessary, unavoidable, or certain. 2 To compel. —**ne·ces′si·ta′tion** *n.* —**ne·ces′si·ta′tive** *adj.*

ne·ces·si·tous (nə·ses′ə·təs) *adj.* 1 Needy; poverty-stricken. 2 Urgent. 3 Essential. —**ne·ces′si·tous·ly** *adv.* —**ne·ces′si·tous·ness** *n.*

ne·ces·si·ty (nə·ses′ə·tē) *n. pl.* **·ties** 1 The quality of being necessary: the *necessity* for sleep. 2 That which is indispensable. 3 *Often pl.* That which is indispensable to a desired end. 4 The condition of being in want; poverty. —**of necessity** Necessarily; unavoidably. [< L *necessitas*] —**Syn.** 1 exigency. 2 essential, requisite, requirement.

neck (nek) *n.* 1 The part of a person or animal that connects the head with the trunk. 2 Something likened to a neck, in position, shape, etc. 3 The part of a violin, or other stringed instrument, between the end and the body. 4 The narrow part of a bottle, flask, etc. 5 A narrow passage of water connecting two larger bodies. 6 A peninsula, isthmus, or cape. 7 That part of a garment that fits about the neck. —**break one's neck** *Slang* To make a tremendous effort. —**get it in the neck** *Slang* To suffer criticism or punishment. —**neck and neck** Keeping abreast. —*v.i.* *Slang* To kiss and caress in making love. —*v.t.* *Slang* To kiss and caress in such a manner. [< OE *hnecca*]

neck·band (nek′band′) *n.* 1 The part of a garment that fits around the neck, esp. the strip on the inside of a collar. 2 A band around the neck.

neck·cloth (nek′klôth′) *n.* A folded cloth worn around the neck and collar; a cravat.

neck·er·chief (nek′ər·chif) *n.* A kerchief or scarf for the neck.

neck·lace (nek′lis) *n.* A string of precious stones, precious metal, beads, or the like, worn around the neck.

neck·line (nek′līn′) *n.* The line formed by the upper edge of a garment around or near the neck.

neck of the woods *Informal* A region or neighborhood.

neck·piece (nek′pēs′) *n.* A scarf, usu. of fur.

neck·tie (nek′tī′) *n.* A band or scarf passing round the neck or collar and tying in front.

neck·wear (nek′wâr′) *n.* 1 Any article worn around the throat. 2 Ties, cravats, mufflers, etc., collectively.

necro- *combining form* 1 Death. 2 Corpse: *necropolis.* [< Gk. *nekros* a corpse]

ne·crol·o·gy (ne·krol′ə·jē) *n. pl.* **·gies** 1 A list of persons who have died in a certain place or time. 2 A treatise on or an account of the dead. [NECRO- + -LOGY] —**nec·ro·log·ic** (nek′rə·loj′ik), **nec′ro·log′i·cal** *adj.* —**nec′ro·log′i·cal·ly** *adv.* —**ne·crol′o·gist** *n.*

nec·ro·man·cy (nek′rə·man′sē) *n.* 1 Divination by means of communication with the dead. 2 Black magic; sorcery. [< L *niger* black + Gk. *mantis* prophet] —**nec′ro·man′cer** *n.* —**nec′ro·man′tic** *adj.*

ne·crop·o·lis (ne·krop′ə·lis) *n.* A cemetery, esp. one belonging to an ancient city. [< NECRO- + Gk. *polis* city]

ne·cro·sis (ne·krō′sis) *n. pl.* **·ses** (-sēz) Localized death of tissue in a plant or animal. [< Gk. *nekrōsis* deadness] —**ne·crot′ic** (-krot′ik) *adj.*

nec·tar (nek′tər) *n.* 1 *Gk. Myth.* The drink of the gods. 2 Any sweet, delicious drink. 3 A sweet liquid secreted by cells at the base of some flowers. [< Gk. *nektar*] —**nec·tar·e·an** (nek·târ′ē·ən), **nec·tar′e·ous** *adj.*

nec·tar·ine (nek′tə·rēn′, nek′tə·rēn) *n.* A variety of peach having a smooth, waxy skin. [< NECTAR]

née (nā) *adj.* Born: noting the maiden name of a married woman: Mrs. Jones, *née* Burney. Also **nee.** [F, p.p. of *naître* be born]

need (nēd) *v.t.* 1 To have want of; require. —*v.i.* 2 To be in want. 3 To be necessary: It *needs* not. 4 To be obliged or compelled: He *need* not go. —*n.* 1 A lack of something requisite or desirable. 2 A situation of want or peril: to be a friend in *need.* 3 The thing needed: His *need* is education. —**have need to** Must; should. —**if need be** If necessary. [< OE *nīed, nēd*] —**need′er** *n.*

need·ful (nēd′fəl) *adj.* 1 Needed; necessary. 2 Needy. —**need′ful·ly** *adv.* —**need′ful·ness** *n.*

nee·dle (nēd′l) *n.* 1 A small, slender, pointed instrument containing an eye at the head, or, in sewing machines, at the point, to carry thread through a fabric in sewing. 2 The straight rod used in knitting. 3 The hooked rod used in crocheting. 4 Any instrument or object shaped like a needle, as a pinnacle or rock, or a leaf, such as that of the pine. 5 A thin pointer, such as a magnetic needle. 6 The sharp-pointed end of a hypodermic syringe. 7 *Informal* A hypodermic syringe. 8 An obelisk. 9 A phonograph stylus. —*v.* **·dled, ·dling** *v.t.* 1 To sew or pierce with a needle. 2 *Informal* To heckle or goad. —*v.i.* 3 To sew or work with a needle. [OE *nædl*]

nee·dle·craft (nēd′l·kraft′, -kräft′) *n.* 1 The art of doing needlework, esp. embroidery. 2 NEEDLEWORK.

nee·dle·point (nēd′l·point′) *n.* 1 Embroidery similar to tapestry, made on a stiff mesh material or canvas and used to cover chair seats, etc. 2 The stitch used in needlepoint. 3 Lace made entirely with a sewing needle rather than bobbins.

need·less (nēd′lis) *adj.* Useless; not required. —**need′less·ly** *adv.* —**need′less·ness** *n.*

needle valve A valve having an opening closed by a thin, needlelike rod.

nee·dle·wom·an (nēd′l·wo͝om′ən) *n. pl.* **·wom·en** (-wim′·in) 1 A woman skilled in needlework. 2 A seamstress.

nee·dle·work (nēd′l·wûrk′) *n.* Work done with a needle; sewing and embroidery. —**nee′dle·work′er** *n.*

needs (nēdz) *adv.* Necessarily; indispensably: often with *must.*

need·y (nē′dē) *adj.* **need·i·er, need·i·est** Being in need, want, or poverty. —**need′i·ly** *adv.* —**need′i·ness** *n.*

ne'er (nâr) *adv.* Contraction of *never.*

ne'er-do-well (nâr′do͞o·wel′) *n.* A useless, unreliable person. —*adj.* Useless; good-for-nothing.

ne·far·i·ous (ni·fâr′ē·əs) *adj.* Wicked in the extreme; heinous. [< L *nefas* a crime] —**ne·far′i·ous·ly** *adv.* —**ne·far′i·ous·ness** *n.* —**Syn.** atrocious, flagrant, infamous, villainous.

neg. negative; negatively.

ne·gate (ni·gāt′) *v.t.* **·gat·ed, ·gat·ing** 1 To make ineffective; nullify. 2 To deny the existence of. [< L *negare* deny]

ne·ga·tion (ni·gā′shən) *n.* 1 The act of denying. 2 Absence of anything affirmative; nullity.

neg·a·tive (neg′ə·tiv) *adj.* 1 Containing contradiction or expressing negation. 2 Characterized by denial or refusal: a *negative* reply. 3 Exhibiting the absence of positive or affirmative character. 4 *Phot.* Showing dark for light and light for dark: a *negative* plate or film. 5 *Math.* Less than zero. 6 *Electr.* Denoting a charge like that carried by an electron. 7 *Biol.* In a direction away from a stimulus: a *negative* response. 8 *Med.* Not showing evidence of a suspected condition: a *negative* biopsy. —*n.* 1 A proposition, word, or act expressing refusal or denial. 2 The side in an argument that denies or is against the affirmative. 3 The right to veto. 4 A photograph having the lights and shades reversed, used for printing positives. 5 *Gram.* A word or particle, such as *non-* or *not,* employing or expressing denial. 6 *Math.* A negative number or sign. —**in the negative** 1 Being on the side against the affirmative. 2 Denying or refusing. —*v.t.* **·tived, ·tiv·ing** 1 To deny; contradict. 2 To refuse to sanction or enact; veto. 3 To prove to be false; disprove. [< L *negare* deny] —**neg′a·tive·ly** *adv.* —**neg′a·tive·ness, neg′a·tiv′i·ty** *n.*

a b

a. negative *def. 4*
b. positive.

negative income tax Payment by the government to those whose incomes fall below a specified level, regarded as a means of replacing or supplementing welfare payments.

neg·a·tiv·ism (neg′ə·tiv·iz′əm) *n.* The tendency to reject or ignore what others suggest or order. —**neg′a·tiv·ist** *n.* —**neg′a·tiv·is′tic** *adj.*

neg·lect (ni·glekt′) *v.t.* 1 To disregard; ignore. 2 To fail to give proper attention to or take proper care of. 3 To fail to do or perform. —*n.* 1 The act of neglecting, or the state of being neglected. 2 Habitual want of attention or care. [< L *nec-* not + *legere* gather, pick up] **—neg·lect′er** *n.* —**Syn.** *v.* 1 slight. 3 overlook. *n.* 2 carelessness, heedlessness, oversight, slackness.

neg·lect·ful (ni·glekt′fəl) *adj.* Exhibiting or indicating neglect. **—neg·lect′ful·ly, neg·lect′ing·ly** *adv.*

neg·li·gée (neg′li·zhā′, neg′li·zhā) *n.* 1 A woman's soft, flowing dressing gown. 2 Any informal, careless, or incomplete attire. *—adj.* Careless or informal in dress. Also **neg′li·gé′.** [< F *négliger* to neglect]

neg·li·gence (neg′lə·jəns) *n.* 1 The act of neglecting or failing to pay proper heed to. 2 Carelessness; lack of interest.

neg·li·gent (neg′lə·jənt) *adj.* 1 Apt to omit what ought to be done; neglectful. 2 Inattentive; careless. [< L *negligere* neglect] **—neg′li·gent·ly** *adv.*

neg·li·gi·ble (neg′lə·jə·bəl) *adj.* That can be disregarded; inconsiderable. **—neg′li·gi·bil′i·ty, neg′li·gi·ble·ness** *n.* **—neg′li·gi·bly** *adv.*

ne·go·ti·a·ble (ni·gō′shē·ə·bəl, -shə·bəl) *adj.* 1 That can be negotiated. 2 *Law* Transferable to a third person, as for the payment of debts. 3 That can be managed or successfully dealt with. **—ne·go′ti·a·bil′i·ty** *n.* **—ne·go′ti·a·bly** *adv.*

ne·go·ti·ate (ni·gō′shē·āt) *v.* **·at·ed, ·at·ing** *v.i.* 1 To treat or bargain with others in order to reach an agreement. —*v.t.* 2 To procure, arrange, or conclude by mutual discussion: to *negotiate* an agreement. 3 To transfer for a value received; assign, as a note or bond. 4 To surmount, cross, or cope with (some obstacle). [< L *negotium* business] **—ne·go′ti·a′tion, ne·go′ti·a′tor** *n.* **—ne·go′ti·a·to′ry** *adj.*

Ne·gress (nē′gris) *n.* A Negro woman or girl: sometimes considered disparaging.

Ne·gri·to (ni·grē′tō) *n. pl.* **·tos** or **·toes** *Anthropol.* One belonging to any of the small Negroid peoples of s Africa, SE Asia, Malaya, and the Philippine Islands. [< Sp. *negro* black] **—Ne·grit′ic** (-grit′ik) *adj.*

Ne·gro (nē′grō) *n. pl.* **·groes** 1 A member of the Negroid racial division of mankind, esp. one belonging to the tribes inhabiting CEN. and s Africa. 2 One who is, in whole or in part, descended from the African and other Negroid peoples. *—adj.* Of, pertaining to, or being, a Negro. [< L *niger* black]

Ne·groid (nē′groid) *adj.* 1 Of or pertaining to the so-called black race, including the peoples originally inhabiting CEN. and s Africa, parts of SE Asia, Malaya, the Philippine Islands, and Melanesia, characterized by skin color varying from light brown to almost black. 2 Resembling, related to, or characteristic of Negroes. *—n.* A member of this racial group.

neigh (nā) *v.i.* To utter the cry of a horse; whinny. *—n.* A whinny. [< OE *hnægan*]

neigh·bor (nā′bər) *n.* 1 One who lives near another. 2 One who is near another. *—adj.* Close at hand; adjacent. *—v.t.* 1 To live or be near to or next to; adjoin. *—v.i.* 2 To be in proximity; lie close. *Brit. sp.* **neigh′bour.** [< OE *nēah* near + *gebūr* farmer]

neigh·bor·hood (nā′bər·hŏŏd) *n.* 1 The region near where one is or resides; vicinity. 2 The people collectively who dwell in the vicinity. 3 Nearness. 4 A district considered with reference to a given characteristic. **—in the neighborhood of** *Informal* About; near. *Brit. sp.* **neigh′bour·hood.**

nei·ther (nē′t͟hər, nī-) *adj.* Not either. *—pron.* Not the one nor the other. *—conj.* 1 Not one nor the other: followed by correlative *nor:* He will *neither* eat nor drink. 2 Nor yet. [< OE *nā* no + *hwæther*]

nem·a·tode (nem′ə·tōd) *n.* Any of a phylum of unsegmented worms, some of which are parasites in man and other animals. [< Gk. *nēma, -atos* a thread]

nem·e·sis (nem′ə·sis) *n.* Retributive justice; retribution. [< Gk. *nemein* distribute]

Nem·e·sis (nem′ə·sis) *Gk. Myth.* The goddess of retributive justice or vengeance.

neo- *combining form* 1 New; recent: *neologism.* 2 A modern or modified form of: *neoclassicism.* [< *Gk. neos* new]

ne·o·clas·si·cism (nē′ō·klas′ə·siz′əm) *n.* A revival of classical style in literature art, etc., esp. the revival in the later 17th and the 18th centuries. **—ne·o·clas·sic** (nē′ō·klas′ik), **ne′o·clas′si·cal** *adj.* **—ne′o·clas′si·cist** *n.*

ne·o·dym·i·um (nē′ō·dim′ē·əm) *n.* A metallic rare-earth element (symbol Nd). [< NEO- + Gk. *didymos* twin]

Ne·o·lith·ic (nē′ə·lith′ik) *adj. Anthropol.* Of or pertaining to the late Stone Age, in which man made polished stone implements and introduced a settled agriculture. [< NEO- + Gk. *lithos* stone]

ne·ol·o·gism (nē·ol′ə·jiz′əm) *n.* 1 A new word or phrase. 2 The use of new words or new meanings for old words. Also **ne·ol′o·gy** (*pl.* **·gies**). [< NEO- + Gk. *logos* word] **—ne·ol′o·gist** *n.* **—ne·ol′o·gis′tic, ne·ol′o·gis′ti·cal** *adj.*

ne·o·my·cin (nē′ə·mī′sin) *n.* An antibiotic obtained from a soil mold, used to treat certain skin and eye infections.

ne·on (nē′on) *n.* A colorless, odorless, gaseous element (symbol Ne) of very low chemical activity, used in neon lamps. [< Gk. *neos* new]

ne·o·nate (nē′ō·nāt) *n.* A newborn infant. [< NEO- + L *natus* born] **—ne′o·na′tal** *adj.*

neon lamp A glass tube containing neon in which an electric discharge produces a red or orange glow.

ne·o·phyte (nē′ə·fīt) *n.* 1 A recent convert. 2 Any novice or beginner. [< Gk. *neophytos* novice]

ne·o·plasm (nē′ə·plaz′əm) *n.* An abnormal growth of tissue; a tumor.

ne·o·prene (nē′ə·prēn) *n.* A synthetic rubber made from chlorinated hydrocarbons.

Ne·pal (ni·pôl′) *n.* A constitutional monarchy located between India and Tibet, 54,362 sq. mi., cap. Katmandu. —**Nep·al·ese** (nep′ə·lēz′, -lēs′) *adj., n.* • See map at INDIA.

ne·pen·the (ni·pen′thē) *n.* 1 A drug or potion used by the ancient Greeks to banish pain and sorrow. 2 Any agent causing oblivion. [< Gk. *nē-* not + *penthos* sorrow] **—ne·pen′the·an, ne·pen′thic** *adj.*

neph·ew (nef′yo͞o, *esp. Brit.* nev′yo͞o) *n.* 1 The son of one's sister or brother. 2 The son of one's sister-in-law or brother-in-law. [< L *nepos*]

ne·phrit·ic (ni·frit′ik) *adj.* 1 Pertaining to the kidneys. 2 Pertaining to or affected with nephritis.

ne·phri·tis (ni·frī′tis) *n.* Any of variously caused acute or chronic inflammations of the kidneys. [< Gk. *nephros* kidney + -ITIS]

ne plus ul·tra (nē′ plus ul′trə) Perfection. [L, lit., nothing more beyond]

nep·o·tism (nep′ə·tiz′əm) *n.* Favoritism by those in power extended toward relatives, esp. by appointing them to desirable positions. [< L *nepos* a grandson, nephew] —**ne·pot·ic** (ni·pot′ik) *adj.* **—nep′o·tist** *n.*

Nep·tune (nep′tyo͞on) *Rom. Myth.* The god of the sea, identified with the Greek Poseidon. *—n.* The planet of the solar system eighth in distance from the sun. • See PLANET. **—Nep·tu′ni·an** *adj.*

nep·tu·ni·um (nep·tyo͞o′nē·əm) *n.* An artificially produced radioactive element (symbol Np).

Ne·re·id (nir′ē·id) *pl.* **Ne·re·i·des** (ni·rē′ə·dēz) or **Ne·re·ids** *Gk. Myth.* One of the sea nymphs who attend Poseidon.

ner·va·tion (nûr·vā′shən) *n.* The arrangement of veins, as in a leaf or an insect's wing.

nerve (nûrv) *n.* 1 A cordlike structure, composed of delicate filaments by which impulses are transmitted between different parts and organs of the body and the central nervous system. 2 Anything likened to a nerve, as a rib or vein of a leaf or of an insect's wing. 3 *Slang* Offensive boldness; effrontery. 4 Fearlessness; intrepidity. 5 *pl.* Nervous excitability; a nervous attack. **—get on one's nerves** To try the patience of; exasperate. *—v.t.* **nerved, nerv·ing** To give strength, vigor, or courage to. [< L *nervus* sinew]

nerve block The injection of an anesthetic into a nerve leading to a definite area, thus producing local anesthesia.

nerve cell A neuron.

nerve center A group of nerve cells having a specific function, as hearing, respiration, etc.

nerve·less (nûrv′lis) *adj.* 1 Without vigor; weak. 2 Showing no stress; self-controlled. **—nerve′less·ly** *adv.*

nerve-rack·ing (nûrv′rak′ing) *adj.* Extremely irritating or exasperating. Also **nerve′-wrack′ing.**

ner·vous (nûr′vəs) *adj.* **1** Of or pertaining to the nerves or the nervous system. **2** Having or made up of nerves. **3** Strong; forceful, as literary style: *nervous* prose. **4** Easily disturbed or agitated. **5** Fearful; timid. —**ner′vous·ly** *adv.* —**ner′vous·ness** *n.* —**Syn. 4** excitable, high-strung, tense. **5** anxious, apprehensive.

nervous prostration NEURASTHENIA.

nervous system The organized network of all the nerve cells in an organism, in vertebrates branching out from the **central nervous system,** which comprises the spinal cord and brain.

ner·vure (nûr′vyŏŏr) *n.* A vein, as on a leaf or an insect's wing. [<L *nervus* sinew]

nerv·y (nûr′vē) *adj.* **nerv·i·er, nerv·i·est 1** Exhibiting force or strength; sinewy. **2** Full of nerve or courage. **3** *Slang* Displaying brazen assurance. **4** *Brit.* Nervous; excitable. —**nerv′i·ness** *n.*

nes·cience (nesh′əns, nēsh′-, -ē·əns) *n.* The state of not knowing; ignorance. [<L *ne-* not + *scire* know] —**nes′cient** *adj.*

-ness *suffix of nouns* **1** State or quality of being: *darkness.* **2** An example of this state or quality: to do someone a *kindness.* [<OE *-nis(s), -nes(s)*]

nest (nest) *n.* **1** The habitation prepared by a bird for the hatching of its eggs and the rearing of its young. **2** The bed or home of certain fish, insects, turtles, mice, etc. **3** Any cozy place or abode; a retreat. **4** A haunt, usu. for evil activities; also, those frequenting it: a *nest* of pirates. **5** A series or set of similar things of graduated sizes, fitting one inside another: a *nest* of bowls. —*v.t.* **1** To place in or as in a nest. **2** To pack or place one inside another. —*v.i.* **3** To build or occupy a nest. **4** To fit compactly inside another. [<OE]

Nests
a. hornet.
b. tailorbird.

nest egg 1 A natural or artificial egg placed in a nest to stimulate a hen to lay eggs there. **2** Something laid by, as a sum of money, for emergencies.

nes·tle (nes′əl) *v.* **·tled, ·tling** *v.i.* **1** To lie closely or snugly; cuddle. **2** To settle down in comfort. **3** To lie as if sheltered; be half-hidden: a lake *nestled* in the valley. —*v.t.* **4** To place or press lovingly or fondly. **5** To shelter in or as in a nest. [<OE *nestlian*] —**nes′tler** *n.*

nest·ling (nest′ling, nes′-) *n.* **1** A bird too young to leave the nest. **2** A young child.

Nes·tor (nes′tər) *Gk. Myth.* The oldest and wisest Greek chief in the Trojan War. —*n.* Any wise old man.

net[1] (net) *n.* **1** An open fabric, woven or tied with meshes, for the capture of fishes, birds, etc. **2** An openwork fabric, as lace. **3** Something constructed with meshes, as a tennis net. —*v.t.* **net·ted, net·ting 1** To catch in or as in a net; ensnare. **2** To make into a net. **3** To cover or enclose with a net. —*adj.* Made of or resembling netting. [<OE]

net[2] (net) *adj.* **1** Free from everything extraneous; obtained after deducting all expenses. **2** Not subject to any discount or deduction. —*n.* A net profit, amount, weight, etc. —*v.t.* **net·ted, net·ting** To earn or yield as clear profit. [<OF, neat]

Neth. Netherlands.

neth·er (neth′ər) *adj.* Situated at the lowest part. [<OE *neothera* under]

Neth·er·lands (neth′ər·landz) *n.* A constitutional monarchy of NW Europe, 15,780 sq. mi., official cap. Amsterdam, de facto cap. The Hague. —**Neth′er·land′er** *n.* —**Neth′er·land·ish** *adj.*

neth·er·most (neth′ər·mōst′) *adj.* Lowest.

nether world The world of the dead, esp. that of punishment after death; hell.

net·ting (net′ing) *n.* **1** A fabric of openwork; a net. **2** The act or operation of making net.

net·tle (net′l) *n.* Any of various plants having stinging hairs or bristles, usu. borne on the leaves. —*v.t.* **·tled, ·tling 1** To sting as the nettle does. **2** To annoy or irritate. [<OE *netle*] —**net′tler** *n.* —**Syn.** *v.* **2** chafe, exasperate, irk, vex.

net·work (net′wûrk′) *n.* **1** NETTING. **2** A system of interlacing lines, tracks, or channels. **3** An interconnection of electric devices. **4** *Telecom.* A chain of broadcasting stations.

neu·ral (n^{y}ŏŏr′əl) *adj.* Of or pertaining to the nerves or nervous system. [<Gk. *neuron* nerve]

neu·ral·gi·a (n^{y}ŏŏ·ral′jē·ə, -jə) *n.* Severe pain along the course of a nerve. [<NEUR(O)- + Gk. *algos* pain] —**neu·ral′gic** *adj.*

neu·ras·the·ni·a (n^{y}ŏŏr′əs·thē′nē·ə, -thēn′yə) *n.* A kind of neurosis marked by headaches, digestive disturbances, depression, etc. [<NEUR(O)- + Gk. *asthenia* weakness] —**neu′ras·then′ic** (-then′ik) *adj., n.*

neu·ri·tis (n^{y}ŏŏ·rī′tis) *n.* Inflammation of a nerve. —**neu·rit′ic** (-rit′ik) *adj.*

neuro- *combining form* Nerve; pertaining to a nerve or system of nerves: *neurology.* [<Gk. *neuron* sinew, nerve]

neu·ro·chem·is·try (nŏŏr′ō·kem′ə·strē) *n.* That branch of chemistry that has to do with chemicals, esp. the neurotransmitters, that affect the nervous system.

neu·rol·o·gy (n^{y}ŏŏ·rol′ə·jē) *n.* The branch of medicine concerned with the nervous system. —**neu·ro·log·i·cal** (n^{y}ŏŏr′ə·loj′i·kəl) *adj.* —**neu·rol′o·gist** *n.*

neu·ron (n^{y}ŏŏr′on) *n.* A nerve cell, consisting of a nucleated central body and two long processes. Also **neu′rone** (-ōn). [<Gk. *neuron* nerve] —**neu·ron·ic** (n^{y}ŏŏ·ron′ik), **neu′ron·al** (-rən·əl) *adj.*

neu·ro·path (n^{y}ŏŏr′ə·path) *n.* One suffering from or subject to neuroses. —**neu′ro·path′ic, neu′ro·path′i·cal** *adj.* —**neu′ro·path′i·cal·ly** *adv.*

neu·ro·psy·chi·a·try (n^{y}ŏŏr′ō·sī·kī′ə·trē) *n.* The study and treatment of diseases involving both neurological and mental factors. —**neu′ro·psy′chi·at′ric** (-sī′kē·at′rik) *adj.* —**neu′ro·psy·chi′a·trist** (-sī·kī′ə·trist) *n.*

neu·rop·ter·ous (n^{y}ŏŏ·rop′tər·əs) *adj.* Of or pertaining to an order of insects having four fine-veined wings and biting mouth parts. [<NEUR(O)- + Gk. *pteron* wing]

neu·ro·sis (n^{y}ŏŏ·rō′sis) *n. pl.* **·ses** (-sēz) Any of several functional mental disorders usu. characterized by anxiety, depression, etc. [<Gk. *neuron* nerve]

neu·rot·ic (n^{y}ŏŏ·rot′ik) *adj.* **1** Of, being, or suffering from neurosis. **2** Having a morbid nature or tendency. —*n.* A person afflicted with neurosis. —**neu·rot′i·cal·ly** *adv.* —**neu·rot′i·cism** *n.*

neut. neuter; neutral.

neu·ter (n^{y}ōō′tər) *adj.* **1** *Gram.* Neither masculine nor feminine in gender. **2** *Biol.* Having functionless or imperfectly developed sex organs. **3** Taking the part of neither side; neutral. —*n.* **1** An animal of no apparent sex, as a worker bee. **2** A eunuch. **3** A castrated animal. **4** *Gram.* **a** The neuter gender. **b** A word in this gender. **5** A neutral in warfare or other conflict. —*v.t. Informal* To castrate or spay, esp. cats; alter. [<L *ne-* not + *uter* either]

neu·tral (n^{y}ōō′tral) *adj.* **1** Refraining from taking the part of either side in a quarrel, contest, or war. **2** Having no decided character; indefinite. **3** Having no decided color; predominantly brownish or grayish. **4** *Biol.* Neuter. **5** *Bot.* Lacking pistils or stamens. **6** *Chem.* Being neither acid nor alkaline. **7** *Electr.* Neither positive nor negative. —*n.* One who or that which is neutral. [<L *neuter* neuter] —**neu′tral·ly** *adv.*

neu·tral·ism (n^{y}ōō′trəl·iz′əm) *n.* A political doctrine holding that neutrality in international relations serves a country's best interests. —**neu′tral·ist** *adj., n.* —**neu′tral·is′tic** *adj.*

neu·tral·i·ty (n^{y}ōō·tral′ə·tē) *n. pl.* **·ties 1** The state of being a neutral nation during a war. **2** The state of being neutral.

neu·tral·ize (n^{y}ōō′trəl·īz) *v.t.* **·ized, ·iz·ing 1** To counteract or destroy by an opposite force or influence; counterbalance. **2** To declare (a nation, area, etc.) to be neutral and not involved in hostilities. **3** *Chem.* To make neutral by adding either acid or base. **4** *Mil.* To render incapable of effective action. *Brit. sp.* **neu′tral·ise.** —**neu·tral·i·za·tion** (n^{y}ōō′trəl·ə·zā′shən), **neu′tral·iz′er** *n.*

neu·tri·no (n^{y}ōō·trē′nō) *n. pl.* **·nos** *Physics* Either of two stable subatomic particles having no electric charge and a theoretical mass of zero when at rest.

neu·tron (n^{y}ōō′tron) *n. Physics* An electrically neutral particle of the atom, having a mass approximately equal to that of the proton. [<NEUTRAL]

neutron star One of a class of objects, identified by some astrophysicists with pulsars, that are produced when fairly massive stars undergo gravitational collapse and form matter so dense that all the electrons and protons are in effect forced together to form neutrons.

Nev. Nevada.

nev·er (nev′ər) *adv.* **1** Not at any time. **2** Not at all; positively not: *Never* fear. [< OE *ne* not + *ǣfre* ever]

nev·er·more (nev′ər·môr′, -mōr′) *adv.* Never again.

nev·er·the·less (nev′ər·thə·les′) *conj. & adv.* None the less; however; yet.

ne·vus (nē′vəs) *n. pl.* **·vi** (-vī) A birthmark or congenital mole. Also **nae·vus.** [< L *naevus* blemish] **—ne′void, nae′·void** (-void) *adj.*

new (nyōō) *adj.* **1** Lately made: a *new* car. **2** Lately discovered or become well known: a *new* invention. **3** Beginning or recurring afresh: the *new* moon. **4** Changed in essence, constitution, etc.: I feel a *new* man. **5** Different from that heretofore known or used; unfamiliar: This game is *new* to me. **6** Up-to-date: *new* styles in clothing. **7** Unaccustomed: a horse *new* to the saddle. **8** Named for another: used to distinguish a place from its namesake: *New* Orleans. **9** Having reached a specified rank, position, etc.: a *new* governor. **10** More; additional: *new* data. *—adv.* Newly; recently. *—n.* Something new: off with the old and on with the *new.* [< OE *nēowe*] **—new′ness** *n.* **—Syn.** *adj.* **2** fresh, novel. **4** better. **6** latest, modern. **10** further.

new·born (nyōō′bôrn) *adj.* **1** Newly born. **2** About to start a new life; reborn. *—n.* A newborn infant or animal.

new·com·er (nyōō′kum′ər) *n.* One who has recently arrived.

New Deal The policies and principles of the U.S. administration under President Franklin D. Roosevelt, embracing various social, economic, and political innovations. **—New Dealer**

new·el (nyōō′əl) *n.* **1** The pillar from which the steps of a spiral staircase radiate. **2** A post supporting the end of a stair rail. Also **newel post.** [< OF *nouel* stone of a fruit]

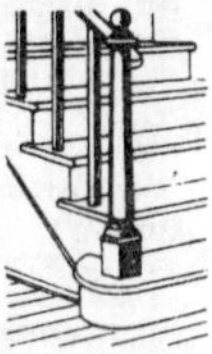

Newel *def. 2*

new-fan·gled (nyōō′fang′gəld) *adj.* **1** Of new fashion: generally in depreciation: *new-fangled* notions. **2** Fond of novelty. **—new′-fan′gled·ness** *n.* [< NEW + OE *fangen* seized]

New·found·land (nyōō′fənd·lənd, nyōō·found′-) *n.* A large dog characterized by a broad head, square muzzle, and usu. black coat, originally bred in Newfoundland.

New France The region settled by the French in North America from 1534 to 1763.

New·gate (nyōō′git, -gāt) *n.* A prison in London, destroyed 1902.

New Jerusalem Heaven. *Rev.* 21:2.

New Latin The Latin in use since about 1500, esp. in scientific nomenclature.

New Left An activist movement in the 1960s made up largely of students and youthful extremist groups, which advocated sweeping political, social, and educational reforms.

new·ly (nyōō′lē) *adv.* **1** In a new or recent manner; lately. **2** In a different way; so as to be or appear new; afresh.

new·ly-wed (nyōō′lē·wed′) *n.* A person recently married.

new moon **1** The phase of the moon when it is between the earth and the sun, and is nearly invisible. **2** The crescent moon. • See MOON.

new-mown (nyōō′mōn′) *adj.* Recently cut or mown, as hay.

news (nyōōz) *n. pl. (construed as sing.)* **1** Fresh information concerning something that has recently taken place. **2** Information about anything new or strange. **—break the news** To make known; tell about. **—Syn. 1** information, intelligence, report, tidings.

news·boy (nyōōz′boi′) *n.* A boy who sells or delivers newspapers.

news·cast (nyōōz′kast′, -käst′) *n.* A radio or television news program. *—v.t. & v.i.* To broadcast (news). **—news′·cast′er** *n.*

news·mag·a·zine (nyōōz′mag′ə·zēn) *n.* A periodical, esp. a weekly, that summarizes the news and reports current events of general interest.

news·man (nyōōz′man′, -mən) *n. pl.* **·men** (-men′, -mən) A newspaper reporter. **—news′wom′an** (-wŏŏm′ən) *n. Fem.*

news·pa·per (nyōōz′pā′pər) *n.* A publication issued for general circulation at frequent, usu. regular, intervals.

news·pa·per·man (nyōōz′pā′pər·man′) *n. pl.* **·men** (-men′, -mən) **1** One who publishes a newspaper. **2** One who writes or edits news for a newspaper. **—news′pa′per·wom′·an** *n. Fem.*

news·print (nyōōz′print′) *n.* The thin, unsized paper on which the ordinary daily or weekly newspaper is printed.

news·reel (nyōōz′rēl′) *n.* A motion picture, usually of short duration, showing events of current interest.

news·stand (nyōōz′stand′) *n.* A stand or stall at which newspapers and periodicals are offered for sale.

news·worth·y (nyōōz′wûr′thē) *adj.* Important enough to be written up in a newspaper; considered to be of current interest. **—news′wor′thi·ness** *n.*

news·y (nyōō′zē) *adj.* **new·si·er, new·si·est** *Informal* Full of news, usu. of a gossipy nature. *—n. Informal* A newsboy.

newt (nyōōt) *n.* A small, amphibious salamander. [< ME *an ewt,* taken as *a newt*]

Newt

New Testament The portion of the Bible containing the life and teachings of Jesus and his followers.

new·ton (nyōō′tən) *n. Physics* A unit of force equal to that which will accelerate a mass of 1 kilogram by 1 meter per second per second. [< Isaac *Newton,* 1642–1727, English mathematician]

new town A planned, new community, often under government auspices or with government support, consisting of various types of housing, schools, parks, and sometimes local industries.

New World The Western Hemisphere, including North and South America.

new year The year just begun or just about to begin.

New Year January 1, the first day of the year, widely observed as a legal holiday. Also **New Year's Day.**

New Year's Eve The evening of December 31, the day before New Year's Day.

next (nekst) *adj.* Being nearest to, in time, space, order, rank, etc.; immediately succeeding or preceding. **—next door to** In the next building, dwelling, etc. **—next to 1** Closest to. **2** Almost: *next to* impossible. *—adv.* In the nearest time, place, or rank, esp. immediately succeeding: when *next* I meet her. *—prep.* Nearest to. [< OE *nēahst,* superl. of *nēah* nigh]

next door In or to the next building, dwelling, etc. **—next door to** Next to. **—next′-door′** *adj.*

next of kin The living person or persons most closely related to one.

nex·us (nek′səs) *n. pl.* **·us·es** or **·us** A bond or tie between the several members of a group or series; link. [< L, pp. of *nectere* to tie]

Nez Per·cé (nez′ pûrs′, *Fr.* nā per·sā′) One of a tribe of North American Indians formerly dwelling in Idaho, Oregon, and Washington. [F, pierced nose]

NF Norman French.

N.F. National Formulary; Newfoundland.

N.G., n.g. no good.

NGk, N.Gk. New Greek.

NH New Hampshire (P.O. abbr.).

N.H. New Hampshire.

N.I., N.Ire. Northern Ireland.

Ni nickel.

ni·a·cin (nī′ə·sin) *n.* The antipellagra factor in the vitamin B complex. [< NI(COTINIC) AC(ID) + -IN]

nib (nib) *n.* **1** A projecting, pointed part. **2** A beak of a bird; neb. **3** The point of a pen. *—v.t.* **nibbed, nib·bing** To furnish with a nib. [Var. of NEB]

nib·ble (nib′əl) *v.* **·bled, ·bling** *v.t.* **1** To eat (food) with small, quick bites. **2** To bite gently or cautiously, as bait. *—v.i.* **3** To bite off or eat little bits. **4** To take gentle or cautious bites: usu. with *at.* —*n.* A little bite. [? < LG *nibbelen*] —**nib'bler** *n.*

nib·lick (nib'lik) *n.* A golf club with a slanted iron head for lifting the ball out of bunkers, long grass, etc. [?]

Nic·a·ra·gua (nik'ə·rä'gwə) *n.* A republic of Central America, 57,100 sq. mi., cap. Managua. —**Nic'a·ra'guan** *adj., n.* • See map at CENTRAL AMERICA.

nice (nīs) *adj.* **nic·er, nic·est** 1 Agreeable or pleasant: *nice* weather. 2 Warm; kindly: a *nice* person. 3 Requiring careful consideration; subtle: a *nice* point. 4 Exact; accurate: a *nice* eye for color. 5 Refined in tastes or habits; fastidious. 6 Suitable: That dress will be *nice* for the party. 7 Scrupulous; honest. 8 Refined or cultivated: *nice* manners. 9 Needing tact, care, etc.: a *nice* situation. 10 Well performed: a *nice* throw. [< L *nescius* ignorant] —**nice'ly** *adv.* —**nice'ness** *n.* —**Syn.** 1 enjoyable. 2 friendly. 5 exacting; particular. 6 fitting; proper.

Ni·cene Creed (nī'sēn, nī·sēn') *Eccl.* A Christian confession of faith, adopted by the first Council of Nicaea in 325 A.D., and now generally accepted by most Christian sects. [< *Nicaea,* ancient town in Asia Minor]

ni·ce·ty (nī'sə·tē) *n. pl.* **·ties** 1 The quality of being nice. 2 A delicate point or distinction; subtlety. 3 A rare or delicious thing; delicacy. 4 Fastidiousness.

niche (nich) *n.* 1 A recessed space or hollow, esp. one in a wall for a statue, etc. 2 Any position specially adapted to its occupant. —*v.t.* **niched, nich·ing** To put in a niche. [< L *nidus* a nest]

Niche

nick (nik) *n.* A slight cut, chip, or indentation in the surface or edge of anything. —**in the nick of time** At the last moment possible to be effective. —*v.t.* 1 To make a nick or nicks in; notch. 2 To cut through or into. 3 *Slang* To cheat or trick. [ME *nyke*] —**nick'er** *n.*

nick·el (nik'əl) *n.* 1 A hard, silver-white metallic element (symbol Ni) widely used in steel and other alloys. 2 A five-cent coin of the U.S. or of Canada. —*v.t.* To plate with nickel. [< G *(Kupfer)nickel,* lit., copper demon; because its ore looks like an ore of copper but contains none]

nick·el·o·de·on (nik'əl·ō'dē·ən) *n.* 1 A former type of motion-picture theater charging an admission fee of five cents. 2 A juke box.

nick·el-plate (nik'əl·plāt') *v.t.* **-plat·ed, -plat·ing** To cover with a thin layer of nickel.

nickel plate A thin layer of nickel on a surface.

nickel silver A hard, silvery alloy of nickel, copper, and zinc that resists corrosion.

nick·er (nik'ər) *v.i.* To neigh or whinny. —*n.* The sound of nickering. [Imit.]

nick-nack (nik'nak') *n.* KNICK-KNACK.

nick·name (nik'nām') *n.* 1 A diminutive, as Tom for Thomas. 2 A descriptive or facetious name given to a person, place, or thing in derision or affection. —*v.t.* **·named, ·nam·ing** 1 To give a nickname to. 2 To misname. [ME *an ekename* an additional name, taken as *a nickname*]

nic·o·tine (nik'ə·tēn, -tin) *n.* A poisonous alkaloid contained in the leaves of tobacco. [< J. *Nicot,* 1530–1604, French courtier, who introduced tobacco into France] —**nic·o·tin·ic** (nik'ə·tin'ik) *adj.*

nicotinic acid NIACIN.

nic·ti·tate (nik'tə·tāt) *v.i.* **·tat·ed, ·tat·ing** To blink. Also **nic'tate.** [< L *nictare* to wink] —**nic'ti·ta'tion, nic·ta'tion** *n.*

nictitating membrane A transparent third eyelid found in certain animals. Also **nic·ta'ting membrane.**

niece (nēs) *n.* 1 The daughter of one's brother or sister. 2 The daughter of one's brother-in-law or sister-in-law. [< L *neptis* niece]

nif·ty (nif'tē) *adj.* **·ti·er, ·ti·est** *Slang* Stylish; pleasing. [?]

Ni·ger (nī'jər, -gər) *n.* A republic of CEN. Africa, 458,976 sq. mi., cap. Niamey. • See map at AFRICA.

Ni·ge·ri·a (nī·jir'ē·ə) *n.* An independent member of the Commonwealth of Nations in w Africa, 339,169 sq. mi., cap. Lagos. —**Ni·ge'ri·an** *adj., n.* • See map at AFRICA.

nig·gard (nig'ərd) *n.* A parsimonious person. —*adj.* Niggardly. [< Scand.]

nig·gard·ly (nig'ərd·lē) *adj.* 1 Avaricious; stingy. 2 Scanty or measly: a *niggardly* portion. —*adv.* Stingily. —**nig'gard·li·ness** *n.* —**Syn.** *adj.* 1 miserly, parsimonious, tight-fisted.

nig·gle (nig'əl) *v.i.* **·gled, ·gling** To occupy oneself with trifles; be too precise. [Prob. < Scand.] —**nig'gler** *n.*

nigh (nī) *adj.* **nigh·er, nigh·est** or, formerly, **next** Being close by; near in time or place. —*adv.* 1 Not remote in time or place. 2 Almost; nearly. —*prep.* Close to; near. [< OE *nēah*]

night (nīt) *n.* 1 The period during which the sun is below the horizon from sunset to sunrise. 2 The dark. 3 A condition of gloom or misfortune. 4 Death. —**night and day** Continuously. —**nights** *Informal* At night. [< OE *niht*]

night blindness Impaired vision in dim light due to vitamin A deficiency.

night-bloom·ing ce·re·us (nīt'blōō'ming sir'ē·əs) Any of several cactuses having fragrant flowers that open at night.

night·cap (nīt'kap') *n.* 1 A headcovering to be worn in bed. 2 *Informal* A drink of liquor taken just before going to bed.

night·clothes (nīt'klōz', -klōthz') *n.pl.* Clothes to be worn in bed, as pajamas and nightgowns.

night·club (nīt'klub') *n.* A restaurant open only at night, providing entertainment, food, and drink.

night·fall (nīt'fôl') *n.* The close of day.

night·gown (nīt'goun') *n.* A long, loose gown worn in bed. Also **night'dress'.**

night·hawk (nīt'hôk') *n.* A bird of nocturnal habits, related to the whippoorwill.

night·in·gale (nī'tən·gāl, nī'·ting-) *n.* A small, Old World thrush noted for the melodious song of the male. [< OE *nihtegale,* lit., night-singer]

Nighthawk

night letter A telegram transmitted at night, usu. at a reduced rate.

night·long (nīt'lông', -long') *adj.* Lasting through the night.

night·ly (nīt'lē) *adj.* Occurring at night or every night. —*adv.* By night; every night.

night·mare (nīt'mâr) *n.* 1 A terrifying dream. 2 Any oppressive or terrifying experience. [< NIGHT + OE *mare* goblin] —**night'mar·ish** *adj.*

night owl *Informal* A person who customarily stays up until late at night.

night school A school that holds classes during the evening.

night·shade (nīt'shād) *n.* Any of various plants related to the tomato and potato; esp., the **common** or **black nightshade,** a poisonous weed with white flowers and black berries; or **deadly nightshade** (belladonna); or **woody nightshade** (bittersweet).

night·shirt (nīt'shûrt') *n.* A loose, shirtlike garment worn in bed, esp. formerly by men or boys.

night spot *Informal* A night club.

night·stick (nīt'stik') *n.* A long, stout club carried by policemen.

night·time (nīt'tīm') *n.* The time from sunset to sunrise, or from dark to dawn.

night·walk·er (nīt'wô'kər) *n.* 1 One who frequents the streets at night. 2 A large earthworm that emerges at night: also **night crawler.**

night watchman A person hired to keep watch and be on guard at night.

ni·hil·ism (nī'əl·iz'əm, ni'hil-) *n.* 1 *Philos.* The doctrine that nothing exists or can be known. 2 The rejection of religious and moral creeds. 3 A political doctrine holding that the existing structure of society should be destroyed. [< L *nihil* nothing + -ISM] —**ni'hil·ist** *n.* —**ni'hil·is'tic** *adj.*

-nik *suffix* One associated, concerned, or connected with: *peacenik.* [< Russ., noun suffix]

Ni·ke (nī'kē) *Gk. Myth.* The winged goddess of victory.

nil (nil) *n.* Nothing. [L, contraction of *nihil* nothing]

Nile green (nīl) Any of several light green tints.

nil·gai (nil'gī) *n. pl.* **·gais** or **·gai** A large, short-maned antelope of India. Also **nil'ghai.** [< Pers. *nīl* blue + *gāu* cow]

nim·ble (nim'bəl) *adj.* **·bler, ·blest 1** Light and quick in motion or action; agile. **2** Intellectually alert or acute. [< OE *numel* quick at learning & *nǣmel* receptive] **—nim'·ble·ness** *n.* **—nim'bly** *adv.* **—Syn. 1** lively, sprightly, spry.

nim·bo·stra·tus (nim'bō·strā'təs, -strat'əs) *n.* A gray cloud at a low altitude, often giving off precipitation.

nim·bus (nim'bəs) *n. pl.* **·bus·es** or **·bi** (-bī) **1** A halo or bright disk encircling the head, as of Jesus, saints, etc., in pictures, on medallions, etc. **2** A cloud of glory about a god, a person, or thing. **3** Any atmosphere or aura of fame, glamour, etc. **4** Formerly, a nimbostratus. [L, rain cloud]

Nim·rod (nim'rod) In the Bible, the grandson of Ham; a mighty hunter. —*n.* A hunter.

nin·com·poop (nin'kəm·pōōp) *n.* A foolish or silly person; simpleton. [?]

nine (nīn) *n.* **1** The sum of eight plus one; 9; IX. **2** A set or group of nine members. [< OE *nigon*] **—nine** *adj., pron.*

nine·fold (nīn'fōld') *adj. & adv.* Nine times as many or as great.

nine·pins (nīn'pinz') *n.pl. (construed as sing.)* A game similar to tenpins, in which nine large wooden pins are set up to be knocked down by a ball.

nine·teen (nīn'tēn') *n.* **1** The sum of 18 plus 1; 19; XIX. **2** A set or group of nineteen members. **—nine'teen'** *adj., pron.*

nine·teenth (nīn'tēnth') *adj. & adv.* Next in order after the 18th. —*n.* The element of an ordered set that corresponds to the number 19. **2** One of 19 equal parts.

nine·ti·eth (nīn'tē·ith) *adj. & adv.* Tenth in order after the 80th. —*n.* **1** The element of an ordered set that corresponds to the number 90. **2** One of 90 equal parts.

nine·ty (nīn'tē) *n. pl.* **·ties 1** The product of nine and ten; 90; XC. **2** A set or group of 90 members. **3** *pl.* The numbers, years, etc., between 90 and 100. **—nine'ty** *adj., pron.*

Nin·e·veh (nin'ə·və) *n.* An ancient city, capital of Assyria.

nin·ny (nin'ē) *n. pl.* **·nies** A simpleton. [? Short for *an innocent*]

ninth (nīnth) *adj. & adv.* Next in order after the eighth. —*n.* **1** The element of an ordered set that corresponds to the number nine. **2** One of nine equal parts.

Ni·o·be (nī'ə·bē) *Gk. Myth.* The mother whose children were killed by the gods because she kept boasting about them; later turned by Zeus into a stone fountain from which her tears continued to flow.

ni·o·bi·um (nī·ō'bē·əm) *n.* A steel-gray, metallic element (symbol Nb), valuable as an alloy metal. [< NIOBE]

nip[1] (nip) *v.t.* **nipped, nip·ping 1** To compress tightly between two surfaces or points; bite. **2** To remove by pinching or clipping. **3** To check or destroy the development of. **4** To benumb: said of cold. **—nip in the bud** To put a stop to at the beginning. —*n.* **1** The act of compressing sharply. **2** A biting, pinching, or clipping off. **3** A sudden blight, as by frost. **—nip and tuck** *Informal* With the outcome undecided; neck and neck. [ME *nippen*] **—nip'ping·ly** *adv.*

nip[2] (nip) *n.* A small dram, esp. of alcoholic liquor. —*v.t. & v.i.* To drink (liquor) in sips. [< earlier *nipperkin* half-pint measure]

nip·per (nip'ər) *n.* **1** One who nips. **2** One of various pincers for nipping. **3** A great claw, as of a crab. **4** *Brit.* A small boy.

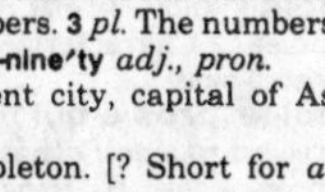

Nipper *def. 2*

nip·ple (nip'əl) *n.* **1** The pigmented cone-shaped process of the breast in humans and other mammals containing the milk duct; teat. **2** A perforated cap on a nursing bottle through which a baby sucks milk. **3** Any nipple-shaped projection. [Earlier *neble,* ? dim. of NEB]

nip·py (nip'ē) *adj.* **·pi·er, ·pi·est 1** Biting; sharp. **2** Chilly; frosty. **—nip'pi·ly** *adv.* **—nip'pi·ness** *n.*

nir·va·na (nir·vä'nə, nər·van'ə) *n.* **1** In Buddhism, the ideal and goal of all religious effort, absorption of the individual into the supreme spirit: also **Nirvana. 2** A place or condition of sublime happiness or fulfillment. [< Skt. *nirvāna* a blowing out]

Ni·sei (nē·sā) *n. pl* **·sei** or **·seis** An American citizen of immigrant Japanese parentage who was born in the U.S.

nit (nit) *n.* **1** The egg of a louse or similar insect. **2** The immature insect itself. [< OE *hnitu*] **—nit'ty** *adj.*

nite (nīt) *n. Nonstand.* NIGHT.

ni·ter (nī'tər) *n.* Potassium or sodium nitrate. Also **ni'tre.** [< Gk. *nitron,* a sodium mineral]

nit·e·ry (nīt'ə·rē) *n. pl.* **·ries** *Slang* A nightclub.

ni·ton (nī'ton) *n.* A former name for radon. [< L *nitere* to shine]

nit-pick·ing (nit'pik·ing) *n. Informal* A fussing over trivial details, usu. with the aim of finding fault. **—nit'-pick'** *v.i.* **—nit'pick·er** *n.* [< NIT + PICKING]

ni·trate (nī'trāt) *v.t.* **·trat·ed, ·trat·ing** To treat with nitric acid; to change into a nitrate. —*n.* **1** A salt or ester of nitric acid: silver *nitrate.* **2** A fertilizer consisting of sodium or potassium nitrate. [< L *nitrum,* a native sodium salt] **—ni·tra'tion** *n.*

ni·tric (nī'trik) *adj.* **1** Of, pertaining to, or obtained from nitrogen. **2** Containing nitrogen in the higher state of valence.

nitric acid A heavy, volatile, unstable, corrosive liquid having strong acid properties in aqueous solution.

ni·tri·fy (nī'trə·fī) *v.t.* **·fied, ·fy·ing 1** To combine with nitrogen. **2** To oxidize, as atmospheric nitrogen, ammonia, etc., into nitric or nitrous acid or into nitrates or nitrites. **3** To treat or impregnate (soil, etc.) with nitrates. **—ni·tri·fi·ca·tion** (nī'trə·fə·kā'shən), **ni'tre·fi'er** *n.* **—ni'tri·fi'a·ble** *adj.*

ni·trite (nī'trīt) *n.* A salt of nitrous acid.

nitro- *combining form Chem.* Containing the univalent nitrous radical: *nitrobenzene.* Also **nitri-.** [< L *nitrum,* a native sodium salt]

ni·tro·ben·zene (nī'trō·ben'zēn, -ben·zēn') *n.* A yellow, poisonous liquid formed by nitrating benzene, used in making dyes.

ni·tro·cel·lu·lose (nī'trō·sel'yə·lōs) *n.* Any of various compounds obtained by treating cellulose with nitric and sulfuric acids, used to make plastics, explosives, etc.

ni·tro·gen (nī'trə·jən) *n.* An odorless, colorless, gaseous element (symbol N) forming 78 percent of the atmosphere and forming essential compounds in all living organisms. [< NITRO- + -GEN] **—ni·trog'e·nous** (-ə·nəs) *adj.*

nitrogen fixation The conversion of atmospheric nitrogen into useful nitrogen compounds, either by certain soil bacteria or by various industrial processes. **—ni'tro·gen-fix'ing** *adj.*

ni·trog·en·ize (nī·troj'ən·īz, nī'trə·jən·īz') *v.t.* **·ized, ·iz·ing** To treat or combine with nitrogen.

ni·tro·glyc·er·in (nī'trō·glis'ər·in) *n.* A pale yellow, oily, explosively unstable liquid, made by nitrating glycerol, used to form dynamite and in medicine. Also **ni'tro·glyc'·er·ine.**

ni·trous (nī'trəs) *adj.* **1** Of, pertaining to, or containing niter. **2** Denoting compounds of nitrogen containing less oxygen than the corresponding nitric compounds.

nitrous acid An unstable compound occurring only in solution.

nitrous oxide An unstable, gaseous compound of nitrogen and oxygen, used as an anesthetic in dentistry.

nit·ty-grit·ty (nit'ē·grit'ē) *Slang. n.* The basic question or details; the heart of the matter. —*adj.* Down-to-earth; basic. [?]

nit·wit (nit'wit') *n.* A silly or stupid person. [Prob. < NIT + WIT]

nix[1] (niks) *n.* In Teutonic mythology, a water spirit. [G] **—nix'ie** *n. Fem.*

nix[2] (niks) *Slang n.* **1** Nothing. **2** No. —*adv.* No. —*interj.* Stop! Watch out!. —*v.t.* To forbid or disagree with. [< G *nichts* nothing]

ni·zam (ni·zäm', -zam', nī-) *n. pl.* **·zam 1** Formerly, a Turkish regular soldier. **2** *Often cap.* The former title of the native ruler of Hyderabad, India. [< Ar. *naẓāma* govern]

NJ New Jersey (P.O. abbr.).

N.J. New Jersey.

NL, NL., N.L. New Latin.

NLRB National Labor Relations Board.

NM New Mexico (P.O. abbr.).

NNW, N.N.W., nnw, n.n.w. north-northwest.

no[1] (nō) *adv.* 1 Nay; not so. 2 Not at all; not in any way. 3 Not: used to express an alternative after *or:* whether or *no.* —*adj.* Not any; not one. —*n. pl.* **noes** 1 A negative reply; a denial. 2 A negative vote or voter: The *noes* have it. [< OE *ne* not + *ā* ever]

no[2] (nō) *n.* The classical drama of Japan, traditionally tragic or noble in theme. Also **Noh.**

No nobelium.

No·ah (nō′ə) In the Bible, a patriarch who, at the command of God, built an ark to save his family and two of every sort of living thing from the Flood.

nob (nob) *n.* 1 *Slang* The head. 2 A knob or protuberance. [Var. of KNOB]

nob·by (nob′ē) *adj.* **·bi·er, ·bi·est** *Brit. Slang* Flashy; showy; stylish. [?]

no·bel·i·um (nō·bel′ē·əm) *n.* An artificially produced radioactive element (symbol No). [< *Nobel* Institute, Stockholm]

No·bel Prizes (nō·bel′) Six prizes usu. awarded annually to those whose work in physics, chemistry, medicine, literature, economics, and world peace is thought of most benefit to humanity. [< Alfred *Nobel,* 1833–96, Swedish philanthropist]

no·bil·i·ty (nō·bil′ə·tē) *n. pl.* **·ties** 1 The state of being noble, as in character or rank. 2 A class composed of nobles. 3 In Great Britain, the peerage. 4 High-mindedness; magnanimity. 5 Great moral excellence. 6 Noble lineage.

no·ble (nō′bəl) *adj.* **·bler, ·blest** 1 Of or pertaining to an aristocracy; of lofty lineage. 2 Characterized by or indicative of virtue or magnanimity; high-minded. 3 Imposing in appearance; grand: a *noble* face. —*n.* A person having hereditary title, rank, and privileges; in Great Britain, a peer. [< L *nobilis* noble, well-known] **—no′ble·ness** *n.* **—no′bly** *adv.* **—Syn.** *adj.* 2 excellent, honorable, worthy, righteous, fine. 3 impressive, magnificent, splendid.

no·ble·man (nō′bəl·mən) *n. pl.* **·men** (-mən) A man of noble rank; in England, a peer. **—no′ble·wom′an** (-wŏŏm′ən) *n. Fem.*

no·blesse o·blige (nō·bles′ ō·blēzh′) The duty of persons of noble birth or high rank to behave courageously, honorably, and generously toward others. [F, lit., nobility obliges]

no·bod·y (nō′bod′ē, -bəd·ē) *pron.* Not anybody. —*n. pl.* **·bod·ies** A person of no importance or influence.

nock (nok) *n.* 1 The notch on the butt end of an arrow. 2 The notch on the horn of a bow for securing the bowstring. —*v.t.* To fit (an arrow) to the bowstring. [ME *nocke*]

noc·tu·id (nok′chŏŏ·id) *n.* Any of a large family of medium-sized moths that usu. fly at night, including many with destructive larvae, as the army worm and the cutworm. —*adj.* Pertaining to these moths. [< L *noctua* night owl]

noc·tur·nal (nok·tûr′nəl) *adj.* 1 Pertaining to night. 2 Occurring or active at night. 3 Seeking food by night, as animals. 4 Having blossoms that open by night. [< L *nocturnus* < *nox* night] **—noc·tur′nal·ly** *adv.*

noc·turne (nok′tûrn) *n.* 1 In painting, a night scene. 2 *Music* A composition evocative of night. [< L *nocturnus* nightly]

nod (nod) *n.* A forward and downward motion of the head, more or less quick or jerky. —*v.* **nod·ded, nod·ding** *v.i.* 1 To make a brief forward and downward movement of the head, as in agreement, invitation, etc. 2 To let the head fall forward involuntarily, as when drowsy. 3 To be inattentive or careless. 4 To incline the top or upper part as if nodding: said of trees, flowers, etc. —*v.t.* 5 To bend (the head) forward and downward briefly. 6 To express or signify by nodding: to *nod* approval. [ME *nodden*] **—nod′der** *n.*

Nod (nod) *n.* 1 The land east of Eden in which Cain settled after killing Abel. *Gen.* 4:16. 2 Sleep. Also **Land of Nod.**

nod·dle (nod′l) *n. Informal* The head: a humorous use. [< NOD]

nod·dy (nod′ē) *n. pl.* **·dies** 1 A dunce; a fool. 2 Any of several terns of warm seas noted for their exceptional tameness. [< NOD]

node (nōd) *n.* 1 A knot or knob; swelling. 2 *Bot.* The joint or knob on the stem of a plant, from which leaves grow. 3 *Astron.* Either of the two points at which the intersection of the planes of two orbits touches the celestial sphere. 4 *Physics* A point, line, or plane in a vibrating body where the amplitude is virtually zero. [< L *nodus* knot] **—no·dal** (nōd′l) *adj.*

Nodes *def. 2*

nod·ule (noj′ōōl) *n.* 1 A little knot, lump, or node. 2 *Bot.* A tubercle. **—nod·u·lar** (noj′·ə·lər) *adj.*

No·ël (nō·el′) *n.* 1 Christmas. 2 A Christmas carol: also **no·el′.** [< L *natalis* birth]

nog (nog) *n.* 1 A strong ale. 2 Eggnog. Also **nogg.** [?]

nog·gin (nog′in) *n.* 1 A small mug, or its contents. 2 A liquid measure equal to about a gill. 3 *Informal* A person's head. [?]

no·how (nō′hou′) *adv. Informal* In no way; not by any means.

noise (noiz) *n.* 1 Any annoying or undesired sound, esp. one that is random. 2 A similar electrical signal. 3 Clamor caused by raised voices and restless moving about. 4 Any sound. —*v.* **noised, nois·ing** *v.t.* 1 To spread by rumor or report; often with *about* or *abroad.* —*v.i.* 2 To make a noise. 3 To talk in a loud manner. [< OF *noyse*]

noise·less (noiz′lis) *adj.* Causing or making little or no noise. **—noise′less·ly** *adv.* **—noise′less·ness** *n.*

noi·some (noi′səm) *adj.* 1 Very offensive, particularly to the sense of smell. 2 Injurious; harmful. [< *noy,* var. of ANNOY + -SOME] **—noi′some·ly** *adv.* **—noi′some·ness** *n.* **—Syn.** 1 fetid, foul, mephitic, stinking. 2 destructive, detrimental, hurtful, noxious.

nois·y (noi′zē) *adj.* **nois·i·er, nois·i·est** 1 Making a loud noise. 2 Characterized by much noise. **—nois′i·ly** *adv.* **—nois′i·ness** *n.*

nol·le pros·e·qui (nol′ē pros′ə·kwī) *Law* An entry of record to signify that the plaintiff or prosecutor will not press a case. [L, to be unwilling to prosecute]

no·lo con·ten·de·re (nō′lō kən·ten′də·rē) *Law* A plea by a defendant in a criminal action, which, while not an admission of guilt, states that he will make no defense. [L, I am unwilling to contend]

nol-pros (nol′pros′) *v.t.* **-prossed, -pros·sing** *Law* To subject to a nolle prosequi.

nol. pros. nolle prosequi.

nom. nomenclature; nominal; nominative.

no·mad (nō′mad, nom′ad) *adj.* Nomadic. —*n.* A rover; one of an unsettled, wandering people, tribe, or race. [< Gk. *nomein* to pasture, feed] **—no′mad·ism** *n.*

no·mad·ic (nō·mad′ik) *adj.* 1 Of or pertaining to nomads. 2 Wandering from one place to another; unsettled. Also **no·mad′i·cal.** **—no·mad′i·cal·ly** *adv.*

no man's land 1 Waste or unowned land. 2 In warfare, the part of a battlefield between the opposing armies.

nom de guerre (nôn də gâr′) An assumed name. [F, lit., war name]

nom de plume (nom′ də plōōm′, *Fr.* nôn də plüm′) A pen name; a writer's assumed name. [F]

no·men·cla·ture (nō′mən·klā′chər) *n.* A system of names used in any art, science, or other specialized field. [L *nomenclatura* list of names]

nom·i·nal (nom′ə·nəl) *adj.* 1 Of or pertaining to a name or names. 2 Existing in name only; not actual: a *nominal* peace. 3 So slight as to be hardly worth naming: a *nominal* sum. [< L *nomen* name] **—nom′i·nal·ly** *adv.*

nom·i·nate (nom′ə·nāt) *v.t.* **·nat·ed, ·nat·ing** 1 To name as a candidate for elective office. 2 To appoint to some office or duty. —*adj.* Nominated. [< L < *nomen, nominis* a name] **—nom·i·na′tion, nom′i·na′tor** *n.*

nom·i·na·tive (nom′ə·nə·tiv, nom′ə·nā′-) *adj.* 1 *Gram.* Designating the case of the subject of a finite verb, or of a word agreeing with, or in apposition to the subject. 2 Appointed by nomination; nominated. —*n. Gram.* 1 The nominative case. 2 A word in this case.

nom·i·nee (nom′ə·nē′) *n.* A person who receives a nomination, esp. for an election.

-nomy *combining form* The science or systematic study of: *astronomy.* [< Gk. *nomos* law]

non- *prefix* Not. [< L *non* not] • **Non-** is the Latin negative adverb adopted as a prefix in English. It denotes in general simple negation or absence of, as in *nonaggression.* Words beginning with *non-* are now usu. written without a hyphen except when one element is a capitalized word: *non-American.* Even words with the initial letter *n* are now often combined with the prefix *non-* to form a solid word: *nonnative.* Following is a list of words beginning with this prefix.

nonabsolute
nonabsorbable
nonabsorbent
nonabstract
nonacceptance
nonachievement
nonachiever
nonacquaintance
nonacquisition
nonaction
nonactive
nonactivist
nonactor
nonactress
nonadherence
nonadherent
nonadjacent
nonadmirer
nonadmission
nonadoption
nonadult
nonadversary
nonaesthetic
nonaffluent
nonagreement
nonalcoholic
nonaligned
nonallegiance
non-American
nonanswer
nonantagonistic
nonapproved
nonarranged
nonarrival
nonart
nonassociative
nonathlete
nonatomic
nonattached
nonattendance
nonattention
nonautomatic
nonbeing
nonbelieving
nonbelligerent
nonbinding
nonbiodegradable
nonblack
nonbook
nonbudding
noncancelable
noncancerous
noncandidacy
noncanonical
noncareer
non-Catholic
noncentral
noncharacter
non-Christian
noncitizen
noncoercive
noncollapsible
noncollege
noncollegiate
noncolonial
noncombustible
noncommercial
noncommunicant
non-Communist
noncompetitive
nonconception
nonconcur
nonconducive
nonconfiguration
nonconflict
nonconfrontation
non-Congressional
nonconnotative
nonconscious
nonconsciousness
nonconsensual
nonconsent
nonconsideration
nonconsumption
noncontagious
noncontest
noncontingent
noncontrolling
noncontroversial
nonconversion
noncriminal
noncritical
noncrystallized
noncurrency
nondefense
nondeliquescent
nondelivery
nondepartmental
nondevelopment
nondifferentiated
nondirective
nondiscrimination
nondissemination
nondistinctive
nondistribution
nondivisible
nondoctrinal
nondrinker
nondurable
noneconomic
noneducational
noneffective
nonefficient
nonego
nonelastic
nonelectoral
nonelectric
nonelectronic
nonemergency
nonempirical
nonenforceable
nonentry
nonequation
nonerotic
noneternal
noneternity
non-Euclidean
non-European
nonexclusive
nonexcusable
nonexecution
nonexempt
nonexercise
nonexistence
nonexistent
nonexisting
nonexpendable
nonexpert
nonexplosive
nonexpressive
nonextant
nonextension
nonextremist
nonfactual
nonfamous
nonfarm
nonfatal
nonferrous
nonfictive
nonfinancial
nonfinite
nonfiscal
nonflammable
nonfood
nonfraternization
nonfreedom
nonfreeman
non-Freudian
nonfunctioning
nonhazardous
non-Hellenic
nonhero
nonholiday
nonhuman
nonidentity
nonideological
nonimperial
nonimprovement
noninductive
noninflammable
nonintellectual
noninterference
noninvolved
noninvolvement
nonionized
nonirritating
non-Jewish
nonjusticiable
nonlethal
nonlinear
nonliterary
nonluminous
nonmagnetic
nonmanagement
nonmaterial
nonmateriality
nonmeaning
nonmechanical
nonmember
nonmembership
nonmilitancy
nonmilitant
nonmodulated
nonmonetary
nonmotile
nonmusical
nonnarcotic
nonnative
nonnatural
nonnegotiable
nonnuclear
nonnucleated
nonnutritive
nonobservance
nonofficial
nonofficially
nonoperative
nonorthodox
nonowner
nonoxidating
nonparallel
nonparasitic
nonparticipant
nonparticipating
nonpaying
nonpayment
nonperformance
nonpermanent
nonperson
nonphysical
nonpigmented
nonpoisonous
nonpolemical
nonpolitical
nonpolluting
nonpossessor
nonpractical
nonprofessional
nonproliferation
nonproperty
nonpropulsive
nonprotection
non-Protestant
nonproven
nonpublic
nonpublication
nonpunishment
nonracial
nonreader
nonrechargeable
nonrecognition
nonrecurring
nonreigning
nonrelative
nonrelevant
nonrenewable
nonreproductive
nonreserved
nonresisting
nonresonant
nonrestraint
nonrestricted
nonreturnable
nonrevolutionary
nonrigid
nonsalaried
nonscientific
nonselective
nonsensitive
nonsentient
nonsequential
nonserious
nonsexual
nonsexually
nonsignificant
nonsmoker
nonsociety
nonsolid
nonspecialist
nonspecific
nonstick
nonstriated
nonstudent
nonsubscriber
nonsubscribing
nonsupporter
nonsupporting
nonsyllabic
nonsympathizer
nonsympathy
nontax
nonteaching
nontechnical
nontenured
nonterminating
nontoxic
nontruth
nonunionization
nonunionized
nonuser
nonvariable
nonvenomous
nonviability
nonviable
nonvolatile
nonvolition
nonvoluntary
nonwar
nonworker
nonworking

non·age (non′ij, nō′nij) *n.* **1** The period of legal minority. **2** An immature or early stage. [< OF *non-* not + *age* age]

non·a·ge·nar·i·an (non′ə·jə·nâr′ē·ən, nō′nə-) *adj.* Pertaining to the nineties in age. —*n.* One between the ages of ninety and a hundred. [< L *nonagenarius* of ninety]

non·ag·gres·sion (non′ə·gresh′ən) *n.* A lack of or abstention from aggression. —**non′ag·gres′sive** *adj.*

non·a·gon (non′ə·gon) *n.* A nine-sided polygon. [< L *nonus* ninth + Gk. *gōnia* angle]

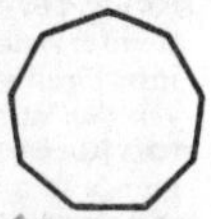
Nonagon

non·ap·pear·ance (non′ə·pir′əns) *n.* Failure to appear, esp. in court in answer to a summons.

nonce (nons) *n.* Present time or occasion. —**for the nonce** For the present time or occasion. [ME *for then ones* for the one (occasion), misread as *for the nones*]

nonce word A word coined for one occasion and usu. not remaining in general use.

non·cha·lance (non′shə·läns′, non′shə·ləns) *n.* Jaunty indifference or unconcern.

non·cha·lant (non′shə·länt′, non′shə·lənt) *adj.* Without concern; casual; indifferent. [< L *non* not + *calere* be warm] —**non′cha·lant·ly** *adv.*

non·com (non′kom′) *Informal adj.* Noncommissioned. —*n.* A noncommissioned officer.

non·com·bat·ant (non′kəm·bat′ənt, -kom′bə·tənt, -kum′-) *n.* **1** One attached to a military force who is not required to fight, as a chaplain or medical officer. **2** Anyone not connected with the military service in time of war; a civilian. —*adj.* Of or pertaining to noncombatants.

non·com·mis·sioned (non′kə·mish′ənd) *adj.* Not holding a military commission, as a corporal or sergeant.

non·com·mit·tal (non′kə·mit′l) *adj.* Not having or expressing a decided opinion. —**non′com·mit′tal·ly** *adv.*

non·com·pli·ance (non′kəm·plī′əns) *n.* Failure, neglect, or refusal to comply. —**non′com·pli′ant** *adj., n.*

non com·pos men·tis (non kom′pəs men′tis) *Latin* Not of sound mind: often shortened to **non compos.**

non·con·duc·tor (non′kən·duk′tər) *n.* A substance or material that offers resistance to the passage of some form of energy.

non·con·form·ist (non′kən·fôr′mist) *n.* One who does not conform to established beliefs and procedures, esp. in religious matters. —**non′con·form′ance** (-məns), **non′con·for′mi·ty** (-fôr′mə·tē) *n.*

non·co·op·er·a·tion (non′kō·op′ə·rā′shən) *n.* Refusal to cooperate; esp. civil resistance to a government. —**non′co·op′er·a·tive** (-kō·op′ə·rə·tiv, -ə·rā′tiv) *adj.* —**non′co·op′er·a·tor** *n.*

non·de·script (non′di·skript) *adj.* Not distinctive enough to be described; difficult to classify. —*n.* A nondescript person or thing. [< NON- + L *descriptus*]

none (nun) *pron.* 1 Not one; no one. 2 No or not one specifically named person or thing. 3 Not any: That is *none* of her business. 4 *(construed as pl.)* Not any (of the persons or things specified). *None* of the apples are rotten. —*adv.* In no respect; not at all: *none* the worse for wear. [< OE *ne* not + *ān* one]

non·en·ti·ty (non·en′tə·tē) *n. pl.* **·ties** 1 A person or thing of small significance. 2 The negation of being; nonexistence.

nones (nōnz) *n.pl.* 1 The ninth day before the ides in the Roman calendar. 2 The fifth of the seven daily canonical hours; also, the service for it. [< L *nonus* ninth]

non·es·sen·tial (non′ə·sen′shəl) *adj.* Not really needed. —*n.* An unneeded person or thing.

none·such (nun′such′) *n.* A person or thing having no equal.

none·the·less (nun′thə·les′) *adv.* In spite of that; however; nevertheless.

non·e·vent (non′i·vent′) *n.* A hoped-for event that either never occurs or fails to come up to expectations.

non·fea·sance (non·fē′zəns) *n. Law* The nonperformance of some act which one is bound by legal or official duty to perform. [< NON- not + OF *faisance* doing] —**non·fea′sor** *n.*

non·fic·tion (non·fik′shən) *n.* 1 A literary work, such as a biography, history, etc., based on actual rather than imaginary persons and events. 2 Such works collectively. —**non·fic′tion·al** *adj.*

non·ful·fill·ment (non′ful·fil′mənt) *n.* 1 Failure to satisfy. 2 Failure to be satisfied. Also **non′ful·fil′ment.**

no·nil·lion (nō·nil′yən) *n. & adj.* See NUMBER. —**no·nil′·lionth** (-yənth) *adj., n.*

non·in·ter·ven·tion (non′in·tər·ven′shən) *n.* 1 A refusal to intervene or interfere. 2 The policy of a nation to avoid interference in the affairs of other nations. —**non′in·ter·ven′tion·ist** *adj., n.*

non·ju·ror (non·jŏŏr′ər) *n.* One who refuses to swear allegiance to a leader or to take any oath.

non·met·al (non·met′l) *n.* Any element, as oxygen, nitrogen, carbon, or sulfur, etc., which forms acids, combines with metals to form salts, and gains, borrows, or shares electrons during chemical reactions.

non·me·tal·lic (non′mə·tal′ik) *adj.* 1 Not metallic. 2 Pertaining to a nonmetal.

non·mor·al (non·môr′əl, -mor′-) *adj.* Having no relation to ethical ideals; neither moral nor immoral.

no-no (nō′nō′) *n. pl.* **-nos** *Informal* Something forbidden or very undesirable.

non·ob·jec·tive (non′əb·jek′tiv) *adj.* 1 Not objective. 2 NONREPRESENTATIONAL.

non·pa·reil (non′pə·rel′) *adj.* Of unequaled excellence. —*n.* 1 Something of unequaled excellence. 2 *Printing* A name for 6-point type. [< OF *non* not + *pareil* equal]

non·par·ti·san (non·pär′tə·zən, -sən) *adj.* 1 Not partisan. 2 Not pertaining or adhering to any established political party. —*n.* A nonpartisan person or group.

non·plus (non·plus′, non′plus) *v.t.* **·plused** or **·plussed, ·plus·ing** or **·plus·sing** To baffle; perplex. —*n.* A mental standstill; perplexity. [< L *non plus* no further] —**Syn.** *v.* confound, embarrass, mystify, puzzle.

non·pro·duc·tive (non′prə·duk′tiv) *adj.* 1 Not producing. 2 Pertaining to those workers not directly involved with production, as clerical help, etc. —**non′pro·duc′tive·ly** *adv.* —**non′pro·duc′tive·ness** *n.*

non·prof·it (non·prof′it) *adj.* 1 Receiving no profit. 2 Established for purposes other than profit: a *nonprofit* organization.

non-pros (non·pros′) *v.t.* **-prossed, -pros·sing** *Law* To enter judgment against (a plaintiff who fails to prosecute).

non pro·seq·ui·tur (non prō·sek′wi·tər) *Law* A judgment entered at common law against a plaintiff who fails to prosecute. [L, he does not prosecute]

non·rep·re·sen·ta·tion·al (non′rep′ri·zen·tā′shən·əl) *adj.* Denoting a form of art that does not attempt to represent the form of objects as they appear in nature; abstract.

non·res·i·dent (non·rez′ə·dənt) *adj.* Not residing in a specified location, esp. where one works, goes to school, etc. —*n.* A nonresident person. —**non·res′i·dence** *n.*

non·re·sis·tant (non′ri·zis′tənt) *adj.* Willing to cooperate; obedient. —*n.* One who believes that authority should not be opposed by force and violence. —**non′re·sis′tance** *n.*

non·re·stric·tive (non′ri·strik′tiv) *adj. Gram.* Denoting a modifier that merely adds descriptive detail and is not essential to the meaning. • See RESTRICTIVE.

non·sched·uled (non·skej′ŏŏld, -əld) *adj.* Not operating in accordance with a formal or regular schedule.

non·sec·tar·i·an (non′sek·târ′ē·ən) *n.* Not allied formally with or restricted to any religious denomination.

non·sense (non′sens, -səns) *n.* 1 That which is without good sense; meaningless or ridiculous language. 2 Things of no importance. 3 Absurd or affected behavior. —*adj.* Consisting of a grouping of letters or sounds that are not intelligible but often formed on a pattern of standard words: "Glip" is a *nonsense* word. —*interj.* How absurd! —**non·sen′si·cal** *adj.* —**non·sen′si·cal·ly** *adv.*

non seq·ui·tur (non sek′wə·tər, -wə·tŏŏr) The fallacy of irrelevant conclusion; an inference that does not follow from the premises. [L, it does not follow]

non·sked (non′sked′) *Informal adj.* Nonscheduled: applied esp. to passenger airplane service. —*n.* Something not operating on or holding to a schedule.

non·skid (non′skid′) *adj.* Having the surface treaded to reduce skidding: said of tires, shoe soles, etc.

nonstand. nonstandard.

non·stand·ard (non′stan′dərd) *adj.* 1 Not standard. 2 Not in accordance with the usage, pronunciation, spelling, grammatical construction, etc., generally accepted by educated speakers and writers of a language.

non·stop (non′stop′) *adj.* Making, having made, or scheduled to make no stops.

non·such (nun′such′) *n.* NONESUCH.

non·suit (non′sŏŏt′) *Law v.t.* To order the dismissal of the suit of. —*n.* A judgment dismissing a suit when the plaintiff abandons it or fails to establish a cause of action.

non·sup·port (non′sə·pôrt′, -pōrt′) *n.* Failure to provide for the support of dependents.

non·un·ion (non·yōōn′yən) *adj.* 1 Not belonging to a trade union. 2 Not employing or recognizing any trade union or its members. —**non·un′ion·ism, non·un′ion·ist** *n.*

non·vi·o·lent (non′vī′ə·lənt) *adj.* 1 Free from violence: a *nonviolent* demonstration. 2 Not given to or believing in violence. —**non′vi′o·lence** *n.* —**non·vi′o·lent·ly** *adv.*

non·vot·er (non·vōt′ər) *n.* One who does not or may not vote. —**non·vot′ing** *adj.*

non·white (non·ʰwīt′) *adj.* 1 Not white. 2 Being other than Caucasian. —*n.* A nonwhite person, as a Negro.

noo·dle[1] (nōōd′l) *n. Slang.* 1 A stupid person: also **noo′·dle·head′.** 2 The head. [?]

noo·dle[2] (nōōd′l) *n.* A thin, flat strip of dried dough, usu. made with egg, used in soup, etc. [< G *Nudel*]

nook (nŏŏk) *n.* 1 A corner or recess, esp. in a room. 2 Any small, cozy or sheltered place. [ME *noke* corner]

noon (nōōn) *n.* 1 That time of day when the sun is on the meridian; the middle of the day. 2 The highest point of any period or career. —*adj.* Of or taking place at noon: the *noon* meal. [< L *nona (hora)* ninth (hour)]

noon·day (nōōn′dā′) *n.* The middle of the day. —*adj.* Pertaining to midday.

no one Not anyone; no person.

noon·time (nōōn′tīm′) *n.* The time of midday; noon. —*adj.* Of or occurring at noon. Also **noon′tide′** (-tīd′).

noose (nōōs) *n.* 1 A loop furnished with a running knot, as in a hangman's halter or a snare. 2 Anything that restricts one's freedom. —*v.t.* **noosed, noos·ing** 1 To capture or secure with a noose. 2 To make a noose in (a rope). [< L *nodus* a knot]

Noose

no-par (nō′pär′) *adj.* Having no par, or face, value, as a share of stock.

nope (nōp) *adv. Slang* No.

nor (nôr) *conj.* And not; likewise not: used chiefly as a correlative of a preceding negative, usu. *neither* or *not.* [Contraction of ME *nother* neither]

nor′ (nôr) *adj., adv. & n.* North: often used in combination: *nor′easter.* Also **nor.**

Nor. Norman; Norway; Norwegian.

Nor., nor. north; northern.

Nor·dic (nôr′dik) *adj.* Pertaining or belonging to a typically blond, tall, long-headed physical type inhabiting N Europe. —*n.* A person of this type. [< F *nord* north]
nor′·east·er (nôr·ēs′tər) *n.* NORTHEASTER.
Nor·folk jacket (nôr′fək) A loose-fitting jacket with side pockets, belt, and two box pleats. [< *Norfolk,* England]
no·ri·a (nō′rē·ə) *n.* In Spain and the Orient, an undershot water wheel having buckets on its rim to raise water. [< Ar. *nā'ūrah*]
norm (nôrm) *n.* 1 A model, type, pattern, or value considered as representative of a specified group. 2 *Psychol.* The average or median of performance in a given function or test. [< L *norma* rule]
nor·mal (nôr′məl) *adj.* 1 Conforming to a type or standard; regular. 2 Constituting a standard; model. 3 *Math.* Perpendicular. 4 Average; mean. 5 *Chem.* Denoting a salt having no replaceable hydrogen. 6 *Psychol.* Of average intelligence or mental health. 7 In good physical health. —*n.* 1 A common or natural condition. 2 A usual or accepted rule or process. 3 The average or mean value of observed quantities. 4 *Math.* A straight line perpendicular to a curve or surface at a point. [< L *norma* rule] —**nor′mal·cy** (-sē), **nor·mal·i·ty** (nôr·mal′ə·tē), **nor′mal·ness** *n.* —**nor′mal·ly** *adv.* —**Syn.** 1 common, everyday, ordinary, typical, usual.
nor·mal·ize (nôr′məl·īz) *v.t.* **·ized, ·iz·ing** To make normal. —**nor′mal·i·za′tion, nor′mal·iz′er** *n.*
normal school A school for the training of elementary-school teachers.
Nor·man (nôr′mən) *adj.* Pertaining to Normandy or to the Normans. —*n.* 1 One of a people of Scandinavian heritage who settled in Normandy, France, in the 10th century. 2 A native or inhabitant of Normandy, France. 3 One of the Norman or French invaders who conquered England in 1066 (the **Norman Conquest**). 4 NORMAN FRENCH.
Norman French The dialect of French spoken by the Norman conquerors in England.
Norse (nôrs) *adj.* 1 Scandinavian. 2 West Scandinavian, i.e., Norwegian, Icelandic, and Faroese. —*n.* 1 The Scandinavians or West Scandinavians collectively: with *the.* 2 The Scandinavian or North Germanic group of the Germanic languages; esp., the language of Norway. 3 The West Scandinavian languages.
Norse·man (nôrs′mən) *n. pl.* **·men** (-mən) A Scandinavian of Viking times.
north (nôrth) *n.* 1 The general direction to the left of sunrise. 2 The point of the compass at 0° or 360°, directly opposite south. 3 Any region north of a given point. 4 *Sometimes cap.* The northern part of any region, country, etc. —**the North** 1 The states in the part of the U.S. north of Maryland, Missouri, and the Ohio river. 2 The states that opposed the Confederacy. —*adj.* 1 Lying toward or in the north. 2 Issuing from or inhabiting the north. 3 Facing or proceeding toward the north. 4 *Usu. cap.* Denoting the northern part of a country, continent, hemisphere, etc.: *North* America. —*adv.* Toward the north. [< OE]
North America The northern continent in the Western Hemisphere, 9,390,000 sq. mi. —**North American**
north-bound (nôrth′bound′) *adj.* Going northward: also **north′bound′.**
north·east (north′ēst′, *in nautical usage* nôr·ēst′) *n.* 1 That point on the compass midway between north and east. 2 Any region lying toward that point on the horizon. —**the Northeast** The NE part of the U.S., including New England and New York, and sometimes New Jersey and Pennsylvania. —*adj.* From the northeast. —*adv.* Toward the northeast. —**north′east′er·ly** *adj., adv.* —**north′east′ern** *adj.*
north·east·er (nôrth′ēs′tər, *in nautical usage* nôr·ēs′tər) *n.* A gale from the northeast.
north·east·ward (nôrth′ēst′wərd) *adv.* Toward the northeast: also **north′east′wards.** —*adj.* Northeast; toward the northeast. —*n.* Northeast. —**north′east′ward·ly** *adj., adv.*
north·er (nôr′thər) *n.* A cold windstorm from the north.
nor·ther·ly (nôr′thər·lē) *adj. & adv.* 1 Toward the north. 2 From the north. —**north′er·li·ness** *n.*
north·ern (nôr′thərn) *adj.* Pertaining to the north or the North. —*n.* 1 A northerner. 2 A north wind. [< OE *northerne*] —**north′ern·most** *adj.*
north·ern·er (nôr′thər·nər) *n.* One born or residing in the north.
North·ern·er (nôr′thər·nər) *n.* One from the northern part of the U.S., as distinguished from a Southerner.
Northern Hemisphere See HEMISPHERE.
northern lights The aurora borealis.
Northern Spy A large, yellow-and-red variety of apple.
North Korea See KOREA.
north·land (nôrth′lənd) *n.* A land in the north. —*adj.* Of or pertaining to a northern land or lands. —**north′land·er** *n.*
North·man (nôrth′mən) *n. pl.* **·men** (-mən) A Scandinavian; esp. a Scandinavian of the Viking period.
North Pole The northern extremity of the earth's axis.

North Pole

North Star POLARIS.
North·um·bri·a (nôr·thum′brē·ə) *n.* An ancient Anglo-Saxon kingdom of Great Britain.
North·um·bri·an (nôr·thum′brē·ən) *adj.* Of the ancient English kingdom of Northumbria, its people, or their dialect. —*n.* 1 A native or inhabitant of Northumbria. 2 The Old English dialect of these people.
North Vietnam See VIETNAM.
north·ward (nôrth′wərd) *adv.* Toward the north. Also **north′wards.** —*adj.* Directed or lying toward the north. —*n.* The northward direction or point of the compass. —**north′ward·ly** *adj., adv.*
north·west (nôrth′west′, *in nautical usage* nôr′west′) *n.* 1 The direction midway between north and west. 2 Any region situated toward that direction. —**the Northwest** 1 The NW part of the U.S., esp. the states of Washington, Oregon, and Idaho. 2 The NW part of Canada. —*adj.* From the northwest. —*adv.* Toward the northwest. —**north′west′er·ly** *adj., adv.* —**north′west′ern** *adj.*
north·west·er (nôrth′wes′tər, *in nautical usage* nôr′wes′tər) *n.* A gale which blows from the northwest.
Northwest Passage A water route from the Atlantic to the Pacific along the northern coast of America.
north·west·ward (nôrth′west′wərd) *adv.* Toward the northwest; also **north′west′wards.** —*adj.* Northwest; toward the northwest. —*n.* Northwest. —**north′west′ward·ly** *adj., adv.*
Norw. Norway; Norwegian.
Nor·way (nôr′wā) *n.* A constitutional monarchy of N Europe, 119,240 sq. mi., cap. Oslo. • See map at SWEDEN.
Nor·we·gian (nôr·wē′jən) *n.* 1 A citizen or native of Norway. —*adj.* Of or pertaining to Norway, its people, or their language.
nor′·west·er (nôr·wes′tər) *n.* An oilskin coat worn by mariners in stormy weather.
Nos., nos. numbers.
nose (nōz) *n.* 1 The part of the face just above the mouth, containing the nostrils and the organ of smell. 2 The power or sense of smelling. 3 Anything resembling a nose, as a ship's prow. 4 The ability to discover: a *nose* for the facts. —**lead by the nose** To control absolutely. —**look down one's nose at** *Informal* To show contempt for. —**pay through the nose** To pay an exorbitant price. —**turn up one's nose at** To reject scornfully. —**under one's (very) nose** In plain sight; obvious. —*v.* **nosed, nos·ing** *v.t.* 1 To perceive or discover by or as by the sense of smell. 2 To examine or touch with the nose. —*v.i.* 3 To

smell; sniff. 4 To pry; meddle. 5 To push (one's way) slowly and carefully. —**nose out** To defeat by a small margin. [< OE *nosu*]

nose bag A canvas bag that hangs over a horse's nose and contains feed.

nose·band (nōz′band′) *n.* That part of a bridle passing over the nose of a horse and attached to the cheek pieces.

nose·bleed (nōz′blēd′) *n.* Bleeding from the nose.

nose cone The conical and separable forward section of a missile or rocket.

nose·dive (nōz′dīv′) *n.* 1 A steep downward plunge of an airplane. 2 Any sudden descent or crash. —*v.i.* **·dived, ·div·ing** To plunge downward.

nose·gay (nōz′gā′) *n.* A small bouquet. [< NOSE + GAY, in obs. sense "a bright object"]

nose·piece (nōz′pēs′) *n.* 1 Any protective covering for the nose. 2 The band fitting across the nose in a pair of spectacles.

nosh (näsh) *Informal n.* A snack; tidbit. —*v.i.* 1 To eat a snack. —*v.t.* 2 To munch on. [< Yiddish] —**nosh′er** *n.*

no-show (nō′shō′) *n.* 1 One who makes a reservation for an airplane flight but fails to claim the seat or make a cancellation. 2 One who buys a ticket for a performance, athletic contest, etc., and fails to attend.

nos·tal·gi·a (nos·tal′jē·ə, -jə) *n.* 1 Severe homesickness. 2 Any longing for something far away or long ago. [< Gk. *nostos* a return home + *algos* a pain] —**nos·tal′gic** *adj.*

nos·tril (nos′trəl) *n.* One of the outer openings in the nose. [< OE *nosu* nose + *thyrel* a hole]

nos·trum (nos′trəm) *n.* 1 A patent medicine; quack recipe. 2 Anything savoring of quackery: political *nostrums.* [< L *noster* our own; because prepared by those selling it]

nos·y (nō′zē) *adj.* **nos·i·er, nos·i·est** *Informal* Prying; snooping; inquisitive. Also **nos′ey.** —**nos′i·ness** *n.*

not (not) *adv.* In no manner, or to no extent or degree. [ME, contraction of NAUGHT]

no·ta be·ne (nō′tə bē′nē) Note well; take notice. [L]

no·ta·ble (nō′tə·bəl) *adj.* Worthy of note; distinguished. —*n.* One who is worthy of note; a distinguished person. [< L *nota* a mark] —**no·ta·bil·i·ty** (nō′tə·bil′ə·tē), **no′ta·ble·ness** *n.* —**no′ta·bly** *adv.*

no·ta·rize (nō′tə·rīz) *v.t.* **·rized, ·riz·ing** To attest to or authenticate as a notary. —**no′ta·ri·za′tion** *n.*

no·ta·ry (nō′tə·rē) *n. pl.* **·ries** An officer empowered to authenticate contracts, administer oaths, take depositions, etc. Also **notary public.** [< L *notarius* a clerk < *notare* to note] —**no·tar·i·al** (nō·târ′ē·əl) *adj.*

no·ta·tion (nō·tā′shən) *n.* 1 The process of designating by figures, etc. 2 Any system of signs, figures, or abbreviations used for convenience in a science or art. 3 A brief note; annotation. —**no·ta′tion·al** *adj.*

notch (noch) *n.* 1 A hollow cut or mark made in anything; a nick. 2 A narrow pass between hills or mountains. 3 *Informal* A degree: He is a *notch* above the others. —*v.t.* 1 To make a notch or notches in. 2 To record by means of notches; tally. [< OF *oschier* to notch] —**notch′er** *n.*

note (nōt) *n.* 1 A brief written record kept as a reminder. 2 *Often pl.* A written summary of a meeting, conversation, etc., to serve as a record for future reference: students taking copious *notes.* 3 A comparatively short letter. 4 An official communication in writing from one government to another. 5 A brief comment in a margin, at the bottom of a page, or at the end of a text. 6 A guarantee in writing to pay a specified sum at a certain time. 7 A government or bank certificate, usu. payable in cash upon pres-

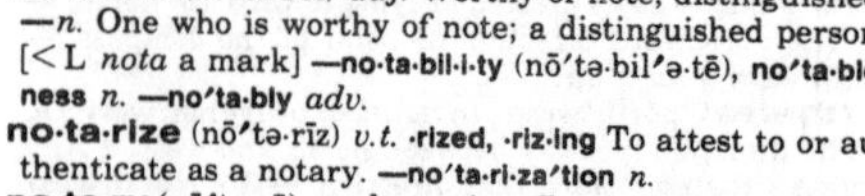

Musical notes
a. whole. b. half. c. quarter. d. eighth. e. sixteenth. f. thirty-second. g. sixty-fourth.

entation. 8 An account or bill. 9 *Music* a A written character used to indicate the pitch and length of a tone. b Any musical sound. c A key of a keyboard instrument. 10 A bird's song. 11 The general tone or quality of something: a *note* of anxiety. 12 High importance or repute: people of *note.* 13 Special notice or attention: He took *note* of the situation. —**compare notes** To exchange opinions; talk over. —*v.t.* **not·ed, not·ing** 1 To take notice or note of; observe. 2 To set down, as in writing; make a note of. 3 To mention specially or separately in the course of writing. 4 To set down in musical notation. [< L *nota* a mark, orig. pp. fem. of *noscere* know] —**not′er** *n.*

note·book (nōt′bŏŏk′) *n.* A book in which to enter memoranda or other notes.

not·ed (nō′tid) *adj.* Well known by reputation or report. —**not′ed·ly** *adv.*

note·pa·per (nōt′pā′pər) *n.* Paper for writing notes or letters.

note·wor·thy (nōt′wûr′thē) *adj.* **·worth·i·er, ·worth·i·est** Worthy of note; significant. —**note′wor′thi·ly** *adv.* —**note′·wor′thi·ness** *n.*

noth·ing (nuth′ing) *n.* 1 Not any being or any particular thing. 2 A state of nonexistence. 3 A person or thing of slight significance, consideration, or value. 4 Zero; naught. —**make nothing of** 1 To be unable to comprehend. 2 To treat as insignificant or worthless. 3 To neglect to use or do. —**think nothing of** To think of as easy to do. —*adv.* In no degree; not at all.

noth·ing·ness (nuth′ing·nis) *n.* 1 A state of nonexistence. 2 Worthlessness. 3 Unconsciousness.

no·tice (nō′tis) *v.t.* **·ticed, ·tic·ing** 1 To pay attention to or take cognizance of. 2 To treat courteously or with favor. 3 To mention or comment on. 4 To serve with a notice; notify. —*n.* 1 The act of noticing or observing. 2 Announcement; warning. 3 Respectful treatment; civility. 4 A formal written or printed notification, instruction, or warning, as of the termination or intended termination of an agreement. 5 A public communication openly displayed. 6 A critique or review: The play closed because of bad *notices.* [< L *notus* known] —**no′tice·a·ble** *adj.* —**no′·tice·a·bly** *adv.*

no·ti·fi·ca·tion (nō′tə·fə·kā′shən) *n.* 1 The act of notifying. 2 Notice given. 3 Written matter that gives information.

no·ti·fy (nō′tə·fī) *v.t.* **·fied, ·fy·ing** 1 To give notice to; inform. 2 To make known. [< L *notus* known + *facere* to make] —**no′ti·fi′er** *n.*

no·tion (nō′shən) *n.* 1 A thought; idea. 2 A hastily formed theory. 3 Intention; inclination. 4 *pl.* Miscellaneous small articles, such as ribbons, thread, pins, needles, etc. [< L *notus,* pp. of *noscere* know]

no·tion·al (nō′shən·əl) *adj.* 1 Pertaining to, expressing, or consisting of notions or concepts. 2 Existing in imagination only. 3 Given to pet ideas or fancies. —**no′tion·al·ly** *adv.*

no·to·ri·e·ty (nō′tə·rī′ə·tē) *n. pl.* **·ties** 1 The character of being notorious. 2 Common knowledge or talk. 3 One who or that which is notorious.

no·to·ri·ous (nō·tôr′ē·əs, -tō′rē-) *adj.* 1 Being publicly and unfavorably known and discussed. 2 Well-known. [< L *notus* known, orig. pp. of *noscere* know] —**no·to′ri·ous·ly** *adv.* —**no·to′ri·ous·ness** *n.* —**Syn. 1** egregious, flagrant, outrageous, unsavory.

not·with·stand·ing (not′with·stan′ding, -wi<u>th</u>-) *adv.* All the same; nevertheless: Though imprisoned, he escaped *notwithstanding.* —*prep.* In spite of: He left *notwithstanding* your orders. —*conj.* In spite of the fact that.

nou·gat (nōō′gət, -gä) *n.* A confection consisting usu. of a honey or sugar paste mixed with chopped almonds, pistachios, etc. [< L *nux, nucis* a nut]

nought (nôt) *n., adj., adv.* NAUGHT.

noun (noun) *Gram. n.* A word used as the name of a thing, quality, or action existing or conceived by the mind; a substantive. —*adj.* Of or used as a noun or nouns: also **noun·al** (noun′əl). [< L *nomen* name]

nour·ish (nûr′ish) *v.t.* 1 To furnish material to sustain the life and promote the growth of (a living organism). 2 To support; maintain: to *nourish* illusions. [< L *nutrire* nourish] —**nour′ish·er** *n.*

nour·ish·ment (nûr′ish·mənt) *n.* 1 Nutriment; food. 2 The act of nourishing or the state of being nourished. 3 Anything that promotes growth and sustains life.

nou·veau riche (nōō′vō′ rēsh′) *pl.* **nou·veaux riches** (nōō′vō′ rēsh′) One recently become rich, esp. one given to vulgar ostentation. [F, lit., new rich]
Nov, Nov. November.
no·va (nō′və) *n. pl.* **·vas** or **·vae** (-vē) A star which suddenly increases in brightness, then fades to its former magnitude after a time. [< L *novus* new]
nov·el (nov′əl) *n.* A fictional prose narrative of considerable length with a plot and characters. —*adj.* New in a striking or unusual way. [Fusion of Ital. *novella* a novel and OF *novel* new] —**Syn.** *adj.* fresh, unfamiliar, unusual. *n.* **1** romance, story, tale.
nov·el·ette (nov′əl·et′) *n.* A short novel.
nov·el·ist (nov′əl·ist) *n.* A writer of novels.
nov·el·is·tic (nov′əl·is′tik) *adj.* Of, pertaining to, characteristic of, or found in novels. —**nov′el·is′ti·cal·ly** *adv.*
no·vel·la (nō·vel′ə) *n. pl.* **·las** or **·le** (-lā) **1** A short tale or narrative, often satirical. **2** A short novel. [Ital.]
nov·el·ty (nov′əl·tē) *n. pl.* **·ties** **1** The quality of being novel. **2** *pl.* Small manufactured articles or trinkets. **3** An innovation.
No·vem·ber (nō·vem′bər) *n.* The 11th month of the year, containing 30 days. [< L *November* ninth month of the Roman calendar]
no·ve·na (nō·vē′nə) *n.* In the Roman Catholic Church, a devotion consisting of a prayer said on nine successive days, asking for some special blessing. [< L *novem* nine]
nov·ice (nov′is) *n.* **1** A beginner in any business or occupation; tyro. **2** *Eccl.* One who enters a religious house or community on probation. [< L *novus* new] —**nov′ice·hood** (-hŏŏd) *n.*
no·vi·ti·ate (nō·vish′ē·it, -āt) *n.* **1** The state of being a novice. **2** *Eccl.* The period of probation of a novice in a religious order. **3** A novice.
No·vo·cain (nō′və·kān) *n.* A local anesthetic containing procaine: a trade name.
now (nou) *adv.* **1** At once. **2** At or during the present time. **3** Nowadays. **4** In the immediate past: He said so just *now.* **5** In the immediate future: He is going just *now.* **6** Things being as they are. **7** At this point in the proceedings, narrative, etc. —*conj.* Since; seeing that. —*n.* The present time or occasion: the here and *now.* —*adj. Informal* **1** Of the present time. **2** Excitingly novel: *now* movies. **3** Practicing and conscious of what is new: the *now* generation. [< OE *nū*]
now·a·days (nou′ə·dāz′) *adv.* In the present time or age.
no·way (nō′wā′) *adv.* In no way, manner, or degree. Also **no′ways′.**
no·where (nō′hwâr′) *adv.* In no place; not anywhere. —*n.* No place. Also *Regional* **no′wheres′.**
no·wise (nō′wīz′) *adv.* In no manner or degree.
nox·ious (nok′shəs) *adj.* Causing, or tending to cause, injury to health or morals; poisonous. [< L *nocere* to hurt] —**nox′ious·ly** *adv.* —**nox′ious·ness** *n.* —**Syn.** deadly, hurtful, pernicious.
noz·zle (noz′əl) *n.* A projecting spout from which something, esp. a fluid, issues. **2** An inlet or outlet pipe. [Dim. of NOSE]

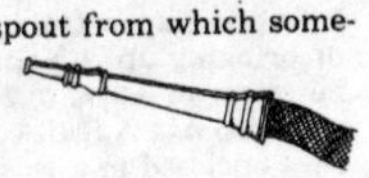

Nozzle of a hose

N.P. Notary Public.
Np neptunium.
N.S. New Style; Nova Scotia.
NT., N.T. New Testament.
nth (enth) *adj.* **1** Of or indicating the element of an ordered set corresponding to a number *n.* **2** Arbitrarily large. —**to the nth degree** To the utmost. —*n.* **1** The *n*th element of an ordered set. **2** One of *n* equal parts.
nt. wt. net weight.
nu (nyōō) *n.* The 13th letter in the Greek alphabet (N, ν).
nu·ance (nyōō′äns, nyōō·äns′) *n.* **1** A shade of difference in tone or color. **2** A slight degree of difference in anything perceptible to the mind. [< OF *nuer* to shade]
nub (nub) *n.* **1** A protuberance; knob. **2** The core of a matter: the *nub* of the story. [< MLG *knobbe* knob]
nub·bin (nub′in) *n.* **1** An imperfectly developed ear of corn. **2** Anything small and stunted. [< NUB]
nu·bile (nyōō′bil, -bīl) *adj.* Of suitable age and physical development to marry: said of young women. [< L *nubere* to wed] —**nu·bil′i·ty** *n.*
nu·cle·ar (nyōō′klē·ər) *adj.* **1** Of, pertaining to, forming, of the nature of, or depending upon a nucleus or nuclei: also **nu′cle·al.** **2** Of or using energy of atomic nuclei.
nuclear energy ATOMIC ENERGY.
nuclear family A family consisting of parents and child or children considered as a discrete group.
nuclear fission FISSION (def. 3).
nuclear physics The branch of physics that studies atomic nuclei.
nuclear reaction REACTION (def. 5).
nuclear reactor REACTOR (def. 2).
nu·cle·ate (nyōō′klē·āt) *adj.* Having a nucleus. Also **nu′cle·at′ed.** —*v.t.* & *v.i.* **·at·ed, ·at·ing** To form or gather into a nucleus. —**nu′cle·a′tion** *n.*
nu·cle·o·lus (nyōō·klē′ə·ləs) *n. pl.* **·li** (-lī) *Biol.* A well-defined particle found within the nucleus of most cells. Also **nu′cle·ole** (-ōl). [< LL, dim. of *nucleus*] —**nu·cle′o·lar** *adj.*
nu·cle·on (nyōō′klē·on) *n. Physics* Any particle that occurs in an atomic nucleus.
nu·cle·on·ics (nyōō′klē·on′iks) *n. pl. (construed as sing.)* The technology based on nuclear energy. —**nu′cle·on′ic** *adj.*
nu·cle·us (nyōō′klē·əs) *n. pl.* **·cle·i** (-klē·ī) **1** A central mass; kernel. **2** *Biol.* A complex, spheroidal body found in plant and animal cells and essential in the vital activities of the cell, as growth, reproduction, etc. **3** *Astron.* A bright central point as in the head of a comet or at the center of a nebula. **4** *Physics & Chem.* The central core of an atom, having a positive charge, composed mainly of protons and neutrons, and containing most of the atomic mass. [L, a kernel, dim. of *nux, nucis* a nut]

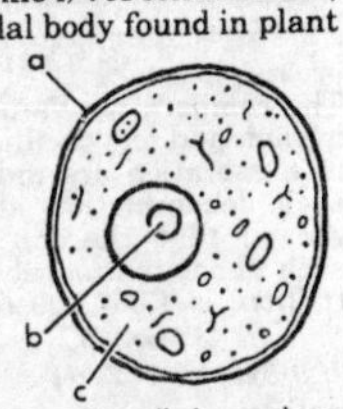

a. cell wall. b. nucleus. c. cell body.

nude (nyōōd) *adj.* Without clothing or covering; naked. —*n.* **1** A nude figure, as in painting or sculpture. **2** The state of being nude: to appear in the *nude.* [< L *nudus* naked] —**nude′ly** *adv.* —**nude′ness** *n.*
nudge (nuj) *v.* **nudged, nudg·ing** *v.t.* **1** To touch or push gently, in order to attract attention. —*v.i.* **2** To give a nudge. —*n.* The act of nudging, as with the elbow. [?]
nud·ism (nyōō′diz·əm) *n.* The practice of living in the state of nudity for hygienic reasons. —**nud′ist** *adj., n.*
nu·di·ty (nyōō′də·tē) *n. pl.* **·ties** **1** The state of being nude. **2** Something that is naked.
nu·ga·to·ry (nyōō′gə·tô′rē, -tō′rē) *adj.* **1** Having no power; inoperative. **2** Having no worth or meaning. [< L *nugae* trifles] —**nu′ga·to′ri·ly** *adv.* —**nu′ga·to′ri·ness** *n.*
nug·get (nug′it) *n.* **1** A lump. **2** A lump of precious metal, as gold. **3** A small amount of anything of value: a *nugget* of good sense. [?]
nui·sance (nyōō′səns) *n.* A person or thing that annoys, vexes, or harms. [< OF *nuire* to harm]
nuisance tax A small tax paid by the consumer and considered a nuisance by both the collector and the payer.
null (nul) *adj.* **1** Of no legal force or effect. **2** Having no existence. **3** Lacking distinction or individuality. **4** Zero. —**null and void** Having no force or effect; invalid. [< L *nullus* no, none]
nul·li·fy (nul′ə·fī) *v.t.* **·fied, ·fy·ing** **1** To bring to nothing; render ineffective or valueless. **2** To deprive of legal force or effect; make void. [< L *nullus* none + *facere* make] —**nul·li·fi·ca·tion** (nul′ə·fə·kā′shən), **nul′li·fi′er** *n.*
nul·li·ty (nul′ə·tē) *n. pl.* **·ties** **1** The state of being null. **2** A nonentity. **3** *Law* A void act or instrument.
Num, Num., Numb. Numbers.
num. number(s); numeral(s).
numb (num) *adj.* Wholly or partially without the power of sensation or of motion. —*v.t.* To make numb. [< ME *nomen* taken, seized] —**numb′ly** *adv.* —**numb′ness** *n.* —**Syn.** *adj.* benumbed, deadened, frozen, insensible.

num·ber (num′bər) *n.* **1** An element of one of various mathematical sets, defined, often by axioms, as having certain properties, esp. with respect to certain operations, as integers, real numbers, imaginary numbers, etc. **2** A collection of units or individuals, whether large or small: a *number* of facts; large *numbers* of people. **3** *pl.* Arithmetic. **4** The character or quality of being numerous: Reliance is placed more on spirit than on *number.* **5** An element of an ordered set. **6** One of the divisions or movements of a piece of music. **7** A series of digits used for identification: a serial *number.* **8** *Often pl.* Poetic measure; rhythm. **9** *Gram.* The form of inflection of a noun, pronoun, adjective, or verb, that indicates whether one thing or more is meant. **10** *Informal* An article of merchandise: our most popular *number.* **11** A single issue, as of a periodical. **12** *Informal* A person or thing set apart: That blouse is a stylish *number.* **—a number of** More than two or three; many. **—get** (or **have**) **someone's number** *Informal* To have insight into a person's motives, character, etc. **—the numbers** NUMBERS POOL. *—v.t.* **1** To determine the total number of; count. **2** To assign a number to. **3** To include as one of a collection or group. **4** To amount to; total: We *number* fifty men. **5** To set or limit the number of: Your days are *numbered.* *—v.i.* **6** To make a count; total. **7** To be included, as in a group: He was *numbered* among the civilians. [< L *numerus*] **—num′ber·er** *n.*

TABLE OF NUMBERS

The comparative values of denominations between one million and one decillion in the U.S. and British systems of numeration are indicated below. In the U.S. system, each denomination above one million is 1,000 times greater than the one preceding. In the British system, each denomination above one billion (equal to one U.S. trillion) is 1,000,000 times greater than the one before.

U.S. System	*Number of Zeros*	*Value as Power of 10*	*British System*
million	6	10^{6}	million
billion	9	10^{9}	milliard
trillion	12	10^{12}	billion
quadrillion	15	10^{15}	(1,000 billions)
quintillion	18	10^{18}	trillion
sextillion	21	10^{21}	(1,000 trillions)
septillion	24	10^{24}	quadrillion
octillion	27	10^{27}	(1,000 quadrillions)
nonillion	30	10^{30}	quintillion
decillion	33	10^{33}	(1,000 quintillions)
	36	10^{36}	sextillion
	42	10^{42}	septillion
	48	10^{48}	octillion
	54	10^{54}	nonillion
	60	10^{60}	decillion

num·ber·less (num′bər·lis) *adj.* **1** Very numerous; innumerable. **2** Having no number. **—Syn. 1** countless, endless, illimitable, measureless, unbounded.

Num·bers (num′bərz) *n.* The fourth book of the Old Testament, giving the two censuses of Israel.

numbers pool A lottery in which wagers are laid on the appearance of some particular, unpredictable number. Also **numbers game, numbers racket.**

nu·mer·a·ble (nyōō′mər·ə·bəl) *adj.* That can be numbered or counted.

nu·mer·a·cy (nyōō′mə·rə·sē) *n.* The acquired ability to reason quantitatively and to apply scientific principles.

nu·mer·al (nyōō′mər·əl) *n.* A symbol, character, letter, or word, used to express a number: Arabic *numerals.* *—adj.* **1** Used in expressing a number. **2** Denoting a number. [< L *numerus* number] **—nu′mer·al·ly** *adv.*

nu·mer·ate (nyōō′mə·rāt) *v.t.* **·at·ed, ·at·ing 1** To enumerate; count. **2** To read, as a numerical expression. [< L *numerus* number] **—nu·mer·a′tion** *n.*

nu·mer·a·tor (nyōō′mə·rā′tər) *n.* **1** *Math.* In a common fraction, the term which stands above or to the left of the line. **2** A person or thing that numbers.

nu·mer·i·cal (nyōō·mer′i·kəl) *adj.* **1** Of, pertaining to or denoting number. **2** Capable of being numbered; numerable. **3** Represented by numbers or figures, as in arithmetic, and not by letters. [< L *numerus* number] **—nu·mer′i·cal·ly** *adv.*

nu·mer·ol·o·gy (nyōō′mə·rol′ə·jē) *n.* A system that purports to explain the occult influence of numbers, as that of the day of one's birth, etc. **—nu′mer·o·log′i·cal** *adj.*

nu·mer·ous (nyōō′mə·rəs) *adj.* Consisting of a great number of units; being many. **—nu′mer·ous·ness** *n.*

Nu·mid·i·a (nyōō·mid′ē·ə) *n.* An ancient kingdom and Roman province in N Africa. **—Nu·mid′i·an** *adj., n.*

nu·mis·mat·ics (nyōō′miz·mat′iks, -mis-) *n.pl. (construed as sing.)* The science of coins and medals. [< L *numisma* a coin] **—nu′mis·mat′ic, nu′mis·mat′i·cal** *adj.* **—nu·mis′ma·tist, nu·mis′ma·tol′o·gist** *n.*

num·skull (num′skul) *n.* A blockhead; a stupid person. Also **numb′skull.**

nun (nun) *n.* A woman devoted to a religious life, and living under vows of poverty, chastity, and obedience, often in a convent. [< Med. L *nonna*] **—nun′nish** *adj.*

nun·ci·o (nun′shē·ō) *n. pl.* **·ci·os 1** An ordinary ambassador of the pope to a foreign court. **2** Any messenger. Also **nun′ci·us** (-shē·əs). [< L *nuntius* messenger]

nun·ner·y (nun′ər·ē) *n. pl.* **·ner·ies** A convent for nuns.

nup·tial (nup′shəl) *adj.* Pertaining to marriage or the marriage ceremony. *—n.pl.* A wedding; marriage ceremony. [< L *nuptus,* pp. of *nubere* marry] **—nup′tial·ly** *adv.*

nurse (nûrs) *n.* **1** A person who cares for the sick, esp. professionally. **2** A female servant who takes care of young children. **3** A person who fosters, protects, or promotes. *—v.* **nursed, nurs·ing** *v.t.* **1** To take care of, as in sickness or infirmity. **2** To feed (an infant) at the breast; suckle. **3** To feed and care for in infancy. **4** To promote the growth and development of. **5** To preserve from injury or undue strain: to *nurse* a weak wrist. **6** To try to cure, as a cold, by taking care of oneself. **7** To clasp or hold carefully or caressingly; fondle. **8** To keep in mind, as a grievance. **9** To use or consume slowly: to *nurse* a drink. *—v.i.* **10** To act or serve as a nurse. **11** To take milk from the breast. **12** To suckle an infant. [< L *nutrix* < *nutrire* nourish, foster] **—nurs′er** *n.*

nurse·maid (nûrs′mād′) *n.* A girl or woman employed to care for children.

nurs·er·y (nûr′sər·ē) *n. pl.* **·er·ies 1** A room set apart for the use of children and babies. **2** A place where trees, shrubs, etc., are raised for sale or transplanting. **3** The place where anything is fostered, bred, or developed.

nurs·er·y·man (nûr′sər·ē·mən) *n. pl.* **·men** (-mən) One who owns or manages a nursery for the cultivation of trees and shrubs.

nursery rhyme A simple story presented in rhymed verse or jingle for children.

nursery school A school for children too young to enter kindergarten.

nursing home A usu. private institution for the care of convalescents, the chronically ill, or the aged who are unable to care for themselves.

nurs·ling (nûrs′ling) *n.* An infant, esp. one that is breastfed. Also **nurse′ling.**

nur·ture (nûr′chər) *v.t.* **·tured, ·tur·ing 1** To feed; nourish. **2** To bring up or train; educate. *—n.* **1** The act of rearing or bringing up. **2** Nourishment. [< L *nutrire* nourish] **—nur′tur·er** *n.* **—Syn.** *v.* **2** cherish, foster, raise, rear.

nut (nut) *n.* **1** A fruit consisting of a usu. edible kernel or seed enclosed in a woody shell. **2** The kernel of such fruit. **3** *Mech.* A small block of metal having an internal screw thread so that it may be fitted upon a bolt, screw, etc. **4** *Slang* The head. **5** *Slang* A crazy or irresponsible person. **6** *Slang* The whole amount of money. *—v.i.* **nut·ted, nut·ting** To seek or gather nuts. [< OE *hnutu*] **—nut′ter** *n.*

Mechanical nuts
a. lock. b. wing.
c. square, plain.

nut·crack·er (nut′krak′ər) *n.* **1** Any of various devices for cracking nuts. **2** One of several crowlike birds that eat nuts.

nut·gall (nut′gôl′) *n.* A nut-shaped gall, as on an oak tree.

nut·hatch (nut′hach′) *n.* Any of various small, short-tailed birds related to the titmouse, having a thin, sharp bill and feeding on nuts and insects.

nut·meg (nut′meg) *n.* **1** The aromatic kernel of the fruit of the nutmeg tree of the Molucca Islands. **2** The tree itself. [< NUT + OF *mugue* musk]

nu·tri·a (nyōō′trē·ə) *n.* **1** A water-inhabiting rodent somewhat like a beaver, of South American origin. **2** Its soft, brown fur. [Sp., an otter < L *lutra*]

nu·tri·ent (nʸōō′trē·ənt) *adj.* **1** Giving nourishment. **2** Conveying nutrition. —*n.* Something that nourishes. [< L *nutrire* nourish]

nu·tri·ment (nʸōō′trə·mənt) *n.* **1** That which nourishes. **2** That which promotes development. [< L *nutrire* nourish] —**nu′tri·men′tal** *adj.* —**Syn. 1** food, meat, nourishment, sustenance.

nu·tri·tion (nʸōō·trish′ən) *n.* **1** The aggregate of all the processes by which food is assimilated in living organisms. **2** Food. —**nu·tri′tion·al** *adj.* —**nu·tri′tion·al·ly** *adv.*

nu·tri·tion·ist (nʸōō·trish′ən·ist) *n.* One who specializes in the processes and problems of nutrition.

nu·tri·tious (nʸōō·trish′əs) *adv.* Nourishing; promoting nutrition. —**nu·tri′tious·ly** *adv.* —**nu·tri′tious·ness** *n.*

nu·tri·tive (nʸōō′trə·tiv) *adj.* **1** Having nutritious properties. **2** Of or relating to nutrition. —**nu′tri·tive·ly** *adv.* —**nu′tri·tive·ness** *n.*

nuts (nuts) *Slang adj.* **1** Crazy; demented. **2** Madly in love: with *about.* **3** Extremely enthusiastic: with *about:* He's *nuts* about baseball. —*interj.* An exclamation of scorn, disapproval, etc. [< NUT]

nut·shell (nut′shel′) *n.* The shell of a nut. —**in a nutshell** In brief and concise statement.

nut·ty (nut′ē) *adj.* **·ti·er, ·ti·est 1** Abounding in nuts. **2** Having the flavor of nuts. **3** *Slang* Crazy. —**nut′ti·ly** *adv.* —**nut′ti·ness** *n.*

nux vom·i·ca (nuks′ vom′i·kə) **1** The seed of an Indian tree containing strychnine and other poisonous alkaloids. **2** The tree producing this fruit. **3** A drug prepared from the seed, sometimes used as a stimulant. [< L *nux* a nut + *vomere* to vomit]

nuz·zle (nuz′əl) *v.* **·zled, ·zling** *v.i.* **1** To rub with the nose. **2** To nestle or snuggle; lie close. —*v.t.* **3** To rub with the nose. [< NOSE] —**nuz′zler** *n.*

NV Nevada (P.O. abbr.).

NW, N.W., nw, n.w. northwest; northwestern.

NWT Northwest Territories.

NY New York (P.O. abbr.).

N.Y. New York.

N.Y.C. New York City.

ny·lon (nī′lon) *n.* **1** A synthetic substance that may be formed into fibers, bristles, sheets, etc., and characterized by extreme toughness, elasticity, and strength. **2** *pl.* Stockings made of nylon thread. [< *Nylon,* a tradename]

nymph (nimf) *Gk. & Rom. Myth.* A beautiful maiden inhabiting groves, forests, fountains, springs, mountains, etc. —*n.* **1** Any lovely young woman. **2** The young of certain insects which undergo incomplete metamorphosis. [< Gk. *nymphē* nymph, bride] —**nymph′al, nym·phe·an** (nim·fē′ən), **nymph′ic, nymph′i·cal** *adj.*

nym·pho·ma·ni·a (nim′fə·mā′nē·ə, -mān′yə) *n.* Abnormal and ungovernable sexual desire in women. [< Gk. *nymphē* nymph + -MANIA] —**nym′pho·ma′ni·ac** *adj., n.*

N.Z., N. Zeal. New Zealand.

O

O, o (ō) *n. pl.* **O's, o's, Os, os** (ōz) **1** The 15th letter of the English alphabet. **2** Any spoken sound representing the letter *O* or *o.* **3** Something shaped like an O. —*adj.* Shaped like an O.

O (ō) *interj.* Oh!

O oxygen.

O. Ocean; October; Ohio; Ontario.

O., o. octavo; old; order.

o ohm.

o′ *prep.* Of: one *o′*clock, man-*o′*-war.

oaf (ōf) *n.* A stupid, vulgar person, esp. a man. [< ON *alfr* elf] —**oaf′ish** *adj.* —**oaf′ish·ly** *adv.* —**oaf′ish·ness** *n.*

oak (ōk) *n.* **1** Any of various hardwood, acorn-bearing trees and shrubs of the beech family. **2** The hard, durable wood or timber of the oak. **3** Any of various other plants having a resemblance or relation to the oak: poison *oak.* [< OE *āc*]

Oak leaves and acorns

oak apple A gall produced on an oak by an insect; a nutgall. Also **oak gall.**

oak·en (ō′kən) *adj.* Made of oak.

oak·um (ō′kəm) *n.* Hemp fiber, sometimes treated with preservative or tar: used in caulking, etc. [< OE *ā-* off + *cemban* to comb]

oar (ôr, ōr) *n.* **1** An implement for propelling or, occasionally, for steering a boat, consisting of a long shaft with a blade at one end. **2** An oarsman. —*v.t.* **1** To propel with or as with oars; row. **2** To make (one's way) or traverse (water) with or as with oars. —*v.i.* **3** To proceed by or as by rowing; row. [< OE *ār*]

oar·lock (ôr′lok′, ōr′-) *n.* A device on the side of a boat for keeping an oar in place.

oars·man (ôrz′mən, ōrz′-) *n. pl.* **·men** (-mən) One who rows, esp. expertly. —**oars′man·ship,** *n.*

OAS Organization of American States.

o·a·sis (ō·ā′sis) *n. pl.* **·ses** (-sēz) **1** An area in a waste or desert made fertile by ground water or by surface irrigation. **2** Any place providing relief or refreshment; refuge: a small city park that provided an *oasis* of quiet amidst the street noises. [< Gk., fertile spot]

oat (ōt) *n. Usu. pl.* A cereal grass extensively cultivated for its edible grain. [< OE *āte*] —**oat′en** *adj.*

oat·cake (ōt′kāk′) *n.* A thin cake of oatmeal, usu. baked hard. Also **oat cake.**

oath (ōth) *n. pl.* **oaths** (ōt͟hz, ōths) **1** A solemn confirmation of a promise, course of action, etc., made by appealing to God or to some person or thing regarded as high and holy. **2** The course of action, promise, etc., so supported, or the form of words used in supporting it. **3** An irreverent or profane use of the name of the Deity or of any sacred name or object. **4** A swearword; curse. [< OE *āth*] —**Syn. 3** blasphemy, curse, imprecation, profanity.

oat·meal (ōt′mēl′) *n.* **1** The meal of oats. **2** Porridge made of it. Also **oat meal.**

ob- *prefix* **1** Toward; to; facing: *obverse.* **2** Against; in opposition to: *obstruct.* **3** Over; upon: *obliterate.* **4** Completely: *obdurate.* [< L *ob* toward, for, against]

Ob, Ob., Obad. Obadiah.

ob. obstetrics; he (or she) died (L *obiit*); in passing (L *obiter*).

ob·bli·ga·to (ob′lə·gä′tō, *Ital.* ôb′blē·gä′tō) *adj. Music* Referring to accompaniments, usu. by a single instrument, that are to be played as written and are not to be omitted. —*n. pl.* **·tos** or **·ti** (-tē) An obbligato accompaniment. [< Ital. *obbligare* obligate]

ob·du·rate (ob′dʸə·rit) *adj.* **1** Unmoved by feelings of humanity or pity; hard. **2** Perversely impenitent. **3** Unyielding; stubborn. [< L *ob-* completely + *durare* harden] —**ob′du·ra·cy** (-rə·sē), **ob′du·rate·ness** *n.* —**ob′du·rate·ly** *adv.*

o·be·di·ence (ō·bē′dē·əns, ə·bē′-) *n.* **1** The state of being obedient; willingness to obey. **2** The act of obeying, or an instance of it.

o·be·di·ent (ō·bē′dē·ənt, ə·bē′-) *adj.* Complying with or submitting to a command, prohibition, law, or duty. [< L *obedire* obey] —**o·be′di·ent·ly** *adv.*

o·bei·sance (ō·bā′səns, ō·bē′-) *n.* **1** An act of courtesy or deference, as a bow or curtsy. **2** Reverent courtesy; deference. [< OF *obeir* obey] —**o·bei′sant** *adj.* —**o·bei′sant·ly** *adv.*

ob·e·lisk (ob′ə·lisk, ō′bə-) *n.* 1 A usu. monumental structure with a square, tapered shaft and a pyramidal top. 2 *Printing* The dagger sign (†) used as a mark of reference: also **ob·e·lus** (ob′ə·ləs). [< Gk. *obeliskos,* dim. of *obelos* a spit, pointed pillar]

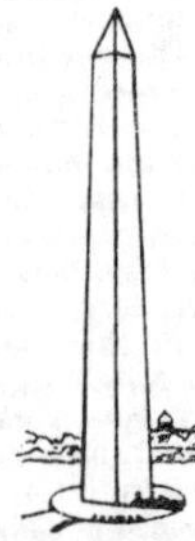
Obelisk

O·ber·on (ō′bə·ron) In medieval folklore, the king of the fairies.

o·bese (ō·bēs′) *adj.* Very fat; corpulent. [< L *ob-* completely + *edere* eat] —**o·be·si·ty** (ō·bē′sə·tē) *n.*

o·bey (ō·bā′, ə·bā′) *v.t.* 1 To do the bidding of; be obedient to. 2 To carry into effect; execute, as a command. 3 To act in accordance with; be guided by: to *obey* the law. —*v.i.* 4 To be obedient. [< L *obedire*] —**o·bey′·er** *n.*

ob·fus·cate (ob′fəs·kāt, ob·fus′-) *v.t.* **·cat·ed, ·cat·ing** 1 To obscure the clarity or meaning of; muddle. 2 To confuse or bewilder. 3 To darken or obscure. [< L *ob-* completely + *fuscare* darken] —**ob′fus·ca′tion** *n.* —**ob·fus·ca·tor·y** (ob·fus′kə·tôr′ē, -tō′rē) *adj.*

o·bi (ō′bē) *n.* A broad sash with a bow in the back, worn with a Japanese kimono. [Japanese]

o·bit (ō′bit, ob′it) *n.* OBITUARY.

ob·i·ter dic·tum (ob′ə·tər dik′təm, ō′bə-) *pl.* **ob·i·ter dic·ta** (dik′tə) 1 A remark made in passing by a judge. 2 An incidental remark. [L]

o·bit·u·ar·y (ō·bich′o͞o·er′ē) *n. pl.* **·ar·ies** A published notice of a person's death, often including a biographical sketch. —*adj.* Of or pertaining to a death. [< L *obitus,* pp. of *obire,* die, go down]

obj. object; objective.

ob·ject[1] (əb·jekt′) *v.i.* 1 To offer arguments or opposition; dissent. 2 To feel or state disapproval or dissent. —*v.t.* 3 To offer as opposition or criticism; charge. [< L *ob-* towards, against + *jacere* to throw] —**ob·jec′tor** *n.*

ob·ject[2] (ob′jikt, -jekt) *n.* 1 Anything that lies within the cognizance of the senses; esp. anything tangible or visible; any material thing. 2 Something to which feeling or action is directed: an *object* of affection. 3 A purpose or goal; aim. 4 *Gram.* A noun or pronoun that receives the action of a verb or is governed by a preposition. [< Med. L *objectum* something thrown in the way]

ob·jec·ti·fy (əb·jek′tə·fī) *v.t.* **·fied, ·fy·ing** To present from an external viewpoint; make objective. —**ob·jec′ti·fi·ca′tion** *n.*

ob·jec·tion (əb·jek′shən) *n.* 1 The act of objecting. 2 An argument, fact, etc., used in dissent or disapproval. 3 A feeling of disapproval or disinclination.

ob·jec·tion·a·ble (əb·jek′shən·ə·bəl) *adj.* Deserving of disapproval; offensive. —**ob·jec′tion·a·bil′i·ty, ob·jec′tion·a·ble·ness** *n.* —**ob·jec′tion·a·bly** *adv.*

ob·jec·tive (əb·jek′tiv) *adj.* 1 Of or belonging to an object; having the nature of an object; esp., being that which is external to the mind or perceived by the senses and subject to verification. 2 Treating of or representing facts or reality without reference to feelings or opinions: an *objective* report or test. 3 Not prejudiced; unbiased. 4 *Gram.* Denoting the case of an object of a transitive verb or preposition. —*n.* 1 A goal or purpose, as of a mission or assignment. 2 Something that is objective. 3 *Gram.* a The objective case. b A word in this case. 4 The lens or lenses of an optical instrument closest to the object observed. —**ob·jec′tive·ly** *adv.* —**ob·jec·tiv·i·ty** (ob′jek·tiv′ə·tē), **ob·jec′·tive·ness** *n.* —**Syn.** *adj.* 2 impersonal. 3 detached, disinterested, fair-minded.

ob·ject lesson (ob′jikt, -jekt) A practical representation or exemplification of a principle or moral.

ob·jet d'art (ôb·zhā där′, ob′-) *pl.* **ob·jets d'art** (ôb·zhā′, ob′- där′) An article, such as a vase, statuette, etc. of artistic value. [F, lit., object of art]

ob·jur·gate (ob′jər·gāt) *v.t.* **·gat·ed, ·gat·ing** To rebuke severely; scold sharply. [< L *ob-* completely + *jurgare* scold] —**ob′jur·ga′tion, ob′jur·ga′tor** *n.* —**ob·jur′ga·to′ry** *adj.*

obl. oblique; oblong.

ob·late (ob′lāt, ob·lāt′) *adj.* Flattened at the poles. [< L *ob-* against + *-latus* carried] —**ob′late·ly** *adv.* —**ob′late·ness** *n.*

ob·la·tion (ob·lā′shən) *n.* 1 Anything offered in worship, esp. the elements of the Eucharist. 2 Any grateful and solemn offering. [< L *oblatus,* carried toward, offered] —**ob·la′tion·al, ob·la·to·ry** (ob′lə·tôr′ē, -tō′rē) *adj.*

ob·li·gate (ob′lə·gāt) *v.t.* **·gat·ed, ·gat·ing** To bind or compel, as by contract, conscience, promise, etc. —*adj.* (ob′lə·git, -gāt) Bound or restricted. [< L *obligare* oblige]

ob·li·ga·tion (ob′lə·gā′shən) *n.* 1 The act of obligating, or state of being obligated. 2 A duty, promise, etc., by which one is bound; responsibility. 3 The constraining power of conscience or law. 4 A requirement imposed by the customs of society or the laws of propriety; what one owes in return for a service, kindness, or favor. 5 A binding legal agreement bearing a penalty. 6 The condition of being indebted for an act of kindness, a service received, etc. —**ob′li·ga′tor** *n.*

ob·lig·a·to·ry (ə·blig′ə·tôr′ē, -tō′rē, ob′lə·gə-) *adj.* 1 In civil or moral law, binding. 2 Of the nature of or constituting a duty or obligation; imperative.

o·blige (ə·blīj′) *v.t.* **o·bliged, o·blig·ing** 1 To obligate; constrain. 2 To place under an obligation, as for a favor or kindness. 3 To do a favor or service for. [< L *ob-* towards + *ligare* to bind] —**o·blig′er** *n.*

o·blig·ing (ə·blī′jing) *adj.* Disposed to do favors; accommodating; kind. —**o·blig′ing·ly** *adv.* —**o·blig′ing·ness** *n.*

ob·lique (ō·blēk′, ə-, *in military usage* ə·blīk′) *adj.* 1 Neither perpendicular nor horizontal; slanting. 2 Acute or obtuse, as an angle. 3 Indirect or allusive rather than straightforward: an *oblique* reference to his uncertain paternity. —*v.i.* **·liqued, ·li·quing** 1 To deviate from the perpendicular; slant. 2 *Mil.* To march or advance in an oblique direction. [< L *ob-* against, completely + *liquis* slanting, awry] —**ob·lique′ly** *adv.* —**ob·lique′ness** *n.*

ob·liq·ui·ty (ə·blik′wə·tē) *n. pl.* **·ties** 1 Oblique quality or state. 2 Inclination from a vertical or horizontal line or plane; also, the amount or the angle of such inclination.

ob·lit·er·ate (ə·blit′ə·rāt) *v.t.* **·at·ed, ·at·ing** 1 To destroy utterly; leave no trace of. 2 To blot or wipe out; erase, as writing. [< L *obliterare* blot out] —**ob·lit′er·a′tion, ob·lit′er·a′tor** *n.* —**ob·lit′er·a′tive** *adj.*

ob·liv·i·on (ə·bliv′ē·ən) *n.* 1 The state or fact of being utterly forgotten. 2 The act or fact of forgetting completely; forgetfulness. [< L *oblivisci* forget]

ob·liv·i·ous (ə·bliv′ē·əs) *adj.* 1 Taking no notice, as though unaware or indifferent: usu. with *of* or *to: oblivious* of the noise. 2 Distracted; forgetful: usu. with *of.* —**ob·liv′i·ous·ly** *adv.* —**ob·liv′i·ous·ness** *n.*

ob·long (ob′lông, -long) *adj.* Longer in one dimension than in another; esp., elongated along the horizontal axis. —*n.* An oblong figure, as a rectangle. [< L *oblongus* somewhat long]

ob·lo·quy (ob′lə·kwē) *n. pl.* **·quies** 1 An expression of severe censure or denunciation. 2 The state of one who is so censured; disgrace. —**Syn.** 1 reprobation, vilification, defamation, calumny, opprobrium. 2 ignominy. [< L *ob-* against + *loqui* speak]

ob·nox·ious (əb·nok′shəs) *adj.* Strongly offensive; disgusting; repulsive; odious. [< L *ob-* towards + *noxa* injury] —**ob·nox′ious·ly** *adv.* —**ob·nox′ious·ness** *n.*

o·boe (ō′bō) *n.* A double-reed wind instrument with a high, penetrating tone. [Ital.] —**o′bo·ist** *n.*

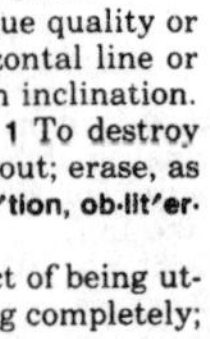
Oboe

obs. obsolete.

ob·scene (ob·sēn′, əb-) *adj.* 1 Offensive to one's sense of modesty or propriety. 2 Intended to provoke lust; licentious; lewd. 3 Disgusting; foul. [< L *obs-,* var of *ob-* towards + *caenum* filth] —**ob·scene′ly** *adv.*

ob·scen·i·ty (ob·sen′ə·tē, -sē′nə-, əb-) *n. pl.* **·ties** 1 The state or quality of being obscene. 2 An obscene remark, act, representation, etc. Also **ob·scene′ness.**

ob·scur·ant·ism (ob·skyo͝or′ənt·iz′əm, əb-) *n.* 1 Opposition to education or popular enlightenment. 2 The practice of being deliberately obscure. —**ob·scur′ant·ist** *adj., n.* [< L *obscurans, obscurare* darken]

ob·scure (ob·skyo͝or′, əb-) *adj.* **·scur·er, ·scur·est** 1 Lacking in light; dim; dark; dusky. 2 Not clear to the mind; vague; abstruse. 3 Faintly marked; hard to discern; undefined. 4 Remote or apart; hidden from view or notice. 5 Little known; unnoticed: an *obscure* hamlet. —*v.t.* **·scured, ·scur·ing** 1 To darken or cloud; dim. 2 To hide from view; conceal. 3 To make unintelligible; confuse. [< L *obscurus*, lit., covered over] **—ob·scure′ly** *adv.* **—ob·scu′ri·ty** (-skyŏŏr′ə·tē), **ob·scure′ness** *n.*

ob·se·qui·ous (ob·sē′kwē·əs, əb-) *adj.* Too eager to please; fawning; servile. [< L *ob-* towards + *sequi* follow] **—ob·se′qui·ous·ly** *adv.* **—ob·se′qui·ous·ness** *n.*

ob·se·quy (ob′sə·kwē) *n. pl.* **·quies** *Usu. pl.* A funeral service. [< L *obsequium* dutiful service]

ob·serv·a·ble (əb·zûr′və·bəl) *adj.* 1 That can be observed; manifest. 2 Deserving of notice. 3 Customary; demanding observance. **—ob·serv′a·ble·ness** *n.* **—ob·serv′a·bly** *adv.*

ob·ser·vance (əb·zûr′vəns) *n.* 1 The act of observing, as a custom or ceremony; compliance, as with law or duty. 2 Any common custom, form, rite, etc. 3 Heedful attention; observation. 4 *Eccl.* The rule or constitution of a religious order.

ob·ser·vant (əb·zûr′vənt) *adj.* 1 Carefully attentive; alert or watchful. 2 Having the habit of keen perception. 3 Strict in observing; heedful: usu. with *of*: *observant* of protocol. **—ob·ser′vant·ly** *adv.*

ob·ser·va·tion (ob′zər·vā′shən) *n.* 1 The act, faculty, or habit of observing. 2 The fact of being observed. 3 The practice of observing and recording, as for scientific study, certain data, events, etc.; also, the record so obtained, or an item within the record. 4 A remark apparently based upon things observed. **—ob′ser·va′tion·al** *adj.*

ob·ser·va·to·ry (əb·zûr′və·tôr′ē, -tō′rē) *n. pl.* **·ries** 1 A building designed and equipped for the systematic observation of astronomical or other natural phenomena. 2 A tower built for obtaining a panoramic view.

ob·serve (əb·zûrv′) *v.* **·served, ·serv·ing** *v.t.* 1 To notice by the sense of sight; see. 2 To watch attentively; keep under surveillance. 3 To make methodical observation of, as for scientific purposes. 4 To abide by or conform to: to *observe* the law. 5 To celebrate or solemnize (an occasion), as with appropriate ritual. 6 To say as a comment or opinion; mention. —*v.i.* 7 To make a remark; comment: often with *on* or *upon.* 8 To take notice. 9 To act as an observer. [< L *ob-* towards + *servare* keep, watch] **—ob·serv′er** *n.* **—ob·serv′ing·ly** *adv.*

ob·sess (əb·ses′) *v.t.* To occupy or trouble the mind of to an excessive degree; preoccupy; harass; haunt. [< L *ob-* towards, against + *sedere* sit]

ob·ses·sion (əb·sesh′ən) *n.* 1 The state of being obsessed with an idea or emotion. 2 An idea or emotion that obsesses one. **—ob·ses′sion·al** *adj.* **—ob·ses′sion·al·ly** *adv.*

ob·ses·sive (əb·ses′iv, ob-) *adj.* 1 Characteristic or of the nature of an obsession. 2 Of or causing an obsession. **—ob·ses′sive·ly** *adv.* **—ob·ses′sive·ness** *n.*

ob·sid·i·an (əb·sid′ē·ən, ob-) *n.* A glassy, usu. black volcanic rock. [< L *Obsius*, a Roman said by Pliny to be its discoverer]

ob·so·les·cent (ob′sə·les′ənt) *adj.* Becoming obsolete. **—ob′so·les′cence** *n.* **—ob′so·les′cent·ly** *adv.*

ob·so·lete (ob′sə·lēt) *adj.* Being out of use or out of fashion, as a word or style. [< L *obsolescere* grow old] **—ob′so·lete′ly** *adv.* **—ob′so·lete′ness** *n.*

ob·sta·cle (ob′stə·kəl) *n.* Something that stands in the way; a hindrance or obstruction. [< L *ob-* before, against + *stare* stand]

ob·ste·tri·cian (ob′stə·trish′ən) *n.* A physician specializing in obstetrics.

ob·stet·rics (əb·stet′riks) *n.pl. (construed as sing.)* The branch of medical science relating to pregnancy and childbirth. [< L *obstetrix* a midwife] **—ob·stet′ri·cal, ob·stet′ric** *adj.* **—ob·stet′ri·cal·ly** *adv.*

ob·sti·nate (ob′stə·nit) *adj.* 1 Persistently and unreasonably resolved in a purpose or opinion; stubborn. 2 Hard to control or cure, as a disease. [< L *obstinare* persist] **—ob′sti·na·cy** (-nə·sē), **ob′sti·nate·ness** *n.* **—ob′sti·nate·ly** *adv.* **—Syn.** 1 dogged, willful, headstrong, obdurate, unyielding.

ob·strep·er·ous (əb·strep′ər·əs, ob-) *adj.* 1 Making a great disturbance; clamorous; boisterous. 2 Unmanageable; unruly. [< L *ob-* against + *strepere* to roar] **—ob·strep′er·ous·ly** *adv.* **—ob·strep′er·ous·ness** *n.*

ob·struct (əb·strukt′) *v.t.* 1 To stop or impede movement through (a way or passage) by obstacles or barriers; choke; clog. 2 To block or retard the progress or way of. 3 To obscure from sight: to *obstruct* a view. [< L *ob-* against + *struere* pile, build] **—ob·struct′er, ob·struc′tor, ob·struc′tive·ness** *n.* **—ob·struc′tive** *adj.* **—ob·struc′tive·ly** *adv.*

ob·struc·tion (əb·struk′shən) *n.* 1 Anything that obstructs; hindrance; obstacle. 2 The act of obstructing, or the state of being obstructed.

ob·struc·tion·ist (əb·struk′shən·ist) *n.* One who obstructs; esp. one who delays the progress of business, as in a legislature. **—ob·struc′tion·ism** *n.* **—ob·struc′tion·is′tic** *adj.*

ob·tain (əb·tān′) *v.t.* 1 To gain possession of, esp. by effort; acquire; get. —*v.i.* 2 To be established or prevail; exist: When the play was made into a film, a different impression *obtained.* [< L *ob-* against + *tenere* hold, keep] **—ob·tain′a·ble** *adj.* **—ob·tain′er, ob·tain′ment** *n.*

ob·trude (əb·trōōd′) *v.* **ob·trud·ed, ob·trud·ing** *v.t.* 1 To thrust or force (oneself, an opinion, etc.) upon others without request or warrant. 2 To push forward or out; eject. —*v.i.* 3 To intrude oneself. [< L *ob-* towards, against + *trudere* to thrust] **—ob·trud′er, ob·tru′sion** *n.*

ob·tru·sive (əb·trōō′siv) *adj.* 1 Forcing itself to the attention; too conspicuous: *obtrusive* colors. 2 Bold or meddlesome in manner; pushing. 3 Tending to obtrude. **—ob·tru′sive·ly** *adv.* **—ob·tru′sive·ness** *n.*

ob·tuse (əb·t*y*ōōs′) *adj.* 1 Blunt or rounded. 2 Lacking alertness or sensitivity; intellectually sluggish or slow. 3 Heavy, dull, and indistinct, as a sound. 4 Having a measure between 90° and 180°: an *obtuse* angle. • See ANGLE. [< L *obtusus* blunt] **—ob·tuse′ly** *adv.* **—ob·tuse′ness** *n.*

ob·verse (ob·vûrs′, ob′vûrs) *adj.* 1 Turned toward or facing one. 2 Narrower at the base than at the apex. 3 Corresponding to something else as its counterpart. —*n.* (ob′·vûrs) 1 The side of a coin or medal bearing the face or main device. 2 The side of any object that is meant to be seen; the front as opposed to the back. 3 A counterpart of a truth or fact. [< L *ob-* towards, against + *vertere* to turn] **—ob·verse′ly** *adv.*

ob·vi·ate (ob′vē·āt) *v.t.* **·at·ed, ·at·ing** To meet or provide for, as an objection or difficulty, by effective measures; make unnecessary: The burglar alarm system *obviated* the need for a guard. [< L *obviare* meet, withstand] **—ob′·vi·a′tion, ob′vi·a′tor** *n.*

ob·vi·ous (ob′vē·əs) *adj.* Immediately evident; easily perceived; manifest. [< L *obvius* in the way, obvious] **—ob′vi·ous·ly** *adv.* **—ob′vi·ous·ness** *n.* **—Syn.** clear, apparent, plain.

Oc., oc. ocean.

o/c overcharge.

oc·a·ri·na (ok′ə·rē′nə) *n.* A small musical wind instrument with a rounded body, a mouthpiece, and holes stopped by the fingers. [Ital., a goose]

oc·ca·sion (ə·kā′zhən) *n.* 1 A particular event or juncture of events. 2 An important event or celebration. 3 A time at which an event occurs. 4 A circumstance that presents some reason, opportunity, or cause for action: no *occasion* for haste. 5 A circumstance that precipitates an event or condition: His confusion was the *occasion* of much merriment. 6 A need or exigency. **—on occasion** Now and then; occasionally. —*v.t.* To cause or bring about; cause accidentally or incidentally. [< L *occasio*, a falling towards, an opportunity]

oc·ca·sion·al (ə·kā′zhən·əl) *adj.* 1 Occurring at irregular intervals. 2 Belonging or suitable to some special occasion. 3 Happening casually or incidentally.

oc·ca·sion·al·ly (ə·kā′zhən·əl·ē) *adv.* Now and then; once in a while.

oc·ci·dent (ok′sə·dənt) *n.* The west. [< OF < L *occidens, -entis* sunset, the west, orig. pr.p. of *occidere* to fall]

Oc·ci·dent (ok′sə·dənt) The countries west of Asia, esp. Europe and the Americas; the West.

oc·ci·den·tal (ok′sə·den′təl) *adj.* Of or belonging to the west, or the countries constituting the Occident. *—n.* One born or living in a western country. Also **Oc'ci·den'tal.** — **oc'ci·den'tal·ly** *adv.*

oc·cip·i·tal (ok·sip'ə·təl) *adj.* Pertaining to the occiput or the occipital bone. *—n.* OCCIPITAL BONE.

occipital bone *Anat.* The bone that forms the back of the skull. • See PARIETAL BONE.

oc·ci·put (ok'sə·pət) *n. pl.* **·ci·puts** or **·cip·i·ta** (-sip'ə·tə) The lower back part of the skull. [< L *ob-* against + *caput* head]

oc·clude (ə·klōōd') *v.* **·clud·ed, ·clud·ing** *v.t.* **1** To shut up or block off: to *occlude* an artery. **2** *Chem.* To absorb or adsorb. *—v.i.* **3** *Dent.* To fit together: said of the upper and lower teeth. [< L *ob-* against, upon + *claudere* to close] — **oc·clu'dent, oc·clu'sive** *adj.* **—oc·clu·sion** (ə·klōō'zhən) *n.*

oc·cult (ə·kult', ok'ult) *adj.* **1** Of or designating those mystic arts involving magic, astrology, alchemy etc. **2** Not divulged; secret. **3** Beyond human understanding; mysterious. *—n.* Occult arts or sciences. *—v.t.* **1** To hide or conceal from view. **2** *Astron.* To block the light from or view of. *—v.i.* **3** To become hidden or concealed from view. [< L *occulere* cover over, hide] **—oc·cult'ism, oc·cult'ist, oc·cult'ness** *n.* **—oc·cult'ly** *adv.*

oc·cul·ta·tion (ok'ul·tā'shən) *n.* **1** The act of occulting, or the state of being occulted. **2** *Astron.* Concealment of one celestial body by another.

oc·cu·pan·cy (ok'yə·pən·sē) *n. pl.* **·cies** **1** The act of occupying; a taking possession. **2** The state of being occupied. **3** The time during which anything is occupied.

oc·cu·pant (ok'yə·pənt) *n.* **1** One who occupies, as an office or position. **2** A resident of a house, building, etc.

oc·cu·pa·tion (ok'yə·pā'shən) *n.* **1** One's regular, principal, or immediate business. **2** The state of being busy. **3** The possession and holding of land by military force. — **oc'cu·pa'tion·al** *adj.* **—oc'cu·pa'tion·al·ly** *adv.*

occupational therapy The treatment of mental or physical disabilities by activities designed to favor recovery. **—occupational therapist**

oc·cu·py (ok'yə·pī) *v.t.* **·pied, ·py·ing** **1** To take and hold possession of, as by conquest. **2** To fill or take up (space or time). **3** To inhabit; dwell in. **4** To hold; fill, as an office or position. **5** To busy; employ: to *occupy* oneself with a hobby. [< L *ob-* against + *capere* take] **—oc'cu·pi'er** *n.*

oc·cur (ə·kûr') *v.i.* **·curred, ·cur·ring** **1** To happen; come about. **2** To be found or met with; appear. **3** To present itself; come to mind. [< L *ob-* towards, against + *currere* run]

oc·cur·rence (ə·kûr'əns) *n.* **1** The act or fact of occurring. **2** An event or incident that occurs; happening.

o·cean (ō'shən) *n.* **1** The great body of salt water that covers over two thirds of the earth's surface. **2** Any one of its five main divisions: the Atlantic, Pacific, Indian, Arctic, or Antarctic Ocean. **3** Any unbounded expanse or quantity. [< Gk. *ōkeanos*] **—o·ce·an·ic** (ō'shē·an'ik) *adj.* — **o'ce·an'ic·al·ly** *adv.*

o·ce·an·og·ra·phy (ō'shən·og'rə·fē) *n.* The branch of physical geography that deals with oceanic life and phenomena. **—o'ce·an·og'ra·pher** *n.* **—o'ce·an·o·graph'ic** (-ə·graf'ik) or **·i·cal** *adj.* **—o'ce·an·o·graph'i·cal·ly** *adv.*

o·cel·lus (ō·sel'əs) *n. pl.* **·li** (-ī) **1** A minute simple eye, as of many invertebrates. **2** An eyelike spot of color, as in the tail of a peacock. [L, dim. of *oculus* eye] **—o·cel'lar** *adj.*

o·ce·lot (os'ə·lot, ō'sə-) *n.* A large, spotted wildcat of the New World. [< Nahuatl *ocelotl* a jaguar]

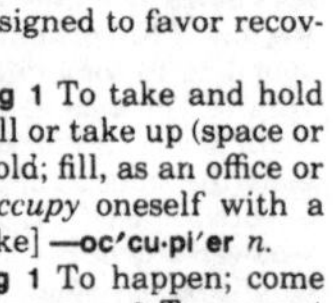
Ocelot

o·cher (ō'kər) *n.* **1** A yellow or rust-colored clay containing iron oxides, used as a pigment. **2** The dark yellow color of ocher. Also **o'chre.** [< Gk. *ōchros* yellow] — **o'cher·ous, o·chre·ous** (ō'krē·əs) *adj.*

o'clock (ə·klok') *adv.* **1** Of, according to, or by the clock. **2** According to the positions of the numbers on a clock face with the number 12 directly ahead or above: aircraft approaching at 3 *o'clock.*

OCS Officer Candidate School.

Oct, Oct. October.

oct. octavo.

oc·ta·gon (ok'tə·gon) *n.* A polygon with eight sides and eight angles. [< Gk. *okta-* eight + *gōnia* an angle] **—oc·tag·o·nal** (ok·tag'ə·nəl) *adj.* **—oc·tag'o·nal·ly** *adv.*

oc·ta·he·dron (ok'tə·hē'drən) *n. pl.* **·drons** or **·dra** (-drə) A solid figure bounded by eight plane faces. [< Gk. *okta-* eight + *hedra* a seat] **—oc·ta·he'dral** *adj.*

oc·tane (ok'tān) *n.* A hydrocarbon containing a chain of eight carbon atoms per molecule. [< OCTO- + -ANE]

octane number A measure of the antiknock properties of a gasoline. Also **octane rating.**

oc·tave (ok'tiv, -tāv) *n.* **1** *Music* The interval between any tone and another having twice or half its frequency. **2** The eighth day from a feast day; also, the lengthening of a festival to include eight days. **3** Any group or series of eight. **4** In prosody, the first eight lines in an Italian sonnet, or a stanza of eight lines. *—adj.* **1** Composed of eight. **2** In prosody, composed of eight lines. Also **oc·ta·val** (ok·tā'·vəl, ok'tə-) *adj.* [< L *octo* eight]

oc·ta·vo (ok·tā'vō, -tä'-) *n. pl.* **·vos** The page size (6 × 9½ inches) of a book made up of printer's sheets folded into eight leaves; also, a book consisting of pages of this size; often written *8vo* or *8°*. *—adj.* In octavo; consisting of pages of this size. [< L, an eighth]

oc·tet (ok·tet') *n.* **1** A musical composition for eight parts. **2** A group of eight musical performers. **3** Any group of eight; esp., OCTAVE (def. 4). Also **oc·tette'.** [< L *octo* eight]

oc·til·lion (ok·til'yən) *n. & adj.* See NUMBER. [< MF < L *octo* eight; on analogy with *million*] **—oc·til'lionth** (-yənth) *adj., n.*

octo- *combining form* Eight: *octopus.* Also **oct-, octa-.** [< L *octo* and Gk. *oktō* eight]

Oc·to·ber (ok·tō'bər) *n.* The tenth month of the year, containing 31 days. [L, the eighth (month) of the Roman calendar]

oc·to·ge·nar·i·an (ok'tə·jə·nâr'ē·ən) *adj.* Being eighty or from eighty to ninety years of age: also **oc·tog·e·nar·y** (ok·toj'ə·ner'ē). *—n.* A person between eighty and ninety years of age. [< L *octoginta* eighty]

oc·to·pus (ok'tə·pəs) *n. pl.* **·pus·es** or **·pi** (-pī) **1** Any of a genus of cephalopods having a saclike body with a mouth on the under surface and eight tentacles covered with suckers. **2** Any organized power with far-reaching influence. [< Gk. *okta-* eight + *pous* a foot]

Octopus

oc·to·roon (ok'tə·rōōn') *n.* A person who is the offspring of a white person and a quadroon. [< OCTO- + (QUAD)ROON]

oc·tu·ple (ok'tyōō·pəl, ok·tyōō'pəl) *adj.* **1** Consisting of eight parts or copies. **2** Multiplied by eight. *—v.t.* **·pled, ·pling** To multiply by eight. *—n.* A number or sum eight times as great as another. [< L *octuplus* eightfold] **—oc'·tu·ply** *adv.*

oc·u·lar (ok'yə·lər) *adj.* Pertaining to, like, derived from, or connected with the eye; visual. *—n.* The eyepiece of an optical instrument. [< L *oculus* eye] **—oc'u·lar·ly** *adv.*

oc·u·list (ok'yə·list) *n.* OPHTHALMOLOGIST. [< L *oculus* eye]

O.D. Doctor of Optometry; Officer of the Day; overdraft; overdrawn.

o.d. olive drab; on demand; outside diameter; overdose.

o·da·lisk (ō'də·lisk) *n.* A female slave or concubine in a harem. Also **o'da·lisque.** [< Turk. *ōdaliq* chambermaid]

ODan. Old Danish.

odd (od) *adj.* **1** Not even; leaving a remainder when divided by two. **2** Marked with an odd number. **3** Left over after a division. **4** Plus an additional number: 200-*odd* miles. **5** Occasional; casual: to work at *odd* jobs. **6** Peculiar; singular; queer; eccentric. **7** Single: an *odd* slipper. [< ON *oddi* a point of land, triangle] **—odd'ly** *adv.* **—odd'ness** *n.* **—Syn. 6** bizarre, extraordinary, fantastic, strange.

odd·ball (od'bôl') *n. Slang* An odd or eccentric person. — *adj.* Habitually odd or eccentric.

odd·i·ty (od'ə·tē) *n. pl.* **·ties** **1** The state or quality of being odd. **2** A person or thing that is odd or peculiar.

odd·ment (od'mənt) *n.* **1** Something left over; a scrap. **2** *pl.* Small belongings; odds and ends.

odds (odz) *n.pl. (sometimes construed as singular)* **1** A difference to the advantage of one side over another: The *odds* are in my favor. 2 The amount of difference in advantage between competing sides: to fight against overwhelming *odds.* 3 The probability or ratio of probabilities that something will happen or be found to be the case. 4 An equalizing allowance based on the apparent chances of success of an opponent or contestant: to give *odds.* **—at odds** At variance; disagreeing. **—by all odds** Far and away; beyond doubt.

odds and ends Fragments; scraps.

odds-on (odz′on′) *adj.* Considered as having the best chance of winning.

ode (ōd) *n.* A lyric poem, originally intended to be sung or chanted, typically marked by lofty tone, dignified theme, and often in the form of an address. [< Gk. *ōidē* a song] **—od·ic** (ō′dik) *adj.*

-ode *combining form* Way; path: *anode, cathode.* [< Gk. *hodos* a way]

O·din (ō′din) In Norse mythology, the supreme deity, god of war and founder of culture.

o·di·ous (ō′dē·əs) *adj.* 1 Exciting hate, repugnance, or disgust. 2 Regarded with aversion or disgust. [< L *odium* hatred] **—o′di·ous·ly** *adv.* **—o′di·ous·ness** *n.*

o·di·um (ō′dē·əm) *n.* 1 The state of being odious; offensiveness; opprobrium. 2 A feeling of extreme repugnance, disgust, or hate. [L, hatred < *odisse* to hate]

o·dom·e·ter (ō·dom′ə·tər) *n.* A device for measuring distance traveled, as by an automobile. [< Gk. *hodos* a way, a road + -METER]

o·don·tol·o·gy (ō′don·tol′ə·jē) *n.* The science that relates to the structure, health, and growth of the teeth. [< Gk. *odous, odontos* tooth + -LOGY]

o·dor (ō′dər) *n.* 1 That quality of a substance that renders it perceptible to the sense of smell. 2 A smell or scent. 3 A quality detected by the mind or feelings; air: an *odor* of righteousness. 4 Regard or estimation: to be in bad *odor.* *Brit. sp.* **o′dour.** [L] **—o′dored** *adj.*

o·dor·if·er·ous (ō′də·rif′ər·əs) *adj.* Diffusing an odor. **—o′dor·if′er·ous·ly** *adv.* **—o′dor·if′er·ous·ness** *n.*

o·dor·less (ō′dər·lis) *adj.* Having no odor. **—o′dor·less·ly** *adv.* **—o′dor·less·ness** *n.*

o·dor·ous (ō′dər·əs) *adj.* Having an odor; fragrant. **—o′dor·ous·ly** *adv.* **—o′dor·ous·ness** *n.*

O·dys·seus (ō·dis′yōōs, -ē·əs) *Gk. Myth.* The king of Ithaca, one of the Greek leaders in the Trojan War; Ulysses.

od·ys·sey (od′ə·sē) *n. pl.* **·seys** *Sometimes cap.* A long, wandering journey or quest. [< ODYSSEY]

Od·ys·sey (od′ə·sē) *n.* An ancient Greek epic poem attributed to Homer, describing the wanderings of Odysseus during the ten years after the fall of Troy.

oe- See also words beginning E-.

OE, OE., O.E. Old English.

oec·u·men·i·cal (ek′yōō·men′i·kəl, *Brit.* ē′kyoo·men′i·kəl) *adj.* ECUMENICAL.

oed·i·pal (ed′ə·pəl, ē′də-) *adj. Often cap.* Of or pertaining to the Oedipus complex.

Oed·i·pus (ed′ə·pəs, ē′də-) *Gk. Myth.* The son of Laius and Jocasta, who unwittingly killed his father, and married his mother, and became king of Thebes.

Oedipus complex A strong, usu. unconscious attachment of a child to the parent of the opposite sex, with antagonism toward the other parent.

o'er (ôr, ōr) *prep. & adv.* Over.

oe·soph·a·gus (i·sof′ə·gəs) *n.* ESOPHAGUS.

oes·trus (es′trəs, ēs′-) *n.* ESTRUS.

oeu·vre (œ′vr′) *n. pl.* **oeu·vres** (œ′vr′) *French* 1 A work, as of art or literature. 2 The totality of works, as of an author.

of (uv, ov; *unstressed* əv) *prep.* 1 Coming from; originating at or from. 2 Associated with; included among: Is he *of* your party? 3 Located at. 4 Away or at a distance from: within six miles *of* home. 5 Named; specified as: the city *of* Athens; a fall *of* ten feet. 6 Characterized by: a man *of* strength. 7 With regard to: a leader *of* men. 8 About; concerning: What do you say *of* that? 9 Because of: dying *of* pneumonia. 10 Possessing: a man *of* means. 11 Belonging to: the lid *of* a box. 12 Pertaining to: the majesty *of* the law. 13 Composed of; made of: a ship *of* steel. 14 Containing: a glass *of* water. 15 Taken from; from the number or class of: one *of* three people. 16 So as to be without: relieved *of* anxiety. 17 Proceeding from; produced by: the plays *of* Shakespeare. 18 Directed toward; exerted upon: a love *of* opera. 19 During or at a specified time or occasion: *of* recent years. 20 Set aside for or devoted to: a program *of* songs. 21 Before; until: used in telling time: ten minutes *of* ten. 22 *Archaic* By: loved *of* all men. [< OE]

OF, OF., O.F. Old French.

off (ôf, of) *adj.* 1 Farther or more distant; remote. 2 In a (specified) circumstance or situation: to be well *off.* 3 Not accurate, wrong: Your figures are *off.* 4 Not up to standard, as in activity or quality: an *off* season. 5 Not in existence; no longer effective: The deal is *off.* 6 Away from work; not on duty: *off* hours. 7 Gone away: *off* to the office. 8 Not in a position to operate; also, not operating. 9 Odd; eccentric. 10 *Naut.* Seaward; farther from the coast. —*adv.* 1 To a distance; so as to be away: My dog ran *off.* 2 To or at a (specified) future time or distance: a week *off;* a mile *off.* 3 So as to be no longer in place, connection, etc.: Take *off* your hat. 4 So as to be no longer functioning, continuing, or in operation: Turn the lights *off.* 5 So as to be away from one's work, duties, etc.: to take the day *off.* 6 So as to be completed, exhausted, etc.: to finish *off* an assignment. —*prep.* 1 So as to be separated, detached, distant, or removed from (a position, source, etc.): Take your feet *off* the table. 2 Not engaged in or occupied with; relieved from: *off* duty. 3 Below standard in: *off* one's game. 4 On or from the substance of: living *off* nuts and berries. 5 *Informal* No longer using, engaging in, or advocating: to be *off* drinking. 6 *Naut.* Opposite to and seaward of. —*n.* The state or condition of being off. [ME, orig. stressed var. of OF]

off. office; officer; official.

of·fal (ô′fəl) *n.* 1 Those parts of a butchered animal that are rejected as worthless. 2 Rubbish or refuse of any kind. [< OFF + FALL]

off·beat (ôf′bēt′, of′-) *n. Music* Any weak beat. —*adj.* (ôf′bēt′, of′-) *Slang* Unconventional; unusual.

off-col·or (ôf′kul′ər, of′-) *adj.* 1 Of doubtful or offensive taste; indelicate or indecent. 2 Unsatisfactory in color, as a gem. 3 *Brit.* Slightly ill; under the weather. *Brit. sp.* **-col·our.**

of·fend (ə·fend′) *v.t.* 1 To give displeasure or offense to; displease; anger. 2 To affect (the senses or sensibilities) in a way that causes displeasure, outrage, etc. —*v.i.* 3 To give displeasure or offense; be offensive. 4 To commit an offense, sin, or crime. [< L *ob-* against + *fendere* to hit, thrust] **—of·fend′er** *n.*

of·fense (ə·fens′) *n.* 1 The act of offending; a fault, sin, or crime. 2 The act of injuring another's feelings, of causing displeasure, etc. 3 That which injures the feelings, causes displeasure, etc. 4 That which affects the senses or sensibilities with displeasure, outrage, etc. 5 The state of being offended. 6 Assault or attack. 7 In sports, the team or team members attempting to score. *Brit. sp.* **of·fence.**

of·fen·sive (ə·fen′siv) *adj.* 1 Giving offense; disagreeable, displeasing, outrageous, etc. 2 Pertaining to or marked by attack; aggressive. —*n.* 1 Aggressive methods, operations, or attitudes: often with *the.* 2 An attack. **—of·fen′sive·ly** *adv.* **—of·fen′sive·ness** *n.*

of·fer (ô′fər, of′ər) *v.t.* 1 To present for acceptance or rejection. 2 To suggest for consideration or action; propose. 3 To present with solemnity or in worship. 4 To show readiness to do or attempt. 5 To attempt or to begin to do or inflict. 6 To suggest as payment; bid. 7 To present for sale. —*v.i.* 8 To present itself; appear. 9 To make an offering in worship or sacrifice. —*n.* 1 The act of offering. 2 Something offered, as a bid, proposal, etc. 3 An attempt or endeavor to do something. [< L *ob-* before + *ferre* bring] **—of′fer·er, of′fer·or** *n.*

of·fer·ing (ô′fər·ing, of′ər-) *n.* 1 The act of making an offer. 2 That which is offered, as the sacrifice presented in an act of religious worship. 3 A gift, esp. a contribution at a religious service.

of·fer·to·ry (ô′fər·tôr′ē, -tō′rē, of′ər-) *n. pl.* **·ries** *Eccl.* 1 *Usu. cap.* A section of the eucharistic liturgy, during which the bread and wine to be consecrated are offered to God. 2 A collection taken during a religious service; also, the part of a service when it is taken. 3 The prayer said or the music played or sung during the offertory.

off·hand (ôf′hand′, of′-) *adv.* Without preparation; extemporaneously. —*adj.* Done, said, or made extemporaneously. Also **off′hand′ed.** —**off′hand′ed·ly** *adv.*

of·fice (ô′fis, of′is) *n.* 1 A particular duty, charge, or trust, esp. a part of one's work. 2 A post or position held officially, esp. a position of trust or authority under a government. 3 That which is performed, assigned, or intended to be done by a particular person or thing. 4 *U.S.* A branch of the federal government, ranking next below the departments. 5 A room or building in which the affairs of a business, profession, or governmental branch are conducted; also, the people employed there. 6 *Eccl.* A prescribed religious or devotional service, esp. that for the canonical hours. 7 Any religious or social ceremony; rite. 8 *pl.* A proffered action of any kind; esp. a service: reinstated through the good *offices* of a friend. [< L *officium* a service]

office boy A boy hired to run errands or do odd jobs in an office.

of·fice-hold·er (ô′fis·hōl′dər, of′-) *n.* One who holds an office under a government.

of·fi·cer (ô′fə·sər, of′ə-) *n.* 1 One elected or appointed to office, as in a business, a society, etc. 2 One appointed to a certain military or naval rank and authority, specifically by commission. 3 On a nonnaval ship, the captain or any of the mates. 4 A policeman. —*v.t.* 1 To furnish with officers. 2 To command; direct; manage.

officer of the day An officer, in a military post or camp, responsible for a 24-hour period for the safety of the command, its property, maintenance of order, etc.

of·fi·cial (ə·fish′əl) *adj.* 1 Of, pertaining to, or holding an office or public trust. 2 Derived from the proper office or officer; authoritative. 3 Formal; studied; ceremonious. —*n.* One holding an office or performing duties of a public nature. —**of·fi′cial·dom, of·fi′cial·ism** *n.* —**of·fi′cial·ly** *adv.*

of·fi·ci·ate (ə·fish′ē·āt) *v.i.* **·at·ed, ·at·ing** 1 To perform the duties or functions of an office. 2 To serve as a priest or minister; conduct a service. [< L *officium* service] —**of·fi′ci·a′tion, of·fi′ci·a′tor** *n.*

of·fic·i·nal (ə·fis′ə·nəl) *adj.* Prepared and on hand in drug stores: *officinal* medicines. —*n.* Any drug or medicine kept ready for sale. [< L *officina* a workshop]

of·fi·cious (ə·fish′əs) *adj.* Volunteering unwanted service or advice, esp. in an unduly forward manner. [< L *officium* service] —**of·fi′cious·ly** *adv.* —**of·fi′cious·ness** *n.* —**Syn.** meddlesome, interfering, obtrusive, nosy.

off·ing (ô′fing, of′ing) *n. Naut.* 1 The distant part of the open sea visible from the shore. 2 A position some distance offshore. —**in the offing** Soon to happen, arrive, etc.

off·ish (ô′fish, of′ish) *adj.* Inclined to be distant in manner; aloof. —**off′ish·ly** *adv.* —**off′ish·ness** *n.*

off-put·ting (ôf′pŏŏt′ing) *adj.* Putting one off; causing hostility, indifference, etc.

off·scour·ing (ôf′skour′ing, of′-) *n.* 1 That which is scoured off; something vile; refuse. 2 An outcast; pariah.

off·set (ôf′set′, of′-) *n.* 1 Anything which counterbalances or compensates for something else. 2 An extension, branch, spur, or offshoot. 3 A ledge in a wall formed by a reduction in its thickness above. 4 A bend in a pipe, bar, etc. that allows it to pass an obstruction. 5 OFFSET PRINTING. 6 An impression made by the offset printing method. —*v.* (ôf′set′, of′-) **·set, ·set·ting** *v.t.* 1 To compensate for; counterbalance. 2 To print by offset printing. 3 *Archit.* To make an offset in. —*v.i.* 4 To make an offset, as in printing. 5 To branch off; project as an offset.

offset printing A method of printing from a lithographic surface to a rubber-surfaced cylinder, and thence onto the paper.

off·shoot (ôf′shōōt′, of′-) *n.* 1 *Bot.* A side shoot or branch from the main stem of a plant. 2 Anything that branches off from a main source.

off·shore (ôf′shôr′, -shōr′, of′-) *adj.* 1 Moving or directed away from the shore. 2 Situated or occurring at some distance from the shore. —*adv.* From or away from the shore.

off·side (ôf′sīd′, of′-) *adv. & adj.* In football, illegally ahead of the ball during a scrimmage.

off·spring (ôf′spring′, of′-) *n.* 1 The progeny of any person, animal, or plant. 2 A result; product. [<OE *of* off + *springan* to spring]

off-stage (ôf′stāj′, of′-) *n.* The area behind or to the side of a stage, out of view of the audience. —*adj.* In or from this area. —*adv.* To this area.

oft (ôft, oft) *adv. Archaic* Often. [<OE]

oft·en (ôf′ən, of′-) *adv.* On frequent or numerous occasions; repeatedly. [ME *ofte* oft]

oft·en·times (ôf′ən·tīmz′, of′-) *adv.* Frequently; often. Also *Archaic* **oft·times** (ôf′tīmz′, of′-).

o·gee (ō′jē, ō·jē′) *n. Archit.* 1 A molding having an S-shaped profile. 2 Such a curve used in any construction. 3 An arch with two such curves meeting at the apex: also **ogee arch.** [<OF *ogive* a kind of arch]

o·give (ō′jīv, ō·jīv′) *n.* 1 A diagonal rib of a vaulted arch or bay. 2 A pointed arch. [MF] —**o·gi′val** *adj.*

Ogive arch

o·gle (ō′gəl) *v.* **o·gled, o·gling** *v.t.* 1 To look at with amorous or impertinent glances. —*v.i.* 2 To look or stare in an amorous or impertinent manner. —*n.* An amorous or coquettish look. [Prob. <LG *oegelen* < *oege* an eye] —**o′gler** *n.*

o·gre (ō′gər) *n.* 1 In fairy tales, a man-eating giant or monster. 2 A dreadful, monstrous, or cruel person. [F] —**o′gre·ish, o′grish** *adj.* —**o·gress** (ō′gris) *n. Fem.*

oh (ō) *interj.* 1 An exclamation expressing surprise, emotion, etc. 2 A word used in direct address: *Oh,* waiter! Would you please bring some water?

OH Ohio (P.O. abbr.)

OHG, OHG. O.H.G. Old High German.

ohm (ōm) *n.* The unit of electrical resistance, equal to the resistance of a conductor in which a current of one ampere is produced by a potential difference of one volt. [< G. S. *Ohm,* 1787–1854, German physicist] —**ohm′ic** *adj.*

ohm·me·ter (ōm′mē′tər) *n.* A meter for measuring the resistance of a conductor.

-oid *suffix* Like; resembling; having the form of: *ovoid.* [< Gk. *eidos* form]

oil (oil) *n.* 1 A slippery, combustible liquid of vegetable, animal, or mineral origin, insoluble in water but soluble in ether. 2 PETROLEUM. 3 An oil paint; also, an oil painting. 4 Anything of an oily consistency. 5 Fawning or flattering speech. —*v.t.* 1 To smear, lubricate, or supply with oil. 2 To bribe; flatter. —*adj.* Of, like, relating to, yielding, or producing oil. [< L *oleum* oil] —**oil′er** *n.*

oil·cake (oil′kāk′) *n.* A mass of compressed seeds of cotton, flax, etc., from which oil has been expressed.

oil·cloth (oil′klôth′, -kloth′) *n.* A cotton fabric waterproofed with an oil or paint preparation, used for table, shelf, or floor coverings, etc.

oil color A pigment ground in linseed or other oil.

oil of vitriol SULFURIC ACID.

oil paint A paint in which the vehicle is an oil, as linseed oil, that forms a tough elastic substance on exposure in thin films to air.

oil painting 1 The art of painting in oil colors. 2 A painting done in pigments mixed in oil.

oil·paper (oil′pā′pər) *n.* Paper treated with oil for transparency and moisture resistance.

oil·skin (oil′skin′) *n.* 1 Cloth made waterproof with oil. 2 *Often pl.* A garment of such material.

oil·stone (oil′stōn′) *n.* A whetstone treated with oil, used for sharpening tools, etc.

oil well A boring into an underground store of petroleum. • See DERRICK.

oil·y (oi′lē) *adj.* **oil·i·er, oil·i·est** 1 Pertaining to or containing oil. 2 Smeared, soaked, or coated with oil. 3 Too smooth; unctuous. —**oil′i·ly** *adv.* —**oil′i·ness** *n.*

oint·ment (oint′mənt) *n.* A medicated fat or oil used to soothe, heal, or protect the skin. [< L *unguentum* an unguent]

O.Ir. Old Irish.

O·jib·wa (ō·jib′wā) *n. pl.* **·wa** or **·was** 1 One of a tribe of North American Indians of Algonquian linguistic stock, formerly inhabiting the regions around Lake Superior. 2 The Algonquian language of this tribe. Also **O·jib′way.**

OK (ō′kā′) *interj., adj., & adv.* All correct; all right: expressing approval, agreement, etc. —*n. pl.* **OK's** An endorsement; approval. —*v.t.* (ō·kā′) **OK'd, OK'ing** To endorse; approve, as by signing with an OK. Also **O.K., o'kay′, o'keh′.** [Prob. < *o(ll) k(orrect),* humorous misspelling of *all correct;* but possibly <The Democratic *O.K.* Club, organized in 1840 to support President Martin Van Buren, nicknamed *Old Kinderhook,* from *Kinderhook,* N.Y., his birthplace]

OK Oklahoma (P.O. abbr.).

o·ka·pi (ō·kä′pē) *n. pl.* **·pi** or **·pis** A small African ruminant related to the giraffe, but with a shorter neck. [< native African name]

Okapi

O·kie (ō′kē) *n.* A migrant farmworker, esp. one from Oklahoma, forced to leave his land during the 1930's.

Okla. Oklahoma.

o·kra (ō′krə) *n.* 1 A tall annual herb cultivated for its edible, mucilaginous pods. 2 Its green pods, used in soups and as a vegetable. [< native African name]

-ol[1] *suffix Chem.* Denoting an alcohol or phenol: *methanol.* [< (ALCOH)OL]

-ol[2] *suffix Chem.* Var. of -OLE.

OL, O.L. Old Latin.

old (ōld) *adj.* **old·er** or **eld·er, old·est** or **eld·est** 1 Having lived or existed for a long time; aged; mature. 2 Of, like, or pertaining to an aged or mature person; exhibiting discretion, judgment, etc. 3 Having some specific age: a child two months *old.* 4 Having been made some time ago; used, or known for a long time; not new. 5 *Sometimes cap.* Belonging to an early or remote period; ancient; antique: the *old* Greeks, *Old* English. 6 Preceding the present; previous; former. 7 *Often cap.* Belonging to the former of two or the earliest of several things: the *Old* Testament. 8 Worthless on account of age; shabby; worn-out: an *old* coat. 9 Stale; trite: an *old* joke. 10 Continued, known, or used for a long time; familiar: an *old* comrade. 11 Having had long experience or practice: an *old* hand at farming. 12 Dear; familiar, through long acquaintance: *old* boy. 13 *Informal* Excellent; great; wonderful: a great *old* time. —*n.* 1 Past time: days of *old.* 2 A long time; long standing: my friend of *old.* 3 A person having some specified age: a two-year-*old.* —**the old** Old persons. [< OE *ald*] —**old′·ness** *n.*

old country The native land of any emigrant.

old·en (ōl′dən) *adj.* Old; ancient.

Old English 1 The English language from about 450 to 1050; Anglo-Saxon. 2 BLACK LETTER.

old-fash·ioned (ōld′fash′ənd) *adj.* Having the characteristics or customs of former times. —**Syn.** dated, obsolete, antiquated, passé.

old fo·gy (fō′gē) A person of extremely conservative or old-fashioned ideas. Also **old fo′gey.** [< Scot., an old soldier] —**old-fo′gy·ish, old-fo′gey·ish** *adj.*

Old French The French language from the 9th to the 16th century, esp. from the 9th to the 13th century.

Old Glory The flag of the United States.

old guard The conservative element in a community, political party, etc. [< trans. of F *Vieille Garde,* the imperial guard formed by Napoleon I in 1804]

Old High German High German as used from about 800 to 1100.

Old Irish The Irish Gaelic language from its origins to about 1100.

old lady *Slang* 1 One's wife. 2 One's mother.

Old Latin The Latin language before the first century B.C.

old-line (ōld′līn′) *adj.* 1 Having a well-established reputation or history. 2 Traditional; conservative.

old maid 1 An elderly single woman; spinster. 2 A fussy, prim, or prudish person. —**old′-maid′ish** *adj.*

old man *Slang* 1 One's father. 2 One's husband. 3 Any man in a position of authority, as the captain of a vessel.

Old Nick The devil.

Old Norse The language of Norway, Denmark, and Iceland before 1400.

Old Persian The Persian language in its oldest form, in use from 700 to 400 B.C.

old rose A grayish or purplish red.

Old Saxon An early form of the West Germanic language, in use during the ninth and tenth centuries.

Old South The South before the Civil War.

old·ster (ōld′stər) *n. Informal* A person of advanced years; an old or elderly person.

old style (ōld′stīl′) *n. Printing* A typeface characterized by slanted serifs and by down-strokes and cross-strokes of nearly the same thickness.

Old Style The old method of reckoning time by the Julian Calendar.

Old Testament The first of the two main divisions of the Bible, containing the early history and the laws and customs of the Jews and including the books of the prophets.

old-time (ōld′tīm′) *adj.* 1 Of or relating to past times. 2 Of long standing.

old-tim·er (ōld′tī′mər) *n. Informal* 1 One who has been a long-time member, resident, or job-holder. 2 An old-fashioned person.

old-world (ōld′wûrld′) *adj.* 1 Of or pertaining to the Old World or Eastern Hemisphere. 2 Charming; picturesque; quaint.

Old World The Eastern Hemisphere, including Europe, Asia, Africa, and Australia. • *Old World* is often used with reference to Europe in particular: *Old World charm.*

-ole *suffix Chem.* Denoting various organic compounds having a ring structure comprising five members. [< L *oleum* oil]

o·le·ag·i·nous (ō′lē·aj′ə·nəs) *adj.* 1 Of or pertaining to oil. 2 Unctuous; oily. [< L *oleaginus* pertaining to the olive] —**o′le·ag′i·nous·ly** *adv.* —**o′le·ag′i·nous·ness** *n.*

o·le·an·der (ō′lē·an′dər) *n.* A poisonous shrub with leathery evergreen leaves and clusters of fragrant flowers. [< Med. L]

o·le·ate (ō′lē·āt) *n.* A salt or ester of oleic acid.

o·le·ic acid (ō·lē′ik, ō·lā′-) An oily compound contained as an ester in most animal and vegetable oils and fats. [< L *oleum* oil]

o·le·in (ō′lē·in) *n.* The colorless, liquid ester of glycerol and oleic acid. Also **o·le·ine** (ō′lē·in, ō′li·ēn). [< L *oleum* oil]

Oleander blossoms

o·le·o (ō′lē·ō) *n.* MARGARINE. [< OLEO(MARGARINE)]

oleo- *combining form* 1 Oil; of oil: *oleoresin.* 2 Olein; oleic: *oleomargarine.* [< L *oleum* oil]

o·le·o·mar·ga·rine (ō′lē·ō·mär′jə·rin, -rēn) *n.* MARGARINE. Also **o′le·o·mar′ga·rin.**

o·le·o·res·in (ō′lē·ō·rez′in) *n.* A compound, either natural or prepared, of an essential oil and a resin.

ol·fac·tion (ol·fak′shən) *n.* 1 The sense of smell. 2 The process of smelling. [< L *olfacere* to smell]

ol·fac·to·ry (ol·fak′tər·ē, -trē) *adj.* Pertaining to the sense of smell. Also **ol·fac′tive.** —*n. pl.* **·ries** 1 *Usu. pl.* The organ of smell. 2 The capacity to smell. [< L *olere* have a smell + *facere* make]

ol·i·garch (ol′ə·gärk) *n.* A ruler in an oligarchy.

ol·i·gar·chy (ol′ə·gär′kē) *n. pl.* **·chies** 1 A form of government in which supreme power is restricted to a few persons. 2 The persons who exercise such power. 3 A state governed by an oligarchy. [< Gk. *oligos* few + *archein* to rule] —**ol′i·gar′chic, ol′i·gar′chal, ol′i·gar′chi·cal** *adj.*

ol·i·go- *combining form* Small; few; scanty: *oligopoly.* [< Gk. *oligos* few]

Ol·i·go·cene (ol′ə·gō·sēn′) *adj., n.* See GEOLOGY.

ol·i·gop·o·ly (ol′ə·gop′ə·lē) *n. pl.* **·lies** A market situation in which the effective control of a market is exercised by a limited number of competitive sellers. [<OLIGO- + (MONO)POLY] **—ol′i·gop′o·list** *n.* **—ol′i·gop′o·lis′tic** *adj.*

o·li·o (ō′lē·ō) *n. pl.* **o·li·os** **1** A medley, as of musical pieces. **2** A highly seasoned meat and vegetable stew. [<Sp. *olla* olla]

ol·ive (ol′iv) *n.* **1** An evergreen tree with leathery leaves. hard yellow wood, and an oily fruit. **2** The fruit of the olive tree. **3** A medium yellowish green color: also **olive green. 4** An olive branch. *—adj.* **1** Of or pertaining to the olive. **2** Having a dull yellowish green color. [<L *oliva*]

Olive

olive branch **1** A branch of the olive tree, as an emblem of peace. **2** An conciliatory proposal.

olive drab **1** A shade of greenish brown. **2** A woolen material of this color, used for uniforms by the U.S. Army. **3** *Often pl.* A uniform of this material. **—ol′ive-drab′** (-drab′) *adj.*

olive oil A pale yellow, edible oil obtained from ripe olives.

ol·la (ol′ə; *Sp.* ô′lyä, ô′yä) *n.* **1** A wide-mouthed pot or jar, usu. of earthenware. **2** A highly spiced stew. [<L, a pot]

ol·o·gy (ol′ə·jē) *n. pl.* **·gies** *Informal* A science or branch of learning: a humorous term. [<-LOGY]

O·lym·pi·ad (ō·lim′pē·ad) *n.* **1** In ancient Greece, the interval of four years between two successive celebrations of the Olympic games. **2** The modern Olympic games.

O·lym·pi·an (ō·lim′pē·ən) *adj.* **1** *Gk. Myth.* Pertaining to Mount Olympus or to the gods who dwelt there. **2** Pertaining to Olympia, a plain in ancient Greece, or to the Olympic games: also **O·lym′pic. 3** Lofty; majestic. *—n.* **1** *Gk. Myth.* One of the twelve higher gods who dwelt on Olympus. **2** A contestant in the Olympic games.

Olympic games **1** Contests of sports, literature, and music held at the chief ancient Pan-Hellenic festival, which was celebrated every four years at Olympia in honor of Zeus. **2** A modern international athletic competition, held every four years at some city chosen for this event. Also **Olympian games, Olympics.**

O·man (ō·män′, ō·man′) *n.* An independent sultanate of SE Arabia, 82,000 sq. mi., cap. Muscat. • See map at SAUDI ARABIA.

o·ma·sum (ō·mā′səm) *n. pl.* **·sa** (-sə) The third division of the stomach of a ruminant. [L, bullock's tripe, paunch]

om·buds·man (om′bo͝odz·mən, -budz-, om·bo͝odz′mən) *n. pl.* **·men** (-mən) A government official appointed to receive and report grievances against the government. [Norw.]

o·me·ga (ō·mē′gə, ō·mā′gə, ō·meg′ə) *n.* **1** The 24th and last letter in the Greek alphabet (Ω, ω). **2** The end.

om·e·let (om′ə·lit, om′lit) *n.* A dish of eggs, beaten together, cooked and then folded, often around a filling, as of cheese, jelly, etc. Also **om′e·lette.** [<OF *alemette,* lit., a thin plate]

o·men (ō′mən) *n.* A phenomenon or incident believed to foretell some future event. *—v.t.* To foretell as or by an omen. [L] **—Syn.** *n.* portent, sign, indication, augury, *v.* indicate, presage, augur, portend.

om·i·cron (om′ə·kron, ō′mə-) *n.* The 15th letter of the Greek alphabet (O, o). Also **om′i·kron.**

om·i·nous (om′ə·nəs) *adj.* Like or marked by an evil omen; sinister; threatening. [<L *omen, ominis* an omen] **—om′i·nous·ly** *adv.* **—om′i·nous·ness** *n.*

o·mis·si·ble (ō·mis′ə·bəl) *adj.* That can be omitted.

o·mis·sion (ō·mish′ən) *n.* **1** The act of omitting or state of being omitted or neglected. **2** Anything omitted or neglected.

o·mit (ō·mit′) *v.t.* **o·mit·ted, o·mit·ting** **1** To leave out; fail to include. **2** To fail to do or use; neglect. [<L *ob-* down, away + *mittere* send]

omni- *combining form* All; totally: *omnipotent.* [<L *omnis* all]

om·ni·bus (om′nə·bəs, -bus) *n.* **1** BUS **2** A printed anthology, either of works by a single author or of works of the same general type. *—adj.* Of, pertaining to, or including many things, classes, situations, etc. [<L, for all]

om·ni·far·i·ous (om′nə·fâr′ē·əs) *adj.* Of all varieties or kinds. [<L *omni-* all + *fari* speak]

om·nip·o·tence (om·nip′ə·təns) *n.* **1** Unlimited and universal power. **2** *Usu. cap.* An omnipotent force, esp. God.

om·nip·o·tent (om·nip′ə·tənt) *adj.* Unlimited in authority or power. **—the Omnipotent** God. **—om·nip′o·tent·ly** *adv.* **—Syn.** mighty, almighty, powerful, authoritative.

om·ni·pres·ence (om′nə·prez′əns) *n.* The quality of being everywhere present at the same time; ubiquity. **—om′ni·pres′ent** *adj.*

om·ni·scient (om·nish′ənt) *adj.* Having infinite knowledge; knowing everything. **—the Omniscient** God. [<L *omni-* all + *sciens* knowing] **—om·ni·science** (om·nish′əns) *n.* **—om·ni′scient·ly** *adv.*

om·ni·um-gath·er·um (om′nē·əm·gath′ər·əm) *n. pl.* **·ums** A miscellaneous collection; a medley. [<L *omnium* of all + GATHER]

om·niv·o·rous (om·niv′ər·əs) *adj.* **1** Eating both animal and vegetable food. **2** Taking in everything; consuming or devouring, as with the mind. [<L *omni-* all + *vorare* devour] **—om·niv′o·rous·ly** *adv.* **—om·niv′o·rous·ness** *n.*

on (on, ôn) *prep.* **1** In contact with the upper surface of; above and supported by. **2** In contact with any surface or part of. **3** So as to be suspended from: a puppet *on* a string. **4** Directed or moving along the course of: Be *on* your way. **5** Near; adjacent to: the store *on* your right. **6** Within the duration of: He arrived *on* my birthday. **7** At the moment or occasion of: *on* the hour. **8** In a state or condition of: *on* fire. **9** By means of: with the support of: *on* wheels. **10** Using as a means of sustenance, activity, etc.: living *on* fruit. **11** In the interest or favor of: betting *on* a horse. **12** Concerning; about: a work *on* economics. **13** Engaged in; occupied or connected with: *on* the job. **14** As a consequence or result of: making a profit *on* tips. **15** In accordance with or relation to: to do something *on* purpose. **16** Directed, tending, or moving toward or against: war *on* the enemy. **17** Following after: disease *on* the heels of famine. **18** *Informal* With; accompanying, as about one's person: Do you have five dollars *on* you? **19** *Informal* At the expense of; paid by: The joke is *on* them. **—have something on** *Informal* To have knowledge, possess evidence, etc., against (a person). *—adv.* **1** In or into a position or condition of contact, adherence, covering, etc.: He put his hat *on.* **2** In the direction of something: He looked *on* while they played. **3** Ahead; forward: They moved *on.* **4** Continuously or in succession: The music went *on.* **5** In or into operation, performance, or existence: to turn the electricity *on.* **—and so on** And like what has gone before; et cetera. **—be on to** *Slang* To be aware of or informed about (someone, something, etc.); understand. **—on and on** Without interruption; continuously. *—adj.* In operation, progress, or application: The radio is *on.* *—n.* The state or fact of being on. [<OE *on, an*] • See UPON.

ON, ON., O.N., Old Norse.

o·nan·ism (ō′nən·iz′əm) *n.* **1** Withdrawal in sexual intercourse before orgasm; incomplete coitus. **2** MASTURBATION. [<*Onān,* son of Judah, + -ISM] **—o′nan·ist** *n.*

once (wuns) *adv.* **1** One time, without repetition. **2** During some past time. **3** At any time; ever; also, at some future time. **4** By one degree or grade of relationship. *—adj.* Former; formerly existing. *—conj.* As soon as; whenever. *—n.* One time. **—all at once** **1** Suddenly. **2** All at the same time. **—at once** **1** Simultaneously. **2** Immediately. **—once (and) for all** Finally. **—once in a while** Occasionally. **—this once** On this occasion only. [<OE *anes,* genitive of *an* one]

once-o·ver (wuns′ō′vər) *n. Slang.* A quick, esp. comprehensive and appraising glance or survey.

on·co·gene (ong′kə·jēn′) *n.* A gene common to all body cells that can cause normal cells to become malignant. [<Gk. *onkos* mass + *-genēs* born]

on·com·ing (on′kum′ing) *adj.* Approaching. *—n.* An approach.

one (wun) *adj.* **1** Being a single person or thing. **2** Being uniquely or preeminently the person or thing indicated. **3** Being a person or thing thought of as indefinite or unspecified. 4 Designating a person, thing, or group as contrasted with another; this; that. 5 Single in kind; the same. 6 Marked by unity; united. —*n.* 1 The number of a set, as of the natural numbers, that when multiplied by any other number of the set give a product equal to that other number; unity. 2 A single person or thing. —*pron.* 1 Someone or something. 2 Anyone or anything. 3 One of certain persons or things already mentioned. —**at one** In harmony; the same. **one another** Each other: said of an action or relation involving two or more persons or things reciprocally: They love *one another.* [<OE *ān*]

-one *suffix Chem.* Denoting a ketone: *acetone.* [<Gk. *-ōnē,* fem. patronymic]

one-horse (wun′hôrs′) *adj.* 1 Drawn or worked by one horse. 2 *Informal* Of small size, importance, etc.

O·nei·da (ō·nī′də) *n. pl.* **·da** or **·das** A member of a tribe of North American Indians of Iroquoian stock.

one-lin·er (wun′lī′nər) *n. Informal* A brief remark, meant to be humorous, clever, critical, etc., often used by a comedian in a performance.

one·ness (wun′nis) *n.* 1 Singleness or unity. 2 Agreement; concord. 3 Sameness; identity.

one-night stand (wun′nīt′) *U.S.* 1 A performance, lecture, etc., given one time only in a particular locality. 2 The place where such a performance, lecture, etc., is given.

on·er·ous (on′ər·əs) *adj.* Imposing or characterized by difficulty, labor, responsibility, etc. [<L *onus, oneris* a burden] —**on′er′ous·ly** *adv.* —**on′er·ous·ness** *n.* —**Syn.** arduous, burdensome, exacting, oppressive.

one·self (wun′self′, wunz′-) *pron.* One's own self; himself or herself. Also **one's self.** —**be oneself** 1 To function in a normal manner. 2 To behave naturally.

one-sid·ed (wun′sī′did) *adj.* 1 On or having one side only. 2 Partial; unfair. 3 Marked by the clear dominance of one side; unequal: a *one-sided* game. 4 Unilateral. 5 Unequal-sided, as elm leaves. —**one′sid′ed·ly** *adv.* —**one′sid′ed·ness** *n.*

one-step (wun′step′) *n.* 1 A dance consisting of quick, walking steps in two-four time. 2 The music for this dance.

one-time (wun′tīm′) *adj.* Former.

one-track (wun′trak′) *adj. Informal* Limited to a single idea or pursuit; undiversified.

one-up (wun′up′) *v.* **-upped, -up·ping** *Informal* To try to gain an advantage over.

one-up·man·ship (wun′up′mən·ship′) *n. Informal* The practice or technique of trying to gain an advantage over another.

one-way (wun′wā′) *adj.* Moving or permitting movement in one direction only.

on·go·ing (on′gō′ing) *adj.* Going on, continuing, or progressing.

on·ion (un′yən) *n.* 1 A plant of the lily family with a pungent, edible bulb. 2 The bulb. [<L *unio* unity, an onion]

Onion

on·ion·skin (un′yən·skin′) *n.* A thin, strong, translucent paper with a glossy surface.

on-line (on′līn′, ôn′līn′) *adj.* Directly connected to a computer.

on·look·er (on′look′ər, ôn′-) *n.* One who looks on; a spectator. —**on′look·ing** *adj., n.*

on·ly (ōn′lē) *adv.* 1 Solely, merely, or exclusively. 2 As recently as: *only* yesterday. 3 Nevertheless in the end: to defeat one contestant, *only* to face a stronger one. —*adj.* 1 Alone in its class; having no fellow or mate; sole; single. 2 Standing alone by reason of excellence. —*conj.* Except that; but. [<OE *ān.* one + *-lic*-ly]

on·o·mat·o·poe·ia (on′ə·mat′ə·pē′ə) *n.* 1 The formation of words in imitation of natural sounds, as *crack, splash,* or *bow-wow.* 2 The use of such words, as in poetry. [<Gk. *onoma* name + *poieein* make] —**on′o·mat′o·poe′ic** or **·i·cal, on′o·mat′o·po·et′ic** (-pō·et′ik) *adj.* —**on′o·mat′o·po·et′i·cal·ly** *adv.*

On·on·da·ga (on′ən·dä′gə) *n.* One of a tribe of North American Indians of Iroquoian stock formerly living in New York and Ontario. —**On′on·da′gan** *adj.*

on·rush (on′rush′, ôn′-) *n.* An onward rush or flow. —**on′rush·ing** *adj.*

on·set (on′set′, ôn′-) *n.* 1 An attack; assault, as of troops. 2 A setting out; start; beginning.

on·shore (on′shôr′, -shōr′, ôn′-) *adv. & adj.* To, toward, or on the shore.

on·side (on′sīd′, ôn′-) *adv. & adj.* In a legal position, according to the rules of a game; not offside.

on·slaught (on′slôt′, ôn′-) *n.* a violent hostile assault. [<Du. *annslag* a striking at] —**Syn.** attack, incursion.

on-the-job (on·thə·job′, ôn-) *adj.* Pertaining to skills acquired, esp. under guidance, while actually doing the job, as distinguished from formal preparation before employment: *on-the-job* training.

on·to (on′tōō, ôn′-) *prep.* To a position on; to and upon: The cat jumped *onto* the table.

onto- *combining form* 1 Being; existence; *ontology.* 2 Organism: *ontogeny.* Also **ont-.** [<Gk. < *ōn, ontos* < *einai* be]

on·tog·e·ny (on·toj′ə·nē) *n. Biol.* The development of an organism from egg cell to maturity. Also **on·to·gen·e·sis** (on′tō·jen′ə·sis). —**on·to·ge·net·ic** (on′tō·jə·net′ik), **on′to·gen′·ic** (-jen′ik) *adj.* —**on·tog′e·nist** *n.*

on·tol·o·gy (on·tol′ə·jē) *n. pl.* **·gies** 1 The branch of metaphysics that deals with the nature of being and reality. 2 A particular theory about being and reality. —**on′to·log′i·cal** *adj.* —**on′to·log′i·cal·ly** *adv.*

o·nus (ō′nəs) *n.* 1 A burden or obligation; duty. 2 Responsibility or blame. [L]

on·ward (on′wərd, ôn′-) *adv.* Toward or at a point that is ahead in space or time; forward. Also **on′wards.** —*adj.* Moving or directed onward.

on·yx (on′iks) *n.* A variety of quartz consisting of layers of different colors. [Gk, a nail or claw, onyx]

oo·dles (ōōd′lz) *n. pl. Informal* A great deal; many; more than plenty. [? var. of HUDDLE, *n.*]

o·ol·o·gy (ō·ol′ə·jē) *n.* The branch of ornithology that treats of birds' eggs. [<Gk. *ōon* egg + -LOGY] —**o·o·log·ic** (ō′ə·log′ik), **o′o·log′i·cal** *adj.* —**o·ol′o·gist** *n.*

oo·long (ōō′lông) *n.* A variety of dark tea that is partly fermented before being dried. [<Chin. *wu* black + *lung* a dragon]

oo·mi·ak (ōō′mē·ak) *n.* UMIAK. Also **oo′mi·ac.**

ooze[1] (ōōz) *v.* **oozed, ooz·ing** *v.i.* 1 To flow or leak out slowly or gradually, as through pores or small holes. 2 To exude moisture. 3 To escape or disappear: His courage *oozed* away. —*v.t.* 4 To emit, give off, or exude. —*n.* 1 A slow, gradual leak; gentle flow. 2 That which oozes. [<OE *wōs* sap, juice] —**oo′zi·ness** *n.* —**oo′zy** *adj.*

ooze[2] (ōōz) *n.* 1 Slimy mud or moist, spongy soil, esp. a deposit of sediment found on the bottom of the ocean, a lake, etc. 2 A piece of muddy or marshy ground; bog; fen. [<OE *wāse*] —**oo′zi·ly** *adv.* —**oo′zi·ness** *n.* —**oo′zy** *adj.*

op. opera; operation; opposite; opus.

o·pac·i·ty (ō·pas′ə·tē) *n. pl.* **·ties** 1 The condition, quality, or degree of being opaque. 2 That which is opaque.

o·pal (ō′pəl) *n.* A colored, translucent silica, softer and less dense than quartz, valued as a gemstone. [<Skt. *upala* a precious stone]

o·pal·esce (ō′pəl·es′) *v.i.* **·esced, ·esc·ing** To exhibit an iridescent play of colors, as in an opal. —**o′pal·es′cence** *n.* —**o′pal·es′cent** *adj.*

o·paque (ō·pak′) *adj.* 1 Impervious to light or other radiation. 2 Loosely, imperfectly transparent. 3 Impervious to reason; unintelligent. 4 Having no luster; dull. 5 Unintelligible; obscure: an *opaque* style. —*n.* Something opaque. [<L *opacus* shaded, darkened] —**o·paque′ly** *adv.* —**o·paque′ness** *n.*

op art (op) A style of art of the 1960's characterized by complex geometric patterns designed to create optical distortions, illusions, etc. [<*optical art*]

op. cit. in the work cited (L *opere citato*).

ope (ōp) *v.t. & v.i.* **oped, op·ing** *Archaic* To open.

o·pen (ō′pən) *adj.* 1 Affording approach, view, passage, or access: unobstructed: an *open* door. **2** Public; accessible to all: the *open* market. **3** Unconcealed; overt; *open* hostility. **4** Expanded; unfolded: an *open* flower. **5** Exposed; uncovered: an *open* car. **6** Ready for business, appointment, etc.: an *open* day in the schedule. **7** Not settled or decided; pending: an *open* question. **8** Available: The job is still *open.* **9** Unbiased; receptive: an *open* mind. **10** Generous; liberal: He gives with an *open* hand. **11** *Phonet.* **a** Pronounced with a wide opening above the tongue; low: said of vowels, as the *a* in *father.* **b** Ending in a vowel or diphthong: said of a syllable. **12** Frank; ingenuous: *open* and aboveboard. **13** Eager or willing to receive: with *open* arms. **14** In hunting or fishing, without prohibition: *open* season. **15** Liable to attack, robbery, temptation, etc. **16** Having openings, or perforations, as woven goods or needlework. **17** Free from ice: *open* water. **18** *Music* **a** Not stopped by a finger, as a string or hole. **b** Having no string or hole stopped. **c** Produced by an open string or instrument. **d** Closed at neither end, as an organ pipe. **19** Unrestricted by union regulations in the employment of labor: an *open* shop. **20** *Informal* Not under control in the sale of intoxicants, gambling, or vice: an *open* town. **21** Out of doors. **22** In elementary education, characterized by an environment designed to encourage self-motivation by giving children freedom of movement within the class or school area: *open* classrooms. **23** *U.S.* Designating a policy of admitting students for matriculation without regard to academic preparedness: *open* admissions. **24** *Mil.* Designating a city that, during a war, is unfortified but safe from enemy attack under international law. —*v.t.* **1** To set open or ajar, as a door. **2** To make passable; free from obstacles. **3** To make or force (a hole, passage, etc.). **4** To remove the covering, lid, etc., of. **5** To expand, as for viewing; unfold, as a map. **6** To make an opening or openings into: to *open* an abscess. **7** To make or declare ready for commerce, use, etc.: to *open* a store. **8** To make or declare public or free of access, as a park. **9** To make less compact; expand: to *open* ranks. **10** To make more receptive to ideas or sentiments; enlighten: to *open* the mind. **11** To bare the secrets of; reveal: to *open* one's heart. **12** To begin; commence, as negotiations. —*v.i.* **13** To become open. **14** To come apart or break open; rupture. **15** To spread out; unroll. **16** To afford access or view: The door *opened* on a courtyard. **17** To become receptive or enlightened. **18** To begin; be started. **19** In the theater, to begin a run, season, etc. —*n.* An open space. —**the open 1** A large, unobstructed clearing. **2** The outdoors. **3** Public view. [< OE] —**o′pen·ly** *adv.* —**o′pen·ness** *n.*

open air The out-of-doors. —**o′pen-air′** *adj.*

o·pen-and-shut (ō′pən·ənd·shut′) *adj.* Simple; easily determinable.

open chain *Chem.* A molecular structure in which atoms, esp. carbon atoms, are linked in a straight or branched chain. —**o′pen-chain′** *adj.*

open door 1 The policy of giving equal and unrestricted opportunities to all nations, esp. for trade. **2** Admission to all without charge. —**o′pen-door′** *adj.*

o·pen-eyed (ō′pən·īd′) *adj.* **1** Having the eyes open; watchful. **2** Amazed: in *open-eyed* wonder.

o·pen-faced (ō′pən·fāst′) *adj.* **1** Possessing a countenance suggestive of frankness and honesty. **2** Denoting a sandwich without a slice of bread on top.

o·pen-hand·ed (ō′pən·han′did) *adj.* Giving freely; generous. —**o′pen-hand′ed·ly** *adv.* —**o′pen-hand′ed·ness** *n.*

o·pen-heart·ed (ō′pən·här′tid) *adj.* Unreserved; candid. —**o′pen-heart′ed·ly** *adj.* —**o′pen-heart′ed·ness** *n.*

o·pen-hearth (ō′pən·härth′) *adj.* *Metall.* Designating a type of reverberatory furnace with a shallow hearth, used in making steel.

open house 1 An informal party in which hospitality is extended to all comers. **2** An occasion when a school, clubhouse, etc., is open to visitors.

o·pen·ing (ō′pən·ing) *n.* **1** The act of becoming open or of causing to be open. **2** A hole, passage, or gap. **3** A clearing in a forest. **4** An aperture in a wall. **5** A formal beginning; prelude. **6** In chess, checkers, etc., the series of initial moves. **7** An opportunity for action, esp. in business.

o·pen-mind·ed (ō′pən·min′did) *adj.* Receptive to new ideas; amenable to reason. —**o′pen-mind′ed·ly** *adv.*

o·pen-mouthed (ō′pən·mouthd′, -moutht′) *adj.* **1** Having the mouth open; gaping, as in wonder or surprise. **2** Noisy; clamorous.

open question A matter as yet undecided.

open sesame An unfailing means or formula for gaining entrance or success. [< the magic words spoken in the story of *Ali Baba and the Forty Thieves*]

open shop An establishment in which union labor and nonunion labor are employed.

o·pen·work (ō′pən·wûrk′) *n.* Numerous small openings decoratively worked in fabric, silver, etc.

op·er·a[1] (op′ər·ə, op′rə) *n.* **1** A musical drama made up of arias, recitatives, choruses, etc., with orchestral accompaniment, scenery, acting, and sometimes dance. **2** A particular musical drama or its music or libretto; also, its performance. **3** The theater in which operas are given: also **opera house.** [< L *opus, operis* work] —**op·er·at·ic** (op′ə·rat′ik) *adj.* —**op′er·at′i·cal·ly** *adv.*

op·er·a[2] (op′ə·re) *n.pl.* of OPUS.

op·er·a·ble (op′ər·ə·bəl) *adj.* **1** Capable of treatment by surgical operation. **2** Feasible. —**op′er·a·bil′i·ty** (-bil′ə·tē), **op′er·a·ble·ness** *n.* —**op′er·a·bly** *adv.*

opera glasses A binocular telescope of small size, suitable for use at the theater. Also **opera glass.**

Opera glasses

opera hat A man's tall hat with a collapsible crown.

op·er·ant (op′ər·ənt) *adj.* **1** Producing a specified effect. **2** *Psychol.* Designating conditioning by which desired behavior is elicited by rewards that reinforce appropriate responses.

op·er·ate (op′ə·rāt) *v.* **·at·ed, ·at·ing** *v.i.* **1** To act or function; work. **2** To bring about or produce the proper effect. **3** To perform a surgical operation. **4** To carry on a military or naval operation: usu. with *against.* —*v.t.* **5** To control the working or function of, as a machine. **6** To conduct the affairs of: to *operate* a business. **7** To bring about or cause. [< L *operari* to work, have an effect < *opus, operis* a work]

op·er·a·tion (op′ə·rā′shən) *n.* **1** The act or process of operating. **2** A method of exercising or applying force. **3** A single specific act or transaction. **4** A series of acts to effect a certain purpose; process. **5** The state of being in action. **6** *Surg.* A manipulation performed on the body to remedy a defect or disorder. **7** *Math.* A process or procedure that associates elements of a set, as numbers, with elements of the same or a different set. **8** A military or naval campaign.

op·er·a·tion·al (op′ə·rā′shən·əl) *adj.* **1** Pertaining to an operation. **2** Organized to carry out assigned tasks. **3** Fit or ready for some specified use. **4** In actual service.

op·er·a·tive (op′ər·ə·tiv, -ə·rā′tiv) *adj.* **1** Exerting force or influence. **2** Moving or working efficiently; effective. **3** Connected with surgical operations: *operative* technique. **4** Concerned with practical work. **5** Engaged in practical activity. —*n.* **1** A person employed as a skilled worker. **2** *Informal* A detective; one who works secretly. —**op′er·a′·tive·ly** *adv.* —**op′er·a·tive′ness** *n.*

op·er·a·tor (op′ə·rā′tər) *n.* **1** One who operates; specifically, a worker at a telephone switchboard, a telegraph, etc. **2** The director of a large industrial organization. **3** *Slang* An aggressive, shrewd person who manages to get what he wants, often by unscrupulous means. **4** *Math.* A symbol that indicates an operation.

o·per·cu·lum (ō·pûr′kyo͞o·ləm) *n. pl.* **·la** (-lə) or **·lums** *Biol.* A lid, cover, or lidlike part in plants or animals, as a gill cover in fishes, etc. [< L *operire* to cover] —**o·per′cu·lar, o·per′cu·late, o·per′cu·lat′ed** *adj.*

op·e·ret·ta (op′ə·ret′ə) *n.* A musical dramatic work with a light or romantic plot, spoken dialogue, many songs, and dancing. [Ital.]

oph·thal·mi·a (of·thal′mē·ə) *n.* Inflammation of the eye or the lining of the eyelids. [< Gk. *ophthalmos* an eye]

oph·thal·mic (of·thal′mik) *adj.* Of, for, or pertaining to the eye: an *ophthalmic* ointment.

ophthalmo- *combining form* Eye; pertaining to the eyes: *ophthalmology.* [< Gk. *ophthalmos* the eye]

oph·thal·mol·o·gy (of′thal·mol′ə·jē) *n.* The study of the structure, functions, and diseases of the eye. **—oph·thal′mo·log′ic** (-mə·loj′ik) or **-i·cal** *adj.* **—oph′thal·mol′o·gist** *n.*

oph·thal·mo·scope (of·thal′mə·skōp) *n.* An optical instrument for illuminating and viewing the inside of the eye. **—oph·thal′mo·scop′ic** (-skop′ik) or **-i·cal** *adj.* **—oph·thal·mos·co·py** (of′thal·mos′kə·pē) *n.*

o·pi·ate (ō′pē·it, -āt) *n.* **1** A preparation of opium or any derivative; a narcotic. **2** Something inducing sleep or relaxation. **—***adj.* **1** Consisting of opium. **2** Inducing sleep or relaxation.

o·pine (ō·pīn′) *v.t. & v.i.* **o·pined, o·pin·ing** To think; conjecture: now usu. humorous. [< L *opinari* think] **—o·pin′er** *n.*

o·pin·ion (ə·pin′yən) *n.* **1** A conclusion or judgment held with confidence, but falling short of positive knowledge. **2** An estimate, judgment, or evaluation. **3** A judgment by an expert: a medical *opinion.* **4** *Law* The formal announcement of the conclusions of a court in a case before it. [< L *opinari* think]

o·pin·ion·at·ed (ə·pin′yən·ā′tid) *adj.* Unwarrantably attached to one's own opinion; obstinate. **—o·pin′ion·at′ed·ly** *adv.* **—o·pin′ion·at′ed·ness** *n.*

o·pin·ion·a·tive (ə·pin′yən·ā′tiv) *adj.* Opinionated. **—o·pin′ion·a′tive·ly** *adv.* **—o·pin′ion·a′tive·ness** *n.*

o·pi·um (ō′pē·əm) *n.* A powerful, addictive narcotic obtained from the seed capsules of the **opium poppy,** the source of a number of substances, including morphine, used in medicine. [< Gk. *opion*]

o·pos·sum (ə·pos′əm, pos′əm) *n.* A tree-dwelling, American marsupial of nocturnal habits. [< Algon.]

opp. oppose; opposed; opposite.

op·po·nent (ə·pō′nənt) *n.* One who opposes another, as in battle or debate; antagonist. **—***adj.* **1** Acting against something or someone; opposing. **2** Opposite. [< L *ob-* against + *ponere* to place]

op·por·tune (op′ər·t^y^ōōn′) *adj.* Meeting some requirement, esp. at the right time; timely. [< L *opportunus* suitable, lit., at the port.] **—op′por·tune′ly** *adv.* **—op′por·tune′·ness** *n.* **—Syn.** auspicious, convenient, favorable, fortunate, well-chosen.

op·por·tun·ism (op′ər·t^y^ōōn′iz·əm) *n.* The governing of one's course of action by opportunities or circumstances rather than by regard for principles. **—op′por·tun′ist** *n.* **—op′por·tu·nis′tic** *adj.*

op·por·tu·ni·ty (op′ər·t^y^ōō′nə·tē) *n. pl.* **·ties** A fit or convenient time; favorable occasion.

op·pos·a·ble (ə·pō′zə·bəl) *adj.* **1** Capable of being placed opposite: said esp. of the thumb in relation to the other fingers. **2** That can be opposed. **—op·pos′a·bil′i·ty** *n.* **—op·pos′a·bly** *adv.*

op·pose (ə·pōz′) *v.* **·posed, ·pos·ing** *v.t.* **1** To act or be in opposition to; resist. **2** To set in opposition or contrast. **3** To place before or in front. **—***v.i.* **4** To act or be in opposition. [< L *oppositus* opposite] **—op·pos′er** *n.* **—op·pos′ing·ly** *adv.*

op·po·site (op′ə·zit) *adj.* **1** Situated or placed on the other side, or on each side, of an intervening space or thing. **2** Facing or moving the other way; contrary. **3** Contrary in tendency or character: *opposite* opinions. **4** *Bot.* Arranged (as similar parts or organs) in pairs, but separated by a stem. **—***n.* **1** Something or someone that is opposite, opposed, or contrary. **2** An antonym. **—***adv.* In an opposite or complementary direction or position. **—***prep.* **1** Across from; facing. **2** Complementary to, as in theatrical roles: He played *opposite* her. [< L *oppositus,* pp. of *opponere* to place against] **—op′po·site·ly** *adv.* **—op′po·site·ness** *n.*

op·po·si·tion (op′ə·zish′ən) *n.* **1** The act of opposing or resisting; antagonism. **2** The state of being opposite or opposed; antithesis. **3** An obstacle to some result: The stream flows without *opposition* . **4** *Often cap.* The political party opposed to the party in power. **5** *Astron.* The relative position of two bodies 180° apart in longitude. **—op′po·si′tion·al** *adj.* **—op′po·si′tion·ist** *n.*

op·press (ə·pres′) *v.t.* **1** To burden or subjugate by use of force or authority. **2** To lie heavy upon physically or mentally; weigh down. [< L *ob-* against + *premere* to press] **—op·pres′sor** *n.* **—Syn. 1** persecute, tyrannize. **2** crush, depress.

op·pres·sion (ə·presh′ən) *n.* **1** The act of oppressing. **2** Subjection to unjust hardships; tyranny. **3** Weariness or dullness of spirits. **4** Hardship; cruelty.

op·pres·sive (ə·pres′iv) *adj.* **1** Characterized by oppression; burdensome; tyrannical. **2** Producing a sense of depression, physical or mental. **—op·pres′sive·ly** *adv.* **—op·pres′sive·ness** *n.*

op·pro·bri·ous (ə·prō′brē·əs) *adj.* **1** Contemptuously abusive; imputing disgrace: *opprobrious* names. **2** Shameful; disgraceful. **—op·pro′bri·ous·ly** *adv.* **—op·pro′bri·ous·ness** *n.*

op·pro·bri·um (ə·prō′brē·əm) *n.* **1** Infamy; public disgrace. **2** A cause of disgrace; shame. [< L *ob-* against + *probum* infamy]

opt (opt) *v.i.* To choose; decide. **—opt out (of)** To decide to withdraw from or discontinue (an organization, activity, etc.) [< L *optare* choose, wish]

op·ta·tive (op′tə·tiv) *adj.* **1** Expressing or indicative of desire or choice. **2** *Gram.* Denoting that mood in Greek and certain other languages which expresses wish or desire. **—***n. Gram.* The optative mood, or a verb in this mood. [< L *optare* to wish] **—op′ta·tive·ly** *adv.*

op·tic (op′tik) *adj.* **1** Pertaining to the eye or to vision. **2** Optical. **—***n. Informal* An eye. [< Gk *optos* seen]

op·ti·cal (op′ti·kəl) *adj.* **1** Pertaining to optics. **2** Of or pertaining to eyesight. **3** Designed to assist or improve vision. **—op′ti·cal·ly** *adv.*

optical art OP ART.

op·ti·cian (op·tish′ən) *n.* One who makes or sells eyeglasses and other optical equipment.

op·tics (op′tiks) *n.pl. (construed as sing.)* The science that deals with the phenomena of light and vision. [< OPTIC]

op·ti·mal (op′tə·məl) *adj.* Most favorable. **—op′ti·mal·ly** *adv.*

op·ti·mism (op′tə·miz′əm) *n.* **1** A disposition to regard with cheerful confidence the course of events and the resolution of present uncertainties or conditions. **2** The philosophical doctrine that everything is ordered for the best. [< L *optimus* best] **—op′ti·mist** *n.* **—op′ti·mis′tic** *adj.* **—op′ti·mis′ti·cal·ly** *adv.*

op·ti·mum (op′tə·məm) *n. pl.* **·ma** (-mə) or **·mums 1** The condition or degree producing the best result. **2** The most favorable degree, conditions, etc. **—***adj.* Producing or conducive to the best results. [L, neut. of *optimus* best]

op·tion (op′shən) *n.* **1** The right, power, or liberty of choosing; the exercise of choice. **2** The purchased privilege of buying or selling something at a specified price within a specified time. **3** A thing that is or can be chosen. [< L *optare* choose]

op·tion·al (op′shən·əl) *adj.* Depending on choice; elective. **—op′tion·al·ly** *adv.*

op·tom·e·trist (op·tom′ə·trist) *n.* One who is skilled in optometry.

op·tom·e·try (op·tom′ə·trē) *n.* The profession of measuring the power of vision and prescribing corrective lenses. [< OPT(IC) + -METER] **—op·to·met·ric** (op′tə·met′rik), **op′to·met′ri·cal** *adj.*

op·u·lence (op′yə·ləns) *n.* **1** Wealth; affluence. **2** Luxuriance. Also **op′u·len·cy.**

op·u·lent (op′yə·lənt) *adj.* **1** Possessing great wealth. **2** Exuberant; profuse. [< L *ops, opis* power, wealth] **—op′u·lent·ly** *adv.*

o·pus (ō′pəs) *n. pl.* **op·er·a** (op′ər·ə, op′rə) or **opus·es** A literary or musical work or composition. [L, a work]

or[1] (ôr, *unstressed* ər) *conj.* **1** Introducing an alternative: stop *or* go. **2** Offering a choice of a series: Will you take milk *or* coffee *or* chocolate? **3** Introducing an equivalent: the culinary art *or* art of cookery. **4** Indicating uncertainty: He lives in Chicago *or* thereabouts. **5** Introducing the second alternative of a choice limited to two: with *either* or *whether:* It must be either black *or* white. **6** Either; whether: *or* in the heart *or* in the head. [< OE *oththe* or]

or[2] (ôr) *n. Her.* Gold. [< L *aurum* gold]

-or[1] *suffix* The person or thing performing the action expressed in the root verb: *competitor.* [< L]

-or[2] *suffix* The quality, state, or condition of: *demeanor. Brit. sp., often* **-our.** [< L]

OR Oregon (P.O. abbr.).

OR, O.R. operating room.

or·a·cle (ôr′ə·kəl, or′-) *n.* **1** The seat of some ancient divinity, as of Apollo at Delphi, where prophecies were given out by the priests. **2** A prophecy thus given. **3** The deity whose prophecies were given. **4** A person of unquestioned wisdom or knowledge; an infallible authority. [< L *orare* speak, pray]

o·rac·u·lar (ô·rak′yə·lər, ō-) *adj.* **1** Pertaining to an oracle. **2** Prophetic. **—o·rac·u·lar·i·ty** (ô·rak′yə·lar′ə·tē), **o·rac′·u·lar·ness** *n.* **—o·rac′u·lar·ly** *adv.*

o·ral (ô′rəl, ō′rəl) *adj.* **1** Uttered through the mouth; spoken. **2** Pertaining to or situated at or near the mouth. **3** Of, pertaining to, or using speech. *—n.* An oral examination, as in a college. [< L *os, oris* mouth] **—o′ral·ly** *adv.* **— o′ral·ness** *n.* • **oral, verbal** Both of these words are commonly used with the sense of "spoken": *an oral* (or *verbal*) *agreement. Verbal,* however, can also mean "composed of or relating to words, as distinguished from ideas or things": *verbal skills. Oral,* derived from the Latin word for *mouth,* suggests the source of expression, whereas *verbal,* from the Latin word for *word,* suggests the form of expression.

or·ange (ôr′inj, or′-) *n.* **1** An edible, round, juicy citrus fruit with a reddish yellow rind. **2** Any of the evergreen trees or related shrubs yielding this fruit. **3** A reddish yellow color. *—adj.* **1** Reddish yellow. **2** Of or pertaining to an orange. [< Pers. *nārang*]

or·ange·ade (ôr′inj·ād′) *n.* A beverage made of orange juice, sugar, and water.

orange pekoe A fine grade of black tea of India, Ceylon, and Java.

or·ange·wood (ôr′inj·wo͝od′, or′-) *n.* The fine-grained, yellowish wood of the orange tree. *—adj.* Of orangewood.

o·rang-u·tan (ō·rang′ə·tan′) *n. pl.* **·tans** or **·tan** A large anthropoid ape of Borneo and Sumatra, having brownish red hair, small ears, a hairless face, and very long arms. Also **o·rang′, o·rang′u·tan′, o·rang′ou·tan′, o·rang′u·tang′** (-ə·tang′). [< Malay *orañ* a man + *utan* a forest]

Orang-utan

o·rate (ô·rāt′, ō·rāt′) *v.i.* **o·rat·ed, o·rat·ing** To deliver an oration; speechify: chiefly humorous. [< L *orare* to speak]

o·ra·tion (ô·rā′shən, ō·rā′-) *n.* A formal public speech delivered on a ceremonial occasion. **—Syn.** address, discourse, talk.

or·a·tor (ôr′ə·tər, or′-) *n.* One who delivers an oration; an eloquent public speaker.

or·a·tor·i·cal (ôr′ə·tôr′ə·kəl, -tō′rə-, or′-) *adj.* Of, like, or characteristic of oratory or an orator. **—or′a·tor′i·cal·ly** *adv.*

or·a·to·ri·o (ôr′ə·tôr′ē·ō, -tō′rē·ō, or′-) *n. pl.* **·os** A narrative musical composition, usu. on a sacred theme, for solo voices, chorus, and orchestra. [Ital., lit., a small chapel]

or·a·to·ry (ôr′ə·tôr′ē, -tō′rē, or′-) *n. pl.* **·ries** **1** The art of public speaking; eloquence. **2** Eloquent language. **3** A place for prayer; a private chapel. [< L *orator* one who speaks]

orb (ôrb) *n.* **1** A sphere or globe. **2** A celestial body, as the sun, moon, etc. **3** A sphere topped by a cross: symbolic of royal power. **4** Eyeball; eye. *—v.t.* To shape into a sphere or circle. [< L *orbis* a circle]

or·bic·u·lar (ôr·bik′yə·lər) *adj.* **1** Having the form of an orb or orbit. **2** Well-rounded. **3** *Bot.* Circular, as a leaf or petal. Also **or·bic′u·late** (-lit, -lāt), **or·bic′u·lat′ed.** [< L *orbiculus,* dim. of *orbis* a circle] **—or·bic′u·lar′i·ty** (-lar′ə·tē) *n.* **—or·bic′u·lar·ly** *adv.*

or·bit (ôr′bit) *n.* **1** *Astron.* The path in space along which a celestial body moves. **2** *Anat.* One of the two sockets of the eyes. **3** *Physics* The path of a body subject to a field of force, esp. that of an electron around the atomic nucleus. **4** A range of influence or action: the *orbit* of imperialism. *—v.t.* **1** To cause to move in an orbit, as an artificial satellite. *—v.i.* **2** To move in an orbit. [< L *orbis* a wheel, a circle] **—or′bi·tal** *adj.*

orch. orchestra; orchestral.

or·chard (ôr′chərd) *n.* A plantation of trees grown for their products, as fruit, nuts, oils, etc.; also, the enclosure or ground containing them. [< Med. L *ortus* a garden + OE *geard* a yard, enclosure]

or·ches·tra (ôr′kis·trə) *n.* **1** A fairly large group of musicians playing together, esp. a symphony orchestra. **2** The instruments on which they play. **3** In theaters, the place immediately before the stage, occupied by the musicians: also **orchestra pit. 4** In the U.S., the main floor of a theater. [< Gk. *orchēstra,* lit., a dancing space] **—or·ches·tral** (ôr·kes′trəl) *adj.* **—or·ches′tral·ly** *adv.*

or·ches·trate (ôr′kis·trāt) *v.t. & v.i.* **·trat·ed, ·trat·ing** **1** To compose or arrange (music) for an orchestra. **2** To arrange or bring about, as by manipulation or careful planning, esp. so as to create a desired effect: a well-*orchestrated* attack on the press. **—or′ches·tra′tion** *n.*

or·chid (ôr′kid) *n.* **1** Any of a widely distributed family of plants having bulbous roots and often very showy flowers. **2** The flower of any of these plants. **3** A delicate, rosy purple color. [< Gk. *orchis* a testicle: so called from the shape of its tubers]

Orchid flower

or·chis (ôr′kis) *n.* An orchid, esp. one having dense spikes of small flowers. [< L, ORCHID]

ord. ordained; order; ordinal; ordinary; ordnance.

or·dain (ôr·dān′) *v.t.* **1** To order or decree; establish. **2** To predestine; destine: said of God, fate, etc. **3** To invest with ministerial or priestly functions. [< L *ordo* an order] **— or·dain′er** *n.*

or·deal (ôr·dēl′, -dē′əl, ôr′dēl) *n.* **1** Any trying or painful experience. **2** An old method of trial in which the accused underwent physical ordeals, as carrying or walking over burning coals, which, if he were innocent, would supposedly leave him unharmed. [< OE *ordāl*]

or·der (ôr′dər) *n.* **1** Methodical and harmonious arrangement, as of successive things in a formation. **2** Proper or working condition. **3** A command or authoritative regulation. **4** *Law* Any direction of a court made to be entered of record in a cause, and not included in the final judgment. **5** A commission or instruction to supply, purchase, or sell something. **6** Established use or customary procedure. **7** Established or existing state of things. **8** *Sometimes cap.* A group of persons united by some common bond: the *Order* of Odd Fellows. **9** A group of persons upon whom a government has conferred an honor and who are thus entitled to affix to their names designated initials and to wear specific insignia; also, the insignia worn. **10** Social rank. **11** A class, kind, or degree: a chef of the first *order.* **12** *Usu. pl.* Any of the various grades or degrees of the Christian ministry: also **holy orders, sacred orders. 13** *Archit.* The general character of a column and its parts as distinguishing a style of architecture: the Ionic *order.* **14** *Biol.* A taxonomic category ranking below the class and above the family. **15** *Math.* A number indicating how many times an operation is performed or implied. **16** *Gram.* The sequence of words in a sentence or construction. **17** The position of the rifle as a result of the command **order arms. 18** Any one of the ancient nine grades of angels. **—call to order** To ask to be quiet in order to start, as a meeting. **—in order** **1** In accordance with rule. **2** Neat; tidy. **—in order that** So that; to the end that. **—in order to** For the purpose of; to the end that. **—in short order** Quickly; without delay. **—on order** Ordered but not yet delivered. **—on the order of** Similar to. **—take orders** **1** To enter the ministry. **2** To obey. **—to order** As specified by the buyer. *—v.t.* **1** To give a command or direction to. **2** To command to go, come, etc. **3** To give an order that (something) be done; prescribe. **4** To give an order for: to *order* a new suit. **5** To put in systematic arrangement. **6** To ordain: He was *ordered* deacon. *—v.i.* **7** To give an order or orders. [< L *ordo* a row, series, an order] **—or′der·er** *n.*

ordered set *Math.* A set in which each element has a unique correspondence with a natural number, beginning with one and proceeding on.

or·der·ly (ôr′dər·lē) *adj.* **1** Neat; systematic. **2** Peaceful and law-abiding: an *orderly* demonstration. **3** Characterized by order. —*n. pl.* **·lies 1** A soldier or noncommissioned officer detailed to carry orders for superior officers. **2** A male hospital attendant. —**or′der·li·ness** *n.* —**Syn.** *adj.* **1** clean, methodical, tidy. **2** peaceful, quiet.

or·di·nal (ôr′də·nəl) *adj.* **1** Denoting position in an order or succession. **2** Pertaining to an order, as of plants, animals, etc. —*n.* **1** ORDINAL NUMBER. **2** *Sometimes cap.* A book of forms for special church services. [< L *ordo, ordinis* an order]

ordinal number A number that shows the order of a unit in a given series, as *first, second, third,* etc.

or·di·nance (ôr′də·nəns) *n.* **1** An authoritative rule; decree. **2** A religious rite or ceremony. **3** A municipal statute. [< L *ordinans* ordained]

or·di·nar·i·ly (ôr′də·ner′ə·lē, ôr′də·nâr′ə·lē) *adv.* In ordinary cases; commonly; usually.

or·di·nar·y (ôr′də·ner′ē) *adj.* **1** Of common or everyday occurrence; usual. **2** According to an established order; regular. **3** Mediocre; commonplace. —*n. pl.* **·nar·ies 1** That which is usual or common. **2** *Brit.* A meal provided regularly at a fixed price. **3** *Brit.* An eating place. **4** One who exercises jurisdiction in his own right, esp. a church official. **5** A rule or book prescribing the form for saying mass. —**in ordinary** In actual and constant service. —**out of the ordinary** Very unusual. [< L *ordinarius* < *ordo* an order] —**or′di·nar′i·ness** *n.*

or·di·nate (ôr′də·nit) *n. Math.* The coordinate that indicates the distance from a point to the *x*-axis, parallel to the *y*-axis; the *y* coordinate. [< L *ordinare* ordain]

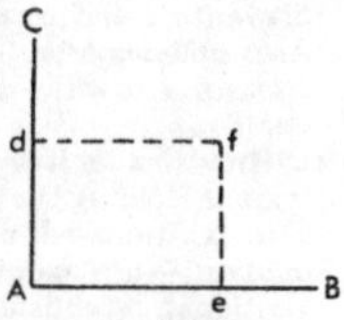

Ordinate

AC: axis of ordinates.
AB: axis of abscissas.
Ad or ef: ordinate of point f.

or·di·na·tion (ôr′də·nā′shən) *n.* **1** The rite of consecration to the ministry. **2** The state of being ordained.

ord·nance (ôrd′nəns) *n. Mil.* **1** All military weapons. **2** Cannon or artillery. [Contraction of ORDINANCE]

Or·do·vi·cian (ôr′də·vish′ən) *adj. & n.* See GEOLOGY. [< L *Ordovices,* an ancient Celtic tribe]

or·dure (ôr′jər, -dyŏŏr) *n.* Excrement; feces. [< L *horridus* HORRID]

ore (ôr, ōr) *n.* A mineral or similar material from which a valuable substance, esp. a metal, can be extracted at reasonable cost. [< OE *ār* brass, copper]

Ore., Oreg. Oregon.

o·reg·a·no (ə·reg′ə·nō) *n.* A species of marjoram having pungent leaves used for seasoning. [< L *origanum*]

O·res·tes (ô·res′tēz, ō-) *Gk. Myth.* The son of Agamemnon and Clytemnestra who, having killed his mother to avenge his father's murder, was pursued by the Furies.

org. organic; organism; organized.

or·gan (ôr′gən) *n.* **1** Any of various keyboard musical instruments capable of sustained tones, esp. a collection of pipes made to sound by means of compressed air; a pipe organ. **2** A musical instrument resembling the pipe organ: a barrel *organ.* **3** A structure of specialized tissue in a plant or animal performing some definite function. **4** A means of making public the opinions and ideas of a person or group, as a periodical. [< Gk. *organon* a tool, a musical instrument]

or·gan·dy (ôr′gən·dē) *n. pl.* **·dies** A thin, crisp, transparent, cotton muslin, used for dresses, collars, etc. Also **or′·gan·die.** [< F *organdi*]

or·gan·elle (ôr′gə·nəl′) *n.* Any of various distinctive submicroscopic structures having specialized functions within a living cell. [Dim. of ORGAN]

or·gan-grind·er (ôr′gən·grīn′dər) *n.* A street musician who plays a hand organ.

or·gan·ic (ôr·gan′ik) *adj.* **1** Of, pertaining to, or of the nature of animals and plants. **2** Having a physical basis in a bodily organ. **3** Serving the purpose of an organ. **4** *Chem.* Of or pertaining to carbon compounds. **5** Inherent in or pertaining to the organization or fundamental structure; structural. **6** Of or characterized by systematic coordination of parts; organized. **7** *Law* Designating the basic laws or principles of a government. **8** Pertaining to foodstuffs grown with only natural fertilizers of animal or plant origin. Also **or·gan′i·cal.** —**or·gan′i·cal·ly** *adv.*

organic chemistry The branch of chemistry that relates to carbon compounds.

organic disease *Pathol.* A disease accompanied by a physical change in an organ or tissue.

or·gan·ism (ôr′gən·iz′əm) *n.* **1** An animal or plant internally organized to maintain vital activities. **2** Anything analogous in structure and function to a living thing. —**or′gan·is′mal** *adj.*

or·gan·ist (ôr′gən·ist) *n.* One who plays the organ.

or·gan·i·za·tion (ôr′gən·ə·zā′shən, -ī·zā′-) *n.* **1** The act of organizing, or the state of being organized. **2** A number of individuals systematically united for some end or work, as a business enterprise, a political party, club, church, etc. **3** The way in which something is organized. —**or′gan·i·za′tion·al** *adj.* —**or′gan·i·za′tion·al·ly** *adv.*

organization man A member of an organization, party, company, etc., who is fully committed to its aims and methods of operation.

or·gan·ize (ôr′gən·īz) *v.* **·ized, ·iz·ing** *v.t.* **1** To arrange systematically; order. **2** To furnish with organic structure. **3** To enlist (workers) in a trade union. **4** To unionize the workers of (a factory, etc.). —*v.i.* **5** To form or join an organization. *Brit sp.* **or′gan·ise.** —**or′gan·iz′er** *n.*

or·gasm (ôr′gaz·əm) *n.* The climax of excitement at the culmination of a sexual act, accompanied in the male by ejaculation of semen and in both sexes followed by relaxation of erectile organs. [< Gk. *orgasmos* a swelling] —**or·gas′mic** *adj.*

or·gy (ôr′jē) *n. pl.* **·gies 1** Wild and drunken revelry; debauch. **2** Any immoderate indulgence in something: an *orgy* of reading. **3** *pl.* In ancient Greece and Rome, the rites honoring certain gods, as Dionysus, marked by frenzied songs and dances. [< Gk. *orgia* secret rites.] —**or′gi·as′tic** (-as′tik) *adj.* —**or′gi·as′ti·cal·ly** *adv.*

o·ri·el (ôr′ē·əl, ō′rē-) *n. Archit.* A bay window, esp. one built out from a wall and resting on a support. [< OF *oriol* a porch, gallery]

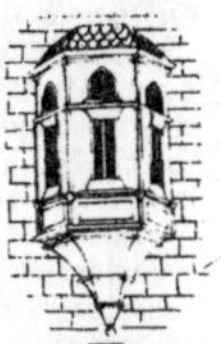

Oriel

o·ri·ent (ôr′ē·ənt, ō′rē-) *n.* **1** The east. **2** The eastern sky. **3** The iridescent luster of a pearl. —*v.t.* **1** To cause to face or turn to the east. **2** To place or adjust, as a map, in exact relation to the points of the compass. **3** To adjust the physical position of. **4** To adjust or adapt according to first principles or recognized facts. —*adj.* **1** Resembling sunrise; bright. **2** Ascending. [< L *oriens* rising sun, east]

O·ri·ent (ôr′ē·ənt, ō′rē-) *n.* Asia, esp. E Asia; the East.

o·ri·en·tal (ôr′ē·en′təl, ō′rē-) *adj.* Eastern. —**o′ri·en′tal·ly** *adv.*

O·ri·en·tal (ôr′ē·en′təl, ō′rē-) *adj.* Of or pertaining to the Orient or to its people. —*n.* An inhabitant of Asia; an Asian.

O·ri·en·tal·ism (ôr′ē·en′təl·iz′əm, ō′rē-) *n.* **1** A quality or character attributed to Orientals. **2** Knowledge or study of Oriental languages, culture, etc. Also **o′ri·en′tal·ism.** —**O′ri·en′tal·ist** *n.*

Oriental rug 1 A one-piece rug, usu. having colorful, intricate designs, woven or knotted by hand in the Orient. **2** Any rug similar in appearance. Also **Oriental carpet.**

o·ri·en·tate (ôr′ē·en·tāt′, ō′rē-) *v.* **·tat·ed, ·tat·ing** *v.t.* **1** To orient. —*v.i.* **2** To face or turn eastward.

o·ri·en·ta·tion (ôr′ē·en·tā′shən, ō′rē-) *n.* **1** The act of orienting, or the state of being oriented. **2** The determination or adjustment of one's position with reference to circumstances, ideals, etc.

o·ri·en·ted (ôr′ē·en·tid, ō′rē-, -ən·tid) *adj.* 1 Directed toward; interested in: *oriented* to the arts. 2 Directed or centered: used in combination: a *child-oriented* family.

or·i·fice (ôr′ə·fis, or′-) *n.* A small opening into a cavity; an aperture. [< L *os, oris* mouth + *facere* make]

or·i·flamme (ôr′ə·flam, or′-) *n.* 1 The ancient banner of the kings of France, red silk split at one end to form flamelike streamers. 2 Any flag or standard. [< L *aurum* gold + *flamma* a flame]

orig. original; originally.

or·i·ga·mi (ôr′i·gä′mē) *n.* The ancient Japanese art of folding paper into animal and other forms. [Jap.]

or·i·gin (ôr′ə·jin, or′-) *n.* 1 The commencement of the existence of anything; primary source. 2 Parentage; ancestry. 3 *Math.* The point at which the axes of a Cartesian coordinate system intersect [< L *origo* a rise < *oriri* to rise]

o·rig·i·nal (ə·rij′ə·nəl) *adj.* 1 Of or belonging to the beginning. 2 Immediately produced by one's own mind; not copied. 3 Able to produce new creations; inventive. 4 Fresh; new: What an *original* idea! —*n.* 1 The first form of anything from which copies, imitations, translations, etc., are made. 2 The language in which a book is first written. 3 A person of unique character or genius; also, an eccentric. 4 Origin. —**o·rig′i·nal·ly** *adv.*

o·rig·i·nal·i·ty (ə·rij′ə·nal′ə·tē) *n. pl.* **·ties** 1 The power of originating; inventiveness. 2 The quality of being original or novel.

original sin *Theol.* The corruption and depravity inherent in mankind as a consequence of Adam's first disobedience.

o·rig·i·nate (ə·rij′ə·nāt) *v.* **·nat·ed, ·nat·ing** *v.t.* 1 To bring into existence; create; initiate. —*v.i.* 2 To come into existence; have origin; arise. —**o·rig′i·na′tion, o·rig′i·na′tor** *n.* —**o·rig′i·na′tive** *adj.* —**o·rig′i·na′tive·ly** *adv.*

o·ri·ole (ôr′ē·ōl, ō′rē-) *n.* 1 Any of a family of black-and-yellow birds related to the crows. 2 One of various American birds building a hanging nest and having yellow or orange and black plumage. [< L *aureus* golden] • See BALTIMORE ORIOLE.

O·ri·on (ō·rī′ən) *Gk. & Rom. Myth.* A giant huntsman who pursued the Pleiades and was killed by Diana. —*n.* An equatorial constellation.

or·i·son (ôr′i·sən, or′-, -zən) *n. Usu. pl.* A devotional prayer. [< L *oratio* a prayer]

Or·lon (ôr′lon) *n.* A synthetic textile fiber with a high resistance to heat, light, and chemicals: a trade name.

or·mo·lu (ôr′mə·lo͞o) *n.* An imitation gold made of an alloy of copper and tin, used in decorating clocks, etc. [< F *or moulu,* lit., ground gold]

or·na·ment (ôr′nə·mənt) *n.* 1 Something that contributes to the beauty or elegance of a thing. 2 Any thing or person considered as a source of honor or credit. 3 *Music* A decorative melodic tone or tones independent of the harmony. —*v.t.* (ôr′nə·ment) To adorn with ornaments. [< L *ornare* adorn] —**or′na·ment′er** *n.* —**Syn.** *v.* beautify, decorate, embellish.

or·na·men·tal (ôr′nə·men′təl) *adj.* Serving to adorn. —*n.* An ornamental object. —**or′na·men′tal·ly** *adv.*

or·na·men·ta·tion (ôr′nə·men·tā′shən, -mən-) *n.* 1 The act of adorning, or the state of being adorned. 2 Ornamental things collectively.

or·nate (ôr·nāt′) *adj.* Ornamented or decorated to a marked degree. [< L *ornatus* adorned] —**or·nate′ly** *adv.* —**or·nate′ness** *n.*

or·ner·y (ôr′nər·ē, ôrn′rē) *adj. Regional* 1 Mean; low. 2 Unruly; stubborn. 3 Common; ordinary. [Alter. of ORDINARY] —**or′ner·i·ness** *n.*

or·ni·thol·o·gy (ôr′nə·thol′ə·jē) *n.* The branch of zoology that deals with the study of birds. [< Gk. *ornis, ornithos* bird + -LOGY] —**or′ni·tho·log′ic** (-thə·loj′ik) or **·i·cal** *adj.* —**or′ni·tho·log′i·cal·ly** *adv.* —**or′ni·thol′o·gist** *n.*

o·rog·e·ny (ō·roj′ə·nē, ō-) *n.* The process of mountain formation. [< Gk. *oros* mountain + -GENY] —**or·o·gen·ic** (ôr′ə·jen′ik, or′-) *adj.*

o·ro·tund (ôr′ə·tund, ō′rə-) *adj.* 1 Full, clear, rounded, and resonant: said of the voice. 2 Pompous; inflated, as a manner of speech. [< L *os, oris* mouth + *rotundus* round] —**o′ro·tun′di·ty** *n.*

or·phan (ôr′fən) *n.* A child whose parents are dead. —*adj.* 1 Having lost one or both parents: said of a child. 2 Pertaining to a child so bereaved. —*v.t.* To bereave of parents or of a parent. [< Gk. *orphanos* bereaved] —**or′phan·hood** (-ho͝od) *n.*

or·phan·age (ôr′fən·ij) *n.* 1 The state of being an orphan. 2 An institution for orphans.

Or·phe·us (ôr′fē·əs) *Gk. Myth.* A singer and lyre player with magical powers. When his wife Eurydice died he was permitted to lead her back from Hades provided he did not look at her, but she disappeared when he glimpsed her. —**Or′phe·an** *adj.*

Or·phic (ôr′fik) *adj.* 1 Belonging, relating, or similar to Orpheus or his music. 2 Oracular; mysterious.

or·pine (ôr′pin) *n.* Any of various small, fleshy-leaved plants with yellow, white or purple flowers, often cultivated in rock gardens. Also **or′pin.** [< OF *orpin*]

Or·ping·ton (ôr′ping·tən) *n.* A variety of domestic fowl. [< *Orpington,* a village in Kent, England]

or·ris (ôr′is, or′-) *n.* Any of the several species of iris having a scented root. [Var. of IRIS]

or·ris·root (ôr′is·ro͞ot′, -ro͝ot′) *n.* The dried rootstock of a species of orris, used in cosmetics, perfumes, etc.

ortho- *combining form* 1 Straight; upright; in line: *orthopteran.* 2 At right angles: *orthogonal.* 3 Correct; proper; *orthography.* 4 *Med.* The correction of irregularities or deformities of: *orthodontia.* [< Gk. *orthos* straight]

or·tho·clase (ôr′thō·klās, -klāz) *n.* A brittle, glassy potassium-aluminum silicate related to feldspar. [< ORTHO- + Gk. *klasis* a fracture] —**or′tho·clas′tic** *adj.*

or·tho·don·tics (ôr′thə·don′tiks) *n.pl. (construed as sing.)* The branch of dentistry which is concerned with preventing and correcting faulty positions of the teeth. Also **or·tho·don′tia** (-shə, -shē·ə). [< ORTHO- + Gk. *odous, odontos* a tooth] —**or′tho·don′tic** (-don′tik) *adj.* —**or′tho·don′tist** *n.*

or·tho·dox (ôr′thə·doks) *adj.* 1 Correct or sound in doctrine. 2 Holding the commonly accepted faith, esp. in religion. 3 Approved; accepted. [< Gk. *orthos* right + *doxa* opinion] —**or′tho·dox′ly** *adv.* —**Syn.** 3 acknowledged, conventional, established, fixed, traditional.

Orthodox *adj.* Designating any church in the Eastern Orthodox Church.

or·tho·dox·y (ôr′thə·dok′sē) *n. pl.* **·dox·ies** 1 Belief in established religious doctrine. 2 Agreement with established or accepted doctrines, ideas, etc. —**or′tho·dox′i·cal** *adj.*

or·tho·e·py (ôr·thō′ə·pē, ôr′thō·ep′ē) 1 The art of correct pronunciation. 2 Pronunciation in general. [< Gk. *orthos* right + *epos* a word] —**or·tho·ep·ic** (ôr′thō·ep′ik) or **·i·cal** *adj.* —**or·tho′e·pist** *n.*

or·thog·o·nal (ôr·thog′ə·nəl) *adj.* Having, meeting at, or determined by right angles. [< Gk. *orthos* right + *gōnia* an angle] —**or·thog′o·nal·ly** *adv.*

or·thog·ra·phy (ôr·thog′rə·fē) *n. pl.* **·phies** 1 A mode or system of spelling, spelling correctly or according to usage. 2 The study of spelling. —**or·thog′ra·pher** *n.* —**or·tho·graph·ic** (or′thə·graf′ik), **or′tho·graph′i·cal** *adj.*

or·tho·pe·dics (ôr′thə·pē′diks) *n.pl. (construed as sing.)* The branch of surgery concerned with treating chronic disorders of the joints, spine, bones, and muscles used in movement. Also **or′tho·pae′dics.** [< Gk. *orthos* right + *paideia* training of children] —**or′tho·pe′dic** or **·di·cal** *adj.* —**or′tho·pe′dist** *n.*

or·thop·ter·an (ôr·thop′tər·ən) *n.* Any of an order of insects with membranous hind wings and hard, narrow forewings, as locusts, crickets, grasshoppers, cockroaches, etc. —*adj.* Of or pertaining to this order. [< ORTHO- + Gk. *pteron* a wing] —**or·thop′ter·al, or·thop′ter·ous** *adj.*

or·to·lan (ôr′tə·lən) *n.* 1 A European bunting esteemed as a table delicacy. 2 Any of several birds of the U.S., as the sora and bobolink. [< Ital. *ortolano* a gardener]

Or·well·i·an (ôr·wel′ē·ən) *adj.* Of, relating to, or typical of the writings of George Orwell (1903–50), British novelist and political satirist.

-ory[1] *suffix* A place or instrument for (performing the action of the main element): *dormitory.* [< L *-orium*]

-ory[2] *suffix* Related to; resembling: *laudatory.* [< L *-orius*]

o·ryx (ôr′iks, or′-, ō′riks) *n. pl.* **o·ryx** or **o·ryx·es** Any of a genus of Asian and African antelopes with long, straight horns, as the gemsbok. [<Gk., a pickax, a kind of antelope; so called from its pointed horns] • See GEMSBOK.

os[1] (os) *n. pl.* **o·ra** (ôr′ə, ō′rə) *Anat.* A mouth or opening into the interior of an organ. [L]

os[2] (os) *n. pl.* **os·sa** (os′ə) *Anat.* A bone. [L]

OS, Os, O.S. Old Saxon.

Os osmium

O·sage orange (ō′sāj) 1 A small, thorny N. American tree related to the mulberry, having glossy leaves and a large, inedible fruit. 2 The fruit of this tree. [<the *Osage*, a tribe of N. American Indians]

Os·car (os′kər) *n.* A gold statuette awarded annually by the Academy of Motion Picture Arts and Sciences for outstanding performances, productions, photography, etc., in motion pictures. [?]

os·cil·late (os′ə·lāt) *v.* **·lat·ed, ·lat·ing** *v.i.* 1 To go periodically through an orderly series or cycle of changes, as a pendulum or other physical system. 2 To vary undecidedly; waver. —*v.t.* 3 To cause to oscillate. [<L *oscillum* a swing] —**os′cil·la′tor** *n.* —**os′cil·la·to′ry** (-lə·tôr′ē, -tō′rē) *adj.*

os·cil·la·tion (os′ə·lā′shən) *n.* 1 The act or state of oscillating. 2 *Physics* A single cycle of an oscillating system.

os·cil·lo·scope (ə·sil′ə·skōp′) *n.* An electronic instrument that displays waveforms corresponding to external signals on the screen of a cathode ray tube.

os·cine (os′īn) *adj.* Of or belonging to a group of perching birds, as thrushes, finches, etc., with very highly developed vocal ability. —*n.* An oscine bird. [<NL <L *ob-* towards + *canere* to sing]

os·cu·late (os′kyə·lāt) *v.t.* & *v.i.* **·lat·ed, ·lat·ing** 1 To kiss. 2 To bring or come into close contact or union. 3 *Biol.* To have (characteristics) in common. [<L *osculari* to kiss] —**os′cu·la′tion** *n.* —**os′cu·la·to′ry** (-lə·tôr′ē, -tō′rē) *adj.*

-ose[1] *suffix* 1 Full of or abounding in: *verbose.* 2 Like; resembling (the main element): *grandiose.* [<L *-osus*]

-ose[2] *suffix Chem.* A carbohydrate: *cellulose.* [<(GLUC)OSE]

o·sier (ō′zhər) *n.* Any of several willows producing long, flexible shoots used in wickerwork. —*adj.* Consisting of shoots of willow, etc. [<Med. L *osaria* a bed of willows]

O·si·ris (o·sī′ris) *Egyptian Myth.* The god of the underworld and lord of the dead.

-osis *suffix* 1 The condition, process, or state of: *metamorphosis.* 2 *Med.* **a** A diseased or abnormal condition of: *melanosis.* **b** A formation of: *sclerosis.* [<Gk. *-ōsis*]

-osity *suffix* Forming nouns corresponding to adjectives in *-ose: verbosity, grandiosity.* [<L *-ositas*]

os·mi·um (oz′mē·əm, os′-) *n.* A hard, heavy, metallic element (symbol Os) of the platinum group. [<Gk. *osmē* an odor]

os·mose (oz′mōs, os′-) *v.t.* & *v.i.* **·mosed, ·mos·ing** To subject to or to undergo the process of osmosis. [<OSMOSIS]

os·mo·sis (oz·mō′sis, os-) *n.* 1 The diffusion of a solvent through a semipermeable membrane in such a manner as to equalize the solution concentration on both sides of the membrane. 2 *Informal* A process resembling diffusion and marked esp. by the absence of effort: Living in Paris, he learned French by *osmosis.* [<Gk. *ōsmos* a thrust, push] —**os·mot·ic** (oz·mot′ik, os-) *adj.* —**os·mot′i·cal·ly** *adv.*

O Sp. Old Spanish.

os·prey (os′prē) *n.* A large hawk that dives and feeds exclusively on fish. [ME *ospray*]

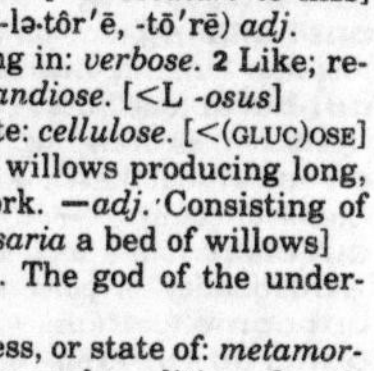

Osprey

OSS, O.S.S. Office of Strategic Services.

os·se·ous (os′ē·əs) *adj.* Pertaining to, of the nature of, or containing bone. [<L *os, ossis* a bone] —**os′se·ous·ly** *adv.*

os·si·fy (os′ə·fī) *v.t.* & *v.i.* **·fied, ·fy·ing** 1 To convert or be converted into bone. 2 To make or become set, conventional, etc. [<L *os, ossis* a bone + -FY] —**os·sif·ic** (o·sif′ik) *adj.* —**os′si·fi·ca′tion** *n.*

os·ten·si·ble (os·ten′sə·bəl) *adj.* Offered as real or having the character represented; seeming; professed or pretended. [<L *ostendere* to show] —**os·ten′si·bly** *adv.*

os·ten·sive (os·ten′siv) *adj.* 1 Exhibiting; showing; revealing. 2 OSTENSIBLE. —**os·ten′sive·ly** *adv.*

os·ten·ta·tion (os′tən·tā′shən) *n.* Elaborate or pretentious display; showiness. [<L *ostendere* to show]

os·ten·ta·tious (os′tən·tā′shəs) *adj.* Marked by a showy or pretentious display. —**os′ten·ta′tious·ly** *adv.* —**os′ten·ta′tious·ness** *n.*

osteo- *combining form* Bone: *osteology.* Also **oste-.** [<Gk. *osteon* a bone]

os·te·ol·o·gy (os′tē·ol′ə·jē) *n.* The study of the functions and structure of bones. —**os′te·o·log′i·cal** (-ə·loj′i·kəl) *adj.* —**os′te·o·log′i·cal·ly** *adv.* —**os′te·ol′o·gist** *n.*

os·te·o·ma (os′tē·ō′mə) *n. pl.* **·ma·ta** (-mə·tə) A tumor consisting of bony substance. [<OSTE(O)- + NL *-oma* tumor]

os·te·o·my·e·li·tis (os′tē·ō·mī′ə·lī′tis) *n.* Inflammation of the bone marrow.

os·te·op·a·thy (os′tē·op′ə·thē) *n.* Therapy based on a theory that most disorders are due to structural abnormalities that may be corrected by manipulation. —**os′te·o·path′, os′te·op′a·thist** *n.* —**os′te·o·path·ic** (-ə·path′ik) *adj.*

os·te·o·po·ro·sis (os′te·ō·pə·rō′sis) *n. Med.* A disease marked by loss of calcium from the bones, causing them to weaken.

os·tler (os′lər) *n.* HOSTLER.

Ost·mark (ôst′märk′) *n.* MARK[2].

os·tra·cism (os′trə·siz′əm) *n.* 1 Exclusion, as from society or common privileges, by general consent. 2 In ancient Greece, banishment by popular vote.

os·tra·cize (os′trə·sīz) *v.t.* **·cized, ·ciz·ing** To exclude, banish, etc., by ostracism. [<Gk. *ostrakon* a potsherd, shell, voting tablet] —**Syn.** reject, expatriate, expel, oust.

os·trich (ôs′trich, os′-) *n.* 1 A large, two-toed bird of Africa and Arabia, with aborted wings and long, powerful legs. 2 RHEA. [<L *avis* a bird + LL *struthio* an ostrich]

Ostrich

Os·tro·goth (os′trə·goth) *n.* A member of the eastern branch of the Goths. —**Os′tro·goth′ic** *adj.*

O.T. Old Testament; overtime.

oth·er (u<u>th</u>′ər) *adj.* 1 Being the remaining one, as of two or more persons or things. 2 Distinct or different from the one or more persons or things first mentioned. 3 Different, as in nature or quality. 4 Additional; further. 5 Former. 6 Second or alternate. —**the other day (night,** etc.) Recently. —*pron.* 1 A different or additional person or thing. 2 The second of two; the other one. —*adv.* Otherwise: with *than.* —*n.* 1 The remaining one or ones of two or more persons or things. 2 A different or additional person or thing. [<OE *ōther*] —**oth′er·ness** *n.*

oth·er·wise (u<u>th</u>′ər·wīz′) *adv.* 1 In another or different manner. 2 In other circumstances or conditions. 3 In all other respects: an *otherwise* sensible writer. —*adj.* Different: How could such notions be *otherwise* than useless?

other world A world after death.

oth·er·world·ly (u<u>th</u>′ər·wûrld′lē) *adj.* 1 Of, pertaining to, or characteristic of a future or ideal world. 2 Concerned with the hereafter or with intellectual or imaginative interests. —**oth′er·world′li·ness** *n.*

-otic *suffix* 1 *Med.* Of, related to, or affected by: *psychotic.* 2 Causing or producing: *narcotic.* [<Gk. *-ōtikos*]

o·ti·ose (ō′shē·ōs, -tē-) *adj.* 1 Being at rest or ease; idle. 2 Futile or useless. [<L *otium* leisure] —**o′ti·ose·ly** *adv.* —**o′ti·os′i·ty** (-os′ə·tē) *n.*

o·ti·tis (ō·tī′tis) *n.* Inflammation of the ear. [<OT(O)- + -ITIS]

oto- *combining form* Ear; pertaining to the ear: *otology.* [<Gk. *ōtos* the ear]

o·tol·o·gy (ō·tol′ə·jē) *n.* The science of the ear and its disorders. —**o·to·log·i·cal** (ō′tə·loj′i·kəl) *adj.* —**o·tol′o·gist** *n.*

OTS, O.T.S. Officer Training School.

ot·ter (ot′ər) 1 A weasel-like, carnivorous, swimming mammal with webbed feet and a flattened, oarlike tail. 2 Its valuable, dark-brown fur. [<OE *oter*]

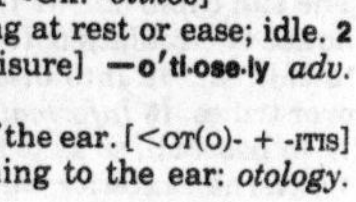

Otter

ot·to·man (ot′ə·mən) *n. pl.* **·mans** 1 An upholstered, often cushioned, backless and armless seat or sofa. 2 A cushioned footstool. [< OTTOMAN]

Ot·to·man (ot′ə·mən) *n. pl.* **·mans** A Turk. —*adj.* Of or pertaining to the Turks or Turkey; Turkish.

Ottoman Empire A former empire (1300–1919) of the Turks in Asia Minor, NE Africa, and SE Europe, cap. Constantinople.

ouch (ouch) *interj.* An exclamation indicating sudden pain.

ought[1] (ôt) *v.* An auxiliary verb used with an infinitive to express: 1 Obligation or moral duty: He *ought* to keep his promises. 2 Advisability or expedience: You *ought* to be careful. 3 Probability or expectation: He *ought* to be here tomorrow. [< OE *āhte,* p.t. of *āgan* owe, possess]

ought[2] (ôt) *n. & adv.* AUGHT.

oui (wē) *adv. French* Yes.

Oui·ja (wē′jə, -jē) *n.* A board inscribed with the alphabet and other characters, and a small, usu. triangular board resting on two casters and a pencil, which is thought to spell out spiritualistic or telepathic communications: a trade name. Also **oui′ja.**

ounce[1] (ouns) *n.* 1 **a** A unit of weight equal to .0625 pound avoirdupois. **b** A unit of weight equal to .0833 pound troy. 2 FLUID OUNCE. 3 A small quantity. [< L *uncia* twelfth part (of a pound or foot)]

ounce[2] (ouns) *n.* A large cat of CEN. Asia, having long, whitish fur with dark spots. [< OF *l'once,* var. of *lonce* the lynx]

our (our) *pronominal adj.* The possessive case of the pronoun *we,* employed attributively. [< OE *ūre*]

ours (ourz) *pron.* 1 The possessive case of *we* used predicatively: That dog is *ours.* 2 The things or persons belonging or pertaining to us: their country and *ours.* —**of ours** Belonging or relating to us; our.

our·self (our·self′) *pron.* Myself: only in formal or regal usage.

our·selves (our·selvz′) *pron. pl.* A form of the first person plural pronoun, used: 1 As a reflexive: We only hurt *ourselves.* 2 As an intensive: We *ourselves* will do it. 3 As the designation of a normal or usual state: We're not *ourselves* today.

-ous *suffix of adjectives* 1 Full of; having; characterized by: *glorious.* 2 *Chem.* Having a lower valence than that indicated by the suffix *-ic: nitrous.* [< L *-osus*]

ou·sel (o͞o′zəl) *n.* OUZEL.

oust (oust) *v.t.* To force from possession or occupancy; eject. [< L *ob-* against + *stare* stand] —**Syn** dispossess, evict, expel, turn out.

oust·er (ous′tər) *n.* 1 The act of putting one out of possession or occupancy; dispossession. 2 One who or that which ousts.

out (out) *adv.* 1 Away from the inside or center: to branch *out.* 2 Away from a specified or usual place: to set *out.* 3 From a source: to pour *out* wine. 4 So as to free of: to thresh *out* grain. 5 From among others: to pick *out* a dress. 6 Into the charge or care of others: to deal *out* cards. 7 So as to project or be extended: to stretch *out.* 8 Into extinction or inactivity: The flame went *out.* 9 To a result or conclusion: to find *out.* 10 Completely; fully: tired *out.* 11 Into existence or manifestation: An epidemic broke *out;* The sun came *out.* 12 Into blossom or leaf. 13 Into public notice or circulation: to bring *out* a new edition. 14 Aloud: to call *out.* 15 Into disagreement; at odds: to be put *out* over trifles. 16 *Informal* Into unconsciousness: to pass *out.* 17 In baseball, so as to be retired from active play. —*adj.* 1 External; exterior; outer. 2 Away from a place regarded as a base: *out* of school. 3 Away at a distance: *out* in the hills. 4 Exposed or bare: *out* at the knees. 5 Manifest; apparent: The stars are *out.* 6 In blossom or leaf. 7 Mistaken; in error. 8 Extinguished; exhausted: The fire is *out.* 9 Finished; at an end: before the week is *out.* 10 At a financial loss: to be *out* five dollars. 11 Not in effective operation. 12 *Informal* Unconscious. 13 In baseball, no longer in active play. 14 *Informal* No longer in fashion. 15 *Informal* Not to be considered; out of the question. —*prep.* From within; outside: *out* the door. —**out of** 1 From or beyond the inside of. 2 Beyond the limits, reach, scope, or proper position of: *out of* view. 3 Without: *out of* breath. 4 Influenced or caused by: *out of* respect. —*n.* 1 Something that is out. 2 An escape; a way to dodge involvement: He had an *out.* 3 *Often pl.* A person not in office or position of power. 4 In baseball, retirement of a batter or base runner. —**on the outs** At odds; in disagreement. —*v.t.* 1 To drive out; expel. —*v.i.* 2 To come or go out; be revealed. —*interj.* Go out! away! begone! [< OE *ūt*]

out- *combining form* 1 Living or situated outside; external; away from the center: *outlying, outpatient.* 2 Going forth: issuing; outward: *outbound, outstretch.* 3 Used to denote the time, place, or result of the action expressed by the root verb: *outcome, outcry.* 4 Excessive; surpassing; more; beyond: *outdo.*

out·age (out′ij) *n.* An interruption or suspension, as in the supply of electric current.

out-and-out (out′ənd·out′) *adj.* Thoroughgoing; blatant: an *out-and-out* lie.

out·back (out′back′) *n.* Rural country remote from settled areas, esp. in Australia.

out·bid (out·bid′) *v.t.* **·bid, ·bid·den** or **·bid, ·bid·ding** To bid more than.

out·board (out′bôrd′, -bōrd′) *adj.* Situated on the outside of a vessel, as a motor for temporary attachment to the stern of a small boat. —*adv.* Away from the center. —*n.* An outboard motor.

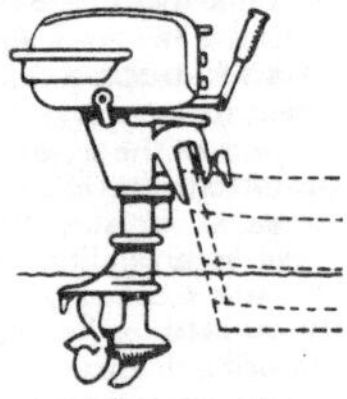

Outboard motor

out·bound (out′bound′) *adj.* Outward bound.

out·break (out′brāk′) *n.* 1 A sudden breaking forth, as of disease or violence. 2 An insurrection. —**Syn.** 1 eruption, outburst. 2 disturbance, uprising.

out·build·ing (out′bil′ding) *n.* A smaller building near a main building, as a woodshed.

out·burst (out′bûrst′) *n.* A bursting out; a violent manifestation, as of feeling.

out·cast (out′kast′, -käst′) *n.* One who is cast out from home or country. —*adj.* Rejected as unworthy or useless.

out·class (out·klas′, -kläs′) *v.t.* To exceed decisively in skill, quality, or powers.

out·come (out′kum′) *n.* A consequence or result.

out·crop (out′krop′) *n.* 1 The exposure of rock at or above the surface of the ground. 2 The rock so exposed. —*v.i.* **·cropped, ·crop·ping** 1 To crop up or out. 2 To appear above the ground, as rocks.

out·cry (out′krī′) *n. pl.* **·cries** 1 A loud cry, as of distress or alarm. 2 A strong protest by several or many sources.

out·dat·ed (out·dā′tid) *adj.* No longer fashionable or popular; old-fashioned. —**out·dat′ed·ness** *n.*

out·dis·tance (out·dis′təns) *v.t.* **·tanced, ·tanc·ing** 1 To outrun; outstrip. 2 To surpass completely; outdo.

out·do (out·do͞o′) *v.t.* **·did, ·done, ·do·ing** To exceed in performance; surpass.

out·door (out′dôr′, -dōr′) *adj.* Being or done in the open air; belonging or occurring outside the house: *outdoor* sports.

out·doors (out·dôrz′, -dōrz′) *adv.* Outside of the doors; out of the house; in the open air. —*n.* 1 The world beyond the house. 2 The open air.

out·door·sy (out′dôr′zē, -dōr′-) *adj.* **·si·er, ·si·est** *Informal* 1 Of or suitable for the outdoors. 2 Fond of engaging in outdoor activities.

out·er (ou′tər) *adj.* 1 Being on the exterior side; external. 2 Farther from a center or the inside.

Outer Mon·go·li·a (mong·gō′lē·ə, mon-) MONGOLIAN PEOPLE'S REPUBLIC.

out·er·most (ou′tər·mōst′) *adj.* Farthest out.

outer space Space beyond the earth's atmosphere.

out·face (out·fās′) *v.t.* **·faced, ·fac·ing** 1 To weaken the confidence of or overcome by or as by an exchange of looks. 2 To defy or confront fearlessly.

out·field (out′fēld′) *n.* In baseball, cricket, etc., the players who take their positions in the outer part of the field, or the field occupied by them. —**out′field′er** *n.*

out·fit (out′fit′) *n.* 1 A set of garments or equipment for a particular purpose, as for a camping trip. 2 A set of clothes worn together and regarded as harmonious. 3 A group of people engaged in a common undertaking: a military *outfit*. —*v.t.* & *v.i.* **-fit·ted, -fit·ting** To provide with or acquire an outfit. —**out′fit′ter** *n.*

out·flank (out·flangk′) *v.t.* 1 To get around and in back of the flank of (an opposing force or army); turn the flank of. 2 To outwit; circumvent.

out·flow (out′flō′) *n.* 1 That which flows out, or the process of flowing out. 2 An outlet.

out·fox (out·foks′) *v.t. Informal* To outwit.

out·gen·er·al (out·jen′ər·əl, -jen′rəl) *v.t.* **-aled** or **-alled, -al·ing** or **-al·ling** To surpass in generalship; outmaneuver.

out·go (out·gō′) *v.t.* **-went, -gone, -go·ing** To go farther than; exceed or outstrip. —*n.* (out′gō′) *pl.* **-goes** 1 That which goes out; esp., cost or expenditure. 2 A going out.

out·go·ing (out′gō′ing) *adj.* 1 Going out; leaving. 2 Retiring, as from an office: the *outgoing* chairman. 3 Friendly; sociable; approachable. —*n.* 1 The act of going out; departure. 2 That which goes out.

out·grow (out·grō′) *v.t.* **-grew, -grown, -grow·ing** 1 To surpass in growth. 2 To grow too large for. 3 To lose or get rid of in the course of time or growth: to *outgrow* a habit.

out·growth (out′grōth′) *n.* 1 That which grows out of something else; an excrescence. 2 A consequence or offshoot; development.

out·guess (out·ges′) *v.t.* To anticipate the actions of; outwit.

out·house (out′hous′) *n. pl.* **-hous·es** A small outbuilding containing a toilet, typically built over a deep pit and without plumbing.

out·ing (ou′ting) *n.* An excursion; short pleasure trip.

out·land (out′land′) *n.* Land lying beyond the limits of occupation or cultivation. —**out′land′er** *n.*

out·land·ish (out·lan′dish) *adj.* 1 Strange, as in appearance or behavior; bizarre; freakish. 2 Situated in an unfamiliar spot; remote. 3 *Archaic* Foreign. [<OE *ūtlandisc* of the outland] —**out·land′ish·ly** *adv.* —**out·land′ish·ness** *n.*

out·last (out·last′, -läst′) *v.t.* To last longer than.

out·law (out′lô′) *n.* 1 A person deprived of the benefit of the law, as for having committed a crime. 2 One who habitually breaks or defies the law. —*v.t.* 1 To declare an outlaw; proscribe. 2 To prohibit; ban. 3 To deprive of legal force or protection, as contracts or debts. [<ON *ūtlagi*] —**out′law·ry** *n.*

out·lay (out′lā′) *n.* 1 The act of laying out or disbursing, as money or effort. 2 That which is laid out; expenditure. —*v.t.* (out·lā′) **-laid, -lay·ing** To expend (money).

out·let (out′let, -lit) *n.* 1 A passage or vent for escape or discharge. 2 A means of expressing needs or desires: an *outlet* for aggression. 3 In trade or commerce, a retail or wholesale market. 4 A point in an electrical wiring system at which an appliance can be connected.

out·line (out′līn′) *n.* 1 A bordering line that defines a figure. 2 A sketch made of such lines without shading. 3 *Often pl.* A preliminary sketch showing the principal features of a thing; general plan. —*v.t.* **-lined, -lin·ing** 1 To draw the outline of; sketch. 2 To describe in general terms; give the main points of.

out·live (out·liv′) *v.t.* **-lived, -liv·ing** 1 To live longer than. 2 To survive.

out·look (out′lŏŏk′) *n.* 1 A view from a particular place. 2 A place having a view. 3 A predicted or probable course; prospect: the *outlook* for the nation's economy. 4 A mental view or position.

out·ly·ing (out′lī′ing) *adj.* Situated away from the main part or center.

out·man (out·man′) *v.t.* **-manned, -man·ning** To surpass in number of men.

out·mo·ded (out·mō′did) *adj.* Out of fashion; obsolete.

out·most (out′mōst′) *adj.* OUTERMOST.

out-of-bounds (out′əv·boundz′) *adv.* Outside the playing area of a ball field. —*adj.* 1 Being outside the proper bounds. 2 Beyond normal or proper limits, as of taste or behavior; uncalled-for.

out of commission Out of order; not working.

out-of-date (out′əv·dāt′) *adj.* Old-fashioned.

out-of-door (out′əv·dôr′, -dōr′) *adj.* OUTDOOR.

out-of-doors (out′əv·dôrz′, -dōrz′) *adv., n.* OUTDOORS.

out-of-the-way (out′əv·thə·wā′) *adj.* 1 Remotely situated; difficult to reach; secluded. 2 Different from what is common.

out·pa·tient (out′pā′shənt) *n.* A patient, not an inmate, treated at a hospital or dispensary.

out·place·ment (out′plās′mənt) *n.* The help in finding other work given to a terminated employee by the former employer.

out·play (out·plā′) *v.t.* To play better than.

out·point (out·point′) *v.t.* 1 To score more points than. 2 *Naut.* To sail closer to the wind than.

out·post (out′pōst′) *n.* 1 A detachment of troops stationed at a distance from the main body as a guard against surprise. 2 The station occupied by them. 3 A settlement in an outlying or frontier area.

out·pour (out·pôr′, -pōr′) *v.t.* & *v.i.* To pour out. —*n.* (out′pôr′, -pōr′) A free outflow; a pouring out. —**out′pour′er, out′pour′ing** *n.*

out·put (out′pŏŏt′) *n.* 1 The quantity put out or produced in a specified time; amount or rate of production. 2 a The useful energy delivered by a machine, system, etc. b The point at which this energy is available. 3 The information derived by a computer from processing a given input.

out·rage (out′rāj′) *n.* 1 An act of shocking violence, cruelty, immorality, or viciousness. 2 A gross insult. 3 Vehement anger or resentment. —*v.t.* **-raged, -rag·ing** 1 To commit outrage upon; wrong or abuse grossly; violate; offend. 2 To make violently angry. 3 To rape. [<OF *ultrage* <L *ultra* beyond]

out·ra·geous (out·rā′jəs) *adj.* 1 Of the nature of an outrage; atrocious. 2 Indifferent to or contemptuous of reasonable authority or decency; violating the limits of tolerable behavior; shocking. 3 Unrestrained; flagrant: an *outrageous* practical joker. —**out·ra′geous·ly** *adv.* —**out·ra′geous·ness** *n.*

ou·tré (ōō·trā′) *adj.* Deviating from conventional usage; strikingly odd or exaggerated. [F]

out·reach (out·rēch′) *v.t.* 1 To reach or go beyond; surpass. 2 To reach out; extend. —*v.i.* 3 To reach out. —*n.* (out′rēch′) 1 The act of reaching out. 2 The outermost extent.

out·ride (out·rīd′) *v.t.* **-rode, -rid·den, -rid·ing** To ride faster, farther, or better than.

out·rid·er (out′rī′dər) *n.* A mounted servant who rides in advance of or beside a carriage.

out·rig·ger (out′rig′ər) *n.* 1 A part built or arranged to project beyond a natural outline, as of a vessel or machine. 2 A projecting contrivance braced to the side of a canoe to prevent capsizing. 3 *Naut.* Any construction that extends beyond the rail of a ship, as a spar for extending a sail or rope, a boom, etc.

Outrigger canoe

out·right (out′rīt′) *adj.* 1 Free from reserve or restraint; downright. 2 Complete; entire. —*adv.* (out′rīt′) 1 Without reservation or limitation; utterly; openly. 2 Without delay; straightaway.

out·sell (out·sel′) *v.t.* **-sold, -sell·ing** 1 To sell more readily; surpass in selling. 2 To sell more goods than.

out·set (out′set′) *n.* A beginning; start; opening. —**Syn.** commencement, inception, origin, initiation.

out·shine (out·shīn′) *v.* **-shone, -shin·ing** *v.t.* 1 To shine brighter than. 2 To surpass, as in excellence. —*v.i.* 3 To shine forth.

out·side (out′sīd′) *n.* 1 The external part of a thing. 2 The part or side that is seen. 3 Superficial appearance. 4 The space beyond a bounding line or surface; outer region. —**at the outside** At the farthest, longest, or most, as in an estimate. —*adj.* 1 Pertaining to, located on, or restricted to the outside; exterior. 2 Originating or situated beyond designated limits; foreign. 3 Reaching the limit; extreme: an *outside* estimate. 4 Slight; inconsequential: an *outside* possibility. —*adv.* 1 On or to the outside; externally. 2 Beyond the outside limts of. 3 In the open air; outdoors. —*prep* (out′sīd′) 1 On or to the exterior of: *outside* the box. 2 Beyond the limit of: Don't tell it *outside* the club. 3 *Informal* Except: No one knows *outside* yourself. —**outside of** 1 *Informal* Except; besides. 2 OUTSIDE (prep.).

out·sid·er (out′sī′dər) *n.* 1 One who is outside; esp., one who is regarded as alien or unfamiliar by the members of a group. 2 A contestant, as in a race, considered to have only a slight chance.

out·size (out′sīz′) *n.* A size, as of clothing, that is larger than the regular sizes. —*adj.* Of unusual size: also **out′·sized′**.

out·skirt (out′skûrt′) *n. Usu. pl.* A place far from the center; an outlying area.

out·smart (out·smärt′) *v.t. Informal* To outwit; fool.

out·spo·ken (out·spō′kən) *adj.* 1 Bold or free of speech; frank. 2 Spoken boldly or frankly. —**out·spo′ken·ly** *adv.* —**out·spo′ken·ness** *n.*

out·spread (out·spred′) *v.t. & v.i.* **·spread, ·spread·ing** To spread out; extend.

out·stand·ing (out·stan′ding) *adj.* 1 Standing prominently forth; preeminent. 2 Standing out; conspicuous. 3 Unsettled; continuing. 4 Still standing, as an unpaid debt.

out·stretch (out·strech′) *v.t.* 1 To stretch out; expand; extend. 2 To extend beyond.

out·strip (out·strip′) *v.t.* **·stripped, ·strip·ping** 1 To leave behind; outrun, as in a race. 2 To excel; surpass.

out·take (out′tāk′) *n.* Something taken out, esp. film deleted in the editing process.

out·ward (out′wərd) *adj.* 1 Of or pertaining to the exterior of an object; outer; external. 2 Tending or directed to the outside. 3 Not inherent; extraneous; superficial. 4 Relating to the physical or bodily as distinguished from the mental. —*adv.* 1 To or in the direction of the outside; away from an inner place. 2 On the surface; superficially. 3 Away from port or home. Also **out′wards**. —**out′ward·ly** *adv.* —**out′ward·ness** *n.*

out·wear (out·wâr′) *v.t.* **·wore, ·worn, ·wear·ing** 1 To wear or stand use better than; outlast. 2 To wear out, as by constant use.

out·weigh (out·wā′) *v.t.* 1 To weigh more than. 2 To exceed in importance, value, etc.

out·wit (out·wit′) *v.t.* **·wit·ted, ·wit·ting** To defeat by superior ingenuity or cunning.

out·work[1] (out·wûrk′) *v.t.* **·worked** or **·wrought, ·work·ing** To work faster or better than; excel in working.

out·work[2] (out′wûrk′) *n. Mil.* Any minor defensive structure built or dug out beyond the main fortifications.

out·worn (out·wôrn′) *p.p.* of OUTWEAR. —*adj.* OUTMODED.

ou·zel (o͞o′zəl) *n.* 1 Any of a genus of European thrushes, as the **ring ouzel.** 2 Any of various related aquatic or diving birds, as the water ouzel. [< OE *ōsle*]

o·va (ō′və) *n.pl.* of OVUM.

o·val (ō′vəl) *adj.* 1 Having the shape of an egg. 2 Elliptical. —*n.* A figure or body of such form or outline. [< L *ovum* egg] —**o′val·ly** *adv.* —**o′val·ness** *n.*

o·va·ry (ō′və·rē) *n. pl.* **·ries** 1 *Biol.* The genital organ of female animals in which are produced the eggs and usu. certain sex hormones. 2 *Bot.* In flowering plants, the enlarged portion of the pistil in which the seed develops. [< L *ovum* an egg] —**o·var′i·al, o·var′i·an** *adj.*

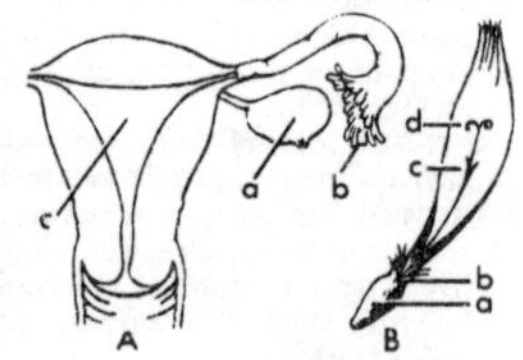

Ovaries
A. human genital tract. a. ovary. b. Fallopian tube. c. uterus. B. floret of dandelion. a. ovary. b. pappus. c. stamen. d. pistil.

o·vate (ō′vāt) *adj. Bot.* Oval: said of leaves. [< L *ovum* egg] —**o′vate·ly** *adv.* • See LEAF.

o·va·tion (ō·vā′shən) *n.* A spontaneous acclamation, as of applause, cheers, etc. [< L *ovare* rejoice, exult] —**o·va′tion·al** *adj.*

ov·en (uv′ən) *n.* An enclosed chamber in which substances are heated, cooked, dried, etc. [< OE *ofen*]

ov·en·bird (uv′ən·bûrd′) *n.* 1 Any of several South American birds having dome-shaped nests. 2 An American warbler that builds a domed nest on the ground.

o·ver (ō′vər) *prep.* 1 In or to a place or position above: the sky *over* our heads. 2 So as to pass or extend across: walking *over* the bridge. 3 On the other side of: lying *over* the ocean. 4 Upon the surface or exterior of: Oil was smeared *over* the axle. 5 Here and there upon or within; throughout all parts of: traveling *over* land and sea. 6 So as to rise above, cover, or submerge: The mud is now *over* my boots. 7 So as to close or cover: a cloth tied *over* the mouth of the jar. 8 During; through: a diary kept *over* the years. 9 Up to the end of and beyond: Stay with us *over* the holidays. 10 More than; in excess of, as in amount, degree, number, extent, etc.: *over* a million dollars in assets. 11 In preference to: chosen *over* all other contenders. 12 Above in rank, authority, power, etc.: They want a strong man *over* them. 13 Upon, as an effect: His influence *over* her is profound. 14 Concerning; with regard to: time wasted *over* trifles. 15 While engaged in or partaking of: a bargain made *over* a bottle of wine. 16 So as to be concerned about the well-being of: a dog watching *over* her puppies. —*adv.* 1 Above; overhead: A plane just flew *over.* 2 So as to close, cover, or be covered: The pond froze *over.* 3 Across an intervening space, brim, or edge: Come on *over* to this side of the room. 4 At or on the other side; at a distance in a specified direction or place: *over* in Europe. 5 From one side, opinion, etc. to another: to be won *over* to a point of view. 6 From one person, condition, or custody to another: to make property *over* to someone. 7 From beginning to end; all through; completely: I'll think the matter *over.* 8 From an upright position, esp. so as to invert, reverse, or transpose: to turn one's hand *over;* to topple *over.* 9 Again: He added his figures *over.* 10 So as to overflow: The cup ran *over.* 11 So as to constitute a surplus; in excess; beyond: enough to have some left *over.* 12 Beyond a stated time; until later: Plan to stay *over.* —**all over** 1 Everywhere. 2 Finished. —*adj.* 1 Finished; complete: The match is *over.* 2 On the other side; having got across: Is the boat *over* yet? 3 Outer, superior, upper, or excessive: usu. in combination: *overhastiness.* 4 In excess or addition; extra: We are three dollars *over.* —*n.* Something remaining or in addition. [< OE *ofer*]

over- *combining form* 1 Above; on top of; superior: *overlord.* 2 Passing above; going beyond the top or limit of: *overflow.* 3 Moving or causing to move downward, as from above: *overthrow.* 4 Excessive or excessively; too or too much. • Following is a list of compounds formed with *over-* in the sense of def. 4.

overabound
overabundance
overabundant
overaccentuate
overaccumulation
overachiever
overactive
overactivity
overadvantaged
overambitious
overanalyze
overanxiety
overanxious
overapplication
overapprehensive
overassertive
overassess
overassessment
overattentive
overbake
overbanked
overbitter
overblame
overboastful
overbold
overbooking
overbright
overbrilliant
overbrush
overbuilding
overburden
overburdensome
overbusy
overbuy
overcall
overcapacity
overcapitalize
overcaptious
overcareful
overcasual
overcaution
overcautious
overcautiously
overcentralization
overcentralize
overcharitable
overcheap
overcivil
overcivilized
overclever
overcold
overcommercial
overcommitment
overcompetitive
overcomplacency
overcomplacent
overcomplex
overcompliant
overcondense
overconfidence
overconfident
overconscientious
overconscious
overconsciousness
overconservatism
overconservative
overconsiderate
overconsume
overconsumption
overcontribute
overcontrol
overcook
overcorrect
overcorrupt
overcostly
overcount
overcourteous
overcredit
overcredulous
overcriticize
overcrop
overcrowd
overcrowded
overcultivate
overcultivation
overcured
overcurious
overcuriousness
overdainty
overdecorate
overdecorative
overdeliberate
overdeliberation
overdelicate
overdelicately
overdemand
overdemocratic
overdepress
overdepressive
overdesign
overdesirous
overdestructive
overdestructiveness
overdetermined
overdevoted
overdevotion
overdiffuse
overdignified

overdiligence
overdiligent
overdilute
overdirected
overdiscipline
overdistant
overdiversification
overdiversify
overdogmatic
overdominate
overdramatic
overdry
overdye
overeager
overearnest
overeasily
overeasy
overeat
overeducate
overelaborate
overelaboration
overelegant
overembellish
overemotional
overemphasis
overemphasize
overemphatic
overenthusiastic
overesteem
overestimate
overestimation
overexcitable
overexcite
overexcitement
overexercise
overexert
overexertion
overexpand
overexpansion
overexpectant
overexpenditure
overexplicit
overexpose
overextended
overexuberant
overfaithful
overfamiliar
overfanciful
overfast
overfastidious
overfastidiousness
overfat
overfatigue
overfatten
overfearful
overfed
overfeed
overfond
overfondness
overfrank
overfree
overfreedom
overfreely
overfrequency
overfrequent
overfull
overfullness
overfunctioning
overfunding
overfurnish
overfussy
overgenerous
overgenial
overgentle
overgracious
overgrasping
overgrateful
overgratify
overgraze
overgreediness
overgreedy
overgrieve
overhandle
overharden
overharsh
overhasty
overhaughty
overhelpful
overhot
overhotly
overidealistic
overillustrate
overimaginative
overimitate
overimitative
overimpress
overinclined
overindividualistic
overindulge
overindulgence
overindulgent
overindustrialization
overindustrialize
overinflate
overinflation
overinfluential
overink
overinsistent
overinsure
overintellectual
overintense
overinterest
overinventoried
overinvest
overirrigate
overirrigation
overissue
overjoyful
overjoyous
overjudicious
overlate
overlavish
overlax
overlaxness
overliberal
overliberality
overlighted
overlinger
overliteral
overliterary
overliveliness
overlively
overlofty
overlogical
overloud
overloyal
overluscious
overlustiness
overlusty
overluxuriant
overluxurious
overmagnify
overmanage
overmeasure
overmechanize
overmelt
overmerciful
overmerry
overmighty
overmild
overminutely
overmix
overmodest
overmoist
overmortgage
overmournful
overmultiply
overmystical
overnarrow
overneat
overneglect
overnegligence
overnegligent
overnervous
overnervousness
overnourish
overnumerous
overobedient
overoblige
overobvious
overoccupied
overoptimism
overoptimistic
overoptimistically
overorganized
overornamented
overpamper
overpartial
overpartiality
overparticular
overpassionate
overpatient
overpatriotic
overpay
overpensive
overpersonal
overpessimism
overpessimistic
overpessimistically
overplentiful
overplenty
overplotted
overplowed
overplump
overpolish
overpopular
overpopulate
overpopulation
overpopulous
overpositive
overpowerful
overpraise
overprecise
overpreciseness
overprecision
overpreoccupation
overprescribe
overpressure
overpretty
overprivileged
overprize
overproductive
overprogramed
overpromise
overproportion
overprotect
overproud
overprovide
overprovision
overpublicity
overpublicize
overpunctuate
overpunish
overpunishment
overqualified
overreadiness
overready
overrealistic
overrefinement
overreflection
overreflective
overregimented
overrelax
overreliant
overreligious
overrepresent
overrepresentation
overreserved
overresolute
overreward
overrighteous
overrighteousness
overrigid
overrigorous
overripe
overroast
overrough
oversalt
oversalty
oversanguine
oversaturate
oversaturation
overschematic
overscrupulous
overseason
overseasoned
oversecure
oversensitive
oversensitivity
oversentimental
overserious
oversevere
overseverely
overseverity
oversharp
overshort
overshorten
overshrink
oversilent
oversimple
oversimplicity
oversimplification
oversimplify
overskeptical
oversoak
oversoft
oversoftness
oversolemn
oversolicitous
oversophisticated
oversophistication
overspacious
overspecialization
overspecialize
overspecific
overspeculate
overspeculation
overspeculative
overspeed
overspeedily
overspend
overstaffed
oversteady
oversteer
overstimulate
overstimulation
overstrain
overstress
overstretch
overstrict
overstriving
overstudious
overstudiousness
oversubtle
oversubtlety
oversuperstitious
oversusceptible
oversuspicious
oversweet
oversystematic
oversystematize
overtalkative
overtalkativeness
overtechnical
overtender
overtenderness
overtense
overtension
overthick
overthin
overthoughtful
overthrifty
overtight
overtimid
overtimorous
overtire
overtrade
overtrain
overurbanization
overurge
overuse
overutilize
overvaluation
overvalue
overvehement
overventilate
overvoltage
overwary
overwealthy
overweary
overwet
overwilling
overwithholding
overzealous
overzealousness

o·ver·act (ō′vər·akt′) *v.t. & v.i.* To act in an exaggerated or flamboyant manner.

o·ver·age[1] (ō′vər·ij) *n.* A surplus or excess.

o·ver·age[2] (ō′vər·āj′) *adj.* 1 Past some specified age. 2 Too old to be of service: *overage* guns.

o·ver·all (ō′vər·ôl′) *adj.* 1 From one end to the other. 2 Including everything. —*adv.* Generally.

o·ver·alls (ō′vər·ôlz′) *n.pl.* Loose, coarse trousers, often with suspenders and a piece extending over the breast, worn over the clothing as protection from soiling.

o·ver·awe (ō′vər·ô′) *v.t.* **·awed, ·aw·ing** To subdue or restrain by awe.

o·ver·bal·ance (ō′vər·bal′əns) *v.* **·anced, ·anc·ing** *v.t.* 1 To exceed in weight, importance, etc. 2 To cause to lose balance. —*n.* Excess of weight or value.

o·ver·bear (ō′vər·bâr′) *v.* **·bore, ·borne, ·bear·ing** *v.t.* 1 To crush or bear down by physical weight or force. 2 To prevail over; dominate. —*v.i.* 3 To be too fruitful.

o·ver·bear·ing (ō′vər·bâr′ing) *adj.* 1 Arrogant; dictatorial. 2 Of greatest importance; dominant. 3 Overwhelming. —**o′ver·bear′ing·ly** *adv.* —**o′ver·bear′ing·ness** *n.* —**Syn.** 1 haughty, arbitrary, domineering, presumptuous, dogmatic, imperious.

o·ver·bid (ō′vər·bid′) *v.t. & v.i.* **·bid, ·bid·den** or **·bid, ·bid·ding** 1 To outbid (someone). 2 To bid more than the fair value of (something). —*n.* A bid that is excessive or higher than one previously made.

o·ver·blown (ō′vər·blōn′) *adj.* 1 Swollen or blown up. 2 Exaggerated. 3 Pretentious; flamboyant.

o·ver·board (ō′vər·bôrd, -bōrd′) *adv.* Over the side of or out of a boat or ship. —**go overboard** *Informal* To be extremely or excessively enthusiastic. —**throw overboard** To get rid of.

o·ver·cast (ō′vər·kast′, -käst′, ō′vər·kast′, -käst′) *v.t.* **·cast, ·cast·ing** 1 To overcloud; darken. 2 To sew, as the edge of a fabric, so as to prevent raveling. —*adj.* 1 Clouded; dark; gloomy. 2 Sewn with long wrapping stitches. —*n.* A covering, esp. of clouds over the sky.

o·ver·charge (ō′vər·chärj′) *v.t.* **·charged, ·charg·ing** 1 To charge (someone) too high a price. 2 To load or fill to excess; overburden. 3 To exaggerate. —*n.* An excessive charge.

o·ver·cloud (ō′vər·kloud′) *v.t.* 1 To cover with clouds. 2 To darken or make gloomy.

o·ver·coat (ō′vər·kōt′) *n.* A warm outdoor coat worn over a suit or other clothing.

o·ver·come (ō′vər·kum′) *v.t.* 1 To get the better of; defeat; conquer. 2 To prevail over or surmount, as difficulties, obstacles, etc. 3 To make helpless, as by emotion, sickness, etc. —*v.i.* 4 To win. [<OE *ofercuman*] —**o′ver·com′er** *n.*

o·ver·com·pen·sate (ō′vər·kom′pən·sāt) *v.* **·sat·ed, ·sat·ing** *v.i.* 1 *Psychol.* To engage in exaggerated or excessive forms of behavior or attitudes in order to compensate for the fact or feeling of inferiority. —*v.t.* 2 To make too great a compensation for. —**o′ver·com′pen·sa′tion** *n.* —**o′ver·com·pen′sa·to·ry** (-kəm·pen′sə·tôr′ē, -tō′rē) *adj.*

o·ver·de·vel·op (ō′vər·di·vel′əp) *v.t.* To develop excessively, esp. to subject (an exposed plate or film) to chemicals to too great a degree. —**o′ver·de·vel′op·ment** *n.*

o·ver·do (ō′vər·dōō′) *v.* **·did, ·done, ·do·ing** *v.t.* 1 To do excessively; carry too far. 2 To overtax; exhaust. 3 To cook too much, as meat. 4 To exaggerate. —*v.i.* 5 To do too much.

o·ver·dose (ō′vər·dōs′) *v.t.* **·dosed, ·dos·ing** To dose to excess. —*n.* (ō′vər·dōs′) An excessive dose.

o·ver·draft (ō′vər·draft′, -dräft′) *n.* 1 The act of overdrawing an account, as at a bank. 2 The amount by which a check or draft exceeds the sum against which it is drawn. Also **o′ver·draught′** (-draft′, -dräft′).

o·ver·draw (ō′vər·drô′) *v.t.* **·drew, ·drawn, ·draw·ing** 1 To draw against (an account) beyond one's credit. 2 To exaggerate.

o·ver·drive (ō′vər·drīv′) *n. Mech.* A gear which causes the driving shaft of a machine to turn at a speed greater than that of the engine.

o·ver·due (ō′vər·dyōō′) *adj.* 1 Remaining unpaid after becoming due. 2 Past due: an *overdue* plane or train.

o·ver·flight (ō′vər·flīt′) *n.* The flight of an aircraft over or beyond a place or area; esp., such a flight made for reconnaissance or espionage purposes.

o·ver·flow (ō′vər·flō′) *v.* **·flowed, ·flown, ·flow·ing** *v.i.* 1 To flow or run over the brim or bank, as water, rivers, etc. 2 To be filled beyond capacity; spill over. 3 To be extremely full. —*v.t.* 4 To flow over the brim or bank of. 5 To flow or spread over; cover. 6 To fill beyond capacity; cause to overflow. —*n.* (ō′vər·flō′) 1 The act of overflowing. 2 That which flows over; excess; surplus. 3 A passage or outlet for liquid. —**o′ver·flow′ing** *adj., n.* —**o′ver·flow′ing·ly** *adv.*

o·ver·grow (ō′vər·grō′) *v.* **·grew, ·grown, ·grow·ing** *v.t.* 1 To grow over; cover with growth. 2 To grow too big for; outgrow. —*v.i.* 3 To grow or increase excessively; grow too large. —**o′ver·grown′** *adj.*

o·ver·growth (ō′vər·grōth′) *n.* 1 Luxuriant or excessive growth. 2 A growth upon or over something.

o·ver·hand (ō′vər·hand′) *adj.* 1 Done with the hand above the level of the elbow or shoulder. 2 In sewing, done by carrying the thread over two edges to sew them together. 3 With the hand above the object which it holds, seizes, or throws. —*adv.* In an overhand manner. —*v.t.* To sew overhand. —*n.* An overhand stroke.

o·ver·hang (ō′vər·hang′) *v.* **·hung, ·hang·ing** *v.t.* 1 To hang or project over (something); jut over. 2 To impend over; threaten. —*v.i.* 3 To hang or jut over something. —*n.* Something that projects over another thing; also, the amount or degree of such projection.

o·ver·haul (ō′vər·hôl′) *v.t.* 1 To examine carefully, as for needed repairs; also, to make such repairs. 2 To catch up with; gain on. —*n.* (ō′vər·hôl′) A thorough inspection and repair. Also **o′ver·haul′ing.**

o·ver·head (ō′vər·hed′) *adj.* 1 Situated, working, or passing above or over the head. 2 Of or pertaining to the overhead of a business. —*n.* General expenditure applicable to all departments of a business, as light, heat, taxes, etc. —*adv.* (ō′vər·hed′) Above one's head; aloft.

o·ver·hear (ō′vər·hir′) *v.t.* **·heard, ·hear·ing** To hear (something said or someone speaking) without the knowledge or intention of the speaker. —**o′ver·hear′er** *n.*

o·ver·heat (ō′vər·hēt′) *v.t.* 1 To heat to excess. —*v.i.* 2 To become too hot.

o·ver·joy (ō′vər·joi′) *v.t.* To delight or please greatly.

o·ver·kill (ō′vər·kil′) *n.* 1 The capacity of a nation's nuclear weapons which is considered in excess of the number needed to demolish all key enemy targets. 2 *Informal* Any action regarded as excessive or extreme.

o·ver·land (ō′vər·land′) *adj.* Journeying or accomplished by or principally by land. —*adv.* Across, over, or via land.

o·ver·lap (ō′vər·lap′) *v.t. & v.i.* **·lapped, ·lap·ping** 1 To lie or extend partly over or upon (another or one another). 2 To extend in time over or into (another period of time, activity, etc.). —*n.* (ō′vər·lap′) The state, extent, or place of overlapping; also, the part that overlaps.

o·ver·lay (ō′vər·lā′) *n.* 1 Anything that overlies, covers, or partly covers something. 2 Something used to overlay something else, as ornamental work on wood. —*v.t.* (ō′vər·lā′) **·laid, ·lay·ing** 1 To cover, as with a decorative pattern or layer. 2 To lay or place over or upon something else.

o·ver·leap (ō′vər·lēp′) *v.t.* 1 To leap over or across. 2 To omit; overlook. 3 To leap farther than; outleap. —**overleap oneself** To miss one's purpose by going too far.

o·ver·lie (ō′vər·lī′) *v.t.* **·lay, ·lain, ·ly·ing** To lie over or upon.

o·ver·load (ō′vər·lōd′) *v.t.* To load excessively. —*n.* (ō′vər·lōd′) An excessive load.

o·ver·look (ō′vər·lŏŏk′) *v.t.* 1 To fail to see or notice; miss. 2 To disregard purposely or indulgently; ignore. 3 To look over or see from a higher place. 4 To afford a view of: The castle *overlooks* the harbor. 5 To supervise; oversee. —*n.* (ō′vər·lŏŏk′) 1 An elevated place from which one may view the surroundings; also, the view from such a place. 2 Oversight; neglect.

o·ver·lord (ō′vər·lôrd′) *n.* 1 A superior lord or chief. 2 One who holds supremacy over another. —**o′ver·lord′ship** *n.*

o·ver·ly (ō′vər·lē) *adv.* To an excessive degree; too much; too.

o·ver·man (ō′vər·man′) *v.t.* **·manned, ·man·ning** To provide with more men than necessary: The ship was *overmanned.*

o·ver·mas·ter (ō′vər·mas′tər, -mäs′-) *v.t.* To overcome; overpower. —**o′ver·mas′ter·ing** *adj.*

o·ver·match (ō′vər·mach′) *v.t.* To be more than a match for; surpass.

o·ver·much (ō′vər·much′) *adj.* Too much. —*adv.* In too great a degree. —*n.* An excess; too much.

o·ver·night (ō′vər·nīt′) *adj.* 1 Of, pertaining to, or caused by the previous evening: *overnight* euphoria that vanished at dawn. 2 Lasting or staying one night: an *overnight* flight; an *overnight* guest. 3 Used for a brief visit: an *overnight* bag. 4 Occurring or appearing quickly or suddenly: *overnight* fame. —*adv.* (ō′vər·nīt′) 1 During or through the night: to stay *overnight.* 2 On or during the previous evening: remembering a joke he'd heard *overnight.* 3 Quickly or suddenly: to achieve success *overnight.*

o·ver·pass (ō′vər·pas′, -päs′) *v.t.* 1 To pass across, over, or through; cross. 2 To surpass or exceed. 3 To overlook; disregard. 4 To transgress. —*n.* (ō′vər·pas′, -päs′) An elevated section of highway or a pedestrian bridge crossing other lines of travel.

o·ver·play (ō′vər·plā′) *v.t.* To play or act (a part or role) to excess; overdo; exaggerate. —**overplay one's hand** To exaggerate one's value, importance, strength, etc., and suffer a defeat as a result.

o·ver·pow·er (ō′vər·pou′ər) *v.t.* 1 To gain supremacy over; subdue; overcome. 2 To supply with more power than necessary. —**o′ver·pow′er·ing** *adj.* —**o′ver·pow′er·ing·ly** *adv.*

o·ver·print (ō′vər·print′) *v.t.* To print additional material on (matter already printed). —*n.* (ō′vər·print′) Anything printed over another impression, as a word, symbol, etc., printed on a stamp.

o·ver·pro·duce (ō′vər·prə·dyōōs′) *v.t.* **·duced, ·duc·ing** To produce too much of or so as to exceed demand.

o·ver·pro·duc·tion (ō′vər·prə·duk′shən) *n.* Production in excess of demand, or of the possibility of profitable sale.

o·ver·rate (ō′vər·rāt′) *v.t.* **·rat·ed, ·rat·ing** To rate or value too highly.

o·ver·reach (ō′vər·rēch′) *v.t.* 1 To reach over or beyond. 2 To spread over; cover. 3 To defeat (oneself), as by trying too hard or being too clever. 4 To get the advantage of, as by cheating; outwit. —*v.i.* 5 To reach too far. —**o′ver·reach′·er** *n.*

o·ver·re·act (ō′vər·rē·akt′) *v.i.* To react to a person, situation, etc., in an excessively emotional or uncontrolled manner. —**o′ver·re·ac′tion** *n.*

o·ver·ride (ō′vər·rīd′) *v.t.* **·rode, ·rid·den, ·rid·ing** 1 To ride over or across. 2 To trample down. 3 To prevail over;

conquer; dominate. 4 To disregard summarily; overrule. 5 To ride (a horse) to exhaustion.

o·ver·rid·ing (ō′vər·rī′ding, ō′vər·rī′-) *adj.* Chief; primary; principal: an *overriding* concern.

o·ver·rule (ō′vər·ro͞ol′) *v.t.* **·ruled, ·rul·ing** 1 To decide or rule against; nullify by superior authority; set aside; invalidate. 2 To prevail over.

o·ver·run (ō′vər·run′) *v.* **·ran, ·run, ·run·ning** *v.t.* 1 To spread or swarm over, esp. harmfully, as vermin or invaders do. 2 To run or flow over so as to cover. 3 To spread rapidly across or throughout: said of fads, ideas, etc. 4 To run or extend beyond; pass the limit of. —*v.i.* 5 To run over; overflow. 6 To pass the usual or desired limit. —*n.* (ō′vər·run′) 1 The act or an instance of overrunning. 2 The amount or extent of overrunning.

o·ver·seas (ō′vər·sēz′) *adv.* Beyond the sea; abroad. —*adj.* Of, with, for, from, or to countries beyond or across the sea: an *overseas* phone call; *overseas* commerce; *overseas* friends.

o·ver·see (ō′vər·sē′) *v.t.* **·saw, ·seen, ·see·ing** 1 To direct or supervise. 2 To survey; watch.

o·ver·se·er (ō′vər·sē′ər) *n.* A person who oversees; esp. one who directs the work of others.

o·ver·sell (ō′vər·sel′) *v.t.* **·sold, ·sell·ing** 1 To sell more than one can deliver. 2 To make exaggerated claims for (a person or thing). 3 To persuade by exaggerated claims.

o·ver·set (ō′vər·set′) *v.* **·set, ·set·ting** *v.t.* 1 To upset mentally or physically. 2 To cause to overturn. —*v.i.* 3 To overturn. —*n.* (ō′vər·set′) A turning over; upset.

o·ver·shad·ow (ō′vər·shad′ō) *v.t.* 1 To render unimportant or insignificant by comparison; loom above; dominate. 2 To throw a shadow over; dim; obscure. —**Syn.** 1 prevail over, master, domineer, control.

o·ver·shoe (ō′vər·sho͞o′) *n.* A shoe, as of rubber, worn for protection over another.

o·ver·shoot (ō′vər·sho͞ot′) *v.* **·shot, ·shoot·ing** *v.t.* 1 To shoot, pass, fly, etc. over or beyond. 2 To go beyond; exceed, as a limit. —*v.i.* 3 To shoot or go too far or beyond a mark.

o·ver·shot (ō′vər·shot′) *adj.* 1 Projecting, as the upper jaw beyond the lower jaw. 2 Driven by water flowing over from above: an *overshot* wheel.

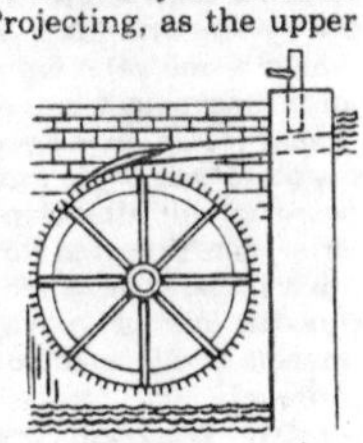

Overshot wheel

o·ver·sight (ō′vər·sīt′) *n.* 1 An error due to inattention; an inadvertent mistake or omission. 2 Watchful supervision.

o·ver·size (ō′vər·sīz′) *adj.* Too large or larger than regular. —*n.* A size that is larger than regular sizes. —**o′ver·sized′** *adj.*

o·ver·skirt (ō′vər·skûrt′) *n.* A skirt worn over another skirt.

o·ver·sleep (ō′vər·slēp′) *v.i.* **·slept, ·sleep·ing** To sleep beyond an intended time for waking.

o·ver·spread (ō′vər·spred′) *v.t.* **·spread, ·spread·ing** To spread or extend over.

o·ver·state (ō′vər·stāt′) *v.t.* **·stat·ed, ·stat·ing** To state in too strong terms; exaggerate. —**o′ver·state′ment** *n.*

o·ver·stay (ō′vər·stā′) *v.t.* To stay beyond the proper limits or duration of.

o·ver·step (ō′vər·step′) *v.t.* **·stepped, ·step·ping** To step over or go beyond; exceed (some limit or restriction).

o·ver·stock (ō′vər·stok′) *v.t.* To stock more than is required or can be handled. —*n.* (ō′vər·stok′) An excessive stock.

o·ver·strung (ō′vər·strung′) *adj.* Too sensitive or highly strung.

o·ver·stuff (ō′vər·stuf′) *v.t.* 1 To stuff excessively. 2 To cover, as a chair or sofa, with deeply stuffed upholstery.

o·ver·sub·scribe (ō′vər·səb·skrīb′) *v.t.* **·scribed, ·scrib·ing** To subscribe for more of than is offered or available.

o·ver·sup·ply (ō′vər·sə·plī′) *n. pl.* **·plies** An excessive supply. —*v.t.* (ō′vər·sə·plī′) **·plied, ·ply·ing** To supply in excess.

o·vert (ō′vûrt, ō·vûrt′) *adj.* Open to view; outwardly manifest. [<OF, pp. of *ovrir* to open] —**o·vert′ly** *adv.* —**Syn.** apparent, evident, obvious, clear, patent.

o·ver·take (ō′vər·tāk′) *v.t.* **·took, ·tak·en, ·tak·ing** 1 To catch up with. 2 To catch up with and go past; leave behind. 3 To come upon suddenly.

o·ver·tax (ō′vər·tax′) *v.t.* 1 To tax too much. 2 To put too heavy a strain on. —**o′ver·tax·a′tion** (-tak·sā′shən) *n.*

o·ver-the-count·er (ō′vər·t͟hə·koun′tər) *adj.* 1 Not sold on the floor of a stock exchange: said of certain stocks and bonds. 2 Sold lawfully without a prescription, as drugs.

o·ver·throw (ō′vər·thrō′) *v.t.* **·threw, ·thrown, ·throw·ing** 1 To throw over or down; upset. 2 To bring down or remove from power by force; defeat; ruin. —*n.* (ō′vər·thrō′) 1 The act of overthrowing. 2 The condition of being overthrown.

o·ver·time (ō′vər·tīm′) *v.t.* **·timed, ·tim·ing** *Phot.* To expose too long, as a plate or film. —*n.* (ō′vər·tīm′) 1 Time spent beyond some specified limit. 2 Wages paid for work done during such time. —*adj.* Of, during, or for extra working time: *overtime* pay. —*adv.* Beyond the stipulated time.

o·ver·tone (ō′vər·tōn′) *n.* 1 *Music* A higher tone heard with and above the fundamental tone produced by a musical instrument or the human voice. 2 The color of the light reflected, as by a painted surface. 3 An association, connotation, implication, etc., as of language, thoughts, etc.

o·ver·top (ō′vər·top′) *v.t.* **·topped, ·top·ping** 1 To rise above the top of; tower over. 2 To surpass; excel.

o·ver·ture (ō′vər·chər) *n.* 1 *Music* An instrumental prelude, as to an opera or other large work. 2 An introductory proposal or offer; approach. [<L *apertura* an opening]

o·ver·turn (ō′vər·tûrn′) *v.t.* 1 To turn or throw over; capsize; upset. 2 To destroy the power of; overthrow; defeat. —*v.i.* 3 To turn over; capsize; upset. —*n.* (ō′vər·tûrn′) The act of overturning or the state of being overturned.

o·ver·view (ō′vər·vyo͞o′) *n.* A broad survey or review of a subject, field of activity, etc.

o·ver·ween·ing (ō′vər·wē′ning) *adj.* Presumptuous; arrogant. [<OE *ofer* over + *wēnan* think] —**o′ver·ween′ing·ly** *adv.* —**o′ver·ween′ing·ness** *n.* —**Syn.** haughty, overbearing, patronizing, pompous.

o·ver·weigh (ō′vər·wā′) *v.t.* 1 To outweigh. 2 To oppress; burden.

o·ver·weight (ō′vər·wāt′) *n.* 1 Excess of weight, as beyond the legal or customary amount. 2 More than normal weight; too much or burdensome weight. —*adj.* Being more than the normal or permitted weight. —*v.t.* (ō′vər·wāt′) To weigh down; burden.

o·ver·whelm (ō′vər·hwelm′) *v.t.* 1 To bury or submerge completely, as with a wave or flood. 2 To overcome or defeat by or as by irresistible force or numbers; crush. —**o′ver·whelm′ing** *adj.* —**o′ver·whelm′ing·ly** *adv.*

o·ver·work (ō′vər·wûrk′) *v.t.* **·worked** or **·wrought, ·work·ing** 1 To cause to work too hard. 2 To work on or use excessively: to *overwork* an argument. —*v.i.* 3 To work too hard or too long. —*n.* (ō′vər·wûrk′) Excessive work.

o·ver·write (ō′vər·rīt′) *v.t.* & *v.i.* **·wrote, ·writ·ten, ·writ·ing** 1 To write over (other writing). 2 To write too much or in too elaborate or labored a style about (a subject).

o·ver·wrought (ō′vər·rôt′) *adj.* 1 Worked up or excited excessively; strained. 2 Having the surface adorned. 3 Too elaborate; overdone.

ovi- *combining form* Egg; of or pertaining to eggs: *oviparous.* [<L *ovum* an egg]

o·vi·duct (ō′vi·dukt) *n.* The passage through which ova are conveyed from an ovary.

o·vi·form (ō′vi·fôrm) *adj.* Egg-shaped.

o·vip·a·rous (ō·vip′ər·əs) *adj.* Reproducing by means of eggs that are hatched outside the body. [<ovi- + L *parere* give birth to] —**o·vip′a·rous·ly** *adv.* —**o·vip′a·rous·ness** *n.*

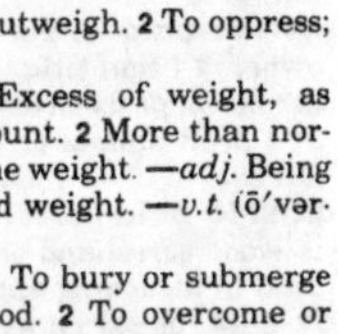

Ovipositor of ichneumon fly

o·vi·pos·i·tor (ō′vi·poz′ə·tər) *n.* A special organ in certain female insects, by which the eggs are deposited.

o·void (ō′void) *adj.* Egg-shaped: also **o·voi′dal.** —*n.* An egg-shaped body.

o·vu·late (ov′yə·lāt, ōv′-) *v.i.* **·lat·**

ed, ·lat·ing To produce and discharge ova from an ovary. —**o′vu·la′tion** *n.*

o·vule (ov′yo͞ol, ōv′-) *n.* **1** *Bot.* The rudimentary body within the ovary which, upon fertilization, becomes the seed. **2** A small egg. [< L *ovum* an egg] —**o′vu·lar, o·vu·lar·y** (ō′vyə·ler′ē) *adj.*

o·vum (ō′vəm) *n. pl.* **o·va** (ō′və) *Biol.* **1** A female reproductive cell; an egg. **2** OVULE. [L]

owe (ō) *v.* **owed, ow·ing** *v.t.* **1** To be indebted to (a person). **2** To be obligated to pay or repay the sum of. **3** To be obligated to render or offer: to *owe* an apology. **4** To have or possess by virtue of gift, labor, etc.: with *to:* He *owes* his success to his own efforts. **5** To cherish (a certain feeling) toward another: to *owe* a grudge. —*v.i.* **6** To be in debt. [< OE *āgan*]

OWI, O.W.I. Office of War Information.

ow·ing (ō′ing) *adj.* Due; yet to be paid: six dollars *owing.* —**owing to** On account of; because of.

owl (oul) *n.* **1** Any of a large order of predatory nocturnal birds having large forward-looking eyes, a short, sharply hooked bill, long powerful claws, and a circular facial disk of radiating feathers. **2** A person having a solemn, thoughtful appearance, nocturnal habits, etc. [< OE *ūle*] —**owl′ish** *adj.* —**owl′ish·ly** *adv.* —**owl′ish·ness** *n.*

owl·et (ou′lit) *n.* **1** A small owl. **2** A young owl.

own (ōn) *adj.* Belonging or relating to oneself or itself: my *own* idea; under its *own* momentum. —*n.* That which belongs to oneself or itself: The success was her *own.* —**come into one's own 1** To obtain possession of one's property. **2** To receive one's reward, as recognition or praise. —**hold one's own** To maintain one's place, position, condition, etc. —**on one's own** Entirely dependent on one's self for support or success. —*v.t.* **1** To have or hold as one's own; possess. **2** To admit or acknowledge. —*v.i.* **3** To confess: with *to.* —**own up (to)** To confess (to). [< OE *āgen,* orig. pp. of *āgan* owe, possess] —**own′a·ble** *adj.* —**own′er** *n.*

own·er·ship (ō′nər·ship) *n.* **1** The state of being an owner. **2** Legal title to something.

ox (oks) *n. pl.* **ox·en** (ok′sən) **1** An adult castrated bull, used as a draft animal or for food. **2** Any bovine mammal. [< OE *oxa*]

ox·al·ic acid (ok·sal′ik) A poisonous organic acid found in wood sorrel and other plants and made synthetically, used in bleaching and dyeing.

ox·a·lis (ok·sal′is) *n.* WOOD SORREL. [< Gk. < *oxys* sharp, acid]

ox·blood (oks′blud′) *n.* A deep red color.

ox·bow (oks′bō′) *n.* **1** A U-shaped piece of wood in an ox yoke, that forms a collar for the ox. **2** A bend in a river shaped like this.

ox·eye (oks′ī′) *n.* **1** Any of various plants having composite flowers with yellow rays and a dark center. **2** The common N. American daisy: also **oxeye daisy.**

ox-eyed (oks′īd′) *adj.* Having large, calm eyes like an ox.

ox·ford (oks′fərd) *n.* **1** A kind of low-cut shoe laced over the instep: also **oxford shoe. 2** A cloth made in a basketlike weave, used for men's shirts, etc.: also **oxford cloth.** [< *Oxford,* England]

oxford gray A very dark gray.

ox·heart (oks′härt′) *n.* A variety of sweet cherry.

ox·i·da·tion (ok′sə·dā′shən) *n. Chem.* **1** The union of a substance with oxygen. **2** The process by which atoms, ions, or radicals lose electrons and gain in positive electric charge. —**ox′i·da′tive** *adj.*

ox·ide (ok′sīd) *n.* Any binary compound of oxygen either with an element or with an organic radical. [< F *ox(ygène)* oxygen + *(ac)ide* acid]

ox·i·dize (ok′sə·dīz) *v.* **·dized, ·diz·ing** *v.t.* **1** To cause the oxidation of. —*v.i.* **2** To undergo oxidation. *Brit. sp.* **·dise.** —**ox′i·diz′a·ble** *adj.* —**ox′i·diz′er** *n.*

ox·lip (oks′lip′) *n.* A species of primrose having yellow flowers. [< OE *oxanslippe,* lit., ox dung]

Oxon. of Oxford (Univ.) (L *Oxoniensis*)

Ox·o·ni·an (ok·sō′nē·ən) *adj.* Of or pertaining to Oxford, England, or to its university. —*n.* **1** A student or graduate of Oxford University. **2** A native or inhabitant of Oxford, England.

ox·tail (oks′tāl′) *n.* The tail of an ox, esp. when skinned for use in soup.

oxy-[1] *combining form* **1** Sharp; keen: *oxymoron.* **2** Acid: *oxygen.* [< Gk. *oxys* sharp, keen]

oxy-[2] *combining form Chem.* Of or containing oxygen: *oxyacetylene.* [< OXYGEN]

ox·y·a·cet·y·lene (ok′sē·ə·set′ə·lēn) *adj.* Designating or pertaining to a mixture of acetylene and oxygen, used as a high-temperature fuel in welding torches.

ox·y·gen (ok′sə·jin) *n.* A highly reactive element (symbol O) essential to life, occurring as an odorless gas in the atmosphere and in chemical combination in water and rocks, and comprising about 50 percent of the material in and above the earth's crust. [< OXY-[1] + -gen]

ox·y·gen·ate (ok′sə·jən·āt′) *v.t.* **·at·ed, ·at·ing** To treat, combine, or mix with oxygen. —**ox′y·gen·a′tion** *n.*

ox·y·gen·ize (ok′sə·jən·īz′) *v.t.* **·ized, ·iz·ing 1** OXIDIZE. **2** OXYGENATE.

oxygen mask A device worn over the nose and mouth to deliver oxygen from a container when atmospheric oxygen is inadequate or absent.

oxygen tent A tentlike chamber placed over a patient's bed and supplied with oxygen as an aid to breathing.

ox·y·hy·dro·gen (ok′si·hī′drə·jən) *adj.* Of, pertaining to, or using a mixture of oxygen and hydrogen, esp. to produce high temperatures.

ox·y·mo·ron (ok′si·môr′on, -mō′ron) *n. pl.* **·mo·ra** (-môr′ə, -mō′rə) A figure of speech in which contradictory or incongruous terms are brought together, as in "solemn jests." [< Gk. *oxys* keen + *mōros* foolish]

o·yez (ō′yez, ō′yā) *interj.* Hear! hear ye! an introductory word to call attention to a proclamation, as by a court crier: usu. repeated three times. Also **o′yes** (ō′yes). [< OF *oyez,* imperative of *oir* hear]

oys·ter (ois′tər) *n.* Any of a family of irregularly shaped marine bivalves, including various edible species. [< Gk. *ostreon*]

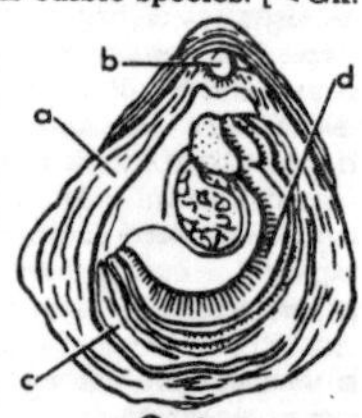

Oyster
a. shell. b. hinge. c. mantle. d. gills.

oyster bed An area on the ocean floor where oysters are cultivated.

oyster crab Any of various minute crabs that live in the gill cavities of oysters, clams, etc.

oyster plant SALSIFY.

oz. (*pl.* **ozs.**) ounce.

o·zone (ō′zōn) *n.* **1** An acrid, unstable, allotropic form of oxygen having three atoms per molecule, formed by electric discharge in air and by high-energy solar radiation in the upper atmosphere. **2** *Informal* Air that is pure and refreshing. [< Gk. *ozein* to smell] —**o·zon·ic** (ō·zon′ik, ō·zō′nik), **o·zo·nous** (ō′zə·nəs) *adj.*

P

P, p (pē) *n. pl.* **P's, p's** or **Ps, ps** (pēz) **1** The 16th letter of the English alphabet. **2** Any spoken sound representing the letter *P* or *p*. **3** Something shaped like a P. —*adj.* Shaped like a P.

P pawn (chess); phosphorus.

P. president.

p. page; part; participle; past; penny; pint; pitcher; softly (Ital. *piano*).

pa (pä) *n. Informal* Papa.

PA Pennsylvania (P.O. abbr.); public address (system).

P.A., P/A power of attorney.

Pa protactinium.

Pa. Pennsylvania.

p.a. participial adjective; per annum.

pab·u·lum (pab′yə·ləm) *n.* Food. [< L *pabulum* fodder]

Pac. Pacific.

pace[1] (pās) *n.* **1** A step in walking. **2** A conventional measure of length approximating the average length of stride in walking, usu. estimated at from 30 to 40 inches. **3** The manner of movement in going on the legs; gait, esp. of a horse. **4** Rate of speed in moving on the legs: a fast *pace.* **5** Rate of movement or work, or of any process or activity. **6** A gait of a horse, etc. in which both feet on the same side are lifted and moved forward at once. —*v.* **paced, pac·ing** *v.t.* **1** To walk back and forth across. **2** To measure by paces. **3** To set or make the pace for. **4** To train to a certain gait or pace. —*v.i.* **5** To walk with slow or regular steps. **6** To move at a pace. [< L *passus* step] —**pac′er** *n.*

pa·ce[2] (pā′sē) *prep.* With the permission of: used to express courteous disagreement. [L, ablative of *pax, pacis* peace, pardon]

pace·mak·er (pās′mā′kər) *n.* **1** One who makes or sets the pace for another in a race. **2** A node of muscle fibers in the heart that regulates the heartbeat. **3** Any of various devices, usu. electronic, used to regulate the heartbeat. —**pace′mak′ing** *adj., n.*

pach·y·derm (pak′ə·dûrm) *n.* Any of certain thick-skinned, hoofed mammals, as an elephant, hippopotamus, or rhinoceros. [< Gk. *pachys* thick + *derma* skin] —**pach′·y·der′ma·tous, pach′y·der′mous** *adj.*

pa·cif·ic (pə·sif′ik) *adj.* **1** Pertaining to the making of peace; leading to peace. **2** Peaceable; calm. [< L < *pax, pacis* peace + *facere* make] —**pa·cif′i·cal·ly** *adv.*

Pa·cif·ic (pə·sif′ik) *adj.* **1** Of, near, in, on, or pertaining to the Pacific Ocean. **2** Of, near, on, or pertaining to the w coast of the U.S. —*n.* The Pacific Ocean.

pac·i·fi·ca·tion (pas′ə·fə·kā′shən) *n.* The act of pacifying, or the state of being pacified. —**pa·cif′i·ca′tor** *n.* —**pa·cif′i·ca·to′ry** (-kə·tôr′ē, -tō′rē) *adj.*

Pacific Standard Time See STANDARD TIME.

pac·i·fi·er (pas′ə·fi′ər) *n.* **1** One who or that which pacifies; a peacemaker. **2** A rubber nipple or ring for a baby to suck.

pac·i·fism (pas′ə·fiz′əm) *n.* Opposition to violence, esp. war, for any purpose, often accompanied by the refusal to bear arms by reason of conscience or religious conviction. —**pac′i·fist** *adj., n.* —**pac′i·fis′tic** *adj.*

pac·i·fy (pas′ə·fī) *v.t.* **·fied, ·fy·ing** **1** To bring peace to; end war or strife in. **2** To allay the anger or agitation of. [< L *pax, pacis* peace + *facere* make] —**Syn. 2** appease, calm, allay, tranquilize.

pack[1] (pak) *n.* **1** A bundle or large package, esp. one to be carried on the back of a man or animal. **2** A full set of like or associated things handled or considered as a unit: a *pack* of cards; a *pack* of lies. **3** A group of animals, as dogs or wolves. **4** Any gang or band. **5** A large area of floating broken ice: also **ice pack. 6** A cosmetic paste spread on the skin and allowed to dry. **7** A wrapping about a patient: a wet or cold *pack.* —*v.t.* **1** To make a pack or bundle of. **2** To place compactly in a trunk, box, etc. **3** To fill compactly, as for storing or carrying. **4** To compress tightly; crowd together. **5** To fill to overflowing; cram. **6** To cover, fill, or surround so as to prevent leakage, damage, etc. **7** To load with a pack; burden. **8** To carry or transport, as on pack animals. **9** To carry habitually: to *pack* a gun. **10** To send or dispatch summarily: with *off* or *away.* **11** To treat (a patient) with a pack. **12** *Slang* To be able to inflict: He *packs* a wallop. —*v.i.* **13** To place one's clothing and belongings in trunks, boxes, etc., for storing or carrying. **14** To crowd together. **15** To settle in a hard, firm mass. **16** To leave in haste: often with *off* or *away.* —**send packing** To send away or dismiss abruptly. [ME *pakke*] —**pack′er** *n.*

pack[2] (pak) *v.t.* To arrange, select, or manipulate to one's own advantage: to *pack* a jury.

pack·age (pak′ij) *n.* **1** Something wrapped up or bound together; a parcel. **2** A receptacle in which something is contained or packed. **3** A combination of items considered as a unit: a salary increase and fringe benefits all in one *package.* —*v.t.* **·aged, ·ag·ing** **1** To bind or make into a package or bundle. **2** To offer as a package. —**pack′ag·er** *n.*

package store *U.S.* A store that sells liquor by the bottle only, for consumption elsewhere.

pack animal An animal, as a horse or mule, used to carry packs or burdens.

pack·et (pak′it) *n.* **1** A small package; parcel. **2** A boat carrying passengers, freight, and mail, esp. along a coast: also **packet boat.**

pack·ing (pak′ing) *n.* **1** The act or process of packing. **2** The canning or putting up of meat, fish, fruit, etc., for market. **3** Material used to protect or insulate something.

packing plant *U.S.* A factory where meats and meat products are processed and packed; also, a similar establishment where other foodstuffs are processed and packed. Also **packing house.**

pack rat **1** Any of various North American rats that collect and store small objects in their nests. **2** *Slang* A person addicted to collecting and saving various, often useless, objects.

pack·sack (pak′sak′) *n.* A canvas or leather sack strapped across the shoulders for those traveling on foot.

pack·sad·dle (pak′sad′l) *n.* A saddle for a pack animal, to which the packs are fastened so as to balance evenly.

pack·thread (pak′thred′) *n.* Strong thread or twine used for binding packages.

pact (pakt) *n.* An agreement, esp. between nations; compact. [< L *pactum* agreement]

pad[1] (pad) *n.* **1** Anything stuffed and soft enough to protect from jarring, friction, etc.; cushion. **2** A launching pad. **3** A soft saddle. **4** A number of sheets of paper gummed together at the edge. **5** A floating leaf of an aquatic plant: a lily *pad.* **6 a** A soft cushion of flesh under the toes of an animal. **b** An animal's footprint. **7** *Slang* A room or apartment; lodgings. —*v.t.* **pad·ded, pad·ding** **1** To stuff, line, or protect with pads or padding. **2** To lengthen (speech or writing) by inserting unnecessary matter. **3** To expand (an expense account) by recording nonexistent expenditures.

pad[2] (pad) *v.i.* **pad·ded, pad·ding** **1** To travel by walking; tramp. **2** To move with soft, almost noiseless footsteps. —*n.* A dull, padded sound.

pad[3] (pad) *n.* An easy-paced road horse. Also **pad horse.** [< LG *pad* path]

pad·ding (pad′ing) *n.* **1** The act of stuffing or forming a pad. **2** Any material used to make a pad. **3** Matter used in writing to fill space.

pad·dle (pad′l) *n.* **1** An implement resembling a short oar with a broad blade at one or both ends, used to propel a canoe or small boat. **2** A similarly shaped implement for inflicting bodily punishment. —*v.* **-dled, -dling** *v.i.* **1** To move a canoe, etc., on or through water by means of a paddle. **2** To row gently or lightly. **3** To swim with short, downward strokes. —*v.t.* **4** To propel by means of a paddle or paddles. **5** To beat with a paddle. [ME *padell* small spade] **—pad′dler** *n.*

pad·dle·ball (pad′l·bôl′) *n.* A game resembling squash in which paddles are used to hit a ball in a walled court.

pad·dle·fish (pad′l·fish′) *n. pl.* **-fish** or **-fish·es** A large fish of the sturgeon family, having a flattened snout.

paddle wheel A wheel having projecting boards for propelling a boat.

pad·dock (pad′ək) *n.* **1** A pasture lot or enclosure for exercising horses. **2** A grassed enclosure at a race-course where horses are walked about and saddled before a race. —*v.t.* To confine, as horses, in a paddock. [< OE *pearruc* enclosure]

Paddle wheel on a steamboat

pad·dy (pad′ē) *n. pl.* **-dies** **1** Rice in the husk, whether gathered or growing. **2** A field in which rice is grown: also **rice paddy.** [< Malay *pādī*]

paddy wagon *Slang* PATROL WAGON. [< *Paddy,* a nickname for Patrick]

pad·lock (pad′lok′) *n.* A detachable lock with a shackle hinged at one end, and devised so as to pass through a staple or chain and lock at the other end. —*v.t.* To fasten with or as with a padlock. [ME *padlocke*]

pa·dre (pä′drā) *n.* **1** Father: a title used in Italy, Spain, and Spanish America in addressing or speaking of priests. **2** An army or navy chaplain. [Sp. & Pg. & Ital. < L *pater* father]

pae·an (pē′ən) *n.* A song of praise, joy, thanksgiving, or exultation. [< Gk. *paian* a hymn addressed to Paian, the god Apollo]

pa·el·la (pī·äl′ə, pī·əl′ə, *Sp.* pī·ä′yə, pī·ä′lyə) *n.* A Spanish dish of rice flavored with saffron, shellfish, chicken and other meats, and vegetables. [Catalan, lit., pot]

pa·gan (pā′gən) *n.* **1** One who is neither a Christian, a Jew, nor a Muslim; a heathen. **2** An irreligious person. —*adj.* Pertaining to pagans; heathenish. [< L *paganus* a rural villager] **—pa′gan·dom, pa′gan·ism** *n.*

pa·gan·ize (pā′gən·īz) *v.t. & v.i.* **-ized, -iz·ing** To make or become pagan. **—pa′gan·iz′er** *n.*

page[1] (pāj) *n.* **1** A male attendant; esp. in chivalry, a lad or young man in training for knighthood. **2** A young person attending legislators while in session, as by delivering messages and doing errands. **3** A man employed in a hotel, club, theater, etc., to perform light duties. —*v.t.* **paged, pag·ing** To seek or summon (a person) by calling his name, as a hotel page does. [< Ital. < Gk. *paidion,* dim. of *pais, paidos* child]

page[2] (pāj) *n.* **1** One side of a leaf of a book, letter, manuscript, etc. **2** The written or printed matter on such a leaf. **3** An entire leaf of a book, magazine, etc.: to tear out a *page.* **4** Something that marks a stage, esp. a memorable one, in a process or sequence: a *page* from one's experience. **5** Any source or record of knowledge. —*v.t.* **paged, pag·ing** To mark the pages of with numbers. [< L *pagina*]

pag·eant (paj′ənt) *n.* **1** A public exhibition, parade, or spectacle, as of floats or other elaborate display. **2** Empty and elaborate display; ostentation. [< Med. L *pagina* a framework]

pag·eant·ry (paj′ən·trē) *n. pl.* **-ries** **1** Pageants collectively. **2** Elaborate and colorful display; splendor. **3** Empty, ostentatious display.

pag·i·nate (paj′ə·nāt) *v.t.* **-nat·ed, -nat·ing** To number the pages of (a book) consecutively. [< L *pagina* page]

pag·i·na·tion (paj′ə·nā′shən) *n.* **1** The numbering of the pages, as of a book. **2** The figures used in paging. **3** The arrangement and number of pages.

pa·go·da (pə·gō′də) *n.* In the countries of the Far East, a tower having several stories, each of which has a roof that curves upward, built as a temple or memorial. [Pg. *pagode*]

Pagoda

paid (pād) *p.t. & p.p. of* PAY.

pail (pāl) *n.* **1** A usu. cylindrical container for carrying liquids, etc. **2** The amount carried in this vessel: also **pail′ful′.** [< L *patella* a small pan]

pain (pān) *n.* **1** A feeling of distress resulting from the stimulation of certain nerve endings by some physical injury or disorder. **2** Mental suffering, as anxiety, grief, etc. **3** *pl.* Care or exertion expended on anything. **4** *pl.* The pangs of childbirth. **5** *Slang* A person or thing that irritates or annoys; nuisance. **—on** (or **upon** or **under**) **pain of** With the penalty of (some specified punishment). —*v.t.* **1** To cause pain to; hurt or grieve; disquiet. —*v.i.* **2** To cause pain. [< Gk. *poinē* a penalty] **—Syn.** *n.* **1** ache, discomfort. **2** anguish, distress, misery, wretchedness.

pain·ful (pān′fəl) *adj.* **1** Giving or attended with pain; distressing. **2** Requiring labor, effort, or care; arduous. **3** Affected with pain: a *painful* toe. **—pain′ful·ly** *adv.* **—pain′ful·ness** *n.*

pain·kill·er (pān′kil′ər) *n. Informal* A medicine that relieves pain; analgesic.

pain·less (pān′lis) *adj.* Free from pain; causing no pain. **—pain′less·ly** *adv.* **—pain′less·ness** *n.*

pains·tak·ing (pānz′tā′king) *adj.* Taking pains; careful; assiduous. —*n.* Diligent and careful endeavor. **—pains′·tak′ing·ly** *adv.*

paint (pānt) *n.* **1** A color or pigment, either dry or mixed with oil, water, etc. **2** A cosmetic, as rouge. —*v.t.* **1** To make a representation of in paints or colors. **2** To make, as a picture, by applying paints or colors. **3** To cover or coat with or as with paint. **4** To describe vividly in words. **5** To apply cosmetics to. **6** To apply (medicine, etc.), as with a swab. —*v.i.* **7** To cover or coat something with paint. **8** To practice the art of painting. **9** To apply cosmetics to the face, etc. [< L *pingere* to paint]

paint·brush (pānt′brush′) *n.* A brush for applying paint.

paint·er[1] (pān′tər) *n.* **1** One whose occupation is painting surfaces with a coat of paint. **2** One who paints pictures; an artist.

paint·er[2] (pān′tər) *n. Naut.* A rope with which to fasten a boat by its bow. [< OF *pentoir* a rope for hanging things]

paint·er[3] (pān′tər) *n. Regional* PUMA. [Var. of PANTHER]

paint·ing (pān′ting) *n.* **1** The act or employment of laying on paints with a brush. **2** The art of applying paint to produce pictures. **3** A painted picture.

pair (pâr) *n.* **1** Two things of a kind that are joined, complementary, or otherwise related, and are used together: a *pair* of socks. **2** Something consisting of two like parts: a *pair* of eyeglasses. **3** Any two persons, animals, or things considered to share certain characteristics or circumstances, as a married couple or mated animals. **4** In legislative bodies, two opposed members who agree to abstain from voting, and so offset each other. —*v.t.* **1** To bring together or arrange in a pair or pairs; match; couple; mate. —*v.i.* **2** To come together as a couple or pair. **3** To marry or mate. **—pair off** **1** To separate into couples. **2** To arrange by pairs. [< L *paria,* neut. plural of *par* equal]

pais·ley (pāz′lē) *adj. Often cap.* **1** Made of or resembling a woolen fabric patterned with colorful, curved shapes. **2** Of or resembling this pattern. —*n.* A paisley fabric or garment, esp. a shawl or necktie. [< *Paisley,* Scotland]

pa·ja·mas (pə·jä′məz, -jam′əz) *n.pl.* **1** Loose trousers with jackets or blouses to match, used as nightwear. **2** Loose trousers worn by both men and women in the Orient. *Brit. sp.* **py·ja·mas.** [< Pers. *pāi* a leg + *jāmah* a garment] **—pa·ja′ma** *adj.*

Pa·ki·stan (pä′ki·stän′, pak′i·stan′) *n.* A republic of the Commonwealth in s Asia, 310, 403 sq. mi., cap. Islamabad. **—Pa′ki·stan′i** *adj., n.* • See map at AFGHANISTAN.

pal (pal) *n. Informal* A close friend; chum. [< Romany *phral* brother < Skt. *bharātṛ*]

pal·ace (pal′is) *n.* **1** A royal residence, or the official residence of some high dignitary. **2** Any splendid residence or stately building. **3** A spacious and often showy place of public entertainment. [< L *palatium,* orig., the Palatine Hill at Rome, on which stood the palace of the Caesars]

pal·a·din (pal′ə·din) *n.* **1** A paragon of knighthood. **2** Any distinguished champion of a cause. [< L *palatinus* of the palace]

pal·an·quin (pal′ən·kēn′) *n.* A type of covered litter borne by poles on the shoulders of two or more men. [< Skt. *palyaṅka* bed]

pal·at·a·ble (pal′it·ə·bəl) *adj.* **1** Agreeable to the taste or palate; savory. **2** Acceptable. **—pal′at·a·bly** *adv.*

pal·a·tal (pal′ə·təl) *adv.* **1** Pertaining to the palate. **2** *Phonet.* Produced by placing the front (not the tip) of the tongue near or against the hard palate, as *y* in English *yoke.* —*n. Phonet.* A palatal sound. **—pal′a·tal·ly** *adv.*

pal·a·tal·ize (pal′ə·təl·īz′) *v.t. & v.i.* **·ized, ·iz·ing** *Phonet.* To change to a palatal sound, as (t) to (ch) in *nature.*

pal·ate (pal′it) *n.* **1** The roof of the mouth, comprising the anterior bony hard palate and the posterior fleshy soft palate. •See MOUTH. **2** The sense of taste; relish: the gourmet's sensitive *palate.* **3** Intellectual taste or preference. [< L *palatum*]

pa·la·tial (pə·lā′shəl) *adj.* Of, like, or befitting a palace; magnificent. **—pa·la′tial·ly** *adv.*

pa·lat·i·nate (pə·lat′ə·nāt, -nit) *n.* The political division ruled over by a prince possessing certain prerogatives of royalty within his own domain. [< ML *palatinus* palatine]

pal·a·tine (pal′ə·tīn, -tin) *adj.* **1** Pertaining to a royal palace or its officials. **2** Possessing royal prerogatives within a certain domain. —*n.* The ruler of a palatinate. [< L *palatinus* of the palace]

pa·lav·er (pə·lav′ər) *n.* **1** A discussion or talk; conference. **2** Originally, a lengthy conference between European explorers and native Africans. —*v.i.* **1** To talk idly and at length. **2** To meet in conference. —*v.t.* **3** To flatter; cajole. [< Pg. *palavra* word, speech < LL *parabola* a story, word]

pale¹ (pāl) *n.* **1** A pointed stick of wood; a fence picket. **2** A territory within established bounds. **3** A defined or delimited area: beyond the *pale* of the law. **4** A boundary; limit. [< L *palus* a stake]

pale² (pāl) *adj.* **1** Of a whitish or ashen appearance. **2** Of any color containing a large proportion of white; lacking in saturation. —*v.t. & v.i.* **paled, pal·ing** To make or turn pale; blanch. [< L *pallidus*] **—pale′ly** *adv.* **—pale′ness** *n.* — **Syn. 1** pallid, wan, ashy, bloodless.

pale·face (pāl′fās) *n.* A white person: a term allegedly originated by North American Indians.

paleo- *combining form* **1** Ancient; old: *paleography.* **2** Primitive: *Paleolithic.* [< Gk. *palaios* old, ancient]

Pa·le·o·cene (pā′lē·ə·sēn′) *adj. & n.* See GEOLOGY.

pa·le·og·ra·phy (pā′lē·og′rə·fē) *n.* **1** An ancient mode of writing, or ancient writing collectively. **2** The science of describing or deciphering ancient writings. **—pa′le·og′ra·pher** *n.* **—pa′le·o·graph′ic** or **·i·cal** *adj.*

Pa·le·o·lith·ic (pā′lē·ō·lith′ik) *adj. Anthropol.* Of, pertaining to, or associated with a period of human culture characterized by increasingly refined stone implements.

pa·le·on·tol·o·gy (pā′lē·on·tol′ə·jē) *n.* The science dealing with fossil organisms. **—pa′le·on′to·log′i·cal, pa′le·on′·to·log′ic** *adv.* **—pa′le·on·tol′o·gist** *n.*

Pa·le·o·zo·ic (pā′lē·ō·zō′ik) *adv. & n.* See GEOLOGY. [< PALEO- + Gk. *zōē* life]

Pal·es·tine (pal′is·tīn) *n.* **1** In biblical times, a territory on the E coast of the Mediterranean, the country of the Jew. **2** A former British mandate west of the Jordan River, from 1923 to 1948 when the state of Israel was established. **—Pal′es·tin′i·an** (-tin′ē·ən) *adj., n.*

pal·ette (pal′it) *n.* **1** A thin tablet providing a surface for the mixing of colors by an artist, usu. designed to be held in the hand. **2** The colors used by an artist in his work as a whole or in a particular work. [F, dim. of *pale* shovel]

palette knife A thin, flat knife with a flexible blade for mixing and applying an artist's colors.

pal·frey (pôl′frē) *n.* A saddle horse, esp. a woman's saddle horse. [< Gk. *para* beside + LL *veredus* post horse]

Pa·li (pä′lē) *n.* The sacred language of the early Buddhist writings, comprising various Indic dialects. [< Skt. *pāli*]

pal·i·mo·ny (pal′ə·mō·nē) *n. Slang* Alimony paid to a person for having lived for a time with another, without being legally married.

pal·imp·sest (pal′imp·sest) *n.* A parchment, tablet, etc. written upon two or three times, the earlier writing having been wholly or partially erased to make room for the next. [< Gk. *palimpsēstos,* lit., scraped again]

pal·in·drome (pal′in·drōm) *n.* A word or phrase that reads the same forward or backward, as "radar." [< Gk. *palindromos* a running back again]

pal·ing (pā′ling) *n.* **1** One of a series of upright pales forming a fence; also, pales collectively. **2** A fence of pales.

pal·i·sade (pal′ə·sād′) *n.* **1** A fence made of strong stakes set in the ground **2** *pl.* A sheer cliff, usu. along a river. —*v.t.* **·sad·ed, ·sad·ing** To enclose or fortify with a palisade. [< MF *palisser* enclose with pales]

pall¹ (pôl) *n.* **1** A heavy cloth fabric, often black, used to cover a coffin. **2** Anything that darkens or dispirits: a *pall* of smoke; The war cast a *pall* over the festivities. **3** *Eccl.* A chalice cover. —*v.t.* To cover with or as with a pall. [< L *pallium* a cover]

pall² (pôl) *v.i.* **1** To become insipid or uninteresting. **2** To have a dulling or displeasing effect: with *on.* —*v.t.* **3** To satiate. [< APPALL]

pal·la·di·um¹ (pə·lā′dē·əm) *n. pl.* **·di·a** (-dē·ə) Any object considered essential to the safety of something; a safeguard. [< GK. *palladios* of Pallas (Athena), whose statue in Troy was believed to protect the city]

pal·la·di·um² (pə·lā′dē·əm) *n.* A rare, white, tarnish-resistant metallic element (symbol Pd) related to platinum. [< *Pallas,* an asteroid]

Pal·las (pal′əs) *Gk. Myth.* ATHENA. Also **Pallas Athena.**

pall·bear·er (pôl′bôr ′ər) *n.* One who escorts or bears a coffin at a funeral.

pal·let¹ (pal′it) *n.* **1** A wooden implement with a flat blade, used for mixing and shaping clay. **2** A movable platform for the storage or transportation of goods. **3** A machine part that changes reciprocating motion to rotary motion or vice versa. [Var. of PALETTE]

pal·let² (pal′it) *n.* A humble or makeshift bed, as a straw mattress or a blanket laid on the floor. [< L *palea* chaff]

pal·li·ate (pal′ē·āt) *v.t.* **·at·ed, ·at·ing 1** To cause (a crime, fault, etc.) to appear less serious or offensive. **2** To relieve the symptoms of without curing, as a disease. [< LL *palliare* to cloak] **—pal′li·a′tion, pal′li·a′tor** *n.* **—Syn. 1** extenuate, excuse. **2** alleviate, mitigate.

pal·li·a·tive (pal′ē·ā′tiv, -ə·tiv) *adj.* Having a tendency to palliate. —*n.* That which serves to palliate.

pal·lid (pal′id) *adj.* **1** Of a pale or wan appearance. **2** Lacking in color or spirit: a *pallid* version of the original show. [< L *pallere* be pale] **—pal′lid·ly** *adv.* **—pal′lid·ness** *n.*

pal·lor (pal′ər) *n.* The state of being pale or pallid.

palm¹ (päm) *n.* **1** The inner surface of the hand between the wrist and the base of the fingers. **2** The breadth (three or four inches) of the hand used as a rough measure. **3** That which covers the palm, as part of a glove. **4** The flattened portion of an antler, as of a moose. **5** The flat expanding end of any armlike projection, as the blade of an oar. —*v.i.* **1** To hide (cards, dice, etc.) in or about the hand, as in sleight of hand. **2** To handle or touch with the palm. **—palm off** To pass off or impose fraudulently. [< L *palma* a hand] **—pal·mar** (pal′mər) *adj.*

palm² (päm) *n.* **1** Any of a large and varied family of tropical trees or shrubs usu. having a branchless trunk topped by large palmate or pinnate leaves. **2** A leaf or branch of the palm, used as a symbol of victory or joy. **3** Supremacy; triumph. [< L *palma*] **—pal·ma·ceous** (pal·mā′shəs) *adj.*

pal·mate (pal′māt) *adj.* **1** Resembling an open hand with fingers spread. **2** Branching out radially from a common center. **3** *Zool.* Webbed, as a bird's foot. Also **pal′mat·ed.** [< L *palma* a hand] **—pal′mate·ly** *adv.*

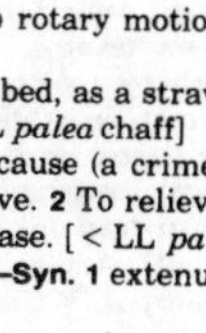

Palm tree

palm·er (pä′mər) *n.* A medieval pilgrim who had visited Palestine and brought back a palm branch as a sign.
pal·met·to (pal·met′ō) *n. pl* ·**tos** or ·**toes** Any of various palms with fanlike leaves, esp. the cabbage palm of the s U.S.
palm·is·try (pä′mis·trē) *n.* The art of reading the past life or future of a person by the lines and marks in the palm of the hand. [< OF *paulme* palm + *maistrie* mastery] —**palm′ist** *n.*
palm oil A yellow or reddish fat obtained from the fruit of various palms, used in making soap, candles, etc.
Palm Sunday The Sunday before Easter, commemorating Christ's triumphal entry into Jerusalem.
palm·y (pä′mē) *adj.* **palm·i·er, palm·i·est 1** Marked by prosperity; flourishing. **2** Abounding in or resembling palms.
pal·my·ra (pal·mī′rə) *n.* A tall, tropical palm yielding wood, edible fruit, and sap. [< Pg. *palmeira* palm tree]
pal·o·mi·no (pal′ə·mē′nō) *n. pl.* ·**nos** A golden brown horse, usu. having a mane and tail of paler color. [< Sp. *paloma* a dove]
palp (palp) *n.* PALPUS.
pal·pa·ble (pal′pə·bəl) *adj.* **1** That may be touched or felt. **2** Readily perceived; apparent. **3** Obvious to the mind; manifest. [< L *palpare* to touch] —**pal′pa·bil′i·ty, pal′pa·ble·ness** *n.* —**pal′pa·bly** *adv.*
pal·pate (pal′pāt) *v.t.* ·**pat·ed,** ·**pat·ing** To examine by touch, esp. for medical diagnosis. —**pal·pa′tion** *n.*
pal·pi·tate (pal′pə·tāt) *v.i.* ·**tat·ed,** ·**tat·ing 1** To quiver; tremble. **2** To throb, usu. at increased speed: said of the heart. [< L *palpitare* to tremble, freq. of *palpare* to touch] —**pal′pi·ta′tion** *n.*
pal·pus (pal′pəs) *n. pl.* ·**pi** (-pī) *Zool.* A feeler, esp. one appended to the oral region of certain insects, lobsters, worms, etc. [< L *palpus* a feeler]
pal·sy (pôl′zē) *n.* Paralysis or trembling due to impairment of nerves controlling voluntary movement. —*v.t.* ·**sied,** ·**sy·ing** To affect with or as if with palsy. [< L *paralysis* paralysis] —**pal′sied** *adj.*
pal·ter (pôl′tər) *v.i.* **1** To speak or act insincerely. **2** To treat something lightly; trifle. **3** To haggle or quibble. [?] —**pal′ter·er** *n.*
pal·try (pôl′trē) *adj.* ·**tri·er,** ·**tri·est** Having little or no worth or value; trifling; trivial [< regional E *palt* a piece of coarse or dirty cloth] —**pal′tri·ly** *adv.* —**pal′tri·ness** *n.*
pam., pamph. pamphlet.
pam·pas (pam′pəz) *n.pl.* The great treeless plains of South America. —*adj.* Pertaining to or growing on the pampas. [< Quechua] —**pam·pe·an** (pam′pē·ən, pam·pē′ən) *adj.*
pam·per (pam′pər) *v.t.* To treat too indulgently; gratify the whims of; coddle. [ME *pamperen*] —**pam′per·er** *n.*
pam·phlet (pam′flit) *n.* A printed publication having relatively few pages and unbound, stapled, or stitched. [< L *Pamphilus seu de Amore,* popular 12th c. love poem]
pam·phlet·eer (pam′flə·tir′) *n.* One who writes pamphlets, esp. on politically controversial subjects. —*v.i.* To write and issue pamphlets.
pan[1] (pan) *n.* **1** A wide, shallow vessel for holding liquids or for cooking. **2** A circular sheet-iron dish with sloping sides, in which gold is separated. **3** The powder cavity of a flintlock. **4** HARDPAN (def. 1). **5** Either of the two receptacles on a pair of scales. **6** *Informal* A severe criticism. —*v.* **panned, pan·ning** *v.t.* **1** To separate (gold) by washing gold-bearing earth in a pan. **2** To wash (earth, gravel, etc.) for this purpose. **3** *Informal* To criticize severely. —*v.i.* **4** To search for gold by washing earth, gravel, etc., in a pan. —**pan out** *Informal* To result or turn out; transpire. [< L *patina* a pan or dish]
pan[2] (pan) *v.t.* **panned, pan·ning** To move (a motion-picture or television camera) across a scene in order to secure a panoramic effect.
Pan (pan) *Gk. Myth.* A horned, goat-footed, pipe-playing god of forests, flocks, and shepherds.
pan- *combining form* **1** All; every; the whole; *panchromatic.* **2** Comprising, including, or applying to all: *Pan-American.* [< Gk., neut. of *pas* all]
pan·a·ce·a (pan′ə·sē′ə) *n.* A remedy for all diseases or ills; a cure-all. [< Gk. *panakeia* a universal remedy] —**pan′a·ce′an** *adj.*
pa·nache (pə·nash′, -näsh′) *n.* **1** A plume or bunch of feathers, esp. as an ornament on a helmet. **2** Dash; spirit; liveliness. [< Ital. *pennacchio* < *penna* feather]
Pan·a·ma (pan′ə·mä, -mô, *Sp.* pä′nä·mä′) *n.* A republic of Central America, 28,575 sq. mi., cap. Panama (also Panama City). —**Pan′a·ma′ni·an** (-mā′nē·ən) *adj., n.* • See map at CENTRAL AMERICA.
Panama hat A hat woven of fine, pale straw obtained from a palmlike plant of Central and South America.
Pan-A·mer·i·can (pan′ə·mer′ə·kən) *adj.* Of or pertaining to the countries of both North and South America. —**Pan′-A·mer′i·can·ism** *n.*
pan·cake (pan′kāk′) *n.* A thin flat batter cake fried in a pan or baked on a griddle; griddlecake.
pan·chro·mat·ic (pan′krō·mat′ik) *adj. Phot.* Sensitive to all the colors in proportion to their brightness, as a film or plate. —**pan·chro′ma·tism** (-krō′mə·tiz′əm) *n.*
pan·cre·as (pan′krē·əs, pang′-) *n.* A large gland situated behind the stomach and manufacturing fat-digesting enzymes and the hormone insulin. [< Gk. *pankreas* sweetbread] —**pan′cre·at′ic** (-at′ik) *adj.*
pan·da (pan′də) *n. pl.* ·**das** or ·**da 1** A small raccoonlike carnivore of the SE Himalayas with reddish fur and ringed tail: also **lesser panda. 2** A large, bearlike, herbivorous mammal of Tibet and China, having a black and white coat: also **giant panda.** [?]
pan·dem·ic (pan·dem′ik) *adj.* Widely epidemic, as a disease. —*n.* An epidemic occurring over a very large area or worldwide. [< Gk. *pan,* neut. of *pas* all + *dēmos* people]
pan·de·mo·ni·um (pan′də·mō′nē·əm) *n.* A tumultuous uproar; wild disorder. —**Syn.** riot, chaos, tumult. [< Gk. *pan,* neut. of *pas* all + *daimōn* an evil spirit]
pan·der (pan′dər) *v.i.* To seek to satisfy another's immoral, vulgar, or uninformed tastes or desires: to *pander* to the mob. —*n.* One who panders; esp., a go-between in sexual intrigues; procurer; pimp. [< *Pandarus,* a character in the Iliad] —**pan′der·er** *n.*
P. and L., P. & L. profit and loss.
Pan·do·ra (pan·dôr′ə, -dō′rə) *Gk. Myth.* The first mortal woman, whose curiosity led her to open a box **(Pandora's box)** from which all human ills escaped.
pan·dow·dy (pan·dou′dē) *n. pl.* ·**dies** A deep-dish pie or pudding made of baked sliced apples. Also **apple pandowdy.** [?]
pane (pān) *n.* **1** A piece of window glass filling one opening in a frame. **2** A piece or compartment, esp. if flat and rectangular. **3** A flat surface or side. [< L *pannus* a piece of cloth] —**paned** *adj.*
pan·e·gyr·ic (pan′ə·jir′ik) *n.* A formal public eulogy, either written or spoken; encomium. [< Gk. < *panēgyris* an assembly] —**pan′e·gyr′i·cal** *adj.* —**pan′e·gyr′i·cal·ly** *adv.* —**pan′e·gyr′ist** *n.*
pan·el (pan′əl) *n.* **1** A rectangular section, as part of a fence or wall, often set in a frame and sometimes raised above or depressed below the surrounding surface. **2** A vertical section of a woman's skirt of a distinctive fabric or color. **3** A tablet of wood used as the surface for a painting; also, a painting on such a surface. **4** A set of instruments and controls displayed in an aircraft, automobile, or other complex system. **5** *Law* **a** The official list of persons called for jury duty; also, the persons so called. **b** The persons composing a jury. **6** A group of people selected to act cooperatively for some purpose, as to conduct a public investigation, judge a contest, participate in a discussion, etc. —*v.t.* ·**eled** or ·**elled,** ·**el·ing** or ·**el·ling 1** To fit, furnish, or adorn with panels. **2** To divide into panels. [< L *pannus* rag]
panel discussion A public discussion by a group of people, usu. selected because they represent divergent points of view or are experts.
pan·el·ing (pan′əl·ing) *n.* Panels collectively, as a series of panels in a wall. Also **pan′el·ling.**
pan·el·ist (pan′əl·ist) *n.* One of a group of people serving on a panel, as to judge a contest or discuss an issue.
pan fish Any little fish that can be fried whole.
pan-fry (pan′frī′) *v.t.* ·**fried,** ·**fry·ing** To fry in a frying pan.
pang (pang) *n.* **1** A sudden, brief, penetrating pain. **2** A sudden feeling of keen mental anguish. [?] —**Syn. 1** stab, ache. **2** throe.

pan·go·lin (pang′gə·lin, pan·gō′lin) *n.* Any of various long-tailed, scale-covered, toothless mammals of Asia and Africa that feed on ants. [< Malay *peng-goling*]

pan·han·dle[1] (pan′han′dəl) *v.i.* **·died, ·dling** *Informal* To beg, esp. on the street. **—pan′han′dler** *n.*

pan·han·dle[2] (pan′han′dəl) *n.* A narrow strip of land projecting from a larger region: from its resemblance to the handle of a pan.

Pan·hel·len·ic (pan′hə·len′ik) *adj.* **1** Of or pertaining to all Greek people. **2** Of or pertaining to fraternities or sororities bearing Greek names.

pan·ic (pan′ik) *n.* **1** A sudden, overpowering fear often affecting many simultaneously and compelling immediate, unreasoning action, esp. flight. **2** Any sudden fear or alarm that provokes unreasonable action, as a sudden loss of confidence in the soundness of the financial system. **3** *Slang* Something extremely funny. **—***adj.* **1** Of, like, or caused by panic. **2** Of or caused by the god Pan, believed to inspire fear. **—***v.* **·icked, ·ick·ing** *v.t.* **1** To affect with panic. **2** *Slang* To cause to laugh or otherwise express pleasure without restraint. **—***v.i.* **3** To become affected with panic. [< Gk. *panikos* of or for the god Pan] **—pan′·ick·y** *adj.*

pan·i·cle (pan′i·kəl) *n. Bot.* A loose, irregularly branched flower cluster. [< L *panus* a swelling] **—pan′i·cled, pa·nic·u·late,** (pə·nik′yə·lāt, -lit), **pa·nic′u·lat′ed** *adj.*

pan·ic-strick·en (pan′ik·strik′ən) *adj.* Overcome by panic. Also **pan′ic-struck′.**

pan·jan·drum (pan·jan′drəm) *n.* A character of exaggerated importance; a pompous personage in a small place. [< a character in a play by Samuel Foote, 1720–1770, English dramatist]

pan·nier (pan′yər) *n.* **1** One of a pair of baskets adapted to be slung on both sides of a beast of burden. **2** A basket for carrying a load on the back. **3** A framework or hoop for extending a woman's dress at the hips. **4** A skirt extended at the hips. [< L *panis* bread]

pa·no·cha (pə·nō′chə) *n.* **1** A coarse Mexican sugar. **2** PENUCHE. [< L *panis* bread]

pan·o·ply (pan′ə·plē) *n. pl.* **·plies 1** The complete equipment of a warrior. **2** Any complete covering that protects or magnificently arrays. [< Gk. *panoplia* full armor] **—pan′o·plied** *adj.*

pan·o·ram·a (pan′ə·ram′ə, -rä′mə) *n.* **1** A complete view in every direction. **2** A complete or comprehensive view of a subject or of constantly passing events. **3** A picture unrolled before the spectator and representing a continuous scene. **4** CYCLORAMA. [< PAN- + Gk. *horama* sight] **—pan′o·ram′ic** *adj.* **—pan′o·ram′i·cal·ly** *adv.*

pan·pipes (pan′pīps′) *n.pl.* A primitive multiple flute made of reeds bound together.

pan·sy (pan′zē) *n. pl.* **·sies 1** A species of garden violet having velvety blossoms of varied colors. **2** *Slang* An effeminate or homosexual boy or man: used contemptuously. [< MF *pensée* thought]

pant (pant) *v.i.* **1** To breathe rapidly or spasmodically; gasp for breath. **2** To emit smoke, steam, etc., in loud puffs. **3** To have a strong desire; yearn: with *for* or *after.* **4** To beat or pulsate rapidly; throb, as the heart. **—***v.t.* **5** To breathe out or utter gaspingly. **—***n.* **1** A short or labored breath. **2** A quick or violent heaving, as of the breast. [< OF *pantoisier* to gasp] **—pant′er** *n.*

pan·ta·lets (pan′tə·lets′) *n. pl.* Long ruffled drawers, formerly worn by women and children. Also **pan′ta·lettes′.** [< PANTALOONS]

Pantalets

pan·ta·loon (pan′tə·lo͞on′) *n.* **1** In pantomimes, an absurd old man on whom the clown plays tricks. **2** *pl.* Trousers; esp., tight-fitting trousers worn in the 19th century. [< Ital. *pantalone* a clown]

Pan·ta·loon (pan′tə·lo͞on′) *n.* In early Italian comedies, an old dotard wearing tight-fitting trousers.

pan·the·ism (pan′thē·iz′əm) *n.* **1** The doctrine that identifies the universe as a whole and the laws that govern it as God. **2** The worship of all gods. **—pan′the·ist** *n.* **—pan′·the·is′tic** or **pan′the·is′ti·cal** *adj.* **—pan′the·is′ti·cal·ly** *adv.*

pan·the·on (pan′thē·on) *n.* **1** All the gods of a people. **2** A mausoleum or temple commemorating the great. [< L *pantheon* < Gk. *pan,* neut. of *pas* all + *theos* a god]

Pan·the·on (pan′thē·on) *n.* A circular temple at Rome, dedicated to all the gods, built about 27 B.C.

pan·ther (pan′thər) *n.* **1** A leopard, esp. one having black fur. **2** MOUNTAIN LION. **3** JAGUAR. [< Gk. *panthēr*]

pant·ies (pan′tēz) *n.pl.* A woman's or child's underpants. Also **pant′ie.**

pan·to·graph (pan′tə·graf, -gräf) *n.* An instrument for copying a drawing, diagram, or map, on the same or an altered scale. [< PAN- + -GRAPH] **—pan′to·graph′ic** or **·i·cal** *adj.* **—pan·tog·ra·phy** (pan·tog′rə·fē) *n.*

pan·to·mime (pan′tə·mīm) *n.* **1** A series of gestures and postures, used without words to express ideas or convey information. **2** Any play in which the actors express themselves without speaking. **3** An ancient, classical play or part of a play in which the actors used gestures or movement only. **—***v.t. & v.i.* **·mimed, ·mim·ing** To act or express in pantomime. [< Gk. *pantomimos* an imitator of all] **—pan′to·mim′ic** (-mim′ik) or **·i·cal** *adj.* **—pan′to·mi′mist** (-mī′·mist) *n.*

pan·try (pan′trē) *n. pl.* **·tries** A room or closet for keeping provisions, dishes, table linen, etc. [< L *panis* bread]

pants (pants) *n.pl.* **1** A garment extending from the waist to the ankles or knees and divided so as to cover each leg separately; trousers. **2** Drawers or panties.

pant·suit (pant′so͞ot′) *n.* A woman's two-piece garment consisting of a jacket and matching pants. Also **pants suit.**

pan·ty·hose (pan′tē·hōz′) *n.pl.* A woman's undergarment combining panties and stockings. Also **panty hose.**

pan·ty·waist (pan′tē·wāst′) *n.* **1** A child's waist with buttons on which to fasten short pants. **2** *Slang* A weak or cowardly youth; sissy.

pan·zer (pan′zər, *Ger.* pän′tsər) *adj.* **1** Armored. **2** Using armored tanks or mechanized troops. [G]

pap (pap) *n.* Any soft food for babies or sick people. [ME *pape*]

pa·pa (pä′pə, pə·pä′) *n.* Father. [< Gk. *papas,* a child's word]

pa·pa·cy (pā′pə·sē) *n. pl.* **·cies 1** The dignity, office, or jurisdiction of the pope of Rome. **2** The succession of popes in the Roman Catholic Church. **3** The tenure of office of the pope. [< L *papa* pope]

Pa·pa·cy (pā′pə·sē) *n.* The Roman Catholic system of church government.

pa·pal (pā′pəl) *adj.* **1** Of or pertaining to the papacy or the pope. **2** Of or pertaining to the Roman Catholic Church.

pa·paw (pə·pô′, pô′pô) *n.* **1** A small, deciduous, North American tree bearing small, pulpy, edible fruit. **2** The fruit of this tree. **3** PAPAYA. [< Sp. *papaya* papaya]

pa·pa·ya (pä·pä′yä, pə·pä′yə) *n.* **1** A tropical American palmlike tree bearing a large, melonlike fruit. **2** Its edible fruit. [Sp.]

pa·per (pā′pər) *n.* **1** A substance typically prepared in thin, flat sheets, made from chemically treated fibrous cellulose, usu. from wood, rags, etc., and used as a writing and printing surface, in packaging, etc. **2** A sheet of paper. **3** A printed or written document. **4** NEWSPAPER. **5** A written essay, report, or examination, as for a school assignment. **6** A scholarly study or treatise read aloud or published in a journal. **7** Written or printed pledges or promises to pay which are negotiable, as bills of exchange, notes, etc.: also **commercial paper. 8** WALLPAPER. **9** *pl.* Personal or business documents, as of identification, permission, agreement, credit, etc. **10** Free tickets, as to a theater; also, the audience so admitted. **—on paper 1** In writing or print. **2** Based upon theoretical sources or superficial evidence. **—***adj.* **1** Of, made of, or like paper. **2** Theoretical rather than actual: *paper* profits. **—***v.t.* **1** To put paper on; cover with wallpaper. **2** To fold or enclose in paper. **3** To issue free tickets of admission to (a place of amusement). [< L *papyrus*] **—pa′per·er** *n.* **—pa′per·y** *adj.*

pa·per·back (pā′pər·bak′) *n.* A book having a paper cover or binding. —*adj.* Being or relating to such a book.
paper boy A boy or man who delivers newspapers.
paper gold SPECIAL DRAWING RIGHTS.
pa·per·hang·er (pā′pər·hang′ər) *n.* One who covers walls, etc., with wallpaper. —**pa′per·hang·ing** *n.*
paper money Currency consisting of paper on which certain fixed values are printed, as banknotes.
paper nautilus A cephalopod named for its thin, paper-like shell.
paper profit A potential profit, as in the stock market, that can be realized only by the sale of an appreciated holding.
paper tiger Something that seems mighty or threatening but is actually ineffectual or trivial.
pa·per·weight (pā′pər·wāt′) *n.* A small, heavy object set on loose papers to hold them in place.
pa·per·work (pā′pər·wûrk′) *n.* Work involving the preparation or handling of reports, letters, etc.
pa·pier-mâ·ché (pā′pər·mə·shā′, *Fr.* pȧ·pyā′mä·shā′) *n.* A tough material molded from paper pulp and a binding material. [F, lit., chewed paper]
pa·pil·la (pə·pil′ə) *n. pl.* **·lae** (-ē) **1** *Anat.* **a** The nipple of a mammary gland. **b** Any small nipplelike process, as on the tongue. **2** *Bot.* A small, nipple-shaped protuberance on a flower or leaf. [L, dim. of *papula* a swelling, pimple] — **pap·il·lar·y** (pap′ə·ler′ē), **pap·il·lose** (pap′ə·lōs) *adj.*
pap·il·lo·ma (pap′ə·lō′mə) *n. pl.* **·mas** or **·ma·ta** (-mə·tə) A small benign tumor on skin or mucous membrane.
pa·pist (pā′pist) *n. & adj.* Roman Catholic: a disparaging usage. [< L *papa* pope] —**pa′pis·try** *n.*
pa·poose (pa·pōōs′) *n.* A North American Indian infant. Also **pap·poose′.** [< Algonquian (Narraganset) *papoos* child]
pap·pus (pap′əs) *n. pl.* **pap·pi** (pap′ī, -ē) *Bot.* A tuft or cluster of hairs, scales, bristles, etc., on the calyx of a floret of the composite family, functioning to disperse the fruit. [< Gk. *pappos* grandfather] —**pap′pose** (-ōs), **pap′·pous** (-əs) *adj.*

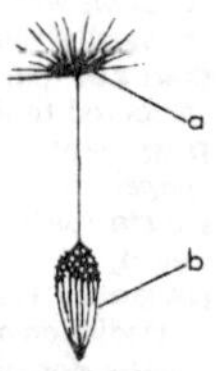

a. pappus.
b. fruit.

pa·pri·ka (pa·prē′kə, pap′rə·kə) *n.* A condiment made from the fruit of a mild red pepper. [< Gk. *peperi* pepper]
Pap smear A method of early detection of cervical cancer, consisting of removal of cervical cell samples, which are stained and examined. Also **Pap test.** [after George *Papanicolaou,* 1883–1962, U.S. scientist]
pa·py·rus (pə·pī′rəs) *n.pl.* **·ruses** or **·ri** (-rē, -rī) **1** A perennial rushlike sedge having stems six to ten feet high. **2** The writing paper of the ancient Egyptians, made from this plant. **3** A manuscript written on this material. [< Gk. *papyros*]
par (pär) *n.* **1** The established value of a national monetary unit defined in monetary units of another country. **2** The value printed on a negotiable document, as a stock certificate or bond. **3** An accepted standard with which to compare variation: not feeling up to *par.* **4** Equivalent level, status, value, etc.; equal basis: on a *par.* **5** In golf, the number of strokes allotted to a round or hole on the basis of faultless play. —*adj.* Equal to par. [L, equal]
par. paragraph; parallel; parenthesis.
para-¹ *prefix* **1** Beside; near by; along with: *paradigm.* **2** Beyond; aside from; amiss: *paradox.* **3** *Med.* **a** Diseased or abnormal: *paranoia.* **b** Similar to: *paratyphoid.* Also **par-.** [< Gk. *para* beside]
para-² *combining form* Shelter or protection against: *parachute.* [< Ital. *parare* defend]
par·a·ble (par′ə·bəl) *n.* A short, simple tale based on familiar things, meant to convey a moral or religious lesson. [< Gk. *parabolē* a placing side by side, a comparison]

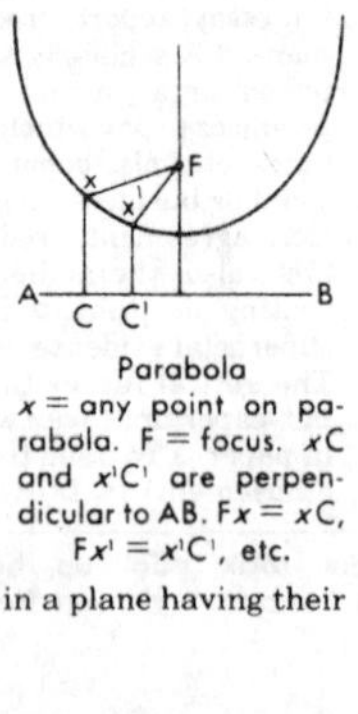

Parabola
x = any point on parabola. F = focus. xC and x'C′ are perpendicular to AB. Fx = xC, Fx' = x'C′, etc.

pa·rab·o·la (pə·rab′ə·lə) *n. Math.* A curve composed of a set of points in a plane having their distances from a fixed point and a fixed straight line equal. [< Gk. *parabolē* a comparison]
par·a·bol·ic (par′ə·bol′ik) *adj.* **1** Pertaining to or having the form of a parabola. **2** Pertaining to a parable.
par·a·chute (par′ə·shōōt) *n.* An apparatus of lightweight fabric that when unfurled assumes the shape of a large umbrella and acts to retard the speed of a body moving or descending through air. —*v.* **·chut·ed, ·chut·ing** *v.t.* **1** To land (troops, materiel, etc.) by means of parachutes. —*v.i.* **2** To descend by parachute. [< F < PARA- + *chute* fall] — **par′a·chut·ist** *n.*
pa·rade (pə·rād′) *n.* **1** A marshaling and maneuvering of troops for display or official inspection. **2** A ceremonious, public procession. **3** A promenade or public walk. **4** Pompous show; ostentation. —*v.* **·rad·ed, ·rad·ing** *v.t.* **1** To walk or march through or about. **2** To display or show off ostentatiously; flaunt. **3** To cause to assemble for military parade or review. —*v.i.* **4** To march formally or with display. **5** To walk in public for the purpose of showing oneself. **6** To assemble in military order for inspection or review. [< LL *parare* adorn, prepare] —**pa·rad′er** *n.*
par·a·digm (par′ə·dim, -dīm) *n.* **1** A pattern or example. **2** *Gram.* A list of the inflected forms of a word, as of a declension or conjugation. [< Gk. *paradeigma* a pattern] —**par′a·dig·mat′ic** (-dig·mat′ik) *adj.*
par·a·dise (par′ə·dīs) *n.* **1** The intermediate place or state where the souls of the saved await the resurrection. **2** Heaven. **3** Any region or state of surpassing delight. [< OPers. *pairidaēza* an enclosure, park] —**par′a·di·sa′ic** (-di·sā′ik) or **·i·cal, par′a·dis′al, par′a·dis′i·ac** (-dis′ē·ak) or **par·a·di·si·a·cal** (par′ə·di·sī′ə·kəl) *adj.*
Par·a·dise (par′ə·dīs) *n.* The garden of Eden.
par·a·dox (par′ə·doks) *n.* **1** A statement that seems to contradict common belief but may nevertheless be true. **2** A self-contradictory statement or proposition. **3** A person or thing that seems to possess contradictory qualities and is thus inexplicable or inscrutable; enigma. [< Gk. *para-* contrary to + *doxa* opinion] —**par′a·dox′i·cal** *adj.* — **par′a·dox′i·cal·ly** *adv.* —**par′a·dox′i·cal·ness.** *n.*
par·af·fin (par′ə·fin) *n.* **1** A white, water-repellent, waxy mixture of hydrocarbons, usu. derived from petroleum, used for making candles, matches, etc.: also **paraffin wax.** **2** Any of a series of saturated, open-chain hydrocarbons analogous to methane in molecular structure. **3** *Brit.* Kerosene. —*v.t.* To treat or impregnate with paraffin. Also **par′af·fine** (-fin, -fēn). [< L *parum* too little + *affinis* related to, because it has little affinity for other bodies]
par·a·gon (par′ə·gon) *n.* **1** A model of excellence: a *paragon* of virtue. **2** A round pearl of exceptional size. [< Gk. *para-* beside + *akonē* whetstone]
par·a·graph (par′ə·graf, -gräf) *n.* **1** A passage in a written work begun on a new and usu. indented line and usu. signaling a distinct thought, statement, or expression. **2** A short article, complete and unified. **3** A mark (¶) used to indicate where a paragraph is to start. —*v.t.* **1** To arrange in or into paragraphs. **2** To comment on or express in a paragraph. [< Gk. *para-* beside + *graphein* write] — **par′a·graph′er, par′a·graph′ist** *n.*
Par·a·guay (par′ə·gwā, -gwī; *Sp.* pä·rä·gwī′) *n.* A republic of CEN. South America, 157,047 sq. mi., cap. Asunción. — **Par′a·guay′an** *adj., n.* • See map at BRAZIL.
Paraguay tea MATÉ.
par·a·keet (par′ə·kēt) *n.* Any of certain small parrots having a long, slender tail. [< Ital. *parrochetto,* dim of *parroco* parson]
par·a·le·gal (par′ə·lē′gəl) *adj.* Of or pertaining to the legal profession at the paraprofessional level. —*n.* A legal paraprofessional.
par·al·lax (par′ə·laks) *n.* **1** The difference in the apparent position of an object, esp. of a celestial body, as would appear if viewed from two points. **2** Any apparent displacement of an object due to an observer's position. [< Gk. *para-* beside + *allassein* change] —**par′al·lac′tic** (-lak′·tik) or **·ti·cal** *adj.*
par·al·lel (par′ə·lel) *adj.* **1** Extending in the same direction and being equidistant at all points: *parallel* rows of seats. **2** *Geom.* Not intersecting, however far extended: said of planes or straight lines in the same plane. **3** Having parallel sides or parts. **4** Of the same kind or form;

functioning in like ways: *parallel* clauses. **5** Displaying the same pattern or course: *parallel* development; *parallel* careers. —*n.* **1** Something essentially similar to another; counterpart. **2** Essential likeness; correspondence. **3** A comparison tracing similarity: to draw a *parallel* between two presidents. **4** *Geom.* A line parallel to another line or to a plane. **5** An imaginary circle parallel to the equator and having all of its points the same latitude. **6** The state of being parallel. —*v.t.* **·leled,** or **·lelled, ·lel·ing** or **·lel·ling 1** To be, go, or extend parallel to. **2** To furnish with a parallel; equal. **3** To be a parallel to; correspond. **4** To compare; liken. **5** To make parallel. [< Gk. *para-* beside + *allēlos* one another]

parallel bars A gymnastic apparatus consisting of two parallel, horizontal bars supported on posts a few feet from the ground.

par·al·lel·e·pi·ped (par′ə·lel′ə·pī′pid, -pip′id) *n.* A prism with six faces, each of which is a parallelogram. Also **par′al·lel′e·pip′e·don** (-pip′ə·don, -pī′pə-). [< Gk. *parallēlos* parallel + *epipedon* a plane surface]

par·al·lel·ism (par′ə·lel·iz′əm) *n.* **1** The state of being parallel. **2** Essential likeness; similarity; correspondence.

par·al·lel·o·gram (par′ə·lel′ə·gram) *n.* A four-sided plane figure whose opposite sides are parallel and equal.

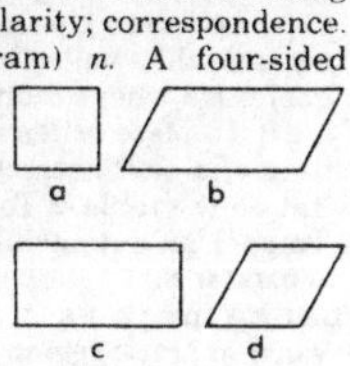

Parallelograms
a. square. b. rhomboid. c. rectangle. d. rhombus.

pa·ral·y·sis (pə·ral′ə·sis) *n. pl.* **·ses** (-sēz) **1** Partial or complete loss of sensation and the power of voluntary motion. **2** Inability to act or respond effectively. [< Gk. < *paralyein* disable]

par·a·lyt·ic (par′ə·lit′ik) *adj.* **1** Of, causing, or affected with paralysis. **2** Subject to paralysis. —*n.* A person subject to or suffering from paralysis.

par·a·lyze (par′ə·līz) *v.t.* **·lyzed, ·lyz·ing 1** To bring about paralysis in. **2** To render powerless, ineffective, or inactive. —**par′a·ly·za′tion, par′a·lyz′er** *n.*

par·a·me·ci·um (par′ə·mē′shē·əm, -sē·əm) *n. pl.* **·ci·a** (-shē·ə, -sē·ə) Any of a genus of slipper-shaped protozoans moving by means of cilia. [< Gk. *paramēkēs* oblong, oval]

par·a·med·ic (par′ə·med′ik) *n.* One trained to assist a physician.

par·a·med·i·cal (par′ə·med′ə·kəl) *adj.* Designating or pertaining to medical personnel trained to assist physicians, as by conducting routine tests, or to attend patients. —**par′a·med′i·cal·ly** *adv.*

pa·ram·e·ter (pə·ram′ə·tər) *n.* **1** *Math.* A variable or constant whose values determine the form of an expression, function, etc. **2** A number expressing some aspect of the behavior of a physical system. **3** A fixed limit or guideline. [< Gk. *para-* beside + *metron* a measure] —**par·a·met·ric** (par′ə·met′rik) *adj.*

par·a·mil·i·tar·y (par′ə·mil′ə·ter′ē) *adj.* Having a military structure and capable of supplementing or becoming a military force; quasi-military.

par·a·mount (par′ə·mount) *adj.* Having the highest title or rank; superior to all others. —*n.* A supreme lord. [< L *per* by + *ad montem* to the hill] —**par′a·mount·ly** *adv.* —**par′a·mount·cy** *n.* —**Syn.** *adj.* chief, foremost, preeminent, supreme.

par·a·mour (par′ə·mo͝or) *n.* A lover, esp. one who unlawfully takes the place of a husband or wife. [< L *per* through + *amor* love]

par·a·noi·a (par′ə·noi′ə) *n. Psychiatry* A mental disorder characterized by delusions, as of persecution or grandeur. [< Gk. *paranoos* distraught]

par·a·noid (par′ə·noid) *adj.* **1** Of, like, or suffering from paranoia: also **par′a·noi′dal. 2** Exhibiting symptoms suggestive of paranoia; esp., suspicious without cause. —*n.* A paranoid person. Also **par′a·noi′ac** (-noi′ak, -ək).

par·a·pet (par′ə·pit, -pet) *n.* **1** A barrier or wall used to shield soldiers from attack; breastwork. **2** A low wall about the edge of a roof, terrace, etc. [< Ital. *parapetto*] —**par′a·pet·ed** *adj.*

par·a·pher·na·li·a (par′ə·fər·nā′lē·ə, -nāl′yə, -fə-) *n.pl. (construed as sing. or pl.)* **1** Personal belongings. **2** Articles or accessories of equipment or adornment; furnishings; trappings. [< Gk. *para-* beside + *phernē* dower]

par·a·phrase (par′ə·frāz) *n.* A restatement of the meaning of a passage, work, etc. —*v.t. & v.i.* **·phrased, ·phras·ing** To express in or make a paraphrase. [< Gk. < *para phrazein* tell the same thing in other words] —**par′a·phras′er** *n.* —**par′a·phras′tic** (-fras′tik) *adj.* —**par′a·phras′ti·cal·ly** *adv.*

par·a·ple·gi·a (par′ə·plē′jē·ə, -jə) *n.* Paralysis of the lower half of the body. [< Gk. *paraplēgia,* a stroke on one side] —**par·a·ple·gic** (par′ə·plē′jik, -plej′ik) *adj., n.*

par·a·pro·fes·sion·al (par′ə·prə·fesh′ə·nəl) *n.* One who assists professionals, as teachers or physicians, by performing tasks not requiring professional skills.

par·a·psy·chol·o·gy (par′ə·sī·kol′ə·jē) *n.* The investigation of psychic phenomena, as extrasensory perception, telepathy, etc.

Pa·ra rubber (pä·rä′) Crude rubber obtained from certain tropical American trees. [< *Pará,* Brazil]

par·a·site (par′ə·sīt) *n.* **1** *Biol.* An animal or plant that lives on or in another living organism from which it takes nourishment, usu. with harm to the host. **2** A person or thing that lives or survives by dependence on and at the expense of another. [< Gk. *parasitos,* lit., one who eats at another's table] —**par′a·sit′ic** (-sit′ik) or **·i·cal** *adj.* —**par′a·sit′i·cal·ly** *adv.* —**par·a·sit·ism** (par′ə·sī′tiz·əm, -sə·tiz′əm) *n.*

par·a·sol (par′ə·sôl, -sol) *n.* A small, light umbrella used as a sunshade, esp. by women. [< Ital. *parasole*]

par·a·sym·pa·thet·ic nervous system (par′ə·sim′·pə·thet′ik) The part of the autonomic nervous system that controls such involuntary actions as the constriction of pupils, dilation of blood vessels, and slowing of heartbeat.

par·a·thi·on (par′ə·thī′on, -ən) *n.* An extremely poisonous synthetic organic compound, used as an agricultural insecticide. [< PARA-[1] + Gk. *theion* sulfur]

par·a·thy·roid (par′ə·thī′roid) *adj.* Pertaining to any of several small endocrine glands on or near the thyroid glands, which produce hormones that regulate calcium and phosphorus metabolism. —*n.* A parathyroid gland.

par·a·troops (par′ə·tro͞ops) *n.pl.* A military force trained to parachute into hostile territory from an airplane. —**par′a·troop** *adj.* —**par′a·troop′er** *n.*

par·a·ty·phoid (par′ə·tī′foid) *adj.* Resembling typhoid fever but due to infection by distinct bacteria. —*n.* Paratyphoid fever.

par·boil (pär′boil′) *v.t.* **1** To boil partially. **2** To make uncomfortable with heat. [< LL *per-* through + *bullire* to bubble]

par·cel (pär′səl) *n.* **1** Anything wrapped up; a package; bundle. **2** An integral part: part and *parcel.* **3** A group or lot of merchandise offered for sale. **4** A group or assortment, as of people or things: a *parcel* of misfits. **5** A distinct portion of land. **6** A separated part of anything. —*v.t.* **·celed** or **·celled, ·cel·ing** or **·cel·ling 1** To divide or distribute in parts or shares: usu. with *out.* **2** To make up into a parcel. [< L *particula,* dim. of *pars, partis* part]

parcel post A postal service for the carrying and delivery of parcels.

parch (pärch) *v.t.* **1** To make extremely dry; shrivel with heat. **2** To dry (corn, peas, etc.) by exposing to great heat; roast slightly. —*v.i.* **3** To become extremely dry; shrivel with heat. [< L *per-* thoroughly + *siccare* dry]

Par·chee·si (pär·chē′zē) *n.* A board game in which moves are regulated by a throw of the dice: a trade name. Also **par·che′si, par·chi′si.**

parch·ment (pärch′mənt) *n.* **1** Animal skin, as of sheep, goats, etc., prepared for writing. **2** A paper resembling this. **3** A college graduation diploma. [< Gk. *Pergamon,* the ancient city of Pergamum, Asia Minor]

pard (pärd) *n. Regional* PARDNER.

pard·ner (pärd′nər) *n. Regional* Chum; friend; mate. [Alter. of PARTNER]

par·don (pär′dən) *v.t.* **1** To remit the penalty of (a crime, insult, etc.). **2** To release from punishment; forgive for an offense. 3 To allow for; forgive. —*n.* 1 The act of pardoning. 2 A waiving of the execution of the penalties of a violated law. 3 Courteous forbearance: used in making polite excuses. 4 An indulgence. [< L *per-* through + *donare* give] —**par′don·a·ble** *adj.* —**par′don·a·bly** *adv.*

par·don·er (pär′dən·ər) *n.* 1 One who pardons. 2 In the Middle Ages, a layman commissioned to collect offerings for promised indulgences.

pare (pâr) *v.t.* **pared, par·ing** 1 To cut off the covering layer or part of. 2 To cut off or trim away (a covering layer or part): often with *off* or *away.* 3 To reduce or diminish, esp. gradually. [< L *parare* prepare] —**par′er** *n.*

par·e·gor·ic (par′ə·gôr′ik, -gōr′ik) *n.* A soothing preparation, esp. a camphorated tincture of opium. [< Gk. *parēgorikos* soothing]

paren. (*pl.* **parens.**) parenthesis.

pa·ren·chy·ma (pə·reng′ki·mə) *n.* 1 *Biol.* The distinctive, functioning tissue in a gland or other organ. 2 *Bot.* A thin-walled, soft, undifferentiated tissue forming the bulk of leaves, fruit pulp, etc. [< Gk. *para-* beside + *enchyma* infusion] —**par·en·chym·a·tous** (par′eng·kim′ə·təs) *adj.*

par·ent (pâr′ənt) *n.* 1 A father or a mother. 2 Any organism that generates another. 3 A source or wellspring; basis; cause. [< L *parens* parent, orig. pr.p. of *parere* beget] —**pa·ren·tal** (pə·ren′təl) *adj.* —**pa·ren′tal·ly** *adv.*

par·ent·age (pâr′ən·tij) *n.* 1 The relation of a parent; parenthood. 2 Descent or derivation from parents.

pa·ren·the·sis (pə·ren′thə·sis) *n. pl.* **·ses** (-sēz) 1 A word, phrase, or clause inserted in a sentence that is grammatically complete without it, separated usually by commas, dashes, or upright curves. 2 Either or both of the upright curves ( ) so used. 3 Any intervening episode or incident. [< Gk. < *parentithenai* put in beside]

pa·ren·the·size (pə·ren′thə·sīz) *v.t.* **·sized, ·siz·ing** 1 To insert as a parenthesis. 2 To insert parentheses in.

par·en·thet·i·cal (par′ən·thet′i·kəl) *adj.* 1 Of or pertaining to a parenthesis. 2 Used within parentheses. 3 Employing parentheses. 4 Added or inserted as a parenthesis; interjected. 5 Employing or including parentheses. Also **par′en·thet′ic.** —**par′en·thet′i·cal·ly** *adv.*

par·ent·hood (pâr′ənt·hŏŏd) *n.* The condition or relation of a parent.

pa·re·sis (pə·rē′sis, par′ə·sis) *n. pl.* **·ses** (-sēz) 1 Weakness or partial paralysis. 2 A brain disease marked by dementia, paralysis, etc., and due to advanced syphilis: also **general paresis.** [< Gk., a letting go < *parienai* let go] —**pa·ret·ic** (pə·ret′ik, -rē′tik) *adj., n.* —**pa·ret′i·cal·ly** *adv.*

par ex·cel·lence (pär ek′sə·läns, *Fr.* pȧr ek·se·läṅs′) Of the highest excellence; beyond comparison. [F, lit., by way of excellence]

par·fait (pär·fā′) *n.* 1 A dessert made with eggs, sugar, whipped cream, brandy or other flavoring, or fruit, frozen in a tall, thin glass called a **parfait glass.** 2 A dessert composed of layers of ice cream and syrup served in a parfait glass. [F, lit., perfect]

pa·ri·ah (pə·rī′ə) *n.* 1 One of a people of low caste in s India and Burma. 2 A social outcast. [< Tamil *paraiyar* drummer, because drummers at festivals came from this caste]

pa·ri·e·tal (pə·rī′ə·təl) *adj.* Of, pertaining to, or forming the walls of any cavity in the body. —*n.* PARIETAL BONE. [< L *paries* wall]

parietal bone Either of two bones forming a part of the top and sides of the cranium.

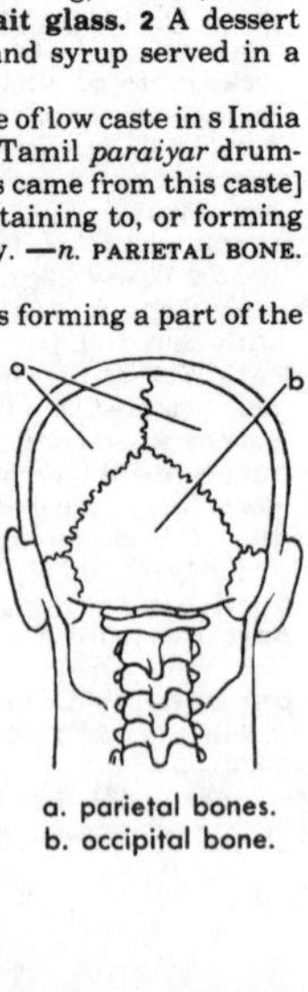

a. parietal bones.
b. occipital bone.

par·i·mu·tu·el (par′i·myŏŏ′chŏŏ·əl) *n.* 1 A system of betting at races in which the winners share in the total amount wagered: also **par′i·mu′tu·el.** 2 A machine for recording bets under this system. [F, a stake or mutual wager]

Par·is (par′is) *Gk. Myth.* A son of Priam who carried off Helen, thus causing the Trojan War.

Paris green A poisonous, emerald-green compound containing arsenic, used largely as an insecticide.

par·ish (par′ish) *n.* 1 *Eccl.* In certain churches, a district in charge of a priest or other clergyman. 2 *U.S.* a A religious congregation, comprising all those who worship at the same church. b The district in which they live. 3 In Louisiana, a civil district corresponding to a county. 4 *Can.* In Quebec and New Brunswick, a political division resembling a township. [< Gk. *paroikia,* orig., a neighborhood]

pa·rish·ion·er (pə·rish′ən·ər) *n.* A member of a parish.

par·i·ty (par′ə·tē) *n. pl.* **·ties** 1 The state or quality of being like or equal, as in rank, value, or position; equivalence. 2 The equivalence of value of currency between two countries, or of the prices of commodities as expressed in a currency. 3 In the U.S., a level for farm prices which gives to the farmer the same purchasing power averaged during a base period. [< L *pars* equal]

park (pärk) *n.* 1 A tract of land for public use in or near a city, usu. laid out with walks, drives, and recreation grounds. 2 An open square or plaza in a city, usu. containing shade trees. 3 A large area of country containing natural scenery, plants, and wildlife, reserved by the government for public enjoyment: a national *park.* 4 A wooded expanse forming part of a country estate. 5 In the w U.S., a plateaulike valley between mountain ranges. 6 *Mil.* An enclosure where munitions, vehicles, etc., are stored. —*v.t.* 1 To place or leave (an automobile, etc.) standing for a time, as on the street. 2 *Informal* To place; set: *Park* your hat on the table. 3 To assemble or mass together. —*v.i.* 4 To park an automobile, etc. [< OF *parc* a game preserve] —**park′er** *n.*

par·ka (pär′kə) *n.* 1 An outer fur garment with a hood, worn in arctic regions. 2 A similar hooded garment, often lined with pile, for sports and casual wear.

Parka *def. 2*

parking lot An area designed for the parking of motor vehicles.

parking meter A device into which a coin is inserted as a fee for parking a vehicle, the time allowed being shown on a scale.

Par·kin·son's disease (pär′kin·sənz) A chronic, progressive nervous disease characterized by muscle tremor when at rest, stiffness, and a rigid facial expression. Also **par′kin·son·ism.** [< James *Parkinson,* 1755–1824, English physician]

park·land (pärk′land′) *n. Often pl.* 1 Land used or designated for use as a park. 2 Grassland with trees, suitable for use as a park.

park·way (pärk′wā′) *n.* A landscaped expressway or large highway.

Parl. Parliament; Parliamentary.

par·lance (pär′ləns) *n.* Manner of speech; language: legal *parlance.* [< OF < *parler* speak]

par·lay (pär·lā′, pär′lē) *v.t.* 1 To place (an original bet and its winnings) on a later race, contest, etc. 2 To increase or exploit (any asset or advantage) successfully. —*n.* 1 The act of parlaying. 2 A bet and its winnings parlayed. [F < Ital., a grand cast at dice < *paro* equal < L *par*]

par·ley (pär′lē) *n.* An oral conference or discussion, as with an enemy. —*v.i.* To hold a conference, esp. with an enemy. [< OF *parler* speak]

par·lia·ment (pär′lə·mənt) *n.* A meeting or assembly for consultation and deliberation; esp., a national legislative body. [< OF *parler* speak]

Par·lia·ment (pär′lə·mənt) *n.* 1 The supreme legislature of Great Britain and Northern Ireland. 2 Any of various other legislatures resembling it.

par·lia·men·ta·ry (pär′lə·men′tər·ē, -men′trē) *adj.* 1 Pertaining to, characterized by, or enacted by a parliament. 2 According to the rules of Parliament. 3 Admissible in a deliberative assembly. —**par′lia·men′tar′i·an** (-men′târ′ē·ən) *adj., n.*

par·lor (pär′lər) *n.* 1 A room for reception of callers or entertainment of guests. 2 A room in an inn, hotel, etc., for private conversation, appointments, etc. 3 A place of business equipped to perform specialized personal services: a beauty *parlor. Brit. sp.* **·lour.** [< LL *parabolare* speak]

parlor car A railway car fitted with individual chairs.

par·lous (pär′ləs) *adj. Archaic* Dangerous or exciting;

perilous. —*adv.* Exceedingly; very. [Var. of PERILOUS] — **par′lous·ly** *adv.*

Par·me·san cheese (pär′mə·zon, -zən, -zan) A hard, dry cheese, usu. grated and served on soups, spaghetti, etc. [after *Parma,* Italy, where originally made]

Par·nas·si·an (pär·nas′ē·ən) *adj.* **1** Belonging or relating to the mountain Parnassus. **2** Of or pertaining to a school of French poetry of the 19th century.

pa·ro·chi·al (pə·rō′kē·əl) *adj.* **1** Pertaining to, supported by, or confined to a parish. **2** Restricted in scope; narrow; provincial. [< LL *parochialis*] —**pa·ro′chi·al·ism** *n.* —**pa·ro′·chi·al·ly** *adv.* —**Syn. 2** limited, uninformed, unenlightened.

parochial school A school supported and directed by a church.

par·o·dy (par′ə·dē) *n. pl.* **·dies 1** A literary composition imitating and ridiculing some serious work. **2** Any burlesque imitation of something serious. **3** A poor imitation. —*v.t.* **·died, ·dy·ing** To make a parody of; travesty. [< Gk. *parōidia* a burlesque poem or song] —**pa·rod·ic** (pə·rod′ik) or **·i·cal** *adj.* —**par′o·dist** *n.*

pa·role (pə·rōl′) *n.* **1** The conditional release of a prisoner from jail prior to the expiration of his term. **2** A pledge of honor by a prisoner of war in return for his release, as that he will not serve against his captors. —*v.t.* **·roled, ·rol·ing** To release on parole. [F *parole (d'honneur)* word (of honor)]

pa·rot·id (pə·rot′id) *adj. Anat.* Situated near the ear. —*n.* PAROTID GLAND. [< Gk. *para-* beside + *ous, ōtos* ear]

parotid gland Either of two large salivary glands located below and in front of the ear.

-parous *suffix* Giving birth to; bearing; producing: *oviparous.* [< L *parere* beget]

par·ox·ysm (par′ək·siz′əm) *n.* **1** A sudden attack or worsening of a disease; a fit. **2** A sudden and violent outburst, as of anger or laughter. [< Gk. *para-* beside + *oxynein* to goad] —**par·ox·ys·mal** (par′ək·siz′məl) *adj.*

par·quet (pär·kā′) *n.* **1** The main-floor space of a theater; orchestra. **2** Flooring of inlaid woodwork; parquetry. —*v.t.* **·queted** (-kād′), **·quet·ing** (-kā′ing) To make of or ornament with parquetry. Also **par·quette** (pär·ket′). [< OF *parchet* a small compartment, dim. of *parc* park]

parquet circle The section of theater seats at the rear of the parquet and under the balcony.

par·quet·ry (pär′kit·rē) *n.* Inlaid woodwork forming geometric patterns, used esp. for floor surfaces.

parr (pär) *n.* A young salmon before its first migration seaward. [?]

par·ra·keet (par′ə·kēt) *n.* PARAKEET.

par·ri·cide (par′ə·sīd) *n.* **1** The murder of a parent, or of a close relative. **2** One who commits such a crime. [< L *paricidium* a killing of a relative] —**par′ri·ci′dal** *adj.*

par·rot (par′ət) *n.* **1** Any of certain birds of warm regions having a hooked bill, usu. brilliant plumage, and, in some, an ability to simulate human speech. **2** A person who repeats or imitates without understanding. —*v.t.* To repeat or imitate without understanding. [? < F *Pierrot,* dim. of *Pierre* Peter, a personal name] —**par′rot·er** *n.*

parrot fever PSITTACOSIS.

parrot fish Any of many small, vividly colored fishes inhabiting warm seas, having beaklike jaws.

par·ry (par′ē) *v.* **·ried, ·ry·ing** *v.t.* **1** To ward off, as a blow or a thrust in fencing. **2** To avoid, esp. by a deft evasion: to *parry* a question. —*v.i.* **3** To make a parry. **4** To avoid something, as by skillful maneuvers. —*n. pl.* **·ries 1** A defensive movement, as in fencing. **2** An evasion or diversion. [< Ital. *parare* defend] —**Syn.** *v.* **2** evade, dodge, sidestep, duck.

parse (pärs) *v.t.* **parsed, pars·ing 1** To describe (a sentence) grammatically by giving the form, function, etc., of each of its components. **2** To describe (a word) as to its part of speech, form, and relation to the other sentence elements. [< L *pars, partis* part] —**pars′er** *n.*

Par·see (pär′sē, pär·sē′) *n.* A Zoroastrian, esp. one whose ancestors fled to India about the eighth century. Also **Par′si.** —**Par′see·ism, Par′si·ism, Par′sism** *n.*

par·si·mo·ni·ous (pär′sə·mō′nē·əs) *adj.* Stingy; niggardly; miserly. —**par′si·mo′ni·ous·ly** *adv.* —**par′si·mo′ni·ous·ness** *n.*

par·si·mo·ny (pär′sə·mō′nē) *n.* Undue reluctance to spend money; stinginess. [< L *parcere* spare]

pars·ley (pärs′lē) *n.* A cultivated edible herb with aromatic, finely divided leaves, used as a garnish and for flavoring. [< Gk. *petra* rock + *selinon* parsley]

pars·nip (pärs′nip) *n.* **1** A cultivated plant related to parsley, with a pale, edible root. **2** The root, used as a vegetable. [< L *pastinaca*]

par·son (pär′sən) *n.* **1** The clergyman of a parish or congregation. **2** Any minister. [< Med. L *persona* a rector]

par·son·age (pär′sən·ij) *n.* A clergyman's residence provided by his church.

part (pärt) *n.* **1** A certain portion or amount of anything; a piece. **2** One of a number of separable elements that together constitute a whole: the *parts* of a motor. **3** An essential portion of a body or an organism; a member. **4** *Usu. pl.* A portion of territory; region: in foreign *parts.* **5** An individual share, as of duty, business, or performance: to do one's *part.* **6** A side, cause, or party opposed to another. **7** The role or lines assigned to an actor. **8** *Usu. pl.* A quality of mind or character; talent: a man of *parts.* **9** *Music* **a** The series of sounds to be made by a single voice or instrument in a concerted piece. **b** The notated version of this. **10** A line formed by dividing the hair. —**for my part** As far as I am concerned. —**for the most part** On the whole; generally. —**in part** Partly. —**on the part of** So far as regards. —**part and parcel** An essential part. —**take part** To participate: usu. with *in.* —**take someone's part** To support someone's position, as in a dispute. —*v.t.* **1** To divide or break (something) into parts. **2** To sever or discontinue (a relationship or connection): to *part* company. **3** To separate by being or coming between. **4** To comb (the hair) so as to leave a dividing line. —*v.i.* **5** To become divided or broken into parts; come apart; divide. **6** To go away from each other; separate. **7** To depart; leave. —**part from** To separate from; leave. —**part with 1** To give up; relinquish. **2** To part from. —*adj.* Of or concerning only a part; partial. —*adv.* In some degree; to some extent; partly. [< L *pars, partis* part] —**Syn.** *n.* **1** segment, section, fraction. **2** component, constituent, ingredient, module.

part. participle.

par·take (pär·tāk′) *v.* **·took, ·tak·en, ·tak·ing** *v.i.* **1** To take part or have a share: with *in.* **2** To receive or take a portion: with *of:* to *partake* of food and drink. **3** To have something of the quality or character: with *of.* —*v.t.* **4** To take or have a part in; share. [< *part taker*] —**par·tak′er** *n.*

part·ed (pär′tid) *adj.* Situated or placed apart; separated; cloven.

par·terre (pär·târ′) *n.* **1** A flower garden having beds arranged in a pattern. **2** PARQUET CIRCLE. [< MF *par terre* on (the) ground]

par·the·no·gen·e·sis (pär′thə·nō·jen′ə·sis) *n.* Reproduction by means of unfertilized eggs, seeds, or spores, as in certain insects, algae, etc. [< Gk. *parthenos* virgin + GENESIS] —**par′the·no·ge·net′ic** (-jə·net′ik), **par′the·no·gen′ic** *adj.* —**par′the·no·ge·net′i·cal·ly** *adv.*

Par·the·non (pär′thə·non) *n.* The Doric temple of Athena on the Acropolis at Athens, built in the fifth century B.C.

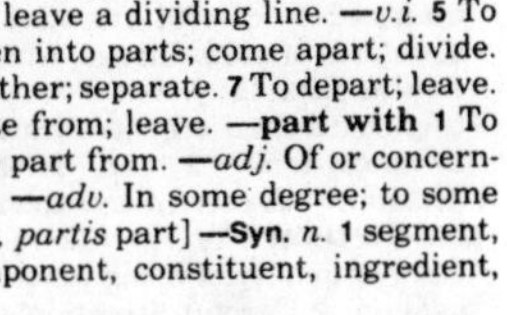

The Parthenon

par·tial (pär′shəl) *adj.* **1** Pertaining to, constituting, or involving a part only; not complete or total. **2** Favoring one side; prejudiced; biased. **3** Having a special liking: with *to.* —**par′tial·ly** *adv.*

par·ti·al·i·ty (pär′shē·al′ə·tē) *n.* **1** The state of being partial. **2** Unfairness; bias. **3** A particular fondness. Also **par′tial·ness.**

partial tone *Music* A fundamental tone or overtone.

add, āce, câre, pälm; end, ēven; it, īce; odd, ōpen, ôrder; to͝ok, po͞ol; up, bûrn; ə = *a* in *above, u* in *focus;* yo͞o = *u* in *fuse;* oil; pout; check; go; ring; thin; this; zh, *vision.* < derived from; ? origin uncertain or unknown.

par·tic·i·pant (pär·tis′ə·pənt) *n.* One who participates. —*adj.* Participating.

par·tic·i·pate (pär·tis′ə·pāt) *v.i.* **·pat·ed, ·pat·ing** To take part or have a share in common with others: with *in.* [< L *pars, partis* a part + *capere* take] —**par·tic′i·pa′tion, par·tic′i·pance, par·tic′i·pa′tor** *n.* —**par·tic′i·pa·to′ry** (-pə·tôr′ē, -tō′rē) *adj.*

par·ti·cip·i·al (pär′tə·sip′ē·əl) *adj. Gram.* Having the nature, form, or use of a participle. —**par′ti·cip′i·al·ly** *adv.*

par·ti·ci·ple (pär′tə·sip′əl) *n. Gram.* A word derived from a verb and functioning as both a verb and an adjective. [<L *participium* a sharing, partaking] • **A dangling participle** is a participle that appears to modify the wrong word and therefore makes no sense, as in *Hopping aboard the train, the whistle blew* (instead of *I heard the whistle blow*). But the meaning of sentences including participles like *concerning* or *considering,* when functioning as prepositions, is perfectly clear, and such usage is well established: *Concerning the debt, you may have a month's extension; Considering everything, he did well.*

par·ti·cle (pär′ti·kəl) *n.* **1** A minute part, piece, or portion. **2** Any very small amount or slight degree: without a *particle* of truth. **3** *Physics* Any of the minute components of matter; esp., an **elementary particle,** one of the elementary constituents of an atom, thought to be irreducible, as an electron, neutron, proton, etc. **4** *Gram.* **a** A short, uninflected part of speech, as a conjunction. **b** A prefix or suffix. [<L *particula,* dim. of *pars, partis* a part]

par·ti-col·ored (pär′tē·kul′ərd) *adj.* Having various colors. [<F *partir* divide + COLORED]

par·tic·u·lar (pər·tik′yə·lər) *adj.* **1** Of, being, or pertaining to a single or separate thing. **2** Having a special character; distinctive: a *particular* way of doing things. **3** More than usual; especial: no *particular* hurry. **4** Comprising all details or circumstances: a *particular* description. **5** Characterized by careful attention to detail; requiring high standards of performance; exacting; fastidious. —**in particular** Especially. —*n.* **1** A specific fact or detail, as distinguished from a generalization. **2** A separate or single instance; item. —**Syn.** *adj.* **1** definite, specific. **2** individual, peculiar. [<L *particularis* concerning a part]

par·tic·u·lar·i·ty (pər·tik′yə·lar′ə·tē) *n. pl.* **·ties** **1** The state or quality of being particular as distinguished from general. **2** Careful attention to detail; fastidiousness. **3** Something that is particular, as a circumstance or detail.

par·tic·u·lar·ize (pər·tik′yə·lə·rīz′) *v.* **·ized, ·iz·ing** *v.t.* **1** To speak of or treat individually or in detail. —*v.i.* **2** To give particulars; be specific. —**par·tic′u·lar·i·za′tion** *n.*

par·tic·u·lar·ly (pər·tik′yə·lər·lē) *adv.* **1** With specific reference. **2** In an unusually great degree: *particularly* difficult. **3** Part by part; in detail.

part·ing (pär′ting) *n.* **1** The act of separating or dividing. **2** A place, line, or point of division. **3** A leave-taking. —*adj.* Occurring while taking leave: a *parting* glance.

par·ti·san (pär′tə·zən, -sən) *n.* **1** One who supports or endorses a party or cause with great devotion or zeal; esp., an overzealous or fanatical devotee. **2** A member of a body of irregular troops; a guerrilla. —*adj.* Pertaining to or characteristic of a partisan. Also **par′ti·zan.** [<Ital. *parte* a part] —**par′ti·san·ship** *n.*

par·tite (pär′tīt) *adj.* Divided into or composed of parts: usu. used in combination: *bipartite, tripartite.* [<L *partire* divide]

par·ti·tion (pär·tish′ən) *n.* **1** The act of parting, or the state of being parted; division; separation. **2** A wall or other barrier dividing an area, esp. an interior space. —*v.t.* **1** To divide into parts, segments, etc. **2** To separate by a partition: with *off.* **3** To divide, as property, into shares or portions. [<L *partire* divide] —**par·ti′tion·er** *n.*

par·ti·tive (pär′tə·tiv) *adj.* **1** Separating into integral parts. **2** *Gram.* Denoting a part as distinct from the whole: *partitive* genitive. —*n. Gram.* A partitive word or case. [< L *partitus,* p.p. of *partire* divide] —**par′ti·tive·ly** *adv.*

part·ly (pärt′lē) *adv.* In some part; in some degree; somewhat.

part·ner (pärt′nər) *n.* **1** One who takes part or is associated with another or others in a business or other enterprise. **2** A husband or wife. **3** Either of two people dancing together. **4** One of two or more people comprising a side or team in a competitive game or sport. [<L *partitio* a share]

part·ner·ship (pärt′nər·ship) *n.* **1** The state of being a partner or partners. **2** Joint interests or ownership. **3** An association founded on a contract between two or more persons to share the profits, expenses, and losses of a business enterprise; also, the contract itself. **4** The group of persons so associated.

part of speech One of the eight traditional classes of words in English, namely: noun, pronoun, verb, adjective, adverb, conjunction, preposition, and interjection.

par·took (pär·to͝ok′) *p.t.* of PARTAKE.

par·tridge (pär′trij) *n.* Any of various chickenlike game birds, as the ruffed grouse, bobwhite, etc. [<Gk. *perdix* a partridge]

Gray partridge

part song A song for two or more voices, esp. without accompaniment.

part-time (pärt′tīm′) *adj.* Working or occupied with an activity for only a part of the time customarily devoted to that activity. —*adv.* On a part-time schedule or basis. —**part′-tim′er** *n.*

par·tu·ri·ent (pär·tyo͝or′ē·ənt) *adj.* **1** Bringing forth or about to bring forth young. **2** Pertaining to childbirth.

par·tu·ri·tion (pär′tyo͞o·rish′ən, -cho͞o-) *n.* The act or process of bringing forth young; childbirth. [<L *parturire* be in labor]

par·ty (pär′tē) *n. pl.* **·ties** **1** A body of persons united for some common purpose, as a political organization. **2** One who participates in or is involved with an action, proceeding, inquiry, etc.: a *party* to the investigation. **3** *Law* One of the persons named on the record in an action. **4** A social gathering: a dinner *party.* **5** A detachment of soldiers. **6** *Informal* A person. —*adj.* **1** Of or pertaining to a political party. **2** Suitable for a social party: a *party* dress. —*v.i.* **·tied, ·ty·ing** *Informal* To attend or give social parties. [<L *pars, partis* a part]

party line **1** A telephone line or circuit serving two or more subscribers: also **party wire.** **2** A boundary line between the properties of two or more owners. **3** A belief or principle of a political party, esp. the Communist party, regarded as an essential conviction of every loyal member. —**par′ty-lin′er** *n.*

par·ve·nu (pär′və·nyo͞o) *n.* One who has suddenly attained wealth or power but lacks the social status commensurate with it; an upstart. —*adj.* **1** Being a parvenu. **2** Like or characteristic of a parvenu. [<L *pervenire* to come through]

par·vo·vi·rus (pär′vō·vī·rəs) *n.* A tiny virus, containing DNA, occurring in various animals, esp. canines. [<L *parvus* small + VIRUS]

pas (pä) *n.* **1** A step. **2** A dance. [F, a step]

pas·chal (pas′kəl) **1** Of or pertaining to the Jewish Passover. **2** Of or pertaining to Easter. [<L *pascha* Passover]

pa·sha (pə·shä′, pash′ə, pä′shə) *n.* **1** A Turkish honorary title placed after the name. **2** A title given a high-ranking official in Turkey.

pasque·flow·er (pask′flou′ər) *n.* Any of several anemones, esp. an early-blooming, crocuslike wildflower of North America with purplish flowers and hairy leaves. Also **pasch′flow′er.** [<OF<*passer* excel + *fleur* flower]

pass (pas, päs) *v.t.* **1** To go by or move past and leave behind. **2** To go across, around, over, or through. **3** To permit to go unnoticed or unmentioned. **4** To undergo; experience: to *pass* a bad night. **5** To meet the requirements of. **6** To go beyond; surpass: It *passes* comprehension. **7** To cause to go or move: to *pass* one's eyes over a book. **8** To cause to go or move past: to *pass* troops in review. **9** To cause or allow to advance or proceed. **10** To spend: to *pass* the night at an inn. **11** To give approval to. **12** To enact, as a law. **13** To be approved by: The bill *passed* the senate. **14** To omit paying (a dividend). **15** To put in circulation: *Pass* the word. **16** To pronounce, esp. judicially, as judgment or sentence. **17** To discharge from the body. **18** To pledge, as one's word. **19** To perform a pass (*n.* def. 6) on or over. **20** In sports, to transfer (the ball, etc.)

to another player on the same side. **21** *Law* To transfer or assign ownership of to another by will, deed, etc. *—v.i.* **22** To go or proceed; move. **23** To have course or direction; extend: The road *passed* under a bridge. **24** To go away; depart. **25** To come to an end; disappear. **26** To elapse or go by; be spent: The day *passed* slowly. **27** To die. **28** To go by; move past in or as in review. **29** To go from person to person; circulate. **30** To be mutually given and received, as greetings. **31** To go or change from one condition, circumstance, etc., to another. **32** To take place; happen. **33** To go unheeded or unpunished. **34** To undergo a test, examination, etc., successfully. **35** To be approved, ratified, enacted, etc. **36** To obtain or force passage. **37** To be excreted or voided. **38** *Law* **a** To give or pronounce judgment, sentence, etc.: with *on* or *upon.* **b** To be transferred or assigned to another by will, deed, etc. **39** In sports, to transfer the ball, etc., to another player on the same side. **40** In fencing, to make a thrust; lunge. **41** In card games, to decline to make a play, bid, etc. **—bring to pass** To cause to happen or to be realized. **—come to pass** To happen; come about. **—pass away 1** To come to an end. **2** To die. **3** To allow (time) to elapse. **—pass for** To be accepted as, usu. fraudulently. **—pass off 1** To come to an end. **2** To give out or circulate as genuine; palm off. **—pass out 1** To distribute. **2** *Informal* To faint. **—pass over** To fail to notice or consider. **—pass up** *Informal* To fail to take advantage of, as an offer. *—n.* **1** The act of passing. **2** A way or opening that affords a passage, as a gap in a mountain range. **3** Permission or a permit to proceed. **4** A state of affairs; crisis. **5** The successful undergoing of an examination, test, or inspection. **6** A sleight-of-hand movement of a hand, wand, etc. **7** A movement made in attempting to stab or strike. **8** In sports, the action of passing the ball, puck, etc., in the course of play. **9** *Slang* **a** An attempt to caress. **b** Any aggressive action intended to lead to sexual familiarity. **—a pretty pass** *Informal* An unpleasant or difficult situation. [< L *passus* a step]— **pass′er** *n.* • **passed, past** *Passed* is the past tense of the verb *to pass,* but unlike many participles, its use as an adjective is restricted to a very few expressions in which the sense is that of an object physically moving by, as in the baseball term *passed ball. Past,* on the other hand, is commonly used as an adjective *(past time),* adverb *(a bird flew past),* noun *(in the past),* or preposition *(ten minutes past the hour),* and is found only in archaic contexts as the past participle of *pass.*

pass·a·ble (pas′ə·bəl, päs′-) *adj.* **1** Capable of being penetrated or traversed. **2** Fairly good or acceptable. **3** Fit for general circulation. **—pass′a·ble·ness** *n.* **—pass′a·bly** *adv.* **—Syn. 2** mediocre, moderate, tolerable, unobjectionable.

pas·sage (pas′ij) *n.* **1** A corridor, hall, or gallery affording access from one part, as of a building, to another. **2** A way through or over. **3** Free entrance, exit, or transit. **4** A passing: the *passage* of the days. **5** A portion of a discourse, writing, etc.: a *passage* from Shakespeare. **6** A journey, as by ship. **7** A navigable route. **8** The enactment of a legislative measure. **9** A personal encounter: a *passage* with swords. **10** Migration, esp. of birds. **11** In music, any short portion of a composition.

pas·sage·way (pas′ij·wā′) *n.* A way affording passage between rooms, areas, etc.

pass·book (pas′bo͝ok′, päs′-) *n.* A bankbook.

pas·sé (pa·sā′, pas′ā) *adj.* **1** Past the prime; faded. **2** Old-fashioned. [F, orig., pp. of *passer*]

passed ball In baseball, a pitch that passes by the catcher and enables a runner to advance a base.

pas·sen·ger (pas′ən·jər) *n.* A person who travels in a car, train, bus, etc. [<OF *passager* < *passage*]

passenger pigeon The wild migratory pigeon of North America, now extinct.

pas·ser-by (pas′ər·bī′, päs′-, pas′ər·bī) *n. pl.* **pas·sers-by** A person who passes by, usu. casually.

pas·ser·ine (pas′ər·īn) *adj.* Pertaining to a very large order of birds having feet adapted to perching and young that are naked and blind when hatched. *—n.* Any of these birds. [< L *passer* sparrow + -INE]

pas·sim (pas′im) *adv.* Here and there; in various passages: used as a bibliographic reference. [L]

pass·ing (pas′ing, päs′-) *adj.* **1** Going by or away. **2** Transitory; fleeting. **3** Happening or occurring; current. **4** Done, said, found, used, or given in or as in passing. **5** Indicating fulfillment of requirements for advancement. *—n.* **1** A going away. **2** Dying. **3** An act of passing or passage. **—in passing** Incidentally; in the course of discussion. *—adv. Archaic* In a surpassing degree; exceedingly.

pas·sion (pash′ən) *n.* **1** Fervent devotion. **2** Ardent sexual feelings and desire; love. **3** The object of such feelings. **4** A fit of intense anger; rage. **5** Any transport of excited feeling. **6** *Archaic* Suffering; agony. [< L *passus,* pp. of *pati* suffer] **—pas′sion·less** *adj.* **—pas′sion·less·ly** *adv.*

Pas·sion (pash′ən) *n.* The sufferings of Christ, esp. in the agony of the garden and on the cross.

pas·sion·ate (pash′ən·it) *adj.* **1** Susceptible to strong emotion; excitable. **2** Easily moved to anger. **3** Expressing or displaying some intense feeling. **4** Ardent in expressing sexual desire. [< L *passio* suffering] **—pas′sion·ate·ly** *adv.* **—pas′sion·ate·ness** *n.*

pas·sion·flow·er (pash′ən·flou′ər) *n.* Any of various tendril-climbing vines or shrubs of tropical America, with showy flowers and sometimes edible fruit.

passion fruit The melonlike fruit of certain cultivated passionflowers.

Passion play A drama representing the Passion of Christ.

pas·sive (pas′iv) *adj.* **1** Acted upon or receiving impressions from external agents or causes. **2** In a state of rest or quiescence; unresponsive. **3** Unresisting; submissive. **4** *Chem.* Inert; inactive. **5** *Gram.* Designating a voice of a verb which indicates that the subject is being acted upon, as *Caesar was killed by Brutus. —n. Gram.* **1** The passive voice. **2** A verb or construction in this voice. [< L *passus,* pp. of *pati* suffer] **—pas′sive·ly** *adv.* **—pas′sive·ness, pas·siv·i·ty** (pa·siv′ə·tē)

passive resistance Opposition to constituted authority expressed typically in voluntary fasting, refusal to obey laws, etc.

pass·key (pas′kē′, päs′-) *n.* A skeleton key or master key.

Pass·o·ver (pas′ō′vər, päs′-) *n.* An annual Jewish feast celebrated in the spring, commemorating the night when the Lord, smiting the firstborn of the Egyptians, "passed over" the houses of the children of Israel. *Ex.* 12.

pass·port (pas′pôrt′, -pōrt′, päs′-) *n.* **1** An official warrant certifying the citizenship of the bearer when traveling abroad. **2** Anything that gives the privilege or right to enter into some place or sphere of action. [< F *passer* pass + *port* harbor]

pass-through (pas′thro͞o′, päs′-) *n.* A wall opening, often with a shelf, as between a kitchen and a dining area, for passing dishes, food, etc.

pass·word (pas′wûrd′, päs′-) *n.* A word identifying one as entitled to pass; a watchword.

past (past, päst) *adj.* **1** Belonging to time gone by. **2** Recently gone by: the *past* week. **3** *Gram.* Denoting a tense or construction which refers to time or action belonging to the past. *—n.* **1** The past life of a person, people, etc. **2** One's record, esp. if disreputable or kept secret. **3** *Gram.* **a** The past tense. **b** A verb or construction in this tense. **—the past** Time gone by; former days collectively. *—adv.* In such manner as to go by and beyond. *—prep.* **1** Beyond in time: It is now *past* noon. **2** Beyond in place or position: walking *past* the house. **3** Beyond the reach or influence of. **4** Beyond in amount or degree: He couldn't count *past* ten. [Orig. pp. of PASS] • See PASS.

pas·ta (päs′tə) *n.* Any of a number of foods made of flour pastes or doughs, as spaghetti, macaroni, etc. [< LL, dough]

paste (pāst) *n.* **1** An adhesive mixture used for joining or affixing paper articles and the like. **2** A mixture of flour and water, often with other materials, for cooking purposes; dough. **3** Any doughy or moist plastic substance: *toothpaste;* almond *paste.* **4** A vitreous composition for making imitation gems. —*v.t.* **past·ed, past·ing** 1 To stick or fasten with paste or the like. 2 *Slang* To strike, as with the fist. [< Gk. *pastē* barley porridge]

paste·board (pāst′bôrd′, -bōrd′) *n.* 1 Paper pulp compressed, or paper pasted together to form a stiff sheet. 2 *Slang* Something made of pasteboard, as a playing card. —*adj.* 1 Made of or resembling pasteboard. 2 Thin and flimsy.

pas·tel (pas·tel′) *n.* 1 A picture drawn with colored crayons. 2 The art of drawing such pictures. 3 A hard crayon made of pipe clay and a pigment, mixed with gum and water. 4 A soft, delicate shade of a color. —*adj.* 1 Of or pertaining to a pastel. 2 Having a delicate, soft tint. [< Ital. *pastello*] —**pas·tel′ist** or **pas·tel′list** *n.*

past·er (pās′tər) *n.* 1 One who pastes. 2 A strip of gummed paper to paste over something.

pas·tern (pas′tərn) *n.* The part of a horse's foot between the fetlock and the hoof. [< OF *pasture* a tether for a grazing animal]

Pastern

paste-up (pāst′up′) *n.* 1 In printing, a layout of a page or pages of columns set in type, illustrations, etc., pasted on a stiff paper backing. 2 A collage.

pas·teur·i·za·tion (pas′tər·ə·zā′shən, -chər-) *n.* A process of controlled heating of milk, beer, etc., to destroy bacteria and arrest spoilage without affecting flavor. *Brit. sp.* **pas′teur·i·sa′tion.** [< Louis *Pasteur,* 1822–95, French chemist] —**pas·teur·ize** (-pas′tə·rīz, -chə·rīz) *v.t.* **(-ized, -iz·ing)**

pas·tille (pas·tēl′, -til′) *n.* 1 A medicated, flavored lozenge. 2 A pellet of combustible aromatic substances for deodorizing or fumigation. Also **pas·til** (pas′til). [F< L *pastillus* a little loaf]

pas·time (pas′tīm′, päs′-) *n.* Something that serves to make time pass agreeably; recreation. [< PASS, *v.* + TIME]

past master 1 One who has held the office of master in certain benevolent organizations. 2 One who has thorough experience in something; an adept.

pas·tor (pas′tər, päs′-) *n.* A Christian minister who has a church or congregation under his official charge. [< L *pastor* a shepherd, lit., a feeder]

pas·tor·al (pas′tər·əl, päs′-) *adj.* 1 Pertaining to shepherds and their work. 2 Describing the conventionalized life of shepherds and rustics: a *pastoral* poem. 3 Having the peaceful simplicity of country life; natural. 4 Pertaining to a pastor and his work. —*n.* 1 A poem, play, etc., set in rustic surroundings. 2 A picture illustrating rural scenes. 3 *Eccl.* A letter from a pastor to his congregation. —**Syn.** *adj.* 3 bucolic, rustic.

pas·tor·ate (pas′tər·it, päs′-) *n.* 1 The office or jurisdiction of a pastor. 2 The duration of a pastoral charge. 3 Pastors collectively.

past participle A verb form used to indicate a time or action completed in the past, as *cooked* in *She has cooked dinner.*

past perfect *Gram.* 1 Denoting the tense of a verb indicating an action completed prior to a specified past time, as *had finished* in *He had finished before the bell rang.* 2 The past perfect tense, or a verb in this tense.

pas·tra·mi (pə·strä′mē) *n.* Smoked beef, heavily seasoned and usu. cut from the shoulder. [< Magyar]

pas·try (pās′trē) *n. pl.* **·tries** 1 Articles of food made with a crust of shortened dough, as pies. 2 Any of various sweet baked goods, as cakes, buns, etc. [< PASTE + -RY]

pas·tur·age (pas′chər·ij, päs′-) *n.* 1 Grass and herbage for cattle. 2 Ground used or suitable for grazing. 3 The business or right of grazing cattle.

pas·ture (pas′chər, päs′-) *n.* 1 Ground for the grazing of domestic animals. 2 Grass or herbage that grazing domestic animals eat. —*v.* **·tured, ·tur·ing** *v.t.* 1 To lead to or put in a pasture to graze. 2 To graze on (grass, land, etc.). —*v.i.* 3 To graze. [< L *pastus,* pp. of *pascere* to feed] —**pas′tur·er** *n.*

past·y[1] (pās′tē) *adj.* **past·i·er, past·i·est** 1 Like paste in consistency. 2 Sickly and pale: a *pasty* complexion. —**past′i·ness** *n.*

past·y[2] (pās′tē, *Brit.* pas′tē, päs′tē) *n. pl.* **past·ies** A meat pie. [< LL *pasta* dough]

pat[1] (pat) *v.* **pat·ted, pat·ting** *v.t.* 1 To touch or tap lightly with the hand. 2 To shape or mold by a pat or pats. 3 To strike with lightly sounding steps, as in running. —*v.i.* 4 To tap or strike gently. 5 To run or walk with light steps. —*n.* 1 A light, caressing stroke. 2 The sound of patting or pattering. 3 A small, molded mass, as of butter. [ME *patte*] —**pat′ter** *n.*

pat[2] (pat) *adj.* 1 Suitable, as a response; fitting. 2 Formulated in a customary way without much thought; facile. —*adv.* In a fit manner. —**stand pat** *Informal* To refuse to reconsider or change, as an opinion, decision, etc. —**pat′ly** *adv.* —**pat′ness** *n.*

pat. patent; patented; patrol; pattern.

patch (pach) *n.* 1 A small piece of material, used to repair a hole, tear, or worn place. 2 A piece of adhesive tape or the like, applied to the skin to hide a blemish or protect a small wound. 3 **a** A small piece of ground. **b** The plants growing on it: a *patch* of corn. 4 A piece of cloth or other material worn over an injured eye. 5 A small piece of cloth sewed on a garment, esp. a uniform, as an emblem or insignia of rank. 6 A shred or scrap. —*v.t.* 1 To put a patch or patches on. 2 To repair or put together hurriedly or crudely: often with *up* or *together.* 3 To make of patches, as a quilt. —**patch (things) up** To resolve or settle, as a quarrel. [ME *pacche*] —**patch′er** *n.*

patch·ou·li (pach′ōō·lē, pə·chōō′lē) *n.* 1 An East Indian herb of the mint family. 2 A fragrant oil or perfume obtained from it. Also **patch′ou·ly.** [< Tamil *paccu* green + *ilai* a leaf]

patch test A skin test for determining hypersensitivity by applying small pads of possibly allergy-producing substances to the skin's surface.

patch·work (pach′wûrk′) *n.* 1 A fabric made of patches of cloth, as for quilts, etc. 2 Work done hastily or carelessly; a jumble.

patch·y (pach′ē) *adj.* **patch·i·er, patch·i·est** 1 Of, containing, or consisting of patches. 2 Occurring here and there rather than uniformly: *patchy* fog. —**patch′i·ly** *adv.* —**patch′i·ness** *n.*

patd. patented.

pate (pāt) *n.* 1 The top of the head, esp. a human head. 2 Brains; intellect: usu. humorous. [ME]

pâté de foie gras (pä·tā′ də fwa grä′) *French* A paste made from the livers of fattened geese.

pa·tel·la (pə·tel′ə) *n. pl.* **·las** or **·tel·lae** (-tel′ē) The flat, movable, oval bone at the front of the human knee joint. [L, dim. of *patina* a pan] —**pa·tel′lar, pa·tel·late** (pə·tel′āt, -it) *adj.*

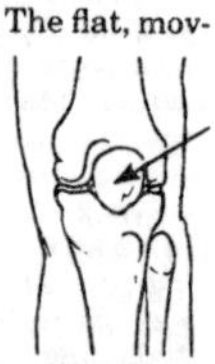

Patella

pat·en (pat′n) *n.* 1 A plate for the eucharistic bread. 2 A thin, metallic plate. [< L *patena* a pan]

pa·ten·cy (pāt′n·sē) *n.* 1 The condition of being evident. 2 The state of being without obstruction.

pat·ent (pat′nt, *Brit.* pāt′nt; *for adj. defs. 2 & 3, usu.* pāt′nt) *n.* 1 A government protection to an inventor, securing to him for a specific time exclusive rights to his invention. 2 The rights so granted. 3 Any official document securing a right. —*v.t.* To obtain a patent on (an invention). —*adj.* 1 Protected or conferred by a patent. 2 Manifest or apparent to everybody. 3 Open; unobstructed, as a duct in the body. [< L *patens* pr.p. of *patere* lie open]

pat·ent leather (pat′nt) Leather finished with a glossy, varnishlike coat: so called from the formerly patented process.

pa·tent·ly (pāt′nt·lē, pat′nt-) *adv.* Manifestly; clearly.

pa·ter (pā′tər) *n. Brit. Informal* Father. [L]

pa·ter·fa·mil·i·as (pā′tər·fə·mil′ē·əs) *n. pl.* **pa·tres·fa·mil·i·as** (pā′trēz-) The father of a family or master of a house. [< L *pater* father + *familia* family]

pa·ter·nal (pə·tûr′nəl) *adj.* 1 Pertaining to a father; fatherly. 2 Derived from one's father; hereditary. 3 Related through one's father: a *paternal* aunt. [< L *pater* a father] —**pa·ter′nal·ly** *adv.*

pa·ter·nal·ism (pə·tûr′nəl·iz′əm) *n.* The control of a country, community, or group in a manner suggestive of a father looking after his children. —**pa·ter′nal·is′tic** *adj.* —**pa·ter′nal·is′ti·cal·ly** *adv.*

pa·ter·ni·ty (pə·tûr′nə·tē) *n.* **1** The condition of being a father. **2** Parentage on the male side. **3** Origin in general.

pa·ter·nos·ter (pā′tər·nos′tər) *n.* **1** The Lord's Prayer, esp. in Latin: also **Pater Noster.** **2** A bead of the rosary representing one recitation of the Lord's Prayer. [< L *pater noster* our father]

path (path, päth) *n. pl.* **paths** (pat͟hz, pät͟hz, paths, päths) **1** A walk or way, as one beaten by the foot, used by men or animals. **2** Any road, track, or course. **3** A way of life or course of action. [< OE *pæth*]

path., pathol. pathology.

Pa·than (pə·tän′, pā′thən) *n.* One of a people of Afghanistan of Indo-Iranian stock and Muslim religion.

pa·thet·ic (pə·thet′ik) *adj.* Inspiring pity; arousing compassion. Also **pa·thet′i·cal.** [< Gk. *pathētikos* sensitive] —**pa·thet′i·cal·ly** *adv.*

pathetic fallacy The attribution of human feelings and emotions to inanimate nature, as in *The November sky wept.*

path·find·er (path′fīn′dər, päth′-) *n.* One skilled in leading or finding a way into unknown regions or in new fields of endeavor.

patho- *combining form* Suffering; disease: *pathogenesis.* [< Gk. *pathos* suffering]

path·o·gen (path′ə·jən) *n.* A disease-producing organism, as a fungus, virus, etc. Also **path′o·gene** (-jēn). —**path′o·gen′ic** *adj.*

path·o·gen·e·sis (path′ə·jen′ə·sis) *n.* The cause or development of a disease. Also **pa·thog·e·ny** (pə·thoj′ə·nē).

pa·thol·o·gist (pə·thol′ə·jist) *n.* A physician or other expert specializing in pathology.

pa·thol·o·gy (pə·thol′ə·jē) *n. pl.* **·gies** **1** The branch of medical science dealing with the causes, nature, and effects of diseases, esp. disease-induced changes in organs, tissues, and body chemistry. **2** A diseased or abnormal condition. —**path·o·log·i·cal** (path′ə·loj′i·kəl) or **path′o·log′ic** *adj.* —**path·o·log′i·cal·ly** *adv.*

pa·thos (pā′thos) *n.* The quality, attribute, or element, in events, speech, or art, that rouses the tender emotions, as compassion or sympathy. [Gk., suffering]

path·way (path′wā′, päth′-) *n.* PATH.

-pathy *combining form* **1** Feeling; emotion: *sympathy.* **2** Disease: *psychopathy.* **3** The treatment of disease: *hydropathy.* [< Gk. *pathos* suffering]

pa·tience (pā′shəns) *n.* **1** The quality of enduring without complaint. **2** The exercise of sustained perseverance. **3** Forbearance toward the faults or infirmities of others. **4** *Brit.* Any solitaire card game. —**Syn.** **1** endurance, fortitude, resignation. **2** steadiness. **3** leniency, tolerance.

pa·tient (pā′shənt) *adj.* **1** Possessing quiet, uncomplaining endurance under distress. **2** Tolerant and forbearing. **3** Capable of tranquilly awaiting events. **4** Persevering. —*n.* A person undergoing medical care. [< L *patiens,* pr.p. of *pati* suffer] —**pa′tient·ly** *adv.*

pat·i·na (pat′ə·nə, pə·tē′nə) *n.* **1** A green coating on copper and its alloys, usu. formed by prolonged weathering. **2** Any surface of antique appearance. [< L *patina* a plate]

pa·ti·o (pä′tē·ō, pat′ē·ō) *n. pl.* **·ti·os** **1** An open inner court of a Spanish dwelling. **2** An outdoor terrace next to a house, used for relaxation, dining, etc. [Sp.]

pat·ois (pat′wä, *Fr.* pȧ·twȧ′) *n. pl.* **pat·ois** (pat′wäz, *Fr.* pȧ·twȧ′) **1** A dialect, esp. one that is provincial and nonstandard. **2** The distinctive language of an occupational group; jargon. [< OF]

pat. pend. patent pending.

patri- *combining form* Father: *patricide.* [< L *pater, -tris* father]

pa·tri·arch (pā′trē·ärk) *n.* **1** The leader of a family or tribe who rules by paternal right. **2** One of the earliest fathers of the human race, as Adam or Noah. **3** One of the fathers of the Hebrew race, as Abraham, Isaac, or Jacob. **4** A venerable man; esp. the founder of a religion. **5** A prelate in the early Roman Catholic church or in the modern Greek Church. [< Gk. *patria* family, clan + *archein* to rule] —**pa′tri·ar′chal, pa′tri·ar′chic** *adj.* —**pa′tri·ar′chal·ly** *adv.*

pa·tri·ar·chate (pā′trē·är′kit) *n.* **1** The office, dominion, or residence of a patriarch. **2** A patriarchal system of government.

pa·tri·ar·chy (pā′trē·är′kē) *n. pl.* **·chies** A social system in which the father rules the family or clan, and in which descent is traced through the male line.

pa·tri·cian (pə·trish′ən) *n.* **1** A member of a nobility; aristocrat. **2** A member of the aristocracy of ancient Rome. —*adj.* **1** Of or pertaining to an aristocracy. **2** Aristocratic; having high rank. **3** Belonging to or suitable for an aristocrat. [< L *pater, -tris* a senator, lit., a father]

pat·ri·cide (pat′rə·sīd) *n.* **1** The killing of a father. **2** One who slays a father; a parricide. —**pat′ri·ci′dal** *adj.*

pat·ri·mo·ny (pat′rə·mō′nē) *n. pl.* **·nies** **1** An inheritance from a father or an ancestor. **2** An endowment of property to a church. **3** Any heritage. [< L *pater* a father] —**pat′ri·mo′ni·al** *adj.* —**pat′ri·mo′ni·al·ly** *adv.*

pa·tri·ot (pā′trē·ət, -ot) *n.* One who loves his country and zealously guards its welfare. [< Gk. *patris* fatherland] —**pa′tri·ot′ic** (-ot′ik) *adj.* —**pa′tri·ot′i·cal·ly** *adv.*

pa·tri·ot·ism (pā′trē·ə·tiz′əm) *n.* Devotion to one's country.

pa·tris·tic (pə·tris′tik) *adj.* Of or pertaining to the early fathers of the Christian church or to their writings. Also **pa·tris′ti·cal.** [< L *pater* father] —**pa·tris′ti·cal·ly** *adv.*

pa·trol (pə·trōl′) *v.t. & v.i.* **·trolled, ·trol·ling** To walk or go through or around (an area, town, etc.) for the purpose of guarding or inspecting. —*n.* **1** One or more soldiers, policemen, etc., patrolling a district. **2** A reconnaissance group of ships, planes, vehicles, or men on foot sent out to observe the enemy. **3** The act of patrolling. **4** A small unit of Boy Scouts. [< MF *patouiller,* orig., paddle in mud] —**pa·trol′ler** *n.*

pa·trol·man (pə·trōl′mən) *n. pl.* **·men** (-mən) A policeman patrolling a specific area.

patrol wagon A police wagon or truck for the conveyance of prisoners.

pa·tron (pā′trən) *n.* **1** One who protects, fosters, or supports some person or thing; benefactor. **2** A regular customer. **3** A saint regarded as one's personal guardian. **4** One who sponsors a charitable entertainment or a cause. [< L *patronus* protector] —**pa′tron·al** *adj.* —**pa′tron·ess** *n. Fem.*

pa·tron·age (pā′trən·ij, pat′rən-) *n.* **1** Encouragement and support given by a patron. **2** Favor or support given with a condescending manner. **3** The power to make appointments to certain positions or offices in public service. **4** Such positions or offices. **5** The financial support given by customers to commercial enterprises.

pa·tron·ize (pā′trən·īz, pat′rən-) *v.t.* **·ized, ·iz·ing** **1** To give support or protection to. **2** To treat in a condescending manner. **3** To trade with as a regular customer. —**pa′tron·iz′er** *n.* —**pa′tron·iz′ing·ly** *adv.*

pat·ro·nym·ic (pat′rə·nim′ik) *n.* A name derived from a father or an ancestor; a family name. Also **pat′ro·nym.** [< Gk. *patēr* father + *onyma* name] —**pat′ro·nym′i·cal·ly** *adv.*

pa·troon (pə·tro͞on′) *n.* Under old Dutch law, a holder of entailed estates, chiefly in New York and New Jersey. [< L *patronus* patron]

pat·ten (pat′n) *n.* A shoe having a thick, wooden sole; a clog. [< OF *patte* a paw, foot]

pat·ter[1] (pat′ər) *v.i.* **1** To make a succession of light, sharp sounds. **2** To move with light, quick steps. —*v.t.* **3** To cause to patter. —*n.* Pattering, or the sound of pattering. [Freq. of PAT[1]]

pat·ter[2] (pat′ər) *v.t. & v.i.* To speak or say glibly or rapidly. —*n.* **1** Glib and rapid talk, as used by comedians, etc. **2** Patois or dialect. [Short for PATERNOSTER; from the rapid repetition of the prayer] —**pat′ter·er** *n.*

pat·tern (pat′ərn) *n.* **1** An original or model proposed for or worthy of imitation. **2** Anything shaped or designed to serve as a model or guide in making something else. **3** Any decorative design or figure worked on something: a vase with a geometrical *pattern.* **4** Arrangement of natural or accidental markings. **5** The stylistic composition or design of a work of art. **6** A complex of integrated parts functioning as a whole: *patterns* of American culture. —*v.t.* 1 To make after a model or pattern: with *on, upon,* or *after.* 2 To decorate or furnish with a pattern. [<L *patronus* patron]

pat·ty (pat′ē) *n. pl.* **·ties** 1 A small pastry shell in which to serve creamed chicken, fish, etc.: also **patty shell.** 2 A flat round cake of food or candy. [Alter. of F *pâté*]

pau·ci·ty (pô′sə·tē) *n.* 1 Smallness of number or quantity. 2 Scarcity; insufficiency. [<L *paucus* few]

Paul Bun·yan (bun′yən) In American folklore, a lumberjack of superhuman size and strength, credited with amazing feats.

Paul·ine (pô′lēn, -līn) *adj.* Of or relating to Saint Paul, his teachings, and his writings.

paunch (pônch) *n.* 1 The abdomen. 2 A protruding abdomen; potbelly. 3 RUMEN. [<L *pantex* belly, bowels] — **paunch′i·ness** *n.* —**paunch′y** *adj.* **(·i·er, ·i·est)**

pau·per (pô′pər) *n.* 1 Any very poor person. 2 A destitute person who receives public charity. [L, poor]

pau·per·ism (pô′pə·riz′əm) *n.* 1 Poverty. 2 Paupers collectively. —**Syn.** 1 beggary, destitution, indigence, penury.

pau·per·ize (pô′pər·īz) *v.t.* **·ized, ·iz·ing** To make a pauper of.

pause (pôz) *v.i.* **paused, paus·ing** 1 To cease action or utterance temporarily. 2 To dwell or linger: with *on* or *upon:* to *pause* on a word. —*n.* 1 A ceasing of action. 2 A holding back because of doubt or irresolution. 3 A momentary cessation in speaking or music for emphasis. 4 A character or sign indicating such cessation. —**give (one) pause** To cause (one) to hesitate or be uncertain, as from trepidation. [<L *pausa* a stop] —**paus′er** *n.*

pave (pāv) *v.t.* **paved, pav·ing** To cover or surface with concrete, macadam, etc., as a road. —**pave the way (for)** To make preparation (for); lead up to. [<L *pavire* ram down]

pave·ment (pāv′mənt) *n.* 1 A hard, solid surface for a road or sidewalk, usu. resting immediately on the ground. 2 A paved road or sidewalk. 3 The material with which a surface is paved.

pa·vil·ion (pə vil′yən) *n.* 1 A movable or open structure for temporary shelter. 2 A related or connected part of a principal building: the dancing *pavilion.* 3 A canopy or tent. 4 A detached building for patients, as at a hospital. —*v.t.* 1 To provide with a pavilion or pavilions. 2 To shelter by a pavilion. [<L *papilio* a butterfly, tent]

pav·ing (pā′ving) *n.* 1 The laying of a pavement. 2 The material used for pavement.

paw (pô) *n.* 1 The foot of an animal having nails or claws. 2 *Informal* A clumsy human hand. —*v.t. & v.i.* 1 To strike or scrape with the feet or paws: to *paw* at the ground. 2 *Informal* To handle rudely or with too great familiarity; maul. [<OF *powe*] —**paw′er** *n.*

pawl (pôl) *n. Mech.* A hinged or pivoted part shaped to engage with ratchet teeth.[?<L *palus* a stake]

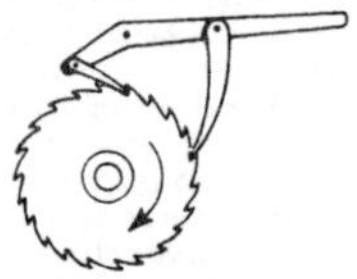
Double pawl

pawn[1] (pôn) *n.* 1 Any of the 16 chessmen of lowest rank. 2 Any insignificant person used at another's will. [<OF *peon, pedon* a foot soldier]

pawn[2] (pôn) *n.* 1 Something, as personal property, pledged to secure a loan. 2 The condition of being held as a pledge for money loaned. —*v.t.* 1 To give (personal property) as security for a loan. 2 To risk or stake; pledge. [<L *pannus* a cloth]

pawn·brok·er (pôn′brō′kər) *n.* One engaged in the business of lending money on pledged personal property. — **pawn′brok′ing** *n.*

Paw·nee (pô·nē′) *n. pl.* **·nee** or **·nees** 1 A member of one of four tribes of North American Indians formerly of Nebraska, now living in Oklahoma. 2 Their language.

pawn·shop (pôn′shop′) *n.* The place of business of a pawnbroker.

pawn ticket A certificate for goods pawned.

paw·paw (pô′pô) *n.* PAPAW.

pay (pā) *v.* **paid, pay·ing** *v.t.* 1 To give to (someone) what is due for a debt, purchase, etc. 2 To give (money, etc.) for a purchase, service rendered, etc. 3 To discharge, as a debt, bill, etc. 4 To yield as return or recompense. 5 To afford profit or benefit to. 6 To defray, as expenses. 7 To answer in kind; requite, as for a favor or an insult. 8 To render or give, as a compliment, attention, etc. 9 To make (a call or visit). —*v.i.* 10 To make recompense or payment. 11 To afford compensation or profit: It *pays* to be honest. —**pay back** To repay. —**pay off** 1 To pay the entire amount of. 2 To pay the wages of and discharge. 3 To gain revenge upon or for. 4 *Informal* To afford full return. 5 *Slang* To bribe. 6 *Naut.* To turn or cause to turn to leeward. —**pay out** 1 To disburse or expend. 2 *Naut.* To let out by slackening, as a rope or cable. —**pay up** To make full payment of. —*n.* 1 That which is given as a recompense or to discharge a debt. 2 That act of paying or the state of being paid. 3 Whatever compensates for labor or loss. —**in the pay of** Employed by: sometimes derogatory. —*adj.* 1 Of or pertainig to payments, persons who pay, or services paid for: *pay* day. 2 Yielding enough metal to be worth mining: *pay* dirt. [<L *pacare* appease<*pax* peace]

pay·a·ble (pā′ə·bəl) *adj.* 1 Due to be paid; owed. 2 That may be paid: *payable* on demand. —**pay′a·bly** *adv.*

pay-as-you-go (pā′əz·yōō·gō′) *adj.* Of or pertaining to a policy of meeting expenses as they occur or become due instead of deferring payment.

pay dirt 1 Soil containing enough metal, esp. gold, to be profitable to mine. 2 *Informal* Anything promising to yield rich rewards.

pay·ee (pā·ē′) *n.* One to whom payment is made.

pay·load (pā′lōd) *n.* 1 That part of a cargo producing revenue. 2 The explosive material in the warhead of a missile. 3 The persons, instruments, etc., carried in a spacecraft that are directly related to the objective of the flight rather than to the operation of the craft.

pay·mas·ter (pā′mas′tər, -mäs′-) *n.* One who has charge of the paying of employees.

pay·ment (pā′mənt) *n.* 1 The act of paying. 2 Something that is paid. 3 Something done in requital.

pay·off (pā′ôf′, -of′) *n.* 1 Payment, as of wages or profits. 2 *Informal* Any reward or punishment. 3 *Informal* The climax of an incident or narrative. 4 *Informal* Anything serving to explain or resolve an issue in dispute or doubt. 5 *Slang* A bribe.

pay·roll (pā′rōl′) *n.* 1 A list of those entitled to receive pay, with the amounts due them. 2 The total sum of money needed to make the payments.

payt. payment.

Pb lead (L *plumbum*)

PBX, P.B.X. private branch (telephone) exchange.

PC (pē′sē) *n.* Personal computer, a microcomputer for use at a table or desk, designed for routine personal or business matters.

pc. piece; price.

pct. percent; precinct.

P.D. Police Department.

P.D., p.d. by the day (L *per diem*).

Pd palladium.

pd. paid.

pea (pē) *n.* 1 A tendril-climbing annual leguminous herb widely cultivated for food and fodder. 2 Its edible seed or green pod. 3 Any of various other plants of the same family or their pods or seeds, as the cowpea. [<L *pisum* pea]

peace (pēs) *n.* 1 The absence or cessation of war. 2 General order and tranquillity. 3 A state of reconciliation after strife or enmity. 4 Freedom from mental agitation or anxiety. —**hold** (or **keep**) **one's peace** To be silent. [< L *pax, pacis*] —**Syn.** 1 amity, concord. 3 agreement, reconciliation. 4 content, relaxation, repose.

peace·a·ble (pē′sə·bəl) *adj.* 1 Inclined to peace; accommodating; not combative. 2 Peaceful; tranquil. —**peace′a·ble·ness** *n.* —**peace′a·bly** *adv.*

Peace Corps A U.S. agency that recruits and trains volunteers who live and work in underdeveloped countries for a period of time.

peace·ful (pēs′fəl) *adj.* 1 Free from war, commotion, or other disturbance. 2 Inclined to be accommodating; not combative or pugnacious: a *peaceful* disposition. 3 Of or characteristic of peace or of a time of peace. 4 Serene; still: a *peaceful* scene. 5 Inclined to or used in peace. —**peace′·ful·ly** *adv.* —**peace′ful·ness** *n.*

peace·mak·er (pēs′mā′kər) *n.* One who effects, or seeks to effect, a reconciliation between unfriendly parties. —**peace′mak′ing** *adj., n.*

peace·nik (pēs′nik) *n. Informal* A person who demonstrates against war or a particular war: a derogatory term. [< PEACE + -NIK]

peace officer A sheriff, constable, or policeman.

peace pipe CALUMET.

peach[1] (pēch) *n.* **1** The fleshy, juicy, edible fruit of the peach tree. **2** The tree, widely cultivated in many varieties. **3** The orange-yellow color of the fruit. **4** *Slang* Any person or thing particularly beautiful or excellent. [< L *persicum (malum)* Persian (apple)]

peach[2] (pēch) *v.i. Slang* To turn informer. [Alter. of IMPEACH]

peach·y (pē′chē) *adj.* **peach·i·er, peach·i·est 1** Resembling a peach. **2** *Slang* Delightfully pleasant. —**peach′i·ness** *n.*

pea·cock (pē′kok) *n.* **1** A male peafowl, having a crested head, long erectile tail feathers marked with eyelike spots, and iridescent greenish blue neck and breast. **2** A person of excessive vanity. [< OE *pēa, pāwa* a peacock + COCK] —**pea′cock·ish** *adj.*

Peacock

pea·fowl (pē′foul) *n.* **1** A peacock or peahen. **2** A large pheasant of s Asia. [< OE *pēa* peacock + FOWL]

pea green Any of several shades of light yellowish green. —**pea′-green′** *adj.*

pea·hen (pē′hen) *n.* A female peafowl.

pea·jack·et (pē′jak·it) *n.* A short coat of thick woolen cloth, worn by seamen. [Prob. < MDu. *pie* a kind of wool + JACKET]

peak (pēk) *n.* **1** A projecting point or edge; an end terminating in a point: the *peak* of a roof. **2 a** A mountain with a pointed summit. **b** The summit itself. **3** The highest point in a pattern of change or development: at the *peak* of his career. **4** A point formed on the forehead by the growth or cut of the hair. —*v.i.* **1** To reach a peak; climax. —*v.t.* **2** To raise to or almost to a vertical position. [?]

peaked[1] (pēkt, pē′kid) *adj.* Having a summit or peak.

peak·ed[2] (pē′kid) *adj.* Having a wan or sickly appearance. [?]

peal (pēl) *n.* **1** A prolonged, sonorous sound, as of a bell, trumpet, or thunder. **2** A set of large bells attuned to the major scale. **3** A change rung on a chime. —*v.t. & v.i.* To sound with a peal or peals. [< OF *apeler* call, appeal]

pe·an (pē′ən) *n.* PAEAN.

pea·nut (pē′nut′) *n.* **1** An annual, leguminous vine that bears underground pods containing one or more oily, edible seeds. **2** The seeds of this plant, with or without the brittle pod. **3** A small or insignificant person.

peanut butter A food product made from ground, roasted peanuts.

pear (pâr) *n.* **1** Any of numerous varieties of a juicy, edible fruit, usu. having a globular shape which narrows into a neck at the stem end. **2** Any of a species of trees of the rose family bearing this fruit. [< L *pirum*]

pearl (pûrl) *n.* **1** A lustrous calcareous concretion found in the shells of various mollusks, and valued as a gem. **2** Something like or likened to such a jewel in form, luster, etc. **3** Nacre or mother-of-pearl. **4** A delicate gray color: also **pearl gray. 5** *Printing* A size of type, smaller than agate, 5 points. —*adj.* **1** Pertaining to or made of pearl or mother-of-pearl: a *pearl* button. **2** Shaped like a pearl. —*v.i.* **1** To seek or fish for pearls. **2** To form beads like pearls. [< OF *perle*] —**pearl′i·ness** *n.* —**pearl′y** *adj.* **(·i·er, ·i·est)**

pearl diver A person occupied in diving for pearl-bearing mollusks. Also **pearl fisher.**

peart (pirt, pûrt) *adj. Regional* In good health and spirits; active; lively. [Var. of PERT] —**peart′ly** *adv.* —**peart′ness** *n.*

peas·ant (pez′ənt) *n.* In Europe and Asia, a small farmer or farm laborer. [< OF *païs* country]

peas·ant·ry (pez′ən·trē) *n.* The peasant class; a body of peasants.

peas·cod (pēz′kod) *n. Archaic* A pea pod. Also **pease′·cod.** [< PEAS(E) + E *cod* pod, husk]

pease (pēz) *n.pl. Archaic* Peas. [< OE *pise*]

peat (pēt) *n.* **1** An accumulation of partly decomposed vegetable material, found usu. in bogs. **2** A block of this substance, pressed and dried for fuel. [< Med. L *peta*] —**peat′y** *adj.* **(·i·er, ·i·est)**

peat moss SPHAGNUM.

pea·vy (pē′vē) *n. pl.* **·vies** An iron-pointed lever fitted with a movable hook and used for handling logs. Also **pea′vey.** [< Joseph *Peavey,* 19th c. American blacksmith]

peb·ble (peb′əl) *n.* **1** A small, rounded fragment of rock, its form being due to the action of water, ice, etc. **2** Leather that has been pebbled. —*v.t.* **·bled, ·bling 1** To impart a rough grain to (leather). **2** To pave, cover, or pelt with pebbles. [< OE *pabol(stān)* a pebble(stone)] —**peb′bly** *adj.*

pe·can (pi·kan′, -kän′, pē′kan) *n.* **1** A species of hickory with olive-shaped, thin-shelled nuts. **2** The nut borne by this tree. [< Algon.]

pec·ca·dil·lo (pek′ə·dil′ō) *n. pl.* **·los** or **·loes** A slight or trifling sin; a fault. [< L *peccare* to sin]

pec·cant (pek′ənt) *adj.* **1** Guilty of sin. **2** Violating some rule or principle. [< L *peccare* to sin] —**pec′can·cy** *n.* —**pec′cant·ly** *adv.*

pec·ca·ry (pek′ər·ē) *n. pl.* **·ries** Either of two species of tropical American animals resembling and related to pigs. [< Cariban *pakira*]

Peccary

peck[1] (pek) *v.t.* **1** To strike with the beak, as a bird does, or with something pointed. **2** To make by striking thus: to *peck* a hole in a wall. **3** To pick up, as food, with the beak. **4** *Informal* To kiss lightly. —*v.i.* **5** To make strokes with the beak. —**peck at** *Informal* **1** To eat by taking small and infrequent bites. **2** To nag; carp at. —*n.* **1** A quick, sharp blow, as with a beak or something pointed. **2** A mark, dent, or hole made by such a blow. [ME *pecken*] —**peck′er** *n.*

peck[2] (pek) *n.* **1** A measure equal to 0.25 bushel, or eight quarts. **2** A vessel for measuring a peck. **3** *Informal* A great quantity. [< OF *pek,* a measure of oats for horses]

pec·tin (pek′tin) *n.* A gummy, water-soluble carbohydrate present in many fruits and used as the basis of fruit jellies. [< Gk. *pēktos* congealed] —**pec·tic** (pek′tik) *adj.*

pec·to·ral (pek′tər·əl) *adj.* **1** Of or pertaining to the breast or chest. **2** Used to treat diseases of the lungs or chest. —*n.* **1** A pectoral fin or muscle. **2** A pectoral medicine. [< L *pectus, -oris* the breast] —**pec′tor·al·ly** *adv.*

pectoral fin Either of the pair of fins located just behind the head of a fish.

pec·u·late (pek′yə·lāt) *v.t. & v.i.* **·lat·ed, ·lat·ing** To appropriate wrongfully (funds, esp. public funds) entrusted to one's care; embezzle. [< L *peculari* embezzle] —**pec′u·la′·tion, pec′u·la′tor** *n.*

pe·cul·iar (pi·kyōōl′yər) *adj.* **1** Odd or strange; queer; singular. **2** Having a character exclusively its own. **3** Select or special. **4** Belonging exclusively to one: a talent *peculiar* to him. [< L *peculiaris* < *peculium* private property] —**pe·cul′iar·ly** *adv.*

pe·cu·li·ar·i·ty (pi·kyōō′lē·ar′ə·tē, -kyōōl′yar′-) *n. pl.* **·ties 1** The quality of being peculiar. **2** Something that is odd or peculiar, as a trait. **3** A distinguishing trait: The thumb is a *peculiarity* of primates. —**Syn. 2** eccentricity, idiosyncrasy, oddity. **3** attribute, characteristic.

pe·cu·ni·ar·y (pi·kyōō′nē·er′ē) *adj.* Consisting of or relating to money; monetary. [< L *pecunia* money < *pecus* cattle] —**pe·cu′ni·ar′i·ly** *adv.*

-ped Var. of -PEDE: *quadruped.*

ped·a·gog·ic (ped′ə·goj′ik, -gō′jik) *adj.* Of or pertaining to teachers and the art of teaching. Also **ped′a·gog′i·cal.** —**ped′a·gog′i·cal·ly** *adv.*

ped·a·gogue (ped′ə·gog, -gôg) *n.* A school teacher, esp.

a pedantic, narrow-minded one. Also **ped′a·gog.** [< Gk. *pais* child + *agōgos* leader]

ped·a·go·gy (ped′ə·gō′jē, -goj′ē) *n.* **1** The science or profession of teaching. **2** The theory or the teaching of how to teach.

ped·al (ped′l) *adj.* Of or relating to a foot, feet, or a foot-like part. —*n.* A lever operated by the foot, as that used to control the tone of a piano, organ, etc., or to govern the rate of movement of an automobile, bicycle, or a mechanical part. —*v.t. & v.i.* **·aled** or **·alled, ·al·ing** or **·al·ling** To move or operate by working pedals. [< L *pes, pedis* the foot]

pedal pushers Women's and girls' trousers reaching to the calf, originally used for bicycling.

ped·ant (ped′ənt) *n.* **1** A scholar who makes needless display of his learning, esp. in trifling points of scholarship. **2** A dull, narrow-minded teacher. [< Ital. *pedante*] —**pe·dan·tic** (pi·dan′tik) *adj.* —**pe·dan′ti·cal·ly** *adv.*

ped·ant·ry (ped′ən·trē) *n. pl.* **·ries 1** Ostentatious display of knowledge. **2** Undue and slavish adherence to forms or rules.

ped·dle (ped′l) *v.* **·dled, ·dling** *v.i.* **1** To travel about selling small wares. —*v.t.* **2** To carry about and offer for sale. **3** *Informal* To put forth or issue as if seeking to sell: to *peddle* an idea. [Back-formation from ME *pedlere* peddler] —**ped′dler, ped′lar** *n.*

-pede *combining form* Footed: *centipede.* [< L *pes, pedis* foot]

ped·er·ast (ped′ə·rast, pē′də-) *n.* One who practices pederasty.

ped·er·as·ty (ped′ə·ras′tē, pē′də-) *n.* Sodomy, esp. as practiced between men and boys. [< Gk. *paiderastēs* a lover of boys] —**ped′er·as′tic** *adj.* —**ped′er·as′ti·cal·ly** *adv.*

ped·es·tal (ped′is·təl) *n.* **1** A base or support for a column, statue, or vase. **2** Any foundation, base, or support, either material or immaterial. —**put on a pedestal** To hold in high estimation; idolize. [< Ital. *piè, pied* foot + *di* of + *stallo* a stall, standing place]

pe·des·tri·an (pə·des′trē·ən) *adj.* **1** Moving on foot. **2** Commonplace, prosaic, or dull. —*n.* One who journeys or moves from place to place on foot; a walker. [< L *pedester* on foot] —**pe·des′tri·an·ism** *n.*

pe·di·at·rics (pē′dē·at′riks, ped′ē-) *n. pl. (construed as sing.)* The branch of medicine dealing with the care and treatment of children and their diseases. [< Gk. *pais, paidos* a child + *iatros* healer] —**pe′di·at′ric** *adj.* —**pe·di·a·tri·cian** (-trish′ən), **pe′di·at′rist** *n.*

ped·i·cel (ped′ə·səl) *n. Biol.* A slender supporting structure, as a stalk supporting a single flower. Also **ped′i·cle** (-kəl). [< L *pediculus,* dim. of *pes, pedis* a foot] —**ped′i·cel′lar** (-sel′ər) *adj.*

ped·i·cure (ped′i·kyŏŏr) *n.* **1** Care of the feet, as by trimming toenails, corns, bunions, etc. **2** PODIATRIST. [< L *pes, pedis* a foot + *cura* care] —**ped′i·cur′ist** *n.*

ped·i·gree (ped′ə·grē) *n.* **1** A line of ancestors; lineage. **2** A genealogical register, esp. of an animal of pure breed. [< MF *pié de grue* a crane's foot; from a mark denoting succession in pedigrees] —**ped′i·greed** *adj.*

ped·i·ment (ped′ə·mənt) *n. Archit.* A broad triangular part above a portico or door. [Earlier *periment,* prob. alter. of PYRAMID] —**ped′i·men′tal** (-men′təl) *adj.*

pe·dom·e·ter (pi·dom′ə·tər) *n.* An instrument that measures distance traveled by recording the number of steps taken by the person who wears it. [< L *pes, pedis* foot + Gk. *metron* measure]

pe·dun·cle (pi·dung′kəl) *n.* **1** *Bot.* The main supporting stalk of an inflorescence. **2** *Anat.* A stalk or stem, as for the attachment of an organ. [< NL *pedunculus* a footstalk, dim. of *pes, pedis* a foot] —**pe·dun′cled, pe·dun′cu·lar, pe·dun′cu·late, pe·dun′cu·lat·ed** *adj.*

peek (pēk) *v.i.* To look furtively, slyly, or quickly. —*n.* A peep; glance. [ME *piken*]

peel[1] (pēl) *n.* The skin of certain fruits, as oranges, etc. —*v.t.* **1** To strip off the bark, skin, etc., of. **2** To strip off; remove. —*v.i.* **3** To lose bark, skin, etc. **4** To come off: said of bark, skin, etc. **5** *Slang* To undress. —**keep one's eye peeled** *Informal* To keep watch; be alert. —**peel off** *Aeron.* To veer off from a flight formation. [< OF *peler* to strip off skin]

peel[2] (pēl) *n.* A broad, thin, long-handled, shovel-like implement used by bakers in moving bread, etc., about an oven. [< L *pala* a spade]

peel·ing (pē′ling) *n.* Something peeled off, as a strip of rind, skin, or outer layer.

peen (pēn) *n.* The end of a hammer head opposite the face, usu. shaped for indenting, chipping, etc. —*v.t.* To beat, bend, or shape with the peen. [?]

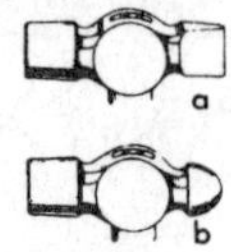

Peens
a. straight.
b. ball.

peep[1] (pēp) *v.i.* **1** To utter a small, sharp cry; chirp; cheep. **2** To speak in a weak, small voice. —*n.* The cry of a small bird or of certain frogs; chirp. [ME *pepen*] —**peep′er** *n.*

peep[2] (pēp) *v.i.* **1** To look furtively or quickly; peek. **2** To begin to appear; be just visible. —*n.* **1** A furtive look. **2** A glimpse or glance. **3** The earliest appearance: the *peep* of day. [ME *pepen*] —**peep′er** *n.*

peep·hole (pēp′hōl) *n.* An aperture, as a hole or small window, through which one may peep.

peeping Tom (tom) One who seeks to look at others clandestinely or from concealment, usu. for sexual pleasure. [< *Peeping Tom,* a tailor in English legend, struck blind because he peeped at the naked Lady Godiva]

peer[1] (pir) *v.i.* **1** To look searchingly, as in an effort to see clearly. **2** To come partially into view. [Var. of APPEAR]

peer[2] (pir) *n.* **1** An equal, as in natural gifts or in social rank. **2** An equal before the law. **3** A noble, as a duke, marquis, earl, viscount, or baron. —**peer of the realm** Any British peer entitled to serve in the House of Lords. [< L *par* equal]

peer·age (pir′ij) *n.* **1** The office or rank of a peer. **2** Peers collectively; the nobility. **3** A book containing a genealogical list of the nobility.

peer·ess (pir′is) *n.* A woman who holds a title of nobility, either in her own right or by marriage with a peer.

peer·less (pir′lis) *adj.* Of unequaled excellence. —**peer′·less·ly** *adv.* —**peer′less·ness** *n.*

peeve (pēv) *v.t. & v.i.* **peeved, peev·ing** *Informal* To make or become peevish or irritable. —*n. Informal* A complaint; grievance. [Back formation < PEEVISH]

pee·vish (pē′vish) *adj.* **1** Irritable or fretful; cross. **2** Showing petulant discontent and vexation. [ME *pevische*] —**pee′vish·ly** *adv.* —**pee′vish·ness** *n.*

pee·wee (pē′wē) *n. Informal* A person or thing esp. small or diminutive. —*adj.* Tiny; insignificant.

peg (peg) *n.* **1** A wooden pin used for fastening articles together. **2** A projecting wooden pin upon which something may be fastened or hung, or which may serve to mark a boundary. **3** A reason or excuse for an action: a *peg* to hang an argument upon. **4** A degree or step, as in rank or estimation. **5** *Brit.* A drink of liquor. **6** *Informal* A leg, often one of wood. —**take (one) down a peg** To lower the conceit of (a person), as by humiliating. —*v.* **pegged, peg·ging** *v.t.* **1** To drive or force a peg into; fasten with pegs. **2** To mark or designate with pegs. **3** To strike or pierce with a peg or sharp instrument. —*v.i.* **4** To work or strive hard and perseveringly: usu. with *away.* [ME *pegge*]

Peg·a·sus (peg′ə·səs) *Gk. Myth.* A winged horse, the symbol of poetic inspiration. —*n. Astron.* A northern constellation.

peg leg *Informal* **1** An artificial leg. **2** A person with such a leg.

peg top 1 A child's spinning top, pear-shaped with a metal tip. **2** *pl.* Trousers that are wide at the hips and taper in at the ankles. —**peg′-top′** *adj.*

pei·gnoir (pān·wär′, pān′wär) *n.* A loose dressing robe worn by women; a negligée. [F < *peigner* to comb]

pe·jo·ra·tion (pē′jə·rā′shən, pej′ə-) *n.* **1** A deterioration. **2** *Ling.* A degeneration in the meaning of a word, as in *silly* (formerly "blessed"). [< L *pejorare* make worse]

pe·jo·ra·tive (pi·jôr′ə·tiv, -jor′-, pej′ər-, pej′ər·ā′tiv, pē′·jər-) *adj.* **1** Tending to disparage; derogatory: the *pejorative* connotations of "huckster." **2** *Ling.* Of or relating to the process of pejoration. —*n.* A pejorative word. —**pe·jo′·ra·tive·ly** *adv.*

Pe·kin·ese (pē′kə·nēz′) *n. pl.* **·ese** A small dog with long silky hair, a snub nose, and short legs. Also **Pe′king·ese′** (-king·ēz′).

pe·koe (pē′kō, *Brit.* pek′ō) *n.* A superior kind of black tea, made from the downy tips of the young white buds of the tea plant. [< Chinese *pek* white + *ho* down]

pe·lag·ic (pə·laj′ik) *adj.* Of, pertaining to, or inhabiting the open sea. [< Gk. *pelagos* the sea]

pelf (pelf) *n.* Money; wealth: often implying ill-gotten gains. [< OF *pelfre* spoil] —**Syn.** affluence, fortune, funds, opulence, riches.

pel·i·can (pel′i·kən) *n.* Any of a genus of large, fish-eating, web-footed birds, having a distensible, membranous pouch on the lower bill for scooping up and holding fish. [< Gk. *pelekan*]

White pelican

pe·lisse (pə·lēs′) *n.* A long outer garment or cloak, esp. one of fur or lined with fur. [< L *pellis* skin]

pel·la·gra (pə·lā′grə, -lag′rə) *n.* A chronic disease due to deficiency of niacin in the diet, marked by gastric disturbance, skin eruptions, and mental derangement. [Ital.] —**pel·la′grous** *adj.*

pel·let (pel′it) *n.* **1** A small round ball, as of wax, paper, bread, etc. **2** A small shot. **3** A very small pill. **4** A bullet. —*v.t.* **1** To make into pellets. **2** To strike with pellets. [< Med. L *pelota, pilota* ball.]

pell-mell (pel′mel′) *adv.* **1** In a confused or disorderly manner. **2** With a headlong rush. —*adj.* Devoid of order or method. —*n.* Confusion; disorder. Also **pell′mell′**. [< OF *pesle-mesle*]

pel·lu·cid (pə·lo͞o′sid) *adj.* **1** Permitting the passage of light; translucent or transparent. **2** Clear; understandable. [< L *perlucere* shine through] —**pel·lu′cid·ly** *adv.* —**pel·lu′cid·ness, pel·lu·cid·i·ty** (pel′o͞o·sid′ə·tē) *n.*

Pel·o·pon·ne·sian (pel′ə·pə·nē′shən, -zhən) *adj.* Of or pertaining to the Peloponnesus, a peninsula of Greece. —*n.* An inhabitant of the Peloponnesus.

pelt[1] (pelt) *n.* **1** An undressed fur skin; raw hide. **2** *Slang* The human skin. [Prob. back formation < PELTRY]

pelt[2] (pelt) *v.t.* **1** To strike repeatedly with or as with missiles or blows. **2** To throw or hurl (missiles). —*v.i.* **3** To beat or descend with violence. **4** To move rapidly; hurry. —*n.* **1** A blow, as one given by something thrown. **2** Speed, esp. in the phrase **at full pelt.** [ME *pelten*] —**pelt′er** *n.* —**Syn.** *v.* **1** assail, attack, beat. **4** rush, speed.

pel·tate (pel′tāt) *adj. Bot.* Forming a shield, as a leaf attached to the stalk near the center of the lower surface. Also **pel′tat·ed.** [< Gk. *peltē* a shield] —**pel′tate·ly** *adv.*

pelt·ry (pel′trē) *n. pl.* **·ries 1** Pelts collectively. **2** A pelt. [< L *pellis* a skin]

pel·vis (pel′vis) *n. pl.* **·vis·es** or **·ves** (-vēz) **1** A basinlike or funnel-shaped structure. **2** The part of the skeleton that forms a bony girdle joining the lower or hind limbs to the body: also **pelvic arch, pelvic girdle.** [L, basin] —**pel′vic** *adj.*

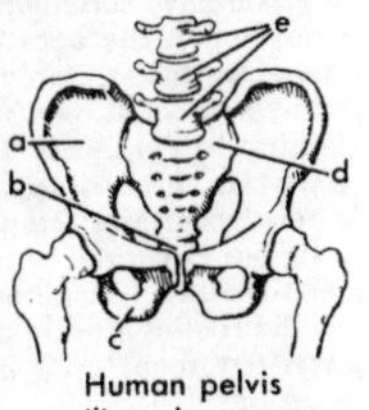

Human pelvis
a. ilium. b. coccyx. c. ischium. d. sacrum. e. lumbar vertebrae.

pem·mi·can (pem′ə·kən) *n.* Venison cut into strips, dried, and pounded into paste with melted fat. Also **pem′i·can.** [< Algon.]

pen[1] (pen) *n.* **1** Any of various instruments for writing with a fluid ink. **2** The profession of writing. **3** Literary style. —*v.t.* **penned, pen·ning** To write. [< L *penna* a feather] —**pen′ner** *n.*

pen[2] (pen) *n.* **1** A small enclosure, as for animals. **2** The animals contained in a pen collectively. **3** Any small place of confinement. —*v.t.* **penned** or **pent, pen·ning** To enclose in or as in a pen; confine. [< OE *penn*]

pen[3] (pen) *n. Slang* A penitentiary.

pen. peninsula.

pe·nal (pē′nəl) *adj.* **1** Of, relating to, or prescribing punishment: a *penal* code; a *penal* institution. **2** Liable, or rendering liable, to punishment. [< L *poena* a penalty]

pe·nal·ize (pē′nəl·īz, pen′əl-) *v.t.* **·ized, ·iz·ing 1** To subject to a penalty, as for a violation. **2** To declare subject to a penalty. *Brit. sp.* **pe·nal·ise.** —**pe′nal·i·za′tion** *n.*

pen·al·ty (pen′əl·tē) *n. pl.* **·ties 1** The consequences that follow the breaking of any law, rule, or custom. **2** Judicial punishment for crime or violation of the law. **3** A handicap imposed for a violation of rules of a game. **4** Any unpleasant consequence: the *penalties* of a misspent life. [< L *poenalis* penal]

pen·ance (pen′əns) *n.* **1** *Eccl.* A sacramental rite involving contrition, confession to a priest, the acceptance of penalties, and absolution. **2** A feeling of sorrow for sin or fault, evinced by some outward act; repentance. —**do penance** To perform an act or acts of penance. [< L *paenitens* penitent]

Pe·na·tes (pə·nā′tēz) *n.pl.* In the ancient Roman religion, the household gods, associated with the Lares.

pence (pens) *Brit. n.pl.* of PENNY.

pen·chant (pen′chənt) *n.* A strong leaning or inclination: a *penchant* for jotting down ideas on scraps of paper. [F < L *pendere* hang]

pen·cil (pen′səl) *n.* **1** A long, pointed strip of graphite, colored chalk, slate, etc., often encased in wood, used for writing or drawing. **2** Any slender instrument used for similar purposes. **3** A set of rays diverging from or converging to a point. **4** A small stick of any substance having caustic or styptic properties. —*v.t.* **·ciled** or **·cilled, ·cil·ing** or **·cil·ling** To mark, write, or draw with or as with a pencil. [< L *penicillum* a paint brush] —**pen′cil·er** or **pen′cil·ler** *n.*

pend (pend) *v.i.* To await or be in process of adjustment or settlement. [< L *pendere* hang]

pen·dant (pen′dənt) *n.* **1** Any hanging ornament, as an earring or locket. **2** A suspended chandelier. **3** An ornament hanging from a ceiling or roof. —*adj.* PENDENT. [< OF *pendre* hang]

pen·dent (pen′dənt) *adj.* **1** Hanging loosely; drooping downward. **2** Projecting or overhanging. **3** Undetermined; pending. —*n.* PENDANT. [< OF *pendre* hang] —**pen′den·cy** *n.* —**pen′dent·ly** *adv.*

pend·ing (pen′ding) *adj.* Remaining unfinished or undecided. —*prep.* **1** During. **2** Awaiting; until: The court adjourned *pending* the jury's verdict. —**Syn.** *adj.* imminent, impending, unsettled.

pen·drag·on (pen·drag′ən) *n.* In ancient Britain, a title used for a supreme ruler or chief, esp. in wartime. [< Welsh]

pen·du·lous (pen′jo͞o·ləs) *adj.* Hanging, esp. so as to swing. [< L *pendere* hang] —**pen′du·lous·ly** *adv.* —**pen′du·lous·ness** *n.*

pen·du·lum (pen′jo͞o·ləm, pen′də-) *n.* **1** A body suspended from a fixed point, and free to swing to and fro. **2** Such a device serving to regulate the rate of a clock. [< L *pendulus* hanging]

Pe·nel·o·pe (pə·nel′ə·pē) In the *Odyssey,* the faithful wife of Odysseus, who, during her husband's absence, kept her many suitors in check for twenty years.

pen·e·trate (pen′ə·trāt) *v.* **·trat·ed, ·trat·ing** *v.t.* **1** To force a way into or through; pierce. **2** To spread or diffuse itself throughout; permeate. **3** To perceive the meaning of; understand. **4** To affect profoundly. —*v.i.* **5** To enter or pass through something. **6** To have effect on the mind or emotions. [< L *penetrare* put within] —**pen′e·tra′tive** *adj.* —**pen′e·tra′tive·ly** *adv.*

pen·e·trat·ing (pen′ə·trā′ting) *adj.* **1** Tending or having power to penetrate; intrusive: a *penetrating* noise or smell. **2** Marked by keen discernment or insight, or having the capacity of such discernment: a *penetrating* analysis; a *penetrating* mind. **3** Deep, as a wound. —**pen′e·trat′ing·ly** *adv.* —**pen′e·trat′ing·ness** *n.* —**Syn. 1** piercing. **2** incisive, shrewd, profound, deep, acute.

pen·e·tra·tion (pen′ə·trā′shən) *n.* **1** The act or power of penetrating physically. **2** Ability to penetrate mentally; acuteness.

pen·e·tra·tive (pen′ə·trā′tiv) *adj.* Tending or having power to penetrate, physically or mentally; a *penetrative* odor; *penetrative* wisdom. —**pen′e·tra′tive·ly** *adv.* —**pen′e·tra′tive·ness** *n.*

pen·guin (pen′gwin, peng′-) *n.* Any of various web-footed, flightless, aquatic birds of the southern hemisphere, with flipperlike wings.

Emperor penguin

pen·hold·er (pen′hōl′dər) *n.* **1** A handle with a device for inserting a metallic pen point. **2** A rack for pens.

pen·i·cil·lin (pen′ə·sil′in) *n.* An antibiotic found in a species of penicillium.

pen·i·cil·li·um (pen′ə·sil′ē·əm) *n. pl.* **·li·a** (-ē·ə) Any of a genus of fungi often seen as blue-green mold on bread, cheese, etc. [< L *penicillus* a brush; from the resemblance of its tufts to small paint brushes]

pe·nin·su·la (pə·nin′sə·lə, -syə-) *n.* An area of land almost surrounded by water, and connected with the mainland by an isthmus. [< L *paene* almost + *insula* an island] **—pe·nin′·su·lar** *adj.* **—pe·nin·su·lar·i·ty** (pən·in′sə·lar′ə·tē, -syə-) *n.*

pe·nis (pē′nis) *n. pl.* **·nis·es** or **·nes** (-nēz) The male organ of sexual intercourse and the excretion of urine. [L, tail, penis]

pen·i·tence (pen′ə·təns) *n.* Sorrow for sin, with desire to amend and atone. [< L *paenitare* repent]

pen·i·tent (pen′ə·tənt) *adj.* Affected by sorrow because of one's own guilt. **—***n.* **1** One who is penitent. **2** One who confesses his sins to a priest and submits himself to the penance prescribed. **—pen′i·tent·ly** *adv.* **—Syn.** *adj.* contrite, remorseful, repentant, regretful.

pen·i·ten·tial (pen′ə·ten′shəl) *adj.* **1** Pertaining to or expressing penitence. **2** Pertaining to penance or punishment. **—***n.* **1** *Eccl.* A book of rules relating to penance. **2** A penitent. **—pen′i·ten′tial·ly** *adv.*

pen·i·ten·tia·ry (pen′ə·ten′shər·ē) *n. pl.* **·ries** A prison, esp. a state or federal prison for those convicted of serious crimes. **—***adj.* **1** Pertaining to penance. **2** Relating to or used for the punishment and discipline of criminals. **3** Rendering the offender liable to imprisonment in a penitentiary. [< L *paenitentia*]

pen·knife (pen′nīf′) *n. pl.* **·knives** (-nīvz′) A small pocket knife. [< former use in sharpening quill pens]

pen·man (pen′mən) *n. pl.* **·men** (-mən) **1** A person considered with regard to the high quality of his handwriting. **2** A writer.

pen·man·ship (pen′mən·ship) *n.* **1** The art of writing by hand. **2** Handwriting; calligraphy.

Penn., Penna. Pennsylvania.

pen name An author's assumed name; pseudonym.

pen·nant (pen′ənt) *n.* **1** A long, narrow flag displayed on ships or used as a signal. **2** A flag symbolizing a championship in certain sports competitions, as baseball. [< PENNON; infl. by PENDANT]

pen·ni·less (pen′i·lis) *adj.* **1** Being without even a penny. **2** Very poor. **—pen′ni·less·ly** *adv.* **—pen′ni·less·ness** *n.*

pen·non (pen′ən) *n.* **1** A small, pointed or swallow-tailed flag, borne by medieval knights on their lances. **2** A wing. **3** A banner or flag of any sort. [< L *penna* a feather]

Penn·syl·va·ni·a Dutch (pen′sil·vā′nyə, -nē·ə) **1** Descendants of immigrants from sw Germany and Switzerland who settled in Pennsylvania in the 17th and 18th centuries. **2** The language spoken by these people. Also **Pennsylvania German. —Penn′syl·va′ni·a-Dutch′** *adj.*

Penn·syl·va·ni·an (pen′sil·vā′nyən, -nē·ən) *adj. & n.* See GEOLOGY.

pen·ny (pen′ē) *n. pl.* **pen·nies** or *Brit.* **pence** (pens) **1** In the U.S. and Canada, a cent. **2** A coin of Great Britain, Ireland, and various members of the Commonwealth. **3** In the United Kingdom, a coin equal in value to 1/100 pound. **4** A piece of money. [< OE *penning, penig*] **—a pretty penny** *Informal* A large sum of money.

pen·ny·roy·al (pen′ē·roi′əl) *n.* **1** Any of various strong-scented herbs of the mint family. **2** An aromatic oil obtained from this plant. [< L *pulegium* fleabane + AF *real* royal]

pen·ny·weight (pen′ē·wāt′) *n.* A unit equal to 1/20 troy ounce.

pen·ny-wise (pen′ē·wīz′) *adj.* Unduly economical in small matters. **—penny-wise and pound-foolish** Economical in small matters, but wasteful in large ones.

pen·ny·worth (pen′ē·wûrth′) *n.* **1** As much as can be bought for a penny. **2** A bargain. **3** A small amount; trifle.

pe·nol·o·gy (pē·nol′ə·jē) *n.* The study dealing with the punishment of crime, the rehabilitation of criminals, and the management of prisons. [< L *poena* a penalty + -LOGY] **—pe·no·log·i·cal** (pē′nə·loj′i·kəl) *adj.* **—pe·nol′o·gist** *n.*

pen·sile (pen′sīl) *adj.* **1** Hanging loosely. **2** Constructing pensile nests: said of birds. [< L *pensus*, pp. of *pendere* hang]

pen·sion[1] (pen′shən) *n.* A periodical and continuing allowance to an individual because of long service, special merit, or injury while serving. **—***v.t.* **1** To grant a pension to. **2** To dismiss with a pension: with *off.* [< L *pensio* payment < *pendere* weigh, pay] **—pen·sion·ar·y** (pen′shən·er′ē) *adj., n.*

pen·sion[2] (päṅ·syôṅ′) *n. French* **1** Room and board. **2** A boarding house. Also *Ital.* **pen·si·on·e** (pen·sē·ō′nā).

pen·sion·er (pen′shən·ər) *n.* **1** One who receives a pension. **2** A boarder, as in a convent or school.

pen·sive (pen′siv) *adj.* **1** Engaged in or accustomed to serious or quiet reflection. **2** Expressive of, suggesting, or causing sad thoughtfulness. [< OF *penser* think] **—pen′·sive·ly** *adv.* **—pen′sive·ness** *n.* **—Syn. 1** meditative, reflective. **2** grave, melancholy, sad, sober.

pent (pent) *p.p. & p.t.* of PEN[2].

penta- *combining form* Five: *pentagon.* [< Gk. *pente* five]

pen·ta·cle (pen′tə·kəl) *n.* A figure composed of five straight lines connecting the vertices of a pentagon and used as a magical symbol. [< Gk. *pente* five]

Pentacle

pen·ta·gon (pen′tə·gon) *n.* A figure with five angles and five sides. **—the Pentagon 1** The military establishment of the U.S. **2** A five-sided building in Arlington, Va., housing the offices of the Department of Defense and the U.S. Armed Forces. [< Gk. *pentagōnon*] **—pen·tag·o·nal** (pen·tag′ə·nəl) *adj.* **—pen·tag′o·nal·ly** *adv.*

pen·ta·he·dron (pen′tə·hē′drən) *n. pl.* **·dra** (-drə) A solid bounded by five plane faces. **—pen′ta·he′dral** *adj.*

pen·tam·e·ter (pen·tam′ə·tər) *n.* **1** A line of verse of five metrical feet. **2** Verse composed of pentameters; heroic verse. **—***adj.* Consisting of five metrical feet.

Pen·ta·teuch (pen′tə·tyo͞ok) *n.* The first five books of the Bible taken collectively. [< Gk. *pente* five + *teuchos* a book, implement] **—Pen′ta·teuch′al** *adj.*

pen·tath·lon (pen·tath′lən) *n.* An athletic contest consisting of five different events in all of which each contestant participates. [< Gk. *pente* five + *athlon* a contest]

Pen·te·cost (pen′tə·kôst, -kost) *n.* **1** A Jewish festival occurring fifty days after the Passover. **2** The feast of Whitsunday, commemorating the descent of the Holy Ghost upon the apostles. *Acts* 2. [< Gk. *pentēkostē (hēmera)* the fiftieth (day)]

Pen·te·cos·tal (pen′tə·kôs′təl, -kos′-) *adj.* **1** Of or pertaining to Pentecost. **2** Of or designating any of various Christian groups typically holding revivalist services where vocal and often emotional expression is given to religious devotion.

pent·house (pent′hous′) *n.* An apartment or dwelling on the roof of a building. [< OF *apentis*]

pent-up (pent′up′) *adj.* Confined; repressed: *pent-up* emotions.

pe·nu·che (pə·no͞o′chē) *n.* A kind of fudge made from brown sugar, milk or cream, butter, and nuts.

pe·nult (pē′nult, pi·nult′) *n.* The syllable next to the last in a word. Also **pe·nul·ti·ma** (pi·nul′tə·mə). [< L *paene* almost + *ultimus* last] **—pe·nul·ti·mate** (pi·nul′tə·mit) *adj., n.*

pe·num·bra (pi·num′brə) *n. pl.* **·brae** (-brē) or **·bras 1** *Astron.* The partial shadow between the umbra, or region of total eclipse, and the region of unobstructed light. **2** The dark fringe around the central part of a sunspot. [< L *paene* almost + *umbra* a shadow] **—pe·num′bral, pe·num′·brous** (-brəs) *adj.*

pe·nu·ri·ous (pə·nyo͝or′ē·əs) *adj.* Excessively sparing or saving in the use of money. **—pe·nu′ri·ous·ly** *adv.* **—pe·nu′·ri·ous·ness** *n.* **—Syn.** frugal, miserly, stingy, tight-fisted.

pen·u·ry (pen′yə·rē) *n.* Extreme poverty or want. [< L *penuria* want]

pe·on (pē′ən) *n.* **1** In Latin America, a laborer. **2** In the sw U.S., a person kept in virtual servitude until he has worked out a debt. [< LL *pedo, -onis* a foot soldier]

pe·on·age (pē′ən·ij) *n.* The condition of a peon, or the system of employing this form of labor. Also **pe′on·ism.**

pe·o·ny (pē′ə·nē) *n. pl.* **·nies 1** Any of a genus of perennial plants having large, usu. double, flowers. **2** Its flower. [< Gk. *paiōnia*]

peo·ple (pē′pəl) *n. pl.* **·ple** or *(for defs. 1 and 2)* **·ples 1** The aggregate of human beings living under the same government: the *people* of England. **2** A body of human beings belonging to the same linguistic stock and having the same culture. **3** The whole body of persons composing a common class or profession. **4** Persons collectively: Who cares what *people* say? **5** The populace; public. **6** Subjects: A ruler cares for his *people.* **7** Family; relatives: Her *people* are from Ohio. **8** Human beings in general: Most *people* are friendly. —*v.t.* **·pled, ·pling** To fill with inhabitants; populate. [< L *populus* the populace] **—peo′pler** *n.*

pep (pep) *Slang n.* Vim; energy; sprightliness. —*v.t.* **pepped, pep·ping** To inspire with energy or pep: usu. with *up.* [Short for PEPPER]

pep·lum (pep′ləm) *n. pl.* **·lums** A short ruffle or flounce attached to a blouse or coat at the waist, and extending down over the hips. [< Gk. *peplos* a kind of shawl]

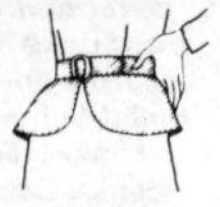
Peplum

pep·per (pep′ər) *n.* **1** A spice made from the black, dried berries of an East Indian climbing shrub. **2** CAYENNE PEPPER. **3** GREEN PEPPER. **4** Any plant yielding pepper. **5** *Informal* Spiciness; pungency; raciness. —*v.t.* **1** To sprinkle or season with pepper. **2** To sprinkle like pepper. **3** To shower, as with missiles; spatter. —*v.i.* **4** To discharge missiles at something. [< Gk. *peperi*]

pep·per-and-salt (pep′ər·ən·sôlt′) *adj.* Mixed white and black, intermingled as to present a speckled grayish appearance.

pep·per·corn (pep′ər·kôrn′) *n.* A dried berry of pepper.

pep·per·grass (pep′ər·gras′, -gräs′) *n.* Any of various small plants of the mustard family with pungent, edible leaves. Also **pep′per·wort** (-wûrt).

pep·per·mint (pep′ər·mint′) *n.* **1** An aromatic herb used in medicine and confectionery. **2** A pungent oil obtained from peppermint. **3** A confection flavored with peppermint.

pep·per·pot (pep′ər·pot′) *n.* Any of several highly seasoned stews or soups.

pep·per·y (pep′ər·ē) *adj.* **1** Pertaining to or like pepper; pungent. **2** Quick-tempered; hasty. **—pep′per·i·ness** *n.*

pep pill *Slang* Any of various pills or tablets that stimulate the central nervous system.

pep·py (pep′ē) *adj.* **·pi·er ·pi·est** *Slang* Full of pep; lively. **—pep′pi·ness** *n.* **—Syn.** active, energetic, spry, vigorous.

pep·sin (pep′sin) *n.* **1** A digestive enzyme that acts on proteins in the stomach. **2** A preparation obtained from the stomachs of pigs, calves, etc., used to aid digestion. Also **pep′sine.** [< Gk. *pepsis* digestion]

pep·tic (pep′tik) *adj.* **1** Of, pertaining to, or promotive of digestion. **2** Of, pertaining to, or producing pepsin. **3** Pertaining to or connected with the action of digestive secretions: *peptic* ulcer. —*n.* An agent that promotes digestion. [< Gk. *peptein* to digest]

peptic ulcer An ulcer of the mucous membrane of the stomach **(gastric ulcer)** or of the small intestine **(duodenal ulcer)** aggravated by acid digestive juices.

pep·tone (pep′tōn) *n.* Any of various soluble protein compounds resulting from the action of pepsin on complex proteins. [< Gk. *peptein* to digest] **—pep·ton·ic** (pep·ton′ik) *adj.*

Pe·quot (pē′kwot) *n.* A member of a tribe of North American Indians of Algonquian stock. Also **Pe′quod** (-kwod).

per (pûr) *prep.* **1** By; by means of; through. **2** For each: ten cents *per* yard. **3** *Informal* According to: *per* your memo. [L, through, by]

per- *prefix* **1** Through; throughout: *pervade.* **2** Thoroughly; completely; very: *perturb.* **3** Away: *pervert.* **4** *Chem.* Denoting an element or radical in a high or the highest valence: *peroxide.* [< L *per* through, by means of]

per. period; person.

per·ad·ven·ture (pûr′əd·ven′chər) *adv. Archaic* Possibly; perhaps. —*n. Archaic* Chance; uncertainty; doubt. [< OF *par aventure* by chance]

per·am·bu·late (pə·ram′byə·lāt) *v.* **·lat·ed, ·lat·ing** *v.t.* **1** To walk through or over; traverse. **2** To walk through or around so as to inspect (a boundary) —*v.i.* **3** To walk about; stroll. [< L *per-* through + *ambulare* to walk] — **per·am′bu·la′tion** *n.* **—per·am′bu·la·to′ry** *adj.*

per·am·bu·la·tor (pə·ram′byə·lā′tər) *n.* **1** One who perambulates. **2** *Chiefly Brit.* A baby carriage.

per an·num (pûr an′əm) *Latin* By the year; annually.

per·cale (pər·kāl′, -kal′) *n.* A closely woven cotton fabric used for sheets, etc. [< Pers. *pergālah* a rag]

per cap·i·ta (pûr kap′ə·tə) For each person. [L, lit., by heads]

per·ceive (pər·sēv′) *v.t. & v.i.* **·ceived, ·ceiv·ing 1** To become aware of (something) through the senses. **2** To come to understand; apprehend with the mind. [< L *per-* thoroughly + *capere* take] **—per·ceiv′a·bly** *adv.* **—per·ceiv′·er** *n.*

per·cent (pər·sent′) *adj. & adv.* For, in, or to every hundred. —*n. pl.* **·cent** or **·cents 1** A one-hundredth part. **2** *Informal* PERCENTAGE. **3** *pl.* Securities bearing a certain percentage of interest. Also **per cent., per cent** [Short for L *per centum* by the hundred]

per·cent·age (pər·sen′tij) *n.* **1** A part considered in its quantitative relation to the whole, expressed in hundredths. **2** A proportion; part. **3** A share or portion, as an allowance, commission, duty, interest, etc., that varies in proportion to some larger sum. **4** *Informal* Advantage; profit.

per·cen·tile (pər·sen′tīl, -til) *n. Stat.* A number indicating the relative position of an individual score per 100 scores ranged in a graded series. —*adj.* Of or pertaining to a percentile.

per·cept (pûr′sept) *n.* A mental event resulting from a sensory stimulus. [< L *percipere* perceive]

per·cep·ti·ble (pər·sep′tə·bəl) *adj.* Capable of being perceived. **—per·cep′ti·bil′i·ty, per·cep′ti·ble·ness** *n.* **—per·cep′·ti·bly** *adv.* **—Syn.** evident, apparent, obvious, visible.

per·cep·tion (pər·sep′shən) *n.* **1** The act, power, process, or product of perceiving. **2** Cognition of fact or truth; appreciation. **3 a** Knowledge acquired through the senses. **b** The process of acquiring such knowledge. **c** The mental product so obtained; percept. **4** Insight or intuitive judgment. [< L *percipere* perceive] **—per·cep′tion·al** *adj.*

per·cep·tive (pər·sep′tiv) *adj.* **1** Perceiving, or having the power of perception. **2** Of or pertaining to perception. **—per·cep′tive·ly** *adv.* **—per·cep′tive·ness, per·cep·tiv·i·ty** (pûr′sep·tiv′ə·tē) *n.*

perch[1] (pûrch) *n.* **1** A pole, slat, or wire, etc., used as a roost by birds. **2** An elevated seat or situation. **3** *Chiefly Brit.* **a** A measure of length: one rod (5½ yds.) **b** A measure of area: a sq. rod (30¼ sq. yards.) **c** Any of several units of measure used in stonework. —*v.i.* **1** To alight or sit on or as on a perch; roost. —*v.t.* **2** To set on or as on a perch. [< L *pertica* pole] **—perch′er** *n.*

perch[2] (pûrch) *n.* **1** A small freshwater food fish with spiny fins. **2** Any of various other similar, usu. marine fishes. [< Gk. *perkē*]

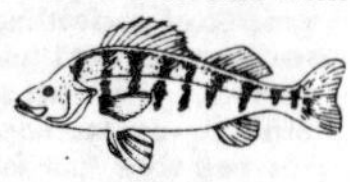
Yellow perch

per·chance (pər·chans′, -chäns′) *adv.* Possibly; perhaps. **2** *Obs.* By chance. [< AF *par chance* by chance]

Per·che·ron (pûr′chə·ron, -shə-) *n.* Any of a breed of large, usu. dapple-gray or black draft horses. [< *Perche,* a region of NW France]

per·cip·i·ent (pər·sip′ē·ənt) *adj.* Having the power to perceive, esp. rapidly or keenly. —*n.* One who perceives. [< L *percipere* perceive] **—per·cip′i·ence** or **·en·cy** *n.*

per·co·late (pûr′kə·lāt) *v.t. & v.i.* **·lat·ed, ·lat·ing 1** To pass or cause to pass through fine pores or openings; filter. **2** To brew (coffee) in a percolator. —*n.* That which has percolated; a filtered liquid. [< L *per-* through + *colare* to strain] —**per'co·la'tion** *n.*

per·co·la·tor (pûr'kə·lā'tər) *n.* **1** One who or that which percolates, as a filter. **2** A coffee pot in which boiling water rises through a tube and repeatedly filters back down through ground coffee contained in a perforated basket.

per·cus·sion (pər·kush'ən) *n.* **1** The impact of one body against another, as that of the hammer against the percussion cap in a firearm. **2** The impression of sound upon the ear. **3** *Med.* A tapping on the back, chest, etc., for diagnosing the condition of the organ beneath. **4** Those musical instruments, collectively, whose tone is produced by striking or hitting, as the timpani, piano, etc. [< L *per-* thoroughly + *quatere* to shake] —**per·cus'sive** (-kus'iv) *adj.* —**per·cus'sive·ly** *adv.* —**per·cus'sive·ness** *n.*

percussion cap CAP (*n.*, def. 4).

percussion instruments Musical instruments played by striking, as cymbals, drums, etc.

per di·em (pər dē'əm, dī'əm) **1** By or for the day. **2** An allowance (of money) for expenses each day. [L]

per·di·tion (pər·dish'ən) *n.* **1** *Theol.* Future misery or eternal death as the condition of the wicked; hell. **2** *Archaic* Utter destruction or ruin. [< L *perdere* destroy, lose]

père (pâr) *n. French* Father: used after a surname to distinguish father from son.

per·e·gri·nate (per'ə·gri·nāt') **·nat·ed, ·nat·ing** *v.i.* **1** To travel from place to place. —*v.t.* **2** To travel through or along. [< L *peregrinari* travel abroad] —**per'e·gri·na'tion** *n.*

per·e·grine (per'ə·grin) *n.* A large, very swift falcon. Also **peregrine falcon.** [< L *pereger* traveling]

per·emp·to·ry (pə·remp'tər·ē) *adj.* **1** *Law* Precluding or putting an end to debate or discussion; final. **2** Not admitting of debate or appeal; decisive; absolute. **3** Opinionated; dogmatic. [< L *peremptorius* destructive] —**per·emp'to·ri·ly** *adv.* —**per·emp'to·ri·ness** *n.*

per·en·ni·al (pə·ren'ē·əl) *adj.* **1** Continuing or enduring through the year. **2** Enduring, unceasing, or recurrent. **3** *Bot.* Lasting more than two years. —*n.* A perennial plant. [< L *per-* through + *annus* a year] —**per·en'ni·al·ly** *adv.*

perf. perfect; perforated.

per·fect (pûr'fikt) *adj.* **1** Having all the qualities or elements requisite to its nature or kind; complete. **2** Thoroughly qualified or informed; skilled: a *perfect* teacher. **3** Correct, exact, or accurate: a *perfect* replica. **4** Meeting all requirements; lacking no essential: a *perfect* antidote. **5** *Informal* Excessive in degree; very great: She has a *perfect* horror of spiders. **6** Total; utter: a *perfect* idiot. **7** *Gram.* Denoting the tense of a verb expressing action completed at the time of speaking or in the past. In English, the perfect tenses include a *present perfect, past perfect* (or *pluperfect*), and a *future perfect* tense. **8** *Music* Denoting a fifth containing seven semitones or a fourth containing five semitones. —*n. Gram.* The perfect tense, or a verb in this tense. —*v.t.* (pər·fekt') **1** To bring to perfection; complete; finish. **2** To make thoroughly skilled or accomplished: to *perfect* oneself in art. [< L *per-* thoroughly + *facere* do, make] —**per·fect'i·bil'i·ty** *n.* —**per·fect'i·ble** *adj.* —**per'fect·ly** *adv.*

per·fec·tion (pər·fek'shən) *n.* **1** The state or condition of being perfect; also, an embodiment of this. **2** The act or process of perfecting.

per·fec·tion·ist (pər·fek'shən·ist) *n.* One who demands perfect or flawless results or performance of himself or others. —**per·fec'tion·ism** *n.*

per·fec·tive (pər·fek'tiv) *adj.* Tending to make perfect. —**per·fec'tive·ly** *adv.* —**per·fec'tive·ness** *n.*

per·fec·to (pər·fek'tō) *n.* A cigar shaped to taper at both ends. [Sp. See PERFECT.]

per·fer·vid (pər·fûr'vid) *adj.* Excessively fervid. [< L *per-* thoroughly + *fervidus* glowing]

per·fid·i·ous (pər·fid'ē·əs) *adj.* Of or characterized by perfidy. —**per·fid'i·ous·ly** *adv.* —**per·fid'i·ous·ness** *n.*

per·fi·dy (pûr'fə·dē) *n. pl.* **·dies** The deliberate violation of faith or trust. [< L *perfidia*] —**Syn.** treachery, disloyalty, betrayal, faithlessness.

per·fo·li·ate (pər·fō'lē·it, -āt) *adj. Bot.* Growing so that the stem seems to pass through it: said of a leaf. [< L *per-* through + *folium* a leaf] —**per·fo'li·a'tion** *n.*

per·fo·rate (pûr'fə·rāt) *v.t.* **·rat·ed, ·rat·ing** **1** To make a hole or holes through, by or as by stamping or drilling. **2** To pierce with holes in rows or patterns, as sheets of stamps, etc. —*adj.* (-rit) Pierced with a hole or a series of holes. [< L *per-* through + *forare* to bore] —**per'fo·rat'ed** *adj.* —**per'fo·ra'tor** *n.*

per·fo·ra·tion (pûr'fə·rā'shən) *n.* **1** A perforating or state of being perforated. **2** A hole or series of holes drilled in or stamped through something.

per·force (pər·fôrs', -fōrs') *adv.* By force; by or of necessity; necessarily. [< OF *par force*]

per·form (pər·fôrm') *v.t.* **1** To execute; do: to *perform* an operation. **2** To act in accord with the requirements or obligations of; fulfill; discharge, as a duty or promise. **3** To act (a part) or give a performance of (a play, piece of music, etc.). —*v.i.* **4** To carry through to completion. **5** To give an exhibition or performance. [< OF *par-* thoroughly + *fournir* accomplish, furnish] —**per·form'er** *n.*

per·form·ance (pər·fôr'məns) *n.* **1** The act of performing. **2** Something performed; deed, feat, etc. **3** The ability to perform; also, the effectiveness of performance. **4** A presentation before spectators; any entertainment: two *performances* daily.

per·fume (pûr'fyōōm, pər·fyōōm') *n.* **1** A pleasant odor, as from flowers; fragrance. **2** A fragrant substance, usu. a volatile liquid, prepared to emit a pleasant odor; scent. —*v.t.* (pər·fyōōm') **·fumed, ·fum·ing** To give a fragrant odor to; scent. [< Ital. *perfumare,* lit., impregnate with smoke]

per·fum·er (pər·fyōō'mər) *n.* **1** One who makes or deals in perfumes. **2** One who or that which perfumes.

per·fum·er·y (pər·fyōō'mər·ē) *n. pl.* **·er·ies** **1** The art or business of making perfume. **2** Perfumes in general, or a specific perfume. **3** A place where perfumes are manufactured.

per·func·to·ry (pər·fungk'tər·ē) *adj.* **1** Done mechanically or routinely; superficial. **2** Without interest or concern; apathetic. [< L *per-* through + *fungi* perform] —**per·func'to·ri·ly** *adv.* —**per·func'to·ri·ness** *n.*

per·go·la (pûr'gə·lə) *n.* An arbor, esp. one with a roof of trelliswork that is supported by columns or posts on which climbing plants are grown. [< L *pergula* a projecting roof, arbor]

per·haps (pər·haps', -aps') *adv.* Maybe; possibly. [< PER + *haps,* pl. of HAP[1]]

pe·ri (pir'ē) *n. Persian Myth.* A fairy or elf.

peri- *prefix* **1** Around; encircling: *periphery.* **2** Situated near; adjoining: *perihelion.* [< Gk. *peri* around]

per·i·anth (per'ē·anth) *n.* The calyx and corolla of a flower. [< Gk. *peri-* around + *anthos* a flower] —**per'i·an'·the·ous** *adj.*

per·i·car·di·um (per'ə·kär'dē·əm) *n. pl.* **·di·a** (-dē·ə) A thin membrane enclosing the heart. [< Gk. *peri-* around + *kardia* heart] —**per'i·car'di·al, per'i·car'di·ac** *adj.*

per·i·carp (per'ə·kärp) *n. Bot.* The wall of a mature ovary. [NL < Gk. *peri-* around + *karpos* fruit] —**per'i·car'·pi·al** *adj.*

per·i·cra·ni·um (per'ə·krā'nē·əm) *n. pl.* **·ni·a** (-nē·ə) A tough membrane covering the skull. [< Gk. *peri-* around + *kranion* skull] —**per'i·cra'ni·al** *adj.*

per·i·gee (per'ə·jē) *n. Astron.* The point in the orbit of the moon or of an artificial earth satellite where it is nearest the earth. [< Gk. *peri-* around + *gē* earth] —**per'i·ge'al, per'i·ge'an** *adj.*

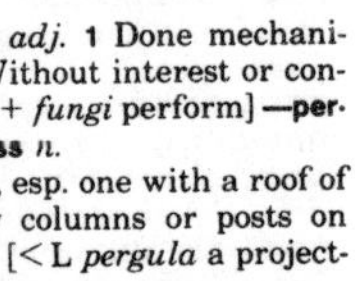

p. perigee.
a. apogee.

per·i·he·li·on (per'ə·hē'lē·ən) *n. pl.* **·li·a** (-lē·ə) *Astron.* The point in the orbit of a planet or comet where it is nearest the sun. [< PERI- + Gk. *hēlios* the sun]

per·il (per'əl) *n.* Exposure to the chance of injury, loss, or destruction. —*v.t.* **·iled** or **·illed, ·il·ing** or **·il·ling** To expose to danger. [< L *periculum* trial, danger] —**Syn.** *n.* danger, jeopardy, risk, insecurity. *v.* imperil, endanger, jeopardize, risk.

per·il·ous (per'əl·əs) *adj.* Full of, involving, or attended with peril. —**per'il·ous·ly** *adv.* —**per'il·ous·ness** *n.*

pe·rim·e·ter (pə·rim'ə·tər) *n.* **1** *Math.* The bounding line or curve of a plane area. **2** *Math.* The measure of this line

PERIODIC TABLE OF THE ELEMENTS

1a	2a	3b	4b	5b	6b	7b	8	8	8	1b	2b	3a	4a	5a	6a	7a	0
1 H																	2 He
3 Li	4 Be											5 B	6 C	7 N	8 O	9 F	10 Ne
11 Na	12 Mg											13 Al	14 Si	15 P	16 S	17 Cl	18 Ar
19 K	20 Ca	21 Sc	22 Ti	23 V	24 Cr	25 Mn	26 Fe	27 Co	28 Ni	29 Cu	30 Zn	31 Ga	32 Ge	33 As	34 Se	35 Br	36 Kr
37 Rb	38 Sr	39 Y	40 Zr	41 Nb	42 Mo	43 Tc	44 Ru	45 Rh	46 Pd	47 Ag	48 Cd	49 In	50 Sn	51 Sb	52 Te	53 I	54 Xe
55 Cs	56 Ba	57* La	72 Hf	73 Ta	74 W	75 Re	76 Os	77 Ir	78 Pt	79 Au	80 Hg	81 Tl	82 Pb	83 Bi	84 Po	85 At	86 Rn
87 Fr	88 Ra	89** Ac															

**Lanthanides*	58 Ce	59 Pr	60 Nd	61 Pm	62 Sm	63 Eu	64 Gd	65 Tb	66 Dy	67 Ho	68 Er	69 Tm	70 Yb	71 Lu
***Actinides*	90 Th	91 Pa	92 U	93 Np	94 Pu	95 Am	96 Cm	97 Bk	98 Cf	99 Es	100 Fm	101 Md	102 No	103 Lr

The properties of the elements are related to the configuration of electrons surrounding the atomic nucleus, and they show a repetitive, cyclic variation when arranged in order of increasing atomic number. They fall into horizontal rows, or *periods*, which usually begin on the left with metals, shade into nonmetals on the right, and end with the group of virtually inert rare gases. The vertical columns comprise *groups* of elements with similar properties. The subgroups, indicated by the letter **b**, comprise elements that resemble each other more closely than they resemble elements in the main groups, marked by the letter **a.** The lanthanide series and the actinide series both consist of elements with almost identical chemical properties. Each box contains an atomic number and the corresponding chemical symbol. See also the table of *Chemical Elements* at ELEMENT.

or curve. **3** A strip or boundary defining or protecting an area. [<Gk. *peri-* around + *metron* a measure] **—per·i·met·ric** (per'ə-met'rik) or **-ri·cal** *adj.* **—per'i·met'ri·cal·ly** *adv.*

per·i·ne·um (per'ə-nē'əm) *n. pl.* **·ne·a** (-nē'ə) *Anat.* The region of the body at the lower end of the trunk, between the genital organs and the rectum. Also **per'i·nae'um.** [< Gk. *perinaion*] **—per'i·ne'al** *adj.*

pe·ri·od (pir'ē-əd) *n.* **1** A portion of time marked and defined by certain events or phenomena, or by the existence of a specific culture. **2** A portion of time between successive occurrences of some astronomical event. **3** A portion of time between certain events: the *period* between the two World Wars. **4** A conclusion or end, as of any sequence of years, events, acts, or phenomena. **5** A portion of time marking one of the divisions of a game, academic day, etc. **6** *Med.* The course of a disease or one of its phases. **7** MENSES. **8** *Gram.* A sentence, esp. a well-constructed complex sentence. **9** The full pause in speaking at the end of a sentence. **10** A dot (.) used in writing as a mark of punctuation after every complete declarative sentence and after most abbreviations. **11** *Geol.* A division of geologic time that may contain two or more epochs. **12** *Physics* The time between two successive similar phases of a wave or oscillation. [<Gk. *periodos* a going around.]

pe·ri·od·ic (pir'ē-od'ik) *adj.* **1** Of, pertaining to, or of the nature of a period. **2** Happening or recurring at regular intervals. **3** Happening now and then; intermittent. **4** Repeating exactly after a given interval, as a mathematical function, physical variable, etc. **5** Of, expressed in, or characterized by periodic sentences.

pe·ri·od·i·cal (pir'ē-od'i-kəl) *adj.* **1** PERIODIC (def. 2). **2** Pertaining to publications, as magazines, professional journals, etc., that are published at fixed intervals of more than one day. **3** Published at such intervals. —*n.* A publication, usu. a magazine, appearing at such fixed intervals. **—pe'ri·od'i·cal·ly** *adv.*

pe·ri·o·dic·i·ty (pir'ē-ə-dis'ə-tē) *n.* The quality or property of being periodic.

periodic law *Chem.* The statement that the properties of the elements are related to their atomic numbers and recur periodically when the elements are arranged in the order of these numbers.

periodic sentence A sentence that leaves the completion of its main clause to the end.

periodic table *Chem.* A chart of elements arranged in rows in order of their atomic numbers, and falling into columns or groups of elements having similar properties.

per·i·o·don·tics (per'ē-ə-don'tiks) *n. pl. (construed as sing.)* The branch of dentistry dealing with the diagnosis and treatment of gum diseases. Also, **per'i·o·don'ti·a** (-shə, -shē-ə) [<PERI- + Gk. *odous* tooth]**—per'i·o·don'tist** *n.*

per·i·os·te·um (per'ē-os'tē-əm) *n.* A tough, fibrous membrane covering the bones. [<Gk. *peri-* around + *osteon* a bone] **—per'i·os'te·al, per'i·os'te·ous** *adj.*

per·i·pa·tet·ic (per'i-pə-tet'ik) *adj.* Walking about; moving from place to place. —*n.* One given to walking about. [<Gk. *peri-* around + *pateein* to walk]

Per·i·pa·tet·ic (per'i-pə-tet'ik) *adj.* Pertaining to the philosophy of Aristotle, who lectured to his disciples while walking in the Lyceum at Athens. —*n.* A disciple of Aristotle.

pe·riph·er·al (pə-rif'ər-əl) *adj.* **1** Of, pertaining to or forming a periphery. **2** Away from the center; external. **3** Of, pertaining to, at, or near the surface of the body. —*n.* Any device not part of the main computing unit, such as a printer, keyboard, modem, etc. **—pe·riph'er·al·ly** *adv.*

pe·riph·er·y (pə-rif'ər-ē) *n. pl.* **·er·ies** **1** The outer bounds of any surface or area. **2** The surface of the body. **3** PERIMETER (def. 1). **4** A surrounding region, country, or area. [<Gk. *periphereia* circumference]

pe·riph·ra·sis (pə-rif'rə-sis) *n. pl.* **·ses** (-sēz) **1** The use of more words than are needed; circumlocution. **2** An instance of this. [<Gk. *peri-* around + *phrazein* speak]

per·i·phras·tic (per'ə-fras'tik) *adj.* **1** Of, pertaining to, or involving periphrasis. **2** *Gram.* Denoting a construction in which a particle or auxiliary verb is substituted for an inflected form of similar function, as, *the hat of John* for *John's hat.* Also **per′i·phras′ti·cal.** —**per′i·phras′ti·cal·ly** *adv.*

per·i·scope (per′ə·skōp) *n.* An instrument capable of reflecting an image down a vertical tube. [< PERI- + -SCOPE] —**per′i·scop′ic** or **·i·cal** (-skop′i·kəl) *adj.*

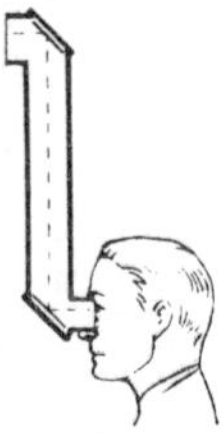

Periscope

per·ish (per′ish) *v.i.* **1** To die, esp. to suffer a violent or untimely death. **2** To be destroyed; pass from existence. [< L *per-* away + *ire* go]

per·ish·a·ble (per′ish·ə·bəl) *adj.* **1** Liable to perish. **2** Liable to speedy decay, as fruit in transportation. —*n.pl.* Goods liable to rapid decay: used chiefly of foods in transit. —**per′ish·a·bil′i·ty, per′ish·a·ble·ness** *n.* —**per′ish·a·bly** *adv.*

per·i·stal·sis (per′ə·stôl′sis, -stal′-) *n. pl.* **·ses** (-sēz) *Physiol.* A rhythmic muscular contraction of any hollow organ of the body, as of the intestines, which propels the contents toward the point of expulsion. [< Gk. *peristellein* surround] —**per′i·stal′tic** *adj.*

per·i·style (per′ə·stīl) *n. Archit.* **1** A system of columns about a building or an internal court. **2** An area or space so enclosed. [< Gk. *peri-* around + *stylos* a pillar] —**per′i·sty′lar** *adj.*

per·i·to·ne·um (per′ə·tə·nē′əm) *n. pl.* **·ne·a** (-nē′ə) The membrane that lines the abdominal cavity and covers the viscera. Also **per′i·to·nae′um.** [< Gk. *peritonos* stretched round] —**per′i·to·ne′al** or **·nae′al** *adj.*

per·i·to·ni·tis (per′ə·tə·nī′tis) *n.* Inflammation of the peritoneum.

per·i·wig (per′ə·wig) *n.* A wig. [< MF *perruque* peruke]

per·i·win·kle[1] (per′ə·wing′kəl) *n.* **1** Any of several small marine snails having a thick, conical shell. **2** The shell of these snails. [< OE *pinewincle*]

per·i·win·kle[2] (per′ə·wing′kəl) *n.* Any of several trailing plants with shining, evergreen leaves and usu. blue flowers. [< L *pervinca*]

per·jure (pûr′jər) *v.t.* **·jured, ·jur·ing** To make (oneself) guilty of perjury. [< L *per-* through, badly + *jurare* swear] —**per′jur·er** *n.*

per·jured (pûr′jərd) *adj.* Guilty of or marked by perjury.

per·ju·ry (pûr′jə·rē) *n. pl.* **·ries 1** *Law* The willful giving of false testimony while under lawfully administered oath. **2** The breaking of any oath, vow, or promise.

perk[1] (pûrk) *v.i.* **1** To recover one's spirits or vigor: with *up.* **2** To carry oneself or lift one's head jauntily. —*v.t.* **3** To raise quickly or smartly, as the ears: often with *up.* **4** To make (oneself) trim and smart in appearance: often with *up* or *out.* [ME *perken*]

perk[2] (pûrk) *v.i. Informal* To percolate.

perk[3] (pûrk) *n. Usu. pl. Chiefly Brit. Slang* PERQUISITE.

perk·y (pûr′kē) *adj.* **·i·er, ·i·est** Brisk, jaunty, spirited, or aggressive. —**perk′i·ly** *adv.* —**perk′i·ness** *n.*

perm. permanent.

per·ma·frost (pûr′mə·frôst, -frost) *n.* A permanently frozen layer of subsoil occurring in frigid climates. [< PERMA(NENT) + FROST]

per·ma·nence (pûr′mə·nəns) *n.* The state of being permanent; durability; fixity.

per·ma·nen·cy (pûr′mə·nən·sē) *n. pl.* **·cies 1** PERMANENCE. **2** Something permanent.

per·ma·nent (pûr′mə·nənt) *adj.* Continuing or intended to continue in the same state or without essential change. —*n.* PERMANENT WAVE. [< L *per-* through + *manere* remain] —**per′ma·nent·ly** *adv.* —**Syn.** durable, stable, fixed, lasting.

permanent wave A persistent curl produced by heat or chemicals in growing hair.

per·man·ga·nate (pər·mang′gə·nāt) *n.* A dark purple salt of permanganic acid.

per·man·gan·ic acid (pûr′man·gan′ik) An unstable acid containing manganese and oxygen.

per·me·a·ble (pûr′mē·ə·bəl) *adj.* Allowing passage, esp. of fluids. —**per·me·a·bil·i·ty** (pûr′mē·ə·bil′ə·tē) *n.* —**per′me·a·bly** *adv.*

per·me·ate (pûr′mē·āt) *v.* **·at·ed, ·at·ing** *v.t.* **1** To spread thoroughly through; pervade. **2** To pass through the pores or interstices of. —*v.i.* **3** To spread itself through something. [< L *per-* through + *meare* to pass] —**per′me·a′tion** *n.* —**per′me·a′tive** *adj.*

Per·mi·an (pûr′mē·ən) *adj. & n.* See GEOLOGY. [< *Perm,* a former E Russian province]

per·mis·si·ble (pər·mis′ə·bəl) *adj.* That can be permitted; allowable. —**per·mis′si·bil′i·ty** *n.* —**per·mis′si·bly** *adv.*

per·mis·sion (pər·mish′ən) *n.* The act of permitting or allowing; formal authorization; consent.

per·mis·sive (pər·mis′iv) *adj.* **1** That permits; granting permission. **2** That is permitted; optional. **3** Tolerant; lenient; indulgent: *permissive* parents. —**per·mis′sive·ly** *adv.* —**per·mis′sive·ness** *n.*

per·mit (pər·mit′) *v.* **·mit·ted, ·mit·ting** *v.t.* **1** To allow the doing of; consent to. **2** To give (someone) leave or consent; authorize. **3** To afford opportunity for: His answer *permits* no misinterpretation. —*v.i.* **4** To afford possibility or opportunity. —*n.* (pûr′mit) **1** Permission or warrant. **2** A formal, written authorization to do something. [< L *per-* through + *mittere* send, let go] —**per·mit′ter** *n.*

per·mu·ta·tion (pûr′myōō·tā′shən) *n.* **1** The act of permuting; transformation. **2** *Math.* **a** Change in the order of the elements of a set. **b** Any one of the set of arrangements that can be produced in this way.

per·mute (pər·myōōt′) *v.t.* **·mut·ed, ·mut·ing 1** To alter; change the order of. **2** *Math.* To subject to permutation. [< L *per-* thoroughly + *mutare* to change]

per·ni·cious (pər·nish′əs) *adj.* **1** Destructive; deadly. **2** *Archaic* Malicious; wicked. [< L *per-* thoroughly + *nex, necis* death] —**per·ni′cious·ly** *adv.* —**per·ni′cious·ness** *n.*

pernicious anemia A severe, progressive anemia of middle age and later, now controllable by administering certain vitamins.

per·nick·e·ty (pər·nik′ə·tē) *adj.* PERSNICKETY.

Pe·ron·ist (pə·rōn′ist) *n.* A follower of Juan Perón or of his policies. Also **Pe·ron·is·ta** (per′ə·nēs′tə).

per·o·rate (per′ə·rāt) *v.i.* **·rat·ed, ·rat·ing 1** To speak at length; harangue. **2** To sum up or conclude a speech. [< L *per-* thoroughly + *orare* speak]

per·o·ra·tion (per′ə·rā′shən) *n.* The concluding portion of an oration; the recapitulation of an argument.

per·ox·ide (pə·rok′sīd) *n.* **1** HYDROGEN PEROXIDE. **2** Any oxide yielding hydrogen peroxide when treated with an acid. —*v.t.* **·id·ed, ·id·ing** To bleach, as hair, with hydrogen peroxide.

per·pen·dic·u·lar (pûr′pən·dik′yə·lər) *adj.* **1** Being at right angles to the plane of the horizon; upright or vertical. **2** *Math.* Meeting a given line or plane at right angles. —*n.* **1** A perpendicular line. **2** A device used to indicate the vertical line from any point. **3** A vertical line or vertical face. **4** Perpendicular position. [< L *perpendiculum* a plumb line] —**per′pen·dic′u·lar′i·ty** (-lar′ə·tē) *n.* —**per′pen·dic′u·lar·ly** *adv.*

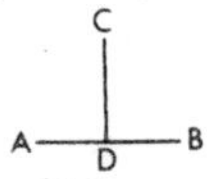

CD is perpendicular to AB

per·pe·trate (pûr′pə·trāt) *v.t.* **·trat·ed, ·trat·ing** To perform or commit (a crime, etc.). [< L *perpetrare* carry through] —**per′pe·tra′tion, per′pe·tra′tor** *n.*

per·pet·u·al (pər·pech′ōō·əl) *adj.* **1** Continuing for all time. **2** Happening continually; repeated ceaselessly. [< L *per-* through + *petere* seek] —**per·pet′u·al·ly** *adv.* —**per·pet′u·al·ness** *n.*

per·pet·u·ate (pər·pech′ōō·āt) *v.t.* **·at·ed, ·at·ing** To make perpetual or enduring. —**per·pet′u·a′tion, per·pet′u·a′tor** *n.*

per·pe·tu·i·ty (pûr′pə·tyōō′ə·tē) *n. pl.* **·ties 1** The quality or state or being perpetual. **2** Something that has perpetual existence or worth, as an annuity that is to be paid for life. **3** Unending or unlimited time.

per·plex (pər·pleks′) *v.t.* **1** To cause to hesitate, as from doubt; confuse; puzzle. **2** To make complicated, intricate, or confusing. [< L *per* thoroughly + *plectere* to twist] —**per·plexed′** *adj.* —**per·plex′ed·ly** (-plek′sid·lē) *adv.*

per·plex·i·ty (pər·plek′sə·tē) *n. pl.* **·ties 1** The state of being perplexed; bewilderment; confusion, etc. **2** That which perplexes; also, an instance of bewilderment.

per·qui·site (pûr′kwə·zit) *n.* **1** Any incidental profit from service beyond salary or wages. **2** A privilege or benefit claimed as due. [< L *perquisitum* a thing diligently sought]

Pers. Persia; Persian.

pers. person; personal.

per se (pûr sā′, sē′) By, in, or of itself, oneself, or themselves; intrinsically. [L]

per·se·cute (pûr′sə·kyōōt) *v.t.* **·cut·ed, ·cut·ing 1** To harass with cruel or oppressive treatment, esp. because of race, religion, or opinions. **2** To annoy or harass persistently. [< L *per-* thoroughly + *sequi* follow] **—per′se·cu′tion, per′·se·cu′tor** *n.* **—per′se·cu′tion·al, per′se·cu′tive** *adj.*

Per·seph·o·ne (pər·sef′ə·nē) *Gk. Myth.* The daughter of Zeus and Demeter, abducted by Pluto and made queen of the kingdom of the dead.

Per·seus (pûr′syōōs, -sē·əs) *Gk. Myth.* The son of Zeus, slayer of Medusa and savior and husband of Andromeda. *—n.* A northern constellation.

per·se·ver·ance (pûr′sə·vir′əns) *n.* **1** The act or habit of persevering. **2** Steadfastness; tenacity.

per·se·vere (pûr′sə·vir′) *v.i.* **·vered, ·ver·ing** To persist in any purpose or enterprise; continue striving in spite of opposition, difficulty, etc. [< L *per-* thoroughly + *severus* strict] **—per′se·ver′ing·ly** *adv.* **—Syn.** endure, carry on, strive, hold out.

Per·sia (pûr′zhə, -shə) *n.* The former name for IRAN.

Per·sian (pûr′zhən, -shən) *adj.* Of or pertaining to ancient Persia or modern Iran, its people, or its language. *—n.* **1** A native or citizen of Persia or Iran. **2** The Iranian language of the Persians.

Persian Empire An ancient empire of sw Asia, extending from the Indus to the Mediterranean: founded by Cyrus the Great (sixth century B.C.) and destroyed by Alexander the Great (331 B.C.).

Persian lamb 1 The young of certain sheep, esp. the karakul. **2** Its skin, used as a fur; astrakhan.

per·si·flage (pûr′sə·fläzh′) *n.* **1** A light, flippant style of talking or writing. **2** Talking or writing of this kind. [< F *persifler* to banter]

per·sim·mon (pər·sim′ən) *n.* **1** A tree related to ebony with astringent, plumlike fruit. **2** The fruit of this tree. [< Algon.]

per·sist (pər·sist′, -zist′) *v.i.* **1** To continue firmly in some course, state, etc., esp. despite opposition or difficulties. **2** To be insistent, as in repeating a statement. **3** To continue to exist; endure. [< L *per-* thoroughly + *sistere* to stand]

per·sis·tence (pər·sis′təns, -zis′-) *n.* **1** The act of persisting. **2** The quality of being persistent; perseverance. **3** The continuance of an effect longer than the cause that first produced it.

per·sis·tent (pər·sis′tənt, -zis′-) *adj.* **1** Firm and persevering in a course or resolve. **2** Continuing to exist; enduring; permanent. **3** Constantly repeated; continual. **—per·sis′tent·ly** *adv.*

per·snick·e·ty (pər·snik′ə·tē) *adj. Informal* **1** Unduly fastidious; fussy; overprecise. **2** Demanding or displaying great care or precision. [< dial. alter. of PARTICULAR] **—per·snick′e·ti·ness** *n.*

per·son (pûr′sən) *n.* **1** A human being; an individual. **2** The body of a human being or its characteristic appearance and condition. **3** The personality of a human being; self. **4** *Law* Any human being, corporation, or other legal entity having legal rights and responsibilities. **5** *Gram.* **a** A modification of the pronoun and verb that distinguishes the speaker **(first person),** the person or thing spoken to **(second person),** and the person or thing spoken of **(third person). b** Any of the forms or inflections indicating this, as *I* or *we, you, he, she, it.* **—in person** Present in the flesh; in bodily presence. [< L *persona* mask for actors]

per·so·na (pər·sō′nə) *n.* **1** *pl.* **·nae** (-nē) A character in a drama, novel, etc.: dramatis *personae.* **2** *pl.* **·nas** *Psych.* The public role adopted by an individual. [L]

per·son·a·ble (pûr′sən·ə·bəl) *adj.* Pleasing in appearance and personality. **—per′son·a·bly** *adv.*

per·son·age (pûr′sən·ij) *n.* **1** A person of importance or rank. **2** Any person. **3** A character in fiction, history, etc. [< L *persona* a person]

per·so·na gra·ta (pər·sō′nə grä′tə, grā′tə) An acceptable person; one who is welcome. [L]

per·son·al (pûr′sən·əl) *adj.* **1** Of, pertaining to, characteristic of, or affecting a person. **2** Performed by or done to the person directly concerned. **3** Carried on directly by the persons concerned. **4** Of or pertaining to the body or appearance: *personal* beauty. **5** Directly relating to a person's character, conduct, personal affairs or habits, etc. **6** Making or tending to make personal remarks or to ask personal questions, esp. of a derogatory nature. **7** *Law* Of, pertaining to, or constituting personal property. **8** *Gram.* Denoting or indicating grammatical person. *—n.* A news item or advertisement that is personal in nature.

per·son·al·ism (pûr′sən·əl·iz′əm) *n.* A doctrine or movement stressing the uniqueness, significance and rights of the individual. **—per·son·al·ist** *adj., n.* **—per·son·al·is·tic** *adj.*

per·son·al·i·ty (pûr′sən·al′ə·tē) *n. pl.* **·ties 1** The state or quality of being a person, esp. a particular person. **2** Those special characteristics that distinguish a person, a group, or a nation. **3** The sum of such characteristics as they impress or tend to impress others. **4** Excellent or distinctive traits of character, sociability, etc. **5** A person having such traits. **6** A person who is famous or notorious. **7** *Usu. pl.* A remark, esp. one that is personally disparaging.

per·son·al·ize (pûr′sən·əl·iz′) *v.t.* **·ized, ·iz·ing 1** To make personal. **2** To personify. **3** To have engraved, monogrammed, etc. with one's name or initials, as stationery. *Brit. sp.* **per′son·al·ise′.**

per·son·al·ly (pûr′sən·əl·ē) *adv.* **1** In person; not through an agent. **2** As a person: I like her *personally.* **3** With reference to one's own opinion: *Personally,* I prefer the theater to the ballet. **4** As if directed at oneself: to take a comment *personally.*

per·son·al·ty (pûr′sən·əl·tē) *n. pl.* **·ties** Personal property.

per·so·na non gra·ta (pər·sō′nə non grä′tə, grā′tə) A person not acceptable. [L]

per·son·ate (pûr′sən·āt) *v.t.* **·at·ed, ·at·ing 1** To act the part of, as a character in a play. **2** To personify, as in poetry, art, etc. **3** *Law* To impersonate with intent to deceive. **—per′son·a′tion, per′son·a′tor** *n.* **—per′son·a′tive** *adj.*

per·son·i·fi·ca·tion (pər·son′ə·fə·kā′shən) *n.* **1** The endowment of inanimate objects or qualities with human attributes. **2** Striking or typical exemplification of a quality in one's person; embodiment: She was the *personification* of joy. **3** The representation of an abstract quality or idea by a human figure.

per·son·i·fy (pər·son′ə·fī) *v.t.* **·fied, ·fy·ing 1** To think of or represent as having life or human qualities. **2** To represent (an abstraction or inanimate object) as a person; symbolize. **3** To be the embodiment of; typify. [< L *persona* a mask, person + *facere* make] **—per·son′i·fi′er** *n.*

per·son·nel (pûr′sə·nel′) *n.* **1** Persons collectively. **2** The persons employed in a business or in military service. • *Personnel,* when it is construed as a unit, takes a singular verb: *The company's personnel has been cut.* When the term refers to the individuals that make up a unit, it takes a plural verb: *All personnel were requested to donate blood.*

per·spec·tive (pər·spek′tiv) *n.* **1** The art or theory of representing, by a drawing made on a flat or curved surface, solid objects or surfaces conceived of as not lying in that surface. **2** The art of conveying the impression of depth and distance by means of correct drawing, shading, etc. **3** The effect of distance upon the appearance of objects, by means of which the eye judges spatial relations. **4** The relative importance of facts or matters from any special point of view; also, the ability to discern this relative importance **5** A distant

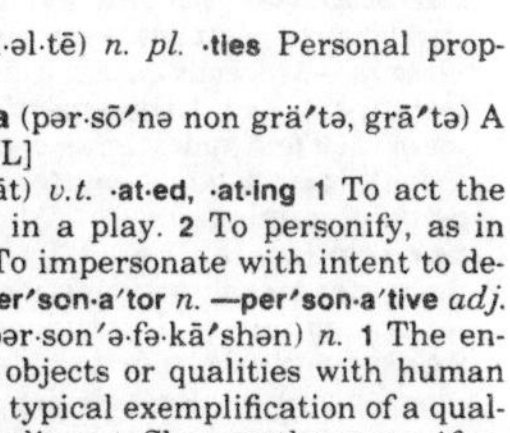

Perspective
ab. horizon. c. vanishing point. dc. line of sight. ef. ground line.

view; vista; prospect. —*adj.* 1 Of or pertaining to perspective. 2 Drawn in perspective. [< L *per-* through + *specere* look] —**per·spec'tive·ly** *adv.*

per·spi·ca·cious (pûr'spə·kā'shəs) *adj.* Keenly discerning or understanding. [< L *perspicax* sharp-sighted] —**per'spi·ca'cious·ly** *adv.* —**per'spi·ca'cious·ness, per'spi·cac'i·ty** (-kas'ə·tē) *n.*

per·spi·cu·i·ty (pûr'spə·kyōō'ə·tē) *n.* Clearness of expression or style; lucidity.

per·spic·u·ous (pər·spik'yōō·əs) *adj.* Having the quality of perspicuity; clear; lucid. [< L *perspicuus* clear, transparent] —**per·spic'u·ous·ly** *adv.* —**per·spic'ous·ness** *n.*

per·spi·ra·tion (pûr'spə·rā'shən) *n.* 1 The exuding of the saline fluid secreted by the sweat glands of the skin. 2 The saline fluid excreted; sweat. —**per·spir·a·to·ry** (pər·spī'rə·tôr'ē, -tō'rē, per'spə-) *adj.*

per·spire (pər·spīr') *v.* **·spired, ·spir·ing** *v.i.* 1 To give off perspiration through the pores of the skin; sweat. —*v.t.* 2 To give off through pores; exude. [< L *per-* through + *spirare* breathe] —**per·spir'a·ble** *adj.*

per·suade (pər·swād') *v.t.* **·suad·ed, ·suad·ing** 1 To move (a person, etc.) to do something by arguments, inducements, pleas, etc. 2 To induce to a belief; convince. [< L *per-* thoroughly + *suadere* advise] —**per·suad'a·ble** *adj.* —**per·suad'er** *n.*

per·sua·sion (pər·swā'zhən) *n.* 1 The act of persuading. 2 The state of being persuaded; conviction. 3 The power to persuade; persuasiveness. 4 A particular sect, denomination, etc. 5 *Informal* Sort; kind: the male *persuasion.*

per·sua·sive (pər·swā'siv) *adj.* Having the power or tendency to persuade. —**per·sua'sive·ly** *adv.* —**per·sua'sive·ness** *n.* —**Syn.** convincing, influential, assuring, cogent.

pert (pûrt) *adj.* 1 Disrespectfully forward or free; impudent. 2 Of fine appearance; comely; sprightly. [< L *apertus* open] —**pert'ly** *adv.* —**pert'ness** *n.*

pert. pertaining.

per·tain (pər·tān') *v.i.* 1 To have reference; relate. 2 To belong as an adjunct, function, quality, etc. 3 To be fitting or appropriate. [< L *pertinere* extend]

per·ti·na·cious (pûr'tə·nā'shəs) *adj.* 1 Marked by a dogged or even perverse firmness, as of purpose. 2 Stubbornly tenacious; hard to get rid of. [< L *per-* thoroughly, very + *tenax* tenacious] —**per'ti·na'cious·ly** *adv.* —**per'ti·na'cious·ness, per'ti·nac'i·ty** (-nas'ə·tē) *n.*

per·ti·nent (pûr'tə·nənt) *adj.* Related to or properly bearing upon the matter in hand; relevant. [< OF *partenir* pertain] —**per'ti·nence, per'ti·nen·cy** *n.* —**per'ti·nent·ly** *adv.*

per·turb (pər·tûrb') *v.t.* 1 To disquiet or disturb greatly; alarm; agitate. 2 To cause confusion or disorder in. [< L *per-* thoroughly + *turbare* disturb] —**per'tur·ba'tion** *n.*

Pe·ru (pə·rōō') *n.* A republic of w South America, 533,916 sq. mi., cap. Lima.

pe·ruke (pə·rōōk') *n.* A wig. [< Ital. *perruca*]

pe·ruse (pə·rōōz') *v.t.* **·rused, ·rus·ing** 1 To read carefully or attentively. 2 To read. 3 To examine; scrutinize. [< PER- + USE, *v.*] —**pe·rus'a·ble** *adj.* —**pe·ru'sal, pe·rus'er** *n.*

Pe·ru·vi·an (pə·rōō'vē·ən) *adj.* Of or pertaining to Peru, its people, or their culture. —*n.* A native or citizen of Peru.

Peruvian bark CINCHONA.

per·vade (pər·vād') *v.t.* **·vad·ed, ·vad·ing** To pass or spread through every part of; be diffused throughout; permeate. [< L *per-* through + *vadere* go] —**per·va'sion** (-zhən) *n.*

per·va·sive (pər·vā'siv) *adj.* Broadly or thoroughly penetrating; widespread. —**per·va'sive·ly** *adv.* —**per·va'sive·ness** *n.*

per·verse (pər·vûrs') *adj.* 1 Different or varying from the correct or normal. 2 Wicked; corrupt. 3 Obstinate and unreasonable in resisting what is reasonable, accepted, etc. 4 Petulant; peevish. [< L *pervertere* turn the wrong way] —**per·verse'ly** *adv.* —**per·verse'ness, per·ver'si·ty** *n.* —**per·ver'sive** *adj.*

per·ver·sion (pər·vûr'zhən, -shən) *n.* 1 The act of perverting, or the state or being perverted. 2 Something perverted. 3 A deviation from the normal, esp. in sexual desires or activities.

per·vert (pər·vûrt') *v.t.* 1 To turn to an improper use or purpose; misapply. 2 To distort the meaning of; misconstrue. 3 To turn from approved opinions or conduct; lead astray; corrupt. —*n.* (pûr'vûrt) A person who is perverted, esp. one affected with or addicted to sexual perversion. [< L *per-* away + *vertere* turn] —**per·vert'er** *n.* —**per·vert'i·ble** *adj.*

per·vert·ed (pər·vûr'tid) *adj.* Of, pertaining to, caused by, or characterized by perversion. —**per·vert'ed·ly** *adv.*

per·vi·ous (pûr'vē·əs) *adj.* 1 Capable of being penetrated; permeable. 2 Having a mind open to argument, suggestion, etc. [< L *per-* through + *via* way] —**per'vi·ous·ly** *adv.* —**per'vi·ous·ness** *n.*

Pe·sach (pā'säkh) *n.* PASSOVER. Also **Pe'sah.**

pe·se·ta (pə·sā'tə, *Sp.* pā·sā'tä) *n.* A silver coin, the basic monetary unit of Spain.

pes·ky (pes'kē) *adj.* **·ki·er, ·ki·est** *Informal* Annoying; troublesome; irksome. [Prob. < PEST] —**pes'ki·ly** *adv.* —**pes'ki·ness** *n.*

pe·so (pā'sō) *n. pl.* **·sos** The basic monetary unit of Argentina, Colombia, Cuba, the Dominican Republic, Mexico, the Philippines, and Uruguay. [Sp.]

pes·sa·ry (pes'ə·rē) *n. pl.* **·ries** Any device worn inside the vagina, as a contraceptive or a support to correct uterine prolapse. [< Gk. *pessos* an oval stone]

pes·si·mism (pes'ə·miz'əm) *n.* 1 A disposition to expect the worst possible conclusion of the course of events or of the resolution of present uncertainties or conditions. 2 The philosophical doctrine that the world as it exists is basically evil. 3 The belief that the evils in life outweigh the good and the happiness. [< L *pessimus* worst + -ISM] —**pes'si·mist** *n.* —**pes'si·mis'tic** *adj.* —**pes'si·mis'ti·cal·ly** *adv.*

pest (pest) *n.* 1 An annoying or harmful person or thing, esp. a destructive or injurious insect. 2 A virulent epidemic; pestilence. [< L *pestis* a plague]

pes·ter (pes'tər) *v.t.* To harass with petty annoyances. [< OF *empestrer* hobble a grazing horse] —**pes'ter·er** *n.*

pest·hole (pest'hōl') *n.* A breeding place for disease.

pest·house (pest'hous') *n. Archaic* A hospital for patients with infectious diseases.

pes·ti·cide (pes'tə·sīd) *n.* A chemical used to destroy weeds or vermin. —**pes'ti·ci'dal** *adj.*

pes·tif·er·ous (pes·tif'ər·əs) *adj.* 1 Carrying pestilence. 2 Threatening or bringing danger or evil. 3 *Informal* Annoying; disagreeable. [< L *pestis* a plague + *ferre* bear] —**pes·tif'er·ous·ly** *adv.* —**pes·tif'er·ous·ness** *n.*

pes·ti·lence (pes'tə·ləns) *n.* 1 Any widespread infectious malady. 2 A dangerous or harmful doctrine, influence, etc. [< L *pestis* a plague] —**pes'ti·lent, pes'ti·len'tial** (-shəl) *adj.* —**pes'ti·lent·ly, pes'ti·len'tial·ly** *adv.*

pes·tle (pes'əl) *n.* 1 An implement used for crushing or mixing substances, as in a mortar. 2 A vertical moving bar employed in pounding, as in a stamp mill, etc. —*v.t. & v.i.* **·tled, ·tling** To pound, grind, or mix with or as with a pestle. [< L *pistillum*]

Pestle

pet[1] (pet) *n.* 1 A tamed or domesticated animal that is treated with affection. 2 Any person who is treated with affection or to whom great attention is paid. —*adj.* 1 Being or treated like a pet. 2 Regarded as a favorite; cherished: my *pet* hobby. —*v.* **pet·ted, pet·ting** —*v.t.* 1 To pamper; indulge. 2 To stroke or caress. —*v.i.* 3 *Informal* To kiss and caress or fondle in making love. [?]

pet[2] (pet) *n.* A fit of pique or ill temper; peevish mood. [?]

pet·al (pet'l) *n. Bot.* A division of a corolla. [< Gk. *petalon* a thin plate, leaf] —**pet'aled** or **pet'alled** *adj.*

pe·tard (pi·tärd') *n.* An explosive device formerly used for making breaches, etc., as in walls. —**hoist with (or by) one's own petard** To undo (one who plots the ruin of others) by ensnaring in his own machinations. [< MF *péter* break wind]

pet·cock (pet'kok') *n. Mech.* A small tap or valve, as for draining a steam cylinder or pump. [? < obs. *pet* a fart + COCK[1] a valve]

pe·ter (pē'tər) *v.i. Informal* To diminish gradually and then cease or disappear; become exhausted: with *out.* [Orig. U.S. mining slang]

pet·i·ole (pet′ē·ōl) *n.* 1 *Bot.* The stalk supporting the blade of a leaf. 2 *Zool.* A stalk or peduncle. [< L *petiolus* a stem, dim. of *pes, pedis* a foot] —**pet′i·o′lar, pet′i·o·late′, pet′i·o·lat′ed** *adj.*

pet·it (pet′ē) *adj.* Small; lesser; minor; trivial: used in legal phrases. [< OF, small]

pe·tite (pə·tēt′) *adj.* Diminutive; little: said of women. [F]

pet·it four (pet′ē fôr′, fōr; *Fr.* pə·tē′ fōōr′) *n. pl.* **pet·its fours** (pet′ē fôrz′, fōrz′; *Fr.* pə·tē′ fōōr′) A small cake, often elaborately frosted. [F, lit., little oven]

pe·ti·tion (pə·tish′ən) *n.* 1 A request, supplication, or prayer; a solemn or formal supplication. 2 A formal request, written or printed, setting forth such a request, addressed to a person or persons in authority and often signed by a group of petitioners. 3 *Law* A formal application in writing made to a court, requesting judicial action concerning some matter therein set forth. 4 That which is requested or asked for. —*v.t.* 1 To make a petition to; entreat. 2 To ask for. —*v.i.* 3 To make a petition. [< L < *petere* seek] —**pe·ti′tion·ar′y** *adj.* —**pe·ti′tion·er** *n.*

petit jury A jury of 12 persons selected to weigh the evidence in and decide upon the facts at issue in a trial in court.

pe·tit mal (pə·tē′ mal′, mäl′) *Pathol.* A minor epileptic seizure characterized by a momentary loss of consciousness. [F, lit., small illness]

pet·rel (pet′rəl) *n.* Any of various small sea birds that fly low over the water with feet hanging. [?]

pet·ri·fy (pet′rə·fī) *v.* **·fied, ·fy·ing** *v.t.* To replace (organic material) with stony minerals. 2 To make fixed and unyielding; harden. 3 To immobilize with fear, surprise, etc. —*v.i.* 4 To become stone or a stony substance. [< L *petra* a rock + *facere* make] —**pet′ri·fac′tion** (-fak′shən), **pet′ri·fi·ca′tion** *n.* —**pet′ri·fac′tive** *adj.*

petro- *combining form* Rock; stone: *petrography.* [Gk. *petros* a stone]

pet·ro·chem·i·cal (pet′rō·kem′i·kəl) *n.* Any compound derived from petroleum or natural gas. —*adj.* Pertaining to petrochemicals. —**pet·ro·chem·is·try** (-is·trē) *n.*

pet·ro·dol·lars (pet′rō·dol′ərz) *n. pl.* Dollars accumulated by oil-producing countries from oil sales, and usually invested in industrial countries.

pe·trog·ra·phy (pə·trog′rə·fē) *n.* The systematic description and classification of rocks. —**pe·trog′ra·pher** *n.* —**pet·ro·graph·ic** (pet′rə·graf′ik) or **·i·cal** *adj.*

pet·rol (pet′rəl) *n. Brit.* GASOLINE. [< F *pétrole*]

pet·ro·la·tum (pet′rə·lā′təm) *n.* A greasy semisolid mixture of hydrocarbons obtained from petroleum, used as a lubricant and in medicinal salves. Also **petroleum jelly.** [< PETROLEUM]

pe·tro·le·um (pə·trō′lē·əm) *n.* An oily, liquid mixture of hydrocarbons found in scattered subterranean deposits, and used as a source of fuels, as gasoline, kerosene, etc. and as raw material for many synthetic products. [< L *petra* rock + *oleum* oil]

pe·trol·o·gy (pə·trol′ə·jē) *n.* The study of the origin and characteristics of rocks. —**pet·ro·log·ic** (pet′rə·loj′ik) or **·i·cal** *adj.* —**pet′ro·log′i·cal·ly** *adv.* —**pe·trol′o·gist** *n.*

pet·ti·coat (pet′ē·kōt) *n.* 1 A skirt, esp. an underskirt worn by young girls and women. 2 *Informal* A girl or woman. —*adj.* Of, pertaining to, or influenced by, women: *petticoat* politics. [< PETTY + COAT]

pet·ti·fog (pet′i·fog, -fôg) *v.i.* **·fogged, ·fog·ging** To be a pettifogger. [Back formation < PETTIFOGGER]

pet·ti·fog·ger (pet′i·fog′ər, -fôg′ər) *n.* 1 A disreputable lawyer, esp. one chiefly employed on mean or petty cases, or resorting to small or tricky methods. 2 A person who quibbles over unimportant details. [< PETTY + obs. *fogger* a trickster for gain] —**pet′ti·fog′ger·y** *n.*

pet·tish (pet′ish) *adj.* Capriciously ill-tempered; petulant. [Prob. < PET²] —**pet′tish·ly** *adv.*

pet·ty (pet′ē) *adj.* **·ti·er, ·ti·est** 1 Having little worth, importance, position, or rank. 2 Having little generosity; small-minded; mean; spiteful. [< OF *petit* small] —**pet′ti·ly** *adv.* —**pet′ti·ness** *n.*

petty cash Money for small incidental expenses.

petty jury PETIT JURY.

petty officer See GRADE.

pet·u·lant (pech·ōō·lənt) *adj.* Displaying or characterized by bad humor, esp. over a minor irritation. [< L *petulans* forward] —**pet′u·lance, pet′u·lan·cy** *n.* —**pet′u·lant·ly** *adv.* —**Syn.** fretful, peevish, grumpy, complaining.

pe·tu·ni·a (pə·tyōō′nē·ə) *n.* A plant of the nightshade family, with funnel-shaped, fragrant flowers in various shades of red, purple, and white. [< F *petun* tobacco; from its close relation to tobacco]

pew (pyōō) *n.* 1 A bench with a back for seating people in church. 2 A boxlike enclosure with seats, for seating a family or other group in a church. [< L *podium* balcony]

pe·wee (pē′wē) *n.* Any of several small flycatchers, including the phoebe. [Imit.]

pe·wit (pē′wit, pyōō′it) *n.* 1 PEWEE. 2 LAPWING.

pew·ter (pyōō′tər) *n.* 1 An alloy of tin with lead and other meals. 2 Tableware, etc., made of pewter. —*adj.* Made of pewter. [< OF *peutre*]

pe·yo·te (pā·ō′tē; *Sp.* pā·yō′tā) *n.* 1 The mescal cactus. 2 The hallucinogen obtained from this cactus. Also **pe·yo′tl** (-yōt′l). [< Nah. *peyotl,* lit., a caterpillar; from the down at its center]

pf. pfennig, preferred.

Pfc, Pfc. private first class.

pfd. preferred.

pfen·nig (fen′ig; *Ger.* pfen′ikh) *n. pl.* **·nigs** or **pfen·ni·ge** (pfen′i·ge) A unit of German currency, equivalent to 1/100 of a Deutsche mark or of a mark or Ostmark.

Pg. Portugal; Portuguese.

pH *Chem.* The symbol used in expressing acidity and alkalinity on a numerical scale such that a pH of 1 represents a strongly acid condition, 7 represents neutrality, and pH values 7 to about 14 indicate increasing alkalinity. [< P(OTENTIAL OF) H(YDROGEN)]

Phae·dra (fē′drə) *Gk. Myth.* The wife of Theseus: she fell in love with her stepson Hippolytus and killed herself because he spurned her.

Pha·e·thon (fē′ə·thon) *Gk. Myth.* The son of Helios, who borrowed his father's chariot of the sun, and would have set heaven and earth on fire if Zeus had not slain him with a thunderbolt.

pha·e·ton (fā′ə·tən; *esp. Brit.* fā′tən) *n.* 1 A light four-wheeled horse-drawn carriage. 2 An early type of open two-seated automobile; usu. with a folding top. [< Phaethon]

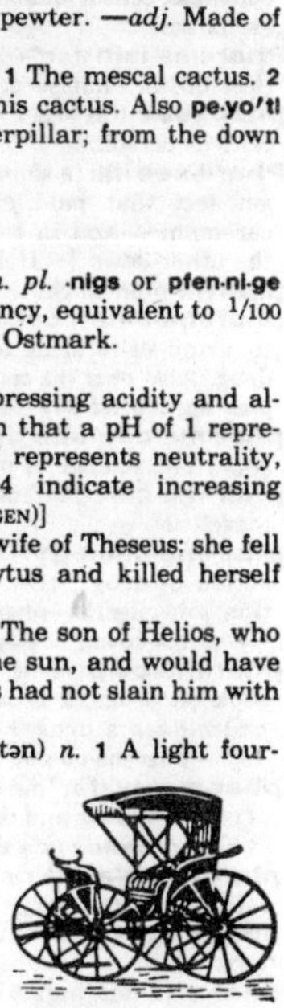
Phaeton *def. 1*

phago- *combining form* Consuming: *phagocyte.* Also **phag-.** [< Gk. *phagein* eat]

phag·o·cyte (fag′ə·sīt) *n.* A leukocyte that engulfs and destroys foreign particles, as bacteria, etc. [< Gk. *phagein* eat + -CYTE] —**phag′o·cyt′ic** (-sit′ik) or **·i·cal** *adj.*

pha·lan·ger (fə·lan′jər) *n.* any of various small arboreal marsupials of Australia and New Guinea. [< NL *phalanx* phalanx (def. 3); in ref. to the peculiar construction of its hind feet]

pha·lanx (fā′langks, *esp. Brit.* fal′angks) *n. pl.* **pha·lanx·es** or **pha·lan·ges** (fə·lan′jēz) 1 In ancient Greece, a dense formation of heavy infantry. 2 Any massed or compact body or corps. 3 *pl* **pha·lan·ges** *Anat.* Any of the bones of the fingers or toes. [Gk., a line of battle] • See FOOT.

phal·li·cism (fal′ə·siz′əm) *n.* Worship of the generative power in nature as symbolized by the phallus.

phal·lus (fal′əs) *n. pl.* **·lus·es** or **·li** (-ī) 1 A figure of the penis as a symbol of male generative power, used in many systems of religion. 2 The penis. [< Gk. *phallos* penis] —**phal′lic** or **phal′li·cal** *adj.*

phan·tasm (fan′taz·əm) *n.* 1 A figment of the imagination, as a ghost or specter. 2 A deceptive likeness or appearance. —**phan·tas′mal, phan·tas′mic,** *adj.*

phan·tas·ma·go·ri·a (fan·taz′mə·gôr′ē·ə, -gō′rē·ə) *n.* A fantastic, rapidly changing series of things, actually seen or imagined.
phan·ta·sy (fan′tə·sē, -zē) *n. pl.* **phan·ta·sies** FANTASY.
phan·tom (fan′təm) *n.* **1** Something that exists only in appearance; illusion. **2** An apparition; specter. **3** Something dreaded or feared. **4** The visible representative of an abstract state or incorporeal person. —*adj.* Of, like, or being a phantom. [< Gk. *phantasma* an appearance]
Phar·aoh (fâr′ō, fā′rō) *n.* Any one of the monarchs of ancient Egypt. [< Egypt. *pr-′ōh* the great house] —**Phar′a·on′ic** (-ā·on′ik) or **·i·cal** *adj.*
phar·i·sa·ic (far′ə·sā′ik) *adj.* Observing the form rather than the spirit of religion; self-righteous; hypocritical. Also **phar′i·sa′i·cal.** —**phar′i·sa′i·cal·ly** *adv.* —**phar′i·sa′i·cal·ness** *n.*
Phar·i·sa·ic (far′ə·sā′ik) *adj.* Of or pertaining to the Pharisees.
phar·i·sa·ism (far′ə·sā·iz′əm) *n.* Formality, self-righteousness, censoriousness, or hypocrisy. Also **phar′i·see·ism** (-sē·iz′əm).
Phar·i·sa·ism (far′ə·sā·iz′əm) *n.* The principles and practices of the Pharisees.
phar·i·see (far′ə·sē) *n.* A formal, sanctimonious, hypocritical person.
Phar·i·see (far′ə·sē) *n.* One of an ancient, exclusive Jewish sect that paid excessive regard to tradition and ceremonies, and in so doing separated themselves from the other Jews. [< Heb. *pārūsh* separated]
pharm. pharmaceutical; pharmacist; pharmacy.
phar·ma·ceu·ti·cal (far′mə·sōō′ti·kəl) *adj.* Pertaining to, using, or relating to pharmacy or pharmacists. —*n.* A drug. Also **phar′ma·ceu′tic.** [< Gk. *pharmakon* a drug] —**phar′ma·ceu′ti·cal·ly** *adv.* —**phar′ma·ceu′tist** *n.*
phar·ma·ceu·tics (fär′mə·sōō′tiks) *n. pl.* (*construed as sing.*) The science of pharmacy.
phar·ma·cist (fär′mə·sist) *n.* A qualified druggist; pharmaceutist.
phar·ma·col·o·gy (fär′mə·kol′ə·jē) *n.* The science of the action of drugs, their nature, preparation, administration, and effects. —**phar′ma·co·log′ic** (-kə·loj′ik) or **·i·cal** *adj.* —**phar′ma·co·log′i·cal·ly** *adv.* —**phar′ma·col′o·gist** *n.*
phar·ma·co·poe·ia (fär′mə·kə·pē′ə) *n.* **1** A reference book on drugs. **2** A stock or collection of drugs. [< Gk. *pharmakon* a drug + *poieein* make] —**phar′ma·co·poe′ial** *adj.* —**phar′ma·co·poe′ist** *n.*
phar·ma·cy (fär′mə·sē) *n. pl.* **·cies** **1** The art or business of compounding and dispensing medicines. **2** A drugstore. [< Gk. *pharmakon* a drug]
pha·ryn·ge·al (fə·rin′jē·əl, far′in·jē′əl) *adj.* Of or pertaining to the pharynx. Also **pha·ryn′gal** (-gəl).
phar·yn·gi·tis (far′in·jī′tis) *n.* Inflammation of the pharynx.
phar·ynx (far′ingks) *n. pl.* **pha·ryn·ges** (fə·rin′jēz) or **phar·ynx·es** The tract between the palate and the esophagus, serving as a passage for air and food. [Gk., throat]

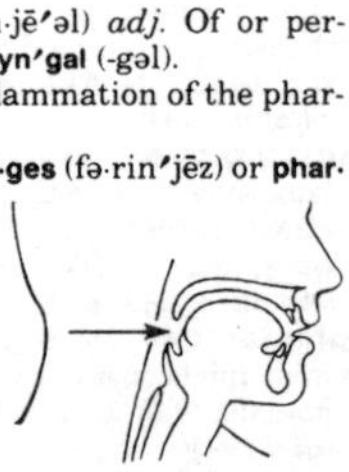
Pharynx

phase (fāz) *n.* **1** Any one of the aspects, parts, etc., that are a distinguishable part of a cycle, development, etc. **2** *Astron.* One of the appearances or forms presented periodically by the moon and planets. **3** *Physics* **a** A stage in a periodic process or phenomenon, as an oscillation, wave, etc. **b** Any homogeneous form of a given substance that may occur alone, or exist independently as a component of a heterogeneous system, as ice in water, etc. **4** *Biol.* Any distinct stage in the reproduction, growth, development, or life pattern of a cell or organism. —**in phase** Having the same phase at a given time and place, as two waves. —*v.t.* **phased, phas·ing** To accomplish in planned phases. —**phase down** To reduce or lessen in planned phases. —**phase in** To introduce in planned phases. —**phase out** To terminate work on, production of, etc., step by step, according to plan. [< Gk. *phasis* an appearance] —**pha·sic** (fā′zik) *adj.*
phase·out (fāz′out′) *n.* A termination, closing down, withdrawal, etc., in planned phases.
Ph.D. Doctor of Philosophy (L *Philosophiae Doctor*).
pheas·ant (fez′ənt) *n.* **1** A long-tailed chickenlike bird noted for the gorgeous plumage of the male. **2** One of various other birds, as the ruffed grouse. [< Gk. *Phasianos (ornis)* (bird) of Phasis, a river in the Caucasus]
phe·nac·e·tin (fə·nas′ə·tin) *n.* A white, synthetic compound used to reduce fever and relieve pain. [< PHEN(O)- + ACET(O)- + -IN]
phe·nix (fē′niks) *n.* PHOENIX.
pheno- *combining form Chem.* Related to or derived from benzene: *phenobarbital.* [< Gk. *phainen* to show, shine]
phe·no·bar·bi·tal (fē′nō·bär′bə·tôl) *n.* A white, odorless powder, used as a sedative.
phe·nol (fē′nōl, -nol) *n.* A derivative of benzene containing a hydroxyl radical; carbolic acid. [< PHEN(O)- + -OL[1]] —**phe·nol′ic** (-nol′ik, -nō′lik) *adj.*
phe·nol·phthal·ein (fē′nōl·thal′ēn, fē′nolf·thal′ē·in) *n.* A whitish crystalline compound that turns red in alkaline solutions, used as an acid-base indicator and in medicine as a laxative.
phe·nom·e·nal (fi·nom′ə·nəl) *adj.* **1** Of, pertaining to, or being a phenomenon. **2** Extraordinary or marvelous. —**phe·nom′e·nal·ly** *adv.*
phe·nom·e·non (fi·nom′ə·non) *n. pl.* **·na** (-nə) or, *for defs. 3 and 4,* **·nons** **1** A fact, event, etc., that can be explained on the basis of scientific principles, as a lunar eclipse. **2** Any fact, appearance, etc., as it is apprehended by the senses, in contrast with or in opposition to the thing in itself. **3** Any unusual fact, thing, occurrence, etc. **4** An unusual, exceptional, or extraordinary person; prodigy. [< Gk. *phainomenon* an appearance]
phen·yl (fen′əl, fē′nəl) *n.* A univalent hydrocarbon radical containing six carbon atoms in a ring linkage, forming the basis of numerous derivatives. [< PHEN(O)- + -YL]
phen·yl·ke·to·nu·ri·a (fen′əl·kēt′n·yōōr′ē·ə, fē′nəl-) *n.* *Pathol.* A rare, inherited metabolic disorder that can cause permanent mental impairment if untreated within a few weeks after birth. [< PHENYL + KETON(E) + Gk. *ouron* urine]
pher·o·mone (fer′ə·mōn′) *n.* An external animal secretion having a taste, smell, or other characteristic that stimulates a behavioral or physiological response in members of the species that produces it. [< Gk. *pherein* carry + (HOR)MONE] —**pher′o·mon′al, ·mon′ic,** *adj.*
phew (fyōō) *interj.* An exclamation of relief, surprise, disgust, etc.
phi (fī, fē) *n.* The 21st letter in the Greek alphabet (Φ,φ).
phi·al (fī′əl) *n.* VIAL.
Phi Be·ta Kap·pa (fī bā′tə kap′ə) **1** An American honorary society composed of college students and graduates of high academic standing. **2** A member of this society.
Phil. Philippians; Philippine.
Philadelphia lawyer *Informal* An unusually clever lawyer, esp. one who is unscrupulous in the application of legal technicalities.
phi·lan·der (fi·lan′dər) *v.i.* To make love casually or without serious intentions. [< Gk. *phileein* to love + *andros* man] —**phi·lan′der·er** *n.*
phi·lan·thro·py (fi·lan′thrə·pē) *n. pl.* **·pies** **1** The disposition or effort to promote the well-being of mankind, as by making donations to charities, working for the improvement of social conditions, etc. **2** A charitable donation, work for the improvement of social conditions, etc. **3** An organization devoted to charity, social improvement, etc. [< Gk. *phileein* love + *anthropos* man] —**phil·an·throp·ic** (fil′ən·throp′ik) or **·i·cal** *adj.* —**phil′an·throp′i·cal·ly** *adv.* —**phi·lan′thro·pist** *n.* —**Syn.** **1** benevolence, charity, generosity, munificence.
phi·lat·e·ly (fi·lat′ə·lē) *n.* The study and collection of postage stamps, stamped envelopes, wrappers, etc.; stamp collecting. [< Gk. *philos* loving + *ateleia* exemption from tax; with ref. to prepaid postage] —**phil·a·tel·ic** (fil′ə·tel′ik) or **·i·cal** *adj.* —**phil′a·tel′i·cal·ly** *adv.* —**phi·lat′e·list** *n.*
-phile *combining form* One who supports or is fond of; one devoted to: *bibliophile.* [< Gk. *phileein* to love]
Phi·le·mon (fi·lē′mən) A Greek converted to Christianity by Paul. —*n.* The epistle addressed by Paul to Philemon, forming a book of the New Testament.

phil·har·mon·ic (fil′här·mon′ik, -ər·mon′-) *adj.* 1 Fond of harmony or music. 2 *Often cap.* Pertaining to a particular musical society or orchestra. —*n. Often cap.* An association sponsoring a symphony orchestra, or the orchestra itself. [< Gk. *philos* loving + *harmonikos* harmony]

-philia *combining form* 1 A tendency toward: *hemophilia.* 2 Abnormal fondness for. [< Gk. *phileein* to love]

Phi·lip·pi·ans (fi·lip′ē·ənz) *n.pl. (construed as sing.)* In the New Testament, an epistle of St. Paul to the Christians at Philippi, an ancient town in N Macedonia.

phi·lip·pic (fi·lip′ik) *n.* An impassioned speech characterized by invective. —**the Philippics** A series of twelve speeches in which Demosthenes denounced Philip of Macedon.

Phil·ip·pines (fil′ə·pēnz′, fil′ə·pēnz′) *n.* A republic located on an island group in the Pacific, SE of China, 115,707 sq. mi., cap. Quezon City, administrative center Manila. Also **Republic of the Philippines.** —**Phil′ip·pine′** *adj.*

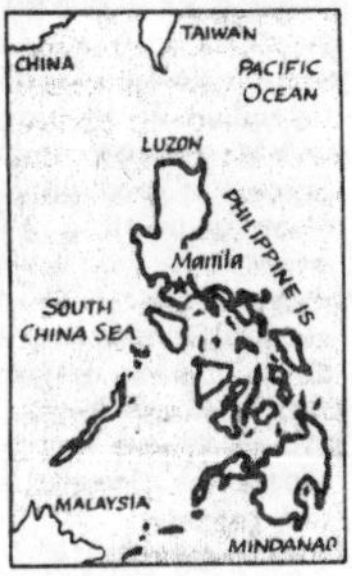

Phi·lis·ti·a (fi·lis′tē·ə) *n.* A region on the Mediterranean, in ancient SW Palestine.

phi·lis·tine (fil′ə·stin, -stēn, fə·lis′tən, -tēn′) *Sometimes cap. n.* An ignorant, narrow-minded person, devoid of culture and indifferent to art. —*adj.* Smugly indifferent to culture and art. —**phi·lis·tin·ism** (fil′ə·stin·iz′əm, -stēn′-) *n.*

Phi·lis·tine (fil′ə·stin, -stēn, fə·lis′tən, tēn′) *n.* One of a warlike race of ancient Philistia. —*adj.* Of or pertaining to the ancient Philistines.

philo- *combining form* Loving; fond of: *philogyny.* [< Gk. *phileein* to love]

phil·o·den·dron (fil′ə·den′drən) *n.* Any of several tropical American climbing plants, with glossy, evergreen leaves, cultivated as an ornamental house plant. [< Gk. *philodendros* fond of trees]

phi·log·y·ny (fi·loj′ə·nē) *n.* Fondness for or devotion to women. [< Gk *philos* fond + *gynē* a woman] —**phi·log′y·nist** *n.* —**phi·log′y·nous** *adj.*

phi·lol·o·gy (fi·lol′ə·jē) *n.* 1 The scientific study of written records, esp. literary works, to determine their meaning, authenticity, etc. 2 LINGUISTICS. 3 Literary scholarship. [< Gk. *philos* fond + *logos* a word] —**phil·o·log·ic** (fil′ə·loj′ik) or **·i·cal** *adj.* —**phil′o·log′i·cal·ly** *adv.* —**phi·lol′o·gist** *n.*

Phil·o·mel (fil′ə·mel) *n.* In poetic usage, the nightingale. Also **Phil·o·me·la** (fil′ə·mē′lə). [< *Philomela,* Greek mythological princess changed into a nightingale]

phi·los·o·pher (fi·los′ə·fər) *n.* 1 A student of or a specialist in philosophy. 2 The creator of a system of philosophy. 3 A person who is reasonable, calm, patient, etc., under all circumstances.

philosopher's stone An imaginary stone thought to have the power of transmuting the baser metals into gold.

phil·o·soph·i·cal (fil′ə·sof′i·kəl) *adj.* 1 Of, pertaining to, or founded on the principles of philosophy or of a philosopher. 2 Learned in or devoted to philosophy. 3 Reasonable, calm, patient, thoughtful, etc. Also **phil′o·soph′ic.** —**phil′o·soph′i·cal·ly** *adv.*

phi·los·o·phize (fi·los′ə·fīz) *v.i.* **·phized, ·phiz·ing** To speculate like a philosopher; seek ultimate causes and principles. —**phi·los′o·phiz′er** *n.*

phi·los·o·phy (fi·los′ə·fē) *n. pl.* **·phies** 1 The search for knowledge of general principles; the study of the elements, powers, or causes and laws that explain facts and existences. 2 A philosophical system or treatise based on such a search or study. 3 The general laws that furnish the rational explanation of anything: the *philosophy* of banking. 4 The system of values adopted by an individual, group, etc. 5 Calm judgment and equable temper; practical wisdom; fortitude. 6 A study of human behavior, ethics, morals, character, etc. [< Gk. *philos* loving + *sophos* wise]

phil·ter (fil′tər) *n.* 1 A charmed draft supposed to have power to excite sexual love. 2 Any magic potion. —*v.t.* To charm with a philter. Also **phil′tre.** [< Gk. *philtron* a love potion]

phle·bi·tis (fli·bī′tis) *n.* Inflammation of a vein. [< Gk. *phleps* vein + -ITIS] —**phle·bit′ic** (-bit′ik) *adj.*

phle·bot·o·mize (fli·bot′ə·mīz) *v.t.* **·mized, ·miz·ing** To treat by phlebotomy.

phle·bot·o·my (fli·bot′ə·mē) *n.* The practice of bloodletting as a remedial measure. [< Gk. *phleps* vein + -TOMY] —**phleb·o·tom·ic** (fleb′ə·tom′ik) or **·i·cal** *adj.* —**phle·bot′o·mist** *n.*

phlegm (flem) *n.* 1 A viscid, stringy mucus secreted in the air passages. 2 Apathy; cold, undemonstrative temper; self-possession. 3 One of the four natural humors in ancient physiology. [< Gk. *phlegma* inflammation]

phleg·mat·ic (fleg·mat′ik) *adj.* Having a sluggish or stolid temperament; not easily moved or excited. Also **phleg·mat′i·cal.** —**phleg·mat′i·cal·ly** *adv.* —**Syn.** indifferent, calm, dull, undemonstrative.

phlo·em (flō′em) *n. Bot.* The food-conducting tissue in the leaves, roots and stems of ferns and seed plants. [< Gk. *phloos* bark]

phlo·gis·ton (flō·jis′tən) *n.* The principle formerly assumed to inhere in combustible bodies, and to be given up by them in burning. [< Gk. *phlogistos* inflammable] —**phlo·gis′tic** *adj.*

phlox (floks) *n.* A plant or flower of a genus of herbs with opposite leaves and clusters of showy flowers. [< Gk. *phlox* wallflower, flame]

Perennial phlox

pho·bi·a (fō′bē·ə) *n.* A compulsive and persistent fear of any specified object or situation. [< Gk. *phobos* fear] —**pho′bic** (-bik) *adj.*

-phobia *combining form* Aversion to; fear of: *claustrophobia.* [< Gk. *phobos* fear]

phoe·be (fē′bē) *n.* Any of a genus of American flycatchers with slightly crested head. [Imit. of its cry]

Phoe·be (fē′bē) *Gk. Myth.* A name for Artemis as goddess of the moon. —*n.* The moon. Also **Phœ′be.**

Phoe·bus (fē′bəs) *Gk. Myth.* Apollo as god of the sun. —*n.* The sun. Also **Phœ′bus.**

Phoe·ni·cia (fə·nē′shə, -nish′ə) *n.* An ancient country of the Mediterranean in the region of modern Syria and Lebanon.

Phoe·ni·cian (fə·nē′shən, -nish′ən) *adj.* Of or pertaining to ancient Phoenicia, its people, or its language. —*n.* 1 One of the people of ancient Phoenicia or any of its colonies. 2 The Semitic language of these people.

phoe·nix (fē′niks) *n.* In Egyptian mythology, a bird which was supposed to live for 500 to 600 years, consume itself by fire, and rise again from its ashes young and beautiful to live through another cycle: a symbol of immortality. Also **phe′nix.** [< Gk. *phoinix*]

pho·nate (fō′nāt) *v.t.* **·nat·ed, ·nat·ing** To make articulate sounds; vocalize. [< Gk. *phōnē* sound + -ATE[1]] —**pho·na′tion** *n.*

phone[1] (fōn) *n. & v. Informal* Telephone.

phone[2] (fōn) *n.* A single sound used in human speech. [< Gk. *phōne* a sound]

-phone *combining form* Voice; sound: often used in names of musical instruments and other sound-transmitting devices: *saxophone, microphone.* [< Gk. *phōnē* voice]

pho·neme (fō′nēm) *n. Ling.* A speech sound or a group of phonetically similar speech sounds comprising one member of a set of the sounds in any language that differentiate between utterances, as /s/ in *sun* and /f/ in *fun.* • The *t* sounds in *tip, stop,* and *pit,* which are not phonetically identical, are members of the phoneme /t/. [< Gk. *phōnē* a voice, sound] —**pho·ne·mic** (fə·nē′mik) *adj.* —**pho·ne′mi·cal·ly** *adv.*

pho·ne·mics (fə·nē′miks) *n.pl. (construed as sing.)* The study of the phonemic system of a language.

pho·net·ic (fə·net′ik) *adj.* 1 Of or pertaining to phonetics, or to speech sounds and their production. 2 Representing speech or speech sounds by characters that refer to specific properties, such as place or manner of articulation. Also **pho·net'i·cal.** [< Gk. *phōnē* sound] —**pho·net'i·cal·ly** *adv.*

pho·ne·ti·cian (fō'nə·tish'ən) *n.* An authority on phonetics.

pho·net·ics (fə·net'iks) *n.pl.* (*construed as sing.*) 1 The branch of linguistics which deals with the analysis, description, and classification of the sounds of speech. 2 The system of sounds of a language or group of languages: the *phonetics* of American English.

pho·ney (fō'nē) *adj.* & *n.* PHONY.

phon·ic (fon'ik, fō'nik) *adj.* 1 Of, pertaining to, or producing sound or the sounds of speech. 2 Of or pertaining to phonics.

phon·ics (fon'iks, fō'niks) *n.pl.* (*construed as sing.*) A method of teaching spelling, pronunciation, and reading by the use of elementary phonetics.

phono- *combining form* Sound; speech; voice: *phonograph.* [< Gk. *phōnē* sound, voice]

pho·no·gram (fō'nə·gram) *n.* A graphic character symbolizing an articulate sound, word, syllable, etc., as in shorthand. —**pho'no·gram'ic** or **·gram'mic** *adj.* —**pho'no·gram'i·cal·ly** or **·gram'mi·cal·ly** *adv.*

pho·no·graph (fō'nə·graf, -gräf) *n.* An apparatus for recording and reproducing sounds on and from plastic disks. —**pho'no·graph'ic** *adj.* —**pho'no·graph'i·cal·ly** *adv.*

pho·nog·ra·phy (fə·nog'rə·fē) *n.* 1 Phonetic spelling or writing. 2 Any of the systems of shorthand based on phonetic transcription of speech. —**pho·nog'ra·pher, pho·nog'·ra·phist** *n.*

pho·nol·o·gy (fə·nol'ə·jē) *n.* 1 Phonetics or phonemics, or both considered together. 2 The historical study of speech sounds, esp. of the sound changes that have taken place in a particular language. —**pho·no·log·i·cal** (fō'nə·loj'i·kəl) **pho'no·log'ic** *adj.* —**pho'no·log'i·cal·ly** *adv.* —**pho·nol'o·gist** *n.*

pho·ny (fō'nē) *Slang adj.* **·ni·er, ·ni·est** Fake; false; spurious; counterfeit. —*n.* 1 Something fake or not genuine. 2 One who pretends to be something he is not. [?] —**pho'ni·ness** *n.*

-phony *combining form* A (specified) type of sound or sounds: *cacophony.* [< Gk. *phōnē* sound, voice]

phos·gene (fos'jēn) *n.* A colorless, highly toxic, volatile liquid, used as a poison gas and in making synthetic chemicals. [< Gk. *phōs* light + -GEN]

phos·phate (fos'fāt) *n.* 1 A salt or ester of phosphoric acid. 2 A fertilizer containing phosphate. 3 A beverage containing small amounts of phosphoric acid. [< PHOSPHORUS] —**phos·phat·ic** (fos·fat'ik) *adj.*

phos·phide (fos'fīd, -fid) *n.* A binary compound of phosphorus with a more positive element: calcium *phosphide.* Also **phos'phid** (-fid).

phos·phite (fos'fīt) *n.* A salt of phosphorous acid.

phos·phor (fos'fər) *n.* A substance that reflects incident radiation as light.

phos·phor·esce (fos'fə·res') *v.i.* **·esced, ·esc·ing** To glow with a faint light while producing negligible heat. [Back formation < PHOSPHORESCENT]

phos·phor·es·cence (for'fə·res'əns) *n.* 1 The emission of light with negligible heat. 2 The light so emitted. [< PHOSPHOR(US) + -ESCENCE] —**phos'phor·es'cent,** *adj.*

phos·phor·et·ed (fos'fə·ret'id) *adj.* Combined or treated with phosphorus. Also **phos'phor·et'ted.**

phos·phor·ic (fos·fôr'ik, -for'-) *adj.* Of, pertaining to or derived from phosphorus, esp. in its highest valence.

phosphoric acid An acid of phosphorus used widely in industrial chemical manufacturing.

phos·pho·rous (fos'fər·əs, fos·fôr'əs, -fō'rəs) *adj.* Of, pertaining to, resembling, containing, or derived from phosphorus, esp. in its lower valence.

phos·pho·rus (fos'fər·əs) *n.* 1 A soft nonmetallic element (symbol P) having three allotropic forms and taking part in various biochemical reactions essential to life. 2 Any phosphorescent substance. [< Gk. *phōs* a light + *phoros* bearing]

pho·to (fō'tō) *n. pl.* **·tos** *Informal* A photograph.

photo- *combining form* 1 Light; of, pertaining to, or produced by light: *photometer.* 2 Photograph; photographic: *photoengrave.* [< Gk. *phōs, phōtos* light]

pho·to·chem·is·try (fō'tō·kem'is·trē) *n.* The branch of chemistry dealing with reactions produced or influenced by light. —**pho'to·chem'i·cal** *adj.*

pho·to·com·po·si·tion (fō'tō·kom'pə·zish'ən) *n.* The composing of printed matter directly on film or photosensitive paper for reproduction.

pho·to·cop·y (fō'tō·kop'ē) *n. pl.* **·cop·ies** A photographic reproduction of printed or other graphic material. —*v.* **·cop·ied, ·cop·y·ing** *v.t.* 1 To make a photocopy of. —*v.i.* 2 To make a photocopy. —**pho'to·cop'i·er** *n.*

pho·to·e·lec·tric (fō'tō·i·lek'trik) *adj.* Of, pertaining to, or indicating the electric effects due to the action of light. Also **pho'to·e·lec'tri·cal.**

photoelectric cell A device in which a flow of light produces or controls a flow of electricity.

pho·to·en·grave (fō'tō·in·grāv') *v.t.* **·graved, ·grav·ing** To reproduce by photoengraving. —**pho'to·en·grav'er** *n.*

pho·to·en·grav·ing (fō'tō·in·grā'ving) *n.* 1 The act or process of producing by the aid of photography a relief plate for printing. 2 A plate so produced. 3 A print produced from such a plate.

photo finish 1 The finish of a race in which the leaders are so close that only a photograph taken as they cross the finish line can determine the winner. 2 A close finish.

pho·to·flash bulb (fō'tō·flash') FLASH BULB.

pho·to·flood lamp (fō'tō·flud') An electric lamp that produces a powerful light for taking photographs and motion pictures.

pho·to·gen·ic (fō'tō·jen'ik) *adj.* 1 Generating or producing light; phosphorescent, as fireflies. 2 Having visually interesting qualities suitable for being photographed: said esp. of a person. —**pho'to·gen'i·cal·ly** *adv.*

pho·to·graph (fō'tə·graf, -gräf) *n.* A picture or image taken by photography. —*v.t.* 1 To take a photograph of. —*v.i.* 2 To practice photography. 3 To undergo photographing. —**pho·tog·ra·pher** (fə·tog'rə·fər) *n.*

pho·to·graph·ic (fō'tə·graf'ik) *adj.* 1 Pertaining to, used in, or produced by photography. 2 Like a photograph; vividly depicted. 3 Capable of precise retention or recall. —**pho'to·graph'i·cal·ly** *adv.*

pho·tog·ra·phy (fə·tog'rə·fē) *n.* The art or process of forming and fixing images by the chemical action of light and other forms of radiant energy on sensitive surfaces.

pho·to·gra·vure (fō'tō·grə·vyŏŏr') *n.* 1 The process of producing prints from an intaglio printing plate or cylinder. 2 A print so produced.

pho·to·lith·o·graph (fō'tō·lith'ə·graf, -gräf) *v.t.* To reproduce by photolithography. —*n.* A picture produced by photolithography.

pho·to·li·thog·ra·phy (fō'tō·li·thog'rə·fē) *n.* Lithography in which the plate for printing is made photographically. —**pho'to·lith'o·graph'ic** (-lith'ə·graf'ik) *adj.*

pho·tol·y·sis (fō·tol'ə·sis) *n.* Decomposition due to the action of light. [< PHOTO- + Gk. *lysis* a loosening] —**pho·to·lyt·ic** (fō'tə·lit'ik) *adj.*

pho·tom·e·ter (fō·tom'ə·tər) *n.* An instrument for measuring the intensity of light.

pho·tom·e·try (fō·tom'ə·trē) *n.* Measurement of the energy, intensity, etc., of light. —**pho·to·met·ric** (fō'tə·met'rik) *adj.* —**pho·tom'e·trist** *n.*

pho·to·mi·cro·graph (fō'tō·mī'krə·graf, -gräf) *n.* A photograph of an object taken through a microscope. —**pho·to·mi·crog·ra·phy** (fō'tō·mī·krog'rə·fē) *n.*

pho·to·mon·tage (fō'tō·mon·täzh', -môn-) *n.* 1 The process of montage with photographs. 2 A picture produced by this process.

pho·to·mu·ral (fō'tō·myŏŏr'əl) *n.* A photograph enlarged to a size suitable for wall decoration.

pho·ton (fō'ton) *n. Physics* A quantum of light or other electromagnetic radiation. [< PHOT(O) + (ELECTR)ON] —**pho·ton'ic** *adj.*

pho·to·off·set (fō'tō·ôf'set, -of'-) *n.* Offset printing from a metal surface on which the text or design has been imprinted by photography.

pho·to·play (fō'tō·plā') *n.* MOTION PICTURE (def. 2).

pho·to·print (fō'tō·print) *n. Phot.* A print produced on photographic paper.

pho·to·sen·si·tive (fō'tō·sen'sə·tiv) *adj.* Sensitive to light. —**pho'to·sen'si·tiv'i·ty** *n.*

pho·to·stat (fō'tə·stat) *v.t. & v.i.* **·stat·ed** or **·stat·ted, ·stat·ing** or **·stat·ting** To make a reproduction (of) with a Photostat. —*n.* The reproduction so produced. —**pho'to·stat'ic** *adj.*

Pho·to·stat (fō'tə·stat) *n.* A device designed to reproduce documents, drawings, etc., directly as positives on special paper: a trade name.

pho·to·syn·the·sis (fō'tō·sin'thə·sis) *n.* The formation of carbohydrates from carbon dioxide and water through the agency of sunlight acting upon chlorophyll. —**pho'to·syn·thet'ic** (-sin·thet'ik) *adj.* —**pho'to·syn·thet'i·cal·ly** *adv.*

pho·tot·ro·pism (fō·tot'rə·piz'əm) *n.* The orientation or movement of an organism in response to light. —**pho·to·trop·ic** (fō'tə·trop'ik) *adj.* —**pho'to·trop'i·cal·ly** *adv.*

pho·to·type·set·ting (fō'tə·tīp'set'ing) *n.* PHOTOCOMPOSITION.

phrase (frāz) *n.* **1** A manner or style of expression; phraseology. **2** *Gram.* A group of words denoting a single idea or forming a separate part of a sentence, but not containing a subject and predicate. **3** A concise, forceful, or colorful expression. **4** *Music* A section of a melody or composition, several measures long. —*v.t. & v.i.* **phrased, phras·ing** **1** To express or be expressed in words or phrases, esp. in a certain way: He *phrased* his objections tactfully. **2** *Music* To execute or divide (music) in or into phrases. [< Gk. *phrazein* point out, tell] —**phras'al** *adj.*

phrase·mak·er (frāz'mā'kər) *n.* **1** A person who coins phrases that are pointed, vivid, incisive, witty, etc. **2** A person who coins phrases that sound pointed, witty, etc., but that often lack meaning or significance. —**phrase'·mak'ing** *n.*

phra·se·ol·o·gy (frā'zē·ol'ə·jē) *n.* The choice and arrangement of words and phrases to express ideas in speech or writing; diction; style. —**phra'se·o·log'i·cal** (-ə·loj'i·kəl) *adj.* —**phra'se·ol'o·gist** *n.*

phre·net·ic (frə·net'ik) *adj.* FRENETIC. Also **phre·net'i·cal.**

phre·nol·o·gy (fri·nol'ə·jē) *n.* The estimation of character and intelligence by the conformation of the skull. [< Gk. *phrēn* mind + -LOGY] —**phren·o·log·ic** (fren'ə·loj'ik) or **·i·cal** *adj.* —**phren'o·log'i·cal·ly** *adv.* —**phre·nol'o·gist** *n.*

Phryg·i·a (frij'ē·ə) *n.* An ancient country in Asia Minor. —**Phryg'i·an** *adj., n.*

PHS Public Health Service.

phthi·sis (thī'sis, tī'-, thi'-, ti'-) *n.* **1** Tuberculosis of the lungs. **2** Progressive emaciation; any continuous destruction of tissue. [< Gk., a wasting away] —**phthis·ic** (tiz'ik) *n., adj.* —**phthis'i·cal. phthis'ick·y** *adj.*

phy·co·my·cete (fī'kō·mī'sēt, -mī·sēt') *n.* Any of a class of fungi resembling algae, but lacking chlorophyll. [< Gk. *phykos* seaweed + *mykēs* a mushroom] —**phy'co·my·ce'·tous** *adj.*

phy·lac·ter·y (fi·lak'tər·ē) *n. pl.* **·ter·ies** **1** A charm or amulet. **2** A small leather case containing slips inscribed with passages of Scripture, one of which is worn on the forehead and another on the left arm by orthodox Jewish men during morning weekday prayers. **3** A reminder. [< Gk. *phylaktēr* a guard]

-phyll *combining form* Leaf: *chlorophyll.*

phyllo- *combining form* Leaf: *phyllotaxy.* [< Gk. *phyllon* a leaf]

phyl·lo·tax·y (fil'ə·tak'sē) *n. Bot.* **1** The arrangement of leaves on a stem. **2** The laws governing this arrangement. Also **phyl'lo·tax'is.** [< PHYLLO- + Gk. *taxis* arrangement] —**phyl'lo·tac'tic** (-tak'tik) *adj.*

phyl·lox·e·ra (fil'ək·sir'ə, fi·lok'sər·ə) *n.* Any of various plant lice, esp. a species of minute aphis or plant louse destructive to grape vines. [< PHYLLO- + Gk. *xēros* dry]

phy·log·e·ny (fī·loj'ə·nē) *n. Biol.* The history of the evolution of a genetically related group of plants or animals. Also **phy·lo·gen·e·sis** (fī'lə·jen'ə·sis). [< Gk. *phylon* a race + *-geneia* birth, origin] —**phy'lo·ge·net'ic** (-jə·net'ik), **phy'·lo·gen'ic** *adj.* —**phy'lo·ge·net'i·cal·ly** *adv.*

phy·lum (fī'ləm) *n. pl.* **·la** (-lə) Any of the main divisions of the animal and plant kingdoms. [< Gk. *phylon* a race]

phys. physical; physician; physicist; physics.

phys·ic (fiz'ik) *n.* **1** A cathartic; a purge. **2** *Archaic* The art or practice of medicine —*v.t.* **phys·icked, phys·ick·ing** **1** To treat with medicine, esp. a cathartic; purge. **2** To cure or relieve. [< Gk. *physikē (epistēmē)* (the knowledge) of nature]

phys·i·cal (fiz'i·kəl) *adj.* **1** Of or relating to the material universe, the natural sciences, or to physics. **2** Of, relating to, or concerned with the human body. [< Gk. *physis* nature] —**phys'i·cal·ly** *adv.*

physical chemistry The branch of chemistry that deals with the physical properties of substances, esp. in relation to energy transformations and chemical change.

physical education Training and development of the human body by athletics and other exercises; also, education in hygiene.

physical geography Geography dealing with the natural, exterior features of the earth, as vegetation, land forms, ocean currents, etc.

phys·i·cal·i·ty (fiz'ə·kal'ə·tē) *n.* **1** The state of being physical, as distinguished from spiritual. **2** Excessive concern with physical sensations or with the body.

physical sciences The sciences that deal with the structure, properties, and energy relations of matter.

physical therapy The treatment of disability or disease by external physical means, as heat, massage, exercise, etc.

phy·si·cian (fi·zish'ən) *n.* **1** A doctor authorized to practice medicine. **2** One engaged in the general practice of medicine as distinguished from a surgeon. **3** Any healer. [< L *physica* natural medicine]

phys·i·cist (fiz'ə·sist) *n.* A scientist whose specialty is physics.

phys·ics (fiz'iks) *n. pl. (construed as sing.)* The science of matter and energy and their mutual interactions.

physio- *combining form* **1** Nature or natural: *physiography.* **2** Physical: *physiotherapy.* Also **phys-.** [< Gk. *physis* nature]

phys·i·og·no·my (fiz'ē·og'nə·mē) *n. pl.* **·mies** **1** The face or features as revealing character or disposition. **2** Outward appearance; external features. **3** The art or practice of reading character by the features of the face or form of the body. [< Gk. *physiognōmonia* the judging of a man's nature (by his features)] —**phys'i·og·nom'ic** (-og·nom'ik) or **·i·cal** *adj.* —**phys'i·og·nom'i·cal·ly** *adv.* —**phys'i·og'no·mist** *n.*

phys·i·og·ra·phy (fiz'ē·og'rə·fē) *n.* **1** A description of nature. **2** PHYSICAL GEOGRAPHY. —**phys'i·og'ra·pher** *n.* —**phys'i·o·graph'ic** (-ə·graf'ik) or **·i·cal** *adj.* —**phys'i·o·graph'i·cal·ly** *adv.*

physiol. physiological; physiology.

phys·i·ol·o·gy (fiz'ē·ol'ə·jē) *n.* **1** The branch of biology that deals with the functions of living organisms or their parts; the science of the vital processes of animals or plants. **2** The aggregate of organic processes of an organism or a part of it: the *physiology* of the frog. [< Gk. *physis* nature + *logos* a word] —**phys'i·ol'o·gist** *n.* —**phys·i·o·log·i·cal** (fiz'ē·ə·loj'i·kəl), **phys'i·o·log'ic** *adj.* —**phys'i·o·log'i·cal·ly** *adv.*

phys·i·o·ther·a·py (fiz'ē·ō·ther'ə·pē) *n.* PHYSICAL THERAPY.

phy·sique (fi·zēk') *n.* The physical structure, organization, appearance, strength, etc., of a person's body.

pi[1] (pī) *n.* **1** The 16th letter in the Greek alphabet (Π,π). **2** The symbol (π) used to designate the ratio of the circumference of a circle to its diameter, 3.14159+ ; also, this ratio.

pi[2] (pī) *n.* **1** *Printing* Type that has been thrown into disorder. **2** Any jumble or disorder. —*v.t.* **pied, pie·ing** To jumble or disorder, as type. [Var. of PIE[1]]

pi·a ma·ter (pī'ə mā'tər, pē'ə mä'tər) The inner vascular membrane that envelops the brain and spinal cord. [Med. L, tender mother]

pi·a·nis·si·mo (pē'ə·nis'i·mō, *Ital.* pyä·nēs'sē·mō) *adj. & adv. Music* Very soft or softly. —*n. pl.* **·mi** (-mē) or **·mos** A section or passage of music rendered pianissimo. [Ital. See PIANO[2]]

pi·an·ist (pē·an′ist, pē′ə·nist) *n.* One who plays the piano; esp. an expert or a professional performer.

pi·an·o[1] (pē·an′ō) *n. pl.* **·an·os** A musical instrument having felt-covered hammers, operated from a manual keyboard, which strike steel wires to produce the tones. [Ital., short for PIANOFORTE]

Grand piano

pi·a·no[2] (pē·ä′nō, *Ital.* pyä′nō) *adj. & adv.* Soft or softly. —*n.* A section or passage of music rendered softly. [Ital. < L *planus* flat, soft (of sound)]

pi·an·o·for·te (pē·an′ə·fôr′tē, -fōr′-, -fôrt′, -fōrt′) *n.* A piano. [Ital. <*piano e forte* soft and loud]

pi·as·ter (pē·as′tər) *n.* **1** The principal monetary unit in South Vietnam. **2** A monetary unit in Lebanon, Syria, Sudan, Turkey, and the United Arab Republic. **3** Formerly, the Spanish peso or dollar. Also **pi·as′tre.** [< Ital. *piastra d'argento* a plate of silver]

pi·az·za (pē·az′ə, *Ital.* pē·at′tsä) *n.* **1** A veranda or porch. **2** In Europe, esp. in Italy, an open square. **3** A covered outer walk or gallery. [Ital. < L *platea* a broad street]

pi·broch (pē′brokh) *n.* A martial or dirgelike air played on the bagpipe. [< Scot. Gaelic *piobair* a piper]

pi·ca[1] (pī′kə) *n.* **1** A size of type, 12-point or about 1/6 inch. **2** A size of typewriter type equivalent to 12-point, with 10 characters to the inch. [Med. L, church book]

pi·ca[2] (pī′kə) *n.* An appetite for substances unfit to eat, as clay, chalk, ashes, etc. [< L *pica* a magpie, with ref. to the bird's omnivorousness] —**pi′cal** *adj.*

pic·a·dor (pik′ə·dôr, *Sp.* pē′kä·thôr′) *n.* In bullfighting, a horseman armed with a lance, whose function it is to prick and thereby weaken the bull's neck muscles. [< Sp. *picar* prick, pierce]

pic·a·resque (pik′ə·resk′) *adj.* **1** Of or pertaining to adventurers or clever rogues. **2** Designating a type of fiction of Spanish origin consisting of loosely connected episodes involving rogues and vagabonds. [< Sp. *picaro* a rogue]

pic·a·yune (pik′i·yōōn′) *adj.* **1** Little; worthless. **2** Concerned with unimportant or petty matters. —*n.* **1** A former small Spanish-American coin; a half-real. **2** *U.S.* A person or thing of trifling value. [< Prov. *picaioun*, dim. of *picalo* money] —**pic′a·yun′ish** *adj.* —**Syn.** *adj.* **1** paltry, worthless, measly. **2** trivial, mean, narrow-minded.

pic·ca·lil·li (pik′ə·lil′ē) *n.* A highly seasoned relish of chopped vegetables. [? < PICKLE]

pic·co·lo (pik′ə·lō) *n. pl.* **·los** A small flute with tones an octave higher than those of the ordinary flute. [Ital., small]

pick[1] (pik) *v.t.* **1** To select; cull, as from a group. **2** To detach; pluck: to *pick* a flower. **3** To harvest: to *pick* cotton. **4** To prepare by removing the feathers, hulls, etc.: to *pick* a chicken. **5** To remove extraneous matter from: to *pick* the teeth. **6** To pull apart, as rags. **7** To penetrate with or as with a pointed instrument. **8** To form or make in this manner: to *pick* a hole. **9** To point out too critically: to *pick* flaws. **10** To bring on purposely; provoke: to *pick* a quarrel. **11** To remove the contents of by stealth: to *pick* a pocket. **12** To open (a lock) by a piece of wire, etc. **13 a** To pluck (the strings) of a musical instrument. **b** To play (an instrument) in this way. —*v.i.* **14** To eat daintily; nibble. —**pick at 1** To touch or irritate with the finger. **2** To eat without appetite. **3** *Informal* To nag at. —**pick off 1** To remove by picking. **2** To shoot one at a time. —**pick on** *Informal* To tease; annoy. —**pick out 1** To choose or select. **2** To distinguish (something) from its surroundings. **3** To grasp (the meaning). —**pick over** To examine one by one. —**pick up 1** To take up, as with the hand. **2** To take up or receive into a vehicle, etc. **3** To acquire by chance. **4** To gain speed. **5** To recover spirits, health, etc. **6** *Informal* To make the acquaintance of, casually or informally. **7** To make orderly; tidy. —*n.* **1** Selection; choice. **2** The choicest part or thing. **3** The quantity of a crop picked at one time. **4** The act of picking. **5** A plectrum for a stringed instrument. [ME *piken*] —**pick′er** *n.* —**Syn.** *v.* **1** choose. **3** collect, gather. **7** pierce.

pick[2] (pik) *n.* **1** A double-headed, pointed metal tool, used for breaking ground, etc.; pickax. **2** Any of various sharp-pointed implements, as an ice pick, toothpick, etc. [ME *pik*]

pick-a-back (pik′ə·bak′) *adj., adv., n.* PIGGYBACK.

pick·ax (pik′aks′) *n.* A tool with one end of the head edged like a chisel and the other pointed, used to break rocks, dirt, etc.: also **pick′·axe′**. [< OF *picois*]

Pickax

picked (pikt) *adj.* **1** Carefully selected. **2** Cleaned by picking out feathers, hulls, etc.

pick·er·el (pik′ər·əl) *n.* **1** Any of various North American pikes, esp. one of the smaller species. **2** A young pike. [Dim. of PIKE[2]]

pick·er·el·weed (pik′ər·əl·wēd′) *n.* Any of several water plants with a spike of blue flowers and long arrow-shaped leaves.

pick·et (pik′it) *n.* **1** A pointed stick, tent peg, bar, fence paling, or stake. **2** *Mil.* A soldier or detachment of soldiers posted to guard a camp, army, etc. **3** A person stationed by a labor union outside a place affected by a strike to attempt to keep out employees or customers. —*v.t.* **1** To fence or fortify with pickets or pointed stakes. **2** *Mil.* **a** To guard by means of a picket. **b** To post as a picket. **3** To station pickets outside of. **4** To tie to a picket, as a horse. —*v.i.* **5** To act as a picket (def. 3). [< OF *piquer* pierce] —**pick′et·er** *n.*

picket fence A fence made of upright pickets.

picket line A line or group of people acting as pickets.

pick·ings (pik′ingz) *n. pl.* **1** An amount picked. **2** That which is left to be picked up or gleaned. **3** Something taken by questionable means; spoils.

pick·le (pik′əl) *n.* **1** A liquid, as brine or vinegar, usu. spiced, for preserving meat, fish, vegetables, etc. **2** A vegetable, esp. a cucumber, preserved in a pickling solution. **3** Diluted acid used in cleaning metal castings, etc. **4** *Informal* An embarrassing condition or position. —*v.t.* **·led, ·ling** To preserve or clean in a pickling solution. [MDu. *pekel*] —**pick′ler** *n.*

pick-me-up (pik′mē·up′) *n. Informal* Something taken to renew one's energy or spirits.

pick·pock·et (pik′pok′it) *n.* One who steals from people's pockets or purses.

pick·up (pik′up′) *n.* **1** Acceleration, as in the speed of an automobile, engine, etc. **2** A device, as that coupled to the stylus of a phonograph, that changes mechanical motion to an electric signal. **3** *Telecom.* **a** In radio, the location of microphones in relation to program elements. **b** The system for broadcasting material gathered outside the studio. **4** *Informal* Gain; improvement: *a pickup* in the stock market. **5** *Slang* A stranger with whom a casual acquaintance is made, as for sexual purposes. **6** One of a group casually enlisted or assembled, as for a sport or game. **7** A small, usu. open, truck for light loads. **8** The act of calling for, as a parcel. **9** *Informal* Something taken to renew energy or spirits; a pick-me-up.

Pick·wick·i·an (pik·wik′ē·ən) *adj.* **1** Having or characterized by the qualities associated with Samuel Pickwick, a character in Dickens' novel *Pickwick Papers;* esp., kind, simple, and generous. **2** Having an esoteric or unusual sense: said of a word or expression.

pick·y (pik′ē) *adj.* **pick·i·er, pick·i·est** *Informal* Choosy; fussy. —**pick′i·ness** *n.*

pic·nic (pik′nik) *n.* **1** An outdoor party, during which a meal is eaten. **2** *Slang* An easy or pleasant time or experience. —*v.i.* **·nicked, ·nick·ing** To have or attend a picnic. Also **pick′nick.** [< F *pique-nique*] —**pic′nick·er** *n.*

pico- *combining form* One trillionth (10^{-12}) times a unit. [?< Ital. *piccolo* small]

pi·cot (pē′kō) *n.* Any of the small loops of an ornamental edging on ribbon, lace, etc. —*v.t. & v.i.* To trim with this edging. [< OF *pic* a point]

pic·ric acid (pik′rik) A yellow, crystalline, organic compound used to make dyes and explosives. [< Gk. *pikros* bitter]

Pict (pikt) *n.* One of an ancient people who inhabited Britain and the Scottish Highlands, conquered in 846 by the Scots. —**Pict′ish** *adj., n.*

pic·to·graph (pik′tə·graf, -gräf) *n.* **1** A picture representing an idea. **2** Writing done in pictographs; picture writing. [< L *pictus* painted + -GRAPH] **—pic′to·graph′ic** *adj.* **—pic′to·graph′i·cal·ly** *adv.* **—pic·tog·ra·phy** (pik·tog′rə·fē) *n.*

pic·to·ri·al (pik·tôr′ē·əl, -tō′rē-) *adj.* **1** Pertaining to or concerned with pictures. **2** Representing in or as if in pictures; graphic. **3** Containing or illustrated by pictures. —*n.* An illustrated publication. [< L *pictor* painter] **—pic·to′ri·al·ly** *adv.*

pic·ture (pik′chər) *n.* **1** A surface representation of an object or scene or a design, as by a painting, drawing, engraving, or photograph. **2** A mental image. **3** A vivid or graphic description. **4** A striking resemblance: She is the *picture* of her mother. **5** TABLEAU. **6** A visual image or scene. **7** MOTION PICTURE. **8** Something beautiful or striking. **9** The sum of significant facts in an event. —*v.t.* **·tured, ·tur·ing 1** To give visible representation to; draw, paint, etc. **2** To describe graphically. **3** To form a mental image of. [< L *pictus,* p.p. of *pingere* to paint]

Pic·ture·phone (pik′chər·fōn′) *n.* A telephone equipped with a television screen: a trade name.

pic·tur·esque (pik′chə·resk′) *adj.* **1** Having pictorial quality; like or suitable for a picture. **2** Having quaintness or charm. **3** Abounding in striking or original expression or imagery; richly graphic. [< L *pictor* painter] **—pic′tur·esque′ly** *adv.* **—pic′tur·esque′ness** *n.*

picture window A large window, usu. in a living room, designed to give a wide view of the outside.

picture writing 1 The use of pictures or pictorial symbols in writing **2** PICTOGRAPH.

pid·dle (pid′l) *v.* **·died, ·dling** *v.t. & v.i.* To trifle; dawdle. [?] **—pid′dler** *n.* **—pid′dling** *adj.*

pidg·in English (pij′in) A jargon composed of English and local native elements, used by English-speaking traders in Melanesia, Northern Australia, w Africa, and formerly in China. Also **pidg′in.** [< pronunciation in this jargon of *business English*]

pie[1] (pī) *n.* **1** A baked food consisting of one or two layers of pastry with a filling, as of fruit, meat, etc. **2** *Slang* Anything very good or very easy.

pie[2] (pī) *n.* A magpie, or a related bird. [< L *pica*]

pie[3] (pī) *n. & v.t.* **pied, pie·ing** *Printing* PI[2].

pie·bald (pī′bôld′) *adj.* Having spots, esp. of white and black. —*n.* A spotted animal, esp. a horse. [< PIE[2] + BALD; because like a magpie's plumage]

piece (pēs) *n.* **1** A portion considered as a distinct part of a whole. **2** A thing existing as an individual entity: a *piece* of paper; a *piece* of music. **3** A single object forming one of a group: a *piece* of furniture. **4** A definite quantity or length in which an article is manufactured or sold. **5** An instance: a *piece* of luck. **6** A firearm. **7** A coin: a fifty-cent *piece.* **8** A single artistic creation, as a literary, dramatic, or musical composition; also, a painting or sculpture. **9** *Regional* A short time, space, or distance: to walk a *piece.* **10** A figure, disk, or counter used in such games as chess, checkers, backgammon, etc. **—a piece of one's mind** Criticism or censure frankly expressed. **—go to pieces 1** To fall apart. **2** To lose self-control. **—in one piece** Unharmed; intact. **—of a piece** Of the same sort or class. —*adj.* Of, made of, or by the piece. —*v.t.* **pieced, piec·ing 1** To add or attach a piece or pieces to. **2** To unite or reunite the pieces of. **3** To find meaning or coherence in by linking elements: often with *together:* to *piece* together a sequence of events from the testimony of eyewitnesses. [< OF *pece*] **—piec′er** *n.*

pièce de ré·sis·tance (pē·es′ də rā·zē′stäns′) *pl.* **pièces** (pē·es′) **de ré·sis·tance 1** The most substantial dish of a dinner. **2** The principal work in a collection, as of art, etc. [F, lit., piece of resistance]

piece goods Dry goods; fabrics, usu. sold by the piece.

piece·meal (pēs′mēl′) *adj.* Made up of pieces or done one piece at a time. —*adv.* **1** Piece by piece; gradually. **2** Into pieces. [< PIECE + OE *mæl* a measure]

piece of eight *pl.* **pieces of eight** An old Spanish silver dollar.

piece·work (pēs′wûrk′) *n.* Work paid for by the piece or quantity completed, rather than by the hour, week, etc. **—piece′work′er** *n.*

pied (pīd) *adj.* Spotted; piebald. [< PIE[2]]

pied·mont (pēd′mont) *adj.* At the foot of a mountain or mountain range: a *piedmont* plain. —*n.* A piedmont region or area. [< *Piedmont,* Italy]

pie·plant (pī′plant′) *n.* The rhubarb, much used for pies.

pier (pir) *n.* **1** A plain, detached mass of masonry, usu. serving as a support: the *pier* of a bridge. **2** An upright projecting portion of a wall. **3** A jetty; projecting wharf. **4** A solid portion of a wall between window openings, etc. [< AF *pere*]

Pier *def. 3*

pierce (pirs) *v.t.* **pierced, pierc·ing 1** To pass into or through; penetrate, as with a pointed object. **2** To make an opening or hole in, into, or through. **3** To force a way into or through: to *pierce* the wilderness. **4** To affect sharply or deeply, as with emotion, pain, etc. **5** To sound suddenly and sharply, as a scream. **6** To penetrate as if seeing; understand: to *pierce* a mystery. [< OF *percer*] **—pierc′er** *n.* **—pierc′ing·ly** *adv.* **—Syn. 1** perforate, puncture.

pier glass A large, high mirror originally intended to fill the space between two openings in the wall.

Pi·e·ri·an (pī·ir′ē·ən) *adj.* Of or pertaining to the Muses, learning, or the arts. [< *Pieria,* region of ancient Macedon where the Muses were worshipped]

Pi·er·rot (pē′ə·rō′) *n.* A comic character wearing white pantaloons and loose white jacket with big buttons, originally a stock figure in French pantomime. Also **pi′er·rot′.** [F, dim. of *Pierre* Peter]

pi·e·tism (pī′ə·tiz′əm) *n.* **1** Piety or godliness; devotion, as distinguished from ritualism. **2** Affected or exaggerated piety. **—pi′e·tist** *n.* **—pi′e·tis′tic** *adj.*

pi·e·ty (pī′ə·tē) *n. pl.* **·ties 1** Religious reverence; devoutness. **2** Filial honor and obedience as due to parents or country, etc. **3** A pious action or belief. [< L < *pius* dutiful]

pi·e·zo·e·lec·tric·i·ty (pē·ā′zō·i·lek′tris′ə·tē) *n.* Electricity or electric phenomena resulting from pressure upon certain bodies, esp. crystals. [< Gk. *piezein* to press + ELECTRICITY] **—pi·e′zo·e·lec′tric** or **·tri·cal** *adj.*

pif·fle (pif′əl) *Informal v.i.* **·fled, ·fling** To talk nonsensically; babble. —*n.* Nonsense. [?]

pig (pig) *n.* **1** A hog or hoglike animal, esp. when small or young. **2** Pork. **3** An oblong mass of metal just run from the smelter and cast in a rough mold. **4** *Informal* A person regarded as like a pig, esp. one who is filthy, gluttonous, or grasping. [ME *pigge*]

pig·eon (pij′ən) *n.* **1** Any of a widely distributed family of birds with small heads; a dove. **2** *Slang* One easily swindled. [< LL *pipio* a young chirping bird]

pigeon breast A deformity associated with rickets in which the breastbone projects forward and outward. **—pig′eon-breast′ed** *adj.*

pigeon hawk A medium-sized American falcon.

pig·eon·hole (pij′ən·hōl′) *n.* **1** A hole for pigeons to nest in, esp. in a compartmented pigeon house. **2** A small compartment, as in a desk, for filing papers. —*v.t.* **·holed, ·hol·ing 1** To place in a pigeonhole; file. **2** To file away and ignore. **3** To place in categories; classify mentally.

pig·eon-toed (pij′ən·tōd′) *adj.* Having the feet turned inward, esp. in walking.

pig·ger·y (pig′ər·ē) *n. pl.* **·ger·ies** PIGPEN (def. 1).

pig·gish (pig′ish) *adj.* Like a pig; greedy, dirty, or selfish. **—pig′gish·ly** *adv.* **—pig′gish·ness** *n.*

pig·gy (pig′ē) *adj.* **·gi·er, ·gi·est** Greedy or dirty.

pig·gy·back (pig′ē·bak′) *adv.* **1** On the back or shoulders. **2** On a railroad flatcar, as a loaded truck body. —*n.* **1** The act of carrying piggyback. **2** The transporting of loaded truck bodies on railroad flatcars. —*adj.* **1** Done up on the back or shoulders: a *piggyback* ride. 2 Of or pertaining to the transporting of loaded truck bodies on railroad flatcars. —*v.t. & v.i.* 1 To carry or be carried on the back or shoulders. 2 To transport or be transported on railroad flat cars. Also **pig′gy-back′**.

pig-head·ed (pig′hed′id) *adj.* Stupidly obstinate. —**pig′-head′ed·ly** *adv.* —**pig′-head′ed·ness** *n.* —**Syn.** headstrong, obdurate, stubborn, unyielding.

pig iron Crude iron obtained by treating ore in a blast furnace.

pig·ment (pig′mənt) *n.* 1 Any of a class of finely powdered, insoluble coloring matters suitable for making paints, enamels, oil colors, etc. 2 Any substance that imparts color to animal or vegetable tissues. [<L *pingere* to paint] —**pig′men·tar′y** *adj.*

pig·men·ta·tion (pig′mən·tā′shən) *n.* 1 Coloration by pigment of plant or animal tissue. 2 *Biol.* Deposition of pigment by cells.

pig·my (pig′mē) *adj. & n.* PYGMY.

Pig·my (pig′mē) *adj. & n. pl.* **·mies** PYGMY.

pig·nut (pig′nut′) *n.* 1 The astringent nut of several species of hickory. 2 Any of these trees.

pig·pen (pig′pen′) *n.* 1 A place for keeping or raising pigs; sty. 2 Any dirty, untidy place.

pig·skin (pig′skin′) *n.* 1 The skin of a pig. 2 Something made of this skin, as a saddle or football.

pig-stick·ing (pig′stik′ing) *n.* The hunting of wild boars with spears.

pig·sty (pig′stī′) *n. pl.* **·sties** PIGPEN.

pig·tail (pig′tāl′) *n.* 1 The tail of a pig. 2 *Informal* A plait of hair. 3 A twist of tobacco. —**pig′tailed′** *adj.*

pike[1] (pīk) *n.* A long pole having a metal spearhead, used by foot soldiers in medieval warfare. —*v.t.* **piked, pik·ing** To run through or kill with a pike. [<MF *piquer* pierce] —**pike′man** (*pl.* **·men**) *n.*

Pike heads

pike[2] (pīk) *n.* Any of a family of large, carnivorous, freshwater food fishes with a long snout, long cylindrical body, and forked tail. [? <PIKE[4]]

pike[3] (pīk) *n.* TURNPIKE.

pike[4] (pīk) *n.* A spike or sharp point, as the central spike in a buckler. [<OE *pīc*]

pik·er (pī′kər) *n. Slang* A person who does things in a small, stingy way; cheapskate. [?<*Pike* County, Missouri]

pike·staff (pīk′staf′, -stäf′) *n. pl.* **·staves** (-stāvz′) The wooden handle of a pike. [<PIKE[4] + STAFF[1]]

pi·las·ter (pi·las′tər) *n. Archit.* A rectangular column, with capital and base, projecting from a wall. [<L *pila* a column]

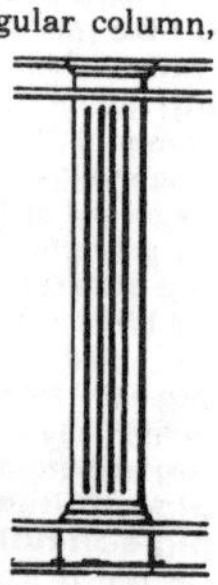

Pilaster

pi·lau (pi·lou′, -lô′) *n.* An Oriental dish of boiled rice, spices, and meat or fish. Also **pi·laf** (pi·läf′), **pi·laff′, pi·law** (pi·lô′). [<Pers. *pilāw*]

pil·chard (pil′chərd) *n.* A small herring-like marine food fish; the commercial sardine. [?]

pile[1] (pīl) *n.* 1 A quantity of anything gathered up together; a heap. 2 A funeral pyre. 3 A large accumulation or number of something. 4 A massive building or group of buildings. 5 *Informal* A great quantity of money. 6 *Physics* A nuclear fission reactor. —**make one's pile** To amass a fortune. —*v.* **piled, pil·ing** *v.t.* 1 To make a heap of: often with *up.* 2 To load with a pile or piles: to *pile* a plate with food. —*v.i.* 3 To form a heap. 4 To proceed or go in a confused mass: to *pile* off a bus. —**pile up** 1 To accumulate; collect, as in a heap: The bills kept *piling up.* 2 *Informal* To reduce or become reduced to a pile or wreck. [<L *pila* a pillar]

pile[2] (pīl) *n.* A heavy timber pointed at one end, forced into the earth to form a foundation —*v.t.* **piled, pil·ing** 1 To drive piles into. 2 To furnish or strengthen with piles. [<L *pilum* a heavy javelin]

pile[3] (pīl) *n.* 1 Soft hair, fur, down, etc. 2 The cut or uncut loops which make the surface of certain fabrics, as velvets, corduroys, carpets, etc. [<L *pilus* hair] —**piled** *adj.*

pi·le·at·ed (pī′lē·ā′tid, pil′ē-) *adj.* Having a crest from the bill to the nape, as some birds. Also **pi′le·ate.** [<L *pileus* a felt cap]

pileated woodpecker A large black and white woodpecker with a red crest.

pile driver A machine for driving piles, usu. a heavy weight raised and released so as to fall, or be driven down, as by steam, to strike the head of the pile.

pi·le·ous (pī′lē·əs) *adj.* PILOSE.

piles (pīlz) *n.pl.* HEMORRHOIDS. [<L *pila* a ball]

pi·le·um (pī′lē·əm, pil′ē-) *n. pl.* **·le·a** (-lē·ə) The top of the head of a bird from bill to nape. [<L *pileus* a felt cap]

pile-up (pīl′up′) *n.* 1 An accumulation: a garbage *pile-up.* 2 A collision involving several or many motor vehicles, usu. causing injury and damage; also, the damaged vehicles. 3 Any group, as of people, piled up after colliding: a *pile-up* on the 40-yard line.

pi·le·us (pī′lē·əs, pil′ē-) *n. pl.* **·le·i** (-lē·ī) The cap of a mushroom. [L, a felt cap]

pil·fer (pil′fər) *v.t. & v.i.* To steal in small quantities. [<OF *pelfre* plunder] —**pil′fer·age** (-ij), **pil′fer·er** *n.*

pil·grim (pil′grim) *n.* 1 One who journeys to some sacred place from religious motives. 2 Any wanderer or wayfarer. [<L *peregrinus* foreigner]

Pil·grim (pil′grim) *n.* One of the English Puritans who founded Plymouth Colony in 1620.

pil·grim·age (pil′grə·mij) *n.* 1 A journey made to a sacred place. 2 Any long journey.

Pilgrim Fathers The Pilgrims.

Pilgrim's Progress A religious allegory in two parts by John Bunyan (1678, 1684).

pil·ing (pī′ling) *n.* 1 Heavy timbers, or piles, driven into the ground. 2 A structure formed of such timbers.

pill (pil) *n.* 1 A medicine in pellet form convenient for swallowing whole. 2 A disagreeable necessity. 3 *Slang* An unpleasant or tiresome person. 4 *Informal* A baseball or golf ball. —**the pill** or **the Pill** Any of various oral contraceptives. —*v.t.* 1 To form into pills. 2 To dose with pills. [<L *pila* a ball]

pil·lage (pil′ij) *n.* 1 The act of pillaging; open robbery, as in war. 2 Spoil; booty. —*v.* **·laged, ·lag·ing** *v.t.* 1 To strip of money or property by violence, esp. in war; loot. 2 To take as loot. —*v.i.* 3 To take plunder. [<OF *piller* to plunder] —**pil′lag·er** *n.*

pil·lar (pil′ər) *n.* 1 A firm, slender, upright column, used to support a roof, etc. 2 A single column designed as a monument. 3 One who or that which strongly supports a work or cause. —**from pillar to post** From one thing to another; hither and thither. —**pillar of society** A person holding an important position. [<L *pila*] —**pil′lared** *adj.*

pill·box (pil′boks′) *n.* 1 A small box for pills. 2 A small concrete emplacement for a machine gun, antitank gun, etc.

pil·lion (pil′yən) *n.* A pad on a horse's back, behind the saddle, on which a second person may ride, esp. a woman. [<L *pellis* a skin]

pil·lo·ry (pil′ər·ē) *n. pl.* **·ries** 1 Formerly, a framework in which an offender was fastened by the neck and wrists and exposed to public scorn. 2 Any public ridicule or disgrace. —*v.t.* **·ried, ·ry·ing** 1 To set in the pillory. 2 To hold up to public scorn or ridicule. [<OF *pellori*]

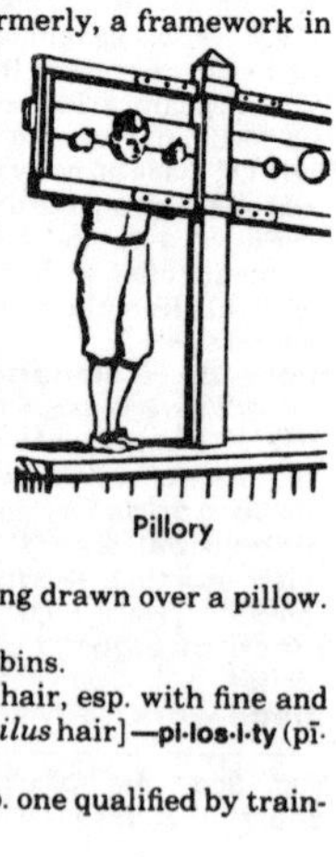

Pillory

pil·low (pil′ō) *n.* 1 A case stuffed with feathers, batting, etc., or inflated with air, used as a support for the head, as in sleeping. 2 Any cushion. —*v.t.* 1 To rest on or as on a pillow. 2 To act as a pillow for. —*v.i.* 3 To recline as on a pillow. [<L *pulvinus* a cushion] —**pil′low·y** *adj.*

pil·low·case (pil′ō·kās′) A covering drawn over a pillow. Also **pil′low·slip′** (-slip′).

pillow lace Lace made with bobbins.

pi·lose (pī′lōs) *adj.* Covered with hair, esp. with fine and soft hair; hairy. Also **pi′lous.** [<L *pilus* hair] —**pi·los·i·ty** (pī·los′ə·tē) *n.*

pi·lot (pī′lət) *n.* 1 A helmsman, esp. one qualified by training and licensed by law to conduct a ship into and out of port. 2 Any guide. 3 One who operates an aircraft or spacecraft. 4 A device for guiding the action of a part of a machine, etc. —*v.t.* 1 To act as the pilot of; steer. 2 To guide. 3 To serve as pilot on, over, or in. [< Ital. *pilota*] —**Syn.** *v.* 2 conduct, direct, lead.

pi·lot·age (pī′lət·ij) *n.* 1 The act of piloting a vessel or aircraft. 2 The fee for such service.

pilot balloon A small balloon sent up to show the direction and velocity of the wind.

pilot bread HARDTACK. Also **pilot biscuit.**

pilot fish A small fish often seen in company with sharks.

pi·lot·house *n.* (pī′lət·hous′) *n.* An enclosed structure, usu. in the forward part of a vessel, containing the steering wheel and compass.

pilot lamp A small electric light used to indicate when a circuit is energized.

pilot light A minute jet of gas kept burning beside a main burner to ignite it when the gas is turned on.

pilot plant An experimental factory, power station, etc.

Pilt·down man (pilt′doun′) A spurious example of prehistoric man based on bone fragments found in gravel beds at Piltdown, Sussex, England in 1911, and exposed as a hoax in 1953.

pi·men·to (pi·men′to) *n. pl.* **·tos** 1 The red fruit of a mild variety of capsicum, used as a garnish: also **pi·mien·to** (pi·myen′to). 2 ALLSPICE. [< Sp. *pimienta* pepper]

pimp (pimp) *n.* A man who finds clients for prostitutes and usu. lives on their earnings. —*v.i.* To act as a pimp. [?]

pim·per·nel (pim′pər·nel) *n.* Any of a genus of plants of the primrose family, as the **scarlet pimpernel,** having usu. red flowers that close in bad weather. [< OF *pimprenele*]

pim·ple (pim′pəl) *n.* A small, usu. inflamed swelling on the skin. [ME *pimplis* pimples] —**pim′pled, pim′ply** *adj.* **(·pli·er, ·pli·est)**

pin (pin) *n.* 1 A short stiff piece of wire, with a sharp point and a round head, used in fastening things together. 2 An ornamental device mounted on a clasp to fasten to a garment; also, a badge. 3 A rigid peg or bar of wood used for a fastening or support. 4 Anything like a pin, as a hairpin, clothespin, rolling pin, belaying pin, etc. 5 *Usu. pl.* A wooden club turned in long, oval, or cylindrical shape, set up as a target in bowling games. 6 *pl.* Legs. 7 The merest trifle. 8 A peg holding the string of a violin, guitar, or other stringed instrument. 9 A peg to keep an oar in place. —**on pins and needles** Anxious; worried. —*v.t.* **pinned, pin·ning** 1 To fasten with a pin or pins. 2 To transfix with a pin, spear, etc. 3 To seize and hold firmly: to *pin* an opponent against a wall. 4 To force (someone) to make a definite statement, abide by a promise, etc.: usu. with *down.* [< OE *pinn* a peg]

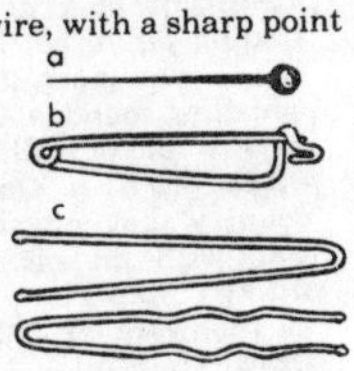

Pins
a. straight. b. safety. c. hairpins.

pin·a·fore (pin′ə·fôr, -fōr) *n.* A sleeveless garment worn as an apron or as a light dress. [< PIN, *v.* + AFORE]

pin·ball (pin′bôl) *n.* A game in which a ball, spring-propelled to the top of an inclined board, contacts in its descent any of various numbered pins, holes, etc.

pince·nez (pans′nā′, pins′-, *Fr.* paṅs·nā′) *n. pl.* **pince·nez** Eyeglasses held upon the nose by a spring. [< F *pincer* to pinch + *nez* nose]

pin·cers (pin′sərz, -chərz) *n.pl. (sometimes construed as sing.)* 1 An instrument having two handles and a pair of jaws working on a pivot, used for holding objects. 2 *Zool.* A grasping organ, as the chela of a lobster. [< OF *pincier* to pinch]

pinch (pinch) *v.t.* 1 To squeeze between two hard edges, or between a finger and thumb. 2 To bind or compress painfully. 3 To affect with pain or distress. 4 To contract or make thin, as from cold or hunger. 5 To limit, as for lack of something: *pinched* for time. 6 *Informal* To distress financially: usu. in the passive. 7 *Slang* To capture or arrest. 8 *Slang* To steal. —*v.i.* 9 To squeeze; hurt. 10 To be stingy. 11 To become narrow or constricted. —**pinch pennies** To be economical or stingy. —*n.* 1 The act of pinching. 2 Painful pressure of any kind. 3 A case of emergency. 4 So much of a loose substance as can be taken between the finger and thumb. 5 *Slang* A theft. 6 *Slang* An arrest or raid. [< OF *pincier*] —**pinch′er** *n.*

pinch·beck (pinch′bek) *n.* 1 An alloy of copper and zinc that resembles gold. 2 Anything spurious or pretentious. —*adj.* 1 Made of pinchbeck. 2 Spurious; false. [< Christopher *Pinchbeck,* 1670?–1732, English inventor]

pinch·ers (pin′chərz) *n.pl.* PINCERS.

pinch-hit (pinch′hit′) *v.i.* **-hit, -hit·ting** 1 In baseball, to go to bat in place of a regular player, as when a hit is needed. 2 *Informal* To substitute for another in an emergency. [< PINCH an emergency + HIT] —**pinch hitter**

pin·cush·ion (pin′kŏŏsh′ən) *n.* A small cushion into which pins and needles are stuck when not in use.

Pin·dar·ic (pin·dar′ik) *adj.* Of or pertaining to an ode written in the complex style of Pindar, Greek lyric poet.

pind·ling (pind′ling) *adj. Informal* 1 Sickly; puny. 2 Trifling; small. [Var. of PIDDLING]

pine[1] (pīn) *n.* 1 Any of several cone-bearing trees having needle-shaped evergreen leaves growing in clusters. 2 The wood of a pine tree. [< L *pinus*]

pine[2] (pīn) *v.i.* **pined, pin·ing** 1 To grow thin or weak with longing, grief, etc.; languish. 2 To have great desire: with *for.* [< OE *pīnian* to torment] —**Syn.** 2 crave, long, yearn.

pin·e·al body (pin′ē·əl) *Anat.* A small, conical, glandlike structure of unknown function found in the brain of vertebrates. Also **pineal gland.** [< L *pinea* pine cone]

pine·ap·ple (pīn′ap′əl) *n.* 1 A tropical plant having spiny leaves and a large cone-shaped fruit. 2 The edible fruit of this plant. 3 *Slang* A bomb or hand grenade. [< OE *pīn* a pine + *æppel* apple]

Pineapple

pine cone The cone-shaped fruit of the pine tree.

pine needle The needle-shaped leaf of a pine tree.

pine tar A dark, viscous tar obtained from the wood of pine trees: used in medicines, disinfectants, etc.

pine·y (pī′nē) *adj.* **pin·i·er, pin·i·est** PINY.

pin·feath·er (pin′feth′ər) *n.* A rudimentary feather just beginning to grow through the skin.

pin·fold (pin′fōld′) *n.* A pound for stray animals; esp. a cattle pound. —*v.t.* To shut in a pinfold; confine. [< OE *pund-* POUND + *fald* FOLD[2]]

ping (ping) *n.* A sharp, metallic, ringing sound. —*v.i.* To make this sound. [Imit.]

Ping-Pong (ping′pong′, -pông′) *n.* TABLE TENNIS: a trade name.

pin·head (pin′hed′) *n.* 1 The head of a pin. 2 *Slang* A brainless or stupid person; a fool. 3 Something insignificant or small. —**pin′head′ed** *adj.*

pin·hole (pin′hōl′) *n.* A minute puncture made by or as by a pin.

pin·ion[1] (pin′yən) *n.* 1 The wing of a bird. 2 A wing feather. 3 The outer segment of a bird's wing, bearing the flight feathers. —*v.t.* 1 To cut off one pinion or bind the wings of (a bird) so as to prevent flight. 2 To bind or hold the arms of. [< L *pinna* feather]

pin·ion[2] (pin′yən) *n. Mech.* A toothed wheel meshing with a larger cogwheel. [< OF *peigne* a comb] • See RACK.

pink[1] (pingk) *n.* 1 A pale hue of red. 2 Any of a genus of garden plants having pink, red, or white flowers with a clovelike scent. 3 The flower of the pink. 4 A type of excellence or perfection. 5 *Often cap.* A person who holds somewhat radical opinions: a derogatory term. —**in the pink** *Informal* In the best of health and spirits. —*adj.* 1 Pale red in color; rose. 2 Somewhat radical in opinion. [?]

pink[2] (pingk) *v.t.* 1 To cut or finish the edges of (cloth) with a notched pattern. 2 To decorate, as cloth or leather, with a pattern of holes. 3 To prick or stab. [ME *pynken*] —**pink'er** *n.*

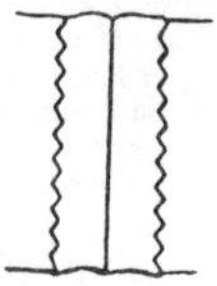

Pinked seam

pink·eye (pingk'ī') *n.* An acute, contagious inflammation of the conjunctiva.

pink·ie (pingk'ē) *n. pl.* **·ies** The fifth, or little, finger. Also **pink'y.**

pinking shears Shears with serrated blades for scalloping the edges of fabrics.

pink·o (pingk'ō) *n. pl.* **·os** PINK[1] (def. 5).

pin money Any trifling sum of money set aside for incidentals.

pin·na (pin'ə) *n. pl.* **pin·nae** (pin'ē) 1 *Bot.* A leaflet of a pinnate leaf. 2 *Anat.* The external ear. 3 *Zool.* A wing, fin, etc. [< L *pinna* feather] —**pin'nal** *adj.*

pin·nace (pin'is) *n. Naut.* 1 A ship's boat. 2 Formerly, a small schooner-rigged vessel. [< Ital. *pinaccia*]

pin·na·cle (pin'ə·kəl) *n.* 1 The topmost point; acme. 2 A small turret or tall ornament, as on a parapet. 3 A mountain peak. —*v.t.* **·cled, ·cling** 1 To place on or as on a pinnacle. 2 To furnish with a pinnacle; crown. [< L *pinna* wing, pinnacle] —**Syn.** *n.* 1 apex, zenith. 3 summit.

pin·nate (pin'āt, -it) *adj.* 1 Resembling a feather. 2 *Bot.* Having leaflets arranged on each side of a common axis: said of compound leaves. Also **pin'nat·ed.** [< L *pinna* a feather, wing] —**pin'nate·ly** *adv.* —**pin·na'tion** *n.*

pi·noch·le (pē'nuk·əl, -nok-) *n.* A card game resembling bezique, played with a double pack of 48 cards, ranking as follows: ace, ten, king, queen, jack, and nine. Also **pi'noc·le.** [?]

pi·ñon (pin'yən, pēn'yōn) *n.* 1 The edible seed of various pines of the Pacific coast. 2 Any of these trees. [Sp., a pine nut]

pin·point (pin'point') *n.* 1 The point of a pin. 2 Something extremely small. —*v.t.* To locate or define precisely. —*adj.* Located or aimed very precisely.

pint (pīnt) *n.* A unit of volume, liquid or dry, equal to ½ quart. [< OF *pinte*]

pin·tail (pin'tāl') *n.* 1 A variety of duck, the male of which has a long, sharp tail. 2 A sharp-tailed grouse.

pin·tle (pin'təl) *n.* A pin upon which anything pivots, as in a hinge, etc. [< OE *pintel* penis]

pin·to (pin'tō) *adj. Regional* Piebald; pied, as an animal. —*n. pl.* **·tos** 1 A pied animal: said esp. of a horse. 2 A kind of spotted bean of the sw U.S.: also **pinto bean.** [< Sp., lit., painted]

pin-up (pin'up') *n. Informal* 1 A picture of an attractive girl hung on a wall or board for display. 2 A lamp fastened on a wall. —*adj.* Designating a photograph or lighting device so affixed.

pin·wheel (pin'hwēl') *n.* 1 A firework that forms a rotating wheel of fire when ignited. 2 A child's plastic or paper toy resembling a windmill revolving on a pin attached to a stick.

pin·worm (pin'wûrm') *n.* A small nematode worm parasitic in the lower intestines and rectum of humans.

pin·y (pī'nē) *adj.* **·i·er, ·i·est** Pertaining to, like, or covered with pines.

pi·o·neer (pī'ə·nir') *n.* 1 One of the first explorers, settlers, or colonists of a new region. 2 One of the first investigators or developers in a new field of research, enterprise, etc. 3 *Mil.* An engineer who goes before the main body building roads, bridges, etc. —*v.t.* 1 To prepare (a way, etc.). 2 To prepare the way for. 3 To be a pioneer of. —*v.i.* 4 To act as a pioneer. [< OF *paonier* a foot soldier]

pi·ous (pī'əs) *adj.* 1 Actuated by religious reverence; godly. 2 Dutiful, respectful, or sanctimonious. 3 Practiced in the name of religion. [< L *pius* dutiful, devout] —**pi'ous·ly** *adv.* —**pi'ous·ness** *n.*

pip[1] (pip) *n.* 1 The seed of an apple, orange, etc. 2 *Slang* A person or thing unusual of its kind. [Short for PIPPIN]

pip[2] (pip) *n.* A spot, as on a playing card, domino, or die. [?]

pip[3] (pip) *v.* **pipped, pip·ping** *v.t.* To break through (the shell), as a chick in the egg. —*v.i.* To peep; chirp. [Prob. var. of PEEP[1]]

pip[4] (pip) *n.* 1 A contagious disease of fowls in which mucus forms in the throat or a scale on the tongue. 2 *Slang* Any mild human ailment. [< L *pituita* mucus, the pip]

pipe (pīp) *n.* 1 An apparatus, usu. a small bowl with a hollow stem, for smoking tobacco, opium, etc. 2 Enough tobacco to fill the bowl of a pipe. 3 A duct of metal, etc., for conveying a fluid. 4 A single section of such a duct. 5 Any hollow or tubular part in an animal or plant body. 6 *Music* **a** A wind instrument consisting of a tube or tubes. **b** Any of the tubular tone-producing parts used in an organ. **c** *pl.* The bagpipe. 7 A high-pitched voice; also, a bird's call. 8 A large cask for wine. 9 A boatswain's whistle. —*v.* **piped, pip·ing** *v.i.* 1 To play on a pipe. 2 To make a shrill sound. 3 *Naut.* To signal the crew by means of a pipe. —*v.t.* 4 To convey by or as by means of pipes, esp. to transmit (television programs) by coaxial cables or wire instead of by airwaves. 5 To provide with pipes. 6 To play, as a tune, on a pipe. 7 To utter shrilly or in a high key. 8 *Naut.* To call to order by means of a boatswain's pipe. 9 To lead, entice, or bring by piping. 10 To trim, as a dress, with piping. —**pipe down** *Slang* To become silent; stop making noise. —**pipe up** 1 To start playing or singing. 2 To speak out, esp. in a shrill voice. [< L *pipare* to cheep]

pipe clay A white clay used for making clay pipes and, formerly, for whitening and cleaning leather.

pipe dream *Informal* Any groundless hope or impractical idea; a daydream.

pipe·line (pīp'līn') *n.* 1 A line of pipe, as for the transmission of water, oil, etc. 2 A channel for the transmission of information.

pipe organ ORGAN (def. 1).

pip·er (pī'pər) *n.* 1 A person who plays a pipe or pipes. 2 A person who makes, installs, or repairs piping (def. 4).

pipe·stem (pīp'stem') *n.* 1 The stem of a tobacco pipe. 2 *pl.* Things of similar shape, as long, thin legs. —*adj.* Shaped like a pipestem; thin.

pi·pette (pī·pet', pi-) *n.* A slender tube for transferring or measuring small portions of a fluid. Also **pi·pet'.** [F, dim. of *pipe* pipe]

pip·ing (pī'ping) *adj.* 1 Playing on the pipe. 2 Hissing or sizzling: *piping* hot. 3 Having a shrill sound. —*n.* 1 The act of one who pipes. 2 The music of pipes. 3 A wailing or whistling sound. 4 A system of pipes, as in plumbing. 5 A narrow fold of cloth for trimming seams.

pip·it (pip'it) *n.* One of various larklike birds of open country that sing in flight and walk with tail bobbing. [Imit.]

American pipit

pip·kin (pip'kin) *n.* A small earthenware jar. [? Dim. of PIPE]

pip·pin (pip'in) *n.* Any of several varieties of apple. [< OE *pepin* seed of a fruit]

pip·sis·se·wa (pip·sis'ə·wə) *n.* A low-growing plant related to wintergreen, having jagged, evergreen leaves and white or pink flowers. [< Algon.]

pip-squeak (pip'skwēk') *n.* A petty and contemptible person or thing.

pi·quant (pē'kənt, -känt') *adj.* 1 Having an agreeably pungent or tart taste. 2 Interesting; tart; racy; also, charmingly lively. [< F *piquer* sting] —**pi'quan·cy** *n.* —**pi'quant·ly** *adv.*

pique (pēk) *n.* A feeling of irritation or resentment. —*v.t.* **piqued, pi·quing** 1 To excite resentment in. 2 To stimulate or arouse; provoke. [< MF *piquer* to sting, prick] —**Syn.** *n.* anger, displeasure. *v.* 1 irritate, nettle, offend.

pi·qué (pē·kā') *n.* A fabric, usu. of cotton, with raised cord or welts running lengthwise. [F, lit., quilted]

pi·quet (pē·ket', pē·kā') *n.* A two-handed game of cards using 32 cards. [F]

pi·ra·cy (pī'rə·sē) *n. pl.* **·cies** 1 Robbery on the high seas. 2 The unauthorized publication, reproduction, or use of another's invention, idea, or literary creation. [< Gk. *peiratēs* a pirate]

pi·ra·nha (pi·rä'nyə) *n.* A small, carnivorous, freshwater fish of South America that, in schools, attacks and severely wounds large animals and man. Also **pi·ra'ya** (-rä'yä). [Tupian, toothed fish]

pi·rate (pī'rit) *n.* 1 A rover and robber on the high seas. 2 A vessel engaged in piracy. 3 A person who appropriates without right the work of another. —*v.t.* & *v.i.* **·rat·ed, ·rat·ing** **1** To practice or commit piracy (upon). **2** To publish or appropriate (the work, ideas, etc., of another) illegally; plagiarize. [< Gk. *peiraein* to attach] **—pi·rat·ic** (pī-rat′ik) or **·i·cal** *adj.* **—pi·rat′i·cal·ly** *adv.*

pi·rogue (pi·rōg′) *n.* A flat-bottomed two-masted boat. [< Cariban *piragua*]

pir·ou·ette (pir′ōō-et′) *n.* A rapid whirling upon the toes in dancing. —*vi.* **·et·ted, ·et·ting** To make a pirouette. [F, a spinning top] **—pir′ou·et′ter** *n.*

pis·ca·to·ri·al (pis′kə-tôr′ē-əl, -tō′rē-) *adj.* Pertaining to fishes, fishermen, or fishing. Also **pis′ca·to′ry.** [< L *piscator* a fisherman] **—pis′ca·to′ri·al·ly** *adv.*

Pis·ces (pī′sēz, pis′ēz) *n. pl.* (*construed as sing*) A constellation and the twelfth sign of the zodiac; the Fishes. [< L *piscis* a fish] • See ZODIAC.

pis·ci·cul·ture (pis′i·kul′chər) *n.* The science or business of hatching and rearing fish. [< L *piscis,* fish + CULTURE] **—pis′ci·cul′tur·al** *adj.* **—pis′ci·cul′tur·ist** *n.*

Pis·gah (piz′gə), **Mount** A mountain of ancient Palestine, now Jordan, NE of the Dead Sea: in the Old Testament, the peak from which Moses beheld the Promised Land: highest peak, Mount Nebo.

pis·mire (pis′mīr) *n.* An ant. [< ME *pisse* urine + *myre* an ant; with ref. to odor of formic acid]

pis·ta·chi·o (pis·tä′shē-ō, -tash′ē-ō) *n. pl.* **·chi·os** **1** A small tree of W Asia and the Levant. **2** Its pale green, edible seed: also **pistachio nut.** **3** The flavor of the pistachio nut. **4** A delicate shade of green. [< Gk. *pistakion*]

pis·til (pis′til) *n.* The seed-bearing organ of flowering plants, composed of the ovary, the stigma, and usu. a style. [< L *pistillum* a pestle] • See OVARY.

pis·til·late (pis′tə-lit, -lāt) *adj.* **1** Having a pistil. **2** having pistils and no stamens. Also **pis′til·lar′y** (-ler′ē).

pis·tol (pis′təl) *n.* A small firearm held and fired by one hand. —*v.t.* **·toled** or **·tolled, ·tol·ing** or **·tol·ling** To shoot with a piston. [< F *pistole*]

pis·tole (pis·tōl′) *n.* An obsolete gold coin of varying value, formerly current in Europe. [F]

pis·ton (pis′tən) *n.* **1** *Mech.* A disk fitted to slide in a cylinder and connected with a rod for receiving the pressure of or exerting pressure upon a fluid in the cylinder. **2** A valve in a wind instrument for altering the pitch of tones. [< Ital. *pistane*]

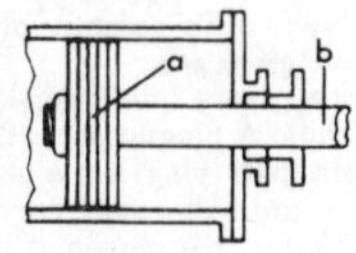

Steam-engine piston a. piston. b. piston rod.

piston ring *Mech.* An open ring fitted on a piston body to prevent leakage between the piston and the cylinder wall.

pit[1] (pit) *n.* **1** A cavity in the ground. **2** A pitfall for animals; snare. **3** A deep abyss. **4** Hell. **5** In Great Britain, the portion of the main floor of the auditorium of a theater under the first balcony. **6** The space just in front of and below the stage, usu. occupied by the orchestra. **7** An enclosed space in which animals engage in fighting: a *cockpit.* **8** Any natural cavity or depression in the body: the *armpit.* **9** A scar like that made by a healed smallpox pustule. **10** That part of the floor of an exchange where a special line of trading is done: the wheat *pit.* **11** A mining excavation. —*v.* **pit·ted, pit·ting** *v.t.* **1** To mark with dents or hollows. **2** To match as antagonists. —*v.i.* **3** To become marked with pits. [< OE *pytt*]

pit[2] (pit) *n.* A hard, single seed of certain fruits, as the plum. —*v.t.* **pit·ted, pit·ting** To remove pits from, as fruits. [< MDu. *pitte* kernel]

pitch[1] (pich) *n.* **1** A sticky nonvolatile residue obtained from the distillation of petroleum, coal tar, etc. **2** Asphalt. **3** A resin exuded by certain conifers. —*v.t.* To caulk, waterproof, cover, or treat with pitch. [< L *pix, picis* pitch]

pitch[2] (pich) *v.t.* **1** To erect or set up (a tent, camp, etc.). **2** To throw or hurl. **3** To set the level, angle degree, etc., of. **4** To put in a definite place or position. **5** In baseball, to deliver (the ball) to the batter. **6** *Music* To set the pitch or key of. —*v.i.* **7** To fall or plunge forward or headlong. **8** to lurch. **9** To rise and fall alternately at the front and back. **10** To incline downward; slope. **11** To encamp. **12** In baseball, to deliver the ball to the batter. **—pitch in** *Informan* To start vigorously. **—pitch into** To attack, assail. —*n* **1** Point or degree of elevation or depression. **2** The degree of descent or inclination of a slope. **3** *Mech.* **a** The amount of advance of a screw thread in a single turn. **b** The distance between two corresponding points on the teeth of a gearwheel. **4** *Music* The subjective characteristic of a tone that correlates essentially with frequency. **5** In games, the act of pitching; a throw. **6** Something pitched. **7** The act of dipping or plunging downward. **8** An attempt to sell or persuade: to make a *pitch.* [ME *picchen*] **—Syn.** *v.* **2** cast, fling, heave, toss.

pitch-black (pich′blak′) *adj.* Intensely black.

pitch·blende (pich′blend′) *n.* A black or brown mineral form of uranium oxide: an ore of uranium and radium. [< G *Pech* pitch[1] + *Blende* blende]

pitch-dark (pich′därk′) *adj.* Very dark.

pitched battle A fierce battle in which the antagonists fight in close contact.

pitch·er[1] (pich′ər) *n.* On who pitches, esp., in baseball, the player who delivers the ball to the batter.

pitch·er[2] (pich′ər) *n.* A vessel with a spout and a handle, used for holding liquids to be poured out. [< Gk. *bikos* a wine jar]

pitcher plant Any of several plants having leaves that form pitcherlike vessels in which insects are trapped and digested.

pitch·fork (pich′fôrk′) *n.* A large fork, often having a long handle for moving about hay, straw, etc. —*v.t.* To lift and throw with a pitchfork. [< PITCH[2] + FORK]

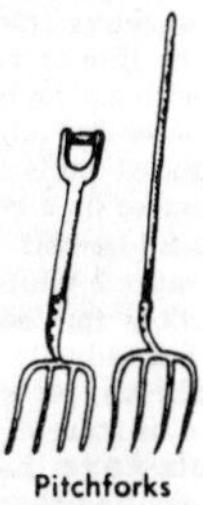

Pitchforks

pitch·man (pich′mən) *n. pl.* **·men** (mən) *Slang* One who sells small articles from a temporary stand, as at a fair, etc.

pitch pine Any of several pines that yield turpentine and pitch.

pitch·y (pich′ē) *adj.* **pitch·i·er, pitch·i·est** **1** Resembling pitch; intensely dark. **2** Full of or daubed with pitch. **3** Sticky. **—pitch′i·ly** *adv.* **—pitch′i·ness** *n.*

pit·e·ous (pit′ē-əs) *adj.* Exciting great pity or sympathy. **—pit′e·ous·ly** *adv.* **—pit′e·ous·ness** *n.* • **piteous, pitiable, pitiful** These words all mean "causing or deserving pity," but they have different shades of meaning. *Piteous* is the strongest, connoting a heart-rending anguish that is keenly felt by the observer: *the piteous cry of a wounded animal.* A *pitiable* thing gives rise to milder compassion mixed with understanding: *his pitiable attempts to appear respectable.* A *pitiful* thing tends to inspire stronger feeling than does a *pitiable* one: *a pitiful account of an unhappy childhood.* The pity suggested by *pitiable* and *pitiful* may be mixed with contempt or condescension.

pit·fall (pit′fôl′) *n.* **1** A pit contrived for entrapping beasts or men. **2** Any hidden danger. [< PIT[1] + OE *fealle* a trap]

pith (pith) *n.* **1** The soft, spongy tissue in the center of the stems and branches of certain plants. **2** Any soft central part, as the marrow of bones. **3** Concentrated force; substance. **4** The essential part; quintessence. —*v.t.* To remove the pith from, as a plant stem. [< OE *pitha*]

Pith·e·can·thro·pus (pith′ə-kan′thrə-pəs, -kan·thrō′pəs) *n. pl.* **·pi** (-pī) The generic name formerly given to Java man as a supposed transitional form between ape and man. [< Gk. *pithēkos* an ape + *anthropos* a man] **—pith′e·can′thro·pine** (-pēn, -pin), **pith′e·can′thro·poid** *adj.*

pith·y (pith′ē) *adj.* **pith·i·er, pith·i·est** **1** Consisting of or like pith. **2** Forcible; effective. **—pith′i·ly** *adv.* **—pith′i·ness** *n.*

pit·i·a·ble (pit′ē-ə-bəl) *adj.* **1** Arousing or meriting pity or compassion; pathetic. **2** Insignificant; contemptible. **—pit′i·a·ble·ness** *n.* **—pit′i·a·bly** *adv.* • See PITEOUS.

pit·i·ful (pit′i-fəl) *adj.* **1** Arousing pity or compassion. **2** Arousing contempt or scorn. **3** *Archaic* Full of pity; compassionate. **—pit′i·ful·ly** *adv.* **—pit′i·ful·ness** *n.* **—Syn. 1** lamentable, miserable, pathetic, touching. **2** abject, contemptible, paltry. • See PITEOUS.

pit·i·less (pit′i·lis) *adj.* Having no pity or mercy; ruthless. —**pit′i·less·ly** *adv.* **pit′i·less·ness** *n.*

pit·man (pit′mən) *n. pl.* **·men** (-mən) One who works in a pit, esp., in mining, the man in charge of the underground machinery.

pit·tance (pit′əns) *n.* **1** A small allowance of money. **2** Any meager income or remuneration. [<OF *pitance,* orig. a monk's food allotment, pity]

pit·ter-pat·ter (pit′ər·pat′ər) *n.* A rapid series of light sounds or taps. —*adv.* With a pitter-patter. [Imit.]

pi·tu·i·tar·y (pi·tʸōō′ə·ter′ē) *adj.* Of or pertaining to the pituitary gland. —*n. pl.* **·tar·ies 1** The pituitary gland. **2** Any of various preparations made from extracts of the pituitary gland. [<L *pituita* phlegm]

pituitary gland *Anat.* A small, bilobate, endocrine gland at the base of the brain in vertebrates which secretes various hormones having specific effects on other glands in the body and on growth, metabolism, etc. Also **pituitary body.**

pit·y (pit′ē) *n. pl.* **pit·ies 1** The feeling of grief or pain awakened by the misfortunes of others; compassion. **2** A cause for compassion or regret: It's a *pity* that their house burned down. —*v.t.* & *v.i.* **pit·ied, pit·y·ing** To feel compassion or pity (for). [<LL *pietas*] —**pit′i·er** *n.* —**pit′y·ing·ly** *adv.*

più (pyōō) *adv. Music* More: *più* allegro: faster. [Ital. < L *plus*]

piv·ot (piv′ət) *n.* **1** *Mech.* Something upon which a related part oscillates or rotates. **2** Something on which an important matter hinges or turns; a turning point. **3** *Mil.* In wheeling troops, the soldier, officer, or point upon which the line turns. —*v.t.* **1** To place on, attach by, or provide with a pivot or pivots. —*v.i.* **2** To turn on a pivot; swing. [F] —**piv′ot·al** *adj.* —**piv′ot·al·ly** *adj.*

pix·el (pik′səl) *n.* A picture element, one of the tiny dots that make up a character or a graphic on a cathode-ray tube.

pix·i·la·ted (pik′sə·lā′tid) *adj.* **1** Somewhat crazy or erratic. **2** Whimsical; droll.

pix·y (pik′sē) *n. pl.* **pix·ies** A fairy or elf. Also **pix′ie.** [< Scand.]

piz·za (pēt′sə) *n.* A doughy crust overlaid and baked with a mixture of cheese, tomatoes, spices, etc. [Ital.]

piz·zazz (pə·zaz′) *n. Slang* A quality of irresistible and exciting charm. Also **pi·zazz′.**

piz·ze·ri·a (pēt′sə·rē′ə) *n.* A place where pizzas are prepared, sold, and eaten.

piz·zi·ca·to (pit′sə·kä′tō) *Music adj.* & *adv.* Plucked or in a plucked manner: used to indicate that the strings of a normally bowed instrument are to be plucked. —*n. pl.* **·ti** (-tē) A pizzicato note, phrase, passage, etc. [<Ital. *pizzicare* to pluck, pinch]

pk. pack; park; peak; peck.

pkg. package(s).

PKU phenylketonuria.

pl. place; plate; plural.

pla·ca·ble (plak′ə·bəl, plā′kə-) *adj.* Appeasable; yielding. [<L *placare* appease] —**pla′ca·bil′i·ty, pla′ca·ble·ness** n.

plac·ard (plak′ərd, plak′ärd) *n.* A printed or written notice to be publicly displayed. —*v.t.* (*usu.* plak′ärd) **1** To announce by means of placards. **2** To post placards on or in. **3** To display as a placard. [<OF *plackart*]

pla·cate (plā′kāt, plak′āt) *v.t.* **·cat·ed, ·cat·ing** To appease the anger of; pacify. [<L *placare* appease] —**pla′cat·er, pla·ca′tion** *n.* —**pla′ca·tive, pla′ca·to′ry** (-tô′rē, -tō′rē) *adj.*

place (plās) *n.* **1** A particular point or portion of space; a definite locality or location. **2** An occupied situation or building; space regarded as abode or quarters. **3** An open space or square in a city; also, a court or street. **4** Position in relative order. **5** Station in life; degree; rank. **6** An office, appointment, or employment; also, rank, position, or station. **7** Room; stead: One thing gives *place* to another. **8** A particular passage, as in a book. **9** The second position among the first three competitors in a horse race. **10** *Math* The position of a digit, and hence its weight, in relation to other digits of a numeral. —**in place 1** In its natural position; also, in a suitable place, position, job, etc. **2** IN SITU. —**in place of** Instead of. —**out of place 1** Not in the appropriate place, order, or relation. **2** Inappropriate; ill-timed. —**take place** To happen; occur. —*v.* **placed, plac·ing** *v.t.* **1** To put in a particular place or position. **2** To put or arrange in a particular relation or sequence. **3** To find a situation, home, etc., for. **4** To appoint to a post or office. **5** To identify; classify: Historians *place* him in the time of Nero. **6** To arrange for: to *place* an order. **7** To bestow or entrust: I *place* my life in your hands. **8** To invest, as funds. **9** To adjust the tones of (the voice) consciously, as in singing. —*v.i.* **10** In racing, to finish among the first three contestants; esp., to finish second. [< L *platea* a wide street] —**Syn.** *v.* **1** lay, locate, set, situate.

pla·ce·bo (plə·sē′bō) *n. pl.* **·bos** or **·boes** Any inactive substance given out as medication either to humor a patient or as a control in testing the effects of other medicines. [<L *placebo* I shall please]

place kick In football, a kick for a goal in which the ball is placed on the ground for kicking. —**place′-kick′** *v.i.*

place·ment (plās′mənt) *n.* **1** The act of placing or the state of being placed. **2** The finding of a suitable situation or job for a person. **3** In football, the putting of the ball in position for a place kick from the field.

pla·cen·ta (plə·sen′tə) *n. pl.* **·tas** or **·tae** (-tē) In higher mammals, the vascular organ of interlocking fetal and maternal tissue by which the fetus is nourished in the uterus. [<NL *placenta (uterina)* (uterine) cake] —**pla·cen′tal, pla·cen′tate** *adj.*

plac·er (plas′ər) *n. Mining* **1** A deposit of sand, gravel, etc., containing gold or other mineral in particles that can be isolated by washing. **2** Any place where deposits are washed for valuable minerals. [<Am. Sp. *placer* a deposit]

plac·id (plas′id) *adj.* Quiet; calm. [<L *placere* to please] —**pla·cid·i·ty** (plə·sid′ə·tē), **plac′id·ness** *n.* —**plac′id·ly** *adv.* —**Syn.** pacific, peaceful, tranquil, unruffled.

plack·et (plak′it) *n.* The opening or slit in the upper part of a skirt, usu. closed by a zipper. Also **placket hole.** [?]

pla·gia·rism (plā′jə·riz′əm, -jē·ə-) *n.* The act of plagiarizing, or something plagiarized. —**pla′gia·rist** *n.* —**pla′gia·ris′tic** *adj.*

pla·gia·rize (plā′jə·rīz, -jē·ə-) *v.* **·rized, ·riz·ing** *v.t.* **1** To appropriate as one's own the writings, ideas, etc., of another). **2** To appropriate and use passages, ideas, etc., from. —*v.i.* **3** To commit plagiarism. *Brit. sp.* **pla′gia·rise.** —**pla′gia·riz′er** *n.*

pla·gia·ry (plā′jər·ē, -jē·ər·ē) *n. pl.* **·ries 1** PLAGIARISM. **2** *Archaic* A plagiarist. [<Gk. *plagios* oblique, treacherous]

plague (plāg) *n.* **1** A pestilence or epidemic disease of man or animals, usu. very deadly and contagious: bubonic *plague.* **2** A person or thing that is troublesome and harassing. —*v.t.* **plague, pla·guing 1** To harass or torment; annoy. **2** To afflict with plague or disaster. [<LL *plaga* a pestilence]

pla·guy (plā′gē) *Informal adj.* Characterized by vexation or annoyance; troublesome. —*adv.* Vexatiously; intolerably. Also **pla·guey.** —**pla′gui·ly** *adv.*

plaice (plās) *n.* Any of various flatfishes of the coasts of Europe and North America. [<Gk. *platys* broad]

plaid (plad) *adj.* Having a tartan pattern; checkered. —*n.* **1** An oblong woolen scarf of tartan or checkered pattern, worn in the Scottish Highlands as a cloak fastened over one shoulder. **2** Any fabric of this pattern. [< Scot. Gaelic *plaide* a blanket]

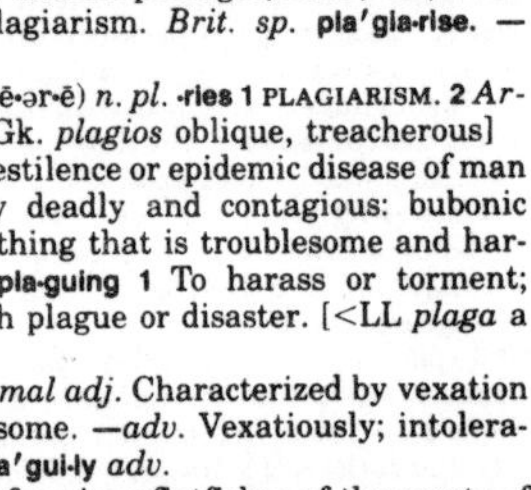

Plaids
a. argyle. b. blanket.
c. tartan. d. tattersall.

plain (plān) *adj.* **1** Presenting few difficulties; easy. **2** Clear; understandable: *plain* English. **3** Lowly in station; humble. **4** Having no conspicuous ornamentation; unadorned. **5** Not figured or twilled: said of textiles. **6** Flat; smooth. **7** Homely. **8** Not rich, as food. —*n.* An expanse of level, treeless land; a prairie. [< L *planus* flat] —**plain′ly** *adv.* —**plain′ness** *n.*

plain·clothes man (plān′klōz′, -klōthz′) A police detective wearing civilian clothes while on duty. Also **plain·clothes·man** (plān′klōz′mən, -klōthz′-) (*pl.* **·men**).

plains·man (plānz′mən) *n. pl.* **·men** (-mən) A dweller on the plains.

plain·song (plān′sông′, -song′) *n.* Ecclesiastical music of the early Christian church, sung in unison, as the Gregorian chant. Also **plain·chant** (plān′chant′, -chänt′).

plain-spo·ken (plān′spō′kən) *adj.* Plainly or frankly speaking or spoken.

plaint (plānt) *n.* 1 COMPLAINT. 2 *Archaic* A lamentation. [< L *plangere* to lament]

plain·tiff (plān′tif) *n.* The person that begins an action at law. [< OF *plaintif* plaintive]

plain·tive (plān′tiv) *adj.* Expressing a subdued sadness; mournful. [< OF *plaintif*] **—plain′tive·ly** *adv.* **—plain′tive·ness** *n.*

plait (plāt, plat) *v.t.* 1 BRAID. 2 PLEAT. 3 To make by pleating or braiding. —*n.* 1 A braid of hair. 2 PLEAT. [< L *plicitum* a folded thing] **—plait′er** *n.*

plan (plan) *n.* 1 A means for the attainment of some object; a scheme. 2 A drawing showing the proportion and relation of parts, as of a building. 3 A mode of action. —*v.t.* **planned, plan·ning** 1 To form a scheme or method for doing, achieving, etc. 2 To make a plan of, as a building; design. 3 To have as an intention or purpose. [< OF, a plane (surface), a ground plan] **—plan′ner** *n.* **—Syn.** *n.* 1 design, method, arrangement, program. *v.* 1 contrive, devise, invent, organize.

plane[1] (plān) *n.* 1 *Geom.* A surface such that a straight line joining any two of its points lies wholly within the surface. 2 Any flat or uncurved surface. 3 A grade of development; stage; level, as of thought, knowledge, rank, etc. 4 *Aeron.* A lifting surface of an airplane; airfoil. 5 An airplane. —*adj.* 1 Of or lying in a plane. 2 Having a flat surface. —*v.i.* **planed, plan·ing** 1 To glide; soar. 2 To rise partly out of the water, as a power boat at high speed. [< L *planus* flat]

plane[2] (plān) *n.* A tool used for smoothing boards or other surfaces of wood. —*v.t.* **planed, plan·ing** 1 To make smooth or even with a plane. 2 To remove with a plane. [< L *planus* flat]

Plane

plane[3] (plān) *n.* Any of a genus of large, deciduous trees with maplelike leaves and bark that is shed in patches. Also **plane tree.** [< Gk. *platys* broad; because of its broad leaves]

plan·er (plā′nər) *n.* A machine for making smooth surfaces on wood or metal. [< PLANE[2]]

plan·et (plan′it) *n.* 1 *Astron.* One of the large bodies that orbit the sun and shine by reflected sunlight. The major solar planets are Mercury, Venus, Earth, Mars, Jupiter, Saturn, Uranus, Neptune, and Pluto. 2 A similar body revolving around another star. 3 In ancient astronomy, one of the seven heavenly bodies (the Sun, Moon, Mercury, Venus, Mars, Jupiter, and Saturn) that have an apparent motion among the fixed stars. 4 In astrology, one of these bodies in relation to its supposed influence on human beings and their affairs. [< Gk. *planētes* wanderer]

plan·e·tar·i·um (plan′ə·târ′ē·əm) *n. pl.* **·tar·i·ums** or **·tar·i·a** 1 An apparatus for exhibiting the features of the heavens as they exist at any time and for any place on earth. 2 A building containing such an apparatus. [< LL *planetarius* planetary]

plan·e·tar·y (plan′ə·ter′ē) *adj.* 1 Of or pertaining to a planet or planets. 2 Mundane; terrestrial. 3 Wandering; erratic: a *planetary* career. 4 *Mech.* Of or denoting a gear in which one or more small wheels mesh with the toothed circumference of a larger wheel, around which they revolve as they rotate. 5 *Physics* Orbiting in the manner of a planet: a *planetary* electron.

plan·e·toid (plan′ə·toid) *n.* ASTEROID. **—plan′e·toi′dal** *adj.*

plan·ish (plan′ish) *v.t.* To condense, smooth, toughen, or polish, as metal, by hammering, rolling, etc. [< L *planus* flat] **—plan′ish·er** *n.*

plank (plangk) *n.* 1 A broad piece of sawed timber, thicker than a board. 2 One of the principles of a political platform. **—walk the plank** To walk off a plank projecting from the side of a ship: a method used by pirates for executing prisoners. —*v.t.* 1 To cover, furnish, or lay with planks. 2 To broil or bake and serve on a plank, as fish. 3 *Informal* To put down emphatically. [< LL *planca* board]

plank·ing (plangk′ing) *n.* 1 The act of laying planks. 2 Planks collectively.

plank·ton (plangk′tən) *n.* The floating or drifting, usu. microscopic, plants and animals living near the surface of bodies of water. [< Gk. *planktos* drifting] **—plank·ton·ic** (plangk·ton′ik) *adj.*

plant (plant, plänt) *n.* 1 Any member of one of the two great kingdoms of organisms, usu. distinguishable from animals by various criteria, as the ability to carry on photosynthesis, the presence of cellulose cell walls, a fixed position, etc. 2 One of the smaller forms of vegetable life, as distinct from shrubs and trees. 3 A set of machines, tools, apparatus, etc., comprising a manufacturing enterprise or other business. 4 A building or buildings used for a manufacturing or industrial process: a packing *plant.* 5 The buildings and equipment needed for any institution, as a college. 6 A sapling; a slip or cutting from a tree or bush. 7 *Slang* A trick; swindle. —*v.t.* 1 To set in the ground for growing. 2 To furnish with plants or seed: to *plant* a field. 3 To place firmly; put in position. 4 To found; establish. 5 To introduce into the mind. 6 To deposit (fish or spawn) in a body of water. 7 *Slang* To deliver, as a blow. 8 *Slang* To place (a person or thing) for purposes of deception. [< L *planta* a sprout]

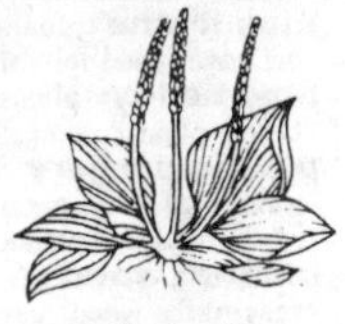
Plantain[1]

Plan·tag·e·net (plan·taj′i·net) *n.* A member of the English royal family from Henry II (1154) to the accession of the House of Tudor (1485).

plan·tain[1] (plan′tin) *n.* Any of a genus of low-growing, weedy plants of temperate regions. [< L *plantago*]

plan·tain[2] (plan′tin) *n.* 1 A tropical tree having coarse, bananalike fruit. 2 Its fruit, usu. eaten cooked. [< Sp. *plátano*]

plan·tar (plan′tər) *adj.* Pertaining to the sole of the foot. [< L *planta* sole of the foot]

plan·ta·tion (plan·tā′shən) *n.* 1 A farm or estate of many acres, esp. in the s U.S., planted in cotton, tobacco, rice, or sugar cane. 2 A newly settled region; a settlement;

PLANETS

Name	*Symbol*	*Distance from sun: miles*	*Mean diameter: miles*	*Period of sidereal revolution*	*Period of rotation*	*Number of satellites*	*Mass: earth considered as 1.*
Mercury	☿	36,000,000	3,000	88 days	88 days?	0	0.0543
Venus	♀	67,000,000	7,600	225 days	20–30 days	0	0.8136
Earth	⊕	93,000,000	7,918	365.25 days	23 hr. 56 min.	1	1.0000
Mars	♂	142,000,000	4,200	687 days	24 hr. 37 min.	2	0.1069
Jupiter	♃	483,000,000	87,000	12 years	9 hr. 50 min.	12	318.35
Saturn	♄	886,000,000	72,000	29.5 years	10 hr. 14 min.	9	95.3
Uranus	♅	1,780,000,000	29,600	84 years	10 hr. 45 min.	5	14.58
Neptune	♆	2,790,000,000	27,700	165 years	15 hr. 48 min.	2	17.26
Pluto	♇	3,670,000,000	4,000	248 years	?	0	.1?

colony. 3 A grove cultivated to provide a certain product. [<L *plantare* to plant]

plant·er (plan′tər) *n.* 1 A person or machine that plants. 2 An owner of a plantation. 3 A decorative container for growing shrubs and flowers, esp. indoors.

plan·ti·grade (plan′tə·grād) *adj.* Walking on the whole sole of the foot, as men, bears, etc. —*n.* A plantigrade animal. [<L *planta* the sole of the foot + *gradi* to walk]

plant louse An aphid or similar insect.

plaque (plak) *n.* 1 A plate, disk, or slab of metal, porcelain, etc., ornamented, as for wall decoration. 2 A brooch. 3 A hardened deposit of microorganisms and mucus on teeth. [<MDu. *placke* flat disk]

plash (plash) *n.* A slight splash. —*v.t.* & *v.i.* To splash lightly. [Prob. imit.] —**plash′y** *adj.*

-plasm *combining form Biol.* The viscous, basic material of organic cells: *protoplasm.* [<Gk. *plasma* a form]

plas·ma (plaz′mə) *n.* 1 The liquid portion of blood, lymph, milk, or similar fluids containing suspended solids. 2 PROTOPLASM. 3 *Physics* An intensely ionized, electrically neutral gas. [<Gk. *plassein* to mold, form] —**plas·mat·ic** (plaz·mat′ik), **plas′mic** *adj.*

plas·ter (plas′tər, pläs′-) *n.* 1 A composition of lime, sand, and water for coating walls and partitions. 2 Plaster of Paris. 3 A viscid substance spread on cloth and applied to the body for healing purposes. —*v.t.* 1 To cover or overlay with plaster. 2 To apply a plaster to, as a part of the body. 3 To apply like plaster: to *plaster* posters on a fence. 4 To cause to adhere or lie flat like plaster. [<Gk. *emplastron*]

plas·ter·board (plas′tər·bôrd′, pläs′-, -bōrd′) *n.* A laminated wallboard of paper and gypsum.

plas·tered (plas′tərd, pläs′-) *adj. Slang* Drunk.

plaster of Paris Calcined gypsum that solidifies readily after mixture with water and is useful in making molds, splints, statuary, etc.

plas·tic (plas′tik) *adj.* 1 Giving form or fashion to matter. 2 Capable of being molded; pliable. 3 Pertaining to modeling or molding; sculptural. 4 Made of plastic. 5 *Slang* Not genuine; sham: *plastic* moral values. —*n.* Any of a class of synthetically produced organic compounds capable of being molded and hardened into any form required by commercial use. [<Gk. *plastos* formed<*plassein* to form, mold] —**plas′ti·cal·ly** *adv.*

Plas·ti·cine (plas′tə·sēn) *n.* A claylike substance with an oil base, used for modeling: a trade name.

plas·tic·i·ty (plas·tis′ə·tē) *n.* The property or quality of being plastic or malleable.

plastic surgery Surgery that deals with structural remodeling or restoration of lost, injured, or deformed parts of the body. —**plastic surgeon**

plastic wood A synthetic paste which when dried resembles wood, used to fill cracks, holes, etc., in wooden articles.

plas·tron (plas′trən) *n.* 1 The under part of the shell of a turtle. 2 An iron breastplate. [<OF] —**plas′tral** *adj.*

plat (plat) *n.* 1 A small piece of ground; a plot. 2 A plotted map, chart, or plan. —*v.t.* **plat·ted, plat·ting** To make a plot or plan of. [<OF]

plat. plateau; platform; platoon.

plate (plāt) *n.* 1 A shallow, usu. round dish upon which food is served. 2 A portion of food; plateful. 3 Service, dishes, food, etc., for one person: a fund-raising dinner at $25 a *plate.* 4 Household utensils covered or lined with a thin coating of silver or gold. 5 Metal in sheets. 6 A cup or other article of silver or gold offered as a prize in a contest. 7 A piece of flat metal bearing an engraved design or inscription. 8 An electrotype or stereotype, esp. a full-page illustration printed on special paper. 9 A horizontal timber for supporting a framework. 10 *Dent.* A device fitted to the mouth and holding one or more artificial teeth. 11 Armor made from metal plates. 12 A thin part of the brisket of beef. 13 A sensitized sheet of glass, metal, or the like, for taking photographs. 14 In baseball, the home base. 15 *Biol.* A platelike structure; a lamina or a lamella. 16 *Geol.* A section of the earth's crust that floats on the surface of the mantle. 17 A dish used in taking up collections, as in churches; also, such a collection. 18 A hinge. 19 The principal anode in an electron tube. —*v.t.* **plat·ed, plat·ing** 1 To coat with a thin layer of gold, silver, etc. 2 To cover or sheathe with metal plates for protection. 3 *Printing* To make an electrotype or stereotype plate from. [<Gk. *platys* broad, flat]

pla·teau (pla·tō′) *n. pl.* **·teaus** or **·teaux** (-tōz′) 1 A stretch of elevated and comparatively level land; tableland. 2 A period of relatively little change in circumstance. 3 A comparatively horizontal area of a graph indicating an unchanging variable. [<OF *platel* a flat piece of metal or wood]

plat·ed (plā′tid) *adj.* 1 Provided with plates of metal, as for defense. 2 Coated with a layer of silver, gold, etc.

plate·ful (plāt′fo͝ol′) *n. pl.* **·fuls** The quantity that fills a plate.

plate glass Glass fabricated in heavy sheets.

plate·let (plāt′lit) *n.* 1 A small disk or flake. 2 Any of the minute, colorless disk-shaped particles found in blood and essential to clot formation. [Dim. of PLATE]

plat·en (plat′n) *n.* The part of a printing press or typewriter on which the paper is supported to receive the impression. [<OF *platine* a flat piece, metal plate]

plat·er (plā′tər) *n.* 1 One who plates articles with a layer of gold, silver, etc. 2 An inferior race horse.

plat·form (plat′fôrm) *n.* 1 Any floor or flat surface raised above the adjacent level, as a stage for public speaking. 2 An enclosed space at the end of a railroad car, etc. 3 A raised walk, usu. of wood, built parallel to the tracks at a railroad station. 4 A statement of principles or objectives put forth by a political party, etc. [<MF *plate* flat + *forme* form]

plat·ing (plā′ting) *n.* 1 A coating of metal of varying thickness: silver *plating.* 2 A sheathing of metal plates, or plate armor for protection. 3 The act or process of sheathing or coating something with plates or metal.

plat·i·nize (plat′ə·nīz) *v.t.* **·nized, ·niz·ing** To coat or combine with platinum.

plat·i·num (plat′ə·nəm) *n.* A heavy, whitish metallic element (symbol Pt) that is highly resistant to corrosion and fusion, and is widely used as a catalyst, for jewelry, etc. [<Sp. *plata* silver]

platinum blonde 1 A very light, almost white blonde hair color, esp. of a woman. 2 A woman whose hair is of this color.

plat·i·tude (plat′ə·t^yo͞od) *n.* 1 A dull or commonplace statement; an obvious truism. 2 Dullness; triteness. [F, flatness] —**plat′i·tu′di·nous** *adj.* —**plat′i·tu′di·nous·ly** *adv.* —**Syn.** 2 banality, flatness, staleness.

plat·i·tu·di·nize (plat′ə·t^yo͞o′də·nīz) *v.i.* **·nized, ·niz·ing** To utter platitudes.

Pla·ton·ic (plə·ton′ik) *adj.* 1 Of, pertaining to Plato or Platonism. 2 Designating love **(Platonic love)** that is spiritual rather than sensual. Also **pla·ton′ic.** —**Pla·ton′i·cal·ly, pla·ton′i·cal·ly** *adv.*

Pla·to·nism (plā′tə·niz′əm) *n.* 1 The philosophy of Plato and his followers. 2 The doctrine or practice of Platonic love. —**Pla′to·nist** *n.*

pla·toon (plə·to͞on′) *n.* 1 A subdivision of a company, troop, or other military unit consisting of two or more squads and commanded by a lieutenant. 2 Any similar company of people. 3 In football, a group of players specializing in either defense or offense and put into or taken from the game as a unit. —*v.t.* In baseball, etc., to use (one player) alternately with another at the same position. [<F *peloton* ball, group of men]

Platt·deutsch (plät′doich′) *n.* The Low German vernacular of N Germany. [G]

plat·ter (plat′ər) *n.* 1 An oblong shallow dish for serving meat or fish. 2 *Informal* A phonograph record. [<AF *plat* dish]

plat·y·pus (plat′ə·pəs) *n. pl.* **·pus·es, ·pi** (-pī) A small, aquatic, egg-laying monotreme of Australia, with a ducklike bill and webbed forepaws. [<Gk. *platys* flat + *pous* foot]

Platypus

plau·dit (plô′dit) *n. Usu. pl.* An expression of applause or praise. [<L *plaudere* applaud]

plau·si·ble (plô′zə·bəl) *adj.* 1 Seeming likely to be true, but open to doubt. 2 Superficially endeavoring or calculated to gain trust: a *plausible* witness. [< L *plausibilis* deserving applause] **—plau′si·bil′·i·ty, plau′si·ble·ness** *n.* **—plau′si·bly** *adv.*

play (plā) *v.i.* **1** To engage in sport or diversion; amuse oneself. **2** To take part in a game or game of skill or chance; gamble. **3** To act in a way which is not to be taken seriously. **4** To act in a specified manner: to *play* false. **5** To deal carelessly or insincerely: with *with.* **6** To make love sportively. **7** To move quickly or irregularly: lights *playing* along a wall. **8** To discharge or be discharged freely or continuously: a fountain *playing* in the square. **9** To perform on a musical instrument. **10** To give forth musical sounds; sound. **11** To be performed: *Hamlet* is *playing* tonight. **12** To act on a stage; perform. **—***v.t.* **13** To engage in (a game, etc.). **14** To imitate in play: to *play* cowboys. **15** To perform sportively: to *play* a trick. **16** To oppose in a game or contest. **17** To move or employ (a piece, card, etc.) in a game. **18** To employ (someone) in a game as a player. **19** To cause; bring about: to *play* hob. **20** To perform upon (a musical instrument). **21** To perform or produce, as a piece of music, a drama, etc. **22** To act the part of: to *play* the fool. **23** To perform in: to *play* Chicago. **24** To cause to move quickly or irregularly: to *play* lights over a surface. **25** To put into or maintain in action; ply. **26** In games of chance: **a** To bet. **b** To bet on. **—play at 1** To take part in. **2** To do half-heartedly. **—play by ear** To play (a musical instrument or composition) without memorization of or reference to written music. **—play down** To minimize. **—play into the hands of** To act to the advantage of (a rival or opponent). **—play it by ear** *Informal* To handle a situation with no prior planning; improvise. **—play it cool** *Slang* To act unconcerned or nonchalant. **—play off 1** To oppose against one another. **2** To decide (a tie) by playing one more game. **—play on** (or **upon**) **1** To exploit (another's hopes, emotions, etc.). **2** To continue: The band *played on.* **—play up** *Informal* To emphasize. **—play up to** *Informal* To curry favor. **—***n.* **1** Activity for diversion, recreation, or sport. **2** A move or turn in a game. **3** The carrying on of a game or sport. **4** The manner of contending in a game: rough *play.* **5** Joking; humor; jest. **6** A dramatic composition; also, a dramatic performance. **7** Action: sword *play.* **8** Light, quick, fitful movement. **9** Freedom of movement. **10** Free motion of a machine part. **11** Active operation. **12** Gambling. **—make a play for** *Informal* To attempt to win or gain by artful means. [< OE *plegan*]

play·back (plā′bak′) *n.* The reproduction of sound or pictures or both from a disk, tape, or film recording.

play·bill (plā′bil′) *n.* **1** A poster advertising a play. **2** A program giving the cast, etc., of a play.

play·boy (plā′boi′) *n.* *Informal* A man, usu. wealthy, whose main interest is the pursuit of pleasure.

play·er (plā′ər) *n.* **1** A participant or a specialist in a game or sport. **2** An actor or actress. **3** A performer on a musical instrument. **4** A gambler. **5** A mechanical device for playing a musical instrument, esp. a piano.

player piano A piano operated by machinery.

play·fel·low (plā′fel′ō) *n.* A playmate.

play·ful (plā′fəl) *adj.* **1** Lively and frolicsome. **2** Humorous; joking. **—play′ful·ly** *adv.* **—play′ful·ness** *n.*

play·go·er (plā′gō′ər) *n.* A frequenter of the theater.

play·ground (plā′ground′) *n.* An outdoor place used esp. by children for play and often equipped for certain activities, as climbing, ball playing, etc.

play·house (plā′hous′) *n.* **1** A theater. **2** A small house for children to play in.

playing card One of any of various decks of cards used in playing a number of games, esp. the pack divided into four suits (spades, hearts, diamonds, clubs) of 13 cards each.

play·mate (plā′māt′) *n.* A companion in sports, games, or recreation.

play-off (plā′ôf′, -of′) *n.* In sports, a decisive game or contest, esp. after a tie.

play·thing (plā′thing′) *n.* A thing to play with.

play·time (plā′tīm′) *n.* Time allowed for or given up to play or amusement.

play·wright (plā′rīt′) *n.* A writer of plays.

pla·za (plä′zə, plaz′ə) *n.* An open square or market place, esp. in a town. [Sp.]

plea (plē) *n.* **1** An act of pleading, or that which is pleaded; an appeal; entreaty. **2** An excuse; pretext or justification. **3** *Law* **a** An allegation made by either party in a cause. **b** In common-law practice, a defendant's answer of fact to the plaintiff's declaration. [< L *placere* seem right, please]

plea-bar·gain·ing (plē′bär′gən·ing) *n.* A process in which a defendant in a law case arranges, as with a district attorney, to plead guilty to a lesser charge in order to avoid standing trial for a more serious one and the risk of severer punishment.

plead (plēd) *v.* **plead·ed** (*Informal* or *Regional* **pled**), **plead·ing** *v.i.* **1** To make earnest entreaty; implore. **2** *Law* **a** To advocate a case in court. **b** To file a pleading. **—***v.t.* **3** To allege as an excuse or defense: to *plead* insanity. **4** *Law* To discuss or maintain (a case) by argument. [< OF *plaider*] **—plead′er** *n.* **—plead′ing·ly** *adv.* **—Syn. 1** ask, beg, beseech, entreat, supplicate.

plead·ings (plē′dingz) *n.pl.* The formal written statements of the parties to a legal action, in which are set forth the allegations of the plaintiff and the answer of the defendant.

pleas·ant (plez′ənt) *adj.* **1** Giving or promoting pleasure; pleasing; agreeable. **2** Conducive to merriment; gay. [< L *placere* please] **—pleas′ant·ly** *adv.* **—pleas′ant·ness** *n.*

pleas·an·try (plez′ən·trē) *n. pl.* **·tries 1** The spirit of playfulness in conversation. **2** A playful or good-natured remark; joke.

please (plēz) *v.* **pleased, pleas·ing** *v.t.* **1** To give pleasure to; gratify. **2** To be the wish or will of: May it *please* you. **—***v.i.* **3** To give satisfaction or pleasure. **4** To have the will or preference; wish: Go when you *please.* [< L *placere* please]

pleas·ing (plē′zing) *adj.* Affording pleasure or satisfaction. **—pleas′ing·ly** *adv.* **—pleas′ing·ness** *n.*

pleas·ur·a·ble (plezh′ər·ə·bəl) *adj.* Affording gratification; pleasant. **—pleas′ur·a·ble·ness** *n.* **—pleas′ur·a·bly** *adv.*

pleas·ure (plezh′ər) *n.* **1** An agreeable sensation or emotion; enjoyment. **2** Sensual gratification. **3** Amusement in general; diversion. **4** One's preference; choice. [< OF *plaisir* please]

pleat (plēt) *n.* A fold of cloth doubled on itself and pressed or sewn in place. **—***v.t.* To make a pleat or pleats in. [Var. of PLAIT] **—pleat′er** *n.*

Pleated skirt

plebe (plēb) *n.* A member of the lowest class in the U.S. Military Academy at West Point, the Naval Academy at Annapolis, or the Air Force Academy at Colorado Springs. [Short for PLEBEIAN]

ple·be·ian (pli·bē′ən) *n.* **1** One of the common people of ancient Rome. **2** One of the common people. **3** A vulgar, crude person **—***adj.* **1** Pertaining to the common people. **2** Vulgar; crude. [< L] **—ple·be′ian·ism** *n.*

pleb·i·scite (pleb′ə·sīt, -sit) *n.* An expression of the popular will by means of a vote by the whole people, usu. resorted to in important changes, as those dealing with the constitution, sovereignty, etc. [< L *plebs* people + *scitum* decree] **—ple·bis·ci·tar·y** (plə·bis′ə·ter′ē), **pleb′i·scit′ic** *adj.*

plec·trum (plek′trəm) *n. pl.* **·trums** or **·tra** (-trə) A small implement with which the player of a guitar, banjo, etc. plucks the strings; pick. Also **plec′tron** (-tron). [< Gk. *plektron* spur]

pled (pled) *Informal or Regional p.t. & p.p.* of PLEAD.

pledge (plej) *v.t.* **pledged, pledg·ing 1** To give or deposit as security for a loan, etc.; pawn. **2** To bind by or as by a pledge. **3** To promise solemnly, as assistance. **4** To offer (one's word, life, etc.) as a guaranty or forfeit. **5** To drink a toast to. **6** To promise to join (a fraternity). **—***n.* **1** A guaranty for the performance of an act, contract or duty. **2** A solemn promise. **3** The drinking of a health or to good cheer. **4** A pawn of personal property. **5** One who has promised to join a fraternity **6** A token. **—take the**

pledge To make a vow to abstain from alcoholic liquor. [< OF *plege* security] **—pledg′ee, pledg′er** *n.*

pledg·or (plej′ər) *n. Law* A person who formally deposits something as a pledge. Also **pledge′or.**

Plei·a·des (plē′ə·dēz, plī′-) *Gk. Myth.* The seven daughters of Atlas, who were set by Zeus among the stars. *—n. Astron.* A cluster of hundreds of stars in the constellation Taurus, six of which are visible to unaided sight.

Plei·o·cene (plī′ə·sēn) *adj. & n.* PLIOCENE. See GEOLOGY.

Pleis·to·cene (plīs′tə·sēn) *adj. & n.* See GEOLOGY. [< Gk. *pleistos* most + -CENE]

ple·na·ry (plē′nə·rē, plen′ə-) *adj.* **1** Full in all respects or requisites. **2** Fully attended by its qualified members: said of an assembly. [< L *plenus* full] **—ple′na·ri·ly** *adv.* **—ple′na·ri·ness** *n.*

plen·i·po·ten·ti·ar·y (plen′i·pə·ten′shē·er′ē, -shə·rē) *adj.* Possessing or conferring full powers. *—n. pl.* **·ar·ies** A person, as an ambassador, minister, or envoy, invested with full powers by a government. [< L *plenus* full + *potens* powerful]

plen·i·tude (plen′ə·tyo͞od) *n.* The state of being full, complete, or abounding. [< L *plenus* full] **—plen·i·tud·i·nous** (plen′ə·tyo͞o′də·nəs) *adj.*

plen·te·ous (plen′tē·əs) *adj.* **1** Characterized by plenty; amply sufficient. **2** Yielding an abundance. **—plen′te·ous·ly** *adv.* **—plen′te·ous·ness** *n.*

plen·ti·ful (plen′ti·fəl) *adj.* Existing in great quantity; abundant. **—plen′ti·ful·ly** *adv.* **—plen′ti·ful·ness** *n.* **—Syn.** abounding, ample, bounteous, copious, lavish, plenteous.

plen·ty (plen′tē) *n. pl.* **·ties 1** The state of having an abundance. **2** As much as can be required: *plenty* of water. *—adj.* Existing in abundance: plentiful. *—adv. Informal* In a sufficient degree: The house is *plenty* large. [< L *plenus* full]

ple·num (plē′nəm) *n. pl.* **·nums** or **·na** (-nə) **1** Space completely filled with matter. **2** A completely attended meeting, as of both houses of a legislature. [< L *plenus* full]

ple·o·nasm (plē′ə·naz′əm) *n.* **1** The use of needless works; redundancy. **2** An unneeded word or phrase. [< Gk. *pleōn* more] **—ple′o·nast** *n.* **—ple′o·nas′tic** (-nas′tik) *adj.* **—ple′o·nas′ti·cal·ly** *adv.*

pleth·o·ra (pleth′ər·ə) *n.* A state of excessive fullness; superabundance. [< Gk. *plēthein* be full] **—ple·thor·ic** (ple·thôr′ik, -thor′-, pleth′ə·rik) *adj.*

pleu·ra (plo͝or′ə) *n. pl.* **pleu·rae** (plo͝or′ē) or **·ras** A thin, slippery, double membrane that covers each lung and lines the chest cavity. [< Gk. *pleura* side] **—pleu′ral** *adj.*

pleu·ri·sy (plo͝or′ə·sē) *n.* Inflammation of the pleura, commonly attended with fever, pain in the chest, difficult breathing, etc. [< Gk. *pleura* side] **—pleu·rit·ic** (plo͝or·rit′ik) *adj.*

Plex·i·glas (plek′si·glas, -gläs) *n.* A thermoplastic synthetic resin used to make transparent objects: a trade name.

plex·us (plek′səs) *n. pl.* **·us·es** or **·us 1** A network. **2** *Anat.* An interlacement of cordlike structures, as blood vessels or nerves. [L, braid]

pli·a·ble (plī′ə·bəl) *adj.* **1** Easily bent or twisted; flexible. **2** Easily persuaded or controlled. **—pli′a·bil′i·ty, pli′a·ble·ness** *n.* **—pli′a·bly** *adv.*

pli·ant (plī′ənt) *adj.* **1** Capable of being bent or twisted with ease. **2** Easily yielding to influence; tractable. [< OF *plier* to fold] **—pli′an·cy, pli′ant·ness** *n.* **—pli′ant·ly** *adv.* **—Syn. 1** limber, lithe, pliable, supple. **2** adaptable, compliant.

pli·cate (plī′kāt) *adj.* Plaited; folded in plaits like a fan, as a leaf. Also **pli′cat·ed. —pli′cate·ly** *adv.* **—pli·ca′tion, plic·a·ture** (plik′ə·cho͞or) *n.*

pli·ers (plī′ərz) *n.pl. (often construed as sing.)* Small pincers for bending, holding, or cutting. Also **pair of pliers.**

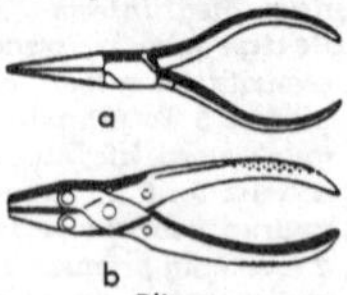

Pliers
a. round-nose.
b. flat-nose.

plight[1] (plīt) *n.* A condition, state, or case, usu. distressed or complicated. [< OF *pleit* a fold]

plight[2] (plīt) *n.* A solemn pledge or promise. *—v.t.* **1** To pledge (one's word, faith, etc.). **2** To promise, as in marriage; betroth. **—plight one's troth 1** To pledge one's solemn word. **2** To promise oneself in marriage. [< OE *pliht* peril] **—plight′er** *n.*

Plim·soll line (plim′sol) A mark painted on the outside of a British vessel's hull to show how deeply she may be loaded; load line. Also **Plimsoll mark.** [< Samuel *Plimsoll,* 1824–98, English legislator]

plinth (plinth) *n. Archit.* The slab, block, or stone on which a column, pedestal, or statue rests. [< Gk. *plinthos* a brick]

Pli·o·cene (plī′ə·sēn) *adj. & n.* See GEOLOGY. [< Gk. *pleiōn* more + -CENE]

plod (plod) *v.* **plod·ded, plod·ding** *v.i.* **1** To walk heavily; trudge. **2** To work in a steady, laborious manner; drudge. *—v.t.* **3** To walk along heavily or laboriously. *—n.* **1** The act of plodding. **2** A heavy step. **3** The sound of a heavy step, as of a horse. [Imit.] **—plod′der** *n.* **—plod′ding·ly** *adv.*

plonk (plonk) *n. & v.* PLUNK.

plop (plop) *v.t. & v.i.* **plopped, plop·ping** To drop with a sound like that of an object striking the water. *—n.* The act or sound of plopping. *—adv.* With the sound of plop. [Imit.]

plo·sive (plō′siv) *Phonet. adj.* Designating a speech sound produced by a total blockage of the breath stream followed by an explosive release, as (p) and (t) before vowels. *—n.* A consonant so produced. [< L *explodere* explode]

plot (plot) *n.* **1** A piece or patch of ground set apart. **2 a** A chart or diagram, as of a building. **b** A surveyor's map. **3** A secret plan; conspiracy. **4** The series of incidents forming the plan of action of a novel, play, etc. *—v.* **plot·ted, plot·ting** *v.t.* **1** To make a map, chart, or plan of. **2** To plan for secretly; conspire. **3** To arrange the plot of (a novel, etc.). **4** To represent or position (something), as on a chart, map, or graph. *—v.i.* **5** To form a plot; conspire. [< OE] **—plot′ter** *n.*

plough (plou) *n. & v.* PLOW.

plov·er (pluv′ər, plō′vər) *n.* Any of various plump, round-headed shore birds with pigeonlike bills and pointed wings. [< AF]

plow (plou) *n.* **1** An implement for cutting, turning over, stirring, or breaking up the soil. **2** Any implement that operates like a plow: a *snowplow. —v.t.* **1** To turn up the surface of (land) with a plow. **2** To make or form (a furrow, ridge, etc.) by means of a plow. **3** To furrow or score the surface of. **4** To dig out or remove with a plow: with *up* or *out.* **5** To move or cut through (water): to *plow* the waves. *—v.i.* **6** To turn up soil with a plow. **7** To undergo plowing, as land. **8** To advance laboriously; plod. **—plow into 1** To start work energetically. **2** To collide with. [< OE *plōh*] **—plow′er** *n.*

plow·man (plou′mən) *n. pl.* **·men** (-mən) **1** One who plows. **2** A farm worker. Also **plough′man.**

plow·share (plou′shâr′) *n.* The cutting blade of a plow. Also **plough′share′.**

ploy (ploi) *n.* A stratagem, as an action or remark, intended to upset or to gain an advantage over someone. [< EMPLOY]

pluck (pluk) *v.t.* **1** To pull out or off; pick: to *pluck* a flower. **2** To pull with force; snatch: with *off, away,* etc. **3** To pull out the feathers, hair, etc., of. **4** To pull and release suddenly. **5** To cause the strings of (a musical instrument) to sound by such action. **6** *Slang* To rob; swindle. *—v.i.* **7** To give a sudden pull; tug: with *at.* **—pluck up** To rouse or summon (one's courage). *—n.* **1** Confidence and spirit in the face of difficulty or danger. **2** A sudden pull; twitch. **3** The act of plucking or state of being plucked. [< OE *pluccian*] **—pluck′er** *n.*

pluck·y (pluk′ē) *adj.* **pluck·i·er, pluck·i·est** Showing bravery; courageous. **—pluck′i·ly** *adv.* **—pluck′i·ness** *n.* **—Syn.** brave, fearless, undaunted, valiant.

plug (plug) *n.* **1** Anything, as a piece of wood or a cork, used to stop a hole. **2** A spark plug. **3** A fireplug. **4** *Electr.* A device for inserting in an outlet, etc., so as to complete a circuit or make contact. **5** A flat cake of pressed or twisted tobacco. **6** Any worn-out or useless thing, esp. an old horse. **7** *Slang* A man's high silk hat: also **plug hat. 8** *Informal* Mention of a product, song, etc., as on a radio or television program; an advertisement. *—v.* **plugged, plug·ging** *v.t.* **1** To stop or close, as a hole, by inserting a plug:

often with *up.* **2** To insert as a plug. **3** *Slang* To shoot a bullet into. **4** *Slang* To advertise frequently or insistently. —*v.i.* **5** *Informal* To work doggedly; persevere. **6** To become stopped or closed: with *up.* —**plug in** To insert the plug of (a lamp, etc.) in an electric outlet. [< MDu. *plugge*]

plug-ug·ly (plug′ug′lē) *n. pl.* **·lies** *Slang* A ruffian.

plum (plum) *n.* **1** The edible, juicy, smooth-skinned fruit of any one of various trees. **2** The tree. **3** A raisin when used in cooking. **4** A choice piece or portion. **5** A desirable post or appointment. **6** A dividend higher than expected. **7** Any of various shades of dull reddish purple or purplish red. —*adj.* Dull reddish purple. [< LL *pruna*]

plum·age (plōō′mij) *n.* The feathers that cover a bird. [< F *plume* feather]

plumb (plum) *n.* **1** A weight hung on a line used to find the exact perpendicular: also **plumb bob. 2** A nautical sounding lead, a sinker on a fishing line, etc. —**off** (or **out of**) **plumb** Not exactly vertical. —*adj.* **1** Vertical or perpendicular. **2** *Informal* Sheer; complete. —*adv.* **1** In a line perpendicular to the plane of the horizon. **2** *Informal* With exactness; correctly. —*v.t.* **1** To test with a plumb. **2** To make vertical; straighten. **3** To learn the facts about; solve. [< L *plumbum* lead]

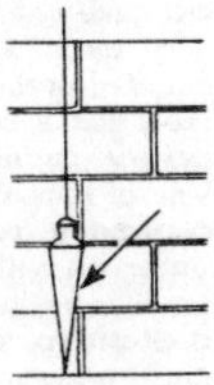

Plumb

plumb·er (plum′ər) *n.* One whose work is plumbing.

plumb·ing (plum′ing) *n.* **1** The art or trade of installing and maintaining tanks, pipes, etc., as for water, gas and sewage. **2** A system of pipes, ducts, etc. **3** The act of sounding for depth, etc., with a plumb line.

plumb line A cord by which a plumb is suspended.

plume (plōōm) *n.* **1** A feather, esp. when long and ornamental. **2** A large feather, tuft of feathers, or flowing tuft of hair, worn as an ornament, esp. on a helmet. **3** Something that resembles this: a *plume* of smoke. **4** A prize. —*v.t.* **plumed, plum·ing 1** To adorn, dress, or furnish with or as with plumes. **2** To smooth or dress (itself or its feathers); preen. —**plume oneself on** (or **upon**) To congratulate oneself on; be proud of. [< L *pluma* small soft feather]

plum·met (plum′it) *n.* PLUMB (def. 1). —*v.i.* To drop straight down; plunge. [< OF *plommet,* dim. of *plom* lead]

plu·mose (plōō′mōs) *adj.* Bearing or resembling feathers. [< L *pluma* feather] —**plu·mos·i·ty** (plōō·mos′ə·tē) *n.*

plump[1] (plump) *adj.* **1** Swelled out or enlarged. **2** Somewhat fat; pudgy. —*v.t. & v.i.* To make or become plump: often with *up* or *out.* [< MDu. *plomp*] —**plump′ness** *n.*

plump[2] (plump) *v.i.* **1** To fall suddenly or heavily. —*v.t.* **2** To drop or throw down heavily or all at once. —**plump for 1** To give one's complete support to. **2** To vote for. —*n.* **1** The act of plumping or falling. **2** The sound made by the impact of a falling object. —*adj.* Blunt; downright. —*adv.* **1** With a sudden impact. **2** Straight down. **3** Directly; bluntly. [< MDu. *plompen*] —**plump′er** *n.* —**plump′ly** *adv.*

plum·y (plōō′mē) *adj.* **plum·i·er, plum·i·est 1** Covered with feathers. **2** Adorned with plumes. **3** Feathery.

plun·der (plun′dər) *v.t.* **1** To rob of goods or property by open violence, as in war. **2** To despoil by robbery or fraud. **3** To take as plunder. —*v.i.* **4** To take plunder; steal. —*n.* **1** That which is taken by plundering; booty. **2** The act of plundering or robbing. **3** *Informal* Personal belongings or goods. **4** Political booty. [< G *plündern*] —**plun′der·age, plun′der·er** *n.* —**plun′der·ous** *adj.*

plunge (plunj) *v.* **plunged, plung·ing** *v.t.* **1** To thrust or force suddenly into a penetrable substance. **2** To force into some condition or state: to *plunge* a nation into debt. —*v.i.* **3** To dive, jump, or fall into a fluid, chasm, etc. **4** To move suddenly or with a rush. **5** To move violently forward and downward, as a horse or ship. **6** To descend abruptly or steeply. **7** *Informal* To gamble or speculate heavily and recklessly. —*n.* **1** The act of plunging. **2** A sudden and violent motion, as of a breaking wave. **3** An exceptionally heavy bet or speculation. —**take the (a) plunge** To begin an uncertain endeavor or enterprise. [< L *plumbum* lead]

plung·er (plun′jər) *n.* **1** One who or that which plunges. **2** A heavy or reckless speculator. **3** *Mech.* A part that has a plunging motion. **4** A cuplike device made of rubber and attached to a stick, used to open clogged drains.

plunk (plungk) *Informal v.t.* **1** To pluck, as a banjo or its strings; strum. **2** To place or throw heavily and suddenly: with *down.* —*v.i.* **3** To emit a twanging sound. **4** To fall heavily or suddenly; plump. —*n.* A heavy blow. [Imit.]

plu·per·fect (plōō·pûr′fikt) *adj. & n.* PAST PERFECT. [Short for L *plus quam perfectum* more than perfect]

plu·ral (plŏŏr′əl) *adj.* **1** Containing, consisting of, or designating more than one. **2** *Gram.* Denoting words or forms that indicate more than one. —*n. Gram.* **1** The plural number. **2** A plural form of a word. [< L *pluralis* < *plus* more] —**plu′ral·ly** *adv.*

plu·ral·ism (plŏŏr′əl·iz·əm) *n.* **1** *Philos.* The doctrine that there is a plurality of ultimate substances, as spirit and matter. **2** The existence within a society of diverse groups, as in religion, race, or ethnic origin, which contribute to the cultural matrix of the society while retaining their distinctive characters; also, a doctrine advocating this. —**plu′ral·ist** *adj., n.* —**plu·ral·is·tic** (plŏŏ′rəl·is′tik) *adj.*

plu·ral·i·ty (plōō·ral′ə·tē) *n. pl.* **·ties 1** The state of being plural. **2** The greater number; majority. **3** In politics: **a** The excess of the highest number of votes cast for any one candidate over the next highest number. **b** In an election involving more than two candidates, the number of votes cast for any one that exceeds that for any of the others, but does not exceed half of the total number of votes cast.

plu·ral·ize (plŏŏr′əl·īz) *v.t.* **·ized, ·iz·ing 1** To make plural. **2** To express in the plural.

plus (plus) *prep.* **1** Added to or to be added to: Three *plus* two equals five. **2** Increased by: salary *plus* commission. —*adj.* **1** Being or indicating more than zero; positive. **2** Extra; supplemental: *plus* value. **3** *Informal* Denoting a value higher than ordinary in a specified grade: B *plus.* —*n. pl.* **plus·es 1** The plus sign. **2** An addition; an extra quantity. **3** A positive quantity. **4** *Informal* Something considered advantageous or desirable. [L, more]

plus fours Knickers, cut very full and four inches longer below the knees than ordinary knickers.

plush (plush) *n.* A fabric having a pile deeper than that of velvet. —*adj.* **1** Of or made of plush. **2** *Slang* Luxurious: a *plush* apartment house. [< L *pilus* hair] —**plush′i·ness** *n.* —**plush′y** *adj.* **(·i·er, ·i·est)**

plus sign The symbol (+) signifying addition or a positive quantity.

Plu·to (plōō′tō) *Gk. & Rom. Myth.* The god of the dead. —*n.* The planet of the solar system furthest from the sun. • See PLANET. —**Plu·to·ni·an** (plōō·tō′nē·ən), **Plu·ton′ic** *adj.*

plu·toc·ra·cy (plōō·tok′rə·sē) *n. pl.* **·cies 1** A class that controls the government by its wealth. **2** Government by the wealthy. **3** A state or nation so governed. [< Gk *ploutos* wealth + *kratein* rule]

plu·to·crat (plōō′tə·krat) *n.* **1** One who exercises power by virtue of his wealth. **2** Any very wealthy person. —**plu′to·crat′ic** or **·i·cal** *adj.* —**plu′to·crat′i·cal·ly** *adv.*

plu·ton·ic (plōō·ton′ik) *adj. Geol.* Deeply subterranean in position or origin. [< PLUTO]

plu·to·ni·um (plōō·tō′nē·əm) *n.* A radioactive metallic element (symbol Pu), used as a nuclear fuel. [< PLUTO (the planet)]

plu·vi·al (plōō′vē·əl) *adj.* **1** Pertaining to rain; rainy. **2** Arising from the action of rain. [< L *pluvia* rain]

ply[1] (plī) *v.* **plied, ply·ing** *v.t.* To bend, mold, or shape. —*n. pl.* **plies 1** A web, layer, fold, or thickness, as in a cloth, etc. **2** A strand, turn, or twist of rope, yarn, thread, etc. **3** A bent or bias; inclination. —*adj.* Having (a specified number of) strands, etc.: used in combination: *two-ply.* [< L *plicare* to fold]

ply[2] (plī) *v.* **plied, ply·ing** *v.t.* **1** To use in working, fighting, etc. **2** To work at: to *ply* a trade. **3** To work steadily, as with a tool. **4** To keep furnishing: to *ply* a child with sweets. **5** To ask urgently; importune: to *ply* a witness with questions. **6** To strike persistently. **7** To traverse regularly: ferryboats that *ply* the river. —*v.i.* **8** To work steadily; be occupied. 9 To make regular trips: usu. with *between.* [< APPLY] **—ply′er** *n.* **—Syn.** 1 employ, wield. 2 follow, practice. 5 urge.

Plym·outh Rock (plim′əth) 1 The rock at Plymouth, Massachusetts, on which the Pilgrim Fathers are said to have landed in 1620. 2 One of a breed of large domestic fowls.

ply·wood (plī′wŏŏd′) *n.* A material composed of a number of thin sheets of wood glued together with the grains of adjacent sheets at right angles.

PM, P.M. Postmaster; Provost Marshal.

P.M. Pacific Mail; Past Master; Paymaster; Police Magistrate; Prime Minister.

P.M., p.m. afternoon (L *post meridiem*); after death (L *post mortem*).

Pm prometheum.

pneu·mat·ic (nʸōō·mat′ik) *adj.* 1 Describing machines that make use of compressed air. 2 Containing air or gas. 3 Pertaining to pneumatics. Also **pneu·mat′i·cal.** —*n.* A tire containing air. [< Gk. *pneuma* breath] **—pneu·mat′i·cal·ly** *adv.*

pneu·ma·tics (nʸōō·mat′iks) *n.pl. (construed as sing.)* The branch of physics that deals with the properties, such as pressure, elasticity, and density, of air and other gases.

pneumo- *combining form* Lung; relating to the lungs: *pneumothorax.* Also **pneum-.** [< Gk. *pneumon* lung]

pneu·mo·coc·cus (nʸōō′mə·kok′əs) *n. pl.* **·coc·ci** (-kok′·sī) Any of a group of bacteria that cause a common type of pneumonia and some other diseases. [< Gk. *pneuma* breath + COCCUS] **—pneu′mo·coc′cal, pneu′mo·coc′cic** (-kok′sik) **pneu′mo·coc′cous** *adj.*

pneu·mo·con·i·o·sis (nʸōō′mō·kon′ē·ō′sis) *n.* Any of various lung disorders, such as silicosis or black lung disease, resulting from the inhalation of dust or other minute particles. Also **pneu′mo·no·con′i·o′sis** (nʸōō′mə·nō-). [< Gk. *pneuma* breath + *konia* dust + -OSIS]

pneu·mon·ia (nʸōō·mōn′yə) *n.* Acute inflammation of the lungs characterized by accumulation of fluid in the alveoli and difficult breathing. [< Gk. *pneumon* lung] — **pneu·mon·ic** (nʸōō·mon′ik) *adj.*

pneu·mo·tho·rax (nʸōō′mō·thôr′aks, -thō′raks) *n.* An accumulation of air or gas within the pleural cavity, causing the lung to collapse, as from injury or disease, or by injection **(artificial pneumothorax)** in the treatment of tuberculosis. [< PNEUMO- + THORAX]

P.O., p.o. personnel officer; petty officer; postal order; post office.

Po polonium.

poach[1] (pōch) *v.t.* To cook (eggs without their shells, fish, etc.) in boiling water, milk, or other liquid. [< OF *pochier* put in a pocket]

poach[2] (pōch) *v.i.* 1 To trespass on another's property, etc., esp. for the purpose of taking game or fish. 2 To take game or fish unlawfully. 3 To become soft and muddy by being trampled: said of land. —*v.t.* 4 To trespass on. 5 To take (game or fish) unlawfully. 6 To make muddy by trampling. [< OF *pochier* thrust one's fingers into] **—poach′er** *n.*

pock (pok) *n.* 1 A pustule in an eruptive disease, as in smallpox. 2 A pockmark. [< OE *poc*]

pock·et (pok′it) *n.* 1 A small bag or pouch; esp. one stitched to a garment. 2 A cavity, opening, or receptacle. 3 *Mining* a A cavity containing gold or other ore. b A small deposit of ore in one spot. 4 One of the pouches in a billiard or pool table. 5 An air pocket. **—in one's pocket** Under one's influence or control. **—line one's pockets** To acquire a lot of money. —*adj.* 1 Small enough to fit into a pocket. 2 Pertaining to, for, or carried in a pocket. —*v.t.* 1 To put into or confine in a pocket. 2 To appropriate as one's own, esp. dishonestly. 3 To enclose as if in a pocket. 4 To accept or endure, as an insult. 5 To conceal or suppress: *Pocket* your pride. [< OF *poque, poche* bag, pouch] **—pock′et·er** *n.* **—Syn.** *v.* 2 embezzle, purloin, steal, take. 5 hide, swallow.

pock·et·book (pok′it·bŏŏk′) *n.* 1 A woman's purse or handbag. 2 A notebook for the pocket. 3 One's financial resources.

pock·et·ful (pok′it·fŏŏl′) *n. pl.* **·fuls** As much as a pocket will hold.

pock·et·knife (pok′it·nīf′) *n. pl.* **·knives** (-nīvz) A knife having one or more blades, tools, etc., which fold into the handle.

Pocketknife

pocket money Money for small expenses.

pocket veto In the U.S., the act of a chief executive who does not sign a bill passed by Congress within ten days of the latter's adjournment and thus simply retains ("pockets") it and achieves an indirect veto.

pock·mark (pok′märk′) *n.* A pit or scar left on the skin by smallpox or similar diseases. **—pock′marked′** *adj.*

po·co (pō′kō) *adv. Music* Slightly. [Ital.]

pod (pod) *n.* 1 A dehiscent seed vessel containing one or more seeds. 2 A housing for an aircraft part that is mounted outboard. —*v.i.* **pod·ded, pod·ding** 1 To fill out like a pod. 2 To produce pods. [?]

podg·y (poj′ē) *adj.* **podg·i·er, podg·i·est** Dumpy and fat. [Var. of PUDGY] **—podg′i·ness** *n.*

po·di·a·try (pə·dī′ə·trē, pō-) *n.* The branch of medicine concerned with disorders of the feet. [< Gk. *pous, podos* foot + *iatros* healer] **—po·di′a·trist** *n.*

po·di·um (pō′dē·əm) *n. pl.* **·di·ums** or **·di·a** (-dē·ə) 1 A raised platform, esp. one for the conductor of an orchestra. 2 *Zool.* A foot, or any footlike structure. [< Gk. *podion,* dim. of *pous, podos* foot]

Po·dunk (pō′dungk) *n. Informal* Any small town regarded as dull and nonprogressive. [?< *Podunk,* Massachusetts]

po·em (pō′əm) *n.* 1 A composition in verse, either in meter or in free verse, characterized by the imaginative treatment of experience, usu. by the use of language more intensive than ordinary speech, and typically presented with the initial letter of each line capitalized. 2 Any composition in verse. 3 Any composition characterized by beauty of language or thought: a prose *poem.* 4 Any beautiful object or experience. [< Gk. *poiēma,* lit., anything made]

po·e·sy (pō′ə·sē, -zē) *n. pl.* **·sies** 1 *Archaic* Poetry taken collectively. 2 *Obs.* A poem. [< Gk. *poiēsis* a making]

po·et (pō′it) *n.* 1 One who writes poems. 2 One esp. endowed with imagination and creativity. [< Gk. *poiētēs*]

po·et·as·ter (pō′it·as′tər) *n.* An inferior poet. [< POET + -ASTER]

po·et·ic (pō·et′ik) *adj.* 1 Of or pertaining to poets or poems. 2 Characteristic of or suitable for poetry: *poetic* language. 3 Highly imaginative: a *poetic* nature. 4 Made up of poems. Also **po·et′i·cal. —po·et′i·cal·ly** *adv.*

poetic justice An outcome in which a person receives what he deserves in a way that is often ironically appropriate.

po·et·ics (pō·et′iks) *n.pl. (construed as sing.)* 1 The principles and nature of poetry. 2 A treatise on poetry.

poet laureate *pl.* **poets laureate** 1 The poet officially invested with the title of laureate by the crown of England. 2 A poet acclaimed as the most eminent of a group, in a locality, etc.

po·et·ry (pō′ə·trē, pō′it·rē) *n.* 1 The writings of a poet; poems. 2 The art of writing poems. 3 Anything resembling poetry in spirit or feeling: Dancing is the *poetry* of motion. 4 Poetic works in general.

po·gey (pō′gē) *n. Can. Slang* 1 Money, food, clothing, and other forms of relief given by the government to people in need. 2 An office providing such relief. **—on the pogey** On relief. Also **po′gy.** [?]

po·go stick (pō′gō) A stiltlike toy with a spring at the base, used to propel oneself in a series of hops.

po·grom (pō′grəm, pō·grom′) *n.* An officially instigated massacre, esp. one directed against Jews. [Russ., destruction]

poi (poi, pō′ē) *n.* A native Hawaiian food made from the ground root of the taro.

poign·ant (poin′yənt, poi′nənt) *adj.* 1 Severely painful or acute to the feelings: *poignant* grief. 2 Keenly piercing: *poignant wit.* 3 Sharp or stimulating to the taste; pungent. [< L *pungere* to prick] **—poign′an·cy** *n.* **—poign′ant·ly** *adv.* **—Syn.** 1 agonizing, excruciating, piercing, sharp.

poi·lu (pwa·lü′) *adj.* Hairy; bearded. —*n.* In World War I, a French soldier. [F]

poin·ci·a·na (poin′sē·ā′nə, -an′ə) *n.* A tropical tree with bright orange and scarlet flowers and large flat pods. [< M. de *Poinci,* a 17th c. governor of French West Indies]

poin·set·ti·a (poin·set′ē·ə) *n.* A shrub of varying size with small yellow flowers surrounded by large vermilion bracts. [< J. R. *Poinsett,* 1779–1851, U.S. diplomat]

Poinsettia

point (point) *n.* **1** The sharp end of a thing, esp. of anything that tapers. **2** A tool or instrument having a sharp, tapering end. **3** A tapering tract of land extending into water. **4** A distinguishing attribute: Her smile is her best *point.* **5** A physical attribute of an animal, used in judging. **6** The main idea under consideration: the *point* of a story. **7** A particular place or position. **8** A position considered as one of a series: to gain a *point.* **9** A precise degree or grade attained, as in a game. **10** A particular juncture in the course of events: at one *point* during the day. **11** A detail or step: Let us go over this *point* by *point.* **12** Purpose; object: There's no *point* in waiting. **13** For students, a unit of credit. **14** The moment when something is about to take place: He is on the *point* of leaving. **15** NEEDLEPOINT (def. 3). **16** A punctuation mark, esp. a period. **17** *Phonet.* A diacritical mark used to indicate a vowel in a Semitic language. **18** A decimal point. **19** A geometric entity having position as its only inherent property. **20** The attitude assumed by a hunting dog when it finds game. **21** In fencing, a thrust. **22** *Printing* A unit measure for type, about 1/72 in.: 8-*point* type. **23** One of the 32 divisions of a compass card. **24** A unit of variation in the price of shares, stocks, etc. **25** A fixed place from which distance is reckoned. **26** *Electr.* Any of a set of contacts controlling current flow in a circuit. **27** *Brit. (Usu. pl.)* A tapering section of a railroad track switch. —**at** (or **on**) **the point of** On the verge of. —**beside the point** Irrelevant. —**in point** Pertinent. —**in point of** In the matter of; as regards. —**make a point of** To treat as vital or essential. —**see the point** To understand the meaning of a story, joke, etc. —**to the point** Relevant. —*v.t.* **1** To direct or aim, as a finger or weapon. **2** To give force or point to, as a meaning or remark. **3** To shape or sharpen to a point. **4** To punctuate. **5** To mark with points, as decimal fractions: with *off.* **6** In hunting, to indicate the presence of (game) by standing rigid: said of dogs. —*v.i.* **7** To call attention or indicate direction by extending the finger: usu. with *at* or *to.* **8** To have a specified direction: with *to* or *toward.* **9** To point game. —**point out** To call attention to. [< L *punctus,* pp. of *pungere* to prick]

point·blank (point′blangk′) *adj.* **1** Aimed directly at the mark. **2** Direct; plain: a *pointblank* question. —*n.* A shot with direct aim. —*adv.* **1** In a horizontal line. **2** Directly; plainly: to object *pointblank.*

point·ed (poin′tid) *adj.* **1** Having or coming to a point. **2** Being to the point; apt; acute. **3** Intended for a particular person or group: a *pointed* remark. —**point′ed·ly** *adv.* —**point′ed·ness** *n.*

point·er (poin′tər) *n.* **1** One who or that which points. **2** An index or hand, as on a clock or scale. **3** A long tapering rod used in classrooms to point out things on wall maps, etc. **4** One of a breed of dogs trained to scent and point out game. **5** A useful suggestion or bit of information.

point lace Lace made entirely with a needle.

point·less (point′lis) *adj.* **1** Without a point; blunt. **2** Having no significance or force: a *pointless* remark. —**point′less·ly** *adv.* —**point′less·ness** *n.* —**Syn. 1** dull. **2** inane, insipid, silly, stupid.

point of honor Something that vitally affects one's honor.

point of order In parliamentary language, a question of procedure under the rules.

point of view **1** The position from which something is evaluated, considered, etc. **2** An attitude or opinion.

poise (poiz) *v.* **poised, pois·ing** *v.t.* **1** To bring into or hold in balance. **2** To hold; support, as in readiness. —*v.i.* **3** To be balanced or suspended; hover. —*n.* **1** Balance; equilibrium. **2** Equanimity and dignity of manner; composure. **3** Suspense; indecision. [< L *pensare,* intens. of *pendere* weigh]

poi·son (poi′zən) *n.* **1** A substance that produces illness or death if swallowed, inhaled, or otherwise introduced into a living organism. **2** Anything that tends to destroy or corrupt. —*v.t.* **1** To kill or injure with poison. **2** To put poison into or on. **3** To affect harmfully. —*adj.* Killing; venomous. [< L *potio* a drink, poisonous draft] —**poi′son·er** *n.*

poison ivy A small shrub or vine of North America having three leaflets and small, green flowers and causing a skin rash on contact.

poison oak **1** A low, nonclimbing shrub related to poison ivy and having similar effects. **2** POISON IVY.

poi·son·ous (poi′zən·əs) *adj.* **1** Containing a poison. **2** Having the effect of a poison; toxic. —**poi′son·ous·ly** *adv.* —**poi′son·ous·ness** *n.*

poison sumac A tall shrub of E North America, related to poison ivy and poisonous to taste or touch.

poke[1] (pōk) *v.* **poked, pok·ing** *v.t.* **1** To push or prod. **2** To make by thrusting: to *poke* a hole. **3** To thrust in, out, through, from, etc.: to *poke* one's head from a window. **4** To stir (a fire, etc.) —*v.i.* **5** To make thrusts. **6** To intrude or meddle. **7** To look curiously; pry. **8** To proceed slowly; dawdle; putter. —**poke one's nose into** To meddle in. —**poke fun at** To ridicule. —*n.* **1** A push; prod. **2** One who dawdles. **3** *Informal* A punch. [ME *poken*]

poke[2] (pōk) *n. Regional* **1** A pocket. **2** A small bag or sack. [< OF *poche* pocket]

poke[3] (pōk) *n.* A large bonnet with projecting front. Also **poke bonnet.** [< POKE[1]]

poke·ber·ry (pōk′ber′ē) *n. pl.* **·ries** **1** A berry of the pokeweed. **2** The plant. [< Algon.]

pok·er[1] (pō′kər) *n.* **1** One who or that which pokes. **2** An iron rod for poking a fire.

pok·er[2] (pō′kər) *n.* Any of several games of cards in which the players bet on the value of the cards dealt to them. [?]

poker face *Informal* A face that reveals no thoughts or feelings. [From the inscrutable face maintained by poker players] —**po·ker-faced** (pō′kər·fāst′) *adj.*

poke·weed (pōk′wēd′) *n.* A stout perennial herb of North America having dark purple berries and poisonous roots. Also **poke, poke′root′** (-rōōt′, -rŏŏt′). [< Algon.]

pok·y (pō′kē) *adj.* **pok·i·er, pok·i·est** **1** Lacking spirit. **2** Shabby. **3** Cramped; stuffy. Also **poke′y.**

pol (pol) *n. Slang* A politician.

Pol. Poland; Polish.

Po·land (pō′lənd) *n.* A republic of CEN. Europe, 120,359 square miles, cap. Warsaw.

po·lar (pō′lər) *adj.* **1** Of, pertaining to, coming from or found near the North or South Pole. **2** Of, pertaining to, or proceeding from a pole or poles, as of a sphere, magnet, etc. **3** Exhibiting polarity. **4** Opposite, as in character, direction, etc. [< L *polus* pole]

polar bear A large, white bear of Arctic coasts and ice floes.

Po·lar·is (pō·lar′is) *n.* **1** The star in the northern sky that is in line with the earth's axis and hence appears to maintain a fixed position as the earth rotates. **2** A U.S. missile designed to be launched from a submerged submarine. [L]

po·lar·i·ty (pō·lar′ə·tē) *n.* **1** The quality or property of having paired but opposed tendencies, as positive and negative. **2** Either of such an opposed pair: a negative *polarity.* **3** *Physics* The property of a body that exhibits a preferred alignment with respect to a field of force.

po·lar·i·za·tion (pō′lər·ə·zā′shən, -ī·zā′-) *n.* 1 The act of polarizing or the property of being polarized. 2 *Physics* A condition of radiation, esp. light or other electromagnetic radiation, in which the direction of any field or disturbance associated with the radiation and transverse to its direction of propagation is not random. 3 *Electr.* A change in the potential of the electrode of a cell due to the accumulation of reaction products. 4 A separation into opposing factions.

po·lar·ize (pō′lə·rīz) *v.* **·ized, ·iz·ing** *v.t.* 1 To cause to acquire polarization or polarity. 2 To separate into opposing factions. —*v.i.* 3 To become polarized. *Brit. sp.* **po′lar·ise.** —**po′lar·iz′er** *n.*

pole[1] (pōl) *n.* 1 Either of the points in which a diameter of a sphere intersects the surface. 2 One of two points where the axis of rotation, as of the earth, meets the surface. 3 *Physics* One of the two points at which opposite physical qualities are concentrated; esp. a point of maximum electric or magnetic force. 4 Either of the ends of any axis. [< Gk. *polos* pivot, pole]

pole[2] (pōl) *n.* 1 A long slender piece of wood or metal: a *flagpole.* 2 In linear and surface measure, a rod or a square rod. —*v.* **poled, pol·ing** *v.t.* To propel, as a boat, with a pole. [< L *palus* stake]

Pole (pōl) *n.* A citizen or native of Poland.

pole·ax (pōl′aks′) *n.* A medieval battleaxe. —*v.t.* To strike or fell with a poleax. Also **pole′axe′.** [< ME *pol* head + AX]

pole·cat (pōl′kat′) *n.* 1 A small, weasellike European carnivore. 2 A skunk. [< F *poule* pullet + CAT]

po·lem·ic (pō·lem′ik) *adj.* Pertaining to controversy. Also **po·lem′i·cal.** —*n.* 1 A controversy. 2 One who engages in controversy. [< Gk. *polemos* war] —**Syn.** *adj.* disputatious. *n.* 1 argument, debate, dispute.

po·lem·ics (pō·lem′iks) *n.pl. (construed as sing.)* 1 The use of aggressive argument to refute errors of doctrine, esp. in theology. 2 A controversy.

pole·star (pōl′stär) *n.* 1 POLARIS. 2 That which governs, guides, or directs.

pole vault A vault for height in which a long, flexible pole is used to help propel one over a crossbar, often a competitive field event. —**pole′-vault′** *v.t.* & *v.i.* —**pole′-vault′er** *n.*

po·lice (pə·lēs′) *n.* 1 A body of persons organized to maintain order and enforce law. 2 The whole system of the department of government that maintains and enforces law and order. 3 The regulation of safety, conduct, and public order in a community. 4 The keeping clean of a camp or garrison. —*v.t.* **·liced, ·lic·ing** 1 To protect, regulate, or maintain order with or as with police. 2 To make clean or orderly, as a military camp. [< Gk. *politeia* polity]

police dog 1 GERMAN SHEPHERD. 2 Any dog trained to assist policemen.

po·lice·man (pə·lēs′mən) *n. pl.* **·men** (-mən) A member of a police force. —**po·lice′wom·an** (*pl.* **·wom·en**) *n. Fem.*

police state A country rigidly supervised by a national police, often working secretly.

pol·i·cy[1] (pol′ə·sē) *n. pl.* **·cies** 1 Prudence or sagacity in the conduct of affairs. 2 A course of administrative action. 3 Any system of management. [< Gk. *politeia*]

pol·i·cy[2] (pol′ə·sē) *n. pl.* **·cies** A written contract of insurance. [< Ital. *polizza*]

policy game NUMBERS POOL. Also **policy racket.**

pol·i·cy·hol·der (pol′ə·sē·hōl′dər) *n.* One who holds a policy of insurance.

pol·i·cy·mak·er (pol′ə·sē·mā′kər) *n.* A person who makes decisions and controls policy at a high level, esp. in a government. —**pol′i·cy·mak′ing** *n.*

po·li·o (pō′lē·ō) *n. Informal* POLIOMYELITIS.

pol·i·o·my·e·li·tis (pol′ē·ō·mī′ə·lī′tis, pō′lē-) *n.* An acute viral disease affecting the central nervous system and often followed by paralysis and atrophy of muscles. [< Gk. *polios* gray + *myelos* marrow + -ITIS]

pol·ish (pol′ish) *n.* 1 Smoothness or glossiness of surface. 2 A substance used to produce such a surface. 3 Refinement of manner or style. 4 The process of polishing. —*v.t.* 1 To make smooth or lustrous. 2 To make refined or elegant. —*v.i.* 3 To take a gloss; shine. 4 To become elegant or refined. —**polish off** *Informal* 1 To do or finish quickly. 2 To dispose of. —**polish up** *Informal* To improve. [< L *polire* make smooth] —**pol′ish·er** *n.*

Po·lish (pō′lish) *n.* The language of Poland. —*adj.* Of or pertaining to Poland, its people, or their language.

Po·lit·bu·ro (po′lit·byŏŏr′ō) *n.* The leading policy-forming committee of the Communist party in the U.S.S.R. until 1952, when it was replaced by the Presidium.

po·lite (pə·līt′) *adj.* 1 Exhibiting in manner or speech a considerate regard for others; courteous. 2 Elegant; refined: *polite* society. [< L *politus,* pp. of *polire* to polish] —**po·lite′ly** *adv.* —**po·lite′ness** *n.* —**Syn.** 1 civil, courtly, gracious, well-mannered. 2 cultivated, genteel, polished.

po·li·tesse (pô·lē·tes′) *n.* Politeness; civility. [F]

pol·i·tic (pol′ə·tik) *adj.* 1 Sagacious and wary in planning; artful. 2 Wisely expedient. 3 Pertaining to the state or its government; political. [< Gk. *politikos* civic] —**pol′i·tic·ly** *adv.*

po·lit·i·cal (pə·lit′i·kəl) *adj.* 1 Concerned in the administration of government. 2 Belonging to the science of government. 3 Having an organized system of government. 4 Pertaining to or connected with a party or parties seeking to control government. —**po·lit′i·cal·ly** *adv.*

political science The science of the form and principles of government.

pol·i·ti·cian (pol′ə·tish′ən) *n.* 1 One engaged in politics. 2 One who engages in politics for personal or partisan aims. 3 *Brit.* One skilled in the science of government; a statesman. 4 One holding a political position.

po·lit·i·cize (pə·lit′ə·sīz′) *v.t.* **·cized, ·ciz·ing** 1 To make politically active or aware. 2 To make into a political issue. Also **po·lit′i·cal·ize′** (-kəl·īz′). —**po·lit′i·ci·za′tion** *n.*

pol·i·tick·ing (pol′ə·tik·ing) *n.* Involvement in political activity. —**pol′i·tick·er** *n.*

po·lit·i·co (pə·lit′i·kō) *n. pl.* **·cos** A politician. [< Sp. *político*]

pol·i·tics (pol′ə·tiks) *n. (construed as sing. or pl.)* 1 The science of government. 2 The administration of political affairs. 3 Political sentiments or beliefs. 4 Political methods or procedures. 5 Participation in political affairs. —**play politics** To scheme for an advantage.

pol·i·ty (pol′ə·tē) *n. pl.* **·ties** 1 The form or method of government of a nation, state, etc. 2 Any community living under some definite form of government. [< OF *politie*]

pol·ka (pōl′kə, pō′-) *n.* 1 A lively round dance. 2 Music for such a dance. —*v.i.* **·kaed, ·ka·ing** To dance the polka. [< Czech *pulka* half (step)]

polka dot 1 One of a series of spots of various sizes and spacing on a textile fabric. 2 A pattern made up of such spots. —**pol′ka-dot′, -dot′ted** *adj.*

poll (pōl) *n.* 1 The head, esp. the top or back of the head. 2 A list of persons, esp. voters. 3 The voting at an election. 4 The number of votes thus cast. 5 *pl.* The place where voting is done and votes are counted. 6 A survey of public opinion on a given subject. —*v.t.* 1 To receive (a specified number of votes). 2 To register for taxation or voting. 3 To cast at the polls. 4 To interview in a poll. 5 To cut off or trim, as hair, horns, etc. —*v.i.* 6 To vote at the polls. [< MDu. *polle* top of the head] —**poll′er** *n.*

pol·len (pol′ən) *n.* The fine yellowish powder borne by the anthers of a flower and consisting of male sex cells. [< L, fine flour]

pol·li·nate (pol′ə·nāt) *v.t.* **·nat·ed, ·nat·ing** To transfer pollen from an anther to a stigma of (a flower). Also **pol′len·ate.** —**pol′li·na′tion** *n.*

pol·li·wog (pol′ē·wog) *n.* TADPOLE. Also **pol′ly·wog.** [ME *polwygle*]

poll·ster (pōl′stər) *n.* One who takes public opinion polls. Also **poll′ist.**

poll tax A tax on a person, as distinguished from that on property, esp. as a prerequisite for voting.

pol·lut·ant (pə·lōō′tənt) *n.* Something that pollutes, esp. a harmful chemical or waste substance introduced into the air, water, or soil.

pol·lute (pə·lōōt′) *v.t.* **·lut·ed, ·lut·ing** 1 To make unclean or impure, as by introducing wastes: fumes *polluting* the air. 2 To desecrate; profane. [< L *polluere* make unclean] —**pol·lut′ed·ly** *adv.* —**pol·lut′ed·ness, pol·lut′er, pol·lu′tion** *n.* —**Syn.** 1 contaminate, foul, befoul. 2 defile.

Pol·lux (pol′əks) *Gk. Myth.* One of the twin sons of Zeus and Leda. —*n. Astron.* One of the two brightest stars in the constellation Gemini.

Pol·ly·an·na (pol′ē·an′ə) *n.* An overly zealous optimist. [< *Polyanna,* heroine of a novel, *Polyanna,* by Eleanor H. Porter, 1868–1920]

po·lo (pō′lō) *n.* A game played on horseback, usu. with a light wooden ball and long-handled mallets. [< Tibetan *pulu* ball] **—po′lo·ist** *n.*

pol·o·naise (pol′ə·nāz′, pō′lə-) *n.* **1** A stately, marchlike Polish dance. **2** The music for this dance. [F]

po·lo·ni·um (pə·lō′nē·əm) *n.* A radioactive element (symbol Po), present in uranium minerals as a disintegration product of radium. [< Med. L *Polonia* Poland]

pol·troon (pol·trōōn′) *n.* A mean-spirited coward. [< Ital. *poltrone* cowardly] **—pol·troon′er·y** *n.*

poly- *combining form* **1** Many; several: *polygamy.* **2** Polymerized, or a polymer of: *polyester.* [< Gk. *polys* much, many]

pol·y·an·dry (pol′ē·an′drē) *n.* The condition of having more than one husband at the same time. [< POLY- + Gk. *anēr, andros* a man] **—pol′y·an′drous** *adj.*

pol·y·an·thus (pol′ē·an′thəs) *n. pl.* **·an·thus·es** or **·an·thi** (-an′thī) **1** A hybrid variety of primrose. **2** A narcissus with clusters of small, fragrant flowers. [< POLY- + Gk. *anthos* flower]

pol·y·clin·ic (pol′i·klin′ik) *n.* A hospital or clinic for treating diverse diseases.

pol·y·es·ter (pol′ē·es′tər) *n.* Any of various polymerized esters of high tensile strength, used esp. in making **polyester fiber** for synthetic fabrics.

pol·y·eth·y·lene (pol′ē·eth′ə·lēn) *n.* A thermoplastic resin made by polymerizing ethylene, used widely to make moisture-proof film, containers, insulators, etc.

po·lyg·a·my (pə·lig′ə·mē) *n.* The condition of having more than one wife or husband at the same time. [< POLY- + Gk. *gamos* marriage] **—po·lyg′a·mist** *n.* **—po·lyg′a·mous** *adj.* **—po·lyg′a·mous·ly** *adv.*

pol·y·glot (pol′i·glot) *adj.* **1** Expressed in several tongues. **2** Speaking several languages. —*n.* A person or book that is polyglot. [< Gk. *polyglōttos*] **—pol·y·glot′tal, pol·y·glot′tic** *adj.*

pol·y·gon (pol′i·gon) *n.* A closed plane figure bounded by straight lines. **—po·lyg·o·nal** (pə·lig′ə·nəl), **po·lyg′o·nous** *adj.* **—po·lyg′o·nal·ly** *adv.*

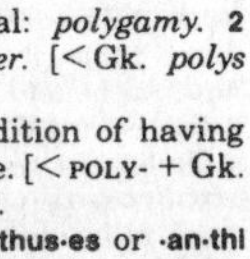

Polygon

pol·y·graph (pol′i·graf, -gräf) *n.* An instrument for the simultaneous recording of various physiological reactions that are influenced by emotion, as pulse, breathing, perspiration, etc. **—pol′y·graph′ic** or **·i·cal** *adj.*

po·lyg·y·ny (pə·lij′ə·nē) *n.* The marriage or cohabitation of one male with more than one female. [< POLY- + Gk. *gynē* woman]

pol·y·he·dron (pol′i·hē′drən) *n. pl.* **·dra** (-drə) or **·drons** *Geom.* A solid bounded by plane faces. **—pol′y·he′dral** *adj.*

Pol·y·hym·ni·a (pol′i·him′nē·ə) *Gk. Myth.* The Muse of sacred song. Also **Po·lym·ni·a** (pə·lim′nē·ə).

pol·y·math (pol′ə·math) *n.* One who is learned in many different fields or disciplines. [< POLY- + Gk. *mathanein* learn] **—pol′y·math′ic** *adj.*

pol·y·mer (pol′i·mər) *n.* **1** Any compound formed by polymerization. **2** Any of a pair or group of polymeric compounds. [< POLY- + Gk. *meros* part]

pol·y·mer·ic (pol′i·mer′ik) *adj.* Having the same percentage composition but different molecular weights and different properties: said of two or more chemical compounds. **—po·lym′er·ism** *n.*

po·lym·er·i·za·tion (pə·lim′ər·ə·zā′shən, pol′i·mər·ə-) *n.* The combination of unit molecules to form large complex molecules that are polymeric with the original molecules. **—po·lym·er·ize (·ized, ·iz·ing)** *v.*

pol·y·mor·phous (pol′i·môr′fəs) *adj.* Occurring in or having several forms. Also **pol′y·mor′phic** (-fik). [< POLY- + Gk. *morphē* form] **—pol′y·mor′phism** (-fiz·əm) *n.*

Pol·y·ne·sian (pol′i·nē′zhən, -shən) *n.* **1** One of the native brown-skinned people of Polynesia. **2** The languages spoken by these people. —*adj.* Of or pertaining to Polynesia, its people, or their languages.

pol·y·no·mi·al (pol′i·nō′mē·əl) *adj.* Of, pertaining to, or consisting of many terms. —*n. Math.* An expression written as a sum of terms. [< POLY- + (BI)NOMIAL]

pol·yp (pol′ip) *n.* **1** Any of various coelenterates having a fringe of tentacles at the end of a cylindrical body, as a hydra, sea anemone, etc. **2** An outgrowth arising from mucous membrane, as of the nose, bladder, uterus, or rectum. [< Gk. *poly-* many + *pous* a foot]

pol·y·phon·ic (pol′i·fon′ik) *adj.* **1** *Phonet.* Representing more than one sound or combination of sounds, as some written characters. **2** Consisting of many sounds or voices. **3** *Music* **a** Designating or involving the simultaneous combination of two or more independent parts or melodies. **b** Denoting an instrument, as a piano, by which two or more tones can be sounded at once. Also **po·lyph·o·nous** (pə·lif′ə·nəs) [< Gk. *polyphōnos* having many tones]

po·lyph·o·ny (pə·lif′ə·nē) *n.* **1** Multiplicity of sounds, as in an echo. **2** Polyphonic music; counterpoint.

pol·y·syl·la·ble (pol′i·sil′ə·bəl) *n.* A word of several syllables, esp. of more than three. **—pol′y·syl·lab′ic** (-si·lab′ik) or **·i·cal** *adj.* **—pol′y·syl′la·bism** or **·syl·lab′i·cism** (pol′i·si·lab′ə·siz′əm) *n.*

pol·y·tech·nic (pol′i·tek′nik) *adj.* Embracing many sciences and technical fields. Also **pol′y·tech′ni·cal.** —*n.* A school of applied science and the industrial arts. [< POLY- + Gk. *technē* an art]

pol·y·the·ism (pol′i·thē·iz′əm) *n.* The belief in and worship of more gods than one. **—pol′y·the′ist** *n.* **—pol′y·the·is′tic** or **·is′ti·cal** *adj.*

pol·y·un·sat·u·rat·ed (pol′ə·un·sach′ə·rā′tid) *adj.* Having many double or triple bonds uniting adjacent carbon atoms and forming potential sites for adding hydrogen or various radicals: used esp. of edible oils and fats.

pol·y·u·re·thane (pol′ē·yŏŏr′ə·thān′) *n.* Any of a group of synthetic, nitrogen-containing polymers with diverse properties, widely used in the manufacture of rigid or flexible solid foams for insulation and upholstery, resins for waterproofing, etc.

pol·y·va·lent (pol′i·vā′lənt) *adj.* **1** *Bacteriol.* Designating a vaccine effective against two or more different strains of one species of microorganism. **2** *Chem.* Multivalent. **—pol′y·va′lence** *n.*

pom·ace (pum′is) *n.* **1** The pulp remaining after the removal of juice from apples or like fruit. **2** The cake left after the expression of oil from nuts, seeds, etc. [< L *pomum* an apple]

po·made (pō·mād′, -mäd′) *n.* A perfumed dressing for the hair. —*v.t.* **·mad·ed, ·mad·ing** To anoint with pomade. [< Ital. *pomo* an apple]

pome (pōm) *n.* A fleshy, many-celled fruit with a core, as an apple, pear, etc. [< L *pomum* apple] **—po·ma·ceous** (pō·mā′shəs) *adj.*

pome·gran·ate (pom′gran·it, pum′-) *n.* **1** A fruit with a leathery rind containing many seeds surrounded with juicy, edible pulp. **2** The tropical shrub bearing this fruit. [< L *pomum* apple + *granum,* a grain, seed]

Pom·e·ra·ni·an (pom′ə·rā′nē·ən) *n.* A small dog with a bushy tail turned over the back and a long, straight, silky coat. [< *Pomerania,* a region of N CEN. Europe]

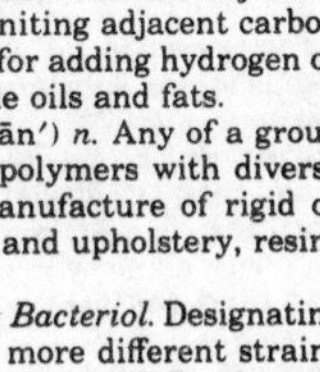

Pomeranian

pom·mel (pum′əl, pom′-) *v.t.* **·meled** or **·melled, ·mel·ing** or **·mel·ling** To beat with or as if with the fists. —*n.* **1** A knob at the front of a saddle. **2** A knob on the hilt of a sword. [< OF *pomel* a rounded knob] • See SADDLE.

po·mol·o·gy (pō·mol′ə·jē) *n.* The science of fruit culture. [< L *pomum* apple + -LOGY] **—po·mo·log·i·cal** (pō′mə·loj′i·kəl) *adj.* **—po′mo·log′i·cal·ly** *adv.* **—po·mol′o·gist** *n.*

pomp (pomp) *n.* **1** Magnificent and majestic display: royal *pomp.* 2 Ostentatious display. [< Gk. *pompē* a parade] — **Syn.** 1 flourish, grandeur, magnificence, splendor. 2 showiness.

pom·pa·dour (pom′pə·dôr, -dōōr, -dōr) *n.* A style of arranging the hair by brushing it up high over the forehead. [< Marquise de *Pompadour,* 1721–64, French courtesan]

pom·pa·no (pom′pə·nō) *n. pl.* **·nos** Any of various spiny-finned food fishes of Caribbean and neighboring coastal waters. [< Sp. *pámpano*]

pom-pom (pom′pom′) *n.* A rapid-fire, automatic cannon used as an antiaircraft weapon. [Imit.]

pom·pon (pom′pon) *n.* 1 A tuft or ball, as of feathers or ribbon, worn on a hat, shoes, etc. 2 A variety of chrysanthemum or dahlia having compact, globular flower heads: also **pom′-pom.** [< OF *pompe* pomp]

pom·pous (pom′pəs) *adj.* 1 Marked by assumed stateliness; overbearing. 2 Magnificent; ceremonious or impressive. —**pom·pos·i·ty** (pom·pos′ə·tē), **pom′pous·ness** *n.* —**pom′pous·ly** *adv.*

pon·cho (pon′chō) *n. pl.* **·chos** A garment shaped like a blanket with a hole in the middle for the head, and often waterproofed. [Sp.]

pond (pond) *n.* A body of still water, smaller than a lake. [ME *ponde*]

pon·der (pon′dər) *v.t.* 1 To weigh in the mind; consider carefully. —*v.i.* 2 To meditate. [< L *pondus* a weight] — **pon′der·er** *n.* —**Syn.** 1 deliberate, examine. 2 muse, reflect.

pon·der·o·sa pine (pon′də·rō′sə) 1 A tall tree of NW U.S. with long, dark green needles. 2 Its strong reddish wood. Also **pon′der·o′sa.** [< L *ponderōsus* ponderous]

pon·der·ous (pon′dər·əs) *adj.* 1 Having great weight; bulky. 2 Dull; lumbering. [< L *pondus* a weight] —**pon′der·os′i·ty** (-də·ros′ə·tē), **pon′der·ous·ness** *n.* —**pon′der·ous·ly** *adv.*

pond·weed (pond′wēd′) *n.* Any of a widely distributed genus of usu. submerged aquatic plants having straplike leaves.

pone (pōn) *n. Regional* 1 Bread made of cornmeal. 2 A small cake or patty of cornbread. [< Algon.]

pon·gee (pon·jē′, pon′jē) *n.* A thin, natural, unbleached silk with a knotty, rough weave.

pon·iard (pon′yərd) *n.* A small dagger. [< L *pugnus* fist]

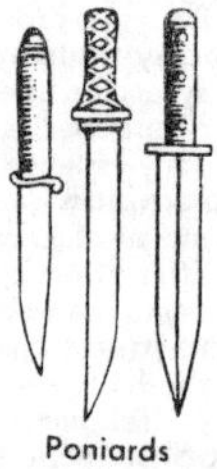
Poniards

pon·tiff (pon′tif) *n.* 1 The pope. 2 A bishop. [< L *pontifex* a high priest of ancient Rome.] —**pon·tif′ic** *adj.*

pon·tif·i·cal (pon·tif′i·kəl) *adj.* 1 Of, pertaining to or appropriate for a pontiff. 2 Having the pomp or dogmatism sometimes ascribed to a pontiff. —*n. Usu. pl.* The vestments, insignia, etc., used by pontiffs on certain ceremonious occasions. — **pon·tif′i·cal·ly** *adv.*

pon·tif·i·cate (pon·tif′ə·kit, -kāt) *n.* 1 The office of a pontiff. 2 A pope's term of office. —*v.i.* (-kāt) **·cat·ed, ·cat·ing** To act or speak pompously or dogmatically.

pon·toon (pon·tōōn′) *n.* 1 A flat-bottomed boat, airtight cylinder, etc., used in the construction of temporary floating bridges. 2 Either of two floats on the landing gear of a seaplane. [< L *ponto* < *pons* a bridge]

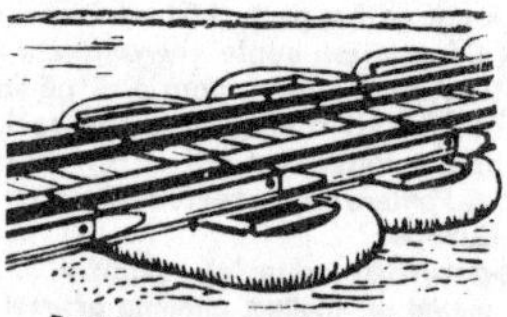
Pontoons supporting bridge

pontoon bridge A bridge supported on pontoons.

po·ny (pō′nē) *n. pl.* **·nies** 1 A horse of any of several small breeds. 2 Anything small of its kind. 3 *Slang* A translation used in the preparation of foreign language lessons. 4 *Informal* A very small glass for alcoholic liquor. —*v.t. & v.i.* **·nied, ·ny·ing** *Slang* 1 To translate (lessons) with the aid of a pony. 2 To pay (money) that is due: with *up.* [< L *pullus* a young animal]

pony express In 1860–61, a postal system by which mail was relayed from Missouri to California by riders mounted on swift ponies.

po·ny·tail (pō′nē·tāl′) *n.* 1 A style of arranging long hair by gathering it tightly at the back of the head and letting it hang down like a pony's tail. 2 Hair worn in this way.

pooch (pōōch) *n. Slang* A dog, esp. a small mongrel. [?]

poo·dle (pōōd′l) *n.* One of a breed of dogs with long, curly hair, usu. clipped short in a conventional pattern. [G *pudel*]

pooh (pōō) *interj.* Bah!: an exclamation of disdain or impatience.

pooh-pooh (pōō′pōō′) *v.t.* To reject or speak of disdainfully. —**pooh′-pooh′er** *n.*

pool[1] (pōōl) *n.* 1 A small body of water. 2 A deep place in a stream. 3 Any small, isolated body of liquid. [< OE *pōl*]

pool[2] (pōōl) *n.* 1 A collective stake in a gambling game. 2 A combination whereby companies or corporations agree to fix rates or prices and divide the collective profits pro rata. 3 Any of various games played on a six-pocket billiard table. 4 A combining of efforts or resources for mutual benefit. 5 The persons forming such a combination. —*v.t.* 1 To combine in a mutual fund or pool. —*v.i.* 2 To form a pool. [< F *poule* a stake, a hen]

pool·room (pōōl′rōōm′, -rŏŏm′) *n.* A place for playing pool, billiards, etc. or for betting on races.

poop[1] (pōōp) *Naut. n.* 1 A short deck built over the after part of the regular deck of a sailing vessel: also **poop deck.** 2 The stern of a ship. —*v.t.* To break over the stern or poop of: said of a wave. [< L *puppis*]

poop[2] (pōōp) *Slang v.t.* To bring to exhaustion: usu. used passively. [?]

poor (pŏŏr) *adj.* 1 Lacking means of comfortable subsistence; needy. 2 Lacking in good qualities. 3 Wanting in strength or spirit; cowardly. 4 Devoid of elegance or refinements. 5 Deserving of pity: the *poor* dog. 6 Devoid of merit; unsatisfactory. [< L *pauper*] —**poor′ly** *adj., adv.* — **poor′ness** *n.* —**Syn.** 1 indigent, penniless, poverty-stricken. 2 deficient. 4 squalid. 5 pitiable, wretched.

poor·house (pŏŏr′hous′) *n.* A public establishment maintained as a dwelling for paupers.

poor-mouth (poor′mouth′) *v.i. Informal* To exaggerate one's financial difficulties. —**poor mouth**

pop[1] (pop) *v.* **popped, pop·ping** *v.i.* 1 To make a sharp, explosive sound. 2 To burst open with such a sound. 3 To move or go suddenly or quickly: with *in, out,* etc. 4 To protrude; bulge. —*v.t.* 5 To cause to burst or explode, as corn by heating. 6 To thrust or put suddenly: with *in, out,* etc. 7 To fire (a gun, etc.). 8 *Slang* To take (habit-forming or harmful drugs) by mouth or injection: to *pop* pills. — **pop the question** *Informal* To make a proposal of marriage. —*n.* 1 A sharp explosive noise, as of a firearm. 2 A nonintoxicating, variously flavored drink, usu. carbonated. 3 A shot, as in basketball. —*adv.* Like, or with the sound of a pop. [Imit.]

pop[2] (pop) *n. Slang* Papa. [Short for *poppa*]

pop[3] (pop) *Informal adj.* 1 Of or pertaining to a pervasive mass culture, esp. that of young persons. 2 Of or pertaining to the music favored by this group. 3 Of or pertaining to pop art. [Short for POPULAR]

pop. popular; population.

pop art A style of painting, the subjects and manner of which resemble those of comic strips and advertising posters. —**pop artist**

pop·corn (pop′kôrn′) *n.* 1 A variety of maize, the kernels of which explode when heated. 2 The fluffy white balls thus formed.

Pope (pōp) *n.* The bishop of Rome, the supreme head of the Roman Catholic Church. Also **pope.** [< Gk. *pappas* father]

pop·eyed (pop′īd′) *adj.* 1 Having bulging or protruding eyes. 2 Amazed.

pop·gun (pop′gun′) *n.* A tube with a piston that expels a pellet with a pop.

pop·in·jay (pop′in·jā) *n.* A silly, vain fellow. [< Ar. *babhagā* a parrot]

pop·ish (pō′pish) *adj.* Pertaining to popes or the Roman Catholic Church; a contemptuous term. —**pop′ish·ly** *adv.* —**pop′ish·ness** *n.*

pop·lar (pop′lər) *n.* 1 Any of a genus of trees and bushes of the willow family. 2 The soft, light wood of any of these trees. [< L *populus*]

pop·lin (pop′lin) *n.* A durable ribbed silk, cotton, or wool fabric. [< F *popeline*]

pop·o·ver (pop′ō′vər) *n.* A very light, hollow muffin that pops up as it bakes.

pop·per (pop′ər) *n.* **1** Anything that makes an explosive noise. **2** A container or device for popping corn.

pop·py (pop′ē) *n. pl.* **·pies 1** Any of a large genus of plants having a milky juice, showy flowers of various colors, and a capsule containing many small seeds. **2** The flower of any poppy plant. **3** An extract, as opium, from the juice of certain species of poppy. **4** The yellowish-red color of certain poppy blossoms: also **poppy red.** [< L *papaver*]

pop·py·cock (pop′ē·kok) *n. & interj. Informal* Nonsense.

Pop·si·cle (pop′sik·əl) *n.* A slab of frozen colored and flavored water at the end of two flat sticks: a trade name. Also **pop′si·cle.**

pop·u·lace (pop′yə·lis) *n.* The mass of common people. [< L *populus* people]

pop·u·lar (pop′yə·lər) *adj.* **1** Of or carried on by the people at large. **2** Possessing many friends. **3** Widely approved or admired. **4** Suitable for the common people. **5** Prevalent among the people. **6** Suited to the means of the people: *popular* prices. **7** Of folk origin: the *popular* ballad. [< L *populus* the people] **—pop′u·lar·ly** *adv.* **—Syn. 2** well-liked. **5** common, universal, widespread.

pop·u·lar·i·ty (pop′yə·lar′ə·tē) *n.* The condition of possessing the confidence and favor of others.

pop·u·lar·ize (pop′yə·lə·rīz′) *v.t.* **·ized, ·iz·ing** To make popular. *Brit. sp.* **·ise′. —pop′u·lar·i·za′tion, pop′u·lar·iz′er** *n.*

pop·u·late (pop′yə·lāt) *v.t.* **·lat·ed, ·lat·ing 1** To furnish with inhabitants; people. **2** To inhabit. [< L *populus* the people]

pop·u·la·tion (pop′yə·lā′shən) *n.* **1** The total group of people or animals of a specified kind in a given area. **2** The number of individuals in such a group. **3** The act or process of populating. **4** The stated experimental base of a statistical study. [< L *populus* the people]

Pop·u·lism (pop′yə·lism) *n.* The platform of a U.S. political party **(People's party)** founded in 1891, that advocated free coinage of silver, public control of railways, an income tax, and limitation of ownership of land. **— Pop′u·list** *adj., n.* **—Pop′u·lis′tic** *adj.*

pop·u·list (pop′yə·list) *n.* A politician who represents or claims to represent the grass roots. **—pop′u·lism** *n.*

pop·u·lous (pop′yə·ləs) *adj.* Having many inhabitants; thickly settled. **—pop′u·lous·ly** *adv.* **—pop′u·lous·ness** *n.*

porce·lain (pôrs′lin, pōrs′-, pôr′sə-, pōr′-) *n.* A white, hard, translucent ceramic ware, usu. glazed, existing in many varieties. [< Ital. *porcellana,* orig. a cowry]

porch (pôrch, pōrch) *n.* **1** A covered structure forming an entrance to a building. **2** A veranda. [< L *porta* a gate]

por·cine (pôr′sīn, -sin) *adj.* Pertaining to, like, or characteristic of pigs or hogs. [< L *porcus* a hog]

por·cu·pine (pôr′kyə·pīn) *n.* Any of various rodents having the back and tail covered with long, sharp, defensive spines. [< OF *porc* a hog + *espin* a thorn]

Canada porcupine

pore[1] (pôr, pōr) *v.i.* **pored, por·ing 1** To study or read with care and application: with *over.* **2** To meditate; ponder. [ME *pouren*]

pore[2] (pôr, pōr) *n.* **1** A small natural opening, as a stoma on a leaf or the open end of a sweat gland. **2** A minute hole in any material. [< Gk. *poros*]

por·gy (pôr′gē) *n. pl.* **·gies** Any of various deep-bodied, saltwater food fishes. [?]

pork (pôrk, pōrk) *n.* **1** The flesh of pigs and hogs, used as food. **2** *Slang* Government money, favors, etc., obtained by political patronage. [< L *porcus* a hog]

pork barrel *Informal* A government appropriation for some local enterprise made to win favor with a representative's constituents.

pork·er (pôr′kər, pōr′-) *n.* A young hog fattened to be butchered.

pork·pie (pôrk′pī, pōrk′-) *n.* **1** A thick-crusted pie with pork filling. **2** A man's hat with a low, flat crown.

pork·y (pôr′kē, pōr′-) *adj.* **pork·i·er, pork·i·est 1** Of or like pork. **2** Obese; fat.

porn (pôrn) *Slang adj.* Pornographic. *—n.* Pornography. Also **por·no** (pôr′nō).

por·no·graph·ic (pôr·nə·graf′ik) *adj.* Of or having the nature of pornography. **—por′no·graph′i·cal·ly** *adv.*

por·nog·ra·phy (pôr·nog′rə·fē) *n.* **1** Depictions of sexual acts or behavior, as in writing, photographs, motion pictures, etc., to stimulate erotic feelings. **2** The material containing such descriptions. [< Gk. *pornē* a harlot + *graphein* write] **—por·nog′ra·pher** *n.*

po·ros·i·ty (pô·ros′ə·tē, pō-) *n.* **1** The property of being porous; porousness. **2** A porous part or structure.

po·rous (pôr′əs, pō′rəs) *adj.* **1** Having pores. **2** Having many tiny holes. **—po′rous·ly** *adv.* **—po′rous·ness** *n.*

por·phy·ry (pôr′fə·rē) *n. pl.* **·ries** An igneous rock that encloses crystals of feldspar or quartz. [< Gk. *porphyros* purple]

por·poise (pôr′pəs) *n. pl.* **·poises** or **·poise 1** Any of various small, usu. gregarious, toothed whales with a blunt snout. **2** A dolphin. [< L *porcus* a hog + *piscis* fish]

Porpoise

por·ridge (pôr′ij, por′-) *n.* A soft food made by boiling oatmeal or other cereal in water or milk. [Alter. of POTTAGE]

por·rin·ger (pôr′in·jər, por′-) *n.* A small, shallow dish, in which soft foods can be served.

port[1] (pôrt, pōrt) *n.* **1** A harbor or haven. **2** A harbor at which ships take on or unload cargo. **2** PORT OF ENTRY. [< L *portus* a harbor]

port[2] (pôrt, pōrt) *n.* **1** An opening in the side of a ship, as for a gun, or for the passage of cargo. **2** PORTHOLE. **3** A passageway into or out of a machine or device. [< L *porta* gate]

port[3] (pôrt, pōrt) *n.* **1** The way in which one bears or carries himself. **2** The position of a rifle when ported. *—v.t.* **1** *Mil.* To carry, as a weapon, diagonally across the body and sloping to the left shoulder. **2** To carry. [< L *portare* carry]

port[4] (pôrt, pōrt) *Naut. n.* The left side of a vessel as one looks from stern to bow. *—v.t. & v.i.* To put or turn (the helm) to the port side. *—adj.* Left. [Prob. < PORT[1]]

port[5] (pôrt, pōrt) *n.* A fortified sweet wine, usu. of a dark red color. [< *Oporto,* Portugal]

Port. Portugal; Portuguese.

port·a·ble (pôr′tə·bəl, pōr′-) *adj.* That can be readily carried or moved. [< L *portare* carry] **—port′a·ble·ness, port′·a·bil′i·ty** *n.* **—port′a·bly** *adv.*

port·age (pôr′tij, pōr′-) *n.* **1** The act of transporting canoes, boats, and goods over land from one navigable water to another. **2** The route over which such transportation is made. **3** The charge for transportation. [< L *portare* carry]

por·tal (pôr′təl, pōr′-) *n.* A passage for gaining entrance; door, esp. one that is grand and imposing. [< L *porta* a gate]

por·tal-to-por·tal pay (pôr′təl·tə·pôr′təl, pōr′-) A wage paid to cover the time a worker spends going to his work location from the entrance to a mine, factory, etc., plus that spent in going back after work.

port·cul·lis (pôrt·kul′is, pōrt-) *n.* A grating made of strong bars of wood or iron that can be let down suddenly to close the portal of a fortified place. [< OF *porte* a gate + *coleis* sliding]

Porte (pôrt, pōrt) *n.* The Turkish government prior to 1923.

porte-co·chère (pôrt′kō·shâr′, pōrt′-) *n.* A porch at the door of a building for sheltering persons entering or leaving vehicles. [F, lit., coach door]

por·tend (pôr·tend′, pōr-) *v.t.* To warn of as an omen; presage. [< L *portendere* < *pro-* forth + *tendere* to stretch]

por·tent (pôr′tent, pōr′-) *n.* 1 Anything that warns of a future event; omen. 2 Ominous significance.

por·ten·tous (pôr·ten′təs, pōr-) *adj.* 1 Full of portents of ill; ominous. 2 Amazing; extraordinary. 3 Pretentiously solemn. **—por·ten′tous·ly** *adv.* **—por·ten′tous·ness** *n.*

por·ter[1] (pôr′tər, pōr′-) *n.* 1 One who carries things, esp. a man hired to carry travelers' luggage, etc. 2 An attendant in a railway parlor car or sleeper. 3 A man who works as a janitor in a hospital, bank, etc. [< L *portare* carry]

por·ter[2] (pôr′tər, pōr′-) *n.* A keeper of a door or gate. [< L *porta* a gate, a door]

por·ter[3] (pôr′tər, pōr′-) *n.* A dark brown, heavy, English malt liquor. [Short for *porter's ale;* formerly drunk chiefly by porters]

por·ter·house (pôr′tər·hous′, pōr′-) *n.* 1 Formerly, a place where porter, ale, etc., were sold. 2 A choice cut of beefsteak including a part of the tenderloin: also **porterhouse steak.**

port·fo·li·o (pôrt·fō′lē·ō, pōrt-) *n. pl.* **·li·os** 1 A portable case for holding documents, etc. 2 The position or office of a minister of state or member of a government. 3 A list of investments. [< L *portare* carry + *folium* leaf]

port·hole (pôrt′hōl′, pōrt′-) *n.* A small round opening in a ship's side to admit air and light.

por·ti·co (pôr′ti·kō, pōr′-) *n. pl.* **·coes** or **·cos** An open porch or place for walking with a roof upheld by columns. [< L *porticus*] **—por′ti·coed** *adj.*

por·tière (pôr·tyâr′, pōr-) *n.* A curtain for a doorway. Also **por·tiere′.** [< F *porte* a door]

por·tion (pôr′shən, pōr′-) *n.* 1 A part of a whole. 2 An allotment; share. 3 The quantity of food served to one person. 4 The part of an estate coming to an heir. 5 A dowry. 6 One's fortune or destiny. *—v.t.* 1 To divide into shares for distribution: often with *out.* 2 To give a dowry to. [< L *portio*] **—por′tion·er** *n.* **—por′tion·less** *adj.* **—Syn.** *n.* 1 division, piece. 3 serving. 4 inheritance. 6 fate, lot.

Portland cement A calcined powder of clay and limestone that hardens when combined with water.

port·ly (pôrt′lē, pōrt′-) *adj.* **·li·er, ·li·est** 1 Rather stout or heavy. 2 Of a stately appearance and carriage. [< PORT[3]] **—port′li·ness** *n.*

port·man·teau (pôrt·man′tō, pōrt-) *n. pl.* **·teaus** or **·teaux** (-tōz) An oblong leather suitcase, hinged at the back, and having two compartments. [< MF *porter* carry + *manteau* coat]

portmanteau word A word blended from two distinct words, as *chortle,* from *chuckle* and *snort.*

port of entry A place, whether on the coast or inland, where customs officials check the entry of foreign persons or goods into a country.

por·trait (pôr′trit, pōr′-, -trāt) *n.* 1 A likeness of a person, esp. of the face. 2 A vivid description of something or someone. [< OF *pourtraire* portray] **—por′trait·ist** *n.*

por·trai·ture (pôr′tri·chər, pōr′-) *n.* 1 A portrait. 2 The art or practice of making portraits.

por·tray (pôr·trā′, pōr-) *v.t.* 1 To represent by drawing, painting, etc. 2 To describe in words. 3 To represent, as in a play. [< L *protrahere* draw forth] **—por·tray′al, por·tray′er** *n.* **—Syn.** 1 delineate. 2 depict, picture, show. 3 act, perform.

Por·tu·gal (pôr′chə·gəl, pōr′-) *n.* A republic of sw Europe, 35,419 sq. mi., cap. Lisbon. • See map at SPAIN.

Por·tu·guese (pôr′chə·gēz′, -gēs′, pōr′-) *n.* 1 A citizen or native of Portugal. 2 The language of Portugal. *—adj.* Of or pertaining to Portugal, its people, or their language.

Portuguese man-of-war A colony of organisms of warm seas, having long, stinging tentacles hanging from a central bladderlike float.

Portuguese West Africa ANGOLA.

por·tu·lac·a (pôr′chə·lak′ə, pōr′-) *n.* Any of a genus of low, fleshy-leaved plants related to purslane, with flowers of many colors. [L, purslane]

pos., posit. position; positive.

pose (pōz) *n.* 1 A position of the whole or part of the body, esp. one held for an artist, photographer, etc. 2 A mental attitude assumed for effect. *—v.* **posed, pos·ing** *v.i.* 1 To assume or hold a position, as for a portrait. 2 To affect attitudes. 3 To represent oneself: to *pose* as an expert. *—v.t.* 4 To cause to assume a position, as for a portrait. 5 To put forward for consideration or discussion: to *pose* a difficult question. [< OF *poser* to pose]

Po·sei·don (pō·sī′dən) *Gk. Myth.* The god of the sea: identified with the Roman Neptune.

pos·er[1] (pō′zər) *n.* One who poses.

pos·er[2] (pō′zər) *n.* A baffling question or problem.

po·seur (pō·zœr′) *n.* One who affects a particular attitude to make an impression on others. [F]

posh (posh) *adj. Brit. Slang* Very luxurious or elegant. [?] **—posh′ly** *adv.* **—posh′ness** *n.*

pos·it (poz′it) *v.t.* To lay down or assume as a fact; postulate. [< L *positus,* pp. of *ponere* to place]

po·si·tion (pə·zish′ən) *n.* 1 The manner in which a thing is placed. 2 The place in which a thing is located. 3 An advantageous location: to jockey for *position.* 4 Disposition of the parts of the body; posture. 5 The manner of being placed: an awkward *position.* 6 Social standing, esp. if high. 7 A job; employment. 8 Point of view; stand. *—v.t.* To place in a particular or appropriate position. [< L *positus,* pp. of *ponere* to place] **—po·si′tion·al** *adj.*

position paper A report from a person or group setting forth a set of principles, a description of policy, or recommendations for action on a specific issue.

pos·i·tive (poz′ə·tiv) *adj.* 1 That is or may be directly affirmed; sure. 2 Inherent in a thing by and of itself, regardless of its relations to other things; absolute. 3 Openly and plainly expressed; emphatic: a *positive* denial. 4 Confident; self-possessed: a *positive* person. 5 Overly confident; arrogant: a *positive* manner. 6 Incontestable: *positive* proof. 7 Helpful; constructive: *positive* suggestions. 8 Noting one of two opposite directions, qualities, properties, etc., which is taken as primary, or as indicating increase or progression. 9 *Math.* Greater than zero. 10 *Electr.* Having a charge or potential capable of attracting electrons. 11 ELECTROPOSITIVE. 12 Tending to move toward a stimulus: a *positive* tropism. 13 Indicating the presence of a specified condition, disease, or microorganism. 14 Having the lights and shades in their natural relation, as in a photograph. 15 *Gram.* Denoting the simple, uncompared degree of the adjective or adverb. *—n.* 1 That which is positive, as a photograph print, a battery terminal, a quality, a degree, a quantity, etc. 2 *Gram.* a The positive degree of an adjective or adverb. b A word in this degree. [< L *positivus* < *positus* placed] **—pos′i·tive·ly** *adv.* **—pos′i·tive·ness** *n.* **—Syn.** *adj.* 1 actual, existing, real. 3 explicit. 6 indisputable.

a b

a. positive *def. 14.* b. negative.

pos·i·tiv·ism (poz′ə·tiv·iz′əm) *n.* 1 A system of philosophy holding that man can have no knowledge of anything but actual phenomena and facts. 2 Certitude; dogmatism. **—pos′i·tiv·ist** *adj., n.* **—pos′i·tiv·is′tic** *adj.*

pos·i·tron (poz′ə·tron) *n. Physics* A positively charged particle with a mass equal to that of the electron. [< POSI(TIVE) + (ELEC)TRON]

poss. possession; possessive; possible; possibly.

pos·se (pos′ē) *n.* A force of men gathered together by a sheriff or other law-enforcement officer to help quell a riot, pursue criminal suspects, etc. [L, be able]

pos·sess (pə·zes′) *v.t.* 1 To have as property; own. 2 To have as a quality, attribute, etc. 3 To exert control over; dominate: his fear *possessed* him. 4 *Archaic* To seize; gain. [< L *possessus,* pp. of *possidere* possess] **—pos·ses′sor** *n.*

pos·sessed (pə·zest′) *adj.* 1 Calm; cool. 2 Controlled by or as if by evil spirits; frenzied. **—possessed of** Having; owning.

pos·ses·sion (pə·zesh′ən) *n.* 1 The act or state of possessing or being possessed; ownership or occupancy. 2 A thing possessed or owned. 3 *pl.* Property; belongings. 4 The state of being dominated by an idea, emotion, evil spirit, etc. 5 Self-possession. 6 A territory under the control of a foreign country.

pos·ses·sive (pə·zes′iv) *adj.* 1 Pertaining to possession or ownership. 2 Overly desirous of owning or controlling. 3 *Gram.* Designating a case of a noun or pronoun indicating possession. *—n. Gram.* 1 The possessive case. 2 A possessive form or construction. **—pos·ses′sive·ly** *adj.* —

pos·ses′sive·ness *n.* • In English the *possessive* is formed in nouns by adding *'s* to the singular and irregular plurals: *Larry's* hammer; *men's* minds, and a simple apostrophe to the regular plural and sometimes to singulars and proper names ending in a sibilant: *boys'* games; *Dickens'* (or *Dickens's*) novels. Pronouns have special possessive forms: *my, mine, your, yours, his, her, hers, our, ours, their, theirs, whose.*

pos·set (pos′it) *n.* A drink of hot milk with liquor, sweetened and spiced. [ME *possot*]

pos·si·bil·i·ty (pos′ə·bil′ə·tē) *n. pl.* **·ties** 1 The fact of being possible. 2 A possible thing.

pos·si·ble (pos′ə·bəl) *adj.* 1 That may be or may become true. 2 That may come about or be done. 3 That may be suitable: a *possible* site for a camp. [< L *posse* be able] —**pos′si·bly** *adv.*

pos·sum (pos′əm) *n. Informal* An opossum. —**play possum** To feign sleep, illness, death, etc.

post[1] (pōst) *n.* 1 An upright piece of timber or other material used as a support. 2 A line serving to mark the starting or finishing point of a racecourse. —*v.t.* 1 To put up (a poster, etc.) in some public place. 2 To fasten posters upon. 3 To announce by or as by a poster. 4 To publish the name of on a list. 5 To forbid trespassing on (land, etc.) by posting signs. [< L *postis* a door post]

post[2] (pōst) *n.* 1 Any fixed place where a soldier or policeman is stationed. 2 A place where troops are garrisoned. 3 The troops occupying a military installation. 4 A local unit of a veterans' organization. 5 An office or employment; position. 6 A trading post, esp. in an undeveloped region. —*v.t.* To assign to a particular position or post. [< L *positum,* pp. neut. of *ponere* to place]

post[3] (pōst) *n.* 1 An established system for transporting and delivering letters, packages, and other mail matter. 2 The mail delivered and carried at one time. 3 Formerly, a courier who traveled over a fixed route carrying letters and dispatches. 4 Formerly, any of the series of stations on such a route, furnishing relays of men and horses, and carriages for travelers. —*v.t.* 1 To place in a mailbox; mail. 2 To inform: He *posted* us on the latest news. 3 In bookkeeping, to transfer (items or accounts) to the ledger. —*v.i.* 4 To travel with post horses. 5 To travel with speed; hasten. 6 In horseback riding, to rise from the saddle in rhythm with a horse's trot. —*adv.* Speedily; rapidly. [< L *posita,* pp. fem. of *ponere* to place]

post- *prefix* After in time or order; following: *postdate, postwar.* [< L *post* behind, after]

post·age (pōs′tij) *n.* The charge levied on mail matter.

postage stamp A small, printed label issued and sold by a government to be affixed to letters, parcels, etc., in payment of postage.

pos·tal (pōs′təl) *adj.* Pertaining to the mails or to mail service. —*n.* A postal card.

postal card A card, issued officially, for carrying a written or printed message through the mails under government stamp.

post-bel·lum (pōst′bel′əm) *adj.* Coming or occurring after the war, esp. the American Civil War. [< L *post* after + *bellum* war]

post box MAILBOX.

post card 1 POSTAL CARD. 2 A card, usu. with a picture on one side, transmissible through the mails on prepayment of the same postage as for a postal card.

post chaise A closed, horse-drawn carriage.

post·date (pōst′dāt′) *v.t.* **·dat·ed, ·dat·ing** 1 To assign or affix a future date to (a check, document, etc.). 2 To follow in time.

post·er (pōs′tər) *n.* A printed sheet for advertising, public information, etc., to be posted on a wall or other surface. —**Syn.** bill, notice, placard, sign.

poster color An opaque water paint, usu. sold in jars, used for making posters, etc.

pos·te·ri·or (pos·tir′ē·ər) *adj.* 1 Situated behind or toward the hinder part. 2 Coming after another in a series. —*n. Often pl.* The buttocks. [< L *posterus* following] —**pos·te·ri·or·i·ty** (pos·tir′ē·ôr′ə·tē, -or′ə-) *n.* —**pos·te′ri·or·ly** *adv.*

pos·ter·i·ty (pos·ter′ə·tē) *n.* 1 A person's descendants. 2 Succeeding generations, collectively. [< L *posterus* following]

pos·tern (pōs′tərn, pos′-) *n.* A back gate or door; a private entrance. —*adj.* Situated at the back; private: a *postern* gate. [< L *posterus* following]

post exchange *Often cap.* An establishment for the sale of merchandise and services to military personnel.

post·gla·cial (pōst′glā′shəl) *adj. Geol.* Existing or occurring later than the glacial epoch.

post·grad·u·ate (pōst′graj′ōō·it, -āt) *adj.* Of or pertaining to studies pursued after receiving a first degree; graduate. —*n.* One who pursues or has completed a postgraduate course.

post·haste (pōst′hāst′) *n.* Great haste or speed. —*adv.* With utmost speed; hurriedly. [?< *Haste, post, haste,* an old direction written on letters]

post horse A horse kept for hire to travelers.

post·hu·mous (pos′chōō·məs) *adj.* 1 Born after the father's death: said of a child. 2 Published after the author's death, as a book. 3 Arising after a person's death: a *posthumous* reputation. [< L *postumus* latest, last] —**post′hu·mous·ly** *adv.*

pos·til·ion (pōs·til′yən, pos-) *n.* A rider of the left-hand horse of a team drawing a vehicle. Also **pos·til′lion.** [< Ital. *posta* a post, station]

post·lude (pōst′lōōd) *n.* An organ solo concluding a church service. [< POST- + (PRE)LUDE]

post·man (pōst′mən) *n. pl.* **·men** (-mən) A man who picks up and delivers letters, parcels, etc.

post·mark (pōst′märk′) *n.* The mark of a post office on mail handled there, serving to cancel stamps, and usu. giving the date and place of mailing. —*v.t.* To stamp with a postmark.

post·mas·ter (pōst′mas′tər, -mäs′-) *n.* An official having charge of a post office. —**post′mis′tress** (-mis′tris) *n. Fem.*

postmaster general *pl.* **postmasters general** The executive head of the postal service of a government.

post·me·rid·i·an (pōst′mə·rid′ē·ən) *adj.* Pertaining to the afternoon.

post me·rid·i·em (pōst mə·rid′ē·əm) After midday.

post-mor·tem (pōst·môr′təm) *adj.* Occurring, done, or made soon after death. —*n.* AUTOPSY. [L]

post·na·tal (pōst·nāt′l) *adj.* Occurring in or pertaining to the period immediately after birth.

post office 1 A branch or agency of a government charged with carrying and delivering the mails. 2 An office for the receipt, transmission, and delivery of mails. 3 A kissing game. —**post-of·fice** (pōst′ôf′is, -of′-) *adj.*

post·paid (pōst′pād′) *adj.* Having postage prepaid.

post·par·tum (pōst′pär′təm) *adj. Med.* Existing or occurring after childbirth: a *postpartum* fever. [< POST- + L *partus* childbirth < *parere* to bear]

post·pone (pōst·pōn′) *v.t.* **·poned, ·pon·ing** To put off to a future time. [< L *post-* after + *ponere* put] —**post·pone′·ment, post·pon′er** *n.* —**Syn.** defer, delay, procrastinate.

post·pran·di·al (pōst·pran′dē·əl) *adj.* After-dinner. [< POST- + L *prandium* lunch]

post·rid·er (pōst′rī′dər) *n.* A person who journeys by relays of horses.

post road A road built and maintained for the transportation of mail, formerly having stations at specified distances.

post·script (pōst′skript′) *n.* 1 A supplemental addition to a written or printed document. 2 Something added to a letter after the writer's signature. [< L *postscribere* write after]

pos·tu·late (pos′chə·lit) *n.* 1 A basis of argument laid down as well known or too plain to require proof. 2 A proposition assumed as true; an axiom. —*v.t.* (pos′chə·lāt) **·lat·ed, ·lat·ing** 1 To claim; demand. 2 To set forth as self-evident or already known. 3 To assume the truth or reality of. [< L *postulare* to demand] —**pos′tu·la′tion, pos′tu·la′tor** *n.*

pos·ture (pos′chər) *n.* 1 The way in which the body is held; bearing. 2 Situation or condition at a given time;

circumstances: the military *posture* of a nation. **3** Frame of mind; attitude. —*v.* **·tured, ·tur·ing** *v.t.* **1** To place in a specific posture; pose. —*v.i.* **2** To assume a specific posture. **3** To pose for effect; attitudinize. [< L *positus,* p.p. of *ponere* to place] **—pos′tur·al** *adj.* **—pos′tur·er, pos′tur·ist** *n.*

post·war (pōst′wôr′) *adj.* After a war.

po·sy (pō′zē) *n. pl.* **·sies 1** A flower. **2** A bunch of flowers. [Contraction of POESY]

pot (pot) *n.* **1** A round earthen, metal, or glass vessel used in cooking. **2** A metal drinking cup; mug. **3** A mug of liquor. **4** The contents of a pot; potful. **5** POTBELLY. **6** The amount of stakes wagered or played for, as in poker. **7** *Informal* A large sum of money. **8** A basketlike trap for catching lobsters, eels, fish, etc. **9** *Slang* Marihuana. **—go to pot** *Informal* To go to ruin; deteriorate. —*v.* **pot·ted, pot·ting** *v.t.* **1** To put into a pot. **2** To preserve in pots or jars. **3** To cook in a pot; stew. **4** To shoot or kill with a pot shot. —*v.i.* **5** To take a pot shot. [< OE *pott*] **—pot′ful** *adj.*

pot. potential.

po·ta·ble (pō′tə·bəl) *adj.* Suitable for drinking. —*n. Usu. pl.* Anything drinkable. [< L *potare* to drink] **—po′ta·bil′i·ty** *n.*

po·tage (pō·täzh′) *n.* A thick soup. [F]

pot·ash (pot′ash′) *n.* **1** POTASSIUM CARBONATE. **2** POTASSIUM HYDROXIDE. **3** The crude mixture of potassium salts obtained by leaching the ashes of plants. [< *pot ashes*]

po·tas·si·um (pə·tas′ē·əm) *n.* A soft, highly reactive metallic element (symbol K) essential to life. [< POTASH]

potassium carbonate A white, alkaline compound found in wood ashes, used in making soap, glass, etc.

potassium chlorate A colorless crystalline salt used in making matches, explosives, etc.

potassium chloride A colorless crystalline salt occurring naturally in mineral deposits and in certain giant kelps of the Pacific coast.

potassium cyanide An intensely poisonous, white, crystalline compound used chiefly in metallurgy.

potassium hydroxide A white, deliquescent, caustic alkali that absorbs carbon dioxide from air.

potassium nitrate A white, crystalline compound used in fertilizers, gunpowder, meat preservatives, etc.

potassium permanganate A purple crystalline salt used as an oxidizing agent, antiseptic, etc.

po·ta·tion (pō·tā′shən) *n.* **1** The act of drinking; a drink. **2** A drinking bout. [< L *potare* to drink]

po·ta·to (pə·tā′tō) *n. pl.* **·toes 1** A starchy, edible tuber of a plant of the nightshade family. **2** The plant. **3** SWEET POTATO. [< Sp. *patata*]

potato beetle A destructive yellowish beetle with black stripes that feeds on the potato, tomato, and other plants. Also **potato bug.**

Potato beetle

potato chip A very thin slice of potato fried crisp and salted.

pot·bel·ly (pot′bel′ē) *n. pl.* **·lies** A protuberant belly. **—pot′bel′lied** *adj.*

pot·boil·er (pot′boi′lər) *n. Informal* A literary or artistic work, often of poor quality, produced simply to earn money. **—pot′boil′ing** *n.*

po·tent (pōt′nt) *adj.* **1** Producing marked effects: a *potent* drug. **2** Convincing: a *potent* argument. **3** Having great authority. **4** Able to perform sexual intercourse: said of males. [< L *potens* pr.p. of *posse* be able, have power] **—po′ten·cy** (*pl.* **·cies**), **po′tence** *n.* **—po′tent·ly** *adv.*

po·ten·tate (pōt′n·tāt) *n.* One having great power or sway; a sovereign.

po·ten·tial (pə·ten′shəl) *adj.* **1** Possible but not actual. **2** Having capacity for existence, but not yet existing. **3** *Physics* Existing by virtue of position: said of energy. **4** *Gram.* Indicating possibility or capability by the use of *can, could, may,* etc. **5** Having force or power. —*n.* **1** Anything that may be possible. **2** *Gram.* The potential mood. **3** *Physics* The work required to move a body from a point infinitely distant to a given point in a field of force. **4** *Electr.* A difference of electric potential; voltage. [< L *potens* potent] **—po·ten·ti·al·i·ty** (pə·ten′shē·al′ə·tē) (*pl.* **·ties**) *n.* **—po·ten′tial·ly** *adv.*

potential energy Energy stored in any of numerous forms, as chemical energy in coal, mechanical energy in a coiled spring, etc.

pot·head (pot′hed′) *n. Slang* A person who habitually smokes marihuana.

poth·er (poth′ər) *n.* Excitement mingled with confusion. —*v.t. & v.i.* To worry; bother. [?] **—Syn.** *n.* ado, bother, bustle, disturbance, fuss.

pot·herb (pot′ûrb′, -hûrb′) *n.* Any plant having leaves or stems used in cookery.

pot·hold·er (pot′hōl′dər) *n.* A padded cloth or mitten used for handling hot cooking pots and pans.

pot·hook (pot′ho͝ok′) *n.* **1** A curved piece of iron for lifting or hanging pots. **2** A curved mark used in teaching penmanship.

pot·house (pot′hous′) *n. Brit.* An alehouse; saloon.

po·tion (pō′shən) *n.* A draft, as of a liquid having medicinal, poisonous, or supposed magical properties. [< L *potare* to drink]

pot luck Whatever happens to be available and ready for a meal: usu. in the phrase **take pot luck.**

pot·pie (pot′pī′) *n.* **1** A pie, baked in a deep dish, containing meat and vegetables. **2** Meat stewed with dumplings.

pot·pour·ri (pō·po͞o·rē′) *n.* **1** A mixture of dried sweet-smelling flower petals used to perfume a room. **2** A collection of various things; miscellany. [F, lit., rotten pot]

pot roast Meat braised and cooked in a pot until tender, often with vegetables.

pot·sherd (pot′shûrd) *n.* A bit of broken pottery. Also **pot′shard** (-shärd). [< POT + SHARD]

pot shot 1 A shot fired within easy range. **2** A random shot. **3** *Informal* A sarcastic or critical remark.

pot·tage (pot′ij) *n.* A thick broth or stew. [< F *pot* pot]

pot·ted (pot′id) *adj.* **1** Placed in a pot. **2** Preserved in a pot or can. **3** *Slang* Drunk.

pot·ter[1] (pot′ər) *v. Chiefly Brit.* PUTTER[2]. **—pot′ter·er** *n.* **—pot′ter·ing·ly** *adv.*

pot·ter[2] (pot′ər) *n.* One who makes earthenware or porcelain. [< OE *potere*]

potter's field A piece of ground appropriated as a burial ground for the destitute or unidentified. [< the Biblical ref. (*Matt.* 27:7) of a potter's field for the burial of strangers]

potter's wheel A usu. horizontal rotating disk used by potters for shaping clay.

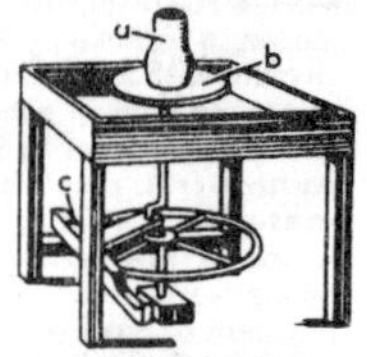

Potter's wheel
a. clay. b. rotating wheel. c. treadle.

pot·ter·y (pot′ər·ē) *n. pl.* **·ter·ies 1** A factory where potters' ware is made. **2** The manufacture of earthenware or porcelain. **3** Clay ware molded and hardened.

pot·ty (pot′ē) **·ti·er, ·ti·est** *adj. Brit. Informal* **1** Insignificant; trivial. **2** Slightly crazy. [Prob. < POT, in the phrase *go to pot* deteriorate]

pouch (pouch) *n.* **1** A small bag or sack. **2** *Zool.* **a** A saclike part for containing or carrying food. **b** MARSUPIUM. —*v.t.* **1** To put in or as in a pouch; pocket. **2** To fashion or arrange in pouchlike form. —*v.i.* **3** To take on a pouchlike shape. [< OF *poche*] **—pouch′y** *adj.* (**·i·er, ·i·est**)

poul·ter·er (pōl′tər·ər) *n. Chiefly Brit.* A dealer in poultry.

poul·tice (pōl′tis) *n.* A warm, pulpy mass applied externally to relieve pain and inflammation. —*v.t.* **·ticed, ·tic·ing** To cover with a poultice. [< L *puls* porridge]

poul·try (pōl′trē) *n.* Domestic fowls, as chickens, ducks, turkeys, and geese. [< OF *poulet* fowl]

pounce (pouns) *v.i.* **pounced, pounc·ing** To swoop, as in seizing prey: with *on, upon,* or *at.* —*n.* The act of pouncing. [?] **—Syn.** *n.,v.* jump, leap, spring. **—pounc′er** *n.*

pound[1] (pound) *n.* **1 a** A unit of avoirdupois weight equal to 0.45359 kilogram or 16 avoirdupois ounces. **b** A unit of troy weight equal to 0.37324 kilogram or 12 troy ounces. **2** The basic monetary unit of the United Kingdom, formerly equal to 20 shillings, but after 1971 equal to 100 pence: also **pound sterling. 3** The basic monetary unit of various other countries, as Cyprus, Gambia, Ireland, Israel, Lebanon, Libya, Malawi, Malta, Nigeria, Rhodesia, Sudan, Syria, Turkey, and Egypt. [< L *pondus* weight]

pound[2] (pound) *n.* **1** A place, enclosed by authority, in which stray animals are kept. **2** An enclosed shelter for cattle or sheep. 3 A trap for wild animals. *—v.t.* To confine in or as in a pound. [< OE *pund*]

pound[3] (pound) *v.t.* 1 To strike heavily and repeatedly. 2 To reduce to a pulp or powder by beating. 3 To teach or impress by constant repetition: to *pound* facts into someone's head. *—v.i.* 4 To strike heavy, repeated blows: with *on, at,* etc. 5 To move or proceed heavily. 6 To throb heavily or resoundingly. *—n.* 1 A heavy blow. 2 The act of pounding. 3 The sound produced by pounding; thump. [< OE *punian*] **—pound′er** *n.*

pound·age (poun′dij) *n.* A tax, rate, etc., of so much per pound sterling or per pound of weight.

pound cake A rich cake having ingredients equal in weight, as a pound each of flour, butter, and sugar, with eggs added.

pound-fool·ish (pound′fōō′lish) *adj.* Extravagant with large sums of money.

pour (pôr, pōr) *v.t.* 1 To cause to flow by gravity in a continuous stream, as water, sand, etc. 2 To emit or utter continuously. *—v.i.* 3 To flow in a continuous stream; gush. 4 To rain heavily. 5 To serve as a hostess at a social tea. 6 To move in great numbers; swarm. *—n.* A pouring or downfall. [ME *pouren*] **—pour′er** *n.* **—pour′ing·ly** *adv.*

pour·boire (pōōr·bwär′) *n.* A gift of money as a tip. [F, lit., for drink]

pout[1] (pout) *v.i.* 1 To thrust out the lips, esp. in ill humor. 2 To be sullen. 3 To swell out; protrude. *—v.t.* 4 To utter with a pout. *—n.* 1 A pushing out of the lips as in petulance. 2 Ill humor; sullenness. [ME *pouten*] **—pout′er** *n.*

pout[2] (pout) *n.* One of various freshwater catfishes having a pouting appearance. [< OE *pūte*]

pout·er (pou′tər) *n.* A breed of pigeon that habitually puffs out the crop. Also **pouter pigeon.**

pov·er·ty (pov′ər·tē) *n.* 1 The state of being poor; need. 2 Scarcity of something needed. 3 Meagerness; inadequacy: *poverty* of language. [< L *pauper* poor]

pov·er·ty-strick·en (pov′ər·tē·strik′ən) *adj.* Suffering from poverty; destitute.

POW, P.O.W. Prisoner of War.

pow·der (pou′dər) *n.* 1 A mass of fine, free particles of a solid substance. 2 A cosmetic preparation. 3 A medicine in the form of powder. 4 GUNPOWDER. **—take a powder** *Slang* To run off; disappear suddenly. *—v.t.* 1 To pulverize. 2 To sprinkle or cover with or as with powder. *—v.i.* 3 To be reduced to powder. 4 To use powder as a cosmetic. [< L *pulvis, pulveris* dust] **—pow′der·er** *n.* **—pow′der·y** *adj.*

powder blue A soft medium blue.

powder horn The hollow horn of an ox or cow, fitted with a cover and formerly used by hunters or soldiers for holding gunpowder.

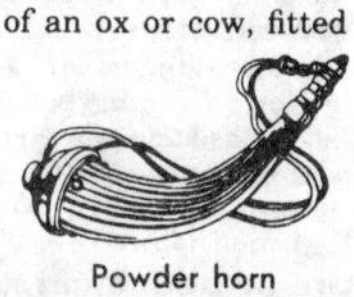
Powder horn

powder puff A soft pad used to apply powder to the skin.

pow·er (pou′ər) *n.* 1 Ability to act; potency. 2 Potential capacity. 3 Strength or force. 4 The right, ability, or capacity to exercise control. 5 Any agent that exercises control or dominion: naval *power.* 6 Great or telling force or effect. 7 Any form of energy that can perform work: water *power.* 8 *Physics* The time rate at which energy is transferred, or work is done. 9 *Math.* a The product of a number taken a given number of times as a factor. b An exponent. 10 *Optics* Magnifying capacity, as of a lens. **—in power** 1 In office. 2 In control. **—the powers that be** Those in control. *—v.t.* 1 To provide with means of propulsion. 2 To force or push, esp. when overcoming resistance: He *powered* his way through for a touchdown. *—v.i.* 3 To force one's way: The truck *powered* through the mud. *—adj.* Operated by a motor or by electricity: *power* tool. [< OF *poeir* be able] **—Syn.** *n.* 1 capacity, efficacy. 3 energy, might. 4 authority, command.

pow·er·boat (pou′ər·bōt′) *n.* A motorboat.

pow·er·ful (pou′ər·fəl) *adj.* 1 Possessing great force. 2 Having great intensity or energy. 3 Exercising great authority. 4 Having great effect on the mind; convincing. *—adv. Informal* Very; exceedingly. **—pow′er·ful·ly** *adv.*

pow·er·house (pou′ər·hous′) *n.* 1 A station where electricity is generated. 2 *Slang* A person or thing of great might or force.

pow·er·less (pou′ər·lis) *adj.* 1 Completely lacking power; helpless or weak. 2 Without authority. **—pow′er·less·ly** *adv.* **—pow′er·less·ness** *n.*

power of attorney *Law* 1 The power to act for another conferred upon an agent. 2 The document by which such authority is conferred.

power play In politics, business, diplomacy, military operations, etc., a maneuver made by the use or threatened use of superior power.

power politics The use or threatened use by nations of superior military or economic force to exact international concessions.

power structure 1 The group of persons who control a political or business organization. 2 The chain of command existing among the members of such a group.

pow·wow (pou′wou′) *n.* 1 A North American Indian ceremony of a medicine man involving a dance, feast, or other demonstration, to cure the sick or effect success in hunting, war, etc. 2 An Indian council. 3 *Informal* Any meeting or conference. *—v.i.* To hold a deliberative council. [< Algon.]

pox (poks) *n.* 1 Any disease characterized by skin eruptions: chicken *pox.* 2 Syphilis. [Var. of *pocks,* pl. of POCK]

P.P., p.p. parcel post; parish priest; postpaid.

pp pianissimo.

p.p., pp., past participle.

pp. pages; privately printed.

ppd. postpaid; prepaid.

pph. pamphlet.

ppl. participle.

ppr., p.pr. present participle.

P.P.S., p.p.s. additional postscript (L *post postscriptum*).

P.Q. Province of Quebec.

PR Puerto Rico (P.O. abbr.)

PR, P.R., p.r. Public Relations.

P.R. Puerto Rico; proportional representation.

Pr praseodymium.

pr. pair; pairs; paper; power; present; price; priest; prince; printing; pronoun.

prac·ti·ca·ble (prak′tə·kə·bəl) *adj.* 1 That can be put into practice; feasible. 2 Usable. **—prac′ti·ca·bil′i·ty, prac′ti·ca·ble·ness** *n.* **—prac′ti·ca·bly** *adv.*

prac·ti·cal (prak′ti·kəl) *adj.* 1 Pertaining to actual use and experience rather than theory. 2 Trained by practice or experience. 3 Useful. 4 Manifested in practice. [< Gk. *praktikos* fit for doing] **—prac′ti·cal′i·ty** (-kal′ə·tē), **prac′ti·cal·ness** *n.*

practical joke A joke involving action instead of wit or words; a trick.

prac·ti·cal·ly (prak′tik·lē) *adv.* 1 In a practical manner. 2 To all intents and purposes.

practical nurse A nurse with practical experience in the care of the sick, but who is not a registered nurse.

prac·tice (prak′tis) *v.* **·ticed, ·tic·ing** *v.t.* 1 To make use of habitually: to *practice* economy. 2 To apply in action: *Practice* what you preach. 3 To work at as a profession: to *practice* law. 4 To do or perform repeatedly in order to acquire skill. *—v.i.* 5 To repeat or rehearse something in order to acquire proficiency. 6 To work at or pursue a profession. *—n.* 1 Any customary action; habit. 2 An established custom or usage. 3 The act or process of executing or accomplishing. 4 The pursuit of a profession; the *practice* of medicine. 5 Frequent and repeated exercise in order to gain skill. 6 The skill so gained: The violinist was out of *practice.* 7 The rules by which legal proceedings are governed. Also **prac′tise.** [< LL *practicus* practical] **—prac′tic·er** *n.* **—Syn.** *v.* 4 drill, exercise, rehearse. • In Britain, *practice* is almost invariably the spelling used for the noun, *practise* for the verb. In the U.S., the noun form is more commonly *practice,* although *practise* is also used; both spellings are widely used as verbs.

prac·ticed (prak′tist) *adj.* 1 Expert by use or habit; experienced. 2 Acquired by practice. Also **prac′tised.**

prac·ti·tion·er (prak·tish′ən·ər) *n.* **1** One who practices an art or profession. **2** A Christian Science healer.

prae·no·men (prē·nō′mən) *n. pl.* **·no·mens** or **·nom·i·na** (-nom′ə·nə) The name prefixed to an ancient Roman family name to mark the individual. [< L *prae* before + *nomen* name]

prae·tor (prē′tər) *n.* A magistrate or judge in ancient Rome, ranking just below a consul. [L] **—prae·to·ri·al** (prē·tôr′ē·əl, -tō′rē-) *adj.* **—prae·tor′i·an** *adj., n.*

prag·mat·ic (prag·mat′ik) *adj.* **1** Practical; dealing with facts. **2** Active rather than thoughtful. **3** Of or pertaining to pragmatism. **4** Officious; interfering. **5** Opinionated. Also **prag·mat′i·cal,** esp. for defs. 1, 2, 4, 5. [< Gk. *pragma* a thing done] **—prag·mat′i·cal·ly** *adv.* **—prag·mat′i·cal·ness** *n.*

prag·ma·tism (prag′mə·tiz′əm) *n. Philos.* The doctrine that ideas have value only in terms of their practical consequences. **—prag′ma·tist** *n.*

prai·rie (prâr′ē) *n.* A level or rolling tract of treeless land covered with coarse grass and generally of rich soil. [< L *pratum* meadow]

prairie chicken A large, henlike grouse of North American grasslands. Also **prairie hen.**

prairie dog A burrowing rodent of the plains of North America, that lives in large communities.

Prairie dog

prairie schooner COVERED WAGON.

prairie wolf COYOTE.

praise (prāz) *v.t.* **praised, prais·ing 1** To express approval of; applaud. **2** To express adoration of; glorify (God, etc.). *—n.* The act of praising or the state of being praised; commendation or adoration. **—sing (one's) praises** To praise highly. [< L *pretium* price] **—prais′er** *n.* **—Syn.** *v.* **1** commend, eulogize, extol, laud. *n.* acclaim, applause, eulogy, plaudit.

praise·wor·thy (prāz′wûr′*th*ē) *adj.* Worthy of praise; commendable. **—praise′wor′thi·ly** *adv.* **—praise′wor′thi·ness** *n.*

pra·line (prä′lēn, prā′-) *n.* A crisp confection made of pecans or other nuts browned in boiling sugar. [< Count Duplessis-*Praslin,* 1598–1675, French soldier]

pram (pram) *n. Brit. Informal* A baby carriage. [Short for PERAMBULATOR]

prance (prans, präns) *v.* **pranced, pranc·ing** *v.i.* **1** To move with high steps, esp. by springing from the hind legs, as a spirited horse. **2** To ride on a prancing horse. **3** To move in an arrogant manner; swagger. **4** To gambol; caper. *—v.t.* **5** To cause to prance. *—n.* The act of prancing. [< Scand.] **—pranc′er** *n.* **—pranc′ing·ly** *adv.*

prank[1] (prangk) *n.* A mischievous act; joke. *—v.i.* To play pranks or tricks. [?] **—prank′ish** *adj.* **—prank′ish·ly** *adv.* **—prank′ish·ness, prank′ster** *n.*

prank[2] (prangk) *v.t.* **1** To decorate gaudily. *—v.i.* **2** To make an ostentatious show. [?]

pra·se·o·dym·i·um (prā′zē·ō·dim′ē·əm, prā′sē-) *n.* A soft, silvery, rare-earth element (symbol Pr). [< Gk. *prasios* light green + (DI)DYMIUM]

prate (prāt) *v.* **prat·ed, prat·ing** *v.i.* **1** To talk idly; chatter. *—v.t.* **2** To utter idly or emptily. *—n.* Idle talk; prattle. [ME *praten*] **—prat′er** *n.* **—prat′ing·ly** *adv.*

prat·fall (prat′fôl′) *n. Slang* A fall on the buttocks, esp. viewed as comical. [< earlier *prat* buttocks + FALL]

prat·tle (prat′l) *v.* **·tled, ·tling** *v.i.* **1** To talk like a child; prate. *—v.t.* **2** To utter in a foolish way: to *prattle* secrets. *—n.* **1** Childish speech; babble. **2** Idle or foolish talk. [Freq. of PRATE] **—prat′tler** *n.* **—prat′tling·ly** *adv.*

prawn (prôn) *n.* Any of various edible, shrimplike shellfish. [ME *prane*]

pray (prā) *v.i.* **1** To address prayers to a deity. **2** To make entreaty; beg. *—v.t.* **3** To ask (someone) earnestly; entreat. **4** To ask for by prayers or entreaty. **5** To effect by prayer. [< L *precari* ask, pray]

prayer (prâr) *n.* **1** The act of offering reverent petitions to a deity. **2** Any earnest request. **3** *Often pl.* A religious service made up largely of prayer. **4** Something prayed for. **5** A form of words appropriate to prayer. [< L *precari* pray] **—prayer′ful** *adj.* **—prayer′ful·ly** *adv.* **—prayer′ful·ness** *n.*

prayer book A book of ritual prescribed for conducting a church service.

praying mantis Any of various predatory, long-bodied insects which grasp their prey with forelegs folded as if in prayer.

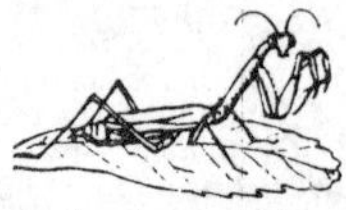
Praying mantis

pre- *prefix* **1** Before in time or order; prior to; preceding: *precancel.* **2** Preliminary to; preparing for: *preschool.* [< L *prae* before]

preach (prēch) *v.i.* **1** To deliver a sermon. **2** To give advice or urge a course of action, esp. in a meddlesome or tedious way. *—v.t.* **3** To advocate or recommend urgently: to *preach* peace. **4** To proclaim; expound upon. **5** To deliver (a sermon, etc.). [< L *prae-* before + *dicare* make known]

preach·er (prē′chər) *n.* One who preaches; specificially, a clergyman.

preach·i·fy (prē′chə·fī) *v.i.* **·fied, ·fy·ing** *Informal* To preach or discourse tediously. **—preach′i·fi·ca′tion** *n.*

preach·ment (prēch′mənt) *n.* A moral lecture, esp. a wearisome one.

preach·y (prē′chē) *adj. Informal* **preach·i·er, preach·i·est** Marked by sanctimony or cant. **—preach′i·ness** *n.*

pre·am·ble (prē′am·bəl) *n.* **1** A statement introductory to and explanatory of what follows, as in a constitution or a contract. **2** A preliminary event or action. [< L *prae-* before + *ambulare* to walk] **—pre·am′bu·lar′y** *adj.*

pre·ar·range (prē′ə·rānj′) **·ranged, ·rang·ing** *v.t.* To plan or arrange ahead of time. **—pre·ar·range′ment** *n.*

preb·end (preb′ənd) *n.* **1** A stipend allotted to a clergyman from the revenues of a cathedral or church. **2** A clergyman who receives a prebend: also **preb·en·dar·y** (preb′ən·der′ē). [< L *prae-* in front of, before + *habere* have] **—preb′en·dal** *adj.*

prec. preceding.

Pre-Cam·bri·an (prē·kam′brē·ən) *adj. & n.* See GEOLOGY. Also **Pre·cam′bri·an.**

pre·can·cel (prē·kan′səl) *v.t.* **·celed** or **·celled, ·cel·ing** or **·cel·ling** To cancel (stamps) before use on mail. *—n.* A stamp so canceled.

pre·car·i·ous (pri·kâr′ē·əs) *adj.* **1** Subject to uncertainty. **2** Subject or leading to danger; hazardous. [< L *precarius* obtained by prayer] **—pre·car′i·ous·ly** *adv.* **—pre·car′i·ous·ness** *n.* **—Syn. 1** doubtful. **2** insecure, perilous, risky.

pre·cau·tion (pri·kô′shən) *n.* **1** Care taken in advance against danger, etc. **2** A provision made for some emergency. [< L *prae-* before + *cavere* take care] **—pre·cau′tion·al, pre·cau·tion·ar·y** (pri·kô′shən·er′ē) *adj.*

pre·cede (pri·sēd′) *v.t. & v.i.* **·ced·ed, ·ced·ing** To go before in order, place, rank, time, etc. [< L *prae-* before + *cedere* go]

pre·ce·dence (pri·sēd′ns, pres′ə·dəns) *n.* **1** The act or right of preceding in place, time, or rank. **2** Higher or superior rank. Also **pre·ce′den·cy.**

prec·e·dent (pres′ə·dənt) *n.* A case that may serve as an example or model for a future action, procedure, etc. *—adj.* (pri·sēd′nt) Previous; preceding. **—prec·e·den·tial** (pres′ə·den′shəl) *adj.* **—prec′e·dent·ly** *adv.*

pre·ced·ing (pri·sē′ding) *adj.* Going before, as in time, place, or rank; foregoing.

pre·cen·tor (pri·sen′tər) *n.* The leader of the musical part of a church service. [< L *prae-* before + *canere* to sing] **—pre·cen·to·ri·al** (prē′sen·tôr′ē·əl, -tō′rē-) *adj.*

pre·cept (prē′sept) *n.* A prescribed rule of conduct or action. [< L *prae-* before + *capere* receive, take]

pre·cep·tor (pri·sep′tər) *n.* A teacher. [< L *praeceptor* teacher] **—pre·cep·to·ri·al** (prē′sep·tôr′ē·əl, -tō′rē-) *adj.*

pre·ces·sion (pri·sesh′ən) *n.* **1** The act of preceding or coming first. **2** The complex motion of a rotating body whose axis is displaced by a torque. **—pre·ces′sion·al** *adj.*

pre·cinct (prē′singkt) *n.* **1** A place definitely marked off by fixed lines. **2** A minor territorial or jurisdictional district. **3** An election district. **4** A police subdivision of a city or town. [< LL *praecingere* gird about]

pre·ci·os·i·ty (presh′ē·os′ə·tē) *n.* Extreme fastidiousness, as in speech, style, or taste. [< L *pretiosus* precious]

pre·cious (presh′əs) *adj.* 1 Highly priced or prized, as for rarity or other value. 2 Beloved; cherished. 3 *Informal* Very considerable. 4 Too refined; fastidious: a *precious* writer. [< L *pretiosus* < *pretium* price] **—pre′cious·ly** *adv.* **—pre′cious·ness** *n.* **—Syn. 1** costly, priceless, valuable.

prec·i·pice (pres′i·pis) *n.* A high, steep place; the brink of a cliff. [< L *praeceps* headlong < *prae-* before + *caput* head]

pre·cip·i·tant (pri·sip′ə·tənt) *adj.* 1 Rushing onward quickly and heedlessly: *precipitant* speed. 2 Rash in thought or action. —*n. Chem.* A substance that causes a precipitate to form. **—pre·cip′i·tance, pre·cip′i·tan·cy** *n.* **—pre·cip′i·tant·ly** *adv.*

pre·cip·i·tate (pri·sip′ə·tit) *adj.* 1 Rushing down headlong. 2 Lacking due deliberation; hasty. 3 Sudden and brief. —*v.* (pri·sip′ə·tāt) **·tat·ed, ·tat·ing** *v.t.* 1 To hasten the occurrence of. 2 To hurl from or as from a height. 3 *Meteorol.* To cause (water vapor) to condense and fall as a liquid or solid. 4 *Chem.* To separate (a constituent) in solid form, as from a solution. —*v.i.* 5 *Meteorol.* To fall as water or ice. 6 *Chem.* To separate out of solution as a solid. 7 To fall headlong; rush. —*n.* (pri·sip′ə·tit, -tāt) *Chem.* A solid precipitated from a solution. [< L *praeceps* headlong] **—pre·cip′i·tate·ly** *adv.* **—pre·cip′i·tate·ness, pre·cip′i·ta′tor** *n.* **—pre·cip′i·ta′tive** *adj.*

pre·cip·i·ta·tion (pri·sip′ə·tā′shən) *n.* 1 The state of being thrown downward. 2 Headlong or rash haste. 3 A falling, flowing, or rushing down with violence or rapidity. 4 *Chem.* **a** The process of precipitating any of the constituents of a solution. **b** PRECIPITATE. 5 *Meteorol.* The depositing of moisture or ice from the atmosphere upon the surface of the earth. 6 Rain, snow, sleet, etc.

pre·cip·i·tous (pri·sip′ə·təs) *adj.* 1 Very steep. 2 Headlong and downward in motion. 3 Headlong in disposition. [< L *praeceps* headlong] **—pre·cip′i·tous·ly** *adv.* **—pre·cip′i·tous·ness** *n.*

pré·cis (prā·sē′, prā′sē) *n. pl.* **·cis** (-sēz′, -sēz) A concise summary. [F, lit., precise]

pre·cise (pri·sīs′) *adj.* 1 Sharply or clearly determined; accurate. 2 No more and no less than. 3 Scrupulously observant of rule; punctilious. [< L *praecisus*, p.p. of *praecidere* cut off short] **—pre·cise′ness** *n.*

pre·cise·ly (pri·sīs′lē) *adv.* In a precise manner. —*interj.* Yes, indeed; quite so.

pre·ci·sion (pri·sizh′ən) *n.* The quality of being precise; accuracy. **—pre·ci′sion·ist** *n.*

pre·clude (pri·klōōd′) *v.t.* **·clud·ed, ·clud·ing** To render impossible or ineffectual by antecedent action; prevent. [< L *prae-* before + *cludere* to shut] **—pre·clu′sion** (-klōō′zhən) *n.* **—pre·clu′sive** (-klōō′siv) *adj.* **—pre·clu′sive·ly** *adv.*

pre·co·cious (pri·kō′shəs) *adj.* 1 Developing before the natural season. 2 Unusually forward or advanced, as a child. [< L *praecox*] **—pre·co′cious·ly** *adv.* **—pre·co′cious·ness, pre·coc′i·ty** (-kos′ə·tē) *n.*

pre·con·ceive (prē′kən·sēv′) *v.t.* **·ceived, ·ceiv·ing** To form an idea or opinion of beforehand. **—pre·con·cep·tion** (prē′kən·sep′shən) *n.*

pre·con·cert (prē′kən·sûrt′) *v.t.* To arrange in advance, as by agreement. **—pre′con·cert′ed·ly** *adv.*

pre·con·di·tion (prē′kən·dish′ən) *n.* Something that is required for something that follows; prerequisite.

pre·cur·sor (pri·kûr′sər) *n.* One who or that which precedes; forerunner. [< L *prae-* before + *currere* to run]

pre·cur·so·ry (pri·kûr′sə·rē) *adj.* 1 Being a precursor. 2 Preliminary; introductory.

pred. predicate; predication; prediction.

pre·da·cious (pri·dā′shəs) *adj.* PREDATORY. Also **pre·da′·ceous.** [< L *praeda* prey] **—pre·da′cious·ness, pre·dac′i·ty** (-das′ə·tē) *n.*

pred·a·to·ry (pred′ə·tôr′ē, -tō′rē) *adj.* 1 Living by preying upon other animals: a *predatory* animal. 2 Characterized by plundering or stealing. [< L *praeda* prey] **—pred′·a·tor, pred′a·to′ri·ness** *n.* **—pred′a·to′ri·ly** *adv.*

pre·de·cease (prē′di·sēs′) *v.t.* **·ceased, ·ceas·ing** To die before, as another person.

pred·e·ces·sor (pred′ə·ses′ər) *n.* 1 One who goes or has gone before another in a position, office, etc. 2 A thing that has preceded another. 3 An ancestor. [< L *prae-* before + *decedere* retire]

pre·des·ti·nate (prē·des′tə·nit, -nāt) *adj.* Foreordained by divine decree. —*v.t.* **·nat·ed, ·nat·ing** (-nāt) To foreordain by divine decree or purpose. [< L *prae-* before + *destinare* destine]

pre·des·ti·na·tion (prē·des′tə·nā′shən) *n.* 1 The act of predestinating; fate. 2 *Theol.* The foreordination of all things by God.

pre·des·tine (prē·des′tin) *v.t.* **·tined, ·tin·ing** 1 To decree or destine beforehand. 2 PREDESTINATE.

pre·de·ter·mine (prē′di·tûr′min) *v.t.* **·mined, ·min·ing** To determine beforehand; decide in advance. **—pre′de·ter′mi·nate** (-mə·nit) *adj.* **—pre′de·ter′mi·na′tion** *n.*

pred·i·ca·ble (pred′i·kə·bəl) *adj.* That may be predicated or affirmed. **—pred′i·ca·bil′i·ty, pred′i·ca·ble·ness** *n.* **—pred′·i·ca·bly** *adv.*

pre·dic·a·ment (pri·dik′ə·mənt) *n.* 1 A trying, embarrassing, or puzzling situation. 2 A specific state, position, or situation. [< LL *praedicamentum* that which is predicated] **—Syn. 1** dilemma, fix, plight, strait.

pred·i·cate (pred′i·kāt) *v.* **·cat·ed, ·cat·ing** *v.t.* 1 To declare; affirm. 2 To affirm concerning the subject of a proposition. 3 To found or base (an argument, proposition, etc.): with *on* or *upon.* —*v.i.* 4 To make a statement or affirmation. —*adj.* 1 Predicated. 2 *Gram.* Belonging to the predicate. In "Trees are leafy," *leafy* is a **predicate adjective**; in "He was king," *king* is a **predicate noun.** —*n.* (pred′i·kit) *Gram.* The word or words in a sentence that express what is affirmed or denied of a subject. In the sentence, "Life is short," "is short" is the predicate. [< L *praedicare* make known] **—pred′i·ca′tion** *n.* **—pred′i·ca′tive** *adj.* **—pred′i·ca′·tive·ly** *adv.*

pre·dict (pri·dikt′) *v.t.* 1 To make known beforehand. 2 To assert on the basis of theory, data, or experience but in advance of proof. —*v.i.* 3 To make a prediction. [< L *prae* before + *dicere* say] **—pre·dict′a·ble** *adj.* **—pre·dict′a·bly** *adv.* **—pre·dic′tor** *n.*

pre·dic·tion (pri·dik′shən) *n.* 1 The act of predicting. 2 The thing predicted; forecast. **—pre·dic′tive** *adj.* **—pre·dic′·tive·ly** *adv.*

pre·di·gest (prē′di·jest′, -dī-) *v.t.* To treat (food), as with digestive enzymes, before introduction into the stomach. **—pre′di·ges′tion** *n.*

pre·di·lec·tion (pred′ə·lek′shən, prē′də-) *n.* A preference or liking: with *for.* [< L *prae-* before + *diligere* love, choose]

pre·dis·pose (prē′dis·pōz′) *v.t.* **·posed, ·pos·ing** To give a tendency to; make susceptible: Exhaustion *predisposes* one to sickness. **—pre·dis·po·si·tion** (prē′dis·pə·zish′ən) *n.*

pre·dom·i·nant (pri·dom′ə·nənt) *adj.* Superior in power, influence, number, or degree. **—pre·dom′in·ance, pre·dom′·in·an·cy** *n.* **—pre·dom′i·nant·ly** *adv.*

pre·dom·i·nate (pri·dom′ə·nāt) *v.i.* **·nat·ed, ·nat·ing** 1 To have influence or control: with *over.* 2 To be superior to all others, as in power, height, number, etc. **—pre·dom′i·nat′ing·ly** *adv.* **—pre·dom′i·na′tion** *n.*

pre·em·i·nent (prē·em′ə·nənt) *adj.* Supremely eminent; distinguished above all others. **—pre·em′i·nent·ly** *adv.* **—pre·em′i·nence** *n.*

pre·empt (prē·empt′) *v.t.* 1 To seize or appropriate beforehand. 2 To occupy (public land) so as to acquire by preemption. **—pre·emp′tor** *n.*

pre·emp·tion (prē·emp′shən) *n.* 1 The right or act of purchasing before others. 2 Public land obtained by exercising this right. [< L *prae-* before + *emptus,* pp. of *emere* buy] **—pre·emp′tive, pre·emp′to·ry** (-tər·ē) *adj.*

preen (prēn) *v.t.* 1 To trim with the beak, as birds their feathers. 2 To dress or adorn (oneself) carefully. —*v.i.* 3 To primp; prink. [ME *preinen*] **—preen′er** *n.*

pref. preface; prefatory; preference; preferred; prefix.

pre·fab (prē′fab′) *Informal n.* A prefabricated structure. —*adj.* Prefabricated. —*v.t.* **·fabbed, ·fab·bing** PREFABRICATE.

pre·fab·ri·cate (prē·fab′rə·kāt) *v.t.* **·cat·ed, ·cat·ing** 1 To fabricate beforehand. 2 To manufacture in sections that can be rapidly assembled, as a building. **—pre·fab′ri·ca′tion** *n.*

pref·ace (pref′is) *n.* 1 A brief explanation to the reader at the beginning of a publication. 2 Any introductory speech, writing, etc. —*v.t.* **·aced, ·ac·ing** 1 To introduce or furnish with a preface. 2 To be or serve as a preface for. [< L *prae-* before + *fari* speak]

pref·a·to·ry (pref′ə·tôr′ē, -tō′rē) *adj.* Of the nature of a preface; introductory. Also **pref′a·to′ri·al. —pref′a·to′ri·ly** *adv.*

pre·fect (prē′fekt) *n.* 1 In ancient Rome, any of various civil and military officials. 2 In France, the chief administrator of a department. [< L *prae-* before + *facere* make, do]

pre·fec·ture (prē′fek·chər) *n.* The office, district, or authority of a prefect. **—pre·fec′tur·al** *adj.*

pre·fer (pri·fûr′) *v.t.* **·ferred, ·fer·ring** 1 To hold in higher regard or esteem; like better. 2 To give priority to. 3 To advance or promote. 4 To offer, as a suit or charge, for consideration or decision before a court. [< L *prae-* before + *ferre* to bear] **—pre·fer′rer** *n.*

pref·er·a·ble (pref′ər·ə·bəl) *adj.* To be preferred; more desirable. **—pref′er·a·bil′i·ty, pref′er·a·ble·ness** *n.* **—pref′er·a·bly** *adv.*

pref·er·ence (pref′ər·əns) *n.* 1 The choice of one thing or person over another. 2 The state of being preferred. 3 An object of favor or choice. 4 The giving of priority to one person over others; favoritism. 5 The right to a prior choice or claim.

pref·er·en·tial (pref′ə·ren′shəl) *adj.* 1 Indicating or arising from partiality. 2 Possessing or giving priority. **—pref′er·en′tial·ism** *n.* **—pref′er·en′tial·ly** *adv.*

preferential shop A shop that gives precedence to union members when hiring, granting promotions, etc.

pre·fer·ment (pri·fûr′mənt) *n.* 1 The act of promoting or appointing to higher office. 2 A superior post or dignity: said esp. of ecclesiastical rank.

pre·ferred (pri·fûrd′) *adj.* 1 Having the first claim: *preferred* bonds or stock. 2 Having gained promotion. 3 Chosen by or as if by preference.

preferred stock The stock of a corporation that assures the holder of dividends before any are paid on common stock.

pre·fig·ure (prē·fig′yər) *v.t.* **·ured, ·ur·ing** 1 To represent in advance; foreshadow. 2 To imagine or picture to oneself beforehand. **—pre·fig′u·ra′tion** *n.* **—pre·fig·ur·a·tive** (prē·fig′yər·ə·tiv) *adj.*

pre·fix (prē′fiks) *n.* 1 *Gram.* A syllable affixed to the beginning of a word to modify or alter the meaning, as *non-* in *nonessential* or *post-* in *postwar.* 2 Something placed before, as a title before a name. —*v.t.* (prē·fiks′) To put before or at the beginning. [< L< *prae-* before + *figere* to fix] **—pre′fix·al** *adj.* **—pre·fix·ion** (prē·fik′shən) *n.*

preg·na·ble (preg′nə·bəl) *adj.* Weak enough to be conquered. [< L *prehendere* seize] **—preg′na·bil′i·ty** *n.*

preg·nan·cy (preg′nən·sē) *n. pl.* **·cies** The condition or a time of being pregnant.

preg·nant (preg′nənt) *adj.* 1 Carrying developing offspring in the uterus. 2 Carrying great weight or significance. 3 Fruitful; teeming with ideas. 4 Implying more than is expressed. [< L *praegnans*] **—preg′nant·ly** *adv.*

pre·hen·sile (pri·hen′sil) *adj.* Adapted for grasping or holding, as the tail of a monkey. [< L *prehendere* seize] **—pre·hen·sil·i·ty** (prē′hen·sil′ə·tē) *n.*

pre·his·tor·ic (prē′his·tôr′ik, -tor′-, prē·is-) *adj.* Of or belonging to a time before that covered by written history. Also **pre′his·tor′i·cal. —pre′his·tor′i·cal·ly** *adv.* **—pre′his′to·ry** *n.*

pre·judge (prē·juj′) *v.t.* **·judged, ·judg·ing** To judge before or without proper inquiry. **—pre·judg′er, pre·judg′ment, pre·judge′ment** *n.*

prej·u·dice (prej′o͞o·dis) *n.* 1 A judgment or opinion formed without due examination of facts, etc. 2 An unreasonable judgment held despite facts to the contrary. 3 Fear of and hatred for other races, religions, etc. 4 Detriment arising from a hasty and unfair judgment. —*v.t.* **·diced, ·dic·ing** 1 To affect or influence with a prejudice; bias. 2 To affect detrimentally by some action or opinion. [< L *prae-* before + *judicium* judgment] **—Syn.** *n.* 1 bias, preconception. 3 bigotry, intolerance, racism.

prej·u·di·cial (prej′o͞o·dish′əl) *adj.* Having power or tendency to injure. **—prej′u·di′cial·ly** *adv.*

prel·a·cy (prel′ə·sē) *n. pl.* **·cies** 1 The system of church government by prelates. 2 The function of a prelate. 3 Prelates collectively.

prel·ate (prel′it) *n.* A member of a higher order of clergy, as a bishop. [< L *praelatus* set over] **—prel′ate·ship** *n.*

prelim. preliminary.

pre·lim·i·nar·y (pri·lim′ə·ner′ē) *adj.* Antecedent or introductory to the main discourse, proceedings, or business; prefatory; preparatory. —*n. pl.* **·ries** 1 A preparatory step or procedure. 2 A preliminary examination. [< PRE- + L *limen, liminis* threshold] **—pre·lim′i·nar′i·ly** *adv.*

prel·ude (prel′yo͞od, prāl-, prā′lo͞od, prē′-) *n.* 1 *Music* **a** An independent instrumental composition of moderate length. **b** An opening piece at the start of a church service. **c** The overture of an opera. **d** An opening section or movement for a composition. 2 Any introductory or opening performance or event. —*v.* **·ud·ed, ·ud·ing** *v.t.* 1 To introduce with a prelude. 2 To serve as a prelude to. —*v.i.* 3 To serve as a prelude. 4 To provide or play a prelude. [< L *prae-* before + *ludere* to play]

prem. premium.

pre·mar·i·tal (prē·mar′ə·təl) *adj.* Occurring or existing before marriage. **—pre·mar′i·tal·ly** *adv.*

pre·ma·ture (prē′mə·cho͝or′, -t(y)o͝or′) *adj.* Existing, arriving, or done before the proper time; untimely. [< L < *prae-* before + *maturus* ripe] **—pre′ma·ture′ly** *adv.* **—pre′ma·tu′ri·ty, pre′ma·ture′ness** *n.*

pre·med·i·cal (prē·med′i·kəl) *adj.* Pertaining to studies required for admission to medical school.

pre·med·i·tate (prē·med′ə·tāt) *v.t.* & *v.i.* **·tat·ed, ·tat·ing** To plan or consider beforehand. **—pre·med′i·tat′ed·ly** *adv.* **—pre·med′i·ta′tive** *adj.* **—pre·med′i·ta′tor** *n.*

pre·med·i·ta·tion (prē·med′ə·tā′shən) *n.* The deliberate intention to do a certain thing, esp. to commit a crime.

pre·mi·er (pri·mir′, -myir′, prē′mē·ər, *esp. Brit.* prem′·yər) *adj.* 1 First in rank or position; principal. 2 First in order of occurrence; earliest. —*n.* 1 The head of government, esp. a prime minister. 2 In Canada, the prime minister of a province. [F< L *primus* first] **—pre′mi·er·ship** *n.*

pre·miere (pri·myâr′, -mir′, -mē·âr′) *adj.* 1 First. 2 Leading; chief: *premiere* ballerina. —*n.* The formal opening of a play, opera, film, ballet, etc. —*v.* **·miered, ·mier·ing** *v.t.* 1 To present publicly for the first time, as a play. —*v.i.* 2 To make one's first public performance. 3 To present a play, opera, etc., publicly for the first time. Also **pre·mière.** [< F *première*]

prem·ise (prem′is) *n.* 1 A proposition laid down that serves as a ground for argument or for a conclusion. 2 *Logic* Either of the two propositions in a syllogism from which the conclusion necessarily follows. 3 *pl.* A distinct portion of real estate; land with its appurtenances, as buildings. —*v.* (prem′is, pri·mīz′) **·ised, ·is·ing** *v.t.* 1 To state beforehand, as by way of introduction or explanation. —*v.i.* 2 To make a premise. [< L *praemissus,* pp. of *praemittere* send before]

pre·mi·um (prē′mē·əm) *n.* 1 A reward or prize. 2 A sum offered or given to secure a loan. 3 The rate at which stocks, shares, or money are valued in excess of their nominal value. 4 The amount paid for insurance. 5 An object offered free or at low cost as an inducement to purchasers of certain goods or services. **—at a premium** Above par; valuable and in demand. [< L *prae-* before + *emere* to buy]

pre·mo·lar (prē·mō′lər) *adj.* Situated in front of a molar tooth. —*n.* A premolar tooth.

pre·mo·ni·tion (prē′mə·nish′ən, prem′ə-) *n.* 1 A warning of something yet to occur. 2 An instinctive foreboding; presentiment. [< L *prae-* before + *monere* warn] **—pre·mon·i·to·ry** (pri·mon′ə·tôr′ē, -tō′rē) *adj.* **—pre·mon′i·to′ri·ly** *adv.*

pre·na·tal (prē·nāt′l) *adj.* Happening, done, or made before birth: *prenatal* care. **—pre·na′tal·ly** *adv.*

pre·oc·cu·py (prē·ok′yə·pī) *v.t.* **·pied, ·py·ing** 1 To engage fully; engross, as the mind. 2 To take possession of in advance of another or others. **—pre·oc′cu·pan·cy** (-pən·sē), **pre·oc·cu·pa·tion** (prē·ok′yə·pā′shən) *n.*

pre·or·dain (prē′ôr·dān′) *v.t.* To decide or decree beforehand; foreordain. **—pre·or·di·na·tion** (prē′ôr·də·nā′shən) *n.*
prep (prep) *adj. Informal* Preparatory: a *prep* school.
prep. preparation; preparatory; prepare; preposition.
pre·pack·age (prē·pak′ij) *v.t.* **·aged, ·a·ging** To package manufactured articles, food, etc., before placing on sale for consumers.
prep·a·ra·tion (prep′ə·rā′shən) *n.* **1** The act, process, or operation of preparing. **2** The fact or state of being prepared; readiness. **3** Something made or prepared, as a compound for a specific purpose; medicinal *preparations.* **4** Preliminary study, as for college or business.
pre·par·a·to·ry (pri·par′ə·tôr′ē, -tō′rē) *adj.* **1** Serving as a preparation; introductory. **2** Occupied in preparation, esp. for higher learning. **—pre·par′a·tor′i·ly** *adv.*
preparatory school A school in which students are prepared for admission to a college or university.
pre·pare (pri·pâr′) *v.* **·pared, ·par·ing** *v.t.* **1** To make ready, fit, or qualified. **2** To provide with what is needed; outfit. **3** To bring to a state of completeness. *—v.i.* **4** To make preparations; get ready. [<L *prae-* before + *parare* make ready] **—pre·par·ed·ly** (pri·pâr′id·lē) *adv.* **—pre·par′er** *n.*
pre·par·ed·ness (pri·pâr′id·nis, -par′-) *n.* **1** Readiness. **2** Military readiness for war.
pre·pay (prē·pā′) *v.t.* **·paid, ·pay·ing** To pay or pay for in advance. **—pre·pay′ment** *n.*
pre·pon·der·ant (pri·pon′dər·ənt) *adj.* Having superior force, weight, importance, number, etc. **—pre·pon′der·ance, pre·pon′der·an·cy** (-ən·sē) *n.* **—pre·pon′der·ant·ly** *adv.*
pre·pon·der·ate (pri·pon′də·rāt) *v.i.* **·at·ed, ·at·ing** **1** To be of greater weight. **2** To be of greater power, importance, quantity, etc.; predominate. [<L *prae-* before + *ponderare* weigh] **—pre·pon′der·a′tion** *n.*
prep·o·si·tion (prep′ə·zish′ən) *n. Gram.* **1** A word such as *for, from, in, to, with,* etc., functioning to indicate certain relations between other words. A preposition is usually placed before its object (whence its name), and together they constitute a prepositional phrase: He sat *beside* the fire; sick *at* heart; a man *of* honor. **2** Any word or construction that functions in a similar manner: He telephoned *in reference to* (equals *about*) your letter. [<L *prae-* before + *ponere* to place] **—prep′o·si′tion·al** *adj.* **—prep′o·si′tion·al·ly** *adv.*
pre·pos·sess (prē′pə·zes′) *v.t.* **1** To preoccupy to the exclusion of other ideas, beliefs, etc. **2** To impress or influence beforehand favorably. **3** To prejudice. **—pre′pos·ses′sion** *n.*
pre·pos·sess·ing (prē′pə·zes′ing) *adj.* Inspiring a favorable opinion from the start. **—pre′pos·sess′ing·ly** *adv.*
pre·pos·ter·ous (pri·pos′tər·əs) *adj.* Contrary to nature, reason, or common sense; ridiculous. [<L *praeposterus* the last first, inverted] **—pre·pos′ter·ous·ly** *adv.* **—pre·pos′ter·ous·ness** *n.* **—Syn.** absurd, foolish, idiotic, irrational, silly.
pre·puce (prē′pyōōs) *n.* FORESKIN. [<L *praeputium*]
pre·quel (prē′kwəl) *n.* A story in the form of a book, movie, or television program that predates the events of an earlier story. [<PRE- + (SE)QUEL]
pre·req·ui·site (prē·rek′wə·zit) *adj.* Required as necessary to something that follows. *—n.* Something that is prerequisite.
pre·rog·a·tive (pri·rog′ə·tiv) *n.* **1** An unquestionable right, esp. a hereditary or official right: the royal *prerogative.* **2** Any generally recognized privilege. *—adj.* Of or holding a prerogative. [<L *praerogativa* right of voting first]
Pres. President.
pres. present; presidency.
pres·age (pres′ij) *n.* **1** An indication of something to come. **2** A presentiment; foreboding. **3** Prophetic meaning or import; prediction. *—v.* (pri·sāj′) **·saged, ·sag·ing** *v.t.* **1** To give a portent of. **2** To have a presentiment of. **3** To predict; foretell. *—v.i.* **4** To make a prediction. [<L *praebefore* + *sagire* be aware of] **—pre·sag′er** *n.* **—pre·sag′ing·ly** *adv.*
pres·by·ter (prez′bə·tər, pres′-) *n.* **1** In the early church, one of the elders. **2** In the Presbyterian church, an ordained clergyman or a layman who is a member of the governing body of a congregation. [<Gk. *presbyteros* an elder] **—pres′by·te′ri·al** (-bə·tir′ē·əl), **pres·byt′er·al** (-bit′ər·əl) *adj.*
Pres·by·te·ri·an (prez′bə·tir′ē·ən, pres′-) *n.* **1** One who believes in the government of the church by presbyters. **2** A member of the Presbyterian church. *—adj.* Of or pertaining to the Presbyterian church. **—Pres′by·te′ri·an·ism** *n.*
pres·by·ter·y (prez′bə·ter′ē, pres′-) *n. pl.* **·ter·ies** **1** In the Presbyterian church, a court having the ecclesiastical rule of a given district. **2** The district so represented. **3** The part of a church set apart for the officiating clergy.
pre·school (prē′skōōl′) *adj.* For or designating a child past infancy but under school age. *—n.* (prē′skōōl′) A nursery school.
pre·school·er (prē′skōōl′ər) *n.* **1** A child under school age. **2** A child attending a nursery school.
pre·sci·ence (presh′ē·əns, prē′shē-) *n.* Knowledge of events before they take place. [<L *prae-* before + *scire* know] **—pre′sci·ent** *adj.* **—pre′sci·ent·ly** *adv.*
pre·scribe (pri·skrīb′) *v.* **·scribed, ·scrib·ing** *v.t.* **1** To set down as a direction or rule to be followed. **2** To order (a medicine or treatment) as a remedy. *—v.i.* **3** To lay down laws or rules. **4** To order medical treatment. [<L *prae-* before + *scribere* write] **—pre·scrib′er** *n.* **—Syn. 1** command, designate, enjoin, ordain.
pre·script (prē′skript) *n.* A prescription or direction, as a rule of conduct. *—adj.* (pri·skript′, prē′skript) Prescribed.
pre·scrip·tion (pri·skrip′shən) *n.* **1** The act of prescribing, directing, or dictating. **2** That which is prescribed. **3 a** A physician's order for a medicine. **b** The remedy so ordered. **—pre·scrip′tive** *adj.* **—pre·scrip′tive·ly** *adv.*
pres·ence (prez′əns) *n.* **1** The state or fact of being present. **2** Vicinity within view or access: He said that in my *presence.* **3** Something invisible, but sensed, as a ghost. **4** Personal appearance; bearing. **5** Personal qualities collectively. **6** A person of high rank: a royal *presence.*
presence of mind Alertness and readiness of thinking in a situation of sudden danger, embarrassment, etc.
pres·ent¹ (prez′ənt) *adj.* **1** Being in a place or company referred to; being at hand. **2** Now going on; current. **3** *Gram.* Relating to or signifying what is going on at the time being: the *present* tense. *—n.* **1** Present time; now. **2** *Gram.* **a** The present tense. **b** A verb in this tense. **—at present** Now. **—by these presents** *Law* By this document. **—for the present** For the time being. [<L *praesens* being in front of or at hand]
pre·sent² (pri·zent′) *v.t.* **1** To bring into the presence or acquaintance of another. **2** To display. **3** To suggest to the mind: This *presents* a problem. **4** To put forward for consideration or action, as a petition. **5** To make a gift to. **6** To offer formally: to *present* a diploma. **7** To exhibit before the public: to *present* a play. **8** To give or send: to *present* a bill. **—present arms 1** To hold a gun vertically in front of and close to the body in salute. **2** This salute. **3** The command for a soldier to salute in this way. *—n.* (prez′ənt) That which is presented or given. [<L *praesentare* set before<*praesens* present] **—pre·sent′er** *n.*
pre·sent·a·ble (pri·zen′tə·bəl) *adj.* **1** Fit to be offered or bestowed. **2** In suitable condition or attire for company. **3** Fit to be shown or seen. **—pre·sent′a·bil′i·ty, pre·sent′a·ble·ness** *n.* **—pre·sent′a·bly** *adv.*
pres·en·ta·tion (prez′ən·tā′shən, prē′zən-) *n.* **1** The offering of a gift. **2** That which is bestowed; a present. **3** A formal introduction, esp. to a superior: *presentation* at court. **4** The bringing before the public, as a play. **5** A submitting for consideration: the *presentation* of a plan.
pres·ent-day (prez′ənt·dā′) *adj.* Of the present time; current.
pre·sen·ti·ment (pri·zen′tə·mənt) *n.* A prophetic sense of something to come; a foreboding. [<L *prae-* before + *sentire* feel]
pres·ent·ly (prez′ənt·lē) *adv.* After a little time; shortly.

pre·sent·ment (pri·zent′mənt) *n.* 1 The act of presenting. 2 A stage representation or a portrait.

present participle *Gram.* A participle expressing present action: *falling* snow.

present perfect *Gram.* The verb tense expressing an action completed by the present time: By now he *has finished* the task.

present tense *Gram.* The tense marking present time: I *go, do go, am going.*

pre·ser·va·tive (pri·zûr′və·tiv) *adj.* Serving or tending to preserve. —*n.* A substance that prevents deterioration or spoilage.

pre·serve (pri·zûrv′) *v.* **·served, ·serv·ing** *v.t.* 1 To keep in safety; guard. 2 To keep intact or unimpaired. 3 To prepare (food) for future consumption, as by drying, salting, pickling, canning, etc. 4 To keep from decomposition: to *preserve* a specimen in alcohol. 5 To keep for one's private use. —*v.i.* 6 To make preserves, as of fruit. —*n.* 1 *Usu. pl.* Fruit which has been cooked, usu. with sugar, to prevent its fermenting. 2 A place set apart for one's own private use. 3 An area set aside for the protection of wildlife. [< L *prae-* before + *servare* keep] **—pre·serv′a·bil′i·ty, pres·er·va·tion** (prez′ər·vā′shən), **pre·serv′er** *n.* **—Syn.** *v.* 1 defend, protect, secure, shield. 2 maintain, uphold.

pre·side (pri·zīd′) *v.i.* **·sid·ed, ·sid·ing** 1 To be in charge of an assembly, government, etc. 2 To exercise control. [< L *praesidere* sit in front of, protect, guard] **—pre·sid′er** *n.*

pres·i·den·cy (prez′ə·dən·sē) *n. pl.* **·cies** 1 The office, function, or term of office of a president. 2 *Often cap.* The office of president of the United States.

pres·i·dent (prez′ə·dənt) *n.* 1 One who is chosen to preside over an organized body, as a corporation, society, college, etc. 2 *Usu. cap.* The chief executive of a republic, as of the United States. **—pres·i·den·tial** (prez′ə·den′shəl) *adj.*

pre·sid·i·um (pri·sid′ē·əm, -zid′-) *n.* Any of several permanent executive committees in the U.S.S.R.

Pre·sid·i·um (pri·sid′ē·əm, -zid′-) *n.* The supreme policy-making committee of the Communist party of the U.S.S.R.

press[1] (pres) *v.t.* 1 To act upon by weight or pressure. 2 To compress so as to extract the juice. 3 To extract by pressure, as juice. 4 To exert pressure upon so as to smooth or shape. 5 To smooth or shape by heat and pressure, as clothes; iron. 6 To embrace closely; hug. 7 To force or impel; drive. 8 To distress or harass: I am *pressed* for time. 9 To urge persistently; importune. 10 To advocate persistently. 11 To put forward insistently: to *press* a gift on a friend. 12 To urge onward; hasten. —*v.i.* 13 To exert pressure; bear heavily. 14 To advance forcibly or with speed: *Press* on! 15 To press clothes, etc. 16 To crowd; cram. 17 To be urgent or importunate. —*n.* 1 A dense throng. 2 The act of crowding together or of straining forward. 3 Hurry or pressure of affairs. 4 An upright closet for clothes, etc.: a linen *press.* 5 An apparatus or machine by which pressure is applied, as for making wine, cider, etc. 6 Newspapers or periodical literature collectively. 7 The body of persons writing for such publications. 8 The art, process, or business of printing. 9 The place of business in which a printing press is set up. 10 Criticism, comments, news, etc., in newspapers and periodicals. [< L *pressare,* freq. of *premere* to press] **—press′er** *n.*

Press *def.5*

press[2] (pres) *v.t.* 1 To force into military or naval service. 2 To put to use in a manner not intended or desired.

press agent A person employed to advance the interests of his client by advertisements and other notices; a publicity agent. **—press-a·gen·try** (pres′ā′jən·trē) *n.*

press conference An interview granted by a celebrity, government official, etc., to a number of journalists at the same time.

press·ing (pres′ing) *adj.* Demanding immediate attention; urgent. **—press′ing·ly** *adv.* **—Syn.** exigent, imperative, important, necessary.

press·man (pres′mən) *n. pl.* **·men** (-mən) A man who operates or manages a printing press.

press release 1 A bulletin prepared by a news service. 2 A statement by a press agent, public relations department, etc., released to the press.

pres·sure (presh′ər) *n.* 1 The act of pressing, or the state of being pressed. 2 *Physics* A force distributed over a surface, expressed as units of force per unit area. 3 Pressure of a fluid exceeding atmospheric pressure: a hose under *pressure.* 4 An impelling or constraining influence: the *pressure* to conform socially. 5 Exigent demand on one's time or energy: to be under daily *pressure.* —*v.t.* **·sured, ·sur·ing** *Informal* To compel, as by forceful persuasion or influence. **—pres′sur·al** *adj.*

pressure cooker A vessel for cooking food at high temperature by means of steam under pressure.

pressure group An organized group which seeks to influence legislators and public opinion in behalf of its own special interests.

pres·sur·ize (presh′ə·rīz) *v.t.* **·ized, ·iz·ing** 1 To maintain near-normal atmospheric pressure in (an aircraft, space vehicle, or other enclosure in a low-pressure environment). 2 To maintain air pressure inside (an underwater vehicle, caisson, etc.) equal to the ambient water pressure. 3 To design (a bathysphere, etc.) to withstand high external pressure. 4 To increase pressure on or in. **—pres′sur·i·za′tion** *n.*

press·work (pres′wûrk′) *n.* 1 The operating or management of a printing press. 2 The work done by the press.

pres·ti·dig·i·ta·tion (pres′tə·dij′ə·tā′shən) *n.* The art of sleight of hand. [< LL *praestus* nimble + *digitus* finger] **—pres′ti·dig′i·ta′tor** *n.*

pres·tige (pres·tēzh′, -tēj′) *n.* Authority or importance based on past achievements or reputation. [< L *praestigium* illusion]

pres·ti·gious (pres·tij′əs, -tē′jəs) *adj.* Having or bestowing prestige or renown. **—pres·ti′gious·ly** *adv.* **—pres·ti′·gious·ness** *n.*

pres·tis·si·mo (pres·tis′i·mō, *Ital.* pres·tēs′sē·mō) *adj. & adv. Music* As fast as possible. —*n.* A prestissimo passage, section, or movement. [Ital., superlative of *presto*]

pres·to (pres′tō) *adv. & adj.* 1 *Music* Very fast. 2 At once; speedily. —*n.* A presto passage or movement. [Ital.]

pre·stressed concrete (prē′strest′) Concrete cast over taut steel cables, etc., to increase its tensile strength.

pre·sume (pri·zōōm′) *v.* **·sumed, ·sum·ing** *v.t.* 1 To take upon oneself without permission. 2 To assume to be true until disproved: I *presume* you are right. —*v.i.* 3 To make excessive demands: with *on* or *upon:* He *presumes* on my good nature. [< L *praesumere* take first] **—pre·sum′a·ble** *adj.* **—pre·sum′a·bly, pre·sum·ed·ly** (pri·zōō′mid·lē) *adv.* **—pre·sum′er** *n.*

pre·sump·tion (pri·zump′shən) *n.* 1 The act of presuming. 2 Something taken for granted. 3 A reason for presuming; probability. 4 Overweening self-assertion; arrogance.

pre·sump·tive (pri·zump′tiv) *adj.* 1 Affording reasonable grounds for belief; probable. 2 Based on presumption or probability: an heir *presumptive.* **—pre·sump′tive·ly** *adv.*

pre·sump·tu·ous (pri·zump′chōō·əs) *adj.* Unduly confident or bold; forward. **—pre·sump′tu·ous·ly** *adv.* **—pre·sump′tu·ous·ness** *n.*

pre·sup·pose (prē′sə·pōz′) *v.t.* **·posed, ·pos·ing** 1 To imply or involve as a necessary antecedent condition. 2 To take for granted. **—pre·sup·po·si·tion** (prē′sup·ə·zish′ən) *n.*

pret. preterit.

pre·tend (pri·tend′) *v.t.* 1 To assume or display a false appearance of. 2 To claim or assert falsely. 3 To feign in play; make believe. —*v.i.* 4 To make believe, as in play or for the purpose of deception. 5 To put forward a claim: with *to.* [< L *prae-* before + *tendere* spread out]

pre·tend·er (pri·ten′dər) *n.* 1 One who pretends. 2 One who advances a dubious claim, esp. to a throne.

pre·tense (prē′tens, pri·tens′) *n.* 1 The act of pretending, as in play; a making believe. 2 Something pretended; ruse. 3 The false assumption of a character or condition. 4 A claim to a right or title. 5 A false claim. *Brit. sp.* **pre·tence.** **—Syn.** 2 pretext, wile. 3 affectation, dissimulation, show.

pre·ten·sion (pri·ten′shən) *n.* 1 A claim put forward, as to a right, title, etc. 2 The making of such a claim. 3 Affectation; display. 4 A bold or presumptuous assertion.

pre·ten·tious (pri·ten′shəs) *adj.* 1 Making unwarranted or exaggerated claims to greatness or importance: a *pretentious* person. 2 Showy or ostentatious: a *pretentious* style of living. —**pre·ten′tious·ly** *adv.* —**pre·ten′tious·ness** *n.*

pret·er·it (pret′ər·it) *Gram. adj.* Signifying past time. —*n.* 1 The past tense. 2 A verb form expressing this tense. *Came* is the preterit of *come* and *called* of *call.* Also **pret′·er·ite.** [< L *praeteritus* past]

pre·ter·nat·u·ral (prē′tər·nach′ər·əl, -rəl) *adj.* 1 Diverging from or exceeding the common order of nature; extraordinary. 2 Supernatural. —**pre′ter·nat′u·ral·ism** *n.* —**pre′ter·nat′u·ral·ly** *adv.*

pre·text (prē′tekst) *n.* A fictitious reason given to conceal a real one; a specious excuse or explanation. [< L *prae-* before + *texere* to weave]

pret·ti·fy (prit′i·fī) *v.t.* **·fied, ·fy·ing** To make pretty, esp. in a fussy way. —**pret′ti·fi·ca′tion** *n.*

pret·ty (prit′ē) *adj.* **·ti·er, ·ti·est** 1 Characterized by delicacy or gracefulness; attractive. 2 Good; nice: often used ironically: A *pretty* mess you've made of it! 3 *Informal* Considerable. —*adv.* 1 Moderately; to a fair extent: He looked *pretty* well. 2 Very; quite: He's grown *pretty* fast. —**sitting pretty** *Informal* In good circumstances. —*n. pl.* **·ties** A pretty thing or person. [< OE *prættig* tricky, cunning] —**pret′ti·ly** *adv.* —**pret′ti·ness** *n.*

pret·zel (pret′səl) *n.* A glazed salted biscuit in the form of a loose knot. [< G *Brezel*]

pre·vail (pri·vāl′) *v.i.* 1 To gain mastery: with *over* or *against.* 2 To be effective; succeed. 3 To be prevalent. 4 To have general or widespread use or acceptance. —**prevail on (upon** or **with)** To persuade; influence. [< L *prae-* before + *valere* be strong]

pre·vail·ing (pri·vā′ling) *adj.* 1 Current; prevalent. 2 Having effective power or influence. —**pre·vail′ing·ly** *adv.* —**pre·vail′ing·ness** *n.*

prev·a·lent (prev′ə·lənt) *adj.* 1 Predominant. 2 Of wide extent or frequent occurrence. [< L *praevalere* prevail] —**prev′a·lence** *n.* —**prev′a·lent·ly** *adv.*

pre·var·i·cate (pri·var′ə·kāt) *v.i.* **·cat·ed, ·cat·ing** To speak or act in a deceptive manner; lie. [< L *praevaricare* walk crookedly] —**pre·var′i·ca′tion, pre·var′i·ca′tor** *n.*

pre·vent (pri·vent′) *v.t.* 1 To keep from happening, as by previous measures: to *prevent* accidents. 2 To keep from doing something; hinder. [< L *prae-* before + *venire* come] —**pre·vent′a·ble** or **·i·ble** *adj.* —**pre·vent′a·bil′i·ty** or **·i·bil′i·ty, pre·vent′er** *n.*

pre·ven·tion (pri·ven′shən) *n.* 1 The act of preventing. 2 A hindrance; obstruction.

pre·ven·tive (pri·ven′tiv) *adj.* Intended or serving to prevent, esp. to ward off a disease. —*n.* That which prevents or hinders, esp. a method of warding off disease. Also **pre·vent·a·tive** (pri·ven′tə·tiv). —**pre·ven′tive·ly** *adv.* —**pre·ven′·tive·ness** *n.*

pre·view (prē′vyōō′) *n.* 1 A showing, to the public, as of a motion picture, etc., before its formal opening. 2 The showing of scenes from a motion picture or television show in advance of its scheduled presentation as a means of advertisement. —*v.t.* (prē·vyōō′) To view in advance.

pre·vi·ous (prē′vē·əs) *adj.* 1 Being or taking place before something else in time or order. 2 *Informal* Acting, occurring, or speaking too soon. —**previous to** Before. [< L *praevius* going before] —**pre′vi·ous·ly** *adv.* —**pre′vi·ous·ness** *n.* —**Syn.** 1 antecedent, former, preceding, prior.

pre·vi·sion (prē·vizh′ən) *n.* 1 Foresight; prescience. 2 A prediction.

pre·vue (prē′vyōō′) *n.* PREVIEW (def. 2). [< F *prévoir* foresee]

pre·war (prē′wôr′) *adj.* Of, pertaining to, or happening in a time before a war.

prey (prā) *n.* 1 Any animal seized by another for food. 2 Booty; pillage. 3 A person or thing made a victim: a *prey* to swindlers. 4 The act of hunting other animals for food: a bird of *prey.* —*v.i.* 1 To seek or take prey for food. 2 To make a victim of someone, as by cheating. 3 To exert a wearing or harmful influence: to *prey* upon impressionable children. [< L *praeda* booty] —**prey′er** *n.*

Pri·am (prī′əm) *Gk. Myth.* The king of Troy during the Trojan War.

price (prīs) *n.* 1 The amount of money or goods given or asked in exchange for something. 2 Anything given or done to obtain something. 3 Worth; cost. 4 A reward for the capture or death of. —**beyond price** 1 So valuable that no adequate price can be set. 2 Not able to be bribed. —**set a price on one's head** To offer a reward for the capture of a person, dead or alive. —*v.t.* **priced, pric·ing** 1 To ask the price of. 2 To set a price on. —**price out of the market** To charge such high prices for goods that no one will buy them. [< L *pretium*] —**Syn.** *n.* 1 charge, cost, outlay. 3 value.

price·less (prīs′lis) *adj.* 1 Beyond price or valuation; invaluable. 2 *Informal* Wonderfully amusing or absurd. —**price′less·ness** *n.*

prick (prik) *v.t.* 1 To pierce slightly, as with a sharp point; puncture. 2 To affect with sharp mental pain. 3 To outline or indicate by punctures. 4 To cause to stick up: often with *up.* 5 To urge on; goad. —*v.i.* 6 To have or cause a stinging or piercing sensation. 7 To stick up; point, as a dog's ears. —*n.* 1 A mark or puncture made by pricking. 2 A stinging or prickling sensation. 3 Something sharply pointed, as a thorn. 4 A mental sting or spur: the *prick* of conscience. [< OE *prica* sharp point] —**prick′er** *n.*

prick·le (prik′əl) *n.* 1 A small, sharp point, as a thorn. 2 A tingling or stinging sensation. —*v.* **·led, ·ling** *v.t.* 1 To prick; pierce. 2 To cause a tingling or stinging sensation in. —*v.i.* 3 To have a tingling sensation. [< OE *pricel*]

prick·ly (prik′lē) *adj.* **·li·er, ·li·est** 1 Furnished with prickles. 2 Stinging; tingling. —**prick′li·ness** *n.*

prickly heat A rash due to inflammation of the sweat glands.

prickly pear 1 Any of a genus of flat-stemmed cactus plants bearing a pear-shaped fruit. 2 The edible fruit.

pride (prīd) *n.* 1 An undue sense of one's own superiority; arrogance; conceit. 2 A proper sense or feeling of personal dignity and worth. 3 That of which one is justly proud. 4 The best part of a group, nation, etc. 5 The best or prime period: in the *pride* of youth. 6 A group or family of lions. —*v.t.* **prid·ed, prid·ing** To take pride in (oneself) for something: with *on* or *upon.* [< OE *prūt* proud] —**pride′ful** *adj.* —**pride′ful·ly** *adv.* —**pride′ful·ness** *n.*

prie-dieu (prē·dyœ′) *n.* A small desk to support a book and with an extension on which to kneel for prayers. [F, pray God]

Prie-dieu

pri·er (prī′ər) *n.* One who pries.

priest (prēst) *n.* 1 One consecrated to the service of a divinity, and serving as mediator between the divinity and his worshipers. 2 In the Anglican, Greek, and Roman Catholic churches, a clergyman ranking next below a bishop, and having authority to administer the sacraments. [< L *presbyter* elder] —**priest′hood′** *n.*

priest·ess (prēs′tis) *n.* A woman or girl who performs sacred rites.

priest·ly (prēst′lē) *adj.* Of, like, or concerning a priest or the priesthood. —**priest′li·ness** *n.*

prig (prig) *n.* A formal and narrow-minded person who assumes superior virtue, wisdom, or learning; pedant. [?] —**prig′gish** *adj.* —**prig′gish·ly** *adv.* —**prig′gish·ness** *n.*

prim (prim) *adj.* Affectedly precise and formal; stiffly proper and neat. —*v.t.* **primmed, prim·ming** To fix in a precise or prim manner. [Prob. < OF *prim* first, prime] —**prim′ly** *adv.* —**prim′ness** *n.*

prim. primary; primitive.

pri·ma·cy (prī′mə·sē) *n. pl.* **·cies** 1 The state of being first, as in rank or excellence. 2 The rank, office, or province of a primate. [< LL *primas, primatis* one of the first]

pri·ma don·na (prē′mə don′ə, prim′ə) *pl.* **pri·ma don·nas** 1 A leading female singer, as in an opera company. 2 *Informal* A temperamental or vain person. [Ital., lit., first lady]

add, āce, câre, pälm; end, ēven; it, īce; odd, ōpen, ôrder; tŏŏk, pōōl; up, bûrn; ə = *a* in *above, u* in *focus;* yōō = *u* in *fuse;* oil; pout; check; go; ring; thin; this; zh, *vision.* < derived from; ? origin uncertain or unknown.

pri·ma fa·ci·e (prī′mə fā′shi·ē, fā′shē) At first view; so far as at first appears. [L]

pri·mal (prī′məl) *adj.* 1 First; original. 2 Most important; chief. [< L *primus* first]

pri·ma·quine (prī′mə·kwīn) *n.* A synthetic chemical used to cure malaria. [< PRIM(E) + A(MINO)- + QUIN(IN)E]

pri·ma·ri·ly (prī·mâr′ə·lē, pri·mâr′-) *adv.* 1 In the first place; originally. 2 Mainly; essentially.

pri·ma·ry (prī′mer·ē, -mər·ē) *adj.* 1 First in time or origin; primitive; original. 2 First in a series or sequence. 3 First in degree, rank, or importance; chief. 4 Constituting the fundamental or original elements of which a whole is comprised; basic; elemental: the *primary* forces of life. 5 Of the first stage of development; elementary: *primary* school. 6 *Electr.* Of or designating the input or input circuit of a transformer or similar device. —*n. pl.* ·**ries** 1 That which is first in rank, dignity, quality, importance, etc. 2 Any of the primary colors. 3 In the U.S. **a** A meeting in which voters belonging to one political party in an election district nominate candidates for office, choose delegates for a party convention, etc. **b** DIRECT PRIMARY. [< L *primus* first]

primary accent See ACCENT.

primary cell *Electr.* A cell for generating electricity which cannot be efficiently recharged after use owing to an irreversible electrochemical reaction.

primary colors Those colors considered basic to the formation of all other colors; loosely, red, blue, and yellow to which black and white may be added.

pri·mate (prī′māt, -mit) *n.* 1 The prelate highest in rank in a nation or province. 2 Any of an order of mammals having five digits with nails on hands and feet, binocular vision, a large brainpan, etc., and including man, apes, monkeys and several monkeylike forms. [< L *primus* first] —**pri·ma·tial** (prī·mā′shəl) *adj.*

prime[1] (prīm) *adj.* 1 First in rank, dignity, or importance; chief. 2 First in value or excellence; first-rate. 3 First in time or order; original; primitive; primeval. 4 *Math.* Having no integral factors other than itself and unity, as certain integers. 5 Not derived from anything else; original; first. —*n.* 1 The period succeeding youth and preceding age. 2 The period of full perfection or vigor in anything. 3 The beginning of anything. 4 The best of anything; a *prime* grade. 5 A mark or accent (′) written above and to the right of a letter or figure to indicate feet, minutes of time, minutes of angle, etc. 6 *Music* The interval of unison. —*v.* **primed, prim·ing** *v.t.* 1 To prepare; make ready for some purpose. 2 To put a primer into (a gun, mine, etc.) preparatory to firing. 3 To pour water into (a pump) so as to displace air and promote suction. 4 To cover (a surface) with sizing, a first coat of paint, etc. 5 To supply beforehand with facts, information, etc.: to *prime* a witness. —*v.i.* 6 To carry water along with the steam into the cylinder: said of a steam boiler or engine. 7 To make a person or thing ready or prepared for something. [< L *primus* first] —**prime′ly** *adv.* —**prime′ness** *n.* —**Syn.** *adj.* 1 main, leading, premiere, head, principal, top.

prime[2] (prīm) *n. Often cap.* 1 The first canonical hour of the day. 2 The office recited at this time. [< LL *prima (hora)* first (hour)]

prime meridian The meridian that passes through Greenwich, England and from which longitude is reckoned east and west.

prime minister The principal minister of a sovereign, or, in parliamentary governments, the chief executive.

prim·er[1] (prim′ər) *n.* 1 An elementary reading and spelling book. 2 A beginner's textbook in any subject. [< Med. L *primarius* basic]

prim·er[2] (prī′mər) *n.* 1 Any device, as a cap, tube, etc., used to detonate the charge of a gun, mine, etc. 2 A first coat of paint or sizing.

prime time In radio and television, the hours which consistently attract the largest audience, usu. the evening hours.

pri·me·val (prī·mē′vəl) *adj.* Of or pertaining to the first ages; primordial. [< L *primus* first + *aevum* age] —**pri·me′val·ly** *adv.*

prim·ing (prī′ming) *n.* 1 The act of one who or that which primes. 2 A substance, as paint or sizing, used as a first coat. 3 A device or substance used to fire an explosive charge.

prim·i·tive (prim′ə·tiv) *adj.* 1 Of or belonging to the earliest ages. 2 Of, like, or belonging to an early period or stage of development: *primitive* Christianity. 3 Characteristic of the earliest ages of man, as in style, manner of living, etc.: a *primitive* tribe of Indians in Brazil. 4 Rough, simple, plain, undeveloped, etc.: *primitive* vacation facilities. 5 Basic; primary. —*n.* 1 A primitive person or thing. 2 A work of art created during the very early, often prehistoric, ages of man; also, a work of art imitative of this. 3 A work of art characterized by a naive, childlike simplicity; also, the artist, often untrained, of such a work. 4 A simple, unsophisticated person. [< L *primitivus* < *primus* first] —**prim′i·tive·ly** *adv.* —**prim′i·tive·ness** *n.*

prim·i·tiv·ism (prim′ə·tiv·iz′əm) *n.* Belief in or adherence to primitive forms and customs.

pri·mo·gen·i·tor (prī′mə·jen′ə·tər) *n.* An earliest ancestor; a forefather. [< L *primus* first + *genitor* a father]

pri·mo·gen·i·ture (prī′mə·jen′ə·chər) *n.* 1 The state of being the first-born of the same parents. 2 The right of inheritance of the eldest son to the exclusion of all other children. [< L *primus* first + *genitura* birth]

pri·mor·di·al (prī·môr′dē·əl) *adj.* 1 First in time; primitive; primeval. 2 Original; fundamental. [< L *primus* first + *ordiri* begin a web] —**pri·mor′di·al·ism′** *n.* —**pri·mor′di·al·ly** *adv.*

primp (primp) *v.t. & v.i.* To groom oneself or dress up, esp. with superfluous attention to detail. [Akin to PRIM] —**primp′er** *n.*

prim·rose (prim′rōz) *n.* 1 Any of a genus of early-blossoming perennials having variously colored, tubular flowers. 2 The flower. 3 A pale yellow color. —*adj.* 1 Pertaining to a primrose. 2 Pale yellow. [< Med. L *primula,* fem. dim. of L *primus* first]

Primrose

prin. principal; principally; principle.

prince (prins) *n.* 1 A nonreigning male member of a royal family, esp. the son of a sovereign. 2 A male ruler of a state or principality. 3 One of a high order of nobility. 4 One of the highest rank of the class to which he belongs: a merchant *prince.* [< L *princeps* first, principal]

Prince Albert A long, double-breasted frock coat. [< *Albert,* Prince of Wales, later Edward VII, 1841–1910]

prince consort The husband of a reigning female sovereign.

prince·ling (prins′ling) *n.* 1 A young prince. 2 A subordinate prince.

prince·ly (prins′lē) *adj.* ·**li·er,** ·**li·est** 1 Of, suitable for, or belonging to a prince. 2 Noble; regal; distinguished: a *princely* bearing. 3 Generous; liberal; kind. 4 Sumptuous; magnificent. —*adv.* In a princely manner. —**prince′li·ness** *n.*

Prince of Darkness SATAN.

Prince of Peace JESUS CHRIST.

Prince of Wales The eldest son or male heir apparent of the British sovereign: a title conferred by the sovereign.

prin·cess (prin′sis, prin·ses′) *n.* 1 A nonreigning female member of a royal family, esp. the daughter of a sovereign or of a son of a sovereign. 2 The wife of a prince. 3 A female sovereign. 4 A woman or girl having the traditional beauty, grace, etc., of a princess.

prin·cesse (prin·ses′, prin′sis) *adj.* Of or designating a woman's close-fitting garment cut in a single piece from shoulder to flared hem. Also **prin′cess.** [F, princess]

prin·ci·pal (prin′sə·pəl) *adj.* First in rank, character, or importance; chief. —*n.* 1 One who takes a leading part in some action. 2 *Law* **a** The actor in a crime, or one present aiding and abetting. **b** The employer of one who acts as an agent. **c** One primarily liable for whom another has become surety. **d** The capital or body of an estate. 3 The head officer or teacher of a school. 4 The leading actor or performer. 5 Any person in authority. 6 The amount of money owed or invested, minus the interest charged or accumulated. 7 The face value: the *principal* of a stock. 8 Any of the chief rafters of a roof. [< L *princeps* chief] —**prin′ci·pal·ly** *adv.* —**prin′ci·pal·ship′** *n.* —**Syn.** *adj.* 1 main, central, foremost, leading.

prin·ci·pal·i·ty (prin'sə·pal'ə·tē) *n. pl.* **·ties** 1 The office or dignity of a prince. 2 A territory ruled by a prince, or one that gives title to a prince.

principal parts The principal inflected forms of a verb from which all other inflected forms may be derived. In English, the principal parts of a verb are the infinitive, the past tense, and the past participle *(walk, walked, walked; go, went, gone).* The present participle (*-ing* added to the infinitive) is sometimes considered a fourth principal part, as *walking, going.*

prin·ci·ple (prin'sə·pəl) *n.* 1 A basic truth, law, force, etc., on which others can be founded: the *principle* of self-government. 2 An essential character or quality of something. 3 A fundamental origin or cause of something. 4 Moral standards or rules of conduct, esp. superior standards or rules: a man of *principle.* 5 In natural phenomena, an established law or mode of action: the *principle* of gravity. 6 The essential mode of operation of something: the *principle* of a digital computer. [<L *principium* a beginning]

prin·ci·pled (prin'sə·pəld) *adj.* Having principles, esp. moral principles.

print (print) *n.* 1 An impression or mark made upon a surface by pressure; imprint. 2 Something having such a mark on it. 3 A device for making such a mark. 4 An impression made by type or plates that have been inked. 5 Type used in printing. 6 Printed matter, as a newspaper. 7 The state of being printed. 8 A photographic reproduction of a work of art. 9 An original picture or design made from an engraved plate, stone, woodblock, etc. 10 A fabric stamped with a design; also, a garment made from such fabric. 11 A positive photographic copy made from a negative. **—in print** Still available at the publisher. **—out of print** No longer available at the publisher, the edition being exhausted. *—v.t.* 1 To mark, as with inked type, a stamp, die, etc. 2 To stamp or impress (a mark, seal, etc.) on or into a surface. 3 To fix as if by impressing: The scene is *printed* on my memory. 4 To produce (a book, newspaper, etc.) by the application of inked type, plates, etc., to paper or similar material. 5 To cause to be put in print; publish: The newspaper *printed* the story. 6 To write in letters similar to those used in print. 7 *Phot.* To produce (a positive picture) by transmitting light through a negative onto a sensitized surface. *—v.i.* 8 To be a printer. 9 To take or give an impression in printing. 10 To form letters similar to printed ones. **—print out** To deliver (information) automatically in printed form, as a computer. [<L *premere* to press]

print·a·ble (print'ə·bəl) *adj.* 1 Capable of being printed. 2 Fit to print or publish.

print·er (prin'tər) *n.* 1 A person who prints or sets type. 2 A mechanism attached to a computer that produces printed information.

printer's devil A printer's apprentice.

print·ing (prin'ting) *n.* 1 The act of one who or that which prints. 2 That which is printed. 3 The art or occupation of a printer. 4 All of the printed copies, as of a book, made at one time or from a single type setting.

printing press A mechanism for printing from inked type, plates, etc.

print·out (print'out') *n.* Material printed automatically, as by a computer.

pri·or (prī'ər) *adj.* Preceding in time, order, or importance. **—prior to** Before in time. *—n.* 1 In an abbey, a monastic officer next in rank below an abbot. 2 The man in charge of a priory. [L, earlier, superior]

pri·or·ess (prī'ər·is) *n.* 1 In an abbey of nuns, a monastic officer next in rank below an abbess. 2 A woman in charge of a priory.

pri·or·i·tize (prī·ôr'ə·tīz) *v.t.* **·tized, ·tiz·ing** *Colloq.* To arrange in order of priority.

pri·or·i·ty (prī·ôr'ə·tē, -or'-) *n. pl.* **·ties** 1 The condition of being prior; precedence. 2 A preferential rating or right to do, buy, or use something. 3 A certificate giving this right. 4 Something that takes precedence over another thing or things.

pri·or·y (prī'ər·ē) *n. pl.* **·or·ies** A monastic house presided over by a prior or prioress.

prism (priz'əm) *n.* 1 *Geom.* A solid whose bases or ends are equal and parallel plane figures, and whose lateral faces are parallelograms. 2 *Optics* An instrument consisting of such a solid, usu. having triangular ends and made of glass or other transparent material. [<Gk. *prisma* something sawed]

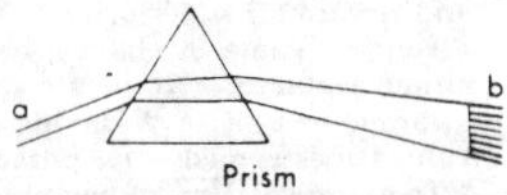

Prism

Beam of white light (a) undergoes refraction in prism and produces its spectrum (b).

pris·mat·ic (priz·mat'ik) *adj.* 1 Refracted or formed by a prism. 2 Exhibiting the colored bands of the spectrum. 3 Pertaining to or shaped like a prism. 4 Variously and brilliantly colored. **—pris·mat'i·cal·ly** *adv.*

pris·on (priz'ən) *n.* 1 A public building for the safekeeping of persons in legal custody, as in punishment for having committed a crime; a penitentiary. 2 Any place of confinement. 3 Imprisonment. *—v.t.* IMPRISON. [<L *praehensio* seizure]

pris·on·er (priz'ənər, -nər) *n.* 1 One who is confined in a prison. 2 Any person whose liberty is forcibly restrained. 3 A person whose freedom is restricted by some cause or condition: a *prisoner* of ignorance.

pris·sy (pris'ē) *adj.* **·si·er, ·si·est** Very precise; prim; fussy. [Blend of PRIM + SISSY] **—priss'i·ly** *adv.* **—priss'i·ness** *n.*

pris·tine (pris'tēn, -tin, pris·tēn') *adj.* 1 Of or pertaining to the earliest state or time; primitive. 2 Uncontaminated; pure. [<L. *pristinus* primitive] **—pris'tine·ly** *adv.*

pri·va·cy (prī'və·sē; *Brit., also* priv'ə·sē) *n. pl.* **·cies** 1 The condition of being private; seclusion. 2 Personal matters that are or should be private. 3 Secrecy.

pri·vate (prī'vit) *adj.* 1 Removed from public view; secluded. 2 Confidential; secret. 3 That is one's own; personal: a *private* sorrow. 4 Not for the public at large: *private* schools. 5 Not in the public or governmental employ: a *private* citizen. 6 Working or conducted independently of other groups, organizations, etc.: a *private* detective; a *private* practice. *—n.* See GRADE. **—in private** In secret; privately. [<L *privus* single, one's own] **—pri'vate·ly** *adv.* **—pri'vate·ness** *n.*

private enterprise FREE ENTERPRISE

pri·va·teer (prī'və·tir') *n.* 1 A vessel privately owned and manned but carrying on maritime war under letters of marque. 2 The commander or one of the crew of privateer: also **pri'va·teers'man.** *—v.i.* To cruise in or as a privateer. **—pri'va·teer'ing** *n.*

private first class See GRADE.

private parts The genitals.

pri·va·tion (prī·vā'shən) *n.* 1 The state of lacking something necessary or desirable. 2 Want of the common comforts or necessities of life. [<L *privare* deprive]

priv·a·tive (priv'ə·tiv) *adj.* 1 Causing privation; depriving. 2 *Gram.* Expressing negation or absence of something. *—n. Gram.* A prefix or suffix indicating negation or absence, as *a-, in-, -less.* **—priv'a·tive·ly** *adv.*

priv·et (priv'it) *n.* 1 An ornamental, bushy shrub with white flowers and black berries, used for hedges. 2 Any of various related shrubs and trees. [?]

priv·i·lege (priv'ə·lij, priv'lij) *n.* 1 A special or peculiar benefit, advantage, right or immunity. 2 A fundamental civil right: the *privilege* of voting. *—v.t.* **·leged, ·leg·ing** To grant a privilege to. [<L *privus* one's own + *lex, legis* law]

priv·i·leged (priv'ə·lijd) *adj.* 1 Having or invested with a privilege or with advantages: a *privileged* class. 2 Exempt from the usual conditions or rules: *privileged* information.

priv·y (priv'ē) *adj.* 1 Participating with another or others in the knowledge of a secret transaction: with *to: privy* to the plot. 2 *Archaic* Secret. *—n. pl.* **priv·ies** A toilet or outhouse. [<L *privatus* private] **—priv'i·ly** *adv.*

privy council A body of confidential advisers, as to a sovereign, executive, etc. **—privy councilor**

prix fixe (prē fēks′) In certain restaurants, a set price for a meal no matter which courses or entrées are chosen. [F, lit., fixed price]

prize[1] (prīz) *n.* **1** That which is offered or won as an honor and reward for superiority. **2** Anything offered or won in a contest, game of chance, etc. **3** Something desirable, either acquired or to be striven for. —*adj.* **1** Offered or awarded as a prize. **2** Having received a prize. **3** Highly valued or esteemed. —*v.t.* **prized, priz·ing 1** To value highly. **2** To appraise. [Var. of PRICE]

prize[2] (prīz) *n.* **1** In international law, property, as a vessel and cargo, lawfully captured by a belligerent at sea. **2** The act of capturing; also, the person or thing captured. —*v.t.* **prized, priz·ing** To seize as a prize, as a ship. [< L *praehendere* seize]

prize·fight (prīz′fīt′) *n.* A boxing match between professional boxers. —**prize′fight′er, prize′fight′ing** *n.*

pro[1] (prō) *n. pl.* **pros 1** An argument or vote in favor of something. **2** One who votes for or favors something. —*adv.* In favor of; for. [L, for]

pro[2] (prō) *n. pl.* **pros** PROFESSIONAL. —*adj.* PROFESSIONAL.

pro-[1] *prefix* **1** Forward; forth: *project.* **2** In place of; substituted for: *procaine.* **3** In favor of: *pro-Russian.* [< L *pro* before, in front]

pro-[2] *prefix* **1** Prior: *prognosis.* **2** Situated in front; forward; before: *prognathous.* [< Gk. *pro* before, in front]

PRO, P.R.O. public relations officer.

pro·a (prō′ə) *n.* A swift Malaysian vessel having a single outrigger and a lateen sail. [< Malay *prāu*]

prob. probable; probably; problem.

prob·a·bil·i·ty (prob′ə·bil′ə·tē) *n. pl.* **·ties 1** The state or quality of being probable; likelihood. **2** Something probable. **3** *Stat.* The ratio of the chances favoring an event to the total number of chances for and against it.

prob·a·ble (prob′ə·bəl) *adj.* **1** Likely to be true or to happen, but leaving room for doubt. **2** That renders something worthy of belief, but fails to prove: *probable* evidence. [< L *probare* prove, test] —**prob′a·bly** *adv.*

pro·bate (prō′bāt) *n.* **1** The act or legal process of proving the genuineness of a document, as a will. **2** The final determination of the genuineness of a will. **3** The authentic copy of a probated will. —*adj.* Of probate or probate court. —*v.t.* **·bat·ed, ·bat·ing** To secure probate of, as a will. [< L *probare* prove]

probate court A court having jurisdiction over probating wills, the settlement of estates, and the guardianship of minors or incompetents.

pro·ba·tion (prō·bā′shən) *n.* **1** A trial or period of testing of a person's character, qualifications, etc. **2** A legal procedure allowing a person convicted of an offense to go at large under suspension of sentence, but usu. under the supervision of a probation officer. **3** The status or condition of one undergoing probation; also, the period of probation. —**pro·ba′tion·al, pro·ba′tion·ar′y** *adj.*

pro·ba·tion·er (prō·bā′shən·ər) *n.* One on probation or trial.

probation officer A person delegated to supervise an offender on probation.

probe (prōb) *v.* **probed, prob·ing** *v.t.* **1** To explore with a probe. **2** To investigate or examine thoroughly. —*v.i.* **3** To investigate; search. —*n.* **1** *Med.* An instrument for exploring wounds, etc. **2** The act of probing. **3** An examination or exploratory search, esp. an investigation or inquiry into crime, malpractice, etc. **4** A spacecraft designed to explore and collect and transmit data to earth about the upper atmosphere, celestial bodies, or outer space. [< L *probare* prove] —**prob′er** *n.*

pro·bi·ty (prō′bə·tē) *n.* Virtue or integrity tested and confirmed; strict honesty. [< L *probus* good, honest]

prob·lem (prob′ləm) *n.* **1** A perplexing question presented for solution. **2** A puzzling or difficult circumstance, situation, person, etc. **3** *Math.* Something to be worked out or solved, as by a series of operations. —*adj.* **1** Presenting and dealing with a problem. **2** Being a problem: a *problem* child. [< Gk. *problēma* something thrown forward (for discussion)]

prob·lem·at·ic (prob′ləm·at′ik) *adj.* **1** Constituting or involving a problem. **2** Uncertain; questionable; contingent. Also **prob′lem·at′i·cal.** —**prob′lem·at′i·cal·ly** *adv.*

pro·bos·cis (prō·bos′is) *n. pl.* **·bos·cis·es** or **·bos·ci·des** (-bos′ə·dēz) **1** An elephant's trunk, or any long flexible snout. **2** A tubular structure used for sucking, sensing, etc., as of certain insects, worms, and mollusks. **3** A human nose: a humorous use. [< Gk. *pro-* before + *boskein* to feed]

Proboscis of elephant

pro·caine (prō·kān′, prō′kān) *n.* A common local anesthetic in dentistry and medicine. [< PRO-[1] + (CO)CAINE]

pro·ce·dure (prə·sē′jər, prō-) *n.* **1** A manner of proceeding or acting. **2** A special course of action. **3** The established methods or forms for the conduct of various proceedings, as in business, legal courts, etc. —**pro·ce′du·ral** *adj.*

pro·ceed (prə·sēd′, prō-) *v.i.* **1** To go on or forward. **2** To begin and carry on an action or process. **3** To issue or come, as from some cause, source, or origin: with *from.* **4** *Law* To institute and carry on legal proceedings. [< L *pro-* forward + *cedere* go]

pro·ceed·ing (prə·sē′ding, prō-) *n.* **1** An act or course of action; a transaction or procedure. **2** The action of issuing forth; emanation. **3** *pl.* The records or minutes of the meetings of a society, etc. **4** *Law* **a** Any action instituted in a court. **b** Any of the various steps taken in a cause by either party.

pro·ceeds (prō′sēdz) *n. pl.* The amount derived from the disposal of goods, a commercial undertaking, etc; return.

proc·ess (pros′es, pros′əs, *esp. Brit.* prō′ses) *n. pl.* **proc·ess·es** (pros′ə·siz, pros′es·əz, pros′ə·sēz′) **1** A course or method of operations in the production of something: a metallurgical *process.* **2** A forward movement or continuous development, as of time, growth, etc. **3** *Law* **a** Any judicial writ or order. **b** A writ issued to bring a defendant into court. **c** The whole course of proceedings in a cause. **4** *Biol.* An accessory outgrowth of an organism. —*adj.* Produced by a special method: *process* cheese. —*v.t.* **1** To treat or prepare by a special method. **2** *Law* **a** To issue or serve a process on. **b** To proceed against. [< L *processus* pp. of *procedere* proceed]

pro·ces·sion (prə·sesh′ən, prō-) *n.* **1** A line, as of persons or vehicles, moving forward in a formal manner; a parade. **2** A continuous course: the *procession* of the stars. **3** The act of proceeding or issuing forth.

pro·ces·sion·al (prə·sesh′ən·əl, prō-) *adj.* Of or pertaining to or moving in a procession. —*n.* **1** A book containing the services in a religious procession. **2** A hymn sung during a religious procession. —**pro·ces′sion·al·ly** *adv.*

process printing Color printing from halftone plates each of which carries one of the primary colors, red, yellow, and blue, with sometimes a fourth plate for black.

pro·claim (prō·klām′, prə-) *v.t.* **1** To announce or make known publicly or officially; declare. **2** To make plain; manifest. **3** To praise; laud. [< L *pro-* before + *clamare* to call] —**pro·claim′er** *n.*

proc·la·ma·tion (prok′lə·mā′shən) *n.* **1** The act of proclaiming. **2** That which is proclaimed.

pro·cliv·i·ty (prō·kliv′ə·tē) *n. pl.* **·ties** Natural disposition or tendency, esp. toward something not desirable. [< L *proclivus* downward]

pro·con·sul (prō·kon′səl) *n.* **1** In ancient Rome, an official who exercised authority over a province or an army. **2** An administrator of a dependency or colony. [< L] —**pro·con′su·lar** (-sə·lər) *adj.* —**pro·con′su·late** (-sə·lit), **pro·con′sul·ship** *n.*

pro·cras·ti·nate (prō·kras′tə·nāt) *v.* **·nat·ed, ·nat·ing** *v.i.* **1** To put off taking action until a future time; be dilatory. —*v.t.* **2** To defer or postpone. [< L *pro-* forward + *cras* tomorrow] —**pro·cras′ti·na′tion, pro·cras′ti·na′tor** *n.*

pro·cre·ate (prō′krē·āt) *v.t. & v.i.* **·at·ed, ·at·ing 1** To engender or beget (offspring). **2** To bring or come into existence; originate. [< L *pro-* before + *creare* create] —**pro′cre·a′tion, pro′cre·a′tor** *n.* —**pro′cre·a′tive, pro′cre·ant** *adj.*

Pro·crus·te·an (prō·krus′tē·ən) *adj.* **1** Of Procrustes. **2** Ruthlessly or violently forcing to conform.

Pro·crus·tes (prō·krus′tēz) *Gk. Myth.* A giant who tied travelers to an iron bed and amputated or stretched their limbs until they fitted it.

proc·tol·o·gy (prok·tol′ə·jē) *n.* The branch of medicine which deals with diseases of the lower colon, rectum, and anus. [< Gk. *proktos* anus + -LOGY] **—proc·to·log·i·cal** (prok′tə·loj′i·kəl) *adj.* **—proc·tol′o·gist** *n.*

proc·tor (prok′tər) *n.* **1** An agent acting for another; proxy. **2** A university or college official charged with maintaining order, supervising examinations, etc. *—v.t. & v.i.* To supervise (an examination). [< PROCURATOR] **—proc·to·ri·al** (prok·tôr′ē·əl, -tō′rē-) *adj.*

proc·to·scope (prok′tə·skōp) *n.* A surgical instrument for examining the interior of the rectum. **—proc·tos·co·py** (prok·tos′kə·pē) *n.*

pro·cum·bent (prō·kum′bənt) *adj.* **1** *Bot.* Lying on the ground; trailing. **2** Lying face down; prone. [< L *pro-* forward + *cubare* lie down]

proc·u·ra·tor (prok′yə·rā′tər) *n.* **1** A person authorized to manage the affairs of another. **2** In ancient Rome, one in charge of imperial revenues, esp. in a province. **—proc′u·ra·to′ri·al** (-rə·tôr′ē·əl, -tō′rē-) *adj.*

pro·cure (prō·kyŏŏr′) *v.* **·cured, ·cur·ing** *v.t.* **1** To obtain by some effort or means; acquire. **2** To bring about; cause. **3** To obtain for the sexual gratification of others. *—v.i.* **4** To obtain women for prostitution. [< L *procurare* look after] **—pro·cur′a·ble** *adj.* **—pro·cure′ment, pro·cur′er** *n.*

Pro·cy·on (prō′sē·on) *n.* The most conspicuous star in the constellation Canis Minor. [< Gk. *pro-* before + *kyōn* dog]

prod (prod) *v.t.* **prod·ded, prod·ding** **1** To punch or poke with or as with a pointed instrument. **2** To arouse mentally; urge; goad. *—n.* **1** Any pointed instrument used for prodding. **2** Something that incites one to action. [?] **—prod′der** *n.*

prod. produce; produced; product.

prod·i·gal (prod′ə·gəl) *adj.* **1** Wastefully extravagant, as of money, time, etc. **2** Yielding in profusion; bountiful. **3** Lavish; profuse. *—n.* One who is wastefully extravagant; a spendthrift. [< L *prodigus* wasteful] **—prod′i·gal′i·ty** (-gal′ə·tē) *n.* **—prod′i·gal·ly** *adv.*

pro·dig·ious (prə·dij′əs, prō-) *adj.* **1** Enormous or extraordinary in size, quantity, or degree. **2** Marvelous; amazing. **—pro·dig′ious·ly** *adv.* **—pro·dig′ious·ness** *n.*

prod·i·gy (prod′ə·jē) *n. pl.* **·gies** **1** Something extraordinary or awe-inspiring. **2** An exceptionally gifted child. **3** A monstrosity of nature. [< L *prodigium*]

pro·duce (prə·dyōōs′) *v.* **·duced, ·duc·ing** *v.t.* **1** To bring forth or bear; yield. **2** To bring forth by mental effort; compose, write, etc. **3** To cause to happen or be: His words *produced* a violent reaction. **4** To bring to view; exhibit; show: to *produce* evidence. **5** To manufacture; make. **6** To bring to performance before the public, as a play. **7** To extend or lengthen, as a line. **8** *Econ.* To create (anything with exchangeable value). *—v.i.* **9** To yield or generate an appropriate product or result. *—n.* (prod′yōōs, prō′dyōōs) That which is produced, esp. farm products collectively. [< L *pro-* forward + *ducere* to lead] **—pro·duc′i·ble** *adj.*

pro·duc·er (prə·dyōō′sər) *n.* **1** One who or that which produces. **2** One who makes things for sale and use. **3** One in charge of the production of a public presentation, as of a play, motion picture, etc.

prod·uct (prod′əkt, -ukt) *n.* **1** Anything produced or obtained as a result of some operation or work. **2** *Math.* The result obtained by multiplication. **3** *Chem.* Any substance resulting from chemical change.

pro·duc·tion (prə·duk′shən) *n.* **1** The act or process of producing. **2** The amount produced. **3** Something produced, esp. an artistic work, as a play, motion picture, etc. **4** In political economy, a producing of goods or services.

pro·duc·tive (prə·duk′tiv) *adj.* **1** Producing easily or abundantly. **2** Characterized by fruitful work and accomplishment: a *productive* meeting. **3** Causing; resulting in: with *of.* **—pro·duc′tive·ly** *adv.* **—pro·duc·tiv·i·ty** (prō′duk·tiv′ə·tē), **pro·duc′tive·ness** *n.*

pro·em (prō′əm) *n.* A preface; prelude. [< Gk. *pro-* before + *oimē* song] **—pro·e·mi·al** (prō·ē′mē·əl) *adj.*

prof (prof) *n. Informal* PROFESSOR.

Prof. Professor. • See PROFESSOR.

prof·a·na·tion (prof′ə·nā′shən, prō·fə-) *n.* The act of profaning or the condition of being profaned.

pro·fane (prō·fān′, prə-) *v.t.* **·faned, ·fan·ing** **1** To treat (something sacred) with irreverence or abuse; desecrate. **2** To put to an unworthy or degrading use; debase. *—adj.* **1** Manifesting irreverence or disrespect toward sacred things. **2** Not sacred or religious in theme, content, use, etc.; secular. **3** Not esoteric; ordinary. **4** Vulgar. [< L *pro-* before + *fanum* temple] **—pro·fan·a·to·ry** (prō·fan′ə·tôr′ē, -tō′rē, prə-) *adj.* **—pro·fane′ly** *adv.* **—pro·fan′er** *n.*

pro·fan·i·ty (prō·fan′ə·tē, prə-) *n. pl.* **·ties** **1** The state of being profane. **2** Profane speech or action. Also **pro·fane′·ness** (-fān′nis).

pro·fess (prə·fes′, prō-) *v.t.* **1** To declare openly; avow; affirm. **2** To assert, usu. insincerely; make a pretense of: to *profess* remorse. **3** To declare or affirm faith in. **4** To have as one's profession: to *profess* the law. **5** To receive into a religious order. *—v.i.* **6** To make open declaration; avow; offer public affirmation. **7** To take the vows of a religious order. [< L *professus,* pp. of *profiteri* avow, confess] **—pro·fessed′** *adj.* **—pro·fess′ed·ly** (-fes′id·lē) *adv.*

pro·fes·sion (prə·fesh′ən) *n.* **1** An occupation that involves a higher education or its equivalent, and mental rather than manual labor, as law, medicine, teaching, etc. **2** The collective body of those following such an occupation. **3** Any calling or occupation requiring special skills, talents, etc.: the acting *profession.* **4** Any occupation. **5** The act of professing or declaring: *professions* of good will. **6** That which is avowed or professed.

pro·fes·sion·al (prə·fesh′ən·əl) *adj.* **1** Connected with, preparing for, engaged in, appropriate, or conforming to a profession: *professional* courtesy; *professional* skill. **2** Performing or doing for pay an activity often engaged in only for pleasure or recreation: a *professional* golfer. **3** Engaged in by performers, players, etc., who are paid: *professional* hockey. **4** Single-minded and zealous, often excessively so: a *professional* do-gooder. *—n.* **1** One who practices any profession or engages in any activity for pay. **2** One who is exceptionally skilled in some activity. **—pro·fes′sion·al·ism′** *n.* **—pro·fes′sion·al·ly** *adv.*

pro·fes·sion·al·ize (prə·fesh′ən·əl·īz′) *v.t.* **·ized, ·iz·ing** To make professional in character or quality: to *professionalize* tourism. **—pro·fes′sion·al·i·za′tion** *n.*

pro·fes·sor (prə·fes′ər) *n.* **1** A teacher of the highest grade in a university or college. **2** One who professes skill and offers instruction in some sport or art: a *professor* of gymnastics. **3** One who makes open declaration of his opinions, religious faith, etc. **—pro·fes·so·ri·al** (prō′fə·sôr′ē·əl, -sō′rē-, prof′ə-) *adj.* **—pro′fes·so′ri·al·ly** *adv.* **—pro′fes·so′ri·ate** (-it), **pro·fes′sor·ship** *n.* • In writing to a college or university professor, one may use either *Professor* or *Prof.* if the name is written in full or if the initials are used with the last name: *Professor Alfred Kern; Prof. C. E. Young.* If only the last name is used, *Professor* is spelled out.

prof·fer (prof′ər) *v.t.* To offer for acceptance. *—n.* The act of proffering, or that which is proffered. [< L *pro-* in behalf of + *offerre* to offer] **—prof′fer·er** *n.*

pro·fi·cien·cy (prə·fish′ən·sē) *n. pl.* **·cies** The fact or quality of being proficient; skill; competence; expertness.

pro·fi·cient (prə·fish′ənt) *adj.* Thoroughly competent; skilled; expert. *—n.* An expert. [< L *proficere* make progress, go forward] **—pro·fi′cient·ly** *adv.*

pro·file (prō′fīl, *esp. Brit.* prō′fēl) *n.* **1** A human head or face, as viewed from the side; also, a drawing of such a side view. **2** A drawing or view of something in outline or contour. **3** A somewhat brief biographical sketch. **4** Degree of exposure to public attention; public image: The army generals who seized control maintained a very low *profile.* **5** A vertical section of stratified soil or rock. *—v.t.* **·filed, ·fil·ing** **1** To draw a profile of; outline. **2** To write a profile of. [< Ital. *proffilare* draw in outline]

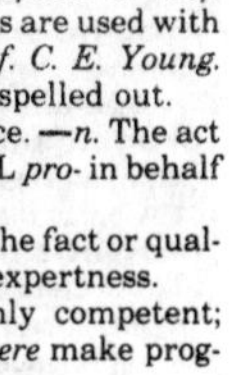

Profile *def. 1*

prof·it (prof′it) *n.* 1 Any benefit, advantage, or return. 2 *Often pl.* Excess of returns over outlay or expenditure. 3 *Often pl.* The gain obtained from invested capital; also, the ratio of gain to the amount of capital invested. 4 Income gained from property, stocks, etc. —*v.i.* 1 To be of advantage or benefit. 2 To derive gain or benefit. —*v.t.* 3 To be of profit or advantage to. [< L *profectus,* p.p. of *proficere* go forward] **—prof′it·less** *adj.*

prof·it·a·ble (prof′it·ə·bəl) *adj.* Bringing profit or gain. **—prof·it·a·bil·i·ty** (prof′ə·tə·bil′ə·tē), **prof′it·a·ble·ness** *n.* **—prof′it·a·bly** *adv.* **—Syn.** advantageous, beneficial, desirable, expedient, gainful, lucrative, productive, useful, worthwhile.

prof·i·teer (prof′ə·tir′) *v.i.* To seek or obtain excessive profits. —*n.* One who makes excessive profits, esp. to the detriment of others. **—prof′i·teer′ing** *n.*

profit sharing A system by which employees are given a percentage of the net profits of a business.

prof·li·ga·cy (prof′lə·gə·sē) *n.* The condition or quality of being profligate.

prof·li·gate (prof′lə·git, -gāt) *adj.* 1 Extremely immoral or dissipated; dissolute. 2 Recklessly extravagant. —*n.* A profligate person. [< L *profligare* strike to the ground, destroy] **—prof′li·gate·ly** *adv.*

pro·found (prə·found′, prō-) *adj.* 1 Intellectually deep or exhaustive: *profound* learning. 2 Reaching to, arising from, or affecting the depth of one's being: a *profound* look; *profound* respect. 3 Reaching far below the surface; deep: a *profound* chasm. 4 Complete; total: a *profound* revision of the book. [< L *pro-* very + *fundus* deep] **—pro·found′ly** *adv.* **—pro·found′ness** *n.*

pro·fun·di·ty (prə·fun′də·tē, prō-) *n. pl.* **·ties** 1 The state or quality of being profound. 2 A deep place. 3 A profound statement, theory, etc.

pro·fuse (prə·fyōōs′, prō-) *adj.* 1 Giving or given forth lavishly; extravagantly generous. 2 Copious; abundant: *profuse* vegetation. [< L *profusus,* pp. of *profundere* pour forth] **—pro·fuse′ly** *adv.* **—pro·fuse′ness** *n.*

pro·fu·sion (prə·fyōō′zhən, prō-) *n.* 1 A lavish supply or condition: a *profusion* of ornaments. 2 The act of pouring forth or supplying in great abundance; prodigality.

prog. progress; progressive.

pro·gen·i·tor (prō·jen′ə·tər) *n.* 1 A forefather or parent. 2 The originator or source of something. [< L *progignere* beget] **—pro·gen′i·tor·ship′** *n.*

prog·e·ny (proj′ə·nē) *n. pl.* **·nies** Offspring; descendants. [< L *progignere* beget]

pro·ges·ter·one (prō·jes′tə·rōn) *n.* An ovarian hormone active in preparing the uterus for reception of the fertilized ovum. Also **pro·ges′tin** (-tin). [< PRO-[1] + GE(STATION) + STER(OL) + -ONE]

prog·na·thous (prog′nə·thəs, prog·nā′-) *adj.* Having projecting jaws. Also **prog·nath·ic** (prog·nath′ik). [< PRO-[2] + Gk. *gnathos* jaw] **—prog·na·thism** (prog′nə·thiz′əm) *n.*

prog·no·sis (prog·nō′sis) *n. pl.* **·ses** (-sēz) A prediction or forecast, esp. as to the future course of a disease. [< Gk. *pro-* before + *gignōskein* know]

prog·nos·tic (prog·nos′tik) *adj.* 1 Predictive. 2 Of or useful in a prognosis. —*n.* 1 A sign of some future occurrence. 2 A basis for a prognosis.

prog·nos·ti·cate (prog·nos′tə·kāt) *v.t.* **·cat·ed, ·cat·ing** 1 To foretell by present indcations. 2 To indicate beforehand; foreshadow. **—prog·nos′ti·ca′tion, prog·nos′ti·ca′tor** *n.* **—prog·nos′ti·ca′tive** (-kā′tiv) *adj.*

pro·gram (prō′gram, -grəm) *n.* 1 A printed list giving in order the items, selections, etc., making up an entertainment; also, the selections, etc., collectively. 2 A printed list of the cast of characters, the performers, the acts or scenes, etc., in a play, opera, or the like. 3 A radio or television show. 4 Any prearranged plan or course of proceedings. 5 A sequence of instructions to be executed by a computer in solving a problem, usu. with means for automatically modifying the sequence depending on conditions that arise. *Brit. sp.* **·gramme.** —*v.t.* **·gramed** or **·grammed, ·gram·ing** or **·gram·ming** 1 To arrange a program of or for: to *program* one's day. 2 To schedule (an act, performer, etc.) for a program. 3 To furnish a program for (a computer). 4 To feed (information, instructions, etc.) into a computer. [< LL *programma* public announcement] **—pro·gram·mat·ic** (prō′grə·mat′ik) *adj.* **—pro′gram·er, pro′·gram·mer** *n.*

programed instruction Instruction in which the learner responds to a prearranged series of questions, items, or statements, using various printed texts, audiovisual means, or a teaching machine. Also **programmed instruction.**

program music Music intended to suggest moods, scenes, or incidents.

prog·ress (prog′res, *esp. Brit.* prō′gres) *n.* 1 A moving forward in space, as toward a destination. 2 Advancement toward something better; improvement. —*v.i.* (prə·gres′) 1 To move forward or onward. 2 To advance toward completion or improvement. [< L *progressus,* pp. of *progredi* go forward]

pro·gres·sion (prə·gresh′ən) *n.* 1 The act of progressing. 2 A successive series of events, happenings, etc. 3 *Math.* A sequence of numbers or elements each of which is derived from the preceding by rule. 4 *Music* **a** An advance from one tone or chord to another. **b** A sequence or succession of tones or chords. 5 Course or lapse of time; passage. **—pro·gres′sion·al** *adj.* **—pro·gres′sion·ism** *n.*

pro·gres·sive (prə·gres′iv) *adj.* 1 Moving forward in space; advancing. 2 Increasing by successive stages: a *progressive* deterioration. 3 Aiming at or characterized by progress toward something better: a *progressive* country. 4 Favoring or characterized by reform, new techniques, etc.: a *progressive* party, jazz, etc. 5 Increasing in severity: said of a disease. 6 *Gram.* Designating an aspect of the verb which expresses continuing action: formed with any tense of the auxiliary *be* and the present participle; as, He *is speaking;* he *had been speaking.* —*n.* One who favors or promotes reforms or changes, as in politics. **—pro·gres′·sive·ly** *adv.* **—pro·gres′sive·ness** *n.*

pro·hib·it (prō·hib′it, prə-) *v.t.* 1 To forbid, esp. by authority or law; interdict. 2 To prevent or hinder. [< L *prohibere*] **—pro·hib′it·er** *n.* **—Syn.** 1 disallow, ban, deny, bar, debar. 2 impede, restrict, constrain, check, block, obstruct.

pro·hi·bi·tion (prō′ə·bish′ən) *n.* 1 A prohibiting or being prohibited. 2 A decree or order forbidding anything. 3 *Often cap.* The forbidding of the manufacture, transportation, and sale of alcoholic liquors as beverages. **—pro′hi·bi′tion·ist** *n.*

pro·hib·i·tive (prō·hib′ə·tiv, prə-) *adj.* Prohibiting or tending to prohibit. Also **pro·hib′i·to′ry** (-tôr′ē, -tō′rē). **—pro·hib′i·tive·ly** *adv.*

proj·ect (proj′ekt) *n.* 1 A course of action; a plan. 2 An organized, usu. rather extensive undertaking: a research *project.* 3 A group of single dwellings or of apartment houses forming a residential complex. —*v.t.* (prə·jekt′) 1 To cause to extend forward or out. 2 To throw forth or forward, as missiles. 3 To cause (an image, shadow, etc.) to fall on a surface. 4 To plan or estimate something in the future: to *project* living expenses. 5 To create or invent in the mind: to *project* an image of one's destiny. 6 To cause (one's voice) to be heard at a distance. 7 To have the ability to communicate (a dramatic role, one's personality, ideas, etc.) effectively, as to an audience. 8 *Psychol.* To ascribe or impute (one's own ideas, feelings, etc.) to another person, group, or object. 9 To make a projection (def. 4) of. —*v.i.* 10 To extend out; protrude. 11 To cause one's voice to be heard at a distance. 12 To communicate effectively, as to an audience. 13 *Psychol.* To impute one's own ideas, feelings, etc., to another person, group, or object. [< L *pro* before + *jacere* throw]

pro·jec·tile (prə·jek′təl, -tīl) *adj.* 1 Projecting, or impelling forward. 2 Capable of being or intended to be projected or shot forth. —*n.* 1 A body projected or thrown forth by force. 2 A missile for discharge from a gun, cannon, etc.

pro·jec·tion (prə·jek′shən) *n.* 1 The act of projecting. 2 That which projects. 3 A prediction or estimation of something in the future based on current information, data, etc. 4 A system of lines drawn on a given fixed plane, as on a map, which represents, point for point, a given terrestrial or celestial surface. 5 *Psychol.* The process or an instance of projecting. 6 The exhibiting of pictures upon a screen. **—pro·jec′tive** *adj.* **—pro·jec′tive·ly** *adv.*

pro·jec·tion·ist (prə·jek′shən·ist) *n.* The operator of a motion-picture or slide projector.

pro·jec·tor (prə·jek′tər) *n.* One who or that which projects, esp. an apparatus for throwing images on a screen: a motion-picture *projector.*

pro·lapse (prō·laps′) *v.i.* **·lapsed, ·laps·ing** *Med.* To fall out of place, as an organ or part. —*n. Med.* (*also* prō′laps) Displacement of a part, esp. toward a natural orifice. [< L *pro-* forward + *labi* glide, fall]

pro·late (prō′lāt) *adj.* **1** Extended lengthwise. **2** Lengthened toward the poles. [< L *prolatus*]

prole (prōl) *n. & adj. Informal* PROLETARIAN.

pro·le·tar·i·an (prō′lə·târ′ē·ən) *adj.* Of the proletariat. —*n.* A member of the proletariat. [< L *proletarius* a Roman citizen of a class that, lacking property, served the state only by having children < *proles* offspring] —**pro′le·tar′i·an·ism** *n.*

pro·le·tar·i·at (prō′lə·târ′ē·ət) *n.* **1** Formerly, the lower classes. **2** The laboring class, esp. industrial wage earners.

pro·lif·er·ate (prō·lif′ə·rāt, prə-) *v.t. & v.i.* **·at·ed, ·at·ing** To create or reproduce in rapid succession. [< L *proles* offspring + *ferre* bear] —**pro·lif′er·a′tion** *n.* —**pro·lif′er·a′tive, pro·lif′er·ous** *adj.*

pro·lif·ic (prō·lif′ik, prə-) *adj.* **1** Producing abundantly, as offspring or fruit. **2** Producing creative or intellectual products abundantly: a *prolific* writer. [< L *proles* offspring + *facere* make] —**pro·lif′i·ca·cy** (-i·kə·sē), **pro·lif′ic·ness** *n.* —**pro·lif′i·cal·ly** *adv.*

pro·lix (prō′liks, prō·liks′) *adj.* **1** Unduly long and wordy. **2** Indulging in long and wordy discourse. [< L *prolixus* extended] —**pro·lix·i·ty** (prō·lik′sə·tē), **pro′lix·ness** *n.* —**pro′·lix·ly** *adv.*

pro·logue (prō′lôg, -log) *n.* **1** A preface, esp. an introduction, often in verse, spoken or sung by an actor before a play or opera. **2** Any anticipatory act or event. —*v.t.* To introduce with a prologue or preface. Also **pro′log.** [< Gk. *pro-* before + *logos* discourse]

pro·long (prə·lông′, -long′) *v.t.* To extend in time or space; continue; lengthen. Also **pro·lon′gate** (-lông′gāt, -long′-). [< L *pro-* forth + *longus* long] —**pro′lon·ga′tion, pro·long′ment, pro·long′er** *n.*

prom (prom) *n. Informal* A formal college or school dance or ball. [Short for PROMENADE]

prom. promenade; promontory.

prom·e·nade (prom′ə·nād′, -näd′) *n.* **1** A leisurely walk taken for pleasure. **2** A place for promenading. **3** A concert or ball opened with a formal march. —*v.* **·nad·ed, ·nad·ing** *v.i.* **1** To take a promenade. —*v.t.* **2** To take a promenade through or along. **3** To take or exhibit on or as on a promenade; parade. [< L *prominare* drive forward] —**prom′e·nad′er** *n.*

Pro·me·theus (prə·mē′thē·əs) *Gk. Myth.* A Titan who stole fire from heaven for mankind and as a punishment was chained to a rock, where an eagle daily devoured his liver. —**Pro·me′the·an** *adj.*

pro·me·thi·um (prə·mē′thē·əm) *n.* A radioactive element (symbol Pm) produced by uranium fission and belonging to the lanthanide series. [< PROMETHEUS]

prom·i·nence (prom′ə·nəns) *n.* **1** The state of being prominent; conspicuousness. **2** Something that extends forth or protrudes. **3** *Astron.* One of the great luminous clouds arising from the sun's surface, seen during total eclipses: also **solar prominence.** Also **prom′i·nen·cy.**

prom·i·nent (prom′ə·nənt) *adj.* **1** Jutting out; projecting; protuberant. **2** Conspicuous. **3** Very well known; eminent: a *prominent* lawyer. [< L *prominere* to project] —**prom′i·nent·ly** *adv.* —**Syn. 3** famous, noted, renowned, celebrated, popular, honored, outstanding.

prom·is·cu·i·ty (prom′is·kyōō′ə·tē, prō′mis-) *n. pl.* **·ties** The state, quality, or an instance of being promiscuous, esp. in sexual relations.

pro·mis·cu·ous (prə·mis′kyōō·əs) *adj.* **1** Composed of persons or things confusedly mingled. **2** Indiscriminate; esp., having sexual relations indiscriminately or casually with various persons. **3** Casual; irregular. [< L *promiscuus* mixed] —**pro·mis′cu·ous·ly** *adv.* —**pro·mis′cu·ous·ness** *n.*

prom·ise (prom′is) *n.* **1** An assurance given that a specified action will or will not be taken. **2** Reasonable ground for hope or expectation of future excellence, satisfaction, etc. **3** Something promised. —*v.* **·ised, ·is·ing** *v.t.* **1** To engage or pledge by a promise: He *promised* to do it. **2** To make a promise of (something) to someone. **3** To give reason for expecting. **4** *Informal* To assure (someone). —*v.i.* **5** To make a promise. **6** To give reason for expectation: often with *well* or *fair.* [< L *promissum,* pp. of *promittere* send forward] —**prom′is·er** *n.*

Promised Land **1** Canaan, promised to Abraham by God. *Gen.* 15:18. **2** Any longed-for place of happiness or improvement.

prom·is·ing (prom′is·ing) *adj.* Giving promise of good results or development. —**prom′is·ing·ly** *adv.*

prom·is·so·ry (prom′ə·sôr′ē, -sō′rē) *adj.* Containing or of the nature of a promise.

promissory note A written promise by one person to pay another unconditionally a certain sum of money at a specified time.

pro·mo (prō′mō) *Slang n.* PROMOTION (def. 3). —*adj.* Of, for, or relating to promotion (def. 3); promotional.

prom·on·to·ry (prom′ən·tôr′ē, -tō′rē) *n. pl.* **·ries** A high point of land extending into a body of water; headland. [< L *promunturium*]

pro·mote (prə·mōt′) *v.t.* **·mot·ed, ·mot·ing** **1** To contribute to the progress, development, or growth of; further; encourage. **2** To advance to a higher position, grade, or rank. **3** To advocate actively. **4** To publicize (a person, product, event, etc.), as by advertising, public appearances, etc. [< L *pro-* forward + *movere* to move] —**pro·mot′a·ble** *adj.*

pro·mot·er (prə·mō′tər) *n.* One who or that which promotes, esp. one who assists, by securing capital, etc., in promoting some enterprise, as a sports event, commercial venture, etc.

pro·mo·tion (prə·mō′shən) *n.* **1** Advancement in dignity, rank, grade, etc. **2** Furtherance or development, as of a cause. **3** Anything, as advertising, public appearances, etc., done to publicize a person, product, event, etc. —**pro·mo′tion·al** *adj.*

pro·mo·tive (prə·mō′tiv) *adj.* Tending to promote.

prompt (prompt) *v.t.* **1** To incite to action; instigate. **2** To suggest or inspire (an act, thought, etc.). **3** To remind of what has been forgotten or of what comes next; give a cue to. —*v.i.* **4** To give help or suggestions. —*adj.* **1** Quick to act, respond, etc.; ready. **2** Taking place at the appointed time; punctual. [< L *promptus* brought forth, hence, at hand] —**promp′ti·tude, prompt′ness** *n.* —**prompt′ly** *adv.*

prompt·er (promp′tər) **1** In a theater, one who follows the lines and prompts the actors. **2** One who or that which prompts.

prom·ul·gate (prom′əl·gāt, prō·mul′gāt) *v.t.* **·gat·ed, ·gat·ing** **1** To make known or announce officially, as a law, dogma, etc. **2** To make known or effective over a wide area or extent. [< L *promulgare* make known] —**prom·ul·ga·tion** (prom′əl·gā′shən, prō′mul-), **prom′ul·gat·or** *n.*

pron. pronoun; pronounced; pronunciation.

prone (prōn) *adj.* **1** Lying flat, esp. with the face, front, or palm downward; prostrate. **2** Leaning forward or downward. **3** Mentally inclined or predisposed: with *to.* [< L *pronus*] —**prone′ly** *adv.* —**prone′ness** *n.*

prong (prông, prong) *n.* **1** A pointed end of a fork. **2** Any pointed and projecting part, as the end of an antler, etc. —*v.t.* To prick or stab with a prong. [ME *pronge*] —**pronged** *adj.*

prong·horn (prông′hôrn′, prong′-) *n. pl.* **·horns** or **·horn** A small, deerlike mammal of w North America.

pro·nom·i·nal (prō·nom′ə·nəl) *adj.* Of, pertaining to, like, or having the nature of a pronoun. —**pro·nom′i·nal·ly** *adv.*

pro·noun (prō′noun) *n.* A word used as a substitute for a noun, as *he, she, that.* [< L *pro-* in place of + *nomen* name, noun]

Pronghorn

pro·nounce (prə·nouns′) *v.*

·nounced, ·nounc·ing *v.t.* 1 To utter or deliver officially or solemnly; proclaim. 2 To assert; declare, esp. as one's judgment: The judge *pronounced* her guilty. 3 To give utterance to; articulate (words, etc.). 4 To articulate in a prescribed manner: hard to *pronounce* his name. 5 To indicate the sound of (a word) by phonetic symbols. —*v.i.* 6 To make a pronouncement or assertion. 7 To articulate words; speak. [< L *pronuntiare* proclaim < *pro-* forth + *nuntiare* announce] **—pro·nounce′a·ble** *adj.* **—pro·nounc′er** *n.*

pro·nounced (prə·nounst′) *adj.* Clearly noticeable; decided. **—pro·nounc·ed·ly** (prə·noun′sid·lē) *adv.*

pro·nounce·ment (prə·nouns′mənt) *n.* 1 The act of pronouncing. 2 A formal declaration or announcement.

pron·to (pron′tō) *adv. Slang* Quickly; promptly; instantly. [< L *promptus*]

pro·nun·ci·a·men·to (prə·nun′sē·ə·men′tō) *n. pl.* **·tos** A public announcement; proclamation; manifesto. [< L *pronuntiare* pronounce]

pro·nun·ci·a·tion (prə·nun′sē·ā′shən) *n.* The act or manner of pronouncing words.

proof (pro͞of) *n.* 1 The act or process of proving; esp., the establishment of a fact by evidence or a truth by other truths. 2 A trial of strength, truth, fact, or excellence, etc.; a test. 3 Evidence and argument sufficient to induce belief. 4 *Law* Anything that serves to convince the mind of the truth or falsity of a fact or proposition. 5 The state or quality of having successfully undergone a proof or test. 6 The standard of strength of alcoholic liquors: see PROOF SPIRIT. 7 *Printing* A printed trial sheet showing the contents or condition of matter in type. 8 In engraving and etching, a trial impression taken from an engraved plate, stone, or block. 9 *Phot.* A trial print from a negative. 10 *Math.* A procedure that shows that a proposition is true. 11 Anything proved true; experience. 12 In philately, an experimental printing of a stamp. —*adj.* 1 Employed in or connected with proving or correcting. 2 Capable of resisting successfully; firm: with *against*: *proof* against bribes. 3 Of standard alcoholic strength, as liquors. —*v.t.* 1 To make a test or proof of. 2 To protect or make impervious: to *proof* a garment against stains. 3 PROOFREAD. [< L *probare* PROVE]

-proof *combining form* 1 Impervious to; not damaged by: *waterproof.* 2 Protected against: *mothproof.* 3 As strong as: *armorproof.* 4 Resisting; showing no effects of: *panic-proof.*

proof·read (pro͞of′rēd′) *v.t. & v.i.* **·read** (-red′), **·read·ing** (-rē′ding) To read and correct (printers' proofs). **—proof′·read′er** *n.*

prop[1] (prop) *v.t.* **propped, prop·ping** 1 To support or keep from falling by or as by means of a prop. 2 To lean or place: usu. with *against.* 3 To support; sustain. —*n.* A support. [< MDu. *proppe* a vine prop]

prop[2] (prop) *n.* PROPERTY (def. 5).

prop[3] (prop) *n. Informal* PROPELLER.

prop. proper; properly; property; proposition; proprietor.

prop·a·gan·da (prop′ə·gan′də) *n.* 1 Any widespread scheme or effort to spread or promote an idea, opinion, or course of action in order to help or do damage to a cause, person, etc. 2 The ideas, opinions, etc., so spread or promoted: now often used disparagingly because of the deceitful or distorted character of much propaganda. [< NL *(congregatio de) propaganda (fide)* (the congregation for) propagating (the faith)]

prop·a·gan·dism (prop′ə·gan′diz·əm) *n.* The art, practice, or system of using propaganda. **—prop′a·gan′dist** *adj., n.* **—prop′a·gan·dis′tic** *adj.* **—prop′a·gan·dis′ti·cal·ly** *adv.*

prop·a·gan·dize (prop′ə·gan′dīz) *v.* **·dized, ·diz·ing** *v.t.* 1 To subject to propaganda. 2 To spread by means of propaganda. —*v.i.* 3 To carry on or spread propaganda.

prop·a·gate (prop′ə·gāt) *v.* **·gat·ed, ·gat·ing** *v.t.* 1 To cause (animals, plants, etc.) to multiply by natural reproduction; breed. 2 To reproduce (itself). 3 To spread abroad or from person to person; disseminate. 4 *Physics* To transmit (a form of energy) through space. —*v.i.* 5 To multiply by natural reproduction; breed. 6 *Physics* To pass or spread through space, as waves, heat, etc. [< L *propago* a slip for transplanting] **—prop′a·ga′tion, prop′a·ga′tor** *n.* **—prop′a·ga′tive** *adj.*

pro·pane (prō′pān) *n.* A gaseous hydrocarbon of the paraffin series. [< PROP(YL) + (METH)ANE]

pro·pel (prə·pel′) *v.t.* **·pelled, ·pel·ling** To cause to move forward or ahead; drive or urge forward. [< L *pro-* forward + *pellere* drive]

pro·pel·lant (prə·pel′ənt) *n.* That which propels, esp. an explosive or fuel that propels a projectile, rocket, etc.

pro·pel·lent (prə·pel′ənt) *adj.* Propelling; able to propel.

pro·pel·ler (prə·pel′ər) *n.* 1 One who or that which propels. 2 Any device for propelling a craft through water or air; esp., a set of rotating vanes operating like a screw. Also **pro·pel′lor.**

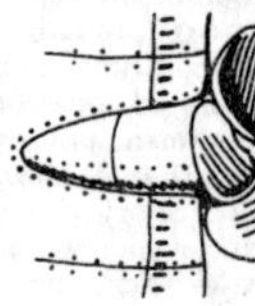
Propeller

pro·pen·si·ty (prə·pen′sə·tē) *n. pl.* **·ties** Natural disposition to or for; tendency. [< L *pro-* forward + *pendere* hang]

PROOFREADER'S MARKS

Symbols in the column headed Margin are used only in the outer margins of the proof; the symbols used within the body of the text are given in the Text column.

Margin		Text
l.c.	Set in lower-case type	circled or /
cap.	Set in capitals	underscored
s.c.	Set in small capitals	underscored
c.+s.c.	Set in caps and small caps	
l.f.	Set in lightface type	circled
b.f.	Set in boldface type	underscored
Rom.	Set in roman type	circled
Ital.	Set in italic type	underscored
⊙	Insert period	^
:/ ;/	Insert colon; semicolon	^ ^
,/	Insert comma	^
’	Insert apostrophe	^
/?/	Insert question mark	^
/!/	Insert exclamation mark	^
/-/	Insert hyphen	^
“ ”	Insert quotation marks	^
∨	Insert superior figure or letter	^
∧	Insert inferior figure or letter	^
1/m	Insert one em-dash	^
ℊ	Take out (delete matter marked)	/
wf	Wrong font	circled or /

Margin		Text
×	Broken letter: examine	circled
tr.	Transpose matter marked	⊓⊔
eq.#	Equalize spacing	^^^
[	Move to left to point marked	[
]	Move to right to point marked	]
⊓	Raise to point marked	⊓
⊔	Lower to point marked	⊔
⊥	Push down space	/
⁀	Close up	⁀
¶	Begin new paragraph	⌐
no ¶	Run on, not a paragraph	~
═	Align type	═
stet	Retain words crossed out	......
ℊ	Take out and close up	ℊ
‖	Line up matter	‖
Out	Omission here; see copy	^
[	Move this to left	
]	Move this to right	
Qu.?	Query: is this right?	^
Sp.	Spell out	circled
#	Insert space	^

proof spirit An alcoholic liquor of a standard strength, in the U.S., containing ethyl alcohol in the amount of 50 percent of its volume, equal to 100 proof.

prop·er (prop′ər) *adj.* 1 Having special fitness; specially suited; appropriate. 2 Conforming to a standard; correct: the *proper* pronunciation. 3 Seemly; right; fitting: the *proper* outfit. **4** Genteel and respectable, often excessively so. **5** Understood in the most correct or strict sense: usu. following the noun modified: Boston *proper.* **6** Naturally belonging to a person or thing: with *to*: Snow is *proper* to winter. —*n. Often cap.* That portion of the breviary or missal containing the prayers and collects suitable to special occasions. [< L *proprius* one's own] —**prop′er·ly** *adv.* —**prop′er·ness** *n.*

proper fraction A fraction in which the denominator exceeds the numerator.

proper noun A noun designating a specific person, place, or thing, always capitalized in English, as *John, Mount Everest, Apollo II.*

proper subset Any subset not identical with the entire set.

prop·er·tied (prop′ər·tēd) *adj.* Owning property.

prop·er·ty (prop′ər·tē) *n. pl.* **·ties 1** Any object that a person may lawfully acquire and own; any possession, esp. land or real estate. **2** A specific piece of land or real estate. **3** The legal right to the possession, use, and disposal of a thing. **4** An inherent quality or characteristic. **5** In the theater, movies, television, ballet, etc., any portable article, except scenery and costumes, used by the performers while performing. [< L *proprius* one's own]

proph·e·cy (prof′ə·sē) *n. pl.* **·cies 1** A prediction made under divine influence. **2** Any prediction. [< Gk. *pro-* before + *phanai* speak]

proph·e·sy (prof′ə·sī) *v.* **·sied, ·sy·ing** *v.t.* **1** To utter or foretell with or as with divine inspiration. **2** To predict (a future event). **3** To point out beforehand. —*v.i.* **4** To speak by divine influence. **5** To foretell the future. [< PROPHECY] —**proph′e·si′er** *n.*

proph·et (prof′it) *n.* **1** One who delivers divine messages or interprets the divine will. **2** One who foretells the future. **3** A religious leader. **4** An interpreter or spokesman for any cause. —**the Prophet** According to Islam, Mohammed. —**the Prophets** The Old Testament books written by the prophets. [< Gk. *pro-* before + *phanai* speak] —**proph′et·ess** *n. Fem.* —**proph′et·hood** (-ho͝od) *n.*

pro·phet·ic (prə·fet′ik) *adj.* **1** Of or pertaining to a prophet or prophecy. **2** Predicting or foreshadowing a future event. Also **pro·phet′i·cal.** —**pro·phet′i·cal·ly** *adv.*

pro·phy·lac·tic (prō′fə·lak′tik, prof′ə-) *adj.* Pertaining to prophylaxis. —*n.* **1** A prophylactic medicine or appliance. **2** A condom.

pro·phy·lax·is (prō′fə·lak′sis, prof′ə-) *n.* Preventive treatment for disease. [< Gk. *pro-* before + *phylaxis* a guarding]

pro·pin·qui·ty (prō·ping′kwə·tē) *n.* **1** Nearness in place or time. **2** Kinship. [< L *propinquus* near]

pro·pi·ti·ate (prō·pish′ē·āt) *v.t.* **·at·ed, ·at·ing** To cause to be favorably disposed; appease; conciliate. [< L *propitiare* render favorable, appease] —**pro·pi·ti·a·ble** (prō·pish′ē·ə·bəl), **pro·pi′ti·a′tive, pro·pi′ti·a·to′ry** *adj.* —**pro·pi·ti·a·tion** (prō·pish′ē·ā′shən), **pro·pi′ti·a′tor** *n.* —**Syn.** pacify, placate, mollify, reconcile.

pro·pi·tious (prō·pish′əs) *adj.* **1** Kindly disposed; gracious. **2** Attended by favorable circumstances; auspicious. [< L *propitius* favorable] —**pro·pi′tious·ly** *adv.* —**pro·pi′tious·ness** *n.* —**Syn. 2** timely, fortunate, lucky, providential, happy, felicitous.

pro·po·nent (prə·pō′nənt) *n.* **1** One who makes a proposal or puts forward a proposition. **2** *Law* One who presents a will for probate. **3** One who advocates or supports a cause or doctrine. [< L *pro-* forth + *ponere* put]

pro·por·tion (prə·pôr′shən, -pōr′-) *n.* **1** Relative magnitude, number, or degree, as existing between parts, a part and a whole, or different things. **2** Balance and harmony; symmetry. **3** A proportionate or proper share. **4** *pl.* Size; dimensions. **5** An equality or identity between ratios. **6** *Math.* An identity or equation involving a pair of fractions, in the general form $4/2 = 8/4$. —*v.t.* **1** To adjust properly as to relative magnitude, amount, or degree. **2** To form with a harmonious relation of parts. [< L *pro-* before + *portio* a share] —**pro·por′tion·a·ble** *adj.* —**pro·por′tion·a·bly** *adv.* —**pro·por′tion·er** *n.*

pro·por·tion·al (prə·pôr′shən·əl, -pōr′-) *adj.* **1** Of, pertaining to, or being in proportion. **2** *Math.* Being the product of a given function or variable and a constant: The area of a circle is *proportional* to the square of the radius. —**pro·por′tion·al·ly** *adv.* —**pro·por′tion·al′i·ty** (-al′ə·tē) *n.*

pro·por·tion·ate (prə·pôr′shən·it, -pōr′-) *adj.* Being in due proportion; proportional. —*v.t.* (-āt) **·at·ed, ·at·ing** To make proportionate. —**pro·por′tion·ate·ly** *adv.* —**pro·por′tion·ate·ness** *n.*

pro·po·sal (prə·pō′zəl) *n.* **1** An offer proposing something to be accepted or adopted. **2** An offer of marriage. **3** Something proposed.

pro·pose (prə·pōz′) *v.* **·posed, ·pos·ing** *v.t.* **1** To put forward for acceptance or consideration. **2** To nominate, as for admission or appointment. **3** To intend; purpose. **4** To suggest the drinking of (a toast or health). —*v.i.* **5** To form or announce a plan or design. **6** To make an offer, as of marriage. [< OF *pro-* forth + *poser* put] —**pro·pos′er** *n.*

prop·o·si·tion (prop′ə·zish′ən) *n.* **1** A scheme or proposal offered for consideration or acceptance. **2** *Informal* Any matter or person to be dealt with: a tough *proposition.* **3** *Informal* A proposal for illicit sexual intercourse. **4** A subject or statement presented for discussion. **5** *Logic* A statement in which the subject is affirmed or denied by the predicate. **6** *Math.* A statement whose truth is assumed or demonstrated. —*v.t. Informal* To make a proposal to (someone) to have illicit sexual intercourse. —**prop′o·si′tion·al** *adj.* —**prop′o·si′tion·al·ly** *adv.*

pro·pound (prə·pound′) *v.t.* To put forward for consideration, solution, etc. [< L *proponere* set forth] —**pro·pound′er** *n.*

pro·pri·e·tar·y (prə·prī′ə·ter′ē) *adj.* **1** Pertaining to a proprietor. **2** Protected as to name, composition, or process of manufacture by copyright, patent, etc. —*n. pl.* **·tar·ies 1** A proprietor or proprietors collectively. **2** Proprietorship. [< LL *proprietas* property]

pro·pri·e·tor (prə·prī′ə·tər) *n.* A person having the exclusive title to anything; owner. —**pro·pri′e·tor·ship′** *n.* —**pro·pri′e·tress** *n. Fem.*

pro·pri·e·ty (prə·prī′ə·tē) *n. pl.* **·ties** The character or quality of being proper; esp., accordance with recognized usage, custom, or principles. —**the proprieties** The standards of good social behavior. [< L *proprius* one's own]

pro·pul·sion (prə·pul′shən) *n.* **1** A propelling or being propelled. **2** Something that propels. [< L *propulsus,* pp. of *propellere* propel] —**pro·pul′sive** (-siv) *adj.*

pro·pyl (prō′pil) *n.* The univalent radical derived from propane.

pro ra·ta (prō rā′tə, rat′ə, rä′tə) Proportionate or proportionately: The loss was shared *pro rata.* [< L *pro rata (parte)* according to the calculated (share)]

pro·rate (prō·rāt′, prō′rāt′) *v.t. & v.i.* **·rat·ed, ·rat·ing** To distribute or divide proportionately. [< PRO RATA] —**pro·rat′a·ble** *adj.* —**pro·ra′tion** *n.*

pro·rogue (prō·rōg′) *v.t.* **·rogued, ·ro·guing** To discontinue a session of (an assembly, esp. the British Parliament). [< L *pro-* forth + *rogare* ask] —**pro·ro·ga·tion** (prō′rō·gā′shən) *n.*

pro·sa·ic (prō·zā′ik) *adj.* **1** Unimaginative; commonplace; dull. **2** Of or like prose. [< L *prosa* prose] —**pro·sa′i·cal·ly** *adv.* —**pro·sa′ic·ness** *n.*

pro·sce·ni·um (prō·sē′nē·əm) *n. pl.* **·ni·ums** or **·ni·a** (-nē·ə) **1** In a modern theater, that part of the stage between the curtain and the orchestra, sometimes including the curtain and its arch (**proscenium arch**). **2** In the ancient Greek or Roman theater, the stage. [< Gk. *proskēnion* < *pro-* before + *skēnē* a stage, orig. a tent]

pro·sciut·to (prō·sho͞o′tō) *n. pl.* **·ti** (-tē) or **·tos** A spicy, dry-cured ham, usu. sliced very thin. [Ital.]

pro·scribe (prō·skrīb′) *v.t.* **·scribed, ·scrib·ing 1** To denounce or condemn; prohibit; interdict. **2** To outlaw or banish. **3** In ancient Rome, to publish the name of (one condemned or exiled). [< L *pro-* before + *scribere* write] —**pro·scrib′er, pro·scrip′tion** (-skrip′shən) *n.* —**pro·scrip′tive** *adj.* —**pro·scrip′tive·ly** *adv.*

prose (prōz) *n.* **1** Speech or writing as found in ordinary conversation, letters, newspapers, etc. **2** Writing, esp. in literature, distinguished from poetry by the lack of conscious rhyme and usu. by rhythms suggesting ordinary speech or by a presentation in the form of a series of sentences with the initial letters capitalized. **3** Commonplace or tedious talk, style, quality, etc. —*adj.* **1** Of or in prose. **2** Tedious. —*v.t. & v.i.* **prosed, pros·ing** To write or speak in prose. [<L *prosa (oratio)* straight-forward (discourse)]

pros·e·cute (pros′ə·kyōōt) *v.* **·cut·ed, ·cut·ing** *v.t.* **1** To go on with so as to complete; pursue to the end: to *prosecute* an inquiry. **2** To carry on or engage in, as a trade. **3** *Law* **a** To bring suit against for redress of wrong or punishment of crime. **b** To seek to enforce or obtain, as a claim or right, by legal process. —*v.i.* **4** To begin and carry on a legal proceeding. [<L *prosequi* pursue]

prosecuting attorney The attorney empowered to act in behalf of the government, whether state, county, or national, in prosecuting for penal offenses.

pros·e·cu·tion (pros′ə·kyōō′shən) *n.* **1** The act or process of prosecuting. **2** *Law* **a** The instituting and carrying forward of a judicial or criminal proceeding. **b** The party instituting and conducting it.

pros·e·cu·tor (pros′ə·kyōō′tər) *n.* **1** One who prosecutes. **2** *Law* **a** One who institutes and carries on a suit, esp. a criminal suit. **b** PROSECUTING ATTORNEY.

pros·e·lyte (pros′ə·līt) *n.* One who has been converted to any opinion, belief, sect, or party. —*v.t. & v.i.* **·lyt·ed, ·lyt·ing** PROSELYTIZE. [<Gk. *prosēlytos* a convert to Judaism] —**pros′e·lyt·ism** (-līt′iz·əm, -lə·tiz′əm), **pros′e·lyt·ist** *n.*

pros·e·lyt·ize (pros′ə·lə·tīz′) *v.t. & v.i.* **·ized, ·iz·ing** To convert or try to convert (a person) to one's religion, opinions, party, etc. —**pros′e·ly·tiz′er** *n.*

pro·sit (prō′sit) *interj.* A toast used in drinking health. [L, lit., may it benefit (you)]

pros·o·dy (pros′ə·dē, proz′-) *n.* The study of poetical forms, including meter, rhyme schemes, structural analysis, etc. [<Gk. *prosōidia* a song sung to music] —**pro·sod·ic** (prə·sod′ik, -zod′-) or **·i·cal** *adj.* —**pros′o·dist** *n.*

pros·pect (pros′pekt) *n.* **1** A future probability or something anticipated. **2** *Usu. pl.* Chances, as for success. **3** A scene; an extended view. **4** The direction in which anything faces; an exposure; outlook. **5** A potential buyer, candidate, etc. **6** The act of observing or examining; survey. **7** *Mining* **a** A place having signs of the presence of mineral ore. **b** The sample of mineral obtained by washing a small portion of ore or dirt. —*v.t. & v.i.* To explore (a region) for gold, oil, etc. [<L *pro-* forward + *specere* look]

pro·spec·tive (prə·spek′tiv) *adj.* **1** Anticipated; expected. **2** Looking toward the future; anticipatory. —**pro·spec′tive·ly** *adv.*

pros·pec·tor (pros′pek·tər) *n.* One who prospects for mineral deposits, oil, etc.

pro·spec·tus (prə·spek′təs) *n.* **1** A paper containing information of a proposed literary or business undertaking. **2** A summary; outline. [L, a look-out, prospect]

pros·per (pros′pər) *v.i.* **1** To thrive; flourish. —*v.t.* **2** To render prosperous. [<OF<L favorable]

pros·per·i·ty (pros·per′ə·tē) *n.* The state of being prosperous; esp., wealth or success.

pros·per·ous (pros′pər·əs) *adj.* **1** Successful; flourishing. **2** Wealthy; well-to-do. **3** Promising; favorable [<L *prosper* favorable] —**pros′per·ous·ly** *adv.* —**pros′per·ous·ness** *n.*

pros·ta·gland·in (pros′tə·glan′din) *n.* A fatty acid, found in many body tissues, including the prostate gland, that regulates many bodily functions.

pros·tate (pros′tāt) *adj.* Of the prostate gland. —*n.* PROSTATE GLAND. [<Gk. *prostatēs* one who stands before]

prostate gland A partly muscular gland at the base of the bladder around the urethra in male mammals.

pros·the·sis (pros·thē′sis, pros′thə-) *n. pl.* **·the·ses** (-thē′·sēz) **1** Replacement of a missing part of the body with an artificial substitute. **2** A device used in prosthesis, as an artificial leg, eye, etc. [<Gk. *pros-* toward, besides + *tithenai* place, put] —**pros·thet·ic** (pros·thet′ik) *adj.*

pros·ti·tute (pros′tə·tyōōt) *n.* **1** A woman who engages in sexual intercourse for money. **2** A person who engages in sexual acts for money: a male *prostitute.* **3** A person who uses his talents or gifts for unworthy or corrupt purposes. —*v.t.* **·tut·ed, ·tut·ing** **1** To put to base or unworthy purposes. **2** To offer (oneself or another) for lewd purposes, esp. for hire. [<L *prostituere* expose publicly, prostitute] —**pros′ti·tu′tion, pros′ti·tu′tor** *n.*

pros·trate (pros′trāt) *adj.* **1** Lying prone, or with the face to the ground. **2** Brought low in mind or body, as from grief, exhaustion, etc. **3** Lying at the mercy of another; defenseless. **4** *Bot.* Trailing along the ground. —*v.t.* **·trat·ed, ·trat·ing** **1** To bow or cast (oneself) down, as in adoration or pleading. **2** To throw flat; lay on the ground. **3** To overthrow or overcome; reduce to helplessness. [<L *prostratus,* pp. of *prosternere* lay flat] —**pros·tra′tion** *n.*

pros·y (prō′zē) *adj.* **pros·i·er, pros·i·est** **1** Like prose. **2** Dull; commonplace. —**pros′i·ly** *adv.* —**pros′i·ness** *n.*

Prot. Protestant.

pro·tac·tin·i·um (prō′tak·tin′ē·əm) *n.* A radioactive element (symbol Pa) occurring in small amounts in uranium ores. [<PROT(O)- + ACTINIUM]

pro·tag·o·nist (prō·tag′ə·nist) *n.* **1** The actor who played the chief part in a Greek drama. **2** A leader in any enterprise or contest. [<Gk. *prōtos* first + *agōnistēs* a contestant, an actor]

pro·te·an (prō′tē·ən, prō·tē′ən) *adj.* Readily assuming different forms or aspects; changeable. [<PROTEUS]

pro·tect (prə·tekt′) *v.t.* **1** To shield or defend from attack, harm, or injury; guard; defend. **2** *Econ.* To assist (domestic industry) by protective tariffs. **3** In commerce, to provide funds to guarantee payment of (a draft, etc.). [<L *pro-* before + *tegere* to cover] —**pro·tec′tive** *adj.* —**pro·tec′tive·ly** *adv.* —**pro·tec′tive·ness, pro·tec′tor** *n.*

pro·tec·tion (prə·tek′shən) *n.* **1** The act of protecting or the state of being protected. **2** That which protects: Our dog is a great *protection.* **3** A system aiming to protect the industries of a country, as by imposing duties. **4** A safe-conduct pass. **5** *Slang* Security purchased under threat of violence from racketeers; also, the money so paid.

pro·tec·tion·ism (prə·tek′shən·iz′əm) *n.* The economic doctrine or system of protection. —**pro·tec′tion·ist** *adj., n.*

protective coloration Any natural coloration of a plant or animal that tends to disguise or conceal it from its enemies.

protective tariff A tariff that is intended to insure protection of domestic industries against foreign competition.

pro·tec·tor·ate (prə·tek′tər·it) *n.* **1** A relation of protection and partial control by a strong nation over a weaker power. **2** A country or region so protected.

pro·té·gé (prō′tə·zhā, prō·tə·zhā′) *n.* One aided, esp. in promoting a career, by another who is older or more powerful. [F, pp. of *protéger* protect] —**pro′té·gée** *n. Fem.*

pro·tein (prō′tēn, -tē·in) *n.* Any of a class of complex nitrogenous compounds found in all living matter and forming an essential part of the diet of animals. —*adj.* Composed of protein.

pro tem·po·re (prō tem′pə·rē) For the time being; temporary: usu. shortened to **pro tem.** [L]

Prot·er·o·zo·ic (prot′ər·ə·zō′ik, prō′tər-) *adj., n.* • See GEOLOGY. [<Gk. *proteros* former + *zōion* animal]

pro·test (prō′test) *n.* **1** An objection, complaint, or declaration of disapproval. **2** A public expression of dissent, esp. if organized. **3** A formal certificate attesting the fact that a note or bill of exchange has not been paid. —*adj.* Of or relating to public protest: *protest* demonstrations. —*v.* (prə·test′) *v.t.* **1** To assert earnestly or positively; state formally, esp. against opposition or doubt. **2** To make a protest against; object to. **3** To declare formally that payment of (a promissory note, etc.) has been duly submitted and refused. —*v.i.* **4** To make solemn affirmation. **5** To make a protest; object. [<L *pro-* forth + *testari* affirm] —**pro·test′er, pro·test′or** *n.*

Prot·es·tant (prot′is·tənt) *n.* Any Christian who is not a member of the Roman Catholic or Eastern Orthodox Churches. —*adj.* Pertaining to Protestants or Protestantism. —**Prot′es·tant·ism** *n.*

Protestant Episcopal Church A religious body in the U.S. which is descended from the Church of England.

prot·es·ta·tion (prot′is·tā′shən, prō′tes-) *n.* **1** The act of protesting. 2 That which is protested. 3 Any protest or objection.

Pro·te·us (prō′tē·əs, -tyōōs) *Gk. Myth.* A sea god who had the power of assuming different forms. **—Pro′te·an** *adj.*

proto- *combining form* 1 First in rank or time; chief; typical: *protozoan.* 2 Primitive; original: *prototype.* Also **prot-.** [< Gk. *prōtos* first]

pro·to·col (prō′tə·kol) *n.* 1 The preliminary draft of an official document, as a treaty. 2 The preliminary draft or report of the negotiations and conclusions arrived at by a diplomatic conference, having the force of a treaty when ratified. 3 The rules of diplomatic and state etiquette and ceremony. —*v.i.* To write or form protocols. [< LGk. *prōtokollon* the first glued sheet of a papyrus roll]

pro·ton (prō′ton) *n.* A stable, positively charged subatomic particle found typically in atomic nuclei, having a charge equal in magnitude to that of an electron and a mass of about 1.672 x 10^{-24} gram. [< Gk. *prōtos* first]

pro·to·plasm (prō′tə·plaz′əm) *n.* The basic living substance of plant and animal cells. [< Gk. *prōtos* first + PLASMA] **—pro′to·plas′mic** *adj.*

pro·to·type (prō′tə·tīp) *n.* A first or original model; an archetype. **—pro′to·typ′al** (-tī′pəl), **pro′to·typ′ic** (-tip′ik), **pro′to·typ′i·cal** *adj.*

pro·to·zo·an (prō′tə·zō′ən) *n. pl.* **·zo·a** (-zō′ə) Any of a phylum of single-celled animals, including free-living, aquatic forms and pathogenic parasites. Also **pro′to·zo′·on.** —*adj.* Pertaining or belonging to the phylum of protozoans: also **pro′to·zo′·ic.** [< PROTO- + Gk. *zōion* animal]

pro·tract (prō·trakt′, prə-) *v.t.* 1 To extend in time; prolong. 2 In surveying, to draw or map by means of a scale and protractor; plot. 3 *Zool.* To protrude or extend. [< L *protractus,* pp. of *protrahere* extend] **—pro·trac′tion** *n.* **—pro·tract′i·ble, pro·trac′tive** *adj.*

pro·tract·ed (prō·trak′tid, prə-) *adj.* Unduly or unusually extended or prolonged. **—pro·tract′ed·ly** *adv.* **—pro·tract′ed·ness** *n.*

pro·trac·tile (prō·trak′til) *adj.* Capable of being protracted or protruded; protrusile.

pro·trac·tor (prō·trak′tər) *n.* 1 An instrument for measuring and laying off angles. 2 One who or that which protracts.

pro·trude (prō·trōōd′, prə-) *v.t.* & *v.i.* **·trud·ed, ·trud·ing** To push or thrust out; project outward. [< L *pro-* forward + *trudere* thrust] **—pro·tru′dent** *adj.* **—pro·tru′sion** (-trōō′·zhən) *n.*

pro·tru·sile (prō·trōō′sil) *adj.* Adapted to being thrust out, as a tentacle, etc. Also **pro·tru′si·ble.**

pro·tru·sive (prō·trōō′siv) *adj.* 1 Tending to protrude. 2 Pushing or driving forward. **—pro·tru′sive·ly** *adv.* **—pro·tru′sive·ness** *n.*

pro·tu·ber·ance (prō·tyōō′bər·əns) *n.* 1 Something that protrudes; a knob; prominence. 2 The state of being protuberant. Also **pro·tu′ber·an·cy.** [< LL *protuberare* bulge out] **—pro·tu′ber·ant** *adj.* **—pro·tu′ber·ant·ly** *adv.*

proud (proud) *adj.* 1 Moved by, having, or exhibiting a due sense of pride; self-respecting. 2 Characterized by excessive or immoderate pride. 3 Being a cause of honorable pride: a *proud* occasion. 4 Appreciative of an honor; glad: *proud* of his heritage. 5 High-mettled, as a horse; spirited. [< OE *prūd*] **—proud′ly** *adv.* **—Syn.** 2 arrogant, haughty, supercilious, disdainful.

proud flesh An excessive growth of tissue at a healing wound or ulcer.

Prov, Prov. Proverbs.

prov. province; provincial; provisional; provost.

prove (prōōv) *v.* **proved, proved** or **prov·en** (prōō′vən), **prov·ing** *v.t.* 1 To show to be true or genuine, as by evidence or argument. 2 To determine the quality or genuineness of; test. 3 To establish the authenticity or validity of, as a will. 4 *Math.* To verify the accuracy of by an independent process. 5 *Printing* To take a proof of or from. 6 *Archaic* To learn by experience. —*v.i.* 7 To turn out to be: His hopes *proved* vain. [< L *probare* to test, try] **—prov′a·ble** *adj.* **—prov′er** *n.*

prov·e·nance (prov′ə·nəns) *n.* Origin or source, as of an archeological find or an object of art. [F< *provenant,* pr.p. of *provenir* come forth]

Pro·ven·çal (prō′vən·säl′, *Fr.* prō·väṅ·sål′) *n.* 1 The Romance language of Provence, France. 2 A native or resident of Provence. —*adj.* Of or pertaining to Provence, its inhabitants, or their language.

prov·en·der (prov′ən·dər) *n.* 1 Dry food for cattle, as hay. 2 Provisions. [< OF *provende* an allowance of food]

pro·ve·ni·ence (prō·vē′nē·əns, -vēn′yəns) *n.* PROVENANCE.

prov·erb (prov′ərb) *n.* 1 A terse expression of a popularly accepted piece of wisdom. 2 Something proverbial; a typical example; byword. [< L *pro-* before + *verbum* a word] **—Syn.** 1 adage, aphorism, maxim, motto, saying, truism.

pro·ver·bi·al (prə·vûr′bē·əl) *adj.* 1 Of the nature of or pertaining to a proverb. 2 Generally known or remarked. **—pro·ver′bi·al·ly** *adv.*

Prov·erbs (prov′ərbz) *n.pl. (construed as sing.)* A book of the Old Testament consisting of moral sayings.

pro·vide (prə·vīd′) *v.* **·vid·ed, ·vid·ing** *v.t.* 1 To acquire for or supply; furnish. 2 To afford; yield: to *provide* pleasure. 3 To set down as a condition; stipulate. —*v.i.* 4 To take measures in advance: with *for* or *against.* 5 To furnish means of subsistence: usu. with *for.* 6 To make a stipulation. [< L *providere* foresee] **—pro·vid′er** *n.*

pro·vid·ed (prə·vī′did) *conj.* On condition that.

prov·i·dence (prov′ə·dəns) *n.* 1 *Often cap.* The care exercised by nature or God's will over the universe. 2 Care exercised for the future; foresight. [< L *providentia* < *providens,* pr.p. of *providere* foresee]

Prov·i·dence (prov′ə·dəns) *n.* God; the Deity.

prov·i·dent (prov′ə·dənt) *adj.* 1 Anticipating and preparing for future wants or emergencies; exercising foresight. 2 Economical; thrifty. **—prov′i·dent·ly** *adv.*

prov·i·den·tial (prov′ə·den′shəl) *adj.* 1 Resulting from or revealing the action of God's providence. 2 As if caused by divine intervention; wonderful. **—prov′i·den′tial·ly** *adv.*

pro·vid·ing (prə·vī′ding) *conj.* Provided; in case that.

prov·ince (prov′ins) *n.* 1 An administrative division within a country: the *provinces* of Canada. 2 A region or country ruled by the Roman Empire. 3 *pl.* Those regions that lie at a distance from the capital or major cities. 4 A sphere of knowledge or activity: the *province* of chemistry. 5 Proper concern or compass, as of responsibilities or duties: The *province* of the judge is to apply the laws. [< L *provincia* an official duty or charge, a province]

pro·vin·cial (prə·vin′shəl) *adj.* 1 Of or characteristic of a province. 2 Confined to a province; rustic. 3 Narrow; unsophisticated; uninformed. —*n.* 1 A native or inhabitant of a province. 2 One who is provincial. **—pro·vin′ci·al′i·ty** (-shē·al′ə·tē) *n.* **—pro·vin′cial·ly** *adv.*

pro·vin·cial·ism (prə·vin′shəl·iz′əm) *n.* 1 The quality of being provincial. 2 Provincial peculiarity, esp. of speech.

pro·vi·sion (prə·vizh′ən) *n.* 1 A measure taken in advance, as against future need. 2 *pl.* Food or a supply of food; victuals. 3 Something provided or prepared in anticipation of need. 4 A stipulation or requirement. —*v.t.* To provide with food or provisions. [< L *provisus,* p.p. of *providere* foresee] **—pro·vi′sion·er** *n.*

pro·vi·sion·al (prə·vizh′ən·əl) *adj.* Provided for a present service or temporary necessity: a *provisional* army. Also **pro·vi′sion·ar′y** (-er′ē). **—pro·vi′sion·al·ly** *adv.*

pro·vi·so (prə·vī′zō) *n. pl.* **·sos** or **·soes** 1 A conditional stipulation. 2 A clause, as in a contract or statute, limiting, modifying, or rendering conditional its operation. [< Med. L *proviso (quod)* it being provided (that)]

pro·vi·so·ry (prə·vī′zər·ē) *adj.* 1 Conditional. 2 Provisional. **—pro·vi′so·ri·ly** *adv.*

pro·vo (prō′vō) *n. pl.* **·vos** A youthful member of any of various groups committed to violent political action. [Du. < F *provocateur*]

prov·o·ca·tion (prov′ə·kā′shən) *n.* 1 The act of provoking. 2 Something that provokes or incites; esp., something that provokes anger or annoyance.

pro·voc·a·tive (prə·vok′ə·tiv) *adj.* Serving to provoke or excite; stimulating: a *provocative* theory. —*n.* That which provokes or tends to provoke. **—pro·voc′a·tive·ly** *adv.* —**pro·voc′a·tive·ness** *n.*

pro·voke (prə·vōk′) *v.t.* **·voked, ·vok·ing 1** To stir to anger or resentment; irritate; vex. **2** To arouse or stimulate to some action. **3** To stir up or bring about: to *provoke* a quarrel. [< L *pro-* forth + *vocare* to call]

prov·ost (prō′vōst, prō′vəst, prov′əst) *n.* **1** A person having charge or authority over others. **2** The chief magistrate of a Scottish burgh. **3** An administrative official in some English and American colleges. **4** *Eccl.* The head of a collegiate chapter or a cathedral; a dean. [< L *praepositus* a prefect] **—prov′ost·ship** *n.*

pro·vost marshal (prō′vō) A military officer commanding a company of military police **(provost guard).**

prow (prou) *n.* **1** The forward part of a ship; the bow. **2** Any pointed projection, as of an airplane. [< Gk. *prōira*]

Prow of a ship

prow·ess (prou′is) *n.* **1** Strength, skill, and courage, esp. in battle. **2** Formidable skill; expertise. [< OF *prou* brave]

prowl (proul) *v.t.* & *v.i.* To roam about stealthily, as in search of prey or plunder. —*n.* The act of prowling. [ME *prollen*] **—prowl′er** *n.*

prowl car SQUAD CAR.

prox·i·mal (prok′sə·məl) *adj.* **1** Relatively nearer the center of the body or point of origin. **2** PROXIMATE. [< L *proximus* nearest] **—prox′i·mal·ly** *adv.*

prox·i·mate (prok′sə·mit) *adj.* Being in immediate relation with something else; next; near. [< L *proximus* nearest, superl. of *prope* near] **—prox′i·mate·ly** *adv.*

prox·im·i·ty (prok·sim′ə·tē) *n.* The state or fact of being near; nearness. [< L *proximus* nearest]

prox·i·mo (prok′sə·mō) *adv.* In or of the next or coming month. [< L *proximo (mense)* in the next (month)]

prox·y (prok′sē) *n. pl.* **prox·ies 1** A person empowered by another to act for him. **2** The means or agency of one so empowered: to vote by *proxy.* **3** The office or right to act for another. **4** A document conferring the authority to act for another. [< L *procurare* procure]

pr.p. present participle.

prude (pro͞od) *n.* One who displays an exaggerated devotion to modesty and propriety, esp. in sexual matters. [F < *prudefemme* an excellent woman] **—prud′ish** *adj.* —**prud′ish·ly** *adv.* **—prud′ish·ness** *n.*

pru·dence (pro͞od′ns) *n.* **1** The exercise of thoughtful care, sound judgment, or discretion; cautious wisdom. **2** Economy; thrift. **—pru·den·tial** (pro͞o·den′shəl) *adj.*

pru·dent (pro͞od′nt) *adj.* **1** Habitually careful to avoid errors and to follow the most reasonable or practical course; politic. **2** Exercising sound judgment; wise; judicious. **3** Characterized by discretion; cautious in manner. **4** Frugal; provident. [< L *prudens* knowing, skilled] **—pru′dent·ly** *adv.* **—Syn. 1** shrewd. **2** sensible, sagacious, thoughtful. **3** circumspect.

prud·er·y (pro͞o′dər·ē) *n. pl.* **·er·ies 1** Exaggerated devotion to modesty and propriety, esp. in sexual matters. **2** An action characteristic of a prude.

prune[1] (pro͞on) *n.* **1** The dried fruit of any of several varieties of plum. **2** *Slang* A stupid or disagreeable person. [< Gk. *prounon* a plum]

prune[2] (pro͞on) *v.t.* & *v.i.* **pruned, prun·ing 1** To trim or cut superfluous branches or parts (from). **2** To cut off (superfluous branches or parts). [< OF *proignier*] **—prun′er** *n.*

pru·ri·ent (pro͝or′ē·ənt) *adj.* **1** Tending to excite lustful thoughts or desires; lewd. **2** Characterized by or having lustful thoughts or desires: *prurient* interest. [< L *prurire* itch, long for] **—pru′ri·ence, pru′ri·en·cy** *n.* **—pru′ri·ent·ly** *adv.*

Prussian blue 1 A dark blue pigment or dye composed of various cyanogen compounds of iron. **2** A strong, blue color.

prussic acid HYDROCYANIC ACID.

pry[1] (prī) *v.i.* **pried, pry·ing** To look or peer carefully, curiously, or slyly; snoop. [ME *prien*]

pry[2] (prī) *v.t.* **pried, pry·ing 1** To raise, move, or open by means of a lever. **2** To obtain by effort. —*n.* **1** A lever, as a bar, stick, or beam. **2** Leverage. [< PRIZE[2]]

pry·er (prī′ər) *n.* PRIER.

P.S. public school.

P.S., p.s. postscript.

Ps, Ps., Psa. Psalms.

psalm (säm) *n.* A sacred song or lyric, esp. one contained in the Old Testament Book of Psalms; a hymn. [< Gk. *psalmos* a song sung to the harp]

psalm·ist (sä′mist) *n.* A composer of psalms. **—the Psalmist** King David, the traditional author of many of the Scriptural psalms.

psalm·o·dy (sä′mə·dē, sal′-) *n. pl.* **·dies 1** The singing of psalms in divine worship. **2** A collection of psalms. [< Gk. *psalmos* a psalm + *ōidē* a song] **—psalm′o·dist** *n.*

Psalms (sämz) *n.pl. (construed as sing.)* A lyrical book of the Old Testament, containing 150 hymns. Also **Book of Psalms.**

psal·ter (sôl′tər) *n.* A version of the Book of Psalms used in religious services. [< L *psalterium* a psaltery]

Psal·ter (sôl′tər) *n.* The Book of Psalms. Also **Psal′ter·y.**

psal·ter·y (sôl′tər·ē) *n. pl.* **·ter·ies** An ancient stringed musical instrument played by plucking. [< Gk. *psaltērion* < *psallein* to twitch, twang]

Psaltery

pseud. pseudonym.

pseu·do (so͞o′dō) *adj.* Pretended; sham; false.

pseudo- *combining form* **1** False; pretended: *pseudonym.* **2** Closely resembling; serving or functioning as: *pseudopodium.* Also **pseud-.** [< Gk. *pseudēs* false]

pseu·do·nym (so͞o′də·nim) *n.* A fictitious name; pen name. [< Gk. *pseudēs* false + *onyma* a name] **—pseu·don·y·mous** (so͞o·don′ə·məs) *adj.* **—pseu·don′y·mous·ly** *adv.* —**pseu·don′y·mous·ness, pseu·do·nym·i·ty** (so͞o′də·nim′ə·tē) *n.*

pseu·do·po·di·um (so͞o′də·pō′dē·əm) *n. pl.* **·di·a** (-dē·ə) A temporary extension of the protoplasm of a cell or unicellular organism, serving for taking in food, locomotion, etc. Also **pseu′do·pod** (-pod). [< PSEUDO- + Gk. *podion* little foot] **—pseu′do·po′di·al, pseu·dop·o·dal** (so͞o·dop′ə·dəl) *adj.*

psf, p.s.f. pounds per square foot.

pshaw (shô) *interj.* & *n.* An exclamation of annoyance, disgust, or impatience.

psi (sī, psī, psē) *n.* The twenty-third letter of the Greek alphabet (Ψ, ψ).

psi, p.s.i. pounds per square inch.

psi·lo·cy·bin (sī′lə·sī′bin) *n.* A hallucinogenic drug derived from a Mexican mushroom. [< *Psilocybe,* generic name of the mushroom + -IN]

psit·ta·co·sis (sit′ə·kō′sis) *n.* A viral infection affecting parrots, pigeons, etc., and sometimes humans, in whom it causes pneumonia, fever, etc. [< Gk. *psittakos* a parrot + -OSIS]

pso·ri·a·sis (sə·rī′ə·sis) *n.* A chronic skin condition characterized by reddish patches and white scales. [< Gk. *psōra* an itch] **—pso·ri·at·ic** (sôr′ē·at′ik, sō′rē-) *adj.*

PST, P.S.T., P.s.t. Pacific standard time.

psych (sīk) *v.t.* **psyched, psych·ing** *Slang* **1** To make mentally ready, as by inducing alertness or tension; key up: often with *up.* **2** To cause to lose self-assurance, esp. in order to place at a competitive disadvantage; demoralize: often with *out:* to *psych* rivals. **3** To manipulate by the use of psychology; esp., to outwit: often with *out: psyched* him into giving me a loan. **4** To understand: with *out:* couldn't *psych* it out. Also **psyche. —Syn. 2** intimidate, distress, put off, disconcert, discountenance.

psych., psychol. psychologist; psychology.

psy·che (sī′kē) *n.* **1** The human soul. **2** The mind. [< Gk. *psychē* the soul < *psychein* breathe, blow]

Psy·che (sī′kē) *Gk. & Rom. Myth.* A maiden beloved by Cupid and regarded as a personification of the soul.

psy·che·de·li·a (sī′kə·dē′lē·ə, -dēl′yə) *n.* Psychedelic drugs and accessories, or things associated with them.

psy·che·del·ic (sī′kə·del′ik) *adj.* Causing or having to do with abnormal alterations of consciousness or perception: *psychedelic* drugs. [< Gk. *psychē* soul + *del(os)* manifest + -IC] **—psy′che·del′i·cal·ly** *adv.*

psy·chi·a·trist (sī·kī′ə·trist) *n.* A medical doctor specializing in the practice of psychiatry.

psy·chi·a·try (sī·kī′ə·trē) *n.* The branch of medicine concerned with mental and emotional disorders. [< PSYCH(O)- + Gk. *iatros* healer] **—psy·chi·at·ric** (sī′kē·at′rik) or **·ri·cal** *adj.* **—psy′chi·at′ri·cal·ly** *adv.*

psy·chic (sī′kik) *adj.* 1 Of or pertaining to the psyche or mind. 2 Inexplicable with reference to present knowledge or scientific theory: *psychic* phenomena. 3 Sensitive or responsive to phenomena apparently independent of normal sensory stimuli: a *psychic* person. Also **psy′chi·cal.** —*n.* 1 A psychic person. 2 A spiritualistic medium. [< Gk. *psychē* soul] **—psy′chi·cal·ly** *adv.*

psy·cho (sī′kō) *n. pl.* **·chos** *Slang* A mentally disturbed person; a neurotic or psychopath. —*adj.* 1 Psychologically disturbed. 2 Psychological or psychiatric. [< PSYCHO(NEUROTIC)]

psycho- *combining form* Mind; soul; spirit: *psychosomatic.* Also **psych-.** [< Gk. *psychē* spirit, soul]

psy·cho·ac·tive (sī′kō·ak′tiv) *adj.* Having an effect on the mind or on behavior.

psy·cho·a·nal·y·sis (sī′kō·ə·nal′ə·sis) *n.* 1 A method of psychotherapeutic treatment developed by Sigmund Freud and others, which seeks to alleviate certain mental and emotional disorders. 2 The theory or practice of such treatment. **—psy′cho·an′a·lyt′ic** (-an′ə·lit′ik) or **·i·cal** *adj.* **—psy′cho·an′a·lyt′i·cal·ly** *adv.*

psy·cho·an·a·lyst (sī′kō·an′ə·list) *n.* One who practices psychoanalysis.

psy·cho·an·a·lyze (sī′kō·an′ə·līz) *v.t.* **·lyzed, ·lyz·ing** To treat by psychoanalysis. *Brit. sp.* **·lyse.**

psy·cho·dra·ma (sī′kō·drä′mə, -dram′ə) *n.* A form of psychotherapy in which the patient acts out, occasionally before an audience, situations involving his problems. **—psy′cho·dra·mat′ic** *adj.*

psy·cho·gen·ic (sī′kō·jen′ik) *adj.* Originating in the mind; caused by a mental or emotional condition. **—psy′·cho·gen′i·cal·ly** *adv.*

psy·cho·log·i·cal (sī′kə·loj′i·kəl) *adj.* 1 Of or pertaining to psychology. 2 Of or in the mind. 3 Suitable for affecting the mind: the *psychological* moment. Also **psy′cho·log′ic.** **—psy′cho·log′i·cal·ly** *adv.*

psy·chol·o·gist (sī·kol′ə·jist) *n.* A specialist in psychology.

psy·chol·o·gize (sī·kol′ə·jīz) *v.* **·gized, ·giz·ing** *v.i.* 1 To theorize psychologically. —*v.t.* 2 To interpret psychologically.

psy·chol·o·gy (sī·kol′ə·jē) *n.* 1 The science of the mind in any of its aspects. 2 The systematic investigation of human or animal learning, behavior, etc. 3 The pattern of mental processes characteristic of an individual or type.

psy·cho·neu·ro·sis (sī′kō·n^y^o͞o·rō′sis) *n. pl.* **·ses** (-sēz) NEUROSIS. **—psy′cho·neu·rot′ic** (-rot′ik) *adj., n.*

psy·cho·path (sī′kō·path) *n.* One exhibiting severely deranged behavior. **—psy′cho·path′ic** *adj.*

psy·cho·pa·thol·o·gy (sī′kō·pə·thol′ə·jē) *n.* The pathology of the mind. **—psy′cho·path′o·log′i·cal** (-path′ə·loj′i·kəl) *adj.* **—psy′cho·pa·thol′o·gist** *n.*

psy·chop·a·thy (sī·kop′ə·thē) *n.* Mental disorder.

psy·cho·sis (sī·kō′sis) *n. pl.* **·ses** (-sēz) A severe mental disorder marked by disorganization of the personality. [< Gk. *psychōsis* a giving of life]

psy·cho·so·mat·ic (sī′kō·sō·mat′ik) *adj.* 1 Of or pertaining to the interrelationships of mind and body, esp. with reference to disease. 2 Designating a physical ailment caused or influenced by emotional stress. [< PSYCHO- + SOMATIC]

psy·cho·sur·ger·y (sī′kō·sûr′jər·ē) *n.* Brain surgery performed to treat a mental disorder or alter behavior. **—psy′cho·sur′geon** (-sûr′jən) *n.* **—psy′cho·sur′gi·cal** *adj.*

psy·cho·ther·a·py (sī′kō·ther′ə·pē) *n.* The treatment of certain nervous and mental disorders by psychological techniques such as counseling, psychoanalysis, etc. Also **psy′cho·ther′a·peu′tics** (-ther′ə·pyo͞o′tiks). **—psy′cho·ther′·a·peu′tic** *adj.* **—psy′cho·ther′a·pist** *n.*

psy·chot·ic (sī·kot′ik) *n.* One suffering from a psychosis. —*adj.* Of psychosis or a psychotic. **—psy·chot′i·cal·ly** *adv.*

Pt platinum.

pt. (*pl.* **pts.**) part; payment; pint; point; port; preterit.

p.t. past tense; for the time being (L *pro tempore*).

PTA, P.T.A. Parent-Teacher Association.

ptar·mi·gan (tär′mə·gən) *n. pl.* **·gans** or **·gan** Any of various species of grouse of northern regions, usu. having white winter plumage. [< Scot. Gaelic *tarmachan*]

PT boat (pē′tē′) A high-speed, easily maneuverable motorboat equipped with torpedoes and, usu. machine guns and depth charges. [< *p(atrol) t(orpedo)*]

pter·i·do·phyte (ter′i·dō·fīt′) *n.* Any of a division of flowerless plants comprising the ferns, horsetails, and related plants with vascular stems, roots, and leaves. [< Gk. *pteris, pteridos* a fern + *phyton* a plant] **—pter′i·do·phyt′ic** (-fit′ik), **pter′i·doph′y·tous** (-dof′ə·təs) *adj.*

ptero- *combining form* Wing; feather; plume; resembling wings: *pterodactyl.* Also **pter-.** [< Gk. *pteron* wing]

pter·o·dac·tyl (ter′ə·dak′til) *n.* PTEROSAUR. [< Gk. *pteron* a wing + *daktylos* a finger]

pter·o·saur (ter′ə·sôr′) *n.* Any of various fossil reptiles having batlike wings. [< Gk. *pteros* wing + *sauros* lizard] **—pter′o·saur′i·an** *adj.*

-pterous *combining form* Having a specified number or kind of wings: *dipterous.* [< Gk. *pteron* wing]

ptg. printing.

Ptol·e·ma·ic (tol′ə·mā′ik) *adj.* Of or pertaining to Ptolemy, the astronomer who lived in the second century A.D., or to the Ptolemies who ruled Egypt.

Ptolemaic system The astronomical system of Ptolemy, which assumed that the earth was the central body around which the sun, planets, stars, etc., moved.

pto·maine (tō′mān, tō·mān′) *n.* Any of a class of usu. nontoxic compounds derived from decomposing protein. Also **pto′main.** [< Gk. *ptōma* a corpse]

ptomaine poisoning FOOD POISONING. • The term is based upon the erroneous idea that ptomaines usually cause food poisoning.

pty. proprietary.

pty·a·lin (tī′ə·lin) *n.* A digestive enzyme converting starch into dextrin and maltose. [< Gk. *ptyalon* saliva + -IN]

Pu plutonium.

pub (pub) *n. Brit.* A tavern or bar. [< PUB(LIC) (HOUSE)]

pub. public; publication; published; publisher.

pu·ber·ty (pyo͞o′bər·tē) *n.* 1 The state in an individual's development when he or she is physically capable of sexual reproduction. 2 The age at which puberty begins, usu. fixed legally at 14 years in boys and 12 in girls. [< L *pubes, puberis* an adult]

pu·bes (pyo͞o′bēz) *n.* 1 The hair that appears on the body at puberty. 2 The genital area that is covered with hair in the adult. [L, pubic hair]

pu·bes·cent (pyo͞o·bes′ənt) *adj.* 1 Arriving or having arrived at puberty. 2 *Biol.* Covered with fine hair or down, as leaves, etc. [< L *pubescere* attain puberty] **—pu·bes′·cence** *n.*

pu·bic (pyo͞o′bik) *adj.* Of or pertaining to the region in the lower part of the abdomen.

pu·bis (pyo͞o′bis) *n. pl.* **·bes** (-bēz) Either of the two bones which join to form the front arch of the pelvis. [< L *(os) pubis* pubic (bone)]

publ. publication; published; publisher.

pub·lic (pub′lik) *adj.* 1 Of, pertaining to, or affecting the people at large. 2 Of or relating to the community as distinguished from private or personal matters. 3 For the use of or open to all; maintained by or for the community: *public* parks. 4 Well-known; open: a *public* scandal. 5 Occupying an official position. 6 Acting before or for the community: a *public* speaker. —*n.* 1 The people collectively. 2 A group of people sharing some attribute or purpose: the church-going *public.* [< L *publicus*] **—pub′lic·ly** *adv.* **—pub′lic·ness** *n.*

pub·li·can (pub′lə·kən) *n.* 1 In England, the keeper of a public house. 2 In ancient Rome, one who collected the public revenues. [< L *publicanus* a tax gatherer]

pub·li·ca·tion (pub′lə·kā′shən) *n.* **1** The act of publishing. **2** That which is published; any printed work placed on sale or otherwise distributed.

public domain **1** Lands owned by a government. **2** The condition of being freely available for unrestricted use and not protected by copyright or patent.

public house **1** An inn, tavern, or hotel. **2** *Brit.* A saloon or bar.

pub·li·cist (pub′lə·sist) *n.* **1** One who publicizes, as an activity, a person, etc. **2** A writer on international law.

pub·lic·i·ty (pub·lis′ə·tē) *n.* **1** The state of being public. **2** Information, news, or promotional material intended to elicit public interest in some person, product, cause, etc.; also the work or business of preparing and releasing such material. **3** The attention or interest of the public.

pub·li·cize (pub′lə·sīz) *v.t.* **·cized, ·ciz·ing** To give publicity to; promote. *Brit. sp.* **pub′li·cise.**

public opinion The prevailing ideas, beliefs, or attitudes of a community.

public relations The business of representing and promoting the interests or reputation of a person or an organization in its relations with the public.

public school **1** A school maintained by public funds for the free education of the children of the community, usu. covering elementary and secondary grades. **2** In England, a private, endowed boarding school preparing students for the universities.

public servant A government official.

pub·lic-spir·it·ed (pub′lik-spir′it·id) *adj.* Showing an enlightened interest in the welfare of the community.

public utility A business organization which performs some public service, as the supplying of water or electric power, and is subject to governmental regulations.

public works Works built with public money, as post offices, roads, etc.

pub·lish (pub′lish) *v.t.* **1** To print and issue (a book, magazine, etc.) to the public. **2** To make known or announce publicly. **3** To print and issue the work of. —*v.i.* **4** To engage in the business of publishing books, magazines, newspapers, etc. **5** To have one's work printed and issued. [< L *publicare* make public] **—pub′lish·a·ble** *adj.* **—Syn. 2** promulgate, proclaim, declare, advertise.

pub·lish·er (pub′lish·ər) *n.* One who makes a business of publishing books, periodicals, etc.

puce (pyōōs) *n.* Dark purplish brown. —*adj.* Of this color. [F, lit., flea < L *pulex*]

puck[1] (puk) *n.* A mischievous sprite or hobgoblin. [< OE *pūca* a goblin] **—puck′ish** *adj.* **—puck′ish·ly** *adv.* **—puck′ish·ness** *n.*

puck[2] (puk) *n.* A hard rubber disk used in playing hockey. [? var. of POKE[1]]

puck·a (puk′ə) *adj.* PUKKA.

puck·er (puk′ər) *v.t.* & *v.i.* To gather or draw up into small folds or wrinkles. —*n.* A wrinkle. [?< POKE[2]]

pud·ding (pŏŏd′ing) *n.* **1** A sweetened and flavored dessert of soft food. **2** A sausage stuffed with seasoned, minced meat, blood, etc. [ME *poding*]

pud·dle (pud′l) *n.* **1** A small pool of water or other liquid. **2** A pasty mixture of clay and water. —*v.t.* **·dled, ·dling** **1** To convert (molten pig iron) into wrought iron by melting and stirring in the presence of oxidizing agents. **2** To mix (clay, etc.) with water to obtain a watertight paste. **3** To line, as canal banks, with such a mixture. **4** To make muddy; stir up. [ME < OE *pudd* a ditch] **—pud′dler** *n.*

pud·dling (pud′ling) *n.* The operation of making wrought iron from pig iron by agitation in a molten state with oxidizing agents present.

pu·den·dum (pyōō·den′dəm) *n. pl.* **·da** (-də) **1** The vulva. **2** *pl.* The external genitals of either sex. [L, neut. of *pudendus* (something) to be ashamed of] **—pu·den′·dal** *adj.*

pudg·y (puj′ē) *adj.* **pudg·i·er, pudg·i·est** Short and thick; fat. [< Scot. *pud* belly] **—pudg′i·ly** *adv.* **—pudg′i·ness** *n.*

Hopi Indian pueblo

pueb·lo (pweb′lō *for def. 1,* pwä′blō *for def. 2*) *n. pl.* **·los** **1** A communal adobe or stone building or group of buildings of the Indians of the sw U.S. **2** A town or village of Indians or Spanish Americans, as in Mexico. [Sp., a town, people < L *populus*]

Pueb·lo (pweb′lō) *n.* A member of one of the Indian tribes of Mexico and the sw U.S.

pu·er·ile (pyōō′ər·il, pwer′il, -īl) *adj.* Childish; immature; silly. [< L *puer* boy] **—pu′er·ile·ly** *adv.* **—pu′er·il′i·ty, pu′er·ile·ness** *n.*

pu·er·per·al (pyōō·ûr′pər·əl) *adj.* Pertaining to or resulting from childbirth. [< L *puer* boy + *parere* bring forth]

Puerto Ri·co (pwer·tə rē′kō, pôr-) An island commonwealth of the West Indies, a part of the U.S., 3,423 sq. mi., cap. San Juan. • See map at DOMINICAN REPUBLIC. **—Puer′to Ri′can** *adj., n.*

puff (puf) *n.* **1** A short, mild explosive force or emission, as a gust of air or expelled breath. **2** The sound of such a force. **3** The air, breath, etc., so felt or emitted: a small *puff* of smoke. **4** The act of sucking in and exhaling in the course of smoking a cigarette, etc. **5** A light, air-filled piece of pastry. **6** A pad for dusting powder on the skin. **7** A small protuberance or swelling. **8** A loose roll of hair. **9** A quilted bed coverlet. **10** A part of a fabric gathered at the edges. **11** A public expression of fulsome praise. —*v.i.* **1** To blow in puffs, as the wind. **2** To breathe hard, as after violent exertion. **3** To emit smoke, steam, etc., in puffs. **4** To smoke a cigarette, etc., with puffs. **5** To move, act, or exert oneself while emitting puffs: with *away, up,* etc. **6** To swell, as with air or pride; dilate: often with *up.* —*v.t.* **7** To send forth or emit with short puffs or breaths. **8** To move, impel, or stir up with or in puffs. **9** To smoke, as a cigarette or pipe, with puffs. **10** To swell or distend. **11** To praise fulsomely. **12** To arrange (the hair) in a puff. [< OE *pyffan*] **—puff′i·ly** *adv.* **—puff′i·ness** *n.* **—puff′y** *adj.* **(·i·er, ·i·est)**

puff adder **1** A large African viper that puffs and hisses when disturbed. **2** HOGNOSE.

puff·ball (puf′bôl′) *n.* A globular fungus that puffs out dustlike spores if broken open when ripe.

puff·er (puf′ər) *n.* **1** One who puffs. **2** Any of various fishes that can inflate themselves with air or water.

puff·er·y (puf′ər·ē) *n.* Excessive praise, esp. to obtain publicity.

puf·fin (puf′in) *n.* Any of various northern sea birds with a chunky body and a large, triangular bill. [ME *poffin*]

Puffin

pug[1] (pug) *v.t.* **pugged, pug·ging** **1** To work (clay) with water in molding pottery or making bricks. **2** To fill in or cover with mortar, clay, felt, etc., to deaden sound. —*n.* A mixture of clay worked with water for brick-making, etc. [< dial. E]

pug[2] (pug) *n.* **1** A short-haired dog with a square body, upturned nose and curled tail. **2** PUG NOSE. [?]

pug[3] (pug) *n.* *Slang* A professional prizefighter. [Short for PUGILIST]

pu·gi·lism (pyōō′jə·liz′əm) *n.* BOXING. [< L *pugil* a boxer] **—pu′gi·list** *n.* **—pu′gi·lis′tic** *adj.* **—pu′gi·lis′ti·cal·ly** *adv.*

pug·na·cious (pug·nā′shəs) *adj.* Disposed or inclined to fight; quarrelsome. [< L *pugnus* fist] **—pug·na′cious·ly** *adv.* **—pug·nac·i·ty** (-nas′ə·tē), **pug·na′cious·ness** *n.*

pug nose A thick, short, upturned nose. [< PUG[2] + NOSE] **—pug′-nosed′** *adj.*

pu·is·sant (pyōō′ə·sənt, pyōō·is′ənt, pwis′ənt) *adj.* Powerful; mighty. [< L *posse* be able] **—pu′is·sance** *n.* **—pu′is·sant·ly** *adv.*

puke (pyōōk) *v.t. & v.i.* **puked, puk·ing,** *n. Informal* VOMIT. [?]

puk·ka (puk′ə) *adj.* Genuine; sound. [< Hind. *pakkā* cooked, ripe]

pul·chri·tude (pul′krə·tyōōd) *n.* Beauty; grace. [< L *pulcher* beautiful] **—pul·chri·tu·di·nous** (-tyōō′də·nəs) *adj.*

pule (pyōōl) *v.i.* **puled, pul·ing** To cry plaintively, as a child; whimper; whine. [< MF *pioler* chirp] **—pul′er** *n.*

Pul·it·zer Prize (po͞ol′it·sər, pyo͞o′lit-) Any of several annual awards for outstanding work in American journalism, literature, drama, and music, established by Joseph Pulitzer, 1847–1911, U.S. journalist.

pull (po͝ol) *v.t.* **1** To apply force to so as to cause motion toward or after the person or thing exerting force; drag; tug. **2** To draw or remove from a natural or fixed place: to *pull* a tooth or plug. **3** To give a pull or tug to. **4** To pluck, as a fowl. **5** To draw asunder; tear; rend: with *to pieces, apart,* etc. **6** To strain so as to cause injury: to *pull* a ligament. **7** In sports, to strike (the ball) so as to cause it to curve obliquely from the direction in which the striker faces. **8** *Informal* To put into effect; carry out: to *pull* off a robbery. **9** *Informal* To make a raid on; arrest. **10** *Informal* To draw out so as to use: to *pull* a knife. **11** To make or obtain by impression from type: to *pull* a proof. **12** In boxing, to deliver (a punch, etc.) with less than full strength. **13** In horse-racing, to restrain (a horse) so as to prevent its winning. **14** To operate (an oar) by drawing toward one. —*v.i.* **15** To use force in hauling, dragging, moving, etc. **16** To move: with *out, in, away, ahead,* etc. **17** To drink or inhale deeply. **18** *Informal* To attract attention or customers: an ad that *pulls.* **19** To row. —**pull for** **1** To strive in behalf of. **2** *Informal* To declare one's allegiance to. —**pull oneself together** To regain one's composure. —**pull through** To survive in spite of illness, etc. —**pull up** To come to a halt. —*n.* **1** The act or process of pulling. **2** Something that is pulled, as a handle. **3** A long swallow or a deep puff. **4** The drawing of an oar in rowing. **5** A steady, continuous effort, as in climbing: a long *pull* to the top. **6** *Informal* Influence, esp. with those in power: political *pull.* **7** An attractive force: the *pull* of gravity. [< OE *pullian* pluck] —**pull′er** *n.*

pull·back (po͝ol′bak′) *n.* A withdrawal, as of troops.

pul·let (po͝ol′it) *n.* A young hen, usu. less than a year old. [< L *pullus* chicken]

pul·ley (po͝ol′ē) *n.* **1** A wheel or wheels grooved to receive a rope, usu. mounted in a block, used singly to reverse the direction of force applied, as in lifting a weight, and in various combinations to increase force at the expense of distance. **2** A flat or flanged wheel driving, carrying, or being driven by a flat belt, used to transmit power. [< Gk. *polos* a pivot, axis]

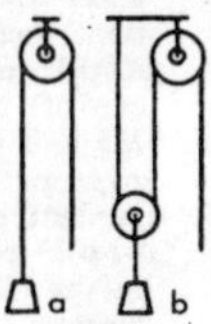

Pulleys
a. single fixed. b. fixed and runner.

Pull·man (po͝ol′mən) *n.* A railroad car with compartments for sleeping or other special accommodations. Also **Pullman car.** [< George M. *Pullman,* 1831–97, U.S. inventor]

pull·out (po͝ol′out′) *n.* **1** A withdrawal or removal, as of troops. **2** Something to be pulled out, as an oversize leaf folded into a magazine.

pull·o·ver (po͝ol′ō′vər) *adj.* Put on by being drawn over the head. —*n.* A garment put on in such a way, as a sweater.

pul·mo·nar·y (po͝ol′mə·ner′ē, pul′-) *adj.* **1** Pertaining to or affecting the lungs. **2** Having lunglike organs. **3** Designating the blood vessels carrying blood between the lungs and heart. Also **pul·mon·ic** (po͝ol·mon′ik, pul-). [< L *pulmo, pulmonis* lung] • See HEART.

Pul·mo·tor (po͝ol′mō′tər, pul′-) *n.* A machine for applying artificial respiration: a trade name.

pulp (pulp) *n.* **1** A moist, soft, slightly cohering mass, as the soft, succulent part of fruit. **2** A mixture of wood fibers or rags, made semifluid and forming the basis from which paper is made. **3** *pl.* Magazines printed on rough, unglazed, wood-pulp paper, and usu. having contents of a sensational nature. **4** Powdered ore mixed with water. **5** The soft tissue of vessels and nerves that fills the central part of a tooth. • See TOOTH. —*v.t.* **1** To reduce to pulp. **2** To remove the pulp from. —*v.i.* **3** To be or become pulp. [< L *pulpa* flesh, pulp] —**pulp′i·ness** *n.* —**pulp′y** *adj.*

pul·pit (po͝ol′pit, pul′-) *n.* **1** An elevated stand or desk for preaching in a church. **2** The office or work of preaching. **3** The clergy. [< L *pulpitum* platform]

pulp·wood (pulp′wo͝od′) *n.* Soft wood used in the manufacture of paper.

pul·que (pul′kē, po͝ol′-; *Sp.* po͞ol′kā) *n.* A fermented Mexican drink made from agave. [Sp.]

pul·sar (pul′sär) *n.* An astronomical object that emits radio waves in pulses whose repetition rate is extremely stable. [< *puls(ating)* + *(st)ar*]

pul·sate (pul′sāt) *v.i.* **·sat·ed, ·sat·ing** **1** To move or throb with rhythmical impulses, as the pulse or heart. **2** To vibrate; quiver. [< L *pulsare,* freq. of *pellere* beat] —**pul·sa′tion, pul′sa·tor** *n.* —**pul′sa·tive** (-sə·tiv), **pul′sa·to′ry** *adj.*

pulse[1] (puls) *n.* **1** The rhythmic pressure in the arteries due to the beating of the heart. **2** Any short, regular throbbing; pulsation. **3** A brief surge of energy, esp. electrical or electromagnetic energy. **4** Feelings and attitudes sensitively perceived as belonging to a group or community; also, an indication of such feelings. —*v.i.* **pulsed, puls·ing** To manifest a pulse; pulsate; throb. [< L *pulsus* p.p. of *pellere* beat]

pulse[2] (puls) *n.* Leguminous plants collectively, as peas, beans, etc., or their edible seeds. [< L *puls* pottage]

pulse·jet (puls′jet′) *n.* A jet engine that operates intermittently and produces power in rapid bursts.

pul·ver·ize (pul′və·rīz) *v.* **·ized, ·iz·ing** *v.t.* **1** To reduce to powder or dust, as by grinding or crushing. **2** To demolish; annihilate. —*v.i.* **3** To become reduced to powder or dust. *Brit. sp.* **·ise.** [< L *pulvis, pulveris* a powder, dust] —**pul′·ver·iz′a·ble, pul′ver·a·ble** (pul′və·rə·bəl) *adj.* —**pul′ver·i·za′·tion, pul′ver·iz′er** *n.*

pu·ma (pyo͞o′mə) *n.* MOUNTAIN LION. [< Quechua]

pum·ice (pum′is) *n.* Porous volcanic lava, used as an abrasive and polisher, esp. when powdered. Also **pumice stone.** —*v.t.* **·iced, ·ic·ing** To smooth, polish, or clean with pumice. [< L *pumex*] —**pu·mi·ceous** (pyo͞o·mish′əs) *adj.*

pum·mel (pum′əl) *v.t.* **·meled** or **·melled, ·mel·ing** or **·mel·ling** POMMEL.

pump[1] (pump) *n.* A device using suction or pressure to raise, circulate, exhaust, or compress a liquid or gas. —*v.t.* **1** To raise (a liquid) with a pump. **2** To remove the water, etc., from. **3** To inflate with air by means of a pump. **4** To propel, discharge, force, etc., from or as if from a pump. **5** To cause to operate in the manner of a pump. **6** To question persistently or subtly. **7** To obtain (information) in such a manner. —*v.i.* **8** To work a pump. **9** To raise water or other liquid with a pump. **10** To move up and down like a pump or pump handle. [< MDu. *pompe*] —**pump′er** *n.*

pump[2] (pump) *n.* A low-cut shoe without a fastening, worn esp. by women. [?]

pum·per·nick·el (pum′pər·nik′əl) *n.* A coarse, dark bread made with rye flour. [G]

pump·kin (pump′kin, pum′-, pung′-) *n.* **1** A coarse trailing vine with gourdlike fruit. **2** Its large, edible, orange-yellow fruit. [< Gk. *pepōn* a melon]

pun (pun) *n.* The humorous use of two words having the same or similar sounds but different meanings, or of a word having two more or less incongruous meanings. —*v.i.* **punned, pun·ning** To make a pun or puns. [? < Ital. *puntiglio* a fine point]

punch[1] (punch) *n.* **1** A tool for perforating or indenting, or for driving an object into a hole. **2** A machine for impressing a design or stamping a die. —*v.t.* To perforate, shape, indent, etc., with a punch. [ME *punchon* puncheon]

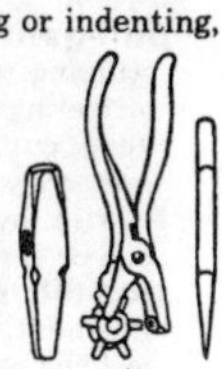

Punches
a. square. b. revolving. c. stamping.

punch[2] (punch) *v.t.* **1** To strike sharply, esp. with the fist. **2** To poke with a stick; prod. **3** To drive (cattle). —*n.* **1** A swift blow with the fist. **2** A thrust or nudge. **3** *Informal* Vitality; effectiveness; force. —**punch in** (or **out**) To activate a time clock and record the hour at the start (or completion) of a period of work. [ME *punchen*] —**punch′er** *n.* —**Syn. 1** hit, pound, pommel, box.

punch[3] (punch) *n.* A hot or cold beverage made with fruit juices, spices, and other ingredients, as tea or soda water, and often mixed with alcoholic spirits. [< Skt. *pañchan* five; from the five original ingredients]

Punch (punch) *n.* The quarrelsome, grotesque hero of a comic puppet show, **Punch and Judy.** —**pleased as Punch** Extremely pleased; highly gratified. [Short for PUNCHINELLO]

punch card In data processing, a card having an arrangement of positions into which holes may be punched for the storage of information. Also **punched card.**

pun·cheon (pun′chən) *n.* **1** An upright supporting timber. **2** A punch or perforating tool. **3** A broad, heavy piece of roughly dressed timber, having one flat, hewed side. **4** A liquor cask of variable capacity, from 72 to 120 gallons. **5** The amount held by such a cask. [< OF *poinçon, poinchon* a punch]

pun·chi·nel·lo (pun′chə·nel′ō) *n. pl.* **·los** or **·loes** **1** *Usu. cap.* A character in an Italian puppet show, the original of the English Punch. **2** A grotesque character; buffoon. [< dial. Ital. *Polcenella*]

punching bag An inflated or stuffed ball, usu. suspended, that is punched for exercise.

punch press A machine equipped with dies for cutting or forming metal.

punch·y (pun′chē) *adj.* **punch·i·er, punch·i·est** *Informal* **1** Dazed or confused, as from having been struck on the head: also **punch-drunk** (punch′drungk′). **2** Lively; snappy. —**punch′i·ly** *adv.* —**punch′i·ness** *n.*

punc·til·i·o (pungk·til′ē·ō) *n. pl.* **·til·i·os** **1** A fine point of etiquette. **2** Preciseness in the observance of etiquette. [< L *punctum* a point]

punc·til·i·ous (pungk·til′ē·əs) *adj.* Very exacting in observing rules or conventions. [< Ital. *puntiglio* small point] —**punc·til′i·ous·ly** *adv.* —**punc·til′i·ous·ness** *n.*

punc·tu·al (pungk′chōō·əl) *adj.* **1** Arriving on time; prompt. **2** Habitually exact as to appointed time. **3** Consisting of or confined to a point. [< L *punctus* a point] —**punc′tu·al′i·ty** *n.* —**punc′tu·al·ly** *adv.*

punc·tu·ate (pungk′chōō·āt) *v.* **·at·ed, ·at·ing** *v.t.* **1** To divide or mark with punctuation. **2** To interrupt at intervals. **3** To emphasize. —*v.i.* **4** To use punctuation. [< L *punctus* a point] —**punc′tu·a′tor** *n.*

punc·tu·a·tion (pungk′chōō·ā′shən) *n.* **1** The use of points or marks in written or printed matter to aid in the better comprehension of the meaning and grammatical relation of the words. **2** The marks so used.

punctuation mark Any of the marks used in punctuating, as the period or comma.

punc·ture (pungk′chər) *v.* **·tured, ·tur·ing** *v.t.* **1** To pierce with a sharp point. **2** To make by pricking, as a hole. **3** To cause to collapse: to *puncture* a cherished illusion. —*v.i.* **4** To be pierced or punctured. —*n.* **1** A small hole, as one made by piercing. **2** The act of puncturing. [< L *punctus,* p.p. of *pungere* prick]

pun·dit (pun′dit) *n.* **1** One who is or assumes the part of an expert in making pronouncements, criticisms, predictions, etc. **2** In India, a Brahmin versed in Sanskrit lore, Hindu religion, etc. [< Skt. *paṇḍita* learned] —**pun′dit·ry** (-rē) *n.*

pun·gent (pun′jənt) *adj.* **1** Causing a sharp pricking, stinging, piercing, or acrid sensation. **2** Affecting the mind or feelings so as to cause pain; piercing; sharp. **3** Caustic; keen; cutting: *pungent* sarcasm. **4** Telling; pointed. [< L *pungere* prick] —**pun′gen·cy** *n.* —**pun′gent·ly** *adv.*

Pu·nic (pyōō′nik) *adj.* Of or pertaining to ancient Carthage or the Carthaginians.

pun·ish (pun′ish) *v.t.* **1** To subject (a person) to pain, confinement, or other penalty for a crime or fault. **2** To subject the perpetrator of (an offense) to a penalty. **3** To treat roughly; injure; hurt. [< L *punire*] —**pun′ish·a·ble** *adj.* —**pun′ish·a·bil′i·ty, pun′ish·er** *n.*

pun·ish·ing (pun′ish·ing) *adj.* Requiring exhausting effort; taxing; demanding: a *punishing* schedule.

pun·ish·ment (pun′ish·mənt) *n.* **1** Penalty imposed, as for a violation of law. **2** Any pain or loss inflicted in response to wrongdoing. **3** The act of punishing. **4** Physical damage or abuse.

pu·ni·tive (pyōō′nə·tiv) *adj.* Pertaining to or inflicting punishment. —**pu′ni·tive·ly** *adv.* —**pu′ni·tive·ness** *n.*

punk[1] (pungk) *n.* **1** Decayed wood, used as tinder. **2** Any substance that smolders when ignited. [< Algon.]

punk[2] (pungk) *Slang n.* **1** Rubbish; nonsense; anything worthless. **2** A petty hoodlum. **3** An inexperienced youth, esp. a young man: usu. contemptuous. —*adj.* Worthless; useless. [?]

pun·ky (pung′kē) *n. pl.* **·kies** Any of various tiny, blood-sucking insects. Also **pun′key, pun′kie.** [< PUNK[1]]

pun·ster (pun′stər) *n.* One who enjoys making puns. Also **pun′ner.**

punt[1] (punt) *n.* A flat-bottomed, square-ended boat for use in shallow waters, and propelled with a pole. —*v.t.* **1** To propel (a boat) by pushing with a pole against the bottom of a shallow stream, lake, etc. **2** To convey in a punt. —*v.i.* **3** To go or hunt in a punt. [< L *ponto*] —**punt′er** *n.*

Punt

punt[2] (punt) *v.i.* To gamble or bet in certain card games, esp. against the banker. [< L *punctum* a point]

punt[3] (punt) *n.* In football, a kick made by dropping the ball from the hands and kicking it before it strikes the ground. —*v.t.* **1** To propel (a football) with a punt. —*v.i.* **2** In football, to make a punt. [?] —**punt′er** *n.*

pu·ny (pyōō′nē) *adj.* **·ni·er, ·ni·est** Small or inferior, as in power, significance, etc. [< OF *puisne* born afterward] —**pu′ni·ly** *adv.* —**pu′ni·ness** *n.* —**Syn.** slight, minor, unimportant, frail.

pup (pup) *n.* The young of certain animals, as a dog, wolf, fox, seal, whale, etc. —*v.i.* **pupped, pup·ping** To bring forth pups. [Short for PUPPY]

pu·pa (pyōō′pə) *n. pl.* **·pae** (-pē) or **·pas** A quiescent stage between larva and adult in the metamorphosis of certain insects. [L, a girl, puppet] —**pu′pal** *adj.*

pu·pate (pyōō′pāt) *v.i.* **·pat·ed, ·pat·ing** To enter upon or undergo the pupal condition. —**pu·pa′tion** *n.*

pu·pil[1] (pyōō′pəl) *n.* A person under the care of a teacher, as in a school. [< L *pupillus* and *pupilla,* dim. of *pupus* boy and *pupa* girl] —**pu′pil·age, pu′pil·lage** *n.* —**Syn.** student, disciple, scholar, learner.

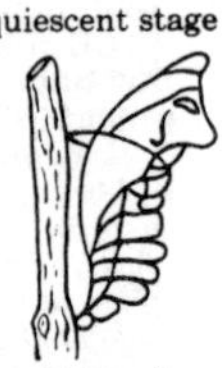

Pupa of a butterfly

pu·pil[2] (pyōō′pəl) *n.* The circular opening in the iris of the eye, through which light reaches the retina. [< L *pupilla* pupil of the eye] • See EYE.

pup·pet (pup′it) *n.* **1** A small figure, as of a person or animal, manipulated usu. by the hands, or by pulling strings or wires attached to its jointed parts. **2** A person controlled by the will or whim of another. **3** A doll. —*adj.* **1** Of puppets. **2** Performing the will of an unseen power; not autonomous: a *puppet* state or government. [< L *pupa* a girl, doll, puppet] —**pup′pet·ry** (-rē) *n.*

pup·pet·eer (pup′i·tir′) *n.* One who manipulates puppets.

pup·py (pup′ē) *n. pl.* **·pies** A young dog. [< L *pupa* a girl, doll]

puppy love Temporary affection or love that a boy and girl feel for each other.

pup tent A small tent providing shelter for one or two people.

pur (pûr) *n. & v.* PURR.

pur·blind (pûr′blind′) *adj.* **1** Partly blind. **2** Having little or no insight. **3** *Obs.* Totally blind. [< ME *pur* totally + *blind* blind] —**pur′blind′ly** *adv.* —**pur′blind′ness** *n.*

pur·chase (pûr′chəs) *v.t.* **·chased, ·chas·ing** **1** To acquire by paying money or its equivalent; buy. **2** To obtain by exertion, sacrifice, flattery, etc. **3** To move, hoist, or hold by a mechanical purchase. —*n.* **1** The act of purchasing. **2** That which is purchased. **3** A mechanical hold or grip. **4** A device that gives a mechanical advantage, as a tackle or lever. [OF *porchacier* seek for] —**pur′chas·er** *n.* —**Syn. 1, 2** get, obtain, procure, secure.

pur·dah (pûr′də) *n.* **1** A curtain or screen used to seclude Muslim and Hindu women, esp. in India. **2** The state of seclusion so secured. [< Pers. *pardah* a veil]

pure (pyŏŏr) *adj.* **pur·er, pur·est** **1** Free from mixture or contact with that which weakens, impairs, or pollutes. **2** Free from adulteration; clear; clean: *pure* water. **3** Faultless; righteous: *pure* motives. **4** Chaste; innocent. **5** Concerned with fundamental research, as distinguished from practical application: *pure* science. **6** Bred from stock having no admixture for many generations. **7** Nothing but; sheer: *pure* luck. [< L *purus* clean, pure] **—pure'ness** *n.*

pu·rée (pyŏŏ·rā', pyŏŏr'ā) *n.* **1** A thick pulp, usu. of vegetables, boiled and strained. **2** A thick soup so prepared. —*v.t.* **·réed, ·rée·ing** To put (cooked or soft food) through a sieve, blender, etc. Also **pu·ree'.** [F< OF *purer* strain< L *purus* pure]

pure·ly (pyŏŏr'lē) *adv.* **1** So as to be free from admixture, taint, or any harmful substance. **2** Chastely; innocently. **3** Merely; only: *purely* as a hobby. **4** Completely: *purely* up to him.

pur·ga·tive (pûr'gə·tiv) *adj.* Purging; cathartic. —*n.* A medication used in purging; cathartic.

pur·ga·to·ry (pûr'gə·tôr'ē, -tō'rē) *n. pl.* **·ries** **1** In Roman Catholic theology, a state or place where the souls of those who have died penitent are made fit for paradise by expiating venial sins. **2** Any place or state of temporary banishment, suffering, or punishment. [< AF < L *purgare* cleanse] **—pur'ga·to'ri·al** *adj.*

purge (pûrj) *v.* **purged, purg·ing** *v.t.* **1** To cleanse of what is impure or extraneous; purify. **2** To remove (impurities, etc.) in cleansing: with *away, off,* or *out.* **3** To rid (a group, nation, etc.) of individuals regarded as undesirable. **4** To remove or kill such individuals. **5** To cleanse or rid of sin, fault, or defilement. **6** *Med.* **a** To cause evacuation of (the bowels, etc.). **b** To induce evacuation of the bowels of. —*v.i.* **7** To become clean or pure. **8** *Med.* To have or induce evacuation of the bowels. —*n.* **1** The action of an organization, esp. a government, in removing from office or positions of power individuals regarded as undesirable. **2** The act of purging. **3** That which purges; a cathartic. [< L *purgare* cleanse] **—pur·ga·tion** (pûr·gā'shən), **purg'er** *n.*

pu·ri·fy (pyŏŏr'ə·fī) *v.* **·fied, ·fy·ing** *v.t.* **1** To make pure or clean; rid of extraneous or noxious matter. **2** To free from sin or defilement. **3** To free of debasing elements. —*v.i.* **4** To become pure or clean. [< L *purus* pure + *facere* make] **—pu·rif·i·ca·to·ry** (pyŏŏ·rif'ə·kə·tôr'ē, -tō'rē) *adj.* **—pu·ri·fi·ca·tion** (pyŏŏr'ə·fə·kā'shən), **pu'ri·fi'er** *n.*

Pu·rim (pʸŏŏr'im; *Hebrew* pōō·rēm') *n.* A Jewish festival commemorating the defeat of Haman's plot to massacre the Jews. *Esth.* 9:26.

pur·ism (pyŏŏr'iz·əm) *n.* **1** Strong endorsement of a strict compliance with standards, rules, or conventions considered correct or pure, as in language. **2** Strict compliance with rules of correctness. **3** An instance of such compliance. **—pur'ist** *n.* **—pu·ris'tic, pu·ris'ti·cal** *adj.* **—pu·ris'ti·cal·ly** *adv.*

pu·ri·tan (pyŏŏr'ə·tən) *n.* One who is unusually or excessively strict regarding adherence to morality or religious practice. —*adj.* Of or characteristic of puritans. [< LL *puritas* purity] **—pu'ri·tan'ic** or **·i·cal** *adj.* **—pu'ri·tan'i·cal·ly** *adv.* **—pu'ri·tan'i·cal·ness, pu'ri·tan·ism** *n.*

Pu·ri·tan (pyŏŏr'ə·tən) *n.* One of a group of English Protestants of the 16th and 17th centuries, many of whom emigrated to the American colonies, who advocated simpler forms of creed and ritual in the Church of England. —*adj.* Of or relating to the Puritans. **—Pu'ri·tan'ic** or **·i·cal** *adj.* **—Pu'ri·tan·ism** *n.*

pu·ri·ty (pyŏŏr'ə·tē) *n.* **1** The character or state of being pure. **2** Absence of admixture or adulteration. **3** Innocence; blamelessness. **4** Degree of absence of white; saturation: said of a color.

purl¹ (pûrl) *v.i.* **1** To whirl; turn. **2** To flow with a bubbling sound. **3** To move in eddies. —*n.* **1** A circling movement of water; an eddy. **2** A gentle murmur, as of a rippling stream. [< Norw. *purla*]

purl² (pûrl) *v.t.* **1** To decorate, as with a border. **2** In knitting, to make (a stitch) backward. **3** To edge with lace, embroidery, etc. —*v.i.* **4** To do edging with lace, etc. —*n.* **1** An edge of lace, embroidery, etc. **2** In lacework, a spiral of gold or silver wire. **3** In knitting, the inversion of the knit stitch. [Earlier *pyrle*]

pur·lieu (pûr'lōō) *n.* **1** *pl.* Outlying districts; outskirts. **2** A place habitually visited; a haunt. **3** *pl.* Bounds. [< OF *puraler* go through]

pur·lin (pûr'lin) *n.* One of several horizontal timbers supporting rafters. Also **pur'line** (-lin). [ME *purlyn*]

pur·loin (pûr·loin') *v.t.* & *v.i.* To steal; filch. [< AF *purloignier* remove, put far off] **—pur·loin'er** *n.*

pur·ple (pûr'pəl) *n.* **1** A color of mingled red and blue, between crimson and violet. **2** Cloth or a garment of this color, an emblem of royalty. **3** Royal power or dignity. **4** Preeminence in rank. —*adj.* **1** Of the color of purple. **2** Imperial; regal. **3** Conspicuously fanciful or ornate: *purple* prose. —*v.t.* & *v.i.* **·pled, ·pling** To make or become purple. [< Gk. *porphyra* purple dye] **—pur'plish** *adj.*

Purple Heart A U.S. military decoration of honor awarded to members of the armed forces wounded in action.

pur·port (pər·pôrt', -pōrt', pûr'pôrt, -pōrt) *v.t.* **1** To have or bear as its meaning; signify; imply. **2** To claim or profess (to be), esp. falsely. —*n.* (pûr'pôrt, -pōrt) **1** That which is conveyed or suggested as the meaning. **2** The substance of a statement, etc., given in other than the exact words. [< L < *pro-* forth + *portare* carry] **—Syn.** *n.* **1** import, significance. **2** gist, meaning. **—pur·port'ed·ly** *adv.*

pur·pose (pûr'pəs) *n.* **1** An end of effort or action; something to be attained; plan; design; aim. **2** Settled resolution; determination. **—on purpose** Intentionally. —*v.t.* & *v.i.* **·posed, ·pos·ing** To intend to do or accomplish; aim. [< OF *porposer*] **—pur'pose·less** *adj.* **—pur'pose·less·ly** *adv.* **—pur'pose·less·ness** *n.*

pur·pose·ful (pûr'pəs·fəl) *adj.* Having, or marked by, purpose; intentional. **—pur'pose·ful·ly** *adv.* **—pur'pose·ful·ness** *n.*

pur·pose·ly (pûr'pəs·lē) *adv.* Intentionally; deliberately; on purpose.

purr (pûr) *n.* An intermittent murmuring sound, such as a cat makes when pleased. —*v.i.* **1** To make such a sound. —*v.t.* **2** To express by purring. [Imit.]

purse (pûrs) *n.* **1** A small bag or pouch for money. **2** A receptacle carried usu. by women for holding personal articles, as a wallet, cosmetics, etc.; pocketbook. **3** Resources or means; a treasury. **4** A sum of money offered as a prize or gift. —*v.t.* **pursed, purs·ing** To contract into wrinkles or folds; pucker. [< Gk. *byrsa* a skin]

purs·er (pûr'sər) *n.* A ship's officer having charge of the accounts, records, payroll, etc.

purs·lane (pûrs'lin, -lān) *n.* Any of various prostrate, weedy plants with fleshy leaves and reddish stems. [< L *porcilaca,* var. of *portulaca*]

pur·su·ance (pər·sōō'əns) *n.* The act of pursuing; a following after or following through: in *pursuance* of the truth.

pur·su·ant (pər·sōō'ənt) *adj.* Pursuing. **—pursuant to** In accordance with; by reason of.

pur·sue (pər·sōō') *v.* **·sued, ·su·ing** *v.t.* **1** To follow in an attempt to overtake or capture; chase. **2** To seek to attain or gain: to *pursue* fame. **3** To advance along the course of, as a path or plan. **4** To apply one's energies to or have as one's profession. **5** To follow persistently; harass; worry. —*v.i.* **6** To follow. **7** To continue. [< L *pro-* forth + *sequi* follow] **—pur·su'er** *n.*

pur·suit (pər·sōōt') *n.* **1** The act of pursuing. **2** A continued employment, vocation, or preoccupation.

pur·sui·vant (pûr'swi·vənt) *n.* **1** An attendant upon a herald. **2** A follower; esp., a military attendant. [< OF *porsievre* pursue]

purs·y (pûr'sē) *adj.* **purs·i·er, purs·i·est** **1** Short-breathed. **2** Fat. [< OF *polser* pant, gasp] **—purs'i·ness** *n.*

pu·ru·lent (pyŏŏr'ə·lənt, -yə·lənt) *adj.* Consisting of or secreting pus; suppurating. [< L *pus, puris* pus] **—pu'ru·lence** or **·len·cy** *n.* **—pu'ru·lent·ly** *adv.*

pur·vey (pər·vā') *v.t.* & *v.i.* To furnish or provide, as provisions. [< L *providere* foresee] **—pur·vey'or** *n.*

pur·vey·ance (pər·vā'əns) *n.* **1** The act of purveying. **2** Provisions.

pur·view (pûr'vyōō) *n.* **1** Extent or scope of anything, as of official authority. **2** Range of view, experience, or understanding; outlook. 3 *Law* The body or the scope or limit of a statute. [< OF *porveier* purvey]

pus (pus) *n.* A viscid, usu. yellowish fluid consisting of bacteria, leukocytes, serum, and dead cells from inflamed tissue.

push (po͝osh) *v.t.* 1 To exert force upon or against (an object) for the purpose of moving. 2 To force (one's way), as through a crowd. 3 To develop, advocate, or promote vigorously and persistently: to *push* a new product. 4 To bear hard upon; press: to be *pushed* for time. 5 *Informal* To approach or come close to: He's *pushing* fifty. 6 *Slang* To sell (narcotic or other drugs) illegally. —*v.i.* 7 To exert pressure against something so as to move it. 8 To move or advance vigorously or persistently. 9 To exert great effort. —*n.* 1 The act of pushing; a propelling or thrusting pressure. 2 Anything pushed to cause action. 3 Determined activity; energy; drive. 4 A vigorous and persistent advance or effort. 5 An emergency; exigency. [< L *pulsare* to push, beat] —**Syn.** *v.* 1 shove, thrust, press, propel, drive.

push button A button or knob which, on being pushed, opens or closes an electric switch. —**push′-but′ton** *adj.*

push·cart (po͝osh′kärt′) *n.* A wheeled cart pushed by hand.

Supermarket pushcart

push·er (po͝osh′ər) *n.* 1 One who or that which pushes; esp., an active, energetic person. 2 *Slang* One who sells narcotic or other drugs illegally.

push·ing (po͝osh′ing) *adj.* 1 Enterprising; energetic. 2 Too aggressive; impertinent. —**push′ing·ly** *adv.*

push·o·ver (po͝osh′ō′vər) *n.* *Slang* 1 Anything that can be done with little or no effort. 2 Someone easily defeated, overcome, outwitted, etc.; one who represents no challenge to one's aims.

push·y (po͝osh′ē) *adj.* **·i·er, ·i·est** Unpleasantly aggressive and persistent. —**push′i·ly** *adv.* —**push′i·ness** *n.*

pu·sil·lan·i·mous (pyo͞o′sə·lan′əməs) *adj.* Weak or cowardly in spirit; lacking strength of mind or courage. [< L *pusillus* very little + *animus* mind] —**pu′sil·la·nim′i·ty** (-lə·nim′ə·tē), **pu′sil·lan′i·mous·ness** *n.* —**pu′sil·lan′i·mous·ly** *adv.*

puss[1] (po͝os) *n.* 1 A cat. 2 A young girl: a term of affection. [?]

puss[2] (po͝os) *n.* *Slang* The mouth; face. [< Ir. *pus* mouth, lips]

pus·sy[1] (po͝os′ē) *n. pl.* **·sies** 1 PUSS[1]. 2 A fuzzy catkin, as of a willow.

pus·sy[2] (pus′ē) *adj.* **pus·si·er, pus·si·est** Full of or like pus. —**pus′si·ness** *n.*

pus·sy·foot (po͝os′ē·fo͝ot′) *v.i.* 1 To move softly and steathily, as a cat does. 2 To act or proceed warily or tentatively, so as to be able to withdraw or change course before one's intentions are apparent. —**pus′sy·foot′er** *n.*

pus·sy willow (po͝os′ē) A small North American willow bearing velvety catkins in early spring.

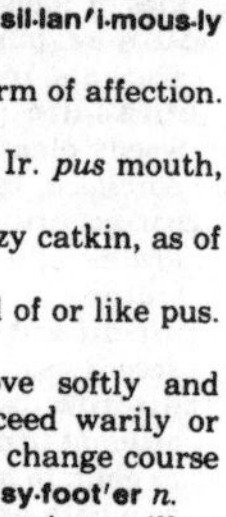
Pussy willow

pus·tu·late (pus′cho͞o·lāt) *v.t. & v.i.* **·lat·ed, ·lat·ing** To form into or become pustules. —*adj.* (-lāt, -lit) Covered with pustules. —**pus′tu·la′tion** *n.*

pus·tule (pus′cho͞ol) *n.* 1 A small, circumscribed elevation of the skin with an inflamed base containing pus. 2 Any elevation resembling a pimple or a blister. [< L *pustula*] —**pus′tu·lar, pus′tu·lous** *adj.*

put (po͝ot) *v.* **put, put·ting** *v.t.* 1 To bring into or set in a specified or implied place or position; lay: *Put* the dishes in the sink. 2 To bring into a specified state, condition, or relation: to *put* someone to work; to *put* merchandise on sale. 3 To order or bring about the establishment or placement of: to *put* a new store in Dallas; to *put* a man on the moon. 4 To send or direct, as by projecting or thrusting: to *put* a dart in the bull's-eye. 5 To throw with a pushing motion: to *put* the shot. 6 To bring to bear; apply: They *put* pressure on her. 7 To impose: to *put* a tax on air travel. 8 To effect; carry out: I'll *put* a stop to that. 9 To express; state: to *put* it simply. 10 To subject: to *put* his loyalty to the test. 11 To incite; prompt: Who *put* him up to it? 12 To ascribe or attribute: to *put* the wrong interpretation on a remark. 13 To propose for debate, consideration, etc.: to *put* the question. 14 To estimate: to *put* the time at five o'clock. 15 To establish; fix, as a price. 16 To risk; bet: to *put* money on a horse. —*v.i.* 17 To go; proceed: to *put* to sea. —**put about** 1 *Naut.* To change to the opposite tack. 2 To change direction. —**put across** 1 To carry out successfully. 2 To manage to be understood. 3 To bring about through deceit. —**put aside** (or **by**) 1 To place in reserve; save. 2 To thrust aside; discard. —**put away** 1 PUT ASIDE. 2 *Informal* To eat or drink. 3 *Informal* To kill, as an injured or sick animal. —**put down** 1 To repress; crush. 2 To degrade; demote. 3 To write. 4 *Slang* To humble or deflate. 5 To preserve or can. —**put forth** 1 To grow, as shoots or buds. 2 To set out; leave port. 3 To proffer; suggest. 4 To publish. 5 To exert. —**put forward** To advance; advocate, as a proposal. —**put in** 1 To submit or advance, as a claim or application. 2 To interject; interpolate. 3 *Naut.* To enter a harbor. 4 *Informal* To devote; expend, as time. —**put off** 1 To delay; postpone. 2 To discard. 3 To make uneasy or uncomfortable; disconcert. —**put on** 1 To clothe oneself in; don. 2 To bring into operation; effectuate: to *put on* a light. 3 To add: to *put on* weight. 4 To stage, as a play. 5 To simulate; pretend: to *put on* a sad face. 6 *Slang* To fool or deceive mischievously. —**put out** 1 To extinguish, as a flame. 2 To expel; eject. 3 To disconcert; embarrass. 4 To inconvenience. 5 PUT FORTH. 6 In baseball, to retire (a batter or base runner). 7 To publish or manufacture, as a book or magazine. 8 *Slang* To use extra effort; exert oneself. —**put over** 1 To delay; postpone. 2 To carry out successfully. 3 To bring about through deceit. —**put through** 1 To bring to successful completion. 2 To cause to perform. 3 To establish a telephone connection for. —**put up** 1 To erect; build. 2 To provide (money, capital, etc.). 3 To preserve or can. 4 To sheathe, as a weapon. 5 To nominate as a candidate. 6 To provide accommodations for. 7 *Informal* To incite. —**put up with** To endure; tolerate. —*n.* The act of putting or casting, esp. the shot. —*adj.* *Informal* Settled in place; fixed: My hat won't stay *put.* [< OE *putian* place] —**put′ter** *n.*

pu·ta·tive (pyo͞o′tə·tiv) *adj.* Supposed; reported; reputed. [< L *putare* think] —**pu′ta·tive·ly** *adv.*

put-down (po͝ot′doun′) *n.* *Slang* Something that humbles or deflates, as a cutting remark.

put-on (po͝ot′on′) *n.* *Slang* A hoax; deception.

put-out (po͝ot′out′) *n.* In baseball, the act of causing an out, as of a batter or base runner.

pu·tre·fac·tion (pyo͞o′trə·fak′shən) *n.* 1 The process of rotting or decomposing, as by bacterial action. 2 The state of being putrefied. —**pu′tre·fac′tive** *adj.*

pu·tre·fy (pyo͞o′trə·fī) *v.t. & v.i.* **·fied, ·fy·ing** To decay or cause to decay; rot. [< L *puter* rotten + *facere* make] —**pu′tre·fi′er** *n.*

pu·tres·cent (pyo͞o·tres′ənt) *adj.* 1 Becoming putrid. 2 Pertaining to putrefaction. [< L *putrescere* grow rotten] —**pu·tres′cence** *n.*

pu·trid (pyo͞o′trid) *adj.* 1 Being in a state of putrefaction; rotten. 2 Indicating or produced by putrefaction: a *putrid* smell. 3 Corrupt. [< L *putridus*] —**pu·trid·i·ty** (pyo͞o′trid′ə·tē), **pu′trid·ness** *n.*

putsch (po͝och) *n.* *Often cap.* An outbreak or rebellion; an attempted coup d'état. [G]

putt (put) *n.* In golf, a light stroke made on a putting green to place the ball in or near the hole. —*v.t. & v.i.* To strike (the ball) with such a stroke. [Var. of PUT]

put·tee (put′ē, pu·tē′) *n.* A strip of cloth or leather gaiter fastened about the leg from knee to ankle. [< Skt. *paṭṭa* a strip of cloth]

put·ter[1] (put′ər) *n.* 1 One who putts. 2 A golf club used in putting. • See GOLF.

put·ter[2] (put′ər) *v.i.* 1 To act, work, or proceed in a dawdling or ineffective manner. —*v.t.* 2 To waste or spend (time, etc.) in dawdling or puttering. [< OE *potion* push, kick]

put·ting green (put′ing) In golf, a smooth area of closely mown grass in which the hole is situated.

put·ty (put′ē) *n.* 1 A doughy mixture of clay and linseed oil, used to cement panes in windows, fill cracks, etc. **2** Any substance similar in properties or uses. —*v.t.* **·tied, ·ty·ing** To fill, stop, fasten, etc., with putty. [< OF *potee* calcined tin, lit., a potful] —**put'ti·er** *n.*

put-up (po͝ot'up') *adj. Informal* Prearranged or contrived; staged: a *put-up* job.

put-up·on (po͝ot'ə·pon') *adj.* Beset or harassed, as by impositions; abused.

puz·zle (puz'əl) *v.* **·zled, ·zling** *v.t.* **1** To confuse or perplex; mystify. **2** To solve by investigation and study, as something perplexing: with *out.* —*v.i.* **3** To be perplexed or confused. —**puzzle over** To attempt to understand or solve. —*n.* **1** Something difficult to understand or explain; an enigma or problem. **2** A device, as a toy, or a problem designed for recreation and requiring ingenuity to solve. **3** The state of being puzzled; perplexity. [?] —**puz'zle·ment, puz'zler** *n.*

Pvt. Private.

PW prisoner of war.

pwt. pennyweight.

PX post exchange.

py·e·mi·a (pī·ē'mē·ə) *n.* Septicemia caused by pus-producing microorganisms. Also **py·ae'mi·a.** [< Gk. *pyon* pus + *haima* blood] —**py·e'mic** *adj.*

pyg·my (pig'mē) *adj.* Diminutive; dwarfish. —*n. pl.* **·mies** **1** Someone of no importance. **2** A dwarfish person or animal.

Pyg·my (pig'mē) *n. pl.* **·mies** A member of a Negroid people of equatorial Africa, ranging in height from four to five feet. [< Gk. *pygmalos* a dwarf]

py·ja·mas (pə·jä'məz, -jam'əz) *n.pl. Brit.* PAJAMAS.

py·lon (pī'lon) *n.* **1** *Archit.* A monumental gateway, as to an Egyptian temple or other large edifice. **2** A tall, mastlike structure, as for supporting high-tension wires or for marking a course for aircraft. [< Gk. *pylōn* a gateway]

py·lo·rus (pī·lôr'əs, -lō'rəs, pi-) *n. pl.* **·ri** (-rī) The muscularly controlled opening between the stomach and the duodenum. [< Gk. *pylōros* a gatekeeper] —**py·lor'ic** (-lôr'ik, -lor'ik) *adj.*

py·or·rhe·a (pī'ə·rē'ə) *n.* A discharge of pus; esp., inflammation and pus discharge affecting the gums and tooth sockets. Also **py'or·rhoe'a.** [< Gk. *pys, pyos* pus + *rheein* flow] —**py'or·rhe'al** *adj.*

pyr·a·mid (pir'ə·mid) *n.* **1** A solid structure of masonry with a square base and triangular sides meeting in an apex, such as those constructed by the ancient Egyptians as royal tombs. **2** Something having the form of a pyramid. **3** *Geom.* A solid having a polygonal base and triangular sides that meet in a common vertex. —*v.i.* **1** To increase in a series of steps; escalate. **2** To buy or sell stock with paper profits used as margin to finance succeeding transactions. —*v.t.* **3** To increase by steps. **4** To buy and sell (stock) with paper profits used as margin to finance succeeding transactions. [< Gk. *pyramis*] —**py·ram·i·dal** (pi·ram'ə·dəl, pir'ə·mid'əl), **pyr'a·mid'ic** or **·i·cal** *adj.* —**pyr'a·mid'i·cal·ly** *adv.*

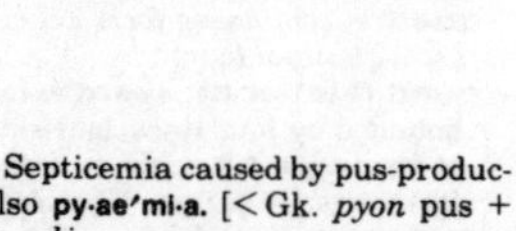

Egyptian pyramids

pyre (pīr) *n.* A heap of combustibles arranged for burning a dead body as a funeral rite. [< Gk. *pyr* a fire]

py·reth·rum (pī·reth'rəm, -rē'thrəm) *n.* **1** A species of chrysanthemum. **2** An insecticide prepared from the powdered flowers of certain chrysanthemums. [L, feverfew]

Py·rex (pī'reks) *n.* A type of heat-resistant glass: a trade name.

pyr·i·dox·ine (pir'ə·dok'sēn, -sin) *n.* A constituent of the vitamin B complex. [< Gk. *pyr* fire + -ID(E) + OX(Y)- + -INE]

py·rite (pī'rīt) *n.* A lustrous, pale yellow, mineral sulfide of iron. [< Gk. *pyritēs* flint]

py·ri·tes (pī·rī'tēz, pī'rīts) *n. pl.* **py·ri·tes** (pī·rī'tēz) Any of various mineral sulfides with a metallic sheen, including pyrite: copper *pyrites.* —**py·rit'ic** (-rit'ik) or **·i·cal** *adj.*

pyro- *combining form* Fire; heat: *pyromania.* Also **pyr-.** [< Gk. *pyr* fire]

py·ro·ma·ni·a (pī'rə·mā'nē·ə, -mān'yə) *n.* A compulsion to commit arson. —**py'ro·ma'ni·ac** (-ak) *adj., n.* —**py·ro·ma·ni·a·cal** (pī'rō·mə·nī'ə·kəl) *adj.*

py·rom·e·ter (pī·rom'ə·tər) *n.* A thermometer designed to measure high temperatures. —**py·ro·met·ric** (pī'rə·met'rik) or **·ri·cal** *adj.* —**py·rom'e·try** *n.*

py·ro·tech·nics (pī'rə·tek'niks) *n. pl. (construed as sing. in def. 1)* **1** The art of making or using fireworks. **2** A display of fireworks. **3** An ostentatious display, as of oratory; virtuosity. [< PYRO- + Gk. *technē* an art] —**py'ro·tech'nic** or **·ni·cal** *adj.*

py·rox·y·lin (pī·rok'sə·lin) *n.* A nitrocellulose that is more stable than guncotton, used in making quick-drying lacquers, etc. Also **py·rox'y·line** (-lēn, -lin). [< Gk. *pyr, pyros* fire + *xylon* wood + -INE]

Pyr·rhic victory (pir'ik) A victory gained at a ruinous cost, such as that of Pyrrhus over the Romans in 279 B.C.

Py·thag·o·re·an theorem (pi·thag'ə·rē'ən) *Math.* The theorem that the sum of the squares of the two sides of a right triangle is equal to the square of the hypotenuse. [< *Pythagoras*, c. 500 B.C., Greek philosopher]

Pyth·i·as (pith'ē·əs) See DAMON AND PYTHIAS.

py·thon (pī'thon, -thən) *n.* A large, nonvenomous snake that crushes its prey. [< Gk. *Pythōn* a serpent slain by Apollo]

Python

py·tho·ness (pī'thə·nis, pith'ə-) *n.* **1** The priestess of the Delphic oracle. **2** Any woman supposed to be possessed of the spirit of prophecy; a witch. [< Gk. *Pytho* a familiar spirit, orig. Delphi]

pyx (piks) *n.* A container for keeping the consecrated wafer of the Eucharist or for carrying it to the sick. [< L *pyxis* a box]

pyx·is (pik'sis) *n. pl.* **pyx·i·des** (pik'sə·dēz) *Bot.* A dehiscent seed vessel with the upper portion separating as a lid. Also **pyx·id·i·um** (pik·sid'ē·əm). [< L, a box]

add, āce, câre, pälm; end, ēven; it, īce; odd, ōpen, ôrder; to͝ok, po͞ol; up, bûrn; ə = *a* in *above*, *u* in *focus;* yo͞o = *u* in *fuse;* oil; pout; check; go; ring; thin; this; zh, *vision.* < derived from; ? origin uncertain or unknown.

Q

Q, q (kyōō) *n. pl.* **Q's, q's** or **Qs, qs** (kyōōz) **1** The 17th letter of the English alphabet. **2** Any spoken sound representing the letter *Q* or *q*. **3** Something shaped like a Q. —*adj.* Shaped like a Q.

Q queen (chess).

Q. Quebec.

q. quart; quarter; quarterly; quarto; quasi; queen; query; question

Qa·tar (kä′tär) *n.* A British protected sheikdom on the w coast of the Persian Gulf, 8,500 sq. mi., cap. Doha. • See map at SAUDI ARABIA.

qb., q.b. quarterback.

Q.C. Quartermaster Corps; Queen's Counsel.

q.e. which is (L *quod est*).

Q.E.D. which was to be demonstrated (L *quod erat demonstrandum*).

Q.E.F. which was to be done (L *quod erat faciendum*).

QM, Q.M. Quartermaster.

QMC, Q.M.C. Quartermaster Corps.

QMG, Q.M.G., Q.M.Gen. Quartermaster General.

Qq. quartos.

qq.v. which see (L *quos vide*).

qr. quarter; quarterly; quire.

q.s. as much as suffices (L *quantum sufficit*).

qt. quart; quantity.

q.t. *Slang* quiet, esp. on the **q.t.** in secret.

qto. quarto.

qts, qts. quarts.

qu. quart; quarter; queen; query; question.

quack[1] (kwak) *v.i.* To utter a harsh, croaking cry, as a duck. —*n.* The sound made by a duck, or a similar croaking noise [Imit.]

quack[2] (kwak) *n.* **1** A pretender to medical knowledge or skill. **2** A charlatan. —*adj.* Of or pertaining to quacks or quackery. —*v.i.* To play the quack. [Short for QUACKSALVER] —**quack′ish** *adj.* —**quack′ish·ly** *adv.*

quack·er·y (kwak′ər·ē) *n. pl.* **·er·ies** The deceitful practices of a quack.

quack·sal·ver (kwak′sal′vər) *n.* QUACK[2]. [< MDu. *quacsalven* use home remedies]

quad[1] (kwod) *n. Informal.* A quadrangle, as of a college or prison.

quad[2] (kwod) *n. Printing* A piece of type metal lower than the letters, used for spacing. [ME *quadrat,* a square instrument]

quad[3] (kwod) *adj.* QUADRAPHONIC.

quad. quadrangle; quadrant; quadrat; quadruple.

Quad·ra·ges·i·ma (kwod′rə·jes′ə·mə) *n.* The first Sunday in Lent. Also **Quadragesima Sunday.** [L, fortieth]

quad·ran·gle (kwod′rang·gəl) *n.* **1** *Geom.* A plane figure having four sides and four angles. **2** An area shaped like a quadrangle, esp. when it is enclosed by buildings. **3** The buildings that enclose such an area. [< L *quattuor* four + *angulus* angle] —**quad·ran′gu·lar** *adj.*

quad·rant (kwod′rənt) *n.* **1** A quarter part of a circle; also, its circumference, having an arc of 90°. **2** An instrument having a graduated arc of 90°, with a movable radius for measuring angles on it. [< L *quattuor* four] —**quad·ran·tal** (kwod·ran′təl) *adj.*

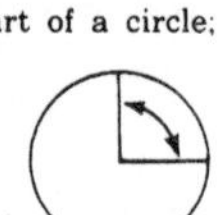

Quadrant

quad·ra·phon·ic (kwod′rə·fon′ik) *adj.* Of, pertaining to, or employing a system of sound reproduction that uses four transmission channels and loudspeakers. [< QUADR(I)- + PHONIC]

quad·rat (kwod′rət) *n.* QUAD[2].

quad·rate (kwod′rāt, -rit) *adj.* Square; four-sided. —*v.* (-rāt) **·rat·ed, ·rat·ing** *v.i.* **1** To correspond or agree: with *with.* —*v.t.* **2** To cause to conform; bring in accordance with. [< L *quadrare* to square < *quattuor* four]

quad·rat·ic (kwod·rat′ik) *adj.* **1** Pertaining to or resembling a square. **2** Of or designating a quadratic equation. —*n. Math.* A quadratic equation.

quadratic equation An equation of the general form $ax^2 + bx + c = 0$, where *a, b, c* are constants.

quad·ra·ture (kwod′rə·chər) *n.* **1** The act or process of squaring. **2** The determining of the area of any surface.

quad·ren·ni·al (kwod·ren′ē·əl) *adj.* **1** Occurring once in four years. **2** Comprising four years. —*n.* A quadrennial period or event. [< QUADR(I)- + L *annus* year]

quadri- *combining form* Four: *quadrilateral.* Also **quadr-.** [< L *quattuor* four]

quad·ri·lat·er·al (kwod′rə·lat′ər·əl) *adj.* Formed or bounded by four lines; four-sided. —*n.* **1** *Geom.* A polygon of four sides. **2** A space or area defended by four enclosing fortresses. [< QUADRI- + L *latus, lateris* side]

qua·drille (kwə·dril′) *n.* **1** A square dance for four couples. **2** Music for such a dance. [< L *quattuor* four]

quad·ril·lion (kwod·ril′yən) *n. & adj.* See NUMBER. [< F *quatre* four + *(m)illion* million]

quad·ri·ple·gi·a (kwod′rə·plē′jē·ə) *n.* Paralysis of the arms and legs.

quad·ri·va·lent (kwod′rə·vā′lənt) *adj. Chem.* Having a valence of four. [< QUADRI- + L *valere* be worth]

quad·roon (kwod·rōōn′) *n.* A person having one Negro and three white grandparents. [< Sp. *cuarto* fourth]

quad·ru·ped (kwod′rōō·ped) *n.* A four-footed animal, esp. a mammal. —*adj.* Having four feet. [< L *quattuor* four + *pes* foot] —**quad·ru·pe·dal** (kwod·rōō′pə·dəl, kwod′·roo·ped′l) *adj.*

quad·ru·ple (kwod·rōō′pəl, -ru′-, kwod′rōō·pəl) *adj.* **1** Four times as great or as many. **2** Having four parts or members. **3** Marked by four beats to the measure. —*n.* A number or sum four times as great as another. —*v.t. & v.i.* **·pled, ·pling** To multiply by four. —*adv.* Fourfold. [< L *quadruplus*]

quad·ru·plet (kwod·rōō′plit, -ru′-, kwod′rōō-) *n.* A combination of four objects. **2** One of four offspring born of the same mother at one birth.

quad·ru·pli·cate (kwod·rōō′plə·kit, -kāt) *adj.* **1** FOURFOLD. **2** Raised to the fourth power. —*v.t.* (-kāt) **·cat·ed, ·cat·ing** To multiply by four; quadruple. —*n.* The fourth of four like things: to file a *quadruplicate.* —**in quadruplicate** In four identical copies. —**quad·ru′pli·ca′tion** *n.*

quaes·tor (kwes′tər, kwēs′-) *n.* Any of a number of public officials in ancient Rome. Also **ques′tor.** [L < *quaerere* seek, inqure] —**quaes′to′ri·al** *adj.* —**quaes′tor·ship** *n.*

quaff (kwaf, kwof, kwôf) *v.t. & v.i.* To drink, esp. copiously or with relish. —*n.* The act of quaffing; also, that which is quaffed. [?] —**quaff′er** *n.*

quag·gy (kwag′ē, kwog′ē) *adj.* **·gi·er, ·gi·est** **1** Yielding to or quaking under the foot, as soft, wet earth; boggy. **2** Soft; yielding; flabby. [< QUAGMIRE]

quag·mire (kwag′mīr′, kwog′-) *n.* **1** Marshy ground that gives way under the foot; bog. **2** A difficult situation. [? < earlier *quab-* wetness + MIRE] —**quag′mired′** *adj.*

qua·haug (kwô′hôg, -hog, kwə·hôg′, -hog′) *n.* An edible, thick-shelled clam of the Atlantic coast of North America. Also **qua′hog.** [< Algon.]

quail[1] (kwāl) *n.* **1** Any of various small game birds related to the partridge. **2** BOBWHITE. [< OF *quaille*]

quail[2] (kwāl) *v.i.* To shrink with fear; lose heart or courage. [ME *quailen*]

quaint (kwānt) *adj.* **1** Pleasingly different, fanciful, or old-fashioned. **2** Unusual; odd; curious. [< L *cognitus* known] —**quaint′ly** *adv.* —**quaint′ness** *n.*

Quail

quake (kwāk) *v.i.* **quaked, quak·ing** **1** To shake, as with violent emotion or cold; shudder; shiver. 2 To shake or tremble, as earth during an earthquake. —*n.* 1 A shaking or shuddering. 2 EARTHQUAKE. [< OE *cwacian* shake]

Quak·er (kwā′kər) *n.* A member of the Society of Friends: originally a term of derision, and still not used within the society. See SOCIETY OF FRIENDS. [< QUAKE, *v.;* with ref. to their founder's admonition to them to tremble at the word of the Lord] —**Quak′er·ish** *adj.* —**Quak′er·ism′** *n.*

quak·y (kwā′kē) *adj.* **quak·i·er, quak·i·est** Shaky; tremulous. —**quak′i·ly** *adv.* —**quak′i·ness** *n.*

qual·i·fi·ca·tion (kwol′ə·fə·kā′shən) *n.* 1 The act of qualifying, or the state of being qualified. 2 That which fits a person or thing for something. 3 A restriction; modification.

qual·i·fied (kwol′ə·fīd) *adj.* 1 Competent or eligible, as for public office. 2 Restricted or modified in some way. —**qual′i·fied′ly** *adv.*

qual·i·fy (kwol′ə·fī) *v.* **·fied, ·fy·ing** *v.t.* 1 To make fit or capable, as for an office, occupation, or privilege. 2 To make legally capable, as by the administration of an oath. 3 To limit, restrict, or lessen somewhat: He *qualified* his enthusiasm with a few criticisms. 4 To attribute a quality to; describe; characterize or name. 5 To make less strong or extreme; soften; moderate. 6 To change the strength or flavor of. 7 *Gram.* To modify. —*v.i.* 8 To be or become qualified. [< L *qualis* of such a kind + *facere* make] —**qual′i·fi′a·ble** *adj.* —**qual′i·fi′er** *n.*

qual·i·ta·tive (kwol′ə·tā′tiv) *adj.* Of or pertaining to quality. —**qual′i·ta′tive·ly** *adv.*

qualitative analysis The chemical identification of the elements or components in a compound or mixture.

qual·i·ty (kwol′ə·tē) *n. pl.* **·ties** 1 That which makes a being or thing such as it is: a distinguishing element or characteristic: a *quality* of gases. 2 The basic nature or character of something: the *quality* of a summer's day. 3 Excellence: striving for *quality.* 4 Degree of excellence; relative goodness; grade: high *quality* of fabric. 5 A personal attribute, trait or characteristic: a woman with good and bad *qualities.* 6 *Archaic* Social rank; also, persons of rank, collectively. 7 *Music* That which distinguishes one tone from another, aside from pitch or loudiness; timbre. —*adj.* Characterized by or having to do with quality: a *quality* product. [< L *qualis* of such a kind]

qualm (kwäm, kwôm) *n.* 1 A twinge of conscience; moral scruple. 2 A sensation of fear or misgiving. 3 A feeling of sickness. [? < OE *cwealm* death] —**qualm′ish, qualm′y** *adj.* —**qualm′ish·ly** *adv.* —**qualm′ish·ness** *n.*

quan·da·ry (kwon′dər·ē, -drē) *n. pl.* **·da·ries** A state of hesitation or perplexity; predicament. [?]

quan·ti·ta·tive (kwon′tə·tā′tiv) *adj.* 1 Of or pertaining to quantity. 2 Capable of being measured. —**quan′ti·ta′tive·ly** *adv.* —**quan′ti·ta′tive·ness** *n.*

quantitative analysis The precise determination of the relative amount of each chemical component in a compound or mixture.

quan·ti·ty (kwon′tə·tē) *n. pl.* **·ties** 1 A definite or indefinite amount or number. 2 *pl.* Large amounts or numbers: *quantities* of food and drink. 3 That property of a thing which admits of exact measurement and numerical statement. 4 In prosody and phonetics, the relative period of time required to produce a given sound. [< L *quantus* how much, how large]

quan·tum (kwon′təm) *n. pl.* **·ta** (-tə) *Physics* A fundamental unit of energy or action as described in the quantum theory. [< L *quantus* how much]

quantum theory *Physics* A physical theory including as one of its essential features the postulate that energy is not continuous but divided into discrete packets, or quanta.

quar·an·tine (kwôr′ən·tēn, kwor′-) *n.* 1 A period of time fixed for the isolation and observation of persons, animals, or plants suspected of harboring an infectious disease. 2 A place for such isolation. 3 The isolation of subjects exposed to or infected with a communicable disease. —*v.t.* **·tined, ·tin·ing** To retain in quarantine. [< L *quadraginta* forty; a ref. to the original 40-day quarantine]

quark (kwärk) *n. Physics* Any of a group of three types of hypothetical fundamental particles proposed as the entities of which all other strongly interacting particles are composed. [Coined by M. Gell-Mann, born 1929, U.S. physicist]

quar·rel[1] (kwôr′əl, kwor′-) *n.* 1 An unfriendly, angry, or violent dispute. 2 A falling out or contention; breach of friendly relations: a lover's *quarrel.* 3 The cause for dispute. —*v.i.* **·reled** or **·relled, ·rel·ing** or **·rel·ling** 1 To engage in a quarrel; dispute; contend; fight: to *quarrel* about money. 2 To break off a mutual friendship; fall out; disagree. 3 To find fault; cavil. [< L *querela* complaint] —**quar′rel·er** or **quar′rel·ler** *n.* —**Syn.** *n.* 1 altercation, bickering, brawl, controversy, feud, fracas, fray. 2 disagreement, fuss, misunderstanding, scene.

quar·rel[2] (kwôr′əl, kwor′-) *n.* 1 A dart or arrow with a four-edged head, formerly used with a crossbow. 2 A stonemason's chisel, glazier's diamond, or other tool having a several-edged point. [< L *quattuor* four]

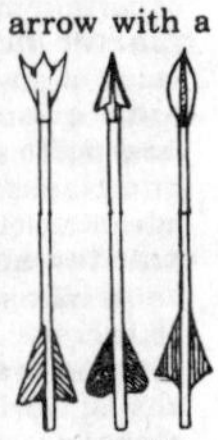

Quarrels *def. 1*

quar·rel·some (kwôr′əl·səm, kwor′-) *adj.* Inclined to quarrel. —**quar′rel·some·ly** *adv.* —**quar′rel·some·ness** *n.*

quar·ri·er (kwôr′ē·ər, kwor′-) *n.* A workman in a stone quarry.

quar·ry[1] (kwôr′ē, kwor′ē) *n. pl.* **·ries** 1 An animal being hunted down; game; prey. 2 Anything hunted, slaughtered, or eagerly pursued. [< L *corium* hide]

quar·ry[2] (kwôr′ē, kwor′ē) *n. pl.* **·ries** An excavation from which stone is taken by cutting, blasting, or the like. —*v.t.* **·ried, ·ry·ing** 1 To cut, dig, or take from or as from a quarry. 2 To establish a quarry in. [< LL *quadraria* place for squaring stone]

quart (kwôrt) *n.* 1 a A U.S. measure of dry capacity equal to 2 pints or 1.10 liters. b A U.S. measure of fluid capacity equal to 2 pints or 0.946 liter. 2 A vessel of such capacity. [< L *quartus* fourth]

quar·ter (kwôr′tər) *n.* 1 One of four equal parts of something; a fourth. 2 Fifteen minutes or the fourth of an hour, or the moment with which it begins or ends. 3 A fourth of a year or three months. 4 A limb of a quadruped with the adjacent parts. 5 In the U.S. and Canada, a coin of the value of 25 cents. 6 *Astron.* a The time it takes the moon to make one fourth of its revolution around the earth. b Either of the phases of the moon between new moon and full moon. 7 *Nav.* One of the four principal points of the compass or divisions of the horizon; also, a point or direction of the compass. 8 A person, persons, or place, esp. as a source or origin of something: gossip coming from all *quarters.* 9 A particular division or district, as of a city. 10 *Usu. pl.* Proper or assigned station, position, or place, as of officers and crew on a warship. 11 *pl.* A place of lodging or residence. 12 *Naut.* The part of a vessel's after side, between the aftermost mast and the stern. 13 *Her.* Any of four equal divisions into which a shield is divided, or a figure or device occupying such a division. 14 Mercy shown to a vanquished foe by sparing his life; clemency. 15 One of the four periods into which a game, as football, is divided. —**at close quarters** Close by; at close range. —*adj.* 1 Consisting of a quarter. 2 Equal to a quarter. —*v.t.* 1 To divide into four equal parts. 2 To divide into a number of parts or pieces. 3 To cut the body of (an executed person) into four parts: He was hanged, drawn, and *quartered.* 4 To range from one side to the other of (a field, etc.) while advancing: The dogs *quartered* the field. 5 To furnish with quarters or shelter; lodge, station, or billet. 6 *Her.* a To divide (a shield) into quarters by vertical and horizontal lines. b To bear or arrange (different coats of arms) upon the quarters of a shield or escutcheon. —*v.i.* 7 To be stationed or lodged. 8 To range from side to side of an area, as dogs in hunting. 9 *Naut.* To blow on a ship's quarter: said of the wind. [< L *quartus* fourth]

quar·ter·back (kwôr′tər·bak′) *n.* In football, one of the backfield, who calls the signals and directs the offensive play of his team.

add, āce, câre, päլm; end, ēven; it, īce; odd, ōpen, ôrder; tŏŏk, pōōl; up, bûrn; ə = *a* in *above, u* in *focus;* yōō = *u* in *fuse;* oil; pout; check; go; ring; thin; this; zh, *vision.* < derived from; ? origin uncertain or unknown.

quarter day A day that begins a new quarter of the year, when quarterly payments, as of rent, etc., are due.

quar·ter-deck (kwôr′tər·dek′) *n. Naut.* The rear part of a ship's upper deck, reserved for officers.

quar·tered (kwôr′tərd) *adj.* **1** Divided into quarters. **2** Having quarters or lodgings. **3** Quartersawed.

quar·ter·ly (kwôr′tər·lē) *adj.* **1** Containing or being a quarter. **2** Occurring at intervals of three months. —*n. pl.* **·lies** A publication issued once every three months. —*adv.* **1** Once in a quarter of a year. **2** In or by quarters.

quar·ter·mas·ter (kwôr′tər·mas′tər, -mäs′-) *n.* **1** The officer on an army post who is responsible for the supply of food, clothing, etc. **2** On shipboard, a petty officer who assists the master or navigator.

quar·tern (kwôr′tərn) *n. Chiefly Brit.* A fourth part, as of certain measures or weights. [< L *quartus* fourth]

quarter note *Music* A note with one fourth the time value of a whole note. • See NOTE.

quar·ter·saw (kwôr′tər·sô′) *v.t.* **·sawed, ·sawed** or **·sawn, ·saw·ing** To saw (a log) lengthwise into quarters and then into planks or boards, in order to show the wood grain advantageously.

quar·ter-sec·tion (kwôr′tər·sek′shən) *n.* A tract of land half a mile square, containing one fourth of a square mile; 160 acres.

quar·ter-ses·sions (kwôr′tər·sesh′ənz) *n.* **1** In the U.S., any of various courts with criminal jurisdiction and, sometimes, administrative functions. **2** In England, a local court held quarterly that has limited criminal and civil jurisdiction and, often, administrative functions.

quar·ter·staff (kwôr′tər·staf′, -stäf′) *n. pl.* **·staves** (-stāvz′) A stout, iron-tipped staff about 6½ feet long, formerly used in England as a weapon.

quar·tet (kwôr·tet′) *n.* **1** A composition for four voices or instruments. **2** The four persons who render such a composition. **3** Any group of four persons or things. Also **quar·tette′.** [< Ital. *quarto* fourth]

quar·to (kwôr′tō) *adj.* Having four leaves or eight pages to the sheet: a *quarto* book. —*n. pl.* **·tos** **1** The size of a piece of paper obtained by folding a sheet into four leaves. **2** Paper of this size; also, a page of this size. **3** A book made of pages of this size. [< L *(in) quarto* (in) fourth]

quartz (kwôrts) *n.* A hard mineral form of silicon dioxide occurring in many varieties, some of which are valued as gems. [< G *Quarz*]

qua·sar (kwā′zär, -sär) *n. Astron.* QUASI-STELLAR OBJECT. [< QUAS(I) - (STELL)AR RADIO SOURCE]

quash[1] (kwosh) *v.t. Law* To make void or set aside, as an indictment; annul. [< LL *cassare* to empty]

quash[2] (kwosh) *v.t.* To put down or suppress forcibly or summarily. [< L *quassare,* freq. of *quatere* shake]

qua·si (kwā′zī, -sī; kwä′zē, -sē) *adj.* More in resemblance than in fact: a *quasi* scholar. [L, as if]

quasi- *combining form* Resembling but not quite; in some ways or to some extent: *quasi-legal, quasi-official.* [< L *quasi* as if]

qua·si-stel·lar object (kwā′zī·stel′ər, -sī-, kwä′zē-, -sē-) Any of various starlike objects emitting vast amounts of radiation over a broad spectrum and having large red shifts. Also **quasi-stellar radio source.**

quas·si·a (kwosh′ē·ə, kwosh′ə) *n.* **1** Any of several tropical trees having bitter wood and bark. **2** A bitter extract obtained from a quassia tree, used to allay fever. **3** An insecticide obtained from the wood of a certain quassia tree. [< Graman *Quassi,* a Surinam Negro who discovered its use in 1730]

qua·ter·na·ry (kwot′ər·ner′ē, kwə·tûr′nə·rē) *adj.* Consisting of four. [< L *quaterni* by fours]

Qua·ter·na·ry (kwot′ər·ner′ē, kwə·tûr′nə·rē) *adj. & n.* See GEOLOGY.

quat·rain (kwot′rān, kwot·rān′) *n.* A stanza of four lines. [< F *quatre* four]

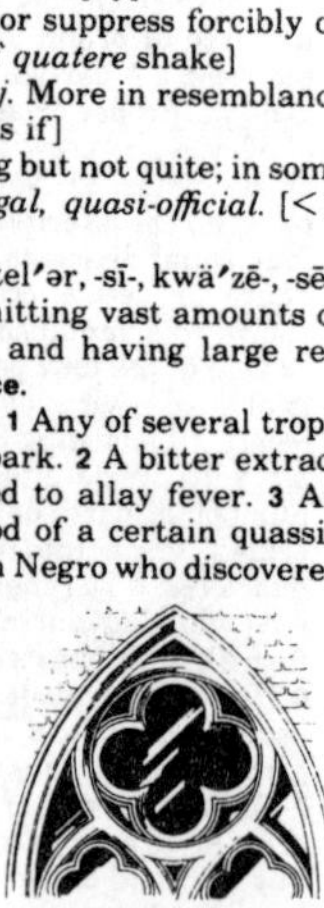

Quatrefoil window

quat·re·foil (kat′ər·foil′, kat′·rə-) *n.* **1** *Bot.* A leaf or flower with four leaflets or petals. **2** *Archit.* An ornament with four foils or lobes. [< OF *quatre* four + *foil* leaf]

quat·tro·cen·to (kwät′trō·chen′tō) *n.* The 15th century, esp. in connection with Italian art and literature. —*adj.* Of or pertaining to the quattrocento. [< Ital., four hundred < *quattro* four + *cento* hundred]

qua·ver (kwā′vər) *v.i.* **1** To tremble or shake: said usu. of the voice. **2** To produce trills or quavers in singing or in playing a musical instrument. —*v.t.* **3** To utter or sing in a tremulous voice. —*n.* **1** A trembling or shaking, as in the voice. **2** A shake or trill, as in singing. **3** An eighth note. [< ME *cwafian* tremble] —**qua′ver·y** *adj.*

quay (kē) *n.* A wharf or artificial landing place where vessels load and unload. [F]

Que. Quebec.

quean (kwēn) *n.* A brazen woman; harlot; prostitute. [< OE *cwene* woman]

quea·sy (kwē′zē) *adj.* **·si·er, ·si·est** **1** Feeling or causing nausea. **2** Easily nauseated; squeamish. **3** Causing or feeling uneasiness or discomfort. [ME *coysy*] —**quea′si·ly** *adv.* —**quea′si·ness** *n.*

Quech·ua (kech′wä) *n.* **1** One of a tribe of South American Indians which dominated the Inca empire prior to the Spanish conquest. **2** The language of the Quechuas. —**Quech′uan** *adj., n.*

queen (kwēn) *n.* **1** The wife of a king. **2** A female sovereign or monarch. **3** A woman preeminent in a given activity, accomplishment, etc. **4** A place or thing of great beauty, excellence, etc. **5** The most powerful piece in chess, capable of moving any number of squares in a straight or diagonal line. **6** A playing card bearing a conventional picture of a queen in her robes. **7** An egg-producing female in a colony of social insects, as bees, ants, etc. —*v.t.* **1** To make a queen of. —*v.i.* **2** To reign as or play the part of a queen: often with *it.* [< OE *cwēn* woman, queen] —**queen′ly** *adj., adv.* —**queen′li·ness** *n.*

Queen Anne's lace The wild carrot, having filmy white flowers resembling lace.

queen consort The wife of a reigning king.

queen dowager The widow of a king.

queen mother A queen dowager who is mother of a reigning sovereign.

queer (kwir) *adj.* **1** Different from the usual; strange; odd. **2** Of questionable character; open to suspicion; mysterious. **3** *Slang* Counterfeit. **4** Mentally unbalanced or eccentric. **5** Queasy or giddy. **6** *Slang* Homosexual: a contemptuous term. —*n. Slang* **1** Counterfeit money. **2** A homosexual, esp. a male homosexual: a contemptuous term. —*v.t. Slang* **1** To jeopardize or spoil. **2** To put into an unfavorable or embarrassing position. [< G *quer* oblique] —**queer′ly** *adv.* —**queer′ness** *n.* —**Syn.** *adj.* **1** bizarre, curious, droll, fantastic, grotesque, peculiar, singular. **2** suspect, suspicious. **4** peculiar, odd, deranged.

quell (kwel) *v.t.* **1** To put down or suppress by force; extinguish. **2** To quiet; allay, as pain. [< OE *cwellan* kill] —**quell′er** *n.*

quench (kwench) *v.t.* **1** To put out or extinguish, as a fire. **2** To slake or satisfy (thirst). **3** To suppress or repress, as emotions. **4** To cool, as heated iron or steel, by thrusting into water or other liquid. [ME *cwenken*] —**quench′a·ble** *adj.* —**quench′er** *n.*

quench·less (kwench′lis) *adj.* Incapable of being quenched; insatiable; irrepressible. —**quench′less·ly** *adv.* —**quench′less·ness** *n.*

quer·u·lous (kwer′ə·ləs, -yə·ləs) *adj.* **1** Disposed to complain or be fretful; faultfinding. **2** Indicating or expressing a complaint. [< L *queri* complain] —**quer′u·lous·ly** *adv.* —**quer′u·lous·ness** *n.* —**Syn.** **1** carping, captious, disparaging, critical, censorious.

que·ry (kwir′ē) *v.t.* **·ried, ·ry·ing** **1** To inquire into; ask about. **2** To ask questions of; interrogate. **3** To express doubt concerning the correctness or truth of, esp., as in printing, by marking with a question mark. —*n. pl.* **·ries** **1** An inquiry; question. **2** A doubt. **3** A question mark. [< L *quaerere* ask]

ques. question.

quest (kwest) *n.* **1** The act of seeking; a looking for something. **2** A search, as an adventure or expedition in medieval romance; also, the person or persons making the search. —*v.i.* To go on a quest. [< L *quaerere* ask, seek] —**quest′er** *n.*

ques·tion (kwes′chən) *n.* **1** An inquiry, esp. to obtain information, test knowledge, etc. **2** A written or vocal expression of such an inquiry; an interrogative sentence, clause, or expression. **3** A subject of debate or dispute. **4** An issue or problem: It's not a *question* of time. **5** A doubt or uncertainty: There is no *question* of his skill. **—out of the question** Not to be considered as a possibility. *—v.t.* **1** To put a question or questions to; interrogate. **2** To be uncertain of; doubt. **3** To make objection to; challenge; dispute. *—v.i.* **4** To ask a question or questions. [< L *quaerere* ask] **—ques′tion·er** *n.*

ques·tion·a·ble (kwes′chən·ə·bəl) *adj.* **1** Open to question; debatable. **2** Dubious or suspect, as regards morality, integrity, respectability, etc.: *questionable* motives. **—ques′tion·a·bil′i·ty, ques′tion·a·ble·ness** *n.* **—ques′tion·a·bly** *adv.*

question mark A punctuation mark (?) indicating that the sentence it closes is a direct question. A question mark is also used to denote that a fact, statement, etc., is uncertain or doubtful.

ques·tion·naire (kwes′chə·nâr′) *n.* A written or printed form comprising a series of questions submitted to one or more persons in order to obtain data, as for a survey or report. [F]

quet·zal (ket·säl′) *n. pl.* **·zals** or **·zal·es** (-sä′lās) A crested bird of Central America having long, upper tail feathers in the male. **2** The monetary unit of Guatemala. Also **que·zal** (kā·säl′). [< Nahuatl]

Quetzal

queue (kyōō) *n.* **1** A braid of hair hanging from the back of the head; a pigtail. **2** A line of persons or vehicles waiting in the order of their arrival. *—v.i.* **queued, queu·ing** To form such a line: usu. with *up.* [< L *cauda* a tail]

quib·ble (kwib′əl) *n.* **1** An evasion of a point or question; an equivocation. **2** A minor objection; cavil. *—v.i.* **·bled, ·bling** To use quibbles. [< L *quibus,* ablative pl. of *qui* who, which] **—quib′bler** *n.*

quiche (kēsh) *n.* Any of various non-dessert, custardlike pies, having meat, cheese, vegetables, etc., as principal ingredients. [F]

quick (kwik) *adj.* **1** Done or occurring in a short time; expeditious; brisk; prompt; speedy: a *quick* answer. **2** Characterized by rapidity or readiness of movement or action; nimble; rapid; swift: a *quick* pace. **3** Alert; sensitive; perceptive: a *quick* ear; *quick* wit. **4** Responding readily; excitable; hasty: *quick-tempered.* **5** Lasting only a short time: a *quick* lunch. *—n.* **1** That which has life; those who are alive: chiefly in the phrase **the quick and the dead. 2** The living flesh; esp., the tender flesh under a nail. **3** The most sensitive feelings: hurt to the *quick.* *—adv.* Quickly; rapidly. [< OE *cwic* alive]

quick bread Any bread, biscuits, etc., whose leavening agent makes immediate baking possible.

quick·en (kwik′ən) *v.t.* **1** To cause to move more rapidly; hasten or accelerate. **2** To make alive or quick; give or restore life to. **3** To excite or arouse; stimulate: to *quicken* the appetite. *—v.i.* **4** To move or act more quickly. **5** To come or return to life; revive. **—quick′en·er** *n.*

quick-freeze (kwik′frēz′) *v.t.* **-froze, -fro·zen, -freez·ing** To preserve by freezing rapidly and storing at a low temperature. **—quick′-fro′zen** *adj.*

quick·ie (kwik′ē) *n. Slang* Anything done hastily, as by short cuts or makeshift methods.

quick·lime (kwik′līm′) *n.* Unslaked lime.

quick·ly (kwik′lē) *adv.* In a quick manner; rapidly; soon.

quick·sand (kwik′sand′) *n.* A deep, wet bed of sand subjected to pressure by water below it and usu. incapable of supporting the weight of a person or animal.

quick·set (kwik′set′) *n.* **1** A slip, as of hawthorn, ready for planting. **2** A hedge made of such slips. *—adj.* Composed of quickset.

quick·sil·ver (kwik′sil′vər) *n.* Elemental mercury.

quick·step (kwik′step′) *n.* **1** A lively tune, esp. one in the rhythm of quick time. **2** A lively dance step, or a combination of such steps.

quick-tem·pered (kwik′tem′pərd) *adj.* Easily angered.

quick time A marching step of 120 paces a minute, each pace of 30 inches.

quick-wit·ted (kwik′wit′id) *adj.* Having a ready wit or quick discernment; keen; alert. **—quick′-wit′ted·ly** *adv.* **—quick′-wit′ted·ness** *n.*

quid[1] (kwid) *n.* A small portion, as of tobacco, to be chewed but not swallowed. [Var. of CUD]

quid[2] (kwid) *n. Brit. Slang* In England, a pound sterling, or a sovereign. [?]

quid·di·ty (kwid′ə·tē) *n. pl.* **·ties 1** The essence of a thing. **2** A quibble; cavil. [< L *quid* which, what]

quid·nunc (kwid′nungk′) *n.* A gossip; busybody. [< L *quid nunc* what now]

quid pro quo (kwid′ prō kwō′) A thing given or received for another thing. [L, lit., something for something]

qui·es·cent (kwī·es′ənt, kwē-) *adj.* Being in a state of repose or inaction; quiet; still. [< L *quiescere* be quiet] **—qui·es′cence** *n.* **—qui·es′cent·ly** *adv.*

qui·et (kwī′ət) *adj.* **1** Being in a state of repose; still; calm; motionless. **2** Free from turmoil, strife, or busyness; tranquil; peaceful. **3** Having or making little or no noise; silent. **4** Gentle or mild, as of disposition. **5** Undisturbed by din or bustle; secluded. **6** Not showy or obtrusive, as dress. *—n.* The condition or quality of being free from motion, disturbance, noise, etc.; peace; calm. *—v.t. & v.i.* To make or become quiet: often with *down.* *—adv.* In a quiet or peaceful manner. [< L *quies* rest, repose] **—qui′et·ly** *adv.* **—qui′et·ness** *n.*

qui·et·en (kwī′ə·tən) *v.t. & v.i. Brit. or Regional* To make or become quiet: often with *down.*

qui·e·tude (kwī′ə·tyōōd) *n.* A state or condition of calm or tranquillity; repose; rest.

qui·e·tus (kwī·ē′təs) *n.* **1** A final discharge or settlement, as of a debt. **2** A release from or extinction of activity or life; death. **3** Something that silences or suppresses. **4** Something that kills. [< L *quietus (est)* (he is) quiet]

quill (kwil) *n.* **1** A large, strong, wing or tail feather. **2** The hollow, horny stem of a feather. **3** Something made from this, as a pen or a plectrum. **4** A spine of a porcupine or hedgehog. [ME *quil*]

Quill

quilt (kwilt) *n.* **1** A bedcover made by stitching together two layers of cloth with a soft padding between them. **2** Any bedcover, esp. if thick. **3** A quilted skirt or other quilted article. *—v.t.* **1** To stitch together (two pieces of material) with a soft substance between. **2** To stitch in ornamental patterns or crossing lines. *—v.i.* **3** To make a quilt or quilted work. [< L *culcita* mattress] **—quilt′work′** *n.*

quilt·ing (kwil′ting) *n.* **1** The act or process of making a quilt, or of stitching as in making a quilt. **2** Material for quiltwork. **3** A quilting bee or party.

quilting bee A social gathering of the women of a community for working on a quilt or quilts. Also **quilting party.**

quince (kwins) *n.* **1** A hard, acid, yellowish fruit, used for preserves. **2** The small tree, related to the apple, which bears quinces. [ME < Gk. *Kydōnia,* a town in Crete]

qui·nine (kwī′nīn, *esp. Brit.* kwi·nēn′) *n.* **1** A bitter alkaloid obtained from cinchona. **2** A medicinal compound of quinine, used to relieve the symptoms of malaria. [< Sp. *quina* cinchona bark + -INE]

Quin·qua·ges·i·ma (kwin′kwə·jes′ə·mə) *n.* The Sunday before Lent. Also **Quinquagesima Sunday.** [< L *quinquagesimus* fiftieth]

quin·sy (kwin′zē) *n.* An acute infection of the throat, esp. when suppurative. [< Gk. *kyōn* dog + *anchein* to choke]

quint (kwint) *n. Informal* A quintuplet. [< L *quinque* five]

quin·tal (kwin′təl) *n.* **1** A hundredweight. **2** In the metric system, 100 kilograms. [< Ar. *qintar*]

quin·tes·sence (kwin·tes′əns) *n.* **1** The essence of anything, esp. in its most pure, concentrated form. **2** The perfect manifestation or embodiment of anything. [< L *quinta essentia* fifth essence] —**quin·tes·sen·tial** (kwin′tə·sen′shəl) *adj.*

quin·tet (kwin·tet′) *n.* **1** A musical composition for five voices or instruments. **2** The five performers of such a composition. **3** Any group of five persons or things. Also **quin·tette′**. [< Ital. *quinto* fifth]

quin·til·lion (kwin·til′yən) *n. & adj.* See NUMBER. [< L *quintus* fifth + MILLION] —**quin·til′lionth** (-yənth) *adj., n.*

quin·tu·ple (kwin·tyōō′pəl, -tup′əl, kwin′tyōō·pəl) *v.t. & v.i.* **·pled, ·pling** To multiply by five; make or become five times as large. —*adj.* **1** Consisting of five. **2** Being five times as much or as many. —*n.* A number or an amount five times as great as another. [< L *quintus* fifth + *-plex* -fold]

quin·tu·plet (kwin·tup′lit, -tyōō′plit, -tyōō′-, kwint′əp·lit) *n.* **1** Five things of a kind considered together. **2** One of five offspring born of the same mother at one birth.

quip (kwip) *n.* **1** A witty or sarcastic remark or retort; gibe. **2** A quibble. **3** An odd, fantastic action or object. —*v.i.* **quipped, quip·ping** To make a quip or quips. [< L *quippe* indeed] —**quip′pish** *adj.* —**quip′ster** *n.*

quire (kwīr) *n.* A set of 24 (or 25) sheets of paper of the same size and quality. [< L *quaterni* by fours]

Quir·i·nal (kwir′ə·nəl) *n.* One of the seven hills on which Rome stands, containing the **Quirinal palace,** formerly a papal residence, after 1870 the royal residence, now the residence of the president of Italy. —*adj.* Pertaining to or situated on the Quirinal.

quirk (kwûrk) *n.* **1** A peculiar mannerism or trait; idiosyncracy. **2** An evasion; quibble. **3** A witticism; quip. **4** An abrupt curve or twist, as a flourish in writing. [?]

quirk·y (kwûrk′ē) *adj.* **quirk·i·er, quirk·i·est** Peculiar, unpredictable, and idiosyncratic: a *quirky* individual. —**quirk′i·ly** *adv.* —**quirk′i·ness** *n.*

quirt (kwûrt) *n.* A short-handled riding whip with a braided rawhide lash. —*v.t.* To strike with a quirt. [?]

quis·ling (kwiz′ling) *n.* One who betrays his country to the enemy and is then given political power by the conquerors. [< Vidkun *Quisling,* 1887–1945, Norwegian politician] —**quis′ling·ism** *n.*

quit (kwit) *v.* **quit** or **quit·ted, quit·ting** *v.t.* **1** To cease or desist from; discontinue. **2** To give up; renounce; relinquish: to *quit* a job. **3** To go away from; leave. **4** To let go of (something held). **5** To free; release. **6** To discharge; pay back. —*v.i.* **7** To resign from a position, etc. **8** To stop; cease; discontinue. **9** To leave; depart. —*adj.* Released, relieved, or absolved from something, as a duty, obligation, encumbrance, or debt; clear; free; rid. —*n.* The act of quitting. [< L *quies* rest, repose]

quit·claim (kwit′klām′) *n. Law* **1** The giving up of a claim, right, title, or interest. **2** An instrument by which one person gives up to another a claim or title to an estate. —*v.t.* To relinquish or give up claim or title to; release from a claim. [< QUIT + CLAIM]

quite (kwīt) *adv.* **1** Completely; fully; totally: not *quite* finished. **2** To a great or considerable extent; very: *quite* ill. **3** Positively; really: *quite* certain. [ME, rid of]

quit·tance (kwit′ns) *n.* **1** Discharge or release, as from a debt or obligation. **2** A document in evidence of this; receipt. **3** Something given or tendered by way of repayment. [< F *quiter* quit]

Quiver of arrows

quit·ter (kwit′ər) *n.* One who quits needlessly; a shirker; slacker; coward.

quiv·er[1] (kwiv′ər) *v.i.* To shake with a slight, tremulous motion; vibrate; tremble. —*n.* The act or fact of quivering; a trembling or shaking. [?< QUAVER]

quiv·er[2] (kwiv′ər) *n.* A portable case or sheath for arrows; also, its contents. [< AF *quiveir*]

qui vive? (kē vēv′) "Who goes there?": used by French sentinels. —**be on the qui vive** To be on the look-out; be wide-awake. [F, who lives?]

quix·ot·ic (kwik·sot′ik) *adj.* **1** Pertaining to or like Don Quixote, the hero of a Spanish romance ridiculing knight-errantry. **2** Ridiculously chivalrous or romantic; having high but impractical sentiments, aims, etc. —**quix·ot′i·cal·ly** *adv.* —**quix·ot·ism** (kwik′sə·tiz′əm) *n.*

quiz (kwiz) *n. pl.* **quiz·zes 1** The act of questioning; specifically, a brief oral or written examination. **2** A person given to ridicule or practical jokes. **3** A hoax; practical joke. —*v.t.* **quizzed, quiz·zing 1** To examine by asking questions; question. **2** To make fun of; ridicule. [?] —**quiz′zer** *n.*

quiz program A television or radio program in which selected contestants or a panel of experts compete in answering questions.

quiz·zi·cal (kwiz′i·kəl) *adj.* **1** Mocking; teasing. **2** Perplexed; puzzled. **3** Queer; odd. —**quiz′zi·cal·ly** *adv.*

quod (kwod) *n. Brit. Slang* A prison. [?]

quoin (koin, kwoin) *n.* **1** An external angle of a building. **2** A large square stone forming such an angle. **3** A wedge-shaped stone, etc., as the keystone of an arch. [Var. of COIN]

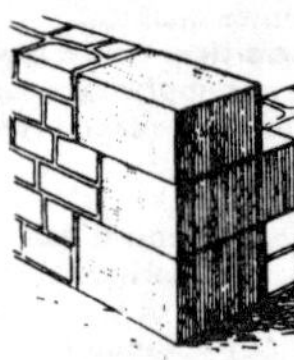
Quoins *def. 2*

quoit (kwoit, *esp. Brit.* koit) *n.* **1** A ring of iron or other material to be thrown over a stake, used in the game of quoits. **2** *pl.* A game played by throwing these disks at a short stake.

quon·dam (kwon′dəm) *adj.* Having been formerly; former. [L]

Quon·set hut (kwon′sit) A prefabricated metal structure in the form of half a cylinder resting lengthwise on its flat surface: a trade name.

Quonset hut

quo·rum (kwôr′əm, kwō′rəm) *n.* The number of members of any deliberative or corporate body that is necessary for the legal transaction of business, usu., a majority. [L, of whom]

quot. quotation.

quo·ta (kwō′tə) *n.* A proportional part or share given to or required from a person, group, etc. [< L *quotus* how great]

quo·ta·tion (kwō·tā′shən) *n.* **1** The act of quoting. **2** The words quoted. **3** A price quoted or current, as of securities, etc. —**quo·ta′tion·al** *adj.* —**quo·ta′tion·al·ly** *adv.*

quotation mark One of a pair of marks (" " or ' ') placed at the beginning and end of a quoted word or passage, the single marks usu. being used to set off a quotation within a quotation.

quote (kwōt) *v.* **quot·ed, quot·ing** *v.t.* **1** To repeat or reproduce the words of. **2** To repeat or cite (a rule, author, etc.), as for authority or illustration. **3** In commerce: **a** To state (a price). **b** To give the current or market price of. —*v.i.* **4** To make a quotation, as from a book. —*n.* **1** QUOTATION. **2** QUOTATION MARK. [< Med. L *quotare* distinguish by number < L *quot* how many] —**quot′a·bil′i·ty, quot′er** *n.* —**quot′a·ble** *adj.*

quoth (kwōth) *v.t. Archaic* Said or spoke; uttered: used only in the first and third persons, the subject always following the verb, as *quoth* he. [< OE *cwethan* say]

quo·tid·i·an (kwō·tid′ē·ən) *adj.* Recurring or occurring every day. —*n.* Something that returns every day, as a fever. [< L *quotidianus* daily]

quo·tient (kwō′shənt) *n. Math.* The result obtained by division; a factor by which a given number must be multiplied to produce a given product. [< L *quotiens* how often]

q.v. which see (L *quod vide*).

qy. query.

R

R, r (är) *n. pl.* **R's, r's, Rs, rs** (ärz) **1** The 18th letter of the English alphabet. **2** Any spoken sound representing the letter *R* or *r*. **3** Something shaped like an R. **—the three R's** Reading, writing, and arithmetic (regarded humorously as spelled *reading, 'riting,* and *'rithmetic*); the essential elements of a primary education. *—adj.* Shaped like an R.

R radical; ratio; Republican; rook (chess); registered (trademark).

R., r. rabbi; railroad; river; road; ruble; rupee.

r roentgen(s); radius.

r. range; rare; received; residence; retired; radius.

Ra (rä) The supreme Egyptian deity, the sun-god.

Ra

Ra radium.

rab·bet (rab'it) *n.* **1** A recess or groove in or near the edge of one piece of wood or other material to receive the edge of another piece. **2** A joint so made. *—v.t.* **1** To cut a rectangular groove in. **2** To unite in a rabbet. *—v.i.* **3** To be jointed by a rabbet. [< OF *rabattre* beat down]

rab·bi (rab'ī) *n. pl.* **·bis 1** A Jew authorized to teach or expound Jewish law. **2** The official head of a Jewish congregation. [< Heb. *rabbī* my master]

rab·bin·i·cal (rə·bin'i·kəl) *adj.* Of or pertaining to the rabbis or to their opinions, languages, writings, etc. Also **rab·bin'ic. —rab·bin'i·cal·ly** *adv.*

rab·bit (rab'it) *n.* **1** Any of numerous small, herbivorous mammals having soft fur, long legs and ears, and a short tail. **2** HARE. **3** The pelt of a rabbit or hare. *—v.i.* To hunt rabbits. [ME *rabette*] **—rab'bit·er** *n.*

rabbit fever TULAREMIA.

rabbit foot The left hind foot of a rabbit carried as a good-luck charm. Also **rabbit's foot.**

rab·ble (rab'əl) *n.* A disorderly crowd; mob. **—the rabble** The common people: a contemptuous term. [?]

rab·ble-rous·er (rab'əl·rou'zər) *n.* One who tries to incite mobs by arousing prejudices and passions. **—Syn.** demagogue, instigator, agitator.

Rab·e·lai·si·an (rab'ə·lā'zē·ən, -zhən) *adj.* **1** Of, pertaining to, or like Rabelais or his works. **2** Humorously coarse and boisterous; bawdy. **—Rab'e·lai'si·an·ism** *n.*

rab·id (rab'id) *adj.* **1** Affected with, arising from, or pertaining to rabies; mad. **2** Unreasonably zealous; fanatical. **3** Furious; raging. [< L *rabere* be mad] **—ra·bid·i·ty** (rə·bid'ə·tē), **rab'id·ness** *n.* **—rab'id·ly** *adv.*

ra·bies (rā'bēz) *n. pl.* **·bies** An acute viral disease affecting the central nervous system of dogs, bats, and other warm-blooded animals and transmissible to man by the bite of an infected animal. [< L *rabere* rave]

rac·coon (ra·ko͞on') *n.* **1** A North American nocturnal, tree-climbing mammal with a black face mask, long gray-brown fur, and a bushy, black-ringed tail. **2** The fur of this animal. Also **ra·coon'.** [< Algon.]

Raccoon

race[1] (rās) *n.* **1** A subdivision of mankind having a relatively constant set of physical traits, such as color of skin and eyes, stature, texture of hair, etc. **2** Any grouping of peoples according to geography, nation, etc. **3** A genealogical or family stock; clan: the *race* of MacGregor. **4** Any class of people having similar activities, interests, etc.: the *race* of lawyers. **5** *Biol.* A group of plants or animals within a species with distinct, inheritable characteristics; a variety. [< Ital. *razza*]

race[2] (rās) *n.* **1** A contest to determine the relative speed of the persons or animals which are in competition. **2** *pl.* A series of such contests, as for horses. **3** Any contest. **4** Duration of life; course; career. **5** A swift current of water or its channel. **6** A swift current or heavy sea. **7** A sluice or channel by which to conduct water to or from a waterwheel or around a dam. **8** Any guide or channel along which some part of a machine moves. **9** SLIPSTREAM. *—v.* **raced, rac·ing** *v.i.* **1** To take part in a race. **2** To move at great or top speed. **3** To move at an accelerated or too great speed, as an engine. *—v.t.* **4** To contend against in a race. **5** To cause to race. [< ON *rās*]

race·course (rās'kôrs', -kōrs') *n.* A course or track for racing.

ra·ceme (rā·sēm', rə-) *n. Bot.* A flower cluster having flowers on short stalks arranged at intervals along a central stalk. [< L *racemus* cluster] **—rac·e·mose** (ras'ə·mōs) *adj.* **—rac'e·mose·ly** *adv.*

rac·er (rā'sər) *n.* **1** One who races. **2** Anything having unusually rapid speed, as a car, yacht, etc. **3** Any of a genus of large, agile snakes of North America.

race riot A riot caused by racial hostility, as between two groups of different races.

race·track (rās'trak') *n.* A course or track for racing, esp. one for horse or dog racing.

Ra·chel (rā'chəl) In the Bible, the wife of Jacob and mother of Joseph.

ra·chi·tis (rə·kī'tis) *n.* RICKETS. [< Gk. *rhachitis* spinal inflammation] **—ra·chit'ic** (-kit'ik) *adj.*

ra·cial (rā'shəl) *adj.* **1** Of, pertaining to, characteristic of a race. **2** Existing between races: *racial* brotherhood. **—ra'cial·ly** *adv.*

ra·cial·ism (rā'shəl·iz'əm) *n.* **1** The belief in or practice of racial superiority. **2** RACISM.

ra·cism (rā'siz·əm) *n.* **1** An excessive and irrational belief in the superiority of one's own racial group. **2** A doctrine, program, or practice based on such belief. **—ra'cist** *adj., n.*

rack[1] (rak) *n.* **1** Something on which various articles can be hung, stored, or canned. **2** A triangular frame for arranging the balls on a billiard table. **3** *Mech.* A bar having teeth that engage those of a gearwheel or pinion. **4** A machine for stretching or making tense; esp., an instrument of torture which stretches the limbs of victims. **5** Intense mental or physical suffering or its cause. **6** A wrenching or straining, as from a storm. **—on the rack** In great physical or mental pain. *—v.t.* **1** To place or arrange in or on a rack. **2** To torture on the rack. **3** To torment. **4** To strain, as with the effort of thinking: to *rack* one's brains. **5** To raise (rents) excessively. **—rack up** *Informal* To gain or achieve: to *rack up* a good score. [Prob. < MDu. *recken* to stretch] **—rack'er** *n.*

Rack *def. 3* and pinion

rack[2] (rak) *n.* SINGLE FOOT. *—v.i.* To proceed or move with this gait. [? Var. of ROCK[2]]

rack[3] (rak) *n.* Thin, flying, or broken clouds. [< Scand.]

rack[4] (rak) *n.* Destruction: obsolete except in the phrase **go to rack and ruin.** [Var. of WRACK]

rack·et[1] (rak'it) *n.* **1** A bat consisting of an oval, wooden or metal hoop strung with catgut, nylon, etc., and having a handle, used in playing tennis, etc. **2** *pl. (construed as sing.)* A game resembling court tennis, played in a court with four walls: also **rac·quets** (rak'its). [< Ar. *rāha* palm of the hand]

rack·et[2] (rak'it) *n.* **1** A loud, clattering or confused noise. **2** *Informal* A scheme for getting money or other benefits by fraud, intimidation, or other illegitimate means. **3**

Slang Any business or occupation. —*v.i.* To make a loud, clattering noise. [?] —**rack′et·y** *adj.*

rack·et·eer (rak′ə·tir′) *n.* One who gets money or other benefits by fraud, intimidation, or other illegitimate means. —**rack′et·eer′ing** *n.*

rac·on·teur (rak′on·tûr′, *Fr.* rà·kôṅ·tœr′) *n.* A skilled storyteller. [F]

rac·y (rā′sē) *adj.* **rac·i·er, rac·i·est 1** Full of spirit and vigor: a *racy* style. **2** Slightly immodest or risqué. **3** Spicy; piquant. [< RACE[1]] —**rac′i·ly** *adv.* —**rac′i·ness** *n.*

rad (rad) *n.* A unit of absorbed radiation equivalent to 100 ergs of absorbed energy per gram of absorbing material. [< R(ADIATION) + A(BSORBED) + D(OSE)]

rad radian.

ra·dar (rā′där) *n. Electronics* A device which detects, locates, and indicates the speed and approximate nature of aircraft, ships, objects, etc., by means of reflected microwaves. [< RA(DIO) D(ETECTING) A(ND) R(ANGING)]

ra·di·al (rā′dē·əl) *adj.* **1** Pertaining to, consisting of, or resembling a ray or radius. **2** Extending from a center like rays. **3** *Anat.* Of, pertaining to, or near the radius or forearm. **4** Developing uniformly on all sides. —*n.* **1** A radiating part. **2** RADIAL TIRE. —**ra′di·al·ly** *adv.*

radial tire A pneumatic tire with plies of fabric laid at right angles to the direction of the tread. Also **ra·di·al-ply tire** (rā′dē·əl·plī′).

ra·di·an (rā′dē·ən) *n.* The angle subtended by an arc equal in length to the radius of the circle of which it is a part: a unit of measure. [< RADIUS]

ra·di·ance (rā′dē·əns) *n.* The quality or state of being radiant. Also **ra′di·an·cy, ra′di·ant·ness.**

ra·di·ant (rā′dē·ənt) *adj.* **1** Emitting rays of light or heat. **2** Beaming with brightness: a *radiant* smile. **3** Resembling rays. **4** Consisting of or transmitted by radiation: *radiant* heat. [< L *radiare* emit rays] —**ra′di·ant·ly** *adv.*

radiant energy *Physics* Energy transmitted by radiation, as electromagnetic waves.

ra·di·ate (rā′dē·āt) *v.* **·at·ed, ·at·ing** *v.i.* **1** To emit rays or radiation; be radiant. **2** To issue forth in rays. **3** To spread out from a center, as the spokes of a wheel. —*v.t.* **4** To send out or emit in rays. **5** To spread or show (joy, love, etc.) as if from a center. —*adj.* (-dē·it) Divided or separated into rays; having rays; radiating. [< L *radiare* emit rays] —**ra′di·a′tive** *adj.*

ra·di·a·tion (rā′dē·ā′shən) *n.* **1** The act or process of radiating or the state of being radiated. **2** That which is radiated, as energy in the form of particles or waves.

radiation sickness Sickness resulting from exposure to X-rays, nuclear explosions, etc.

ra·di·a·tor (rā′dē·ā′tər) *n.* **1** That which radiates. **2** A device for distributing heat, partly by radiation, as in heating or cooling systems.

rad·i·cal (rad′i·kəl) *adj.* **1** Thoroughgoing; extreme: *radical* measures. **2** Of, pertaining to, or professing policies and practices of extreme change, as in government. **3** Of or pertaining to the root or foundation; essential; basic. —*n.* **1** One who holds radical or extreme convictions. **2** In politics, one who advocates extreme governmental changes. **3** The primitive or underived part of a word; root. **4** *Math.* An indicated root of a number, expression, etc. **5** *Chem.* A group of atoms that act as a unit in a compound and remain together during a chemical reaction. [< L *radix, radicis* root] —**rad′i·cal·ly** *adv.* —**rad′i·cal·ness** *n.*

rad·i·cal·ism (rad′i·kəl·iz′əm) *n.* **1** The state of being radical. **2** Advocacy of radical or extreme measures.

rad·i·cal·ize (rad′i·kə·līz′) *v.t.* **·ized, ·iz·ing** To make radical, as in politics. —**rad·i·cal·i·za·tion** (rad′i·kə·lə·zā′shən) *n.*

radical sign *Math.* The symbol $\sqrt{\;}$ placed around a number or expression to indicate that its root is to be taken. A number above it, not written when equal to 2, shows what root is to be taken; thus $\sqrt[n]{a}$ stands for the *n*th root of *a*.

rad·i·cle (rad′i·kəl) *n. Bot.* The embryonic root of a sprouting seed. [< L *radix, radicis* root]

ra·di·o (rā′dē·ō) *n. pl.* **·os 1** The technology and process of communicating by means of radio waves. **2** A transmitter or receiver used in such communication. **3** The process, business, or industry of producing programs to be communicated in this way. —*adj.* Of, pertaining to, designating, employing, or produced by radiant energy, esp. electromagnetic waves: a *radio* beam. —*v.t.* & *v.i.* **·di·oed, ·di·o·ing 1** To transmit (a message, etc.) by radio. **2** To communicate with (someone) by radio. [< RADIO(TELEGRAPHY)]

radio- *combining form* Radiation: *radioscopy.* [< L *radius* a ray]

ra·di·o·ac·tive (rā′dē·ō·ak′tiv) *adj.* Of, pertaining to, exhibiting, caused by, or characteristic of radioactivity.

ra·di·o·ac·tiv·i·ty (rā′dē·ō·ak·tiv′ə·tē) *n. Physics* The spontaneous disintegration of nuclei of certain elements and isotopes, with the emission of particles or rays.

radio astronomy The branch of astronomy which studies celestial phenomena by means of radio waves received from stars and other objects in space.

radio beacon A stationary radio transmitter which sends out signals for the guidance of ships and aircraft.

radio beam 1 A steady flow of radio signals concentrated along a given course or direction. **2** The narrow zone marked out for the guidance of aircraft by radio beacons.

ra·di·o·broad·cast (rā′dē·ō·brôd′kast′, -käst′) *v.t.* & *v.i.* **·cast** or **·cast·ed, ·cast·ing** To broadcast by radio. —*n.* BROADCAST. —**ra′di·o·broad′cast′er** *n.* —**ra′di·o·broad′cast′·ing** *n.*

ra·di·o·car·bon (rā′dē·ō·kär′bən) *n.* CARBON 14.

radio frequency Any wave frequency from about 10 kilohertz to about 30,000 megahertz.

ra·di·o·gram (rā′dē·ō·gram′) *n.* **1** A message sent by wireless telegraphy. **2** RADIOGRAPH.

ra·di·o·graph (rā′dē·ō·graf′, -gräf′) *n.* An image made by means of X-rays or the products of radioactivity. —*v.t.* To make a radiograph of. —**ra′di·og′ra·pher** (-og′rə·fər), **ra′di·og′ra·phy** *n.* —**ra′di·o·graph′ic** or **·i·cal** *adj.*

ra·di·o·i·so·tope (rā′dē·ō·ī′sə·tōp) *n.* A radioactive isotope, usu. one of an element having also a stable isotope.

ra·di·ol·o·gy (rā′dē·ol′ə·jē) *n.* That branch of science concerned with radioactivity, X-rays, etc., esp. in diagnostic and therapeutic applications. —**ra·di·o·log·i·cal** (rā′dē·ə·loj′i·kəl) or **ra′di·o·log′ic** *adj.* —**ra′di·ol′o·gist** *n.*

ra·di·om·e·ter (rā′dē·om′ə·tər) *n.* An instrument for detecting and measuring radiant energy by noting the speed of rotation of blackened disks suspended in a partially evacuated chamber.

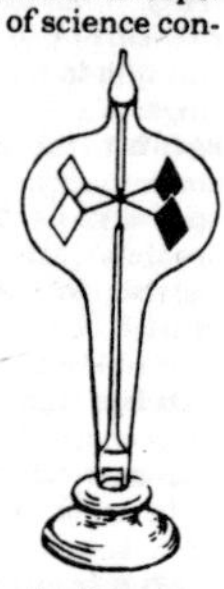

Radiometer

ra·di·o·phone (rā′dē·ō·fōn′) *n.* RADIOTELEPHONE.

ra·di·o·pho·to (rā′dē·ō·fō′tō) *n.* A photograph or image transmitted by radio. Also **ra′di·o·pho′to·graph.**

ra·di·o·scope (rā′dē·ō·skōp′) *n.* An apparatus for detecting radioactivity or X-rays.

ra·di·os·co·py (rā′dē·os′kə·pē) *n.* Examination of bodies opaque to light by X-rays or other penetrating radiation. —**ra′di·o·scop′ic** (-skop′ik) or **·i·cal** *adj.*

ra·di·o·sonde (rā′dē·ō·sond′) *n. Meteorol.* A device, usu. attached to a small balloon and sent aloft, which measures the pressure, temperature, and humidity of the upper air and radios the data to the ground. [< RADIO + F *sonde* sounding]

Radiosonde

radio star A star that emits a sizable part of its energy as radio waves.

ra·di·o·tel·e·gram (rā′dē·ō·tel′ə·gram) *n.* A message sent by radiotelegraphy.

ra·di·o·te·leg·ra·phy (rā′dē·ō·tə·leg′rə·fē) *n.* Telegraphic communication by means of radio waves. Also **ra′di·o·tel′e·graph** (-tel′ə·graf, -gräf). —**ra′di·o·tel′e·graph′ic** *adj.*

ra·di·o·tel·e·phone (rā′dē·ō·tel′ə·fōn) *n.* A telephone set that uses radio waves to carry messages. —**ra′di·o·te·leph′o·ny** (-tə·lef′ə·nē) *n.*

radio telescope A sensitive radio receiver designed to receive radio waves from space.

ra·di·o·ther·a·py (rā′dē·ō·ther′ə·pē) *n.* The use of X-rays and radioactivity in the treatment of disease.

ra·dio wave Any electromagnetic wave of radio frequency.

rad·ish (rad′ish) *n.* **1** A tall, branching herb of the mustard family. **2** Its pungent, edible root, commonly eaten raw. [< L *radix, radicis* root]

ra·di·um (rā′dē·əm) *n.* A radioactive metallic element (symbol Ra) found in pitchblende as a disintegration product of uranium. [< L *radius* ray]

radium therapy The treatment of disease, esp. cancer, by means of radium.

ra·di·us (rā′dē·əs) *n. pl.* **·di·i** (-dē·ī) or **·di·us·es** **1** A straight line segment joining the surface of a sphere or circumference of a circle with its center. **2** *Anat.* The shorter of the two bones of the forearm. **3** *Zool.* A corresponding bone in the forelimb of other vertebrates. **4** *Bot.* A ray floret of a composite flower. **5** A raylike part, as a wheel spoke. **6** A circular area or boundary measured by its radius. **7** Sphere, scope, or limit, as of activity. **8** A fixed or circumscribed area or distance of travel. [L, spoke of a wheel, ray]

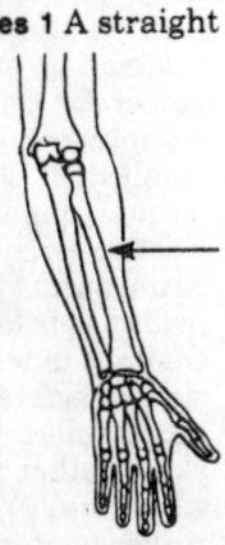

Radius *def. 2*

radius vector *pl.* **radius vectors** or **ra·di·i vec·to·res** (rā′dē·ī vek·tôr′ēz, -tō′rēz) *Math.* The distance in an indicated direction from a fixed origin to any point.

ra·dix (rā′diks) *n. pl.* **rad·i·ces** (rad′ə·sēz, rā′də-) or **ra·dix·es** *Math.* A number or symbol used as the base of a system of numeration. [L, root]

ra·dome (rā′dōm) *n.* A housing, transparent to microwaves, for a radar assembly. [< RA(DAR) + DOME]

ra·don (rā′don) *n.* A gaseous, radioactive element (symbol Rn) resulting from the decay of radium and having a half-life of about four days. [< RAD(IUM) + (NE)ON]

RAF, R.A.F. Royal Air Force.

raf·fi·a (raf′e·ə) *n.* **1** A cultivated palm of Madagascar. **2** Fiber made from the leaves of this palm, used for weaving baskets, etc. [< Malagasy *rafia*]

raff·ish (raf′ish) *adj.* **1** Tawdry; gaudy; vulgar. **2** Disreputable. [< ME *raf* rubbish + -ISH]

raf·fle (raf′əl) *n.* A form of lottery in which a number of people buy chances on an object. —*v.* **·fled, ·fling** *v.t.* **1** To dispose of by a raffle: often with *off.* —*v.i.* **2** To take part in a raffle. [< OF *rafle* a game of dice] —**raf′fler** *n.*

raft[1] (raft, räft) *n.* **1** A float of logs, planks, etc., fastened together for transportation by water. **2** A flat, often inflatable object, as of rubber, that floats on water. —*v.t.* **1** To transport on a raft. **2** To form into a raft. —*v.i.* **3** To travel by or work on a raft. [< ON *raptr* log] —**rafts′man** *n.*

raft[2] (raft, räft) *n. Informal* A large number or an indiscriminate collection of any kind. [< ME *raf* rubbish]

raft·er (raf′tər, räf′-) *n.* A timber or beam giving form, slope, and support to a roof. [< OE *ræfter*]

rag[1] (rag) *v.t.* **ragged, rag·ging** *Slang* **1** To tease or irritate. **2** To scold. —*n. Brit.* A prank. [?]

rag[2] (rag) *n.* **1** A waste, usu. torn piece of cloth. **2** A fragment of anything. **3** *pl.* Tattered or shabby clothing. **4** *pl.* Any clothing: a jocular use. **5** *Slang* A newspaper. —**chew the rag** *Slang* To talk or argue at length. —**glad rags** *Slang* One's best clothes. [< ON *rögg* tuft or strip of fur]

rag[3] (rag) *n.* RAGTIME. —*v.t.* **ragged, rag·ging** To compose or play in ragtime.

ra·ga (rä′gə) *n.* One of a large number of traditional melodic patterns, used by Hindu musicians as the basis for improvisation. [< Skt. *rāga* (musical) color]

rag·a·muf·fin (rag′ə·muf′in) *n.* Anyone, esp. a child, wearing very ragged clothes. [< *Ragamoffyn,* demon in *Piers Plowman* (1393), a long allegorical poem]

rag-bag (rag′bag′) *n.* **1** A bag in which rags or scraps of cloth are kept. **2** A miscellaneous collection; potpourri.

rage (rāj) *n.* **1** Violent anger; wrath; fury. **2** Any great violence or intensity, as of a fever or a storm. **3** Extreme eagerness or emotion. **4** Something that arouses great enthusiasm; craze; vogue. —*v.i.* **raged, rag·ing** **1** To feel or show violent anger. **2** To act or proceed with great violence. **3** To spread or prevail uncontrolled, as an epidemic. [< L *rabies* madness]

rag·ged (rag′id) *adj.* **1** Torn or worn into rags; frayed. **2** Wearing worn, frayed, or shabby garments. **3** Of rough or uneven character or aspect: a *ragged* performance. **4** Naturally of a rough or shabby appearance. —**rag′ged·ly** *adv.* —**rag′ged·ness** *n.*

rag·ged·y (rag′id·ē) *adj.* Ragged in appearance.

rag·lan (rag′lən) *n.* An overcoat or topcoat, the sleeves of which extend in one piece up to the collar. —*adj.* Of or designating such a sleeve or a garment with such sleeves. [< Lord Fitzroy *Raglan,* 1788–1855, Eng. field marshal]

rag·man (rag′man′, -mən) *n. pl.* **·men** (-men′, -mən) One who buys and sells old rags and other waste; a ragpicker.

ra·gout (ra·gōō′) *n.* A highly seasoned dish of stewed meat and vegetables. —*v.t.* **ra·gouted** (-gōōd′), **ra·gout·ing** (-gōō′·ing) To make into a ragout. [< F *ragoûter* revive the appetite]

rag·pick·er (rag′pik′ər) *n.* One who picks up and sells rags and other junk for a livelihood.

rag·time (rag′tīm′) *n.* **1** A kind of American dance music, popular 1890 to 1920, highly syncopated and in quick tempo. **2** The rhythm of this dance. [< *ragged time*]

rag·weed (rag′wēd′) *n.* Any of a genus of coarse, composite plants having pollen that often induces hay fever.

rag·wort (rag′wûrt′) *n.* GROUNDSEL (def. 1).

rah (rä) *interj.* Hurrah!: a cheer used esp. in school yells.

raid (rād) *n.* **1** A hostile or predatory attack, as by a rapidly moving body of troops. **2** AIR RAID. **3** Any sudden breaking into, invasion, or capture, as by the police. **4** A manipulative attempt to make stock prices fall by concerted selling. —*v.t.* **1** To make a raid on. —*v.i.* **2** To participate in a raid. [< OE *rād* a ride] —**raid′er** *n.*

rail[1] (rāl) *n.* **1** A bar, usu. of wood or metal, resting on supports, as in a fence, at the side of a stairway or roadway, or capping the bulwarks of a ship; a railing. **2** One of a series of parallel bars, of iron or steel, resting upon cross-ties, forming a support and guide for wheels, as of a railway. **3** A railroad: to ship by *rail.* —*v.t.* To furnish or shut in with rails; fence. [< L *regula* ruler]

rail[2] (rāl) *n.* Any of various small marsh and shore birds having short wings and tail. [< OF *raale, ralle*]

Rail

rail[3] (rāl) *v.i.* To use scornful, insolent, or abusive language: with *at* or *against.* [< MF *railler* to mock]

rail·ing (rā′ling) *n.* **1** A series of rails; a balustrade. **2** Rails or material from which rails are made.

rail·ler·y (rā′lər·ē) *n. pl.* **·ler·ies** Merry jesting or teasing. [< F *raillerie* jesting]

rail·road (rāl′rōd′) *n.* **1** A graded road, having metal rails supported by ties, for the passage of trains or other rolling stock drawn by locomotives. **2** The system of tracks, stations, etc., used in transportation by rail. **3** The corporation or persons owning or operating such a system. —*v.t.* **1** To transport by railroad. **2** *Informal* To rush or force with great speed or without deliberation: to *railroad* a bill through Congress. **3** *Slang* To cause to be imprisoned on false charges or without fair trial. —*v.i.* **4** To work on a railroad. —**rail′road′er** *n.*

railroad flat An apartment having rooms arranged one after another in a straight line without hallways.

rail-split·ter (rāl′split′ər) *n.* One who splits logs into fence rails.

rail·way (rāl′wā′) *n.* **1** A railroad, esp. one using comparatively light vehicles. **2** *Brit.* RAILROAD. **3** Any track having rails for wheeled equipment.

rai·ment (rā′mənt) *n.* Wearing apparel; clothing; garb. [< ARRAY + -MENT]

rain (rān) *n.* **1** The condensed water vapor of the atmosphere falling in drops. **2** The fall of such drops. **3** A fall or shower of anything in the manner of rain. **4** A rainstorm; shower. **5** *pl.* The rainy season in a tropical country. —*v.i.* **1** To fall from the clouds in drops of water. **2** To fall like rain. **3** To send or pour down rain. —*v.t.* **4** To send down like rain; shower. [<OE *regn*]

rain·bow (rān′bō′) *n.* **1** An arch of light formed in the sky opposite the sun and exhibiting the colors of the spectrum. It is caused by refraction, reflection, and dispersion of sunlight in raindrops or mist. **2** Any brilliant display of color. **3** Any unfounded hope.

rain check **1** The stub of a ticket to an outdoor event entitling the holder to future admission if for any reason the event is called off. **2** Any postponed invitation.

rain·coat (rān′kōt′) *n.* A water-resistant coat giving protection against rain.

rain·drop (rān′drop′) *n.* A drop of rain.

rain·fall (rān′fôl′) *n.* **1** A fall of rain. **2** *Meteorol.* The amount of water precipitated in a given region over a stated time.

rain gauge An instrument for measuring rainfall.

rain·proof (rān′pro͞of′) *adj.* Shedding rain. —*v.t.* To make rainproof.

rain·storm (rān′stôrm′) *n.* A storm accompanied by heavy rain.

rain·wa·ter (rān′wô′tər, -wot′ər) *n.* Water that falls or has fallen as rain.

rain·y (rā′nē) *adj.* **rain·i·er, rain·i·est** Of, abounding in, or bringing rain. —**rain′i·ly** *adv.* —**rain′i·ness** *n.*

rainy day A time of need; hard times.

raise (rāz) *v.* **raised, rais·ing** *v.t.* **1** To cause to move upward or to a higher level; lift; elevate. **2** To place erect; set up. **3** To construct or build; erect. **4** To make greater in amount, size, or value: to *raise* the price of corn. **5** To advance or elevate in rank, estimation, etc. **6** To increase the strength, intensity, or degree of. **7** To breed; grow: to *raise* chickens or tomatoes. **8** To rear (children, a family, etc.). **9** To cause to be heard: to *raise* a hue and cry. **10** To cause; occasion, as a smile or laugh. **11** To stir to action or emotion; arouse. **12** To waken; animate or reanimate: to *raise* the dead. **13** To obtain or collect, as an army, capital, etc. **14** To bring up for consideration, as a question. **15** To cause to swell or become lighter; leaven. **16** To put an end to, as a siege. **17** In card games, to bid or bet more than. **18** *Naut.* To cause to appear above the horizon, as land or a ship, by approaching nearer. —*v.i.* **19** *Regional* To rise or arise. **20** In card games, to increase a bid or bet. —**raise Cain** (or **the devil, the dickens, a rumpus,** etc.) *Informal* to make a great disturbance; stir up confusion. —*n.* **1** The act of raising. **2** An increase, as of wages or a bet. [<ON *reisa* lift, set up]

raised (rāzd) *adj.* **1** Elevated in low relief. **2** Made with yeast or leaven.

rai·sin (rā′zən) *n.* A grape of a special sort dried in the sun or in an oven. [<L *racemus* bunch of grapes]

rai·son d'ê·tre (re·zôn′ de′tr′) *French* A reason or excuse for existing.

raj (räj) *n.* In India, sovereignty; rule [<Hind. *rāj*]

ra·ja (rä′jə) *n.* **1** A prince or chief of India. **2** A Malay or Javanese ruler. Also **ra′jah.** [<Skt. *rājan* king]

rake[1] (rāk) *n.* A long-handled, toothed implement for drawing together loose material, making a surface smooth, etc. —*v.* **raked, rak·ing** *v.t.* **1** To gather together with or as with a rake. **2** To smooth, clean, or prepare with a rake. **3** To gather by diligent effort. **4** To search or examine carefully. **5** To direct heavy gunfire along the length of. —*v.i.* **6** To use a rake. **7** To scrape or pass roughly or violently: with *across, over, etc.* **8** To make a search. —**rake in** *Informal* To earn or acquire (money, etc.) in large quantities. —**rake up** *Informal* To make public or bring to light: to *rake up* old gossip. [<OE *raca*]

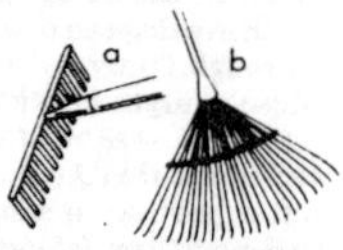

Rakes
a. garden. b. broom.

rake[2] (rāk) *v.* **raked, rak·ing** *v.i.* **1** To lean from the perpendicular, as a ship's masts. —*v.t.* **2** To cause to lean; incline. —*n.* Inclination from the perpendicular or horizontal, as the edge of a cutting tool. [?] —**raked** *adj.*

rake[3] (rāk) *n.* A dissolute, lewd man. [Orig. *rakehell* < ME *rakel* rash, wild] —**Syn.** roué, libertine, lecher, profligate.

rake-off (rāk′ôf′, -of′) *n. Slang* A percentage, as of profits; commission or rebate, usu. illegitimate.

rak·ish[1] (rā′kish) *adj.* **1** Dashing; jaunty. **2** *Naut.* Having the masts unusually inclined, usu. connoting speed. [<RAKE[2]] —**rak′ish·ly** *adv.* —**rak′ish·ness** *n.*

rak·ish[2] (rā′kish) *adj.* Like a rake; dissolute. —**rak′ish·ly** *adv.* —**rak′ish·ness** *n.*

ral·len·tan·do (ral′ən·tan′dō, *Ital.* râl′len·tän′dō) *adj. & adv. Music* Gradually slower. [Ital., pr.p. of *rallentare* slow down]

ral·ly[1] (ral′ē) *v.* **·lied, ·ly·ing** *v.t.* **1** To bring together and restore to effective discipline: to *rally* fleeing troops. **2** To summon up or revive: to *rally* one's spirits. **3** To bring together for common action. —*v.i.* **4** To return to effective discipline or action: The enemy *rallied.* **5** To unite for common action. **6** To make a partial or complete return to a normal condition. **7** In tennis, badminton, etc. to engage in a rally. —*n. pl.* **·lies** **1** An assembly of people, esp. to arouse enthusiasm. **2** A quick recovery or improvement, as of health, spirits, vigor, etc. **3** A reassembling, as of scattered troops. **4** In tennis, badminton, etc., an exchange of several strokes before one side wins the point. **5** A competition for automobiles that emphasizes driving and navigational skills rather than speed. [<F *re-* again + *allier* join]

ral·ly[2] (ral′ē) *v.t. & v.i.* To tease or ridicule; banter. [<F *railler* banter]

ram (ram) *n.* **1** A male sheep. **2** BATTERING-RAM. **3** Any device for forcing or thrusting, as by heavy blows. **4** A device for raising water by pressure of its own flow; a hydraulic ram. —*v.t.* **rammed, ram·ming** **1** To strike with or as with a ram; dash against. **2** To drive or force down or into something. **3** To cram; stuff. [<OE]

Ram (ram) *n.* ARIES.

RAM Random access memory, a kind of computer memory in which information may be stored and/or erased repeatedly.

ram·ble (ram′bəl) *v.i.* **·bled, ·bling** **1** To walk about freely and aimlessly; roam. **2** To write or talk aimlessly or without sequence of ideas. **3** To proceed with turns and twists; meander. —*n.* **1** The act of rambling. **2** A meandering path; maze. [?]

ram·bler (ram′blər) *n.* **1** One who or that which rambles. **2** Any of several varieties of climbing roses.

ram·bunc·tious (ram·bungk′shəs) *adj. Informal* Difficult to control or manage; unruly. [?]

ram·e·kin (ram′ə·kin) *n.* **1** Any of various food mixtures, usu. containing cheese, baked and served in individual dishes. **2** Any small or individual baking dish. Also **ram′e·quin.** [<F *ramequin*]

ram·i·fi·ca·tion (ram′ə·fə·kā′shən) *n.* **1** The act or process of ramifying. **2** An offshoot or branch. **3** A result or consequence; ougrowth, as of an action.

ram·i·fy (ram′ə·fī) *v.t. & v.i.* **·fied, ·fy·ing** To divide or spread out into or as into branches. [<L *ramus* branch + *facere* make]

ram·jet (ram′jet′) *n.* A type of jet engine consisting of a duct whose forward motion provides compressed air which mixes with fuel that burns and provides an exhaust velocity high enough to create thrust.

ra·mose (rā′mōs, rə·mōs′) *adj.* **1** Branching. **2** Consisting of or having branches. [<L *ramus* branch]

ramp[1] (ramp) *n.* **1** An inclined passageway or roadway that connects different levels. **2** A movable stairway or passageway for entering or leaving an airplane. **3** *Archit.* A concave part at the top or cap of a railing, wall, or coping. [<F *ramper* to climb]

ramp[2] (ramp) *v.i.* **1** To rear up on the hind legs and stretch out the forepaws. **2** To act in a violent or threatening manner. —*n.* The act of ramping. [<OF *ramper* to climb]

ram·page (ram′pāj) *n.* An outbreak of boisterous or angry agitation or violence. —*v.i.* (ram·pāj′) **·paged, ·pag·ing** To rush or act violently; storm; rage [Orig. Scot.,? < RAMP[2]]

Rampant lion

ram·pant (ram′pənt) *adj.* **1** Exceeding all bounds; unrestrained; wild. **2** Widespread; unchecked, as an erroneous belief. **3** Standing on the hind legs; rearing: said of a quadruped. **4** *Her.* Standing on the hind legs, with both forelegs elevated. [<OF *ramper* to climb] —**ram′pan·cy** *n.* —**ram′pant·ly** *adv.*

ram·part (ram′pärt, -pərt) *n.* 1 The embankment surrounding a fort, on which the parapet is raised. 2 A bulwark or defense. —*v.t.* To supply with or as with ramparts; fortify. [<OF *re-* again + *emparer* prepare]

ram·pike (ram′pīk′) *n. Can.* A bare, dead tree, esp. one destroyed by fire. [?]

ram·rod (ram′rod′) *n.* 1 A rod used to compact the charge of a muzzleloading firearm. 2 A similar rod used for cleaning the barrel of a rifle, etc.

ram·shack·le (ram′shak′əl) *adj.* About to go to pieces from age and neglect. [?] —**Syn.** dilapidated, unsteady, shaky, battered.

ran (ran) *p.t.* of RUN.

ranch (ranch) *n.* 1 An establishment for rearing or grazing cattle, sheep, horses, etc., in large herds. 2 The buildings, personnel, and lands connected with it. 3 A large farm. —*v.i.* To manage or work on a ranch. [<Sp. *rancho* group eating together, mess] —**ranch′er, ranch′man** *n.*

ranch house 1 A long, one-story residence having a low-pitched roof. 2 The main house on a ranch.

ran·cid (ran′sid) *adj.* Having the bad taste or smell of spoiled fats. [<L *rancere* be rancid] —**ran·cid·i·ty** (ran·sid′ə·tē), **ran′cid·ness** *n.*

ran·cor (rang′kər) *n.* Bitter and vindictive enmity. *Brit. sp.* **ran·cour.** [<L *rancere* be rank] —**ran′cor·ous** *adj.* —**ran′cor·ous·ly** *adv.* —**ran′cor·ous·ness** *n.* —**Syn.** malice, spite, hatred, hostility.

ran·dom (ran′dəm) *n.* Lack of definite purpose or intention: now chiefly in the phrase **at random,** without careful thought, planning, intent, etc.; haphazardly. —*adj.* 1 Done or chosen without deliberation or plan; chance; casual. 2 Chosen, determined, or varying without pattern, rule, or bias. [<OF *randonner, rander* move rapidly, gallop] —**ran′dom·ly** *adv.* —**ran′dom·ness** *n.*

ra·nee (rä′nē) *n.* RANI.

rang (rang) *p.t.* of RING².

range (rānj) *n.* 1 The area over which anything moves, operates, or is distributed. 2 An extensive tract of land over which cattle, sheep, etc., roam and graze. 3 Extent or scope: the whole *range* of political influence. 4 The extent of variation of anything: the temperature *range.* 5 A line, row, or series, as of mountains. 6 The horizontal distance between a gun and its target. 7 The horizontal distance covered by a projectile. 8 The maximum distance for which an airplane, ship, vehicle, etc., can be fueled. 9 The maximum effective distance, as of a weapon. 10 *Math.* The entire set of possible values of a dependent variable. 11 A place for shooting at a mark: a rifle *range.* 12 A large cooking stove. —*adj.* Of or pertaining to a range. —*v.* **ranged, rang·ing** *v.t.* 1 To place or arrange in definite order, as in rows. 2 To assign to a class, division, or category; classify. 3 To move about or over (a region, etc.), as in exploration. 4 To put (cattle) to graze on a range. 5 To adjust or train, as a telescope or gun. —*v.i.* 6 To move over an area in a thorough, systematic manner. 7 To rove; roam. 8 To occur; extend; be found: forests *ranging* to the east. 9 To vary within specified limits. 10 To lie in the same direction, line, etc. 11 To have a specified range. [<OF *ranger* arrange <*renc* row]

rang·er (rān′jər) *n.* 1 One who or that which ranges. 2 One of a group of mounted troops that protect large tracts of country. 3 One of a herd of cattle that feeds on a range. 4 A warden employed in patrolling forest tracts. 5 *Brit.* A government official in charge of a royal forest or park. 6 One of a group of soldiers trained esp. for raiding and close combat.

rang·y (rān′jē) *adj.* **rang·i·er, rang·i·est** 1 Disposed to roam, or adapted for roving, as cattle. 2 Having long, slender limbs. 3 Roomy; spacious.

ra·ni (rä′nē) *n.* 1 The wife of a raja or prince. 2 A reigning Hindu queen or princess.

rank¹ (rangk) *n.* 1 A series of objects ranged in a line or row. 2 A degree of official standing: the *rank* of colonel. 3 A line of soldiers side by side in close order. 4 *pl.* An army; also, the common body of soldiers: to rise from the *ranks.* 5 Relative position in a scale; degree; grade: a writer of low *rank.* 6 A social class or stratum: from all *ranks* of life. 7 High degree or position: a lady of *rank.* —*v.t.* 1 To place or arrange in a rank or ranks. 2 To assign to a position or classification. 3 To outrank: Sergeants *rank* corporals. —*v.i.* 4 To hold a specified place or rank. 5 To have the highest rank or grade. [<OF *ranc, renc*]

rank² (rangk) *adj.* 1 Flourishing and luxuriant in growth: *rank* weeds. 2 Strong and disagreeable to the taste or smell. 3 Utter; total: *rank* injustice. 4 Indecent; gross; vulgar. [<OE *ranc* strong] —**rank′ly** *adv.* —**rank′ness** *n.*

rank and file 1 The common soldiers of an army. 2 Those who form the main body of any organization, as distinguished from its leaders.

rank·ing (rangk′ing) *adj.* Taking precedence (over others): a *ranking* senator, officer, etc. —**Syn.** superior, senior.

ran·kle (rang′kəl) *v.* **·kled, ·kling** *v.i.* 1 To cause continued resentment, sense of injury, etc. 2 To become irritated or inflamed. —*v.t.* 3 To irritate; embitter. [<OF *rancler*]

ran·sack (ran′sak) *v.t.* 1 To search through every part of. 2 To search for plunder; pillage. [<ON *rann* house + *sækja* seek] —**ran′sack·er** *n.*

ran·som (ran′səm) *v.t.* 1 To secure the release of (a person, property, etc.) for a required price, as from captivity or detention. 2 To set free on payment of ransom. —*n.* 1 The price paid to ransom a person or property. 2 Release purchased, as from captivity. [<L *redimere* redeem] —**ran′som·er** *n.*

rant (rant) *v.i.* 1 To speak in loud, violent, or extravagant language. —*v.t.* 2 To exclaim or utter in a ranting manner. —*n.* Declamatory and bombastic talk. [<MDu. *ranten*] —**rant′er** *n.* —**rant′ing·ly** *adv.*

rap¹ (rap) *v.* **rapped, rap·ping** *v.t.* 1 To strike sharply and quickly; hit. 2 To utter in a sharp manner: with *out.* 3 *Slang* To criticize severely. —*v.i.* 4 To strike sharp, quick blows. 5 *Slang* To have a frank discussion; talk. —*n.* 1 A sharp blow. 2 A sound caused by or as by knocking. 3 *Slang* A severe criticism. 4 *Slang* Blame or punishment, as for wrongdoing: to take the *rap.* 5 *Slang* A prison sentence. 6 *Slang* A talk; discussion. —*adj. Slang* Marked by frank discussion: a *rap* session. [Imit.] —**rap′per** *n.*

rap² (rap) *n. Informal* The least bit: I don't care a *rap.* [?]

ra·pa·cious (rə·pā′shəs) *adj.* 1 Given to plunder or rapine. 2 Greedy; grasping. 3 Subsisting on prey seized alive, as hawks, etc. [<L *rapere* seize] —**ra·pa′cious·ly** *adv.* —**ra·pac·i·ty** (rə·pas′ə·tē), **ra·pa′cious·ness** *n.*

rape¹ (rāp) *v.* **raped, rap·ing** *v.t.* 1 To commit rape on. 2 To plunder or sack (a city, etc.). —*v.i.* 3 To commit rape. —*n.* 1 The act of a man who has sexual intercourse with a woman against her will or (called **statutory rape**) with a girl below the age of consent. 2 Any unlawful sexual intercourse or sexual connection by force or threat: homosexual *rape* in prison. 3 The plundering or sacking of a city, etc. 4 Any gross violation, assault, or abuse: the *rape* of natural forests. [<L *rapere* seize] —**rap′ist** *n.*

rape² (rāp) *n.* A plant related to mustard, grown for forage. [<L *rapum* turnip]

rape oil An oil obtained from seeds of the rape, used as a lubricant, etc. Also **rape·seed oil** (rāp′sēd′).

rap·id (rap′id) *adj.* 1 Having or done with great speed; swift; fast. 2 Marked or characterized by rapidity. —*n. Usu. pl.* A swift-flowing descent in a river. [<L *rapidus* <*rapere* seize, rush] —**ra·pid·i·ty** (rə·pid′ə·tē), **rap′id·ness** *n.* —**rap′id·ly** *adv.*

rap·id-fire (rap′id·fīr′) *adj.* 1 Firing or designed to fire shots rapidly. 2 Characterized by speed: *rapid-fire* repartee. Also **rap′id-fir′ing.**

rapid transit An urban passenger railway system.

Rapier

ra·pi·er (rā′pē·ər, rāp′yər) *n.* 1 A long, pointed, two-edged sword with a large cup hilt, used in dueling, chiefly for thrusting. 2 A shorter straight sword without cutting edge and therefore used for thrusting only. [<F *rapière*]

rap·ine (rap′in) *n.* The taking of property by force, as in war. [<L *rapere* seize] **—Syn.** plunder, pillage, looting, spoiling.

rap·pel (ra·pel′) *n.* A way of lowering oneself down a vertical surface, using a rope attached at the top and to the climber's body. —*v.i.* To lower oneself using a rappel. [<F]

rap·port (rə·pôr′, -pōr′, *Fr.* rȧ·pôr′) *n.* Harmonious, sympathetic relationship; accord. **—en rapport** (äṅ rȧ·pôr′) *French* In close accord. [<F *rapporter* refer, bring back]

rap·proche·ment (rȧ·prôsh·mäṅ′) *n.* A state of harmony or reconciliation; restoration of cordial relations. [F]

rap·scal·lion (rap·skal′yən) *n.* A scamp; rascal. [Earlier *rascallion*<RASCAL]

rapt (rapt) *adj.* **1** Carried away with lofty emotion; enraptured; transported. **2** Deeply engrossed or intent. [<L *raptus,* pp. of *rapere* seize]

rap·to·ri·al (rap·tôr′ē·əl, -tō′rē-) *adj.* **1** Seizing and devouring living prey; predatory. **2** Having talons adapted for seizing prey: said esp. of hawks, vultures, eagles, owls, etc. [<L *raptus,* pp. of *rapere* seize]

rap·ture (rap′chər) *n.* **1** The state of being rapt or transported; ecstatic joy; ecstasy. **2** An expression of excessive delight. —*v.t.* **·tured, ·tur·ing** To enrapture; transport with ecstasy. **—rap′tur·ous** *adj.* **—rap′tur·ous·ly** *adv.*

rare[1] (râr) *adj.* **rar·er, rar·est 1** Occurring infrequently; not common, usual, or ordinary. **2** Excellent in quality, merit, etc. **3** Rarefied: now said chiefly of the atmosphere. [<L *rarus*] **—Syn. 2** extraordinary, distinctive, fine, choice.

rare[2] (râr) *adj.* **rar·er, rar·est** Not thoroughly cooked, as roasted or broiled meat retaining its redness and juices. [<OE *hrēre* lightly boiled]

rare·bit (râr′bit) *n.* WELSH RABBIT. [Alter. of (WELSH) RABBIT]

rare earth Any of the oxides of the rare-earth elements.

rare-earth elements The series of metallic elements comprising atomic numbers 57 through 71. See PERIODIC TABLE OF ELEMENTS. Also **rare-earth metals.**

rar·e·fy (râr′ə·fī) *v.t.* & *v.i.* **·fied, ·fy·ing 1** To make or become rare, thin, or less dense. **2** To make or become more refined, pure, subtle, etc. [<L *rarus* rare + *facere* make] **—rar′e·fac′tion** (-fak′shən) *n.* **—rar′e·fac′tive** *adj.*

rare·ly (râr′lē) *adv.* **1** Not often; infrequently. **2** With unusual excellence or effect; finely. **3** Exceptionally; extremely.

rar·ing (râr′ing) *adj. Informal* Full of enthusiasm; intensely desirous; eager: used with an infinitive: *raring* to go. [<dial. E, var. of REAR[2], to raise]

rar·i·ty (râr′ə·tē) *n. pl.* **·ties 1** The quality or state of being rare, uncommon, or infrequent. **2** That which is exceptionally valued because scarce. **3** Thinness; tenuousness.

ras·cal (ras′kəl) *n.* **1** An unscrupulous person; scoundrel. **2** A mischievous person; tease; scamp. [<OF *rasque* filth, shavings] **—ras·cal′i·ty** (-kal′ə·tē) *n.* **—ras′cal·ly** *adj.* & *adv.*

rash[1] (rash) *adj.* **1** Acting without due caution or regard of consequences; reckless. **2** Exhibiting recklessness or precipitancy. [ME *rasch*] **—rash′ly** *adv.* **—rash′ness** *n.*

rash[2] (rash) *n.* A patch of redness, itchiness, or other usu. temporary skin lesion.

rash·er (rash′ər) *n.* **1** A thin slice of meat, esp. of bacon. **2** A serving of several such slices.[?]

rasp (rasp, räsp) *n.* **1** A filelike tool having coarse, pointed projections. **2** The act or sound of rasping. —*v.t.* **1** To scrape with or as with a rasp. **2** To affect unpleasantly; irritate. **3** To utter in a rough voice. —*v.i.* **4** To grate; scrape. **5** To make a harsh, grating sound. [<OF *rasper* to scrape] **—rasp′er** *n.* **—rasp′y** *adj.* **(·i·er, ·i·est)**

rasp·ber·ry (raz′ber′ē, -bər·ē, räz′-) *n. pl.* **·ries 1** A sweet, edible fruit, composed of drupelets clustered around a fleshy receptacle. **2** Any of a genus of brambles yielding this fruit. **3** *Slang* BRONX CHEER. [Earlier *rasp, raspis* raspberry + BERRY]

rat (rat) *n.* **1** Any of a genus of long-tailed rodents of worldwide distribution, larger and more aggressive than the mouse. **2** Any of various similar animals. **3** *Slang* A contemptible person, esp. one who deserts or betrays his associates. **4** A pad over which a woman's hair is combed to give more fullness. —*v.i.* **rat·ted, rat·ting 1** To hunt rats. **2** *Slang* To desert one's party, companions, etc. **3** *Slang* To betray or inform: with *on.* [<OE *ræt*]

rat·a·ble (rā′tə·bəl) *adj.* That may be rated or valued. Also **rate′a·ble. —rat′a·bil′i·ty** *n.* **—rat′a·bly** *adv.*

ra·tan (ra·tan′) *n.* RATTAN.

ratch·et (rach′it) *n.* **1** A mechanism consisting of a notched wheel, the teeth of which engage with a pawl, permitting relative motion in one direction only. **2** The pawl or the wheel thus used. Also **ratchet wheel.** [<Ital. *rochetto* bobbin]

a. ratchet. b. pawl.

rate[1] (rāt) *n.* **1** The quantity, quality, degree, etc., of a thing in relation to units of something else: a typing *rate* of 50 words per minute. **2** A price or value, esp. the unit cost of a commodity or service: the *rate* for electricity. **3** Rank or class: to be of the first *rate.* **4** A fixed ratio: the *rate* of exchange. **5** *Brit.* A local tax on property. **—at any rate** In any case; anyhow. —*v.* **rat·ed, rat·ing** *v.t.* **1** To estimate the value or worth of; appraise. **2** To place in a certain rank or grade. **3** To consider; regard: He is *rated* as a great statesman. **4** To fix the rate for the transportation of (goods), as by rail, water, or air. —*v.i.* **5** To have rank, rating, or value. [<L *ratus,* pp. of *reri* reckon] **—rat′·r** *n.*

rate[2] (rāt) *v.t.* & *v.i.* **rat·ed, rat·ing** To reprove with vehemence; scold.[?]

rath·er (rath′ər, rä′thər) *adv.* **1** More willingly; preferably. **2** With more reason, justice, wisdom, etc.: We, *rather* than they, should leave first. **3** More accurately or precisely: my teacher, or *rather* my friend. **4** Somewhat; to a certain extent: *rather* tired. **5** On the contrary. —*interj. Chiefly Brit.* (ra′thûr′, rä′-) Most assuredly; absolutely. [<OE *hrathor* sooner]

raths·kel·ler (rath′skel·ər, räts′kel·ər) *n.* A beer hall or restaurant, often located below the street level. [<G *Rat* town hall + *Keller* cellar]

rat·i·fy (rat′ə·fī) *v.t.* **·fied, ·fy·ing** To give sanction to, esp. official sanction. [<L *ratus* fixed, reckoned + *facere* make] **—rat′i·fi·ca′tion, rat′i·fi′er** *n.* **—Syn.** confirm, approve, endorse, validate.

rat·ing (rā′ting) *n.* **1** A classification or evaluation based on a standard; grade; rank. **2** An evaluation of the financial standing of a business firm or an individual. **3** A classification of men in the armed services based on their specialties. **4** In radio and television, the popularity of a program as determined by polling public opinion. **5** Any of several classifications given a motion picture regarding the content or treatment of its subject matter.

ra·tio (rā′shō, -shē·ō) *n. pl.* **·tios 1** Relation of degree, number, etc., between two similar things; proportion; rate. **2** A fraction or indicated quotient, esp. one used to compare the magnitudes of numbers. [L, computation<*reri* think]

ra·ti·oc·i·nate (rash′ē·os′ə·nāt, -os′-, rat′ē-) *v.i.* **·nat·ed, ·nat·ing** To make a deduction from premises; reason. [<L *ratiocinari* calculate, deliberate] **—ra′ti·oc′i·na′tion, ra′ti·oc′i·na′tor** *n.* **—ra′ti·oc′i·na′tive** *adj.*

ra·tion (rash′ən, rā′shən) *n.* **1** A portion; share. **2** A fixed allowance or portion of food or provisions, as alloted daily to a soldier, etc. **3** *pl.* Food or provisions, as for an army, expedition, etc. —*v.t.* **1** To issue rations to, as an army. **2** To give out or allot in rations. [<L *ratio* computation]

ra·tion·al (rash′ən·əl) *adj.* **1** Of, pertaining to, or attained by reasoning. **2** Able to reason; mentally sound; sane. **3** Sensible; judicious. **4** *Math.* **a** Of or being a rational number. **b** Denoting an algebraic expression, as $\sqrt{x^2 - y^2}$, containing a radical that can be solved. [<L *ratio* reckoning] **—ra′tion·al′i·ty** (-al′ə·tē) *n.* **—ra′tion·al·ly** *adv.*

ra·tion·ale (rash′ən·al′) *n.* **1** A logical basis or reason for something. **2** A rational exposition of principles.

ra·tion·al·ism (rash′ən·əl·iz′əm) *n.* **1** The formation of opinions by relying upon reason alone. **2** *Philos.* The theory that truth and knowledge are attainable through reason alone rather than through experience or sense perception. **—ra′tion·al·ist** *adj., n.* **—ra′tion·al·is′tic** *adj.*

ra·tion·al·ize (rash′ən·əl·īz′) *v.* **·ized, ·iz·ing** *v.t.* **1** To explain (one's behavior) plausibly without recognizing the actual motives. **2** To explain or treat from a rationalistic point of view. **3** To make rational or reasonable. **4** *Math.*

To solve the radicals of (an expression or equation containing variables). —*v.i.* **5** To think in a rational or rationalistic manner. **6** To rationalize one's behavior. —**ra′tion·al·i·za′tion** (-ə·zā′shən, -ī·zā′shən) *n.*

rational number A number expressible as a quotient of two integers; a fraction.

rat·ite (rat′īt) *adj.* Designating any of various large, flightless birds, as ostriches, kiwis, emus, etc. [< L *ratis* raft, in ref. to lack of a keel on the sternum]

rat·line (rat′lin) *n. Naut.* One of the small ropes fastened across the shrouds of a ship, used as a ladder for going aloft or descending. Also **rat′lin** (-lin), **rat′ling** (-ling). [?]

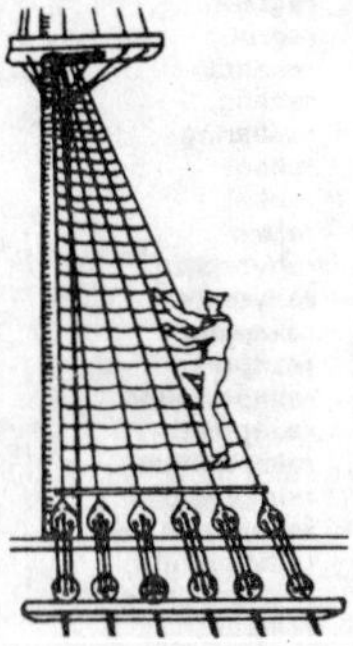

Ratlines

rat race *Slang* Frantic, usu. competitive activity or strife.

rats·bane (rats′bān′) *n.* Rat poison.

rat·tan (ra·tan′) *n.* **1** The long, tough, flexible stem of various climbing palms, used in wickerwork, etc. **2** Any of these palms. [< Malay *rotan*]

rat·ter (rat′ər) *n.* **1** A dog or cat that catches rats. **2** *Slang* A deserter or traitor.

rat·tle (rat′l) *v.* **·tled, ·tling** *v.i.* **1** To make a series of sharp noises in rapid succession. **2** To move or act with such noises. **3** To talk rapidly and foolishly; chatter. —*v.t.* **4** To cause to rattle. **5** To utter or perform rapidly or noisily. **6** *Informal* To confuse; disconcert. —*n.* **1** A series of short, sharp sounds in rapid succession. **2** A plaything, implement, etc., adapted to produce a rattling noise. **3** The series of jointed horny rings in the tail of a rattlesnake, or one of these. **4** Rapid and noisy talk; chatter. **5** A sound caused by the passage of air through mucus in the throat. [< ME *ratelen*]

rat·tle·brain (rat′l·brān′) *n.* A talkative, flighty person; foolish chatterer. Also **rat′tle·head′** (-hed′), **rat′tle·pate′** (-pāt′). —**rat′tle·brained′** *adj.*

rat·tler (rat′lər) *n.* **1** RATTLESNAKE. **2** One who or that which rattles.

rat·tle·snake (rat′l·snāk′) *n.* Any of various venomous American snakes with a tail ending in a series of horny rings that rattle when the tail is vibrated.

rat·tle·trap (rat′l·trap′) *n.* Any rickety, clattering, or worn-out vehicle or article.

rat·ty (rat′ē) *adj.* **·ti·er, ·ti·est** **1** Ratlike, or abounding in rats. **2** *Slang* Disreputable; treacherous. **3** *Slang* Rundown; shabby. —**rat′ti·ness** *n.*

rau·cous (rô′kəs) *adj.* **1** Rough in sound; hoarse; harsh. **2** Noisy and rowdy. [< L *raucus*] —**rau′cous·ly** *adv.* —**rau′cous·ness** *n.*

raunch·y (rôn′chē, rän′-) *adj. Slang* **raunch·i·er, raunch·i·est** **1** Sloppy; slovenly. **2** Sexually vulgar; lewd. **3** Lustful. [?] —**raunch′i·ly** *adv.* —**raunch′i·ness** *n.*

rav·age (rav′ij) *v.* **·aged, ·ag·ing** *v.t.* **1** To lay waste, as by pillaging or burning; despoil; ruin. —*v.i.* **2** To wreak havoc; be destructive. —*n.* Violent and destructive action, or its result; ruin. [< F *ravir* ravish] —**rav′ag·er** *n.*

rave (rāv) *v.* **raved, rav·ing** *v.i.* **1** To speak wildly or incoherently. **2** To speak with extravagant enthusiasm. **3** To make a wild, roaring sound; rage. —*v.t.* **4** To utter wildly or incoherently. —*n.* **1** The act or state of raving. **2** *Informal* A highly favorable review. —*adj. Informal* Extravagantly enthusiastic: *rave* reviews. [< L *rabere* to rage] —**Syn. 1** babble, rant, gibber.

rav·el (rav′əl) *v.* **·eled** or **·elled, ·el·ing** or **·el·ling** *v.t.* **1** To separate the threads or fibers of; unravel. **2** To make clear or plain; explain: often with *out.* —*v.i.* **3** To become separated, as threads or fibers; unravel; fray. —*n.* A raveled part or thread; a raveling. [? < MDu. *ravelen* to tangle] —**rav′el·er** or **rav′el·ler** *n.*

rav·el·ing (rav′əl·ing) *n.* A thread or threads raveled from a fabric. Also **rav′el·ling.**

ra·ven (rā′vən) *n.* A large, crowlike bird. —*adj.* Black and shining. [< OE *hræfn*]

Raven

rav·en·ing (rav′ən·ing) *adj.* **1** Seeking eagerly for prey; rapacious. **2** Mad. [< OF *raviner* ravage]

rav·en·ous (rav′ən·əs) *adj.* **1** Violently hungry; voracious. **2** Extremely eager; greedy; grasping: *ravenous* for praise. [< OF *ravine* rapine] —**rav′en·ous·ly** *adv.* —**rav′en·ous·ness** *n.*

ra·vine (rə·vēn′) *n.* A deep gorge or gully, esp. one worn by a flow of water. [F, small gully or torrent]

rav·ing (rā′ving) *adj.* **1** Furious; delirious; frenzied. **2** *Informal* Extraordinary; remarkable: a *raving* beauty. —*n.* Frenzied or irrational speech.

ra·vi·o·li (rä·vyō′lē, rä′vē·ō′lē, rav′ē-) *n.pl. (usu. construed as sing.)* Little envelopes of dough encasing meat, cheese, etc., which are boiled in broth and sauced. [Ital.]

rav·ish (rav′ish) *v.t.* **1** To fill with strong emotion, esp. delight; enrapture. **2** To rape. **3** To carry off by force. [< L *rapere* seize] —**rav′ish·er, rav′ish·ment** *n.*

rav·ish·ing (rav′ish·ing) *adj.* Very attractive, pleasing, etc. —**rav′ish·ing·ly** *adv.*

raw (rô) *adj.* **1** Not changed or prepared by cooking; uncooked. **2** In its original state or condition; not refined, processed, etc.: *raw* wool; *raw* sugar. **3** Having the skin torn or abraded: a *raw* wound. **4** Bleak; chilling: a *raw* wind. **5** Newly done; fresh: *raw* paint; *raw* work. **6** Inexperienced; undisciplined: a *raw* recruit. **7** Vulgar; off-color: a *raw* joke. **8** *Informal* Brutally harsh or unfair: a *raw* deal. —*n.* A sore or abraded spot. —**in the raw** **1** In a raw, unspoiled, or unrefined state. **2** *Informal* Nude. [< OE *hrēaw*] —**raw′ly** *adv.* —**raw′ness** *n.*

raw-boned (rô′bōnd′) *adj.* Bony; gaunt.

raw·hide (rô′hīd′) *n.* **1** An untanned cattle hide. **2** A whip made of such hide.

ray[1] (rā) *n.* **1** A narrow beam of light. **2** Any of several lines radiating from an object. **3** *Geom.* A straight line emerging from a point and extending in one direction only. **4** A slight amount or indication: a *ray* of hope. **5** *Zool.* **a** A supporting spine of a fish's fin. **b** Any of numerous parts radiating from a common center, as the arms of a starfish. **6** *Bot.* **a** RAY FLOWER. **b** One of the flower stalks of an umbel. **7** *Physics* A stream of particles or waves. —*v.i.* **1** To emit rays; shine. **2** To radiate. —*v.t.* **3** To send forth as rays. **4** To mark with rays or radiating lines. [< L *radius*]

ray[2] (rā) *n.* Any of an order of marine fishes having a cartilaginous skeleton and a horizontally flattened body, dorsally placed eyes, and a thin, usu. long tail. [< L *raia*]

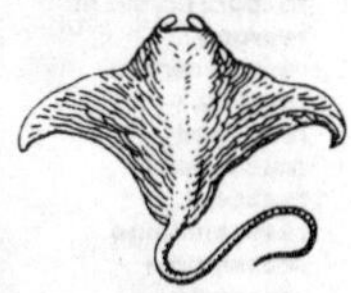

Ray

ray flower *Bot.* Any of the straplike flowers encircling certain composite flower heads, as in the daisy or sunflower. Also **ray floret.**

ray·on (rā′on) *n.* **1** A synthetic fiber made from a cellulose solution that is forced through spinnerets to produce solidified filaments. **2** A fabric made from these fibers. [F, ray; in ref. to its sheen]

raze (rāz) *v.t.* **razed, raz·ing** **1** To tear down; demolish. **2** To scrape or shave off. [< L *rasum,* pp. of *radere* scrape]

ra·zor (rā′zər) *n.* A sharp cutting implement used for shaving off the beard or hair. [< OF *raser* to scrape]

ra·zor·back (rā′zər·bak′) *n.* **1** FINBACK WHALE. **2** A lean half-wild hog of SE U.S. **3** A sharp ridge. —**ra′zor-backed′** *adj.*

razz (raz) *n. Slang* BRONX CHEER. —*v.t.* To heckle; deride. [< RASPBERRY]

raz·zle-daz·zle (raz′əl·daz′əl) *n. Slang* Any bewildering, exciting, or dazzling activity or performance. [Varied reduplication of DAZZLE]

Rb rubidium.

RBI, rbi, r.b.i. run(s) batted in.

R.C. Red Cross; Roman Catholic.

RCAF, R.C.A.F. Royal Canadian Air Force.
RCMP, R.C.M.P. Royal Canadian Mounted Police.
RCN, R.C.N. Royal Canadian Navy.
RCP, R.C.P. Royal College of Physicians.
RCS, R.C.S. Royal College of Surgeons
R.D. Rural Delivery.
R & D, R. & D., R and D research and development.
re[1] (rā) *n. Music* In solmization, the second tone of a diatonic scale. [< L *re(sonare)* resound. See GAMUT.]
re[2] (rē, rā) *prep.* Concerning; about; in the matter of: used in business letters, etc. [L, ablative of *res* thing]
re- *prefix* **1** Back: *remit* (to send back). **2** Again; anew; again and again: *regenerate.* [< L *re-, red-* back, again] • In the list of words below, *re-* is used solely to mean *again, anew, again and again.* These words are for the most part written solid. A hyphen, however, is sometimes used: **a** To prevent confusion with a similarly spelled word having a different meaning, as in *retreat* (to go back) and *re-treat* (to treat again). **b** In the formation of nonce words, as "We *reread* the contract and then *re-reread* it." Formerly, a hyphen was the rule before words beginning with *e,* as *re-edit,* but such words are now often written solid.

reabsorb
reabsorption
reaccess
reaccommodate
reaccredit
reaccuse
readapt
readdict
readdress
readjourn
readjournment
readjust
readjustment
readopt
readorn
readvance
readvertise
reaffirm
realign
realignment
reanoint
reappear
reappearance
reapply
reappoint
reappointment
reapportion
reapportionment
reargue
reargument
rearrest
reascend
reascension
reascent
reassemblage
reassemble
reassert
reassertion
reassign
reassignment
reassimilate
reassimilation
reassociate
reattach
reattachment
reattempt
reavow
reawake
reawakening
rebaptism
rebaptize
rebid
rebill
rebind
rebloom
reblossom
reboil
reborn
rebottle
rebuild
recalibrate
recapitalize
recharge
recharter
recheck
rechoose
rechristen
reclose
reclothe
recoin
recoinage
recolonize
recolor
recombination
recombine
recommence
recommission
recompose
recompute
reconcentrate
recondensation
recondense
reconfirm
reconjoin
reconquer
reconquest
reconsecrate
reconsecration
reconsign
reconsolidate
reconsolidation
reconvene
reconvey
recopy
recross
recrystallization
recrystallize
recultivate
recultivation
redecorate
rededicate
rededication
redefine
redeliberate
redeliver
redemand
redemonstrate
redeposit
redescend
redescent
redesign
redesignate
redetermine
redial
redigest
redirect
rediscover
rediscovery
redispose
redissolve
redistill
redistribute
redistribution
redivide
redo
redraft
redraw
redrive
reecho
reedit
reelect
reelection
reelevate
reembark
reembarkation
reemerge
reemergence
reemit
reemphasize
reenact
reenaction
reenactment
reencourage
reencouragement
reendow
reengage
reengagement
reengrave
reenjoy
reenjoyment
reenlist
reenlistment
reenslave
reenslavement
reenter
reenthrone
reenthronement
reentrance
reequip
reestablish
reestablishment
reevaluate
reevaluation
reexamination
reexamine
reexchange
reexhibit
reexpel
reexperience
reexport
reexportation
reexpulsion
reface
refashion
refasten
refertilize
refind
reflavor
reflight
reflorescence
reflourish
reflow
reflower
refluctuation
refold
reformulate
refortification
refortify
refreeze
refuel
refurbish
refurnish
regalvanize
regather
regerminate
regermination
regild
regrade
regraft
regrant
regroup
rehandle
rehang
rehearing
reheat
reheel
rehire
rehybridize
rehydrate
reimplant
reimport
reimportation
reimpose
reimposition
reimpress
reimprison
reinaugurate
reincorporate
reincur
reinduce
reinfect
reinfection
reinflame
reinform
reinfuse
reingratiate
reinhabit
reinjure
reinoculate
reinoculation
reinscribe
reinsert
reinsertion
reinspect
reinspection
reinspire
reinstall
reinstruct
reinsure
reintegrate
reintegration
reinter
reinterment
reintroduce
reintroduction
reinvest
reinvestigate
reinvestment
reinvigorate
reinvigoration
reinvitation
reinvite
reinvolve
reinvolvement
reissue
rekindle
reknit
reland
relaunch
relet
reliquidate
reliquidation
reload
reloan
relocate
relocation
reman
remarriage
remarry
remast
remaster
remeasure
remelt
remigrate
remigration
remilitarize
remix
remold
rename
renationalize
renavigate
renegotiate
renominate
renomination
renumber
renumerate
reobtain
reoccupation
reoccupy
reopen
reoppose
reordain
reorder
reordination
reorient
reorientation
reossify
repacify
repack
repackage
repaint
repartition
repass
repassage
repeople
rephrase
replant
replantation
replaster
repledge
replunge
repolish
repoll
repopulate
repopulation
repossess
repour
re-press
reprocess
reprogram
repropose
re-prove
republish
repurchase
repurify
reread
re-record
re-refer
re-release
resail
resale
resalute
re-search
reseat
reschool
resegregate
reseize
reseizure
resell
resensitize
reseparate
re-serve
reset
resettle
resettlement
reshape
resharpen
reshoot
reshuffle
re-sign
resite
resolder
resole
re-solve
re-sound
resow
respeak
respell
restart
restock
restoke
re-store
restrengthen
restress
restrike
resubject
resubjection
resubjugate
resubmit
resummon
resummons
resupply
resurprise
resurvey
retake
retarget
retell
retool
retrace
retrain
re-treat
retrial
retrim
retry
retune
re-turn
reunification
reunify
reurge
reuse
reutilize
reutter
revaccinate
revaccination
revaluation
revalue
revarnish
revest
re-view
revindication
revisit
reweave
reweigh
rewin
rewind
rewire
reword
rework

Re rhenium.
reach (rēch) *v.t.* **1** To stretch out or forth, as the hand. **2** To present or deliver; hand over. **3** To touch, grasp, or extend as far as: Can you *reach* the top shelf? **4** To arrive at or come to by motion or progress. **5** To achieve communication with; gain access to. **6** To amount to; total. **7** To have an influence on; affect. *—v.i.* **8** To stretch the hand, foot, etc., out or forth. **9** To attempt to touch or obtain something: He *reached* for his wallet. **10** To have extent in space, time, amount, influence, etc.: The ladder *reached* to the ceiling. **11** *Naut.* To sail on a tack with the wind on or forward of the beam. *—n.* **1** The act or power of reaching. **2** The distance one is able to reach, as with

the hand, an instrument, or missile. 3 An extent or result attained by thought, influence, etc.; scope; range. 4 An unbroken stretch, as of a stream; a vista or expanse. 5 *Naut.* The sailing, or the distance sailed, by a vessel on one tack. [< OE *ræcan*] **—reach′er** *n.*

re·act (rē·akt′) *v.i.* 1 To act in response, as to a stimulus. 2 To act in a manner contrary to some preceding act. 3 To be affected by a circumstance, influence, act, etc. 4 *Chem.* To undergo chemical change.

re-act (rē′akt′) *v.t.* To act again.

re·ac·tance (rē·ak′təns) *n. Electr.* The component of impedance that results from the presence of capacitance or inductance.

re·ac·tion (rē·ak′shən) *n.* 1 Any response, as to a stimulus, event, influence, etc. 2 A trend or tendency toward a former state of things; esp., a trend toward an earlier, usu. outmoded social, political, or economic policy or condition. 3 Any change in an organism effected by an agent, as a drug, food, allergen, etc., or an environmental condition, as heat, cold, etc. 4 *Physics* The force exerted on an agent by the body acted upon. 5 Any process involving a change in the composition or structure of an atomic nucleus, as fission, fusion, or radioactive decay. 6 *Chem.* A molecular change undergone by two or more substances in contact. **—re·ac′tion·al** *adj.* **—re·ac′tion·al·ly** *adv.*

re·ac·tion·ar·y (rē·ak′shən·er′ē) *adj.* Of, relating to, favoring, or characterized by reaction (def. 2). *—n. pl.* **·ar·ies** One who generally opposes change or liberalism in political or social matters. Also **re·ac′tion·ist.**

re·ac·ti·vate (rē·ak′tə·vāt) *v.t.* **·vat·ed, ·vat·ing** To make active or effective again. **—re·ac′ti·va′tion** *n.*

re·ac·tive (rē·ak′tiv) *adj.* 1 Tending to react, or resulting from reaction. 2 Responsive to a stimulus. **—re·ac′tive·ly** *adv.* **—re·ac′tiv′i·ty, re·ac′tive·ness** *n.*

re·ac·tor (rē·ak′tər) *n.* 1 One who or that which reacts. 2 An assembly of fissionable material, moderator, coolant, shielding, and other accessories, designed to control and utilize the energy released by atomic fission.

read (rēd) *v.* **read** (red), **read·ing** (rē′ding) *v.t.* 1 To apprehend the meaning of (a book, writing, etc.) by perceiving the form and relation of the printed or written characters. 2 To utter aloud (something printed or written). 3 To understand the significance of as if by reading: to *read* the sky. 4 To apprehend the meaning of something printed or written in (a foreign language). 5 To make a study of: to *read* law. 6 To discover the nature or significance of (a person, character, etc.) by observation or scrutiny. 7 To interpret (something read) in a specified manner. 8 To take as the meaning of something read. 9 To have or exhibit as the wording: The passage *reads* "principal," not "principle." 10 To indicate or register: The meter *reads* zero. 11 To extract (data) from storage: said of a computer or other information-retrieval system. 12 To bring into a specified condition by reading: I *read* her to sleep. *—v.i.* 13 To apprehend the characters of a book, musical score, etc. 14 To utter aloud the words or contents of a book, etc. 15 To gain information by reading: with *of* or *about.* 16 To learn by means of books; study. 17 To have a specified wording: The contract *reads* as follows. 18 To admit of being read in a specified manner. 19 To give a public reading or recital. **—read between the lines** To perceive or infer what is not expressed or obvious. **—read into** To discern (implicit meanings or implications) in a statement or position. **—read out** To expel from a religious body, political party, etc., by proclamation or concerted action. **—read up** (or **up on**) To learn by reading. *—adj.* (red) Informed by or acquainted with books or literature: *well-read.* [< OE *rædan* advise, read]

read·a·ble (rē′də·bəl) *adj.* 1 That can be read; legible. 2 Easy and pleasant to read. 3 MACHINE-READABLE. **—read′a·bil′i·ty, read′a·ble·ness** *n.* **—read′a·bly** *adv.*

read·er (rē′dər) *n.* 1 One who reads. 2 Any of various devices that provide readable images, as by projection on a screen, of material or microfilm, microcards, etc. 3 One who reads and criticizes manuscripts offered to publishers. 4 PROOFREADER. 5 A layman authorized to read the lesson in church services. 6 A professional reciter. 7 A textbook containing matter for exercises in reading.

read·ing (rē′ding) *n.* 1 The act or practice of one who reads. 2 The public recital of literary works. 3 Matter that is read or is designed to be read. 4 The datum indicated by an instrument, as a thermometer. 5 The form in which any passage or word appears in any copy of a work. 6 An interpretation, as of a musical composition. *—adj.* 1 Pertaining to or suitable for reading. 2 Inclined to read.

read·out (rēd′out′) *n.* 1 A display in intelligible form of specific items of information derived from data that have been recorded automatically or processed by computer. 2 The information so displayed.

read·y (red′ē) *adj.* **read·i·er, read·i·est** 1 Prepared for use or action. 2 Prepared in mind; willing. 3 Likely or liable: with *to: ready* to sink. 4 Quick to act, follow, occur, or appear; prompt. 5 Immediately available; convenient; handy. 6 Designating the standard position in which a rifle is held just before aiming. 7 Quick to understand; alert; quick; facile: a *ready* wit. *—n.* The position in which a rifle is held before aiming. *—v.t.* **read·ied, read·y·ing** To make ready; prepare. [< OE *ræde, geræde*] **—read′i·ly** *adv.* **—read′i·ness** *n.*

read·y-made (red′ē·mād′) *adj.* 1 Not made to order: *ready-made* clothing. 2 Not impromptu or original: *ready-made* opinions.

re·a·gent (rē·ā′jənt) *n.* Any substance used to induce a chemical reaction. [< RE- + AGENT]

re·al[1] (rē′əl, rēl) *adj.* 1 Having existence or actuality as a thing or state; not imaginary: a *real* event. 2 Not artificial or counterfeit; genuine. 3 Representing the true or actual, as opposed to the apparent or ostensible: the *real* reason. 4 Unaffected; unpretentious: a *real* person. 5 *Philos.* Having actual existence, and not merely possible, apparent, or imaginary. 6 *Law* Of or pertaining to things permanent and immovable: *real* property. 7 *Math.* Of or being a real number. *—n.* That which is real. *—adv. Informal* Very; extremely: to be *real* glad. [< Med. L *realis* < L *res* thing] **—re′al·ness** *n.*

re·al[2] (rē′əl, *Sp.* rā·äl′) *n. pl.* **re·als** or **re·a·les** (rā·ä′lās) 1 A former small silver coin of Spain. 2 *pl.* **reis** (rās) A former Portuguese and Brazilian coin; one thousandth of a milreis. [Sp., lit., royal]

real estate Land, including whatever is made part of or attached to it by man or nature, as trees, houses, etc. **—re′al-es·tate′** *adj.*

re·al·ism (rē′əl·iz′əm) *n.* 1 A disposition to deal solely with facts and reality and to reject the impractical or visionary. 2 In literature and art, the principle of depicting persons and scenes as they actually exist, without any idealization. 3 *Philos.* a The doctrine that universals or abstract concepts have actual, objective existence. b The doctrine that things have reality apart from the conscious perception of them. **—re′al·ist** *adj., n.* **—re′al·is′tic** *adj.* **—re′al·is′ti·cal·ly** *adv.*

re·al·i·ty (rē·al′ə·tē) *n. pl.* **·ties** 1 The fact, state, or quality of being real, genuine, or true to life. 2 That which is real; an actual thing, situation, or event. 3 *Philos.* The absolute or the ultimate.

re·al·ize (rē′əl·īz) *v.* **·ized, ·iz·ing** *v.t.* 1 To understand or appreciate fully. 2 To make real or concrete. 3 To cause to appear real. 4 To obtain as a profit or return. 5 To obtain money in return for: He *realized* his holdings for a profit. *—v.i.* 6 To sell property for cash. **—re′al·iz′a·ble** *adj.* **—re′al·i·za′tion, re′al·iz′er** *n.*

re·al·ly (rē′ə·lē, rē′lē) *adv.* 1 In reality; actually. 2 Truly; genuinely: a *really* fine play. *—interj.* Oh: used to express surprise, doubt, etc.

realm (relm) *n.* 1 A kingdom. 2 Domain; sphere: the *realm* of imagination. [< L *regalis* royal]

real number A number whose square is greater than or equal to zero.

re·al·tor (rē′əl·tər, -tôr) *n.* 1 A person engaged in the real-estate business. 2 *Usu. cap.* A member of the National Association of Real Estate Boards: a trade name.

re·al·ty (rē′əl·tē) *n. pl.* **·ties** REAL ESTATE.

ream[1] (rēm) *n.* 1 A quantity of paper equal to 20 quires and consisting of 480, 500, or 516 sheets. 2 *pl. Informal* A prodigious amount. [< Ar. *rizmah* packet]

ream[2] (rēm) *v.t.* 1 To increase the size of (a hole), as with a rotating cutter or reamer. 2 To get rid of (a defect) by reaming. [< OE *rēman* enlarge, make room]

ream·er (rē′mər) *n.* 1 One who or that which reams. 2 A rotary tool with cutting edges for reaming. 3 A device with a ridged cone for extracting juice from citrus fruits.

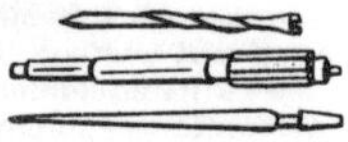

Reamers

re·an·i·mate (rē·an′ə·māt) *v.t.* **·mat·ed, ·mat·ing** 1 To bring back to life; resuscitate. 2 To revive; encourage. **—re′an·i·ma′tion** *n.*

reap (rēp) *v.t.* 1 To cut and gather (grain) with a scythe, reaper, etc. 2 To harvest a crop from: to *reap* a field. 3 To obtain as the result of action or effort. *—v.i.* 4 To harvest grain, etc. 5 To receive a return or result. [< OE *repan*] **—reap′a·ble** *adj.* **—reap′ing** *n.*

reap·er (rē′pər) *n.* 1 One who reaps. 2 A machine for reaping grain.

rear[1] (rir) *n.* 1 The back or hind part. 2 A place or position at the back of or behind anything. 3 That division of a military force which is farthest from the front. *—adj.* Being in the rear. [< ARREAR]

rear[2] (rir) *v.t.* 1 To place upright; raise. 2 To build; erect. 3 To care for and bring to maturity. 4 To breed or grow. *—v.i.* 5 To rise upon its hind legs, as a horse. 6 To rise high; tower, as a mountain. [< OE *ræran* set upright] **—rear′er** *n.*

rear admiral See GRADE.

rear guard A body of troops to protect the rear of an army.

re·arm (rē·ärm′) *v.t. & v.i.* 1 To arm again. 2 To arm with more modern weapons. **—re·ar′ma·ment** *n.*

rear·most (rir′mōst′) *adj.* Coming or stationed last.

re·ar·range (rē′ə·ranj′) *v.t. & v.i.* **·ranged, ·rang·ing** To arrange again or in some new way. **—re′ar·range′ment** *n.* **—Syn.** reorder, redispose, reorganize, readjust.

rear·ward (rir′wərd) *adj.* Coming last or toward the rear; hindward. *—adv.* Toward or at the rear; backward: also **rear′wards.** *—n.* The rear; end.

rea·son (rē′zən) *n.* 1 A motive or basis for an action, opinion, etc. 2 A statement which explains or accounts for an action, belief, etc. 3 The ability to think logically and rationally. 4 Sound thinking or judgment; common sense. 5 Sanity. **—by reason of** Because of. **—in** (or **within**) **reason** Within reasonable limits or bounds. **—it stands to reason** It is logical. **—with reason** Justifiably. *—v.i.* 1 To think logically; obtain inferences or conclusions from known or presumed facts. 2 To talk or argue logically. *—v.t.* 3 To think out carefully and logically; analyze: with *out.* 4 To influence or persuade by means of reason. 5 To argue; debate. [< L *ratio* computation] **—rea′son·er** *n.*

rea·son·a·ble (rē′zən·ə·bəl, rēz′nə-) *adj.* 1 Conformable to reason. 2 Having the faculty of reason; rational. 3 Governed by reason. 4 Not extreme or excessive; moderate. **—rea′son·a·bil′i·ty, rea′son·a·ble·ness** *n.* **—rea′son·a·bly** *adv.*

rea·son·ing (rē′zən·ing) *n.* 1 The act or process of using one's rational faculties to draw conclusions from known or assumed facts. 2 The reasons or proofs resulting from this process.

re·as·sure (rē′ə·shŏŏr′) *v.t.* **·sured, ·sur·ing** 1 To restore to courage or confidence. 2 To assure again. 3 To reinsure. **—re′as·sur′ance** *n.* **—re′as·sur′ing·ly** *adv.*

re·bate (rē′bāt, ri·bāt′) *v.t.* **·bat·ed, ·bat·ing** 1 To allow as a deduction. 2 To make a deduction from. *—n.* A deduction from a gross amount; discount: also **re·bate′·ment.** [< OF *rabattre* beat down] **—re′bat·er** *n.*

re·bec (rē′bek) *n.* A medieval bowed instrument, somewhat like a violin. Also **re′beck.** [< Ar. *rabāb*]

Rebec

Re·bec·ca (ri·bek′ə) In the Bible, wife of Isaac and mother of Esau and Jacob.

re·bel (ri·bel′) *v.i.* **·belled, ·bel·ling** 1 To resist or fight against any authority, established custom, etc. 2 To react with violent aversion: usu. with *at.* *—n.* (reb′əl) One who rebels. *—adj.* (reb′əl) 1 Rebellious; refractory. 2 Of rebels. [< L *re-* again + *bellare* make war]

re·bel·lion (ri·bel′yən) *n.* 1 The act of rebelling. 2 Organized resistance to a government or to any lawful authority.

re·bel·lious (ri·bel′yəs) *adj.* 1 Being in a state of rebellion; insubordinate. 2 Of or pertaining to a rebel or rebellion. 3 Resisting control; refractory: a *rebellious* temper. **—re·bel′lious·ly** *adv.* **—re·bel′lious·ness** *n.*

re·birth (rē·bûrth′, rē′bûrth′) *n.* 1 A new birth. 2 A revival or renaissance.

re·bound (ri·bound′) *v.i.* 1 To bounce or spring back after or as after hitting something. 2 To recover, as from a difficulty. 3 To reecho. *—v.t.* 4 To cause to rebound. *—n.* (rē′bound′, ri·bound′) 1 A bounding back; recoil. 2 Something that rebounds, as a basketball from a backboard. 3 Reaction after a disappointment: to fall in love on the *rebound.* [< F *re-* back + *bondir* bound]

re·broad·cast (rē·brôd′kast′, -käst′) *v.t.* **·cast** or **·cast·ed, ·cast·ing** To broadcast (the same program) again. *—n.* A program so transmitted.

re·buff (ri·buf′) *v.t.* 1 To reject or refuse abruptly or rudely. 2 To drive or beat back; repel. *—n.* 1 A sudden repulse; curt denial. 2 A sudden check; defeat. 3 A beating back. [< Ital. *ribuffare*]

re·buke (ri·byŏŏk′) *v.t.* **·buked, ·buk·ing** To reprove sharply; reprimand. *—n.* A strong expression of disapproval. [< OF *re-* back + *bucher* beat] **—re·buk′er** *n.*

re·bus (rē′bəs) *n.* A representation of a word, phrase, or sentence by letters, numerals, pictures, etc., whose names suggest the same sounds as the words or phrases they represent. [L, ablative pl. of *res* thing]

Rebus meaning *I can see.*

re·but (ri·but′) *v.t.* **·but·ted, ·but·ting** To dispute or show the falsity of, as by argument or by contrary evidence. [< OF *re-* back + *bouter* push, strike] **—re·but′ter** *n.* **—Syn.** disprove, refute, contradict.

re·but·tal (ri·but′l) *n.* The act of rebutting; refutation.

rec. receipt; recipe; record; recording.

re·cal·ci·trant (ri·kal′sə·trənt) *adj.* Not complying; obstinate; rebellious; refractory. *—n.* One who is recalcitrant. [< L *re-* back + *calcitrare* to kick] **—re·cal′ci·trance, re·cal′·ci·tran·cy** *n.*

re·call (ri·kôl′) *v.t.* 1 To call back; order or summon to return. 2 To summon back in awareness or attention. 3 To recollect; remember. 4 To take back; revoke; countermand. *—n.* (ri·kôl′, rē′kôl′) 1 A calling back. 2 An ability to remember. 3 Revocation, as of an order. 4 A system whereby public officials may be removed from office by popular vote.

re·cant (ri·kant′) *v.t.* 1 To withdraw formally one's belief in (something previously believed or maintained). *—v.i.* 2 To disavow an opinion or belief previously held. [< L *re-* again + *cantare* sing] **—re·can·ta·tion** (rē′kan·tā′shən), **re·cant′er** *n.*

re·cap[1] (rē′kap′, rē·kap′) *v.t.* **·capped, ·cap·ping** 1 To provide (a worn pneumatic tire) with a tread of new rubber. 2 To replace a cap on. *—n.* (rē′kap′) A tire which has been so treated. [< RE- + CAP]

re·cap[2] (rē′kap′) *v.t. & v.i.* **·capped, ·cap·ping** RECAPITULATE. *—n.* RECAPITULATION (def. 2).

re·ca·pit·u·late (rē′kə·pich′ŏŏ·lāt) *v.t. & v.i.* **·lat·ed, ·lat·ing** To restate or review briefly; sum up. [< LL *re-* again + *capitulare* draw up in chapters]

re·ca·pit·u·la·tion (rē′kə·pich′ŏŏ·lā′shən) *n.* 1 The act of recapitulating. 2 A brief summary. **—re′ca·pit′u·la′tive, re′·ca·pit′u·la·to′ry** (-lə·tôr′ē, -tō′rē) *adj.*

re·cap·ture (rē·kap′chər) *v.t.* **·tured, ·tur·ing** 1 To capture again. 2 To recall; remember. *—n.* The act of recapturing or the state of being recaptured.

re·cast (rē·kast′, -käst′) *v.t.* **·cast, ·cast·ing** 1 To form anew; cast again. 2 To fashion anew by changing style, arrangement, etc., as a sentence. 3 To calculate anew. *—n.* (rē′kast′, -käst′) Something which has been recast.

recd. received.
re·cede (ri·sēd′) *v.i.* **·ced·ed, ·ced·ing** 1 To move back; withdraw, as flood waters. 2 To withdraw, as from an assertion, position, agreement, etc. 3 To slope backward: a *receding* forehead. 4 To become more distant or smaller. [< L *re-* back + *cedere* go]
re-cede (rē′sēd′) *v.t.* **-ced·ed, -ced·ing** To cede back; grant or yield to a former owner.
re·ceipt (ri·sēt′) *n.* 1 The act or state of receiving anything: to be in *receipt* of good news. 2 *Usu. pl.* That which is received: cash *receipts.* 3 A written acknowledgment of the payment of money, of the delivery of goods, etc. 4 RECIPE. —*v.t.* 1 To give a receipt for the payment of. 2 To write acknowledgment of payment on, as a bill. —*v.i.* 3 To give a receipt, as for money paid. [< L *receptus,* pp. of *recipere* take back, receive]
re·ceiv·a·ble (ri·sē′və·bəl) *adj.* 1 Capable of being received; fit to be received, as legal tender. 2 Due to be paid. —*n. pl.* Outstanding accounts listed as business assets.
re·ceive (ri·sēv′) *v.* **·ceived, ·ceiv·ing** *v.t.* 1 To take into one's hand or possession (something given, offered, delivered, etc.). 2 To gain knowledge or information of. 3 To take from another by hearing or listening. 4 To bear; support. 5 To experience; meet with: to *receive* abuse. 6 To undergo; suffer: He *received* a wound in his arm. 7 To contain; hold. 8 To allow entrance to; admit; greet. 9 To perceive mentally: to *receive* a bad impression. 10 To regard in a specified way: The play was well *received.* —*v.i.* 11 To be a recipient. 12 To welcome visitors or callers. 13 *Telecom.* To convert incoming signals, as radio waves, into intelligible sounds or shapes, as in a radio or television set. [< L *re-* back + *capere* take]
re·ceived (ri·sēvd′) *adj. Chiefly Brit.* Accepted by established opinion or authority; standard.
re·ceiv·er (ri·sē′vər) *n.* 1 One who receives; a recipient. 2 An official assigned to receive money due. 3 *Law* A person appointed by a court to take into his custody the property or funds of another pending litigation. 4 One who knowingly buys or receives stolen goods. 5 Something which receives; a receptacle. 6 *Telecom.* An instrument designed to receive electric or electromagnetic signals and process them or transmit them to another stage.
re·ceiv·er·ship (ri·sē′vər·ship) *n.* 1 The office and functions pertaining to a receiver. 2 *Law* The state of being in the hands of a receiver.
re·cent (rē′sənt) *adj.* 1 Of or pertaining to a time not long past. 2 Occurring, formed, or characterized by association with a time not long past; modern; fresh; new. [< L *recens*] —**re′cent·ly** *adv.* —**re′cen·cy, re′cent·ness** *n.*
Re·cent (rē′sənt) *adj. & n.* See GEOLOGY.
re·cep·ta·cle (ri·sep′tə·kəl) *n.* 1 Anything that serves to contain or hold other things. 2 *Bot.* The base on which the parts of a flower grow. 3 An electric outlet. [< L *receptare,* freq. of *recipere* receive]
re·cep·tion (ri·sep′shən) *n.* 1 The act of receiving, or the state of being received. 2 A formal social entertainment of guests: a wedding *reception.* 3 The manner of receiving a person or persons: a warm *reception.* 4 *Telecom.* The act or process of receiving or, esp., the quality of reproduction achieved: poor radio *reception.*
re·cep·tion·ist (ri·sep′shən·ist) *n.* A person employed to receive callers, etc., as in a place of business.
re·cep·tive (ri·sep′tiv) *adj.* 1 Able or inclined to receive favorably: *receptive* to new ideas. 2 Able to contain or hold. —**re·cep′tive·ly** *adv.* —**re·cep·tiv·i·ty** (rē′sep·tiv′ə·tē), **re·cep′tive·ness** *n.*
re·cep·tor (ri·sep′tər) *n.* A sensory nerve ending adapted to receiving stimuli. [L, receiver]
re·cess (rē′ses, ri·ses′) *n.* 1 A depression or indentation in any otherwise continuous line or surface, esp. in a wall; niche. 2 A time of cessation from employment or occupation. 3 *Usu. pl.* A quiet and secluded spot; withdrawn or inner place: the *recesses* of the mind. —*v.* (*usu.* ri·ses′) *v.t.* 1 To place in or as in a recess. 2 To make a recess in. 3 To interrupt for a recess. —*v.i.* 4 To take a recess. [< L *recessus,* pp. of *recedere* go back]
re·ces·sion (ri·sesh′ən) *n.* 1 The act of receding; a withdrawal. 2 The procession of the clergy, choir, etc., as they leave the chancel after a church service. 3 A temporary economic setback occurring during a period of generally rising prosperity.
re-ces·sion (rē′sesh′ən) *n.* The act of ceding back, as to a former owner.
re·ces·sion·al (ri·sesh′ən·əl) *adj.* Of or pertaining to recession. —*n.* A hymn sung as the choir or clergy leave the chancel.
re·ces·sive (ri·ses′iv) *adj.* 1 Having a tendency to recede or go back. 2 *Genetics* Designating a hereditary factor that remains latent unless it is present in both members of a pair of chromosomes. —*n. Genetics* 1 A recessive factor or trait. 2 An organism having such factors or traits. —**re·ces′sive·ly** *adv.* —**re·ces′sive·ness** *n.*
re·cher·ché (rə·sher·shā′) *adj.* 1 Much sought after; choice; rare. 2 Elegant or refined, usu. to an excessive degree. [F]
re·cid·i·vism (rə·sid′ə·viz′əm) *n.* A tendency to relapse into a former state or condition, esp. into crime. [< L *recidivus* falling back] —**re·cid′i·vist** *adj., n.* —**re·cid′i·vis′tic, re·cid′i·vous** *adj.*
rec·i·pe (res′ə·pē) *n.* 1 A list of ingredients and directions for combining them, as in cooking, pharmacy, etc. 2 The means prescribed for attaining an end. [< L, imperative of *recipere* take]
re·cip·i·ent (ri·sip′ē·ənt) *adj.* Receiving or ready to receive; receptive. —*n.* One who or that which receives. —**re·cip′i·ence, re·cip′i·en·cy** *n.*
re·cip·ro·cal (ri·sip′rə·kəl) *adj.* 1 Done or given by each of two to the other; mutual. 2 Mutually interchangeable. 3 Related or corresponding, but in an inverse manner; opposite. 4 *Gram.* Expressive of mutual relationship or action: *One another* is a *reciprocal* phrase. 5 *Math.* Having a product of 1, as a pair of numbers. —*n.* 1 That which is reciprocal. 2 *Math.* Either of a pair of numbers having 1 as their product. [< L *reciprocus*] —**re·cip′ro·cal·ly** *adv.*
re·cip·ro·cate (ri·sip′rə·kāt) *v.* **·cat·ed, ·cat·ing** *v.t.* 1 To cause to move backward and forward alternately. 2 To give and receive mutually; interchange. 3 To give, feel, do, etc., in return. —*v.i.* 4 To move backward and forward. 5 To make a return in kind. 6 To give and receive favors, gifts, etc., mutually. [< L *reciprocare* move to and fro] —**re·cip′ro·ca′tion, re·cip′ro·ca′tor** *n.* —**re·cip′ro·ca′tive, re·cip′ro·ca·to′ry** (-kə·tôr′ē, -kə·tō′rē) *adj.*
rec·i·proc·i·ty (res′ə·pros′ə·tē) *n.* 1 Reciprocal obligation, action, or relation. 2 A trade relation between two countries by which each makes concessions favoring the importation of the products of the other.
re·cit·al (ri·sīt′l) *n.* 1 A retelling in detail of an event, etc.; a narration; also, that which is retold. 2 A public delivery of something memorized. 3 A musical or dance program by a single performer or by a small group.
rec·i·ta·tion (res′ə·tā′shən) *n.* 1 The act of publicly reciting something that has been memorized. 2 That which is recited. 3 The reciting of a lesson in school or the time during a class when this takes place.
rec·i·ta·tive (res′ə·tə·tēv′, rə·sit′ə·tiv) *n. Music* 1 A style of singing that approaches ordinary speech in its rhythms and lack of melodic variation, used in opera and oratorio. 2 A passage so sung. Also *Italian* **re·ci·ta·ti·vo** (rā′chē·tä·tē′vō) —*adj.* Having the character of a recitative. [< Ital. *recitativo*]
re·cite (ri·sīt′) *v.* **·cit·ed, ·cit·ing** *v.t.* 1 To declaim or say from memory, esp. formally, as in public or in a class. 2 To tell in particular detail; relate. 3 To enumerate. —*v.i.* 4 To declaim or speak something from memory. 5 To repeat or be examined in a lesson or part of a lesson in class. [< L *re-* again + *citare* cite] —**re·cit′er** *n.*
reck (rek) *v.t. & v.i. Archaic* 1 To heed; mind. 2 To be of concern or interest (to). [< OE *rēccan*]
reck·less (rek′lis) *adj.* 1 Foolishly heedless of danger; rash. 2 Careless; irresponsible. [< OE *recceléas*] —**reck′less·ly** *adv.* —**reck′less·ness** *n.*
reck·on (rek′ən) *v.t.* 1 To count; compute; calculate. 2 To

look upon as being; regard. 3 *Regional* To suppose or guess; expect. —*v.i.* 4 To make computation; count up. 5 To rely or depend: with *on* or *upon.* —**reckon with** 1 To settle accounts with. 2 To take into consideration; consider. [< OE *recenian* explain] —**reck′on·er** *n.*

reck·on·ing (rek′ən·ing) *n.* 1 The act of counting; computation. 2 A settlement of accounts. 3 Account; bill, as at a hotel. 4 An appraisal or estimate. 5 *Naut.* The calculation of a ship's position.

re·claim (ri·klām′) *v.t.* 1 To bring (a swamp, desert, etc.) into a condition to support cultivation or life, as by draining or irrigating. 2 To obtain (a substance) from used or waste products. 3 To cause to reform. —*n.* The act of reclaiming or state of being reclaimed. [< L *re-* against + *clamare* cry out] —**re·claim′a·ble** *adj.* —**re·claim′er, re·claim′ant** *n.*

re-claim (rē′klām′) *v.t.* To claim again.

rec·la·ma·tion (rek′lə·mā′shən) *n.* 1 The act of reclaiming. 2 Restoration, as to ownership, usefulness, etc.

re·cline (ri·klīn′) *v.t.* & *v.i.* **·clined, ·clin·ing** To assume or cause to assume a recumbent position; lie or lay down or back. [< L *re-* back + *clinare* lean] —**rec·li·na·tion** (rek′lə·nā′shən), **re·clin′er** *n.*

rec·luse (rek′lo͞os, ri·klo͞os′) *n.* One who lives in solitude and seclusion; hermit. —*adj.* Secluded or retired from the world. [< L *recludere* shut off] —**re·clu′sion** *n.* —**re·clu′sive** *adj.*

rec·og·ni·tion (rek′əg·nish′ən) *n.* 1 The act of recognizing or the condition of being recognized. 2 Special notice or acknowledgment; attention: His work has received much *recognition.* 3 Acknowledgment and acceptance on the part of one government of the independence and validity of another. —**re·cog·ni·to·ry** (ri·kog′nə·tôr′ē, -tō′rē), **re·cog′ni·tive** *adj.*

re·cog·ni·zance (ri·kog′nə·zəns, -kon′ə-) *n. Law* 1 An acknowledgment or obligation of record, with condition to do some particular act, as to appear and answer. 2 A sum of money deposited as surety for fulfillment of such act or obligation, and forfeited by its nonperformance. [< L *recognoscere* call to mind] —**re·cog′ni·zant** *adj.*

rec·og·nize (rek′əg·nīz) *v.t.* **·nized, ·niz·ing** 1 To perceive as identical with someone or something previously known. 2 To identify or know, as by previous experience or knowledge: I *recognize* the symptoms. 3 To perceive as true; realize: I *recognize* my error. 4 To acknowledge the independence and validity of, as a newly constituted government. 5 To indicate appreciation or approval of. 6 To regard as valid or genuine: to *recognize* a claim. 7 To give (someone) permission to speak, as in a legislative body. 8 To admit the acquaintance of; greet. [Back formation < RECOGNIZANCE] —**rec·og·niz·a·ble** (rek′əg·nīz′ə·bəl) *adj.* —**rec′og·niz′a·bly** *adv.* —**rec′og·niz′er** *n.* —**Syn.** 3 acknowledge, admit, allow.

re·coil (ri·koil′) *v.i.* 1 To start back, as in fear or loathing; shrink. 2 To spring back, as from force of discharge or impact. 3 To return to the source; react: with *on* or *upon.* 4 To move; retreat. —*n.* (rē′koil′) 1 A backward movement or impulse, as of a gun at the moment of firing. 2 A shrinking. [< OF *reculer*] —**re·coil′er** *n.*

re-coil (rē′koil′) *v.t.* & *v.i.* To coil again.

rec·ol·lect (rek′ə·lekt′) *v.t.* 1 To call back to the mind; remember. —*v.i.* 2 To have a recollection of something. [< L *recollectus,* pp. of *recolligere* gather together again]

re-col·lect (rē′kə·lekt′) *v.t.* 1 To collect again, as things scattered. 2 To collect or recover (one's thoughts, strength, etc.). 3 To compose (oneself). Also, for defs. 2 & 3, **rec·ol·lect** (rek′ə·lekt′). —**re′-col·lec′tion** *n.*

rec·ol·lec·tion (rek′ə·lek′shən) *n.* 1 The act or power of recollecting. 2 Something remembered. —**rec′ol·lec′tive** *adj.* —**rec′ol·lec′tive·ly** *adv.* —**rec′ol·lec′tive·ness** *n.*

rec·om·mend (rek′ə·mend′) *v.t.* 1 To commend or praise as desirable, worthy, etc. 2 To make attractive or acceptable. 3 To advise; urge. 4 To give in charge; commend. —**rec′om·mend′a·ble, rec′om·men′da·to′ry** (-də·tôr′ē, -tōr′ē) *adj.* —**rec′om·mend′er** *n.*

rec·om·men·da·tion (rek′ə·mən·dā′shən, -men-) *n.* 1 The act of recommending. 2 Something that recommends, as a letter or statement.

re·com·mit (rē′kə·mit′) *v.t.* **·mit·ted, ·mit·ting** 1 To commit again. 2 To refer back to a committee, as a bill. —**re′com·mit′ment, re′com·mit′tal** *n.*

rec·om·pense (rek′əm·pens) *v.t.* **·pensed, ·pens·ing** 1 To give compensation to; pay or repay; reward. 2 To give compensation for, as a loss. —*n.* An equivalent for anything given, done, or suffered; payment; compensation; reward. [< L *re-* again + *compensare* compensate]

rec·on·cil·a·ble (rek′ən·sī′lə·bəl, rek′ən·sī′-) *adj.* Capable of being reconciled, adjusted, or harmonized. —**rec′on·cil′a·bil′i·ty, rec′on·cil′a·ble·ness** *n.* —**rec′on·cil′a·bly** *adv.*

rec·on·cile (rek′ən·sīl) *v.t.* **·ciled, ·cil·ing** 1 To bring back to friendship after estrangement. 2 To settle or adjust, as a quarrel. 3 To bring to acquiescence, content, or submission. 4 To make or show to be consistent or congruous; harmonize. [< L *re-* again + *conciliare* unite] —**rec′on·cile′ment, rec′on·cil′er, rec·on·cil·i·a·tion** (rek′ən·sil′ē·a′·shən) *n.* —**rec′on·cil′i·a·to′ry** (-sil′ē·ə·tôr′ē, -tō′rē) *adj.*

rec·on·dite (rek′ən·dīt, ri·kon′dīt) *adj.* 1 Beyond ordinary or easy understanding or perception; abstruse. 2 Dealing in difficult matters. 3 Hidden; obscure. [< L *recondere* put away, hide] —**rec′on·dite′ly** *adv.* —**rec′on·dite′·ness** *n.*

re·con·di·tion (rē·kən·dish′ən) *v.t.* To put back into good or working condition, as by making repairs.

re·con·nais·sance (ri·kon′ə·səns, -säns) *n.* 1 An exploratory examination or survey, as of territory. 2 *Mil.* The act of obtaining information regarding the position, strength, and movement of enemy forces. [F]

re·con·noi·ter (rē′kə·noi′tər, rek′ə-) *v.t.* 1 To examine or survey, as for military, engineering, or geological purposes. —*v.i.* 2 To make a reconnaissance. *Brit. sp.* **·noi′tre.** [< OF *reconoistre*] —**re′con·noi′ter·er, re′con·noi′trer** *n.*

re·con·sid·er (rē′kən·sid′ər) *v.t.* & *v.i.* To consider again, esp. with a view to a reversal of a previous action. —**re′·con·sid′er·a′tion** *n.*

re·con·sti·tute (rē·kon′stə·to͞ot) *v.t.* **·tut·ed, ·tut·ing** To constitute again, esp. to add water to a dehydrated or condensed substance. —**re·con′sti·tu′tion** *n.*

re·con·struct (rē′kən·strukt′) *v.t.* To construct again. —**Syn.** rebuild, refashion, reestablish, remodel.

re·con·struc·tion (rē′kən·struk′shən) *n.* 1 The act of reconstructing. 2 Something reconstructed. 3 *Usu. cap.* **a** The restoration of the seceded s States as members of the Union after the American Civil War. **b** The period of this restoration, from 1867–1877. —**re′con·struc′tive** *adj.*

re·con·vert (rē′kən·vûrt′) *v.t.* To change back, as to a former condition, form, religion, etc. —**re′con·ver′sion** (-vûr′zhən) *n.*

rec·ord (rek′ərd) *n.* 1 An account in written or other permanent form serving as evidence of a fact or event. 2 Something on which such an account is made, as a monument. 3 Information preserved and handed down: the heaviest rainfall on *record.* 4 The known career or performance of a person, animal, organization, etc. 5 The best listed achievement, as in a competitive sport. 6 *Law* **a** A written account of an act, statement, or transaction made by an officer acting under authority of law. **b** An official written account of a judicial or legislative proceeding. 7 A disk or cylinder, grooved so as to reproduce sounds that have been registered on its surface. —**go on record** To state publically or officially. —**off the record** Not for quotation or publication. —*adj.* Surpassing any previously recorded achievement or performance of its kind. —**re·cord** (ri·kôrd′) *v.t.* 1 To write down or otherwise inscribe, as for preservation, evidence, etc. 2 To indicate; register. 3 To offer evidence of. 4 To register and make permanently reproducible, as on tape, a phonograph record, etc. —*v.i.* 5 To record something. [< L *recordari* call to mind]

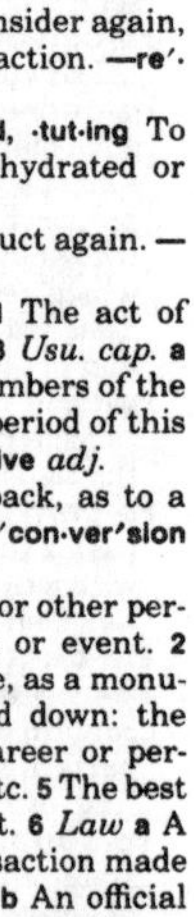

Recorder *def. 3*

re·cord·er (ri·kôr′dər) *n.* 1 One who records. 2 A magistrate having criminal jurisdiction in a city or borough. 3 A type of flute blown at one end. 4 A device that records, as a tape recorder.

re·cord·ing (ri·kôr′ding) *n.* 1 The act or process of making a representation from which sound, video, data, etc., can be reproduced. 2 The material so represented.

record player A machine for reproducing sound from a record (def. 7).
re·count[1] (ri·kount′) *v.t.* **1** To relate the particulars of; narrate in detail. **2** To enumerate; recite. [< OF *reconter* relate] **—re·count′er** *n.*
re·count[2] (rē′kount′) *v.t.* To count again. **—***n.* (rē′kount′) An additional count, esp. a second count of votes cast.
re·count·al (ri·koun′təl) *n.* A detailed narrative.
re·coup (ri·ko͞op′) *v.t.* **1** To recover or make up for, as a loss. **2** To regain, as health. **3** To repay or reimburse. **—***n.* The act of recouping. [< F *re-* again + *couper* to cut] **—re·coup′a·ble** *adj.* **—re·coup′ment** *n.*
re·course (rē′kôrs, -kōrs, ri·kôrs′, -kōrs′) *n.* **1** Resort to or application for help or security in trouble. **2** The person or thing resorted to. [< L *recursus* a running back]
re·cov·er (ri·kuv′ər) *v.t.* **1** To obtain again, as after losing; regain. **2** To make up for; retrieve, as a loss. **3** To restore (oneself) to natural balance, health, etc. **4** To reclaim, as land. **5** *Law* To gain or regain in judicial proceedings. **—***v.i.* **6** To regain health, composure, etc. **7** *Law* To succeed in a lawsuit. [< L *recuperare*] **—re·cov′er·a·ble** *adj.*
re-cov·er (rē′kuv′ər) *v.t.* To cover again.
re·cov·er·y (ri·kuv′ər·ē) *n. pl.* **·er·ies** **1** The act, process, or an instance of recovering. **2** The duration of recovering. **3** Restoration from sickness or from any undesirable or abnormal condition. **4** The extraction of usable substances and materials from byproducts, waste, etc. **5** The retrieval of a flying object, as a balloon, space vehicle, meteorite, etc., after it has fallen to earth.
rec·re·ant (rek′rē·ənt) *adj.* **1** Unfaithful to a cause or pledge; false. **2** Craven; cowardly. **—***n.* A cowardly or faithless person; also, a deserter. [< L *re-* back + *credere* believe] **—rec′re·ance, rec′re·an·cy** *n.* **—rec′re·ant·ly** *adv.*
rec·re·ate[1] (rek′rē·āt) *v.* **·at·ed, ·at·ing** *v.t.* **1** To impart fresh vigor to; refresh, esp. after toil. **—***v.i.* **2** To take recreation. [< L *recreare* create anew] **—rec′re·a′tive** *adj.*
re-cre·ate[2] (rē′krē·āt′) *v.t.* **·at·ed, ·at·ing** To create anew. **—re′cre·a′tion** *n.*
rec·re·a·tion (rek′rē·ā′shən) *n.* **1** Refreshment of body or mind, esp. after work; diversion; amusement. **2** Any pleasurable exercise or occupation. **—rec′re·a′tion·al** *adj.*
re·crim·i·nate (ri·krim′ə·nāt) *v.* **·nat·ed, ·nat·ing** *v.t.* **1** To accuse in return. **—***v.i.* **2** To repel one accusation by making another in return. [< L *re-* again + *criminare* accuse] **—re·crim′i·na′tor** *n.* **—re·crim′i·na′tive, re·crim·i·na·to·ry** (ri·krim′ə·nə·tôr′ē, -tō′rē) *adj.*
re·crim·in·a·tion (ri·krim′ə·nā′shən) *n.* **1** The act of recriminating. **2** An accusation made in response to another.
re·cru·desce (rē′kro͞o·des′) *v.i.* **·desced, ·desc·ing** To reappear after lying dormant. [< L *re-* again + *crudescere* become harsh, break out] **—re′cru·des′cence** *n.* **—re′cru·des′cent** *adj.*
re·cruit (ri·kro͞ot′) *v.t.* **1** To enlist (men or women) for service, as in a military organization or a police force. **2** To muster; raise, as an army, by enlistment. **3** To enlist the aid, services, or support of: to *recruit* new members for a political party. **4** To replenish. **—***v.i.* **5** To enlist new personnel for service, as in an army or other organization. **6** To gain or raise new supplies of anything lost or needed. **—***n.* **1** A newly enlisted person, as a soldier or sailor. **2** Any new adherent of a cause, organization, or the like. [< F *recrute*] **—re·cruit′er, re·cruit′ment** *n.*
rec. sec. recording secretary.
rect. receipt; rectangle; rector; rectory.
rec·tal (rek′təl) *adj.* Pertaining to, for, or in the region of the rectum.
rec·tan·gle (rek′tang′gəl) *n.* A parallelogram with all angles right angles. [< L *rectus* straight + *angulus* angle] • See PARALLELOGRAM.
rec·tan·gu·lar (rek·tang′gyə·lər) *adj.* **1** Having right angles. **2** Resembling a rectangle. **—rec·tan′gu·lar′i·ty** (-lar′ə·tē) *n.* **—rec·tan′gu·lar·ly** *adv.*
recti- *combining form* Straight: *rectilinear.* [< L *rectus* straight]
rec·ti·fi·er (rek′tə·fī′ər) *n.* **1** One who or that which rectifies. **2** *Electr.* A device that conducts in only one direction.
rec·ti·fy (rek′tə·fī) *v.t.* **·fied, ·fy·ing** **1** To make right; correct; amend. **2** *Chem.* To refine or purify, as a liquid, by distillation. **3** *Electr.* To change (an alternating current) into a direct current. **4** To allow for errors or inaccuracies in, as a compass reading. [< L *rectus* right + *facere* make] **—rec′ti·fi′a·ble** *adj.* **—rec′ti·fi·ca′tion** (-tə·fə·kā′shən) *n.*
rec·ti·lin·e·ar (rek′tə·lin′ē·ər) *adj.* Pertaining to, consisting of, moving in, or bounded by a straight line or lines; straight. Also **rec′ti·lin′e·al.** **—rec′ti·lin′e·ar·ly** *adv.*
rec·ti·tude (rek′tə·tʸo͞od) *n.* **1** Uprightness in principles and conduct. **2** Correctness of judgment, method, etc. [< L *rectus* right]
rec·tor (rek′tər) *n.* **1** In the Church of England, a priest who has full charge of a parish. **2** In the Protestant Episcopal Church, a priest in charge of a parish. **3** In the Roman Catholic Church: **a** A priest in charge of a congregation or church. **b** The head of a seminary or university. **4** In certain universities, colleges, and schools, the headmaster or principal. [< L *rectus,* pp. of *regere* rule] **—rec′tor·ate** (-it) *n.* **—rec·to·ri·al** (rek·tôr′ē·əl, -tō′rē-) *adj.*
rec·to·ry (rek′tər·ē) *n. pl.* **·ries** **1** A rector's dwelling. **2** In England, a parish domain with its buildings, revenue, etc.
rec·tum (rek′təm) *n. pl.* **·tums** or **·ta** (-tə) The terminal part of the large intestine ending at the anus. [< NL *rectum (intestinum)* straight (intestine)]
re·cum·bent (ri·kum′bənt) *adj.* **1** Lying down, wholly or partly. **2** Resting; inactive. [< L *re-* back + *cumbere* lie] **—re·cum′bence, re·cum′ben·cy** *n.* **—re·cum′bent·ly** *adv.*
re·cu·per·ate (ri·kʸo͞o′pə·rāt) *v.* **·at·ed, ·at·ing** *v.i.* **1** To regain health or strength. **2** To recover from loss, as of money. **—***v.t.* **3** To obtain again after loss; recover. **4** To restore to vigor and health. [< L *recuperare*] **—re·cu′per·a′tion, re·cu′per·a′tor** *n.* **—re·cu′per·a′tive** *adj.*
re·cur (ri·kûr′) *v.i.* **·curred, ·cur·ring** **1** To happen again or repeatedly. **2** To come back or return, as to the memory, in conversation, etc. [< L *re-* back + *currere* run]
re·cur·rent (ri·kûr′ənt) *adj.* **1** Happening or appearing again or repeatedly; recurring. **2** Turning back toward the source, as certain arteries and nerves. **—re·cur′rence, re·cur′ren·cy** *n.* **—re·cur′rent·ly** *adv.*
re·curve (ri·kûrv′) *v.t. & v.i.* **·curved, ·curv·ing** To curve or bend backward. [< L *re-* back + *curvus* curved] **—re·cur′·vate** (-kûr′vit, -vāt) *adj.*
re·cy·cle (rē·sī′kəl) *v.t.* **·cy·cled, ·cy·cling** To reclaim (waste materials, as used newsprint, glass bottles, etc.) by using in the manufacture of new products. **—re·cy′cla·ble** *adj.*
red (red) *adj.* **red·der, red·dest** **1** Having or being of a bright color resembling blood. **2** Of a hue approximating red: *red* hair. **3** Ultraradical in politics, esp. communistic. **—***n.* **1** One of the primary colors, occurring at the opposite end of the spectrum from violet; the color of fresh human blood. **2** A hue or tint that approximates primary red. **3** Any pigment or dye having or giving this color. **4** A red animal or object. **5** *Often cap.* An ultraradical or revolutionary in politics, esp. a communist: from the red banner of revolution. **—in the red** *Informal* Operating at a loss; owing money. **—see red** To be very angry. [< OE *rēad*] **—red′dish** *adj.* **—red′ly** *adv.* **—red′ness** *n.*
red. reduce; reduction.
re·dact (ri·dakt′) *v.t.* **1** To prepare, as for publication; edit; revise. **2** To draw up or frame, as a message or edict. [< L *redactus,* pp. of *redigere* lead back, restore] **—re·dac′·tion, re·dac′tor** *n.*
red algae A class of marine algae having predominantly red pigment and usu. mosslike growth.
red·bait (red′bāt′) *v.t.* To denounce as being communist. **—red′bait′er** *n.*
red·bird (red′bûrd′) *n.* Any of various birds with red plumage in the male, as cardinals, certain tanagers, etc.
red-blood·ed (red′blud′id) *adj.* Having vitality and vigor. **—red′-blood′ed·ness** *n.*
red·breast (red′brest′) *n.* A robin.
red·cap (red′kap′) *n.* A porter, as in a railroad or airline terminal.

red carpet A long red carpet traditionally used for important guests to walk on. **—red′-car′pet** *adj.*

Red China *Informal* The People's Republic of China.

red·coat (red′kōt′) *n.* **1** A British soldier during the American Revolution and the War of 1812. **2** *Can.* MOUNTIE.

red corpuscle ERYTHROCYTE.

Red Cross **1** An international society for bringing aid to victims of a war or disaster. **2** Any national branch of this society. **3** Their emblem, a red Greek cross on a white ground, symbol of neutrality.

red deer **1** A common deer of Europe and Asia. **2** The white-tailed deer in its summer coat.

red·den (red′n) *v.t.* **1** To make red. —*v.i.* **2** To grow red, esp. to blush.

re·deem (ri·dēm′) *v.t.* **1** To regain possession of by paying a price. **2** To pay off, as a promissory note. **3** To convert into cash or a premium: to *redeem* stocks or trading stamps. **4** To set free; ransom. **5** *Theol.* To rescue from sin and its penalties. **6** To fulfill, as an oath or promise. **7** To make worthwhile. [< L *re-* back + *emere* buy] **—re·deem′a·ble, re·demp′ti·ble** (-demp′tə·bəl) *adj.*

re·deem·er (ri·dē′mər) *n.* One who redeems. **—the Redeemer** Jesus Christ.

re·demp·tion (ri·demp′shən) *n.* **1** The act of redeeming, or the state of being redeemed. **2** The recovery of what is mortgaged or pawned. **3** The payment of a debt or obligation, esp. the paying of the value of its notes, warrants, etc., by a government. **4** Deliverance or rescue, as by paying a ransom. **—re·demp′tive, re·demp′to·ry** *adj.*

re·de·ploy (rē′di·ploi′) *v.t.* To transfer (troops) from one zone of combat to another. **—re′de·ploy′ment** *n.*

re·de·vel·op (rē′di·vel′əp) *v.t.* **1** To develop again. **2** To rebuild, as a slum area. **3** *Phot.* To intensify with chemicals and put through a second developing process. —*v.i.* **4** To develop again. **—re′de·vel′op·er, re′də·vel′op·ment** *n.*

red·eye (red′ī′) *n. Slang* Inferior whiskey.

red-hand·ed (red′han′did) *adj.* **1** Having just committed any crime. **2** Caught in the act of doing some particular thing. **—red′-hand′ed·ly** *adv.* **—red′-hand′ed·ness** *n.*

red·head (red′hed′) *n.* **1** A person with red hair. **2** A North American duck, the male of which has a red head. **—red′head′ed** *adj.*

redheaded woodpecker A North American woodpecker having a red head and neck.

red herring **1** Smoked herring. **2** An irrelevant topic introduced in order to divert attention from the main point under discussion.

red-hot (red′hot′) *adj.* **1** Heated to redness. **2** New; fresh. **3** Marked by excitement, agitation, or enthusiasm.

red·in·gote (red′ing·gōt) *n.* An outer coat with long full skirts. [F< E *riding coat*]

re·dis·trict (rē′dis′trikt) *v.t.* To redraw the district boundaries of.

red lead (led) An oxide of lead, used as a red pigment.

red-let·ter (red′let′ər) *adj.* Happy or memorable: from the use on calendars of red letters to indicate holidays.

red light A traffic signal light meaning stop.

red-light district (red′līt′) That part of a city or town in which brothels are numerous: from the former use of red lights to mark brothels.

red man An American Indian.

red·neck (red′nek′) *n.* A white, usu. uneducated laborer of the South: a disparaging term. Also **red′-neck′.**

red·o·lent (red′ə·lənt) *adj.* **1** Fragrant; odorous. **2** Smelling: with *of:* a swamp *redolent* of decay. **3** Evocative: with *of: redolent* of the past. [< L *redolere* emit a smell] **—red′o·lence, red′o·len·cy** *n.* **—red′o·lent·ly** *adv.*

re·doub·le (rē·dub′əl) *v.t. & v.i.* **·led, ·ling** **1** To make or become double. **2** To increase greatly. **3** To echo or re-echo. **4** To fold or double back again. **5** In bridge, to double (an opponent's double).

re·doubt (ri·dout′) *n.* **1** A temporary fortification, as to defend a pass, a hilltop, etc. **2** Any place providing protection; stronghold. [< Med. L *reductus,* lit., a refuge]

re·doubt·a·ble (ri·dou′tə·bəl) *adj.* **1** Inspiring fear; formidable. **2** Deserving respect or deference. Also **re·doubt′·ed.** [< L *re-* thoroughly + *dubitare* doubt] **—re·doubt′a·ble·ness** *n.* **—re·doubt′a·bly** *adv.*

re·dound (ri·dound′) *v.i.* **1** To have an effect or result. **2** To return; reflect. —*n.* A return by way of consequence; result. [< L *redundare* to overflow]

red pepper **1** Any of various capsicums having fruit that is red when ripe. **2** Such a fruit, or a condiment made from it, as cayenne, pimiento, etc.

red·poll (red′pōl′) *n.* A small finch of northern regions, having a reddish crown.

re·dress (ri·dres′) *v.t.* **1** To set right or make reparation for, as a wrong, by compensation or by punishment. **2** To make reparation to; compensate. **3** To remedy; correct. —*n.* (rē′dres, ri·dres′) **1** Satisfaction for wrong done; reparation; amends. **2** A restoration; correction. [< F *redresser* straighten] **—re·dress′er** or **re·dres′sor** *n.*

red shift *Astron.* Displacement toward the red or low-frequency end of the spectrum of light or radio waves from a celestial body that is receding at high velocity.

red snapper Any of various reddish, marine fish highly esteemed as food.

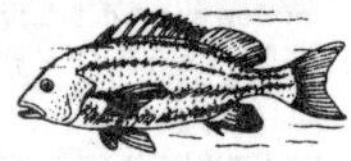
Red snapper

red·start (red′stärt′) *n.* Any of various small warblers having red markings. [< RED + obs. *start* tail]

red tape Rigid official regulations, forms, or procedure involving delay or inaction: from the former practice of tying public documents with red tape.

red·top (red′top′) *n.* Any of certain grasses used for lawns and pasturage.

re·duce (ri·d^{y}ōōs′) *v.* **·duced, ·duc·ing** *v.t.* **1** To make less in size, amount, number, intensity, etc.; diminish. **2** To bring into a certain system or order; classify. **3** To bring to a lower condition; degrade. **4** To bring to submission; subdue; conquer. **5** To bring to a specified condition or state: with *to:* to *reduce* rock to powder; *reduced* to tears. **6** To thin (paint, etc.) with oil or turpentine. **7** *Math.* To change (an expression) to a more elementary form. **8** *Chem.* **a** To remove oxygen from (a compound). **b** To add electrons to (an atom). **c** To decrease the positive valence of (an atom). **9** *Phot.* To diminish the density of (a photographic negative). —*v.i.* **10** To become less in any way. **11** To decrease one's weight, as by dieting. [< L *re-* back + *ducere* lead] **—re·duc′er, re·duc′i·bil′i·ty** *n.* **—re·duc′i·ble** *adj.* **—re·duc′i·bly** *adv.*

reducing agent *Chem.* Any substance that reduces another substance and is thereby oxidized in a chemical reaction.

re·duc·ti·o ad ab·sur·dum (ri·duk′tē·ō ad ab·sûr′dəm, -shē·ō) Disproof of a proposition by showing that it is self-contradictory. [L, lit., reduction to absurdity]

re·duc·tion (ri·duk′shən) *n.* **1** The act or process of reducing. **2** Something that results from reducing. **3** The amount by which something is reduced. **—re·duc′tion·al, re·duc′tive** *adj.*

re·dun·dan·cy (ri·dun′dən·sē) *n. pl.* **·cies** **1** The condition or quality of being redundant. **2** Something redundant, esp. unnecessary repetition. **3** Excess; surplus. **4** In information theory, repeated information in a message, used to lessen the probability of error. Also **re·dun′dance.**

re·dun·dant (ri·dun′dənt) *adj.* **1** Being more than is required; constituting an excess. **2** Unnecessarily repetitive or verbose. [<L *redundare* to overflow] **—re·dun′dant·ly** *adv.* **—Syn. 1** superfluous, excessive, inordinate, undue. **2** repetitious, iterative, reiterative, wordy.

re·du·pli·cate (ri·d^{y}ōō′plə·kāt) *v.* **·cat·ed, ·cat·ing** *v.t.* **1** To repeat again and again; copy; iterate. **2** *Ling.* To affix a reduplication to. —*v.i.* **3** To undergo reduplication. —*adj.* (-kit) Repeated again and again; duplicated. **—re·du′pli·ca′tive** *adj.*

re·du·pli·ca·tion (ri·d^{y}ōō′plə·kā′shən) *n.* **1** The act of reduplicating, or the state of being reduplicated; a redoubling. **2** *Ling.* **a** The repetition of an initial element or elements in a word. **b** The doubling of all or part of a word, often with vowel or consonant change, as in *fiddle-faddle.*

red·wing (red′wing′) *n.* **1** A North American blackbird with red and yellow wing patches in the male: also **red-winged blackbird.** **2** An Old World thrush with reddish orange on its wings.

red·wood (red′wŏŏd′) *n.* **1** SEQUOIA. **2** Its wood.

reed (rēd) *n.* **1** The slender, frequently jointed stem of certain tall grasses growing in wet places; also, the grasses themselves. **2** *Music* **a** A thin, elastic plate of reed, wood, or metal nearly closing an opening, as in a pipe, used in reed organs, reed pipes of pipe organs, and some woodwind instruments, to produce a musical tone when vibrated by air. **b** An instrument having such a reed or reeds. **3** A crude musical pipe made of the hollow stem of a plant. **4** *Archit.* REEDING. **5** A comblike device on a loom that keeps the warp yarns evenly separated. —*v.t.* **1** To fashion into or decorate with reeds. **2** To thatch with reeds. —*adj. Music* Equipped with a reed or reeds. [< OE *hrēod*]

reed·ing (rē′ding) *n. Archit.* **1** Small, convex molding. **2** Parallel ornamentation using such molding.

reed organ A keyboard musical instrument sounding by means of reeds that vibrate freely in response to air currents.

re·ed·u·cate (rē·ej′ōō·kāt) *v.t.* **·cat·ed, ·cat·ing 1** To educate again. **2** To rehabilitate, as a criminal, by education. **—re′ed·u·ca′tion** *n.*

reed·y (rē′dē) *adj.* **reed·i·er, reed·i·est 1** Full of reeds. **2** Like a reed. **3** Having a tone like that of a reed instrument. **—reed′i·ness** *n.*

reef[1] (rēf) *n.* **1** A ridge of sand or rocks, or esp. of coral, at or near the surface of the water. **2** A lode, vein, or ledge. [< ON *rif* rib, reef] **—reef′y** *adj.* • See ATOLL.

reef[2] (rēf) *Naut. n.* **1** The part of a sail that is folded and secured or untied and let out in regulating its size on the mast. **2** The tuck taken in a sail when reefed. —*v.t.* **1** To reduce (a sail) by folding a part and tying it to a yard or boom. **2** To shorten or lower, as a topmast, by taking part of it in. [Prob. < ON *rif* rib]

reef·er[1] (rē′fər) *n.* **1** One who reefs. **2** A short, double-breasted coat or jacket.

reef·er[2] (rē′fər) *n. Slang* A marihuana cigarette. [?]

reef knot SQUARE KNOT.

reek (rēk) *v.i.* **1** To give off smoke, vapor, etc. **2** To give off a strong, offensive smell. **3** To be pervaded with anything offensive. —*v.t.* **4** To expose to smoke or its action. **5** To give off; emit. [< OE *rēocan*] **—reek′er** *n.* **—reek′y** *adj.* **(·i·er, ·i·est)**

reel[1] (rēl) *n.* **1** A rotatory device or frame for winding rope, cord, photographic film, or other flexible substance. **2** Such a device attached to a fishing rod. **3** The length of wire, film, thread, etc., wound on one reel. —*v.t.* **1** To wind on a reel or bobbin, as a line. **2** To draw in by reeling a line: with *in:* to *reel* a fish in. **3** To say, do, etc., easily and fluently: with *off.* [< OE *hrēol*] **—reel′a·ble** *adj.* **—reel′er** *n.*

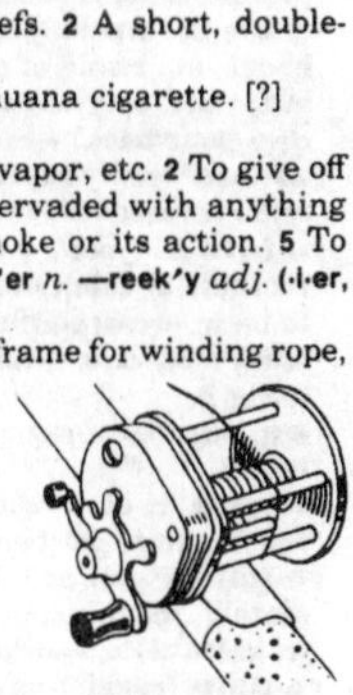

Fishing reel

reel[2] (rēl) *v.i.* **1** To stagger, sway, or lurch, as when giddy or drunk. **2** To whirl round and round. **3** To have a sensation of giddiness or whirling: My head *reels.* **4** To waver or fall back, as attacking troops. —*v.t.* **5** To cause to reel. —*n.* A staggering motion; giddiness. [< REEL[1]] **—reel′er** *n.*

reel[3] (rēl) *n.* **1** A lively Scottish dance. **2** The music for such a dance. [?< REEL[1]]

re·en·force (rē′in·fôrs′, -en-, -fōrs′) *v.* **·forced, ·forc·ing** REINFORCE.

re·en·try (rē·en′trē) *n.* **1** The act of entering again. **2** In whist and bridge, a card by which a player can regain the lead. **3** The return into the atmosphere of an object launched into space from the earth.

reeve[1] (rēv) *v.t.* **reeved** or **rove** (*for p.p. also* **rov·en**), **reev·ing** *Naut.* **1** To pass, as a rope or rod, through a hole, block, or aperture. **2** To fasten in such manner. **3** To pass a rope, etc., through (a block or pulley). [?< Du. *reven* reef a sail]

reeve[2] (rēv) *n.* In Canada, an elected official who presides over the council in certain villages and townships. [< OE *gerēfa* steward]

ref. referee; reference; referred; refining; reformed.

re·fec·tion (ri·fek′shən) *n.* **1** Refreshment by food and drink. **2** A light meal. [< L *refectus,* pp. of *reficere* remake, refresh]

re·fec·to·ry (ri·fek′tər·ē) *n. pl.* **·ries** A room for eating, esp. in a monastery, convent, or college. [< Med. L *refectorium*]

re·fer (ri·fûr′) *v.* **·ferred, ·fer·ring** *v.t.* **1** To direct or send for information or other purpose. **2** To hand over for consideration, settlement, etc. **3** To assign or attribute to a source, cause, group, class, etc. —*v.i.* **4** To make reference; allude. **5** To turn, as for information, help, or authority. [< L *re-* back + *ferre* bear, carry] **—ref·er·a·ble** (ref′ər·ə·bəl, ri·fûr′-), **re·fer′ra·ble** or **re·fer′ri·ble** *adj.* **—re·fer′rer** *n.*

ref·e·ree (ref′ə·rē′) *n.* **1** A person to whom a thing is referred for judgment or decision. **2** An official who sees that the rules of certain sports events are observed. —*v.t. & v.i.* To judge as a referee.

ref·er·ence (ref′ər·əns, ref′rəns) *n.* **1** The act of referring. **2** An incidental allusion or direction of the attention. **3** A note or other indication in a book, referring to some other book or passage. **4** One who or that which is or may be referred to. **5** A book or other source intended to be referred to for information, as a dictionary. **6** Relation: in *reference* to your inquiry. **7** A person to whom an employer may refer for information about a potential employee. **8** A written statement or testimonial referring to character or dependability. **—ref′er·en′tial** (-ər·en′shəl) *adj.* **—ref′er·en′tial·ly** *adv.*

ref·er·en·dum (ref′ə·ren′dəm) *n. pl.* **·dums** or **·da** (-də) **1** The submission of a proposed public measure or law, which has been passed upon by a legislature or convention, to a vote of the people for ratification or rejection. **2** The vote itself. [L, gerund of *referre* refer]

ref·er·ent (ref′ər·ənt) *n.* Something referred to, esp. the thing to which reference is made in any verbal statement.

re·fer·ral (ri·fûr′əl) *n.* **1** The act of referring or the condition of being referred. **2** One who has been referred.

re·fill (rē·fil′) *v.t. & v.i.* To fill or become filled again. —*n.* (rē′fil′) Any commodity packaged to fit and fill a container originally containing that commodity. **—re·fill′a·ble** *adj.*

re·fine (ri·fīn′) *v.* **·fined, ·fin·ing** *v.t.* **1** To make fine or pure. **2** To make more elegant, polished, etc. **3** To improve or perfect. —*v.i.* **4** To become fine or pure. **5** To become more polished or cultured. **6** To make fine distinctions; use subtlety in thought or speech. [< RE- + FINE[1], *v.*] **—re·fin′er** *n.*

re·fined (ri·fīnd′) *adj.* **1** Characterized by refinement or polish. **2** Free from impurity. **3** Exceedingly precise or exact; subtle.

re·fine·ment (ri·fīn′mənt) *n.* **1** The act or process of refining. **2** The result of refining, esp. an improvement. **3** Fineness of thought, taste, language, etc.; freedom from coarseness or vulgarity. **4** A nice distinction; subtlety.

re·fin·er·y (ri·fī′nər·ē) *n. pl.* **·er·ies** A plant for extracting useful products from raw material, as metal from ore, etc.

re·fit (rē·fit′) *v.t. & v.i.* **·fit·ted, ·fit·ting** To make or be made fit or ready again, as by making or obtaining repairs, replacing equipment, etc. —*n.* The repair of damages or wear, esp. of a ship.

refl. reflection; reflex; reflexive.

re·flect (ri·flekt′) *v.t.* **1** To turn or throw back, as rays of light, heat, or sound. **2** To produce a symmetrically reversed image of, as a mirror. **3** To cause or bring as a result: with *on*: He *reflects* credit on his teacher. **4** To show or manifest: His writings *reflect* great imagination. —*v.i.* **5** To send back rays, as of light or heat. **6** To return in rays. **7** To give back an image; also, to be mirrored. **8** To think carefully; ponder. **9** To bring blame, discredit, etc.: with *on* or *upon.* [< L *re-* back + *flectere* bend]

re·flec·tion (ri·flek′shən) *n.* **1** The act of reflecting, or the state of being reflected. **2** *Physics* The throwing off or back (from a surface) of impinging light, heat, sound, or any form of radiant energy. **3** Reflected rays or an image thrown by reflection. **4** Careful, serious thought or consideration. **5** The result of such thought. **6** Censure; discredit; also, a remark or action tending to discredit. **—re·flec′tion·al** *adj.*

re·flec·tive (re·flek′tiv) *adj.* **1** Given to reflection or thought; meditative. 2 Of or caused by reflection. 3 That reflects. **—re·flec'tive·ly** *adv.* **—re·flec'tive·ness, re'flec·tiv'i·ty** *n.*

re·flec·tor (ri·flek'tər) *n.* One who or that which reflects, esp. a device for reflecting light, heat, sound, etc.

re·flex (rē'fleks) *adj.* 1 Turned, bent, directed, or thrown backward. 2 *Physiol.* Of, pertaining to, or produced by an involuntary action or response. *—n.* 1 Reflection, as of light, or an image produced by reflection. 2 *Physiol.* An involuntary response to a stimulus: also **reflex action.** 3 A habitual or automatic reaction. [< L *reflexus* reflected, pp. of *reflectere* bend back]

re·flex·ive (ri·flek'siv) *adj.* 1 REFLEX. 2 *Gram.* a Designating a verb whose object is identical with its subject, as "dresses" in "He dresses himself." b Designating a pronoun which is the direct object of a reflexive verb. *—n.* A reflexive verb or pronoun. **—re·flex'ive·ly** *adv.* **—re·flex'ive·ness, re·flex·iv·i·ty** (rē'flek·siv'ə·tē) *n.*

ref·lu·ent (ref'lo͞o·ənt) *adj.* Flowing back; ebbing, as the tide. [< L *re-* back + *fluere* flow] **—ref'lu·ence, ref'lu·en·cy** *n.*

re·flux (rē'fluks') *n.* A flowing back; ebb; return. [< L *refluxus,* pp. of *refluere* flow back]

re·for·est (rē·fôr'ist, -for'-) *v.t. & v.i.* To replant (an area) with trees. **—re'for·es·ta'tion** *n.*

re·form (ri·fôrm') *v.t.* 1 To make better by removing abuses, malpractice, etc. 2 To make better morally; persuade or educate from a sinful to a moral life. 3 To put an end to; stop (an abuse, malpractice, etc.). *—v.i.* 4 To give up sin or error; become better. *—n.* A correction or improvement of social or personal evils or errors. [< L *re-* again + *formare* to form] **—re·form'a·tive** *adj.* **—re·form'er** *n.* **—re·form'ist** *adj., n.*

re-form (rē'fôrm') *v.t. & v.i.* To form again. **—re'-for·ma'tion** *n.*

ref·or·ma·tion (ref'ər·mā'shən) *n.* 1 The act of reforming. 2 The state of being reformed.

Ref·or·ma·tion (ref'ər·mā'shən) *n.* The religious revolution of the 16th century that began by trying to reform Catholicism and ended with the establishment of Protestantism.

re·form·a·to·ry (ri·fôr'mə·tôr'ē, -tō'rē) *adj.* Tending or aiming to reform. *—n. pl.* **·ries** An institution for the reformation and instruction of juvenile offenders: also **reform school.**

re·fract (ri·frakt') *v.t.* 1 To deflect (a ray) by refraction. 2 *Optics* To determine the degree of refraction of (an eye or lens). [< L *refractus,* pp. of *refringere* turn aside]

re·frac·tion (ri·frak'shən) *n.* *Physics* The change of direction of a ray, as of light or heat, in oblique passage between media of different densities. **—re·frac'tive** *adj.* **—re·frac'tive·ness, re·frac·tiv·i·ty** (rē'frak·tiv'ə·tē), **re·frac'tor** *n.*

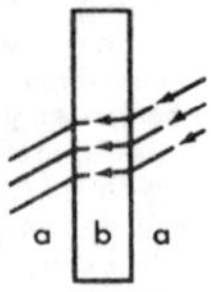

Light refraction a. air. b. glass prism.

re·frac·to·ry (ri·frak'tər·ē) *adj.* 1 Hard to control; stubborn; obstinate. 2 Resisting heat. 3 Resisting treatment, as a disease. *—n. pl.* **·ries** 1 A refractory or obstinate person or thing. 2 Any of various highly heat-resistant materials. [< L *refractarius*] **—re·frac'to·ri·ly** *adv.* **—re·frac'to·ri·ness** *n.*

re·frain[1] (ri·frān') *v.i.* To hold oneself back. [< L *refrenare* curb] **—re·frain'er** *n.* **—Syn.** abstain, forbear, forgo, renounce.

re·frain[2] (ri·frān') *n.* 1 A phrase or verse repeated at intervals in a poem or a song. 2 The music for a refrain. [< OF *refraindre* to check, repeat]

re·fran·gi·ble (ri·fran'jə·bəl) *adj.* Capable of being refracted, as light. [< RE- + L *frangere* to break] **—re·fran'gi·bil'i·ty, re·fran'gi·ble·ness** *n.*

re·fresh (ri·fresh') *v.t.* 1 To revive (a person), as with food or rest. 2 To make fresh, clean, cool, etc. 3 To stimulate, as the memory. 4 To renew or replenish with or as with new supplies. *—v.i.* 5 To become fresh again; revive. 6 To take refreshment. **—re·fresh'er** *n.*

refresher course A course for reviewing and learning of recent developments in a profession or field of study.

re·fresh·ing (ri·fresh'ing) *adj.* 1 Serving to refresh. 2 Pleasing because new or unusual. **—re·fresh'ing·ly** *adv.*

re·fresh·ment (ri·fresh'mənt) *n.* 1 The act of refreshing, or the state of being refreshed. 2 That which refreshes. 3 *pl.* Food, or food and drink, served as a light meal.

re·frig·er·ant (ri·frij'ər·ənt) *adj.* 1 Cooling or freezing. 2 Allaying heat or fever. *—n.* 1 Any medicine or material that reduces fever. 2 A substance used to produce refrigeration.

re·frig·er·ate (ri·frij'ə·rāt) *v.t.* **·at·ed, ·at·ing** 1 To keep or cause to become cold; cool. 2 To freeze or chill for preservative purposes, as foodstuffs. [< L *re-* thoroughly + *frigerare* to cool] **—re·frig'er·a'tion** *n.* **—re·frig'er·a'tive** *adj., n.* **—re·frig'er·a·to'ry** *adj.*

re·frig·er·a·tor (ri·frij'ə·rā'tər) *n.* A box, cabinet, room, railroad car, etc., equipped with a cooling apparatus for preserving the freshness of perishable foods, etc.

ref·uge (ref'yo͞oj) *n.* 1 Shelter or protection, as from danger or distress. 2 A safe place; asylum. 3 Something that brings relief, lessens difficulties, etc. [< L *refugere* to retreat]

ref·u·gee (ref'yo͞o·jē', ref'yo͞o·jē') *n.* One who flees to find refuge in another land or place, as from persecution or political danger.

re·ful·gent (ri·ful'jənt) *adj.* Shining; radiant; resplendent. [< L *refulgere* reflect light] **—re·ful'gence, re·ful'gen·cy** *n.* **—re·ful'gent·ly** *adv.*

re·fund[1] (ri·fund') *v.t.* 1 To give or pay back (money, etc.). 2 To repay (a person). *—v.i.* 3 To make repayment. *—n.* (rē'fund) A repayment; refunding; also, the amount repaid. [< L *refundere* pour back] **—re·fund'er, re·fund'ment** *n.*

re·fund[2] (rē'fund') *v.t.* To fund anew.

re·fus·al (ri·fyo͞o'zəl) *n.* 1 The act of refusing. 2 The privilege or opportunity of accepting or rejecting before others.

re·fuse[1] (ri·fyo͞oz') *v.* **·fused, ·fus·ing** *v.t.* 1 To decline to do, permit, take, or yield. 2 To decline to fulfill the request or desire of (a person). 3 To balk at jumping over (a ditch, hedge, etc.): said of a horse. *—v.i.* 4 To decline to do, permit, take, or yield something. [< L *refusus,* pp. of *refundere* pour back] **—re·fus'er** *n.*

ref·use[2] (ref'yo͞os) *n.* Anything worthless; rubbish. [< OF *refus* refused]

re·fute (ri·fyo͞ot') *v.t.* **·fut·ed, ·fut·ing** 1 To prove the incorrectness or falsity of (a statement). 2 To prove (a person) to be in error; confute. [< L *refutare*] **—re·fut'a·ble** *adj.* **—re·fut'a·bly** *adv.* **—ref·u·ta·tion** (ref'yə·tā'shən), **re·fu'tal, re·fut'er** *n.*

reg. regiment; region; register; registered; regular; regulation.

re·gain (ri·gān') *v.t.* 1 To get possession of again. 2 To reach again; get back to. **—re·gain'er** *n.*

re·gal (rē'gəl) *adj.* Belonging to or fit for a king; royal, stately, magnificent, etc. [< L *rex, regis* king] **—re·gal·i·ty** (ri·gal'ə·tē) *n.* **—re'gal·ly** *adv.*

re·gale (ri·gāl') *v.* **·galed, ·gal·ing** *v.t.* 1 To give unusual pleasure to; delight. 2 To entertain royally or sumptuously; feast. *—v.i.* 3 To feast. [< F *régaler*] **—re·gale'ment** *n.*

re·ga·li·a (ri·gā'lē·ə, -gāl'yə) *n. pl.* 1 The insignia and emblems of royalty, as the crown, scepter, etc. 2 The distinctive symbols, insignia, etc., of any society, order, or rank. 3 Fine clothes; fancy trappings.

re·gard (ri·gärd') *v.t.* 1 To look at or observe attentively. 2 To look on or think of in a certain way. 3 To take into account; consider. 4 To have relevance to. *—v.i.* 5 To pay attention. 6 To gaze or look. *—n.* 1 A look; gaze. 2 Careful attention; consideration. 3 Respect; esteem. 4 *Usu. pl.* Greetings; good wishes. 5 Reference; relation: with *regard* to your letter. [< OF *regarder* look at]

re·gard·ful (ri·gärd'fəl) *adj.* 1 Having or showing regard; heedful. 2 Respectful. **—re·gard'ful·ly** *adv.* **—re·gard'ful·ness** *n.*

re·gard·ing (ri·gär'ding) *prep.* In reference to; with regard to.

re·gard·less (ri·gärd'lis) *adj.* Having no regard or consideration; heedless; negligent. *—adv. Informal* In spite of everything. **—re·gard'less·ly** *adv.*

re·gat·ta (ri·gat'ə, -gä'tə) *n.* A boat race, or a series of such races. [Ital.]

re·gen·cy (rē'jən·sē) *n. pl.* **·cies** 1 The government or office of a regent or body of regents. 2 The period during which a regent or body of regents governs. 3 A body of regents. 4 The district under the rule of a regent. Also **re′gent·ship.**

re·gen·er·ate (ri·jen′ə·rāt) *v.* **·at·ed, ·at·ing** *v.t.* 1 To cause moral and spiritual reformation in. 2 To produce or form anew; reestablish; recreate. 3 *Biol.* To replace (a lost organ or tissue) with new growth. —*v.i.* 4 To form anew; be reproduced. 5 To become spiritually regenerate. 6 To effect regeneration. —*adj.* (ri·jen′ər·it) 1 Having new life; restored. 2 Spiritually renewed; regenerated. —**re·gen′er·a·cy** (-ər·ə·sē), **re·gen′er·a′tion, re·gen′er·a′tor** *n.*

re·gent (rē′jənt) *n.* 1 One who rules in the name and place of a sovereign. 2 One of various officers having charge of education, as of a university or state. [<L *regens,* pr.p. of *regere* rule]

reg·gae (reg′ā, rā′gā) *n.* A popular music of West Indian origin having a rhythm that suggests both blues and rock.

reg·i·cide (rej′ə·sīd) *n.* 1 The killing of a king. 2 The killer of a king. [<L *rex, regis* king + -CIDE] —**reg′i·ci′dal** *adj.*

re·gime (ri·zhēm′) *n.* 1 System of government or administration. 2 A particular government or its duration of rule. 3 A social system. 4 REGIMEN. Also **ré·gime** (rā·zhēm′). [<F<L *regimen*]

reg·i·men (rej′ə·mən) *n.* A system of diet, exercise, etc., used for therapeutic purposes. [<L *regimen*<*regere* to rule]

reg·i·ment (rej′ə·mənt) *n.* A military unit larger than a battalion and smaller than a division. —*v.t.* 1 To form into a regiment or regiments; organize. 2 To assign to a regiment. 3 To form into well-defined or specific units or groups; systematize. 4 To make uniform. [<LL *regimentum*<L *regere* to rule] —**reg′i·men′tal** *adj.* —**reg′i·men·ta′tion** *n.*

reg·i·men·tals (rej′ə·men′təlz) *n. pl.* 1 Military uniform. 2 The uniform worn by the men and officers of a regiment.

re·gion (rē′jən) *n.* 1 An indefinite, usu. large portion of territory or space. 2 A specific area or place. 3 A specified area of activity, interest, etc.: the *region* of art. 4 A portion of the body. [<L *regio*<*regere* to rule]

re·gion·al (rē′jən·əl) *adj.* 1 Of or pertaining to a particular region; sectional; local: *regional* planning. 2 Of or pertaining to an entire region or section. —**re′gion·al·ly** *adv.* • In this dictionary the label *Regional* is applied to terms used chiefly or exclusively within a particular region of the U.S., and constituting a part of that region's distinctive variety of speech or dialect. A user of regional speech should be aware that terms so labeled may be misunderstood or considered odd or illiterate in other parts of the country.

reg·is·ter (rej′is·tər) *n.* 1 An official record, as of names, events, transactions, etc. 2 The book containing such a record. 3 An item in such a record. 4 Any of various devices for adding or recording: a cash *register.* 5 REGISTRAR. 6 A device for regulating the admission of heated air to a room. 7 *Music* **a** The range or compass of a voice or instrument. **b** A series of tones of a particular quality or belonging to a particular portion of the compass of a voice or instrument. 8 *Printing* **a** Exact correspondence of the lines and margins on the opposite sides of a printed sheet. **b** Correct imposition of the colors in color printing. —*v.t.* 1 To enter in or as in a register; enroll or record officially. 2 To indicate on a scale. 3 To express or indicate: His face *registered* disapproval. 4 *Printing* To effect exact correspondence or imposition of. 5 To cause (mail) to be recorded, on payment of a fee, so as to insure delivery. —*v.i.* 6 To enter one's name in a register, poll, etc. 7 To have effect; make an impression. 8 *Printing* To be in register. [<L *regestus,* pp. of *regerere* record] —**reg·is·tra·ble** (rej′is·trə·bəl) *adj.* —**reg′is·trant** (-trənt) *n.*

reg·is·tered (rej′is·tərd) *adj.* 1 Recorded, as a birth, a voter, an animal's pedigree, etc. 2 Officially or formally qualified.

reg·is·trar (rej′is·trär) *n.* An authorized keeper of a register or of records, esp. of a college or court.

reg·is·tra·tion (rej′is·trā′shən) *n.* 1 The act of registering, as of voters, students, etc. 2 The number of persons registered. 3 An entry in a register.

reg·is·try (rej′is·trē) *n. pl.* **·tries** 1 REGISTRATION. 2 A register, or the place where it is kept. 3 The nationality of a ship as entered in a register.

reg·nant (reg′nənt) *adj.* 1 Reigning in one's own right. 2 Predominant. 3 Widespread. [<L *regnum* reign]

re·gress (ri·gres′) *v.i.* To go back; move backward; return. —*n.* (rē′gres) 1 A going back; return. 2 A return to a less perfect or lower state; retrogression. [<L *regressus,* pp. of *regredi* go back] —**re·gres′sive** *adj.* —**re·gres′sive·ly** *adv.* —**re·gres′sor** *n.*

re·gres·sion (ri·gresh′ən) *n.* 1 The act of regressing. 2 A return to a less perfect or lower state; retrogression. 3 *Psychoanal.* A retreat to earlier or infantile behavior.

re·gret (ri·gret′) *v.t.* **·gret·ted, ·gret·ting** 1 To look back upon with a feeling of distress or loss. 2 To feel sorrow or grief concerning. —*n.* 1 Distress of mind in recalling some past event, act, loss, etc. 2 Remorseful sorrow; compunction. 3 *pl.* A polite refusal in response to an invitation. [<OF *regreter*] —**re·gret′ter** *n.*

re·gret·ful (ri·gret′fəl) *adj.* Feeling, expressive of, or full of regret. —**re·gret′ful·ly** *adv.* —**re·gret′ful·ness** *n.* —**Syn.** sorry, remorseful, contrite, apologetic.

re·gret·ta·ble (ri·gret′ə·bəl) *adj.* Deserving regret; unfortunate. —**re·gret′ta·bly** *adv.*

regt. regiment.

reg·u·lar (reg′yə·lər) *adj.* 1 Made, formed, or arranged according to a rule, standard, or type; symmetrical; normal. 2 Methodical; orderly: *regular* habits. 3 Conforming to a fixed or proper procedure or principle. 4 Customary; habitual: his *regular* breakfast. 5 Officially authorized. 6 Without variation or abnormality: His pulse is *regular.* 7 Thorough; unmitigated: a *regular* bore. 8 *Informal* Pleasant, good, honest, etc.: a *regular* guy. 9 *Gram.* Undergoing the inflection that is normal or most common. 10 *Bot.* Having all similar parts or organs of the same shape and size: said mainly of flowers. 11 *Eccl.* Belonging to a religious order: the *regular* clergy. 12 *Mil.* Pertaining or belonging to the permanent army. 13 In politics, designating, nominated by, or loyal to the official party organization or platform. 14 *Geom.* Having equal sides and angles. 15 *Math.* Controlled or formed by one law or operation throughout. —*n.* 1 A soldier belonging to a permanent or standing army. 2 In sports, a starting member of a team. 3 An habitual customer, patron, etc. 4 A clothing size for those of average height and weight. 5 *Eccl.* A member of a religious order. 6 A person loyal to a certain political party. [<L *regula* rule] —**reg′u·lar′i·ty** *n.* —**reg′u·lar·ly** *adv.*

reg·u·lar·ize (reg′yə·lə·rīz′) *v.t.* **·ized, ·iz·ing** To make regular. —**reg′u·lar·i·za′tion** *n.*

reg·u·late (reg′yə·lāt) *v.t.* **·lat·ed, ·lat·ing** 1 To direct, manage, or control according to certain rules, principles, etc. 2 To adjust according to a standard, degree, etc.: to *regulate* currency. 3 To adjust to accurate operation. 4 To put in order; set right. [<L *regula* a rule<*regere* rule, lead straight] —**reg′u·la′tive, reg′u·la·to′ry** (-lə·tôr′ē, -tō′rē) *adj.*

reg·u·la·tion (reg′yə·lā′shən) *n.* 1 The act of regulating, or the state of being regulated. 2 A prescribed rule of conduct or procedure. —*adj.* 1 Required by rule or regulation. 2 Normal; customary.

reg·u·la·tor (reg′yə·lā′tər) *n.* 1 One who or that which regulates. 2 A device for regulating the speed of a watch. 3 A contrivance for controlling motion, flow, voltage, etc.

re·gur·gi·tate (rē·gûr′jə·tāt) *v.* **·tat·ed, ·tat·ing** *v.i.* 1 To flow backward. —*v.t.* 2 To cause to surge back, as partially digested food to the mouth from the stomach. [<LL *re-* back + *gurgitare* flood, engulf] —**re·gur′gi·tant** *adj.* —**re·gur′gi·ta′tion** *n.*

re·ha·bil·i·tate (rē′hə·bil′ə·tāt, rē′ə-) *v.t.* **·tat·ed, ·tat·ing** 1 To restore to a former state, capacity, privilege, rank, etc.; reinstate. 2 To restore to health or normal activity. [<Med. L *rehabilitare*] —**re′ha·bil′i·ta′tion** *n.*

re·hash (rē·hash′) *v.t.* To work into a new form; go over again. —*n.* (rē′hash′) The act or result of rehashing.

re·hears·al (ri·hûr′səl) *n.* 1 The act of rehearsing, as for a play. 2 The act of reciting or telling over again.

re·hearse (ri·hûrs′) *v.* **·hearsed, ·hears·ing** *v.t.* 1 To practice privately in preparation for public performance, as a play or song. 2 To instruct or direct (a person) by way of preparation. 3 To say over again; repeat aloud; recite. 4 To give an account of; relate. —*v.i.* 5 To rehearse a play, song, dance, etc. [< OF *reherser* harrow over, repeat] —**re·hears′er** *n.*

Reich (rīk, *Ger.* rīkh) *n.* Formerly, Germany, the German government, or its territory. —**Third Reich** The Nazi state under Adolf Hitler, 1933–45. [G]

reichs·mark (rīks′märk′, *Ger.* rīkhs′-) *n. pl.* **·marks** or **·mark** A monetary unit of Germany from 1924–48.

Reichs·tag (rīks′täg′, *Ger.* rīkhs′täkh′) *n.* The former legislative assembly of Germany.

reign (rān) *n.* 1 Sovereign power or rule; sovereignty. 2 The time or duration of a sovereign's rule. 3 Domination; sway: the *reign* of rationalism. —*v.i.* 1 To hold and exercise sovereign power. 2 To hold sway; prevail: Winter *reigns.* [< L *regnum* rule]

Reign of Terror The period of the French Revolution from May, 1793, to August, 1794, during which Louis XVI, Marie Antoinette, and thousands of others were guillotined.

re·im·burse (rē′im·bûrs′) *v.t.* **·bursed, ·burs·ing** 1 To pay back (a person) an equivalent for what has been spent or lost; recompense. 2 To pay back; refund. [< RE- + < L *in-* in + *bursa* purse] —**re′im·burs′a·ble** *adj.* —**re′im·burse′ment** *n.*

rein (rān) *n.* 1 *Usu. pl.* A strap attached to each end of a bit to control a horse or other draft animal. 2 Any means of restraint or control. —*v.t.* 1 To guide, check, or halt with or as with reins. —*v.i.* 2 To check or halt a horse by means of reins: with *in* or *up.* [< OF *resne*]

re·in·car·nate (rē′in·kär′nāt) *v.t.* **·nat·ed, ·nat·ing** To cause to undergo reincarnation.

re·in·car·na·tion (rē′in·kär·nā′shən) *n.* 1 The rebirth of a soul in a new body. 2 The Hindu doctrine that the soul, upon the death of the body, returns to earth in another body or a new form.

rein·deer (rān′dir′) *n. pl.* **·deer** A European form of caribou, often domesticated. [< ON *hreinn* reindeer + *dyr* deer]

re·in·force (rē′in·fôrs′, -fōrs′) *v.t.* **·forced, ·forc·ing** 1 To give new force or strength to. 2 *Mil.* To strengthen with more troops or ships. 3 To add some strengthening part or material to. 4 To increase the number of. [< RE- + *inforce,* var. of ENFORCE]

reinforced concrete Concrete containing metal bars, rods, or netting to increase its strength and durability.

re·in·force·ment (rē′in·fôrs′mənt, -fōrs′-) *n.* 1 The act of reinforcing. 2 Something that reinforces. 3 *Often pl. Mil.* A fresh body of troops or additional vessels.

re·in·state (rē′in·stāt′) *v.t.* **·stat·ed, ·stat·ing** To restore to a former state, position, etc. —**re′in·state′ment** *n.*

reis (rās) *n.pl.* of REAL² (def. 2).

re·it·er·ate (rē·it′ə·rāt) *v.t.* **·at·ed, ·at·ing** To say or do again and again. [< L *re-* again + *iterare* say] —**re·it′er·a′tion** *n.* —**re·it′er·a′tive** *adj.* —**re·it′er·a′tive·ly** *adv.* —**Syn.** iterate, repeat, retell, recapitulate.

re·ject (ri·jekt′) *v.t.* 1 To refuse to accept, recognize, believe, etc. 2 To refuse to grant; deny, as a petition. 3 To refuse (a person) recognition, acceptance, etc. 4 To expel; react against physiologically. 5 To cast away as worthless; discard. —*n.* (rē′jekt) A person or thing that has been rejected. [< L *re-* back + *jacere* to throw] —**re·ject′er** or **re·jec′tor, re·jec′tion** *n.*

re·joice (ri·jois′) *v.* **·joiced, ·joic·ing** *v.i.* 1 To feel joyful; be glad. —*v.t.* 2 To fill with joy; gladden. [< L *re-* again + *ex-* thoroughly + *gaudere* be joyous] —**re·joic′er, re·joic′ing** *n.* —**re·joic′ing·ly** *adv.*

re·join¹ (ri·join′) *v.t.* 1 To say in reply; answer. —*v.i.* 2 To answer. [< F *rejoindre*]

re·join² (rē′join′) *v.t.* 1 To come again into company with. 2 To join together again; reunite. —*v.i.* 3 To come together again.

re·join·der (ri·join′dər) *n.* 1 An answer to a reply. 2 Any reply or retort. [< F *rejoindre* to answer, reply]

re·ju·ve·nate (ri·jo͞o′və·nāt) *v.t.* **·nat·ed, ·nat·ing** To make young; give new vigor or youthfulness to. [< RE- again + L *juvenis* young + -ATE] —**re·ju′ve·na′tion** *n.*

rel. relating; relative; released; religion; religious.

re·lapse (ri·laps′) *v.i.* **·lapsed, ·laps·ing** 1 To lapse back, as into disease after partial recovery. 2 To return to bad habits or sin; backslide. —*n.* (*also* rē′laps) 1 The act or an instance of relapsing. 2 The return of an illness after apparent recovery. [< L *relapsus,* pp. of *relabi* slide back] —**re·laps′er** *n.*

re·late (ri·lāt′) *v.* **·lat·ed, ·lat·ing** *v.t.* 1 To tell the events or the particulars of; narrate. 2 To bring into connection or relation. —*v.i.* 3 To have relation: with *to.* 4 To have reference: with *to.* [< L *relatus,* pp. of *referre* to carry back] —**re·lat′er** *n.*

re·lat·ed (ri·lā′tid) *adj.* 1 Standing in relation; connected. 2 Of common ancestry; connected by blood or marriage; akin. 3 Narrated. —**re·lat′ed·ly** *adv.* —**re·lat′ed·ness** *n.*

re·la·tion (ri·lā′shən) *n.* 1 The fact or condition of being related or connected: the *relation* between poverty and disease. 2 Connection by blood or marriage; kinship. 3 A person connected by blood or marriage; a relative. 4 Reference; regard; allusion: in *relation* to your request. 5 *pl.* The contacts or dealings between or among individuals, groups, nations, etc.: race *relations;* political *relations.* 6 The act of relating or narrating; also, that which is related or told. —**re·la′tion·al** *adj.*

re·la·tion·ship (ri·lā′shən·ship) *n.* 1 The state or quality of being related; connection. 2 Kinship. 3 The kind or quality of association between people: a healthy *relationship.*

rel·a·tive (rel′ə·tiv) *adj.* 1 Having connection; pertinent: an inquiry *relative* to one's health. 2 Resulting from or depending upon a relation to or comparison with something else; comparative: a *relative* truth. 3 Intelligible only in relation to something else; not absolute. 4 *Gram.* Referring to or qualifying an antecedent: a *relative* pronoun. —*n.* 1 One who is related; a kinsman. 2 A relative word or term. —**rel′a·tive·ly** *adv.* —**rel′a·tive·ness** *n.*

relative clause *Gram.* A dependent clause introduced by a relative pronoun.

relative humidity At any given temperature, the percentage of the maximum possible water vapor content actually present in the air.

relative pronoun *Gram.* A pronoun that refers to an antecedent and introduces a dependent clause, as *who* in *We who knew him admired him.*

rel·a·tiv·i·ty (rel′ə·tiv′ə·tē) *n.* 1 The quality or condition of being relative; relativeness. 2 *Philos.* Existence viewed only as an object of, or in relation to, a thinking mind. 3 A condition of dependence or of close relation of one thing on or to another. 4 *Physics* The principle of the interdependence of matter, energy, space, and time, as mathematically formulated by Albert Einstein. The **special theory of relativity** states that the speed of light is the same in all frames of reference and that the same laws of physics hold in all frames of reference that are not accelerated. The **general theory of relativity** extends these principles to accelerated frames of reference and gravitational phenomena.

re·lax (ri·laks′) *v.t.* 1 To make lax or loose; make less tight or firm. 2 To make less stringent or severe, as discipline. 3 To abate; slacken, as efforts. 4 To relieve from strain or effort. —*v.i.* 5 To become lax or loose; loosen. 6 To become less stringent or severe. 7 To rest. 8 To unbend; become less formal. [< L *re-* again + *laxare* loosen] —**re·lax′a·ble** *adj.* —**re′lax·a′tion, re·lax′er** *n.*

re·lax·ant (ri·laks′ənt) *adj.* Pertaining to or causing relaxation. —*n.* A drug or other agent that reduces tension, esp. of muscles.

re·lay¹ (rē′lā) *n.* 1 A fresh set, as of men, horses, or dogs, to replace or relieve a tired set. 2 A supply of anything kept in store for anticipated use or need. 3 A relay race, or one of its laps or legs. 4 *Electr.* An electronically controlled switch. —*v.t.* (*also* ri·lā′) **·layed, ·lay·ing** 1 To send onward by or as by relays. 2 To provide with relays. 3 *Telecom.* To retransmit (a message or signal). [< Ital. *rilasciare* leave behind]

re·lay² (rē′lā′) *v.t.* **·laid, ·lay·ing** To lay again.

re·lay race (rē′lā) A race between teams, each runner of which runs only a set part of the course and is relieved by a teammate.

re·lease (ri·lēs′) *v.t.* **·leased, ·leas·ing 1** To set free; liberate. **2** To deliver from worry, pain, obligation, etc. **3** To free from something that holds, binds, etc. **4** To permit the circulation, sale, performance, etc., of, as a motion picture, phonograph record, or news item. —*n.* **1** The act of releasing or setting free, or the state of being released. **2** A discharge from responsibility or penalty; also, a document authorizing this. **3** *Law* An instrument of conveyance by which one person surrenders and relinquishes all claims or rights to another person. **4** The releasing of something to the public; also, that which is released, as a news item, motion picture, etc. **5** *Mech.* Any catch or device to hold and release something. [< L *relaxare* relax] —**re·leas′er** *n.*

re-lease (rē′lēs′) *v.t.* **·leased, ·leas·ing** To lease again.

rel·e·gate (rel′ə·gāt) *v.t.* **·gat·ed, ·gat·ing 1** To send off or consign, as to an obscure position or place. **2** To assign, as to a particular class or sphere. **3** To refer (a matter) to someone for decision, action, etc. **4** To banish; exile. [< L *re-* away, back + *legare* send] —**rel′e·ga′tion** *n.*

re·lent (ri·lent′) *v.i.* To soften in temper; become more gentle or compassionate. [< L *relentescere* grow soft]

re·lent·less (ri·lent′lis) *adj.* **1** Unremitting; continuous. **2** Not relenting; pitiless. —**re·lent′less·ly** *adv.* —**re·lent′less·ness** *n.*

rel·e·vant (rel′ə·vənt) *adj.* Fitting; pertinent; applicable. [< Med. L *relevare* bear upon] —**rel′e·vance, rel′e·van·cy** *n.* —**rel′e·vant·ly** *adv.*

re·li·a·ble (ri·lī′ə·bəl) *adj.* That may be relied upon; worthy of confidence. —**re·li′a·bil′i·ty, re·li′a·ble·ness** *n.* —**re·li′a·bly** *adv.* —**Syn.** trustworthy, dependable, loyal, constant.

re·li·ance (ri·lī′əns) *n.* **1** The act of relying. **2** Confidence; trust; dependence. **3** That upon which one relies.

re·li·ant (ri·lī′ənt) *adj.* **1** Having or manifesting reliance. **2** Dependent: with *on.* —**re·li′ant·ly** *adv.*

rel·ic (rel′ik) *n.* **1** Some remaining portion or fragment of that which has vanished or is destroyed. **2** A custom, habit, etc., from the past. **3** A keepsake or memento. **4** The body or part of the body of a saint, or any sacred memento. **5** *pl.* A corpse; remains. [< L *reliquiae* remains < *relinquere* leave]

re·lief (ri·lēf′) *n.* **1** The act of relieving, or the state of being relieved. **2** That which relieves. **3** Charitable aid, as money or food. **4** Release, as from a post or duty; also, the person or persons who take over for those released. **5** In architecture and sculpture, the projection of a figure, ornament, etc., from a surface; also, any such figure. **6** In painting, the apparent projection of forms and masses. **7** *Geog.* **a** The unevenness of land surface, as caused by mountains, hills, etc. **b** The parts of a map which portray such unevenness.

Relief *def. 5*

re·lieve (ri·lēv′) *v.t.* **·lieved, ·liev·ing 1** To free wholly or partly from pain, stress, pressure, etc. **2** To lessen or alleviate, as pain or pressure. **3** To give aid or assistance to. **4** To free from obligation, injustice, etc. **5** To release from duty by providing a substitute. **6** To make less monotonous, harsh, or unpleasant; vary. **7** To bring into prominence; display by contrast. [< L *relevare* lift up] —**re·liev′a·ble** *adj.* —**re·liev′er** *n.*

re·lig·ion (ri·lij′ən) *n.* **1** A belief in a divine or superhuman power or principle, usu. thought of as the creator of all things. **2** The manifestation of such a belief in worship, ritual, conduct, etc. **3** Any system of religious faith or practice: the Jewish *religion.* **4** The religious or monastic life: to enter *religion.* **5** Anything that elicits devotion, zeal, dedication, etc.: Politics is his *religion.* [< L *religio*]

re·lig·i·os·i·ty (ri·lij′ē·os′ə·tē) *n.* The state or quality of being religious, esp. excessively or affectedly so.

re·lig·ious (ri·lij′əs) *adj.* **1** Feeling and manifesting religion; devout; pious. **2** Of or pertaining to religion: a *religious* teacher. **3** Faithful and strict in performance; conscientious: a *religious* loyalty. **4** Belonging to the monastic life. —*n. pl.* **·ious** A monk or nun. —**re·lig′ious·ly** *adv.* —**re·lig′ious·ness** *n.*

re·lin·quish (ri·ling′kwish) *v.t.* **1** To give up; abandon. **2** To renounce: to *relinquish* a claim. **3** To let go (a hold or something held). [< L *re-* back, from + *linquere* leave] —**re·lin′quish·er, re·lin′quish·ment** *n.*

rel·i·quar·y (rel′ə·kwer′ē) *n. pl.* **·quar·ies** A casket, shrine, or other repository for relics. [< L *reliquiae* remains]

rel·ish (rel′ish) *n.* **1** Appetite; appreciation; liking. **2** The flavor, esp. when agreeable, in food and drink. **3** The quality in anything that lends spice or zest: Danger gives *relish* to adventure. **4** A savory food or condiment served with other food to lend it flavor or zest. **5** A hint, trace, or suggestion of some quality or characteristic. —*v.t.* **1** To like; enjoy: to *relish* a dinner or a joke. —*v.i.* **2** To have an agreeable flavor; afford gratification. [< OF *relaisser* leave behind] —**rel′ish·a·ble** *adj.*

re·live (rē·liv′) *v.t.* **·lived, ·liv·ing** To experience again, as in one's memory.

re·luc·tance (ri·luk′təns) *n.* **1** The state of being reluctant; unwillingness. **2** *Electr.* Capacity for opposing magnetic induction. Also **re·luc′tan·cy.**

re·luc·tant (ri·luk′tənt) *adj.* **1** Disinclined; unwilling. **2** Marked by unwillingness. [< L *reluctari* fight back] —**re·luc′tant·ly** *adv.*

re·ly (ri·lī′) *v.i.* **·lied, ·ly·ing** To place trust or confidence: with *on* or *upon.* [< L *re-* again + *ligare* to bind] —**Syn.** lean, depend, count, bank (all with *on* or *upon*).

re·main (ri·mān′) *v.i.* **1** To stay or be left behind after the removal, departure, or destruction of other persons or things. **2** To continue in one place, condition, or character. **3** To be left as something to be done, dealt with, etc. **4** To endure or last; abide. [< L *re-* back + *manere* stay, remain]

re·main·der (ri·mān′dər) *n.* **1** That which remains; something left over. **2** *Math.* **a** The result of subtraction; difference. **b** The difference of the product of the quotient and divisor subtracted from the dividend in division. **3** *Law* An estate in expectancy, but not in actual possession and enjoyment. **4** A copy or copies of a book remaining with a publisher after sales have fallen off or ceased. —*adj.* Left over; remaining. —*v.t.* To sell as a remainder (def. 4).

re·mains (ri·mānz′) *n. pl.* **1** That which is left after a part has been removed or destroyed; remnants. **2** A corpse. **3** Unpublished writings at the time of an author's death. **4** Survivals of the past, as fossils, monuments, etc.

re·make (rē·māk′) *v.t.* **·made, ·mak·ing** To make again or in a different form: to *remake* a silent film. —*n.* (rē′māk) Something that is remade, esp. a motion picture.

re·mand (ri·mand′, -mänd′) *v.t.* **1** To order or send back. **2** *Law* **a** To recommit to custody, as an accused person after a preliminary examination. **b** To send (a case) back to a lower court. —*n.* The act of remanding or the state of being remanded. [< L *re-* back + *mandare* to order] —**re·mand′ment** *n.*

re·mark (ri·märk′) *n.* **1** A comment or saying; casual observation. **2** The act of noticing, observing, or perceiving. —*v.t.* **1** To say or write by way of comment. **2** To take particular notice of. —*v.i.* **3** To make remarks: with *on* or *upon.* [< F *re-* again + *marquer* to mark] —**re·mark′er** *n.*

re·mark·a·ble (ri·mär′kə·bəl) *adj.* **1** Worthy of special notice. **2** Extraordinary; unusual. —**re·mark′a·ble·ness** *n.* —**re·mark′a·bly** *adv.*

re·me·di·a·ble (ri·mē′dē·ə·bəl) *adj.* Capable of being cured or remedied. —**re·me′di·a·bly** *adv.*

re·me·di·al (ri·mē′dē·əl) *adj.* Of the nature of or adapted to be used as a remedy: *remedial* measures. —**re·me′di·al·ly** *adv.*

rem·e·dy (rem′ə·dē) *v.t.* **·died, ·dy·ing 1** To cure or heal, as by medicinal treatment. **2** To make right; repair; correct. **3** To overcome or remove (an evil or defect). —*n. pl.* **·dies 1** A medicine or remedial treatment. **2** A means of correcting an evil, fault, etc. **3** *Law* A legal mode for enforcing a right or redressing or preventing a wrong. [< L *re-* thoroughly + *mederi* heal, restore]

re·mem·ber (ri·mem′bər) *v.t.* **1** To bring back or present again to the mind or memory; recall. **2** To keep in mind carefully, as for a purpose. **3** To bear in mind with affection, respect, awe, etc. **4** To reward (someone) with a gift, legacy, tip, etc. —*v.i.* **5** To bring something back to or keep something in the mind. **6** To have or use one's memory. —**remember (one) to** To inform a person of the regard of: *Remember* me *to* your wife. [< L *re-* again + *memorare* bring to mind] —**re·mem′ber·er** *n.*

re·mem·brance (ri·mem′brəns) *n.* **1** The act or power of remembering or the state of being remembered. **2** The period within which one can remember. **3** That which is remembered. **4** A gift, memento, or keepsake. **5** An observance in commemoration.

re·mind (ri·mīnd′) *v.t.* To bring to (someone's) mind; cause to remember. —**re·mind′er** *n.* —**re·mind′ful** *adj.*

rem·i·nisce (rem′ə·nis′) *v.i.* **·nisced, ·nisc·ing** To recall incidents or events of the past; indulge in reminiscences. [Back formation < REMINISCENCE]

rem·i·nis·cence (rem′ə·nis′əns) *n.* **1** The recalling to mind of past incidents and events. **2** A written or oral account of past experiences. **3** Anything that serves as a reminder of something else. [< L *reminisci* recollect] —**rem′i·nis′cent** *adj.* —**rem′i·nis′cent·ly** *adv.*

re·miss (ri·mis′) *adj.* Lax or careless in matters requiring attention; negligent. [< L *remittere* send back, slacken] —**re·miss′ness** *n.*

re·mis·si·ble (ri·mis′ə·bəl) *adj.* Capable of being remitted or pardoned, as sins. —**re·mis′si·bil′i·ty** *n.*

re·mis·sion (ri·mish′ən) *n.* **1** The act of remitting, or the state of being remitted. **2** Pardon, as of sins or a crime. **3** Release from a debt, penalty, or obligation. **4** Temporary abatement, as of pain, symptoms, etc.

re·mit (ri·mit′) *v.* **·mit·ted, ·mit·ting** *v.t.* **1** To send, as money in payment for goods; transmit. **2** To refrain from exacting or inflicting, as a penalty. **3** To pardon; forgive. **4** To slacken; relax, as vigilance. **5** To restore; replace. **6** To put off; postpone. **7** *Law* To refer (a legal proceeding) to a lower court for further consideration. —*v.i.* **8** To send money, as in payment. **9** To diminish; abate. [< L *re-* back + *mittere* send] —**re·mit′ter** or **re·mit′tor** *n.*

re·mit·tal (ri·mit′l) *n.* REMISSION.

re·mit·tance (ri·mit′ns) *n.* **1** The act of remitting money or credit. **2** That which is remitted, as money.

re·mit·tent (ri·mit′nt) *adj.* Having temporary abatements: a *remittent* fever. —*n.* A remittent fever. [< L *remittere* remit] —**re·mit′tent·ly** *adv.*

rem·nant (rem′nənt) *n.* **1** That which remains of anything. **2** A piece of cloth, etc., left over after the last cutting. **3** A remaining trace or survival of anything: a *remnant* of faith. **4** A small remaining number or quantity, as of people. —*adj.* Remaining. [< OF *remaindre* remain]

re·mod·el (rē·mod′l) *v.t.* **·eled** or **·elled, ·el·ing** or **·el·ling** **1** To model again. **2** To make over or anew.

re·mon·e·tize (ri·mon′ə·tīz) *v.t.* **·tized, ·tiz·ing** To reinstate, esp. silver, as lawful money. [< RE- + L *moneta* money + -IZE] —**re·mon′e·ti·za′tion** *n.*

re·mon·strance (ri·mon′strəns) *n.* The act or an instance of remonstrating; protest.

re·mon·strant (ri·mon′strənt) *adj.* Protesting or opposing; expostulatory. —*n.* One who remonstrates.

re·mon·strate (ri·mon′strāt) *v.* **·strat·ed, ·strat·ing** *v.t.* **1** To say or plead in protest or opposition. —*v.i.* **2** To protest; object. [< L *re-* again + *monstrare* show] —**re·mon·stra·tion** (rē′mon·strā′shən, rem′ən-), **re·mon′stra′tor** *n.* —**re·mon′·stra·tive** (-strə·tiv) *adj.*

re·morse (ri·môrs′) *n.* The keen or hopeless anguish caused by a sense of guilt; distressing self-reproach. [< LL *remorsus* a biting back] —**re·morse′ful** *adj.* —**re·morse′ful·ly** *adv.* —**re·morse′ful·ness** *n.*

re·morse·less (ri·môrs′lis) *adj.* Having no remorse or compassion. —**re·morse′less·ly** *adv.* —**re·morse′less·ness** *n.* —**Syn.** pitiless, cruel, merciless, ruthless.

re·mote (ri·mōt′) *adj.* **1** Located far from a specified place. **2** Removed far from present time. **3** Having slight bearing on or connection with: a problem *remote* from our discussion. **4** Distant in relation: a *remote* cousin. **5** Not obvious; faint; slight: a *remote* likeness. **6** Cold; aloof: a *remote* manner. [< L *remotus,* p.p. of *removere* remove] —**re·mote′ly** *adv.* —**re·mote′ness** *n.*

remote control Control from a distance, as of a machine, apparatus, aircraft, etc.

re·mount (rē·mount′) *v.t.* & *v.i.* To mount again or anew. —*n.* (rē′mount′) **1** A new setting or framing. **2** A fresh riding horse.

re·mov·a·ble (ri·mōō′və·bəl) *adj.* Capable of being removed. —**re·mov′a·bil′i·ty, re·mov′a·ble·ness** *n.*

re·mov·al (ri·mōō′vəl) *n.* **1** The act of removing or the state of being removed. **2** Dismissal, as from office. **3** Changing of place, esp. of habitation.

re·move (ri·mōōv′) *v.* **·moved, ·mov·ing** *v.t.* **1** To take or move away or from one place to another. **2** To take off. **3** To get rid of; do away with: to *remove* abuses. **4** To kill. **5** To displace or dismiss, as from office. **6** To take out; extract: with *from.* —*v.i.* **7** To change one's place of residence or business. **8** To go away; depart. —*n.* **1** The act of removing. **2** The distance or degree of difference between things: He is only one *remove* from a fool. [< L *re-* again + *movere* move] —**re·mov′er** *n.*

re·moved (ri·mōōvd′) *adj.* Separated, as by intervening space, time, or relationship, or by difference in kind: a cousin twice *removed.* —**re·mov·ed·ness** (ri·mōō′vid·nis) *n.*

re·mu·ner·ate (ri·myōō′nə·rāt) *v.t.* **·at·ed, ·at·ing** **1** To pay (a person) for something, as for services, losses, etc. **2** To compensate or reward for (work, diligence, etc.). [< L *remunerari*] —**re·mu′ner·a′tion, re·mu′ner·a′tor** *n.* —**re·mu′·ner·a·tive** (-nər·ə·tiv, -nə·rā′tiv) *adj.* —**re·mu′ner·a·tive·ly** *adv.*

Re·mus (rē′məs) *Rom. Myth.* The twin brother of Romulus, by whom he was killed.

ren·ais·sance (ren′ə·säns′, -zäns′, ri·nā′səns) *n.* A new birth; resurrection; renascence. [F< *renaître* be reborn]

Ren·ais·sance (ren′ə·säns′, -zäns′, ri·nā′səns) *n.* **1** The revival of letters and art in Europe, marking the transition from the medieval to the modern world. **2** The period of this revival, from the 14th to the 16th century. **3** The style of art, literature, etc., marked by a classical influence, that was developed in and characteristic of this period. —*adj.* **1** Of, pertaining to, or characteristic of the Renaissance. **2** Pertaining to a style of architecture originating in Italy in the 15th century and based on the classical Roman style.

re·nal (rē′nəl) *adj.* Of or situated near the kidneys. [< L *renes* kidneys]

re·nas·cence (ri·nās′əns, -nas′-) *n.* A rebirth; revival. [< L *re-* again + *nasci* be born] —**re·nas′cent** *adj.*

Re·nas·cence (ri·nās′əns, -nas′-) *n.* RENAISSANCE.

rend (rend) *v.* **rent** or **rend·ed, rend·ing** *v.t.* **1** To tear apart forcibly. **2** To pull or remove forcibly: with *away, from, off,* etc. **3** To pass through (the air) violently and noisily. **4** To distress (the heart, etc.), as with grief or despair. —*v.i.* **5** To split; part. [< OE *rendan* tear, cut down] —**rend′er** *n.*

ren·der (ren′dər) *v.t.* **1** To give, present, or submit for action, approval, payment, etc. **2** To provide or furnish; give: to *render* aid. **3** To give as due: to *render* obedience. **4** To perform; do: to *render* great service. **5** To give or state formally. **6** To give by way of requital or retribution: to *render* good for evil. **7** To represent or depict, as in music or painting. **8** To cause to be: to *render* someone helpless. **9** To express in another language; translate. **10** To melt and clarify, as lard. **11** To give back; return: often with *back.* **12** To surrender; give up. [< L *reddere* give back] —**ren′der·a·ble** *adj.* —**ren′der·er** *n.*

ren·dez·vous (rän′dā·vōō, -də-) *n. pl.* **·vous** (-vōōz) **1** An appointed place of meeting. **2** A meeting or an appointment to meet. —*v.t.* & *v.i.* **·voused** (-vōōd), **·vous·ing** (-vōō′·ing) To assemble or cause to assemble at a certain place or time. [< F *rendez-vous,* lit., betake yourself]

ren·di·tion (ren·dish′ən) *n.* **1** A version or interpretation of a text. **2** A performance or interpretation, as of a musical composition, role, etc. **3** The act of rendering. [< OF *rendre* render]

ren·e·gade (ren′ə·gād) *n.* **1** One who abandons a previous loyalty, as to a religion, political party, etc. **2** One who gives up conventional or lawful behavior. —*adj.* Traitorous. [< Sp. *renegar* deny]

re·nege (ri·nig′, -neg′, -nēg′) *v.i.* **·neged, ·neg·ing 1** In card games, to fail to follow suit when able or required by rule to do so. **2** To fail to fulfill a promise. [< L *re-* again + *negare* deny] **—re·neg′er** *n.*

re·new (ri·nyōō′) *v.t.* **1** To make new or as if new again. **2** To begin again; resume. **3** To repeat: to *renew* an oath. **4** To regain (vigor, strength, etc.). **5** To cause to continue in effect; extend: to *renew* a subscription. **6** To revive; reestablish. **7** To replenish or replace, as provisions. *—v.i.* **8** To become new again. **9** To begin or commence again. [< RE- + NEW] **—re·new′a·ble** *adj.* **—re·new′al, re·new′er** *n.* **—re·new′ed·ly** *adv.*

ren·i·form (ren′ə·fôrm, rē′nə-) *adj.* Kidney-shaped. [< L *renes* kidneys + -FORM]

ren·net (ren′it) *n.* **1** The mucous membrane lining the fourth stomach of a suckling calf or lamb. **2** An extract of this, used to curdle milk in making cheese, etc. **3** RENNIN. [< OE *rinnan* run together, coagulate]

ren·nin (ren′in) *n.* **1** A milk-curdling enzyme present in gastric juice. **2** This enzyme in partially purified form obtained from rennet.

re·nounce (ri·nouns′) *v.t.* **·nounced, ·nounc·ing 1** To give up, esp. by formal statement. **2** To disown; repudiate. [< L *renuntiare* protest against] **—re·nounce′ment, re·nounc′·er** *n.* **—Syn. 1** abjure, disavow, disclaim, forswear.

ren·o·vate (ren′ə·vāt) *v.t.* **·vat·ed, ·vat·ing 1** To make as good as new, as by repairing, cleaning, etc. **2** To renew; refresh; reinvigorate. [< L *re-* again + *novare* make new] **—ren′o·va′tion, ren′o·va′tor** *n.*

re·nown (ri·noun′) *n.* The state of being widely known for great achievements; fame. [< L *re-* again + *nominare* to name] **—re·nowned′** *adj.*

rent[1] (rent) *n.* Compensation, esp. payment in money, made by a tenant to a landlord or owner for the use of property, as land, a house, etc., usu. due at specified intervals. **—for rent** Available in return for a rent. *—v.t.* **1** To obtain the temporary possession and use of in return for paying rent. **2** To grant the temporary use of for a rent. *—v.i.* **3** To be let for rent. [< L *reddita* what is given back or paid] **—rent′a·ble** *adj.* **—rent′er** *n.*

rent[2] (rent) A *p.t. & p.p.* of REND. *—n.* **1** A hole or slit made by rending or tearing. **2** A violent separation; schism.

rent·al (ren′təl) *n.* **1** An amount paid or due to be paid as rent. **2** The revenue derived from rented property. **3** The act of renting. *—adj.* **1** Of or pertaining to rent. **2** Engaged in the business of renting or supervising rents.

re·nun·ci·a·tion (ri·nun′sē·ā′shən, -shē-) *n.* **1** The act of renouncing; repudiation. **2** A declaration in which something is renounced. **—re·nun′ci·a′tive** (-sē·ā′tiv), **re·nun′ci·a·to′ry** *adj.*

re·o·pen (rē·ō′pən) *v.t. & v.i.* **1** To open again. **2** To begin again; resume.

re·or·gan·i·za·tion (rē′ôr·gən·ə·zā′shən, -ī·zā′-) *n.* **1** The act of reorganizing. **2** The legal reconstruction of a corporation, usu. to avert a failure.

re·or·gan·ize (rē·ôr′gən·īz) *v.t. & v.i.* **·ized, ·iz·ing** To organize anew. **—re·or′gan·iz′er** *n.*

rep[1] (rep) *n.* A silk, cotton, rayon, or wool fabric having a crosswise rib. [< F *reps*]

rep[2] (rep) *n. Slang* **1** REPERTORY. **2** REPRESENTATIVE. **3** REPUTATION.

Rep. Representative; Republic; Republican.

re·pair[1] (ri·pâr′) *v.t.* **1** To restore to sound or good condition after damage, injury, decay, etc. **2** To make up, as a loss; compensate for. *—n.* **1** The act or instance of repairing. **2** Condition after use or after repairing: in good *repair.* [< L *re-* again + *parare* prepare] **—re·pair′er** *n.*

re·pair[2] (ri·pâr′) *v.i.* To betake oneself; go: to *repair* to the garden. [< LL *repatriare* repatriate]

re·pair·man (ri·pâr′man′, -mən) *n. pl.* **·men** (-men′, -mən) A man whose work is to make repairs.

rep·a·ra·ble (rep′ər·ə·bəl) *adj.* Capable of being repaired. **—rep′a·ra·bly** *adv.*

rep·a·ra·tion (rep′ə·rā′shən) *n.* **1** The act of making amends; atonement. **2** That which is done or paid by way of making amends. **3** *pl.* Indemnities paid by defeated countries for acts of war. **4** The act of repairing, or the state of being repaired. **—re·par·a·tive** (ri·par′ə·tiv) *adj.*

rep·ar·tee (rep′är·tē′, -ər-, -tā′) *n.* **1** Conversation marked by quick and witty replies. **2** Skill in such conversation. **3** A witty reply. [< F *re-* again + *partir* depart]

re·past (ri·past′, -päst′, rē′past) *n.* Food taken at a meal; a meal. [< LL *repascere* feed again]

re·pa·tri·ate (rē·pā′trē·āt) *v.t. & v.i.* **·at·ed, ·at·ing** To send back to the country of birth, citizenship, or allegiance, as prisoners of war. *—n.* (rē·pā′trē·it) A person who has been repatriated. [< L *re-* again + *patria* native land] **—re·pa′·tri·a′tion** *n.*

re·pay (ri·pā′) *v.* **·paid, ·pay·ing** *v.t.* **1** To pay back; refund. **2** To pay back or refund something to. **3** To make compensation or retaliation for. *—v.i.* **4** To make repayment or requital. **—re·pay′ment** *n.*

re·peal (ri·pēl′) *v.t.* To withdraw the authority to effect; rescind; revoke. *—n.* The act of repealing; revocation. [< OF *rapeler* recall] **—re·peal′a·ble** *adj.* **—re·peal′er** *n.*

re·peat (ri·pēt′) *v.t.* **1** To say again; reiterate. **2** To recite

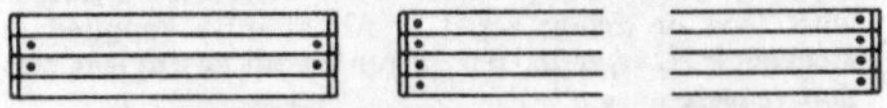

Repeats *def. 2a*

from memory. **3** To say (what another has just said). **4** To tell, as a secret, to another. **5** To do, make, or experience again. *—v.i.* **6** To say or do something again. **7** To vote more than once at the same election. *—n.* **1** The act of repeating. **2** *Music* **a** A sign indicating that a passage is to be repeated. **b** A passage meant to be repeated. [< L *repetere* do or say again] **—re·peat′a·ble** *adj.*

re·peat·ed (ri·pē′tid) *adj.* Occurring or spoken again and again. **—re·peat′ed·ly** *adv.*

re·peat·er (ri·pē′tər) *n.* **1** One who or that which repeats. **2** A firearm that can discharge several shots without being reloaded. **3** One who illegally votes more than once at the same election. **4** One who has been repeatedly imprisoned for criminal offenses.

re·pel (ri·pel′) *v.* **·pelled, ·pel·ling** *v.t.* **1** To force or drive back; repulse. **2** To reject; refuse, as a suggestion. **3** To cause to feel distaste or aversion. **4** To fail to mix with or adhere to. *—v.i.* **5** To act so as to drive something back or away. **6** To cause distaste or aversion. [< L *re-* back + *pellere* drive] **—re·pel′ler** *n.*

re·pel·lent (ri·pel′ənt) *adj.* **1** Serving, tending, or having power to repel. **2** Exciting disgust; repugnant; repulsive. *—n.* Something that repels, as a substance that repels water, insects, etc. **—re·pel′len·cy, re·pel′lence** *n.*

re·pent (ri·pent′) *v.i.* **1** To feel remorse or regret, as for something done or undone; be contrite. **2** To change one's mind concerning past action: with *of.* *—v.t.* **3** To feel remorse or regret for (an action, sin, etc.). [< L *re-* again + *poenitere* cause to repent] **—re·pent′er** *n.*

re·pen·tance (ri·pen′təns) *n.* The act of repenting; sorrow for having done wrong. **—re·pen′tant** *adj.* **—re·pen′tant·ly** *adv.*

re·per·cus·sion (rē′pər·kush′ən) *n.* **1** *Usu. pl.* A long-range or unpredictable result, as of an event; aftereffect. **2** A reverberation; echo. [< L *repercussus,* p.p. of *repercutere* rebound] **—re′per·cus′sive** *adj.*

rep·er·toire (rep′ər·twär) *n.* **1** A list of works, as of music or drama, that a company or person is prepared to perform. **2** Such works collectively. **3** The aggregate of devices, methods, etc., used in a particular line of activity: the teacher's *repertoire* of visual aids. [< LL *repertorium* inventory]

rep·er·to·ry (rep′ər·tôr′ē, -tō′rē) *n. pl.* **·ries 1** A theatrical group having a repertoire of productions: also **repertory company, repertory theater. 2** REPERTOIRE. **3** A place where things are gathered in readiness for use. [< L *repertus,* p.p. of *reperire* find, discover]

rep·e·ti·tion (rep′ə·tish′ən) *n.* **1** The doing, making, or saying of something again. **2** That which is repeated; a copy. **—re·pet·i·tive** (ri·pet′ə·tiv) *adj.* **—re·pet′i·tive·ly** *adv.*

rep·e·ti·tious (rep′ə·tish′əs) *adj.* Characterized by or containing repetition, esp. useless or tedious repetition. —**rep'e·ti'tious·ly** *adv.* —**rep'e·ti'tious·ness** *n.*

re·pine (ri·pīn') *v.i.* **·pined, ·pin·ing** To be discontented or fretful. [< RE- + PINE[2]] —**re·pin'er** *n.*

re·place (ri·plās') *v.t.* **·placed, ·plac·ing** **1** To put back in place. **2** To take or fill the place of; supersede. **3** To refund; repay. —**re·place'a·ble** *adj.* —**re·plac'er** *n.*

re·place·ment (ri·plās'mənt) *n.* **1** The act of replacing, or the state of being replaced. **2** Something used to replace, as a substitute.

re·play (rē·plā') *v.t.* **1** To play again. **2** To show a replay of. —*n.* (rē'plā') **1** The act of playing again. **2** The playing of a television tape, often in slow motion and usu. immediately following the live occurrence of the action shown. **3** The action shown in such a replay.

re·plen·ish (ri·plen'ish) *v.t.* **1** To fill again. **2** To bring back to fullness or completeness, as diminished supplies. [< L *re-* again + *plenus* full] —**re·plen'ish·er, re·plen'ish·ment** *n.*

re·plete (ri·plēt') *adj.* **1** Full to the uttermost. **2** Gorged with food or drink; sated. **3** Abundantly supplied or stocked. [< L *repletus,* p.p. of *replere* fill again] —**re·ple'·tion, re·plete'ness** *n.*

rep·li·ca (rep'lə·kə) *n.* **1** A duplicate, as of a picture, executed by the original artist. **2** Any close copy or reproduction. [< L *replicare* to reply]

rep·li·cate (rep'lə·kāt) *v.t.* **·cat·ed, ·cat·ing** **1** To make an indeterminate number of copies of; duplicate. **2** To fold over. —**rep'li·ca'tion** *n.*

re·ply (ri·plī') *v.* **·plied, ·ply·ing** *v.i.* **1** To give an answer. **2** To respond by some act, gesture, etc. **3** To echo. **4** *Law* To file a pleading in answer to the statement of the defense. —*v.t.* **5** To say in answer: She *replied* that she would do it. —*n. pl.* **·plies** Something said, written, or done by way of answer. [< L *replicare* fold back, make a reply] —**re·pli'er** *n.*

re·port (ri·pôrt', -pōrt') *v.t.* **1** To make or give an account of; relate, as information obtained by investigation. **2** To bear back or repeat to another, as an answer. **3** To complain about, esp. to the authorities. **4** To state the result of consideration concerning: The committee *reported* the bill. —*v.i.* **5** To make a report. **6** To act as a reporter. **7** To present oneself, as for duty. —*n.* **1** That which is reported. **2** A formal statement of the result of an investigation. **3** Common talk; rumor. **4** Fame, reputation, or character. **5** A record of the transactions of a deliberative body. **6** An account prepared for publication in the press. **7** An explosive sound: the *report* of a gun. [< L *re-* back + *portare* carry] —**re·port'a·ble** *adj.* —**Syn** *v.* **1** describe, record, transcribe. *n.* **1, 2, 5, 6** account, statement, announcement. **3** gossip, hearsay.

re·port·age (ri·pôr'tij, -pōr'-, rep'ôr·täzh') *n.* **1** The act or art of reporting, as for publication. **2** Reports that deal with events in a journalistic style. [F]

report card A periodic statement of a pupil's scholastic record.

re·port·ed·ly (ri·pôr'tid·lē, -pōr'-) *adv.* According to report.

re·port·er (ri·pôr'tər, -pōr'-) *n.* **1** One who reports. **2** One employed to gather and report news for publication or broadcasting. —**rep·or·to·ri·al** (rep'ər·tôr'ē·əl, -tō'rē-) *adj.*

re·pose[1] (ri·pōz') *n.* **1** The state of being at rest. **2** Sleep. **3** Freedom from excitement or anxiety; composure. **4** Dignified calmness; serenity; peacefulness. —*v.* **·posed, ·pos·ing** *v.t.* **1** To lay or place in a position of rest. —*v.i.* **2** To lie at rest. **3** To lie in death. **4** To rely; depend: with *on, upon,* or *in.* [< LL *re-* again + *pausare* to pause] —**re·pose'ful** *adj.* —**re·pose'ful·ly** *adv.*

re·pose[2] (ri·pōz') *v.t.* **·posed, ·pos·ing** To place, as confidence or hope: with *in.* [< L *repositus,* p.p. of *reponere* put back]

re·pos·i·to·ry (ri·poz'ə·tôr'ē, -tō'rē) *n. pl.* **·ries** **1** A place in which goods may be stored; a depository. **2** Anything considered as a place of storage or assembly: a *repository* of Indian lore. **3** A person to whom a secret is entrusted. [< L *repositorium*]

re·pos·sess (rē'pə·zes') *v.t.* To regain possession of, esp. as a result of the default of payments due. —**re'pos·ses'·sion** *n.*

rep·re·hend (rep'ri·hend') *v.t.* To criticize sharply; find fault with. [< L *re-* back + *prehendere* hold] —**rep're·hen'·sion** *n.* —**rep're·hen'sive** *adj.* —**rep're·hen'sive·ly** *adv.*

rep·re·hen·si·ble (rep'ri·hen'sə·bəl) *adj.* Deserving blame or censure. —**rep're·hen'si·bil'i·ty, rep're·hen'si·ble·ness** *n.* —**rep're·hen'si·bly** *adv.*

rep·re·sent (rep'ri·zent') *v.t.* **1** To serve as the symbol, expression, or designation of; symbolize: The dove *represents* peace. **2** To serve as an example, specimen, type, etc., of; typify: They *represent* the best in America. **3** To set forth a likeness or image of; depict; portray. **4** To serve as or be the delegate, agent, etc., of, as by legal authority or by election. **5** To act the part of; impersonate. **6** To bring before the mind; present clearly: Goya etchings that *represent* the horrors of war. **7** To set forth in words, esp. in a forceful and persuasive manner. **8** To describe as being of a specified character or condition: to *represent* a signature as authentic. [< L *re-* again + *praesentare* to present]

rep·re·sen·ta·tion (rep'ri·zen·tā'shən) *n.* **1** The act of representing, or the state of being represented. **2** A likeness or model. **3** A statement usu. purporting to be descriptive that represents a point of view and is intended to influence judgment. **4** A dramatic performance. **5** Representatives collectively.

rep·re·sen·ta·tive (rep'ri·zen'tə·tiv) *adj.* **1** Typifying a group or class. **2** Acting or having the power to act as an agent. **3** Made up of representatives. **4** Based on the political principle of representation. **5** Presenting, portraying, or representing. —*n.* **1** One who or that which is typical of a group or class. **2** One who is authorized as an agent or delegate. **3** *Often cap.* A member of a legislative body, esp., in the U.S., a member of the lower house of Congress or of a state legislature. —**rep're·sen'ta·tive·ly** *adv.* —**rep're·sen'ta·tive·ness** *n.*

re·press (ri·pres') *v.t.* **1** To keep under restraint or control. **2** To block the expression of: to *repress* a groan. **3** To put down; quell, as a rebellion. [< L *repressus,* p.p. of *reprimere* press back] —**re·press'er, re·pres'sive·ness** *n.* —**re·press'i·ble, re·pres'sive** *adj.* —**re·pres'sive·ly** *adv.* —**Syn. 1** curb, rein. **2** suppress, hold in.

re·pres·sion (ri·presh'ən) *n.* **1** The act of repressing, or the condition of being repressed. **2** *Psychoanal.* The exclusion from consciousness of painful desires, memories, etc., and consequent manifestation through the unconscious.

re·prieve (ri·prēv') *v.t.* **·prieved, ·priev·ing** **1** To suspend temporarily the execution of a sentence upon. **2** To relieve for a time from suffering or trouble. —*n.* **1** The temporary suspension of a sentence. **2** Temporary relief or cessation of pain; respite. [< F *reprendre* take back]

rep·ri·mand (rep'rə·mand) *v.t.* To reprove sharply or formally. —*n.* Severe reproof or formal censure. [< L *reprimendus* to be repressed]

re·print (rē'print') *n.* A printing that is an exact copy of a work already printed. —*v.t.* (rē·print') To print again, esp. without alteration. —**re·print'er** *n.*

re·pri·sal (ri·prī'zəl) *n.* Any action done in retaliation for harm or injuries received, esp. an action involving the use of force and sanctioned by a government or political group. [< OF *reprendre* take back]

re·proach (ri·prōch') *v.t.* To charge with or blame for something wrong; rebuke. —*n.* **1** The act of or an expression of reproaching; censure; reproof. **2** A cause of blame or disgrace. **3** Disgrace; discredit. [< OF *reprochier*] —**re·proach'ful** *adj.* —**re·proach'ful·ly** *adv.* —**re·proach'ful·ness** *n.*

rep·ro·bate (rep'rə·bāt) *adj.* **1** Utterly depraved; profligate; corrupt. **2** *Theol.* Abandoned in sin; condemned. —*n.* One who is reprobate. —*v.t.* **·bat·ed, ·bat·ing** **1** To disapprove of heartily; condemn. **2** *Theol.* To abandon to damnation. [< LL *reprobare* reprove] —**rep'ro·ba'tion** *n.* —**rep'·ro·ba'tive** *adj.*

re·pro·duce (rē'prə·d^yōōs') *v.* **·duced, ·duc·ing** *v.t.* **1** To make a copy or image of. **2** To bring (offspring) into existence by sexual or asexual generation. **3** To replace (a lost part or organ) by regeneration. **4** To cause the reproduction of (plant life, etc.). **5** To produce again. **6** To recall to the mind; recreate mentally. —*v.i.* **7** To produce offspring. **8** To undergo copying, reproduction, etc. —**re'pro·duc'er** *n.* —**re'pro·duc'i·ble** *adj.*

re·pro·duc·tion (rē′prə·duk′shən) *n.* **1** The act or process of reproducing. **2** Any process by which animals or plants give rise to new organisms. **3** Something reproduced, as a photocopy. **—re′pro·duc′tive** *adj.* **—re′pro·duc′tive·ly** *adv.* **—re′pro·duc′tive·ness** *n.*

re·prog·ra·phy (rē·prog′rə·fē) *n.* The reproduction of graphic material, esp. by electronic devices.

re·proof (ri·pro͞of′) *n.* The act or an expression of reproving; censure.

re·prove (ri·pro͞ov′) *v.t.* **·proved, ·prov·ing 1** To censure, as for a fault; rebuke. **2** To express disapproval of (an act). [< L *re-* again + *probare* to test] **—re·prov′er** *n.* **—re·prov′ing·ly** *adv.* **—Syn. 1** admonish, chasten, chide, reproach, scold.

rep·tile (rep′tīl, -til) *n.* **1** Any of a class of cold-blooded, air-breathing vertebrates having a scaly skin, as crocodiles, lizards, snakes, turtles, etc. **2** A groveling, abject person. *—adj.* **1** Of, like, or characteristic of a reptile. **2** Groveling, sly, base, etc. [< L *reptus*, p.p. of *repere* creep] **—rep·til·i·an** (rep·til′ē·ən) *adj., n.*

Reptile (crocodile)

re·pub·lic (ri·pub′lik) *n.* **1** A state in which the sovereignty resides in the people entitled to vote for officers who represent them in governing. **2** This form of government. [< L *res* thing + *publicus* public]

re·pub·li·can (ri·pub′li·kən) *adj.* Pertaining to, of the nature of, or suitable for a republic. *—n.* An advocate of a republican form of government. **—re·pub′li·can·ism** *n.*

Re·pub·li·can (ri·pub′li·kən) *n.* A member of the Republican Party in the U.S. **—Re·pub′li·can·ism** *n.*

Republican Party One of the two major political parties in the U.S.

re·pu·di·ate (re·pyo͞o′dē·āt) *v.t.* **·at·ed, ·at·ing 1** To refuse to accept as valid, true, or authorized; reject. **2** To refuse to acknowledge or pay. **3** To cast off; disown, as a son. [< L *repudium* divorce] **—re·pu′di·a′tion, re·pu′di·a′tor** *n.*

re·pug·nance (ri·pug′nəns) *n.* **1** A feeling of strong distaste or aversion. **2** Contradiction; inconsistency.

re·pug·nant (ri·pug′nənt) *adj.* **1** Offensive to taste or feeling; exciting aversion. **2** Contradictory; inconsistent. [< L *re* back + *pugnare* to fight] **—re·pug′nant·ly** *adv.*

re·pulse (ri·puls′) *v.t.* **·pulsed, ·puls·ing 1** To drive back; repel, as an attacking force. **2** To repel by coldness, discourtesy, etc.; rebuff. **3** To excite disgust in. *—n.* **1** The act of repulsing, or the state of being repulsed. **2** Rejection; refusal. [< L *repulsus*, p.p. of *repellere* repel] **—re·puls′er** *n.*

re·pul·sion (ri·pul′shən) *n.* **1** The act of repelling, or the state of being repelled. **2** Aversion; repugnance. **3** *Physics* The mutual action of two bodies that tends to drive them apart.

re·pul·sive (ri·pul′siv) *adj.* **1** Exciting strong feelings of dislike or disgust; offensive. **2** Such as to discourage approach; forbidding. **3** Acting to repulse. **—re·pul′sive·ly** *adv.* **—re·pul′sive·ness** *n.*

rep·u·ta·ble (rep′yə·tə·bəl) *adj.* **1** Having a good reputation; estimable; honorable. **2** Complying with the usage of the best writers. **—rep′u·ta·bil′i·ty** *n.* **—rep′u·ta·bly** *adv.*

rep·u·ta·tion (rep′yə·tā′shən) *n.* **1** The general estimation in which a person or thing is held by others, either good or bad. **2** High regard or esteem. **3** A particular credit ascribed to a person or thing: a *reputation* for honesty. [< L *reputare* be reputed.]

re·pute (ri·pyo͞ot′) *v.t.* **·put·ed, ·put·ing** To regard or consider: usu. in the passive: *reputed* to be clever. *—n.* REPUTATION (defs. 1 & 2). [< L *re-* again + *putare* think, count]

re·put·ed (ri·pyo͞o′tid) *adj.* Generally thought or supposed. **—re·put′ed·ly** *adv.*

re·quest (ri·kwest′) *v.t.* **1** To express a desire for, esp. politely. **2** To ask a favor of. *—n.* **1** The act of requesting; entreaty; petition. **2** That which is requested, as a favor. **3** The state of being requested: in *request.* [< L *requisitus*, p.p. of *requirere* seek again]

re·qui·em (rek′wē·əm, rē′kwē-) *n.* **1** *Often cap.* Any musical composition or service for the dead. **2** *Often cap.* A musical setting for such a service. [< L *Requiem* rest, the first word of a Roman Catholic mass for the dead]

req·ui·es·cat (rek′wē·es′kat) *n.* A prayer for the repose of the dead. [L, may he (or she) rest]

re·quire (ri·kwīr′) *v.* **·quired, ·quir·ing** *v.t.* **1** To have need of; find necessary. **2** To call for, demand: Hunting *requires* patience. **3** To insist upon: to *require* absolute silence. **4** To command; order. *—v.i.* **5** To make a demand or request. [< L *re-* again + *quaerere* ask, seek] **—re·quir′er** *n.*

re·quire·ment (ri·kwīr′mənt) *n.* **1** That which is required, as to satisfy a condition; a requisite. **2** A need or necessity.

req·ui·site (rek′wə·zit) *adj.* Required by the nature of things or by circumstances; indispensable. *—n.* That which cannot be dispensed with. **—req′ui·site·ly** *adv.* **—req′ui·site·ness** *n.*

req·ui·si·tion (rek′wə·zish′ən) *n.* **1** A formal request, as for supplies or equipment. **2** The act of requiring or demanding, as that something be supplied. **3** The state of being required. *—v.t.* To make a requisition for or to.

re·qui·tal (ri·kwīt′l) *n.* **1** The act of requiting. **2** Adequate return for good or ill; reward, compensation, or retaliation.

re·quite (ri·kwīt′) *v.t.* **·quit·ed, ·quit·ing 1** To make equivalent return for, as kindness, service, or injury. **2** To compensate or repay in kind. [< RE- + *quite*, obs. var. of QUIT] **—re·quit′er** *n.*

rere·dos (rir′ə dos, rer′ə-, rir′dos) *n.* An ornamental screen behind an altar. [< OF *arere* at the back + *dos* back]

re·run (rē′run′) *n.* A running over again, esp. a showing of a film of videotape after the initial showing. *—v.t.* (rē·run′) **·ran, ·run·ning** To run again.

res. research; reserve; residence; resolution.

re·scind (ri·sind′) *v.t.* To cancel or make void, as an order or an act. [< L *re-* back + *scindere* to cut] **—re·scind′ment, re·scind′er** *n.*

re·scis·sion (ri·sizh′ən) *n.* The act of rescinding. **—re·scis′si·ble, re·scis′so·ry** *adj.*

res·cue (res′kyo͞o) *v.t.* **·cued, ·cu·ing 1** To save or free from danger, captivity, evil, etc. **2** *Law* To take or remove forcibly from the custody of the law. *—n.* The act of rescuing. [< L *re-* again + *excutere* shake off] **—res′cu·er** *n.*

re·search (ri·sûrch′, rē′sûrch) *n.* Studious, systematic investigation or inquiry to ascertain, uncover, or assemble facts, used as a basis for conclusions or the formulation of theory. *—v.t.* **1** To do research on or for: to *research* an article. *—v.i.* **2** To do research; investigate. [< F *recherche*] **—re·search′er** *n.*

re·sect (ri·sekt′) *v.t.* To perform a resection on. [< L *re-* back + *secare* cut, amputate]

re·sec·tion (ri·sek′shən) *n.* The surgical removal of a part of a bone, organ, etc.

re·sem·blance (ri·zem′bləns) *n.* **1** The quality of similarlity in nature, appearance, etc.; likeness. **2** A point or degree of similarity. **3** That which resembles a person or thing; semblance.

re·sem·ble (ri·zem′bəl) *v.t.* **·bled, ·bling** To be similar to in appearance, quality, or character. [< OF *re-* again + *sembler* seem]

re·sent (ri·zent′) *v.t.* To be indignant at, as an injury or insult. [< L *re-* again + *sentire* feel] **—re·sent′ful** *adj.* **—re·sent′ful·ly** *adv.* **—re·sent′ful·ness** *n.*

re·sent·ment (ri·zent′mənt) *n.* Anger and ill will caused by a feeling of injury or mistreatment.

res·er·va·tion (rez′ər·vā′shən) *n.* **1** A feeling of doubt or skepticism, expressed or unexpressed. **2** A qualification; condition; limitation. **3** An agreement to hold something back, as a hotel room, restaurant table, etc., for use at a particular time; also, a record of such an agreement. **4** The act of reserving. **5** A tract of public land set aside for some special purpose, as for the use of Indians or for the preservation of wildlife.

re·serve (ri·zûrv′) *v.t.* **·served, ·serv·ing, 1** To hold back or set aside for special or future use. **2** To arrange for ahead of time; have set aside for one's use. 3 To hold back or delay the determination or disclosure of: to *reserve* judgment. 4 To keep as one's own; retain: to *reserve* the right to quit. —*n.* 1 Something stored up for future use or set aside for a particular purpose. 2 A restrained quality of character or manner; reluctance to divulge one's feelings, thoughts, etc. 3 *Usu. pl.* a A military force held back from active duty to meet possible emergencies. b Members or units of such a force. 4 A substitute player on an athletic team. 5 Funds held back from investment, as in a bank, to meet regular demands. 6 The act of reserving; stint; qualification: without *reserve.* —**in reserve** Subject to or held for future use when needed. —*adj.* Constituting a reserve: a *reserve* supply. [< L *re-* back + *servare* keep] —**re·serv'er** *n.* —**Syn.** *n.* 2 reticence, diffidence, aloofness, modesty, restraint.

reserve clause In professional sports, the stipulation in a contract that commits a player to work for a particular team until released or traded by the employer or until retirement.

re·served (ri·zûrvd') *adj.* 1 Showing or characterized by reserve of manner; undemonstrative. 2 Kept in reserve; held ready for use. —**re·serv·ed·ly** (ri·zûr'vid·lē) *adv.* —**re·serv'ed·ness** *n.*

re·serv·ist (ri·zûr'vist) *n.* A member of a military reserve.

res·er·voir (rez'ər·vwär, -vwôr -vôr) *n.* 1 A place where some material is stored for use, esp. a lake, usu. artificial, for collecting and storing water. 2 A receptacle for a fluid. 3 An extra supply; store.

re·shape (rē·shāp') *v.t.* **·shaped, ·shap·ing** To give new form to; reorder the elements or structure of.

re·side (ri·zīd') *v.i.* **·sid·ed, ·sid·ing** 1 To dwell for a considerable time; live. 2 To exist as an attribute or quality: with *in.* 3 To be vested: with *in.* [< L *residere* sit back]

res·i·dence (rez'ə·dəns) *n.* 1 The place or the house where one resides. 2 The act of residing. 3 The length of time one resides in a place. 4 The act or fact of residing. 5 The condition of residing in a particular place to perform certain duties or to pursue studies, often for a specified length of time.

res·i·den·cy (rez'ə·dən·sē) *n. pl.* **·cies** 1 RESIDENCE. 2 A period of advanced training in a hospital, usu. in a medical specialty.

res·i·dent (rez'ə·dənt) *n.* 1 One who resides or dwells in a place. 2 A physician engaged in residency. 3 A diplomatic representative residing at a foreign seat of government. —*adj.* 1 Having a residence; residing. 2 Living in a place in connection with one's official work. 3 Not migratory: said of certain birds.

res·i·den·tial (rez'ə·den'shəl) *adj.* 1 Of, characteristic of, or suitable for residences. 2 Used by residents.

re·sid·u·al (ri·zij'ōō·əl) *adj.* 1 Pertaining to or having the nature of a residue or remainder. 2 Left over as a residue. —*n.* 1 That which is left over from a total, as after subtraction. 2 *Often pl.* A payment made to a performer for each rerun of taped or filmed TV material in which he or she has appeared. —**re·sid'u·al·ly** *adv.*

re·sid·u·ar·y (ri·zij'ōō·er'ē) *adj.* Entitled to receive the residue of an estate.

res·i·due (rez'ə·dyōō) *n.* 1 A remainder after a part has been separated or removed. 2 *Chem.* Matter left unaffected after combustion, distillation, evaporation, etc. 3 *Law* That portion of an estate which remains after all charges, debts, and particular bequests have been satisfied. [< L *residuus* remaining]

re·sid·u·um (ri·zij'ōō·əm) *n. pl.* **·sid·u·a** (-zij'ōō·ə) 1 RESIDUAL (def. 1). 2 RESIDUE (def. 3). [L]

re·sign (ri·zīn') *v.t.* 1 To give up, as a position, office, or trust. 2 To relinquish (a privilege, claim, etc.). 3 To give over (oneself, one's mind, etc.), as to fate or domination. —*v.i.* 4 To resign a position, etc. [< OF< L *re-* back + *signare* to sign] —**re·sign'er** *n.*

res·ig·na·tion (rez'ig·nā'shən) *n.* 1 The act of resigning. 2 A formal notice of resigning. 3 The quality of being submissive; unresisting acquiescence.

re·signed (ri·zīnd') *adj.* Characterized by resignation; submissive. —**re·sign·ed·ly** (ri·zī'nid·lē) *adv.* —**re·sign'ed·ness** *n.*

re·sil·ience (ri·zil'yəns) *n.* 1 The quality of being resilient; elasticity. 2 Cheerful buoyancy. Also **re·sil'ien·cy.**

re·sil·ient (ri·zil'yənt) *adj.* 1 Springing back to a former shape or position after being bent, compressed, etc. 2 Able to recover quickly; buoyant. [< L *resilire* to rebound] —**re·sil'ient·ly** *adv.*

res·in (rez'in) *n.* 1 A solid or semisolid, usu. translucent substance exuded from certain plants, used in varnishes, plastics, etc. 2 Any of various substances resembling this made by chemical synthesis. 3 ROSIN. —*v.t.* To apply resin to. [< Gk. *rhētinē*] —**res·i·na·ceous** (rez'ə·nā'shəs), **res'in·ous** *adj.*

re·sist (ri·zist') *v.t.* 1 To stay the effect of; withstand; hold off: Steel *resists* corrosion. 2 To fight or struggle against; seek to foil or frustrate: to *resist* arrest; to *resist* temptation. —*v.i.* 3 To offer opposition. [< L *re-* back + *sistere,* causative of *stare* stand] —**re·sist'er, re·sist'i·bil'i·ty** *n.* —**re·sist'i·ble, re·sis'tive** *adj.* —**re·sist'i·bly** *adv.*

re·sis·tance (ri·zis'təns) *n.* 1 The act of resisting. 2 Any force tending to hinder motion. 3 The capacity of an organism to ward off the effects of potentially harmful substances, as toxins. 4 *Electr.* The opposition of a body to the passage through it of an electric current. 5 The underground and guerrilla movement in a conquered country opposing the occupying power. —**re·sis'tant** *adj.*

re·sis·tor (ri·zis'tər) *n. Electr.* A device whose principal property is resistance.

res·o·lute (rez'ə·lōōt) *adj.* Having a fixed purpose; determined. [< L *resolutus,* p.p. of *resolvere* to resolve] —**res'o·lute·ly** *adv.* —**res'o·lute·ness** *n.* —**Syn.** steady, constant, firm, decisive.

res·o·lu·tion (rez'ə·lōō'shən) *n.* 1 The act of resolving or of reducing to a simpler form. 2 The making of a resolve. 3 The purpose or course resolved upon. 4 Firmness of purpose. 5 An outcome or result that serves to settle a problem, uncertainty, or conflict. 6 A statement expressing the intention or judgment of an assembly or group. 7 *Music* a The conventional replacement of a dissonant tone, chord, etc., by one that is consonant. b The tone or chord replacing the dissonant one. 8 The capacity of a telescope, microscope, etc., to give separate images of objects close together.

re·solve (ri·zolv') *v.* **·solved, ·solv·ing** *v.t.* 1 To decide; determine (to do something). 2 To cause to decide or determine. 3 To separate or break down into constituent parts; analyze. 4 To clear away or settle, as a problem, uncertainty, or conflict; explain or solve. 5 To state or decide by vote. 6 *Music* To cause (a dissonant tone, chord, etc.) to undergo resolution. 7 To make distinguishable, as with a telescope or microscope. —*v.i.* 8 To make up one's mind: with *on* or *upon.* 9 To become separated into constituent parts. 10 *Music* To undergo resolution. —*n.* 1 Fixity of purpose; determination. 2 Something resolved upon; a decision. 3 A formal expression of the intention or judgment of an assembly or group. [< L *resolvere* loosen again] —**re·solv'a·ble** *adj.* —**re·solv'er** *n.*

res·o·nance (rez'ə·nəns) *n.* 1 The state or quality of being resonant; resonant sound. 2 Prolongation and amplification of a sound or tone by reverberation. 3 *Physics* A property of oscillatory systems whereby excitation at certain frequencies produces response of greater amplitude than at other frequencies.

res·o·nant (rez'ə·nənt) *adj.* 1 Having the quality of prolonging and amplifying sound by reverberation; producing resonance. 2 Resounding; displaying resonance. 3 Full of or characterized by resonance: a *resonant* voice. [< L *resonare* resound, echo] —**res'o·nant·ly** *adv.*

res·o·nate (rez'ə·nāt) *v.i.* **·nat·ed, ·nat·ing** To exhibit or produce resonance.

res·o·na·tor (rez'ə·nā'tər) *n.* Any device used to produce resonance or to increase sound by resonance.

re·sor·cin·ol (ri·zôr'sin·ōl, -ol) *n.* A derivative of phenol, used as an antiseptic and in making dyes, plastics, etc. Also **re·sor'cin.** [< RES(IN) + *orcinol* a phenol]

re·sort (ri·zôrt') *v.i.* 1 To go frequently or habitually; repair. 2 To have recourse: with *to.* —*n.* 1 A hotel or other place that provides recreational facilities and sometimes entertainment, esp. for those on vacation. 2 The use of something as a means; a recourse; refuge. 3 A person looked to for help. 4 A place frequented regularly. [< OF *re-* again + *sortir* go out] **—re·sort'er** *n.*

re·sound (ri·zound') *v.i.* 1 To be filled with sound; echo; reverberate. 2 To make a loud, prolonged, or echoing sound. 3 To ring; echo. 4 To be famed or extolled. —*v.t.* 5 To give back (a sound, etc.); re-echo. 6 To celebrate; extol. [< L *resonare*]

re·source (rē'sôrs, -sōrs, -zôrs, -zōrs, ri·sôrs', -sōrs', -zôrs', -zōrs') *n.* 1 *Usu. pl.* That which can be drawn upon as a means of help or support. 2 *Usu. pl.* Natural advantages, esp. of a country, as forests, oil deposits, etc. 3 *pl.* Available wealth or property. 4 Skill or ingenuity in meeting any situation. 5 Any way or method of coping with a difficult situation. [< L *re-* back + *surgere* to rise, surge]

re·source·ful (ri·sôrs'fəl, -sōrs'-, -zôrs', -zōrs') *adj.* Having the ability to meet the demands of any situation; ingenious. **—re·source'ful·ly** *adv.* **—re·source'ful·ness** *n.*

re·spect (ri·spekt') *v.t.* 1 To have deferential regard for; esteem. 2 To treat with propriety or consideration. 3 To avoid intruding upon; regard as inviolable. 4 To have reference to; concern. —*n.* 1 A high regard for and appreciation of worth; esteem. 2 Due regard or consideration: *respect* for the law. 3 *pl.* Expressions of consideration; compliments: to pay one's *respects.* 4 The condition of being honored or respected. 5 A specific aspect or detail: In some *respects* the plan is impractical. 6 Reference or relation: usu. with *to:* with *respect* to profits. [< L *respectus,* p.p. of *respicere* look back, consider] **—re·spect'er** *n.*

re·spect·a·ble (ri·spek'tə·bəl) *adj.* 1 Deserving of respect. 2 Conventionally correct; socially acceptable. 3 Having a good appearance; presentable. 4 Moderate in quality, size, or amount; fair: a *respectable* talent. **—re·spect'a·bil'i·ty, re·spect'a·ble·ness** *n.* **—re·spect'a·bly** *adv.*

re·spect·ful (ri·spekt'fəl) *adj.* Characterized by or showing respect. **—re·spect'ful·ly** *adv.* **—re·spect'ful·ness** *n.*

re·spect·ing (ri·spek'ting) *prep.* In relation to.

re·spec·tive (ri·spek'tiv) *adj.* Relating separately to each of those under consideration; several.

re·spec·tive·ly (ri·spek'tiv·lē) *adv.* Singly in the order designated: to describe the duties of the judge and jury *respectively.*

res·pi·ra·tion (res'pə·rā'shən) *n.* 1 The act of inhaling air and expelling it; breathing. 2 The process by which an organism takes in and uses oxygen and gives off carbon dioxide and other waste products. **—re·spir·a·to·ry** (res'pər·ə·tôr'ē, ri·spīr'ə·tôr'ē) *adj.*

res·pi·ra·tor (res'pə·rā'tər) *n.* 1 A screen, as of fine gauze, worn over the mouth or nose, as a protection against dust, etc. 2 An apparatus for artificial respiration.

re·spire (ri·spīr') *v.* **·spired, ·spir·ing** *v.i.* 1 To inhale and exhale air; breathe. —*v.t.* 2 To breathe. [< L *re-* again + *spirare* breathe]

res·pite (res'pit) *n.* 1 Postponement; delay. 2 Temporary relief from labor or effort; an interval of rest. [< Med. L *respectus* delay]

re·splen·dent (ri·splen'dənt) *adj.* Shining with brilliant luster; splendid; gorgeous. [< L *re-* again + *splendere* to shine] **—re·splen'dence, re·splen'den·cy** *n.* **—re·splen'dent·ly** *adv.*

re·spond (ri·spond') *v.i.* 1 To give an answer; reply. 2 To act in reply or return. 3 To react favorably: to *respond* to treatment. —*v.t.* 4 To say in answer; reply. [< L *re-* back + *spondere* to pledge] **—re·spond'er** *n.*

re·spon·dent (ri·spon'dənt) *n.* 1 One who responds or answers. 2 *Law* The party called upon to answer an appeal or petition; a defendant. **—re·spon'dence, re·spon'den·cy** *n.*

re·sponse (ri·spons') *n.* 1 Words or acts called forth as a reaction; an answer or reply. 2 *Eccl.* A portion of a church service said or sung by the congregation in reply to the officiating priest. 3 *Biol.* Any reaction resulting from a stimulus. 4 The action of a physical system when energized or disturbed.

re·spon·si·bil·i·ty (ri·spon'sə·bil'ə·tē) *n. pl.* **·ties** 1 The state of being responsible or accountable. 2 That for which one is responsible; a duty or trust. Also **re·spon'si·ble·ness.**

re·spon·si·ble (ri·spon'sə·bəl) *adj.* 1 Subject to being called upon to account or answer for something; accountable. 2 Able to discriminate between right and wrong. 3 Able to account or answer for something; able to meet one's obligations. 4 Being the cause: Rain was *responsible* for the delay. **—re·spon'si·bly** *adv.*

re·spon·sive (ri·spon'siv) *adj.* 1 Constituting a response. 2 Inclined to react with sympathy or understanding. 3 Containing responses. **—re·spon'sive·ly** *adv.* **—re·spon'sive·ness** *n.*

rest[1] (rest) *v.i.* 1 To cease working or exerting oneself for

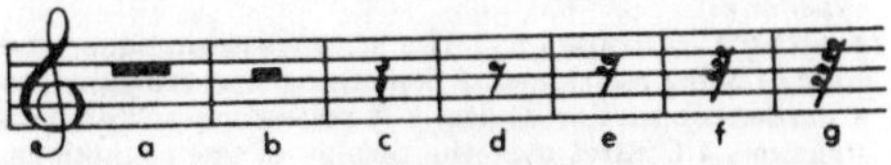

Rests *def. 8b*

a. whole. b. half. c. quarter. d. eighth. e. sixteenth. f. thirty-second. g. sixty-fourth.

a time; cease activity. 2 To obtain ease or refreshment by lying down, sleeping, etc. 3 To sleep. 4 To be still or quiet; cease all motion. 5 To be dead. 6 To be or lie in a specified place: The blame *rests* with me. 7 To be supported; stand, lean, lie, or sit: The rifle *rested* on the mantel. 8 To be founded or based: That *rests* on the assumption of his innocence. 9 To be directed, as the eyes. —*v.t.* 10 To give rest to; refresh by rest. 11 To put, lay, lean, etc., as for support or rest. 12 To found; base. 13 To direct (the gaze, eyes, etc.). 14 *Law* To cease presenting evidence in (a case). —*n.* 1 The act or state of resting. 2 A period of resting. 3 Freedom from disturbance or disquiet; peace; tranquillity. 4 Sleep. 5 Death. 6 That on which anything rests; a support; basis. 7 A place for stopping or resting. 8 *Music* a A measured interval of silence. b A character representing this. **—at rest** In a state of rest; motionless, peaceful, asleep, or dead. [< OE *restan*] **—rest'er** *n.* **—Syn.** *n.* 1 repose, quiet, inactivity, relaxation. 2 respite. 3 serenity, peacefulness, calmness. 6 base, foundation.

rest[2] (rest) *n.* That which remains or is left over. **—the rest** That or those which remain; the remainder; the others. —*v.i.* To be and remain: *Rest* content. [< L *restare* stop, stand]

re·state (rē·stāt') *v.t.* **·stat·ed, ·stat·ing** To state again or in a new way. **—re·state'ment** *n.*

res·tau·rant (res'tə·ränt, -tränt, -tər·ənt) *n.* A place where meals are prepared for sale and served on the premises. [F, lit., restoring]

res·tau·ra·teur (res'tər·ə·tûr') *n.* The proprietor of a restaurant. [F]

rest·ful (rest'fəl) *adj.* 1 Full of or giving rest. 2 Being at rest; quiet. **—rest'ful·ly** *adv.* **—rest'ful·ness** *n.*

res·ti·tu·tion (res'tə·tyōō'shən) *n.* 1 The act of restoring something that has been taken away or lost. 2 Restoration or return to a rightful owner. 3 The act of making good for injury or loss. [< L *restituere* restore]

res·tive (res'tiv) *adj.* 1 Restless; fidgety: The audience grew *restive.* 2 Unwilling to submit to control; unruly; balky. [< F *rester* remain, balk] **—res'tive·ly** *adv.* **—res'tive·ness** *n.*

rest·less (rest'lis) *adj.* 1 Affording no rest or little rest; disturbed: a *restless* sleep. 2 Uneasy; impatient; unquiet: to feel *restless.* 3 Never resting; unending: the *restless* waves. 4 Constantly seeking change or activity; unable or unwilling to rest. **—rest'less·ly** *adv.* **—rest'less·ness** *n.*

res·to·ra·tion (res'tə·rā'shən) *n.* 1 The act of restoring, or the state of being restored. 2 The bringing back to an original or earlier condition, as a work of art or a building; also, the object so restored. **—the Restoration** 1 The return of Charles II to the English throne in 1660. 2 The period following his return up to the revolution in 1688.

re·sto·ra·tive (ri·stôr'ə·tiv, -stō'rə-) *adj.* Tending or able to restore consciousness, strength, health, etc. —*n.* A restorative substance. **—re·sto'ra·tive·ly** *adv.* **—re·sto'ra·tive·ness** *n.*

re·store (ri·stôr', -stōr') *v.t.* **·stored, ·stor·ing** 1 To bring into existence or effect again: to *restore* peace. **2** To bring back to a former or original condition, as a work of art or a building. **3** To put back in a former place or position; reinstate. **4** To bring back to health and vigor. **5** To give back (something lost or taken away); return. [< L *restaurare*] **—re·stor′er** *n.*

re·strain (ri·strān′) *v.t.* **1** To hold back from acting, proceeding, or advancing. **2** To restrict or limit. **3** To deprive of liberty, as by placing in a prison. [< L *re-* back + *stringere* draw tight] **—re·strain′ed·ly** (-strān′id·lē) *adv.* **—re·strain′er** *n.*

re·straint (ri·strānt′) *n.* **1** The act of restraining, or the state of being restrained. **2** Something that restrains, as a harness or similar device. **3** A restriction on conduct; stricture. **4** Control over the display of one's emotions, opinions, etc.; self-control.

re·strict (ri·strikt′) *v.t.* To hold or keep within limits or bounds; confine. [< L *re-* back + *stringere* draw tight]

re·strict·ed (ri·strik′tid) *adj.* **1** Limited or confined. **2** Available for use by certain persons or groups; also, excluding certain persons or groups.

re·stric·tion (ri·strik′shən) *n.* **1** The act of restricting, or the state of being restricted. **2** That which restricts; a limitation or restraint.

re·stric·tive (ri·strik′tiv) *adj.* **1** Serving, tending, or operating to restrict. **2** *Gram.* Limiting: a *restrictive* clause. **—re·stric′tive·ly** *adv.* • In *Will the man who spoke just now please stand up, who spoke just now* is a restrictive clause because it limits the application of *man,* which it modifies. It is not set off by commas, and is to be distinguished from a nonrestrictive clause, as in *The president, who will be 60 years old tomorrow, held a press conference today.*

rest room In a public building, a room or rooms provided with toilet facilities.

re·struc·ture (rē·struk′chər) *v.t.* **·tured, ·tur·ing** To reorganize on a different basis or into a new pattern.

re·sult (ri·zult′) *n.* **1** The outcome of an action, course, or process. **2** A quantity or value derived by calculation. *—v.i.* **1** To be a result or outcome; follow: with *from.* **2** To have as a consequence; end: with *in.* [< L *resultare* spring back]

re·sul·tant (ri·zul′tənt) *adj.* Arising or following as a result. *—n.* **1** That which results; a consequence. **2** *Physics* A vector representing the sum of two or more other vectors.

re·sume (ri·zo͞om′) *v.* **·sumed, ·sum·ing** *v.t.* **1** To begin again after an interruption. **2** To take or occupy again: *Resume* your places. *—v.i.* **3** To continue after an interruption. [< L *resumere* take up again] **—re·sum′er** *n.*

rés·u·mé (rez′o͝o·mā, rez′o͝o·mā′) *n.* A summary, as of one's employment record, education, etc., used in applying for a new position. Also **res·u·mé′, res·u·me′.** [F]

re·sump·tion (ri·zump′shən) *n.* The act of resuming; a beginning again.

re·sur·face (rē·sûr′fis) *v.t.* **·faced, ·fac·ing 1** To provide with a new surface. *—v.i.* **2** To come into view again; become evident.

re·sur·gence (ri·sûr′jəns) *n.* A rising again, as from death, obscurity, or defeat; a surging back. Also **re·sur′·gen·cy. —re·sur′gent** *adj.*

res·ur·rect (rez′ə·rekt′) *v.t.* **1** To bring back to life. **2** To bring back into use or to notice.

res·ur·rec·tion (rez′ə·rek′shən) *n.* **1** Any revival or renewal, as of a practice or custom. **2** *Theol.* **a** A rising from the dead. **b** The state of those who have risen from the dead. **—the Resurrection 1** The rising of Christ from the dead. **2** The rising again of all the dead at the day of final judgment. [< L *resurrectus,* p.p. of *resurgere* < *re-* again + *surgere* rise] **—res′ur·rec′tion·al** *adj.*

re·sus·ci·tate (ri·sus′ə·tāt) *v.t. & v.i.* **·tat·ed, ·tat·ing** To revive from unconsciousness or apparent death. [< L *re-* again + *suscitare* revive] **—re·sus′ci·ta′tion, re·sus′ci·ta′tor** *n.* **—re·sus′ci·ta′tive** *adj.*

ret (ret) *v.t.* **ret·ted, ret·ting** To steep or soak, as flax, to separate the fibers. [ME *reten*]

ret. retired.

re·tail (rē′tāl) *n.* The selling of goods in small quantities directly to the consumer. **—at retail 1** In small quantities to the consumer. **2** At retail prices. *—adj.* Of, pertaining to, or engaged in the sale of goods at retail. *—adv.* AT RETAIL. *—v.t.* **1** To sell in small quantities directly to the consumer. **2** (ri·tāl′) To repeat, as gossip. *—v.i.* **3** To be sold at retail. [< OF *retailler* cut up] **—re′tail·er** *n.*

re·tain (ri·tān′) *v.t.* **1** To keep in one's possession; hold. **2** To maintain in use, practice, etc.: to *retain* one's standards. **3** To keep in a fixed condition or place. **4** To keep in mind; remember. **5** To hire or engage, as an attorney. [< L *re-* back + *tenere* to hold]

re·tain·er[1] (ri·tā′nər) *n.* **1** One employed in the service of a person of rank; servant. **2** One who or that which retains.

re·tain·er[2] (ri·tā′nər) *n.* **1** The fee paid to retain the services of an attorney or other adviser. **2** The act of retaining the services of an attorney, etc. [< OF *retenir* hold back]

retaining wall A wall to prevent a side of an embankment or cut from sliding.

re·tal·i·ate (ri·tal′ē·āt) *v.* **·at·ed, ·at·ing** *v.i.* **1** To return like for like; esp., to repay evil with evil. *—v.t.* **2** To repay (an injury, wrong, etc.) in kind; revenge. [< L *re-* back + *talio* punishment in kind] **—re·tal′i·a′tion** *n.* **—re·tal′i·a′tive, re·tal′i·a·to·ry** *adj.*

re·tard (ri·tärd′) *v.t.* **1** To hinder the advance or course of; impede; delay. *—v.i.* **2** To be delayed. *—n.* Delay; retardation. [< L *re-* back + *tardus* slow] **—re′tar·da′tion, re·tard′er** *n.* **—re·tard′a·tive** *adj.*

re·tard·ant (ri·tär′dənt) *n.* Something that retards: a fire *retardant.* *—adj.* Tending to retard.

re·tar·date (ri·tär′dāt) *n.* A mentally retarded person.

re·tard·ed (ri·tärd′id) *adj.* Abnormally slow in development, esp. mental development.

retch (rech) *v.i.* To make an effort to vomit; strain; heave. [< OE *hræcan* bring up (blood or phlegm)]

retd. retained; returned; retired.

re·ten·tion (ri·ten′shən) *n.* **1** The act of retaining, or the state of being retained. **2** The ability to retain data, images, etc., in the mind subject to later recall. **3** *Med.* A retaining within the body of materials normally excreted.

re·ten·tive (ri·ten′tiv) *adj.* Having the power or tendency to retain, esp. to retain in the mind: a *retentive* memory. **—re·ten′tive·ly** *adv.* **—re·ten′tive·ness, re·ten·tiv′i·ty** *n.*

re·think (rē·thingk′) *v.t.* **·thought** (-thôt), **·think·ing** To think about again, esp. in order to reassess; reconsider.

ret·i·cent (ret′ə·sənt) *adj.* **1** Reluctant to speak or speak freely; habitually silent; reserved. **2** Subdued or restrained; shunning bold statement: *reticent* prose. [< L *re-* again + *tacere* be silent] **—ret′i·cence, ret′i·cen·cy** *n.* **—ret′i·cent·ly** *adv.*

re·tic·u·lar (ri·tik′yə·lər) *adj.* **1** Like a net. **2** Intricate. **3** Of or pertaining to a reticulum. [< L *reticulum* network]

re·tic·u·late (ri·tik′yə·lāt) *v.* **·lat·ed, ·lat·ing** *v.t.* **1** To make a network of. **2** To cover with or as with lines of network. *—v.i.* **3** To form a network. *—adj.* (-lit, -lāt) Having the form or appearance of a network: also **re·tic′u·lat′ed. —re·tic′u·late·ly** *adv.* **—re·tic′u·la′tion** *n.*

ret·i·cule (ret′ə·kyo͞ol) *n.* A small handbag closed with a drawstring, formerly used by women. [< L *reticulum* network]

re·tic·u·lum (ri·tik′yə·ləm) *n. pl.* **·lums** or **·la** (-lə) The second stomach of a ruminant. [L, dim. of *rete* net]

ret·i·na (ret′ə·nə, ret′nə) *n. pl.* **·nas** or **·nae** (-nē) The light-sensitive membrane lining the back of the eyeball at the distal end of the optic nerve. [< L *rete* net] **—ret′i·nal** *adj.*

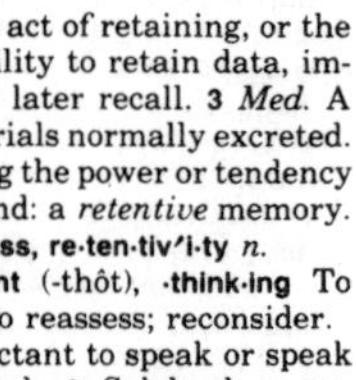

a. retina. b. lens. c. pupil. d. cornea. e. iris. f. optic nerve.

ret·i·nue (ret′ə·n^y^o͞o) *n.* The group of retainers attending a person of rank. [< F *retenir* retain]

re·tire (ri·tīr′) *v.* **·tired, ·tir·ing** *v.i.* **1** To withdraw oneself from business, public life, or active service. **2** To go away or withdraw, as for privacy, shelter, or rest. **3** To go to bed. **4** To fall back; retreat. **5** To move back; recede. *—v.t.* **6** To remove from active service. **7** To pay off and withdraw from circulation: to *retire* bonds. **8** To withdraw (troops, etc.) from action. **9** In baseball, to put out, as a batter. [< F *re-* back + *tirer* draw]

re·tired (ri·tīrd′) *adj.* 1 Withdrawn from business, public life, or active service; esp., no longer actively engaged in one's occupation or profession because of having reached a certain age. 2 Of or for those in retirement. 3 Withdrawn from public view; secluded.

re·tir·ee (ri·tīr′ē′) *n.* A person who is retired.

re·tire·ment (ri·tīr′mənt) *n.* 1 The act of retiring, or the state of being retired. 2 A withdrawal from active engagement in one's occupation or profession, esp. because of age. 3 An age or date at which retirement is planned. 4 A secluded place.

re·tir·ing (ri·tīr′ing) *adj.* Shy; modest; reserved. —**re·tir′·ing·ly** *adv.*

re·tort[1] (ri·tôrt′) *v.t.* 1 To direct (a word or deed) back upon the originator. 2 To reply to, as an accusation or argument, by a similar one. 3 To say in reply. —*v.i.* 4 To answer, esp. sharply. 5 To respond to an accusation, etc., in kind. —*n.* A sharp or witty reply that turns back a previously expressed accusation, insult, etc., upon its originator. [<L *retorquere* twist back] —**re·tort′er** *n.* —**Syn.** *n.* rejoinder, riposte, comeback.

re·tort[2] (ri·tôrt′) *n.* A stoppered vessel with a side tube, for heating or distilling substances. [<L *retortus* bent back]

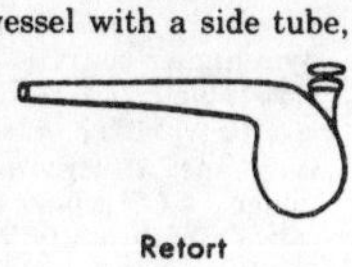
Retort

re·touch (rē·tuch′) *v.t.* 1 To modify by changing details; touch up, as a painting. 2 To change or improve, as a photographic print, by a hand process. —*n.* (*also* rē′·tuch′) A retouching, as of a picture. · —**re·touch′er** *n.*

re·tract (ri·trakt′) *v.t.* & *v.i.* 1 To take back (an assertion, accusation, admission, etc.); disavow. 2 To draw back or in, as the claws of a cat. [<F<L *retractare* draw back] —**re·tract′a·ble, re·trac′tive** *adj.* —**re·trac′tion, re·trac′tor** *n.*

re·trac·tile (ri·trak′til) *adj. Zool.* Capable of being drawn back or in. —**re·trac·til·i·ty** (rē′trak·til′ə·tē) *n.*

re·tread (rē′tred′) *n.* A tire furnished with a new tread to replace a worn one. —*v.t.* (rē·tred′) To fit or furnish (a tire) with a new tread.

re·treat (ri·trēt′) *v.i.* 1 To go back or backward; withdraw. 2 To curve or slope backward. —*n.* 1 The act of retreating or drawing back, as from danger or conflict. 2 The retirement of an armed force from a position of danger. 3 In the armed forces, a signal, as by bugle, for the lowering of the flag at sunset. 4 A place of retirement or security; a refuge. 5 A period of religious contemplation and prayer by a group withdrawn from regular society. [<L *re-* again + *trahere* draw]

re·trench (ri·trench′) *v.t.* 1 To cut down or curtail (expenditures). 2 To cut off or away. —*v.i.* 3 To economize. [<MF *re-* back + *trencher* to cut] —**re·trench′er, re·trench′ment** *n.*

ret·ri·bu·tion (ret′rə·byōō′shən) *n.* 1 The impartial infliction of punishment, as for evil done. 2 That which is done or given in requital, as a reward or, esp., a punishment. [<L *re-* back + *tribuere* to pay] —**re·trib·u·tive** (ri·trib′yə·tiv), **re·trib′u·to′ry** *adj.* —**re·trib′u·tive·ly** *adv.*

re·triev·al (ri·trē′vəl) *n.* 1 The act or process of retrieving. 2 The power to restore or retrieve.

re·trieve (ri·trēv′) *v.* **·trieved, ·triev·ing** *v.t.* 1 To get back; regain. 2 To restore; revive, as flagging spirits. 3 To make up for; remedy the consequences of. 4 To call to mind; remember. 5 To locate and provide access to (data) in computer storage. 6 In tennis, etc., to return (a ball, etc.) after a run. 7 To find and bring in (wounded or dead game): said of dogs. —*v.i.* 8 To retrieve game. —*n.* The act of retrieving; recovery. [<OF *re-* again + *trouver* find] —**re·triev′a·bil′i·ty** *n.* —**re·triev′a·ble** *adj.*

re·triev·er (ri·trē′vər) *n.* 1 Any of various breeds of dog usu. trained to retrieve game. 2 A person who retrieves.

retro- *prefix* Back; backward: *retrograde.* [<L *retro* backward]

ret·ro·ac·tive (ret′rō·ak′tiv, rē′trō-) *adj.* Effective or applicable to a period prior to the time of enactment: a *retroactive* ruling granting wage increases as of last May. —**ret′ro·ac′tive·ly** *adv.* —**ret′ro·ac·tiv′i·ty** *n.*

ret·ro·grade (ret′rə·grād) *adj.* 1 Going, moving, or tending backward. 2 Declining toward a worse state or character. 3 Inverted in order. —*v.* **·grad·ed, ·grad·ing** *v.i.* 1 To move or appear to move backward. 2 To grow worse; decline; degenerate. [<L *retrogradus* a step backward] —**ret′ro·gra·da′tion** (-grā·dā′shən) *n.*

ret·ro·gress (ret′rə·gres) *v.i.* To go back to a more primitive or worse condition. [<L *retro-* backward + *gradi* walk] —**ret′ro·gres′sion** *n.* —**ret′ro·gres′sive** *adj.*

ret·ro·rock·et (ret′rō·rok′it) *n.* An auxiliary rocket that provides a backward thrust, as for reducing speed.

ret·ro·spect (ret′rə·spekt) *n.* A looking back on things past. —**in retrospect** In recalling or reviewing the past. [<L<*retro-* back + *specere* look] —**ret′ro·spec′tion** *n.*

ret·ro·spec·tive (ret′rə·spek′tiv) *adj.* 1 Looking back on the past. 2 RETROACTIVE. —*n.* An exhibition of works representing the entire period of an artist's productivity. —**ret′ro·spec′tive·ly** *adv.*

ret·ro·vi·rus (ret′rō·vī′rəs) *n.* A member of a family of viruses that contain RNA instead of DNA.

re·turn (ri·tûrn′) *v.i.* 1 To come or go back, as to or toward a former place or condition. 2 To come back or revert in thought or speech. 3 To revert to a former owner. 4 To answer; respond. —*v.t.* 5 To bring, carry, send, or put back; restore; replace. 6 To give in return, esp. with an equivalent: to *return* a favor. 7 To yield or produce, as a profit. 8 To send back; reflect, as light or sound. 9 To render (a verdict, etc.). 10 In sports, to throw, hit, or carry back (a ball). 11 In card games, to lead (a suit previously led by one's partner). —*n.* 1 The act of bringing back or restoring something to a former place or condition; restoration or replacement. 2 An appearing again; recurrence. 3 Something given or sent back, esp. in kind or as an equivalent; repayment. 4 Something, as an article of merchandise, returned for exchange or reimbursement. 5 *Often pl.* Profit or revenue; yield. 6 A response; answer; retort. 7 A formal or official report: a tax *return.* 8 *pl.* A report of the tabulated votes of an election. 9 In sports, the act of returning a ball. —**in return** in repayment; as an equivalent —*adj.* 1 Of or for a return: a *return* ticket. 2 Constituting a return or recurrence: a *return* engagement. 3 Returning. 4 Used for return: a *return* address. [<OF] —**re·turn′er** *n.*

re·un·ion (rē·yōōn′yən) *n.* 1 The act of reuniting. 2 A social gathering of persons who have been separated.

re·u·nite (rē′yōō·nīt′) *v.t.* & *v.i.* **·nit·ed, ·nit·ing** To bring or come together after separation. —**re′u·nit′er** *n.*

rev (rev) *Informal n.* A revolution, as of a motor. —*v.t.* **revved, rev·ving** 1 To increase the speed of (an engine, motor, etc.,): often with *up.* 2 To increase in tempo or intensity with *up.* 3 To stimulate or excite: with *up.* —*v.i.* 4 To increase the speed of an engine, etc.: often with *up.* 5 To become stimulated or excited: with *up.*

Rev, Rev. Revelation; Reverend.

rev. revenue; reverse; review; revised; revision; revolution.

re·vamp (rē·vamp′) *v.t.* To make over or renovate.

re·vanch·ism (ri·vänsh′iz′əm) *n.* The revengeful desire to reacquire the land and power lost by a nation through war. [<F *revanche* revenge + -ISM] —**re·vanch′ist** *adj., n.*

re·veal (ri·vēl′) *v.t.* 1 To make known; disclose; divulge. 2 To make visible; expose to view. [<L *revelare* unveil]

rev·eil·le (rev′i·lē) *n.* A morning signal by drum or bugle, notifying soldiers or sailors to rise. [<F *reveillez-vous,* imperative of *se reveiller* wake up]

rev·el (rev′əl) *v.i.* **·eled** or **·elled, ·el·ing** or **·el·ling** 1 to take delight: with *in:* He *revels* in his freedom. 2 To make merry; engage in boisterous festivities. —*n.* 1 A boisterous festivity; celebration. 2 Merrymaking. [<OF<L *rebellare* to rebel] —**rev′el·er** or **rev′el·ler** *n.*

rev·e·la·tion (rev′ə·lā′shən) *n.* 1 The act of revealing. 2 That which is revealed, esp. news of a surprising nature. 3 *Theol.* a The act of revealing divine truth. b That which is so revealed.

Rev·e·la·tion (rev′ə·lā′shən) *n.* The Book of Revelation, the last book of the New Testament; the Apocalypse. Also **Rev′e·la′tions.**

rev·el·ry (rev′əl·rē) *n. pl.* **·ries** Noisy or boisterous merriment.

re·venge (ri·venj′) *n.* **1** The act of returning injury for injury to obtain satisfaction. **2** A means of avenging oneself or others. **3** The desire for vengeance. **4** An opportunity to obtain satisfaction, esp. to make up for a prior defeat, humiliation, etc. —*v.t.* **·venged, ·veng·ing 1** To inflict punishment, injury, or loss in return for. **2** To take or seek vengeance in behalf of. [MF< L *re-* again + *vindicare* vindicate] **—re·venge′ful** *adj.* **—re·venge′ful·ly** *adv.* **—re·veng′er** *n.*

rev·e·nue (rev′ə·nʸōō) *n.* **1** Total current income of a government. **2** Income from any property or investment. **3** A source or an item of income. [<F *revenir* to return]

re·ver·ber·ate (ri·vûr′bə·rāt) *v.* **·at·ed, ·at·ing** *v.i.* **1** To resound or reecho. **2** To be reflected or repelled. **3** To rebound or recoil. —*v.t.* **4** To echo back (a sound); reecho. **5** To reflect. [<L *reverberare* strike back, cause to rebound < *re-* back + *verberare* to beat] **—re·ver′ber·ant** *adj.* **—re·ver′ber·a′tor** *n.*

re·ver·ber·a·tion (ri·vûr′bə·rā′shən) *n.* **1** The act of reverberating, or the state of being reverberated. **2** The rebound or reflection of light, heat, or sound waves. **—re·ver′ber·a′tive, re·ver′ber·a·to′ry** *adj.*

re·vere (ri·vir′) *v.t.* **·vered, ·ver·ing** To regard with profound respect and awe; venerate. [<L *re-* again and again + *vereri* to fear] **—re·ver′er** *n.*

rev·er·ence (rev′ər·əns) *n.* **1** A feeling of profound respect often mingled with awe and affection. **2** An act of respect; an obeisance, as a bow or curtsy. **3** The state of being revered. **4** A reverend person: used as a title. —*v.t.* **·enced, ·enc·ing** To regard with reverence. **—Syn.** *n.* **1** adoration, awe, homage, honor, veneration.

rev·er·end (rev′ər·ənd) *adj.* **1** Worthy of reverence. **2** *Usu. cap.* Being a clergyman: used as a title. **3** Of or pertaining to the clergy. —*n.* A clergyman. • In formal usage, *Reverend* follows *the* and precedes the clergyman's full name or title of address and last name: *the Reverend Donald Smith; the Rev. Mr.* (or *Dr.*) *Smith.* Less formally, *Reverend* is used as a title of address: *Reverend Smith.* The use of *reverend* as a noun should be avoided, esp. in writing: *The reverend's sermon was much admired.*

rev·er·ent (rev′ər·ənt) *adj.* Feeling or expressing reverence. **—rev′er·ent·ly** *adv.*

rev·er·en·tial (rev′ə·ren′shəl) *adj.* Proceeding from or expressing reverence. **—rev′er·en′tial·ly** *adv.*

rev·er·ie (rev′ər·ē) *n. pl.* **·er·ies 1** Abstracted musing; daydreaming. **2** DAYDREAM. Also **rev′er·y.** [<F *rêver* dream]

re·vers (rə·vir′, -vâr′) *n. pl.* **·vers** (-virz′, -vârz′) A part of a garment folded over to show the inside, as the lapel of a coat. [<OF]

re·ver·sal (ri·vûr′səl) *n.* **1** The act of reversing. **2** A change to an opposite direction or course.

re·verse (ri·vûrs′) *adj.* **1** Turned backward; contrary or opposite in direction, order, etc. **2** Having the other side or back in view. **3** Causing backward motion. —*n.* **1** That which is directly opposite or contrary. **2** The back, rear, or secondary side or surface. **3** A change to an opposite position, direction, or state; reversal. **4** A change for the worse; a misfortune. **5** *Mech.* A gear that causes reverse motion. —*v.* **·versed, ·vers·ing** *v.t.* **1** To turn upside down or inside out. **2** To turn in an opposite direction. **3** To transpose; exchange. **4** To change completely or into something opposite: to *reverse* one's stand. **5** To set aside; annul: The higher court *reversed* the decision. **6** To apply (the charges for a telephone call) to the party receiving the call. **7** *Mech.* To cause to have an opposite motion or effect. —*v.i.* **8** To move or turn in the opposite direction. **9** To reverse its action: said of engines, etc. [<L *reversus,* p.p. of *revertere* turn around] **—re·verse′ly** *adv.* **—re·vers′er** *n.*

re·vers·i·ble (ri·vûr′sə·bəl) *adj.* **1** Capable of being worn or used with either side open to view, as a fabric, coat, rug, etc. **2** Capable of being reversed, as a chemical reaction. —*n.* A reversible coat, fabric, etc. **—re·vers′i·bil′i·ty** *n.* **—re·vers′i·bly** *adv.*

re·ver·sion (ri·vûr′zhən, -shən) *n.* **1** A return to some former condition or practice. **2** The act of reversing, or the state of being reversed. **3** *Biol.* The recurrence of ancestral characteristics; atavism. **4** *Law* The return of an estate to the grantor or his heirs after the expiration of the grant. **—re·ver′sion·ar′y, re·ver′sion·al** *adj.*

re·vert (ri·vûrt′) *v.i.* **1** To go or turn back to a former place, condition, attitude, topic, etc. **2** *Biol.* To return to or show characteristics of an earlier, primitive type. [<L *re-* back + *vertere* to turn]

re·vet·ment (ri·vet′mənt) *n.* A facing or retaining wall, as of masonry, for protecting earthworks, river banks, etc. [<F *revêtement*]

re·view (ri·vyōō′) *v.t.* **1** To go over or examine again: to *review* a lesson. **2** To look back upon, as in memory. **3** To study carefully; survey or evaluate: to *review* test scores. **4** To write or make a critical evaluation of, as a new book or film. **5** *Law* To examine (something done or adjudged by a lower court) so as to determine its legality or correctness. —*v.i.* **6** To go over material again. **7** To review books, films, etc. —*n.* **1** An examination or study of something; a retrospective survey. **2** A lesson studied again. **3** A careful study or survey. **4** A critical evaluation, as of a new book or film. **5** A periodical featuring critical reviews. **6** A formal inspection, as of troops. **7** *Law* The process by which the proceedings of a lower court are reexamined by a higher court. [<MF <L *re-* again + *videre* see] **—re·view′a·ble** *adj.* **—re·view′er** *n.*

re·vile (ri·vīl′) *v.* **·viled, ·vil·ing** *v.t.* **1** To assail with abusive language; attack verbally. —*v.i.* **2** To use abusive language. [<OF *reviler* treat as vile] **—re·vile′ment, re·vil′er** *n.* **—Syn.** abuse, vilify, malign, slander, defame.

re·vise (ri·vīz′) *v.t.* **·vised, ·vis·ing 1** To read over so as to correct errors, make changes, etc. **2** To change; alter: to *revise* one's opinion. —*n.* **1** An instance of revising. **2** A corrected proof after having been revised. [<L *revisere* look back, see again] **—re·vis′er** or **re·vi′sor** *n.*

re·vi·sion (ri·vizh′ən) *n.* **1** The act or process of revising. **2** A revised version or edition. **—re·vi′sion·ar′y, re·vi′sion·al** *adj.*

re·vi·sion·ist (ri·vizh′ən·ist) *n.* **1** One who proposes a course of action regarded as a deviation from accepted ideas or established policy, as of a Communist state. **2** One who advocates revision. —*adj.* Of or characteristic of a revisionist. **—re·vi′sion·ism** *n.* **—re·vi′sion·is′tic** *adj.*

re·vi·tal·ize (rē·vī′təl·īz) *v.t.* **·ized, ·iz·ing** To restore vitality to; revive. **—re·vi′tal·i·za′tion** *n.*

re·vi·val (ri·vī′vəl) *n.* **1** The act of reviving, or the state of being revived. **2** A restoration or renewal after neglect or obscurity: the *revival* of radio drama. **3** An awakening of interest in religion. **4** A series of often emotional evangelical meetings.

re·vi·val·ist (ri·vī′vəl·ist) *n.* A preacher or leader of religious revivals. **—re·vi′val·ism** *n.* **—re·vi′val·is′tic** *adj.*

re·vive (ri·vīv′) *v.* **·vived, ·viv·ing** *v.t.* **1** To bring to life or consciousness again. **2** To give new vigor, health, etc., to. **3** To bring back into use or currency, as after a period of neglect or obscurity: to *revive* an old play. **4** To renew in the mind or memory. —*v.i.* **5** To return to consciousness or life. **6** To assume new vigor, health, etc. **7** To come back into use or currency. [<F <L *revivere* < *re-* again + *vivere* live] **—re·viv′er** *n.*

re·viv·i·fy (ri·viv′ə·fī) *v.t.* **·fied, ·fy·ing** To give new life or spirit to. [<L *re-* again + *vivificare* vivify] **—re·viv′i·fi·ca′tion, re·viv′i·fi·er** *n.*

rev·o·ca·ble (rev′ə·kə·bəl) *adj.* Capable of being revoked. **—rev′o·ca·bil′i·ty** *n.* **—rev′o·ca·bly** *adv.*

rev·o·ca·tion (rev′ə·kā′shən) *n.* The act of revoking, or the state of being revoked; repeal.

re·voke (ri·vōk′) *v.* **·voked, ·vok·ing** *v.t.* **1** To annul or make void; rescind. —*v.i.* **2** In card games, to fail to follow suit when possible and required by the rules. —*n.* In card games, neglect to follow suit. [<L *re-* back + *vocare* call] **—re·vok′er** *n.*

re·volt (ri·vōlt′) *n.* **1** An uprising against authority, esp. a government; a rebellion or insurrection. **2** An act of protest or refusal. —*v.i.* **1** To rise in rebellion against constituted authority. **2** To turn away in disgust or abhorrence. —*v.t.* **3** To cause to feel disgust or revulsion; repel. [<L *revolutus,* p.p. of *revolvere* revolve] **—re·volt′er** *n.*

re·volt·ing (ri·vōl′ting) *adj.* Abhorrent; loathsome; nauseating. **—re·volt′ing·ly** *adv.*

rev·o·lu·tion (rev′ə·lōō′shən) *n.* **1** The act or state of revolving. 2 A motion in a closed curve around a center, or a complete or apparent circuit made by a body in such a course. 3 Any turning, winding, or rotation about an axis. 4 A round or cycle of successive events or changes. 5 The period of space or time occupied by a cycle. 6 The overthrow and replacement of a government or political system by those governed. 7 Any extensive or drastic change.

rev·o·lu·tion·ar·y (rev'ə·lōō'shən·er'ē) *adj.* 1 Pertaining to or of the nature of revolution. 2 Causing or tending to produce a revolution. —*n. pl.* **·ar·ies** One who advocates or takes part in a revolution: also **rev'o·lu'tion·ist.**

Revolutionary War AMERICAN REVOLUTION.

rev·o·lu·tion·ize (rev'ə·lōō'shən·īz) *v.t.* **·ized, ·iz·ing** To bring about a radical or complete change in.

re·volve (ri·volv') *v.* **·volved, ·volv·ing** *v.i.* 1 To move in a circle or closed path about a center. 2 To rotate. 3 To recur periodically. —*v.t.* 4 To cause to move in a circle or closed path. 5 To cause to rotate. 6 To turn over mentally. [< L *re-* back + *volvere* roll, turn]

re·volv·er (ri·vol'vər) *n.* A handgun with a cylinder that revolves to make possible successive discharges without reloading.

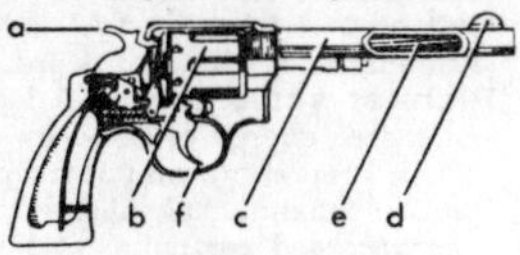

Revolver
a. hammer. b. cylinder. c. barrel. d. front sight. e. rifling. f. trigger.

revolving door A door rotating like a turnstile and consisting of three or four adjustable panels.

re·vue (ri·vyōō') *n.* A series of skits, songs, dances, etc., often comical or satirical in nature. [F, review]

re·vul·sion (ri·vul'shən) *n.* 1 A sudden change of feeling; a strong reaction. 2 Complete disgust or aversion; loathing. [< L *revulsus*, p.p. of *revellere* pluck away] —**re·vul'·sive** *adj.*

re·ward (ri·wôrd') *n.* 1 Something given or done in return, esp. to acknowledge and encourage merit, service, or achievement. 2 Money offered, as for the return of lost goods. —*v.t.* To give a reward to or for; recompense. [< AF *rewarder* look at] —**re·ward'er** *n.*

re·ward·ing (ri·wôrd'ing) *adj.* Yielding intangible rewards; satisfying: a *rewarding* career.

re·write (rē·rīt') *v.t.* **·wrote, ·writ·ten, ·writ·ing** 1 To write over again. 2 To revise or put into publishable form, as for a newspaper. —*n.* (rē'rīt') A news item rewritten for publication.

RF, R.F., r.f. radio frequency.

RFD, R.F.D. Rural Free Delivery.

RH, R.H., r.h. right hand.

R.H. Royal Highness.

Rh rhodium.

r.h. relative humidity.

rhap·so·dize (rap'sə·dīz) *v.t. & v.i.* **·dized, ·diz·ing** To express or recite with exaggerated sentiment and enthusiasm. —**rhap'so·dist** *n.*

rhap·so·dy (rap'sə·dē) *n. pl.* **·dies** 1 Any rapturous or highly enthusiastic utterance or writing. 2 *Music* An instrumental composition of free form. [< Gk. *rhaptein* stitch together + *ōidē* song] —**rhap·sod'ic** (rap·sod'ik) or **·i·cal** *adj.* —**rhap·sod'i·cal·ly** *adv.*

rhe·a (rē'ə) *n.* A ratite bird of South America, resembling but smaller than an ostrich, and having three toes. [NL]

rhe·ni·um (rē'nē·əm) *n.* A rare metallic element (symbol Re). [< L *Rhenus* Rhine]

rhe·o·stat (re'ə·stat) *n. Electr.* A variable resistor used to control or limit current. [< Gk. *rheos* current + *statos* standing]

rhe·sus (rē'səs) *n.* A small macaque of India, widely used in research. Also **rhesus monkey.** [NL]

Rhesus

Rhe·sus factor (rē'səs) RH FACTOR.

rhet·o·ric (ret'ə·rik) *n.* 1 Skill in the use of language, as in writing or speech. 2 The pretentious use of language. [< Gk. *rhētorikē (technē)* rhetorical (art)]

rhe·tor·i·cal (ri·tôr'i·kəl, -tor'-) *adj.* 1 Of the nature of rhetoric. 2 Designed for showy oratorical effect. —**rhe·tor'·i·cal·ly** *adv.* —**rhe·tor'i·cal·ness** *n.*

rhetorical question A question put only for effect, the answer being implied in the question.

rhet·o·ri·cian (ret'ə·rish'ən) *n.* A master or teacher of rhetoric.

rheum (rōōm) *n.* 1 A watery discharge from the nose or eyes. 2 A cold in the head. [< Gk. *rheuma* a flow] —**rheum'y** *adj.* **(·i·er, ·i·est)**

rheu·mat·ic (rōō·mat'ik) *adj.* Of, causing, or affected with rheumatism. —*n.* One affected with rheumatism.

rheumatic fever A disease chiefly affecting young persons following streptococcal infection, characterized by swollen joints and fever.

rheu·ma·tism (rōō'mə·tiz'əm) *n.* Any of various painful disorders of the joints. [< Gk. *rheuma* rheum] —**rheu'ma·toid** (-toid) *adj.*

rheumatoid arthritis A chronic, crippling disease of the joints.

Rh factor (är'āch') A genetically transmitted substance in the blood of most individuals **(Rh positive)** and which may cause hemolytic reactions under certain conditions, as during pregnancy, or following transfusions with blood lacking this factor **(Rh negative).** [< RH(ESUS) monkey, the laboratory animal used in discovering this substance]

rhine·stone (rīn'stōn') *n.* A highly refractive, colorless glass or paste, used as an imitation gemstone.

Rhine wine (rīn) A light, dry, white wine produced in the region of the Rhine River in W. CEN. Europe.

rhi·ni·tis (rī·nī'tis) *n.* Inflammation of the mucous membrane of the nose. [< Gk. *rhis, rhinos* nose + -ITIS]

rhi·no (rī'nō) *n. pl.* **·nos** *Informal* A rhinoceros.

rhi·noc·e·ros (rī·nos'ər·əs) *n. pl.* **·ros·es** or **·ros** Any of various large, herbivorous, three-toed mammals of Africa and Asia, with one or two horns on the snout and a thick hide. [< Gk. *rhis, rhinos* nose + *keras* horn]

Indian rhinoceros

rhi·zome (rī'zōm) *n.* A specialized trailing or underground stem, producing roots from its lower surface and leaves or shoots from its upper surface or upturned tip. [< Gk. *rhizōma* mass of roots] —**rhi·zom·a·tous** (rī·zom'ə·təs, -zō'mə-) *adj.*

rho (rō) *n.* The 17th letter in the Greek alphabet (P,ρ).

Rhode Island Red (rōd) An American breed of chicken having reddish brown feathers.

Rho·de·sia (rō·dē'zhə, -zhē·ə) *n.* A British colony in CEN. Africa; unilaterally declared independence in 1965; 150,333 sq. mi., cap. Salisbury. —**Rho·de'sian** *adj., n.* • See map at AFRICA.

rho·di·um (rō'dē·əm) *n.* A hard, silvery metallic element (symbol Rh). [< Gk. *rhodon* rose; from the color of its salts]

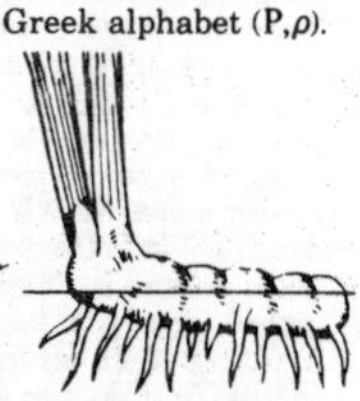

Rhizome of bearded iris

rho·do·den·dron (rō'də·den'drən) *n.* Any of a genus of usu. evergreen shrubs or small trees with profuse clusters of flowers. [< Gk. *rhodon* rose + *dendron* tree]

rhom·boid (rom'boid) *n. Geom.* A parallelogram, esp. one with oblique angles, having unequal adjacent sides. —*adj.* Having the shape of a rhomboid or rhombus: also **rhom·boi'dal.** • See PARALLELOGRAM.

rhom·bus (rom'bəs) *n. pl.* **·bus·es** or **·bi** (-bī) *Geom.* An equilateral parallelogram, esp. one with oblique angles. [< Gk. *rhombos* spinning top, rhombus] —**rhom'bic** *adj.* • See PARALLELOGRAM.

rhu·barb (rōō'bärb) *n.* 1 Any of a genus of large-leaved perennial herbs. 2 The fleshy stalks of a species of rhubarb used in cooking. 3 *Slang* A heated argument or quarrel. [< Gk. *rha* rhubarb + *barbaron* foreign]

rhum·ba (rum′bə) *n.* & *v.* RUMBA.

rhyme (rīm) *n.* **1** A similarity of sounds of two or more words, esp. at the ends of lines of poetry. **2** A word wholly or partly similar in sound to another word. **3** A poem or verse employing such words, esp. at the ends of lines. **4** Poetry or verse in general. —*v.* **rhymed, rhy·ming** *v.i.* **1** To make rhymes or verses. **2** To be a rhyme. **3** To end in rhymes: said of verses. —*v.t.* **4** To write in rhyme. **5** To use as a rhyme. **6** To cause to be a rhyme or rhymes. [< Gk. *rhythmos* rhythm] —**rhym′er** *n.*

rhyme·ster (rīm′stər) *n.* A writer of light or inferior verse.

rhythm (rith′əm) *n.* **1** Movement or process characterized by the regular or harmonious recurrence of a beat, sound, action, development, etc.: the *rhythm* of the pulse; the *rhythm* of the seasons; the *rhythms* of speech. **2 a** The property of music that arises from comparison of the relative duration and accents of sounds. **b** A particular arrangement of durations and accents: a dance *rhythm.* **3** In literature, drama, etc., a forward-moving or compelling development toward a particular end, effect, etc.: The *rhythm* of the play was all off. **4** In art, the regular or harmonious recurrence of colors, forms, etc. **5** In prosody: **a** The cadenced flow of sound as determined by the succession of accented and unaccented syllables. **b** A particular arrangement of such syllables: iambic *rhythm.* [< Gk. *rhythmos* < *rheein* flow] —**rhyth′mic** or **·mi·cal** *adj.* —**rhyth′mi·cal·ly** *adv.* —**rhyth′mist** *n.*

rhythm method A method of birth control that consists of sexual abstinence during the woman's monthly period of ovulation.

RI Rhode Island (P.O. abbr.).

R.I. King and Emperor (L *Rex et Imperator*); Queen and Empress (L *Regina et Imperatrix*); Rhode Island.

ri·al (rī′al) *n.* A silver coin, the basic monetary unit of Iran. [< OF *rial, real* royal]

ri·al·to (rē·al′tō) *n. pl.* **·tos** A market or place of exchange. [< *Rialto,* an island of Venice]

rib (rib) *n.* **1** *Anat.* One of the series of curved bones attached to the spine of most vertebrates, and enclosing the chest cavity. **2** Something, as a structural element, likened to a rib: the *rib* of an umbrella. **3** The curved piece of an arch; also, one of the intersecting arches in vaulting. **4** A curved side timber bending away from the keel in a boat or ship. **5** A raised wale or stripe in cloth or knit goods. **6** A vein or nerve of a leaf or insect's wing. **7** A cut of meat including one or more ribs. **8** A wife: in jocular allusion to the creation of Eve from Adam's rib. *Gen.* 2:22. **9** *Slang* A practical joke. —*v.t.* **ribbed, rib·bing 1** To make with ridges: to *rib* a piece of knitting. **2** To strengthen by or enclose within ribs. **3** *Slang* To make fun of; tease. [< OE *ribb*]

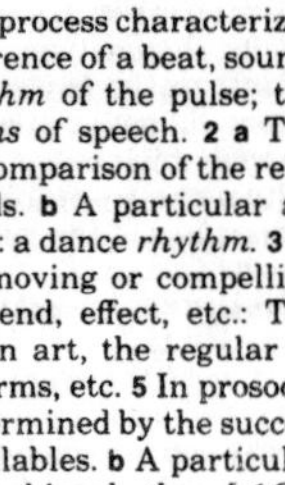

Human ribs

rib·ald (rib′əld) *adj.* Of or indulging in coarse, vulgar language or jokes. —*n.* A ribald person. [< OF *ribauld*] —**Syn.** *adj.* improper, unseemly, gross, obscene, impure.

rib·ald·ry (rib′əl·drē) *n. pl.* **·ries** Ribald language or jokes.

rib·bing (rib′ing) *n.* An arrangement of ribs, as in ribbed cloth, etc.

rib·bon (rib′ən) *n.* **1** A narrow strip of fabric made in a variety of weaves, used as trimming, for tying, etc. **2** Something shaped like or suggesting a ribbon. **3** *pl.* A narrow strip; a shred: torn to *ribbons.* **4** An ink-bearing strip of cloth in a typewriter. **5** A colored strip of cloth worn to signify the award of a prize, etc. **6** *Mil.* A strip of cloth worn to indicate campaigns served in, medals won, etc. —*v.t.* **1** To ornament with ribbons. **2** To tear into ribbons. [< OF *riban*]

ri·bo·fla·vin (rī′bō·flā′vin) *n.* A vitamin of the B complex found in many foods and essential for normal growth.

ri·bo·nu·cle·ic acid (rī′bō·nyōō·klē′ik, -klā′ik) A substance that controls various processes within living cells, esp. the synthesis of proteins.

rice (rīs) *n.* **1** A cereal grass widely cultivated on wet land in warm climates. **2** The edible, starchy seeds of this plant. —*v.t.* **riced, ric·ing** To reduce (a food) to ricelike grains. [< Gk. *oryza*]

rice paper 1 A thin paper made from rice straw. **2** A similar paper made from the pith of a Chinese shrub, the **rice-paper plant.**

ric·er (rī′sər) *n.* A utensil consisting of a perforated container through which cooked potatoes, etc., are pressed.

rich (rich) *adj.* **1** Having large possessions, as of money, goods, or lands; wealthy. **2** Abundantly supplied: with *in* or *with.* **3** Yielding abundant returns; plentiful: a *rich* source of oil. **4** Of precious materials, fine workmanship, etc.: *rich* fabrics. **5** Luxuriant; sumptuous. **6** Having many choice ingredients, as butter, cream, etc.: a *rich* dessert. **7** Pleasingly full and resonant: a *rich* tone. **8** Deep; intense: a *rich* color. **9** Very fragrant; pungent: a *rich* perfume. **10** Containing a high percentage of fuel to air: said of fuel mixtures. **11** Abounding in desirable qualities: *rich* soil. **12** *Informal* Very funny: a *rich* joke. [< OE *rīce*] —**rich′ly** *adv.* —**rich′ness** *n.*

rich·es (rich′iz) *n. pl.* **1** Abundant possessions; wealth. **2** Abundance of whatever is precious.

Rich·ter scale (rik′tər) A logarithmic measure of the estimated energy released by earthquakes according to which 1 represents an imperceptible tremor and 10 a theoretical maximum about one thousand times greater than any recorded earthquake. [< Charles R. *Richter,* born 1900, U.S. seismologist]

rick (rik) *n.* A stack, as of hay, having the top rounded and thatched to protect the interior from rain. —*v.t.* To pile in ricks. [< OE *hrēac*]

rick·ets (rik′its) *n. pl.* (*construed as sing.*) A children's disease in which the bones do not harden normally, usu. due to vitamin D deficiency. [?]

rick·ett·si·a (rik·et′sē·ə) *n. pl.* **·si·ae** (-si·ē) Any of a genus of pathogenic bacterialike organisms parasitic in certain ticks and lice and transmissible to other animals and man. [< H. T. *Ricketts,* 1871–1910, U.S. pathologist] —**rick·ett′si·al** *adj.*

rick·et·y (rik′it·ē) *adj.* **1** Ready to fall; tottering. **2** Affected with rickets. **3** Feeble; infirm. —**rick′et·i·ly** *adv.* —**rick′et·i·ness** *n.*

rick·ey (rik′ē) *n. pl.* **rick·eys** A drink consisting of liquor, usu. gin, sweetened lime juice, and carbonated water. [?]

rick·rack (rik′rak′) *n.* Flat braid in zigzag form, used as trimming. [Reduplication of RACK[1]]

rick·shaw (rik′shô) *n.* JINRIKSHA. Also **rick′sha.**

ric·o·chet (rik′ə·shā′, *esp. Brit.* -shet′) *v.i.* **·cheted** (-shād′) or **·chet·ted** (-shet′id), **·chet·ing** (-shā′ing) or **·chet·ting** (-shet′ing) To glance or rebound obliquely from a surface. —*n.* **1** A richocheting. **2** Something that ricochets. [< OF]

ri·cot·ta (ri·kot′ə; *Ital.* rē·kôt′tä) *n.* An unripened cheese, Italian in origin and similar to cottage cheese but smoother. [< L *recoquere* to cook again]

rid (rid) *v.t.* **rid** or **rid·ded, rid·ding** To free, as from a burden or annoyance: usu. with *of.* —*adj.* Free; clear; quit: with *of:* We are well *rid* of him. [< ON *rythja* clear (land) of trees]

rid·dance (rid′ns) *n.* **1** A removal of something undesirable. **2** The state of being rid.

rid·den (rid′n) *p.p.* of RIDE.

rid·dle[1] (rid′l) *v.t.* **·dled, ·dling 1** To perforate in numerous places, as with shot. **2** To sift through a coarse sieve. **3** To damage, injure, refute, etc., as if by perforating: to *riddle* a theory. —*n.* A coarse sieve. [< OE *hriddel* sieve] —**rid′dler** *n.*

rid·dle[2] (rid′l) *n.* **1** A puzzling question or conundrum. **2** Any mysterious object or person. —*v.* **·dled, ·dling** *v.t.* **1** To solve; explain. —*v.i.* **2** To utter or solve riddles; speak in riddles. [< OE *rædels*]

ride (rīd) *v.* **rode** (*Regional* **rid**), **rid·den** (*Regional* **rid**), **rid·ing** *v.i.* **1** To sit on and be borne along by a horse or other animal. **2** To be borne along as if on horseback. **3** To travel or be carried on or in a vehicle or other conveyance. **4** To be supported in moving: The wheel *rides* on a shaft. **5** To float; be borne: The ship *rides* on the waves. **6** To carry a rider, etc., in a specified manner: This car *rides* well. **7** To seem to float in space, as a star. **8** To lie at anchor, as a ship. **9** To overlap or overlie, as broken bones. **10** To depend: with *on:* Everything *rides* on him. **11** To be a bet: with *on:* They let their money *ride* on the filly. **12** *Informal* To continue unchanged: Let it *ride.* —*v.t.* **13** To sit on and control the motion of (a horse, bicycle, etc.). **14** To be borne or supported upon. **15** To overlap or overlie. **16** To travel or traverse (an area, certain distance, etc.) on a horse, in an automobile, etc. **17** To harass or bother oppressively: usu. in the past participle: *ridden* with shame. **18** To accomplish by riding: to *ride* a race. **19** To convey. **20** *Informal* To tease or torment by ridicule, criticisms, etc. **21** To keep somewhat engaged, usu. unnecessarily: to *ride* the brake. —**ride for a fall** To be headed for trouble, failure, etc. —**ride herd on** To control or supervise closely. —**ride out** To survive; endure successfully. —**ride up** To move upward out of place, as clothing. —*n.* **1** An excursion by any means of conveyance. **2** A means of transportation: to ask for a *ride.* **3** A manner of riding: a smooth *ride.* **4** A mechanical contrivance for riding, as at an amusement park. —**take for a ride** *Slang* **1** To remove (a person) to a place with the intent to murder. **2** To cheat; swindle. [< OE *rīdan*] —**rid'a·ble** *adj.*

rid·er (rī'dər) *n.* **1** One who or that which rides. **2** A piece of writing added to a document, contract, etc. **3** An addition to a legislative bill.

rid·er·less (rī'dər·lis) *adj.* Without a rider.

ridge (rij) *n.* **1** A raised mass of land long in proportion to its width and height. **2** A long, raised or top part of something, as the backbone of an animal, crest of a wave or mountain, ribbed part of a fabric, etc. **3** That part of a roof where the rafters meet the ridgepole. —*v.* **ridged, ridg·ing** *v.t.* **1** To mark with ridges. **2** To form into ridges. —*v.i.* **3** To form ridges. [< OE *hrycg* spine, ridge]

ridge·pole (rij'pōl') *n.* A horizontal timber at the ridge of a roof. Also **ridge'beam', ridge'·piece', ridge'plate'.**

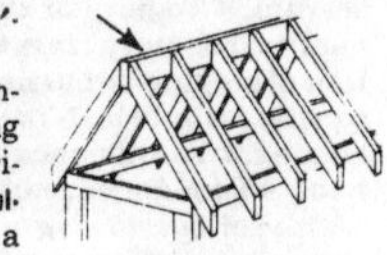

Ridgepole

rid·i·cule (rid'ə·kyōōl) *n.* Language or actions expressing amused contempt or scorn; derision; mockery. —*v.t.* **·culed, ·cul·ing** To make fun of; hold up as a laughingstock; deride. [< L *ridiculum* a jest] —**rid'i·cul'er** *n.* —**Syn.** *v.* banter, chaff, jeer, mock, taunt, satirize, scoff.

ri·dic·u·lous (ri·dik'yə·ləs) *adj.* **1** Absurdly comical: a *ridiculous* costume. **2** Unworthy of consideration; preposterous. —**ri·dic'u·lous·ly** *adv.* —**ri·dic'u·lous·ness** *n.* —**Syn. 1** droll, funny, grotesque, laughable. **2** absurd, nonsensical, foolish, stupid, asinine, senseless.

rid·ing[1] (rī'ding) *n.* The act of one who rides. —*adj.* **1** Suitable for riding: a *riding* horse. **2** To be used while riding: *riding* boots.

rid·ing[2] (rī'ding) *n.* **1** One of the three administrative divisions of Yorkshire, England. **2** Any similar administrative or electoral division, as in Canada, New Zealand, etc. [< OE *thrithing* the third part (of a county)]

rife (rīf) *adj.* **1** Prevalent; widespread. **2** Plentiful; abundant. **3** Containing in abundance: with *with.* [< OE *rīfe*]

riff (rif) *n.* In jazz music, a melodic phrase or motif played repeatedly as background or used as the main theme. —*v.i.* To perform a riff. [? Alter. of REFRAIN]

rif·fle (rif'əl) *n.* **1** A shoal or rocky obstruction lying beneath the surface of a stream and causing a stretch of choppy water. **2** Such a stretch of water. **3** A way of shuffling cards. —*v.t.* & *v.i.* **·fled, ·fling 1** To cause or form a riffle. **2** To shuffle (cards) by bending up adjacent corners of two halves of the pack, and permitting the cards to slip together as they are released. **3** To thumb through (the pages of a book). [?]

riff·raff (rif'raf') *n.* **1** Low, disreputable persons; rabble. **2** Miscellaneous rubbish. [< OF *rif et raf* every bit]

ri·fle[1] (rī'fəl) *n.* **1** A firearm having spiral grooves on the surface of the bore for imparting rotation to the projectile. **2** Such a weapon fired from the shoulder. **3** *pl.* A body of soldiers equipped with rifles. —*v.t.* **·fled, ·fling** To cut a spirally grooved bore in (a firearm, etc.). [< OF *rifler* to scratch]

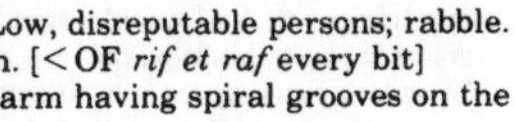

Automatic rifle (M-14)

ri·fle[2] (rī'fəl) *v.t.* **·fled, ·fling 1** To search through and rob, as a safe. **2** To search and rob (a person). **3** To take away by force. [< OF *rifler* to scratch, plunder] —**ri'fler** *n.*

ri·fle·man (rī'fəl·mən) *n. pl.* **·men** (-mən) One armed or skilled with the rifle.

ri·fling (rī'fling) *n.* **1** The operation of forming the grooves in a rifle. **2** Such grooves collectively. • See REVOLVER.

rift (rift) *n.* **1** An opening made by splitting; a cleft; fissure. **2** A break in friendly relations. —*v.t.* & *v.i.* To rive; burst open; split. [< Scand.]

rig[1] (rig) *v.t.* **rigged, rig·ging 1** To fit out; equip. **2** *Naut.* **a** To fit, as a ship, with rigging. **b** To fit (sails, stays, etc.) to masts, yards, etc. **3** *Informal* To dress; clothe, esp. in finery: usu. with *out.* **4** To construct hurriedly or by makeshifts: often with *up.* **5** To prepare or arrange for special operation: controls *rigged* for the left hand only. —*n.* **1** The arrangement of sails, spars, etc., on a vessel. **2** *Informal* Dress or costume. **3** Gear, machinery, or equipment: an oil-well *rig.* **4** A carriage and its horse or horses. [< Scand.]

rig[2] (rig) *v.t.* **rigged, rig·ging** To control fraudulently: manipulate: to *rig* an election. [?]

rig·ger (rig'ər) *n.* One who rigs, esp. one who fits the rigging of ships, assembles lifting or hoisting gear, etc.

rig·ging (rig'ing) *n.* **1** *Naut.* The entire cordage system of a vessel. **2** Equipment or gear used in lifting, hauling, etc.

right (rīt) *adj.* **1** In accordance with some moral, just, or equitable law or standard; virtuous; upright. **2** Conformable to truth or fact; correct; accurate. **3** Proper; fitting; suitable. **4** Most desirable or preferable: to go to the *right* parties. **5** In an orderly or satisfactory state or condition: to put things *right.* **6** Sound; healthy; normal, as in mind or body. **7 a** Designating, being, or closest to that side of the body which is toward the south when one faces the sunrise. **b** Designating a corresponding side of anything. **8** Designating that surface or part of something designed to be worn outward or, when used, to be seen. **9** Politically conservative or reactionary. **10.** *Geom.* Formed by lines, segments, or planes perpendicular to a base. —*adv.* **1** According to some moral, just, or equitable law or standard. **2** Correctly; accurately. **3** In a straight line; directly: Go *right* home. **4** Precisely: He stood *right* in the doorway. **5** Suitably; properly: I can't fix it *right.* **6** Completely: burned *right* to the ground. **7** Thoroughly: He felt *right* at home. **8** Immediately: *right* after the storm. **9** Very: used regionally or in certain titles: a *right* nice day; the *Right* Reverend. **10** On or toward the right: to go *right.* —*n.* **1** That which is right, good, just, true, proper, etc. **2** *Often pl.* Any power or privilege to which a person has a moral, legal, or just claim: the *right* to vote. **3** *pl.* A claim or title to, or interest in, anything that is enforceable by law or custom: *rights* to property; fishing *rights.* **4** Something a person feels belongs justly or properly to him: a *right* to leave. **5** The correct or factual report or interpretation of something. **6** The right hand or side of a person or thing. **7** A direction to or a location on the right. **8** Something adapted for right-hand use or position. **9** In boxing: **a** A blow delivered with the right hand. **b** The right hand. **10** *Often cap.* In politics, a conservative or reactionary position, or a party or group advocating such a position, so designated because of the views of the party occupying seats on the right side of the presiding officer in certain European legislative bodies. —**by right** (or **rights**) Justly; properly. —**to rights** *Informal* Into a proper or orderly condition. —*v.t.* **1** To restore to an upright or normal position. **2** To put in order; set right. **3** To make correct or in accord with facts. **4** To make reparation for; redress or avenge: to *right* a wrong. **5** To make reparation to (a person); do justice to. —*v.i.* **6** To regain an upright or normal position. —*interj.* I agree! I understand! —**right on** *Informal* An interjectory phrase expressing enthusiastic agreement or encouragement: also used adjectivally: He was *right on* in that speech. [< OE *riht*]

add, āce, câre, pälm; end, ēven; it, īce; odd, ōpen, ôrder; tŏŏk, pōōl; up, bûrn; ə = *a* in *above,* *u* in *focus;* yōō = *u* in *fuse;* oil; pout; check; go; ring; thin; this; zh, *vision.* < derived from; ? origin uncertain or unknown.

right·a·bout (rīt′ə·bout′) *n.* A turning in or to the opposite direction, physically or mentally: also **right′a·bout′-face′** (-fās′).

right angle An angle with a measure of 90°. **—right′-an′·gled** *adj.* • See ANGLE.

right·eous (rī′chəs) *adj.* **1** Morally right and just. **2** Virtuous; blameless: a *righteous* man. **3** Justifiable; defensible: *righteous* anger. [< OE *riht* right + *wīs* wise] **—right′·eous·ly** *adv.* **—right′eous·ness** *n.*

right·ful (rīt′fəl) *adj.* **1** Owned or held by just or legal claim: *rightful* heritage. **2** Having a just or legal claim: the *rightful* heir. **3** Fair; upright; just. **4** Proper; suitable. **—right′ful·ly** *adv.* **—right′ful·ness** *n.*

right-hand (rīt′hand′) *adj.* **1** Of, pertaining to, or situated on the right side. **2** Of or for the right hand. **3** Most dependable or helpful: He was my *right-hand* man.

right-hand·ed (rīt′han′did) *adj.* **1** Using the right hand habitually or more easily than the left. **2** Done with the right hand. **3** Turning or moving from left to right, as the hands of a clock. **4** Adapted for use by the right hand, as a tool. **—right′-hand′ed·ness** *n.*

right·ism (rī′tiz·əm) *n.* Politically conservative or reactionary policies or principles. **—right′ist** *adj., n.*

right·ly (rīt′lē) *adv.* **1** Correctly. **2** Honestly; uprightly. **3** Properly; aptly.

right-mind·ed (rīt′mīn′did) *adj.* Having feelings or opinions that are right or sound.

right·ness (rīt′nis) *n.* The quality or condition of being right.

right of search **1** In international law, the right of a belligerent vessel in time of war to verify the nationality of a vessel and to ascertain, if neutral, whether it carries contraband goods. **2** A similar right in time of peace exercised to prevent piracy or to enforce revenue laws.

right of way **1** *Law* **a** The right, general or special, of a person to pass over the land of another. **b** The land over which such passage is made. **2** The strip of land over which a railroad, public highway, or high-tension power line is built. **3** The legal or customary precedence which allows one vehicle to cross in front of another. **4** Any right of precedence. Also **right′-of-way′.**

right triangle A triangle containing one right angle. • See TRIANGLE.

right whale Any of various large-headed, toothless whales that feed by straining water through whalebone plates in the mouth.

right wing **1** A political party or group advocating conservative or reactionary policies. **2** That part of any group advocating such policies. Also **Right Wing.** **—right′-wing′** *adj.* **—right′-wing′er** *n.*

rig·id (rij′id) *adj.* **1** Resisting change of form; stiff. **2** Rigorous; inflexible; severe; strict. **3** Precise; exact, as reasoning. [< L *rigere* be stiff] **—rig′id·ly** *adv.* **—ri·gid′i·ty, rig′id·ness** *n.*

rig·ma·role (rig′mə·rōl, rig′ə·mə-) *n.* Incoherent or uselessly complicated talk, writing, procedures, etc. [Alter. of *ragman roll* catalog, long list]

rig·or (rig′ər) *n.* **1** Harshness; strictness; severity, as of opinions, methods, temperament, etc. **2** Severe hardship, discomfort, etc. **3** Inclemency, as of the weather. **4** Exactitude; precision. **5** The condition of being stiff or rigid. *Brit. sp.* **rig′our.** [< L *rigere* be stiff] **—rig′or·is′tic** *adj.*

rig·or mor·tis (rig′ər môr′tis, rī′gər) The muscular stiffening that ensues within a few hours after death. [L, stiffness of death]

rig·or·ous (rig′ər·əs) *adj.* **1** Marked by or acting with rigor; severe. **2** Rigidly accurate; exact; strict. **3** Extremely difficult, arduous, or demanding. **4** Extremely variable, as weather; inclement. **—rig′or·ous·ly** *adv.* **—rig′or·ous·ness** *n.*

rile (rīl) *v.t. Informal* **1** To vex; irritate. **2** To roil; make muddy. [Var. of ROIL]

rill (ril) *n.* A small stream; rivulet. [< Du. *ril* or G *rille*]

rim (rim) *n.* **1** The edge or border of an object, usu. of a circular object. **2** The circumference of a wheel, esp., on an automobile wheel, the detachable, metal band over which the tire is fitted. **—*v.t.*** **rimmed, rim·ming** **1** To provide with or serve as a rim; border. **2** In sports, to roll around the edge of (the basket, cup, etc.) without falling in. [< OE *rima*]

rime[1] (rīm) *n., v.* **rimed, rim·ing** RHYME.

rime[2] (rīm) *n.* HOARFROST. **—*v.t.* & *v.i.*** **rimed, rim·ing** To cover with rime. [< OE *hrīm* frost] **—rim′y** *adj.*

rind (rīnd) *n.* The skin or outer coat that may be peeled or taken off, as of fruit, cheese, bacon, plants, etc. [< OE *rind* bark, crust]

ring[1] (ring) *n.* **1** Any object, line, or figure having the form of a circle or similar closed curve. **2** A rim or border of something circular. **3** A circular band of precious metal, worn on a finger. **4** Any metal or wooden band used for holding or carrying something: a napkin *ring.* **5** A group of persons or things in a circle. **6** A group of persons engaged in some common, often corrupt activity, business, etc.: a dope *ring.* **7** A place where the bark has been cut away around a branch or tree trunk. **8** A concentric layer of wood formed during a single year's growth in most trees and shrubs: also **annual ring.** **9** An area or arena, usu. circular, for exhibitions, etc.: a circus *ring.* **10** **a** A square area, usu. bordered with ropes, for boxing or wrestling matches. **b** The sport of prizefighting: with *the.* **11** Any field of competition or rivalry: He tossed his hat into the *ring.* **—*v.*** **ringed, ring·ing** *v.t.* **1** To surround with a ring; encircle. **2** To form into a ring or rings. **3** To provide or decorate with a ring or rings. **4** To cut a ring of bark from (a branch or tree); girdle. **5** To put a ring in the nose of (a pig, bull, etc.). **6** To hem in (cattle, etc.) by riding in a circle around them. **7** In certain games, to cast a ring over (a peg or pin). **—*v.i.*** **8** To form a ring or rings. **9** To move or fly in rings or spirals; circle. [< OE *hring*]

ring[2] (ring) *v.* **rang, rung, ring·ing** *v.i.* **1** To give forth a resonant sound, as a bell when struck. **2** To sound loudly or be filled with sound or resonance; reverberate; resound. **3** To cause a bell or bells to sound, as in summoning a servant. **4** To have or suggest, as by sounding, a specified quality: His story *rings* true. **5** To have a continued sensation of ringing or buzzing: My ears *ring.* **—*v.t.*** **6** To cause to ring, as a bell. **7** To produce, as a sound, by or as by ringing. **8** To announce or proclaim by ringing: to *ring* the hour. **9** To summon, escort, usher, etc., by or as by ringing: with *in* or *out*: to *ring* out the old year. **10** To strike (coins, etc.) on something so as to test their quality. **11** To call on the telephone: often with *up.* **—*n.*** **1** The sound produced by a bell. **2** A sound suggesting this: the *ring* of laughter. **3** Any loud, reverberating sound. **4** A telephone call. **5** A sound that is characteristic or indicative: with *of:* His words have the *ring* of truth. [< OE *hringan*] **—Syn.** *v.* **1** clang, resound, peal, toll, chime.

ring bolt A bolt having a ring through an eye in its head.

ringed (ringd) *adj.* **1** Wearing a ring or rings. **2** Encircled or marked by a ring or rings. **3** Composed of rings.

ring·er[1] (ring′ər) *n.* **1** One who or that which rings a bell, chime, etc. **2** *Slang* An athlete, horse, etc., illegally entered in a sports competition. **3** *Slang* A person who bears a marked resemblance to another.

ring·er[2] (ring′ər) *n.* **1** One who or that which rings or encircles. **2** A quoit or horseshoe that falls around one of the posts.

ring·lead·er (ring′lē′dər) *n.* A leader of any undertaking, esp. of an unlawful one.

ring·let (ring′lit) *n.* A long, spiral lock of hair; a curl.

ring·mas·ter (ring′mas′tər, -mäs′-) *n.* One who has charge of a circus ring and of the performances in it.

ring·side (ring′sīd′) *n.* **1** The space or seats immediately surrounding a ring, as at a prize fight. **2** Any area for close viewing.

ring·worm (ring′wûrm′) *n.* A contagious skin disease caused by certain fungi and marked by itchy lesions that spread ringlike from the site of infection.

rink (ringk) *n.* **1** A smooth surface of ice, used for sports, as ice-skating, hockey, curling, etc. **2** A smooth floor, used for roller-skating. **3** A building containing a surface for ice-skating or roller-skating. [< OF *renc* row, rank]

rinse (rins) *v.t.* **rinsed, rins·ing** **1** To remove soap, dirt, impurities, etc., from by immersing in or flooding with clear water. **2** To remove (soap, dirt, etc.) in this manner. **3** To wash lightly: often with *out.* **4** To use a rinse on (the hair). **—*n.*** **1** The act of rinsing. **2** A solution used for coloring the hair. [? < L *recens* recent, fresh] **—rins′er** *n.*

rins·ing (rin′sing) *n.* **1** A rinse. **2** *Usu. pl.* **a** The liquid in which anything is rinsed. **b** That which is removed by rinsing; dregs.

ri·ot (rī′ət) *n.* **1** A violent or tumultuous public disturbance by a large number of persons; uproar; tumult. **2** Any boisterous outburst: a *riot* of laughter. **3** A vivid show or display: a *riot* of color. **4** *Informal* An uproariously amusing person, thing, or performance. **—run riot 1** To act or move wildly and without restraint. **2** To grow profusely, as vines. *—v.i.* **1** To take part in a riot. **2** To live a life of unrestrained revelry. *—v.t.* **3** To spend (time, money, etc.) in riot or revelry. [< OF *riote*] **—ri′ot·er** *n.*

riot act Any forceful or vigorous warning or reprimand. **—read the riot act to** To reprimand bluntly and severely.

ri·ot·ous (rī′ət·əs) *adj.* **1** Of, pertaining to, like, or engaged in a riot. **2** Loud; boisterous. **3** Profligate: *riotous* spending. **—ri′ot·ous·ly** *adv.* **—ri′ot·ous·ness** *n.*

rip[1] (rip) *v.* **ripped, rip·ping** *v.t.* **1** To tear or cut apart, often roughly or violently. **2** To tear or cut from something else, often in a rough or violent manner: with *off, away, out,* etc. **3** To saw or split (wood) in the direction of the grain. *—v.i.* **4** To be torn or cut apart; split. **5** *Informal* To rush headlong. **—rip into** *Informal* To attack violently, as with blows or words. **—rip off** *Slang* **1** To steal or steal from. **2** To cheat, swindle, or dupe. **—rip out** *Informal* To utter with vehemence. *—n.* **1** A tear or split. **2** The act of ripping. [ME *rippen*] **—rip′per** *n.*

rip[2] (rip) *n.* **1** A ripple; a rapid in a river. **2** A riptide.

R.I.P. may he (she, or they) rest in peace (L *requiescat in pace*).

ri·par·i·an (ri·pâr′ē·ən, rī-) *adj.* Pertaining to, growing, or located on the banks of a river or other watercourse. [< L *ripa* bank of a river]

rip·cord (rip′kôrd′) *n.* The cord by which the canopy of a parachute is released from its pack.

ripe (rīp) *adj.* **rip·er, rip·est 1** Grown to maturity and fit for food, as fruit or grain. **2** Brought to a condition for use: *ripe* cheese. **3** Fully developed; matured; also, advanced, as in years. **4** In full readiness to do or try; prepared; ready: *ripe* for mutiny. **5** Resembling ripe fruit; rosy; luscious. **6** Ready for surgical treatment, as an abscess. [< OE *rīpe* ready for reaping] **—ripe′ly** *adv.* **—ripe′ness** *n.*

rip·en (rī′pən) *v.t. & v.i.* To make or become ripe; mature. **—rip′en·er** *n.*

rip-off (rip′of′, -ôf′) *n. Slang* **1** The act of ripping off; an act of stealing or cheating. **2** Anything dishonest, illegal, or exploitative.

ri·poste (ri·pōst′) *n.* **1** A return thrust, as in fencing. **2** A quick, clever reply or retort. Also **ri·post′**. [< L *respondere* to answer]

rip·ping (rip′ing) *adj. Brit. Slang* Splendid; excellent.

rip·ple (rip′əl) *v.* **·pled, ·pling** *v.i.* **1** To become slightly agitated on the surface, as water. **2** To flow with small waves or undulations. **3** To make a sound like water flowing in small waves. *—v.t.* **4** To cause to form ripples. *—n.* **1** A small wave or undulation on the surface of water. **2** Anything suggesting this in appearance. **3** Any sound like that made by rippling. [?] **—rip′pler** *n.* **—rip′pling** *adj.* **—rip′pling·ly** *adv.*

rip-roar·ing (rip′rôr′ing, -rōr′-) *adj. Slang* Excellent; exciting; boisterous.

rip·saw (rip′sô′) *n.* A saw designed for cutting wood in the direction of the grain.

rip·tide (rip′tīd′) *n.* Water violently agitated by conflicting tides or currents.

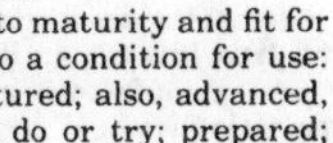

Ripsaw

rise (rīz) *v.* **rose, ris·en, ris·ing** *v.i.* **1** To move upward; go from a lower to a higher position. **2** To slope gradually upward: The ground *rises* here. **3** To have height or elevation; extend upward: The city *rises* above the plain. **4** To gain elevation in rank, status, fortune, or reputation. **5** To swell up: Dough *rises.* **6** To become greater in force, intensity, height, etc. **7** To become greater in amount, value, etc. **8** To become elated or more optimistic: Their spirits *rose.* **9** To become erect after lying down, sitting, etc.; stand up. **10** To get out of bed. **11** To return to life. **12** To revolt; rebel: The people *rose* against the tyrant. **13** To adjourn: The House passed the bill before *rising.* **14** To appear above the horizon: The sun *rose.* **15** To come to the surface, as a fish after a lure. **16** To have origin; begin. **17** To become perceptible to the mind or senses: The scene *rose* in his mind. **18** To occur; happen. **19** To be able to cope with an emergency, danger, etc.: Will he *rise* to the occasion? *—v.t.* **20** To cause to rise. **—rise above** To prove superior to; show oneself indifferent to. *—n.* **1** A moving or sloping upward; ascent. **2** An elevated place, as a small hill. **3** Appearance above the horizon. **4** The height of a stair step or of a flight of stairs. **5** Advance, as in rank, status, prosperity, etc. **6** Increase, as in price, volume, intensity, etc. **7** An origin, source, or beginning. **8** *Informal* An emotional reaction; a response or retort, esp. in the phrase **get a rise out of** (someone). **9** *Brit.* An increase in salary. [< OE *rīsan*]

ris·er (rī′zər) *n.* **1** One who rises or gets up, as from bed: an early *riser.* **2** The vertical part of a step or stair.

ris·i·bil·i·ty (riz′ə·bil′ə·tē) *n. pl.* **·ties 1** A tendency to laughter. **2** *Usu. pl.* Appreciation of what seems laughable or ridiculous.

ris·i·ble (riz′ə·bəl) *adj.* **1** Having the power of laughing. **2** Of a nature to excite laughter. **3** Pertaining to laughter. [< L *risus,* p.p. of *ridere* to laugh] **—ris′i·bly** *adv.*

ris·ing (rī′zing) *adj.* **1** Increasing in wealth, rank, fame, etc. **2** Ascending: the *rising* moon. **3** Sloping upward: a *rising* hill. **4** Advancing to adult years; maturing: the *rising* generation. *—n.* **1** The act of one who or that which rises. **2** That which rises. **3** An uprising or revolt.

risk (risk) *n.* **1** A chance of encountering harm or loss; hazard; danger. **2** In insurance: **a** Chance of loss. **b** Degree of exposure to loss or injury. **c** An applicant for an insurance policy considered with regard to the hazard of insuring him. *—v.t.* **1** To expose to a chance of injury or loss; hazard. **2** To incur the risk of. [< Ital. *risicare* to dare] **—risk′er** *n.*

risk·y (ris′kē) *adj.* **risk·i·er, risk·i·est** Attended with risk; hazardous; dangerous. **—Syn.** perilous, ticklish, unsafe, uncertain, critical.

ris·qué (ris·kā′) *adj.* Bordering on or suggesting impropriety; somewhat daring or improper. [F] **—Syn.** indelicate, lewd, smutty, dirty, unseemly, unbecoming.

ri·tar·dan·do (rē′tär·dän′dō) *adj. & adv. Music* In a gradually slower tempo. [< Ital. *ritardare* to delay]

rite (rīt) *n.* **1** A solemn ceremony performed in a prescribed manner. **2** The words or acts accompanying such a ceremony. **3** Any formal practice or custom. [< L *ritus*]

rit·u·al (rich′o͞o·əl) *n.* **1** A prescribed form or method for the performance of a rite. **2** The use or performing of such rites. **3** A book setting forth such a system of rites or observances. **4** Any act, observance, or custom performed somewhat regularly or formally. *—adj.* Of, pertaining to, or consisting of a rite or rites. **—rit′u·al·ly** *adv.*

rit·u·al·ism (rich′o͞o·əl·iz′əm) *n.* **1** The use or performance of ritual. **2** Slavish devotion to ritual. **—rit′u·al·ist** *n.* **—rit′u·al·is′tic** *adj.* **—rit′u·al·is′ti·cal·ly** *adv.*

ritz·y (rit′sē) *adj.* **ritz′i·er, ritz·i·est** *Slang* Smart; elegant; luxurious. [< C. *Ritz,* 1850–1918, Swiss hotelier] **—Syn.** classy, posh, swank, chic.

ri·val (rī′vəl) *n.* **1** One who strives to equal or excel another; a competitor. **2** A person or thing equaling or nearly equaling another, in any respect. *—v.t.* **·valed** or **·valled, ·val·ing** or **·val·ling 1** To strive to equal or excel; compete with. **2** To be the equal of or a match for. *—adj.* Being a rival or rivals; competing. [< L *rivalis*]

ri·val·ry (rī′vəl·rē) *n. pl.* **·ries 1** The act of rivaling. **2** The state of being a rival or rivals; competition.

rive (rīv) *v.* **rived, rived** or **riv·en, riv·ing** *v.t.* **1** To split asunder by force; cleave. **2** To break (the heart, etc.). *—v.i.* **3** To become split. [< ON *rifa* tear, rend] **—riv·er** (rī′vər) *n.*

riv·er (riv′ər) *n.* **1** A large, natural stream of water, usu. fed by converging tributaries along its course and discharging into a larger body of water. **2** A large stream of any kind; copious flow. **—sell down the river** To betray;

deceive. **—send up the river** *Slang* To send to a penitentiary. [<L *riparius*]

river basin An area of land drained by a river and its branches.

riv·er·side (riv′ər·sīd′) *n.* The land adjacent to a river.

riv·et (riv′it) *n.* A metal bolt, having a head on one end, used to join objects, as metal plates, by passing the shank through holes and forming a head by flattening out the plain end. *—v.t.* **1** To fasten with or as with a rivet. **2** To fasten firmly. **3** To engross or attract (the eyes, attention, etc.). [<OF *river* to clench] **—riv′et·er** *n.*

riv·u·let (riv′yə·lit) *n.* A small stream or brook. [<L *rivus* brook]

RM, R.M., RM., r.m. Reichsmark(s).

rm. ream; room.

rms. reams; rooms.

R.N. registered nurse; Royal Navy.

Rn radon.

RNA ribonucleic acid.

R.N.R. Royal Naval Reserve.

R.N.W.M.P. Royal Northwest Mounted Police.

roach[1] (rōch) *n.* **1** A European freshwater fish of the carp family. **2** One of other related fishes, as the American freshwater sunfish. [<OF *roche*]

roach[2] (rōch) *n.* **1** COCKROACH. **2** *Slang* The butt of a marihuana cigarette.

road (rōd) *n.* **1** An open way for public passage; a highway. **2** Any course followed in a journey or a project. **3** A railroad. **—on the road 1** On tour: said of circuses, theatrical companies, athletic teams, etc. **2** Traveling, as a canvasser or salesman. [<OE *rād* a ride, a riding]

road·bed (rōd′bed′) *n.* The foundation of a railroad track or of a road.

road·block (rōd′blok′) *n.* **1** An obstruction, as of men or materials, for blocking passage, as along a road. **2** Any obstacle to progress or advancement.

road·house (rōd′hous′) *n.* A restaurant, bar, etc., located at the side of a suburban or rural road.

road·metal Broken stone or the like, used for making or repairing roads.

road·run·ner (rōd′run′ər) *n.* A long-tailed, very agile, crested ground cuckoo of SW North America.

road·stead (rōd′sted) *n. Naut.* A place of anchorage offshore, less sheltered than a harbor.

road·ster (rōd′stər) *n.* A light, open automobile having seats for two persons.

road·way (rōd′wā′) *n.* A road, esp. that part over which vehicles pass.

Roadrunner

roam (rōm) *v.i.* **1** To move about purposelessly from place to place; wander; rove. *—v.t.* **2** To wander over; range: to *roam* the fields. *—n.* The act of roaming. [ME *romen*] **—roam′er** *n.*

roan (rōn) *adj.* Of a color consisting of brown, reddish brown, black, or gray thickly interspersed with white hairs, as a horse. *—n.* **1** A roan color. **2** An animal of a roan color. [<Sp. *roano*]

roar (rôr, rōr) *v.i.* **1** To utter a deep, prolonged cry, as of rage or distress. **2** To make a loud noise or din, as a cannon. **3** To laugh loudly. **4** To move, proceed, or act noisily. *—v.t.* **5** To utter or express by roaring: The crowd *roared* its disapproval. *—n.* **1** A full, deep, resonant cry. **2** Any loud, prolonged sound, as of wind or waves. **3** Loud, boisterous laughter. [<OE *rārian*] **—roar′er** *n.*

roast (rōst) *v.t.* **1** To cook by subjecting to the action of heat, as in an oven or by placing in hot ashes, embers, etc. **2** To heat to an extreme degree. **3** To dry and parch: to *roast* coffee. **4** *Informal* To criticize or ridicule severely. *—v.i.* **5** To roast food in an oven, etc. **6** To be cooked or prepared by this method. **7** To be uncomfortably hot. *—n.* **1** Something prepared for roasting, or that is roasted. **2** A social gathering where food is roasted: a corn *roast.* **3** *Informal* Severe criticism or ridicule. *—adj.* Roasted. [<OHG *rōsten*]

roast·er (rōs′tər) *n.* **1** A person who roasts. **2** A pan for roasting. **3** Something suitable for roasting, as a chicken.

rob (rob) *v.* **robbed, rob·bing** *v.t.* **1** To seize and carry off the property of by unlawful violence or threat of violence. **2** To deprive (a person) of something belonging, necessary, due, etc.: *robbed* him of his honor. **3** To take something unlawfully from: to *rob* a store. **4** To steal: to *rob* gold. *—v.i.* **5** To commit robbery. [<OHG *roubon*] **—rob′ber** *n.*

rob·ber·y (rob′ər·ē) *n. pl.* **·ber·ies** The act of robbing, esp. the taking away of the property of another unlawfully by using force or intimidation.

robe (rōb) *n.* **1** A long, loose, flowing, outer garment. **2** *pl.* Such a garment worn as a badge of office or rank. **3** A bathrobe or dressing gown. **4** A blanket or covering: lap *robe.* *—v.* **robed, rob·ing** *v.t.* **1** To put a robe upon; clothe; dress. *—v.i.* **2** To put on robes. [<OHG *roub* robbery]

rob·in (rob′in) *n.* **1** A large North American thrush with reddish brown breast and underparts. **2** A small European songbird with cheeks and breast yellowish red. [Dim. of *Robert*]

American robin

Robin Hood A legendary, English outlaw of great skill in archery, who robbed the rich to relieve the poor.

rob·in's-egg blue (rob′inz·eg′) A pale greenish blue.

Rob·in·son Cru·soe (rob′in·sən krōō′sō) The hero of Daniel Defoe's *Robinson Crusoe* (1719), a sailor shipwrecked on a tropical island.

ro·bot (rō′bət, ·bot) *n.* **1** A machine designed to resemble a person and perform human tasks. **2** Any mechanical device that performs complex, often humanlike actions automatically or by remote control. **3** A person who lives or works mechanically, without spontaneity, etc. [<Czech *robota* work, compulsory service]

robot bomb An early form of jet-powered guided missile having an explosive charge.

ro·bot·ics (rō·bot′iks) *n.* The science of robots, their design, manufacture, and purposes.

ro·bust (rō·bust′, rō′bust) *adj.* **1** Possessing or characterized by great strength or endurance. **2** Requiring strength. **3** Boisterous; rude: *robust* humor. **4** Rich, as in flavor: a *robust* soup. [<L *robur, roboris,* a hard variety of oak, strength] **—ro·bust′ly** *adv.* **—ro·bust′ness** *n.*

roc (rok) *n.* In Arabian and Persian legend, an enormous and powerful bird of prey.

Ro·chelle salt (rō·shel′) A potassium and sodium salt of tartaric acid, used as a cathartic, etc. [<La *Rochelle,* France]

rock[1] (rok) *n.* **1** A large mass of stone or stony matter, often forming a peak or cliff. **2** A piece of stone of any size. **3** *Geol.* Solid mineral matter, such as that forming an essential part of the earth's crust. **4** Any strong, solid person or thing, often acting as a support, refuge, defense, etc. **5** *Slang* A precious gem, esp. a diamond. **—on the rocks** *Informal* **1** In a ruined or disastrous condition. **2** Bankrupt; destitute. **3** Served with ice cubes: said of an alcoholic beverage. *—adj.* Made or composed of rock; hard; stony. [<OF *roque*]

rock[2] (rok) *v.i.* **1** To move backward and forward or from side to side; sway. **2** To sway, reel, or stagger, as from a blow. *—v.t.* **3** To move backward and forward or from side to side, esp. so as to soothe or put to sleep. **4** To cause to sway or reel. *—n.* **1** The act of rocking or a rocking motion. **2** A type of popular music whose origins lie in jazz, country music, and blues, characterized by a strong, persistent rhythm, simple, often repeated melodies, and usu. performed by small, electronically amplified instrumental-singing groups: also **rock and roll, rock-and-roll, rock'n' roll.** [<OE *roccian*]

rock·a·by (rok′ə·bī) *interj.* Go to sleep: used to lull a child to slumber. Also **rock′a·bye, rock′-a-bye.**

rock bottom 1 The very bottom; the lowest possible level. **2** The basis of any issue. **—rock′-bot′tom** *adj.*

rock-bound (rok′bound′) *adj.* Encircled by or bordered with rocks.

rock candy Sugar candied in hard, clear crystals.

rock crystal Colorless transparent quartz.

rock·er (rok′ər) *n.* **1** One who or that which rocks. **2** One of the curved pieces on which a rocking chair or a cradle rocks. 3 ROCKING CHAIR.

rock·et (rok′it) *n.* 1 a A usu. cylindrical firework, projectile, missile, or other device propelled by the reaction of ejected matter. b An engine that develops thrust by ejecting matter. 2 A vehicle propelled by rockets and designed for space travel. —*v.i. & v.t.* 1 To move or cause to move rapidly, as a rocket. 2 To rise or cause to rise rapidly: Her career *rocketed.* [< Ital. *rocchetta* spool]

rock·et·ry (rok′it·rē) *n.* The science and technology of rocket flight, design, and construction.

rock garden A garden with flowers and plants growing in rocky ground or among rocks arranged to imitate this.

rocking chair A chair having the legs set on rockers.

rocking horse A toy horse mounted on rockers.

rock 'n' roll (rok′ən·rōl′) ROCK[2] *n.* (def. 2).

rock-ribbed (rok′ribd′) *adj.* 1 Surrounded or edged by rocks. 2 Inflexible; unchangeable.

rock salt Salt found in large, rocklike masses; halite.

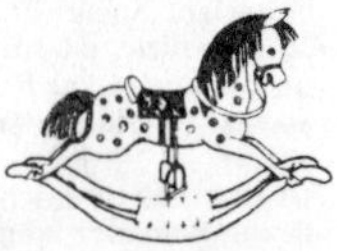

Rocking horse

rock·y[1] (rok′ē) *adj.* **rock·i·er, rock·i·est** 1 Consisting of, abounding in, or resembling rocks. 2 Marked by difficulties, obstacles, etc. 3 Tough; unfeeling; hard. —**rock′i·ness** *n.*

rock·y[2] (rok′ē) *adj.* **rock·i·er, rock·i·est** 1 Not firm; shaky; wobbly. 2 *Informal* Unsteady; dizzy. —**rock′i·ness** *n.*

Rocky Mountain goat MOUNTAIN GOAT.

ro·co·co (rə·kō′kō, rō′kə·kō′) *n.* 1 A style of decoration and architecture distinguished by profuse, elaborate, and delicately executed ornament, esp. prevalent during the 18th century. 2 Anything sometimes considered overly elaborate or delicate, as in literature, music, etc. —*adj.* 1 Having, or built in, the style of rococo. 2 Overelaborate; florid. [< F *rocaille* shellwork]

rod (rod) *n.* 1 A straight, usu. slim piece of wood, metal, etc. 2 A stick used to inflict punishment; also, the punishment itself. 3 A staff, wand, or scepter used as a badge of office, rank, rule, etc. 4 Dominion; rule; power, esp. if harsh. 5 FISHING ROD. 6 LIGHTNING ROD. 7 A measure of length, equal to 5.5 yards or 16.5 feet, or 5.03 meters. 8 A measuring rule. 9 One of the rodlike bodies of the retina sensitive to faint light. 10 *Slang* A pistol. [< OE *rod.*]

rode (rōd) *p.t.* of RIDE.

ro·dent (rōd′nt) *n.* Any of an order of gnawing mammals having incisors that grow continually, as a squirrel, beaver, or rat. —*adj.* 1 Gnawing. 2 Pertaining to the rodents. [< L *rodere* gnaw]

ro·de·o (rō′dē·ō, rō·dā′ō) *n. pl.* **·de·os** 1 A roundup of cattle. 2 A public performance in which the riding of broncos or bulls, roping of calves, lariat-throwing, etc., are presented. [< Sp. *rodear* go around]

rod·o·mon·tade (rod′ə·mon·tād′, rō′də-, -täd′) *n.* Vain boasting; bluster. —*adj.* Bragging. [< Ital. *rodomontata*]

roe[1] (rō) *n.* A mass of eggs of fish or of certain crustaceans, as lobsters. [< MDu. *roge*]

roe[2] (rō) *n.* A small, graceful deer of Europe and w Asia. Also **roe deer.** [< OE *rā*]

roe·buck (rō′buk′) *n.* The male of the roe deer.

Roent·gen ray (rent′gən, runt′-, ren′chən) X-RAY. [< W. K. *Roentgen,* 1845–1923, German physicist]

Ro·ga·tion days (rō·gā′shən) *Eccl.* The three days immediately preceding Ascension Day, observed by litanies, processions, etc. [< L *rogare* ask]

rog·er (roj′ər) *interj.* 1 *Often cap.* Message received: a code signal used in radiotelephone communication. 2 *Informal* All right; O.K. [< *Roger,* code word for *r* used in telecommunication]

rogue (rōg) *n.* 1 A dishonest and unprincipled person; scoundrel. 2 One who is innocently mischievous or playful. 3 A dangerous animal separated from the herd: also used adjectively: a *rogue* elephant. —*v.* **rogued, ro·guing** *v.t.* 1 To practice roguery upon; defraud. —*v.i.* 2 To live or act like a rogue. [?] —**Syn.** ne'er-do-well, dastard, good-for-nothing, scamp, knave, rascal.

ro·guer·y (rō′gər·ē) *n. pl.* **·guer·ies** 1 Knavery, cheating, or dishonesty. 2 Playful mischievousness.

rogues' gallery A collection of photographs of criminals taken to aid the police in their future identification.

ro·guish (rō′gish) *adj.* 1 Playfully mischievous. 2 Knavish; dishonest. —**ro′guish·ly** *adv.* —**ro′guish·ness** *n.*

roil (roil) *v.t.* 1 To make muddy, as a liquid, by stirring up sediment. 2 To irritate or anger. [?< F *rouiller* rust, make muddy] —**roil′y** *adj.*

roist·er (rois′tər) *v.i.* 1 To act in a blustery manner; swagger. 2 To engage in revelry. [< L *rusticus* rustic] —**roist′·er·er** *n.* —**roist′er·ing** *adj.*

ROK Republic of (South) Korea.

role (rōl) *n.* 1 A part or character taken by an actor. 2 Any assumed office or function. 3 A specific or acceptable pattern of behavior expected from those in a certain social status, profession, etc. Also **rôle.** [< F < Med. L *rotulus* roll of parchment]

roll (rōl) *v.i.* 1 To move upon a surface by turning round and round, as a wheel. 2 To move, be moved, travel about, etc., on or as on wheels. 3 To rotate wholly or partially: Her eyes *rolled.* 4 To assume the shape of a ball or cylinder by turning over and over upon itself. 5 To move or appear to move in undulations or swells, as waves or plains. 6 To sway or move from side to side, as a ship. 7 To rotate on a front-to-rear axis, as a projectile. 8 To walk with a swaying motion. 9 To make a sound as of heavy, rolling wheels; rumble: Thunder *rolled* across the sky. 10 To become spread or flat because of pressure applied by a roller, etc. 11 To perform a periodic revolution, as the sun. 12 To move ahead; progress. —*v.t.* 13 To cause to move by turning round and round or turning on an axis: to *roll* a ball; to *roll* a log. 14 To move, push forward, etc., on wheels or rollers. 15 To impel or cause to move onward with a steady, surging motion. 16 To begin to operate: *Roll* the presses. 17 To rotate, as the eyes. 18 To impart a swaying motion to. 19 To spread or make flat by means of a roller. 20 To wrap round and round upon itself. 21 To cause to assume the shape of a ball or cylinder by means of rotation and pressure: to *roll* a cigarette. 22 To wrap or envelop in or as in a covering. 23 To utter with a trilling sound: to *roll* one's r's. 24 To emit in a full and swelling manner, as musical sounds. 25 To beat a roll upon, as a drum. 26 To cast (dice) in the game of craps. 27 *Slang* To rob (a drunk or unconscious person). —**roll back** To cause (prices, wages, etc.) to return to a previous, lower level, as by government order. —**roll in** 1 To arrive, usu. in large amounts: Money *rolled in.* 2 *Informal* To have large amounts of: *rolling in* money. —**roll out** 1 To unroll. 2 *Informal* To get out of (bed, etc.). 3 To flatten by means of rollers. —**roll up** 1 To assume or cause to assume the shape of a ball or cylinder by turning over and over upon itself. 2 To accumulate; amass: to *roll up* large profits. 3 To arrive, as in an automobile. —*n.* 1 The act or an instance of rolling. 2 Anything rolled up. 3 A list of names, a register of items, etc.: an honor *roll.* 4 A long strip of something rolled upon itself: a *roll* of carpet. 5 Any food rolled up in preparation for eating or cooking, esp. small, variously shaped pieces of baked bread dough. 6 A roller. 7 A rolling gait or movement. 8 A rotation on an axis from front to rear, as of an aircraft. 9 A reverberation, as of thunder. 10 A trill. 11 A rapid beating of a drum. 12 An undulation or swell, as of waves or land. 13 *Slang* A wad of paper money; also, money in general. [< L *rota* wheel]

roll·a·way (rōl′ə·wā′) *adj.* Mounted on rollers for easy movement into storage.

roll·back (rōl′bak′) *n.* A return, esp. by government order, to a lower level, as of prices, wages, or rents.

roll call 1 The act of calling out a list of names to ascertain who is present. 2 The time of or signal for this.

roll·er (rō′lər) *n.* 1 One who or that which rolls anything. 2 Any cylindrical device that rolls, as for smoothing, crushing, imprinting, etc. 3 The wheel of a caster or roller skate. 4 A rod on which something is rolled up, as a curtain, map, hair, etc. 5 One of a series of long, swelling waves which break on a coast.

roller bearing A bearing employing rollers to lessen friction between parts.

roller coaster A railway having many steep inclines and sharp curves over which open cars run, as at an amusement park.

roller derby A race between two teams on roller skates, in which points are scored when a player overtakes opponents after skating around a track within a given time.

roll·er-skate (rō′lər·skāt′) *v.i.* **-skat·ed, -skat·ing** To go on roller skates. **—roller skater**

roller skate A metal frame on wheels, designed to be clamped to a shoe, or a shoe with wheels attached, for skating over a sidewalk, a wood floor, etc.

Roller skate

rol·lick·ing (rol′ik·ing) *adj.* Carelessly gay and frolicsome. Also **rol′lick·some** -(səm). [<earlier *rollick*, blend of ROMP and FROLIC]

rolling mill A machine or factory in which metal is rolled into sheets, bars, etc.

rolling pin A cylindrical roller of wood, glass, etc., for rolling out dough, etc.

rolling stock The wheeled transport equipment of a railroad.

roll·top (rōl·top′) *adj.* Having a flexible cover which slides back: a *rolltop* desk.

ro·ly-po·ly (rōl′lē-pō′lē) *adj.* Short and fat; pudgy; dumpy. *—n.* **1** *Brit.* A pudding made of a sheet of pastry dough spread with fruit, preserves, etc., rolled up and cooked. **2** A pudgy person.

ROM Read-only memory, a kind of computer memory from which information may only be read, not altered or erased.

Ro·ma·ic (rō·mā′ik) *adj.* Pertaining to the language or people of modern Greece. *—n.* Modern Greek. [<Gk. *Rhōmaikos* Roman]

ro·maine (rō·mān′) *n.* A variety of lettuce having long leaves clustered in a head. [F, fem. of *romain* Roman]

ro·man (rō′mən) *adj. Printing* Designating a much-used style of type having serifs, and upright strokes thicker than horizontal strokes. *—n.* Roman type.

Ro·man (rō′mən) *adj.* **1** Of, pertaining to, or characteristic of Rome or its people. **2** Of the Roman Catholic Church. **3** LATIN. **4** Having a prominent, aquiline bridge: a *Roman* nose. *—n.* **1** A native, resident, or citizen of modern Rome or a citizen of ancient Rome. **2** A Roman Catholic.

ro·man à clef (rō·män′ ä·klā′) *n. pl.* **romans à clef** (-manz-) *French* A novel in which real persons or events appear under disguise; literally, novel with a key.

Roman calendar A calendar used by the ancient Romans. The day of the new moon (the calends), the full moon (the ides), and the ninth day before the ides (the nones) provided the bases for reckoning the day of the month.

Roman candle A tubular firework which discharges colored balls and sparks of fire.

Roman Catholic **1** A member of the Roman Catholic Church. **2** Of the Roman Catholic Church.

Roman Catholic Church The Christian church which recognizes the Pope as its supreme head on earth.

ro·mance (rō·mans′, rō′mans) *n.* **1** Adventurous, fascinating, or picturesque nature or appeal: the *romance* of faraway places. **2** A disposition to delight in the mysterious, adventurous, sentimental, etc.: a child of *romance.* **3** A love affair. **4** A long narrative from medieval legend, usu. involving heroes in strange adventures and affairs of love. **5** Any fictitious narrative embodying adventure, love affairs, etc. **6** The class of literature consisting of romances (defs. 4 and 5). **7** An extravagant falsehood. *—v.* (rō·mans′) **-manced, -manc·ing** *v.i.* **1** To tell romances. **2** To think or act in a romantic manner. **3** *Informal* To make love. *—v.t.* **4** *Informal* To make love to; woo. [<OF *romans* a story written in French] **—ro·manc′er** *n.*

Ro·mance languages (rō·mans′) The languages developed from the vulgar Latin speech, including French, Italian, Spanish, Portuguese, and Rumanian.

Roman Empire The empire of ancient Rome, established in 27 B.C. and continuing until A.D. 395.

Ro·man·esque (rō′mən·esk′) *adj.* Of, pertaining to, or designating the style of architecture prevalent from the 5th to 12th centuries and characterized by the use of rounded arches and general massiveness. *—n.* Romanesque architecture.

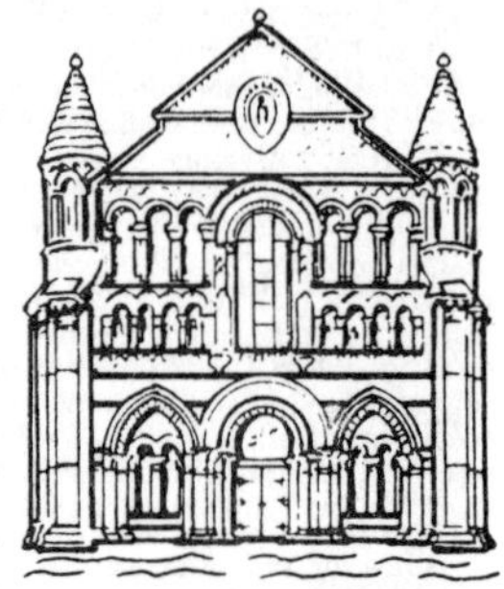
Romanesque façade

Roman holiday Enjoyment or profit derived from the sufferings of others. [< gladiatorial contests of ancient Rome]

Ro·ma·nia (rō·mā′·nē·ə, -mān′yə) *n.* RUMANIA. **—Ro·man′ian** *adj. n.*

Ro·man·ic (rō·man′ik) *adj.* **1** Roman. **2** Of or pertaining to the Romance languages.

Ro·man·ism (rō′mən·iz′əm) *n.* The dogmas, forms, etc., of the Roman Catholic Church: a term used chiefly in disparagement. **—Ro′man·ist** *adj., n.*

Ro·man·ize (rō′mən·īz) *v.t. & v.i.* **-ized, -iz·ing** **1** To make or become Roman or Roman Catholic. **2** To write or speak in a Latinized style. **—Ro′man·i·za′tion** *n.*

Roman numerals The letters used until the tenth century as symbols in arithmetical notation. The basic letters are I (1), V (5), X (10), L (50), C (100), D (500), and M (1000). Intermediate and higher numbers are formed according to the following rules: Any symbol following another of equal or greater value adds to its value, as II = 2, XI = 11; any symbol preceding one of greater value subtracts from its value, as IV = 4, IX = 9, XC = 90; when a symbol stands between two of greater value, it is subtracted from the second and the remainder added to the first, as XIV = 14, LIX = 59.

ro·man·tic (rō·man′tik) *adj.* **1** Of, like, characterized or influenced by romance. **2** Given to feelings or thoughts of romance, adventure, idealism, etc. **3** Characterized by or conducive to love or amorousness. **4** Visionary; fantastic; impractical: a *romantic* scheme. **5** Strangely wild or picturesque: *romantic* scenery. **6** Of, pertaining to, or characteristic of romanticism (def. 1). *—n.* **1** An adherent of romanticism; a romanticist. **2** A romantic person. [<F *romance* romance, novel] **—ro·man′ti·cal·ly** *adv.*

ro·man·ti·cism (rō·man′tə·siz′əm) *n.* **1** *Often cap.* In the late 18th and early 19th centuries, a social and esthetic movement, beginning as a reaction to neo-classicism, and characterized, in art, literature, music, etc., by freedom of form, spontaneity of feeling, flights of lyricism and imagination, and a fascination with the remote past, nature, the strange and picturesque, etc. **2** The quality or characteristic of being romantic. **—ro·man′ti·cist** *n.*

ro·man·ti·cize (rō·man′tə·sīz) *v.t.* **-cized, -ciz·ing** To regard or interpret in a romantic manner.

Romantic Movement ROMANTICISM (def. 1).

Rom·a·ny (rom′ə·nē) *n. pl.* **-nies** **1** GYPSY. **2** The Indic language of the Gypsies. [<Romany *romani* < *rom* man]

Ro·me·o (rō′mē·ō) *n.* **1** In Shakespeare's tragedy *Romeo and Juliet*, the hero of the play. **2** Any ardent male lover.

romp (romp) *v.i.* **1** To play boisterously. **2** To win easily. *—n.* **1** One, esp. a girl, who romps. **2** Noisy, exciting frolic or play. **3** An easy victory. [Var. of RAMP[2]]

romp·er (rom′pər) *n.* **1** One who romps. **2** *pl.* A combination of waist and bloomers, as worn by young children.

Rom·u·lus (rom′yə·ləs) *Rom. Myth.* The founder of Rome, who, with his twin brother Remus, was reared by a she-wolf.

ron·do (ron′dō, ron·dō′) *n. pl.* **-dos** *Music* A composition or movement having a main theme that is repeated after each of several subordinate themes. [Ital., round]

rood (rōōd) *n.* **1** A cross or crucifix. **2** A square land measure, equivalent to one fourth of an acre, or 40 square rods. [<OE *rōd* rod]

roof (rōōf, rŏŏf) *n.* **1** The exterior upper covering of a building. **2** Any top covering, as of the mouth, a car, etc. **3** A house; home. **4** The most elevated part of anything; top; summit. —*v.t.* To cover with or as with a roof. [< OE *hrōf*] —**roof′er** *n.*

roof garden **1** A garden on the roof of a building. **2** A gardenlike space on a roof used for a nightclub, restaurant, etc.

roof·ing (ro͞o′fing, ro͝of′ing) *n.* **1** Roofs collectively. **2** Material for roofs. **3** The act of covering with a roof.

rook[1] (ro͝ok) *n.* **1** An Old World bird similar to a crow. **2** A sharper; cheat; trickster. —*v.t. & v.i.* To cheat; defraud. [< OE *hrōc*]

rook[2] (ro͝ok) *n.* One of a pair of castle-shaped chessmen; a castle. [< Pers. *rukh*]

rook·er·y (ro͝ok′ər·ē) *n. pl.* **·er·ies** **1** A place where rooks flock together and breed. **2** A breeding place of sea birds, seals, etc.

rook·ie (ro͝ok′ē) *n. Slang* **1** A raw recruit in the army, police, or any other service. **2** A first-year player in a major professional sport. [Prob. alter. of RECRUIT]

room (ro͞om, ro͝om) *n.* **1 a** A space for occupancy or use enclosed on all sides, as in a building. **b** The people in a room. **2** Space available or sufficient for some specified purpose: *room* to park. **3** Suitable or warrantable occasion; opportunity: *room* for doubt. **4** *pl.* Lodgings. —*v.i.* To occupy a room; lodge. [< OE *rūm* space]

room·er (ro͞o′mər, ro͝om′ər) *n.* A lodger.

room·ette (ro͞o·met′, ro͝om·et′) *n.* A compartment with a single bed in some railroad sleeping-cars.

room·ful (ro͞om′fo͝ol′, ro͝om′-) *n.* **1** As many or as much as a room will hold. **2** The number of persons in a room.

rooming house A house for roomers.

room·mate (ro͞om′māt′, ro͝om′-) *n.* One who occupies a room with another or others.

room·y (ro͞o′mē, ro͝om′ē) *adj.* **room·i·er, room·i·est** Having abundant room; spacious. —**room′i·ly** *adv.* —**room′i·ness** *n.*

roor·back (ro͝or′bak) *n. U.S.* A fictitious report circulated for political purposes. [< *Roorback,* purported author of a (nonexistent) book of travel]

roost (ro͞ost) *n.* **1 a** A perch upon which fowls rest at night. **b** Any place where birds resort to spend the night. **2** Any temporary resting place. —*v.i.* **1** To sit or perch upon a roost. **2** To come to rest; settle. [< OE *hrōst*]

roost·er (ro͞os′tər) *n.* The male of the chicken; cock. [< ROOST + -ER[1]]

root[1] (ro͞ot, ro͝ot) *n.* **1** The descending axis of a plant, usu. growing underground, providing support and absorbing moisture from the soil. **2** Any underground growth, as a tuber or bulb. **3** Some rootlike part of an organ or structure: the *root* of a tooth, hair, nerve, etc. • See TOOTH. **4** That from which something derives its origin, growth, life, etc.: Money is the *root* of all evil. **5.** *pl.* A mental or emotional attachment to some place or people, as through birth, childhood, etc. **6** The essence or basic part: the *root* of the problem. **7** *Ling.* A word or word part serving as the basic constituent element of a related group of words, as *know* in *unknown, knowledge, knowable,* and *knowingly.* **8** *Math.* A number or element that, taken a specified number of times as a factor, will produce a given number or element. **9** *Music* The principal tone of a chord. —*v.i.* **1** To put forth roots and begin to grow. **2** To be or become firmly fixed or established. —*v.t.* **3** To fix or implant by or as by roots. **4** To pull, dig, or tear up by or as by the roots; extirpate; eradicate: with *up* or *out.* [< OE *rōt*] —**root′y** *adj.*

Rooster

root[2] (ro͞ot, ro͝ot) *v.t.* **1** To turn up or dig with the snout or nose, as swine. —*v.i.* **2** To turn up the earth with the snout. **3** To search for something; rummage. **4** To work hard; toil. [< OE *wrōtan* root up] —**root′er** *n.*

root[3] (ro͞ot, ro͝ot) *v.i. Informal* To give one's moral support to a contestant, team, cause, etc.: with *for.* [? < ROOT[2]] —**root′er** *n.*

root beer A carbonated beverage flavored with the extracts of several roots.

root hair Any of numerous minute outgrowths on plant roots, having an absorbent function.

root·less (ro͞ot′lis, ro͝ot′-) *adj.* **1** Without roots. **2** Having no permanent or secure emotional attachment to a place, community, or culture. —**root′less·ness** *n.*

root·let (ro͞ot′lit, ro͝ot′-) *n.* A small root.

root·stock (ro͞ot′stok′, ro͝ot′-) *n.* RHIZOME.

rope (rōp) *n.* **1** An assembly of intertwined strands of fiber, wire, plastic, etc., forming a thick cord. **2** A collection of things plaited or united in a line. **3** A sticky or glutinous filament or thread of something, as of beaten egg yolks. **4 a** A cord or halter used in hanging. **b** Death by hanging. **5** LASSO. —*v.t.* **roped, rop·ing** **1** To tie or fasten with or as with rope. **2** To enclose, border, or divide with a rope: usu. with *off:* He *roped* off the arena. **3** To catch with a lasso. **4** *Informal* To deceive: with *in.* [< OE *rāp*]

rop·y (rō′pē) *adj.* **rop·i·er, rop·i·est** **1** That may be drawn into threads, as a glutinous substance; stringy. **2** Resembling ropes or cordage. —**rop′i·ly** *adv.* —**rop′i·ness** *n.*

Roque·fort cheese (rōk′fərt, *Fr.* rôk·fôr′) A strong cheese with a blue mold, made from ewe's and goat's milk. [< *Roquefort,* France, where first made]

ror·qual (rôr′kwəl) *n.* Any of various whales having a dorsal fin and marked lengthwise creases at the throat. [< Norw. *röyrkval*]

Rorqual

Ror·schach test (rôr′shäk, -shäkh, rōr′-) A psychological test based on the subject's interpretation of inkblot patterns. [< H. *Rorschach,* 1884–1922, Swiss psychiatrist]

ro·sa·ceous (rō·zā′shəs) *adj.* **1** Of, pertaining to, or designating the rose and related plants, as apple, hawthorn, etc. **2** Resembling a rose; rosy.

ro·sa·ry (rō′zə·rē) *n. pl.* **·ries** *Eccl.* **1** A string of beads for keeping count of a series of prayers, used esp. in Roman Catholicism. **2** The prayers. [< LL *rosarium* a rose garden]

rose[1] (rōz) *n.* **1** Any of a genus of hardy, erect or climbing shrubs with prickly stems and flowers of pink, red, white, yellow, etc. **2** The flower. **3** Any of various other plants or flowers having a likeness to the true rose. **4** A pinkish or purplish red color. **5** An ornamental knot, as of ribbon or lace; a rosette. **6** A form in which gems, esp. diamonds, are often cut. —*adj.* **1** Of, containing, or used for roses. **2** Of the color rose. **3** Rose-scented. [< L *rosa* < Gk. *rhodon*]

rose[2] (rōz) *p.t.* of RISE.

ro·se·ate (rō′zē·it, -āt) *adj.* **1** Of a rose color. **2** Optimistic; rosy. —**ro′se·ate·ly** *adv.*

rose·bud (rōz′bud′) *n.* The bud of a rose.

rose·bush (rōz′bo͝osh′) *n.* A rose-bearing shrub.

rose chafer A hairy, fawn-colored beetle that feeds on the blossoms of roses and related plants. Also **rose beetle.**

rose fever A kind of hay fever that occurs in early summer when roses are in bloom. Also **rose cold.**

rose·mar·y (rōz′mâr′ē) *n. pl.* **·mar·ies** **1** An evergreen, fragrant shrub related to mint. **2** Its leaves, used for their taste and aroma in cooking, perfumery, etc. [< L *ros* dew + *marinus* marine; infl. by *rose, Mary*]

rose of Sharon **1** In the Bible, an unidentified flower. **2** A species of hibiscus; althea. **3** A species of St. Johnswort.

ro·se·o·la (rō·zē·ō′lə, -zē′ə·lə) *n.* **1** A pink rash occurring as a symptom of various diseases. **2** A mild disease of infants, marked by fever and a pink rash. [< L *roseus* rosy]

Ro·set·ta stone (rō·zet′ə) A tablet containing an inscription in Egyptian hieroglyphics and in Greek, found near Rosetta, Egypt, in 1799. It supplied the key to the ancient inscriptions of Egypt.

ro·sette (rō·zet′) *n.* **1** A painted or sculptured architectural ornament with parts circularly arranged. **2** A ribbon badge shaped like a rose and worn to indicate possession of a certain military decoration. **3** Any flowerlike cluster as of leaves, markings, etc. [F, little rose]

rose water An aqueous extract of rose petals, used in perfumery and cooking. **—rose′-wa′ter** *adj.*

rose window A circular window filled with tracery that radiates from the center.

Rose window

rose·wood (rōz′wo͝od′) *n.* **1** The hard, dense, dark-colored wood of various tropical leguminous trees, valued for cabinet work. **2** Any tree yielding such a wood.

Rosh Ha·sha·na (rosh hə·shä′·nə, rōsh) The Jewish New Year, celebrated in September or early October. Also **Rosh Ha·sho′nah** (-shō′-). [<Hebrew *rōsh* head of + *hash-shānāh* the year]

ros·in (roz′in) *n.* A hard, usu. amber-colored resin obtained from turpentine. —*v.t.* To apply rosin to. [Var. of RESIN] **—ros′in·y** *adj.*

ros·ter (ros′tər) *n.* **1** A list of officers and men enrolled for duty. **2** Any list of names. [<Du. *rooster* list]

ros·trum (ros′trəm) *n. pl.* **·trums** or **·tra** (-trə) **1** A stage or platform for public speaking. **2** Those speaking publically on a rostrum. **3** *pl.* **ros·tra** The orators' platform in the Roman forum. **4** A beak or snout. **5** One of various beak-like parts, as the prow of an ancient war galley. [<L *rostrum* beak]

ros·y (rō′zē) *adj.* **ros·i·er, ros·i·est** **1** Like a rose in color. **2** Blushing. **3** Fresh and blooming. **4** Favorable; optimistic. **—ros′i·ly** *adv.* **—ros′i·ness** *n.*

rot (rot) *v.* **rot·ted, rot·ting** *v.i.* **1** To undergo decomposition. **2** To fall or pass by decaying: with *away, off,* etc. **3** To become morally rotten. —*v.t.* **4** To cause to decompose; decay. —*n.* **1** The process of rotting or the state of being rotten. **2** Any of various plant and animal diseases characterized by destruction of tissue. **3** *Informal* Nonsense; bosh. —*interj.* Nonsense. [<OE *rotian*]

rot. rotating; rotation.

ro·ta·ry (rō′tər·ē) *adj.* **1** Turning on an axis, as a wheel. **2** Having some part that so turns: a *rotary* press. [<L *rota* wheel]

rotary engine An engine, as a turbine, in which rotary motion is directly produced without reciprocating parts.

ro·tate (rō′tāt, rō·tāt′) *v.t. & v.i.* **·tat·ed, ·tat·ing** **1** To turn or cause to turn on or as on its axis. **2** To alternate in a definite order or succession. [<L *rota* wheel] **—ro·tat′a·ble, ro′ta·tive** (-tə·tiv) *adj.* **—ro′ta·tor** *n.*

ro·ta·tion (rō·tā′shən) *n.* **1** The act or state of rotating. **2** Alternation or succession in some fixed order. **3** *Agric.* The practice of planting a field with a series of various crops to preserve the fertility of the field: also **crop rotation. —ro·ta′tion·al** *adj.*

ro·ta·to·ry (rō′tə·tôr′ē, -tō′rē) *adj.* **1** Of, pertaining to, or producing rotation. **2** Alternating or recurring.

ROTC, R.O.T.C. Reserve Officers' Training Corps.

rote (rōt) *n.* A routine, mechanical way of doing something. **—by rote** Mechanically; without intelligent attention: to learn *by rote.* [ME]

ro·ti·fer (rō′tə·fər) *n.* Any of numerous many-celled, aquatic microorganisms having rows of cilia at one end, which in motion resemble revolving wheels. [<L *rota* wheel + *ferre* to bear] **—ro·tif·er·al** (rō·tif′ər·əl), **ro·tif′er·ous** *adj.*

Rotifer

ro·tis·se·rie (rō·tis′ə·rē) *n.* **1** An establishment where meat is roasted and sold. **2** A device for roasting meat by rotating it on a spit before or over a source of heat. [<F *rôtir* to roast]

ro·to·gra·vure (rō′tə·grə·vyo͝or′) *n.* **1** A printing process in which an impression is produced by rotating cylinders which have been etched from photographic plates. **2** Something printed by this process. [<L *rota* wheel + GRAVURE]

ro·tor (rō′tər) *n.* **1** A rotary part of a machine. **2** *Aeron.* The horizontally rotating airfoil assembly of a helicopter. [Contraction of ROTATOR]

rot·ten (rot′n) *adj.* **1** Decomposed; spoiled. **2** Smelling of decomposition or decay; putrid. **3** Untrustworthy; dishonest. **4** Weak or unsound, as if decayed. **5** *Informal* Disagreeable or very bad: a *rotten* disposition; a *rotten* movie. [<ON *rotinn*] **—rot′ten·ly** *adv.* **—rot′ten·ness** *n.*

rot·ter (rot′ər) *n. Chiefly Brit. Slang* A worthless or objectionable person.

ro·tund (rō·tund′) *adj.* **1** Rounded out, spherical, or plump. **2** Full-toned, as a voice or utterance. [<L *rota* wheel] **—ro·tun′di·ty, ro·tund′ness** *n.* **—ro·tund′ly** *adv.*

ro·tun·da (rō·tun′də) *n.* A circular building, room, hall, etc., esp. one with a dome. [<L *rotundus* round]

Rotunda

rou·ble (ro͞o′bəl) *n.* RUBLE.

rouche (ro͞osh) *n.* RUCHE.

rou·é (ro͞o·ā′) *n.* A dissolute man; sensualist. [<F *rouer* break on the wheel]

rouge[1] (ro͞ozh) *n.* **1** Any cosmetic used for coloring the cheeks or lips. **2** A red powder, mainly ferric oxide, used in polishing. —*v.* **rouged, roug·ing** *v.t. & v.i.* To color with or apply rouge. [<L *rubeus* ruby]

rouge[2] (ro͞ozh) *n. Can.* A member of the Liberal party in Quebec. —*adj.* Of or pertaining to the Liberal party in Quebec.

rough (ruf) *adj.* **1** Having an uneven surface: a *rough* pavement. **2** Coarse in texture; shaggy: a *rough* tweed. **3** Disordered or ragged: a *rough* shock of hair. **4** Characterized by rude or violent action: *rough* sports. **5** Agitated; stormy: a *rough* passage. **6** Rude; coarse: a *rough* manner. **7** Lacking finish and polish; crude: a *rough* gem. **8** Done or made hastily and without attention to details: a *rough* sketch. **9** *Phonet.* Uttered with an aspiration, or *h* sound. **10** Harsh to the senses: *rough* sounds. **11** Without comforts or conveniences: the *rough* life of the poor. **12** Requiring physical strength: *rough* work. **13** *Informal* Difficult; trying: It's been a *rough* day. **—in the rough** In an unpolished or crude condition. —*n.* **1** Any rough ground. **2** A crude, incomplete, or unpolished object, material, or condition. **3** Any part of a golf course on which tall grass, bushes, etc., grow. **4** *Chiefly Brit.* A rude or violent person; ruffian. —*v.t.* **1** To make rough; roughen. **2** To treat roughly: often with *up.* **3** To make, cut, or sketch roughly: to *rough* in the details of a plan. —*v.i.* **4** To become rough. **5** To behave roughly. **—rough it** To live under or endure conditions that are hard, rustic, inconvenient, etc. —*adv.* In a rude manner. [<OE *rūh*] **—rough′ly** *adv.* **—rough′ness** *n.* **—Syn.** *adj.* **3** unkempt. **6** boorish, uncultivated.

rough·age (ruf′ij) *n.* Food containing bulky, indigestible constituents that stimulate peristalsis.

rough-and-read·y (ruf′ən·red′ē) *adj.* Crude or rough in quality but effective for a particular purpose.

rough-and-tum·ble (ruf′ən·tum′bəl) *adj.* Disregarding all rules of fighting; disorderly and violent. —*n.* A fight in which anything goes; a brawl.

rough-cast (ruf′kast′, -käst′) *v.t.* **-cast, -cast·ing** **1** To shape or prepare in a preliminary or incomplete form. **2** To coat, as a wall, with coarse plaster. —*n.* **1** Very coarse plaster for the outside of buildings. **2** A rude model of a thing in its first rough stage. **—rough′-cast′er** *n.*

rough-dry (ruf′drī′) *v.t.* **-dried, -dry·ing** To dry (laundry) without ironing it afterward. —*adj.* Washed and dried but unironed.

rough·en (ruf′ən) *v.t. & v.i.* To make or become rough.

rough-hew (ruf′ʰyo͞o′) *v.t.* **-hewed, -hewed** or **-hewn, -hew·ing** **1** To hew or shape roughly without smoothing. **2** To make crudely.

rough·house (ruf′hous′) *Slang n.* A noisy, boisterous disturbance; rough play. —*v.* (ruf′hous′, -houz′) **·housed, ·hous·ing** *v.i.* **1** To engage in roughhouse. —*v.t.* **2** To handle or treat roughly, usu. without hostile intent.

rough·neck (ruf′nek′) *n. Slang* A rowdy.

rough·rid·er (ruf′rī′dər) *n.* One skilled in breaking horses for riding, or accustomed to hard, rough riding.

Rough Riders The 1st U.S. Volunteer Cavalry in the Spanish-American War of 1898, commanded by Theodore Roosevelt.

rough-shod (ruf′shod′) *adj.* Shod with rough shoes to prevent slipping, as a horse. **—ride rough-shod (over)** To treat harshly and without consideration.

rou·lette (rōō·let′) *n.* 1 A gambling game in which participants place bets on which compartment of a rotating shallow bowl a small ball will fall into. 2 A toothed wheel for making marks or holes, as the tiny slits in a sheet of postage stamps. —*v.t.* **·let·ted, ·let·ting** To use a roulette upon. [< L *rota* wheel]

Rou·ma·ni·a (rōō·mā′nē·ə, -mān′yə) *n.* RUMANIA. —**Rou·ma′ni·an** *adj., n.*

round (round) *adj.* 1 Having a shape like a ball, ring, or cylinder; spherical, circular, or cylindrical. 2 Semicircular: a *round* arch. 3 Plump. 4 Formed or moving in rotation or a circle: a *round* dance. 5 Approximate to the nearest ten, hundred, thousand, etc., as a number. 6 Pronounced with the lips forming a circle, as the vowel *o.* 7 Full; complete: a *round* dozen. 8 Large; ample; liberal: a good *round* fee. 9 Full in tone or resonance. 10 Free and easy; brisk: a *round* pace. —*n.* 1 Something round, as a globe, ring, or cylinder. 2 *Often pl.* A circular course or range; circuit; beat: to make one's *rounds.* 3 Motion in a circular path. 4 A series of recurrent actions; a routine: the daily *round* of life. 5 An outburst, as of applause. 6 In some sports and games, a division based on action or time. 7 A short canon for several voices. 8 A single shot fired by a weapon or by each of a number of weapons. 9 The ammunition used for such a shot. 10 ROUND DANCE (def. 1). 11 The state of being carved out on all sides: opposed to *relief.* 12 The state or condition of being circular; roundness. 13 A portion of a hind leg of beef, between the rump and lower leg. 14 A rung of a chair or ladder. —**go the rounds** To pass from person to person, as gossip, a rumor, etc. —*v.t.* 1 To make round or plump. 2 *Phonet.* To utter (a vowel) with the lips in a rounded position. 3 To travel or go around; make a circuit of. —*v.i.* 4 To become round or plump. 5 To make a circuit; travel a circular course. 6 To turn around. —**round off** (or **out**) 1 To make or become round. 2 To bring to perfection or completion. —**round up** 1 To collect (cattle, etc.) in a herd, as for driving to market. 2 *Informal* To gather together; assemble. —*adv.* 1 On all sides; in such a manner as to encircle: A crowd gathered *round.* 2 In a circular path, or with a circular motion: The plane circled *round;* The wheel turns *round.* 3 To each of a number, one after the other: provisions enough to go *round.* 4 In circumference: a log three feet *round.* 5 From one position to another; here and there. 6 In the vicinity: to loiter *round.* 7 So as to complete a period of time: Will spring ever come *round* again? 8 In a circuitous or indirect way: Come *round* by way of the shopping center. 9 In the opposite direction: to turn *round.* —*prep.* 1 Enclosing; encircling: a belt *round* his waist. 2 On every side of; surrounding. 3 Toward every side of; about: He peered *round* him. 4 In the vicinity of: farms *round* the town. 5 To all or many parts of: driving friends *round* the city. 6 Here and there in: to look *round* a room. 7 So as to get to the other side of: walking *round* the corner. 8 In a group or mass surrounding: a rich socialite with hangers-on *round* him. [< L *rotundus*] —**round′ness** *n.*

round·a·bout (round′ə·bout′) *adj.* 1 Circuitous; indirect. 2 Encircling. —*n.* 1 A short, tight-fitting jacket for men and boys. 2 *Brit.* A merry-go-round.

round dance 1 A country dance in which the dancers form or move in a circle. 2 A dance with revolving or circular movements, as a waltz or polka, performed by two persons.

roun·de·lay (roun′də·lā) *n.* A simple song with a recurrent refrain. [< OF *rond* round]

round·er (roun′dər) *n.* 1 *Informal* A dissolute person; wastrel. 2 A tool for rounding a surface or edge.

Round·head (round′hed′) *n.* A member of the Parliamentary party in England in the civil war of 1642–49.

round·house (round′hous′) *n.* 1 A cabin on the after part of the quarter-deck of a vessel. 2 A round building with a turntable in the center, used for housing and repairing locomotives.

round·ly (round′lē) *adv.* 1 In a round manner or form. 2 Severely; vigorously; bluntly. 3 Thoroughly; completely.

round robin 1 A petition, protest, etc., on which signatures are written in a circle to avoid revealing the order of signing. 2 A tournament, as in tennis or chess, in which each player is matched with every other player.

round-shoul·dered (round′shōl′dərd) *adj.* Having the back rounded or the shoulders stooping.

round table 1 A group of persons meeting for a discussion. 2 Such a discussion. —**round′-ta′ble** *adj.*

Round Table 1 The table of King Arthur, made exactly circular so as to avoid any question of precedence among his knights. 2 King Arthur and his body of knights.

round trip A trip to a place and back again. —**round′-trip′** *adj.*

round·up (round′up′) *n.* 1 The bringing together of cattle scattered over a range for inspection, branding, etc. 2 The cowboys, horses, etc., employed in this work. 3 A bringing together, as of persons or things: a *roundup* of hobos.

round·worm (round′wûrm′) *n.* Any of a large phylum of worms with thin, cylindrical, unsegmented bodies; nematode worm.

rouse (rouz) *v.* **roused, rous·ing** *v.t.* 1 To cause to awaken from slumber, repose, unconsciousness, etc. 2 To excite to vigorous thought or action; stir up. 3 To startle or drive (game) from cover. —*v.i.* 4 To awaken from sleep or unconsciousness. 5 To become active. 6 To start from cover: said of game. —*n.* The act of rousing. [?] —**rous′er** *n.* —**Syn.** *v.* 2 animate, incite, arouse, stimulate.

rous·ing (rou′zing) *adj.* 1 Able to rouse or excite: a *rousing* speech. 2 Lively; vigorous: a *rousing* trade. 3 Exceptional; remarkable: a *rousing* success. —**rous′ing·ly** *adv.*

roust·a·bout (rous′tə·bout′) *n.* 1 A deck hand or dock worker. 2 An unskilled, semiskilled, or transient worker, as on an oil field or ranch. 3 A worker at a circus who helps to set up and dismantle tents, etc. [< *roust,* blend of ROUSE and ROUT]

rout[1] (rout) *n.* 1 A disorderly retreat or flight. 2 A boisterous and disorderly crowd; rabble. 3 An overwhelming defeat; debacle. —*v.t.* 1 To defeat disastrously. 2 To put to flight. [< L *ruptus,* p.p. of *rumpere* to break]

rout[2] (rout) *v.i.* 1 To turn up the earth with the snout, as swine. 2 To search; rummage. —*v.t.* 3 To dig or turn up with the snout. 4 To disclose to view; turn up as if with the snout: with *out.* 5 To hollow, gouge, or scrape, as with a scoop. 6 To drive or force out. [Var. of ROOT[2]]

route (rōōt, rout) *n.* 1 A course or way taken in passing from one point to another. 2 A road; highway. 3 The established passage which is regularly traveled by a person who delivers mail, milk, etc. 4 A way or means of approach: the *route* to success. —*v.t.* **rout·ed, rout·ing** 1 To send by a certain way, as passengers, goods, etc. 2 To arrange an itinerary for. [< L *rupta (via)* broken (road)] —**rout′er** *n.*

rou·tine (rōō·tēn′) *n.* 1 A detailed method of procedure, prescribed or regularly followed. 2 Anything that has become customary or habitual. —*adj.* 1 Customary; habitual. 2 Uninspired; dull: a *routine* performance. [< F *route* way, road] —**rou·tine′ly** *adv.*

rove[1] (rōv) *v.* **roved, rov·ing** *v.i.* 1 To go from place to place without any definite destination. —*v.t.* 2 To roam over, through, or about. —*n.* The act of roving or roaming. [? < Du. *rooven* rob] —**Syn.** 1 ramble, roam, wander.

rove[2] (rōv) A *p.t.* & *p.p.* of REEVE[1].

row[1] (rō) *n.* An arrangement or series of persons or things in a continued line, as a street lined with buildings on both sides, or a line of seats in a theater. —**a long row to hoe** A hard task or undertaking. —*v.t.* To arrange in a row: with *up.* [< OE *rāw* line]

row[2] (rō) *v.i.* 1 To use oars, sweeps, etc., in propelling a boat. 2 To be propelled by or as if by oars. —*v.t.* 3 To propel across the surface of the water with oars, as a boat. 4 To transport by rowing. 5 To be propelled by (a specific number of oars): said of boats. 6 To take part in (a rowing race). 7 To row against in a race. —*n.* 1 A trip in a rowboat; also, the distance covered. 2 The act of rowing, or an instance of it. [< OE *rōwan*]

row[3] (rou) *n.* A noisy disturbance or quarrel; dispute; brawl; clamor. —*v.t.* & *v.i.* To engage in a row. [?]

row·an (rō′ən, rou′-) *n.* 1 Any of various related trees having compound pinnate leaves, white flowers and red berries, as the European or American mountain ash. 2 The fruit of these trees: also **row′an·ber′ry.** [< Scand.]
row·boat (rō′bōt′) *n.* A boat propelled by oars.
row·dy (rou′dē) *n. pl.* **·dies** One inclined to create disturbances or engage in rows; a rough, quarrelsome person. —*adj.* **·di·er, ·di·est** Rough and loud; disorderly. [?] **—row′di·ly** *adv.* **—row′di·ness, row′dy·ism** *n.* **—row′dy·ish** *adj.*
row·el (rou′əl) *n.* A spiked or toothed wheel, as on a spur. —*v.t.* **·eled** or **·elled, ·el·ing** or **·el·ling** To prick with a rowel; spur. [< L *rota* wheel]

Rowel of spur

row·lock (rō′lok′) *n. Brit.* OARLOCK.
roy. royal.
roy·al (roi′əl) *adj.* 1 Of, pertaining to, or being a king, queen, or other sovereign. 2 Of, pertaining to, or under the patronage or authority of a sovereign. 3 Like or suitable for a sovereign. 4 Of superior quality or size: *royal* octavo. —*n.* A small sail or mast next above the topgallant. [< L *regalis* kingly] **—roy′al·ly** *adv.* **—Syn.** *adj.* 3 imperial, kingly, noble, regal, stately.
royal blue A vivid purplish or reddish blue.
roy·al·ist (roi′əl·ist) *n.* A supporter of a king, queen, or other sovereign. **—roy′al·ism** *n.*
roy·al·ty (roi′əl·tē) *n. pl.* **·ties** 1 The rank, status, or authority of a sovereign. 2 A royal personage; also, royal persons collectively. 3 Royal nature or quality. 4 A share of proceeds paid to a proprietor, author, inventor, etc.
rpm, r.p.m. revolutions per minute.
rps, r.p.s. revolutions per second.
rpt. report.
R.R. railroad; Right Reverend.
R.S. Recording Secretary; Reformed Spelling; Revised Statutes.
R.S.F.S.R. Russian Soviet Federated Socialist Republic.
RSV Revised Standard Version (of the Bible).
R.S.V.P., r.s.v.p. please reply (F *répondez s'il vous plaît*).
Rt. Hon. Right Honorable.
Rt. Rev. Right Reverend.
Rts. rights.
Ru ruthenium.
rub (rub) *v.* **rubbed, rub·bing** *v.t.* 1 To move or pass over the surface of with pressure and friction. 2 To cause (something) to move or pass with friction. 3 To cause to become frayed, worn, or sore from friction: This collar *rubs* my neck. 4 To clean, shine, dry, etc., by means of pressure and friction, or by means of a substance applied thus. 5 To apply or spread with pressure and friction: to *rub* polish on a table. 6 To force by rubbing: with *in* or *into:* to *rub* oil into wood. 7 To remove or erase by friction: with *off* or *out.* —*v.i.* 8 To move along a surface with friction; scrape. 9 To exert pressure and friction. 10 To become frayed, worn, or sore from friction; chafe. 11 To undergo rubbing or removal by rubbing: with *off, out,* etc. **—rub down** To massage. **—rub it in** *Slang* To harp on someone's errors, faults, etc. **—rub out** *Slang* To kill. **—rub the wrong way** To irritate; annoy. —*n.* 1 A subjection to frictional pressure; rubbing: Give it a *rub.* 2 A hindrance or doubt: There's the *rub.* 3 Something that injures the feelings; a sarcasm. [ME *rubben*]
ru·ba·to (rōō·bä′tō) *Music adj. & adv.* With certain notes lengthened or shortened at the performer's discretion. —*n. pl.* **·tos** A rubato passage or manner of playing [Ital.]
rub·ber¹ (rub′ər) *n.* 1 A tough, resilient, elastic material made from the latex of certain tropical plants, or synthesized from coal, petroleum, etc. 2 An article made of this material, as: **a** A rubber overshoe. **b** A condom. 3 One who or that which rubs. —*adj.* Made of rubber. [< RUB] —**rub′ber·y** *adj.*
rub·ber² (rub′ər) *n.* 1 In bridge, whist, and other card games, a series of games (3, 5, or 7) played by the same partners against the same adversaries, terminated when one side has won a majority (2 out of 3, etc.). 2 The odd game which breaks a tie between the players. [?]
rubber band A continuous elastic band of rubber, stretched to encircle and bind articles, etc.
rub·ber·ize (rub′ər·īz) *v.t.* **·ized, ·iz·ing** To coat, impregnate, or cover with rubber or a rubber solution.
rub·ber·neck (rub′ər·nek′) *n. Slang* One who is extremely curious or inquisitive, as a tourist. —*v.i.* To look or listen with great curiosity.
rubber plant 1 Any of several plants yielding latex. 2 An Asian tree related to the fig, with oblong, leathery leaves, often kept as a house plant.
rub·ber-stamp (rub′ər·stamp′) *v.t.* 1 To endorse, initial, or approve with the mark made by a rubber stamping device. 2 *Informal* To pass or approve as a matter of course or routine.
rubber stamp 1 A stamp made of rubber which, when coated with ink, is used to print names, dates, etc. 2 A person or group of persons that approves something, as a policy or program, with little or no discussion, debate, etc. 3 Any routine approval.
rub·bish (rub′ish) *n.* 1 Waste refuse; garbage; trash. 2 Silly or worthless ideas, talk, etc.; nonsense. [?] **—rub′bish·y** *adj.* **—Syn.** 1 debris, litter. 2 absurdness, foolishness.
rub·ble (rub′əl) *n.* 1 Rough, irregular pieces of broken stone, brick, etc. 2 The debris to which buildings of brick, stone, etc., have been reduced by destruction or decay. 3 Masonry composed of irregular or broken stone: also **rub′ble·work′.**
rub·down (rub′doun′) *n.* A massage.
rube (rōōb) *n. Slang* An unsophisticated country person; rustic. [Abbr. of *Reuben*]
ru·bel·la (rōō·bel′ə) *n.* A contagious viral disease benign in children but linked to birth defects of children born of women infected in early pregnancy; German measles. [< L *rubellus* reddish, dim. of *ruber* red]
ru·be·o·la (rōō′bē·ō′lə, rōō·bē′ə·lə) *n.* A contagious viral disease usu. affecting children, marked by catarrh, fever, and a rash that persists for about a week; measles. [< L *rubeus* red] **—ru·be′o·lar** *adj.*
Ru·bi·con (rōō′bi·kon) *n.* A river in N CEN. Italy that formed the boundary separating Julius Caesar's province of Gaul from Italy; by crossing it under arms he committed himself to a civil war. **—cross the Rubicon** To commit oneself irrevocably to some course of action.
ru·bi·cund (rōō′bə·kənd) *adj.* Red, or inclined to redness; ruddy. [< L *rubicundus*] **—ru′bi·cun′di·ty** *n.*
ru·bid·i·um (rōō·bid′ē·əm) *n.* A soft, rare, metallic element (symbol Rb) resembling potassium. [< L *rubidus* red]
ru·ble (rōō′bəl) *n.* The basic monetary unit of the Soviet Union.
ru·bric (rōō′brik) *n.* 1 In early manuscripts and books, the heading of a chapter, an initial letter, etc., that appears in red, or in some distinctive type. 2 Any heading or title, as that of a statute. 3 A direction or rule as in a prayer book, missal, or breviary. [< L *ruber* red] **—ru′bri·cal** *adj.* **—ru′bri·cal·ly** *adv.*
ru·by (rōō′bē) *n. pl.* **·bies** 1 A translucent gemstone of a deep red color, a variety of corundum. 2 A rich red color like that of a ruby. —*adj.* Deep red. [< L *rubeus* red]
ruche (rōōsh) *n.* A pleated or gathered strip of fine fabric, worn about the neck or wrists of a woman's costume. [F < Med. L *rusca* tree bark]
ruch·ing (rōō′shing) *n.* 1 Material for ruches. 2 Ruches collectively.
ruck·sack (ruk′sak′, rŏŏk′-) *n.* KNAPSACK. [G, lit., back sack]
ruck·us (ruk′əs) *n. Slang* An uproar; commotion. [? blend of RUMPUS and *ruction,* alter. of INSURRECTION]
rud·der (rud′ər) *n.* 1 *Naut.* A broad, flat device hinged vertically at the stern of a vessel to direct its course. 2 Anything that guides or directs a course. 3 *Aeron.* A hinged or pivoted surface, used to turn an aircraft about its vertical axis. [< OE *rōthor* oar, scull] **—rud′der·less** *adj.*

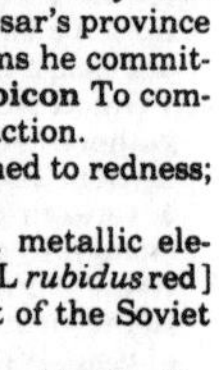

a. rudder *def. 1.* b. screw.

rud·dy (rud′ē) *adj.* **·di·er, ·di·est** 1 Red or tinged with red. 2 Having a healthy glow; rosy: a *ruddy* complexion. [< OE *rudig*] **—rud′di·ly** *adv.* **—rud′di·ness** *n.*
rude (rōōd) *adj.* **rud·er, rud·est** 1 Offensively blunt or uncivil; impolite. 2 Characterized by lack of polish or refinement; uncouth. 3 Unskilfully made or done; crude. 4 Characterized by robust vigor; strong: *rude* health. 5 Barbarous; savage. 6

Jarring to the ear; harsh; discordant. 7 Lacking skill, training, accuracy, etc. [< L *rudis* rough] **—rude'ly** *adv.* —**rude'ness** *n.* **—Syn.** 1 discourteous, impertinent. 2 boorish, uncultivated. 5 uncivilized.

ru·di·ment (rōō'də·mənt) *n.* 1 A first step, stage, or condition. 2 That which is undeveloped or partially developed. [< L *rudis* rough]

ru·di·men·ta·ry (rōō'də·men'tər·ē) *adj.* 1 Introductory; elementary: *rudimentary* knowledge. 2 Being in an imperfectly developed state; undeveloped. 3 Vestigial. Also **ru'di·men'tal.** **—ru'di·men'ta·ri·ly** *adv.* **—ru'di·men'ta·ri·ness** *n.*

rue[1] (rōō) *v.* **rued, ru·ing** *v.t.* 1 To feel sorrow or remorse for; regret extremely. *—v.i.* 2 To feel sorrow or remorse. *—n. Archaic* Sorrowful remembrance; regret. [< OE *hrēowan* be sorry] **—ru'er** *n.*

rue[2] (rōō) *n.* 1 A small, pungent shrub with bitter, evergreen leaves. 2 An infusion of rue leaves. [< Gk. *rhytē*]

rue·ful (rōō'fəl) *adj.* 1 Feeling or expressing sorrow, regret, or pity. 2 Causing sympathy or pity; pitiable. **—rue'·ful·ly** *adv.* **—rue'ful·ness** *n.*

ruff[1] (ruf) *n.* 1 A pleated, round, heavily starched collar popular in the 16th century. 2 A natural collar of projecting feathers or hair around the neck of a bird or mammal. 3 The male of a European species of sandpiper, which has a large ruff in the breeding season. [Short for RUFFLE[1]] **—ruffed** *adj.*

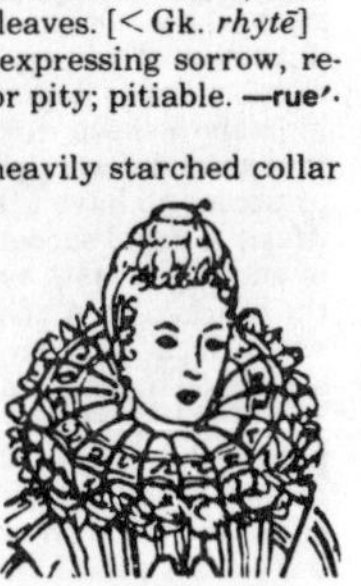
Ruff

ruff[2] (ruf) *n.* In a card game, the act of trumping. *—v.t. & v.i.* To trump. [< OF *roffle*]

ruffed grouse (ruft) A North American grouse having in the male a fan-shaped tail and a black ruff.

ruf·fi·an (ruf'ē·ən, ruf'yən) *n.* A lawless, brutal person. *—adj.* Lawlessly or recklessly brutal or cruel. [< MF *rufian*] **—ruf'fi·an·ism** *n.* **—ruf'fi·an·ly** *adj.*

ruf·fle[1] (ruf'əl) *n.* 1 A pleated strip; frill, as for trim or ornament. 2 Anything resembling this, as a bird's ruff. 3 A disturbance; discomposure. 4 A ripple. *—v.* **·fled, ·fling** *v.t.* 1 To disturb or destroy the smoothness or regularity of: The wind *ruffles* the lake. 2 To draw into folds or ruffles; gather. 3 To furnish with ruffles. 4 To erect (the feathers) in a ruff, as a bird when frightened. 5 To disturb or irritate; upset. 6 a To riffle (the pages of a book). b To shuffle (cards). *—v.i.* 7 To be or become rumpled or disordered. 8 To become disturbed or irritated. [ME *ruffelen* to ruffle]

ruf·fle[2] (ruf'əl) *n.* A low, continuous beat of a drum, not as loud as a roll. *—v.t.* **·fled, ·fling** To beat a ruffle upon, as a drum. [?]

rug (rug) *n.* 1 A covering for all or part of a floor, made of some heavy, durable fabric, strips of rag, animal skins, etc. 2 A warm covering, as of cloth, fur, etc., for the lap and feet.

rug·by (rug'bē) *n. Often cap.* A form of football. [< *Rugby* School, Rugby, England, where first played]

rug·ged (rug'id) *adj.* 1 Having a surface that is rough or uneven. 2 Rough; harsh: a *rugged* life. 3 Furrowed and irregular: *rugged* features. 4 Lacking polish and refinement. 5 Tempestuous; stormy: *rugged* weather. 6 Robust; sturdy: *rugged* health. [< Scand.] **—rug'ged·ly** *adv.* **—rug'·ged·ness** *n.*

ru·in (rōō'in) *n.* 1 Destruction, downfall, or decay. 2 A person or thing that has decayed, fallen, or been destroyed. 3 *Usu. pl.* That which remains of something that has decayed or been destroyed: the *ruins* of Dresden. 4 That which causes destruction, downfall, or decay: Gambling was his *ruin.* 5 The state of being destroyed, fallen, decayed, etc: to fall into *ruin.* *—v.t.* 1 To bring to ruin; destroy. 2 To bring to disgrace or bankruptcy. 3 To deprive of chastity; seduce. *—v.i.* 4 To fall into ruin. [< L *ruere* to fall] **—ru'in·er** *n.* **—Syn.** *n.* 1 collapse, devastation, dilapidation. *v.* 1 demolish, ravage, raze.

ru·in·a·tion (rōō'in·ā'shən) *n.* 1 The act of ruining. 2 The state of being ruined. 3 Something that ruins.

ru·in·ous (rōō'in·əs) *adj.* 1 Causing or tending to ruin. 2 Falling to ruin. **—ru'in·ous·ly** *adv.* **—ru'in·ous·ness** *n.*

rule (rōōl) *n.* 1 Controlling power, or its possession and exercise; government; reign; also, the period of time during which a ruler or government is in power. 2 A method or principle of action; regular course of procedure: I make early rising my *rule.* 3 An authoritative direction or regulation about something to do or the way of doing it. 4 The body of directions laid down by or for a religious order: the *rule* of St. Francis. 5 A procedure or formula for solving a given class of mathematical problems. 6 An established usage fixing the form of words: a *rule* for forming the plural. 7 Something in the ordinary course of events or condition of things: In some communities illiteracy is the *rule.* 8 *Law* A judicial decision on some specific question or point of law. 9 A straight-edged instrument for use in measuring, or as a guide in drawing lines; a ruler. 10 *Printing* A strip of type-high metal for printing a rule or line. **—as a rule** Ordinarily; usually. *—v.* **ruled, rul·ing** *v.t.* 1 To have authority or control over; govern. 2 To influence greatly; dominate. 3 To decide judicially or authoritatively. 4 To restrain; keep in check. 5 To mark lines on, as with a ruler. *—v.i.* 6 To have authority or control. 7 To form and express a decision: The judge *ruled* on that point. **—rule out** 1 To eliminate or exclude. 2 To preclude; prevent. [< L *regula* ruler, rule]

rule of thumb 1 A rule based on experience or common sense instead of scientific knowledge. 2 A method of procedure that is practical but not precise.

rul·er (rōō'lər) *n.* 1 One who rules or governs, as a sovereign. 2 A straight-edged strip of wood, metal, etc., used in drawing lines and in measuring.

rul·ing (rōō'ling) *adj.* 1 Exercising control. 2 Prevalent; predominant. *—n.* A decision, as of a judge or chairman.

rum[1] (rum) *n.* 1 An alcoholic liquor distilled from fermented molasses. 2 Any alcoholic liquor. [?]

rum[2] (rum) *adj. Brit. Slang* Queer; strange. [?]

Rum. Rumania; Rumanian.

Ru·ma·ni·a (rōō·mā'nē·ə, -mān'yə) *n.* A republic of SE Europe, 91,671 sq. mi., cap. Bucharest. • See map at BALKAN STATES.

Ru·ma·ni·an (rōō·mā'nē·ən, -mān'yən) *adj.* Of or pertaining to Rumania, its people, or their language. *—n.* 1 A native or citizen of Rumania. 2 The Romance language of the Rumanians.

rum·ba (rum'bə, *Sp.* rōōm'bä) *n.* 1 A dance originated by Cuban Negroes. 2 A ballroom dance based on this. 3 Music for such a dance. *—v.i.* To dance the rumba. [Sp.]

rum·ble (rum'bəl) *v.* **·bled, bling** *v.i.* 1 To make a low, heavy, rolling sound, as thunder. 2 To move or proceed with such a sound. *—v.t.* 3 To cause to make a low, heavy, rolling sound. 4 To utter with such a sound. *—n.* 1 A continuous low, heavy, rolling sound; a muffled roar. 2 A seat or baggage compartment in the rear of an automobile or carriage: also **rumble seat.** 3 *Slang* A street fight involving a group, usu. deliberately provoked. [< MDu. *rommelen*]

ru·men (rōō'men) *n. pl.* **ru·mi·na** (rōō'mə·nə) or **ru·mens** The first chamber of the stomach of a ruminant. [L, throat]

ru·mi·nant (rōō'mə·nənt) *n.* Any of a division of even-toed ungulates, as a deer, sheep, cow, etc., that graze and chew the cud, which is temporarily stored in the first of the four chambers of the stomach. *—adj.* 1 Chewing the cud. 2 Of or pertaining to ruminants. 3 Meditative or thoughtful. [< L *ruminare* chew the cud, think over]

ru·mi·nate (rōō'mə·nāt) *v.t. & v.i.* **·nat·ed, ·nat·ing** 1 To chew (food previously swallowed and regurgitated) over again; chew (the cud). 2 To meditate or reflect (upon). **—ru'mi·nat'ing·ly, ru'mi·na'tive·ly** *adv.* **—ru'mi·na'tion, ru'mi·na'tor** *n.* **—Syn.** 2 brood, consider, contemplate, muse.

rum·mage (rum'ij) *v.* **·maged, ·mag·ing** *v.t.* 1 To search through (a place, box, etc.) by turning over and disarranging the contents; ransack. 2 To find or bring out by searching: with *out* or *up.* *—v.i.* 3 To make a thorough search. *—n.* 1 Any act of rummaging, esp., disarranging things by searching thoroughly. 2 Odds and ends. [< MF *arrumer* pack or arrange cargo] **—rum'mag·er** *n.*

rummage sale A sale of donated miscellaneous objects to raise money, as for some charity.
rum·my[1] (rum′ē) *n.* Any of several card games the object of which is to match cards into sets of three or four of the same denomination or into sequences in the same suit. [?]
rum·my[2] (rum′ē) *n. pl.* **·mies** *Slang* A drunkard. —*adj.* Of, pertaining to, or affected by rum.
ru·mor (ro͞o′mər) *n.* **1** A story or report circulating without known foundation or authority. **2** Common gossip; hearsay. —*v.t.* To tell or spread as a rumor; report abroad. *Brit. sp.* **ru′mour.** [L, noise]
rump (rump) *n.* **1** The upper part of the hindquarters of an animal. **2** A cut of beef from this part. **3** The buttocks. **4** A last, often unimportant or undesirable part.
rum·ple (rum′pəl) *v.t. & v.i.* **·pled, ·pling** To form into creases or folds; wrinkle. —*n.* An irregular fold or crease; wrinkle. [< MDu. *rumpelen*]
rum·pus (rum′pəs) *n. Informal* A usu. noisy disturbance or commotion. [?]
rumpus room A room used for recreation, games, etc.
rum-run·ner (rum′run′ər) *n.* A person or ship involved in smuggling alcoholic liquor ashore or across a border.
run (run) *v.* **ran, run, run·ning** *v.i.* **1** To move by rapid steps, faster than walking. **2** To move rapidly; go swiftly. **3** To flee; take flight. **4** To make a brief or rapid journey: We *ran* over to Staten Island last night. **5** To make regular trips: This steamer *runs* between New York and Liverpool. **6 a** To take part in a race. **b** To be a candidate or contestant: to *run* for dogcatcher. **7** To finish a race in a specified position: I *ran* a poor last. **8** To move or pass easily: The rope *runs* through the pulley. **9** To pass or flow rapidly: watching the tide *run* out. **10** To proceed in direction or extent: This road *runs* north. **11** To flow: His nose *runs.* **12** To become liquid and flow, as wax; also, to spread or mingle confusedly, as colors when wet. **13** To move or roam about freely and easily: to *run* around town with friends. **14** To pass into a specified condition: to *run* to seed. **15** To unravel, as a fabric. **16** To give forth a discharge or flow. **17** To leak. **18** To continue or proceed without restraint: The conversation *ran* on and on. **19** To be operative; work: Will the engine *run?* **20** To continue or extend, as in time or space: Our property *runs* down to the sea. **21** To be reported or expressed: The story *runs* as follows. **22** To migrate, as salmon from the sea to spawn. **23** To occur or return to the mind: An idea *ran* through his head. **24** To occur with specified variation of size, quality, etc.: The corn is *running* small this year. **25** To be performed or repeated in continuous succession: The play *ran* for forty nights. **26** To pass or spread, as from mouth to mouth or point to point: rumors *running* wild. **27** To creep or climb, as a vine. —*v.t.* **28** To run or proceed along, as a route or path. **29** To make one's way over, through, or past: to *run* rapids. **30** To perform or accomplish by or as by running: to *run* a race or an errand. **31** To compete against in or as in a race. **32** To become subject to; incur: to *run* the risk of failure. **33** To present and support as a candidate. **34** To hunt or chase, as game. **35** To bring to a specified condition by or as by running: to *run* oneself out of breath. **36** To drive or force: with *out of, off, into, through,* etc. **37** To cause to move, as in some manner or direction: They *ran* the ship into port. **38** To move (the eye, hand, etc.) quickly or lightly: He *ran* his hand over the table. **39** To cause to move, slide, etc., as into a specified position: to *run* up a flag. **40** To transport or convey in a vessel or vehicle. **41** To smuggle. **42** To cause to flow: to *run* water into a pot. **43** To trace back: trying to *run* a bit of gossip to its source. **44** To mold, as from melted metal; found. **45** To sew (cloth) in a continuous line, usu. by taking a number of stitches with the needle at a time. **46** To control the motion or operation of; operate: to *run* an engine. **47** To direct or control; manage. **48** To allow to continue or mount up, as a bill. **49** In games, to make (a number of points, strokes, etc.) successively. **50** To publish in a magazine or newspaper: to *run* an ad. **51** To mark, set down, or trace, as a boundary line. **52** To suffer from (a fever, etc.). —**run across** To meet by chance. —**run down 1** To pursue and overtake, as a fugitive. **2** To strike down while moving. **3** To exhaust or damage, as by abuse or overwork. **4** To speak of disparagingly. —**run for it** To run to avoid something, to escape, seek safety, etc. —**run in 1** To insert; include. **2** *Slang* To arrest and place in confinement. —**run into 1** To meet by chance. **2** To collide with. —**run off 1** To produce on a typewriter, printing press, etc. **2** To decide (a tied race, game, etc.) by the outcome of another, subsequent race, game, etc. —**run out** To be exhausted, as supplies. —**run out of** To exhaust one's supply of. —**run over 1** To ride or drive over; run down. **2** To overflow. **3** To go over, examine, or rehearse. —**run through 1** To squander. **2** To stab or pierce. **3** To rehearse quickly. —**run up** To make hurriedly, as on a sewing machine. —*n.* **1** The act, or an act, of running or going rapidly. **2** A running pace: to break into a *run.* **3** Flow; movement; sweep: the *run* of the tide. **4** A distance covered by running. **5** A journey or passage, esp. between two points, made by a vessel, train, etc. **6** A rapid journey or excursion: take a *run* into town. **7** A swift stream or brook. **8** A migration of fish, esp. to up-river spawning grounds; also, the fish that so migrate. **9** A grazing or feeding ground for animals: a sheep *run.* **10** The regular trail or path of certain animals: an elephant *run.* **11** The privilege of free use or access: to have the *run* of the place. **12** A runway. **13** *Music* A rapid succession of tones. **14** A series, sequence, or succession. **15** A trend or tendency: the general *run* of the market. **16** A continuous spell (of some condition): a *run* of luck. **17** A surge of demands, as those made upon a bank or treasury to meet its obligations. **18** A period of continuous performance, occurrence, popularity, etc.: a play with a long *run.* **19** Class or type; also, the usual or general class or type. **20** A period of operation of a machine or device: an experimental *run.* **21** The output during such a period. **22** A period during which a liquid is allowed to run. **23** The amount of liquid allowed to flow at one time. **24** A narrow, lengthwise ravel, as in a sheer stocking. **25** An approach to a target made by a bombing plane. **26** In baseball, a score made by a player who completes a circuit of the bases from home plate before three outs are made. **27** An unbroken series of successful shots, strokes, etc., as in billiards. —**in the long run** As the ultimate outcome of any train of circumstances. —**on the run 1** Hastily: to eat *on the run.* **2** Running, running away, or retreating. —*adj.* **1** Made liquid; melted. **2** That has been melted or cast: *run* metal. [< OE *rinnan* to flow]
run·a·bout (run′ə·bout′) *n.* **1** A light, open automobile. **2** A light, open wagon. **3** A small motorboat. **4** A person who wanders or runs about from place to place; gadabout.
run·a·round (run′ə·round′) *n. Informal* Evasive or deceptive action or treatment: to get the *runaround* from someone.
run·a·way (run′ə·wā′) *adj.* **1** Escaping or escaped from restraint or control. **2** Brought about by running away: a *runaway* marriage. **3** Easily won, as a horse race. —*n.* **1** One who or that which runs away or flees, as a fugitive or deserter, or a horse of which the driver has lost control. **2** An act of running away.
run·down (run′doun′) *n.* **1** A summary; resumé. **2** In baseball, a play attempting to put out a base runner who is trapped between two bases.
run-down (run′doun′) *adj.* **1** Debilitated; tired out. **2** Dilapidated; shabby. **3** Stopped because not wound, as a watch. —**Syn. 1** exhausted, weary. **2** decayed, ruined.
rune (ro͞on) *n.* **1** A character of an ancient Germanic alphabet. **2** A Finnish or Old Norse poem; also, one of the sections of such a poem. **3** An obscure or mystic mark, song, poem, verse, or saying. [< ON *rūn* mystery, rune] —**ru′nic** *adj.*

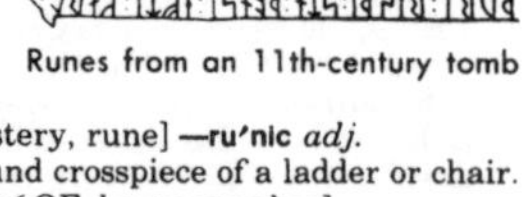
Runes from an 11th-century tomb

rung[1] (rung) *n.* **1** A round crosspiece of a ladder or chair. **2** A spoke of a wheel. [< OE *hrung* crossbar]
rung[2] (rung) *p.p.* of RING[2].
run-in (run′in′) *n.* **1** A quarrel; bicker. **2** *Printing* Inserted or added matter. —*adj.* (run′in′) *Printing* That is inserted or added.
run·nel (run′əl) *n.* A little stream; a brook. Also **run′let** (-lit). [< OE *rinnan* to run]
run·ner (run′ər) *n.* **1** One who or that which runs. **2** One who operates or manages anything. **3** One who runs er-

rands or goes about on any kind of business, as a messenger. 4 That part on which an object runs or slides: the *runner* of a skate. 5 *Bot.* A slender horizontal stem that takes root at the nodes to produce new plants, as in the strawberry. 6 A smuggler. 7 A long, narrow rug or carpeting, used in hallways, etc. 8 A narrow strip of cloth, usu. of fine quality, used on tables, dressers, etc.

run·ner-up (run′ər·up′) *n. pl.* **·ners-up** or **·ner-ups** A contestant or team finishing second in a contest.

run·ning (run′ing) *adj.* 1 Inclined or trained to a running gait, as certain horses. 2 Done in or started with a run: a *running* jump. 3 Following one another without intermission; successive: He talked for three hours *running.* 4 Continuous: a *running* battle. 5 Characterized by easy flowing curves; cursive: a *running* hand. 6 Discharging, as pus from a sore. 7 Fluid or flowing. 8 In operation, as an engine. 9 Measured in a straight line: the cost per *running* foot. —*n.* 1 The act or movement of one who or that which runs. 2 That which runs or flows. —**in the running** Having a chance to win. —**out of the running** Having no chance to win.

running board A footboard, as on the side of a locomotive, certain automobiles, etc.

running head A heading or title at the top of each page or of every other page of a book, etc.: also **running title.**

running knot A knot made so as to slip along a noose and tighten when pulled upon.

running mate A candidate running with another but for a lesser position, as one seeking to be vice-president.

run·ny (run′ē) *adj.* **·ni·er, ·ni·est** Having a tendency to discharge: a *runny* nose. —**run′ni·ness** *n.*

run·off (run′ôf′ -of′) *n.* 1 Rainfall that drains from a particular area rather than soaking into the soil. 2 A final, deciding contest, game, etc.

run-of-the-mill (run′əv·thə·mil′) *adj.* Average; ordinary.

run-on (run′on′, -ôn′) *Printing n.* Appended or added matter. —*adj.* That is appended or added.

runt (runt) *n.* 1 A stunted animal, esp. the smallest of a litter. 2 A small or stunted person. [?] —**runt′i·ness** *n.* —**runt′y** *adj.* **(·i·er, ·i·est)**

run-through (run′thrōō′) *n.* A rapid reading through or rehearsal, as of a musical composition or a dramatic work.

run·way (run′wā′) *n.* 1 A way on, in, along, or over which something runs. 2 The path over which animals pass to and from their places of feeding or watering. 3 An enclosed place, as for chickens. 4 A strip of surfaced ground used for the takeoff and landing of airplanes. 5 A long, narrow platform extending from a stage into an auditorium.

ru·pee (rōō·pē′, rōō′pe) *n.* The basic monetary unit of India, Pakistan, and Sri Lanka. [< Skt. *rūpya* silver]

ru·pi·ah (rōō·pē′ä) *n.* The basic monetary unit of Indonesia.

rup·ture (rup′chər) *n.* 1 The act of breaking apart or the state of being broken apart. 2 HERNIA. 3 Breach of peace and agreement between individuals or nations. —*v.t. & v.i.* **·tured, ·tur·ing** 1 To break apart. 2 To affect with or suffer a rupture. [< L *ruptus,* p.p. of *rumpere* to break]

ru·ral (rŏŏr′əl) *adj.* Of or pertaining to the country, country people, country life, or agriculture. [< L *rus, ruris* country] —**ru′ral·ism, ru′ral·ist, ru′ral·ness** *n.* —**ru′ral·ly** *adv.*

rural free delivery Free mail delivery by carrier in rural districts.

ru·ral·ize (rŏŏr′əl·īz) *v.* **·ized, ·iz·ing** *v.t.* To make rural. —*v.i.* To go into or live in the country; rusticate. —**ru′ral·i·za′tion** *n.*

Rus., Russ. Russia; Russian.

ruse (rōōs, rōōz) *n.* An action intended to mislead or deceive; a stratagem; trick. [< F *ruser* dodge, detour]

rush[1] (rush) *v.i.* 1 To move or go swiftly, impetuously, forcefully, or violently. 2 To make an attack; charge: with *on* or *upon.* 3 To proceed recklessly or rashly; plunge: with *in* or *into.* 4 To come, go, pass, act, etc. with suddenness or haste: Ideas kept *rushing* to her mind. 5 To advance a football in a running play. —*v.t.* 6 To move, push, drive, etc. with haste, impetuosity, or violence. 7 To do, perform, deliver, etc. hastily or hurriedly: to *rush* one's work. 8 To make a sudden assault upon. 9 *Slang* To seek the favor of with assiduous attentions. 10 To advance (a football) in a running play. —*n.* 1 The act of rushing; a sudden turbulent movement, drive, surge, etc. 2 Frantic activity; haste: the *rush* of city life. 3 A sudden pressing demand; a run: a *rush* on foreign bonds. 4 A sudden exigency; urgent pressure: a *rush* of business. 5 A sudden flocking of people, as to some new location. 6 A general contest or scrimmage between students from different classes. 7 In football, an attempt to take the ball through the opposing linemen and toward the goal. 8 *Usu. pl.* In motion pictures, the first film prints of a scene or series of scenes, before editing or selection. —**with a rush** Suddenly and hastily. —*adj.* Requiring urgency or haste: a *rush* order. [< AF *russher* to push] —**rush′er** *n.* —**Syn.** *v.* 1 dash, hasten, hurry.

rush[2] (rush) *n.* 1 Any of various grasslike plants common in marshy ground. 2 The pliant stem of certain rush plants, used for mats, basketry, etc. [< OE *rysc*] —**rush′y** *adj.* **(·i·er, ·i·est)**

rush hour A time when large numbers of people are traveling, as to or from work. —**rush′-hour′** *adj.*

rush·light (rush′līt′) *n.* A candle made by dipping a rush in tallow: also **rush light, rush candle.**

rusk (rusk) *n.* 1 Plain or sweet bread that is sliced after baking and then toasted or baked a second time until it is brown and crisp. 2 A light, soft, sweet biscuit. [< Sp. *rosca,* twisted loaf of bread]

rus·set (rus′it) *n.* 1 Reddish brown or yellowish brown. 2 A coarse homespun cloth, russet in color, formerly used by country people. 3 A winter apple of russet color. —*adj.* 1 Reddish brown or yellowish brown. 2 Made of russet. [< L *russus* reddish] —**rus′set·y** *adj.*

Rus·sia (rush′ə) *n.* 1 Loosely, the Union of Soviet Socialist Republics. 2 The Russian Soviet Federated Socialist Republic.

Rus·sian (rush′ən) *n.* 1 Loosely, a citizen or native of the Union of Soviet Socialist Republics. 2 A citizen or native of Russia. 3 The language of Russia and the official language of the Union of Soviet Socialist Republics. —*adj.* 1 Loosely, of or pertaining to the Union of Soviet Socialist Republics. 2 Of or pertaining to Russia or its people. 3 Of or pertaining to Russian, the language.

Russian dressing Mayonnaise combined with chili sauce, chopped pickles, etc.

Rus·sian·ize (rush′ən·īz) *v.t.* **·ized, ·iz·ing** To make Russian. —**Rus′sian·i·za′tion** *n.*

Russian leather A smooth, well-tanned, high-grade leather, often dark red, of calfskin or light cattle hide, dressed with birch oil and having a characteristic odor.

Russian Orthodox Church An autonomous branch of the Eastern Orthodox Church.

Russian Revolution The uprising of 1917 that resulted in the overthrow of the czarist regime. The revolution had two phases: first, the establishment of a moderate, provisional government under Kerensky (the **February Revolution**), and, second, the seizure of power by the Bolsheviks (Communists) under Lenin (the **October Revolution**).

Russian thistle A large tumbleweed common on the central plains of North America.

Russian wolfhound BORZOI.

Russo- *combining form* 1 Russia. 2 Russian and: *Russo-*Egyptian.

rust (rust) *n.* 1 A reddish or yellow coating on iron or iron alloys due to spontaneous oxidation. 2 A corroded spot or film of oxide on any metal. 3 Any of various parasitic fungi living on higher plants. 4 A plant disease caused by such fungi, which form spots on stems and leaves. 5 Any spot or film resembling rust on metal. 6 Any of several shades of reddish brown. —*v.t. & v.i.* 1 To become or cause to become coated with rust. 2 To contract or cause to contract the plant disease rust. 3 To become or cause to become weakened because of disuse. [< OE *rūst*]

rus·tic (rus′tik) *adj.* 1 Of or pertaining to the country;

rural. **2** Uncultured; rude; awkward. **3** Unsophisticated; artless. **4** Made of the rough limbs of trees with the bark on them: *rustic* furniture. —*n.* **1** One who lives in the country. **2** An unsophisticated, coarse, or ignorant person, esp. one from a rural area. [< L *rus* country] **—rus′ti·cal·ly** *adv.*

rus·ti·cate (rus′tə·kāt) *v.* **·cat·ed, ·cat·ing** *v.i.* **1** To go to or live in the country. —*v.t.* **2** To send or banish to the country. **3** *Brit.* To suspend (a student) temporarily from a college for punishment. **—rus′ti·ca′tion, rus′ti·ca′tor** *n.*

rus·tic·i·ty (rus·tis′ə·tē) *n. pl.* **·ties 1** The condition or quality of being rustic. **2** A rustic trait or peculiarity.

rus·tle[1] (rus′əl) *v.t. & v.i.* **·tled, ·tling** To move or cause to move with a quick succession of small, light, rubbing sounds, as dry leaves or sheets of paper. —*n.* A rustling sound. [ME *rustelen*] **—rus′tler** *n.* **—rus′tling·ly** *adv.*

rus·tle[2] (rus′əl) *v.t. & v.i.* **·tled, ·tling 1** *Informal* To act with or obtain by energetic or vigorous action. **2** *Informal* To steal (cattle, etc.). [? Blend of RUSH and HUSTLE]

rus·tler (rus′lər) *n.* **1** *Slang* A person who is active and bustling. **2** *Informal* A cattle thief.

rust·y (rus′tē) *adj.* **rust·i·er, rust·i·est 1** Covered or affected with rust. **2** Consisting of or produced by rust. **3** Having the color or appearance of rust; discolored; faded, etc. **4** Not working well or freely; lacking nimbleness; stiff. **5** Impaired or deficient by neglect or want of practice: *rusty* in math. **—rust′i·ly** *adv.* **—rust′i·ness** *n.*

rut[1] (rut) *n.* **1** A sunken track worn by a wheel, as in a road. **2** A groove, furrow, etc., in which something runs. **3** A settled and tedious routine. —*v.t.* **rut·ted, rut·ting** To wear or make a rut or ruts in. [? Var. of ROUTE] **—rut′ti·ness** *n.* **—rut′ty** *adj.* **(·i·er, ·i·est)**

rut[2] (rut) *n.* The sexual excitement of various animals, esp. the male deer; also, the period during which it lasts. —*v.i.* **rut·ted, rut·ting** To be in rut. [< L *rugire* to roar]

ru·ta·ba·ga (rōō′tə·bā′gə) *n.* A variety of turnip having a large, yellowish root. [< dial. Sw. *rotabagge*]

ruth (rōōth) *n.* **1** Compassion; pity, mercy. **2** Grief; sorrow; remorse. [< OE *hrēow* sad]

Ruth (rōōth) In the Bible, a widow from Moab who left her people to live with her mother-in-law, Naomi. —*n.* The Old Testament book that tells her story.

ru·the·ni·um (rōō·thē′nē·əm) *n.* A rare metallic element (symbol Ru). [< *Ruthenia,* a region in the Ukraine]

ruth·less (rōōth′lis) *adj.* Having no compassion; merciless. **—ruth′less·ly** *adv.* **—ruth′less·ness** *n.*

R.V. Revised Version (of the Bible).

R.W. Right Worshipful; Right Worthy.

Rwan·da (rwän′də) *n.* A republic of CEN. Africa, 10,169 sq. mi., cap. Kigali. • See map at AFRICA.

Rx *symbol Med.* Take: the conventional heading for a prescription or formula. [Abbr. of L *recipe* take]

-ry Var. of -ERY.

Ry., ry. railway.

rye (rī) *n.* **1** A hardy, cultivated cereal grass. **2** The seeds of this grass. **3** Flour made from these seeds. **4** Whiskey consisting of a blend of bourbon and neutral spirits: also **rye whiskey.** [< OE *ryge*]

rye·grass (rī′gras′, -gräs′) *n.* A weedy grass sometimes cultivated for forage.

S

S, s (es) *n. pl.* **S's, s's, Ss, ss** (es′iz) **1** The 19th letter of the English alphabet. **2** Any spoken sound representing the letter *S* or *s.* **3** Something shaped like an S. —*adj.* Shaped like an S.

S Seaman; sulfur.

S. Sabbath; Saturday; Saxon; Senate; September; Signor; Sunday.

S., s. saint; school; senate; south; southern.

s. second; section; shilling; semi; series; shilling; son; southern; steamer; substantive; sun; surplus.

SA Seaman Apprentice.

S.A. Salvation Army; South Africa; South America.

Sab. Sabbath.

Sab·bath (sab′əth) *n.* **1** The seventh day of the week, a day of rest observed in Judaism and some Christian sects; Saturday. **2** The first day of the week as observed as a day of rest by Christians; Sunday. [< Heb. *shābath* to rest]

sab·bat·i·cal (sə·bat′i·kəl) *adj. Often cap.* Of the nature of or suitable for the Sabbath: also **sab·bat′ic.** —*n.* SABBATICAL YEAR (def. 2).

sabbatical year 1 In the ancient Jewish economy, every seventh year, in which the people were required to refrain from tillage. **2** In the U.S., a year of leave, or a shorter period, to be used for study and travel with full or partial salary, awarded to college faculty members, usu. every seven years: also **sabbatical leave.**

sa·ber (sā′bər) *n.* A heavy one-edged cavalry sword, often curved. —*v.t.* **·bered** or **·bred, ·ber·ing** or **·bring** To strike, wound, kill, or arm with a saber. Also, and *Brit. sp.,* **sa′bre.** [< MHG *sabel*]

Saber

Sa·bine (sā′bīn) *n.* A member of an ancient people of CEN. Italy, conquered and absorbed by Rome in 290 B.C. —*adj.* Of or pertaining to the Sabines.

sa·ble (sā′bəl) *n.* **1** A N Eurasian species of marten bearing costly fur. **2** The dressed fur of a sable. **3** *pl.* Garments made wholly or partly of this fur. **4** The color black. —*adj.* **1** Black; dark. **2** Made of sable fur. [< Med. L *sabelum*]

sa·bot (sab′ō, *Fr.* sȧ·bō′) *n.* **1** A wooden shoe, as of a French peasant. **2** A shoe having a wooden sole but flexible shank. [F]

sab·o·tage (sab′ə·täzh) *n.* **1** A wasting of materials or damage to machinery, tools, etc., by workmen to make management comply with their demands. **2** The destruction of bridges, railroads, supply depots, etc., either by enemy agents or by underground resisters. **3** Any deliberate effort to obstruct plans or aims. —*v.t. & v.i.* **·taged, ·tag·ing** To engage in, damage, or destroy by sabotage. [F < *saboter* work badly, damage]

sab·o·teur (sab′ə·tûr′, *Fr.* sȧ·bô·tœr′) *n.* One who engages in sabotage. [F]

sa·bra (sä′brə) *n. Often cap.* An Israeli born in Israel. [< Heb.]

sac (sak) *n.* A membranous pouch or cavity, often fluid-filled, in a plant or animal. [< L *saccus*]

SAC (sak) Strategic Air Command.

sac·cha·rin (sak′ər·in) *n.* A sweet compound derived from coal tar, used as a substitute for sugar. [< Gk. *sakcharon* sugar]

sac·cha·rine (sak′ər·in, -ə·rīn′, -ə·rēn′) *adj.* **1** Very sweet. **2** Cloyingly sweet: a *saccharine* voice. —*n.* SACCHARIN. **—sac′cha·rine·ly** *adv.* **—sac′cha·rin′i·ty** *n.*

sac·er·do·tal (sas′ər·dōt′l, sak′-) *adj.* Pertaining to a priest or priesthood; priestly. [< L *sacerdos* priest] **—sac′·er·do′tal·ism** (-iz·əm) *n.* **—sac′er·do′tal·ly** *adv.*

sa·chem (sā′chəm) *n.* A North American Indian hereditary chief. [< Algon.]

sa·chet (sa·shā′) *n.* **1** A small bag for perfumed powder, used to scent closets, dresser drawers, etc. **2** The perfumed powder so used. [< L *saccus* a sack]

sack[1] (sak) *n.* **1** A large bag for holding heavy articles. **2** Such a bag and its contents: a *sack* of potatoes. **3** A measure or weight of varying amount. **4** A loosely hanging dress without a waistline, often worn without a belt: also **sack dress. 5** A short, loosely fitting coatlike garment worn by women and children. **6** *Slang* Dismissal, esp. in the phrases **get the sack, give (someone) the sack. 7** In baseball slang, a base. **8** *Slang* A bed; mattress. **—hit the sack** *Slang* To go to bed; retire for the night. —*v.t.* **1** To put into a sack or sacks. 2 *Slang* To dismiss, as an employee. [< Gk. *sakkos* < Heb. *saq* sackcloth]

sack[2] (sak) *v.t.* To plunder or pillage (a town or city) after capturing. —*n.* The pillaging of a captured town or city. [< L *saccus* a sack (for carrying off plunder)] —**sack′er** *n.*

sack[3] (sak) *n.* Any of several strong, light-colored, dry Spanish wines, esp. sherry. [< L *siccus* dry]

sack·but (sak′but) *n.* 1 An early instrument resembling the trombone. 2 In the Bible, a stringed instrument. [< OF *saquer* to pull + *bouter* to push]

sack·cloth (sak′klôth′, -kloth′) *n.* 1 A coarse cloth used for making sacks. 2 Coarse cloth or haircloth worn in penance or mourning.

sack coat A man's short, loose-fitting coat with no waist seam, for informal wear.

sack·ful (sak′fo͝ol′) *n. pl.* **·fuls** Enough to fill a sack.

sack·ing (sak′ing) *n.* A coarse cloth made of hemp or flax and used for sacks.

sacque (sak) *n.* A jacket for a baby.

sac·ra·ment (sak′rə·mənt) *n.* 1 A rite ordained by Christ or by the church as an outward sign of grace, as baptism, confirmation, marriage, etc. 2 *Often cap.* **a** The Eucharist. **b** The consecrated bread and wine of the Eucharist: often with *the.* 3 Any solemn covenant or pledge. 4 Anything considered to have sacred significance. [< L *sacramentum* oath, pledge] —**sac′ra·men′tal** *adj.* —**sac′ra·men′tal·ly** *adv.*

sa·cred (sā′krid) *adj.* 1 Dedicated to religious use; hallowed. 2 Pertaining or related to religion: *sacred* books. 3 Consecrated by love or reverence: *sacred* to the memory of his father. 4 Dedicated to a person or purpose: a memorial *sacred* to those killed in battle. 5 Not to be profaned; inviolable: a *sacred* promise. [< L *sacer* holy] —**sa′cred·ly** *adv.* —**sa′cred·ness** *n.*

Sacred College COLLEGE OF CARDINALS.

sac·ri·fice (sak′rə·fīs) *n.* 1 The act of making an offering to a deity. 2 That which is sacrificed; a victim. 3 A giving up of something cherished or desired. 4 Loss incurred or suffered without return. 5 A reduction of price that leaves little profit or involves loss. 6 In baseball, a hit by which the batter is put out, but the base runner is advanced: also **sacrifice hit.** —*v.* **·ficed, ·fic·ing** *v.t.* 1 To give up (something valued) for the sake of something else: to *sacrifice* one's principles for expediency. 2 To sell or part with at a loss. 3 To make an offering, as to a god. 4 In baseball, to advance (one or more runners) by means of a sacrifice. —*v.i.* 5 To make a sacrifice. [< L *sacer* holy + *facere* to make] —**sac′ri·fic′er** *n.* —**sac′ri·fic′ing·ly** *adv.*

sac·ri·fi·cial (sak′rə·fish′əl) *adj.* Pertaining to, performing, or of the nature of a sacrifice. —**sac′ri·fi′cial·ly** *adv.*

sac·ri·lege (sak′rə·lij) *n.* The act of violating or profaning anything sacred. [< L *sacer* holy + *legere* to plunder]

sac·ri·le·gious (sak′rə·lij′əs, -lē′jəs) *adj.* Disrespectful or injurious to sacred persons or things. —**sac′ri·le′gious·ly** *adv.* —**sac′ri·le′gious·ness** *n.* —**Syn.** blasphemous, godless, impious, irreligious, profane.

sac·ris·tan (sak′ris·tən) *n.* A church official having charge of a sacristy and its contents. Also **sa′crist** (sā′·krist). [< L *sacer* sacred]

sac·ris·ty (sak′ris·tē) *n. pl.* **·ties** A room in a church for the sacred vessels and vestments; a vestry. [< Med. L *sacrista* sacristan]

sac·ro·il·i·ac (sak′rō·il′ē·ak) *adj.* Pertaining to the sacrum and the ilium and the joint between them.

sac·ro·sanct (sak′rō·sangkt) *adj.* Exceedingly sacred; inviolable: sometimes used ironically. [< L *sacer* holy + *sanctus* made holy] —**sac′ro·sanc′ti·ty** *n.*

sa·crum (sā′krəm, sak′rəm) *n. pl.* **·cra** (-krə) A triangular bone formed of fused vertebrae at the lower end of the spinal column and articulating with the hip bone. [< L *(os) sacrum* sacred (bone); from its being offered in sacrifices] • See PELVIS.

sad (sad) *adj.* **sad·der, sad·dest** 1 Sorrowful or depressed in spirits; mournful. 2 Causing sorrow or pity; distressing. 3 *Informal* Very bad; awful: a *sad* situation. 4 Dark-hued; somber. [< OE *sæd* sated] —**sad′ly** *adv.* —**sad′ness** *n.* —**Syn.** 1 dejected, despondent, disconsolate, miserable, unhappy, depressed. 2 deplorable, grievous, lamentable, pitiful.

sad·den (sad′n) *v.t. & v.i.* To make or become sad.

sad·dle (sad′l) *n.* 1 A seat or pad for a rider, as on the back of a horse, bicycle, motorcycle, etc. 2 A padded cushion for a horse's back, as part of a harness or to support a pack, etc. 3. The two hindquarters and part of the backbone of a carcass, as of mutton, venison, etc. 4 Some part or object like or likened to a saddle, as in form or position. —**in the saddle** In a position of control. —*v.t.* **·dled, ·dling** 1 To put a saddle on. 2 To load, as with a burden. 3 To place (a burden or responsibility) on a person. [< OE *sadol*]

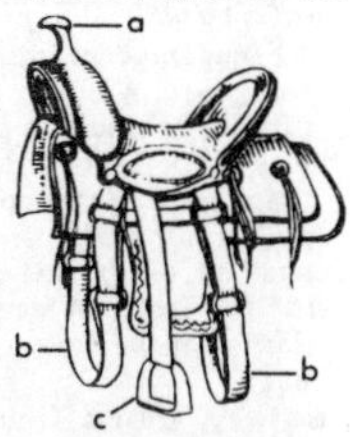

American stock saddle
a. pommel or saddle horn. b. cinches. c. stirrup.

sad·dle·bag (sad′l·bag′) *n.* A large pouch, usu. one of a pair connected by a strap or band and slung over an animal's back behind the saddle.

saddle block A form of anesthesia used esp. during childbirth, in which the patient is injected in the lower spinal cord.

sad·dle·bow (sad′l·bō′) *n.* The arched front upper part of a saddle.

sad·dle·cloth (sad′l·klôth′, -kloth′) *n.* A thick cloth laid on an animal's back under a saddle.

saddle horse A horse used or trained for riding.

sad·dler (sad′lər) *n.* A maker of saddles, harness, etc.

sad·dler·y (sad′lər·ē) *n. pl.* **·dler·ies** 1 Saddles, harness, and fittings, collectively. 2 A shop or the work of a saddler.

saddle shoe A white sport shoe with a dark band of leather across the instep.

saddle soap A softening and preserving soap for leather, containing neat's-foot oil.

Sad·du·cee (saj′o͞o·sē, sad′yo͞o·sē) *n.* A member of an ancient Jewish sect, which during the time of Jesus rejected doctrines of the oral tradition, as resurrection, and adhered strictly to the Mosaic law. —**Sad′du·ce′an, Sad′du·cae′an** *adj.* —**Sad′du·cee′ism** *n.*

sad·i·ron (sad′ī′ərn) *n.* A heavy flatiron pointed at each end. [< SAD, in obs. sense "heavy" + IRON]

sad·ism (sā′diz·əm, sad′iz·əm) *n.* 1 The obtaining of sexual gratification by inflicting pain. 2 A morbid delight in cruelty. [< Comte Donatien de *Sade,* 1740–1814, French writer] —**sad·ist** (sā′dist, sad′ist) *n., adj.* —**sa·dis·tic** (sə·dis′tik, sā-) *adj.* —**sa·dis′ti·cal·ly** *adv.*

sad·o·mas·o·chism (sā′dō·mas′ə·kiz′m, sad′ō-, -maz′-) *n.* A tendency in one individual to be both a sadist and a masochist. [< SAD (ISM) + -O- + MASOCHISM] —**sad′o·mas′o·chist** *n.* —**sad′o·mas′o·chis′tic** *adj.*

sad sack *Slang* A well-meaning but bungling person, esp. a soldier.

sa·fa·ri (sə·fä′rē) *n. pl.* **·ris** A hunting expedition or journey, esp. in E Africa. [< Ar. *safara* travel]

safe (sāf) *adj.* **saf·er, saf·est** 1 Free or freed from danger. 2 Having escaped injury or damage. 3 Not involving risk or loss: a *safe* investment. 4 Not likely to disappoint: It is *safe* to promise. 5 Not likely to cause or do harm or injury: Is this ladder *safe?* 6 No longer in a position to do harm: a burglar *safe* in jail. 7 In baseball, having reached base without being retired. —*n.* 1 A strong iron-and-steel receptacle, usu. fireproof, for protecting valuables. 2 Any place of safe storage. [< L *salvus* whole, healthy] —**safe′·ly** *adv.* —**safe′ness** *n.* —**Syn.** 1 secure. 2 unharmed, unscathed. 3 dependable, reliable.

safe-con·duct (sāf′kon′dukt) *n.* 1 Permission to travel in foreign or enemy territories without risking arrest or injury. 2 An official document assuring such protection.

safe·crack·er (sāf′krak′ər) *n.* One who breaks into safes to rob them. —**safe′crack′ing** *n.*

safe-de·pos·it box (sāf′di·poz′it) A box, safe, or drawer, usu. fireproof, for valuable jewelry, papers, etc., generally located in a bank. Also **safe′ty-de·pos′it box.**

safe·guard (sāf′gärd′) *n.* 1 One who or that which guards or keeps in safety. 2 A mechanical device designed to prevent accident or injury. —*v.t.* To defend; guard.

safe·keep·ing (sāf′kē′ping) *n.* The act or state of keeping or being kept in safety; protection.

safe·ty (sāf′tē) *n. pl.* **·ties** 1 Freedom from danger or risk. 2 Freedom from injury. 3 A device or catch designed as a safeguard. 4 In football, the touching of the ball to the ground behind the player's own goal line when the ball was propelled over the goal line by a member of his own team, scoring two points for the opposing team. 5 In baseball, a fair hit by which the batter reaches first base: also **base hit.** —*adj.* Providing protection.

safety belt 1 A strap that gives a workman needed freedom of movement and protection against falling. 2 SEAT BELT.

safety glass Glass strengthened by any of various methods to reduce the likelihood of its shattering upon impact.

safety match A match that ignites only if struck on a chemically prepared surface.

safety pin 1 A pin whose point springs into place within a protecting sheath. • See PIN. 2 A pin which prevents the premature detonation of a hand grenade.

safety razor A razor in which the blade is fixed and provided with a guard to reduce the risk of cuts.

safety valve 1 *Mech.* A valve for automatically relieving excessive pressure. 2 Any outlet for pent-up energy or emotion.

saf·flow·er (saf′lou′ər) *n.* A thistlelike herb with composite orange-red flowers and seeds that yield edible **safflower oil.** [< Ital. *saffiore* saffron]

saf·fron (saf′rən) *n.* 1 A species of crocus with orange stigmas. 2 The dried stigmas, used in cookery. 3 A deep yellow orange: also **saffron yellow.** —*adj.* Of the color or flavor of saffron. [< Ar. *za'farān*]

S. Afr. South Africa; South African.

sag (sag) *v.* **sagged, sag·ging** *v.i.* 1 To droop from weight or pressure, esp. in the middle. 2 To hang unevenly. 3 To lose firmness; weaken, as from exhaustion, age, etc. 4 To decline, as in price or value. —*v.t.* 5 To cause to sag. —*n.* 1 A sagging. 2 A depressed or sagging place: a *sag* in a roof. [ME *saggen*] **—sag′ging·ly** *adv.*

sa·ga (sä′gə) *n.* 1 A medieval Scandinavian narrative dealing with legendary and heroic exploits. 2 A story having the saga form or manner. [ON, history, narrative]

sa·ga·cious (sə·gā′shəs) *adj.* 1 Ready and apt to apprehend and to decide on a course; intelligent. 2 Shrewd and practical. [< L *sagax* wise] **—sa·ga′cious·ly** *adv.* **—sa·ga′cious·ness** *n.* **—Syn.** 1 acute, discerning, clear-sighted, keen, perspicacious.

sa·gac·i·ty (sə·gas′ə·tē) *n. pl.* **·ties** The quality or an instance of being sagacious; discernment or shrewdness.

sag·a·more (sag′ə·môr, -mōr) *n.* A lesser chief among the Algonquian Indians of North America. [< Algon.]

sage[1] (sāj) *n.* A venerable man of profound wisdom, experience, and foresight. —*adj.* 1 Characterized by or proceeding from calm, far-seeing wisdom and prudence: a *sage* observation. 2 Profound; learned; wise. [< L *sapere* be wise] **—sage′ly** *adv.* **—sage′ness** *n.*

sage[2] (sāj) *n.* 1 A plant of the mint family with aromatic, gray-green leaves that are used for flavoring meats, etc. 2 Any of various related plants. 3 SAGEBRUSH. [< L *salvia*]

sage·brush (sāj′brush′) *n.* Any of various small, aromatic shrubs with composite flowers, native to the w U.S.

sage grouse A large grouse of the plains of the w U.S.

sage hen The sage grouse, esp. the female.

Sag·it·ta·ri·us (saj′ə·târ′ē·əs) *n.* A constellation and the ninth sign of the zodiac; the Archer. • See ZODIAC.

sag·it·tate (saj′ə·tāt) *adj.* Shaped like an arrowhead, as certain leaves. [< L *sagitta* an arrow] • See LEAF.

sa·go (sā′gō) *n. pl.* **·gos** 1 Any of several varieties of East Indian palm. 2 The powdered pith of this palm, used as a thickening agent in puddings, etc. [< Malay *sāgū*]

sa·gua·ro (sə·gwä′rō, -wä′-) *n. pl.* **·ros** A giant cactus of the sw U.S.: also **sa·hua′ro** (-wä′-). [< Sp.]

sa·hib (sä′ib) *n.* Master; lord; Mr.; sir: formerly used in India by natives in speaking of or addressing Europeans. Also **sa′heb.** [< Ar. *sāhib* a friend]

said (sed) *p.t. & p.p.* of SAY. —*adj. Law* Previously mentioned.

sail (sāl) *n.* 1 *Naut.* A piece of canvas, etc., attached to a mast, spread to catch the wind, and thus to propel a craft through the water. 2 Sails collectively. 3 *pl.* **sail** A sailing vessel or craft. 4 A trip in any watercraft. 5 Anything resembling a sail in form or use, as a windmill arm. **—set sail** To begin a voyage. **—take in sail** To lower the sails of a craft. **—under sail** With sails spread and driven by the wind. —*v.i.* 1 To move across the surface of water by the action of wind or steam. 2 To travel over water in a ship or boat. 3 To begin a voyage. 4 To manage a sailing craft: Can you *sail?* 5 To move, glide, or float in the air; soar. 6 To move along in a stately or dignified manner: She *sailed* by haughtily. 7 *Informal* To pass rapidly. 8 *Informal* To proceed boldly into action: with *in.* —*v.t.* 9 To move or travel across the surface of (a body of water) in a ship or boat. 10 To navigate. **—sail into** 1 To begin with energy. 2 To attack violently. [< OE *segl*]

sail·boat (sāl′bōt′) *n.* A small boat propelled by a sail or sails.

sail·cloth (sāl′klôth′, -kloth′) *n.* A very strong, firmly woven, cotton canvas suitable for sails.

sail·fish (sāl′fish′) *n. pl.* **·fish** or **·fish·es** Any of a genus of marine fishes allied to the swordfish, having a large dorsal fin likened to a sail.

Sailfish

sail·or (sā′lər) *n.* 1 An enlisted man in any navy. 2 One whose work is sailing. 3 One who works on a ship. 4 One skilled in sailing. 5 A passenger on a ship or boat, esp. in reference to seasickness: a good *sailor.* 6 A low-crowned, flat-topped hat with a brim. **—sail′or·ly** *adj.*

sail·plane (sāl′plān′) *n.* A light maneuverable glider used for soaring. —*v.i.* **·planed, ·plan·ing** To fly a sailplane.

saint (sānt) *n.* 1 A holy or sanctified person. 2 Such a person who has died and been canonized by certain churches, as the Roman Catholic. 3 *Often cap.* A member of any of certain religious sects calling themselves saints. 4 A very patient, unselfish person. —*v.t.* To canonize; venerate as a saint. —*adj.* Holy; canonized. [< L *sanctus* holy, consecrated] **—saint′hood** *n.*

Saint Ber·nard (bər·närd′) A working dog of great size and strength, originally bred in Switzerland to rescue travelers in the Swiss Alps.

saint·ed (sān′tid) *adj.* 1 Canonized. 2 Of holy character; saintly.

saint·ly (sānt′lē) *adj.* **·li·er, ·li·est** 1 Like a saint; godly; holy. 2 Unusually good, kind, etc. **—saint′li·ness** *n.* **—Syn.** 1 pious, sacred, blessed. 2 benevolent, charitable, kindly, righteous.

saith (seth, sā′ith) *Archaic* Present indicative third person singular of SAY.

sake[1] (sāk) *n.* 1 Purpose; motive; end: for the *sake* of peace and quiet. 2 Interest, regard, or consideration: for the *sake* of your children. [< OE *saccu* a (legal) case]

sa·ke[2] (sä′kē) *n.* A Japanese fermented alcoholic liquor made from rice: also **sa′ki.**

sal (sal) *n.* Salt: used esp. as a pharmaceutical term. [L]

sa·laam (sə·läm′) *n.* 1 An Oriental salutation resembling a low bow, the palm of the right hand being held to the forehead. 2 A respectful or ceremonious greeting. —*v.t. & v.i.* To make a salaam. [< Ar. *salām* peace]

sal·a·ble (sā′lə·bəl) *adj.* Such as can be sold; marketable. **—sal′a·bil′i·ty, sal′a·ble·ness** *n.* **—sal′a·bly** *adv.*

sa·la·cious (sə·lā′shəs) *adj.* Lascivious; lustful; lecherous. [< L *salire* to leap] **—sa·la′cious·ly** *adv.* **—sa·la′cious·ness, sa·lac′i·ty** (-las′ə·te) *n.*

sal·ad (sal′əd) *n.* 1 A dish of vegetables such as lettuce, cucumbers, tomatoes, etc., usu. uncooked and served with a dressing, sometimes mixed with chopped cold meat, fish, hard-boiled eggs, etc. 2 Any green vegetable that can be eaten raw. [< L *salare* to salt]

salad days Days of youth and inexperience.

salad dressing A sauce used on salads, as mayonnaise, oil and vinegar, etc.

sal·a·man·der (sal′ə·man′dər) *n.* 1 Any of an order of tailed amphibians having a smooth, moist skin. 2 A fabled reptile purportedly able to live in fire. [< L *salamandra*] —**sal′a·man′drine** (-drin) *adj.*

Salamander

sa·la·mi (sə·lä′mē) *n. pl.* **·mis** A salted, spiced sausage, originally Italian. [< L *sal* salt]

sal ammoniac AMMONIUM CHLORIDE. [L]

sal·a·ried (sal′ər·ēd) *adj.* 1 In receipt of a salary. 2 Yielding a salary.

sal·a·ry (sal′ər·ē) *n. pl.* **·ries** A periodic payment as compensation for official or professional services. —*v.t.* **·ried, ·ry·ing** To pay or allot a salary to. [< L *salarium* money paid Roman soldiers for their salt]

sale (sāl) *n.* 1 The exchange or transfer of property for money or its equivalent. 2 A selling of merchandise at prices lower than usual. 3 An auction. 4 Opportunity of selling; market: Stocks find no *sale.* 5 *Usu. pl.* The amount sold: last year's *sales.* —**for sale** Offered or ready for sale. —**on sale** For sale at bargain rates. [< OE *sala*]

sale·a·ble (sā′lə·bəl) *adj.* SALABLE.

sal·e·ra·tus (sal′ə·rā′təs) *n.* BAKING SODA. [< NL *sal aëratus* aerated salt]

sales·girl (sālz′gûrl′) *n.* A woman or girl hired to sell merchandise, esp. in a store.

sales·la·dy (sālz′lā′dē) *n. pl.* **·dies** *Informal* A woman or girl hired to sell merchandise, esp. in a store.

sales·man (sālz′mən) *n. pl.* **·men** (-mən) A man hired to sell goods, stock, etc., in a store or by canvassing.

sales·man·ship (sālz′mən·ship) *n.* 1 The work of a salesman. 2 Skill in selling.

sales·peo·ple (sālz′pē′pəl) *n.pl.* Salespersons.

sales·per·son (sālz′pûr′sən) *n.* A person hired to sell merchandise, esp. in a store: also **sales′clerk′** (-klûrk′).

sales resistance A resistance on the part of a potential customer to buying certain goods.

sales·room (sālz′ro͞om′, -ro͝om′) *n.* A room where merchandise is displayed for sale.

sales tax A tax on money received from sales of goods, usu. passed on to the buyer.

sales·wom·an (sālz′wo͝om′ən) *n. pl.* **·wom·en** (-wim′in) A woman or girl hired to sell merchandise, esp. in a store.

Sal·ic (sal′ik) *adj.* Characterizing a law (the **Salic Law**) derived from Germanic sources in the fifth century, and providing that males only could inherit lands: later applied to the succession to the French and Spanish thrones.

sa·lic·y·late (sə·lis′ə·lāt, sal′ə·sil′āt) *n.* A salt or ester of salicylic acid.

sal·i·cyl·ic acid (sal′ə·sil′ik) A crystalline organic compound used in making aspirin and various analgesics. [< L *salix* willow]

sa·li·ent (sā′lē·ənt) *adj.* 1 Standing out prominently: a *salient* feature. 2 Extending outward; projecting: a *salient* angle. 3 Leaping; springing. —*n.* An extension, as of a fortification or a military line protruding toward the enemy. [< L *salire* to leap] —**sa′li·ence, sa′li·en·cy** *n.* —**sa′li·ent·ly** *adv.* —**Syn.** 1 conspicuous, noticeable, significant. 2 jutting.

sa·line (sā′lēn, sā′līn) *adj.* Constituting, consisting of, or characteristic of salt; salty. —*n.* 1 A metallic salt, esp. a salt of one of the alkalis or of magnesium. 2 A solution of sodium chloride or other salt. 3 A natural deposit of salt. [< L *sal* salt] —**sa·lin·i·ty** (sə·lin′ə·tē) *n.*

Salis·bur·y steak (sôlz′ber·ē, -brē) Ground beef mixed with bread crumbs, onion, seasoning, etc., cooked as patties and usu. served with gravy. [< J. H. *Salisbury,* 19th-century English physician]

Sa·lish (sā′lish) *n.* 1 A family of Indian languages of the NW U.S. and SW Canada. 2 A member of a tribe speaking any of these languages. —*adj.* Of or pertaining to the Salish languages or the people speaking them. Also **Sa′lish·an** (-ən).

sa·li·va (sə·lī′və) *n.* A mixture of mucus and fluid secreted by glands in the cheeks and lower jaw. [L] —**sal·i·var·y** (sal′ə·ver′ē) *adj.*

sal·i·vate (sal′ə·vāt) *v.* **·vat·ed, ·vat·ing** *v.i.* 1 To secrete saliva. —*v.t.* 2 To cause to secrete saliva, esp. excessively. —**sal′i·va′tion** *n.*

sal·low (sal′ō) *adj.* Of an unhealthy yellowish color or complexion. —*v.t.* To make sallow. [< OE *salo*] —**sal′low·ness** *n.*

sal·ly (sal′ē) *v.i.* **·lied, ·ly·ing** 1 To rush out suddenly. 2 To set out energetically. 3 To go out, as from a room or building. —*n. pl.* **·lies** 1 A rushing forth, as of besieged troops against besiegers; sortie. 2 A going forth, as on a walk. 3 A witticism or bantering remark. [< L *salire* to leap]

sal·ma·gun·di (sal′mə·gun′dē) *n.* 1 A dish of chopped meat, anchovies, eggs, onions, etc., mixed and seasoned. 2 Any medley or miscellany. [?< Ital. *salami conditi* pickled meats]

salm·on (sam′ən) *n.* 1 Any of various anadromous food and game fishes inhabiting cool ocean waters and certain landlocked lakes. 2 The pinkish orange color of the flesh of certain salmon: also **salm′on-pink′.** —*adj.* Having the color salmon: also **salm′on-pink′.** [< L *salmo*]

Salmon

sal·mo·nel·la (sal′mō·nel′ə) *n. pl.* **·lae** (lē) or **·las** Any of a genus of aerobic bacteria that cause food poisoning and some diseases, including typhoid fever. [< D. E. *Salmon,* U.S. pathologist, 1850–1914]

salmon trout Any of various salmonlike fish, as the European sea trout, the namaycush, etc.

Sa·lo·me (sə·lō′mē, sal·ə·mā′) The daughter of Herodias, who asked from Herod the head of John the Baptist in return for her dancing.

sa·lon (sə·lon′, sal′on, *Fr.* sȧ·lôn′) *n.* 1 A room in which guests are received; a drawing-room. 2 The periodic gathering of noted persons, under the auspices of some distinguished personage. 3 A hall or gallery used for exhibiting works of art. 4 An establishment devoted to some specific purpose: a beauty *salon.* [< Ital. *sala* a room, hall]

sa·loon (sə·lo͞on′) *n.* 1 A place where alcoholic drinks are sold; a bar. 2 A large room for public use, as on a passenger ship: a dining *saloon.* [< F *salon* salon] • In the U.S., *saloon* (def. 1) is now used mainly in historical contexts dealing with the American western frontier or as a rough equivalent of *dive* in describing a squalid bar.

sa·loon-keep·er (sə·lo͞on′kē′pər) *n.* One who keeps a saloon (def. 1).

sal·si·fy (sal′sə·fē, ·fī) *n.* A plant with purple, composite flowers and a white, edible root of an oysterlike flavor. [< F *salsifis*]

sal soda Sodium carbonate; washing soda.

salt (sôlt) *n.* 1 A white, soluble, crystalline compound of sodium and chlorine, widely distributed in nature and found in all living organisms: also **table salt, common salt.** 2 *Chem.* Any compound derived from an acid by replacement of all or part of the hydrogen by an electropositive radical or a metal. 3 *pl.* Any of various mineral compounds in common use, as Epsom salts, smelling salts, etc. 4 Piquant humor; dry wit. 5 That which preserves, corrects, or purifies: the *salt* of criticism. 6 A sailor. 7 A saltcellar. —**salt of the earth** A person or persons regarded as being fine, honest, kindly, etc. —**take with a grain of salt** To allow for exaggeration; have doubts about. —**worth one's salt** Worth one's pay or keep; hardworking. —*adj.* 1 Seasoned with salt; salty. 2 Cured or preserved with salt. 3 Containing, or growing or living in or near, salt water. —*v.t.* 1 To season with salt. 2 To preserve or cure with salt. 3 To furnish with salt: to *salt* cattle. 4 To add zest or piquancy to. 5 To add something to so as fraudulently to increase the value: to *salt* a mine with gold. —**salt away** 1 To pack in salt for preserving. 2 *Informal* To store up; save. [< OE *sealt*] —**salt′er** *n.*

SALT, S.A.L.T. (sôlt) Strategic Arms Limitation Talks.

salt·cel·lar (sôlt′sel′ər) *n.* A small receptacle for table salt. [< ME *salt saler* < *salt* salt + *saler* saltcellar < OF *saliere;* form infl. by CELLAR]

salt chuck *Can. Regional* The sea.
salt·ed (sôl′tid) *adj.* 1 Treated or preserved with salt. 2 *Informal* Experienced or expert.
salting out The injection of a saline solution into the amniotic fluid to terminate a pregnancy.
salt lick A place to which animals go to lick salt from superficial natural deposits.
salt marsh Low coastal land frequently overflowed by the tide, usu. covered with coarse grass: also **salt meadow.**
salt·pe·ter (sôlt′pē′tər) *n.* 1 POTASSIUM NITRATE. 2 CHILE SALTPETER. Also **salt′pe′tre.** [< L *sal* salt + *petra* rock]
salt·shak·er (sôlt′shā′kər) *n.* A container with small apertures for sprinkling table salt.
salt·wa·ter (sôlt′wô′tər, -wot′ər) *adj.* Of, composed of, or living in salt water.
salt·works (sôlt′wûrks′) *n. pl.* **·works** An establishment where salt is made commercially.
salt·wort (sôlt′wûrt′) *n.* Any of a genus of weedy plants adapted to saline soils.
salt·y (sôl′tē) *adj.* **salt·i·er, salt·i·est** 1 Tasting of or containing salt. 2 Piquant; sharp, as speech, etc. **—salt′i·ly** *adv.* **—salt′i·ness** *n.*
sa·lu·bri·ous (sə·lo͞o′brē·əs) *adj.* Conducive to health; healthful; wholesome. [< L *salus* health] **—sa·lu′bri·ous·ly** *adv.* **—sa·lu′bri·ty, sa·lu′bri·ous·ness** *n.*
sal·u·tar·y (sal′yə·ter′ē) *adj.* 1 Beneficial. 2 Wholesome; healthful. [< L *salus* health] **—sal′u·tar′i·ly** *adv.* **—sal′u·tar′i·ness** *n.*
sal·u·ta·tion (sal′yə·tā′shən) *n.* 1 The act of saluting. 2 Any form of greeting. 3 The opening words of a letter, as *Dear Sir* or *Dear Madam.*
sa·lu·ta·to·ri·an (sə·lo͞o′tə·tôr′ē·ən, -tō′rē-) *n.* In colleges and schools, the graduating student who delivers the salutatory at commencement.
sa·lu·ta·to·ry (sə·lo͞o′tə·tôr′ē, -tō′rē) *n. pl.* **·ries** An opening oration, as at a college commencement. *—adj.* Of or relating to a salutatory address. [< L *salutare* SALUTE]
sa·lute (sə·lo͞ot′) *v.* **·lut·ed, ·lut·ing** *v.t.* 1 To greet with an expression or sign of welcome, respect, etc.; welcome. 2 To honor in some prescribed way, as by raising the hand to the cap, presenting arms, firing cannon, etc. *—v.i.* 3 To make a salute. *—n.* 1 An act of saluting; a greeting, show of respect, etc. 2 The attitude assumed in giving a military hand salute. [< L *salutare* < *salus* health] **—sa·lut′er** *n.*
Sal·va·dor (sal′və·dôr′, *Sp.* säl′vä·t͟hôr′) *n.* EL SALVADOR.
Sal·va·do·ri·an (sal′və·dôr′ē·ən, -dō′rē-) *n.* A citizen or native of El Salvador. *—adj.* Of or pertaining to El Salvador or its people: also **Sal′va·do′ran.**
sal·vage (sal′vij) *v.t.* **·vaged, ·vag·ing** 1 To save, as a ship or its cargo, from wreck, capture, etc. 2 To save (material) from something damaged or discarded for reuse: to *salvage* aluminum. *—n.* 1 The saving of a ship, cargo, etc., from loss. 2 Any act of saving property. 3 The compensation allowed to persons by whose exertions a vessel, its cargo, or the lives of those sailing on it are saved from loss. 4 That which is saved from a wrecked or abandoned vessel or from or after a fire. 5 Anything saved from destruction. [< OF *salver* to save] **—sal′vag·er** *n.*
sal·va·tion (sal·vā′shən) *n.* 1 The process or state of being saved. 2 A person or thing that delivers from evil, danger, or ruin. 3 *Theol.* Deliverance from sin and penalty; redemption. [< LL *salvare* to save]
Salvation Army A religious and charitable organization founded on semimilitary lines by William Booth in England in 1865. **—Sal·va′tion·ist** *n.*
salve[1] (sav, säv) *n.* 1 An emollient preparation for burns, cuts, etc. 2 Anything that heals, soothes, or mollifies. *—v.t.* **salved, salv·ing** 1 To dress with salve or ointment. 2 To soothe; appease, as conscience, pride, etc. [< OE *sealf*]
salve[2] (salv) *v.t.* **salved, salv·ing** To save from loss; salvage. [Back formation < SALVAGE]
sal·ver (sal′vər) *n.* A tray, as of silver. [< Sp. *salva,* orig. the foretasting of food, as for a king]
sal·vi·a (sal′vē·ə) *n.* 1 An ornamental species of sage with red flowers. 2 Any plant of the sage genus. [L]
sal·vo (sal′vō) *n. pl.* **·vos** or **·voes** 1 A simultaneous discharge of artillery, or of two or more bombs from an aircraft. 2 A sudden discharge or burst: a *salvo* of hail. 3 Tribute; praise. [< Ital. *salva* a salute]
sal vo·lat·i·le (sal vō·lat′ə·lē) Ammonium carbonate; smelling salts. [NL, volatile salt]
SAM (sam) surface-to-air missile.
S. Am., S. Amer. South America; South American.
sam·a·ra (sam′ər·ə, sə·mâr′ə) *n.* An indehiscent winged fruit, as of the elm or maple. [L, elm seed]
sa·mar·i·um (sə·mâr′ē·əm) *n.* A metallic element (symbol Sm) of the lanthanide series. [NL < Col. *Samarski,* 19th-century Russian mining official]
sam·ba (sam′bə, säm′bä) *n.* A dance of Brazilian origin in two-four time. *—v.i.* To dance the samba. [< a native African name]
Sam Browne belt (sam′ broun′) A military belt, with one or two light shoulder straps running diagonally across the chest from right to left. [< Sir Samuel J. Browne, 1824–1901, British army general]
same (sām) *adj.* 1 Identical; equal: They both are the *same* price. 2 Exactly alike; not different: The two children have the *same* first name. 3 Aforementioned; just spoken of. 4 Equal in degree of preference; indifferent. 5 Unchanged: The old place looks the *same.* **—all the same** 1 Nevertheless. 2 Equally acceptable or unacceptable. **—just the same** 1 Nevertheless. 2 Exactly identical or corresponding; unchanged. *—pron.* The identical person, thing, event, etc. *—adv.* In like manner; equally: with *the.* [< ON *samr, sami*] **—same′ness** *n.*
sam·i·sen (sam′i·sen) *n.* A three-stringed Japanese musical instrument played with a plectrum.
sa·mite (sā′mīt, sam′īt) *n.* A rich medieval fabric of silk, often interwoven with gold or silver. [< Gk. *hexamitos* woven with six threads]
Sa·mo·an (sə·mō′ən) *adj.* Of or pertaining to Samoa, its people, their language, culture, etc. *—n.* 1 A native or citizen of Samoa. 2 The language of the Samoans.
sam·o·var (sam′ə·vär) *n.* A metal urn containing a tube for charcoal for heating water, as for making tea. [Russ. < *samo-* self + *varit* boil]

Samovar

Sam·o·yed (sam′ə·yed′) *n.* 1 One of a Mongoloid people inhabiting the Arctic coasts of Siberia. 2 A large Siberian dog with a thick white coat. *—adj.* Of or pertaining to the Samoyed people. Also **Sam′o·yede′** (-yed′). **—Sam′o·yed′ic** *adj.*
samp (samp) *n.* Coarsely ground Indian corn; also, a porridge made of it. [< Algon.]
sam·pan (sam′pan) *n.* Any of various small flat-bottomed boats used along rivers and coasts of China and Japan. [< Chin. *san* three + *pan* board]

Sampan

sam·ple (sam′pəl) *n.* 1 A portion, part, or piece taken or shown as a representative of the whole. 2 An instance: This is a *sample* of his kindness. *—v.t.* **·pled, ·pling** To test or examine by means of a portion or sample. *—adj.* Serving as a sample: a *sample* dress. [< OF *essample* example]
sam·pler (sam′plər) *n.* 1 One who tests by samples. 2 A device for removing a portion of a substance for testing. 3 A piece of needlework, designed to show a beginner's skill. [< L *exemplum* example]
Sam·son (sam′sən) In the Bible, a Hebrew judge of great physical strength, betrayed to the Philistines by Delilah.
sam·u·rai (sam′o͝o·rī) *n. pl.* **·rai** Under the Japanese feudal system, a member of the soldier class of the lower nobility; also, the class itself. [Jap.]
san·a·tive (san′ə·tiv) *adj.* Healing; health-giving. [< L *sanare* heal]
san·a·to·ri·um (san′ə·tôr′ē·əm, -tō′rē-) *n. pl.* **·to·ri·ums** or **·to·ri·a** (-tôr′ē·ə, -tō′rē·ə) An institution for the treatment of chronic disorders, as mental illness, alcoholism, etc. [< LL *sanatorius* healthy]
sanc·ti·fy (sangk′tə·fī) *v.t.* **·fied, ·fy·ing** 1 To set apart as holy; consecrate. 2 To free of sin; purify. 3 To render sacred or inviolable, as a vow. [< L *sanctus* holy + *facere* to make] **—sanc′ti·fi·ca′tion, sanc′ti·fi′er** *n.*
sanc·ti·mo·ni·ous (sangk′tə·mō′nē·əs) *adj.* Making an

ostentatious display or a hypocritical pretense of sanctity. **—sanc'ti·mo'ni·ous·ly** *adv.* **—sanc'ti·mo'ni·ous·ness** *n.*

sanc·ti·mo·ny (sangk'tə·mō'nē) *n.* Assumed or outward sanctity; a show of devoutness. [< L *sanctimonia* holiness]

sanc·tion (sangk'shən) *v.t.* **1** To approve authoritatively; confirm; ratify. **2** To countenance; allow. **—***n.* **1** Final and authoritative confirmation; justification or ratification. **2** A formal decree. **3** A provision for securing conformity to law, as by the enactment of rewards or penalties or both. **4** *pl.* In international law, a coercive measure adopted by several nations to force a nation to obey international law, by limiting trade relations, by military force and blockade, etc. [< L *sanctus,* p.p. of *sancire* make sacred]

sanc·ti·ty (sangk'tə·tē) *n. pl.* **·ties 1** The state of being sacred or holy. **2** Saintliness; holiness. **3** Something sacred or holy.

sanc·tu·ar·y (sangk'cho͞o·er'ē) *n. pl.* **·ar·ies 1** A holy or sacred place, esp. one devoted to the worship of a deity. **2** The most sacred part of a place in a sacred structure; esp. the part of a church where the principal altar is situated. **3** A place of refuge: a wildlife *sanctuary.* **4** Immunity from the law or punishment. [< L *sanctus* holy] **—Syn. 1** church, shrine, temple. **3** preserve, shelter.

sanc·tum (sangk'təm) *n. pl.* **·tums** or **·ta** (-tə) **1** A sacred place. **2** A private room where one is not to be disturbed. [L < *sanctus* holy]

sanc·tum sanc·to·rum (sangk'təm sangk·tôr'əm, -tō'rəm) **1** HOLY OF HOLIES. **2** A place of great privacy: often used humorously. [LL, holy of holies]

sand (sand) *n.* **1** A hard, granular rock material finer than gravel and coarser than dust. **2** *pl.* Stretches of sandy desert or beach. **3** *pl.* Sandy grains, as those of the hourglass. **4** *Slang* Endurance; grit. **—***v.t.* **1** To sprinkle or cover with sand. **2** To smooth or abrade with sand or sandpaper. [< OE]

san·dal (san'dəl) *n.* **1** A foot covering, consisting usu. of a sole only, held to the foot by thongs or straps. **2** A light, openwork slipper. [< Gk. *sandalion*] **—san'daled** *adj.*

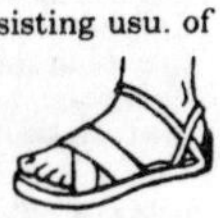
Sandal

san·dal·wood (san'dəl·wo͝od') *n.* **1** The fine-grained, dense, fragrant wood of any of several East Indian trees. **2** The similar wood of other trees. **3** Any tree yielding this wood. [< Med. L *sandalum* sandalwood + WOOD]

sand·bag (sand'bag') *n.* **1** A bag filled with sand, used for building fortifications, for ballast, etc. **2** A small bag filled with sand and used as a club. **—***v.t.* **·bagged, ·bag·ging 1** To fill or surround with sandbags. **2** To strike or attack with a sandbag. **—sand'bag'ger** *n.*

sand·bank (sand'bangk') *n.* A mound or ridge of sand.

sand·bar (sand'bär') *n.* A ridge of silt or sand in rivers, along beaches, etc., formed by the action of currents or tides.

sand·blast (sand'blast', -bläst') *n.* **1** An apparatus for propelling a jet of sand, as for etching glass or cleaning stone. **2** The jet of sand. **—***v.t.* To clean or engrave by means of a sandblast. **—sand'blast'er** *n.*

sand·box (sand'boks') *n.* A box of sand for children to play in.

sand·er (san'dər) *n.* A device, esp. a machine powered by electricity, that smooths and polishes surfaces by means of a disk or belt coated with an abrasive: also **sanding machine.**

sand flea 1 CHIGOE. **2** Any of various tiny crustaceans that jump like fleas.

sand·hog (sand'hôg', -hog') *n.* One who works under air pressure, as in sinking caissons, building tunnels, etc.: also **sand hog.**

sand·lot (sand'lot') *n.* A vacant lot in or near an urban area. **—***adj.* Of or played in such a lot: *sandlot* baseball.

sand·man (sand'man') *n.* In nursery lore, a mythical person supposed to make children sleepy by casting sand in their eyes.

sand·pa·per (sand'pā'pər) *n.* Strong paper coated with abrasive for smoothing or polishing. **—***v.t.* To rub or polish with sandpaper.

sand·pi·per (sand'pī'pər) *n.* Any of certain small wading birds having long, thin bills and frequenting shores and marsh lands.

Sandpiper

sand·stone (sand'stōn') *n.* A rock consisting chiefly of quartz sand cemented with other materials.

sand·storm (sand'stôrm') *n.* A high wind by which clouds of sand or dust are carried along.

sand·wich (sand'wich, san'-) *n.* **1** Two or more slices of bread, having between them meat, cheese, etc. **2** Any combination of alternating dissimilar things pressed together. **—***v.t.* To place between other persons or things. [< John Montagu, fourth Earl of *Sandwich,* 1718–92]

sandwich man *Informal* A man carrying boards, called **sandwich boards,** one in front and one behind, for the purpose of advertising or picketing.

sand·y (san'dē) *adj.* **sand·i·er, sand·i·est 1** Consisting of or characterized by sand; containing, covered with, or full of sand. **2** Yellowish red: a *sandy* beard. **—sand'i·ness** *n.*

sane (sān) *adj.* **san·er, san·est 1** Mentally sound; not deranged. **2** Proceeding from a sound mind. **3** Sensible; wise. [< L *sanus* whole, healthy] **—sane'ly** *adv.* **—sane'ness** *n.*

San·for·ize (san'fə·rīz) *v.t.* **·ized, ·iz·ing** To treat (cloth) by a special process so as to prevent more than slight shrinkage. [Back formation < *Sanforized,* a trade name]

sang (sang) *p.t.* of SING.

sang-froid (säng'frwä', *Fr.* säṅ·frwä') *n.* Calmness amid trying circumstances; composure. [F, lit., cold blood]

san·gui·nar·y (sang'gwə·ner'ē) *adj.* **1** Attended with bloodshed. **2** Prone to shed blood; bloodthirsty. [< L *sanguis* blood] **—san'gui·nar'i·ly** *adv.* **—san'gui·nar'i·ness** *n.*

san·guine (sang'gwin) *adj.* **1** Of buoyant disposition; hopeful. **2** Having the color of blood; ruddy: a *sanguine* complexion. **3** *Obs.* Bloodthirsty; sanguinary. Also **san·guin·e·ous** (sang·gwin'ē·əs). [< L *sanguis* blood] **—san'guine·ly** *adv.* **—san'guine·ness** *n.* **—Syn. 1** ardent, confident, enthusiastic, optimistic. **2** rubicund.

San·he·drin (san·hed'rən, -hēd'-, san'hi·drin, san'i-) *n.* In ancient times, the supreme council and highest court of the Jewish nation. Also **Great Sanhedrin.** [< Heb.]

san·i·tar·i·an (san'ə·târ'ē·ən) *n.* A person skilled in matters relating to sanitation and public health.

san·i·tar·i·um (san'ə·târ'ē·əm) *n. pl.* **·i·ums** or **·i·a** (-ē·ə) **1** A health resort. **2** SANATORIUM. [< L *sanitas* health]

san·i·tar·y (san'ə·ter'ē) *adj.* **1** Relating to the preservation of health and prevention of disease: *sanitary* measures. **2** Free from filth; clean; hygienic. **—***n. pl.* **·tar·ies** A public toilet. [< L *sanitas* health] **—san'i·tar'i·ly** *adv.*

sanitary napkin An absorbent pad used by women during menstruation.

san·i·ta·tion (san'ə·tā'shən) *n.* **1** The science or process of establishing sanitary conditions, esp. as regards public health. **2** The removal of sewage, garbage, etc.

san·i·ta·tion·man (san'i·tā'shən·man') *n. pl.* **·men** (-mən) A person, esp. a municipal employee, whose work is the collection of refuse and trash.

san·i·tize (san'ə·tīz) *v.t.* **·tized, ·tiz·ing 1** To make sanitary, as by scrubbing, washing, or sterilizing. **2** To make acceptable or unobjectionable, as by deleting offensive parts: a *sanitized* fairy tale. **—san'i·tiz·er** *n.*

san·i·ty (san'ə·tē) *n.* **1** The state of being sane or sound; mental health. **2** Sane moderation or reasonableness. [< L *sanus* healthy] **—Syn. 1** rationality, saneness. **2** common sense, level-headedness, sensibleness.

sank (sangk) *p.t.* of SINK.

San Ma·ri·no (mä·rē'nō) *n.* A republic located in an enclave of NE Italy, 23 sq. mi., cap. San Marino.

sans (sanz, *Fr.* säṅ) *prep.* Without. [< OF *sens, sanz*]

sans·cu·lotte (sanz'kyo͞o·lot', *Fr.* säṅ·kü·lôt') *n.* **1** A revolutionary: used by the aristocrats as a term of contempt for the poorly clad republicans who started the French Revolution of 1789. **2** Any revolutionary republican or radical. [F, lit., without knee breeches] **—sans′cu·lot′tic** *adj.* **—sans′cu·lot′tism** *n.*

san·se·vi·e·ri·a (san′sə·vir′ē·ə, -vi·ē′rē·ə) *n.* Any of a genus of succulent plants of the lily family with a cluster of tall, lance-shaped leaves. [< the Prince of *Sanseviero,* 1710–71, Italian scholar]

San·skrit (san′skrit) *n.* The ancient and classical language of the Hindus of India, belonging to the Indic branch of the Indo-Iranian subfamily of Indo-European languages: also **San′scrit.** [< Skt. *samskrita* well-formed]

sans ser·if (sanz ser′if) *Printing* A style of type without serifs.

San·ta Claus (san′tə klôz′) In folklore, a friend of children who brings presents at Christmas time: usu. represented as a fat, jolly old man in a red suit; St. Nicholas. [< dial. Du. *Sante Klaus* Saint Nicholas]

Santa Fe Trail The trade route, important from 1821 to 1880, between Independence, Missouri and Santa Fe, New Mexico.

sap[1] (sap) *n.* **1** The juices of plants, which contain and transport the materials necessary to growth. **2** Any vital fluid; vitality. **3** Sapwood. **4** *Slang* A foolish, stupid, or ineffectual person. [< OE *sæp*]

sap[2] (sap) *v.* **sapped, sap·ping** *v.t.* **1** To weaken or destroy gradually and insidiously. **2** To approach or undermine (an enemy fortification) by digging trenches. *—v.i.* **3** To dig a sap or saps. *—n.* A deep, narrow trench dug so as to approach or undermine a fortification. [< MF *sappe* a spade] **—Syn.** *v.* **1** debilitate, disable, enervate, enfeeble.

sap·head (sap′hed′) *n. Slang* A stupid person; simpleton. **—sap′head′ed** *adj.*

sa·pi·ent (sā′pē·ənt, sap′ē-) *adj.* Wise; sagacious: often ironical. [< L *sapere* know, taste] **—sa′pi·ence, sa′pi·en·cy** *n.* **—sa′pi·ent·ly** *adv.*

sap·ling (sap′ling) *n.* **1** A young tree. **2** A young person. [Dim. of SAP[1]]

sap·o·dil·la (sap′ə·dil′ə) *n.* **1** A large tropical American evergreen tree which yields chicle and an edible fruit. **2** Its apple-shaped fruit: also **sapodilla plum.** [< Nahuatl *zapotl*]

sap·o·na·ceous (sap′ə·nā′shəs) *adj.* Soapy. [< L *sapo* soap] **—sap′o·na′ceous·ness** *n.*

sa·pon·i·fy (sə·pon′ə·fī) *v.t.* **·fied, ·fy·ing** To convert (a fat or oil) into soap by the action of an alkali. [< L *sapo* soap + *facere* to make] **—sa·pon′i·fi·ca′tion, sa·pon′i·fi′er** *n.*

sap·per (sap′ər) *n.* A soldier employed in making trenches, tunnels, and underground fortifications. [< SAP[2]]

sap·phire (saf′īr) *n.* **1** Any one of the hard, transparent, colored varieties of corundum, esp. a blue variety valued as a gem. **2** Deep blue. **—star sapphire** A sapphire cut without facets, showing six rays on the dome. *—adj.* Deep blue. [< Gk. *sappheiros* a gemstone]

sap·py (sap′ē) *adj.* **·pi·er, pi·est 1** Full of sap; juicy. **2** *Slang* Immature; silly. **3** Vital; pithy. **—sap′pi·ness** *n.*

sap·ro·phyte (sap′rə·fīt) *n.* An organism that lives on dead or decaying organic matter, as certain bacteria, fungi, etc. [< Gk. *sapros* rotten + -PHYTE] **—sap′ro·phyt′ic** (-fit′ik) *adj.*

sap·suck·er (sap′suk′ər) *n.* A small woodpecker that taps trees and drinks sap.

Yellow-bellied sapsucker

sap·wood (sap′wŏŏd′) *n.* The new wood beneath the bark of a tree.

S.A.R. Sons of the American Revolution.

sar·a·band (sar′ə·band) *n.* **1** A stately Spanish dance in triple time, of the 17th and 18th centuries. **2** Music for this dance. Also **sar′a·bande.** [< Sp. *zarabanda*]

Sar·a·cen (sar′ə·sən) *n.* **1** Formerly, a Muslim enemy of the Crusaders. **2** An Arab. *—adj.* Of or pertaining to the Saracens. **—Sar′a·cen′ic** (-sen′ik) or **·i·cal** *adj.*

Sar·ah (sâr′ə) In the Bible, the wife of Abraham and the mother of Isaac.

Sa·ran (sə·ran′) *n.* A synthetic plastic material used as a textile fiber and as a transparent, moistureproof wrapping: a trade name.

sar·casm (sär′kaz·əm) *n.* **1** The use of keenly ironic or scornful remarks. **2** Such a remark. [< Gk. *sarkazein* tear flesh, speak bitterly] **—Syn. 2** gibe, sneer, taunt.

sar·cas·tic (sär·kas′tik) *adj.* **1** Characterized by or of the nature of sarcasm. **2** Taunting. Also **sar·cas′ti·cal. —sar·cas′ti·cal·ly** *adv.*

sarce·net (särs′net) *n.* A fine, thin silk, used for linings. [< OF *drap sarrasinois,* lit. Saracen cloth]

sar·co·carp (sär′kō·kärp) *n.* The fleshy, usu. edible part of a drupe. [< Gk. *sarx* flesh + *karpos* a fruit]

sar·co·ma (sär·kō′mə) *n. pl.* **·mas** or **·ma·ta** (-mə·tə) A malignant tumor originating in connective tissue. [< Gk. *sarkaein* become fleshy] **—sar·co′ma·tous** (-kō′mə·təs) *adj.*

sar·coph·a·gus (sär·kof′ə·gəs) *n. pl.* **·gi** (-jī) or **·gus·es 1** A stone coffin or tomb. **2** A large ornamental coffin of marble or other stone placed in a crypt or exposed to view. [< Gk. *sarx* flesh + *phagein* eat]

sard (särd) *n.* A deep brownish red variety of chalcedony, used as a gem. [< L *sarda*]

sar·dine (sär·dēn′) *n.* **1** A small fish preserved in oil as a delicacy. **2** The young of the herring or some like fish similarly prepared. [< Gk. *sarda* a kind of fish]

sar·don·ic (sär·don′ik) *adj.* Scornful or derisive; sneering; mocking; cynical. [< Gk. *sardanios* bitter, scornful] **—sar·don′i·cal·ly** *adv.* **—sar·don′i·cism** *n.*

sar·do·nyx (sär·don′iks, sär′də·niks) *n.* A variety of onyx, containing layers of light-colored chalcedony and sard. [< Gk. *sardios* sard + *onyx* onyx]

sar·gas·so (sär·gas′ō) *n.* Any of a genus of large, floating brown seaweed: also **sargasso weed, sar·gas′sum.** [< Pg. *sarga,* a kind of grape]

sa·ri (sä′rē) *n. pl.* **·ris** A length of cloth, constituting the principal garment of Hindu women, one end falling to the feet, and the other crossed over the bosom, shoulder, and sometimes over the head: also **sa′ree.** [< Skt. *śāṭī*]

Sari

sa·rong (sə·rong′) *n.* A rectangular piece of colored cloth worn as a skirt by both sexes in the Malay Archipelago. [< Malay *sārung*]

sar·sa·pa·ril·la (sas′pə·ril′ə, sär′sə·pə·ril′ə) *n.* **1** A tropical American vine with fragrant roots. **2** An extract of these roots, used as flavoring. **3** Any of various plants resembling sarsaparilla. [< Sp. *zarza* a bramble + *parilla* little vine]

sar·to·ri·al (sär·tôr′ē·əl, -tō′rē-) *adj.* **1** Pertaining to a tailor or his work. **2** Pertaining to men's clothes. [< L *sartor* tailor] **—sar·to′ri·al·ly** *adv.*

sash[1] (sash) *n.* An ornamental band or scarf, worn around the waist or over the shoulder. [< Ar. *shāsh* muslin, turban]

sash[2] (sash) *n.* A frame, as of a window, in which glass is set. *—v.t.* To furnish with a sash. [Alter. of CHASSIS, taken as a pl.]

sa·shay (sa·shā′) *v.i. Informal* To move or glide about, esp. ostentatiously. [< Fr. *chassé* a dance movement]

Sask. Saskatchewan.

sass (sas) *Informal n.* Impudence; back talk. *—v.t.* To talk to impudently. [Dial. alter. of SAUCE]

sas·sa·fras (sas′ə·fras) *n.* **1** A small North American tree related to laurel. **2** A flavoring agent made from the bark of its roots. [< Sp. *sasafrás*]

sas·sy (sas′ē) *adj.* **·si·er, ·si·est** *Informal* Saucy; impertinent. **—sas′si·ly** *adv.* **—sas′si·ness** *n.*

sat (sat) *p.t.* of SIT.

SAT Scholastic Aptitude Test.

Sat. Saturday; Saturn.

Sa·tan (sā′tən) In the Bible, the great adversary of God and tempter of mankind; the Devil. [< Heb. *sātān* an enemy] **—sa·tan·ic** (sā·tan′ik, sə-), **sa·tan′i·cal** *adj.* **—sa·tan′i·cal·ly** *adv.*

satch·el (sach′əl) *n.* A small bag for carrying books, clothing, etc. [< L *sacellus* little sack]

sate[1] (sāt) *v.t.* **sat·ed, sat·ing 1** To satisfy the appetite of. **2** To indulge with too much so as to weary or sicken; satiate. [< OE *sadian*] **—Syn 1** gratify. **2** cloy, glut, stuff, surfeit.

sate[2] (sāt) Archaic *p.t.* of SIT.

sa·teen (sa·tēn′) *n.* A smooth, shiny cotton fabric resembling satin. [Alter. of SATIN]

sat·el·lite (sat′ə·līt) *n.* 1 A body held in orbit about a more massive one; a moon. 2 An artificial body propelled into orbit, esp. around the earth. 3 One who attends upon a person in power. 4 Any obsequious attendant. 5 A small nation dependent on a great power. [< L *satelles* an attendant]

sa·ti·a·ble (sā′shē·ə·bəl, -shə·bəl) *adj.* Capable of being satiated. **—sa′ti·a·bil′i·ty, sa′ti·a·ble·ness** *n.* **—sa′ti·a·bly** *adv.*

sa·ti·ate (sā′shē·āt) *v.t.* **·at·ed, ·at·ing** 1 To satisfy the appetite or desire of; gratify. 2 To fill or gratify excessively; glut. —*adj.* Filled to satiety; satiated. [< L *satis* enough] **—sa′ti·a′tion** *n.*

sa·ti·e·ty (sə·tī′ə·tē, sā′shē·ə·tē) *n. pl.* **·ties** The state of being satiated; surfeit. [< L *satis* enough]

sat·in (sat′ən) *n.* A fabric of silk, rayon, etc., with glossy face and dull back. —*adj.* Of or similar to satin; glossy; smooth. [< OF] **—sat′in·y** *adj.*

sat·in·wood (sat′ən·wo͝od′) *n.* 1 The smooth, hard wood of various trees, used in cabinetwork. 2 Any tree yielding such wood.

sat·ire (sat′īr) *n.* 1 The use of sarcasm, irony, or wit in ridiculing and denouncing abuses, follies, customs, etc. 2 A literary work that ridicules in this manner. [< L *satira*]

sa·tir·i·cal (sə·tir′i·kəl) *adj.* 1 Given to or characterized by satire: a *satirical* writer. 2 Sarcastic; caustic; biting. Also **sa·tir′ic. —sa·tir′i·cal·ly** *adv.* **—sa·tir′i·cal·ness** *n.*

sat·i·rist (sat′ə·rist) *n.* 1 A writer of satire. 2 A person fond of satirizing or ridiculing.

sat·i·rize (sat′ə·rīz) *v.t.* **·rized, ·riz·ing** To subject to or criticize in satire. **—sat′i·riz′er** *n.*

sat·is·fac·tion (sat′is·fak′shən) *n.* 1 The act of satisfying, or the state of being satisfied. 2 The making of amends, reparation, or payment. 3 That which satisfies; compensation.

sat·is·fac·to·ry (sat′is·fak′tər·ē) *adj.* Giving satisfaction; answering expectations or requirements. **—sat′is·fac′to·ri·ly** *adv.* **—sat′is·fac′to·ri·ness** *n.* **—Syn.** adequate, gratifying, pleasing, sufficient.

sat·is·fy (sat′is·fī) *v.* **·fied, ·fy·ing** *v.t.* 1 To supply fully with what is desired, expected, or needed. 2 To please; gratify. 3 To free from doubt or anxiety; convince. 4 To give what is due to. 5 To pay or discharge (a debt, obligation, etc.). 6 To answer sufficiently or convincingly, as a question or objection. 7 To make reparation for; expiate. —*v.i.* 8 To give satisfaction. [< L *satis* enough + *facere* do] **—sat′is·fi′er** *n.* **—sat′is·fy′ing·ly** *adv.*

sa·to·ri (sä·tō′rē) *n.* The sudden change of consciousness which is the goal of Zen Buddhism. [Jap.]

sa·trap (sā′trap, sat′rap) *n.* 1 A governor of a province in ancient Persia. 2 Any petty ruler under a despot. 3 A subordinate ruler or governor. [< O Pers. *shathraparan*, lit., a protector of a province]

sa·trap·y (sā′trə·pē, sat′rə·pē) *n. pl.* **·trap·ies** The territory or the jurisdiction of a satrap. Also **sa·trap·ate** (sā′·trə·pit, sat′rə-).

sat·u·rate (sach′ə·rāt) *v.t.* **·rat·ed, ·rat·ing** To soak or imbue thoroughly to the utmost capacity for absorbing or retaining. —*adj.* Saturated. [< L *satur* full] **—sat′u·ra′tor** or **sat′u·rat′er** *n.*

sat·u·rat·ed (sach′ə·rā′tid) *adj.* 1 Replete; incapable of holding more of a substance: a *saturated* solution. 2 *Chem.* Designating an organic compound having no free or multiple valence bonds available for direct union with additional atoms. 3 Tending to increase the cholesterol content of the blood: said of some edible fats.

sat·u·ra·tion (sach′ə·rā′shən) *n.* 1 A saturating or being saturated. 2 A massive concentration, in any given area, as of advertising, military force, etc., for a specific purpose: often used attributively: *saturation* bombing.

saturation point 1 The maximum possible degree of impregnation of one substance with another. 2 A condition in which a person has reached the limit of patience, toleration, etc.

Sat·ur·day (sat′ər·dē, -dā) *n.* The seventh or last day of the week; the day of the Jewish Sabbath. [< OE *Sæternesdæg* Saturn's day]

Sat·urn (sat′ərn) *Rom. Myth.* The god of agriculture. —*n.* The planet of the solar system sixth in distance from the sun. • See PLANET. **—Sa·tur·ni·an** (sə·tûr′nē·ən) *adj.* [< L *Saturnus*]

sat·ur·na·li·a (sat′ər·nā′lē·ə) *n.pl.* *(usu. construed as sing.)* Any season or period of general license or revelry. **—sat′ur·na′li·an** *adj.*

Sat·ur·na·li·a (sat′ər·nā′lē·ə) *n.pl.* The feast of Saturn held in ancient Rome in mid-December, and marked by wild reveling and abandon. **—Sat′ur·na′li·an** *adj.*

sat·ur·nine (sat′ər·nīn) *adj.* 1 Having a grave, gloomy, or morose disposition or character. 2 In astrology, born under the supposed dominance of Saturn. [< L *Saturnus* Saturn] **—sat′ur·nine·ly** *adv.* **—sat′ur·nine′ness** *n.*

sat·yr (sā′tər, sat′ər) *Gk. Myth.* A wanton woodland deity with a man's body and goatlike legs. —*n.* A lascivious man. [< Gk. *satyros*] **—sa·tyr·ic** (sə·tir′ik) or **·i·cal** *adj.*

sat·y·ri·a·sis (sat′ə·rī′ə·sis) *n.* An abnormally strong, insatiable sexual drive in males. [< Gk. *satyros* a satyr]

sauce (sôs) *n.* 1 An appetizing, usu. liquid relish for food to improve its taste. 2 A dish of fruit pulp stewed and sweetened: cranberry *sauce.* 3 *Informal* Pert or impudent language. 4 *Slang* Alcoholic liquor. —*v.t.* **sauced, sauc·ing** 1 To flavor or dress with sauce. 2 *Informal* To be saucy to. [< L *salsus* salted]

sauce·pan (sôs′pan′) *n.* A pan, usu. of metal or enamel, with projecting handle, for cooking food.

sau·cer (sô′sər) *n.* 1 A small dish for holding a cup. 2 Any round, shallow thing of similar shape. [< OF *sauce* sauce]

sau·cy (sô′sē) *adj.* **·ci·er, ci·est** 1 Disrespectful to superiors; impudent. 2 Piquant; sprightly; amusing. **—sau′ci·ly** *adv.* **—sau′ci·ness** *n.*

Sau·di A·ra·bi·a (sou′dē ə·rā′bē·ə, sä·o͞o′dē) A kingdom

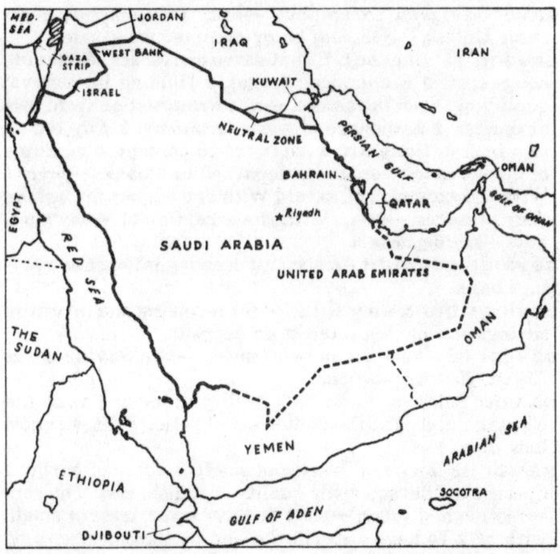

of N CEN. Arabia, 927,000 sq. mi., cap. Riyadh. **—Sau′di A·ra′bi·an** *adj., n.*

sauer·kraut (sour′krout′) *n.* Shredded and salted cabbage fermented in its own juice. [< G *sauer* sour + *kraut* cabbage]

Saul (sôl) In the Bible, the first king of Israel.

sau·na (sou′nə, sô′-) *n.* 1 A Finnish steam bath in which the steam is produced by running water over heated stones. 2 A bath in which the bather is exposed to very hot, dry air. 3 A room or enclosure for a sauna. [Finnish]

saun·ter (sôn′tər) *v.i.* To walk in a leisurely or lounging way; stroll. —*n.* 1 A slow, aimless manner of walking. 2 An idle stroll. [< ME *santren* muse] **—saun′ter·er** *n.* **—saun′ter·ing·ly** *adv.*

sau·ri·an (sôr′ē·ən) *n.* Any of the suborder of reptiles comprising the lizards. —*adj.* Pertaining to or having the characteristics of lizards. [< Gk. *sauros* a lizard]

-saurus *combining form Zool.* Lizard: *brontosaurus.* [< Gk. *sauros* a lizard]

sau·sage (sô′sij) *n.* Finely chopped and highly seasoned meat, commonly stuffed into a prepared animal intestine or other casing. [< L *salsus* salted]

sau·té (sô·tā′, sō-) *v.t.* **·téed, ·té·ing** To fry quickly in a little fat. —*n.* A sautéed dish. [F, p.p. of *sauter* to leap]

sau·terne (sô·tûrn′, sō-; *Fr.* sō·tern′) *n.* A sweet, white wine. [< *Sauternes,* district in sw France]

sav·age (sav′ij) *adj.* **1** Of a wild and untamed nature; not domesticated. **2** Fierce; ferocious. **3** Living in or belonging to the most primitive condition of human society; uncivilized. **4** Remote and wild: *savage* mountain country. —*n.* **1** A primitive or uncivilized human being. **2** A brutal and cruel person. —*v.t.* **sav·aged, sav·a·ging** To beat or maul cruelly. [< L *silva* a wood] —**sav′age·ly** *adv.* —**Syn.** *adj.* **1** undomesticated, feral. **2** brutal, bloodthirsty, barbarous. **3** uncultivated.

sav·age·ry (sav′ij·rē) *n. pl.* **·ries 1** The state of being savage. **2** Cruelty in disposition or action. **3** A savage act.

sa·van·na (sə·van′ə) *n.* A tract of level land covered with low vegetation; a treeless plain, esp. in or near the tropics: also **sa·van′nah.** [< Cariban]

sa·vant (sə·vänt′, sav′ənt; *Fr.* sà·väṅ′) *n.* A person of exceptional learning. [F < L *sapere* be wise]

save[1] (sāv) *v.* **saved, sav·ing** *v.t.* **1** To preserve or rescue from danger, harm, etc. **2** To keep from being spent, expended, or lost. **3** To set aside for future use; accumulate: often with *up.* **4** To treat carefully so as to avoid fatigue, harm, etc.: to *save* one's eyesight. **5** To prevent by timely action: A stitch in time *saves* nine. **6** *Theol.* To deliver from the consequences of sin; redeem. —*v.i.* **7** To be economical. **8** To preserve something from harm, etc. **9** To accumulate money. [< L *salvus* safe] —**sav′er** *n.*

save[2] (sāv) *prep.* Except; but. —*conj.* **1** Except; but. **2** *Archaic* Unless. [< OF *sauf* being excepted, orig. safe]

sav·ing (sā′ving) *adj.* **1** That saves or rescues: *lifesaving* equipment. **2** Economical; frugal. **3** Holding in reserve; qualifying: a *saving* clause. —*n.* **1** Preservation from loss or danger. **2** Avoidance of waste; economy. **3** Any reduction in cost, time, etc.: a *saving* of 16 percent. **4** *pl.* Sums of money saved, esp. those deposited in a bank. —*prep.* **1** With the exception of; save. **2** With due respect for: *saving* your presence. —*conj.* With the exception of. —**sav′ing·ly** *adv.* —**sav′ing·ness** *n.*

savings account An account drawing interest at a savings bank.

savings bank An institution for receiving and investing savings and paying interest on deposits.

sav·ior (sāv′yər) *n.* One who saves. —**the Savior** Jesus Christ. *Brit. sp.* **sav′iour.**

sa·voir faire (sà·vwàr fâr′) Ability to see and to do the right thing; esp., sophisticated social poise. [F, lit., to know how to act]

sa·vor (sā′vər) *n.* **1** Taste and smell: a *savor* of garlic. **2** Specific or characteristic quality. **3** Relish; zest: The conversation had *savor.* —*v.i.* **1** To have savor; taste or smell: with *of.* **2** To have a specified savor or character: with *of.* —*v.t.* **3** To give flavor to; season. **4** To taste or enjoy with pleasure; relish. **5** To have the savor or character of. *Brit. sp.* **sa′vour.** [< L *sapere* taste, know] —**sa′vor·er** *n.* —**sa′vor·ous** *adj.*

sa·vor·less (sā′vər·lis) *adj.* Tasteless; insipid.

sa·vor·y[1] (sā′vər·ē) *adj.* **1** Of an agreeable taste and odor; appetizing. **2** In good repute. —*n. pl.* **·vor·ies** *Brit.* A small, hot serving of tasty food, usu. eaten at the end of a dinner. *Brit. sp.* **sa′vour·y.** [< OF *savourer* to taste] —**sa′vor·i·ly** *adv.* —**sa′vor·i·ness** *n.* —**Syn.** *adj.* **1** flavorful, palatable, piquant, tasty, toothsome. **2** respectable.

sa·vor·y[2] (sā′vər·ē) *n.* A hardy, annual herb of the mint family used for seasoning. Also **summer savory.** [< OF *savoreie*]

sa·voy (sə·voi′) *n.* A variety of cabbage with wrinkled leaves and a compact head. [< F *(chou de) Savoie* (cabbage of) Savoy]

Sa·voy·ard (sə·voi′ərd, sav′oi·ärd′) *n.* An actor or actress in or an admirer or producer of the Gilbert and Sullivan operas. [< the *Savoy,* London theater]

sav·vy (sav′ē) *Slang v.i.* **·vied, ·vy·ing** To understand; comprehend. —*n.* Understanding; know-how. —*adj.* Having good sense or know-how. [Alter. of Sp. *¿ Sabe (usted)?* Do (you) know?]

saw[1] (sô) *n.* **1** A cutting tool with pointed teeth arranged continuously along the edge of a blade or disk. **2** A tool or machine having such teeth: a power *saw.* —*v.* **sawed, sawed** or **sawn, saw·ing** *v.t.* **1** To cut or divide with or as with a saw. **2** To shape or fashion with a saw. **3** To make a motion as if sawing: The speaker *saws* the air. —*v.i.* **4** To use a saw. **5** To cut: said of a saw. **6** To be cut with a saw: This wood *saws* easily. [< OE *sagu*] —**saw′er** *n.*

saw[2] (sô) *n.* A proverbial or familiar saying; old maxim. [< OE *sagu*]

saw[3] (sô) *p.t.* of SEE[1].

saw·bones (sô′bōnz′) *n. Slang* A surgeon.

saw·buck (sô′buk′) *n.* **1** A frame consisting of two X-shaped ends joined by connecting bars, for holding sticks of wood for sawing. **2** *Slang* A ten-dollar bill: from the resemblance of X, Roman numeral ten, to the ends of a sawbuck.

Sawbuck *def. 1*

saw·dust (sô′dust′) *n.* Tiny particles of wood cut or torn out by sawing.

saw·fish (sô′fish′) *n. pl.* **·fish** or **·fish·es** Any of a genus of large tropical fishes related to rays and having an elongated snout with teeth on each edge.

saw·fly (sô′flī′) *n. pl.* **·flies** A hymenopterous insect having in the female a pair of sawlike organs for piercing plants, wood, etc., in which to lay eggs.

saw·horse (sô′hôrs′) *n.* A frame consisting of a long wooden bar or plank supported by four extended legs.

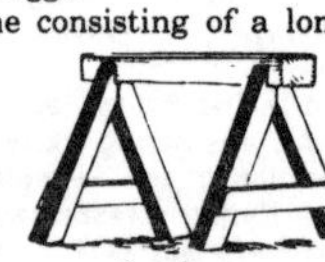

Sawhorse

saw·mill (sô′mil′) *n.* **1** An establishment for sawing logs with power-driven machinery. **2** A large sawing machine.

sawn (sôn) A *p.p.* of SAW[1].

saw-toothed (sô′tōōtht′) *adj.* Having teeth or toothlike processes similar to those of a saw; serrate. Also **saw′tooth′** (-tōōth′).

saw·yer (sô′yər) *n.* One who saws logs, esp. a lumberman who fells trees by sawing, or one who works in a sawmill.

sax (saks) *n. Informal* A saxophone.

sax·i·frage (sak′sə·frij) *n.* Any of numerous perennial plants usu. having a basal rosette of leaves and growing in rocky places. [< L *(herba) saxifraga,* lit., stone-breaking (herb)]

Sax·on (sak′sən) *n.* **1** A member of a Germanic tribal group living in NW Germany in the early centuries of the Christian era. With the Angles and Jutes, the Saxons conquered England in the fifth and sixth centuries. **2** The language of the early Saxons. **3** An inhabitant of modern Saxony in Germany. —*adj.* Of or pertaining to the early Saxons, or to their language.

sax·o·phone (sak′sə·fōn) *n.* Any of a group of reed instruments having a straight metal body equipped with finger keys and terminating in a curved, conical bore. [< A. J. *Sax,* 1814–94, Belgian instrument maker] —**sax′o·phon′ist** *n.*

Saxophone

say (sā) *v.* **said, say·ing** *v.t.* **1** To speak. **2** To express in words; tell. **3** To state positively: *Say* which you prefer. **4** To recite; repeat: to *say* one's prayers. **5** To allege: They *say* that he lied. **6** To assume: He is worth, *say,* a million. —*v.i.* **7** To make a statement; speak. —**say nothing of** Without mentioning. —**that is to say** In other words. —*n.* **1** What one has said or has to say: Let him have his *say.* **2** *Informal* Right or turn to speak or choose: Now it is my *say.* —**the say** *Informal* Authority: Who has *the say* in this office? —*interj.* A hail or exclamation to command attention: also *Brit.* **I say!** [< OE *secgan*] —**say′er** *n.* —**Syn.** *v.* **1** articulate, pronounce, utter. **2** declare, affirm. **5** assert.

say·ing (sā′ing) *n.* 1 An utterance. 2 A maxim or saw. —**go without saying** To be so evident as to require no explanation.

say-so (sā′sō′) *n. Informal* 1 An unsupported assertion or decision. 2 Right or power to make decisions: He has the *say-so.*

Sb antimony (L *stibium*).

SBA Small Business Administration.

SbE south by east.

SbW south by west.

SC Security Council (of the United Nations); South Carolina (P.O. abbr.).

S.C. Signal Corps; South Carolina; Supreme Court.

Sc scandium; stratocumulus.

sc. he (or she) carved or engraved it (L *sculpsit*); namely (L *scilicet*); scale; scene; science; screw; scruple (weight).

s.c. small capitals (printing).

scab (skab) *n.* 1 A crust on a wound or sore. 2 A contagious disease of sheep. 3 Any of certain plant diseases marked by a roughened or warty exterior. 4 A worker who will not join a labor union. 5 A worker who does the job of a person on strike. —*v.i.* **scabbed, scab·bing** 1 To form or become covered with a scab. 2 To act or work as a scab. [< Scand.] —**scab′bi·ly** *adv.* —**scab′bi·ness** *n.* —**scab′by** *adj.* (**·i·er, ·i·est**)

scab·bard (skab′ərd) *n.* A sheath for a weapon, as for a bayonet or a sword. —*v.t.* To sheathe in a scabbard. [< OHG *scar* a sword + *bergan* hide, protect]

sca·bi·es (skā′bēz) *n.* A skin disease affecting man and various animals, caused by infestation by certain mites; the itch. [< L *scabere* to scratch, scrape] —**sca·bi·et·ic** (skā′bē·et′ik), **sca′bi·ous** (-əs) *adj.*

sca·bi·o·sa (skā′bē·ō′sə) *n.* Any of various plants related to the teasel, with showy, usu. prickly flowers. Also **sca′bi·ous** (-əs). [< Med. L *(herba) scabiosa* herb for scabies]

sca·brous (skā′brəs) *adj.* 1 Roughened with minute points. 2 Difficult to handle tactfully. 3 Suggestive; salacious. [< L *scabere* to scratch] —**sca′brous·ly** *adv.* —**sca′brous·ness** *n.*

scads (skadz) *n.pl. Informal* A large amount or quantity. [?]

scaf·fold (skaf′əld, -ōld) *n.* 1 A temporary elevated structure for the support of workmen, materials, etc., as in constructing, painting, or repairing a building. 2 A platform for the execution of criminals. 3 Any raised platform. —*v.t.* To furnish or support with a scaffold. [< OF *escadafaut*]

scaf·fold·ing (skaf′əl·ding) *n.* 1 A scaffold, or system of scaffolds. 2 The materials for constructing scaffolds.

scag (skag) *n. Slang* Heroin.

sca·lar (skā′lər) *adj.* Defined by a single number, as a quantity having only magnitude. —*n.* A scalar quantity. [< L *scala* a ladder]

scal·a·wag (skal′ə·wag) *n.* 1 *Informal* A worthless person; rascal. 2 A Southern white who became a Republican during the Reconstruction period: a contemptuous term. Also **scal′la·wag, scal′ly·wag.** [?]

scald[1] (skôld) *v.t.* 1 To burn with hot liquid or steam. 2 To cleanse or treat with boiling water. 3 To heat (a liquid) to a point just short of boiling. 4 To cook in a liquid which is just short of the boiling point. —*v.i.* 5 To be or become scalded. —*n.* 1 A burn due to a hot fluid or steam. 2 Surface injury of plant tissue due to various causes, as exposure to sun, fungi, etc. [< L *ex-* very + *calidus* hot]

scald[2] (skôld, skäld) *n.* SKALD. —**scal·dic** (skôl′dik, skäl′-) *adj.*

scale[1] (skāl) *n.* 1 One of the thin, horny, usu. overlapping, protective plates covering most fishes, reptiles, etc. 2 SCALE INSECT. 3 A specialized leaf, as of a pine cone. 4 A flaky coating on metal, as from corrosion, etc. 5 Any thin, scalelike piece, as of skin. —*v.* **scaled, scal·ing** *v.t.* 1 To strip or clear of scale or scales. 2 To form scales on; cover with scales. 3 To take off in layers or scales; pare off. —*v.i.* 4 To come off in layers or scales; peel. 5 To shed scales. 6 To become incrusted with scales. [< OF *escale* a husk] —**scal′er** *n.*

scale[2] (skāl) *n.* 1 An object bearing accurately spaced

Ascending chromatic scale *def. 6*

marks for use in measurement, or the series of marks so used. 2 Any system of units of measurement. 3 A proportion used in representing distances, as on a map or blueprint. 4 *Math.* A system of numeration in which the successive places determine the value of digits, as the decimal system. 5 Any progressive or graded series; a graduation: the social *scale.* 6 *Music* A series of tones arranged in a sequence of ascending or descending pitches according to any of various systems of intervals. 7 *Phot.* The range of light values which may be reproduced by a photographic paper. 8 A succession of steps or degrees: a salary *scale.* 9 A relative degree or extent: to live on a modest *scale.* —*v.* **scaled, scal·ing** *v.t.* 1 To climb to the top of. 2 To make according to a scale. 3 To regulate or adjust according to a scale or ratio: with *up, down,* etc. —*v.i.* 4 To climb; ascend. 5 To rise, as in steps or stages: mountains *scaling* to the skies. [< L *scala* a ladder] —**scal′er** *n.*

scale[3] (skāl) *n.* 1 The bowl, scoop, or platform of a weighing instrument or balance. 2 *Usu. pl.* The balance itself. —**the Scales** LIBRA. —**turn the scales** To determine; decide. —*v.* **scaled, scal·ing** *v.t.* 1 To weigh in scales. 2 To amount to in weight. —*v.i.* 3 To be weighed. [< ON *skāl* a bowl]

scale insect Any of numerous plant-feeding insects of which the adult female is sedentary under a scalelike, waxy shield.

sca·lene (skā′lēn, skā·lēn′) *adj. Geom.* Having no two sides equal: said of a triangle. [< Gk. *skalēnos* uneven] • See TRIANGLE.

scal·lion (skal′yən) *n.* 1 A young, tender onion with a small white bulb. 2 A shallot or leek. [< L *(caepa) Ascalonia* (onion) of Ashkelon, a Palestinian seaport]

scal·lop (skal′əp, skol′-) *n.* 1 Any of various mollusks having a hinged shell with radiating ribs and wavy edge. 2 The edible abductor muscle of certain scallops. 3 A scallop shell. 4 One of a series of semicircular curves along an edge, as for ornament. —*v.t.* 1 To shape the edge of with scallops for ornamentation. 2 To bake (food) in a casserole with a sauce, usu. topped with bread crumbs. [< MF *escalope* shell] —**scal′lop·er** *n.*

Scallop shell

scalp (skalp) *n.* 1 The skin of the top and back of the skull, usu. covered with hair. 2 A portion of this, cut or torn away as a trophy among certain North American Indians. —*v.t.* 1 To cut or tear the scalp from. 2 *Informal* To buy (tickets) and sell again at prices exceeding the established rate. 3 *Informal* To buy and sell again quickly to make a small profit. —*v.i.* 4 *Informal* To scalp bonds, tickets, etc. [< Scand.] —**scalp′er** *n.*

scal·pel (skal′pəl) *n.* A small, sharp, surgical knife. [< L *scalpere* to cut]

scal·y (skā′lē) *adj.* **scal·i·er, scal·i·est** 1 Having a covering of scales or flakes. 2 Of the nature of a scale. 3 Incrusted with a flaking deposit. —**scal′i·ness** *n.*

scamp[1] (skamp) *n.* A confirmed rogue; rascal. [< obs. *scamp* to roam] —**scamp′ish** *adj.* —**scamp′ish·ness** *n.*

scamp[2] (skamp) *v.t.* To perform (work) carelessly or dishonestly. [?] —**scamp′er** *n.*

scam·per (skam′pər) *v.i.* To run quickly or hastily. —*n.* A hurried flight. [< L *ex* out + *campus* a plain, battlefield] —**scam′per·er** *n.*

scam·pi (skam′pē) *n.pl.* Large shrimp, usu. served in a garlic sauce. [Ital.]

scan (skan) *v.* **scanned, scan·ning** *v.t.* **1** To examine in detail; scrutinize closely. **2** To pass the eyes over quickly; glance at. **3** To separate (verse) into metrical feet. **4** *Electronics* To cause a beam, as of light, electrons, microwaves, etc., to pass systematically over a surface or through a region. —*v.i.* **5** To scan verse. **6** To conform to metrical rules: said of verse. [< LL *scandere* scan verses] **—scan′ner** *n.*

Scan., Scand. Scandinavia; Scandinavian.

scan·dal (skan′dəl) *n.* **1** A discreditable action or circumstance offensive to public morals or feelings. **2** Injury to reputation. **3** General criticism that injures reputation; malicious gossip. **4** A person whose conduct arouses public censure. [< Gk. *skandalon* a snare] **—Syn. 2** discredit, disgrace, disrepute. **3** calumny, defamation, slander.

scan·dal·ize (skan′dəl·īz) *v.t.* **·ized, ·iz·ing** To shock the moral feelings of; outrage. **—scan′dal·i·za′tion, scan′dal·iz′·er** *n.*

scan·dal·ous (skan′dəl·əs) *adj.* **1** Causing or being a scandal; disgraceful. **2** Consisting of evil or malicious reports. **—scan′dal·ous·ly** *adv.* **—scan′dal·ous·ness** *n.*

Scan·di·na·vi·a (skan′də·nā′vē·ə) *n.* The region of NW Europe occupied by Sweden, Norway, and Denmark; 315,156 sq. mi; Finland, Iceland, and the Faroe Islands are often included: total area, 485,539 sq. mi. **—Scan′di·na′vi·an** *adj., n.*

scan·di·um (skan′dē·əm) *n.* A rare metallic element of low density. [< L *Scandia* Scandinavia]

scan·sion (skan′shən) *n.* The act or art of scanning verse to show its metrical parts.

scant (skant) *adj.* **1** Meager in measure or quantity. **2** Being just short of the measure specified: a *scant* half-hour; a *scant* five yards. **—scant of** Insufficiently supplied with: to be *scant of* breath from running. —*v.t.* **1** To restrict or limit in supply; stint. **2** To treat briefly or inadequately. —*adv. Regional* Scarcely; barely. [< ON *skammr* short] **—scant′ly** *adv.* **—scant′ness** *n.*

scant·ling (skant′ling) *n.* **1** A small beam or timber, esp. an upright timber in a structure. **2** Such timbers collectively. [< OF *eschantillon* specimen]

scant·y (skan′tē) *adj.* **scant·i·er, scant·i·est 1** Too little; not enough: a *scanty* meal. **2** Scarcely enough for what is needed; insufficient. [< SCANT] **—scant′i·ly** *adv.* **—scant′i·ness** *n.* **—Syn. 1** deficient, poor, sparse. **2** limited, restricted.

scape·goat (skāp′gōt′) *n.* **1** In the Bible, the goat upon whose head Aaron symbolically laid the sins of the people on the day of atonement, after which it was led away into the wilderness. *Lev.* 16. **2** Any person bearing blame for the misdeeds of others. —*v.t. Informal* To make a scapegoat of. [< ESCAPE + GOAT]

scape·grace (skāp′grās′) *n.* A mischievous or incorrigible person.

s. caps. small capitals (printing).

scap·u·la (skap′yə·lə) *n. pl.* **·las** or **·lae** (-lē) Either of the two large, flat bones of the upper back; shoulder blade. [< L *scapulae* shoulder blades]

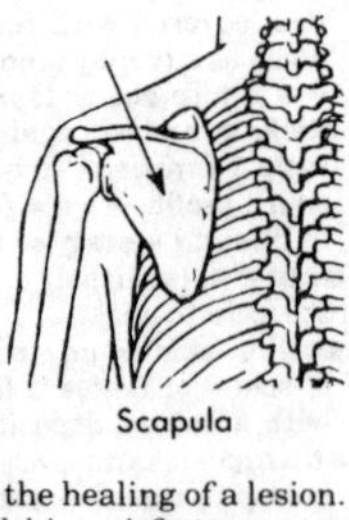

Scapula

scap·u·lar (skap′yə·lər) *n.* **1** A garment of certain religious orders consisting of two strips of cloth hanging down front and back. **2** Two small rectangular pieces of cloth connected by strings, worn as a badge of membership by certain religious orders. Also **scap′u·lar′y** (-ler′ē). [< L *scapula* shoulder]

scar (skär) *n.* **1** The mark left after the healing of a lesion. **2** Any lingering sign, as from hardship, misfortune, etc.: the *scars* of poverty. —*v.t. & v.i.* **scarred, scar·ring** To mark or become marked with a scar. [< LL *eschara* a scab]

scar·ab (skar′əb) *n.* **1** Any of various beetles, esp. a large, black beetle held sacred by the ancient Egyptians. **2** A gemstone or other ornament in the form of this beetle. Also **scar·a·bee** (skar′ə·bē). [< L *scarabaeus*] **—scar′a·boid** (-boid) *adj.*

scar·a·bae·us (skar′ə·bē′əs) *n. pl.* **·bae·us·es** or **·bae·i** (-bē′ī) SCARAB. Also **scar′a·be′us —scar·a·bae′id** *adj., n.*

scar·a·mouch (skar′ə·mouch, -mōōsh) *n.* **1** A boastful, cowardly person. **2** *Usu. cap.* A similar character in old Italian comedy. Also **scar′a·mouche.** [< Ital. *Scaramuccia*, lit., a skirmish]

scarce (skârs) *adj.* **scarc·er, scarc·est 1** Rare and unusual: *scarce* antiques. **2** Scant; insufficient. **—make oneself scarce** *Informal* To go or stay away. [< OF *eschars* scanty, insufficient] **—scarce′ness** *n.*

scarce·ly (skârs′lē) *adv.* **1** Only just; barely: so weary he could *scarcely* walk. **2** Rarely: He *scarcely* goes out now. **3** Certainly not; probably not: That's *scarcely* possible.

scar·ci·ty (skâr′sə·tē) *n. pl.* **·ties 1** Scantiness; insufficiency: a *scarcity* of truffles. **2** Rarity: the *scarcity* of genius.

scare (skâr) *v.* **scared, scar·ing** *v.t.* **1** To strike with sudden fear; frighten. **2** To drive or force by frightening: with *off* or *away.* —*v.i.* **3** To take fright; become scared. **—scare up** *Informal* To get together hurriedly; produce: *to scare up* a meal from leftovers. —*n.* A sudden fright; alarm. —*adj. Informal* Intended to provoke alarm or concern: *scare* tactics. [< ON *skiarr* shy] **—scar′er** *n.* **—scar′ing·ly** *adv.* **—Syn.** *v.* **1** alarm, startle, terrify. *n.* fright, panic.

scare·crow (skâr′krō′) *n.* **1** Any effigy set up to scare crows and other birds from growing crops. **2** A cause of false alarm. **3** A person who is ragged and tattered or thin and gangling.

scare·head (skâr′hed′) *n. Informal* A newspaper headline in large type for sensational news.

scarf[1] (skärf) *n. pl.* **scarfs 1** In carpentry, a lapped joint made as by notching two timbers at the ends, and bolting them together to form a single piece: also **scarf joint. 2** The notched end of either of the timbers so cut. —*v.t.* **1** To unite with a scarf joint. **2** To cut a scarf in. [ME]

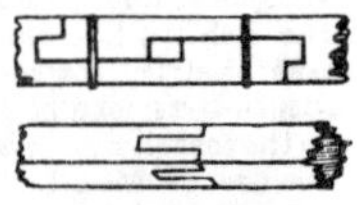

Scarf joints

scarf[2] (skärf) *n. pl.* **scarfs** or **scarves** (skärvz) **1** A long and wide band, worn about the head, neck, shoulders, or waist. **2** A necktie or cravat with dangling ends. **3** A runner for a bureau or table. —*v.t.* To cover or decorate with a scarf. [< OF *escharpe*]

scar·i·fy (skar′ə·fī) *v.t.* **·fied, ·fy·ing 1** To make shallow scratches in, as the skin. **2** To criticize severely. **3** To stir the surface of, as soil. [< Gk. *skariphasthai* scratch an outline] **—scar′i·fi′er, scar′i·fi·ca′tion** *n.*

scar·la·ti·na (skär′lə·tē′nə) *n.* A mild form of scarlet fever.

scar·let (skär′lit) *n.* **1** A brilliant red, inclining to orange. **2** Cloth or clothing of a scarlet color. —*adj.* Brilliant red. [< Pers. *saqalāt* a rich, scarlet cloth]

scarlet fever An acute streptococcal infection marked by fever, sore throat, and a red rash.

scarlet letter A scarlet "A" which adulterous women were once condemned to wear.

scarlet runner A climbing bean with vivid red flowers and long seed pods. Also **scarlet runner bean.**

scarp (skärp) *n.* **1** Any steep slope. **2** A steep artificial slope, esp. the inner slope, about a fortification. —*v.t.* To cut to a steep slope. [< Ital. *scarpa*]

scarves (skärvz) A *pl.* of SCARF[2].

scar·y (skâr′ē) *adj.* **scar·i·er, scar·i·est** *Informal* **1** Easily scared. **2** Giving cause for alarm. **—scar′i·ness** *n.*

scat[1] (skat) *v.i.* **scat·ted, scat·ting** *Informal* To go away quickly: usu. in the imperative. [?]

scat[2] (skat) *n.* Jazz singing that employs improvised nonsense syllables. —*v.i.* **scat·ted, scat·ting** To sing scat. [?]

scathe (skāth) *v.t.* **scathed, scath·ing 1** To criticize severely. **2** *Archaic* To injure severely. [< ON *skatha*]

scathe·less (skāth′lis) *adj.* Without harm or injury.

scath·ing (skā′thing) *adj.* Blasting; withering: a *scathing* rebuke. **—scath′ing·ly** *adv.*

sca·tol·o·gy (ska·tol′ə·jē, skə-) *n.* **1** The scientific study of excrement. **2** Preoccupation with obscenity or with excrement, as in literature. [< Gk. *skōr, skatos* dung + -LOGY] **—scat·o·log·i·cal** (skat′ə·loj′i·kəl) *adj.* **—sca·tol′o·gist** *n.*

scat·ter (skat′ər) *v.t.* **1** To throw about in various places; strew. **2** To disperse; rout. **3** *Physics* To reflect (radiation) in more than one direction. —*v.i.* **4** To separate and go in different directions. —*n.* The act of scattering or the condition of being scattered. [ME *scateren*] **—scat′ter·er** *n.* — **Syn.** *v.* **1** disseminate, sow, spread, sprinkle. **2** drive away.

scat·ter·brain (skat′ər·brān′) *n.* A heedless, flighty person. **—scat′ter-brained′** *adj.*

scat·ter·site (skat′ər·sīt) *adj.* Of or describing housing sponsored by government, esp. for low-income groups, located in various communities to avoid ghettoization.

scaup (skôp) *n.* A North American wild duck related to the canvasback, having the head and neck black in the male: also **scaup duck.** [Obs. var. of SCALP + DUCK]

scav·enge (skav′inj) *v.* **·enged, ·eng·ing** *v.t.* **1** To remove filth, rubbish, and refuse from, as streets. —*v.i.* **2** To act as a scavenger. **3** To search for food. [Back formation < SCAVENGER]

scav·en·ger (skav′in·jər) *n.* **1** Any organism that feeds on refuse, carrion, etc. **2** A person who removes refuse or unwanted things, as a garbage collector or a junkman. [< AF *scawage* inspection]

sce·nar·i·o (si·nâr′ē·ō, -nä′rē·ō) *n. pl.* **·nar·i·os** **1** The plot or outline of a dramatic work. **2** The written plot and arrangement of incidents of a motion picture. **3** An outline or plan of a projected series of actions or events. [< LL *scenarius* of stage scenes] **—sce·nar′ist** *n.*

scene (sēn) *n.* **1** A locality and all connected with it, as presented to view; a landscape. **2** The setting for a dramatic action. **3** The place and surroundings of any event, as in literature or art. **4** A division of an act of a play. **5** A specific incident or episode in a play, novel, motion picture, etc.: the ghost *scene* in *Hamlet.* **6** The painted canvas, hangings, etc., for the background for a play. **7** An unseemly display of anger or excited feeling, esp. in public. **8** *Slang* A place or realm of a currently popular activity: the country music *scene.* **—behind the scenes** **1** Out of sight of a theater audience; backstage. **2** Privately; in secret. [< Gk. *skēnē* a tent, a stage]

scen·er·y (sē′nər·ē) *n. pl.* **·er·ies** **1** The features of a landscape; view. **2** The painted backdrops, etc., used in the theater to represent a setting in a play.

sce·nic (sē′nik, sen′ik) *adj.* **1** Of or relating to beautiful natural scenery: a *scenic* spot. **2** In art, representing a situation, action, etc. **3** Relating to stage scenery. **—sce′·ni·cal·ly** *adv.*

scent (sent) *n.* **1** An odor. **2** The effluvium by which an animal can be tracked. **3** A clue aiding investigation. **4** A fragrant, fluid essence; perfume. **5** The sense of smell. —*v.t.* **1** To perceive by the sense of smell. **2** To form a suspicion of. **3** To cause to be fragrant; perfume. —*v.i.* **4** To hunt by the sense of smell. [< L *sentire* to sense]

scep·ter (sep′tər) *n.* **1** A staff or wand carried as the badge of command or sovereignty. **2** Kingly office or power. —*v.t.* To confer the scepter on; invest with royal power. Also, *esp. Brit.,* **scep′tre** (-tər). [< Gk. *skēptron* a staff]

Head of scepter

scep·tic (skep′tik) *n.* SKEPTIC.

sched·ule (skej′ōōl, *Brit.* shed′yōōl) *n.* **1** A list specifying the details of some matter. **2** A timetable. **3** A detailed and timed plan for the steps in a procedure. —*v.t.* **·uled, ·ul·ing** **1** To place in or on a schedule. **2** To appoint or plan for a specified time or date: He *scheduled* his appearance for five o'clock. [< LL *scedula*]

sche·ma (skē′mə) *n. pl.* **sche·ma·ta** (skē′·mə·tə) A synopsis, summary, diagram, etc. [< Gk. *schēma*]

sche·mat·ic (skē·mat′ik) *adj.* Of or relating to a scheme, diagram, or plan. —*n.* A schematic diagram or drawing.

scheme (skēm) *n.* **1** A plan of something to be done; program. **2** An underhand plot: a *scheme* to defraud consumers. **3** A systematic arrangement: a color *scheme.* **4** An outline drawing; diagram. —*v.* **schemed, schem·ing** *v.t.* **1** To make a scheme for; plan. **2** To plan or plot in an underhand manner. —*v.i.* **3** To make schemes; plan. **4** To plot underhandedly. [< Gk. *schēma* a form, plan] **—schem′er** *n.*

scher·zo (sker′tsō) *n. pl.* **·zos** or **·zi** (-tsē) *Music* A playful or light movement, as in a symphony. [Ital., a jest]

Schick test (shik) A test that indicates susceptibility to diphtheria if reddening of the skin occurs at the site of an injection of toxin. [< B. *Schick,* 1877–1967, Austrian physician]

schil·ling (shil′ing) *n.* The basic monetary unit of Austria.

schism (siz′əm, skiz′əm) *n.* **1** A division of a church into factions because of differences in doctrine. **2** A splitting into antagonistic groups. [< Gk. *schizein* to split]

schis·mat·ic (siz·mat′ik, skiz′-) *adj.* **1** Of or being a schism. **2** Promoting or guilty of schism. Also **schis·mat′·i·cal.** —*n.* One who makes or participates in a schism. — **schis·mat′i·cal·ly** *adv.* **—schis·mat′i·cal·ness** *n.*

schist (shist) *n.* Any crystalline rock that readily splits or cleaves. [< Gk. *schizein* to split] **—schist′ous, schist·ose** (shis′tōs) *adj.*

schizo- *combining form* Split; divided: *schizophrenia.* [< Gk. *schizein* to split]

schiz·oid (skit′soid) *adj.* Pertaining to or resembling schizophrenia. —*n.* One having schizoid characteristics.

schiz·o·phre·ni·a (skit′sō·frē′nē·ə) *n.* Mental illness characterized in varying degrees by irrational thinking, disturbed emotions, bizarre behavior, etc. [< SCHIZO- + Gk. *phrēn* mind] **—schiz′o·phren′ic** (-fren′ik) *adj., n.*

schle·miel (shlə·mēl′) *n. Slang* An inept, easily duped person. Also **schle·mihl′.** [Yiddish, an unlucky person]

schlep (shlep) *Slang v.* **schlepped, schlep·ping** *v.t.* **1** To drag awkwardly; lug. —*v.i.* **2** To drag something awkwardly. **3** To proceed wearily or heavily: to *schlep* uptown. —*n.* **1** A difficult journey. **2** A stupid, awkward person. Also **schlepp.** [Yiddish *shleppen* to drag] **—schlep′per** *n.*

schlock (shlok) *Slang n.* Shoddy, inferior merchandise. —*adj.* Of inferior quality; tawdry. [Yiddish] **—schlock′y** *adj.* **(·i·er, ·i·est)**

schmaltz (shmälts) *n. Slang* **1** Anything which is overly sentimental, as in music or literature. **2** Extreme sentimentalism. [< G *Schmalz,* lit., melted fat] **—schmaltz′y** *adj.* **(·i·er, ·i·est)**

schnapps (shnäps, shnaps) *n.* **1** A strong gin. **2** Any strong alcoholic liquor. Also **schnaps.** [G, a dram, a nip]

schnau·zer (shnou′zər) *n.* A breed of terrier having a wiry coat. [< G *Schnauze* snout]

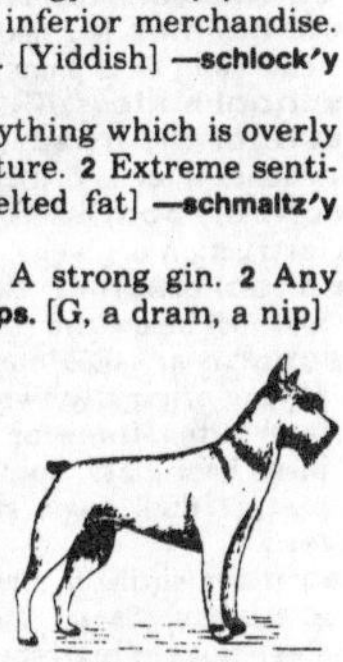

Schnauzer

schnor·kel (shnôr′kəl) *n.* SNORKEL.

schnoz·zle (shnoz′əl) *n. Slang* Nose. [< G *Schnauze*]

schol·ar (skol′ər) *n.* **1** A person eminent for learning. **2** An authority or specialist in an academic disicipline. **3** The holder of a scholarship. **4** One who learns under a teacher; a pupil. [< L *schola* school]

schol·ar·ly (skol′ər·lē) *adj.* **1** Of or characteristic of a scholar: a *scholarly* mind. **2** Exhibiting great learning. **3** Devoted to learning. —*adv.* After the manner of a scholar. **—schol′ar·li·ness** *n.* **—Syn.** *adj.* **2** erudite, intellectual, learned, lettered. **3** bookish, studious.

schol·ar·ship (skol′ər·ship) *n.* **1** Learning; erudition. **2** A stipend or other aid given to a student to enable him to continue his studies.

scho·las·tic (skō·las′tik, skə-) *adj.* **1** Pertaining to or characteristic of scholars, education, or schools. **2** Pertaining to or characteristic of the medieval schoolmen. Also **scho·las′ti·cal.** —*n. Often cap.* **1** A schoolman of the Middle ages. **2** An advocate of scholasticism. [< Gk. *scholazein* devote leisure to study] **—scho·las′ti·cal·ly** *adv.*

scho·las·ti·cism (skō·las′tə·siz′əm, skə-) *n.* **1** *Often cap.* The systematized logic, philosophy, and theology of medieval scholars. **2** Any system of teaching which insists on traditional doctrines and forms.

school[1] (skōōl) *n.* **1** An educational institution. **2** The building or group of buildings in which formal instruction is given. **3** A period or session of an educational institution: *School* begins tomorrow. 4 The pupils and teachers in an educational institution. 5 A subdivision of a university devoted to a special branch of higher education: a medical *school.* 6 The training of any branch of the armed services: gunnery *school.* 7 A body of disciples of a teacher or a group of persons whose work shows a common style or influence: a painting of the Flemish *school.* 8 Any sphere or means of instruction: the *school* of hard knocks. 9 A group of people having similar opinions, patterns of behavior, interests, etc.: He belongs to the old *school.* —*v.t.* 1 To instruct in a school; train. 2 To subject to rule or discipline. [< Gk. *scholē* leisure, school]

school² (sko͞ol) *n.* A congregation of fish, whales, etc., that feed or swim together. —*v.i.* To come together in a school. [< MDu. *schōle*]

school board A legal board or committee in charge of public schools

school·book (sko͞ol′bo͝ok′) *n.* A book for use in school; textbook.

school·boy (sko͞ol′boi′) *n.* A boy attending school. —*adj.* Like or characteristic of a schoolboy.

school·fel·low (sko͞ol′fel′ō) *n.* A fellow pupil.

school·girl (sko͞ol′gûrl′) *n.* A girl attending school. —*adj.* Like or characteristic of a schoolgirl.

school·house (sko͞ol′hous′) *n.* A building in which a school is conducted.

school·ing (sko͞o′ling) *n.* 1 Instruction given at school. 2 The cost of educating and maintaining a student at a school. 3 The training of horses and riders.

school·man (sko͞ol′mən) *n. pl.* **·men** (-mən) One of the theologians of the Middle Ages.

school·marm (sko͞ol′märm′) *n. Informal* A woman schoolteacher, esp. one considered to be prudish.

school·mas·ter (sko͞ol′mas′tər, -mäs′-) *n.* A man who teaches in or is principal of a school.

school·mate (sko͞ol′māt′) *n.* A fellow pupil.

school·mis·tress (sko͞ol′mis′tris) *n.* A woman who teaches in or is principal of a school.

school·room (sko͞ol′ro͞om′, -ro͝om′) *n.* A room in which instruction is given.

school·teach·er (sko͞ol′tē′chər) *n.* One who teaches in a school below the college level.

schoon·er (sko͞o′nər) *n.* 1 A fore-and-aft rigged vessel having originally two masts, but later often three or more. 2 A large beer glass, holding about a pint. [< dial. *scoon* skim on water.]

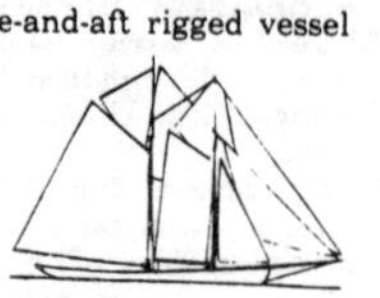
Schooner

schtick (shtik) *n.* SHTICK.

schuss (sho͝os) *v.i.* To ski down a steep slope at high speed. —*n.* 1 A straight, steep ski course. 2 The act of skiing down such a course. [G, lit., a shot] —**schuss′er** *n.*

schwa (shwä, shvä) *n.* 1 A weak or obscure central vowel sound occurring in most of the unstressed syllables in English speech, as that of the *a* in *alone* or the *u* in *circus.* 2 The symbol (ə) for this sound. [< Heb. *shewa*]

sci. science; scientific.

sci·at·ic (sī·at′ik) *adj.* Pertaining to, in the area of, or affecting the hip. —*n.* A large leg nerve originating at the hip: also **sciatic nerve.** [< Gk. *ischion* hip, hip joint]

sci·at·i·ca (sī·at′i·kə) *n.* 1 Severe pain affecting the sciatic nerve. 2 Any painful affection of the hip and leg.

sci·ence (sī′əns) *n.* 1 Knowledge as of facts, phenomena, laws, and proximate causes, gained and verified by exact observation, organized experiment, and analysis. 2 Any of the various branches of such knowledge, as biology, chemistry, physics **(natural sciences)**; economics, history, sociology **(social sciences)**; agriculture, engineering **(applied sciences).** 3 Any department of knowledge in which the results of investigation have been systematized in the form of hypotheses and general laws subject to verification. 4 Expertness; skill: the *science* of statesmanship. 5 Originally, knowledge. [< L *scire* know]

Sci·ence (sī′əns) *n.* CHRISTIAN SCIENCE.

science fiction Novels and short stories dealing with actual or imaginary scientific developments and their effect on society or individuals. —**sci′ence-fic′tion** *adj.*

sci·en·tif·ic (sī′ən·tif′ik) *adj.* 1 Of, pertaining to, discovered by, derived from, or used in science. 2 Agreeing with the rules, principles, or methods of science; systematic. 3 Versed in science or a science. —**sci′en·tif′i·cal·ly** *adv.*

sci·en·tist (sī′ən·tist) *n.* One trained or learned in science or devoted to scientific study or investigation.

Sci·en·tist (sī′ən·tist) *n.* A Christian Scientist.

sci·en·tol·o·gy (sī′ən·tol′ə·jē) *n. Often cap.* A religious and psychotherapeutic cult purporting to solve personal problems, cure mental and physical disorders, and increase intelligence. [< L *scientia* science + -LOGY] —**sci′en·tol′o·gist** *n.*

sci-fi (sī′fī′) *Informal n.* Science fiction. —*adj.* Science-fiction.

scil·i·cet (sil′ə·set) *adv.* Namely; that is to say. [< L *scire licet* it is permitted to know]

scim·i·tar (sim′ə·tər) *n.* A curved sword or saber used by Turks. Also **scim′i·ter.** [MF < Pers. *shamshīr*]

Scimitar

scin·til·la (sin·til′ə) *n.* 1 A spark. 2 A trace; iota: a *scintilla* of truth. [L]

scin·til·late (sin′tə·lāt) *v.* **·lat·ed, ·lat·ing** *v.i.* 1 To give off sparks. 2 To be witty and brilliant in conversation. 3 To twinkle, as a star. —*v.t.* 4 To give off as a spark or sparks. [< L *scintilla* a spark] —**scin′til·la′ting·ly** *adv.* —**scin′til·la′tion** *n.* —**Syn. 1, 2** glitter, glow, shine, sparkle.

sci·o·lism (sī′ə·liz′əm) *n.* Pretentious, superficial knowledge. [< LL *sciolus* a smatterer] —**sci′o·list** *n.* —**sci′o·lis′tic** *adj.*

sci·on (sī′ən) *n.* 1 A child or descendant. 2 A bud or shoot from a plant or tree, used in grafting. [< OF *cion*]

scis·sion (sizh′ən, sish′-) *n.* 1 The act of cutting or splitting, or the state of being cut. 2 Any division. [< L *scissus,* p.p. of *scindere* to cut]

scis·sor (siz′ər) *v.t. & v.i.* To cut with scissors.

scis·sors (siz′ərz) *n.pl.* 1 A cutting implement with handles and a pair of blades pivoted face to face: sometimes a **pair of scissors.** 2 *(construed as sing.)* In wrestling, a hold secured by clasping the legs about the body or head of the opponent. [< LL *cisorium* a cutting instrument]

scissors kick In swimming, a kick in which both legs, bent at the knee, are thrust apart, then straightened and brought sharply together.

scis·sor·tail (siz′ər·tāl′) *n.* A flycatcher of the sw U.S. and Mexico having a forked tail.

scle·ra (skler′ə, sklir′ə) *n.* The firm, fibrous, white outer coat of the eyeball, continuous with the cornea: also **scle·rot·i·ca** (sklə·rot′i·kə). [< Gk. *sklēros* hard]

scle·ren·chy·ma (sklə·reng′kə·mə) *n. Bot.* Tissue composed of cells with hard, thick walls. [< Gk. *sklēros* hard + *enchyma* an infusion] —**scle·ren·chym·a·tous** (skler′en·kim′ə·təs, sklir′-, -kī′mə-) *adj.*

scle·ro·sis (sklə·rō′sis) *n.* Abnormal thickening and hardening of tissue. [< Gk. *sklēros* hard] —**scle·ro′sal** *adj.*

scle·rot·ic (sklə·rot′ik) *adj.* 1 Dense; firm, as the white of the eye. 2 Pertaining to or affected with sclerosis: also **scle·rosed** (-rōst′) [< Gk. *sklērotēs* hardness]

scoff (skôf, skof) *v.i.* 1 To speak with contempt or derision: often with *at.* —*v.t.* 2 To deride; mock. —*n.* 1 Words or actions of contempt. 2 A person or thing held in contempt. [ME *scof*] —**scoff′er** *n.* —**scoff′ing·ly** *adv.* —**Syn.** *v.* **1, 2** gibe, jeer, scorn, sneer, taunt.

scoff·law (skôf′lô, skof′-) *n.* A habitual or deliberate violator of traffic, safety, or public-health regulations.

scold (skōld) *v.t.* 1 To find fault with harshly. —*v.i.* 2 To find fault harshly or continuously. —*n.* One who scolds constantly: also **scold′er.** [< ON *skāld* a poet, satirist] —**scold′ing·ly** *adv.*

scol·lop (skol′əp) *n. & v.* SCALLOP.

sconce (skons) *n.* An ornamental wall bracket for holding a candle or other light. [< L *abscondere* to hide]

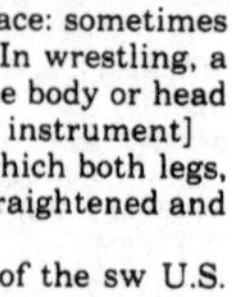
Wall sconce

scone (skōn, skon) *n.* 1 A thin oatmeal cake, baked on a griddle. 2 A teacake or soda biscuit. [?< MDu. *schoonbrot* fine bread]

scoop (sko͞op) *n.* 1 The part of a dredge or steam shovel that lifts earth, sand, coal, etc. 2 A small shovellike implement for flour, sugar, ice cream, etc. 3 An implement for bailing, as water from a boat. 4 A spoon-shaped instrument for using in a cavity: a surgeon's *scoop.* 5 An act of scooping. 6 A scooping motion. 7 The amount scooped at once: a *scoop* of ice cream. 8 *Informal* A news story obtained and published ahead of rival papers. —*v.t.* 1 To take or dip out with a scoop. 2 To hollow out, as with a scoop; excavate. 3 *Informal* To heap up or gather in as if in scoopfuls; amass. 4 *Informal* To obtain and publish a news story before (a rival). [< MDu. *schōpe* a vessel for bailing out water] —**scoop′er** *n.*

scoop·ful (sko͞op′fo͝ol′) *n. pl.* **·fuls** As much as a scoop will hold.

scoot (sko͞ot) *v.i. Informal* To go quickly; dart off. —*n.* The act of scooting. [? < Scand.]

scoot·er (sko͞o′tər) *n.* 1 A child's vehicle consisting of a board mounted on two wheels and steered by a handle attached to the front axle, the rider standing with one foot on the board, using the other to push. 2 A similar vehicle powered by an internal-combustion engine and having a driver's seat: also **motor scooter.**

scope (skōp) *n.* 1 A range of view or action. 2 Capacity for achievement. 3 End in view; aim. 4 *Informal* A telescope, microscope, oscilloscope, etc. [< Gk. *skopos* a watcher]

-scope *combining form* An instrument for viewing, observing, or indicating: *microscope.* [< Gk. *skopos* a watcher]

sco·pol·a·mine (skō·pol′ə·mēn, -min, skō′pə·lam′ēn, -in) *n.* A depressant drug related to belladonna which blocks the formation of memories and various other functions of the brain. [< G. A. *Scopoli,* 1723–88, Italian naturalist]

-scopy *combining form* Observation; viewing: *microscopy.* [< Gk. *skopeein* to watch]

scor·bu·tic (skôr·byo͞o′tik) *adj.* Of, like, or affected with scurvy. Also **scor·bu′ti·cal.** [< Med. L *scorbutus* scurvy] —**scor·bu′ti·cal·ly** *adv.*

scorch (skôrch) *v.t.* 1 To change the color, taste, etc., of, by slight burning. 2 To wither or shrivel by heat. 3 To criticize severely. —*v.i.* 4 To become scorched. 5 *Informal* To go at high speed. —*n.* 1 A superficial burn. 2 A mark caused by a slight burn. [ME *scorchen*] —**scorch′ing·ly** *adv.*

scorched-earth policy (skôrcht′ûrth′) The policy of destroying all crops, industrial equipment, dwellings, etc., before the arrival of an advancing enemy.

scorch·er (skôr′chər) *n.* 1 A person or thing that scorches. 2 *Informal* A very hot day. 3 *Informal* One who moves at great speed.

score (skôr, skōr) *n.* 1 The record of the winning points, counts, runs, etc., in competitive games. 2 A record of indebtedness; bill. 3 *Music* A printed or written copy of a musical composition in which all vocal and instrumental parts are shown on two or more connected staves one above another. 4 A group of 20. 5 *pl.* An indefinite large number. 6 A value assigned to an individual or group response to a test or series of tests, as of intelligence or performance. 7 *Slang* A success, esp. in making a purchase of narcotics. —**to pay off** (or **settle**) **old scores** To get even with someone for past wrongs, injuries, etc. —*v.* **scored, scor·ing** *v.t.* 1 To mark with notches, cuts, or lines. 2 To mark with cuts or lines for the purpose of keeping a tally. 3 To delete by means of a line drawn through: with *out.* 4 To make or gain, as points, runs, etc. 5 To count for a score of, as in games: A touchdown *scores* six points. 6 To rate or grade, as an examination paper. 7 *Music* a To orchestrate. b To arrange or adapt for an instrument. 8 *Informal* To criticize severely; scourge. 9 In cooking, to make superficial cuts in (meat, etc.). —*v.i.* 10 To make points, runs, etc., as in a game. 11 To keep score. 12 To make notches, cuts, etc. 13 To achieve a success. 14 *Slang* To purchase marihuana or narcotics. 15 *Slang* To succeed in having sexual intercourse with someone. [< ON *skor* a notch] —**scor′er** *n.*

sco·ri·a (skôr′ē·ə, skō′rē·ə) *n. pl.* **·ri·ae** (-i·ē) 1 The refuse of melted metal or reduced ore. 2 Lava that is loose and cinderlike. [< Gk. *skōr* dung] —**sco′ri·a′ceous** (-ā′shəs) *adj.*

scorn (skôrn) *n.* 1 A feeling of contempt. 2 An object of supreme contempt. —*v.t.* 1 To hold in or treat with contempt; despise. 2 To reject with scorn; spurn. [< OF *escarn*] —**scorn′er, scorn′ful·ness** *n.* —**scorn′ful** *adj.* —**scorn′ful·ly** *adv.* —**Syn.** *n.* 1 disdain, scoffing. *v.* 1 contemn, detest.

Scor·pi·o (skôr′pē·ō) *n.* A constellation and the eighth sign of the zodiac; the Scorpion. Also **Scor·pi·us** (-əs). [< Gk. *skorpios*] • See ZODIAC.

scor·pi·on (skôr′pē·ən) *n.* 1 Any of an order of arachnids with long segmented tails bearing a poisonous sting. 2 In the Bible, a whip or scourge. [< Gk. *skorpios*]

Indian scorpion

Scorpion *n.* SCORPIO.

scot (skot) *n.* An assessment or tax. [< ON *skot*]

Scot (skot) *n.* A native of Scotland. • See SCOTCH.

Scot. Scotland; Scots; Scottish.

scotch (skoch) *v.t.* 1 To cut; scratch. 2 To wound so as to maim or cripple. 3 To quash or suppress: to *scotch* a rumor. —*n.* 1 A superficial cut; a notch. 2 A line traced on the ground, as for hopscotch. [?]

Scotch (skoch) *n.* 1 The people of Scotland collectively. 2 One or all of the dialects spoken by the people of Scotland. 3 Scotch whisky. —*adj.* Of or pertaining to Scotland, its inhabitants, or their dialects. • **Scotch, Scots, Scottish; Scot, Scotchman, Scotsman** Of the three proper adjectives, the form *Scotch* is accepted in Scotland only as applying to *Scotch plaid, Scotch terriers, Scotch whisky,* etc. In Scotland and northern England, the forms *Scots* and *Scottish* are preferred as applying to the people, language, culture, and institutions of Scotland: *Scots* or *Scottish English, the Scottish church.* In referring to an inhabitant of Scotland, *Scot* and *Scotsman* are preferred over the chiefly U.S. term *Scotchman.*

Scotch·man (skoch′mən) *n. pl.* **·men** (-mən) A Scot; Scotsman. • See SCOTCH.

Scotch tape A rolled strip of transparent adhesive tape: a trade name.

Scotch terrier A small terrier with compact body, short legs, and a grizzled coat.

Scotch terrier

Scotch whisky Whiskey made in Scotland from malted barley and having a rather smoky flavor. • Scotch whisky is traditionally spelled without the "e."

sco·ter (skō′tər) *n.* Any of several large ducks of northern regions, having black or dark brown plumage. [?< dial. E *scote,* var. of SCOOT]

scot-free (skot′frē′) *adj.* 1 Free from any penalty, blame, or punishment. 2 Free from scot.

Scotland Yard 1 The headquarters of the London police: in full, **New Scotland Yard.** 2 The London police force, esp. the detective bureau.

Scots (skots) *adj.* SCOTTISH. —*n.* The Scottish dialect of English. • See SCOTCH.

Scots·man (skots′mən) *n. pl.* **·men** (-mən) A Scot. • See SCOTCH.

Scot·ti·cism (skot′ə·siz′əm) *n.* A verbal usage or idiom peculiar to the Scottish people.

Scot·tish (skot′ish) *adj.* Pertaining to or characteristic of Scotland, its inhabitants, or their language. —*n.* 1 The dialect of English spoken in Scotland. 2 The people of Scotland collectively: with *the.* • See SCOTCH.

Scottish Gaelic The language of the Scottish Highlands.

Scottish terrier SCOTCH TERRIER. Also *Informal* **scot·tie** (skot′ē), **scot′ty.**

scoun·drel (skoun′drəl) *n.* An unscrupulous, dishonest person; villain. —*adj.* Villainous; base. [?] —**scoun′drel·ly** *adj.*

scour[1] (skour) *v.t.* 1 To clean or brighten by thorough washing and rubbing. **2** To remove dirt, grease, etc., from; clean. **3** To clear by means of a strong current of water; flush. —*v.i.* **4** To rub something vigorously so as to clean or brighten it. **5** To become bright or clean by rubbing. —*n.* **1** The act of scouring. **2** A cleanser used in scouring. **3** *Usu. pl.* A dysentery affecting cattle. [<OF *escurer*] —**scour'er** *n.* —**Syn.** *v.* **1** polish, scrub. **2** cleanse.

scour[2] (skour) *v.t.* **1** To range over or through, as in making a search. **2** To move or run swiftly over or along. —*v.i.* **3** To range swiftly about, as in making a search. [ME *scoure*]

scourge (skûrj) *n.* **1** A whip for inflicting suffering or punishment. **2** Any severe punishment. **3** Any means for causing suffering or death: the *scourge* of cholera. —*v.t.* **scourged, scourg·ing 1** To whip severely; flog. **2** To punish severely; afflict. [<LL *excoriare* flay] —**scourg'er** *n.*

scout[1] (skout) *n.* **1** A person, plane, etc., sent out to observe and get information, as of the position or strength of an enemy in war. **2** The act of scouting. **3** A person in search of promising performers in athletics, entertainment, etc.: a talent *scout.* **4** A member of the Girl Scouts or the Boy Scouts. **5** A fellow; guy: usu. in the phrase **a good scout.** —*v.t.* **1** To observe or spy upon for the purpose of gaining information. —*v.i.* **2** To go or act as a scout. —**scout around** To go in search. [<L *auscultare* to listen] —**scout'er** *n.*

scout[2] (skout) *v.t.* & *v.i.* To reject with disdain. [<Scand.]

scout·mas·ter (skout'mas'tər, -mäs'-) *n.* The adult leader of a troop of Boy Scouts.

scow (skou) *n.* A large boat with a flat bottom and square ends, chiefly used to carry freight, garbage, etc. [<Du. *schouw*]

scowl (skoul) *n.* **1** A lowering of the brows, as in anger. **2** Gloomy aspect. —*v.i.* **1** To contract the brows in anger, sullenness, or disapproval. **2** To look threatening; lower. —*v.t.* **3** To affect or express by scowling. [?<Scand.]

scr. scrip; script; scruple (weight).

scrab·ble (skrab'əl) *v.* **·bled, ·bling** *v.i.* **1** To scratch, scrape, or paw. **2** To scribble. **3** To struggle or strive. —*v.t.* **4** To scrible on. **5** To scrape together. —*n.* **1** The act of scrabbling; a moving on hands and feet or knees. **2** A scrambling effort. [<Du. *schrabbelen*] —**scrab'bler** *n.*

scrag (skrag) *v.t.* **scragged, scrag·ging** *Informal* To wring the neck of; garrote. —*n.* **1** *Slang* The neck. **2** A lean, bony person or animal. [?<Scand.]

scrag·gly (skrag'lē) *adj.* **·gli·er, ·gli·est** Uneven; irregular; jagged: a *scraggly* beard.

scrag·gy (skrag'ē) *adj.* **·gi·er, ·gi·est 1** SCRAGGLY. **2** Lean; scrawny. —**scrag'gi·ly** *adv.* —**scrag'gi·ness** *n.*

scram (skram) *v.i.* **scrammed, scram·ming** *Slang* To go away; leave quickly. [Short for SCRAMBLE]

scram·ble (skram'bəl) *v.* **·bled, ·bling** *v.i.* **1** To move by clambering or crawling. **2** To struggle in a disorderly manner; scuffle. **3** To strive for something in such a manner. —*v.t.* **4** To mix together haphazardly or confusedly. **5** To gather or collect hurriedly or confusedly. **6** To cook (eggs) with the yolks and whites stirred together. **7** *Telecom.* To encode (a message) so that a special decoder is needed to make it intelligible. —*n.* **1** A difficult climb, as over rough terrain. **2** A struggle for possession: a *scramble* for power. [?] —**scram'bler** *n.*

scrap[1] (skrap) *n.* **1** A small piece; fragment. **2** A small part of something written. **3** *pl.* Bits of unused food. **4** Old or refuse metal. —*v.t.* **scrapped, scrap·ping 1** To break up into scrap. **2** To discard. —*adj.* Having the form of scraps: *scrap* metal. [<ON *skrap* scraps] —**Syn. 1** bit, chip, segment, shard. **3** leftovers.

scrap[2] (skrap) *Informal v.i.* **scrapped, scrap·ping** To fight; quarrel. —*n.* A fight; quarrel; squabble. [?<SCRAPE, *n.* (def. 2)] —**scrap'per** *n.*

scrap·book (skrap'bŏŏk') *n.* **1** A blank book in which to paste pictures, cuttings from periodicals, etc. **2** A personal notebook.

scrape (skrāp) *v.* **scraped, scrap·ing** *v.t.* **1** To rub, as with something rough or sharp, so as to abrade. **2** To remove an outer layer thus: with *off, away,* etc. **3** To rub (a rough or sharp object) across a surface. **4** To rub roughly across or against (a surface). **5** To dig or form by scratching or scraping. **6** To gather or accumulate with effort or difficulty. —*v.i.* **7** To scrape something. **8** To rub with a grating noise. **9** To make a grating noise. **10** To draw the foot backward along the ground in bowing. **11** To manage or get along with difficulty. **12** To be very or overly economical. —*n.* **1** The act or effect of scraping; also, the noise made by scraping. **2** A difficult situation. **3** A quarrel or fight. **4** A scraping or drawing back of the foot in bowing. [<ON *skrapa*] —**scrap'er** *n.*

scrap·ing (skrā'ping) *n.* **1** The act of one who or that which scrapes. **2** The sound so produced. **3** *Usu. pl.* Something scraped off or together.

scrap·ple (skrap'əl) *n.* Cornmeal cooked with scraps of pork and spices and molded into a firm loaf to be sliced for frying.

scrap·py[1] (skrap'ē) *adj.* **·pi·er, ·pi·est** Composed of scraps; fragmentary. —**scrap'pi·ly** *adv.* —**scrap'pi·ness** *n.*

scrap·py[2] (skrap'ē) *adj.* **·pi·er, ·pi·est** *Informal* **1** Ready and willing to fight. **2** Strongly competitive; gritty; tough. —**scrap'pi·ly** *adv.* —**scrap'pi·ness** *n.*

scratch (skrach) *v.t.* **1** To tear or mark the surface of with something sharp or rough. **2** To scrape or dig with something sharp or rough. **3** To scrape lightly with the nails, etc., as to relieve itching. **4** To rub with a grating sound; scrape. **5** To write or draw awkwardly or hurriedly. **6** To erase or cancel by scratches or marks. **7** To withdraw (an entry) from a competition, race, etc. —*v.i.* **8** To use the nails or claws, as in fighting or digging. **9** To scrape the skin, etc., lightly, as to relieve itching. **10** To make a grating noise. **11** To manage or get along with difficulty. **12** To withdraw from a game, race, etc., —*n.* **1** A mark or incision made on a surface by scratching. **2** A slight flesh wound or cut. **3** The sound of scratching. **4** The line from which contestants start, as in racing. **5** *Slang* Money. —**from scratch** From the beginning; from nothing. —**up to scratch** *Informal* Meeting the standard or requirement. —*adj.* **1** Done by chance; haphazard. **2** Made for hurried notes, figuring, etc.: a *scratch* pad. **3** Chosen hastily and at random: a *scratch* team. [<MDu. *cratsen*] —**scratch'er** *n.*

scratch·y (skrach'ē) *adj.* **scratch·i·er, scratch·i·est 1** Consisting of scratches: *scratchy* handwriting. **2** Making a scratching noise. **3** Causing itching: a *scratchy* sweater. —**scratch'i·ly** *adv.* —**scratch'i·ness** *n.*

scrawl (skrôl) *v.t.* & *v.i.* To write hastily or illegibly. —*n.* Irregular or careless writing. [?] —**scrawl'er** *n.*

scraw·ny (skrô'nē) *adj.* **·ni·er, ·ni·est** Lean and bony. [?] —**scraw'ni·ness** *n.*

scream (skrēm) *v.i.* **1** To utter a prolonged, piercing cry, as of pain, terror, or surprise. **2** To make a piercing sound: the wind *screamed* in the trees. **3** To laugh loudly or immoderately. **4** To use heated, hysterical language. —*v.t.* **5** To utter with a scream. —*n.* **1** A loud, shrill, prolonged cry or sound. **2** *Informal* A hugely entertaining person or thing. [<ON *skraema* to scare] —**scream'ing·ly** *adv.*

scream·er (skrē'mər) *n.* **1** One who or that which screams. **2** A South American wading bird, related to the ducks. **3** *Slang* A sensational headline in a newspaper.

screech (skrēch) *n.* A shrill, harsh cry; shriek. —*v.t.* **1** To utter with a screech. —*v.i.* **2** To shriek. [<ON *skrækja*] —**screech'er** *n.* —**screech'y** *adj.* **(·i·er, ·i·est)**

screech owl 1 Any of various small owls emitting a high-pitched wail. **2** The barn owl.

screed (skrēd) *n.* A prolonged spoken or written tirade; harangue. [<OE *scrēade*]

screen (skrēn) *n.* **1** Something that separates or shelters, as a light partition. **2** A coarse or fine metal mesh used for sifting, or as protection: a window *screen.* **3** Something that serves to conceal or protect: a smoke *screen.* **4** A surface, as a canvas or curtain, on which motion pictures and slides may be shown. **5** The surface of a cathode-ray tube, on which television pictures, computer information or graphics, etc., may be viewed. —**the screen** Motion pictures. —*v.t.* **1** To shield or conceal with or as with a screen. **2** To pass through a screen or sieve; sift. **3** To classify or scan for suitability, qualifications, etc.: to *screen* applicants for a job. **4** To project on a motion-picture screen. **5** To photograph (a motion picture); shoot. **6** To adapt (a play, novel, story, etc.) for motion pictures. —*v.i.* **7** To be suitable for representation as a motion picture. [<OF *escren*]

screen·ing (skrēn′ing) *n.* 1 A meshlike material, as for a window screen. 2 A showing of a motion picture. 3 *pl.* The parts of anything passed through or retained by a sieve; siftings.

screw (skrōō) *n.* 1 A device resembling a nail but having a slotted head and a tapering or cylindrical spiral for driving into wood, metal, plaster, etc., or for insertion into a corresponding threaded part. 2 A cylindrical socket with a spiral groove or thread 3 Anything having the form of a screw. 4 SCREW PROPELLER • See RUDDER. 5 A turn of or as of a screw. 6 Pressure; force. 7 *Slang* A prison guard. 8 *Brit. Slang* An old, worn-out, or bad-tempered horse. **—have a screw loose** *Slang* To be mentally deranged, eccentric, etc. **—put the screws on** (or to) *Slang* To exert pressure or force upon. *—v.t.* 1 To tighten, fasten, attach, etc., by a screw or screws. 2 To turn or twist. 3 To force; urge: to *screw* one's courage to the sticking point. 4 To contort, as one's features. 5 To practice oppression or extortion on; defraud. 6 To obtain by extortion. 7 *Slang* To act maliciously toward; harm. *—v.i.* 8 To turn as a screw. 9 To become attached or detached by means of twisting: with *on, off,* etc. 10 To twist or wind. 11 To practice oppression or extortion. **—screw up** *Slang* To botch; make a mess of: He *screwed up* his career. [< OF *escroue* nut] **—screw′er** *n.*

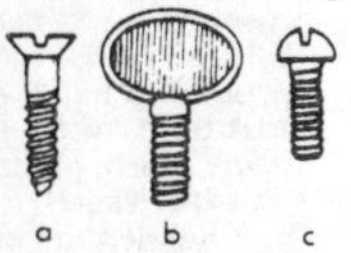

Screws
a. wood screw.
b. thumbscrew.
c. round-headed screw.

screw·ball (skrōō′bôl′) *n.* 1 In baseball, a pitch thrown with a wrist motion opposite to that used for the outcurve. 2 *Slang* An unconventional or erratic person.

screw cap A cap or lid designed to screw onto the threaded top of a bottle, jar, or the like.

screw·driv·er (skrōō′drī′vər) *n.* A tool for turning screws.

screwed-up (skrōōd′up′) *adj. Slang* 1 Disorganized or disorderly. 2 Mentally ill or emotionally distressed.

screw propeller An array of radial blades set at an angle on a rotary shaft to produce a spiral action in a fluid, used to propel ships, etc. • See RUDDER

screw thread The spiral ridge of a screw or nut.

screw·y (skrōō′ē) *adj.* **screw·i·er, screw·i·est** *Slang* Irrational; eccentric. **—screw′i·ly** *adv.* **—screw′i·ness** *n.*

scrib·ble (skrib′əl) *v.* **·bled, ·bling** *v.t.* 1 To write hastily and carelessly. 2 To cover with careless or illegible writing. *—v.i.* 3 To write carelessly or hastily. 4 To make illegible or meaningless marks. *—n.* 1 Hasty, careless writing. 2 Meaningless lines and marks; scrawl. [<L *scribere* write] **—scrib′bler** *n.* **—scrib′bly** *adj.*

scribe (skrīb) *n.* 1 One who copied manuscripts and books before printing was invented. 2 A clerk, public writer, or amanuensis. 3 An author: used humorously. 4 An ancient Jewish teacher of the Mosaic law. [<L *scribere* write] **—scrib′al** *adj.*

scrim (skrim) *n.* A lightweight, open-mesh, usu. cotton fabric, used for curtains, etc. [?]

scrim·mage (skrim′ij) *n.* 1 A rough-and-tumble contest; fracas. 2 In American football, a mass play from the line of scrimmage after the ball has been placed on the ground and snapped back, the play ending when the ball is dead. **—line of scrimmage** In football, the hypothetic line, parallel to the goal lines, on which the ball rests and along which the opposing linemen take position at the start of play. *—v.t. & v.i.* **·maged, ·mag·ing** To engage in a scrimmage. [Var. of SKIRMISH]

scrimp (skrimp) *v.i.* 1 To be very economical or stingy. *—v.t.* 2 To be overly sparing toward; skimp. 3 To cut too small, narrow, etc. [?] **—scrimp′er** *n.*

scrim·py (skrim′pē) *adj.* **·i·er, ·i·est** Skimpy or meager. **—scrimp′i·ly** *adv.* **—scrimp′i·ness** *n.*

scrim·shaw (skrim′shô) *n.* 1 The carving and engraving of usu. whalebone or whale ivory, as by American sailors. 2 An article so made. *— v.t.* 1 To make into scrimshaw by carving or engraving. *— v.i.* 2 To create scrimshaw. [?]

scrip (skrip) *n.* 1 Writing. 2 Any of various certificates showing that a person is entitled to receive something, as a fractional share of stock, a share of jointly owned property, etc. 3 A piece of paper money less than a dollar, formerly issued during emergencies in the U.S. [<SCRIPT]

Scrip. Scriptural; Scripture(s).

script (skript) *n.* 1 Handwriting; also, a particular style of

This line is in script.

handwriting. 2 Printed matter in imitation of handwriting. 3 A manuscript or text. 4 The written text of a play, TV show, etc. [<L *scribere* write]

scrip·ture (skrip′chər) *n.* 1 The sacred writings of any people. 2 Any authoritative book or writing. [<L *scribere* write] **—scrip′tur·al** *adj.* **—scrip′tur·al·ly** *adv.*

Scripture (skrip′chər) *n.* 1 *Usu. pl.* The books of the Old and New Testaments; the Bible; also **(the) Holy Scripture.** 2 A passage from the Bible.

scriv·en·er (skriv′ən·ər, skriv′nər) *n.* 1 A clerk or scribe. 2 A notary. [<L *scribere* write]

scrod (skrod) *n.* A young codfish, esp. when split and prepared for broiling. [<MDu. *schrode*]

scrof·u·la (skrof′yə·lə) *n.* Tuberculosis of the lymph glands. [<LL *scrofa* a breeding sow] **—scrof′u·lous** *adj.* **—scrof′u·lous·ly** *adv.* **—scrof′u·lous·ness** *n.*

scroll (skrōl) *n.* 1 A roll of parchment, paper, etc., esp. one containing or intended for writing. 2 The writing on such a roll. 3 Anything resembling a parchment roll, as a convoluted ornament or part. *—v.i.* To move one or more lines of copy off the top of a computer screen, so that additional lines may be displayed at the bottom, or vice versa. [<AF *escrowe*]

scroll saw A narrow-bladed saw for cutting thin sheets of wood into curved or convoluted shapes.

scrooge (skrōōj) *n.* A miserly, misanthropic person. [<Ebenezer *Scrooge,* a miserly character in Dickens' *A Christmas Carol*]

scro·tum (skrō′təm) *n. pl.* **·ta** (tə) or **·tums** The pouch that contains the testes. [L] **—scro′tal** *adj.*

scrounge (skrounj) *v.t. & v.i.* **scrounged, scoung·ing** *Slang* 1 To hunt about and take (something); pilfer. 2 To mooch; sponge. [?] **—scroung′er** *n.*

scrub[1] (skrub) *v.* **scrubbed, scrub·bing** *v.t.* 1 To rub vigorously in washing. 2 To remove (dirt, etc.) by such action. *—v.i.* 3 To rub something vigorously in washing. *—n.* The act of scrubbing. [<MDu. *schrobben*] **—scrub′ber** *n.*

scrub[2] (skrub) *n.* 1 A stunted tree. 2 A tract of stunted trees or shrubs. 3 A domestic animal of inferior breed. 4 A poor, insignificant person. 5 In sports, a player not on the varsity or regular team. 6 A game of baseball contrived hastily by a few players. *—adj.* 1 Undersized or inferior. 2 Consisting of or participated in by untrained players or scrubs: *scrub* team. [Var. of SHRUB]

scrub·by (skrub′ē) *adj.* **·bi·er, ·bi·est** 1 Of stunted growth. 2 Covered with or consisting of scrub or underbrush. **—scrub′bi·ly** *adv.* **—scrub′bi·ness** *n.*

scrub oak Any of various dwarf oaks.

scruff (skruf) *n.* The nape or outer back part of the neck. [Earlier *scuff* < ON *skopt* hair]

scruf·fy (skruf′ē) *adj.* **·i·er, ·i·est** 1 Shabby; seedy. 2 Worthless. [<OE *scruf* scurf] **—scruf′fi·ly** *adv.* **—scruf′fi·ness** *n.*

scrump·tious (skrump′shəs) *adj. Slang* Elegant or stylish; splendid. [? Var. of SUMPTUOUS] **—scrump′tious·ly** *adv.*

scru·ple (skrōō′pəl) *n.* 1 Doubt or uncertainty about what one should do. 2 Reluctance arising from conscientious disapproval. 3 An apothecaries' weight of 20 grains. 4 A minute quantity. *—v.t. & v.i.* **·pled, ·pling** To hesitate (doing) from considerations of right or wrong. [<L *scrupus* a sharp stone]

scru·pu·lous (skrōō′pyə·ləs) *adj.* 1 Cautious in action for fear of doing wrong; conscientious. 2 Resulting from the exercise of scruples; careful. **—scru′pu·lous·ly** *adv.* **—scru′·pu·los′i·ty** (-los′ə·tē), **scru′pu·lous·ness** *n.* **—Syn.** 1 ethical, honest, upright. 2 exact, precise.

scru·ti·neer (skrōō′tə·nir′) *n.* 1 One who scrutinizes. 2

Brit. & Can. One who oversees a polling place, checking voters against the registry, etc.

scru·ti·nize (skro͞o′tə·nīz) *v.t.* **·nized, ·niz·ing** To observe carefully; examine in detail. **—scru′ti·niz′er** *n.* **—scru′ti·niz′ing·ly** *adv.*

scru·ti·ny (skro͞o′tə·nē) *n. pl.* **·nies** Close investigation; careful inspection. [< L *scrutari* examine]

scu·ba (skʸo͞o′bə) *n.* A device worn by a free-swimming diver to provide a supply of air for breathing. [< *s(elf-) c(ontained) u(nderwater) b(reathing) a(pparatus)*]

scuba diving Swimming under water with the aid of a scuba. **—scuba diver**

scud (skud) *v.i.* **scud·ded, scud·ding** To move, run, or fly swiftly. *—n.* **1** The act of scudding. **2** Light clouds driven rapidly before the wind. [?]

scuff (skuf) *v.i.* **1** To drag the feet in walking; shuffle. — *v.t.* **2** To scrape (the floor, ground, etc.) with the feet. **3** To roughen the surface by rubbing or scraping: to *scuff* one's shoes. *—n.* The act of scuffing; also, the noise so made. [? < ON *skūfa* shove]

scuf·fle (skuf′əl) *v.i.* **·fled, ·fling** **1** To struggle roughly or confusedly. **2** To drag one's feet; shuffle. *—n.* A disorderly struggle; fracas. [? < Scand.] **—scuf′fler** *n.*

scull (skul) *n.* **1** A long oar worked from side to side over the stern of a boat. **2** A light oar, used in pairs by one person. **3** A small boat for sculling. *—v.t. & v.i.* To propel (a boat) by a scull or sculls. [ME *sculle*] **—scull′er** *n.*

scul·ler·y (skul′ər·ē) *n. pl.* **·ler·ies** A room where kitchen utensils are kept and cleaned. [< L *scutella* a tray]

scul·lion (skul′yən) *n. Archaic* A servant who scours dishes, pots, and kettles. [< OF *escouillon* a mop]

scul·pin (skul′pin) *n.* Any of a family of spiny fishes having a large head and fanlike pectoral fins. [< L *scorpaena,* a scorpionlike fish]

sculpt (skulpt) *v.t. & v.i. Informal* SCULPTURE.

sculp·tor (skulp′tər) *n.* A person who sculptures. — **sculp′tress** (-tris) *n. Fem.*

sculp·ture (skulp′chər) *n.* **1** The art of fashioning three-dimensional figures, busts, abstract pieces, etc., of stone, wood, clay, bronze, or other material. **2** A piece or group produced by sculpture. *—v.t.* **·tured, ·tur·ing** **1** To fashion, (stone, wood, metal, etc.) into sculpture. **2** To represent or portray by sculpture. **3** To embellish with sculpture. **4** To change (features on the surface of the earth) by erosion. *—v.i.* **5** To work as a sculptor. [< L *sculpere* carve in stone] **—sculp′tur·al** *adj.* **—sculp′tur·al·ly** *adv.*

scum (skum) *n.* **1** A layer of impure or extraneous matter on the surface of a liquid. **2** Low, contemptible people. — *v.* **scummed, scum·ming** *v.t.* **1** To take scum from; skim. — *v.i.* **2** To become covered with or form scum. [< MDu. *schuum*] **—scum′mi·ness** *n.* **—scum′my** *adj.* **(·mi·er, ·mi·est)**

scup (skup) *n.* A small porgy of the E coast of the U.S. [< Algon.]

scup·per (skup′ər) *n.* A hole or gutter bordering a ship's deck, to let water run off. [? < OF *escope* a bailing scoop]

scup·per·nong (skup′ər·nong) *n.* **1** A light-colored grape of the S U.S. **2** A sweet wine made from this grape. [< the *Scuppernong* River in N.C.]

scurf (skûrf) *n.* **1** Loose scales thrown off by the skin, as dandruff. **2** Any scaly matter adhering to a surface. [< OE] **—scurf′i·ness** *n.* **—scurf′y** *adj.* **(·i·er, ·i·est)**

scur·ri·lous (skûr′ə·ləs) *adj.* Grossly offensive or indecent; coarse and abusive: a *scurrilous* attack. [< L *scurra* a buffoon] **—scur·ril·i·ty** (skə·ril′ə·tē) (*pl.* **·ties**), **scur′ri·lous·ness** *n.* **—scur′ri·lous·ly** *adv.*

scur·ry (skûr′ē) *v.i.* **·ried, ·ry·ing** To move or go hurriedly: scamper. *—n. pl.* **·ries** The act or sound of scurrying. [?] — **Syn.** *v.* dart, dash, scoot, scuttle.

scur·vy (skûr′vē) A disease due to lack of vitamin C, marked by weakness, spotted skin, and bleeding gums. — *adj.* **·vi·er, ·vi·est** Low or contemptible. [< SCURF] **—scur′vi·ly** *adv.* **—scur′vi·ness** *n.*

scut (skut) *n.* A short tail, as of a rabbit or deer. [ME, a tail, a hare]

scutch·eon (skuch′ən) *n.* ESCUTCHEON.

scu·tel·late (skyo͞o·tel′it, skyo͞o′tə·lāt) *adj. Zool.* Covered with small plates or scales: also **scu′tel·lat′ed** (-lā′tid). [< L *scutum* a shield]

scu·tel·lum (skyo͞o·tel′əm) *n. pl.* **·la** (-ə) A small protective plate or scale, as on the tarsus of a bird. [< L *scutum* a shield] **—scu·tel′lar** *adj.*

scut·tle[1] (skut′l) *n.* **1** A small opening or hatchway with movable lid or cover, esp. in the roof or wall of a house, or in the deck or side of a ship. **2** The lid closing such an opening. *—v.t.* **·tled, ·tling** **1** To sink (a ship) by making holes below the water line. **2** To wreck or destroy. [< MF *escoutille* a hatchway]

scut·tle[2] (skut′l) *n.* A metal vessel or hod for coal. [< OE *scutel* a dish, platter]

scut·tle[3] (skut′l) *v.i.* **·tled, ·tling** To run in haste; scurry. — *n.* A hurried run or departure. [?] **—scut′tler** *n.*

scut·tle·butt (skut′l·but) *n.* **1** A drinking fountain aboard ship. **2** *Slang* Rumor; gossip. [Orig. *scuttled butt,* a lidded cask for drinking water]

scu·tum (skyo͞o′təm) *n. pl.* **·ta** (-tə) **1** A large shield carried by Roman foot soldiers. **2** *Zool.* A large, horny protective plate or scale: also **scute.** [L] **—scu·tate** (skyo͞o′tāt) *adj.*

Scyl·la (sil′ə) *Gk. Myth.* A sea monster who dwelt in a cave on the Italian coast opposite the whirlpool Charybdis. **—between Scylla and Charybdis** Between two equally menacing situations, one of which must be dealt with.

scythe (sīth) *n.* A tool composed of a long curved blade fixed at an angle to a long handle, used for mowing, reaping, etc. *—v.t.* **scythed, scyth·ing** To cut with a scythe. [< OE *sīthe*]

Scyth·i·a (sith′ē·ə) *n.* An ancient region of SE Europe, lying N of the Black Sea. **—Scyth′i·an** *adj., n.*

SD South Dakota (P.O. abbr.).

S.D., S. Dak. South Dakota.

SDR, S.D.R., SDRs, S.D.R.s Special Drawing Rights.

SE, S.E., se, s.e. southeast; southeastern.

Se selenium.

sea (sē) *n.* **1** The great body of salt water covering most of the earth's surface; the ocean. **2** A large body of salt water partly or wholly enclosed by land: the Adriatic *Sea.* **3** An inland body of water, esp. if salty: the *Sea* of Galilee. **4** The state of the ocean with regard to the course, flow, swell, or turbulence of the waves. **5** A heavy wave or swell. **6** Anything vast or boundless that resembles or suggests the sea. **—at sea** **1** On the ocean. **2** Bewildered. **—follow the sea** To follow the occupation of a sailor. **—put to sea** To sail away from the land [< OE *sæ*]

sea anemone Any of various soft-bodied, sessile marine polyps with tentacles resembling the petals of a flower.

sea bass Any of various carnivorous food fishes of U.S. coastal waters.

Sea·bee (sē′bē′) *n.* A member of one of the construction battalions of the U.S. Navy. [< *c(onstruction) b(attalion)*]

sea·board (sē′bôrd′, -bōrd′) *adj.* Bordering on the sea. *—n.* The seashore or seacoast and the adjoining region. [< SEA + *board* a border < OE *bord*]

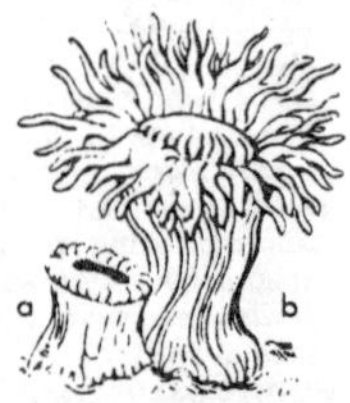

Sea anemone
a. tentacles contracted. b. extended.

sea bread HARDTACK.

sea breeze A breeze blowing from the sea toward land.

sea calf A spotted seal of the E U.S. coast.

sea·coast (sē′kōst′) *n.* The land on or close to the sea.

sea cow **1** Any of various large aquatic mammals, as the manatee or the dugong. **2** WALRUS.

sea cucumber Any of various cylindrical echinoderms having a rosette of tentacles at the mouth.

sea dog **1** SEAL[2]. **2** DOGFISH. **3** A sailor with long experience at sea.

sea eagle Any of various fish-eating birds related to the bald eagle.

sea·far·er (sē′fâr′ər) *n.* A sailor; mariner.

sea·far·ing (sē′fâr′ing) *n.* **1** The occupation of a sailor. **2** Traveling over the sea. *—adj.* Of, pertaining to, given to, or engaged in seafaring.

sea·food (sē′fo͞od′) *n.* Edible saltwater fish or shellfish.

sea·girt (sē′gûrt′) *adj.* Surrounded by the sea.

sea·go·ing (sē′gō′ing) *adj.* **1** Designed or adapted for use on the ocean. **2** SEAFARING.

sea green Bluish green.

sea gull A gull, esp. one of a widely distributed gregarious species.

sea horse 1 Any of various small fishes found in warm seas, having a long curled tail and a head resembling that of a horse. 2 A walrus. 3 A mythical creature, half horse and half fish.

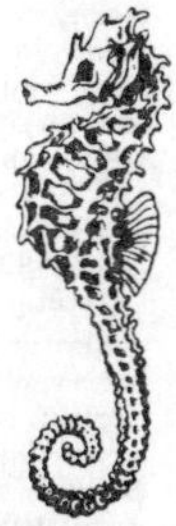

Sea horse

sea king A viking pirate chief of the Middle Ages.

seal[1] (sēl) *n.* 1 An impression made on a letter, document, etc., to prove its authenticity. 2 A wax wafer, piece of paper, etc., bearing such an authenticating impression. 3 A device with a raised or cut initial, word, or design, used to make such an impression. 4 A stamp, ring, etc., bearing such a device. 5 Something used to close or secure a letter, door, lid, wrapper, joint, passage, etc., firmly. 6 Anything that confirms, ratifies, or guarantees; pledge. 7 A sign or indication; token. 8 An ornamental stamp for packages, etc. —*v.t.* 1 To affix a seal to, as to prove authenticity or prevent tampering. 2 To stamp or otherwise impress a seal upon in order to attest to weight, quality, etc. 3 To fasten or close with a seal: to *seal* a glass jar. 4 To confirm the genuineness or truth of, as a bargain. 5 To establish or settle finally. 6 To secure, set, or fill up, as with plaster. [< L *sigillum* a small picture, seal] **—seal'a·ble** *adj.* **—seal'er** *n.*

Great Seal of the United States

seal[2] (sēl) *n.* 1 Any of various species of sea mammals with a short tail and four webbed flippers, with which it swims and waddles ashore. 2 The commercially valued fur of the **fur seal.** 3 Leather made from the hide of a seal. —*v.i.* To hunt seals. [< OE *seolh*] **—seal'er** *n.*

Seal

sea legs The ability to walk aboard a ship in motion without losing one's balance or suffering from seasickness.

sea level The average level of the surface of the ocean.

sea lily CRINOID.

sealing wax A pigmented mixture of shellac and resin with turpentine that is fluid when heated but becomes solid as it cools: used to seal papers, etc.

sea lion One of various large, eared seals, esp. the California sea lion.

seal ring SIGNET RING.

seal·skin (sēl'skin') *n.* 1 The pelt or fur of the fur seal, often dyed dark brown or black. 2 An article made of this fur. —*adj.* Made of sealskin.

Sea·ly·ham terrier (sē'lē·ham, -əm) One of a breed of terriers with short legs, a wide skull, square jaws, and a wiry white coat. [Orig. bred in *Sealyham,* Wales]

seam (sēm) *n.* 1 A visible line of junction between parts, as the edges of two pieces of cloth sewn together. • See PINK[2]. 2 A line, ridge, or groove marking joined edges, as of boards. 3 Any similar line, ridge, etc., as that formed by a scar, wrinkle, etc. 4 A thin layer or stratum, as of rock or ore. —*v.t.* 1 To unite by means of a seam. 2 To mark with a cut, furrow, wrinkle, etc. —*v.i.* 3 To crack open; become fissured. [< OE *sēam*] **—seam'er** *n.*

sea·man (sē'mən) *n. pl.* **·men** (-mən) 1 An enlisted man in the navy or in the coast guard, graded according to his rank. 2 A mariner; sailor. **—sea'man·like'** (-līk') *adj.* **—sea'man·ly** *adj., adv.*

sea·man·ship (sē'mən·ship) *n.* The skill of a seaman in handling sea craft.

sea mew A gull, esp. the European mew.

sea·mount (sē'mount') *n.* A submarine mountain.

seam·stress (sēm'stris) *n.* A woman whose occupation is sewing. [< OE *sēam* seam + -ST(E)R + -ESS]

seam·y (sē'mē) *adj.* **seam·i·er, seam·i·est** 1 Like, formed by, or characterized by seams. 2 Showing an unworthy, unpleasant, or unpresentable aspect. **—seam'i·ness** *n.* **—Syn.** 2 sordid, degraded, squalid, disagreeable.

sé·ance (sā'äns) *n.* 1 A session or sitting. 2 A meeting of persons seeking to receive communications from spirits of the dead. [F < OF *seoir* sit]

sea·plane (sē'plān') *n.* An airplane that can take off from and land on the water.

sea·port (sē'pôrt', -pōrt') *n.* 1 A harbor or port accessible to seagoing ships. 2 A town or city located at such a place.

sea purse The leathery egg case of certain sharks, rays, etc.

sear (sir) *v.t.* 1 To wither; dry up. 2 To burn the surface of; scorch. 3 To burn or cauterize; brand. 4 To make callous; harden. —*v.i.* 5 To become withered; dry up. —*adj.* Dried or blasted; withered. —*n.* A scar or brand. [< OE *sēar* dry]

search (sûrch) *v.t.* 1 To look through or explore thoroughly in order to find something. 2 To subject (a person) to a search. 3 To examine with close attention; probe. 4 To penetrate or pierce: The wind *searches* my clothes. 5 To learn by examination or investigation: with *out.* —*v.i.* 6 To make a search. —*n.* 1 The act of searching. 2 An act of boarding and inspecting a ship in pursuance of the right to search. [< LL *circare* go round, explore] **—search'a·ble** *adj.* **—search'er** *n.*

search·ing (sûr'ching) *adj.* 1 Investigating thoroughly. 2 Keenly penetrating. **—search'ing·ly** *adv.* **—search'ing·ness** *n.*

search·light (sûrch'līt') *n.* 1 An apparatus consisting of a powerful light equipped with a reflector and mounted so that it can be projected in various directions. 2 The light so projected.

search warrant A warrant authorizing a police officer to search a house or other specified place, as for stolen goods.

sea·scape (sē'skāp') *n.* 1 A view of the sea. 2 A picture presenting such a view.

sea·shell (sē'shel') *n.* The shell of a marine mollusk.

sea·shore (sē'shôr', -shōr') *n.* Land bordering on the sea.

sea·sick (sē'sik') *adj.* Suffering from seasickness.

sea·sick·ness (sē'sik'nis) *n.* Nausea, dizziness, etc., caused by the motion of a ship at sea.

sea·side (sē'sīd') *n.* SEASHORE.

sea·son (sē'zən) *n.* 1 A division of the year as determined by the earth's position with respect to the sun: spring, summer, autumn, and winter. 2 A period of time. 3 A period of special activity or when a specified place is frequented: usu. with *the:* the opera *season;* the Palm Beach *season.* 4 A fit or suitable time. 5 The time of and surrounding a major holiday. **—in season** 1 At a time of availability and fitness, as for eating: Clams are *in season* during the summer. 2 In or at the right time. 3 Able to be killed or taken by permission of the law. 4 Ready to mate or breed: said of animals. —*v.t.* 1 To increase the flavor or zest of (food), as by adding spices, etc. 2 To add zest or piquancy to. 3 To render more suitable for use. 4 To make fit, as by discipline; harden. 5 To mitigate or soften; moderate. —*v.i.* 6 To become seasoned. [< LL *satio* sowing time] **—sea'son·er** *n.*

sea·son·a·ble (sē'zən·ə·bəl) *adj.* 1 Being in keeping with the season or circumstances. 2 Done or occurring at the proper or best time. **—sea'son·a·ble·ness** *n.* **—sea'son·a·bly** *adv.* **—Syn.** 1 timely, well-timed. 2 opportune, favorable, propitious, advantageous.

sea·son·al (sē'zən·əl) *adj.* Of, pertaining to, characteristic of, or happening during a season or the seasons. **—sea'son·al·ly** *adv.*

sea·son·ing (sē'zən·ing) *n.* 1 The process by which something is rendered fit for use. 2 Something added to give relish; esp., a condiment. 3 Something added to increase enjoyment, give zest, etc.

season ticket A ticket entitling the holder to something specified, as train trips, admission to entertainments, etc., during a certain period of time.

seat (sēt) *n.* **1** The thing on which one sits; a chair, bench, stool, etc. **2** That part of a thing upon which one rests in sitting, or upon which an object or another part rests. **3** That part of the person which sustains the weight of the body in sitting; buttocks. **4** That part of a garment which covers the buttocks. **5** The place where anything is situated or established: the *seat* of pain, the *seat* of a government. **6** A place of abode, esp. a large estate. **7** The privilege or right of membership in a legislative body, stock exchange, or the like. **8** The manner of sitting, as on horseback. **9** A surface or part upon which the base of anything rests. —*v.t.* **1** To place on a seat or seats; cause to sit down. **2** To have seats for; furnish with seats: The theater *seats* only 299 people. **3** To put a seat on or in; renew or repair the seat of. **4** To locate, settle, or center: usu. in the passive: The French government is *seated* in Paris. **5** To fix, set firmly, or establish in a certain position, place, etc. [< ON *sæti*]

seat belt A strap or harness that holds a passenger firmly in the seat, as while riding in a car or airplane.

seat·ing (sē′ting) *n.* **1** The act of providing with seats; also, the arrangement of such seats. **2** Fabric for upholstering seats. **3** A fitted support or base; a seat.

SEATO (sē′tō) Southeast Asia Treaty Organization.

sea urchin Any of various echinoderms shielded within a spine-covered, rounded case.

sea wall A wall for preventing erosion of the shore by the sea or for breaking the force of waves. —**sea-walled** (sē′·wôld′) *adj.*

sea·ward (sē′wərd) *adj.* **1** Going or situated toward the sea. **2** Blowing, as wind, from the sea. —*adv.* In the direction of the sea: also **sea′wards.** —*n.* A direction or position toward the sea, away from land.

sea·way (sē′wā′) *n.* **1** A way or route over the sea. **2** An inland waterway that receives ocean shipping. **3** The headway made by a ship. **4** A rough sea.

sea·weed (sē′wēd′) *n.* Any marine plant or vegetation, esp. any multicellular alga.

sea·wor·thy (sē′wûr′thē) *adj.* In fit condition for a sea voyage. —**sea′wor′thi·ness** *n.*

se·ba·ceous (si·bā′shəs) *adj.* **1** Of, pertaining to, or resembling fat. **2** Secreting sebum. [< L *sebum* tallow]

se·bum (sē′bəm) *n.* An oily substance secreted by special glands in the skin. [L, tallow]

sec (sek) *adj.* *French* Dry: said of wines. Also *Italian* **sec·co** (sek′kō).

SEC, S.E.C. Securities and Exchange Commission.

sec. second(s); secondary; secretary; section(s); sector.

se·cant (sē′kant, -kənt) *adj.* Cutting, esp. into two parts; intersecting. —*n.* **1** *Geom.* A straight line intersecting a given curve. **2** *Trig.* A function equal to the reciprocal of the cosine. [< L *secare* to cut]

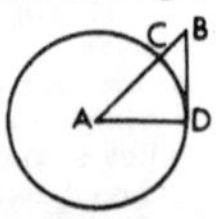

Ratio of AB to AD is the secant of angle BAD. AB is secant of arc CD.

se·cede (si·sēd′) *v.i.* **·ced·ed, ·ced·ing** To withdraw formally from a union, fellowship, etc., esp. from a political or religious organization. [< L *se-* apart + *cedere* go] —**se·ced′er** *n.*

se·ces·sion (si·sesh′ən) *n.* **1** The act of seceding. **2** *Usu. cap. U.S.* The withdrawal of the Southern States from the Union in 1860–61. —**se·ces′sion·al** *adj.* —**se·ces′·sion·ism, se·ces′sion·ist** *n.*

Seck·el (sek′əl, sik′əl) *n.* A variety of small, sweet pear. Also **Seckel pear.** [< the Pennsylvania farmer who introduced it]

se·clude (si·klōōd′) *v.t.* **·clud·ed, ·clud·ing** **1** To remove and keep apart from the society of others; isolate. **2** To screen or shut off, as from view. [< L *se-* apart + *claudere* to shut]

se·clud·ed (si·klōō′did) *adj.* **1** Separated; living apart from others. **2** Protected or screened. —**se·clud′ed·ly** *adv.* —**se·clud′ed·ness** *n.*

se·clu·sion (si·klōō′zhən) *n.* **1** The act of secluding, or the state or condition of being secluded; solitude; retirement. **2** A secluded place. —**se·clu′sive** *adj.* —**se·clu′sive·ly** *adv.* —**se·clu′sive·ness** *n.*

sec·ond[1] (sek′ənd) *n.* **1** A unit of time, 1/60 of a minute. **2** A unit of angular measure, 1/60 of a minute. **3** An instant; moment: Wait a *second.* [< Med. L *seconda (minuta),* lit., second (minute), i.e., the result of the second sexagesimal division]

sec·ond[2] (sek′ənd) *adj.* **1** Next in order, authority, responsibility, etc., after the first. **2** Ranking next below the first or best. **3** Of lesser quality or value; inferior; subordinate. **4** Identical with another or preceding one; other. **5** *Music* Lower in pitch, or rendering a secondary part. —*n.* **1** The one next after the first, as in order, rank, importance, etc. **2** The element of an ordered set that corresponds to the number two. **3** An attendant who supports or aids another, as in a duel. **4** *Often pl.* An article of merchandise of inferior quality. **5** *Music* **a** The interval between any tone and another a whole step or half step away from or below it. **b** A subordinate part, instrument, or voice. **6** In parliamentary law, the act or declaration by which a motion is seconded: Do I hear a *second*? **7** *pl. Informal* A second portion of food. —*v.t.* **1** To act as a supporter or assistant of; promote; stimulate; encourage. **2** To support formally, as a motion, resolution, etc. —*adv.* In the second order, place, rank, etc. [< L *secundus* following]

sec·on·dar·y (sek′ən·der′ē) *adj.* **1** Of second rank, grade, or influence; subordinate. **2** Depending on, resulting from, or following what is primary. **3** Second in order of occurrence or development. **4** *Electr.* Of or pertaining to the output of a transformer. —*n. pl.* **·dar·ies** **1** One who or that which is secondary or subordinate. **2** *Electr.* A secondary circuit or coil. —**sec′on·dar′i·ly** *adv.*

secondary accent See ACCENT.

secondary education Education beyond the elementary or primary, and below the college, level.

secondary school A school providing secondary education.

second best One who or that which is next after the best. —**sec′ond-best′** *adj.*

second childhood A time or condition of dotage; senility.

sec·ond-class (sek′ənd·klas′, -kläs′) *adj.* **1** Ranking next below the first or best; inferior, inadequate, etc. **2** Of, pertaining to, or belonging to a class next below the first: *second-class* mail, *second-class* ticket, etc. —*adv.* By using second-class travel accommodations or second-class mail.

sec·ond-guess (sek′ənd·ges′) *v.t.* **1** To use hindsight in criticizing (an action, decision, etc., or the person responsible for it). **2** OUTGUESS. —**sec′ond-guess′er** *n.*

sec·ond·hand (sek′ənd·hand′) *adj.* **1** Previously owned, worn, or used by another; not new. **2** Received from another; not direct from the original source: *secondhand* information. **3** Of, pertaining to, or dealing in merchandise that is not new. —*adv.* Indirectly.

second hand The hand that marks the seconds on a clock or a watch.

second lieutenant See GRADE.

sec·ond·ly (sek′ənd·lē) *adv.* In the second place; second.

second nature An acquired trait or habit so ingrained as to seem innate.

sec·ond-rate (sek′ənd·rāt′) *adj.* Second or inferior in quality, size, rank, importance, etc.; second-class. —**sec′·ond-rat′er** *n.*

second sight The supposed capacity to see objects not actually present, to see into the future, etc. —**sec′ond-sight′ed** *adj.*

sec·ond·sto·ry man (sek′ənd·stôr′ē, -stō′rē) *Informal* A burglar who enters a building through an upstairs window. Also **sec′ond·sto′ry-man.**

sec·ond-string (sek′ənd·string′) *adj.* *Informal* **1** In sports, being a substitute rather than a regular or starting player. **2** SECOND-RATE.

second thought A reevaluation or reconsideration of something following one's initial response or decision.

second wind **1** The return of easy breathing after a period of exertion or exercise. **2** A renewed capacity for the continuation of any effort.

se·cre·cy (sē′krə·sē) *n. pl.* **·cies** **1** The condition or quality of being secret; concealment. **2** The character of being secretive.

se·cret (sē′krit) *adj.* **1** Kept separate or hidden from view or knowledge, or from all persons except the individuals concerned; unseen. **2** Affording privacy; secluded. **3** Good at keeping secrets; close-mouthed. **4** Unrevealed or unavowed: a *secret* partner. **5** Not revealed to everyone; mysterious; esoteric. —*n.* **1** Something known only by a few people. **2** Something that is not explained or is kept hidden; mystery. **3** An underlying reason; key. —**in secret** In privacy; in a hidden place. [< L *se-* apart + *cernere* to separate] —**se′cret·ly** *adv.*

sec·re·tar·i·at (sek′rə·târ′ē·it, -at) *n.* **1** A secretary's position. **2** The place where a secretary transacts business and keeps records. **3** The entire staff of secretaries in an office; esp., a department headed by a secretary-general.

sec·re·tar·y (sek′rə·ter′ē) *n. pl.* **·tar·ies** **1** An employee who deals with correspondence, records, and clerical business for a person, business, committee, etc. **2** An official in a business, club, etc., who has overall responsibility for somewhat similar work. **3** An executive officer presiding over and managing a department of government. **4** A writing desk with a bookcase on top. [< L *secretum* a secret] —**sec′re·tar′i·al** (-târ′ē·əl) *adj.*

secretary bird A large, predatory African bird having a crest resembling quill pens stuck behind the ear.

secretary general *pl.* **secretaries general** A chief administrative officer, esp. the head of a secretariat.

sec·re·tar·y·ship (sek′rə·ter′ē·ship) *n.* The work or position of a secretary.

se·crete (si·krēt′) *v.t.* **·cret·ed, ·cret·ing** **1** To remove or keep from observation; conceal; hide. **2** *Biol.* To form and release (an enzyme, hormone, etc.). [Alter. of obs. *secret,* to conceal] —**se·cre′tor** *n.*

se·cre·tion (si·krē′shən) *n.* **1** *Biol.* The cellular process by which materials are separated from blood or sap and converted into new substances: the *secretion* of milk, urine, etc. **2** The substance secreted. **3** The act of concealing or hiding.

se·cre·tive (sē′krə·tiv, si·krē′tiv) *adj.* **1** Having or showing a disposition to secrecy. **2** (si·krē′tiv) SECRETORY. —**se′cre·tive·ly** *adv.* —**se′cre·tive·ness** *n.*

se·cre·to·ry (si·krē′tər·ē) *adj.* Of, pertaining to, causing, or produced by secretion (def. 1).

secret service A department of the government concerned with work of a secret nature.

Secret Service A division of the U.S. Treasury Department concerned with the suppression of counterfeiting, the protection of the President, etc.

sect (sekt) *n.* **1** A religious denomination, esp. a body of dissenters from an established or older form of faith. **2** Adherents of a particular philosophical system or teacher, esp. a faction of a larger group. [< L *sequi* follow]

sect. section; sectional.

sec·tar·i·an (sek·târ′ē·ən) *adj.* **1** Of, pertaining to, or characteristic of a sect. **2** Having devotion to or prejudice in favor of a sect. **3** Narrow-minded; limited; parochial. —*n.* **1** A member of a sect. **2** A person who is blindly devoted to a sect or factional viewpoint. —**sec·tar′i·an·ism′** *n.*

sec·ta·ry (sek′tər·ē) *n. pl.* **·ries** A member of a sect.

sec·tion (sek′shən) *n.* **1** The act of cutting; a separating by cutting. **2** A slice or portion separated by or as if by cutting. **3** A separate part or division, as of a book or chapter. **4** A distinct part of a country, community, etc. **5** *U.S.* An area of land one square mile in extent and constituting 1/36 of a township. **6** A portion of a railroad's right of way under the care of a particular crew of men. **7** In a sleeping-car, a space containing two berths. **8** A representation of an object, as if cut by an intersecting plane. —*v.t.* **1** To divide into sections. **2** To shade (a drawing) so as to designate a section or sections. [< L *sectus,* p.p. of *secare* to cut]

sec·tion·al (sek′shən·əl) *adj.* **1** Of, pertaining to, or characteristic of a section. **2** Made up of sections. —**sec′tion·al·ly** *adv.*

sec·tion·al·ism (sek′shən·əl·iz′əm) *n.* Exaggerated concern for a particular section of a country rather than the whole. —**sec′tion·al·ist** *n.*

sec·tor (sek′tər) *n.* **1** *Geom.* A part of a circle bounded by two radii and the arc subtended by them. **2** *Mil.* **a** A part of a front in contact with the enemy. **b** Any of the subdivisions of a defensive position. **3** A distinct part, as of a society. —*v.t.* To divide into sectors. [< L *sectus,* p.p. of *secare* to cut] —**sec·to·ri·al** (-tôr′ē·əl, -tō′rē-) *adj.*

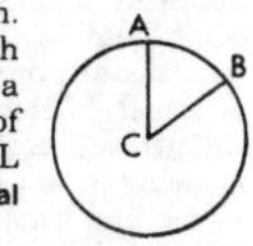

ACB is a sector of the circle.

sec·u·lar (sek′yə·lər) *adj.* **1** Of or pertaining to this world; temporal; worldly. **2** Not controlled by the church; civil; not ecclesiastical. **3** Not concerned with religion; not sacred: *secular* art. **4** Not bound by monastic vows, and not living in a religious community. **5** Of or describing a trend or process continuing for a long, indefinite period of time. —*n.* **1** A member of the clergy who is not bound by monastic vows and who does not live in a religious community. **2** A layman as distinguished from a member of the clergy. [< L *saeculum* generation, age]

sec·u·lar·ism (sek′yə·lə·riz′əm) *n.* **1** Regard for worldly as opposed to spiritual matters. **2** The belief that religion should not be introduced into public education or public affairs. —**sec′u·lar·ist** *n.* —**sec′u·lar·is′tic** *adj.*

sec·u·lar·ize (sek′yə·lə·rīz′) *v.t.* **·ized, ·iz·ing** **1** To make secular; convert from sacred to secular possession or uses. **2** To make worldly. **3** To change (a regular clergyman) to a secular. —**sec′u·lar·i·za′tion** *n.*

se·cure (si·kyŏŏr′) *adj.* **·cur·er, ·cur·est** **1** Free from or not likely to be exposed to danger, theft, etc.; safe. **2** Free from fear, apprehension, etc. **3** Confident; certain. **4** In a state or condition that will not break, come unfastened, etc.: Is the door *secure?* **5** Reliable; steady; dependable: a *secure* job. —*v.* **·cured, ·cur·ing** *v.t.* **1** To make secure; protect. **2** To make firm, tight, or fast; fasten. **3** To make sure or certain; insure; guarantee. **4** To obtain possession of; get. —*v.i.* **5** To stop working: said of a ship's crew. **6** To berth; moor: said of a ship. [< L *se-* without + *cura* care] —**se·cur′a·ble** *adj.* —**se·cure′ly** *adv.* —**se·cure′ness, se·cur′er** *n.*

se·cur·i·ty (si·kyŏŏr′ə·tē) *n. pl.* **·ties** **1** The state of being secure; freedom from danger, risk, care, poverty, doubt, etc. **2** One who or that which secures or guarantees; surety. **3** *pl.* Written promises or something deposited or pledged for payment of money, as stocks, bonds, etc. **4** Defense or protection against espionage, attack, escape, etc. **5** Measures calculated to provide such defense or protection. **6** An organization or division of one charged with providing for safety and protection.

Security Council A permanent organ of the United Nations charged with the maintenance of international peace and security.

secy., sec'y. secretary.

se·dan (si·dan′) *n.* **1** A closed automobile having one compartment, front and rear seats, and two or four doors. **2** A closed chair, for one passenger, carried by two men by means of poles at the sides: also **sedan chair.** [?]

Sedan *def. 2*

se·date (si·dāt′) *adj.* Not disturbed by excitement, passion, etc. [< L *sedare* make calm, settle] —**se·date′ly** *adv.* —**se·date′ness** *n.* —**Syn.** calm, composed, staid.

se·da·tion (si·dā′shən) *n.* The reduction of sensitivity to pain, stress, etc., by administering a sedative.

sed·a·tive (sed′ə·tiv) *adj.* Tending to calm or soothe; esp., acting to allay nervousness or emotional agitation. —*n.* A sedative medicine.

sed·en·tar·y (sed′ən·ter′ē) *adj.* **1** Accustomed to sit much or to work in a sitting posture. **2** Characterized by sitting. **3** Remaining in one place; not migratory. **4** Attached or fixed to an object. [< L *sedere* sit] —**sed′en·tar′i·ly** *adv.* —**sed′en·tar′i·ness** *n.*

Se·der (sā′dər) *n. pl.* **Se·da·rim** (sə·där′im) or **Se·ders** In Judaism, a ceremonial dinner commemorating the Exodus, held on the eve of the first day of Passover, and traditionally on the eve of the second day by Jews outside of Israel. [< Heb. *sēdher* order]

sedge (sej) *n.* Any of a large family of grasslike plants growing in wet ground and usu. having triangular, solid stems and tiny flowers in spikes. [< OE *secg*] **—sedged, sedg′y** *adj.*

sed·i·ment (sed′ə·mənt) *n.* **1** Matter that settles to the bottom of a liquid; dregs; lees. **2** *Geol.* Fragmentary material deposited by water, ice, or air. [< L *sedere* sit, settle] **sed′i·men·ta′tion** *n.*

sed·i·men·ta·ry (sed′ə·men′tər·ē) *adj.* **1** Of, pertaining to, or having the character of sediment. **2** *Geol.* Designating rocks composed of compacted sediment. Also **sed′i·men′tal.**

se·di·tion (si·dish′ən) *n.* The incitement and act of resistance to or revolt against lawful authority. [< L *sed-* aside + *itio* a going]

se·di·tious (si·dish′əs) *adj.* **1** Of, pertaining to, or having the character of sedition. **2** Inclined to, taking part in, or guilty of sedition. **—se·di′tious·ly** *adv.* **—se·di′tious·ness** *n.*

se·duce (si·dyōōs′) *v.t.* **·duced, ·duc·ing 1** To lead astray, as from a proper or right course: *seduced* by quick profits. **2** To entice into wrong, disloyalty, etc.; tempt. **3** To induce to have sexual intercourse. [< L *se-* apart + *ducere* lead] **—se·duc′er** *n.* **—se·duc′i·ble** or **se·duce′a·ble** *adj.*

se·duc·tion (si·duk′shən) *n.* **1** The act of seducing or the condition of being seduced. **2** Something which seduces; an enticement. Also **se·duce′ment.**

se·duc·tive (si·duk′tiv) *adj.* Tending to seduce. **—se·duc′tive·ly** *adv.* **—se·duc′tive·ness** *n.*

sed·u·lous (sej′ōō·ləs) *adj.* **1** Constant in application or attention; assiduous. **2** Diligent; industrious. [< L *se dolo* without guile] **—sed′u·lous·ly** *adv.* **—sed′u·lous·ness** *n.*

se·dum (sē′dəm) *n.* Any of a large genus of chiefly creeping or mat-forming plants with fleshy leaves, adapted to rocky terrain. [L, house leek]

see[1] (sē) *v.* **saw, seen, see·ing** *v.t.* **1** To perceive with the eyes; gain knowledge or awareness of by means of one's vision. **2** To perceive with the mind; comprehend. **3** To find out or ascertain; inquire about: *See* who is at the door. **4** To have experience or knowledge of; undergo: We have *seen* more peaceful times. **5** To encounter; chance to meet: I *saw* your husband today. **6** To have a meeting or interview with; visit or receive as a guest, visitor, etc.: The doctor will *see* you now. **7** To attend as a spectator; view. **8** To accompany; escort. **9** To take care; be sure: *See* that you do it! **10** In poker, to accept (a bet) or equal the bet of (a player) by betting an equal sum. *—v.i.* **11** To have or exercise the power of sight. **12** To find out; inquire. **13** To understand; comprehend. **14** To think; consider. **15** To take care; be attentive: *See* to your work. **16** To gain certain knowledge, as by awaiting an outcome: We will *see* if you are right. **—see about 1** To inquire into the facts, causes, etc., of. **2** To take care of; attend to. **—see through 1** To perceive the real meaning or nature of. **2** To aid or protect, as throughout a period of danger. **3** To finish. [< OE *sēon*]

see[2] (sē) *n.* **1** The official seat from which a bishop exercises jurisdiction. **2** The authority or jurisdiction of a bishop. [< L *sedes* a seat]

seed (sēd) *n.* **1** The ovule containing an embryo from which a plant may be reproduced. **2** That from which anything springs; source. **3** Offspring; children. **4** The male fertilizing element; semen; sperm. **5** Any small granular fruit, singly or collectively. *—v.t.* **1** To sow with seed. **2** To sow (seed). **3** To remove the seeds from: to *seed* raisins. **4** To strew (moisture-bearing clouds) with crystals, as of dry ice, silver iodide, etc., in order to initiate precipitation. **5** In sports: **a** To arrange (the drawing for positions in a tournament, etc.) so that the more skilled competitors meet only in the later events. **b** To rank (a skilled competitor) thus. *—v.i.* **6** To sow seed. **7** To grow to maturity and produce or shed seed. **—go to seed 1** To develop and shed seed. **2** To become shabby, useless, etc.; deteriorate. [< OE *sæd*] **—seed′er** *n.* **—seed′less** *adj.*

seed·bed (sēd′bed′) *n.* **1** A protected bed of earth planted with seeds for later transplanting. **2** A place of early growth or nurture.

seed·case (sēd′kās′) *n.* SEED VESSEL.

seed coat The integument of a seed. • See EMBRYO.

seed leaf COTYLEDON.

seed·ling (sēd′ling) *n.* **1** Any plant grown from seed. **2** A very small or young tree or plant.

seed oyster A young oyster, esp. one transplanted from one bed to another.

seed pearl A small pearl, esp. one used for ornamenting bags, etc., or in embroidery.

seed plant A plant which bears seeds.

seed vessel A pericarp, esp. one that is dry, as a pod.

seed·y (sē′dē) *adj.* **seed·i·er, seed·i·est 1** Abounding with seeds. **2** Gone to seed. **3** Poor and ragged; shabby. **4** Feeling or looking wretched. **—seed′i·ly** *adv.* **—seed′i·ness** *n.*

see·ing (sē′ing) *conj.* Since; in view of the fact; considering.

Seeing Eye dog The name used for a dog trained to lead the blind, esp. one trained by an organization **(Seeing Eye)** in New Jersey: a trade name.

seek (sēk) *v.* **sought, seek·ing** *v.t.* **1** To go in search of; look for. **2** To strive for; try to get. **3** To endeavor or try: He *seeks* to mislead me. **4** To ask or inquire for; request: to *seek* information. **5** To go to; betake oneself to: to *seek* a warmer climate. *—v.i.* **6** To make a search or inquiry. [< OE *sēcan*] **—seek′er** *n.*

seem (sēm) *v.i.* **1** To give the impression of being; appear. **2** To appear to oneself: I *seem* to remember her face. **3** To appear to exist: There *seems* no reason for hesitating. **4** To be evident or apparent: It *seems* to be raining. [< ON *sæma* honor, conform to]

seem·ing (sē′ming) *adj.* Having the appearance of reality but often not so: Her *seeming* nonchalance was solely due to three martinis. *—n.* Appearance; semblance; esp., false show. **—seem′ing·ly** *adv.* **—seem′ing·ness** *n.*

seem·ly (sēm′lē) *adj.* **·li·er, ·li·est 1** Befitting the proprieties; becoming; proper; decorous. **2** Handsome; attractive. *—adv.* Becomingly; appropriately. [< ON *sæmr* fitting] **—seem′li·ness** *n.*

seen (sēn) *p.p.* of SEE.

seep (sēp) *v.i.* To soak through pores or small openings; ooze. [< OE *sipian* soak] **—seep′y** *adj.*

seep·age (sē′pij) *n.* **1** The act or process of seeping; oozing; leakage. **2** The fluid that seeps.

seer (sē′ər *for def. 1*; sir *for def. 2*) *n.* **1** One who sees. **2** One who foretells events; a prophet. [< SEE[1] + -ER]

seer·suck·er (sir′suk′ər) *n.* A thin fabric, often striped, with crinkled surface. [< Pers. *shīr o shakkar*, lit., milk and sugar]

see·saw (sē′sô′) *n.* **1** A game or contest in which persons sit or stand on opposite ends of a board balanced at the middle and make it move up and down. **2** A board balanced for this sport. **3** Any up-and-down or to-and-fro movement, tendency, change, etc. *—v.t. & v.i.* To move on or as if on a seesaw. *—adj.* Moving up and down or to and fro. [Reduplication of SAW[1]]

seethe (sēth) *v.* **seethed, seeth·ing** *v.i.* **1** To boil. **2** To foam or bubble as if boiling. **3** To be agitated, as by rage. *—v.t.* **4** To soak in liquid; steep. **5** *Archaic* To boil. *—n.* The act or condition of seething. [< OE *sēothan*]

seg·ment (seg′mənt) *n.* **1** A part cut off or distinct from the other parts of anything: a section. **2** *Geom.* A part of a line or curve lying between two of its points. *—v.t. & v.i.* To divide into segments. [< L *secare* to cut] **—seg·men·tal** (seg·men′təl) *adj.* **—seg·men′tal·ly** *adv.* **—seg·men·tar·y** (seg′mən·ter′ē) *adj.*

seg·men·ta·tion (seg′mən·tā′shən) *n.* **1** Division into segments. **2** The process of repeated cleavage whereby a complex organism develops from a single cell.

se·go (sē′gō) *n. pl.* **·gos 1** A perennial plant of the lily family, having bell-shaped flowers. **2** Its edible bulb. Also **sego lily.** [< Ute]

seg·re·gate (seg′rə·gāt) *v.* **·gat·ed, ·gat·ing** *v.t.* **1** To place apart from others or the rest; isolate. **2** To cause the separation of (a race, social class, etc.) from the general mass of society or from a larger group. *—v.i.* **3** To separate from a mass and gather about nuclei, as in crystallization. *—adj.* (-git) Separated or set apart from others; segregated.

[< L *se-* apart + *grex* a flock] **—seg′re·ga′tive** *adj.* **—seg′re·ga′tor** *n.*

seg·re·ga·tion (seg′rə·gā′shən) *n.* **1** A segregating or being segregated or process of segregating. **2** The act or policy of separating a race, social class, etc., from the general mass of society or from a larger group.

Seid·litz powders (sed′lits) An effervescent mixture of salts, used as a laxative. Also **Seidlitz powder.** [< similarity to spring water in *Seidlitz*, Czechoslovakia]

sei·gnior (sān·yôr′, sān′yər) *n.* A man of rank, esp. a feudal lord. Also **sei·gneur** (sān′yər). [< L *senior* older] — **sei·gnio′ri·al** *adj.*

seign·ior·y (sān′yər·ē) *n. pl.* **·ior·ies** The territory, rights, or jurisdiction of a seignior.

seine (sān) *n.* Any long fishing net, having floats at the top edge and weights at the bottom. *—v.t. & v.i.* **seined, sein·ing** To fish or catch with a seine. [< Gk. *sagēnē* a fishing net]

seis·mic (sīz′mik, sīs′-) *adj.* Of, pertaining to, subject to, or produced by an earthquake or earthquakes. Also **seis′mal, seis′mi·cal.** [< Gk. *seismos* earthquake.]

seismo- *combining form* Earthquake: *seismograph.* [< Gk. *seismos* an earthquake]

seis·mo·gram (sīz′mə·gram, sīs′-) *n.* The record made by a seismograph.

seis·mo·graph (sīz′mə·graf, -gräf, sīs′-) *n.* An instrument for automatically recording the movements of the earth's crust. **—seis′mo·graph′ic** *adj.* — **seis·mog·ra·pher** (sīz·mog′rə·fər, sīs-), **seis·mog′ra·phy** *n.*

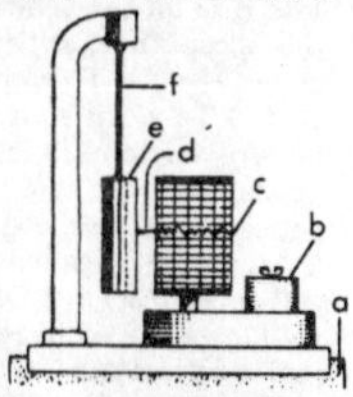

Seismograph
a. concrete base. b. clock. c. seismogram. d. stylus. e. weight. f. spring suspension.

seis·mol·o·gy (sīz·mol′ə·jē, sīs-) *n.* The science dealing with earthquakes and related phenomena. **—seis·mo·log·ic**(sīz′mə·loj′ik,sīs′-) or **·i·cal** *adj.* **—seis′mo·log′i·cal·ly** *adv.* **—seis·mol′o·gist** *n.*

seize (sēz) *v.* **seized, seiz·ing** *v.t.* **1** To take hold of suddenly and forcibly; clutch; grasp. **2** To grasp mentally; understand. **3** To take possession of by authority or right. **4** To take possession of by or as by force. **5** To take prisoner; capture. **6** To act upon with sudden and powerful effect; attack; strike. **7** To take advantage of immediately, as an opportunity. **8** *Naut.* To fasten or bind by turns of cord, line, or small rope; lash. *—v.i.* **9** To take hold or make use: usu. with *on* or *upon.* [< OF *saisir, seisir*] **—seiz′a·ble** *adj.* **—seiz′er** *n.*

sei·zure (sē′zhər) *n.* **1** The act of seizing or the state of being seized. **2** A sudden incapacitation, as by disease.

se·lah (sē′lə) *n.* A Hebrew word of unknown meaning in the Psalms, usu. considered as a direction to readers or musicians.

sel·dom (sel′dəm) *adv.* At widely separated intervals, as of time or space; infrequently; rarely. *—adj.* Infrequent; rare. [< OE *seldan*]

se·lect (si·lekt′) *v.t.* **1** To take in preference to another or others; pick out; choose. *—v.i.* **2** To choose. *—adj.* **1** Chosen in preference to others. **2** Excellent; superior; choice. **3** Exclusive. **4** Very particular in selecting. [< L *se-* apart + *legere* choose] **—se·lect′ness, se·lec′tor** *n.*

se·lec·tee (si·lek′tē′) *n.* One called up for military service under selective service.

se·lec·tion (si·lek′shən) *n.* **1** A selecting or being selected. **2** Anything selected. **3** *Biol.* Any process, natural or artificial, which determines the survival of specific characteristics.

se·lec·tive (si·lek′tiv) *adj.* **1** Of, pertaining to, or characterized by selection. **2** Having the power or tendency to select. **3** Having or characterized by good selectivity, as a radio receiver. **—se·lec·tive·ly** *adv.* **—se·lec′tive·ness** *n.*

selective service Compulsory military service according to specified conditions of age, fitness, etc. **—se·lec′·tive-ser′vice** *adj.*

se·lec·tiv·i·ty (si·lek′tiv′ə·tē) *n.* **1** The state or condition of being selective. **2** *Telecom.* That characteristic of a radio receiver or filter by which frequencies can be sharply discriminated.

se·lect·man (si·lekt′mən) *n. pl.* **·men** (-mən) One of a board of town officers, elected annually in New England, except in Rhode Island, to manage local affairs.

sel·e·nite (sel′ə·nīt) *n.* A crystalline form of gypsum. [< Gk. *selēnitēs (lithos),* lit., moon(stone); so called because it was thought to wax and wane with the moon]

se·le·ni·um (si·lē′nē·əm) *n.* A nonmetallic element (symbol Se) of variable electrical resistance under the influence of light and having several allotropic forms. [< Gk. *selēnē* the moon]

self (self) *n. pl.* **selves 1** One's own person known or considered as the subject of his own consciousness. **2** The distinct and characteristic individuality or identity of any person or thing. **3** Personal interest or advantage. *—adj.* **1** Being uniform or of the same quality throughout. **2** Of the same kind (as in material, color, etc.,) as something else: a coat with a *self*belt. *—pron.* Myself, yourself, himself, or herself. [< OE]

self- *combining form* **1** Of oneself or itself: *self-analysis.* **2** By oneself or itself: *self-employed.* **3** In oneself or itself: *self-absorbed.* **4** To, with, for, or toward oneself: *self-satisfied.* **5** In or of oneself or itself inherently: *self-evident.*

self-ab·ne·ga·tion (self′ab′ni·gā′shən) *n.* The complete putting aside of self-interest. **—Syn.** self-sacrifice, self-denial, self-control, self-restraint.

self-a·buse (self′ə·byōōs′) *n.* **1** The disparagement of one's own person or powers. **2** MASTURBATION.

self-ad·dressed (self′ə·drest′) *adj.* Addressed to oneself.

self-as·sured (self′ə·shōōrd′) *adj.* Confident in one's own abilities. **—self′-as·sur′ance** *n.*

self-cen·tered (self′sen′tərd) *adj.* Concerned exclusively with oneself and one's own needs and desires.

self-com·mand (self′kə·mand′, -mänd′) *n.* SELF-CONTROL.

self-con·fi·dence (self′kon′fə·dəns) *n.* Confidence in oneself or in one's own unaided powers, judgment, etc. — **self′-con′fi·dent** *adj.* **—self′-con′fi·dent·ly** *adv.*

self-con·scious (self′kon′shəs) *adj.* **1** Uncomfortably conscious that one is observed by others; ill at ease. **2** Displaying such consciousness: a *self-conscious* giggle. **3** Conscious of one's existence. **—self′-con′scious·ly** *adv.* — **self′-con′scious·ness** *n.*

self-con·tained (self′kən·tānd′) *adj.* **1** Keeping one's thoughts and feelings to oneself; impassive. **2** Exercising self-control. **3** Having within oneself or itself all that is necessary for independent existence or operation.

self-con·tra·dic·tion (self′kon′trə·dik′shən) *n.* **1** The contradicting of oneself or itself. **2** A statement, proposition, etc., that contradicts itself. **—self′-con′tra·dic′to·ry** *adj.*

self-con·trol (self′kən·trōl′) *n.* Control of one's impulses, emotions, etc.

self-de·fense (self′di·fens′) *n.* Defense of oneself, one's property, one's reputation, etc. **—self′-de·fen′sive** *adj.*

self-de·ni·al (self′di·nī′əl) *n.* The restraining of one's desires, impulses, etc. **—self′-de·ny′ing** *adj.*

self-de·ter·mi·na·tion (self′di·tûr′mə·nā′shən) *n.* **1** The principle of free will; decision by oneself without extraneous force or influence. **2** Decision by the people of a country or section as to its future political status. **—self′-de·ter′mined, self′-de·ter′min·ing** *adj.*

self-de·vo·tion (self′di·vō′shən) *n.* The devoting of oneself to the service of a person or a cause.

self-ed·u·cat·ed (self′ej′ōō·kā′tid) *adj.* Educated through one's own efforts with little or no formal instruction. **—self′-ed′u·ca′tion** *n.*

self-es·teem (self′es·tēm′) *n.* **1** A good or just opinion of oneself. **2** An overestimate of oneself; conceit.

self-ev·i·dent (self′ev′ə·dənt) *adj.* Requiring no proof of its truth or validity. **—self′-ev′i·dence** *n.* **—self′-ev′i·dent·ly** *adv.*

self-ex·ist·ence (self′ig·zis′təns) *n.* Existence that is independent, without external cause. —**self′-ex·ist′ent** *adj.*

self-ex·plan·a·to·ry (self′ik·splan′ə·tôr·ē, -tō′rē) *adj.* Explaining itself; needing no explanation.

self-ex·pres·sion (self′ik·spresh′ən) *n.* Expression of one's own personality or individuality, as in art.

self-fer·til·i·za·tion (self′fûr′təl·ə·zā′shən, -ī·zā′shən) *n.* Fertilization of an organism by its own sperm or pollen.

self-gov·ern·ment (self′guv′ərn·mənt, -ər·mənt) *n.* **1** Self-control. **2** Government of a country or region by its own people. —**self′-gov′ern·ing, self′-gov′erned** *adj.*

self·heal (self′hēl′) *n.* A weedy perennial herb reputed to cure disease.

self-im·age (self′im′ij) *n.* The image or idea one has of oneself or of one's position in life.

self-im·por·tance (self′im·pôr′təns) *n.* An excessively high appraisal of one's own importance; conceit. —**self′-im·por′tant** *adj.*

self-in·duced (self′in·dyōōst′) *adj.* **1** Induced by oneself or by itself. **2** Produced by self-induction.

self-in·duc·tion (self′in·duk′shən) *n.* The production of an induced voltage in a circuit by the variation of the current in that circuit.

self-in·ter·est (self′in′trist, -in′tər·ist) *n.* Personal interest or advantage, or concern for it; selfishness. —**self′-in′ter·est·ed** *adj.*

self·ish (sel′fish) *adj.* **1** Motivated by personal needs and desires to the disregard of the welfare or wishes of others. **2** Proceeding from or characterized by undue concern for self. —**self′ish·ly** *adv.* —**self′ish·ness** *n.*

self·less (self′lis) *adj.* Having, showing, or prompted by a lack of concern for self. —**Syn.** unselfish, altruistic, self-sacrificing, self-denying.

self-load·ing (self′lō′ding) *adj.* Automatically reloading: said of a gun using the energy of recoil to eject and reload.

self-love (self′luv′) *n.* Love of oneself; the desire or tendency to seek to promote one's own well-being.

self-made (self′mād′) *adj.* **1** Having attained honor, wealth, etc., by one's own efforts. **2** Made by oneself.

self-pol·li·na·tion (self′pol′ə·nā′shən) *n.* Pollen transfer from stamens to pistils of the same flower, plant, or clone. —**self′-pol′li·na·ted** *adj.*

self-pos·ses·sion (self′pə·zesh′ən) *n.* The full possession or control of one's powers or faculties; presence of mind; self-control. —**self′-pos·sessed′** *adj.*

self-pres·er·va·tion (self′prez′ər·vā′shən) *n.* **1** The protection of oneself from injury or death. **2** The instinctive drive to protect oneself.

self-pro·nounc·ing (self′prə·noun′sing) *adj.* Having marks of pronunciation and stress applied to a word without phonetic alteration of the spelling.

self-re·li·ance (self′ri·lī′əns) *n.* Reliance on one's own abilities, resources, or judgment. —**self′-re·li′ant** *adj.* —**self′-re·li′ant·ly** *adv.*

self-re·spect (self′ri·spekt′) *n.* A proper respect for oneself, one's standing, position, etc. —**self′-re·spect′ing, self′-re·spect′ful,** *adj.* —**self′-re·spect′ful·ly** *adv.*

self-re·straint (self′ri·strānt′) *n.* Restraint imposed by the force of one's own will; self-control. —**self′-re·strained′** *adj.*

self-right·eous (self′rī′chəs) *adj.* Having or showing a high, usu. smug, opinion of one's own moral superiority. —**self′-right′eous·ly** *adv.* —**self′-right′eous·ness** *n.*

self-ris·ing (self′rī′zing) *adj.* Rising without the addition of leaven, as some flours.

self-sac·ri·fice (self′sak′rə·fīs) *n.* The subordination of one's self or one's personal welfare or wishes for others' good, for duty, etc. —**self′-sac′ri·fic′ing** *adj.*

self·same (self′sām′) *adj.* Exactly the same; identical. —**self′same′ness** *n.*

self-sat·is·fac·tion (self′sat′is·fak′shən) *n.* Satisfaction with one's own actions, characteristics, etc.; conceit. —**self′-sat′is·fied** *adj.* —**self′-sat′is·fy′ing** *adj.*

self-seek·ing (self′sē′king) *adj.* Given to the exclusive pursuit of one's own interests or gain. —*n.* Such a pursuit; selfishness. —**self′-seek′er** *n.*

self-ser·vice (self′sûr′vis) *adj.* Designating a particular type of café, restaurant, or store where patrons serve themselves.

self-serv·ing (self′sûr′ving) *adj.* Tending to justify or advance oneself, often at the expense of others.

self-start·er (self′stär′tər) *n.* **1** An engine or device with an automatic or semi-automatic starting mechanism; also, such a mechanism. **2** *Slang* One who requires no outside stimulus to start or accomplish work. —**self′-start′ing** *adj.*

self-styled (self′stīld′) *adj.* Characterized (as such) by oneself: a *self-styled* gentleman.

self-suf·fi·cient (self′sə·fish′ənt) *adj.* **1** Able to support or maintain oneself without aid or cooperation from others. **2** Having too much confidence in oneself. Also **self′-suf·fic′ing** (-sə·fī′sing). —**self′-suf·fi′cien·cy** *n.*

self-sup·port·ing (self′sə·pôrt′ing) *adj.* **1** Capable of supporting itself or its own weight. **2** Able to provide for oneself, as with money, lodging, clothing, etc.

self-will (self′wil′) *n.* Persistent adherence to one's own will or wish, esp. with disregard of the wishes of others; obstinacy. —**self′-willed′** *adj.*

self-wind·ing (self′wīn′ding) *adj.* Having an automatic winding mechanism, as some watches.

sell (sel) *v.* **sold, sell·ing** *v.t.* **1** To transfer (property) to another for a consideration; dispose of by sale. **2** To deal in; offer for sale. **3** To deliver, surrender, or betray in violation of duty or trust: often with *out*: to *sell* one's country. **4** *Informal* To cause to accept or approve something: They *sold* him on the scheme. **5** *Informal* To cause or promote the acceptance, approval, or sale of. **6** *Slang* To deceive; cheat. —*v.i.* **7** To engage in selling. **8** To be on sale or be sold. **9** To work as a salesperson. **10** To be popular with buyers, customers, etc. —**sell out 1** To get rid of (one's goods, etc.) by sale. **2** *Informal* To betray one's trust, cause, associates, etc. —*n.* **1** *Slang* A trick; joke; swindle. **2** An act or instance of selling. [< OE *sellan* give]

sell·er (sel′ər) *n.* **1** One who sells: **2** An item that is being sold, considered in reference to its sales.

sell-out (sel′out′) *n.* *Informal* **1** An act of selling out. **2** A performance for which all seats have been sold.

selt·zer (selt′sər) *n.* An artificially prepared mineral water that contains carbon dioxide. [< SELTZER]

Selt·zer (selt′sər) *n.* An effervescing mineral water. Also **Seltzer water.** [< Nieder *Selters,* a village in sw Prussia]

sel·vage (sel′vij) *n.* The edge of a woven fabric so finished that it will not ravel. Also **sel′vedge.** [< SELF + EDGE]

Sem. Seminary; Semitic.

se·man·tic (si·man′tik) *adj.* **1** Of or pertaining to meaning. **2** Of, relating to, or according to semantics. [< Gk. *sēmainein* signify]

se·man·tics (si·man′tiks) *n. pl. (construed as sing.)* **1** *Ling.* The study of the meanings of speech forms, esp. of the development and changes in meaning of words and word groups. **2** *Logic* The study of the relation between signs or symbols and what they signify. —**se·man′ti·cist** *n.*

sem·a·phore (sem′ə·fôr, -fōr) *n.* An apparatus for giving signals, as with movable arms, disks, flags, or lanterns. —*v.t.* To send by semaphore. [< Gk. *sēma* a sign + *pherein* carry] —**sem′a·phor′ic** (-fôr′ik, -for′ik) or **·i·cal** *adj.*

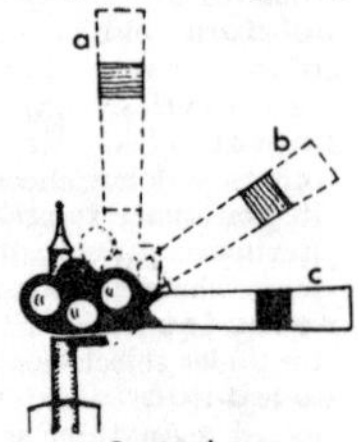

Semaphore
a. clear. b. approach. c. stop.

sem·blance (sem′bləns) *n.* **1** An outward, sometimes deceptive appearance; look. **2** A representation, likeness, or resemblance. **3** The barest trace; modicum. [< OF *sembler* seem]

se·men (sē′mən) *n.* The sperm-containing fluid of male animals. [< L *serere* sow]

se·mes·ter (si·mes′tər) *n.* Either of the two periods of approximately 18 weeks into which an academic year is divided. [< L *sex* six + *mensis* month] —**se·mes′tral** *adj.*

semi- *prefix* **1** Partly; not fully: *semicivilized.* **2** Exactly half: *semicircle.* **3** Occurring twice (in the period specified): *semiweekly.* [< L]

sem·i·an·nu·al (sem′ē·an′yōō·əl, sem′ī-) *adj.* Occurring, issued, etc., twice a year or every six months. —**sem′i·an′nu·al·ly** *adv.*

sem·i·breve (sem′ē·brēv′, sem′ī-) *n. Music* WHOLE NOTE.

sem·i·cir·cle (sem′i·sûr′kəl, sem′ē-) *n.* **1** A half-circle; an arc of 180°. **2** Anything formed or arranged in a half-circle. —**sem′i·cir′cu·lar** *adj.* —**sem′i·cir′cu·lar·ly** *adv.*

semicircular canal Any of three fluid-filled tubes in the inner ear which serve as the organ of balance. • See EAR.

sem·i·civ·i·lized (sem′ē·siv′ə·līzd, sem′ī-) *adj.* Partly civilized.

sem·i·co·lon (sem′i·kō′lən, sem′ē-) *n.* A mark (;) of punctuation, indicating a greater degree of separation than the comma but less than the period.

sem·i·con·duc·tor (sem′ē·kən·duk′tər, sem′ī-) *n.* **1** One of a class of crystalline solids, as germanium or silicon, having an electrical conductivity intermediate between conductors and insulators, used in making transistors and related devices. **2** A transistor or related device.

sem·i·con·scious (sem′ē·kon′shəs, sem′ī-) *adj.* Partly conscious; not fully aware or responsive. —**sem′i·con′scious·ly** *adv.* —**sem′i·con′scious·ness** *n.*

sem·i·de·tached (sem′ē·di·tacht′, sem′ī-) *adj.* Joined to another on one side only, as two houses built side by side with one common wall.

sem·i·fi·nal (sem′ē·fī′nəl, sem′ī-) *adj.* Next before the final, as in a series of competitions. —*n.* **1** A semifinal match. **2** A semifinal round. —**sem′i·fi′nal·ist** *n.*

sem·i·flu·id (sem′ē·floo͞′id, sem′ī-) *adj.* Fluid, but thick and viscous. —*n.* A thick, viscous fluid.

sem·i·liq·uid (sem′ē·lik′wid, sem′ī-) *adj. & n.* SEMIFLUID.

sem·i·month·ly (sem′ē·munth′lē, sem′ī-) *adj.* Taking place, issued, etc., twice a month. —*n. pl.* **·lies** A publication issued twice a month. —*adv.* Twice monthly.

sem·i·nal (sem′ə·nəl) *adj.* **1** Of, pertaining to, or containing seed or semen. **2** Like seed in having or contributing to the potential for future development. [< L *semen* semen, seed] —**sem′i·nal·ly** *adv.* —**Syn. 2** original, originative, germinal, germinative.

sem·i·nar (sem′ə·när) *n.* **1** A group of students at a college or university, meeting regularly with a professor for informal discussion of research problems. **2** A course thus conducted. **3** A room in which such a course is conducted. **4** Any informal meeting to discuss a particular topic, problem, etc. [< L *seminarium* seed plot]

sem·i·nar·y (sem′ē·ner′ē) *n. pl.* **·nar·ies** **1** A school of theology. **2** A boarding school, esp. for young women. **3** A place where anything is nurtured. [< L *seminarium* a seed plot]

sem·i·na·tion (sem′ə·nā′shən) *n.* **1** The act of sowing or spreading seeds. **2** Propagation. [< L *semen* a seed, semen]

sem·i·nif·er·ous (sem′ə·nif′ər·əs) *adj.* **1** Carrying or containing semen. **2** Seed-bearing.

Sem·i·nole (sem′ə·nōl) *n. pl.* **·noles** or **·nole** One of a Florida tribe of North American Indians of Muskhogean linguistic stock.

sem·i·of·fi·cial (sem′ē·ə·fish′əl, sem′ī-) *adj.* Having partial official authority or sanction; official to some extent. —**sem′i·of·fi′cial·ly** *adv.*

sem·i·per·me·a·ble (sem′ē·pûr′mē·ə·bəl, sem′ī-) *adj.* Selectively permeable; preventing passage of larger molecules, as membranes in osmosis.

sem·i·pre·cious (sem′ē·presh′əs, sem′ī-) *adj.* Designating a gem that is not as valuable as one classified precious.

sem·i·pri·vate (sem′ē·prī′vit, sem′ī-) *adj.* Partly private: said esp. of a hospital room with two, three, or four beds.

sem·i·pro (sem′ē·prō′, sem′ī-) *adj. & n.* SEMIPROFESSIONAL.

sem·i·pro·fes·sion·al (sem′ē·prə·fesh′ən·əl, sem′ī-) *adj.* **1** Taking part in a sport or other activity for pay but not on a full-time basis. **2** Engaged in by semiprofessional players. —*n.* A semiprofessional player, etc.

sem·i·qua·ver (sem′ē·kwā′vər, sem′ī-) *n.* SIXTEENTH NOTE.

sem·i·skilled (sem′ē·skild′, sem′ī-) *adj.* Partly skilled.

sem·i·sol·id (sem′ē·sol′id, sem′ī-) *adj.* Partly solid; highly viscous. —*n.* A semisolid substance.

Sem·ite (sem′īt, *esp. Brit.* sē′mīt) *n.* **1** A person considered as a descendant of Shem. **2** One of a people of sw Asia, now represented by the Jews and Arabs, but originally including the ancient Babylonians, Assyrians, Arameans, Phoenicians, etc.

Se·mit·ic (sə·mit′ik) *adj.* Of, pertaining to, or characteristic of the Semites or their languages. —*n.* **1** The Semitic family of languages. **2** Any of these languages, including Arabic, Hebrew, Amharic, Aramaic, etc.

Sem·i·tism (sem′ə·tiz′əm) *n.* **1** A Semitic word or idiom. **2** Semitic practices, opinions, or customs collectively. **3** Any political or economic policy favoring the Jews.

sem·i·tone (sem′ē·tōn′, sem′ī-) *n. Music* **1** The tone at an interval equal to half a tone in the standard diatonic scale. **2** Such an interval; a half step. —**sem′i·ton′ic** (-ton′·ik) *adj.*

sem·i·trop·i·cal (sem′ē·trop′i·kəl, sem′ī-) *adj.* Somewhat characteristic of the tropics.

sem·i·vow·el (sem′i·vou′əl) *n.* A vowellike sound used as a consonant, as (w), (y), and (r).

sem·i·week·ly (sem′ē·wēk′lē, sem′ī-) *adj.* Issued, occurring, done, etc., twice a week. —*n. pl.* **·lies** A publication issued twice a week. —*adv.* Twice a week.

sem·o·li·na (sem′ə·lē′nə) *n.* Coarse-ground wheat flour, used in making pasta. [< L *simila* fine flour]

sem·per fi·de·lis (sem′pər fi·dā′lis) *Latin* Always faithful: motto of the U.S. Marine Corps.

sem·per pa·ra·tus (sem′pər pə·rä′təs, -pə·rā′-) *Latin* Always prepared: motto of the U.S. Coast Guard.

sem·pi·ter·nal (sem′pə·tûr′nəl) *adj.* Enduring or existing to all eternity; everlasting. [< L *semper* always] —**sem′·pi·ter′nal·ly** *adv.* —**sem′pi·ter′ni·ty** *n.*

sen (sen) *n.* A Japanese coin or unit of currency, equal to 1/100 of a yen.

Sen., sen. senate; senator; senior.

sen·ate (sen′it) *n.* **1** *Usu. cap.* The upper branch of many national or state legislative bodies, as in the U.S. **2** A legislative body, as at a university; council. **3** A body of distinguished or venerable men often possessing legislative functions. **4** The highest governing body of the ancient Roman state. [< L *senatus,* lit., a council of old men]

sen·a·tor (sen′ə·tər) *n.* A member of a senate. —**sen′a·to′ri·al** *adj.* —**sen′a·to′ri·al·ly** *adv.* —**sen′a·tor·ship′** *n.*

send (send) *v.* **sent, send·ing** *v.t.* **1** To cause or enable to go: to *send* a messenger; to *send* one's daughter to medical school. **2** To cause to be conveyed; transmit; forward: to *send* a letter. **3** To cause to issue; emit or discharge, as heat, smoke, etc.: with *forth, out,* etc. **4** To drive by force; impel. **5** To cause to come, happen, etc.; grant: God *send* us peace. **6** To bring into a specified state or condition: The decision *sent* him into a panic. **7** To transmit, as an electric or magnetic signal. **8** *Slang* To thrill or delight. —*v.i.* **9** To dispatch an agent, messenger, or message. —**send for** To summon or order by a message or messenger. —**send packing** To dismiss abruptly or roughly. [< OE *sendan*] —**send′er** *n.*

send-off (send′ôf′, -of′) *n.* **1** The act of sending off; a start given to someone or something. **2** *Informal* A demonstration of friendship, enthusiasm, etc., toward someone beginning a new venture.

send-up (send′up′) *n. Brit. Slang* A parody; takeoff.

Sen·e·ca (sen′ə·kə) *n.* One of a tribe of North American Indians of Iroquoian stock, the largest tribe of the Five Nations, still living in New York and Ontario.

se·nes·cent (si·nes′ənt) *adj.* Growing old. [< L *senex* old] —**se·nes′cence** *n.*

sen·e·schal (sen′ə·shəl) *n.* A steward or major-domo in charge of the household of a medieval prince or noble. [< OF]

se·nile (sē′nīl, sen′īl) *adj.* Of, pertaining to, proceeding from, or characteristic of old age, esp. pertaining to or exhibiting certain mental infirmities often resulting from old age. [< L *senex* old] —**se′nile·ly** *adv.* —**se·nil·i·ty** (sə·nil′·ə·tē) *n.*

sen·ior (sēn′yər) *adj.* **1** Older in years; elder; after personal names (usu. abbreviated *Sr.*), to denote the elder of two related persons of the same name, esp. a father and his son. 2 Longer in service or superior in rank or dignity. 3 Of or pertaining to a senior or seniors. —*n.* 1 One older in years, longer in office, or more advanced in rank or dignity than another. 2 Any elderly person. 3 A member of a graduating class. [< L *senior* older]

senior citizen An elderly person, esp. one of or over the age of retirement.

sen·ior·i·ty (sēn·yôr′ə·tē, -yor′-) *n. pl.* **·ties** 1 The state or condition of being senior. 2 The status or priority one achieves by length of service (as in a business firm).

sen·na (sen′ə) *n.* 1 A cathartic obtained from certain species of cassia. 2 Any of various cassia plants. [< Ar. *sanā*]

se·ñor (sā·nyôr′) *n. pl.* **·ño·res** (-nyō′rās) *Spanish* 1 A title of courtesy equivalent to *Mr.* or *Sir.* 2 A man; gentleman.

se·ño·ra (sā·nyō′rä) *n. Spanish* 1 A title of courtesy equivalent to *Mrs.* or *Madam.* 2 A woman; lady.

se·ño·ri·ta (sā′nyō·rē′tä) *n. Spanish* 1 A title of courtesy equivalent to *Miss.* 2 An unmarried woman; young lady.

sen·sa·tion (sen·sā′shən) *n.* 1 **a** A mental event due to stimulation of a sense organ, as hearing, taste, etc. **b** The capacity to respond to such stimulation. 2 A state of mind induced by indeterminate stimuli: a *sensation* of fear. 3 A state of interest or excitement. 4 That which produces such a state of interest or excitement. [< L *sensus* sense]

sen·sa·tion·al (sen·sā′shən·əl) *adj.* 1 Of or pertaining to the senses or sensation. 2 Causing excitement; startling; thrilling. 3 Tending to shock, startle, etc., esp. by lurid or melodramatic details, techniques, etc. 4 *Informal* Excellent, great, etc. —**sen·sa′tion·al·ly** *adv.*

sen·sa·tion·al·ism (sen·sā′shən·əl·iz′əm) *n.* 1 *Philos.* The theory that all knowledge has a sensory basis. 2 The use of details, techniques, etc., that are intended to shock, or startle, as in literature, motion pictures, etc. —**sen·sa′tion·al·ist** *n.* —**sen·sa′tion·al·is′tic** *adj.*

sense (sens) *n.* 1 Any of the faculties of man and animals, specialized to receive and transmit external or internal stimuli, as sound, hunger, etc.; sight, touch, taste, hearing, and smell. 2 A perception or feeling produced by the senses. 3 A special capacity to perceive, appreciate, estimate, etc.: a *sense* of humor. 4 A somewhat vague perception or feeling; a *sense* of danger. 5 Rational perception or discrimination; awareness; realization: a *sense* of wrong. 6 Normal power of mind or understanding: The fellow has no *sense.* 7 That which is in accord with reason and good judgment: to talk *sense.* 8 Signification; meaning. 9 One of several meanings of the same word or phrase. 10 The opinion or judgment, as of a majority: the *sense* of the meeting. —*v.t.* **sensed, sens·ing** 1 To perceive; become aware of. 2 *Informal* To comprehend; understand. [< L *sensus* perception, p.p. of *sentire* feel]

sense·less (sens′lis) *adj.* 1 Unconscious; incapable of feeling or perception. 2 Devoid of good sense, knowledge, or meaning: a *senseless* remark. 3 Without apparent cause or reason: a *senseless* crime. —**sense′less·ly** *adv.* —**sense′less·ness** *n.*

sense organ A structure specialized to receive sense impressions, as the eye, nose, ear, etc.

sen·si·bil·i·ty (sen′sə·bil′ə·tē) *n. pl.* **·ties** 1 The power to receive physical sensations. 2 A special susceptibility or sensitiveness to outside influences or mental impressions, as of pleasure or pain. 3 An awareness of and ability to respond to something (as an emotion or moral value). 4 Discriminating or excessive sensitivity in taste and emotion, with especial responsiveness to pathos.

sen·si·ble (sen′sə·bəl) *adj.* 1 Possessed of good mental perception; wise. 2 Capable of physical sensation; sensitive: *sensible* to pain. 3 Perceptible through the senses: *sensible* heat. 4 Perceptible to the mind. 5 Emotionally or mentally sensitive; aware. 6 Great enough to be perceived; appreciable. [< L *sensus,* p.p. of *sentire* feel, perceive] —**sen′si·ble·ness** *n.* —**sen′si·bly** *adv.*

sen·si·tive (sen′sə·tiv) *adj.* 1 Of or pertaining to the senses or sensation. 2 Receptive and responsive to sensations. 3 Responding readily to sensations, esp. of a particular kind: a *sensitive* ear. 4 Acutely receptive or responsive to the quality or strength of attitudes, feelings, or relationships. 5 Capable of appreciating aesthetic or intellectual subtleties. 6 Easily irritated; tender: *sensitive* skin. 7 Hurt; sore. 8 Reacting excessively, as to an agent or substance: *sensitive* to insect bites. 9 Apt to take offense on slight provocation; touchy. 10 Capable of indicating very slight changes or differences; delicate: a *sensitive* barometer. 11 Readily fluctuating or tending to fluctuate: a *sensitive* stock market. [< L *sensus* sense] —**sen′si·tive·ly** *adv.* —**sen′si·tive·ness, sen′si·tiv′i·ty** *n.*

sensitive plant A tropical species of mimosa whose leaves close at a touch.

sen·si·tize (sen′sə·tīz) *v.t.* **·tized, ·tiz·ing** 1 To make sensitive, esp., in photography, to make sensitive to light, as a plate or film. 2 *Med.* To make susceptible to an allergen. —**sen′si·ti·za′tion, sen′si·tiz′er** *n.*

sen·so·ri·um (sen·sôr′ē·əm, -sō′rē-) *n. pl.* **·ri·a** (-ē·ə) The entire sensory apparatus of an organism. [< L *sensus* sense]

sen·so·ry (sen′sər·ē) *adj.* 1 Of or pertaining to the senses or sensation. 2 AFFERENT. Also **sen·so·ri·al** (sen·sôr′ē·əl, -sō′rē-).

sen·su·al (sen′shōō·əl) *adj.* 1 Of or pertaining to the senses or their gratification; fleshly; carnal. 2 Unduly indulgent to the appetites or senses. 3 Caused by or preoccupied with bodily or sexual pleasure. [< L *sensus* perception] —**sen′su·al·ly** *adv.*

sen·su·al·ism (sen′shōō·əl·iz′əm) *n.* 1 Frequent or excessive indulgence in sensual pleasures. 2 *Philos.* A system of ethics holding that sensual pleasures are the highest good. —**sen′su·al·ist** *n.* —**sen′su·al·is′tic** *adj.*

sen·su·al·i·ty (sen′shōō·al′ə·tē) *n.* 1 The state of being sensual. 2 Sensual indulgence; lewdness; lasciviousness.

sen·su·al·ize (sen′shōō·əl·īz′) *v.t.* **·ized, ·iz·ing** To make sensual. *Brit. sp.* **sen′su·al·ise′.** —**sen′su·al·i·za′tion** *n.*

sen·su·ous (sen′shōō·əs) *adj.* 1 Of, pertaining to or appealing to, or perceived or caused by the senses. 2 Keenly appreciative of or susceptible to the pleasures of sensation. —**sen′su·ous·ly** *adv.* —**sen′su·ous·ness** *n.*

sent (sent) *p.t. & p.p.* of SEND.

sen·tence (sen′təns) *n.* 1 A determination; opinion, esp. one expressed formally. 2 A final judgment, esp. one pronounced by a court. 3 The penalty pronounced upon a convicted person. 4 *Gram.* A word or group of words expressing a complete thought in the form of a declaration, a question, a command, a wish or an exclamation, usu. beginning with a capital letter and concluding with proper end punctuation. —*v.t.* **·tenced, ·tenc·ing** To pass sentence upon; condemn to punishment. [< L *sententia* opinion < *sentire* feel, be of opinion] —**sen′tenc·er** *n.* —**sen·ten·tial** (sen·ten′shəl) *adj.*

sen·ten·tious (sen·ten′shəs) *adj.* 1 Saying much in few words; terse; pithy. 2 Habitually using or full of aphoristic language. 3 Habitually using or full of moralistic language. [< L *sententia* opinion] —**sen·ten′tious·ly** *adv.* —**sen·ten′tious·ness** *n.*

sen·ti·ent (sen′shē·ənt, -shənt) *adj.* Possessing the powers of feeling or perception. [< L *sentire* feel] —**sen′ti·ence** *n.* —**sen′ti·ent·ly** *adv.*

sen·ti·ment (sen′tə·mənt) *n.* 1 Noble, tender, or refined feeling; delicate sensibility, esp. as expressed in a work of art. 2 A complex of opinions and feelings used as a basis for judgment or action. 3 A mental attitude, judgment, or thought often conditioned by feeling more than reason. 4 SENTIMENTALITY. 5 The meaning of something said, as distinguished from its expression. 6 A thought or wish phrased in conventional language, as a toast. [< L *sentire* feel]

sen·ti·men·tal (sen′tə·men′təl) *adj.* 1 Of, pertaining to, caused by, having, or showing sentiment. 2 Experiencing, displaying, or given to sentiment in an extravagant or maudlin manner. —**sen′ti·men′tal·ism, sen′ti·men′tal·ist** *n.* —**sen′ti·men′tal·ly** *adv.*

sen·ti·men·tal·i·ty (sen′tə·men·tal′ə·tē) *n. pl.* **·ties.** 1 The state or quality of being overly sentimental, esp. in a superficial or maudlin way. 2 An expression of this.

sen·ti·men·tal·ize (sen′tə·men′təl·īz) *v.* **·ized, ·iz·ing** *v.t.* 1 To regard or treat with sentiment. —*v.i.* 2 To behave sentimentally.

sen·ti·nel (sen′tə·nəl) *n.* A guard, esp. a sentry. —*v.t.* **·neled** or **·nelled, ·nel·ing** or **·nel·ling** 1 To watch over as a sentinel. **2** To protect or furnish with sentinels. **3** To station or appoint as a sentinel. [< LL *sentinare* avoid danger < *sentire* perceive]

sen·try (sen′trē) *n. pl.* **·tries 1** A guard, esp. a soldier placed on guard to see that only authorized persons pass his post and to give warning of approaching danger. **2** The guard kept by a sentry. [? var. of SENTINEL]

Sep. September; Septuagint.

sep. sepal; separate; separated.

se·pal (sē′pəl) *n. Bot.* Any of the individual leaves of a calyx. [< NL *sepa* covering + *petalum* a petal] **—sep·a·line** (sep′ə·lin, -līn), **sep′a·lous, se′paled, se′palled** *adj.*

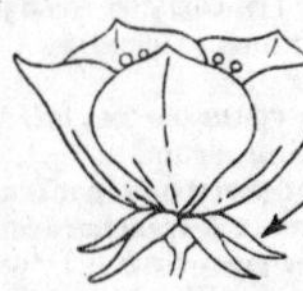
Sepals of flower

sep·a·ra·ble (sep′ər·ə·bəl, sep′rə-) *adj.* Capable of being separated or divided. **—sep′a·ra·bil′i·ty, sep′a·ra·ble·ness** *n.* **—sep′a·ra·bly** *adv.*

sep·a·rate (sep′ə·rāt) *v.* **·rat·ed, ·rat·ing** *v.t.* **1** To set apart; sever; disjoin. **2** To keep apart; divide: The Hudson River *separates* New York from New Jersey. **3** To divide into components, parts, etc. **4** To isolate or obtain from a compound, mixture, etc.: to *separate* the wheat from the chaff. **5** To consider separately; distinguish between. **6** *Law* To part by separation. *—v.i.* **7** To become divided or disconnected; draw apart. **8** To part company; sever an association. **9** To cease living together as man and wife. **10** To break up into component parts, as a mixture. *—adj.* (sep′ər·it, sep′rit) **1** Existing or considered apart from others; distinct; individual. **2** Detached; disunited. **3** Existing independently; not related. *—n.pl.* Garments to be worn in various combinations, as skirts and blouses. [< L *se-* apart + *parare* prepare] **—sep′a·rate·ly** *adv.* **—sep′a·rate·ness, sep′a·ra′tor** *n.* **—sep′a·ra′tive** (-rā′tiv, -ə·rə·tiv) *adj.*

sep·a·ra·tion (sep′ə·rā′shən) *n.* **1** The act or process of separating. **2** The state of being separated. **3** A gap or dividing line. **4** *Law* Relinquishment of cohabitation between husband and wife by mutual consent.

sep·a·ra·tist (sep′ər·ə·tist, sep′rə-) *n.* One who advocates or upholds separation, esp. political, racial, or religious separation. Also **sep′a·ra′tion·ist. —sep′a·ra·tism** *n.*

Sep·a·ra·tist (sep′ər·ə·tist, sep′rə-) *n. Can.* One who believes in or supports the withdrawal of a province, esp. Quebec, from Confederation.

Se·phar·dim (si·fär′dim) *n. pl.* The Spanish and Portuguese Jews or their descendants. Also **Se·phar′a·dim** (-ə·dim). [< Hebrew *sephārādhīm* < *Sephāradh, Obad.* 1:20, a country identified with Spain] **—Se·phar′dic** *adj.*

se·pi·a (sē′pē·ə) *n.* **1** A reddish brown pigment prepared from the ink of certain cuttlefish. **2** The color of this pigment. **3** A picture done in this color. *—adj.* Executed in or colored like sepia. [< Gk. *sēpia* cuttlefish]

se·poy (sē′poi) *n.* Formerly, a native Indian soldier in the British or other European army. [< Pers. *sipāh* army]

sep·sis (sep′sis) *n.* The presence of pathogenic microorganisms or their toxins in the blood or tissues. [< Gk. *sēpein* make putrid]

sep·ta (sep′tə) *n. pl.* of SEPTUM.

Sep·tem·ber (sep·tem′bər) *n.* The ninth month of the year, containing 30 days. [< L *septem* seven]

sep·te·nar·y (sep′tə·ner′ē) *adj.* Consisting of, pertaining to, or being seven. *—n. pl.* **·nar·ies** A group of seven things of any kind. [< L *septeni* seven each]

sep·ten·ni·al (sep·ten′ē·əl) *adj.* **1** Recurring every seven years. **2** Continuing or capable of lasting seven years. **—sep·ten′ni·al·ly** *adv.*

sep·tet (sep·tet′) *n.* **1** A group or set of seven, esp. seven musical performers. **2** *Music* A composition for such a group. Also **sep·tette′**. [< L *septem* seven]

sep·tic (sep′tik) *adj.* **1** Of, pertaining to, or caused by sepsis. **2** Productive of putrefaction; putrid. Also **sep′ti·cal.**

sep·ti·ce·mi·a (sep′tə·sē′mē·ə) *n.* BLOOD POISONING. Also **sep′ti·cae′mi·a.** [< Gk. *sēptikos* putrefactive + *haima* blood] **—sep′ti·ce′mic** (-sē′mik) *adj.*

septic tank A tank in which sewage is held until decomposed by anaerobic bacteria.

sep·til·lion (sep·til′yən) *n. & adj.* See NUMBER. [< L *sept(em)* + F *(m)illion* a million] **—sep·til′lionth** *adj., n.*

sep·tu·a·ge·nar·i·an (sep′tyōō·ə·jə·nâr′ē·ən, sep′tə·wäj′ə-) *n.* A person 70 years old, or between 70 and 80. [< L *septuaginta* seventy]

Sep·tu·a·ges·i·ma (sep′tə·wə·jes′ə·mə, -jā′zə-) *n.* The third Sunday before Lent. Also **Septuagesima Sunday.** [< L, seventieth]

Sep·tu·a·gint (sep′tyōō·ə·jint′, sep′tə·wə-) *n.* An ancient Greek version of the Old Testament, made between 280 and 130 B.C. [< L *septuaginta* seventy < a tradition that it was produced in 70 days by a group of 72 scholars]

sep·tum (sep′təm) *n. pl.* **·ta** (-tə) A partition between two masses of tissue or two cavities: the nasal *septum.* [< L *sepes* a hedge] **—sep′tal** *adj.*

sep·tu·ple (sep′tyōō·pəl, sep·tyōō′-) *adj.* **1** Consisting of seven; sevenfold. **2** Multiplied by seven; seven times repeated. *—v.t. & v.i.* **·pled, ·pling** To multiply by seven. *—n.* A number or sum seven times as great as another. [< L *septem* seven]

sep·ul·cher (sep′əl·kər) *n.* **1** A burial place; tomb; vault. **2** A receptacle for relics, esp. in an altar slab. *—v.t.* **·chered** or **·chred, ·cher·ing** or **·chring** To place in a grave; entomb; bury. Also **sep′ul·chre** (-kər). [< L *sepulcrum*]

se·pul·chral (si·pul′krəl) *adj.* **1** Of a sepulcher. **2** Dismal in color or aspect. **3** Low or melancholy in sound. **—se·pul′chral·ly** *adv.*

seq. sequel.

seq., seqq. the following (L *sequens, sequentia*).

se·quel (sē′kwəl) *n.* **1** Something which follows; a continuation; development. **2** A narrative which, though entire in itself, develops from a preceding one. **3** A consequence; result. [< L *sequi* follow]

se·quence (sē′kwəns) *n.* **1** The process or fact of following in space, time, or thought; succession or order. **2** Order of succession; arrangement. **3** A number of things following one another, considered collectively; a series. **4** An effect or consequence. **5** A section of motion-picture film presenting a single episode, without time lapses or interruptions. [< L *sequi* follow]

se·quent (sē′kwənt) *n.* That which follows; a consequence; result. *—adj.* **1** Following in the order of time; succeeding. **2** Consequent; resultant. [< L *sequi* follow]

se·quen·tial (si·kwen′shəl) *adj.* **1** Characterized by or forming a sequence, as of parts. **2** SEQUENT. **—se·quen·ti·al·i·ty** (si·kwen′shē·al′ə·tē) *n.* **—se·quen′tial·ly** *adv.* **—Syn. 1** consecutive, orderly, serial.

se·ques·ter (si·kwes′tər) *v.t.* **1** To place apart; separate. **2** To seclude; withdraw: often used reflexively. **3** *Law* To take (property) into custody until a controversy, claim, etc., is settled. **4** In international law, to confiscate and control (enemy property) by preemption. [< LL *sequestrare* remove, lay aside] **—se·ques′tered** *adj.*

se·ques·trate (si·kwes′trāt) *v.t.* **·trat·ed, ·trat·ing** SEQUESTER. **—se·ques·tra·tor** (sē′kwes·trā′tər, si·kwes′trā·tər) *n.*

se·quin (sē′kwin) *n.* A spangle or small coinlike ornament sewn on clothing. *—v.t.* **se·quined** or **se·quinned, se·quin·ing** or **se·quin·ning** To decorate with sequins. [< Ar. *sikka* a coining-die]

se·quoi·a (si·kwoi′ə) *n.* Either of two species of gigantic coniferous evergreen trees of the western U.S. [< *Sikwayi,* 1770?–1843, American Indian who invented the Cherokee alphabet]

Sequoia

ser. serial; series; sermon.

se·ra (sir′ə) A *pl.* of SERUM.

se·ra·glio (si·ral′yō, -räl′-) *n. pl.* **·glios 1** That part of a sultan's palace where his harem lives. **2** The palace of a sultan. Also **se·rail** (se·rāl′). [< Ital. *serraglio* an enclosure]

se·ra·pe (se·rä′pē) *n.* A shawl or blanketlike outer garment worn in Latin America. [Sp.]

Serape

ser·aph (ser′əf) *n. pl.* **ser·aphs** or **ser·a·phim** (ser′ə·fim) An angel of the highest order, usu. represented as having six wings. [< Heb. *serāphīm,* pl.] **—se·raph·ic** (si·raf′ik) *adj.* **—se·raph′i·cal·ly** *adv.*

Ser·bo-Cro·a·tian (sûr′bō·krō·ā′shən) *n.* **1** The South Slavic language of Yugoslavia. **2** Any person whose native tongue is Serbo-Croatian. *—adj.* Of this language or people.

sere (sir) *adj.* Withered; dried up.

ser·e·nade (ser′ə·nād′) *n.* An evening piece, usu. the song of a lover beneath his lady's window. *—v.t. & v.i.* **·nad·ed, ·nad·ing** To entertain with a serenade. [< L *serenus* clear, serene] **—ser′e·nad′er** *n.*

ser·en·dip·i·ty (ser′ən·dip′ə·tē) *n.* The faculty of making fortunate discoveries by accident. [Coined by Horace Walpole (1754) after fairy tale characters] **—ser′en·dip′i·tous** *adj.*

se·rene (si·rēn′) *adj.* **1** Clear, bright, and fair; cloudless; untroubled. **2** Tranquil; calm; peaceful. **3** *Usu. cap.* Of exalted rank: used chiefly in royal titles: His *Serene* Highness. [< L *serenus*] **—se·rene′ly** *adv.* **—se·ren·i·ty** (si·ren′ə·tē), **se·rene′ness** *n.* **—Syn. 2** composed, collected, placid.

serf (sûrf) *n.* **1** In feudal times, a person attached to the estate on which he lived. **2** Any person in servile subjection. [< L *servus* a slave] **—serf′dom, serf′age, serf′hood** *n.*

serge (sûrj) *n.* **1** A strong twilled woolen fabric woven with a diagonal rib on both sides. **2** A twilled silk or synthetic lining fabric. [< L *serica (lana)* (wool) of the Seres, an eastern Asian people]

ser·geant (sär′jənt) *n.* **1** See GRADE. **2** A police officer of rank next below a captain or lieutenant. **3** SERGEANT AT ARMS. [< L *servire* serve] **—ser′gean·cy, ser′geant·cy, ser′geant·ship** *n.*

sergeant at arms *pl.* **sergeants at arms** An officer in a legislative body, court, etc. who enforces order.

sergeant major *pl.* **sergeants major** See GRADE.

se·ri·al (sir′ē·əl) *adj.* **1** Of, like, or arranged in a series. **2** Published or presented in a series at regular intervals. **3** Of a serial or serials. **4** Of, pertaining to, or being atonal music consisting of a fixed series of tones based on the twelve-tone chromatic scale. *—n.* **1** A novel or other story regularly presented in successive installments, as in a magazine, on radio or television, or in motion pictures. **2** A periodical. **—se′ri·al·ly** *adv.*

se·ri·al·ism (sir′ē·əl·izm) *n.* Serial music. **—se′ri·al·ist** *n.*

se·ri·al·ize (sir′ē·əl·īz′) *v.t.* **·ized, ·iz·ing** To present in serial form. **—se′ri·al·i·za′tion** *n.*

serial number An identifying number assigned to a person, object, item of merchandise, etc.

se·ri·a·tim (sir′ē·ā′tim, ser′ē-) *adv.* One after another; in connected order; serially. [< L *series* series]

se·ries (sir′ēz) *n. pl.* **se·ries** **1** An arrangement or connected succession of related things placed in space or happening in time one after the other: a *series* of games; a *series* of lakes. **2** *Math.* The indicated sum of any finite set of terms or of an ordered infinite set of terms. **3** *Chem.* A group of related compounds or elements showing an orderly succession of changes in composition or structure. **4** *Electr.* An arrangement of electric devices in which the current flows through each in order. [L < *serere* join]

ser·if (ser′if) *n.* *Printing* A light line or stroke crossing or projecting from the end of a main line or stroke in a letter. [< L *scribere* write]

se·ri·o·com·ic (sir′ē·ō·kom′ik) *adj.* Mingling the comic with the serious. Also **se′ri·o·com′i·cal.** **—se′ri·o·com′i·cal·ly** *adv.*

se·ri·ous (sir′ē·əs) *adj.* **1** Grave and earnest in quality, feeling, or disposition; thoughtful; sober. **2** Being or done in earnest; not jesting or joking. **3** Involving much work, thought, difficulty, etc.: a *serious* problem. **4** Of grave importance; weighty. **5** Attended with considerable danger or loss: a *serious* accident. [< L *serius*] **—se′ri·ous·ly** *adv.* **—se′ri·ous·ness** *n.* **—Syn. 1** sedate, staid, solemn, grim. **3** complex, complicated, involved, hard, troublesome.

ser·jeant (sär′jənt) *n. Brit.* SERGEANT.

ser·mon (sûr′mən) *n.* **1** A discourse, usu. based on a passage or text of the Bible, delivered as part of a church service. **2** Any serious talk or exhortation, as on duty, morals, etc. [< L *sermo* talk] **—ser·mon·ic** (sər·mon′ik) *adj.*

ser·mon·ize (sûr′mən·īz) *v.t. & v.i.* **·ized, ·iz·ing** To deliver sermons (to). **—ser′mon·iz′er** *n.*

Sermon on the Mount The discourse of Jesus found recorded in *Matt.* 5–7.

se·rol·o·gy (si·rol′ə·jē) *n.* The science of serums and their actions. [< SER(UM) + -LOGY] **—se·ro·log·i·cal** (sir′ə·loj′i·kəl) *adj.*

se·rous (sir′əs) *adj.* Pertaining to, producing, or resembling serum.

ser·pent (sûr′pənt) *n.* **1** A snake, esp. a poisonous or large one. **2** A treacherous person. [< L *serpere* to creep]

ser·pen·tine (sûr′pən·tīn, -tēn) *adj.* **1** Of or like a serpent. **2** Winding; zigzag. **3** Subtle; cunning. *—n.* A massive or fibrous, often mottled green or yellow, magnesium silicate.

ser·rate (ser′āt, -it) *adj.* Having sawlike teeth, as the margins of certain leaves. Also **ser′rat·ed.** [< L *serra* a saw] • See LEAF.

ser·ra·tion (se·rā′shən) *n.* **1** The state of being edged as with saw teeth. **2** A single projection of a serrate edge, or a series of such projections. Also **ser·ra·ture** (ser′ə·chər). [< L *serra* a saw]

ser·ried (ser′ēd) *adj.* Compacted in rows or ranks, as soldiers in company formation. [< LL *serrare* to lock]

se·rum (sir′əm) *n. pl.* **se·rums** or **se·ra** (sir′ə) **1** The fluid constituent of blood. **2** The serum of the blood of an animal which has developed immunity to a specific pathogen. **3** WHEY. **4** Any watery plant or animal secretion. [L, whey]

ser·vant (sûr′vənt) *n.* **1** A person employed to assist in domestic matters, sometimes living within the employer's house. **2** A government worker. [< OF *servir* to serve]

serve (sûrv) *v.* **served, serv·ing** *v.t.* **1** To work for as a servant. **2** To be of service to; wait on. **3** To promote the interests of; aid; help: to *serve* one's country. **4** To obey and give homage to: to *serve* God. **5** To satisfy the requirements of; suffice for. **6** To perform the duties connected with, as a public office. **7** To go through (a period of enlistment, term of punishment, etc.). **8** To furnish or provide, as with a regular supply. **9** To offer or bring food or drink to (a guest, etc.); wait on at table. **10** To bring and place on the table or distribute among guests, as food or drink. **11** To operate or handle; tend: to *serve* a cannon. **12** To copulate with: said of male animals. **13** In tennis, etc., to put (the ball) in play by hitting it to one's opponent. **14** *Law* **a** To deliver (a summons or writ) to a person. **b** To deliver a summons or writ to. **15** *Naut.* To wrap (a rope, stay, etc.), as with wire, cordage, etc., so as to strengthen or protect. *—v.i.* **16** To be a servant. **17** To perform the duties of any employment, office, etc. **18** To go through a term of service, as in the army or navy. **19** To offer or give food or drink, as to guests. **20** To wait on customers. **21** To be suitable or usable, as for a purpose; perform a function. **22** To be favorable, as weather. **23** In tennis, etc., to put the ball in play. *—n.* In tennis, etc.: **a** The delivering of the ball by striking it toward an opponent. **b** The turn of one who serves. [< L *servus* a slave]

serv·er (sûr′vər) *n.* **1** One who serves, as an attendant aiding a priest at low mass. **2** That which is used in serving, as a tray.

ser·vice (sûr′vis) *n.* **1** The act or occupation of serving. **2** The manner in which one serves or is served. **3** A division of employment, esp. of public or governmental employment: the diplomatic *service.* **4** Any branch of the armed forces. **5** A facility for meeting some public need: electric *service.* **6** Installation, maintenance, and repair provided for the buyer of something. **7** Assistance; aid; benefit: to be of *service.* **8** *Often pl.* A useful result or product of labor which is not a tangible commodity: a doctor's *services.* **9** *Often pl.* A public exercise of worship. **10** A religious or civil ritual: the marriage *service.* **11** The music for a liturgical office or rite. **12** A set of articles for a particular purpose: a tea *service.* **13** *Naut.* The protective wire, cordage, etc., wrapped around a rope. **14** *Law* The legal communication of a writ, process, or summons to a designated person. **15** In animal husbandry, the copulation of a female. —*adj.* **1** Pertaining to or for service. **2** Of, for, or used by servants or tradespeople: a *service* entrance. **3** Of, pertaining to, or belonging to a military service: a *service* flag. **4** For rough or everyday usage. —*v.t.* **·viced, ·vic·ing** **1** To maintain or repair: to *service* a car. **2** To supply service to. **3** SERVE (def. 12). [< L *servus* a slave]

ser·vice·a·ble (sûr′vis·ə·bəl) *adj.* **1** That can serve a useful purpose; beneficial. **2** Capable of rendering long service; durable. —**ser′vice·a·ble·ness, ser′vice·a·bil′i·ty** *n.* —**ser′vice·a·bly** *adv.* —**Syn. 1** practical, practicable, utilitarian, helpful.

ser·vice·man (sûr′vis·man′) *n. pl.* **·men** (-men′) **1** A member of one of the armed forces. **2** A man who performs services of maintenance, supply, repair, etc.: also **service man.**

service station 1 A place for supplying motor vehicles with gasoline, oil, etc., and often for doing auto maintenance and repair work. **2** A place for adjusting, repairing, or supplying parts for electrical and mechanical appliances.

ser·vi·ette (sûr′vē·et′, -vyet′) *n.* A table napkin. [< MF *servir* serve]

ser·vile (sûr′vīl, -vil) *adj.* **1** Having the spirit of a slave; slavish; abject. **2** Of, pertaining to, or appropriate for slaves or servants: *servile* employment. [< L *servus* a slave] —**ser′vile·ly** *adv.* —**ser·vil′i·ty, ser′vile·ness** *n.* —**Syn. 1** obsequious, fawning, groveling, cowering, submissive, cringing.

serv·ing (sûr′ving) *n.* **1** A portion of food for one person. **2** The act of one who or that which serves. —*adj.* Used for dealing out food.

ser·vi·tor (sûr′və·tər) *n.* One who waits upon and serves another; an attendant; follower; servant.

ser·vi·tude (sûr′və·tyōōd) *n.* **1** The condition of a slave; slavery; bondage. **2** Enforced service as a punishment for crime: penal *servitude.* [< L *servus* a slave]

ser·vo·mech·a·nism (sûr′vō·mek′ə·niz′əm) *n.* Any of various devices using feedback in which a small input is amplified and used to control a machine, operation, process, etc. [< L *servus* slave + MECHANISM]

ses·a·me (ses′ə·mē) *n.* An East Indian plant bearing edible, oily seeds **(sesame seed)** that yield an oil **(sesame oil)** used in cooking. [< Gk. *sēsamon*]

ses·qui·cen·ten·ni·al (ses′kwi·sen·ten′ē·əl) *adj.* Of or pertaining to a century and a half. —*n.* A 150th anniversary, or its celebration. [< L *sesqui-* one half more + CENTENNIAL]

ses·sile (ses′īl, -əl) *adj.* **1** *Bot.* Attached without a stalk, as a leaf. **2** *Zool. & Anat.* Attached at the base; sedentary. [< L *sessilis* sitting down, stunted] —**ses·sil′i·ty** *n.*

ses·sion (sesh′ən) *n.* **1** The sitting together of a legislative assembly, court, etc., for the transaction of business. **2** A single meeting or series of meetings of an assembly, court, etc. **3** In some schools, a term. **4** Any period of some specified activity: a *session* with the boss. [< L *sessus,* p.p. of *sedere* sit] —**ses′sion·al** *adj.* —**ses′sion·al·ly** *adv.*

ses·tet (ses·tet′) *n.* **1** The last six lines of a sonnet; also, any six-line stanza. **2** *Music* SEXTET. [< L *sextus* sixth]

set[1] (set) *v.* **set, set·ting** *v.t.* **1** To put in a certain place or position; place. **2** To put into a fixed, firm, or immovable position, condition, or state: to *set* brick; to *set* one's jaw. **3** To bring to a specified condition or state: *Set* your mind at ease; He *set* the barn afire; She has *set* her heart on being a doctor. **4** To restore to proper position for healing, as a broken bone. **5** To place in readiness for use: to *set* a trap. **6** To adjust according to a standard: to *set* a clock. **7** To adjust (an instrument, dial, etc.) to a particular calibration or position. **8** To place knives, forks, etc., on (a table) for a meal. **9** To bend the teeth of (a saw) to either side alternately. **10** To appoint or establish; prescribe: to *set* boundaries, regulations, fashions, etc. **11** To fix or establish a time for: We *set* our departure for noon. **12** To assign for performance, completion, etc.; to *set* a task. **13** To assign to some specific duty or function; appoint; station: to *set* a guard. **14** To cause to sit. **15** To present or perform so as to be copied or emulated: to *set* the pace. **16** To give a specified direction to: He *set* his course for the Azores. **17** To put in place so as to catch the wind: to *set* the jib. **18** To place in a mounting or frame, as a gem. **19** To stud or adorn with gems: to *set* a crown with rubies. **20** To place (a hen) on eggs to hatch them. **21** To place (eggs) under a fowl or in an incubator for hatching. **22** To place (a price or value): with *by* or *on:* to *set* a price on an outlaw's head. **23** To arrange (hair), as with curlers, lotions, etc. **24** *Printing* **a** To arrange (type) for printing; compose. **b** To put into type, as a sentence, manuscript, etc. **25** *Music* To compose music for (words) or write words for (existing music). **26** To describe (a scene) as taking place: to *set* the scene in Monaco. **27** In the theater, to arrange (a stage) so as to depict a scene. **28** In some games, as bridge, to defeat. —*v.i.* **29** To go or pass below the horizon, as the sun. **30** To wane; decline. **31** To sit on eggs, as fowl. **32** To become firm; solidify; congeal. **33** To become fast, as a dye. **34** To begin to move, as on a journey: with *forth, out, off,* etc. **35** To begin: *Set* to work. **36** To have a specified direction; tend. **37** To hang or fit, as clothes. **38** To mend, as a broken bone. **39** *Regional* To sit. **40** *Bot.* To begin development or growth, as a rudimentary fruit. —**set against 1** To balance; compare. **2** To make unfriendly to; prejudice against. —**set off 1** To put apart by itself. **2** To serve as a contrast or foil for; enhance. **3** To make begin; set in motion. **4** To cause to explode. —**set out 1** To display; exhibit. **2** To lay out or plan. **3** To begin a journey. **4** To begin any enterprise. **5** To plant. —**set to 1** To start; begin. **2** To start fighting. —**set up 1** To place in an upright or high position. **2** To raise. **3** To place in power, authority, etc. **4 a** To construct or build. **b** To put together; assemble. **c** To found; establish. **5** To provide with the means to start a new business. **6** To cause to be heard: to *set up* a cry. **7** To propose or put forward (a theory, etc.). **8** To cause. **9** To work out a plan for. **10** To claim to be. **11 a** To pay for the drinks, etc., of; treat. **b** To pay for (drinks, etc.). **12** To encourage; exhilarate. —**set upon** To attack; assail. —*adj.* **1** Established by authority or agreement; prescribed; appointed: a *set* time or method. **2** Customary; conventional: a *set* phrase. **3** Deliberately and systematically conceived; formal: a *set* speech. **4** Fixed and motionless; rigid. **5** Firm in consistency. **6** Fixed in opinion or disposition; obstinate. **7** Formed; built; made: deep-*set* eyes. **8** Ready; prepared: to get *set.* —*n.* **1** The act or condition of setting. **2** Permanent change of form, as by bending, pressure, strain, etc. **3** The arrangement, tilt, or hang of a garment, hat, sail, etc. **4** Carriage or bearing: the *set* of his shoulders. **5** The sinking of a heavenly body below the horizon. **6** The direction of a current or wind. **7** A young plant ready for setting out. **8** Inclination of the mind; bent. **9** *Psychol.* A temporary condition assumed by an organism preparing for a particular response or activity. **10** An arrangement of the hair, as by curling. **11** In tennis, a group of games completed when one side wins six games, or, if tied at five games, wins either two more games consecutively or wins a tie breaker. [< OE *settan* cause to sit]

set[2] (set) *n.* **1** A number of persons regarded as associated through status, common interests, etc.: a new *set* of customers. **2** A social group having some exclusive character; coterie; clique: the fast *set.* **3** A number of things belonging together or customarily used together: a *set* of instruments. **4** A group of books or periodicals issued together or related by common authorship, subject, etc. **5** In jazz performances, the music played during one period of time without an intermission; also, the period of time. **6** In the theatre, motion pictures, etc., the complete assembly of properties, structures, etc., required in a scene. **7** Radio or television receiving equipment assembled for use. **8** *Math.* Any collection of elements, objects, or numbers. [< L *secta* a sect]

se·ta (sē′tə) *n. pl.* **·tae** (-tē) *Biol.* A bristle or bristlelike process. [< L] —**se·ta·ceous** (si·tā′shəs), **se′tose** *adj.*

set·back (set′bak′) *n.* **1** A misfortune or reversal, as in progress. **2** An indentation or steplike arrangement of the upper levels of a tall building.

Seth (seth) In the Bible, the third son of Adam.

set·off (set′ôf′, -of′) *n.* **1** Something that offsets, balances, or compensates for something else. **2** Something that contrasts with or sets off something else. **3** A counterclaim or the discharge of a debt by a counterclaim. **4** *Archit.* A ledge; offset.

set piece **1** Something, as a passage in literature, music, etc., aimed at creating a brilliant effect. **2** A fireworks display. **3** A piece of scenery for the stage.

set·screw (set′skrōō′) *n.* **1** A screw so made that it can be screwed tightly against or into another surface to prevent movement. **2** A screw for regulating the tension of a spring or the opening of a valve.

set·tee (se·tē′) *n.* **1** A long wooden seat with a high back. **2** A sofa suitable for two or three people. [?< SETTLE]

set·ter (set′ər) *n.* **1** One who or that which sets. **2** One of a breed of medium-sized, silky-coated dogs trained to indicate the location of game birds while standing rigid.

set·ting (set′ing) *n.* **1** The position, degree, etc., at which something is set. **2** A frame or mounting, as for a jewel. **3** Physical environment or surroundings. **4** The scene, time, background, etc., as of a novel or play. **5** A number of eggs placed together for hatching. **6** The music composed for a poem, set of words, etc. **7** The tableware set out for one person.

set·tle (set′l) *v.* **·tled, ·tling** *v.t.* **1** To put in order; set to rights; to *settle* affairs. **2** To establish or fix permanently or as if permanently: He *settled* himself on the couch. **3** To calm; quiet: to *settle* one's nerves. **4** To cause (sediment or dregs) to sink to the bottom. **5** To make firm or compact: to *settle* dust or ashes. **6** To make clear or transparent, as by causing sediment or dregs to sink. **7** To make quiet or orderly: One blow *settled* him. **8** To decide or determine finally, as an argument, legal case, etc. **9** To pay, as a debt; satisfy, as a claim. **10** To establish residents or residence in (a country, town, etc.). **11** To establish as residents. **12** To establish in a permanent occupation, home, etc. **13** *Law* To make over or assign (property) by legal act: with *on* or *upon.* —*v.i.* **14** To come to rest. **15** To sink gradually; subside. **16** To become clear by the sinking of sediment. **17** To become more firm by sinking. **18** To become established or located: The pain *settled* in his arm. **19** To establish one's abode or home. **20** To come to a decision; determine; resolve: with *on, upon,* or *with.* **21** To pay a bill, etc. —**settle down** **1** To start living a regular, orderly life, esp. after a period of wandering or irresponsibility. **2** To become quiet or orderly. —*n.* A long, wooden, high-backed bench, usu. with arms and sometimes having a chest from seat to floor. [< OE *setl* a seat]

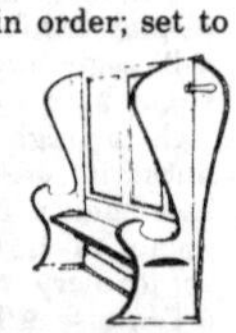

Settle

set·tle·ment (set′l·mənt) *n.* **1** The act of settling or the condition of being settled. **2** An area newly colonized. **3** A small, usu. remote village. **4** *Law* **a** The act of assigning property, money, etc., to someone. **b** That which is thus assigned. **5** An agreement or adjustment, as of differences. **6** An urban welfare institution that provides various educational or recreational services to a community or neighborhood: also **settlement house.**

set·tler (set′lər) *n.* **1** One who establishes himself in a colony or new country. **2** One who settles or decides.

set·tlings (set′lingz) *n.pl.* Dregs; sediment.

set-to (set′tōō′) *n.* A bout at fighting, arguing, etc.

set·up (set′up′) *n.* **1** A system or plan, as of a business operation, etc. **2** The arrangement or assembly of a machine, piece of equipment, etc. **3** The elements or circumstances of a situation or plan. **4** Carriage of the body; posture. **5** Ice, soda water, etc., provided for those who furnish their own liquor. **6** A table setting. **7** *Informal* **a** A contest or match arranged so as to result in an easy victory. **b** Anything easy to accomplish.

sev·en (sev′ən) *n.* **1** The sum of six plus one; 7; VII. **2** A set or group of seven members. [< OE *seofon*] —**sev′en** *adj., pron.*

seven deadly sins Pride, lust, envy, anger, covetousness, gluttony, and sloth.

sev·en·fold (sev′ən·fōld′) *adj.* **1** Seven times as many or as great. **2** Made up of seven; septuple. **3** Folded seven times. —*adv.* In sevenfold manner or degree.

seven seas All the oceans of the world.

sev·en·teen (sev′ən·tēn′) *n.* **1** The sum of 16 plus 1; 17; XVII. **2** A set or group of 17 members. —**sev′en·teen′** *adj., pron.*

sev·en·teenth (sev′ən·tēnth′) *adj. & adv.* Next in order after the 16th. —*n.* **1** The element of an ordered set that corresponds to the number 17. **2** One of seventeen equal parts.

sev·enth (sev′ənth) *adj. & adv.* Next in order after the sixth. —*n.* **1** The element of an ordered set that corresponds to the number seven. **2** One of seven equal parts. **3** *Music* The interval between any tone and the seventh tone above or below in the diatonic scale. —*adv.* In the seventh order, place, or rank: also, in formal discourse, **sev′enth·ly.**

seventh heaven The highest condition of happiness. [< the highest heaven according to certain ancient cosmologies]

sev·en·ti·eth (sev′ən·tē·ith) *adj.* & *adv.* Tenth in order after the 60th. —*n.* **1** The element of an ordered set that corresponds to the number 70. **2** One of seventy equal parts.

sev·en·ty (sev′ən·tē) *n. pl.* **·ties** **1** The product of seven and ten; 70; LXX. **2** A set or group of 70 members. **3** *pl.* The numbers, years, etc., between 70 and 80. —**sev′en·ty** *adj., pron.*

sev·er (sev′ər) *v.t.* **1** To put or keep apart; separate. **2** To cut or break into two or more parts. **3** To break off; dissolve, as a relationship. —*v.i.* **4** To come or break apart or into pieces. **5** To go away or apart; separate. [< L *separare* separate] —**sev′er·a·ble** *adj.* —**sev′er·er** *n.*

sev·er·al (sev′ər·əl, sev′rəl) *adj.* **1** Being of an indefinite number, more than one or two, yet not large; divers. **2** Considered individually; single; separate. **3** Individually different; various or diverse. [< L *separ* separate]

sev·er·al·ly (sev′ər·əl·ē, sev′rəl·ē) *adv.* **1** Individually; separately. **2** Respectively.

sev·er·ance (sev′ər·əns, sev′rəns) *n.* The act of severing, or the condition of being severed.

severance pay Additional pay sometimes given to an employee who has been discharged.

se·vere (si·vir′) *adj.* **·ver·er, ·ver·est** **1** Difficult; trying. **2** Unsparing; harsh; merciless: a *severe* punishment. **3** Conforming to rigid rules; extremely strict or accurate. **4** Serious and austere in disposition or manner; grave. **5** Austerely plain and simple, as in style, design, etc. **6** Causing sharp pain or anguish; extreme: *severe* hardship. —**se·vere′ness** *n.* [< L *severus*] —**se·vere′ly** *adv.*

se·ver·i·ty (si·ver′ə·tē) *n. pl.* **·ties** The quality or condition of being severe.

sew (sō) *v.* **sewed, sewed** or **sewn, sew·ing** *v.t.* **1** To make, mend, or fasten with needle and thread. **2** To enclose or secure by sewing. —*v.i.* **3** To work with needle and thread. —**sew up** **1** To mend by sewing. **2** *Informal* **a** To achieve absolute control or use of. **b** To make or be totally successful. [< OE *siwan, siowian*]

sew·age (sōō′ij) *n.* The waste matter carried off in sewers. [< SEW(ER) + -AGE]

sew·er (sōō′ər) *n.* **1** A conduit, usu. laid underground, to carry off drainage and excrement. **2** Any large public drain. [< OF *seuwiere* a channel from a fish pond]

sew·er·age (sōō′ər·ij) *n.* **1** A system of sewers. **2** Systematic draining by sewers. **3** SEWAGE.

sew·ing (sō′ing) *n.* **1** The act, business, or occupation of one who sews. **2** Material worked with needle and thread; needlework.

sewing circle A group of women meeting periodically to sew, usu. for some charitable purpose.

sewing machine A machine for stitching or sewing cloth, leather, etc.

sewn (sōn) A *p.p.* of SEW.

sex (seks) *n.* **1** Either of two divisions, male and female, by which organisms are distinguished with reference to the reproductive functions. **2** Males or females collectively. **3** The character of being male or female. **4** The activity or phenomena of life concerned with sexual desire or reproduction. 5 *Informal* Any act affording sexual gratification, as sexual intercourse. —*adj. Informal* SEXUAL. [< L *sexus*]

sex·a·ge·nar·i·an (sek′sə·jə·nâr′ē·ən) *adj.* Sixty years old, or between sixty and seventy. —*n.* A person of this age. [< L *sexageni* sixty each]

Sex·a·ges·i·ma (sek′sə·jes′ə·mə, -jā′zə-) *n.* The second Sunday before Lent. [L, sixtieth]

sex·a·ges·i·mal (sek′sə·jes′ə·məl) *adj.* Of or based on the number 60. [< L *sexagesimus* < *sexaginta* sixty]

sex appeal A physical quality or charm which attracts sexual interest.

sex chromosome Either of a pair of chromosomes associated with the determination of sex in plants and animals.

sex·ism (seks′iz·əm) *n.* Prejudice or discrimination against women. [< SEX + -ISM, on analogy with *racism*] —**sex′ist** *n, adj.*

sex·less (seks′lis) *adj.* 1 Having no sex; neuter. 2 Without sexual interest or qualities. —**sex′less·ly** *adv.* —**sex′less·ness** *n.*

sex linkage The presence on a sex chromosome of genes for certain nonsexual characteristics, resulting in the development of those characteristics in one sex only. —**sex-linked** (seks′lingkt′) *adj.*

sex·ol·o·gy (seks·ol′ə·jē) *n.* The study of human sexual behavior. —**sex·o·log·ic** (sek′sə·loj′ik) or **·i·cal** *adj.* —**sex·ol′o·gist** *n.*

sex·ploi·ta·tion (seks′ploi·tā′shən) *n.* The commercial exploitation of interest in sex, as by means of pornography. [Blend of SEX + EXPLOITATION]

sex·pot (seks′pot) *n. Slang* A very sexy woman.

sext (sekst) *n.* One of the canonical hours; the office for the sixth hour or noon. [< L *sex* six]

sex·tant (seks′tənt) *n.* An instrument for measuring the angular distance between two objects, as between a heavenly body and the horizon, used esp. in determining latitude at sea. [< L *sextus* sixth]

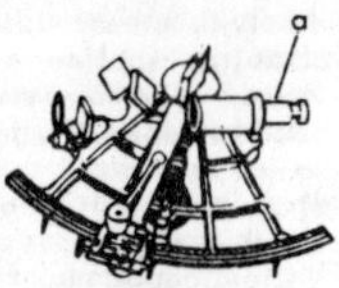

Sextant
a. eyepiece.

sex·tet (seks·tet′) *n.* 1 A group of six musical performers. 2 A musical composition for such a group. 3 Any collection of six persons or things. Also **sex·tette′**. [Alter. of SESTET]

sex·til·lion (seks·til′yən) *n. & adj.* See NUMBER. [< L *sex* six + F *(m)illion* a million]

sex·ton (seks′tən) *n.* An officer of a church having charge of maintenance and also of ringing the bells, overseeing burials, etc. [< Med. L *sacristanus* sacristan]

sex·tu·ple (sek·styo͞o′pəl, -stup′-, seks′too·pəl) *adj.* 1 Sixfold. 2 Multiplied by six; six times repeated. 3 *Music* Having six beats to the measure. —*v.t.* **·pled, ·pling** To multiply by six. —*n.* A number or sum six times as great as another. [< L *sextus* sixth] —**sex′tu·ply** *adv.*

sex·tu·plet (seks·tup′lit, -tyo͞o′plit, seks′too·plit) *n.* 1 A set of six similar things. 2 One of six offspring produced at a single birth.

sex·u·al (sek′sho͞o·əl) *adj.* 1 Of, pertaining or peculiar to, characteristic of, or affecting sex, the sexes, or the organs or functions of sex. 2 Characterized by or having sex. [< L *sexus* sex] —**sex′u·al′i·ty** (-al′ə·tē) *n.* —**sex′u·al·ly** *adv.*

sexual intercourse 1 The sexual act, esp. between humans, in which the erect penis is introduced into the vagina for the ejaculation of semen and sexual gratification. 2 Any act of sexual connection, esp. between humans.

sex·y (sek′sē) *adj.* **sex·i·er, sex·i·est** 1 *Informal* Provocative of sexual desire: a *sexy* dress; a *sexy* woman. 2 *Informal* Concerned in large or excessive degree with sex: a *sexy* novel. 3 *Slang* Interesting, exciting, or stimulating: Crime was the *sexiest* issue of the political campaign.

sf., sfz. sforzando.

sfor·zan·do (sfôr·tsän′do) *adj. & adv. Music* Accented with sudden explosive force. —*n.* A sforzando note or chord. Also **sfor·za′to** (-tsä′tō). [Ital. < *sforzare* to force]

sg. s.g. senior grade; specific gravity.

sgd. signed.

Sgt. Sergeant.

sh (sh) *interj.* An exclamation requesting silence.

sh. share; sheep; sheet; shilling.

Shab·bat (shä·bät′, shä′bəs) *n. pl.* **Shab·bat·im** (-bä′təm, -bô′səm) The Jewish Sabbath. [< Heb. *shabbāth*]

shab·by (shab′ē) *adj.* **·bi·er, ·bi·est** 1 Threadbare, ragged. 2 Characterized by worn or ragged garments. 3 Mean; paltry. [< OE *sceabb* a scab] —**shab′bi·ly** *adv.* —**shab′bi·ness** *n.*

Sha·bu·oth (shä·vo͞o′ōth, shə·vo͞o′əs) *n.* The Jewish festival of Pentecost.

shack (shak) *n.* 1 A crudely built cabin or hut. 2 *Informal* A poorly built or designed house. —*v.i. Slang* To live or stay, usu. briefly, at a specific place. [?]

shack·le (shak′əl) *n.* 1 A bracelet or fetter for encircling and confining a limb or limbs. 2 *Usu. pl.* Any impediment or restraint. 3 One of various forms of fastenings, as a link for coupling railway cars. —*v.t.* **·led, ·ling** 1 To restrain or confine with shackles; fetter. 2 To keep or restrain from free action or speech. 3 To connect or fasten with a shackle. [< OE *sceacul*] —**shack′ler** *n.*

Shackles

shad (shad) *n. pl.* **shad** Any of various anadromous fish related to the herring. [< OE *sceadd*]

shad·ber·ry (shad′ber′ē) *n. pl.* **·ries** 1 SHADBUSH. 2 The fruit of the shadbush.

shad·bush (shad′bo͝osh′) *n.* Any of various early-blooming shrubs with white flowers and edible purple berries. Also **shad′blow′** (-blō). [So called because it flowers when the shad appear in U.S. rivers]

shade (shād) *v.* **shad·ed, shad·ing** *v.t.* 1 To screen from light or heat. 2 To make dim with or as with a shadow; darken; 3 To screen or protect with or as with a shadow. 4 To cause to change, pass, blend, or soften, by gradations. 5 **a** To represent (degrees of shade, colors, etc.) by gradations of light or shading. **b** To represent varying shades, colors, etc., in (a picture of painting). 6 To make slightly lower, as a price. —*v.i.* 7 To change or vary by degrees. —*n.* 1 Relative darkness caused by the interception or partial absence of rays of light. 2 A place having such relative darkness. 3 That part of a drawing, painting, etc. represented as being relatively dark or in shadow. 4 A gradation of darkness or blackness in a color. 5 A minute difference, variation, or degree: *shades* of meaning. 6 A screen or cover that partially or totally shuts off light: a lamp *shade.* 7 A ghost or phantom. 8 *pl. Slang* SUNGLASSES. —**in** (or **into**) **the shade** 1 In or into a shady place. 2 In or into a condition of inferiority, defeat, obscurity, etc. [< OE *sceadu* a shade]

shad·ing (shā′ding) *n.* 1 Protective against light or heat. 2 The representation pictorially of darkness, color, or depth. 3 A slight difference or variation.

shad·ow (shad′ō) *n.* 1 A comparative darkness within an illuminated area caused by the interception of light by an opaque body. 2 The dark figure or image thus produced on a surface: the *shadow* of a man. 3 The shaded portion of a picture. 4 A mirrored image: to see one's *shadow* in a pool. 5 A phantom, ghost, etc. 6 A faint representation or indication; a symbol: the *shadow* to things to come. 7 A remnant; vestige: *shadows* of his former glory. 8 An insignificant trace or portion: not a *shadow* of evidence. 9 Gloom or a saddening influence. 10 An inseparable companion. 11 One who trails or follows another, as a detective or spy. 12 A slight growth of beard, esp. in the phrase **five o'clock shadow.** —*v.t.* 1 To cast a shadow upon; shade. 2 To darken or make gloomy. 3 To represent or foreshow dimly or vaguely: with *forth* or *out.* 4 To follow closely or secretly; spy on. 5 To shade in painting, drawing, etc. —*adj.* Of or pertaining to a shadow cabinet. [< OE *sceadu* a shade] —**shad′ow·er** *n.*

shad·ow·box (shad′ō·boks′) *v.i.* To spar with an imaginary opponent as a form of exercise. —**shad′ow·box′ing** *n.*

shadow box A small, open, framed cabinet, usu. hung on a wall to display knickknacks, etc.

shadow cabinet In the British or other parliamentary government, a group of opposition leaders who would assume specific cabinet positions if the government in power should fall.

shad·ow·y (shad′ō·ē) *adj.* **·ow·ier, ·ow·i·est 1** Dark; shady. **2** Vague; dim. **3** Unreal; ghostly. **—shad′ow·i·ness** *n.*

shad·y (shā′dē) *adj.* **shad·i·er, shad·i·est 1** Full of shade; casting a shade. **2** Shaded or sheltered. **3** Morally questionable; suspicious. **4** Quiet; hidden. **—shad′i·ness** *n.*

shaft (shaft, shäft) *n.* **1** The long narrow rod of an arrow, spear, lance, harpoon, etc. **2** An arrow or spear. **3** Something hurled like or having the effect of an arrow or spear: *shafts* of ridicule. **4** A beam of light. **5** A long handle, as of a hammer, ax, etc. **6** *Mech.* A long and usu. cylindrical bar, esp. if rotating and transmitting motion. **7** *Archit.* **a** The portion of a column between capital and base. **b** A slender column, as an obelisk. **8** The stem of a feather. **9** The slender portion of a bone or the portion of a hair from root to the end. **10** A tall, narrow building or spire. **11** A narrow, vertical passage, as the entrance to a mine or an opening through a building for an elevator. **12** A conduit for the passage of air, heat, etc. **13** *Slang* Malicious or abusive treatment: with *the,* esp. in the phrases **get the shaft, give (someone) the shaft.** *—v.t. Slang* To act maliciously or abusively toward. [< OE *sceaft*]

shag (shag) *n.* **1** A rough coat or mass, as of hair. **2** A long, rough nap on cloth. **3** Cloth having a rough or long nap. **4** A coarse, strong tobacco: also **shag tobacco.** *—v.* **shagged, shag·ging** *v.t.* **1** To make shaggy or rough. *—v.i.* **2** To become shaggy or rough. [< OE *sceacga* wool]

shag·bark (shag′bärk′) *n.* **1** A species of hickory with rough, flaking bark. **2** Its edible nut. **3** Its wood.

shag·gy (shag′ē) *adj.* **·gi·er, ·gi·est 1** Having, consisting of, or resembling rough hair or wool. **2** Covered with any rough, tangled growth; fuzzy. **3** Unkempt. **—shag′gi·ly** *adv.* **—shag′gi·ness** *n.*

sha·green (shə·grēn′) *n.* **1** An abrasive leather made of the skin of various sharks and rays. **2** A rough-grained rawhide. [< Turk. *sāghrī* horse's hide]

shah (shä) *n.* An eastern ruler, esp. of Iran. [< Pers.]

shake (shāk) *v.* **shook, shak·en, shak·ing** *v.t.* **1** To cause to move to and fro or up and down with short, rapid movements. **2** To affect by or as by vigorous action: with *off, out, from,* etc.: to *shake* out a sail; to *shake* off a tackler. **3** To cause to tremble or quiver; vibrate: The blows *shook* the door. **4** To cause to stagger or totter. **5** To weaken or disturb: to *shake* one's determination. **6** To agitate or rouse; stir: often with *up.* **7** *Informal* To get rid of or away from. **8** To clasp (hands) as a form of greeting, agreement, etc. **9** *Music* TRILL. *—v.i.* **10** To move to and fro or up and down in short, rapid movements. **11** To be affected by vigorous action: with *off, out, from,* etc. **12** To tremble or quiver, as from cold or fear. **13** To become unsteady; totter. **14** To clasp hands. **15** *Music* TRILL. **—shake down 1** To cause to fall by shaking. **2** To cause to settle by shaking. **3** To test or become familiar with (new equipment, etc.). **4** *Slang* To extort money from. **—shake up 1** To mix or blend by shaking. **2** To agitate or rouse; stir. **3** To jar or jolt. **4** To effect or cause rather extensive changes or reorganization in. **5** *Slang* To cause to lose one's composure; disconcert. *—n.* **1** The act or an instance of shaking: a *shake* of the hand. **2** A tight fissure in rock or timber. **3** *pl. Informal* A fit of bodily shaking or trembling: usu. with *the.* **4** MILKSHAKE. **5** *Informal* EARTHQUAKE. **6** *Informal* An instant; jiffy. **7** *Informal* A deal: to get a fair *shake.* **8** *Music* TRILL. **—give (someone** or **something) the shake** To get away from (someone or something). [< OE *scacan*]

shake·down (shāk′doun′) *n.* **1** A thorough search. **2** *Slang* Extortion of money. **3** A testing or becoming familiar with something, as with a new ship. *—adj.* For the purpose of testing mechanical parts or familiarizing personnel: a *shakedown* cruise.

shak·er (shā′kər) *n.* One who or that which shakes: a *saltshaker,* cocktail *shaker,* etc.

Shak·er (shā′kər) *n.* One of a sect practicing celibacy and communal living: so called from their trembling movements during religious meetings. **—Shak′er·ism** *n.*

Shake·spear·i·an (shāk·spir′ē·ən) *adj.* Of, pertaining to, or characteristic of Shakespeare, his work, or his style. *—n.* A specialist on Shakespeare or his writings. Also **Shake·spear′e·an.**

shake-up (shāk′up′) *n.* A rather extensive change or reorganization, as in a business office, etc.

shak·o (shak′ō, shāk′-, shäk′-) *n. pl.* **·os** A high, stiff military headdress, having a visor and an upright plume. [< Hung. *csākō*]

Shako

shak·y (shā′kē) *adj.* **shak·i·er, shak·i·est 1** Not firm or solid. **2** Not well founded, thought out, etc.: a *shaky* theory. **3** Not dependable or reliable. **4** Characterized by shaking. **5** Weak; unsound, as in body. **—shak′i·ly** *adv.* **—shak′i·ness** *n.*

shale (shāl) *n.* A rock resembling slate, with fragile, uneven layers. [< G *Schale* shale] **—shal′y** *adj.*

shall (shal) *v. p.t.* **should.** Used now only as an auxiliary, *shall* expresses: **1** Simple futurity: I *shall* go next week. **2** That which seems inevitable or certain: I know I *shall* never leave. **3** Determination, promise, threat, or command: They *shall* not pass; You *shall* pay for this; You *shall* have it. **4** In laws, resolutions, etc., that which is obligatory: It *shall* be required to have identification. [< OE *sceal* I am obliged] • **shall, will** The traditional rule is that to express simple futurity *shall* is used with the first person and the auxiliary *will* with the second and third. To express determination, obligation, command, etc., *will* is used with the first person and *shall* with the second and third. This rule is now widely ignored, both in speech and in writing. *Will,* by far the more common auxiliary, occurs with all subjects and in all contexts. *Shall* is still often used with the first person, less so with the second and third, where its use is likely to appear stilted.

shal·lop (shal′əp) *n.* An open boat propelled by oars or sails. [< Du. *sloep* sloop]

shal·lot (shə·lot′, shal′ət) *n.* **1** A mild, onionlike vegetable allied to garlic. **2** SCALLION. [< OF *eschalotte*]

shal·low (shal′ō) *adj.* **1** Lacking depth. **2** Not extending far inwards or outwards: a *shallow* room. **3** Lacking intellectual depth; superficial. *—n. Usu. pl. but construed as sing. or pl.* A shallow place in a body of water; shoal. *—v.t. & v.i.* To make or become shallow. [ME *schalowe*] **—shal′low·ly** *adv.* **—shal′low·ness** *n.*

shalt (shalt) *v. Archaic* second person singular, present tense of SHALL: used with *thou.*

sham (sham) *adj.* False; pretended; counterfeit; mock. *—n.* **1** A person who shams. **2** A hoax; deception. **3** An imitation; counterfeit. **4** Cheap artificiality or pretension. **5** A decorative cover or the like for use over a household article: a pillow *sham.* *—v.* **shammed, sham·ming** *v.t.* **1** To counterfeit; feign. *—v.i.* **2** To make false pretenses; feign something. [? dial. var. of SHAME]

sha·man (shä′mən, shā′-, sham′ən) *n.* A priest of shamanism. [< Skt. *śamana* ascetic]

sha·man·ism (shä′mən·iz′əm, shā′-, sham′ən-) *n.* **1** A religion of NE Asia holding that supernatural spirits, etc., work for the good or ill of mankind only through the shamans. **2** Any similar religion, such as that practiced by certain Indians of the American Northwest. **—sha′man·ist** *n.* **—sha′man·is′tic** *adj.*

sham·ble (sham′bəl) *v.i.* **·bled, ·bling** To walk with shuffling or unsteady gait. [?]

sham·bles (sham′bəlz) *n.pl. (usu. construed as sing.)* **1** SLAUGHTERHOUSE. **2** Any place of carnage or execution. **3** A place marked by great destruction, disorder, or confusion. [< OE *scamel* a bench.]

shame (shām) *n.* **1** A painful feeling caused by a sense of guilt, unworthiness, impropriety, etc. **2** Disgrace; humiliation. **3** A person or thing causing disgrace or humiliation. **4** Misfortune; outrage: It's a *shame* they didn't go. **—put to shame 1** To disgrace; make ashamed. **2** To surpass or eclipse. *—v.t.* **shamed, sham·ing 1** To cause to feel shame. **2** To bring shame upon; disgrace. **3** To impel by a sense of shame: with *into* or *out of.* [< OE *scamu*]

shame·faced (shām′fāst′) *adj.* **1** Showing shame; ashamed. **2** Bashful; modest. [< OE *scamfæst* abashed] —

shame·fac·ed·ly (shām′fā′sid·lē, shām′fāst′lē) *adv.* —**shame′fac′ed·ness** *n.*

shame·ful (shām′fəl) *adj.* 1 Bringing shame or disgrace; disgraceful; scandalous. 2 Indecent. —**shame′ful·ly** *adv.* —**shame′ful·ness** *n.* —**Syn.** 1 disreputable, dishonorable, ignoble, ignominious, base, despicable, contemptible, deplorable, vile, odious.

shame·less (shām′lis) *adj.* 1 Impudent; brazen; immodest. 2 Done without shame, indicating a want of decency. —**shame′less·ly** *adv.* —**shame′less·ness** *n.*

sham·my (sham′ē) *n.* CHAMOIS.

sham·poo (sham·pōō′) *v.t.* 1 To lather and wash (the hair and scalp) thoroughly. 2 To cleanse by rubbing. —*n.* The act or process of shampooing, or a preparation used for it. [< Hind. *chāmpnā* to press] —**sham·poo′er** *n.*

sham·rock (sham′rok) *n.* Any of several plants, with trifoliate leaves, accepted as the national emblem of Ireland, esp. the wood sorrel. [< Irish *seamar* trefoil]

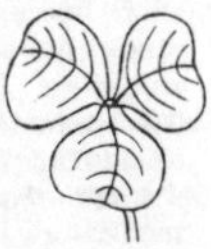

Shamrock (wood sorrel)

shang·hai (shang′hī, shang·hī′) *v.t.* **·haied, ·hai·ing** 1 To drug or render unconscious and kidnap for service aboard a ship. 2 To cause to do something by force or deception. [< *Shanghai*]

Shan·gri-la (shang′gri·lä′) *n.* Any imaginary hidden utopia or paradise. [< *Shangri-la,* name of a utopian place in James Hilton's novel *Lost Horizon,* 1933]

shank (shangk) *n.* 1 The leg between the knee and the ankle. 2 The entire leg. 3 A cut of meat from the leg of an animal; the shin. 4 The stem, as of a tobacco pipe, key, anchor, etc. 5 The part of a tool connecting the handle with the working part; shaft. 6 The projecting piece or loop in the back of some buttons by which they are attached. 7 *Printing* The body of a type. 8 The narrow part of a shoe sole in front of the heel. • See SHOE. —**shank of the evening** *Informal* The early part of the evening. [< OE *sceanca*] —**shanked** *adj.*

shanks' mare One's own legs as a means of conveyance.

shan't (shant, shänt) Contraction of *shall not.*

shan·tung (shan′tung, shan·tung′) *n.* A fabric with a rough, nubby surface, originally made in China of silk, now often made of synthetic or cotton fiber. [< *Shantung,* China]

shan·ty[1] (shan′tē) *n. pl.* **·ties** A small, rickety shack or cabin. [< F (Canadian) *chantier* lumberer's shack]

shan·ty[2] (shan′tē) *n.* CHANTEY.

shape (shāp) *n.* 1 Outward form or contour. 2 Appearance of a body with reference only to its contour; figure. 3 Something that gives or determines shape, as a pattern or mold. 4 An assumed aspect or appearance; guise. 5 A developed or final expression or form: to put an idea into *shape.* 6 Any embodiment or form in which a thing may exist: the *shape* of a novel. 7 A ghost or phantom. 8 *Informal* The condition of a person or thing as regards health, orderliness, etc. —**in shape** In good physical condition or appearance. —**out of shape** In bad physical condition or appearance. —**take shape** To begin to have or assume definite form. —*v.* **shaped, shap·ing** *v.t.* 1 To give shape to; mold; form. 2 To adjust or adapt; modify. 3 To devise; prepare. 4 To give direction or character to: to *shape* one's course of action. 5 To put into or express in words. —*v.i.* 6 To take shape; develop; form: often with *up* or *into.* —**shape up** 1 To develop fully or appropriately; work out. 2 *Informal* To do, work, behave, etc., properly. [< OE *gesceap* creation] —**shap′er** *n.*

SHAPE (shāp) Supreme Headquarters Allied Powers, Europe.

shape·less (shāp′lis) *adj.* 1 Having no definite shape. 2 Lacking a pleasing shape or symmetry. —**shape′less·ly** *adv.* —**shape′less·ness** *n.*

shape·ly (shāp′lē) *adj.* **·li·er, ·li·est** Having a pleasing shape; well-formed. —**shape′li·ness** *n.*

shape-up (shāp′up′) *n.* The selection of a work crew, usu. on a day-to-day basis, from among a number of men assembled for a work shift.

shard (shärd) *n.* 1 A broken piece of a brittle substance, as of an earthen vessel. 2 *Zool.* A stiff covering, as the wing cover of a beetle. [< OE *sceard*]

share (shâr) *n.* 1 A portion alloted or due to a person or contributed by a person. 2 One of the equal parts into which the capital stock of a company or corporation is divided. 3 An equitable part of something used, done, or divided in common. —*v.* **shared, shar·ing** *v.t.* 1 To divide and give out in shares or portions; apportion. 2 To enjoy, use, participate in, endure, etc., in common. —*v.i.* 3 To have a part; participate: with *in.* 4 To divide something in equal parts: with *out* or *with.* [< OE *scearu*] —**shar′er** *n.*

share·crop·per (shâr′krop′ər) *n.* A tenant farmer who pays a share of his crop as rent for his land.

share·hold·er (shâr′hōl′dər) *n.* An owner of a share or shares of a company's stock.

sha·rif (shə·rēf′) *n.* SHERIF.

shark[1] (shärk) *n.* Any of a large order of mostly marine fishes having a cartilaginous skeleton, lateral gill slits, and a tough skin. —*v.i.* To fish for sharks. [?]

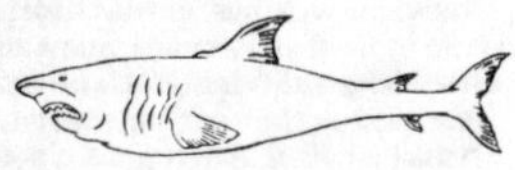

Great white shark

shark[2] (shärk) *n.* 1 A dishonest person, esp. a swindler. 2 *Slang* A person of exceptional skill or ability. [?< SHARK[1]]

shark·skin (shärk′skin′) *n.* 1 Leather made of a shark's skin. 2 A summer fabric with a smooth surface. 3 A fabric with a pebbly surface.

sharp (shärp) *adj.* 1 Having a keen edge or an acute point; capable of cutting or piercing. 2 Not rounded; pointed; angular: *sharp* features. 3 Abrupt in change of direction: a *sharp* curve. 4 Distinct; well-defined: a *sharp* contrast. 5 Keen or quick in perception or discernment. 6 Keen or acute, as in seeing or hearing. 7 Shrewd, as in bargaining. 8 Quickly aroused; harsh: a *sharp* temper. 9 Heated; fiery: a *sharp* debate. 10 Vigilant; attentive: a *sharp* watch. 11 Quick; vigorous. 12 Keenly felt: *sharp* hunger pangs. 13 Intense or penetrating in effect; incisive to the point of being unsettling or wounding: a *sharp* look; a *sharp* tongue. 14 Shrill: a *sharp* sound. 15 Having an acid or pungent taste or smell. 16 *Slang* Stylishly dressed or well groomed. 17 *Music* Being above the proper or indicated pitch. —*adv.* 1 In a sharp manner. 2 Promptly; exactly: at 4 o'clock *sharp.* 3 *Music* Above the proper pitch. —*n.* 1 *Music* A character (#) used on a natural degree of the staff to make it represent a tone a half-step higher; also, the tone so indicated. 2 A sewing needle of long, slender shape. 3 A cheat; sharper: a *cardsharp.* —*v.t.* 1 *Music* To raise in pitch, as by a half-step. —*v.i.* 2 *Music* To sing, play, or sound above the right pitch. [< OE *scearp*] —**sharp′ly** *adv.* —**sharp′ness** *n.*

sharp·en (shär′pən) *v.t. & v.i.* To make or become sharp. —**sharp′en·er** *n.*

sharp·er (shär′pər) *n.* A swindler; cheat.

sharp·ie (shär′pē) *n.* 1 A long, flat-bottomed sailboat having a centerboard and one or two masts. 2 *Informal* A shrewd, clever person, esp. in bargaining. [< SHARP]

sharp·shoot·er (shärp′shōō′tər) *n.* A skilled marksman. —**sharp′shoot′ing** *n.*

sharp-sight·ed (shärp′sī′tid) *adj.* Having keen vision. —**sharp′-sight′ed·ly** *adv.* —**sharp′-sight′ed·ness** *n.*

sharp-tongued (shärp′tungd′) *adj.* Bitter or caustic in speech.

sharp-wit·ted (shärp′wit′id) *adj.* Acutely intelligent; discerning.

Shas·ta daisy (shas′tə) A cultivated, daisylike variety of chrysanthemum having white-rayed flowers. [< Mt. *Shasta,* California]

shat·ter (shat′ər) *v.t.* 1 To break into pieces suddenly, as by a blow. 2 To break the health or well-being of, as the body or mind. 3 To damage or demolish. —*v.i.* 4 To break into pieces; burst. —*n. pl.* Shattered pieces or fragments, esp. in the phrase **in shatters.** [ME *schateren* to scatter]

shave (shāv) *v.* **shaved, shaved** or **shav·en, shav·ing** *v.i.* 1 To cut hair or beard close to the skin with a razor. —*v.t.* **2** To remove hair or beard from (the face, head, etc.) with a razor. **3** To cut (hair or beard) close to the skin with a razor: often with *off.* **4** To trim closely as if with a razor: to *shave* a lawn. **5** To cut thin slices or pieces from. **6** To touch or scrape in passing; graze; come close to. **7** *Informal* To lower or deduct from (a price, amount, etc.). —*n.* **1** The act or operation of shaving with a razor. **2** A thin slice or piece; shaving. **3** *Informal* The act of barely grazing something. [< OE *scafan*]

shav·en (shā′vən) A *p.p.* of SHAVE. —*adj.* **1** Shaved; also, tonsured. **2** Trimmed closely.

shav·er (shā′vər) *n.* **1** One who shaves. **2** An instrument for shaving: an electric *shaver.* **3** *Informal* A lad.

shave·tail (shāv′tāl′) *n. Slang* A second lieutenant, esp. one recently commissioned. [In allusion to young, unbroken army mules with bobbed tails]

Sha·vi·an (shā′vē·ən) *n.* An admirer of George Bernard Shaw, his writings, or his theories. —*adj.* Of or characteristic of George Bernard Shaw or his work.

shav·ing (shā′ving) *n.* **1** The act of one who or that which shaves. **2** A thin paring shaved from anything.

shawl (shôl) *n.* A wrap, as a square cloth, or large broad scarf, worn over the head or shoulders. [< Pers. *shāl*]

Shaw·nee (shô·nē′) *n.* One of a tribe of North American Indians of Algonquian stock, formerly living in Tennessee and South Carolina, now in Oklahoma. [< Algon.]

shay (shā) *n.* A light carriage; chaise. [Back formation < CHAISE, mistaking it for a plural]

she (shē) *pron.* **1** The female person or being previously mentioned or understood, in the nominative case. **2** Any woman. **3** Something personified as female: *She* is a great little car. —*n.* A female person or animal: often used in combination: a *she-lion.* [< OE *sēo*]

sheaf (shēf) *n. pl.* **sheaves** (shēvz) **1** Stalks of cut grain or the like, bound together. **2** Any collection of things, as papers, held together by a band or tie. —*v.t.* To bind in a sheaf; sheave. [< OE *scēaf*]

shear (shir) *n.* **1** Either of the blades of a pair of shears. **2** A cutting machine for sheet metal. **3** *Physics* **a** A deformation of a solid body, equivalent to a sliding over each other of adjacent layers. **b** A force or system of forces tending to cause this. **4** The act or result of shearing. —*v.* **sheared** (*Archaic* **shore**), **sheared** or **shorn, shear·ing** *v.t.* **1** To cut the hair, fleece, etc., from. **2** To remove by cutting or clipping: to *shear* wool. **3** To deprive; strip, as of power or wealth. **4** To cut or clip with shears or other sharp instrument: to *shear* a cable. —*v.i.* **5** To use shears or other sharp instrument. **6** To slide or break from a shear (def. 3). **7** To proceed by or as by cutting a way: with *through.* [< OE *sceran* to shear] —**shear′er** *n.*

shears (shirz) *n.pl.* Any large cutting or clipping instrument worked by the crossing of cutting edges. Also **pair of shears.**

shear·wa·ter (shir′wô′tər, -wot′ər) *n.* Any of various web-footed, far-ranging sea birds that usu. skim the water when flying.

sheath (shēth) *n.* **1** An envelope or case, as for a sword; scabbard. **2** *Biol.* Any structure that enfolds or encloses. [< OE *scæth*]

sheathe (shē<u>th</u>) *v.t.* **sheathed, sheath·ing** **1** To put into a sheath. **2** To plunge (a sword, etc.) into flesh. **3** To draw in, as claws. **4** To protect or conceal, as by covering: to *sheathe* plasterboard; to *sheathe* one's anger.

sheath·ing (shē′<u>th</u>ing) *n.* **1** An outer covering, as of a building or ship's hull. **2** The material used for this. **3** The act of one who sheathes.

sheave[1] (shēv) *v.t.* **sheaved, sheav·ing** To gather into sheaves; collect.

sheave[2] (shēv) *n.* A grooved pulley wheel; also, a pulley wheel and its block. [ME]

sheaves (shēvz) *n.pl.* of SHEAF.

she·bang (shi·bang′) *n. Slang* Matter; concern; affair: tired of the whole *shebang.* [?]

shed[1] (shed) *v.* **shed, shed·ding** *v.t.* **1** To pour forth in drops; emit, as tears or blood. **2** To cause to pour forth. **3** To send forth or abroad; radiate: to *shed* light on a subject. **4** To throw off without allowing to penetrate, as rain; repel. **5** To cast off by natural process, as hair, skin, a shell, etc. —*v.i.* **6** To cast off or lose hair, skin, etc., by natural process. **7** To fall or drop, as leaves or seed. —*n.* That which sheds, as a sloping surface or watershed. [< OE *scēadan* separate, part]

shed[2] (shed) *n.* **1** A small low building or lean-to, used for storage, etc. **2** A large hangarlike building, often with open front or sides. [Var. of SHADE]

she'd (shēd) Contraction of *she had* or *she would.*

shed·der (shed′ər) *n.* **1** One who sheds. **2** An animal that molts.

sheen (shēn) *n.* **1** A glistening brightness, as if from reflection. **2** Bright, shining attire. —*v.i.* To shine; gleam; glisten. [< OE *scēne* beautiful] —**sheen′y** *adj.*

sheep (shēp) *n. pl.* **sheep** **1** Any of a genus of woolly, medium-sized ruminants, esp. domesticated species grown for their fleece, flesh, and hide. **2** A meek or timid person. [< OE *scēap*]

Sheep

sheep·cote (shēp′kōt′) *n.* SHEEPFOLD. Also **sheep′cot′** (-kot′).

sheep dip Any insecticidal, medicinal, or cleansing solution used to bathe sheep.

sheep dog Any dog trained to guard and control sheep.

sheep·fold (shēp′fōld′) *n.* A pen for sheep.

sheep·herd·er (shēp′hûr′dər) *n.* A herder of sheep. —**sheep′herd′ing** *n.*

sheep·ish (shē′pish) *adj.* **1** Embarrassed; chagrined. **2** Meek; timid. —**sheep′ish·ly** *adv.* —**sheep′ish·ness** *n.*

sheep·skin (shēp′skin′) *n.* **1** A sheep's hide, or anything made from it, as parchment, an outdoor coat, etc. **2** A document written on parchment. **3** *Informal* A diploma.

sheep sorrel A low-growing weed related to buckwheat.

sheer[1] (shir) *v.i.* **1** To swerve from a course; turn aside. —*v.t.* **2** To cause to swerve. —*n.* **1** *Naut.* **a** The slight rise of the lengthwise lines of a vessel's hull. **b** A position of a vessel that enables it to swing clear of a single anchor. **2** A swerving course. [< SHEAR]

sheer[2] (shir) *adj.* **1** Having no modifying conditions; absolute; utter: *sheer* folly. **2** Exceedingly thin and fine: said of fabrics. **3** Perpendicular; steep: a *sheer* precipice. **4** Pure; pellucid. —*n.* Any very thin fabric used for clothes. —*adv.* **1** Entirely; utterly. **2** Perpendicularly. [ME *schere*] —**sheer′ly** *adv.* —**sheer′ness** *n.*

sheet (shēt) *n.* **1** A thin, broad, usu. rectangular piece of any material, as metal, glass, etc. **2** A broad, flat surface or expanse: a *sheet* of flame. **3** A large, usu. rectangular piece of cotton, linen, silk, etc., used as bedding. **4** A usu. rectangular piece of paper, used esp. for writing, printing, etc. **5** *Usu. pl. Printing* A printed signature for a book. **6** *Informal* A newspaper. **7** A sail: a literary use. **8** *Naut.* A rope or chain attached to the lower corner of a sail, used to regulate the angle of the sail to the wind. **9** The large, unseparated block of stamps printed by one impression of a plate. —*v.t.* To cover with, wrap in, or form into a sheet or sheets. —*adj.* Formed or cut into sheets: *sheet* metal. [< OE *scēte* linen cloth]

sheet anchor **1** An anchor used only in emergency. **2** A person or thing depended upon in an emergency.

sheet·ing (shē′ting) *n.* **1** Material for bed sheets. **2** Any material used for lining or covering a surface.

sheet metal Metal rolled and pressed into sheets.

sheet music Music printed on unbound sheets of paper.

sheik (shēk, shāk) *n.* The chief of an Arab tribe or family. Also **sheikh.** [< Ar. *shakha* grow old] —**sheik′dom, sheikh′dom** *n.*

shek·el (shek′əl) *n.* **1** An ancient, esp. Hebrew unit of weight. **2** A coin having this weight. **3** *pl. Slang* Money; riches.

shel·drake (shel′drāk′) *n.* **1** Any of various Old World wild ducks with varicolored plumage. **2** MERGANSER. [< dial. E *sheld* dappled + DRAKE]

shelf (shelf) *n. pl.* **shelves** (shelvz) **1** A piece of material set horizontally into or against a wall, cabinet, closet, etc., to support articles. **2** The contents of a shelf. **3** Any flat projecting ledge, as of rock. **4** A reef; shoal. [< LG *schelf* set of shelves]

shell (shel) *n.* **1** The hard outer covering of a mollusk, lobster, egg, nut, etc. • See OYSTER. 2 Something like a shell in shape or function, as the outer framework of a building, a ship's hull, a hollow pastry or pie crust for filling, etc. 3 A sleeveless blouse or sweater. 4 A very light, long, and narrow racing rowboat. 5 A hollow metallic projectile filled with an explosive or chemical. 6 A metallic or paper cartridge case containing the powder, bullet, or shot for breechloading small arms. 7 Any case used to contain the explosives of fireworks. 8 A reserved or impersonal attitude: to come out of one's *shell.* —*v.t.* 1 To divest of or remove from a shell, husk, or pod. 2 To separate from the cob, as Indian corn. 3 To bombard with shells, as a fort. 4 To cover with shells. —*v.i.* 5 To shed or become freed from the shell or pod. 6 To fall off, as a shell or scale. [< OE *scell* shell] **—shell'er** *n.* **—shell'y** *adj.* **(·i·er, ·i·est)**

she'll (shēl) Contraction of *she will* or *she shall.*

shel·lac (shə·lak') *n.* 1 A purified lac in the form of thin flakes, used in varnish, insulators, etc. 2 A varnish made of shellac dissolved in alcohol. —*v.t.* **·lacked, ·lack·ing** 1 To cover or varnish with shellac. 2 *Slang* **a** To beat. **b** To defeat utterly. Also **shel·lack'.** [< SHELL + LAC[1]]

shel·lack·ing (shə·lak'ing) *n. Slang* 1 A beating; assault. 2 A thorough defeat.

shell·back (shel'bak') *n.* 1 A veteran sailor. 2 Anyone who has crossed the equator on a ship.

shell·bark (shel'bärk') *n.* SHAGBARK.

shell·fire (shel'fīr') *n.* The firing of artillery shells.

shell·fish (shel'fish') *n. pl.* **·fish** or **·fish·es** An aquatic mollusk or crustacean, esp. if edible, as a clam, shrimp, etc.

shell game 1 A swindling game in which the victim bets on the location of a pea covered by one of three nutshells; thimblerig. 2 Any game in which the victim cannot win.

shell·proof (shel'pro͞of') *adj.* Built to resist the destructive effect of projectiles and bombs.

shell shock COMBAT FATIGUE. **—shell-shocked** (shel'shokt') *adj.*

shel·ter (shel'tər) *n.* 1 That which covers or shields from exposure, danger, etc. 2 The state of being covered, protected, or shielded. —*v.t.* 1 To provide protection or shelter for; shield, as from danger or inclement weather. —*v.i.* 2 To take shelter. [?] **—shel'ter·er** *n.*

shelve (shelv) *v.* **shelved, shelv·ing** *v.t.* 1 To place on a shelf. 2 To postpone indefinitely; put aside. 3 To retire. 4 To provide or fit with shelves. —*v.i.* 5 To incline gradually.

shelves (shelvz) *n. pl.* of SHELF.

shelv·ing (shel'ving) *n.* 1 Shelves collectively. 2 Material for the construction of shelves.

Shem (shem) In the Bible, the eldest son of Noah.

Shem·ite (shem'īt) *n.* SEMITE.

she·nan·i·gan (shi·nan'ə·gən) *n. Usu. pl. Informal* 1 Trickery; foolery. 2 Deceitful or underhanded actions. [?]

She·ol (shē'ōl) *n.* In the Old Testament, a place where the dead were believed to go. [< Heb. *shā'al* dig]

shep·herd (shep'ərd) *n.* 1 A keeper or herder of sheep. 2 Figuratively, a pastor, leader, or guide. —*v.t.* To herd, guide, protect, or direct, as a shepherd. [< OE *scēaphyrde*] **—shep'herd·ess** *n. Fem.*

shepherd dog SHEEP DOG.

shepherd's purse A common weed related to mustard, bearing small white flowers and pouchlike pods.

Sher·a·ton (sher'ə·tən) *adj.* Denoting a style of furniture characterized by simplicity and pleasing proportions. [< T. *Sheraton,* 1751–1806, English designer]

sher·bet (shûr'bit) *n.* 1 A frozen dessert, usu. fruit-flavored, made with water or milk, gelatin, etc. 2 Originally, a Turkish drink, made of fruit juice sweetened and diluted with water. Also **sher'bert** (-bərt). [< Ar. *sharbah* a drink]

she·rif (shə·rēf') *n.* 1 A member of a princely Muslim family which claims descent from Mohammed. 2 The chief magistrate of Mecca. 3 An Arab chief. [< Ar. *sharīf* noble]

sher·iff (sher'if) *n.* 1 The chief law-enforcement officer of a county, who executes the mandates of courts, keeps order, etc. 2 In Canada, an official whose job is to enforce minor court orders, such as the eviction of persons for nonpayment of rent. [< OE *scīr-gerēfa* shire reeve] **—sher'iff·dom** *n.*

sher·ry (sher'ē) *n. pl.* **·ries** A fortified wine originally made in Spain. [< *Xeres,* former name of Jerez, Spain]

she's (shēz) Contraction of *she is* or *she has.*

Shet·land pony (shet'lənd) A small, shaggy breed of pony originally bred on the Shetland Islands.

shew (shō) *n. & v. Archaic* SHOW.

shew·bread (shō'bred') *n.* Unleavened bread formerly placed as an offering in Jewish temples.

SHF, S.H.F., shf, s.h.f. superhigh frequency.

shib·bo·leth (shib'ə·leth) *n.* A test word or pet phrase of a party; a watchword. [< Heb. *shibbōleth,* a word mispronounced by certain Hebrew spies, betraying them as aliens. *Judges* 12:4–6]

shied (shīd) *p.t. & p.p.* of SHY.

shield (shēld) *n.* 1 A broad piece of defensive armor, commonly carried on the left arm; a large buckler. 2 Anything that protects or defends. 3 Any of various devices that afford protection, as from machinery, electricity, radiation, etc. 4 Anything shaped like a shield, as a policeman's badge, decorative emblem, etc. 5 A heraldic escutcheon. —*v.t.* 1 To protect from danger; defend; guard. 2 To hide or screen from view. —*v.i.* 3 To act as a shield or safeguard. **—shield'er** *n.*

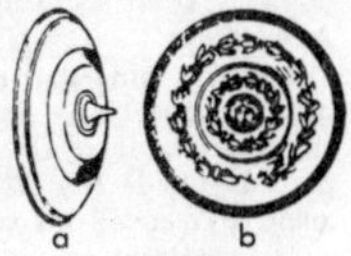

a b
Shields
a. Anglo-Saxon.
b. Greek.

shield·ing (shēld'ing) *n.* A protective device or screen: radiation *shielding.*

shi·er (shī'ər) Comparative of SHY.

shi·est (shī'ist) Superlative of SHY.

shift (shift) *v.t.* 1 To change or move from one position, arrangement, place, etc., to another. 2 To change for another or others of the same class. —*v.i.* 3 To change position, place, attitude, etc. 4 To manage or get along. 5 To evade; equivocate. —*n.* 1 The act of shifting. 2 A change in position, place, direction, etc. 3 A change in attitude, loyalty, etc. 4 An action or recourse taken in an emergency; expedient. 5 A trick or evasion. 6 GEARSHIFT. 7 A relay of workers or their period of work: the night *shift.* 8 A woman's dress that is not belted or fitted at the waist. 9 *Archaic* A chemise or undergarment. [< OE *sciftan* divide] **—shift'er** *n.*

shift·less (shift'lis) *adj.* 1 Unable or unwilling to work or accomplish something; inefficient or lazy. 2 Inefficiently or incompetently done. **—shift'less·ly** *adv.* **—shift'less·ness** *n.*

shift·y (shif'tē) *adj.* **shift·i·er, shift·i·est** 1 Characterized by or showing deceit or trickery. 2 Full of expedients; resourceful. **—shift'i·ly** *adv.* **—shift'i·ness** *n.*

shill (shil) *n. Slang* The ally of a sidewalk peddler or gambler who makes a purchase or bet to encourage onlookers to buy or bet. [?]

shil·le·lagh (shi·lā'lē, -lə) *n.* In Ireland, a stout cudgel made of oak or blackthorn. Also **shil·la'lah, shil·lea'lah, shil·le'lah.** [< *Shillelagh,* a town in Ireland famed for its oaks]

shil·ling (shil'ing) *n.* 1 A current silver coin of Great Britain, equal to five (new) pence or 1/20 of a pound. 2 A former colonial American coin, varying in value from 12 to 16 cents. [< OE *scilling*]

shil·ly-shal·ly (shil'ē·shal'ē) *v.i.* **·lied, ·ly·ing** To act with indecision; vacillate. —*adj.* Irresolute; hesitating. —*n.* Weak or foolish vacillation; irresolution. —*adv.* In an irresolute manner. [Redupl. of *Shall I?*] **—shil'ly-shal'li·er** *n.*

shim (shim) *n.* A thin wedge of metal, wood, etc., used to fill out space. —*v.t.* **shimmed, shim·ming** To wedge up, fill out, or level by inserting a shim. [?]

shim·mer (shim'ər) *v.i.* To shine faintly; give off or emit a tremulous light; glimmer. —*n.* A tremulous shining or gleaming; glimmer. [< OE *scimerian*] **—shim'mer·y** *adj.*

shim·my (shim'ē) *n. pl.* **·mies** 1 A jazz dance accompanied by shaking movements. 2 Undesired oscillation or vibration, as of automobile wheels. —*v.i.* **·mied, ·my·ing** 1 To vibrate or wobble. 2 To dance the shimmy. [Alter. of CHEMISE]

shin (shin) *n.* 1 The front part of the leg below the knee; also, the shinbone. 2 The lower foreleg: a *shin* of beef. —*v.t. & v.i.* **shinned, shin·ning** To climb (a pole) by gripping with the hands or arms and the shins or legs: usu. with *up.* [< OE *scinu*]

shin·bone (shin′bōn′) *n.* TIBIA.

shin·dig (shin′dig) *n. Slang* A dance or noisy party. [?]

shine (shīn) *v.i.* **shone** or *(esp. for def. 5)* **shined, shin·ing** 1 To emit light; beam; glow. 2 To show or be conspicuous. 3 To excel; be preeminent. —*v.t.* 4 To cause to shine. 5 To brighten by rubbing or polishing. —*n.* 1 Radiance; luster; sheen. 2 Fair weather; sunshine. 3 *Informal* A liking or fancy. 4 *Informal* A smart trick or prank. 5 A gloss or polish, as on shoes. [< OE *scīnan*]

shin·er (shī′nər) *n.* 1 One who or that which shines. 2 Any of various species of minnows with silvery scales. 3 *Slang* A black eye.

shin·gle[1] (shing′gəl) *n.* 1 A thin, tapering piece of wood or other material, used in courses to cover roofs. 2 A small signboard bearing the name of a doctor, lawyer, etc., and placed outside his office. 3 A short haircut. —*v.t.* **·gled, ·gling** 1 To cover (a roof, building, etc.) with shingles. 2 To cut (the hair) short. [< L *scandula* a shingle] —**shin′gler** *n.*

shin·gle[2] (shing′gəl) *n.* 1 Rounded, stones, coarser than gravel, found on the seashore. 2 A place strewn with shingle, as a beach. [?] —**shin′gly** *adj.*

shin·gles (shing′gəlz) *n. pl. (construed as sing.)* A painful viral disease marked by inflammation of sensory nerves and blistering, chiefly affecting the torso. [< L *cingulum* girdle]

shin·ing (shī′ning) *adj.* 1 Emitting or reflecting a continuous light; gleaming. 2 Of unusual excellence; conspicuous. —**shin′ing·ly** *adv.*

shin·ny[1] (shin′ē) *n.* A game resembling hockey, or one of the sticks or clubs used by the players. Also **shin′ney.** [< *shin ye,* a cry used in the game]

shin·ny[2] (shin′ē) *v.i* **·nied, ·ny·ing** *Informal* To climb using one's shins: usu. with *up.*

Shin·to (shin′tō) *n.* The primary religion of Japan, consisting chiefly in ancestor worship, and formerly in the worship of the Emperor as a divinity. Also **Shin′to·ism.** [< Chin. *shin* god + *tao* way] —**Shin′to·ist** *n.*

shin·y (shī′nē) *adj.* **shin·i·er, shin·i·est** 1 Glistening; glossy; polished. 2 Full of sunshine; bright. —**shin′i·ness** *n.*

ship (ship) *n.* 1 Any large vessel suitable for deep-water navigation. 2 The crew and officers of such a vessel. 3 An aircraft or spacecraft. —*v.* **shipped, ship·ping** *v.t.* 1 To transport by ship. 2 To send by any means of transportation, as by rail, truck, or air. 3 To hire and receive for service on board a vessel, as sailors. 4 To draw (oars) inside a boat. *Naut.* To receive over the side: to *ship* a wave. —*v.i.* 6 To go on board ship; embark. 7 To enlist as a seaman. [< OE *scip*]

-ship *suffix* 1 The state or quality of: *friendship.* 2 Office, rank, or dignity of: *kingship.* 3 The art or skill of: *marksmanship.* [< OE *-scipe*]

ship biscuit A hard, crackerlike biscuit; hardtack.

ship·board (ship′bôrd′, -bōrd′) *n.* A ship. —**on shipboard** In or on a ship.

ship·build·er (ship′bil′dər) *n.* One who designs or works at building ships. —**ship′build′ing** *n.*

ship·load (ship′lōd′) *n.* A load that a ship can carry.

ship·mas·ter (ship′mas′tər, -mäs′-) *n.* The captain or master of a merchant ship.

ship·mate (ship′māt′) *n.* A fellow sailor.

ship·ment (ship′mənt) *n.* 1 The act of shipping. 2 Goods shipped; a consignment.

ship·per (ship′ər) *n.* One who ships goods.

ship·ping (ship′ing) *n.* 1 The act, process, or business of shipping goods. 2 Ships collectively, esp. with respect to nationality or tonnage.

ship·shape (ship′shāp′) *adj.* Trim; orderly; neat. —*adv.* In a seamanlike manner; neatly.

ship·worm (ship′wûrm′) *n.* Any of various wormlike marine mollusks that undermine wooden piers, ships, etc., by boring into them.

ship·wreck (ship′rek′) *n.* 1 A ship or parts of it after being wrecked. 2 The partial or total destruction of a ship at sea. 3 Utter destruction; ruin. —*v.t.* 1 To wreck, as a vessel. 2 To bring to disaster; destroy.

ship·wright (ship′rīt′) *n.* One whose work is to construct or repair ships.

ship·yard (ship′yärd′) *n.* An enclosure where ships are built or repaired.

shire (shīr) *n.* A territorial division of Great Britain; a county. [< OE *scīr*]

shirk (shûrk) *v.t.* 1 To avoid doing (something that should be done). —*v.i.* 2 To avoid work or evade obligation. —*n.* One who shirks: also **shirk′er.** [?]

shirr (shûr) *v.t.* 1 To gather (cloth) by parallel rows of small stitches. 2 To bake with crumbs in a buttered dish, as eggs. —*n.* A gathering of cloth made by shirring. [?]

shirt (shûrt) *n.* 1 A garment for the upper part of the body, usu. having a collar and cuffs and buttoning along the front. 2 UNDERSHIRT. —**lose one's shirt** *Slang* To lose everything. [< OE *scyrte* shirt, short garment]

shirt·ing (shûr′ting) *n.* Material used for making shirts, blouses, etc.

shirt-sleeve (shûrt′slēv′) *adj.* 1 Not wearing a jacket or coat; informally dressed: a *shirt-sleeve* audience. Also **shirt-sleeved.** 2 Straightforward; plain; simple and direct in technique, approach, manner, etc.: *shirt-sleeve* diplomacy.

shirt·waist (shûrt′wāst′) *n.* A tailored blouse or shirt worn by women.

Shi·va (shē′və) SIVA.

shiv·er[1] (shiv′ər) *v.i.* To tremble, as with cold or fear. —*n.* The act of shivering; a shaking or quivering. —**shiv′er·y** *adj.* [ME *shiveren*]

shiv·er[2] (shiv′ər) *v.t. & v.i.* To break suddenly into fragments; shatter. —*n.* A splinter; silver. [ME *schivere*]

shlock (shlok) *n.* SCHLOCK. —**shlock′y** *adj.* **(·i·er, ·i·est)**

shoal[1] (shōl) *n.* 1 A shallow place in any body of water. 2 A bank or bar of sand, esp. one seen at low water. —*v.i.* To become shallow. [< OE *sceald* shallow]

shoal[2] (shōl) *n.* A thing or school, as of fish. —*v.i.* To gather in shoals. [< OE *scolu* shoal of fish.]

shoat (shōt) *n.* A young hog. [ME *shote*]

shock[1] (shok) *n.* 1 A violent collision or concussion; impact; blow. 2 The result of such a collision. 3 A sudden, severe effect on the mind or emotions; jolt: the *shock* of recognition. 4 Something causing such an effect. 5 An acute impairment of vital functions associated with failure of the circulatory system following grave trauma such as burns, poisoning, brain injury, massive bleeding, etc. 6 Involuntary muscular contraction caused by the passage of an electric current through the body. —*v.t.* 1 To disturb the emotions or mind of; horrify; disgust. 2 To subject to an electric shock. 3 To shake by sudden collison; jar. [< OF *choc*] —**shock′er** *n.* —**Syn.** *v.* 1 appall, take aback, surprise, astound.

shock[2] (shok) *n.* A number of sheaves of grain, stalks of corn, or the like, stacked for drying upright in a field. —*v.t. & v.i.* To gather (grain) into a shock or shocks. [ME *schokke*] —**shock′er** *n.*

shock[3] (shok) *adj.* Shaggy; bushy. —*n.* A coarse, tangled mass, as of hair. [?]

shock absorber *Mech.* A device designed to absorb the energy of sudden impacts, as in the suspension of an automobile.

shock·ing (shok′ing) *adj.* Causing sudden and violent surprise, horror, etc.: *shocking* news. —**shock′ing·ly** *adv.*

shock therapy A method of treating mental illness by inducing convulsions and unconsciousness with electric current or certain drugs. Also **shock treatment.**

shock wave *Physics* A powerful compression wave produced by a body moving faster than the speed of sound.

shod (shod) *p.t. & p.p.* of SHOE.

shod·dy (shod′ē) *n. pl.* **·dies** 1 Reclaimed wool obtained by shredding waste materials. 2 Fiber or cloth manufactured of inferior material. 3 Vulgar display; sham. 4 Refuse; waste. —*adj.* **·di·er, ·di·est** 1 Poorly made; inferior. 2 Made of or containing shoddy. 3 Cheaply pretentious; vulgar. 4 Nasty; mean: a *shoddy* remark. [?] —**shod′di·ly** *adv.* —**shod′di·ness** *n.* —**Syn.** *adj.* 1 tawdry, cheap, sloppy, second-rate.

shoe (shōō) *n.* **1** An outer covering, usu. of leather, for the human foot. **2** Something resembling a shoe in position or use. **3** A rim or plate of iron to protect the hoof of an animal. **4** The tread or outer covering of a pneumatic tire. **5** A braking device that stops or retards the motion of an object. —*v.t.* **shod** or **shoed, shoe·ing** To furnish with shoes or the like. [< OE *scōh*] —**sho'er** *n.*

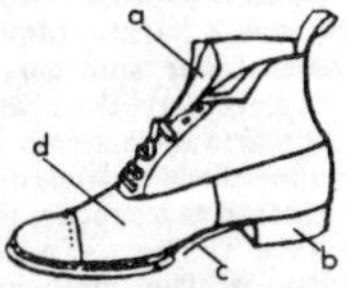

Shoe
a. tongue. b. heel.
c. shank. d. vamp.

shoe·horn (shōō'hôrn') *n.* A smooth curved implement as of metal, horn, etc., shaped to aid in putting on a shoe.
shoe·lace (shōō'lās) *n.* A cord or string used to fasten a shoe.
shoe·mak·er (shōō'mā'kər) *n.* One who makes or repairs shoes. —**shoe'mak'ing** *n.*
shoe·shine (shōō'shīn') *n.* The waxing and polishing of a pair of shoes.
shoe·string (shōō'string) *n.* SHOELACE. —**on a shoestring** With meager or inadequate financial resources.
shoe·tree (shōō'trē') *n.* A rigid form inserted in a shoe to hold its shape or to stretch it.
sho·far (shō'fär) A ram's horn used in Jewish ritual, sounded on solemn occasions. [< Heb. *shōphār*]
sho·gun (shō'gun) *n.* The hereditary commander in chief of the Japanese army until 1868. [< Chin. *chiang-chün* leader of an army] —**sho'gun·ate** (-it, -āt) *n.*
shone (shōn, shon) *p.t. & p.p.* of SHINE.
shoo (shōō) *interj.* Get away! —*v.t.* **1** To drive away by crying "shoo." —*v.i.* **2** To cry "shoo."
shoo-in (shōō'in') *n. Informal* One who is virtually certain to win, as an election.
shook (shŏŏk) *p.t.* of SHAKE.
shoot (shōōt) *v.* **shot, shoot·ing** *v.t.* **1** To hit, wound, or kill with a missile discharged from a weapon. **2** To discharge (a missile or weapon): to *shoot* an arrow or a gun. **3** To send forth, as questions, glances, etc. **4** To pass over or through swiftly: to *shoot* rapids. **5** To photograph or film. **6** To thrust out; dart; flick: with *out:* He *shot* out an arm in gesture. **7** To push into or out of the fastening, as the bolt of a door. **8** To propel, discharge, or dump, as down a chute or from a container. **9** *Slang* To inject (a drug, esp. a narcotic). **10** In games: **a** To score (a goal, point, total score, etc.). **b** To play (golf, craps, pool, etc.). **c** To propel (a basketball, puck, marble, etc.) to attempt a score. **d** To cast (dice). —*v.i.* **11** To discharge a missile from a firearm, bow, etc. **12** To go off; discharge. **13** To move swiftly; dart. **14** To extend or project. **15** To put forth buds, leaves, etc. **16** To record photographically. **17** In games, to make a play by propelling the ball, puck, etc., in a certain manner. —**shoot at** (or **for**) *Informal* To strive for; seek to attain. —**shoot the works** *Informal* To risk everything. —*n.* **1** A young branch or growth; offshoot. **2** The process of early growth. **3** A narrow passage in a stream; a rapid. **4** An inclined passage down which anything may be shot. **5** The act of shooting; a shot. **6** A shooting match, hunting party, etc. [< OE *scēotan*] —**shoot'er** *n.*
shooting star METEOR.
shoot-out (shōōt'out') *n.* A battle involving an exchange of gunfire.
shop (shop) *n.* **1** A place where goods and services are sold at retail: also **shoppe. 2** A place for the carrying on of any skilled work: a machine *shop.* —**talk shop** To discuss one's work. —*v.i.* **shopped, shop·ping** To visit shops or stores to purchase or look at goods. [< OE *sceoppa* booth] —**shop'per** *n.* • *Shoppe* is an archaic spelling but is still used in the names of some establishments to suggest a quaint, old-fashioned character. However, the spelling *shop* has been in use since at least 1600, so it is hardly a novelty.
shop·keep·er (shop'kē'pər) *n.* One who owns or runs a shop.
shop·lift·er (shop'lif'tər) *n.* One who steals goods displayed for sale in a shop. —**shop'lift'ing** *n.*
shopping center A group of retail stores, restaurants, etc., including an ample parking area, usu. built as a unit and accessible chiefly by automobile.
shop steward A union worker elected to represent the union in conferences, etc., with management.
shop·worn (shop'wôrn', -wōrn') *adj.* **1** Soiled or damaged from having been handled or on display in a store. **2** Lacking freshness or originality: *shopworn* ideas.
sho·ran (shôr'an, shō'ran) *n.* A short-range electronic navigation system for ships and aircraft. [< *sho(rt) ra(nge) n(avigation)*]
shore[1] (shôr, shōr) *n.* **1** The land adjacent to an ocean, sea, lake, or large river. **2** Land, as distinguished from a body of water. [ME]
shore[2] (shôr, shōr) *v.t.* **shored, shor·ing** To prop, as a wall, by a vertical or sloping timber: usu. with *up.* —*n.* A beam set endwise as a prop, as against the side of a building. [ME *shoren*]
shore bird Any of various birds that feed and nest along the edges of lakes, oceans, rivers, etc.
shore·line (shôr'līn', shōr'-) *n.* The line or contour of a shore.
shore patrol A detail of the U.S. Navy, Coast Guard, or Marine Corps assigned to police duties ashore.
shore·ward (shôr'wərd, shōr'-) *adj. & adv.* Toward the shore. Also **shore'wards.**
shor·ing (shôr'ing, shō'ring) *n.* **1** The act of propping, as with shores. **2** Shores or their manner of use.
shorn (shôrn, shōrn) A *p.p.* of SHEAR.
short (shôrt) *adj.* **1** Having relatively little linear extension; not long. **2** Being below the average stature; not tall. **3** Having relatively little extension in time; brief. **4** Of no great distance: a *short* trip. **5** Less than the usual or standard duration, quantity, extent, etc.: on *short* notice; a *short* letter. **6** Having few items: a *short* list. **7** Not reaching or attaining a goal or requirement: an effort *short* of the mark. **8** Not retentive: a *short* memory. **9** Abrupt in manner; curt. **10** Having an inadequate supply: *short* of cash. **11** Quickly aroused or agitated: a *short* temper. **12** *Phonet.* **a** Of relatively brief duration. **b** Describing any vowel sound that contrasts with a long vowel, as the vowel sound in *mat* contrasted with that in *mate.* **13** In finance: **a** Not having in one's possession when selling, as stocks or commodities. **b** Describing a sale of stocks or commodities that the seller does not possess but anticipates procuring subsequently at a lower price for delivery as contracted. **14** In English prosody, unaccented. **15** Flaky or crisp: pastry made *short* with lard. —**for short** For brevity and ease of expression: The University of Connecticut is called Uconn *for short.* —**in short** In summary; briefly. —**in short order** Without delay; forthwith; promptly. —*n.* **1** Something short, as a garment, vowel, syllable, etc. **2** *pl.* Short trousers extending to the knee or above the knee. **3** *pl.* A man's undergarment resembling short trousers. **4** SHORT CIRCUIT. **5** SHORT SUBJECT. —*adv.* **1** Abruptly: to stop *short.* **2** In a curt manner. **3** So as to be short of a goal or mark. **4** By means of a short sale. —*v.t. & v.i.* **1** To give (someone) less than the amount due. **2** SHORT-CIRCUIT. [< OE *sceort*] —**short'ness** *n.*
short·age (shôr'tij) *n.* An inadequate supply; deficiency.
short·bread (shôrt'bred') *n.* A rich, dry cake or cooky made with shortening.
short·cake (shôrt'kāk') *n.* A dessert consisting of a cake or biscuit served with fruit and often topped with whipped cream.
short·change (shôrt'chānj') *v.t.* **·changed, ·chang·ing 1** To give less change than is due to. **2** To give less than what is rightfully due; cheat. —**short'chang'er** *n.*
short-cir·cuit (shôrt'sûr'kit) *v.t. & v.i.* To make a short circuit (in).
short circuit *Electr.* An electrical connection of low resistance or impedance, esp. when accidental or unintended.
short·com·ing (shôrt'kum'ing) *n.* A defect; imperfection.
short·cut (shôrt'kut') *n.* **1** A route between two places

shorter than the regular way. 2 A means or method that saves time, effort, etc.

short·en (shôr′tən) *v.t.* 1 To make short or shorter; reduce; lessen. 2 To make flaky or crisp, as pastry. —*v.i.* 3 To become short or shorter. —**short′en·er** *n.*

short·en·ing (shôr′tən·ing, shôrt′ning) *n.* 1 Edible fat, esp. as used in bakery products. 2 An abbreviation.

short·fall (shôrt′fôl′) *n.* 1 A failure to meet an expectation or requirement. 2 The amount or extent of such a failure: a *shortfall* of 20 percent.

short·hand (shôrt′hand′) *n.* 1 Any of various systems of recording speech by writing symbols, abbreviations, etc.; stenography. 2 Any method of quick communication. —*adj.* 1 Written in shorthand. 2 Using shorthand.

short-hand·ed (shôrt′han′did) *adj.* Not having a sufficient number of assistants or workmen.

short·horn (shôrt′hôrn′) *n.* One of a breed of cattle with short horns.

short-lived (shôrt′līvd′, -livd′) *adj.* Living or lasting but a short time.

short·ly (shôrt′lē) *adv.* 1 In a short time; soon. 2 In few words; briefly. 3 Curtly; abruptly.

short shrift Little or no mercy or delay in dealing with a person or disposing of a matter.

short·sight·ed (shôrt′sī′tid) *adj.* 1 NEARSIGHTED. 2 Resulting from or characterized by lack of foresight. —**short′-sight′ed·ly** *adv.* —**short′-sight′ed·ness** *n.*

short·stop (shôrt′stop′) *n.* In baseball, an infielder stationed between second and third bases.

short story A narrative prose story shorter than a novel or novelette.

short subject A relatively brief film, as a documentary or animated cartoon.

short-tem·pered (shôrt′tem′pərd) *adj.* Easily aroused to anger.

short-term (shôrt′tûrm′) *adj.* Payable a short time after issue, as securities.

short ton 2,000 pounds avoirdupois.

short wave A radio wave having a wavelength of about 100 meters or less. —**short′-wave′** *adj.*

short-wind·ed (shôrt′win′did) *adj.* Becoming easily out of breath. —**short′-wind′ed·ness** *n.*

Sho·sho·ne (shō·shō′nē) *n.* One of a large tribe of North American Indians, formerly occupying parts of Wyoming, Idaho, Nevada, and Utah. Also **Sho·sho′ni.**

Sho·sho·ne·an (shō·shō′nē·ən, shō′shə·nē′ən) *n.* The largest branch of the Uto-Aztecan linguistic family of North American Indians. —*adj.* Of or pertaining to this linguistic branch. Also **Sho·sho′ni·an.**

shot[1] (shot) *n.* 1 The act of shooting, as a firearm. 2 Something likened to a shot, as a cutting remark. 3 *pl.* **shot** a Any of the lead pellets that comprise ammunition for a shotgun; also, the pellets collectively. b A solid missile, as a ball of iron, fired from a cannon or other gun. 4 A solid metal ball thrown for distance in sports competitions. 5 The range of a projectile. 6 One who shoots; a marksman. 7 A single effort, attempt, or opportunity to do a specific thing: to have a *shot* at getting the job. 8 In certain sports and games, the act or manner of shooting the ball, puck, etc., as in attempting a score. 9 A conjecture; guess. 10 A hypodermic injection, as of a drug, or the dose so administered. 11 An action or scene recorded on film. 12 The taking of a photograph; also, a photograph. 13 A blast, as in mining. —**like a shot** Very quickly. —*adj.* 1 Having a changeable or variegated appearance: purple fabric *shot* with gold. 2 *Informal* Utterly exhausted or ruined; washed-up. [< OE *scot*]

shot[2] (shot) *p.t. & p.p.* of SHOOT.

shote (shōt) *n.* SHOAT.

shot·gun (shot′gun′) *n.* A smoothbore gun, often double-barreled, adapted for the discharge of shot at short range. —*adj.* Coerced with, or as with, a shotgun.

Repeating shotgun

should (sho͝od) 1 *p.t.* of SHALL. 2 An auxiliary expressing: a Obligation: You *should* write that letter. b Condition: If I *should* go, he would go too. c Futurity, as viewed from the past: She wondered how she *should* dress for the party. d Expectation: I *should* be at home by noon. e Politeness or modesty in requests or statements of doubt: I *should* hardly think so. [< OE *scolde,* p.t. of *sculan* owe]

shoul·der (shōl′dər) *n.* 1 The part of the trunk between the neck and the arm or forelimb. 2 The joint connecting the arm or forelimb with the body. 3 *pl.* The area of the upper back including both shoulders. 4 The shoulders considered as a support for burdens or the seat of responsibility. 5 The part of a garment designed to cover the shoulder. 6 The forequarter of an animal. 7 Something resembling a shoulder in form, as the broadened part of a bottle below the neck. 8 Either edge of a road or highway. —**straight from the shoulder** *Informal* Candidly; straightforwardly. —*v.t.* 1 To assume as something to be borne: to *shoulder* the blame. 2 To bear upon the shoulders. 3 To push with or as with the shoulder. —*v.i.* 4 To push with the shoulder. —**shoulder arms** To rest a rifle against the shoulder, holding the butt with the hand on the same side. [< OE *sculder* shoulder]

shoulder blade SCAPULA.

should·n't (sho͝od′nt) Contraction of *should not.*

shout (shout) *n.* A sudden and loud outcry. —*v.t.* 1 To utter with a shout; say loudly. —*v.i.* 2 To utter a shout; cry out loudly. [ME *shouten*] —**shout′er** *n.*

shove (shuv) *v.t. & v.i.* **shoved, shov·ing** 1 To push, as along a surface. 2 To press forcibly (against); jostle. —**shove off** 1 To push along or away, as a boat. 2 *Informal* To depart. —*n.* The act of pushing or shoving. [< OE *scūfan*] —**shov′er** *n.*

shov·el (shuv′əl) *n.* A flattened scoop with a handle, as for digging, lifting earth, rock, etc. —*v.* **·eled** or **·elled, ·el·ing** or **·el·ling** *v.t.* 1 To take up and move or gather with a shovel. 2 To toss hastily or in large quantities as if with a shovel. 3 To clear or clean with a shovel, as a path. —*v.i.* 4 To work with a shovel. [< OE *scofl*] —**shov′el·er, shov′el·ler, shov′el·ful** *n.*

show (shō) *v.* **showed, shown** or **showed, show·ing** *v.t.* 1 To cause or permit to be seen; present to view. 2 To cause or allow (something) to be understood or known; explain. 3 To make known by behavior or expression; reveal: to *show* emotion. 4 To cause (someone) to understand or see; explain something to. 5 To confer; bestow: to *show* favor. 6 To make evident by the use of logic; prove. 7 To guide; lead, as into a room: Please *show* them in. 8 To enter in a show or exhibition. —*v.i.* 9 To become visible or known. 10 To appear; seem. 11 To make one's or its appearance. 12 To give a theatrical performance; appear. 13 In racing, to finish third or better. —**show off** To exhibit proudly; display ostentatiously. —**show up** 1 To expose or be exposed, as faults. 2 To be evident or prominent. 3 To make an appearance. 4 *Informal* To be better than. —*n.* 1 A presentation, as of a film, television program, or live entertainment, for viewing by spectators. 2 An exhibition, as of merchandise or art. 3 A competition at which certain animals, as dogs, are displayed and judged. 4 Someone or something regarded as a spectacle to be viewed, as in wonder or amusement. 5 An act of showing; display or manifestation: a *show* of strength. 6 Pretense or semblance; also, ostentation: mere *show.* 7 A sign of metal, oil, etc., in a mining or drilling operation. 8 In racing, a finish of third place or better. [< OE *scēawian*] —**show′er** *n.* —**Syn.** *v.* 1 exhibit, manifest, display. 4 convince, teach. *n.* 1 viewing, showing. 5 mark, sign, indication.

show biz *Slang* SHOW BUSINESS.

show·boat (shō′bōt′) *n.* A boat on which an acting troupe gives performances in river towns.

show business The entertainment industry, esp. the theater, motion pictures, and television.

show·case (shō′kās′) *n.* A glass case for exhibiting and protecting articles for sale.

show·down (shō′doun′) *n.* *Informal* Any action that forces a resolution of an issue or dispute.

show·er (shou′ər) *n.* 1 A fall of rain, hail, or sleet, esp. of short duration. 2 A copious fall, as of tears, sparks, or other small objects. 3 A bath in which water is sprayed from an overhead nozzle: also **shower bath.** 4 A party for the giving of gifts, as to a bride. —*v.t.* 1 To sprinkle or wet with or as with showers. 2 To discharge in a shower; pour out. 3 To bestow upon in large numbers; overwhelm: to

shower her with gifts. —*v.i.* 4 To fall as in a shower. 5 To take a shower bath. [< OE *scūr*] —**show′er·y** *adj.*
show·ing (shō′ing) *n.* 1 An act of presenting for public view, as a film. 2 A result of being shown, as in competition; record: a fine *showing.* 3 Presentation; statement, as of a subject.
show·man (shō′mən) *n. pl.* **·men** (-mən) 1 One who exhibits or produces shows. 2 One who is skilled at the art of effective performance. —**show′man·ship** *n.*
shown (shōn) *p.p.* of SHOW.
show·off (shō′ôf′) *n.* One who makes a pretentious display of himself.
show·piece (shō′pēs′) *n.* A prized object considered worthy of special exhibit.
show·place (shō′plās′) *n.* A place exhibited or noted for its beauty, historic interest, etc.
show·room (shō′ro͞om′) *n.* A room for the display of merchandise.
show·y (shō′ē) *adj.* **show·i·er, show·i·est** 1 Striking; splendid; brilliant. 2 Brilliant or conspicuous in a superficial or tasteless way; gaudy; meretricious. —**show′i·ly** *adv.* —**show′i·ness** *n.*
shpt. shipment.
shrank (shrangk) *p.t.* of SHRINK.
shrap·nel (shrap′nəl) *n. pl.* **·nel** 1 A projectile for use against personnel, containing metal balls and a charge that expels them in mid-air. 2 Shell fragments. [< Henry *Shrapnel,* 1761–1842, British artillery officer]
shred (shred) *n.* 1 A long, irregular strip torn or cut off. 2 A fragment; particle. —*v.t.* **shred·ded** or **shred, shred·ding** To tear or cut into shreds. [< OE *scrēade* cutting] —**shred′der** *n.*
shrew (shro͞o) *n.* 1 Any of numerous tiny mouselike mammals having a long pointed snout and soft fur. 2 A vexatious or nagging woman. [< OE *scrēawa*] —**shrew′ish** *adj.* —**shrew′ish·ly** *adv.* —**shrew′ish·ness** *n.*

Shrew

shrewd (shro͞od) *adj.* 1 Having keen insight, esp. in practical matters; clever; able. 2 Artful; sly. [< ME *shrew* malicious person] —**shrewd′ly** *adv.* —**shrewd′ness** *n.*
shriek (shrēk) *n.* A sharp, shrill cry or scream. —*v.i.* 1 To utter a shriek. —*v.t.* 2 To utter with a shriek. [< ON *skrækja*] —**shriek′er** *n.*
shrift (shrift) *n. Archaic* The act of shriving; confession. [< OE *scrift*]
shrike (shrīk) *n.* Any of various predatory birds with hooked bill and a slim tail. [< OE *scrīc* thrush]
shrill (shril) *adj.* 1 High-pitched and piercing, as a sound. 2 Emitting a sharp, piercing sound. 3 Harsh and immoderate: *shrill* criticism. —*v.t.* 1 To cause to utter a shrill sound. —*v.i.* 2 To make a shrill sound. [ME *shrille*] —**shrill′·ness** *n.* —**shril′y** *adv.* —**Syn.** 1 penetrating. 3 intemperate, hysterical, bitter.
shrimp (shrimp) *n. pl.* **shrimp** or **shrimps** 1 Any of numerous small, long-tailed crustaceans having ten legs and a fused head and thorax covered with a carapace, esp. various edible marine species. 2 *Informal* A small or insignificant person. [ME *shrimpe*]

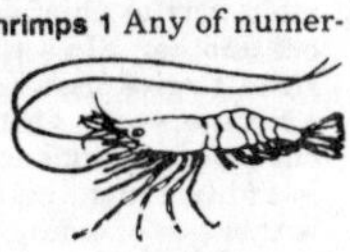
Shrimp

shrine (shrīn) *n.* 1 A receptacle for sacred relics. 2 A sacred tomb or chapel. 3 A thing or spot made sacred by historic or other association. [< L *scrinium* case]
shrink (shringk) *v.* **shrank** or **shrunk, shrunk** or **shrunk·en, shrink·ing** *v.i.* 1 To draw together; contract as from heat, cold, etc. 2 To become less or smaller; diminish. 3 To draw back, as from disgust or horror; recoil: with *from.* —*v.t.* 4 To cause to shrink, contract, or draw together. —*n.* 1 The act of shrinking. 2 *Slang* A psychiatrist or psychoanalyst. [< OE *scrincan*] —**shrink′a·ble** *adj.* —**shrink′er** *n.*
shrink·age (shringk′ij) *n.* 1 The act or process of shrinking; contraction. 2 The amount lost by contraction. 3 Decrease in value; depreciation.
shrive (shrīv) *v.* **shrove** (shrōv) or **shrived, shriv·en** (shriv′-) or **shrived, shriv·ing** *Archaic v.t.* 1 To receive the confession of and give absolution to. —*v.i.* 2 To make confession. 3 To hear confession. [< OE *scrīfan*] —**shriv′er** *n.*
shriv·el (shriv′əl) *v.t. & v.i.* **·eled** or **·elled, ·el·ing** or **·el·ling** 1 To contract into wrinkles; shrink and wrinkle. 2 To make or become helpless or impotent; wither. [?]
shroud (shroud) *n.* 1 A cloth used to wrap a corpse for burial. 2 Something that envelops or conceals. 3 *Naut.* One of a set of ropes or wires stretched from a masthead to the sides of a ship, serving to strengthen the mast laterally. —*v.t.* 1 To clothe in a shroud. 2 To envelop or conceal; block from view. [< OE *scrūd* a garment]
shrove (shrōv) *p.t.* of SHRIVE.
Shrove·tide (shrōv′tīd′) *n.* The three days immediately preceding Ash Wednesday, on which confession is made in preparation for Lent.
shrub (shrub) *n.* A woody perennial of low stature, usu. with several stems. [< OE *scrybb* brushwood] —**shrub′bi·ness** *n.* —**shrub′by** *adj.* (**·bi·er, ·bi·est**)
shrub·ber·y (shrub′ər·ē) *n. pl.* **·ber·ies** A group of shrubs, as in a garden.
shrug (shrug) *v.t. & v.i.* **shrugged, shrug·ging** To draw up (the shoulders), as in displeasure, doubt, surprise, etc. —*n.* The act of shrugging the shoulders. [?]
shrunk (shrungk) *p.t. & p.p.* of SHRINK.
shrunk·en (shrungk′ən) *p.p.* of SHRINK. —*adj.* Contracted and atrophied.
shtick (shtik) *n. Slang* Something contrived to make one's personality distinct or memorable, as an actor's characteristic mannerism or a comedian's routine. [< Yiddish < G *stück* piece, bit]
sh. tn. short ton.
shuck (shuk) *n.* 1 A husk, shell, or pod, as of corn. • See WALNUT. 2 A shell of an oyster or a clam. 3 *Informal* Something of little or no value: not worth *shucks.* —*v.t.* 1 To remove the husk or shell from (corn, oysters, etc.). 2 *Informal* To take off or cast off, as an outer covering. [?] —**shuck′er** *n.*
shucks (shuks) *interj. Informal* A mild exclamation of annoyance, disgust, etc.
shud·der (shud′ər) *v.i.* To tremble or shake, as from fright or cold. —*n.* A convulsive shiver, as from horror or fear. [ME *shudren*] —**Syn.** *v.* shiver, quake. *n.* tremor.
shuf·fle (shuf′əl) *v.* **·fled, ·fling** *v.t.* 1 To shift about so as to mix up or confuse; disorder. 2 To change the order of by mixing, as cards in a pack. 3 To move (the feet) along with a dragging gait. 4 To change or move from one place to another. —*v.i.* 5 To scrape the feet along. 6 To change position; shift ground. 7 To resort to indirect or deceitful methods; prevaricate. 8 To shuffle cards. —*n.* 1 A dragging of the feet. 2 The act of shuffling, as cards. 3 A deceitful or evasive course; artifice. [< LG *schuffeln*] —**shuf′fler** *n.*
shuf·fle·board (shuf′əl·bôrd′, -bōrd′) *n.* A game in which disks are slid by means of a pronged cue along a smooth surface toward numbered spaces.
shun (shun) *v.t.* **shunned, shun·ning** To keep clear of; avoid. [< OE *scunian*] —**shun′ner** *n.*
shunt (shunt) *v.t.* 1 To turn aside. 2 In railroading, to switch, as a train or car, from one track to another. 3 *Electr.* a To connect a shunt in parallel with. b To be connected as a shunt for or of. 4 To put off on someone else, as a task. —*v.i.* 5 To move to one side. 6 *Electr.* To be diverted by a shunt: said of current. 7 To move back and forth; shuttle. —*n.* 1 The act of shunting. 2 A railroad switch. 3 *Electr.* A conductor joining two points in a circuit and diverting part of the current. —**shunt′er** *n.*
shush (shush) *interj.* Keep quiet! —*v.t.* To try to quiet.
shut (shut) *v.* **shut, shut·ting** *v.t.* 1 To bring into such position as to close an opening. 2 To close (an opening) so as to prevent passage or movement in or out. 3 To close and fasten securely, as with a lock. 4 To keep from entering or leaving: with *out* or *in.* 5 To close, fold, or bring together, as extended parts: to *shut* an umbrella. —*v.i.* 6 To be or become closed or in a closed position. —**shut down** 1 To cease from operating, as a factory. 2 To lower;

come down close: The fog *shut down.* **—shut off** 1 To cause to stop operating: to *shut off* a light. 2 To separate: usu. with *from: shut off* from all companionship. **—shut out** In sports, to keep (an opponent) from scoring during the course of a game. **—shut up** 1 *Informal* To stop talking or cause to stop talking. 2 To close all the entrances to, as a house. 3 To imprison; confine. *—adj.* 1 Made fast or closed. 2 *Regional* Freed, as from something disagreeable; rid: with *of.* [< OE *scyttan*]

shut·down (shut′doun′) *n.* The closing of a mine, industrial plant, etc.

shut-eye (shut′ī′) *n. Slang* Sleep.

shut-in (shut′in′) *n.* An invalid who has to stay at home. *—adj.* 1 Obliged to stay at home. 2 Inclined to avoid people.

shut·out (shut′out′) *n.* In sports, a game in which one side is prevented from scoring.

shut·ter (shut′ər) *n.* 1 A hinged screen or cover, as for a window. 2 *Phot.* A mechanism for momentarily admitting light through a camera lens to a film or plate. 3 One who or that which shuts. *—v.t.* To furnish, close, or divide off with shutters.

shut·tle (shut′l) *n.* 1 A device used in weaving to carry the weft to and fro between the warp threads. 2 A similar device in a sewing machine. 3 A system of transportation for moving goods or passengers in both directions between two nearby points; also, the vehicle, as a bus, train, or airplane, operating between these points, usu. frequently. *—v.t. & v.i.* **·tled, ·tling** To move back and forth frequently or like a shuttle. [< OE *scytel* missile]

shut·tle·cock (shut′l·kok′) *n.* A rounded piece of cork, with a crown of feathers, that is hit back and forth in the game of badminton.

Shuttlecock

shy[1] (shī) *adj.* **shy·er, shy·est,** or **shi·er, shi·est** 1 Easily frightened or startled; timid. 2 Uneasy in the company of others; bashful; reserved. 3 Circumspect; watchful; wary. 4 Expressing or suggesting diffidence or reserve: a *shy* look. 5 *Informal* Having less than is called for or expected; short. *—v.t.* **shied, shy·ing** 1 To start suddenly to one side, as a horse. 2 To draw back, as from doubt or caution: with *off* or *away.* *—n.* A starting aside, as in fear. [< OE *scēoh* timid] **—shy′ly** *adv.* **—shy′ness** *n.*

shy[2] (shī) *v.t. & v.i.* **shied, shy·ing** To throw with a swift, sidelong motion. *—n. pl.* **shies** A careless throw; a fling. [?]

shy·ster (shīs′tər) *n. Informal* Anyone, esp. a lawyer, who conducts his business in an unscrupulous or tricky manner. [?]

SI International System of Units (Le Système International d'Unités).

Si silicon.

Si·am (sī·am′) *n.* The former name for THAILAND. **—Si·a·mese** (sī′ə·mēz′, -mēs′) *adj., n.*

Siamese cat A breed of short-haired cat, typically fawn-colored or pale cream, with dark ears, tail, feet, and face, and blue eyes.

Siamese twins Any twins conjoined at birth. [< Eng and Chang (1811–74), conjoined twins born in Siam.]

sib (sib) *n.* 1 A blood relation, esp. a brother or sister. 2 Kinsmen collectively; relatives. *—adj.* Related by blood; akin. [< OE *sibb*]

sib·i·lant (sib′ə·lənt) *adj.* 1 Hissing. 2 *Phonet.* Describing those consonants which are uttered with a hissing sound, as (s), (z), (sh), and (zh). *—n. Phonet.* A sibilant consonant. [< L *sibilare* to hiss] **—sib′i·lance** *n.* **—sib′i·lant·ly** *adv.*

sib·ling (sib′ling) *n.* A brother or sister. [< OE, a relative]

sib·yl (sib′əl) *n.* 1 In ancient Greece and Rome, any of several women who prophesied future events. 2 A fortune-teller; sorceress. **—si·byl·ic** (si·bil′ik) or **si·byl′lic, sib′yl·line** (-īn) *adj.*

sic[1] (sik) *adv.* So; thus: used within brackets after something quoted, to indicate that the quotation is exactly reproduced, even though questionable or incorrect. [L]

sic[2] (sik) *v.t.* **sicked, sick·ing** 1 To urge to attack: to *sic* a dog on a burglar. 2 To seek out or attack: used in the imperative esp. to a dog. [Var. of SEEK]

sick[1] (sik) *adj.* 1 Affected with disease; ill; ailing. 2 Of or used by sick persons. 3 Affected by nausea; nauseated. 4 Sickly; weak: a *sick* laugh. 5 Mentally or emotionally upset or ill: *sick* with grief. 6 Disposed to find offensive or wearisome from being surfeited: with *of: sick* of hearing transistor radios in public places. [< OE *sēoc*] **—sick′ish** *adj.* **—sick′ish·ly** *adv.* **—sick′ish·ness** *n.*

sick[2] (sik) *v.t.* SIC[2].

sick·bay (sik′bā′) *n.* That part of a ship or naval base set aside for the care of the sick.

sick·bed (sik′bed′) *n.* The bed upon which a sick person lies.

sick·en (sik′ən) *v.t. & v.i.* To make or become sick or disgusted. **—sick′en·er** *n.*

sick·en·ing (sik′ən·ing) *adj.* Disgusting; nauseating. **—sick′en·ing·ly** *adv.*

sick headache MIGRAINE.

sick·le (sik′əl) *n.* A cutting or reaping implement with a long, curved blade mounted on a short handle. *—v.t.* **·led, ·ling** To cut with a sickle, as grass, hay, etc. [< OE *sicel*]

Sickle

sick·le-cell anemia (sik′əl·sel′) A severe, hereditary anemia occurring among the offspring of parents who both have sickle-cell trait.

sickle-cell trait A tendency in erythrocytes to become deformed into a sickle shape and to clog small blood vessels, occurring chiefly among Negroes and due to the presence of a genetic hemoglobin abnormality inherited from one parent. Also **sickl·e·mi·a** (sik′əl·ē′mē·ə).

sick·ly (sik′lē) *adj.* **·li·er, ·li·est** 1 Habitually ailing; unhealthy; feeble. 2 Marked by the prevalence of sickness. 3 Nauseating; disgusting; sickening. 4 Of or characteristic of sickness: a *sickly* appearance. 5 Lacking in conviction; weak; unconvincing: a *sickly* excuse. 6 Faint; pallid. *—adv.* In a sick manner; poorly. *—v.t.* **·lied, ·ly·ing** To make sickly, as in color. **—sick′li·ly** *adv.* **—sick′li·ness** *n.*

sick·ness (sik′nis) *n.* 1 The state of being sick; illness. 2 A particular form of disease. 3 Nausea. 4 Any disordered and weakened state.

side (sīd) *n.* 1 Any of the boundary lines of a surface or any of the surfaces of a solid: the *side* of a box. 2 A boundary line or surface, distinguished from the top and bottom or front and back. 3 Either of the surfaces of an object of negligible thickness, as a sheet of paper or a coin. 4 The right half or the left half of a human body, esp. of the torso, or of any animal. 5 The space beside someone. 6 A lateral part of a surface or object: the right *side* of a room. 7 The lateral half of a slaughtered animal: a *side* of beef. 8 One of two or more contrasted surfaces, parts, or places: the far *side* of a river. 9 A slope, as of a mountain. 10 An opinion, aspect, or point of view: the conservative *side* of the issue. 11 A group of competitors or partisans of a point of view. 12 Family connection, esp. by descent through one parent: my father's *side.* **—on the side** In addition to the main part or chief activity. **—side by side** 1 Alongside one another. 2 In a spirit of cooperation; together. **—take sides** To give one's support to one of two sides engaged in a dispute. *—adj.* 1 Situated at or on one side. 2 Being from one side: a *side* glance. 3 Incidental: a *side* issue. 4 Being in addition to the main dish: a *side* order. *—v.t.* To provide with a side or sides. **—side with** To range oneself on the side of; support, esp. in a dispute. [< OE]

side arms Weapons worn at the side, as pistols.

side·board (sīd′bôrd′, -bōrd′) *n.* 1 A piece of dining-room furniture for holding tableware. 2 *pl. Brit.* SIDEBURNS.

side·burns (sīd′bûrnz′) *n.pl.* 1 Whiskers grown on the cheeks; burnsides. 2 The hair growing on the sides of a man's face in front of the ears.

side·car (sīd′kär′) *n.* A one-wheeled passenger car attached to the side of a motorcycle.

side effect A secondary, often harmful effect, as of a drug.

side·kick (sīd′kik′) *n. Slang* A faithful subordinate or friend.

side·light (sīd′līt′) *n.* 1 A light coming from the side. 2 Incidental illustration or information.

side·line (sīd′līn′) *n.* 1 An auxiliary line of goods. 2 Any additional or secondary work differing from one's main job. 3 One of the lines bounding the two sides of an athletic field or court, as in football or tennis. **4** *pl.* The area just outside these lines. —*v.t.* **·lined, ·lin·ing** To make unfit or unavailable for active participation: Injuries *sidelined* him.

side·long (sīd′lông′, -long′) *adj.* Inclining or tending to one side; lateral. —*adv.* **1** In a lateral or oblique direction. **2** On the side.

side·man (sīd′man′) *n. pl.* **·men** (-men′) One of the supporting musicians, as distinguished from the featured performers, of a band, esp. a jazz band.

si·de·re·al (sī·dir′ē·əl) *adj.* **1** Of or relating to the stars. **2** Measured by means of the stars: *sidereal* time. [< L *sidus* star] —**si·de′re·al·ly** *adv.*

sid·er·ite (sid′ə·rīt) *n.* **1** A glassy ferrous carbonate mineral. **2** An iron meteorite. [< Gk. *sidēros* iron] —**sid′er·it′ic** (-rit′ik) *adj.*

side·sad·dle (sīd′sad′l) *n.* A saddle for a woman wearing skirts, designed to be ridden facing sideways, with both legs on the same side of the horse.

side·show (sīd′shō′) *n.* **1** A small show incidental to a major one, as in a circus. **2** Any subordinate issue or attraction.

side·split·ting (sīd′split′ing) *adj.* Provoking wild laughter; hilarious.

side·step (sīd′step′) *v.* **·stepped, ·step·ping** *v.i.* **1** To step to one side. **2** To avoid responsibility. —*v.t.* **3** To avoid, as an issue; dodge. —**side′step′per** *n.*

side step A step or movement to one side.

side·swipe (sīd′swīp′) *v.t.* & *v.i.* **·swiped, ·swip·ing** To strike or scrape along the side: to *sideswipe* a car while passing it. —*n.* **1** A glancing collision along the side. **2** *Informal* An oblique or parenthetical criticism.

side·track (sīd′trak′) *v.t.* & *v.i.* **1** To move to a siding, as a railroad train. **2** To divert from the main issue or subject. —*n.* A railroad siding.

side·walk (sīd′wôk′) *n.* A pavement at the side of the street for pedestrians.

side·ward (sīd′wərd) *adj.* Directed or moving toward or from the side; lateral. —*adv.* Toward or from the side: also **side′wards.**

side·ways (sīd′wāz′) *adv.* **1** From one side. **2** So as to incline with the side forward: Hold it *sideways.* **3** Toward one side; askance; obliquely. —*adj.* Moving to or from one side. Also **side′way′, side′wise′** (-wīz′).

side-wheel (sīd′hwēl′) *adj.* Describing a steamboat having a paddle wheel on either side. —**side′-wheel′er** *n.*

sid·ing (sī′ding) *n.* **1** A railway track by the side of the main track. **2** A material used to cover the side of a frame building, as paneling or shingles.

si·dle (sīd′l) *v.i.* **·dled, ·dling** To move sideways, esp. in a cautious or stealthy manner. —*n.* A sideways step or movement. [< obs. *sidling* sidelong] —**si′dler** *n.*

siege (sēj) *n.* **1** The surrounding of a town or fortified place in an effort to seize it, as after a blockade. **2** A steady attempt to win something. **3** A trying time: a *siege* of illness. —*v.t.* **sieged, sieg·ing** BESIEGE. [< L *sedere* sit]

si·en·na (sē·en′ə) *n.* **1** A yellowish brown pigment consisting of clay containing oxides of iron and manganese. **2** A yellowish brown color. **3** BURNT SIENNA. [< Ital. *(terra di) Siena* (earth of) Siena]

si·er·ra (sē·er′ə) *n.* A mountain range or chain, esp. one having a jagged outline. [< L *serra* a saw]

Si·er·ra Le·one (sē·er′ä lē·ōn′, sir′ə-) An independent member of the Commonwealth of Nations in w Africa, 27,925 sq. mi., cap. Freetown. • See map at AFRICA.

si·es·ta (sē·es′tə) *n.* A nap or rest taken in the afternoon. [Sp.< L *sexta (hora)* sixth (hour), noon]

sieve (siv) *n.* A utensil or apparatus for sifting, consisting of a frame provided with a bottom of mesh wire. —*v.t.* & *v.i.* **sieved, siev·ing** To sift. [<OE *sife* sieve]

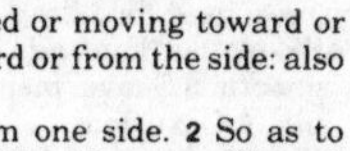

Sieve

sift (sift) *v.t.* **1** To pass through a sieve in order to separate the fine parts from the coarse. **2** To scatter by or as by a sieve. **3** To examine carefully. **4** To separate as if with a sieve; distinguish: to *sift* fact from fiction. —*v.i.* **5** To use a sieve. **6** To fall or pass through or as through a sieve: The light *sifts* through the trees. [<OE *siftan* sift] —**sift′er** *n.*

Sig., sig. signal; signature; signor.

sigh (sī) *v.i.* **1** To draw in and exhale a deep, audible breath, as in expressing sorrow, weariness, pain, or relief. **2** To make a sound suggestive of a sigh, as the wind. **3** To yearn; long: with *for.* —*v.t.* **4** To express with a sigh. —*n.* **1** The act of sighing. **2** A sound of sighing or one suggestive of sighing. [ME *sighen*] —**sigh′er** *n.*

sight (sīt) *n.* **1** The act or faculty of seeing; vision. **2** Something seen; an image perceived by the eye; spectacle: an inspiring *sight;* an ugly *sight.* **3** A view; glimpse: to catch *sight* of someone. **4** The range or scope of vision. **5** *Informal* Something remarkable or strange in appearance. **6** *Usu. pl.* A place or thing of particular interest, as to a tourist: seeing the *sights.* **7** A point of view; estimation. **8** Mental perception or awareness: Don't lose *sight* of the facts. **9** A device to assist aiming, as a gun or a leveling instrument. **10** An aim or observation taken with a telescope or other sighting instrument. —**at** (or **on**) **sight 1** As soon as seen. **2** On presentation for payment. —**out of sight 1** Beyond range of sight. **2** *Informal* Beyond expectation; too great or too much. **3** *Slang* Extraordinarily good. —*v.t.* **1** To catch sight of; discern with the eyes: to *sight* shore. **2** To look at through a sight, as a telescope; observe. **3** To adjust the sights of, as a gun. **4** To take aim with. —*v.i.* **5** To take aim. **6** To make an observation or sight. —*adj.* **1** Understood or performed on sight without previous familiarity or preparation: *sight* reading of music. **2** Payable when presented: a *sight* draft. [<OE *gesiht*]

sight·ed (sīt′əd) *adj.* Having (a specified kind of) sight or vision: *far-sighted.*

sight·less (sīt′lis) *adj.* **1** Blind. **2** Invisible. —**sight′less·ly** *adv.* —**sight′less·ness** *n.*

sight·ly (sīt′lē) *adj.* **·li·er, ·li·est 1** Pleasant to the view; comely. **2** Affording a grand view. —**sight′li·ness** *n.*

sight·see·ing (sīt′sē′ing) *n.* The practice of going to see places or things of interest, as in touring. —*adj.* Engaged in or for the purpose of sightseeing. —**sight′se′er** *n.*

sig·ma (sig′mə) *n.* The 18th letter in the Greek alphabet (Σ, σ, ς).

sign (sīn) *n.* **1** Anything that directs the mind or attention toward something: a *sign* of aging; a *sign* of intelligence. **2** A telltale mark or indication; trace: the first *sign* of spring. **3** A motion or action used to communicate a thought, desire, or command. **4** A symbol; token: black armbands as a *sign* of grief. **5** A conventional written or printed symbol representing a word or relation: $ is a dollar *sign;* = is an equal *sign.* **6** Information, directions, advertising, etc., publicly displayed. **7** A structure on which such information is printed or posted. **8** An occurrence taken to be miraculous and proof of divine commission. **9** One of the twelve equal divisions of the zodiac. —*v.t.* **1** To write one's signature on, esp. in acknowledging or attesting to the validity of a document. **2** To write (one's name). **3** To indicate or represent by a sign. **4** To mark or consecrate with a sign, esp. with a cross. **5** To engage by obtaining the signature of to a contract. **6** To hire (oneself) out for work: often with *on.* —*v.i.* **7** To write one's signature. **8** To make signs or signals. —**sign off** To announce the end of a program from a broadcasting station and stop transmission. —**sign up** To enlist, as in a branch of military service. [< L *signum*] —**sign′er** *n.* —**Syn.** *n.* **2** vestige, evidence, spoor.

sig·nal (sig′nəl) *n.* **1** A sign or event agreed upon or understood as a call to action. **2** Any device, sound, gesture, etc., used to convey information or give direction or warning. **3** An event that incites to action or movement: His yawn was our *signal* to leave. **4** *Telecom.* A flow of energy that varies so as to transmit information. —*adj.* **1** Out of the ordinary; notable; distinguished. **2** Used to signal. —*v.* **·naled** or **·nalled, ·nal·ing** or **·nal·ling** *v.t.* **1** To inform or notify by signals. **2** To communicate by signals. —*v.i.* **3** To make a signal or signals. [< L *signum* sign] —**sig′nal·er** or **sig′nal·ler** *n.*

sig·nal·ize (sig′nəl·īz) *v.t.* **·ized, ·iz·ing 1** To make notable or distinguished. **2** To point out with care.

sig·nal·ly (sig′nəl·ē) *adv.* In a signal manner; extraordinarily.

sig·nal·man (sig′nəl·mən) *n. pl.* **·men** (-mən) One who operates or is responsible for signals, as for a railroad.

sig·na·to·ry (sig′nə·tôr′ē, -tō′rē) *n. pl.* **·ries** One who has signed or is bound by a document, esp. a nation so bound. —*adj.* Being a signatory. [< L *signum* a sign]

sig·na·ture (sig′nə·chər) *n.* **1** The name of a person written by himself. **2** The act of signing one's name. **3** Any identifying mark or sign, as a musical theme to signal the beginning and end of a television show. **4** *Printing* **a** A distinguishing mark or number on the first page of each sheet of pages to be gathered as a guide to the binder. **b** A printed sheet that when folded and trimmed constitutes a section of a book, as 32 pages. **5** *Music* A symbol or group of symbols at the beginning of a staff, indicating time or key. [< L *signum* sign]

sign·board (sīn′bôrd′, -bōrd′) *n.* A board displaying a sign, as an advertisement.

sig·net (sig′nit) *n.* **1** A seal used instead of a signature on a document to indicate its official nature. **2** An impression made by or as if by a seal. —*v.t.* To mark wth a signet or seal. [< L *signum* sign]

signet ring A finger ring bearing a signet, as a monogram.

sig·nif·i·cance (sig·nif′ə·kəns) *n.* **1** Importance; consequence. **2** That which is signified or intended to be expressed; meaning. **3** The state or character of being significant. Also **sig·nif′i·can·cy.**

sig·nif·i·cant (sig·nif′ə·kənt) *adj.* **1** Having or expressing a meaning; esp., rich in meaning: *significant* details. **2** Important; momentous. **—sig·nif′i·cant·ly** *adv.* **—Syn. 1** meaningful, suggestive. **2** weighty, consequential.

sig·ni·fi·ca·tion (sig′nə·fə·kā′shən) *n.* **1** That which is signified; meaning; sense; import. **2** The act of signifying; communication.

sig·nif·i·ca·tive (sig·nif′ə·kā′tiv) *adj.* **1** Signifying. **2** Conveying a meaning; significant.

sig·ni·fy (sig′nə·fī) *v.* **·fied, ·fy·ing** *v.t.* **1** To represent; mean; suggest. **2** To make known by signs or words; express. —*v.i.* **3** To have some meaning or importance; matter. [< L *signum* sign + -FY] **—sig′ni·fi′er** *n.*

sign language A system of communication by means of signs, largely manual.

si·gnor (sēn·yôr′) *n. pl.* **si·gno·ri** (-ē) or **si·gnors** *Italian* **1** A title of courtesy equivalent to *Mr.* or *Sir.* **2** A man; gentleman. Also **si·gnior′.** [< L *senior* senior]

si·gno·ra (sē·nyō′rä) *n. pl.* **si·gno·re** (-rā) or **·ras** *Italian* **1** A title of courtesy equivalent to *Mrs.* or *Madam.* **2** A woman; lady.

si·gno·ri·na (sē′nyō·rē′nä) *n. pl.* **·ri·ne** (-nā) or **·nas** *Italian* **1** A title of courtesy equivalent to *Miss.* **2** An unmarried woman; young lady.

sign·post (sīn′pōst′) *n.* A post bearing a sign.

Sikh (sēk) *n.* An adherent of a religion of India characterized by monotheism and the rejection of caste. —*adj.* Of or pertaining to the Sikhs. [Hind., lit., disciple] **—Sikh′·ism** *n.*

si·lage (sī′lij) *n.* Succulent fodder stored in a silo.

si·lence (sī′ləns) *n.* **1** Absence of sound; stillness. **2** Abstinence from speech or from making any sound. **3** Failure to mention; oblivion; secrecy. —*v.t.* **·lenced, ·lenc·ing 1** To make silent. **2** To stop the activity or expression of; put to rest. —*interj.* Be silent. [< L *silere* be silent]

si·lenc·er (sī′lən·sər) *n.* **1** A device attached to the muzzle of a firearm to muffle the report. **2** One who or that which imposes silence.

si·lent (sī′lənt) *adj.* **1** Not making any sound or noise; noiseless. **2** Not speaking; mute. **3** Disinclined to talk; taciturn. **4** Present but not audible: *silent* tears. **5** Characterized by the absence of comment: His statement was *silent* on that point. **6** Free from activity, motion, or disturbance. **7** Written but not pronounced, as the *e* in *bake.* **8** Not accompanied by a sound track: a *silent* film. [< L *silere* be silent] **—si′lent·ly** *adv.* **—si′lent·ness** *n.*

silent partner A partner who shares in the financing of an enterprise but has no part in its management.

sil·hou·ette (sil′o͞o·et′) *n.* **1** A profile drawing or portrait having its outline filled in with uniform color, usu. black. **2** The outline of a solid figure. —*v.t.* **·et·ted, ·et·ting** To cause to appear in silhouette; outline. [< Étienne de *Silhouette,* 1709–1767, French minister]

Silhouette of Abraham Lincoln

sil·i·ca (sil′i·kə) *n.* The dioxide of silicon, occurring pure as quartz and as an important constituent of rocks, sand, and clay. [< L *silex, silicis* flint]

sil·i·cate (sil′ə·kāt, -i·kit) *n.* Any of various compounds consisting of an oxide of silicon and a metallic radical.

si·li·ceous (si·lish′əs) *adj.* Pertaining to or containing silica. Also **si·li′cious.**

si·lic·ic (si·lis′ik) *adj.* Pertaining to or derived from silica or silicon.

silicic acid Any of several gelatinous compounds of silica and water.

sil·i·con (sil′ə·kon′, -kən) *n.* A nonmetallic element (symbol Si) comprising about 25 percent of the earth's crust and forming many compounds analogous to those of carbon. [< L *silex, silicis* flint]

sil·i·cone (sil′ə·kōn′) *n.* Any of various synthetic compounds composed of chains of alternate silicon and oxygen atoms with hydrocarbon branches joined to the silicon.

sil·i·co·sis (sil′ə·kō′sis) *n.* A chronic lung disease due to inhalation of silica dust produced by stonecutting, etc.

silk (silk) *n.* **1** A soft, shiny fiber produced by various insect larvae, as silkworms, to form their cocoons. **2** Cloth or thread made of this fiber. **3** Anything resembling silk, as the fine strands of an ear of corn. **4** *Usu. pl.* A garment of silk, as the uniform of a jockey. —*adj.* Consisting of or like silk; silken. [< OE *seoloc*]

silk cotton The silky covering of the seeds of certain trees, used for filling cushions, etc.; kapok.

silk·en (sil′kən) *adj.* **1** Made of silk. **2** Like silk; glossy; smooth. **3** Suave; insinuating: *silken* speech. **4** Dressed in silk. **5** Luxurious.

silk-screen (silk′skrēn′) *adj.* Describing or made by a printing process which forces ink through the meshes of a silk screen prepared so that ink penetrates only in those areas to be printed. —*v.t.* To make or print by the silk-screen process.

silk-stock·ing (silk′stok′ing) *adj.* Marked by patrician elegance or extreme wealth. —*n.* A member of a silk-stocking social class.

silk·worm (silk′wûrm′) *n.* The larva of a moth that produces a dense silken cocoon.

silk·y (sil′kē) *adj.* **silk·i·er, silk·i·est 1** Like silk; soft; lustrous. **2** Made or consisting of silk; silken. **3** Smooth or insinuating. **—silk′i·ly** *adv.* **—silk′i·ness** *n.*

sill (sil) *n.* **1** A horizontal member or beam forming the foundation, or part of the foundation, of a structure, as at the bottom of a casing in a building. **2** The horizontal part at the bottom of a door or window frame. [< OE *syll*]

sil·ly (sil′ē) *adj.* **·li·er, ·li·est 1** Showing a lack of ordinary sense or judgment; foolish. **2** Trivial; frivolous. **3** *Informal* Stunned; dazed, as by a blow. —*n. pl.* **·lies** *Informal* A silly person. [< OE *gesælig* happy] **—sil′li·ly** or **sil′ly** *adv.* **—sil′li·ness** *n.*

si·lo (sī′lō) *n. pl.* **·los 1** A pit or tower in which fodder is stored. **2** An underground structure for the housing and launching of guided missiles. —*v.t.* **·loed, ·lo·ing** To put or preserve in a silo. [< Gk. *siros* pit for corn]

silt (silt) *n.* **1** An earthy sediment consisting of extremely fine particles suspended in and carried by water. **2** A deposit of such sediment. —*v.t. & v.i.* To fill or become filled or choked with silt: usu. with *up.* [ME *sylte*] **—sil·ta·tion** (sil·tā′shən) *n.* **—silt′y** *adj.* **(·i·er, ·i·est)**

Si·lu·ri·an (si·lo͝or′ē·ən, sī-) *adj. & n.* See GEOLOGY.

sil·van (sil′vən) *adj.* SYLVAN.

sil·ver (sil′vər) *n.* **1** A pale gray, lustrous, malleable metallic element (symbol Ag), having great electric and thermal conductivity and forming various photosensitive salts. **2** Silver regarded as a commodity or as a standard of currency. **3** Silver coin considered as money. **4** Articles, as tableware, made of or plated with silver; silverware. **5**

A luster or color resembling that of silver. —*adj.* 1 Made of or coated with silver. 2 Resembling silver; having a silvery grey color. 3 Relating to, connected with, or producing silver. 4 Having a soft, clear, bell-like tone. 5 Designating a 25th wedding anniversary. 6 Favoring the use of silver as a monetary standard. —*v.t.* 1 To coat or plate with silver or something resembling silver. —*v.i.* 2 To become silver or white, as with age. [< OE *siolfor*] —**sil′·ver·er** *n.* —**sil′ver·ly** *adv.*

sil·ver·fish (sil′vər·fish′) *n. pl.* **·fish** or **·fish·es** Any of numerous silvery, wingless insects having bristles on the tail and long feelers, usu. found in damp and dark places.

silver fox 1 A fox with white-tipped black fur. 2 The fur, or a garment made of it.

silver nitrate The salt of silver and nitric acid, used in industry, photography, and in medicine as an antiseptic.

sil·ver·smith (sil′vər·smith′) *n.* A maker of silverware.

silver standard A monetary standard or system based on silver.

sil·ver·ware (sil′vər·wâr′) *n.* Articles made of or plated with silver, esp. tableware.

sil·ver·y (sil′vər·ē) *adj.* 1 Containing silver. 2 Resembling silver, as in luster or hue. 3 Having a soft, clear, bell-like tone. —**sil′ver·i·ness** *n.*

sim·i·an (sim′ē·ən) *adj.* Like or pertaining to the apes and monkeys. —*n.* An ape or monkey. [< L *simia* ape]

sim·i·lar (sim′ə·lər) *adj.* 1 Bearing resemblance to one another or to something else. 2 Having like characteristics, nature, or degree. 3 *Geom.* Shaped alike, but differing in measure. [< L *similis* like] —**sim′i·lar·ly** *adv.*

sim·i·lar·i·ty (sim′ə·lar′ə·tē) *n. pl.* **·ties** 1 The quality or state of being similar. 2 A point in which compared objects are similar.

sim·i·le (sim′ə·lē) *n.* A figure of speech expressing comparison or likeness by the use of such terms as *like* or *as.* [< L *similis* similar] • See METAPHOR.

si·mil·i·tude (si·mil′ə·tyōōd) *n.* 1 Similarity; correspondence. 2 One who or that which is similar; counterpart. 3 A point of similarity. [< L *similis* like]

sim·i·tar (sim′ə·tər) *n.* SCIMITAR.

sim·mer (sim′ər) *v.i.* 1 To boil gently; be or stay at or just below the boiling point. 2 To be on the point of breaking forth, as with rage. —*v.t.* 3 To cook in a liquid at or just below the boiling point. —*n.* The state of simmering. [?]

si·mo·le·on (si·mō′lē·ən) *n. Slang* A dollar. [?]

Si·mon Le·gree (sī′mən li·grē′) A harsh or brutal taskmaster. [< a character in Harriet Beecher Stowe's *Uncle Tom's Cabin,* 1851]

si·mon-pure (sī′mən·pyŏŏr′) *adj.* Real; genuine; authentic. [< a character in Susanna Centlivre's play, *A Bold Stroke for a Wife,* 1718]

si·mo·ny (sī′mə·nē, sim′ə-) *n.* The purchase or sale of sacred things, as ecclesiastical preferment. [< *Simon* (Magus), who offered Peter money for the gift of the Holy Spirit *Acts* 8:9–24]

si·moom (si·mōōm′, sī-) *n.* A hot, dry, dustladen, exhausting wind of the African and Arabian deserts. Also **si·moon′** (-mōōn′). [< Ar. *samūm*]

simp (simp) *n. Slang* A simpleton.

sim·per (sim′pər) *v.i.* 1 To smile in a silly, self-conscious manner; smirk. —*v.t.* 2 To say with a simper. —*n.* A silly, self-conscious smile. —**sim′per·er** *n.* —**sim′per·ing·ly** *adv.*

sim·ple (sim′pəl) *adj.* **·pler, ·plest** 1 Easy to comprehend or do: a *simple* problem or task. 2 Not complex or complicated. 3 Without embellishment; plain; unadorned: a *simple* dress. 4 Having nothing added; mere: the *simple* truth. 5 Not luxurious or elaborate: a *simple* meal. 6 Consisting of one thing; single. 7 Free from affectation; artless: a *simple* soul. 8 Weak in intellect; silly or foolish. 9 Of humble rank or condition; ordinary. 10 *Bot.* Not divided: a *simple* leaf. —*n.* 1 One who is foolish or ignorant; simpleton. 2 A medicinal plant. [< L *simplex*] —**sim′ple·ness** *n.* —**Syn.** 4 bare, sheer. 5 frugal, austere. 7 guileless, unsophisticated.

simple fraction A fraction in which both numerator and denominator are integers.

simple interest Interest computed on the original principal alone.

simple machine Any one of certain basic mechanical devices, as the lever, the wedge, the inclined plane, the screw, the wheel and axle, and the pulley.

sim·ple-mind·ed (sim′pəl·mīn′did) *adj.* 1 Weak in intellect; foolish or feeble-minded. 2 Artless or unsophisticated. —**sim′ple-mind′ed·ly** *adv.* —**sim′ple-mind′ed·ness** *n.*

simple sentence A sentence consisting of one independent clause, without subordinate clauses.

sim·ple·ton (sim′pəl·tən) *n.* A weak-minded or silly person.

sim·plic·i·ty (sim·plis′ə·tē) *n. pl.* **·ties** 1 The state of being simple; freedom from complexity or difficulty. 2 Freedom from ornament or ostentation. 3 Freedom from affectation; artlessness; sincerity. 4 Foolishness; stupidity.

sim·pli·fy (sim′plə·fī) *v.t.* **·fied, ·fy·ing** To make more simple or less complex. —**sim′pli·fi·ca′tion, sim′pli·fi′er** *n.*

sim·plis·tic (sim·plis′tik) *adj.* Tending to ignore or overlook underlying questions, complications, or details. —**sim·plis′ti·cal·ly** *adv.*

sim·ply (sim′plē) *adv.* 1 In a simple manner. 2 Merely; only. 3 Really; absolutely: *simply* adorable.

sim·u·la·crum (sim′yə·lā′krəm, -lak′rəm) *n. pl.* **·cra** (-krə) 1 A likeness; image. 2 An imaginary or shadowy semblance. [< L, image]

sim·u·late (sim′yə·lāt) *v.t.* **·lat·ed, ·lat·ing** 1 To make a pretense of; imitate, esp. to deceive. 2 To assume or have the appearance or form of, without the reality. [< L *similis* like] —**sim′u·la′tive** *adj.* —**sim′u·la′tor** *n.*

sim·u·la·tion (sim′yə·lā′shən) *n.* 1 The act of simulating. 2 Something given the form or function of another, as in order to test or determine capability; model.

si·mul·cast (sī′məl·kast′, -käst′) *v.t.* **·cast, ·cast·ing** To broadcast by radio and television simultaneously. —*n.* A broadcast so transmitted.

si·mul·ta·ne·ous (sī′məl·tā′nē·əs, sim′əl-) *adj.* Occurring, done, or existing at the same time. [< L *simul* at the same time] —**si′mul·ta′ne·ous·ly** *adv.* —**si′mul·ta′ne·ous·ness, si′mul·ta·ne′i·ty** (-tə·nē′ə·tē) *n.*

sin (sin) *n.* 1 A transgression against moral or religious law or divine authority, esp. when deliberate. 2 The state of having thus transgressed; wickedness. 3 Any action or condition regarded as morally wrong or deplorable. —*v.* **sinned, sin·ning** *v.i.* 1 To commit a sin. 2 To do wrong. [< OE *synn*]

Si·nai (sī′nī), **Mount** The mountain where Moses received the law from God. *Ex.* 19.

since (sins) *adv.* 1 From a past time up to the present: traveling *since* last Monday. 2 At some time between the past and the present: He has *since* recovered from the illness. 3 Before now: long *since* forgotten. —*prep.* During the time following (a time in the past): Times have changed *since* you left. —*conj.* 1 During or within the time after which. 2 Continuously from the time when: She has been ill ever *since* she arrived. 3 Because of; inasmuch as. [< OE *siththan* afterwards]

sin·cere (sin·sir′) *adj.* **·cer·er, ·cer·est** Free from hypocrisy, deceit, or calculation; honest; genuine: a *sincere* friend; *sincere* regrets. [< L *sincerus* uncorrupted] —**sin·cere′ly** *adv.* —**sin·cere′ness** *n.*

sin·cer·i·ty (sin·ser′ə·tē) *n.* The state or quality of being sincere; honesty of purpose or character; freedom from hypocrisy.

sine (sīn) *n.* A function of an acute angle in a right triangle expressible as the ratio of the side opposite the angle to the hypotenuse. [< L *sinus* a bend]

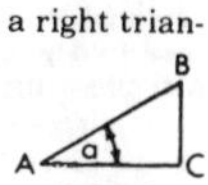

BC/AB = sine of angle a

si·ne·cure (sī′nə·kyŏŏr, sin′ə-) *n.* A position or office providing compensation or other benefits but requiring little or no responsibility or effort. [< L *sine* without + *cura* care]

si·ne di·e (sī′nē dī′ē, sin′ā dē′ā) Without setting a date, as for another meeting; indefinitely: an adjournment *sine die.* [L, without a day]

si·ne qua non (sin′ə kwä nōn′, non′, sī′nē kwā non′) That which is absolutely indispensable; an essential element. [L, without which not]

sin·ew (sin′yo͞o) *n.* 1 TENDON. 2 Strength or power. 3 *Often pl.* A source of strength. —*v.t.* To strengthen, as with sinews. [<OE *sinu, seonu*] —**sin′ew·less** *adj.*

sin·ew·y (sin′yo͞o·ē) *adj.* 1 Of, like, or having sinews. 2 Having many sinews; tough. 3 Strong; brawny. 4 Vigorous; forceful.

sin·ful (sin′fəl) *adj.* Tainted with, full of, or characterized by sin. —**sin′ful·ly** *adv.* —**sin′ful·ness** *n.* —**Syn.** wicked, bad, immoral, evil.

sing (sing) *v.* **sang** or *(now less commonly)* **sung, sung, sing·ing** *v.i.* 1 To produce musical sounds with the voice. 2 To perform vocal compositions professionally or in a specified manner. 3 To produce melodious sounds, as a bird. 4 To make a continuous, melodious sound suggestive of singing, as a teakettle, the wind, etc. 5 To buzz or hum; ring: My ears are *singing*. 6 To be suitable for singing. 7 To relate or celebrate something in song or verse. 8 To compose poetry. 9 *Slang* To confess the details of a crime, esp. so as to implicate others. 10 To be joyous; rejoice. —*v.t.* 11 To perform (music) vocally. 12 To chant; intone. 13 To bring to a specified condition or place by singing: *Sing* me to sleep. 14 To relate, proclaim, praise, etc., in or as in verse or song. —*n. Informal* A singing, esp. by a group. [<OE *singan*] —**sing′a·ble** *adj.*

sing. singular.

singe (sinj) *v.t.* **singed, singe·ing** 1 To burn slightly. 2 To remove bristles or feathers from by passing through flame. 3 To burn the ends of (hair, etc.). —*n.* A slight or superficial burn; scorch. [<OE *sengan*] —**sing′er** *n.*

sing·er (sing′ər) *n.* 1 One who sings, esp. as a profession. 2 A poet. 3 A songbird.

Sin·gha·lese (sing′gə·lēz′, -lēs′) *adj.* Of or pertaining to a group of people in Sri Lanka or to their language. —*n.* 1 One of the Singhalese people. 2 Their language.

sin·gle (sing′gəl) *adj.* 1 Consisting of only one. 2 With no other or others; solitary; lone; alone. 3 Unmarried; also, pertaining to the unmarried state. 4 Of, pertaining to or involving only one person. 5 Consisting of only one part; simple. 6 Upright; sincere; honest. 7 Designed for use by only one person: a *single* bed. 8 *Bot.* Having only one row of petals, as a flower. —*n.* 1 One who or that which is single. 2 In baseball, a hit by which the batter reaches first base. 3 In cricket, a hit which scores one run. 4 *pl.* In tennis or similar games, a match with only one player on each side —*v.* **·gled, ·gling** *v.t.* 1 To choose or select (one) from others: usually with *out*. —*v.i.* 2 In baseball, to make a single. [<L *singulus*] —**sin′gle·ness** *n.* —**sin′gly** *adv.*

sin·gle-breast·ed (sing′gəl·bres′tid) *adj.* Overlapping at the center of the front of the body just enough to allow for fastening by a single button or row of buttons.

single file 1 A line of people, animals, etc., moving one behind the other. 2 In such a line: to walk *single file*.

sin·gle-foot (sing′gəl·fo͝ot′) *n.* The gait of a horse in which the sequence in which the feet leave the ground is right hind, right fore, left hind, left fore. —*v.i.* To go at this gait.

sin·gle-hand·ed (sing′gəl·han′did) *adj.* 1 Done or working alone; without assistance; unaided. 2 Having but one hand. 3 Capable of being used with a single hand. —**sin′·gle-hand′ed·ly** *adv.*

sin·gle-heart·ed (sing′gəl·här′tid) *adj.* Sincere and undivided, as in purpose, dedication, feeling, etc. —**sin′gle-heart′ed·ly** *adv.*

sin·gle-mind·ed (sing′gəl·mīn′did) *adj.* 1 Having only one purpose or end in view. 2 Free from duplicity; ingenuous; sincere. —**sin′gle-mind′ed·ly** *adv.* —**sin′gle-mind′ed·ness** *n.*

sin·gle·stick (sing′gəl·stik′) *n.* 1 A wooden, swordlike stick used in fencing. 2 The art or an instance of fencing with such sticks.

sin·gle·ton (sing′gəl·tən) *n.* 1 A single card of a suit originally held in the hand of a player. 2 Any single thing, distinct from two or more of its group.

sin·gle-track (sing′əl·trak′) *adj.* 1 Having only one track. 2 Having a limited scope, outlook, flexibility, etc.

sin·gle·tree (sing′gəl·trē′) *n.* WHIFFLETREE.

sing·song (sing′sông′, -song′) *n.* 1 Monotonous regularity of rhythm and rhyme in verse. 2 Verse characterized by such regularity. 3 A voice, speech tones, etc., characterized by a monotonous rise and fall of pitch. —*adj.* Having a monotonous rhythm or rise and fall of pitch.

sin·gu·lar (sing′gyə·lər) *adj.* 1 Being the only one of its type; unique; separate; individual. 2 Extraordinary; remarkable; uncommon: a *singular* honor. 3 Odd; not customary or usual. 4 *Gram.* Of, pertaining to, or being a word form which denotes one person or thing. —*n. Gram.* The singular number, or a word form having this number. —**sin′gu·lar·ly** *adv.* —**sin′gu·lar·ness** *n.* —**Syn.** 1 peculiar, distinctive. 3 strange, conspicuous.

sin·gu·lar·i·ty (sing′gyə·lar′ə·tē) *n. pl.* **·ties** 1 The state or quality of being singular. 2 Something of uncommon or remarkable character.

sin·gu·lar·ize (sing′gyə·lə·rīz′) *v.t.* **·ized, ·iz·ing** To make singular.

Sin·ha·lese (sin′hə·lēz′, -lēs′) *adj., n.* SINGHALESE.

sin·is·ter (sin′is·tər) *adj.* 1 Malevolent; evil: a *sinister* expression on the face. 2 Boding or attended with misfortune or disaster; inauspicious. 3 Of, pertaining to, or situated on the left side or hand. 4 *Her.* On the wearer's left, the spectator's right. [L, left, unlucky] —**sin′is·ter·ly** *adv.* —**sin′is·ter·ness** *n.*

sink (singk) *v.* **sank** or **sunk, sunk** (*Obs.* **sunk·en**), **sink·ing** *v.i.* 1 To go beneath the surface or to the bottom, as of water or snow. 2 To go down, esp. slowly or by degrees. 3 To seem to descend, as the sun. 4 To incline downward; slope gradually, as land. 5 To pass into a specified state: to *sink* into a coma. 6 To approach death: He's *sinking* fast. 7 To become less in force, volume, or degree: His voice *sank* to a whisper. 8 To become less in value, price, etc. 9 To decline in quality or condition; retrogress; degenerate: usu. with *into* or *to*. 10 To penetrate or be absorbed: The oil *sank* into the wood. 11 To be impressed or fixed, as in the heart or mind: I think that lesson will *sink* in. —*v.t.* 12 To cause to go beneath the surface or to the bottom: to *sink* a fence post. 13 To cause or allow to fall or drop; lower. 14 To cause to penetrate or be absorbed. 15 To make (a mine shaft, well, etc.) by digging or excavating. 16 To reduce in force, volume, or degree. 17 To debase or degrade. 18 To suppress or hide; restrain. 19 To defeat; ruin. 20 To invest. 21 To invest and subsequently lose. 22 To pay up; liquidate. 23 In certain sports, to cause (a ball or other object) to go through or into a receptacle or hole. —*n.* 1 A basinlike receptacle with a drainpipe and usu. a water supply. 2 A sewer or cesspool. 3 A place where corruption and vice gather or are rampant. 4 A hollow place or depression in a land surface, esp. one in which water collects or disappears by evaporation or percolation. 5 A body or mechanism by which matter or energy is absorbed or dissipated: a heat *sink*. [<OE *sincan*] —**sink′a·ble** *adj.* —**Syn.** 2 descend, dwindle, diminish, lessen.

sink·er (singk′ər) *n.* 1 One who or that which sinks. 2 A weight for sinking a fishing or sounding line. 3 *Informal* A doughnut.

sinking fund A fund accumulated to pay off a debt at maturity.

sin·less (sin′lis) *adj.* Having no sin; guiltless; innocent. —**sin′less·ly** *adv.* —**sin′less·ness** *n.*

sin·ner (sin′ər) *n.* One who has sinned.

Sino- *combining form* 1 Of or pertaining to the Chinese people, language, etc. 2 Chinese and: *Sino-Tibetan*. [<LL *Sinae* the Chinese]

Si·no-Ti·bet·an (sī′nō·ti·bet′n) *n.* A family of languages spoken over a wide area in CEN. and SE Asia, including the languages of China, Burma, Tibet, and Thailand.

sin·u·ate (sin′yo͞o·it, -āt) *adj.* 1 Winding in and out; wavy. 2 *Bot.* Having a strongly indented, wavy margin, as some leaves. —*v.i.* (sin′yo͞o·āt) **·at·ed, ·at·ing** To curve in and out; turn; wind. [<L *sinus* curve] —**sin′u·ate·ly** *adv.* —**sin′u·a′·tion** *n.*

sin·u·ous (sin′yo͞o·əs) *adj.* 1 Characterized by turns or curves; winding; undulating; tortuous: a *sinuous* path. 2 Devious; indirect; not straightforward. [<L *sinus* bend] —**sin′u·ous·ly** *adv.* —**sin·u·os·i·ty** (sin′yo͞o·os′ə·tē), **sin′u·ous·ness** *n.*

si·nus (sī′nəs) *n.* **1** Any of the natural cavities in the skull that contain air and usu. connect with the nostrils. **2** A dilated part of a blood vessel. **3** Any narrow opening leading to an abscess. **4** *Bot.* A recess or depression between two adjoining lobes, as of a leaf. [L, curve, hollow]

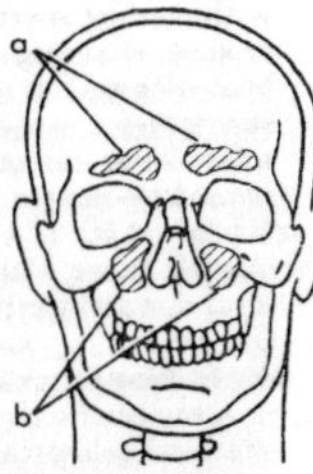

Sinuses
a. frontal.
b. maxillary.

si·nu·si·tis (sī′nə·sī′tis) *n.* Inflammation of a sinus or the sinuses of the skull.

Si·on (sī′ən) *n.* ZION.

Siou·an (so͞o′ən) *n. pl.* **Siouan** or **Siouans 1** A large family of languages spoken by Indians who formerly inhabited parts of CEN. and E North America. **2** A member of any of the peoples speaking a language of this family. —*adj.* Of or pertaining to this language family.

Sioux (so͞o) *n. pl.* **Sioux** One of a group of North American Indian tribes of Siouan linguistic stock formerly occupying parts of the Great Plains area in the Dakotas, Minnesota, and Nebraska.

sip (sip) *v.* **sipped, sip·ping** *v.t.* **1** To imbibe in small quantities. **2** To drink from by sips. **3** To take in; absorb. —*v.i.* **4** To drink in sips. —*n.* **1** A very small amount sipped. **2** The act of sipping. [< OE *sypian* drink in] —**sip·per** *n.*

si·phon (sī′fən) *n.* **1** A bent tube for transferring liquids from a higher to a lower level over an intervening barrier. **2** SIPHON BOTTLE. **3** *Zool.* A tubular structure in certain aquatic animals, as the squid, for drawing in or expelling liquids. —*v.t.* **1** To draw off by or cause to pass through or as through a siphon. —*v.i.* **2** To pass through a siphon. [< Gk. *siphōn*] —**si′phon·al** *adj.*

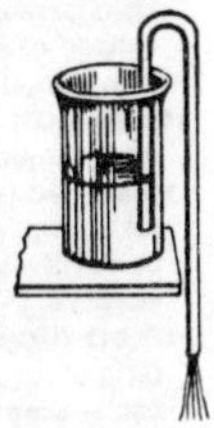
Siphon

siphon bottle A bottle containing aerated or carbonated water, which is expelled through a bent tube in the neck of the bottle by the pressure of the gas when a valve in the tube is opened.

sir (sûr) *n.* The conventional term of respectful address to a man: not followed by a proper name. [< SIRE]

Sir (sûr) *n.* A title of baronets and knights, used before the given name or the full name.

sire (sīr) *n.* **1** *Archaic* A father or forefather. **2** The male parent of an animal, esp. a domestic animal. **3** *Archaic* A man of high rank; also a form of address to a superior used esp. in addressing a king. —*v.t.* **sired, sir·ing** To beget; procreate: used chiefly of domestic animals. [< L *senior* older]

si·ren (sī′rən) *n.* **1** *Often cap. Gk. Myth.* One of a group of sea nymphs who lured sailors to destruction by their sweet singing. **2** A seductive, enticing woman. **3** A device for producing a series of loud tones, as for a warning, often consisting of a perforated rotating disk or disks through which sharp puffs of steam or compressed air are permitted to escape. —*adj.* Of or pertaining to a siren; seductive; enticing. [< Gk. *seirēn*]

Sir·i·us (sir′ē·əs) *n.* The Dog Star, the brightest star in the night sky, in the constellation of Canis Major. [< Gk. *seirios* scorching]

sir·loin (sûr′loin) *n.* A cut of meat, esp. of beef, from the upper portion of the loin. [< OF *sur-* above + *longe* loin]

si·roc·co (si·rok′ō) *n. pl.* **·cos 1** A hot, dry, and dusty wind blowing from the Libyan deserts into S Europe, esp. to Italy, Sicily, and Malta. **2** Any hot or warm wind, esp. one blowing toward a center of low barometric pressure. [< Ar. *sharq* the east]

sir·up (sir′əp) *n.* SYRUP.

sis (sis) *n. Informal* Sister.

si·sal (sī′səl, -zəl, sis′əl) *n.* **1** A tough fiber obtained from the leaves of a species of agave. **2** The plant itself. Also **sisal hemp.** [< *Sisal,* town in Yucatán, Mexico]

sis·sy (sis′ē) *n. pl.* **·sies** *Informal* **1** An effeminate man or boy. **2** A timid person; weakling; coward. —*adj.* **·si·er, ·si·est** Being a sissy.[< SIS]

sis·ter (sis′tər) *n.* **1** A female person having the same parents as another person. **2** A female of the lower animals having one parent in common with another. **3 a** HALF SISTER. **b** SISTER-IN-LAW. **c** A foster sister. **4** A woman or girl allied to another or others by race, creed, a common interest, membership in a society, etc. **5** *Eccl.* A member of a sisterhood; nun. **6** *Chiefly Brit.* A head nurse in the ward or clinic of a hospital; also, any nurse. **7** A person or thing having similar characteristics to another. —*adj.* Bearing the relationship of a sister or one suggestive of sisterhood. [< OE *swostor*] —**sis′ter·ly** *adj.*

sis·ter·hood (sis′tər·ho͝od) *n.* **1** A body of women united by some bond. **2** *Eccl.* A community of women forming a religious order. **3** The sisterly relationship.

sis·ter-in-law (sis′tər·in·lô′) *n. pl.* **sis·ters-in-law 1** A sister of one's husband or wife. **2** A brother's wife. **3** A brother-in-law's wife.

Sis·y·phus (sis′ə·fəs) *Gk. Myth.* A king of Corinth, condemned in Hades forever to roll uphill a huge stone that always rolled down again.

sit (sit) *v.* **sat, sit·ting** *v.i.* **1** To rest on the buttocks or haunches; be seated. **2** To perch or roost, as a bird. **3** To cover eggs so as to give warmth for hatching. **4** To pose, as for a portrait. **5** To be in session; hold a session. **6** To occupy a seat in a deliberative body. **7** To have or exercise judicial authority. **8** To fit or hang: That dress *sits* well. **9** To rest; lie: an obligation that *sat* heavily on her. **10** To be situated or located. **11** BABY-SIT. —*v.t.* **12** To have or keep a seat or a good seat upon: to *sit* a horse. **13** To seat (oneself): *Sit* yourself down. —**sit in (on) 1** To join; participate: to *sit in on* a game of cards or a business deal. **2** To attend or take part in a discussion or music session. **3** To take part in a sit-in. —**sit on** (or **upon**) **1** To belong to (a jury, commission, etc.) as a member. **2** To hold discussions about or investigate. **3** *Informal* To suppress, squelch, or delay action on or consideration of. —**sit out 1** To remain until the end of. **2** To sit during or take no part in: They *sat out* a dance. **3** To stay longer than. —**sit up 1** To assume a sitting position. **2** To maintain an erect posture while seated. **3** To stay up later than usual at night. **4** To be startled or show interest. [< OE *sittan*]

si·tar (si·tär′) *n.* A stringed instrument used in Hindu music, somewhat resembling the lute, having a long neck, a resonating gourd or gourds, and a variable number of strings, some of which are plucked, others vibrating sympathetically. [< Hind. *sitār*]

Sitar

sit·com (sit′kom′) *n. Slang* A situation comedy. [< SIT(UATION) + COM(EDY)]

sit-down (sit′doun′) *n.* **1** A strike during which strikers refuse to work or leave their place of employment until agreement is reached: also **sit-down strike. 2** A form of civil disobedience in which demonstrators obstruct some activity by sitting down and refusing to move.

site (sīt) *n.* **1** A plot of ground used for or considered for some specific purpose. **2** The place, scene, or location of something: the battle *site.* [< L *situs* position]

sit-in (sit′in′) *n.* **1** SIT-DOWN (def. 2). **2** An organized demonstration in which a protesting group occupies an area prohibited to them, as by taking seats in a restricted restaurant, etc. —**sit′-in·ner** *n.*

sit·ter (sit′ər) *n.* One who sits, esp. a baby sitter.

sit·ting (sit′ing) *n.* **1** The act or position of one who sits. **2** An uninterrupted period of being seated, as for the painting of a portrait. **3** A session or term. **4** An incubation; period of hatching. **5** The number of eggs on which a bird sits at one incubation. —*adj.* That sits or is seated.

sitting duck *Informal* An easy target or victim.

sit·ting room (sit′ting·ro͞om′, -ro͝om′) LIVING ROOM.

sit·u·ate (sich′o͞o·āt) *v.t.* **·at·ed, ·at·ing** To place in a certain position; locate. [< L *situs* a place]

sit·u·at·ed (sich′o͞o·ā′tid) *adj.* **1** Having a fixed location. **2** Placed in certain circumstances or conditions, esp. financially: He is well *situated.*

sit·u·a·tion (sich′o͞o·ā′shən) *n.* **1** The way in which something is situated, relative to its surroundings; position; location. **2** A locality; site. **3** Condition as modified or determined by circumstances. **4** A salaried post of employment. **5** A combination of circumstances at a specific time; state of affairs. **6** An unusual, difficult, critical, or otherwise significant state of affairs. **—sit′u·a′tion·al** *adj.*

situation comedy A television or radio show typically centered about a few characters involved in comical situations and presented in separate episodes.

Si·va (sē′və, shē′-) The Hindu god of destruction and reproduction. **—Si′va·ism** *n.* **—Si′va·is′tic** *adj.*

six (siks) *n.* **1** The sum of five plus one; 6; VI. **2** A set or group of six members. **—at sixes and sevens** In a state of confusion and indecision. [< OE] **—six** *adj., pron.*

six-pack (siks′pak′) *n.* **1** A group of six cans or bottles packaged as a unit. **2** The contents of such a unit.

six·pence (siks′pəns) *n.* **1** A British coin worth six pence. **2** The sum of six pence.

six·pen·ny (siks′pen′ē, -pən·ē) *adj.* **1** Worth, or sold for sixpence. **2** Cheap; trashy. **3** Denoting a size of nails, usu. two inches long.

six-shoot·er (siks′sho͞ot′ər) *n.* A revolver that will fire six shots without reloading.

six·teen (siks′tēn′) *n.* **1** The sum of 15 plus 1; 16; XVI. **2** A set or group of sixteen members. **—six′teen′** *adj., pron.*

six·teenth (siks′tēnth′) *adj. & adv.* Next in order after the 15th. **—***n.* **1** The element of an ordered set that corresponds to the number 16. **2** One of 16 equal parts.

sixteenth note *Music* A note of one sixteenth of the time value of a whole note. • See NOTE.

sixth (siksth) *adj. & adv.* Next in order after the fifth. **—** *n.* **1** The element of an ordered set that corresponds to the number six. **2** One of six equal parts. **3** *Music* The interval between a tone and another five steps away in a diatonic scale.

sixth sense The power of intuitive perception, thought of as independent of the five senses.

six·ti·eth (siks′tē·ith) *adj. & adv.* Tenth in order after the 50th. **—***n.* **1** The element of an ordered set that corresponds to the number 60. **2** One of sixty equal parts.

six·ty (siks′tē) *n. pl.* **·ties 1** The product of six and ten; 60; LX. **2** A set or group of 60 members. **3** *pl.* The numbers, years, etc., between 60 and 70. **—six′ty** *adj., pron.*

six·ty-fourth note (siks′tē·fôrth, -fōrth) *Music* A note of one sixty-fourth of the time value of a whole note. • See NOTE.

siz·a·ble (sī′zə·bəl) *adj.* Comparatively large. Also **size′a·ble.** **—siz′a·ble·ness** *n.* **—siz′a·bly** *adv.*

size[1] (sīz) *n.* **1** The dimensions of a thing as compared with some standard; physical magnitude or bulk. **2** Considerable amount, dimensions, etc. **3** One of a series of graded measures, as of hats, shoes, etc. **4** *Informal* State of affairs; true situation: That's the *size* of it. **—***v.t.* **sized, siz·ing 1** To arrange or classify according to size. **2** To cut or otherwise make (an article) to a required size. **—size up** *Informal* **1** To form an opinion of. **2** To meet specifications. [< OF *assise* ASSIZE]

size[2] (sīz) *n.* A liquid preparation used to give a smooth finish to cloth, paper, or other porous surface. **—***v.t.* **sized, siz·ing** To treat with size. [?< SIZE[1]]

size[3] (sīz) *adj.* SIZED (def. 1).

sized (sīzd) *adj.* **1** Having graded dimensions or a definite size: usu. in combination: large-*sized.* **2** Arranged according to size.

siz·ing (sī′zing) *n.* **1** SIZE[2]. **2** The act or process of adding size to a fabric, yarn, etc.

siz·zle (siz′əl) *v.* **·zled, ·zling** *v.i.* **1** To emit a hissing sound under the action of heat. **2** To seethe with rage, resentment, etc. **—***v.t.* **3** To cause to sizzle. **—***n.* A hissing sound, as from frying. [Imit.]

S.J. Society of Jesus.

skald (skôld, skäld) *n.* A Scandinavian poet or bard of ancient times. [< ON *skāld* poet]

skate[1] (skāt) *n.* **1** A metal runner attached to a frame, with clamps or straps for fastening it to the sole of a boot or shoe, enabling the wearer to glide over ice. **2** A shoe or boot with such a runner permanently attached. **3** ROLLER SKATE. **—***v.i.* **skat·ed, skat·ing** To glide or move over ice or some other smooth surface, on or as on skates. [< Du. *schaats*] **—skat′er** *n.*

skate[2] (skāt) *n.* Any of various flat-bodied, cartilaginous marine fishes with enlarged pectoral fins and ventral gill slits. [< ON *skata*]

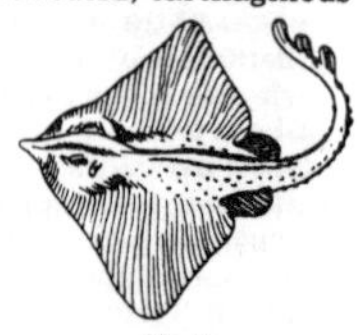

Skate

skate·board (skāt′bôrd′, -bōrd′) *n.* A toy consisting of two pairs of skate wheels attached to a narrow board serving as a platform for riding. **—skate′board′er** *n.*

ske·dad·dle (ski·dad′l) *Informal v.i.* **·dled, ·dling** To flee in haste. **—***n.* A hasty flight. [?]

skeet (skēt) *n.* A variety of trapshooting in which clay targets, hurled in such a way as to resemble the flight of birds, are fired at from various angles. [?]

skein (skān) *n.* **1** A fixed quantity of yarn, thread, silk, wool, etc., wound in a loose coil. **2** Something like this: a *skein* of hair. [< OF *escaigne*]

skel·e·ton (skel′ə·tən) *n.* **1** The supporting framework of a vertebrate, composed of bone and cartilage. **2** Any framework constituting the main supporting parts of a structure. **3** A mere sketch or outline of anything. **4** A very thin person or animal. **—skeleton in the closet** A secret source of shame or discredit. **—***adj.* Of, pertaining to, or like a skeleton. [< Gk. *skeletos* dried up] **—skel·e·tal** *adj.*

skeleton key A key having a large part of the bit filed away to enable it to open many simple locks.

skep·tic (skep′tik) *n.* **1** A person characterized by skepticism, esp. in regard to religion. **2** A person who advocates or believes in philosophical skepticism. *Chiefly Brit. sp.* **scep′tic.** [< Gk. *skeptikos* reflective]

skep·ti·cal (skep′ti·kəl) *adj.* Of, pertaining to, characteristic of, or marked by skepticism. *Chiefly Brit. sp.* **scep′ti·cal.** **—skep′ti·cal·ly** *adv.* **—skep′ti·cal·ness** *n.*

skep·ti·cism (skep′tə·siz′əm) *n.* **1** A doubting or incredulous state of mind. **2** Doubt about basic religious doctrines such as immortality, revelation, etc. **3** The philosophical doctrine that absolute knowledge in any given area is unattainable, and that relative certainty can be approximated only by a continuous process of doubt, criticism, and suspended judgment. *Chiefly Brit. sp.* **scep′ti·cism.**

sketch (skech) *n.* **1** A rough or undetailed drawing or design, often done as a preliminary study. **2** A brief plan, description, or outline. **3** A short literary or musical composition. **4** A short scene, play, comical act, etc. **—***v.t.* **1** To make a sketch or sketches of. **—***v.i.* **2** To make a sketch or sketches. [< Gk. *schedios* impromptu] **—sketch′er** *n.*

sketch·book (skech′bo͝ok′) *n.* **1** A pad or book of drawing paper for sketching. **2** A printed volume of sketches.

sketch·y (skech′ē) *adj.* **sketch·i·er, sketch·i·est 1** Like or in the form of a sketch; roughly suggested without detail. **2** Incomplete; superficial. **—sketch′i·ly** *adv.* **—sketch′i·ness** *n.*

skew (skyo͞o) *v.i.* **1** To take an oblique direction. **2** To look sideways; squint. **—***v.t.* **3** To give an oblique form or direction to. **4** To give a bias to; misrepresent; distort. **—***adj.* **1** Placed, turned or running to one side; oblique; slanting. **2** ASYMMETRIC. **—***n.* A deviation from straightness; an oblique direction or course. [< AF *eskiuer*]

skew·er (skyo͞o′ər) *n.* **1** A long pin of wood or metal, used for fastening meat while roasting. **2** Any of various articles of similar shape or use. **—***v.t.* To run through or fasten with or as with a skewer. [?]

ski (skē, *Brit. also* shē) *n. pl.* **skis 1** One of a pair of flat, narrow runners of wood, metal, or other material, worn clamped to boots for gliding over snow. **2** WATER SKI. **—***v.* **skied, ski·ing** *v.i.* **1** To glide or travel on skis. **—***v.t.* **2** To glide or travel over on skis. [Norw.< ON *skidh* snowshoe] **—ski′er** *n.*

skid (skid) *n.* **1** A log, plank, etc., often one of a pair, used to support or elevate something or as an incline on which heavy objects can be rolled or slid. **2** A low, movable platform that holds material to be moved, temporarily stored, etc. 3 A shoe, drag, etc., used to prevent a wheel from turning. 4 A runner used in place of a wheel in the landing gear of an airplane or helicopter. 5 The act of skidding. —**on the skids** *Slang* Rapidly declining in prestige, power, etc. —*v.* **skid·ded, skid·ding** *v.i.* 1 To slide instead of rolling, as a wheel over a surface. 2 To slide due to loss of traction, as a vehicle. 3 *Aeron.* To slip sideways when turning. —*v.t.* 4 To put, drag, haul, or slide on skids. 5 To brake or hold back with a skid. [?] —**skid′der** *n.*

skid row *Slang* An urban section frequented by vagrants, derelicts, etc.

skiff (skif) *n.* 1 A light rowboat. 2 A small, light sailing vessel. [< OHG *scif* ship]

skill (skil) *n.* 1 Ability or proficiency in execution or performance. 2 A specific art, craft, trade, or job; also such an art, craft, etc., in which one has a learned competence. [< ON *skil* knowledge]

skilled (skild) *adj.* 1 Having skill. 2 Having or requiring a specialized ability, as in a particular occupation, gained by training or experience.

skil·let (skil′it) *n.* A frying pan. [ME *skelet*] • See APPLIANCE.

skill·ful (skil′fəl) *adj.* 1 Having skill. 2 Done with or requiring skill. Also **skil′ful.** —**skill′fully** *adv.* —**skill′ful·ness** *n.*

skim (skim) *v.* **skimmed, skim·ming** *v.t.* 1 To remove floating matter from the surface of (a liquid): to *skim* milk. 2 To remove (floating matter) from the surface of a liquid: to *skim* cream from milk. 3 To cover with a thin film, as of ice. 4 To move lightly and quickly across or over. 5 To cause to bounce and ricochet swiftly and lightly, as a coin across a pond. 6 To read or glance over hastily or superficially. —*v.i.* 7 To move quickly and lightly across or near a surface; glide. 8 To make a hasty and superficial perusal; glance: with *over* or *through.* 9 To become covered with a thin film. —*n.* 1 The act of skimming. 2 That which is skimmed off. 3 A thin layer or coating. —*adj.* Skimmed: *skim* milk. [< OF *escume* scum, foam] —**skim′mer** *n.*

skim milk Milk from which the cream has been removed. Also **skimmed milk.**

skimp (skimp) *v.i.* 1 To provide too little; scrimp. 2 To keep expenses at a minimum. —*v.t.* 3 To do poorly, hastily, or carelessly. 4 To be stingy in providing for. —*adj.* Scant; meager. [?] —**skimp′ing·ly** *adv.*

skimp·y (skim′pē) *adj.* **skimp·i·er, skimp·i·est** Scanty; insufficient. —**skimp′i·ly** *adv.* —**skimp′i·ness** *n.*

skin (skin) *n.* 1 The membranous outer covering of an animal body. 2 The pelt or hide of an animal. 3 A vessel for holding liquids, made of the skin of an animal. 4 Any outside layer, coat, or covering resembling skin, as fruit rind. —**by the skin of one's teeth** *Informal* Very closely or narrowly; barely. —**get under one's skin** 1 To provoke one. 2 To be a source of excitement, emotion, etc., to one. —**have a thick (thin) skin** To be very insensitive (or sensitive), as to insult, criticism, etc. —**save one's skin** *Informal* To avoid harm or death. —*v.* **skinned, skin·ning** *v.t.* 1 To remove the skin of; peel. 2 To cover with or as with skin. 3 To remove as if taking off skin: to *skin* a dollar from a roll of bills. 4 *Informal* To cheat or swindle. —*v.i.* 5 To become covered with skin. 6 To climb up or down; shin. [< ON *skinn*] —**skin·ner** *n.*

skin-deep (skin′dēp′) *adj.* 1 Penetrating only as deep as the skin. 2 Of little significance; superficial.

skin diving Underwater swimming in which the swimmer is equipped with a breathing apparatus, as a snorkel, goggles, and with various other equipment as foot fins, rubber garments, etc. —**skin diver**

skin·flint (skin′flint) *n.* One who tries to get or save money in any possible way. —**Syn.** miser, niggard, scrooge.

skink (skingk) *n.* One of a group of lizards with short limbs and smooth, flat, shiny scales. [< Gk. *skinkos,* a kind of lizard]

skin·ner (skin′ər) *n.* 1 One who strips or processes the skins of animals. 2 A dealer in skins. 3 *Informal* A mule driver.

skin·ny (skin′ē) *adj.* **·ni·er, ·ni·est** 1 Consisting of or like skin. 2 Without sufficient flesh; too thin. 3 Lacking the normal or desirable quality, quantity, size, etc. —**skin′ni·ly** *adv.* —**skin′ni·ness** *n.*

skin·ny-dip (skin′ē·dip′) *Informal v.i.* **·dipped, ·dip·ping** To swim in the nude. —*n.* A swim in the nude. —**skin·ny-dip·per** *n.*

skin-tight (skin′tīt′) *adj.* Fitting tightly to the skin, as a garment.

skip (skip) *v.* **skipped, skip·ping** *v.i.* 1 To move with springing steps, esp. by a series of light hops on alternate feet. 2 To be deflected from a surface; ricochet. 3 To pass from one point to another without noticing what lies between. 4 *Informal* To leave or depart hurriedly; flee. 5 To be advanced in school beyond the next grade in order —*v.t.* 6 To leap lightly over. 7 To cause to ricochet. 8 To pass over or by without notice. 9 *Informal* To leave (a place) hurriedly. 10 To fail to attend a session or sessions of (church, school, etc.) 11 To cause to be advanced in school beyond the next grade in order —*n.* 1 A light bound or spring, esp. any of a series of light hops on alternate feet. 2 A passing over without notice. [Prob. < Scand.]

skip·jack (skip′jak) *n.* Any of various fishes that jump above or play along the surface of the water.

skip·per[1] (skip′ər) *n.* 1 One who or that which skips. 2 Any of various insects that make erratic, skipping movements.

skip·per[2] (skip′ər) *n.* 1 The master or captain of a vessel, esp. of a small ship or boat. 2 One who is in charge of any endeavor. —*v.t.* To act as the skipper of (a vessel, etc.) [< Du. *schip* ship]

skirl (skûrl, skirl) *v.i.* 1 To shriek shrilly, as a bagpipe. —*v.t.* 2 To play on the bagpipe. —*n.* A high, shrill sound, as of a bagpipe. [< Scand.]

skir·mish (skûr′mish) *n.* 1 A minor fight or encounter, usu. an incident in a larger conflict. 2 Any unimportant dispute, argument, etc. —*v.i.* To take part in a skirmish. [< OF *eskermir* to fence, fight] —**skir′mish·er** *n.*

skirt (skûrt) *n.* 1 That part of a dress, gown, etc., that hangs from the waist down. 2 A separate garment for women or girls that hangs from the waist down. • See PLEAT. 3 Anything that hangs or covers like a skirt: the *skirt* of a dressing table. 4 *Slang* A girl; woman. 5 The margin, border, or outer edge of anything. 6 *pl.* The border, fringe, or edge of a particular area; outskirts. —*v.t.* 1 To lie along or form the edge of; to border. 2 To surround or border: with *with.* 3 To pass around or about, usu. to avoid crossing: to *skirt* the town. —*v.i.* 4 To be on or pass along the edge or border. [< ON *skyrt* shirt]

skit (skit) *n.* 1 A short theatrical sketch, usu. humorous or satirical. 2 A short piece of writing, humorous or satirical in tone. [?]

skit·ter (skit′ər) *v.i.* 1 To glide or skip along a surface lightly and quickly. 2 To draw a lure or baited hook along the surface of the water with a skipping or twitching movement. —*v.t.* 3 To cause to skitter.

skit·tish (skit′ish) *adj.* 1 Easily frightened, as a horse. 2 Very playful or lively. 3 Unreliable; fickle. [ME] —**skit′tish·ly** *adv.* —**skit′tish·ness** *n.*

skit·tle (skit′l) *n.* 1 *pl. (construed as sing.)* A British version of the game of ninepins, in which a wooden disk or ball is thrown to knock down the pins. 2 One of the pins used in this game. —**beer and skittles** Carefree, unruffled enjoyment: usu. with a negative: Life is not all *beer and skittles.* [?]

skiv·vy (skiv′ē) *n. pl.* **·vies** *Slang* 1 A man's T-shirt. 2 *pl.* Men's underwear. [?]

skoal (skōl) *interj.* Good health, good luck, etc.: used as a toast. [< Dan. and Norw. *skaal* cup < ON *skāl* bowl]

Skr. Sanskrit.

Skt. Sanskrit.

sku·a (skyōō′ə) *n.* A predatory sea bird. Also **skua gull.** [< ON *skūfr*]

skul·dug·ger·y (skul·dug′ər·ē) *n.* Dishonesty; trickery; underhandedness. [?]

skulk (skulk) *v.i.* 1 To move about furtively or slily; sneak. 2 *Chiefly Brit.* To shirk; evade work or responsibility. —*n.* One who skulks. [< Scand.] —**skulk′er** *n.*

skull (skul) *n.* **1** The bony framework of the head of a vertebrate animal; the cranium. **2** The head considered as the seat of intelligence; mind. [< Scand.]

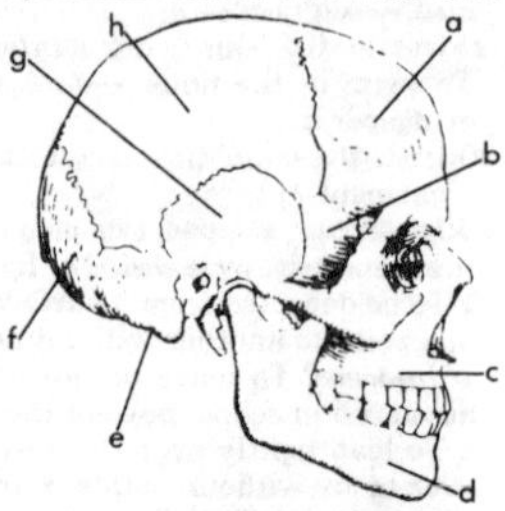

Bones of the human skull a. frontal. b. sphenoid. c. superior maxillary. d. inferior maxillary. e. mastoid process. f. occipital. g. temporal. h. parietal.

skull and cross-bones A representation of the human skull over two crossed thighbones, used as a warning label on poison and, formerly, as an emblem of piracy.

skull·cap (skul′kap′) *n.* A cap closely fitting the skull and having no brim or peak.

skunk (skungk) *n.* **1** A small nocturnal carnivore of North America, usu. black with a white stripe down the back, and ejecting an offensive odor when attacked. **2** *Informal* A low, contemptible person. —*v.t.* *Slang* To defeat, as in a contest, esp. to defeat so thoroughly as to keep from scoring. [< Algon. *seganku*]

Skunk

skunk cabbage A stemless perennial herb growing in marshy terrain and having a strong, skunklike odor. Also **skunk′weed′** (-wēd′).

sky (skī) *n. pl.* **skies** **1** The blue vault that seems to bend over the earth; the firmament. **2** *Often pl.* The upper atmosphere, esp. in regard to its appearance: cloudy *skies.* **3** The celestial regions; heaven. **4** Climate; weather. —**out of a clear** (or **blue**) **sky** Without any warning. —**to the skies** Without reservations: to praise something *to the skies.* —*v.t.* **skied** or **skyed, sky·ing** *Informal* **1** To hit, throw, bat, etc., high into the air. **2** To hang, as a picture, esp. at an exhibition, above eye level. [< ON *skȳ* cloud]

sky blue A blue like the color of the sky; azure. —**sky′-blue′** *adj.*

sky·dive (skī′dīv′) *v.i.* **·dived, ·div·ing** To engage in skydiving. —**sky′div′er** *n.*

sky·div·ing (skī′dī′ving) *n.* The sport of jumping from an airplane and performing various maneuvers before opening a parachute.

sky·jack (skī′jak′) *v.t.* HIJACK (def. 3). [< SKY + (HI)JACK] —**sky′jack′er** *n.*

sky·lark (skī′lärk′) *n.* A lark noted for singing as it flies. —*v.i.* To indulge in hilarious or boisterous frolic. —**sky′·lark′er** *n.*

sky·light (skī′līt′) *n.* A window facing skyward.

sky·line (skī′līn′) *n.* **1** The line where earth and sky appear to meet; horizon. **2** The outline of buildings, trees, etc., against the sky.

sky·rock·et (skī′rok′it) *n.* A rocket that is shot high into the air. —*v.t.* & *v.i.* To rise or cause to rise or ascend steeply, like a skyrocket, as wages, prices, etc.

sky·sail (skī′səl, -sāl′) *n.* *Naut.* A small sail above the royal in a square-rigged vessel.

sky·scrap·er (skī′skrā′pər) *n.* A very high building.

sky·ward (skī′wərd) *adv.* Toward the sky. Also **sky′·wards.** —**sky′ward** *adj.*

sky·writ·ing (skī′rī′ting) *n.* The forming of words in the air by the release of a substance, as a jet of vapor, from an airplane. —**sky′writ′er** *n.*

slab (slab) *n.* **1** A fairly thick, flat piece or slice, as of metal, stone, meat, etc. **2** An outer piece cut from a log. —*v.t.* **slabbed, slab·bing** **1** To saw slabs from, as a log. **2** To form into a slab or slabs. [ME]

slack[1] (slak) *adj.* **1** Hanging loosely. **2** Careless; remiss; slovenly; slow. **3** Weak; loose: a *slack* mouth. **4** Lacking activity; not brisk or busy; slow or sluggish: a *slack* season. **5** Listless; limp: a *slack* grip. **6** Flowing sluggishly, as water. —*v.t.* **1** To make slack. **2** To slake, as lime. —*v.i.* **3** To be or become slack. **4** To become less active or less busy: usu. with *off.* —*n.* **1** The part of anything, as a rope, that is slack. **2** A period of inactivity. **3** A cessation of movement, as in a current. —*adv.* In a slack manner. [< OE *slæc*] —**slack′ly** *adv.* —**slack′ness** *n.*

slack[2] (slak) *n.* A mixture of coal dust, dirt, and small pieces of coal left after coal has been screened. [ME *sleck*]

slack·en (slak′ən) *v.t.* & *v.i.* To make or become slack.

slack·er (slak′ər) *n.* One who shirks his duties, esp. one who avoids military service in wartime.

slacks (slaks) *n.pl.* Trousers, esp. for informal wear.

slag (slag) *n.* **1** *Metall.* The fused residue separated in the reduction of ores. **2** Volcanic scoria. —*v.t.* & *v.i.* **slagged, slag·ging** To form into slag. [< MLG *slagge*] —**slag′gy** *adj.*

slain (slān) *p.p.* of SLAY.

slake (slāk) *v.* **slaked, slak·ing** *v.t.* **1** To lessen the force of; quench: to *slake* thirst or flames. **2** To mix (an oxide, as lime, etc.) with water; to hydrate. —*v.i.* **3** To become hydrated; said of lime. [< OE *slacian* retard]

slaked lime Calcium hydroxide produced by mixing calcium oxide and water.

sla·lom (slä′ləm, slā′-) *n.* In skiing, a race over a zigzag course laid out between upright obstacles. —*v.i.* To ski in or as in a slalom. [Norw.]

slam[1] (slam) *v.* **slammed, slam·ming** *v.t.* **1** To shut with violence and noise. **2** To put, dash, throw, etc., with violence. **3** *Slang* To strike with the fist. **4** *Informal* To criticize severely. —*v.i.* **5** To shut or move with force. —*n.* **1** A closing or striking with a bang; the act or noise of slamming. **2** *Informal* Severe criticism. [? < Scand.]

slam[2] (slam) *n.* **1** GRAND SLAM (def. 1). **2** LITTLE SLAM. [?]

slam-bang (slam′bang′) *Informal adv.* Vigorously, violently, or noisily. —*adj.* Vigorous, violent, or noisy.

slan·der (slan′dər) *n.* **1** The uttering of false statements or misrepresentations which defame and injure the reputation of another. **2** Such a statement. —*v.t.* **1** To injure by uttering a false statement, etc.; defame. —*v.i.* **2** To utter slander. [< L *scandalum* scandal] —**slan′der·er** *n.* • Popularly, *slander* and *libel* are used synonymously to mean defamation. Legally, however, *slander* refers to oral defamation and *libel* to defamation by any other means, as writing, pictures, effigies, etc.

slan·der·ous (slan′dər·əs) *adj.* **1** Uttering slander. **2** Containing or constituting slander. —**slan′der·ous·ly** *adv.* —**slan′der·ous·ness** *n.*

slang (slang) *n.* **1** A type of popular language comprised of words and phrases of a vigorous, colorful, or facetious nature, which are invented or derived from the unconventional use of the standard vocabulary. **2** The special vocabulary of a certain class, group, profession, etc.; argot; jargon. [?] —**slang′i·ness** *n.* —**slang′y** *adj.*

slant (slant) *v.t.* **1** To give a sloping direction to. **2** To write or edit (news or other literary matter) so as to express a special attitude or appeal to a particular group, interest, etc. —*v.i.* **3** To have or take an oblique or sloping direction. —*adj.* Sloping —*n.* **1** A slanting direction, course, line, etc.; incline. **2** A point of view, esp. one that is personal or peculiar. [< Scand.] —**slant′ing** *adj.* —**slant′ing·ly** *adv.* —**slant′ing·ness** *n.*

slant·wise (slant′wīz) *adj.* Slanting; oblique. —*adv.* At a slant or slope; obliquely. Also **slant′ways′** (-wāz′).

slap (slap) *n.* **1** A blow delivered with the open hand or with something flat. **2** The sound made by such a blow, or a sound like it. **3** An insult or rebuff. —*v.* **slapped, slap·ping** *v.t.* **1** To strike with the open hand or with something flat. **2** To put, place, throw, etc., violently or carelessly. —*adv.* **1** Suddenly; abruptly. **2** Directly; straight: *slap* into his face. [< LG *slapp*] —**slap′per** *n.*

slap-dash (slap′dash′) *adj.* Done or acting in a hasty or careless way. —*n.* Something done in a hasty or careless manner. —*adv.* In a slap-dash manner.

slap-hap·py (slap′hap′ē) *adj.* *Slang* **1** Confused or dazed, as by blows to the head. **2** Giddy or silly.

slap·jack (slap′jak) *n.* PANCAKE.

slap·stick (slap′stik′) *n.* **1** A flexible, double paddle formerly used in farces and pantomimes to make a loud report when an actor was struck with it. **2** The type of comedy which depends on farce, violent activity, etc. —*adj.* Using or suggestive of such comedy.

slash (slash) *v.t.* 1 To cut violently with or as with an edged instrument; gash. 2 To strike with a whip; lash; scourge. 3 To slit, as a garment, so as to expose ornamental material or lining in or under the slits. 4 To criticize severely. 5 To reduce sharply, as salaries. —*v.i.* 6 To make a long sweeping stroke with or as with something sharp; cut. —*n.* 1 The act of slashing. 2 The result of slashing; cut; slit; gash. 3 An ornamental slit cut in a garment. 4 An opening in a forest, covered with debris, as from cutting timber. 5 Such debris. [? < OF *esclashier* to break] —**slash′er** *n.*

slash·ing (slash′ing) *adj.* 1 Severely critical; merciless. 2 Spirited; dashing; impetuous. 3 *Informal* Tremendous; great. —*n.* A slash. —**slash′ing·ly** *adv.* —**slash′ing·ness** *n.*

slat (slat) *n.* Any thin, narrow strip of wood or metal; lath. —*v.t.* **slat·ted, slat·ting** To provide or make with slats. [< OF *esclat* splinter, chip]

slat (slāt) *n.* 1 A rock that splits readily into thin and even sheets or layers. 2 A piece, slab, or plate of slate used for roofing, writing upon, etc. 3 A list of candidates, as for nomination or election. 4 A dull bluish gray color resembling that of slate: also **slate gray.** —**a clean slate** A record unmarred by dishonor or dishonesty. —*v.t.* **slat·ed, slat·ing** 1 To cover with or as with slate. 2 To put on a political slate or a list of any sort. [< OF *esclat* a chip, splinter] —**slat′er** *n.* —**slat′y** *adj.* **(·i·er, ·i·est)**

slat·tern (slat′ərn) *n.* An untidy or slovenly woman. [?]

slat·tern·ly (slat′ərn·lē) *adj.* Of, pertaining to, characteristic of, or fit for a slattern. —*adv.* In the manner of a slattern. —**slat′tern·li·ness** *n.* —**Syn.** *adj.* untidy, dowdy, frowzy, sluttish.

slaugh·ter (slô′tər) *n.* 1 The act of killing, esp. the butchering of animals for market. 2 The wanton or savage killing of one or more human beings, esp. of a great number in battle. —*v.t.* 1 To kill for the market; butcher. 2 To kill wantonly or savagely, esp. in large numbers. [< ON *slātr* butcher's meat] —**slaugh′ter·er** *n.* —**slaugh′ter·ous** *adj.* —**slaugh′ter·ous·ly** *adv.*

slaugh·ter·house (slô′ter·hous′) *n.* A place where animals are butchered.

Slav (släv, slav) *n.* A member of any of the Slavic-speaking peoples of E, SE, or CEN. Europe.

Slav. Slavic.

slave (slāv) *n.* 1 A person who is owned by and completely subject to another; one bound by slavery. 2 A person who is totally subject to some habit, influence, etc. 3 One who labors like a slave; drudge. 4 A machine or device that is controlled by another machine or device. 5 SLAVE ANT. —*v.i.* **slaved, slav·ing** To work like a slave; toil; drudge. [< Med. L *sclavus* Slav]

slave ant An ant enslaved by members of a slave-making ant species.

slave-driv·er (slāv′drī′vər) *n.* 1 An overseer of slaves at work. 2 Any severe or exacting taskmaster.

slave·hold·er (slāv′hōl′dər) *n.* An owner of slaves. —**slave′hold′ing** *adj. n.*

slav·er[1] (slā′vər) *n.* A person or a vessel engaged in the slave trade.

slav·er[2] (slav′ər) *v.i.* To dribble saliva; drool. —*n.* Saliva dribbling from the mouth. [? < ON *slafra*] —**slav′er·er** *n.*

slav·er·y (slā′vər·ē, slāv′rē) *n.* 1 The legalized social institution in which humans are held as property or chattels. 2 The condition of being a slave. 3 Submission to some habit, influence, etc. 4 Slavish toil; drudgery.

slave trade The business of dealing in slaves, esp. the procurement, transportation, and sale of black Africans.

slav·ey (slā′vē, slav′ē) *n. pl.* **slav·eys** *Chiefly Brit. Informal* A drudge, usu. a maidservant.

Slav·ic (slä′vik, slav′ik) *adj.* Of or pertaining to the Slavs or their languages. —*n.* A branch of the Indo-European language family including Byelorussian, Bulgarian, Czech, Polish, Serbo-Croatian, Slovene, Russian, and Ukainian.

slav·ish (slā′vish) *adj.* 1 Of, pertaining to, or characteristic of a slave; servile. 2 Having no originality; imitative. —**slav′ish·ly** *adv.* —**slav′ish·ness** *n.*

slaw (slô) *n.* COLESLAW. [< Du. *sla*, short for *salade* salad]

slay (slā) *v.t.* **slew, slain, slay·ing** 1 To kill violently; slaughter. 2 *Informal* To amuse, impress, etc., in an overwhelming way. [< OE *slēan*] —**slay′er** *n.*

slea·zy (slē′zē, slā′-) *adj.* **·zi·er, ·zi·est** 1 Lacking firmness of texture or substance. 2 Cheap in character or quality; shoddy, shabby, etc.: a *sleazy* novel; a *sleazy* dress. [?] —**slea′zi·ly** *adv.* —**slea′zi·ness** *n.*

sled (sled) *n.* 1 A vehicle on runners, designed for carrying people or loads over snow and ice. 2 A small sled used esp. by children for sliding on snow and ice. —*v.* **sled·ded, sled·ding** *v.t.* 1 To convey on a sled. —*v.i.* 2 To ride on or use a sled. [< MLG *sledde*] —**sled′der** *n.*

sled·ding (sled′ing) *n.* 1 The act of using or riding on a sled. 2 The conditions under which one uses a sled. 3 *Informal* The conditions under which one pursues any goal; going; progress.

sledge[1] (slej) *n.* A vehicle mounted on low runners for moving loads, esp. over snow and ice. —*v.t.* & *v.i.* **sledged, sledg·ing** To travel or convey on a sledge. [< MDu. *sleedse*]

Sledge

sledge[2] (slej) *n.* & *v.t.*, *v.i.* **sledged, sledg·ing** SLEDGEHAMMER. [< OE *slecg*]

sledge·ham·mer (slej′ham′ər) *n.* A long, heavy hammer, usu. wielded with both hands. —*v.t.* & *v.i.* To strike with or as with such a hammer. —*adj.* Like a sledgehammer; extremely powerful; crushing.

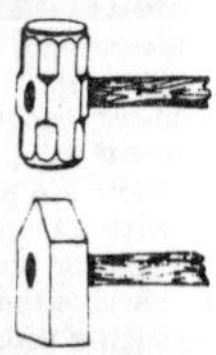
Sledge-hammers

sleek (slēk) *adj.* 1 Smooth and glossy. 2 Well-groomed or well-fed. 3 Smooth-spoken and polished in behavior, esp. in a specious way. —*v.t.* 1 To make smooth or glossy; polish. 2 To soothe; mollify. [Var. of SLICK] —**sleek′ly** *adv.* —**sleek′ness** *n.*

sleep (slēp) *n.* 1 A natural, recurrent physiological state characterized by cessation of voluntary movement and inattention to external stimuli. 2 A period of sleep. 3 Any condition of inactivity or rest. —**last sleep** Death. —*v.* **slept, sleep·ing** *v.i.* 1 To be or fall asleep; slumber. 2 To be in a state resembling sleep. —*v.t.* 3 To rest or repose in: to *sleep* the sleep of the dead. 4 To provide with sleeping quarters; lodge: The hotel can *sleep* a hundred guests. —**sleep away** To pass or spend in sleeping. —**sleep in** To sleep in the house where one works. —**sleep off** To get rid of by sleeping: He *slept off* a headache. —**sleep on** To postpone a decision upon. [< OE *slēp*]

sleep·er (slē′pər) *n.* 1 One who or that which sleeps. 2 A railroad sleeping car. 3 A heavy beam resting on or in the ground, as a support for a roadway, rails, etc. 4 *Informal* Someone or something thought to be unpromising that unexpectedly attains value, importance, notoriety, etc.

sleeping bag A large, warmly-lined bag, usu. zippered and often padded, for sleeping in esp. outdoors.

sleeping car A passenger railroad car with accommodations for sleeping.

sleeping sickness 1 Any of several often fatal tropical diseases caused by protozoans transmitted by the bites of certain insects, as the tsetse fly in Africa, and marked by fever and progressive lethargy. 2 A form of encephalitis.

sleep·less (slēp′lis) *adj.* 1 Unable to sleep; wakeful; restless. 2 Marked by or giving no sleep. 3 Always active or moving. —**sleep′less·ly** *adv.* —**sleep′less·ness** *n.*

sleep·walker (slēp′wô′kər) *n.* A person who walks in his sleep; somnambulist. —**sleep′walk′ing** *n.*

sleep·y (slē′pē) *adj.* **sleep·i·er, sleep·i·est** 1 Inclined to or ready for sleep; drowsy. 2 Lethargic, inactive, sluggish, or dull. 3 Conducive to sleep. —**sleep′i·ly** *adv.* —**sleep′i·ness** *n.*

sleet (slēt) *n.* 1 A mixture of snow or hail and rain. 2 Partly frozen rain. 3 A thin coating of ice, as on rails, wires, roads, etc. —*v.i.* To pour or shed sleet. [ME *slete*] —**sleet′y** *adj.*

sleeve (slēv) *n.* 1 The part of a garment that serves as a covering for the arm. **2** *Mech.* A tube or tubelike part surrounding another part or into which another part fits. **—up one's sleeve** Hidden but at hand **—***v.t.* **sleeved, sleev·ing** To furnish with a sleeve or sleeves. [< OE *slēfe*]

sleigh (slā) *n.* A light vehicle with runners, used esp. for transporting people on snow and ice. **—***v.i.* To ride or travel in a sleigh. [< Du. *slee,* contraction of *slede* sledge[1]] **—sleigh'er** *n.*

Sleigh

sleight (slīt) *n.* **1** Deftness; skill; dexterity. **2** Craft; cunning. [< ON *slægdh* slyness]

sleight of hand **1** Skill in performing magical tricks or in juggling. **2** An instance of such skill in performing.

slen·der (slen'dər) *adj.* **1** Having a small width or circumference, in proportion to length or height; long and thin. **2** Having a slim figure; attractively slight. **3** Having slight force or foundation. **4** Small or inadequate. [ME *slendre*] **—slen'der·ly** *adv.* **—slen'der·ness** *n.*

slen·der·ize (slen'də·rīz) *v.t. & v.i.* **·ized, ·iz·ing** To make or become slender.

slept (slept) *p.t. & p.p.* of SLEEP.

sleuth (slōōth) *n.* **1** *Informal* A detective. **2** A bloodhound: also **sleuth'hound.** **—***v.i.* To act as a detective. [< ON *slōdh* track]

slew[1] (slōō) *p.t.* of SLAY.

slew[2] (slōō) *n.* SLOUGH[1] (def. 2).

slew[3] (slōō) *n. Informal* A large number or amount. [< Ir. *sluagh*]

slew[4] (slōō) *v. & n.* SLUE[1].

slice (slīs) *n.* **1** A thin, broad piece cut off from a larger body. **2** A share or portion. **3** Any of various implements with a thin, broad blade, as a spatula. **4 a** The course of a ball so hit that it curves in the direction of the dominant hand of the player who propels it. **b** The ball that follows such a course. **—***v.* **sliced, slic·ing** *v.t.* **1** To cut or remove from a larger piece: often with *off, from,* etc. **2** To cut, separate, or divide into parts, shares, or thin, broad pieces. **3** To stir, spread, etc. with a slice. **4** To hit (a ball) so as to produce a slice. **—***v.i.* **5** To cut with or as with a knife. **6** To slice a ball, as in golf. [< OHG *slizan* to slit] **—slic'er** *n.*

slick (slik) *adj.* **1** Smooth, slippery, or sleek. **2** *Informal* Deceptively clever; tricky; smooth. **3** Clever; deft; adept. **4** *Informal* Technically skillful but shallow and insignificant: a *slick* novel. **5** *Slang* Very good, attractive, enjoyable, etc. **—***n.* **1** A smooth place on a surface of water, as from oil. **2** A film of oil on the surface of water. **3** *Informal* A magazine printed on glossy paper. **—***adv. Slang* In a slick or smooth manner; deftly, cleverly, smoothly, etc. **—** *v.t.* **1** To make smooth, trim, or glossy. **2** *Informal* To make smart or presentable: often with *up.* [< OE *slician* make smooth]

slick·er (slik'ər) *n.* **1** A long, loose waterproof coat of oilskin. **2** *Informal* A clever, deceptive, crooked person.

slide (slīd) *v.* **slid, slid** or **slid·den, slid·ing** *v.i.* **1** To pass along a surface with a smooth movement. **2** To move smoothly over snow or ice. **3** To move or pass stealthily or imperceptibly. **4** To proceed in a natural way; drift: to let the matter *slide.* **5** To pass or fall gradually (into a specified condition). **6** To slip from a position: The cup *slid* off the saucer. **7** To slip or fall by losing one's equilibrium or foothold. **8** In baseball, to throw oneself along the ground toward a base. **—***v.t.* **9** To cause to slide, as over a surface. **10** To move, put, enter, etc., with quietness or dexterity: with *in* or *into.* **—***n.* **1** An act of sliding. **2** An inclined plane, channel, etc., on which persons, goods, logs, etc., slide downward to a lower level. **3** A small plate of glass on which a specimen is mounted and examined through a microscope. **4** A small plate of transparent material bearing a single image for projection on a screen. **5** A part or mechanism that slides, as the U-shaped portion of the tubing which is pushed in and out to vary the pitch of a trombone. **6** The slipping of a mass of earth, snow, etc., from a higher to a lower level. **7** The mass that slips down. [< OE *slīdan*] **—slid'er** *n.*

slide fastener ZIPPER.

slide rule A device consisting of a rigid ruler with a central sliding piece, both graduated, used in calculation.

sliding scale A schedule affecting imports, prices, or wages, varying under conditions of consumption, demand, or market price.

slight (slīt) *adj.* **1** Of small importance or degree: a *slight* illness. **2** Slender in build: a *slight* figure. **3** Frail; fragile: a *slight* structure. **—***v.t.* **1** To omit due courtesy toward or respect for: to *slight* a friend. **2** To do carelessly or thoughtlessly; shirk. **3** To treat as trivial or insignificant. **—***n.* An act of discourtesy or disrespect. [< ON *slēttr* smooth] **—slight'er, slight'ness** *n.* **—slight'ly** *adv.*

sli·ly (slī'lē) *adv.* SLYLY.

slim (slim) *adj.* **slim·mer, slim·mest** **1** Small in thickness in proportion to height or length. **2** Slight; meager: a *slim* chance of survival. **—***v.t. & v.i.* **slimmed, slim·ming** To make or become thin or thinner. [< Du. *slim* bad] **—slim'ly** *adv.* **—slim'ness** *n.*

slime (slīm) *n.* **1** Soft, moist, adhesive mud or earth; muck. **2** A mucous exudation from the bodies of certain organisms. **3** An offensive, digusting substance or quality. **—***v.t.* **slimed, slim·ing** **1** To smear with or as with slime. **2** To remove slime from, as fishes. [< OE *slīm*]

slim·y (slī'mē) *adj.* **slim·i·er, slim·i·est** **1** Covered with slime. **2** Containing slime. **3** Filthy; foul. **—slim'i·ly** *adv.* **—slim'i·ness** *n.*

sling (sling) *n.* **1** A strap or pocket with a string attached to each end, for hurling a stone. **2** One of various devices for holding up an injured arm. **3** A device, as a band or chain, for lifting or moving heavy objects. **4** The act of slinging; a sudden throw. **5** A drink made of sugar, liquor, and water: a gin *sling.* **—***v.t.* **slung, sling·ing** **1** To fling; hurl. **2** To move or hoist, as by a rope or tackle. **3** To suspend loosely in a sling. [? < ON *slyngva* hurl] **—sling'er** *n.*

sling·shot (sling'shot') *n.* A forked stick with an elastic strap attached to the prongs for hurling small missiles.

slink (slingk) *v.* **slunk** or **slinked, slink·ing** *v.i.* To move or go furtively or stealthily. [< OE *slincan*] **—slink'ing·ly** *adv.* **— Syn.** creep, steal, sneak, skulk.

slink·y (slingk'ē) *adj.* **slink·i·er, slink·i·est** **1** Sneaking; stealthy. **2** *Slang* Sinuous or feline in movement or form. **—slink'i·ly** *adv.* **—slink'i·ness** *n.*

slip[1] (slip) *v.* **slipped, slip·ping** *v.t.* **1** To cause to glide or slide. **2** To put on or off easily, as a loose garment. **3** To convey slyly or secretly. **4** To free oneself or itself from. **5** To unleash, as hounds. **6** To release from its fastening and let run out, as a cable. **7** To dislocate, as a bone. **8** To escape or pass unobserved: It *slipped* my mind. **—***v.i.* **9** To slide so as to lose one's footing. **10** To fall into an error. **11** To escape. **12** To move smoothly and easily. **13** To go or come stealthily: often with *off, away,* or *from.* **14** To overlook: to let an opportunity *slip.* **—let slip** To say without intending to. **—slip one over on** *Informal* To take advantage of by trickery. **—slip up** *Informal* To make a mistake. **—***n.* **1** A sudden slide. **2** A slight mistake. **3** A narrow space between two wharves. **4** A pier. **5** An inclined plane leading down to the water, on which vessels are repaired or constructed. **6** A woman's undergarment approximately the length of a dress. **7** A pillowcase. **8** A leash containing a device which permits quick release of the dog. **9** Undesired relative motion, as between a wheel and the road; also, the amount of this. **—give (someone) the slip** To elude (someone). [< MLG *slippen*]

slip[2] (slip) *n.* **1** A cutting from a plant for planting or grafting. **2** A small, slender person, esp. a youthful one. **3** A small piece of something, as of paper. **—***v.t.* **slipped, slip·ping** To cut off for planting; make a slip or slips of. [< MDu. *slippe*]

slip·cov·er (slip'kuv'ər) *n.* A fitted cloth cover for a piece of furniture, that can be readily removed.

slip·knot (slip'not') *n.* **1** A knot so made that it will slip along the rope or cord around which it is formed. **2** A knot easily untied by pulling. Also **slip knot.**

slip-on (slip'on', -ôn') *adj.* **1** Designating a garment or accessory that can be easily donned or taken off. **2** Designating a garment, esp. a sweater, that is put on and taken off over the head: also **slip'o'ver** (-ō'vər). **—***n.* A slip-on garment, glove, shoe, etc.

slip·per (slip'ər) *n.* A low, light shoe into or out of which the foot is easily slipped. **—slip'pered** *adj.*

slip·per·y (slip′ər·ē) *adj.* **·per·i·er, ·per·i·est 1** Having a surface so smooth that bodies slip or slide easily on it. **2** That evades one's grasp; elusive. **3** Unreliable; tricky. **—slip′per·i·ness** *n.*

slippery elm 1 A species of small elm with mucilaginous inner bark. **2** Its wood or inner bark.

slip·shod (slip′shod′) *adj.* **1** Wearing shoes or slippers down at the heels. **2** Slovenly; sloppy. **3** Performed carelessly: *slipshod* work.

slip·stream (slip′strēm′) *n. Aeron.* The stream of air driven backwards by the propeller of an aircraft.

slip-up (slip′up′) *n. Informal* A mistake; error.

slit (slit) *n.* A relatively straight cut or a long, narrow opening. *—v.t.* **slit, slit·ting 1** To make a long incision in; slash. **2** To cut lengthwise into strips. **3** To sever. [ME *slitten*] **—slit′ter** *n.*

slith·er (slit͟h′ər) *v.i.* **1** To slide; slip, as on a loose surface. **2** To glide, as a snake. *—v.t.* **3** To cause to slither. *—n.* A sinuous, gliding movement. [< OE *slidrian*] **—slith′er·y** *adj.*

sliv·er (sliv′ər) *n.* **1** A slender piece, as of wood, cut or torn off lengthwise; a splinter. **2** Corded textile fibers drawn into a fleecy strand. *—v.t. & v.i.* To cut or be split into long thin pieces. [< ME *sliven* to cleave] **—sliv′er·er** *n.*

slob (slob) *n.* **1** Mud; mire. **2** *Slang* A careless or unclean person. [< Ir. *slab*]

slob·ber (slob′ər) *v.t.* **1** To wet with liquids oozing from the mouth. **2** To shed or spill, as liquid food, in eating. *—v.i.* **3** To drivel; slaver. **4** To talk or act gushingly. *—n.* **1** Liquid spilled as from the mouth. **2** Gushing, sentimental talk. [ME *sloberen*] **—slob′ber·er** *n.* **—slob′ber·y** *adj.*

sloe (slō) *n.* **1** A small, plumlike, astringent fruit. **2** The shrub that bears it; the blackthorn. [< OE *slā*]

sloe gin A cordial with a gin base, flavored with sloes.

slog (slog) *v.t. & v.i.* **slogged, slog·ging 1** To slug, as a pugilist. **2** To plod (one's way). *—n.* A heavy blow. [?] **—slog′ger** *n.*

slo·gan (slō′gən) *n.* **1** A catchword or motto adopted by a political party, advertiser, etc. **2** A battle or rallying cry. [< Scot. Gael. *sluagh* army + *gairm* yell]

slo·gan·eer (slō′gə·nir′) *Informal n.* One who coins or uses slogans. *—v.i.* To coin or use slogans.

sloop (slo͞op) *n.* A small sailboat with a single mast and at least one jib. [< Du. *sloep*]

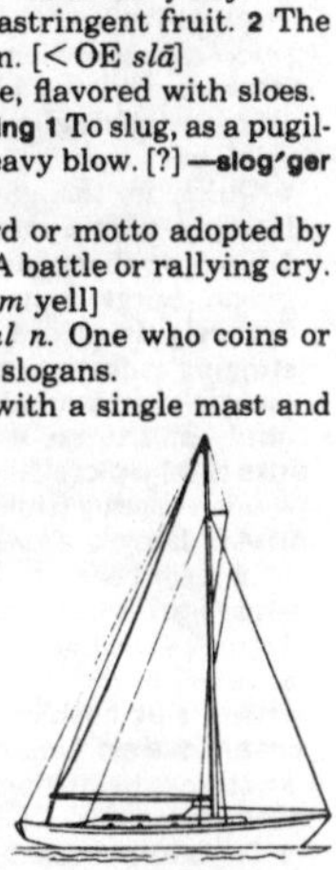
Sloop

slop[1] (slop) *v.* **slopped, slop·ping** *v.i.* **1** To splash or spill. **2** To walk or move through slush. *—v.t.* **3** To cause (a liquid) to spill or splash. **4** To feed (a domestic animal) with slops. **—slop over 1** To overflow and splash. **2** *Slang* To show too much zeal, emotion, etc. *—n.* **1** Slush or watery mud. **2** An unappetizing liquid or watery food. **3** *pl.* Refuse liquid. **4** *pl.* Waste food or swill. [< ME *sloppe* mud]

slop[2] (slop) **1** A loose outer garment, as a smock. **2** *pl.* Articles of clothing and other merchandise sold to sailors on shipboard. [ME *sloppe*]

slope (slōp) *v.* **sloped, slop·ing** *v.i.* **1** To be inclined from the level; slant downward or upward. **2** To go obliquely. *—v.t.* **3** To cause to slope. *—n.* **1** Any slanting surface or line. **2** The degree of inclination of a line or surface from the plane of the horizon. [< OE *aslupan* slip away] **—slop′er, slop′ing·ness** *n.* **—slop′ing·ly** *adv.*

slop·py (slop′ē) *adj.* **·pi·er, ·pi·est 1** Slushy; splashy; wet. **2** Watery or pulpy. **3** Splashed with liquid or slops. **4** *Informal* Messy; slovenly; careless. **5** *Informal* Maudlin; overly sentimental. **—slop′pi·ly** *adv.* **—slop′pi·ness** *n.*

slosh (slosh) *v.t.* **1** To throw about, as a liquid. *—v.i.* **2** To splash; flounder: to *slosh* through a pool. *—n.* Slush. [Var. of SLUSH]

slot (slot) *n.* **1** A long narrow groove or opening; slit. **2** A narrow depression cut to receive some corresponding part in a mechanism. **3** *Informal* An opening or position, as in an organization, or a place in a sequence. *—v.t.* **slot·ted, slot·ting** To cut a slot or slots in. [< OF *esclot* the hollow between the breasts]

sloth (slōth, slôth, sloth) *n.* **1** Disinclination to exertion; laziness. **2** Any of several slow-moving, arboreal mammals of South America. [< SLOW]

Three-toed sloth

sloth·ful (slōth′fəl, slôth′-, sloth′-) *adj.* Inclined to or characterized by sloth. **—sloth′ful·ly** *adv.* **—sloth′ful·ness** *n.* **—Syn.** lazy, indolent, sluggish, shiftless.

slot machine A vending machine or gambling machine having a slot in which a coin is dropped to cause operation.

slouch (slouch) *v.i.* **1** To have a downcast or drooping gait, look, or posture. **2** To hang or droop carelessly. *—n.* **1** A drooping movement or appearance caused by depression or carelessness. **2** An awkward or incompetent person. [?] **—slouch′y** *adj.* **(·i·er, ·i·est) —slouch′i·ly** *adv.* **—slouch′i·ness** *n.*

slough[1] (slou; slo͞o *esp. for def. 2*) *n.* **1** A place of deep mud or mire. **2** A stagnant swamp, backwater, etc. **3** A state of great despair or degradation. [< OE *slōh*] **—slough′y** *adj.*

slough[2] (sluf) *n.* **1** Dead tissue separated and thrown off from living tissue. **2** The skin of a serpent that has been or is about to be shed. *—v.t.* **1** To cast off; shed. **2** To discard; shed, as a habit or a growth. *—v.i.* **3** To be cast off. **4** To cast off a slough or tissue. [ME *slouh*] **—slough′y** *adj.*

Slo·vak (slō′väk, slō′vak) *n.* **1** One of a Slavic people of NW Hungary and parts of Moravia. **2** The language spoken by the Slovaks. *—adj.* Of or pertaining to the Slovaks or to their language. Also **Slo·vak′i·an.**

slov·en (sluv′ən) *n.* One who is habitually untidy, careless, or dirty. [ME *sloveyn*]

Slo·vene (slō′vēn, slō·vēn′) *n.* One of a group of s Slavs now living in NW Yugoslavia. *—adj.* Of or pertaining to the Slovenes or to their language. **—Slo·ve′ni·an** *adj., n.*

slov·en·ly (sluv′ən·lē) *adj.* **·li·er, ·li·est** Untidy and careless in appearance, work, habits, etc. *—adv.* In a slovenly manner. **—slov′en·li·ness** *n.*

slow (slō) *adj.* **1** Taking a long time to move, perform, or occur. **2** Behind the standard time: said of a timepiece. **3** Not hasty: *slow* to anger. **4** Dull in comprehending: a *slow* student. **5** Uninteresting; tedious: a *slow* drama. **6** Denoting a condition of a racetrack that retards the horses' speed. **7** Heating or burning slowly; low: a *slow* flame. **8** Not brisk; slack: Business is *slow*. *—v.t. & v.i.* To make or become slow or slower: often with *up* or *down*. *—adv.* In a slow manner. [< OE *slāw*] **—slow′ly** *adv.* **—slow′ness** *n.*

slow-mo·tion (slō′mō′shən) *adj.* **1** Moving or acting at less than normal speed. **2** Denoting a television or motion picture filmed at greater than standard speed so that the action appears slow in normal projection.

sludge (sluj) *n.* **1** Soft, water-soaked mud. **2** A slush of snow or broken or half-formed ice. **3** Muddy or pasty refuse, sediment, etc. [?] **—sludg′y** *adj.* **(·i·er, ·i·est)**

slue[1] (slo͞o) *v.* **slued, slu·ing** *v.t.* **1** To cause to swing, slide, or skid to the side. **2** To cause to twist or turn. *—v.i.* **3** To move sidewise. *—n.* The act of skidding or pivoting. [?]

slue[2] (slo͞o) *n. Informal* SLEW[3].

slue[3] (slo͞o) *n.* SLOUGH[1] (def. 2).

slug[1] (slug) *n.* **1** A bullet. **2** *Printing* **a** A strip of type metal between words or letters. **b** A metal strip bearing a line of type in one piece. **3** Any small chunk of metal; esp., one used in place of a coin in automatic machines.

slug[2] (slug) *n.* **1** Any of numerous land mollusks related to the snail, having an elongated body and a rudimentary shell. **2** The sluglike larvae of certain insects. [ME *slugge* a sluggard]

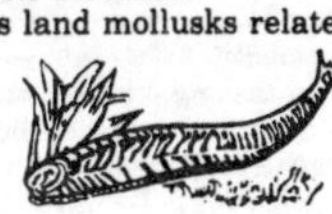
Slug

slug[3] (slug) *Informal n.* A heavy blow, as with the fist. *—v.t.* **slugged, slug·ging** To strike heavily, as with the fist. [?] **—slug′ger** *n.*

slug[4] (slug) *n. Slang* A single drink, esp. of undiluted alcoholic liquor. [< Du. *sluck* a swallow]
slug·gard (slug′ərd) *n.* A person habitually lazy. —*adj.* Lazy; sluggish. [< SLUG[2]] —**slug′gard·ly** *adv.*
slug·gish (slug′ish) *adj.* **1** Having little motion; inactive; torpid. **2** Habitually idle and lazy. —**slug′gish·ly** *adv.* — **slug′gish·ness** *n.*
sluice (slōōs) *n.* **1** Any artificial channel for conducting water. **2** A device for controlling the flow of water; a floodgate: also **sluice gate.** **3** The water held back by such a gate. **4** Something through which anything issues or flows. **5** A sloping trough in which gold is washed from sand. —*v.* **sluiced, sluic·ing** *v.t.* **1** To drench or cleanse by a flow of water. **2** To wash in or by a sluice. **3** To draw out or conduct by or through a sluice. **4** To send (logs) down a sluiceway. —*v.i.* **5** To flow out or issue from a sluice. [< L *excludere* shut out]
sluice·way (slōōs′wā′) *n.* An artificial channel for the passage of water.
slum (slum) *n.* A squalid, dirty, overcrowded street or section of a city. —*v.i.* **slummed, slum·ming** To visit slums, as for reasons of curiosity. [?] —**slum′mer** *n.*
slum·ber (slum′bər) *v.i.* **1** To sleep lightly or quietly. **2** To be inactive; stagnate. —*v.t.* **3** To spend or pass in sleeping. —*n.* Quiet sleep. [< OE *slūma* sleep] —**slum′ber·er** *n.* — **slum′ber·ing·ly** *adv.*
slum·ber·ous (slum′bər·əs) *adj.* **1** Inviting to slumber. **2** Drowsy; sleepy. **3** Quiet; peaceful: a hot, *slumberous* afternoon. Also **slum·brous** (slum′brəs). —**slum′ber·ous·ly** *adv.* —**slum′ber·ous·ness** *n.*
slum·lord (slum′lôrd′) *n.* A landlord who derives high profits from run-down property, esp. housing. [< SLUM + (LAND)LORD]
slump (slump) *v.i.* **1** To fall or fail suddenly. **2** To stand, walk, or proceed with a stooping posture; slouch. —*n.* **1** The act of slumping. **2** A collapse or decline: a *slump* in the stock market. [Prob. < Scand.]
slung (slung) *p.t. & p.p.* of SLING.
slunk (slungk) *p.t. & p.p.* of SLINK.
slur (slûr) *v.t.* **slurred, slur·ring 1** To slight; disparage; depreciate. **2** To pass over lightly or hurriedly. **3** To pronounce hurriedly and indistinctly. **4** *Music* **a** To sing or play as indicated by the slur. **b** To mark with a slur. —*n.* **1** A disparaging remark or insinuation. **2** *Music* **a** A curved line (‿ or ⁀) indicating that tones so tied are to be performed without a break between them. **b** The legato effect indicated by this mark. **3** A slurred pronunciation. [< ME *sloor* mud] —**slur′ring·ly** *adv.*
slurb (slûrb) *n. Slang* A suburban area so poorly planned and developed as to seem like a slum. [< SL(UM) + (SUB)URB]
slurp (slûrp) *v.t. & v.i. Slang* To sip noisily. [Imit.]
slush (slush) *n.* **1** Soft, sloppy material, as melting snow or soft mud. **2** Greasy material used for lubrication, etc. **3** Sentimental talk or writing. [ME *sloche*] —**slush′y** *adj.*
slush fund Money collected or spent for bribery, lobbying, political pressure, etc.
slut (slut) *n.* **1** A slatternly woman. **2** A sexually promiscuous woman; whore. **3** A female dog. [?] —**slut′tish** *adj.* — **slut′tish·ly** *adv.* —**slut′tish·ness** *n.*
sly (slī) *adj.* **sli·er** or **sly·er, sli·est** or **sly·est 1** Artfully dexterous in doing things secretly. **2** Playfully clever; roguish. **3** Meanly or stealthily clever; crafty. **4** Done with or marked by artful secrecy: a *sly* trick. —**on the sly** In a stealthy way. [< ON *slægr*] —**sly′ly** *adv.* —**sly′ness** *n.*
Sm samarium.
smack[1] (smak) *n.* **1** A quick, sharp sound, as of the lips when separated rapidly. **2** A noisy kiss. **3** A sounding blow or slap. —*v.t.* **1** To separate (the lips) rapidly. **2** To kiss noisily. **3** To slap. —*v.i.* **4** To make a smacking noise, as in tasting, kissing, striking, etc.; slap. —*adv.* Directly; exactly: also **smack′-dab′** (-dab′). [< MDu. *smack* a blow]
smack[2] (smak) *v.i.* **1** To have a slight taste or flavor: usu. with *of.* **2** To have, keep, or disclose a slight suggestion: with *of.* —*n.* **1** A suggestive flavor. **2** A mere taste; smattering. [< OE *smæc* a taste]
smack[3] (smak) *n.* A small sailing vessel used chiefly for fishing; esp. one having a well for fish in its hold. [< Du. *smak, smacke*]
smack[4] (smak) *n. Slang* HEROIN.
smack·er (smak′ər) *n.* **1** One who or that which smacks. **2** *Slang* A dollar.
smack·ing (smak′ing) *adj.* Brisk; lively, as a breeze.
small (smôl) *adj.* **1** Not as large as other things of the same kind; little. **2** Being of slight degree, weight, or importance. **3** Ignoble; mean: a *small* nature. **4** Of humble background; poor. **5** Acting or transacting business in a limited way: a *small* shopkeeper. **6** Weak in characteristic properties: *small* beer. **7** Having little body or volume. **8** Not capital: said of letters. —**feel small** To feel humiliated or ashamed. —*adv.* **1** In a low or faint tone: to sing *small.* **2** Into small pieces. **3** In a small way; trivially. —*n.* **1** A small or slender part: the *small* of the back. **2** A small thing or quantity. [< OE *smæl*] —**small′ness** *n.*
small arms Arms that may be carried on the person, as a rifle, automatic pistol, or revolver.
small calorie See CALORIE.
small capital A capital letter cut slightly larger than the lower-case letters of a specified type and slightly smaller than the regular capital.
small fry 1 Small, young fish. **2** Young children. **3** Small or insignificant people or things.
small hours The early hours after midnight.
small-minded (smôl′mīn′did) *adj.* Having a petty mind; intolerant; ungenerous.
small potatoes *Informal* Unimportant, insignificant persons or things.
small·pox (smôl′poks′) *n.* An acute, highly contagious viral disease characterized by a rash that leaves pitted scars.
small talk Unimportant or casual conversation.
small-time (smôl′tīm′) *adj. Slang* Petty; unimportant: a *small-time* gambler.
smart (smärt) *v.i.* **1** To experience a stinging sensation. **2** To cause a stinging sensation. **3** To experience remorse, grief, hurt feelings, etc. —*v.t.* **4** To cause to smart. —*adj.* **1** Quick in thought; clever. **2** Impertinently witty. **3** Harsh; severe: a *smart* slap. **4** Brisk: to go at a *smart* pace. **5** Keen or sharp, as at trade; shrewd. **6** *Informal* or *Regional* Large; considerable: a *smart* crop of wheat. **7** Sprucely dressed. **8** Fashionable; chic. —*n.* **1** An acute stinging sensation, as from a scratch or an irritant. **2** Any mental or emotional suffering. [< OE *smeortan*] —**smart′ly** *adv.* —**smart′ness** *n.*
smart al·eck (al′ik) *Informal* A cocky, conceited person. —**smart-al·eck·y** (smärt′al′ik·ē) *adj.*
smart bomb *Slang* A bomb capable of being guided, as by a laser beam, to a target.
smart·en (smär′tən) *v.t.* **1** To improve in appearance. **2** To make alert or lively. —*v.i.* **3** To improve one's appearance: with *up.*
smart set Fashionable, sophisticated society.
smart·weed (smärt′wēd′) *n.* Any of several species of knotgrass having an acrid taste, growing usu. in wet soil.
smash (smash) *v.t.* **1** To break in many pieces suddenly. **2** To flatten; crush. **3** To dash or fling violently so as to break in pieces. **4** To strike with a sudden blow. **5** To destroy; ruin. **6** In tennis, to strike (the ball) with a hard, swift, overhand stroke. —*v.i.* **7** To be ruined; fail. **8** To move or be moved with force; collide. —**go to smash** *Informal* To be ruined; fail. —*n.* **1** An instance or sound of smashing. **2** Any disaster or sudden collapse, esp. financial ruin. **3** In tennis, a strong overhand shot. **4** *Informal* An outstanding public success. —*adj.* Outstandingly successful: a *smash* hit. [?] —**smash′er** *n.*
smash·ing (smash′ing) *adj.* **1** That smashes: a *smashing* blow. **2** *Informal* Extremely impressive; overwhelmingly good. —*interj. Chiefly Brit.* An exclamation expressing approval, enthusiasm, etc.
smash-up (smash′up′) *n.* A violent collision; a wreck.
smat·ter (smat′ər) *n.* A slight knowledge. [< ME *smateren* to dabble]
smat·ter·ing (smat′ər·ing) *n.* **1** A superficial or fragmentary knowledge. **2** A little bit or a few.
sm. c., sm. caps small capitals (printing).
smear (smir) *v.t.* **1** To rub or soil with grease, paint, dirt, etc. **2** To spread or apply in a thick layer or coating. **3** To harm the reputation of; slander. **4** *Slang* To defeat utterly. —*v.i.* **5** To become smeared. —*n.* **1** A soiled spot; stain. **2**

A specimen, as of blood, tissue cells, etc., spread on a slide for microscopic examination. **3** A slanderous attack. [< OE *smeoru* grease] **—smear′y** *adj.* **—smear′i·ness** *n.*

smell (smel) *v.* **smelled** or **smelt, smell·ing** *v.t.* **1** To perceive by means of the nose and its olfactory nerves. **2** To perceive the odor of. **3** To test by odor or smell. **4** To discover or detect, as if by smelling. *—v.i.* **5** To give off a particular odor: to *smell* of roses. **6** To have an unpleasant odor. **7** To give indications of: to *smell* of treason. **8** To use the sense of smell. *—n.* **1** The sense by means of which odors are perceived. **2** That which is smelled; odor. **3** An unpleasant odor. **4** A faint suggestion; hint. **5** An act of smelling. [ME *smellen*] **—smel′ler** *n.* **—smel′ly** *adj.* **(·i·er, ·i·est) —Syn.** *n.* **2** aroma, fragrance, scent. **3** reek, stench, stink.

smelling salts A pungent preparation, as ammonium carbonate, used to relieve faintness, etc.

smelt[1] (smelt) *v.t. Metall.* **1** To reduce (ores) by fusion in a furnace. **2** To obtain (a metal) from the ore by a process including fusion. *—v.i.* **3** To melt or fuse, as a metal. [< MDu. *smelten* melt]

smelt[2] (smelt) *n. pl.* **smelts** or **smelt** Any of various small, silvery, anadromous or landlocked food fishes. [< OE]

smelt[3] (smelt) A *p.t. & p.p.* of SMELL.

smelt·er (smel′tər) *n.* **1** One engaged in smelting ore. **2** An establishment for smelting: also **smelt′er·y.**

smidg·en (smij′ən) *n. Informal* A tiny bit or part. [?]

smi·lax (smī′laks) *n.* **1** Any of a large genus of woody vines having oval leaves and globular fruit. **2** A twining plant of the lily family, with greenish flowers, used for bouquets, etc. [< Gk. *smilax* yew]

Smilax

smile (smīl) *n.* **1** A pleased or amused expression of the face, formed by curling the corners of the mouth upward. **2** A favorable appearance or aspect: the *smile* of fortune. *—v.* **smiled, smil·ing** *v.i.* **1** To exhibit a smile; appear cheerful. **2** To show approval or favor: often with *upon.* *—v.t.* **3** To express by means of a smile. [ME *smilen.*] **—smil′er** *n.* **—smil′ing·ly** *adv.*

smirch (smûrch) *v.t.* **1** To soil, as by contact with grime; smear. **2** To defame; dishonor: to *smirch* a reputation. *—n.* **1** A smutch; smear. **2** A moral stain. [ME *smorchen*]

smirk (smûrk) *v.i.* To smile in a self-complacent, affected manner. *—n.* An affected or artificial smile. [< OE *smercian*] **—smirk′er** *n.* **—smirk′ing·ly** *adv.*

smite (smīt) *v.* **smote, smit·ten** or **smote, smit·ing** *v.t.* **1** To strike (something) hard. **2** To strike a blow with (something); cause to strike. **3** To kill with a sudden blow. **4** To strike with disaster; afflict. **5** To affect or impress suddenly and powerfully. *—v.i.* **6** To strike a blow with or as if with sudden force. [< OE *smītan*] **—smit′er** *n.*

smith (smith) *n.* **1** One whose work is shaping metals, esp. a blacksmith. **2** A maker: used in combination: *gunsmith; wordsmith.* [< OE]

smith·er·eens (smith̲′ə·rēnz′) *n.pl. Informal.* Fragments produced as by a blow. Also **smith′ers.** [< Ir. *smidirin* a fragment]

smith·y (smith′ē, smith̲′ē) *n. pl.* **smith·ies** A blacksmith's shop.

smit·ten (smit′n) A *p.p.* of SMITE.

smock (smok) *n.* A loose outer garment worn to protect one's clothes. *—v.t.* To decorate (fabric) with smocking. [< OE *smoc*]

smock·ing (smok′ing) *n.* Shirred work; stitching that forms a gathered pattern.

smog (smog) *n.* A noxious mist resulting from the action of sunlight on atmospheric pollutants. [< SM(OKE) + (F)OG]

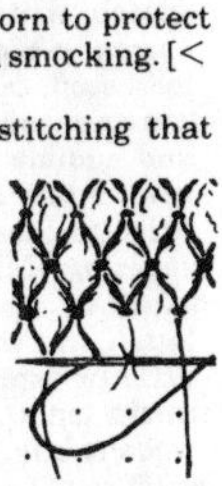

Smocking

smoke (smōk) *n.* **1** The vaporous products of the combustion of an organic compound, as coal, wood, etc., charged with fine particles of carbon or soot. **2** Any system of solid particles dispersed in a gas. **3** The act of or time taken in smoking tobacco. **4** *Informal* A cigarette, cigar, or pipeful of tobacco. *—v.* **smoked, smok·ing** *v.i.* **1** To emit or give out smoke. **2** To emit smoke excessively, as a stove or lamp. **3** To inhale and exhale the smoke of tobacco. *—v.t.* **4** To inhale and exhale the smoke of (tobacco, opium, etc.). **5** To use, as a pipe, for this purpose. **6** To treat, cure, or flavor with smoke. **7** To drive away or force out of hiding by or as if by the use of smoke: *smoke* bees; *smoke* out the enemy. **8** To change the color of (glass, etc.) by darkening with smoke. [< OE *smoca*]

smoke·house (smōk′hous′) *n.* A building or room in which meat, fish, hides, etc., are smoked.

smoke·less (smōk′lis) *adj.* Having or emitting little or no smoke: *smokeless* powder.

smok·er (smō′kər) *n.* **1** One who smokes tobacco habitually. **2** A railroad car in which smoking is allowed. **3** A social gathering for men only.

smoke screen **1** A dense cloud of smoke emitted to screen an attack or cover a retreat. **2** Anything intended to conceal or mislead.

smoke·stack (smōk′stak′) *n.* An upright pipe through which combustion gases from a furnace are discharged into the air.

smok·y (smō′kē) *adj.* **smok·i·er, smok·i·est** **1** Giving forth smoke, esp. excessively or unpleasantly. **2** Containing smoke: *smoky* air. **3** Like or suggestive of smoke: a *smoky* flavor. **4** Discolored by smoke. **5** Smoke-colored. **—smok′i·ly** *adv.* **—smok′i·ness** *n.*

smol·der (smōl′dər) *v.i.* **1** To burn showing little smoke and no flame. **2** To show suppressed feeling. **3** To exist in a latent state or inwardly. *—n.* A smoldering fire or thick smoke. *Brit. sp.* **smoul′der.** [ME *smolderen*]

smolt (smōlt) *n.* A young salmon on its first descent from the river to the sea. [ME]

smooch (smo͞och) *v.i. Slang* To kiss and caress; neck. **—smooch′er** *n.* [?]

smooth (smo͞oth̲) *adj.* **1** Having no surface irregularities; continuously even. **2** Free from obstructions, shocks, or jolts. **3** Without lumps; well blended. **4** Free from hair. **5** Flowing or moving evenly and without interruption. **6** Mild-mannered; calm. **7** Suave and flattering, usu. in a deceitful way: a *smooth* talker. **8** Pleasant-tasting; mild: a *smooth* wine. **9** *Phonet.* Having no aspiration. *—adv.* Calmly; evenly. *—v.t.* **1** To make smooth or even on the surface. **2** To free from obstructions. **3** To soften the worst features of: usu. with *over.* **4** To make calm; mollify. *—v.i.* **5** To become smooth. *—n.* **1** The smooth portion or surface of anything. **2** The act of smoothing. [< OE *smōth*] **—smooth′er, smooth′ness** *n.* **—smooth′ly** *adv.* **—Syn.** *adj.* **1** glossy, polished, sleek. **6** collected, placid, unruffled. *v.* **3** extenuate, palliate. **4** soothe.

smooth·bore (smo͞oth̲′bôr′, -bōr′) *n.* A firearm with an unrifled bore: also **smooth bore.** *—adj.* Having no rifling: said of firearms.

smooth muscle Muscle tissue consisting of flat sheets of spindle-shaped cells, by which involuntary movement is effected in blood vessels, viscera, etc.

smor·gas·bord (smôr′gəs·bôrd; *Sw.* smœr′gōs·bōrd) *n.* A Scandinavian buffet. Also **smör′gås·bord.** [Sw.]

smote (smōt) *p.t.* of SMITE.

smoth·er (smuth̲′ər) *v.t.* **1** To prevent (someone) from breathing. **2** To kill by such means; suffocate. **3** To cover, or cause to smolder, as a fire. **4** To hide or suppress: to *smother* a scandal. **5** To cook in a covered pan or under a blanket of some other substance. *—v.i.* **6** To be covered without vent or air, as a fire. **7** To be hidden or suppressed, as wrath. *—n.* That which smothers, as stifling vapor or dust. [< OE *smorian*] **—smoth′er·er** *n.* **—smoth′er·y** *adj.*

smudge (smuj) *v.* **smudged, smudg·ing** *v.t.* **1** To smear; soil. *—v.i.* **2** To be or become smudged. *—n.* **1** A smear; stain. **2** A smoky fire or smoke for driving away insects, preventing frost, etc. [? var. of SMUTCH] **—smudg′i·ly** *adv.* **—smudg′i·ness** *n.* **—smudg′y** *adj.* **(·i·er, ·i·est)**

smug (smug) *adj.* **smug·ger, smug·gest** **1** Self-satisfied or extremely complacent. **2** Trim; neat; spruce. [?< LG *smuk* neat] **—smug′ly** *adv.* **—smug′ness** *n.*

smug·gle (smug′əl) *v.* **·gled, ·gling** *v.t.* **1** To take (merchandise) into or out of a country illegally. 2 To bring in or introduce illicitly or secretly. —*v.i.* 3 To engage in or practice smuggling. [< LG *smuggeln*] **—smug′gler** *n.*

smut (smut) *n.* 1 The blackening made by soot, smoke, etc. 2 Obscene writing, speech, or illustration. 3 Any of various fungus diseases of plants, characterized by patches of powdery black spores. 4 The parasitic fungus causing such a disease. —*v.t.* & *v.i.* **smut·ted, smut·ting** To make or become smutty. [< LG *schmutt* dirt]

smutch (smuch) *n.* A stain or smear. —*v.t.* To smear; smudge. [?] **—smutch·y** *adj.* **(·i·er, ·i·est)**

smut·ty (smut′ē) *adj.* **·ti·er, ·ti·est** 1 Soiled with smut; stained. 2 Affected by smut: *smutty* corn. 3 Obscene; indecent. **—smut′ti·ly** *adv.* **—smut′ti·ness** *n.* **—Syn.** 1 blackened, dirty. 3 coarse, earthy, suggestive.

Sn tin (L *stannum*).

Sn. sanitary.

snack (snak) *n.* A light meal. —*v.i.* To eat a snack. [< MDu. *snacken* to bite, snap]

snaf·fle (snaf′əl) *n.* A horse's bit without a curb, jointed in the middle. —*v.t.* **·fled, ·fling** To control with a snaffle. [?< Du. *snavel* muzzle]

sna·fu (sna fōō′) *Slang adj.* In a state of utter confusion; chaotic. —*v.t.* **·fued, ·fu·ing** To put into a confused or chaotic condition. —*n.* A confused or chaotic situation. [< S(ITUATION) N(ORMAL) A(LL) F(UCKED) U(P)]

snag (snag) *n.* 1 A jagged or sharp protuberance, esp. the stumpy base of a branch left in pruning. 2 A snaggletooth. 3 The trunk of a tree fixed in a river, bayou, etc., which presents a danger to navigation. 4 Any hidden obstacle or difficulty. —*v.t.* **snagged, snag·ging** To injure, destroy, or impede by or as by a snag. [< Scand.] **—snag′gy** *adj.*

snag·gle·tooth (snag′əl·tōōth′) *n.* A tooth that is broken or out of alignment with the others. **—snag′gle-toothed′** (-tōōtht′, -tōōthd′) *adj.*

snail (snāl) *n.* 1 Any of numerous slow-moving, terrestrial or aquatic gastropod mollusks with a spiral shell. 2 A slow or lazy person. [< OE *snægl*]

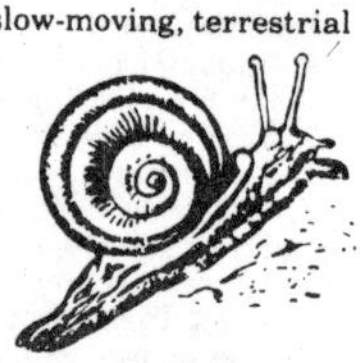

Snail

snake (snāk) *n.* 1 Any of a large variety of limbless reptiles having a scaly body, no eyelids, and a specialized swallowing apparatus. 2 A treacherous person. 3 A flexible wire used to clean clogged drains, etc. —*v.* **snaked, snak·ing** *v.t. Informal* 1 To drag or pull forcibly; haul, as a log. —*v.i.* 2 To wind or move like a snake. [< OE *snaca*]

snake·bird (snāk′bûrd′) *n.* Any of several birds with a long sinuous neck, frequenting southern U.S. swamps.

Snakebird

snak·y (snā′kē) *adj.* **snak·i·er, snak·i·est** 1 Of or like a snake. 2 Cunning; treacherous. 3 Full of snakes. 4 Winding; serpentine. **—snak′i·ly** *adv.* **—snak′i·ness** *n.*

snap (snap) *v.* **snapped, snap·ping** *v.i.* 1 To make a sharp, quick sound, as of twigs breaking. 2 To break suddenly with a crackling noise. 3 To close, fasten, etc., with a snapping sound. 4 To bite or snatch with a sudden, grasping motion: often with *up* or *at.* 5 To speak sharply: often with *at.* 6 To move or act with sudden, neat gestures: He *snapped* to attention. 7 To give way suddenly, as under mental pressure. —*v.t.* 8 To seize suddenly or eagerly; snatch: often with *up.* 9 To sever with a snapping sound. 10 To cause to make a sharp, quick sound. 11 To close, fasten, etc., with a snapping sound. 12 To take (a photograph). **—snap out of it** *Informal* 1 To recover quickly. 2 To change a mood, attitude, etc., quickly. —*n.* 1 The act of snapping or a sharp, quick sound produced by it. 2 A sudden breaking or release of anything or the sound so produced. 3 Any catch, fastener, etc., that closes or springs into place with a snapping sound. 4 A small, thin, crisp cake, esp. a gingersnap. 5 Brisk energy; zip. 6 A brief spell: said chiefly of cold weather. 7 Any easy task or duty. 8 A snapshot. —*adj.* 1 Made or done suddenly: a *snap* judgment. 2 Fastening with a snap. 3 *Informal* Easy. —*adv.* Briskly; quickly. [< MDu. *snappen* bite at]

snap·drag·on (snap′drag′ən) *n.* Any of several varieties of plants having racemes of flowers with a saclike, double-lipped corolla.

snap·per (snap′ər) *n.* 1 One who or that which snaps. 2 Any of various voracious marine food fishes. • See RED SNAPPER. 3 A snapping turtle.

snapping turtle Any of various large voracious freshwater turtles having powerful jaws, a small plastron, and a tail with erect bony scales.

Snapping turtle

snap·pish (snap′ish) *adj.* 1 Apt to speak crossly. 2 Disposed to snap or bite, as a dog. **—snap′·pish·ly** *adv.* **—snap′pish·ness** *n.*

snap·py (snap′ē) *adj.* **·pi·er, ·pi·est** 1 *Informal* Brisk and energetic. 2 *Informal* Smart or stylish. 3 Snappish. **—snap′pi·ly** *adv.* **—snap′pi·ness** *n.*

snap·shot (snap′shot′) *n.* A photograph taken with a small, simple camera.

snare[1] (snâr) *n.* 1 A device, as a noose, for catching birds or other animals; a trap. 2 Anything that misleads, entangles, etc. —*v.t.* **snared, snar·ing** 1 To catch with a snare; entrap. 2 To capture by trickery; entice. [< ON *snara*] **—snar′er** *n.*

snare[2] (snâr) *n.* 1 A cord that produces a rattling on a drumhead. 2 A snare drum. [< MDu. *snare* a string]

snare drum A small drum to be beaten on one head and having snares stretched across the other. • See DRUM.

snarl[1] (snärl) *n.* A sharp, angry growl. —*v.i.* 1 To growl harshly, as a dog. 2 To speak angrily and resentfully. —*v.t.* 3 To utter or express with a snarl. [< MLG *snarren* to growl] **—snarl′er** *n.* **—snarl′ing·ly** *adv.* **—snarl′y** *adj.*

snarl[2] (snärl) *n.* 1 A tangle, as of hair or yarn. 2 Any complication or entanglement. —*v.i.* 1 To become entangled or confused. —*v.t.* 2 To put into a snarl. [?< SNARE[1]] **—snarl′er** *n.* **—snarl′y** *adj.*

snatch (snach) *v.t.* 1 To seize, take, grasp, etc., suddenly or eagerly. 2 To take or obtain as the opportunity arises: to *snatch* a few hours of sleep. —*v.i.* 3 To attempt to seize swiftly and suddenly: with *at.* —*n.* 1 A hasty grab or grasp: usu. with *at.* 2 A small amount; fragment: *snatches* of a conversation. [ME *snacchen*] **—snatch′er** *n.*

snatch·y (snach′ē) *adj.* **snatch·i·er, snatch·i·est** Interrupted; spasmodic.

sneak (snēk) *v.i.* 1 To move or go in a stealthy manner. 2 To act slyly or with cowardice. —*v.t.* 3 To put, give, move, etc., secretly or stealthily. 4 *Informal* To pilfer. —**sneak out of** To avoid (work, etc.) by sly means. —*n.* 1 One who sneaks; a stealthy, despicable person. 2 *pl. Informal* Sneakers. 3 A stealthy movement. —*adj.* Stealthy; covert: a *sneak* attack. [?] **—sneak′i·ly, sneak′ing·ly** *adv.* **—sneak′i·ness** *n.* **—sneak′y** *adj.* **(·i·er, ·i·est)**

sneak·er (snē′kər) *n.* 1 *pl.* Rubber-soled canvas shoes. 2 One who sneaks; a sneak.

sneer (snir) *n.* 1 A grimace of contempt or scorn. 2 A mean or contemptuous sound, word, etc. —*v.i.* 1 To show contempt or scorn by a sneer. 2 To express contempt in speech, writing, etc. —*v.t.* 3 To utter with a sneer. [ME *sneren*] **—sneer′er** *n.* **—sneer′ing·ly** *adv.* **—Syn.** *v.* 2 gibe, jeer, scoff, taunt.

sneeze (snēz) *v.i.* **sneezed, sneez·ing** To drive air forcibly and audibly out of the mouth and nose by a spasmodic involuntary action. **—not to be sneezed at** *Informal* Entitled to consideration; not to be ignored. —*n.* An act of sneezing. [ME *fnesen*] **—sneez′er** *n.*

snick·er (snik′ər) *n.* A half-suppressed or smothered laugh, usu. scornful. —*v.i.* 1 To utter a snicker. —*v.t.* 2 To utter or express with a snicker. [Imit.]

snide (snīd) *adj.* **snid·er, snid·est** Malicious; nasty. [?] **—snide′ly** *adv.* **—snide′ness** *n.*

sniff (snif) *v.i.* 1 To breathe through the nose in short, quick, audible inhalations. 2 To express contempt, etc., by sniffing: often with *at.* 3 To inhale a scent in sniffs. —*v.t.* 4 To inhale. 5 To smell or attempt to smell with sniffs. 6 To perceive as if by sniffs. —*n.* 1 An act or the sound of sniffing. 2 Something perceived by sniffing; an odor. [ME *sniffen*]

snif·fle (snif′əl) *v.i.* **·fled, ·fling** 1 To breathe through a partially obstructed nose noisily and with difficulty. 2 To snivel or whimper. —*n.* The act of sniffling, or the sound made by it. —**the sniffles** A clogged condition of the nose caused by a cold, allergy, etc. [Freq. of SNIFF] —**snif′fler** *n.*

snig·ger (snig′ər) *n.* SNICKER. —*v.i.* SNICKER. [Var. of SNICKER] —**Syn.** *n.,v.* giggle, smirk, snort, titter.

snip (snip) *v.* **snipped, snip·ping** *v.t.* 1 To clip, remove, or cut with a short, light stroke or strokes, as of shears: often with *off.* —*v.i.* 2 To cut with small, quick strokes. —*n.* 1 An act of snipping. 2 A small piece snipped off. 3 *Informal* A small or insignificant person. [< Du. *snippen*] —**snip′per** *n.*

snipe (snīp) *n. pl.* **snipe** or **snipes** Any of various marsh and shore birds having a long, flexible bill. —*v.i.* **sniped, snip·ing** 1 To hunt or shoot snipe. 2 To shoot at individuals, as of an enemy force, from a place of concealment. 3 To attack a person in an underhanded, malicious manner: with *at.* [< ON *snīpa*]

snip·er (snī′pər) *n.* One who shoots at individuals, as of an enemy force, from a place of concealment.

snip·pet (snip′it) *n.* 1 A small piece snipped off. 2 A small or insignificant person.

snip·py (snip′ē) *adj.* **·pi·er, ·pi·est** *Informal* 1 Supercilious; impertinent. 2 Fragmentary. —**snip′pi·ly** *adv.* —**snip′pi·ness** *n.*

snit (snit) *n. Informal* A state of irritability or agitation.

snitch (snich) *Slang v.t.* 1 To grab quickly; steal. —*v.i.* 2 To inform; tattle: usu. with *on.* [?]

sniv·el (sniv′əl) *v.i.* **·eled** or **·elled, ·el·ing** or **·el·ling** To cry in a snuffling manner. —*n.* The act of sniveling. [< OE (assumed) *snyflan*] —**sniv′el·er** or **sniv′el·ler** *n.*

snob (snob) *n.* 1 One who regards wealth and elevated social position as of paramount importance and who typically seeks to improve his station by associating with the rich or powerful or popular and by avoiding or behaving with condescension to those with whom association is inexpedient. 2 One who affects to be superior, as in taste or learning: an intellectual *snob.* [?] —**snob′ber·y** (*pl.* **·ies**), **snob′bish·ness** *n.* —**snob′bish** *adj.* —**snob′bish·ly** *adv.*

snood (snōōd) *n.* A small meshlike cap or bag worn by women to keep the hair in place at the back of the head. —*v.t.* To bind with a snood. [< OE *snōd*]

snoop (snōōp) *Informal v.i.* To pry into things with which one has no business. —*n.* One who snoops. [< Du. *snoepen* eat goodies on the sly] —**snoop′er** *n.* —**snoop′y** *adj.* (**·i·er, ·i·est**)

snoot (snōōt) *n. Informal* The nose or face. [Var. of SNOUT]

snoot·y (snōō′tē) *adj.* **snoot·i·er, snoot·i·est** *Informal* Haughty; snobbish. —**snoot′i·ly** *adv.* —**snoot′i·ness** *n.*

snooze (snōōz) *Informal v.i.* **snoozed, snooz·ing** To sleep lightly; doze. —*n.* A short, light sleep. [?]

snore (snôr, snōr) *v.i.* **snored, snor·ing** To breathe with loud, snorting noises while asleep. —*n.* An act or sound of snoring. [Imit.] —**snor′er** *n.*

snor·kel (snôr′kəl) *n.* 1 A long ventilating tube capable of extending from a submerged submarine to the surface of the water. 2 A similar device used for underwater breathing. —*v.i.* To swim with a snorkel. [< G *Schnorchel*] —**snor′kel·er** *n.*

snort (snôrt) *v.i.* 1 To force the air violently and noisily through the nostrils, as a horse. 2 To express indignation, ridicule, etc., by a snort. —*v.t.* 3 To utter or express by snorting. —*n.* 1 The act or sound of snorting. 2 *Slang* A small drink of liquor. [ME *snorten*] —**snort′er** *n.*

snot (snot) *n.* 1 Mucus from or in the nose: a vulgar usage. 2 *Slang* A snotty person. [< OE *gesnot*]

snot·ty (snot′ē) *adj.* **·ti·er, ·ti·est** 1 Dirtied with snot: a vulgar usage. 2 *Slang* Contemptible; nasty. 3 *Slang* Impudent. —**snot′ti·ly** *adv.* —**snot′ti·ness** *n.*

snout (snout) *n.* 1 The projecting muzzle of a vertebrate. 2 Some similar anterior prolongation of the head, as that of a gastropod, skate, weevil, etc. 3 A person's nose, esp. a large one. [ME *snute*]

snow (snō) *n.* 1 Precipitation in the form of ice crystals formed from water vapor in the air when the temperature is below 32° F., usu. falling in irregular masses or flakes. 2 A fall of snow. 3 Flickering light or dark spots appearing on a television or radar screen. 4 *Slang* Cocaine. —*v.i.* 1 To fall as snow. —*v.t.* 2 To cause to fall as or like snow. 3 *Slang* To overpower with insincere or flattering talk. —**snow in** To close in or obstruct with snow. —**snow under** 1 To cover with snow. 2 *Informal* To overwhelm: *snowed under* with work. [< OE *snāw*]

Snow crystals

snow·ball (snō′bôl′) *n.* 1 A small round mass of snow to be thrown. 2 A shrub related to honeysuckle, having globular clusters of sterile white flowers: also **snowball bush** or **tree.** —*v.i.* 1 To throw snowballs. 2 To gain in size, importance, etc. —*v.t.* 3 To throw snowballs at.

snow bank A large mound or heap of snow.

snow·ber·ry (snō′ber′ē) *n. pl.* **·ries** Any of various shrubs bearing white berries.

snow·bird (snō′bûrd′) *n.* 1 A junco. 2 SNOW BUNTING.

snow blindness A temporary or partial impairment of vision, caused by long exposure to the glare of snow. —**snow′-blind′** *adj.*

snow-bound (snō′bound′) *adj.* Forced to remain in a place because of heavy snow.

snow bunting A sparrowlike bird of northern regions, having white plumage with black or rust-colored markings.

snow-capped (snō′kapt′) *adj.* Having its top covered with snow, as a mountain.

snow·drift (snō′drift′) *n.* A pile of snow heaped up by the wind.

snow·drop (snō′drop′) *n.* A low, early-blooming bulbous plant bearing a single, white, drooping flower.

snow·fall (snō′fôl′) *n.* 1 A fall of snow. 2 The amount of snow that falls in a given period.

snow·flake (snō′flāk′) *n.* 1 A flake or crystal of snow. 2 Any of various plants allied to and resembling the snowdrop.

snow job *Slang* An attempt to overpower with a flow of insincere talk, esp. flattery.

snow line The limit of perpetual snow on the sides of mountains. Also **snow limit.**

snow·mo·bile (snō′mō·bēl) *n.* A motorized vehicle used for traveling over snow, ice, etc. —**snow′mo·bil′er, snow′·mo·bil′ing** *n.*

snow·plow (snō′plou′) *n.* Any large, plowlike device for removing snow from roads, railroad tracks, etc.

snow·shoe (snō′shōō′) *n.* A device, usu. a network of sinew in a wooden frame, to be fastened on the foot and used to prevent sinking in soft snow when walking. —*v.i.* **·shoed, ·shoe·ing** To walk on snowshoes.

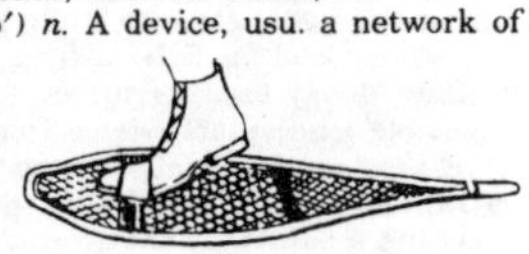

Snowshoe

snow·slide (snō′slīd′) *n.* An avalanche of snow.

snow·storm (snō′stôrm′) *n.* A storm with a heavy fall of snow.

snow·y (snō′ē) *adj.* **·i·er, ·i·est** 1 Abounding in or covered with snow. 2 White as snow. —**snow′i·ly** *adv.* —**snow′i·ness** *n.*

snub (snub) *v.t.* **snubbed, snub·bing** 1 To treat with contempt or disdain. 2 To stop or check, as the movement of a rope in running out. —*n.* 1 An act of snubbing; a deliberate slight. 2 A sudden checking, as of a running rope or cable. —*adj.* Short and slightly turned-up: said of the nose. [< ON *snubba*] —**snub′ber** *n.* —**Syn.** *v.* 1 cut, high-hat, ignore, rebuff, slight.

snub-nosed (snub′nōzd′) *adj.* Having a snub nose.

snuff[1] (snuf) *v.t.* 1 To draw in (air, etc.) through the nose.

2 To smell; sniff. —*v.i.* 3 To snort; sniff. —*n.* An act of snuffing. [?< MDu. *snuffen*] **—snuf′fi·ness** *n.* **—snuf′fy** *adj.*

snuff[2] (snuf) *n.* The charred portion of a wick. —*v.t.* 1 To crop the snuff from (a wick). 2 To put out or extinguish: with *out.* [ME *snoffe*]

snuff[3] (snuf) *n.* 1 Pulverized tobacco to be inhaled into the nostrils. 2 The quantity of it taken at one time. **—up to snuff** *Informal* Meeting the usual standard, as in quality, health, etc. —*v.i.* To take or use snuff. [< Du. *snuf*]

snuf·fer (snuf′ər) *n.* 1 One who or that which snuffs (a candle). 2 *pl.* A scissorlike instrument for removing the snuff from a candle.

snuf·fle (snuf′əl) *v.* **·fled, ·fling** *v.i.* 1 SNIFFLE. 2 To talk through the nose. —*v.t.* 3 To utter in a nasal tone. —*n.* An act of snuffling, or the sound made by it. **—the snuffles** THE SNIFFLES. See SNIFFLE. [Freq. of SNUFF[1]] **—snuf′fler** *n.*

snug (snug) *adj.* **snug·ger, snug·gest** 1 Comfortable and cozy. 2 Well-built and compact; trim: said of a ship. 3 Fitting closely, as a garment. —*v.* **snugged, snug·ging** —*v.t.* 1 To make snug. —*v.i.* 2 SNUGGLE. **—snug down** To prepare (a vessel) for a storm, as by lashing down movables. [?] **—snug′ly** *adv.* **—snug′ness** *n.*

snug·gle (snug′əl) *v.t. & v.i.* **·gled, ·gling** To nestle; cuddle; often with *up* or *together.* [Freq. of SNUG]

so[1] (sō) *adv.* 1 To this or that or such a degree; to this or that extent: Don't talk *so* much. 2 In this, that, or such a manner: Hold the flag *so.* 3 To such a great extent: I love him *so.* 4 Just as said, directed, suggested, or implied; consequently; therefore. 5 To an extreme degree; very: He is *so* tall. 6 About as many or as much as stated; thereabouts: I shall stay a day or *so.* 7 Too; also: and *so* do I. 8 According to the truth of what is sworn to or averred: *So* help me God. —*adj.* True: It isn't *so.* —*conj.* 1 With the purpose that: often with *that.* 2 As a consequence of which: He consented, *so* they went away. —*interj.* An expression of surprise, disapproval, triumph, etc. [< OE *swā*]

so[2] (sō) *n.* SOL.

So. South; southern.

soak (sōk) *v.t.* 1 To place in liquid till thoroughly saturated; steep. 2 To wet thoroughly; drench. 3 *Informal* To drink, esp. to excess. 4 *Slang* To charge exorbitantly. —*v.i.* 5 To remain or be placed in liquid till saturated. 6 To penetrate; pass: with *in* or *into.* 7 *Slang* To drink to excess. **—soak up** 1 To take up; absorb. 2 *Informal* To take eagerly into the mind. —*n.* 1 The process or act of soaking, or state of being soaked. 2 Liquid in which something is soaked. 3 *Slang* A hard drinker. [< OE *socian*] **—soak′er** *n.* **—soak′ing·ly** *adv.*

so-and-so (sō′ən·sō′) *n. pl.* **·sos** An unnamed or undetermined person or thing: often a euphemism for offensive epithets.

soap (sōp) *n.* 1 *Chem.* A metallic salt of a fatty acid. 2 A cleansing agent consisting of a sodium or potassium salt of a fatty acid made by boiling a fat or oil with a lye. 3 *Slang* Money used for bribes. **—no soap** *Slang* It's not possible or acceptable. —*v.t.* To rub or treat with soap. [< OE *sāpe*] **—soap′i·ly** *adv.* **—soap′i·ness** *n.* **—soap′y** *adj.*

soap·ber·ry (sōp′ber′ē) *n. pl.* **·ries** 1 A berrylike fruit containing a substance that forms a detergent lather with water. 2 Any of various related trees of s U.S. and tropical America that yield soapberries.

soap·box (sōp′boks′) *n.* Any box or crate used as a platform by street orators. —*adj.* Of or pertaining to such orators or oratory. —*v.i.* To make a speech to a street audience.

soap opera A daytime television or radio drama presented serially and usu. dealing with highly emotional domestic themes.

soap·stone (sōp′stōn′) *n.* STEATITE.

soap·suds (sōp′sudz′) *n.pl.* Soapy water, esp. when worked into a foam.

soar (sôr, sōr) *v.i.* 1 To float aloft through the air on wings, as a bird. 2 To sail or glide through the air. 3 To rise above any usual level: Prices *soared.* —*n.* 1 An act of soaring. 2 A range of upward flight. [< L *ex* out + *aura* breeze, air] **—soar′er** *n.* **—soar′ing·ly** *adv.*

sob (sob) *v.* **sobbed, sob·bing** *v.i.* 1 To weep with audible, convulsive catches of the breath. 2 To make a sound like a sob, as the wind. —*v.t.* 3 To utter with sobs. 4 To bring to a specified condition by sobbing: to *sob* oneself to sleep. —*n.* The act or sound of sobbing. [Imit.] **—sob′bing·ly** *adv.*

so·ber (sō′bər) *adj.* 1 Moderate in or abstaining from the use of alcoholic beverages. 2 Not drunk. 3 Temperate in action or thought; rational. 4 Not frivolous; straightforward. 5 Solemn; serious: a *sober* expression. 6 Of subdued or modest color. —*v.t.* 1 To make sober. —*v.i.* 2 To become sober, as after intoxication: with *up.* [< L *sobrius*] **—so′ber·ly** *adv.* **—so′ber·ness** *n.* **—Syn.** *n.* 1 abstemious. 3 calm, dispassionate, staid, steady.

so·bri·e·ty (sō·brī′ə·tē) *n. pl.* **·ties** 1 The state or quality of being moderate, serious, or sedate. 2 Abstinence from alcoholic drink.

so·bri·quet (sō′bri·kā, sō·bri·kā′) *n.* A fanciful or humorous appellation; a nickname. [F]

sob story *Slang* A sad personal narrative told to elicit pity or sympathy.

soc. socialist; society.

so-called (sō′kôld′) *adj.* 1 Popularly or generally named or known (by the following term): the *so-called* black market. 2 Called (by the following term): an ironic use, implying that the designated term is unjustified or unsuitable: his *so-called* wittiness.

soc·cer (sok′ər) *n.* A form of football in which the ball is propelled toward the opponents' goal by kicking or by striking with the body or head, but never with the hands. [Alter. of *association (football),* original name]

so·cia·ble (sō′shə·bəl) *adj.* 1 Inclined to seek company; friendly. 2 Characterized by or affording occasion for agreeable conversation and friendliness. —*n.* An informal social gathering. [< L *socius* friend] **—so′cia·bil′i·ty, so′cia·ble·ness** *n.* **—so′cia·bly** *adv.*

so·cial (sō′shəl) *adj.* 1 Of or pertaining to society or its organization: *social* questions. 2 Friendly toward others; sociable. 3 Living in a society: *social* beings. 4 Of or pertaining to public welfare: *social* work. 5 Pertaining to or characteristic of fashionable, wealthy people: the *social* register. 6 Living in communities: *social* ants. 7 Grouping compactly, as individual plants. 8 Partly or wholly covering a large area of land: said of plant species. —*n.* An informal social gathering. [< L *socius* ally]

social disease Venereal disease: a euphemism.

so·cial·ism (sō′shəl·iz′əm) *n.* 1 The theory of public collective ownership or control of the basic means of production, distribution, and exchange, with the avowed aim of operating for use rather than for profit. 2 A political system or party advocating or practicing this theory. **—so′cial·ist** *adj., n.* **—so′cial·is′tic** *adj.*

Socialist party A political party advocating socialism, esp. a U.S. party formed in 1901.

so·cial·ite (sō′shəl·īt) *n.* A person prominent in fashionable society.

so·cial·ize (sō′shəl·īz) *v.* **·ized, ·iz·ing** *v.t.* 1 To make friendly, cooperative, or sociable. 2 To put under group control; esp. to regulate according to socialistic principles. 3 To adopt for the uses and needs of society. —*v.i.* 4 To take part in social activities. *Brit. sp.* **so′cial·ise. —so′cial·i·za′tion** *n.*

socialized medicine The provision of comprehensive medical services at public expense.

social register A directory of persons prominent in fashionable society.

social science 1 The body of knowledge dealing with society, its members, organizations, interrelationships, etc. 2 Any of the fields into which this body of knowledge is divided, as economics, history, sociology, politics, etc.

social security A federal program of old-age pensions, unemployment benefits, disability insurance, survivors' benefits, etc., paid jointly by workers, employers, and the U.S. government.

social work Any of various activities for improving community welfare, as services for health, rehabilitation, counseling, recreation, adoptions, etc. Also **social service. —social worker**

so·ci·e·ty (sə·sī′ə·tē) *n. pl.* **·ties** 1 A group of people, usu. having geographical boundaries and sharing certain characteristics, as language, culture, etc. 2 The people making up such a group. 3 The fashionable, usu. wealthy portion of a community. 4 A body of persons associated for a common purpose; an association, club, or fraternity. **5** Association based on friendship or intimacy: to enjoy the *society* of one's neighbors. [< L *socius* a friend]

Society of Friends A Christian religious group, founded in seventeenth-century England, noted for its repudiation of ritual and its opposition to military service and to violence.

Society of Jesus The Jesuits.

socio- *combining form* **1** Society; social: *sociology.* **2** Sociology; sociological: *socioeconomic.* [< F < L *socius* a companion]

so·ci·o·bi·ol·o·gy (sō′sē·ō·bī·ol′ə·jē) *n.* The study of social behavior in animals and humans, as determined by their biological characteristics.

so·ci·o·ec·o·nom·ic (sō′sē·ō·ek′ə·nom′ik, sō′shē-, -ē′kə-) *adj.* Based upon the interrelationship of social and economic factors. **—so′ci·o·ec′o·nom′i·cal·ly** *adv.*

so·ci·o·lin·guis·tics (sō′sē·ō·ling·gwis′tiks, sō′shē-) *n. pl. (construed as sing.)* The study of language as a social instrument and in its social context. [< SOCIO- + LINGUISTICS] **—so′ci·o·lin·guis′tic** *adj.* **—so′ci·o·lin·guis′ti·cal·ly** *adv.*

so·ci·ol·o·gy (sō′sē·ol′ə·jē, sō′shē-) *n.* The science dealing with the origin, evolution, and development of human society and its organization, institutions, and functions. **—so′ci·o·log′i·cal** *adj.* **—so′ci·o·log′i·cal·ly** *adv.* **—so′ci·ol′o·gist** *n.*

sock[1] (sok) *n.* A short stocking reaching part way to the knee. [< L *soccus* slipper]

sock[2] (sok) *Slang v.t.* To strike or hit, esp. with the fist. *—n.* A hard blow. [?]

sock·et (sok′it) *n.* A cavity into which a corresponding part fits: an electric light *socket;* the eye *socket.* [< OF *soc* a plowshare]

sock·eye (sok′ī′) *n.* A red salmon of the Pacific coast, highly valued as a food fish. [Alter. of Salishan *sukkegh*]

So·crat·ic method (sə·krat′ik, sō-) The method of instruction by questions and answers, as adopted by Socrates in his disputations, leading the pupil either to a foreseen conclusion or to contradict himself.

sod (sod) *n.* **1** Grassy surface soil held together by the matted roots of grass and weeds. **2** A piece of such soil. *—v.t.* **sod·ded, sod·ding** To cover with sod. [< MDu. *sode* piece of turf]

so·da (sō′də) *n.* **1** Any of several sodium compounds in common use, as sodium bicarbonate, carbonate, hydroxide, etc. **2** SODA WATER **3** A soft drink containing soda water and flavoring and sometimes ice cream. [< Ital. *soda (cenere)* solid (ash)]

soda ash Anhydrous sodium carbonate.

soda cracker A thin, crisp, usu. salted wafer of flour leavened with baking soda.

soda fountain **1** An apparatus from which soda water is drawn, usu. containing receptacles for syrups, ice, and ice cream. **2** A counter at which soft drinks and ice cream are dispensed.

soda jerk *Slang* A clerk who serves at a soda fountain.

so·dal·i·ty (sō·dal′ə·tē) *n. pl.* **·ties** A brotherhood or fraternity; esp., one for devotional or charitable purposes. [< L *sodalis* companion]

soda water An effervescent drink consisting of water charged under pressure with carbon dioxide, formerly generated from sodium bicarbonate.

sod·den (sod′n) *adj.* **1** Soaked; saturated. **2** Doughy; soggy, as undercooked bread. **3** Dull or stupid, as from drink. [ME *sothen,* pp. of *sethen* seethe] **—sod′den·ly** *adv.*

so·di·um (sō′dē·əm) *n.* A soft, silver-white, highly reactive metallic element (symbol Na) whose compounds are abundant in nature and essential to life. [< Med. L *soda* soda]

sodium bicarbonate A white crystalline compound that reacts with acids to liberate carbon dioxide; baking soda.

sodium carbonate The strongly alkaline sodium salt of carbonic acid, in crystalline hydrated form known as washing soda.

sodium chloride Common salt.

sodium cyanide A white, very poisonous salt of hydrocyanic acid, used in electroplating, as a fumigant, etc.

sodium hydroxide A white, deliquescent compound forming a strongly alkaline solution in water; caustic soda.

sodium hypochlorite An unstable compound of sodium, oxygen, and chlorine, used in weak aqueous solution as a laundry bleach.

sodium nitrate A white compound occurring naturally and produced synthetically, used as a fertilizer and in the manufacture of nitric acid and explosives.

sodium thiosulfate A crystalline compound of sodium, sulfur, and oxygen, used in photography as a fixing agent. Also, erroneously, **sodium hyposulfite.**

Sod·om (sod′əm) *n.* In the Bible, a city on the Dead Sea, destroyed with Gomorrah because of the wickedness of its people. *Gen.* 13:10.

sod·om·ite (sod′əm·īt) *n.* A person who practices sodomy.

sod·om·y (sod′əm·ē) *n.* Anal copulation, esp. between male persons or with animals. [< LL *Sodoma* Sodom]

so·ev·er (sō·ev′ər) *adv.* To or in any degree at all. • *Soever* is usu. added to *who, which, what, where, when, how,* etc., to form the compounds *whosoever,* etc., giving them emphasis or specific force. When used separately, as in "how great *soever* he might be," *soever* tends to sound stilted and literary.

so·fa (sō′fə) *n.* A long upholstered couch having a back and arms. [< Ar. *soffah* a part of a floor raised to form a seat]

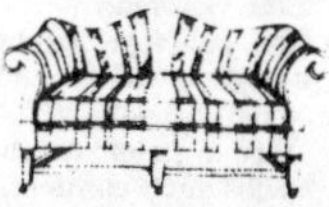

Sofa

soft (sôft, soft) *adj.* **1** Easily changed in shape by pressure. **2** Easily worked: *soft* wood. **3** Less hard than other things of the same kind: *soft* rock. **4** Smooth and delicate to the touch: *soft* skin. **5** Not loud or harsh: a *soft* voice. **6** Mild; gentle: a *soft* breeze. **7** Not glaring; subdued: *soft* colors. **8** Expressing mildness or sympathy: *soft* words. **9** Easily touched in feeling: a *soft* heart. **10** Out of condition: *soft* muscles. **11** *Informal* Weak-minded: *soft* in the head. **12** *Informal* Overly lenient: a judge *soft* on criminals. **13** Free from mineral salts that form insoluble compounds with soap: said of water. **14** Biodegradable: said of detergents. **15** Regarded as being nonaddicting and less harmful than hard narcotics: said of drugs, esp. marihuana. **16** *Phonet.* Describing *c* and *g* when articulated fricatively as in *cent* and *gibe.* **17** *Informal* Easy: a *soft* job. *—n.* That which is soft; a soft part or material. *—adv.* **1** Softly. **2** Quietly; gently. *—interj. Archaic* Hush! Stop!. [< OE *sōfte*] **—soft′ly** *adv.* **—soft′ness** *n.* **—Syn.** *adj.* **1** flexible, malleable, pliable. **5** low. **9** compassionate, kind, sympathetic.

soft·back (sôft′bak′, soft′-) *adj.* SOFT-COVER. *—n.* A soft-cover book.

soft·ball (sôft′bôl′, soft′-) *n.* **1** A variation of baseball requiring a smaller diamond and a larger, softer ball. **2** The ball used in this game.

soft-boiled (sôft′boild′) *adj.* Boiled so that the yolk and white are soft or semiliquid: said of eggs.

soft coal Bituminous coal.

soft-cov·er (sôft′kuv′ər, soft′-) *adj.* Designating a book having flexible sides, as of paper. Also **soft′bound′** (-bound′).

soft drink A nonalcoholic beverage, esp. a carbonated drink.

sof·ten (sôf′ən, sof′-) *v.t. & v.i.* To make or become soft or softer. **—sof′ten·er** *n.*

soft·heart·ed (sôft′här′tid, soft′-) *adj.* Full of kindness, tenderness, and compassion. **—soft′heart′ed·ly** *adv.*

soft palate The fleshy back part of the roof of the mouth. • See MOUTH.

soft-shell (sôft′shel′, soft′-) *adj.* Having a soft shell, as a crab after shedding its shell: also **soft′-shelled′**. *—n.* A crab that has shed its shell: also **soft-shelled crab.**

soft-soap (sôft′sōp′, soft′-) *v.t. Informal* To flatter.

soft soap **1** Fluid or semifluid soap. **2** *Informal* Flattery.

soft·ware (sôft′wâr′, soft′-) *n.* In a digital computer, any of the programs designed to control various aspects of the operation of the machine, such as input and output operations.

soft·wood (sôft′wŏŏd′, soft′-) *n.* 1 A coniferous tree or its wood. 2 Any light, loosely structured wood, or any tree with such wood.

soft·y (sôf′tē, sof′-) *n. pl.* **soft·ies** *Informal* 1 An extremely sentimental person. 2 A person who is easily taken advantage of. Also **soft′ie.**

sog·gy (sog′ē) *adj.* **·gi·er, ·gi·est** 1 Saturated with water or moisture; soaked. 2 Heavy and wet: said of pastry. [< dial. E *sog* a swamp, bog] **—sog′gi·ly** *adv.* **—sog′gi·ness** *n.*

soil[1] (soil) *n.* 1 Finely divided rock mixed with decayed vegetable or animal matter, constituting the portion of the surface of the earth in which plants grow. 2 Region, land, or country. [< L *solium* a seat, mistaken for *solum* the ground]

soil[2] (soil) *v.t.* 1 To make dirty; smudge. 2 To disgrace; defile. *—v.i.* 3 To become dirty. *—n.* A spot or stain. [< L *suculus,* dim. of *sus* a pig]

soi·rée (swä·rā′) *n.* An evening party or reception. Also **soi·ree′.** [F < *soir* evening]

so·journ (sō′jûrn, sō·jûrn′) *v.i.* To stay or live temporarily. *—n.* (sō′jûrn) A temporary residence or short visit. [< OF *sojourner*] **—so′journ·er** *n.*

sol (sōl) *n. Music* In solmization, the fifth note of a diatonic scale. [See GAMUT.]

Sol (sol) *Rom. Myth.* The god of the sun. *—n.* The sun. [L]

Sol. Solomon.

sol. solicitor; soluble; solution.

sol·ace (sol′is) *v.t.* **·aced, ·ac·ing** 1 To comfort in trouble or grief; console. 2 To alleviate, as grief; soothe. *—n.* 1 Comfort in grief, trouble, or calamity. 2 Anything that supplies such comfort. [< L *solacium*] **—sol′ac·er** *n.* **—Syn.** *v.* 2 assuage, ease, mitigate. *n.* 1 cheer, consolation.

so·lar (sō′lər) *adj.* 1 Of, from, reckoned by, or pertaining to the sun. 2 Using energy from the sun: *solar* heat. [< L *sol* sun]

solar energy 1 Energy emitted by the sun as radiation over the entire electromagnetic spectrum. 2 Radiation from the sun, esp. in the infrared range, technologically convertible to domestic and industrial uses.

so·lar·i·um (sō·lâr′ē·əm) *n. pl.* **·i·a** (-ē·ə) or **·ums** A room, porch, etc., in which people can sit in the sun. [L]

solar plexus 1 A network of sympathetic nerves serving the abdominal viscera. 2 *Informal* The pit of the stomach.

solar system The sun and the bodies that orbit it. • See PLANET.

sold (sōld) *p.t. & p.p.* of SELL.

sol·der (sod′ər) *n.* 1 An easily melted alloy used for joining metal parts. 2 Anything that unites or cements. *—v.t.* 1 To unite or repair with solder. 2 To join together; bind. *—v.i.* 3 To work with solder. 4 To be united by or as by solder. [< L *solidus* firm, hard] **—sol′der·er** *n.*

sol·dier (sōl′jər) *n.* 1 A person serving in an army. 2 An enlisted man in an army, as distinguished from a commissioned officer. 3 A brave, skillful, or experienced warrior. 4 One who serves a cause loyally. *—v.i.* 1 To be or serve as a soldier. 2 To shirk: to *soldier* on the job. [< LL *solidus*] **—sol′dier·ly** *adj.* **—sol′dier·li·ness** *n.*

soldier of fortune A soldier willing to serve any government for money or adventure.

sol·dier·y (sōl′jər·ē) *n. pl.* **·ies** 1 Soldiers collectively. 2 Military service.

sole[1] (sōl) *n.* 1 The bottom surface of the foot. 2 The bottom surface of a shoe, boot, etc. 3 The lower part or bottom of anything. *—v.t.* **soled, sol·ing** To furnish with a new sole, as a shoe. [< L *solea* a sandal]

sole[2] (sōl) *n.* Any of several marine flatfishes allied to the flounders, highly esteemed as food. [< L *solea* sole[1], fish]

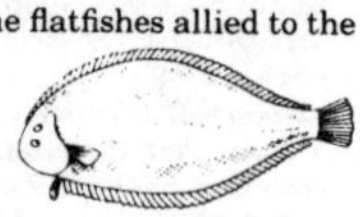

Sole

sole[3] (sōl) *adj.* 1 Being the only one: a *sole* survivor. 2 Only: His *sole* desire was for sleep. 3 *Law* Unmarried; single. 4 Of or for only one person or group. 5 Acting or accomplished without another. [< L *solus* alone] **—sole′ness** *n.*

sol·e·cism (sol′ə·siz′əm) *n.* 1 A grammatical error or a violation of approved idiomatic usage. 2 Any impropriety or incongruity. [< Gk *soloikos* speaking incorrectly] **—sol′e·cist** *n.* **—sol′e·cis′tic** or **·ti·cal** *adj.*

sole·ly (sōl′lē) *adv.* 1 By oneself or itself alone; singly. 2 Completely; entirely. 3 Only.

sol·emn (sol′əm) *adj.* 1 Characterized by majesty, mystery, or power; awe-inspiring. 2 Characterized by ceremonial observances; sacred. 3 Marked by gravity; earnest. [< L *solemnis*] **—sol′emn·ly** *adv.* **—sol′emn·ness** *n.* **—Syn.** 1 impressive. 3 grave, sedate, serious, somber.

so·lem·ni·ty (sə·lem′nə·tē) *n. pl.* **·ties** 1 The state or quality of being solemn. 2 A solemn rite or observance.

sol·em·nize (sol′əm·nīz) *v.t.* **·nized, ·niz·ing** 1 To perform according to legal or ritual forms: to *solemnize* a marriage. 2 To celebrate with formal ritual. 3 To make solemn, grave, or serious. **—sol′em·ni·za′tion, sol′em·niz′er** *n.*

so·le·noid (sō′lə·noid) *n. Electr.* A conducting wire in the form of a cylindrical coil, used to produce a magnetic field. [< Gk. *sōlēn* a channel + -OID] **—so′le·noi′dal** *adj.* **—so′le·noi′dal·ly** *adv.*

Solenoid

sol-fa (sōl′fä′) *Music v.t. & v.i.* **-faed, -fa·ing** To sing using the sol-fa instead of words. *—n.* 1 The syllables used in solmization. 2 The act of singing them. [< Ital. *solfa.* See GAMUT.] **—sol′fa′ist** *n.*

sol·feg·gio (sōl·fej′ō) *n. pl.* **·feg·gi** (-fej′ē) or **·feg·gios** *Music* 1 A florid singing exercise using arbitrary vowels and consonants. 2 Solmization. [< Ital. *solfa* sol-fa]

so·lic·it (sə·lis′it) *v.t.* 1 To ask for earnestly; beg or entreat. 2 To seek to obtain, as by persuasion. 3 To entice (one) to an unlawful or immoral act. *—v.i.* 4 To make a petition. [< L *sollicitare* agitate] **—so·lic′i·ta′tion** *n.*

so·lic·i·tor (sə·lis′ə·tər) *n.* 1 A person who solicits money for causes, subscriptions, etc. 2 The chief law officer of a city, town, etc. 3 In England, a lawyer who may appear as an advocate in the lower courts only. **—so·lic′i·tor·ship′** *n.*

Solicitor General *pl.* **Solicitors General** 1 A law officer ranking below the Attorney General and assisting him. 2 The principal law officer in some of the states, corresponding to the Attorney General in others.

so·lic·i·tous (sə·lis′ə·təs) *adj.* 1 Full of anxiety or concern. 2 Full of eagerness. **—so·lic′i·tous·ly** *adv.* **—so·lic′i·tous·ness** *n.*

so·lic·i·tude (sə·lis′ə·t^{y}ŏŏd) *n.* 1 The state of being solicitous. 2 That which makes one solicitous.

sol·id (sol′id) *adj.* 1 Having a definite shape and volume; resistant to stress; not fluid. 2 Filling the whole of the space occupied by its form; not hollow. 3 Of the same substance throughout: *solid* marble. 4 Three-dimensional. 5 Well-built; firm: a *solid* building. 6 United or unanimous: a *solid* base of support. 7 Financially safe; sound. 8 Continuous; unbroken: a *solid* hour. 9 Written without a hyphen: said of a compound word. 10 Carrying weight or conviction: a *solid* argument. 11 Serious; reliable: a *solid* citizen. 12 *Informal* Being on good terms: They were *solid* with the boss. 13 *Slang* Excellent. 14 *Printing* Having no leads or slugs between the lines; not open. *—n.* 1 A mass of matter that has a definite shape which resists change. 2 A three-dimensional figure or object. [< L *solidus*] **—sol′id·ly** *adv.* **—so·lid′i·ty** (*pl.* **·ties**), **sol′id·ness** *n.*

solid angle The angle formed at the vertex of a cone or subtended at the point of intersection of three or more planes.

sol·i·dar·i·ty (sol′ə·dar′ə·tē) *n. pl.* **·ties** Unity of purpose, relations, or interests, as of a race, class, etc.

solid geometry The geometry of a space of three dimensions.

so·lid·i·fy (sə·lid′ə·fī) *v.t. & v.i.* **·fied, ·fy·ing** 1 To make or become solid, hard, firm, or compact. 2 To bring or come together in unity. **—so·lid′i·fi·ca′tion** *n.*

solid state physics The physics of solid substances, esp. their properties and structure.

sol·i·dus (sol′ə·dəs) *n. pl.* **·di** (-dī) 1 A gold coin of the Byzantine Empire. 2 The sign (/) used to divide shillings from pence: 10/6 (10*s.* 6*d.*) or sometimes used to express fractions: 3/4. [L, solid]

so·lil·o·quize (sə·lil′ə·kwīz) *v.i.* **·quized, ·quiz·ing** To utter a soliloquy. **—so·lil′o·quist** (-kwist), **so·lil′o·quiz′er** *n.* **—so·lil′o·quiz′ing·ly** *adv.*

so·lil·o·quy (sə·lil′ə·kwē) *n. pl.* **·quies** **1** A talking to oneself. **2** A speech made by an actor while alone on the stage, revealing his thoughts to the audience. [< L *solus* alone + *loqui* to talk]

sol·ip·sism (sol′ip·siz′əm) *n.* The theory that only knowledge of the self is possible, that, for each individual, only the self exists, and therefore that reality is subjective. **—sol′ip·sist** *n.* **—sol′ip·sis′tic** *adj.*

sol·i·taire (sol′ə·târ′) *n.* **1** A diamond or other gem set alone. **2** Any of various card games played by one person. [< L *solitarius* solitary]

sol·i·tar·y (sol′ə·ter′ē) *adj.* **1** Living, being, or going alone. **2** Made, done, or passed alone: a *solitary* life. **3** Remote; secluded. **4** Lonesome; lonely. **5** Single; one; sole: Not a *solitary* soul was there —*n.* **1** *pl.* **·tar·ies** One who lives alone; a hermit. **2** *Informal* Solitary confinement in prison, usu. directed as a punishment. [< L *solus* alone] **—sol′i·tar′i·ly** *adv.* **—sol′i·tar′i·ness** *n.*

sol·i·tude (sol′ə·t*y*o͞od) *n.* **1** A being alone; seclusion. **2** Loneliness. **3** A deserted or lonely place. [< L *solus* alone] **—Syn. 1** privacy, retirement. **2** isolation, lonesomeness.

sol·mi·za·tion (sol′mə·zā′shən) *n. Music* The use of syllables as names for the tones of the scale, now commonly *do, re, mi, fa, sol, la, ti.* [< SOL + MI]

so·lo (sō′lō) *n. pl.* **·los** or **·li** (-lē) **1** A musical composition or passage for a single voice or instrument, with or without accompaniment. **2** Any of several card games, esp. one in which a player plays alone against others. **3** Any performance accomplished alone or without assistance. —*adj.* **1** Performed or composed to be performed as a solo. **2** Done by a single person alone: a *solo* flight. —*v.i.* **·loed, ·lo·ing** To fly an airplane alone, esp. for the first time. [< L *solus* alone] **—so′lo·ist** *n.*

Sol·o·mon (sol′ə·mən) In the Bible, king of Israel, successor to his father David. —*n.* Any very wise man.

Sol·o·mon's-seal (sol′ə·mənz·sēl′) *n.* Any of several perennial herbs of the lily family, having tubular greenish flowers.

so long *Informal* Good-by.

sol·stice (sol′stis) *n.* Either of the times of year when the sun is farthest from the celestial equator, either north or south. In the northern hemisphere the **summer solstice** occurs about June 22, the **winter solstice** about December 22. [< L *solstitium*] **—sol·sti·tial** (sol·stish′əl) *adj.*

sol·u·ble (sol′yə·bəl) *adj.* **1** Capable of being dissolved. **2** Capable of being solved or explained. [< L *solvere* solve, dissolve] **—sol′u·bil′i·ty, sol′u·ble·ness** *n.* **—sol′u·bly** *adv.*

sol·ute (sol′yo͞ot, sō′lo͞ot) *n.* The dissolved substance in a solution.

so·lu·tion (sə·lo͞o′shən) *n.* **1** A homogeneous mixture of varying proportions, formed by dissolving one or more substances, whether solid, liquid, or gaseous, in another substance, usu. liquid but sometimes gaseous or solid. **2** The act or process by which such a mixture is made. **3** The act or process of explaining, settling, or solving a difficulty, problem, or doubt. **4** The answer or explanation reached in such a process. [< L *solutus,* pp. of *solvere* dissolve]

solve (solv) *v.t.* **solved, solv·ing** To arrive at or work out the correct solution or the answer to; resolve. [< L *solvere* solve, loosen] **—sol′va·ble** *adj.* **—sol′va·bil′i·ty, sol′ver** *n.*

sol·vent (sol′vənt) *adj.* **1** Having means sufficient to pay all debts. **2** Capable of dissolving. —*n.* **1** That which solves. **2** A substance, usu. a liquid, capable of dissolving other substances. [< L *solvere* solve, loosen] **—sol′ven·cy** *n.*

Som. Somaliland.

So·ma·lia (sō·mä′lyə) *n.* A republic of E Africa, 262,000 sq. mi., cap. Mogadiscio. • See map at AFRICA. **—So·ma′li** (-lē) *adj., n.*

so·mat·ic (sō·mat′ik) *adj.* **1** Of or relating to the body; corporeal. **2** Of or pertaining to the walls of a body, as distinguished from the viscera. **3** Pertaining to those elements or processes of an organism which are concerned with the maintenance of the individual as distinguished from the reproduction of the species: *somatic* cells. [< Gk. *sōma* body] **—so·mat′i·cal·ly** *adv.*

som·ber (som′bər) *adj.* **1** Dark; gloomy. **2** Somewhat melancholy; sad. *Brit. sp.* **som′bre.** [< F *sombre*] **—som′ber·ly** *adv.* **—som′ber·ness** *n.* **—Syn. 1** cloudy, dusky, murky.

som·bre·ro (som·brâr′ō) *n. pl.* **·ros** A broad-brimmed hat, usu. of felt, worn in Spain and Latin America. [< Sp. *sombra* shade]

Sombrero

some (sum) *adj.* **1** Of indeterminate quantity: Have *some* candy. **2** Of an unspecified number: It happened *some* days ago. **3** Not definitely specified: *Some* people dislike cats. **4** *Informal* Worthy of notice; extraordinary: That was *some* cake. —*pron.* **1** A certain undetermined quantity or part: Please take *some.* **2** Certain ones not named: *Some* believe it is true. —*adv.* **1** *Informal* Approximately; about: *Some* eighty people were present. **2** *Informal* Somewhat. [< OE *sum* some]

-some[1] *suffix of adjectives* Characterized by, or tending to be: *blithesome.* [< OE *-sum* like, resembling]

-some[2] *suffix of nouns* A group consisting of (a specified number): *twosome.* [< SOME]

some·bod·y (sum′bod′ē, -bəd·ē) *pron.* An unknown or unnamed person. —*n. pl.* **·bod·ies** *Informal* A person of consequence or importance.

some·day (sum′dā′) *adv.* At some future time.

some·how (sum′hou′) *adv.* In some unspecified way.

some·one (sum′wun′, -wən) *pron.* Some person; somebody.

som·er·sault (sum′ər·sôlt) *n.* An acrobatic roll in which a person turns heels over head. —*v.i.* To perform a somersault. [< OF *sobresault*]

some·thing (sum′thing) *n.* **1** A thing not determined or stated. **2** A person or thing of importance. **3** An indefinite quantity or degree: He is *something* of an artist. —*adv.* Somewhat: *something* like his brother.

some·time (sum′tīm′) *adv.* **1** At some future time not precisely stated. **2** At some indeterminate time or occasion. —*adj.* **1** Former: a *sometime* student at Oxford. **2** *Informal* Occasional; sporadic: a *sometime* thing.

some·times (sum′tīmz′) *adv.* At times; occasionally.

some·way (sum′wā′) *adv.* In some way; somehow: also **some way, some′ways′.**

some·what (sum′hwot′, -hwət) *adv.* To some degree. —*n.* An uncertain quantity or degree.

some·where (sum′hwâr′) *adv.* **1** In, at, or to some unspecified or unknown place. **2** At some unspecified time: *somewhere* around noon. **3** Approximately. —*n.* An unspecified or unknown place.

some·wheres (sum′hwârz′) *adv. Chiefly Regional* Somewhere.

som·nam·bu·late (som·nam′byə·lāt) *v.* **·lat·ed, ·lat·ing** *v.i.* To walk about while asleep. [< L *somnus* sleep + AMBULATE] **—som·nam′bu·la′tion** *n.*

som·nam·bu·lism (som·nam′byə·liz′əm) *n.* The act or state of walking during sleep. **—som·nam′bu·lant** (-lənt), **som·nam′bu·lis′tic** *adj.* **—som·nam′bu·list** *n.*

som·nif·er·ous (som·nif′ər·əs) *adj.* Tending to produce sleep; narcotic. [< L *somnus* sleep + -FEROUS]

som·no·lent (som′nə·lənt) *adj.* **1** Inclined to sleep; drowsy. **2** Tending to induce drowsiness. [< L *somnus* sleep] **—som′no·lence** or **·len·cy** *n.* **—som′no·lent·ly** *adv.*

son (sun) *n.* **1** A male child considered in his relationship to one parent or both. **2** Any male descendant. **3** One who occupies the place of a son, as by adoption, marriage, or regard. **4** Any male associated with a particular country, place, or idea: a *son* of liberty; a native *son.* **5** A familiar term of address to a young man or boy. **—the Son** Jesus Christ. [< OE *sunu*]

so·nant (sō′nənt) *Phonet. adj.* Voiced. —*n.* **1** A voiced speech sound. **2** A syllabic sound. [< L *sonare* resound]

so·nar (sō′när) *n.* A system or device for using underwater sound waves for sounding, range finding, detection of submerged objects, communication, etc. [< *so(und) na(vigation and) r(anging)*]

so·na·ta (sə·nä′tä) *n. Music* An instrumental composition written in three or four movements. [< Ital. *sonare* to sound]

song (sông, song) *n.* **1** The act of singing. **2** Any melodious utterance, as of a bird. **3** A short musical composition for voice. **4** A short poem; a lyric or ballad. **5** Poetry; verse. —**for a song** At a very low price. —**song and dance** *Slang* A long, usu. repetitive statement or explanation, often untrue or not pertinent to the subject under discussion. [< OE]

song·bird (sông′bûrd′, song′-) *n.* Any of a large number of small, perching birds, having complex musical songs characteristic of each species.

Song of Solomon A book of the Old Testament, consisting of a dramatic love poem, attributed to Solomon. Also **Song of Songs.**

song sparrow A common North American sparrow noted for its song.

song·ster (sông′stər, song′-) *n.* **1** A person or bird given to singing. **2** A writer of songs. —**song′stress** (-stris) *n. Fem.*

son·ic (son′ik) *adj.* Of, pertaining to, determined, or affected by sound: *sonic* speed. [< L *sonus* sound]

sonic barrier *Aeron.* The effects, such as drag and turbulence, that hinder flight at or near the speed of sound.

son-in-law (sun′in·lô′) *n. pl.* **sons-in-law** The husband of one's daughter.

son·net (son′it) *n.* A poem of 14 lines in any of several fixed verse and rhyme schemes. [< Prov. *son* a sound]

son·net·eer (son′ə·tir′) *n.* A composer of sonnets. —*v.i.* To compose sonnets.

son·ny (sun′ē) *n. pl.* **·nies** *Informal* Little boy: a familiar form of address.

so·no·rous (sə·nôr′əs, -nō′rəs, son′ə·rəs) *adj.* **1** Productive or capable of producing sound vibrations. **2** Loud and full-sounding; resonant. **3** High-sounding: *sonorous* verse. [< L *sonare* resound] —**so·nor·i·ty** (sə·nôr′ə·tē, -nor-, son′·ôr′ə·tē), **so·nor′ous·ness** *n.* —**so·no′rous·ly** *adv.*

soon (so͞on) *adv.* **1** In the near future; shortly. **2** Without delay. **3** Early: He awoke too *soon.* **4** In accord with one's inclination; willingly: I would as *soon* go as not; I'd *sooner* quit than accept a demotion. —**had sooner** Would rather. —**sooner or later** Eventually; in time; sometime. [< OE *sōna* immediately]

soot (so͝ot, so͞ot) *n.* A black deposit of finely divided carbon from the incomplete combustion of wood, coal, etc. —*v.t.* To soil or cover with soot. [< OE *sōt*] —**soot′i·ness** *n.* —**soot′y** *adj.* **(·i·er, ·i·est)**

sooth (so͞oth) *Archaic adj.* True; real. —*n.* Truth. —**in sooth** *Archaic* Truly. [< OE *sōth*] —**sooth′ly** *adv.*

soothe (so͞oth) *v.* **soothed, sooth·ing** *v.t.* **1** To restore to a quiet or normal state; calm. **2** To mitigate, soften, or relieve, as pain or grief. —*v.i.* **3** To afford relief. [< OE *sōthian* verify] —**sooth′er** *n.* —**sooth′ing·ly** *adv.* —**Syn. 1** compose, pacify, tranquilize. **2** allay, alleviate, ease.

sooth·say·er (so͞oth′sā′ər) *n.* A person who claims to be able to foretell events. —**sooth′say′ing** *n.*

sop (sop) *v.* **sopped, sop·ping** *v.t.* **1** To dip or soak in a liquid. **2** To take up by absorption: often with *up.* —*v.i.* **3** To be absorbed; soak in. **4** To become saturated or drenched. —*n.* **1** Anything softened in liquid, as bread. **2** Anything given to pacify, as a bribe. [< OE *sopp*]

SOP, S.O.P. standard operating procedure; *(Mil.)* standing operating procedure.

sop. soprano.

soph·ism (sof′iz·əm) *n.* **1** A false argument seemingly correct but actually misleading. **2** A fallacy. [< Gk. *sophos* wise]

soph·ist (sof′ist) *n.* **1** A learned person; thinker. **2** One who argues cleverly and deviously. **3** *Often cap.* A member of a certain school of early Greek philosophy, preceding the Socratic school. **4** *Often cap.* One of the later Greek teachers of philosophy and rhetoric, skilled in subtle disputation. [< Gk. *sophos* wise] —**so·phis′tic** or **·ti·cal** *adj.* —**so·phis′ti·cal·ly** *adv.* —**so·phis′ti·cal·ness** *n.*

so·phis·ti·cate (sə·fis′tə·kāt) *v.* **·cat·ed, ·cat·ing** *v.t.* **1** To make less simple or ingenuous; render worldly-wise. **2** To mislead or corrupt. —*v.i.* **3** To indulge in sophistry. —*n.* (-kit, -kāt) A sophisticated person. [< Gk. *sophos* wise] —**so·phis′ti·ca′tor** *n.*

so·phis·ti·cat·ed (sə·fis′tə·kā′tid) *adj.* **1** Worldly-wise. **2** Of a kind that appeals to the worldly-wise. **3** Very complicated in design, function, etc.: a *sophisticated* machine.

so·phis·ti·ca·tion (sə·fis′tə·kā′shən) *n.* **1** Worldly experience; urbanity, usu. with a loss of simplicity. **2** The state of being sophisticated. **3** Sophistry.

soph·is·try (sof′is·trē) *n. pl.* **·tries** **1** Subtly fallacious reasoning or disputation. **2** The art or methods of the Sophists.

soph·o·more (sof′ə·môr, -mōr) *n.* A second-year student in an American high school or college. —*adj.* Of or pertaining to second-year students or studies. [Earlier *sophomer* a dialectician < *sophom,* var. of SOPHISM]

soph·o·mor·ic (sof′ə·môr′ik, -mōr′-) *adj.* **1** Of, pertaining to, or like a sophomore. **2** Shallow and pretentious. **3** Immature; inexperienced. Also **soph′o·mor′i·cal.** —**soph′o·mor′i·cal·ly** *adv.*

-sophy *combining form* Knowledge or a system of knowledge: *philosophy.* [< Gk. *sophia* wisdom]

sop·o·rif·ic (sop′ə·rif′ik, sō′pə-) *adj.* **1** Causing or tending to cause sleep. **2** Drowsy; sleepy. —*n.* A medicine that produces sleep. [< L *sopor* sleep]

sop·ping (sop′ing) *adj.* Drenched; soaking.

sop·py (sop′ē) *adj.* **·pi·er, ·pi·est** Saturated and softened with moisture; soft and sloppy. —**sop′pi·ness** *n.*

so·pran·o (sə·pran′ō, -prä′nō) *n. pl.* **so·pran·os** or **so·pra·ni** (sə·prä′nē) **1** A part or singing voice of the highest range. **2** The music for such a voice. **3** A person having such a voice or singing such a part. —*adj.* Of or pertaining to a soprano voice or part. [< Ital. *sopra* above]

so·ra (sôr′ə, sō′rə) *n.* A grayish brown crake with a short yellow bill. Also **sora rail.** [?< N. Am. Ind.]

sor·cer·er (sôr′sər·ər) *n.* A wizard; magician.

sor·cer·ess (sôr′sər·es) *n.* A woman who practices sorcery; witch.

sor·cer·y (sôr′sər·ē) *n. pl.* **·cer·ies** Use of supernatural agencies; magic; witchcraft. [< L *sors* fate] —**sor′cer·ous** *adj.* —**sor′cer·ous·ly** *adv.*

sor·did (sôr′did) *adj.* **1** Of degraded character; vile; base. **2** Dirty; squalid. **3** Mercenary; selfish. [< L *sordidus* squalid] —**sor′did·ly** *adv.* —**sor′did·ness** *n.*

sore (sôr, sōr) *n.* **1** A place on an animal body where the skin or flesh is bruised, broken, or inflamed. **2** Anything that causes pain or trouble. —*adj.* **sor·er, sor·est** **1** Having a sore or sores; tender. **2** Pained or distressed. **3** Irritating; distressing. **4** Very great; extreme: in *sore* need of money. **5** *Informal* Offended; angry. —*adv. Archaic* Sorely. [< OE *sār*] —**sore′ness** *n.* —**Syn.** *n.* **1** cut, scrape, wound.

sore·head (sôr′hed′, sōr′-) *n. Informal.* A disgruntled person.

sore·ly (sôr′lē, sōr′-) *adv.* **1** Grievously; distressingly. **2** Greatly: His aid was *sorely* needed.

sor·ghum (sôr′gəm) *n.* **1** A canelike tropical grass cultivated for fodder and its sugary sap. **2** Syrup prepared from the sap of the plant. [< L *Syricus* of Syria, where originally grown]

Sorghum

so·ror·i·ty (sə·rôr′ə·tē, -ror′-) *n. pl.* **·ties** A women's organization having chapters at colleges, universities, etc. [< L *soror* a sister]

sor·rel[1] (sôr′əl, sor′-) *n.* Any of various plants with acid leaves. [< OF *sur* sour]

sor·rel[2] (sôr′əl, sor′-) *n.* **1** A reddish brown color. **2** An animal of this color. —*adj.* Reddish brown. [< OF *sor* a hawk with red plumage]

sor·row (sor′ō, sôr′ō) *n.* **1** Pain or distress because of loss, injury, misfortune, or grief. **2** An event that causes such pain or distress; affliction. **3** The expression of grief; mourning. —*v.i.* To feel or express sorrow; grieve. [< OE *sorg* care] —**sor′row·er** *n.*

sor·row·ful (sor′ə·fəl, sôr′-) *adj.* **1** Full of or showing sorrow or grief. **2** Causing sorrow: a *sorrowful* occasion. —**sor′row·ful·ly** *adv.* —**sor′row·ful·ness** *n.*

sor·ry (sor′ē, sôr′ē) *adj.* **·ri·er, ·ri·est 1** Feeling or showing regret or remorse. **2** Affected by sorrow; grieved. **3** Causing sorrow; melancholy. **4** Pitiable or worthless; paltry. [< OE *sārig* < *sār* sore] **—sor′ri·ly** *adv.* **—sor′ri·ness** *n.*

sort (sôrt) *n.* **1** A collection of persons or things characterized by similar qualities; a kind. **2** Character; nature. **3** Manner; way; style. **4** A person of a certain type: He's a good *sort.* **—of sorts** Of a poor or unsatisfactory kind: an actor *of sorts.* **—out of sorts** Slightly ill or ill-humored. **—sort of** *Informal* Somewhat. —*v.t.* To arrange or separate into grades, kinds, or sizes; assort. [< L *sors* lot, condition] **—sort′er** *n.*

sor·tie (sôr′tē) *n.* **1** A sudden attack by troops from a besieged place. **2** A single trip of an aircraft on a military mission. [< F *sortir* go forth]

S O S (es′ō·es′) **1** The international signal of distress in the Morse code (. . . – – – . . .), used by airplanes, ships, etc. **2** *Informal* Any call for assistance.

so-so (sō′sō′) *adj.* Passable; mediocre. —*adv.* Indifferently; tolerably. Also **so′so′, so so.**

sot (sot) *n.* A habitual drunkard. [< OE *sott* a fool] **—sot′tish** *adj.* **—sot′tish·ly** *adv.* **—sot′tish·ness** *n.*

sot·to vo·ce (sot′ō vō′chē, *Ital.* sôt′tō vō′chā) Softly; in an undertone; privately. [Ital., lit., under the voice]

sou (sōō) *n.* **1** Any of several former French coins of varying value, esp. one equal to 12 deniers. **2** A coin equal to five centimes. [< LL *solidus,* a gold coin]

sou·brette (sōō·bret′) *n.* **1** The part of a frivolous or flirtatious young woman, often a maidservant, in a play or light opera. **2** An actress who portrays such parts. [< Prov. *soubret* shy] **—sou·bret′tish** *adj.*

sou·bri·quet (sōō′bri·kā, sōō·bri·kā′) *n.* SOBRIQUET.

souf·flé (sōō·flā′) *adj.* Made light and frothy, and fixed in that condition by heat: also **souf·fléed′** (-flād′). —*n.* A light, baked dish made of a sauce, beaten egg whites, and various flavorings and ingredients. [F < L *sub-* under + *flare* to blow]

sough (suf, sou) *v.i.* To make a sighing sound, as the wind. —*n.* A deep, murmuring sound. [< OE *swōgan* sound]

sought (sôt) *p.t. & p.p.* of SEEK.

soul (sōl) *n.* **1** That essence or entity of the human person which is regarded as being immortal, invisible, and the source or origin of spirituality, emotion, volition, etc. **2** The moral or spiritual part of man. **3** Emotional or spiritual force, vitality, depth, etc.: His acting lacks *soul.* **4** The most essential or vital element or quality of something: Justice is the *soul* of law. **5** The leading figure or inspirer of a cause, movement, etc. **6** Embodiment: the *soul* of generosity. **7** A person: Every *soul* trembled at the sight. **8** The disembodied spirit of one who has died. **9** Among U.S. Negroes: **a** The awareness of a black African heritage. **b** A strongly emotional pride and solidarity based on this awareness. **c** The qualities that arouse such feelings, esp. as exemplified in black culture and art. **10** SOUL MUSIC. **11** SOUL FOOD. —*adj.* Of or pertaining to soul (def. 9). [< OE *sāwol*]

soul brother A Negro male: used by other Negroes.

soul food Any of various Southern foods or dishes popular with American Negroes, as fried chicken, ham hocks, chitterlings, yams, etc.

soul·ful (sōl′fəl) *adj.* Full of emotion or feeling. **—soul′ful·ly** *adv.* **—soul′ful·ness** *n.* **—Syn.** deep-felt, heartfelt, deep, profound, moving, emotional.

soul kiss A kiss with the mouth open and the tongues touching.

soul·less (sōl′lis) *adj.* **1** Having no soul. **2** Without feeling or emotion; cold. **—soul′less·ly** *adv.* **—soul′less·ness** *n.*

soul music A type of popular music strongly emotional in character and influenced chiefly by the blues and gospel hymns.

soul-search·ing (sōl′sûrch′ing) *n.* A deep examination of one's motives, desires, actions, etc.

soul sister A Negro female: used by other Negroes.

sound[1] (sound) *n.* **1** Energy in the form of a disturbance, usually periodic, in the pressure and density of a fluid or the elastic strain of a solid, detectable by human organs of hearing when between about 20Hz and 20kHz in frequency. **2** The sensation produced by such energy. **3** Any noise, tone, voice, etc., of a specified quality or source: the *sound* of a door slamming shut. **4** Sounding or hearing distance; earshot: within *sound* of the battle. **5** Significance; implication: The story has a sinister *sound.* **6** Mere noise without significance: full of *sound* and fury. —*v.i.* **1** To give forth a sound or sounds. **2** To give a specified impression; seem: The story *sounds* true. —*v.t.* **3** To cause to give forth sound: to *sound* a bell; also, to give forth the sound of: to *sound* A on the violin. **4** To give a signal or order for or announcement of: to *sound* retreat. **5** To utter audibly; pronounce. **6** To make known or celebrated. **7** To test or examine by sound; auscultate. [< OF *son* < L *sonus*]

sound[2] (sound) *adj.* **1** Functioning without impairment; healthy. **2** Free from injury, flaw, or decay: *sound* timber. **3** Correct, logical, or sensible in reasoning, judgment, etc.: *sound* advice. **4** Not unorthodox; established: a *sound* belief. **5** Financially solid or solvent. **6** Stable; safe; secure: a *sound* investment. **7** Complete and effectual; thorough: a *sound* beating. **8** Deep; unbroken: *sound* sleep. **9** Legally valid. [< OE *gesund*] **—sound′ly** *adv.* **—sound′ness** *n.*

sound[3] (sound) *n.* **1** A long, narrow body of water connecting larger bodies of water or separating an island from the mainland. **2** The air bladder of a fish. [< OE *sund* sea and ON *sund* a strait]

sound[4] (sound) *v.t.* **1** To test the depth of (water, etc.), esp. by means of a lead weight at the end of a line. **2** To measure (depth) thus. **3** To explore or examine (the bottom of the sea, the atmosphere, etc.) by means of various probing devices. **4** To discover or try to discover the views and attitudes of (a person) by means of conversation, subtle questions, etc.: usu. with *out.* **5** To try to ascertain or determine (beliefs, attitudes, etc.) in such a manner. **6** *Surg.* To examine, as with a sound. —*v.i.* **7** To measure depth, as with a sounding lead. **8** To dive down suddenly and deeply, as a whale when harpooned. **9** To make investigation; inquire. —*n. Surg.* An instrument for exploring a cavity; a probe. —*adv.* Deeply: *sound* asleep. [< OF *sonder*] **—sound′a·ble** *adj.* **—sound′er** *n.*

sound barrier SONIC BARRIER.

sound effects In motion pictures, radio, on the stage, etc., the imitative sounds, as of rain, hoofbeats, fire, etc., produced by various methods.

sound·ing[1] (soun′ding) *adj.* **1** Giving forth a full sound; sonorous. **2** Noisy and empty. **—sound′ing·ly** *adv.*

sound·ing[2] (soun′ding) *n.* **1** Measurement of the depth of water. **2** *pl.* The depth of water as sounded. **3** Water of such depth that the bottom may be reached by sounding. **4** Measurement or examination of the atmosphere, space, etc. at various heights. **5** A sampling of public opinion.

sounding board 1 A structure over a pulpit or speaker's platform to amplify and clarify the speaker's voice. **2** A thin board, as the belly of a violin, used to increase the resonance of the sound: also **sound′board′. 3** Any person, group, device, etc., used to propagate opinions. **4** A person or group on whom one tests the validity or effectiveness of something.

sound·less (sound′lis) *adj.* Making no sound; silent. **—sound′less·ly** *adv.* **—sound′less·ness** *n.*

sound·man (sound′man′) *n. pl.* **·men′** (-men′) A man who has charge of sound effects.

sound·proof (sound′prōōf′) *adj.* Resistant to the penetration or spread of sound. —*v.t.* To make soundproof.

sound track That portion along the edge of a motion-picture film which carries the sound record.

soup (sōōp) *n.* **1** A food made of meat or fish, vegetables, etc., cooked and served, either whole or puréed, in water, stock, or other liquid. **2** *Slang* A heavy fog. **3** *Slang* Nitroglycerin. **—in the soup** *Slang* In difficulties; in a quandary. **—soup up** *Slang* To supercharge or otherwise modify (an engine) for high speed. [< F *soupe*]

soup·çon (sōōp·sôn′) *n.* A minute quantity; a taste. [F, lit., a suspicion]

soup·y (sōō′pē) *adj.* **soup·i·er, soup·i·est 1** Like soup in consistency. **2** Very foggy or cloudy. **3** Overly sentimental.

sour (sour) *adj.* 1 Sharp, acid, or tart to the taste, like vinegar. 2 Having an acid or rancid taste or smell as the result of fermentation. 3 Of or pertaining to fermentation. 4 Cross; morose: a *sour* smile. 5 Bitterly disenchanted. 6 Bad in quality, performance, etc.: an athlete gone *sour.* 7 Wrong or unpleasant in pitch or tone: a *sour* note. 8 Unpleasant. 9 Acid: said of soil. —*v.t. & v.i.* To become or make sour. —*n.* 1 Something sour. 2 A cocktail, made usu. with lemon juice, fruit garnishes, etc.: a whiskey *sour.* [< OE *sūr*] —**sour′ly** *adv.* —**sour′ness** *n.* —**Syn.** 4 dour, acid, bitter, unhappy.

source (sôrs, sōrs) *n.* 1 That from which something originates or is derived. 2 A cause or agency: a *source* of joy. 3 The spring or fountain from which a stream of water originates. 4 A person, writing, or agency from which information is obtained. [< L *surgere* to rise]

sour cream A food product made of cream soured and thickened by the action of lactic acid bacteria.

sour·dough (sour′dō′) *n.* 1 Fermented dough for use as leaven in making bread. 2 A pioneer or prospector in Alaska or Canada: from the practice of carrying fermented dough to make bread.

sour grapes That which a person affects to despise, because it is unattainable: an allusion to Aesop's fable of the fox and the grapes.

sour·gum (sour′gum′) *n.* TUPELO.

sour·puss (sour′pōōs′) *n. Slang* A person with a sullen, peevish expression or disposition.

souse (sous) *v.t. & v.i.* **soused, sous·ing** 1 To dip or steep in a liquid. 2 To pickle. 3 To make or become thoroughly wet. 4 *Slang* To make or get drunk. —*n.* 1 Pickled meats, esp. the feet and ears of a pig. 2 A plunge in water. 3 Brine. 4 *Slang* A drunkard. [< OHG *sulza* brine]

sou·tane (sōō·tän′, -tan′) *n.* CASSOCK. [< Ital. *sottana*]

south (south) *n.* 1 The general direction to the right of sunrise. 2 The point of the compass at 180°, directly opposite north. 3 A region or point lying in this direction. —*adj.* 1 Situated in a southern direction relatively to the observer or to any given place or point. 2 Facing south. 3 Belonging to or proceeding from the south. —*v.i.* To turn southward. —*adv.* 1 Toward or at the south. 2 From the south. —**the South** 1 In the U.S., those states lying south of Pennsylvania and the Ohio River and east of the Mississippi. 2 The Confederacy. [< OE *sūth*]

South Africa A republic of s Africa, 472,359 sq. mi., cap. Pretoria, legislative center Cape Town.

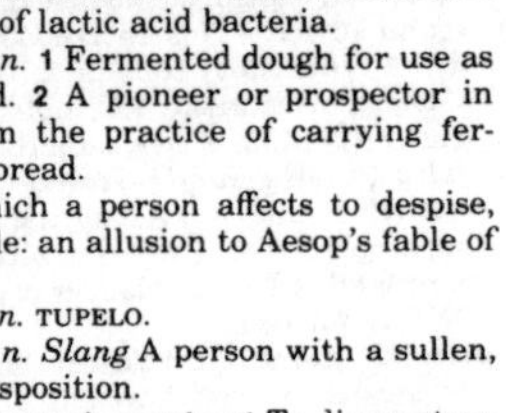

South African A native or citizen of South Africa, esp. an Afrikaner. —*adj.* Of or pertaining to South Africa or its people.

South African Dutch AFRIKAANS.

South America The southern continent of the western hemisphere, about 6,900,000 square miles. —**South American**

south·bound (south′bound′) *adj.* Going southward.

south·east (south′ēst′, *in nautical usage* sou′ēst′) *n.* 1 The direction or compass point midway between south and east. 2 Any region lying in this direction. —*adj.* Of, pertaining to, toward, or from the southeast. —*adv.* Toward or from the southeast. —**south′east′ern, south′east′ern·most** *adj.*

south·east·er (south′ēs′tər, *in nautical usage* sou′ēs′tər) *n.* A gale from the southeast.

south·east·er·ly (south′ēs′tər·lē, *in nautical usage* sou′ēs′tər·lē) *adj. & adv.* 1 Toward the southeast. 2 From the southeast: said of wind.

south·east·ward (south′ēst′wərd) *adj. & adv.* Toward the southeast. —*n.* A southeastward point or direction —**south′east′ward·ly, south′east′wards** *adv.*

south·er (sou′thər) *n.* A strong wind from the south.

south·er·ly (suth′ər·lē) *adj.* 1 Situated in or tending toward the south. 2 From the south: a *southerly* wind. —*adv.* Toward or from the south. —**south′er·li·ness** *n.*

south·ern (suth′ərn) *adj.* 1 Of, in, or facing the south. 2 From the south, as a wind. 3 *Often cap.* Of, from, or characteristic of the South: *southern* cooking. —**south′ern·ly** *adv.* —**south′ern·most** *adj.*

Southern Cross A southern constellation having four bright stars in the form of a cross.

South·ern·er (suth′ərn·ər) *n.* A native or inhabitant of the s regions of the U.S.

Southern Hemisphere See HEMISPHERE.

southern lights AURORA AUSTRALIS.

Southern Yemen YEMEN, PEOPLE'S DEMOCRATIC REPUBLIC OF.

South Korea See KOREA.

south·land (south′land′) *n.* 1 A region situated to the south. 2 *Often cap.* The southern U.S. —**south′land′er** *n.*

south·paw (south′pô′) *Slang n.* 1 In baseball, a left-handed pitcher. 2 Any left-handed person or player. —*adj.* Left-handed.

South Pole The southern extremity of the earth's axis; the 90th degree of south latitude.

south-south·east (south′south′ēst′, *in nautical usage* sou′sou′ēst′) *n.* The direction or compass point midway between south and southeast. —*adj.* Of, pertaining to, toward, or from this direction. —*adv.* Toward or from this direction.

south-south·west (south′south′west′, *in nautical usage* sou′sou′west′) *n.* The direction or compass point midway between south and southwest. —*adj.* Of, pertaining to, toward, or from this direction. —*adv.* Toward or from this direction.

South Vietnam See VIETNAM.

south·ward (south′wərd, *in nautical usage* suth′ərd) *adj.* Situated in or toward the south. —*adv.* In a southerly direction: also **south′ward·ly, south′wards.** —*n.* The direction of south; also, a region to the south.

south·west (south′west′, *in nautical usage* sou′west′) *n.* 1 The direction or compass point midway between south and west. 2 Any region lying in this direction. —*adj.* Of, pertaining to, toward or from the southwest. —*adv.* Toward or from the southwest. —**the Southwest** The sw part of the U.S., generally including Oklahoma, Texas, New Mexico, Arizona, and southern California. —**south′west′ern, south′west′ern·most** *adj.*

south·west·er (south′wes′tər, *in nautical usage* sou′wes′tər) *n.* 1 A wind, gale, or storm from the southwest. 2 A waterproof hat of oilskin, canvas, etc., with a broad protective brim behind. Also **sou′west′er.**

Southwester *def. 2*

south·west·er·ly (south′wes′tər·lē, *in nautical usage* sou′wes′tər·lē) *adj. & adv.* 1 Toward the southwest. 2 From the southwest: said of wind.

south·west·ward (south′west′wərd) *adj. & adv.* Toward the southwest. —*n.* A southwestward point or direction. —**south′west′ward·ly, south′west′wards** *adv.*

sou·ve·nir (sōō′və·nir′, sōō′və·nir) *n.* A token of remembrance; memento. [< L *subvenire* come to mind]

sov·er·eign (sov′rin, -ə·rən, -ərn, suv′-) *adj.* 1 Exercising or possessing supreme jurisdiction or power. 2 Free; independent; autonomous: a *sovereign* state. 3 Supremely excellent, great, or exalted. 4 Extremely potent or effective: a *sovereign* remedy. 5 Total; unmitigated: *sovereign* hate. 6 Of chief importance, supremacy, etc.: *sovereign* claims. —*n.* 1 One who possesses sovereign authority; a monarch. 2 A body of persons in whom sovereign power is vested. 3 An English gold coin equivalent to one pound sterling. [< L *super* above] —**sov′er·eign·ly** *adv.*

sov·er·eign·ty (sov′rin·tē, -ə·rən-, -ərn-, suv′-) *n. pl.* **·ties** 1 The state or quality of being sovereign. 2 The ultimate, supreme power in a state. 3 A sovereign state. 4 The status or power of a sovereign.

so·vi·et (sō′vē·et, sō′vē·et′, sov′ē-, -ē·it) *n.* 1 In the Soviet Union, any of the elected legislative councils existing at various governmental levels. 2 Any of various similar socialist legislative councils. [< Russ. *sovyet* a council]

So·vi·et (sō′vē·et, sō′vē·et′, sov′ē-, -ē·it) *adj.* Of or pertaining to the Union of Soviet Socialist Republics. —*n.pl.* The Soviet people, esp. the officials of the government.

so·vi·et·ize (sō′vē·ə·tīz′, sov′ē-) *v.t.* **·ized, ·iz·ing** To bring under a soviet form of government. **—so′vi·et·i·za′tion** *n.*

Soviet Russia **1** UNION OF SOVIET SOCIALIST REPUBLICS. **2** RUSSIAN SOVIET FEDERATED SOCIALIST REPUBLIC.

Soviet Union UNION OF SOVIET SOCIALIST REPUBLICS.

sow[1] (sō) *v.* **sowed, sown** or **sowed, sow·ing** *v.t.* **1** To scatter (seed) over land for growth. **2** To scatter seed over (land). **3** To disseminate; implant: to *sow* the seeds of distrust. —*v.i.* **4** To scatter seed. [< OE *sāwan*] **—sow′er** *n.*

sow[2] (sou) *n.* A female hog. [< OE *sū*]

sow·bel·ly (sou′bel′ē) *n. Informal* SALT PORK.

soy (soi) *n.* A dark brown salty liquid condiment made from fermented soybeans. Also **soy sauce.** [Japanese]

soy·bean (soi′bēn) *n.* **1** A small leguminous forage plant native to Asia. **2** Its edible bean, a source of oil, flour, and other products. Also, *esp. Brit.,* **soy·a** (soi′ə).

SP Shore Patrol; Submarine Patrol.

Sp. Spain; Spaniard; Spanish.

sp. special; specialist; species; specific; spelling; spirit(s).

s.p. without issue (L *sine prole*).

spa (spä) *n.* **1** Any locality frequented for its mineral springs. **2** A mineral spring. **3** A fashionable resort or resort hotel. [< *Spa,* a Belgian watering town]

space (spās) *n.* **1** The three-dimensional expanse that is considered as coextensive with the universe. **2** A limited or measurable distance or area, as that between or within points or objects. **3** A specific area designated for a particular purpose: landing *space.* **4** OUTER SPACE. **5** An interval or period of time. **6** One of the degrees of a musical staff between two lines. **7** *Printing* **a** A blank piece of type metal, used for spacing between lines, characters, etc. **b** The area occupied by such pieces. **8** Reserved accommodations, as on a ship or airliner. —*adj.* Of or pertaining to space, esp. to outer space. —*v.t.* **spaced, spac·ing 1** To separate by spaces. **2** To divide into spaces. [< L *spatium*] —**space′less** *adj.* **—spac′er** *n.*

space·craft (spās′kraft′, -kräft′) *n.* Any vehicle, manned or unmanned, designed for flight in outer space.

spaced-out (spāst′out′) *adj. Slang* Dazed or drugged, by or as by the use of narcotics.

space·flight (spās′flīt′) *n.* Flight in outer space.

space·ship (spās′ship′) *n.* Any vehicle designed to travel outside the earth's atmosphere.

space station A large, usu. manned satellite orbiting the earth and used for observation, experiments, as a relay station, etc.

space-time (spās′tīm′, -tīm′) *n.* A four-dimensional continuum in which each point is identified by three position coordinates and one coordinate of time. Also **space-time continuum.**

spa·cial (spā′shəl) *adj.* SPATIAL.

spac·ing (spā′sing) *n.* **1** The arrangement of spaces. **2** A space or spaces, as in a line of print.

spa·cious (spā′shəs) *adj.* **1** Of large or ample extent; not cramped or crowded; roomy. **2** Large or great in scale or scope. **—spa′cious·ly** *adv.* **—spa′cious·ness** *n.* **—Syn. 1** extensive, ample, sizable, capacious, commodious.

spack·le (spak′əl) *v.t.* **·led, ·ling** To apply Spackle to.

Spack·le (spak′əl) *n.* A powder which, moistened to form a paste, is used for filling cracks, etc. before painting: a trade name.

spade[1] (spād) *n.* An implement used for digging in the ground, heavier than a shovel and having a flatter blade. **—call a spade a spade 1** To call a thing by its right name. **2** To speak the plain truth. —*v.t.* **spad·ed, spad·ing** To dig or cut with a spade. [< OE *spadu*] **—spade′ful, spad′er** *n.*

spade[2] (spād) *n.* **1** A figure, resembling a heart with a triangular handle, on a playing card. **2** A card so marked. **3** *Usu. pl.* The suit of cards so marked. [< Gk. *spathē* broad sword]

spade·work (spād′wûrk′) *n.* Any preliminary work necessary to get a project under way.

spa·dix (spā′diks) *n. pl.* **spa·di·ces** (spā′də·sēz) *Bot.* A spike of tiny flowers on a fleshy axis, usu. enclosed within a spathe. [L, branch torn from palm tree < Gk.]

spa·ghet·ti (spə·get′ē) *n.* **1** A thin, cordlike pasta. **2** Insulated tubing through which bare wire is passed, as in a radio circuit. [< Ital. *spago* a small cord]

Spain (spān) *n.* A nominal constitutional monarchy in sw Europe, 194,368 sq. mi., capital Madrid.

spake (spāk) *Archaic p.t.* of SPEAK.

span[1] (span) *v.t.* **spanned, span·ning 1** To measure, esp. with the hand with the thumb and little finger extended. **2** To extend in time across: His influence *spanned* two centuries. **3** To extend over or from side to side of: This road *spans* the continent. **4** To provide with something that stretches across or extends over. —*n.* **1** The distance or measure between two points, ends, or extremities: the *span* of an eagle's wing. **2** The space or distance between the supports of an arch, abutments of a bridge, etc. **3** The part that spans such a space or distance: the graceful *spans* of Brooklyn Bridge. **4** A period of time or duration: life *span.* **5** The extreme space over which the hand can be expanded, usu. considered to be nine inches. [< OE *spann* distance]

span[2] (span) *n.* A pair of matched horses, oxen, etc., used as a team. [< MDu. *spannen* join together]

span·gle (spang′gəl) *n.* **1** A small bit of brilliant metal foil, plastic, etc., used for decoration, esp. on theatrical costumes. **2** Any small sparkling object. —*v.* **·gled, ·gling** *v.t.* **1** To adorn with or as with spangles; cause to glitter. —*v.i.* **2** To sparkle as spangles; glitter. [< MDu. *spang* a clasp, brooch] **—span′gly** *adj.*

Span·iard (span′yərd) *n.* A native or citizen of Spain.

span·iel (span′yəl) *n.* **1** A small or medium-sized dog having large pendulous ears and long silky hair. • See SPRINGER. **2** An obsequious follower. [< OF *espaignol* Spanish (dog)]

Span·ish (span′ish) *n.* **1** The language of Spain and many of the countries of the Western Hemisphere. **2** The people of Spain collectively: used with *the.* —*adj.* Of or pertaining to Spain, its people, their language, etc.

Spanish America Those countries of the Western Hemisphere in which Spanish is the common language. **—Span′ish-A·mer′i·can** *adj.*

Spanish American A native or inhabitant of Spanish America.

Spanish moss An epiphytic plant related to pineapple, growing in pendulous tufts on trees in s U.S. and tropical America.

spank (spangk) *v.t.* **1** To slap or strike, esp. on the buttocks with the open hand as a punishment. —*v.i.* **2** To move briskly. —*n.* A smack on the buttocks. [Imit.]

spank·er (spangk′ər) *n.* **1** One who spanks. **2** *Naut.* A fore-and-aft sail extended by a boom and a gaff from the mizzenmast of a ship or bark.

spank·ing (spangk′ing) *adj.* **1** Moving or blowing rapidly; swift; lively. **2** *Informal* Uncommonly large or fine. —*n.* A series of slaps on the buttocks. —*adv. Informal* Very: a *spanking* new bike. [?]

span·ner (span′ər) *n.* **1** One who or that which spans. **2** *Brit.* WRENCH.

spar[1] (spär) *n.* **1** *Naut.* A pole for extending a sail, as a mast, yard, or boom. **2** A similar heavy, round beam forming part of a derrick, crane, etc. **3** That part of an airplane wing which supports the ribs. —*v.t.* **sparred, spar·ring** To furnish with spars. [< ON *sparri* a beam]

spar[2] (spär) *v.i.* **sparred, spar·ring 1** To box, esp. with care and adroitness, as in practice. **2** To bandy words; wrangle. **3** To fight, as cocks, by striking with spurs. —*n.* The act or practice of boxing: also **spar′ring.** [< L *parare* prepare]

spar[3] (spär) *n.* Any of various vitreous, crystalline, easily cleavable, lustrous minerals. [< MDu.]

Spar (spär) *n.* A member of the women's reserve of the U.S. Coast Guard. Also **SPAR.** [< L *s(emper) par(atus)* always ready, the motto of the U.S. Coast Guard]

spare (spâr) *v.* **spared, spar·ing** *v.t.* 1 To refrain from injuring, molesting, or killing; treat mercifully. 2 To free or relieve (someone) from (pain, expense, etc.): *Spare* us the sight. 3 To use frugally; refrain from using or exercising. 4 To dispense or dispense with; do without: Can you *spare* a dime? —*v.i.* 5 To be frugal. 6 To be lenient or forgiving. —*adj.* **spar·er, spar·est** 1 That is over and above what is necessary, used, filled, etc.: *spare* time. 2 Held in reserve; additional; extra. 3 Thin; lean. 4 Not abundant or plentiful; scanty. 5 Not elaborate or fussy: a *spare* style of writing. —*n.* 1 A duplicate of something that has been saved for future use. 2 An extra tire usu. carried in or on a vehicle as a replacement in the event of a flat tire: also **spare tire.** 3 In bowling, the act of overturning all the pins with the first two balls; also, the score thus made. [< OE *sparian* to spare] —**spare′ly** *adv.* —**spare′ness, spar′er** *n.*

spare·ribs (spâr′ribz′) *n.pl.* A cut of pork ribs somewhat closely trimmed.

spar·ing (spâr′ing) *adj.* 1 Scanty; slight. 2 Frugal; stingy. —**spar′ing·ly** *adv.* —**spar′ing·ness** *n.*

spark (spärk) *n.* 1 An incandescent particle, esp. one thrown off by a fire. 2 Any similar glistening or brilliant point or particle. 3 A small trace or indication: a *spark* of wit. 4 Anything that kindles or animates. 5 *Electr.* The luminous effect of an electric discharge, or the discharge itself. —*v.i.* 1 To give off sparks. 2 In an internal-combustion engine, to have the electric ignition operating. —*v.t.* 3 To activate or cause: The shooting *sparked* a revolution. [< OE *spearca*] —**spark′er** *n.*

spar·kle (spär′kəl) *v.i.* **·kled, ·kling** 1 To give off flashes or bright points of light; glitter. 2 To emit sparks. 3 To effervesce, as certain wines, etc. 4 To be brilliant or vivacious. —*n.* 1 A spark; gleam. 2 Brilliance; vivacity. [Freq. of SPARK]

spar·kler (spär′klər) *n.* 1 One who or that which sparkles. 2 *Informal* A sparkling gem, as a diamond. 3 A thin, rodlike firework that emits sparks.

spark plug A device for igniting the charge in an internal-combustion engine by means of an electric spark.

spar·row (spar′ō) *n.* 1 Any of various small, plainly colored, passerine birds related to the finches, as the English sparrow. 2 Any of numerous similar birds, as the song sparrow. [< OE *spearwa*]

sparrow hawk 1 A small North American falcon with rufous back and tail. 2 A small European hawk.

sparse (spärs) *adj.* **spars·er, spars·est** Thinly spread or scattered; not dense: a *sparse* crowd. [< L *sparsus*, pp. of *spargere* sprinkle] —**sparse′ly** *adv.* —**sparse′ness, spar·si·ty** (spär′sə·tē) *n.*

Spar·ta (spär′tə) *n.* An ancient city in the Peloponnesus, s Greece, capital of ancient Laconia.

Spar·tan (spär′tən) *adj.* 1 Of Sparta or the Spartans. 2 Characterized by austerity, simplicity, self-denial, self-discipline, etc. 3 Heroically brave and enduring. —*n.* 1 A native or citizen of Sparta. 2 One of exceptional valor and fortitude. —**Spar′tan·ism** *n.*

spasm (spaz′əm) *n.* 1 A sudden, involuntary muscular contraction. 2 Any sudden action or effort. [< Gk. *spasmos* < *spaein* draw, pull]

spas·mod·ic (spaz·mod′ik) *adj.* 1 Of the nature of a spasm; intermittent; temporary; transitory. 2 Violent or impulsive. Also **spas·mod′i·cal.** —**spas·mod′i·cal·ly** *adv.*

spas·tic (spas′tik) *adj.* Of, pertaining to, or characterized by spasms. —*n.* A person afflicted with cerebral palsy or similar disability. —**spas′ti·cal·ly** *adv.*

spat[1] (spat) *p.t. & p.p.* of SPIT[1].

spat[2] (spat) *n.* 1 Spawn of a bivalve mollusk, esp. the oyster. 2 A young oyster, or young oysters collectively. [?]

spat[3] (spat) *n.* 1 *Informal* A petty dispute or quarrel. 2 A splash, as of rain; spatter. —*v.* **spat·ted, spat·ting** *v.i.* 1 To strike with a slight sound. 2 *Informal* To engage in a petty quarrel. —*v.t.* 3 To slap. [Imit.]

spat[4] (spat) *n.* A short gaiter worn over a shoe and fastened underneath with a strap. [Short for SPATTERDASH]

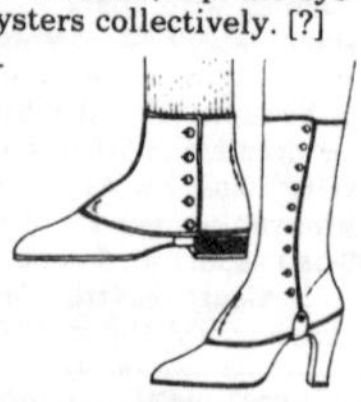

Spats[4]

spate (spāt) *n.* 1 A flood or overflow. 2 A large amount or incidence. 3 A sudden outpouring, as of words. [?]

spathe (spāth) *n. Bot.* A large bract or pair of bracts sheathing a flower cluster, as a spadix. [< Gk. *spathē* broad sword]

spa·tial (spā′shəl) *adj.* Of, involving, occupying, or having the nature of space. [< L *spatium* space] —**spa·ti·al·i·ty** (spā′shē·al′ə·tē) *n.* —**spa′tial·ly** *adv.*

spat·ter (spat′ər) *v.t.* 1 To scatter in drops or splashes, as mud or paint. 2 To splash with such drops; bespatter. 3 To defame. —*v.i.* 4 To throw off drops or splashes. 5 To fall in a shower, as raindrops. —*n.* 1 The act of spattering or the condition of being spattered. 2 The mark or soiled place caused by spattering. 3 The sound of spattering. 4 A small amount or number. [?< OE *spatlian* spit out]

spat·ter·dash (spat′ər·dash′) *n.* A knee-high legging worn as a protection from mud, esp. when riding.

spat·u·la (spach′ōō·lə) *n.* A knifelike instrument with a dull, flexible, rounded blade, used to spread plaster, cake icing, etc. [L]

spav·in (spav′in) *n.* A laming disease of the hock joint of horses. [< OF *espavain*] —**spav′ined** *adj.*

spawn (spôn) *n.* 1 The eggs of fishes, amphibians, mollusks, etc., esp. in masses. 2 A great number of offspring: usu. derisive. 3 Any large quantity or yield. —*v.i.* 1 To produce spawn; deposit eggs or roe. 2 To come forth as or like spawn. —*v.t.* 3 To produce (spawn). 4 To give rise to; originate. [< L *expandere* expand]

spay (spā) *v.t.* To remove the ovaries from (a female animal). [< OF *espeer* cut with a sword]

S.P.C.A. Society for the Prevention of Cruelty to Animals.

speak (spēk) *v.* **spoke** (*Archaic* **spake**), **spo·ken** (*Archaic* **spoke**), **speak·ing** *v.i.* 1 To employ the vocal organs in ordinary speech; utter words. 2 To express or convey ideas, opinions, etc., in or as in speech: Actions *speak* louder than words. 3 To make a speech; deliver an address. 4 To converse. 5 To make a sound; also, to bark, as a dog. —*v.t.* 6 To express or make known in or as in speech. 7 To utter in speech: to *speak* words of love. 8 To use or be capable of using (a language) in conversation. —**so to speak** In a manner of speaking. —**speak for** 1 To speak in behalf of; represent officially. 2 To reserve or request: usu. used in the passive voice: Has that appointment been *spoken for?* [< OE *specan*] —**speak′a·ble** *adj.*

speak-eas·y (spēk′ē′zē) *n. pl.* **-eas·ies** A place where liquor is sold contrary to law, esp. such a place in the U.S. during prohibition.

speak·er (spē′kər) *n.* 1 One who speaks, esp. in public. 2 The presiding officer in a legislative body. 3 LOUDSPEAKER.

speak·ing (spē′king) *adj.* 1 Able to speak. 2 Of, pertaining to, or for speech. 3 Using a specified language: a French-*speaking* colony. 4 Vividly lifelike: the *speaking* image of his father. —*n.* 1 The act or technique of one who speaks. 2 Something spoken. —**speak′ing·ly** *adv.*

spear (spir) *n.* 1 A weapon consisting of a pointed head on a long shaft. 2 A similar instrument, barbed and usu. forked, as for spearing fish. 3 A leaf or slender stalk, as of grass. —*v.t.* 1 To pierce or capture with or as with a spear. —*v.i.* 2 To pierce or wound with or as with a spear. 3 To send forth spears, as a plant. [< OE *spere*] —**spear′er** *n.*

spear·head (spir′hed′) *n.* 1 The point of a spear or lance. 2 The person, group, etc., that leads an action or undertaking. —*v.t.* To be in the lead of (an attack, etc.).

spear·man (spir′mən) *n. pl.* **·men** (-mən) A man armed with a spear. Also **spears′man.**

spear·mint (spir′mint′) *n.* An aromatic herb similar to peppermint.

spe·cial (spesh′əl) *adj.* 1 Out of the ordinary; uncommon; unique; different: a *special* problem. 2 Designed for or assigned to a specific purpose, occasion, etc.: a *special* permit. 3 Memorable; notable: a very *special* occasion. 4 Extra or additional: a *special* bonus. 5 Intimate; esteemed; beloved: a *special* favorite. —*n.* 1 Something made, detailed for, or appropriated to a specific service, occasion, etc., as a train, newspaper edition, sales item, featured dish, etc. 2 A television show produced and scheduled for a single presentation only. [< L *species* kind, species] —**spe′cial·ly** *adv.* —**Syn.** *adj.* 1 peculiar, particular, distinctive, singular, original, unusual. 3 noteworthy, unforgettable, extraordinary, exceptional, rare.

special delivery Mail delivery by special courier for an additional fee.

Special Drawing Rights International monetary credit that can be drawn by member nations from the International Monetary Fund to be used in lieu of gold.

spe·cial·ist (spesh′əl·ist) *n.* A person devoted to one line of study, occupation, or professional work. **—spe′cial·ism** *n.* **—spe′cial·is′tic** *adj.*

spe·ci·al·i·ty (spesh′ē·al′ə·tē) *n. pl.* **·ties** *Chiefly Brit.* SPECIALTY.

spe·cial·ize (spesh′əl·īz) *v.* **·ized, ·iz·ing** *v.i.* 1 To concentrate on one particular activity or subject. 2 To take on a form or forms adapted to special conditions or functions. —*v.t.* 3 To make specific or particular; particularize. 4 To adapt for or direct toward some special use or purpose. *Brit. sp.* **·ise.** **—spe′cial·i·za′tion** *n.*

spe·cial·ty (spesh′əl·tē) *n. pl.* **·ties** 1 Something, as a trade, study, activity, etc., in which one specializes. 2 A product or article possessing a special quality, excellence, character, etc.: Fish is the *specialty* of this restaurant. 3 A special mark, quality, or characteristic. 4 The state of being special.

spe·cie (spē′shē) *n.* Coined money; coin. **—in specie** 1 In coin. 2 In kind. [< L *(in) specie* (in) kind]

spe·cies (spē′shēz, -shiz) *n. pl.* **·cies** 1 A category of animals or plants subordinate to a genus and comprising similar organisms usu. with the capacity of interbreeding only among themselves. 2 A group of individuals or objects having in common certain attributes and designated by a common name. 3 A kind; sort; variety; form. 4 *Eccl.* **a** The visible form of bread or of wine retained by the eucharistic elements after consecration. **b** The consecrated elements of the Eucharist. [L, kind]

spe·cif·ic (spi·sif′ik) *adj.* 1 Distinctly and plainly set forth; explicit. 2 Special; definite; particular; distinct: He took no *specific* action. 3 Belonging to or distinguishing a species. 4 Having some distinct medicinal or pathological property: a *specific* germ. 5 Designating a particular property, composition, ratio, or quantity serving to identify a given substance or phenomenon: *specific* gravity. —*n.* 1 Anything adapted to effect a specific result. 2 A medicine affecting a specific condition or pathogen. 3 *Usu. pl.* A particular item or detail. [< L *species* kind + -FIC] **—spe·cif′i·cal·ly** *adv.* **—spec·i·fic·i·ty** (spes′ə·fis′ə·tē) *n.*

spec·i·fi·ca·tion (spes′ə·fə·kā′shən) *n.* 1 The act of specifying. 2 A definite and complete statement, as in a contract; also, one detail in such a statement. 3 In patent law, the detailed description of an invention. 4 *Usu. pl.* A description of dimensions, types of material, capabilities, etc., of a device, building project, etc. 5 A single item in such a description.

specific gravity The ratio of the mass of a substance to that of an equal volume of some standard substance, water in the case of solids and liquids, and air or hydrogen in the case of gases.

spec·i·fy (spes′ə·fī) *v.t.* **·fied, ·fy·ing** 1 To mention or state in full and explicit detail. 2 To include as an item in a specification.

spec·i·men (spes′ə·mən) *n.* 1 A person or thing regarded as representative of a class. 2 A sample, as of blood, sputum, etc., for laboratory analysis. 3 *Informal* A person of a specified type or character. [< L *specere* look at]

spe·cious (spē′shəs) *adj.* Apparently good, right, logical, etc., but actually without merit or foundation: *specious* reasoning. [< L *speciosus* fair] **—spe′cious·ly** *adv.* **—spe′cious·ness** *n.*

speck (spek) *n.* 1 A small spot or stain. 2 Any very small thing; particle. —*v.t.* To mark with specks. [< OE *specca*]

speck·le (spek′əl) *v.t.* **·led, ·ling** To mark with specks. —*n.* A speck.

specs (speks) *n.pl. Informal* 1 EYEGLASSES. 2 Specifications. See SPECIFICATION (def. 4).

spec·ta·cle (spek′tə·kəl) *n.* 1 A grand or unusual sight or public display, as a pageant, parade, natural phenomenon, etc. 2 An embarrassing or deplorable exhibition. 3 *pl.* EYEGLASSES. [< L *specere* see] **—spec′ta·cled** (-kəld) *adj.*

spec·tac·u·lar (spek·tak′yə·lər) *adj.* Of or like a spectacle; unusually wonderfully, exciting, etc. —*n.* Something spectacular, esp. a lavish television production. **—spec·tac′u·lar·ly** *adv.* **—spec·tac′u·lar′i·ty** (-lar′ə·tē) *n.*

spec·ta·tor (spek′tā·tər, spek·tā′-) *n.* 1 One who beholds; an eyewitness. 2 One who is present at and views a show, game, spectacle, etc. [L < *spectare* look at]

spec·ter (spek′tər) *n.* A phantom; apparition. Also *esp. Brit.* **spec′tre.** [< L *spectrum* vision]

spec·tra (spek′trə) A *pl.* of SPECTRUM.

spec·tral (spek′trəl) *adj.* 1 Pertaining to a specter; ghostly. 2 Pertaining to a spectrum. **—spec′tral·ly** *adv.*

spectro- *combining form* Spectrum: *spectroscope.*

spec·tro·gram (spek′trə·gram) *n.* A photograph or other record of a spectrum.

spec·tro·graph (spek′trə·graf, -gräf) *n.* A device for displaying and recording spectra.

spec·tro·scope (spek′trə·skōp) *n.* An instrument for sorting out into a spectrum the wavelengths in a beam of light or other radiation. **—spec′tro·scop′ic** (-skop′ik) or **·i·cal** *adj.* **—spec′tro·scop′i·cal·ly** *adv.*

spec·tros·co·py (spek·tros′kə·pē) *n.* 1 The science treating of the phenomena observed with the spectroscope. 2 The art of using the spectroscope.

spec·trum (spek′trəm) *n. pl.* **·tra** (-trə) or **·trums** 1 The continuous band of colors observed when a beam of white light is diffracted, as by a prism, according to wavelength, ranging from red, the longest visible rays, to violet, the shortest. 2 Any array of radiant energy ordered according to a varying characteristic, as frequency, wavelength, etc. 3 A band of wave frequencies: the radio *spectrum.* 4 A series or range within limits: a wide *spectrum* of activities. [L, a vision]

spec·u·late (spek′yə·lāt) *v.i.* **·lat·ed, ·lat·ing** 1 To weigh mentally or conjecture; ponder; theorize. 2 To make a risky investment with hope of gain. [< L *speculari* look at, examine] **—spec′u·la′tor** *n.* **—spec′u·la·to′ry** (-lə·tôr′ē, -tō′rē) *adj.* **—Syn.** 1 guess, presume, surmise, venture, hazard.

spec·u·la·tion (spek′yə·lā′shən) *n.* 1 The act of speculating or conjecturing. 2 A theory or conjecture. 3 An investment or business transaction involving risk with hope of large profit.

spec·u·la·tive (spek′yə·lə·tiv, -lā′tiv) *adj.* 1 Of, pertaining to, engaged in, or given to speculation or conjecture. 2 Strictly theoretical; not practical. 3 Engaging in or involving financial speculation. 4 Risky; doubtful. **—spec′u·la·tive·ly** *adv.* **—spec′u·la·tive·ness** *n.*

spec·u·lum (spek′yə·ləm) *n. pl.* **·la** (-lə) or **·lums** 1 A mirror usu. of polished metal, used for telescope reflectors, etc. 2 *Med.* An instrument that dilates a passage of the body for examination. [L, mirror < *specere* see]

sped (sped) A *p.t. & p.p.* of SPEED.

speech (spēch) *n.* 1 The act of speaking; faculty of expressing thought and emotion by spoken words. 2 The power or capability of speaking. 3 That which is spoken; conversation; talk. 4 A public address. 5 A characteristic manner of speaking. 6 A particular language, idiom, or dialect: American *speech.* 7 The study or art of oral communication. [< OE *specan* speak]

speech·i·fy (spē′chə·fī) *v.i.* **·fied, ·fy·ing** To make speeches: often used derisively. **—speech′i·fi′er** *n.*

speech·less (spēch′lis) *adj.* 1 Temporarily unable to speak because of physical weakness, strong emotion, etc.: *speechless* with rage. 2 Mute; dumb. 3 Silent; reticent. 4 Inexpressible in words: *speechless* joy. **—speech′less·ly** *adv.* **—speech′less·ness** *n.*

speed (spēd) *n.* 1 Rapidity of motion; swiftness. 2 Rate of motion: *speed* of light. 3 Rate or rapidity of any action or performance. 4 A transmission gear in a motor vehicle. 5 *Informal* A characteristic interest, life style, etc. 6 *Slang* An amphetamine drug, esp. methamphetamine. 7 *Archaic* Good luck; success: They wished him good *speed.* —*v.* **sped** or **speed·ed, speed·ing** *v.i.* 1 To move or go with speed. 2 To exceed the legal driving limit, esp. on highways. —*v.t.* 3 To promote the forward progress of: *speed* a letter. 4 To cause to move or go with speed. 5 To promote the success of. 6 To wish Godspeed to: *Speed* the parting guest. —**speed up** To accelerate in speed or action. —*adj.* Of, pertaining to, or indicating speed. [< OE *spēd* power]

speed·boat (spēd′bōt′) *n.* A motorboat capable of high speed.

speed·er (spē′dər) *n.* A person or thing that speeds; esp., a motorist who drives at a speed exceeding a safe or legal limit.

speed·om·e·ter (spi·dom′ə·tər) *n.* A device for indicating the speed of a vehicle.

speed·ster (spēd′stər) *n.* A speeder.

speed·up (spēd′up′) *n.* An acceleration in work, output, movement, etc.

speed·way (spēd′wā′) *n.* 1 A racetrack for automobiles or motorcycles. 2 A road for vehicles traveling at high speed.

speed·well (spēd′wel) *n.* Any of various herbs of the figwort family, usu. bearing blue or white flowers.

speed·y (spē′dē) *adj.* **speed·i·er, speed·i·est** 1 Characterized by speed. 2 Without delay. —**speed′i·ly** *adv.* —**speed′·i·ness** *n.*

spe·le·ol·o·gy (spē′lē·ol′ə·jē, spel′ē-) *n.* 1 The scientific study of caves. 2 The exploration of caves. [< L *spelaeum* a cave + -LOGY] —**spe′le·o·log′i·cal** (-ə·loj′i·kəl) *adj.* —**spe′le·ol′o·gist** *n.*

spell[1] (spel) *v.* **spelled** or **spelt, spell·ing** *v.t.* 1 To pronounce or write the letters of (a word); esp., to do so correctly. 2 To form or be the letters of: C-a-t *spells* cat. 3 To signify; mean. —*v.i.* 4 To form words out of letters, esp. correctly. —**spell out** 1 To read each letter of, usu. with difficulty. 2 To puzzle out and learn. 3 To make explicit and detailed. [< OF *espeler*]

spell[2] (spel) *n.* 1 A magical word or formula. 2 A state of enchantment. 3 An irresistible power or fascination. [< OE, story]

spell[3] (spel) *n.* 1 *Informal* A period of time, usu. of short duration. 2 *Informal* A continuing type of weather. 3 *Informal* A short distance. 4 *Informal* A fit of illness, debility, etc. 5 A turn of duty in relief of another. 6 A period of work or employment. —*v.t.* 1 To relieve temporarily from some work or duty. 2 *Austral.* To give a rest to, as a horse. —*v.i.* 3 *Austral.* To take a rest. [< OE *gespelia* a substitute]

spell·bind (spel′bīnd′) *v.t.* **·bound, ·bind·ing** To bind or enthrall, as if by a spell. —**spell′bind·er** *n.*

spell·bound (spel′bound′) *adj.* Enthralled or fascinated by or as by a spell. —**Syn.** astonished, amazed, aghast, agog, bewitched, enchanted, charmed.

spell·er (spel′ər) *n.* 1 One who spells. 2 A spelling book.

spell·ing (spel′ing) *n.* 1 The act of one who spells. 2 The art of correct spelling; orthography. 3 The way in which a word is spelled.

spelling bee A spelling competition.

spelt[1] (spelt) A *p.t.* & *p.p.* of SPELL[1].

spelt[2] (spelt) *n.* A species of wheat. [< OE]

spe·lun·ker (spē·lung′kər) *n.* An enthusiast in the exploration and study of caves; a speleologist. [< L *spelunca* a cave]

spend (spend) *v.* **spent, spend·ing** *v.t.* 1 To pay out or disburse (money). 2 To expend by degrees; use up. 3 To apply or devote, as thought or effort, to some activity, purpose, etc. 4 To pass: to *spend* one's life in jail. 5 To use wastefully; squander. —*v.i.* 6 To pay out or disburse money, etc. [< OE *aspendan*] —**spend′er** *n.*

spend·thrift (spend′thrift′) *n.* One who is wastefully lavish of money. —*adj.* Excessively lavish; prodigal.

spent (spent) *p.t.* & *p.p.* of SPEND. —*adj.* 1 Worn out or exhausted. 2 Deprived of force.

sperm[1] (spûrm) *n.* 1 The male fertilizing fluid; semen. 2 A male reproductive cell; spermatozoon. [< Gk. *sperma* a seed]

sperm[2] (spûrm) *n.* 1 SPERM WHALE. 2 SPERMACETI. 3 SPERM OIL.

-sperm *combining form Bot.* A seed (of a specified kind): *gymnosperm.* [< Gk. *sperma* a seed]

sper·ma·ce·ti (spûr′mə·sē′tē, -set′ē) *n.* A white, waxy substance separated from the oil contained in the head of the sperm whale, used for making candles, ointments, etc. [< L *sperma ceti* seed of a whale]

sper·mat·ic (spûr·mat′ik) *adj.* Of or pertaining to sperm or the male sperm-producing gland.

sper·ma·to·phyte (spûr′mə·tə·fīt′) *n.* Any seed-bearing plant; an angiosperm or a gymnosperm. [< Gk. *sperma* seed + *phylos* plant] —**sper′ma·to·phyt′ic** (-fit′ik) *adj.*

sper·ma·to·zo·on (spûr′mə·tə·zō′on) *n. pl.* **·zo·a** (-zō′ə) A male reproductive cell of an animal, which carries half the complement of genetic material normal for its species. [< Gk. *sperma* seed + *zōion* an animal] —**sper′ma·to·zo′al, sper′ma·to·zo′an, sper′ma·to·zo′ic** *adj.*

sperm oil A pale yellow lubricating oil obtained from the sperm whale.

sperm whale A large, toothed whale of warm seas, having a huge truncate head containing a reservoir of sperm oil.

Sperm whale

spew (spyo͞o) *v.i.* 1 To throw up; vomit. 2 To come or issue forth. —*v.t.* 1 To throw up; vomit. 2 To eject or send forth. —*n.* That which is spewed. [< OE *spīwan*]

sp. gr. specific gravity.

sphag·num (sfag′nəm) *n.* 1 Any of a genus of whitish gray mosses; peat moss. 2 This moss in dried form, used by florists for potting plants, etc. [< Gk. *sphagnos* kind of moss] —**sphag′nous** *adj.*

sphe·noid (sfē′noid) *n.* An irregular, wedge-shaped bone forming part of the orbit. —*adj.* Wedge-shaped. [< Gk. *sphēn* wedge] —**sphe·noi·dal** (sfi·noid′l) *adj.* • See SKULL.

sphere (sfir) *n.* 1 A round body in which every point on its surface is equidistant from the center; globe. 2 A planet, sun, star, etc. 3 CELESTIAL SPHERE. 4 The apparent outer dome of the sky. 5 The field or place of activity, experience, influence, etc.; scope; province. 6 Social rank or position. —*v.t.* **sphered, spher·ing** 1 To place in or as in a sphere; encircle. 2 To set among the celestial spheres. 3 To make spherical. [< Gk. *sphaira* a ball]

-sphere *combining form* Denoting an enveloping spherical mass: *atmosphere.*

spher·i·cal (sfer′i·kəl) *adj.* 1 Shaped like a sphere; globular. 2 Pertaining to a sphere or spheres. Also **spher′ic.** —**spher′i·cal·ly** *adv.* —**spher′i·cal·ness** *n.*

sphe·roid (sfir′oid) *n.* A body having approximately the form of a sphere; an ellipsoid. —**sphe·roi′dal** (sfi·roid′l), **sphe·roi′dic** or **·di·cal** *adj.* —**sphe·roi′dal·ly** *adv.*

sphinc·ter (sfingk′tər) *n. Anat.* A ring of muscle serving to open and close an opening in the body. [< Gk. *sphingein* to close] —**sphinc′ter·al** *adj.*

sphinx (sfingks) *n. pl.* **sphinx·es** or **sphin·ges** (sfin′jēz) 1 *Egypt. Myth* A wingless monster with a lion's body and the head of a man, a ram, or a hawk. 2 *Gk. Myth. Usu. cap.* A winged monster with a woman's head and breasts and a lion's body, that destroyed those unable to guess her riddle. 3 A mysterious or enigmatical person. [< Gk.]

Sphinx *def. 2*

sphyg·mo·ma·nom·e·ter (sfig′mō·mə·nom′ə·tər) *n.* An instrument for measuring blood pressure. Also **sphyg·mom′e·ter** (-mom′ə·tər). [< Gk. *sphygmos* pulse + MANOMETER]

spi·cate (spī′kāt) *adj.* 1 Arranged in spikes: said of flowers. 2 Having a spur, as the legs of some birds. Also **spi′·cat·ed.** [< L *spica* spike]

spice (spīs) *n.* 1 An aromatic vegetable substance, as cinnamon, cloves, etc., used for flavoring. 2 Such substances collectively. 3 That which gives zest or adds interest. 4 An aromatic odor; an agreeable perfume. —*v.t.* **spiced, spic·ing** 1 To season with spice. 2 To add zest or piquancy to. [< L *species* kind] —**spic′er** *n.*

spice·bush (spīs′bo͝osh′) *n.* An aromatic deciduous shrub related to laurel. Also **spice′wood′** (-wo͝od′).

spick-and-span (spik′ən·span′) *adj.* 1 Neat and clean. 2 Perfectly new, or looking as if new. Also **spic′-and-span′.** [Var. of SPIKE[1] + ON *spānn* chip]

spic·ule (spik′yōōl) *n.* 1 A small, slender, sharp-pointed body; a spikelet. 2 *Zool.* One of the small, hard, needlelike growths supporting the soft tissues of certain invertebrates, as sponges. Also **spic·u·la** (spik′yə·lə). [< L *spicum* point, spike] **—spic′u·lar, spic′u·late** (-lāt, -lit) *adj.*

spic·u·lum (spik′yə·ləm) *n. pl.* **·la** (-lə) 1 SPICULE. 2 *Zool.* A small, pointed organ, as a spine of a sea urchin. [L]

spic·y (spī′sē) *adj.* **spic·i·er, spic·i·est** 1 Containing, flavored, or fragrant with spices. 2 Producing spices. 3 Full of spirit and zest; lively. 4 Somewhat improper or risqué. **—spic′i·ly** *adv.* **—spic′i·ness** *n.*

spi·der (spī′dər) *n.* 1 Any of numerous wingless arachnids capable of spinning silk into webs for the capture of prey. 2 A long-handled iron frying pan, often having legs. 3 Any of various devices with radiating, leglike projections. [< OE *spīthra*] **—spi′der·y** *adj.*

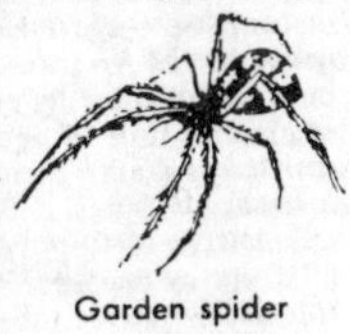

Garden spider

spider crab Any of various ocean crabs with long legs and spiny growths on the carapace.

spider monkey An arboreal Central and South American monkey with very long, slender limbs and a long prehensile tail.

spi·der·wort (spī′dər·wûrt′) *n.* Any of several plants with grasslike leaves and usu. blue, three-petaled flowers.

spiel (spēl) *Slang n.* An informal but purposeful speech or talk, usu. rehearsed, as by a politician or salesman. —*v.i.* To deliver a spiel. [< G *spielen* to play]

spi·er (spī′ər) *n.* One who spies.

spif·fy (spif′ē) *adj.* **·fi·er, ·fi·est** *Slang* Smartly dressed; spruce. **—spif′fi·ness** *n.* [?]

spig·ot (spig′ət, spik′-) *n.* 1 A plug for the bunghole of a cask. 2 A turning plug or valve fitting into a faucet; also, the faucet itself. [ME *spigote*]

spike[1] (spīk) *n.* 1 A very large, thick nail. 2 A slender, pointed piece of metal, as used along the top of an iron fence. 3 A projecting, pointed piece of metal in the soles of shoes to keep the wearer from slipping. 4 A very high, slender heel on a woman's shoe. 5 A straight, unbranched antler, as of a young deer. —*v.t.* **spiked, spik·ing** 1 To fasten with spikes. 2 To set or provide with spikes. 3 To block; put a stop to. 4 To pierce with or impale on a spike. 5 *Informal* To add alcoholic liquor to. [ME] **—spik′er** *n.* **—spik′y** *adj.*

spike[2] (spīk) *n.* 1 An ear of corn, barley, wheat, or other grain. 2 *Bot.* A flower cluster in which the flowers are closely attached to the stalk. [< L *spica* ear of grain]

spike·let (spīk′lit) *n. Bot.* A small spike.

spike·nard (spīk′nərd, -närd) *n.* 1 An ancient fragrant and costly ointment. 2 A perennial East Indian herb of the valerian family yielding this ointment. [< L *spica* spike + *nardus* nard]

spile (spīl) *n.* 1 A large timber or stake driven into the ground as a foundation; a pile. 2 A wooden spigot or plug used in a cask. 3 A spout driven into a sugar-maple tree to lead the sap to a bucket. —*v.t.* **spiled, spil·ing** 1 To pierce for and provide with a spile. 2 To drive spiles into. [< MDu., skewer]

spill[1] (spil) *v.* **spilled** or **spilt, spill·ing** *v.t.* 1 To allow or cause to fall or run out or over, as a liquid or a powder. 2 To shed, as blood. 3 *Naut.* To empty (a sail) of wind. 4 *Informal* To cause to fall, as from a horse. 5 *Informal* To divulge; make known, as a secret. —*v.i.* 6 To fall or run out or over: said of liquids, etc. —*n.* 1 The act of spilling. 2 That which is spilled. 3 *Informal* A fall to the ground, as from a horse or vehicle. 4 SPILLWAY. [< OE *spillan* destroy] **—spill′age, spill′er** *n.*

spill[2] (spil) *n.* 1 A slip of wood, or rolled strip of paper, used for lighting lamps, etc. 2 A splinter. 3 A slender peg, pin, or bar of wood, esp. for stopping up a hole. [Var. of SPILE[1]]

spill·way (spil′wā′) *n.* 1 A passageway in or about a dam to release the water in a reservoir. 2 The paved upper surface of a dam over which surplus water escapes.

spilt (spilt) A *pt. & p.p.* of SPILL[1].

spin (spin) *v.* **spun, spin·ning** *v.t.* 1 To draw out and twist into threads; also, to draw out and twist fiber into (threads, yarn, etc.). 2 To make or produce (a web or cocoon) as if by spinning. 3 To tell, as a story or yarn. 4 To protract; prolong, as a story by additional details: with *out.* 5 To cause to whirl rapidly. —*v.i.* 6 To make thread or yarn. 7 To extrude filaments of a viscous substance from the body: said of spiders, etc. 8 To whirl rapidly; rotate. 9 To seem to be whirling, as from dizziness. 10 To move rapidly. —*n.* 1 An act or instance of spinning. 2 A rapid whirling. 3 Any rapid movement or action. 4 A ride, as in an automobile. 5 The uncontrolled, spiral descent of an airplane after a stall. [< OE *spinnan*]

spin·ach (spin′ich) *n.* 1 An edible garden plant of the goosefoot family. 2 Its edible leaves. [< Ar. *isbānah*]

spi·nal (spī′nəl) *adj.* 1 Of or pertaining to the spine or spinal cord. 2 Of or pertaining to spines or a spiny process.

spinal column A series of hollow, articulated bones that enclose the spinal cord and form the axis of the skeleton of a vertebrate animal.

spinal cord The thick, soft cord of nerve tissue enclosed by the spinal column.

spin·dle (spin′dəl) *n.* 1 In hand spinning, a notched, tapered rod used to twist into thread the fibers pulled from the distaff. 2 The slender rod in a spinning wheel by the rotation of which the thread is twisted and wound on a spool or bobbin on the same rod. 3 A small rod or pin bearing the bobbin of a spinning machine. 4 A rotating rod, pin, axis, arbor, or shaft, esp. when small and bearing something that rotates: the *spindle* of a lathe. 5 The tapering end of a vehicle axle that enters the hub. 6 A small shaft passing through the lock of a door and bearing the knobs or handles. 7 Any decorative, often tapered rod, used in the back of a chair, etc. 8 A needlelike rod mounted on a weighted base, for impaling bills, checks, etc. —*v.* **·dled, ·dling** *v.i.* 1 To grow into a long, slender stalk or body. —*v.t.* 2 To form into or as into a spindle. 3 To provide with a spindle. [< OE *spinel*]

spin·dle-leg·ged (spin′dəl·leg′id, -legd′) *adj.* Having long, slender legs. Also **spin′dle-shanked′** (-shangkt′).

spin·dle-legs (spin′dəl·legz′) *n.* 1 Long, slender legs. 2 *Informal* A person having long, slender legs. Also **spin′·dle-shanks′** (-shangks′).

spin·dling (spind′ling) *adj.* SPINDLY.

spin·dly (spind′lē) *adj.* **·dli·er, ·dli·est** Of a slender, lanky growth or form, suggesting weakness.

spin·drift (spin′drift) *n.* Blown spray or scud. [Var. of SPOONDRIFT]

spine (spīn) *n.* 1 SPINAL COLUMN. 2 Any of various hard, pointed outgrowths on the bodies of certain animals, as the porcupine and starfish. 3 A thorny projection on the stems of certain plants, as the cactus. 4 The back of a bound book. 5 A projecting eminence or ridge. [< L *spina* spine, thorn]

spi·nel (spi·nel′, spin′əl) *n.* Any of various hard minerals, a red variety, the **ruby spinel,** being used as a gem. [< Ital. *spina* thorn]

spine·less (spīn′lis) *adj.* 1 Having no spine or backbone; invertebrate. 2 Lacking spines. 3 Having a very flexible backbone; limp. 4 Weak-willed; irresolute. **—spine′less·ness** *n.*

spin·et (spin′it) *n.* 1 A small harpsichord. 2 A small upright piano. 3 A small electronic organ. [< Ital. *spinetta*]

spin·na·ker (spin′ə·kər) *n. Naut.* A large jib-shaped sail set on the mainmast of a racing vessel, opposite the mainsail, and used when sailing before the wind. [?]

spin·ner (spin′ər) *n.* 1 One who or that which spins, as a spider or a machine. 2 In angling, a whirling spoon bait.

spin·ner·et (spin′ə·ret′) *n.* 1 An organ, as of spiders and silkworms, for spinning their silky threads. 2 A metal plate pierced with holes through which filaments of plastic material are forced, as in the making of rayon fibers.

spin·ning (spin′ing) *n.* 1 The action of converting fibers into thread or yarn. **2** The product of spinning. *—adj.* That spins or is used in the process of spinning.

spinning jenny A machine for spinning more than one strand of yarn at a time.

spinning wheel A former household implement for spinning yarn or thread, consisting of a rotating spindle operated by a treadle and flywheel.

Spinning wheel

spin-off (spin′ôf′, -of′) *n.* **1** A secondary product, application, or result derived from another product or activity; by-product: industrial *spin-offs* from military technological research. **2** The distribution by a corporation to its stockholders of stocks or assets obtained from a subsidiary company. Also **spin′off′.**

spi·nose (spī′nōs) *adj.* Bearing, armed with, or having spines. Also **spi·nous** (-nəs). **—spi′nose·ly** *adv.* **—spi·nos′i·ty** (-nos′ə·tē) *n.*

spin·ster (spin′stər) *n.* **1** A woman who has never married, esp. an elderly one. **2** A woman who spins; a spinner. [< SPIN + -STER] **—spin′ster·hood** *n.* **—spin′ster·ish** *adj.*

spin·y (spī′nē) *adj.* **spin·i·er, spin·i·est 1** Having spines; thorny. **2** Difficult; perplexing. **—spin′i·ness** *n.*

spiny anteater ECHIDNA.

spir·a·cle (spir′ə·kəl, spī′rə-) *n.* **1** Any of numerous external openings through which air enters the tracheae of insects, etc. **2** The blowhole of a cetacean. [< L *spiraculum* airhole]

spi·ral (spī′rəl) *adj.* **1** Winding about and constantly receding from or advancing toward a center. **2** Winding and advancing; helical. **3** Winding and rising in a spire, as some springs. **4** Continuously increasing or developing. *—n.* **1** *Geom.* Any plane curve formed by a point that moves around a fixed center at a distance that is always increasing. **2** A curve winding like a screw thread. **3** Something wound as a spiral or having a spiral shape. **4** A continuously developing increase or decrease: price *spirals.* *—v.* **·raled** or **·ralled, ·ral·ing** or **·ral·ling** *v.t.* **1** To cause to take a spiral form or course. *—v.i.* **2** To take a spiral form or course. **3** To increase or decrease continuously or sharply, as prices, costs, etc. [< L *spira* coil] **—spi′ral·ly** *adv.* • The use of the intransitive verb (def. 3) without any accompanying modifier almost always means "to increase," as *Prices spiraled in June.* If "to decrease" is meant, an adverb should be used to prevent ambiguity, as *Prices spiraled downward in June.*

spi·rant (spī′rənt) *n.* & *adj.* *Phonet.* FRICATIVE. [< L *spirare* breathe]

spire (spīr) *n.* **1** The tapering or pyramidal roof of a tower; also, a steeple. **2** A slender stalk or blade. **3** The summit or tapering end of anything. *—v.* **spired, spir·ing** *v.t.* **1** To furnish with a spire or spires. *—v.i.* **2** To shoot or point up in or as in a spire. **3** To put forth a spire or spires; sprout. [< OE *spīr* stem] **—spired** *adj.*

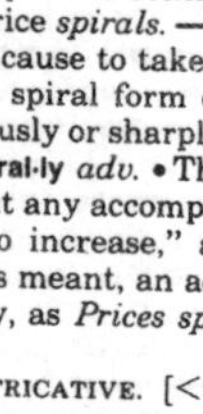

Spire

spi·re·a (spī·rē′a) *n.* Any of a genus of ornamental shrubs of the rose family, having small, white or pink flowers. Also **spi·rae′a.** [< Gk. *speira* coil]

spir·it (spir′it) *n.* **1** The animating principle of life and energy in man and animals. **2** SOUL (def. 1). **3** That part of a human being characterized by intelligence, emotion, will, etc.; the mind. **4 a** A supernatural being without a material body, as an angel, demon, etc. **b** Such a being regarded as having a certain character, abode, etc.: an evil *spirit.* **c** A supernatural being regarded as having a visible form, power of speech, etc.; ghost; specter. **5** A state of mind; mood; disposition: low *spirits.* **6** Vivacity, energy, courage, positiveness, etc.: to have *spirit.* **7** A characteristic or prevailing feeling, attitude, motivation, quality, etc.: in the *spirit* of fun; the *spirit* of the Reformation. **8** A person regarded with reference to any specific activity, characteristic, or temper: a blithe *spirit.* **9** True intent or meaning: the *spirit* of the law. **10** Ardent loyalty or devotion: school *spirit.* **11** *pl.* A strong alcoholic liquor or liquid obtained by distillation. **12** *Usu. pl.* A distilled extract: *spirits* of turpentine. **13** *Usu. pl.* A solution of a volatile principle in alcohol; essence: *spirits* of ammonia. **—the Spirit** HOLY GHOST. *—v.t.* **1** To carry off secretly or mysteriously: with *away, off,* etc. **2** To infuse with spirit or animation; inspirit. *—adj.* **1** Of or pertaining to ghosts or disembodied entities. **2** Operated by the burning of alcohol: a *spirit* lamp. [< L *spiritus* breathing, breath of a god]

spir·it·ed (spir′it·id) *adj.* **1** Full of spirit; lively; animated. **2** Having a specific characteristic, temper, etc.: *high-spirited, mean-spirited.* **—spir′it·ed·ly** *adv.* **—spir′it·ed·ness** *n.*

spir·it·less (spir′it·lis) *adj.* Lacking enthusiasm, energy, or courage. **—spir′it·less·ly** *adv.* **—spir′it·less·ness** *n.*

spirit level An instrument for indicating the horizontal or perpendicular by reference to the position of a bubble of air in a tube of liquid.

spir·it·ous (spir′i·təs) *adj.* SPIRITUOUS.

spir·i·tu·al (spir′i·chōō·əl, -ich·əl) *adj.* **1** Of or pertaining to spirit, as distinguished from matter. **2** Of or consisting of spirit; incorporeal. **3** Of, pertaining to, or affecting the highest or purest moral or intellectual qualities of man; not earthly or sensual. **4** Sacred or religious; not lay or temporal. **5** Supernatural. *—n.* **1** Anything pertaining to spirit or to sacred matters. **2** A religious folk song originating among the Negroes of the s U.S. **—spir′i·tu·al′i·ty, spir′i·tu·al·ness** *n.* **—spir′i·tu·al·ly** *adv.* **—Syn.** *adj.* **3** otherworldly, unworldly, unearthly, pure, heavenly, angelic.

spir·i·tu·al·ism (spir′i·chōō·əl·iz′əm) *n.* **1** The belief that the spirits of the dead can communicate with the living, usu. through the agency of a person called a medium. **2** *Usu. cap.* A religious movement based on this belief. **3** A philosophy that identifies ultimate reality as basically spiritual. **—spir′i·tu·al·ist** *n.* **—spir′i·tu·al·is′tic** *adj.*

spir·i·tu·al·ize (spir′i·chōō·əl·īz′, -ich·ə·līz′) *v.t.* **·ized, ·iz·ing 1** To make spiritual. **2** To treat as having a spiritual meaning or sense. *Brit. sp.* **·ise.** **—spir′i·tu·al·i·za′tion, spir′i·tu·al·iz′er** *n.*

spir·i·tu·el (spir′i·chōō·el′, *Fr.* spē·rē·tü·el′) *adj.* Characterized by esprit, or wit, and by the higher and finer qualities of the mind generally. [F] **—spir′i·tu·elle′** *adj. Fem.*

spir·i·tu·ous (spir′i·chōō·əs, -ich·əs, -ət·əs) *adj.* Containing alcohol, esp. distilled alcohol. **—spir′i·tu·ous·ness** *n.*

spiro- *combining form* Spiral; coiled: *spirochete.* [< Gk. *speira* a coil]

spi·ro·chete (spī′rə·kēt) *n.* **1** Any of a genus of spiral-shaped bacteria usu. found in water. **2** Any similar microorganisms including those which cause syphilis, yaws, etc. Also **spi′ro·chaete.** [< Gk. *speira* coil + *chaitē* bristle] **—spi′ro·che′tal** *adj.* • See BACTERIUM.

spirt (spûrt) *n.* & *v.* SPURT.

spit[1] (spit) *v.* **spat** or **spit, spit·ting** *v.t.* **1** To eject (saliva, blood, etc.) from the mouth. **2** To throw off, eject, or utter by or as if by spitting: often with *out:* to *spit* out an oath. **3** To light, as a fuse. *—v.i.* **4** To eject saliva from the mouth. **5** To make a hissing noise, as an angry cat. **6** To fall in scattered drops or flakes, as rain or snow. **—spit on** *Informal* To treat with contempt. *—n.* **1** Spittle; saliva. **2** An act of spitting or expectorating. **3** A frothy, spitlike secretion of a spittle insect; also, a spittle insect. **4** A light, scattered fall of snow or rain. **5** *Informal* SPITTING IMAGE. [< OE *spittan*] **—spit′ter** *n.*

spit[2] (spit) *n.* **1** A pointed rod on which meat is skewered and roasted before a fire. **2** A point of low land, or a long, narrow shoal, extending into the water. *—v.t.* **spit·ted, spit·ting** To transfix or impale with or as with a spit. [< OE *spitu*]

spit·ball (spit′bôl′) *n.* **1** Paper chewed in the mouth and shaped into a ball for use as a missile. **2** In baseball, an illegal pitch of a ball moistened on one side with saliva, etc.

spite (spīt) *n.* **1** Malicious bitterness or resentment, usu. resulting in mean or vicious acts. **2** That which is done in spite. **—in spite of** (or **spite of**) In defiance of; notwithstanding. *—v.t.* **spit·ed, spit·ing** To show one's spite toward; vex maliciously; thwart. [Short for DESPITE] **—spite′ful** *adj.* **—spite′ful·ly** *adv.* **—spite′ful·ness** *n.*

spit·fire (spit′fīr′) *n.* A quick-tempered person.
spitting image *Informal* An exact likeness or counterpart. Also **spit and image.**
spit·tle (spit′l) *n.* 1 SALIVA. 2 SPIT[1] *n.* (def. 3). [< OE *spātl*]
spittle insect Any of various jumping insects whose nymphs excrete frothy matter.
spit·toon (spi·to͞on′) *n.* A receptacle for spit; a cuspidor.
spitz (spitz) *n.* One of a breed of small dogs with a tapering muzzle; a Pomeranian. Also **spitz dog.** [G, pointed]
spiv (spiv) *n. Brit. Informal* A flashy chiseler, sharper, or one who lives by his wits. [?]
splash (splash) *v.t.* 1 To dash or spatter (a liquid, etc.) about. 2 To spatter, wet, or soil with a liquid dashed about. 3 To make with splashes: to *splash* one's way. 4 To decorate or mark with or as with splashed colors. 5 To display prominently: His name was *splashed* all over the front page. —*v.i.* 6 To make a splash or splashes. 7 To move, fall, or strike with a splash or splashes. —*n.* 1 The act or noise of splashing liquid. 2 Something splashed, as a spot of liquid. 3 A small area or spot of color, light, etc. 4 A small amount; dash: a *splash* of bitters. 5 A brilliant or ostentatious display. —**make a splash** *Informal* To attract notice or become conspicuous, usu. briefly. [Var. of PLASH]—**splash′er** *n.* —**splash′y** *adj.* (**·i·er, ·i·est**)
splash·down (splash′doun′) *n.* The landing of a spacecraft, or a part of it, in the seas following its flight.
splat (splat) *n.* A thin, broad piece of wood, as that forming the middle of a chair back. [?]
splat·ter (splat′ər) *v.t. & v.i.* To spatter or splash. —*n.* A spatter; splash. [Blend of SPLASH and SPATTER]
splay (splā) *adj.* 1 Spread or turned outward. 2 Clumsily formed; ungainly. —*n. Archit.* A slanted surface or beveled edge. —*v.t.* 1 To make with a splay. 2 To open to sight; spread out. —*v.i.* 3 To spread out; open. 4 To slant; slope. [Var. of DISPLAY]
splay·foot (splā′fo͝ot′) *n.* 1 Abnormal flatness and turning outward of a foot or feet. 2 A foot so affected. —**splay′·foot′ed** *adj.*
spleen (splēn) *n. Anat.* 1 A highly vascular, ductless organ near the stomach of most vertebrates, which modifies, filters, and stores blood. 2 Ill temper; spitefulness: to vent one's *spleen.* [< Gk. *splēn*]
spleen·ful (splēn′fəl) *adj.* Irritable; peevish; ill-tempered. Also **spleen′ish, spleen′y.** —**spleen′ful·ly** *adv.*
splen·did (splen′did) *adj.* 1 Magnificent; imposing. 2 Conspicuously great or illustrious; glorious: a *splendid* achievement. 3 Giving out or reflecting brilliant light; shining. 4 *Informal* Very good; excellent: a *splendid* offer. [< L *splendere* to shine] —**splen′did·ly** *adv.* —**splen′did·ness** *n.* —**Syn.** 1 majestic, dazzling, sublime, superb, grand. 2 outstanding, renowned, celebrated, marvelous.
splen·dif·er·ous (splen·dif′ər·əs) *adj. Informal* Exhibiting great splendor; very magnificent: a facetious usage.
splen·dor (splen′dər) *n.* 1 Exceeding brillance or brightness. 2 Magnificence; greatness; grandeur. *Brit. sp.* **·dour.** —**splen′dor·ous, splen′drous** *adj.*
sple·net·ic (spli·net′ik) *adj.* Fretfully spiteful; peevish; irritable. —*n.* A peevish person. —**sple·net′i·cal·ly** *adv.*
splen·ic (splen′ik, splē′nik) *adj.* Of or pertaining to the spleen.
splice (splīs) *v.t.* **spliced, splic·ing** 1 To unite, as two ropes or parts of a rope, so as to form one continuous piece, by intertwining the strands. 2 To connect, as timbers, by beveling, scarfing, or overlapping at the ends. 3 *Slang* To join in marriage. —*n.* A joining or joint made by splicing. [< MDu. *splissen*] —**splic′er** *n.*

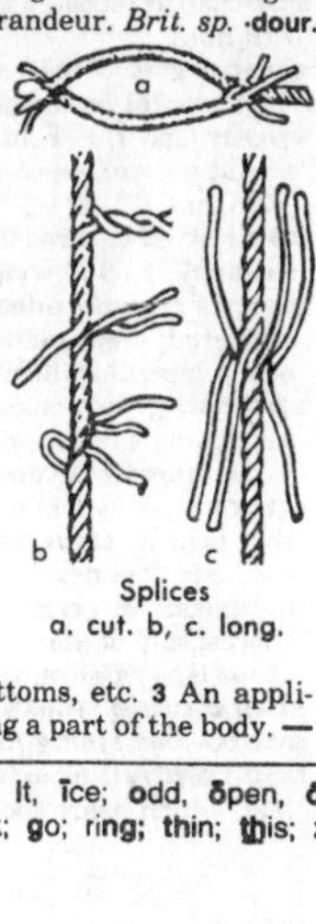

Splices
a. cut. b, c. long.

splint (splint) *n.* 1 SPLINTER. 2 A thin, flexible strip of split wood used for basket-making, chair bottoms, etc. 3 An appliance for supporting or immobilizing a part of the body. —*v.t.* To confine, support, or brace, as a fractured limb, with or as with splints. [< MDu. *splinte*]
splin·ter (splin′tər) *n.* 1 A thin, sharp piece of wood, glass, metal, etc., split or torn off lengthwise; a sliver. 2 SPLINTER GROUP. —*v.t. & v.i.* 1 To split into thin sharp pieces or fragments; shatter; shiver. 2 To separate into smaller groups or factions. [< MDu.] —**splin′ter·y** *adj.*
splinter group A group or faction that has broken away from a parent group or organization, usu. because of disagreements.
split (split) *v.* **split, split·ting** *v.t.* 1 To separate into two or more parts by or as by force. 2 To break or divide lengthwise or along the grain. 3 To divide or separate: The mountains *split* the state down the middle. 4 To divide and distribute by portions or shares. 5 To divide into groups or factions. 6 To cast (a vote) for candidates of different parties. 7 To act upon as if by splitting or breaking: Thunder *split* the air. —*v.i.* 8 To break apart or divide lengthwise or along the grain. 9 To become divided through disagreement, etc. 10 To share something with others. 11 *Slang* To leave quickly or abruptly. —**split off** 1 To break off by splitting. 2 To separate by or as by splitting. —**split up** 1 To separate into parts and distribute. 2 To cease association; separate. —*n.* 1 The act of splitting. 2 The result of splitting, as a crack, tear, rent, etc. 3 A separation into factions or groups, usu. because of disagreements. 4 A sliver; splinter. 5 A share or portion, as of loot or booty. 6 A small, usu. six-ounce, bottle of wine, soft drink, etc. 7 A wooden strip, as of osier, used in weaving baskets. 8 A confection made of a sliced banana, ice cream, syrup, chopped nuts, and whipped cream. 9 A single thickness of a skin or hide split horizontally. 10 In bowling, the position of two or more pins left standing on such spots that a spare is nearly impossible. 11 An acrobatic trick in which the legs are fully extended to the front and back and at right angles to the body. 12 *Slang* A quick departure. —*adj.* 1 Divided or separated longitudinally or along the grain. 2 Divided, as to agreement, unanimity, etc.: a *split* ballot; a *split* decision. [< MDu. *splitten*] —**split′ter** *n.*
split infinitive A verbal phrase in which the sign of the infinitive "to" is separated from its verb by an intervening word, usu. an adverb, as in "to quickly return." • Although this construction is often condemned by purists, it is sometimes justified to avoid ambiguity or awkwardness.
split-lev·el (split′lev′əl) *adj.* Designating a type of dwelling in which the floors of adjoining parts are at different levels, connected by short flights of stairs. —*n.* A split-level dwelling.
split pea A dried, hulled pea that has split naturally into two parts, used mainly for soup.
split personality A psychological condition in which a person intermittently exhibits traits, mannerisms, attitudes, etc., of two or more unrelated personalities.
split second A very small instant of time. —**split′-sec′·ond** *adj.*
split ticket A ballot on which the voter has distributed his vote among candidates of different parties.
split·ting (split′ing) *adj.* Acute or extreme in kind or degree: a *splitting* headache.
splotch (sploch) *n.* A spot or daub, as of ink, etc. —*v.t.* To soil or mark with a splotch or splotches. [?] —**splotch′y** *adj.*
splurge (splûrj) *Informal n.* 1 An ostentatious display. 2 An extravagant expenditure. —*v.i.* **splurged, splurg·ing** 1 To show off; be ostentatious. 2 To spend money lavishly or wastefully. [?]
splut·ter (splut′ər) *v.i.* 1 To make a series of slight, explosive sounds, or throw off small particles, as meat frying in fat. 2 To speak hastily, confusedly, or incoherently, as from surprise or indignation. —*v.t.* 3 To utter excitedly or confused; sputter. 4 To spatter or bespatter. —*n.* A spluttering noise or utterance. [Blend of SPLASH and SPUTTER] —**splut′ter·er** *n.*
spoil (spoil) *v.* **spoiled** or **spoilt, spoil·ing** *v.t.* 1 To impair or destroy the value, usefulness, beauty, enjoyment, etc., of.

2 To weaken or impair the character or personality of, esp. by overindulgence. —*v.i.* 3 To lose normal or useful qualities; specifically, to become tainted or decayed, as food. —*n.* 1 *Usu. pl.* Plunder seized by violence; booty; loot. 2 *Usu. pl.* The jobs in government awarded by a winning political party to its faithful supporters. 3 An object of plunder. 4 Material removed in digging. [< L *spolium* booty] —**spoil'er** *n.* —**Syn.** *v.* 1 damage, injure, harm, mar, mutilate, disfigure, maim, botch, bungle. 2 indulge, humor. 3 decay, decompose, mold, rot, putrefy.

spoil·age (spoi'lij) *n.* 1 The act or process of spoiling. 2 Something spoiled. 3 Waste or loss due to spoilage.

spoils·man (spoilz'mən) *n. pl.* **·men** (-mən) One who works for a political party for spoils.

spoil·sport (spoil'spôrt', -spōrt') *n.* A person who spoils the pleasures of others.

spoils system The practice of giving public offices or other awards to supporters of a victorious political party.

spoke[1] (spōk) *n.* 1 One of the members of a wheel which brace the rim by connecting it to the hub. 2 One of the radial handles of a ship's steering wheel. 3 A rung of a ladder. —*v.t.* **spoked, spok·ing** To provide with spokes. [< OE *spāca*]

spoke[2] (spōk) *p.t.* & a *p.p.* of SPEAK.

spo·ken (spō'kən) *p.p.* of SPEAK. —*adj.* 1 Uttered as opposed to written. 2 Having a specified kind of speech: *smooth-spoken.*

spoke·shave (spōk'shāv') *n.* A wheelwright's tool having a blade set between two handles, used with a drawing motion in rounding and smoothing wooden surfaces.

spokes·man (spōks'mən) *n. pl.* **·men** (-mən) One who speaks in the name and on behalf of another or others. —**spokes'wom'an** (-wo͝om'ən) *n. Fem.*

spo·li·a·tion (spō'lē·ā'shən) *n.* 1 The act of plundering or robbing. 2 The act of spoiling or damaging. [< L *spoliare* despoil] —**spo'li·a'tor** *n.*

spon·dee (spon'dē) *n.* A metrical foot consisting of two long or accented syllables. [< Gk. *spondeios (pous)* libation (meter)] —**spon·da'ic** (-dā'ik) *adj.*

sponge (spunj) *n.* 1 Any of a phylum of plantlike animals having a fibrous skeleton and growing underwater in large colonies. 2 The light, porous, extremely absorbent skeleton of such animals, used for bathing, cleaning, etc. 3 Any of various absorbent substances or materials used to clean, soak up liquids, etc. 4 Leavened dough. 5 A porous mass of metal, as platinum. 6 *Informal* SPONGER (def. 3). —**throw** (or **toss**) **up** (or **in**) **the sponge** *Informal* To yield; give up; abandon the struggle. —*v.* **sponged, spong·ing** *v.t.* 1 To wipe, wet, or clean with a sponge. 2 To wipe out; expunge; erase. 3 To absorb; suck in, as a sponge does. 4 *Informal* To get by imposing or at another's expense. —*v.i.* 5 To be absorbent. 6 To gather or fish for sponges. 7 *Informal* To be a sponger (def. 3): often with *off* or *on.* [< OE < Gk. *spongos*] —**spong'i·ness** *n.* —**spong'y** *adj.*

sponge cake A light cake of sugar, eggs, flour, etc., but containing no shortening.

spong·er (spun'jər) *n.* 1 One who uses a sponge, as for cleaning, etc. 2 A person or vessel that gathers sponges. 3 *Informal* A person who obtains something from others by taking advantage of their generosity, good nature, etc.

spon·son (spon'sən) *n.* 1 A curved projection from the hull of a vessel or seaplane, to increase its stability or surface area. 2 A similar protuberance on a ship or tank, for storage purposes or for the training of a gun. 3 An air tank built into the side of a canoe, to improve stability and prevent sinking. [?]

spon·sor (spon'sər) *n.* 1 A person who acts as surety for another, as in a loan, debt, etc. 2 A person or group who helps establish or finance something, as a club, activity, etc. 3 GODPARENT. 4 A business firm or enterprise that assumes all or part of the costs of a radio or television program which advertises its product or service. —*v.t.* To act as a sponsor for. [< L *spondere* to pledge] —**spon·so·ri·al** (spon·sôr'ē·əl, -sō'rē-) *adj.* —**spon'sor·ship** *n.*

spon·ta·ne·i·ty (spon'tə·nē'ə·tē, -nā-) *n. pl.* **·ties** 1 The state or quality of being spontaneous. 2 Something spontaneous, as an action, manner of behavior, etc.

spon·ta·ne·ous (spon·tā'nē·əs) *adj.* 1 Acting or arising naturally and without constraint from an inner impulse, prompting, or desire; not planned or contrived. 2 Apparently arising independently without external cause, stimulus, influence, or condition. 3 Produced without human labor; wild; indigenous. [< L *sponte* of free will] —**spon·ta'ne·ous·ly** *adv.* —**spon·ta'ne·ous·ness** *n.*

spontaneous combustion Ignition resulting from the accumulation of heat generated by slow oxidation.

spontaneous generation *Biol.* ABIOGENESIS.

spoof (spo͞of) *Informal v.t.* & *v.i.* 1 To deceive or hoax; joke. 2 To satirize in a good-natured manner. —*n.* 1 A deception; hoax. 2 A playful parody or satire. [< a game invented by A. Roberts, 1852-1933, English comedian]

spook (spo͝ok) *Informal n.* A ghost; apparition; specter. —*v.t.* 1 To haunt (a person or place). 2 To frighten, disturb, or annoy. 3 To startle or frighten (an animal) into flight, stampeding, etc. [< Du.] —**spook'ish** *adj.*

spook·y (spo͞o'kē) *adj.* **spook·i·er, spook·i·est** *Informal* 1 Of or like a spook; ghostly; eerie. 2 Frightened; nervous; skittish. —**spook'i·ly** *adv.* —**spook'i·ness** *n.*

spool (spo͞ol) *n.* 1 A cylinder having a projecting rim at each end, on which is wound thread, wire, etc., and a hole from one end to the other, as for mounting on a spindle. 2 The quantity of thread, wire, etc., held by a spool. 3 Anything resembling a spool in shape or purpose. —*v.t.* To wind on a spool. [< MLG *spole*]

spoon (spo͞on) *n.* 1 A utensil having a shallow, generally ovoid bowl and a handle, used in preparing, serving, or eating food. 2 Something resembling a spoon or its bowl. 3 A metallic lure attached to a fishing line: also **spoon bait.** 4 A wooden golf club with lofted face and comparatively short, stiff shaft. —*v.t.* 1 To lift up or out with a spoon. 2 To play or hit (a ball) with a weak shoving or scooping movement. —*v.i.* 3 To spoon a ball. 4 *Informal* To kiss and caress, as lovers. [< OE *spōn* chip]

spoon·bill (spo͞on'bil') *n.* 1 A wading bird related to the ibis, having a spoon-shaped bill. 2 A duck having the bill broad and flattened; a shoveler. —**spoon'-billed'** *adj.*

Spoonbill *def. 1*

spoon·drift (spo͞on'drift) *n.* SPINDRIFT. [< *spoon,* var. of SPUME + DRIFT]

spoon·er·ism (spo͞o'nə·riz'əm) *n.* The unintentional transposition of sounds or of parts of words in speaking, as in "half-*w*armed *f*ish" for "half-*f*ormed *w*ish". [< W. A. *Spooner,* 1844-1930, of New College, Oxford]

spoon·feed (spo͞on'fēd') *v.t.* **·fed, ·feed·ing** 1 To feed with a spoon. 2 To pamper; spoil. 3 To present (information) in such a manner that little or no thought, initiative, etc., is required of the recipient. 4 To instruct or inform (a person or group) in this manner.

spoon·ful (spo͞on'fo͝ol') *n. pl.* **·fuls** As much as a spoon will hold.

spoon·y (spo͞o'nē) *adj.* **spoon·i·er, spoon·i·est** *Informal* Sentimental or silly, as in lovemaking. Also **spoon'ey.**

spoor (spo͝or) *n.* Footprints, droppings, or other traces of a wild animal. —*v.t.* & *v.i.* To track by or follow a spoor. [< MDu.]

spo·rad·ic (spə·rad'ik) *adj.* 1 Occurring infrequently; occasional. 2 Not widely diffused; occurring in isolated cases: a *sporadic* infection. Also **spo·rad'i·cal.** [< Gk. *sporas* scattered] —**spo·rad'i·cal·ly** *adv.* —**spo·rad'i·cal·ness** *n.* —**Syn.** 1 irregular, fitful, spasmodic, intermittent.

spo·ran·gi·um (spô·ran'jē·əm, spō-) *n. pl.* **·gi·a** (-jē·ə) A sac or single cell in which spores are produced. [< SPOR(O)- + Gk. *angeion* a vessel] —**spo·ran'gi·al** *adj.*

spore (spôr, spōr) *n.* 1 The reproductive body in plants that bear no seeds, as bacteria, algae, ferns, etc. 2 A minute body that develops into a new individual; any minute organism; a germ. —*v.i.* **spored, spor·ing** To develop spores: said of plants. [< Gk. *spora* seed, sowing] —**spo·ra·ceous** (spô·rā'shəs, spō-) *adj.*

spore case SPORANGIUM.

sporo- *combining form* Seed; spore: *sporophyte.*

spo·ro·phyll (spôr'ə·fil, spō'rə-) *n.* A leaf, or modified leaf, which bears sporangia. Also **spo'ro·phyl.**

spo·ro·phyte (spôr′ə·fīt, spō′rə-) *n.* The spore-bearing generation in plants which have a distinct reproductive phase.

spor·ran (spor′ən, spôr′-) *n.* A skin pouch, usu. with the fur on, worn in front of the kilt by Highlanders. [< Scots Gaelic *sporan*] • See KILT.

sport (spôrt, spōrt) *n.* **1** A diversion; pastime. **2** A particular game or physical activity pursued for diversion, esp. an outdoor or athletic game, as baseball, football, track, tennis, swimming, etc. **3** A spirit of jesting or raillery. **4** An object of derision; a laughingstock; butt. **5** An animal or plant that exhibits sudden variation from the normal type; a mutation. **6** *Informal* A gambler. **7** *Informal* One who lives a fast, gay, or flashy life. **8** A person characterized by his observance of the rules of fair play, or by his ability to get along with others: a good *sport.* **9** *Archaic* Amorous or sexual play. —*v.i.* **1** To amuse oneself; play; frolic. **2** To participate in games. **3** To make sport or jest; trifle. **4** To vary suddenly or spontaneously from the normal type; mutate. **5** *Archaic & Regional* To make love, esp. in a trifling manner. —*v.t.* **6** *Informal* To display or wear ostentatiously. —*adj.* Of, pertaining to, or fitted for sports; also, appropriate for casual wear: a *sport* coat: also **sports.** [Var. of DISPORT] —**sport′ful** *adj.* —**sport′ful·ly** *adv.*

sport·ing (spôr′ting, spōr′-) *adj.* **1** Pertaining to, engaged in, or used in athletic games or field sports. **2** Characterized by or conforming to the spirit of sportsmanship. **3** Interested in or associated with gambling or betting. —**sport′ing·ly** *adv.*

sporting chance *Informal* A chance involving the likelihood of loss but also the possibility of success.

spor·tive (spôr′tiv, spōr′-) *adj.* **1** Relating to or fond of sport or play; frolicsome. **2** Interested in, active in, or related to sports. —**spor′tive·ly** *adv.* —**spor′tive·ness** *n.*

sports·man (spôrts′mən, spōrts′-) *n. pl.* **·men** (-mən) **1** One who pursues field sports, esp. hunting and fishing. **2** One who abides by a code of fair play. —**sports′man·like′, sports′man·ly** *adj.*

sports·man·ship (spôrts′mən·ship, spōrts′-) *n.* **1** The art or practice of field sports. **2** Honorable or sportsmanlike conduct.

sports·wear (spôrts′wâr′, spōrts′-) *n.* Clothes made for informal or outdoor activities.

sports·wom·an (spôrts′wo͝om′ən, spōrts′-) *n. pl.* **·wom·en** (-wim′in) A woman who participates in sports.

sport·y (spôr′tē, spōr′-) *adj.* **sport·i·er, sport·i·est** *Informal* **1** Relating to or characteristic of a sport. **2** Colorful; gay; loud, as clothes. —**sport′i·ly** *adv.* —**sport′i·ness** *n.*

spor·ule (spôr′yo͞ol, spor′-) *n.* A little spore. [Dim. of SPORE]

spot (spot) *n.* **1** A particular place or locality. **2** Any small portion of a surface differing as in color from the rest, as a mark, speck, blotch, etc. **3** A stain or blemish on character; a fault; a reproach. **4** A food fish of the Atlantic coast of the U.S. **5** One of the figures or pips with which a playing card is marked; also, a card having (a certain number of) such marks: the five *spot* of clubs. **6** *Slang* Paper money having a specified value: a ten *spot.* **7** *Chiefly Brit.* A portion or bit: a *spot* of tea. **8** *Informal* Place or allotted time, as on a list, schedule, etc. **9** *Informal* Position, job, or situation. **10** *Informal* SPOTLIGHT. **11** *Slang* NIGHTCLUB. **12** *Informal* A brief commercial or announcement, usu. scheduled between regular radio or television programs. —**hit the spot** *Slang* To gratify an appetite or need. —**in a spot** *Slang* In a difficult or embarrassing situation; in trouble. —**on the spot** **1** At once; immediately. **2** At the very place of occurrence. **3** *Slang* **a** In trouble, danger, difficulty, etc. **b** Accountable for some action, mistake, etc. —*v.* **spot·ted, spot·ting** *v.t.* **1** To mark or soil with spots. **2** To remove spots from. **3** To place or locate in or at a designated spot or spots. **4** To recognize or detect; identify; see. **5** To sully or disgrace, as the reputation of. **6** To schedule or list. **7** To shine a spotlight on. **8** *Informal* To yield (an advantage or handicap) to someone. —*v.i.* **9** To become marked or soiled with spots. **10** To make a stain or discoloration. —*adj.* **1** Paid or ready to be paid for at once: *spot* cash. **2** Ready for instant delivery following sale. **3** Involving cash payment only. **4** Made or selected at random or according to a prearranged plan: a *spot* check. **5** Broadcast between regular programs: a *spot* announcement. **6** Televised or broadcast on the spot or from a specific spot. [< LG] —**spot′ta·ble** *adj.*

spot-check (spot′chek′) *v.t. & v.i.* To sample or examine at random or according to a prearranged plan.

spot·less (spot′lis) *adj.* **1** Free from spots, dirt, etc.: a *spotless* house. **2** Pure; unsullied: a *spotless* life. —**spot′less·ly** *adv.* —**spot′less·ness** *n.*

spot·light (spot′līt′) *n.* **1** A bright, powerful beam of light used to illuminate a person, group, building, etc. **2** A device that produces such a light. **3** Public notice or acclaim. —*v.t.* To light up or make prominent with or as with a spotlight.

spot·ted (spot′id) *adj.* **1** Discolored in spots; soiled. **2** Characterized or marked by spots.

spotted fever Any of various infectious diseases marked by fever and skin rash.

spot·ter (spot′ər) *n.* **1** In drycleaning, one who removes spots. **2** A detective hired to watch for theft, etc., as in a department store. **3** Anyone who keeps watch for something.

spot·ty (spot′ē) *adj.* **·ti·er, ·ti·est** **1** Having many spots. **2** Uneven or irregular, as in quality, performance, etc. —**spot′ti·ly** *adv.* —**spot′ti·ness** *n.*

spous·al (spou′zəl) *adj.* Pertaining to marriage. —*n.* Marriage; espousal.

spouse (spouz, spous) *n.* A partner in marriage; one's husband or wife. [< L *sponsus,* pp. of *spondere* to promise, betroth]

spout (spout) *v.i.* **1** To pour out copiously and forcibly, as a liquid under pressure. **2** To speak pompously, somewhat angrily, or at length. —*v.t.* **3** To cause to pour or shoot forth. **4** To utter pompously, somewhat angrily, or at length. —*n.* **1** A tube, trough, etc., for the discharge of a liquid. **2** A continuous stream of fluid. [ME *spoute*] —**spout′er** *n.*

spp. species (plural).

sprain (sprān) *n.* **1** A violent straining or twisting of the ligaments surrounding a joint. **2** The condition due to such strain. —*v.t.* To cause a sprain in. [< OF *espreindre* to squeeze]

sprang (sprang) A *p.t.* of SPRING.

sprat (sprat) *n.* Any of various small herringlike fish. [< OE *sprott*]

sprawl (sprôl) *v.i.* **1** To sit or lie with the limbs stretched out ungracefully. **2** To be stretched out ungracefully, as the limbs. **3** To move with awkward motions of the limbs. **4** To spread out in a straggling manner, as handwriting, vines, etc. —*v.t.* **5** To cause to spread or extend awkwardly or irregularly. —*n.* **1** The act or position of sprawling. **2** An unplanned or disorderly group, as of houses, spread out over a broad area: urban *sprawl.* [< OE *sprēawlian* move convulsively] —**sprawl′er** *n.*

spray[1] (sprā) *n.* **1** Liquid dispersed in fine particles. **2** An instrument for discharging small particles of liquid; an atomizer. **3** Something like a spray of liquid. —*v.t.* **1** To disperse (a liquid) in fine particles. **2** To apply spray to. —*v.i.* **3** To send forth or scatter spray. **4** To go forth as spray. [< MDu. *sprayen*] —**spray′er** *n.*

spray[2] (sprā) *n.* **1** A small branch bearing dependent branchlets or flowers. **2** Any ornament or pattern like this. [ME]

spread (spred) *v.* **spread, spread·ing** *v.t.* **1** To open or unfold to full width, extent, etc., as wings, sail, a map, etc. **2** To distribute over a surface, esp. in a thin layer. **3** To cover with something. **4** To force apart or farther apart. **5** To distribute over a period of time or among a group. **6** To make more widely known, active, etc.; promulgate or diffuse: to *spread* a rumor. **7** To set (a table, etc.), as for a meal. **8** To arrange or place on a table, etc., as a meal or feast. **9** To set forth or record in full. —*v.i.* **10** To be extended or expanded; increase in size, width, etc. **11** To be distributed or dispersed, as over a surface or area; scatter.

12 To become more widely known, active, etc. 13 To be forced farther apart; separate. —*n.* 1 The act of spreading. 2 The limit, distance, or extent of spreading, expansion, etc. 3 A cloth or covering for a table, bed, etc. 4 Something used for spreading: a cheese *spread.* 5 *Informal* A feast or banquet; also, a table with a meal set out on it. 6 A prominent presentation in a periodical. 7 Two pages of a magazine or newspaper facing each other and covered by related material; also, the material itself. —*adj.* Expanded; outstretched. [<OE *spraedan*] —**spread'er** *n.*

spread·ea·gle (spred'ē'gəl) *adj.* 1 Having the arms and legs spread wide apart. 2 Extravagant; bombastic: said of excessively patriotic oratory in the U.S. —*v.* **-ea·gled, -ea·gling** *v. t.* 1 To force to assume a spread-eagle position.

spread eagle 1 The figure of an eagle with extended wings, used as an emblem of the U.S. 2 Any position or movement resembling this, as a figure in skating.

spread·sheet (spred'shēt') *n.* A kind of computer program that processes numerical data for detailed financial calculations of various kinds.

spree (sprē) *n.* 1 A period of heavy drinking. 2 Any period of fun, activity, etc. [?]

sprig (sprig) *n.* 1 A shoot or sprout of a plant. 2 An ornament in this form. 3 An heir or offspring of a family, esp. a young man. [ME *sprigge*] —**sprig'ger** *n.*

spright·ly (sprīt'lē) *adj.* **-li·er, -li·est** Full of animation and spirits; vivacious; lively. —*adv.* Spiritedly; briskly; gaily. [<*spright,* var. of SPRITE] —**spright'li·ness** *n.*—**Syn.** *adj.* animated, brisk, bustling, cheerful, nimble, spry, quick.

spring (spring) *v.* **sprang** or **sprung, sprung, spring·ing** *v.i.* 1 To move or rise suddenly and rapidly; leap; dart. 2 To move suddenly as by elastic reaction; snap. 3 To happen or occur suddenly or immediately: An angry retort *sprang* to his lips. 4 To work or snap out of place, as a mechanical part. 5 To become warped or bent, as boards. 6 To rise above surrounding objects. 7 To come into being: New towns have *sprung* up. 8 To originate; proceed, as from a source. 9 To develop; grow, as a plant. 10 To be descended: He *springs* from good stock. —*v.t.* 11 To cause to spring or leap. 12 To cause to act, close, open, etc., unexpectedly or suddenly, as by elastic reaction: to *spring* a trap. 13 To cause to happen, become known, or appear suddenly: to *spring* a surprise. 14 To leap over; vault. 15 To start (game) from cover; flush. 16 To explode (a mine). 17 To warp or bend; split. 18 To cause to snap or work out of place. 19 To force into place, as a beam or bar. 20 To suffer (a leak). 21 *Slang* To obtain the release of (a person) from prison or custody. —*n.* 1 *Mech.* An elastic device that yields under stress, and returns to normal form when the stress is removed. 2 Elastic quality or energy. 3 The act of flying back from a position of tension; recoil. 4 A cause of action; motive. 5 Any source or origin. 6 A flow or fountain, as of water. 7 The act of leaping up or forward suddenly; a jump; bound. 8 The season in which vegetation starts anew; in the north temperate zone, the three months of March, April, and May; in the astronomical year, the period from the vernal equinox to the summer solstice. —*adj.* 1 Of or pertaining to the season of spring. 2 Resilient; acting like or having a spring. 3 Hung on springs. 4 Coming from or housing a spring of water. [<OE *springan*]

Springs

spring·board (spring'bôrd', -bōrd') *n.* 1 A flexible board used to give impetus, as to a dive, acrobatic leap, etc. 2 Anything that gives impetus, as to an activity.

spring·bok (spring'bok') *n. pl.* **-bok** or **-boks** A small African gazelle noted for its ability to leap high in the air. Also **spring'buck'** (-buk'). [<Afrikaans]

Springbok

spring chicken 1 A young chicken. 2 *Informal* A young person, esp. a girl: usu. with a negative: She's no *spring chicken.*

spring·er (spring'ər) *n.* 1 One who or that which springs. 2 A young chicken. 3 A spaniel valuable for flushing game; also **springer spaniel.**

Springer spaniel

spring fever The listlessness that overtakes a person with the first warm days of spring.

spring tide 1 A high tide occurring about new moon and full moon. 2 Any great wave of feeling, etc.

spring·time (spring'tīm') *n.* 1 The season of spring. 2 Any early or youthful period. Also **spring'tide'** (-tīd').

spring·y (spring'ē) *adj.* **spring·i·er, spring·i·est** 1 Elastic; resilient. 2 Having many water springs; wet. —**spring'i·ly** *adv.* —**spring'i·ness** *n.*

sprin·kle (spring'kəl) *v.* **-kled, -kling** *v.t.* 1 To scatter in drops or small particles. 2 To scatter over or upon: *Sprinkle* the top with flour. —*v.i.* 3 To fall or rain in scattered drops. —*n.* 1 The act of sprinkling. 2 A small quantity. 3 A light rain. [ME *sprenkelen*] —**sprin'kler** *n.*

sprin·kling (spring'kling) *n.* 1 The act of one who or that which sprinkles. 2 A small amount or number: a *sprinkling* of people.

sprint (sprint) *n.* 1 The act of sprinting. 2 A short race run at top speed. 3 A brief period, as of speed. —*v.i.* To go or run fast, as in a sprint. [<Scand.] —**sprint'er** *n.*

sprit (sprit) *n.* A small spar reaching diagonally from a mast to the peak of a fore-and-aft sail. [<OE *sprēot* pole] • See SPRITSAIL.

sprite (sprīt) *n.* 1 A fairy, elf, or goblin. 2 A small, elflike person. 3 A ghost. [<L *spiritus*]

sprit·sail (sprit'səl, sprit'sāl') *n.* A sail extended by a sprit.

a. spritsail. b. sprit.

sprock·et (sprok'it) *n.* 1 A projection, as on the rim of a wheel, for engaging with the links of a chain. 2 A wheel bearing such projections: also **sprocket wheel.** [?]

sprout (sprout) *v.i.* 1 To put forth shoots; begin to grow; germinate. 2 To develop or grow rapidly. —*v.t.* 3 To cause to sprout. 4 To remove shoots from. —*n.* 1 A new shoot or bud on a plant. 2 Something like or suggestive of a sprout, as a young person. 3 *pl.* BRUSSELS SPROUTS. [<OE *sprūtan*]

spruce[1] (sprōōs) *n.* 1 Any of a genus of evergreen trees of the pine family, having needle-shaped leaves and pendulous cones. 2 The wood of any of these trees. [<Med. L *Prussia* Prussia]

spruce[2] (sprōōs) *adj.* **spruc·er, spruc·est** Smart, trim, and neat in appearance. —*v.* **spruced, spruc·ing** *v.t.* 1 To make spruce: often with *up.* —*v.i.* 2 To make oneself spruce: usu. with *up.* [<earlier *spruce,* a kind of superior Prussian leather] —**spruce'ly** *adv.* —**spruce'ness** *n.*

sprung (sprung) *p.p.* & a *p.t.* of SPRING.

spry (sprī) *adj.* **spri·er** or **spry·er, spri·est** or **spry·est** Quick and active; agile. [<Scand.] —**spry'ly** *adv.* —**spry'ness** *n.*

spt. seaport.

spud (spud) *n.* 1 A spadelike tool with narrow blade or prongs for uprooting weeds. 2 *Informal* A potato. —*v.t.* **spud·ded, spud·ding** To remove, as weeds, with a spud. [ME *spuddle*]

spume (spyōōm) *n.* Froth; foam; scum. —*v.i.* **spumed, spum·ing** To foam; froth. [<L *spuma* foam] —**spu'mous, spum'y** *adj.*

spu·mo·ni (spyōō·mō'nē) *n.* A frozen dessert of Italian origin, containing ice cream in layers of various colors and usu. candied fruit and nuts. Also **spu·mo'ne.** [<L *spuma* foam]

spun (spun) *p.t.* & *p.p.* of SPIN.

spunk (spungk) *n.* 1 A slow-burning tinder, as punk. 2 *Informal* Mettle; pluck; courage. [<L *spongia* sponge]

spunk·y (spungk'ē) *adj.* **spunk·i·er, spunk·i·est** *Informal* Spirited; courageous. —**spunk'i·ly** *adv.* —**spunk'i·ness** *n.*

spur (spûr) *n.* 1 Any of various pricking or goading instruments worn on the heel of a horseman. 2 Anything that incites or urges; incentive. 3 A part or attachment like a spur, as a steel gaff fastened to a gamecock's leg, a climbing iron used by linemen, etc. 4 A stiff, sharp spine on the legs or wings of certain birds. 5 A crag or ridge extending laterally from a mountain or range. 6 A branch of a railroad, lode, etc. 7 A buttress or other offset from a wall. 8 A brace reinforcing a rafter or post. 9 A tubular extension of a part of a flower, usu. containing the nectar. **—on the spur of the moment** Hastily; impulsively. **—win one's spurs** To gain recognition or reward, esp. for the first time. *—v.* **spurred, spur·ring** *v.t.* 1 To prick or urge with or as with spurs. 2 To furnish with spurs. 3 To injure or gash with the spur, as a gamecock. *—v.i.* 4 To spur one's horse. 5 To hasten; hurry. [< OE *spura*] **—spur'rer** *n.*

spurge (spûrj) *n.* Any of several flowering shrubs yielding a milky juice of bitter taste. [< OF *espurgier* to purge]

spu·ri·ous (spyŏŏr'ē·əs) *adj.* 1 Seemingly real or genuine, but actually not; false; counterfeit. 2 Illegitimate, as of birth. [< L *spurius*] **—spu'ri·ous·ly** *adv.* **—spu'ri·ous·ness** *n.*

spurn (spûrn) *v.t.* 1 To reject with disdain; scorn. 2 To strike with the foot; kick. *—v.i.* 3 To reject something with disdain. *—n.* The act or an instance of spurning. [< OE *spurnan*] **—spurn'er** *n.*

spurred (spûrd) *adj.* Wearing or having spurs.

spurt (spûrt) *n.* 1 A sudden gush of liquid. 2 Any sudden, short-lived outbreak, as of anger, energy, etc. *—v.i.* 1 To come out in a jet; gush forth. 2 To make a sudden, forceful effort. *—v.t.* 3 To squirt. [< OE *spryttan* come forth]

sput·nik (spŏŏt'nik, sput'-) *n.* An artificial earth satellite, esp. the first, called Sputnik I, launched in October, 1957, by the U.S.S.R. [Russ., lit., fellow traveler]

sput·ter (sput'ər) *v.i.* 1 To throw off solid or fluid particles in a series of slight explosions. 2 To speak excitedly and incoherently. 3 To make crackling or popping sounds, as burning wood, frying fat, etc. *—v.t.* 4 To throw off in small particles. 5 To utter excitedly or incoherently *—n.* 1 The act or sound of sputtering; esp. excited talk; jabbering. 2 That which is thrown out in sputtering. [< Du. *sputteren*] **—sput'ter·er** *n.*

spu·tum (spyōō'təm) *n. pl.* **·ta** (-tə) Mucus from the respiratory tract, usu. mixed with saliva; expectorated matter. [< L *spuere* to spit]

spy (spī) *n. pl.* **spies** 1 One who is hired to get secret information from or about an enemy, another government, etc.; a secret agent. 2 One who watches another or others secretly. *—v.* **spied, spy·ing** *v.i.* 1 To keep watch closely or secretly; act as a spy. 2 To make careful examination; pry: with *into*. *—v.t.* 3 To observe stealthily and usu. with hostile intent: often with *out*. 4 To catch sight of; see; espy. [< OF *espier* espy]

spy·glass (spī'glas', -gläs') *n.* A small telescope.

Sq. Squadron; Square (street).

sq. square; sequence; the following (L *sequentia*).

sq. ft. square foot; square feet.

sq. in. square inch(es).

sq. mi. square mile(s).

squab (skwob) *n.* 1 A young nestling pigeon about four weeks old. 2 A fat, short person. *—adj.* 1 Fat and short; squat. 2 Unfledged or but half-grown. [< Scand.]

squab·ble (skwob'əl) *v.i.* **·bled, ·bling** To engage in a petty quarrel; bicker. *—n.* A petty quarrel. [< Scand.] **—squab'·bler** *n.*

squad (skwod) *n.* 1 A small group of persons organized to do a special job; esp., the smallest tactical unit in the infantry of the U.S. Army. 2 A team: a football *squad*. *—v.t.* **squad·ded, squad·ding** 1 To form into a squad or squads. 2 To assign to a squad. [< L *quattuor* four]

squad car An automobile used by police for patrolling, and equipped with radiotelephone for communicating with headquarters.

squad·ron (skwod'rən) *n.* 1 An assemblage of war vessels smaller than a fleet. 2 A division of a cavalry regiment. 3 The basic unit of the U.S. Air Force, usu. consisting of two or more flights operating as a unit. 4 Any regularly arranged or organized group. *—v.t.* To arrange in a squadron or squadrons. [< Ital. *squadra* squad]

squal·id (skwol'id) *adj.* 1 Having a dirty, neglected, or poverty-stricken appearance. 2 Sordid; base. [< L *squalere* be foul] **—squal'id·ly** *adv.* **—squal'id·ness, squa·lid·i·ty** (skwo·lid'ə·tē) *n.* **—Syn.** 1 foul, filthy, wretched, untidy.

squall[1] (skwôl) *n.* A loud, screaming outcry. *—v.i.* To cry loudly; scream; bawl. [< Scand.] **—squall'er** *n.*

squall[2] (skwôl) *n.* 1 A sudden, violent burst of wind, often accompanied by rain or snow. 2 A brief disturbance or commotion. *—v.i.* To blow a squall. [< Scand.] **—squall'y** *adj.* **(·i·er, ·i·est)**

squal·or (skwol'ər) *n.* The state of being squalid; wretched filth or poverty.

squa·ma (skwā'mə) *n. pl.* **·mae** (-mē) A thin, scalelike structure; a scale. [L] **—squa'mate** (-māt), **squa'mose, squa'mous** *adj.*

squan·der (skwon'dər) *v.t.* To spend (money, time, etc.) wastefully. *—n.* Prodigality; wastefulness. [?] **—squan'·der·er** *n.* **—squan'der·ing·ly** *adv.* **—Syn.** *v.* dissipate, waste, lavish, run through, throw away.

square (skwâr) *n.* 1 A parallelogram having four equal sides and four right angles. 2 Any object, part, or surface that is square or nearly so, as one of the spaces on a checkerboard. 3 An L- or T-shaped instrument by which to test or lay out right angles. 4 An open area bordered by streets or formed by their intersection. 5 A town or city block; also, the distance between one street and the next. 6 *Math.* The product of a number or element multiplied by itself. 7 *Slang* A person of excessively conventional tastes or habits. **—on the square** 1 At right angles. 2 *Informal* Honest, fair, true, etc.; also, honestly, fairly, truly, etc. **—out of square** Not at right angles; obliquely. *—adj.* **squar·er, squar·est** 1 Having four equal sides and four right angles. 2 Approaching a square or a cube in form: a *square* box. 3 Forming a right angle: a *square* nook. 4 Adapted to forming squares or computing in squares: a *square* measure. 5 Being a square with each side of specified length: two inches *square*. 6 Perfectly adjusted, aligned, balanced, etc. 7 Even; settled: said of debts, etc. 8 Tied, as a score. 9 Honest; fair; just. 10 *Informal* Solid; full; satisfying: a *square* meal. 11 Broad; solid; muscular: a *square* build. 12 *Slang* Excessively conventional or conservative; not sophisticated. 13 *Naut.* At right angles to the mast and keel. *—v.* **squared, squar·ing** *v.t.* 1 To make square. 2 To shape or adjust so as to form a right angle. 3 To mark with or divide into squares. 4 To test for the purpose of adjusting to a straight line, right angle, or plane surface. 5 To bring to a position suggestive of a right angle: *Square* your shoulders. 6 To make satisfactory settlement or adjustment of: to *square* accounts. 7 To make equal, as a game score. 8 To cause to conform; adapt: to *square* one's opinions to the times. 9 To reconcile or set right. 10 *Math.* **a** To multiply (a number or element) by itself. **b** To determine the area of. 11 *Slang* To bribe. *—v.i.* 12 To be at right angles. 13 To conform; agree; harmonize: with *with*. **—square away** 1 *Naut.* To set (the yards) at right angles to the keel. 2 To put into good order; make ready. 3 SQUARE OFF. **—square off** To assume a position for attack or defense; prepare to fight. **—square up** To adjust or settle satisfactorily. *—adv.* 1 So as to be square, or at right angles. 2 Honestly; fairly. 3 Directly; firmly. [< OF *esquarre*] **—square'ness, squar'er** *n.* • See PARALLELOGRAM.

square dance Any dance, as a quadrille, in which the couples form sets in squares.

square knot A common knot, formed of two overhand knots. • See KNOT.

square·ly (skwâr'lē) *adv.* 1 In a direct or straight manner: He looked her *squarely* in the eyes. 2 Honestly; fairly. 3 Plainly; unequivocally. 4 In a square form: *squarely* built. 5 At right angles (to a line or plane).

square measure A unit or system of units for measuring areas. • See MEASURE.

square-rigged (skwâr'rigd') *adj.* Having the principal sails extended by horizontal yards at right angles to the masts.

square-rig·ger (skwâr'rig'ər) *n.* A square-rigged ship.

square root *Math.* A number or element whose square is equal to a given quantity.
square sail A four-sided sail usu. rigged on a horizontal yard set at right angles to the mast.
square shooter *Informal* One who acts honestly and justly.
squash[1] (skwosh) *v.t.* **1** To squeeze or press into a pulp or soft mass; crush. **2** To quell or suppress. **3** *Informal* To silence or humiliate quickly and thoroughly; squelch. —*v.i.* **4** To be smashed or squashed. **5** To make a splashing or sucking sound. —*n.* **1** A crushed mass. **2** The sudden fall of a heavy, soft, or bursting body; also, the sound made by such a fall. **3** The sucking, squelching sound made by walking through ooze or mud. **4** Either of two games played on an indoor court with rackets and a ball. In one **(squash rackets),** a slow rubber ball is used; in the other **(squash tennis),** a livelier, smaller ball. **5** *Brit.* A fruit-flavored beverage. —*adv.* With a squelching, oozy sound. [< L *ex-* thoroughly + *quassare* crush] **—squash′er** *n.*
squash[2] (skwosh) *n.* **1** Any of various edible gourds usu. cooked and served as a vegetable. **2** The plant that bears it. [< Algon.]
squash·y (skwosh′ē) *adj.* **squash·i·er, squash·i·est 1** Soft and moist. **2** Easily squashed. **—squash′i·ly** *adv.* **—squash′·i·ness** *n.*
squat (skwot) *v.* **squat·ted** or **squat, squat·ting** *v.i.* **1** To sit on the heels or hams, or with the legs near the body. **2** To crouch or cower down, as to avoid being seen. **3** To settle on a piece of land without title or payment. **4** To settle on government land in accordance with certain government regulations that will eventually give title. —*v.t.* **5** To cause (oneself) to squat. —*adj.* **squat·ter, squat·test 1** Short and thick. **2** Being in a squatting position. —*n.* A squatting attitude or position. [< OF *esquatir*] **—squat′ter** *n.*
squat·ty (skwot′ē) *adj.* **·ti·er, ·ti·est** Short and thickset; squat.
squaw (skwô) *n.* An American Indian woman or wife.
squawk (skwôk) *v.i.* **1** To utter a shrill, harsh cry, as a parrot. **2** *Slang* To utter loud complaints or protests. —*n.* **1** A shrill, harsh cry. **2** *Slang* A shrill complaint. [Imit.] —**squawk′er** *n.*
squeak (skwēk) *n.* **1** A thin, sharp, penetrating sound. **2** *Informal* An escape, esp. in the phrase **a narrow** (or **close**) **squeak.** —*v.i.* **1** To make a squeak. **2** *Informal* To let out information; squeal. **3** To succeed or otherwise progress after narrowly averting failure: to *squeak* through. —*v.t.* **4** To utter or effect with a squeak. **5** To cause to squeak. [Prob. < Scand.] **—squeak′y** *adj.* **(·i·er, ·i·est) —squeak′i·ly** *adv.* **—squeak′i·ness** *n.*
squeal (skwēl) *v.i.* **1** To utter a sharp, shrill, somewhat prolonged cry. **2** *Slang* To turn informer; betray an accomplice or a plot. —*v.t.* **3** To utter with or cause to make a squeal. —*n.* A shrill, prolonged cry, as of a pig. [Imit.] —**squeal′er** *n.*
squeam·ish (skwē′mish) *adj.* **1** Easily disgusted or shocked. **2** Overly scrupulous. **3** Nauseated; also, easily nauseated. [< AF *escoymous*] **—squeam′ish·ly** *adv.* —**squeam′ish·ness** *n.*
squee·gee (skwē′jē) *n.* **1** An implement having a straight-edged strip of rubber, etc., used for removing water from window panes, etc., after washing them. **2** *Phot.* A smaller similar implement, often made in the form of a roller, used for pressing a film closer to its mount, etc. —*v.t.* **·geed, ·gee·ing** To use a squeegee on. [Var. of SQUEEZE]
squeeze (skwēz) *v.* **squeezed, squeez·ing** *v.t.* **1** To press hard upon; compress. **2** To extract something from by pressure: to *squeeze* oranges. **3** To get or draw forth by pressure: to *squeeze* juice from apples. **4** To force, push, maneuver, etc., by or as by squeezing: He *squeezed* his car into the narrow space. **5** To oppress, as with burdensome taxes. **6** To exert pressure upon (someone) to act as one desires, as by blackmailing. **7** To embrace; hug. —*v.i.* **8** To apply pressure. **9** To force one's way; push: with *in, through,* etc. **10** To be pressed; yield to pressure. —**squeeze by, through,** etc. *Informal* To avoid failure, defeat, trouble, etc., by the narrowest margin. —*n.* **1** The act or process of squeezing; pressure. **2** A handclasp; also, an embrace; hug. **3** A quantity of something, as juice, extracted or expressed. **4** The state or condition of being squeezed; crush. **5** A time of trouble, scarcity, difficulty, etc. **6** SQUEEZE PLAY. **7** *Informal* Pressure exerted for the extortion of money or favors; also, financial pressure. [< OE *cwēsan* to crush] **—squeez′a·ble** *adj.* **—squeez′er** *n.*
squeeze play 1 In baseball, a play in which the batter bunts the ball so that a man on third base may score by starting while the pitcher is about to deliver the ball. **2** Any attempt or maneuver to realize some end or goal by coercion.
squelch (skwelch) *v.t.* **1** To crush; squash. **2** *Informal* To subdue utterly; silence, as with a crushing reply. —*v.i.* **3** To make or move with a splashing or sucking noise. —*n.* **1** A noise, as made when walking in wet boots. **2** A heavy fall or blow. **3** *Informal* A crushing retort or reply. [Imit.] **—squelch′er** *n.*
squib (skwib) *n.* **1** A brief news item. **2** A short witty or satirical speech or writing. **3** A broken firecracker that burns with a spitting sound. —*v.* **squibbed, squib·bing** *v.i.* **1** To write or use squibs. **2** To fire a squib. **3** To explode or sound like a squib. —*v.t.* **4** To attack with squibs; lampoon. [?]
squid (skwid) *n.* One of various ten-armed marine cephalopods with a long, slender body, ink sac, and broad caudal fins. [?]

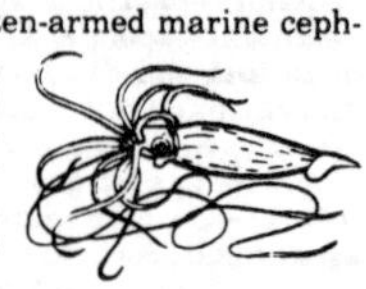

Squid

squill (skwil) *n.* **1** A bulbous plant of the lily family. **2** Its bulb, containing various medicinal and poisonous alkaloids. [< Gk. *skilla* sea onion]
squint (skwint) *v.i.* **1** To look with half-closed eyes, as into bright light. **2** To look with a side glance; look askance. **3** To be cross-eyed. **4** To incline or tend: with *toward,* etc. —*v.t.* **5** To hold (the eyes) half shut, as in glaring light. **6** To cause to squint. —*adj.* **1** Affected with strabismus. **2** Looking obliquely or askance; indirect. —*n.* **1** An affection of the eyes in which their axes are differently directed; strabismus. **2** The act or habit of squinting. [?] **—squint′er** *n.*
squire (skwīr) *n.* **1** A knight's attendant; an armor bearer. **2** In England, the chief landowner of a district. **3** In the U.S., a title applied esp. to village lawyers and justices of the peace. **4** A gentleman who escorts a lady in public; a gallant. —*v.t.* **squired, squir·ing** To be a squire to (someone); escort. [Var. of ESQUIRE]
squirm (skwûrm) *v.i.* **1** To bend and twist the body; wriggle; writhe. **2** To show signs of pain or distress. —*n.* A squirming motion. [?] **—squirm′y** *adj.* **(·i·er, ·i·est)**
squir·rel (skwûr′əl *Brit.* skwir′əl) *n.* **1** Any of various slender rodents with a long bushy tail, living mainly in trees and feeding chiefly on nuts. The **red squirrel,** the **gray squirrel,** and the **fox squirrel** are North American types. **2** One of various related rodents, as the woodchuck, ground squirrel, etc. **3** The fur of a squirrel. —*v.t.* **squir·reled** or **·relled, squir·rel·ing** or **·rel·ling** To take away and hide (something) for possible use in the future: often with *away.* [< Gk. *skia* shadow + *oura* tail]

Gray squirrel

squirt (skwûrt) *v.i.* **1** To come forth in a thin stream or jet; spurt out. —*v.t.* **2** To eject (water or other liquid) forcibly and in a jet. **3** To wet or bespatter with a squirt or squirts. —*n.* **1** The act of squirting or spurting; also, a jet of liquid squirted forth. **2** A syringe or squirt gun. **3** *Informal* A youngster, esp. a mischievous one. [ME *swirten*] **—squirt′·er** *n.*
squirt gun An instrument or toy shaped like a gun and used for squirting.
squish (skwish) *v.t.* & *v.i.* SQUASH[1]. —*n.* A squashing sound. [Var. of SQUASH[1]] **—squish′y (·i·er, ·i·est)** *adj.*
sq. yd. square yard(s).
Sr strontium.
Sr. Senior; Señor; Sir; Sister.
sr steradian.
Sra. Señora.
Sri Lank·a (srē langk′ə) An island south of India, an independent state of the Commonwealth of Nations, 25,332 sq. mi., cap. Colombo: formerly Ceylon. • See map at INDIA.

S.R.O. standing room only.
Srta. Señorita.
SS, SS. Nazi special police (G *Schutzstaffel*).
SS, S.S., S/S steamship.
SS. Saints.
S.S. Sunday School; written above (L *supra scriptum*).
ss, ss., s.s. shortstop.
SSA, S.S.A. Social Security Administration.
SSB, S.S.B. Social Security Board.
SSE, S.S.E., sse, s.s.e. south-southeast.
S.Sgt., S/Sgt Staff Sergeant.
SSR, S.S.R. Soviet Socialist Republic.
SSS Selective Service System.
SST supersonic transport.
SSW, S.S.W., ssw, s.s.w. south-southwest.
St. Saint; Strait; Street.
St., st. statute(s); stratus (clouds).
st. stanza; stet; stitch; stone (weight); street.
s.t. short ton.
Sta. Santa; Station.
sta. station; stationary.

stab (stab) *v.* **stabbed, stab·bing** *v.t.* **1** To pierce with a pointed weapon; wound, as with a dagger. **2** To thrust (a dagger, etc.), as into a body. **3** To penetrate; pierce. —*v.i.* **4** To thrust or wound with or as with a pointed weapon. —*n.* **1** A thrust or wound made with a pointed weapon. **2** A sharp painful or poignant sensation: a *stab* of grief. **3** *Informal* An effort; attempt. [ME *stabbe*] —**stab'ber** *n.*

sta·bile (stā'bil, -bīl) *adj.* **1** Stable; fixed. **2** *Med.* Not affected by moderate heat. —*n.* (stā'bēl) A piece of stationary abstract sculpture, usu. of sheet metal, wood, wire, etc. [< L *stabilis*]

sta·bil·i·ty (stə·bil'ə·tē) *n. pl.* **·ties 1** The condition of being stable; steadiness. **2** Steadfastness of purpose or resolution; constancy. **3** *Physics* The ability of an object or system to resume equilibrium after a disturbance.

sta·bi·lize (stā'bə·līz) *v.* **·lized, ·liz·ing** *v.t.* **1** To make stable. **2** To keep from fluctuating, as currency: to *stabilize* prices. —*v.i.* **3** To become stable. —**sta'bi·li·za'tion** *n.*

sta·bi·liz·er (stā'bə·lī'zər) *n.* Something that stabilizes, esp. an auxiliary airfoil of an aircraft. • See AIRPLANE.

sta·ble[1] (stā'bəl) *adj.* **·bler, ·blest 1** Standing firmly in place; not easily moved, shaken, or overthrown; fixed. **2** Marked by firmness of purpose; steadfast. **3** Having durability or permanence; abiding. **4** Resistant to chemical change. **5** *Physics* Of, having, or exhibiting stability. [< L *stabilis*] —**sta'bly** *adv.* —**sta'ble·ness** *n.*

sta·ble[2] (stā'bəl) *n.* **1** A building for lodging and feeding horses or cattle. **2** Racehorses belonging to a particular owner; also, the personnel who take care of such racehorses. **3** *Informal* Those performers, writers, athletes, etc., who are under the same management or agency. —*v.t. & v.i.* **·bled, ·bling** To put or lodge in or as in a stable. [< L *stabulum*]

sta·ble·boy (stā'bəl·boi') *n.* A boy employed in a stable.

stac·ca·to (stə·kä'tō) *adj.* **1** *Music* Played, or to be played, with brief pauses between each note. **2** Marked by abrupt, sharp sounds or emphasis: a *staccato* style of speaking. —*adv.* So as to be staccato. —*n.* Something staccato. [< Ital. *staccare* detach]

stack (stak) *n.* **1** A large, orderly pile of unthreshed grain, hay, or straw, usu. conical. **2** Any pile or heap of things arranged somewhat neatly or systematically. **3** A group of rifles (usu. three) set upright and supporting one another. **4** *pl.* That part of a library where most of the books are shelved; also, the bookshelves. **5** A chimney; smokestack; also, a collection of such chimneys or flues. **6** *Informal* A great amount; plenty. —*v.t.* **1** To gather or pile up in a stack. **2** To plan or arrange dishonestly beforehand so as to assure a certain result or outcome. **3** To assign (an airplane) to a pattern of designated altitudes while awaiting clearance to land: often with *up.* —**stack up 1** To total. **2** To compare: often with *against.* [< ON *stakkr*] —**stack'er** *n.*

sta·di·um (stā'dē·əm) *n. pl.* **·di·ums,** *for def. 2* **·di·a** (-dē·ə) **1** A large modern structure for sports events, having seats arranged in tiers. **2** In ancient Greece and Rome: **a** A course for footraces, with banked seats for spectators. **b** A measure of length, equaling 606.75 feet. [< Gk. *stadion,* a measure of length]

staff (staf) *n. pl.* **staffs;** *also for defs. 1–3* **staves** (stāvz). **1** A stick or piece of wood carried for some special purpose, as an aid in climbing, as a cudgel, or as an emblem of authority. **2** A shaft or pole that forms a support or handle: the *staff* of a flag. **3** A stick used in measuring or testing, as a surveyor's leveling rod. **4** A group of people who function as assistants or advisors to a leader, director, president, etc. **5** A body of persons working together in some specific task, occupation, or enterprise: the hospital *staff;* the editorial *staff.* **6** *Mil.* A body of officers not having command but attached in an executive or advisory capacity to a military unit as assistants to the officer in command. **7** *Music* The five horizontal lines and the spaces between them on which notes are written. —*v.t.* To provide (an office, etc.) with a staff. [< OE *stæf* stick]

staff·er (staf'ər) *n.* A member of a staff, as of a periodical.

staff officer An officer serving on a military staff.

stag (stag) *n.* **1** The adult male of various deer, esp. the red deer. **2** A castrated bull or boar. **3** A man at a party, dance, etc., who is unaccompanied by a woman. **4** A social gathering for men only. —*adj.* Of or for men only. [< OE *stagga*]

Stag head

stage (stāj) *n.* **1** The platform on which plays, operas, etc., are given. **2** The area on the adjacent sides and in back of this platform, including the wings, backstage, etc. **3** The profession of acting: with *the.* **4** Any of the activities or occupations having to do with the theater or drama: with *the.* **5** Any raised platform or floor, esp. a scaffold for workmen. **6** A horizontal level, section, or story of a building. **7** The scene of, or plan of action for, an event or events. **8** A center of attention. **9** A distinct period or step in some development, progress, or process. **10** A water level: flood *stage.* **11** A regular stopping place on a journey, esp. a journey by stagecoach. **12** STAGECOACH. **13** The distance traveled between two stopping points; leg. **14** *Electronics* One of a series of modules through which a signal passes. **15** One of the series of propulsion units used by a rocket vehicle. —*v.t.* **staged, stag·ing 1** To put or exhibit on the stage. **2** To plan, conduct, or carry out: to *stage* a rally. **3** To organize, perform, or carry out so as to appear authentic, legitimate, or spontaneous, when actually not so: The entire incident was *staged* for the press photographers. [< OF *estage*]

stage·coach (stāj'kōch') *n.* A horse-drawn, passenger and mail vehicle having a regular route between towns.

stage·craft (stāj'kraft', -kräft') *n.* Skill in writing or staging plays.

stage door A door to a theater which leads to the stage or behind the scenes.

stage·hand (stāj'hand') *n.* A worker in a theater who handles scenery and props, etc.

stage-man·age (stāj'man'ij) *v.t.* **·aged, ·ag·ing 1** To be a stage manager for. **2** To direct, organize, or carry out so as to achieve maximum effectiveness, publicity, etc.

stage manager One who assists a director in the production of a play and, during its performance, superintends the stage area, actors, and technicians.

stage·struck (stāj'struk') *adj.* **1** Fascinated by the theater. **2** Longing to become an actor or actress.

stage whisper A loud whisper, as one uttered on the stage for the audience to hear.

stag·fla·tion (stag'flā'shən) *n. Econ.* Inflation combined with abnormally slow economic growth, resulting in high unemployment. [< *stag(nation)* + *(in)flation*]

stag·ger (stag'ər) *v.i.* **1** To move unsteadily; totter; reel. **2** To become less confident or resolute; waver; hesitate. —*v.t.* **3** To cause to stagger. **4** To affect strongly; overwhelm, as with surprise or grief. **5** To place in alternating rows or groups. **6** To arrange or distribute so as to prevent congestion or confusion: to *stagger* lunch hours. —*n.* The act of staggering. **—the (blind) staggers** Any of various diseases of domestic animals marked by staggering, falling, etc. [<ON *stakra*] **—stag′ger·er** *n.* **—stag′ger·ing·ly** *adv.*

stag·ing (stā′jing) *n.* **1** A scaffolding or temporary platform. **2** The act of putting a play, opera, etc., upon the stage. **3** The act of jettisoning a rocket stage from a space vehicle. **4** The business of running stagecoaches. **5** Traveling by stagecoach.

stag·nant (stag′nənt) *adj.* **1** Standing still; not flowing: said of water. **2** Foul from long standing. **3** Dull; inert; sluggish. [< L *stagnum* a pool] **—stag′nan·cy** *n.* **—stag′nant·ly** *adv.*

stag·nate (stag′nāt) *v.i.* **·nat·ed, ·nat·ing** To be or become stagnant. **—stag·na′tion** *n.*

stag·y (stā′jē) *adj.* **stag·i·er, stag·i·est** **1** Of or suited to the stage. **2** Excessively theatrical; artificial. **—stag′i·ly** *adv.* **—stag′i·ness** *n.*

staid (stād) *adj.* Sedate; sober; serious. [Orig. p.t. and p.p. of STAY[1]] **—staid′ly** *adv.* **—staid′ness** *n.*

stain (stān) *n.* **1** A discoloration or spot from foreign matter. **2** A dye or thin pigment used in staining. **3** A moral blemish or taint. *—v.t.* **1** To make a stain upon; discolor; soil. **2** To color with a dye or stain. **3** To bring a moral stain upon; blemish. *—v.i.* **4** To take or impart a stain. [<OF *desteindre* to deprive of color] **—stain′a·ble** *adj.* **—stain′er** *n.*

stained glass Glass colored by the addition of pigments, usu. in the form of metallic oxides which are fused throughout the glass or burned onto its surface. **—stained′-glass′** *adj.*

stain·less (stān′lis) *adj.* **1** Without a stain. **2** Resistant to stain. **3** Made of stain-resistant materials. *—n.* Tableware made of stainless steel. **—stain′less·ly** *adv.*

stainless steel A corrosion-resistant steel alloyed with chromium and often other elements, esp. nickel.

stair (stâr) *n.* **1** A step, or one of a series of steps, for mounting or descending from one level to another. **2** *Usu. pl.* A series of steps. [<OE *stæger*]

stair·case (stâr′kās′) *n.* A flight of stairs, complete with the supports, balusters, etc.

stair·way (stâr′wā′) *n.* One or more flights of stairs.

stair·well (stâr′wel′) *n.* A vertical shaft enclosing a staircase.

stake (stāk) *n.* **1** A stick or post, as of wood or metal, sharpened for driving into the ground. **2** A post to which a person is bound to be burned alive; also, death by burning at the stake. **3** A post or stick set upright in the floor of a car or wagon, to confine loose material. **4** *Often pl.* Something wagered or risked, as the money bet on a race. **5** *Often pl.* A prize in a contest. **6** An interest or share, as in an enterprise. **7** GRUBSTAKE. **—at stake** In hazard or jeopardy. *—v.t.* **staked, stak·ing** **1** To fasten or support by means of a stake. **2** To mark the boundaries of with stakes: often with *off* or *out.* **3** *Informal* To wager; risk. **4** *Informal* To supply with money, equipment, etc.; back. [<OE *staca*]

sta·lac·tite (stə·lak′tīt′, stal′ək-) *n.* **1** An elongated, hanging cone of calcium carbonate formed by slow dripping from the roof of a cave. **2** Any similar formation. [<Gk. *stalaktitos* dripping] **—stal·ac·tit·ic** (stal′ək·tit′ik) or **·i·cal** *adj.*

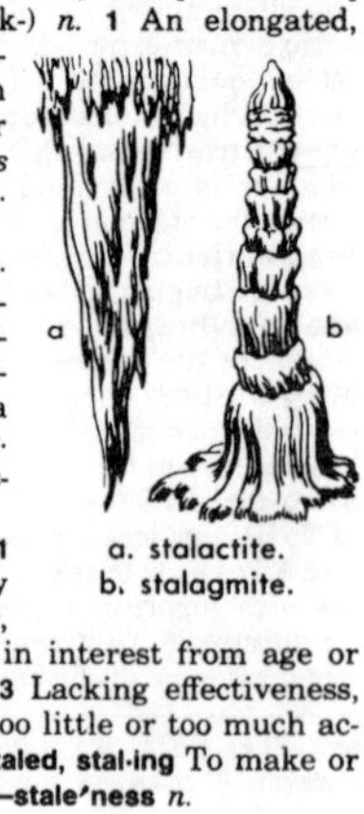

a. stalactite.
b. stalagmite.

sta·lag·mite (stə·lag′mīt′, stal′əg-) *n.* **1** A usu. conical mound deposited on a cave floor by dripping from a stalactite. **2** Any similar formation. [<Gk. *stalagmos* a dripping] **—stal·ag·mit·ic** (stal′əg·mit′ik) or **·i·cal** *adj.* • See STALACTITE.

stale (stāl) *adj.* **stal·er, stal·est** **1** Having lost freshness; slightly changed or deteriorated, as air, beer, old bread, etc. **2** Lacking in interest from age or familiarity; trite: a *stale* joke. **3** Lacking effectiveness, energy, spontaneity, etc., from too little or too much activity or practice. *—v.t. & v.i.* **staled, stal·ing** To make or become stale. [?] **—stale′ly** *adv.* **—stale′ness** *n.*

stale·mate (stāl′māt′) *n.* **1** In chess, a position in which a player can make no move without putting his king in check. The result is a draw. **2** Any tie, standstill, or deadlock. *—v.t.* **·mat·ed, ·mat·ing** **1** To put into a condition of stalemate. **2** To bring to a standstill. [<AF *estale* a fixed position + MATE[2]]

stalk[1] (stôk) *n.* **1** The stem or axis of a plant. **2** Any support on which an organ is borne, as a pedicel. **3** A supporting part or stem: the *stalk* of a quill. **4** Any stem or main axis, as of a goblet. [ME *stalke*] **—stalked, stalk′less** *adj.*

stalk[2] (stôk) *v.i.* **1** To approach game, etc., stealthily. **2** To walk in a stiff or haughty manner. *—v.t.* **3** To approach (game, etc.) stealthily. **4** To invade or permeate: Famine *stalked* the countryside. *—n.* **1** The act of stalking game. **2** A stalking step or walk. [<OE *bestealcian* move stealthily] **—stalk′er** *n.*

stalk·ing-horse (stô′king·hôrs′) *n.* **1** A horse behind which a hunter conceals himself in stalking game. **2** Anything serving to conceal one's intention.

stall (stôl) *n.* **1** A compartment in which a horse or bovine animal is confined and fed. **2** A small booth or compartment in a street, market, etc., for the sale or display of small articles. **3** A partially enclosed seat, as in the choir of a cathedral. **4** *Brit.* A seat very near the stage of a theater. **5** A small compartment, as for showering. **6** An evasive or delaying action. **7** A condition in which a motor temporarily stops functioning. **8** A condition in which an airplane loses the air speed needed to produce sufficient lift to keep it flying. *—v.t.* **1** To place or keep in a stall. **2** To bring to a standstill; halt the progress of. **3** To stop, usu. unintentionally, the operation or motion of. **4** To put (an airplane) into a stall. **5** To cause to stick fast in mud, snow, etc. *—v.i.* **6** To come to a standstill; stop, esp. unintentionally. **7** To stick fast in mud, snow, etc. **8** To make delays; be evasive: to *stall* for time. **9** To live or be kept in a stall. **10** *Aeron.* To go into a stall. [<OE *steall*]

stall-feed (stôl′fēd′) *v.t.* **-fed, -feed·ing** To feed (cattle) in a stall so as to fatten them. **—stall′-fed′** *adj.*

stal·lion (stal′yən) *n.* An uncastrated male horse. [<OHG *stal* stable]

stal·wart (stôl′wərt) *adj.* **1** Strong and robust. **2** Resolute: determined. **3** Brave; courageous. *—n.* **1** An uncompromising partisan, as in politics. **2** One who is stalwart. [<OE *stæl* place + *wierthe* worth] **—stal′wart·ly** *adv.* **—stal′wart·ness** *n.*

sta·men (stā′mən) *n. pl.* **sta·mens** or **stam·i·na** (stam′ə·nə) One of the pollen-bearing organs of a flower, consisting of a filament supporting an anther. [L, warp, thread] **—stam·i·nal** (stam′ə·nəl) *adj.*

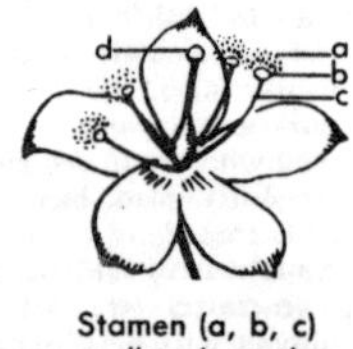

Stamen (a, b, c)
a. pollen. b. anther.
c. filament. d. pistil.

stam·i·na (stam′ə·nə) *n.* Strength and endurance, as in withstanding hardship or difficulty. [L, pl. of *stamen* warp, thread] **—stam′i·nal** *adj.*

stam·i·nate (stam′ə·nit, -nāt) *adj.* **1** Having stamens but no pistil, as male flowers. **2** Having stamens.

stam·mer (stam′ər) *v.t. & v.i.* To speak or utter with nervous repetitions or prolongations of a sound or syllable, and involuntary pauses. *—n.* The act or habit of stammering. [<OE *stamerian*] **—stam′mer·er** *n.*

stamp (stamp) *v.t.* **1** To strike heavily with the sole of the foot. **2** To bring down (the foot) heavily and noisily. **3** To affect in a specified manner by or as by stamping with the foot: to *stamp* out opposition. **4** To make, form, cut out, etc., with a stamp or die: often with *out:* to *stamp* out a circle from the steel. **5** To imprint or impress with a die, stamp, etc.: to *stamp* the date on a letter. **6** To fix or imprint permanently: The deed was *stamped* on his memory. **7** To characterize; brand: to *stamp* a story false. **8** To affix an official seal, stamp, etc., to. **9** To crush or pulverize, as ore. *—v.i.* **10** To strike the foot heavily on the ground. **11** To walk with heavy, resounding steps. *—n.* **1** The act of stamping. **2** A machine or tool, as a die, that cuts out or shapes a form. **3** An implement or device that imprints a design, character, mark, etc., on something; also, the design, character, mark, etc., so imprinted. **4** A printed device of paper to be attached to something to show that a tax or fee has been paid: a postage *stamp.* **5** TRADING STAMP. **6** A specific impression or effect: the *stamp* of genius. **7** Characteristic quality or form; kind; sort: I dislike men of his *stamp.* [ME *stampen*] **—stamp′er** *n.*

stam·pede (stam·pēd′) *n.* **1** A sudden starting and rushing off through panic: said primarily of a herd of cattle, horses, etc. **2** Any sudden, impulsive rush or movement of a crowd, as of a mob. **3** A spontaneous mass impulse, trend, or movement, as toward the support of a political candidate. **4** *Can.* RODEO. *—v.* **·ped·ed, ·ped·ing** *v.t.* **1** To cause a stampede in. *—v.i.* **2** To engage in a stampede. [< Am. Sp. *estampar* to stamp] **—stam·ped′er** *n.*

stamping ground A favorite or habitual gathering place.

stance (stans) *n.* **1** Mode of standing; posture, esp. with reference to the placing of the feet. **2** Attitude; point of view: a moral *stance.* [< L *stans* pr. p. of *stare* to stand]

stanch (stanch, stänch) *v.t.* **1** To stop or check the flow of (blood, tears, etc.). **2** To stop the flow of blood from (a wound). **3** To check or put an end to. *—adj.* STAUNCH. [< OF *estanchier* to halt] **—stanch′er** *n.* • The spelling *stanch* is usu. preferred for the verb in both England and the U.S., and *staunch* for the adjective. Many writers, however, use one or the other spelling for both.

stan·chion (stan′shən) *n.* **1** An upright bar forming a principal support. **2** A device that fits around a cow's neck, used to restrain movement in a stall. *—v.t.* To provide, restrain, or support with stanchions. [< OF *estanchon*]

stand (stand) *v.* **stood, stand·ing** *v.i.* **1** To assume or maintain an erect position on the feet. **2** To be in a vertical position: The oars *stood* in the corner. **3** To measure a specified height when standing: He *stands* six feet. **4** To assume a specified position: to *stand* aside. **5** To be situated; have position or location; lie: The factory *stands* on a hill. **6** To have or be in a specified state, condition, or relation: We *stand* to gain everything by not fighting; He *stood* in fear of his life. **7** To assume an attitude for defense or offense: *Stand* and fight! **8** To maintain one's attitude, opinions, etc.: *Stand* firm. **9** To be or exist in a printed or written form: Photograph the letter just as it *stands.* **10** To remain unimpaired, unchanged, or valid: My decision still *stands.* **11** To collect and remain: Tears *stood* in her eyes. **12** To be of a specified rank or class: He *stands* third. **13** To stop or pause; halt. **14** *Naut.* To take a direction; steer. **15** *Brit.* To be a candidate, as for election. *—v.t.* **16** To place upright; set in an erect position. **17** To put up with; endure; tolerate. **18** To be subjected to; undergo: He must *stand* trial. **19** To withstand or endure successfully: to *stand* the test of time. **20** To carry out the duty of: to *stand* watch. **21** *Informal* **a** To treat: I'll *stand* you to a drink. **b** To bear the expense of: to *stand* a dinner. **—stand a chance** To have a chance. **—stand by 1** To stay near and be ready to help or operate. **2** To help; support. **3** To abide by; make good; adhere to. **4** To remain passive, as when help is needed. **5** *Telecom.* To keep tuned in, as for the continuance of an interrupted transmission. **—stand for 1** To represent; symbolize. **2** To put up with; tolerate. **—stand in for** To act as a substitute for. **—stand off 1** To keep at a distance. **2** To fail to agree or comply. **3** To put off; evade, as a creditor. **—stand on 1** To be based on or grounded in; rest. **2** To insist on observance of: to *stand on* ceremony. **3** *Naut.* To keep on the same tack or course. **—stand out 1** To stick out; project or protrude. **2** To be prominent or conspicuous. **3** To be outstanding, remarkable, etc. **4** To refuse to consent or agree. **—stand pat 1** In poker, to play one's hand as dealt, without drawing new cards. **2** To resist change. **—stand to reason** To conform to reason. **—stand up 1** To stand erect. **2** To withstand wear, criticism, analysis, etc. **3** *Slang* To fail, usu. intentionally, to keep an appointment with. **—stand up for** To side with; take the part of. **—stand up to** To confront courageously; face. *—n.* **1** The act or condition of standing, esp. of halting or stopping, as: **a** A stopping or halt, as in a retreat, to fight back or resist. **b** A stop for a performance, made by a theatrical company while on tour; also, the place stopped at. **2** The place or location where one stands or is assigned to stand; position. **3** Any place where something stands: a taxi *stand.* **4** An opinion, attitude, point of view, etc.: to take a *stand.* **5** A structure upon which persons may sit or stand, as: **a** *Often pl.* A series of raised seats or benches, as at an athletic contest. **b** A platform: a reviewing *stand.* **c** A small platform in court from which a witness testifies. **6** A small table. **7** A rack or other structure for holding something: an umbrella *stand.* **8** A stall, counter, or the like where merchandise is displayed or sold. **9** A vertical growth of trees or plants. [< OE *standan*] **—stand′er** *n.*

stan·dard (stan′dərd) *n.* **1** A flag, ensign, or banner, used as an emblem of a government, body of men, head of state, etc. **2** A figure or image adopted as an emblem or symbol. **3** Something established and generally accepted as a model, example, or test of excellence, attainment, etc.; criterion. **4** Something established as a measure or reference of weight, extent, quantity, quality, or value. **5** In coinage, the established proportion by weight of pure gold or silver and an alloy. **6** The measurable basis of value in a monetary system. **7** An upright structure, timber, post, etc., used as a support. **8** A musical composition whose popularity has become firmly established over the years. **9** A plant growing on a vigorous, unsupported, upright stem. *—adj.* **1** Having the accuracy or authority of a standard; serving as a gauge or criterion. **2** Of recognized excellence, popularity, reliability, etc.: the *standard* repertoire of symphonies. **3** Not unusual or special in any way; ordinary; typical; regular: *standard* procedure; *standard* equipment. [< OF *estandard* banner]

stan·dard-bear·er (stan′dərd·bâr′ər) *n.* **1** The person who carries the flag or standard of a group, esp. of a regiment or other military body. **2** The official leader or representative of a group, as a presidential nominee.

standard gauge 1 A railroad track width of 56½ inches, considered as standard. **2** A railroad having such a gauge. **—stan′dard-gauge′** *adj.*

stan·dard·ize (stan′dər·dīz) *v.t.* **·ized, ·iz·ing** To make conform to, regulate, or test by a standard. **—stan′dard·i·za′tion, stan′dard·iz′er** *n.*

standard of living The average manner of day-to-day living of a country, group, or person, with reference to food, housing, clothing, comforts, etc.

standard time The official time for any region or country. Mean solar time is reckoned, east or west, from the meridian of Greenwich, England, each time zone comprising a sector of 15 degrees of longitude and representing a time interval of one hour. In the conterminous U.S., the four time zones, **Eastern Standard Time, Central Standard Time, Mountain Standard Time,** and **Pacific Standard Time** represent the 75th, 90th, 105th, and 120th meridians west of Greenwich, and are accordingly 5, 6, 7, and 8 hours earlier than Greenwich time. Therefore, noon in London corresponds to 7 A.M. in New York, 6 A.M. in Chicago, 5 A.M. in Denver, and 4 A.M. in San Francisco.

stand·by (stand′bī′) *n. pl.* **·bys 1** A person who can be relied on, as in an emergency. **2** Something that always pleases, is always effective, etc. **3** A person or thing waiting and ready to replace another person or thing; substitute.

stand·ee (stan·dē′) *n.* A person who must stand for lack of chairs or seats, as at a theater or on a train.

stand-in (stand′in′) *n.* **1** A person who substitutes for a motion-picture or television performer while lights are arranged, camera angles set, etc. **2** Any substitute for another person.

stand·ing (stan′ding) *adj.* **1** That is upright or erect. **2** Continuing for regular or permanent use; not special or temporary: a *standing* rule. **3** Stagnant; not flowing: *standing* water. **4** Begun or done while standing: a *standing* ovation; a *standing* high jump. **5** Not in use; idle: *standing* machinery. **6** Not movable. *—n.* **1** The act or condition of one who stands. **2** A place to stand in. **3** Relative place or position, as on a graded list of excellence, achievement, etc. 4 Reputation, esp. good reputation. 5 Duration; continuance: a feud of long *standing.*

standing room Place in which to stand, as in a theater when the seats are all occupied.

stand·off (stand′ôf′, -of′) *n.* 1 A draw or tie, as in a game. 2 A counterbalancing or neutralizing effect. —*adj.* 1 That stands off. 2 STANDOFFISH.

stand·off·ish (stand′ôf′ish) *adj.* Aloof; cool. —**stand′off′·ish·ly** *adv.* —**stand′off′ish·ness** *n.*

stand·out (stand′out′) *Informal n.* A person or thing that is unusually good or excellent. —*adj.* Unusually good or excellent.

stand·pat (stand′pat′) *adj. Informal* Resistant to change; conservative. —**stand′pat′ter, stand′pat′tism** *n.*

stand·pipe (stand′pīp′) *n.* A high vertical pipe or water tower, as at a reservoir, into which the water is pumped to create pressure.

stand·point (stand′point′) *n.* Point of view; position; stance.

stand·still (stand′stil′) *n.* A stopping; cessation; halt.

stand-up (stand′up′) *adj.* 1 Having an erect or vertical position: a *stand-up* collar. 2 Done, consumed, etc., while standing.

stan·hope (stan′hōp) *n.* A light, open, one-seated carriage. [< F. *Stanhope,* 1787–1864, English clergyman]

stank (stangk) *p.t.* of STINK.

stan·nic (stan′ik) *adj. Chem.* Of, pertaining to, or containing tin, esp. in its higher valence. [< L *stannum* tin]

stan·nous (stan′əs) *adj.* Of, pertaining to, or containing tin, esp. in its lower valence. [< L *stannum* tin]

stan·za (stan′zə) *n.* A certain number of lines of verse grouped together and forming a definite division of a poem. [Ital., room, stanza] —**stan·za·ic** (stan·zā′ik) *adj.*

sta·pes (stā′pēz) *n. pl.* **sta·pes** or **sta·pe·des** (stə·pē′dēz, stā′pə·dēz′) *Anat.* The innermost small bone of the middle ear of mammals. [LL, a stirrup] —**sta·pe·di·al** (stə·pē′·dē·əl) *adj.*

staph (staf) *n.* STAPHYLOCOCCUS.

staph·y·lo·coc·cus (staf′ə·lō·kok′əs) *n. pl.* **·coc·ci** (-kok′sī, -sē, -ī, -ē) Any of a group of spherical bacteria occurring singly, in pairs, or in irregular clusters and often acting as infective agents. [< Gk. *staphylos* bunch of grapes + *kokkos* a berry] —**staph′y·lo·coc′cic** (-kok′sik, -kok′ik) *adj.* • See BACTERIUM.

sta·ple[1] (stā′pəl) *n.* 1 A principal commodity or product of a country or region. 2 A chief item, element, or main constituent of anything. 3 A product that is constantly sold and used, as sugar or salt. 4 Raw material. 5 The corded or combed fiber of cotton, wool, or flax, with reference to its length. 6 A source of supply; storehouse. —*adj.* 1 Regularly and constantly produced, consumed, or sold. 2 Main; chief. —*v.t.* **·pled, ·pling** To sort or classify according to length, as wool fiber. [< MDu. *stapel* market]

sta·ple[2] (stā′pəl) *n.* A U-shaped piece of metal or thin wire, having pointed ends and driven into a surface, as wood or paper, to serve as a fastening. —*v.t.* **·pled, ·pling** To fix or fasten by a staple or staples. [< OE *stapol* post]

sta·pler[1] (stā′plər) *n.* 1 A person who staples wool, etc. 2 A person who deals in staple goods.

sta·pler[2] (stā′plər) *n.* A device for driving staples into a surface.

star (stär) *n.* 1 *Astron.* Any of the numerous celestial objects that emit radiant energy, including visible light, generated by nuclear reactions. 2 Loosely, any of the luminous bodies regularly seen as points of light in the night sky. 3 A conventional figure having five or more radiating points. 4 Something resembling such a figure, as an emblem or device. 5 An asterisk (*). 6 A person of outstanding talent or accomplishment and a quality of personality that attracts wide public interest or attention. 7 A performer who plays the leading role in a play, opera, etc. 8 *Often pl.* Any of the planets or their configuration considered as influencing one's fate. 9 Fortune; destiny. —*v.* **starred, star·ring** *v.t.* 1 To set, mark, or adorn with stars. 2 To mark with an asterisk. 3 To present as a star in an entertainment. —*v.i.* 4 To be prominent or brilliant. 5 To play the leading part; be the star. —*adj.* 1 Of or pertaining to a star or stars. 2 Prominent; brilliant: a *star* football player. [< OE *steorra*] —**star′less, star′like** *adj.*

star·board (stär′bərd) *n.* The right-hand side of a vessel or aircraft as one faces the front or forward. —*adj.* Of, pertaining to, or on the starboard. —*adv.* Toward the starboard side. —*v.t.* To put, move, or turn (the helm) to the starboard side. [< OE *steorbord* steering side]

starch (stärch) *n.* 1 A complex, insoluble carbohydrate produced by photosynthesis and usu. stored in roots, tubers, seeds, etc. 2 A white, powdery substance consisting of purified starch extracted from potatoes, corn, etc. 3 Any starchy foodstuff. 4 A fabric stiffener made of starch suspended in water. 5 A stiff or formal manner. 6 *Informal* Energy; vigor. —*v.t.* To apply starch to; stiffen with or as with starch. [< OE *stearc* stiff]

starch·y (stär′chē) *adj.* **starch·i·er, starch·i·est** 1 Stiffened with starch; stiff. 2 Primly formal or stiff. 3 Containing a large proportion of starch: a *starchy* vegetable. —**starch′·i·ly** *adv.* —**starch′i·ness** *n.*

star-crossed (stär′krôst′, -krost′) *adj.* Doomed; ill-fated: a *star-crossed* love affair.

star·dom (stär′dəm) *n.* 1 The status of a person who is a star. 2 Stars of the stage, screen, etc., collectively.

stare (stâr) *v.* **stared, star·ing** *v.i.* 1 To gaze fixedly, usu. with the eyes open wide, as from admiration, fear, or insolence. 2 To be conspicuously or unduly apparent; glare. —*v.t.* 3 To gaze fixedly at. 4 To affect in a specified manner by a stare: to *stare* a person into silence. —**stare down** To gaze back fixedly (at a person) until he turns his eyes away. —**stare one in the face** To be perfectly plain or obvious. —*n.* A steady, fixed gaze. [< OE *starian*] —**star′er** *n.*

star·fish (stär′fish′) *n. pl.* **·fish** or **·fish·es** Any of various radially symmetrical echinoderms with a star-shaped body having five or more arms.

Starfish

star·gaze (stär′gāz′) *v.i.* **·gazed, ·gaz·ing** 1 To gaze at or study the stars. 2 To daydream. —**star′gaz′·er** *n.*

stark (stärk) *adj.* 1 Deserted; barren; bleak: a *stark* landscape. 2 Severe; difficult: *stark* measures. 3 With little or no ornamentation, color, etc.: a *stark* room. 4 Blunt; grim; pitiless: *stark* reality. 5 Complete; utter: *stark* madness. 6 Stiff or rigid, as in death. 7 Sharp and bare, as of outline. —*adv.* 1 In a stark manner. 2 Completely; utterly: *stark* naked. [< OE *stearc* stiff] —**stark′ly** *adv.* —**stark′ness** *n.*

star·let (stär′lit) *n. Informal* A young movie actress being prepared for stardom.

star·light (stär′līt) *n.* The light given by a star or stars. —*adj.* Lighted by or only by the stars: also **star′lit′** (-lit′).

star·ling (stär′ling) *n.* 1 A chubby, gregarious, aggressive bird with iridescent black plumage, introduced from Europe and now common in North America. 2 Any of various related European birds. [< OE *stærling*]

star of David The six-pointed star used as a symbol of Judaism.

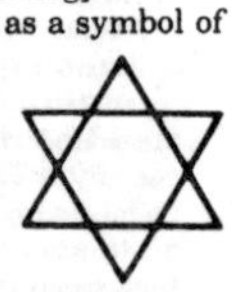

Star of David

starred (stärd) *adj.* 1 Spangled or marked with stars. 2 Marked with an asterisk. 3 Affected by astral influence: used chiefly in combination: *ill-starred.* 4 Presented or advertised as the star of an entertainment.

star·ry (stär′ē) *adj.* **·ri·er, ·ri·est** 1 Set or marked with stars. 2 Shining as or like stars. 3 Star-shaped. 4 Lighted by or abounding in stars. 5 Of, from, having to do with, or like stars. —**star′ri·ness** *n.*

star·ry-eyed (stär′ē·īd′) *adj.* Excited by or given to fanciful thoughts of romance, adventure, etc.

Stars and Stripes The flag of the U.S., having 13 alternating horizontal stripes of red and white, and in the upper left-hand corner 50 white stars against a blue ground.

star-span·gled (stär′spang′gəld) *adj.* Spangled with stars or starlike spots or points.

Star-Spangled Banner 1 The flag of the U.S. 2 The national anthem of the U.S., with words written by Francis Scott Key in 1814.

start (stärt) *v.i.* 1 To make an involuntary, startled movement, as from fear or surprise. 2 To move suddenly, as with a spring, leap, or bound. 3 To begin an action, undertaking, trip, etc.: They *started* early on their vacation. 4 To become active, operative, etc.: School *starts* in the fall. 5 To be on the team, lineup, etc., that begins a game or contest. 6 To protrude; seem to bulge: His eyes *started* from his head. 7 To be displaced or dislocated; become loose, warped, etc. —*v.t.* 8 To set in motion, activity, etc.: to *start* an engine; to *start* a rumor. 9 To begin; commence: to *start* a lecture. 10 To put on the team, lineup, etc., that begins a game or contest: I'm *starting* the new players today. 11 To set up; establish. 12 To introduce (a subject) or propound (a question). 13 To displace or dislocate; loosen, warp, etc.: The collision *started* the ship's seams. 14 To rouse from cover; cause to take flight; flush, as game. 15 To draw the contents from; tap, as a cask. **—start up** 1 To rise or appear suddenly. 2 To begin; come into being. 3 To begin the operation of (a motor, etc.). **—to start with** In the first place. —*n.* 1 A quick, startled movement or reaction. 2 A temporary or spasmodic action or attempt: by fits and *starts.* 3 A beginning or commencement, as of an action, undertaking, etc. 4 Advantage; lead, as in a race. 5 A place or time of beginning. 6 A loosened place or condition; crack: a *start* in a ship's planking. [ME *sterten* start, leap]

start·er (stär′tər) *n.* 1 One who or that which starts, esp.. a A competitor or member of a team at the start of a race or contest. b A person giving the starting signal for a race or contest. c A person whose job is to see to it that buses, trolleys, etc., leave on schedule. d Any mechanical device that initiates movement in an engine or the like. 2 A substance or mixture that initiates a chemical reaction, esp. in food: a *starter* for bread.

star·tle (stärt′əl) *v.* **·tled, ·tling** *v.t.* 1 To arouse or excite suddenly; alarm. —*v.i.* 2 To be aroused or excited suddenly; take alarm. —*n.* A sudden fright or shock; a scare. [< OE *steartlian* to kick] **—star′tler** *n.*

star·tling (stärt′ling) *adj.* Rousing sudden surprise, alarm, or the like. **—star′tling·ly** *adv.*

star·va·tion (stär·vā′shən) *n.* 1 The act of starving. 2 The state of being starved. —*adj.* Insufficient to sustain life or to purchase basic necessities: a *starvation* diet; *starvation* wages.

starve (stärv) *v.* **starved, starv·ing** *v.i.* 1 To die or perish from lack of food. 2 To suffer from extreme hunger. 3 To suffer from lack or need: to *starve* for friendship. —*v.t.* 4 To cause to die of hunger. 5 To deprive of food. 6 To bring to a specified condition by starving: to *starve* an enemy into surrender. [< OE *steorfan* die] **—starv′er** *n.*

starve·ling (stärv′ling) *n.* A person or animal that is starving, starved, or emaciated.

stash (stash) *v.t. Informal* To hide or conceal (money or valuables), for future use or safe-keeping: often with *away.* —*n. Slang* 1 A place where things are stashed away. 2 Something stashed away. [?]

-stat *combining form* A device which stops or makes constant: *thermostat.* [< Gk. *-statēs* causing to stand]

state (stāt) *n.* 1 A mode or condition of being or existing: a *state* of war. 2 A particular physical or chemical stage or condition of something: Ice is the solid *state* of water. 3 Frame of mind: a *state* of utter peace. 4 Any extreme mental condition, as of excitement, nervousness, etc. 5 Social status or position. 6 A grand, ceremonious, or luxurious style of living or doing: to arrive in *state.* 6 A sovereign political community; nation. 7 A political and territorial unit within such a community: the *state* of Maine. **—lie in state** To be placed on public view before burial. —*adj.* 1 Of or pertaining to a state, nation, or government. 2 Intended for use on occasions of ceremony. —*v.t.* **stat·ed, stat·ing** 1 To set forth explicitly in speech or writing; declare. 2 To fix; settle: to *state* terms. [< L *status* condition, state < *stare* to stand] **—state′hood** *n.* **—Syn.** *n.* 1 circumstances. 5 standing. *v.* 1 affirm, assert, aver.

state·craft (stāt′kraft′, -kräft′) *n.* The art of conducting affairs of state.

stat·ed (stā′tid) *adj.* 1 Regular; fixed. 2 Told; asserted: a *stated* fact. **—stat′ed·ly** *adv.*

state·house (stāt′hous′) *n. Often cap.* A building used for sessions of a state legislature. Also **state house.**

state·ly (stāt′lē) *adj.* **·li·er, ·li·est** 1 Dignified; majestic: a *stately* mansion. 2 Slow; measured: a *stately* march. —*adv.* Loftily. **—state′li·ness** *n.* **—Syn.** 1 imposing, grand, awesome, impressive.

state·ment (stāt′mənt) *n.* 1 The act of stating. 2 That which is stated. 3 A summary of assets and liabilities, showing the balance due. 3 A major or dominant idea expressed in the composition of a creative work, as in art, music, or design; motif. 4 The expression of such an idea.

state·room (stāt′ro͞om′, -ro͝om′) *n.* A small private bedroom on a passenger ship or railroad train.

state's evidence Testimony for the prosecution in a U.S. federal or state court, esp. that of a criminal against his accomplices. **—turn state's evidence** To offer state's evidence.

state·side (stāt′sīd′) *adj. Informal* Of or in the continental U.S. —*adv.* In or to the continental U.S.

states·man (stāts′mən) *n. pl.* **·men** (-mən) A person skilled in the science of government and prominent in national and foreign affairs. **—states′man·ly** *adv.* **—states′·man·ship** *n.*

state socialism A political theory advocating government ownership of utilities and industries.

States' rights The powers not vested in the U.S. federal government by the Constitution nor prohibited by it to the states. Also **State rights.**

states·wom·an (stāts′wo͝om′ən) *n. pl.* **·wom·en** (-wim′in) A woman skilled in the science of government and prominent in national and foreign affairs.

state-wide (stāt′wīd′) *adj. & adv.* Throughout a state.

stat·ic (stat′ik) *adj.* 1 Pertaining to bodies at rest or forces in equilibrium. 2 *Physics* Not involved in or with motion: *static* pressure. 3 *Electr.* Of or caused by stationary electric charges. 4 At rest; not active. 5 Of or pertaining to nonactive elements. 6 Dealing with fixed or stable conditions. Also **stat′i·cal.** —*n. Electronics* Electrical noise, esp. atmospheric, that interferes with radio communications. [< Gk *statikos* causing to stand] **—stat′i·cal·ly** *adv.*

stat·ics (stat′iks) *n.pl. (construed as sing.)* The mechanics of bodies at rest.

sta·tion (stā′shən) *n.* 1 A place where a person or thing usu. stands. 2 The headquarters of some official person or body of men: a police *station.* 3 A starting point or stopping place of a railroad or bus line. 4 A building for the accommodation of passengers or freight, as on a railroad or bus line; depot. 5 Social rank; standing. 6 *Mil.* The place to which an individual, unit, or ship is assigned for duty. 7 The installations of a radio or television broadcasting unit. —*v.t.* To assign to a station; set in position. [< L *stare* to stand]

sta·tion·ar·y (stā′shə·ner′ē) *adj.* 1 Remaining in one place. 2 Fixed; not portable. 3 Exhibiting no change of character or condition.

sta·tion·er (stā′shə·nər) *n.* A dealer in stationery and related goods. [< Med. L *stationarius* stationary, having a fixed location (for business)]

sta·tion·er·y (stā′shə·ner′ē) *n.* Paper, pens, pencils, ink, notebooks, and other related goods.

station wagon An automotive vehicle with one or more rows of seats behind the front seat and with a hinged tailgate for admitting luggage, etc.

stat·ism (stā′tiz·əm) *n.* A theory of government which advocates the concentration of economic planning, control, etc., in a centralized government. **—stat′ist** *n.*

sta·tis·tic (stə·tis′tik) *n.* Any element entering into a statistical statement. —*adj.* STATISTICAL.

sta·tis·ti·cal (stə·tis′tə·kəl) *adj.* 1 Of or pertaining to statistics. 2 Composed of statistics. **—sta·tis′ti·cal·ly** *adv.*

stat·is·ti·cian (stat′is·tish′ən) *n.* One skilled in collecting and tabulating statistical data.

sta·tis·tics (stə·tis′tiks) *n.pl.* 1 A collection of quantitative data or facts. 2 *(construed as sing.)* The branch of mathematics that deals with the collection and analysis of quantitative data. [< L *status* position, state]

stat·u·ar·y (stach′o͞o·er′ē) *n. pl.* **·ar·ies** Statues collectively. —*adj.* Of or suitable for statues. [< L *statua* statue]

stat·ue (stach′o͞o) *n.* A three-dimensional representation of a human or animal figure modeled in clay or wax, cast in bronze or plaster, or carved in wood or stone. [< L *status,* pp. of *stare* stand]

stat·u·esque (stach′o͞o·esk′) *adj.* 1 Resembling a statue, as in grace or dignity. 2 Shapely; comely. —**stat′u·esque′ly** *adv.* —**stat′u·esque′ness** *n.*

stat·u·ette (stach′o͞o·et′) *n.* A small statue. [F]

stat·ure (stach′ər) *n.* 1 The natural height of a body. 2 The height of anything, as a tree. 3 Status or reputation resulting from development or growth: artistic *stature.* [< L *status* condition, state]

sta·tus (stā′təs, stat′əs) *n.* 1 State, condition, or relation. 2 Relative position or rank. [< L *stare* to stand]

sta·tus quo (stā′təs kwō, stat′əs) The actual or existing condition or state. Also **status in quo.** [L]

stat·ute (stach′o͞ot) *n.* 1 *Law* A legislative enactment. 2 An established law or regulation. [< L *statutus,* pp. of *statuere* constitute]

statute law The law as set forth in statutes.

statute mile MILE (def. 1).

statute of limitations A statute which imposes time limits upon the right of action in certain cases.

stat·u·to·ry (stach′ə·tôr′ē, -tō′rē) *adj.* 1 Pertaining to a statute. 2 Created by or based upon legislative enactment.

statutory rape See RAPE.

staunch (stônch, stänch) *adj.* 1 Firm in principle; constant; trustworthy. 2 Stout; seaworthy: a *staunch* ship. —*v.t.* STANCH. [< OF *estanchier* make stand] —**staunch′ly** *adv.* —**staunch′ness** *n.* —**Syn.** *adj.* 1 faithful, loyal, trusty. 2 sound, trim. • See STANCH.

stave (stāv) *n.* 1 A curved strip of wood, forming a part of the sides of a barrel, tub, or the like. 2 *Music* A staff. 3 A stanza; verse. 4 A rod, cudgel, or staff. 5 A rung of a rack or ladder. —*v.* **staved** or **stove, stav·ing** *v.t.* 1 To break or make (a hole) by crushing or collision. 2 To furnish with staves. —*v.i.* 3 To be broken in, as a vessel's hull. —**stave off** To ward off: to *stave off* bankruptcy. [< *staves,* pl. of STAFF]

Barrel stave

staves (stāvz) *n.* 1 A *pl.* of STAFF. 2 *pl.* of STAVE.

stay[1] (stā) *v.i.* 1 To stop; halt: *Stay* where you are. 2 To continue in a specified place or condition: to *stay* home; to *stay* healthy. 3 To remain temporarily as a guest or resident. 4 To tarry: I'll *stay* a few more minutes. 5 *Informal* To have endurance; last. 6 *Informal* To keep pace with a competitor, as in a race. —*v.t.* 7 To bring to a stop; halt. 8 To hinder; delay. 9 To put off; postpone. 10 To satisfy the demands of temporarily; appease: to *stay* the pangs of hunger. 11 To remain for the duration of: to *stay* the night. —*n.* 1 The act or time of staying: a week's *stay* at the beach. 2 A deferment or suspension of judicial proceedings: The court granted a *stay* of sentencing. 3 *Informal* Staying power; endurance. [< L *stare* stand] —**stay′er** *n.*

stay[2] (stā) *v.t.* To be a support to; prop or hold up. —*n.* 1 Anything which props or supports. 2 *pl.* A corset stiffened, as with steel strips or whalebone. [< OF *estayer*]

stay[3] (stā) *Naut. n.* 1 A large, strong rope or wire, used to brace a mast or spar. 2 Any rope having a similar use. —*v.t.* 1 To support with a stay or stays. 2 To put (a vessel) on the opposite tack. —*v.i.* 3 To tack: said of vessels. [< OE *stæg*]

staying power The ability to endure.

stay·sail (stā′sāl′, -səl) *n. Naut.* A sail, usu. triangular, extended on a stay.

Ste. Sainte (female) (F *Sainte*).

stead (sted) *n.* Place of another person or thing as assumed by a substitute or a successor: My sister went in my *stead.* —**stand (one) in good stead** To give (one) good service, support, etc. [< OE *stede* place]

stead·fast (sted′fast′, -fäst′, -fəst) *adj.* 1 Firmly fixed in faith or devotion to duty. 2 Directed fixedly at one point, as the gaze. [< OE *stedefæst*] —**stead′fast′ly** *adv.* —**stead′fast′ness** *n.*

stead·y (sted′ē) *adj.* **stead·i·er, stead·i·est** 1 Stable; not liable to shake or totter: a *steady* ladder. 2 Unfaltering; constant: a *steady* light; *steady* loyalty. 3 Calm; unruffled: *steady* nerves. 4 Free from intemperance and dissipation: *steady* habits. 5 Regular: a *steady* customer. 6 Of a ship, keeping more or less upright in rough seas. —**go steady** *Informal* To date exclusively. —*v.t. & v.i.* **stead·ied, stead·y·ing** To make or become steady. —*interj.* Not so fast; keep calm. —*n. Slang* A sweetheart or constant companion. [< STEAD] —**stead′i·ly** *adv.* —**stead′i·ness** *n.*

steak (stāk) *n.* A slice of meat or fish, esp. of beef, usu. broiled or fried. [< ON *steik*]

steal (stēl) *v.* **stole, sto·len, steal·ing** *v.t.* 1 To take from another without right or permission. 2 To take or obtain in a subtle manner: He has *stolen* the hearts of the people. 3 In baseball, to reach (another base) without the aid of a hit or error: said of a base runner. —*v.i.* 4 To move quietly and stealthily: to *steal* away in the night. 5 To commit theft. 6 To move secretly or furtively. —*n. Informal* 1 The act of stealing or that which is stolen. 2 Any underhanded financial deal that benefits the originators. 3 A bargain: a *steal* at $3.99. [< OE *stelan*] —**steal′er** *n.* —**Syn.** *v.* 1 filch, pilfer, purloin. 4 skulk, slink.

stealth (stelth) *n.* Secret or furtive action, movement, or behavior. [< OE *stelan* steal]

stealth·y (stel′thē) *adj.* **stealth·i·er, stealth·i·est** Marked by stealth; designed to elude notice. —**stealth′i·ly** *adv.* —**stealth′i·ness** *n.*

steam (stēm) *n.* 1 Water in the form of a gas, esp. above the boiling point of the liquid. 2 The visible mist formed by sudden cooling of hot steam. 3 Any kind of vaporous exhalation. 4 Energy or power derived from hot water vapor under pressure. 5 *Informal* Vigor; force; speed. —**let off steam** To give expression to pent-up emotions or opinions. —*v.i.* 1 To emit steam or vapor. 2 To rise or pass off as steam. 3 To become covered with condensed water vapor: often with *up.* 4 To generate steam. 5 To move or travel by the agency of steam. —*v.t.* 6 To treat with steam, as in softening, cooking, cleaning, etc. —*adj.* 1 Of, driven, or operated by steam. 2 Producing or containing steam: a *steam* boiler; a *steam* pipe. 3 Treated by steam. 4 Using steam: *steam* heat. [< OE *stēam*] —**steam′i·ness** *n.* —**steam′y** *adj.* **(·i·er, i·est)**

steam·boat (stēm′bōt′) *n.* A boat propelled by steam.

steam engine An engine that derives its force from the pressure of hot steam.

steam·er (stē′mər) *n.* 1 A steamship or steamboat. 2 A pot or container in which something is steamed.

steam·fit·ter (stēm′fit′ər) *n.* A man who sets up or repairs steam pipes and their fittings. —**steam′fit′ting** *n.*

steam·roll·er (stēm′rōl′ər) *n.* 1 A machine having a heavy roller for flattening asphalt surfaces. 2 *Informal* Any force that ruthlessly overcomes opposition. —*v. Informal v.t.* 1 To crush ruthlessly. —*v.i.* 2 To move with crushing force. Also **steam′roll′.**

steam·ship (stēm′ship′) *n.* A large vessel used for ocean traffic and propelled by steam.

steam shovel A power-operated machine for digging and excavation.

ste·ap·sin (stē·ap′sin) *n.* A pancreatic enzyme that aids in the digestion of fat. [< STEA(RIN) + (PE)PSIN]

ste·ar·ic acid (stē·ar′ik, stir′ik) A fatty acid common in solid animal fats, used in making soap. Also **ste′a·rin.** [< Gk. *stear* suet]

ste·a·tite (stē′ə·tīt) *n.* Massive talc found in extensive beds and used for electric insulation. [< Gk. *stear, steatos* suet, tallow] —**ste′a·tit′ic** (-tit′ik) *adj.*

sted·fast (sted′fast′, -fäst′, -fəst) *adj.* STEADFAST.

steed (stēd) *n.* A horse; esp., a spirited horse. [< OE *stēda* studhorse]

steel (stēl) *n.* 1 Any of various alloys of iron containing carbon in amounts up to about 2 percent, often with other components that give special properties. 2 Something made of steel, as an implement or weapon. 3 Hardness of character. 4 *Can.* A railway track or line. —*adj.* 1 Made or composed of steel. 2 Adamant; unyielding. —*v.t.* 1 To cover with steel. 2 To make strong; harden: to *steel* one's heart against misery. [< OE *stēl*] —**steel′i·ness** *n.* —**steel′y** *adj.* **(·i·er, ·i·est)**

steel wool Steel fibers matted together for use in cleaning and polishing.

steel·work·er (stēl′wûr′kər) *n.* One who works in a steel mill.

steel·yard (stēl′yärd′, stil′yərd) *n.* A device for weighing, consisting of a scaled beam, a movable counterpoise, and hooks to hold the article to be weighed. Also **steel′·yards.**

steen·bok (stēn′bok, stān′) *n. pl.* **·bok** or **·boks** A small African antelope with short horns in the male. [< MDu. *steen* stone + *boc* buck]

Steenbok

steep[1] (stēp) *adj.* **1** Sloping sharply; precipitous. **2** *Informal* Exorbitant; high, as a price. —*n.* A cliff; a precipitous place. [< OE *stēap*] —**steep′ly** *adv.* —**steep′ness** *n.* —**Syn.** *adj.* **1** abrupt, high, sharp, sheer.

steep[2] (stēp) *v.t.* **1** To soak in a liquid, as for softening, cleansing, etc. **2** To imbue thoroughly: *steeped* in crime. —*v.i.* **3** To undergo soaking in a liquid. —*n.* **1** The process of steeping, or the state of being steeped. **2** A liquid or bath in which anything is steeped. [< ON *steypa* pour] —**steep′er** *n.*

steep·en (stē′pən) *v.t. & v.i.* To make or become steep or steeper.

stee·ple (stē′pəl) *n.* A lofty structure rising above the roof of a church, usu. having a spire. [< OE *stēpel*]

stee·ple·chase (stē′pəl·chās′) *n.* **1** A race on horseback across country. **2** A race over a course with hedges, rails, and water jumps. —**stee′ple·chas′er** *n.*

stee·ple·jack (stē′pəl·jak′) *n.* A man whose occupation is to climb steeples and other tall structures to inspect or make repairs.

steer[1] (stir) *v.t.* **1** To direct the course of (a vessel or vehicle). **2** To follow (a course). **3** To direct; guide; control. —*v.i.* **4** To direct the course of a vessel, vehicle, etc. **5** To undergo guiding or steering. **6** To follow a course: to *steer* for land. —**steer clear of** To avoid; keep away from. —*n. Slang* A tip; piece of advice. [< OE *stēoran*] —**steer′er** *n.*

steer[2] (stir) *n.* **1** A young castrated bovine. **2** Any male cattle raised for beef. [< OE *stēor*]

steer·age (stir′ij) *n.* That part of an ocean passenger vessel allotted to passengers paying the lowest fares.

steers·man (stirz′mən) *n. pl.* **·men** (-mən) One who steers a boat or a ship; a helmsman.

stein (stīn) *n.* A beer mug. [G]

stein·bok (stīn′bok) *n.* STEENBOK.

stel·lar (stel′ər) *adj.* **1** Of or pertaining to the stars; astral. **2** Chief; principal: a *stellar* role in a play. [< L *stella* star]

stel·late (stel′it, -āt) *adj.* Star-shaped; having rays pointing outward from a center. Also **stel·lat·ed** (stel′ā·tid). [< L *stella* star] —**stel′late·ly** *adv.*

St. El·mo's fire (sānt el′mōz) A luminous discharge of static electricity sometimes appearing on the superstructure of ships, on the tips of airplane wings, etc. Also **St. El·mo's light.**

stem[1] (stem) *n.* **1** The main ascending axis of a plant, serving to transport water and nutrients, to hold up the leaves to air and light, etc. **2** A subsidiary stalk supporting a fruit, flower, or leaf. **3** The slender upright support of a goblet, wine glass, vase, etc. **4** In a watch, the small projecting rod used for winding the mainspring. **5** *Music* The line attached to the head of a written musical note. **6** *Ling.* The unchanged element common to all the members of a given inflection. **7** The bow of a boat. —**from stem to stern 1** From one end of a ship to the other. **2** Throughout; thoroughly. —*v.t.* **stemmed, stem·ming** To remove the stems of or from. —**stem from** To be descended or derived. [< OE *stemm, stemn*] —**stem′mer** *n.*

stem[2] (stem) *v.t.* **stemmed, stem·ming 1** To stop, hold back, or dam up, as a current. **2** To make progress against, as a current, opposing force, etc. [< ON *stemma* stop]

stem·wind·er (stem′wīn′der) *n.* **1** A stemwinding watch. **2** *Slang* A very superior person or thing.

stem·wind·ing (stem′wīn′ding) *adj.* Wound, as a watch, by turning a knob at the outermost end of the stem.

stench (stench) *n.* A foul or offensive odor. [< OE *stenc*] —**stench′y** *adj.* —**Syn.** fetidness, miasma, reek, stink.

sten·cil (sten′səl) *n.* **1** A thin sheet or plate in which a written text or a pattern is cut through which applied paint or ink penetrates to a surface beneath. **2** Produced by stenciling. —*v.t.* **·ciled** or **·cilled, ·cil·ing** or **·cil·ling** To mark with a stencil. [< OF *estenceler*] —**sten′·cil·er** or **sten′cil·ler** *n.*

sten·o (sten′ō) *n. pl.* **sten·os 1** STENOGRAPHER. **2** STENOGRAPHY.

steno- *combining form* Tight; contracted: *stenography,* [< Gk. *stenos* narrow]

steno., stenog. stenographer; stenography.

ste·nog·ra·pher (stə·nog′rə·fər) *n.* One who is skilled in shorthand.

ste·nog·ra·phy (stə·nog′rə·fē) *n.* **1** The method of rapid writing by the use of contractions or arbitrary symbols; shorthand. **2** The act of using stenography. —**sten·o·graph·ic** (sten′ə·graf′ik) or **·i·cal** *adj.* —**sten′o·graph′i·cal·ly** *adv.*

sten·o·type (sten′ə·tīp) *n.* A keyboard-operated machine for recording on paper tape symbols representing speech.

sten·o·typ·y (sten′ə·tī′pē) *n.* A system of shorthand utilizing a keyboard-operated machine to record letters in various combinations that represent sounds, words, or phrases. —**sten′o·typ′ist** *n.*

sten·to·ri·an (sten·tôr′ē·ən, -tō′rē-) *adj.* Extremely loud. [< *Stentor,* a herald in the *Iliad,* famous for his loud voice] —**sten·to′ri·an·ly** *adv.*

step (step) *n.* **1** A change in location or position accomplished by lifting the foot and putting it down in a different place. **2** The distance passed over in making such a motion. **3** Any space easily traversed. **4** A stair or ladder rung. **5** A single action or proceeding regarded as leading to something. **6** A grade or degree: They advanced him a *step.* **7** The sound of a footfall. **8** A footprint; track. **9** *pl.* Progression by walking. **10** A combination of foot movements in dancing. **11** *Music* An interval approximately equal to that between the first two tones of a diatonic scale. —**in step 1** Walking or dancing evenly with another by taking corresponding steps. **2** Conforming; in agreement. —**out of step 1** Not in step. **2** Not conforming or agreeing. —**step by step** In slow stages. —**take steps** To adopt measures, as to attain an end. —**watch one's step** To be cautious. —*v.* **stepped, step·ping** *v.i.* **1** To move forward or backward by taking a step or steps. **2** To walk a short distance. **3** To move with measured, dignified, or graceful steps. **4** To move or act quickly or briskly. **5** To pass into a situation, circumstance, etc.: He *stepped* into a fortune. —*v.t.* **6** To take (a pace, stride, etc.). **7** To perform the steps of: to *step* a quadrille. **8** To place or move (the foot) in taking a step. **9** To measure by taking steps: often with *off.* **10** To cut or arrange in steps. —**step down 1** To decrease gradually. **2** To resign from an office or position; abdicate. —**step in** To begin to take part; intervene. —**step on** (or **upon**) **1** To tread upon. **2** To put the foot on so as to activate, as a brake or treadle. **3** *Informal* To reprove or subdue. —**step on it** *Informal* To hurry; hasten. —**step out 1** To go outside. **2** *Informal* To go out for fun or entertainment. **3** To step down. **4** To walk with long strides. —**step up** To increase; raise. [< OE *stæpe*] —**Syn.** *n.* **6** stage, level, position, notch.

step- *combining form* Related through the previous marriage of a parent or spouse, but not by blood: *stepchild.* [< OE *steop-*]

step·broth·er (step′bruth′ər) *n.* The son of one's stepparent by a former marriage.

step·child (step′chīld′) *n. pl.* **·chil·dren** The child of one's husband or wife by a former marriage.

step·daugh·ter (step′dô′tər) *n.* A female stepchild.

step-down (step′doun′) *adj.* 1 That decreases gradually. 2 *Electr.* Designating a transformer whose output voltage is less than its input voltage. 3 Designating a speed-reducing gear.
step·fa·ther (step′fä′thər) *n.* A man who has married one's mother after the decease or divorce of one's own father.
step-in (step′in′) *adj.* Put on, as undergarments or shoes, by being stepped into.
step·lad·der (step′lad′ər) *n.* A set of portable, usu. flat steps with a hinged frame at the back for support.
step·moth·er (step′muth′ər) *n.* A woman who has married one's father after the decease or divorce of one's own mother.
step·par·ent (step′pâr′ənt) *n.* A stepfather or stepmother.
steppe (step) *n.* 1 A vast plain devoid of forest. 2 One of the extensive plains in SE Europe and Asia. [< Russ. *step′*]
stepped-up (stept′up′) *adj. Informal* Speeded up; increased: *stepped-up* production.
step·per (step′ər) *n.* 1 One who or that which steps. 2 *Slang* A dancer.
step·ping·stone (step′ing·stōn′) *n.* 1 A stone forming a footrest, as for crossing a stream, etc. 2 That by which one advances or rises.
step·sis·ter (step′sis′tər) *n.* The daughter of one's stepparent by a former marriage.
step·son (step′sun′) *n.* A male stepchild.
step-up (step′up′) *adj.* 1 Increasing by stages. 2 Designating a transformer whose output voltage exceeds its input voltage. 3 Designating a speed-increasing gear. —*n.* An increase, as in intensity, amount, etc.
-ster *suffix of nouns* 1 One who makes or is occupied with: *songster.* 2 One who belongs or is related to: *gangster.* 3 One who is: *youngster.* [< OE *-estre*]
ster., stg. Sterling.
ste·ra·di·an (sti·rā′dē·ən) *n.* A solid angle with its vertex at the center of a sphere which encloses a surface equivalent to the square of the radius of the sphere: a unit of measure. [< Gk. *stereos* solid + RADIAN]
stere (stir) *n.* A cubic meter. [< Gk. *stereos* solid]
ster·e·o (ster′ē·ō, stir′-) *n. pl.* **·e·os** 1 A stereophonic record player, record, tape, etc. 2 Stereophonic sound. 3 STEREOTYPE (defs. 1 & 2). 4 A stereoscopic method; also, a steroscopic photograph. —*adj.* 1 STEREOPHONIC. 2 STEREOTYPED (def. 1). 3 Of or pertaining to the stereoscope; stereoscopic.
stereo- *combining form* Solid; firm; three-dimensional: *stereoscope.* [< Gk. *stereos* hard]
ster·e·o·phon·ic (ster′ē·ə·fon′ik, stir′-) *adj.* Of, for, or designating a system of sound reproduction in which two independent channels are used so as to present different sounds to each of a listener's ears. —**ster′e·o·phon′i·cal·ly** *adv.*
ster·e·o·scope (ster′ē·ə·skōp, stir′-) *n.* An instrument for presenting different images of an object to each eye, so as to produce a three-dimensional illusion. —**ster′e·o·scop′ic** (-skop′ik) or **·i·cal** *adj.* —**ster′e·o·scop′i·cal·ly** *adv.* —**ster·e·os·co·pist** (ster′ē·os′kə·pist, stir-) *n.*
ster·e·o·type (ster′ē·ə·tīp′, stir′-) *n.* 1 A printing plate cast in metal from a matrix molded from a raised surface, as type. 2 Anything made or processed in this way. 3 A conventional or hackneyed expression, custom, or mode of thought. —*v.t.* **·typed, ·typ·ing** 1 To make a stereotype of. 2 To print from stereotypes. 3 To give a fixed or unalterable form to. —**ster′e·o·typ′er, ster′e·o·typ′ist** *n.*
ster·e·o·typed (ster′ē·ə·tīpt′, stir′-) *adj.* 1 Produced from a stereotype. 2 Hackneyed; without originality.
ster·ile (ster′əl, *Chiefly Brit.* -īl) *adj.* 1 Having no reproductive power; barren. 2 Lacking productiveness: *sterile* soil. 3 Containing no microorganisms; aseptic: a *sterile* fluid. 4 Lacking vigor or interest; *sterile* prose. 5 Without results; futile: *sterile* hopes. [< L *sterilis*] —**ster′ile·ly** *adv.* —**ste·ril·i·ty** (stə·ril′ə·tē), **ster′ile·ness** *n.*
ster·il·ize (ster′əl·īz) *v.t.* **·ized, ·iz·ing** 1 To render incapable of reproduction, esp. by surgery. 2 To destroy microorganisms. 3 To make barren. —**ster′i·li·za′tion, ster′il·iz′er** *n.*
ster·ling (stûr′ling) *n.* 1 British money. 2 The official standard of fineness for British coins. 3 Sterling silver as used in manufacturing articles, as tableware, etc. 4 Articles made of sterling silver collectively. —*adj.* 1 Made of or payable in sterling: pounds *sterling.* 2 Made of sterling silver. 3 Having great worth; genuine: *sterling* qualities. [Prob. < OE *steorra* star + -LING]
sterling silver An alloy of 92.5 percent silver and usu. 7.5 percent copper.
stern[1] (stûrn) *adj.* 1 Marked by severity or harshness: a *stern* command. 2 Having an austere disposition: a *stern* judge. 3 Inspiring fear. 4 Resolute: a *stern* resolve. [< OE *styrne*] —**stern′ly** *adv.* —**stern′ness** *n.*
stern[2] (stûrn) *n.* 1 *Naut.* The aft part of a ship, boat, etc. 2 The hindmost part of any object. —*adj.* Situated at or belonging to the stern. [< ON *styra* steer] —**stern′most′** (-mōst′) *adj.*
ster·num (stûr′nəm) *n. pl.* **·na** (-nə) or **·nums** The structure of bone and cartilage that forms the ventral support of the ribs in vertebrates. [< Gk. *sternon* breast] —**stern·al** (stûr′nal) *adj.*
ster·nu·ta·tion (stûr′nyə·tā′shən) *n.* 1 The act of sneezing. 2 A sneeze or the noise produced by it. [< L *sternuere* to sneeze] —**ster·nu·ta·to·ry** (ster·nyōō′tə·tôr′ē, -tō′ri) *adj.*
stern-wheel·er (stûrn′hwē′lər) *n.* A steamboat propelled by one large paddle wheel at the stern.
ster·oid (ster′oid) *n.* Any of a large group of structurally similar organic compounds found in plants and animals, including many hormones and the precursors of certain vitamins. [< STER(OL) + -OID]
ster·ol (ster′ōl, -ol) *n.* Any of a class of steroids comprising solid, fat-soluble alcohols, as cholesterol. [Contraction of CHOLESTEROL]
ster·tor·ous (stûr′tər·əs) *adj.* Characterized or accompanied by a snoring sound: *stertorous* breathing. [< L *stertere* to snore] —**ster′tor·ous·ly** *adv.* —**ster′tor·ous·ness** *n.*
stet (stet) Let it stand: a direction used in proofreading to indicate that a word, letter, etc., marked for omission is to remain. —*v.t.* **stet·ted, stet·ting** To mark for retention with the word *stet.* [< L *stare* to stand]
steth·o·scope (steth′ə·skōp) *n.* An apparatus for conducting sounds from the human body to the ears of an examiner. [< Gk. *stēthos* breast + -SCOPE] —**steth′o·scop′ic** (-skop′ik) *adj.* —**steth′o·scop′i·cal·ly** *adv.* —**ste·thos·co·py** (ste·thos′kə·pē) *n.*
stet·son (stet′sən) *n. Often cap.* A man's hat, usu. of felt, with a high crown and a broad brim, popular in the w U.S. [< *Stetson*, a trade name]
ste·ve·dore (stē′və·dôr, -dōr) *n.* One whose business is loading or unloading ships. —*v.t. & v.i.* **·dored, ·dor·ing** To load or unload (a vessel or vessels). [< L *stipare* compress, stuff]
stew (styōō) *v.t. & v.i.* 1 To boil slowly and gently. 2 *Informal* To worry. —*n.* 1 Stewed food, esp. a preparation of meat or fish and vegetables cooked by stewing. 2 *Informal* Mental agitation; worry. [< OF *estuver*]
stew·ard (styōō′ərd) *n.* 1 A person entrusted with the management of the affairs of others. 2 A person put in charge of services for a club, ship, railroad train, etc. 3 On shipboard, a person who waits on table and takes care of passengers' staterooms. 4 SHOP STEWARD. [< OE *stī* hall + *weard* ward, keeper] —**stew′ard·ship** *n.*
stew·ard·ess (styōō′ər·dis) *n.* A woman whose occupation is that of a steward, esp. one who is employed on an airplane to attend passengers.
stewed (styōōd) *adj.* 1 Cooked by stewing. 2 *Slang* Drunk.
stge. storage.
stick (stik) *n.* 1 A stiff shoot or branch cut or broken off from a tree or bush. 2 Any relatively long and thin piece of wood. 3 A piece of wood fashioned for a specific use: a walking *stick;* a hockey *stick.* 4 Anything resembling a stick in form: a *stick* of dynamite. 5 A piece of wood of any size, cut for fuel, lumber, or timber. 6 *Aeron.* The lever of an airplane that controls pitching and rolling. 7 A poke, stab, or thrust with a stick or pointed implement. 8 The state of being stuck together; adhesion. 9 *Informal* A stiff, inert, or dull person. —**the sticks** *Informal* An obscure rural district. —*v.* **stuck, stick·ing** *v.t.* 1 To pierce or penetrate with a pointed object. 2 To stab. 3 To thrust or force, as a sword or pin, into or through something else. 4 To force the end of (a nail, etc.) into something. 5 To fasten

in place with or as with pins, nails, etc. **6** To cover with objects piercing the surface: a paper *stuck* with pins. **7** To impale; transfix. **8** To put or thrust: He *stuck* his hand into his pocket. **9** To fasten to a surface by or as by an adhesive substance. **10** To bring to a standstill: We were *stuck* in Rome. **11** *Informal* To smear with something sticky. **12** *Informal* To baffle; puzzle. **13** *Slang* To cheat. **14** *Slang* To force great expense, an unpleasant task, responsibility, etc., upon. —*v.i.* **15** To be or become fixed in place by being thrust in: The pins are *sticking* in the cushion. **16** To adhere; cling. **17** To come to a standstill; halt. **18** *Informal* To be baffled or disconcerted. **19** To hesitate; scruple: with *at* or *to.* **20** To persevere, as in a task or undertaking: with *at* or *to.* **21** To remain faithful, as to an ideal or bargain. **22** To protrude: with *out, through, up,* etc. —**be stuck on** *Informal* To be enamored of. —**stick around** *Slang* To remain near or near at hand. —**stick by** To remain loyal to. —**stick it out** To persevere to the end. —**stick up** *Slang* To stop and rob. —**stick up for** *Informal* To take the part of; defend. [< OE *sticca*]

stick·er (stik′ər) *n.* **1** One who or that which sticks. **2** A gummed label. **3** *Informal* Anything that confuses; a puzzle. **4** A prickly stem, thorn, or bur.

sticking plaster An adhesive material for covering slight cuts, etc.

stick·le (stik′əl) *v.i.* **·led, ·ling 1** To contend about trifles. **2** To hesitate for petty reasons. [< OE *stihtan* arrange]

stick·le·back (stik′əl·bak′) *n.* Any of various small, nest-building fresh- or salt-water fishes having sharp dorsal spines.

Stickleback

stick·ler (stik′lər) *n.* **1** One who insists upon exacting standards, as of behavior: with *for:* a *stickler* for punctuality. **2** A baffling problem.

stick·pin (stik′pin′) *n.* An ornamental pin for a necktie.

stick-to-it·ive·ness (stik′to͞o′ə·tiv·nis) *n. Informal* Perseverance; diligence.

stick-up (stik′up′) *n. Slang* A robbery or hold-up.

stick·y (stik′ē) *adj.* **stick·i·er, stick·i·est 1** Adhering to a surface; adhesive. **2** Warm and humid. **3** *Informal* Unpleasant or complicated: a *sticky* situation. —**stick′i·ly** *adv.* —**stick′i·ness** *n.* —**Syn. 1** gluey, mucilaginous, viscous.

stiff (stif) *adj.* **1** Resistant to bending; rigid. **2** Not easily worked or moved: a *stiff* bolt. **3** Moving with difficulty or pain: a *stiff* back. **4** Not natural, graceful, or easy: a *stiff* bow. **5** Taut; tightly drawn: a *stiff* rope. **6** Strong and steady: a *stiff* breeze. **7** Thick; viscous: a *stiff* batter. **8** Harsh; severe: a *stiff* penalty. **9** High; dear: *stiff* prices. **10** Difficult; hard: a *stiff* examination. **11** Stubborn; unyielding: *stiff* resistance. **12** Awkward or noticeably formal; not relaxed or easy; wooden. **13** Strong; potent: a *stiff* drink. **14** Difficult; arduous: a *stiff* climb. —*n. Slang* **1** A corpse. **2** An awkward or unresponsive person. **3** A person; fellow: a working *stiff.* **4** A rough person. [< OE *stīf*] —**stiff′ly** *adv.* —**stiff′ness** *n.*

stiff·en (stif′ən) *v.t.* & *v.i.* To make or become stiff or stiffer. —**stiff′en·er** *n.*

stiff-necked (stif′nekt′) *adj.* **1** Suffering from a stiff neck. **2** Stubborn; obstinate.

sti·fle (stī′fəl) *v.* **·fled, ·fling** *v.t.* **1** To kill by stopping respiration; choke. **2** To suppress or repress, as sobs. —*v.i.* **3** To die of suffocation. **4** To experience difficulty in breathing, as in a stuffy room. [ME *stufflen*] —**sti′fler** *n.* —**sti′fling·ly** *adv.*

stig·ma (stig′mə) *n. pl.* **stig·ma·ta** (stig·mä′tə, stig′mə·tə) or (*esp. for def. 2*) **stig·mas 1** A mark of disgrace. **2** *Bot.* That part of a pistil which receives the pollen. **3** *Biol.* Any spot or small opening. **4** A spot or scar on the skin. **5** *Med.* Any physical sign of diagnostic value. **6** *pl.* The wounds that Christ received at the Crucifixion. [L, mark, brand] —**stig·mat·ic** (-mat′ik) *adj.* —**Syn. 1** blemish, blot, stain.

stig·ma·tize (stig′mə·tīz) *v.t.* **·tized, ·tiz·ing 1** To characterize as disgraceful. **2** To mark with a stigma. *Brit. sp.* **stig′ma·tise.** —**stig′ma·ti·za′tion, stig′ma·tiz′er** *n.*

stile (stīl) *n.* A step, or series of steps, on each side of a fence or wall to enable one to climb over. [< OE *stigel*]

Stile

sti·let·to (sti·let′ō) *n. pl.* **·tos** or **·toes** A small dagger with a slender blade. —*v.t.* **·toed, ·to·ing** To pierce with a stiletto; stab. [< Ital. *stilo* dagger]

still[1] (stil) *adj.* **1** Being without movement; motionless. **2** Free from disturbance or agitation. **3** Making no sound; silent. **4** Low in sound; hushed. **5** Subdued; soft. **6** Dead; inanimate. **7** Having no effervescence: said of wines. **8** *Phot.* Not capable of showing movement. —*n.* **1** Absence of sound or noise. **2** *Phot.* A still photograph; esp. one taken on a motion-picture set, for advertising purposes. —*adv.* **1** Up to this or that time; yet: He is *still* here. **2** After or in spite of something; nevertheless. **3** In increasing degree; even yet: *still* more. **4** *Archaic* or *Regional* Always; constantly. —*conj.* Nevertheless. —*v.t.* **1** To cause to be still or calm. **2** To silence or hush. **3** To allay, as fears. —*v.i.* **4** To become still. [< OE *stille*] —**still′ness** *n.* —**Syn.** *adj.* **2** peaceful, tranquil, undisturbed. *v.* **1** soothe, tranquilize. **2** quiet.

Still[2]

still[2] (stil) *n.* **1** An apparatus for distilling liquids, esp. alcoholic liquors. **2** DISTILLERY. —*v.t.* & *v.i.* To distill. [< L *stilla* a drop]

still·born (stil′bôrn′) *adj.* Dead at birth. —**still′birth′** (-bûrth′) *n.*

still life *pl.* **lifes 1** In painting, the representation of inanimate objects. **2** A picture of such objects. —**still′-life′** *adj.*

Still·son wrench (stil′sən) A wrench resembling a monkey wrench, but with one serrated jaw capable of slight angular movement, so that the grip is tightened by pressure on the handle: a trade name. [< D. *Stillson,* its U.S. inventor in 1869]

Stillson wrench

still·y (stil′ē) *adj.* **·i·er, ·i·est** Quiet; calm. —*adv.* (stil′lē) Calmly; quietly.

stilt (stilt) *n.* **1** One of a pair of slender poles made with a projection above the ground to support the foot in walking. **2** A tall post or pillar used as a support for a dock or building. **3** Any of various shore birds with thin bills and long legs. [ME *stilte*]

stilt·ed (stil′tid) *adj.* Excessively formal or stuffy: *stilted* prose. —**stilt′ed·ly** *adv.* —**stilt′ed·ness** *n.*

stim·u·lant (stim′yə·lənt) *n.* **1** A drug that stimulates the rate or intensity of vital functions, esp. in the central nervous system. **2** Something that stimulates one to activity.

stim·u·late (stim′yə·lāt) *v.* **·lat·ed, ·lat·ing** *v.t.* **1** To rouse to activity; spur. **2** To increase action in by applying some form of stimulus: to *stimulate* the heart. **3** To affect by intoxicants. —*v.i.* **4** To act as a stimulus or stimulant. [< L *stimulus* a goad] —**stim′u·lat′er, stim′u·la′tor, stim′u·la′·tion** *n.*

stim·u·la·tive (stim′yə·lā′tiv) *adj.* Having the power to stimulate. —*n.* Something that stimulates.

stim·u·lus (stim′yə·ləs) *n. pl.* **·li** (-lī, -lē) **1** Anything that rouses to activity, as a stimulant, incentive, etc. **2** Any agent that influences activity in an organism. [< L]

sting (sting) *v.* **stung, sting·ing** *v.t.* **1** To pierce or prick painfully: The bee *stung* me. **2** To cause to suffer sharp, smarting pain. **3** To cause to suffer mentally: to be *stung* with remorse. **4** To stimulate or rouse as if with a sting; goad. **5** *Slang* To overcharge. —*v.i.* **6** To have or use a sting, as a bee. **7** To suffer a sharp, smarting pain. **8** To suffer mental distress. —*n.* **1** A sharp offensive or defensive organ, as of a bee, capable of introducing an allergen or a venom into a victim's skin. 2 The act of stinging. 3 A wound made by a sting. 4 The pain caused by such a wound. 5 Any sharp, smarting sensation. 6 A keen stimulus; spur. [< OE *stingan*] **—sting'er** *n.* **—sting'ing·ly** *adv.*

sting ray Any of various flat-bodied fishes with a whiplike tail having one or more stinging spines. Also **sting'ray, sting·a·ree** (sting'ə·rē, sting'rē')

Sting ray

stin·gy (stin'jē) *adj.* **·gi·er, ·gi·est** 1 Extremely penurious or miserly. 2 Scanty; meager: a *stingy* portion. [?] **—stin'gi·ly** *adv.* **—stin'·gi·ness** *n.* **—Syn. 1** avaricious, niggardly, parsimonious, tightfisted.

stink (stingk) *n.* A strong, foul odor; stench. *—v.* **stank** or **stunk, stunk, stink·ing** *v.i.* 1 To give forth a foul odor. 2 To be extremely offensive or hateful. *—v.t.* 3 To cause to stink. [< OE *stincan*] **—stink'er** *n.* **—stink'ing·ly** *adv.* **—stink'y** *adj.* **(·i·er, ·i·est)**

stink·bug (stingk'bug') *n.* Any of certain hemipterous insects with a sickening odor.

stink·weed (stingk'wēd') *n.* Any of various plants with foul-smelling flowers or leaves.

stint (stint) *v.t.* 1 To limit, as in amount. *—v.i.* 2 To be frugal or sparing. *—n.* 1 A task to be performed within a specified time: a weekly *stint.* 2 A bound; restriction. [< OE *styntan* stupefy] **—stint'er** *n.* **—stint'ing·ly** *adv.*

stipe (stīp) *n.* A stalklike support, esp. that of a fern frond, a pistil, or a mushroom cap. [< L *stipes* branch]

sti·pend (stī'pend, -pənd) *n.* A regular, fixed allowance or salary. [< L *stips* payment in coin + *pendere* weigh, pay out]

sti·pen·di·ar·y (stī·pen'dē·er'ē) *adj.* 1 Receiving a stipend. 2 Performing services for a fixed payment. *—n. pl.* **·ar·ies** One who receives a stipend.

stip·ple (stip'əl) *v.t.* **·pled, ·pling** To draw, paint, or engrave with dots. *—n.* 1 In painting, etching, etc., a method of representing light and shade by employing dots instead of lines. 2 The effect resulting from this method. 3 Stippled work. Also **stip'pling.** [< Du. *stip* dot] **—stip'pler** *n.*

stip·u·late (stip'yə·lāt) *v.* **·lat·ed, ·lat·ing** *v.t.* 1 To specify as the terms of an agreement, contract, etc. 2 To specify as a requirement for agreement. *—v.i.* 3 To demand something as a requirement or condition. [< L *stipulari* to bargain] **—stip'u·la'tor** *n.* **—stip'u·la·to'ry** (-lə·tôr'ē, -tō'rē) *adj.*

stip·u·la·tion (stip'yə·lā'shən) *n.* 1 The act of stipulating. 2 An agreement or contract.

stip·ule (stip'yo͞ol) *n.* One of a pair of leaflike appendages at the base of the petiole of certain leaves. [< L *stipula* stalk] **—stip'u·lar, stip'u·late, stip'u·lat'ed** *adj.*

stir[1] (stûr) *v.* **stirred, stir·ring** *v.t.* 1 To mix thoroughly by giving a circular motion to, as with a spoon, fork, etc.: to *stir* soup. 2 To cause to move, esp. slightly. 3 To move vigorously; bestir: *Stir* yourself! 4 To rouse, as from sleep, indifference, or inactivity. 5 To incite; provoke: often with *up.* 6 To affect strongly; move with emotion. *—v.i.* 7 To move, esp. slightly: The log wouldn't *stir.* 8 To be active; move about. 9 To take place; happen. 10 To undergo stirring: This molasses *stirs* easily. *—n.* 1 The act of stirring. 2 Movement. 3 Public interest; excitement. 4 A poke; nudge. [< OE *styrian*] **—stir'rer** *n.*

stir[2] (stûr) *n. Slang* A jail; prison. [?]

stir·ring (stûr'ing) *adj.* 1 Stimulating; inspiring. 2 Full of activity. **—stir'ring·ly** *adv.* **—Syn. 1** exciting, rousing. **2** animated, lively, sprightly.

stir·rup (stûr'əp, stir'-) *n.* 1 A loop of metal or wood suspended from a saddle to support a horseback rider's foot. 2 A similar device used as a support, as for a beam. [< OE *stigrāp* mounting rope] • See SADDLE.

stirrup bone STAPES.

stitch (stich) *n.* 1 A single passage of a threaded needle or other implement through fabric and back again, as in sewing. 2 A single turn of thread or yarn around a needle or other implement, as in knitting or crocheting. 3 Any individual arrangement of a thread or threads used in sewing: a chain *stitch.* 4 A sharp sudden pain. 5 *Informal* A garment: I haven't a *stitch* to wear. **—be in stitches** To be overcome with laughter. *—v.t.* 1 To join together with stitches. 2 To ornament with stitches. *—v.i.* 3 To make stitches; sew. [< OE *stice* prick]

sti·ver (stī'vər) *n.* 1 A small Dutch coin, 1/20 of a guilder. 2 Anything of little value.

St. Johns·wort (sānt jonz'wûrt') Any of various small, woody perennials, usu. with yellow flowers. Also **Saint Johnswort, St. John's-wort.**

stk. stock.

sto·a (stō'ə) *n. pl.* **sto·ae** (stō'ē) or **sto·as** In Greek architecture, a covered colonnade, portico, cloister, or promenade. [Gk., porch]

stoat (stōt) *n. pl.* **stoats** or **stoat** The ermine, esp. in its brown summer coat. [ME *stote*]

stock (stok) *n.* 1 The goods a store or merchant has on hand. 2 A quantity of something acquired or kept for future use: a *stock* of provisions. 3 LIVESTOCK. 4 The original, as a man, race, or language, from which others are descended or derived. 5 A line of familial descent. 6 An ethnic group; race. 7 A related group of plants or animals. 8 A group of related languages; also, a language family. 9 The trunk or main stem of a tree or other plant. 10 **a** A plant stem from which cuttings are taken for grafting. **b** A plant stem upon which a graft is made. 11 In finance: **a** The capital raised by a corporation through the sale of shares that entitle the holder to interest or dividends. **b** The part of this capital credited to an individual stock holder. **c** The certificate or certificates indicating this. 12 A fund or debt owed (as by a nation, city, etc.) to individuals who receive a fixed interest rate. 13 The part of a device that functions as a support and to which other parts are attached, as the wooden portion or handle of a firearm, whip, etc. 14 Raw material: paper *stock.* 15 The broth from boiled vegetables, meat, or fish, used in preparing soups, gravies, etc. 16 Something lacking life, feeling, or motion. 17 The group of plays produced by a theatrical company at one theater. 18 A broad, heavily starched band, formerly worn as a cravat. **—in stock** Available for purchase. **—out of stock** Not available; all sold out. **—stock in trade** One's abilities, talents, or resources. **—take stock** 1 To take an inventory. 2 To size up a situation. **—take stock in** *Informal* To have trust or belief in. **—the stocks** 1 A former device for public punishment consisting of a timber frame for confining the ankles, or the ankles and wrists. 2 The timber frame on which a ship or boat is built. *—v.t.* 1 To supply with cattle, as a farm. 2 To supply (a store) with merchandise. 3 To keep for sale: to *stock* avocados. 4 To supply with wildlife: to *stock* a pond. 5 To put aside for future use. 6 To provide with a handle or stock. *—v.i.* 7 To lay in supplies or stock: often with *up.* *—adj.* 1 Kept on hand: a *stock* size. 2 Banal; commonplace: a *stock* phrase. 3 Of or pertaining to the breeding and raising of livestock. 4 Employed in handling or caring for the stock: a *stock* clerk. 5 Of or pertaining to a stock or stocks (def. 9). [< OE *stocc*]

stock·ade (sto·kād') *n.* 1 A defense consisting of a strong, high barrier of upright posts, stakes, etc. 2 The area enclosed by such a barrier. 3 A similar area used to confine prisoners, esp. in military installations. *—v.t.* **·ad·ed, ·ad·ing** To surround or fortify with a stockade. [< OF *estaque* a stake]

stock·bro·ker (stok'brō'kər) *n.* One who buys and sells stocks or securities for others.

stock car 1 An automobile, usu. a sedan, modified for racing. 2 A railroad car used for transporting cattle.

stock company 1 An incorporated company that issues stock. 2 A theatrical company under one management that presents a series of plays.

stock exchange 1 A place where securities are bought and sold. 2 An association of stockbrokers

stock farm A farm that specializes in the breeding of livestock.

stock·hold·er (stok'hōl'dər) *n.* One who holds stocks or shares in a company.

stock·i·net (stok'i·net') *n.* An elastic knitted fabric used chiefly for undergarments. [< STOCKING]

stock·ing (stok'ing) *n.* 1 A close-fitting knitted covering for the foot and leg. 2 Something resembling such a covering. [< STOCK, in obs. sense of "a stocking"]

stocking cap A long knitted cap, tapered and often having a pompon or tassel at the end.

stock·man (stok′mən) *n. pl.* **·men** (-mən) **1** One who raises or owns livestock; a cattleman. **2** A man having charge of goods, as in a warehouse.

stock market **1** STOCK EXCHANGE. **2** The business transacted in such a place: The *stock market* was active.

stock·pile (stok′pīl′) *n.* A storage pile of materials or supplies. Also **stock pile.** —*v.t. & v.i.* **·piled, ·pil·ing** To accumulate a supply or stockpile (of).

stock raising The breeding and raising of livestock.

stock·room (stok′rōōm′, -rŏŏm′) *n.* A room where reserve stocks of goods are stored.

stock·still (stok′stil′) *adj.* Completely motionless.

stock·y (stok′ē) *adj.* **stock·i·er, stock·i·est** Short and stout. —**stock′i·ly** *adv.* —**stock′i·ness** *n.*

stock·yard (stok′yärd′) *n.* A large yard with pens, stables, etc., where cattle are kept ready for shipping, slaughter, etc.

stodg·y (stoj′ē) *adj.* **stodg·i·er, stodg·i·est** **1** Dull; boring. **2** Indigestible; heavy. [?] —**stodg′i·ly** *adv.* —**stodg′i·ness** *n.*

sto·gy (stō′gē) *n. pl.* **·gies** A long, slender, inexpensive cigar. Also **sto′gie.** [< *Conestoga,* Pennsylvania]

sto·ic (stō′ik) *n.* A person apparently unaffected by pleasure or pain. —*adj.* Indifferent to pleasure or pain; impassive: also **sto′i·cal.** [< STOIC] —**sto′i·cal·ly** *adv.* —**sto′i·cal·ness** *n.*

Sto·ic (stō′ik) *n.* A member of a school of Greek philosophy founded by Zeno about 308 B.C., holding the belief that wisdom lies in being superior to passion, joy, grief, etc. —*adj.* Of or pertaining to the Stoics or Stoicism. [< Gk. *Stoa,* the colonnade at Athens where Zeno taught]

sto·i·cism (stō′ə·siz′əm) *n.* Indifference to pleasure or pain.

Sto·i·cism (stō′ə·siz′əm) *n.* The doctrines of the Stoics.

stoke (stōk) *v.t.* **stoked, stok·ing** **1** To supply (a furnace) with fuel. **2** To stir up; intensify. —*v.i.* **3** To tend a fire. [Back formation < STOKER]

stoke·hole (stōk′hōl′) *n.* **1** The space about the mouth of a furnace; the fireroom. **2** The mouth of a furnace.

stok·er (stō′kər) *n.* **1** A person who tends a furnace or boiler. **2** A mechanical device for feeding coal to a furnace. [< Du. *stoken* stir a fire]

STOL, S.T.O.L. short takeoff and landing.

stole[1] (stōl) *n.* **1** *Eccl.* A long, narrow band, usu. of decorated silk or linen, worn about the shoulders by priests and bishops. **2** A fur, scarf, or garment resembling a stole, worn by women. [< Gk. *stolē* a garment] —**stoled** *adj.*

Stole

stole[2] (stōl) *p.t.* of STEAL.

sto·len (stō′lən) *p.p.* of STEAL.

stol·id (stol′id) *adj.* Expressing no feeling; impassive. [< L *stolidus* dull] —**sto·lid·i·ty** (stə·lid′ə·tē), **stol′id·ness** *n.* —**stol′id·ly** *adv.*

sto·ma (stō′mə) *n. pl.* **sto·ma·ta** (stō′mə·tə, stom′ə·tə) or **sto·mas** A small, mouthlike opening, esp. any of the minute epidermal breathing pores on a plant leaf. Also **sto′mate** (stō′māt′). [< Gk. *stoma* mouth] —**sto′ma·tal** *adj.*

stom·ach (stum′ək) *n.* **1** A pouchlike dilation of the alimentary canal, situated in most vertebrates next to the esophagus and serving as one of the principal organs of digestion. **2** Any digestive cavity, as of an invertebrate. **3** The abdomen; belly. **4** Desire for food; appetite. **5** Any desire or inclination. —*v.t.* **1** To put up with; endure. **2** To take into and retain in the stomach; digest. [< Gk. *stomachos*] —**stom′ach·al** *adj.* —**sto·mach·ic** (stō·mak′ik), **sto·mach′i·cal** *adj., n.* • See LIVER.

stom·ach·er (stum′ək·ər) *n.* A former article of clothing worn, esp. by women, over the breast and stomach.

stomp (stomp) *v.t. & v.i.* To stamp; tread heavily (upon). —*n.* A jazz dance involving heavy stamping. [Var of STAMP] —**stomp′er** *n.*

stone (stōn) *n. pl.* **stones** or *for def. 8* **stone** **1** ROCK (def. 3). **2** A small piece of rock, as a pebble. **3** A piece of shaped or hewn rock, as a gravestone. **4** A jewel; gem. **5** Something like a stone in shape or hardness: a *hailstone.* **6** An abnormal, hard concretion in the body. **7** The hard inner part of a drupe. **8** *Brit.* A measure of weight equal to 14 pounds. —**cast the first stone** To be the first to blame (someone). —**leave no stone unturned** To do everything within possibility. —*adj.* **1** Made of stone: a *stone* ax. **2** Made of coarse, hard earthenware: a *stone* bottle. —*v.t.* **stoned, ston·ing** **1** To hurl stones at. **2** To kill by throwing stones at. **3** To remove the stones or pits from. **4** To furnish or line with stone. [< OE *stān*] —**ston′er** *n.*

Stone Age The earliest known period of human cultural evolution, marked by the creation of stone implements.

stone-blind (stōn′blīnd′) *adj.* Completely blind.

stone-broke (stōn′brōk′) *adj. Informal* Without any money; having no funds. Also **ston′y-broke′.**

stone·crop (stōn′krop′) *n.* SEDUM.

stone·cut·ter (stōn′kut′ər) *n.* One who or that which cuts stone; esp. a machine for facing stone. —**stone′cut′·ting** *n.*

stoned (stōnd) *adj. Slang* **1** Drunk. **2** Under the influence of a drug or narcotic.

stone-deaf (stōn′def′) *adj.* Completely deaf.

stone·ma·son (stōn′mā′sən) *n.* One whose trade is to prepare and lay stones in building. —**stone′ma′son·ry** *n.*

stone's throw (stōnz) **1** The distance a stone may be cast by hand. **2** A short distance.

stone·wall (stōn′wôl′) *Slang v.i.* **1** To act in a calculatedly obstructive way, as by lying or failing to respond to inquiry. —*v.t.* **2** To respond to in such a way.

stone·ware (stōn′wâr′) *n.* A very hard, glazed pottery, made from siliceous clay or clay mixed with flint or sand.

stone·work (stōn′wûrk′) *n.* **1** The art or process of cutting or setting stone. **2** Work built or made of stone. **3** *pl.* A place where stone is shaped. —**stone′work′er** *n.*

ston·y (stō′nē) *adj.* **ston·i·er, ston·i·est** **1** Abounding in stone or stones. **2** Made or consisting of stone. **3** Hard as stone; unfeeling. **4** Like stone. **5** *Slang* Having no money. —**ston′i·ly** *adv.* —**ston′i·ness** *n.* —**Syn. 3** chilly, cold, pitiless.

stood (stŏŏd) *p.t. & p.p.* of STAND.

stooge (stōōj) *n.* **1** *Informal* An actor who feeds lines to the principal comedian, acts as a foil for his jokes, etc. **2** Anyone who acts as or is the tool or dupe of another. —*v.i.* **stooged, stoog·ing** To act as a stooge: usu. with *for.* [?]

stool (stōōl) *n.* **1** A backless and armless seat intended for one person. **2** A low bench or portable support for the feet or for kneeling. **3** A seat or place used as a toilet. **4** The matter evacuated from the bowels; feces. **5** A stump or root from which suckers or sprouts shoot up. [< OE *stōl*]

stool pigeon **1** A living or artificial pigeon used to decoy others into a trap. **2** *Slang* An informer, as for the police.

stoop[1] (stōōp) *v.i.* **1** To lean the body forward and down. **2** To stand or walk with the upper part of the body habitually bent forward; slouch. **3** To bend: said of trees, cliffs, etc. **4** To lower or degrade oneself. —*v.t.* **5** To bend (one's head, shoulders, etc.) forward. —*n.* **1** A downward and forward bending of the body. **2** A habitual forward inclination of the head and shoulders. [< OE *stūpian*]

stoop[2] (stōōp) *n.* A small porch or platform at the entrance to a house. [< Du. *stoep*]

stop (stop) *v.* **stopped, stop·ping** *v.t.* **1** To bring (something in motion) to a halt: to *stop* an automobile. **2** To prevent the doing or completion of: to *stop* a revolution. **3** To prevent (a person) from doing something; restrain. **4** To withhold or cut off, as wages or supplies. **5** To cease doing: *Stop* that! **6** To check, as a flow of blood from a wound. **7** To obstruct (a passage, road, etc.). **8** To fill in or otherwise close, as a hole, cavity, etc. **9** To close (a bottle, barrel, etc.) with a cork, plug, etc. **10** To order a bank not to pay or honor: to *stop* a check. **11** *Music* To press down (a string) or close (a finger hole) to change the pitch of. **12** In boxing, etc., to parry. —*v.i.* **13** To come to a halt; cease progress or motion. **14** To cease doing something. **—stop off** To stop for a brief stay before continuing on a trip. **—stop over** *Informal* To stop briefly, as for a visit or a rest during a journey. *—n.* **1** The act of stopping, or the state of being stopped. **2** That which stops or limits the range or time of a movement; an obstruction. **3** *Music* **a** The pressing down of a string or the closing of an aperture to change the pitch. **b** A key, lever, or handle for stopping a string or an aperture. **4** *Music* In an organ, a set of pipes producing tones of the same timbre. **5 a** *Brit.* A punctuation mark; a period. **b** In cables, etc., a period. **6** *Phonet.* **a** Complete blockage of the breath stream, as with the lips or tongue, followed by a sudden release. **b** A consonant so produced, as *p, b, t, d, k,* and *g.* **—put a stop to** To end; terminate. [< OE *-stoppian*] **—Syn** *v.* **2** deter, quash. **4** discontinue.

stop·cock (stop′kok′) *n.* A faucet or valve.

stop·gap (stop′gap′) *n.* A person or thing serving as a temporary substitute. *—adj.* Being a stopgap.

stop·o·ver (stop′ō′vər) *n.* The act of stopping over, or permission to stop over on a journey and continue later, using the ticket issued for the whole journey.

stop·page (stop′ij) *n.* **1** The act of stopping or the state of being stopped. **2** A blocking or obstruction.

stop·per (stop′ər) *n.* **1** One who or that which stops or brings to a stop. **2** A plug or cork for a container, as a bottle. *—v.t.* To secure or close with a stopper.

stop·ple (stop′əl) *n.* A stopper, plug, cork, or bung. *—v.t.* **·pled, ·pling** To close with or as with a stopple. [< ME *stoppen* stop]

stop·watch (stop′woch′) *n.* A watch with a hand indicating fractions of a second which may be stopped or started instantly, used for timing races, etc.

stor·age (stôr′ij, stō′rij) *n.* **1** The depositing of articles in a place for their safekeeping. **2** Space for storing goods. **3** A charge for storing. **4** A section of a computer in whch data is held for later use; memory.

storage battery A connected group of two or more electrolytic cells that can be reversibly charged and discharged.

store (stôr, stōr) *v.t.* **stored, stor·ing** **1** To put away for future use. **2** To furnish or supply; provide. **3** To place in a warehouse or other place for safekeeping. *—n.* **1** That which is stored or laid up against future need. **2** *pl.* Supplies, as of food, arms, or clothing. **3** A storehouse; warehouse. **4** A place where merchandise of any kind is kept for sale; a shop. **—in store** Set apart for the future; impending. **—set store by** To value or esteem. [< L *instaurare* restore, erect]

store·front (stôr′frunt′, stōr′-) *n.* **1** The front or facade of a store, usu. opening directly out onto a pedestrian sidewalk. **2** A public service or other facility, often temporary, situated on the site of a former store. *—adj.* Characteristic of or being a storefront.

store·house (stôr′hous′, stōr′-) *n.* A place in which goods are stored; depository.

store·keep·er (stôr′kē′pər, stōr′-) *n.* A person who keeps a retail store or who is in charge of supplies.

store·room (stôr′rōōm′, -rōōm′, stōr′-) *n.* A room in which things are stored.

sto·rey (stôr′ē, stōr′ē) *n. pl.* **·reys** *Chiefly Brit.* STORY[2].

sto·ried[1] (stôr′ēd, stōr′ēd) *adj.* Having or consisting of stories: a *six-storied* house.

sto·ried[2] (stôr′ēd, stōr′ēd) *adj.* **1** Having a notable history. **2** Ornamented with designs representing scenes from history or story.

stork (stôrk) *n.* A large wading bird with a long neck and long legs, related to the herons. [< OE *storc*]

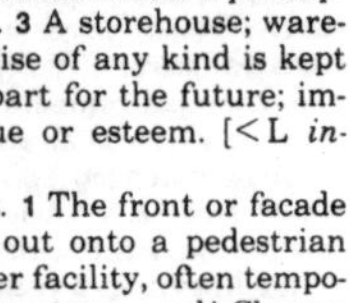

White stork

storm (stôrm) *n.* **1** A disturbance of the atmosphere that creates strong winds, often with heavy precipitation of rain, snow, dust, etc. **2** Any heavy, prolonged precipitation of snow, rain, etc. **3** Anything similar to a storm: a *storm* of missiles. **4** A violent outburst: a *storm* of applause. **5** A violent and rapid assault. *—v.i.* **1** To blow with violence; rain, snow, hail, etc., heavily. **2** To be very angry; rage. **3** To rush with violence or rage: He *stormed* about the room. *—v.t.* **4** To attack: to *storm* a fort. [< OE]

storm cellar An underground shelter adapted for use during cyclones, hurricanes, etc.

storm door An additional outer door used to conserve heat during cold weather.

storm petrel Any of certain petrels thought to portend storm.

storm troops A Nazi party militia unit, the *Sturmabteilung,* established in 1924. **—storm trooper**

storm window An extra window outside the ordinary one for greater insulation against cold.

storm·y (stôr′mē) *adj.* **storm·i·er, storm·i·est** **1** Characterized by storms; turbulent. **2** Violent; rough. **—storm′i·ly** *adv.* **—storm′i·ness** *n.* **—Syn. 1** blustery, tempestuous. **2** disturbed, passionate, vehement.

stormy petrel **1** STORM PETREL. **2** A person thought to portend or foment trouble.

sto·ry[1] (stôr′ē, stōr′ē) *n. pl.* **·ries** **1** A narrative or recital of an event, or a series of events. **2** A narrative intended to entertain a reader or hearer. **3** An account of the facts relating to a particular person, thing, or incident. **4** A news article in a newspaper or magazine. **5** The material for a news article. **6** An anecdote. **7** *Informal* A lie; falsehood. **8** The series of events in a novel, play, etc. *—v.t.* **·ried, ·ry·ing** **1** *Archaic* To relate as a story. **2** To adorn with designs representing scenes from history, legend, etc. [< L *historia*]

sto·ry[2] (stôr′ē, stōr′ē) *n. pl.* **·ries** **1** A division in a building comprising the space between two successive floors. **2** All the rooms on one level of a building. [< Med. L *historia* story (painted on a row of windows)]

sto·ry·tell·er (stôr′ē·tel′ər, stōr′ē-) *n.* **1** One who relates stories or anecdotes. **2** *Informal* A prevaricator; fibber. **—sto′ry·tell′ing** *n., adj.*

stoup (stōōp) *n.* **1** *Eccl.* A basin for holy water at the entrance of a church. **2** A flagon, tankard, or large drinking glass. [< ON *staup* bucket]

stout (stout) *adj.* **1** Fat; thick-set. **2** Firmly built; strong: a *stout* fence. **3** Courageous: a *stout* heart. **4** Stubborn; unyielding: a *stout* denial. *—n.* **1** A stout person. **2** *Usu. pl.* Clothing made for stout or big people. **3** A strong, very dark porter or ale. [< OF *estout* bold, strong] **—stout′ly** *adv.* **—stout′ness** *n.*

stout·heart·ed (stout′här′tid) *adj.* Brave; courageous. **—stout′heart′ed·ly** *adv.* **—stout′heart′ed·ness** *n.*

stove[1] (stōv) *n.* An apparatus, usu. of metal, in which fuel is consumed for heating or cooking. [< OE *stofa* a heated room]

stove[2] (stōv) A *p.t. & p.p.* of STAVE.

stove·pipe (stōv′pīp′) *n.* **1** A pipe for conducting the smoke from a stove to a chimney flue. **2** *Informal* A tall silk hat: also **stovepipe hat.**

stow (stō) *v.t.* **1** To place or arrange compactly; pack. **2** To fill by packing. **—stow away** **1** To put in a place of safekeeping, hiding, etc. **2** To be a stowaway. [< OE *stōw* a place]

stow·age (stō′ij) *n.* **1** The act of stowing. **2** Space for stowing goods. **3** Charge for stowing goods. **4** The goods stowed.

stow·a·way (stō′ə·wā′) *n.* One who conceals himself on a ship, train, airplane, etc., to obtain free passage, to escape, or to cross a border illegally.

STP (es′tē′pē′) *n.* A hallucinogenic drug chemically related to mescaline and amphetamine. [< STP, a trade name for a gasoline additive supposed to increase engine power.]

STP standard temperature and pressure.

str. steamer; strait; string(s).

stra·bis·mus (strə·biz′məs) *n.* Inability to focus the eyes simultaneously on the same spot because of a disorder of the eye muscles. [< Gk. *strabizein* to squint] **—stra·bis′mal, stra·bis′mic** or **·mi·cal** *adj.*

strad·dle (strad′l) *v.* **·dled, ·dling** *v.i.* **1** To stand, walk, or sit with the legs spread apart. **2** To be spread wide apart: said of the legs. **3** *Informal* To appear to favor both sides of an issue. *—v.t.* **4** To stand, walk, or sit with the legs on either side of. **5** To spread (the legs) wide apart. **6** *Informal* To appear to favor both sides of (an issue). *—n.* **1** The act of straddling. **2** The distance between the legs in straddling. **3** *Informal* A noncommital position on an issue. [Freq. of STRIDE] **—strad'dler** *n.* **—strad'dling·ly** *adv.*

Strad·i·var·i·us (strad'i·vâr'ē·əs) *n.* One of the violins, cellos, etc., made by Antonio Stradivari (1644–1737), Italian violin maker.

strafe (strāf, sträf) *v.t.* **strafed, straf·ing 1** To attack (troops, emplacements, etc.) with machine-gun fire from low-flying airplanes. **2** To bombard or shell heavily. **3** *Slang* To punish. [< G *strafen* punish] **—straf'er** *n.*

strag·gle (strag'əl) *v.i.* **·gled, ·gling 1** To wander from the road, main body, etc.; stray. **2** To wander aimlessly about; ramble. **3** To occur at irregular intervals. [ME *straglen*] **—strag'gler** *n.* **—strag'gling·ly** *adv.* **—strag'gly** *adj.* **(·i·er, ·i·est)**

straight (strāt) *adj.* **1** Extending uniformly in the same direction without curve or bend. **2** Free from kinks; not curly, as hair. **3** Not stooped; erect. **4** Not deviating from truth, fairness, or honesty. **5** Free from obstruction; uninterrupted. **6** Correctly ordered or arranged. **7** Sold without discount for number or quantity taken. **8** *Informal* Accepting the whole, as of a plan, party, or policy: a *straight* ticket. **9** In poker, consisting of five cards forming a sequence. **10** Having nothing added: *straight* whiskey. **11** *Slang* Conforming to what is accepted as usual, normal, or conventional, esp. according to middle-class standards. **12** *Slang* HETEROSEXUAL. **—n. 1** A straight part or piece. **2** The part of a racecourse between the winning post and the last turn. **3** In poker, a numerical sequence of five cards. **4** *Slang* A conventional person. **5** *Slang* HETEROSEXUAL. **—adv. 1** In a straight line or a direct course. **2** Closely in line; correspondingly. **3** At once: Go *straight* to bed. **4** Uprightly: to live *straight.* **5** Correctly: I can't think *straight.* **6** Without restriction or qualification: Tell it *straight.* **—go straight** To reform after having led the life of a criminal. **—straight away** or **off** At once; right away. [< OE *streht,* pp. of *streccan* stretch] **—straight'ness** *n.*

straight angle An angle of 180°.

straight·a·way (strāt'ə·wā') *adj.* Having no curve or turn. **—n.** A straight course or track. **—adv.** At once; straightway.

straight·en (strāt'n) *v.t.* **1** To make straight. **—v.i. 2** To become straight. **—straighten out** To restore order to; rectify. **—straighten up 1** To make neat; tidy. **2** To stand in erect posture. **3** To reform. **—straight'en·er** *n.*

straight face A sober, expressionless, or unsmiling face. **—straight-faced** (strāt'fāst') *adj.*

straight·for·ward (strāt'fôr'wərd) *adj.* **1** Candid; honest. **2** Proceeding in a straight course. **—adv.** In a straight course or direct manner: also **straight'for'wards** (-wərdz). **—straight'for'ward·ly** *adv.* **—straight'for'ward·ness** *n.* **—Syn. 1** aboveboard, frank, open, sincere. **2** direct.

straight man *Informal* An entertainer who acts as a foil for a comedian.

straight-out (strāt'out') *adj. Informal* **1** Unreserved; unrestrained. **2** Thorough; complete.

straight·way (strāt'wā') *adv.* Immediately.

strain¹ (strān) *v.t.* **1** To pull or draw tight. **2** To exert to the utmost. **3** To injure by overexertion; sprain. **4** To deform in structure or shape as a result of stress. **5** To stretch beyond the true intent, proper limit, etc.: to *strain* a point. **6** To embrace tightly; hug. **7** To pass through a strainer. **8** To remove by filtration. **—v.i. 9** To make violent efforts; strive. **10** To be or become wrenched or twisted. **13** To filter, trickle, or percolate. **—strain at 1** To push or pull with violent efforts. **2** To strive for. **3** To scruple or balk at accepting. **—n. 1** An act of straining or the state of being strained. **2** Any very taxing demand on strength, emotions, etc.: the *strain* of city life. **3** Any violent effort or exertion. **4** The injury resulting from excessive tension or effort. **5** *Physics* The change of shape or structure of a body produced by the action of a stress. [< L *stringere* bind tight]

strain² (strān) *n.* **1** Line of descent, or the individuals, collectively, in that line. **2** Inborn or hereditary disposition; natural tendency. **3** A line of plants or animals selectively bred to perpetuate distinctive traits. **4** *Often pl.* A melody; tune. **5** Prevailing tone, style, or manner. [< OE *strēon* offspring]

strain·er (strā'nər) *n.* A utensil or device that filters, strains, or sifts.

strait (strāt) *n.* **1** *Often pl.* A narrow passage of water connecting two larger bodies of water. **2** Any narrow pass or passage. **3** *Often pl.* Distress; embarrassment: financial *straits.* **—adj.** *Archaic* **1** Narrow. **2** Strict. [< L *strictus,* p.p. of *stringere* bind tight.] **—strait'ly** *adv.* **—strait'ness** *n.*

strait·en (strāt'n) *v.t.* **1** To make strait or narrow; restrict. **2** To embarrass, or restrict, as in finances.

strait·jack·et (strāt'jak'it) *n.* **1** A jacket with long, closed sleeves for confining the arms of a violent patient or prisoner. **2** Anything that unduly confines or restricts. **—v.t.** To confine in or as if in a straitjacket.

strait-laced (strāt'lāst') *adj.* **1** Formerly, tightly laced, as corsets. **2** Strict, esp. in morals or manners; prudish.

strand¹ (strand) *n.* A shore or beach, esp. on the ocean. **—v.t. & v.i. 1** To drive or run aground, as a ship. **2** To leave or be left in difficulties or helplessness: *stranded* in a strange city. [< OE]

strand² (strand) *n.* **1** Any of the fibers, wires, or threads twisted or plaited together to form a rope, cable, cord, etc. **2** A single hair or similar filament. **3** Any of various ropelike objects: a *strand* of pearls. **—v.t.** To break a strand of (a rope). [ME *strond*]

strange (strānj) *adj.* **strang·er, strang·est 1** Previously unknown, unseen, or unheard of. **2** Peculiar; out of the ordinary: a *strange* experience. **3** Foreign; alien. **4** Out of place: to feel *strange* in a new school. **5** Inexperienced: *strange* to a new job. [< L *extraneus* foreign] **—strange'ly** *adv.* **—strange'ness** *n.* **—Syn. 1** unfamiliar. **2** odd, queer, unusual. **4** unaccustomed.

stran·ger (strān'jər) *n.* **1** One who is not an acquaintance. **2** An unfamiliar visitor; guest. **3** A foreigner. **4** One unacquainted with something specified: with *to:* a *stranger* to higher mathematics.

stran·gle (strang'gəl) *v.* **·gled, ·gling** *v.t.* **1** To choke to death; throttle. **2** To repress; suppress. **—v.i. 3** To suffer or die from strangulation. [< Gk. *strangalaein*] **—stran'gler** *n.*

stran·gle·hold (strang'gəl·hōld') *n.* **1** In wrestling, an illegal hold which chokes one's opponent. **2** Anything that chokes freedom or progress.

stran·gu·late (strang'gyə·lāt) *v.t.* **·lat·ed, ·lat·ing 1** STRANGLE. **2** *Pathol.* To constrict so as to cut off circulation of the blood. [< L *strangulare*] **—stran'gu·la'tion** *n.*

strap (strap) *n.* **1** A long, narrow, and flexible strip of leather, webbing, etc., for binding or fastening things together. **2** A razor strop. **3** Something used as a strap: a shoulder *strap.* **—v.t. strapped, strap·ing 1** To fasten or bind with a strap. **2** To beat with a strap. **3** To sharpen or strop. **4** To embarrass financially. [Var. of STROP]

strap·hang·er (strap'hang'ər) *n. Informal* A standing passenger on a bus or train who keeps his balance by holding on to a strap, bar, etc.

strap·ping (strap'ing) *adj. Informal* Large and muscular; robust.

stra·ta (strā'tə, strat'ə) *n.pl.* of STRATUM.

strat·a·gem (strat'ə·jəm) *n.* **1** A maneuver designed to deceive or outwit an enemy. **2** Any device or trick for obtaining advantage. [< Gk. *stratēgēma* piece of generalship] **—Syn. 2** artifice, deception, ruse, trick.

stra·te·gic (strə·tē'jik) *adj.* **1** Of or based on strategy. **2** Important in strategy. **3** Having to do with materials essential for conducting a war. **4** Assigned to destroy important enemy installations: a *strategic* air force. Also **stra·te'gi·cal.** **—stra·te'gi·cal·ly** *adv.*

strat·e·gist (strat'ə·jist) *n.* One skilled in strategy.

strat·e·gy (strat'ə·jē) *n. pl.* **·gies 1** The science of planning and conducting military campaigns on a broad scale. **2** Any plan based on this. **3** The use of stratagem or artifice, as in business, politics, etc. **4** Skill in management. **5** An ingenious plan or method. [< Gk. *stratēgos* general]

strat·i·fy (strat'ə·fī) *v.* **·fied, ·fy·ing** *v.t.* **1** To form or arrange in strata or layers. **—v.i. 2** To form in strata. **3** To be formed in strata. [< L *stratum* layer + -FY] **—strat′i·fi·ca′tion** *n.*

stra·to·cu·mu·lus (strā′tō·kyo͞o′myə·ləs, strat′-) *n. pl.* **·li** (-lī) *Meteorol.* A type of dark, low-lying cloud, characterized by horizontal bases and high, rounded summits.

strat·o·sphere (strat′ə·sfir) *n. Meteorol.* The portion of the atmosphere beginning at about six miles above the earth, where a more or less uniform temperature prevails. **—strat′o·spher′ic** (-sfer′ik) or **·i·cal** *adj.*

stra·tum (strā′təm, strat′əm) *n. pl.* **·ta** (-tə) or **·tums 1** A natural or artificial layer. **2** *Geol.* A more or less homogeneous layer of rock. **3** A level of society, having similar educational, cultural, and usu. economic backgrounds. [< L *stratus,* p.p. of *sternere* to spread]

Rock strata

stra·tus (strā′təs, strat′əs) *n. pl.* **·ti** (-tī) *Meteorol.* A low-lying, foglike cloud. [L, orig. p.p. of *sternere* to spread]

straw (strô) *n.* **1** A dry stalk of grain. **2** Stems or stalks of grain after being threshed, used for fodder, etc. **3** A mere trifle. **4** A slender tube made of paper, glass, etc., used to suck up a beverage. **—catch** (or **grab**) **at a straw** To try anything as a last resort. **—straw in the wind** A sign of the course of future events. **—*adj.* 1** Made of or like straw, as in color. **2** Worthless; sham. [< OE *strēaw* straw]

straw·ber·ry (strô′ber′ē, -bər·ē) *n. pl.* **·ries 1** Any of a genus of stemless perennials of the rose family, with trifoliolate leaves, usu. white flowers and slender runners by which it propagates: also **strawberry vine. 2** Its edible fruit, consisting of a red, fleshy receptacle bearing many achenes. [< STRAW + BERRY]

strawberry blond A person having reddish blond hair.

straw boss *Informal* A worker acting as an assistant foreman.

straw vote An unofficial test vote.

stray (strā) *v.i.* **1** To wander from the proper course; roam. **2** To deviate from right or goodness; go astray. **—*adj.* 1** Having strayed; straying: a *stray* dog. **2** Irregular; occasional: He made a few *stray* remarks. **—*n.*** A domestic animal that has strayed. [< L *extra vagare* wander outside] **—stray′er** *n.*

streak (strēk) *n.* **1** A long, narrow mark or stripe: a *streak* of lightning. **2** A trace or characteristic: a *streak* of meanness. **3** A layer or strip: meat with a *streak* of fat and a *streak* of lean. **4** *Informal* A period or interval: a winning *streak.* **5** *Slang* The act or an instance of streaking (*v.* def. 3). **—like a streak** *Informal* As rapidly as possible. **—*v.i.* 1** To form a streak or streaks. **2** To move at great speed. **3** *Slang* To appear naked in a public place, usu. briefly and esp. while running, as for a thrill. **—*v.t.* 4** To form streaks in or on. **5** *Slang* To appear naked in (a public place), usu. briefly and esp. while running, as for a thrill. [< OE *strica*] **—streak′y** *adj.* **(·i·er, ·i·est) —streak′i·ly** *adv.* **—streak′er, streak′i·ness** *n.*

stream (strēm) *n.* **1** A current or flow of water, esp. a small river. **2** Any continuous flow or current: a *stream* of invective. **—*v.i.* 1** To pour forth or issue in a stream. **2** To pour forth in a stream: eyes *streaming* with tears. **3** To proceed uninterruptedly, as a crowd. **4** To float with a waving movement, as a flag. **5** To move with a trail of light, as a meteor. **6** To come or arrive in large numbers. [< OE *strēam*] **—Syn.** *n.* **1** brook, course, creek, rill, rivulet.

stream·er (strē′mər) *n.* **1** An object that streams forth, or hangs extended. **2** A long, narrow flag or standard. **3** A stream or shaft of light. **4** A newspaper headline that runs across the whole page.

stream·let (strēm′lit) *n.* RIVULET.

stream·line (strēm′līn′) *n.* **1** A line in a mass of fluid such that each of its tangents coincides with the local velocity of the fluid. **2** Any shape or contour designed to lessen resistance to motion of a solid in a fluid. **—*adj.* 1** Designating an uninterrupted flow or drift. **2** Denoting a form or body designed to minimize turbulence in the flow of fluid around it. **—*v.t.* ·lined, ·lin·ing 1** To design with a streamline shape. **2** To make more up-to-date, esp. by reorganization.

stream·lined (strēm′līnd′) *adj.* **1** STREAMLINE. **2** Improved in efficiency; modernized.

street (strēt) *n.* **1** A public way in a city, town, or village, usu. with buildings on one or both sides. **2** Such a public way as set apart for vehicles: Don't play in the *street.* **3** *Informal* The people living on a specific street. **—*adj.* 1** Working in the streets: a *street* musician. **2** Opening onto the street: a *street* door. **3** Performed or taking place on the street: *street* crime. **4** Habituated to the ways of life in the streets, esp. in cities: *street* people. [< LL *strata (via)* paved (road)]

street Arab A homeless or outcast child who lives in the streets; gamin.

street·car (strēt′kär′) *n.* A passenger car that runs on rails laid on the surface of the streets.

street people Young people, esp. of the late 1960s, usu. without a permanent residence and having a life style marked by the rejection of middle-class values and by the use of drugs.

street·walk·er (strēt′wô′kər) *n.* A prostitute who solicits in the streets. **—street′walk′ing** *n.*

strength (strength) *n.* **1** The quality or property of being physically strong: the *strength* of a weight lifter. **2** The capacity to sustain the application of force without yielding or breaking. **3** Effectiveness: the *strength* of an argument. **4** Binding force or validity, as of a law. **5** Vigor or force of style: a drama of great *strength.* **6** Available numerical force in a military unit or other organization. **7** Degree of intensity, as of color, light, or sound. **8** Potency, as of a drug, chemical, or liquor; concentration. **9** A support; aid: He is our *strength.* **—on the strength of** Relying on; on the basis of. [< OE *strang* strong] **—Syn. 1** force, power, vigor. **2** solidity, tenacity, toughness.

strength·en (streng′thən) *v.t.* **1** To make strong. **2** To encourage; hearten. **—*v.i.* 3** To become or grow strong or stronger. **—strength′en·er** *n.*

stren·u·ous (stren′yo͞o·əs) *adj.* Necessitating or marked by strong effort or exertion. [< L *strenuus*] **—stren′u·ous·ly** *adv.* **—stren′u·ous·ness** *n.*

strep throat (strep) A streptococcal throat infection.

strep·to·coc·cus (strep′tə·kok′əs) *n. pl.* **·coc·ci** (-kok′sī, -sē, -ī, -ē) Any of a large group of spherical bacteria that grow together in long chains, including a few pathogens. [< Gk. *streptos* twisted + COCCUS] **—strep′to·coc′cal** (-kok′əl), **strep′to·coc′cic** (-kok′sik, -kok′ik) *adj.*

strep·to·my·cin (strep′tō·mī′sin) *n.* A potent antibiotic isolated from a mold. [< Gk. *streptos* twisted + *mykēs* fungus]

stress (stres) *n.* **1** Special weight, importance, or significance. **2** Physical or emotional tension. **3** *Mech.* A force tending to deform a body on which it acts. **4** Emphasis. **5** In pronunciation, the relative force with which a sound, syllable, or word is uttered. **—*v.t.* 1** To subject to stress. **2** To accent, as a syllable. **3** To give emphasis or weight to. [< L *strictus,* p.p. of *stringere* draw tight] **—stress′ful** *adj.*

-stress *suffix of nouns* Feminine form of -STER: *songstress.*

stretch (strech) *v.t.* **1** To extend or draw out, as to full length or width. **2** To draw out forcibly, esp. beyond normal or proper limits. **3** To cause to reach, as from one place to another. **4** To put forth, hold out, or extend (the hand, an object, etc.). **5** To tighten, strain, or exert to the utmost: to *stretch* every nerve. **6** To adjust or adapt to meet specific needs, circumstances, etc.: to *stretch* the truth; to *stretch* food. **7** *Slang* To fell with a blow. **—*v.i.* 8** To reach or extend from one place to another. **9** To become extended, esp. beyond normal limits. **10** To extend one's body or limbs, as in relaxing. **11** To lie down: usu. with *out.* **—*n.* 1** An act of stretching, or the state of being stretched. **2** Extent to which something can be stretched. **3** A continuous extent of space or time: a *stretch* of woodland; a *stretch* of two years. **4** In racing, the straight part of the track. **5** *Slang* A term of imprisonment. **—*adj.*** Capable of being easily stretched, as clothing: *stretch* socks. [< OE *streccan* stretch] **—stretch′i·ness** *n.* **—stretch′y** *adj.*

stretch·er (strech′ər) *n.* **1** Any device for stretching: a shoe *stretcher.* **2** A portable, often webbed frame for carrying the injured, sick, or dead.

stretch-out (strech′out′) *n. Informal* A system of industrial operation in which employees are required to perform more work per unit of time worked, usu. without increase in pay.

strew (stro͞o) *v.t.* **strewed, strewed** or **strewn, strew·ing 1** To spread about at random; sprinkle. **2** To cover with something scattered or sprinkled. **3** To be scattered over (a surface). [< OE *strēawian*]

stri·a·ted (strī′ā·tid) *adj.* Striped, grooved, or banded: *striated* muscle. [< L *striatus,* p.p. of *striare* to groove] —**stri′a·tion** *n.*

strick·en (strik′ən) *adj.* **1** Struck down by injury, disease, calamity, remorse, etc. **2** Advanced or far gone, as in age: *stricken* in years. [< OE *stricen,* p.p. of *strican* to strike]

strict (strikt) *adj.* **1** Observing or enforcing rules exactly: a *strict* church. **2** Containing severe rules or provisions; exacting. **3** Harsh; stern: a *strict* teacher. **4** Exactly defined or applied: the *strict* truth. **5** Devout; orthodox: a *strict* Catholic. **6** Absolute: in *strict* confidence. [< L *strictus,* p.p. of *stringere* draw tight] —**strict′ly** *adv.* —**strict′·ness** *n.*

stric·ture (strik′chər) *n.* **1** Severe criticism. **2** Something that checks or restricts. **3** Closure or narrowing of a duct or passage of the body. [< L *strictus* strict]

stride (strīd) *n.* **1** A long and measured step. **2** The space passed over by such a step. —**hit one's stride** To attain one's normal speed. —**make rapid strides** To make quick progress. —**take (something) in one's stride** To do or accept (something) without undue effort or without becoming upset. —*v.* **strode, strid·den, strid·ing** *v.i.* **1** To walk with long steps, as from haste. —*v.t.* **2** To walk through, along, etc., with long steps. **3** To pass over with a single stride. **4** To straddle; bestride. [< OE *strīdan* to stride] —**strid′er** *n.*

stri·dent (strīd′nt) *adj.* Having a loud and harsh sound; grating. [< L *stridere* to creak] —**stri′dence, stri′den·cy** *n.* —**stri′dent·ly** *adv.*

strid·u·late (strij′o͞o·lāt) *v.i.* **·lat·ed, ·lat·ing** To make a chirping, nonvocal noise, as a cricket, etc. [< L *stridere* to rattle, rasp] —**strid′u·la′tion** *n.* —**strid′u·la·to′ry** (-lə·tôr′ē, -tō′rē), **strid′u·lous** *adj.*

strife (strīf) *n.* **1** Angry contention; fighting. **2** Any contest or rivalry. **3** The act of striving; strenuous endeavor. [< OF *estriver* strive]

strike (strīk) *v.* **struck, struck** (*chiefly Archaic* **strick·en**), **strik·ing** *v.t.* **1** To hit with a blow; deal a blow to. **2** To crash into: The car *struck* the wall. **3** To deal (a blow, etc.). **4** To cause to hit forcibly: He *struck* his hand on the table. **5** To attack; assault. **6** To ignite (a match, etc.) **7** To form by stamping, printing, etc. **8** To announce; sound: The clock *struck* two. **9** To reach: A sound *struck* his ear. **10** To affect suddenly or in a specified manner: He was *struck* speechless. **11** To occur to: An idea *strikes* me. **12** To impress in a specified manner. **13** To attract the attention of: The dress *struck* her fancy. **14** To assume: to *strike* an attitude. **15** To cause to enter deeply or suddenly: to *strike* dismay into one's heart. **16** To lower or haul down, as a sail or a flag. **17** To cease working at in order to compel compliance to a demand, etc. **18** To make and confirm, as a bargain. —*v.i.* **19** To come into violent contact; crash; hit. **20** To deal or aim a blow or blows. **21** To make an assault or attack. **22** To sound from a blow or blows. **23** To be indicated by the sound of blows or strokes: Noon has just *struck.* **24** To ignite. **25** To lower a flag in token of surrender. **26** To take a course; start and proceed: to *strike* for home. **27** To cease work in order to enforce demands, etc. **28** To snatch at or swallow the lure: said of fish. —**strike camp** To take down the tents of a camp. —**strike down 1** To fell with a blow. **2** To incapacitate completely. —**strike dumb** To astonish; amaze. —**strike home 1** To deal an effective blow. **2** To have telling effect. —**strike it rich 1** To find a valuable pocket of ore. **2** To come into wealth or good fortune. —**strike off 1** To remove or take off by or as by a blow or stroke. **2** To deduct. —**strike oil 1** To find oil while drilling. **2** *Slang* To meet with unexpected good fortune. —**strike out 1** To aim a blow or blows. **2** To cross out or erase. **3** To begin; start. **4** In baseball, to put out (the batter) by pitching three strikes. —**strike up 1** To begin to play, as a band. **2** To start up; begin, as a friendship. —*n.* **1** An act of striking. **2** In baseball, an unsuccessful attempt by the batter to hit the ball. **3** In bowling, the knocking down of all the pins with the first bowl. **4** The quitting of work by a body of workers to secure some demand from management. **5** A new discovery, as of oil or ore. **6** Any unexpected or complete success. **7** The sudden rise and taking of the bait by a fish. —**on strike** Refusing to work in order to secure higher pay, better working conditions, etc. [< OE *strīcan* stroke, move]

strike·break·er (strīk′brā′kər) *n.* One who takes the place of a worker on strike or who seeks to intimidate or replace the strikers with other workers. —**strike′break′ing** *n.*

strik·er (strī′kər) *n.* **1** One who or that which strikes. **2** An employee who is on strike.

strik·ing (strī′king) *adj.* **1** Notable; impressive: a *striking* girl. **2** On strike. **3** That strikes: a *striking* clock. —**strik′ing·ly** *adv.* —**strik′ing·ness** *n.*

string (string) *n.* **1** A slender line, thinner than a cord and thicker than a thread, used for tying parcels, lacing, etc. **2** A cord of catgut, nylon, wire, etc., for musical instruments, bows, tennis rackets, etc. **3** A stringlike formation, as of certain vegetables. **4** A series of things hung on a small cord: a *string* of pearls. **5** A connected series or succession, as of things, acts, or events. **6** A drove or small collection of stock, esp. of saddle horses. **7** *pl.* Stringed instruments, esp., the section of violins, cellos, etc., in a symphony orchestra. **8** In sports, a group of contestants ranked as to skill. **9** *Informal Often pl.* A condition or restriction attached to an offer or gift. —**on a string** Under control or domination. —**pull strings 1** To control the actions of others, usu. secretly. **2** To influence others to gain an advantage. —*v.* **strung, string·ing** *v.t.* **1** To thread, as beads, on or as on a string. **2** To fit with a string or strings, as a guitar or bow. **3** To bind, fasten, or adorn with a string or strings. **4** To tune the strings of (a musical instrument). **5** To brace; strengthen. **6** To make tense or nervous. **7** To arrange or extend like a string. **8** To remove the strings from (vegetables). —*v.i.* **9** To extend or proceed in a line or series. **10** To form into strings. —**string along** *Slang* **1** To cooperate with. **2** To deceive; cheat. **3** To keep (someone) on tenterhooks. —**string out** *Informal* To protract; prolong: to *string out* an investigation. —**string up** *Informal* To hang. [< OE *streng* string]

string bean 1 The unripe edible seed pod of several varieties of bean. **2** The plants bearing these pods. **3** *Informal* A tall, skinny person.

stringed instrument (stringd) A musical instrument provided with strings or wires, as a violin, guitar, etc.

strin·gent (strin′jənt) *adj.* **1** Rigid; severe, as regulations. **2** Hampered by scarcity of money: said of a market. **3** Convincing; forcible. [< L *stringens,* pr.p of *stringere* draw tight] —**strin′gen·cy, strin′gent·ness** *n.* —**strin′gent·ly** *adv.*

string·er (string′ər) *n.* **1** One who strings. **2** A heavy timber supporting other members of a structure. **3** A newsman employed on a free-lance basis, often in out-of-town or foreign locations. **4** A person having a specific rating as to excellence, skill, etc.: used in combination: a *second-stringer.*

string·halt (string′hôlt′) *n.* In horses, lameness marked by spasmodic movement of the hind legs.

string·y (string′ē) *adj.* **string·i·er, string·i·est 1** Of or like a string or strings: *stringy* hair. **2** Containing fibrous strings. **3** Forming in strings, as thick glue; ropy. **4** Tall and wiry in build. —**string′i·ly** *adv.* —**string′i·ness** *n.*

strip[1] (strip) *n.* **1** A narrow piece, comparatively long, as of cloth, wood, etc. **2** A number of stamps attached in a row. **3** A narrow piece of land used as a runway for airplanes. **4** A comic strip. [?]

strip[2] (strip) *v.* **stripped** or **stript, strip·ping** *v.t.* **1** To pull the covering, clothing, leaves, etc., from; lay bare. **2** To pull off (the covering, etc.). **3** To rob or plunder; spoil. **4** To make bare or empty. **5** To take away. **6** To deprive of something; divest. **7** To damage the teeth, thread, etc., of (a gear, bolt, etc.). —*v.i.* **8** To undress. [< OE *bestrȳpan* plunder]

stripe[1] (strīp) *n.* **1** A line, band, or long strip of material differing in color or finish from its adjacent surfaces. **2** Distinctive quality or character: a man of artistic *stripe.* **3** Striped cloth. **4** *pl.* Prison uniform. **5** A piece of material or braid on a uniform to indicate rank. —*v.t.* **striped, strip·ing** To mark with a stripe or stripes. [< MDu.]

stripe[2] (strīp) *n.* **1** A blow struck with a whip or rod. **2** A weal or welt on the skin caused by such a blow. [Prob. < LG]

strip·ling (strip′ling) *n.* A mere youth; a lad. [?]

strip mine A mine, esp. a coal mine, the seams of which are close to the surface of the earth and which is worked by stripping away the topsoil and the material beneath it. —**strip′-mine′** *v.t.* **(-mined, -min·ing)** —**strip miner**

strip·per (strip′ər) *n.* **1** One who or that which strips. **2** *Slang* A female performer of a striptease.

strip·tease (strip′tēz′) *n.* An act, usu. in burlesque, in which a female performer gradually disrobes before an audience. —**strip′teas′er** *n.*

strive (strīv) *v.i.* **strove, striv·en** (striv′ən) or **strived, striv·ing 1** To make earnest effort. **2** To engage in strife; fight: to *strive* against an enemy. [< OF *estriver*] —**striv′er** *n.* — **Syn. 1** endeavor, try. **2** contend, struggle.

strobe (strōb) *n.* **1** STROBOSCOPE. **2** An electronically controlled device that emits light in very brief, brilliant flashes, used in photography, in the theater, etc.: also **strobe light.**

strob·o·scope (strōb′ə·skōp) *n.* An instrument for studying the motion of an object by making the object appear to be stationary, as by periodic instantaneous illumination or observation. [< Gk. *strobos* twirling + -SCOPE] —**strob′o·scop′ic** (-skop′ik) or **·i·cal** *adj.* —**strob·os·co·py** (strō·bos′kə·pē) *n.*

strode (strōd) *p.t.* of STRIDE.

stroke (strōk) *n.* **1** The act or movement of striking. **2** One of a series of recurring movements, as of oars, arms in swimming, a piston, etc. **3** A rower who sets the pace for the rest of the crew. **4** A single movement of a pen or pencil. **5** A mark made by such a movement. **6** Any ill effect: a *stroke* of misfortune. **7** APOPLEXY. **8** A sound of a striking mechanism, as of a clock. **9** A sudden or brilliant mental act: a *stroke* of wit. **10** A light caressing movement; a stroking. —**keep stroke** To make strokes simultaneously, as oarsmen. —*v.t.* **stroked, strok·ing 1** To pass the hand over gently or caressingly. **2** To set the pace for (a rowboat or its crew). [< OE *strācian* strike] —**strok′er** *n.*

stroll (strōl) *v.i.* **1** To walk in a leisurely manner; saunter. **2** To go from place to place. —*n.* A leisurely walk. [?]

stroll·er (strō′lər) *n.* **1** A small, light baby carriage, often collapsible. **2** One who strolls. **3** An actor who travels from place to place to perform.

strong (strông, strong) *adj.* **1** Physically powerful; muscular. **2** Healthy; robust: a *strong* constitution. **3** Resolute; courageous. **4** Mentally powerful or vigorous. **5** Especially competent or able: *strong* in mathematics. **6** Abundantly supplied: *strong* in trumps. **7** Solidly made or constituted: *strong* walls. **8** Powerful, as a rival or combatant. **9** Easy to defend: a *strong* position. **10** In numerical force: an army 20,000 *strong.* **11** Well able to exert influence, authority, etc. **12** Financially sound: a *strong* market. **13** Powerful in effect: *strong* poison. **14** Not diluted or weak: *strong* coffee. **15** Containing much alcohol: a *strong* drink. **16** Powerful in flavor or odor: a *strong* breath. **17** Intense in degree or quality: a *strong* light. **18** Loud and firm: a *strong* voice. **19** Firm; tenacious: a *strong* will. **20** Fervid: a *strong* desire. **21** Cogent; convincing: *strong* evidence. **22** Distinct; marked: a *strong* resemblance. **23** Extreme: *strong* measures. **24** Emphatic: *strong* language. **25** Moving with great force: said of a wind, stream, or tide. **26** *Phonet.* Stressed. **27** *Gram.* Of verbs, indicating changes in tense by means of vowel changes, rather than by inflectional endings, as *drink, drank, drunk.* —*adv.* In a firm, vigorous manner. [< OE] —**strong′ly** *adv.* —**strong′ness** *n.*

strong-arm (strông′ärm′, strong′-) *Informal adj.* Using physical or coercive power: *strong-arm* tactics. —*v.t.* **1** To use physical force upon; assault. **2** To coerce; compel.

strong·box (strông′boks′, strong′-) *n.* A chest or safe for keeping valuables.

strong drink Alcoholic liquors.

strong·hold (strông′hōld′, strong′-) *n.* A strongly defended place; fortress.

strong·man (strông′man′, strong′-) *n. pl.* **·men** (-mən) A political leader having preeminent power, as from a military coup or other extralegal means.

strong-mind·ed (strông′mīn′did, strong′-) *adj.* **1** Having an active, vigorous mind. **2** Determined; resolute. —**strong′-mind′ed·ly** *adv.* —**strong′-mind′ed·ness** *n.*

strong-willed (strông′wild′, strong′-) *adj.* Having a strong will; obstinate.

stron·ti·um (stron′chē·əm, -chəm, -tē·əm) *n.* A metallic element (symbol Sr) chemically resembling calcium, used in pyrotechnics. [< *Strontian,* Argyll, Scotland, where first discovered] —**stron′tic** (-tik) *adj.*

strop (strop) *n.* A strip of leather on which to sharpen a razor. —*v.t.* **stropped, strop·ping** To sharpen on a strop. [< Gk. *strophos* band]

Strop

stro·phe (strō′fē), *n.* **1** In ancient Greece, the verses sung by the chorus in a play while moving from right to left. **2** A stanza of a poem. [< Gk. *strophē* a turning, twist] —**stroph·ic** (strof′ik, strō′fik) or **·i·cal** *adj.*

strove (strōv) *p.t.* of STRIVE.

struck (struk) *p.t. & p.p.* of STRIKE.

struc·tur·al (struk′chər·əl) *adj.* **1** Of, pertaining to, or characterized by structure. **2** Used in or essential to construction. —**struc′tur·al·ly** *adv.*

structural steel Rolled steel shaped and adapted for use in construction.

struc·ture (struk′chər) *n.* **1** That which is constructed, as a building. **2** Something based upon or organized according to a plan or design: the political *structure* of a republic. **3** The manner of such organization: a hierarchical *structure.* **4** The arrangement and relationship of the parts of a whole, as organs in a plant or animal, atoms in a molecule, etc. —*v.t.* **·tured, ·tur·ing 1** To form or organize into a structure; build. **2** To conceive as a structural whole. [< L *structus,* p.p. of *struere* build]

stru·del (strōōd′l) *n.* A kind of pastry with a filling of fruit, nuts, etc. [G, lit., eddy]

strug·gle (strug′əl) *n.* **1** A violent effort or series of efforts. **2** A war; battle. —*v.i.* **·gled, ·gling 1** To contend with an adversary in physical combat; fight. **2** To strive: to *struggle* against odds. **3** To make one's way by violent efforts: to *struggle* through mud. [ME *strogelen*] —**strug′·gler** *n.* —**strug′gling·ly** *adv.*

strum (strum) *v.t. & v.i.* **strummed, strum·ming** To play idly or carelessly (on a stringed instrument). —*n.* The act of strumming. [Prob. Imit.] —**strum′mer** *n.*

strum·pet (strum′pit) *n.* A whore; prostitute. [ME]

strung (strung) *p.t. & p.p.* of STRING.

strung out *Slang* **1** Sick or in weakened health from prolonged use of drugs. **2** Addicted to narcotics.

strut (strut) *n.* **1** A proud or pompous step or walk. **2** A supporting piece in a framework, keeping two others from approaching nearer together. —*v.* **strut·ted, strut·ting** *v.i.* **1** To walk pompously and affectedly. —*v.t.* **2** To brace or support with a brace or strut. [< OE *strūtian* be rigid, stand stiffly] —**strut′ter** *n.* —**strut′ting·ly** *adv.*

strych·nine (strik′nīn, -nən, -nēn) *n.* A poisonous alkaloid obtained from nux vomica, used in medicine as a stimulant. Also **strych′ni·a** (-nē·ə) [< Gk. *strychnos* nightshade] —**strych′nic** *adj.*

stub (stub) *n.* **1** Any short remnant, as of a pencil, candle, cigarette, cigar, or broken tooth. **2** In a checkbook, the short piece on which the amount of a check is recorded and that remains when the check is detached. **3** A tree stump. —*v.t.* **stubbed, stub·bing 1** To strike, as the toe, against a low obstruction or projection. **2** To clear or remove the stubs or roots from. [< OE *stubb*] —**stub′ber** *n.*

stub·ble (stub′əl) *n.* **1** The stubs of plants covering a field after reaping. **2** The field itself. **3** Any surface or growth resembling stubble, as short bristly hair or beard. [< L *stipula* stalk] —**stub′bly** *adj.* **(·bli·er, ·bli·est)**

stub·born (stub′ərn) *adj.* 1 Inflexible in opinion or intention. 2 Determined to have one's own way. 3 Not easily handled, bent, or overcome. 4 Characterized by perseverance or persistence: *stubborn* fighting. [ME *stoborne*] —**stub′born·ly** *adv.* —**stub′born·ness** *n.* —**Syn.** 1 opinionated, unyielding. 2 headstrong, obdurate, obstinate.

stub·by (stub′ē) *adj.* **·bi·er, ·bi·est** 1 Short, stiff, and bristling: a *stubby* beard. 2 Short and thick: a *stubby* pencil. 3 Short and thick-set: a *stubby* man. —**stub′bi·ly** *adv.* —**stub′bi·ness** *n.*

stuc·co (stuk′ō) *n. pl.* **·coes** or **·cos** 1 Any plaster or cement used for the external coating of buildings. 2 Work done in stucco: also **stuc′co·work′**. —*v.t.* **·coed, ·co·ing** To apply stucco to; decorate with stucco. [Ital.] —**stuc′co·er** *n.*

stuck (stuk) *p.t. & p.p.* of STICK.

stuck-up (stuk′up′) *adj. Informal* Conceited; very vain.

stud[1] (stud) *n.* 1 Any of a series of small knobs, round-headed nails, or small protuberant ornaments. 2 A small, removable button such as is used in a shirt front. 3 A post to which laths are nailed in a building frame. 4 STUD POKER. —*v.t.* **stud·ded, stud·ding** 1 To set thickly with small points, projections, or knobs. 2 To be scattered over: Daisies *stud* the meadows. 3 To support or stiffen by means of studs or upright props. [< OE *studu* post]

stud[2] (stud) *n.* 1 A collection of horses and mares for breeding, riding, hunting, or racing. 2 The place where they are kept. 3 A stallion. —**at stud** Available for breeding purposes: said of male animals. —*adj.* Of or pertaining to a stud. [< OE *stōd*]

stu·dent (styōōd′nt, -ənt) *n.* 1 A person engaged in a course of study, esp. in an educational institution. 2 One who closely examines or investigates. [< L *studere* be eager, apply oneself, study]

stud·horse (stud′hôrs′) *n.* A stallion kept for breeding. Also **stud horse.**

stud·ied (stud′ēd) *adj.* 1 Deliberately planned; premeditated: a *studied* insult. 2 Acquired or prepared by study. —**stud′ied·ly** *adv.* —**stud′ied·ness** *n.*

stu·di·o (styōō′dē·ō) *n. pl.* **·di·os** 1 The workroom of an artist, photographer, etc. 2 A place where motion pictures are filmed. 3 A room or rooms where radio or television programs are broadcast or recorded. 4 A room or place in which music is recorded. [< L *studere* apply oneself, be diligent]

stu·di·ous (styōō′dē·əs) *adj.* 1 Given to or fond of study. 2 Considerate; careful; attentive. —**stu′di·ous·ly** *adv.* —**stu′di·ous·ness** *n.*

stud poker A game of poker in which the cards of the first round are dealt face down and the rest face up.

stud·y (stud′ē) *v.* **stud·ied, stud·y·ing** *v.t.* 1 To acquire a knowledge of: to *study* physics. 2 To examine; search into: to *study* a problem. 3 To scrutinize: to *study* one's reflection. 4 To memorize, as a part in a play. —*v.i.* 5 To apply the mind in acquiring knowledge. 6 To be a student. —**study up on** To acquire more complete information concerning. —*n. pl.* **stud·ies** 1 The process of acquiring information. 2 A particular instance or form of mental work. 3 A branch or department of knowledge. 4 A specific product of studious application: his *study* of plankton. 5 An examination or consideration of a problem, proposal, etc. 6 In art, a first sketch. 7 A careful literary treatment of a subject. 8 A room set aside for study, reading, etc. 9 A thoughtful state of mind: a brown *study.* 10 *Music* A composition designed to develop technique; an étude. [< L *studium* zeal] —**Syn.** *v.* 1 grasp, learn. 2 investigate, ponder, analyze.

stuff (stuf) *v.t.* 1 To fill completely; pack. 2 To plug. 3 To obstruct or stop up. 4 To fill with padding, as a cushion. 5 To fill (a fowl, roast, etc.) with stuffing. 6 In taxidermy, to fill the skin of (a bird, animal, etc.) with a material preparatory to mounting. 7 To fill too full; cram: He *stuffed* himself with cake. 8 To fill with knowledge, ideas, or attitudes, esp. unsystematically. —*v.i.* 9 To eat to excess. —*n.* 1 The material or matter out of which something is or may be shaped or made. 2 The fundamental element of anything: the *stuff* of genius. 3 *Informal* A specific skill, field of knowledge, etc.: That editor knows her *stuff.* 4 Personal possessions generally. 5 Unspecified material, matter, etc.: They carried away tons of the *stuff.* 6 A miscellaneous collection of things. 7 Nonsense; foolishness. 8 Woven material, esp. of wool. 9 Any textile fabric. [< OF *estoffer* cram] —**stuff′er** *n.*

stuffed shirt *Informal* A pretentious, pompous person.

stuff·ing (stuf′ing) *n.* 1 The material with which anything is stuffed. 2 A mixture, as of crumbs with seasoning, used in stuffing fowls, etc. 3 The process of stuffing anything.

stuff·y (stuf′ē) *adj.* **stuff·i·er, stuff·i·est** 1 Badly ventilated. 2 Filled up so as to impede respiration: a *stuffy* nose. 3 Dull; uninspired: a *stuffy* speech. 4 Strait-laced; stodgy. —**stuff′i·ly** *adv.* —**stuff′i·ness** *n.*

stul·ti·fy (stul′tə·fī′) *v.t.* **·fied, ·fy·ing** 1 To cause to appear absurd. 2 To make useless or futile. [< L *stultus* foolish + -FY] —**stul′ti·fi·ca′tion, stul′ti·fi′er** *n.*

stum·ble (stum′bəl) *v.* **·bled, ·bling** *v.i.* 1 To miss one's step in walking or running; trip. 2 To speak or act in a blundering manner: The student *stumbled* through his recitation. 3 To happen upon something by chance: with *across, on, upon,* etc. 4 To do wrong; err. —*v.t.* 5 To cause to stumble. —*n.* The act of stumbling. [ME *stumblen*] —**stum′bler** *n.* —**stum′bling·ly** *adv.*

stum·bling·block (stum′bling·blok′) *n.* Any obstacle or hindrance.

stump (stump) *n.* 1 That portion of the trunk of a tree left standing when the tree is felled. 2 The part of a limb, etc., that remains when the main part has been removed. 3 *pl. Informal* The legs. 4 A place or platform where a political speech is made. 5 A short, thick-set person or animal. 6 A heavy step; a clump. —**take the stump** To electioneer in a political campaign. —**up a stump** In trouble or in a dilemma. —*adj.* 1 Being or resembling a stump. 2 Of or pertaining to political oratory or campaigning: a *stump* speaker. —*v.t.* 1 To reduce to a stump; lop. 2 To remove stumps from (land). 3 To canvass (a district) by making political speeches. 4 *Informal* To bring to a halt by real or fancied obstacles. 5 To stub, as one's toe. —*v.i.* 6 To walk heavily. [< MLG] —**stump′i·ness** *n.* —**stump′y** *adj.*

stun (stun) *v.t.* **stunned, stun·ning** 1 To render unconscious or incapable of action. 2 To astonish; astound. 3 To daze or overwhelm. —*n.* The act of stunning or the condition of being stunned. [< OF *estoner*]

stung (stung) *p.t. & p.p.* of STING.

stunk (stungk) *p.p.* and alternative *p.t.* of STINK.

stun·ner (stun′ər) *n.* 1 A person or blow that stuns. 2 *Slang* A person or thing of extraordinary qualities, such as beauty.

stun·ning (stun′ing) *adj.* 1 That stuns or astounds. 2 *Informal* Surprising; impressive; beautiful. —**stun′ning·ly** *adv.*

stunt[1] (stunt) *v.t.* To check the natural development of; dwarf; cramp. —*n.* 1 A check in growth, progress, or development. 2 A stunted animal or person. [< OE, dull, foolish] —**stunt′ed·ness** *n.*

stunt[2] (stunt) *Informal n.* 1 A sensational feat, as of bodily skill. 2 Any remarkable feat. —*v.i.* 1 To perform a stunt or stunts. —*v.t.* 2 To perform stunts with (an airplane, etc.). [?]

stunt man In motion pictures, a person employed to substitute for an actor when dangerous jumps, falls, etc., must be made.

stu·pe·fac·tion (styōō′pə·fak′shən) *n.* The act of stupefying or state of being stupefied.

stu·pe·fy (styōō′pə·fī′) *v.t.* **·fied, ·fy·ing** 1 To dull the senses or faculties of; stun. 2 To amaze; astound. [< L *stupere* be stunned + -FY] —**stu′pe·fi′er** *n.*

stu·pen·dous (styōō·pen′dəs) *adj.* 1 Of prodigious size, bulk, or degree. 2 Astonishing; marvelous. [< L *stupere* be stunned] —**stu·pen′dous·ly** *adv.* —**stu·pen′dous·ness** *n.*

stu·pid (styōō′pid) *adj.* 1 Very slow in understanding; lacking in intelligence; dull-witted. 2 Affected with stupor; stupefied. 3 Dull and profitless; tiresome: to regard rote learning as *stupid.* 4 Resulting from slowness in understanding or a lack of intelligence. **5** *Informal* Annoying; bothersome: This *stupid* nail won't go in straight. [< L *stupidus* struck dumb] **—stu·pid·i·ty** (styōō·pid′ə·tē) (*pl.* **·ties**), **stu′pid·ness** *n.* **—stu′pid·ly** *adv.*

stu·por (styōō′pər) *n.* **1** Abnormal lethargy due to shock, drugs, etc. **2** Extreme intellectual dullness. [< L *stupere* be stunned] **—stu′por·ous** *adj.*

stur·dy (stûr′dē) *adj.* **·di·er, ·di·est 1** Possessing rugged health and strength. **2** Firm and resolute: a *sturdy* defense. [< OF *estourdir* stun, amaze] **—stur′di·ly** *adv.* **—stur′di·ness** *n.* **—Syn. 1** hardy, lusty, robust, vigorous. **2** determined, unyielding.

stur·geon (stûr′jən) *n.* Any of various large edible fishes of northern regions, valued as the source of caviar. [< Med. L *sturio*]

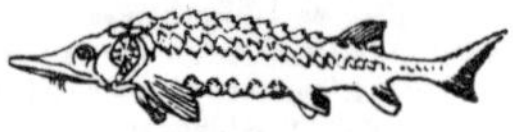
Sturgeon

stut·ter (stut′ər) *v.t.* & *v.i.* To utter or speak with spasmodic repetition, blocking, and prolongation of sounds and syllables. **—*n.*** The act or habit of stuttering. [Freq. of ME *stutten* stutter] **—stut′ter·er** *n.* **—stut′ter·ing·ly** *adv.*

St. Vi·tus's dance (sānt vī′təs·iz) CHOREA. Also **St. Vitus dance.** [< *St. Vitus,* third-century Christian child martyr]

sty[1] (stī) *n. pl.* **sties 1** A pen for swine. **2** Any filthy habitation. [< OE *stī, stig*]

sty[2] (stī) *n. pl.* **sties** A pustule on the edge of an eyelid. Also **stye.** [< OE *stīgan* rise + *ye* eye]

Styg·i·an (stij′ē·ən) *adj.* **1** Pertaining to or like the river Styx or the lower world. **2** Dark and gloomy.

style (stīl) *n.* **1** A fashionable manner or appearance: to be in *style.* **2** Fashion: the latest *style* in shirts. **3** A particular fashion in clothing. **4** A distinctive form of expression: a florid *style.* **5** An effective way of expression: His drawings have *style.* **6** Manner: a church in the Romanesque *style* of architecture. **7** A way of living or behaving: Domestic life is not his *style.* **8** A pointed instrument for marking or engraving. **9** An indicator on a dial. **10** *Printing* The typography, spelling, design, etc., used in a given published text. **11** *Bot.* The slender part of a carpel between stigma and ovary. **12** A system of arranging the calendar years so as to average that of the true solar year. Our calendar, adopted in 1752, is called **New Style,** while **Old Style** dates are 13 days earlier. **—*v.t.*** **styled, styl·ing 1** To name; give a title to: Richard I was *styled* "the Lion-Hearted." **2** To cause to conform to a specific style: to *style* a manuscript. [< L *stylus* writing instrument] **—styl′er** *n.*

style·book (stīl′bŏŏk′) *n.* A book setting forth rules of capitalization, punctuation, etc., for the use of printers, writers, and editors. Also **style manual.**

styl·ish (stī′lish) *adj.* **1** Having style. **2** Very fashionable. **—styl′ish·ly** *adv.* **—styl′ish·ness** *n.*

styl·ist (stī′list) *n.* **1** One who is a master of style: a literary *stylist.* **2** An adviser on or a creator of styles: a hair *stylist.* **—sty·lis′tic** *adj.* **—sty·lis′ti·cal·ly** *adv.*

styl·ize (stī′līz) *v.t.* **·ized, ·iz·ing** To conform to or create in a distinctive or specific style. *Brit. sp.* **styl′ise. —styl′i·za′·tion** (stī′lə·zā′shən), **styl′iz·er** *n.*

sty·lus (stī′ləs) *n. pl.* **·lus·es** or **·li** (lī) **1** An ancient instrument for writing on wax tablets. **2** A tiny, usu. jewel-tipped needle whose vibrations in tracing the groove in a phonograph record transmit sound. [L]

sty·mie (stī′mē) *n.* A condition in golf in which an opponent's ball lies in the line of the player's putt on the green. **—*v.t.*** **·mied, ·my·ing 1** To block (an opponent) by or as by a stymie. **2** To baffle or perplex. [?]

styp·tic (stip′tik) *adj.* Tending to halt bleeding; astringent: also **styp′ti·cal.** **—*n.*** A styptic substance. [< Gk. *stypsis* a contraction] **—styp·tic·i·ty** (stip·tis′ə·tē) *n.*

Sty·ro·foam (stī′rə·fōm) *n.* A lightweight, rigid, cellular material formed from a synthetic hydrocarbon polymer: a trade name.

Styx (stiks) *n. Gk. Myth.* The river across which the dead were ferried to Hades.

sua·sion (swā′zhən) *n.* The act of persuading: usu. in the phrase **moral suasion.** [< L *suadere* persuade] **—sua·sive** (swā′siv), **sua·so·ry** (swā′sər·ē) *adj.* **—sua′sive·ly** *adv.* **—sua′sive·ness** *n.*

suave (swäv) *adj.* Smooth and pleasant in manner, often superficially so. [< L *suavis* sweet] **—suave′ly** *adv.* **—suave′ness, suav′i·ty** (*pl.* **·ties**) *n.*

sub (sub) *n. Informal* **1** SUBSTITUTE. **2** A subordinate or subaltern. **3** SUBMARINE. **—*v.i.*** **subbed, sub·bing** To act as a substitute for someone.

sub- *prefix* **1** Under; beneath; below: *subcutaneous.* **2** Almost; nearly: *subtropical.* **3** Further; again: *subdivide.* **4** Lower in rank or grade: *subordinate.* **5** Having less importance; secondary: *subtitle.* **6** Forming a further division: *subcommittee.* [< L *sub* under] • See TAXONOMY.

sub. subaltern; submarine; subscription; substitute; suburb; suburban.

sub·al·tern (sub·ôl′tərn, *esp. Brit.* sub′əl·tərn) *adj.* **1** *Brit. Mil.* Ranking below a captain. **2** Of inferior rank or position. **—*n.*** **1** A person of subordinate rank or position. **2** *Brit. Mil.* An officer ranking below a captain. [< L *sub-* under + *alternus* alternate]

sub·ant·arc·tic (sub′ant·ärk′tik, -är′tik) *adj.* Denoting or pertaining to a region surrounding the Antarctic Circle.

sub·arc·tic (sub·ärk′tik, -är′tik) *adj.* Denoting or pertaining to a region surrounding the Arctic Circle.

sub·a·tom·ic (sub′ə·tom′ik) *adj.* **1** Of or pertaining to the constituent parts of an atom. **2** Smaller than an atom.

sub·com·mit·tee (sub′kə·mit′ē) *n.* A small committee appointed from a larger committee for special work.

sub·con·scious (sub·kon′shəs) *adj.* **1** Only dimly conscious; not fully aware. **2** Not attended by full awareness, as an automatic action. **—*n.*** That portion of mental activity not in the focus of consciousness. **—sub·con′scious·ly** *adv.* **—sub·con′scious·ness** *n.*

sub·con·tract (sub·kon′trakt) *n.* A contract subordinate to another contract and assigning part of the work to a third party. **—*v.t.* & *v.i.*** (sub′kən·trakt′) To make a subcontract (for). **—sub·con·trac·tor** (sub′kon′trak′tər, sub′·kən·trak′-) *n.*

sub·cul·ture (sub′kul·chər) *n.* A group having specific patterns of behavior that set it off from other groups within a culture or society.

sub·cu·ta·ne·ous (sub′kyōō·tā′nē·əs) *adj.* Situated or applied beneath the skin. [< L *sub-* under + *cutis* skin] **—sub′cu·ta′ne·ous·ly** *adv.*

subd. subdivision.

sub·deb (sub′deb′) *n. Informal* **1** A young girl during the period before she becomes a debutante. **2** Any young girl of the same age.

sub·di·vide (sub′di·vīd′, sub′di·vīd′) *v.t.* & *v.i.* **·vid·ed, ·vid·ing 1** To divide again. **2** To divide (land) into lots for sale or improvement.

sub·di·vi·sion (sub′di·vizh′ən, sub′di·vizh′ən) *n.* **1** Division following upon division. **2** A part, as of land, resulting from subdividing.

sub·due (sub·dyōō′) *v.t.* **·dued, ·du·ing 1** To gain dominion over, as by war or force. **2** To overcome by training, influence, or persuasion. **3** To repress (emotions, impulses, etc.). **4** To reduce the intensity of. [< L *subducere* lead away] **—sub·du′ed·ly** *adv.* **—sub·du′er** *n.* **—Syn. 1** conquer, subjugate, vanquish. **2** master, tame. **4** lessen, soften.

sub·group (sub′grōōp′) *n.* A subdivision of a group.

sub·head (sub′hed′) *n.* **1** A heading or title of a subdivision of a chapter, etc. **2** A subordinate title. Also **sub′·head·ing.**

sub·hu·man (sub·hyōō′mən) *adj.* Less than or imperfectly human.

subj. subject; subjective; subjunctive.

sub·ja·cent (sub·jā′sənt) *adj.* Situated underneath; underlying. [< L *sub-* under + *jacere* to lie] **—sub·ja′cen·cy** *n.* **—sub·ja′cent·ly** *adv.*

sub·ject (sub′jikt) *adj.* **1** Being under the power of another. **2** Exposed: *subject* to criticism. **3** Having a tendency: *subject* to colds. **4** Conditional upon: *subject* to your consent. **—*n.*** **1** One who is under the governing power of another, as of a ruler. • See CITIZEN. **2** One who or that which is employed or treated in a specified way, as in an experiment. **3** The theme or topic of a discussion. **4** Something described or depicted in a literary or artistic work. **5** *Gram.* The word, phrase, or clause of a sentence about which something is stated or asked in the predicate. **6**

Music The melodic phrase on which a composition or a part of it is based. 7 A branch of learning. —*v.t.* (səb·jekt′) 1 To bring under dominion or control; subjugate. 2 To cause to undergo some experience or action. 3 To make liable; expose: His inheritance was *subjected* to heavy taxation. [<L *sub-* under + *jacere* throw] —**sub·jec′tion** *n.*

sub·jec·tive (səb·jek′tiv) *adj.* 1 Of or belonging to that which is within the mind and not subject to independent verification. 2 Expressing very personal feelings or opinions: a *subjective* piece of writing. 3 Highly influenced by the emotions or by prejudice. 4 *Med.* Of the kind of which only the patient is aware: said of symptoms. 5 *Gram.* Designating the case and function of the subject of a sentence. —**sub·jec′tive·ly** *adv.* —**sub·jec′tive·ness, sub·jec·tiv·i·ty** (sub′-jek·tiv′ə·tē) *n.*

sub·join (sub·join′) *v.t.* To add at the end; affix. [<L *sub-* in addition + *jungere* join] —**sub·join′der** (-dər) *n.*

sub·ju·gate (sub′jŏŏ·gāt) *v.t.* **·gat·ed, ·gat·ing** 1 To bring under dominion; conquer. 2 To make subservient or submissive. [<L *sub-* under + *jugum* a yoke] —**sub′ju·ga′tion, sub′ju·ga′tor** *n.*

sub·junc·tive (səb·jungk′tiv) *Gram. adj.* Of or pertaining to that mood of the finite verb that is used to express a future contingency, a supposition, or a wish or desire. —*n.* 1 The subjunctive mood. 2 A verb form or construction in this mood. [<L *subjunctus.* p.p. of *subjungere* subjoin] —**sub·junc′tive·ly** *adv.*

sub·lease (sub·lēs′) *v.t.* **·leased, ·leas·ing** To obtain or let (property) on a sublease. —*n.* (sub′lēs′) A lease of property from a tenant.

sub·let (sub·let′, sub′let′) *v.t.* **·let, ·let·ting** 1 To let to another (property held on a lease). 2 To let (work that one has contracted to do) to a subordinate contractor. —*n.* Property, esp. dwellings, that is subleased or available for subleasing.

sub·li·mate (sub′lə·māt) *v.* **·mat·ed, ·mat·ing** *v.t.* 1 To refine; purify. 2 *Psychol.* To convert (a primitive impulse) into socially acceptable behavior. 3 *Chem.* SUBLIME. —*v.i.* 4 To undergo or engage in sublimation. —*adj.* Sublimated; refined. —*n. Chem.* The product of sublimation. [<L *sublimis* uplifted, sublime]

sub·li·ma·tion (sub′lə·mā′shən) *n.* 1 The act or process of sublimating. 2 *Chem.* A change of state from solid to vapor or from vapor to solid without liquefaction.

sub·lime (sə·blīm′) *adj.* 1 Characterized by or eliciting feelings of grandeur, nobility, or awe. 2 *Informal* Outstandingly excellent; supreme: a *sublime* meal. —*v.* **·limed, ·lim·ing** *v.t.* 1 To make sublime; ennoble. 2 *Chem.* To purify by the process of sublimation. —*v.i.* 3 *Chem.* To undergo sublimation. [<L *sublimis* lofty] —**sub·lime′ly** *adv.* —**sub·lim·i·ty** (sə·blim′ə·tē), **sub·lime′ness** *n.* —**Syn.** *adj.* 1 grand, magnificent, solemn. 2 noble.

sub·lim·i·nal (sub·lim′ə·nəl) *adj.* 1 Below or beyond the threshold of consciousness: a *subliminal* stimulus. 2 Too slight or weak to be felt or perceived. [<L *sub-* under + *limen* threshold] —**sub·lim′i·nal·ly** *adv.*

sub·ma·chine gun (sub′mə·shēn′) A lightweight, automatic or semi-automatic gun, designed for firing from the shoulder or hip.

sub·mar·gin·al (sub·mär′jən·əl) *adj.* 1 Below the margin. 2 Not productive enough to develop, cultivate, etc.: *submarginal* land.

sub·ma·rine (sub′mə·rēn′) *adj.* Existing, done, or operating beneath the surface of the sea. —*n.* (sub′mə·rēn) 1 A vessel, usu. a warship, designed to operate both on and below the surface of the water. 2 HERO (def. 5).

sub·max·il·lar·y (sub·mak′sə·ler′ē) *adj.* Of, pertaining to, or situated in the lower jaw. —*n. pl.* **·lar·ies** A submaxillary salivary gland, nerve, artery, etc.

sub·merge (səb·mûrj′) *v.* **·merged, ·merg·ing** *v.t.* 1 To place under or plunge into water. 2 To cover; hide. —*v.i.* 3 To sink or dive beneath the surface of water. [<L *sub-* under + *mergere* to plunge] —**sub·mer′gence** *n.*

sub·merse (səb·mûrs′) *v.t.* **·mersed, ·mers·ing** SUBMERGE. [<L *submergere* submerge] —**sub·mer′sion** *n.*

sub·mers·i·ble (səb·mûr′sə·bəl) *adj.* That may be submerged. —*n.* 1 SUBMARINE (def. 1). 2 Any of various, usu. small, underwater craft used for naval observation, scientific study, etc.

sub·mis·sion (səb·mish′ən) *n.* 1 A yielding to the power or authority of another. 2 Acquiescence or obedience. 3 The act of referring a matter of controversy to consideration, arbitration, etc. —**Syn.** 1 surrender. 2 compliance, humbleness.

sub·mis·sive (səb·mis′iv) *adj.* Willing or inclined to submit; docile. —**sub·mis′sive′ly** *adv.* —**sub·mis′sive·ness** *n.*

sub·mit (səb·mit′) *v.* **·mit·ted, ·mit·ting** *v.t.* 1 To place under or yield to the authority of another. 2 To present for the consideration of others; refer. 3 To present as one's opinion; suggest. —*v.i.* 4 To give up; surrender. 5 To be obedient. [<L *sub-* under + *mittere* send] —**sub·mit′tal** *n.*

sub·nor·mal (sub·nôr′məl) *adj.* Below the normal; of less than normal intelligence, development, etc. —*n.* A subnormal individual. —**sub·nor·mal·i·ty** (sub′nôr·mal′ə·tē) *n.* —**sub·nor′mal·ly** *adv.*

sub·or·di·nate (sə·bôr′də·nit) *adj.* 1 Secondary; minor. 2 Lower in rank. 3 Subject or subservient to another. 4 *Gram.* Used within a sentence as a noun, adjective, or adverb: said of a clause. —*n.* One who or that which is subordinate. —*v.t.* (-nāt) **·nat·ed, ·nat·ing** 1 To assign to a lower order or rank. 2 To make subject or subservient. [<L *sub-* under + *ordinare* to order] —**sub·or′di·nate·ly** *adv.* —**sub·or′di·nate·ness, sub·or′di·na′tion** *n.*

sub·orn (sə·bôrn′) *v. t.* 1 To bribe (someone) to commit perjury. 2 To incite or instigate to an evil act. [<L *sub-* secretly + *ornare* equip] —**sub·orn′er, sub·or·na·tion** (sub′ôr·nā′shən) *n.*

sub·poe·na (sə·pē′nə) *n.* A writ requiring a person to appear at court at a specified time and place. —*v.t.* **·naed, ·na·ing** To summon by subpoena. Also **sub·pe′na.** [<L *sub-* under + *poena* penalty]

sub·ro·gate (sub′rō·gāt) *v.t.* **·gat·ed, ·gat·ing** To substitute (one person, esp. one creditor) for another. [<L *sub-* in place of + *rogare* ask] —**sub′ro·ga′tion** *n.*

sub ro·sa (sub rō′zə) Confidentially; in secret. [L, under the rose, a symbol of silence]

sub·rou·tine (sub′rōō·tēn′) *n.* A part of a computer program, especially a sequence of instructions to perform a specific task.

sub·scribe (səb·skrīb′) *v.* **·scribed, ·scrib·ing** *v.t.* 1 To write, as one's name, at the end of a document; sign. 2. To sign one's name to as an expression of assent. 3 To promise, esp. in writing, to pay or contribute (a sum of money). —*v.i.* 4 To write one's name at the end of a document. 5 To give approval; agree. 6 To promise to contribute money. 7 To pay in advance for a series of periodicals, tickets to performances, etc. with *to.* [<L *sub-* under + *scribere* write] —**sub·scrib′er** *n.*

sub·script (sub′skript) *adj.* 1 Written following and slightly beneath, as a small letter or number. —*n.* A subscript number, symbol, or letter, as the *2* in H_2O. [<L *subscriptus,* p.p. of *subscribere* subscribe]

sub·scrip·tion (səb·skrip′shən) *n.* 1 The act of subscribing; confirmation or agreement. 2 That which is subscribed; a signed paper or statement. 3 A signature written at the end of a document. 4 The total subscribed for any purpose. 5 The purchase in advance of a series of periodicals, tickets to performances, etc.

sub·sec·tion (sub·sek′shən, sub′sek′shən) *n.* A subdivision of a section.

sub·se·quent (sub′sə·kwənt) *adj.* Following in time, place, or order, or as a result. —**subsequent to** Following; after. [<L *sub-* next below + *sequi* follow] —**sub·se·quence** (sub′sə·kwəns), **sub′se·quen·cy, sub′se·quent·ness** *n.* —**sub′·se·quent·ly** *adv.*

sub·serve (səb·sûrv′) *v.t.* **·served, ·serv·ing** 1 To be of use or help in furthering (a process, cause, etc.); promote. 2 To serve as a subordinate to (a person). [<L *sub-* under + *servire* serve]

sub·ser·vi·ent (səb·sûr′vē·ənt) *adj.* 1 Servile; obsequious; truckling. 2 Adapted to promote some end or purpose, esp. in a subordinate capacity. —*n.* One who or that which subserves. **—sub·ser′vi·ent·ly** *adv.* **—sub·ser′vi·ent·ness, sub·ser′vi·ence, sub·ser′vi·en·cy** *n.*

sub·set (sub′set) *n. Math.* A set comprising some or all of the elements of another set.

sub·side (səb·sīd′) *v.i.* **·sid·ed, ·sid·ing 1** To sink to a lower level. **2** To become calm or quiet; abate. **3** To sink to the bottom, as sediment; settle. [< L *sub-* under + *sidere* to settle] **—sub·sid·ence** (səb·sīd′ns, sub′sə·dəns) *n.* **—Syn. 1** fall. **2** decrease, diminish, ebb, wane.

sub·sid·i·ar·y (səb·sid′ē·er′ē, -sid′ə·rē) *adj.* **1** Assisting; supplementary; auxiliary. **2** Of, pertaining to, or in the nature of a subsidy. —*n. pl.* **·ar·ies 1** One who or that which furnishes supplemental aid or supplies. **2** A business enterprise with over half of its assets or stock owned by another company. **—sub·sid·i·ar·i·ly** (səb·sid′ē·er′ə·lē) *adv.*

sub·si·dize (sub′sə·dīz) *v.t.* **·dized, ·diz·ing 1** To grant a regular allowance or financial aid to. **2** To obtain the assistance of by a subsidy. *Brit. sp.* **sub′si·dise. —sub′si·di·za′tion, sub′si·diz′er** *n.*

sub·si·dy (sub′sə·dē) *n. pl.* **·dies 1** Financial aid directly granted by government to a person or commercial enterprise whose work is deemed beneficial to the public. **2** Any financial assistance granted by one government to another. [< L *subsidium* auxiliary forces, aid < *subsidere* subside]

sub·sist (səb·sist′) *v.i.* **1** To continue to exist. **2** To remain alive; manage to live: to *subsist* on a meatless diet. **3** To continue unchanged; abide. [< L *sub-* under + *sistere* cause to stand] **—sub·sist′er** *n.*

sub·sis·tence (səb·sis′təns) *n.* **1** The act of subsisting. **2** That on which or by which one subsists; sustenance; livelihood. [< LL *subsistentia* < *subsistere* SUBSIST] **—sub·sis′tent** *adj.*

sub·soil (sub′soil′) *n.* The stratum of earth just beneath the surface soil.

sub·son·ic (sub·son′ik) *adj.* Designating those sound waves beyond the lower limits of human audibility.

subst. substantive; substitute.

sub·stance (sub′stəns) *n.* **1** The material of which anything is made or constituted. **2** The essential meaning of anything said or written. **3** Material possessions; wealth; property. **4** The quality of stability or solidity: an argument lacking *substance.* **5** A distinct but unidentified kind of matter: a gaseous *substance.* **6** Essential components or ideas: The *substance* of the two arguments is the same. —**in substance 1** Essentially; chiefly. **2** Really; actually. [< L *substare* be present]

sub·stan·dard (sub·stan′dərd) *adj.* **1** Below an accepted standard; inferior: *substandard* housing. **2** Lower than the established legal standard. **3** Not conforming to the standard language usage of educated speakers and writers: "He don't want none" is *substandard.*

sub·stan·tial (səb·stan′shəl) *adj.* **1** Solid; strong; firm: a *substantial* bridge. **2** Of real worth and importance: a *substantial* profit. **3** Possessed of wealth or sufficient means. **4** Having real existence; not illusory. **5** Containing or conforming to the essence of a thing: in *substantial* agreement. **6** Ample and nourishing: a *substantial* meal. **—sub·stan′ti·al′i·ty** (-shē·al′ə·tē), **sub·stan′tial·ness** *n.* **—sub·stan′tial·ly** *adv.*

sub·stan·ti·ate (səb·stan′shē·āt) *v.t.* **·at·ed, ·at·ing 1** To establish by evidence; verify. **2** To give form or substance to. [< L *substantia* substance] **—sub·stan′ti·a′tion** *n.* **—sub·stan′ti·a′tive** *adj.*

sub·stan·tive (sub′stən·tiv) *n.* **1** A noun or pronoun. **2** A verbal form, phrase, or clause used in place of a noun. —*adj.* **1** Capable of being used as a noun. **2** Expressive of or denoting existence: The verb "to be" is called the *substantive* verb. **3** Having substance or reality. **4** Being an essential part or constituent. **5** Having distinct individuality. **6** Independent. [< L *substantia* substance] **—sub·stan·ti·val** (sub′stən·tī′vəl) *adj.* **—sub′stan·ti′val·ly, sub′stan·tive·ly** *adv.* **—sub′stan·tive·ness** *n.*

sub·sta·tion (sub′stā′shən) *n.* A subsidiary station, as for electric power or postal service.

sub·sti·tute (sub′stə·t(y)ōōt) *v.* **·tut·ed, ·tut·ing** *v.t.* **1** To put in the place of another person or thing. **2** To take the place of. —*v.i.* **3** To act as a substitute. —*n.* One who or that which takes the place of another. —*adj.* Situated in or taking the place of another: a *substitute* teacher. [< L *sub-* in place of + *statuere* set up]

sub·sti·tu·tion (sub′stə·t(y)ōō′shən) *n.* **1** The act of substituting, or the state of being substituted. **2** A substitute. **—sub′sti·tu′tion·al** *adj.* **—sub′sti·tu′tion·al·ly** *adv.*

sub·stra·tum (sub·strā′təm, -strat′əm) *n. pl.* **·stra·ta** (-strā′tə, -strat′ə) or **·stra·tums 1** An underlying stratum or layer, as of earth or rock. **2** A foundation or basis. [< L, p.p. neut. of *substernere* spread underneath] **—sub·stra′tal, sub·stra′tive** *adj.*

sub·struc·ture (sub′struk′chər, sub·struk′-) *n.* A structure serving as a foundation. **—sub·struc′tur·al** *adj.*

sub·ten·ant (sub·ten′ənt) *n.* A person who rents or leases from a tenant. **—sub·ten′an·cy** *n.*

sub·tend (sub·tend′) *v.t.* **1** *Geom.* To extend under or opposite to, as the chord of an arc or the side of a triangle opposite to an angle. **2** *Bot.* To enclose in its axil: A leaf *subtends* a bud. [< L *sub-* underneath + *tendere* stretch]

sub·ter·fuge (sub′tər·fyōōj′) *n.* Any plan or trick to escape something unpleasant. [< L *subter-* below, in secret + *fugere* flee, take flight]

sub·ter·ra·ne·an (sub′tə·rā′nē·ən) *adj.* **1** Situated or occurring below the surface of the earth. **2** Hidden. Also **sub′ter·ra′ne·ous.** [< L *sub-* under + *terra* earth] **—sub′ter·ra′ne·an·ly, sub′ter·ra′ne·ous·ly** *adv.*

sub·tile (sut′l, sub′til) *adj.* **1** Elusive; subtle. **2** Crafty; cunning. [< L *subtilis*] **—sub′tile·ly** *adv.* **—sub′tile·ness, sub·til·i·ty** (sub·til′ə·tē) *n.*

sub·ti·tle (sub′tī′tl) *n.* **1** A subordinate or explanatory title, as in a book, play, or document. **2** *pl.* In motion pictures, printed translations of foreign-language dialogue, usu. appearing at the bottom of the screen.

sub·tle (sut′l) *adj.* **sub·tler** (sut′lər, sut′l·ər), **sub·tlest 1** Not easily detected; elusive; delicate: a *subtle* aroma. **2** Characterized by or requiring keenness of mind, vision, hearing, etc.: *subtle* humor; *subtle* variations in sound. **3** Very skillful or ingenious: a *subtle* craftsman. **4** Not direct or obvious: a *subtle* hint. [< L *subtilis* fine] **—sub′tle·ness** *n.* **—sub′tly** *adv.*

sub·tle·ty (sut′l·tē) *n. pl.* **·ties 1** The state or quality of being subtle. **2** Something that is subtle.

sub·tract (səb·trakt′) *v.t. & v.i.* To take away or deduct, as a portion from the whole, or one quantity from another. [< L *sub-* away + *trahere* draw] **—sub·tract′er, sub·trac′tion** *n.* **—sub·trac′tive** *adj.*

sub·tra·hend (sub′trə·hend) *n. Math.* That which is to be subtracted from a number or quantity to give the difference.

sub·treas·ur·y (sub·trezh′ər·ē) *n. pl.* **·ur·ies 1** A branch office of the U.S. Treasury Department. **2** Any branch treasury. **—sub·treas′ur·er** *n.*

sub·trop·i·cal (sub·trop′i·kəl) *adj.* Of, pertaining to, or designating regions adjacent to the tropical zone. Also **sub·trop′ic. —sub·trop′ics** *n.pl.*

sub·urb (sub′ûrb) *n.* **1** A district or town adjacent to a city. **2** Outlying districts; environs. **—the suburbs** Residential areas near or within commuting distance of a city. [< L *sub-* near to + *urbs* a city]

sub·ur·ban (sə·bûr′bən) *adj.* Of or pertaining to a suburb or its residents.

sub·ur·ban·ite (sə·bûr′bən·īt) *n.* A resident of a suburb.

sub·ur·ban·ize (sə·bûr′bə·nīz′) *v.t.* **·ized, ·iz·ing** To make suburban or give a suburban character to. **—sub·ur′ban·i·za′tion** *n.*

sub·ur·bi·a (sə·bûr′bē·ə) *n.* **1** The social and cultural world of suburbanites. **2** Suburbs or suburbanites collectively.

sub·ven·tion (səb·ven′shən) *n.* A grant of money made, esp. by a government, to an institution, cause, or study; subsidy. [< L *subvenire*] **—sub·ven′tion·ar′y** (-er′ē) *adj.*

sub·ver·sion (səb·vûr′shən, -zhən) *n.* **1** The act of subverting; demolition; overthrow. **2** A cause of ruin. **—sub·ver′sion·ar′y** (-er′ē) *adj.*

sub·ver·sive (səb·vûr′siv) *adj.* Tending to subvert or overthrow. —*n.* A person regarded as desiring to weaken or overthrow a government, organization, etc. **—sub·ver′sive·ly** *adv.* **—sub·ver′sive·ness** *n.*

sub·vert (səb·vûrt′) *v.t.* **1** To overthrow from the very foundation; destroy utterly. **2** To corrupt; undermine the principles or character of. [< L *subvertere* overturn] —**sub·vert′er** *n.*

sub·way (sub′wā) *n.* 1 A passage below the surface of the ground. 2 An underground railroad beneath city streets for local transportation; also, the tunnel through which it runs. 3 UNDERPASS.

suc·ceed (sək·sēd′) *v.i.* 1 To accomplish what is attempted or intended. 2 To come next in order or sequence. 3 To come after another into office, ownership, etc. —*v.t.* 4 To be the successor or heir of. 5 To come after in time or sequence; follow. [< L *succedere* go under, follow after] —**suc·ceed′er** *n.*

suc·cess (sək·ses′) *n.* 1 A favorable course or termination of anything attempted. 2 The gaining of position, fame, wealth, etc. 3 A person or thing that is successful. 4 The degree of succeeding: Did you have any *success* in getting an appointment? [< L *succedere* succeed] —**Syn.** 1 achievement, satisfaction. 2 prosperity, eminence, station.

suc·cess·ful (sək·ses′fəl) *adj.* 1 Having achieved success. 2 Ending in success: a *successful* venture. —**suc·cess′ful·ly** *adv.* —**suc·cess′ful·ness** *n.*

suc·ces·sion (sək·sesh′ən) *n.* 1 The act of following consecutively. 2 A group of things that succeed in order; a series or sequence. 3 The act or right of legally or officially coming into a predecessor's office, possessions, position, etc. 4 A group or hierarchy of persons having the right to succeed. —**in succession** One after another. —**suc·ces′·sion·al** *adj.* —**suc·ces′sion·al·ly** *adv.*

suc·ces·sive (sək·ses′iv) *adj.* Following in succession; consecutive. —**suc·ces′sive·ly** *adv.* —**suc·ces′sive·ness** *n.*

suc·ces·sor (sək·ses′ər) *n.* One who or that which follows in succession; esp. a person who succeeds to an office, position, or property.

suc·cinct (sək·singkt′) *adj.* Reduced to a minimum number of words; concise; terse. [< L *sub-* underneath + *cingere* gird] —**suc·cinct′ly** *adv.* —**suc·cinct′ness** *n.*

suc·cor (suk′ər) *n.* 1 Help rendered in danger, difficulty, or distress. 2 One who or that which affords relief. —*v.t.* To go to the aid of; help. *Brit. sp.* **suc′cour.** [< L *sub-* up from under + *currere* to run] —**suc′cor·er** *n.* —**Syn.** *n.* 1 aid, rescue, relief, support.

suc·co·tash (suk′ə·tash) *n.* A dish of corn kernels and beans, usu. lima beans, cooked together. [< Algon.]

suc·cu·bus (suk′yə·bəs) *n. pl.* **·bi** (-bī, -bē) One of a class of demons in female form fabled to have intercourse with sleeping men. [< LL *succuba* a strumpet]

suc·cu·lent (suk′yə·lənt) *adj.* 1 Juicy; full of juice. 2 *Bot.* Composed of fleshy, juicy tissue: a *succulent* leaf. 3 Absorbing; interesting. —*n.* A succulent plant. [< L *succus* juice] —**suc′cu·lence, suc′cu·len·cy** *n.* —**suc′cu·lent·ly** *adv.*

suc·cumb (sə·kum′) *v.i.* 1 To give way; yield, as to force or persuasion. 2 To die. [< L *sub-* underneath + *cumbere* lie]

such (such) *adj.* 1 Being the same or similar in kind or quality; of a kind mentioned or indicated: a book *such* as this; screws, bolts, and other *such* items. 2 Indicated but not specified: some *such* place. 3 Extreme in degree, quality, etc.: *such* an uproar. —**such as** As an example or examples of the kind indicated: flowers *such as* dandelions. —*pron.* 1 Such a person or thing or such persons or things. 2 The same as implied or indicated: *Such* was the result. —**as such** As the particular thing or kind it is, regardless of others: People *as such* deserve compassion. —*adv.* 1 So: *such* destructive criticism. 2 Especially; very: She's in *such* good spirits today. [< OE *swelc, swylc*]

such and such Understood to be specific but not specified: to consult *such and such* an expert.

such·like (such′līk′) *adj.* Of a like or similar kind. —*pron.* Persons or things of that kind.

suck (suk) *v.t.* 1 To draw into the mouth by means of a partial vacuum created by action of the lips and tongue. 2 To draw in or take up by suction. 3 To draw liquid or nourishment from with the mouth: to *suck* an orange or a lollipop. 4 To take and hold in the mouth as if to do this: to *suck* one's thumb. 5 To pull or draw into an association: with *in* or *into:* The lure of quick profits *sucked* him in. —*v.i.* 6 To draw in liquid, air, etc., by suction. 7 To draw in milk from a breast or udder by sucking. 8 To make a sucking sound. —*n.* 1 The act or sound of sucking. 2 That which is sucked. [< OE *sūcan*]

suck·er (suk′ər) *n.* 1 One who or that which sucks. 2 Any of various freshwater fishes having thick, fleshy lips. 3 A mouth adapted for clinging and sucking, as that of a leech, tapeworm, etc. 4 *Slang* A person easily deceived. 5 *Bot.* An adventitious shoot. 6 A tube or pipe used for suction. 7 A lollipop. —*v.t.* 1 To strip (a plant) of suckers. —*v.i.* 2 To form or send out suckers or shoots.

Sucker *def. 2*

suck·le (suk′əl) *v.* **·led, ·ling** *v.t.* 1 To nourish at the breast; nurse. 2 To bring up; nourish. —*v.i.* 3 To suck at the breast. —**suck′ler** *n.*

suck·ling (suk′ling) *n.* An unweaned mammal.

su·cre (so͞o′krā) *n.* The monetary unit of Ecuador.

su·crose (so͞o′krōs) *n.* The sweet, soluble, crystalline carbohydrate familiar as the common white sugar of commerce, and consisting of fructose and glucose in chemical combination. [< F *sucre* sugar]

suc·tion (suk′shən) *n.* 1 The act or process of sucking. 2 The production of a partial vacuum in a space connected with a fluid or gas under reduced pressure. —*adj.* Creating or operating by suction.

suc·to·ri·al (suk·tôr′ē·əl, -tōr′-) *adj.* 1 Adapted for sucking or suction. 2 *Zool.* Living by sucking; having organs for sucking.

Su·dan (so͞o·dan′) *n.* A republic of NE Africa, 967,500 sq. mi., cap. Khartoum. —**Su·da·nese** (so͞o′də·nēz′) *adj., n.* • See map at AFRICA.

sud·den (sud′n) *adj.* 1 Happening quickly and without warning. 2 Causing surprise; unexpected: a *sudden* development. 3 Hurried; hasty; rash. —**all of a sudden** Without warning; suddenly. [< L *subitus,* p.p. of *subire* come or go stealthily] —**sud′den·ly** *adv.* —**sud′den·ness** *n.*

suds (sudz) *n.pl.* 1 Soapy water. 2 Froth; foam. 3 *Slang* Beer. [< MDu. *sudde, sudse* a marsh] —**suds′y** *adj.*

sue (so͞o) *v.* **sued, su·ing** *v.t.* 1 To institute legal proceedings against, as for the redress of some wrong. 2 To prosecute (a legal action). —*v.i.* 3 To institute legal proceedings. 4 To seek to persuade someone by entreaty: with *for:* to *sue* for peace. [< AF *suer* pursue, sue] —**su′er** *n.*

suede (swād) *n.* Leather or a fabric having a napped surface. Also **suède.** [< F *gants de Suède* Swedish gloves]

su·et (so͞o′it) *n.* The white, solid fatty tissue of beef, lamb, etc. [< L *sebum* fat] —**su′et·y** *adj.*

suf., suff. suffix.

suf·fer (suf′ər) *v.i.* 1 To feel pain or distress. 2 To sustain loss, injury, or detriment. 3 To undergo punishment, esp. death. —*v.t.* 4 To have inflicted on one; sustain, as an injury or loss: to *suffer* a fracture of the arm; to *suffer* a business reversal. 5 To undergo; pass through, as change. 6 To bear; endure: He never could *suffer* incompetence. 7 To allow; permit. [< L *sub-* up from under + *ferre* bear] —**suf′fer·a·ble** *adj.* —**suf′fer·a·bly** *adv.* —**suf′fer·er** *n.*

suf·fer·ance (suf′ər·əns, suf′rəns) *n.* 1 Permission given or implied by failure to prohibit. 2 The capacity for suffering or tolerating pain or distress. —**on sufferance** Tolerated or suffered but not encouraged.

suf·fer·ing (suf′ər·ing, suf′ring) *n.* 1 The state of anguish or pain of one who suffers. 2 The pain suffered; loss; injury.

suf·fice (sə·fīs′, -fīz′) *v.* **·ficed, ·fic·ing** *v.i.* To be sufficient or adequate. [< L *sub-* under + *facere* make]

suf·fi·cien·cy (sə·fish′ən·sē) *n. pl.* **·cies** 1 The state of being sufficient. 2 That which is sufficient; esp., adequate means or income.

suf·fi·cient (sə·fish′ənt) *adj.* Being all that is needed; adequate; enough. [< L *sufficere* substitute, suffice] —**suf·fi′cient·ly** *adv.* —**Syn.** ample, satisfactory, fitting.

suf·fix (suf′iks) *n.* A letter or letters added to the end of a word or root, forming a new word or functioning as an inflectional element, as *-ful* in faithful and *-ed* in loved.

—*v.t.* To add as a suffix. [< L *suffixus,* p.p. of *suffigere* fasten underneath] —**suf′fix·al** *adj.*

suf·fo·cate (suf′ə·kāt′) *v.* **·cat·ed, ·cat·ing** *v.t.* **1** To kill by obstructing respiration in any manner. **2** To cause distress in by depriving of an adequate supply or quality of air. **3** To stifle or smother, as a fire. —*v.i.* **4** To die from suffocation. **5** To be distressed by an inadequate supply or quality of air. [< L *sub-* under + *fauces* throat] —**suf′fo·cat′ing·ly** *adv.* —**suf′fo·ca′tion** *n.* —**suf′fo·ca′tive** *adj.*

suf·fra·gan (suf′rə·gən, -jən) *n.* **1** An auxiliary or assistant bishop. **2** Any bishop subordinate to an archbishop. —*adj.* Assisting; auxiliary. [< L *suffragium* vote] —**suf′fra·gan·ship′** *n.*

suf·frage (suf′rij) *n.* **1** A vote in support of someone or something. **2** The right or privilege of voting; franchise. **3** Any short intercessory prayer. [< L *suffragium* a vote]

suf·fra·gette (suf′rə·jet′) *n.* A woman who advocates female suffrage. —**suf′fra·get′tism** *n.*

suf·fra·gist (suf′rə·jist) *n.* An advocate of suffrage, esp. for women.

suf·fuse (sə·fyo͞oz′) *v.t.* **·fused, ·fus·ing** To spread over, as with a fluid, light, or color. [< L *suffusus,* p.p. of *suffundere* pour underneath] —**suf·fu′sion** *n.* —**suf·fu′sive** *adj.*

sug·ar (sho͝og′ər) *n.* **1** A sweet, crystalline foodstuff obtained chiefly from sugar cane and sugar beets; sucrose. **2** Any of a large class of mostly sweet and water-soluble carbohydrates widely distributed in plants and animals, as lactose, glucose, fructose, etc. —*v.t.* **1** To sweeten, cover, or coat with sugar. **2** To make less distasteful, as by flattery. —*v.i.* **3** To make maple sugar by boiling down maple syrup: usu. with *off.* **4** To form or produce sugar; granulate. [< Ar. *sukkar*] —**sug′ar·less** *adj.*

sugar beet A variety of beet cultivated as a commercial source of sugar.

sugar cane A tall tropical grass with a solid jointed stalk rich in sugar.

sug·ar-coat (sho͝og′ər·kōt′) *v.t.* **1** To cover with sugar. **2** To cause to appear attractive or less distasteful. —**sug′ar-coat′ing** *n.*

sug·ar-cured (sho͝og′ər·kyo͝ord′) *adj.* Treated with a sweetened brine, as ham or pork.

sug·ar·plum (sho͝og′ər·plum′) *n.* A small ball or disk of candy.

sug·ar·y (sho͝og′ər·ē) *adj.* **1** Of, like, or composed of sugar; sweet. **2** Honeyed or complaisant; esp., excessively sweet or sentimental. —**sug′ar·i·ness** *n.*

sug·gest (səg·jest′, sə·jest′) *v.t.* **1** To bring or put forward for consideration, action, or approval; propose. **2** To arouse in the mind by association or connection: Gold *suggests* wealth. **3** To give a hint of; intimate: Her gesture *suggested* indifference. [< L *suggerere* carry underneath, suggest] —**sug·gest′er** *n.*

sug·gest·i·ble (səg·jes′tə·bəl, sə-) *adj.* **1** That can be suggested. **2** Responding readily to suggestions; easily led. —**sug·gest′i·bil′i·ty** *n.*

sug·ges·tion (səg·jes′chən, sə·jes′-) *n.* **1** The act of suggesting. **2** Something suggested. **3** A hint; trace; touch: a *suggestion* of irony. **4** An association of thoughts or ideas, esp. if based upon incidental or fortuitous similarities rather than a logical or rational relationship.

sug·ges·tive (səg·jes′tiv, sə-) *adj.* **1** Tending to suggest; stimulating thought or reflection. **2** Suggesting or hinting at something improper or indecent. —**sug·ges′tive·ly** *adv.* —**sug·ges′tive·ness** *n.*

su·i·cide (s^yo͞o′ə·sīd) *n.* **1** The intentional taking of one's own life. **2** One who takes or tries to take one's own life. **3** Personal or professional ruin brought on by one's own actions. [< L *sui* of oneself + *caedere* kill] —**su·i·ci·dal** (s^yo͞o′ə·sīd′l) *adj.* —**su′i·ci′dal·ly** *adv.*

su·i gen·e·ris (so͞o′ī jen′ər·is, so͞o′ē, gen′-) Of his (her, its) particular kind; unique. [L]

suit (s^yo͞ot) *n.* **1** A set of garments worn together; esp., a coat and trousers or skirt, made of the same fabric. **2** An outfit or garment for a particular purpose: a bathing *suit.* **3** A group of like things; a set. **4** Any of the four sets of thirteen cards each that make up a deck of cards. **5** A proceeding in a court of law for the recovery of a right or the redress of a wrong. **6** The courting of a woman. —**follow suit 1** To play a card identical in suit to the card led. **2** To follow an example set by another. —*v.t.* **1** To meet the requirements of or be appropriate to; befit. **2** To please; satisfy. **3** To render appropriate; adapt. **4** To furnish with clothes. —*v.i.* **5** To agree; accord. **6** To be or prove satisfactory. **7** To put on a protective suit or uniform: with *up:* ballplayers *suiting up* before a game. [< OF *sieute* < L *sequi* follow]

suit·a·ble (s^yo͞o′tə·bəl) *adj.* Appropriate; proper; fitting. —**suit′a·bil′i·ty, suit′a·ble·ness** *n.* —**suit′a·bly** *adv.*

suit·case (s^yo͞ot′kās′) *n.* A case for carrying clothing, etc., esp. one that is flat and rectangular.

suite (swēt; *for def. 2, also* so͞ot) *n.* **1** A set of things intended to go or be used together, as a number of connected rooms forming an apartment or leased as a unit in a hotel. **2** A set of matched furniture. **3** A company of attendants; a retinue. **4** *Music* An instrumental composition consisting of a series of short pieces. [< OF *sieute.* See SUIT.]

suit·ing (s^yo͞o′ting) *n.* Cloth used in making suits of clothes.

suit·or (s^yo͞o′tər) *n.* **1** One who institutes a suit in court. **2** A man who courts a woman. **3** A petitioner.

su·ki·ya·ki (so͞o′kē·yä′kē, skē·yä′kē) *n.* A Japanese dish of thinly sliced meat and vegetables fried together and served with condiments. [Jap.]

Suk·koth (so͞ok′ōth, so͞ok′ōs) *n.* A Jewish holiday, originally a harvest festival, occurring in late September or in October. Also **Suk′kos, Suk′kot.** [< Hebrew *sūkōth* tabernacles, booths]

sulfa- *combining form Chem.* Sulfur; related to or containing sulfur. Also **sulf-, sulfo-.** [< SULFUR]

sul·fa drug (sul′fə) Any of various sulfonamide derivatives effective in the treatment of certain bacterial infections.

sul·fate (sul′fāt) *n.* A salt of sulfuric acid. —*v.* **·fat·ed, ·fat·ing** *v.t.* **1** To convert into a sulfate. **2** To treat with a sulfate or sulfuric acid. **3** *Electr.* To form a coating of lead sulfate on (the plate of a storage battery). —*v.i.* **4** To become sulfated. Also **sul′phate.** [< L *sulfur* sulfur] —**sul·fa′tion** *n.*

sul·fide (sul′fīd) *n.* A compound of sulfur with an element or radical. Also **sul′phide.**

sul·fite (sul′fīt) *n.* A salt or ester of sulfurous acid. Also **sul′phite.** —**sul·fit′ic** (-fit′ik) *adj.*

sul·fon·a·mide (sul·fon′ə·mīd, -mid) *n.* Any of a group of organic sulfur compounds containing a univalent amide radical.

sul·fur (sul′fər) *n.* **1** An industrially important, abundant nonmetallic element (symbol S), occurring in three allotropic forms and found in both free and combined states. **2** Any of various small yellow butterflies. Also, and for def. 2 always, **sul′phur.** —**sul′fur·y** *adj.*

sul·fu·rate (sul′f^yə·rāt) *v.t.* **·rat·ed, ·rat·ing** SULFURIZE. —**sul′fu·ra′tion** *n.*

sulfur dioxide A colorless gas with a sharp odor, very soluble in water, used in manufacturing sulfuric acid, in bleaching, etc.

sul·fu·re·ous (sul·fyo͝or′ē·əs) *adj.* **1** Of or like sulfur. **2** Greenish yellow.

sul·fu·ret (sul′f^yə·ret) *v.t.* **·ret·ed** or **·ret·ted, ·ret·ing** or **·ret·ting** SULFURIZE. —*n.* SULFIDE.

sul·fu·ric (sul·fyo͝or′ik) *adj.* Pertaining to or derived from sulfur, esp. in its higher valence.

sulfuric acid A colorless, exceedingly corrosive, syrupy liquid with a strong affinity for water, used extensively in the chemical industry.

sul·fur·ize (sul′f^yə·rīz) *v.t.* **·ized, ·iz·ing** To impregnate, treat with, or subject to the action of sulfur. —**sul′fur·i·za′tion** *n.*

sul·fur·ous (sul′fər·əs, *for def. 1 esp.* sul·fyo͝or′əs) *adj.* **1** Pertaining to or derived from sulfur, esp. in its lower valence. **2** Resembling burning sulfur; fiery. **3** Biting; vitriolic: *sulfurous* criticism. **4** Blasphemous, as language. —**sul′fur·ous·ly** *adv.* —**sul′fur·ous·ness** *n.*

sulfurous acid (sul·fyo͝or′əs) An unstable acid formed by dissolving sulfur dioxide in water.

sulk (sulk) *v.i.* To be sullen in mood and tend to shun others. —*n.* A sulky mood or humor. [Back formation < SULKY]

sulk·y[1] (sul′kē) *adj.* **sulk·i·er, sulk·i·est** Sulking or tending to sulk. [? < OE *(ā)seolcan* be weak or slothful]—**sulk′i·ly** *adv.* —**sulk′i·ness** *n.*

sulk·y[2] (sul′kē) *n. pl.* **sulk·ies** A light, two-wheeled, one-horse vehicle for one person. [< SULKY[1]; so called because one rides alone]

Sulky

sul·len (sul′ən) *adj.* **1** Showing ill-humor, as from dwelling upon a grievance; morose; glum. **2** Depressing; somber: *sullen* clouds. **3** Slow; sluggish. **4** Melancholy; mournful. [< AF *solein* sullen, alone] —**sul′len·ly** *adv.* —**sul′len·ness** *n.* —**Syn. 1** gloomy, sad, sulky, moody.

sul·ly (sul′ē) *v.* **·lied, ·ly·ing** *v.t.* To mar the brightness or purity of; soil; defile. [< MF *souiller* to soil]

sulph- For all words so spelled, see SULF-.

sul·tan (sul′tən) *n.* A Muslim ruler. [< Ar. *sulṭān* a sovereign, dominion]

sul·tan·a (sul·tan′ə, -tä′nə) *n.* **1** A sultan's wife, daughter, sister, or mother. **2** A white, seedless variety of grape or raisin.

sul·tan·ate (sul′tən·āt, -it) *n.* **1** The authority of a sultan. **2** The domain of a sultan. Also **sul′tan·ship.**

sul·try (sul′trē) *adj.* **·tri·er, ·tri·est 1** Hot, moist, and still; close: said of weather. **2** Oppressively hot; burning. **3** Inflamed with passion. **4** Expressing or tending to excite sexual interest; sensual. [< obs. *sulter,* var. of SWELTER] —**sul′tri·ly** *adv.* —**sul′tri·ness** *n.*

sum (sum) *n.* **1** An amount of money. **2** The result obtained by the addition of numbers or quantities. **3** A problem in arithmetic. **4** The entire quantity, number, or substance; the whole: The *sum* of his effort came to naught. **5** Essence or core; summary: In *sum,* the issue is one of trust; the *sum* of an argument. **6** The highest or furthest point; summit. —*v.* **summed, sum·ming** *v.t.* **1** To present as a summary; recapitulate; summarize: usu. with *up.* **2** To add into one total: often with *up.* —*v.i.* **3** To give a summary; recapitulate: usu. with *up.* **4** To calculate a sum: often with *up.* [< L *summa (res)* highest (thing)]

su·mac (so͞o′mak, sho͞o′-) *n.* **1** Any of a genus of woody plants related to the cashew. **2** A species of sumac with hairy red fruit and compound leaves turning brilliant red in autumn: also **smooth sumac. 3** The dried and powdered leaves of certain species of sumac, used for tanning and dyeing. Also **su′mach.** [< Ar. *summāq*]

sum·ma cum lau·de (soom′ə koom lou′də, -dē, so͞o′mə, sum′ə kum lô′dē) *Latin* With the greatest praise: to be graduated *summa cum laude.*

sum·ma·rize (sum′ə·rīz) *v.t.* **·rized, ·riz·ing** To make a summary of. *Brit. sp.* **·rise.** —**sum′ma·ri·za′tion** *n.*

sum·ma ·ry (sum′ər·ē) *n. pl.* **·ries** A brief account of the substance or essential points of something spoken or written; recapitulation. —*adj.* **1** Giving the substance or essential points; concise. **2** Performed without ceremony or delay; instant: *summary* execution. [< L *summa.* See SUM.] —**Syn.** *n.* condensation, abridgment, epitome, précis, compendium. —**sum·ma·ri·ly** (sə·mer′ə·lē, sum′ər·ə·lē) *adv.*

sum·ma·tion (sum·ā′shən) *n.* **1** The act or operation of obtaining a sum; addition. **2** A sum or total. **3** A summing up of the main points of an argument, as the final speech in behalf of one of the parties in a court trial.

sum·mer (sum′ər) *n.* **1** The warmest season of the year, including, in the northern hemisphere, June, July, and August. **2** A year of life. **3** A bright or prosperous period. —*v.i.* **1** To pass the summer. —v.t. **2** To keep or care for through the summer. —*adj.* **1** Of, pertaining to, or occurring in summer. **2** Used or intended for use in the summer: a *summer* house. [OE *sumor, sumer*] —**sum′mer·y** *adj.*

sum·mer·sault (sum′ər·sôlt) *n. v.i.* SOMERSAULT.

summer squash Any of various small squashes with a soft rind, usu. eaten before they ripen.

sum·mer·time (sum′ər·tīm′) *n.* Summer; the summer season.

sum·mit (sum′it) *n.* **1** The highest part; the top; vertex. **2** The highest degree; maximum. **3** The highest level or office, as of a government or business organization. **4** A meeting of executives of the highest level, as heads of government. —*adj.* Of or involving those at the highest level: a *summit* conference. [< L *summus* highest]

sum·mit·ry (sum′it·rē) *n.* **1** Meetings of officials of the highest rank, as heads of government. **2** The use or dependency upon such meetings to solve international problems.

sum·mon (sum′ən) *v.t.* **1** To order to come; send for. **2** To call together; cause to convene, as a legislative assembly. **3** To order (a person) to appear in court by a summons. **4** To call forth or into action; arouse: usu. with *up:* to *summon* up courage. **5** To call on for a specific act. [< L *summonere* suggest, hint]—**sum′mon·er** *n.*

sum·mons (sum′ənz) *n. pl.* **sum·mons·es 1** An order or call to attend or act at a particular place or time. **2** *Law* **a** A notice to a defendant summoning him to appear in court. **b** A notice to appear in court as a witness or as a juror. [< OF *somondre* summon]

su·mo (so͞o′mō) *n.* A highly stylized form of wrestling popular in Japan. [< Japanese *sumō*]

sump (sump) *n.* A pit or reservoir in which liquids are received by drainage, as a cesspool. [< MDu. *somp, sump* a marsh]

sump·ter (sump′tər) *n.* A pack animal. [< OF *sometier* a driver of a pack horse]

sump·tu·ar·y (sump′cho͞o·er′ē) *adj.* Limiting or regulating expenditure. [< L *sumptus* expenditure < *sumere* take]

sump·tu·ous (sump′cho͞o·əs) *adj.* **1** Involving or showing lavish expenditure. **2** Luxurious; magnificent. [< L *sumptus* expense] —**sump′tu·ous·ly** *adv.* —**sump′tu·ous·ness** *n.*

sun (sun) *n.* **1** The star that is the gravitational center and the main source of energy for the solar system, about 93,000,000 miles distant from the earth, with a diameter of 864,000 miles and a mass 332,000 times that of the earth. **2** Any star, esp. one with a planetary system. **3** The light and heat from the sun; sunshine. **4** Anything brilliant and magnificent; a source of splendor. **5** A day or a year. —*v.* **sunned, sun·ning** *v.t.* **1** To expose to the light or heat of the sun. —*v.i.* **2** To bask in the sun; sun oneself. [< OE *sunne*]

Sun. Sunday.

sun-bathe (sun′bāth′) *v.i.* **-bathed, -bath·ing** To bask in the sun. —**sun′-bath′er** *n.*

sun·beam (sun′bēm′) *n.* A ray or beam of the sun.

Sun·belt (sun′belt′) *n.* The southeastern and southwestern states of the U.S., ranging from Virginia south to Florida and west to California.

sun·bon·net (sun′bon′it) *n.* A wide-brimmed bonnet sometimes having a flap covering the neck.

sun·burn (sun′bûrn′) *n.* Injury to the skin by ultraviolet radiation from the sun. —*v.t. & v.i.* **·burned** or **·burnt** (bûrnt), **·burn·ing** To affect or be affected with sunburn.

sun·dae (sun′dē) *n.* Ice cream topped with crushed fruit, flavoring, syrup, nuts, etc. [? < *Sunday*]

Sun·day (sun′dē, -dā) *n.* The first day of the week; the Christian Sabbath. [< OE *sunnan dæg* day of the sun]

Sunday school A school meeting on Sundays for religious instruction, esp. of the young.

sun·der (sun′dər) *v.t. & v.i.* To break apart; sever. [< OE *syndrian, sundrian*]

sun·di·al (sun′dī′əl, -dīl) *n.* A device that shows the time of day by the shadow of a style or gnomon cast on a dial in sunlight.

Sundial

sun·down (sun′doun′) *n.* SUNSET (def. 2).

sun·dries (sun′drēz) *n. pl.* Various or miscellaneous articles. [< SUNDRY]

sun·dry (sun′drē) *adj.* Various; several; miscellaneous. [< OE *syndrig* separate]

sun·fish (sun′fish′) *n. pl.* **·fish** or

·fish·es 1 Any of several North American freshwater perchlike fishes, usu. with narrow bodies. 2 Any of various large fishes of warm seas, having a deep compressed body.

sun·flow·er (sun′flou′ər) *n.* Any of a genus of tall plants with large leaves and large composite flower heads encircled with a ring of bright yellow ray flowers.

Sunflower

sung (sung) *p.p.* of SING.

sun·glasses (sun′glas′iz, -gläs′-) *n. pl.* Eyeglasses having colored lenses that protect the eyes from the glare of the sun.

sunk (sungk) *p.p. & a p.t.* of SINK.

sunk·en (sung′kən) A *p.p.* of SINK. —*adj.* 1 Lying at the bottom of a body of water. 2 Located beneath a surface. 3 Lower than the surrounding or usual level: *sunken* gardens. 4 Deeply depressed or fallen in: *sunken* cheeks.

sun·lamp (sun′lamp′) *n.* An electric lamp radiating ultraviolet rays, used esp. for the therapeutic treatments.

sun·less (sun′lis) *adj.* Dark; cheerless. —**sun′less·ness** *n.*

sun·light (sun′līt′) *n.* The light of the sun.

sun·lit (sun′lit′) *adj.* Lighted by the sun.

sun·ny (sun′ē) *adj.* **·ni·er, ·ni·est** 1 Characterized by bright sunlight. 2 Filled with sunlight: a *sunny* room. 3 Cheerful; genial: a *sunny* smile. —**sun′ni·ly** *adv.* —**sun′ni·ness** *n.*

sun parlor A room enclosed in glass and having a sunny exposure. Also **sun porch, sun room.**

sun·rise (sun′rīz′) *n.* 1 The daily first appearance of the sun above the horizon. 2 The time at which the sun rises.

sun·set (sun′set′) *n.* 1 The apparent daily descent of the sun below the horizon. 2 The time at which the sun sets. 3 A final period or decline, as of life.

sun·shade (sun′shād′) *n.* Something used as protection from the sun, as a parasol or an awning.

sun·shine (sun′shīn′) *n.* 1 The direct light of the sun. 2 The light and warmth of sunlight. 3 Brightness or warmth, as of feeling. —**sun′shin′y** *adj.*

sun·spot (sun′spot′) *n.* One of many dark irregular spots appearing sometimes on the surface of the sun.

sun·stroke (sun′strōk′) *n.* Prostration and fever induced by heat and exposure to the sun. —**sun′struck′** (-struk′) *adj.*

sun·tan (sun′tan′) *n.* A darkened coloration of the skin induced by exposure to ultraviolet light. —**sun′tanned′** (-tand′) *adj.*

sun·up (sun′up′) *n.* SUNRISE.

sun·ward (sun′wərd) *adj.* Facing toward the sun. —*adv.* Toward the sun: also **sun′wards.**

sup¹ (sup) *v.t. & v.i.* **supped, sup·ping** To take (fluid food) a little at a time; sip. —*n.* A mouthful or sip of liquid or semiliquid food. [<OE *sūpan* drink]

sup² (sup) *v.* **supped, sup·ping** *v.i.* To eat supper. [<OF *soper*<*soupe* soup]

sup. above (L *supra*); superior, superlative; supplement; supplementary; supply.

su·per (so͞o′pər) *adj.* 1 Surpassing others of its class, as in power or size: a *super* bomb; a *super* city. 2 *Informal* Outstanding; superb: a *super* performance. 3 *Slang* Great; wonderful: He's *super!* 4 More than normal or warranted. —*n.* 1 A superintendent (def. 2). 2 SUPERNUMERARY (esp. def. 2). 3 An article of superior size or quality.

super- *prefix* 1 Above in position; over: *superstructure.* 2 More than; above or beyond: *supersonic.* 3 More than normal or warranted; inordinate or inordinately: *superintelligent; superpatriot.* 4 Surpassing others in its class, as in power, size, or skill; superior: *superhighway.* 5 Extra: *supertax.* [<L *super* above, beyond] • See TAXONOMY.

su·per·a·ble (so͞o′pər·ə·bəl) *adj.* That can be surmounted, overcome, or conquered. [<L *superare* overcome<*super* over] —**su′per·a·bil′i·ty** *n.* —**su′per·a·bly** *adv.*

su·per·a·bound (so͞o′pər·ə·bound′) *v.i.* To abound to excess. [<L *super-* exceedingly + *abundare* overflow]

su·per·a·bun·dant (so͞o′pər·ə·bun′dənt) *adj.* More than sufficient; excessive. [<LL *superabundare* to superabound] —**su′per·a·bun′dance** *n.* —**su′per·a·bun′dant·ly** *adv.*

su·per·an·nu·at·ed (so͞o′pər·an′yo͞o·wāt′id) *adj.* 1 Relieved of active work on account of age; retired. 2 Set aside or discarded as obsolete or too old. [<L *super* beyond + *annus* a year]

su·perb (so͞o·pûrb′, so͞o-) *adj.* 1 Extraordinarily good; excellent: a *superb* wine. 2 Having grand, impressive beauty; majestic: a *superb* cathedral. 3 Luxurious; elegant. [<L *superbus* proud] —**su·perb′ly** *adv.* —**su·perb′ness** *n.*

su·per·block (so͞o′pər·blok′) *n.* A large block of commercial buildings or residences from which motor traffic is barred, often landscaped as a unit and joined by pedestrian walks.

su·per·car·go (so͞o′pər·kär′gō) *n. pl.* **·goes** or **·gos** An officer on board ship in charge of the cargo and its sale and purchase.

su·per·charge (so͞o′pər·chärj′) *v.t.* **·charged, ·charg·ing** 1 To adapt (an engine) to develop more power, as by fitting with a supercharger. 2 To charge excessively, as with emotion.

su·per·charg·er (so͞o′pər·chär′jər) *n.* A compressor for supplying extra air or fuel mixture to an internal-combustion engine.

su·per·cil·i·ous (so͞o′pər·sil′ē·əs) *adj.* Haughtily contemptuous; arrogant. [<L *supercilium* eyebrow, pride] —**su′per·cil′i·ous·ly** *adv.* —**su′per·cil′i·ous·ness** *n.*

su·per·col·lid·er (so͞o′pər·kə·līd·er) *n.* A very large particle accelerator.

su·per·con·duc·ting (so͞o′pər·kən·duk′ting) *adj.* Having the property, when cooled to temperatures near absolute zero, of conducting electricity continuously without resistance: said of certain metals and alloys. —**su′per·con·duc′tive** *adj.* —**su′per·con′duc·tiv′i·ty** (-kon′duk·tiv′ə·tē), **su′per·con·duc′tor** *n.*

su·per·e·go (so͞o′pər·ē′gō, -eg′ō) *n. pl.* **·gos** *Psychoanal.* A largely unconscious element of the personality, acting principally as conscience and critic.

su·per·er·o·ga·tion (so͞o′pər·er′ə·gā′shən) *n.* The performance of an act in excess of the demands or requirements of duty. [<L *super-* above + *erogare* pay out]

su·per·e·rog·a·to·ry (so͞o′pər·ə·rog′ə·tôr′ē, -tō′rē) *adj.* 1 Of the nature of supererogation. 2 SUPERFLUOUS.

su·per·fi·cial (so͞o′pər·fish′əl) *adj.* 1 Of, lying near, or on the surface: a *superficial* wound. 2 Of or pertaining to only the ordinary and the obvious; not profound; shallow. 3 Hasty; cursory: a *superficial* examination. 4 Apparent only; not real or genuine. [<L *super-* above + *facies* a face] —**su′per·fi′ci·al′i·ty** (-fish′ē·al′ə·tē), **su′per·fi′cial·ness** *n.* —**su′per·fi′cial·ly** *adv.*

su·per·fine (so͞o′pər·fīn′) *adj.* 1 Of the best quality; very fine and delicate. 2 Unduly elaborate. —**su′per·fine′ness** *n.*

su·per·flu·i·ty (so͞o′pər·flo͞o′ə·tē) *n. pl.* **·ties** 1 The state of being superfluous. 2 That which is superfluous.

su·per·flu·ous (so͞o·pûr′flo͞o·əs) *adj.* Exceeding what is needed; surplus. [<L *super-* above + *fluere* to flow] —**su·per′flu·ous·ly** *adv.* —**su·per′flu·ous·ness** *n.*

su·per·heat (so͞o′pər·hēt′) *v.t.* 1 OVERHEAT. 2 To raise the temperature of (a vapor not in contact with its liquid) above the saturation point for a given pressure. 3 To heat (a liquid) above the boiling point without conversion into vapor. —**su′per·heat′er** *n.*

su·per·het·er·o·dyne (so͞o′pər·het′ər·ə·dīn′) *adj. Electronics* Pertaining to or designating radio reception in which the incoming signals are converted to an intermediate frequency, and are then amplified and demodulated. —*n.* A radio receiver of this type. [<SUPER(SONIC) + HETERODYNE]

su·per·high·way (so͞o′pər·hī′wā′) *n.* A highway for high-speed traffic, usu. with four or more lanes.

su·per·hu·man (so͞o′pər·ʰyo͞o′mən) *adj.* 1 Above and beyond what is human; miraculous; divine. 2 Beyond normal human ability or power. —**su′per·hu′man·ly** *adv.*

su·per·im·pose (so͞o′pər·im·pōz′) *v.t.* **·posed, ·pos·ing** 1 To lay or impose something else. 2 To add as an incidental or superfluous feature. —**su′per·im′po·si′tion** (-im′pə·zish′ən) *n.*

su·per·in·duce (so͞o′pər·in·dʸo͞os′) *v.t.* **·duced, ·duc·ing** To introduce additionally. [<L *super-* over + *inducere* lead in] —**su′per·in·duc′tion** (-duk′shən) *n.*

su·per·in·tend (so͞o′pər·in·tend′) *v.t.* To have the charge and direction of; supervise. [<LL *super-* over + *intendere*

direct, aim at] **—su′per·in·ten′dence, su′per·in·ten′den·cy** *n.*

su·per·in·ten·dent (sōō′pər·in·ten′dənt) *n.* 1 One who has charge of an institution or undertaking; director. 2 One responsible for the maintenance and repair of a building. *—adj.* Superintending.

su·pe·ri·or (sə·pir′ē·ər, sōō-) *adj.* 1 Higher in rank, quality, or degree; better or excellent: *superior* vision; *superior* talent. 2 Greater in quantity: a *superior* supply. 3 Higher in relation to other things; upper. 4 *Printing* Set above the line, as 1 in x^1. 5 Serenely unaffected or indifferent: with *to: superior* to pettiness. 6 Affecting or suggesting an attitude of contemptuous indifference or disdain: *superior* airs. *—n.* 1 One who is superior, as in rank or excellence. 2 The head of an abbey, convent, or monastery. [< L *superus* higher < *super* above] **—su·pe·ri·or·i·ty** (sə·pir′ē·ôr′ə·tē, -or′-, sōō-) *n.* **—su·pe′ri·or·ly** *adv.*

su·per·la·tive (sə·pûr′lə·tiv, sōō-) *adj.* 1 Being of the highest degree; most excellent or eminent. 2 *Gram.* Expressing the highest or extreme degree of the quality expressed by the positive degree of an adjective or adverb: "Wisest" is the *superlative* form of "wise." 3 Exaggerated. *—n.* 1 That which is superlative. 2 The highest degree; apex. 3 *Gram.* a The superlative degree. b A form in the superlative degree. [< L *superlatus* excessive < *super-* above + *latus* carried] **—su·per′la·tive·ly** *adv.* **—su·per′la·tive·ness** *n.*

su·per·man (sōō′pər·man′) *n. pl.* **·men** (-men′) 1 A man of superhuman powers. 2 An intellectually and morally superior man.

su·per·mar·ket (sōō′pər·mär′kit) *n.* A large, chiefly self-service store selling food and household supplies.

su·per·nal (sōō·pûr′nəl) *adj.* 1 Heavenly; celestial. 2 Coming from above or from the sky. [< L *supernus* < *super* over] **—su·per′nal·ly** *adv.*

su·per·nat·u·ral (sōō′pər·nach′ər·əl, -rəl) *adj.* 1 Existing or occurring through some agency beyond the known forces of nature. 2 Of or concerning phenomena of this kind: *supernatural* tales. 3 Believed to be miraculous or divine. 4 Suggestive of ghosts, demons, or other agents unconstrained by natural law. *—n.* That which is supernatural. [< L *super-* above + *natura* nature] **—su′per·nat′u·ral·ism, su′per·nat′u·ral·ness** *n.* **—su′per·nat′u·ral·ist** *adj., n.* **—su′per·nat′u·ral·is′tic** *adj.* **—su′per·nat′u·ral·ly** *adv.*

su·per·nu·mer·ar·y (sōō′pər·n^yōō′mə·rer′ē) *adj.* 1 Being beyond a fixed or usual number. 2 Beyond a necessary number; superfluous. *—n. pl.* **·ar·ies** 1 A supernumerary person or thing. 2 A stage performer without any speaking part. [< L *super* over + *numerus* a number]

su·per·pa·tri·ot (sōō′pər·pā′trē·ət, -ot) *n.* A person who is or claims to be a great patriot, often one whose patriotic fervor is marked by a readiness to regard dissent as unpatriotic or subversive. **—su′per·pa′tri·ot′ic** *adj.* **—su′per·pa′tri·ot·ism** *n.*

su·per·pose (sōō′pər·pōz′) *v.t.* **·posed, ·pos·ing** To lay over or upon something else. **—su′per·pos′a·ble** *adj.* **—su′per·po·si′tion** (-pə·zish′ən) *n.*

su·per·pow·er (sōō′pər·pou′ər) *n.* One of a few great, dominant nations characterized by superior economic or military strength and by large population.

su·per·sat·u·rate (sōō′pər·sach′ōō·rāt) *v.t.* **·rat·ed, ·rat·ing** To cause (a solution) to hold more of a solute than it can normally hold at the given temperature. **—su′per·sat′u·ra′tion** *n.*

su·per·scribe (sōō′pər·skrīb′) *v.t.* **·scribed, ·scrib·ing** 1 To write or engrave on the outside or on the upper part of. 2 To address, as a letter. [< L *super-* over + *scribere* write] **—su′per·scrip′tion** (-skrip′shən) *n.*

su·per·script (sōō′pər·skript′) *adj.* Written above or overhead. *—n.* A letter, index, or other mark following and above a letter or figure, as in a^3 or c'. [< LL *superscriptus,* p.p. of *superscribere* superscribe]

su·per·sede (sōō′pər·sēd′) *v.t.* **·sed·ed, ·sed·ing** 1 To take the place of, as by reason of superiority or right; replace. 2 To put something in the place of; set aside. [< L *super-* above + *sedere* sit] **—su′per·sed′er, su′per·se′dure** (-sē′jər) *n.*

su·per·son·ic (sōō′pər·son′ik) *adj.* 1 Of or capable of moving at a speed greater than that of sound. 2 Moving at such a speed. 3 ULTRASONIC. **—su′per·son′i·cal·ly** *adv.*

su·per·star (sōō′pər·stär′) *n.* A public performer, as an actor, singer, or professional athlete, regarded as one of the best or most popular. **—su′per·star′dom** *n.*

su·per·sti·tion (sōō′pər·stish′ən) *n.* 1 An ignorant or irrational belief, often provoked by fear, and based upon assumptions of cause and effect contrary to known scientific facts and principles. 2 Any practice inspired by such belief. 3 Any unreasonable belief or impression. [< L *superstitio* excessive fear of the gods, amazement]

su·per·sti·tious (sōō′pər·stish′əs) *adj.* 1 Disposed to believe in or be influenced by superstitions. 2 Of, based upon, or manifesting superstition. **—su′per·sti′tious·ly** *adv.* **—su′per·sti′tious·ness** *n.*

su·per·struc·ture (sōō′pər·struk′chər) *n.* 1 Any structure above the basement or considered in relation to its foundation. 2 Any structure built on top of another. 3 The parts of a ship's structure above the main deck.

su·per·tank·er (sōō′pər·tangk′ər) *n.* A very large tanker capable of carrying a vast cargo, as of oil.

su·per·tax (sōō′pər·taks′) *n.* An extra tax in addition to the normal tax; a surtax.

su·per·vene (sōō′pər·vēn′) *v.i.* **·vened, ·ven·ing** To follow closely upon something as an extraneous or additional circumstance. [< L *super-* over and above + *venire* come] **—su′per·ven′ient** (-vēn′yənt) *adj.* **—su′per·ven′tion** (-ven′shən) *n.*

su·per·vise (sōō′pər·vīz) *v.t.* **·vised, ·vis·ing** To have charge of; direct. [< L *super-* over + *videre* see] **—Syn.** manage, run, oversee, superintend.

su·per·vi·sion (sōō′pər·vizh′ən) *n.* The act or process of supervising; direction, control, or guidance.

su·per·vi·sor (sōō′pər·vī′zər) *n.* 1 One who supervises; a superintendent or manager. 2 In education, an official supervising teachers and responsible for curricula, etc., in a particular subject. **—su′per·vi′sor·ship** *n.* **—su·per·vi·sor·y** (sōō′pər·vī′zər·ē) *adj.*

su·pine (sōō·pīn′, sə-) *adj.* 1 Lying on the back, or with the face turned upward. 2 Having no interest or care; listless. [< L *supinus*] **—su·pine′ly** *adv.* **—su·pine′ness** *n.*

supp., suppl. supplement; supplementary.

sup·per (sup′ər) *n.* 1 The last meal of the day; the evening meal. 2 A social event including the serving of supper: a church *supper.* [< OF *soper* sup] **—sup′per·less** *adj.*

sup·plant (sə·plant′, -plänt′) *v.t.* 1 To take the place of, as of something inferior or out of date; displace. 2 To take the place of (someone) by scheming, treachery, etc. 3 To replace (one thing) with another: to *supplant* naive expectations with realistic goals. [< L *supplantare* trip up] **—sup·plan·ta·tion** (sup′lan·tā′shən), **sup·plant′er** *n.*

sup·ple (sup′əl) *adj.* **sup·pler** (sup′lər, -əl·ər), **sup·plest** 1 Easily bent; flexible; pliant: *supple* leather. 2 Agile or graceful in movement; limber. 3 Yielding readily to the wishes of others; compliant. 4 Servile; obsequious. 5 Quick to respond or adjust, as the mind; adaptable. *—v.t. & v.i.* **·pled, ·pling** To make or become supple. [< L *supplex,* lit., bending under] **—sup′ple·ly** (sup′əl·ē, sup′lē) or **sup′ply** (sup′lē) *adv.* **—sup′ple·ness** *n.* **—Syn. 2** lithe, deft, nimble.

sup·ple·ment (sup′lə·mənt) *n.* 1 Something added that supplies a deficiency. 2 An addition to a publication, as a section providing additional information added to a book. *—v.t.* To make additions to; provide for what is lacking in. [< L *supplere.* See SUPPLY.] **—sup·ple·ment·al** (sup′lə·men′təl) *adj.* • Both *supplement* and *complement* refer to something added to make up for a lack or deficiency. *Complement* (not to be confused with *compliment,* an expression of praise) emphasizes the correction or adjustment of something unfinished or imperfect, and often implies a balancing of elements: *The design of the housing project called for low buildings to complement the high-rises.* In the case of *supplement,* the fact of being added is more emphatic, and the expected result is one of improvement rather than completion: *Student teachers supplemented the regular teaching staff, freeing them to give more individual help to slow learners.*

sup·ple·men·ta·ry (sup′lə·men′tər·ē, -trē) *adj.* Added as a supplement; additional.

sup·pli·ant (sup′lē·ənt) *adj.* Entreating earnestly and humbly. —*n.* One who supplicates. [< L *supplicare* supplicate] —**sup′pli·ant·ly** *adv.* —**sup′pli·ant·ness** *n.*

sup·pli·cant (sup′lə·kənt) *n.* One who supplicates. —*adj.* Asking or entreating humbly. [< L *supplicare* supplicate]

sup·pli·cate (sup′lə·kāt) *v.* **·cat·ed, ·cat·ing** *v.t.* **1** To ask for humbly or by earnest prayer. **2** To beg something of; entreat. —*v.i.* **3** To make an earnest request. [< L *sub-* under + *plicare* bend, fold] —**sup′pli·ca′tion** *n.* —**sup′pli·ca·to′ry** (-kə·tôr′ē, -tō′rē) *adj.*

sup·ply (sə·plī′) *v.* **·plied, ·ply·ing** *v.t.* **1** To make available; provide or furnish: to *supply* electricity to a remote area. **2** To furnish with what is needed: to *supply* an army with weapons. **3** To provide for adequately; satisfy. **4** To make up for; compensate for. **5** To fill (the place of another). —*v.i.* **6** To take the place of another temporarily. —*n. pl.* **·plies 1** That which is or can be supplied. **2** A store or quantity on hand. **3** *pl.* Accumulated stores, as for an army. **4** The amount of a commodity offered at a given price or available for meeting a demand. **5** The act of supplying. [< L *supplere* < *sub-* up from under + *plere* fill] —**sup·pli′·er** *n.*

sup·port (sə·pôrt′, -pōrt′) *v.t.* **1** To bear the weight of, esp. from underneath; hold in position; keep from falling, sinking, etc. **2** To bear or sustain (weight, etc.). **3** To provide money or necessities for; provide with the means of subsistence. **4** To give approval or assistance to; uphold. **5** To serve to uphold or corroborate; substantiate: His testimony *supports* our position. **6** To endure patiently; tolerate. **7** To provide with the means to endure; keep from collapsing or yielding: Faith *supported* her. **8** To carry on; keep up: to *support* a war. **9** In the theater, etc., to act in a subordinate role to. —*n.* **1** The act of supporting. **2** One who supports. **3** That which supports, as a brace or girdle for the body. [< L *sub-* up from under + *portare* carry] —**sup·port′a·ble** *adj.* —**sup·port′a·bly** *adv.* —**Syn. 4** advocate, endorse, help, aid, assist. **5** verify, bear out. **6** bear, suffer. **7** sustain.

sup·port·er (sə·pôr′tər, -pōr′-) *n.* **1** One who or that which supports. **2** An elastic or other support for some part of the body.

sup·por·tive (sə·pôr′tiv, -pōr′-) *adj.* **1** Tending or intended to support. **2** Contributing importantly to the stability of one's physical or emotional health: *supportive* treatment. —**sup·por′tive·ly** *adv.*

sup·pose (sə·pōz′) *v.* **·posed, ·pos·ing** *v.t.* **1** To believe to be true or probable; presume. **2** To assume as true for the sake of argument or illustration. **3** To expect: I am *supposed* to follow. **4** To presuppose; imply: Mercy *supposes* a sense of compassion. —*v.i.* **5** To make a supposition. [< L *supponere* substitute, put under] —**sup·pos′a·ble** *adj.* —**sup·pos′a·bly** *adv.* —**sup·pos′er** *n.*

sup·posed (sə·pōzd′) *adj.* **1** Accepted as genuine; believed. **2** Imagined only, instead of actually experienced. —**sup·pos·ed·ly** (sə·pō′zid·lē) *adv.*

sup·po·si·tion (sup′ə·zish′ən) *n.* **1** Something supposed; a conjecture or hypothesis. **2** The act of supposing. —**sup′po·si′tion·al** *adj.* —**sup′po·si′tion·al·ly** *adv.*

sup·pos·i·to·ry (sə·poz′ə·tôr′ē, -tō′rē) *n. pl.* **·ries** A small mass of a usu. medicated substance that melts at body temperature, for introduction into a body cavity, as the rectum or vagina. [< LL *suppositorius* placed underneath or up < L *supponere* put under]

sup·press (sə·pres′) *v.t.* **1** To put an end or stop to; crush, as a rebellion. **2** To stop or prohibit the activities of. **3** To withhold from knowledge or publication, as a book, news, etc. **4** To hold back or repress. **5** To stop or check (a hemorrhage, etc.). [< L *suppressus,* p.p. of *supprimere* press down] —**sup·press′er, sup·pres′sor** *n.* —**sup·press′i·ble, sup·pres′sive** *adj.*

sup·pres·sion (sə·presh′ən) *n.* **1** The act of suppressing, or the state of being suppressed. **2** The deliberate exclusion from consciousness of unacceptable ideas, memories, etc.

sup·pu·rate (sup′yə·rāt) *v.i.* **·rat·ed, ·rat·ing** To discharge or generate pus. [< L *sub-* under + *pus, puris* pus] —**sup′·pu·ra′tion** *n.* —**sup′pu·ra·tive** (-rə·tiv, -rā′-) *adj.*

su·pra (sōō′prə) *adv.* Above. [L]

supra- *prefix* Above; beyond: *supranational.* [< L *supra* above, beyond]

su·pra·na·tion·al (sōō′prə·nash′ə·nəl) *adj.* Of or concerning several or a number of nations; involving more than one nation. —**su′pra·na′tion·al·ism** *n.* —**su′pra·na′tion·al·ist** *adj., n.*

su·pra·re·nal (sōō′prə·rē′nəl) *adj.* Situated above the kidneys; adrenal. —*n.* An adrenal gland. [< L *supra-* above + *renalis* renal]

su·prem·a·cy (sə·prem′ə·sē, sōō-) *n. pl.* **·cies 1** The state of being supreme. **2** Supreme power or authority.

su·preme (sə·prēm′, sōō-) *adj.* **1** Highest in power or authority; dominant. **2** Highest or greatest, as in degree; utmost: *supreme* devotion. **3** Ultimate; last and greatest. [< L *supremus,* superl. of *superus* < *super* above] —**su·preme′ly** *adv.* —**su·preme′ness** *n.*

Supreme Being God.

Supreme Court 1 The highest Federal court. **2** The highest court in many states.

Supreme Soviet The legislature of the Soviet Union.

supt. superintendent.

sur- *prefix* Over; beyond: *surtax.* [< OF *sur-* < L *super-*]

su·rah (sōōr′ə) *n.* A soft, usu. twilled, silk or silk and rayon fabric. [< *Surat,* India]

sur·base (sûr′bās′) *n.* A border or molding above the top of a base, as of a pedestal.

sur·cease (sûr·sēs′, sûr′sēs) *n.* Cessation; end. —*v.t.* & *v.i.* **·ceased, ·ceas·ing** To end. [< AF *surseoir* to refrain < L *supersedere* to sit above]

sur·charge (sûr′chärj′) *n.* **1** An additional amount charged or imposed. **2** An excessive burden, load, or charge. **3** OVERCHARGE. **4** A new valuation or something additional printed on a postage or revenue stamp. —*v.t.* (sûr·chärj′) **·charged, ·charg·ing 1** OVERCHARGE. **2** To fill or load to excess. **3** To imprint a surcharge on (postage stamps). —**sur·charg′er** *n.*

sur·cin·gle (sûr′sing·gəl) *n.* A strap encircling the body of a horse, for holding a saddle, blanket, etc. [< SUR- + L *cingulum* a belt]

sur·coat (sûr′kōt′) *n.* An outer coat or garment, esp., in the Middle Ages, one worn over armor.

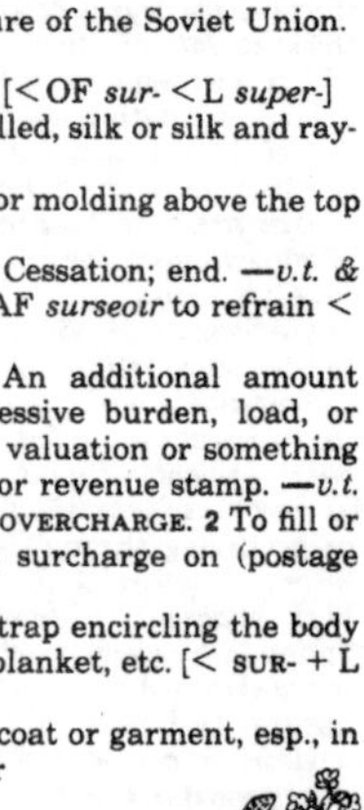

Surcoat

surd (sûrd) *n.* **1** *Math.* An irrational number, esp. an indicated root, as $\sqrt{2}$. **2** *Phonet.* A voiceless speech sound. —*adj.* **1** *Math.* IRRATIONAL. **2** *Phonet.* VOICELESS. [< L *surdus* deaf, silent]

sure (shōōr) *adj.* **sur·er, sur·est 1** Not subject to uncertainty or doubt; beyond all question; indisputable. **2** Characterized by freedom from doubt or uncertainty; firm: *sure* convictions; a *sure* grasp of his subject. **3** Certain or confident; positive: I was *sure* I had seen her before. **4** Not liable to fail or disappoint; reliable; sound: a *sure* memory. **5** Bound to happen or be: a *sure* winner. **6** *Obs.* Safe; secure. —*adv.* *Informal* Surely; certainly. —**for sure** Certainly; beyond all question. —**to be sure** Indeed; certainly; quite so. [< L *securus*] —**sure′ness** *n.* —**Syn. 1** unquestionable, unimpeachable, indubitable. **4** trustworthy, dependable, true.

sure-foot·ed (shōōr′fōōt′id) *adj.* Not liable to fall or stumble. —**sure′-foot′ed·ly** *adv.* —**sure′-foot′ed·ness** *n.*

sure·ly (shōōr′lē) *adv.* **1** In a sure manner. **2** Without doubt; certainly. **3** Really; certainly: used as an intensive to express strong probability: He *surely* knew that.

sure·ty (shōōr′ə·tē, shōōr′tē) *n. pl.* **·ties 1** The state of being sure; certainty. **2** Security against loss or damage. **3** One who assumes the debts, responsibilities, etc., of another; a guarantor. [< L *securus* secure] —**sure′ty·ship** *n.*

surf (sûrf) *n.* **1** The swell of the sea that breaks upon a shore. **2** The foam caused by the billows. —*v.i.* To ride the surf on a surfboard; engage in surfing. [?] —**surf′er** *n.*

sur·face (sûr′fis) *n.* **1** The outer part or face of an object. **2** That which has area but not thickness. **3** A superficial aspect; external appearance. —*v.* **·faced, ·fac·ing** *v.t.* **1** To put a surface on; esp., to make smooth, even, or plain. **2** To cause to rise to the surface, as a submarine. —*v.i.* **3** To rise to the surface. **4** To come to public notice, esp. something formerly kept secret. [< SUR- + FACE] **—sur′fac·er** *n.*

sur·face-ac·tive (sûr′fis·ak′tiv) *adj.* Effective in changing the properties of a substance, esp. surface tension, at the area of contact with another substance: *surface-active* detergents.

surface tension That property of a liquid by which the surface molecules exert a strong cohesive force, thus forming an elastic skin that tends to contract.

sur·fac·tant (sûr·fak′tənt) *n.* A surface-active substance, as a detergent. [< SURF(ACE)-ACT(IVE) + -ANT]

surf·board (sûrf′bôrd′, -bōrd′) *n.* A long, narrow board used in surfing. —*v.i.* SURF. **—surf′board′er** *n.*

surf·boat (sûrf′bōt′) *n.* A boat of extra strength and buoyancy, for launching and landing through surf.

sur·feit (sûr′fit) *v.t.* **1** To feed or supply to fullness or to excess. —*v.i.* **2** To overindulge in food or drink. —*n.* **1** Excess in eating or drinking. **2** The result of such excess; satiety. **3** Any excessive amount: a *surfeit* of praise. [< OF *surfaire* overdo]

surf·ing (sûrf′ing) *n.* A water sport in which a person standing on a surfboard is borne by the surf toward the shore. Also **surf·rid·ing** (sûrf′rī′ding).

surg. surgeon; surgery; surgical.

surge (sûrj) *v.* **surged, surg·ing** *v.i.* **1** To rise and roll with a powerful, swelling motion, as waves. **2** To be tossed about by waves. **3** To move or go in a powerful, wavelike motion: The mob *surged* through the square. **4** To increase or vary suddenly, as an electric current. —*n.* **1** A large swelling wave; billow. **2** A great swelling or rolling movement, as of waves. **3** *Electr.* A sudden, transient rise in current flow. **4** Any sudden, sharp increase. [< L *surgere*]

sur·geon (sûr′jən) *n.* One who practices surgery. [< OF *cirurgie* surgery] **—sur′geon·cy** (-sē) *n.*

sur·ger·y (sûr′jər·ē) *n. pl.* **·ger·ies** **1** The treatment of disease, injury, etc., by manual and operative means. **2** The branch of medicine concerned with surgical treatment. **3** A place where surgery is performed; an operating room. **4** *Brit.* A physician's office. [< Gk. *cheirourgia* a handicraft < *cheir* the hand + *ergein* to work] **—sur·gi·cal** (sûr′·ji·kəl) *adj.* **—sur′gi·cal·ly** *adv.*

sur·ly (sûr′lē) *adj.* **·li·er, ·li·est** Rude and ill-humored, esp. in response; gruff or insolent. [Earlier *sirly* like a lord < *sir* a lord] **—sur′li·ly** *adv.* **—sur′li·ness** *n.*

sur·mise (sər·mīz′) *v.* **·mised, ·mis·ing** *v.t.* & *v.i.* To infer (something) on slight evidence; guess. —*n.* (sər·mīz′, sûr′·mīz) A conjecture made on slight evidence; supposition. [< OF *surmettre* accuse < *sur-* upon + *mettre* put] **—Syn.** *v.* suppose, assume, conjecture.

sur·mount (sər·mount′) *v.t.* **1** To overcome; prevail over (a difficulty, etc.). **2** To mount to the top or cross to the other side of, as an obstacle. **3** To be or lie over or above. **4** To place something above or on top of; cap. [< L *super-* over + *mons, montis* a hill, mountain]

sur·name (sûr′nām′) *n.* **1** A last name; family name. **2** A name added to one's real name, as Ethelred *the Unready.* —*v.t.* (sûr′nām′, sûr·nām′) **·named, ·nam·ing** To give a surname to; call by a surname. [< OF *sur-* above, beyond + *nom* a name]

sur·pass (sər·pas′, -päs′) *v.t.* **1** To go beyond or past in degree or amount; exceed or excel. **2** To be beyond the reach or powers of; transcend. **—sur·pass′a·ble** *adj.* **—sur·pass′er** *n.* **—Syn. 1** eclipse, outdo, outstrip.

sur·pass·ing (sər·pas′ing, -päs′-) *adj.* Exceptional; excellent. **—sur·pass′ing·ly** *adv.*

sur·plice (sûr′plis) *n.* A loose white vestment with full sleeves, worn over the cassock by the clergy and choristers of some churches. [< Med. L *superpellicium (vestimentum)* an overgarment]

Surplice

sur·plus (sûr′plus) *n.* **1** That which remains over and above what is used or required. **2** Assets in excess of liabilities. —*adj.* Being in excess of what is used or needed. [< L *super-* over and above + *plus* more] **—sur′plus·age** (-ij) *n.*

sur·prise (sər·prīz′, sə-) *v.t.* **·prised, ·pris·ing** **1** To cause to feel wonder or astonishment, esp. because unusual or unexpected. **2** To come upon suddenly or unexpectedly; take unawares. **3** To attack suddenly and without warning. **4** To lead unawares, as into doing something not intended: with *into.* —*n.* **1** The state of being surprised; astonishment. **2** Something that causes surprise, as a sudden and unexpected event. **3** A sudden attack or capture. [< L *super-* over + *prehendere* take] **—sur·pris′er** *n.*

sur·pris·ing (sər·prī′zing, sə-) *adj.* Causing surprise or wonder. **—sur·pris′ing·ly** *adv.* **—Syn.** amazing, startling.

sur·re·al·ism (sə·rē′əl·iz′əm) *n.* A 20th-century movement in art and literature characterized chiefly by the incongruous juxtaposition or use of dreamlike elements, in theory an expression of the unconscious mind. **—sur·re′al·ist** *adj., n.* **—sur·re′al·is′tic** *adj.* **—sur·re′al·is′ti·cal·ly** *adv.*

sur·ren·der (sə·ren′dər) *v.t.* **1** To yield possession of or power over to another because of demand or compulsion. **2** To give up or relinquish, esp. in favor of another; resign; abandon. **3** To give (oneself) over to a passion, influence, etc. —*v.i.* **4** To give oneself up, as to an enemy in warfare. —*n.* The act of surrendering. [< OF *surrendre* < *sur-* over + *rendre* give, render]

sur·rep·ti·tious (sûr′əp·tish′əs) *adj.* **1** Accomplished by secret or improper means; clandestine. **2** Acting secretly or by stealth. [< L *subreptus,* p.p. of *subripere* steal] **—sur′rep·ti′tious·ly** *adv.* **—sur′rep·ti′tious·ness** *n.*

sur·rey (sûr′ē) *n.* A vehicle having two seats facing forward and sometimes a top. [< *Surrey,* England]

Surrey

sur·ro·gate (sûr′ə·gāt, -git) *n.* **1** Someone or something taking the place of another; substitute. **2** In some U.S. states, a probate court judge. —*v.t.* (sûr′ə·gāt) **·gat·ed, ·gat·ing** To put in the place of another; deputize or substitute. [< L *subrogare* < *sub-* in place of another + *rogare* ask]

sur·round (sə·round′) *v.t.* **1** To extend or place completely around; encircle or enclose. **2** To enclose on all sides so as to cut off communication or retreat. **3** To be or cause something to become a significant part of the environment or experience of: *surrounded* by lies; to *surround* oneself with the best legal talent. —*n.* *Chiefly Brit.* That which surrounds, as a border. [< LL *super-* over + *undare* rise in waves]

sur·round·ings (sə·roun′dingz) *n.pl.* The conditions, objects, etc., that constitute one's environment.

sur·tax (sûr′taks′) *n.* An extra or additional tax.

sur·tout (sər·tōō′, sûr′tōō′) *n.* A man's long, close-fitting overcoat. [F < *sur-* above + *tout* all]

sur·veil·lance (sər·vā′ləns, -vāl′yəns) *n.* A careful watching of someone or something, usu. carried on secretly or discreetly: to keep a suspect under *surveillance.* [F < *sur-* over + *veiller* watch] **—sur·veil′lant** *adj.*

sur·vey (sər·vā′, sûr′vā) *v.t.* **1** To look at in its entirety; view comprehensively, as from a height. **2** To look at carefully and minutely; scrutinize. **3** To determine accurately the area, contour, or boundaries of according to the principles of geometry and trigonometry. **4** To make a survey of. —*v.i.* **5** To survey land. —*n.* (*usu.* sûr′vā) **1** The operation, act, process, or results of surveying land. **2** A systematic inquiry to collect data for analysis, used esp. for the preparation of a comprehensive report or summary. **3** The result of such an inquiry; a comprehensive report. **4** A general or overall view; overview: a *survey* of contemporary theater. [< L *super-* over + *videre* look]

sur·vey·ing (sər·vā′ing) *n.* **1** The science and art of surveying portions of the surface of the earth and representing them on maps. **2** The work of one who surveys.

sur·vey·or (sər·vā′ər) *n.* One who surveys, esp. one engaged in land surveying.

sur·viv·a·ble (sûr·vī′və·bəl) *adj.* Not precluding survival: a *survivable* accident. **—sur·viv′a·bil′i·ty** *n.*

sur·viv·al (sər·vī′vəl) *n.* **1** The act or fact of surviving; a continuation of life or existence. **2** The fact of living or lasting beyond another. **3** One who or that which survives.

sur·vive (sər·vīv′) *v.* **·vived, ·viv·ing 1** *v.i.* To live or continue beyond the death of another, the occurrence of an event, etc.; remain alive or in existence. *—v.t.* **2** To live or exist beyond the death, occurrence, or end of; outlive or outlast. **3** To go on living after or in spite of: to *survive* a flood. [< L *super-* above, beyond + *vivere* live] **—sur·vi′vor, sur·viv′er** *n.*

sus·cep·ti·ble (sə·sep′tə·bəl) *adj.* **1** Readily affected; especially subject or vulnerable: with *to: susceptible* to infection; lax supervision *susceptible* to abuse. **2** Capable of being influenced or determined; liable: with *of* or *to: susceptible* of proof. **3** Easily affected in feeling or emotion; sensitive. [< L *suscipere* receive, undertake] **—sus·cep·ti·bil·i·ty** (sə·sep′tə·bil′ə·tē), **sus·cep′ti·ble·ness** *n.* **—sus·cep′ti·bly** *adv.* **—Syn. 1** unresistant, open. **2** admitting. **3** tender, impressionable.

sus·pect (sə·spekt′) *v.t.* **1** To think (a person) guilty without evidence or proof. **2** To have distrust of; doubt: to *suspect* one's motives. **3** To have an inkling or suspicion of; think possible. *—v.i.* **4** To have suspicions. *—adj.* (sus′pekt, sə·spekt′) Suspected; exciting suspicion. *—n.* (sus′pekt) A person suspected, esp. of a crime. [< F *suspecter* < L *suspectus,* p.p. of *suspicere* look under, mistrust] **—sus·pect′er** *n.*

sus·pend (sə·spend′) *v.t.* **1** To bar for a time from a privilege or office as a punishment. **2** To cause to cease for a time; interrupt: to *suspend* telephone service. **3** To withhold or defer action on: to *suspend* a sentence. **4** To hang from a support so as to allow free movement. **5** To keep in suspension, as dust particles in the air. *—v.i.* **6** To stop for a time. **7** To fail to meet obligations; stop payment. [< L *sub-* under + *pendere* hang]

sus·pend·er (sə·spen′dər) *n.* **1** One who or that which suspends. **2** *pl.* A pair of straps for supporting trousers. **3** *Brit.* A garter.

sus·pense (sə·spens′) *n.* **1** Anxiety caused by an uncertainty, as to the outcome of an event. **2** Excited interest caused by the progressive unfolding of events or information leading to a climax or resolution. **3** The state of being uncertain or indecisive. [< L *suspensus,* p.p. of *suspendere* suspend]

sus·pen·sion (sə·spen′shən) *n.* **1** The act of suspending, or the state of being suspended. **2** A temporary removal from office or position or withdrawal of privilege. **3** An interruption; cessation: *suspension* of normal procedure. **4** A deferment of action. **5** The state of hanging freely from a support. **6** A dispersion in a liquid or gas of insoluble particles that slowly settle on standing; also, a substance in this condition. **7** *Mech.* A system, as of springs or other absorbent parts, by which the chassis and body of a vehicle is insulated against shocks when moving. **8 a** *Music* The prolongation of one or more tones of a chord into the succeeding chord, causing a transient dissonance. **b** The note so prolonged.

suspension bridge A bridge having its roadway suspended from cables supported by towers and anchored at either end.

sus·pen·sive (sə·spen′siv) *adj.* **1** Tending to suspend or keep in suspense. **2** Suspending or deferring operation or effect: a *suspensive* veto. **—sus·pen′sive·ly** *adv.*

sus·pen·so·ry (sə·spen′sər·ē) *adj.* **1** Acting to support or sustain. **2** Suspending or delaying. *—n. pl.* **·ries** Something that supports or sustains, esp. a truss for the scrotum.

sus·pi·cion (sə·spish′ən) *n.* **1** The act of suspecting; an uncertain but often tenacious feeling or belief in the likelihood of another's guilt, wrongdoing, etc., without evidence or proof. **2** *Informal* A slight amount; trace, as of a flavor. *—v.t. Regional* To suspect. [< L *suspicere.* See SUSPECT.]

sus·pi·cious (sə·spish′əs) *adj.* **1** Tending to arouse suspicion; questionable. **2** Having or disposed to have suspicions. **3** Indicating suspicion. **—sus·pi′cious·ly** *adv.* **—sus·pi′cious·ness** *n.*

sus·tain (sə·stān′) *v.t.* **1** To keep up or maintain; keep in effect or being. **2** To maintain by providing with food and other necessities. **3** To keep from sinking or falling, esp. by bearing up from below. **4** To endure without succumbing; withstand. **5** To suffer, as a loss or injury; undergo. **6** To uphold or support as being true or just. **7** To prove the truth or correctness of; confirm. [< L *sub-* up from under + *tenere* to hold] **—sus·tain′a·ble** *adj.* **—sus·tain′er, sus·tain′ment** *n.* **—Syn. 7** corroborate, establish.

sus·te·nance (sus′tə·nəns) *n.* **1** The act or process of sustaining; esp., maintenance of life or health; subsistence. **2** That which sustains, as food. **3** Means of support; livelihood.

sut·ler (sut′lər) *n.* Formerly, a peddler or tradesman who followed an army to sell goods and food to the soldiers. [< Du. *soeteler*] **—sut′ler·ship** *n.*

sut·tee (su·tē′, sut′ē) *n.* **1** The former custom in which a Hindu woman willingly cremated herself on the funeral pyre of her husband: also **sut·tee′ism. 2** The widow so cremated. [< Hind. *satī* < Skt., faithful wife, fem. of *sat* good, wise]

su·ture (sōō′chər) *n.* **1** The junction of two edges by or as by sewing. **2** *Anat.* The fusion of two bones at their edges, as in the skull. **3** *Surg.* **a** The act or operation of joining the edges of an incision, wound, etc. **b** The thread, wire, or other material used in this operation. *—v.t.* **·tured, ·turing** To unite by means of sutures; sew together. [< L *sutus,* p.p. of *suere* sew] **—su′tur·al** *adj.* **—su′tur·al·ly** *adv.*

su·ze·rain (sōō′zə·rin, -rān) *n.* **1** A feudal lord. **2** A nation having paramount control over a locally autonomous state. [< L *susum* upwards] **—su′ze·rain·ty** *n.* (*pl.* **·ties**)

svelte (svelt) *adj.* **1** Slender; willowy: a *svelte* fashion model. **2** Sophisticated; smart; chic. [< Ital. *svelto* stretched, slender]

SW, S.W., sw, s.w. southwest; southwestern.

Sw. Sweden; Swedish.

swab (swob) *n.* **1** A soft, absorbent substance, as of cotton or gauze, usu. secured at the end of a small stick, for applying medication, cleansing a body surface, etc. **2** *Med.* A specimen of mucus, etc., taken for examination with a swab. **3** A mop for cleaning decks, floors, etc. **4** A cylindrical brush for cleaning firearms. **5** *Slang* An oaf; lout. *—v.t.* **swabbed, swab·bing** To clean or apply with a swab. [< MDu. *zwabben* swab] **—swab′ber** *n.*

swad·dle (swod′l) *v.t.* **·dled, ·dling 1** To wrap (an infant) in swaddling clothes. **2** To wrap with or as if with a bandage; swathe; bind. *—n.* A band or cloth used for swaddling. [< OE *swathian* swathe]

swaddling clothes Bands or strips of linen or cloth formerly wound around a newborn infant. Also **swaddling bands.**

swag (swag) *n.* **1** A curved decoration, as a hanging fastened at either end or a carved motif on a building. **2** *Slang* Property obtained by robbery or theft; plunder. **3** *Austral.* A bundle or pack containing belongings. **4** A swaying; a lurch. [? < Scand.]

swage (swāj) *n.* A tool or form for shaping metal by hammering or pressure. *—v.t.* **swaged, swag·ing** To shape (metal) with or as with a swage. [< OF *souage*]

swag·ger (swag′ər) *v.i.* **1** To walk with an air of conspicuous self-satisfaction and usu. of masculine vanity. **2** To behave in a blustering or self-satisfied manner. **3** To boast; brag. *—n.* **1** A swaggering gait or manner. **2** Verve; dash; bravado. *—adj.* Showy or stylish; smart. [< SWAG] **—swag′ger·er** *n.* **—swag′ger·ing·ly** *adv.*

swagger stick A short, lightweight stick, usu. tipped with metal, carried by some military officers as a mark of elegance or authority.

Swa·hi·li (swä·hē′lē) *n. pl.* **·hi·li** or **·hi·lis 1** One of a Bantu people of Zanzibar and the adjacent coast. **2** The language of this people, now widely used in E and central Africa.

swain (swān) *n.* **1** A rustic youth. **2** A lover; wooer. [< ON *sveinn* a boy, servant]

swal·low[1] (swol′ō) *v.t.* 1 To cause (food, etc.) to pass from the mouth into the stomach by means of muscular action of the esophagus. 2 To take in or engulf in a manner suggestive of this; absorb; envelop: often with *up.* 3 To put up with or endure; submit to, as insults. 4 To refrain from expressing; suppress: to *swallow* one's pride. 5 To take back: to *swallow* one's words. 6 *Informal* To believe (something improbable or incredible) to be true. —*v.i.* 7 To perform the act or the motions of swallowing. —*n.* 1 The act of swallowing. 2 An amount swallowed at once; a mouthful. [< OE *swelgan* swallow] —**swal′low·er** *n.*

swal·low[2] (swol′ō) *n.* 1 Any of various small birds with short bill, long, pointed wings, and forked tail, noted for swiftness of flight and migratory habits. 2 A similar bird, as the swift. [< OE *swealwe*]

swal·low·tail (swol′ō·tāl′) *n.* 1 A man's dress coat with two long, tapering skirts or tails. 2 A butterfly having a tapering prolongation on each hind wing. —**swal′low-tailed′** *adj.*

swam (swam) *p.t.* of SWIM.

swa·mi (swä′mē) *n. pl.* **·mis** Master; lord: a Hindu title of respect, esp. for a religious teacher.

swamp (swomp, swômp) *n.* A tract or region of low land saturated with water; a bog. Also **swamp′land′** (-land′). —*v.t.* 1 To drench or submerge with water or other liquid. 2 To overwhelm with difficulties; crush; ruin. 3 To sink or fill (a boat) with water. —*v.i.* 4 To sink in water, etc.; become swamped. [?< LG] —**swamp′y** *adj.* **(·i·er, ·i·est)**

swamp fever MALARIA.

swan (swon, swôn) *n.* Any of several large, web-footed, long-necked birds allied to but heavier than the goose. [< OE]

Trumpeter swan

swan dive A dive performed with the head tilted back and the arms held sideways and brought together as the water is entered.

swank (swangk) *n.* 1 Ostentatious display, as in taste or manner; swagger. 2 Stylishness; smartness. —*adj.* 1 Ostentatiously fashionable. 2 Stylish; smart. —*v.i. Slang* To swagger; bluster. [?< MHG *swanken* sway]

swank·y (swangk′ē) *adj.* **swank·i·er, swank·i·est** *Informal* Ostentatiously or extravagantly fashionable. —**swank′i·ly** *adv.* —**swank′i·ness** *n.*

swan's-down (swonz′doun′, swônz′-) *n.* 1 The down of a swan, used for trimming, powder puffs, etc. 2 Any of various fine, soft fabrics, usu. with a nap. Also **swans′·down′.**

swan song A last work, utterance, or performance, as before retirement or death. [< the ancient fable that the swan sings a last song before dying]

swap (swop) *v.t. & v.i.* **swapped, swap·ping** *Informal* To exchange (one thing for another); trade. —*n.* The act or an instance of swapping. [< ME *swappen* strike (a bargain), slap] —**swap′per** *n.*

sward (swôrd) *n.* Land thickly covered with grass; turf. —*v.t.* To cover with sward. [< OE *sweard* a skin]

swarm[1] (swôrm) *n.* 1 A large number of bees moving together with a queen to form a new colony. 2 A hive of bees. 3 A large crowd or mass, esp. one in apparent overall movement; throng. —*v.i.* 1 To leave the hive in a swarm: said of bees. 2 To come together, move, or occur in great numbers: The crowd *swarmed* out of the stadium; gnats *swarming* about. 3 To be crowded or overrun; teem: with *with: swarming* with tourists. —*v.t.* 4 To fill with a swarm or crowd. [< OE *swearm*] —**swarm′er** *n.*

swarm[2] (swôrm) *v.t. & v.i.* To climb (a tree, etc.) by clasping it with the hands and limbs. [?]

swart (swôrt) *adj.* Swarthy. [< OE *sweart*] —**swart′ness** *n.*

swarth·y (swôr′thē) *adj.* **swarth·i·er, swarth·i·est** Having a dark complexion; tawny. [Var. of obs. *swarty* < SWART] —**swarth′i·ly** *adv.* —**swarth′i·ness** *n.*

swash (swosh, swôsh) *v.i.* 1 To move with a splashing sound, as waves. —*v.t.* 2 To splash (water, etc.). 3 To splash or dash water, etc., upon or against. —*n.* The splash of a liquid. [Imit.] —**swash′er** *n.* —**swash′ing·ly** *adv.*

swash·buck·ler (swosh′buk′lər, swôsh′-) *n.* A swaggering soldier, adventurer, daredevil, etc. [< SWASH + BUCKLER] —**swash′buck′ler·ing** *n.* —**swash′buck′ling** *adj., n.*

swas·ti·ka (swos′ti·kə) *n.* 1 A primitive ornament or symbol in the form of a cross with arms of equal length, bent at the ends at right angles. 2 Such a figure with the arms extended clockwise, used as the emblem of the Nazis. Also **swas′ti·ca.** [< Skt. *sú* good + *asti* being < *as* be]

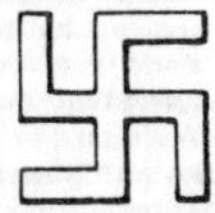

Nazi swastika

swat (swot) *v.t.* **swat·ted, swat·ting** To hit with a sharp, quick, or violent blow. —*n.* A sharp, quick, or violent blow. [Var. of SQUAT] —**swat′ter** *n.* —**Syn** *v.* smack, strike, whack.

swatch (swoch) *n.* A strip, as of fabric, esp. one cut off for a sample. [?]

swath (swoth, swôth) *n.* 1 A row or line of cut grass or grain. 2 The space cut by a machine or implement in a single course. 3 A strip, track, row, etc. —**cut a wide swath** To make a fine impression. [< OE *swæth* a track]

swathe[1] (swāth, swäth) *v.t.* **swathed, swath·ing** 1 To bind or wrap, as in bandages; swaddle. 2 To envelop; enwrap. —*n.* A bandage for swathing. [< OE *swathian*] —**swath′er** *n.*

swathe[2] (swāth, swäth) *n.* SWATH.

sway (swā) *v.i.* 1 To swing from side to side or to and fro; oscillate. 2 To bend or incline to one side. 3 To incline in opinion, sympathy, etc. 4 To control; rule. —*v.t.* 5 To cause to swing from side to side. 6 To cause to bend or lean to one side. 7 To cause (a person, opinion, etc.) to tend in a given way; influence. 8 To deflect or divert, as from a course of action. —*n.* 1 Power; influence. 2 A sweeping, swinging, or turning from side to side. [Prob. < ON *sveigja* bend] —**Syn.** *v.* 2 lean, veer. 4 govern, influence. *n.* 1 control, dominion.

sway·back (swā′bak′) *n.* A hollow or sagging condition of the back, as in a horse. —*adj.* Having such a back: also **sway′backed′** (-bakt).

Swa·zi·land (swä′zē·land) *n.* An independent kingdom of the Commonwealth of Nations in SE Africa, 6,704 sq. mi., cap. Mbabane. • See map at AFRICA.

swear (swâr) *v.* **swore, sworn, swear·ing** *v.i.* 1 To make a solemn affirmation with an appeal to God or some other deity or to something held sacred. 2 To make a vow. 3 To use profanity; curse. 4 *Law* To give testimony under oath. —*v.t.* 5 To affirm or assert solemnly by invoking sacred beings or things. 6 To promise with an oath; vow. 7 To declare or affirm, earnestly or emphatically: I *swear* he's a liar. 8 To take or utter (an oath). —**swear by** 1 To appeal to by oath. 2 To have complete confidence in. —**swear in** To administer a legal oath to. —**swear off** *Informal* To promise to give up: to *swear off* drink. —**swear out** To obtain (a warrant for arrest) by making a statement under oath. [< OE *swerian*] —**swear′er** *n.*

swear·word (swâr′wûrd′) *n.* A word used in profanity or cursing.

sweat (swet) *v.* **sweat** or **sweat·ed, sweat·ing** *v.i.* 1 To exude or excrete salty moisture from the pores of the skin; perspire. 2 To exude moisture in drops. 3 To gather and condense moisture in drops on its surface. 4 To pass through pores or interstices in drops. 5 To ferment, as tobacco leaves. 6 To come forth, as through a porous surface; ooze. 7 *Informal* To work hard; toil; drudge. 8 *Informal* To suffer, as from anxiety. —*v.t.* 9 To exude (moisture) from the pores or a porous surface. 10 To gather or condense drops of (moisture). 11 To soak or stain with sweat. 12 To cause to sweat. 13 To cause to work hard. 14 *Informal* To force (employees) to work for low wages and under unfavorable conditions. 15 To heat (solder, etc.) until it melts. 16 To join, as metal objects with solder. 17 *Metall.* To heat so as to extract an element that is easily fusible; also, to extract thus. 18 To subject to fermentation, as hides or tobacco. 19 *Slang* To subject to torture or rigorous interrogation to extract information. —**sweat (something) out** *Slang* To wait through anxiously; endure. —*n.* 1 Moisture in minute drops on the skin. 2 The act or state of sweating. 3 Hard labor; drudgery. 4 *Informal* Impatience, anxiety, or hurry. [< OE *swǣtan*] —**sweat'i·ly** *adv.* —**sweat'i·ness** *n.* —**sweat'y** *adj.* (**·i·er, ·i·est**)

sweat·band (swet'band') *n.* 1 A band, usu. of leather, inside a hat to protect it from sweat. 2 An absorbent cloth band worn over the forehead or around the wrist.

sweat·er (swet'ər) *n.* 1 One who or that which sweats. 2 A knitted or crocheted garment with or without sleeves.

sweat gland One of the numerous minute subcutaneous glands that secrete sweat.

sweat shirt A loose-fitting, usu. long-sleeved pullover of soft, absorbent material, sometimes hooded.

sweat·shop (swet'shop') *n.* A place where work is done under poor conditions, for insufficient wages, and for long hours.

sweat·suit (swet'so͞ot') *n.* A sweat shirt and matching pants (**sweat pants**) worn esp. by athletes when warming up or just after competing.

Swed. Sweden; Swedish.

Swede (swēd) *n.* A native or citizen of Sweden.

Swe·den (swē'dən) *n.* A constitutional monarchy of N Europe, 173,577 sq. mi., cap. Stockholm.

Swed·ish (swē'dish) *adj.* Of or pertaining to Sweden, the Swedes, or their language. —*n.* 1 The North Germanic language of Sweden. 2 The inhabitants of Sweden collectively: with *the.*

sweep (swēp) *v.* **swept, sweep·ing** *v.t.* 1 To collect or clear away with a broom, brush, etc. 2 To clear or clean with a broom, etc.: to *sweep* a floor. 3 To touch or brush with a motion as of sweeping: to *sweep* the strings of a harp. 4 To pass over swiftly: The searchlight *swept* the sky. 5 To move, carry, bring, etc., with force: The flood *swept* the bridge away. 6 To move over or through with force: The gale *swept* the bay. 7 To drag the bottom of (a body of water, etc.). 8 To win totally or overwhelmingly. —*v.i.* 9 To clean a floor or other surface with a broom, etc. 10 To move or go strongly and evenly: The train *swept* by. 11 To walk with great dignity: She *swept* into the room. 12 To trail, as a skirt. 13 To extend with a long reach or curve: The road *sweeps* along the lake shore on the north. —*n.* 1 The act or result of sweeping. 2 A long stroke or movement: a *sweep* of the hand. 3 The act of clearing out or getting rid of. 4 An unbroken stretch or extent: a *sweep* of beach. 5 A total or overwhelming victory, as in an election. 6 The range, area, or compass reached by sweeping. 7 One who sweeps chimneys, streets, etc. 8 A curving line; flowing contour. 9 A long, heavy oar. 10 A long pole on a pivot, having a bucket suspended from one end, for use in drawing water. 11 *pl.* Sweepings. 12 *pl. Informal* Sweepstakes. [< OE *swāpan*] —**sweep'er** *n.*

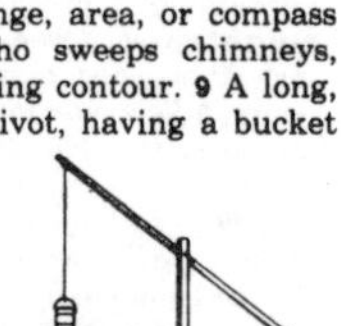
Sweep *def. 10*

sweep·ing (swē'ping) *adj.* 1 Extending in a long line or over a wide area: a *sweeping* glance. 2 Covering a wide area; comprehensive: *sweeping* reforms. —*n.* 1 The action of one who or that which sweeps. 2 *pl.* Things swept up, as refuse. —**sweep'·ing·ly** *adv.* —**sweep'ing·ness** *n.*

sweep·stakes (swēp'stāks') *n. pl.* **·stakes** *(construed as sing. or pl.)* 1 A type of lottery in which all the sums staked may be won by one or by a few of the betters, as in a horse race. 2 A race, contest, etc., to determine the outcome of such a lottery. 3 A prize in such a lottery. Also **sweep'stake'**.

sweet (swēt) *adj.* 1 Having a flavor like that of sugar, often due to the presence of sugar in some form. 2 Not salted, sour, rancid, or spoiled. 3 Gently pleasing to the senses; agreeable to the taste, smell, etc. 4 Agreeable or delightful to the mind or the emotions. 5 Having gentle, pleasing, and winning qualities. 6 Sound; rich; productive: said of soil. —*n.* 1 The quality of being sweet; sweetness. 2 Something sweet, agreeable, or pleasing. 3 *Usu. pl.* Confections, preserves, candy, etc. 4 A beloved person. 5 *Brit.* DESSERT. [< OE *swēte*] —**sweet'ly** *adv.* —**sweet'ness** *n.*

sweet alyssum A small plant related to mustard having spikes of fragrant white blossoms.

sweet·bread (swēt'bred') *n.* The pancreas (**stomach sweetbread**) or the thymus (**neck sweetbread** or **throat sweetbread**) of a calf or other animal, when used as food.

sweet·bri·er (swēt'brī'ər) *n.* A species of rose with dense, prickly branches and fragrant leaves. Also **sweet'·bri'ar.**

sweet clover Any of several leguminous forage plants having fragrant white or yellow flowers.

sweet corn Any of several varieties of maize rich in sugar, cultivated for use as a vegetable.

sweet·en (swēt'n) *v.t.* 1 To make sweet or sweeter. 2 To make more endurable; alleviate; lighten. 3 To make pleasant or gratifying. —**sweet'en·er** *n.*

sweet·en·ing (swēt'n·ing) *n.* 1 The act of making sweet. 2 That which sweetens.

sweet flag A marsh-dwelling plant with sword-shaped leaves and a fragrant rhizome.

sweet gum 1 A large North American tree with maple-like leaves and bark exuding a fragrant gum. 2 The balsam or gum yielded by it.

sweet·heart (swēt'härt') *n.* 1 Darling: a term of endearment. 2 A lover.

sweetheart contract An agreement made between an employer and union officials, the terms of which are disadvantageous to union members. Also **sweetheart agreement.**

sweet·meat (swēt'mēt') *n. Usu. pl.* A highly sweetened food, as candy, cake, candied fruit, etc.

sweet pea A climbing leguminous plant cultivated for its fragrant, varicolored flowers.

sweet pepper A mild variety of capsicum used for pickling and as a vegetable.

sweet potato 1 A perennial tropical vine of the morning-glory family, with a fleshy tuberous root. 2 The sweet yellow or orange root, eaten as a vegetable.

sweet-talk (swēt'tôk') *Informal v.t.* 1 To persuade by coaxing or flattering. —*v.i.* 2 To flatter or coax someone. —**sweet talk**

sweet tooth *Informal* A fondness for candy or sweets.

sweet wil·liam (wil'yəm) A perennial species of pink with fragrant, closely clustered flowers. Also **sweet William.**

swell (swel) *v.* **swelled, swelled** or **swol·len, swell·ing** *v.i.* 1 To increase in size or volume, as by inflation with air or by absorption of moisture. 2 To increase in amount, degree, force, intensity, etc. 3 To rise above the usual or surrounding level, surface, etc. 4 To rise in waves or swells, as the sea. 5 To bulge. 6 *Informal* To become puffed up with pride. —*v.t.* 7 To cause to increase in size or volume. 8 To cause to increase in amount, degree, force, intensity, etc. 9 To cause to bulge. 10 To puff with pride. —*n.* 1 The act, process, or effect of swelling; expansion. 2 A long continuous wave without a crest. 3 A rise of, or undulation in, the land. 4 Any bulge or protuberance. 5 *Music* A crescendo and diminuendo in succession; also, the signs (< >) indicating it. 6 A device by which the loudness of an organ may be varied. 7 *Informal* A person who is very fashionable, elegant, or social. —*adj.* 1 *Informal* Very fashionable, elegant, or social. 2 *Slang* Very fine; first-rate; excellent. [< OE *swellan*] —**Syn.** *v.* 1 bulge, dilate, distend, enlarge, expand.

swell·ing (swel'ing) *n.* 1 The act or process by which a person or thing swells. 2 The condition of being swollen. 3 Something swollen, esp. an abnormal enlargement of a part of the body. —*adj.* That swells; increasing, bulging, puffing up, etc.

swel·ter (swel'tər) *v.i.* 1 To perspire or suffer from oppressive heat. —*v.t.* 2 To cause to swelter. —*n.* A sweltering condition; oppressive heat. [< OE *sweltan* die] **—swel′·ter·ing·ly** *adv.*

swept (swept) *p.t. & p.p.* of SWEEP.

swept·back (swept′bak′) *adj. Aeron.* Having the front edge (of a wing) tilted backward from the lateral axis, as an airplane.

swerve (swûrv) *v.t. & v.i.* **swerved, swerv·ing** To turn or cause to turn aside from a course; deflect. *—n.* The act of swerving; a sudden turning aside. [< OE *sweorfan* file or grind away]

swift[1] (swift) *adj.* **1** Moving with great speed; rapid; quick. **2** Capable of quick motion; fleet. **3** Happening, coming, finished, etc., in a brief time. **4** Quick to act or respond; prompt. *—adv.* In a swift manner. [< OE] **—swift′ly** *adv.* **—swift′ness** *n.*

swift[2] (swift) *n.* Any of various swallowlike birds with extraordinary powers of flight, as the chimney swift. [< SWIFT[1]]

Chimney swift

swig (swig) *n. Informal* A great gulp; deep draft. *—v.t. & v.i.* **swigged, swig·ging** *Informal* To take swigs (of). [?]

swill (swil) *v.t.* **1** To drink greedily or to excess. **2** To drench, as with water; rinse; wash. **3** To fill with, as drink. *—v.i.* **4** To drink greedily or to excess. *—n.* **1** Semiliquid food for domestic animals, as the mixture of edible refuse and liquid fed to pigs. **2** Garbage. **3** Unappetizing food. **4** A great gulp; swig. [< OE *swillan* to wash]

swim[1] (swim) *v.* **swam** (*Regional* **swum**), **swum, swim·ming** *v.i.* **1** To move through water by working the legs, arms, fins, etc. **2** To float. **3** To move with a smooth or flowing motion. **4** To be flooded. *—v.t.* **5** To cross or traverse by swimming. **6** To cause to swim. *—n.* **1** The action or pastime of swimming. **2** The distance swum or to be swum. **3** The air bladder of a fish: also **swim bladder, swimming bladder. —in the swim** Active in current affairs, esp. those involved with fashion, socializing, etc. [< OE *swimman*] **—swim′mer** *n.*

swim[2] (swim) **swam** (*Regional* **swum**), **swum, swim·ming** *v.i.* **1** To be dizzy. **2** To seem to go round; reel. [< OE *swima* dizziness]

swimming hole A deep hole or pool in a stream, used for swimming.

swim·ming·ly (swim′ing·lē) *adv.* Easily and successfully.

swim·suit (swim′so͞ot′) *n.* A garment designed to be worn while swimming.

swin·dle (swin′dəl) *v.* **·dled, ·dling** *v.t.* **1** To cheat; defraud. **2** To obtain by such means. *—v.i.* **3** To practice fraud. *—n.* The act or process of swindling. [< G *schwindeln* cheat] **—swin′dler** *n.* **—Syn.** *v.* **1** deceive, dupe, rook.

swine (swīn) *n. pl.* **swine 1** A pig or hog: usu. used collectively. **2** A low, greedy, or vicious person. [< OE *swīn*] **—swin′ish** *adj.* **—swin′ish·ly** *adv.* **—swin′ish·ness** *n.*

swine·herd (swīn′hûrd′) *n.* A tender of swine.

swing (swing) *v.* **swung, swing·ing** *v.i.* **1** To move to and fro or backward and forward rhythmically, as something suspended. **2** To ride in a swing. **3** To move with an even, swaying motion. **4** To turn; pivot: We *swung* around and went home. **5** To be suspended; hang. **6** *Informal* To be executed by hanging. **7** *Slang* To be very up-to-date and sophisticated, esp. in one's amusements and pleasures. **8** *Informal* To sing or play with or to have a compelling, usu. jazzlike rhythm. **9** *Slang* To be sexually promiscuous. *—v.t.* **10** To cause to move to and fro or backward and forward. **11** To brandish; flourish: to *swing* an ax. **12** To cause to turn on or as on a pivot or central point. **13** To lift, hoist, or hang: They *swung* the mast into place. **14** *Informal* To bring to a successful conclusion: to *swing* a deal. **15** *Informal* To sing or play in the style of swing (*n.*, def. 8). *—n.* **1** The action process, or manner of swinging. **2** A free swaying motion. **3** A contrivance of hanging ropes with a seat on which a person may move to and fro through the air. **4** Freedom of action. **5** The arc or range of something that swings. **6** A swinging blow or stroke. **7** A trip or tour: a *swing* through the west. **8** A type of jazz music played by big bands, achieving its effect by lively, compelling rhythms, contrapuntal styles, and arranged ensemble playing: also **swing music. —in full swing** In full and lively operation. [< OE *swingan* scourge, beat up]

swinge (swinj) *v.t.* **swinged, swinge·ing** *Archaic* To flog; chastise. [< OE *swengan* shake, beat] **—swing′er** *n.*

swinge·ing (swin′jing) *adj. Chiefly Brit. Informal* Very large, good, or first-rate. [< SWINGE]

swing·er (swing′ər) *n. Slang* **1** A lively and up-to-date person. **2** A person who indulges freely in sex.

swing·ing (swing′ing) *adj. Slang* **1** Lively and compelling in effect: a *swinging* jazz quartet. **2** Modern; modish.

swin·gle (swing′gəl) *n.* A large, knifelike wooden implement for beating and cleaning flax: also **swing′knife.** *—v.t.* **·gled, ·gling** To cleanse, as flax, by beating with a swingle. [< MDu. *swinghel*]

swin·gle·tree (swing′gəl·trē′) *n.* WHIFFLETREE.

swing shift An evening work shift, usu. lasting from about 4 p.m. to midnight. **—swing shifter**

swipe (swīp) *v.* **swiped, swip·ing** *—v.t.* **1** *Informal* To strike with a sweeping motion. **2** *Slang* To steal; snatch. *—v.i.* **3** To hit with a sweeping motion. *—n. Informal* A hard blow. [Var. of SWEEP]

swirl (swûrl) *v.t. & v.i.* To move or cause to move along in irregular eddies; whirl. *—n.* **1** A whirling along, as in an eddy. **2** A curl or twist; spiral. [ME *swyrl*] **—swirl′y** *adj.*

swish (swish) *v.i.* **1** To move with a hissing or whistling sound. *—v.t.* **2** To cause to swish. *—n.* **1** A swishing sound. **2** A movement producing such a sound. [Imit.]

Swiss (swis) *n.* **1** A citizen or native of Switzerland. **2** The people of Switzerland collectively: used with *the.* *—adj.* Of or pertaining to Switzerland or its people.

Swiss chard Chard.

Swiss cheese A pale yellow cheese with many large holes, originally made in Switzerland.

Swiss steak A cut of steak floured and cooked, often with a sauce of tomatoes, onions, etc.

Swit., Switz., Swtz. Switzerland.

switch (swich) *n.* **1** A small flexible rod, twig, or whip. **2** A tress of false hair, worn by women in building a coiffure. **3** A mechanism for shifting a railway train from one track to another. **4** The act or operation of switching, shifting, or changing. **5** The tuft of hair at the end of the tail in certain animals, as a cow. **6** *Electr.* A device used to start or stop a flow of current. **7** A blow with or as with a switch. *—v.t.* **1** To whip or lash. **2** To move, jerk, or whisk suddenly or sharply. **3** To turn aside or divert; shift. **4** To exchange: They *switched* plates. **5** To shift, as a railroad car, to another track. **6** *Electr.* To connect or disconnect with a switch. *—v.i.* **7** To turn aside; change; shift. **8** To swing back and forth or from side to side. **9** To shift from one track to another. [?] **—switch′er** *n.*

switch·back (swich′bak′) *n.* **1** A zigzag road or railroad up a steep incline. **2** *Brit.* ROLLER COASTER.

switch·board (swich′bôrd′, -bōrd′) *n.* A panel bearing switches or controls for several electric circuits, as a telephone exchange.

switch·man (swich′mən) *n. pl.* **·men** (-mən) One who handles switches, esp. on a railroad.

switch·yard (swich′yärd′) *n.* A railroad yard in which trains are stored, maintained, assembled, etc.

Swit·zer·land (swit′sər·lənd) *n.* A republic of CEN. Europe, 15,940 sq. mi., cap. Bern. • See map at ITALY.

swiv·el (swiv′əl) *n.* **1** A coupling or pivot that permits parts, as of a mechanism, to rotate independently. **2** Anything that turns on a pin or headed bolt. **3** A cannon that swings on a pivot: also **swivel gun.** *—v.* **·eled** or **·elled, ·el·ing** or **·el·ling** *v.t.* **1** To turn on or as on a swivel. **2** To provide with or secure by a swivel. *—v.i.* **3** To turn or swing on or as on a swivel. [< OE *swīfan* revolve]

swivel chair A chair whose seat turns freely on a swivel.

swob (swob) *n. & v.* **swobbed, swob·bing** SWAB.

swol·len (swō′lən) A *p.p.* of SWELL.

swoon (swo͞on) *v.i.* To faint. *—n.* A fainting fit. [< OE *swōgan* suffocate]

swoop (swōōp) *v.i.* 1 To drop or descend suddenly, as a bird pouncing on its prey. —*v.t.* 2 To take or seize suddenly; snatch. —*n.* The act of swooping. [< OE *swāpan* sweep]

swop (swop) *n.* & *v.* **swopped, swop·ping** SWAP.

sword (sôrd, sōrd) *n.* A weapon consisting of a long blade fixed in a hilt. —**at swords' points** Very unfriendly; hostile. —**cross swords** 1 To quarrel; argue. 2 To fight. —**put to the sword** To kill with a sword. —**the sword** 1 Military power. 2 War. [< OE *sweord*]

sword·fish (sôrd′fish′, sōrd′-) *n. pl.* **·fish** or **·fish·es** A large fish of the open sea having the upper jaw elongated into a swordlike process.

Swordfish

sword·grass (sôrd′gras′, -gräs′, sōrd′-) *n.* Any of several grasses or sedges with serrated or swordlike leaves.

sword·knot (sôrd′not′, sōrd′-) *n.* An ornamental tassel of leather, cord, etc., tied to a sword hilt.

sword play The act, technique, or skill of using a sword, esp. in fencing. —**sword′-play′er** *n.*

swords·man (sôrdz′mən, sōrdz′-) *n. pl.* **·men** (-mən) One skilled in the use of or armed with a sword, esp. a fencer. Also **sword′man.** —**swords′man·ship, sword′man·ship** *n.*

swore (swôr, swōr) *p.t.* of SWEAR.

sworn (swôrn, swōrn) *p.p.* of SWEAR.

swot (swot) *n.* & *v.* **swot·ted, swot·ting** SWAT.

swounds (zwoundz, zoundz) *interj.* ZOUNDS.

swum (swum) *p.p.* & *regional p.t.* of SWIM.

swung (swung) *p.t.* & *p.p.* of SWING.

syb·a·rite (sib′ə·rīt) *n.* A person devoted to luxury or sensuality; voluptuary. [< *Sybaris,* an ancient Greek city in southern Italy] —**syb·a·rit·ic** (sib′ə·rit′ik), **syb′a·rit′i·cal** *adj.* —**syb′a·rit′i·cal·ly** *adv.*

syc·a·more (sik′ə·môr, -mōr) *n.* 1 A medium-sized tree of Syria and Egypt allied to the fig. 2 Any of various plane trees widely distributed in North America. 3 An ornamental maple tree: also **sycamore maple.** [< Gk. *sykon* a fig + *moron* a mulberry]

syc·o·phant (sik′ə·fənt, -fant) *n.* A servile flatterer; toady. [< Gk. *sykon* fig + *phainein* to show] —**syc′o·phan·cy** (-sē) (*pl.* **·cies**) *n.* —**syc′o·phan′tic** (-fan′tik), **syc′o·phan′ti·cal** *adj.* —**syc′o·phan′ti·cal·ly** *adv.*

syl·la·bar·y (sil′ə·ber′ē) *n. pl.* **·bar·ies** A list of syllables; esp., a list of written characters representing syllables.

syl·lab·ic (si·lab′ik) *adj.* 1 Of, pertaining to, or consisting of syllables. 2 *Phonet.* Designating a consonant capable of forming a complete syllable, as *l* in *middle* (mid′l). 3 Having every syllable distinctly pronounced. Also **syl·lab′i·cal.** —*n. Phonet.* A syllabic sound. —**syl·lab′i·cal·ly** *adv.*

syl·lab·i·cate (si·lab′ə·kāt) *v.t.* **·cat·ed, ·cat·ing** SYLLABIFY. —**syl·lab′i·ca′tion** *n.*

syl·lab·i·fy (si·lab′ə·fī) *v.t.* **·fied, ·fy·ing** To form or divide into syllables. —**syl·lab′i·fi·ca′tion** *n.*

syl·la·ble (sil′ə·bəl) *n.* 1 *Phonet.* A word or part of a word uttered in a single vocal impulse. 2 A part of a written or printed word corresponding to the spoken division. 3 The least detail or mention: Please don't repeat a *syllable* of what you've heard here. —*v.* **·bled, ·bling** *v.t.* 1 To pronounce the syllables of. —*v.i.* 2 To pronounce syllables. [< Gk. *syn-* together + *lambanein* take]

syl·la·bus (sil′ə·bəs) *n. pl.* **·bus·es** or **·bi** (-bī) A concise statement or outline, esp. of a course of study. [< Gk. *sittyba* label on a book] —**Syn.** abstract, epitome, synopsis.

syl·lo·gism (sil′ə·jiz′əm) *n.* 1 *Logic* A form of reasoning consisting of three propositions. The first two propositions, called *premises,* have one term in common furnishing a relation between the two other terms, which are linked in the third, called the *conclusion.* Example: All men are mortal *(major premise);* kings are men *(minor premise);* therefore, kings are mortal *(conclusion).* 2 Reasoning that makes use of this form; deduction. [< Gk. *syn-* together + *logizesthai* infer] —**syl′lo·gis′tic, syl′lo·gis′ti·cal** *adj.* —**syl′lo·gis′ti·cal·ly** *adv.*

sylph (silf) *n.* 1 A being, mortal but without a soul, living in and on the air. 2 A slender, graceful young woman or girl. [< NL *sylphus*]

syl·van (sil′vən) *adj.* 1 Of, pertaining to, or located in a forest or woods. 2 Composed of or abounding in trees or woods. —*n.* A person or animal living in or frequenting forests or woods. [< L *silva* a wood]

sym. symbol; symmetrical; symphony.

sym·bi·o·sis (sim′bī·ō′sis, -bē-) *n.* An intimate and mutually advantageous partnership of dissimilar organisms, as of algae and fungi in lichens. [< Gk. *syn-* together + *bios* life] —**sym′bi·ot′ic** (-ot′ik) or **·i·cal** *adj.* —**sym′bi·ot′i·cal·ly** *adv.*

sym·bol (sim′bəl) *n.* 1 Something chosen to stand for or represent something else, as an object used to typify a quality, idea, etc.: The lily is a *symbol* of purity. 2 A character, mark, abbreviation, letter, etc., that represents something else. —*v.t.* **sym·boled** or **·bolled, sym·bol·ing** or **·bol·ling** SYMBOLIZE. [< Gk. *syn-* together + *ballein* throw]

sym·bol·ic (sim·bol′ik) *adj.* 1 Of, pertaining to, or expressed by a symbol. 2 Used as a symbol: with *of.* 3 Characterized by or involving the use of symbols or symbolism: *symbolic* poetry. Also **sym·bol′i·cal.** —**sym·bol′i·cal·ly** *adv.* —**sym·bol′i·cal·ness** *n.*

sym·bol·ism (sim′bəl·iz′əm) *n.* 1 The use of symbols to represent things; the act or art of investing things with a symbolic meaning. 2 A system of symbols or symbolical representation. 3 Symbolic meaning or character.

sym·bol·ist (sim′bəl·ist) *n.* One who uses symbols or symbolism, esp. an artist or writer skilled in the use of symbols.

sym·bol·is·tic (sim′bəl·is′tik) *adj.* Of or pertaining to symbolism or symbolists. —**sym′bol·is′ti·cal·ly** *adv.*

sym·bol·ize (sim′bəl·īz) *v.* **·ized, ·iz·ing** *v.t.* 1 To be a symbol of; represent symbolically; typify. 2 To represent by a symbol or symbols. 3 To treat as symbolic or figurative. —*v.i.* 4 To use symbols. *Brit. sp.* **sym′bol·ise.** —**sym′bol·i·za′tion, sym′bol·i·zer** *n.*

sym·me·try (sim′ə·trē) *n. pl.* **·tries** 1 Corresponding arrangement or balancing of the parts or elements of a whole in respect to size, shape, and position on opposite sides of an axis or center. 2 The element of beauty and harmony in nature or art that results from such arrangement and balancing. 3 *Math.* An arrangement of points in a system such that the system appears unchanged after certain partial rotations. [< Gk. *syn-* together + *metron* a measure] —**sym·met·ric** (si·met′rik), **sym·met′ri·cal** *adj.* —**sym·met′ri·cal·ly** *adv.* —**sym·met′ri·cal·ness** *n.*

sym·pa·thet·ic (sim′pə·thet′ik) *adj.* 1 Pertaining to, expressing, or proceeding from sympathy. 2 Having a compassionate feeling for others; sympathizing. 3 Being in accord or harmony; congenial. 4 Of, proceeding from, or characterized by empathy. 5 Referring to sounds produced by responsive vibrations. Also **sym′pa·thet′i·cal.** —**sym′pa·thet′i·cal·ly** *adv.*

sympathetic nervous system The part of the autonomic nervous system that controls such involuntary actions as the dilation of pupils, constriction of blood vessels and salivary glands, and increase of heartbeat.

sym·pa·thize (sim′pə·thīz) *v.i.* **·thized, ·thiz·ing** 1 To experience or understand the sentiments or ideas of another. 2 To feel or express compassion, as for another's sorrow or affliction: with *with.* 3 To be in harmony or agreement. *Brit. sp.* **sym′pa·thise.** —**sym′pa·thiz′er** *n.* —**sym′pa·thiz′ing·ly** *adv.*

sym·pa·thy (sim′pə·thē) *n. pl.* **·thies** 1 The fact or condition of an agreement in feeling: The *sympathy* between husband and wife was remarkable. 2 A feeling of compassion for another's sufferings. 3 Agreement or accord: to be in *sympathy* with an objective. 4 Support; loyalty; approval: trying to enlist my *sympathies.* [< Gk. *syn-* together + *pathos* a feeling, passion] —**Syn.** 1 affinity, concord. 2 commiseration, condolence, pity.

sympathy strike A strike in which the strikers support the demands of another group of workers. Also **sympathetic strike.**

sym·pho·ny (sim′fə·nē) *n. pl.* **·nies** 1 A harmonious or agreeable mingling of sounds. 2 Any harmony or agreeable blending, as of color. 3 A composition for orchestra, consisting usu. of four extensive movements. 4 SYMPHONY ORCHESTRA. [< Gk. *syn-* together + *phōnē* a sound] —**sym·phon·ic** (sim·fon′ik) *adj.* —**sym·phon′i·cal·ly** *adv.*

symphony orchestra A large orchestra composed usu. of string, brass, woodwind, and percussion instruments.

sym·po·si·um (sim·pō′zē·əm) *n. pl.* **·si·ums, ·si·a** (-zē·ə) **1** A meeting for discussion of a particular subject or subjects. **2** A collection of comments, opinions, essays, etc. on the same subject. [< Gk. *syn-* together + *posis* drinking] —**sym·po′si·ac** (-ak) *adj.*

symp·tom (simp′təm) *n.* **1** An organic or functional condition indicating the presence of disease, esp. when regarded as an aid in diagnosis. **2** A sign or indication that serves to point out the existence of something else: *symptoms* of civil unrest. [< Gk. *syn-* together + *piptein* fall] —**symp′to·mat′ic** (-tə·mat′ik), **symp′to·mat′i·cal** *adj.* —**symp′to·mat′i·cal·ly** *adv.* —**Syn. 2** earmark, mark, signal, token.

syn- *prefix* With; together; associated; at the same time: *syncarp.* [< Gk. *syn* together]

syn. synchronize; synonym; synonymous; synonymy.

syn·a·gogue (sin′ə·gôg, -gog) *n.* **1** A place of meeting for Jewish worship and religious instruction. **2** A Jewish congregation or assemblage for religious instruction and observances. Also **syn′a·gog.** [< Gk. *synagōgē* an assembly]

syn·apse (sin′aps′, sə·naps′) *n.* The junction point of two neurons, across which a nerve impulse passes. Also **syn·ap·sis** (sə·nap′səs) *pl.* **·ap·ses** (-sēz). [< Gk. *syn-* together + *hapsis* a joining] —**syn·ap·tic** (-nap′tik) *adj.*

sync (singk) *n. & v.* **synced, sync·ing** SYNCH.

syn·carp (sin′kärp) *n.* A multiple or fleshy aggregate fruit, as the blackberry. [< Gk. *syn-* together + *karpos* a fruit] —**syn·car·pous** (sin·kär′pəs) *adj.*

Syncarp (blackberry)

synch (singk) *Slang v.i. & v.t.* **synched, synch·ing** To synchronize or cause to be synchronized. —*n.* Synchronization: usu. in phrases **in synch** and **out of synch.** [< SYNCHRONIZATION]

syn·chro·mesh (sing′kro·mesh′, sin′-) *n. Mech.* **1** A gear system in which parts are synchronized before engagement. **2** The synchronizing mechanism thus used.

syn·chro·nism (sing′krə·niz′əm, sin′-) *n.* **1** The state of being synchronous; concurrence. **2** A grouping of historic personages or events according to their dates. —**syn′chro·nis′tic, syn′chro·nis′ti·cal** *adj.* —**syn′chro·nis′ti·cal·ly** *adv.*

syn·chro·ni·za·tion (sing′·krə·nə·zā′shən) *n.* **1** The state of being synchronous. **2** The act of synchronizing, or the state of being synchronized.

syn·chro·nize (sing′krə·nīz, sin′-) *v.* **·nized, ·niz·ing** *v.i.* **1** To occur at the same time; coincide. **2** To move or operate in unison. —*v.t.* **3** To cause to operate synchronously: to *synchronize* watches. **4** To cause (the appropriate sound of a motion picture) to coincide with the action. **5** To assign the same date or period to; make contemporaneous. [< SYNCHRONOUS] —**syn′chro·niz′er** *n.*

syn·chro·nous (sing′krə·nəs, sin′-) *adj.* **1** Occurring at the same time; concurrent; simultaneous. **2** *Physics* Having the same period or frequency. **3** *Electr.* Normally operating at a speed proportional to the frequency of the current in the power line, as a motor. Also **syn′chro·nal.** [< Gk. *syn-* together + *chronos* time] —**syn′chro·nous·ly** *adv.* —**syn′chro·nous·ness** *n.*

syn·cline (sin′klīn) *n. Geol.* A trough or fold of stratified rock in which the layers dip downward on each side toward the axis of the fold. [< Gk. *syn-* together + *klinein* to incline] —**syn·cli′nal** (sin·klī′nəl) *adj.*

syn·co·pate (sing′kə·pāt, sin′-) *v.t.* **·pat·ed, ·pat·ing 1** To contract, as a word, by syncope. **2** *Music* To treat or modify (a rhythm, melody, etc.) by syncopation. [< LL *syncope* syncope]

syn·co·pa·tion (sing′kə·pā′shən, sin′-) *n.* **1** The act of syncopating or state of being syncopated; also, that which is syncopated. **2** *Music* The suppression of an expected rhythmic accent by the continuation of an unaccented tone that begins just before it. **3** Any music featuring syncopation, as ragtime, jazz, etc. **4** Syncope of a word, or an example of it.

syn·co·pe (sing′kə·pē, sin′-) *n.* **1** The elision of a sound or syllable in the middle part of a word, as *e'er* for *ever.* **2** *Music* Syncopation. **3** Temporary loss of consciousness; fainting. [< Gk. *syn-* together + *koptein* to cut] —**syn′co·pal, syn·cop·ic** (sin·kop′ik) *adj.*

syn·cre·tize (sin′krə·tīz, sing′-) *v.t.* **·tized, ·tiz·ing** To attempt to blend and reconcile. [< Gk. *synkrētizein* combine] —**syn′cre·tism** *n.*

syn·dic (sin′dik) *n.* **1** The business agent of a university or other corporation. **2** A government official, as a civil magistrate, with varying powers in different countries. [< Gk. *syn-* together + *dikē* judgment] —**syn′di·cal** *adj.*

syn·di·cal·ism (sin′di·kəl·iz′əm) *n.* A social and political theory proposing the taking over of the means of production by federations of labor unions through the staging of general strikes, etc. [< F *(chambre) syndicale* a labor union] —**syn′di·cal·ist** *n.* —**syn′di·cal·is′tic** *adj.*

syn·di·cate (sin′də·kit) *n.* **1** An association of individuals united to negotiate some business or to engage in some enterprise, often one requiring large capital. **2** An association for purchasing feature articles, etc., and selling them again to a number of periodicals, as newspapers, for simultaneous publication. **3** The office or jurisdiction of a syndic; also, a body of syndics. —*v.t.* (-kāt) **·cat·ed, ·cat·ing 1** To combine into or manage by a syndicate. **2** To sell for publication in many newspapers or magazines. [< F *syndic* syndic] —**syn′di·ca′tion, syn′di·ca′tor** *n.*

syn·drome (sin′drōm) *n.* **1** The aggregate of symptoms and signs characteristic of a specific disease or condition. **2** A group of traits regarded as being characteristic of a certain type, condition, etc. [< Gk. *syn-* together + *dramein* run] —**syn·drom·ic** (sin·drom′ik) *adj.*

sy·nec·do·che (si·nek′də·kē) *n.* A figure of speech in which a part stands for a whole or a whole for a part, a material for the thing made of it, etc., as *bronze* for a *statue.* [< Gk. *syn-* together + *ekdechesthai* take from]

syn·er·gism (sin′ər·jiz′əm) *n.* The mutually reinforcing action of separate substances, organs, agents, etc., which together produce an effect greater than that of all of the components acting separately. Also **syn′er·gy.** [< Gk. *synergos* working together] —**syn′er·gis′tic** or **·ti·cal** *adj.*

syn·fu·el (sin′fyōō′əl) *n.* Synthetic fuel.

syn·od (sin′əd, -od) *n.* **1** An ecclesiastical council. **2** Any assembly, council, etc. [< Gk. < *syn-* together + *hodos* a way]

sy·nod·i·cal (si·nod′i·kəl) *adj.* **1** Of, pertaining to, or of the nature of a synod; transacted in a synod. **2** *Astron.* Pertaining to the conjunction of two celestial bodies or to the interval between two successive conjunctions of the same celestial bodies. Also **syn·od·al** (sin′ə·dəl, si·nod′əl), **sy·nod′ic.** —**sy·nod′i·cal·ly** *adv.*

syn·o·nym (sin′ə·nim) *n.* **1** A word having the same or almost the same meaning as some other or others in the same language. **2** A word used in metonymy to substitute for another. [< Gk. *syn-* together + *onyma* a name] —**syn′o·nym′ic, syn′o·nym′i·cal** *adj.* —**syn′o·nym′i·ty** *n.*

sy·non·y·mous (si·non′ə·məs) *adj.* Being equivalent or similar to meaning. —**sy·non′y·mous·ly** *adv.*

sy·non·y·my (si·non′ə·mē) *n. pl.* **·mies 1** The quality of being synonymous. **2** The study of synonyms. **3** The discrimination of synonyms. **2** A list or collection discriminating the meanings of synonyms or of allied terms.

sy·nop·sis (si·nop′sis) *n. pl.* **·ses** (-sēz) A general view or condensation, as of a story, book, etc.; summary. [< Gk. *syn-* together + *opsis* a view] —**Syn.** abridgment, abstract, digest, précis.

sy·nop·tic (si·nop′tik) *adj.* **1** Giving a general view. **2** Presenting the same or a similar point of view: said of the first three Gospels **(Synoptic Gospels).** Also **sy·nop′ti·cal.** —**sy·nop′ti·cal·ly** *adv.*

sy·no·vi·a (si·nō′vē·ə) *n.* The viscid, transparent, lubricating fluid secreted by a membrane in the interior of joints. [< Gk. *syn-* together + L *ovum* an egg] —**sy·no′vi·al** *adj.*

syn·tax (sin′taks) *n.* 1 The arrangement and interrelationship of words in grammatical constructions. 2 The branch of grammar which deals with this. [< Gk. *syn-* together + *tassein* arrange] —**syn·tac·tic** (sin·tak′tik), **syn·tac′ti·cal** *adj.* —**syn·tac′ti·cal·ly** *adv.*

syn·the·sis (sin′thə·sis) *n. pl.* **·ses** (-sēz) 1 The assembling of separate or subordinate parts into a new form. 2 The complex whole resulting from this. 3 *Chem.* The building up of a compound by the direct union of its elements or of simpler compounds. [< Gk. *syn-* together + *tithenai* to place] —**syn′the·sist** *n.*

syn·the·size (sin′thə·sīz) *v.t.* **·sized, ·siz·ing** 1 To unite or produce by synthesis. 2 To apply synthesis to. *Brit. sp.* **syn′the·sise.**

syn·the·siz·er (sin′thə·sīz′ər) *n.* Any of various complex electronic devices by which a musician can create and manipulate a wide variety of tones.

syn·thet·ic (sin·thet′ik) *adj.* 1 Of, pertaining to, or using synthesis. 2 Produced artificially by chemical synthesis. 3 Artificial; spurious. Also **syn·thet′i·cal.** —*n.* Anything produced by synthesis, esp. by chemical synthesis, as a material. [< Gk. *syn-* together + *tithenai* to place] —**syn·thet′i·cal·ly** *adv.*

syph·i·lis (sif′ə·lis) *n.* An infectious, chronic, venereal disease caused by a spirochete transmissible by direct contact or congenitally. [< *Syphilus,* a shepherd in a 16th-century Latin poem who had the disease] —**syph·i·lit·ic** (sif′ə·lit′ik) *adj., n.*

syphon (sī′fən) *n. & v.* SIPHON.

Syr. Syria; Syriac; Syrian.

syr. syrup (pharmacy).

Syr·i·a (sir′ē·ə) *n.* A republic of sw Asia, 72,234 sq. mi., cap. Damascus. • See map at JORDAN.

Syr·i·ac (sir′ē·ak) *n.* The language of the ancient Syrians, a dialect of Aramaic.

Syr·i·an (sir′ē·ən) *adj.* Of or pertaining to Syria, its people, or their language. —*n.* 1 A citizen or native of Syria. 2 The Arabic dialect spoken in modern Syria.

sy·rin·ga (si·ring′gə) *n.* 1 LILAC (defs. 1 and 2) 2 MOCK ORANGE. [< Gk. *syrinx* a pipe]

syr·inge (si·rinj′, sir′inj) *n.* 1 An instrument used to remove fluids from or inject fluids into body cavities. 2 HYPODERMIC SYRINGE. —*v.t.* **·inged, ·ing·ing** To spray, cleanse, inject, etc. with a syringe. [< Gk. *syrinx* a pipe]

syr·inx (sir′ingks) *n. pl.* **sy·rin·ges** (sə·rin′jēz), **syr·inx·es** 1 A modification of the windpipe in songbirds serving as the vocal organ. 2 *pl.* PANPIPES. [Gk., a pipe] —**sy·rin·ge·al** (si·rin′jē·əl) *adj.*

syr·up (sir′əp) *n.* A thick, sweet liquid, as the boiled juice of fruits, sugar cane, etc. [< OF sirop < Turkish *sharbat* sherbet] —**syr′up·y** *adj.*

syst. system; systematic.

sys·tem (sis′təm) *n.* 1 A group or arrangement of parts, facts, phenomena, etc., that relate to or interact with each other in such a way as to form a whole: the solar *system;* the nervous *system.* 2 Any orderly group of logically related facts, principles, beliefs, etc.: the democratic *system.* 3 An orderly method, plan, or procedure: a betting *system* that really works. 4 A method of classification, organization, arrangement, etc.: books classified according to the Dewey decimal *system.* 5 The body, considered as a functional whole. —**the system** The dominant political, economic, and social institutions and their leaders, regarded as resistant to change or to effective influence. [< Gk. *systēma* an organized whole]

sys·tem·at·ic (sis′tə·mat′ik) *adj.* 1 Of, pertaining to, or characterized by system or classification. 2 Acting by or carried out with system or method; methodical. 3 Forming or based on a system. Also **sys′tem·at′i·cal.** —**sys′tem·at′i·cal·ly** *adv.* —**Syn.** 2 orderly, organized, procedural, routine. 3 organizational, bureaucratic.

sys·tem·a·tize (sis′tə·mə·tīz′) *v.t.* **·tized, ·tiz·ing** To make into a system; organize methodically. Also **sys′tem·ize.** *Brit. sp.* **sys′tem·a·tise′.** —**sys′tem·a·ti·za′tion, sys′tem·i·za′tion** *n.* —**sys′tem·a·tiz′er, sys′tem·iz′er** *n.*

sys·tem·ic (sis·tem′ik) *adj.* 1 Of or pertaining to a system; systematic. 2 Pertaining to or affecting the body as a whole: a *systemic* poison. —**sys·tem′i·cal·ly** *adv.*

systems analysis The technique of reducing complex processes, as of industry, government, research, etc., to basic operations that can be treated quantitatively and reordered into sequences amenable to control.

sys·to·le (sis′tə·lē) *n.* 1 The rhythmic contraction of the heart, esp. of the ventricles, that impels the blood outward. 2 The shortening of a syllable that is naturally or by position long. [< Gk. *syn-* together + *stellein* send] —**sys·tol·ic** (sis·tol′ik) *adj.*

T

T, t (tē) *n. pl.* **T's, t's** or **Ts, ts, tees** (tēz) 1 The 20th letter of the English alphabet. 2 Any spoken sound representing the letter *T* or *t.* 3 Something shaped like a T. —**to a T** Precisely; perfectly. —*adj.* Shaped like a T.

't Contraction of IT: used initially, as in *'tis,* and finally, as in *on't.*

-t Inflectional ending used to indicate past participles and past tenses, as in *bereft, lost, spent:* equivalent to *-ed.*

T Technician; temperature (absolute); tension (surface); time (of firing or launching).

T. tablespoon (s); Testament; Tuesday.

t. in the time of (L *tempore*); teaspoon(s); time; ton(s); transitive; troy.

Ta tantalum.

tab[1] (tab) *n.* A flap, strip, tongue, or projection of something, as a garment, file card, etc. —*v.t.* **tabbed, tab·bing** To provide with a tab or tabs. [?]

tab[2] (tab) *n. Informal* 1 A check or bill; also, the total cost of something. 2 Close watch: to keep *tabs* on someone's activities. [? Short for TABULATION]

tab. table(s); tablet(s).

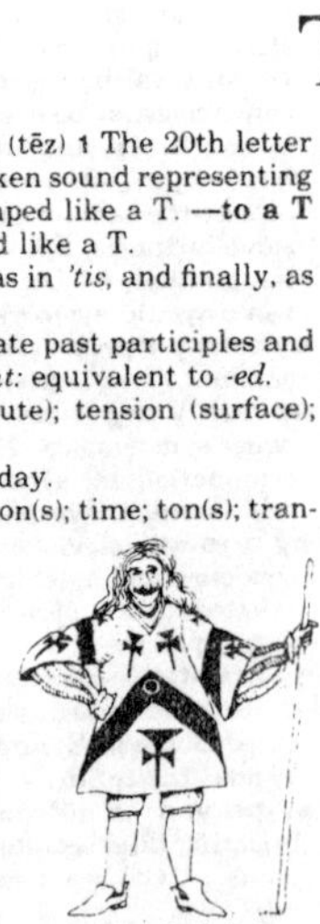

Tabard *def. 3*

tab·ard (tab′ərd) *n.* 1 Formerly, a short, sleeveless or short-sleeved outer garment. 2 A knight's cape or cloak, worn over his armor and emblazoned with his own arms. 3 A similar garment worn by a herald and embroidered with his lord's arms. [< OF]

Ta·bas·co (tə·bas′kō) *n.* A pungent sauce made from capsicum: a trade name.

tab·by (tab′ē) *n. pl.* **·bies** 1 A silk taffeta, esp. one that is striped or watered. 2 A brown or gray domestic cat with dark stripes. 3 Any domestic cat, esp. a female. 4 A gossiping woman. —*adj.* 1 Of, pertaining to, or made of tabby. 2 Brindled. [< *Attabi,* a quarter of Baghdad where it was manufactured]

tab·er·nac·le (tab′ər·nak′əl) *n.* 1 A tent or similar temporary structure. 2 *Usu. cap.* In the Old Testament, the portable sanctuary used by the Israelites in the wilderness. 3 *Usu. cap.* The Jewish temple. 4 Any house of worship, esp. one of large size. 5 The human body as the dwelling place of the soul. 6 The ornamental receptacle for the consecrated eucharistic elements. [< L *taberna* shed] —**tab·er·nac·u·lar** (tab′ər·nak′yə·lər) *adj.*

ta·ble (tā′bəl) *n.* 1 An article of furniture with a flat top, usu. fixed on legs. 2 Such a table on which food is set for a meal. 3 The food served at a meal. 4 The persons present at a meal. 5 A gaming table, as for roulette. 6 A collection of related numbers, values, signs, or items of any kind, arranged for ease of reference or comparison, often in parallel columns. 7 A compact listing: *table* of contents. 8 A tableland; plateau. 9 Any flat horizontal rock, surface, etc. **10** A tablet or slab bearing an inscription. **—the Tables** Laws inscribed on tablets, as the Ten Commandments. **—turn the tables** To reverse a situation. *—v.t.* **·bled, ·bling 1** To place on a table. **2** To postpone discussion of (a resolution, bill, etc.). [< L *tabula* board]

tab·leau (tab′lō, ta·blō′) *n. pl.* **·leaux** (-lōz) or **·leaus** (-lōz) **1** Any picture or picturesque representation. **2** A scene reminiscent of a picture, usu. presented by persons motionless on a stage. [F, lit., small table]

ta·ble·cloth (tā′bəl·klôth′, -kloth′) *n.* A cloth covering for a table.

tab·le d'hôte (tab′əl dōt′, tä′bəl) *pl.* **tab·les d'hote** (tab′·əlz dōt′, tä′bəlz) A complete meal of several specified courses, served in a restaurant at a fixed price. [F, lit., table of the host]

ta·ble·land (tā′bəl·land′) *n.* A broad, level, elevated region; a plateau.

ta·ble·spoon (tā′bəl·spōōn′, -spōōn′) *n.* **1** A measuring spoon with three times the capacity of a teaspoon. **2** A tablespoonful.

ta·ble·spoon·ful (tā′bəl·spōōn·fōōl′, -spōōn-) *n. pl.* **·fuls** The amount a tablespoon will hold; ½ fluid ounce.

tab·let (tab′lit) *n.* **1** A small, flat or nearly flat piece of some prepared substance, as a drug. **2** A pad, as of writing paper or note paper. **3** A small flat surface designed for or containing an inscription or design. **4** A thin leaf or sheet of ivory, wood, etc., for writing, painting, or drawing. **5** A set of such leaves joined together at one end. [< OF *tablete,* lit., small table]

table tennis A game resembling tennis in miniature, played indoors with a small celluloid ball and wooden paddles on a large table.

ta·ble·ware (tā′bəl·wâr′) *n.* Dishes, knives, forks, spoons, etc., used to set a table.

tab·loid (tab′loid) *n.* A newspaper, usu. one half the size of an ordinary newspaper, in which the news is presented concisely, often sensationally, and with many pictures. —*adj.* Compact; concise. [< TABL(ET) + -OID]

ta·boo (tə·bōō′, ta-) *n. pl.* **·boos 1** A religious or social prohibition against touching or mentioning someone or something or doing something because such persons or things are considered sacred, dangerous, etc. **2** The practice of such prohibitions. **3** Any restriction or ban based on custom or convention. —*adj.* Restricted, prohibited, or excluded by taboo, custom, or convention. —*v.t.* **1** To place under taboo. **2** To avoid as taboo. Also **ta·bu′.** [< Tongan]

ta·bor (tā′bər) *n.* A small drum on which a fife player beats his own accompaniment. Also **ta′bour.** [< Pers. *tabīrah* drum]

tab·o·ret (tab′ə·ret′, -rā′) *n.* **1** A small tabor. **2** A stool or small seat, usu. without arms or back. **3** A small table or stand. **4** An embroidery frame. Also **tab′ou·ret.**

tab·u·lar (tab′yə·lər) *adj.* **1** Of, pertaining to, rranged in a table or list. **2** Computed from or with a matnematical table. **3** Having a flat surface. **—tab′u·lar·ly** *adv.*

tab·u·late (tab′yə·lāt) *v.t.* **·lat·ed, ·lat·ing** To arrange in a table or list. —*adj.* Having a flat surface or surfaces; broad and flat. **—tab′u·la′tion, tab′u·la′tor** *n.*

tac·a·ma·hac (tak′ə·mə·hak′) *n.* **1** A resinous substance with a strong odor, used in ointments and incense. **2** Any of the trees producing this substance. Also **tac′a·ma·hac′a** (-hak′ə), **tac′ma·hack′.** [< Nahuatl *tecomahca*]

ta·chom·e·ter (tə·kom′ə·tər) *n.* A device for indicating the speed of rotation of an engine, centrifuge, etc. [< Gk. *tachos* speed + -METER]

tach·y·car·di·a (tak′i·kär′dē·ə) *n.* Abnormal rapidity of the heartbeat. [< Gk. *tachys* swift + *kardia* heart]

tac·it (tas′it) *adj.* **1** Existing, inferred, or implied without being directly stated. **2** Not spoken; silent. **3** Emitting no sound. [< L *tacitus,* pp. of *tacere* be silent] **—tac′it·ly** *adv.*

tac·i·turn (tas′ə·tûrn) *adj.* Habitually silent or reserved. [< L *tacitus.* See TACIT.] **—tac·i·tur·ni·ty** (tas′ə·tûr′nə·tē) *n.* **—tac′i·turn·ly** *adv.* **—Syn.** uncommunicative, reticent.

tack (tak) *n.* **1** A small sharp-pointed nail, usu. with a relatively broad, flat head. **2** *Naut.* **a** A rope which holds down the lower outer corner of some sails. **b** The corner so held. **c** The direction in which a vessel sails when sailing closehauled, considered in relation to the position of its sails. **d** A change in a ship's direction made by a change in the position of its sails. **3** A policy or course of action. **4** A temporary fastening, as any of various stitches in sewing. —*v.t.* **1** To fasten or attach with tacks. **2** To secure temporarily, as with long stitches. **3** To attach as supplementary; append. **4** *Naut.* **a** To change the course of (a vessel) by turning into the wind. **b** To navigate (a vessel) to windward by making a series of tacks. —*v.i.* **5** *Naut.* **a** To tack a vessel. **b** To sail to windward by a series of tacks. **6** To change one's course of action. **7** ZIGZAG. [< OF *tache* a nail] **—tack′er** *n.*

tack·le (tak′əl) *n.* **1** A rope and pulley or combination of ropes and pulleys, used for hoisting or moving objects. **2** The rigging of a ship. **3** The equipment used in any work or sport; gear. **4** The act of tackling. **5** In football, either of two linemen stationed between the guard and end. —*v.t.* **·led, ·ling 1** To fasten with or as if with tackle. **2** To harness (a horse). **3** To undertake to master, accomplish, or solve: *tackle* a problem. **4** To seize suddenly and forcefully. **5** In football, to seize and stop (an opponent carrying the ball). [< MLG *taken* seize] **—tack′ler** *n.*

Tackles

tack·y[1] (tak′ē) *adj.* **tack·i·er, tack·i·est** Slightly sticky, as partly dried varnish. [< TACK, *v.*]

tack·y[2] (tak′ē) *adj.* **tack·i·er, tack·i·est 1** *Informal* Unfashionable; in bad taste. **2** Without good breeding; common. [?]

ta·co (tä′kō) *n. pl.* **·cos** A fried tortilla folded around any of several fillings, as chopped meat or cheese. [< Sp., wad]

tact (takt) *n.* **1** A quick or intuitive appreciation of what is fit, proper, or right; facility in saying or doing the proper thing. **2** A delicate sense of discrimination, esp. in aesthetics. [< L *tactus* sense of touch, pp. of *tangere* touch]

tact·ful (takt′fəl) *adj.* Having or showing tact. **—tact′ful·ly** *adv.* **—tact′ful·ness** *n.*

tac·ti·cal (tak′ti·kəl) *adj.* **1** Of or pertaining to tactics. **2** Showing adroitness in planning and maneuvering. **—tac′·ti·cal·ly** *adv.*

tac·ti·cian (tak·tish′ən) *n.* An expert in tactics.

tac·tics (tak′tiks) *n.pl.* **1** *(construed as sing.)* The science and art of handling troops in securing military and naval objectives. **2** Any adroit maneuvering to gain an end. [< Gk. *taktikos* suitable for arranging]

tac·tile (tak′təl, -tīl) *adj.* **1** Of, pertaining to, or having the sense of touch. **2** That may be touched; tangible. [< L *tactus.* See TACT.] **—tac·til·i·ty** (tak·til′ə·tē) *n.*

tact·less (takt′lis) *adj.* Showing or characterized by a lack of tact. **—tact′less·ly** *adv.* **—tact′less·ness** *n.*

tad·pole (tad′pōl) *n.* The aquatic larva of an amphibian, as a frog or toad, having gills and a tail. [< ME *tadde* toad + *pol* head, poll]

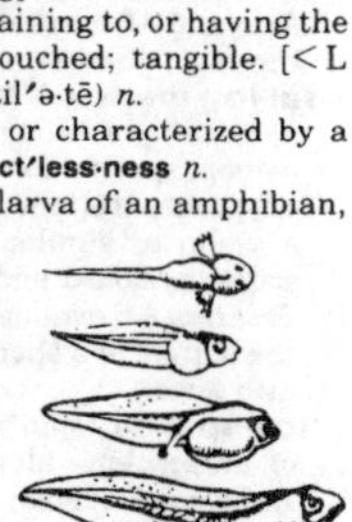

Development of a tadpole

tael (tāl) *n.* **1** Any of several units of weight of E Asia. **2** A Chinese monetary unit. [< Pg. < Malay *tahil*]

taf·fe·ta (taf′ə·tə) *n.* A fine, glossy, somewhat stiff fabric woven of silk, rayon, nylon, etc. —*adj.* Made of or resembling taffeta. [< Pers. *tāftah*]

taff·rail (taf′rāl′) *n.* The rail around a vessel's stern. [< MDu. *tafereel* panel, lit., small table]

taf·fy (taf′ē) *n. pl.* **taf·fies 1** A chewy confection made usu. of brown sugar or molasses, boiled down, and pulled until it cools. **2** *Informal* Flattery; blarney. [?]

tag[1] (tag) *n.* **1** Something attached to something else, to identify, price, classify, etc.; a label. **2** A loose, ragged edge, esp. of a piece of cloth. **3** The metal sheath at the end of a lace, cord etc. **4** The final lines of a speech, song, or poem. —*v.* **tagged, tag·ging** *v.t.* **1** To supply, adorn, fit, mark, or label with a tag. 2 *Informal* To follow closely or persistently. —*v.i.* 3 *Informal* To follow closely at one's heels: with *along, behind,* etc. [? <Scand.]

tag² (tag) *n.* A children's game in which a player, called "it," chases other players until he touches one of them, that person in turn becoming the one who must pursue another. —*v.t.* **tagged, tag·ging** To overtake and touch, as in the game of tag. [?]

Ta·ga·log (tə·gäl′əg, -gä′lôg) *n.* 1 A member of a people native to the Philippines. 2 The Austronesian language of this people, the official language of the Philippines.

tail¹ (tāl) *n.* 1 The rear end of an animal's body, esp. when prolonged to form a flexible appendage. 2 Anything similar in appearance, as a pigtail. 3 *Astron.* The luminous cloud extending from a comet. 4 The hind, back, or inferior portion of anything. 5 *Often pl. Informal* The reverse side of a coin. 6 A body of persons in single file. 7 A group of attendants; retinue. 8 *Aeron.* A system of airfoils placed some distance to the rear of the main bearing surfaces of an airplane. 9 *pl. Informal* A man's full-dress suit; also, a swallow-tailed coat. 10 *Informal* A person, as a detective, who follows another in surveillance. 11 *Informal* A trail or course, as one taken by a fugitive. —*v.t.* 1 To furnish with a tail. 2 To cut off the tail of. 3 To be the tail or end of. 4 To join (one thing) to the end of another. 5 To insert and fasten by one end. 6 *Informal* To follow secretly and stealthily; shadow. —*v.i.* 7 To form or be part of a tail. 8 *Informal* To follow close behind. 9 To diminish gradually: with *off.* —*adj.* 1 Rearmost; hindmost: the *tail* end. 2 Coming from behind: a *tail* wind. [<OE *tægl*]

tail² (tāl) *Law adj.* Restricted in some way, as to particular heirs: an estate *tail.* —*n.* A limiting of the inheritance of an estate, as to particular heirs. [<OF *taillié,* p.p. of *taillier* to cut]

tail·gate (tāl′gāt′) *n.* A hinged or removable board or gate closing the back end of a truck, wagon, etc. Also **tail·board** (tāl′bôrd′, -bōrd′). —*v.t.* & *v.i.* **·gat·ed, ·gat·ing** To drive too close for safety behind (another vehicle).

tail·light (tāl′līt′) *n.* A warning light, usu. red, attached to the rear of a vehicle. Also **tail lamp.**

tai·lor (tā′lər) *n.* One who makes or repairs garments. —*v.i.* 1 To do a tailor's work. —*v.t.* 2 To fit with garments. 3 To make, work at, or style by tailoring. 4 To form or adapt to meet certain needs or conditions. [<LL *taliare* split, cut] —**tai′lor·ing** *n.*

tai·lor·bird (tā′lər·bûrd′) *n.* Any of various small birds of Asia and Africa that stitch leaves together so as to conceal the nest. • See NEST.

tai·lor-made (tā′lər·mād′) *adj.* 1 Made by or looking as if made by a tailor. 2 Right or suitable for a particular person, specific conditions, etc.

tail·piece (tāl′pēs′) *n.* 1 Any endpiece or appendage. 2 In a violin or similar instrument, a piece of wood at the sounding-board end, having the strings fastened to it. 3 *Printing* An ornamental design at the end of a chapter or the bottom of a short page. 4 A short beam or rafter tailed into a wall.

tail·spin (tāl′spin′) *n.* 1 *Aeron.* The uncontrolled descent of an airplane along a helical path at a steep angle. 2 *Informal* A sudden, sharp, mental or emotional upheaval.

tail wind A wind blowing in the same direction as the course of an aircraft or ship.

taint (tānt) *v.t.* 1 To affect with decay or contamination. 2 To render morally corrupt. —*v.i.* 3 To be or become tainted. —*n.* A cause or result of contamination or corruption. [<OF *teint,* pp. of *teindre* to tinge, color]

take (tāk) *v.* **took, tak·en, tak·ing** *v.t.* 1 To lay hold of; grasp. 2 To get possession of; seize; capture; catch. 3 To gain, capture, or win, as in a game or in competition. 4 To choose; select. 5 To buy. 6 To rent or hire; lease. 7 To subscribe to, as a periodical. 8 To assume occupancy of: to *take* a chair. 9 To assume the responsibilities of: to *take* office. 10 To accept into some relation to oneself: He *took* a wife. 11 To assume as a symbol or badge: to *take* the veil. 12 To subject oneself to: to *take* a vow. 13 To remove or carry off: with *away.* 14 To steal. 15 To remove by death. 16 To subtract or deduct. 17 To be subjected to; undergo: to *take* a beating. 18 To submit to; accept passively: to *take* an insult. 19 To become affected with; contract: He *took* cold. 20 To affect: The fever *took* him at dawn. 21 To captivate; charm or delight: The dress *took* her fancy. 22 To react to: How did she *take* the news? 23 To undertake to deal with; contend with; handle: to *take* an examination. 24 To consider; deem: I *take* him for an honest man. 25 To understand; comprehend: I couldn't *take* the meaning of her remarks. 26 To hit: The blow *took* him on the forehead. 27 *Informal* To aim or direct: He *took* a shot at the target. 28 To carry with one: *Take* your umbrella! 29 To lead: This road *takes* you to town. 30 To escort. 31 To receive into the body, as by eating, inhaling, etc.: *Take* a deep breath. 32 To accept or assume as if due or granted: to *take* credit. 33 To require: it *takes* courage. 34 To let in; admit; accommodate: The car *takes* only six people. 35 To occupy oneself in; enjoy: to *take* a nap. 36 To perform, as an action: to *take* a stride. 37 To confront and get over: The horse *took* the hurdle. 38 To avail oneself of (an opportunity, etc.). 39 To put into effect; adopt: to *take* measures. 40 To use up or consume: The piano *takes* too much space. 41 To make use of; apply: to *take* pains. 42 To travel by means of: to *take* a train. 43 To seek: to *take* cover. 44 To ascertain by measuring, computing, etc.: to *take* a census. 45 To obtain or derive from some source. 46 To write down or copy: to *take* notes. 47 To obtain (a likeness or representation of) by photographing. 48 To conceive or feel: She *took* a dislike to him. 49 *Slang* To cheat; deceive. 50 *Gram.* To require by construction or usage: The verb *takes* a direct object. —*v.i.* 51 To get possession. 52 To engage; catch, as mechanical parts. 53 To begin to grow; germinate. 54 To have the intended effect: The vaccination *took.* 55 To gain favor, as a play. 56 To detract: with *from.* 57 To become (ill or sick). —**take after** 1 To resemble. 2 To follow in pursuit. —**take amiss** To be offended by. —**take back** To retract. —**take down** 1 To humble. 2 To write down. —**take for** To consider to be. —**take in** 1 To admit; receive. 2 To lessen in size or scope. 3 To include; embrace. 4 To understand. 5 To cheat or deceive. 6 To visit. —**take it** To endure hardship, abuse, etc. —**take off** 1 To mimic; burlesque. 2 To rise from a surface, esp. to begin a flight, as an airplane or rocket. 3 To leave; depart. 4 To begin: often used to refer to that point in an economic venture when growth becomes a self-generating and self-sustaining process. —**take on** 1 To hire; employ. 2 To undertake to deal with. 3 *Informal* To exhibit violent emotion. —**take over** To assume control of (a business, nation, etc.) —**take place** To happen. —**take to** 1 To become fond of. 2 *Informal* To adopt a way of doing, using, etc.: He has *taken* to walking to work. 3 To flee: to *take to* the hills. —**take up** 1 To make smaller or less; shorten or tighten. 2 To pay, as a note or mortgage. 3 To accept as stipulated: to *take up* an option. 4 To begin or begin again. 5 To occupy, engage, or consume, as space or time. 6 To develop an interest in or devotion to: to *take up* a cause. —**take up with** *Informal* To become friendly with; associate with. —*n.* 1 The act of taking or that which is taken. 2 *Slang* An amount of money received; receipts; profit. 3 A quantity collected at one time: the *take* of fish. 4 An uninterrupted run of the camera in photographing a movie or television scene. 5 A scene so photographed. 6 The process of making a sound recording. 7 A recording made in a single recording session. [<OE *tacan* <ON *taka*] —**tak′er** *n.* • See BRING.

take-home pay (tāk′hōm′) Net wages after tax and other deductions.

take·off (tāk′ôf′, -of′) *n.* 1 *Informal.* A satirical representation; caricature. 2 The act of taking off, as in flight. 3 The place from which one takes off. 4 A point at which something begins.

take·o·ver (tak′ō′vər) *n.* The act or an instance of taking over, esp. the assumption of power in a business, nation, etc.

tak·ing (tā′king) *adj.* Fascinating; captivating. —*n.* 1 The act of one who takes. 2 The thing or things taken; catch. 3 *pl.* Receipts, as of money. —**tak′ing·ly** *adv.* —**tak′ing·ness** *n.*

talc (talk) *n.* A soft mineral magnesium silicate, used in making talcum powder, lubricants, etc. —*v.t.* **talcked** or **talced, talck·ing** or **talc·ing** To treat with talc. [<Ar. *talq*]

tal·cum (tal′kəm) *n.* TALC.

talcum powder Finely powdered, purified, and usu. perfumed talc, used as a face and body powder.

tale (tāl) *n.* **1** A story that is told or written; a narrative of real or fictitious events. **2** An idle or malicious piece of gossip. **3** A lie. **4** *Archaic* A tally or amount; total. [< OE *talu* speech, narrative]

tale·bear·er (tāl′bâr′ər) *n.* One who gossips, spreads rumors, tells secrets, etc. **—tale′bear′ing** *adj., n.* **—Syn.** gossip, scandalmonger, newsmonger.

tal·ent (tal′ənt) *n.* **1** *pl.* A person's natural abilities. **2** A particular aptitude for some special work, artistic endeavor, etc. **3** A person, or people collectively with skill or ability. **4** Any of various ancient weights and denominations of money, used in ancient Greece, Rome, and the Middle East. [< L *talentum,* a sum of money] **—tal′ent·ed** *adj.*

ta·ler (tä′lər) *n.* A former German silver coin. [< G *Taler*]

tales·man (tālz′mən) *n. pl.* **·men** (-mən) One summoned to fill a vacancy in a jury when the regular panel has become deficient in number. [< ML *tales (de circumstantibus)* such (of the bystanders) + MAN]

tale·tel·ler (tāl′tel′ər) *n.* **1** RACONTEUR. **2** TALEBEARER. **—tale′tell′ing** *adj., n.*

ta·li (tā′lī) *n.pl.* of TALUS[1].

tal·i·pes (tal′ə·pēz) *n.* Congenital deformity of one or both feet. [< L *talus* ankle + *pes* foot]

tal·i·pot (tal′ə·pot) *n.* An East Indian palm crowned by large leaves often used as fans, umbrellas, etc. Also **talipot palm.** [< Skt. *tālī* fan palm + *pattra* leaf]

tal·is·man (tal′is·mən, -iz-) *n. pl.* **·mans 1** An object, as a ring or amulet, supposed to ward off evil, bring good luck, etc. **2** Anything supposed to have a magical effect. [< LGk. *telesma* a sacred rite] **—tal′is·man′ic** (·man′ik) *adj.*

talk (tôk) *v.i.* **1** To express or exchange thoughts in audible words; speak or converse. **2** To communicate by means other than speech: to *talk* with one's fingers. **3** To chatter. **4** To confer; consult. **5** To gossip. **6** To make sounds suggestive of speech. **7** *Informal* To give information; inform. —*v.t.* **8** To express in words; utter. **9** To converse in: to *talk* Spanish. **10** To discuss: to *talk* business. **11** To bring to a specified condition or state by talking: to *talk* one into doing something. **—talk back** To answer impudently. **—talk down** To silence by talking. **—talk down to** To speak to patronizingly. **—talk shop** To talk about one's work. —*n.* **1** The act of talking; conversation; speech. **2** A speech, either formal or informal. **3** Report; rumor: *talk* of war. **4** A subject of conversation. **5** A conference or discussion. **6** Mere words; empty conversation, discussion, etc. **7** A special kind of speech; lingo: baseball *talk.* **8** Sounds suggestive of speech, as made by a bird or animal. [Prob. < OE *talian* reckon, tell]

talk·a·thon (tô′kə·thon′) *n. Informal* A prolonged session of talking, debating, etc. [< TALK + (MAR)ATHON]

talk·a·tive (tô′kə·tiv) *adj.* Given to or fond of much talking. **—talk′a·tive·ly** *adv.* **—talk′a·tive·ness** *n.* **—Syn.** garrulous, loquacious, voluble, windy.

talk·ie (tô′kē) *n.* Formerly, a motion picture with a sound track, as distinguished from a silent film.

talk·ing-to (tô′king·tōō′) *n. pl.* **·tos** *Informal* A scolding.

tall (tôl) *adj.* **1** Having more than average height; high. **2** Having a specified height: five feet *tall.* **3** *Informal* Extravagant; boastful; exaggerated: a *tall* story. **4** Large; extensive: a *tall* order. —*adv. Informal* Proudly: to walk *tall.* [< OE *getæl* swift, prompt] **—tall′ish** *adj.* **—tall′ness** *n.*

tal·lith (tal′ith, tä′lis) *n. pl.* **tal·li·thim** (tal′ə·sēm′, -thēm) A fringed shawl worn by Jewish men during morning prayer. [< Heb. *tallīth* cover]

tal·low (tal′ō) *n.* Solid, rendered animal fats, as of beef or mutton, refined for making candles, soaps, etc. —*v.t.* To smear with tallow. [< MLG *talg, talch*] **—tal′low·y** *adj.*

tal·ly (tal′ē) *n. pl.* **·lies 1** A piece of wood on which notches or scores are cut as marks of number. **2** A score or mark. **3** A reckoning; account. **4** A counterpart; duplicate. **5** A mark indicative of number. **6** A label; tag. —*v.* **·lied, ·ly·ing** *v.t.* **1** To score on a tally; mark. **2** To reckon; count: often with *up.* **3** To register, as points in a game; score. **4** To cause to correspond. —*v.i.* **5** To make a tally. **6** To agree precisely: His story *tallies* with yours. **7** To keep score. **8** To score, as in a game. [< L *talea* rod, cutting] **—tal′li·er** *n.*

tal·ly·ho (tal′ə·hō′) *interj.* A huntsman's cry to hounds when the quarry is sighted. —*n.pl.* **·hos 1** The cry of "tallyho." **2** A kind of coach drawn by four horses. —*v.t.* **1** To urge on, as hounds, with the cry of "tallyho." —*v.i.* **2** To cry "tallyho." [? < F *taïaut,* a hunting cry]

Tal·mud (tal′mud, täl′mōōd) *n.* The written body of Jewish civil and religious law. [< Heb. *talmūdh* instruction] **—Tal·mud′ic** or **·i·cal** *adj.* **—Tal′mud·ist** *n.*

tal·on (tal′ən) *n.* **1** The claw of a bird or other animal, esp. a bird of prey. **2** A human finger or hand thought of as resembling a claw. [< L *talus* heel] **—tal′oned** *adj.*

ta·lus[1] (tā′ləs) *n. pl.* **·li** (-lī) or **·lus·es 1** The upper, pivotal bone of the ankle. **2** The entire ankle. [L, ankle]

ta·lus[2] (tā′ləs, tal′əs) *n.* **1** A slope, as of a tapering wall. **2** *Geol.* The sloping mass of rock fragments at the foot of a cliff. **3** The slope given to the face of a wall, as in a fortification. [F < L *talutium* slope bearing signs of the presence of gold]

tam (tam) *n.* TAM-O'-SHANTER.

ta·ma·le (tə·mä′lē) *n.* A Mexican dish made of ground meat seasoned with red pepper, rolled in cornmeal, wrapped in corn husks, and steamed. [< Nahuatl *tamalli*]

tam·a·rack (tam′ə·rak) *n.* **1** A species of larch common in N North America. **2** Its wood. [< Algon.]

tam·a·rind (tam′ə·rind) *n.* **1** A tropical tree of the bean family, with yellow flowers. **2** The edible fruit of this tree, a pod with acid pulp. [< Ar. *tamr hindi* Indian date]

tam·bour (tam′bōōr) *n.* **1** A drum. **2** A light wooden frame, usu. circular, esp. a set of two hoops between which fabric is stretched for embroidering. —*v.t. & v.i.* To embroider on a tambour. [< Ar. *tanbūr* drum]

tam·bou·rine (tam′bə·rēn′) *n.* A musical instrument like the head of a drum, with metal disks in the rim, played by striking it with the hand. [F, lit., small tambour]

tame (tām) *adj.* **tam·er, tam·est 1** Having lost its native wildness; domesticated. **2** Docile; tractable; subdued; submissive. **3** Lacking in spirit; uninteresting; dull. —*v.t.* **tamed, tam·ing 1** To make tame; domesticate. **2** To bring into subjection or obedience. **3** To tone down; soften. [< OE *tam*] **—tam′a·ble** or **tame′a·ble** *adj.* **—tame′ly** *adv.* **—tame′ness, tam′er** *n.*

tame·less (tām′lis) *adj.* Untamable or not tamed.

Tam·il (tam′əl) *n.* **1** A member of a Dravidian people of S India and N Sri Lanka. **2** Their language.

Tam·ma·ny (tam′ə·nē) *n.* A fraternal society in New York City (founded 1789) serving as the central organization of the city's Democratic party, located in **Tammany Hall.** [< *Tamanend,* a 17th c. Delaware Indian chief]

tam-o'-shan·ter (tam′ə·shan′tər) *n.* A Scottish cap with a round flat top, sometimes with a center pompon. [< the hero of a poem by Robert Burns]

tamp (tamp) *v.t.* **1** To force down or pack closer by repeated blows. **2** In blasting, to pack matter around a charge in order to increase the explosive effect. [Back formation < TAMPION] **—tam′per** *n.*

tam·per (tam′pər) *v.i.* **1** To meddle; interfere: usu. with *with.* **2** To make changes, esp. so as to damage, falsify, etc.: with *with.* **3** To use secret or improper measures, as bribery. [Var. of TEMPER] **—tam′per·er** *n.*

tam·pi·on (tam′pē·ən) *n.* A plug or cover for the muzzle of a gun. [< OF *tapon, tape* a bung]

tam·pon (tam′pon) *n.* A plug of absorbent material for insertion in a body cavity or wound to stop bleeding or absorb secretions. —*v.t.* To plug up, as a wound, with a tampon. [< OF *tapon, tape* a bung]

tan (tan) *v.* **tanned, tan·ning** *v.t.* **1** To convert into leather, as hides or skins, by treating with tannin. **2** To darken, as the skin, by exposure to sunlight. **3** *Informal.* To thrash; flog. —*v.i.* **4** To become tanned. —*n.* **1** TANBARK. **2** TANNIN. **3** A yellowish brown color tinged with red. **4** A dark coloring of the skin, resulting from exposure to the sun. —*adj.*

1 Of the color tan. 2 Of, pertaining to, or used for tanning. [< Med. L *tanum* tanbark]

tan tangent.

tan·a·ger (tan′ə·jər) *n.* Any of a family of American songbirds related to finches and noted for the brilliant plumage of the male. [< Pg. *tangara* < Tupi] **—tan′a·grine** (-grēn) *adj.*

tan·bark (tan′bärk′) *n.* 1 The bark of certain trees used as a source of tannin. 2 Shredded bark from which the tannin has been removed, used on circus rings, racetracks, etc.

tan·dem (tan′dəm) *adv.* One behind the other. —*n.* 1 A team, as of horses, harnessed one behind the other. 2 A two-wheeled carriage drawn in such a way. 3 A bicycle with two or more seats one behind the other. —*adj.* Having parts or things arranged one behind another. [L, at length (of time)]

Tandem bicycle

tang (tang) *n.* 1 A sharp, penetrating taste, flavor or odor. 2 Any distinctive quality or flavor. 3 A trace or hint. 4 A slender shank or tongue projecting from the end of a sword blade, chisel, etc., for fitting into a handle, hilt, etc. [< ON *tongi* a point] **—tang′y** *adj.* **(·i·er, ·i·est)**

tan·gent (tan′jənt) *adj.* 1 *Geom.* Coinciding at a point or along a line without intersection, as a curve and line, surface and plane, etc. 2 Touching; in contact. —*n.* 1 *Geom.* A line tangent to a curve at any point. 2 *Trig.* A function of an angle, equal to the quotient of its sine divided by its cosine. 3 A sharp change in course or direction. **—fly** (or **go**) **off on a tangent** *Informal* To make a sharp or sudden change, as in a course of action or train of thought. [< L *tangere* to touch] **—tan·gen·cy** (tan′jən·sē) *n.*

tan·gen·tial (tan·jen′shəl) *adj.* 1 Of, pertaining to, like, or in the direction of a tangent. 2 Touching slightly. 3 Divergent. **—tan·gen′ti·al′i·ty** (-shē·al′ə·tē) *n.* **—tan·gen′tial·ly** *adv.*

tan·ger·ine (tan′jə·rēn′, tan′jə·rēn′) *n.* 1 A variety of orange with a loose skin and easily separated segments. 2 A burnt orange color like that of the tangerine. [< *Tangier,* a city in Morocco]

tan·gi·ble (tan′jə·bəl) *adj.* 1 Perceptible by touch. 2 Not elusive or unreal; objective; concrete: *tangible* evidence. 3 Having value that can be appraised. —*n. pl.* Things having value that can be appraised. [< L *tangere* to touch] — **tan′gi·bil′i·ty, tan′gi·ble·ness** *n.* **—tan′gi·bly** *adv.*

tan·gle (tang′gəl) *v.* **·gled, ·gling** *v.t.* 1 To twist in a confused and not readily separable mass. 2 To ensnare as in a tangle; trap; enmesh. 3 To involve in such a way as to confuse, obstruct, etc. —*v.i.* 4 To be or become entangled. **—tangle with** *Informal* To become involved or fight with. —*n.* 1 A confused intertwining, as of threads or hairs; a snarl. 2 State of confusion or complication. 3 A state of bewilderment. [Prob. < Scand.] **—tan′gler** *n.*

tan·go (tang′gō) *n. pl.* **·gos** 1 A Latin American dance characterized by deliberate gliding steps and low dips. 2 The music for such a dance. —*v.i.* To dance the tango. [< Sp.]

tank (tangk) *n.* 1 A large vessel, basin, or receptacle for holding a fluid. 2 A natural or artificial pool or pond. 3 An armored combat vehicle that rides on treads and has mounted guns. 4 *Slang* A jail cell, esp. one for receiving prisoners. —*v.t.* To place or store in a tank. [? < Pg. *estanque*]

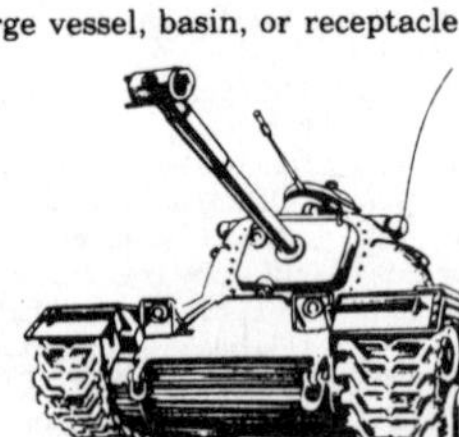

U.S. Army tank

tank·age (tangk′ij) *n.* 1 The act or process of storing in tanks. 2 The price for storage in tanks. 3 The capacity or contents of a tank. 4 Slaughterhouse waste from which the fat has been rendered in tanks, used, when dried, as fertilizer or feed.

tank·ard (tangk′ərd) *n.* A large, one-handled drinking cup, often with a cover. [ME]

tank·er (tangk′ər) *n.* 1 A cargo ship for the transport of oil or other liquids. 2 A cargo plane used to carry gasoline and to refuel other planes in flight.

tank farm An area where oil is stored in tanks.

tan·ner (tan′ər) *n.* One who tans hides.

tan·ner·y (tan′ər·ē) *n. pl.* **·ner·ies** A place where leather is tanned.

tan·nic (tan′ik) *adj.* Of, pertaining to, or derived from tannin or tanbark.

tan·nin (tan′in) *n.* A yellowish, astringent substance extracted from tanbark, gallnut, etc., used in dyeing, tanning, etc. Also **tannic acid.** [< F *tanin* < *tanner* to tan]

tan·sy (tan′zē) *n. pl.* **·sies** Any of a genus of coarse perennial herbs, esp. a species with yellow flowers and pungent foliage. [< Gk. *athanasia* immortality]

tan·ta·lize (tan′tə·līz′) *v.t.* **·lized, ·liz·ing** To tease or torment by promising or showing something desirable and then denying access to it. *Brit. sp.* **·lise′.** [< TANTALUS] — **tan′ta·li·za′tion, tan′ta·liz′er** *n.* **—tan′ta·liz′ing·ly** *adv.*

tan·ta·lum (tan′tə·ləm) *n.* A hard, corrosion-resistant metallic element (symbol Ta). [< TANTALUS, from its inability to react with most acids]

Tan·ta·lus (tan′tə·ləs) *Gk. Myth.* A king who was punished in Hades by being made to stand in water that receded when he tried to drink and under fruit-laden branches he could not reach.

tan·ta·mount (tan′tə·mount) *adj.* Equivalent: with *to.* [< L *tantus* as much + OF *amonter* to amount]

tan·trum (tan′trəm) *n.* A violent fit of temper. [?]

Tan·za·ni·a (tan′zə·nē′ə) *n.* A republic of the Commonwealth of Nations in E Africa, 362,800 sq. mi., cap. Dar es Salaam. **—Tan′za·ni′an** *adj., n.* • See map at AFRICA.

Tao·ism (dou′iz·əm, tou′-) *n.* One of the principal religions or philosophies of China, founded in the sixth century B.C. by Lao-tse. [< Chin. *tao* way] **—Tao′ist** *adj., n.* — **Tao·is′tic** *adj.*

tap[1] (tap) *n.* 1 A spout through which liquid is drawn, as from a cask. 2 FAUCET. 3 A plug or stopper to close an opening, as in a cask. 4 Liquor drawn from a tap, esp. of a particular quality or brew. 5 A tool for cutting internal screw threads. 6 A point of connection for an electrical circuit. 7 The act or an instance of wiretapping. **—on tap** 1 Contained in a cask; ready for tapping: beer *on tap.* 2 *Informal* Available; ready. —*v.t.* **tapped, tap·ping** 1 To provide with a tap or spigot. 2 To pierce or open so as to draw liquid from. 3 To draw (liquid) from a container, body cavity, etc. 4 To make connection with: to *tap* a gas main. 5 To draw upon; utilize: to *tap* new sources of energy. 6 To make connection with secretly: to *tap* a telephone wire. 7 To make an internal screw thread in with a tap. [< OE *tæppa*]

tap[2] (tap) *v.* **tapped, tap·ping** *v.t.* 1 To touch or strike gently. 2 To strike gently with. 3 To make or produce by tapping. 4 To apply a tap to (a shoe) —*v.i.* 5 To strike a light blow or blows, as with the finger tip. 6 To walk with a light, tapping sound. 7 TAP-DANCE. —*n.* 1 The act or sound of striking gently. 2 Leather, metal, etc., affixed to a shoe sole or heel, for repair or tap-dancing. 3 *pl.* A military signal sounded on a trumpet or drum for the extinguishing of all lights in soldiers' quarters. [< OF *taper*]

ta·pa (tä′pä) *n.* 1 The inner bark of an Asian tree related to the mulberry. 2 A cloth made of this bark: also **tapa cloth.** [< native Polynesian name]

tap-dance (tap′dans′, -däns′) *v.i.* **-danced, -danc·ing** To dance a tap dance. **—tap′-danc′er** *n.*

tap dance A dance in which the dancer taps out a rhythm with the heels and toes of shoes.

tape (tāp) *n.* 1 A narrow strip of woven fabric. 2 Any long, narrow, flat strip of paper, metal, plastic, etc., as the magnetic strip used in a tape recorder. 3 TAPE MEASURE. 4 A string stretched across the finishing point of a racetrack and broken by the winner of the race. —*v.t.* **taped, tap·ing** 1 To wrap or secure with tape. 2 To measure with a tape measure. 3 To record on magnetic tape. [< OE *tæppe* strip of cloth] —**tap'er** *n.*

tape deck An assembly of magnetic head, tape reels, and drive for tape recording and playback.

tape measure A tape marked in inches, feet, etc., for measuring. Also **tape·line** (tāp'līn') *n.*

ta·per (tā'pər) *n.* 1 A slender candle. 2 A long wax-coated wick used to light candles, lamps, etc. 3 A weak light. 4 A gradual diminution of size in an elongated object; also, any tapering object, as a cone. 5 Any gradual decrease. —*v.t. & v.i.* 1 To make or become smaller or thinner toward one end. 2 To lessen gradually: with *off.* —*adj.* Growing smaller toward one end. [< OE]

tape-re·cord (tāp'ri·kôrd') *v.t.* TAPE (*v.*, def. 3).

tape recorder An electromagnetic apparatus which can record sound on magnetic tape and play it back.

tap·es·try (tap'is·trē) *n. pl.* **·tries** 1 A heavy woven textile with a pictorial design, used for hangings, upholstery, etc. 2 Something like this, as in complexity of design. —*v.t.* **·tried, ·try·ing** 1 To hang or adorn with tapestry. 2 To depict or weave in a tapestry. [< Gk. *tapētion,* dim. of *tapēs* rug]

tape·worm (tāp'wûrm') *n.* Any of various long flatworms parasitic in the intestines of man and various animals.

tap·i·o·ca (tap'ē·ō'kə) *n.* A starchy, granular foodstuff obtained from cassava, used in puddings, as a thickener for soups, etc. [< Tupi *tipioca*]

ta·pir (tā'pər) *n.* Any of various hoofed, herbivorous mammals of tropical America and SE Asia, having short stout limbs and a flexible snout. [< Tupi *tapy'ra*]

tap·room (tap'ro͞om', -ro͝om') *n.* BARROOM.

tap·root (tap'ro͞ot', -ro͝ot') *n.* A type of plant root having one main descending part. —**tap'root'ed** *adj.*

tar[1] (tär) *n.* A dark, usu. pungent, viscid mixture of hydrocarbons obtained by the dry distillation of wood, coal, etc. —*v.t.* **tarred, tar·ring** To cover with or as with tar. —**tar and feather** To smear with tar and then cover with feathers as a punishment. —*adj.* Made of, derived from, or resembling tar. [< OE *teru*]

tar[2] (tär) *n. Informal* A sailor. [Short for TARPAULIN]

tar·an·tel·la (tar'ən·tel'ə) *n.* 1 A lively Neapolitan dance. 2 Music for this dance. [< *Taranto,* a port in SE Italy]

ta·ran·tu·la (tə·ran'cho͞o·lə, -tə·lə) *n. pl.* **·las** or **·lae** (-lē) 1 A large, hairy, venomous spider of S Europe. 2 Any of various large, hairy American spiders capable of inflicting a painful but not dangerous bite. [< *Taranto,* Italy]

Tarantula *def. 1*

tar·dy (tär'dē) *adj.* **·di·er, ·di·est** 1 Not coming, happening, etc., at the scheduled or proper time. 2 Moving, acting, etc., at a slow pace. [< L *tardus* slow] —**tar'di·ly** *adv.* —**tar'di·ness** *n.* —**Syn.** 1 late, dilatory, overdue, delayed. 2 slow, sluggish, leisurely, torpid.

tare[1] (târ) *n.* 1 In the Bible, a weed that grows among wheat, supposed to be the darnel. 2 Any one of various species of vetch. [?]

tare[2] (târ) *n.* 1 The deduction of the weight of a container, used to calculate the weight of its contents if the gross weight of the container and contents is determined. 2 The weight of the container. —*v.t.* **tared, tar·ing** To weigh, as a vessel or package, in order to determine the tare. [< Ar. *tarḥah*]

tar·get (tär'git) *n.* 1 An object presenting a usu. marked surface that is to be aimed and shot at, as in archery practice. 2 Anything that is shot at. 3 One who or that which is made an object of ridicule, criticism, etc.; butt. 4 A goal; objective. 5 A small round shield. —*v.t.* 1 To make a target of. 2 To establish as a goal. [< OF *targe* shield] —**tar'get·a·ble** *adj.*

tar·iff (tar'if) *n.* 1 A schedule of government-imposed duties to be paid for the importation or exportation of goods. 2 A duty of this kind, or its rate. 3 Any schedule of charges, prices, etc. —*v.t.* 1 To make a list of duties on. 2 To fix a price or tariff on. [< Ar. *ta'rif* information]

tarn (tärn) *n.* A small mountain lake. [< ON *tjörn*]

tar·nish (tär'nish) *v.t.* 1 To dim the luster of. 2 To sully, mar, debase, etc. —*v.i.* 3 To become tarnished. —*n.* 1 The condition of being tarnished; stain, blemish, loss of luster, etc. 2 The thin discolored film on the surface of tarnished metal. [< OF *ternir*] —**tar'nish·a·ble** *adj.*

ta·ro (tä'rō, tar'ō) *n. pl.* **·ros** Any of several tropical plants having starchy, edible rootstocks. [< native Polynesian name]

tar·ot (tar'ō, -ət, tar·ō') *n.* Any of a set of old Italian figured playing cards, now used chiefly in fortunetelling.

tar·pau·lin (tär·pô'lin, tär'pə-) *n.* A waterproof material, esp. canvas, used as a covering for exposed objects. [?< TAR[1] + *palling,* pr.p. of PALL[1]]

tar·pon (tär'pon, -pən) *n. pl.* **·pon** or **·pons** A large game fish of the West Indies and the coast of Florida. [?]

tar·ra·gon (tar'ə·gon) *n.* 1 A European perennial plant allied to wormwood. 2 The fragrant leaves of this plant, used for seasoning. [< Ar. *tarkhun*]

tar·ry[1] (tar'ē) *v.* **·ried, ·ry·ing** *v.i.* 1 To put off going or coming; linger. 2 To remain in the same place; stay. 3 To wait. —*v.t.* 4 *Archaic* To wait for. [< L *tardare* to delay]

tar·ry[2] (tär'ē) *adj.* **tar·ri·er, tar·ri·est** Of, like, or covered with tar. —**tar'ri·ness** *n.*

tar·sal (tär'səl) *adj.* Of, pertaining to, or situated near the tarsus or ankle. —*n.* A tarsal part, as a bone.

tar·si·er (tär'sē·ər) *n.* A small, arboreal, nocturnal East Indian primate with large eyes and ears, long tail, and elongated digits. [< F < *tarse* tarsus]

Tarsier

tar·sus (tär'səs) *n. pl.* **·si** (-sī) 1 *Anat.* **a** The ankle. **b** In man, the seven bones of the ankle and heel. 2 *Zool.* **a** The shank of a bird's leg. **b** The distal part of the leg of certain arthropods. [< Gk. *tarsos* flat of the foot, any flat surface]

tart[1] (tärt) *adj.* 1 Having a sharp, sour taste. 2 Severe; caustic: a *tart* remark. [< OE *teart*] —**tart'ly** *adv.* —**tart'ness** *n.* —**Syn.** 1 acid, bitter. 2 cutting, biting, acrimonious, sarcastic.

tart[2] (tärt) *n.* 1 A small open pastry shell filled with fruit, jelly, custard, etc. 2 *Slang* A girl or woman of loose morality. [< OF *tarte*]

tar·tan (tär'tən) *n.* 1 A woolen plaid fabric, esp. one with a pattern distinctive to a particular clan of the Scottish Highlands. 2 A fabric made to look like this. 3 Any plaid. —*adj.* Made of or like tartan. [? < OF *tiretaine* linsey-woolsey] • See PLAID.

tar·tar[1] (tär'tər) *n.* 1 A hard deposit of potassium tartrate that forms in wine casks. 2 A yellowish incrustation on teeth, chiefly calcium phosphate. [< Med. Gk. *tartaron*] —**tar·tar'e·ous** *adj.*

tar·tar[2] (tär'tər) *n.* A person of intractable or violent disposition.

Tar·tar (tär'tər) *n.* TATAR. —*adj.* Of or pertaining to the Tatars or Tatary.

tartar emetic A poisonous tartrate of antimony and potassium, used in medicine and in dyeing.

tar·tar·ic (tär·tar'ik, -tär'ik) *adj.* Pertaining to or derived from tartar or tartaric acid.

tartaric acid A white, crystalline organic acid present in grapes and other fruits.

Tar·ta·rus (tär'tər·əs) *Gk. Myth.* 1 The abyss below Hades where Zeus confined the Titans. 2 HADES (def. 2).

Tar·ta·ry (tär'tər·ē) *n.* TATARY.

task (task, täsk) *n.* 1 A piece of work, esp. one imposed by authority or required by duty or necessity. 2 Any unpleasant or difficult assignment; burden. —**take to task** To reprove; lecture. —*v.t.* 1 To assign a task to. 2 To burden. [< L *taxare* appraise]

task force 1 A military unit specially trained to execute a specific mission. 2 Any group assigned to handle a specific task.

task·mas·ter (task'mas'tər, täsk'mäs'tər) *n.* One who assigns tasks, esp. burdensome ones.

tas·sel (tas′əl) *n.* **1** A tuft of loosely hanging threads or cords used as an ornament for curtains, cushions, etc. **2** Something resembling a tassel, as the inflorescence on Indian corn. —*v.* **·seled** or **·selled, ·sel·ing** or **·sel·ling** *v.t.* **1** To provide or adorn with tassels. **2** To form in a tassel or tassels. —*v.i.* **3** To put forth tassels, as Indian corn. [< OF, clasp]

taste (tāst) *v.* **tast·ed, tast·ing** *v.t.* **1** To perceive the flavor of (something) by taking into the mouth or touching with the tongue. **2** To eat or drink a little of. **3** To recognize by the sense of taste. **4** To experience. —*v.i.* **5** To recognize a flavor by the sense of taste. **6** To take a small quantity into the mouth: usu. with *of.* **7** To have experience or enjoyment: with *of: taste* of great sorrow. **8** To have a specified flavor when in the mouth: Sugar *tastes* sweet. —*n.* **1** The sensation associated with stimulation of the taste buds by foods or other substances. **2** The quality thus perceived; flavor. **3** A small quantity tasted. **4** A slight experience; sample. **5** Special fondness and aptitude; inclination: a *taste* for music. **6** Appreciation of the beautiful in nature, art, and literature. **7** Style or form with respect to the rules of propriety or etiquette. **8** Individual preference or liking. **9** The act of tasting. [< L *taxare* touch, handle, appraise]

taste bud Any of numerous clusters of receptors located on the tongue and capable of stimulation by sweet, salt, sour or bitter substances.

taste·ful (tāst′fəl) *adj.* Having, showing, or conforming to good taste. **—taste′ful·ly** *adv.* **—taste′ful·ness** *n.* **—Syn.** elegant, aesthetic, artistic, graceful.

taste·less (tāst′lis) *adj.* **1** Having no flavor; insipid; dull. **2** Uninteresting; dull. **3** Lacking or showing a lack of good taste. **—taste′less·ly** *adv.* **—taste′less·ness** *n.*

tast·er (tās′tər) *n.* **1** One who tastes, esp. to test the quality of something. **2** A device for testing or sampling, as the small, shallow, metal vessel used in testing wines.

tast·y (tās′tē) *adj.* **tast·i·er, tast·i·est** **1** Having a fine flavor. **2** Tasteful. **—tast′i·ly** *adv.* **—tast′i·ness** *n.*

tat (tat) *v.* **tat·ted, tat·ting** *v.t.* **1** To make (edging) by tatting. —*v.i.* **2** To make tatting. [Back formation < TATTING] —**tat′ter** *n.*

Ta·tar (tä′tər) *n.* **1** A member of any of the Mongolian and Turkic tribes that invaded much of W Asia and E Europe in the Middle Ages. **2** A member of a chiefly Turkic people now living in the Russian Soviet Federated Socialist Republic and Soviet Central Asia. **3** Any of the Turkic languages of the Tatars, as Uzbek. —*adj.* Of or pertaining to the Tatars or Tatary. **—Ta·tar′i·an** (tä·târ′ē·ən) *adj., n.* **—Ta·tar′ic** *adj.*

Ta·ta·ry (tä′tər·ē) *n.* A region of indefinite extent in Asia and E Europe invaded and inhabited by Tatars in the Middle Ages.

tat·ter (tat′ər) *n.* **1** A torn and hanging shred; rag. **2** *pl.* Ragged clothing. —*v.t.* **1** To tear into tatters. —*v.i.* **2** To become ragged. [< ON *töturr* rags]

tat·ting (tat′ing) *n.* **1** A kind of lace made by looping and knotting a single thread that is wound on a shuttle. **2** The act or process of making it. [?]

tat·tle (tat′l) *v.* **·tled, ·tling** *v.i.* **1** To talk idly; chatter. **2** To tell secrets, plans, etc.; gossip. —*v.t.* **3** To reveal by gossiping. —*n.* Idle talk or gossip. [< MDu. *tatelen*] **—tat′tler** *n.*

tat·tle·tale (tat′l·tāl′) *n.* A talebearer; tattler. —*adj.* Revealing; betraying.

tat·too[1] (ta·to͞o′) *v.t.* **·tooed, ·too·ing** **1** To mark (the skin) in patterns with indelible pigments. **2** To mark the skin with (designs, etc.) in this way. —*n. pl.* **·toos** **1** A pattern or design so made. **2** The act of tattooing or the condition of being tattooed. [< Polynesian] **—tat·too′er** *n.*

tat·too[2] (ta·to͞o′) *n. pl.* **·toos** **1** A continuous beating or drumming. **2** A signal by drum or bugle to soldiers to repair to quarters. —*v.t. & v.i.* **·tooed, ·too·ing** To beat or rap on (a drum, etc.). [< Du. < *tap* tap, faucet + *toe* shut]

tau (tou) *n.* The nineteenth letter in the Greek alphabet (Τ, τ).

taught (tôt) *p.t. & p.p.* of TEACH.

taunt (tônt) *n.* A sarcastic, biting remark; insult; jibe. —*v.t.* **1** To reproach or challenge with sarcastic or contemptuous words. **2** To provoke with taunts. [? < OF *tanter* provoke] **—taunt′er** *n.* **—taunt′ing·ly** *adv.*

taupe (tōp) *n.* The color of moleskin; dark brownish gray. [< L *talpa* mole]

Tau·rus (tôr′əs) *n.* A constellation and the second sign of the zodiac; the Bull. [L, bull] • See ZODIAC.

taut (tôt) *adj.* **1** Stretched tight. **2** In proper shape; trim; tidy. **3** Tense; tight: *taut* muscles. [? < OE *togian,* to pull, tow] **—taut′ly** *adv.* **—taut′ness** *n.*

tau·tog (tô·tôg′, -tog′) *n.* Any of various blackish, edible fishes of the North American Atlantic coast. [< Algon.]

tau·tol·o·gy (tô·tol′ə·jē) *n. pl.* **·gies** **1** Unnecessary repetition of the same idea in different words. **2** An instance of this. [< Gk. *tautos* identical + *logos* discourse] **—tau·to·log·ic** (tô′tə·loj′ik) or **·i·cal** *adj.* **—tau′to·log′i·cal·ly** *adv.*

tav·ern (tav′ərn) *n.* **1** An inn. **2** A place licensed to sell liquor, beer, etc., to be drunk on the premises. [< OF < L *taberna* hut, booth]

taw (tô) *n.* **1** A game of marbles. **2** The line from which marble players shoot. **3** A fancy marble used for shooting. [?]

taw·dry (tô′drē) *adj.* **·dri·er, ·dri·est** Pretentiously showy without taste or quality. [< *St. Audrey,* designating a cheap type of lace sold at St. Audrey's Fair at Ely, England] **—taw′dri·ly** *adv.* **—taw′dri·ness** *n.* **—Syn.** cheap, gaudy, meretricious, flashy.

taw·ny (tô′nē) *adj.* **·ni·er, ·ni·est** Tan-colored; brownish yellow. —*n.* The color tan or brownish yellow. [< OF *tanner* to tan] **—taw′ni·ness** *n.*

tax (taks) *n.* **1** A compulsory contribution levied upon persons, property, or business for the support of government. **2** A heavy demand, as on one's powers or resources; a burden. —*v.t.* **1** To impose a tax on. **2** To settle or fix (amounts) chargeable in any judicial matter. **3** To impose a burden upon; task. **4** To charge; blame: usu. with *with.* [< L *taxare* estimate, appraise]

tax·a·ble (taks′ə·bəl) *adj.* Liable to be taxed: *taxable* income. **—tax′a·bil′i·ty** *n.*

tax·a·tion (tak·sā′shən) *n.* **1** The act of taxing. **2** The amount assessed as a tax. **3** Revenue raised from taxes.

tax·i (tak′sē) *n. pl.* **tax·is** or **tax·ies** TAXICAB. —*v.* **tax·ied, tax·i·ing** or **tax·y·ing** *v.i.* **1** To ride in a taxicab. **2** To move along the ground or on the surface of the water, as an airplane before taking off or after landing. —*v.t.* **3** To cause (an airplane) to taxi.

tax·i·cab (tak′sē·kab′) *n.* A passenger vehicle, usu. fitted with a taximeter, available for hire. [< TAXIMETER + CAB]

tax·i·der·my (tak′sə·dûr′mē) *n.* The art of stuffing and mounting the skins of dead animals to simulate their appearance when alive. [< Gk. *taxis* arrangement + *derma* skin] **—tax′i·der′mal, tax′i·der′mic** *adj.* **—tax′i·der′·mist** *n.*

tax·i·me·ter (tak′si·mē′tər) *n.* An instrument for recording fares in a taxicab. [< F < *taxe* tariff + *mètre* a meter]

tax·on·o·my (tak·son′ə·mē) *n.* **1** The laws and principles of classification. **2** *Biol.* The systematic classification of plant and animal life into successive subgroups, as kingdom, phylum or division, class, order, family, genus, and species. [< Gk. *taxis* arrangement + *nomos* law] **—tax·o·nom·ic** (tak′sə·nom′ik) or **·i·cal** *adj.* **—tax′o·nom′i·cal·ly** *adv.* **—tax·on′o·mist** *n.* • The prefixes *sub-,* meaning next below, and *super-,* meaning next above, are often used with the taxonomic categories specified in def. 2. Thus a *suborder* ranks next below an order but above a family (or a *superfamily*), whereas a *superorder* ranks above an order but below a class (or a *subclass*).

tax·pay·er (taks′pā′ər) *n.* One who pays or is liable to pay taxes.

TB, T.B., tb, t.b. tubercle bacillus; tuberculosis.

Tb terbium.

tbs. tbsp. tablespoon(s).

Tc technetium.

Te tellurium.

tea (tē) *n.* **1** An evergreen Asian plant having white flowers. **2** The prepared leaves of this plant, or an infusion of them used as a beverage. **3** A similar potable infusion of plant leaves or animal extract: beef *tea.* **4** *Brit.* A light evening or afternoon meal. **5** A social gathering at which tea is served. **6** *Slang* MARIHUANA. [< dial. Chinese *t'e*]

tea bag A small porous sack of cloth or paper containing tea leaves, which is immersed in water to make tea.

teach (tēch) *v.* **taught, teach·ing** *v.t.* 1 To give instruction to: *teach* a class. 2 To give instruction in: *teach* French. 3 To train by example, practice, or exercise. —*v.i.* 4 To act as a teacher; impart knowledge or skill. [< OE *tæcan*] —**teach′a·bil′i·ty, teach′a·ble·ness** *n.* —**teach′a·ble** *adj.*

teach·er (tē′chər) *n.* One who teaches, esp. as an occupation.

teach-in (tēch′in′) *n.* An extended meeting, as at a college or university, during which faculty and students participate in lectures, discussions, etc., on a controversial issue, esp. as a form of social protest.

teach·ing (tē′ching) *n.* 1 The act or occupation of a teacher. 2 That which is taught.

teaching machine Any of various mechanical devices that present educational material to a student, enabling him to learn at his own rate by a system of corrective feedback.

tea·cup (tē′kup′) *n.* 1 A small cup suitable for serving tea. 2 The amount a teacup will hold: also **tea′cup·ful′** (-fŏŏl′)

teak (tēk) *n.* 1 A large tree of SE Asia yielding a hard, durable timber highly prized for furniture, etc. 2 The wood of this tree: also **teak′wood.** [< Pg. *teca* < Malayalam *tēkka*]

tea·ket·tle (tē′ket′l) *n.* A kettle with a spout, used for boiling water.

teal (tēl) *n.* Any of several small, short-necked, wild ducks. [ME *tele*]

team (tēm) *n.* 1 Two or more beasts of burden harnessed together. 2 A group of people working or playing together as a unit, esp. a group forming one side in a contest. —*v.t.* 1 To convey with a team. 2 To harness together in a team. —*v.i.* 3 To drive a team. 4 To form or work as a team: to *team* up. [< OE *tēam* offspring, team]

team·mate (tēm′māt′) *n.* A fellow player on a team.

team·ster (tēm′stər) *n.* One who drives a team or a truck, esp. as an occupation.

team·work (tēm′wûrk′) *n.* 1 Work done by a team. 2 Unity of action, as by the players on a team.

tea·pot (tē′pot′) *n.* A vessel with a spout, handle, and lid, in which tea is brewed and from which it is served.

tear[1] (târ) *v.* **tore, torn, tear·ing** *v.t.* 1 To pull apart, as cloth; rip. 2 To make by tearing: *tear* a hole in. 3 To injure or lacerate. 4 To divide or disrupt: a party *torn* by dissension. 5 To distress or torment: The sight *tore* his heart. —*v.i.* 6 To become torn or rent. 7 To move with haste and energy. —**tear down** 1 To demolish, as a building. 2 To take apart, as a machine for repair. 3 *Informal* To attack or abuse verbally. —**tear into** To attack violently or with impetuous haste. —*n.* 1 The act of tearing. 2 A fissure made by tearing. 3 *Slang* A spree; frolic. 4 A rushing motion. 5 A violent outburst, as of anger. [< OE *teran*]

tear[2] (tir) *n.* 1 A drop of the saline liquid that normally lubricates the eyeball and in weeping flows from the eyes. 2 Something resembling this. 3 *pl.* Sorrow. 4 *pl.* The act of weeping: to burst into *tears.* —*v.i.* To fill with tears. [< OE *tēar*] —**tear′less, tear′y** *adj.*

tear·drop (tir′drop′) *n.* A tear. —*adj.* Shaped like a falling tear: a *teardrop* earring.

tear·ful (tir′fəl) *adj.* 1 Weeping. 2 Causing tears. 3 Accompanied by tears: a *tearful* confession. —**tear′ful·ly** *adv.* —**tear′ful·ness** *n.* —**Syn.** 1 sobbing, crying, blubbering. 2 sad, pathetic, mournful.

tear gas (tir) A gas or other agent that causes the eyes to tear.

tear-jerk·er (tir′jûr′kər) *n. Slang* A story, play, film, etc., charged with sentimental sadness.

tea·room (tē′rōōm′, -rŏŏm′) *n.* A restaurant serving tea and other light refreshments.

tease (tēz) *v.* **teased, teas·ing** *v.t.* 1 To annoy or harass; pester. 2 To raise the nap, as with teasels. 3 To coax or beg. 4 To comb or card, as wool or flax. 5 To comb (hair) in such a way as to form fluffy layers. —*v.i.* 6 To annoy a person in a facetious or petty way. —*n.* 1 One who teases. 2 The act of teasing or the state of being teased. [< OE *tæsan* tease, pluck apart] —**teas′er** *n.* —**teas′ing·ly** *adv.*

tea·sel (tē′zəl) *n.* 1 Any of various coarse, prickly herbs having the flower heads covered with hooked bracts, esp. the **fuller's teasel.** 2 The dried flower head of this plant, or a mechanical substitute, used to raise a nap on cloth. —*v.t.* **·seled** or **·selled, ·sel·ing** or **·sel·ling** To raise the nap of with a teasel. Also **tea′zel, tea′zle.** [< OE *tæsel*] —**tea′sel·er** or **tea′sel·ler** *n.*

Teasel

tea·spoon (tē′spōōn′, -spŏŏn′) *n.* 1 A small spoon used for stirring tea, etc. 2 The amount a teaspoon will hold, 1/3 of a tablespoon: also **tea′spoon·ful** (-fŏŏl′).

teat (tit, tēt) *n.* 1 The protuberance on the breast or udder of most female mammals, through which milk is drawn; a nipple. 2 A small protuberance like a teat. [< OF *tete*]

teched (techt) *adj.* TETCHED.

tech·ne·ti·um (tek·nē′shē·əm) *n.* A synthetic radioactive metallic element (symbol Tc) occupying a former gap after molybdenum in the periodic table. [< Gk. *technētos* artificial]

tech·nic (tek′nik) *n.* TECHNIQUE —*adj.* TECHNICAL.

tech·ni·cal (tek′ni·kəl) *adj.* 1 Of or pertaining to some particular art, science, or trade, esp. to the practical arts or applied sciences. 2 Of, characteristic of, used or skilled in a particular art, science, profession, etc. 3 Of, in, or exhibiting technique. 4 According to an accepted body of rules and regulations: a *technical* defeat. [< Gk. *technē* art] —**tech′ni·cal·ly** (-kə·lē, -klē) *adv.* —**tech′ni·cal·ness** *n.*

tech·ni·cal·i·ty (tek′ni·kal′ə·tē) *n. pl.* **·ties** 1 The state or quality of being technical. 2 A technical point peculiar to some art, trade, etc. 3 A petty, formal, or highly specialized distinction or detail.

technical sergeant See GRADE.

tech·ni·cian (tek·nish′ən) *n.* One skilled in carrying out operations in a specific field.

tech·ni·col·or (tek′ni·kul′ər) *n.* Brilliant or realistic color. [< *Technicolor*] —**tech′ni·col′ored** *adj.*

Tech·ni·col·or (tek′ni·kul′ər) *n.* A process used in making color films: a trade name. Also **tech′ni·col′or.**

tech·nics (tek′niks) *n.pl. (construed as sing.)* The principles or study of an art or of the arts, esp. the industrial or mechanical arts.

tech·nique (tek·nēk′) *n.* 1 The way in which an artist, craftsman, scientist, etc., handles technical details or uses basic skills. 2 The degree of excellence in doing these things. 3 Any method of accomplishing something. [< Gk. *technikos* technical]

tech·noc·ra·cy (tek·nok′rə·sē) *n. pl.* **·cies** A government controlled by technicians, as scientists, engineers, etc. —**tech′no·crat** (tek′nə·krat) *n.* —**tech′no·crat′ic** *adj.*

tech·nol·o·gy (tek·nol′ə·jē) *n.* 1 The sum total of the technical means employed to meet the material needs of a society. 2 Applied science. 3 The technical terms used in a science, art, etc. [< Gk. *technē* skill + -LOGY] —**tech′no·log′ic** or **·i·cal** *adj.* —**tech′no·log′i·cal·ly** *adv.* —**tech·nol′o·gist** *n.*

tec·ton·ics (tek·ton′iks) *n.pl. (construed as singular)* 1 The science or art of constructing buildings or things. 2 The branch of geology relating to the continuing structural evolution of the earth's crust. [< Gk. *tektōn* carpenter] —**tec·ton′ic** *adj.* —**tec·ton′i·cal·ly** *adv.*

ted (ted) *v.t.* **ted·ded, ted·ding** To scatter or spread for drying, as newly mown grass. [? < ON *tethja* spread manure]

ted·dy bear (ted′ē) A toy bear. [< *Teddy,* a nickname of Theodore Roosevelt, 26th U.S. president, 1858–1919]

Te De·um (tē dē′əm) 1 An ancient Christian hymn beginning with the words *Te Deum.* 2 The music for this hymn. [< L *Te Deum (laudamus)* (we praise) Thee, O God]

te·di·ous (tē′dē·əs) *adj.* Fatiguing or boring, as because of lack of interest or repetitiousness. [< L *taedium* tedium] —**te′di·ous·ly** *adv.* —**te′di·ous·ness** *n.*

te·di·um (tē′dē·əm) *n.* The quality or state of being boring, wearisome, monotonous, etc. [< L *taedere* vex, weary]

tee[1] (tē) *n.* 1 The letter T. 2 Something resembling the form of the letter T. —*adj.* Shaped like a T.

tee[2] (tē) *n.* 1 A little peg or cone-shaped mound on which a golf ball is placed in making the first play to a hole. 2 In golf, the area from which a player makes his first stroke at the beginning of play for each hole. —*v.t. & v.i.* **·teed, tee·ing** To place (the ball) on the tee before striking it. —**tee off** 1 To strike (a golf ball) in starting play. 2 To begin. 3 *Slang* To make angry or resentful.[?]

tee[3] (tē) *n.* In certain games, a mark toward which the balls, quoits, etc., are directed. [?<TEE[1]]

teem (tēm) *v.i.* To be full to overflowing; abound. [<OE *tīeman*]

teen·age (tēn'āj') *adj.* Of, being in, or related to the years from 13 to 19 inclusive. —**teen'ag'er** *n.*

teens (tēnz) *n. pl.* 1 The numbers from 13 to 19 inclusive. 2 The years of one's age from 13 to 19 inclusive. [<OE *tēne* ten]

tee·ny (tē'nē) *adj.* **·ni·er, ·ni·est** *Informal* Tiny. [Alter. of TINY]

teen·y·bop·per (tē'nē·bop'ər) *n. Slang* A modern, hip teen-ager of the 1960's, esp. a girl.

tee·pee (tē'pē) *n.* TEPEE.

tee shirt (tē) T-SHIRT.

tee·ter (tē'tər) *v.i.* 1 SEESAW. 2 To walk or move with a swaying or tottering motion. 3 To vacillate; waver. —*v.t.* 4 To cause to teeter. —*n.* SEESAW. [?<ON *titra* tremble]

tee·ter-tot·ter (tē'tər·tot'ər) *n.* SEESAW.

teeth (tēth) *n. pl.* of TOOTH.

teethe (tēth) *v.i.* **teethed, teeth·ing** To develop teeth; cut one's teeth.

tee·to·tal (tē'tōt'l) *adj.* 1 Of, pertaining to, or practicing total abstinence from alcoholic beverages. 2 Total; entire. [<TOTAL, with emphatic repetition of initial letter] —**tee·to'tal·ism** *n.* —**tee·to'tal·ly** *adv.*

tee·to·tal·er (tē·tōt'l·ər) *n.* One who abstains totally from alcoholic beverages. Also **tee·to'tal·ist, tee·to'tal·ler.**

Tef·lon (tef'lon) *n.* A tough, slippery, heat-resistant, chemically inert, synthetic polymer having many industrial and household applications: a trade name.

tel. telegram; telegraph; telephone.

tele- *combining form* 1 At, from, over, or to a distance; distant: *telegraph.* 2 Of, in, pertaining to, or transmitted by television: *telecast.* [<Gk. *tēle* far]

tel·e·cast (tel'ə·kast, -käst) *v.t. & v.i.* **·cast** or **·cast·ed, ·cast·ing** To broadcast by television. —*n.* A program broadcast by television.

tel·e·com·mu·ni·ca·tion (tel'ə·kə·myōō'nə·kā'shən) *n.* The technology of communicating at a distance, as in radio, television, telegraphy, etc. Also **tel'e·com·mu'ni·ca'·tions** (*construed as sing.* or *pl.*).

tel·e·com·mut·ing (tel'ə·kə·myōōt'ing) *n.* Working at home by means of a home computer terminal connected by telephone line to a main computer.

tel·e·gram (tel'ə·gram) *n.* A message sent by telegraph.

tel·e·graph (tel'ə·graf, -gräf) *n.* Any of various devices, systems, or processes for transmitting messages to a distance, esp. by means of coded electric impulses conducted by wire. —*v.t.* 1 To send (a message) by telegraph. 2 To communicate with by telegraph. —*v.i.* 3 To transmit a message by telegraph. —**te·leg·ra·pher** (tə·leg'rə·fər) *n.*

tel·e·graph·ic (tel'ə·graf'ik) *adj.* 1 Of, pertaining to, or transmitted by the telegraph. 2 Concise, as a telegram. Also **tel'e·graph'i·cal.** —**tel'e·graph'i·cal·ly** *adv.*

te·leg·ra·phy (tə·leg'rə·fē) *n.* 1 The process of conveying messages by telegraph. 2 The technology used in doing this.

Te·lem·a·chus (tə·lem'ə·kəs) *Gk. Myth.* The son of Odysseus and Penelope, who helped his father kill his mother's suitors.

tel·e·mar·ket·ing (tel'ə·mär'kə·ting) *n.* The marketing of products and services over the telephone or on television.

te·lem·e·ter (tel'ə·mē'tər, tə·lem'ə·tər) *n.* An apparatus for indicating or measuring various quantities and for transmitting the data to a distant point. —*v.t. & v.i.* To transmit by telemeter. —**te·lem'e·try** *n.*

tel·e·ol·o·gy (tel'ē·ol'ə·jē, tē'lē-) *n.* 1 The study of final causes. 2 The belief that natural phenomena can be explained in terms of an overall design as well as by mechanical causes. 3 The study of evidence supporting this belief. 4 The explanation of nature in terms of utility or purpose. [<Gk. *telos, teleos* end + -LOGY] —**tel'e·o·log'i·cal** (-ə·loj'i·kəl) *adj.* —**tel'e·ol'o·gist** *n.*

te·lep·a·thy (tə·lep'ə·thē) *n.* The supposed communication of one mind with another by other than normal sensory means. —**tel·e·path·ic** (tel'ə·path'ik) *adj.* —**tel'e·path'i·cal·ly** *adv.* —**te·lep'a·thist** *n.*

tel·e·phone (tel'ə·fōn) *n.* An instrument for reproducing sound or speech at a distant point, using electric impulses transmitted by wire. —*v.* **·phoned, ·phon·ing** —*v.t.* 1 To send by telephone, as a message. 2 To communicate with by telephone. —*v.i.* 3 To communicate by telephone. —**tel'e·phon'ic** (-fon'ik) *adj.* —**tel'e·phon'i·cal·ly** *adv.*

te·leph·o·ny (tə·lef'ə·nē) *n.* The technology of telephone communication.

tel·e·pho·to (tel'ə·fō'tō) *adj.* 1 Denoting a system of lenses which produces a large image of a distant object in a camera. 2 Of, pertaining to, or being telephotography.

tel·e·pho·to·graph (tel'ə·fō'tə·graf, -gräf) *n.* 1 A picture transmitted by wire or radio. 2 A picture made with a telephoto lens. —*v.t. & v.i.* To take or transmit (photographs) by telephotography. —**tel'e·pho'to·graph'ic** *adj.*

tel·e·pho·tog·ra·phy (tel'ə·fə·tog'rə·fē) *n.* 1 The technique of producing magnified photographs of distant objects. 2 The transmission of photographs or other visual material by radio or wire.

tel·e·proc·ess·ing (tel'ə·pros'es·ing) *n.* Data processing by a computer which collects data from distant locations by means of communications lines.

Tel·e·prompt·er (tel'e·promp'tər) *n.* A prompting device for television whereby a magnified script, unseen by the audience, is unrolled for a speaker or performer, line by line: a trade name.

tel·e·scope (tel'ə·skōp) *n.* An optical instrument for enlarging the image of a distant object. —*v.* **·scoped, ·scop·ing** *v.t.* 1 To put together so that one part fits into another. 2 To shorten, condense, or compress. —*v.i.* 3 To slide or be forced one into another, as the cylindrical tubes of a collapsible telescope or railroad cars in a collision.

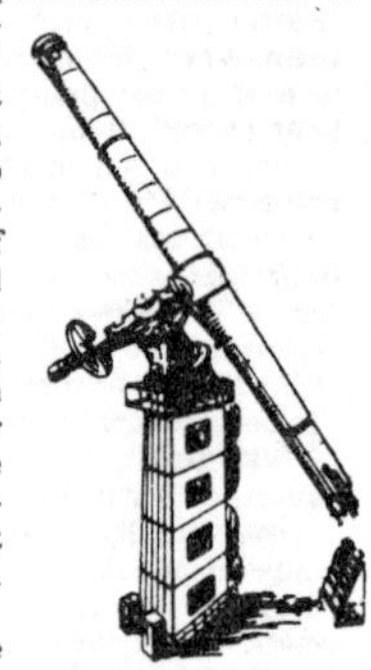

Refracting telescope

tel·e·scop·ic (tel'ə·skop'ik) *adj.* 1 Of, pertaining to, or done with a telescope. 2 Visible through or obtained by a telescope. 3 Visible only through a telescope. 4 Far-seeing. 5 Having sections that slide within or over one another. Also **tel'e·scop'i·cal.**

te·les·co·py (tə·les'kə·pē) *n.* The technology of using or making telescopes. —**te·les'co·pist** *n.*

tel·e·text (tel'ə·tekst') *n.* A communications system that transmits information over a television broadcast signal, to be viewed on a television screen.

tel·e·thon (tel'ə·thon) *n.* A long telecast, usu. to raise funds for a charity. [<TELE- + (MARA)THON]

Tel·e·type (tel'ə·tīp) *n.* A teletypewriter: a trade name.

tel·e·type·writ·er (tel'ə·tīp'rī'tər) *n.* A telegraphic instrument resembling a typewriter, by which the work done on one is simultaneously typed on others, electrically connected but a distance away.

tel·e·view (tel'ə·vyōō) *v.t. & v.i.* To observe by means of television. —**tel'e·view'er** *n.*

tel·e·vise (tel'ə·vīz) *v.t. & v.i.* **·vised, ·vis·ing** To transmit or receive by television.

tel·e·vi·sion (tel'ə·vizh'ən) *n.* 1 An optical and electric system for continuous transmission of visual images and sound that may be instantaneously received at a distance. 2 The technology of television transmission. 3 A television receiving set. 4 Television as an industry, an art form, or a medium of communications. 5 A show transmitted by television: to watch *television.*

tel·ex (tel'eks) *n.* 1 A communication system using teletypewriters connected by wire through exchanges which operate automatically. **2** A message sent by such a system. —*v.t.* To send by telex. [< TEL(ETYPEWRITER) + EX(CHANGE)]

tell (tel) *v.* **told, tell·ing** *v.t.* **1** To relate in detail; narrate, as a story. **2** To make known by speech or writing; express in words; communicate; utter; say. **3** To divulge; reveal; disclose: to *tell* secrets. **4** To decide; ascertain: I cannot *tell* who is to blame. **5** To distinguish; recognize: to *tell* right from wrong. **6** To command; direct; order: I *told* him to go home. **7** To let know; report to; inform. **8** To state or assure emphatically: It's cold out, I *tell* you! **9** To count; enumerate: to *tell* one's beads. —*v.i.* **10** To give an account or description: usu. with *of.* **11** To serve as indication or evidence: with *of:* Their rags *told* of their poverty. **12** To produce a marked effect: Every blow *told.* —**tell off 1** To count and set apart. **2** *Informal* To reprimand severely. —**tell on 1** To wear out; tire; exhaust. **2** *Informal* To tattle on; inform against. [< OE *tellan*] —**Syn. 1** recount, recite. **2** state, aver. **4** discriminate.

tell·er (tel′ər) *n.* **1** One who tells, as a story; narrator. **2** One who receives or pays out money, as in a bank. **3** One who counts, esp. one appointed to count votes.

tell·ing (tel′ing) *adj.* Producing a great effect. —**tell′ing·ly** *adv.* —**Syn.** striking, effective, impressive, forceful.

tell·tale (tel′tāl′) *adj.* Betraying or revealing. —*n.* **1** One who gives information about others; a tattler. **2** That which conveys information; an outward sign or indication. **3** An instrument or device for giving or recording information, as a time clock.

tel·lu·ri·um (te·lo͝or′ē·əm, tel·yo͝or′-) *n.* A rare, very poisonous, semimetallic element (symbol Te) resembling sulfur and selenium. [< L *tellus* the earth]

tel·ly (tel′ē) *n. pl.* **tel·lies** *Chiefly Brit. Informal* Television.

Tel·star (tel′stär′) *n.* Any of several U.S. comsats, the first of which was launched July 10, 1962.

te·mer·i·ty (tə·mer′ə·tē) *n.* Foolish boldness; rashness; foolhardiness. [< L *temeritas*] —**Syn.** audacity, heedlessness, recklessness, presumption, venturesomeness.

temp. temperature; temporary; in the time of (L *tempore*).

tem·per (tem′pər) *n.* **1** A fit of anger; rage. **2** A tendency to become easily angered. **3** State of mind or feeling; mood. **4** TEMPERAMENT (def. 1). **5** Equanimity; self-control: now only in the phrases **lose** (or **keep**) **one's temper. 6** The hardness and strength of a metal, esp. when produced by heat treatment. **7** Something used to temper a substance or mixture. —*v.t.* **1** To moderate or make suitable, as by adding another quality; free from excess; mitigate: to *temper* justice with mercy. **2** To bring to the proper consistency, texture, etc., by moistening and working: to *temper* clay. **3** To bring (metal) to a required hardness and elasticity by controlled heating and cooling. **4** To make experienced; toughen, as by difficulties, hardships, etc. **5** *Music* To tune (an instrument) by temperament. —*v.i.* **6** To be or become tempered. [< L *temperare* combine in due proportion] —**tem′per·a·bil′i·ty** *n.* —**tem′per·a·ble** *adj.*

tem·per·a (tem′pər·ə) *n.* **1** An aqueous painting medium in which the pigment is laid down in a matrix of casein, size, egg, etc. **2** The method of painting in this medium; also a painting done in tempera. **3** A water-soluble paint used for posters. [< Ital. *temperare* to temper]

tem·per·a·ment (tem′pər·ə·mənt, -prə-) *n.* **1** The characteristic nature or disposition of a person. **2** A nature or disposition that is exceedingly dramatic, excitable, moody, etc. **3** *Music* The tuning of an instrument of fixed intonation to a slightly modified chromatic scale so that it is in tune for all keys. [< L *temperamentum* proper mixture]

tem·per·a·men·tal (tem′pər·ə·men′təl, -prə-) *adj.* **1** Of or pertaining to temperament. **2** Exceedingly excitable, moody, capricious, etc. **3** Unpredictable or erratic, as in performance. —**tem′per·a·men′tal·ly** *adv.*

tem·per·ance (tem′pər·əns) *n.* **1** Habitual moderation and self-control, esp. in the indulgence of any appetite. **2** The principle and practice of moderation or total abstinence from intoxicants. —*adj.* Of, relating to, practicing, or promoting total abstinence from intoxicants. [< L *temperare* mix in due proportions]

tem·per·ate (tem′pər·it, tem′prət) *adj.* **1** Characterized by moderation or the absence of extremes; not excessive. **2** Calm; restrained; self-controlled. **3** Observing moderation or self-control, esp. in the use of intoxicating liquors. **4** Moderate as regards temperature; mild. [< L *temperare* mix in due proportions] —**tem′per·ate·ly** *adv.* —**tem′·per·ate·ness** *n.*

temperate zone Either of two zones of the earth, the one between the Tropic of Capricorn and the Antarctic Circle and the other between the Tropic of Cancer and the Arctic Circle. • See ZONE.

tem·per·a·ture (tem′pər·ə·chər, -prə-) *n.* **1** The degree of heat in the atmosphere as measured on a thermometer.

TEMPERATURE CONVERSION TABLE

This table provides approximate conversion figures from the Fahrenheit to the Celsius temperature scales and vice versa. On the Celsius scale, water boils at about 100° and freezes at about 0°. On the Fahrenheit scale, water boils at about 212° and freezes at about 32°. One Fahrenheit degree = 5/9° Celsius. To convert from Fahrenheit to Celsius, subtract 32 from the Fahrenheit reading, multiply by 5, and divide the product by 9. *Example:* 65°F − 32 = 33; 33 × 5 = 165; 165 ÷ 9 = 18.3°C. To convert from Celsius to Fahrenheit, multiply the Celsius reading by 9, divide the product by 5, and add 32. *Example:* 35°C × 9 = 315; 315 ÷ 5 = 63; 63 + 32 = 95°F.

Fahrenheit	*Celsius*	*Fahrenheit*	*Celsius*
500	260.0	0	−17.8
400	204.4	−10	−23.3
300	149.0	−20	−28.9
212	100.0	−30	−34.4
200	93.3	−40	−40.0
100	37.8	−50	−45.6
90	32.2	−60	−51.1
80	26.7	−70	−56.7
70	21.1	−80	−62.2
60	15.6	−90	−67.8
50	10.0	−100	−73.3
40	4.4	−200	−129.0
32	0.0	−300	−184.0
30	−1.1	−400	−240.0
20	−6.6	−459.4*	−273.0
10	−12.2		**Absolute zero.*

Celsius	*Fahrenheit*	*Celsius*	*Fahrenheit*
500	932	0	32
400	752	−10	14
300	572	−20	−4
200	392	−30	−22
100	212	−40	−40
90	194	−50	−58
80	176	−60	−76
70	158	−70	−94
60	140	−80	−112
50	122	−90	−130
40	104	−100	−148
30	86	−200	−328
20	68	−273*	−459.4
10	50		**Absolute zero.*

2 The degree or intensity of heat in a living body; also, the excess of this above the normal. **3** The intensity of heat or cold in any substance. [< L *temperatura* due measure]

tem·pered (tem′pərd) *adj.* **1** Having a particular kind of temper: used mostly in combination: *quick-tempered, ill-tempered.* **2** Moderated or changed by the addition of something else: love *tempered* with discipline. **3** *Music* Adjusted in pitch to some temperament. **4** Having the right degree of hardness, elasticity, etc.

tem·pest (tem′pist) *n.* **1** An extensive and violent wind, usu. attended with rain, snow, or hail. **2** A violent commotion or tumult. [< L *tempestas* space of time, weather < *tempus* time]

tem·pes·tu·ous (tem·pes′cho͞o·əs) *adj.* Stormy; turbulent; violent. —**tem·pes′tu·ous·ly** *adv.* —**tem·pes′tu·ous·ness** *n.*

add, āce, câre, pälm; end, ēven; it, īce; odd, ōpen, ôrder; to͝ok, po͞ol; up, bûrn; ə = *a* in *above, u* in *focus;* yo͞o = *u* in *fuse;* oil; pout; check; go; ring; thin; th̸is; zh, *vision.* < derived from; ? origin uncertain or unknown.

Tem·plar (tem′plər) *n.* KNIGHT TEMPLAR.

tem·plate (tem′plit) *n.* **1** A pattern, as of wood or metal, used as a guide in shaping or making something. **2** In building, a stout stone or timber for distributing weight or thrust. [< OF *temple* small timber]

tem·ple[1] (tem′pəl) *n.* **1** An edifice consecrated to the worship of one or more deities. **2** An edifice dedicated to public worship; esp., in the U.S.: **a** A synagogue. **b** A Mormon church. **3** Any usu. large or imposing building dedicated or used for a special purpose: a *temple* of learning. [< L *templum* temple]

tem·ple[2] (tem′pəl) *n.* The region on each side of the head above the cheek bone. [< L *tempus* temple]

tem·po (tem′pō) *n. pl.* **·pos** or **·pi** (-pē) **1** *Music* Relative speed at which a composition is played or is supposed to be played. **2** Characteristic rate of speed; pace. [< L *tempus* time]

tem·po·ral[1] (tem′pər·əl) *adj.* **1** Of or pertaining to the present as opposed to a future life. **2** Worldly; material, as opposed to spiritual. **3** Ephemeral; transitory, as opposed to eternal. **4** Of or relating to time. **5** *Gram.* Of, pertaining to, or denoting time: *temporal* conjunctions. [< L *tempus, temporis* time] **—tem·po·ral·i·ty** (tem′pə·ral′ə·tē), **tem′po·ral·ness** *n.* **—tem′po·ral·ly** *adv.*

tem·po·ral[2] (tem′pər·əl) *adj.* Of, pertaining to, or situated at the temple or temples of the head.

temporal bone The compound bone forming either side of the skull. • See SKULL.

tem·po·rar·y (tem′pə·rer′ē) *adj.* Lasting, to be used, etc., for a time only; not permanent. [< L *tempus, temporis* time] **—tem′po·rar′i·ly** *adv.* **—tem′po·rar′i·ness** *n.*

tem·po·rize (tem′pə·rīz) *v.i.* **·rized, ·riz·ing** **1** To act evasively so as to gain time or put off commitment. **2** To comply with or yield to the situation, circumstances, etc.; compromise. [< L *tempus, temporis* time] **—tem′po·ri·za′tion, tem′po·riz′er** *n.* **—tem′po·riz′ing·ly** *adv.*

tempt (tempt) *v.t.* **1** To attempt to persuade (a person) to do wrong, as by promising pleasure or gain. **2** To be attractive to; invite: Your offers do not *tempt* me. **3** To provoke or risk provoking: to *tempt* fate. **4** To incline or dispose: They were *tempted* to leave at once. [< L *temptare, tentare* test, try] **—tempt′a·ble** *adj.* **—tempt′er** *n.* **—tempt′ress** *n. Fem.*

temp·ta·tion (temp·tā′shən) *n.* **1** That which tempts. **2** The state of being tempted.

tempt·ing (temp′ting) *adj.* Alluring; attractive; seductive. **—tempt′ing·ly** *adv.* **—tempt′ing·ness** *n.*

tem·pu·ra (tem·po͝or′ə, tem′po͝or′ə, -po͞o·rä′) *n.* A Japanese dish of seafood or vegetables, dipped in batter and deep-fried. [Jap., fried food]

tem·pus fu·git (tem′pəs fyo͞o′jit) *Latin* Time flies.

ten (ten) *n.* **1** The sum of nine plus one; 10; X. **2** A set or group of ten members. [< OE *tēne*] **—ten** *adj., pron.*

ten. tenement; tenor; tenuto (music).

ten·a·ble (ten′ə·bəl) *adj.* Capable of being held, maintained, or defended. [< L *tenere* to hold] **—ten′a·bil′i·ty, ten′a·ble·ness** *n.* **—ten′a·bly** *adv.*

te·na·cious (ti·nā′shəs) *adj.* **1** Having great cohesiveness; tough. **2** Adhesive; sticky. **3** Stubborn; obstinate; persistent. **4** Strongly retentive: a *tenacious* memory. [< L *tenax* holding fast] **—te·na′cious·ly** *adv.* **—te·na′cious·ness, te·nac·i·ty** (tə·nas′ə·tē) *n.*

ten·an·cy (ten′ən·sē) *n. pl.* **·cies** **1** The holding of lands or estates by any form of title; occupancy. **2** The period of being a tenant. **3** The property occupied by a tenant.

ten·ant (ten′ənt) *n.* **1** A person who rents a house, land, etc., for his own use. **2** One who holds or possesses lands or property by any kind of title. **3** A dweller in any place; an occupant. —*v.t.* **1** To hold as tenant; occupy. —*v.i.* **2** To be a tenant. [< F *tenir* to hold] **—ten′ant·a·ble** *adj.*

tenant farmer One who farms land owned by another and pays rent either in cash or in a share of the crops.

ten·ant·ry (ten′ən·trē) *n. pl.* **·ries** **1** Tenants collectively. **2** The state of being a tenant.

ten-cent store (ten′sent′) FIVE-AND-TEN-CENT STORE.

Ten Commandments In the Old Testament, the ten rules of conduct given by God to Moses on Mount Sinai.

tend[1] (tend) *v.i.* **1** To have an aptitude, tendency, or disposition; incline. **2** To lead or conduce: Education *tends* to refinement. **3** To go in a certain direction. [< L *tendere* extend, tend]

tend[2] (tend) *v.t.* **1** To attend to the needs or requirements of; take care of; minister to: to *tend* children. **2** To watch over or be in charge of: to *tend* a store. —*v.i.* **3** To be in attendance; serve or wait: with *on* or *upon.* **4** To give attention or care: with *to.* [Alter. of ATTEND]

ten·den·cy (ten′dən·sē) *n. pl.* **·cies** **1** Inclination; propensity; bent: a *tendency* to lie. **2** A movement or course toward some purpose, end, or result. **3** The purpose or trend of a speech or story. [< L *tendere* extend, tend] **—Syn. 1** aptitude, proclivity, disposition, leaning, predilection.

ten·den·tious (ten·den′shəs) *adj.* Disposed to promote a particular view or opinion; lacking in detachment. **—ten·den′tious·ly** *adv.* **—ten·den′tious·ness** *n.*

ten·der[1] (ten′dər) *adj.* **1** Easily crushed, bruised, broken, etc.; delicate; fragile. **2** Easily chewed or cut: said of food. **3** Physically weak; not strong or hardy. **4** Youthful and delicate; not strengthened by maturity: a *tender* age. **5** Characterized by gentleness, care, consideration, etc.: a *tender* respect for the aged. **6** Kind; affectionate; loving: a *tender* father. **7** Sensitive to impressions, feelings, etc.: a *tender* conscience. **8** Sensitive to pain, discomfort, roughness, etc.: a *tender* skin. **9** Of delicate quality: a *tender* color. **10** Capable of arousing sensitive feelings; touching: *tender* memories. **11** Requiring deft or delicate treatment; ticklish; touchy: a *tender* subject. —*v.t.* To make tender; soften. [< L *tener*] **—ten′der·ly** *adv.* **—ten′der·ness** *n.*

ten·der[2] (ten′dər) *v.t.* **1** To present for acceptance, as a resignation; offer. **2** To proffer, as money, in payment of a debt, etc. —*n.* **1** The act of tendering; an offer. **2** That which is offered as payment, esp. money. [< L *tendere* extend, tend] **—ten′der·er** *n.*

tend·er[3] (ten′dər) *n.* **1** A boat used to bring supplies, passengers, and crew to and from a ship anchored near the shore. **2** A vessel that services ships at sea, lighthouses, seaplanes, etc. **3** A vehicle attached to the rear of a steam locomotive to carry fuel and water for it. **4** One who tends or ministers to.

ten·der·foot (ten′dər·fo͝ot′) *n. pl.* **·feet** (-fēt′) or **·foots** **1** A newcomer, esp. to a rough or unsettled region. **2** Any inexperienced person or beginner. **3** A Boy Scout in the beginning group. —*adj.* Inexperienced.

ten·der·heart·ed (ten′dər·här′tid) *adj.* Compassionate; sympathetic. **—ten′der·heart′ed·ly** *adv.* **—ten′der·heart′ed·ness** *n.*

ten·der·ize (ten′də·rīz) *v.t.* **·ized, ·iz·ing** To make (meat) tender by some process or substance that softens the tough fibers and connective tissues. **—ten′der·iz′er** *n.*

ten·der·loin (ten′dər·loin′) *n.* **1** The tender part of the loin of beef, pork, etc., that lies parallel to the backbone. **2** *Often cap.* A city district noted for its high incidence of crime, corruption, and police leniency.

ten·don (ten′dən) *n.* One of the bands of tough, fibrous tissue attaching a voluntary muscle to a bone. [< Gk. *tenōn* a sinew < *tenein* stretch] **—ten′di·nous** *adj.*

ten·dril (ten′dril) *n.* One of the slender, threadlike, usu. coiling organs serving to attach a climbing plant to a supporting surface. [< OF *tendron* sprout] **—ten′driled** or **ten′drilled, ten′dril·ous** *adj.*

ten·e·ment (ten′ə·mənt) *n.* **1** A room, or set of rooms, designed for one family; apartment; flat. **2** TENEMENT HOUSE. **3** *Law* Anything, as land, houses, offices, franchises, etc., held of another by tenure. [< LL *tenementum* tenure < L *tenere* to hold] **—ten′e·men′ta·ry** (-men′tər·ē), **ten′e·men′tal** (-men′təl) *adj.*

tenement house A run-down building or house, usu. an apartment house, situated in a poor section of a city.

ten·et (ten′it, tē′nit) *n.* A principle, dogma, or doctrine, esp. one held by a group or profession. [L, he holds]

ten·fold (ten′fōld′) *adj.* **1** Made up of ten. **2** Ten times as many or as much. —*adv.* In a tenfold manner or degree.

Tenn. Tennessee.

ten·nis (ten′is) *n.* **1** A game in which two opposing players or pairs of players strike a ball with rackets over a low net on a court (**tennis court**), as of clay or synthetic materials, usu. outdoors. **2** An old form of tennis played in an interior space: also **court tennis.** [< AF *tenetz* take, receive, imperative of *tenir* hold]

ten·on (ten′ən) *n.* A projection on the end of a timber, etc., for inserting into a mortise to form a joint. —*v.t.* **1** To form a tenon on. **2** To join by a mortise and tenon. [< OF *tenir* to hold] • See MORTISE.

ten·or (ten′ər) *n.* **1** General intent or purport; substance: the *tenor* of the speech. **2** General course or tendency: the even *tenor* of their ways. **3** General character or nature. **4** A man's voice singing higher than a baritone and lower than an alto; also, a singer having, or a part to be sung by, such a voice. —*adj.* **1** Of or pertaining to a tenor. **2** Having a range of or similar to a tenor voice. [< L, a course < *tenere* to hold]

ten·pins (ten′pinz′) *n.pl.* **1** *(construed as sing.)* A game of bowling in which the players attempt to bowl down ten pins. **2** The pins.

tense[1] (tens) *adj.* **tens·er, tens·est 1** Stretched tight; taut. **2** Under mental or nervous strain; apprehensive. **3** *Phonet.* Pronounced with the tongue and its muscles taut, as (ē) and (o͞o). —*v.t. & v.i.* **tensed, tens·ing** To make or become tense. [< L *tensus*, pp. of *tendere* to stretch] —**tense′ly** *adv.* —**tense′ness** *n.* —**Syn. 2** anxious, nervous, restless, jittery, restive, fidgety.

tense[2] (tens) *n.* **1** Any of the forms of a verb that indicate when or how long the expressed action took place or the state of being existed. **2** A specific set of such verb forms: the past *tense* of *to see.* [< L *tempus* time, tense]

ten·sile (ten′sil, *Brit.* ten′sīl) *adj.* **1** Of or pertaining to tension. **2** Capable of tension. —**ten·sil·i·ty** (ten·sil′ə·tē) *n.*

tensile strength The resistance of a material to forces of rupture and longitudinal stress: usu. expressed in pounds or tons per square inch.

ten·sion (ten′shən) *n.* **1** The act of stretching or the condition of being stretched tight; tautness. **2** Mental or nervous strain or anxiety. **3** Any strained relation, as between governments. **4** *Physics* **a** A stress that tends to lengthen a body. **b** The condition of a body when acted on by such stress. **5** A device to regulate the tightness or tautness of something, esp. the thread in a sewing machine. **6** A condition of balance or symmetry produced by opposing elements, as in an artistic work. **7** Electric potential. —**ten′sion·al** *adj.*

ten·sor (ten′sər, -sôr) *n.* Any muscle that makes tense or stretches a part.

tent (tent) *n.* A shelter of canvas or the like, supported by poles and fastened by cords to pegs (called **tent pegs**) driven into the ground. —*v.t.* **1** To cover with or as with a tent. —*v.i.* **2** To pitch a tent; camp out. [< L *tendere* stretch]

ten·ta·cle (ten′tə·kəl) *n.* **1** *Zool.* Any of various long, slender, flexible appendages of animals, esp. invertebrates, functioning as organs of touch, motion, etc. • See SEA ANEMONE. **2** *Bot.* A sensitive hair, as on the leaves of some plants. [< L *tentaculum* < *tentare* to touch, try] —**ten·tac′u·lar** (ten·tak′yə·lər) *adj.*

ten·ta·tive (ten′tə·tiv) *adj.* **1** Not definite or final; subject to change. **2** Somewhat uncertain or timid: a *tentative* glance. [< L *tentatus*, pp. of *tentare* to try, probe] —**ten′ta·tive·ly** *adv.* —**ten′ta·tive·ness** *n.*

tent caterpillar The gregarious larva of several moths that form colonies in large silken webs in the branches of trees, etc.

ten·ter (ten′tər) *n.* A frame or machine for stretching cloth to prevent shrinkage while drying. [< L *tentus* extended]

ten·ter·hook (ten′tər·ho͝ok′) *n.* A sharp hook for holding cloth while being stretched on a tenter. —**be on tenterhooks** To be in a state of anxiety or suspense.

tenth (tenth) *adj. & adv.* Next in order after the ninth. —*n.* **1** The element of an ordered set that corresponds to the number ten. **2** One of ten equal parts.

ten·u·ous (ten′yo͞o·əs) *adj.* **1** Without much substance; slight; weak: *tenuous* arguments. **2** Thin; slender. **3** Having slight density; rare. [< L *tenuis* thin] —**ten′u·ous·ly** *adv.* —**ten′u·ous·ness, ten·u·i·ty** (te·nʸo͞o′ə·tē, tə-) *n.*

ten·ure (ten′yər) *n.* **1** The act, right, length of time, or manner of holding something, as land, elected office, or a position. **2** The permanent status of a teacher, civil servant, etc., after fulfilling certain requirements. [< L *tenere* to hold] —**ten′ured, ten·u·ri·al** (ten·yo͝or′ē·əl) *adj.* —**ten·u′ri·al·ly** *adv.*

te·pee (tē′pē) *n.* A conical tent of the North American Plains Indians, usu. covered with skins.

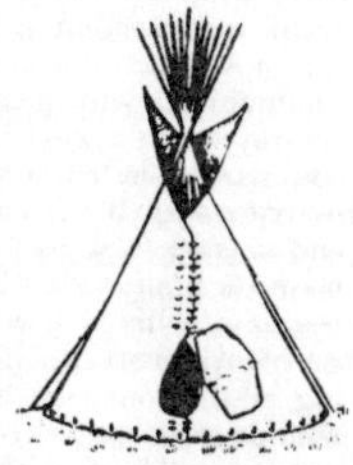

Tepee

tep·id (tep′id) *adj.* **1** Moderately warm, as a liquid. **2** Not enthusiastic. [< L *tepere* be lukewarm] —**te·pid·i·ty** (tə·pid′ə·tē), **tep′id·ness** *n.* —**tep′id·ly** *adv.*

te·qui·la (tə·kē′lə) *n.* A Mexican alcoholic liquor made from the maguey. [< *Tequila*, a district in Mexico]

ter., terr. terrace; territorial; territory.

ter·a·tism (ter′ə·tiz′əm) *n. Biol.* A monstrosity, esp. a malformed human or animal fetus. [< Gk. *teras* monster]

ter·a·to·gen·ic (ter′ə·tō·jen′ik) *adj.* Tending to cause malformations, as in a developing fetus.

ter·bi·um (tûr′bē·əm) *n.* A rare-earth metal (symbol Tb). [< *Ytterby*, a town in Sweden] —**ter′bic** *adj.*

ter·cen·te·nar·y (tûr′sen′ten′ər·ē, -sent′ən·er′ē) *adj.* Of or pertaining to a 300th anniversary. —*n. pl.* **·nar·ies** The 300th anniversary. Also **ter·cen·ten·ni·al** (tûr′sen·ten′ē·əl).

ter·gi·ver·sate (tər′jiv′ər·sāt′, -giv′-) *v.i.* **·sat·ed, ·sat·ing 1** To be evasive; equivocate. **2** To change sides, attitudes, etc.; apostatize. [< L *tergum* back + *versare* to turn] —**ter′gi′ver·sa′tor, ter′gi′ver·sa′tion** *n.*

ter·i·ya·ki (ter′ē·yä′kē) *n.* A Japanese dish of meat or fish marinated in soy sauce, ginger, etc., then fried, broiled, or grilled. [< Jap.]

term (tûrm) *n.* **1** A word or expression used to designate some definite thing in a science, profession, art, etc.: a medical *term.* **2** *Often pl.* Any word or expression conveying some conception or thought: a *term* of reproach; to speak in general *terms.* **3** *pl.* The conditions or stipulations according to which something is to be done or acceded to: the *terms* of a contract; peace *terms.* **4** *pl.* Mutual relations; footing: usu. preceded by *on* or *upon:* to be on friendly *terms.* **5** *Math.* **a** The numerator or denominator of a fraction. **b** One of the units of an algebraic expression that are connected by the plus and minus signs. **6** *Logic* **a** In a proposition, either of the two parts, the subject and predicate, which are joined by a copula. **b** Any of the three elements of a syllogism. **7** A fixed or definite period of time, esp. of duration: a *term* of office. **8** A school semester or quarter. **9** End; conclusion. **10** *Law* **a** One of the prescribed periods of the year during which a court may hold a session. **b** A specific extent of time during which an estate may be held. **c** A space of time allowed a debtor to meet his obligation. **11** *Med.* The time for the normal termination of a pregnancy. —**in terms of** With respect to; as relating to. —*v.t.* To designate by means of a term; name or call. [< L *terminus* a limit]

term. terminal; termination; terminology.

ter·ma·gant (tûr′mə·gənt) *n.* A scolding or abusive woman; shrew. —*adj.* Violently abusive and quarrelsome; vixenish. [< ME < *Termagant*, an imaginary Muslim deity] —**ter′ma·gan′cy** *n.*

term·er (tûr′mər) *n.* A person serving or attending a certain term, as in a prison or school: used in combination: a *second-termer.*

ter·mi·na·ble (tûr′mə·nə·bəl) *adj.* That may be terminated; not perpetual. —**ter′mi·na·bil′i·ty, ter′mi·na·ble·ness** *n.* —**ter′mi·na·bly** *adv.*

ter·mi·nal (tûr′mə·nəl) *adj.* **1** Situated at or forming the end, limit, or boundary of something: a *terminal* bus station. **2** Situated or occurring at the end of a series or period of time; final: a *terminal* experiment. **3** At, undergoing, or causing the termination of life: *terminal* cancer; a *terminal* patient. **4** Of or occurring regularly in or at the end of a term or period of time: *terminal* payments. **5**

add, **ā**ce, c**â**re, p**ä**lm; **e**nd, **ē**ven; **i**t, **ī**ce; **o**dd, **ō**pen, **ô**rder; t**o͝o**k, p**o͞o**l; **u**p, b**û**rn; **ə** = *a* in *above*, *u* in *focus;* **yo͞o** = *u* in *fuse;* **oi**l; **pou**t; **ch**eck; **g**o; ri**ng**; **th**in; **th**is; **zh**, *vision.* < derived from; ? origin uncertain or unknown.

Borne at the end of a stem or branch. —*n.* **1** A terminating point or part; termination; end. **2 a** Either end of a railroad line, bus line, airline, etc. **b** A passenger or freight station located at these end points. **c** Any large passenger or freight station serving an area of considerable size. **3 a** A point in an electric circuit at which it is usual to make or break a connection. **b** A connector designed to facilitate this. **4** An electronic device by means of which a user may communicate with a computer, usually including a cathode-ray tube, a keyboard, and a printer. [<L *terminus* boundary] —**ter'mi·nal·ly** *adv.*

ter·mi·nate (tûr'mə·nāt) *v.* **·nat·ed, ·nat·ing** *v.t.* **1** To put an end or stop to. **2** To form the conclusion of; finish. **3** To bound or limit. —*v.i.* **4** To have an end; come to an end. [<L *terminus* a limit] —**ter'mi·na'tive** *adj.*

ter·mi·na·tion (tûr'mə·nā'shən) *n.* **1** The act of terminating or the condition of being terminated. **2** That which bounds or limits in time or space; close; end. **3** Outcome; result; conclusion. **4** The final letters or syllable of a word; a suffix. —**ter'mi·na'tion·al** *adj.*

ter·mi·na·tor (tûr'mə·nā'tər) *n.* **1** One who or that which terminates. **2** *Astron.* The boundary between the illuminated and dark portions of the moon or of a planet.

ter·mi·nol·o·gy (tûr'mə·nol'ə·jē) *n. pl.* **·gies** The technical terms relating to a particular subject, as a science, art, trade, etc. [<L *terminus* a limit + -LOGY] —**ter'mi·no·log'·i·cal** (-nə·loj'i·kəl) *adj.* —**ter'mi·no·log'i·cal·ly** *adv.*

ter·mi·nus (tûr'mə·nəs) *n. pl.* **·nus·es** or **·ni** (-nī, -nē) **1** The final point or goal; end; terminal. **2** Either end of a railroad or bus line, airline, etc.; also, a town or station located at either end [L]

ter·mite (tûr'mīt) *n.* Any of an order of whitish, soft-bodied insects resembling ants and noted for boring into and destroying wooden structures, furniture, etc. [<L *termes, termitis*]

tern (tûrn) *n.* Any of several birds resembling gulls, but smaller, with a sharply pointed bill and a deeply forked tail. [<Scand.]

ter·na·ry (tûr'nər·ē) *adj.* **1** Formed or consisting of three; grouped in threes. **2** Third in order, importance, etc. —*n. pl.* **·ries** A group of three; a triad. [<L *terni* by threes]

ter·pene (tûr'pēn) *n.* Any of various isomeric hydrocarbons contained in essential oils, resins, etc. [<*terp(entin)*, earlier form of TURPENTINE + -ENE]

Terp·sich·o·re (tûrp·sik'ə·rē) *Gk. Myth.* The Muse of dancing. [<Gk. *terpsis* enjoyment + *choros* dance]

terp·si·cho·re·an (tûrp'si·kə·rē'ən, -sə·kôr'ē-, -kō'rē-) *adj.* Of or relating to dancing. Also **terp'si·cho·re'al.**

ter·race (ter'is) *n.* **1** A raised level space, as of lawn, usu. with sloping sides; also, such levels collectively. **2** A raised street supporting a row of houses; also, the houses occupying such a street. **3** A flat roof, esp. of an Oriental or Spanish house. **4** An open, paved area connected to a house, apartment, or building, usu. with places for seating, plantings, etc. **5** A balcony. **6** A parklike area extending down the middle of a wide street or boulevard. **7** A relatively narrow step in the face of a steep natural slope. —*v.t.* **·raced, ·rac·ing** To form into or provide with a terrace or terraces. [<L *terra* earth]

ter·ra cot·ta (ter'ə kot'ə) **1** A hard, kiln-burnt clay, reddish brown and usu. unglazed, used for pottery, sculpture, etc. **2** A statue made of this clay. **3** A brownish red color. [Ital., lit, cooked earth]

ter·ra fir·ma (ter'ə fûr'mə) Solid ground, as distinguished from the sea or the air. [L]

ter·rain (te·rān', ter'ān) *n.* **1** Battleground, or a region suited for defense, fortifications, etc. **2** A land area viewed with regard to some particular characteristic: marshy *terrain.* [<L *terrenus* earthen < *terra* earth]

Ter·ra·my·cin (ter'ə·mī'sin) *n.* An antibiotic effective against a wide variety of pathogenic organisms: a trade name.

ter·ra·pin (ter'ə·pin) *n.* **1** One of the several North American edible tortoises, esp. the diamond-back. **2** Its flesh. [<Algon.]

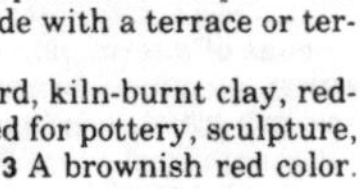

Terrapin

ter·rar·i·um (te·râr'ē·əm) *n. pl.* **·rar·i·ums** or **·rar·i·a** (-râr'ē·ə) **1** A glass enclosure for growing a collection of small plants. **2** A vivarium for small land animals. [<L *terra* earth + -arium, on analogy with *aquarium*]

ter·res·tri·al (tə·res'trē·əl) *adj.* **1** Belonging to the planet earth. **2** Pertaining to land or earth. **3** Living on or growing in earth. **4** Belonging to or consisting of land, as distinct from water, air, etc. **5** Worldly; mundane. —*n.* An inhabitant of the earth. [<L *terra* land] —**ter·res'tri·al·ly** *adv.*

ter·ret (ter'it) *n.* One of two metal rings on a harness, through which the reins are passed. [<OF *touret* small wheel]

ter·ri·ble (ter'ə·bəl) *adj.* **1** Causing extreme fear, dread, or terror. **2** Severe; extreme: a *terrible* headache. **3** Awesome: a *terrible* burden of guilt. **4** Very bad; dreadful; awful: a *terrible* play. [<L *terribilis* < *terrere* terrify] —**ter'ri·ble·ness** *n.* —**ter'ri·bly** *adv.*

ter·ri·er (ter'ē·ər) *n.* Any of several breeds of small, active, wiry dogs, formerly used to hunt burrowing animals. [<L *terrarius* pertaining to earth]

ter·rif·ic (tə·rif'ik) *adj.* **1** Arousing great terror or fear; frightening. **2** *Informal* **a** Very great; extraordinary; tremendous. **b** Unusually good; excellent. —**ter·rif'i·cal·ly** *adv.*

ter·ri·fy (ter'ə·fī) *v.t.* **·fied, ·fy·ing** To fill with terror; frighten severely. [<L *terrere* frighten + -FY]

ter·ri·to·ri·al (ter'ə·tôr'ē·əl, -tō'rē-) *adj.* **1** Of or pertaining to a territory or territories. **2** Of, restricted to, or under the jurisdiction of a particular territory, region, or district. **3** *Often cap.* Organized or intended primarily for home defense: the British *Territorial* Army. —**ter'ri·to'ri·al·ism',** **ter'ri·to'ri·al·ist** *n.* —**ter'ri·to'ri·al·ly** *adv.*

ter·ri·to·ri·al·i·ty (ter'ə·tôr'ē·al'ə·tē, -tō'rē-) *n.* Territorial condition, status, or position.

ter·ri·to·ry (ter'ə·tôr'ē, -tō'rē) *n. pl.* **·ries 1** The domain over which a nation, state, etc., exercises jurisdiction. **2** Any considerable tract of land; a region; district. **3** A region having a certain degree of self-government, but not having the status of a state or province. **4** A special sphere or province of activity, knowledge, etc. **5** A specific area used by or assigned to a person, group, etc.: a salesman's *territory.* [<L *terra* earth]

ter·ror (ter'ər) *n.* **1** Overwhelming fear. **2** A person or thing that causes extreme fear. **3** *Informal* A difficult or annoying person, esp. a child. **4** TERRORISM. [<L *terrere* frighten]

ter·ror·ism (ter'ə·riz'əm) *n.* The act or practice of terrorizing, esp. by violence committed for political purposes, as by a government seeking to intimidate a populace or by revolutionaries seeking to overthrow a government, compel the release of prisoners, etc. —**ter'ror·ist** *n.* —**ter'ror·is'tic** *adj.*

ter·ror·ize (ter'ə·rīz) *v.t.* **·ized, ·iz·ing 1** To reduce to a state of terror; terrify. **2** To coerce or intimidate through terrorism. —**ter'ror·i·za'tion, ter'ror·iz'er** *n.*

ter·ry (ter'ē) *n. pl.* **·ries** A very absorbent pile fabric in which the loops are uncut, used for towels, etc. Also **terry cloth.** [?]

terse (tûrs) *adj.* **ters·er, ters·est** Short and to the point; succinct. [<L *tersus,* pp. of *tergere* rub off, rub down] —**terse'ly** *adv.* —**terse'ness** *n.* —**Syn.** brief, concise, pithy, curt, laconic.

ter·tian (tûr'shən) *adj.* Recurring every other day: said of a fever or disease causing such a fever, as certain forms of malaria. [<L *tertius* third (recurring every third day, reckoned inclusively)]

ter·ti·ar·y (tûr'shē·er'ē, -shə·rē) *adj.* Third in point of time, importance, rank, or value. —*n. pl.* **·ar·ies** Any of the third row of wing feathers of a bird. [<L *tertius* third]

Ter·ti·ar·y (tûr'shē·er'ē, -shə·rē) *n. & adj.* See GEOLOGY.

tes·sel·late (tes'ə·lāt) *v.t.* **·lat·ed, ·lat·ing** To lay or adorn with small squares or mosaic tiles, as pavement. —*adj.* Adorned or laid with mosaic patterns: also **tes'sel·lat'ed.** [<L *tessellatus* checkered] —**tes'sel·la'tion** *n.*

tes·si·tu·ra (tes'i·to͝or'ə) *n.* The average range of a melody or vocal composition. [Ital., lit., texture]

test (test) *v.t.* **1** To subject to an examination or proof; try. —*v.i.* **2** To undergo or give an examination or test: usu. with *for:* to *test* for accuracy. **3** To receive a rating as a result of testing: The alcohol *tested* 75 percent. —*n.* **1** An examination or observation to find out the real nature of something or to prove or disprove its value or validity. 2 A method or technique employed to do this. 3 A criterion or standard of judgment or evaluation. 4 An undergoing of or subjection to certain conditions that disclose the character, quality, nature, etc., of a person or thing: a *test* of will. 5 A series of questions, problems, etc., intended to measure knowledge, aptitudes, intelligence, etc. 6 *Chem.* **a** A reaction by means of which a compound or ingredient may be identified. **b** Its agent or the result. [< L *testum* an earthen vessel < *testa* potsherd, shell] **—test′a·ble** *adj.* **—test′er** *n.*

Test. Testament.

tes·ta (tes′tə) *n. pl.* **·tae** (-tē) The outer, usu. hard and brittle coat of a seed. [L, shell]

tes·ta·ment (tes′tə·mənt) *n.* 1 The written declaration of one's last will: now usu. in the phrase **last will and testament.** 2 A statement testifying to some belief or conviction; credo. 3 Proof; evidence: a *testament* to their courage. 4 In Biblical use, a covenant; dispensation. [< L *testari* testify] **—tes′ta·men′tal, tes′ta·men′ta·ry** (-men′tər·ē) *adj.*

Tes·ta·ment (tes′tə·mənt) *n.* Either of the two parts of the Bible, distinguished as the **Old** and the **New Testament.**

tes·tate (tes′tāt) *adj.* Having made a will before decease. [< L *testari* be a witness]

tes·ta·tor (tes·tā′tər, tes′tā·tər) *n.* One who has died leaving a will. [< L] **—tes·ta′trix** (-triks) *n. Fem.*

tes·ti·cle (tes′ti·kəl) *n.* One of the two sex glands of the male which secrete sex hormones and spermatozoa. [< L *testiculus,* dim. of *testis* testicle]

tes·ti·fy (tes′tə·fī) *v.* **·fied, ·fy·ing** *v.i.* 1 To make solemn declaration of truth or fact. 2 *Law* To give testimony; bear witness. 3 To serve as evidence or indication. *—v.t.* 4 To bear witness to; affirm. 5 *Law* To state or declare on oath or affirmation. 6 To be evidence or indication of. 7 To make known publicly; declare. [< L *testis* witness + -FY] **—tes′ti·fi·ca′tion, tes′ti·fi′er** *n.*

tes·ti·mo·ni·al (tes′tə·mō′nē·əl) *n.* 1 A statement, often a letter, recommending the character, value, etc., of a person or thing. 2 An act, statement, event, etc., that gives public acknowledgment of esteem or appreciation. *—adj.* Pertaining to or constituting testimony or a testimonial.

tes·ti·mo·ny (tes′tə·mō′nē) *n. pl.* **·nies** 1 An oral statement of a witness under oath in a court, usu. made in answer to questioning by a lawyer or judge. 2 Any public acknowledgment or declaration, as of a religious experience. 3 Proof of something; evidence. [< L *testimonium* < *testis* a witness]

tes·tis (tes′tis) *n. pl.* **·tes** (-tēz) TESTICLE. [L]

tes·tos·ter·one (tes·tos′tə·rōn) *n.* A natural or synthetic male sex hormone. [< TESTIS + STER(OL) + -ONE]

test-tube (tes′tyo͞ob′) *adj.* 1 Experimental in nature. 2 Produced by artificial insemination.

test tube A tubular glass vessel used in making chemical or biological tests.

tes·ty (tes′tē) *adj.* **·ti·er, ·ti·est** Irritable; touchy. [< AF *testif* heady < OF *teste* head] **—tes′ti·ly** *adv.* **—tes′ti·ness** *n.* **—Syn.** irascible, peevish, petulant, querulous, snappish, crabby, grouchy.

tet·a·nus (tet′ə·nəs) *n.* An acute and often fatal infectious bacterial disease marked by spasmodic contraction of voluntary muscles, esp. the muscles of the jaw. [< Gk. *tetanos* spasm < *teinein* to stretch] **—te·tan·ic** (ti·tan′ik) *adj.*

tetched (techt) *adj. Regional* Slightly unbalanced mentally. [Alter. of *touched*]

tetch·y (tech′ē) *adj.* **tetch·i·er, tetch·i·est** Irritable; peevish; touchy. [< OF *teche* mark, quality] **—tetch′i·ly** *adv.* **—tetch′i·ness** *n.*

tête-à-tête (tāt′ə·tāt′, *Fr.* tet·à·tet′) *adj.* Confidential, as between two persons. *—n.* 1 A confidential chat between two persons. 2 An S-shaped sofa on which two persons may face each other. *—adv.* In private or personal talk. [F, lit., head to head]

teth·er (teth′ər) *n.* 1 Something used to check or confine, as a rope for fastening an animal. 2 The limit of one's powers or field of action. **—at the end of one's tether** At the extreme limit of one's resources, patience, etc. [< Scand.]

tetra- *combining form* Four; fourfold: *tetrachloride.* [< Gk.]

tet·ra·chlo·ride (tet′rə·klôr′īd, -id, -klō′rīd, -rid) *n.* A compound containing four atoms of chlorine per molecule.

tet·ra·eth·yl lead (tet′rə·eth′il led) A poisonous organic antiknock compound.

tet·ra·he·dron (tet′rə·hē′drən) *n. pl.* **·drons** or **·dra** (-drə) A solid bounded by four plane triangular faces. [< Gk. *tetra-* four + *hedra* base] **—tet′ra·he′dral** *adj.*

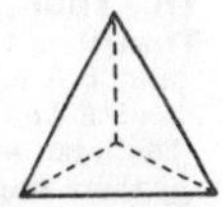

Tetrahedron

te·tral·o·gy (te·tral′ə·jē, -tral′-) *n. pl.* **·gies** 1 A group of four dramas presented together at the festivals of Dionysus at Athens. 2 Any series of four related novels, plays, operas, etc. [< TETRA- + -LOGY]

te·tram·e·ter (te·tram′ə·tər) *n.* In English verse, a line having four metrical feet. [< TETRA + -METER]

tet·rarch (tet′rärk, tē′trärk) *n.* 1 In the Roman Empire, the governor of one of four divisions of a province. 2 A subordinate ruler. [< Gk. *tetra-* four + *archos* ruler] **—tet·rar·chy** (tet′rär·kē, tē′trär-), **tet·rarch·ate** (tet′rär·kāt, -kit, tē′trär-) *n.*

tet·ra·va·lent (tet′rə·vā′lənt) *adj.* QUADRIVALENT. **—tet′·ra·va′lence, tet′ra·va′len·cy** *n.*

te·trox·ide (te·trok′sīd, -sid) *n.* Any oxide having four atoms of oxygen per molecule. [< TETR(A)- + OXIDE]

Teu·ton (tyo͞ot′n) *n.* 1 One of an ancient German tribe that dwelt in Jutland north of the Elbe, appearing in history as **Teu·to·nes** (tyo͞o′tə·nēz). 2 One belonging to any of the Teutonic peoples, esp. a German.

Teu·ton·ic (tyo͞o·ton′ik) *adj.* 1 Of or pertaining to the Teutons. 2 Of or pertaining to Germany or the Germans. 3 Of or pertaining to the peoples of northern Europe, including the English, Scandinavians, Dutch, etc. **—Teu·ton′i·cal·ly** *adv.*

Tex. Texan; Texas.

Texas leaguer In baseball, a looping fly ball that falls safe between an infielder and an outfielder.

text (tekst) *n.* 1 The actual or original words of an author or speaker, as distinguished from notes, commentary, illustrations, etc. 2 Any of the written or printed versions or editions of a piece of writing. 3 The main body of written or printed matter of a book or a single page, as distinguished from notes, indexes, illustrations, etc. 4 The words of a song, opera, etc. 5 A verse of Scripture, esp. when cited as the basis of a sermon. 6 Any subject of discourse; a topic; theme. 7 One of several styles of letters or types. 8 TEXTBOOK. [< L *textus* fabric, structure < *texere* to weave]

text·book (tekst′bo͝ok′) *n.* A book used as a standard work or basis of instruction in any branch of knowledge; schoolbook; manual.

tex·tile (teks′tīl, -til) *adj.* 1 Pertaining to weaving or woven fabrics. 2 Such as may be woven; manufactured by weaving. *—n.* 1 A fabric, esp. if woven or knitted; cloth. 2 Material, as a fiber, yarn, etc., capable of being woven. [< L *textus* fabric. See TEXT.]

tex·tu·al (teks′cho͞o·əl) *adj.* 1 Pertaining to, contained in, or based on a text. 2 Literal; word for word. **—tex′tu·al·ly** *adv.*

tex·ture (teks′chər) *n.* 1 The arrangement or characteristics of the threads, etc., of a fabric: a tweed having a rough *texture.* 2 The arrangement or characteristics of the constituent elements of anything, esp. as regards surface appearance or tactile qualities: the *texture* of bread. 3 The overall or characteristic structure, form, or interrelatedness of parts of a work of art, music, literature, etc.: the tightly-knit *texture* of his poems. 4 The basic nature or structure of something: the *texture* of rural life. [< L *textus* fabric. See TEXT.] **—tex′tur·al** *adj.* **—tex′tur·al·ly** *adv.*

T-group (tē′gro͞op) *n.* A group of people, often business or industrial personnel, who meet with a trained leader whose function is to guide them to a more insightful awareness of themselves and others through the free and uninhibited expression of their thoughts, feelings, prejudices, etc. [< *t(raining) group*]

-th[1] *suffix of nouns* **1** The act or result of the action: *growth.* **2** The state or quality of being or having: *health.* [< OE *-thu, -tho*]

-th[2] *suffix* Used in ordinal numbers: *tenth.* Also **-eth.** [< OE *-tha, -the*]

-th[3] See -ETH[1].

Th thorium.

Th., Thur., Thurs. Thursday.

Thai (tī) *n.* **1** *pl.* **Thai** or **Thais a** A native or citizen of Thailand. **b** A member of the majority ethnic group of Thailand. **2** Any one of a group of related languages used in Thailand. —*adj.* Of or pertaining to Thailand, its people, or their languages.

Thai·land (tī′land) *n.* A constitutional monarchy in SE Asia, 198,404 sq. mi., cap. Bangkok. • See map at INDOCHINA.

thal·a·mus (thal′ə·məs) *n. pl.* **·mi** (-mī, mē) **1** A mass of gray matter at the base of the brain, involved in sensory transmission. **2** The receptacle of a flower. [< Gk. *thalamos* chamber] **—tha·lam·ic** (thə·lam′ik) *adj.*

Tha·li·a (thə·lī′ə, thā′lē·ə, thāl′yə) *Gk. Myth.* **1** The Muse of comedy and pastoral poetry. **2** One of the three Graces. [< Gk. *thallein* to bloom]

thal·li·um (thal′ē·əm) *n.* A soft, rare, highly poisonous metallic element (symbol Tl), used in rat poison, insecticides, and in making optical glass. [< Gk. *thallos* a green shoot; from the bright green line in its spectrum]

thal·lo·phyte (thal′ə·fīt) *n.* Any of a major division of plants without roots, stems, or leaves, comprising the bacteria, fungi, algae, and lichens. [< THALLUS + -PHYTE] **—thal′lo·phyt′ic** (-fit′ik) *adj.*

thal·lus (thal′əs) *n. pl.* **·lus·es** or **·li** (-ī) *Bot.* A plant body without true root, stem, or leaf, as in thallophytes. [< Gk. *thallos* a shoot]

than (t͟han, *unstressed* t͟hən) *conj.* **1** When, as, or if compared with: after an adjective or adverb to express comparison between what precedes and what follows: I am stronger *than* he (is); I know her better *than* (I know) him. **2** Except; but: used after *other, else,* etc: no other *than* you. **3** When: usu. used after *scarcely, hardly, barely:* Scarcely had we got settled *than* we had to leave. —*prep.* Compared to: used only in the phrases *than whom, than which:* An eminent judge *than whom* no other is finer. [< OE *thanne*] • The case of a word following *than* can be either nominative or objective, depending on the word's function in the elliptical clause introduced by *than: You owe him more money than I (owe him)* or *You owe him more money than (you owe) me.* However, in informal writing and speech, the objective case is acceptable following *than* whether or not it agrees with the ellipsis: *He is younger than me.*

thane (thān) *n.* **1** In Anglo-Saxon England, a man who ranked above an ordinary freeman but below an earl or nobleman and who held land of the king or a noble in exchange for military service. **2** The chief of a Scottish clan, a baron in the service of the king. [< OE *thegn*]

thank (thangk) *v.t.* **1** To express gratitude to; give thanks to. **2** To hold responsible; blame: often used ironically: We have him to *thank* for this mess. **—thank you** An expression of gratitude or in acknowledgment of a service rendered. [< OE *thancian*]

thank·ful (thangk′fəl) *adj.* Feeling or manifesting thanks or gratitude; grateful. **—thank′ful·ly** *adv.* **—thank′ful·ness** *n.*

thank·less (thangk′lis) *adj.* **1** Not feeling or expressing gratitude; ungrateful. **2** Not gaining or likely to gain thanks; unappreciated. **—thank′less·ly** *adv.* **—thank′less·ness** *n.*

thanks (thangks) *n.pl.* An expression of gratitude or appreciation. —*interj.* I thank you. **—thanks to 1** Thanks be given to. **2** Because of.

thanks·giv·ing (thangks′giv′ing) *n.* **1** The act of giving thanks. **2** A manner of expressing thanks, as a prayer, public celebration, etc.

Thanksgiving Day 1 In the U.S., the fourth Thursday in November, set apart as a legal holiday for giving thanks for the year's blessings. Also **Thanksgiving. 2** In Canada, a similar holiday celebrated the second Monday in October.

that (t͟hat, *unstressed* t͟hət) *adj. pl.* **those 1** Pertaining to some person or thing previously mentioned, understood, or specifically designated: *that* man. **2** Denoting something more remote in place, time, or thought than the thing with which it is being compared: This winter was colder than *that* one. —*pron. pl.* **those 1** As a demonstrative pronoun: **a** The person or thing implied, mentioned, or understood. **b** The thing further away or more remote: This will happen sooner than *that* will. **2** As a relative pronoun, *that* is used to introduce restrictive clauses and, as such, has a variety of meanings, as *who, whom, which, where, at which, with which,* etc.: The man *that* (whom) I saw is not here; The house *that* (which) you lived in was torn down. **3** Something: There is *that* to be said for him. —*adv.* **1** To that extent; so: I can't see *that* far. **2** *Informal* In such a manner or degree: It really is *that* bad! —*conj. That* is used primarily to connect a subordinate clause with its principal clause, with the following meanings: **1** As a fact that: introducing a fact: I tell you *that* it is so. **2** So that; in order that: I tell you *that* you may know. **3** For the reason that; because: She wept *that* she was growing old. **4** As a result: introducing a result, consequence, or effect: He bled so profusely *that* he died. **5** At which time; when: It was only yesterday *that* I saw him. **6** Introducing an exclamation: O *that* he would come! **—so that 1** To the end that. **2** With the result that. **3** Provided. [< OE *thæt*] • See WHO.

thatch (thach) *n.* **1** A covering of reeds, straw, etc., arranged on a roof so as to shed water. **2** Any of various palm leaves or coarse grasses so used. Also **thatching.** —*v.t.* To cover with a thatch. [< OE *thæc* cover] **—thatch′er** *n.* **—thatch′y** *adj.* **(thatch·i·er, thatch·i·est)**

thau·ma·tur·gy (thô′mə·tûr′jē) *n.* Magic; the performance or working of wonders or miracles. [< Gk. *thauma* wonder + *ergon* work] **—thau′ma·turge, thau′ma·tur′gist** *n.* **—thau′ma·tur′gic** or **·gi·cal** *adj.*

thaw (thô) *v.i.* **1** To melt or dissolve, as snow or ice. **2** To lose the effects of coldness or of having been frozen: often with *out.* **3** To rise in temperature so as to melt ice and snow: said of weather: It *thawed* last night. **4** To become less aloof, unsociable, rigid in opinions, etc. —*v.t.* **5** To cause to thaw. —*n.* **1** The act of thawing. **2** Warmth of weather such as melts things frozen. **3** A becoming less aloof, unsociable, etc. [< OE *thāwian*] **—thaw′er** *n.*

Th.B. Bachelor of Theology.

Th.D. Doctor of Theology.

the[1] (*stressed* t͟hē; *unstressed before a consonant* t͟hə; *unstressed before a vowel* t͟hē, t͟hi) *definite article. The* is opposed to the indefinite article *a* or *an,* and is used specifically: **1** When reference is made to a particular person, thing, or group: *The* children are getting restless; He left *the* room. **2** To give an adjective substantive force, or render a notion abstract: *the* quick and *the* dead; *the* doing of the deed. **3** Before a noun to make it generic: *The* dog is a friend of man. **4** With the force of a possessive pronoun: He kicked me in *the* (my) leg. **5** To give distributive force: equivalent to *a, per, each,* etc.: a dollar *the* bushel. **6** To designate the whole of a specific time period: in *the* Middle Ages; in *the* forties. **7** To designate a particular one as emphatically outstanding: usu. stressed in speech and italicized in writing: He is *the* officer for the command. **8** As part of a title: *The* Duke of York. **9** Before the name of a well-known place, thing, etc.: *the* Grand Canyon; *the* Eiffel Tower. [< OE]

the[2] (t͟hə) *adv.* By that much; to this extent: *the* more, *the* merrier: used to modify words in the comparative degree. [< OE *thȳ*]

the·a·ter (thē′ə·tər) *n.* **1** A structure for the indoor or outdoor presentation of plays, operas, motion pictures, etc. **2** A place resembling such a structure, used for lectures, surgical demonstrations, etc. **3** The theatrical world and everything relating to it, esp.: **a** The legitimate stage, as distinguished from motion pictures, television, etc. **b** The works written for or the arts connected with the theater. **4** Theatrical effectiveness: The play was not good *theater.* **5** Any place that is the scene of events or action:

a *theater* of war operations. Also **the'a·tre.** [< Gk. *theatron* < *theasthai* behold]

the·a·ter-in-the-round (thē'ə·tər·in·t͟hə·round') *n.* A theater having a central stage and no proscenium, with seats surrounding the stage.

theater of the absurd A form of drama that concerns itself with the tragic or comic absurdities of man's condition and his futile efforts to deal with or resolve such absurdities.

the·at·ri·cal (thē·at'ri·kəl) *adj.* **1** Of or pertaining to the theater or things of the theater, as plays, actors, costumes, etc. **2** Dramatically effective or compelling. **3** Artificially dramatic, esp. in a pretentious or showy way. Also **the·at'ric.** —*n.pl.* Dramatic performances, esp. when given by amateurs. **—the·at'ri·cal·ism, the·at'ri·cal'i·ty** *n.* **—the·at'ri·cal·ly** *adv.*

the·at·rics (thē·at'riks) *n.pl.* **1** *(construed as sing.)* The art of the theater. **2** Exaggeratedly dramatic or showy behavior, mannerisms, etc.

thee (t͟hē) *pron.* **1** The objective case of *thou.* **2** Thou: used generally by Quakers with a verb in the third person singular: *Thee* knows my mind. [< OE *thē*]

theft (theft) *n.* **1** The act or an instance of stealing; larceny. **2** That which is stolen. [< OE *thēoft*]

the·ine (thē'ən) *n.* The alkaloid identical with caffeine, found in tea. [< NL *thea* tea]

their (t͟hâr) *pronominal adj.* The possessive case of the pronoun *they* used attributively; belonging or pertaining to them: *their* homes. [< ON *theirra* of them]

theirs (t͟hârz) *pron.* **1** The possessive case of *they,* used predicatively; belonging or pertaining to them: That house is *theirs.* **2** The things or persons belonging or relating to them: our country and *theirs.* **—of theirs** Belonging or pertaining to them.

the·ism (thē'iz·əm) *n.* **1** Belief in a god or gods. **2** Belief in a personal God as creator and supreme ruler of the universe. [< Gk. *theos* god] **—the'ist** *n.* **—the·is'tic** or **·ti·cal** *adj.* **—the·is'ti·cal·ly** *adv.*

them (them, *unstressed* t͟həm) *pron.* The objective case of *they.* [< ON *theim*]

theme (thēm) *n.* **1** A main subject or topic, as of a poem, novel, play, speech, etc. **2** A short essay, often written as an exercise. **3** In a musical composition, a melodic, harmonic, or rhythmic subject or phrase, usu. developed with variations. **4** THEME SONG. [< Gk. *thema*] **—the·mat'ic** (-mat'ik) or **·i·cal** *adj.* **—the·mat'i·cal·ly** *adv.*

theme song **1** A musical motif recurring in a film, television presentation, etc. **2** The brief melody identifying a radio or television presentation, a dance band, etc.

them·selves (t͟hem'selvz', *unstressed* t͟həm-) *pron.* A form of the third person, plural pronoun, used: **1** As a reflexive: They forced *themselves* to go. **2** As an intensive: They *themselves* are responsible. **3** As an indication of their normal, true, or proper selves: They were not *themselves* when they said it.

then (t͟hen) *adv.* **1** At that time. **2** Soon afterward; next in time: We dressed and *then* ate. **3** Next in space or order: Add the flour, *then* the butter. **4** At another time: often introducing a sequential statement following *now, at first,* etc.: At first she laughed, *then* she cried. —*conj.* **1** For that reason; as a consequence; accordingly: If we leave now, *then* you can go to bed. **2** In that case: I will *then,* since you won't. —*adj.* Being or acting in, or belonging to, that time: the *then* secretary of state. —*n.* A specific time already mentioned or understood; that time: We will be gone by *then.* [< OE *thanne*]

thence (t͟hens) *adv.* **1** From that place. **2** From the circumstance, fact, or cause; therefore. **3** From that time; after that time. [< OE *thanon* from there]

thence·forth (t͟hens'fôrth', -fōrth') *adv.* From that time on; thereafter. Also **thence'for'ward** (-fôr'wərd), **thence'·for'wards.**

theo- *combining form* God or a god: *theocracy.* [< Gk. *theos* a god]

the·o·cen·tric (thē'ə·sen'trik) *adj.* Having God for its center; proceeding from God.

the·oc·ra·cy (thē·ok'rə·sē) *n. pl.* **·cies** **1** A state, polity, or group of people that claims a deity as its ruler. **2** Government by a priestly class claiming to have divine authority, as in the Papacy. [< Gk. *theos* god + *krateein* rule] **—the·o·crat** (thē'ə·krat) *n.* **—the·o·crat·ic** (thē'ə·krat'ik) or **·i·cal** *adj.* **—the'o·crat'i·cal·ly** *adv.*

the·od·o·lite (thē·od'ə·līt) *n.* A surveying instrument having a small telescope for measuring angles. [?]

theol. theologian; theological; theology.

the·o·lo·gi·an (thē'ə·lō'jən) *n.* One versed in theology.

the·o·log·i·cal (thē'ə·loj'i·kəl) *adj.* Of, pertaining to, based on, or teaching theology. Also **the'o·log'ic.** **—the'o·log'i·cal·ly** *adv.*

the·ol·o·gize (thē·ol'ə·jīz) *v.* **·gized, ·giz·ing** *v.t.* **1** To devise or fit (something) into a system of theology. —*v.i.* **2** To reason theologically.

the·ol·o·gy (thē·ol'ə·jē) *n. pl.* **·gies** **1** The study of God, his attributes, and his relationship with man and the universe, esp. such studies as set forth by a specific church, religious group, or theologian. **2** The study of religion and religious doctrine, culminating in a synthesis or philosophy of religion. [< Gk. *theos* god + *logos* discourse]

the·o·rem (thē'ər·əm, thir'əm) *n.* **1** A proposition demonstrably true or so universally acknowledged as such as to become part of a general theory. **2** *Math.* A proposition to be proved or which has been proved. [< Gk. *theōrēma* sight, theory] **—the·o·re·mat·ic** (thē'ər·ə·mat'ik) *adj.*

the·o·ret·i·cal (thē'ə·ret'i·kəl) *adj.* **1** Of, relating to, or consisting of theory. **2** Existing only in theory; not applied; speculative; hypothetical. **3** Addicted to theorizing. Also **the'o·ret'ic.** **—the'o·ret'i·cal·ly** *adv.*

the·o·re·ti·cian (thē'ər·ə·tish'ən) *n.* One who theorizes. Also **the·o·rist** (thē'ər·ist).

the·o·rize (thē'ə·rīz) *v.i.* **·rized, ·riz·ing** To form or express theories; speculate. **—the'o·ri·za'tion, the'o·riz'er** *n.*

the·o·ry (thē'ər·ē, thir'ē) *n. pl.* **·ries** **1** A plan, scheme, or procedure used or to be used as a basis or technique for doing something. **2** A merely speculative or an ideal circumstance, principle, mode of action, etc.: often with *in:* In *theory,* the plan worked. **3** A body of fundamental or abstract principles underlying a science, art, etc.: a *theory* of modern architecture. **4** A proposed explanation or hypothesis designed to account for any phenomenon. **5** Loosely, mere speculation, conjecture, or guesswork. [< Gk. *theōria* view, speculation]

theos. theosophical; theosophist; theosophy.

the·os·o·phy (thē·os'ə·fē) *n.* **1** Any of several religious or philosophical systems claiming to have mystical insight into the nature of God and the universe. **2** *Usu. cap.* The religious system of a modern religious sect (**Theosophical Society**) that is strongly Buddhist or Brahmanic in character and claims to have and to be able to teach such mystical insights. [< Gk. *theos* god + *sophos* wise] **—the·o·soph·ic** (thē'ə·sof'ik) or **·i·cal** *adj.* **—the'o·soph'i·cal·ly** *adv.* **—the·os'o·phist** *n.*

ther·a·peu·tic (ther'ə·pyōō'tik) *adj.* **1** Having healing qualities; curative. **2** Pertaining to therapeutics. Also **ther'a·peu'ti·cal.** [< Gk. *therapeuein* serve, take care of] **—ther'a·peu'ti·cal·ly** *adv.*

ther·a·peu·tics (ther'ə·pyōō'tiks) *n.pl.* *(construed as sing.)* The branch of medicine that treats of remedies for disease. **—ther'a·peu'tist** *n.*

ther·a·py (ther'ə·pē) *n. pl.* **·pies** **1** The treatment of disease or any bodily disorder or injury by drugs, physical exercise, etc. **2** PSYCHOTHERAPY. [< Gk. *therapeuein* take care of] **—ther'a·pist** *n.*

there (t͟hâr) *adv.* **1** In or at that place; in a place other than that of the speaker. **2** To, toward, or into that place; thither. **3** At that stage or point of action or proceeding. **4** In that respect, relation, or connection. —*n.* That place, position, or point: We moved it from *there* to here. [< OE *thǣr*] • *There* is also used: **a** As a pronominal expletive introducing a clause or sentence, the subject usually following the verb: *There* once lived three bears. **b** With independent phrases or clauses, as an equivalent of *that,* expressing encouragement, approval, etc.: *There's* a little

add, āce, câre, pälm; end, ēven; it, īce; odd, ōpen, ôrder; tŏŏk, pōōl; up, bûrn; ə = *a* in *above, u* in *focus;* yōō = *u* in *fuse;* oil; pout; check; go; ring; thin; t͟his; zh, *vision.* < derived from; ? origin uncertain or unknown.

dear. **c** As an exclamation expressing triumph, etc.: *There!* I told you so.

there·a·bouts (t͟hâr′ə·bouts′, t͟hâr′ə·bouts′) *adv.* Near that number, quantity, degree, place, or time; approximately. Also **there′a·bout′** (-bout′).

there·af·ter (t͟hâr′af′tər, -äf′-) *adv.* **1** Afterward; from that time on. **2** Accordingly.

there·at (t͟hâr′at′) *adv.* At that event, place, or time; at that incentive; upon that.

there·by (t͟hâr′bī′, t͟hâr′bī′) *adv.* **1** Through the agency of that. **2** Connected with that. **3** Conformably to that. **4** Nearby; thereabout. **5** By it or that; into possession of it or that: How did you come *thereby?*

there·for (t͟hâr′fôr′) *adv.* For this, that, or it; in return or requital for this or that: We return thanks *therefor.*

there·fore (t͟hâr′fôr′, -fōr′) *adv. & conj.* **1** For that or this reason. **2** Consequently: He did not run fast enough; *therefore* he lost the race.

there·from (t͟hâr′frum′, -from′) *adv.* From this, that, or it; from this or that time, place, state, event, or thing.

there·in (t͟hâr′in′) *adv.* **1** In that place. **2** In that time, matter, or respect.

there·in·af·ter (t͟hâr′in·af′tər, -äf′-) *adv.* In a subsequent part of that (book, document, speech, etc.).

there·in·to (t͟hâr′in·to͞o′, t͟hâr·in′to͞o) *adv.* Into this, that, or it.

there·of (t͟hâr′uv′, -ov′) *adv.* **1** Of or relating to this, that, or it. **2** From or because of this or that cause or particular; therefrom.

there·on (t͟hâr′on′, -ôn′) *adv.* **1** On this, that, or it. **2** Thereupon; thereat.

there's (t͟hârz) Contraction of *there is.*

there·to (t͟hâr′to͞o′) *adv.* **1** To this, that, or it. **2** In addition; furthermore. Also **there·un·to** (t͟hâr′un′to͞o, -un·to͞o′).

there·to·fore (t͟hâr′tə·fôr′, -fōr′, t͟hâr′tə·fôr′, -fōr′) *adv.* Before this or that; previously to that.

there·un·der (t͟hâr′un′dər) *adv.* **1** Under this or that. **2** Less, as in number. **3** In a lower or lesser status or rank.

there·up·on (t͟hâr′ə·pon′, -pôn′, t͟hâr′ə·pon′, -ə·pôn′) *adv.* **1** Upon that; upon it. **2** Following upon or in consequence of that. **3** Immediately following; at once.

there·with (t͟hâr′with′, -wit͟h′) *adv.* **1** With this, that, or it. **2** Thereupon; thereafter; immediately afterward.

there·with·al (t͟hâr′wit͟h·ôl′) *adv.* With all this or that; besides.

ther·mal (thûr′məl) *adj.* **1** Of, coming from, or having hot springs. **2** Of, relating to, or caused by heat. **3** Hot or warm: a *thermal* draft. **4** Aiding to conserve body heat: *thermal* fabrics. Also **ther′mic.** —*n.* A rising current of warm air in the atmosphere. [< Gk. *thermē* heat]

thermo- *combining form* Heat; of, related to, or caused by heat: *thermodynamics.* [< Gk. *thermos* heat, warmth]

ther·mo·dy·nam·ics (thûr′mō·dī·nam′iks, -di-) *n.pl.* *(construed as sing.)* The branch of physics that deals with the relations between heat, other forms of energy, and work. **—ther′mo·dy·nam′ic** or **·i·cal** *adj.* **—ther′mo·dy·nam′i·cist** (-nam′ə·sist) *n.*

ther·mo·e·lec·tric·i·ty (thûr′mō·i·lek′tris′ə·tē) *n.* Electricity generated by heat. **—ther′mo·e·lec′tric** or **·tri·cal** *adj.* **—ther′mo·e·lec′tri·cal·ly** *adv.*

ther·mo·gram (thûr′mə·gram) *n.* The record made by a thermograph.

ther·mo·graph (thûr′mə·graf, -gräf) *n.* **1** An instrument for detecting and recording temperature gradations across a surface. **2** A self-registering thermometer.

ther·mog·ra·phy (thər·mog′rə·fē) *n.* **1** The process of recording temperature variations with a thermograph. **2** A process that produces raised lettering on paper, as on stationery, by applying a powder to the lettering and then subjecting it to heat. **—ther·mo·graph·ic** (thûr′mə·graf′ik) *adj.*

ther·mom·e·ter (thər·mom′ə·tər) *n.* An instrument for measuring temperature, often consisting of a tube with a bulb containing a liquid which expands or contracts so that its height in the tube is proportional to the temperature. **—ther·mo·met·ric** (thûr′mō·met′rik) or **·ri·cal** *adj.* **—ther′mo·met′ri·cal·ly** *adv.*

ther·mo·nu·cle·ar (thûr′mō·nʸo͞o′klē·ər) *adj. Physics* Pertaining to or characterized by reactions involving the fusion of light atomic nuclei subjected to very high temperatures.

ther·mo·plas·tic (thûr′mō·plas′tik) *adj.* Becoming soft when heated, as certain synthetic resins. —*n.* A thermoplastic substance or material.

Ther·mop·y·lae (thər·mop′ə·lē) *n.* A narrow mountain pass in Greece; scene of a battle, 480 B.C., in which the Spartans held off the Persians and finally died to the last man rather than yield.

ther·mos (thûr′məs) *n.* A container having two walls separated by a vacuum which serves to retard transfer of heat to or from the contents. Also **thermos bottle.** [< *Thermos,* a trade name]

ther·mo·set·ting (thûr′mō·set′ing) *adj.* Permanently assuming a fixed shape when heated, as certain synthetic resins.

ther·mo·stat (thûr′mə·stat) *n.* An automatic control device used to maintain a desired temperature. [< THERMO- + Gk. *statos* standing] **—ther′mo·stat′ic** *adj.* **—ther′mo·stat′i·cal·ly** *adv.*

ther·mot·ro·pism (thər·mot′rə·piz′əm) *n. Biol.* Movement or growth in a direction determined by the location of a heat source. **—ther·mo·trop·ic** (thûr′mō·trop′ik) *adj.* **—ther′mo·trop′i·cal·ly** *adv.*

the·sau·rus (thi·sôr′əs) *n. pl* **·sau·ri** (-sôr′ī) or **sau′rus·es** **1** A book containing words and their synonyms grouped together. **2** A book containing words or facts dealing with a specific subject or field. [< Gk. *thēsauros* treasure]

these (t͟hēz) *pl.* of THIS.

The·seus (thē′so͞os, -sē·əs) *Gk. Myth.* The chief hero of Attica, celebrated chiefly for killing the Minotaur, and for unifying Attica with Athens as its capital. **—The′se·an** (-sē·ən) *adj.*

the·sis (thē′sis) *n. pl.* **·ses** (-sēz) **1** A proposition, esp. a formal proposition advanced and defended by argumentation. **2** A formal treatise on a particular subject, esp. a dissertation presented by a candidate for an advanced academic degree. **3 a** *Logic* An affirmative proposition. **b** An unproved premise or postulate, as opposed to a hypothesis. [< Gk., a placing, proposition]

thes·pi·an (thes′pē·ən) *adj. Often cap.* Of or relating to drama; dramatic. —*n.* An actor or actress. [< *Thespis,* 6th-c. B.C. Gk. poet]

Thess. Thessalonians.

Thes·sa·lo·ni·ans (thes′ə·lō′nē·ənz) *n.pl. (construed as sing.)* Either of two epistles in the New Testament (**First** and **Second Thessalonians**) written by St. Paul to the Christians of Thessalonica.

Thes·sa·lo·ni·ca (thes′ə·lə·nī′kə, -lon′i·kə) *n.* An ancient city of N Greece.

the·ta (thā′tə, thē′tə) *n.* The eighth letter in the Greek alphabet (Θ, ϑ, θ).

thew (thyo͞o) *n.* **1** A sinew or muscle. **2** *pl.* Bodily strength or vigor. [< OE *thēaw* habit, characteristic quality]

they (t͟hā) *pron.* **1** The persons, beings, or things previously mentioned or understood: the nominative plural of *he, she, it.* **2** People in general: *They* say that the fishing is excellent in this area. [< ON *their*]

they'd (t͟hād) Contraction of *they had* or *they would.*

they'll (t͟hāl) Contraction of *they shall* or *they will.*

they're (t͟hâr) Contraction of *they are.*

they've (t͟hāv) Contraction of *they have.*

T.H.I., T.-H.I. temperature-humidity index.

thi·a·mine (thī′ə·min, -mēn) *n.* Vitamin B_1, a compound found in cereal grains, liver, egg yolk, etc., and also made synthetically. Also **thi′a·min** (-min). [< THI(O)- + -AMINE]

thick (thik) *adj.* **1** Relatively large in depth or extent from one surface to its opposite; not thin. **2** Having a specified dimension of this kind, whether great or small: an inch *thick.* **3** Having the constituent or specified elements growing, packed, arranged, etc., close together: a field *thick* with daisies. **4** Viscous in consistency: a *thick* sauce. **5** Heavy; dense: a *thick* fog. **6** Foggy, hazy, smoky, etc. **7** Very dark; impenetrable: a *thick* gloom. **8** Indistinct; muffled; guttural, as speech. **9** Very noticeable; decided: a *thick* German accent. **10** *Informal* Dull; stupid. **11** *Informal* Very friendly; intimate. **12** *Informal* Going beyond what is tolerable; excessive. —*adv.* In a thick manner. —

n. The thickest or most intense time or place of anything: the *thick* of the fight. [<OE *thicce*] **—thick′ish** *adj.* **—thick′ly** *adv.* **—thick′ness** *n.*

thick·en (thik′ən) *v.t. & v.i.* **1** To make or become thick or thicker. **2** To make or become more intricate or intense: The plot *thickens.* **—thick′en·er** *n.*

thick·en·ing (thik′ən·ing) *n.* **1** The act of making or becoming thick. **2** Something added to a liquid to make it thicker. **3** That part which is or has been thickened.

thick·et (thik′it) *n.* A thick growth, as of underbrush. [< OE *thiccet* < *thicce* thick]

thick·head (thik′hed′) *n.* A stupid person. **—thick′head′·ed** *adj.* **—thick′head′ed·ness** *n.*

thick·set (thik′set′) *adj.* **1** Having a short, thick body; stocky. **2** Closely planted.

thick-skinned (thik′skind′) *adj.* **1** Having a thick skin, as a pachyderm. **2** Insensitive; callous to hints or insults.

thick-wit·ted (thik′wit′id) *adj.* Stupid; obtuse.

thief (thēf) *n. pl.* **thieves** (thēvz) One who takes something belonging to another, esp. secretly. [<OE *thēof*]

thieve (thēv) *v.* **thieved, thiev·ing** *v.t.* To take by theft; purloin; steal. *—v.i.* To be a thief; commit theft. [<OE *thēofian*]

thiev·er·y (thē′vər·ē) *n. pl.* **·er·ies** The practice or act of thieving; theft; also, an instance of thieving. **—thiev′ish** *adj.* **—thiev′ish·ly** *adv.* **—thiev′ish·ness** *n.*

thigh (thī) *n.* **1** The human leg between the hip and the knee. **2** The corresponding portion in other animals. [< OE *thēoh*]

thigh·bone (thī′bōn′) *n.* FEMUR. Also **thigh bone.**

thim·ble (thim′bəl) *n.* **1** In sewing, a pitted cover worn to protect the finger that pushes the needle. **2** Any similar device, esp. a ring on a rope to prevent chafing. [<OE *thȳmel* < *thūma* thumb]

thin (thin) *adj.* **thin·ner, thin·nest** **1** Having opposite surfaces relatively close to each other; being of little depth or width; not thick. **2** Lean and slender of figure. **3** Having the component parts or particles scattered or diffused; rarefied: a *thin* gas. **4** Not large or abundant, as in number: a *thin* audience. **5** Lacking thickness of consistency: a *thin* sauce. **6** Not dense or heavy: a *thin* fog. **7** Having little intensity or richness: a *thin* red. **8** Having little volume or resonance; shrill, as a voice. **9** Of a loose or light texture: *thin* clothing. **10** Insufficient; flimsy: a *thin* excuse. **11** Lacking essential ingredients or qualities: *thin* blood. **12** Meager; scant: *thin* hair. **13** Lacking vigor, force, substance, complexity, etc.; superficial; slight: *thin* humor. *—adv.* In a thin way: Slice the sausage *thin.* *—v.t. & v.i.* **thinned, thin·ning** To make or become thin or thinner. [<OE *thynne*] **—thin′ly** *adv.* **—thin′ness** *n.*

thine (t͟hīn) *pron. Archaic* The things or persons belonging to thee: thou and *thine.* *—pronominal adj. Archaic* Thy: *thine* eyes. [<OE *thīn*]

thing (thing) *n.* **1** That which exists or is conceived to exist as a separate entity: all the *things* in the world. **2** That which is designated, as contrasted with the word or symbol used to denote it. **3** A matter or circumstance: *Things* have changed. **4** An act, deed, event, etc.: That was a shameless *thing* to do. **5** A procedure or step, as in an ordered course or process: the first *thing* to do. **6** An item, particular, detail, etc.: each *thing* on the schedule. **7** A statement or expression; utterance: to say the right *thing.* **8** An idea; opinion; notion: Stop putting *things* in her head. **9** A quality; attribute; characteristic: Kindness is a precious *thing.* **10** An inanimate object. **11** An object that is not or cannot be described or particularized: What kind of *thing* is that? **12** A person, regarded in terms of pity, affection, or contempt: that poor *thing.* **13** *pl.* Possessions; belongings: to pack one's *things.* **14** *pl.* Clothes; esp. outer garments. **15** A piece of clothing, as a dress: not a *thing* to wear. **16** A piece of literature, art, music, etc.: He read a few *things* by Byron. **17** The proper or befitting act or result: with *the:* That was not the *thing* to do. **18** The important point, attitude, etc.: with *the:* The *thing* one learns from travel is how to combat fatigue. **19** *Informal* A point; issue; case: He always makes a big *thing* out of dividing up the bill. **20** *Informal* A strong liking, disliking, fear, attraction, etc.: to have a *thing* for tall girls. **21** *Law* A subject or property or dominion, as distinguished from a person. **—do one's (own) thing** *Slang* To express oneself by doing what one wants to do or can do well or is in the habit of doing. [<OE, thing, cause, assembly]

thing·a·ma·bob (thing′ə·mə·bob′) *n. Informal* THINGAMAJIG. Also **thing′um·a·bob′, thing′um·bob.**

thing·a·ma·jig (thing′ə·mə·jig′) *n. Informal* A thing the specific name of which is unknown or forgotten. Also **thing′um·a·jig′.**

think[1] (thingk) *v.* **thought** (thôt), **think·ing** *v.t.* **1** To produce or form in the mind; conceive mentally: to *think* evil thoughts. **2** To examine in the mind; meditate upon, or determine by reasoning: to *think* a plan through. **3** To believe; consider: I *think* him guilty. **4** To expect; anticipate: They did not *think* to meet us. **5** To bring to mind; remember; recollect: I cannot *think* what he said. **6** To have the mind preoccupied by: to *think* business morning, noon, and night. **7** To intend; purpose: Do they *think* to rob me? *—v.i.* **8** To use the mind or intellect in exercising judgment, forming ideas, etc.; engage in rational thought; reason. **9** To have a particular opinion, sentiment, or feeling: I don't *think* so. **—think of** (or **about**) **1** To bring to mind; remember; recollect. **2** To conceive in the mind; invent; imagine. **3** To have a specified opinion or attitude toward; regard. **4** To be considerate of; have regard for. **—think over** To reflect upon; ponder. **—think up** To devise, arrive at, or invent by thinking. *—n. Informal* The act of thinking. [<OE *thencan*] **—think′er** *n.*

think[2] (thingk) *v.i.* To seem; appear: now obsolete except with the pronoun as indirect object in the combinations *methinks, methought.* [<OE *thyncan* seem]

think·a·ble (thingk′ə·bəl) *adj.* **1** Susceptible of being thought; conceivable. **2** Possible.

think·ing (thingk′ing) *adj.* Using or given to using the mind; intellectually active. *—n.* **1** The act or process of using the mind to think. **2** A result of thought; opinion or position. **—think′ing·ly** *adv.*

think tank *Informal* **1** A group of people (**think tankers**), usu. academics, business executives, or government employees, organized for the investigation and study of social, scientific, and technological problems. **2** The place in which such a group works.

thin·ner (thin′ər) *n.* One who or that which thins, esp. a liquid added to a viscid substance to thin it.

thin-skinned (thin′skind′) *adj.* **1** Having a thin skin. **2** Easily offended; sensitive.

thio- *combining form* Containing sulfur: *thiosulfate.* [< Gk. *theion* sulfur]

thi·o·sul·fate (thī′ō·sul′fāt) *n.* Any salt of thiosulfuric acid, esp. sodium thiosulfate.

thi·o·sul·fu·ric acid (thī′ō·sul·fyŏŏr′ik) An unstable acid, known chiefly by its salts, which are used in bleaching and photography.

third (thûrd) *adj. & adv.* **1** Next in order after the second. **2** Being one of three equal parts. *—n.* **1** The element of an ordered set that corresponds to the number three. **2** One of three equal parts. **3** *Music* The interval between any tone and another two steps away in a diatonic scale. **4** In baseball, the third base. [<OE *thridda*]

third-class (thûrd′klas′, -kläs′) *adj.* **1** Ranking next below the second or second best. **2** Of, pertaining to, or belonging to a class next below the second: *third-class* mail. *—adv.* By third-class accommodations or mail.

third degree *Informal* Severe or brutal examination of a prisoner for the purpose of securing information or a confession.

third estate The common people, traditionally ranked after the nobility and the clergy.

third·ly (thûrd′lē) *adv.* Third.

third person The form of the pronoun, as *he, she, it,* to indicate the person or thing spoken of, or the grammatical form of the verb referring to such person or thing.

third rail An insulated rail on an electric railway for supplying current to the trains or cars.

third-rate (thûrd′rāt′) *adj.* 1 Third in rating or class. 2 Of poor quality; inferior.

third world 1 Any or all of the underdeveloped countries in the world, esp. such countries in Asia or Africa that are not aligned with either the Communist or non-Communist nations. 2 Those not resident in the countries of the third world but collectively identified with their peoples, as because of ideology, ethnic background, or disadvantaged status. Also **Third World.**

thirst (thûrst) *n.* 1 Discomfort or distress due to a need for water. 2 A craving or taste for any specified liquid: a *thirst* for alcohol. 3 Any longing or craving: a *thirst* for glory. —*v.i.* 1 To feel thirst; be thirsty. 2 To have an eager desire or craving. [< OE *thurst*] —**thirst′er** *n.*

thirst·y (thûrs′tē) *adj.* **thirst·i·er, thirst·i·est** 1 Affected with thirst. 2 Lacking moisture; arid; parched. 3 Eagerly desirous. 4 *Informal* Causing thirst. [< OE *thurstig*] —**thirst′i·ly** *adv.* —**thirst′i·ness** *n.*

thir·teen (thûr′tēn′) *n.* 1 The sum of 12 plus 1; 13; XIII. 2 A set or group of 13 members. [< OE *thrēotēne*] —**thir′·teen′** *adj., pron.*

thir·teenth (thûr′tēnth′) *adj.* & *adv.* Next in order after the 12th. —*n.* 1 The element of an ordered set that corresponds to the number 13. 2 One of 13 equal parts.

thir·ti·eth (thûr′tē·ith) *adj.* & *adv.* Tenth in order after the 20th. —*n.* 1 The element of an ordered set that corresponds to the number 30. 2 One of 30 equal parts.

thir·ty (thûr′tē) *n. pl.* **·ties** 1 The product of three and ten. 2 A set or group of 30 members. 3 *pl.* The numbers, years, etc. from 30 to 40. [< OE *thrītig*] —**thir′ty** *adj., pron.*

thir·ty-sec·ond note (thûr′tē·sek′ənd) *Music* A note having one thirty-second of the time value of a whole note. • See NOTE.

this (this) *adj. pl.* **these** 1 That is near or present, either actually or in thought: *This* house is for sale; I shall be there *this* evening. 2 That is understood or has just been mentioned: *This* offense justified my revenge. 3 That is nearer than or contrasted with something else: opposed to *that: This* tree is still alive, but that one is dead. —*pron. pl.* **these** 1 The person or thing near or present, being understood or just mentioned: *This* is where I live; *This* is the guilty man. 2 The person or thing nearer than or contrasted with something else: opposed to *that: This* is a better painting than that. 3 The idea, statement, etc., about to be made clear: I will say *this:* he is a hard worker. —*adv.* To this degree; thus or so: I was not expecting you *this* soon. [< OE]

this·tle (this′əl) *n.* Any of various prickly plants with cylindrical or globular heads of composite flowers. [< OE *thistel*] —**this′tly** *adj.*

Thistle

this·tle·down (this′əl·doun′) *n.* The silky fibers of the ripening flower of a thistle.

thith·er (thith′ər, thith′-) *adv.* To that place; in that direction. —*adj.* Situated or being on the other side; more distant. [< OE *thider*]

thith·er·to (thith′ər·to͞o′, thith′-) *adv.* Up to that time.

thith·er·ward (thith′ər·wərd, thith′-) *adv.* In that direction; toward that place. Also **thith′er·wards.**

tho (thō) *conj.* & *adv.* THOUGH.

thole (thōl) *n.* A pin or pair of pins serving as a fulcrum for an oar in rowing. Also **thole pin.** [< OE *thol*]

Tho·mism (tō′miz·əm) *n.* The theological and philosophical doctrines of St. Thomas Aquinas. [< St. *Thomas* Aquinas] —**Tho′mist** *adj., n.*

thong (thông, thong) *n.* 1 A narrow strip, usu. of leather, as for fastening. 2 A lash of a whip. [< OE *thwang* thong]

Thor (thôr, tôr) *Norse Myth.* The god of war and thunder and son of Odin.

tho·rax (thôr′aks, thō′raks) *n. pl.* **tho·rax·es** or **tho·ra·ces** (thôr′ə·sēz, thō′rə-) 1 The part of the body between the neck and the abdomen, enclosed by the ribs. 2 The middle segment between the head and abdomen of an insect. • See INSECT. [< Gk. *thōrax*] —**tho·rac·ic** (thô·ras′ik) *adj.*

tho·ri·um (thôr′ē·əm, thō′rē-) *n.* A rare, radioactive, metallic element (symbol Th), used as a fuel in certain nuclear reactors. [< THOR] —**tho′ric** *adj.*

thorn (thôrn) *n.* 1 A sharp, rigid outgrowth from a plant stem. 2 Any of various thorn-bearing shrubs or trees. 3 A cause of discomfort, pain, or annoyance. 4 The name of the Old English rune þ, equivalent to *th,* as in *thorn,* from which it derives its name. —*v.t.* To pierce or prick with a thorn. [< OE] —**thorn′less** *adj.*

thorn apple 1 JIMSONWEED. 2 HAW[2].

thorn·y (thôr′nē) *adj.* **thorn·i·er, thorn·i·est** 1 Full of thorns; spiny. 2 Sharp like a thorn. 3 Full of difficulties or trials; painful; vexatious. —**thorn′i·ness** *n.*

tho·ron (thôr′on, thō′ron) *n.* A radioactive isotope of radon, resulting from the disintegration of thorium and having a half-life of 54.5 seconds.

thor·ough (thûr′ō, thûr′ə) *adj.* 1 Complete; exhaustive: a *thorough* search. 2 Attentive to details and accuracy; painstaking: a *thorough* worker. 3 Completely (such and such); through and through: a *thorough* nincompoop. [Emphatic var. of THROUGH] —**thor′ough·ly** *adv.* —**thor′ough·ness** *n.* —**Syn.** 1 comprehensive, sweeping, out-and-out, total. 2 exact, precise, meticulous, careful, conscientious. 3 absolute, downright, utter, unmitigated, perfect.

thor·ough·bred (thûr′ə·bred′) *adj.* 1 Bred from pure stock; pedigreed. 2 Possessing or showing excellence, as in training, education, manners, culture, etc.; first-rate. —*n.* 1 A thoroughbred animal. 2 A person of culture and good breeding.

Thor·ough·bred (thûr′ə·bred′) *n.* A breed of English race horse, originally developed by mating Arabian stallions with English mares.

thor·ough·fare (thûr′ō·fâr′, thûr′ə-) *n.* 1 A much frequented road or street through which the public have unobstructed passage. 2 A passage: now chiefly in the phrase **no thoroughfare.** [< OE *thurh* through + *faru* going]

thor·ough·go·ing (thûr′ō·gō′ing, thûr′ə-) *adj.* 1 Characterized by extreme thoroughness or efficiency. 2 Unmitigated; out-and-out.

those (thōz) *adj.* & *pron. pl.* of THAT. [< OE *thās*]

thou (thou) *pron.* The person spoken to, as denoted in the nominative case: archaic except in religious or poetic language, or in certain dialects. [< OE *thū*]

though (thō) *conj.* 1 Notwithstanding the fact that; although: *Though* he was sleepy, he stayed awake. 2 Granting that; even if: *Though* she may win, she will have lost her popularity. 3 And yet; still; however: I am well, *though* I do not feel very strong. —*adv.* Notwithstanding; nevertheless: It's not a good play, but I like it *though.* [< ON *thō*]

thought[1] (thôt) *n.* 1 The act or process of thinking. 2 The product of thinking, as an idea, concept, judgment, opinion, or the like. 3 Intellectual activity of a specific kind, time, place, etc.: Greek *thought.* 4 Consideration; attention; heed: Give the plan some *thought.* 5 Intention; plan; design: All *thought* of returning was abandoned. 6 Expectation; anticipation: He had no *thought* of finding her there. 7 A trifle; a small amount: Be a *thought* more cautious. [< THOUGHT[2]]

thought[2] (thôt) *p.t.* & *p.p.* of THINK. [< OE *thōht*]

thought·ful (thôt′fəl) *adj.* 1 Full of thought; meditative. 2 Showing, characterized by, or promoting thought. 3 Attentive; careful, esp. manifesting regard for others; considerate. —**thought′ful·ly** *adv.* —**thought′ful·ness** *n.*

thought·less (thôt′lis) *adj.* 1 Manifesting lack of thought or care; careless. 2 Not considerate of others. 3 Giddy; flighty. —**thought′less·ly** *adv.* —**thought′less·ness** *n.*

thou·sand (thou′zənd) *n.* 1 The product of ten times a hundred. 2 *Usu. pl.* An indefinitely large number. —*adj.* Consisting of a hundred times ten. [< OE *thūsend*] —**thou′sand·fold′** (-fōld′) *adj., adv.*

thou·sandth (thou′zəndth) *adj.* 1 Last in a series of a thousand. 2 Being one of a thousand equal parts. —*n.* 1 The element of an ordered set that corresponds to the number 1000. 2 One of a thousand equal parts.

thrall (thrôl) *n.* 1 A person in bondage; a slave; serf. 2 One controlled by a passion or vice. 3 Slavery. [< ON *thræl*]

thrall·dom (thrôl′dəm) *n.* 1 The state of being a thrall. 2 Any sort of bondage or servitude. Also **thral′dom.**

thrash (thrash) *v.t.* 1 To thresh, as grain. 2 To beat as if with a flail; flog; whip. 3 To move or swing with flailing, violent motions. 4 To defeat utterly. —*v.i.* 5 To move or swing about with flailing, violent motions. 6 To make one's way by thrashing. —**thrash out** (or **over**) To discuss fully and usu. come to a conclusion. —*n.* The act of thrashing. [Dial. var. of THRESH]

thrash·er[1] (thrash′ər) *n.* 1 One who or that which thrashes. 2 A machine for threshing grain. 3 THRESHER (def. 2).

thrash·er[2] (thrash′ər) *n.* Any of several long-tailed American songbirds resembling the thrushes and related to the mockingbirds. [?< THRUSH[1]]

thread (thred) *n.* 1 A very slender cord or line composed of two or more filaments, as of flax, cotton, silk, nylon, etc., twisted together. 2 A filament of metal, glass, etc. 3 A fine beam: a *thread* of light. 4 Something that runs a continuous course through a series or whole: the *thread* of his discourse. 5 *Mech.* The helical ridge of a screw. —*v.t.* 1 To pass a thread through the eye of: to *thread* a needle. 2 To string on a thread, as beads. 3 To cut a thread on or in, as a screw. 4 To make one's way through or over: to *thread* a maze. 5 To make (one's way) carefully. —*v.i.* 6 To make one's way carefully. 7 To fall from a fork or spoon in a fine thread: said of boiling syrup. [< OE *thræd*] —**thread′er** *n.*

thread·bare (thred′bâr′) *adj.* 1 Worn so that the threads show, as a rug or garment. 2 Clad in worn garments. 3 Commonplace; hackneyed. —**thread′bare′ness** *n.* —**Syn.** 2 shabby. 3 common, stale, stereotyped, trite.

thread·y (thred′ē) *adj.* **thread·i·er, thread·i·est** 1 Like a thread; stringy. 2 Forming threads, as some liquids. 3 Weak; lacking vigor: a *thready* pulse. —**thread′i·ness** *n.*

threat (thret) *n.* 1 A declaration of an intention to inflict injury or pain. 2 Any menace or danger. [< OE *threat* crowd, oppression]

threat·en (thret′n) *v.t.* 1 To utter threats against. 2 To be menacing or dangerous to. 3 To portend (something unpleasant or dangerous). 4 To utter threats of (injury, vengeance, etc.). —*v.i.* 5 To utter threats. 6 To have a menacing aspect; lower. —**threat′en·er** *n.* —**threat′en·ing·ly** *adv.*

three (thrē) *n.* 1 The sum of two plus one; 3, III. 2 A set or group of three members. [< OE *thrī*] —**three** *adj., pron.*

three-D (thrē′dē′) *adj.* THREE-DIMENSIONAL. —*n.* A technique, medium, or process giving the appearance of three dimensions to visual images. Also **3-D.**

three-deck·er (thrē′dek′ər) *n.* 1 A vessel having three decks or gun decks. 2 Anything having three levels.

three-di·men·sion·al (thrē′də·men′shən·əl) *adj.* 1 Of or having three dimensions. 2 Appearing to have depth as well as height and width.

three·fold (thrē′fōld′) *adj.* 1 Made up of three parts. 2 Having three times as many or as much. —*adv.* Triply; in a threefold manner.

three-mile limit (thrē′mīl′) A distance of three geographic miles from the shore line seaward, allowed by international law for territorial jurisdiction.

three·pence (thrip′əns, threp′-, thrup′-) *n. Brit.* 1 The sum of three pennies. 2 A small coin of Great Britain worth three pennies: also **thrip′pence** (thrip′əns).

three-ply (thrē′plī′) *adj.* Consisting of three thicknesses, strands, layers, etc.

three R's Reading, writing, and arithmetic.

three·score (thrē′skôr′, -skōr′) *adj. & n.* Sixty.

three·some (thrē′səm) *n.* 1 A group of three people. 2 A game played by three people; also, the players.

thren·o·dy (thren′ə·dē) *n. pl.* **·dies** An ode or song of lamentation; a dirge. Also **thren′ode** (-ōd). [< Gk. *thrēnos* lament + *ōidē* song] —**thre·nod·ic** (thri·nod′ik) *adj.* —**thren′o·dist** *n.*

thresh (thresh) *v.t.* 1 To beat stalks of (ripened grain) with a flail so as to separate the grain from the husks. —*v.i.* 2 To thresh grain. 3 To move or thrash about. —**thresh out** To discuss fully and to a conclusion. —**thresh over** To discuss over and over. [< OE *therscan*]

thresh·er (thresh′ər) *n.* 1 One who or that which threshes, esp. a machine for threshing. 2 A large shark having an extremely long tail: also **thresher shark.**

thresh·old (thresh′ōld, -hōld) *n.* 1 The plank, timber, or stone lying under the door of a building; doorsill. 2 The entering point or beginning of anything: the *threshold* of the 20th century. 3 The minimum degree of stimulation necessary to produce a response or to be perceived. [< OE *therscold*]

threw (thrōō) *p.t.* of THROW.

thrice (thrīs) *adv.* 1 Three times. 2 Fully; extremely. [< OE *thriwa* thrice]

thrift (thrift) *n.* Care and wisdom in the management of one's resources; frugality. [< ON] —**thrift′less** *adj.* —**thrift′less·ly** *adv.* —**thrift′less·ness** *n.*

thrift·y (thrif′tē) *adj.* **thrift·i·er, thrift·i·est** 1 Displaying thrift or good management; frugal. 2 Prosperous; thriving. —**thrift′i·ly** *adv.* —**thrift′i·ness** *n.* —**Syn** 1 economical, provident, prudent, saving.

thrill (thril) *v.t.* 1 To cause to feel a great or tingling excitement. —*v.i.* 2 To feel a sudden wave of emotion. 3 To vibrate or tremble; quiver. —*n.* 1 A feeling of excitement. 2 A thrilling quality. 3 A pulsation; quiver. [< OE *thyrlian* pierce] —**thrill′ing·ly** *adv.*

thrill·er (thril′ər) *n.* 1 One who or that which thrills. 2 *Informal* An exciting book, play, etc.

thrive (thrīv) *v.i.* **throve** (thrōv) or **thrived, thrived** or **thriv·en** (thriv′ən), **thriv·ing** 1 To prosper; be successful. 2 To flourish. [< ON *thrīfast* reflexive of *thrīfa* grasp] —**thriv′er** *n.* —**thriv′ing·ly** *adv.*

throat (thrōt) *n.* 1 The front part of the neck. 2 The passage extending from the back of the mouth and containing the epiglottis, larynx, trachea, and pharynx. 3 Any narrow passage resembling a throat. —**jump down one's throat** To scold or criticize with sudden violence. —**lump in the throat** A feeling of tightness in the throat, as from strong emotion. —**stick in one's throat** To be difficult or painful to say. [< OE *throte*]

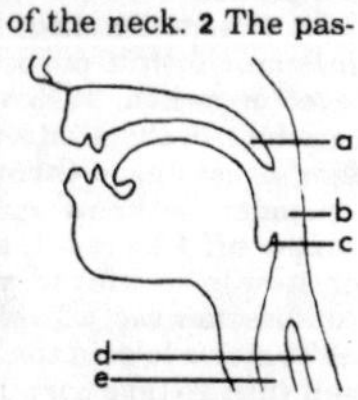

Throat
a. soft palate. b. pharynx. c. epiglottis. d. esophagus. e. trachea.

throat·y (thrō′tē) *adj.* **throat·i·er, throat·i·est** Uttered in the throat; guttural. —**throat′i·ly** *adv.* —**throat′i·ness** *n.*

throb (throb) *v.i.* **throbbed, throb·bing** 1 To pulsate rhythmically, as the heart. 2 To feel or show emotion by trembling. —*n.* 1 The act or state of throbbing. 2 A pulsation, esp. one caused by excitement or emotion. [Imit.] —**throb′ber** *n.*

throe (thrō) *n.* 1 A violent pang or pain. 2 *pl.* The pains of death or childbirth. 3 Any agonized or agonizing activity. [< OE *thrawe*]

throm·bin (throm′bin) *n.* An enzyme in blood serum that promotes clotting. [< Gk. *thrombos* clot]

throm·bo·sis (throm·bō′sis) *n.* The formation of a blood clot inside the heart or a blood vessel. [< Gk. *thrombos* clot] —**throm·bot′ic** (-bot′ik) *adj.*

throne (thrōn) *n.* 1 The chair occupied by a king, pope, etc., on state occasions. 2 The rank or authority of a king, queen, etc. —*v.t. & v.i.* **throned, thron·ing** To enthrone; exalt. [< Gk. *thronos* seat]

throng (thrông, throng) *n.* 1 A closely crowded multitude. 2 Any numerous collection. —*v.t.* 1 To crowd into and occupy fully; jam. 2 To crowd upon. —*v.i.* 3 To collect or move in a throng. [< OE *gethrang*] —**Syn.** *n.* 1 crowd, host, jam, mass, press.

throt·tle (throt′l) *n.* 1 A valve controlling the supply of fuel or steam to the cylinders of an engine: also **throttle valve.** 2 The lever which operates the throttle valve: also **throttle lever.** —*v.t.* **·tled, ·tling** 1 To strangle, choke, or suffocate. 2 To silence, stop, or suppress. 3 To reduce or shut off the flow of (steam or fuel to the cylinders of an engine). 4 To reduce the speed of by means of a throttle. —*v.i.* 5 To suffocate; choke. [Dim. of ME *throte* throat] —**throt′tler** *n.*

through (thrōō) *prep.* 1 From end to end, side to side, or limit to limit of; into at one side, end, or point, and out of at another. 2 Covering, entering, or penetrating all parts of; throughout. 3 From the first to the last of: *through* the day. 4 Here and there upon or in. 5 By way of: He departed *through* the door. 6 By the instrumentality or aid of. 7 Having reached the end of: He got *through* his examinations. —*adv.* 1 From one end, side, surface, etc., to or beyond another. 2 From beginning to end. 3 To a termination or conclusion: to pull *through.* 4 Completely; entirely: He is wet *through.* —**through and through** Thoroughly; completely. —*adj.* 1 Going to its destination without stops: a *through* train. 2 Usable or valid for an entire trip: a *through* ticket. 3 Extending from one side or surface to another. 4 Allowing unobstructed or direct passage: a *through* road. 5 Finished: Are you *through* with my pen? [< OE *thurh*]

through·out (thrōō·out′) *adv.* Through or in every part. —*prep.* All through; everywhere in.

throve (thrōv) *p.t.* of THRIVE.

throw (thrō) *v.* **threw** (thrōō), **thrown, throw·ing** *v.t.* 1 To propel through the air by means of a sudden straightening or whirling of the arm. 2 To propel or hurl. 3 To put hastily or carelessly: He *threw* a coat over his shoulders. 4 To direct or project (light, shadow, a glance, etc.). 5 To bring to a specified condition or state: to *throw* the enemy into a panic. 6 To cause to fall: The horse *threw* its rider. 7 In wrestling, to force the shoulders of (an opponent) to the ground. 8 To cast (dice). 9 To make (a specified cast) with dice. 10 To shed; lose: The horse *threw* a shoe. 11 *Informal* To lose purposely, as a race. 12 To move, as a lever or switch. 13 *Slang* To give (a party, etc.). 14 In ceramics, to shape on a potter's wheel. —*v.i.* 15 To cast or fling something. —**throw away** 1 To cast off; discard. 2 To squander. —**throw cold water on** To discourage. —**throw off** 1 To reject; spurn. 2 To rid oneself of. 3 To do or utter in an offhand manner. 4 To emit; discharge. 5 To confuse; mislead. 6 To elude (a pursuer). —**throw oneself at** To strive to gain the affection or love of. —**throw oneself into** To take part in vigorously. —**throw oneself on** (or **upon**) To rely on utterly. —**throw open** 1 To open suddenly, as a door. 2 To free from restrictions or obstacles. —**throw out** 1 To emit. 2 To discard; reject. 3 To utter as if accidentally: to *throw out* hints. 4 In baseball, to retire (a runner) by throwing the ball to the base toward which he is advancing. —**throw over** 1 To overturn. 2 To jilt. —**throw together** To put together carelessly. —**throw up** 1 To vomit. 2 To erect hastily. 3 To give up. 4 *Informal* To mention (something) repeatedly and reproachfully; taunt. —*n.* 1 An act of throwing. 2 The distance over which a missile may be thrown: a long *throw.* 3 A cast of dice, or the resulting number. 4 A scarf or other light covering. 5 In wrestling, a flooring of one's opponent so that both his shoulders touch the mat simultaneously for ten seconds. [< OE *thrāwan* to turn, twist, curl] —**throw′er** *n.* —**Syn.** *v.* 1 fling, heave, hurl, pitch.

throw·back (thrō′bak′) *n.* 1 An atavism. 2 A throwing back.

thru (thrōō) *adj., adv. & prep.* THROUGH.

thrum (thrum) *v.* **thrummed, thrum·ming** *v.t.* 1 To play on (a stringed instrument), esp. idly; strum. 2 To drum on monotonously with the fingers. —*v.i.* 3 To strum a stringed instrument. —*n.* The sound made by thrumming. [Prob. imit.]

thrush[1] (thrush) *n.* Any of many species of migratory songbirds, usu. having long wings and spotted under parts, as the **hermit thrush,** the **wood thrush,** the robin, and the bluebird. [< OE *thrysce*]

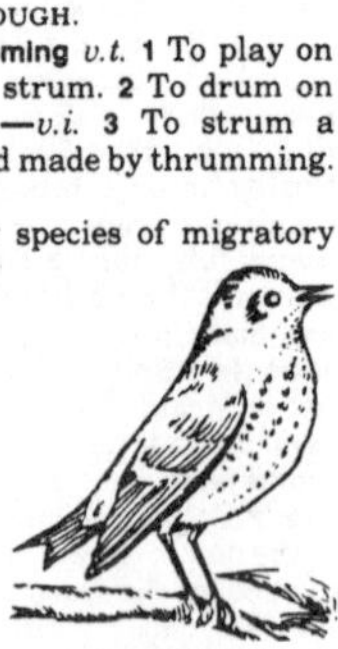
Wood thrush

thrush[2] (thrush) *n.* A disease of the mouth, lips, and throat caused by a yeastlike fungus. [?]

thrust (thrust) *v.* **thrust, thrust·ing** *v.t.* 1 To push or shove with force. 2 To pierce with a sudden forward motion, as with a sword. 3 To interpose. —*v.i.* 4 To make a sudden push or thrust. 5 To force oneself on or ahead: to *thrust* through a crowd. —*n.* 1 A sudden and forcible push, esp. with a pointed weapon. 2 A vigorous attack; sharp onset. 3 A force that drives or propels. 4 Salient force or meaning: the *thrust* of his remarks. [< ON *thrȳsta*] —**thrust′er** *n.* —**Syn.** *v.* 1 lunge. 2 stab, stick. *n.* 4 import, intention, significance, sense, gist.

thru·way (thrōō′wā′) *n.* EXPRESSWAY.

thud (thud) *n.* 1 A dull, heavy sound. 2 A blow causing such a sound; a thump. —*v.i.* **thud·ded, thud·ding** To strike or fall with a thud. [< OE *thyddan* strike, thrust, press]

thug (thug) *n.* 1 Formerly, one of an organization of religious assassins in India. 2 Any assassin or ruffian. [< Skt. *sthaga* swindler]

thu·li·um (thōō′lē·əm) *n.* A metallic element (symbol Tm) of the lanthanide series. [< *Thule,* the northernmost limit of the habitable world in ancient geography]

thumb (thum) *n.* 1 The short, thick digit of the human hand. 2 A similar part in certain animals. 3 The division in a glove or mitten that covers the thumb. —**all thumbs** Clumsy with the hands. —**thumbs down** A signal of negation or disapproval. —**thumbs up** A signal of approval. —**under one's thumb** Under one's influence or power. —*v.t.* 1 To rub, soil, or wear with the thumb in handling. 2 To handle clumsily. 3 To run through the pages of (a book, etc.) rapidly. —**thumb a ride** To get a ride by signaling with the thumb. [< OE *thūma*]

thumb index A series of scalloped indentations cut along the front edge of a book and labeled to indicate its various sections. —**thumb′-in′dex** *v.t.*

thumb·nail (thum′nāl′) *n.* 1 The nail of the thumb. 2 Anything as small as a thumbnail. —*adj.* Very brief: a *thumbnail* sketch.

thumb·screw (thum′skrōō′) *n.* 1 A screw to be turned by thumb and fingers. • See SCREW. 2 An instrument of torture for compressing the thumb or thumbs.

thumb·tack (thum′tak′) *n.* A broad-headed tack that may be pushed in with the thumb.

thump (thump) *n.* 1 A blow with a blunt or heavy object. 2 The sound made by such a blow; a thud. —*v.t.* 1 To beat or strike so as to make a heavy thud or thuds. 2 *Informal* To beat or defeat severely. —*v.i.* 3 To strike with a thump. 4 To pound or throb, as the heart. [Imit.] —**thump′er** *n.*

thun·der (thun′dər) *n.* 1 The sound that accompanies lightning, caused by the explosive effect of the electric discharge. 2 Any loud noise resembling thunder. 3 A vehement or powerful utterance. —**steal one's thunder** To undermine the effectiveness of an opponent by anticipating his next move, argument, etc. —*v.i.* 1 To give forth peals of thunder: It is *thundering.* 2 To make a noise like thunder. 3 To utter vehement denunciations. —*v.t.* 4 To utter or express with a noise like thunder: The cannon *thundered* defiance. [< OE *thunor*] —**thun′der·er** *n.*

thun·der·bolt (thun′dər·bōlt′) *n.* 1 A lightning flash accompanied by a clap of thunder. 2 A person or thing acting with great force, speed, or destructiveness.

thun·der·clap (thun′dər·klap′) *n.* 1 A sharp, violent detonation of thunder. 2 Anything violent or sudden.

thun·der·cloud (thun′dər·kloud′) *n.* A dark, heavy mass of electrically charged cloud.

thun·der·head (thun′dər·hed′) *n.* A rounded mass of silvery cumulus cloud, often developing into a thundercloud.

thun·der·ous (thun′dər·əs) *adj.* Producing or emitting thunder or a sound like thunder. —**thun′der·ous·ly** *adv.*

thun·der·show·er (thun′dər·shou′ər) *n.* A shower of rain with thunder and lightning.

thun·der·storm (thun′dər·stôrm′) *n.* A local storm accompanied by lightning and thunder.

thun·der·struck (thun′dər·struk′) *adj.* Amazed, astonished, or confounded. Also **thun′der·strick′en** (-strik′ən).

Thur., Thurs. Thursday.

thu·ri·ble (thŏŏr′ə·bəl) *n.* CENSER. [< L *thus, thuris* frankincense]

Thurs·day (thûrz′dē, -dā) *n.* The fifth day of the week. [< OE *Thunres dæg* day of Thor]

thus (thus) *adv.* 1 In this or that or the following way. 2 To such degree or extent; so: *thus* far. 3 In this case; therefore. [< OE]

thwack (thwak) *v.t.* To strike heavily with something flat; whack. —*n.* A blow with something flat. [Prob. imit.] —**thwack′er** *n.*

thwart (thwôrt) *v.t.* To obstruct (a plan, a person, etc.) as by interposing an obstacle; frustrate. —*n.* 1 An oarsman's seat extending athwart a boat. 2 A brace athwart a canoe. —*adj.* Lying, moving, or extending across something; transverse. —*adv. & prep.* Athwart. [<ON *thvert,* neut. of *thverr* transverse] —**thwart'er** *n.*

thy (t̲h̲ī) *pronominal adj.* Belonging or pertaining to thee: *Thy* kingdom come. [<OE *thīn* THINE]

thyme (tīm) *n.* 1 Any of various small shrubby plants of the mint family, having aromatic leaves. 2 The dried leaves of certain thyme plants, used for seasoning in cookery. [<Gk. *thymon*] —**thy·mic** (-mik), **thym'y** *adj.*

thy·mus (thī'məs) *n.* A ductless glandlike structure situated at the root of the neck and usu. becoming atrophied after early childhood. [<Gk. *thymos*] • See THYROID.

thy·roid (thī'roid) *adj.* 1 Of or pertaining to the cartilage of the larynx which forms the Adam's apple. 2 Of, pertaining to, or describing a large ductless gland situated near the larynx on each side of the trachea and secreting thyroxin. —*n.* 1 The thyroid cartilage. 2 The thyroid gland. [<Gk. *thyreoeidēs* shield-shaped]

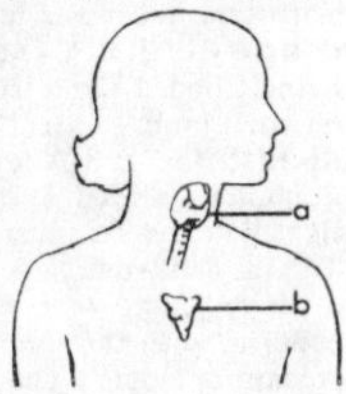

a. thyroid. b. thymus.

thy·rox·in (thī·rok'sin) *n.* 1 A vital hormone, secreted by the thyroid gland, which regulates growth and metabolism. 2 A white, crystalline compound, obtained from the thyroid glands of animals and also made synthetically, used in the treatment of thyroid disorders. Also **thy·rox'ine** (-sēn, -sin).

thyr·sus (thûr'səs) *n. pl.* **·si** (-sī, -sē) A staff wreathed in ivy and crowned with a pine cone or a bunch of ivy leaves, borne by Dionysus and the satyrs. [<Gk. *thyrsos*]

thy·self (t̲h̲ī·self') *pron.* Emphatic or reflexive form of *thou:* I love thee for *thyself.*

ti (tē) *n. Music* In solmization, the seventh note of a diatonic scale. [Ital. See GAMUT.]

Ti titanium.

ti·ar·a (tē·âr'ə, -är'ə) *n.* 1 The pope's triple crown. 2 The upright headdress worn by the ancient Persian kings. 3 A jeweled head ornament or coronet worn by women on very formal or state occasions. [Gk., Persian headdress]

Ti·bet·an (ti·bet'n) *adj.* Of or pertaining to Tibet, the Tibetans, or to their language. —*n.* 1 An inhabitant or citizen of Tibet. 2 The language of Tibet.

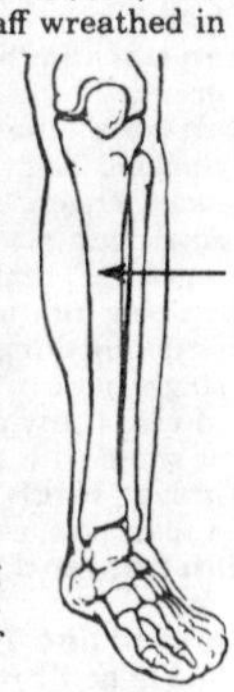
Tibia

tib·i·a (tib'ē·ə) *n. pl.* **tib·i·as** or **tib·i·ae** (tib'·ē·ē, -ē·ī) The inner and larger of the two bones of the leg below the knee; the shinbone. —**tib'i·al** *adj.*

tic (tik) *n.* Any involuntary, recurrent muscular spasm. [F]

tick[1] (tik) *n.* 1 A light recurring sound made by a watch, clock, etc. 2 *Informal* The time elapsing between two ticks of a clock; an instant. 3 A mark, as a dot or dash, used in checking off something. —*v.i.* 1 To sound a tick or ticks. —*v.t.* 2 To mark or check with ticks. [Prob. imit.]

tick[2] (tik) *n.* 1 Any of numerous small, bloodsucking arachnids, parasitic on warm-blooded animals and often harboring and transmitting pathogenic microorganisms. 2 Any of certain usu. wingless parasitic insects. [<OE *ticia*]

Tick

tick[3] (tik) *n.* 1 The stout outer covering of a mattress; also, the material for such covering. 2 *Informal* Ticking. [<Gk. *thēke* a case]

tick[4] (tik) *n. Brit. Informal* Credit; trust: to buy merchandise on *tick.* [Short for TICKET]

tick·er (tik'ər) *n.* 1 One who or that which ticks. 2 Formerly, a telegraphic instrument that printed stock quotations on paper ribbon (**ticker tape**). 3 *Slang* The heart.

tick·et (tik'it) *n.* 1 A printed card showing that the holder is entitled to something, as transportation in a public vehicle, admission to a theater, etc. 2 A label or tag: a price *ticket.* 3 A list of candidates of a single party on a ballot: the Democratic *ticket.* 4 *Informal* A court summons for a traffic violation, usu. involving a fine. —*v.t.* 1 To fix a ticket to; label. 2 To furnish with a ticket. [<OF *estiquette*]

ticket of leave *Brit.* Formerly, a written permit granted to a convict to be at large before the expiration of his sentence.

tick·ing (tik'ing) *n.* A strong, closely woven cotton or linen fabric, used for mattress covering, awnings, etc. [<TICK[3]]

tick·le (tik'əl) *v.* **·led, ·ling** *v.t.* 1 To excite the nerves of by touching or scratching on some sensitive spot, producing a sensation resulting in spasmodic laughter or twitching. 2 To please: Compliments *tickle* our vanity. 3 To amuse or entertain; delight. 4 To move, stir, or get by tickling. —*v.i.* 5 To have a tingling sensation: My foot *tickles.* 6 To be ticklish. —*n.* 1 The sensation produced by tickling. 2 The touch or action producing such sensation. [ME *tikelen*]

tick·ler (tik'lər) *n.* 1 One who or that which tickles. 2 A memorandum book or file used as a reminder to attend to matters on certain dates in the future.

tick·lish (tik'lish) *adj.* 1 Sensitive to tickling. 2 Liable to be upset. 3 Easily offended; sensitive. 4 Requiring tact in handling; delicate: a *ticklish* situation. —**tick'lish·ly** *adv.* —**tick'lish·ness** *n.*

tick-tock (tik'tok') *n.* The oscillating sound of a clock. —*v.i.* To make this sound. [Imit.]

tick·y tack·y (tik'ē tak'e) *Slang* 1 Shoddy, inferior materials: rows of little houses built of *ticky tacky.* 2 Dull, tedious uniformity. —**tick'y-tack'y** *adj.*

tid·al (tīd'l) *adj.* 1 Of, pertaining to, or influenced by the tides. 2 Dependent on the tide.

tidal wave 1 A great incoming rise of waters along a shore, caused by heavy winds and very high tides. 2 TSUNAMI. 3 A great upsurge, as of popular sentiment.

tid·bit (tid'bit') *n.* A choice bit, as of food. [<dial. E *tid* a small object + BIT[1]]

tide (tīd) *n.* 1 The periodic rise and fall of the surface of the ocean caused by the gravitational attraction of moon and sun. 2 Anything that comes like the tide at flood. 3 The natural drift or tendency of events. 4 A current; stream: the *tide* of public feeling. 5 Season; time: *Eastertide.* —**turn the tide** To reverse a condition completely. —*v.i.* **tid·ed, tid·ing** To ebb and flow like the tide. —**tide over** 1 To give or act as temporary help, as in a difficulty. 2 To surmount. [<OE *tīd* a period, season]

tide·land (tīd'land') *n.* 1 Land alternately covered and uncovered by the tide. 2 *Often pl.* Offshore land lying completely under the ocean, but within the limits of a nation's territorial waters.

tide·wa·ter (tīd'wô'tər, -wot'ər) *n.* 1 Water affected by the tide on the seacoast or in a river. 2 A region in which water is affected by the tide. —*adj.* Pertaining to or along a tidewater.

ti·dings (tī'dingz) *n.pl. (sometimes construed as sing.)* Information; news. [<OE *tīdung*]

ti·dy (tī'dē) *adj.* **·di·er, ·di·est** 1 Neat in appearance; orderly: a *tidy* desk. 2 Keeping things in order: a *tidy* housekeeper. 3 *Informal* Moderately large: a *tidy* sum. 4 *Informal* Fairly good. —*v.t. & v.i.* **ti·died, ti·dy·ing** To put (things) in order. —*n. pl.* **·dies** An antimacassar. [<OE *tīd* time] —**ti'di·ly** *adv.* —**ti'di·ness** *n.* —**Syn.** *adj.* 1 shipshape, spruce, trim, well-kept.

tie (tī) *v.* **tied, ty·ing** *v.t.* 1 To fasten with cord, rope, etc., the ends of which are then knotted. 2 To draw the parts of together by a cord fastened with a knot: to *tie* one's shoes. 3 To form (a knot). 4 To form a knot in, as string. 5 To fasten, or join in any way. 6 To restrict; bind. 7 a To equal (a competitor) in score or achievement. b To equal (a competitor's score). 8 *Informal* To unite in marriage. 9 *Music* To unite by a tie. —*v.i.* 10 To make a tie or connection. 11 To make the same score; be equal. —**tie down** To hinder;

restrict. —**tie up** 1 To fasten with rope, string, etc. 2 To wrap, as with paper, and fasten with string, cord, etc. 3 To moor (a vessel). 4 To block; hinder. 5 To be previously committed, so as to be unavailable: His money is *tied up* in real estate. —*n.* 1 A flexible bond or fastening secured by drawing the ends into a knot or loop. 2 Any bond or obligation. 3 In a contest, a draw; also, the point at which this occurs. 4 Something that is tied or intended for tying, as a shoelace, necktie, etc. 5 *Engin.* A structural member fastening parts together. 6 *Music* A curved line joining two notes of the same pitch to make them represent one tone. 7 One of a set of timbers laid crosswise on the ground as supports for railroad tracks. 8 *pl.* Low shoes with laces. [< OE *tīgan* bind] —**ti′er** *n.*

tie-dye (tī′dī′) *v.t.* **-dyed, -dye·ing** To create designs on fabric by tying parts of it in clumps that will not absorb the dye. —*n.* 1 The process of decorating fabrics by tie-dyeing. 2 Fabric so decorated; also, a design so made.

tie-in (tī′in′) *n.* Something that connects or associates.

tier (tir) *n.* A rank or row in a series of things placed one above another. —*v.t. & v.i.* To place or rise in tiers. [< OF, a sequence]

tierce (tirs) *n.* 1 Formerly, a third of anything. 2 The third canonical hour. [< OF, a third < L *tertius*]

tie-up (tī′up′) *n.* 1 A temporary stoppage of services, operations, progress of traffic, etc. 2 *Informal* Connection; linkage.

tiff (tif) *n.* A slight quarrel; a spat. —*v.i.* To be in or have a tiff. [?]

tif·fin (tif′ən) *Brit. n.* Midday luncheon. —*v.i.* To lunch. [< Anglo-Indian *tiffing* drinking]

ti·ger (tī′gər) *n.* 1 A large carnivorous feline of Asia, with black stripes on a tawny body. 2 A fiercely determined, spirited, or energetic person or quality. [< Gk. *tigris*] —**ti′·gress** *n. Fem.* —**ti′ger·ish, ti′grish** *adj.*

tiger beetle Any of certain active, usu. striped or spotted beetles having larvae that feed on other insects.

ti·ger·eye (tī′gər·ī′) *n.* A semiprecious stone, usu. shimmering yellow and brown. Also **ti′ger's-eye′**.

tiger lily Any of various lilies having orange flowers with recurved petals spotted with black. • See LILY.

tiger moth A stout-bodied moth with striped or spotted wings.

tight (tīt) *adj.* 1 Impervious to fluids; not leaky: often used in combination: *watertight.* 2 Firmly fixed or fastened in place; secure. 3 Fully stretched; taut: *tight* as a drum. 4 Strict; stringent: a *tight* schedule. 5 Fitting closely; esp. too closely: *tight* shoes. 6 *Informal* Difficult to cope with; troublesome: a *tight* spot. 7 *Informal* Stingy. 8 *Slang* Intoxicated. 9 Evenly matched: said of a race or contest. 10 Difficult to obtain because of scarcity or financial restrictions: said of money or of commodities. —*adv.* 1 Firmly; securely· Hold on *tight.* 2 With much constriction: The dress fits too *tight.* —**sit tight** To remain firm in one's position or opinion. [?< ON *thēttr* dense] —**tight′ly** *adv.* —**tight′ness** *n.*

tight·en (tīt′n) *v.t. & v.i.* To make or become tight or tighter. —**tight′en·er** *n.*

tight-fist·ed (tīt′fis′tid) *adj.* Stingy.

tight-lipped (tīt′lipt′) *adj.* 1 Having the lips held tightly together. 2 Reticent; uncommunicative.

tight·rope (tīt′rōp′) *n.* A tightly stretched rope on which acrobats perform. —*adj.* Pertaining to or performing on a tightrope.

tights (tīts) *n.pl.* A close-fitting garment for the lower torso and legs, worn by dancers, acrobats, etc.

tight·wad (tīt′wod′) *n. Slang* A miser.

tike (tīk) *n.* TYKE.

til·bur·y (til′ber·ē) *n. pl.* **·bur·ies** A light, two-wheeled carriage seating two persons. [< *Tilbury,* 19th-c. London coachmaker]

til·de (til′də, -dē) *n.* A sign (˜) used in Spanish over *n* to indicate the sound of *ny,* as in *cañon,* canyon. [Sp.< L *titulus* superscription, title]

tile (tīl) *n.* 1 A thin piece of baked clay, stone, etc., used for covering roofs, floors, etc., and as an ornament. 2 A thin piece of linoleum, plastic, cork, etc., for covering walls and floors. 3 A short earthenware pipe, as used in forming sewers. 4 Tiles collectively; tiling. 5 Any of the pieces in the game of mah jong. —*v.t.* **tiled, til·ing** To cover with tiles. [< L *tegula* < *tegere* to cover] —**til′er** *n.*

til·ing (tī′ling) *n.* 1 The work of one who covers with tiles. 2 Tiles collectively. 3 Something made of or faced with tiles.

till[1] (til) *v.t. & v.i.* To put and keep (soil) in order for the production of crops, as by plowing, hoeing, etc.; cultivate. [< OE *tilian* strive, acquire] —**till′er** *n.*

till[2] (til) *prep & conj.* UNTIL. [< OE *til*] • *Till* and *until* have exactly the same meaning and may usu. be used interchangeably. However, *until* is the preferred form at the beginning of a sentence: *Until today, the weather has been bad; It won't be long till winter.*

till[3] (til) *n.* 1 A money drawer behind the counter of a store. 2 The money in such a drawer; also, available cash. 3 Formerly, a drawer for holding valuables. [ME *tillen*]

till·age (til′ij) *n.* 1 The cultivation of land. 2 The state of being tilled. 3 Land that has been tilled. 4 Crops growing on such land. [< TILL[1] + -AGE]

till·er (til′ər) *n.* 1 A lever to turn a rudder. 2 A means of guidance. [< Med. L *telarium* a weaver's beam]

tilt (tilt) *v.t.* 1 To cause to rise at one end or side; slant. 2 To aim or thrust, as a lance. 3 To charge or overthrow in a tilt or joust. —*v.i.* 4 To incline at an angle; lean. 5 To contend with the lance; joust. 6 To argue; debate. —*n.* 1 A slant or slope. 2 The act of tilting something. 3 A medieval sport in which mounted knights, charging with lances, endeavored to unseat each other. 4 A quarrel or dispute. 5 *Can.* In certain provinces, a seesaw. —**at full tilt** At full speed. [ME *tylten* be overthrown, totter] —**tilt′er** *n.*

tilth (tilth) *n.* 1 The act of tilling; cultivation. 2 Cultivated land.

tim·bal (tim′bəl) *n.* A kettledrum. [< Ar. *aṭ ṭabl* the drum]

tim·bale (tim′bəl, *Fr.* tań·bál′) *n.* 1 A dish made of chicken, fish, cheese, or vegetables, mixed with eggs, sweet cream, etc., cooked in a drum-shaped mold. 2 A small cup made of fried pastry, in which food may be served. [F, timbal]

tim·ber (tim′bər) *n.* 1 Wood suitable for building or constructing things. 2 Growing or standing trees; forests. 3 A single piece of squared wood prepared for use or already in use. 4 Any principal beam in a ship. —*v.t.* To provide or shore with timber. [< OE] —**tim′ber·er** *n.*

timber hitch A knot by which a rope is fastened around a spar, post, etc.

tim·ber·land (tim′bər·land′) *n.* Land covered with forests.

timber line The boundary of tree growth on mountains and in arctic regions; the line above which no trees grow. —**tim′ber-line′** (-līn′) *adj.*

timber wolf The large gray wolf of northern forest areas. • See WOLF.

tim·bre (tam′bər, tim′-; *Fr.* tań′br′) *n.* The distinctive quality of sound, produced chiefly by overtones, that characterizes or identifies a singing voice, a musical instrument, or a voiced speech sound. [F < L *tympanum* a kettledrum]

tim·brel (tim′brəl) *n.* An ancient Hebrew instrument resembling a tambourine. [< OF *timbre,* a small bell]

time (tīm) *n.* 1 The general idea, relation, or fact of continuous or successive existence; the past, present, and future. 2 A definite moment, hour, period, etc.: The *time* is 3:30. 3 Epoch; era: the *time* of the Vikings. 4 The portion of duration allotted to some specific happening, condition, etc. 5 Leisure: He has no *time* to play golf. 6 Experience on a specific occasion: to have a good *time.* 7 A point in duration; occasion: Your *time* has come! 8 A period considered as having some quality of its own: *Times* are hard. 9 A system of reckoning or measuring duration: daylight-saving *time.* 10 A case of recurrence or repetition: three *times* a day. 11 *Music* The division of a musical composition into measures; meter. 12 Period during which work has been or remains to be done; also, the amount of pay due one: *time* and a half for overtime. 13 Rate of movement, as in dancing, marching, etc.; tempo. 14 Fit or proper occasion: This is no *time* to quibble. —**against time** As quickly as possible so as to finish within the allotted time. —**at the same time** 1 At the same moment. 2

Despite that; nevertheless. **—at times** Now and then. —**behind the times** Out-of-date; passé. **—for the time being** For the present time. **—from time to time** Now and then; occasionally. **—in good time** 1 Soon. 2 At the right time. **—in time** 1 While time permits or lasts. 2 Ultimately. **—keep time** 1 To indicate time correctly, as a clock. 2 To make regular or rhythmic movements in unison with another or others. 3 To render a musical composition in proper time or rhythm. 4 To make a record of the number of hours worked by an employee. **—on time** 1 Promptly. 2 Paid for, or to be paid for, later or in installments. **—time after time** Again and again. *—adj.* 1 Of or pertaining to time. 2 Devised so as to operate, explode, etc., at a specified time: a *time* bomb, *time* lock. 3 Payable at, or to be paid for at, a future date. *—v.t.* **timed, tim·ing** 1 To record the speed or duration of: to *time* a race. 2 To cause to correspond in time: They *timed* their steps to the music. 3 To arrange the time or occasion for: He *timed* his arrival for five o'clock. 4 To mark the rhythm or measure of. [<OE *tīma*]

time·card (tīm'kärd') *n.* A card for recording the arrival and departure times of an employee.

time clock A clock equipped to record times of arrival and departure of employees.

time exposure A long film exposure made by two separate manual operations of the shutter.

time-hon·ored (tīm'on'ərd) *adj.* Honored or accepted because of long-established usage or custom.

time·keep·er (tīm'kē'pər) *n.* 1 One who or that which keeps time. 2 TIMEPIECE.

time·less (tīm'lis) *adj.* 1 Eternal; unending. 2 Not assigned or limited to any special time, era, or epoch. —**time'less·ly** *adv.* —**time'less·ness** *n.*

time·ly (tīm'lē) *adj.* **·li·er, ·li·est** Being or occurring in good or proper time. —**time'li·ness** *n.* —**Syn.** convenient, fitting, opportune, suitable.

time·piece (tīm'pēs') *n.* A clock or watch.

tim·er (tī'mər) *n.* 1 A timekeeper. 2 A stopwatch. 3 A device similar to a stopwatch for timing various processes: a kitchen *timer.* 4 A device that begins operations in sequence or after measured intervals of time.

times (tīmz) *prep.* Multiplied by: four *times* two is eight.

time·serv·ing (tīm'sûr'ving) *adj.* Conducting oneself so as to conform to the demands and opinions of the times and of those in power, usu. for personal advantage. *—n.* The actions of a timeserving person. —**time'serv'er** *n.*

time-shar·ing (tīm'shâr'ing) *n.* The simultaneous use of a single large computer by many people at once, by means of individual terminals.

time signature A sign, usu. two numerals placed one above the other on a musical staff, to indicate meter.

time·ta·ble (tīm'tā'bəl) *n.* A schedule showing the times at which trains, boats, airplanes, buses, etc., arrive and depart.

time-worn (tīm'wôrn, -worn') *adj.* Made worn and ineffective by long existence or use.

time zone One of the 24 established divisions or sectors into which the earth is divided for convenience in reckoning time: each sector represents 15 degrees of longitude, or a time interval of 1 hour.

tim·id (tim'id) *adj.* 1 Easily frightened; fearful. 2 Lacking self-confidence. [<L *timere* to fear] —**ti·mid·i·ty** (ti·mid'ə·tē), **tim'id·ness** *n.* —**tim'id·ly** *adv.* —**Syn.** 2 retiring, shrinking, shy, timorous.

tim·ing (tī'ming) *n.* The art or act of regulating the speed at which something is performed to secure maximum effects.

tim·or·ous (tim'ər·əs) *adj.* Fearful and anxious; timid. [<L *timor* fear] —**tim'or·ous·ly** *adv.* —**tim'or·ous·ness** *n.*

tim·o·thy (tim'ə·thē) *n.* A perennial fodder grass having its flowers in a dense cylindrical spike. Also **timothy grass.** [<*Timothy* Hanson, who took the seed from New York to the Carolinas about 1720]

Tim·o·thy (tim'ə·thē) A convert and companion of the apostle Paul. *—n.* Either of two epistles in the New Testament, written to Timothy by Paul.

tim·pa·ni (tim'pə·nē) *n. pl. (construed as sing. or pl.)* Kettledrums. [<Ital., pl. of *timpano* a kettledrum <L *tympanum* a drum] —**tim'pa·nist** *n.*

tin (tin) *n.* 1 A soft, silvery white, corrosion-resistant metallic element (symbol Sn) usu. found combined with oxygen; used in making alloys. 2 Tin plate. 3 *Chiefly Brit.* A can, as of preserved food. *—v.t.* **tinned, tin·ning** 1 To coat or cover with tin, solder, or tin plate. 2 *Chiefly Brit.* To pack or preserve (food) in cans. *—adj.* Made of tin. [<OE]

tinc·ture (tingk'chər) *n.* 1 A medicinal solution, usu. in alcohol. 2 A tinge of color; tint. 3 A slight trace. [<L *tinctura* a dyeing]

tin·der (tin'dər) *n.* Any dry, readily combustible substance that will ignite on contact with a spark. [<OE *tynder*] —**tin'der·y** *adj.*

tin·der·box (tin'dər·boks') *n.* 1 A box containing tinder, flint, and steel for starting a fire. 2 A highly flammable mass of material. 3 An excitable, temperamental person.

tine (tīn) *n.* A spike or prong, as of a fork or of an antler. [<OE *tind*] —**tined** *adj.*

tin·foil (tin'foil') *n.* 1 Tin or an alloy of tin made into very thin sheets. 2 A similar sheeting made of rolled aluminum, commonly used as wrapping material.

ting (ting) *n.* A high metallic sound, as of a small bell.

tinge (tinj) *v.t.* **tinged, tinge·ing** or **ting·ing** 1 To imbue with a faint trace of color. 2 To impart a slight trace of a quality to. *—n.* 1 A faint trace of added color. 2 A slight trace, as of a quality. [<L *tingere* to dye] —**Syn.** *n.* **1, 2** dash, hint, soupçon, tincture, touch.

tin·gle (ting'gəl) *v.* **·gled, ·gling** *v.i.* 1 To experience a prickly, stinging sensation. 2 To cause such a sensation. 3 To jingle; tinkle. *—v.t.* 4 To cause to tingle. *—n.* 1 A prickly, stinging sensation. 2 A jingle or tinkling. [Appar. var. of TINKLE] —**tin'gler** *n.* —**tin'gly** *adj.*

tin·horn (tin'hôrn') *adj. Slang* Cheap, vulgar, and pretentious: a *tinhorn* politician. [With ref. to the fine appearance but poor sound of a tin horn]

tink·er (tingk'ər) *n.* 1 A mender of pots and pans, etc. 2 A clumsy workman; a botcher. 3 Work done hastily and carelessly. *—v.i.* 1 To work as a tinker. 2 To work in a clumsy, makeshift fashion. 3 To potter; fuss. *—v.t.* 4 To mend as a tinker. 5 To repair clumsily or inexpertly. [Var. of earlier *tinekere* a worker in tin]

tinker's damn *Slang* Any useless or worthless thing: usu. in the phrase **not worth a tinker's damn.** Also **tinker's dam.** [<TINKER + DAMN; with ref. to the reputed profanity of tinkers]

tin·kle (ting'kəl) *v.* **·kled, ·kling** *v.i.* 1 To produce slight, sharp, metallic sounds, as a small bell. *—v.t.* 2 To cause to tinkle. 3 To summon or signal by a tinkling. *—n.* A sharp, clear, tinkling sound. [Imit.] —**tin'kly (·kli·er, ·kli·est)** *adj.*

tin·ner (tin'ər) *n.* 1 A miner employed in tin mines. 2 A tinsmith.

tin·ni·tus (ti·nī'təs) *n.* A ringing, buzzing, or clicking sound in the ears, not caused by external stimuli. [<L *tinnire* to ring]

tin·ny (tin'ē) *adj.* **·ni·er, ·ni·est** 1 Made of or containing tin. 2 Like tin in cheapness and brightness. 3 Having a thin, flat sound like that of tin being struck. —**tin'ni·ly** *adv.* —**tin'ni·ness** *n.*

Tin Pan Alley 1 A section of a city, esp. New York, frequented by musicians, song writers, and publishers of popular music. 2 The musicians, writers, publishers, etc., of popular music.

tin plate Sheet iron or steel plated with tin. —**tin'-plate' (-plat·ed, -plat·ing)** *v.t.* —**tin'-plat'er** *n.*

tin·sel (tin'səl) *n.* 1 Very thin glittering bits of metal or plastic used for display and ornament. 2 Anything sparkling and showy, but with little real worth. *—adj.* 1 Made or covered with tinsel. 2 Like tinsel; superficially brilliant. *—v.t.* **·seled** or **·selled, ·sel·ing** or **·sel·ling** 1 To adorn or decorate with or as with tinsel. 2 To give a false attractiveness to. [<L *scintilla* a spark]

tin·smith (tin'smith') *n.* One who works with tin or tin plate.

tint (tint) *n.* 1 A variety of color; tinge: red with a blue *tint.* 2 A gradation of a color made by dilution with white. 3 A pale or delicate color. 4 In engraving, uniform shading produced by parallel lines or hatching. —*v.t.* To give a tint to. [< L *tinctus* a dyeing] —**tint′er** *n.*

tin·tin·nab·u·la·tion (tin′ti·nab′yə·lā′shən) *n.* The pealing, tinkling, or ringing of bells. [< L *tintinnare* to ring]

tin·type (tin′tīp′) *n.* An old type of photograph taken on a sensitized plate of enameled tin or iron.

tin·ware (tin′wâr′) *n.* Articles made of tin plate.

ti·ny (tī′nē) *adj.* **·ni·er, ·ni·est** Very small; minute. [< obs. *tine* a small amount, bit] —**ti′ni·ness** *n.*

-tion *suffix of nouns* 1 Action or process of: *rejection.* 2 Condition or state of being: *completion.* 3 Result of: *connection.* [< L *-tio, -tionis*]

tip[1] (tip) *n.* A slanting position; a tilt. —*v.* **tipped, tip·ping** *v.t.* 1 To cause to lean; tilt. 2 To put at an angle: to *tip* one's hat. 3 To overturn or upset: often with *over.* —*v.i.* 4 To become tilted; slant. 5 To overturn; topple: with *over.* [ME *tipen* overturn] —**tip′per** *n.*

tip[2] (tip) *v.t.* **tipped, tip·ping** 1 To strike lightly; tap. 2 In baseball, to strike (the ball) a light, glancing blow. —*n.* A tap; light blow. [Prob. < LG *tippe*]

tip[3] (tip) *n.* 1 A small gift of money for services rendered. 2 A helpful hint. 3 A piece of confidential information: a *tip* on a horse race. —*v.* **tipped, tip·ping** *v.t.* 1 To give a small gratuity to. 2 *Informal* To give secret information to, as in betting, etc. —*v.i.* 3 To give gratuities. —**tip off** *Informal* 1 To give secret information to. 2 To warn. [? < TIP[2]] —**tip′per** *n.*

tip[4] (tip) *n.* 1 The point or extremity of anything tapering: the *tip* of the tongue. 2 A piece made to form the end of something, as a nozzle, ferrule, etc. 3 The uppermost part; top: the *tip* of a flagpole. —*v.t.* **tipped, tip·ping** 1 To furnish with a tip. 2 To form the tip of. 3 To cover or adorn the tip of. [Prob. < MDu., a point]

tip-off (tip′ôf′, -of′) *n. Informal* A hint or warning, usu. given confidentially.

tip·pet (tip′it) *n.* 1 Formerly, a long hanging strip of cloth attached to the sleeve or hood. 2 A covering, usu. of fur, velvet, etc., for the neck and shoulders, hanging well down in front. [Prob. dim. of TIP[4]]

Tippet *def. 1*

tip·ple (tip′əl) *v.t. & v.i.* **·pled, ·pling** To drink (alcoholic beverages) frequently and habitually. —*n.* Liquor consumed in tippling. [< earlier *tipler* bartender]

tip·ster (tip′stər) *n. Informal* One who sells tips for betting, as on a race.

tip·sy (tip′sē) *adj.* **·si·er, ·si·est** 1 Mildly intoxicated. 2 Shaky; unsteady. [< TIP[1]] —**tip′si·ly** *adv.* —**tip′si·ness** *n.*

tip·toe (tip′tō′, -tō′) *n.* The tip of a toe, or the tips of all the toes. —**on tiptoe** 1 On one's tiptoes. 2 Expectantly; eagerly. 3 Stealthily; quietly. —*v.i.* **·toed, ·toe·ing** To walk on tiptoe; go stealthily or quietly. —*adv.* On tiptoe.

tip-top (tip′top′) *adj.* 1 At the very top. 2 *Informal* Best of its kind; first-rate. —*n.* The highest point. —**tip′-top′per** *n.*

ti·rade (tī′rād, tī·rād′) *n.* A prolonged declamatory outpouring, as of censure. [< Ital. *tirata* a volley]

tire[1] (tīr) *v.* **tired, tir·ing** *v.t.* 1 To reduce the strength of, as by exertion. 2 To reduce the interest or patience of, as with monotony. —*v.i.* 3 To become weary or exhausted. 4 To lose patience, interest, etc. —**tire of** To become bored or impatient with. —**tire out** To weary completely. [< OE *tīorian*] —**Syn.** 1 exhaust, fag, fatigue, wear out, weary.

tire[2] (tīr) *n.* 1 A band or hoop surrounding the rim of a wheel. 2 A tough, flexible tube, usu. of inflated rubber, set around the rims of the wheels of automobiles, bicycles, etc. —*v.t.* **tired, tir·ing** To put a tire on. *Brit. sp.* **tyre.** [Prob. < obs. *tire* to attire]

tired (tīrd) *adj.* Weary; fatigued. [Orig. pp. of TIRE[1]] —**tired′ly** *adv.* —**tired′ness** *n.*

tire·less (tīr′lis) *adj.* 1 Not becoming easily fatigued; untiring. 2 Ceaseless; *tireless* zeal. —**tire′less·ly** *adv.* —**tire′less·ness** *n.*

tire·some (tīr′səm) *adj.* Tending to tire, or causing one to tire; tedious. —**tire′some·ly** *adv.* —**tire′some·ness** *n.*

ti·ro (tī′rō) *n.* TYRO.

'tis (tiz) Contraction of *it is.*

tis·sue (tish′o͞o) *n.* 1 Any light or gauzy textile fabric. 2 *Biol.* An aggregate of cells and intercellular material having a particular function: nerve *tissue.* 3 A network; chain: a *tissue* of lies. 4 TISSUE PAPER. 5 A disposable square of soft absorbent paper for use as a handkerchief, etc. [< OF *tistre* to weave]

tissue paper Very thin, unsized, translucent paper for wrapping delicate articles, protecting engravings, etc.

tit[1] (tit) *n.* A titmouse, titlark, etc.

tit[2] (tit) *n.* Teat; breast; nipple. [< OE *titt*]

ti·tan (tīt′n) *n.* Any person having gigantic strength or size; a giant. —**ti·tan′ic** *adj.* [< TITAN]

Ti·tan (tīt′n) *Gk. Myth.* One of a race of giant gods, who were succeeded by the Olympian gods. —**Ti·tan′ic** *adj.*

Ti·ta·ni·a (ti·tā′nē·ə, tī-, -tan′yə) In folklore, the queen of fairyland and wife of Oberon.

ti·ta·ni·um (tī·tā′nē·əm) *n.* A widely distributed lightweight metallic element (symbol Ti) resembling aluminum in appearance, used to make tough, heat-resistant alloys. [< L *Titani* the Titans]

tit·bit (tit′bit′) *n.* TIDBIT.

tit for tat Retaliation in kind; blow for blow. [?]

tithe (tīth) *n.* 1 One tenth. 2 *Usu. pl.* A tax of one tenth part of yearly income arising from lands and from the personal industry of the inhabitants, for the support of the clergy and the church. 3 A small part. 4 Loosely, any tax or levy. —*v.t.* **tithed, tith·ing** 1 To give or pay a tithe, or tenth part of. 2 To tax with tithes. [< OE *tēotha, tēogotha* a tenth] —**tith′er** *n.*

ti·tian (tish′ən) *n.* A reddish yellow color much used by Titian, esp. in painting women's hair. —*adj.* Having the color titian. [< *Titian,* Venetian artist, 1477–1576]

tit·il·late (tit′ə·lāt) *v.t.* **·lat·ed, ·lat·ing** 1 To cause a tickling sensation in. 2 To excite pleasurably. [< L *titillare* to tickle] —**tit′il·lat′er, tit′il·la′tion** *n.* —**tit′il·la′tive** *adj.*

tit·i·vate (tit′ə·vāt) *v.t. & v.i.* **·vat·ed, ·vat·ing** *Informal* To smarten; dress up. Also **tit′ti·vate.** [Earlier *tidivate* ? < TIDY, on analogy with *cultivate*] —**tit′i·va′tion, tit′i·va′tor** *n.*

tit·lark (tit′lärk′) *n.* A pipit. [ME *tit* a little thing + LARK]

ti·tle (tīt′l) *n.* 1 The name of a book, play, motion picture, song, etc. 2 A title page, as of a book. 3 A descriptive name; epithet. 4 **a** An appellation showing rank, office, profession, station in life, etc. **b** In some countries, a designation of nobility or one conferred for unusual distinction. 5 In some sports, championship: to win the *title.* 6 *Law* **a** The legal right to own property. **b** Legal evidence of such a right. **c** A document setting forth such evidence. —*v.t.* **·tled, ·tling** To give a name to; entitle. [< L *titulus* a label, inscription]

ti·tled (tīt′ld) *adj.* Having a title, esp. of nobility.

title page A page containing the title of a work, its author, its publisher, etc.

title role The character in a play, opera, or motion picture for whom it is named.

tit·mouse (tit′mous′) *n. pl.* **·mice** (-mīs′) Any of numerous small birds related to the nuthatches. [< Me *tit-* little + *mose* < OE *mase* a titmouse]

Titmouse

ti·trate (tī′trāt) *v.t. & v.i.* **·trat·ed, ·trat·ing** To analyze (a substance) by titration. [< F *titrer*]

ti·tra·tion (tī·trā′shən, ti-) *n.* Quantitative analysis of a substance in solution by the completion of a specific reaction with a measured volume of a standard solution.

tit·ter (tit′ər) *v.i.* To laugh in a suppressed way. —*n.* The act of tittering. [Imit.] —**tit′ter·er** *n.* —**tit′ter·ing·ly** *adv.* —**Syn.** *v.* chuckle, giggle, snicker, snigger, snort.

tit·tle (tit′l) *n.* 1 The minutest quantity; iota. 2 A very small diacritical mark in writing, as the dot over an *i,* etc. [< L *titulus* title]

tit·tle-tat·tle (tit′l·tat′l) *n.* 1 Trivial talk; gossip. 2 An idle talker. —*v.i.* **·tled, ·tling** To gossip; chatter. [Reduplication of TATTLE]

tit·u·lar (tich′ōō·lər, tit′yə-) *adj.* 1 Existing in name or title only: a *titular* ruler. 2 Pertaining to a title. 3 Having a title. [< L *titulus* a title] —**tit′u·lar·ly** *adv.*

Ti·tus (tī′təs) A disciple of the apostle Paul. —*n.* The epistle in the New Testament addressed to Titus and attributed to Paul.

tiz·zy (tiz′ē) *n. pl.* **·zies** *Slang* A bewildered or excited state of mind; a dither. [?]

TKO, T.K.O., t.k.o. technical knockout.

Tl thallium.

T.L. trade last.

T/L time loan.

Tm thulium.

TN Tennessee (P.O. abbr.).

Tn thoron.

tn. ton; train.

tng. training.

TNT, T.N.T. trinitrotoluene.

to (tōō, *unstressed* tə) *prep.* 1 Toward or terminating in: going *to* town. 2 Opposite or near: face *to* face; Hold me *to* your breast. 3 Intending or aiming at: Come *to* my rescue. 4 Resulting in: frozen *to* death. 5 Belonging with; of: the key *to* the barn. 6 In honor of: Drink *to* our victory. 7 In comparison with: 9 is *to* 3 as 21 is *to* 7. 8 Until: five minutes *to* one. 9 For the utmost duration of: a miser *to* the end of his days. 10 Concerning: blind *to* her faults. 11 In close application toward: Get down *to* work. 12 For: The contest is open *to* everyone. 13 Noting action toward: Give the ring *to* me. 14 By: known *to* the world. 15 From the point of view of: It seems *to* me. 16 About; involved in: That's all there is *to* it. 17 On; against: Nail the sign *to* the post. 18 In: four quarts *to* a gallon. 19 Into: The house was reduced *to* ashes. —*adv.* 1 Forward: He wore his sweater back side *to.* 2 In a direction or position, esp. closed: Pull the door *to.* 3 Into a normal condition or consciousness: She soon came *to.* 4 Into action or operation: They fell *to* eagerly. —**to and fro** In opposite or different directions; back and forth. [< OE *tō*] • *To* is also used before a verb to indicate the infinitive: It is good *to* see you; You can go if you want *to* (go).

toad (tōd) *n.* 1 Any of various tailless, jumping, insectivorous amphibians resembling the frog but usu. having a warty skin and resorting to water only to breed. 2 A contemptible or loathsome person. [< OE *tādige*]

Toad

toad·fish (tōd′fish′) *n. pl.* **·fish** or **·fish·es** Any of a family of fishes with scaleless skin and a toadlike head.

toad·stool (tōd′stōōl′) *n.* An inedible or poisonous mushroom.

toad·y (tō′dē) *n. pl.* **toad·ies** An obsequious flatterer; a sycophant. —*v.t.* & *v.i.* **toad·ied, toad·y·ing** To act the toady (to). [< earlier *toad-eater,* a charlatan's attendant who pretended to eat toads] —**toad′y·ism** *n.*

to-and-fro (tōō′ən·frō′) *adj.* Moving back and forth or from one position to another. —*adv.* In a to-and-fro motion.

toast[1] (tōst) *v.t.* 1 To brown the outside of (a piece of bread, etc.) by heating in an oven, toaster, etc. 2 To warm thoroughly. —*v.i.* 3 To become warm or toasted. —*n.* Toasted bread. [< L *tostus* < *torrere* parch, roast]

toast[2] (tōst) *n.* 1 The act of drinking to someone's health or to some thing. 2 The person or thing thus named. —*v.t.* & *v.i.* To drink a toast or toasts (to). [< TOAST[1], from a custom of flavoring a drink with a spiced piece of toast] —**toast′er** *n.*

toast·er (tōst′ər) *n.* An electrical device for toasting bread.

toast·mas·ter (tōst′mas′tər, -mäs′tər) *n.* A person who, at public dinners, announces the toasts, calls upon the speakers, etc.

to·bac·co (tə·bak′ō) *n. pl.* **·cos** or **·coes** 1 Any of various plants of the nightshade family, with large sticky leaves and yellow, white, or purple flowers. 2 The leaves of several of these plants, processed for smoking, chewing, etc. 3 The various products prepared from tobacco leaves, as cigarettes, cigars, etc. [< Sp. *tabaco*]

Tobacco plant

to·bac·co·nist (tə·bak′ə·nist) *n. Brit.* One who deals in tobacco.

To·bit (tō′bit) *n.* A book of the Apocrypha of the Old Testament. Also **To·bi·as** (tō·bī′əs).

to·bog·gan (tə·bog′ən) *n.* A long sledlike vehicle without runners, consisting of thin boards curved upward in front. —*v.i.* 1 To coast on a toboggan. 2 To descend swiftly: Wheat prices *tobogganed.* [< Algon.] —**to·bog′gan·er, to·bog′gan·ist** *n.*

to·by (tō′bē) *n. pl.* **·bies** *Often cap.* A mug or jug for ale or beer, often made in the form of an old man wearing a three-cornered hat. Also **toby jug.** [< *Toby,* dim. of the name *Tobias*]

toc·ca·ta (tə·kä′tə, *Ital.* tôk·kä′tä) *n.* An elaborate composition for piano, organ, etc. often preceding a fugue. [Ital., lit., a touching]

To·char·i·an (tō·kâr′ē·ən, -kär′-) *n.* 1 One of an ancient people who inhabited central Asia in the first Christian millennium. 2 The language of the Tocharians, two dialects of which are known.

to·coph·er·ol (tō·kof′ə·rōl, -rol) *n.* Vitamin E. [< Gk. *tokos* offspring + *pherein* to bear]

toc·sin (tok′sin) *n.* 1 A signal sounded on a bell; alarm. 2 An alarm bell. [< Prov. *tocar* to strike, touch + *senh* a bell]

to·day (tə·dā′) *adv.* 1 On or during this present day. 2 At the present time. —*n.* The present day or age. Also **to-day′.** [< OE *tō* to + *daeg* day]

tod·dle (tod′l) *v.i.* **·dled, ·dling** To walk unsteadily and with short steps, as a little child. —*n.* The act of toddling. —**tod′dler** *n.*

tod·dy (tod′ē) *n. pl.* **·dies** 1 A drink made with whiskey, brandy, etc., and hot water and sugar. 2 The fermented sap of certain East Indian palms (**toddy palms**). [< Skt. *tāla* a palm tree]

to-do (tə·dōō′) *n. Informal* A stir; fuss. —**Syn.** bustle, commotion, confusion, disturbance.

toe (tō) *n.* 1 One of the five digits of the foot. 2 The forward part of the foot. 3 That portion of a shoe, boot, sock, etc., that covers or corresponds to the toes. 4 Anything resembling a toe in contour, function, position, etc. —**on one's toes** Alert. —**tread on (someone's) toes** To trespass on (someone's) feelings, prejudices, etc. —*v.* **toed, toe·ing** *v.t.* 1 To touch or kick with the toes. 2 To furnish with a toe. 3 To drive (a nail or spike) obliquely. 4 To attach by nails driven thus. —*v.i.* 5 To stand or walk with the toes pointing in a specified direction: to *toe* out. —**toe the mark** (or **line**) 1 To touch a certain line with the toes preparatory to starting a race. 2 To conform to a discipline or a standard. [< OE *tā*]

toed (tōd) *adj.* 1 Having (a specified kind or number of) toes: used in combination: *pigeon-toed; three-toed.* 2 Fastened or fastening by obliquely driven nails. 3 Driven in obliquely, as a nail.

toe dance Dancing on the tips of the toes, as in ballet. —**toe′-dance′ (-danced, -danc·ing)** *v.i.* —**toe′-danc′er** *n.*

toe·hold (tō′hōld′) *n.* 1 In climbing, a small space which supports the toes. 2 Any means of entrance, support, or the like; a footing. 3 A hold in which a wrestler bends back the foot of his opponent.

toe·nail (tō′nāl′) *n.* 1 The nail growing on a toe. 2 A nail driven obliquely. —*v.t.* To fasten with obliquely driven nails.

tof·fee (tôf′ē, tof′ē) *n.* TAFFY. Also **tof′fy.**

tog (tog) *Informal n. pl.* Clothes. —*v.t.* **togged, tog·ging** To clothe: often with *up* or *out.* [< L *toga* toga]

to·ga (tō′gə) *n. pl.* **·gas** or **·gae** (-gī) **1** The loose, flowing outer garment worn in public by a citizen of ancient Rome. **2** Any robe characteristic of a calling. [< L < *tegere to* cover] **—to′·gaed** (tō′gəd) *adj.*

Roman toga

to·geth·er (too͝-geth′ər, tə-) *adv.* **1** In company: We were sitting *together.* **2** In or into one group, mass, unit, etc.: They put the jigsaw puzzle *together.* **3** Into contact with each other: Glue these two pieces *together.* **4** Simultaneously: Let's sing it *together.* **5** With one another; mutually: They discussed it *together.* **6** In agreement or harmony: The tie and shirt go well *together.* **7** Considered collectively: He has more courage than all of us *together.* **8** Without cessation: He talked for hours *together.* **—get it all together** *Slang* To achieve a positive outlook on life; free oneself from anxiety. **—together with** Along with. [< OE *tōgædere*]

tog·ger·y (tog′ər·ē) *n. Informal* Clothing; togs.

tog·gle (tog′əl) *n.* **1** A pin, or short rod, properly attached in the middle, as to a rope, and designed to be passed through a hole or eye and turned. **2** A toggle joint. **—***v.t.* **·gled, ·gling** To fix, fasten, or furnish with a toggle or toggles. [?]

toggle joint A joint having a central hinge like an elbow, and operable by applying the force at the junction, thus changing the direction of motion.

Toggle joint

toggle switch *Electr.* A switch connected to its actuating lever by a toggle joint loaded by a spring.

To·go (tō′gō) *n.* A republic of w Africa, 21,500 sq. mi., cap. Lomé. **—To′go·lese′** (-lēs, -lēz) *adj., n.* • See map at AFRICA.

toil[1] (toil) *n.* **1** Fatiguing work; labor. **2** Any work accomplished by great labor. **—***v.i.* **1** To work strenuously and tiringly. **2** To make one's way laboriously: to *toil* up a hill. **—***v.t.* **3** To accomplish with great effort: to *toil* one's way. [< L *tudiculare* stir about] **—toil′er** *n.* **—Syn.** *v.* **1** drudge, labor, slave, travail.

toil[2] (toil) *n.* **1** *Archaic* A net, snare, or other trap. **2** *pl.* Anything that binds or entraps: the *toils* of remorse. [< L *tela* a web]

toi·let (toi′lit) *n.* **1** A fixture in the shape of a bowl, used for urination and defecation and equipped with a device for flushing and discharging with water. **2** A room containing such a fixture or fixtures. **3** PRIVY. **4** The act or process of bathing, grooming, and dressing oneself. **5** Formerly, a woman's attire or costume: also **toi·lette** (twa·let′). **—***adj.* Used in dressing or grooming: *toilet* articles. [< F *toilette* orig. a cloth dressing gown, dim. of *toile* cloth]

toi·let·ry (toi′lit·rē) *n. pl.* **·ries** Soap, powder, cologne, etc., used in bathing and grooming oneself.

toilet water A scented liquid applied after the bath, after shaving, etc.

toil·some (toil′səm) *adj.* Involving hard work; laborious; difficult. **—toil′some·ly** *adv.* **—toil′some·ness** *n.*

toil·worn (toil′wôrn′, -wōrn′) *adj.* Exhausted by toil; showing the effects of toil.

To·kay (tō·kā′) *n.* **1** A large, sweet grape originally from Tokay, Hungary. **2** A wine made from it.

to·ken (tō′kən) *n.* **1** A visible sign; indication: This gift is a *token* of my affection. **2** Some tangible proof or evidence of one's identity, authority, etc. **3** A keepsake; souvenir. **4** A characteristic mark or feature. **5** A piece of metal issued as currency and having a face value greater than its actual value: a bus *token.* **—by the same token** Moreover; furthermore. **—in token of** As a sign or evidence of. **—***adj.* **1** Having only the appearance of; nominal; minimal: *token* resistance; *token* integration. **2** Partial or very small: a *token* payment. [< OE *tācen*]

to·ken·ism (tō′kən·iz·əm) *n.* The policy of attempting to meet certain obligations or conditions by partial, symbolic, or token efforts.

To·khar·i·an (tō·kâr′ē·ən, -kär′-) *n.* TOCHARIAN.

told (tōld) *p.t. & p.p.* of TELL.

To·le·do (tə·lē′dō) *n. pl.* **·dos** A sword or sword blade from Toledo, Spain. Also **to·le′do.**

tol·er·a·ble (tol′ər·ə·bəl) *adj.* **1** Endurable; bearable. **2** Fairly good: *tolerable* health. [< L *tolerare* endure] **—tol′·er·a·ble·ness** *n.* **—tol′er·a·bly** *adv.*

tol·er·ance (tol′ər·əns) *n.* **1** The character, state, or quality of being tolerant. **2** Freedom from prejudice; open-mindedness. **3** The act of enduring, or the capacity for endurance. **4** An allowance for variations from specified measure, as of machine parts. **5** *Med.* Ability to withstand large or increasing amounts of a specified substance or stimulus.

tol·er·ant (tol′ər·ənt) *adj.* **1** Of a long-suffering disposition. **2** Indulgent; liberal. **3** *Med.* Resistant to the effects of a specific substance or stimulus. [< L *tolerare* endure] **—tol′er·ant·ly** *adv.*

tol·er·ate (tol′ə·rāt) *v.t.* **·at·ed, ·at·ing** **1** To allow without opposition. **2** To concede, as the right to opinions or participation. **3** To bear or be capable of bearing. **4** *Med.* To be tolerant. [< L *tolerare* endure] **—tol′er·a′tive** *adj.* **—tol′·er·a′tion, tol′er·a′tor** *n.* **—Syn. 1** permit. **3** endure, sustain.

toll[1] (tōl) *n.* **1** A tax or charge for some privilege granted, esp. for passage on a bridge or turnpike. **2** The right to levy such a charge. **3** A charge for a special service, as for a long-distance telephone call. **4** The number or amount lost, as in a disaster: The wreck took a *toll* of nine lives. **—***v.t.* **1** To take as a toll. **—***v.i.* **2** To exact a toll. [< OE]

toll[2] (tōl) *v.t.* **1** To sound (a church bell) slowly and at regular intervals. **2** To announce (a death, funeral, etc.) by tolling a church bell. **3** To call or summon by tolling. **—***v.i.* **4** To sound slowly and at regular intervals. **—***n.* **1** The act of tolling. **2** The sound of a bell rung slowly and regularly. [ME *tollen*] **—toll′er** *n.*

toll bridge A bridge at which toll for passage is paid.

toll call A long-distance telephone call.

toll·gate (tōl′gāt′) *n.* A gate at the entrance to a bridge, or on a road, at which toll is paid.

toll·keep·er (tōl′kē′pər) *n.* One who collects the tolls at a tollgate.

Tol·tec (tōl′tek, tol′-) *n.* Any of certain ancient Nahuatlan tribes that dominated Mexico about 900–1100 before the Aztecs. **—***adj.* Of or pertaining to the Toltecs: also **Tol′tec·an.**

tol·u·ene (tol′yo͞o·ēn) *n.* A hydrocarbon obtained from coal tar, used in making dyes, drugs, and explosives. Also **tol′u·ol** (-yo͞o·wôl, -wōl).

tom (tom) *n.* **1** The male of various animals, esp. the cat. **2** *Often cap. Slang* UNCLE TOM. **—***adj.* Male: a *tom* turkey.

tom·a·hawk (tom′ə·hôk) *n.* An ax used as a tool and as a war weapon by the Algonquian Indians. **—***v.t.* To strike or kill with a tomahawk. [< Algon.]

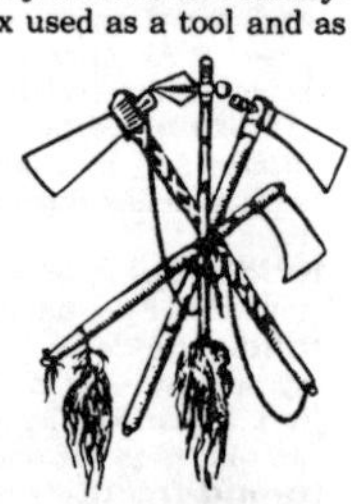

North American Indian tomahawks

to·ma·to (tə·mā′tō, -mä′-) *n. pl.* **·toes** **1** The pulpy edible berry, yellow or red when ripe, of a tropical American plant related to the potato, used as a vegetable. **2** The plant itself. **3** *Slang* An attractive girl or woman. [< Nah. *tomatl*]

tomb (to͞om) *n.* **1** A burial place; grave. **2** A tombstone or monument. **—the tomb** Death. **—***v.t.* To entomb; bury. [< Gk. *tymbos* a mound]

tom·boy (tom′boi′) *n.* A young girl who behaves like a lively, active boy. [< TOM + BOY] **—tom′boy′ish** *adj.* **—tom′boy′ish·ness** *n.*

tomb·stone (to͞om′stōn′) *n.* A stone, usu. inscribed, marking a place of burial.

tom·cat (tom′kat′) *n.* A male cat. **—***v.i.* **·cat·ted, ·cat·ting** *Slang* To engage in sexual relations indiscriminately: said of a man. [< *Tom,* hero of *The Life and Adventures of a Cat,* 1760, a popular anonymous work]

tome (tōm) *n.* A large, heavy book. [< Gk. *tomos* a fragment, volume]

tom·fool (tom′fo͞ol′) *n.* An idiotic or silly person. **—***adj.* Foolish; stupid. [< *Tom Fool,* a name formerly applied to mental defectives]

tom·fool·er·y (tom′fo͞o′lər·ē) *n. pl.* **·er·ies** Nonsensical behavior; silliness.

tom·my (tom′ē) *n. pl.* **·mies** A British soldier. Also **Tom′·my.** [Short for TOMMY ATKINS]

Tommy At·kins (at′kinz) A British private of the regular army. [< *Thomas Atkins,* a name used on British Army specimen forms]

Tommy gun *Informal* A type of submachine gun. [< J. *Thompson,* d. 1940, U.S. army officer]

to·mor·row (tə·môr′ō, -mor′ō) *adv.* On or for the next day after today. —*n.* The next day after today. Also **to·mor′row.** [< OE *tō* to + *morgen* morning, morrow]

Tom Thumb 1 In English folklore, a hero as big as his father's thumb. 2 Any midget or dwarf.

tom·tit (tom′tit′) *n.* A titmouse or other small bird. [< the name *Tom* + TIT[1]]

tom-tom (tom′tom′) *n.* Any of various drums, as of American Indian and African tribes, usu. beaten with the hands. [< Hind. *tamtam,* imit.]

-tomy *combining form* A cutting of a (specified) part or tissue: *lobotomy.* [< Gk. *tomē* a cutting]

ton (tun) *n.* 1 Any of several measures of weight; esp. the **short ton** of 2000 pounds avoirdupois; the **long ton** of 2240 pounds; or the **metric ton** of 1000 kilograms. 2 A unit for reckoning the displacement of vessels, equal to 35 cubic feet, or about one long ton of sea water: called **displacement ton.** 3 A unit for reckoning the freight capacity of a ship, usu. equivalent to 40 cubic feet of space: called **freight ton, measurement ton.** 4 A unit for reckoning the capacity of merchant vessels for purposes of registration, equivalent to 100 cubic feet or 2.832 cubic meters: called **register ton.** 5 *Informal* Any large amount, weight, etc. [Var. of TUN]

to·nal (tō′nəl) *adj.* 1 Of or pertaining to tone or tonality. 2 Having a keynote or tonic. —**to′nal·ly** *adv.*

to·nal·i·ty (tō·nal′ə·tē) *n. pl.* **·ties** 1 The existence of a keynote or tonic in music; also a key or mode. 2 The general color scheme or collective tones of a painting.

tone (tōn) *n.* 1 A vocal or musical sound; also, the quality of such a sound. 2 *Music* **a** A sound having a definite pitch, loudness, and timbre. **b** WHOLE STEP. 3 A predominating disposition; mood. 4 Characteristic tendency; quality: a want of moral *tone.* 5 Style or elegance: The party had *tone.* 6 Vocal inflection: a *tone* of pity. 7 The acoustical pitch, or change in pitch, of a phrase or sentence: A question is indicated by a rising *tone.* 8 The effect of light, shade, and color as combined in a picture. 9 A shade of a particular color: a deep *tone* of yellow. 10 Tonicity. —*v.* **toned, ton·ing** *v.t.* 1 To give tone to; modify in tone. 2 INTONE. —*v.i.* 3 To assume a certain tone or hue. 4 To blend or harmonize, as in tone or shade. —**tone down** 1 To subdue the tone of. 2 To moderate in quality or tone. —**tone up** 1 To raise in quality or strength. 2 To elevate in pitch. 3 To gain in vitality. [< Gk. *tonos* a pitch of voice, a stretching] —**ton′er** *n.*

tone·less (tōn′lis) *adj.* Lifeless; flat: a *toneless* voice. —**tone′less·ly** *adv.* —**tone′less·ness** *n.*

tong (tông, tong) *n.* 1 A Chinese association or closed society. 2 In the U.S., a former secret society composed of Chinese. [< Chin. *t'ang* a hall, meeting place]

Ton·ga (tong′gə) *n.* An independent kingdom in the Commonwealth of Nations situated on an archipelago E of Fiji, 270 sq. mi., cap. Nukualofa.

Ton·gan (tong′gən) *n.* 1 One of the Polynesian inhabitants of Tonga. 2 The language of Tonga.

tongs (tôngz, tongz) *n.pl. (sometimes construed as sing.)* An implement for grasping, holding, or lifting objects, consisting usu. of a pair of pivoted levers. Also **pair of tongs.** [< OE *tange*]

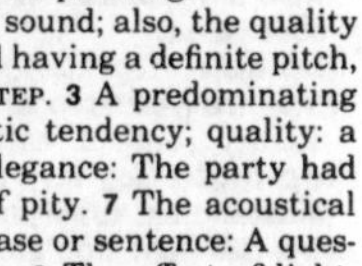

Tongs
a. blacksmith's.
b. ice.

tongue (tung) *n.* 1 A muscular organ attached to the floor of the mouth of most vertebrates, important in masticating and tasting food, and in man as an organ of speech. • See MOUTH. 2 A similar organ in various insects, etc. 3 An animal's tongue, as of beef, prepared as food. 4 The power of speech: Have you lost your *tongue?* 5 Manner or style of speaking: a smooth *tongue.* 6 Utterance; talk. 7 A language or dialect. 8 Anything resembling a tongue in appearance, shape, or function. 9 A slender projection of land. 10 A long narrow bay or inlet. 11 A jet of flame. 12 A strip of leather for closing the gap in front of a laced shoe. • See SHOE. 13 The free or vibrating end of a reed in a wind instrument. 14 The clapper of a bell. 15 The harnessing pole of a horse-drawn vehicle. 16 The projecting edge of a tongue-and-groove joint. —**hold one's tongue** To keep silent. —**on the tip of one's tongue** On the verge of being remembered or uttered. —**with tongue in cheek** Facetiously, insincerely, or ironically. —*v.* **tongued, tongu·ing** *v.t.* 1 To use the tongue to attack or separate (notes) in playing a wind instrument. 2 To touch or lap with the tongue. 3 In carpentry: **a** To cut a tongue on (a board). **b** To join by a tongue-and-groove joint. —*v.i.* 4 To use the tongue to attack or separate notes in playing a wind instrument. 5 To extend as a tongue. [< OE *tunge*]

tongue-and-groove joint (tung′ən·gro͞ov′) In carpentry, a joint in which a projecting edge, or tongue, of one board is inserted into a corresponding groove of another board.

Tongue-and-groove joint

tongue-in-cheek (tung′ən·chēk′) *adj.* Said or meant insincerely, ironically, or facetiously.

tongue-tie (tung′tī′) *n.* Abnormal shortness of the membrane under the tongue, whereby its motion is impeded. —*v.t.* **·tied, ·ty·ing** 1 To deprive of speech or the power of speech. 2 To bewilder or amaze so as to render speechless.

tongue twister A word or phrase difficult to articulate quickly: "Miss Smith's fish-sauce shop" is a *tongue-twister.*

ton·ic (ton′ik) *adj.* 1 Having power to invigorate or build up; bracing. 2 Pertaining to tone or tones; in music, of the principal tone of a scale or tonal system. 3 *Physiol.* Of or pertaining to tension, esp. muscular tension. 4 *Pathol.* Rigid; unrelaxing: *tonic* spasm. 5 Of or pertaining to musical intonations or modulations of words, sentences, etc. 6 *Phonet.* Accented or stressed. —*n.* 1 *Med.* A medicine that promotes physical well-being. 2 Whatever imparts vigor or tone. 3 The basic tone of a key or tonal system. [< Gk. *tonos* sound, tone]

to·nic·i·ty (tō·nis′ə·tē) *n.* 1 The state of being tonic; tone. 2 The normal tension of muscle tissue. 3 Health and vigor.

to·night (tə·nīt′) *adv.* In or during the present or coming night. —*n.* The night that follows this day; also, the present night. Also **to-night′.** [< OE *tō* to + *niht* night]

ton·nage (tun′ij) *n.* 1 Weight, as expressed in tons. 2 Capacity, as of a vessel or vessels, expressed in tons. 3 A tax levied at a given rate per ton. [< OF *tonne* a ton, tun]

ton·neau (tu·nō′) *n. pl.* **·neaus** (-nōz′) or **·neaux** (-nōz′) The rear part of an early type of automobile enclosing the seats for passengers. [F, lit., barrel]

ton·sil (ton′səl) *n.* Either of two oval lymphoid organs situated on either side of the passage from the mouth to the pharynx. [< L *tonsillae* tonsils] —**ton′sil·lar, ton′sil·ar** *adj.* • See MOUTH.

ton·sil·lec·to·my (ton′sə·lek′tə·mē) *n. pl.* **·mies** Removal of the tonsils by surgery.

ton·sil·li·tis (ton′sə·lī′tis) *n.* Inflammation of the tonsils. —**ton′sil·lit′ic** (-lit′ik) *adj.*

ton·so·ri·al (ton·sôr′ē·əl, -sō′rē-) *adj.* Pertaining to a barber or to barbering: chiefly humorous. [< L *tonsor* a barber]

ton·sure (ton′shər) *n.* 1 The shaving of the head, or of the crown of the head, as of a priest or monk. 2 That part of a priest's or monk's head left bare by shaving. —*v.t.* **·sured, ·sur·ing** To shave the head of. [< L *tonsura* a shearing]

ton·tine (ton′tēn, ton·tēn′) *n.* A form of collective life annuity, the individual profits of which increase as the number of survivors diminishes, the final survivor taking

the whole. —*adj.* Of or pertaining to such an annuity. [< Lorenzo *Tonti,* a 17th-c. Neapolitan banker]
to·nus (tō′nəs) *n. Physiol.* The slightly contracted state of a muscle at rest. [L, tone]
ton·y (tō′nē) *adj.* **ton·i·er, ton·i·est** *Informal* Aristocratic; fashionable. [< TONE]
too (to͞o) *adv.* **1** In addition; also. **2** In excessive quantity or degree: *too* long. **3** Very; extremely: I am *too* happy for you. **4** *Informal* Indeed: an intensive: You are *too* going! [< OE *tō* to]
took (to͝ok) *p.t.* of TAKE.
tool (to͞ol) *n.* **1** A simple implement, as a hammer, saw, spade, chisel, etc., used in work. **2** A power-driven apparatus used for cutting, shaping, boring, etc. **3** The active part of such an apparatus. **4** *Often pl.* Something necessary to the performance of a profession, vocation, etc.: Paints and brushes are an artist's *tools.* **5** A person used to carry out the designs of another or others, esp. when such designs are unethical or unlawful. —*v.t.* **1** To shape or work with a tool. **2** To provide, as a factory, with machinery and tools. **3** In bookbinding, to ornament or impress designs upon with a tool. —*v.i.* **4** To work with a tool. **5** *Informal* To drive or travel in a vehicle: usu. with *along.* **6** To install, as in a factory, equipment, tools, etc; usu. with *up.* [< OE *tōl*] —**tool′er** *n.* —**Syn.** *n.* **1** appliance, device, instrument, utensil. **5** dupe, stooge.
tool·ing (to͞o′ling) *n.* Ornamentation or work done with tools.
toot (to͞ot) *v.i.* **1** To blow a horn, whistle, etc., with short blasts. **2** To give forth a short blast. —*v.t.* **3** To sound (a horn, etc.) with short blasts. **4** To sound (a blast, etc.). —*n.* **1** A short blast on a horn, whistle, etc. **2** *Slang* A drinking spree. [? < MLG *tūten*] —**toot′er** *n.*
tooth (to͞oth) *n. pl.* **teeth** (tēth) **1** One of the hard, dense

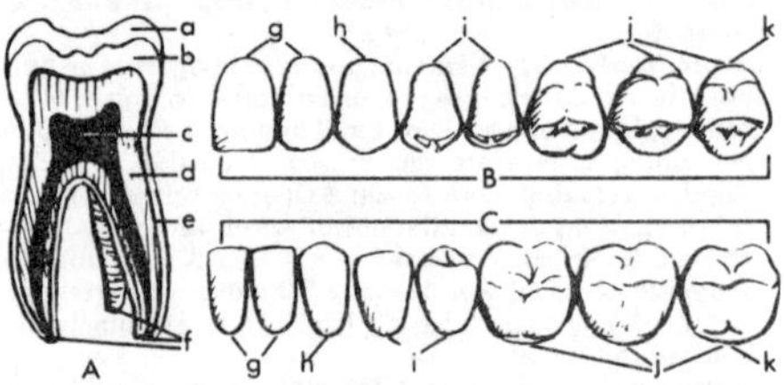

Teeth of human adult
A. cross-section of a molar. B. left upper jaw. C. left lower jaw. A.a. crown. b. enamel. c. pulp cavity. d. dentine. e. cement. f. roots. B. & C. g. incisors. h. canines. i. bicuspids. j. molars. k. wisdom teeth.

structures in the mouth of most vertebrates, used for seizing and chewing food, as offensive and defensive weapons, etc. **2** One of various hard bodies of the oral or gastric regions of invertebrates. **3** Something resembling a tooth in form or use, as a projection on a saw, comb, rake, or gearwheel. **4** Appetite or taste (for something): She has a sweet *tooth.* —**armed to the teeth** Completely or heavily armed. —**in the teeth of** Counter to or in defiance of. —**put teeth into** To make effective: to *put teeth into* a law. —**tooth and nail** With all one's strength and skill. —*v.t.* **1** To supply with teeth, as a rake or saw. **2** To give a serrated edge to; indent. —*v.i.* **3** To become interlocked, as gearwheels. [< OE *tōth*]
tooth·ache (to͞oth′āk′) *n.* Pain in a tooth or in the nearby area.
tooth·brush (to͞oth′brush′) *n.* A small brush used for cleaning the teeth.
toothed (to͞otht, to͞othd) *adj.* **1** Having (a specified type or number of teeth): used in combination: *sharp-toothed.* **2** Notched; serrated.
tooth·paste (to͞oth′pāst′) *n.* A paste applied to a toothbrush and used in cleaning the teeth.
tooth·pick (to͞oth′pik′) *n.* A small sliver, as of wood, used for removing particles of food from between the teeth.
tooth·some (to͞oth′səm) *adj.* Having a pleasant taste. —**tooth′some·ly** *adv.* —**tooth′some·ness** *n.* —**Syn.** appetizing, delicious, savory, tasty.
too·tle (to͞ot′l) *v.i.* **·tled, ·tling** **1** To toot lightly or continuously, as on a flute, whistle, etc. —*v.t.* **2** To toot (a flute, whistle, etc.) lightly and continuously. —*n.* The sound of tootling. [Freq. of TOOT]
top[1] (top) *n.* **1** The uppermost or highest part: the *top* of a hill. **2** The higher or upper surface: the *top* of a bureau. **3** A lid or cover: a bottle *top.* **4** The roof of a vehicle, as an automobile. **5** The crown of the head. **6** *pl.* The aboveground part of a root vegetable. **7** The highest degree or reach: at the *top* of one's voice. **8** The most prominent place or rank: at the *top* of one's profession. **9** One who is highest in rank: the *top* of one's class. **10** The choicest or best part: the *top* of the crop. **11** The upper part of a shoe or boot. —**blow one's top** *Slang* To break out in a rage. —**from top to toe** **1** From head to foot. **2** Completely. —**on top** **1** Successful. **2** With success; victoriously. —**over the top** Over the upper edge of a trench so as to attack. —*adj.* **1** Of or pertaining to the top. **2** Forming or comprising the top. **3** Most important; chief: *top* authors. **4** Greatest in amount or degree: *top* prices; *top* speed. —*v.* **topped, top·ping** *v.t.* **1** To remove the top of; prune: to *top* a tree. **2** To provide with a top, cap, etc. **3** To form the top of. **4** To reach the top of; surmount: to *top* a wave. **5** To surpass or exceed: Can you *top* this? **6** In golf, tennis, etc., to hit the upper part of (the ball) in making a stroke. —*v.i.* **7** To top someone or something. —**top off** To complete, esp. with a finishing touch. [< OE]
top[2] (top) *n.* A toy of wood, plastic, metal, etc., with a point on which it is made to spin, as by the unwinding of a string. [< OE]
to·paz (tō′paz) *n.* **1** A yellow or brownish yellow crystalline mineral, valued as a gemstone. **2** A yellow sapphire. **3** A yellow variety of quartz resembling topaz. [< Gk. *topazos*]
top boot A boot with a high top, sometimes ornamented with materials different from the rest of the boot. —**top′-boot′ed** *adj.*
top·coat (top′kōt′) *n.* A lightweight overcoat.
top-drawer (top′drôr′) *adj. Informal* Of the highest quality, rank, or status.
top·flight (top′flīt′) *adj. Informal* Of the highest quality; outstanding; superior.
top·gal·lant (top′gal′ənt, tə·gal′ənt) *Naut. n.* The mast, sail, yard, or rigging immediately above the topmast and topsail. —*adj.* Pertaining to the topgallants.
top hat A man's formal hat, usu. black and made of silk, having a tall, cylindrical crown.
top·heav·y (top′hev′ē) *adj.* **·heav·i·er, ·heav·i·est** **1** Too heavy at the top and liable to topple: a *topheavy* bookcase. **2** Having too many in positions of high rank, as an organization. —**top′heav′i·ly** *adv.* —**top′heav′i·ness** *n.*
top·ic (top′ik) *n.* **1** A subject treated of in speech or writing. **2** A theme for discussion. **3** A subdivision of an outline or a treatise. [< L *Topica,* title of a work by Aristotle] —**Syn.** **1** issue, matter, point, question.
top·i·cal (top′i·kəl) *adj.* **1** Of or belonging to a place or spot; local. **2** Of or relating to matters of present or local interest; limited in relevance to a time or place. **3** Of or pertaining to a topic. **4** *Med.* Pertaining to a restricted area of the body. —**top′i·cal·ly** *adv.*
top kick *Slang* A top sergeant.
top·knot (top′not′) *n.* **1** A tuft or knot of hair or feathers on the top of the head. **2** A bow or other ornament worn as a headdress.
top·less (top′lis) *adj.* **1** Lacking a top. **2** Nude from the waist up. **3** Being without a covering for the breasts. **4** Presenting topless waitresses, dancers, etc., as a bar. **5** So high that no top can be seen. —**top′less·ness** *n.*
top-lev·el (top′lev′əl) *adj.* Of the highest rank or importance.
top·loft·y (top′lôf′tē) *adj.* **·i·er, ·i·est** Very proud or haughty. —**top′-loft′i·ness** *n.*
top·mast (top′mast′, -məst) *n. Naut.* The mast next above the lower mast.
top·most (top′mōst′) *adj.* Being at the very top.
top-notch (top′noch′) *adj. Informal* Best or highest, as in quality, merit, or performance. —**top′-notch′er** *n.*
to·pog·ra·phy (tə·pog′rə·fē) *n. pl.* **·phies** **1** The art of representing on a map or chart the physical features of

a place, as mountains, lakes, canals, usu. with indications of elevation. 2 The physical features of a region. 3 Topographic surveying. [< Gk. *topos* place + -GRAPHY] —**to·pog′ra·pher** *n.* —**top·o·graph·ic** (top′ə·graf′ik) or **·i·cal** *adj.* —**top′o·graph′i·cal·ly** *adv.*

top·per (top′ər) *n.* 1 One who or that which tops. 2 *Slang* One who or that which is of supreme quality. 3 *Informal* A top hat. 4 *Informal* A topcoat.

top·ping (top′ing) *adj.* 1 Towering high above. 2 Eminent; distinguished. 3 *Brit. Informal* Excellent; first-rate. —*n.* That which forms a top.

top·ple (top′əl) *v.* **·pled, ·pling** *v.i.* 1 To fall, top foremost, by or as if by its own weight. 2 To seem to be about to fall; totter. —*v.t.* 3 To cause to totter or fall. 4 To cause to collapse; overthrow: to *topple* a government. [Freq. of TOP¹, *v.*]

tops (tops) *adj. Slang* Excellent; first-rate.

top·sail (top′sāl′, -səl) *n. Naut.* 1 In a square-rigged vessel, a square sail set next above the lowest sail of a mast. 2 In a fore-and-aft-rigged vessel, a sail above the gaff of a lower sail.

top-se·cret (top′sē′krit) *adj.* Designating information requiring the strictest secrecy.

top sergeant *Informal* FIRST SERGEANT. See GRADE.

top·side (top′sīd′) *n.* 1 The portion of a ship above the main deck. 2 *pl.* The side of a ship above the waterline. —*adv.* To or on the upper parts of a ship.

top·soil (top′soil′) *n.* The surface soil of land.

top·sy-tur·vy (top′sē·tûr′vē) *adv.* 1 Upside down. 2 In utter confusion. —*adj.* 1 Being in an upset or disordered condition. 2 Upside-down. —*n.* A state of being topsy-turvy; disorder. [Earlier *topsy-tervy*, ? < TOP¹ + obs. *terve* overturn] —**top′sy-tur′vi·ly** *adv.* —**top′sy-tur′vi·ness** *n.*

toque (tōk) *n.* 1 A small, close-fitting, brimless hat worn by women. 2 TUQUE. [< Sp. *toca*]

To·rah (tôr′ə, tō′rə) *n.* In Judaism: 1 The Pentateuch. 2 A scroll, as of parchment, containing the Pentateuch. 3 The whole of Jewish law, including the Old Testament and the Talmud. [< Hebrew *tōrāh* an instruction, law]

torch (tôrch) *n.* 1 A stick of wood or some material dipped in tallow or oil and set ablaze at the end to provide a light that can be carried about. 2 Anything that illuminates or brightens. 3 A portable device giving off an intensely hot flame and used for burning off paint, melting solder, etc. 4 *Brit.* A flashlight. [< OF *torche*]

torch·bear·er (tôrch′bâr′ər) *n.* 1 One who carries a torch. 2 One who conveys knowledge, truth, etc. 3 A leader of a cause or movement.

torch·light (tôrch′līt′) *n.* The light of a torch or torches. —*adj.* Lighted by torches.

torch song A popular love song, usu. melancholy and expressing hopeless yearning. —**torch singer**

tore (tôr, tōr) *p.t.* of TEAR¹.

tor·e·a·dor (tôr′ē·ə·dôr′, tō′rē-) *n.* One who engages in a bullfight, esp. on horseback. [< Sp. < *toro* a bull]

to·ri·i (tôr′ē·ē, tōr′-) *n. pl.* **to·ri·i** The gateway of a Shinto shrine. [Jap.]

tor·ment (tôr′ment, -mənt) *n.* 1 Intense bodily pain or mental anguish. 2 A source of pain or anguish, or a persistent annoyance. 3 The inflicting of torture. —*v.t.* (tôr·ment′) 1 To subject to intense or persistent physical or mental pain; make miserable. 2 To harass or vex. 3 To disturb; agitate; stir up. [< L *tormentum* a rack] —**tor·men′tor, tor·men′ter** *n.* —**Syn.** *n.* 1 agony, torture, suffering, misery.

Japanese torii

torn (tôrn, tōrn) *p.p. of* TEAR¹.

tor·na·do (tôr·nā′dō) *n. pl.* **·does** or **·dos** 1 A whirling wind of exceptional force and violence, accompanied by a funnel-shaped cloud marking the narrow path of greatest destruction. 2 Any hurricane or violent windstorm. [Alter. of Sp. *tronada* a thunderstorm < *tronar* to thunder] —**tor·nad′ic** (-nad′ik) *adj.*

tor·pe·do (tôr·pē′dō) *n. pl.* **·does** 1 A self-propelled, tube-shaped underwater missile with an explosive warhead. 2 Any of various devices containing an explosive, as a submarine mine. —*v.t.* **·doed, ·do·ing** 1 To damage or sink (a vessel) with a torpedo. 2 *Informal* To destroy utterly; demolish: Publicity could *torpedo* the agreement. 3 ELECTRIC RAY. [L, stiffness, numbness < *torpere* be numb]

torpedo boat A swift, lightly armed boat equipped to discharge torpedoes.

tor·pid (tor′pid) *adj.* 1 Having lost sensibility or power of motion, partially or wholly, as a hibernating animal; dormant; numb. 2 Slow to act or respond; sluggish. 3 Apathetic; spiritless; dull. [< L *torpidus* < *torpere* be numb] —**tor·pid·i·ty** (tôr·pid′ə·tē), **tor′pid·ness** *n.* —**tor′pid·ly** *adv.*

tor·por (tôr′pər) *n.* 1 Complete or partial loss of sensibility or power of motion; stupor. 2 Apathy; listlessness; dullness. [< L *torpere* be numb] —**tor·po·rif·ic** (tôr′pə·rif′ik) *adj.*

torque (tôrk) *n.* That which causes or tends to cause twisting or rotational acceleration; the moment of a force. [< L *torquere* to twist]

tor·rent (tôr′ənt, tor′-) *n.* 1 A stream of liquid, esp. water, flowing rapidly and turbulently. 2 Any violent or tumultuous flow; a gush: a *torrent* of abuse. [< L *torrens*, lit., boiling, burning, pr.p. of *torrere* parch]

tor·ren·tial (tô·ren′shəl, to-) *adj.* 1 Of, like, or resulting in a torrent. 2 Resembling a torrent —**tor·ren′tial·ly** *adv.*

tor·rid (tôr′id, tor′-) *adj.* 1 Parched or hot from exposure to heat, esp. of the sun. 2 Intensely hot and dry; scorching. 3 Passionate. [< L *torridus* < *torrere* parch] —**tor·rid·i·ty** (tô·rid′ə·tē, to-), **tor′rid·ness** *n.* —**tor′rid·ly** *adv.*

torrid zone That part of the earth's surface on both sides of the equator between the tropics of Cancer and Capricorn. • See ZONE.

tor·sion (tôr′shən) *n.* 1 The act of twisting, or the state of being twisted. 2 *Mech.* Deformation or stress caused by twisting. [< L *tortus*, p.p. of *torquere* twist] —**tor′sion·al** *adj.* —**tor′sion·al·ly** *adv.*

tor·so (tôr′sō) *n. pl.* **·sos** or **·si** (-sē) 1 The trunk of a human body. 2 The part of a sculptured human figure corresponding to the trunk, esp. when the head and limbs are missing. [Ital., a stalk, trunk of a body]

tort (tôrt) *n. Law* Any civil wrong by act or omission for which a suit can be brought, exclusive of a breach of contract. [< L *tortus* twisted]

torte (tôrt, tôr′tə) *n. pl.* **tortes** or **tor·ten** (tôr′tən) A rich cake variously made of butter, eggs, fruits, and nuts. [G]

tor·til·la (tôr·tē′ə) *n.* A small, flat cake made of coarse cornmeal and baked on a griddle, common in Mexico. [Sp., dim. of *torta* a cake]

tor·toise (tôr′təs) *n.* A turtle, esp. one living on land. [< Med. L *tortuca*]

tortoise shell 1 The mottled yellow and brown shell of certain turtles, formerly used to make eyeglass frames, combs, etc. 2 A plastic imitation of this. —**tor′toise-shell′** *adj.*

Giant tortoise

tor·tu·ous (tôr′chōō·əs) *adj.* 1 Abounding in bends, twists, or turns; winding. 2 Not straightforward; devious: *tortuous* logic. [< L *tortus* twisted. See TORSION.] —**tor′tu·ous·ly** *adv.* —**tor′tu·ous·ness** *n.*

tor·ture (tôr′chər) *n.* 1 The infliction of extreme pain on one held captive, as in punishment, to obtain a confession or information, or to deter others from a course of action. 2 Intense physical or mental suffering; agony. 3 Something that causes severe pain. 4 *Informal* Something intensely annoying, embarrassing, or intolerable: Sitting through his speech was sheer *torture*. —*v.t.* **·tured, ·tur·ing** 1 To inflict extreme pain upon; subject to torture. 2 To cause to suffer keenly in body or mind. 3 To twist or turn into an abnormal form; distort; wrench. [< L *tortura*, lit., a twisting < *tortus*. See TORSION.] —**tor′tur·er** *n.*

To·ry (tôr′ē, tō′rē) *n. pl.* **To·ries** **1** A historical English political party, opposed to the Whigs, now called the Conservative party. **2** One who adhered to the British cause at the time of the American Revolution. **3** A very conservative person: also **tory.** —**To′ry·ism** *n.*

toss (tôs, tos) *v.t.* **1** To throw, pitch, or fling about: *tossed* in a small boat on the open sea. **2** To throw or cast upward or toward another: to *toss* a ball. **3** To throw, esp. casually or indifferently: to *toss* clothes on a chair. **4** To remove from abruptly or violently: with *out:* He was *tossed* out of a job. **5** To throw (a coin) in the air to decide a question by comparing the side facing up, upon landing, with a previous call. **6** To lift with a quick motion, as the head. **7** To insert or interject casually or carelessly: to *toss* in impressive but irrelevant statistics. **8** To utter, write, or do easily or in an offhand manner: with *off.* **9** To bandy about, as something discussed. **10** To turn over and mix the contents of: to *toss* a salad. **11** To make restless; agitate. **12** To drink at one draft: often with *off.* —*v.i.* **13** To be moved or thrown about, as a ship in a storm. **14** To roll about restlessly or from side to side, as in sleep. **15** To go quickly or angrily, as with a toss of the head. **16** To toss a coin. —*n.* **1** The act of tossing, as a throw or pitch. **2** A quick movement, as of the head. **3** The state of being tossed. **4** TOSS-UP (def. 1). [Prob. < Scand.] —**toss′er** *n.* —**Syn.** *v.* **2** flip, flick, hurl. **12** quaff, swallow, gulp.

toss-up (tôs′up′, tos′-) *n.* **1** The tossing of a coin to decide a question. **2** An even chance.

tot[1] (tot) *n.* A little child; toddler. [Prob. < Scand.]

tot[2] (tot) *v.* **tot·ted, tot·ting** *Informal v.t.* **1** To add; total: with *up.* —*v.i.* **2** To add. [Short for TOTAL]

to·tal (tōt′l) *n.* The whole sum or amount. —*adj.* **1** Constituting or comprising a whole. **2** Complete: a *total* loss. —*v.* **·taled** or **·talled, ·tal·ing** or **·tal·ling** *v.t.* **1** To ascertain the total of. **2** To come to or reach as a total; amount to. **3** *Slang* To wreck completely; demolish, esp. a car. —*v.i.* **4** To amount: often with *to.* [< L *totus* all] —**to′tal·ly** *adv.*

to·tal·i·tar·i·an (tō·tal′ə·târ′ē·ən) *adj.* **1** Designating or characteristic of a government controlled exclusively by one party or faction that suppresses political dissent by force or intimidation and whose power to control the economic, social, and intellectual life of the individual is virtually unlimited. **2** Tyrannical; despotic. —*n.* An adherent of totalitarian government. —**to·tal′i·tar′i·an·ism** *n.*

to·tal·i·ty (tō·tal′ə·tē) *n. pl.* **·ties** **1** A total amount; aggregate; sum. **2** The state of being whole or entire.

tote (tōt) *Informal v.t.* **tot·ed, tot·ing** **1** To carry or bear on the person; transport; haul. **2** To carry habitually: He *totes* a gun. —*n.* **1** The act of toting. **2** A load or haul. [?] —**tot′er** *n.*

tote bag A large handbag for personal articles, carried esp. by women.

to·tem (tō′təm) *n.* **1** An animal, plant, or other natural object believed to be ancestrally related to a tribe, clan, or family group, and serving as its emblem, as among the North American Indians. **2** A representation of such an emblem. [< Algon.] —**to·tem·ic** (tō·tem′ik) *adj.* —**to′·tem·ism** *n.*

totem pole A pole carved or painted with totemic symbols, erected outside the houses of Indians along the NW coast of North America.

tot·ter (tot′ər) *v.i.* **1** To shake or waver, as if about to fall; be unsteady. **2** To walk unsteadily. —*n.* An unsteady or wobbly manner of walking. [Prob. < Scand.] —**tot′ter·er** *n.* —**tot′ter·ing·ly** *adv.* —**tot′ter·y** *adj.*

tou·can (to͞o′kan, to͞o·kän′) *n.* A fruit-eating bird of tropical America with brilliant plumage and a very large beak. [< Tupi *tucana*]

Toucan

touch (tuch) *v.t.* **1** To place the hand, finger, or other body part in contact with; perceive by feeling. **2** To be or come in contact with. **3** To bring into contact with something else. **4** To hit or strike lightly; tap. **5** To lay the hand or hands on: Please don't *touch* the paintings. **6** To border on; adjoin. **7** To come to; reach: The temperature *touched* 90°. **8** To rival or equal: As a salesman, nobody could *touch* him. **9** To color slightly: The sun *touched* the clouds with gold. **10** To affect the emotions of, esp. so as to feel compassion or gratitude; move: She was *touched* by their concern for her health. **11** To hurt the feelings of. **12** To relate to; concern; affect: The war *touches* us all. **13** To have to do with, use, or partake of: He never *touches* anything stronger than ginger ale. **14** To affect injuriously; taint: vegetables *touched* by frost. **15** *Slang* To borrow money from. —*v.i.* **16** To touch someone or something. **17** To come into or be in contact. —**touch at** To stop briefly at (a port or place) in the course of a journey or voyage. —**touch down** To land after flight. —**touch off** **1** To cause to explode; detonate; fire. **2** To provoke or initiate, esp. a violent reaction. —**touch on** (or **upon**) **1** To relate to; concern: That *touches on* another question. **2** To treat or discuss briefly or in passing. —**touch up** To add finishing touches or corrections to, as a work of art or writing. —*n.* **1** The act or fact of touching; a coming into contact, as a tap. **2** The sense stimulated by touching; the tactile sense by which a surface or its characteristics, as of pressure or texture, may be perceived. **3** A sensation conveyed by touching: a silky *touch.* **4** Communication or contact: Let's keep in *touch.* **5** A distinctive manner or style, as of an artist, author, or craftsman: a master's *touch.* **6** Delicate sensitivity, appreciation, or understanding: a fine *touch* for collecting rare china. **7** Any slight or delicate detail that helps to finish or perfect something, as a work of art or writing: to apply the finishing *touches.* **8** A trace; hint: a *touch* of irony. **9** A slight attack; twinge: a *touch* of rheumatism. **10** A small quantity; dash: a *touch* of perfume. **11** The resistance to motion offered by the keys of a piano, typewriter, etc. **12** The manner in which something is struck or touched, as the keys of a piano. **13** *Slang* Borrowed money, or a request to borrow money. **14** *Slang* A person from whom money may be borrowed, esp. easily: a soft *touch.* [< OF *tochier*] —**touch′a·ble** *adj.* —**touch′er** *n.*

touch and go An uncertain, risky, or precarious state of things. —**touch′-and-go′** *adj.*

touch·back (tuch′bak′) *n.* In football, the act of touching the ball to the ground behind the player's own goal line when the ball was propelled over the goal line by an opponent.

touch·down (tuch′doun′) *n.* **1** A scoring play in football in which a player has possession of the ball on or over the opponent's goal line. **2** The act of touching down, as an aircraft or spacecraft.

tou·ché (to͞o·shā′) *interj.* A term used in fencing to indicate a touch scored by one's opponent, and otherwise to acknowledge the wit or effectiveness of a point made in argument or conversation. [F]

touched (tucht) *adj.* **1** Affected emotionally; moved. **2** Slightly unbalanced in mind; crack-brained.

touch·ing (tuch′ing) *adj.* Appealing to the emotions; esp., inspiring tenderness or sympathy. —*prep.* With regard to; concerning. —**touch′ing·ly** *adv.* —**touch′ing·ness** *n.*

touch-me-not (tuch′mē·not′) *n.* Any of various plants, the ripe seed capsules of which explode when touched.

touch·stone (tuch′stōn′) *n.* **1** A dark stone formerly used to test the purity of gold by the color of the streak made on the stone by the metal. **2** Any criterion or standard by which quality or value may be tested.

touch·wood (tuch′wo͝od′) *n.* PUNK[1] (def. 1).

touch·y (tuch′ē) *adj.* **touch·i·er, touch·i·est** **1** Apt to take offense on very little provocation. **2** Liable to cause hurt feelings or contention: a *touchy* subject. —**touch′i·ly** *adv.* —**touch′i·ness** *n.* —**Syn.** **1** sensitive, thin-skinned, volatile. **2** delicate, sensitive.

tough (tuf) *adj.* **1** Capable of bearing tension or strain without breaking, esp. because strong in texture or composition. **2** Difficult to cut or chew. **3** Strong in body or mind, esp. in resisting or enduring stress. **4** Requiring determined or intense effort; difficult: a *tough* assignment. **5** Resolute; unyielding; inflexible: a *tough* stand in the negotiations. **6** Severe; harsh: a *tough* punishment. **7** Given to or characterized by violence or rowdyism: a *tough* neighborhood. **8** *Informal* Unfortunate; regrettable. **9** *Slang* Great; fine. —*n.* A ruffian; rowdy. —*v.t. Informal* To manage to get through; endure: often with *out:* to *tough out* a recession. [< OE *tōh*] —**tough′ly** *adv.* —**tough′·ness** *n.* —**Syn.** **5** uncompromising, stubborn, militant.

tough·en (tuf′ən) *v.t. & v.i.* To make or become tough or tougher. **—tough′en·er** *n.*

tou·pee (to͞o·pā′) *n.* A man's small wig worn to cover a bald spot. [<OF *toup, top* a tuft of hair]

tour (to͝or) *n.* **1** An excursion or journey, as for sightseeing. **2** A trip, usu. over a planned course, as to conduct business, present theatrical performances, etc. **3** A set period of time, as of service in a particular place; turn or shift. **4** A brief survey; circuit: a *tour* of the grounds. *—v.t.* **1** To make a tour of; travel. **2** To present on a tour: to *tour* a play. *—v.i.* **3** To go on a tour. [<OF *tor* a turn <L *tornus* a lathe]

tour de force (to͝or də fôrs′) *pl.* **tours de force** (to͝or) A remarkable feat, as of skill, creativity, or industry. [F, lit., feat of strength]

touring car An old type of large, open automobile with a capacity for five or more passengers.

tour·ism (to͝or′iz·əm) *n.* **1** Recreational travel, considered esp. as an industry or source of income. **2** The organization and guidance of tourists. **—tour·is′tic** *adj.*

tour·ist (to͝or′ist) *n.* One who makes a tour or a pleasure trip. *—adj.* Of or suitable for tourists. **—tour′ist·y** *adj.*

tour·ma·line (to͝or′mə·lən, -lēn′) *n.* A complex mineral with a vitreous to resinous luster, found in various colors and valued in its transparent varieties as a gemstone. Also **tour′ma·lin** (-lin). [<F]

tour·na·ment (tûr′nə·mənt, to͝or′-) *n.* **1** A series of competitive sports events or games for prizes or cash awards and often for a championship: a golf or bridge *tournament.* **2** In medieval times, a pageant in which two opposing parties of men in armor contended on horseback with blunted weapons, esp. lances. [<OF <*torneier* to tourney]

tour·ney (tûr′nē, to͝or′-) *v.i.* To take part in a tournament. *—n.* TOURNAMENT. [<OF *torneier*]

tour·ni·quet (to͝or′nə·kit, tûr′-) *n.* A device for controlling arterial bleeding by tightening a nooselike bandage. [<F *tourner* to turn]

tou·sle (tou′zəl) *v.t.* **·sled, ·sling** To disarrange or dishevel; rumple. *—n.* A tousled mass, esp. of hair. [Freq. of ME *tousen*]

tout (tout) *Informal v.i.* **1** To solicit patronage, customers, votes, etc. **2** To sell information, as to a bettor, about horses entered in a race. *—v.t.* **3** To solicit; importune. **4** To praise highly or proclaim: *touted* as the world's fastest human. **5** To sell information concerning (a race horse). *—n.* **1** One who touts. **2** One who solicits business. [<OE *tōtian, tȳtan* peep, look out]

tout à fait (to͞o tȧ fe′) *French* Entirely; quite.

tout de suite (to͞ot swēt) Immediately; at once. [F]

tout en·sem·ble (to͞o täṅ säṅ′bl′) *French* All in all; everything considered.

tow[1] (tō) *n.* A short, coarse hemp or flax fiber prepared for spinning. [Prob. <OE *tōw-* spinning]

tow[2] (tō) *v.t.* To pull or drag, as by a rope or chain. *—n.* **1** The act of towing, or the state of being towed. **2** That which is towed, as a barge. **3** TOWLINE. **—in tow 1** In the condition of being towed. **2** Drawn along as if being towed: a film star with her fans *in tow.* **3** Under one's protection or care: took the orphan *in tow.* [<OE *togian*]

tow·age (tō′ij) *n.* **1** The charge for towing. **2** The act of towing.

to·ward (tôrd, tōrd, tə·wôrd′) *prep.* **1** In the direction of; facing. **2** With respect to; regarding. **3** In anticipation of or as a contribution to; for: He is saving *toward* his education. **4** Near in point of time; approaching: *toward* evening. **5** Tending or designed to result in. Also **to·wards′.** *—adj.* (tôrd, tōrd) Impending or imminent. [<OE *tō* to + *-weard* -ward] **—to·ward′ness** *n.*

tow·el (toul, tou′əl) *n.* A cloth or paper for drying anything by wiping. *—v.t.* **·eled** or **·elled, ·el·ing** or **·el·ling** To wipe or dry with a towel. [<OF *toaille*]

tow·el·ing (tou′ling, tou′əl·ing) *n.* Material for towels. Also **tow·el·ling.**

tow·er (tou′ər) *n.* **1** A structure very tall in proportion to its other dimensions, and either standing alone or forming part of a building. **2** A place of security or defense; citadel. **3** Someone or something likened to a tower in strength or command. *—v.i.* To rise or stand like a tower; extend to a great height. [<L *turris*]

tow·er·ing (tou′ər·ing) *adj.* **1** Very high or very great: a *towering* figure in modern drama. **2** Rising to a high pitch of violence or intensity: a *towering* rage.

tow·head (tō′hed′) *n.* **1** A head of very light-colored or flaxen hair. **2** A person having such hair. [<TOW[1] + HEAD] **—tow′-head′ed** *adj.*

tow·hee (tō′ē, tō′hē) *n.* Any of various American finches related to the buntings and the sparrows. Also **towhee bunting.** [Imit.]

Towhee

tow·line (tō′līn′) *n.* A line, rope, or chain used in towing.

town (toun) *n.* **1** Any collection of dwellings and other buildings larger than a village and smaller than a city. **2** A closely settled urban district, as contrasted with less populated or suburban areas or with the open country. **3** A city of any size. **4** The inhabitants or voters of a town. **5** TOWNSHIP. **6** Those residents of a town who are not associated educationally or administratively with a college or university situated in the town: *town* and gown. **—go to town** *Slang* To work or proceed with dispatch; get busy. **—on the town** *Slang* On a round of bars, nightclubs, etc., in the city in search of diversion or excitement. **—paint the town red** *Slang* To go on a spree; carouse. *—adj.* Of, situated in, or for a town. [<OE *tūn, tuun* an enclosure, group of houses]

town clerk An official who keeps the records of a town.

town crier Formerly, a person appointed to make proclamations through the streets of a town.

town hall A building in a town containing the public offices and often a place for meetings.

town house 1 A residence in a town or city, esp. when owned by one who also owns a house in the country. **2** A two- or three-story house, usu. for one family, contiguous to one or more similar houses.

town meeting A meeting of residents or voters of a town for the purpose of transacting town business.

town·ship (toun′ship) *n.* **1** In the U.S. and Canada, a territorial subdivision of a county with certain corporate powers of municipal government for local purposes. **2** In New England, a local political unit governed by a town meeting.

towns·man (tounz′mən) *n. pl.* **·men** (-mən) **1** A resident of a town. **2** A fellow citizen of a town. **3** A permanent resident of a town, as contrasted with a student or teacher in a school or college situated in the town.

towns·peo·ple (tounz′pē′pəl) *n.pl.* People who live in towns or in a particular town or city. Also **towns′folk′** (-fōk′).

town·y (toun′ē) *n. pl.* **town·ies** *Informal* TOWNSMAN (def. 3). Also **town′ie.**

tow·path (tō′path′, -päth′) *n.* A path along a river or canal used by men, horses, or mules towing boats.

tow·rope (tō′rōp′) *n.* A heavy rope or cable for towing.

tow truck (tō) A truck equipped to tow other vehicles.

tox·e·mi·a (tok·sē′mē·ə) *n.* The presence in the blood of toxins from a local source of infection. Also **tox·ae′mi·a.** [<TOX(IC) + Gk. *haima* blood] **—tox·e′mic** *adj.*

tox·ic (tok′sik) *adj.* **1** Poisonous. **2** Due to or caused by poison or a toxin. [<Gk. *toxicon (pharmakon)* (a poison) for arrows <*toxon* a bow] **—tox′i·cal·ly** *adv.* **—tox·ic′i·ty** (-sis′ə·tē) *n.*

toxico- *combining form* Poison; of or pertaining to poison or poisons: *toxicology.* Also **toxic-.** [<Gk. *toxicon* poison]

tox·i·col·o·gy (tok′sə·kol′ə·jē) *n.* The science that deals with poisons, their detection, antidotes, etc. **—tox′i·co·log′ic** (-kə·loj′ik) or **·i·cal** *adj.* **—tox′i·co·log′i·cal·ly** *adv.* **—tox′i·col′o·gist** *n.*

tox·in (tok′sin) *n.* **1** Any of various poisonous compounds produced by living organisms and acting as causative agents in many diseases. **2** Any toxic matter generated in living or dead organisms. [<TOX(IC) + -IN]

toy (toi) *n.* 1 Something designed or serving as a plaything for children. 2 Something trifling or unimportant. 3 An ornament; trinket. 4 A small animal, esp. one of a breed characterized by small size. —*v.i.* 1 To act or consider something without seriousness or conviction; trifle: to *toy* with an idea. 2 To use someone or something for one's amusement. 3 To act flirtatiously. —*adj.* 1 Designed as a toy. 2 Resembling a toy; esp., of miniature size: a *toy* dog. [Prob. < ME *toye* flirtation, sport] —**toy'er** *n.*

tp. township.

tpk. turnpike.

tr. translated; translation; translator; transpose; transitive; treasurer.

trace[1] (trās) *n.* 1 A vestige or mark left by some past event or by a person or thing no longer present. 2 An imprint or mark indicating the passage of a person or thing, as a footprint, etc. 3 A path or trail beaten down by men or animals. 4 A barely detectable quantity, quality, or characteristic. 5 A lightly drawn line; something traced. —*v.* **traced, trac·ing** *v.t.* 1 To follow the tracks or trail of. 2 To follow the course or development of, esp. by investigation of a series of events. 3 To find out or determine by investigation. 4 To follow (tracks, a course of development, etc.). 5 To draw; sketch. 6 To copy (a drawing, etc.) on a superimposed transparent sheet. 7 To form (letters, etc.) painstakingly. —*v.i.* 8 To have its origin; go back in time. 9 To follow a track, course of development, etc. [< OF *tracier* to trace] —**trace'a·bil'i·ty, trace'a·ble·ness** *n.* —**trace'a·ble** *adj.* —**trace'a·bly** *adv.* —**Syn.** 1 remnant, sign, aftermath, token, clue.

trace[2] (trās) *n.* One of two side straps or chains connected to a draft animal's harness and to the vehicle to be pulled. —**kick over the traces** To throw off control; become unmanageable. [< OF *trait* a dragging, a leather harness]

trac·er (trā'sər) *n.* 1 One who or that which traces. 2 An inquiry forwarded from one point to another, to trace missing mail, etc. 3 A substance, as a radioisotope, introduced into a system in minute amount as an indicator of the course of a process, reaction, disease, etc. 4 A bullet or shell that indicates its course by leaving a trail of smoke or fire.

trac·er·y (trā'sər·ē) *n. pl.* **·er·ies** 1 Ornamental stonework formed of branching lines, as in a Gothic window. 2 Any delicate ornamentation resembling this.

tra·che·a (trā'kē·ə) *n. pl.* **·che·ae** (-kē·ē, -kē·ī) or **·che·as** 1 In vertebrates, the duct by which air passes from the larynx to the bronchi and the lungs; the windpipe. 2 Any of the air passages in air-breathing arthropods. [< Gk. *(artēria) tracheia* a rough (artery)] —**tra'che·al** *adj.*

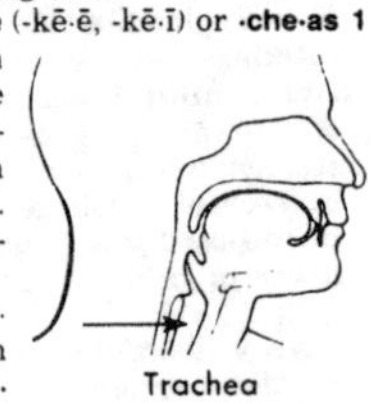

Trachea

tra·che·ot·o·my (trā'kē·ot'ə·mē) *n. pl.* **·mies** *Surg.* An incision into the trachea. Also **tra'che·ost'·o·my** (-ost'ə·mē).

tra·cho·ma (trə·kō'mə) *n.* A contagious virus disease of the eye characterized by granular excrescences on the inner surface of the eyelids. [< Gk. *trachōma* roughness] —**tra·chom·a·tous** (trə·kom'ə·təs) *adj.*

trac·ing (trā'sing) *n.* 1 The act of one who traces. 2 Something traced, as a copy made by tracing on transparent paper. 3 A record made by a self-registering instrument.

track (trak) *n.* 1 A mark or trail left by the passage of anything, as a series of footprints. 2 A path or way marked or worn out by the repeated passage of people, animals, or vehicles. 3 Any course or path, esp. one describing movement: the *track* of a missile or a comet. 4 A pair of parallel rails, usu. including the ties, that guide the wheels of a train, trolley, etc. 5 A usu. elliptical course for racing. 6 A sport in which footraces of various distances are held on a track. 7 TRACK AND FIELD. 8 A sequence of events; a succession of ideas. 9 Awareness of the progress or sequence; count; record: to lose *track* of an old friend; to keep *track* of expenses. 10 An endless metal belt, usu. one of a pair, by means of which certain vehicles are capable of moving over soft, slippery, or uneven surfaces. 11 The distance between the front or rear wheels of a vehicle, usu. measured from the center of the treads. 12 SOUND TRACK. 13 In education, any of two or more classes covering the same course of study in which students are placed according to their preparation and ability. —**in one's tracks** Right where one is; on the spot. —**make tracks** *Informal* To run away in haste; hurry. —**on** (or **off**) **the track** Keeping in view (or losing sight of) the subject or objective. —*v.t.* 1 To follow the tracks of; trail. 2 To discover or apprehend by following up marks, clues, or other evidence: with *down:* to *track* down a suspect; to *track* down a shipment of contaminated canned food. 3 To observe or plot the course of (an aircraft, spacecraft, etc.). 4 To make tracks upon or with: to *track* mud into a house. 5 To go through or traverse, as on foot: to *track* the wilderness. 6 To furnish with rails or tracks. —*v.i.* 7 To measure a certain distance between front or rear wheels. 8 To run in the same track or groove; be in alignment. 9 To leave tracks. —*adj.* Pertaining to or performed on a track, esp. a track for racing: *track* events. [< OF *trac*] —**track'er** *n.* —**track'less** *adj.*

track·age (trak'ij) *n.* 1 Railroad tracks collectively. 2 The right of one company to use the tracks of another. 3 The charge for this right.

track and field A sport consisting of footraces on a track and contests on a field, as in hurling, throwing, or leaping. —**track'-and-field'** *adj.*

trackless trolley TROLLEY BUS.

track record *Informal* A record of achievements.

tract[1] (trakt) *n.* 1 An extended area, as of land or water; stretch or expanse. 2 A system of parts or organs in an animal, having a distinct function: the alimentary *tract.* [< L *tractus* a drawing out < *trahere* draw]

tract[2] (trakt) *n.* A short treatise or pamphlet, as on religion or morals. [< L *tractatus* a handling]

tract·a·ble (trak'tə·bəl) *adj.* 1 Easily led or controlled; docile. 2 Readily worked or handled; malleable. [< L *tractare* handle, freq. of *trahere* draw] —**tract'a·bly** *adv.* —**tract'a·ble·ness, tract'a·bil'i·ty** *n.* —**Syn.** 1 manageable, compliant, mild, submissive.

trac·tile (trak'til, tīl) *adj.* That can be drawn out; ductile. [< L *tractus.* See TRACT[1]] —**trac·til'i·ty** *n.*

trac·tion (trak'shən) *n.* 1 The act of drawing, as by motive power over a surface. 2 The state of being pulled or drawn: to place a fractured limb in *traction.* 3 The power employed in pulling or drawing. 4 Adhesive or rolling friction, as of tires on a road. [< L *tractus.* See TRACT[1].] —**trac'tion·al, trac·tive** (trak'tiv) *adj.*

trac·tor (trak'tər) *n.* 1 A powerful, self-propelled vehicle used to pull farm machinery. 2 An automotive vehicle with a driver's cab, used to haul trailers, etc. 3 An airplane with the propeller or propellers situated in front of the lifting surfaces. [< L *tractus.* See TRACT[1].]

Tractor *def. 1*

trad (trad) *adj. Slang* Traditional: *trad* jazz.

trade (trād) *n.* 1 A business or occupation. 2 A skilled or specialized line of work, as a craft. 3 The people or companies engaged in a particular business. 4 The buying and selling or exchange of commodities; also, an instance of such commerce. 5 A firm's customers. 6 An exchange of personal articles; swap. 7 Any exchange of things or people having negotiable value: a baseball *trade.* 8 *Usu. pl.* TRADE WIND. —*adj.* 1 Of or pertaining to a trade. 2 Used by or intended for the members of a particular trade: a *trade* journal. —*v.t.* **trad·ed, trad·ing** 1 To give in exchange for something else. 2 To barter or exchange. —*v.i.* 3 To engage in commerce or in business transactions. 4 To make an exchange. 5 *Informal* To do one's shopping: with *at:* to *trade* at a store. —**trade in** To give in exchange as payment or part payment. —**trade off** To match or correlate, as incompatible elements or objectives, in the process of reaching a solution or compromise. —**trade on** To take advantage of. [< MLG, a track] —**trad'er** *n.*

trade-in (trād'in') *n.* Used merchandise accepted in payment or part payment for other, esp. new, merchandise.

trade-last (trād'last', -läst') *n. Informal* A favorable remark that one has heard and offers to repeat to the person complimented in return for a similar remark.

trade·mark (trād′märk′) *n.* 1 A name, symbol, design, device, or word used by a merchant or manufacturer to identify his product and distinguish it from that of others. 2 Any distinctive or characteristic feature. —*v.t.* 1 To label with a trademark. 2 To register and bring under legal protection as a trademark.

trade name 1 The name by which an article, process, etc., is designated in trade. 2 A name given by a manufacturer to designate a proprietary article, sometimes having the status of a trademark. 3 The name of a business concern.

trade-off (trād′ôf′, -of′) *n.* 1 A giving up of something, as an objective or advantage, in exchange for something else: a *trade-off* of higher pay for longer vacations. 2 The relationship that characterizes such an exchange; a compromise or adjustment between opposing elements or positions: the *trade-off* between taxation and improved public services.

trade school A school where practical skills or trades are taught.

trades·man (trādz′mən) *n. pl.* **·men** (-mən) A retail dealer; shopkeeper. —**trades′wom·an** *n. Fem.*

trade union LABOR UNION. Also **trades union.** —**trade unionism** —**trade unionist**

trade wind Either of two steady winds blowing toward the equator, one from the northeast on the north, the other from the southeast on the south side of the equatorial line.

trading post A building or small settlement in unsettled territory used as a station for barter, as for furs.

trading stamp A stamp of fixed value given as a premium with a purchase and exchangeable, in quantity, for merchandise.

tra·di·tion (trə·dish′ən) *n.* 1 The transmission of knowledge, opinions, customs, practices, etc., from generation to generation, esp. by word of mouth and by example. 2 The body of beliefs and usages so transmitted; also, any particular story, belief, or usage of this kind. 3 A custom so long continued that it has almost the force of a law. [< L *traditus,* p.p. of *tradere* deliver] —**tra·di′tion·al** *adj.* —**tra·di′tion·al·ly** *adv.*

tra·duce (trə·d^y^ōōs′) *v.t.* **·duced, ·duc·ing** To misrepresent willfully the conduct or character of; defame; slander. [< L *traducere* transport, bring into disgrace] —**tra·duce′·ment, tra·duc′er** *n.*

traf·fic (traf′ik) *n.* 1 The passing of pedestrians, vehicles, aircraft, messages, etc., in a limited space or between certain points. 2 The people, vehicles, messages, etc., so moving. 3 The business of buying and selling commodities; trade. 4 Unlawful or improper trade: *traffic* in stolen goods. 5 The people or freight transported by a carrier, as a railroad. 6 The business of transportation. 7 Communication or contact; connection. —*v.i.* **·ficked, ·fick·ing** 1 To engage in buying and selling illegally: with *in:* to *traffic* in narcotic drugs. 2 To have dealings: with *with.* [< MF < Ital. *traffico*] —**traf′fick·er** *n.*

traffic light A set of colored signal lights used to control the passage of automotive traffic.

tra·ge·di·an (trə·jē′dē·ən) *n.* 1 An actor of tragedy. 2 A writer of tragedies.

tra·ge·di·enne (trə·jē′dē·en′) *n.* An actress of tragedy.

trag·e·dy (traj′ə·dē) *n. pl.* **·dies** 1 A form of drama in which the protagonist comes to disaster, as through a flaw in character, and in which the ending is usu. marked by sorrow or pity. 2 A play, film, etc., of this kind. 3 Any tragic or disastrous incident or series of incidents. 4 *Informal* A misfortune. [< Gk. *tragōidia*]

trag·ic (traj′ik) *adj.* 1 Of or having the nature of tragedy. 2 Appropriate to or suggestive of tragedy: a *tragic* manner. 3 Causing or likely to cause suffering, sorrow, or death: a *tragic* accident. [< Gk. *tragikos* pertaining to tragedy] —**trag′i·cal·ly** *adv.*

trag·i·com·e·dy (traj′i·kom′ə·dē) *n. pl.* **·dies** 1 A drama having characteristics of both tragedy and comedy. 2 An incident or series of incidents of this nature. —**trag′i·com′ic** or **·i·cal** *adj.* —**trag′i·com′i·cal·ly** *adv.*

trail (trāl) *v.t.* 1 To draw along lightly over a surface. 2 To drag or draw after: to *trail* oars; to *trail* an injured leg. 3 To follow the track of; trace: to *trail* game. 4 To be or come along behind. 5 To follow behind, as in pursuit or to keep under surveillance: to *trail* a suspect. —*v.i.* 6 To hang or extend loosely so as to drag over a surface. 7 To grow extensively and usu. irregularly along the ground or over rocks, etc. 8 To be or come along behind. 9 To move or walk heavily or ponderously; trudge. 10 To lag behind: to *trail* by 30,000 votes; to *trail* in the development of auto safety standards. 11 To flow or extend, as in a stream. —*n.* 1 The track left by something that has moved or been drawn or dragged over a surface. 2 The track, scent, etc., indicating the passage of someone or something. 3 The path worn by persons or by animals, esp. through a wilderness. 4 Something that trails or is trailed behind, as the train of a dress or the track of a meteor. 5 A sequence of results or conditions following after something: left a *trail* of broken hearts. [< AF *trailler* haul, tow a boat]

trail·er (trā′lər) *n.* 1 One who or that which trails. 2 A vehicle drawn by a cab or tractor having motive power. 3 A vehicle usu. drawn by an automobile or truck and equipped to serve as living quarters. 4 PREVIEW (def. 2).

trailing arbutus A prostrate evergreen shrub bearing clusters of fragrant pink flowers.

train[1] (trān) *n.* 1 A series of connected railway cars, often drawn by a locomotive. 2 Anything drawn along behind, as a trailing part of a skirt. 3 A line or group of followers; retinue. 4 A moving line of people, animals, vehicles, etc.; procession. 5 A series, succession, or set of connected things; sequence: a *train* of thought. 6 Something, as a period of time or set of circumstances, following after something else; aftermath: The argument left bitter feelings in its *train.* 7 *Mech.* A series of parts acting on each other, as for transmitting motion. —*v.t.* 1 To bring to a desired standard by careful instruction; esp., to guide in morals or manners. 2 To make skillful or proficient: to *train* soldiers. 3 To make obedient to orders or capable of performing tricks, as an animal. 4 To lead into taking a particular course; develop into a fixed shape: to *train* a plant on a trellis; to *train* the hair to lie flat. 5 To put or point in an exact direction; aim: to *train* a rifle or a gaze on someone. —*v.i.* 6 To undergo a course of training. [< OF *trahiner* to draw] —**train′a·ble** *adj.* —**train′er** *n.* —**Syn.** *v.* 1 educate, instruct, rear, bring up, mold.

train[2] (trān) *n. Can.* A large sled, having a shape like a toboggan. [< F *traineau* sled]

train·ee (trā·nē′) *n.* One who is being trained, as a new employee.

train·ing (trā′ning) *n.* 1 Systematic instruction and drill. 2 The method or action of one who trains, as for an athletic contest.

train·man (trān′mən) *n. pl.* **·men** (-mən) A railway employee serving on a train.

traipse (trāps) *v.i.* **traipsed, traips·ing** To walk or wander about; gad. —*n.* The act of traipsing. [Prob. < OF *trapasser,* var. of *trespasser* trespass]

trait (trāt) *n.* A distinguishing feature or quality, as of character. [< L *tractus* a drawing out < *trahere* draw]

trai·tor (trā′tər) *n.* 1 One who commits treason. 2 One who betrays a trust or acts deceitfully and disloyally. [< L *tradere* betray] —**trai′tress** (-tris) *n. Fem.*

trai·tor·ous (trā′tər·əs) *adj.* 1 Of, constituting, or resembling treason. 2 Of or characteristic of a traitor; treacherous. —**trai′tor·ous·ly** *adv.* —**trai′tor·ous·ness** *n.*

tra·jec·to·ry (trə·jek′tər·ē) *n. pl.* **·ries** The path described by an object or body moving in space, as of a comet or a bullet. [< L *trajectus,* p.p. of *trajicere* throw over]

tram (tram) *n.* 1 *Brit.* STREETCAR. 2 An open vehicle running on rails, used to carry coal in a mine. Also **tram′car′** (-kär′). [< dial. *tram* a rail]

tram·mel (tram′əl) *n.* 1 *Usu. pl.* That which limits freedom or activity; hindrance. 2 A fetter or shackle, esp. one used in teaching a horse to amble. 3 An instrument for drawing ellipses. 4 An adjustable hook used to suspend cooking pots from a fireplace crane. 5 A net formed of three layers, the central one of finer mesh, to trap fish passing through either of the others: also **trammel net.** —*v.t.* **·meled** or **·melled, ·mel·ing** or **·mel·ling** 1 To hinder or obstruct; restrict. 2 To entangle in or as in a snare; imprison. [< LL *tremaculum* net < L *tri-* three + *macula* a mesh] —**tram′mel·er** or **tram′mel·ler** *n.*

tramp (tramp) *v.i.* 1 To walk or wander about, esp. as a tramp or hobo. 2 To walk heavily or firmly. —*v.t.* 3 To walk or wander through. 4 To walk on heavily; trample. —*n.* 1 One who travels from place to place, usu. on foot and destitute and dependent on charity for a living. 2 The sound of heavy marching or walking. 3 A long stroll; hike. 4 A steam vessel that goes from port to port picking up freight wherever it can: also **tramp steamer.** 5 *Slang* A sexually promiscuous woman. [ME *trampen*] —**tramp′er** *n.* —**Syn** *n.* 1 vagrant, vagabond, hobo, bum.

tram·ple (tram′pəl) *v.* **·pled, ·pling** *v.i.* 1 To tread heavily, esp. so as to crush. 2 To injure or encroach upon someone or something by or as by tramping: with *on:* to *trample* on someone's rights. —*v.t.* 3 To tread heavily or ruthlessly on. —*n.* The sound of treading under foot. [< ME *trampen* tramp] —**tram′pler** *n.*

tram·po·line (tram′pə·lēn′, tram′pə·lēn′) *n.* A heavy canvas stretched to a frame by springs and used for its resiliency in tumbling. Also **tram′po·lin.** [< Ital. *trampoli* stilts]

tram·way (tram′wā′) *n. Brit.* A streetcar line.

trance (trans, träns) *n.* 1 A state in which one appears to be unable to act consciously, as though hypnotized or governed by a supernatural force. 2 A dreamlike or sleepy state, as that induced by hypnosis. 3 A state of profound concentration marked by lack of awareness of one's surroundings; deep abstraction. [< OF *transir* pass, die]

tran·quil (trang′kwil) *adj.* 1 Free from agitation or disturbance; calm: a *tranquil* mood. 2 Quiet and motionless: a *tranquil* scene. [< L *tranquillus* quiet] —**tran′quil·ly** *adv.* —**tran′quil·ness** *n.* —**Syn.** 1 relaxed, serene. 2 placid.

tran·quil·ize (trang′kwəl·īz) *v.t.* & *v.i.* **·ized, ·iz·ing** To make or become tranquil, esp. by using a drug. Also **tran′·quil·lize.** *Brit. sp.* **·lise.** —**tran′quil·i·za′tion** *n.*

tran·quil·iz·er (trang′kwəl·ī′zər) *n.* 1 One who or that which tranquilizes. 2 Any of various drugs that calm mental agitation without impairing consciousness. Also **tran′·quil·liz′er.**

tran·quil·li·ty (trang·kwil′ə·tē) *n.* The state of being tranquil; peacefulness; quiet. Also **tran·quil′i·ty.**

trans- *prefix* 1 Across; beyond; on the other side of: *transatlantic; transmigrate.* 2 Through: *transfix.* 3 Through and through; changing completely: *transform.* [< L *trans* across, beyond, over]

trans. transactions; transferred; transitive; translated; translation; translator.

trans·act (trans·akt′, tranz-) *v.t.* 1 To carry through; accomplish; do. —*v.i.* 2 To do business. [< L *transactus,* p.p. of *transigere* drive through, accomplish] —**trans·ac′tor** *n.*

trans·ac·tion (trans·ak′shən, tranz-) *n.* 1 The act or process of transacting. 2 Something transacted; esp., a business deal. 3 *pl.* Published reports, as of a society. —**trans·ac′tion·al** *adj.*

trans·at·lan·tic (trans′ət·lan′tik, tranz′-) *adj.* 1 Across or crossing the Atlantic Ocean: a *transatlantic* flight. 2 On the other side of the Atlantic.

tran·scend (tran·send′) *v.t.* 1 To go or pass beyond the limits of: knowledge that *transcends* reason. 2 To rise above in excellence or degree. —*v.i.* 3 To be surpassing; excel. [< L *trans-* beyond, over + *scandere* to climb]

tran·scen·dent (tran·sen′dənt) *adj.* 1 TRANSCENDENTAL (def. 1). 2 *Theol.* Existing apart from and above the material universe: said of God. [< L *transcendere* transcend] —**tran·scen′dence, tran·scen′den·cy** *n.* —**tran·scen′dent·ly** *adv.*

tran·scen·den·tal (tran′sen·den′təl) *adj.* 1 Rising above or going beyond ordinary limits; surpassing. 2 Beyond natural experience; supernatural. 3 Of or pertaining to transcendentalism. —**tran′scen·den′tal·ly** *adv.*

tran·scen·den·tal·ism (tran′sen·den′təl·iz′əm) *n.* The philosophical doctrine that man can attain knowledge which goes beyond or transcends appearances or sensory phenomena. —**tran′scen·den′tal·ist** *adj., n.* —**tran′scen·den′·tal·is′tic** *adj.*

transcendental number An irrational number, such as pi, that cannot result from any finite set of algebraic equations having rational coefficients.

trans·con·ti·nen·tal (trans′kon·tə·nen′təl) *adj.* Extending or passing across a continent.

tran·scribe (tran·skrīb′) *v.t.* **·scribed, ·scrib·ing** 1 To write over again; copy from an original. 2 To make a record of in handwriting or typewriting, as of something spoken. 3 To translate (shorthand notes, etc.) into standard written form. 4 To make a recording of for use in a later broadcast. 5 To adapt (a musical composition) for a change of instrument or voice. [< L *trans-* over + *scribere* write] —**tran·scrib′er** *n.*

tran·script (tran′skript) *n.* 1 Something transcribed, as from a stenographer's notes. 2 Any copy, esp., an official copy of a student's academic record. [< L *transcribere* transcribe]

tran·scrip·tion (tran·skrip′shən) *n.* 1 The act of transcribing. 2 Something transcribed; a copy; transcript. 3 A recording made for a later broadcast. 4 *Music* The adaptation of a composition for a different instrument or voice. —**tran·scrip′tion·al** *adj.*

tran·sept (tran′sept) *n.* A projecting part of a cruciform church crossing at right angles to the longer part and situated between the nave and choir; also, its projecting ends. [< L *transversus* transverse + *septum* an enclosure] —**tran·sep′tal** *adj.*

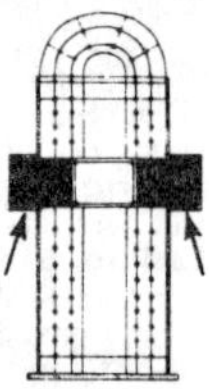

Transepts

trans·fer (trans·fûr′, trans′fər) *v.* **·ferred, ·fer·ring** *v.t.* 1 To carry, or cause to pass, from one person, place, etc., to another. 2 To make over possession of to another. 3 To convey (a drawing) from one surface to another. —*v.i.* 4 To transfer oneself. 5 To be transferred. 6 To change from one vehicle or line to another. —*n.* (trans′fər) 1 The act of transferring, or the state of being transferred. 2 That which is transferred, as a design conveyed from one surface to another. 3 A place, method, or means of transfer. 4 A ticket entitling a passenger on one vehicle to ride on another. 5 A delivery of title or property from one person to another. 6 A person transferred from one organization or position to another. [< L *trans-* across + *ferre* carry] —**trans·fer′a·bil′i·ty, trans·fer′ence, trans·fer′rer** *n.* —**trans·fer′a·ble, trans·fer′ra·ble** *adj.*

trans·fer·al (trans·fûr′əl) *n.* The act or an instance of transferring. Also **trans·fer′ral.**

trans·fig·ur·a·tion (trans′fig·yə·rā′shən) *n.* A change in shape or appearance. —**the Transfiguration** 1 The supernatural transformation of Christ on the mount. 2 A festival commemorating this, August 6.

trans·fig·ure (trans·fig′yər) *v.t.* **·ured, ·ur·ing** 1 To change the outward form or appearance of. 2 To make glorious. [< L *trans-* across + *figura* shape] —**trans·fig′ure·ment** *n.*

trans·fix (trans·fiks′) *v.t.* 1 To pierce through, as with a pointed implement; impale. 2 To fix in place by impaling. 3 To make motionless, as with horror, amazement, etc. [< L *trans-* through, across + *figere* fasten] —**trans·fix′ion** (-fik′shən) *n.*

trans·form (trans·fôrm′) *v.t.* 1 To change the form or appearance of. 2 To change the nature or character of; convert. 3 *Electr.* To subject to the action of a transformer. —*v.i.* 4 To be or become changed in form or character. [< L *trans-* over + *forma* a form] —**trans·form′a·ble, trans·form′a·tive** *adj.*

trans·for·ma·tion (trans′fər·mā′shən) *n.* 1 The act of transforming or the state of being transformed. 2 *Ling.* Any of the systematic processes by which grammatical sentences of a language may be derived from underlying constructions. —**trans′for·ma′tion·al** *adj.*

trans·form·er (trans·fôr′mər) *n.* 1 One who or that which transforms. 2 *Electr.* A device that couples electricity from one alternating-current circuit to another by electromagnetic induction, often with a change in the ratio of current to voltage and always with a small power loss.

trans·fuse (trans·fyo͞oz′) *v.t.* **·fused, ·fus·ing** 1 To cause to flow or pass from one person or thing to another. 2 *Med.* a To transfer (blood, plasma, etc.) from one person or animal to another. b To give a transfusion to. 3 To pass into; permeate. [< L *transfusus,* p.p. of *transfundere*] — **trans·fus′er** *n.* —**trans·fus′i·ble, trans·fu·sive** (trans·fyōō′siv) *adj.*

trans·fu·sion (trans·fyōō′zhən) *n.* 1 The act or an instance of transfusing. 2 *Med.* The introduction of a fluid, as saline solution, blood, blood plasma, etc., into the blood stream.

trans·gress (trans·gres′, tranz-) *v.t.* 1 To disregard and go beyond the bounds of, as a divine or traditional law; violate. 2 To pass beyond or over (limits); exceed. —*v.i.* 3 To break a law; sin. [< L *transgressus,* p.p. of *transgredi* step across] —**trans·gres′sor** *n.*

trans·gres·sion (trans·gresh′ən, tranz-) *n.* The act or an instance of transgressing, esp. a sin.

tran·ship (tran·ship′) *v.t.* **·shipped, ·shipping** TRANSSHIP. — **tran·ship′ment** *n.*

tran·sient (tran′shənt, tranch′ənt, tranz′ē·ənt) *adj.* 1 Occurring or existing only for a time; not permanent; transitory. 2 Brief; fleeting; momentary. 3 Residing or staying in a place temporarily: a large *transient* population. —*n.* One who or that which is transient, esp. a temporary resident. [< L *transire* go across] —**tran′sience, tran′·sien·cy** *n.* —**tran′sient·ly** *adv.* —**Syn.** 1 temporary, passing. 2 ephemeral, fugitive, evanescent. 3 casual.

tran·sis·tor (tran·zis′tər, -sis′-) *n.* *Electronics* 1 A semiconductor device having three terminals and the property that the current between one pair of them is a function of the current between another pair. 2 A transistorized radio. [< TRANS(FER) (RES)ISTOR]

tran·sis·tor·ize (tran·zis′tər·īz, -sis′-) *v.t.* **·ized, ·iz·ing** To equip with transistors. —**tran·sis′tor·i·za′tion** *n.*

tran·sit (tran′sit, -zit) *n.* 1 The act of passing over or through; passage. 2 The process of change; transition. 3 The act of carrying across or through; conveyance. 4 Transportation, esp. for carrying large numbers of people, as in a city: public *transit.* 5 *Astron.* a The passage of one celestial body over the disk of another. b The passage of a celestial body across the meridian. 6 A surveying instrument resembling a theodolite. [< L *transire* go across]

tran·si·tion (tran·sish′ən, tranz-) *n.* 1 Passage from one place, condition, or stage to another; change. 2 Something, as a period of time or a situation, that leads from one stage or period to another. 3 *Music* A passage or modulation connecting sections of a composition. —**tran·si′tion·al** *adj.* —**tran·si′tion·al·ly** *adv.*

tran·si·tive (tran′sə·tiv) *adj.* 1 *Gram.* Having, requiring, or completed by a direct object: said of a verb. 2 Of or pertaining to transition. —*n.* *Gram.* A transitive verb. [< L *transitus* transit] —**tran′si·tive·ly** *adv.* —**tran′si·tive·ness, tran′si·tiv′i·ty** *n.*

tran·si·to·ry (tran′sə·tôr′ē, -tō′rē) *adj.* 1 Existing for a short time only; soon extinguished or annulled. 2 Brief; ephemeral. —**tran′si·to′ri·ly** *adv.* —**tran′si·to′ri·ness** *n.*

trans·late (trans·lāt′, tranz-, trans′lāt, tranz′-) *v.* **·lat·ed, ·lat·ing** *v.t.* 1 To change into another language. 2 To change from one form, condition, or place to another. 3 To explain in other words; interpret. 4 *Mech.* To change the position of in space, esp. without rotation. —*v.i.* 5 To change the words of one language into those of another, esp. as an occupation. 6 To admit of translation. [< L *translatus,* lit., carried across] —**trans·lat′a·ble** *adj.* —**trans·la′tor** *n.*

trans·la·tion (trans·lā′shən, tranz-) *n.* 1 The act of translating, or the state of being translated. 2 Something translated; esp., a reproduction of a work in a language different from the original. 3 *Mech.* Motion in which all the parts of a body follow identical courses. —**trans·la′tion·al** *adj.*

trans·lit·er·ate (trans·lit′ə·rāt, tranz-) *v.t.* **·at·ed, ·at·ing** To represent, as a word, by the characters of another alphabet. [< TRANS- + L *litera* a letter] —**trans·lit′er·a′tion** *n.*

trans·lu·cent (trans·lōō′sənt, tranz-) *adj.* Allowing the passage of light, but not permitting a clear view of any object. [< L *trans-* through, across + *lucere* to shine] — **trans·lu′cence, trans·lu′cen·cy** *n.* —**trans·lu′cent·ly** *adv.*

trans·mi·grate (trans·mī′grāt, tranz-, trans′mī-, tranz′·mī-) *v.i.* **·grat·ed, ·grat·ing** 1 To pass into another body, as the soul at death. 2 To migrate, as from one country or jurisdiction to another. —**trans·mi·gra·tion** (trans′mī·grā′·shən, tranz′-), **trans·mi′gra·tor** *n.* —**trans·mi′gra·to′ry** (-mī′·grə·tôr′ē, -tō′rē) *adj.*

trans·mis·si·ble (trans·mis′ə·bəl, tranz-) *adj.* Capable of being transmitted. —**trans·mis′si·bil′i·ty** *n.*

trans·mis·sion (trans·mish′ən, tranz-) *n.* 1 The act of transmitting, or the state of being transmitted. 2 That which is transmitted. 3 *Mech.* A device that transmits power from its source to its point of application, as from the engine of an automobile to the wheels. —**trans·mis′sive** *adj.*

trans·mit (trans·mit′, tranz-) *v.t.* **·mit·ted, ·mit·ting** 1 To send from one place or person to another; convey. 2 To pass on (a gene, a virus, etc.) from one organism to another. 3 To cause (light, sound, etc.) to pass through space or a medium. 4 To send out, as by means of radio waves. 5 To serve as a medium of passage for; conduct: Iron *transmits* heat. 6 *Mech.* To convey (force, motion, etc.) from one part or mechanism to another. [< L *trans-* across + *mittere* send] —**trans·mit′ta·ble** *adj.* —**trans·mit′tal, trans·mit′·tance** *n.*

trans·mit·ter (trans·mit′ər, tranz-) *n.* 1 One who or that which transmits. 2 The part of a telephone into which a person talks. 3 The part of a telegraph for sending messages. 4 *Telecom.* A device that modulates a carrier with a signal and sends the carrier forth, as in radio, telephony, or telegraphy.

trans·mog·ri·fy (trans·mog′rə·fī, tranz-) *v.t.* **·fied, ·fy·ing** To make into something altogether different; transform radically: often used humorously. [?] —**trans·mog′ri·fi·ca′·tion** *n.*

trans·mu·ta·tion (trans′myōō·tā′shən, tranz′-) *n.* 1 The act of transmuting, or the state of being transmuted. 2 The conversion of an atom of an element into an atom of a different element, as by radioactive decay, nuclear fission, etc. 3 The supposed conversion of a base metal into gold or silver. —**trans′mu·ta′tion·al, trans·mut·a·tive** (trans·myōō′tə·tiv, tranz-) *adj.*

trans·mute (trans·myōōt′, tranz-) *v.t.* **·mut·ed, ·mut·ing** To change in nature or form. Also **trans·mu′tate.** [< L *trans-* across + *mutare* to change] —**trans·mut′a·ble** *adj.* —**trans·mut′a·bil′i·ty, trans·mut′a·ble·ness, trans·mut′er** *n.* —**trans·mut′a·bly** *adv.*

trans·o·ce·an·ic (trans′ō·shē·an′ik, tranz′-) *adj.* 1 Crossing or traversing the ocean. 2 Lying beyond or over the ocean.

tran·som (tran′səm) *n.* 1 A horizontal piece framed across an opening; a lintel. 2 A small window above and often hinged to such a bar, usu. situated above a door. 3 The horizontal crossbar of a gallows or cross. [< L *transtrum* a crossbeam] —**tran′somed** *adj.*

transp. transportation.

trans·pa·cif·ic (trans′pə·sif′ik) *adj.* 1 Across or crossing the Pacific Ocean. 2 On the other side of the Pacific.

trans·par·en·cy (trans·pâr′ən·sē, -par′-) *n. pl.* **·cies** 1 The state or quality of being transparent. 2 Something whose transmission of light defines an image, esp. a piece of photographic film, often mounted as a slide and viewed by projecting its image on a screen or other surface.

trans·par·ent (trans·pâr′ənt, -par′-) *adj.* 1 Allowing the passage of light and of clear views of objects beyond. 2 Having a texture fine enough to be seen through; diaphanous. 3 Easy to understand. 4 Without guile; frank; candid. 5 Easily detected; obvious: a *transparent* lie. [< L *trans-* across + *parere* appear, be visible] —**trans·par′ent·ly** *adv.* —**trans·par′ence, trans·par′ent·ness** *n.*

tran·spi·ra·tion (trans′pə·rā′shən) *n.* A transpiring or exhalation, as the loss of water from a plant by evaporation.

tran·spire (trans·pīr′) *v.* **·spired, ·spir·ing** *v.t.* 1 To give off through permeable tissues, as of the skin and lungs or of leaf surfaces. —*v.i.* 2 To be emitted, as through the skin; be exhaled, as moisture or odors. 3 To become known. 4 To happen; occur. [< L *trans-* across, through + *spirare* breathe] • An accepted meaning of *transpire* is to become known or leak out: *It transpired that he had died penniless.* The word is more commonly used today, however, with the sense of "to happen": *We shall never know what transpired at that meeting.* The latter usage still strikes the more traditionally inclined as improper or ignorant. That judgment may be unduly harsh, but as a matter of style the usage is almost always inelegant and often pretentious.

trans·plant (trans·plant′) *v.t.* 1 To remove and plant in another place. 2 To remove and settle for residence in another place. 3 *Surg.* To transfer (an organ or tissue) from its original site to another part of the body or to another individual. —*v.i.* 4 To admit of being transplanted. —*n.* (trans′plant′) 1 That which is transplanted, as a seedling or an organ of the body. 2 The act of transplanting. **—trans′plan·ta′tion, trans·plant′er** *n.*

trans·port (trans·pôrt′, -pōrt′) *v.t.* 1 To carry or convey from one place to another. 2 To carry away with emotion, as with delight; enchant. 3 To banish to another country. —*n.* (trans′pôrt, -pōrt) 1 The act or a means of transporting; transportation. 2 A state of emotional rapture; intense delight. 3 A ship, train, truck, etc., used to transport troops, supplies, etc. 4 A system of transportation. 5 A deported convict. [< L *trans-* across + *portare* carry] — **trans·port′a·bil′i·ty, trans·port′er** *n.* **—trans·port′able** *adj.*

trans·por·ta·tion (trans′pər·tā′shən) *n.* 1 The act of transporting. 2 A means of transporting or traveling. 3 The conveying of passengers or freight, esp. as an industry. 4 Money, a pass, etc., used for being transported.

trans·pose (trans·pōz′) *v.t.* **·posed, ·pos·ing** 1 To reverse the order or change the place of: to *transpose* two numerals or a word in a sentence. 2 *Math.* To transfer (a term) from one side of an algebraic equation to the other with reversed sign. 3 *Music* To write or play in a different key. [< L *trans-* over + OF *poser* put] **—trans·pos′a·ble** *adj.* — **trans·po′sal, trans·pos′er, trans·po·si·tion** (trans′pə·zish′ən) *n.*

trans·sex·u·al (trans·sek′shōō·əl, -sek′shəl) *n.* A person who is genetically and physically of one sex but who identifies psychologically with the other and may seek treatment by surgery or with hormones to bring the physical sexual characteristics into conformity with the psychological preference. —*adj.* Of, for, or characteristic of transsexuals. **—trans·sex′u·al·ism** *n.*

trans·ship (trans·ship′) *v.t.* & *v.i.* **·shipped, ·ship·ping** To transfer from one conveyance or means of transport to another for further shipment. **—trans·ship′ment** *n.*

tran·sub·stan·ti·ate (tran′səb·stan′shē·āt) *v.t.* **·at·ed, ·at·ing** 1 To change from one substance into another; transmute; transform. 2 *Theol.* To change the substance of (bread and wine) in the rite of transubstantiation.

tran·sub·stan·ti·a·tion (tran′səb·stan′shē·ā′shən) *n.* In the Roman Catholic and Eastern Orthodox churches, the conversion of the substance of the bread and wine of the Eucharist into that of Christ's body and blood.

trans·u·ra·ni·um (trans′yōō·rā′nē·əm, tranz′-) *adj.* Of or pertaining to elements having an atomic number greater than that of uranium. Also **trans′u·ran′ic** (-ran′ik).

trans·ver·sal (trans·vûr′səl, tranz-) *adj.* TRANSVERSE. — *n. Geom.* A straight line intersecting a system of lines.

trans·verse (trans·vûrs′, tranz-) *adj.* Lying or being across or from side to side. —*n.* (*also* trans′vûrs, tranz′-) That which is transverse. [< L *transversus* lying across] — **trans·verse′ly** *adv.*

trans·ves·tite (trans·ves′tīt, tranz-) *n.* One who wears the clothes of the opposite sex. [< L *trans-* over + *vestire* to clothe + -ITE] **—trans·ves′tism, trans·ves′ti·tism** (-ves′tə·tiz′əm) *n.*

trap[1] (trap) *n.* 1 A device for catching game or other animals, as a pitfall or a baited contrivance set to spring shut on being slightly jarred or moved. 2 A devious plan or trick by which a person may be caught or taken unawares. 3 A device for hurling clay pigeons into the air, used in trapshooting. 4 Any of various devices that collect residual material or that form a seal to stop a return flow of noxious gas, etc., as a water-filled U- or S-bend in a pipe. 5 In golf, an obstacle or hazard: a sand *trap.* 6 TRAPDOOR. 7 A light, two-wheeled carriage suspended by springs. 8 *pl.* Percussion instruments, as drums, cymbals, etc. 8 *Slang* The mouth. —*v.* **trapped, trap·ping** *v.t.* 1 To catch in or as if in a trap. 2 To provide with a trap. 3 To stop or hold by the formation of a seal. 4 To catch (a ball) just as or after it strikes the ground. —*v.i.* 5 To set traps for game; be a trapper. [< OE *træppe*]

trap[2] (trap) *n. Geol.* A dark, fine-grained igneous rock, often of columnar structure, as basalt. Also **trap′rock′.** [< Sw. *trappa* a stair]

trap·door (trap′dôr′, -dōr′) *n.* A door, hinged or sliding, to cover an opening, as in a floor or roof.

tra·peze (tra·pēz′, trə-) *n.* A short swinging bar suspended by two ropes, for gymnastic exercises and acrobatic stunts. [< NL *trapezium* a trapezium]

tra·pe·zi·um (trə·pē′zē·əm) *n. p.* **·zi·ums** or **·zi·a** (-zē·ə) *Geom.* 1 A four-sided plane figure of which no two sides are parallel. 2 *Brit.* TRAPEZOID (def. 1). [< Gk. *trapeza* a table, lit., a four-footed (bench)]

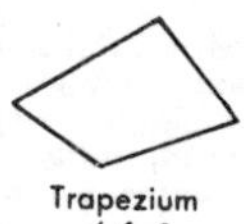

Tropezium *def. 1*

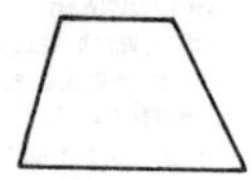

Tropezoid *def. 1*

trap·e·zoid (trap′ə·zoid′) *n. Geom.* 1 A quadrilateral of which two sides are parallel. 2 *Brit.* TRAPEZIUM (def. 1). [< Gk. *trapeza* a table + *eidos* a form] **—trap′e·zoi′dal** *adj.*

trap·per (trap′ər) *n.* One whose occupation is the trapping of fur-bearing animals.

trap·pings (trap′ingz) *n. pl.* 1 An ornamental covering or harness for a horse; caparison. 2 Adornments of any kind; embellishments. 3 The superficial signs or perquisites; marks: the *trappings* of success. [< ME *trappe*]

Trap·pist (trap′ist) *n.* A monk belonging to an ascetic order noted for silence. —*adj.* Of this order. [< *La Trappe,* France, site of the order's establishment in 1664]

trap·shoot·ing (trap′shōō′ting) *n.* The sport of shooting clay pigeons sent up from spring traps. **—trap′shoot′er** *n.*

trash (trash) *n.* 1 Worthless or waste matter; rubbish. 2 That which is broken or lopped off, as twigs and branches. 3 Foolish or idle talk. 4 Anything worthless, shoddy, or without merit: literary *trash.* 5 A person regarded as worthless or of no account. —*v.t.* & *v.i. Slang* To wreck or destroy (something) purposefully but often indiscriminately as an expression of alienation or rebellion. [?] — **trash′i·ness** *n.* **—trash′y (·i·er, ·i·est)** *adj.*

trau·ma (trou′mə, trô′-) *n. pl.* **·mas** or **·ma·ta** (-mə·tə) 1 Any physical injury resulting from force. 2 A severe emotional shock having a deep effect upon the personality. [< Gk., a wound] **—trau·mat·ic** (trou·mat′ik, trô-) *adj.* **—trau·mat′i·cal·ly** *adv.*

trau·ma·tize (trô′mə·tīz) *v.t.* **·tized, ·tiz·ing** To cause trauma to or in.

trav·ail (trə·vāl′, trav′āl) *n.* 1 Pain, anguish, or distress encountered in an effort or achievement. 2 Labor in childbirth. 3 Hard or wearisome labor. 4 Physical agony. —*v.i.* 1 To suffer the pangs of childbirth. 2 To toil; labor. [< OF < *travailler* to labor, toil]

trav·el (trav′əl) *v.* **trav·eled** or **·elled, trav·el·ing** or **·el·ling** *v.i.* 1 To go from one place to another or from place to place; make a journey or tour. 2 To proceed; advance. 3 To go about from place to place as a traveling salesman. 4 *Informal* To move with speed. 5 To pass or be transmitted, as light, sound, etc. 6 *Mech.* To move in a fixed path, as a machine part. 7 In basketball, to commit the infraction of failing to dribble while moving with the ball. —*v.t.* 8 To move or journey across or through: traverse. —*n.* 1 The act of traveling. 2 *Often pl.* A journey or tour, usu. extensive. 3 Passage to, over, or past a certain place. 4 Distance traveled, as by a machine part. [< OF *travailler* to travail]

trav·eled (trav′əld) *adj.* 1 Having made many journeys. 2 Frequented or used by travelers. Also **trav′elled.**

trav·e·logue (trav·ə·lôg, -log) *n.* 1 A documentary film about a traveled place. 2 A lecture or talk on travel, usu. illustrated pictorially. Also **trav′e·log.**

tra·verse (trə·vûrs′, tra-) *u.* **·ersed, ·ers·ing** *v.t.* 1 to pass over, across, or through. 2 To move back and forth over or along. 3 To examine carefully; scrutinize. 4 To oppose; thwart. 5 *Law* To make denial of. —*v.i.* 6 To move back and forth. 7 To move across; cross. —**trav·erse** (trav′ərs) *n.* 1 Something that traverses, as a crosspiece of a machine or structure. 2 Something serving as a screen or barrier. 3 The act of traversing or denying; a denial. —*adj.* (trav′·ərs) Lying or being across; transverse. [< L *transversus* transverse] —**tra·vers′a·ble** *adj.* —**tra·vers′al, tra·vers′er** *n.*

trav·erse rod (trav′ərs) A curtain rod equipped with a sliding mechanism for drawing a pair of curtains together or apart with a cord.

trav·es·ty (trav′is·tē) *n. pl.* **·ties** 1 A grotesque imitation, as of a lofty subject; burlesque. 2 A distorted or absurd rendering or example, as if in mockery: a *travesty* of justice. —*v.t.* **·tied, ·ty·ing** To make a travesty of; burlesque; parody. [< Ital. *travestire* to disguise]

trawl (trôl) *n.* 1 A large net for towing on the bottom of the ocean by a fishing boat. 2 A stout fishing line, anchored and buoyed, from which many lines bearing baited hooks may be secured. —*v.i.* 1 To fish with a trawl. —*v.t.* 2 To drag, as a net, to catch fish. [?]

trawl·er (trô′lər) *n.* A boat used for trawling.

tray (trā) *n.* 1 A flat, shallow utensil with raised edges, used to hold or carry several or a number of articles, as dishes. 2 A tray and the articles on it. 3 A shallow, topless box serving as a compartment, as in a tool or sewing box. [< OE *trēg* a wooden board] —**tray′ful** (-fo͝ol′) *n.*

treach·er·ous (trech′ər·əs) *adj.* 1 Likely to betray allegiance or confidence; untrustworthy. 2 Of the nature of treachery; perfidious. 3 Apparently safe or secure, but in fact dangerous or unreliable: *treacherous* footing. —**treach′er·ous·ly** *adv.* —**treach′er·ous·ness** *n.*

treach·er·y (trech′ər·ē) *n. pl.* **·er·ies** Violation of allegiance, confidence, or faith; treason. [< OF *tricher* cheat]

trea·cle (trē′kəl) *n.* 1 Molasses, esp. that obtained in refining sugar. 2 Saccharine speech or sentiments. 3 Formerly, a compound used as an antidote for poison. [< Gk. *thēriakē* a remedy for poisonous bites] —**trea′cly** *adj.*

tread (tred) *v.* **trod, trod·den** or **trod, tread·ing** *v.t.* 1 To step or walk on, over, along, etc. 2 To press with the feet; trample. 3 To crush or oppress harshly. 4 To accomplish in walking or in dancing: to *tread* a measure. 5 To copulate with: said of male birds. —*v.i.* 6 To place the foot down; walk. 7 To press the ground or anything beneath the feet: usu. with *on.* —**tread water** In swimming, to keep the body erect and the head above water by moving the feet and arms. —*n.* 1 The act, manner, or sound of treading; a walking or stepping. 2 The part of a wheel or automobile tire that comes into contact with the road or rails. 3 The impression made by a foot, a tire, etc. 4 The horizontal part of a step in a stairway. [< OE *tredan*] —**tread′er** *n.*

tread·le (tred′l) *n.* A lever operated by the foot, usu. to cause rotary motion. —*v.i.* **·led, ·ling** To work a treadle. [< OE *tredel* < *tredan* tread] • See POTTER'S WHEEL.

tread·mill (tred′mil′) *n.* 1 A mechanism rotated by the walking motion of one or more persons or animals. 2 Monotonous routine; tedious and unrewarding effort.

treas. treasurer; treasury.

trea·son (trē′zən) *n.* 1 Betrayal, treachery, or breach of allegiance toward a sovereign or government. 2 A breach of faith; treachery. [< L *traditio* a betrayal, delivery] —**trea′son·ous** *adj.* —**trea′son·ous·ly** *adv.*

trea·son·a·ble (trē′zən·ə·bəl) *adj.* Of, involving, or characteristic of treason. —**trea′son·a·ble·ness** *n.* —**trea′son·a·bly** *adv.*

treas·ure (trezh′ər) *n.* 1 Riches accumulated or possessed, as a store of precious metals, jewels, or money. 2 Someone or something very precious. —*v.t.* **·ured, ·ur·ing** 1 To set a high value upon; prize. 2 To lay up in store; accumulate. [< L *thesaurus*] —**Syn.** *v.* 1 cherish, esteem, value, venerate. 2 hoard.

treas·ur·er (trezh′ər·ər) *n.* 1 An officer authorized to receive, care for, and disburse revenues, as of a government, business corporation, or society. 2 A similar custodian of the funds of a society or a corporation.

treas·ure-trove (trezh′ər·trōv′) *n.* 1 *Law* Money, gold, etc., found hidden, the owner being unknown. 2 Any rich or rewarding discovery. Also **treasure trove.** [< AF *tresor* treasure + *trover* to find]

treas·ur·y (trezh′ər·ē) *n. pl.* **·ur·ies** 1 A place of receipt and disbursement of public revenue or private funds. 2 The revenue or funds. 3 The place where a treasure is stored. 4 A department of government concerned with finances, the issuance of money, etc. [< OF *tresor* treasure]

treat (trēt) *v.t.* 1 To conduct oneself toward (a person, animal, etc.) in a specified manner. 2 To look upon or regard in a specified manner: They *treat* it as a childhood prank. 3 To give medical or surgical attention to. 4 To deal with in writing or speaking. 5 To depict or express artistically in a specified style. 6 To pay for the entertainment, food, or drink of. —*v.i.* 7 To deal with a subject in writing or speaking: usu. with *of.* 8 To carry on negotiations; negotiate. 9 To pay for another's entertainment. —*n.* 1 Something that gives unusual pleasure. 2 Entertainment of any kind furnished gratuitously to another. 3 *Informal* One's turn to pay for refreshment or entertainment. [< OF *tretier, traitier*] —**treat′er** *n.*

trea·tise (trē′tis) *n.* A formal, systematic, written exposition of a serious subject: a *treatise* on labor relations. [< OF *traitier*]

treat·ment (trēt′mənt) *n.* 1 The act, manner, or process of treating anything. 2 The therapeutic measures designed to cure a disease or abnormal condition.

trea·ty (trē′tē) *n. pl.* **·ties** A formal agreement or compact between two or more nations. [< OF *traitié,* p.p. of *traitier* treat]

treb·le (treb′əl) *v.t.* & *v.i.* **·led, ·ling** To multiply by three; triple. —*adj.* 1 Threefold. 2 *Music* **a** Of the highest range. **b** Soprano. —*n.* 1 **a** *Music* A part or instrument of the highest range. **b** A soprano singer. 2 High, piping sound. [< L *triplus* triple] —**treb′ly** *adv.*

tree (trē) *n.* 1 A woody perennial plant having a distinct trunk with branches and foliage at some distance above the ground. 2 Any shrub or plant with a treelike shape or dimensions. 3 Something whose outline resembles the spreading branches of a tree, as a diagram: a genealogical *tree.* 4 A timber, post, or piece of wood used for a particular purpose. —*v.t.* **treed, tree·ing** 1 To force to climb or take refuge in a tree: to *tree* an opossum. 2 *Informal* To get the advantage of; corner. [< OE *trēow*]

tree fern Any of various treelike ferns with woody trunks.

tree frog Any of various arboreal frogs having adhesive disks on the toes. Also **tree toad.**

tree·nail (trē′nāl′, tren′əl, trun′əl) *n.* A wooden peg or nail of dry, hard wood which swells when moist, used for fastening timbers.

Trefoil *def. 2*

tree of heaven AILANTHUS.

tree surgery The treatment of damaged trees by pruning, cementing cavities, etc. —**tree surgeon**

tre·foil (trē′foil) *n.* 1 Any of various plants having threefold leaves, as clover. 2 An architectural ornament having the form of a three-lobed leaf. [< L *trifolium*]

trek (trek) *v.* **trekked, trek·king** *v.i.* 1 To move along with effort or slowly, esp. on foot. 2 To make a journey; travel. 3 In South Africa, to travel by ox wagon. —*v.t.* 4 To transport. 5 In South Africa, to draw (a vehicle or load): said of an ox. —*n.* 1 A journey or a stage in a journey. 2 The act of trekking. 3 In South Africa, an organized migration. [< Du. *trekken* draw, travel < MDu. *trecken*] —**trek′ker** *n.*

trel·lis (trel′is) *n.* A grating or lattice, often of wood, used as a screen or a support for vines, etc.

Trellis

add, āce, câre, pälm; end, ēven; it, īce; odd, ōpen, ôrder; to͝ok, po͞ol; up, bûrn; ə = *a* in *above,* *u* in *focus;* yo͞o = *u* in *fuse;* oil; pout; check; go; ring; thin; this; zh, *vision.* < derived from; ? origin uncertain or unknown.

—*v.t.* 1 To interlace so as to form a trellis. 2 To furnish with or fasten on a trellis. [<L *trilix* of three threads]

trem·a·tode (trem′ə·tōd, trē′mə-) *n.* Any of a class of parasitic flatworms, as the liver fluke. [<Gk. *trēma* a hole + *eidos* form] —**trem′a·toid** (-toid) *adj.*

trem·ble (trem′bəl) *v.i.* **·bled, ·bling** 1 To shake involuntarily, as with fear or weakness. 2 To move slightly or vibrate, as from some jarring force: The building *trembled.* 3 To feel anxiety or fear. 4 To quaver, as the voice. —*n.* The act or state of trembling. [<LL *tremulus* tremulous] —**trem′bler** *n.* —**trem′bling·ly** *adv.* —**trem′bly** *adj.* —**Syn.** *v.* 2 quiver, shake, totter, quake.

tre·men·dous (tri·men′dəs) *adj.* 1 Extraordinarily large or extensive; enormous; great. 2 Causing astonishment by its magnitude, force, etc.; awe-inspiring. 3 *Informal* Wonderful; marvelous. [<L *tremendus* to be trembled at] —**tre·men′dous·ly** *adv.* —**tre·men′dous·ness** *n.*

trem·o·lo (trem′ə·lō) *n. pl.* **·los** *Music* 1 A rapid, periodic variation in the loudness of a tone. 2 The mechanism for causing this in organ tones. [Ital., trembling]

trem·or (trem′ər, trē′mər) *n.* 1 A quick, vibratory movement; a shaking. 2 Any involuntary quivering or trembling, as of a muscle. 3 A state of agitation or excitement, as in anticipation of something. [<OF *tremour* fear, a trembling]

trem·u·lous (trem′yə·ləs) *adj.* 1 Characterized or affected by trembling: *tremulous* speech. 2 Showing timidity and irresolution. 3 Characterized by mental excitement. Also **trem′u·lant.** [<L *tremulus*] —**trem′u·lous·ly** *adv.* —**trem′u·lous·ness** *n.*

tre·nail (trē′nāl, tren′əl, trun′əl) *n.* TREENAIL.

trench (trench) *n.* 1 A long narrow ditch, esp. one lined with a parapet of the excavated earth, to protect troops. 2 A long, narrow region much deeper than the adjacent surfaces, as along the ocean floor. —*v.t.* 1 To dig a trench or trenches in. 2 To fortify with trenches. 3 To cut deep furrows in. —*v.i.* 4 To cut or dig trenches. 5 To cut; carve. 6 To encroach. [<OF *trenchier* to cut] —**trench′er** *n.*

trench·ant (tren′chənt) *adj.* 1 Clear, vigorous, and effective: a *trenchant* rebuttal. 2 Cutting, as sarcasm; biting. 3 Incisive; sharp; keen: *trenchant* wit. 4 *Archaic* Cutting deeply and quickly: a *trenchant* sword. [<OF *trenchier*]

trench coat A raincoat with a belt, straps on the shoulders, and several pockets.

trench·er (tren′chər) *n.* A wooden plate or board used to serve food or as a surface for cutting it. [<OF *trenchier* to cut]

trench·er·man (tren′chər·mən) *n. pl.* **·men** (-mən) A person who eats heartily.

trench fever A relapsing fever transmitted by body lice.

trench foot A foot condition resembling frostbite, due to continued dampness and cold.

trench mouth A mildly contagious disease of the gums, and sometimes the larynx and tonsils, caused by a soil bacillus.

trend (trend) *n.* 1 A prevailing or probable tendency; predominant or likely course or direction; drift: a *trend* toward smaller families; investment *trends;* to study *trends* in education. 2 A popular preference or inclination: fashion *trends.* 3 The general course or direction, as of a coast; bent. —*v.i.* 1 To have or follow a general course or direction. 2 To exhibit a tendency; move: wheat prices *trending* upward. [<OE *trendan* to roll]

trend·y (tren′dē) *adj. Slang* **trend·i·er, trend·i·est** In step with current fashion; voguish. —*n. pl.* **trend·ies** *Chiefly Brit.* A trendy person or thing. —**trend′i·ness** *n.*

tre·pan (tri·pan′) *n.* 1 An early form of the trephine. 2 A large rock-boring tool —*v.t.* **·panned, ·pan·ning** To use a trepan upon. [<Gk. *trypanon* a borer]

tre·phine (tri·fīn′, -fēn′) *n. Surg.* A cylindrical saw for removing a disk of tissue, as from the skull, cornea, etc. —*v.t.* **·phined, ·phin·ing** To operate on with a trephine. [<L *tres fines* three ends]

trep·i·da·tion (trep′ə·dā′shən) *n.* 1 Tremulous agitation caused by fear; apprehension. 2 *Archaic* An involuntary trembling; tremor. [<L *trepidare* hurry, be alarmed]

tres·pass (tres′pəs, -pas′) *v.i.* 1 To violate the personal or property rights of another; esp., to go unlawfully onto another's land. 2 To go beyond the bounds of what is right or proper; transgress. 3 To intrude; encroach: to *trespass* on one's privacy. —*n.* 1 *Law* a Any act accompanied by actual or implied force in violation of another's person, property, or rights. b An action for injuries sustained because of this. 2 Any transgression of law or moral duty. 3 An intrusion; encroachment. [<Med. L *trans-* across, beyond + *passare* to pass] —**tres′pass·er** *n.*

tress (tres) *n.* 1 A lock or curl of human hair. 2 *pl.* The hair of a woman or girl, esp. when long and worn loose [<OF *tresce*] —**tressed** (trest) *adj.*

tres·tle (tres′əl) *n.* 1 A beam or bar braced by two pairs of divergent legs, used to support tables, platforms, etc. 2 A braced framework functioning like a bridge in supporting a roadway or railway over a short span. [<L *transtrum* crossbeam]

trey (trā) *n.* A card, domino, or die having three spots or pips. [<L *tres* three]

tri- *prefix* 1 Three; threefold; thrice: *tricycle.* 2 *Chem.* Containing three atoms, radicals, groups, etc.: *trioxide.* 3 Occurring three times within a (specified) interval: *triweekly.* [<L *tri-* threefold]

tri·ad (trī′ad) *n.* 1 A group of three persons or things. 2 *Music* A chord of three tones, esp. a tone with its third and fifth. [<Gk. *trias*<*treis* three] —**tri·ad′ic** *adj., n.*

tri·al (trī′əl, trīl) *n.* 1 The examination in a court of law, often before a jury, of the facts of a case in order to determine its disposition. 2 The act of testing or proving by experience or use. 3 The state of being tried or tested. 4 An experience, person, or thing that puts strength, patience, or faith to the test. 5 An attempt or effort to do something. 6 Hardship; difficulty: the *trials* of poverty. —**on trial** In the process of being tried or tested. —**trial and error** The trying of one thing after another until something succeeds. —*adj.* 1 Of or pertaining to a trial or trials. 2 Made or used in the course of trying or testing. [<AF<*trier* to try] —**Syn.** *n.* 2 examination, experiment. 5 endeavor. 6 misfortune, trouble.

trial balance In double-entry bookkeeping, a draft of the debit and credit balances of each account in the ledger.

trial jury A jury of 12 persons impaneled to decide a civil or criminal case; petit jury.

tri·an·gle (trī′ang′gəl) *n.* 1 *Geom.* A figure, esp. a plane figure, bounded by three sides, and having three angles. 2 Something resembling such a figure in shape. 3 A situation involving three persons: the eternal *triangle.* 4 *Music* A percussion instrument consisting of a resonant metal bar bent into a triangle and sounded by striking with a small metal rod. [<L *tri-* three + *angulus* an angle]

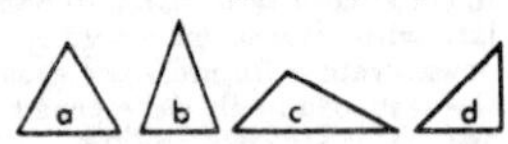

Triangles
a. equilateral. b. isosceles. c. scalene. d. right-angle.

tri·an·gu·lar (trī·ang′gyə·lər) *adj.* 1 Pertaining to, like, or bounded by a triangle. 2 Concerned with or pertaining to three things, parties, or persons. —**tri·an′gu·lar′i·ty** (-lar′ə·tē) *n.* —**tri·an′gu·lar·ly** *adv.*

tri·an·gu·late (trī·ang′gyə·lāt) *v.t.* **·lat·ed, ·lat·ing** 1 To divide into triangles. 2 To measure or determine by means of trigonometry. 3 To give triangular shape to. —*adj.* Marked with triangles. —**tri·an·gu·la′tion** *n.*

Tri·as·sic (trī·as′ik) *adj. & n.* See GEOLOGY. [<LL *trias* triad]

tri·ath·lon (trī′ath′lon) *n.* An athletic event comprising swimming, bicycle riding, and long-distance running. [<Gk. *tri-* three + *athlon* a contest]

tri·bal·ism (trī′bəl·iz′əm) *n.* Tribal organization, culture, or relations.

tribe (trīb) *n.* 1 A group of people, under one chief or ruler, united by common ancestry, language, and culture. 2 In ancient Israel, any of the 12 divisions of the Hebrews. 3 In ancient Rome, any of the three clans making up the Roman people. 4 A number of persons of any class or profession taken together: often contemptuous. 5 *Biol.* a A group of closely related genera. b Any group of plants or animals. [<L *tribus*] —**tri′bal** *adj.* —**tri′bal·ly** *adv.*

tribes·man (trībz′mən) *n. pl.* **·men** (-mən) A member of a tribe.

trib·u·la·tion (trib′yə·lā′shən) *n.* 1 A condition of distress; suffering. 2 The cause of such distress. [< L *tribulare* thrash] —**Syn.** 1 misery, oppression, sorrow, trouble.

tri·bu·nal (trī·byo͞o′nəl, tri-) *n.* 1 A court of justice. 2 Any judicial body, as a board of arbitrators. 3 The seat set apart for judges, magistrates, etc. [< L *tribunus* tribune]

trib·une[1] (trib′yo͞on, trib·yo͞on′) *n.* 1 In ancient Rome, a magistrate chosen by the plebeians to protect them against patrician oppression. 2 Any champion of the people. [< L *tribunus,* lit., head of a tribe < *tribus* a tribe] —**trib′u·nar′y** (-yə·ner′ē), **trib′u·ni′tial** (-yə·nish′əl) *adj.*

trib·une[2] (trib′yo͞on) *n.* A rostrum or platform. [< L *tribunal* a tribunal]

trib·u·tar·y (trib′yə·ter′ē) *adj.* 1 Supplying a larger body, as a stream flowing into a river. 2 Paying tribute. —*n. pl.* **·tar·ies** 1 A stream flowing into a larger one. 2 A person or state paying tribute. [< L *tributum.* See TRIBUTE.]

trib·ute (trib′yo͞ot) *n.* 1 Money or other valuables paid by one state to another as the price of peace and protection, or by virtue of some treaty. 2 Any obligatory payment, as a tax. 3 Anything given that is due to worth, affection, or duty: a *tribute* of praise. [< L *tributum,* neut. p.p. of *tribuere* pay, allot]

trice (trīs) *v.t.* **triced, tric·ing** To raise with a rope: usu. with *up.* —*n.* An instant: only in the phrase **in a trice.** [< MDu. *trisen* to hoist]

tri·ceps (trī′seps) *n. pl.* **·cep·ses** (-sep·sēz) or **·ceps** The large muscle at the back of the upper arm which straightens the arm when it contracts. [L, three-headed]

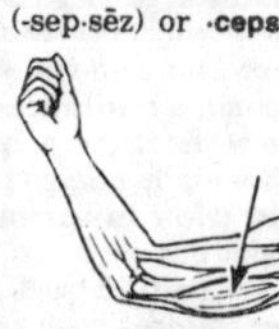

Triceps

tri·chi·na (tri·kī′nə) *n. pl.* **·nae** (-nē) or **·nas** A roundworm whose larvae cause trichinosis. [< Gk. *trichinos* of hair]

trich·i·no·sis (trik′ə·nō′sis) *n.* A disease usu. resulting from eating undercooked infected pork and marked by encysted trichina larvae in the muscles. Also **trich′i·ni′a·sis** (-nī′ə·sis). —**trich′i·nosed** (-nōzd, -nōst), **trich′i·nous** (-ə·nəs) *adj.*

trick (trik) *n.* 1 A deception; a petty artifice. 2 A malicious or annoying act: a dirty *trick.* 3 A practical joke; prank. 4 A particular characteristic; trait: a *trick* of tapping her foot. 5 A peculiar skill or knack. 6 A feat of jugglery. 7 In card games, the whole number of cards played in one round. 8 A turn or spell of duty. 9 *Informal* A child or young girl. —**do** (or **turn**) **the trick** *Slang* To produce the desired result. —*v.t.* 1 To deceive or cheat; delude. —*v.i.* 2 To practice trickery or deception. [< OF *trichier* cheat] —**trick′er** *n.* —**Syn.** *n.* 1 ruse, stratagem, subterfuge, device.

trick·er·y (trik′ər·ē) *n. pl.* **·er·ies** The practice of tricks; artifice; wiles.

trick·le (trik′əl) *v.* **·led, ·ling** *v.i.* 1 To flow or run drop by drop or in a very thin stream. 2 To move, come, go, etc., bit by bit. —*v.t.* 3 To cause to trickle. —*n.* 1 The act or state of trickling. 2 A thin stream. [ME *triklen*]

trick·ster (trik′stər) *n.* One who plays tricks.

trick·y (trik′ē) *adj.* **trick·i·er, trick·i·est** 1 Given to tricks; crafty; deceitful. 2 Intricate; requiring adroitness or skill. —**trick′i·ly** *adv.* —**trick′i·ness** *n.*

tri·col·or (trī′kul′ər) *adj.* Having or characterized by three colors: also **tri′col′ored.** —*n.* The French national flag. *Brit. sp.* **tri′col′our.**

tri·corn (trī′kôrn) *n.* A hat with the brim turned up on three sides. —*adj.* Three-horned; three-pronged. [< L *tricornis* three-horned]

tri·cot (trē′kō, trī′kət) *n.* 1 A hand-knitted or woven fabric, or a machine-made imitation thereof. 2 A soft ribbed cloth. [< F *tricoter* knit]

tri·cus·pid (trī·kus′pid) *adj.* 1 Having three cusps or points, as a molar tooth: also **tri·cus′pi·date.** 2 Having three segments, as the valve between the right auricle and right ventricle of the heart: also **tri·cus′pi·dal.** [< L *tricuspis* three-pointed]

tri·cy·cle (trī′sik·əl) *n.* A three-wheeled vehicle worked by pedals, esp. one used by children.

tri·dent (trīd′nt) *n.* A three-pronged implement or weapon, the emblem of Neptune (Poseidon). —*adj.* Having three teeth or prongs: also **tri·den·tate** (trī·den′tāt), **tri·den′tat·ed.** [< L *tri-* three + *dens* a tooth]

tried (trīd) *p.t. & p.p.* of TRY. —*adj.* 1 Tested; trustworthy. 2 Freed of impurities.

tri·en·ni·al (trī·en′ē·əl) *adj.* 1 Taking place every third year. 2 Lasting three years. —*n.* 1 A ceremony celebrated every three years. 2 A plant lasting three years. [< L *tri-* three + *annus* year] —**tri·en′ni·al·ly** *adv.*

tri·fle (trī′fəl) *v.* **·fled, ·fling** *v.i.* 1 To treat or speak of something as of no value or importance: with *with.* 2 To play; toy. —*v.t.* 3 To spend (time, money, etc.) idly and purposelessly: He *trifled* away his entire fortune. —*n.* 1 Anything of very little value or importance. 2 A dessert, popular in England, made of layers of macaroons or ladyfingers with sugared fruit, custard, and meringue or whipped cream. 3 A small amount: It costs only a *trifle.* —**a trifle** Slightly; to a small extent: a *trifle* short. [< OF *truffer* deceive, jeer at] —**tri′fler** *n.*

tri·fling (trī′fling) *adj.* 1 Frivolous. 2 Insignificant. —**tri′·fling·ly** *adv.*

tri·fo·cal (trī·fō′kəl) *adj. Optics* Of or describing a lens with three segments, for near, intermediate, and far vision respectively. —*n.* A trifocal lens.

tri·fo·li·ate (trī·fō′lē·it, -āt) *adj. Bot.* Having three leaves or leaflike processes. Also **tri·fo′li·at′ed.**

tri·fo·li·o·late (trī·fō′lē·ə·lāt′) *adj. Bot.* Having three leaflets, as a clover leaf.

tri·fo·ri·um (trī·fôr′ē·əm, -fō′rē-) *n. pl.* **·fo·ri·a** (-fôr′ē·ə, -fō′rē·ə) *Archit.* A gallery above the arches of the nave or transept in a church. [< L *tri-* three + *foris* a door] —**tri·fo′ri·al** *adj.*

Triforium

trig[1] (trig) *adj.* 1 Characterized by tidiness; trim; neat. 2 Strong; sound; firm. —*v.t.* **trigged, trig·ging** To make trig or neat; often with *out* or *up.* [< ON *tryggr* true, trusty] —**trig′ly** *adv.* —**trig′ness** *n.*

trig[2] (trig) *n.* TRIGONOMETRY.

trig., trigon. trigonometric; trigonometry.

trig·ger (trig′ər) *n.* 1 A lever of a gun activating the firing mechanism when moved by a finger. • See REVOLVER. 2 Any one of various devices designed to activate other devices or systems. —**quick on the trigger** 1 Quick to shoot a gun. 2 Quick-witted; alert. —*v.t. Informal* To cause or set off (an action). [< Du. *trekken* pull, tug at]

trigonometric functions *Math.* Any of various functions of an angle or arc, principally the sine, cosine, tangent, cotangent, secant, and cosecant.

trig·o·nom·e·try (trig′ə·nom′ə·trē) *n.* The branch of mathematics based on the use of trigonometric functions, as in studying the relations of the sides and angles of triangles. [< Gk. *trigōnon* a triangle + *metron* measure] —**trig·o·no·met·ric** (trig′ə·nə·met′rik) or **·ri·cal** *adj.* —**trig′o·no·met′ri·cal·ly** *adv.*

tri·he·dron (trī·hē′drən) *n. pl.* **·dra** (-drə) *Geom.* A figure having three plane surfaces meeting at a point. [< Gk. *tri-* three + *hedra* a base] —**tri·he′dral** *adj.*

tri·lat·er·al (trī·lat′ər·əl) *adj.* Having three sides. [< L *tri-* three + *latus, lateris* a side] —**tri·lat′er·al·ly** *adv.*

trill (tril) *v.t.* 1 To sing or play in a quavering or tremulous tone. 2 *Phonet.* To articulate with a trill. —*v.i.* 3 To utter a quavering or tremulous sound. 4 *Music* To execute a trill. —*n.* 1 A tremulous utterance of successive tones, as of certain insects or birds; a warble. 2 *Music* A quick alternation of two notes either a tone or a semitone apart. 3 *Phonet.* A rapid vibration of a speech organ, as of the tip of the tongue. 4 A consonant or word so uttered. [< Ital. *trillare*] —**trill′er** *n.*

tril·lion (tril′yən) *n. & adj.* See NUMBER. [< MF *tri-* three + *million* million] —**tril′lionth** *adj., n.*

tril·li·um (tril′ē·əm) *n.* Any of a genus of perennial plants of the lily family, bearing a whorl of three leaves and a solitary flower. [< L *tri-* three]

tri·lo·bate (trī·lō′bāt, trī′lə·bāt) *adj.* Having three lobes. Also **tri·lo′bal, tri·lo′bat·ed, tri·lobed** (trī′lōbd′).

tri·lo·bite (trī′lə·bīt) *n.* Any of various fossilized extinct marine arthropods found in abundance in Paleozoic rocks, characterized by two lengthwise grooves forming three ridges. [< Gk. *tri-* three + *lobos* a lobe] **—tri′lo·bit′ic** (-bit′ik) *adj.*

tril·o·gy (tril′ə·jē) *n. pl.* **·gies** A group of three literary or dramatic compositions, each complete in itself, but connected into a whole through theme and subject matter. [< Gk. *tri-* three + *logos* a discourse]

trim (trim) *v.* **trimmed, trim·ming** *v.t.* **1** To make neat by clipping, pruning, etc. **2** To remove by cutting: usu. with *off* or *away.* **3** To put ornaments on; decorate. **4** In carpentry, to smooth; dress. **5** *Informal* **a** To chide; rebuke. **b** To punish. **c** To defeat. **6** *Naut.* **a** To adjust (sails or yards) for sailing. **b** To cause (a ship) to sit well in the water by adjusting cargo, ballast, etc. **7** To bring (an airplane) to stable flight by adjusting controls. —*v.i.* **8** *Naut.* **a** To be or remain in equilibrium. **b** To adjust sails or yards for sailing. **9** To act so as to appear to favor opposing sides in a controversy. —*n.* **1** State of adjustment or preparation; fitting condition. **2** Good physical condition: in *trim* to play tennis. **3** *Naut.* Fitness for sailing. **4** *Naut.* Actual or comparative degree of immersion. **5** The moldings, etc., as about the doors of a building. **6** Ornament, as on a dress; trimming. **7** The attitude of an aircraft in flight. —*adj.* **trim·mer, trim·mest** Having a smart appearance; spruce. —*adv.* In a trim manner: also **trim′ly.** [< OE *trymman* arrange, strengthen] **—trim′ness** *n.* **—Syn.** *v.* **1** cut, lop. **2** pare. **3** adorn, garnish.

tri·mes·ter (trī·mes′tər, trī′mes·tər) *n.* **1** A three-month period; quarter, as of an academic year. **2** Any of the three three-month periods used to identify the progress of a pregnancy. [< L *trimestris* < *tri-* three + *mensis* a month] **—tri·mes′tral, tri·mes′tri·al** *adj.*

trim·e·ter (trim′ə·tər) *adj.* In prosody, consisting of three measures or of lines containing three measures. —*n.* A line of verse having three measures.

trim·ming (trim′ing) *n.* **1** Something added for ornament or to give a finished appearance or effect. **2** *pl. Informal* The proper accompaniments or condiments of an article or food. **3** Parts or pieces trimmed away. **4** A severe reproof or a chastisement. **5** *Informal* A defeat.

tri·month·ly (trī·munth′lē) *adj. & adv.* Done or occurring every third month.

Trin·i·dad and To·ba·go (trin′ə·dad, tō·bā′gō) An independent member of the Commonwealth of Nations on two islands N of Venezuela, 1,980 sq. mi., cap. Port-of-Spain.

Trin·i·tar·i·an (trin′ə·târ′ē·ən) *adj.* **1** Of or pertaining to the Trinity. **2** Holding or professing belief in the Trinity. —*n.* A believer in the doctrine of the Trinity. **—Trin′i·tar′·i·an·ism** *n.*

tri·ni·tro·tol·u·ene (trī·nī′trō·tol′yōō·ēn) *n.* An explosive made by treating toluene with nitric acid. Also **tri·ni′tro·tol′u·ol** (-yōō·ōl, -ol). [< TRI- + NITRO- + TOLUENE]

trin·i·ty (trin′ə·tē) *n. pl.* **·ties** **1** The state or character of being three. **2** The union of three parts or elements in one; a triad. [< L *trinitas* a triad]

Trin·i·ty (trin′ə·tē) *n.* In Christian theology, the union in one divine nature of Father, Son, and Holy Spirit.

trin·ket (tring′kit) *n.* **1** Any small ornament, as of jewelry. **2** A trifle; trivial object. [< AF *trenquet*]

tri·no·mi·al (trī·nō′mē·əl) *adj.* **1** *Biol.* Of, having, or employing three terms or names. **2** *Math.* Expressed as a sum of three terms. —*n.* **1** *Math.* A trinomial expression in algebra. **2** A trinomial name. Also **tri·nom′i·nal** (-nom′ə·nəl). [< TRI- + (BI)NOMIAL] **—tri·no′mi·al·ly** *adv.*

tri·o (trē′ō) *n. pl.* **tri·os** **1** Any three things grouped or associated together. **2** *Music* **a** A composition for three performers. **b** A group of three musicians who perform trios. [< Ital. *tre* three]

tri·ox·ide (trī·ok′sīd) *n.* An oxide containing three atoms of oxygen per molecule.

trip (trip) *n.* **1** A journey; excursion. **2** A misstep or stumble. **3** An active, nimble step or movement. **4** A catch or similar device for starting or stopping a movement, as in a mechanism. **5** A sudden catch of the legs or feet to make a person fall. **6** A blunder; mistake. **7** *Slang* **a** The hallucinations and other sensations experienced by a person taking a psychedelic drug. **b** Any intense, usu. personal experience. —*v.* **tripped, trip·ping** *v.i.* **1** To stumble. **2** To move quickly and lightly. **3** To make an error. **4** To run past the nicks or dents of the ratchet escape wheel of a timepiece. **5** *Slang* To experience the effects of a psychedelic drug: often with *out.* —*v.t.* **6** To cause to stumble or make a mistake: often with *up.* **7** To perform (a dance) lightly. **8** *Mech.* To activate by releasing a catch, trigger, etc. **—trip it** To dance. [< OF *treper, triper* leap, trample] **—Syn.** *n.* **1** jaunt, tour, sojourn, voyage.

tri·par·tite (trī·pär′tīt) *adj.* **1** Divided into three parts. **2** Having three corresponding parts or copies. **3** Made between three persons: a *tripartite* pact. [< L *tri-* three + *partitus,* p.p. of *partiri* to divide] **—tri·par′tite·ly** *adv.* **—tri′·par·ti′tion** (-tish′ən) *n.*

tripe (trīp) *n.* **1** A part of the stomach wall of a ruminant used for food. **2** *Informal* Contemptible or worthless stuff; nonsense. [< OF]

trip·ham·mer (trip′ham′ər) *n.* A heavy power hammer that is raised mechanically and allowed to drop by a tripping action.

tripl. triplicate.

trip·le (trip′əl) *v.* **·led, ·ling** *v.t.* **1** To make threefold in number or quantity. —*v.i.* **2** To be or become three times as many or as large. **3** In baseball, to make a triple. —*adj.* **1** Consisting of three things united. **2** Multiplied by three; thrice said or done. —*n.* **1** A set or group of three. **2** In baseball, a fair hit that enables the batter to reach third base without the help of an error. [< Gk. *triploos* threefold] **—trip′ly** *adv.*

triple play In baseball, a play during which three men are put out.

trip·let (trip′lit) *n.* **1** A group of three of a kind. **2** Any of three children born at one birth. **3** *Music* A group of three notes that divide the time usu. taken by two. [< TRIPLE]

triple time *Music* A rhythm having three beats to the measure with the accent on the first beat.

trip·li·cate (trip′lə·kit) *adj.* Threefold; made in three copies. —*n.* One of three precisely similar things. **—in triplicate** In three identical copies. —*v.t.* (-kāt) **·cat·ed, ·cat·ing** To make three times; triple. [< L *triplicare* to triple] **—trip′li·cate·ly** *adv.* **—trip′li·ca′tion** *n.*

tri·pod (trī′pod) *n.* A three-legged frame or stand, as for supporting a camera, etc. [< Gk. *tri-* three + *pous* foot] **—trip·o·dal** (trip′ə·dəl), **tri·pod·ic** (tri·pod′ik) *adj.*

Tripod

trip·per (trip′ər) *n.* **1** A person or thing that trips. **2** *Brit. Informal* A tourist or traveler. **3** *Mech.* A trip or tripping mechanism, as a cam, pawl, etc. **4** *Slang* A person who frequently uses psychedelic drugs.

trip·ping (trip′ing) *adj.* Light; nimble. **—trip′ping·ly** *adv.*

trip·tych (trip′tik) *n.* **1** A picture, carving, or work of art on three panels side by side. **2** A writing tablet in three sections. [< Gk. *tri-* three + *ptyx, ptychos* a fold]

tri·reme (trī′rēm′) *n.* An ancient warship with three banks of oars on each side. [< L *tri-* three + *remus* an oar]

tri·sect (trī·sekt′) *v.t.* To divide into three parts, esp., as in geometry, into three equal parts. [< TRI- + L *sectus,* p.p. of *secare* to cut] **—tri·sec′tion** (-sek′shən), **tri·sec′tor** *n.*

triste (trēst) *adj.* Sorrowful; sad. [F]

tri·syl·la·ble (trī·sil′ə·bəl) *n.* A word of three syllables. **—tri·syl·lab·ic** (trī·si·lab′ik) *adj.* **—tri′syl·lab′i·cal·ly** *adv.*

trite (trīt) *adj.* **trit·er, trit·est** Made commonplace or hackneyed by frequent repetition. [< L *tritus,* p.p. of *terere* to rub] **—trite′ly** *adv.* **—trite′ness** *n.* **—Syn.** stale, stereotyped, threadbare, cliché, shopworn, tired, stock.

trit·i·um (trit′ē·əm, trish′ē·əm) *n.* The radioactive hydrogen isotope of atomic mass 3, having a half-life of 12.5 years. [< Gk. *tritos* third]

tri·ton (trīt′n) *n.* A marine snail with a trumpet-shaped shell. [< TRITON]

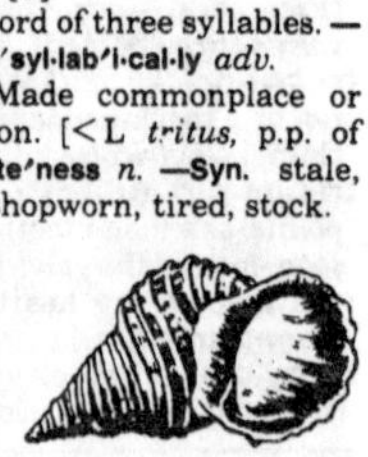
Triton

Tri·ton (trī′n) *Gk. Myth.* A sea god having a man's head and upper body and a dolphin's tail.

trit·u·rate (trich′ə·rāt) *v.t.* **·rat·ed, ·rat·ing** To reduce to a fine powder or pulp by grinding or rubbing; pulverize. —*n.* That which has been triturated. [< L *tritura* a rubbing, threshing < *tritus.* See TRITE.] *adj.* **—trit′u·ra′tor, trit′u·ra′·tion** *n.*

tri·umph (trī′əmf) *v.i.* **1** To win a victory. **2** To be successful. **3** To rejoice over a victory; exult. —*n.* **1** A victory or conquest: a *triumph* of will power. **2** An important success: the *triumphs* of modern medicine. **3** Exultation over a victory. **4** In ancient Rome, a pageant welcoming a victorious general. [< Gk. *thriambos* a processional hymn to Dionysus] **—tri·um·phal** (trī·um′fəl) *adj.* **—tri·um′phal·ly** *adv.* **—tri′umph·er** *n.*

tri·um·phant (trī·um′fənt) *adj.* **1** Exultant for or as for victory. **2** Crowned with victory; victorious. **—tri·um′phant·ly** *adv.*

tri·um·vir (trī·um′vər) *n. pl.* **·virs** or **·vi·ri** (-və·rī′, -rē′) In ancient Rome, one of three men united in public office or authority. [< L *trium virorum* of three men] **—tri·um′vi·ral** *adj.*

tri·um·vi·rate (trī·um′vər·it, -və·rāt) *n.* **1** A group or coalition of three men who govern. **2** The office of a triumvir. **3** The triumvirs collectively. **4** A group of three persons; a trio. [< L *triumvir* triumvir]

tri·une (trī′yōōn) *adj.* Three in one: said of the Godhead. [< TRI- + L *unus* one] **—tri·un·i·ty** (trī·yōō′na·tē) *n.*

tri·va·lent (trī·vā′lənt) *adj. Chem.* Having a valence or combining value of three. [< TRI- + L *valens,* pr.p. of *valere* be strong] **—tri·va′lence, tri·va′len·cy** *n.*

triv·et (triv′it) *n.* A short, usu. three-legged stand for holding cooking vessels in a fireplace, a hot dish on a table, or a heated iron. [< L *tri-* three + *pes, pedis* a foot]

triv·i·a (triv′ē·ə) *n.pl.* Insignificant or unimportant matters; trifles. [< L *trivialis* trivial]

triv·i·al (triv′ē·əl) *adj.* **1** Of little value or importance; insignificant. **2** *Archaic* Ordinary; commonplace. [< L *trivialis* of the crossroads, commonplace] **—triv′i·al·ism** *n.* **—triv′i·al·ly** *adv.* **—Syn. 1** slight, mean, paltry, inconsiderable, piddling.

triv·i·al·i·ty (triv′ē·al′ə·tē) *n. pl.* **·ties 1** The state or quality of being trivial. **2** A trivial matter.

triv·i·al·ize (triv′ē·ə·līz) *v.t.* **·ized, ·iz·ing** To treat as or make trivial; regard as unimportant. **—triv′i·al·i·za′tion** *n.*

tri·week·ly (trī·wēk′lē) *adj. & adv.* **1** Occurring three times a week. **2** Done or occurring every third week. —*n. pl.* **·lies** A triweekly publication.

tro·che (trō′kē) *n.* A small medicated lozenge, usu. circular. [< Gk. *trochiskos* a small wheel, a lozenge]

tro·chee (trō′kē) *n.* In prosody, a foot comprising a long and short syllable (¯ ˘), or an accented syllable followed by an unaccented one. [< Gk. *trochaios (pous)* a running (foot) < *trechein* to run] **—tro·cha·ic** (trō·kā′ik) *adj.*

trod (trod) *p.t. & alternative p.p.* of TREAD.

trod·den (trod′n) *p.p.* of TREAD.

trog·lo·dyte (trog′lə·dīt) *n.* **1** A prehistoric cave man. **2** A person with primitive habits. **3** A hermit. [< Gk. *trōglodytēs*] **—trog′lo·dyt′ic** (-dit′ik), **trog′lo·dyt′i·cal** *adj.*

Tro·jan (trō′jən) *n.* **1** A native of Troy. **2** A brave, persevering person. —*adj.* Of or pertaining to ancient Troy or to its people.

Trojan horse 1 *Gk. Myth.* During the Trojan War, a large, hollow wooden horse filled with Greek soldiers and brought within the walls of Troy, thus bringing about the downfall of the city. **2** *Mil.* The infiltration of military men into enemy territory to commit sabotage against industry and military installations.

Trojan War *Gk. Myth.* The ten years' war waged by the Greeks against the Trojans to recover Helen, the wife of Menelaus, who had been abducted by Paris.

troll[1] (trōl) *v.t.* **1** To sing in succession, as in a round. **2** To sing in a full, hearty manner. **3** To fish for with a moving lure, as from a moving boat. —*v.i.* **4** To roll; turn. **5** To sing a tune, etc., in a full, hearty manner. **6** To fish with a moving lure. —*n.* **1** A song taken up at intervals by several voices; round. **2** A rolling movement or motion. **3** In fishing, a spoon or other lure. [?] **—troll′er** *n.*

troll[2] (trōl) *n.* In Scandinavian folklore, a giant or dwarf living in caves or underground. [< ON]

trol·ley (trol′ē) *n. pl.* **·leys 1** A device that rolls or slides along an electric conductor to carry current to an electric vehicle. **2** A trolley car; also, a system of trolley cars. **3** A small truck or car suspended from an overhead track and used to convey material, as in a factory, mine, etc. —*v.t. & v.i.* To convey or travel by trolley. [< TROLL[1]]

trolley bus A passenger conveyance operating without rails, propelled electrically by current taken from an overhead wire by means of a trolley.

trolley car A car arranged with a trolley and motor for use on an electric railway.

trol·lop (trol′əp) *n.* **1** A slatternly woman. **2** A prostitute. [?]

trom·bone (trom·bōn′, trom′bōn) *n.* A brass wind instrument of the trumpet family in the tenor range, usu. equipped with a slide for changing pitch. [< Ital. *tromba* a trumpet] **—trom·bon′ist** *n.*

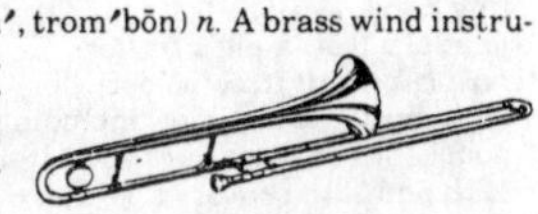

Trombone

troop (trōōp) *n.* **1** A gathering of people. **2** A flock or herd, as of animals. **3** A unit of cavalry having 60 to 100 men and corresponding to a company in other military branches. **4** *pl.* Soldiers. **5** A unit of Boy Scouts or Girl Scouts. —*v.i.* **1** To move along as a group: shoppers *trooping* through a store. **2** To go: to *troop* across the street. —*v.t.* **3** To form into troops. [< LL *troppus* a flock] **—Syn. 1** company, crowd, multitude, throng.

troop·er (trōō′pər) *n.* **1** A cavalryman. **2** A mounted policeman. **3** A troop horse. **4** *Informal* A state policeman.

troop·ship (trōōp′ship′) *n.* A ship for carrying troops.

trope (trōp) *n.* **1** The figurative use of a word or phrase. **2** A figure of speech. **3** Figurative language in general. [< L *tropus* a figure of speech < Gk. *tropos* a turn]

tro·phy (trō′fē) *n. pl.* **·phies 1** Anything taken from an enemy and displayed or treasured in proof of victory. **2** A prize representing victory or achievement: a tennis *trophy.* **3** An animal skin, mounted head, etc., kept to show skill in hunting. **4** Any memento. [< Gk. *tropē* a defeat, turning] **—tro′phied** *adj.*

trop·ic (trop′ik) *n.* **1** *Geog.* Either of two parallels of latitude, the **tropic of Cancer** at 23° 27′ north of the equator and the **tropic of Capricorn** 23° 27′ south of the equator, between which lies the torrid zone. **2** *Astron.* Either of two corresponding parallels in the celestial sphere similarly named, and respectively 23° 27′ north or south from the celestial equator. **3** *pl.* The regions in the torrid zone. —*adj.* Of or pertaining to the tropics; tropical. [< Gk. *tropikos (kyklos)* the tropical (circle), pertaining to the turning of the sun at the solstice.]

-tropic *combining form* Having a (specified) tropism: *geotropic.* [< Gk. *tropos* a turn]

trop·i·cal (trop′i·kəl) *adj.* **1** Of, pertaining to, or characteristic of the tropics. **2** Of the nature of a trope or metaphor. **—trop′i·cal·ly** *adv.*

tropical fish Any of various small, usu. brightly colored fishes originating in the tropics and adapted to living in an aquarium (**tropical aquarium**) kept at a constant warm temperature.

tro·pism (trō′piz·əm) *n.* **1** A tendency in an organism to grow or move toward or away from a given stimulus. **2** An instance of such growth or movement. [< Gk. *tropē* a turning] **—tro·pis·tic** (trō·pis′tik) *adj.*

-tropism *combining form* A (specified) tropism: *phototropism.* Also **-tropy.**

trop·o·sphere (trōp′ə·sfir, trop′-) *n. Meteorol.* The region of the atmosphere extending from six to twelve miles above the earth's surface, characterized by decreasing temperature with increasing altitude. [< Gk. *tropos* a turning + SPHERE]

trot (trot) *n.* **1** The gait of a quadruped, in which each diagonal pair of legs is moved alternately. 2 The sound of this gait. 3 A slow running gait of a person. 4 A little child. 5 *Informal* A literal translation of a foreign-language text, used by students, often dishonestly. **—the trots** *Slang* Diarrhea. **—***v.* **trot·ted, trot·ting** *v.i.* 1 To go at a trot. 2 To go quickly; hurry. **—***v.t.* 3 To cause to trot. 4 To ride at a trotting gait. **—trot out** *Informal* To bring forth for inspection, approval, etc. [< OHG *trottōn* to tread]

troth (trôth, trōth) *n.* 1 Good faith; fidelity. 2 The act of pledging fidelity. 3 Truth; verity. **—plight one's troth** To promise to marry or be faithful to. [< OE *trēowth* truth]

Trot·sky·ism (trot′skē·iz′əm) *n.* The doctrines of Trotsky and his followers who opposed Stalin and believed that Communism to succeed must be international. [< L. *Trotsky,* 1879–1940, Russian Bolshevist leader] **— Trot′sky·ist, Trot′sky·ite** *n., adj.*

trot·ter (trot′ər) *n.* 1 One who or that which trots; a trotting horse, esp. one trained to trot in races. 2 *Informal* An animal's foot: a pig's *trotters.*

trou·ba·dour (trōō′bə·dôr, -dōr, -dōōr) *n.* One of a class of lyric poets, sometimes including wandering minstrels, flourishing in parts of France, Italy, and Spain during the 12th and 13th centuries. [< Prov. *trobador* < *trobar* compose, invent]

troub·le (trub′əl) *n.* 1 The state of being distressed or worried. 2 A person, circumstance, or event that occasions difficulty or perplexity. 3 A condition of difficulty: to be in *trouble* at school; money *troubles.* 4 A disease or ailment: heart *trouble.* 5 Bother; effort: They took the *trouble* to drive me home. 6 Agitation; unrest: *trouble* in the streets. **—***v.* **·led, ·ling** *v.t.* 1 To distress; worry. 2 To stir up or roil, as water. 3 To inconvenience. 4 To annoy. 5 To cause physical pain or discomfort to. **—***v.i.* 6 To take pains; bother. [< OF *turbler* to trouble] **—troub′ler** *n.*

troub·le·mak·er (trub′əl·mā′kər) *n.* One who habitually stirs up trouble for others.

troub·le-shoot·er (trub′əl·shōō′tər) *n.* 1 A skilled workman able to analyze and repair breakdowns in machinery, electronic equipment, etc. 2 A person assigned to eliminate sources of difficulty or to mediate disputes, esp. in diplomacy and politics. **—troub′le-shoot′ing** *n.*

troub·le·some (trub′əl·səm) *adj.* 1 Causing trouble; trying. 2 Difficult: a *troublesome* task. **—troub′le·some·ly** *adv.* **—troub′le·some·ness** *n.* **—Syn.** 1 burdensome, disturbing, galling, harassing.

troub·lous (trub′ləs) *adj.* 1 Uneasy; restless: *troublous* times. 2 Troublesome.

trough (trôf, trof) *n.* 1 A long, narrow receptacle for food or water for animals. 2 A similarly shaped receptacle, as for mixing dough. 3 A long, narrow depression, as between waves. 4 A gutter for rain water fixed under the eaves of a building. 5 *Meteorol.* An elongated region of relatively low atmospheric pressure. [< OE *trog*]

trounce (trouns) *v.t.* **trounced, trounc·ing** 1 To beat or thrash severely; punish. 2 *Informal* To defeat. [?]

troupe (trōōp) *n.* A company of actors or other performers. **—***v.i.* **trouped, troup·ing** To travel as one of a company of actors or entertainers. [< OF *trope* troop]

troup·er (trōōp′ər) *n.* 1 A member of a theatrical company. 2 An older actor of long experience.

trou·sers (trou′zərz) *n.pl.* A two-legged garment, covering the body from the waist to the ankles or knees. [Blend of obs. *trouse* breeches and DRAWERS]

trous·seau (trōō′sō, trōō·sō′) *n. pl.* **·seaux** (-sōz, -sōz′) or **·seaus** A bride's outfit, esp. of clothing. [F < OF, dim. of *trousse* a packed collection of things]

trout (trout) *n.* Any of various fishes of the salmon family found mostly in fresh waters and esteemed as a game and food fish. [< OE *trūht*]

Trowels
a. garden. b. plastering. c. brick.

trow·el (trou′əl, troul) *n.* 1 A flat-bladed, sometimes pointed implement, used by masons, plasterers, and molders. 2 A small concave scoop with a handle, used in digging about small plants. **—***v.t.* **·eled** or **·elled, ·el·ing** or **·el·ling** To apply, smooth, or dig with a trowel. [< L *trulla,* dim. of *trua* a stirring spoon] **—trow′el·er** or **trow′el·ler** *n.*

troy (troi) *adj.* Measured or expressed in troy weight. [< *Troyes,* France; with ref. to a weight used at a fair held there]

troy weight A system of weights in which 12 ounces or 5,760 grains equal a pound, and the grain is identical with the avoirdupois grain. • See MEASURE.

tru·ant (trōō′ənt) *n.* 1 A pupil who stays away from school without leave. 2 A person who shirks responsibilities or work. **—play truant** 1 To be absent from school without leave. 2 To shirk responsibilities or work. **—***adj.* 1 Being truant; idle. 2 Relating to or characterizing a truant. [< OF, a vagabond] **—tru·an·cy** (trōō′ən·sē) *n.* (*pl.* **·cies**)

truce (trōōs) *n.* 1 An agreement for a temporary suspension of hostilities; an armistice. 2 A temporary stopping, as from pain, etc.; respite. [< OE *truwa* faith, a promise]

Tru·cial States (trōō′shəl) A group of sheikdoms, bound by treaties with Great Britain, in E Arabia, 32,300 sq. mi.

truck[1] (truk) *n.* 1 Any of several types of strongly built motor vehicles designed to transport heavy loads, bulky articles, freight, etc. 2 A two-wheeled barrowlike vehicle for moving barrels, boxes, etc., by hand. 3 A small wheeled vehicle used for moving baggage, goods, etc. 4 A disk at the upper extremity of a mast or flagpole through which the halyards of signals are run. 5 A small wheel. **—***v.t.* 1 To carry on a truck. **—***v.i.* 2 To carry goods on a truck. 3 To drive a truck. [< Gk. *trochos* a wheel]

truck[2] (truk) *v.t. & v.i.* To exchange or barter. **—***n.* 1 Commodities for sale. 2 Garden produce for market. 3 *Informal* Rubbish; worthless articles. 4 Barter. 5 *Informal* Dealings: I will have no *truck* with him. [< OF *troquer* to barter]

truck·age (truk′ij) *n.* 1 The conveyance of goods on trucks. 2 The charge for this. [< TRUCK[1]]

truck·er (truk′ər) *n.* One who drives or supplies trucks or moves commodities in trucks.

truck farm A farm on which vegetables are produced for market. **—truck farmer, truck farming**

truck·ing (truk′ing) *n.* The act or business of transportation by trucks.

truck·le (truk′əl) *v.* **·led, ·ling** *v.i.* 1 To yield or submit weakly: with *to.* 2 To move on rollers or casters. **—***v.t.* 3 To cause to move on rollers or casters. **—***n.* A small wheel. [< L *trochlea* system of pulleys] **—truck′ler** *n.*

truckle bed TRUNDLE BED.

truck·man (truk′mən) *n. pl.* **·men** (mən) 1 A truck driver. 2 One engaged in the business of trucking.

truc·u·lent (truk′yə·lənt) *adj.* Of savage character; cruel; ferocious. [< L *trux, trucis* fierce] **—truc·u·lence** (truk′yə·ləns), **truc′u·len·cy** *n.* **—truc′u·lent·ly** *adv.* **—Syn.** barbarous, brutal, fierce, ruthless, vicious.

trudge (truj) *v.i.* **trudged, trudg·ing** To walk wearily or laboriously; plod. **—***n.* A tiresome walk or tramp. [?] **— trudg′er** *n.*

true (trōō) *adj.* **tru·er, tru·est** 1 Faithful to fact or reality. 2 Being real; genuine, not counterfeit: *true* gold. 3 Faithful to friends, promises, or principles; loyal. 4 Exact: a *true* copy. 5 Accurate, as in shape, or position: a *true* fit. 6 Faithful to the requirements of law or justice; legitimate: the *true* king. 7 Faithful to truth; honest: a *true* man. 8 Faithful to the promise or predicted event: a *true* sign. 9 *Biol.* Possessing all the attributes of its class: a *true* root. 10 *Music* Exactly in tune. **—come true** To turn out as hoped for or imagined. **—***n.* The state or quality of being true; also, something that is true: usu. with *the.* **—in** (or **out of**) **true** In (or not in) line of adjustment. **—***adv.* 1 In truth; truly. 2 Within proper tolerances: The wheel runs *true.* **—***v.t.* **trued, tru·ing** To bring to conformity with a standard or requirement: to *true* a frame. [< OE *trēowe*] **—true′ness** *n.*

true bill *Law* A bill of indictment found by a grand jury to be sustained by the evidence.

true-blue (trōō′blōō′) *adj.* Staunch; faithful.

true·love (trōō′luv′) *n.* One truly beloved; a sweetheart.

truf·fle (truf′əl, trōō′fəl) *n.* Any of various fleshy underground edible fungi regarded as a delicacy. [< OF *truffe*]

tru·ism (trōō′iz·əm) *n* An obvious or self-evident truth; a platitude.

trull (trul) *n.* A prostitute. [< G *Trolle*]

tru·ly (tro͞o′lē) *adv.* **1** In conformity with fact. **2** With accuracy. **3** With loyalty.

trump (trump) *n.* **1** In various card games, a card of the suit selected to rank above all others temporarily. **2** The suit thus determined. **3** *Informal* A fine, reliable person. —*v.t.* **1** To take (another card) with a trump. **2** To surpass; excel; beat. —*v.i.* **3** To play a trump. —**trump up** To invent for a fraudulent purpose. [Alter. of TRIUMPH]

trump·er·y (trum′pər·ē) *n. pl.* **·er·ies 1** Worthless finery. **2** Rubbish; nonsense. —*adj.* Having a showy appearance, but valueless. [< OF *tromper* to cheat]

trum·pet (trum′pit) *n.* **1** A soprano brass wind instrument with a flaring bell and a long metal tube. **2** Something resembling a trumpet in form. **3** A tube for collecting and conducting sounds to the ear; an ear trumpet. **4** A loud penetrating sound like that of a trumpet. —*v.t.* **1** To sound or publish abroad. —*v.i.* **2** To blow a trumpet. **3** To give forth a sound as if from a trumpet, as an elephant. [< OF *trompette*]

Trumpet

trum·pet·er (trum′pə·tər) *n.* **1** One who plays a trumpet. **2** One who publishes something loudly abroad. **3** A large South American bird, related to the cranes. **4** A large North American wild swan having a clarionlike cry: also **trumpeter swan.** • See SWAN. **5** A breed of domestic pigeons.

trun·cate (trung′kāt) *v.t.* **·cat·ed, ·cat·ing** To cut the top or end from. —*adj. Biol.* Ending abruptly, as though cut off: a *truncate* leaf. [< L *truncare*] —**trun′cate·ly** *adv.* —**trun·ca·tion** (trung·kā′shən) *n.*

trun·cheon (trun′chən) *n.* **1** A short, heavy stick, esp. a policeman's club. **2** Any baton of office or authority. —*v.t.* To beat as with a truncheon; cudgel. [< OF *tronchon* a stump]

trun·dle (trun′dəl) *n.* **1** A small broad wheel, as of a caster. **2** The act, motion, or sound of trundling. **3** TRUNDLE BED. —*v.* **·dled, ·dling** *v.t.* **1** To propel by rolling along: to *trundle* a wheelbarrow. **2** To haul or carry in a wheeled vehicle. —*v.i.* **3** To move ahead by revolving. **4** To progress on wheels. [< OE *trendel* a circle] —**trun′dler** *n.*

trundle bed A bed with very low frame resting upon casters, so that it may be rolled under another bed.

trunk (trungk) *n.* **1** The main stem or stock of a tree. **2** An animal or human body, apart from the head and limbs; the torso. **3** The thorax of an insect. **4** The main stem of a nerve, blood vessel, or lymphatic. **5** A main line of communication or transportation, as the circuit connecting two telephone exchanges. **6** A proboscis, as of an elephant. **7** A large box or case used for packing and carrying clothes or other articles. **8** *pl.* Very short, close-fitting trousers worn by swimmers, athletes, etc. **9** *Archit.* The shaft of a column. **10** A compartment in an automobile, opposite the end housing the motor, for carrying luggage, tools, etc. —*adj.* Being or belonging to a trunk or main body: a *trunk* railroad. [< L *truncus* stem, trunk]

trunk·fish (trungk′fish′) *n. pl.* **·fish** or **·fish·es** Any of a family of fishes characterized by a body covering of hard, bony plates.

truss (trus) *n.* **1** A supporting framework, as for a roof or bridge. **2** A bandage or support for a hernia. **3** A bundle or package. **4** *Naut.* A heavy iron piece by which a lower yard is attached to a mast. —*v.t.* **1** To tie or bind; fasten: often with *up.* **2** To support or brace (a roof, bridge, etc.) with trusses. **3** To fasten the wings of (a fowl) before cooking. [< OF *trousser, trusser* pack up, bundle] —**truss′er** *n.*

trust (trust) *n.* **1** A reliance on the integrity, veracity, or reliability of a person or thing. **2** Something committed to one's care for use or safekeeping. **3** The state or position of one who has received an important charge. **4** Confident expectation; hope. **5** In commerce, credit. **6** *Law* **a** The confidence reposed in a person to whom the legal title to property is conveyed for the benefit of another. **b** The property or thing held in trust. **c** The relation subsisting between the holder and the property so held. **7** A combination of business firms formed to control production and prices of some commodity. —**in trust** In the charge or care of another or others. —**on trust 1** On credit. **2** Without investigating: to accept a statement *on trust.* —*v.t.* **1** To rely upon. **2** To commit to the care of another; entrust. **3** To commit something to the care of: with *with.* **4** To allow to do something without fear of the consequences. **5** To expect; hope. **6** To believe. **7** To allow business credit to. —*v.i.* **8** To place trust or confidence; rely: with *in.* **9** To allow business credit. —**trust to** To depend upon; confide in. —*adj.* Held in trust: *trust* property. [< ON *traust,* lit., firmness] —**trust′er** *n.* —**Syn.** *n.* **1** confidence, credence, faith.

trus·tee (trus·tē′) *n.* **1** One who is entrusted with the property of another. **2** One of a body of persons, often elective, who hold the property and manage the affairs of a company or institution.

trus·tee·ship (trus·tē′ship) *n.* **1** The post or function of a trustee. **2** Supervision and control of a trust territory by a country or countries commissioned by the United Nations.

trust·ful (trust′fəl) *adj.* Disposed to trust. —**trust′ful·ly** *adv.* —**trust′ful·ness** *n.*

trust fund Money, securities, or similar property held in trust.

trust·ing (trus′ting) *adj.* Having trust; trustful. —**trust′·ing·ly** *adv.* —**trust′ing·ness** *n.*

trust territory An area, usu. a former colonial possession, governed by a member state of the United Nations.

trust·wor·thy (trust′wûr′t͟hē) *adj.* Worthy of confidence; reliable. —**trust′wor′thi·ly** (-wûr′t͟hə·lē) *adv.* —**trust′wor′thi·ness** *n.*

trust·y (trus′tē) *adj.* **trust·i·er, trust·i·est 1** Faithful to duty or trust. **2** Staunch; firm. —*n. pl.* **trust·ies** A trustworthy person; esp. a convict to whom special privileges are granted. —**trust′i·ly** *adv.* —**trust′i·ness** *n.*

truth (tro͞oth) *n. pl.* **truths** (tro͞ot͟hz, tro͞oths) **1** The state or character of being true. **2** That which is true. **3** Conformity to fact or reality. **4** The quality of being true; fidelity; constancy. —**in truth** Indeed; in fact. [< OE *treowe* true]

truth·ful (tro͞oth′fəl) *adj.* **1** Conforming to fact; veracious. **2** Telling the truth. —**truth′ful·ly** *adv.* —**truth′ful·ness** *n.*

try (trī) *v.* **tried, try·ing** *v.t.* **1** To make an attempt to do or accomplish. **2** To make experimental use or application of: to *try* a new pen. **3** To subject to a test; put to proof. **4** To put severe strain upon; tax: to *try* one's patience. **5** To subject to trouble or tribulation. **6** To extract by rendering or melting; refine. **7** *Law* To determine the guilt or innocence of by judicial trial. —*v.i.* **8** To make an attempt; put forth effort. **9** To make an examination or test. —**try on** To put on (a garment) to test it for fit or appearance. —**try out 1** To attempt to qualify: He *tried out* for the team. **2** To test the result or effect of. —*n. pl.* **tries** The act of trying; trial. [< OF *trier* sift, pick out] —**tri′er** *n.* • **try and, try to** These constructions are both standard in modern English: *Try and meet me at six; Try to finish your work on time.* However, *try to* is usu. preferable in precise, formal writing.

try·ing (trī′ing) *adj.* Testing severely; hard to endure. —**try′ing·ly** *adv.* —**try′ing·ness** *n.* —**Syn.** arduous, difficult, onerous, troublesome.

try·out (trī′out′) *n. Informal* A test of ability, as of an actor or athlete.

tryp·sin (trip′sin) *n.* A pancreatic enzyme that helps to digest proteins. [< Gk. *tripsis* a rubbing + (PEP)SIN] —**tryp′tic** (-tik) *adj.*

try square A device for marking off right angles and testing the accuracy of anything square.

tryst (trist, trīst) *n.* **1** An appointment to meet at a specified time or place. **2** The meeting place agreed upon. **3** The meeting so agreed upon. [< OF *triste, tristre* an appointed station in hunting]

tsar (zär, tsär) *n.* CZAR.

tset·se (tset′sē, tsē′tsē) *n.* Any of several bloodsucking flies of Africa, including species that carry and transmit pathogenic organisms to humans and animals. Also **tsetse fly.** [< Bantu]

T. Sgt., T/Sgt Technical Sergeant.

T-shirt (tē′shûrt′) *n.* A knitted cotton undershirt with short sleeves.

tsp. teaspoon(s); teaspoonful(s).

T-square (tē′skwâr′) *n.* A device used to measure out right angles or parallel lines, consisting usu. of a flat strip with a shorter head at right angles to it.

tsu·na·mi (tsōō·nä′mē) *n.* An immense wave generated by a submarine earthquake. [Jap. < *tsu* port, harbor + *nami* wave]

Tu., Tues. Tuesday.

tub (tub) *n.* **1** A broad, open-topped vessel of metal, wooden staves, etc., for washing and bathing. **2** A bathtub. **3** *Informal* A bath taken in a tub. **4** The amount that a tub contains. **5** Anything resembling a tub, as a broad, clumsy boat. **6** *Informal* A small cask. —*v.t. & v.i.* **tubbed, tub·bing** To wash or bathe in a tub. [< MDu. *tubbe*] —**tub′ber** *n.*

tu·ba (tʸōō′bə) *n. pl.* **·bas** or **·bae** (-bē) A large bass instrument of the bugle family. [< L, a war trumpet]

Tuba

tub·by (tub′ē) *adj.* **·bi·er, ·bi·est** Resembling a tub in form; round and fat. —**Syn.** chubby, chunky, corpulent, rotund.

tube (tʸōōb) *n.* **1** A long hollow cylindrical body of metal, glass, rubber, etc., generally used to convey or hold a liquid or gas. **2** Any device having a tube or tubelike part, as a telescope. **3** *Biol.* Any elongated hollow part or organ. **4** A subway or subway tunnel. **5** An electron tube. **6** A collapsible metal or plastic cylinder for containing paints, toothpaste, glue, and the like. —**the tube** *Slang* Television. —*v.t.* **tubed, tub·ing 1** To fit or furnish with a tube. **2** To make tubular. [< L *tubus*] —**tu′bal** *adj.*

tu·ber (tʸōō′bər) *n.* **1** A short, thickened portion of an underground stem, as a potato. **2** A tubercle. [L, a swelling]

tu·ber·cle (tʸōō′bər·kəl) *n.* **1** A small rounded eminence or nodule. **2** *Bot.* A small wartlike swelling, usu. due to symbiotic microorganisms, as on the roots of certain legumes. **3** *Pathol.* A small granular tumor within an organ. [< L *tuber* a swelling]

tubercle bacillus The rod-shaped bacterium that causes tuberculosis.

tu·ber·cu·lar (tʸōō·bûr′kyə·lər) *adj.* **1** Affected with tubercles. **2** Tuberculous. —*n.* One affected with tuberculosis.

tu·ber·cu·lin (tʸōō·bûr′kyə·lin) *n.* A substance derived from tubercle bacilli, used in a diagnostic test for tuberculosis. [< L *tuberculum* TUBERCLE + -IN]

tu·ber·cu·lo·sis (tʸōō·bûr′kyə·lō′sis) *n.* A communicable disease caused by the tubercle bacillus and characterized by tubercles in the lungs or other organs or tissues of the body. —**tu·ber′cu·lous** (tʸōō·bûr′kyə·ləs) *adj.*

tube·rose (tʸōōb′rōz′, tʸōō′bə·rōs′) *n.* A bulbous plant of the amaryllis family, bearing a spike of fragrant white flowers. [< L *tuberosus* knobby < *tuber* a swelling]

tu·ber·ous (tʸōō′bər·əs) *adj.* **1** Bearing projections or prominences. **2** Resembling tubers. **3** *Bot.* Bearing tubers: also **tu′ber·ose.** —**tu·ber·os·i·ty** (tʸōō′bə·ros′ə·tē) *n.* (*pl.* **·ties**)

tub·ing (tʸōō′bing) *n.* **1** Tubes collectively. **2** A piece of tube or material for tubes.

tu·bu·lar (tʸōō′byə·lər) *adj.* **1** Having the form of a tube. **2** Of or pertaining to a tube or tubes.

tuck (tuk) *v.t.* **1** To thrust or press in the ends or edges of: to *tuck* in a blanket. **2** To wrap or cover snugly. **3** To thrust or press into a close place; cram. **4** To make tucks in, by folding and stitching. —*v.i.* **5** To contract; draw together. **6** To make tucks. —*n.* **1** A fold sewed into a garment. **2** Any inserted or folded thing. **3** A position in diving in which the knees are bent and the upper legs pressed against the chest. [< OE *tūcian* ill-treat, lit., tug]

tuck·er[1] (tuk′ər) *n.* **1** One who or that which tucks. **2** A covering of muslin, lace, etc., formerly worn over the neck and shoulders by women. **3** A device on a sewing machine to make tucks.

tuck·er[2] (tuk′ər) *v.t. Informal* To weary completely; exhaust: usu. with *out.* [?]

Tu·dor (tʸōō′dər) *adj.* **1** Of or pertaining to the English royal family (1485–1603) descended from Sir Owen Tudor. **2** Designating or pertaining to the architecture, poetry, etc., developed during the reigns of the Tudors.

Tues·day (tʸōōz′dē, -dā) *n.* The third day of the week. [< OE *tīwesdæg* day of Tiw, a god of war]

tuft (tuft) *n.* **1** A collection or bunch of small, flexible parts, as hair, grass, or feathers, held together at the base. **2** A clump or knot. —*v.t.* **1** To provide (a mattress, upholstery, etc.) with tightly drawn tufts or buttons to keep the padding in place. **2** To cover or adorn with tufts. —*v.i.* **3** To form or grow in tufts. [< OF *tuffe*] —**tuft′er** *n.*

tuft·ed (tuf′tid) *adj.* **1** Having or adorned with a tuft or crest. **2** Forming a tuft or dense cluster.

tug (tug) *v.* **tugged, tug·ging** *v.t.* **1** To pull at with effort; strain at. **2** To pull or drag with effort. **3** To tow with a tugboat. —*v.i.* **4** To pull strenuously: to *tug* at an oar. **5** To strive; struggle. —*n.* **1** A violent pull. **2** A strenuous contest. **3** A tugboat. **4** A trace of a harness. [< OE *tēon* tow] —**tug′ger** *n.* —**Syn.** *v.* **2** draw, haul, heave, lug.

tug·boat (tug′bōt′) *n.* A small, compact, ruggedly built vessel designed for towing or pushing barges and larger vessels.

tug of war 1 A contest in which a number of persons at one end of a rope pull against a like number at the other end. **2** A laborious effort; supreme contest. Also **tug-of-war** (tug′uv·wôr′, tug′ə-) *n.* (*pl.* **tugs-of-war**).

tu·i·tion (tʸōō·ish′ən) *n.* **1** The act or business of teaching. **2** The charge or payment for instruction. [< L *tuitio* a guard, guardianship] —**tu·i′tion·al, tu·i′tion·ar′y** (-er′ē) *adj.*

tu·la·re·mi·a (tōō′lə·rē′mē·ə) *n.* An acute bacterial infection that can be transmitted to man from infected rabbits, squirrels, or other animals by the bite of certain flies or by direct contact. Also **tu′la·rae′mi·a.** [< *Tulare* County, California + Gk. *haima* blood]

tu·lip (tʸōō′lip) *n.* **1** Any of numerous bulbous plants of the lily family, bearing variously colored cup-shaped flowers. **2** A bulb or flower of this plant. [< Turkish *tuliband* turban]

tulip tree A large North American forest tree related to magnolia, with greenish cup-shaped flowers.

tu·lip·wood (tʸōō′lip·wŏŏd′) *n.* **1** The soft, light wood of the tulip tree. **2** Any of several ornamental cabinet woods. **3** Any of the trees yielding these woods.

tulle (tōōl, *Fr.* tül) *n.* A fine, silk, open-meshed material, used for veils, etc. [< *Tulle,* a city in sw France]

tum·ble (tum′bəl) *v.* **·bled, ·bling** *v.i.* **1** To roll or toss about. **2** To perform acrobatic feats, as somersaults, etc. **3** To fall violently or awkwardly. **4** To move in a careless or headlong manner; stumble. **5** *Informal* To understand; comprehend: with *to.* —*v.t.* **6** To toss carelessly; cause to fall. **7** To throw into disorder; rumple. —*n.* **1** The act of tumbling; a fall. **2** A state of disorder or confusion. [< OE *tumbian* fall, leap]

tum·ble·bug (tum′bəl·bug′) *n.* Any of several beetles that roll up a ball of dung to enclose their eggs.

tum·ble-down (tum′bəl·doun′) *adj.* Rickety, as if about to fall in pieces; dilapidated.

tum·bler (tum′blər) *n.* **1** A drinking glass without a foot or stem; also, its contents. **2** One who or that which tumbles, as an acrobat or contortionist. **3** One of a breed of domestic pigeons noted for turning somersaults during flight. **4** In a lock, a latch that engages and immobilizes a bolt unless raised by the key bit. **5** A revolving device the contents of which are tumbled about, as certain dryers for clothes.

Tumbrel

tum·ble·weed (tum′bəl·wēd′) *n.* Any of various plants which break off in autumn and are driven about by the wind.

tum·brel (tum′bril) *n.* **1** A farmer's cart. **2** A rude cart in which prisoners were taken to the guillotine during the French

Revolution. 3 A military cart for carrying tools, ammunition, etc. Also **tum′bril.** [< OE *tomberel*]

tu·me·fy (t^yōō′mə·fī) *v.t. & v.i.* **·fied, ·fy·ing** To swell or puff up. [< L *tumere* swell + *facere* make] **—tu·me·fac·tion** (t^yōō′mə·fak′shən) *n.*

tu·mes·cent (t^yōō·mes′ənt) *adj.* Swelling; somewhat tumid. [< L *tumescere* to swell up] **—tu·mes′cence** *n.*

tu·mid (t^yōō′mid) *adj.* 1 Swollen; enlarged, protuberant. 2 Inflated or pompous. [< L *tumidus* < *tumere* swell] **—tu·mid′i·ty, tu′mid·ness** *n.*

tum·my (tum′ē) *n. pl.* **-mies** *Colloq.* The stomach or abdomen.

tu·mor (t^yōō′mər) *n.* A local swelling on or in the body, esp. from growth of tissue having no physiological function. *Brit. sp.* **tu′mour.** [< L *tumere* to swell] **—tu′mor·ous** *adj.*

tu·mult (t^yōō′mult) *n.* 1 The commotion, disturbance, or agitation of a multitude; an uproar. 2 Any violent commotion. 3 Mental or emotional agitation. [< L *tumultus* < *tumere* swell] **—Syn.** ferment, hubbub, racket, turbulence.

tu·mul·tu·ous (t^yōō·mul′chōō·əs) *adj.* 1 Characterized by tumult; disorderly; violent. 2 Greatly agitated or disturbed. 3 Stormy; tempestuous. **—tu·mul′tu·ous·ly** *adv.* **—tu·mul′tu·ous·ness** *n.*

tun (tun) *n.* 1 A large cask. 2 A varying measure of capacity for wines, etc., usu. equal to 252 gallons. *—v.t.* **tunned, tun·ning** To put into a cask or tun. [< OE *tunne*]

tu·na (t^yōō′nə) *n. pl.* **tu·na** or **tu·nas** Any of various large marine food and game fishes related to mackerel. Also **tuna fish.** [Am. Sp., ult. < *thunnus* tunny]

tun·dra (tun′drə, tōōn′-) *n.* A rolling, treeless, often marshy plain of Siberia, arctic North America, etc. [Russ.]

tune (t^yōōn) *n.* 1 A coherent succession of musical tones; a melody or air. 2 Correct musical pitch or key. 3 Fine adjustment: the *tune* of an engine. 4 State of mind; humor: He will change his *tune.* 5 Concord; agreement: to be out of *tune* with the times. **—sing a difficult tune** To assume a different style or attitude. **—to the tune of** *Informal* To the amount of: *to the tune of* ten dollars. *—v.* **tuned, tun·ing** *v.t.* 1 To put into tune; adjust precisely. 2 To adapt to a particular tone, expression, or mood. 3 To bring into harmony or accord. *—v.i.* 4 To be in harmony. **—tune in** 1 To adjust a radio or television receiver to (a station, program, etc.). 2 *Slang* To become or cause to become aware, knowing, or sophisticated. **—tune out** 1 To adjust a radio or television receiver to exclude (interference, a station, etc.). 2 *Slang* To turn one's interest or attention away from. **—tune up** 1 To bring (musical instruments) to a common pitch. 2 To adjust (a machine, engine, etc.) to proper working order. [< ME *tone* tone] **—tun′er** *n.*

tune·ful (t^yōōn′fəl) *adj.* Melodious; musical. **—tune′ful·ly** *adv.* **—tune′ful·ness** *n.*

tune·less (t^yōōn′lis) *adj.* 1 Not being in tune. 2 Lacking in melody. **—tune′less·ly** *adv.* **—tune′less·ness** *n.*

tune-up (t^yōōn′up′) *n.* A precise adjustment of an engine or other device.

tung oil (tung) A fast-drying oil extracted from the seeds of the subtropical **tung tree,** used in paints, varnishes, etc. [Chin. *t'ung* the tung tree]

tung·sten (tung′stən) *n.* A hard, heavy metallic element (symbol W), having a high melting point, used to make filaments for electric lamps and various alloys. [Sw. < *tung* weighty + *sten* stone]

tu·nic (t^yōō′nik) *n.* 1 Among the ancient Greeks and Romans, a loose body garment, with or without sleeves, reaching to the knees. 2 A modern outer garment gathered at the waist, as a short overskirt or a blouse. 3 A short coat worn as part of a uniform. 4 *Biol.* A mantle of tissue covering an organism or a part: also **tu′ni·ca** (-kə) [< L *tunica*]

tuning fork A fork-shaped piece of steel that produces a fixed tone when struck.

Tu·ni·sia (t^yōō·nē′zhə, -nish′ə, -nish′ē·ə) *n.* A republic of N Africa, 48,195 sq. mi., cap. Tunis. **—Tu·ni′sian** *adj., n.* • See map at AFRICA.

tun·nage (tun′ij) *n. Brit.* TONNAGE.

tun·nel (tun′əl) *n.* 1 An underground passageway or gallery, as for a railway or roadway. 2 Any similar passageway under or through something. 3 A burrow. *—v.* **·neled** or **·nelled, ·nel·ing** or **·nel·ling** *v.t.* 1 To make a tunnel or similar passage through or under. 2 To proceed by digging or as if by digging a tunnel. *—v.i.* 3 To make a tunnel. [< OF *tonne* a cask] **—tun′nel·er** or **tun′nel·ler** *n.*

tun·ny (tun′ē) *n. pl.* **·nies** or **·ny** TUNA. [< Gk. *thynnos*]

tup (tup) *n.* A ram, or male sheep. *—v.t. & v.i.* **tupped, tup·ping** To copulate with (a ewe). [Prob. < Scand.]

tu·pe·lo (t^yōō′pə·lō) *n. pl.* **·los** Any of several North American gum trees having smooth, oval leaves and brilliant red autumn foliage. [< Muskhogean]

Tu·pi (tōō′pē′, tōō′pē′) *n. pl.* **Tu·pis** or **Tu·pi** 1 A member of any of a group of South American Indian tribes comprising the N branch of the Tupian stock. 2 The language spoken by the Tupis: also **Tu·pi′-Gua·ra·ni′** (-gwä·rä·nē′).

Tu·pi·an (tōō·pē′ən) *adj.* Of or pertaining to the Tupis or their language. *—n.* A large linguistic stock of South American Indians.

tup·pence (tup′əns) *n.* TWOPENCE.

tuque (t^yōōk) *n. Can.* A knitted stocking cap. [F (Canadian) < F *toque* < Sp. *toca*]

tur·ban (tûr′bən) *n.* 1 A head covering consisting of a sash or shawl, twisted about the head or about a cap, worn by men in the Orient. 2 Any similar headdress. [< Pers. *dulband* < *dul* a turn + *band* a band] **—tur′baned** (-bənd) *adj.*

tur·bid (tûr′bid) *adj..* 1 Muddy or opaque: a *turbid* stream. 2 Dense; heavy: *turbid* clouds of smoke. 3 Confused; disturbed. [< L *turbidus* < *turbare* to trouble] **—tur′bid·ly** *adv.* **—tur′bid·ness, tur·bid·i·ty** (tûr·bid′ə·tē) *n.* • **turbid, turgid** Because these words sound alike, they are often confused: *Turbid* usu. refers to water, smoke, etc., so filled with sediment or particles as to be opaque. *Turgid* means abnormally swollen or inflated.

tur·bine (tûr′bin, -bīn) *n.* An engine consisting of one or more rotary units, mounted on a shaft and provided with a series of vanes, actuated by steam, water, gas, or other fluid under pressure. [< L *turbo* a whirlwind, top]

turbo- *combining form* Pertaining to, consisting of, or driven by a turbine: *turbojet.* [< L *turbo* a top]

tur·bo·fan (tûr′bō·fan′) *n. Aeron.* A jet engine with turbine-driven fans that augment its thrust.

tur·bo·jet (tûr′bō·jet′) *n. Aeron.* A jet engine that uses a gas turbine to drive the air compressor.

tur·bo·prop (tûr′bō·prop′) *n. Aeron.* A jet engine in which part of the thrust is produced by a turbine-driven propeller.

tur·bot (tûr′bət) *n. pl.* **·bot** or **·bots** 1 A large, edible European flatfish. 2 Any of various flatfishes, as the flounder, halibut, etc. [< OF *tourbout*]

tur·bu·lent (tûr′byə·lənt) *adj.* 1 Violently disturbed or agitated: a *turbulent* sea. 2 Inclined to rebel; insubordinate. 3 Having a tendency to disturb. [< L *turbulentus* full of disturbance] **—tur′bu·lence, tur′bu·len·cy** *n.* **—tur′bu·lent·ly** *adv.* **—Syn. 1** stormy, tumultuous, wild. **2** obstreperous, unruly.

tu·reen (t^yōō·rēn′) *n.* A large, deep, covered dish, as for soup. [< F *terrine*]

turf (tûrf) *n. pl.* **turfs** (*Archaic* **turves**) 1 A mass of grass and its matted roots. 2 A plot of grass. 3 Peat. 4 *Slang* **a** A home territory, esp. that of a youthful street gang, defended against invasion by rival gangs. **b** Any place regarded possessively as the center of one's activity or interest: Philadelphia is his home *turf.* **—the turf** 1 A racecourse. 2 Horse racing. *—v.t.* To cover with turf; sod. [< OE]

turf·man (tûrf′mən) *n. pl.* **·men** (-mən) A man who is connected with horseracing.

tur·ges·cent (tur·jes′ənt) *adj.* Being or becoming swollen or inflated. [< L *turgere* swell] **—tur·ges′cence, tur·ges′cen·cy** *n.* **—tur·ges′cent·ly** *adv.*

tur·gid (tûr′jid) *adj.* 1 Unnaturally distended; swollen. 2 Using high-flown laguage; bombastic: *turgid* prose. [< L *turgere* swell] **—tur·gid·i·ty** (tər·jid′ə·tē), **tur′gid·ness** *n.* **—tur′gid·ly** *adv.* • See TURBID.

Turk (tûrk) *n.* A citizen or native of Turkey.

Turk. Turkey; Turkish.

tur·key (tûr′kē) *n. pl.* **·keys 1** A large North American bird related to the pheasant, having the head naked and a spreading tail. **2** The edible flesh of this bird. **3** *Slang* A play or a motion picture that fails. [From mistaken identification with a guinea fowl originating in *Turkey*]

Turkey

Tur·key (tûr′kē) *n.* A republic of s Eurasia, 296,108 sq. mi., cap. Ankara.

turkey buzzard A black vulture of temperate and tropical America with a naked red head and neck. Also **turkey vulture.**

Turk·ic (tûr′kik) *n.* A subfamily of the Altaic family of languages. *—adj.* Pertaining to this linguistic subfamily, or to any of the peoples speaking its languages.

Turk·ish (tûr′kish) *n.* The language of Turkey. *—adj.* Of or pertaining to Turkey, its people, or their language.

Turkish bath A bath in which sweating is induced by exposure to high temperature, usu. in a room heated by steam.

Turkish Empire OTTOMAN EMPIRE.

Turkish towel A heavy, rough towel with loose, uncut pile. Also **turkish towel.**

tur·mer·ic (tûr′mər·ik, tyōō′mə·rik) *n.* **1** The orange-red, aromatic root of an East Indian plant; used as a condiment, dyestuff, etc. **2** The plant. **3** Any of several plants resembling turmeric. [? < F *terre mérite* deserving earth]

tur·moil (tûr′moil) *n.* Confused motion; disturbance; tumult. [?]

turn (tûrn) *v.t.* **1** To cause to rotate, as about an axis. **2** To change the position of, as by rotating: to *turn* a trunk on its side. **3** To move so that the upper side becomes the under: to *turn* a page. **4** To reverse the arrangement or order of; cause to be upside down. **5** To ponder: often with *over.* **6** To sprain or strain: to *turn* one's ankle in running. **7** To make sick or disgusted: The sight *turns* my stomach. **8** To shape in a lathe. **9** To give rounded or curved form to. **10** To give graceful or finished form to: to *turn* a phrase. **11** To perform by revolving: to *turn* cartwheels. **12** To bend, curve, fold, or twist. **13** To bend or blunt (the edge of a knife, etc.). **14** To change or transform: to *turn* water into wine. **15** To translate: to *turn* French into English. **16** To exchange for an equivalent: to *turn* stocks into cash. **17** To cause to become as specified: The sight *turned* him sick. **18** To make sour or rancid; ferment or curdle. **19** To change the direction of. **20** To change the direction or focus of (thought, attention, etc.). **21** To deflect or divert: to *turn* a blow. **22** To repel: to *turn* a charge. **23** To go around: to *turn* a corner. **24** To pass or go beyond: to *turn* twenty-one. **25** To compel to go; drive: to *turn* a beggar from one's door. *—v.i.* **26** To rotate; revolve. **27** To move completely or partially on or as if on an axis: He *turned* and ran. **28** To change position, as in bed. **29** To take a new direction: We *turned* north. **30** To reverse position; become inverted. **31** To reverse direction or flow: The tide has *turned.* **32** To change the direction of one's thought, attention, etc.: Let us *turn* to the next problem. **33** To depend; hinge: with *on* or *upon.* **34** To be affected with giddiness; whirl, as the head. **35** To become upset, as the stomach. **36** To change attitude, sympathy, or allegiance: to *turn* on one's neighbors. **37** To become transformed; change: The water *turned* into ice. **38** To become as specified: His hair *turned* gray. **39** To change color: said esp. of leaves. **40** To become sour or fermented, as milk or wine. **—turn against** To become or cause to become opposed or hostile to. **—turn down 1** To diminish the flow, volume, etc., of: *Turn down* the gas. **2** *Informal.* **a** To reject or refuse, as a proposal, or request. **b** To refuse the request, proposal, etc., of. **—turn in 1** To fold or double. **2** To bend or incline inward. **3** To deliver; hand over. **4** *Informal* To go to bed. **—turn off 1** To stop the operation, flow, etc., of. **2** To leave the direct road; make a turn. **3** To deflect or divert. **4** *Slang* To cause (a person) to lose interest in or liking for. **—turn on 1** To set in operation, flow, etc.: to *turn on* an engine. **2** *Slang* To experience the effects of taking a psychedelic drug. **3** *Slang* To arrange for (someone) to take such a drug. **4** *Slang* To evoke in (someone) a profound or rapt response. **—turn out 1** To turn inside out. **2** To eject or expel. **3** To bend or incline outward. **4** To produce or make. **5** To come or go out: to *turn out* for a meeting. **6** To prove (to be). **7** To equip or fit; dress. **8** *Informal* To get out of bed. **—turn over 1** To change the position of. **2** To upset; overturn. **3** To hand over; transfer. **4** To do business to the amount of. **5** To invest and get back (capital). **—turn to 1** To set to work. **2** To seek aid from. **3** To refer or apply to. **—turn up 1** To fold the under side upward. **2** To incline upward. **3** To find or be found: to *turn up* new evidence. **4** To increase the flow, volume, etc., of. **5** To arrive. *—n.* **1** The act of turning, or the state of being turned. **2** A change to another direction or position: a *turn* of the tide. **3** A deflection from a course; a bend. **4** The point at which a change takes place: a *turn* for the better. **5** A rotation or revolution: the *turn* of a crank. **6** A regular time or chance in some sequence of action: It's his *turn* at bat. **7** Characteristic form or style. **8** Disposition; tendency: a humorous *turn.* **9** A deed: an ill *turn.* **10** A walk or drive: a *turn* in the park. **11** A round in a skein or coil. **12** *Music* An ornament in which the main tone alternates with the seconds above and below. **13** *Informal* A spell of dizziness or nervousness: The explosion gave me quite a *turn.* **14** A variation or difference in type or kind. **15** A short theatrical act. **16** A twist, as of a rope, around a tree or post. **17** A business transaction. **—at every turn** On every occasion; constantly. **—by turns 1** In alternation or sequence: also **turn by turn. 2** At intervals. **—in turn** One after another. **—out of turn** Not in proper order or sequence. **—to a turn** Just right: meat browned *to a turn.* **—take turns** To act, play, etc. in proper order. [< L *tornare* turn in a lathe < *turnus* a lathe] **—turn′er** *n.*

turn·a·bout (tûrn′ə·bout′) *n.* **1** The act of turning about so as to face the opposite direction. **2** An about-face in allegiance, opinion, etc.

turn·a·round (tûrn′ə·round′) *n.* **1** The time required for maintenance, refueling, discharging or loading cargo, etc., during a round trip of a ship, aircraft, etc. **2** A space, as in a driveway, large enough for the turning around of a vehicle. **3** A shift or reversal of a trend, procedure, development, etc.

turn·buck·le (tûrn′buk′əl) *n. Mech.* A threaded coupling that receives a threaded rod at each end so that it may be turned to regulate the distance between them.

turn·coat (tûrn′kōt′) *n.* One who goes over to the opposite side or party; a renegade.

turn·down (tûrn′doun′) *adj.* Folded down or able to be folded down, as a collar. *—n.* **1** A rejection. **2** A decline: a *turndown* in prices.

turn·ing (tûr′ning) *n.* **1** The art of shaping wood, metal, etc., in a lathe. **2** *pl.* Spiral shavings produced by turning wood or metal on a lathe. **3** A winding; bend.

turning point The point of decisive change, as in progress, decline, etc.

tur·nip (tûr′nip) *n.* **1** The fleshy, yellow or white edible root of certain plants related to cabbage. **2** Any of these plants. [< Earlier *turnepe*]

turn·key (tûrn′kē′) *n.* One who has charge of the keys of a prison; a jailer. *—adj.* Of, pertaining to, or being, by prearrangement with a buyer, a product or service in complete readiness for use when purchased: a *turnkey* housing project.

turn·out (tûrn′out′) *n.* **1** A turning out. **2** An assemblage of persons, as at a meeting: a good *turnout.* **3** A quantity produced; output. **4** Array; equipment; outfit. **5** A railroad siding. **6** A carriage or wagon with its horses and equipage.

turn·o·ver (tûrn′ō′vər) *n.* **1** An upset. **2** A change or revolution: a *turnover* in affairs. **3** A tart made by covering half of a circular crust with fruit, jelly, etc., and turning the other half over on top. **4** The amount of money taken in and paid out in a business within a given period. **5** The selling out and restocking of goods, as in a store. **6** The rate at which persons hired within a given period are replaced by others; also, the number of persons hired. —*adj.* Turning over, or capable of being turned over.

turn·pike (tûrn′pīk′) *n.* **1** A road on which there are, or formerly were, tollgates: also **turnpike road.** **2** TOLLGATE. [ME *turnpyke* a spiked road barrier < TURN, *v.* + PIKE[1]]

turn·stile (tûrn′stīl′) *n.* A kind of gate consisting of a vertical post and horizontal arms which by revolving permit persons to pass.

turn·stone (tûrn′stōn′) *n.* A ploverlike migratory bird that turns over stones when searching for food.

turn·ta·ble (tûrn′tā′bəl) *n.* **1** A rotating platform, usu. circular, on which to turn a locomotive or other vehicle around. **2** The revolving disk of a phonograph on which records are played.

tur·pen·tine (tûr′pən·tīn) *n.* **1** A resinous, oily liquid obtained from any of several coniferous trees. **2** The colorless essential oil **(oil of turpentine)** formed when turpentine is distilled, widely used in industry, medicine, and in mixing paints. —*v.t.* **·tined, ·tin·ing** To treat or saturate with turpentine. [< L *terebinthus* a Mediterranean tree]

tur·pi·tude (tûr′pə·tyo͞od) *n.* Inherent baseness; depravity. [< L *turpis* vile] —**Syn.** corruption, degeneracy, vileness, wickedness.

tur·quoise (tûr′koiz, -kwoiz) *n.* **1** A blue or blue-green stone, esteemed as a gemstone when highly polished. **2** A light, greenish blue: also **turquoise blue.** —*adj.* Light, greenish blue. [< MF *(pierre) turquoise* Turkish (stone)]

tur·ret (tûr′it) *n.* **1** A small projecting tower, usu. at the corner of a building. **2** *Mil.* A rotating armed structure containing guns and gunners, forming part of a warship or tank. **3** A structure for a gunner on a combat airplane, usu. enclosed in transparent plastic material. [< OF *tor* tower] —**tur′ret·ed** *adj.*

tur·tle (tûr′təl) *n.* **1** Any of numerous four-limbed, terrestrial or aquatic reptiles having a toothless beak and a soft body encased in a shell. **2** The edible flesh of certain turtles. —**turn turtle** To overturn; capsize. [?< Sp. *tortuga* < Med. L *tortuca* tortoise] • See SNAPPING TURTLE.

Turtle

tur·tle·dove (tûr′təl·duv′) *n.* **1** A dove noted for its plaintive cooing. **2** The mourning dove. [< L *turtur* turtledove]

tur·tle·neck (tûr′təl·nek′) *n.* **1** A pullover sweater or knitted shirt with a high, close-fitting, turnover collar. **2** Such a collar.

tusk (tusk) *n.* A long, projecting tooth, as in the boar, walrus, or elephant. —*v.t.* To use the tusks to gore, root up, etc. [< OE *tūx*]

tus·sah (tus′ə) *n.* **1** An Asian silkworm that spins large cocoons of brownish or yellowish silk. **2** The silk, or the fabric woven from it. [< Skt. *tasara* a shuttle]

tus·sle (tus′əl) *v.t. & v.i.* **·sled, ·sling** **1** To scuffle or struggle. **2** To argue. —*n.* **1** A scuffle or struggle. **2** An argument. [Var. of TOUSLE]

tus·sock (tus′ək) *n.* **1** A tuft or clump of grass or sedge. **2** A tuft, as of hair or feathers. [?] —**tus′sock·y** *adj.*

tut (tut) *interj.* An exclamation to express impatience.

tu·te·lage (tyo͞o′tə·lij) *n.* **1** The state of being under the care of a tutor or guardian. **2** The act or office of a guardian. **3** The act of tutoring; instruction. [< L *tutela* a watching, guardianship]

tu·te·lar·y (tyo͞o′tə·ler′ē) *adj.* **1** Watching over; protecting. **2** Of or pertaining to a guardian. Also **tu′te·lar.** —*n.* *pl.* **·ar·ies** A guardian spirit, divinity, etc.

tu·tor (tyo͞o′tər) *n.* **1** A private teacher. **2** A college teacher who gives individual instruction. **3** *Brit.* A college official entrusted with the tutelage and care of undergraduates assigned to him. —*v.t.* **1** To act as tutor to; train. **2** To treat sternly; discipline. —*v.i.* **3** To do the work of a tutor. **4** To be tutored or instructed. [< L, a watcher, guardian]

tu·to·ri·al (tyo͞o·tôr′ē·əl) *adj.* Of or involving tutors, or based upon their participation: the *tutorial* system. —*n.* A small class of students guided by a tutor.

tut·ti (to͞o′tē) *Music adj.* All: used to indicate that all performers take part. —*n.* A passage or section to be performed by all the voices and instruments together. [< Ital. *tutto* all]

tut·ti-frut·ti (to͞o′tē·fro͞o′tē) *n.* A confection, chewing gum, ice cream, etc., made or flavored with mixed fruits. —*adj.* Flavored with mixed fruits. [Ital., all fruits]

tu·tu (to͞o′to͞o; *Fr.* tü′tü) *n.* A short, projecting, layered skirt worn by ballet dancers. [F]

tux·e·do (tuk·sē′dō) *n. pl.* **·dos** **1** A man's semiformal dinner or evening jacket without tails. **2** The suit of which the jacket is a part. Also **Tux·e′do.** [< *Tuxedo* Park, N.Y.]

TV (tē′vē′) *n.* TELEVISION.

TV terminal velocity.

TVA, T.V.A. Tennessee Valley Authority.

TV dinner A frozen meal in a partitioned tray, ready to be heated and served.

twad·dle (twod′l) *v.t. & v.i.* **·dled, ·dling** To talk foolishly and pretentiously. —*n.* Pretentious, silly talk. [?] —**twad′·dler** *n.*

twain (twān) *adj. & n. Archaic* Two. [< OE *twēgen* two]

twang (twang) *v.t. & v.i.* **twanged, twang·ing** **1** To make or cause to make a sharp, vibrant sound. **2** To utter or speak with a harsh, nasal sound. —*n.* **1** A sharp, vibrating sound. **2** A sharp, nasal sound of the voice. **3** A sound resembling these. [Imit.] —**twang′y** *adj.* **(·i·er, ·i·est)**

tweak (twēk) *v.t.* To pinch and twist sharply. —*n.* A twisting pinch. [< OE *twiccan* twitch]

tweed (twēd) *n.* **1** A woolen fabric often woven in two or more colors to effect a check or plaid pattern. **2** *pl.* Clothes made of tweed. [< Scot. *tweel,* var. of TWILL]

twee·dle (twēd′l) *v.* **·dled, ·dling** *v.t.* **1** To play (a musical instrument) casually or carelessly. —*v.i.* **2** To produce a series of shrill tones. **3** To play a musical instrument casually or carelessly. —*n.* A sound so produced. [Imit. of the sound of a reed pipe]

tweet (twēt) *v.i.* To utter a thin, chirping note. —*n.* A twittering or chirping. [Imit.]

tweet·er (twē′tər) *n.* A loudspeaker specially designed to reproduce only high-frequency sounds.

tweeze (twēz) *v.t.* **tweezed, tweez·ing** *Informal* To handle, pinch, pluck, etc., with tweezers.

tweez·ers (twē′zərz) *n.pl. (construed as sing. or pl.)* Small pincers for picking up or extracting tiny objects. Also **pair of tweezers.** [< F *étui* a small case]

twelfth (twelfth) *adj. & adv.* Next in order after the 11th. —*n.* **1** The element of an ordered set that corresponds to the number 12. **2** One of 12 equal parts. [< OE *twelfta*]

Twelfth Day The twelfth day after Christmas; Epiphany.

twelve (twelv) *n.* **1** The sum of eleven plus one; 12; XII. **2** A set or group of 12 members. —**the Twelve** The twelve apostles. [< OE *twelf*] —**twelve** *adj., pron.*

Twelve Apostles The twelve original disciples of Jesus.

twelve·month (twelv′munth′) *n.* A year.

twelve-tone (twelv′tōn′) *adj. Music* Of, pertaining to, or composed in a system in which any series of all twelve tones of the chromatic scale is used as the basis of composition.

twen·ti·eth (twen′tē·ith) *adj. & adv.* Tenth in order after the tenth. —*n.* **1** The element of an ordered set that corresponds to the number 20. **2** One of 20 equal parts.

twen·ty (twen′tē) *n. pl.* **·ties** **1** The sum of 19 plus 1; 20; XX. **2** A set or group of 20 members. **3** The numbers, years, etc., from 20 to 30. [< OE *twentig*] —**twen′ty** *adj., pron.*

twen·ty-one (twen′tē·wun′) *n.* BLACKJACK (def. 3).

twice (twīs) *adv.* **1** Two times. **2** In double measure; doubly. [< OE *twiga*]

twid·dle (twid′l) *v.* **·dled, ·dling** *v.t.* **1** To twirl idly; play with. —*v.i.* **2** To toy with something idly. **3** To be busy about trifles. —**twiddle one's thumbs** **1** To rotate one's thumbs around each other. **2** To do nothing; be idle. —*n.* A gentle twirling. [Prob. < ON *tridla* stir] —**twid′dler** *n.*

twig (twig) *n.* A small shoot or branch of a woody plant. [< OE *twigge*]

twi·light (twī′līt′) *n.* **1** The light diffused over the sky after sunset and before sunrise. **2** The period during which this light prevails. **3** Any faint light; shade. **4** An obscure condition following the waning of past glory, achievements, etc. —*adj.* Pertaining or peculiar to twilight. [< OE < *twa* two + LIGHT]

twilight sleep A light anesthesia induced by morphine and scopolamine, formerly used in childbirth.

twill (twil) *n.* **1** Cloth woven in such a way as to produce diagonal, parallel ribs or lines. **2** The pattern formed by such weaving. —*v.t.* To weave (cloth) with a twill. [< OE *twili* a twilled fabric]

Twill

twin (twin) *n.* **1** Either of two young produced at the same birth. **2** Either of two persons or things greatly alike. —**the Twins** GEMINI. —*adj.* **1** Being a twin or twins: *twin* boys. **2** Being one of a pair of similar and closely related people or things. —*v.* **twinned, twin·ning** *v.i.* **1** To bring forth twins. **2** To be matched or equal. —*v.t.* **3** To bring forth as twins. **4** To couple; match. [< OE *twinn, getwinn*]

twine (twīn) *v.* **twined, twin·ing** *v.t.* **1** To twist together, as threads. **2** To form by such twisting. **3** To coil or wrap about something. **4** To encircle by winding or wreathing. —*v.i.* **5** To interlace. **6** To proceed in a winding course; meander. —*n.* **1** A string composed of two or more strands twisted together. **2** The act of twining or entwining. **3** A thing produced by twining. [< OE *twīn* a twisted double thread < *twa* two] —**twin′er** *n.* —**twin′ing·ly** *adv.*

twinge (twinj) *v.t.* & *v.i.* **twinged, twing·ing** To affect with or suffer a sudden pain. —*n.* **1** A sharp, darting, local pain. **2** A mental pang. [< OE *twengan* pinch] —**Syn.** *n.* **1** ache, cramp, throe.

twin·kle (twing′kəl) *v.* **·kled, ·kling** *v.i.* **1** To shine with fitful, intermittent gleams. **2** To be bright, as with amusement: Her eyes *twinkled.* **3** To wink or blink. **4** To move rapidly to and fro; flicker: *twinkling* feet. —*v.t.* **5** To cause to twinkle. **6** To emit (light) in fitful, intermittent gleams. —*n.* **1** A tremulous gleam of light; glimmer. **2** A quick or repeated movement of the eyelids. **3** An instant; a twinkling. [< OE *twinclian*] —**twin′kler** *n.*

twin·kling (twing′kling) *n.* **1** The act of something that twinkles. **2** A wink or twinkle. **3** An instant; moment. —**twink′ling·ly** *adv.*

twirl (twûrl) *v.t.* & *v.i.* **1** To whirl or rotate rapidly. **2** To twist or curl. **3** In baseball, to pitch. —*n.* **1** A whirling motion. **2** A curl; twist; coil. [?] —**twirl′er** *n.*

twist (twist) *v.t.* **1** To wind (strands, etc.) around each other. **2** To form by such winding: to *twist* thread. **3** To give a spiral shape to. **4** To deform or distort, esp. by means of torque. **5** To distort the meaning of. **6** To confuse; perplex. **7** To wreathe, twine, or wrap. **8** To cause to revolve or rotate. **9** To impart spin to (a ball) so that it moves in a curve. —*v.i.* **10** To become twisted. **11** To move in a winding course. **12** To squirm; writhe. —*n.* **1** The act, manner, or result of twisting. **2** The state of being twisted. **3** *Physics* A torsional strain. **4** A curve; turn; bend. **5** A wrench; strain, as of a joint or limb. **6** A peculiar inclination or attitude: a mind with a criminal *twist.* **7** An unexpected turn or development. **8** A variant or novel approach or method: a mystery novel with a new *twist.* **9** Thread or cord made of tightly twisted or braided strands. **10** A twisted roll of bread. **11** A spin given to a ball by a certain stroke or throw. [< OE *-twist* a rope]

twist·er (twis′tər) *n.* **1** One who or that which twists. **2** In baseball, a curve. **3** A tornado; cyclone.

twit (twit) *v.t.* **twit·ted, twit·ting** To taunt. —*n.* A taunting allusion; reproach. [< OE *ætwitan*] —**twit′ter** *n.* —**Syn.** *v.* gibe, jeer, scoff, tease.

twitch (twich) *v.t.* **1** To pull sharply; pluck with a jerky movement. —*v.i.* **2** To move with a quick, spasmodic jerk, as a muscle. —*n.* **1** A sudden involuntary contraction of a muscle. **2** A sudden jerk or pull. [ME *twicchen*]

twit·ter (twit′ər) *v.i.* **1** To utter a series of light chirping or tremulous notes, as a bird. **2** To titter. **3** To be excited. —*v.t.* **4** To utter or express with a twitter. —*n.* **1** A succession of light, tremulous sounds. **2** A state of excitement. [Imit.]

′twixt (twikst) *prep.* Betwixt.

two (to͞o) *n.* **1** The sum of one plus one; 2; II. **2** A set or group of two members. —**in two** Bisected; asunder —**put two and two together** To draw an obvious conclusion by considering the facts. [< OE *twā, tū*] —**two** *adj., pron.*

two-base hit (to͞o′bās′) In baseball, a hit in which the batter reaches second base without benefit of an error. Also **two′-bag′ger** (-bag′ər).

two-bit (to͞o′bit′) *adj. Slang* Cheap; small-time: a *two-bit* gambler.

two bits *Informal* Twenty-five cents.

two-by-four (to͞o′bī·fôr′, -fōr′) *adj.* **1** Measuring two inches by four inches. **2** *Slang* Narrow or cramped: a *two-by-four* kitchen. —*n.* (to͞o′bī·fôr′, -fōr′) A timber measuring two inches in thickness and four inches in width before finishing.

two-edged (to͞o′ejd′) *adj.* **1** Having an edge on each side; cutting both ways. **2** Having a double meaning.

two-faced (to͞o′fāst′) *adj.* **1** Having two faces. **2** Double-dealing; insincere. —**two′-fac′ed·ly** (-fā′sid·lē, -fāst′lē) *adv.* —**two′fac′ed·ness** *n.*

two·fer (to͞o′fər) *n.* **1** An article sold at two for the price of one. **2** A free coupon entitling the holder to buy two theater tickets for the price of one.

two·fold (to͞o′fōld′) *adj.* Double. —*adv.* In a twofold manner or degree; doubly.

two-hand·ed (to͞o′han′did) *adj.* **1** Requiring the use of both hands at once. **2** Constructed for use by two persons: a *two-handed* saw. **3** Ambidextrous. **4** Having two hands. **5** Played by two people: a *two-handed* card game.

two·pence (tup′əns) *n. Brit.* **1** Two pennies. **2** A silver coin of the same value, now issued only for alms money on Maundy Thursday. **3** A trifle; small amount.

two·pen·ny (tup′ən·ē) *adj. Brit.* **1** Of the value of twopence. **2** Cheap; worthless.

two-ply (to͞o′plī′) *adj.* **1** Woven double: a *two-ply* carpet. **2** Made of two strands or thicknesses of material.

two·some (to͞o′səm) *n.* **1** Two persons together. **2** A game played by two persons. **3** The players.

two-step (to͞o′step′) *n.* **1** A ballroom dance step in 2/4 time. **2** The music for it. —*v.i.* To do the two-step.

two-time (to͞o′tīm′) *v.t.* **-timed, -tim·ing** *Slang* **1** To be unfaithful to. **2** DOUBLE-CROSS. —**two′-tim′er** *n.*

two-way (to͞o′wā′) *adj.* **1** Permitting vehicles to go in opposite directions simultaneously: a *two-way* street. **2** Involving mutual or reciprocal exchanges, duties, obligations, etc.: a *two-way* agreement. **3** Involving two persons, groups, etc.: a *two-way* contest. **4** Capable of both sending and receiving communications: a *two-way* radio. **5** Made or fashioned so as to be used or worn in two ways: a *two-way* jacket.

twp. township.

TX Texas (P.O. abbr.).

-ty[1] *suffix of nouns* The state or condition of being: *sanity.* [< L *-tas*]

-ty[2] *suffix* Ten; ten times: used in numerals, as *thirty, forty,* etc. [< OE *-tig* ten]

Ty. Territory.

ty·coon (tī·ko͞on′) *n.* **1** *Informal* A wealthy and powerful business leader. **2** A Japanese shogun. [< Japanese *taikun* a mighty lord]

ty·ing (tī′ing) *pr.p.* of TIE.

tyke (tīk) *n.* **1** A mongrel dog. **2** *Informal* A small mischievous child. [< ON *tik* bitch]

tym·pa·ni (tim′pə·nē) *n.pl.* TIMPANI.

tympanic membrane The membrane separating the middle ear from the external ear; the eardrum.

tym·pa·nist (tim′pə·nist) *n.* One who plays the timpani.

tym·pa·num (tim′pə·nəm) *n. pl.* **·na** (-nə) or **·nums** **1** *Anat.* **a** The cavity of the middle ear lined with the tympanic membrane. **b** TYMPANIC MEMBRANE. **2** A drum. **3** *Archit.* **a** A recessed, usu. triangular, space bounded by the sides of a pediment or gable at the end of a building. **b** A similar space over a door or window, between the lintel and the arch. [< Gk. *tympanon* a drum] —**tym·pan·ic** (tim·pan′ik) *adj.*

typ., typo., typog. typographer; typographic; typography.

type (tīp) *n.* **1** A class or group having traits and characteristics in common: an old *type* of car. **2** A standard or model. **3** The characteristic plan, form, style, etc., of a given class or group. **4** A person, animal, or object embodying the characteristics of a class or group. **5** *Printing* **a** A piece or block of metal or of wood bearing, usu. in relief, a letter or character for use in printing. **b** Such pieces collectively. **6** Typewritten or printed letters and numerals. **7** The characteristic device on either side of a medal or coin. —*v.* **typed, typ·ing** *v.t.* **1** To represent; typify. **2** To determine the type of; identify: to *type* a blood sample. **3** TYPEWRITE. **4** To prefigure. —*v.i.* **5** TYPEWRITE. [< Gk. *typos* an impression, figure, type]

-type *combining form* **1** Representative form; stamp; type: *prototype.* **2** Used in or produced by duplicating processes or by type: *Linotype.* [< Gk. *typos* stamp]

type·face (tīp′fās′) *n.* **1** A set of type of a particular design. **2** The face or impression of a type.

type·set·ter (tīp′set′ər) *n.* **1** One who sets type. **2** A machine for setting type. **—type′set′ting** *adj., n.*

type·write (tīp′rīt′) *v.t. & v.i.* **·wrote, ·writ·ten, ·writ·ing** To write with a typewriter.

type·writ·er (tīp′rī′tər) *n.* **1** A keyboard machine for producing characters, as letters, numbers, etc., that have the appearance of printer's type. **2** A typist.

ty·phoid (tī′foid) *adj.* **1** Pertaining to or resembling typhoid fever: also **ty·phoi′dal.** **2** Resembling typhus. —*n.* TYPHOID FEVER.

typhoid fever A serious infectious disease caused by a bacillus transmitted in contaminated water or food and characterized by high fever, severe intestinal disturbances, and prostration.

ty·phoon (tī·fo͞on′) *n.* A violent tropical storm, occurring in the w Pacific. [< Chin. *tai feng,* lit., big wind]

ty·phus (tī′fəs) *n.* Any of a group of contagious rickettsial diseases marked by high fever, a rash, nervous and mental disorders, and extreme prostration. [< Gk. *typhos* smoke, a stupor] **—ty′phous** *adj.*

typ·i·cal (tip′i·kəl) *adj.* **1** Having the nature or character of a type: a *typical* schoolboy. **2** Characteristic or representative of a group, class, etc.: *typical* middle-class values. [< Gk. *typos* TYPE] **—typ′i·cal·ly** *adv.* **—typ′i·cal·ness** *n.*

typ·i·fy (tip′ə·fī) *v.t.* **·fied, ·fy·ing** **1** To represent by a type. **2** To serve as a characteristic example of. **—typ′i·fi·ca′tion** (-fə·kā′shən), **typ′i·fi′er** *n.*

typ·ist (tī′pist) *n.* **1** One who uses a typewriter. **2** A person whose work is operating a typewriter.

ty·po (tī′pō) *n. pl.* **ty·pos** *Informal* An error made by a printer or a typist. [< *typo(graphical error)*]

ty·pog·ra·pher (tī·pog′rə·fər) *n.* An expert in typography, esp. a printer or compositor.

ty·po·graph·i·cal (tī′pə·graf′i·kəl) *adj.* Of or pertaining to printing. Also **ty′po·graph′ic.** **—ty′po·graph′i·cal·ly** *adv.*

ty·pog·ra·phy (tī·pog′rə·fē) *n.* **1** The arrangement, style, and appearance of printed matter. **2** The act or art of composing and printing from types.

typw. typewriter; typewritten.

ty·ran·ni·cal (ti·ran′i·kəl, tī-) *adj.* Of or like a tyrant; despotic; arbitrary. Also **ty·ran′nic.** **—ty·ran′ni·cal·ly** *adv.* **—ty·ran′ni·cal·ness** *n.*

ty·ran·ni·cide (ti·ran′ə·sīd, tī-) *n.* **1** The slayer of a tyrant. **2** The slaying of a tyrant.

tyr·an·nize (tir′ə·nīz) *v.* **·nized, ·niz·ing** *v.i.* **1** To exercise power cruelly or unjustly. **2** To rule as a tyrant; have absolute power. —*v.t.* **3** To treat tyrannically; domineer. **—tyr′an·niz′er** *n.*

tyr·an·nous (tir′ə·nəs) *adj.* Despotic; tyrannical. **—tyr′an·nous·ly** *adv.* **—tyr′an·nous·ness** *n.*

tyr·an·ny (tir′ə·nē) *n. pl.* **·nies** **1** The office, power, or jurisdiction of a tyrant. **2** A government or ruler having absolute power; despot or despotism. **3** Power used in a cruel or oppressive manner. **4** Harsh rigor; severity. **5** A tyrannical act. [< L *tyrannus* a tyrant]

ty·rant (tī′rənt) *n.* **1** One who rules oppressively or cruelly; a despot. **2** Any person who exercises power or authority in a harsh, cruel manner. [< Gk. *tyrannos* a master, a usurper]

tyre (tīr) *n. Brit. sp.* of TIRE[2].

Tyre (tīr) *n.* A port and capital of ancient Phoenicia, now in sw Lebanon.

ty·ro (tī′rō) *n. pl.* **·ros** One who is beginning to learn or study something; novice. [< L *tiro* a recruit]

tzar (tsär) *n.* CZAR.

tzet·ze (tset′sē) *n.* TSETSE.

tzi·gane (tsē·gän′) *n.* A Gypsy, esp. a Hungarian Gypsy. [F < Hung. *czigány*]

U

U, u (yo͞o) *n. pl.* **U's, u's, Us, us** (yo͞oz) **1** The twenty-first letter of the English alphabet. **2** Any spoken sound representing the letter *U* or *u.* **3** Something shaped like a U. —*adj.* Shaped like a U.

U uranium.

U., u. uncle; union; unit; university.

U.A.R. United Arab Republic.

UAW, U.A.W. United Automobile Workers; (officially) United Automobile, Aerospace, and Agricultural Implement Workers of America.

u·biq·ui·tous (yo͞o·bik′wə·təs) *adj.* Existing, or seeming to exist, everywhere at once; omnipresent. **—u·biq′ui·tous·ly** *adv.* **—u·biq′ui·tous·ness** *n.*

u·biq·ui·ty (yo͞o·bik′wə·tē) *n.* The state of being or seeming to be everywhere at the same time; omnipresence, real or seeming. [< L *ubique* everywhere]

U-boat (yo͞o′bōt′) *n.* A German submarine. [< G *U-boot,* contraction of *Unterseeboot,* lit., undersea boat]

u.c. upper case (printing).

ud·der (ud′ər) *n.* A large, pendulous, milk-secreting gland having nipples or teats for the suckling of offspring, as in cows. [< OE *ūder*]

UFO (yo͞o′ef·ō′) *n. pl.* **UFOs, UFO's** Any of various unidentified flying objects alleged to have been seen traveling at speeds and following courses that would be impossible for any aircraft to duplicate. [< *u(nidentified) f(lying) o(bject)*]

U·gan·da (yo͞o·gan′də, o͞o·gän′dä), *n.* An independent member of the Commonwealth of Nations in CEN. Africa, 93,981 sq. mi., cap. Kampala. • See map at AFRICA.

ugh (ug, ukh, u, o͝okh, o͝o) *interj.* An exclamation of repugnance or disgust. [Imit.]

ug·li·fy (ug′lə·fī′) *v.t.* **·fied, ·fy·ing** To make ugly. **—ug′li·fi·ca′tion** (-fə·kā′shən) *n.*

ug·ly (ug′lē) *adj.* **·li·er, ·li·est** **1** Distasteful in appearance; unsightly. **2** Distasteful to any of the senses. **3** Morally revolting or repulsive. **4** Bad in character or consequences, as a rumor or a wound. **5** Ill-tempered; quarrelsome. **6** Portending storms; threatening. [< ON *uggligr* dreadful < *uggr* fear] **—ug′li·ly** *adv.* **—ug′li·ness** *n.* **—Syn. 1** homely, ill-looking, unlovely, unseemly. **2** repulsive, repellent, repugnant, revolting, abhorrent, disgusting. **5** ill-humored, irascible, irritable, testy, querulous.

ugly duckling Any ill-favored or unpromising child who unexpectedly grows into a beauty or a wonder. [< *The Ugly Duckling,* a story by Hans Christian Andersen]

U·gri·an (o͞o′grē·ən, yo͞o′-) *n.* **1** A member of any of the Finno-Ugric peoples of Hungary and w Siberia. **2** UGRIC.

—*adj.* Of or pertaining to the Ugrians or their languages.

U·gric (ōō′grik, yōō′-) *n.* A branch of the Finno-Ugric subfamily of languages including Magyar (Hungarian). —*adj.* UGRIAN.

UHF, U.H.F., uhf, u.h.f. ultrahigh frequency.

uit·land·er (īt′lan·dər, oit′-; *Afrikaans* œit′län·dər) *n.* *Often cap.* A foreigner; outlander. [Afrikaans]

U.K. United Kingdom.

u·kase (yōō·kās′, -kāz′, yōō′kās, ōō·koz′) *n.* **1** In imperial Russia, an edict or decree of the czar. **2** Any official decree. [<Russ. *ukaz*]

U·krain·i·an (yōō·krā′nē·ən, -krī′-) *adj.* Of or pertaining to the Ukraine, its people, or their language. —*n.* **1** A native or inhabitant of the Ukraine. **2** An East Slavic language spoken in the Ukraine.

u·ku·le·le (yōō′kə·lā′lē; *Hawaiian* ōō′kōō·lā′lā) *n.* A small, guitarlike musical instrument having four strings. [Hawaiian <*uku* insect + *lele* jump; from the movements of the fingers in playing]

Ukulele

ul·cer (ul′sər) *n.* **1** An open sore on skin or mucous membrane with disintegration of tissue. **2** Any evil or corrupt condition or vice. [<L *ulcus, ulceris*] —**ul′cer·ous** *adj.* —**ul′cer·ous·ly** *adv.*

ul·cer·ate (ul′sə·rāt) *v.t.* & *v.i.* **·at·ed, ·at·ing** To make or become ulcerous. —**ul′cer·a′tion** *n.* —**ul′·cer·a′tive** *adj.*

-ule *suffix* Small; little: used to form diminutives: *granule.* [<L *-ulus*]

-ulent *suffix* Abounding in; full of (what is indicated in the main element): *opulent, truculent.* [<L *-ulentus*]

ul·na (ul′nə) *n. pl.* **·nae** (-nē) or **·nas** **1** The larger of the two bones of the forearm on the same side as the little finger. **2** The homologous bone in the foreleg of a quadruped. [<L, elbow] —**ul′nar** *adj.* • See HUMERUS.

ul·ster (ul′stər) *n.* A long, loose overcoat, sometimes belted at the waist, made originally of Irish frieze. [<*Ulster,* Ireland]

ult. ultimate; ultimately.

ul·te·ri·or (ul·tir′ē·ər) *adj.* **1** Not so pertinent as something else: *ulterior* considerations. **2** Intentionally unrevealed; hidden: *ulterior* motives. **3** Later in time, or secondary in importance; following; succeeding. **4** Lying beyond or on the farther side of a certain bounding line. [<L, compar. of *ulter* beyond] —**ul·te′ri·or·ly** *adv.*

ul·ti·ma (ul′tə·mə) *n.* The last syllable of a word. [<L, fem. of *ultimus* last]

ul·ti·mate (ul′tə·mit) *adj.* **1** Beyond which there is no other; maximum, greatest, utmost, etc. **2** Last; final, as of a series. **3** Most distant or remote; farthest. **4** Not susceptible of further analysis; elementary; primary. —*n.* The best, latest, most fundamental, etc., of something. [<L *ultimus* farthest, last, superl. of *ulter* beyond] —**ul′ti·mate·ness** *n.*

ul·ti·mate·ly (ul′tə·mit·lē) *adv.* In the end; at last; finally.

ul·ti·ma Thu·le (ul′tə·mə thōō′lē, tōō′lē) **1** In ancient geography, Thule, the northernmost habitable regions of the earth. **2** Any distant, unknown region. **3** The farthest possible point, degree, or limit.

ul·ti·ma·tum (ul′tə·mā′təm, -mä′-) *n. pl.* **·tums** or **·ta** (-tə) A final statement of terms, demands, or conditions, the rejection of which usu. results in a breaking off of all negotiations, a resorting to force, etc. [<L *ultimus* last, ultimate]

ul·ti·mo (ul′tə·mō) *adv.* In the month preceding the present month. [L]

ul·tra (ul′trə) *adj.* Going beyond the bounds of moderation; extreme. —*n.* One who holds extreme opinions. [<L, beyond, on the other side]

ultra- *prefix* **1** On the other side of; beyond in space: *ultramarine.* **2** Going beyond the limits or range of: *ultrasonic.* **3** Beyond what is usual or natural; extremely or excessively; *ultraconservative.*

ul·tra·high frequency (ul′trə·hī′) Any wave frequency between 300 and 3,000 megahertz.

ul·tra·ist (ul′trə·ist) *n.* One who goes to extremes in opinions, conduct, etc.; extremist. —*adj.* Radical; extreme: also **ul′tra·is′tic.** —**ul′tra·ism** *n.*

ul·tra·light (ul′trə·līt′) *adj.* Extremely light in weight. —*n.* An extremely lightweight airplane.

ul·tra·ma·rine (ul′trə·mə·rēn′) *n.* **1** A deep purplish blue pigment. **2** The color of ultramarine. —*adj.* Beyond or across the sea. [<L *ultra* beyond + *mare* sea]

ul·tra·mi·cro·scope (ul′trə·mī′krə·skōp′) *n.* A microscope in which objects too small to be seen by the transmitted light of an ordinary microscope are examined against a dark background by means of refracted light.

ul·tra·mi·cro·scop·ic (ul′trə·mī′krə·skop′ik) *adj.* **1** Too minute to be seen by an ordinary microscope. **2** Relating to the ultramicroscope. Also **ul′tra·mi′cro·scop′i·cal.**

ul·tra·mod·ern (ul′trə·mod′ərn) *adj.* Extremely modern, as in tastes, design, etc. —**ul′tra·mod′ern·ist** *n.*

ul·tra·son·ic (ul′trə·son′ik) *adj.* Pertaining to or designating sound waves having a frequency above the limits of audibility.

ul·tra·vi·o·let (ul′trə·vī′ə·lit) *adj.* Having wavelengths shorter than those of visible violet light and longer than those of X-rays.

ul·u·late (ul′yə·lāt′, yōōl′yə·lāt′) *v.i.* **·lat·ed, ·lat·ing** To howl, hoot, or wail. [<L *ululare*] —**ul′u·lant** *adj.*

U·lys·ses (yōō·lis′ēz) ODYSSEUS.

um·bel (um′bəl) *n.* A flower cluster having pedicels arising from a single point. [<L *umbella* a parasol, dim. of *umbra* shadow] —**um·bel·late** (um′bə·lit, -lāt), **um′bel·lat′ed** *adj.*

um·ber (um′bər) *n.* **1** A chestnut- to liver-brown iron oxide earth, used as a pigment. **2** The color of umber, either in its natural state (**raw umber**), or heated, so as to produce a reddish brown (**burnt umber**). —*adj.* **1** Of or pertaining to umber. **2** Of the color of umber. —*v.t.* To color with umber. [<F *(terre d′)ombre*<Ital. *ombra*<L *umbra* shade, shadow]

um·bil·i·cal (um·bil′i·kəl) *adj.* **1** Pertaining to or situated near the umbilicus. **2** Placed near the navel; central. —*n.* **1** A long, flexible tube that serves as a connecting device, conduit for air, power, communication, etc., for an astronaut or aquanaut when outside the craft. **2** A similar device used as a source of fuel, etc., for a spacecraft before launching. [<L *umbilicus* navel]

umbilical cord **1** The ropelike structure connecting the navel of a fetus with the placenta. **2** UMBILICAL *(n.).*

um·bil·i·cus (um′bə·lī′kəs, -bil′i-) *n. pl.* **·ci** (-kī, -sī) **1** NAVEL. **2** A navel-shaped depression. [<L]

um·bra (um′brə) *n. pl.* **·bras** or **·brae** (-brē, -brī) **1** A shadow. **2** The cone of shadow cast at all times by a celestial body in the solar system. When the umbra of the moon strikes the earth, it creates an area of total solar eclipse. **3** The inner dark portion of a sunspot. [L, shadow]

um·brage (um′brij) *n.* **1** A feeling of anger or resentment, esp. in the phrase **take umbrage,** to have such feelings. **2** That which gives shade, as a leafy tree. **3** Shade or shadow. [<L *umbraticus* shady<*umbra* shade] —**um·bra′geous** (-brā′jəs) *adj.* —**um·bra′geous·ly** *adv.*

um·brel·la (um·brel′ə) *n.* **1** A light portable canopy on a folding frame, carried as a protection against sun or rain. **2** A usu. radial formation of military aircraft, used as a protective screen for operations on the ground or on water. **3** Something serving as a cover or shield, or as a means of linking together various things under a common name or sponsor: the expanding *umbrella* of nuclear power. [<L *umbella* parasol, dim. of *umbra* shadow]

umbrella tree A magnolia of the s U.S., with white flowers and umbrellalike whorls of leaves at the ends of the branches.

u·mi·ak (ōō′mē·ak′) *n.* A large, open boat made of skins on a wooden frame. Also **u′mi·ack.** [Eskimo]

Umiak

um·laut (o͝om′lout) *n.* 1 *Ling.* a The change in quality of a vowel sound caused by its partial assimilation to a vowel or semivowel (often later lost) in the following syllable. b A vowel which has been so altered, as *ä, ö,* and *ü* in German. 2 In German, the two dots (ö) put over a vowel modified by umlaut. —*v.t.* To modify by umlaut. [G, change of sound < *um* about + *laut* sound]

um·pir·age (um′pīr·ij, -pə·rij) *n.* The office, function, or decision of an umpire. Also **um′pire·ship.**

um·pire (um′pīr) *n.* 1 A person called upon to settle a disagreement or dispute. 2 In various games, as baseball, a person chosen to enforce the rules of the game and to settle disputed points. —*v.t. & v.i.* **·pired, ·pir·ing** To act as umpire (of or in). [Alter. of ME *noumpere*]

ump·teen (ump′tēn′) *adj. Slang* Indeterminately large in number; very many. —**ump′teenth′** *adj.*

UMW, U.M.W. United Mine Workers.

un-[1] *prefix* Used in forming adjectives, adverbs, and less often nouns, to indicate: 1 Not; opposed or contrary to: *unable, unmannerly.* 2 Lack of: *unease.* [<OE] • See UN-[2].

un-[2] *prefix* Used in forming verbs to indicate: 1 Reversal of an action: *untie.* 2 Removal from something: *unearth.* 3 Deprivation of a condition or quality: *unman; unnerve.* 4 Intensification: *unloose.* [<OE *un-, on-, and-*] • Beginning at the bottom of this page is a partial list of words formed with **un-**[1] and **un-**[2]. Other words formed with these prefixes, having strongly positive, specific, or special meanings, will be found in vocabulary place.

UN, U.N. United Nations.

un·a·ble (un·ā′bəl) *adj.* 1 Not able; incompetent. 2 Helpless; ineffectual.

un·ac·count·a·ble (un′ə·koun′tə·bəl) *adj.* 1 Impossible to be explained or accounted for; inexplicable. 2 Not responsible. —**un′ac·count′a·ble·ness** *n.* —**un′ac·count′a·bly** *adv.*

un·ac·cus·tomed (un′ə·kus′təmd) *adj.* 1 Not accustomed or familiar: usu. with *to: unaccustomed* to hardship. 2 Not common; strange: an *unaccustomed* sight. —**un′ac·cus′tomed·ness** *n.*

un·ad·vised (un′əd·vīzd′) *adj.* 1 Not having received advice. 2 Rash or imprudent. —**un′ad·vis′ed·ly** (-vī′zid·lē) *adv.* —**un′ad·vis′ed·ness** *n.*

un·af·fect·ed (un′ə·fek′tid) *adj.* 1 Not showing affectation; natural; sincere. 2 Not influenced or changed. —**un′af·fect′ed·ly** *adv.* —**un′af·fect′ed·ness** *n.*

un-A·mer·i·can (un′ə·mer′ə·kən) *adj.* Not American, esp. not consistent with or opposed to the institutions, ideals, objectives, etc. of the U.S. —**un′-A·mer′i·can·ism** *n.*

u·nan·i·mous (yo͞o·nan′ə·məs) *adj.* 1 Sharing the same views or sentiments. 2 Showing or resulting from the assent of all concerned: the *unanimous* voice of the jury. [< L *unus* one + *animus* mind] —**u·na·nim·i·ty** (yo͞o′nə·nim′ə·tē) *n.* —**u·nan′i·mous·ly** *adv.*

un·ap·proach·a·ble (un′ə·prō′chə·bəl) *adj.* 1 Not easy to know or contact; aloof; reserved. 2 Inaccessible. —**un′ap·proach′a·bil′i·ty, un′ap·proach′a·ble·ness** *n.* —**un′ap·proach′a·bly** *adv.*

un·armed (un·ärmd′) *adj.* Having no firearms, esp. on one's person.

un·as·sail·a·ble (un′ə·sāl′ə·bəl) *adj.* 1 That cannot be disproved or contested successfully. 2 Resistant to attack; impregnable. —**un′as·sail′a·ble·ness, un′as·sail′a·bil′i·ty** *n.* —**un′as·sail′a·bly** *adv.*

un·as·sum·ing (un′ə·so͞o′ming) *adj.* Not pretentious; modest. —**un′as·sum′ing·ly** *adv.*

un·at·tached (un′ə·tacht′) *adj.* 1 Not attached. 2 Not connected with any particular group; independent. 3 Not married or engaged. 4 *Law* Not held or seized, as in satisfaction of a judgment.

un·a·vail·ing (un′ə·vā′ling) *adj.* Not effective; futile. —**un′a·vail′ing·ly** *adv.*

un·a·void·a·ble (un′ə·voi′də·bəl) *adj.* That cannot be avoided; inevitable. —**un′a·void′a·ble·ness** *n.* —**un′a·void′a·bly** *adv.*

---

unabashed
unabated
unabridged
unaccented
unacceptable
unaccommodating
unaccompanied
unaccredited
unachievable
unacknowledged
unacquainted
unadorned
unadulterated
unadvisable
unaesthetic
unaffiliated
unafraid
unaggressive
unaided
unaligned
unalike
unallied
unalloyed
unalluring
unalterable
unaltered
unambiguous
unambitious
unamusing
unannealed
unannounced
unanswerable
unanswerably
unanswered
unanticipated
unapparent
unappeasable
unappeased
unappetizing
unappreciative
unappropriated
unapproved
unarguable
unarm
unarmored
unashamed
unashamedly
unasked
unaspirated
unassailable
unassailably
unassignable
unassigned
unassimilable
unassimilated
unassisted
unathletic
unattainable
unattained
unattempted
unattended
unattested
unattractive
unauthenticated
unauthorized
unavailable
unavenged
unavowed
unavowedly
unawakened
unawed
unbacked
unbaked
unbanked
unbaptized
unbeaten
unbelt
unbetrayed
unbetrothed
unbleached
unblemished
unblest
unblinking
unblinkingly
unbloody
unboastful
unboned
unbought
unbound
unbranched
unbranded
unbreakable
unbreathable
unbridgeable
unbridle
unbudging
unburied
unburnt
unbusinesslike
unbuttoned
uncage
uncalculating
uncalendered
uncanceled
uncared-for
uncaring
uncarpeted
uncastrated
uncaught
uncaused
unceasing
unceasingly
uncensored
uncensured
uncertified
unchallenged
unchangeable
unchanged
unchanging
unchangingly
unchaperoned
uncharged
uncharted
unchartered
unchaste
unchastened
unchastity
unchecked
unchewed
unchilled
unchivalrous
unchlorinated
unchristened
unclaimed
unclassifiable
unclassified
uncleaned
unclear
unclench
unclog
unclogged
unclouded
uncoated
uncock
uncoerced
uncoined
uncollectable
uncollected
uncollectible
uncolored
uncombed
uncomforted
uncommercial
uncommissioned
uncommitted
uncompetitive
uncomplaining
uncompleted
uncomplicated
uncomplimentary
uncomprehending
uncomprehendingly
uncompressed
uncompromised
uncomputed
unconcealable
unconcealed
unconfined
unconfirmed
uncongeal
uncongealed
uncongenial
unconnected
unconnectedly
unconquerable
unconquerably
unconquered
unconscientious
unconsecrated
unconsenting
unconsidered
unconsoled
unconsolidated
unconstituted
unconstrained
unconsumed
uncontaminated
uncontested
uncontradicted
uncontrite
uncontrollable
uncontrollably
uncontrolled
unconversant
unconverted
unconvinced
unconvincing
uncooked
uncooperative
uncoordinated
uncorked
uncorrected
uncorroborated
uncorrupt
uncorrupted
uncounseled
uncountable
uncourteous
uncourtly
uncovered
uncreated
uncredited
uncritical
uncross
uncrowded
uncrown
uncrowned
uncrystalline
uncrystallizable
uncrystallized
uncultivated
uncultured
uncurbed
uncurdled
uncured
uncurl
uncurled
uncursed
uncurtained
uncushioned
undamaged
undamped
undated
undecayed
undecaying
undecipherable
undeciphered
undeclared
undeclinable
undeclined
undecomposed
undecorated
undefaced
undefeated
undefended
undefiled
undefinable
undefined
undeformed
undelayed
undeliverable
undelivered

un·a·ware (un′ə·wâr′) *adj.* 1 Not aware or cognizant, as of something specified. 2 Carelessly unmindful; inattentive; heedless. —*adv.* UNAWARES.

un·a·wares (un′ə·wârz′) *adv.* 1 Unexpectedly. 2 Without premeditation; unwittingly.

un·bal·ance (un·bal′əns) *v.t.* **·anced, ·anc·ing** 1 To deprive of balance. 2 To disturb or derange mentally. —*n.* The state or condition of being unbalanced.

un·bal·anced (un·bal′ənst) *adj.* 1 Not in a state of equilibrium. 2 In bookkeeping, not adjusted so as to balance. 3 Lacking mental balance; unsound; erratic.

un·bar (un·bär′) *v.t.* **·barred, ·bar·ring** To remove the bar from.

un·bear·a·ble (un′bâr′ə·bəl) *adj.* Not to be borne; intolerable; insufferable. **—un′bear′a·bly** *adv.*

un·beat·a·ble (un·bēt′ə·bəl) *adj.* 1 Not to be defeated. 2 *Slang* First-rate; excellent.

un·be·com·ing (un′bi·kum′ing) *adj.* 1 Not becoming or appropriate, as a dress. 2 Not fitting or decorous; improper. **—un′be·com′ing·ly** *adv.* **—un′be·com′ing·ness** *n.*

un·be·known (un′bi·nōn′) *adj.* Unknown: used with *to.* Also **un′be·knownst′** (-nōnst′).

un·be·lief (un′bi·lēf′) *n.* 1 Absence of positive belief; incredulity. 2 A refusal to believe; disbelief, as in religion.

un·be·liev·a·ble (un′bə·lēv′ə·bəl) *adj.* Too unusual or astonishing to be believed; incredible. **—un′be·liev′a·bly** *adv.* **—Syn.** inconceivable, untenable, staggering, improbable.

un·be·liev·er (un′bi·lē′vər) *n.* 1 One who does not believe; skeptic; doubter. 2 One who has no religious belief.

un·be·liev·ing (un′bi·lē′ving) *adj.* Doubting; skeptical. **—un′be·liev′ing·ly** *adv.* **—un′be·liev′ing·ness** *n.*

un·bend (un·bend′) *v.* **·bent, ·bend·ing** *v.t.* 1 To relax, as from exertion or formality. 2 To straighten (something bent or curved). 3 To relax, as a bow, from tension. 4 *Naut.* To loose or detach, as a rope or sail. —*v.i.* 5 To become free of restraint or formality; relax. 6 To become straight or nearly straight again.

un·bend·ing (un·ben′ding) *adj.* 1 Not bending easily. 2 Resolute; firm. 3 Not relaxed socially; stiff. **—un·bend′ing·ly** *adv.* **—un·bend′ing·ness** *n.*

un·bi·ased (un·bī′əst) *adj.* Having no bias; not prejudiced; impartial. Also **un·bi′assed. —un·bi′ased·ly** *adv.* **—un·bi′ased·ness** *n.*

un·bid·den (un·bid′n) *adj.* 1 Not commanded or invited. 2 Spontaneous: *unbidden* thoughts.

un·blush·ing (un·blush′ing) *adj.* Not blushing; immodest; shameless. **—un·blush′ing·ly** *adv.*

un·born (un·bôrn′) *adj.* 1 Not yet born. 2 Of a future time or generation; future. 3 Not in existence.

un·bos·om (un·bŏŏz′əm, -bōō′zəm) *v.t.* 1 To reveal, as one's thoughts or secrets: often used reflexively. —*v.i.* 2 To say what is troubling one; tell one's thoughts, feelings, etc.

un·bound·ed (un·boun′did) *adj.* 1 Having no bounds or limits; boundless. 2 Going beyond bounds; unrestrained. **—un·bound′ed·ly** *adv.* **—un·bound′ed·ness** *n.*

un·bowed (un·boud′) *adj.* 1 Not bent or bowed. 2 Not broken or subdued by defeat or adversity.

un·brace (un·brās′) *v.t.* **·braced, ·brac·ing** 1 To free from bands or braces. 2 To free from tension; loosen. 3 To weaken.

un·bri·dled (un·brīd′ld) *adj.* 1 Having no bridle on. 2 Without restraint; unrestrained: an *unbridled* tongue.

un·bro·ken (un·brō′kən) *adj.* 1 Not broken; whole; entire. 2 Not violated: an *unbroken* promise. 3 Uninterrupted; continuous. 4 Not tamed or trained. 5 Not bettered or surpassed. 6 Not disarranged or thrown out of order.

un·bur·den (un·bûr′dən) *v.t.* 1 To free from a burden. 2 To relieve (oneself, one's mind, etc.) from cares, worries, etc. 3 To make known (one's cares, worries, guilt, etc.) in order to gain relief.

un·called-for (un·kôld′fôr′) *adj.* 1 Not needed; unnecessary. 2 Not justified by circumstances; unprovoked.

un·can·ny (un·kan′ē) *adj.* 1 Weird; unnatural; eerie. 2 So

---

undemocratic
undemonstrable
undemonstrative
undenominational
undependable
underived
underserved
undeservedly
undeserving
undesignated
undesigned
undesirable
undesirably
undesired
undesirous
undetached
undetected
undetermined
undeterred
undeveloped
undeviating
undifferentiated
undiffused
undigested
undignified
undilated
undiluted
undiminished
undimmed
undiplomatic
undirected
undiscernible
undiscerning
undischarged
undisciplined
undisclosed
undiscouraged
undiscoverable
undiscovered
undiscriminating
undiscussed
undisguised
undismayed
undispelled
undisputed
undissected
undisseminated
undissolved
undistilled
undistinguished
undistracted
undistributed
undisturbed
undiversified
undiverted
undivided
undivorced
undocking
undogmatic
undomesticated
undoubting
undramatic
undramatized
undrape
undraped
undreamed
undreamt
undried
undrinkable
undutiful
undyed
uneatable
uneaten
uneconomic
uneconomical
unedifying
uneducable
uneducated
unelectrified
unembarrassed
unembellished
unemotional
unemotionally
unemphatic
unencumbered
unendangered
unending
unendingly
unendorsed
unendowed
unendurable
unenforceable
unenforced
unenfranchised
unengaged
unengaging
un-English
unenjoyable
unenlightened
unenlivened
unenriched
unenrolled
unenslaved
unentangled
unentered
unenterprising
unenthralled
unenthusiastic
unenthusiastically
unenviable
unenvied
unenvious
unequipped
unerased
unerotic
unestablished
unethical
unexaggerated
unexalted
unexamined
unexcavated
unexcelled
unexchangeable
unexcited
unexciting
unexcused
unexpanded
unexpended
unexpiated
unexpired
unexplainable
unexplained
unexploded
unexploited
unexplored
unexported
unexposed
unexpressed
unexpressive
unexpurgated
unextended
unextinguished
unfaded
unfading
unfallen
unfaltering
unfashionable
unfashionably
unfastened
unfathomable
unfavored
unfeared
unfearing
unfeasible
unfed
unfederated
unfelt
unfeminine
unfenced
unfermented
unfertilized
unfetter
unfettered
unfilled
unfilmed
unfiltered
unfinished
unfired
unfixed
unflattered
unflattering
unflavored
unfocus
unforbidden
unforced
unfordable
unforeseeable
unforetold
unforfeited
unforged
unforgetful
unforgetting
unforgivable
unforgiven
unforgiving
unforgotten
unformed
unformulated
unforsaken
unfortified
unfought
unfound
unfractured
unframed
unfranchised
unfree
unfreedom
unfrozen
unfruitful
unfulfilled
unfunded
unfunny
unfurnished
unfussy
ungallant
ungarnished
ungenerous
ungentle
ungentlemanly
ungently
ungenuine
ungifted
ungird
ungirt
unglazed
unglossed
unglove
ungloved
unglue
ungoverned
ungraced
ungraceful
ungraded
ungrafted
ungrained
ungrammatical
ungrammatically
ungranted
ungratified
ungrounded
ungrudging
unguided
unhackneyed
unhampered
unhang
unhanged
unharbored
unharmed
unharnessed
unharrowed
unharvested
unhasty
unhatched
unhealed
unhealthful
unheated
unheeded
unheedful
unheeding
unheedingly
unhelpful
unheralded
unheroic
unhesitating
unhesitatingly
unhindered
unhired
unhistoric
unhomogeneous
unhonored
unhousebroken
unhoused
unhurried
unhurt
unhusk
unhygienic
unhyphenated
unhypocritical
unidentified
unidiomatic

good as to seem almost supernatural in origin: *uncanny* accuracy. —**un·can′ni·ly** *adv.* —**un·can′ni·ness** *n.*

un·cer·e·mo·ni·ous (un′ser·ə·mō′nē·əs) *adj.* **1** Not ceremonious; informal. **2** Abruptly rude or discourteous. —**un′cer·e·mo′ni·ous·ly** *adv.* —**un′cer·e·mo′ni·ous·ness** *n.*

un·cer·tain (un·sûr′tən) *adj.* **1** Not yet determined; indefinite: The date is *uncertain.* **2** Not to be relied upon; unpredictable: *uncertain* weather. **3** Not definitely or exactly known. **4** Not sure or convinced; doubtful; dubious. **5** Not constant; fitful; changeable. **6** Not clear, forceful, steady, etc.: His delivery of the speech was very *uncertain.* —**un·cer′tain·ly** *adv.*

un·cer·tain·ty (un·sûr′tən·tē) *n. pl.* **·ties** **1** The state of being uncertain; doubt. **2** Something uncertain.

un·char·i·ta·ble (un·char′ə·tə·bəl) *adj.* Not forgiving or charitable, as in judgment; censorious. —**un·char′i·ta·ble·ness** *n.* —**un·char′i·ta·bly** *adv.*

un·char·ted (un·chär′tid) *adj.* **1** Not marked or charted on a map. **2** Not explored; unknown.

un·chris·tian (un·kris′chən) *adj.* **1** Not according with Christian principles, attitudes, etc. **2** Not Christian.

un·church (un·chûrch′) *v.t.* **1** To deprive of membership in a church; excommunicate. **2** To deny the status of a church to (a sect, etc.).

un·cir·cum·cised (un·sûr′kəm·sīzd) *adj.* **1** Not circumcised. **2** Not Jewish; Gentile.

un·civ·il (un·siv′əl) *adj.* Wanting in civility; discourteous; ill-bred. —**un·civ′il·ly** *adv.*

un·civ·i·lized (un·siv′ə·līzd) *adj.* **1** Not civilized; barbarous. **2** Uncouth; rude; gross. **3** Remote from civilization. —**Syn. 1** savage, brutish, brutal, ferocious. **2** crude, cross, boorish, churlish, vulgar, coarse.

un·clad (un·klad′) *adj.* Without clothes; naked.

un·cle (ung′kəl) *n.* **1** The brother of one's father or mother. **2** The husband of one's aunt. **3** *Informal* An elderly man; used in direct address. **4** *Slang* A pawnbroker. [< L *avunculus* a mother's brother]

un·clean (un·klēn′) *adj.* **1** Not clean; foul. **2** Morally impure. **3** Ceremonially impure. —**un·clean′ness** *n.*

un·clean·ly[1] (un·klen′lē) *adj.* **1** Lacking cleanliness. **2** Morally impure. —**un·clean′li·ness** *n.*

un·clean·ly[2] (un·klēn′lē) *adv.* In an unclean manner.

Uncle Sam The personification of the government or the people of the U.S., represented as a tall, lean man with chin whiskers, wearing a plug hat, blue swallow-tailed coat, and red-and-white striped pants.

Uncle Tom *Informal* A Negro who acts in an obsequious or servile manner towards whites: a contemptuous term. —*v.i.* **Uncle Tommed, Uncle Tom·ming** To behave like an Uncle Tom. [< *Uncle Tom,* the faithful Negro slave in H. B. Stowe's *Uncle Tom's Cabin*] —**Uncle Tom′ism** *n.*

un·cloak (un·klōk′) *v.t.* **1** To remove the cloak or covering from. **2** To unmask; expose.

un·close (un·klōz′) *v.t. & v.i.* **·closed, ·clos·ing** **1** To open or set open. **2** To reveal; disclose.

un·clothe (un·klō*th*′) *v.t.* **·clothed** or **·clad, ·cloth·ing** **1** To remove the clothes from; undress. **2** To divest; uncover.

un·com·fort·a·ble (un·kum′fər·tə·bəl, -kumf′tə·bəl) *adj.* **1** Not at ease; feeling discomfort. **2** Causing uneasiness; disquieting. —**un·com′fort·a·ble·ness** *n.* —**un·com′fort·a·bly** *adv.*

un·com·mon (un·kom′ən) *adj.* **1** Not usual or common. **2** Strange; remarkable. —**un·com′mon·ly** *adv.* —**un·com′mon·ness** *n.*

un·com·mu·ni·ca·tive (un′kə·myōō′nə·kə·tiv, -kāt′iv) *adj.* Not communicative; not disposed to talk, to give information, etc.; reserved; taciturn. —**un′com·mu′ni·ca·tive·ly** *adv.* —**un′com·mu′ni·ca·tive·ness** *n.*

un·com·pro·mis·ing (un·kom′prə·mī′zing) *adj.* Making or admitting of no compromise; inflexible; strict. —**un·com′pro·mis′ing·ly** *adv.* —**Syn.** resolute, steadfast, firm, indomitable, inexorable, tenacious, obstinate.

un·con·cern (un′kən·sûrn′) *n.* **1** Lack of anxiety, concern, or worry. **2** Lack of interest; indifference.

---

unilluminated
unillumined
unillustrated
unimaginable
unimaginably
unimaginative
unimagined
unimbued
unimitated
unimmunized
unimpaired
unimpeded
unimportance
unimportant
unimposing
unimpressed
unimpressionable
unimpressive
unincorporated
unindemnified
unindustrialized
uninfected
uninfested
uninflammable
uninflected
uninfluenced
uninformed
uninhabitable
uninhabited
uninhibited
uninitiated
uninjured
uninspired
uninspiring
uninstructed
uninsurable
uninsured
unintellectual
unintelligent
unintelligible
unintelligibly
unintended
unintentional
unintentionally
uninteresting
uninterpreted
uninterrupted
unintimidated
unintoxicated
uninvited
uninviting
uninvoked
uninvolved
unissued
unitemized
unjaded
unjoined
unjointed
unjustifiable
unjustifiably
unkennel
unkept
unkindled
unkissed
unknowable
unknowing
unlabeled
unlabored
unladylike
unlamented
unlash
unlasting
unlaundered
unleaded
unleased
unlevel
unlevied
unlicensed
unlifelike
unlighted
unlikable
unlikeable
unlined
unlink
unlisted
unlit
unliteral
unliveliness
unlively
unlocked
unlovable
unloved
unlovely
unloving
unlubricated
unmagnified
unmanageable
unmanful
unmanicured
unmannerly
unmarked
unmarketable
unmarred
unmarriageable
unmarried
unmasculine
unmastered
unmatched
unmated
unmatted
unmeant
unmechanical
unmedicated
unmemorable
unmercenary
unmerited
unmethodical
unmilitary
unmilled
unmindful
unmistaken
unmixed
unmodified
unmodish
unmodulated
unmoistened
unmold
unmolested
unmollified
unmortgaged
unmotivated
unmounted
unmourned
unmoved
unmown
unmuffle
unmusical
unmuzzle
unmuzzled
unnamable
unnameable
unnamed
unnaturalized
unnavigable
unnavigated
unneeded
unneighborly
unnoted
unnoticed
unobjectionable
unobliging
unobservant
unobserved
unobserving
unobstructed
unobtainable
unobtrusive
unobtrusively
unobtrusiveness
unoffending
unoffered
unoiled
unopen
unopened
unopposed
unoppressed
unordained
unoriginal
unorthodox
unostentatious
unostentatiously
unowned
unoxidized
unpacified
unpaginated
unpaid
unpaired
unpalatable
unpardonable
unpardonably
unparliamentary
unparted
unpartisan
unpasteurized
unpatched
unpatented
unpatriotic
unpaved
unpeaceable
unpeaceful
unpedigreed
unpensioned
unpeopled
unperceived
unperfected
unperforated
unperformed
unpersuaded
unpersuasive
unperturbed
unphilosophical
unphonetic
unphotogenic
unphysical
unpicturesque
unpile
unpitying
unplaced
unplait
unplanned
unplanted
unplayed
unpleasing
unpledged
unplowed
unplucked
unplugged
unpoetic
unpoetical
unpointed
unpolarized
unpolished
unpolitical
unpolluted
unpopulated
unposted
unpractical
unpredictable
unpredictably
unprejudiced
unpremeditated
unprepared
unprepossessing
unpressed
unpretentious
unpretentiously
unpretentiousness
unpriced
unprimed
unprinted
unprivileged
unprocessed
unproductive
unprofitable
unprofitably
unprogramed
unpromising
unpronounceable
unpropitious
unprosperous
unprotected
unproved

---

add, āce, câre, pälm; end, ēven; it, īce; odd, ōpen, ôrder; to͝ok, po͞ol; up, bûrn; ə = *a* in *above,* *u* in *focus;* yo͞o = *u* in *fuse;* oil; pout; check; go; ring; thin; *th*is; zh, *vision.* < derived from; ? origin uncertain or unknown.

un·con·cerned (un′kən·sûrnd′) *adj.* 1 Not anxious or worried. 2 Not interested; indifferent. **—un′con·cern′ed·ly** (-sûr′nid·lē) *adj.* **—un′con·cern′ed·ness** *n.*

un·con·di·tion·al (un′kən·dish′ən·əl) *adj.* Limited by no conditions; absolute. **—un′con·di′tion·al·ly** *adv.*

un·con·di·tioned (un′kən·dish′ənd) *adj.* 1 Not restricted; unconditional. 2 *Psychol.* Not acquired; natural.

un·con·scion·a·ble (un·kon′shən·ə·bəl) *adj.* 1 Unbelievably bad, wrong, inequitable, etc.: an *unconscionable* error. 2 Wholly unscrupulous. **—un·con′scion·a·ble·ness** *n.* **—un·con′scion·a·bly** *adv.*

un·con·scious (un·kon′shəs) *adj.* 1 Temporarily deprived of consciousness. 2 Not cognizant; unaware: with *of*: *unconscious* of his charm. 3 Not produced or accompanied by conscious effort; not intended or known: an *unconscious* pun. 4 Not endowed with consciousness or a mind. 5 Of or having to do with the unconscious. *—n.* That area of the psyche which is not in the immediate field of awareness and whose content may become manifest through dreams, morbid fears and compulsions, etc.: with *the*. **—un·con′scious·ly** *adv.* **—un·con′scious·ness** *n.*

un·con·sti·tu·tion·al (un′kon·sti·t^yōō′shən·əl) *adj.* Contrary to or violating the precepts of a constitution. **—un′·con·sti·tu′tion·al′i·ty** *n.* **—un·con′sti·tu′tion·al·ly** *adv.*

un·con·ven·tion·al (un′kən·ven′shən·əl) *adj.* Not adhering to conventional rules, practices, etc.; informal; free. **—un′con·ven′tion·al′i·ty** *n.* **—un′con·ven′tion·al·ly** *adv.*

un·count·ed (un·koun′tid) *adj.* 1 Not counted. 2 Beyond counting; innumerable.

un·coup·le (un·kup′əl) *v.t.* **·led, ·ling** 1 To disconnect or unfasten. 2 To set loose; unleash (dogs). **—un·coup′led** (-kup′əld) *adj.*

un·couth (un·kōōth′) *adj.* 1 Marked by awkwardness or oddity; outlandish. 2 Coarse, boorish, or unrefined, as in manner or speech. [< OE *uncūth* unknown] **—un·couth′ly** *adv.* **—un·couth′ness** *n.*

un·cov·er (un·kuv′ər) *v.t.* 1 To remove a covering from. 2 To make known; disclose. *—v.i.* 3 To remove a covering. 4 To raise or remove the hat, as in token of respect.

unc·tion (ungk′shən) *n.* 1 The act of anointing, as for religious or medicinal purposes. 2 A substance used in anointing, as oil. 3 Anything that soothes or palliates. 4 A quality of speech, esp. in religious discourse, that awakens or is intended to awaken deep sympathetic feeling. 5 Excessive or affected sincerity or sympathy in speech or manner. [< L *unctio* < *ungere* anoint]

unc·tu·ous (ungk′chōō·əs) *adj.* 1 Like an unguent; greasy. 2 Greasy or soapy to the touch, as certain minerals. 3 Characterized by excessive or affected sincerity, sympathy, concern, etc. 4 Unduly smooth or suave in speech or manner. 5 Having plasticity, as clay. [< L *unctum* ointment, orig. neut. p.p. of *ungere* anoint] **—unc′tu·ous·ly** *adv.* **—unc′tu·ous·ness, unc′tu·os′i·ty** (-chōō·os′ə·tē) *n.*

un·cut (un·kut′) *adj.* 1 Not cut. 2 In bookbinding, having untrimmed margins. 3 Not ground, as a gem. 4 Not shortened or abridged.

un·daunt·ed (un·dôn′tid, -dän′-) *adj.* Not daunted; fearless; intrepid. **—un·daunt′ed·ly** *adv.* **—un·daunt′ed·ness** *n.*

un·de·cid·ed (un′di·sī′did) *adj.* 1 Not having the mind made up; irresolute. 2 Not decided upon or determined. **—un′de·cid′ed·ly** *adv.*

un·de·ni·a·ble (un′di·nī′ə·bəl) *adj.* 1 That cannot be denied; indisputably true. 2 Unquestionably good; excellent: His reputation was *undeniable*. **—un′de·ni′a·bly** *adv.*

un·der (un′dər) *prep.* 1 Beneath; covered by: dust *under* the rug. 2 In a place lower than; at the foot or bottom of: *under* the hill. 3 Beneath the shelter of: *under* the paternal roof. 4 Beneath the concealment, guise, or assumption of: *under* a false name. 5 Less than in number, degree, age, value, or amount: *under* 10 tons. 6 Inferior to in quality, character, or rank. 7 Beneath the domination of; subordinate or subservient to: *under* the British flag. 8 Subject to the guidance, tutorship, or direction of: He studied *under* Mendelssohn. 9 Subject to the moral obligation of: a state-

---

unproven
unprovided
unprovoked
unpruned
unpublishable
unpublished
unpunctual
unpunished
unpurified
unpuritanical
unqualifying
unquenchable
unquestioning
unrated
unratified
unreachable
unreadable
unrealizable
unrealized
unrebuked
unreceipted
unreceivable
unreceived
unreceptive
unreciprocated
unreclaimed
unrecognizable
unrecognized
unreconciled
unrecorded
unrecounted
unredeemed
unrefined
unreflecting
unreflective
unreformable
unreformed
unrefreshed
unregistered
unregretted
unregulated
unrehearsed
unrelated
unrelaxed
unrelievable
unrelieved
unremarkable
unremarked
unremedied
unremembered
unremitted
unremorseful
unremunerated
unremunerative
unrenewed
unrented
unrepaid
unrepairable
unrepaired
unrepealed
unrepeatable
unrepentant
unrepented
unrepenting
unreplaced
unreplenished
unreported
unrepresentative
unrepresented
unrepressed
unrequested
unrequited
unresented
unreserve
unresigned
unresistant
unresisting
unresistingly
unresolved
unrespectful
unresponsive
unresting
unrestless
unrestrained
unrestrainedly
unrestraint
unrestricted
unretentive
unretracted
unreturned
unrevealed
unrevenged
unrevised
unrevoked
unrewarded
unrhymed
unrhythmic
unrhythmical
unrighted
unripened
unrisen
unroasted
unromantic
unromantically
unroof
unruled
unsafe
unsafely
unsafeness
unsaintly
unsalability
unsalable
unsalaried
unsaleability
unsaleable
unsalted
unsalvageable
unsanctified
unsanctioned
unsanitary
unsated
unsatiated
unsatiating
unsatisfactorily
unsatisfactory
unsatisfied
unsatisfying
unsaved
unsayable
unscaled
unscanned
unscarred
unscenic
unscented
unscheduled
unscholarly
unschooled
unscientific
unscratched
unscreened
unsealed
unseamed
unseasoned
unseaworthy
unseconded
unsecret
unsecretive
unsectarian
unsecured
unseeing
unseen
unsegmented
unselected
unselective
unself-conscious
unselfish
unselfishly
unselfishness
unsent
unsentimental
unserviceable
unset
unsew
unsewn
unsexual
unshaded
unshakable
unshaken
unshaven
unsheathed
unsheltered
unshod
unshorn
unshrinkable
unshriven
unshrouded
unshut
unsifted
unsighted
unsigned
unsinkable
unsized
unskeptical
unslaked
unsling
unsmiling
unsmilingly
unsmoked
unsnobbish
unsocial
unsoiled
unsold
unsoldierly
unsolicited
unsolicitous
unsoluble
unsolvable
unsolved
unsorted
unsought
unsown
unspecialized
unspecified
unspectacular
unspent
unspilled
unspiritual
unspoiled
unspoken
unsponsored
unsportsmanlike
unstack
unstained
unstamped
unstandardized
unstarched
unstarred
unstartling
unstatesmanlike
unstemmed
unstereotyped
unsterile
unsterilized
unstick
unstimulating
unstitched
unstopped
unstopper
unstrap
unstratified
unstressed
unstriated
unstriped
unstructured
unstuck
unstudied
unstuffed
unsubsidized
unsubstantiated
unsubtle
unsuccessful
unsuccessfully
unsuited
unsullied
unsupportable
unsupported
unsuppressed
unsure
unsurmountable
unsurpassed
unsurprising
unsurveyed
unsurvivable
unsusceptible
unsuspected
unsuspecting
unsuspicious
unswathe
unswear
unsweetened
unswept
unsworn
unsymmetrical
unsympathetic
unsympathetically
unsystematic
untack
untactful
untactfully
untainted

ment *under* oath. **10** With the liability or certainty of incurring: *under* penalty of the law. **11** Subject to the influence or pressure of: *under* the circumstances. **12** Swayed or impelled by: *under* fear of death. **13** Driven or propelled by: *under* sail. **14** Included in the group or class of; found in the matter titled or headed: See *under* History. **15** Being the subject of: the matter *under* discussion. **16** During the period of; in the reign of. **17** By virtue of; authorized, substantiated, attested, or warranted by: *under* his own signature. **18** In conformity to or in accordance with; having regard to. **19** Planted or sowed with: an acre *under* wheat. —*adv.* **1** In or into a position below something; underneath. **2** In or into an inferior or subordinate condition, rank, etc. **3** So as to be covered or hidden. **4** Less in amount, value, time, etc.: We did it in ten minutes or *under.* —*adj.* **1** Situated or moving under something else; lower or lowermost: an *under* layer. **2** Subordinate; lower in rank or authority. **3** Less than usual, standard, or prescribed. **4** Held in subjection or restraint: used predicatively. [< OE]

under- *combining form* **1** Below in position; situated or directed beneath; on the underside: *undercarriage.* **2** Below or beneath another surface or covering: *undergarment.* **3** Inferior in rank or importance; subordinate: *undergraduate.* **4** Less than is usual or proper; not enough; insufficient(ly): *underdeveloped.* **5** At a lower rate; less in degree or amount: *underpay.*

un·der·a·chieve (un′dər·ə·chēv′) *v.i.* **·chieved, ·chiev·ing** To fail to achieve the approximate level of performance, esp. in school studies, commensurate with one's abilities as indicated by testing. —**un′der·a·chieve′ment, un′der·a·chiev′er** *n.*

un·der·act (un′dər·akt′) *v.t. & v.i.* To perform (a role, scene, etc.) in a somewhat less dramatic or emphatic way than might naturally be expected.

un·der·age (un′dər·āj′) *adj.* Not of a requisite or legal age.

un·der·arm (un′dər·ärm′) *adj.* **1** Situated, placed, or used under the arm. **2** UNDERHAND (def. 2). —*n.* ARMPIT.

un·der·bid (un′dər·bid′) *v.t.* **·bid, ·bid·ding 1** To bid lower than, as in a competition. **2** In bridge, to fail to bid the full value of (a hand). —**un′der·bid′der** *n.*

un·der·brush (un′dər·brush′) *n.* Small trees and shrubs growing beneath forest trees; undergrowth. Also **un′der·bush′** (-bo͝osh′).

un·der·buy (un′dər·bī′) *v.t.* **·bought, ·buy·ing 1** To buy at a price lower than that paid by (another). **2** To pay less than the value for. **3** To buy less of (something) than is required.

un·der·car·riage (un′dər·kar′ij) *n.* **1** The framework supporting the body of a structure, as an automobile. **2** The principal landing gear of an aircraft.

Undercarriage *def. 2*

un·der·charge (un′dər·chärj′) *v.t.* **·charged, ·charg·ing 1** To make an inadequate charge for. **2** To load with an insufficient charge, as a gun. —*n.* (un′dər·chärj′) An inadequate or insufficient charge.

un·der·class·man (un′dər·klas′mən, -kläs′-) *n. pl.* **·men** (-mən) A freshman or sophomore.

un·der·clothes (un′dər·klōz′, -klōthz′) *n.pl.* UNDERWEAR. Also **un′der·cloth′ing.**

un·der·coat (un′dər·kōt′) *n.* **1** A coat worn under another. **2** A layer of paint, varnish, etc., beneath another layer; also, a protective coating applied to the undersurface of a vehicle: also **un′der·coat′ing.** —*v.t.* To provide with an undercoat (def. 2).

un·der·cov·er (un′dər·kuv′ər) *adj.* Secret; surreptitious; esp., engaged in spying.

un·der·cur·rent (un′dər·kûr′ənt) *n.* **1** A current, as of water or air, below another or below the surface. **2** A hidden drift or tendency, as of popular sentiments.

un·der·cut (un′dər·kut′) *n.* **1** The act or result of cutting away a part, section, etc., from the lower or under surface of something. **2** *Brit.* TENDERLOIN. **3** A notch cut in the side of a tree so that it will fall toward that side when sawed through. **4** In sports, a cut or backspin imparted to the ball by an underhand stroke. —*v.t.* (un′dər·kut′) **·cut, ·cut·ting 1** To cut away the underpart of. **2** To cut away a lower portion of so as to leave a part overhanging. **3** To work or sell for lower payment than (a rival). **4** In sports, to hit (a ball) with an oblique downward or underhand stroke so as to give the ball a backspin. **5** To lessen or destroy the effectiveness or impact of; undermine. —*adj.* **1** Having the parts in relief cut under. **2** Done by undercutting.

un·der·de·vel·oped (un′dər·di·vel′əpt) *adj.* **1** Not sufficiently developed. **2** Below a normal or adequate standard in the development of industry, resources, agriculture, etc.: an *underdeveloped* country.

un·der·dog (un′dər·dôg′, -dog′) *n.* **1** The one that is losing, has lost, or is at a disadvantage in a contest. **2** The weaker, subservient, or exploited person.

un·der·done (un′dər·dun′) *adj.* Not cooked to the fullest degree.

un·der·em·ployed (un′dər·əm·ploid′) *adj.* Employed only part of the time or for too few hours to assure an adequate income. —**un′der·em·ploy′ment** *n.*

un·der·es·ti·mate (un′dər·es′tə·māt) *v.t.* **·mat·ed, ·mat·ing** To put too low an estimate or valuation upon (things or people). —*n.* (-mit) An estimate below the just value, expense, opinion, etc. —**un′der·es′ti·ma′tion** *n.*

un·der·ex·pose (un′dər·ik·spōz′) *v.t.* **·posed, ·pos·ing** *Phot.* To expose (a film) to less light than is required for a clear image. —**un′der·ex·po′sure** (-spō′zhər) *n.*

un·der·feed (un′dər·fēd′) *v.t.* **·fed, ·feed·ing** To feed insufficiently.

un·der·foot (un′dər·fo͝ot′) *adv.* **1** Beneath the feet; down on the ground. **2** In the way.

un·der·gar·ment (un′dər·gär′mənt) *n.* A garment to be worn beneath outer garments.

un·der·go (un′dər·gō′) *v.t.* **·went, ·gone, ·go·ing 1** To be

untaken
untalented
untamable
untame
untameable
untamed
untangled
untaped
untapped
untarnished
untasted
untaxable
untaxed
unteachable
untechnical
untempered
untenable
untenanted
untended
untenured
untested
untether
unthatched
untheatrical
unthinkable
unthoughtful
unthreshed
unthrifty
unthrone
untilled
untinged
untired
untiring
untiringly
untitled
untouched
untracked
untrained
untrammeled
untransferable
untransferred
untranslatable
untranslated
untrapped
untraveled
untraversed
untread
untreatable
untreated
untried
untrim
untrodden
untroubled
untrustworthy
untuck
untufted
untuned
untuneful
unturned
untwilled
untwisted
untypical
unusable
unutilized
unuttered
unvaccinated
unvalued
unvanquished
unvaried
unvarying
unvaryingly
unveiled
unventilated
unverifiable
unverified
unversed
unvitrified
unvocal
unvoiced
unvolatilized
unvulcanized
unwakened
unwalled
unwanted
unwarlike
unwarmed
unwarned
unwarranted
unwashed
unwasted
unwatched
unwavering
unwaveringly
unweakened
unweaned
unwearable
unweary
unwearying
unweathered
unweave
unwed
unwedded
unweeded
unwelcome
unwelded
unwhetted
unwhipped
unwilled
unwished
unwithered
unwitnessed
unwomanly
unwooded
unwooed
unworkable
unworked
unworkmanlike
unworldly
unworn
unworshiped
unwounded
unwoven
unwrinkled
unwrought
unyielding
unzealous

subjected to; have experience of; suffer. 2 To bear up under; endure.

un·der·grad·u·ate (un′dər·graj′ōō·it) *n.* A student of a university or college who has not taken the bachelor's degree. *—adj.* Of, being, or for an undergraduate.

un·der·ground (un′dər·ground′) *adj.* 1 Situated, done, or operated beneath the surface of the ground. 2 Done in secret; clandestine. 3 Of, relating to, or characterized by the underground (defs. 3 and 4), their works, actions, etc. *—n.* 1 That which is beneath the surface of the ground, as a passage or space. 2 *Brit.* SUBWAY. 3 A group secretly organized to resist or oppose those in control of a government or country: usu. with *the.* 4 An avant-garde movement in art, cinema, journalism, etc., generally considered to be in opposition to conventional culture or society and whose works are usu. experimental, erotic, or radical in style, content, or purpose: usu. with *the.* *—adv.* (un′dər·ground′) 1 Beneath the surface of the ground. 2 In or into hiding, secrecy, etc.

Underground Railroad A system of cooperation among antislavery people, before 1861, for assisting fugitive slaves to escape to Canada and the free states.

un·der·growth (un′dər·grōth′) *n.* UNDERBRUSH.

un·der·hand (un′dər·hand′) *adj.* 1 Done or acting in a sly or treacherously secret manner. 2 In certain sports, done or delivered with the hand and forearm lower than the elbow or shoulder. *—adv.* 1 In a secret, sly manner. 2 With an underhand motion.

un·der·hand·ed (un′dər·han′did) *adj. & adv.* UNDERHAND. **—un′der·hand′ed·ly** *adv.* **—un′der·hand′ed·ness** *n.*

un·der·lay (un′dər·lā′) *v.t.* **·laid, ·lay·ing** 1 To place (one thing) under another. 2 To furnish with a base or lining. 3 To support or elevate with something placed beneath. *—n.* (un′dər·lā′) Something laid beneath something else, esp., in printing, a piece of paper, etc., placed under type, etc., in order to raise it.

un·der·lie (un′dər·lī′) *v.t.* **·lay, ·lain, ·ly·ing** 1 To lie below or under. 2 To be the basis or reason for: What motives *underlie* his refusal to go? 3 To constitute a first or prior claim or lien over.

un·der·line (un′dər·līn′) *v.t.* **·lined, ·lin·ing** 1 To mark with a line underneath; underscore. 2 To emphasize. *—n.* A line underneath a word or passage, as for emphasis.

un·der·ling (un′dər·ling) *n.* A subordinate; inferior.

un·der·ly·ing (un′dər·lī′ing) *adj.* 1 Lying under: *underlying* strata. 2 Basic; fundamental: *underlying* principles. 3 Not obvious, but implicit: *underlying* reasons.

un·der·mine (un′dər·mīn′, un′dər·mīn) *v.t.* **·mined, ·min·ing** 1 To excavate beneath; dig a mine or passage under. 2 To weaken by wearing away at the base. 3 To weaken or impair secretly, insidiously, or by degrees.

un·der·most (un′dər·mōst′) *adj.* Having the lowest place or position.

un·der·neath (un′dər·nēth′) *adv.* 1 In a place below. 2 On the under or lower side. *—prep.* 1 Beneath; under; below. 2 Under the form or appearance of. 3 Under the authority of; in the control of. *—adj.* Lower. *—n.* The lower or under part or side. [< OE *underneothan*]

un·der·nour·ish (un′dər·nûr′ish) *v.t.* To provide with insufficient nourishment. **—un′der·nour′ished** *adj.* **—un′der·nour′ish·ment** *n.*

un·der·pass (un′dər·pas′, -päs′) *n.* A road, passageway, etc., that runs beneath something, esp. a road that passes under railway tracks or under another road.

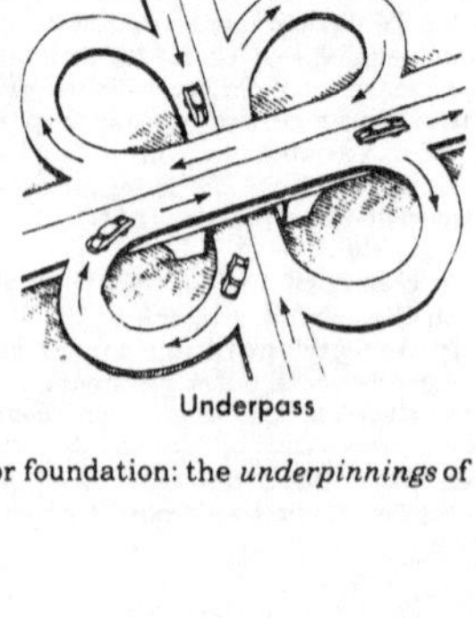

Underpass

un·der·pay (un′dər·pā′) *v.t.* **·paid, ·pay·ing** To pay insufficiently.

un·der·pin·ning (un′dər·pin′ing) *n.* 1 Material or framework used to support a wall or building from below. 2 *Often pl.* Something used or functioning as a basis or foundation: the *underpinnings* of guilt in our society.

un·der·play (un′dər·plā′) *v.t. & v.i.* 1 UNDERACT. 2 To behave, react to, etc., in a deliberately restrained manner.

un·der·priv·i·leged (un′dər·priv′ə·lijd) *adj.* 1 Deprived socially and economically of enjoying certain fundamental rights theoretically possessed by all members of a community or nation. 2 Of or pertaining to people who are underprivileged.

un·der·rate (un′dər·rāt′) *v.t.* **·rat·ed, ·rat·ing** To rate too low; underestimate.

un·der·score (un′dər·skôr′, -skōr′) *v.t.* **·scored, ·scor·ing** To draw a line below, as for emphasis; underline. *—n.* (un′dər·skôr′, -skōr′) A line drawn beneath a word, etc., as for emphasis.

un·der·sea (un′dər·sē′) *adj.* Being, carried on, or designed for use beneath the surface of the sea. *—adv.* (un′dər·sē′) Beneath the surface of the sea: also **un·der·seas** (un′dər·sēz′).

under secretary The assistant secretary of a principal secretary in government.

un·der·sell (un′dər·sel′) *v.t.* **·sold, ·sell·ing** 1 To sell at a lower price than. 2 To present or promote, as a point of view or commodity, in an understated manner.

un·der·shirt (un′dər·shûrt′) *n.* A collarless undergarment, usu. without sleeves, worn beneath a shirt.

un·der·shoot (un′dər·shōōt′) *v.* **·shot, ·shoot·ing** *v.t.* 1 To shoot short of or below (a target). 2 To land an airplane short of (the runway). *—v.i.* 3 To shoot or land short of the mark.

un·der·shot (un′dər·shot′) *adj.* 1 Propelled by water that flows underneath, as a water wheel. 2 Having a projecting lower jaw or teeth.

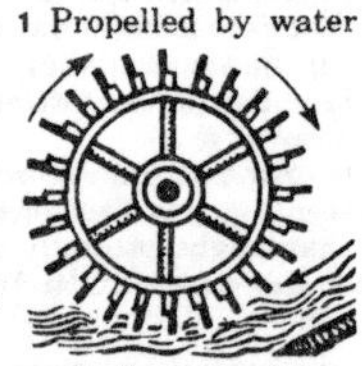

Undershot water wheel

un·der·side (un′dər·sīd′) *n.* The lower or under side or surface.

un·der·signed (un′dər·sīnd′) *n.* The person or persons who have signed their names at the end of a document, letter, etc.

un·der·sized (un′dər·sīzd′) *adj.* Of less than the normal, legal, or average size.

un·der·slung (un′dər·slung′) *adj.* Having the springs fixed to the axles from below, as certain automobiles.

un·der·stand (un′dər·stand′) *v.* **·stood, ·stand·ing** *v.t.* 1 To come to know the meaning or import of. 2 To perceive the nature or character of: I do not *understand* her. 3 To have comprehension or mastery of: Do you *understand* German? 4 To be aware of; realize: She *understands* her position. 5 To have been told; believe: I *understand* that she went home. 6 To take or interpret: How am I to *understand* that remark? 7 To accept as a condition or stipulation: It is *understood* that the tenant will provide his own heat. *—v.i.* 8 To have understanding; comprehend. 9 To grasp the meaning, significance, etc., of something. 10 To believe or assume something to be the case. 11 To have a sympathetic attitude or tolerance toward something. [< OE *under-* under + *standan* stand] **—un′der·stand′a·ble** *adj.* **—un′der·stand′a·bly** *adv.*

un·der·stand·ing (un′dər·stan′ding) *n.* 1 An intellectual grasp of something; comprehension. 2 The power or capacity to think, acquire and retain knowledge, interpret experience, etc.; intelligence. 3 An agreement or settlement of differences. 4 An informal or confidential compact or agreement. 5 An individual viewpoint, interpretation, or opinion. 6 A sympathetic comprehension of or tolerance for the feelings, actions, attitudes, etc., of others. *—adj.* Possessing or characterized by comprehension, compassion, etc. **—un′der·stand′ing·ly** *adv.*

un·der·state (un′dər·stāt′) *v.t.* **·stat·ed, ·stat·ing** 1 To state with less force than the actual truth warrants. 2 To state or describe in a deliberately restrained manner in order to achieve greater force or effectiveness. **—un′der·state′·ment** *n.*

un·der·stat·ed (un′dər·stāt′əd) *adj.* Stated, executed, designed, etc., in an unemphatic, restrained, or simple manner.

un·der·stood (un′dər·stŏŏd′) *p.t. & p.p.* of UNDERSTAND. *—adj.* 1 Grasped mentally; comprehended. 2 Taken for granted. 3 Agreed upon by all.

un·der·stud·y (un′dər·stud′ē) *v.t. & v.i.* **·stud·ied, ·stud·y·ing** **1** To study (a part) in order to be able, if necessary, to substitute for the actor playing it. **2** To act as an understudy to (another actor). —*n. pl.* **·stud·ies** **1** An actor or actress who can substitute for another actor in a given role. **2** A person prepared to perform the work or fill the position of another.

un·der·take (un′dər·tāk′) *v.t.* **·took, ·tak·en, ·tak·ing** **1** To take upon oneself; agree or attempt to do. **2** To contract to do; pledge oneself to. **3** To guarantee or promise. **4** To take under charge or guidance.

un·der·tak·er (un′dər·tā′kər *for def. 1;* un′dər·tā′kər *for def. 2*) *n.* **1** One who undertakes any work or enterprise; esp. a contractor. **2** One whose business it is to prepare a dead person for burial and to conduct funerals.

un·der·tak·ing (un′dər·tā′king, *esp. for def. 3;* un′dər·tā′·king) *n.* **1** The act of one who undertakes any task or enterprise. **2** The thing undertaken; an enterprise; task. **3** The business of an undertaker (def. 2). **4** An engagement, promise, or guarantee.

un·der·tone (un′dər·tōn′) *n.* **1** A low or subdued tone, esp. a vocal tone, as a whisper. **2** A subdued color, esp. one with other colors imposed on it. **3** A meaning, suggestion, quality, etc., that is implied but not expressed.

un·der·tow (un′dər·tō′) *n.* A flow of water beneath and in a direction opposite to the surface current, esp. such a flow moving seaward beneath surf.

un·der·val·ue (un′dər·val′yōō) *v.t.* **·ued, ·u·ing** **1** To value or rate below the real worth. **2** To regard or esteem as of little worth. —**un′der·val′u·a′tion** *n.*

un·der·wa·ter (un′dər·wô′tər, -wot′ər) *adj.* **1** Being, occurring, used, etc., below the surface of a body of water: *underwater* research. **2** Below the water line of a ship. —*adv.* Below the surface of water.

under way **1** In progress: The meeting was already *under way.* **2** Into operation or motion: to get the fund drive *under way.*

un·der·wear (un′dər·wâr′) *n.* Garments worn underneath the ordinary outer garments.

un·der·weight (un′dər·wāt′) *adj.* Having less than the normal, desired, or permitted weight. —*n.* Weight less than normal, permitted, or desired.

un·der·went (un′dər·went′) *p.t.* of UNDERGO.

un·der·wood (un′dər·wŏŏd′) *n.* UNDERBRUSH.

un·der·world (un′dər·wûrld′) *n.* **1** The mythical abode of the dead; Hades. **2** The world of organized crime and vice.

un·der·write (un′dər·rīt′) *v.* **·wrote, ·writ·ten, ·writ·ing** *v.t.* **1** To write beneath or sign something, as a document. **2** To agree or subscribe to, esp. to agree to pay for (an enterprise, etc.). **3** In insurance: **a** To sign one's name to (an insurance policy), thereby assuming liability for certain designated losses or damage. **b** To insure. **c** To assume (a risk or a liability for a certain sum) by way of insurance. **4** To engage to buy, at a determined price and time, all or part of the stock in (a new enterprise or company) that is not subscribed for by the public. —*v.i.* **5** To act as an underwriter; esp., to issue a policy of insurance.

un·der·writ·er (un′dər·rī′tər) *n.* **1** A person or company in the insurance business; also, an insurance employee who determines the risks involved, the amount of the premiums, etc., for a specific applicant or policy. **2** One who underwrites something.

un·de·sir·a·ble (un′di·zīr′ə·bəl) *adj.* Not desirable; objectionable. —*n.* An undesirable person. —**un′de·sir′a·bil′i·ty** *n.* —**un′de·sir′a·bly** *adv.*

un·do (un·dōō′) *v.t.* **·did, ·done, ·do·ing** **1** To cause to be as if never done; reverse, annul, or cancel. **2** To loosen or untie. **3** To unfasten and open. **4** To bring to ruin; destroy. **5** To disturb emotionally. [< OE *undōn*] —**un·do′er** *n.*

un·do·ing (un·dōō′ing) *n.* **1** A reversal of what has been done. **2** Destruction; ruin; disgrace; also, the cause of such ruin or disgrace. **3** The action of unfastening, loosening, opening, etc.

un·done[1] (un·dun′) *adj.* **1** Untied; unfastened. **2** Ruined; disgraced. **3** Extremely disturbed or upset. [Orig. p.p. of UNDO]

un·done[2] (un·dun′) *adj.* Not done.

un·doubt·ed (un·dou′tid) *adj.* **1** Not doubted; assured; certain. **2** Not viewed with distrust; unsuspected. —**un·doubt′ed·ly** *adv.*

un·draw (un·drô′) *v.t. & v.i.* **·drew, ·drawn, ·draw·ing** To draw open, away, or aside.

un·dreamed-of (un·drēmd′uv′, -dremt′-) *adj.* Never imagined; wholly unforeseen: *undreamed-of* joy. Also **un·dreamt′-of′** (-dremt′-).

un·dress (un·dres′) *v.t.* **1** To divest of clothes; strip. **2** To remove the dressing or bandages from, as a wound. **3** To divest of special attire; disrobe. —*v.i.* **4** To remove one's clothing. —*n.* **1** The state of being nude or in only partial attire, as in undergarments, dressing robe, etc. **2** The military or naval uniform worn by officers when not in full dress.

un·due (un·dyōō′) *adj.* **1** Excessive; immoderate. **2** Not justified by law; illegal. **3** Not yet due, as a bill. **4** Not appropriate; improper.

un·du·lant (un′dyə·lənt, -jə-) *adj.* Undulating; fluctuating.

undulant fever A persistent bacterial disease usu. transmitted to man by contact with infected cattle and characterized by recurrent fever, exhaustion, neuralgic pains, etc.

un·du·late (un′dyə·lāt, -jə-) *v.* **·lat·ed, ·lat·ing** *v.t.* **1** To cause to move like a wave or in waves. **2** To give a wavy appearance or surface to. —*v.i.* **3** To move like a wave or waves. **4** To have a wavy form or appearance. —*adj.* (-lit, -lāt) Having a wavelike appearance, surface, or markings: also **un′du·lat′ed.** [< L *unda* wave]

un·du·la·tion (un′dyə·lā′shən, -jə-) *n.* **1** A waving or sinuous motion. **2** An appearance as of waves; a gentle rise and fall. —**un′du·la·to′ry** (-lə·tôr′ē, -tō′rē) *adj.*

un·du·ly (un·dyōō′lē) *adv.* **1** Excessively. **2** Improperly; unjustly.

un·dy·ing (un·dī′ing) *adj.* Immortal; eternal.

un·earned (un·ûrnd′) *adj.* **1** Not earned by labor, skill, etc. **2** Undeserved.

unearned increment An increase in the value of land or property independent of any efforts of the owner, as through an increase of population that creates demand.

un·earth (un·ûrth′) *v.t.* **1** To dig or root up from the earth. **2** To reveal; discover.

un·earth·ly (un·ûrth′lē) *adj.* **1** Not, or seemingly not, of this earth. **2** Supernatural; terrifying; weird; terrible. **3** *Informal* Ridiculous, absurd, preposterous, etc. —**un·earth′li·ness** *n.*

un·ease (un·ēz′) *n.* Mental or emotional discomfort, dissatisfaction, anxiety, etc.

un·eas·y (un·ē′zē) *adj.* **·eas·i·er, ·eas·i·est** **1** Deprived of ease; disturbed; unquiet. **2** Not comfortable; causing discomfort. **3** Showing embarassment or constraint; strained. **4** Not stable or secure; precarious: an *uneasy* peace. —**un·eas′i·ly** *adv.* —**un·eas′i·ness** *n.*

un·em·ploy·a·ble (un′əm·ploi′ə·bəl) *adj.* Not employable because of illness, age, physical incapacity, etc. —*n.* An unemployable person.

un·em·ployed (un′əm·ploid′) *adj.* **1** Having no employment; out of work. **2** Not put to use or turned to account; idle. —**the unemployed** People who have no jobs. —**un′·em·ploy′ment** *n.*

un·e·qual (un·ē′kwəl) *adj.* **1** Not equal in size, importance, weight, ability, duration, etc. **2** Inadequate; insufficient: with *to.* **3** Not balanced or uniform; variable; irregular. **4** Involving poorly matched competitors or contestants: an *unequal* contest. —**un·e′qual·ly** *adv.*

un·e·qualed (un·ē′kwəld) *adj.* Not equaled or matched; unrivaled. Also **un·e′qualled.**

un·e·quiv·o·cal (un′i·kwiv′ə·kəl) *adj.* Understandable in only one way; not ambiguous; clear. —**un′e·quiv′o·cal·ly** *adv.* —**un′e·quiv′o·cal·ness** *n.*

un·err·ing (un·ûr′ing, -er′-) *adj.* **1** Making no mistakes. **2** Certain; accurate; infallible. —**un·err′ing·ly** *adv.*

UNESCO (yōō·nes′kō) United Nations Educational, Scientific, and Cultural Organization.

un·es·sen·tial (un′ə·sen′shəl) *adj.* Not essential; not needed. —*n.* Something not essential; an extra.

un·e·ven (un·ē′vən) *adj.* **1** Not even, smooth, or level; rough. **2** Not straight, parallel, or perfectly horizontal. **3** Not equal or even, as in length, width, etc. **4** Not balanced or matched equally. **5** Not uniform; variable; fluctuating. **6** Not fair or just. **7** Not divisible by two without remainder; odd: said of numbers. —**un·e′ven·ly** *adv.* —**un·e′ven·ness** *n.*

un·e·vent·ful (un′i·vent′fəl) *adj.* Devoid of any noteworthy or unusual events or incidents; quiet. —**un′e·vent′·ful·ly** *adv.* —**un′e·vent′ful·ness** *n.*

un·ex·am·pled (un′ig·zam′pəld) *adj.* Without a parallel example; unprecedented; unique.

un·ex·cep·tion·a·ble (un′ik·sep′shən·ə·bəl) *adj.* That cannot be objected to; without any flaw; irreproachable. —**un′ex·cep′tion·a·bly** *adv.*

un·ex·cep·tion·al (un′ik·sep′shən·əl) *adj.* **1** Not unusual or exceptional; ordinary. **2** Subject to no exception.

un·ex·pect·ed (un′ik·spek′tid) *adj.* Coming without warning; not expected; unforeseen. —**un′ex·pect′ed·ly** *adv.* —**un′ex·pect′ed·ness** *n.* —**Syn.** unanticipated, sudden.

un·fail·ing (un·fā′ling) *adj.* **1** Giving or constituting a supply that never fails; inexhaustible: an *unfailing* spring. **2** Always fulfilling requirements or expectation. **3** Sure; infallible. —**un·fail′ing·ly** *adv.* —**un·fail′ing·ness** *n.*

un·fair (un·fâr′) *adj.* **1** Marked by injustice, deception, or bias; not fair. **2** Not honest or ethical in business affairs. —**un·fair′ly** *adv.* —**un·fair′ness** *n.*

un·faith·ful (un·fāth′fəl) *adj.* **1** Not faithful to or abiding by a vow, agreement, duty, etc.; disloyal. **2** Not accurate or exact; unreliable. **3** Not true to marriage vows; adulterous. —**un·faith′ful·ly** *adv.* —**un·faith′ful·ness** *n.*

un·fa·mil·iar (un′fə·mil′yər) *adj.* **1** Not knowing well or at all: with *with: unfamiliar* with his plays. **2** Not familiarly known; strange: an *unfamiliar* face. —**un′fa·mil′i·ar′·i·ty** (-mil′ē·ar′ə·tē) *n.* —**un′fa·mil′iar·ly** *adv.*

un·fast·en (un·fas′ən, -fäs′-) *v.t.* To untie or undo; loosen or open.

un·fa·vor·a·ble (un·fā′vər·ə·bəl) *adj.* **1** Not favorable; adverse. **2** Not propitious. —**un·fa′vor·a·bly** *adv.*

un·feel·ing (un·fē′ling) *adj.* **1** Not sympathetic; hard; callous. **2** Having no feeling or sensation. —**un·feel′ing·ly** *adv.* —**un·feel′ing·ness** *n.*

un·feigned (un·fānd′) *adj.* Not feigned; sincere; genuine. —**un·feign′ed·ly** (-fān′id·lē) *adv.*

un·fit (un·fit′) *v.t.* **·fit·ed** or **·fit, ·fit·ting** To deprive of requisite fitness, skill, etc.; disqualify. —*adj.* **1** Not able to meet the requirements or needs; unsuitable. **2** Not physically or mentally sound or fit. **3** Not appropriate or proper for a given purpose. —**un·fit′ly** *adv.* —**un·fit′ness** *n.*

un·fix (un·fiks′) *v.t.* **1** To unfasten; loosen; detach. **2** To unsettle.

un·flag·ging (un·flag′ing) *adj.* Not diminishing or failing; tireless. —**un·flag′ging·ly** *adv.*

un·flap·pa·ble (un·flap′ə·bəl) *adj. Informal* Characterized by unshakable composure; imperturbable. —**un·flap′·pa·bil′i·ty** *n.*

un·fledged (un·flejd′) *adj.* **1** Not yet fledged, as a young bird. **2** Inexperienced or immature.

un·flinch·ing (un·flin′ching) *adj.* Done without shrinking; steadfast. —**un·flinch′ing·ly** *adv.*

un·fold (un·fōld′) *v.t.* **1** To open or spread out (something folded). **2** To unwrap. **3** To reveal or make clear, as by explaining or disclosing gradually. **4** To develop. —*v.i.* **5** To become opened; expand. **6** To become manifest or develop fully.

un·fore·seen (un′fôr·sēn′, -fōr-) *adj.* Unexpected.

un·for·get·ta·ble (un′fər·get′ə·bəl) *adj.* Difficult or impossible to forget; memorable. —**un′for·get′ta·bly** *adv.*

un·for·tu·nate (un·fôr′chə·nit) *adj.* **1** Not fortunate or lucky. **2** Causing, attended by, or resulting from misfortune; disastrous. **3** Not suitable or proper; bad; regrettable: an *unfortunate* thing to say. —*n.* One who is unfortunate. —**un·for′tu·nate·ly** *adv.* —**un·for′tu·nate·ness** *n.*

un·found·ed (un·foun′did) *adj.* **1** Not based on fact; groundless; baseless. **2** Not established.

un·fre·quent·ed (un′fri·kwen′tid) *adj.* Rarely or never visited or frequented.

un·friend·ly (un·frend′lē) *adj.* **1** Not friendly or sympathetic. **2** Not favorable or propitious. —**un·friend′li·ness** *n.*

un·frock (un·frok′) *v.t.* **1** To remove a frock or gown from. **2** To depose, as a priest, from ecclesiastical rank.

un·furl (un·fûrl′) *v.t. & v.i.* **1** To unroll, as a flag; spread out. **2** To unfold. —**un·furled′** *adj.*

un·gain·ly (un·gān′lē) *adj.* **1** Awkward; clumsy. **2** Not attractive. —**un·gain′li·ness** *n.*

un·glued (un·glo͞od′) *adj.* No longer glued together; separated. —**come unglued** *Slang* To become mentally or emotionally upset.

un·god·ly (un·god′lē) *adj.* **1** Without reverence for God; impious. **2** Unholy; sinful. **3** *Informal* Outrageous. —*adv. Informal* Outrageously. —**un·god′li·ness** *n.*

un·gov·ern·a·ble (un·guv′ər·nə·bəl) *adj.* That cannot be governed; wild; unruly. —**un·gov′ern·a·bly** *adv.*

un·gra·cious (un·grā′shəs) *adj.* **1** Lacking in graciousness of manner; unmannerly. **2** Not pleasing; offensive. —**un·gra′cious·ly** *adv.* —**un·gra′cious·ness** *n.* —**Syn. 1** discourteous, rude, impolite, uncivil, ill-mannered, ill-bred.

un·grate·ful (un·grāt′fəl) *adj.* **1** Feeling or showing a lack of gratitude; not thankful. **2** Not pleasant; disagreeable. **3** Unrewarding; yielding no return. —**un·grate′ful·ly** *adv.* —**un·grate′ful·ness** *n.*

un·guard·ed (un·gär′did) *adj.* **1** Having no guard; unprotected. **2** Thoughtless; careless. **3** Without guile; direct; open. —**un·guard′ed·ly** *adv.*

un·guent (ung′gwənt) *n.* An ointment or salve. [< L *unguere* anoint] —**un′guen·tar′y** (-gwən·ter′ē) *adj.*

un·guis (ung′gwis) *n. pl.* **·gues** (-gwēz) A hoof, claw, nail, or talon. [L, nail]

un·gu·late (ung′gyə·lit, -lāt) *adj.* Having hoofs. —*n.* A hoofed mammal. [< L *ungula* hoof]

un·hand (un·hand′) *v.t.* To remove one's hand from; release from the hand or hands; let go.

un·hand·y (un·han′dē) *adj.* **·di·er, ·di·est 1** Hard to get to or use; inconvenient. **2** Clumsy; lacking in manual skill. —**un·hand′i·ly** *adv.*

un·hap·py (un·hap′ē) *adj.* **·pi·er, ·pi·est 1** Sad; depressed. **2** Causing or constituting misery, unrest, or dissatisfaction: *unhappy* circumstances. **3** Unfortunate; unpropitious. **4** Exhibiting lack of tact or judgment; inappropriate. —**un·hap′pi·ly** *adv.* —**un·hap′pi·ness** *n.*

un·health·y (un·hel′thē) *adj.* **·health·i·er, ·health·i·est 1** Lacking health, vigor, or wholesomeness; sickly. **2** Causing sickness; injurious to health. **3** Morally harmful. **4** Dangerous; risky. —**un·health′i·ly** *adv.* —**un·health′i·ness** *n.*

un·heard (un·hûrd′) *adj.* **1** Not perceived by the ear. **2** Not granted a hearing. **3** Obscure; unknown.

un·heard-of (un·hûrd′uv′, -ov′) *adj.* **1** Not known of before; unknown or unprecedented. **2** Outrageous; unbelievable.

un·hinge (un·hinj′) *v.t.* **·hinged, ·hing·ing 1** To take from the hinges. **2** To remove the hinges of. **3** To detach; dislodge. **4** To throw into confusion; unsettle, as the mind.

un·hitch (un·hich′) *v.t.* To unfasten.

un·ho·ly (un·hō′lē) *adj.* **·ho·li·er, ·ho·li·est 1** Not hallowed. **2** Wicked; sinful. **3** *Informal* Frightful; outrageous. —**un·ho′li·ly** *adv.* —**un·ho′li·ness** *n.*

uni- *combining form* One; single; one only: *unifoliate.* [< L *unus* one]

U·ni·ate (yo͞o′nē·at, -it) *n.* A member of any community of Eastern Christians that acknowledges the supremacy of the pope at Rome, but retains its own liturgy, ceremonies, and rites. —*adj.* Of the Uniates or their faith. Also **U′ni·at** (-it).

u·ni·cam·er·al (yo͞o′nə·kam′ər·əl) *adj.* Consisting of but one chamber, as a legislature.

Unicorn

UNICEF (yo͞o′nə·sef) United Nations Children's Fund. [< *U(nited) N(ations) I(nternational) C(hildren's) E(mergency) F(und),* its former name]

u·ni·cel·lu·lar (yo͞o′nə·sel′yə·lər) *adj.* Consisting of a single cell, as a protozoan.

u·ni·corn (yo͞o′nə·kôrn′) *n.* A mythical, horselike animal with one horn growing from the middle of its forehead. [< L *unicornis* one-horned]

u·ni·cy·cle (yo͞o′nə·sī′kəl) *n.* A bicyclelike vehicle having only a single wheel propelled by pedals.

u·ni·form (yo͞o′nə·fôrm′) *adj.* **1** Being always the same or alike; not varying: *uniform* temperature. **2** Having the same form, color, character, etc. as others: a line of *uniform* battleships. **3** Being the same throughout in appearance, color, surface, etc.: a *uniform* texture. **4** Consistent in effect, action, etc.: a *uniform* law for all drivers. —*n.* A distinctive dress or suit worn, esp. when on duty, by members of the same organization, service, etc., as soldiers, sailors, postmen, etc. —*v.t.* To put into or clothe with a uniform. [< L *unus* one + *forma* form] **—u′ni·form·ly** *adv.*

u·ni·form·i·ty (yo͞o′nə·fôr′mə·tē) *n. pl.* **·ties 1** The state or quality of being uniform. **2** An instance of it.

u·ni·fy (yo͞o′nə·fī) *v.t.* **·fied, ·fy·ing** To cause to be one; make uniform; unite. [< L *unus* one + *facere* make] **—u′ni·fi·ca′·tion** (-fə·kā′shən), **u′ni·fi′er** *n.*

u·ni·lat·er·al (yo͞o′nə·lat′ər·əl) *adj.* **1** Of, relating to, or affecting one side only; one-sided. **2** Made, undertaken, done, or signed by only one of two or more people or parties. **3** Growing on or turning toward one side only. **—u′ni·lat′er·al·ism** *n.* **—u′ni·lat′er·al·ly** *adv.*

un·im·peach·a·ble (un′im·pē′chə·bəl) *adj.* Not impeachable; beyond question as regards truth, honesty, etc.; faultless; blameless. **—un′im·peach′a·bly** *adv.*

un·im·proved (un′im·pro͞ovd′) *adj.* **1** Not improved; not bettered or advanced. **2** Having no improvements; not cleared, cultivated, or built upon. **3** Not made anything of; unused.

un·in·tel·li·gi·ble (un′in·tel′ə·jə·bəl) *adj.* Impossible to understand; incomprehensible. **—un′in·tel′li·gi·bil′i·ty** *n.* **—un′in·tel′li·gi·bly** *adv.*

un·in·ter·es·ted (un·in′tər·is·tid, -tris-) *adj.* Not interested; indifferent; unconcerned. • See DISINTERESTED.

un·ion (yo͞on′yən) *n.* **1** The act or an instance of uniting two or more things into one, as: **a** A political joining together, as of states or nations. **b** Marriage; wedlock. **2** The condition of being united or joined; junction. **3** Something formed by uniting or combining parts, as: **a** A confederation, coalition, or league, as of nations, states, or individuals. **b** LABOR UNION. **4** A device for joining mechanical parts, esp. a coupling device for pipes or rods. **5** A college or university organization that provides facilities for recreation, meetings, light meals, etc.: also **student union. 6** A device emblematic of union used in a flag or ensign, as the blue field with white stars in the flag of the U.S. —*adj.* Of, being, or relating to a union. —**the Union** The United States of America. [< L *unus* one]

un·ion·ism (yo͞on′yən·iz′əm) *n.* **1** The principle of union. **2** Labor unions collectively; also, their principles and practices. **—un′ion·ist** *n.* **—un′ion·is′tic** *adj.*

Un·ion·ism (yo͞on′yən·iz′əm) *n.* During the U.S. Civil War, the advocacy of political union between the States, as opposed to secession. **—Un′ion·ist** *n.*

un·ion·ize (yo͞on′yən·īz) *v.* **·ized, ·iz·ing** *v.t.* To cause to join or to organize into a labor union. —*v.i.* To become a member of or organize a labor union. **—un′ion·i·za′tion** *n.*

Union Jack The British national flag.

Union of Soviet Socialist Republics A federal union of 15 republics in N Eurasia, 8,646,400 sq. mi., cap. Moscow.

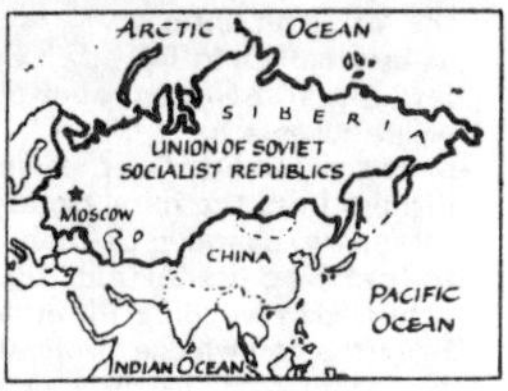

union shop A factory, office, hospital, etc., in which only members of a labor union are employed.

union suit A one-piece, man's or boy's undergarment consisting of shirt and drawers.

u·nique (yo͞o·nēk′) *adj.* **1** Being the only one of its kind; single; sole. **2** Being without equal; unparalleled. **3** Very unusual or remarkable; exceptional, extraordinary, etc. [< L *unicus* < *unus* one] **—u·nique′ly** *adv.* **—u·nique′ness** *n.*

u·ni·sex (yo͞o′nə·seks′) *Informal adj.* For, appropriate to, or having characteristics of both sexes: *unisex* fashions. —*n.* The embodiment or integration of qualities, characteristics, etc., of both sexes, as in appearance, clothes, or activities.

u·ni·sex·u·al (yo͞o′nə·sek′sho͞o·əl) *adj.* **1** Of only one sex; dioecious: a *unisexual* plant. **2** *Informal* Of or having to do with unisex. **—u′ni·sex′u·al′i·ty** *n.* **—u′ni·sex′u·al·ly** *adv.*

u·ni·son (yo͞o′nə·sən, -zən) *n.* **1** A condition of perfect agreement and accord; harmony. **2** *Music* **a** The interval between tones of identical pitch. **b** The simultaneous sounding of the same tones by two or more parts. —**in unison 1** So that identical tones are sounded simultaneously by two or more parts. **2** So that identical words or sounds are uttered simultaneously. **3** In perfect agreement. [< L *unisonus* having a single sound]

u·nit (yo͞o′nit) *n.* **1** A predetermined quantity, as of time, length, work, value, etc., used as a standard of measurement or comparison. **2** A fixed amount of work or classroom hours used in calculating a scholastic degree. **3** The quantity, as of a drug or antigen, required to produce a given effect or result. **4** A person or group considered both singly and as a constituent part of a whole: a military *unit.* **5** Something, as a mechanical part or device, having a specific function and serving as part of a whole: the electrical *unit* of a percolator. **6** *Math.* A quantity whose measure is represented by the number 1. —*adj.* Of or being a unit: the *unit* value of an article of merchandise. [Short for UNITY]

U·ni·tar·i·an (yo͞o′nə·târ′ē·ən) *n.* A member of a Protestant denomination which rejects the doctrine of the Trinity, but accepts the ethical teachings of Jesus and emphasizes complete freedom of religious opinion and the independence of each local congregation. —*adj.* Pertaining to the Unitarians, or to their teachings. **—U′ni·tar′i·an·ism** *n.*

u·ni·tar·y (yo͞o′nə·ter′ē) *adj.* **1** Of a unit or units. **2** Characterized by, based on, or pertaining to unity. **3** Having the nature of or used as a unit.

u·nite (yo͞o·nīt′) *v.* **u·nit·ed, u·nit·ing** *v.t.* **1** To join together so as to form a whole; combine. **2** To bring into close connection, as by legal, physical, marital, social, or other ties: to be *united* in marriage; allies *united* by a common interest. **3** To have or possess in combination: to *unite* courage with wisdom. **4** To cause to adhere; combine. —*v.i.* **5** To become or be merged into one; be consolidated by or as if by adhering. **6** To join together for action. [< L *unus* one]

u·nit·ed (yo͞o·nī′tid) *adj.* **1** Incorporated into one; combined. **2** Of or resulting from joint action. **3** Harmonious; in agreement. **—u·nit′ed·ly** *adv.* **—u·nit′ed·ness** *n.*

United Kingdom A constitutional monarchy located on several islands off the coast of N Europe, comprising Great Britain, Northern Ireland, and nearby islands, 94,284 sq. mi., cap. London.

United Kingdom

United Nations 1 A coalition to resist the military aggression of the Axis Powers in World War II, formed of 26 national states in January, 1942. **2** An international organization of sovereign states (originally called the **United Nations Organization**) created by the United Nations Charter adopted at San Francisco in 1945.

United States of America A federal republic including 50 states (49 in North America, and Hawaii, an archipelago in the Pacific Ocean), and the District of Columbia, 3,615,222 sq. mi., cap. Washington, D.C.

u·ni·ty (yōō′nə·tē) *n. pl.* **·ties** 1 The state or quality of being one or united; oneness. 2 The product or result of being one or united. 3 Singleness of purpose or action. 4 A state of mutual understanding. 5 The quality or fact of being a whole through the unification of separate or individual parts. 6 In a literary or artistic production, a combination of parts that exhibits a prevailing oneness of purpose, thought, spirit, and style; also, the cohesive or harmonious effect so produced. 7 *Math.* **a** The number one. **b** The element of a number system that leaves any number unchanged under multiplication. [< L *unus* one]

Univ. Universalist; University.

univ. universal; universally; university.

u·ni·va·lent (yōō′nə·vā′lənt) *adj. Chem.* Having a valence or combining value of one; monovalent. **—u′ni·va′·lence, u′ni·va′len·cy** *n.*

u·ni·valve (yōō′nə·valv′) *adj.* Having the shell in one piece, as a snail. Also **u′ni·val′vate, u′ni·valved′**. *—n.* 1 A mollusk having a univalve shell; a gastropod. 2 A shell of a single piece. **—u′ni·val′vu·lar** (-val′vyə·lər) *adj.*

u·ni·ver·sal (yōō′nə·vûr′səl) *adj.* 1 Prevalent or common everywhere or among all things or persons. 2 Of, applicable to, for, or including all things, persons, cases, etc., without exception. 3 Accomplished or interested in a vast variety of subjects, activities, etc.: Leonardo da Vinci was a *universal* genius. 4 Adapted or adaptable to a great variety of uses, shapes, etc. 5 *Logic* Including or designating all the members of a class. *—n.* 1 *Logic* A universal proposition. 2 Any general or universal notion or idea. 3 A behavioral trait common to all men or cultures. **—u′ni·ver′sal·ly** *adv.* **—u′ni·ver′sal·ism, u′ni·ver′sal·ness** *n.*

u·ni·ver·sal·i·ty (yōō′nə·vər·sal′ə·tē) *n.* 1 The quality, condition, or an instance of being universal. 2 Limitlessness, as of range, occurrence, etc.

u·ni·ver·sal·ize (yōō′nə·vûr′səl·īz) *v.t.* **·ized, ·iz·ing** To make universal. **—u′ni·ver′sal·i·za′tion** *n.*

universal joint *Mech.* A coupling for connecting two shafts, etc., so as to permit angular motion in all directions. Also **universal coupling.**

u·ni·verse (yōō′nə·vûrs) *n.* 1 The aggregate of all existing things; the whole creation embracing all celestial bodies and all of space; the cosmos. 2 In restricted sense, the earth. 3 Something regarded as being a universe in its comprehensiveness, as a field of thought or activity. [< L *universus* turned, combined into one < *unus* one + *versus,* p.p. of *vertere* turn]

u·ni·ver·si·ty (yōō′nə·vûr′sə·tē) *n. pl.* **·ties** 1 An educational institution for higher instruction, usu., in the U.S., an institution that includes an undergraduate college or colleges and professional schools granting advanced degrees in law, medicine, the sciences, academic subjects, etc. 2 The buildings, grounds, etc., of a university. 3 The students, faculty, and administration of a university.

un·just (un·just′) *adj.* Not legitimate, fair, or just; wrongful. **—un·just′ly** *adv.*

un·kempt (un·kempt′) *adj.* 1 Not combed: said of hair. 2 Not neat or tidy. 3 Without polish; rough. [< UN-[1] + *kempt* combed, p.p. of *kemb,* dial. var. of COMB]

un·kind (un·kīnd′) *adj.* Lacking kindness; unsympathetic; harsh; cruel. **—un·kind′ly** *adj.* **(·li·er, ·li·est)** *& adv.* **— un·kind′li·ness, un·kind′ness** *n.*

un·known (un·nōn′) *adj.* 1 Not known; not apprehended mentally; not recognized, as a fact or person. 2 Not determined or identified: an *unknown* substance. *—n.* An unknown person, thing, or quantity.

un·lace (un·lās′) *v.t.* **·laced, ·lac·ing** To loosen or unfasten the lacing of; untie.

un·law·ful (un·lô′fəl) *adj.* 1 Contrary to or in violation of law; illegal. 2 Not moral or ethical. **—un·law′ful·ly** *adv.* **— un·law′ful·ness** *n.*

un·learn (un·lûrn′) *v.t.* **·learned** or **·learnt, ·learn·ing** 1 To dismiss from the mind (something learned); forget. 2 To attempt to abandon the habit of.

un·learn·ed (un·lûr′nid) *adj.* 1 Not possessed of or characterized by learning; illiterate; ignorant. 2 Characterized by lack of knowledge, professional skill, etc. 3 (un·lûrnd′) Not acquired by learning or study.

un·leash (un·lēsh′) *v.t.* To set free from or as from a leash: He *unleashed* his rage.

un·less (un·les′) *conj.* If it be not a fact that; except that: *Unless* we persevere, we shall lose. *—prep.* Save; except; excepting: with an implied verb: *Unless* a miracle, he'll not be back in time. [Earlier *onlesse (that)* in a less case < ON + LESS]

un·let·tered (un·let′ərd) *adj.* Not educated; not lettered; illiterate.

un·like (un·līk′) *adj.* Having little or no resemblance; different. —*prep.* 1 Not like; different from. 2 Not characteristic of: It's *unlike* her to complain. —**un·like′ness** *n.*

un·like·ly (un·līk′lē) *adj.* 1 Improbable. 2 Not inviting or promising success. —*adv.* Improbably. —**un·like′li·hood, un·like′li·ness** *n.*

un·lim·it·ed (un·lim′it·id) *adj.* 1 Having no limits in space, number, or time. 2 Not restricted or limited.

un·load (un·lōd′) *v.t.* 1 To remove the load or cargo from. 2 To take off or discharge (cargo, etc.). 3 To relieve of something burdensome or oppressive. 4 To withdraw the charge of ammunition from. 5 *Informal* To dispose of, esp. by selling in large quantities. —*v.i.* 6 To discharge freight, cargo, etc.

un·lock (un·lok′) *v.t.* 1 To unfasten (something locked). 2 To open; release. 3 To lay open; reveal or disclose. —*v.i.* 4 To become unlocked.

un·looked-for (un·lo͝okt′fôr′) *adj.* Not anticipated; unexpected.

un·loose (un·lo͞os′) *v.t.* **·loosed, ·loos·ing** To make loose; set free; undo, release, etc. Also **un·loos′en** (-lo͞o′sən).

un·luck·y (un·luk′ē) *adj.* **·luck·i·er, ·luck·i·est** 1 Not favored by luck; unfortunate. 2 Resulting in or attended by ill luck; disastrous. 3 Likely to prove unfortunate; inauspicious. —**un·luck′i·ly** *adv.* —**un·luck′i·ness** *n.*

un·make (un·māk′) *v.t.* **·made, ·mak·ing** 1 To reduce to the original condition or form. 2 To ruin; destroy. 3 To deprive of rank, power, etc.

un·man (un·man′) *v.t.* **·manned, ·man·ning** 1 To cause to lose courage; dishearten. 2 To deprive of manly qualities; make weak or timid. 3 To castrate; emasculate.

un·man·ly (un·man′lē) *adj.* Not manly; weak, cowardly, effeminate, etc. —**un·man′li·ness** *n.*

un·mask (un·mask′, -mäsk′) *v.t.* 1 To remove a mask from. 2 To expose the true nature of. —*v.i.* 3 To remove one's mask or disguise.

un·mean·ing (un·mē′ning) *adj.* 1 Having no meaning: an *unmeaning* speech. 2 Having no expression: an *unmeaning* stare. —**un·mean′ing·ly** *adv.* —**un·mean′ing·ness** *n.*

un·men·tion·a·ble (un·men′shən·ə·bəl) *adj.* Not fit to be mentioned or discussed; embarrassing. —*n.pl.* Things not ordinarily mentioned or discussed, esp. undergarments. —**un·men′tion·a·ble·ness** *n.* —**un·men′tion·a·bly** *adv.*

un·mer·ci·ful (un·mûr′sə·fəl) *adj.* 1 Showing no mercy; cruel; pitiless. 2 Extreme; exorbitant. —**un·mer′ci·ful·ly** *adv.* —**un·mer′ci·ful·ness** *n.*

un·mis·tak·a·ble (un′mis·tā′kə·bəl) *adj.* That cannot be mistaken for something else; evident; obvious. —**un′mis·tak′a·bly** *adv.*

un·mit·i·gat·ed (un·mit′ə·gā′tid) *adj.* 1 Not relieved or lessened: *unmitigated* sorrow. 2 Absolute; thoroughgoing: an *unmitigated* liar. —**un·mit′i·gat′ed·ly** *adv.*

un·mor·al (un·môr′əl, -mor′-) *adj.* 1 Incapable of distinguishing between right and wrong; not guided by moral considerations. 2 Outside the realm of morality or ethics. —**un·mo·ral·i·ty** (un′mə·ral′ə·tē) *n.* • *Unmoral, amoral,* and *immoral* are alike in meaning not moral. However, *unmoral* and *amoral* are synonomous in referring to objects or acts (or people involved with such objects or acts) which stand outside the realm of morality whereas *immoral* infers a conflict with accepted standards of morality.

un·nat·u·ral (un·nach′ər·əl, -nach′rəl, un′-) *adj.* 1 Contrary to the norm. 2 Contrary to the common laws of morality or decency; monstrous; inhuman. 3 Contrived; artificial. —**un·nat′u·ral·ly** *adv.* —**un·nat′u·ral·ness** *n.*

un·nec·es·sary (un·nes′ə·ser′ē, un′-) *adj.* Not required; not necessary. —**un·nec·es·sar·i·ly** (un′nes′ə·ser′ə·lē) *adv.*

un·nerve (un·nûrv′) *v.t.* **·nerved, ·nerv·ing** 1 To deprive of strength, firmness, courage, etc. 2 To make nervous.

un·num·bered (un·num′bərd) *adj.* 1 Not counted. 2 Innumerable. 3 Not numbered.

un·oc·cu·pied (un·ok′yə·pīd′, un′-) *adj.* 1 Empty; uninhabited: an *unoccupied* house. 2 Idle; unemployed; at leisure.

un·of·fi·cial (un·ə·fish′əl) *adj.* Not official; not authoritative. —**un·of·fi′cial·ly** *adv.*

un·or·gan·ized (un·ôr′gən·īzd) *adj.* 1 Not organized. 2 Without form or structure. 3 Not unionized.

un·pack (un·pak′) *v.t.* 1 To open and take out the contents of. 2 To take out of the container, as something packed. —*v.i.* 3 To take the contents out of a suitcase, etc.

un·par·al·leled (un·par′ə·leld) *adj.* Without parallel; unmatched; unprecedented.

un·peg (un·peg′) *v.t.* **·pegged, ·peg·ging** To unfasten by removing the peg or pegs from.

un·peo·ple (un·pē′pəl) *v.t.* **·pled, ·pling** To depopulate; deprive of inhabitants.

un·per·son (un′pûr′sən) *n.* One reduced to a state of oblivion, as by official action or the loss of position, after a period of fame or public importance.

un·pin (un·pin′) *v.t.* **·pinned, ·pin·ning** 1 To remove a pin or pins from. 2 To unfasten by removing pins.

un·pleas·ant (un·plez′ənt) *adj.* Disagreeable; objectionable. —**un·pleas′ant·ly** *adv.* —**un·pleas′ant·ness** *n.*

un·plug (un·plug′) *v.t.* **·plugged, ·plug·ging** 1 To remove a plug from. 2 To remove an obstruction from, as a drain. 3 To break an electrical connection by pulling out a plug.

un·plumbed (un·plumd′) *adj.* Not measured or explored fully; unfathomed; unknown.

un·polled (un·pōld′) *adj.* 1 Not cast or registered: said of a vote. 2 Not canvassed in a poll.

un·pop·u·lar (un·pop′yə·lər) *adj.* Generally disliked, unaccepted, etc. —**un·pop′u·lar·ly** *adv.* —**un·pop′u·lar′i·ty** (-lar′ə·tē) *n.*

un·prac·ticed (un·prak′tist) *adj.* 1 Not skilled; inexperienced. 2 Not used or tried.

un·prec·e·dent·ed (un·pres′ə·den′tid) *adj.* Being without precedent; preceded by no similar case; novel.

un·prej·u·diced (un·prej′o͞o·dist) *adj.* 1 Free from prejudice or bias; impartial. 2 Not impaired, as a right.

un·prin·ci·pled (un·prin′sə·pəld) *adj.* Without moral principles; unscrupulous.

un·print·a·ble (un·prin′tə·bəl) *adj.* Not fit for printing, esp. because of profanity, obscenity, etc.

un·pro·fes·sion·al (un′prə·fesh′ən·əl) *adj.* 1 Not pertaining to, characteristic of, or belonging to a particular profession. 2 Violating the standards, ethical code, etc., of a profession. —**un′pro·fes′sion·al·ly** *adv.*

un·qual·i·fied (un·kwol′ə·fīd) *adj.* 1 Being without the proper qualifications; unfit. 2 Without limitation or restrictions; absolute: *unqualified* approval.

un·ques·tion·a·ble (un·kwes′chən·ə·bəl) *adj.* Too certain or sure to be open to question, doubt, etc.; indisputable. —**un·ques′tion·a·bly** *adv.*

un·qui·et (un·kwī′ət) *adj.* 1 Turbulent; agitated; tumultuous. 2 Disturbed physically, mentally or emotionally; restless; uneasy. —**un·qui′et·ly** *adv.* —**un·qui′et·ness** *n.*

un·quote (un·kwōt′) *v.t.* & *v.i.* **·quot·ed, ·quot·ing** To close (a quotation).

un·rav·el (un·rav′əl) *v.* **·eled** or **·elled, ·el·ing** or **·el·ling** *v.t.* 1 To separate the threads of, as a tangled skein or knitted article. 2 To unfold; explain, as a mystery or a plot. —*v.i.* 3 To become unraveled.

un·read (un·red′) *adj.* 1 Having read very little; uninformed; unlearned. 2 Not yet read or examined.

un·read·y (un·red′ē) *adj.* Not ready; unprepared, as for speech, action, etc. —**un·read′i·ly** *adv.* —**un·read′i·ness** *n.*

un·re·al (un·rē′əl, -rēl′) *adj.* 1 Having no reality, actual existence, or substance. 2 Not true or sincere; false. 3 Fanciful; imaginary. —**un·re·al·i·ty** (un′rē·al′ə·tē) *n.*

un·rea·son·a·ble (un·rē′zən·ə·bəl, -rēz′nə-) *adj.* 1 Acting without or contrary to reason. 2 Immoderate; exorbitant. —**un·rea′son·a·ble·ness** *n.* —**un·rea′son·a·bly** *adv.*

un·rea·son·ing (un·rē′zən·ing) *adj.* Marked by the absence of reason; irrational. —**un·rea′son·ing·ly** *adv.*

un·reel (un·rēl′) *v.t.* & *v.i.* To unwind from a reel.

un·re·gen·er·ate (un′ri·jen′ər·it) *adj.* 1 Not changed spiritually by regeneration; unrepentant. 2 Not convinced by or converted to a particular doctrine, theology, cause, etc. **3** Stubborn; recalcitrant.

un·re·lent·ing (un'ri·lent'ing) *adj.* **1** Not relenting; inflexible. **2** Not diminishing in pace, effort, speed, etc. —**un're·lent'ing·ly** *adv.*

un·re·li·a·ble (un'ri·lī'ə·bəl) *adj.* Not to be relied upon; undependable. —**un're·li'a·bil'i·ty, un're·li'a·ble·ness** *n.* —**un're·li'a·bly** *adv.*

un·re·lig·ious (un'ri·lij'əs) *adj.* **1** IRRELIGIOUS. **2** Not related to or connected with religion.

un·re·mit·ting (un'ri·mit'ing) *adj.* Incessant; not stopping or relaxing. —**un're·mit'ting·ly** *adv.* —**un're·mit'ting·ness** *n.*

un·re·served (un'ri·zûrvd') *adj.* **1** Not qualified; unrestricted. **2** Not reticent; informal; open. **3** Not set aside, as seats. —**un·re·serv·ed·ly** (un'ri·zûr'vid·lē) *adv.* —**un're·serv'·ed·ness** *n.*

un·rest (un'rest', un'rest') *n.* **1** Restlessness, esp. of the mind. **2** Angry dissatisfaction, bordering on revolt.

un·rid·dle (un·rid'l) *v.t.* **·dled, ·dling** To solve, as a mystery.

un·right·eous (un·rī'chəs) *adj.* **1** Not righteous; wicked; sinful. **2** Unfair; inequitable. —**un·right'eous·ly** *adv.* —**un·right'eous·ness** *n.*

un·ripe (un·rīp') *adj.* **1** Not arrived at maturity; not ripe; immature. **2** Not ready; not prepared. —**un·ripe'ness** *n.*

un·ri·valed (un·rī'vəld) *adj.* Having no rival; peerless.

un·roll (un·rōl') *v.t.* **1** To spread or open (something rolled up). **2** To exhibit to view. —*v.i.* **3** To become unrolled.

un·ruf·fled (un·ruf'əld) *adj.* **1** Not disturbed or agitated; calm. **2** Not ruffled; smooth.

un·ru·ly (un·ro͞o'lē) *adj.* Disposed to resist rule or discipline; ungovernable. —**un·ru'li·ness** *n.*

un·sad·dle (un·sad'l) *v.* **·dled, ·dling** *v.t.* **1** To remove a saddle from. **2** To remove from the saddle. —*v.i.* **3** To take the saddle off a horse.

un·said (un·sed') *adj.* Not said; not spoken.

un·sat·u·rat·ed (un·sach'ə·rā'tid) *adj.* **1** Capable of dissolving more solute. **2** Having at least one free or multiple valence bond available for direct union with an atom or radical: said of organic compounds.

un·sa·vor·y (un·sā'vər·ē) *adj.* **1** Having a disagreeable taste or odor. **2** Having no savor; tasteless. **3** Disagreeable or offensive, esp. morally. —**un·sa'vor·i·ness** *n.*

un·say (un·sā') *v.t.* **·said, ·say·ing** To retract (something said).

un·scathed (un·skāthd') *adj.* Not injured.

un·scram·ble (un·skram'bəl) *v.t.* **·bled, ·bling** *Informal* To resolve the confused, scrambled, or disordered condition of.

un·screw (un·skro͞o') *v.t.* **1** To remove the screw or screws from. **2** To remove or detach by withdrawing screws, or by turning. —*v.i.* **3** To become unscrewed or permit of being unscrewed.

un·scru·pu·lous (un·skro͞o'pyə·ləs) *adj.* Not scrupulous; having no scruples; unprincipled. —**un·scru'pu·lous·ly** *adv.* —**un·scru'pu·lous·ness** *n.*

un·seal (un·sēl') *v.t.* **1** To break or remove the seal of. **2** To open (that which has been sealed or closed).

un·search·a·ble (un·sûr'chə·bəl) *adj.* That cannot be searched into or explored; mysterious. —**un·search'a·ble·ness** *n.* —**un·search'a·bly** *adv.*

un·sea·son·a·ble (un·sē'zən·ə·bəl) *adj.* **1** Not suitable to the season: *unseasonable* weather. **2** Untimely; inopportune. —**un·sea'son·a·ble·ness** *n.* —**un·sea'son·a·bly** *adv.*

un·seat (un·sēt') *v.t.* **1** To remove from a seat. **2** To throw (a rider) from a horse. **3** To deprive of office or rank; depose.

un·seem·ly (un·sēm'lē) *adj.* **·li·er, ·li·est** Unbecoming, indecent, unattractive, or inappropriate. —*adv.* In an unseemly fashion. —**un·seem'li·ness** *n.*

un·set·tle (un·set'l) *v.* **·tled, ·tling** *v.t.* **1** To move from a fixed or settled condition. **2** To confuse, upset, or disturb. —*v.i.* **3** To become unsettled. —**un·set'tling·ly** *adv.*

un·sex (un·seks') *v.t.* To deprive of sex, sexual power, or the distinctive qualities of one's sex.

un·shack·le (un·shak'əl) *v.t.* **·led, ·ling 1** To unfetter; free from shackles. **2** To free, as from restraint.

un·sheathe (un·shēth') *v.t.* **·sheathed, ·sheath·ing** To take from or as from a scabbard or sheath; bare.

un·ship (un·ship') *v.t.* **·shipped, ·ship·ping** To unload from a ship or other vessel.

un·sight·ly (un·sīt'lē) *adj.* **·li·er, ·li·est** Offensive to the sight; ugly. —**un·sight'li·ness** *n.*

un·skilled (un·skild') *adj.* **1** Without special skill or training: an *unskilled* worker. **2** Requiring no special skill or training.

un·skill·ful (un·skil'fəl) *adj.* Lacking or not evincing skill; awkward; incompetent. Also **un·skil'ful.** —**un·skill'ful·ly** *adv.* —**un·skill'ful·ness** *n.*

un·snap (un·snap') *v.t.* **·snapped, ·snap·ping** To undo the snap or snaps of.

un·snarl (un·snärl') *v.t.* To undo snarls; disentangle.

un·so·cia·ble (un·sō'shə·bəl) *adj.* **1** Not sociable; not inclined to seek the society of others. **2** Lacking or not conducive to sociability. —**un·so·cia·bil·i·ty** (un·sō'shə·bil'ə·tē), **un·so'cia·ble·ness** *n.* —**un·so'cia·bly** *adv.*

un·sol·der (un·sod'ər) *v.t.* **1** To take apart (something soldered). **2** To separate; divide.

un·so·phis·ti·cat·ed (un'sə·fis'tə·kā'tid) *adj.* **1** Showing inexperience or naiveté; artless. **2** Genuine; pure. **3** Not complicated; simple. —**un'so·phis'ti·cat'ed·ly** *adv.* —**un'so·phis'ti·cat'ed·ness, un'so·phis'ti·ca'tion** *n.*

un·sound (un·sound') *adj.* **1** Not strong or solid: *unsound* construction. **2** Unhealthy in body or mind. **3** Untrue or logically invalid: *unsound* arguments. **4** Not deep; disturbed: said of sleep. —**un·sound'ly** *adv.* —**un·sound'ness** *n.*

un·spar·ing (un·spâr'ing) *adj.* **1** Not sparing or saving; lavish. **2** Showing no mercy. —**un·spar'ing·ly** *adv.* —**un·spar'ing·ness** *n.*

un·speak·a·ble (un·spē'kə·bəl) *adj.* **1** That cannot be expressed; unutterable: *unspeakable* joy. **2** Extremely bad or objectionable: an *unspeakable* crime. —**un·speak'a·ble·ness** *n.* —**un·speak'a·bly** *adv.*

un·sta·ble (un·stā'bəl) *adj.* **1** Lacking in stability or firmness; liable to move, sway, shake, etc. **2** Having no fixed purpose; easily influenced: an *unstable* character. **3** Emotionally unsteady. **4** Liable to change; fluctuating; variable: an *unstable* economy. **5** *Chem.* Easily decomposed, as certain compounds. —**un·sta'ble·ness** *n.* —**un·sta'bly** *adv.*

un·stead·y (un·sted'ē) *adj.* **·stead·i·er, ·stead·i·est** Not steady, as: **a** Not stable; liable to move or shake. **b** Variable; fluctuating. **c** Undependable or irregular. —**un·stead'·i·ly** *adv.* —**un·stead'i·ness** *n.*

un·stop (un·stop') *v.t.* **·stopped, ·stop·ping 1** To remove a stopper from. **2** To open by removing obstructions; clear.

un·stop·pa·ble (un·stop'ə·bəl) *adj.* Impossible to stop or check. —**un·stop'pa·bly** *adv.*

un·strap (un·strap') *v.t.* **·strapped, ·strap·ping** To undo or loosen the strap or straps of.

un·string (un·string') *v.t.* **·strung, ·string·ing 1** To remove from a string, as pearls. **2** To take the string or strings from. **3** To loosen the string or strings of, as a bow or guitar. **4** To make unstable or nervous.

un·struc·tured (un·struk'chərd) *adj.* Not having a definite organization or plan.

un·strung (un·strung') *adj.* **1** Having the strings removed or loosened. **2** Emotionally upset.

un·stud·ied (un·stud'ēd) *adj.* **1** Not stiff or artificial; natural; unaffected. **2** Not acquainted through study.

un·sub·stan·tial (un'səb·stan'shəl) *adj.* **1** Lacking solidity or strength; unstable; weak. **2** Having no valid basis in fact. **3** Unreal; fanciful. —**un'sub·stan'tial·ly** *adv.* —**un'sub·stan'ti·al'i·ty** (-shē·al'ə·tē) *n.*

un·suit·a·ble (un·s^yo͞o'tə·bəl) *adj.* Not suitable; unfitting. —**un·suit·a·bil·i·ty** (un's^yo͞o·tə·bil'ə·tē), **un·suit'a·ble·ness** *n.* —**un·suit'a·bly** *adv.*

un·sung (un·sung') *adj.* **1** Not celebrated, as in song or poetry; obscure. **2** Not sung.

un·swerv·ing (un·swûr'ving) *adj.* **1** Not changing or wavering; consistent: *unswerving* loyalty. **2** Not swerving from a path or course. —**un·swerv'ing·ly** *adv.*

un·tan·gle (un·tang'gəl) *v.t.* **·gled, ·gling 1** To free from tangles; disentangle. **2** To clear up or straighten out (a perplexing or confused situation, etc.).

un·taught (un·tôt') *adj.* **1** Not having been instructed; ignorant. **2** Known without having been taught; natural.

un·thank·ful (un·thangk'fəl) *adj.* **1** Not grateful. **2** Not appreciated. —**un·thank'ful·ly** *adv.* —**un·thank'ful·ness** *n.*

un·think·ing (un·thingk′ing) *adj.* Lacking thoughtfulness, care, or attention. —**un·think′ing·ly** *adv.* —**un·think′ing·ness** *n.*

un·thread (un·thred′) *v.t.* 1 To remove the thread from, as a needle. 2 To unravel; disentangle. 3 To find one's way out of, as a maze.

un·ti·dy (un·tī′dē) *adj.* **·di·er, ·di·est** Not tidy; messy; disorderly. —**un·ti′di·ly** *adv.* —**un·ti′di·ness** *n.*

un·tie (un·tī′) *v.* **·tied, ·ty·ing** *v.t.* 1 To loosen or undo, as a knot. 2 To free from that which binds or restrains. —*v.i.* 3 To become loosened or undone.

un·til (un·til′) *prep.* 1 Up to the time of; till: We will wait *until* midnight. 2 Before: used with a negative: The music doesn't begin *until* nine. —*conj.* 1 To the time when: *until* I die. 2 To the place or degree that: Walk east *until* you reach the river. 3 Before: with a negative: He couldn't leave *until* the car came for him. [< ME *und-* up to, as far as + TILL] • See TILL[2].

un·time·ly (un·tīm′lē) *adj.* Coming before time or not in proper time; premature or inopportune. —*adv.* Before time or not in the proper time; inopportunely.

un·to (un′tōō) *prep. Archaic* 1 To. 2 Until. [< ME *und-* up to, as far as + TO, on analogy with *until*]

un·told (un·tōld′) *adj.* 1 Not told, revealed, or described. 2 Of too great a number or extent to be counted or measured.

un·touch·a·ble (un·tuch′ə·bəl) *adj.* 1 Inaccessible to the touch; out of reach. 2 Forbidden to the touch. 3 Unpleasant, disgusting, or dangerous to touch. —*n.* In India, formerly, a member of the lowest caste.

un·to·ward (un·tôrd′, -tōrd′, -tə·wôrd′) *adj.* 1 Causing or characterized by difficulty or unhappiness; unfavorable. 2 Not easily managed; refractory. 3 Improper; unseemly. —**un·to·ward′ly** *adv.* —**un·to·ward′ness** *n.*

un·true (un·trōō′) *adj.* 1 Not true; false or incorrect. 2 Not conforming to rule or standard. 3 Disloyal; faithless. —**un·tru′ly** *adv.*

un·truth (un·trōōth′, un′trōōth′) *n. pl.* **·truths** (-trōōths, -trōōthz) 1 The quality or character of being untrue. 2 Something that is not true; a falsehood; lie.

un·truth·ful (un·trōōth′fəl) *adj.* 1 Not truthful; not telling the truth. 2 Not consistent with the truth. —**un·truth′ful·ly** *adv.* —**un·truth′ful·ness** *n.*

un·tu·tored (un·tyōō′tərd) *adj.* Not educated; untaught.

un·twine (un·twīn′) *v.* **·twined, ·twin·ing** *v.t.* 1 To undo (something twined); unwind by disentangling. —*v.i.* 2 To become undone.

un·twist (un·twist′) *v.t.* 1 To separate by a movement the reverse of twisting; untwine. —*v.i.* 2 To become untwined.

un·used (un·yōōzd′) *adj.* 1 Not used. 2 Never having been used. 3 Not accustomed: with *to.*

un·u·su·al (un·yōō′zhōō·əl) *adj.* Not usual; odd, rare, or extraordinary. —**un·u′su·al·ly** *adv.* —**un·u′su·al·ness** *n.*

un·ut·ter·a·ble (un·ut′ər·ə·bəl) *adj.* Too great, deep, etc., to be expressed or described in words. —**un·ut′ter·a·ble·ness** *n.* —**un·ut′ter·a·bly** *adv.*

un·var·nished (un·vär′nisht) *adj.* 1 Not varnished. 2 Not embellished or adorned; simple: the *unvarnished* truth.

un·veil (un·vāl′) *v.t.* 1 To remove the veil or covering from; disclose to view; reveal. —*v.i.* 2 To remove one's veil; reveal oneself.

un·war·rant·a·ble (un·wôr′ən·tə·bəl, -wor′-) *adj.* That cannot be justified; inexcusable; indefensible. —**un·war′rant·a·bly** *adv.*

un·war·y (un·wâr′ē) *adj.* **·war·i·er, ·war·i·est** Not careful; incautious. —**un·war′i·ly** *adv.* —**un·war′i·ness** *n.* —**Syn.** careless, heedless, reckless, unguarded.

un·well (un·wel′) *adj.* Sick; ailing.

un·wept (un·wept′) *adj.* 1 Not lamented or wept for. 2 Not shed, as tears.

un·whole·some (un·hōl′səm) *adj.* 1 Harmful to physical, mental, or moral health. 2 Sickly in health or in appearance. —**un·whole′some·ly** *adv.* —**un·whole′some·ness** *n.*

un·wield·y (un·wēl′dē) *adj.* **·i·er, ·i·est** Difficult to move, manage, or control, as because of great size or awkward shape. —**un·wield′i·ly** *adv.* —**un·wield′i·ness** *n.*

un·will·ing (un·wil′ing) *adj.* 1 Not willing; reluctant; loath. 2 Done, said, granted, etc., with reluctance. —**un·will′ing·ly** *adv.* —**un·will′ing·ness** *n.*

un·wind (un·wīnd′) *v.* **·wound, ·wind·ing** *v.t.* 1 To reverse the winding of; untwist or wind off. 2 To disentangle. —*v.i.* 3 To become disentangled or untwisted. 4 To free oneself from tension or anxieties; relax.

un·wise (un·wīz′) *adj.* Acting with, or showing, lack of wisdom or good sense. —**un·wise′ly** *adv.*

un·wit·ting (un·wit′ing) *adj.* 1 Having no knowledge or awareness; ignorant; unconscious. 2 Not intentional. —**un·wit′ting·ly** *adv.*

un·wont·ed (un·wôn′tid, -won′-) *adj.* Not ordinary or customary; unusual; uncommon. —**un·wont′ed·ly** *adv.* —**un·wont′ed·ness** *n.*

un·wor·thy (un·wûr′thē) *adj.* 1 Not worthy or deserving: often with *of.* 2 Not befitting or becoming: usu. with *of:* conduct *unworthy* of a gentleman. 3 Lacking worth or merit. 4 Not deserved or merited. —**un·wor′thi·ly** *adv.* —**un·wor′thi·ness** *n.*

un·wrap (un·rap′) *v.t.* **·wrapped, ·wrap·ping** To take the wrapping from; open; undo.

un·writ·ten (un·rit′n) *adj.* 1 Not written down; traditional. 2 Having no writing upon it; blank.

unwritten law A law or rule of conduct, procedure, etc., whose authority stems from custom and tradition rather than from a written command, decree, or statute.

un·yoke (un·yōk′) *v.t.* **·yoked, ·yok·ing** 1 To release from a yoke. 2 To separate; part.

up (up) *adv.* 1 Toward a higher place or level. 2 In or on a higher place. 3 To or at that which is literally or figuratively higher, as: **a** To or at a higher price: Barley is going *up.* **b** To or at a higher rank: people who have come *up* in the world. **c** To or at a greater size or amount: to swell *up.* **d** To or at a greater degree, intensity, volume, etc.: Turn *up* the radio. **e** To or at a place regarded as higher up: *up* north. **f** To a position above the horizon: when the sun comes *up.* **g** To a later point in time or life: from her childhood *up* to her teens. 4 In or into a vertical position; on one's feet. 5 Out of bed: to get *up.* 6 So as to be level or even (with) in time, degree, amount, etc.: *up* to the brim. 7 In or into commotion or activity: to be *up* in arms. 8 Into or in a place of safekeeping: to lay *up* provisions. 9 Completely; wholly: Houses were burned *up.* 10 In baseball, at bat. 11 In some sports: **a** In the lead. **b** Apiece; alike: said of a score. 12 So as to be compact, secure, etc.: Fold *up* the linen. 13 In or into view, existence, etc.: to bring *up* a subject; It will turn *up.* 14 *Naut.* Shifted to windward, as a tiller. 15 Into an aggregate number or quantity: Add *up* these figures. 16 To a source, conclusion, etc.: to follow *up* a rumor. —**be up against** *Informal* To meet with something to be dealt with. —**be up against it** *Informal* To be in trouble, usu. financial trouble. —**be up to** 1 *Informal* To be doing or about to do: What is he *up to?* 2 To be equal to or capable of: I'm not *up to* playing golf today. 3 To be incumbent upon: It's *up to* her to help us. —*adj.* 1 Moving or directed upward. 2 In, at, or to a high level, condition, etc.: Is the river *up* today? 3 Above the ground or horizon: The jonquils are *up.* 4 In a raised or erect position or condition: The new school is finally *up.* 5 At an end: Your time is *up.* 6 *Informal* Going on; taking place: What's *up?* 7 *Informal* Informed; up-to-date: *up* on the newest movies. 8 Characterized by or showing agitation or excitement: Tempers are *up.* 9 In baseball, at bat. 10 *Informal* Alert; ready: to be *up* for a meeting. —**up and doing** Busy; bustling. —**up for** 1 Being considered or presented for: *up for* reelection. 2 Charged with or on trial for: *up for* manslaughter. —*prep.* 1 To, toward, or at a higher point, position, etc., on or along: monkeys scampering *up* a tree; *up* the social ladder. 2 To or at a point farther above or along: The farm is *up* the road. 3 From the coast toward the interior of (a country). 4 From the mouth toward the source of (a river). —*n. Usu. pl.* 1 An ascent or upward movement. 2 A state of prosperity. —**on the up and up**

Slang Honest; genuine. **—ups and downs** Changes of fortune or circumstance. *—v.* **upped, up·ping** *Informal v.t.* 1 To increase; cause to rise: to *up* one's price. 2 To put, lift, or take up. *—v.i.* 3 To rise. 4 To do quickly and abruptly: usu. followed by another verb: Then she *up* and left. [OE]

up-and-com·ing (up′ən·kum′ing) *adj.* Enterprising; energetic; promising.

u·pas (yōō′pəs) *n.* 1 A tall Asian and East Indian tree related to mulberry, with an acrid, milky, poisonous juice. 2 The sap of this tree, used to make arrow poison. [< Malay *(phon) upas* poison (tree)]

up·beat (up′bēt′; *for adj., also* up′bēt′) *n. Music* An unaccented beat, esp. the last beat in a measure. *—adj.* Optimistic; confident.

up·braid (up·brād′) *v.t* To reproach for some wrongdoing; scold. [< OE *up-* up + *bregdan* weave; twist] **—up·braid′er** *adj.* **—up·braid′ing·ly** *adv.* **—Syn.** admonish, chastise, rebuke, reprimand.

up·bring·ing (up′bring′ing) *n.* Rearing and training received during childhood.

up·chuck (up′chuk′) *Informal v.t. & v.i.* To vomit. *—n.* Vomit.

up·coun·try (up′kun′trē) *Informal n.* Inland country. *—adj.* In, from, or characteristic of inland places. *—adv.* (up′kun′trē) In, into or toward the interior.

up·date (up′dāt′) *v.t.* **·dat·ed, ·dat·ing** To bring up to date, as a textbook or manual.

up·end (up′end′) *v.t. & v.i.* To stand on end.

up·front (up′frunt′) *adj. Colloq.* Out in the open; unconcealed.

up·grade (up′grād′; *for v., also* up′grād′) *n.* An upward incline or slope. *—vt.* **·grad·ed, ·grad·ing** To raise to a higher rank, responsibility, value, importance, etc., as an employee or job.

up·heav·al (up·hē′vəl) *n.* 1 The act of upheaving, or the state of being upheaved. 2 A violent change or disturbance, as of the established social order.

up·heave (up·hēv′) *v.* **·heaved** or **·hove, ·heav·ing** *v.t.* 1 To heave or raise up. *—v.i.* 2 To be raised or lifted.

up·hill (up′hil′) *adv.* Up or as up a hill or an ascent. *—adj.* 1 Going up hill or an ascent; sloping upward. 2 Attended with difficulty or exertion. 3 Situated on high ground. *—n.* (up′hil′) An upward slope; rising ground; a steep rise.

up·hold (up·hōld′) *v.t.* **·held, ·hold·ing** 1 To hold up; keep from falling or sinking. 2 To raise; lift up. 3 To aid, encourage, sustain, or confirm. **—up·hold′er** *n.*

up·hol·ster (up·hōl′stər) *v.t.* To fit, as furniture, with coverings, cushioning, springs, etc. [ult. < ME *upholder* tradesman] **—up·hol′ster·er** *n.*

up·hol·ster·y (up·hōl′stər·ē, ·strē) *n. pl.* **·ster·ies** 1 The materials used in upholstering. 2 The act, art, or business of upholstering.

UPI, U.P.I. United Press International.

up·keep (up′kēp′) *n.* 1 The act of keeping in good condition. 2 The state of being kept in good condition. 3 The cost of keeping in good condition.

up·land (up′lənd, -land′) *n.* High land, esp. such land located far from the sea. *—adj.* Pertaining to or situated in an upland.

up·lift (up·lift′) *v.t.* 1 To lift up, or raise aloft; elevate. 2 To put on a higher plane, mentally, morally, culturally, or socially. *—n.* (up′lift′) 1 The act of lifting up raising. 2 An elevation to a higher mental, spiritual, moral, or social plane. 3 A social movement aiming to improve, esp. morally or culturally. 4 A brassiere designed to lift and support the breasts. **—up·lift′er** *n.*

up·most (up′mōst′) *adj.*, UPPERMOST.

up·on (ə·pon′, ə·pôn′) *prep.* On: *upon* the throne. *—adv.* On: The paper has been written *upon.* • *Upon* no longer differs in meaning from *on,* but it is sometimes preferred for reasons of euphony. When *upon* has its original meaning of *up* + *on,* it is written and pronounced as two words: *Let's go up on the roof.*

up·per (up′ər) *adj.* 1 Higher, as in location or position. 2 Higher in station, rank, authority, etc.: the *upper* house. 3 *Geol. Usu. cap.* Being a later division of a specified period or series. *—n.* 1 Something that is above another similar or related thing, part, etc., as an upper berth. 2 That part of a boot or shoe above the sole. 3 *Slang* Any of various drugs that stimulate the central nervous system, as amphetamines. **—on one's uppers** *Informal* 1 Having worn out the soles of one's shoes. 2 At the end of one's resources; destitute. [ME, orig. compar. of UP]

up·per·case (up′ər·kās′) *adj.* Of, in, or designating capital letters. *—v.t.* **·cased, ·cas·ing** To set in capital letters.

upper case 1 A case in which are kept capital letters and some auxiliary type for use in printing. 2 Capital letters.

upper class The socially or economically superior group in any society. **—up′per-class′** (-klas′, -kläs′) *adj.*

up·per·class·man (up′ər·klas′mən, -kläs′-) *n. pl.* **·men** (-mən) A junior or senior in a high school or college.

up·per·cut (up′ər·kut′) *n.* In boxing, a swinging blow directed upward, as to an opponent's jaw. *—v.t & v.i.* **·cut, ·cut·ting** To strike with an uppercut.

upper hand The advantage; control.

Upper House The branch, in a bicameral legislature, where membership is more restricted, as the U.S. Senate.

up·per·most (up′ər·mōst′) *adj.* Highest in place, rank, authority, importance, etc.; foremost. *—adv.* In the highest place, rank, importance, etc.

Upper Vol·ta (vol′tə) A republic of w Africa, 105,900 sq. mi., cap. Ouagadougou. • See map at AFRICA.

up·pish (up′ish) *adj. Informal* UPPITY. **—up′pish·ly** *adv.* **—up′pish·ness** *n.*

up·pi·ty (up′ə·tē) *adj. Informal* Arrogant; snobbish; haughty. **—up′pi·ti·ness** *n.*

up·raise (up·rāz′) *v.t.* **·raised, ·rais·ing** To lift up; elevate.

up·right (up′rīt′) *adj.* 1 Being in a vertical position; erect. 2 Righteous; just. *—n.* 1 The state of being upright: a post out of *upright.* 2 Something having an upright position, as a vertical timber. 3 An upright piano. 4 In a football, a goal post. *—adv.* In an upright position; vertically. [< OE *up-* up + *riht* right] **—up′right′ly** *adv.* **—up′right′ness** *n.*

upright piano A piano having the strings mounted vertically within a rectangular, upright case.

up·ris·ing (up′rī′zing) *n.* 1 The act of rising up; esp., a revolt or insurrection. 2 An ascent; upward slope; acclivity.

up·roar (up′rôr′, -rōr′) *n.* 1 A state of confusion, disturbance, excitement, tumult, etc. 2 A loud, boisterous noise; din. [< Du. *op-* up + *roeren* stir]

up·roar·i·ous (up·rôr′ē·əs, -rō′·rē-) *adj.* 1 Accompanied by or making uproar. 2 Very loud and boisterous. 3 Provoking loud laughter. **—up·roar′i·ous·ly** *adv.* **—up·roar′ous·ness** *n.*

up·root (up·rōōt′, -rŏŏt′) *v.t.* 1 To tear up by the roots. 2 To destroy utterly; eradicate. **—up·root′er** *n.*

up·set (up·set′) *v.* **·set, ·set·ting** *v.t.* 1 To overturn. 2 To throw into confusion or disorder. 3 To disconcert, derange, or disquiet. 4 To defeat (an opponent favored to win): The amateur team *upset* the professionals. *—v.i.* 5 To become overturned. *—adj.* (*also* up′set′) 1 Overturned. 2 Physically ill or mentally disturbed. *—n.* (up′set′) 1 The act of overturning. 2 A physical or emotional disorder. 3 A defeat of an opponent favored to win. **—up·set′ter** *n.*

up·shot (up′shot′) *n.* The outcome; result.

up·side (up′sīd′) *n.* The upper side or part.

upside down 1 So that the upper part is underneath: to turn a table *upside down.* 2 In or into disorder or confusion: to turn a room *upside down* looking for something.

up·si·lon (yōōp′sə·lon, up′sə·lon) *n.* The twentieth letter in the Greek alphabet (Υ, υ). [< Gk. *u* u + *psilon* simple]

up·stage (up′stāj′) *adj.* 1 Of or pertaining to the back half of a stage. 2 *Informal* Conceited; haughty; snobbish. *—adv.* Toward or at the back half of a stage. *—n.* That part of a stage farthest from the audience. *—v.* (up′stāj′) **·staged, ·stag·ing** 1 To force (a fellow actor) to face away from the audience by moving or remaining upstage. 2 To try to outdo (someone), as in a professional or social encounter.

up·stairs (up′stârz′) *adj.* Of or on an upper story. *—n.* The part of a building above the ground floor; an upper story or stories. *—adv.* To or on an upper story.

up·stand·ing (up·stan′ding) *adj.* 1 Standing up; erect. 2 Honest, straightforward, etc. **—up·stand′ing·ness** *n.*

up·start (up′stärt′) *n.* A person who has suddenly risen from a humble position to one of consequence; esp., such a person who behaves in a way that is presumptuous, arrogant, etc.

up·state (up′stāt′) *adj.* Of, from, or designating that part of a state lying outside, usu. north, of a principal city. —*n.* The outlying, usu. northern, sections of a state. —*adv.* In or toward the outlying or northern sections of a state. —**up′stat′er** *n.*

up·stream (up′strēm′) *adv. & adj.* Toward or at the upper part or source of a stream.

up·sweep (up′swēp′) *n.* **1** A sweeping up or upward. **2** A hairdo in which the hair is piled on the top of the head and held there by pins or combs.

up·swing (up′swing′) *n.* **1** A swinging upward. **2** An increase or improvement.

up·take (up′tāk′) *n.* **1** The act of lifting or taking up. **2** Mental comprehension; understanding.

up·thrust (up′thrust′) *n.* **1** An upward thrust. **2** A sharp upward movement of rock in the earth's crust.

up·tight (up′tīt′) *adj. Slang* Uneasy, anxious, or nervous. Also **up′-tight′, up tight.** —**up′tight′ness** *n.*

up-to-date (up′tə·dāt′) *adj.* **1** Extending to the present; including the latest information, data, etc.: an *up-to-date* census report. **2** Abreast of the latest fashions, ideas, outlook, etc. —**up′-to-date′ness** *n.*

up·town (up′toun′) *adj. & adv.* Of, in, to, or toward the upper part of a town or city. —*n.* An uptown area.

up·turn (up′tûrn′, up′tûrn′) *v.t.* To turn up or over. —*n.* (up′tûrn′) A turn upward, as to improved business conditions.

up·ward (up′wərd) *adv.* **1** In or toward a higher place, position, or part. **2** Toward a source or interior part. **3** In the upper parts. **4** To or toward a higher, greater, or better condition. Also **up′wards.** —**upward of** or **upwards of** Higher than or in excess of. —*adj.* Turned, directed toward, or located in a higher place. —**up′ward·ly** *adv.*

u·rae·mi·a (yo͞o·rē′mē·ə) *n.* UREMIA.

U·ral-Al·ta·ic (yo͞or′əl·al·tā′ik) *n.* A family of languages of Europe and N Asia, comprising the Uralic and Altaic subfamilies. —*adj.* Of or pertaining to these languages or the peoples speaking them.

U·ral·ic (yo͞o·ral′ik) *n.* A family of languages comprising the Finno-Ugric and Samoyedic subfamilies. —*adj.* Of or pertaining to this linguistic family. Also **U·ra·li·an** (yo͞o·rā′·lē·ən).

U·ra·ni·a (yo͞o·rā′nē·ə) *Gk. Myth.* The Muse of astronomy.

u·ra·ni·um (yo͞o·rā′nē·əm) *n.* A heavy, radioactive, metallic element (symbol U), found only in combination and in association with radium, used in the generation of atomic energy. [< URANUS]

U·ra·nus (yo͞or′ə·nəs, yo͞or·ā′nəs) *Gk. Myth.* The son and husband of Gaea (Earth) and father of the Titans, Furies, and Cyclopes. —*n.* The planet of the solar system seventh in distance from the sun. • See PLANET. —**U·ra′ni·an** *adj.*

ur·ban (ûr′bən) *adj.* **1** Of, pertaining to, characteristic of, constituting, or including a city. **2** Living or located in a city or cities. [See URBANE.]

ur·bane (ûr·bān′) *adj.* Characterized by or having refinement, esp. in manner; polite; courteous; suave. [< L *urbs, urbis* a city] —**ur·bane′ly** *adv.* —**ur·bane′ness** *n.*

ur·ban·ism (ûr′bən·iz′əm) *n.* **1** Life in the cities. **2** The study of urban life. **3** The advocacy of living in a city. —**ur′ban·ist** *n.* —**ur′ban·is′tic** *adj.*

ur·ban·ite (ûr′bən·īt) *n.* One who lives in a city.

ur·ban·i·ty (ûr·ban′ə·tē) *n. pl.* **·ties 1** The character or quality of being urbane. **2** *pl.* Urbane acts or behavior; courtesies, amenities, etc.

ur·ban·i·za·tion (ûr′bə·nə·zā′shən) *n.* **1** The act or process of urbanizing an area or a rural group of people. **2** The quality or state of being urbanized. *Brit. sp.* **·i·sa′tion.**

ur·ban·ize (ûr′bən·īz) *v.t.* **·ized, ·iz·ing 1** To cause (an area) to assume the characteristics of a city. **2** To cause (people) to adopt an urban life style. *Brit. sp.* **·ise.**

ur·ban·ol·o·gy (ûr′bə·nol′ə·jē) *n.* The study of problems peculiar to cities. —**ur′ban·ol′o·gist** *n.*

urban renewal A program for rebuilding or replacing substandard housing and improving public facilities in distressed urban areas.

urban sprawl The uncontrolled spread of urban housing, shopping centers, etc., into rural or undeveloped areas close to a city.

ur·chin (ûr′chin) *n.* **1** A roguish, mischievous child. **2** A ragged street child. **3** HEDGEHOG. **4** SEA URCHIN. [< L *ericius* hedgehog]

Ur·du (o͞or′do͞o, o͞or·do͞o′, ûr′do͞o) *n.* An Indic language, a variety of Hindi that is the official language of Pakistan and is also spoken by some of the population of India.

-ure *suffix of nouns* **1** The act, process, or result of: *pressure.* **2** The condition of being: *exposure.* **3** The function, rank, or office of: *prefecture.* **4** The means or instrument of: *ligature.* [< L *-ura*]

u·re·a (yo͞o·rē′ə) *n.* A soluble colorless crystalline compound excreted in urine and also made synthetically; used in the making of plastics. [< L *urina* urine] —**u·re′al** *adj.*

u·re·mi·a (yo͞o·rē′mē·ə) *n.* A toxic condition of the blood due to the presence of substances ordinarily excreted by the kidneys. —**u·re′mic** *adj.*

u·re·ter (yo͞or′ə·tər, yo͞o·rē′-) *n.* The duct by which urine passes from the kidney to the bladder or the cloaca. [< Gk *ourein* urinate] —**u·re·ter·al** (yo͞o·rē′tə·rəl), **u·re·ter·ic** (yo͞or′·ə·ter′ik) *adj.* • See KIDNEY.

u·re·thra (yo͞o·rē′thrə) *n. pl.* **·thrae** (-thrē), **·thras** The duct by which urine is discharged from the bladder and which, in males, carries the seminal discharge. [< Gk. *ouron* urine] —**u·re′thral** *adj.*

urge (ûrj) *v.* **urged, urg·ing** *v.t.* **1** To drive or force forward. **2** To plead with or entreat earnestly: He *urged* them to accept the plan. **3** To advocate earnestly: to *urge* reform. **4** To move or force to some course or action. —*v.i.* **5** To present or press arguments, claims, etc. **6** To exert an impelling or prompting force. —*n.* **1** A strong impulse to perform a certain act. **2** The act of urging. [< L *urgere* to drive, urge] —**Syn.** *v.* **1** impel, press. **2** exhort, importune.

ur·gen·cy (ûr′jən·sē) *n. pl.* **·cies 1** The quality of being urgent; insistence: the *urgency* of her plea. **2** Something urgent: to prepare for any possible *urgencies.*

ur·gent (ûr′jənt) *adj.* **1** Requiring prompt attention; pressing; imperative. **2** Eagerly importunate or insistent. [< L *urgere* drive] —**ur′gent·ly** *adv.*

-urgy *combining form* Development of or work with a (specified) material or product: *metallurgy.* [< Gk. *ergon* work]

u·ric (yo͞or′ik) *adj.* Of, relating to, or derived from urine.

uric acid A white, odorless substance found in small quantity in urine.

u·ri·nal (yo͞or′ə·nəl) *n.* **1** A fixture for men's use in urination; also, a place containing such a fixture or fixtures. **2** A receptacle for urine.

u·ri·nal·y·sis (yo͞or′ə·nal′ə·sis) *n. pl.* **·ses** (-sēz) Chemical analysis of the urine.

u·ri·nar·y (yo͞or′ə·ner′ē) *adj.* Of or pertaining to urine or to the organs concerned in its production and excretion.

u·ri·nate (yo͞or′ə·nāt) *v.i.* **·nat·ed, ·nat·ing** To void or pass urine. —**u′ri·na′tion** *n.*

u·rine (yo͞or′in) *n.* A usu. fluid substance secreted by the kidneys of vertebrates and some invertebrates and containing nitrogenous and saline wastes. [< L *urina*]

u·ri·no·gen·i·tal (yo͞or′ə·nō·jen′ə·təl) *adj.* UROGENITAL.

urn (ûrn) *n.* **1** A vase, usu. having a foot or pedestal, variously used as a receptacle for the ashes of the dead, or ornament, etc. **2** A vase-shaped receptacle having a faucet, designed to make and serve tea, coffee, etc. [< L *urna*]

Urn

uro- *combining form* Urine; pertaining to urine or to the urinary tract: *urology.* [< Gk. *ouron* urine]

u·ro·gen·i·tal (yo͞or′ō·jen′ə·təl) *adj.* Of or pertaining to the urinary and genital organs and their functions.

u·rol·o·gy (yo͞o·rol′ə·jē) *n.* The branch of medicine relating to the urogenital or urinary system. —**u·ro·log·ic** (yo͝or′·ə·loj′ik) or **·i·cal** *adj.* —**u·rol′o·gist** *n.*

u·ros·co·py (yo͞o·ros′kə·pē) *n.* Examination of the urine, as for diagnosis. —**u·ro·scop·ic** (yo͝or′ə·skop′ik) *adj.* —**u·ros′·co·pist** *n.*

Ur·sa Major (ûr′sə) *Astron.* The Great Bear, a large northern constellation containing seven conspicuous stars, including two which point to the polestar. [L]

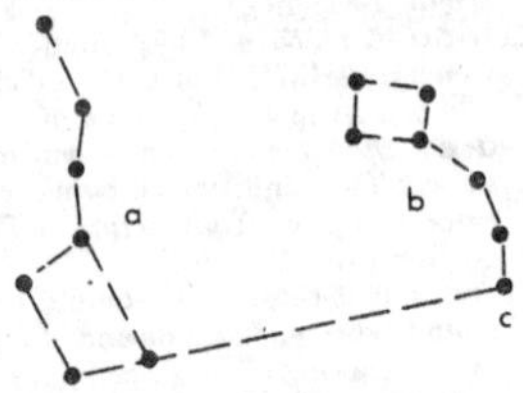

Ursa Major and Ursa Minor
a. Ursa Major. b. Ursa Minor.
c. Polaris.

Ursa Minor *Astron.* The Little Bear, a northern constellation including the polestar. [L]

ur·sine (ûr′sīn, -sin) *adj.* Of, pertaining to, or like a bear. [<L *ursus* bear]

ur·ti·car·i·a (ûr′tə·kâr′ē·ə) *n.* A skin eruption of systemic origin characterized by evanescent wheals and itching; hives. [<L *urtica* nettle] —**ur′ti·car′i·al, ur′ti·car′i·ous** *adj.*

Uru. Uruguay.

U·ru·guay (yo͝or′ə·gwā, *Sp.* o͞o′ro͞o·gwī) *n.* A republic of SE South America, 72,172 sq. mi., cap. Montevideo. —**U′ru·guay′an** *adj., n.* • See map at ARGENTINA.

us (us) *pron.* The objective case of WE. [<OE *ūs*]

US, U.S. United States.

USA, U.S.A. United States of America; United States Army.

us·a·ble (yo͞o′zə·bəl) *adj.* **1** Capable of being used. **2** That can be used conveniently. Also **use′a·ble.** —**us′a·ble·ness** *n.* —**us′a·bly** *adv.*

USAF, U.S.A.F. United States Air Force.

us·age (yo͞o′sij, -zij) *n.* **1** The act or manner of using; treatment. **2** Customary or habitual practice; custom; habit. **3** The accepted and established way of using words, speech patterns, etc.

USCG, U.S.C.G. United States Coast Guard.

use (yo͞oz) *v.* **used, us·ing** *v.t.* **1** To put into service: to *use* a hammer. **2** To borrow; avail oneself of: May I *use* your pen? **3** To put into practice or employ habitually: to *use* diligence in business. **4** To conduct oneself toward; treat: to *use* one badly. **5** To partake of: He does not *use* tobacco. **6** To take advantage of; exploit: to *use* one's friends. **7** To expend, exhaust, or consume: usu. with *up.* —*v.i.* **8** To be accustomed: used in the past tense with an infinitive: We *used* to go to the theater regularly. —*n.* (yo͞os) **1** The act of using, or the state of being used. **2** Function: He has lost the *use* of his legs. **3** Way or manner of using: to make good *use* of one's time. **4** Habitual practice or employment; custom; usage. **5** The ability or right to use, or the privilege of using. **6** Advantage; benefit; usefulness. **7** The purpose for which something is used. **8** *Law* The benefit or profit of property to which legal title is vested in another in trust for the beneficiary. —**have no use for 1** To have no need of. **2** To have dislike or contempt for. —**in use** Being used or occupied. —**make use of** To have occasion to use; use. —**put to use** To utilize; employ. [<L *usus,* pp. of *uti* to use] —**us′er** *n.*

used (yo͞ozd) *adj.* **1** That has been employed in some way. **2** SECONDHAND. **3** Accustomed; experienced. —**used to** (yo͞ost) Accustomed to; habituated.

use·ful (yo͞os′fəl) *adj.* Capable of being used; serviceable; helpful. —**use′ful·ly** *adv.* —**use′ful·ness** *n.*

use·less (yo͞os′lis) *adj.* Being of or having no use; serving no function. —**use′less·ly** *adv.* —**use′less·ness** *n.*

us·er-friend·ly (yo͞o′zər-frend′lē) *adj.* of a computer, program, software, etc., easy to use.

ush·er (ush′ər) *n.* **1** One who acts as doorkeeper, as of a court. **2** One who conducts persons to seats, etc., as in a church or theater. —*v.t.* **1** To act as an usher to; escort; conduct. **2** To precede as a harbinger; be a forerunner of. [<L *ostiarius* doorkeeper]

USM, U.S.M. United States Mail; United States Mint.

USMA, U.S.M.A. United States Military Academy.

USMC, U.S.M.C. United States Marine Corps; United States Maritime Commission.

USN, U.S.N. United States Navy.

USNA, U.S.N.A. United States Naval Academy.

USNG, U.S.N.G. United States National Guard.

USNR, U.S.N.R. United States Naval Reserve.

USO, U.S.O. United Service Organizations.

USS United States Ship, Steamer, or Steamship.

U.S.S. United States Senate.

USSR, U.S.S.R. Union of Soviet Socialist Republics.

usu. usual; usually.

u·su·al (yo͞o′zho͞o·əl) *adj.* Such as occurs in the ordinary course of events; customary; common. [<L *usus* use] —**u′su·al·ly** *adv.* —**u′su·al·ness** *n.* —**Syn.** everyday, general, ordinary, prevalent.

u·su·fruct (yo͞o′zə·frukt, yo͞o′sə-) *n. Law* The right of using the fruits or profits of another's property. [<L *usus et fructus* use and fruit]

u·su·rer (yo͞o′zhər·ər) *n.* One who practices usury. [<L *usura* use, usury]

u·su·ri·ous (yo͞o·zho͝or′ē·əs) *adj.* **1** Practicing usury. **2** Of, relating to, or having the nature of usury. —**u·su′ri·ous·ly** *adv.* —**u·su′ri·ous·ness** *n.*

u·surp (yo͞o·sûrp′, -zûrp′) *v.t.* To seize and hold (an office, rights, powers, etc.) without right or legal authority; take possesion of by force. [<L *usurpare* make use of, usurp]

u·sur·pa·tion (yo͞o′sər·pā′shən, -zər-) *n.* The act of usurping, esp. the unlawful seizure of sovereign power.

u·su·ry (yo͞o′zhər·ē) *n. pl.* **·ries 1** The act or practice of lending money and charging interest that is excessive or unlawfully high. **2** Interest that is excessive or unlawfully high. [<L *usura* < *usus,* pp. of *uti* to use]

UT Utah (P.O. abbr.).

Ut. Utah.

u·ten·sil (yo͞o·ten′səl) *n.* A vessel, tool, implement, etc., serving a useful purpose, esp. for domestic or farming use. [<L *utensilis* fit for use]

u·ter·ine (yo͞o′tər·in, -in) *adj.* **1** Of or pertaining to the uterus. **2** Born of the same mother, but having a different father. [<LL *uterinus* born of the same mother]

u·ter·us (yo͞o′tər·əs) *n. pl.* **u·ter·i** (yo͞o′tər·ī), **u·ter·us·es** The organ of a female mammal in which the fertilized ovum is deposited and develops until birth; womb. [L] • See OVARY.

u·til·i·tar·i·an (yo͞o·til′ə·târ′ē·ən) *adj.* **1** Of or pertaining to utility; esp., placing utility above beauty, the amenities of life, etc. **2** Of, pertaining to, or advocating utilitarianism. —*n.* An advocate of utilitarianism.

u·til·i·tar·i·an·ism (yo͞o·til′ə·târ′ē·ən·iz′əm) *n.* **1** The doctrine that holds usefulness to be the end and criterion of action. **2** The doctrine that the greatest happiness of the greatest number should be the sole end and criterion of all action.

u·til·i·ty (yo͞o·til′ə·tē) *n. pl.* **·ties 1** Fitness for some desirable, practical purpose; usefulness. **2** Fitness to supply the needs of people. **3** Something useful. **4** A public service, as a telephone system, gas, water, etc. **5** A company that provides such a service. [<L *utilis* useful < *uti* use]

u·til·ize (yo͞o′təl·īz) *v.t.* **·ized, ·iz·ing** To make use of. *Brit. sp.* **u′til·ise.** —**u′til·i·za′tion, u′til·iz′er** *n.*

ut·most (ut′mōst) *adj.* **1** Of the highest or greatest degree. **2** Being at the farthest limit or most distant point; most remote; extreme. —*n.* The most possible. [<OE *ūtmost*]

U·to-Az·tec·an (yo͞o′tō·az′tek·ən) *n.* One of the chief linguistic stocks of North American Indians formerly occupying NW and SW U.S., Mexico, and Central America. —*adj.* Of or pertaining to this linguistic stock.

u·to·pi·a (yo͞o·tō′pē·ə) *n.* **1** Any state, condition, or place of ideal perfection. **2** A visionary, impractical scheme for social improvement. [<UTOPIA] —**u·to′pi·an** *adj., n.* —**u·to′·pi·an·ism** *n.*

U·to·pi·a (yo͞o·tō′pē·ə) *n.* An imaginary island described as the seat of a perfect social and political life in the book by Sir Thomas More, published in 1516. [<Gk. *ou* not + *topos* a place] —**U·to′pi·an** *adj., n.*

u·tri·cle (yo͞o′tri·kəl) *n.* A small sac or cavity. [<L *uter* skin bag] —**u·tric·u·lar** (yo͞o·trik′yə·lər) *adj.*

ut·ter[1] (ut′ər) *v.t.* **1** To say, express, give out, or send forth, as in words or sounds. **2** To put in circulation; esp., to deliver or offer (something forged or counterfeit). [< ME *out* say, speak out] **—ut'ter·er** *n.*

ut·ter² (ut'ər) *adj.* **1** Complete; absolute; total: *utter* misery. **2** Unqualified; final: an *utter* denial. [< OE *ūttra,* orig. compar. of *ūt* out] **—ut'ter·ly** *adv.*

ut·ter·ance (ut'ər·əns) *n.* **1** The act of uttering. **2** A manner of speaking. **3** A thing uttered.

ut·ter·most (ut'ər·mōst') *adj. & n.* UTMOST.

U-turn (yōō'tûrn') *n.* A complete turn which reverses the direction of movement, as of a vehicle on a road.

u·vu·la (yōō'vyə·lə) *n. pl.* **·las** or **·lae** (-lē) The pendent fleshy portion of the soft palate in the back of the mouth. [LL, dim. of *uva* grape] • See MOUTH.

u·vu·lar (yōō'vyə·lər) *adj.* **1** Pertaining to the uvula. **2** *Phonet.* Articulated with the back of the tongue near the uvula. *—n. Phonet.* A uvular sound.

ux. wife (L *uxor*).

ux·o·ri·ous (uk·sôr'ē·əs, -sō'rē-, ug·zôr'ē-, -zō'rē-) *adj.* Excessively devoted to or dominated by one's wife. [< L *uxor* wife] **—ux·o'ri·ous·ly** *adv.* **—ux·o'ri·ous·ness** *n.*

Uz·bek (ōōz'bek, uz'-) *n.* **1** A member of a Turkic people living in the Uzbek S.S.R. **2** The Turkic language of the Uzbeks.

V

V,v (vē) *n. pl.* **V's, v's, Vs, vs** (vēz) **1** The 22nd letter of the English alphabet. **2** Any spoken sound representing the letter *V* or *v.* **3** Something shaped like a V. **4** In Roman notation, the symbol for five. *—adj.* Shaped like a V.

V vanadium; vector; velocity; victory; volume.

V.,v. volt; volume.

v. valve; verb; verse; version; versus; vicar; village; vocative; voice; voltage; von.

VA Virginia (P.O. abbr.).

VA, V.A. Veterans Administration.

Va. Virginia.

va·can·cy (vā'kən·sē) *n. pl.* **·cies 1** The state of being vacant; emptiness. **2** An apartment, room, etc., that is available for rent. **3** An unoccupied post, place, or office.

va·cant (vā'kənt) *adj.* **1** Containing or holding nothing; empty. **2** Not lived in or occupied. **3** Not being used; free: a *vacant* hour. **4** Being or appearing without intelligence: a *vacant* stare. **5** Having no incumbent, officer, or possessor. [< L *vacans* pr.p. of *vacare* be empty] **—va'cant·ly** *adv.* **—va'cant·ness** *n.* **—Syn. 1** blank, void. **4** vapid, dull, vacuous, witless, obtuse, blank.

va·cate (vā'kāt', vā'kāt') *v.* **·cat·ed, ·cat·ing** *v.t.* **1** To make vacant, as a dwelling, position, etc. **2** To set aside; annul. *—v.i.* **3** To leave an office, dwelling, place, etc. **4** *Informal* To go away; leave. [< L *vacare* be empty]

va·ca·tion (vā·kā'shən) *n.* A time set aside from work, study, etc., for recreation or rest; a holiday. *—v.i.* To take a vacation. [See VACATE.] **—va·ca'tion·er, va·ca'tion·ist** *n.*

vac·ci·nate (vak'sə·nāt) *v.* **·nat·ed, ·nat·ing** *v.t.* **1** To inoculate with a vaccine as a preventive or therapeutic measure; esp., to inoculate against smallpox. *—v.i.* **2** To perform the act of vaccination. **—vac'ci·na'tor** *n.*

vac·ci·na·tion (vak'sə·nā'shən) *n.* **1** The act or process of vaccinating. **2** A scar produced at the site of inoculation with a vaccine.

vac·cine (vak·sēn', vak'sēn) *n.* **1** The virus of cowpox, as prepared for inoculation to produce immunity to smallpox. **2** Any modified virus or bacterium used to give immunity against a specific disease. [< L *vaccinus* pertaining to a cow] **—vac'ci·nal** (-sə·nəl) *adj.*

vac·il·late (vas'ə·lāt) *v.i.* **·lat·ed, ·lat·ing 1** To move one way and the other; waver. **2** To waver in mind; be irresolute. [< L *vacillare* waver] **—vac'il·la'tion** *n.* **—vac'il·la·to'ry** (-ə·lə·tô'rē, -tō'rē) *adj.* **—Syn. 1** fluctuate, oscillate, sway.

va·cu·i·ty (va·kyōō'ə·tē) *n. pl.* **·ties 1** The state of being a vacuum: emptiness. **2** Vacant space; a void. **3** Lack of intelligence; stupidity. **4** An inane or stupid thing, statement, etc. [< L *vacuus* empty]

vac·u·ole (vak'yōō·ōl) *n.* A small cavity within a cell containing air or fluid or food particles. [< L *vacuus* empty]

vac·u·ous (vak'yōō·əs) *adj.* **1** Having no contents; empty. **2** Lacking intelligence; blank. [< L *vacuus*] **—vac'u·ous·ly** *adv.* **—vac'u·ous·ness** *n.*

vac·u·um (vak'yōō·əm, -yōōm) *n. pl.* **·u·ums** or **·u·a** (-yōō·ə) **1** *Physics* A space devoid, or nearly devoid, of matter. **2** A reduction of the pressure in a space below atmospheric pressure. **3** A void; an empty feeling. **4** *Informal* A vacuum cleaner. *—v.t. & v.i. Informal* To clean with a vacuum cleaner. [L, neut. of *vacuus* empty]

vacuum bottle THERMOS.

vacuum cleaner A machine for cleaning floors, carpets, etc., by means of suction.

vacuum pump A pump designed to remove gas or air from a sealed space.

vacuum tube *Electronics* An electron tube containing a negligible amount of gas.

va·de me·cum (vā'dē mē'kəm) Anything carried for constant use, as a guidebook, manual, etc. [L, go with me]

vag·a·bond (vag'ə·bond) *n.* **1** One who wanders from place to place without visible means of support; a tramp. **2** A shiftless, irresponsible person. *—adj.* **1** Wandering; nomadic. **2** Having no definite residence; irresponsible. **3** Driven to and fro; aimless. [< L *vagus* wandering] **—vag'a·bond'age, vag'a·bond'ism** *n.*

va·gar·y (vā'gə·rē, və·gâr'ē) *n. pl.* **·gar·ies** A wild fancy; extravagant notion. [< L *vagari* wander]

va·gi·na (və·jī'nə) *n. pl.* **·nas** or **·nae** (-nē) **1** The canal leading from the external genital orifice in female mammals to the uterus. **2** A sheath or sheathlike covering. [L, a sheath] **—vag·i·nal** (vaj'ə·nəl) *adj.*

va·gran·cy (vā'grən·sē) *n. pl.* **·cies 1** The condition of being a vagrant. **2** The offense of being a vagrant: arrested for *vagrancy.*

va·grant (vā'grənt) *n.* A person who wanders from place to place without a settled home or job and who exists usu. by begging or stealing; a tramp. *—adj.* **1** Wandering about aimlessly; wayward. **2** Pertaining to or characteristic of a vagrant. [< OF *wacrer* to walk, wander] **—va'grant·ly** *adv.* **—va'grant·ness** *n.*

vague (vāg) *adj.* **vagu·er, vagu·est 1** Lacking definiteness; not clearly stated: *vague* rumors; *vague* promises. **2** Indistinct; hard to perceive: *vague* shapes in the fog. **3** Not thinking or expressing oneself clearly. [< L *vagus* wandering] **—vague'ly** *adv.* **—vague'ness** *n.*

va·gus (vā'gəs) *n. pl.* **·gi** (-jī) *Anat.* Either of the pair of cranial nerves sending branches to the lungs, heart, stomach, and most of the abdominal viscera. Also **vagus nerve.** [L, wandering]

vain (vān) *adj.* **1** Having or showing excessive pride in oneself; conceited. **2** Unproductive; useless: *vain* efforts. **3** Without substantial foundation; unreal. **—in vain 1** To no purpose; without effect. **2** Irreverently: to take the Lord's name *in vain.* [< L *vanus* empty] **—vain'ly** *adv.* **—vain'ness** *n.* **—Syn. 1** boastful, egotistical, narcissistic.

vain·glo·ry (vān'glôr'ē, -glōr-, vān·glôr'ē) *n.* **1** Excessive or groundless vanity; boastfulness. **2** Empty, showy pomp. [< Med. L *vana gloria* empty pomp, show] **—vain·glo'ri·ous** *adj.* **—vain·glo'ri·ous·ly** *adv.* **—vain·glo'ri·ous·ness** *n.*

val·ance (val'əns, vā'ləns) *n.* **1** A drapery hanging from the tester of a bedstead. **2** A short, full drapery across the top of a window. [Prob. < OF *avaler* descend] **—val'anced** *adj.* • See CANOPY.

vale[1] (vāl) *n.* VALLEY. [< L *vallis*]

va·le[2] (vā′lē) *interj.* Farewell. [L, lit., be in good health]

val·e·dic·tion (val′ə·dik′shən) *n.* **1** A bidding farewell. **2** VALEDICTORY. [< L *valedicere* say farewell]

val·e·dic·to·ri·an (val′ə·dik·tôr′ē·ən, -tō′rē-) *n.* A student, usu. the highest in scholastic rank, who delivers a valedictory at the graduating exercises of an educational institution.

val·e·dic·to·ry (val′ə·dik′tər·ē) *adj.* Pertaining to a leave-taking. —*n. pl.* **·ries** A parting address, as by a member (ordinarily the first in rank) of a graduating class.

va·lence (vā′ləns) *n. Chem.* The combining capacity of an atom or radical as measured by the number of electrons gained or lost or shared in forming a bond with another atom or radical. [< L *valens,* pr.p. of *valere* be well, be strong]

val·en·tine (val′ən·tīn) *n.* **1** A card or small gift sent as a token of affection on Valentine's Day. **2** A sweetheart.

Valentine's Day February 14, a day observed in honor of St. Valentine, and on which valentines are sent to sweethearts, etc.

va·le·ri·an (və·lir′ē·ən) *n.* **1** Any of various plants with small pink or white flowers and a strong odor. **2** A sedative derived from the roots of some of these plants. [< Med. L *valeriana*]

val·et (val′it, val′ā, val·ā′) *n.* **1** A man's personal servant. **2** A manservant in a hotel who cleans and presses clothes. —*v.t. & v.i.* To act as a valet. [F < OF *vaslet, varlet,* dim. of *vasal* vassal]

val·e·tu·di·nar·i·an (val′ə·tyōō′də·nâr′ē·ən) *n.* **1** A chronic invalid. **2** A person unduly concerned about his health. —*adj.* **1** Infirm; ailing. **2** Unduly concerned about one's health. [< L *valetudo,* health, ill health < *valere* be well] —**val′e·tu′di·nar′i·an·ism** *n.*

Val·hal·la (val·hal′ə) *n. Norse Myth.* The great hall in which the souls of heroes, borne by the Valkyries, are received and feasted by Odin.

val·iant (val′yənt) *adj.* **1** Strong and intrepid; powerful and courageous. **2** Performed with valor; heroic. [< OF *valoir* be strong] —**val′iant·ly** *adv.* —**val′i·an·cy** or **val′i·ance, val′iant·ness** *n.*

val·id (val′id) *adj.* **1** Based on facts or evidence; sound: a *valid* argument. **2** Legally binding: a *valid* will. [< L *validus* powerful] —**val′id·ly** *adv.* —**va·lid·i·ty** (və·lid′ə·tē), **val′id·ness** *n.*

val·i·date (val′ə·dāt) *v.t.* **·dat·ed, ·dat·ing** **1** To confirm by facts or authority. **2** To declare legally valid; legalize. —**val′i·da′tion** *n.*

va·lise (və·lēs′) *n.* A traveling bag; suitcase. [< Ital. *valigia*]

Val·kyr·ie (val·kir′ē, val′kir·ē) *n. pl.* **·kyr·ies** or **·kyr·ie** *Norse Myth.* One of the maidens who ride through the air and choose heroes from among those slain in battle, and carry them to Valhalla. Also **Val′kyr** (-kir). —**Val·kyr′i·an** *adj.*

val·ley (val′ē) *n.* **1** A long, wide area drained by a large river system: the Hudson *valley.* **2** Low land lying between mountains or hills. **3** Any hollow or depression shaped like a valley. [< L *vallis*]

val·or (val′ər) *n.* Marked courage; personal heroism; bravery. *Brit. sp.* **val′our.** [< L *valere* be strong] —**val′or·ous** *adj.* —**val′or·ous·ly** *adv.* —**val′or·ous·ness** *n.*

val·or·i·za·tion (val′ər·ə·zā′shən, -ī·zā′-) *n.* The maintenance by governmental action of an artificial price for any product. [< Pg. *valor* value] —**val·or·ize** (val′ə·rīz) *v.t.*

val·u·a·ble (val′yōō·ə·bəl, val′yə·bəl) *adj.* **1** Having financial worth, price, or value. **2** Very costly. **3** Worthy; estimable: a *valuable* friend. —*n. Usu. pl.* An article of value, as a piece of jewelry. —**val′u·a·ble·ness** *n.* —**val′u·a·bly** *adv.*

val·u·a·tion (val′yōō·ā′shən) *n.* **1** The act of estimating the value of something; evaluation. **2** Estimated value; appraisement. —**val′u·a′tion·al** *adj.*

val·ue (val′yōō) *n.* **1** The desirability or worth of a thing; merit: the *value* of self-discipline. **2** Something regarded as desirable, worthy, or right, as a belief or ideal. **3** Worth in money; market price. **4** A bargain. **5** Purchasing power: a decline in the *value* of the dollar. **6** Exact meaning: the *value* of a word. **7** *Music* The relative length of a tone. **8** *Math.* The number assigned to or represented by a symbol or expression. **9** In art, the relative lightness or darkness of a color. **10** The relation, as of light and shade, of one part to another in a work of art. —*v.t.* **·ued, ·u·ing** **1** To assess; appraise. **2** To regard highly; prize. **3** To place a relative estimate of value upon: to *value* health above all else. [< L *valere*] —**val′u·er** *n.*

val·ue-add·ed tax (val′yōō·ad′id) A tax levied on each stage of a product's manufacture and marketing, from the raw material to the final retailer, the ultimate burden being placed on the consumer in the form of higher prices.

val·ued (val′yōōd) *adj.* **1** Highly esteemed: a *valued* friend. **2** Having a specified value: *valued* at ten dollars.

val·ue·less (val′yōō·lis) *adj.* Having no value; worthless. —**val′ue·less·ness** *n.*

valve (valv) *n.* **1** *Mech.* Any device used to block, direct, or otherwise control motion of a fluid. **2** *Anat.* A membranous structure inside a vessel or other organ, allowing fluid to flow in one direction only. **3** *Zool.* One of the parts of a shell, as of a clam, etc. **4** *Bot.* One of the parts into which a seed capsule splits. —*v.t.* **valved, valv·ing** To control the flow of by means of a valve. [< L *valva* leaf of a door]

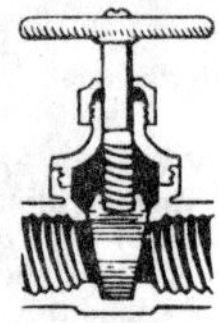

Gate valve in closed position (cross section)

val·vu·lar (val′vyə·lər) *adj.* **1** Pertaining to valves, as of the heart. **2** Having valves. **3** Having the form of a valve.

va·moose (va·mōōs′) *v.t. & v.i.* **·moosed, ·moos·ing** *Slang* To leave or depart hastily. Also **va·mose′** (-mōs′) [< Sp. *vamos* let us go]

vamp[1] (vamp) *n.* **1** The piece of leather forming the upper front part of a boot or shoe. • See SHOE. **2** Something added to give an old thing a new appearance. —*v.t.* **1** To provide with a vamp. **2** To repair or patch. [< OF *avant* before + *pied* foot] —**vamp′er** *n.*

vamp[2] (vamp) *Slang n.* A seductive woman who entices and exploits men. —*v.t. & v.i.* To seduce (a man) by acting as a vamp. [Short for VAMPIRE]

vam·pire (vam′pīr) *n.* **1** In folklore, a reanimated corpse that rises from its grave at night to suck the blood of persons who are asleep. **2** A person who preys upon those of the opposite sex; esp. a woman who degrades or impoverishes her lover. **3** A bat of tropical America that drinks the blood of mammals: also **vampire bat. 4** An insect- or fruit-eating bat mistakenly thought to suck blood: also **false vampire.** [< Slavic] —**vam′pir·ism** *n.*

van[1] (van) *n.* **1** A large covered wagon or truck for transporting furniture, household goods, etc. **2** *Brit.* A closed railway car for luggage, etc. [Short for CARAVAN]

van[2] (van) *n.* VANGUARD. [Short for VANGUARD]

va·na·di·um (və·nā′dē·əm) *n.* A rare, silver-white metallic element (symbol V), used to produce **vanadium steel,** a tough, resilient alloy. [L < ON *Vanadís,* a name of the Norse goddess Freya]

Van Al·len belt (van al′ən) An extensive region of intense radiation consisting of charged atomic particles trapped by the earth's magnetic field and surrounding the earth in inner and outer belts. [< J. A. *Van Allen,* 1914–, U.S. physicist]

van·dal (van′dəl) *n.* One who engages in vandalism. [< VANDAL]

Van·dal (van′dəl) *n.* A member of a Germanic people that laid waste to Gaul, Spain, and North Africa in the fifth century and conquered Rome in 455.

van·dal·ism (van′dəl·iz′əm) *n.* Willful destruction or defacement of public or private property.

Van·dyke beard (van·dīk′) A small pointed beard. [< Anthony *Van Dyck,* 1599–1641, Flemish painter]

vane (vān) *n.* **1** A thin plate, pivoted on a vertical rod, to indicate the direction of the wind; a weathercock. **2** An arm or blade, as of a windmill, propeller, projectile, turbine, etc. **3** The web, or flat portion, of a feather. [< OE *fana* a flag] —**vaned** (vānd) *adj.*

Windmill vanes

van·guard (van′gärd) *n.* **1** The forward part of an advancing army. **2** The foremost position in a movement, trend, etc. **3** The leaders of a movement, trend, etc. [< OF *avant* before + *garde* guard]

va·nil·la (və·nil′ə) *n.* **1** Any of a genus of tall climbing orchids of tropical America. **2** The long seed capsule of one species: also **vanilla bean. 3** A flavoring extracted from these capsules or made synthetically. [< Sp. *vaina* sheath, pod] **—va·nil′lic** *adj.*

Vanilla a. flower. b. bean. c. pod.

va·nil·lin (və·nil′in) *n.* The organic compound which gives vanilla flavoring its distinct odor and taste.

van·ish (van′ish) *v.i.* **1** To disappear; fade away. **2** To pass out of existence. [< L *evanescere* fade away] **—van′ish·er** *n.*

vanishing point **1** In perspective, the point at which receding parallel lines appear to meet. • See PERSPECTIVE. **2** The point at which something approaches an end.

van·i·ty (van′ə·tē) *n. pl.* **·ties** **1** Excessive pride in one's talents, looks, possessions, etc. **2** Worthlessness; futility. **3** Something that is worthless or futile. **4** A low table with an attached mirror, for use while dressing the hair or putting on makeup. **5** VANITY CASE. [< L *vanus* empty, vain]

vanity case A small case holding face powder, rouge, puff, mirror, etc. Also **vanity box.**

van·quish (vang′kwish, van′-) *v.t.* **1** To defeat in battle; conquer. **2** To suppress or overcome (a feeling): to *vanquish* fear. **3** To defeat in any encounter. [< L *vincere*] **—van′quish,·er van′quish·ment** *n.* **—Syn. 1** beat, overcome, overpower, overwhelm, upset.

van·tage (van′tij) *n.* **1** Superiority, as over a competitor; advantage. **2** A position, place, situation, etc., that gives superiority or an advantage. [< OF *avantage* advantage]

vantage ground A position or condition which gives one an advantage.

van·ward (van′wərd) *adj. & adv.* Toward or in the front.

vap·id (vap′id, vā′pəd) *adj.* **1** Having lost sparkle and flavor. **2** Flat; insipid. [< L *vapidus* insipid] **—va·pid·i·ty** (və·pid′ə·tē), **vap′id·ness** *n.* **—vap′id·ly** *adv.*

va·por (vā′pər) *n.* **1** Moisture in the air; esp. visible floating moisture, as light mist. **2** Any cloudy substance in the air, as smoke. **3** The gaseous phase of any substance. **4** Something that is fleeting and unsubstantial. **5** A remedial agent applied by inhalation. **—the vapors** *Archaic* Depression of spirits. **—***v.t.* **1** VAPORIZE. **—***v.i.* **2** To emit vapor. **3** To pass off in vapor; evaporate. *Brit. sp.* **va′·pour.** [< L *vapor* steam] **—va′por·er** *n.*

va·por·ize (vā′pə·rīz) *v.t. & v.i.* **·ized, ·iz·ing** To convert or be converted into vapor. **—va′por·i·za′tion** *n.*

va·por·iz·er (vā′pə·rī′zər) *n.* **1** One who or that which vaporizes. **2** A device for boiling water or a medicated liquid to form a vapor for inhalation.

va·por·ous (vā′pər·əs) *adj.* **1** Of or like vapor; misty. **2** Emitting or forming vapor. **3** Whimsical; fanciful. **—va·por·os·i·ty** (vā′pə·ros′ə·tē), **va′por·ous·ness** *n.*

va·que·ro (vä·kā′rō) *n. pl.* **·ros** (-rōz, *Sp.* -rōs) A herdsman; cowboy. [< Sp. *vaca* cow]

var. variant; variation; variety; various.

var·i·a·ble (vâr′ē·ə·bəl, var′-) *adj.* **1** Having the capacity of varying; alterable. **2** Having a tendency to change; not constant. **3** Having no definite value as regards quantity. **4** *Biol.* Prone to deviate from a type. **—***n.* **1** That which is liable to change. **2** *Math.* **a** A quantity that may be equal to any one of a specified set of numbers. **b** A symbol representing such a quantity. **3** A shifting wind. **—var′i·a·bil′i·ty, var′i·a·ble·ness** *n.* **—var′i·a·bly** *adv.* **—Syn.** *adj.* **2** fluctuating, unstable, unsteady, wavering.

variable zone TEMPERATE ZONE.

var·i·ance (vâr′ē·əns, var′-) *n.* **1** The act of varying or the state of being varied. **2** Discrepancy; difference. **3** A dispute; quarrel. **4** A license or official permission to do something contrary to official regulations. **—at variance** Not in agreement; disagreeing.

var·i·ant (vâr′ē·ənt, var′-) *adj.* **1** Varying; differing, esp. differing from a standard or type. **2** *Archaic* Variable; changeable. **—***n.* **1** A person or thing that differs from another in form only. **2** One of several different spellings, pronunciations, or forms of the same word.

var·i·a·tion (vâr′ē·ā′shən, var′-) *n.* **1** The act or process of varying; modification. **2** The extent to which a thing varies. **3** A thing changed in form from others of the same type. **4** *Music* A repetition of a theme or melody with changes in key, rhythm, harmony, etc. **5** *Biol.* Deviation from the typical structure or function. **—var′i·a′tion·al** *adj.*

var·i·col·ored (vâr′i·kul′ərd, var′-) *adj.* Variegated in color; parti-colored.

var·i·cose (var′ə·kōs) *adj.* **1** Abnormally dilated, as veins. **2** Having or resulting from varicose veins: *varicose* ulcer. [< L < *varix* a varicose vein] **—var′i·cos′i·ty** (-kos′ə·tē) *n.*

var·ied (vâr′ēd, var′-) *adj.* **1** Consisting of diverse sorts; assorted. **2** Altered; changed. **—var′ied·ly** *adv.*

var·i·e·gate (vâr′ē·ə·gāt′, var′-) *v.t.* **·gat·ed, ·gat·ing** **1** To mark with different colors; dapple; streak. **2** To make varied; diversify. **—***adj.* VARIEGATED. [< L *varius* various + *agere* to drive, do] **—var′i·e·ga′tion** *n.*

var·i·e·gat·ed (vâr′ē·ə·gā′tid, var′-) *adj.* **1** Varied in color, as with streaks or blotches. **2** Having or exhibiting different forms, styles, or varieties.

va·ri·e·ty (və·rī′ə·tē) *n. pl.* **·ties** **1** Absence of sameness or monotony; diversity; variation; difference. **2** Sort; kind: a sweet *variety* of pickle. **3** A collection of diverse kinds; assortment: a *variety* of flowers. **4** A subdivision of a species. **5** Vaudeville: also **variety show.** [< L *varius* various]

va·ri·o·la (ver′ē·ō′lə, və·rī′ə·lə) *n.* SMALLPOX. [< L *varius* speckled] **—va·ri′o·lar** *adj.*

var·i·o·rum (vâr′ē·ôr′əm, -ō′rəm, var′-) *n.* **1** An edition of a work containing various versions of the text. **2** An edition of a work with notes by different critics or editors. **—***adj.* Of or pertaining to such an edition. [< L *(cum notis) variorum* (with the notes) of various persons]

var·i·ous (vâr′ē·əs, var′-) *adj.* **1** Characteristically different from one another; diverse: *various* customs. **2** Being more than one and easily distinguishable; several: *various* friends. **3** Separate; particular; identifiable: He shook hands with *various* people. **4** Differing in nature or appearance; dissimilar. **5** Versatile; multifaceted. [< L *varius*] **—var′i·ous·ly** *adv.* **—var′i·ous·ness** *n.*

var·let (vär′lit) *n. Archaic* A scoundrel. [OF, a groom] **—var′let·ry** *n.*

var·mint (vär′mənt) *n. Regional* Any person or animal considered as troublesome, esp. vermin. [Alter. of VERMIN]

var·nish (vär′nish) *n.* **1** A solution of certain gums or resins in alcohol, linseed oil, etc., used to produce a shining, transparent coat on a surface. **2** The glossy, hard finish made by this solution when dry. **3** Any substance or finish resembling varnish. **4** Outward show; deceptive appearance. **—***v.t.* **1** To cover with varnish. **2** To give a glossy appearance to. **3** To hide by a deceptive appearance; gloss over. [< Med. L *vernicium,* a kind of resin] **—var′nish·er** *n.*

var·si·ty (vär′sə·tē) *n. pl.* **·ties** *Informal* **1** *Brit.* UNIVERSITY. **2** The team that represents a university, college, or school in any competition. [Alter. of UNIVERSITY]

var·y (vâr′ē, var′-) *v.* **var·ied, var·y·ing** *v.t.* **1** To change the form, nature, substance, etc., of; modify. **2** To cause to be different from one another. **3** To diversify. **4** *Music* To systematically alter (a melody or other thematic element). **—***v.i.* **5** To become changed in form, substance, etc. **6** To differ. **7** To deviate; depart: with *from.* **8** To alternate. **9** *Math.* To be subject to change. **10** *Biol.* To show variation. [< L *varius* various, diverse] **—var′y·ing·ly** *adv.*

vas (vas) *n. pl.* **va·sa** (vā′sə) *Biol.* A vessel or duct. [L, vessel, dish] **—va′sal** *adj.*

vas·cu·lar (vas′kyə·lər) *adj.* Of, pertaining to, or having vessels or ducts, as blood vessels, phloem tissue, etc. [< L *vasculum,* dim. of *vas* vessel] **—vas′cu·lar′i·ty** (-lar′ə·tē) *n.* **—vas′cu·lar·ly** *adv.*

vas def·er·ens (vas def′ər·ənz) The duct by which spermatozoa pass from the testicle to the penis. [<L *vas* vessel + *deferens* leading down]

vase (vās, vāz, väz) *n.* An urnlike vessel used as an ornament or for holding flowers. [<L *vas* vessel]

va·sec·to·my (və·sek′tə·mē) *n. pl.* **·to·mies** Surgical removal of a portion of the vas deferens, thus producing sterilization by preventing semen from reaching the seminal vesicles. [<VAS(O)- + -ECTOMY]

Vas·e·line (vas′ə·lēn, vas·ə·lēn′) *n.* PETROLATUM: a trade name.

vaso- *combining form* A vessel, esp. a blood vessel: *vasomotor.* [<L *vas* a vessel]

vas·o·mo·tor (vas′ō·mō′tər) *adj.* Producing contraction or dilation of blood vessels.

vas·sal (vas′əl) *n.* **1** In feudalism, a man who held land from a superior lord to whom he rendered, in return, military or other service. **2** A person who is in a position that is subordinate, lowly, servile, slavish, etc. —*adj.* Of or pertaining to a vassal. [<LL *vassus* a servant]

vas·sal·age (vas′əl·ij) *n.* **1** The condition, duties, and obligations of a vassal. **2** A position of servitude, dependence, or subjection.

vast (vast, väst) *adj.* **1** Of great extent; immense: a *vast* desert. **2** Very great in number, quantity, or amount. **3** Very great in degree, intensity, or importance. [<L, waste, empty, vast] —**vast′ly** *adv.* —**vast′ness** *n.* —**Syn. 1, 2** enormous, extensive, huge, tremendous.

vat (vat) *n.* A large vessel, tub, or cistern, esp. for holding liquids during some process, as heating, fermenting, etc. —*v.t.* **vat·ted, vat·ting** To treat in a vat. [<OE *fæt*]

VAT value-added tax.

Vat. Vatican.

vat dye Any of a class of fast dyes in which the color develops, as by oxidation in air, subsequent to treatment of the fabric in a usu. colorless dye solution. —**vat′dyed′** *adj.*

Vat·i·can (vat′ə·kən) *n.* **1** The papal palace in Vatican City, Rome. **2** The papal government.

Vatican City A sovereign papal state included in Rome. 108.7 acres.

vau·de·ville (vô′də·vil, vōd′vil) *n.* A theatrical entertainment consisting of short dramatic sketches, songs, dances, acrobatic feats, etc.; a variety show. [<F *(chanson de) Vau de Vire* (song of) the valley of the Vire river (in Normandy)]

vault[1] (vôlt) *n.* **1** An arched roof or ceiling, usu. of masonry. **2** Any vaultlike covering, as the sky. An arched passage or room. **4** An underground room or compartment for storage. **5** A place for keeping valuables: bank *vault.* **6** A burial chamber.—*v.t.* **1** To cover with or as with a vault. **2** To construct in the form of a vault. [<OF *volte, vaute*]

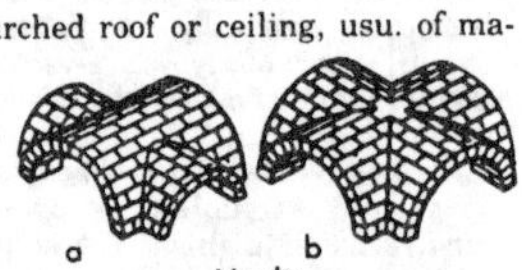
a b
Vaults
a. barrel. b. groined.

vault[2] (vôlt) *v.i.* **1** To leap, as over an object, by the use of one's hands on the object or by the use of a pole. —*v.t.* **2** To leap over. —*n.* **1** The act of vaulting. **2** A leap. [<OF *volter* to leap, gambol] —**vault′er** *n.*

vault·ing[1] (vôl′ting) *n.* The construction that forms a vault.

vault·ing[2] (vôl′ting) *adj.* **1** That leaps or leaps over. **2** Unduly confident or presumptuous. **3** Used for leaping and leaping over.

vaunt (vônt, vänt) *v.i.* **1** To boast. —*v.t.* **2** To boast of. —*n.* A brag or boast. [<LL *vanitare* brag<L *vanus* empty, vain]

vb. verb; verbal.

V.C. Victoria Cross; Vietcong.

VCR Videocassette recorder, a recorder utilizing videotape to record programs, movies, etc., for replay by means of a television set.

VD, V.D., v.d. venereal disease.

VDT Video (or visual) display terminal, a computer terminal with attached keyboard for the display of data; cathode-ray tube; terminal.

veal (vēl) *n.* **1** A calf, esp. one grown or suitable for food. **2** The flesh of a calf as food. [<L *vitellus,* dim. of *vitulus* calf]

vec·tor (vek′tər) *n.* **1** *Math.* A quantity defined by its magnitude and direction. **2** *Med.* An insect or other living carrier of pathogenic organisms from one host to another. [<L, carrier<*vehere* carry]

Ve·da (vā′də, vē′-) *n.* Any of four collections of ancient Hindu sacred writings. [Skt., knowledge] —**Ve·da·ic** (vi·dā′ik), **Ve′dic** *adj.* —**Ve·da·ism** (vā′də·iz′əm, vē′-) *n.*

V-E Day (vē′ē′) May 8, 1945, the official date of the Allied victory in Europe in World War II.

veep (vēp) *n. Slang* A vice president, esp. the vice president of the U.S. [<*V.P.*, abbr. of vice president]

veer (vir) *v.i.* **1** To shift or turn in position or direction: The wind *veered* to the east. **2** To shift from one opinion, belief, etc., to another. —*v.t.* **3** To change the direction of. —*n.* A change in direction. [<F *virer* to turn]

veer·y (vir′ē) *n. pl.* **veer·ies** A melodious tawny thrush that breeds in CEN. North America. [Prob. imit.]

veg. vegetable; vegetation.

Ve·ga (vē′gə, vā′-) *n.* A bright star in the constellation Lyra. [<Ar. *(al-Nasr) al-Waqi* the falling (vulture)]

veg·e·ta·ble (vej′ə·tə·bəl, vej′tə-) *n.* **1** A plant, esp. one cultivated for food. **2** The edible part of a plant, raw or cooked. **3** *Informal* A person who is mindless, apathetic, or passive. —*adj.* **1** Pertaining to plants, as distinct from animals: the *vegetable* kingdom. **2** Derived from, of the nature of, or resembling plants. **3** Made from or pertaining to edible vegetables: *vegetable* soup. **4** *Informal* Showing little mental activity; apathetic, passive, etc. [<L *vegetus* vigorous, lively<*vegere* be lively]

veg·e·tal (vej′ə·təl) *adj.* **1** Of or pertaining to plants or vegetables. **2** Pertaining to nonreproductive aspects of plant life.

veg·e·tar·i·an (vej′ə·târ′ē·ən) *n.* A person whose diet is made up of vegetables, fruits, grain, nuts, and sometimes animal products, as milk, eggs, etc. —*adj.* **1** Pertaining to or advocating the eating of only vegetable foods. **2** Made up exclusively of vegetables, fruits, grain, etc. —**veg′e·tar′i·an·ism** *n.*

veg·e·tate (vej′ə·tāt) *v.i.* **·tat·ed, ·tat·ing 1** To grow, as a plant. **2** To live in a monotonous, passive way.

veg·e·ta·tion (vej′ə·tā′shən) *n.* **1** The process or condition of vegetating. **2** Plant life in the aggregate.

veg·e·ta·tive (vej′ə·tā′tiv) *adj.* **1** Of or pertaining to vegetation and plant growth. **2** Growing or capable of growing as plants; productive. **3** VEGETABLE (def. 4). **4** Concerned with nonreproductive life processes.

ve·he·ment (vē′ə·mənt) *adj.* **1** Arising from or marked by strong feeling or passing. **2** Acting with great force; violent. [<L *vehemens, -entis* impetuous, rash] —**ve′he·mence, ve′he·men·cy** *n.* —**ve′he·ment·ly** *adv.* —**Syn. 1** ardent, fervent, zealous, fierce. **2** energetic, forceful, intense, powerful.

ve·hi·cle (vē′ə·kəl, vē′hi-) *n.* **1** Any device for carrying or transporting persons or things, as a car, spacecraft, etc. **2** A neutral medium for administering a medicine, etc. **3** The medium with which pigments are mixed in painting. **4** Any means by which thoughts or ideas are transmitted or communicated. [<L *vehiculum*<*vehere* to carry, ride] —**ve·hic·u·lar** (vi·hik′yə·lər) *adj.*

veil (vāl) *n.* **1** A piece of thin and light fabric, worn over the face or head for concealment, protection, or ornament. **2** A piece of cloth, as a curtain, that covers, conceals, etc. **3** Anything that conceals or covers. —**take the veil** To become a nun. —*v.t.* **1** To cover with a veil. **2** To conceal, cover, hide, disguise, etc. [<L *velum* piece of cloth, sail]

veil·ing (vā′ling) *n.* **1** The act of covering with a veil. **2** Material for veils. **3** A veil.

vein (vān) *n.* **1** Any of the tubular vessels that convey blood to the heart. **2** One of the radiating supports of an insect's wing. **3** One of the slender vascular bundles that form the framework of a leaf. **4** LODE. **5** A long, irregular, colored streak, as in wood, marble, etc. **6** A distinctive tendency or disposition. —*v.t.* **1** To furnish or fill with veins. **2** To streak or ornament with veins. **3** To extend over or throughout as veins. [<L *vena* blood vessel]

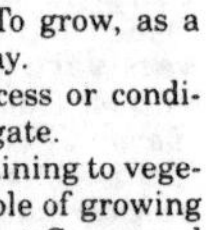
Veining of maple leaf

veined (vānd) *adj.* 1 Having veins, esp. many veins. 2 Marked with streaks of another color: *veined* marble.
vein·ing (vā′ning) *n.* 1 A vein or network of veins. 2 A streaked or veined surface.
vein·let (vān′lit) *n.* A small vein.
ve·lar (vē′lər) *adj.* 1 Of or pertaining to a velum, esp. the soft palate. 2 *Phonet.* Formed with the back of the tongue touching or near the soft palate, as (k) in *cool.* —*n. Phonet.* A velar sound. [< L *velum* sail, curtain]
veld (velt, felt) *n.* In South Africa, open country having few shrubs or trees. Also **veldt.** [< MDu. *velt* field]
vel·lum (vel′əm) *n.* 1 Fine parchment made from the skins of calves; used for expensive binding, printing, etc. 2 A manuscript written on vellum. 3 Paper or cloth made to resemble vellum. [< OF *veel, viel* calf]
ve·loc·i·pede (və·los′ə·pēd) *n.* 1 An early form of bicycle or tricycle. 2 A child's tricycle. [< L *velox* swift + -PEDE]
ve·loc·i·ty (və·los′ə·tē) *n. pl.* **·ties** 1 Quickness of motion; speed; swiftness. 2 *Physics* A vector representing the rate of change of position of a body. [< L *velox* swift]
ve·lour (və·lo͝or′) *n. pl.* **·lours** 1 A soft, velvetlike, cotton or wool fabric having a short, thick pile. 2 A type of felt with a velvety nap, used esp. for hats. Also **ve·lours** (və·lo͝or′. [See VELURE.]
ve·lum (vē′ləm) *n. pl.* **·la** (-lə) 1 SOFT PALATE. 2 A thin membranous covering or partition. [L, veil]
ve·lure (və·lyo͝or′) *n. Archaic* A heavy fabric resembling velvet, formerly used for hangings, etc. [< F *velours* < L *villosus* shaggy]
vel·vet (vel′vit) *n.* 1 A fabric of silk, rayon, nylon, etc., having on one side a short, smooth pile. 2 Something resembling velvet. 3 *Slang* Unexpected profit or gain. —*adj.* 1 Made of velvet. 2 Smooth and soft to the touch like velvet. [Ult. < L *villus* shaggy hair] —**vel′vet·y** *adj.*
vel·vet·een (vel′və·tēn′) *n.* 1 A fabric, usu. of cotton, with a short, close pile like velvet. 2 Clothes, esp. slacks, made of velveteen.
Ven. Venerable; Venice; Venus.
ve·na ca·va (vē′nə kā′və) *pl.* **ve·nae ca·vae** (vē′nē kā′vē) Either of the two great veins that deliver blood to the right auricle of the heart. [< L, hollow vein] • See HEART.
ve·nal (vē′nəl) *adj.* 1 Capable of being corrupted or bribed. 2 Characterized by corruption or bribery. [< L *venum* sale] —**ve·nal·i·ty** (vē·nal′ə·tē) *n.* —**ve′nal·ly** *adv.*
ve·na·tion (ve·nā′shən, vē-) *n.* 1 Veins collectively. 2 NERVATION. [< L *vena* a vein]
vend (vend) *v.t.* 1 To sell, as by peddling. 2 To sell by means of a vending machine. 3 To give expression to in public —*v.i.* 4 To sell merchandise. [< L *vendere*] —**Syn.** *v.t.* 1 dispense, hawk, market, peddle.
ven·dee (ven·dē′) *n.* The person or party to whom something is sold.
ven·det·ta (ven·det′ə) *n.* Private warfare or feud, as in revenge for a murder, injury, etc. [< L *vindicta* vengeance]
vend·i·ble (ven′də·bəl) *adj.* Salable; marketable. —*n.* A thing for sale. —**vend′i·bil′i·ty, vend′i·ble·ness** *n.* —**vend′i·bly** *adv.*
vending machine A machine that makes candy, stamps, etc., available when a coin is inserted.
ven·dor (ven′dər) *n.* 1 One who vends; seller. 2 VENDING MACHINE. Also **vender.**
ve·neer (və·nir′) *n.* 1 A thin layer, as of choice wood, upon a cheaper surface. 2 Mere surface or outside show: a *veneer* of politeness. —*v.t.* 1 To cover (a surface) with veneers. 2 To conceal, as something disagreeable or coarse, with an attractive and deceptive surface. [< G *furnieren* inlay < F *fournir* furnish] —**ve·neer′er** *n.*
ven·er·a·ble (ven′ər·ə·bəl) *adj.* Meriting or commanding veneration because of dignity, age, religious or historical associations, etc. [< L *venerari* revere] —**ven′er·a·bil′i·ty, ven′er·a·ble·ness** *n.* —**ven′er·a·bly** *adv.*
ven·er·ate (ven′ə·rāt) *v.t.* **·at·ed, ·at·ing** To regard with respect and deference; revere. [< L *venerari* revere]
ven·er·a·tion (ven′ə·rā′shən) *n.* 1 Profound respect combined with awe. 2 The act of worshiping; worship.
ve·ne·re·al (və·nir′ē·əl) *adj.* 1 Pertaining to or proceeding from sexual intercourse. 2 Communicated by sexual relations with an infected person: a *venereal* disease. 3 Pertaining to or curative of diseases so communicated. 4 Infected with syphilis, gonorrhea, or other venereal disease. [< L *Venus* goddess of love] —**ve·ne′re·al·ly** *adv.*
venereal disease Any of several diseases transmitted by sexual intercourse, as syphilis, gonorrhea, etc.
ven·er·y[1] (ven′ər·ē) *n.* The pursuit of sexual gratification. [< L *Venus,* goddess of love]
ven·er·y[2] (ven′ər·ē) *Archaic n. pl.* **·er·ies** The hunting of game; the chase. [< L *venari* to hunt]
Ve·ne·tian (və·nē′shən) *adj.* Pertaining to Venice or to its people. —*n.* A citizen or inhabitant of Venice.
Venetian blind A flexible window screen having movable, overlapping slats so fastened on webbing or tape as to exclude or admit light.
Ven·e·zue·la (ven′ə·zwā′lə, -zo͞o·ē′lə) *n.* A republic of N South America, 352,143 sq. mi, cap. Caracas. —**Ven′e·zue′lan** *adj., n.*

ven·geance (ven′jəns) *n.* The infliction of a deserved penalty; retributive punishment. —**with a vengeance** 1 With great force or violence. 2 Extremely; to an unusual extent. [< L *vindicare* defend, avenge]
venge·ful (venj′fəl) *adj.* Seeking to inflict vengeance; vindictive. —**venge′ful·ly** *adv.* —**venge′ful·ness** *n.*
ve·ni·al (vē′nē·əl, vēn′yəl) *adj.* So slight or trivial as to be overlooked, as a fault. [< L *venia* forgiveness, mercy] —**ve′ni·al′i·ty** (-al′ə·tē), **ve′ni·al·ness** *n.* —**ve′ni·al·ly** *adv.* —**Syn.** excusable, forgivable, pardonable.
ve·ni·re (vi·nī′rē) *n. Law* A panel of people from which a jury is selected. [< L *venire facias* that you cause to come]
ve·ni·re·man (vi·nī′rē·mən) *n. pl.* **·men** (-mən) A member of a venire.
ven·i·son (ven′ə·zən, -sən) *n.* The flesh of a wild animal, esp. a deer, used for food. [< L *venari* to hunt]
ve·ni, vi·di, vi·ci (vā′nē, vē′dē, vē′chē; wā′nē, wē′dē, wē′kē) *Latin* I came, I saw, I conquered: Julius Caesar's report to the Roman Senate of a victory.
ven·om (ven′əm) *n.* 1 The poison secreted by certain reptiles, insects, etc., which is transferred to a victim by a bite or sting. 2 Ill will; spite. [< L *venenum* poison] —**Syn.** 2 hate, malice, rancor, spitefulness.
ven·om·ous (ven′əm·əs) *adj.* 1 Able to give a poisonous sting. 2 Malicious; spiteful. —**ven′om·ous·ly** *adv.* —**ven′om·ous·ness** *n.*
ve·nous (vē′nəs) *adj.* 1 Of, pertaining to, contained, or carried in a vein or veins. 2 Designating the blood carried by the veins back to the heart and lungs. 3 Marked with or having veins: also **ve′nose.** [< L *vena* vein] —**ve′nous·ly** *adv.* —**ve·nos·i·ty** (vē·nos′ə·tē, və-), **ve′nous·ness** *n.*
vent (vent) *n.* 1 An outlet; means of escape. 2 An opening for the passage of liquids, gases, etc. 3 A slit in a garment, as a coat. 4 *Zool.* An opening through which wastes are eliminated. —**give vent to** To utter or express: to *give vent to* one's anger. —*v.t.* 1 To give expression to. 2 To permit to escape at a vent, as a gas. 3 To make a vent in. [< OF < *fendre* cleave < L *findere* split]
ven·ti·late (ven′tə·lāt) *v.t.* **·lat·ed, ·lat·ing** 1 To produce a free circulation of air in, as by means of open windows, doors, etc. 2 To provide with a vent. 3 To expose to examination and discussion. 4 To oxygenate, as blood. [< L *ventus* wind] —**ven′ti·la′tion** *n.* —**ven′ti·la′tive** *adj.*
ven·ti·la·tor (ven′tə·lā′tər) *n.* 1 One who or that which ventilates. 2 A device or opening for replacing stale air with fresh air.
ven·tral (ven′trəl) *adj.* Toward, near, in, or on the abdomen. [< L *venter, ventris* belly] —**ven′tral·ly** *adv.*
ven·tri·cle (ven′trə·kəl) *n.* Any cavity in the body, esp. either of the two lower chambers of the heart, from which blood is forced into the arteries. [< L *venter, ventris* belly] —**ven·tric·u·lar** (-trik′yə·lər) *adj.* • See HEART.

add, āce, câre, pälm; end, ēven; it, īce; odd, ōpen, ôrder; to͝ok, po͞ol; up, bûrn; ə = *a* in *above, u* in *focus;* yo͞o = *u* in *fuse;* oil; pout; check; go; ring; thin; this; zh, *vision.* < derived from; ? origin uncertain or unknown.

ven·tril·o·quism (ven·tril′ə·kwiz′əm) *n.* The art of speaking in such a way that the sound seems to come from some source other than the person speaking. Also **ven·tril′·o·quy** (-kwē). [< L *venter* belly + *loqui* speak] **—ven·tri·lo·qui·al** (ven′trə·lō′kwē·əl), **ven·tril′o·quis′tic** *adj.* **—ven′tri·lo′·qui·al·ly** *adv.* **—ven·tril′o·quist** *n.* **—ven·tril′o·quize′** (-kwīz) **(·quized, ·qui·zing)** *v.i. & v.t.*

ven·ture (ven′chər) *v.* **·tured, ·tur·ing** *v.t.* **1** To expose to chance or risk; stake. **2** To run the risk of. **3** To express at the risk of denial or refutation: to *venture* a suggestion. **4** To place or send on a chance, as in a speculative investment. —*v.i.* **5** To take risk in going, coming, etc.: to *venture* into deep water. —*n.* **1** A risk; hazard. **2** An undertaking attended with risk. **3** That which is ventured, esp. property risk. **—at a venture** At random; haphazardly. [Alter. of ADVENTURE] **—ven′tur·er** *n.*

ven·ture·some (ven′chər·səm) *adj.* **1** Bold; daring. **2** Involving hazard; risky. **—ven′ture·some·ly** *adv.* **—ven′ture·some·ness** *n.*

ven·tur·ous (ven′chər·əs) *adj.* **1** Adventurous; bold. **2** Hazardous; risky; dangerous. **—ven′tur·ous·ly** *adv.* **—ven′·tur·ous·ness** *n.*

ven·ue (ven′yōō) *n. Law* **1** The place or neighborhood where a crime is committed or a cause of action arises. **2** The county or political division from which the jury must be summoned and in which the trial must be held. **—change of venue** The change of the place of trial, for good cause shown, from one county to another. [< OF *venir* come]

Ve·nus (vē′nəs) *Rom. Myth.* The goddess of love and beauty. —*n.* **1** A beautiful woman. **2** The planet of the solar system second in distance from the sun. • See PLANET.

Venus fly·trap (flī′trap′) An insectivorous plant of the SE U.S., with a basal rosette of leaves that entrap anything that touches certain sensitive hairs on their surface. Also **Ve′nus's-fly′trap** (vē′nəs·iz-).

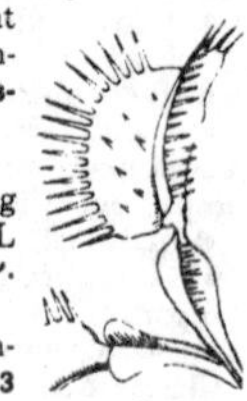
Venus flytrap

ver. verse(s); version.

ve·ra·cious (və·rā′shəs) *adj.* **1** Speaking the truth; truthful. **2** True; accurate. [< L *verus* true] **—ve·ra′cious·ly** *adv.* **—ve·ra′·cious·ness** *n.*

ve·rac·i·ty (və·ras′ə·tē) *n. pl.* **·ties 1** Honesty; truthfulness. **2** Accuracy; trueness. **3** That which is true; truth. [< L *verax*] **—Syn. 1** candor, frankness, integrity.

ve·ran·da (və·ran′də) *n.* An open porch, usu. roofed, along one or more sides of a building. Also **ve·ran′dah.** [< Pg. *varanda* railing, balustrade]

verb (vûrb) *n. Gram.* **1** One of a class of words which express existence, action, or occurrence, or that function as a copula or an auxiliary. **2** Any word or construction functioning similarly. [< L *verbum* word]

ver·bal (vûr′bəl) *adj.* **1** Of, in, or pertaining to words: a *verbal* contract; a *verbal* image. **2** Of, pertaining to, or concerned with words rather than the ideas they convey. **3** Word for word; verbatim; literal: a *verbal* translation. **4** *Gram.* **a** Partaking of the nature of or derived from a verb: a *verbal* noun. **b** Used to form verbs: a *verbal* prefix. **5** *Informal* Adept at using words, as in choice or range of vocabulary: She's very *verbal* for her age. —*n. Gram.* A noun directly derived from a verb, in English often having the form of the present participle, as, "There shall be *weeping* and *wailing* and *gnashing* of teeth"; also, an infinitive used as a noun, as, "*To err* is human": also **verbal noun.** [< L *verbum* word] **—ver′bal·ly** *adv.* • See ORAL.

ver·bal·ism (vûr′bəl·iz′əm) *n.* **1** A verbal phrase or expression. **2** A meaningless form of words; verbiage.

ver·bal·ist (vûr′bəl·ist) *n.* **1** One who is skilled in the use and meanings of words. **2** A person overly concerned with words rather than facts or concepts.

ver·bal·ize (vûr′bəl·īz) *v.* **·ized ·iz·ing** *v.t.* **1** *Gram.* To change (a noun, etc.) into a verb. **2** To express in words. —*v.i.* **3** To speak or write verbosely. **—ver′bal·i·za′tion, ver′bal·iz′er** *n.*

ver·ba·tim (vər·bā′tim) *adj. & adv.* In the exact words; word for word. [< L *verbum* word]

ver·be·na (vər·bē′nə) *n.* Any of a genus of plants having spikes of showy, often fragrant flowers. [< L, foliage, vervain]

ver·bi·age (vûr′bē·ij) *n.* **1** Use of too many words. **2** Manner of verbal expression. [< F *verbe* word]

ver·bose (vər·bōs′) *adj.* Using or containing an unnecessary number of words; wordy. [< L *verbum* word] **—ver·bose′ly** *adv.* **—ver·bose′ness, ver·bos′i·ty** (-bos′ə·tē) *n.* **—Syn.** garrulous, long-winded, prolix.

ver·bo·ten (vər·bōt′n, fər-) *adj. German* Forbidden.

ver·dant (vûr′dənt) *adj.* **1** Green with vegetation; fresh. **2** Immature in experience. [< F *verdoyer* grow green] **—ver′dan·cy** *n.* **—ver′dant·ly** *adv.*

ver·dict (vûr′dikt) *n.* **1** The decision of a jury in an action. **2** A conclusion expressed; an opinion. [< L *vere dictum* truly said]

ver·di·gris (vûr′də·grēs, -gris, -grē) *n.* **1** A green or greenish blue acetate of copper obtained by treating copper with acetic acid. **2** The blue-green crust formed by corrosion of copper, bronze, or brass in air, sea water, etc. [< OF *vert de Grece,* lit., green of Greece]

ver·dure (vûr′jər) *n.* **1** The fresh greenness of growing vegetation. **2** Green vegetation. [< F *verd* green]

verge[1] (vûrj) *n.* **1** The extreme edge; brink: on the *verge* of bankruptcy. **2** A bounding or enclosing line surrounding something. —*v.i.* **verged, verg·ing 1** To be contiguous or adjacent. **2** To form the limit or verge. [< L *virga* twig]

verge[2] (vûrj) *v.i.* **verged, verg·ing 1** To come near; approach: a remark *verging* on rudeness. **2** To tend; incline. [< L *vergere* to bend, turn]

ver·i·fi·ca·tion (ver′ə·fə·kā′shən) *n.* **1** The act of verifying, or the state of being verified. **2** A proof or confirmation, as by examination. **—ver′i·fi·ca′tive** *adj.*

ver·i·fy (ver′ə·fī) *v.t.* **·fied, ·fy·ing 1** To prove to be true or accurate; confirm. **2** To test the accuracy or truth of. **3** *Law* To affirm under oath. [< L *verus* true + *facere* make] **—ver′i·fi′er** *n.* **—Syn. 1** authenticate, corroborate, substantiate. **2** ascertain.

ver·i·ly (ver′ə·lē) *adv.* In truth; certainly. [< VERY]

ver·i·sim·i·lar (ver′ə·sim′ə·lər) *adj.* Appearing or seeming to be true; likely; probable. [< L *verus* true + *similis* like] **—ver′i·sim′i·lar·ly** *adv.*

ver·i·si·mil·i·tude (ver′ə·si·mil′ə·tyōōd) *n.* **1** Appearance of truth; likelihood. **2** That which resembles truth. [< L *verisimilitudo*]

ver·i·ta·ble (ver′ə·tə·bəl) *adj.* Genuine; true; real. [< F *vérité* truth] **—ver′i·ta·ble·ness** *n.* **—ver′i·ta·bly** *adv.*

ver·i·ty (ver′ə·tē) *n. pl.* **·ties 1** Truth; correctness. **2** A true statement; a fact. [< L *veritas* truth < *verus* true]

vermi- *combining form* A worm; of or related to a worm: *vermicide.* [< L *vermis* a worm]

ver·mi·cel·li (vûr′mə·chel′ē, -sel′ē) *n.* A food paste made into slender wormlike cords thinner than spaghetti. [Ital., lit., little worms]

ver·mi·cide (vûr′mə·sīd) *n.* Any substance that kills worms, esp. a drug destructive of intestinal worms. **—ver′mi·cid′al** *adj.*

ver·mi·form (vûr′mə·fôrm) *adj.* Like a worm in shape.

vermiform appendix A slender, wormlike sac protruding from the large intestine. • See INTESTINE.

ver·mi·fuge (vûr′mə·fyōōj′) *n.* Any remedy that destroys intestinal worms. [< L *vermis* a worm + *fugare* expel]

ver·mil·ion (vər·mil′yən) *n.* **1** A brilliant, durable red pigment obtained from cinnabar or made synthetically. **2** An intense orange-red color. —*adj.* Of a bright orange-red color. —*v.t.* To color with vermilion. [< OF *vermeil*]

ver·min (vûr′min) *n. pl.* **·min 1** Noxious small animals or parasitic insects, as lice, worms, mice, etc. **2** *Brit.* Certain animals injurious to game, as weasels, owls, etc. **3** A repulsive person or persons. [< L *vermis* a worm] **—ver′min·ous** *adj.* **—ver′min·ous·ly** *adv.* **—ver′min·ous·ness** *n.*

ver·mouth (vər·mōōth′) *n.* A fortified white wine flavored with aromatic herbs. [< G *Wermuth* wormwood]

ver·nac·u·lar (vər·nak′yə·lər) *n.* **1** The native language of a locality. **2** The common daily speech of any people. **3** The specialized vocabulary of a profession or trade. **4** An idiomatic word or phrase. —*adj.* **1** Belonging to one's native land; indigenous: said of a language, idiom, etc. **2** Using the colloquial native tongue: *vernacular* poets. **3** Written in the language indigenous to a people: a *vernacu-*

lar translation of the Bible. [< L *vernaculus* domestic, native] **—ver·nac′u·lar·ly** *adv.*

ver·nal (vûr′nəl) *adj.* 1 Belonging to, appearing in, or appropriate to spring. 2 Youthful; fresh. [< L *vernus* belonging to spring] **—ver′nal·ly** *adv.*

vernal equinox The equinox that occurs on or about March 21.

ver·ni·er (vûr′nē·ər) *n.* A small, movable, auxiliary scale for obtaining fractional parts of the subdivisions of a main scale. Also **vernier scale.** [< Pierre *Vernier*, 1580–1637, French mathematician]

Ver·o·nal (ver′ə·nəl) *n.* BARBITAL: a trade name.

ve·ron·i·ca (və·ron′i·kə) *n.* SPEEDWELL. [< St. *Veronica*, a legendary follower of Christ]

ver·sa·tile (vûr′sə·til, -tīl) *adj.* 1 Having many aptitudes or talents. 2 Having many uses: a *versatile* fabric. 3 Movable in more than one direction, as the toe of a bird. 4 *Bot.* Turning about freely on the support to which it is attached: said of an anther. [< L *versare*, freq. of *vertere* turn] **—ver′sa·tile·ly** *adv.* **—ver′sa·til′i·ty** (-til′ə·tē) *n.*

verse (vûrs) *n.* 1 A single line of a poem. 2 A group of lines in a poem; stanza. 3 Metrical composition as distinguished from prose; poetry. 4 A specified type of metrical composition: iambic *verse.* 5 One of the short divisions of a chapter of the Bible. [< L *versus* a turning, a verse]

versed (vûrst) *adj.* Having ready skill and knowledge; proficient. [< L *versari* occupy oneself] **—Syn.** experienced, practiced, seasoned, skillful.

ver·si·fy (vûr′sə·fī) *v.* **·fied, ·fy·ing** *v.t.* 1 To turn prose into verse. 2 To narrate or treat in verse. *—v.i.* 3 To write poetry. **—ver·si·fi·ca·tion** (vûr′sə·fə·kā′shən), **ver′si·fi′er** *n.*

ver·sion (vûr′zhən, -shən) *n.* 1 A translation or rendition from one language into another. 2 A description of an event, occurrence, etc., from a personal viewpoint. [< Med. L *versio* a turning < L *vertere* to turn] **—ver′sion·al** *adj.*

vers li·bre (ver lē′br′) *French* Free verse. **—vers li·brist** (lē′brist).

ver·so (vûr′sō) *n. pl.* **·sos** 1 A left-hand page of a book, leaflet, etc. 2 The reverse of a coin or medal. [< L *verso (folio)* a turned (leaf)]

verst (vûrst) *n.* A Russian measure of distance equal to about two thirds of a mile. [< Russ. *versta*]

ver·sus (vûr′səs) *prep.* 1 In law, sports, and contests, against. 2 Considered as the alternative of: free trade *versus* high tariffs. [L, toward, turned toward]

ver·te·bra (vûr′tə·brə) *n. pl* **·brae** (-brē, -brā) or **·bras** Any of the individual bones of the spinal column. [L, a joint, vertebra < *vertere* to turn] **—ver′te·bral** *adj.*

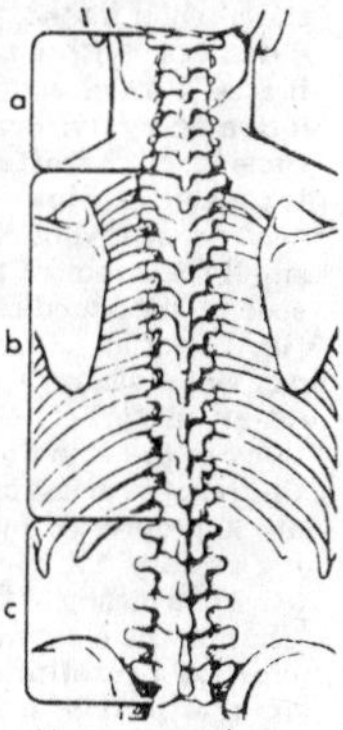

Human vertebrae
a. cervical.
b. thoracic. c. lumbar.

ver·te·brate (vûr′tə·brit, -brāt) *adj.* 1 Having a backbone or spinal column. 2 Pertaining to or characteristic of vertebrates. 3 Pertaining to, having, or composed of vertebrae. *—n.* Any of a division of animals characterized by a spinal column, as fishes, birds, and mammals. [< L *vertebratus* jointed] **—ver′te·brat′ed** *adj.*

ver·tex (vûr′teks) *n. pl.* **·tex·es** or **·ti·ces** (-tə·sēz′) 1 The highest point of anything; apex. 2 *Astron.* **a** ZENITH. **b** The point in the sky toward or from which a group of stars appears to be moving. 3 *Geom.* **a** The point of intersection of the sides of an angle. **b** The point farthest from the base. [L, the top < *vertere* to turn]

ver·ti·cal (vûr′ti·kəl) *adj.* 1 Perpendicular; upright. 2 Of or pertaining to the vertex. 3 Occupying a position directly overhead; at the highest point. 4 Of or pertaining to a business concern that undertakes a process from raw material to consumer: a *vertical* trust. *—n.* 1 A vertical line, plane, or circle. 2 An upright beam or rod in a truss. **—ver′ti·cal′i·ty** (-kal′ə·tē), **ver′ti·cal·ness** *n.* **—ver′ti·cal·ly** *adv.*

vertical angle Either one of two angles which lie on opposite sides of two intersecting lines.

ver·tig·i·nous (vər·tij′ə·nəs) *adj.* 1 Affected by vertigo; dizzy. 2 Turning round; whirling. 3 Liable to cause giddiness. **—ver·tig′i·nous·ly** *adv.* **—ver·tig′i·nous·ness** *n.*

ver·ti·go (vûr′tə·gō′) *n. pl.* **·goes** or **ver·tig·i·nes** (vər·tij′ə·nēz) A disorder in which a person or his surroundings seem to whirl about in such a way as to make the person dizzy and usu. sick. [L, lit., a turning around]

ver·vain (vûr′vān) *n.* A species of verbena supposedly having medicinal properties. [< L *verbena* verbena]

verve (vûrv) *n.* Enthusiasm or energy. [< L *verba*, pl. of *verbum* a word] **—Syn.** élan, liveliness, spirit, vigor.

ver·y (ver′ē) *adv.* 1 In a high degree; extremely: *very* generous. 2 Exactly: They both had the *very* same thought. *—adj.* **ver·i·er, ver·i·est** 1 Absolute; complete: the *very* truth. 2 Suitable; right: the *very* tool we need. 3 Unqualified; complete: a *very* scoundrel. 4 Selfsame; identical: my *very* words. 5 The (thing) itself: used as an intensive: The *very* stones cry out. [< L *verus* true]

very high frequency Any wave frequency from 30 to 300 megahertz.

very low frequency Any wave frequency from 3 to 30 kilohertz.

ves·i·cant (ves′i·kənt) *adj.* Blister-producing. *—n.* That which produces blisters, esp. a chemical warfare agent which attacks the skin on contact or lung tissue if inhaled. [< L *vesica* a blister, bladder]

ves·i·cate (ves′i·kāt) *v.* **·cat·ed, ·cat·ing** *v.t.* 1 To raise blisters on. *—v.i.* 2 To blister, as the skin. **—ves′i·ca′tion** *n.*

ves·i·ca·to·ry (ves′i·kə·tôr′ē, və·sik′ə·tôr′ē, -tō′rē) *adj., n. pl.* **·ries** VESICANT.

ves·i·cle (ves′i·kəl) *n.* Any small bladderlike cavity, cell, cyst, or blister. [< L *vesica* a bladder] **—ve·sic·u·lar** (və·sik′yə·lar) *adj.* **—ve·sic′u·lar·ly** *adv.*

ves·per (ves′pər) *n. Archaic* EVENING. *—adj.* Of or pertaining to evening. [L, the evening star]

Ves·per (ves′pər) *n.* EVENING STAR. [L]

ves·pers (ves′pərz) *n.pl. Often cap. Eccl.* 1 The sixth in order of the canonical hours. 2 A service of worship in the late afternoon or evening.

ves·sel (ves′əl) *n.* 1 A hollow receptacle capable of holding a liquid, as a pot, tub, pitcher, etc. 2 A ship or large boat. 3 Any of several aircraft. 4 *Biol.* A duct or canal for containing or transporting a fluid. [< L *vas* a vessel]

vest (vest) *n.* 1 A short sleeveless jacket worn, esp. under a suit coat, by men. 2 A similar garment worn by women. 3 A vestee. 4 *Chiefly Brit.* UNDERSHIRT. *—v.t.* 1 To confer (ownership, authority, etc.) upon some person or persons. 2 To place ownership, control, or authority with (a person or persons). 3 To clothe or robe, as with church vestments. *—v.i.* 4 To clothe oneself, as in vestments. 5 To be or become legally vested, as property. [< L *vestis* clothing, a garment]

Ves·ta (ves′tə) *Rom. Myth.* The goddess of the hearth and the hearth fire.

ves·tal (ves′təl) *n.* 1 One of the virgin priestesses of Vesta: also **vestal virgin.** 2 A chaste woman, esp. a virgin. *—adj.* 1 Of or relating to Vesta or her priestesses. 2 Chaste. [< L *Vesta* Vesta]

vest·ed (ves′tid) *adj.* 1 Wearing clothes, esp. church vestments. 2 Not dependent on any contingency; fixed; inalienable; absolute: a *vested* right.

vested interest 1 A special interest, as in an economic or political system or arrangement, often pursued by the holder at the expense of others. 2 A person or group that pursues such an interest.

vest·ee (ves·tē′) *n.* A garment worn by women to fill in the neckline of a jacket, blouse, etc. [Dim. of VEST]

ves·ti·bule (ves′tə·byōōl) *n.* 1 A small antechamber leading into a building or another room. 2 An enclosed passage from one railway passenger car to another. 3 *Anat.* Any cavity leading to another cavity: the *vestibule* of the ear. —*v.t.* **·buled, ·bul·ing** To provide with a vestibule or vestibules. [< L *vestibulum* an entrance hall] **—ves·tib′u·lar** (-tib′yə·lər) *adj.*

ves·tige (ves′tij) *n.* **1** A trace of something absent, lost, or gone. **2** *Biol.* A remnant of an organ that is no longer functional. [< F < L *vestigium* a footprint] **—Syn. 1** hint, remnant, tinge, touch.

ves·tig·i·al (ves·tij′ē·əl) *adj.* Of, or of the nature of a vestige; surviving in small or degenerate form. **—ves·tig′i·al·ly** *adv.*

vest·ment (vest′mənt) *n.* **1** An article of clothing. **2** Any of several ritual garments of the clergy. [< L *vestire* clothe] **—vest·ment·al** (vest·men′təl) *adj.*

vest-pock·et (vest′pok′it) *adj.* **1** Small enough to fit in a vest pocket. **2** Much smaller than standard or usual size: a *vest-pocket* battleship.

vest-pocket park A small urban park, often on a vacant lot.

ves·try (ves′trē) *n. pl.* **·tries 1** In a church, a room where vestments are put on or kept. **2** A room in a church used for Sunday school, meetings, etc. **3** In the Anglican and Episcopal churches, a body administering the affairs of a parish or congregation. [< L *vestis* a garment]

ves·try·man (ves′trē·mən) *n. pl.* **·men** (-mən) A member of a vestry.

ves·ture (ves′chər) *n. Archaic* **1** Garments; clothing. **2** A covering or envelope. —*v.t.* **·tured, ·tur·ing** To cover or clothe. [< L *vestire* clothe] **—ves′tur·al** *adj.*

vet[1] (vet) *Informal n.* VETERINARIAN. —*v.t. & v.i.* **vet·ted, vet·ting** To treat (animals) as a veterinarian does. [Short for VETERINARIAN]

vet[2] (vet) *n. Informal* A veteran.

vet. veteran; veterinarian; veterinary.

vetch (vech) *n.* Any of a genus of trailing, leguminous vines grown for fodder. [< L *vicia*]

vet·er·an (vet′ər·ən, vet′rən) *n.* **1** An experienced soldier or an ex-soldier. **2** A member of the armed forces who has been in active service. **3** A person with long experience in an occupation, calling, etc. —*adj.* **1** Having had long experience or practice. **2** Of, pertaining to, or for veterans. [< L *vetus, veteris* old]

Veterans Day The fourth Monday in October, a U.S. holiday honoring veterans of the armed forces, formerly celebrated November 11.

vet·er·i·nar·i·an (vet′ər·ə·nâr′ē·ən, vet′rə-) *n.* A practitioner of medical and surgical treatment of animals.

vet·er·i·nar·y (vet′ər·ə·ner′ē, vet′rə-) *adj.* Of, pertaining to, or designating the science or practice of preventing, curing, or alleviating the diseases and injuries of animals, esp. domestic animals. —*n. pl.* **·nar·ies** VETERINARIAN. [< L *veterinarius* pertaining to beasts of burden < *veterina* beasts of burden]

ve·to (vē′tō) *v.t.* **·toed, ·to·ing 1** To refuse approval of (a bill passed by a legislative body). **2** To forbid or refuse to consent to. —*n. pl.* **·toes 1** The right of one branch of government to cancel, prohibit, postpone, etc., the projects of another branch; esp., the right of a chief executive, as the president or a governor, to refuse to approve a legislative enactment by withholding his signature. **2** A message giving the reasons of a chief executive for refusing to approve a bill. **3** The exercise of the right to veto. **4** Any authoritative prohibition. [< L, I forbid] **—ve′to·er** *n.*

vex (veks) *v.t.* **1** To annoy by petty irritations. **2** To trouble or afflict. **3** To baffle, puzzle, or confuse. [< L *vexare* to shake] **—vex·ed·ly** (vek′sid·lē) *adv.* **—vex′ed·ness, vex′er** *n.* **—Syn. 1** chagrin, irritate, pester, pique.

vex·a·tion (vek·sā′shən) *n.* **1** The act of vexing, or the state of being vexed. **2** Trouble, annoyance, affliction, etc.

vex·a·tious (vek·sā′shəs) *adj.* Annoying; harassing. **—vex·a′tious·ly** *adv.* **—vex·a′tious·ness** *n.*

VFW, V.F.W. Veterans of Foreign Wars.

VHF, V.H.F., vhf, v.h.f. very high frequency.

VI Virgin Islands (P.O. abbr.).

V.I. Virgin Islands.

v.i. see below (L *vide infra*); verb intransitive.

vi·a (vī′ə, vē′ə) *prep.* **1** By way of; by a route passing through. **2** By means of. [< L *via* a way]

vi·a·ble (vī′ə·bəl) *adj.* **1** Capable of living and developing normally, as a newborn infant, a seed, etc. **2** Workable; practicable: a *viable* plan. [< L *vita*] **—vi′a·bil′i·ty** *n.* **—vi′a·bly** *adv.*

vi·a·duct (vī′ə·dukt) *n.* A bridgelike structure, esp. a large one of arched masonry, to carry a road or railroad over a valley, section of a city, etc. [< L *via* a way + (AQUE)DUCT]

Viaduct

vi·al (vī′əl) *n.* A small bottle, usu. of glass, for medicines and other liquids. [< Gk. *phialē* a shallow cup]

vi·a me·di·a (vī′ə mē′dē·ə, vē′ə mā′-) *Latin* A middle way.

vi·and (vī′ənd) *n.* **1** An article of food, esp. meat. **2** *pl.* Provisions; food. [< OF *viande*]

vi·at·i·cum (vī·at′ə·kəm) *n. pl.* **·ca** (-kə) or **·cums 1** *Often cap.* The Eucharist, as given on *the verge of death.* **2** The provisions needed for a journey. [L, traveling money < *via* a way]

vibes (vībz) *n.pl. (usu. construed as sing. for def. 2) Slang* **1** Vibrations. See VIBRATION (def. 3). **2** VIBRAPHONE.

vi·brant (vī′brənt) *adj.* **1** Having, showing, or resulting from vibration; resonant. **2** Throbbing; pulsing: *vibrant* with enthusiasm. **3** Energetic; vigorous. **4** *Phonet.* VOICED (def. 3). —*n. Phonet.* A voiced sound. [< L *vibrare* to shake] **—vi′bran·cy** (-sē) *n. (pl.* **·cies) —vi′brant·ly** *adv.*

vi·bra·phone (vī′brə·fōn) *n.* A musical instrument like the marimba in which a vibrato is produced by rotating disks in electrically powered resonators.

vi·brate (vī′brāt) *v.* **·brat·ed, ·brat·ing** *v.i.* **1** To move back and forth, as a pendulum. **2** To move back and forth rapidly. **3** To resound: The note *vibrates* on the ear. **4** To be emotionally moved. —*v.t.* **5** To cause to move back and forth. **6** To cause to quiver. **7** To send forth (sound, etc.) by vibration. [< L *vibrare* to shake]

vi·bra·tile (vī′brə·til, -tīl) *adj.* **1** Pertaining to vibration. **2** Capable of vibration. **3** Having a vibratory motion. **—vi′bra·til′i·ty** (-til′ə·tē) *n.*

vi·bra·tion (vī·brā′shən) *n.* **1** The act of vibrating; oscillation. **2** *Physics* **a** A periodic, back-and-forth motion of a particle or body. **b** Any physical process characterized by cyclic changes in a variable, as wave motion. **c** A single cycle of such a process. **3** *pl. Slang* One's emotional response to an aura felt to surround a person or thing, esp. when considered in or out of harmony with oneself. **—vi·bra′tion·al** *adj.*

vi·bra·to (vē·brä′tō) *n. pl.* **·tos** *Music* A cyclic variation in the pitch of a tone. [Ital. < *vibrare* vibrate]

vi·bra·tor (vī′brā·tər) *n.* **1** One who or that which vibrates. **2** An electrically operated massaging apparatus.

vi·bra·to·ry (vī′brə·tôr′ē, -tō′rē) *adj.* **1** Pertaining to, causing, or characterized by vibration. **2** That vibrates or is capable of vibration.

vi·bur·num (vī·bûr′nəm) *n.* **1** Any of a genus of shrubs or small trees related to honeysuckle. **2** The bark of several species, used medicinally. [L, the wayfaring tree]

Vic. Victoria.

vic. vicar; vicarage; vicinity.

vic·ar (vik′ər) *n.* **1** One who is authorized to perform functions in the stead of another; deputy. **2** In the Anglican Church, the priest of a parish of which the main revenues are appropriated by a layman, the priest himself receiving a salary. **3** In the Roman Catholic Church, a representative of a bishop or the pope. **4** In the Protestant Episcopal Church, the clergyman who is the head of a chapel. [< L *vicarius* a substitute < *vicis* a change]

vic·ar·age (vik′ər·ij) *n.* **1** The benefice, office, or duties of a vicar. **2** A vicar's residence.

vic·ar-gen·er·al (vik′ər·jen′ər·əl, -jen′rəl) *n.* **1** In the Roman Catholic Church, a priest appointed by the bishop as assistant in administering a diocese. **2** In the Anglican church, an official assisting the bishop or archbishop.

vi·car·i·ous (vī·kâr′ē·əs, vi-) *adj.* **1** Suffered or done in place of another: a *vicarious* sacrifice. **2** Felt through identifying with another's experience: *vicarious* pleasure in his wife's talent. **3** Filling the office of or acting for another. **4** Delegated: *vicarious* authority. [< L *vicarius*] **—vi·car′i·ous·ly** *adv.* **—vi·car′i·ous·ness** *n.*

vice[1] (vīs) *n.* **1** Moral depravity; evil. **2** An immoral action, trait, etc. **3** A habitual, usu. trivial, failing or defect; shortcoming. [<L *vitium* a fault] —**Syn. 1** corruption, dissoluteness, profligacy.

vice[2] (vīs) *n.* & *v.t.* **viced, vic·ing** *Chiefly Brit.* VISE.

vice[3] (vī'sē) *prep.* Instead of; in place of. [<L *vicis* change]

vice- *prefix* One who acts for or takes the place of. [<L *vice*, abl. of *vicis* change]

vice admiral See GRADE. —**vice'-ad'mir·al·ty** (-mər·əl·tē) *n.*

vice-con·sul (vīs'kon'səl) *n.* A person who acts as a substitute for or a subordinate to a consul. —**vice-con·su·lar** (vīs'kon'sə·lər) *adj.* **vice-con·su·late** (vīs'kon'sə·lit), **vice'-con'sul·ship** *n.*

vice·ge·rent (vīs·jir'ənt) *n.* One duly authorized to exercise the powers of another; a deputy. —*adj.* Acting in the place of another. [<L VICE + *gerere* carry, manage] —**vice-ge'ren·cy** (-sē) *n.* (*pl.* **·cies**).

vice president **1** An officer ranking next below a president, and acting, on occasion, in his place. **2** In the U.S. government, an officer of this rank designated by the Constitution to succeed the president if necessary. —**vice-pres·i·den·cy** (vīs'prez'·ə·dən·sē) (*pl.* **·cies**) *n.* —**vice'-pres'i·den'·tial** (-prez'ə·den'shəl) *adj.*

vice·re·gal (vīs·rē'gəl) *adj.* Of or relating to a viceroy. —**vice·re'gal·ly** *adv.*

vice-re·gent (vīs'rē'jənt) *n.* A person who acts in the place of a regent when necessary. —*adj.* Of or pertaining to a vice-regent. —**vice'-re'gen·cy** *n.*

vice·roy (vīs'roi) *n.* One who rules a country, colony, or province by the authority of his sovereign. [<VICE- + F *roi* a king] —**vice·roy'al** (-roi'əl) *adj.* —**vice'roy'al·ty** (*pl.* **·ties**), **vice'roy·ship'** *n.*

vice squad A police division charged with combating prostitution, gambling, and other vices.

vi·ce ver·sa (vī'sē vûr'sə, vī'sə vûr'sə, vīs'vûr'sə) With the relation of terms being reversed; conversely. [L]

vi·chy·ssoise (vē'shē·swäz', vē'shē·swäz', vish'-) *n.* A potato cream soup flavored with leeks, celery, etc., usu. served cold with a sprinkling of chives. [<*Vichy*, France]

Vi·chy water (vish'ē) **1** The effervescent mineral water from the springs at Vichy, France. **2** Any mineral water resembling it.

vi·cin·i·ty (vi·sin'ə·tē) *n. pl.* **·ties 1** A region adjacent or near; neighborhood. **2** Nearness; proximity. [<L *vicinus* nearby]

vi·cious (vish'əs) *adj.* **1** Corrupt in conduct or habits; depraved; immoral. **2** Of the nature of vice: *vicious* acts. **3** Unruly or dangerous, as an animal: a *vicious* dog. **4** Marked by evil intent; malicious; spiteful: a *vicious* lie. **5** Worthless or invalidated because defective; full of errors or faults: *vicious* arguments. **6** *Informal* Unusually severe or punishing: a *vicious* blow. **7** *Informal* Savage; heinous: a *vicious* crime. [<OF<L *vitiosus*<*vitium* a fault] —**vi'cious·ly** *adv.* —**vi'cious·ness** *n.*

vicious circle **1** The predicament that arises when the solution of a problem creates a new problem, etc. **2** *Logic* A fallacy in reasoning created when a conclusion is based upon a premise which depends upon the conclusion.

vi·cis·si·tude (vi·sis'ə·t[y]ōōd) *n.* **1** *Usu. pl.* Irregular changes or variations, as of conditions or fortune: the *vicissitudes* of life. **2** A change or alteration; also, the condition or quality of being changeable. [<L *vicis* a turn, change] —**vi·cis·si·tu·di·nary** (və·sis'ə·t[y]ōō'də·ner'ē), **vi·cis'·si·tu'di·nous** *adj.*

vic·tim (vik'tim) *n.* **1** A person injured or killed by circumstances beyond his control: a *victim* of a flood. **2** A sufferer from any diseased condition: a *victim* of arthritis. **3** One who is swindled; a dupe. **4** A living creature killed as a sacrifice to a deity. [<L *victima* a beast for sacrifice]

vic·tim·ize (vik'tim·īz) *v.t.* **·ized, ·iz·ing 1** to make a victim of; cause suffering to. **2** To cheat; dupe: *victimized* by loan sharks. —**vic·tim·i·za·tion** (vik'tə·mə·zā'shən) *n.* —**vic'·tim·iz'er** *n.*

vic·tor (vik'tər) *n.* One who wins any struggle or contest. —*adj.* Victorious: the *victor* nation. [<L *victus*, p.p. of *vincere* conquer]

vic·to·ri·a (vik·tôr'ē·ə, -tō'rē·ə) *n.* A low, light, four-wheeled carriage, with a folding top, a seat for two persons, and a raised driver's seat. [<*Victoria*, 1819–1901, Queen of England]

Victoria

Victoria Cross The highest British military decoration, awarded for outstanding valor.

Victoria Day In Canada, a national holiday celebrated on the first Monday preceding May 25th.

Vic·to·ri·an (vik·tôr'ē·ən, -tō'rē-) *adj.* **1** Of or relating to Queen Victoria of England, or to her reign. **2** Pertaining to or characteristic of the standards of morality and taste prevalent during that era. **3** Prudish; prim; priggish. —*n.* A person living during the time of Queen Victoria's reign; also, a person exhibiting the characteristic qualities, behavior, etc., of her era. —**Vic·to'ri·an·ism** *n.*

vic·to·ri·ous (vik·tôr'ē·əs, -tō'rē-) *adj.* **1** Having won victory; triumphant. **2** Characterized by or relating to victory. —**vic·to'ri·ous·ly** *adv.* —**vic·to'ri·ous·ness** *n.*

vic·to·ry (vik'tər·ē) *n. pl.* **ries 1** The overcoming of an enemy or adversary; triumph, as in war. **2** An overcoming of any difficulty or obstacle, considered as an achievement earned through effort. [<L *victor* victor]

vict·ual (vit'l) *n.* **1** Food fit for consumption by man. **2** *pl.* Food prepared for consumption. **3** *pl.* A supply of food; provisions. [<L *victualis* of food<*victus* food]

vi·cu·ña (vi·kōōn'yə, -kyōō'nə, vī-) *n.* **1** A small llamalike ruminant of the Andes having fine wool. **2** A textile made from this wool or some substitute: also **vicuña cloth.** Also **vi·cu'na.** [<Quechua]

Vicuña

vi·de (vī'dē, vē'dā') *v.* See: used to direct attention to: *vide* p. 36. [L, imperative sing. of *videre* see]

vi·de in·fra (vī'dē in'frə) *Latin* See below.

vi·de·li·cet (vi·del'ə·sit, vī-, vi·dā'·li·ket') *adv.* That is to say; namely. [L<*videre licet* it is permitted to see]

vid·e·o (vid'ē·ō) *adj.* **1** Of or pertaining to television, esp. to the picture. **2** Producing a signal convertible into a television picture: a *video* recording —*n.* **1** Television image or the electric signal corresponding to it. **2** Videotape. [L, I see]

vid·e·o·cas·sette (vid'ē·ō·kas·et') *n.* A cassette that contains videotape for recording programs, movies, etc.

vid·e·o·disc (vid'ē·ō·disk') *n.* A disc for recording both image and sound for replay through a television.

vid·e·o·tape (vid'ē·ō·tāp') *n.* A recording of a television program on magnetic tape. —*v.t.* **·taped, ·tap·ing** To make such a recording.

vi·de su·pra (vī'dē, sōō'prə) *Latin* See above.

vie (vī) *v.* **vied, vy·ing** *v.i.* To put forth effort to excel or outdo others. [<MF *envier* invite, challenge] —**vi'er** *n.*

Vi·en·nese (vē'ə·nēz', -nēs') *adj.* Of or pertaining to Vienna, its inhabitants, culture, etc. —*n. pl.* **·ese 1** A native or inhabitant of Vienna. **2** The German dialect spoken in Vienna.

Vi·et·nam (vē·et·näm') *n.* A country of SE Asia, cap. Hanoi; from 1954 to 1976 divided into: **Democratic Republic of Vietnam,** 63,344 sq. mi., cap. Hanoi: also **North Vietnam;** and **Republic of Vietnam,** 65,749 sq. mi., cap. Saigon: also **South Vietnam.** • See map at INDOCHINA.

Vi·et·nam·ese (vēet'nəm·ēz', vyet'-, -ēs') *adj.* Of or pertaining to Vietnam, its people, or their language. —*n. pl.* **·ese 1** a native or citizen of Vietnam. **2** The language of Vietnam.

view (vyōō) *n.* **1** The act of seeing or examining; survey; examination; inspection. **2** Range of vision. **3** Something seen: a *view* of the harbor. **4** A representation of a scene, esp. a landscape. 5 Something regarded as the object of action; purpose. 6 Opinion; judgment; belief: What are your *views* on this subject? 7 The immediate or forseeable future: no end in *view*. **—in view of** In consideration of. **—on view** Set up for public inspection. **—with a view to** With the aim or purpose of. *—v.t.* 1 To look at; behold. 2 To scrutinize; examine. 3 To survey mentally; consider. 4 To regard in a certain way. [< OF *veoir* see < L *videre*]

view·er (vyōō′ər) *n.* 1 One who views; esp., one who watches television. 2 A device for viewing, esp. one for viewing photographic transparencies.

view·less (vyōō′lis) *adj.* 1 That cannot be viewed. 2 Having no opinions. **—view′less·ly** *adv.*

view·point (vyōō′point′) *n.* The position from which one views or evaluates something; point of view.

vi·ges·i·mal (vī·jes′ə·məl) *adj.* 1 Of, pertaining to, or based on the number 20. 2 Twentieth. [< L *vicesimus*]

vig·il (vij′əl) *n.* 1 An act or period of keeping awake. 2 An act or period of keeping watch. 3 *Eccl.* **a** The eve of a holy day. **b** *pl.* Religious devotions on such an eve. [< L *vigil* awake]

vig·i·lance (vij′ə·ləns) *n.* The quality of being vigilant; alertness to threat or danger.

vigilance committee A body of men self-organized and without official legal sanction, with the professed purpose of maintaining order and punishing crime.

vig·i·lant (vij′ə·lənt) *adj.* Alert to danger; wary. [< L *vigilare* keep awake < *vigil* awake] **—vig′i·lant·ly** *adv.* **—Syn.** cautious, circumspect, heedful, watchful.

vig·i·lan·te (vij′ə·lan′tē) *n.* A member of a vigilance committee. **—vig′i·lant′ism** *n.*

vi·gnette (vin·yet′) *n.* 1 A short, subtly wrought picture in words; sketch. 2 A decorative design before the title page of a book, at the end or beginning of a chapter, etc. 3 An engraving, photograph, etc., that shades off gradually into the background. *—v.t.* **·gnet·ted, ·gnet·ting** To finish, as an engraving or photograph, in the manner of a vignette. [< F *vigne* a vine]

vig·or (vig′ər) *n.* 1 Active bodily or mental strength; energy. 2 Vital or natural growth, as in a healthy plant. 3 Intensity or force. 4 Legal force; validity. *Brit. sp.* **vig′·our.** [< L < *vigere* be lively, thrive]

vig·or·ous (vig′ər·əs) *adj.* Possessing, characterized by, or done with vigor. **—vig′or·ous·ly** *adv.* **—vig′or·ous·ness** *n.*

vi·king (vī′king) *n.* *Often cap.* One of the Scandinavian sea rovers who harried the coasts of Europe from the eighth to the tenth centuries.

vil. village.

vile (vīl) *adj.* **vil·er, vil·est** 1 Morally base; corrupt. 2 Disgusting; loathsome. 3 Very bad: *vile* food. [< L *vilis* cheap] **—vile′ly** *adv.* **—vile′ness** *n.*

vil·i·fy (vil′ə·fī) *v.t.* **·fied, ·fy·ing** To speak of abusively or slanderously; defame. [< L *vilis* cheap + *facere* make] **—vil′i·fi·ca′tion** (-fə·kā′shən), **vil′i·fi′er** *n.* **—Syn.** denigrate, malign, revile, traduce.

vil·la (vil′ə) *n.* A house, usu. large and imposing, in the country or suburbs or at the seashore. [L, a country house, farm]

vil·lage (vil′ij) *n.* 1 A collection of houses in a rural district, smaller than a town but larger than a hamlet. 2 Such a settlement incorporated as a municipality. 3 The inhabitants of a village, collectively. [< L *villaticus* pertaining to a villa < *villa* a villa]

vil·lag·er (vil′ij·ər) *n.* One who lives in a village.

vil·lain (vil′ən) *n.* 1 One who has committed crimes or evil deeds; scoundrel: now often used humorously. 2 A character in a novel, play, etc., who is the opponent of the hero. 3 VILLEIN. [< OF *vilain* a farm servant]

vil·lain·ous (vil′ən·əs) *adj.* 1 Wicked; evil. 2 *Informal* Very bad; abominable. **—vil′lain·ous·ly** *adv.* **—vil′lain·ous·ness** *n.* **—Syn.** 1 detestable, heinous, notorious, shameful.

vil·lain·y (vil′ən·ē) *n. pl.* **·lain·ies** 1 The quality or condition of being villainous. 2 A villainous act; crime.

vil·lein (vil′ən) *n.* In feudal England, a member of a class of serfs who, by the 13th century, were regarded as freemen in their legal relations with all persons except their lord. [< OF *vilain*. See VILLAIN.] **—vil′lein·age, vil′len·age** *n.*

vil·lus (vil′əs) *n. pl.* **vil·li** (vil′ī, -ē) 1 *Anat.* Any of numerous tiny projections from mucous membrane, as the absorptive processes in the small intestine. 2 *Bot.* Any of the soft hairs on the surface of certain plants. [L, a tuft of hair, shaggy hair] **—vil′lous** *adj.*

vim (vim) *n.* Force or vigor; energy; spirit. [L, accusative of *vis* power]

vin (vaṅ) *n.* *French* Wine.

vi·na·ceous (vī·nā′shəs) *adj.* 1 Of or pertaining to wine or grapes. 2 Wine-colored; red. [< L *vinum* wine]

vin·ai·grette (vin′ə·gret′) *n.* 1 An ornamental box or bottle for holding vinegar, smelling salts, etc. 2 Vinaigrette sauce. [< F *vinaigre* vinegar]

vinaigrette sauce A sauce made of vinegar and oil with herbs, onions, parsley, etc., served usu. on cold meats or fish.

Vin·cent's infection (vin′səntz) TRENCH MOUTH. Also **Vincent's angina, Vincent's disease.** [< J. H. *Vincent*, 1862–1950, French physician]

vin·ci·ble (vin′sə·bəl) *adj.* That can be conquered or overcome; conquerable. [< L *vincere* conquer] **—vin′ci·bil′i·ty, vin′ci·ble·ness** *n.*

vin·di·ca·ble (vin′də·kə·bəl) *adj.* That can be vindicated; justifiable.

vin·di·cate (vin′də·kāt) *v.t.* **·cat·ed, ·cat·ing** 1 To clear of accusation, censure, suspicion, etc. 2 To defend or maintain, as a right or claim, against challenge or attack and show to be just, right, and reasonable. 3 To provide justification for; justify. [< L *vindicare* avenge, claim] **—vin·di·ca·tive** (vin·dik′ə·tiv, vin′də·kā′tiv), **vin′di·ca·to′ry** (-kə·tôr′ē, -tō′rē) *adj.* **—vin′di·ca′tor** *n.*

vin·di·ca·tion (vin′də·kā′shən) *n.* 1 The act of vindicating, or the state of being vindicated. 2 A justification; defense.

vin·dic·tive (vin·dik′tiv) *adj.* Having or characterized by a vengeful spirit. [< L *vindicta* a revenge] **—vin·dic′tive·ly** *adv.* **—vin·dic′tive·ness** *n.* **—Syn.** retaliatory, revengeful, spiteful.

vine (vīn) *n.* 1 Any climbing plant. 2 The flexible stem of such a plant. 3 GRAPEVINE (def. 1). [< L *vinum* wine]

vin·e·gar (vin′ə·gər) *n.* 1 A variously flavored solution of acetic acid obtained by the fermentation of cider, wine, etc., and used as a condiment and preservative. 2 Acerbity, as of speech. [< OF *vin* wine + *aigre* sour] **—vin′e·gar·y** *adj.*

vin·er·y (vī′nər·ē) *n. pl.* **·er·ies** A building or area where vines are grown.

vine·yard (vin′yərd) *n.* An area devoted to the growing of grapevines. [< OE *wīngeard*] **—vine′yard·ist** *n.*

vingt-et-un (vaṅ·tā·œṅ′) *n.* BLACKJACK (def. 3). [F, twenty-one]

vin·i·cul·ture (vin′ə·kul′chər) *n.* The cultivation of grapes for making wine. [< L *vinum* wine] **—vin′i·cul′tur·al** *adj.*

vi·nous (vī′nəs) *adj.* 1 Pertaining to, characteristic of, or having the qualities of wine. 2 Caused by, affected by, or addicted to wine. [< L *vinum* wine] **—vi·nos·i·ty** (vī·nos′ə·tē) *n.*

vin·tage (vin′tij) *n.* 1 The yield of grapes or wine from a vineyard or wine-growing district for one season. 2 The harvesting of a vineyard and the making of wine; also, the season when these things are done. 3 Wine, esp. fine wine of a particular region and year. 4 The year or the region in which a particular wine is produced. 5 *Informal* The type or kind current at a particular time: a joke of ancient *vintage*. *—adj.* Of a fine vintage: *vintage* wines. [< OF *vendage* < L *vinum* wine + *demere* remove]

vint·ner (vint′nər) *n.* 1 A wine merchant. 2 A maker of wine. [< OF *vin* wine]

vin·y (vī′nē) *adj.* **·i·er, ·i·est** Pertaining to, like, of, full of, or yielding vines.

vi·nyl (vī′nəl) *n.* An organic radical derived from ethylene and entering into the composition of numerous plastics. [< L *vinum* wine + -YL]

vi·ol (vī′əl, -ōl′) *n.* Any of a family of stringed musical instruments, predecessors of the violin family. [< Med. L *vidula, vitula*]

vi·o·la (vē·ō′lə, vī-) *n.* A four-stringed musical instrument of the violin family, somewhat larger than the violin, and tuned a fifth lower. [Ital., orig., a viol]

vi·o·la·ble (vī′ə·lə·bəl) *adj.* That can or is likely to be violated. **—vi′o·la·ble·ness, vi′o·la·bil′i·ty** *n.* **—vi′o·la·bly** *adv.*

vi·o·la da gam·ba (vē·ō′lə·də·gäm′bə) An early bass of the viol family, held between the legs, and having a range similar to that of the cello. [Ital., viola of the leg]

vi·o·late (vī′ə·lāt) *v.t.* **·lat·ed, ·lat·ing 1** To break or infringe, as a law, oath, agreement, etc. **2** To profane, as a holy place. **3** To break in on; interfere with: to *violate* one's privacy. **4** To ravish; rape. **5** To offend or treat contemptuously: to *violate* a person's beliefs. [< L *violare* use violence < *vis* force] **—vi′o·la′tion, vi′o·la′tor** *n.* **—vi′o·la′tive** *adj.* **—Syn. 2** desecrate, pollute. **3** disturb; interrupt.

vi·o·lence (vī′ə·ləns) *n.* **1** Physical force exercised to injure, damage, or destroy. **2** An instance of such exercise of physical force; an injurious or destructive act. **3** Intensity; severity; force: the *violence* of a tornado. **4** Injury or damage, as by irreverence, distortion, or alteration: editing that did *violence* to the original text.

vi·o·lent (vī′ə·lənt) *adj.* **1** Proceeding from or marked by great physical force or activity. **2** Caused by or exhibiting intense emotional or mental excitement; passionate: a *violent* rabble-rouser. **3** Characterized by intensity of any kind: *violent* heat. **4** Marked by the unjust or illegal exercise of force: to take *violent* measures. **5** Resulting from external force or injury; unnatural: a *violent* death. [< L *violentus* < *vis* force] **—vi′o·lent·ly** *adv.*

vi·o·let (vī′ə·lit) *n.* **1** Any of a widely distributed genus of perennial herbs, bearing irregular flowers usu. of a bluish purple color. **2** Any of several plants having violet-colored flowers. **3** A bluish purple color. *—adj.* Bluish purple. [< L *viola*]

vi·o·lin (vī′ə·lin′) *n.* **1** A musical instrument having four strings and a sounding box of wood, and played by means of a bow. **2** A violinist, esp. in an orchestra. [< Ital. *viola* a viola]

Violin
a. bridge.
b. chin rest.

vi·o·lin·ist (vī′ə·lin′ist) *n.* One who plays the violin.

vi·ol·ist (vī′əl·ist) *n.* **1** One who plays the viol. **2** (vē·ō′list) One who plays the viola.

vi·o·lon·cel·lo (vī′ə·lən·chel′ō, vē′ə-) *n. pl.* **·los** CELLO. [< Ital. *violone* a bass viol, aug. of *viola*] **—vi′o·lon·cel′list** *n.*

VIP, V.I.P. *Informal* very important person.

vi·per (vī′pər) *n.* **1** Any of a family of venomous Old World snakes, including the African puff adder. **2** Any of a family of typically American poisonous snakes, the **pit vipers,** including the rattlesnake, copperhead, etc., which are characterized by a small depression between the nostril and the eye. **3** Any poisonous or allegedly poisonous snake. **4** A malicious, treacherous, or spiteful person. [< L *vipera*] **—vi·per·ine** (vī′pə·rīn) *adj.*

vi·per·ous (vī′pər·əs) *adj.* **1** Of, pertaining to, or composed of vipers. **2** Malicious, treacherous, or spiteful. **—vi′per·ous·ly** *adv.*

vi·ra·go (vi·rä′gō, -rā′-, vī-) *n. pl.* **·goes** or **·gos** A loud, ill-tempered woman; shrew; scold. [L, manlike woman]

vi·ral (vī′rəl) *adj.* Of, pertaining to, or caused by a virus.

vir·e·o (vir′ē·ō) *n. pl.* **·os** Any of various inconspicuous, insectivorous songbirds of North America. [L, a kind of small bird]

vi·res·cent (vī·res′ənt) *adj.* Greenish or becoming green. [< L *virescere* grow green] **—vi·res′cence** *n.*

vir·gin (vûr′jin) *n.* **1** A person, esp. a young woman, who has never had sexual intercourse. **2** A maiden or unmarried woman. *—adj.* **1** Being a virgin. **2** Consisting of virgins: a *virgin* band. **3** Pertaining or suited to a virgin; chaste; maidenly. **4** Uncorrupted; pure; clean: *virgin* whiteness. **5** Not hitherto used, touched, tilled, or worked upon: *virgin* forest. **6** Not previously processed or manufactured; new: *virgin* wool. **7** Occurring for the first time; initial: a *virgin* effort. [< L *virgo* a maiden]

Vir·gin (vûr′jin) VIRGIN MARY. *—n.* VIRGO.

vir·gin·al[1] (vûr′jin·əl) *adj.* **1** Of, pertaining to, like, or suited to a virgin; modest; maidenly. **2** Pure; pristine; unsullied. **—vir′gin·al·ly** *adv.*

vir·gin·al[2] (vûr′jin·əl) *n. Often pl.* A small, rectangular harpsichord with no legs. Also **pair of virginals.**

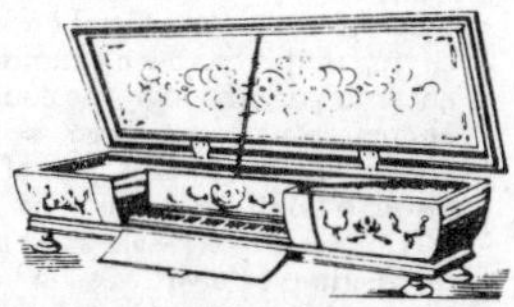
Virginal

virgin birth *Usu. cap. Theol.* The doctrine that Jesus Christ was conceived by divine agency and born without impairment of the virginity of his mother Mary.

Vir·gin·i·a cowslip (vər·jin′yə) A perennial herb of the E U.S. with clusters of blue or purple tubular flowers. Also **Virginia bluebell.**

Virginia creeper A woody vine of the grape family, with compound leaves, small green flowers, and inedible blue berries.

Virginia deer WHITE-TAILED DEER.

Virginia reel 1 A country dance performed by couples who stand initially in two parallel lines facing one another. **2** The music for such a dance.

vir·gin·i·ty (vər·jin′ə·tē) *n. pl.* **·ties 1** The state of being a virgin; maidenhood; virginal chastity. **2** The state of being fresh, untouched, etc.

Virgin Mary Mary, the mother of Jesus.

vir·gin's-bow·er (vûr′jinz·bou′ər) *n.* A species of clematis bearing white flowers in leafy clusters.

Vir·go (vûr′gō) *n.* A constellation and the sixth sign of the Zodiac; the Virgin. • See ZODIAC.

vir·gule (vûr′gyōōl) *n.* A slanting line (/) used to indicate a choice between two alternatives, as in the phrase *and/or.* [< L *virga* a rod]

vir·i·des·cent (vir′ə·des′ənt) *adj.* Greenish; turning green. [< L *viridis* green] **—vir′i·des′cence** *n.*

vir·ile (vir′əl, īl) *adj.* **1** Having the characteristics of manhood. **2** Having the vigor or strength of manhood. **3** Able to procreate. [< L *vir* a man] **—vi·ril·i·ty** (və·ril′ə·tē) *n.*

vi·rol·o·gy (və·rol′ə·jē, vī-) *n.* The study of viruses, esp. in relation to disease. **—vi·rol′o·gist** *n.*

vir·tu (vər·tōō′, vûr′tōō) *n.* **1** Rare, curious, or artistic quality: often in the phrase **objects (or articles) of virtu. 2** A taste for or knowledge of such objects. **3** Such objects collectively. [< L *virtus*]

vir·tu·al (vûr′chōō·əl) *adj.* Being so in essence or effect, but not in form or fact. [< Med. L *virtualis* < L *virtus* strength] **—vir′tu·al′i·ty** (-al′ə·tē) *n.* **—vir′tu·al·ly** *adv.*

vir·tue (vûr′chōō) *n.* **1** General moral excellence; uprightness; goodness. **2** A particular moral excellence. **3** Any admirable quality or merit: Patience is a *virtue.* **4** Sexual purity; chastity. **5** Efficacy; potency, as of a medicine. **—by** (or **in**) **virtue of** By or through the force or authority of. **—make a virtue of necessity** To do willingly what one has to do anyhow. [< L *virtus* strength, bravery < *vir* man] **—Syn. 1** integrity, rectitude, righteousness, worthiness.

vir·tu·os·i·ty (vûr′chōō·os′ə·tē) *n. pl.* **·ties** The technical mastery of an art, as music.

vir·tu·o·so (vûr′chōō·ō′sō) *n. pl.* **·si** (-sē) or **·sos 1** A master of technique in some fine art, esp. in musical performance. **2** A knowledgeable collector or lover of curios or works of art. *—adj.* Of or characteristic of a virtuoso. [< LL *virtuosus* full of excellence]

vir·tu·ous (vûr′chōō·əs) *adj.* **1** Righteous; upright; dutiful. **2** Pure and chaste. **—vir′tu·ous·ly** *adv.* **—vir′tu·ous·ness** *n.*

vir·u·lent (vir′yə·lənt) *adj.* **1** Extremely harmful; noxious; deadly. **2** Severe and rapid in its progress: said of a disease. **3** Very infectious: said of a pathogenic microorganism. **4** Full of bitter hatred; hostile. [< L *virulentus* full of poison < *virus* a poison] **—vir′u·lence, vir′u·len·cy** *n.* **—vir′·u·lent·ly** *adv.*

vi·rus (vī′rəs) *n.* **1** Any of a class of ultramicroscopic filter-passing pathogens capable of reproduction only within specific living cells. 2 Venom, as of a snake. 3 Any evil influence: the *virus* of greed. [L, poison, slime]

vis (vis) *n. pl.* **vi·res** (vī′rēz) Force. [L]

Vis., Visc., Visct. Viscount; Viscountess.

vi·sa (vē′zə) *n.* An official endorsement on a passport certifying that it has been examined and that the bearer may enter or pass through the country which has granted the endorsement. —*v.t.* **·saed, ·sa·ing** 1 To put a visa on. 2 To give a visa to. [F< L < p.p. of *videre* see]

vis·age (viz′ij) *n.* 1 The face. 2 Appearance; aspect; look. [< L *visus* a look] —**vis′aged** *adj.*

vis-à-vis (vēz′ə·vē′, vēs-, -ä·vē′) *adj. & adv.* Face to face. —*prep.* 1 Opposite. 2 In relation to; toward. [F, face to face]

vis·cer·a (vis′ər·ə) *n.pl. sing.* **vis·cus** (vis′kəs) 1 The internal organs of the body, as the stomach, lungs, heart, etc. 2 Commonly, the intestines. [L, pl. of *viscus* an internal organ]

vis·cer·al (vis′ər·əl) *adj.* 1 Of or pertaining to the viscera. 2 Instinctive or emotional: a *visceral* reaction. —**vis′cer·al·ly** *adv.*

vis·cid (vis′id) *adj.* Glutinous in consistency; adhesive; syrupy; viscous. [< L *viscum* birdlime] —**vis·cid·i·ty** (vi·sid′·ə·tē), **vis′cid·ness** *n.* —**vis′cid·ly** *adv.*

vis·cose (vis′kōs) *n.* A viscid substance produced from cellulose as a step in the manufacture of rayon, cellophane, etc. —*adj.* 1 VISCOUS. 2 Of, pertaining to, containing, or made from viscose.

vis·cos·i·ty (vis·kos′ə·tē) *n. pl.* **·ties** 1 The property of fluids by which they offer resistance to flow or to change in the arrangement of their molecules. 2 The measure of this property.

vis·count (vī′kount) *n.* A nobleman ranking below an earl or count and above a baron. [< OF *visconte*] —**vis′·count·cy, vis′count·ship, vis′count·y** *n.*

vis·count·ess (vī′koun·tis) *n.* The wife of a viscount, or a peeress holding the title in her own right.

vis·cous (vis′kəs) *adj.* 1 Greatly resistant to flow; of high viscosity. 2 VISCID. [< L *viscum* birdlime] —**vis′cous·ly** *adv.* —**vis′cous·ness** *n.*

vise (vīs) *n.* A clamping device, usu. of two jaws made to be closed together with a screw, lever, or the like, for grasping and holding a piece of work. —*v.t.* **vised, vis·ing** To hold, force, or squeeze in or as in a vise. [< OF *vis* a screw < L *vitis* vine]

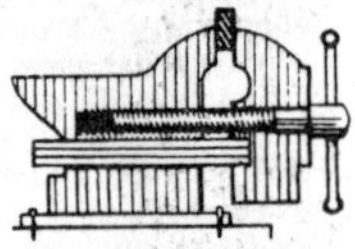

Machinist's vise (cross section)

vi·sé (vē′zā) *n., v.t.* **vi·séed** or **vi·séd, vi·sé·ing** VISA.

Vish·nu (vish′nōō) In Hindu theology, the second god of the trinity (Brahma, Vishnu, and Siva), known as "the Preserver."

vis·i·bil·i·ty (viz′ə·bil′ə·tē) *n. pl.* **·ties** 1 The fact, condition, or degree of being visible. 2 *Meteorol.* The clearness of the atmosphere in terms of the distance at which objects can be seen distinctly.

vis·i·ble (viz′ə·bəl) *adj.* 1 Capable of being seen. 2 That can be perceived mentally; evident. [< L *visus,* p.p. of *videre* see] —**vis′i·ble·ness** *n.* —**vis′i·bly** *adv.* —**Syn.** 1 perceptible. 2 clear, distinct, obvious, plain.

Vis·i·goth (viz′ə·goth) *n.* A member of the western Goths, a Teutonic people that invaded the Roman Empire in the late fourth century and established a monarchy in France and Spain. —**Vis′i·goth′ic** *adj.*

vi·sion (vizh′ən) *n.* 1 The act or power of seeing; sense of sight. 2 That which is seen. 3 A beautiful person, landscape, etc. 4 A mental representation of external objects or scenes, as in sleep. 5 A conception in the imagination; mental image: *visions* of power and wealth. 6 The ability to perceive, discern, and anticipate; foresight; imagination. —*v.t.* To see in or as in a vision. [< L *visus,* p.p. of *videre* see] —**vi′sion·al** *adj.* —**vi′sion·al·ly** *adv.*

vi·sion·ar·y (vizh′ən·er′ē) *adj.* 1 Not founded on fact; existing in the imagination; imaginary. 2 Able or disposed to see visions; affected by fantasies; dreamy. 3 Impractical, speculative, utopian, etc. 4 Of, pertaining to, characterized by, or seen in a vision or visions. —*n. pl.* **·ar·ies** 1 One who has visions. 2 One whose plans, projects, etc., are unrealistic or impractical; dreamer. —**vi′sion·ar′i·ness** *n.*

vis·it (viz′it) *v.t.* 1 To go or come to see (a person) from friendship, courtesy, on business, etc. 2 To go or come to (a place, etc.), as for transacting business or for touring: to *visit* the Louvre. 3 To be a guest of; stay with temporarily: I *visited* them for several days. 4 To come upon or afflict. 5 To inflict upon. —*v.i.* 6 To pay a visit; call. 7 To stay with someone temporarily. 8 *Informal* To converse; chat. —*n.* 1 The act of visiting a person, place, or thing. 2 A social call or short stay. 3 *Informal* A friendly chat. 4 An official call, as for inspection, medical examination, etc. [< L *visare* < *visus,* p.p. of *videre* see]

vis·i·tant (viz′ə·tənt) *n.* 1 A visitor. 2 A migratory bird at a particular region for a limited period.

vis·i·ta·tion (viz′ə·tā′shən) *n.* 1 The act of visiting; esp., an official inspection, examination, etc. 2 A dispensation of punishment or reward, as by God. —**the Visitation** 1 The visit of the Virgin Mary to her cousin, Elizabeth. *Luke* 1:39–56. 2 A church feast, observed on July 2, commemorating this event. —**vis′i·ta′tion·al** *adj.*

visiting card CALLING CARD.

vis·i·tor (viz′ə·tər) *n.* One who visits; guest.

vi·sor (vī′zər) *n.* 1 A projecting piece on a cap shielding the eyes. 2 In armor, the front piece of a helmet which protected the upper part of the face and could be raised or lowered. 3 A movable device over the inside of the windshield of a car, serving to reduce glare. [< OF *vis* face] —**vi′sored** (-zərd) *adj.*

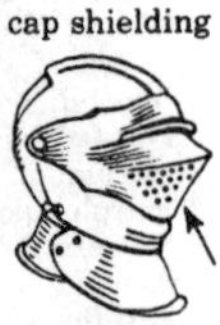

Visor *def. 2*

vis·ta (vis′tə) *n.* 1 A view, esp. one seen through a long, narrow space, as along an avenue, between rows of trees, etc. 2 The space itself. 3 A mental view embracing a series of events. [Ital., sight < L *videre* see] —**vis′taed** (vis′təd) *adj.*

vis·u·al (vizh′ōō·əl) *adj.* 1 Of or pertaining to the sense of sight. 2 Perceptible by sight; visible. 3 Done or perceived by sight only. 4 Instructing through the sense of sight: *visual* aids. [< L *visus* a sight < *videre* see] —**vis′u·al·ly** *adv.*

visual aids Charts, diagrams, slides, motion pictures, etc., used as aids in teaching and lecturing.

vis·u·al·ize (vizh′ōō·əl·īz′, vizh′əl-) *v.* **·ized, ·iz·ing** *v.t.* 1 To form a mental image of; picture in the mind. —*v.i.* 2 To form mental images. *Brit. sp.* **vis·u·al·ise.** —**vis′u·al·i·za′·tion, vis′u·al·iz′er** *n.*

vi·tal (vīt′l) *adj.* 1 Of or pertaining to life. 2 Essential to or supporting life. 3 Affecting life in a destructive way; fatal: a *vital* wound. 4 Of the utmost importance or interest. 5 Full of life; vigorous; energetic; dynamic. —*n.pl.* 1 The organs necessary to life, as the brain, heart, etc. 2 The necessary parts of anything. [< L *vitalis* < *vita* life] —**vi′tal·ly** *adv.*

vi·tal·ism (vīt′l·iz′əm) *n.* The doctrine that the life and functions of a living organism depend upon a vital force that differs in kind from all chemical and physical forces. —**vi′tal·ist** *n.* —**vi′tal·is′tic** *adj.*

vi·tal·i·ty (vī·tal′ə·tē) *n.* 1 The power to live and develop. 2 Power of continuing in force or effect. 3 Physical or mental energy; vigor; strength.

vi·tal·ize (vīt′l·īz) *v.t.* **·ized, ·iz·ing** To make vital; endow with life or energy; animate. —**vi′tal·i·za′tion, vi′tal·iz′er** *n.*

vital statistics Data relating to births, deaths, marriages, health, etc.

vi·ta·min (vī′tə·min) *n.* Any of a group of organic substances whose presence in the diet in minute quantities is essential for the maintenance of specific physiological functions. [< L *vita* life + AMINE] —**vi′ta·min′ic** *adj.*

vitamin A The fat-soluble vitamin essential to vision and occurring in all animal tissues and many vegetables.

vitamin B complex A varied group of water-soluble vitamins having distinct functions.

vitamin B_1 THIAMINE.

vitamin B_2 RIBOFLAVIN.

vitamin B_6 PYRIDOXINE.

vitamin B_{12} A vitamin normally produced in the intestine and essential for the production of erythrocytes.

vitamin C ASCORBIC ACID.

vitamin D A substance essential in the formation of bone and the metabolism of calcium, occurring in fish-liver oils and formed from sterols in the skin when exposed to sunshine.

vitamin E An oily substance present in most foods and essential to fertility in experimental animals.

vitamin G RIBOFLAVIN.

vitamin H BIOTIN.

vitamin K$_1$ A vitamin, found in green leafy vegetables, which promotes the clotting of blood.

vitamin K$_2$ A form of vitamin K$_1$ prepared from fishmeal.

vitamin P A factor present in citrus juices that promotes the normal permeability of capillary walls.

vi·ti·ate (vish′ē·āt) *v.t.* **·at·ed, ·at·ing 1** To impair the use or value of; spoil. **2** To debase or corrupt. **3** To render weak, ineffective, legally invalid, etc.: Fraud *vitiates* a contract. [< L *vitium* a fault] **—vi′ti·a′tion, vi′ti·a′tor** *n.*

vit·i·cul·ture (vit′ə·kul′chər, vī′tə-) *n.* The science and art of grape-growing; cultivation of grapes. [< L *vitis* a vine + CULTURE] **—vit′i·cul′tur·al** *adj.* **—vit′i·cul′tur·er, vit′i·cul′tur·ist** *n.*

vit·i·li·go (vit′ə·lī′gō) *n.* A skin disorder characterized by partial loss of pigment resulting in white spots. [L, a vesicular skin disease]

vit·re·ous (vit′rē·əs) *adj.* **1** Of, pertaining to, or like glass; glassy. **2** Obtained from glass. **3** Of or pertaining to the vitreous humor. [< L *vitrum* glass] **—vit′re·os′i·ty** (-os′ə·tē), **vit′re·ous·ness** *n.*

vitreous humor The transparent jellylike tissue that fills the eyeball. Also **vitreous body.**

vit·ri·fy (vit′rə·fī) *v.t.* & *v.i.* **·fied, ·fy·ing** To change into glass or a vitreous substance; make or become vitreous. [< L *vitrum* glass + *facere* make] **—vit′ri·fac′tion** (-fak′shən), **vit′ri·fi·ca′tion** *n.*

vit·ri·ol (vit′rē·ōl, -əl) *n.* **1** Any sulfate of a heavy metal, as **green vitriol** (iron); **blue vitriol** (copper); **white vitriol** (zinc). **2** Sulfuric acid: also **oil of vitriol. 3** Anything sharp or caustic, as sarcasm. **—***v.t.* **·oled** or **·olled, ·ol·ing** or **·ol·ling** To subject (anything) to the agency of vitriol. [< L *vitrum* glass]

vit·ri·ol·ic (vit′rē·ol′ik) *adj.* **1** Of, like, or derived from vitriol. **2** Biting, sharp, or caustic: *vitriolic* remarks.

vit·tle (vit′l) *n.* VICTUAL.

vi·tu·per·ate (vī·t*y*ōō′pə·rāt, vi-) *v.t.* **·at·ed, ·at·ing** To find fault with abusively; rail at; berate; scold. [< L *vituperare* blame, scold < *vitium* a fault + *parare* prepare] **—vi·tu′per·a′tion, vi·tu′per·a′tor** *n.* **—vi·tu′per·a′tive** *adj.* **—vi·tu′per·a′tive·ly** *adv.*

viv. *Music* lively (It. *vivace*).

vi·va (vē′vä) *interj.* Live; long live (the person or thing specified): used in acclamation. [Ital. < *vivere* live < L]

vi·va·ce (vē·vä′chā) *adv. Music* Lively; quickly; briskly. [< L *vivax*]

vi·va·cious (vi·vā′shəs, vī-) *adj.* Full of life and spirits; lively; active. [< L *vivax* < *vivere* live] **—vi·va′cious·ly** *adv.* **—vi·va′cious·ness** *n.* **—Syn.** animated, brisk, cheerful, sparkling, spirited.

vi·vac·i·ty (vi·vas′ə·tē, vī-) *n. pl.* **·ties 1** The state or quality of being vivacious. **2** A vivacious act, expression, etc.

vi·var·i·um (vī·vâr′ē·əm) *n. pl.* **·var·i·a** (-vâr′ē·ə) or **·var·i·ums** A place for keeping or raising animals or plants for observation or research. Also **viv·a·ry** (viv′ər·ē). [< L *vivus* alive < *vivere* live]

vi·va vo·ce (vī′və vō′sē, vē′və vō′chā) By spoken word; orally or oral. [L]

vive (vēv) *interj. French* Live; long live (the person or thing specified): used in acclamation.

viv·id (viv′id) *adj.* **1** Having an appearance of vigorous life; lively; spirited. **2** Very strong; intense: said of colors. **3** Producing or suggesting lifelike images. **4** Producing a sharp impression on the senses: a *vivid* description. [< L *vividus* lively < *vivere* to live] **—viv′id·ly** *adv.* **—viv′id·ness** *n.*

viv·i·fy (viv′ə·fī) *v.t.* **·fied, ·fy·ing 1** To give life to; animate; vitalize. **2** To make more vivid or striking. [< L *vivus* alive + *facere* make] **—viv′i·fi·ca′tion** (-fə·kā′shən), **viv′i·fi′er** *n.*

vi·vip·a·rous (vī·vip′ər·əs) *adj.* Bringing forth young that have developed from eggs within the mother's body. [< L *vivus* alive + *parere* bring forth] **—vi·vip′a·rous·ly** *adv.* **—vi·vip′a·rous·ness, viv·i·par·i·ty** (viv′ə·par′ə·tē) *n.*

viv·i·sect (viv′ə·sekt) *v.t.* **1** To perform vivisection on. **—***v.i.* **2** To practice vivisection. **—viv′i·sec′tor** *n.*

viv·i·sec·tion (viv′ə·sek′shən) *n.* Cutting, dissection, or other operation on a living animal, esp. in experiments designed to promote knowledge of physiological and pathological processes. [< L *vivus* living, alive + *sectio* a cutting] **—viv′i·sec′tion·al** *adj.* **—viv′i·sec′tion·ist** *n., adj.*

vix·en (vik′sən) *n.* **1** A female fox. **2** A turbulent, quarrelsome woman; shrew. [< ME *fixen* a she-fox] **—vix′en·ish** *adj.* **—vix′en·ly** *adj., adv.*

viz, viz. namely (L *videlicet*).

viz·ard (viz′ərd) *n.* A mask or visor. [Alter. of VISOR]

vi·zier (vi·zir′) *n.* A high official of a Muslim country, as in the old Turkish Empire. Also **vi·zir′.** [< Ar. *wazīr* a counselor]

vi·zor (vī′zər) *n.* VISOR.

V-J Day (vē′jā′) Sept. 2, 1945, the official date of the Allied victory over Japan in World War II.

VL, V.L. Vulgar Latin.

VLF, V.L.F., vlf, v.l.f. very low frequency.

V-mail (vē′māl′) *n.* Mail transmitted overseas in World War II on microfilm, and enlarged at point of reception for final delivery. [< V(ICTORY) + MAIL[1]]

V.M.D. Doctor of Veterinary Medicine (L *Veterinariae Medicinae Doctor*).

vo. verso.

voc. vocative.

vocab. vocabulary.

vo·ca·ble (vō′kə·bəl) *n.* A word viewed as a combination of sounds and letters apart from its meaning. [< L *vocabulum* a name, appellation < *vocare* to call]

vo·cab·u·lar·y (vō·kab′yə·ler′ē) *n. pl.* **·lar·ies 1** A list of words or of words and phrases, esp. one arranged in alphabetical order and defined or translated; a lexicon; glossary. **2** All the words of a language. **3** All the words used or understood by a particular person, class, profession, etc. **4** The range of expression at a person's disposal, esp. in art. [< L *vocabulum.* See VOCABLE.]

vo·cal (vō′kəl) *adj.* **1** Of or pertaining to the voice or the production of the voice. **2** Having voice; able to speak or utter sounds: *vocal* creatures. **3** Composed for, uttered by, or performed by the voice: a *vocal* score. **4** Full of voices or sounds; resounding: The air was *vocal* with their cries. **5** Freely expressing oneself in speech: the *vocal* segment of the populace. [< L *vocalis* speaking, sounding] **—vo·cal·i·ty** (vō·kal′ə·tē), **vo′cal·ness** *n.* **—vo′cal·ly** *adv.*

vocal cords Two ligaments extending across the larynx, which, when tense, are caused to vibrate by the passage of air, thereby producing voice.

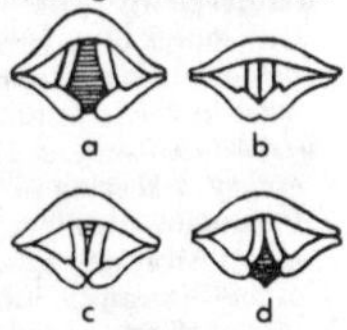

Vocal cords
a. open. b. closed.
c. voice. d. whisper.

vo·cal·ic (vō·kal′ik) *adj.* **1** Of, pertaining to, or like a vowel sound. **2** Characterized by or consisting of vowel sounds.

vo·cal·ist (vō′kəl·ist) *n.* A singer.

vo·cal·ize (vō′kəl·īz) *v.* **·ized, ·iz·ing** *v.t.* **1** To make vocal; utter, say, or sing. **2** *Phonet.* **a** To change to or use as a vowel: to *vocalize* y. **b** To voice. **—***v.i.* **3** To produce sounds with the voice, as in speaking or singing. **4** *Phonet.* To be changed to a vowel. **—vo′cal·i·za′tion, vo′cal·iz′er** *n.*

vo·ca·tion (vō·kā′shən) *n.* **1** A stated or regular occupation. **2** A call to, or fitness for, a certain career. **3** The work or profession for which one has or believes one has a special fitness. [< L *vocare* to call] **—vo·ca′tion·al** *adj.* **—vo·ca′tion·al·ly** *adv.*

voc·a·tive (vok′ə·tiv) *Gram. adj.* In some inflected languages, denoting the case of a noun, pronoun, or adjective used in direct address. **—***n.* **1** The vocative case. **2** A word in this case. [< L *vocare* to call]

vo·cif·er·ant (vō·sif′ər·ənt) *adj.* Vociferous; uttering loud cries. **—vo·cif′er·ance** *n.*

vo·cif·er·ate (vō·sif′ə·rāt) *v.t. & v.i.* **·at·ed, ·at·ing** To cry out with a loud voice; shout. [< L *vox* a voice + *ferre* carry] **—vo·cif′er·a′tion, vo·cif′er·a′tor** *n.* **—Syn.** bawl, bellow, clamor, scream, yell.

vo·cif·er·ous (vō·sif′ər·əs) *adj.* Making or characterized by a loud outcry; noisy; clamorous. **—vo·cif′er·ous·ly** *adv.* **—vo·cif′er·ous·ness** *n.*

vod·ka (vod′kə) *n.* A colorless alcoholic liquor originally made in Poland and Russia, distilled from a mash, as of rye, wheat, or potatoes. [< Russ. *voda* water]

vogue (vōg) *n.* **1** Fashion or style. **2** Popular favor; popularity. [F, fashion, orig., rowing] **—vogu′ish** *adj.*

voice (vois) *n.* **1** The sound produced by the vocal organs of a vertebrate, esp. by a human being in speaking, singing, etc. **2** The quality or character of such sound: a melodious *voice.* **3** The power or ability to make such a sound: to lose one's *voice.* **4** Something suggesting the sound of vocal utterance: the *voice* of the wind. **5** Expressed opinion, choice, etc. **6** The right to express an opinion, choice, etc. **7** A person or agency by which the thought, wish, or purpose of another is expressed: This journal is the *voice* of the teaching profession. **8** Expression: to give *voice* to one's ideals. **9** *Phonet.* The sound produced by vibration of the vocal cords, as heard in the utterance of vowels and certain consonants, as *b, d,* and *z.* **10** A singer: Caruso was a great *voice.* **11** In a musical composition, a part for a singer or an instrument. **12** *Gram.* A form of a verb which indicates whether its subject is active or passive. **—in voice** Having the voice in good condition for singing and speaking. **—lift up one's voice 1** To shout or sing loudly. **2** To protest. **—with one voice** With one accord; unanimously. **—***v.t.* **voiced, voic·ing 1** To put into speech; give expression to; utter. **2** *Music* To regulate the tones of, as the pipes of an organ. **3** *Phonet.* To utter with voice. [< L *vox, vocis*] • When the subject of a verb performs the action, the verb is in the **active voice:** *My aunt baked a chocolate cake; Her father gave her a bicycle.* When the subject of a verb is acted upon, the verb is in the **passive voice:** *The chocolate cake was baked by my aunt; She was given a bicycle by her father.*

voiced (voist) *adj.* **1** Having a voice or a specified kind of voice: often used in combination: *high-voiced, soft-voiced.* **2** Expressed by voice. **3** *Phonet.* Uttered with vibration of the vocal cords, as (b), (d), (z).

voice·less (vois′lis) *adj.* **1** Having no voice, speech, or vote. **2** *Phonet.* Produced without voice, as (p), (t), (s). **—voice′less·ly** *adv.* **—voice′less·ness** *n.*

voice-o·ver (vois′ō′vər) *n.* In motion pictures and television programs, the voice of a narrator or announcer speaking off camera.

voice·print (vois′print′) *n.* A graphic representation of the sound of a person's voice, consisting of a complex pattern of wavy lines corresponding to the various pitches used in the utterance.

void (void) *adj.* **1** Containing nothing; without content; empty. **2** Having no legal force or validity; not binding. **3** Producing no effect; useless. **—void of** Lacking; without. **—***n.* **1** An empty space; vacuum. **2** The quality or condition of feeling empty, lonely, lost, etc. **—***v.t.* **1** To make void or of no effect; annul. **2** To empty or remove (contents); evacuate. **—***v.i.* **3** To eliminate waste from the body; urinate or defecate. [< L *vacuus* empty] **—void′er, void′ness** *n.* **—void′ly** *adv.*

voi·là (vwȧ·lȧ′) *interj. French* There! behold! literally, see there.

voile (voil) *n.* A fine, sheer fabric, as of cotton, silk, wool, or rayon. [< OF *veile* veil]

vol. volcano; volume; volunteer.

vo·lant (vō′lənt) *adj.* **1** Flying, or capable of flying. **2** Agile; quick; nimble. **3** *Her.* Represented as flying, as a bird or bee. [< L *volare* to fly]

vol·a·tile (vol′ə·til; *chiefly Brit.* -tīl) *adj.* **1** Evaporating rapidly; capable of being vaporized. **2** Inconstant; changeable. **3** Transient; fleeting. [< L *volatilis* < *volare* fly] **—vol′a·tile·ness, vol·a·til·i·ty** (vol′ə·til′ə·tē) *n.*

vol·a·til·ize (vol′ə·til·īz′) *v.t. & v.i.* **·ized, ·iz·ing** To pass off or cause to pass off in vapor. **—vol′a·til·i·za′tion** *n.*

vol·can·ic (vol·kan′ik) *adj.* **1** Of, pertaining to, produced by, or characterized by a volcano or volcanoes. **2** Like a volcano; explosive; violent. **—vol·can′i·cal·ly** *adv.* **—vol·can·ic·i·ty** (vol′kə·nis′ə·tē) *n.*

vol·can·ism (vol′kən·iz′əm) *n.* The power or action of volcanoes.

vol·ca·no (vol·kā′nō) *n. pl.* **·noes** or **·nos** *Geol.* An opening in the earth's surface from which hot matter is or has been ejected, often surrounded by a hill or mountain of ejected material. [< L *Vulcanus* Vulcan]

vole (vōl) *n.* Any of various short-tailed, mouselike or ratlike rodents. [Short for earlier *vole mouse* field mouse]

vo·li·tion (və·lish′ən) *n.* **1** The act of willing; exercise of the will. **2** The power of willing; willpower. [< L *velle* to will] **—vo·li′tion·al, vo·li′tion·ar·y** (-ən·er·ē), **vol·i·tive** (vol′ə·tiv) *adj.* **—vo·li′tion·al·ly** *adv.*

vol·ley (vol′ē) *n.* **1** A simultaneous discharge of many guns. **2** A discharge of many bullets, stones, arrows, etc. **3** Any discharge of many things at once: a *volley* of oaths. **4** In tennis, the flight of the ball before it touches the ground; also, a return of the ball before it touches the ground. **—***v.t. & v.i.* **·leyed, ·ley·ing 1** To discharge or be discharged in a volley. **2** In tennis, to return (the ball) without allowing it to touch the ground. [< MF *voler* to fly] **—vol′ley·er** *n.*

vol·ley·ball (vol′ē·bôl′) *n.* **1** A game in which a number of players on both sides of a high net use their hands to hit a ball back and forth over the net without letting it drop. **2** The ball used in this game.

vol·plane (vol′plān) *v.i.* **·planed, ·plan·ing** To glide down in an airplane with the engine turned off. **—***n.* An airplane glide. [< F *vol plané* gliding flight]

vols. volumes.

volt[1] (vōlt) *n.* A unit equal to the difference of electric potential which, when steadily applied to a conductor whose resistance is one ohm, will produce a current of one ampere. [< A. *Volta,* 1745–1827, Italian physicist]

volt[2] (vōlt) *n.* **1** In horse-training, a gait in which the horse moves sidewise round a center with the head turned out. **2** In fencing, a sudden leap to avoid a thrust. [< Ital. *volta,* p.p. fem. of *volvere* to turn]

volt·age (vōl′tij) *n.* Electromotive force expressed in volts.

vol·ta·ic (vol·tā′ik) *adj.* Pertaining to electricity developed through chemical action; galvanic.

voltaic battery A set of voltaic cells which operate as a unit.

voltaic cell A cell that generates electricity by a chemical reaction and that cannot be efficiently recharged.

volt·me·ter (vōlt′mē′tər) *n.* An instrument for measuring differences of electric potential.

vol·u·ble (vol′yə·bəl) *adj.* Having a flow of words or fluency in speaking; talkative. [< L *volubilis* easily turned < *volutus,* p.p. of *volvere* to turn] **—vol′u·bil′i·ty** (vol′yə·bil′ə·tē), **vol′u·ble·ness** *n.* **—vol′u·bly** *adv.*

vol·ume (vol′yo͞om, -yəm) *n.* **1** A collection of sheets of paper bound together; a book. **2** A book that is part of a set. **3** A quantity or amount: a large *volume* of sales. **4** A measure of quantity in terms of space occupied, as cubic inch, cubic centimeter, liter, pint, etc. **5** *Acoustics* Fullness or quantity of sound or tone. **—speak volumes** To be full of meaning; express a great deal. [< L *volumen* a roll, scroll] **—vol′umed** *adj.*

vol·u·met·ric (vol′yə·met′rik) *adj.* Of, based on, or pertaining to measurement of substances by volume. Also **vol′u·met′ri·cal. —vol′u·met′ri·cal·ly** *adv.*

vo·lu·mi·nous (və·lo͞o′mə·nəs) *adj.* **1** Consisting of or capable of filling volumes: a *voluminous* correspondence. **2** Writing or speaking much. **3** Having great volume or bulk; large. [< L *volumen* a roll] **—vo·lu·mi·nos·i·ty** (və·lo͞o′mə·nos′ə·tē), **vo·lu′mi·nous·ness** *n.* **—vo·lu′mi·nous·ly** *adv.*

vol·un·tar·y (vol′ən·ter′ē) *adj.* **1** Done, made, or given by one's own free will or choice: a *voluntary* contribution. **2** Endowed with or exercising will or free choice. **3** Acting without constraint: a *voluntary* donor. **4** Subject to or directed by the will, as a muscle or movement. **5** Intentional; volitional: *voluntary* manslaughter. **—***n. pl.* **·tar·ies 1** Voluntary action or work. **2** A solo, usu. on the organ, often improvised, played before, during, or after a church service. [< L *voluntas* will] **—vol·un·tar·i·ly** (vol′ən·ter′ə·lē, vol′ən·ter′-) *adv.* **—vol′un·tar′i·ness** *n.*

vol·un·teer (vol'ən·tir') *n.* 1 One who enters into any service of his own free will. 2 One who voluntarily enters military service. —*adj.* 1 Of, pertaining to, or composed of volunteers; voluntary. 2 Serving as a volunteer. —*v.t.* 1 To offer or give voluntarily: to *volunteer* one's services. —*v.i.* 2 To enter or offer to enter into some service or undertaking of one's free will. [< OF *voluntaire* voluntary]

vo·lup·tu·ar·y (və·lup'chōō·er'ē) *n. pl.* **·ar·ies** One addicted to luxury and sensual indulgence. [< L *voluptas* pleasure] —**Syn.** hedonist, sensualist, sybarite.

vo·lup·tu·ous (və·lup'chōō·əs) *adj.* 1 Pertaining to, inclining to, producing, or produced by sensuous or sensual gratification. 2 Devoted to the enjoyment of pleasures or luxuries. 3 Suggesting the satisfaction of sensual desire. [< L *voluptas* pleasure] —**vo·lup'tu·ous·ly** *adv.* —**vo·lup'tu·ous·ness** *n.*

vo·lute (və·lōōt') *n.* 1 *Archit.* A spiral scroll-like ornament, as in Ionic capitals. 2 *Zool.* One of the whorls or turns of a spiral shell. 3 A spiral or twisted form. —*adj.* Having a spiral form; scroll-shaped. [< L *voluta* a scroll < p.p. of *volvere* to turn] —**vo·lut'ed** *adj.* —**vo·lu'tion** *n.*

Volute

vom·it (vom'it) *v.i.* 1 To disgorge the contents of the stomach; throw up. 2 To issue with violence from any hollow place; be ejected. —*v.t.* 3 To disgorge (the contents of the stomach). 4 To discharge or send forth copiously or forcibly: The volcano *vomited* smoke. —*n.* 1 The act of vomiting. 2 Matter ejected from the stomach in vomiting. [< L *vomere*] —**vom'it·er** *n.*

vom·i·tive (vom'ə·tiv) *adj.* Of, pertaining to, or causing vomiting. —*n.* EMETIC.

von (von; *Ger.* fōn, *unstressed* fən) *prep. German* Of; from: used in German and Austrian family names as an attribute of nobility.

voo·doo (vōō'dōō) *n.* 1 A primitive religion of African origin, found among Haitian and West Indian Negroes and the Negroes of the s U.S., characterized by belief in sorcery and the use of charms, fetishes, witchcraft, etc. 2 A person who practices voodoo. 3 A voodoo charm or fetish. —*adj.* Of or pertaining to the beliefs, ceremonies, etc., of voodoo. —*v.t.* To practice voodoo upon; bewitch. Also **vou'dou.** —**voo'doo·ism, voo'doo·ist** *n.* —**voo'doo·is'tic** *adj.*

vo·ra·cious (vô·rā'shəs, vō-, və-) *adj.* 1 Eating with greediness; ravenous. 2 Very eager, as in some desire; insatiable. 3 Immoderate: a *voracious* appetite. [< L *vorax* < *vorare* devour] —**vo·ra'cious·ly** *adv.* —**vo·rac·i·ty** (-ras'ə·tē), **vo·ra'cious·ness** *n.*

-vorous *combining form* Consuming; eating or feeding upon: *omnivorous, carnivorous.* [< L *vorare* devour]

vor·tex (vôr'teks) *n. pl.* **·tex·es** or **·ti·ces** (-tə·sēz) 1 A mass of rotating or whirling fluid, esp. one spiraling in toward a center; a whirlpool or whirlwind. 2 Something resembling a vortex, as an activity or situation from which it is difficult to escape. [< L, var. of *vertex* top, point] —**vor'ti cal** (-ti·kəl) *adj.* —**vor'ti·cal·ly** *adv.*

vo·ta·ry (vō'tər·ē) *n. pl.* **·ries** 1 One who is bound by vows, as a nun or priest. 2 One devoted to some particular worship, pursuit, study, etc. Also **vo'ta·rist.** —*adj.* 1 Of, pertaining to, or like a vow. 2 Consecrated by a vow. [< L *votus*, p.p. of *vovere* vow]

vote (vōt) *n.* 1 A formal expression of choice or opinion, as in electing officers, passing resolutions, etc. 2 That by which such choice or opinion is expressed, as the ballot, a show of hands, etc. 3 The number of ballots cast, hands raised, etc., to indicate such choice or opinion. 4 The votes of a specified group; also, the group itself. 5 The right to vote. 6 A voter. —*v.* **vot·ed, vot·ing** *v.t.* 1 To enact or determine by vote. 2 To cast one's vote for: to *vote* the Democratic ticket. 3 To elect or defeat by vote. 4 *Informal* To declare by general agreement: to *vote* a concert a success. —*v.i.* 5 To cast one's vote. —**vote down** To defeat or suppress by voting against. —**vote in** To elect. [< L *votum* a vow, wish, orig. p.p. neut. of *vovere* vow]

vot·er (vōt'ər) *n.* 1 A person who votes. 2 A person having the right to vote.

vo·tive (vō'tiv) *adj.* Performed, offered, lit, etc., as fulfillment of a vow, as an act of worship, in gratitude, etc. [< L *votum.* See VOTE.] —**vo'tive·ly** *adv.* —**vo'tive·ness** *n.*

vouch (vouch) *v.i.* 1 To give one's own assurance or guarantee: with *for:* I will *vouch* for their honesty. 2 To serve as assurance or proof: with *for:* The evidence *vouches* for his innocence. —*v.t.* 3 To bear witness to; attest or affirm. 4 To cite as support or justification, as a precedent, authority, etc. 5 To uphold by satisfactory proof or evidence; substantiate. [< L *vocare* call < *vox, vocis* a voice]

vouch·er (vou'chər) *n.* 1 A document that serves to vouch for the truth of something, or attest an alleged act, esp. the expenditure or receipt of money. 2 One who vouches for another; a witness.

vouch·safe (vouch'sāf') *v.* **·safed, ·saf·ing** *v.t.* 1 To grant, as with condescension; permit; deign. —*v.i.* 2 To condescend; deign. [< VOUCH + SAFE] —**vouch'safe'ment** *n.*

vous·soir (vōō·swär') *n. Archit.* A wedge-shaped stone in an arch. [< OF *vausoir, volsoir* curvature of a vault]

vow (vou) *n.* 1 A solemn promise, as to God or a god. 2 A pledge of faithfulness: marriage *vows.* 3 A solemn and emphatic affirmation. —**take vows** To enter a religious order. —*v.t.* 1 To promise solemnly. 2 To declare with assurance or solemnity. 3 To make a solemn promise or threat to do, inflict, etc. —*v.i.* 4 To make a vow. [< L *votum.* See VOTE.] —**vow'er** *n.*

vow·el (vou'əl, voul) *n.* 1 *Phonet.* A voiced speech sound produced by the relatively unimpeded passage of air through the mouth. 2 A letter indicating such a sound, as *a, e, i, o,* or *u.* —*adj.* Of or pertaining to a vowel or vowels. [< L *vocalis (littera)* vocal (letter)]

vox pop. voice of the people (L *vox populi*).

vox po·pu·li (voks pop'yə·lī, -lē) The voice of the people; public sentiment. [L]

voy·age (voi'ij) *n.* 1 A journey by water, esp. by sea. 2 Any journey, as one by aircraft. —*v.* **·aged, ·ag·ing** *v.i.* 1 To make a voyage; travel. —*v.t.* 2 To traverse. [< L *viaticum*] —**voy'ag·er** *n.* —**Syn.** *n.* 1 crossing, cruise, sail, trip.

vo·ya·geur (vwà·yà·zhœr') *n. pl.* **·geurs** (-zhœr') *Can.* Formerly, a man engaged by a fur company to carry men, supplies, etc., between remote trading posts. [F]

vo·yeur (vwä·yûr') *n.* One who is sexually gratified by looking at sexual objects or acts. [< F *voir* see] —**vo·yeur'·ism** *n.*

V.P. Vice President.

vs. versus.

v.s. see above (L *vide supra*).

VSS versions.

VT Vermont (P.O. abbr.).

Vt. Vermont.

v.t. verb transitive.

VTOL vertical takeoff and landing.

Vul., Vulg. Vulgate.

Vul·can (vul'kən) *Rom. Myth.* The god of fire and of metallurgy. —**Vul·ca·ni·an** (-kā'nē·ən) *adj.*

vul·can·ite (vul'kən·īt) *n.* A dark-colored, hard, vulcanized rubber. [< VULCAN]

vul·can·ize (vul'kən·īz) *v.t. & v.i.* **·ized, ·iz·ing** To heat (natural rubber) with sulfur in order to increase strength and elasticity. [< VULCAN] —**vul'can·i·za'tion, vul'can·iz'er** *n.*

vul·gar (vul'gər) *adj.* 1 Lacking good manners, taste, etc.; coarse; unrefined. 2 Offensive or obscene in expression: a *vulgar* usage. 3 Of or pertaining to the common people; general; popular. 4 Written in or translated into the common language or dialect; vernacular. [< L *vulgus* the common people] —**vul'gar·ly** *adv.* —**Syn.** 1 boorish, crude, tasteless. 2 indecent, taboo. 3 ordinary, plebeian.

vul·gar·i·an (vul·gâr'ē·ən) *n.* A person of vulgar tastes or manners; esp., a wealthy person with coarse habits.

vul·gar·ism (vul'gə·riz'əm) *n.* 1 A word, phrase, or expression generally considered to be incorrect or coarse and indicative of ignorance or ill breeding on the part of the user. 2 VULGARITY.

vul·gar·i·ty (vul·gar′ə·tē) *n. pl.* **·ties 1** The state, quality, or character of being vulgar. **2** Something vulgar, as an act or expression.

vul·gar·ize (vul′gə·rīz) *v.t.* **·ized, ·iz·ing** To make vulgar. *Brit. sp.* **vul′gar·ise. —vul′gar·i·za′tion, vul′gar·iz′er** *n.*

Vulgar Latin The popular, informal speech of the ancient Romans, considered to be the chief source of the Romance languages.

vul·gate (vul′gāt) *adj.* Popular; accepted. *—n.* **1** Everyday speech. **2** A popularly accepted text. [<L *vulgare* make common < *vulgus* the common people]

Vul·gate (vul′gāt) *n.* A Latin version of the Bible, translated in the 4th century, since revised and used as the authorized version by Roman Catholics. *—adj.* Of or in the Vulgate.

vul·ner·a·ble (vul′nər·ə·bəl) *adj.* **1** That may be wounded; capable of being hurt. **2** Open to attack; assailable. **3** In contract bridge, having won one game of a rubber, and therefore subject to doubled penalities if contract is not fulfilled. [<L *vulnerare* to wound < *vulnus* a wound] **—vul′ner·a·bil′i·ty, vul′ner·a·ble·ness** *n.* **—vul′ner·a·bly** *adv.*

vul·pine (vul′pin, -pīn) *adj.* **1** Of or pertaining to a fox. **2** Like a fox; sly; crafty; cunning. [<L *vulpes* a fox]

vul·ture (vul′chər) *n.* **1** Any of various large birds related to hawks and falcons, having a naked head and dark plumage, and feeding on carrion. **2** Something or someone that preys upon others. [<L *vultur*] **—vul′tur·ous** *adj.*

Vulture

vul·va (vul′və) *n. pl.* **·vae** (-vē) The external genital parts of the female. [L, a covering, womb] **—vul′val, vul′var, vul′vi·form** (-və·fôrm) *adj.*

vy·ing (vī′ing) *pr.p.* of VIE. *—adj.* That vies or competes. **—vy′ing·ly** *adv.*

W

W, w (dub′əl·yōō, -yōō) *n. pl.* **W's, w's, Ws, ws** (dub′əl·yōōz, -yōōz) **1** The 23rd letter of the English alphabet. **2** Any spoken sound representing the letter *W* or *w*. **3** Something shaped like a W. *—adj.* Shaped like a W.

W tungsten (G *wolfram*).

W, W., w, w. watt; west; western.

w. warden; week(s); weight; wife; with; word; work.

WA Washington (P.O. abbr.).

wab·ble (wob′əl) *n., v.t. & v.i.* **·bled, ·bling** WOBBLE. [Var. of WOBBLE] **—wab′bler** *n.* **—wab′bly** *adj.*

Wac (wak) *n.* A member of the **WAC**, the women's division of the U.S. Army. [< *W(omen's) A(rmy) C(orps)*]

wack·y (wak′ē) *adj.* **wack·i·er, wack·i·est** *Slang* Extremely irrational or erratic; crazy. Also **whack′y.** [Prob. < WHACK] **—wack′i·ly** *adv.* **—wack′i·ness** *n.*

wad (wod) *n.* **1** A small compact mass of any soft or flexible substance, esp. as used for stuffing, packing, or lining. **2** A lump; mass: a *wad* of tobacco. **3** A small plug used to hold in a charge of powder in a muzzleloading gun. **4** A pasteboard or paper disk to hold powder and shot in place in a shotgun shell. • See CARTRIDGE. **5** Fibrous material for stopping up breaks, leakages, etc.; wadding. **6** *Informal* A large amount, esp. of money. **7** *Informal* A roll of banknotes. *—v.* **wad·ded, wad·ding** *v.t.* **1** To press (fibrous substances, as cotton) into a mass or wad. **2** To roll or fold into a tight wad, as paper. **3** To pack or stuff with wadding for protection, as valuables. **4** To place a wad in (a gun, etc.). **5** To hold in place with a wad. *—v.i.* **6** To form into a wad. [?] **—wad′der** *n.*

wad·ding (wod′ing) *n.* **1** Wads collectively. **2** Any substance used as wads.

wad·dle (wod′l) *v.i.* **·dled, ·dling 1** To walk with short steps, swaying from side to side. **2** To move clumsily; totter. *—n.* A clumsy rocking walk, like that of a duck. [Freq. of WADE] **—wad′dler** *n.* **—wad′dly** *adj.*

wade (wād) *v.* **wad·ed, wad·ing** *v.i.* **1** To walk through water or any substance more resistant than air, as mud, sand, etc. **2** To proceed slowly or laboriously: to *wade* through a lengthy book. *—v.t.* **3** To pass or cross, as a river, by walking on the bottom; walk through; ford. **—wade in** (or **into**) *Informal* To attack or begin energetically or vigorously. *—n.* An act of wading. [<OE *wadan* go]

wad·er (wā′dər) *n.* **1** One who wades. **2** A long-legged wading bird, as a snipe, plover, or stork. **3** *pl.* High waterproof boots or pants, worn esp. by anglers.

wa·di (wä′dē) *n. pl.* **·dies 1** In Arabia and N Africa, a ravine containing the bed of a watercourse, usu. dry except in the rainy season. **2** The stream of water flowing through a wadi. Also **wa′dy.** [< Ar. *wādī*]

Waf (waf, wäf) *n.* A member of the **WAF**, the women's division of the U.S. Air Force. [< *W(omen in the) A(ir) F(orce)*]

wa·fer (wā′fər) *n.* **1** A very thin crisp biscuit, cooky, or cracker; also, a small disk of candy. **2** *Eccl.* A small flat disk of unleavened bread, used in the Eucharist in some churches. **3** A thin hardened disk of dried paste, gelatin, etc., used for sealing letters, attaching papers, or receiving the impression of a seal. *—v.t.* To attach, seal, or fasten with a wafer. [<AF *wafre* <MLG *wafel*]

waf·fle[1] (wof′əl, wô′fəl) *n.* A batter cake, crisper than a pancake, baked in a waffle iron. [< Du. *wafel* a wafer]

waf·fle[2] (wof′əl, wô′fəl) *v.i.* **·fled, ·fling 1** *Chiefly Brit. Informal* To speak or write nonsense. **2** *Informal* To avoid giving a direct answer; hedge. *—n. Chiefly Brit. Informal* Nonsense; twaddle. [< obs. *woff, waff* to yelp]

waffle iron A utensil for cooking waffles, consisting of two indented metal griddles, hinged together, between which the waffle is baked.

waft (waft, wäft) *v.t.* **1** To carry or bear gently or lightly over air or water; float. **2** To convey as if on air or water. *—v.i.* **3** To float, as on the wind. **4** To blow gently, as a breeze. *—n.* **1** The act of one who or that which wafts. **2** A breath or current of air. **3** A passing sound or odor. **4** A waving motion. [< Du. *wachten* to guard] **—waft′er** *n.*

wag (wag) *v.* **wagged, wag·ging** *v.t.* **1** To cause to move lightly and quickly from side to side or up and down, as a dog's tail. **2** To move (the tongue) in talking. *—v.i.* **3** To move lightly and quickly from side to side or up and down. **4** To move busily in animated talk or gossip: said of the tongue. *—n.* **1** The act or motion of wagging: a *wag* of the head. **2** A droll or humorous person; wit. [Prob. < Scand.]

wage (wāj) *n.* **1** *Often pl.* Payment for service rendered, esp. such payment calculated by the hour, day, or week, or for a certain amount of work. **2** *Usu. pl. (construed as sing. or pl.)* Reward: the *wages* of sin. *—v.t.* **waged, wag·ing** To engage in and maintain vigorously; carry on: to *wage* war. [< AF *wagier* pledge] **—Syn.** *n.* **1** compensation, earnings, pay, remuneration.

wage earner One who works for wages.

wa·ger (wā′jər) *v.t. & v.i.* To bet. *—n.* **1** A bet. **2** The thing bet on. [< AF *wagier*] **—wa′ger·er** *n.*

wage·worker (wāj′wûr′kər) *n.* An employee receiving wages. **—wage′work′ing** *n., adj.*

wag·ger·y (wag′ər·ē) *n. pl.* **·ger·ies 1** Mischievous joking. **2** A practical joke. [< WAG]

wag·gish (wag′ish) *adj.* **1** Being or acting like a wag; humorous. **2** Said or done as a joke. **—wag′gish·ly** *adv.* **—wag′gish·ness** *n.* **—Syn. 1** droll, facetious, funny, jocose.

wag·gle (wag′əl) *v.* **·gled, ·gling** *v.t.* To wag; swing: The duck *waggles* its tail. *—n.* The act of waggling. [Freq. of WAG] **—wag′gling·ly** *adv.* **—wag′gly** *adj.* **(·i·er, ·i·est)**

Wag·ne·ri·an (väg·nir′ē·ən) *adj.* **1** Of or pertaining to Richard Wagner or to his music, style, or theories. **2** Specializing in the performance of Wagner's music. *—n.* One who admires the music or the theories of Richard Wagner.

wag·on (wag′ən) *n.* 1 Any of various four-wheeled, usu. horse-drawn vehicles for carrying heavy loads. 2 A child's open, four-wheeled cart, pulled and steered by a long handle. 3 PATROL WAGON. 4 STATION WAGON. 5 *Brit.* A railway freight car. 6 A stand on wheels or casters for serving food or drink: a tea *wagon.* —**on** (or **off**) **the (water) wagon** *Informal* Abstaining (or no longer abstaining) from alcoholic beverages. —**fix (someone's) wagon** *Slang* To even scores with; get revenge on. —*v.t.* To carry or transport in a wagon. *Brit. sp.* **wag′gon.** [< Du. *wagen*]

Wagon

wag·on·er (wag′ən·ər) *n.* One whose business is driving wagons. *Brit. sp.* **wag·gon·er.**

wag·on·load (wag′ən·lōd′) *n.* The amount that a wagon can carry. *Brit. sp.* **wag·gon·load.**

wagon train A line of wagons traveling together.

wag·tail (wag′tāl′) *n.* Any of various birds that habitually jerk the tail, as certain pipits.

Wa·ha·bi (wä·hä′bē) *n.* A member of a strict orthodox Muslim sect. Also **Wah·ha′bi.** —**Wa·ha′bism, Wah·ha′bism** (-biz·əm) *n.*

waif (wāf) *n.* 1 A homeless, neglected person, esp. a child. 2 A stray animal. [Prob. < Scand.]

wail (wāl) *v.i.* 1 To grieve with mournful cries; lament. 2 To make a mournful, crying sound, as the wind. —*v.t.* 3 To mourn; lament. 4 To cry out in sorrow. —*n.* 1 A prolonged, high-pitched sound of lamentation. 2 Any mournful sound, as of the wind. [< ON *vei* woe] —**wail′er** *n.* —**wail′ful** *adj.* —**wail′ful·ly, wail′ing·ly** *adv.*

Wailing Wall A high wall in Jerusalem reputedly containing fragments of Solomon's temple and traditionally a place for Jews to pray and mourn.

wain (wān) *n.* An open, four-wheeled wagon for hauling heavy loads. [< OE *wægn, wæn*]

wain·scot (wān′skət, -skōt, -skot) *n.* 1 A facing for inner walls, usu. of paneled wood. 2 The lower part of an inner wall, when finished with material different from the rest of the wall. —*v.t.* **·scot·ed** or **·scot·ted, ·scot·ing** or **·scot·ting** To face or panel with wainscot. [< MLG *wagen* a wagon + *schot* a wooden partition]

wain·scot·ing (wān′skət·ing, -skot-) *n.* 1 WAINSCOT. 2 Material for a wainscot. Also **wain′scot·ting.**

wain·wright (wān′rīt) *n.* A maker of wagons.

waist (wāst) *n.* 1 The part of the body between the lower ribs and the hips. 2 The middle part of any object, esp. if narrower than the ends: the *waist* of a violin. 3 That part of a woman's dress covering the body from the waistline to the shoulders. 4 BLOUSE. 5 WAISTLINE (def. 2). [ME *wast*]

waist·band (wāst′band′) *n.* A band encircling the waist, esp. such a band inside a skirt or trousers.

waist·coat (wes′kit, wāst′kōt′) *n. Chiefly Brit.* VEST (def. 1).

waist·line (wāst′līn′) *n.* 1 The so-called line that encircles the middle of the waist. 2 That part of a garment covering this line or extending above or below it according to the dictates of fashion.

wait (wāt) *v.i.* 1 To stay in expectation, as of an anticipated action or event: with *for, until,* etc. 2 To be or remain in readiness. 3 To remain temporarily neglected or undone. 4 To perform duties of personal service; esp. to act as a waiter or waitress. —*v.t.* 5 To stay or remain in expectation of: to *wait* one's turn. 6 *Informal* To put off or postpone: Don't *wait* breakfast for me. —**wait on** (or **upon**) 1 To act as a clerk or attendant to. 2 To go to see; visit. 3 To attend as a result or consequence. —**wait up** 1 To delay going to bed in anticipation of someone's arrival or of something happening. 2 *Informal* To stop until someone catches up. —*n.* The act of waiting, or the time spent in waiting; delay. —**lie in wait** To remain hidden in order to make a surprise attack. [< AF *waitier*] —**Syn.** *v.* 1 abide, linger, remain, tarry.

wait·er (wā′tər) *n.* 1 A man employed to wait on table, as in a restaurant. 2 One who awaits something. 3 A tray for dishes, etc.

wait·ing (wā′ting) *n.* The act of one who waits. —**in waiting** In attendance, esp. at court.

waiting room A room for the use of persons waiting, as for a train, a doctor, etc.

wait·ress (wā′tris) *n.* A woman employed to wait on table, as in a restaurant.

waive (wāv) *v.t.* **waived, waiv·ing** 1 To give up or relinquish a claim to. 2 To refrain from insisting upon or taking advantage of; forgo. 3 To put off; postpone; delay. [< OF *gaiver* abandon]

waiv·er (wā′vər) *n. Law* 1 The voluntary relinquishment of a right, privilege, or advantage. 2 The instrument which evidences such relinquishment. [< AF *weyver* abandon, waive]

wake[1] (wāk) *v.* **woke** or **waked, waked** (*Regional* **wok·en**), **wak·ing** *v.i.* 1 To emerge from sleep: often with *up.* 2 To be or remain awake. 3 To become aware or alert. 4 *Regional* To keep watch at night; esp., to hold a wake. —*v.t.* 5 To rouse from sleep or slumber; awake: often with *up.* 6 To rouse or stir up; excite. 7 To make aware; alert. 8 *Regional* To hold a wake over. —*n.* A vigil, esp. a watch over the body of a dead person through the night, just before the burial. [Fusion of OE *wacan* awaken and *wacian* be awake]

wake[2] (wāk) *n.* 1 The trail of turbulence left by a moving ship, aircraft, etc. 2 Any course passed over. —**in the wake of** Following close behind. [< ON *vök* an opening in ice]

wake·ful (wāk′fəl) *adj.* 1 Not sleeping or sleepy. 2 Watchful; alert. 3 Sleepless; restless: a *wakeful* time. —**wake′·ful·ly** *adv.* —**wake′ful·ness** *n.* —**Syn.** 1 awake. 2 cautious, vigilant, wary.

wak·en (wā′kən) *v.t.* 1 To rouse from sleep; awake. 2 To rouse or urge to alertness or activity. —*v.i.* 3 To cease sleeping; wake up. [< OE *wacnian*] —**wak′en·er** *n.*

wake-rob·in (wāk′rob′in) *n.* 1 TRILLIUM. 2 JACK-IN-THE-PULPIT.

Wal·dorf salad (wôl′dôrf) A salad made of chopped celery, apples, walnuts, and mayonnaise. [< the first *Waldorf*-Astoria Hotel, New York City]

wale (wāl) *n.* 1 WELT (def. 1). 2 A ridge or rib on the surface of cloth, as on corduroy. 3 *Usu. pl.* One of several planks on the outer sides of a wooden ship. —*v.t.* **waled, wal·ing** 1 To raise wales on by striking. 2 To manufacture (cloth) with ridges or ribs. [< OE *walu*]

walk (wôk) *v.i.* 1 To advance on foot in such a manner that one part of a foot is always on the ground, or, in quadrupeds, that two or more feet are always on the ground. 2 To go on foot for exercise or amusement. 3 To move in a manner suggestive of walking, as certain inanimate objects. 4 To act or live in some manner: to *walk* in peace. 5 In baseball, to advance to first base after being pitched four balls. —*v.t.* 6 To pass through, over, or across at a walk: to *walk* the floor. 7 To lead, ride, or drive at a walk: to *walk* a horse. 8 To force or help to walk. 9 To accompany on a walk: I'll *walk* you to school. 10 To bring to a specified condition by walking. 11 To cause to move with a motion resembling a walk: to *walk* a trunk on its corners. 12 In baseball, to allow to advance to first base by pitching four balls. —**walk away from** 1 To outrun or outdo (someone). 2 To sustain little or no injury in an accident. —**walk off** 1 To depart, esp. abruptly. 2 To get rid of (fat, etc.) by walking. —**walk off with** 1 To win, esp. with little difficulty. 2 To steal. —**walk out** *Informal* 1 To go out on strike. 2 To depart suddenly. —**walk out on** *Informal* To forsake; desert. —**walk over** 1 To defeat easily. 2 To treat with contempt. —*n.* 1 The act of walking, as for enjoyment. 2 Manner of walking; gait. 3 A place prepared for walking, as a sidewalk. **4** The distance covered or time spent in walking. **5** A piece of ground set apart for the feeding and exercise of domestic animals. **6** In baseball, the act of walking a batter; also, a being walked. **—walk of life** One's social or financial status. [< OE *wealcan* roll, toss] **—walk'er** *n.* **—Syn.** *v.* **1** saunter, step, stride, tread.

walk·a·way (wôk'ə·wā') *n. Informal* A contest won without serious opposition. Also **walk'o'ver** (-ō'vər).

walk·ie-talk·ie (wô'kē·tô'kē) *n.* A portable radio transmitting and receiving set.

walking papers *Informal* Notice of dismissal from employment, office, etc.

walking stick **1** A staff or cane. **2** Any of various insects having legs and body resembling twigs.

walk-on (wôk'on', -ôn') *n.* A very small, usu. non-speaking role in a play, etc.

walk·out (wôk'out') *n. Informal* A workmen's strike.

walk-up (wôk'up') *Informal n.* **1** An apartment house or building of two or more stories having no elevator. **2** An apartment located higher than the ground floor in such an apartment house.

wall (wôl) *n.* **1** A continuous structure designed to enclose an area, to be the surrounding exterior of a building, or to be a partition between rooms or halls. **2** A fence of stone or brickwork, surrounding or separating yards, fields, etc. **3** *Usu. pl.* A barrier or rampart constructed for defense. **4** A sea wall; levee. **5** A barrier enclosing a cavity, vessel, or receptacle: the *wall* of the abdomen. **6** Something suggestive of a wall: a *wall* of bayonets. **—drive (push** or **thrust) to the wall** To force (one) to an extremity; crush. **—drive** (or **send**) **up the wall** *Informal* To make extremely nervous, tense, etc. —*v.t.* **1** To provide, surround, protect, etc., with or as with a wall or walls. **2** To fill or block with a wall: often with *up.* —*adj.* **1** Of or pertaining to a wall. **2** Hanging from, growing on, or built into a wall. [< OE *weall* < L *vallum* a rampart]

wal·la·by (wol'ə·bē) *n. pl.* **·bies** Any of various small to medium-sized kangaroos. [< Australian *wolaba*]

wall·board (wôl'bôrd', -bōrd') *n.* A material of varied composition pressed into sheets and used for walls, ceilings, etc.

wal·let (wol'it) *n.* A small, usu. folding case, as of leather, for holding paper money, cards, etc., and sometimes change, carried in a pocket or purse. [ME *walet*]

wall·eye (wôl'ī') *n.* **1** An eye with a light-colored or white iris. **2** A kind of strabismus in which the eyes diverge. **3** Any of several walleyed fishes. [Back formation < WALLEYED]

wall·eyed (wôl'īd') *adj.* **1** Having a walleye or walleyes. **2** Having large, staring eyes, as certain fish. [< ON *vagl* a film on the eye + *auga* eye]

walleyed pike A large freshwater game fish of North America. Also **walleyed perch.**

wall·flow·er (wôl'flou'ər) *n.* **1** Any of various cultivated perennials related to mustard having fragrant yellow, orange, or red flowers. **2** *Informal* A person who because of unpopularity or shyness does not participate in some social activity, as a party or dance.

Wal·loon (wo·lōōn') *n.* **1** One of a people of s Belgium and adjoining regions of France. **2** Their language, a dialect of French. —*adj.* Of or pertaining to the Walloons or their dialect.

wal·lop (wol'əp) *Informal v.t.* **1** To beat soundly; thrash. **2** To hit with a hard blow. —*n.* A hard blow. [< AF *waloper*] **—wal'lop·er** *n.*

wal·lop·ing (wol'əp·ing) *Informal adj.* Very large; whopping. —*n.* A beating; whipping or crushing defeat.

wal·low (wol'ō) *v.i.* **1** To roll about, as in mud, snow, etc. **2** To move with a heavy, rolling motion, as a ship in a storm. **3** To indulge oneself wantonly: to *wallow* in sensuality. —*n.* **1** The act of wallowing. **2** A depression or hollow made by wallowing. [< OE *wealwian*] **—wal'low·er** *n.*

wall·pa·per (wôl'pā'pər) *n.* Decorative paper for covering walls. —*v.t.* To cover with wallpaper.

Wall Street **1** A street in lower Manhattan, New York City, famous as the financial center of the U.S. **2** The U.S. financial world.

wall-to-wall (wôl'tə·wôl') *adj.* Completely covering a floor: *wall-to-wall* carpeting.

wal·nut (wôl'nut', -nət) *n.* **1** Any of various deciduous trees cultivated as ornamental shade trees and valued for their timber and their edible nuts. **2** The wood or nut of any of these trees. **3** The shagbark or its nut. **4** The color of the wood of any of these trees, esp. of the black walnut, a very dark brown: also **walnut brown.** [< OE *wealh* foreign + *hnutu* a nut]

Black walnut
a. shuck. b. nut.

Wal·pur·gis Night (väl·pŏŏr'·gis) The night before May 1, thought to be the occassion of a gathering of witches for demonic rites and orgies. [< St. *Walpurga,* 8th-cent. English missionary in Germany]

wal·rus (wôl'rəs, wol'-) *n.* A very large, seallike mammal of arctic seas, with flexible hind limbs, projecting tusklike canines in the upper jaw, a bushy, bristly mustache on the muzzle, and a very tough hide. —*adj.* **1** Belonging or pertaining to a walrus. **2** Designating a type of bushy mustache drooping at the ends. [< Scand.]

Walrus

waltz (wôlts) *n.* **1** A dance to music in triple time. **2** Music for or in the style of such a dance. —*v.i.* **1** To dance a waltz. **2** To move quickly: She *waltzed* out of the room. —*v.t.* **3** To cause to waltz. —*adj.* Pertaining to the waltz. [< G *walzen* to waltz, roll] **—waltz'er** *n.*

wam·pum (wom'pəm, wôm'-) *n.* **1** Beads made of shells, formerly used as jewelry and currency among North American Indians. **2** *Informal* Money. [< Algon. *wampom(peag),* lit., a white (string of beads)]

wan (won) *adj.* **wan·ner, wan·nest** **1** Pale, as from sickness; careworn. **2** Faint; feeble: a *wan* smile. [< OE *wann* dark, gloomy] **—wan'ly** *adv.* **—wan'ness** *n.* **—Syn.** **1** ashen, livid, pallid. **2** weak.

wand (wond) *n.* **1** A slender, flexible rod waved by a magician. **2** Any rod symbolizing authority, as a scepter. **3** A musician's baton. [< ON *vöndr*]

wan·der (won'dər) *v.i.* **1** To travel about without destination or purpose; roam. **2** To go casually or by an indirect route; stroll. **3** To twist or meander. **4** To stray. **5** To deviate in conduct or opinion; go astray. **6** To be delirious. —*v.t.* **7** To wander through or across. [< OE *wandrian*] **—wan'der·er** *n.* **—wan'der·ing·ly** *adv.* **—Syn.** **1** range, rove.

wan·der·lust (won'dər·lust') *n.* An impulse to travel; restlessness. [< G *wandern* to travel + *Lust* joy]

wane (wān) *v.i.* **waned, wan·ing** **1** To diminish in size and brilliance. **2** To decline or decrease gradually. **3** To draw to an end. —*n.* **1** A waning or decreasing. **2** The period of such decrease. **—on the wane** Decreasing; declining. [< OE *wanian* lessen]

wan·gle (wang'gəl) *v.* **·gled, ·gling** *Informal v.t.* **1** To obtain or make by indirect, manipulatory, or dishonest methods; finagle. —*v.i.* **2** To resort to indirect, irregular, or dishonest methods. [?] **—wan'gler** *n.*

Wan·kel engine (väng'kəl, wäng'-) A light, compact type of internal-combustion engine having combustion chambers bounded by the wall of a shallow cylinder and the sides of a triangular piston that rotates in one direction inside it. Also **Wan'kel.** [< F. *Wankel,* 1902–, German inventor]

want (wont, wônt) *v.t.* **1** To feel a desire or wish for. **2** To wish; desire: used with the infinitive: to *want* to help. **3** To be deficient in, esp. to a required or customary extent. **4** To desire to see, speak to, arrest, etc.: He *wants* you on the phone; *wanted* by the police. **5** *Chiefly Brit.* To need; require. —*v.i.* **6** To have need: usu. with *for.* **7** To be needy or destitute. —*n.* **1** Lack; scarcity; shortage. **2** Poverty; destitution. **3** Something lacking; a need or craving. [Prob. < ON *vanta* be lacking] **—want'er** *n.* **—Syn.** *n.* **1** dearth, deficiency, insufficiency. **2** indigence, privation.

want ad *Informal* A classified advertisement, as in a newspaper, for something wanted, as an employee, a job, a lodging, etc.

want·ing (won′ting, wôn′-) *adj.* **1** Missing; lacking: One juror is still *wanting.* **2** Not coming up to some standard, need, or expectation: He was found *wanting.* **—wanting in** Deficient in. *—prep.* **1** Lacking; without. **2** Less; minus.

wan·ton (won′tən) *adj.* **1** Licentious; lewd; lustful. **2** Heartless or unjust; malicious: *wanton* savagery. **3** Unprovoked; senseless: a *wanton* murder. **4** Extravagant; unrestrained: *wanton* speech. **5** Not bound or tied; loose: *wanton* curls. **6** Capricious; frolicsome. *—v.i.* **1** To act in a wanton manner; be wanton. *—v.t.* **2** To waste or squander carelessly. *—n.* A lewd or licentious person. [<OE *wan* deficient + *tēon* bring up, educate] **—wan′ton·ly** *adv.* **—wan′ton·ness** *n.*

wap·i·ti (wop′ə·tē) *n. pl.* **·tis** or **·ti** A large North American deer; the American elk. [<Algon.] • See ELK.

war (wôr) *n.* **1** Armed strife or conflict between nations or states, or between different parties in the same nation. **2** Any act or state of conflict, struggle, or strife: a *war* against poverty. **3** Military science or strategy. *—v.i.* **warred, war·ring 1** To wage war; fight or take part in a war. **2** To be in any state of active opposition. *—adj.* Of, pertaining to, used in, or resulting from war. [<OHG *werra* strife, confusion]

War Between the States CIVIL WAR.

war·ble (wôr′bəl) *v.* **·bled, ·bling** *v.t.* **1** To sing (something) with trills and runs or with tremulous vibrations. *—v.i.* **2** To sing with trills, etc. **3** To make a liquid, murmuring sound, as a stream. **4** YODEL. *—n.* The act or sound of warbling. [<OF *werble* a warble]

war·bler (wôr′blər) *n.* **1** One who or that which warbles. **2** Any of a family of small, mostly Old World birds noted for their song. **3** Any of a large and varied family of small, migratory, New World birds, usu. having brilliant springtime plumage and distinctive songs.

war bonnet The ceremonial headdress of the North American Plains Indians.

war crime *Usu. pl.* Any of various crimes committed during or as a result of war, as maltreatment of prisoners, atrocities against civilians, genocide, etc. **—war criminal**

war cry A rallying cry or slogan used by combatants in a war, or by participants in any contest.

ward (wôrd) *n.* **1** In a hospital: **a** A large room for six or more patients. **b** A division for specific illnesses or groups of patients: the children's *ward.* **2** A division of a city for administrative or electoral purposes. **3** *Law* A person, as a minor, who is in the charge of a guardian or court. **4** The act of guarding or the state of being guarded. **5** A division or subdivision of a prison. **6** Any means of defense or protection. *—v.t.* To repel or turn aside, as a thrust or blow: usu. with *off.* [<OE *weardian* to watch, guard]

-ward *suffix* Toward; in the direction of: *upward, homeward.* Also **-wards.** [<OE *-weard*]

war dance A dance of certain tribes before going to war or in celebration of a victory.

war·den (wôr′dən) *n.* **1** A supervisor or custodian of something: a game *warden;* prison *warden.* **2** *Brit.* The head of certain colleges. **3** CHURCHWARDEN (def 1). [<AF *wardein*] **—war′den·ry** (*pl.* **·ries**), **war′den·ship** *n.*

ward·er (wôr′dər) *n.* **1** A guard or sentinel. **2** *Chiefly Brit.* A prison official; warden. [<OF *guarder* guard, keep]

ward heeler *Slang* A hanger-on of a political boss in a ward or other local area, who does minor tasks, canvasses votes, etc.

ward·robe (wôrd′rōb′) *n.* **1** A large upright cabinet for wearing apparel. **2** All the garments belonging to any one person. **3** The clothes for a particular season: a spring *wardrobe.* **4** The costumes of a theater, theatrical troupe, motion-picture company, etc.; also, the place where such costumes are kept. [<AF *warder* keep + *robe* a robe]

ward·room (wôrd′ro͞om′, -ro͝om′) *n.* **1** On a warship, the eating or living quarters allotted to the commissioned officers, excepting the commander. **2** These officers regarded as a group.

ward·ship (wôrd′ship) *n.* **1** The state of being a ward of a guardian or court. **2** Custody; guardianship.

ware (wâr) *n.* **1** Articles of the same class: used collectively in compounds: *glassware.* **2** *pl.* Articles for sale; merchandise. **3** Pottery; earthenware. [<OE *waru*]

ware·house (wâr′hous′) *n.* **1** A storehouse for goods or merchandise. **2** *Chiefly Brit.* A large wholesale shop. *—v.t.* **·housed** (-houzd′), **·hous·ing** (-hou′zing) To place or store in a warehouse.

ware·house·man (wâr′hous′mən) *n. pl.* **·men** (-mən) One who owns or works in a warehouse.

war·fare (wôr′fâr′) *n.* **1** The waging or carrying on of war. **2** Struggle; strife.

war game 1 *pl.* Practice maneuvers imitating the conditions of actual warfare. **2** A simulated military conflict organized to test tactical procedures and concepts by discussion and analysis.

war·head (wôr′hed′) *n.* The chamber in the nose of a bomb, guided missile, etc., containing an explosive, incendiary, or chemical charge.

war horse 1 A heavy horse used in warfare. **2** *Informal* A veteran of many struggles or contests, esp. political contests.

war·like (wôr′līk′) *adj.* **1** Fond of or ready for war. **2** Relating to, used in, or suggesting war. **3** Threatening war. **—Syn. 1** bellicose, belligerent. **2** martial, military.

war·lock (wôr′lok′) *n.* **1** A male witch; sorcerer. **2** A magician or conjurer. [<OE *wær* a covenant + *lēogen* lie, deny]

warm (wôrm) *adj.* **1** Moderately hot; having heat somewhat greater than temperate: *warm* water; a *warm* climate. **2** Imparting heat: a *warm* fire. **3** Imparting or preserving warmth: a *warm* coat. **4** Having the natural temperature of most living persons or animals: *warm* blood. **5** Heated, as from exertion. **6** Ardent; enthusiastic; fervent: *warm* interest. **7** Lively; agitated: a *warm* argument. **8** Cordial; friendly: a *warm* welcome. **9** Amorous; loving: a *warm* glance. **10** Excitable; fiery: a *warm* temper. **11** Having predominating tones of red or yellow. **12** Recently made; fresh: a *warm* trail. **13** Near to finding a hidden object or fact, as in certain games. **14** *Informal* Uncomfortable by reason of annoyances or danger: They made the town *warm* for him. *—v.t.* **1** To make warm. **2** To make ardent or enthusiastic; interest. **3** To fill with kindly feeling. *—v.i.* **4** To become warm. **5** To become ardent or enthusiastic: often with *up* or *to.* **6** To become kindly disposed or friendly: with *to* or *toward.* **—warm up 1** To warm. **2** To exercise the body, voice, etc., as before a game or performance. **3** To run an engine, etc., in order to attain correct operating temperature. *—n. Informal* A warming or being warm. [<OE *wearm*] **—warm′er, warm′ness** *n.* **—warm′ly** *adv.*

warm-blood·ed (wôrm′blud′id) *adj.* **1** Having a nearly uniform and warm body temperature, whatever the surrounding medium. **2** Enthusiastic; ardent; passionate.

warm-heart·ed (wôrm′här′tid) *adj.* Kind; affectionate.

warming pan A closed metal pan with a long handle, containing live coals or hot water, used for warming a bed.

war·mon·ger (wôr′mung′gər, -mong′-) *n.* One who favors or tries to incite war. **—war′mon′ger·ing** *adj., n.*

warmth (wôrmth) *n.* **1** The state, quality, or sensation of being warm. **2** Ardor or excitement of disposition or feeling. **3** Sympathetic friendliness, affection, or understanding. **4** The effect produced by warm colors.

warm-up (wôrm′up′) *n.* The act or an instance of warming up.

warn (wôrn) *v.t.* **1** To make aware of possible harm; caution. **2** To advise; counsel. **3** To give notice in advance. **4** To notify (a person) to go or stay away. *—v.i.* **5** To give warning. [<OE *wearnian*] **—warn′er** *n.*

warn·ing (wôr′ning) *n.* **1** The act of one who warns or the state of being warned. **2** That which warns. *—adj.* Serving as a warning. **—warn′ing·ly** *adv.* **—Syn.** *n.* **2** admonition, advice, recommendation.

War of 1812 A war between the U.S. and Great Britain (1812–15).

War of Independence AMERICAN REVOLUTION.

add, āce, câre, pälm; end, ēven; it, īce; odd, ōpen, ôrder; to͝ok, po͞ol; up, bûrn; ə = *a* in *above, u* in *focus;* yo͞o = *u* in *fuse;* oil; pout; check; go; ring; thin; this; zh, *vision.* < derived from; ? origin uncertain or unknown.

warp (wôrp) *v.t.* **1** To turn or twist out of shape, as by shrinkage or heat. **2** To corrupt; pervert: a mind *warped* by bigotry. **3** *Naut.* To move (a vessel) by hauling on a rope or line fastened to something stationary. —*v.i.* **4** To become turned or twisted out of shape, as wood in drying. **5** To deviate from a correct or proper course: go astray. **6** *Naut.* To move by means of ropes fastened to a pier, anchor, etc. —*n.* **1** The state of being warped, twisted out of shape, or biased. **2** The threads that run the long way of a fabric, crossing the woof. **3** *Naut.* A rope or line used for warping. [< OE *weorpan* to throw] **—warp′er** *n.*

war paint **1** Paint applied to faces and bodies of primitive peoples as a sign of going to war. **2** *Informal* Cosmetics, as rouge, lipstick, etc. **3** *Informal* Official garb or regalia.

war·path (wôr′path′, -päth′) *n.* The route taken by an attacking party of American Indians. **—on the warpath** **1** On a warlike expedition. **2** Ready for a fight; thoroughly angry.

war·plane (wôr′plān′) *n.* An airplane used in war.

war·rant (wôr′ənt, wor′-) *n.* **1** *Law* A judicial writ or order authorizing arrest, search, seizure, etc. **2** Something which assures or attests; guarantee. **3** That which gives authority for some course or act; sanction; justification. **4** A certificate of appointment given to a naval or military warrant officer. **5** A document giving a certain authority, esp. for the receipt or payment of money. —*v.t.* **1** To assure or guarantee the quality, accuracy, certainty, or sufficiency of: to *warrant* a title to property. **2** To guarantee the character or fidelity of; pledge oneself for. **3** To guarantee against injury, loss, etc. **4** To be sufficient grounds for; justify. **5** To give legal authority or power to; authorize. **6** *Informal* To say confidently; feel sure. [< AF *warant*] **—war′rant·er** *n.*

war·ran·tee (wôr′ən·tē′, wor′-) *n. Law* The person to whom a warranty is given.

warrant officer See GRADE.

war·rant·or (wôr′ən·tôr, wor′-) *n. Law* One who makes or gives a warranty to another.

war·ran·ty (wôr′ən·tē, wor′-) *n. pl.* **·ties** **1** *Law* A guarantee by the seller of property, a product, etc., that whatever is sold is or shall be as represented. **2** An official authorization or warrant. [< AF *warant* a warrant]

war·ren (wôr′ən, wor′-) *n.* **1** A place where rabbits live and breed. **2** Any building or area overcrowded with people. [< AF *warenne* a game park, a rabbit warren]

war·ri·or (wôr′ē·ər, wôr′yər, wor′-) *n.* A man engaged in or experienced in warfare or conflict.

war·ship (wôr′ship′) *n.* Any vessel used in naval combat.

wart (wôrt) *n.* **1** A small, usu. hard, benign excrescence on the skin, caused by a virus. **2** Any of various natural protuberances on certain plants and animals. [< OE *wearte*] **—wart′y** *adj.* **(·i·er, ·i·est)**

wart hog An African wild hog having large tusks and warty excrescences on the face.

Wart hog

war whoop A yell, as made by American Indians, as a signal for attack, etc.

war·y (wâr′ē) *adj.* **war·i·er, war·i·est** **1** Carefully watching and guarding. **2** Shrewd; wily. [< OE *wær*] **—war′i·ly** *adv.* **—war′i·ness** *n.*

was (woz, wuz, *unstressed* wəz) First and third person sing , past indicative of BE. [< OE *wæs*]

wash (wosh, wôsh) *v.t.* **1** To cleanse with water or other liquid, as by immersing, scrubbing, etc. **2** To wet or cover with water or other liquid. **3** To flow against or over: a beach *washed* by the ocean. **4** To remove or carry by the use or action of water: with *away, off, out,* etc. **5** To form or wear by erosion. **6** To purify, as gas, by passing through a liquid. **7** To coat with a thin layer of color. **8** To cover with a thin coat of metal. **9** *Mining* **a** To subject (gravel, earth, etc.) to the action of water so as to separate the ore, etc. **b** To separate (ore, etc.) thus. —*v.i.* **10** To wash oneself. **11** To wash clothes, etc., in water or other liquid. **12** To withstand the effects of washing: That calico will *wash.* **13** *Informal* To undergo testing successfully: That story won't *wash.* **14** To flow with a lapping sound, as waves. **15** To be carried away or removed by the use or action of water: with *away, off, out,* etc. **16** To be eroded by the action of water. **—wash out** *Slang* To fail and be dropped from a course, esp. in military flight training. —*n.* **1** The act or an instance of washing. **2** A number of articles, as of clothing, set apart for washing. **3** Liquid or semiliquid refuse; swill. **4** Any preparation used in washing or coating, as a mouthwash. **5** A paint, as water color, spread lightly on a surface. **6** The breaking of a body of water upon the shore, or the sound made by this. **7** Erosion of soil or earth by the action of running water. **8** Material collected and deposited by water, as along a river bank. **9** Agitation or turbulence in water or air caused by something passing through it. **10** An area washed by a sea or river; a marsh; bog. **11** In the w U.S., the dry bed of a stream. —*adj.* Washable without injury: *wash* fabrics. [< OE *wascan*]

Wash. Washington.

wash·a·ble (wosh′ə·bəl, wôsh′-) *adj.* That can be washed without damage.

wash-and-wear (wosh′ən·wâr′, wôsh′-) *adj.* Designating a garment or fabric so treated as to require little or no ironing after washing.

wash·board (wosh′bôrd′, -bōrd′, wôsh′-) *n.* A board having a corrugated surface on which to rub clothes while washing them.

wash·bowl (wosh′bōl, wôsh′-) *n.* A basin or bowl used for washing the hands and face. Also **wash′ba′sin** (-bā′sən).

wash·cloth (wosh′klôth′, -kloth′, wôsh′-) *n.* A small cloth used for washing the body.

washed-out (wosht′out′, wôsht′-) *adj.* **1** Faded; pale. **2** *Informal* Exhausted; tired.

washed-up (wosht′up′, wôsht′-) *adj. Informal* **1** Finished; done with; through. **2** Exhausted.

wash·er (wosh′ər, wô′shər) *n.* **1** One who washes. **2** *Mech.* A small, flat, perforated disk of metal, rubber, etc., used to make a nut or joint tight. **3** WASHING MACHINE.

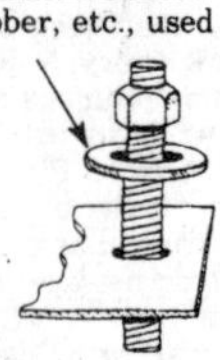

Washer *def 2*

wash·er·wom·an (wosh′ər·wo͝om′ən, wô′shər-) *n. pl.* **·wom·en** (-wim′in) LAUNDRESS.

wash·ing (wosh′ing, wô′shing) *n.* **1** The act of one who or that which washes. **2** Things (as clothing) washed or to be washed at one time. **3** A thin coating of metal: forks with only one *washing* of silver. **4** That which is obtained by washing: a *washing* of ore.

washing machine A machine that washes and usu. rinses automatically, used to clean clothes, linens, etc.

washing soda SODIUM CARBONATE.

Washington's Birthday (wash′ing·tənz, wô′shing-) The third Monday in February, a U.S. holiday observed in honor of the anniversary of George Washington's birth, February 22.

wash·out (wosh′out′, wôsh′-) *n.* **1** A considerable erosion of earth by the action of water; also, the excavation thus made. **2** *Slang* A hopeless or total failure.

wash·room (wosh′ro͞om′, -ro͝om′, wôsh′-) *n.* A restroom or lavatory.

wash·stand (wosh′stand′, wôsh′-) *n.* **1** A stand for washbowl, pitcher, etc. **2** A bathroom sink.

wash·tub (wosh′tub′, wôsh′-) *n.* A usu. stationary tub used for laundry.

wash·wom·an (wosh′wo͝om′ən, wôsh′-) *n. pl.* **·wom·en** (-wim′in) LAUNDRESS.

wash·y (wosh′ē, wô′shē) *adj.* **wash·i·er, wash·i·est** **1** Watery; diluted. **2** Weak; feeble.

was·n't (woz′ənt, wuz′-) Contraction of *was not.*

wasp (wosp, wôsp) *n.* Any of numerous insects related to bees, having membranous wings, biting mouth parts, and effective stings, and including both social and solitary species. [< OE *wæsp*]

WASP (wosp, wôsp) *n. Slang* A white Protestant American, esp. one of N European ancestry. Also **Wasp.** [< *w(hite) A(nglo)-S(axon) P(rotestant)*] **—WASP′ish, Wasp′ish** *adj.*

wasp·ish (wos′pish, wôs′-) *adj.* **1** Of or like a wasp. **2** Irritable; bad-tempered. **—wasp′ish·ly** *adv.* **—wasp′ish·ness** *n.*

wasp waist A very slim, narrow waist. —**wasp-waist·ed** (wosp′wās′tid, wôsp′-) *adj.*

was·sail (wos′əl, was′-, wo·sāl′) *n.* **1** An ancient toast, esp. to one's health. **2** The spiced drink, usu. ale and wine, prepared for a wassail. **3** An occasion of much drinking; a carousal. —*v.i.* **1** To take part in a wassail; carouse. —*v.t.* **2** To drink the health of; toast. [< ON *ves heill* be whole] —**was′sail·er** *n.*

Was·ser·mann test (wäs′ər·mən) A diagnostic test for syphilis, based on the detection of certain antibodies in the blood. Also **Wassermann reaction.** [< August von *Wassermann*, 1866–1925, German bacteriologist]

wast (wost, *unstressed* wəst) *Archaic* Were: used with THOU.

wast·age (wās′tij) *n.* That which is lost by leakage, waste, etc.

waste (wāst) *v.* **wast·ed, wast·ing** *v.t.* **1** To use or expend thoughtlessly; squander. **2** To make weak or feeble. **3** To use up; consume. **4** To fail to use or take advantage of, as an opportunity. **5** To lay waste; devastate. **6** *Slang* To kill; destroy. —*v.i.* **7** To lose strength, vigor, or bulk: often with *away.* **8** To diminish or dwindle gradually. **9** To pass gradually: said of time. —*n.* **1** Thoughtless or unnecessary expenditure, consumption, etc. **2** Failure to benefit or gain from something, as an opportunity. **3** A desolate or devastated place or region; wilderness; desert. **4** A continuous, gradual wearing away of strength, vigor, or substance. **5** Something discarded or rejected as worthless or unneeded, esp. tangled spun cotton thread. **6** Something that escapes without being used, as steam. **7** Garbage; rubbish; trash. **8** Something excreted from the body, as urine or excrement. —**lay waste** To destroy or devastate. —*adj.* **1** Cast aside as worthless; discarded. **2** Excreted from the body. **3** Not cultivated or inhabited; wild; barren. **4** Superfluous: *waste* energy. **5** Containing or conveying waste products. [< L *vastare* lay waste] —**wast′er** *n.* —**Syn.** *v.* **1** dissipate. **2** debilitate, enfeeble.

waste·bas·ket (wāst′bas′kit, -bäs′-) *n.* A container for paper scraps and other waste. Also **wastepaper basket.**

waste·ful (wāst′fəl) *adj.* **1** Prone to waste; extravagant. **2** Causing waste. —**waste′ful·ly** *adv.* —**waste′ful·ness** *n.*

waste·land (wāst′land′) *n.* A barren or desolate land.

waste·pa·per (wāst′pā′pər) *n.* Paper thrown away as worthless. Also **waste paper.**

waste pipe A pipe for carrying off waste water, etc.

wast·ing (wās′ting) *adj.* **1** Destructive; devastating. **2** Destructive to health; enfeebling.

wast·rel (wās′trəl) *n.* **1** A profligate; spendthrift. **2** An idler or loafer. [Dim. of *waster* one who wastes]

watch (woch, wôch) *v.i.* **1** To look attentively; observe closely. **2** To be on the alert. **3** To wait expectantly for something: with *for.* **4** To do duty as a guard or sentinel. **5** To keep vigil. —*v.t.* **6** To look at attentively; observe. **7** To keep informed concerning. **8** To be alert for; to *watch* one's opportunity. **9** To keep watch over; guard. —**watch out** To be careful. —*n.* **1** Close and continuous attention; careful observation. **2** Service as a guard or sentry. **3** The period of time during which a guard is on duty. **4** The person or persons set to guard or watch. **5** A small, portable timepiece worn on the wrist or carried in a pocket. **6** A vigil or wake. **7** *Naut.* **a** A spell of duty on board ship, usu. four hours. **b** The division of a crew on duty during such a period. [< OE *wæccan*] —**watch′er** *n.*

watch·case (woch′kās′, wôch′-) *n.* A metal covering for the mechanism of a watch.

watch·dog (woch′dôg′, -dog′, wôch′-) *n.* **1** A dog kept to guard a building or other property. **2** A person who keeps a vigilant lookout.

watch·ful (woch′fəl, wôch′-) *adj.* Watching carefully; vigilant; alert. —**watch′ful·ly** *adv.* —**watch′ful·ness** *n.*

watch·mak·er (woch′mā′kər, wôch′-) *n.* One who makes or repairs watches.

watch·man (woch′mən, wôch′-) *n. pl.* **·men** (-mən) A man employed to guard a building, etc., at night.

watch·tow·er (woch′tou′ər, wôch′-) *n.* A tower upon which a sentinel is stationed.

watch·word (woch′wûrd′, wôch′-) *n.* **1** PASSWORD. **2** A slogan or maxim.

wa·ter (wô′tər, wot′ər) *n.* **1** The colorless liquid that covers over 70 percent of the earth's surface, is capable of wetting and dissolving many different substances, and is an essential constituent of all organisms. **2** A chemical compound of hydrogen and oxygen which occurs as a solid, a liquid, or a vapor, depending upon its temperature. **3** *Often pl.* Any body of water, as a lake, river, or a sea. **4** Any liquid or liquid secretion of the body, as perspiration, tears, urine, etc. **5** Any preparation of water holding a substance in solution: mineral *water.* **6** An undulating sheen given to certain fabrics, as silk, etc. **7** In commerce and finance, stock issued without an increase of assets or earning power to back it. —**above water** Out of danger, debt, etc.; secure. —**hold water** To be logical, valid, or dependable. —**like water** Freely; prodigally. —**of the first water** Of the finest quality. —*v.t.* **1** To provide (land, plants, etc.) with water, as by sprinkling or irrigating. **2** To provide with water for drinking. **3** To dilute or weaken with water: often with *down.* **4** To give an undulating sheen to the surface of (silk, linen, etc.). **5** To enlarge the number of shares of (a stock company) without increasing the company assets in proportion. —*v.i.* **6** To secrete or discharge water, tears, etc. **7** To fill with saliva, as the mouth, from desire for food. **8** To drink water. [< OE *wæter*] —**wa′ter·er** *n.*

Water Bearer AQUARIUS.

wa·ter·bed (wô′tər·bed′, wot′ər-) *n.* A bed with a water-filled container serving as a mattress.

water bird Any bird living on or near water.

water bomber In Canada, an aircraft equipped to drop water on forest fires. Also **fire bomber.**

wa·ter-borne (wô′tər·bôrn′, -bōrn′, wot′ər-) *adj.* **1** Floating on water. **2** Transported in a ship, etc.

wa·ter·buck (wô′tər·buk′, wot′ər-) *n.* Either of two species of large African antelope, frequenting rivers, etc.

water buffalo A large, slow, oxlike animal of s Asia with curved horns, often domesticated as a draft animal.

water chestnut **1** The hard, nutlike, edible fruit of an aquatic plant native to Asia. **2** The plant itself: also **water cal·trop** (kal′trəp).

wa·ter·clock (wô′tər·klok′, wot′ər-) *n.* A device for measuring time by the fall or flow of water.

water closet TOILET (defs. 1 & 2).

wa·ter·col·or (wô′tər·kul′ər, wot′ər-) *n.* **1** A pigment or coloring matter prepared for painting with water as the medium. **2** A picture or painting done in watercolors. Also **water color.** —*adj.* Of or painted with watercolors.

wa·ter-cool (wô′tər·kōōl′, wot′ər-) *v.t.* To cool by means of water, as by a jacket or pipe.

water cooler A vessel or apparatus for cooling and dispensing drinking water.

wa·ter·course (wô′tər·kôrs′, -kōrs′, wot′ər-) *n.* **1** A stream of water, as a river or brook. **2** A channel for a stream of water.

wa·ter·craft (wô′tər·kraft′, -kräft′, wot′ər-) *n.* **1** Skill in sailing boats or in aquatic sports. **2** A boat or ship. **3** Boats and ships collectively.

wa·ter·cress (wô′tər·kres′, wot′ər-) *n.* An edible perennial herb of the mustard family, usu. growing in running water and cultivated for use as salad.

water cure HYDROPATHY.

wa·ter·fall (wô′tər·fôl′, wot′ər-) *n.* A fall of water over a precipice.

wa·ter·fowl (wô′tər·foul′, wot′ər-) *n. pl.* **·fowl** or **·fowls** A water bird, esp. a swimming game bird.

wa·ter·front (wô′tər·frunt′, wot′ər-) *n.* **1** Property abutting on or overlooking a natural body of water. **2** That part of a town which fronts on a body of water, usu. a commercial area of docks, warehouses, etc.

water gap A deep ravine in a mountain ridge giving passage to a stream.

water gas A poisonous fuel gas containing hydrogen and carbon monoxide produced by forcing steam over white-hot coke.

wa·ter·gate (wô′tər·gāt′, wot′ər-) *n.* FLOODGATE.

water gauge A gauge for indicating the level of water in a boiler, reservoir, etc.

wa·ter·glass (wô′tər·glas′, -gläs′, wot′ər-) *n.* **1** A drinking glass. **2** WATER GAUGE. **3** A glass-bottomed tube for examining objects lying under water. **4** A water-soluble silicate, as of sodium or potassium, used as an adhesive, for preserving eggs, etc. Also **water glass.**

water hole A pond or pool of water, esp. one used by animals for drinking.

water ice *Chiefly Brit.* SHERBET.

watering place **1** A place where water can be obtained, as a spring. **2** *Chiefly Brit.* A health resort having mineral springs; also, a pleasure resort near the water.

water jacket A casing containing water for cooling, as one surrounding a cylinder of an internal-combustion engine.

water level **1** The level of water in a body of water. **2** A ship's waterline.

wa·ter·lil·y (wô′tər·lil′ē, wot′ər-) *n. pl.* **·lil·ies** Any of various aquatic plants with large floating leaves and showy white or colored flowers.

Waterlily

wa·ter·line (wô′tər·līn′, wot′ər-) *n.* **1** *Naut.* **a** A line on the hull of a ship which shows where the water surface reaches. **b** Short, horizontal lines on a ship's hull which correspond with the surface of the water when the ship is unloaded, partly loaded, or fully loaded. **2** Any line or mark showing to what level water has risen.

wa·ter·logged (wô′tər·lôgd′, -logd′, wot′ər-) *adj.* **1** So saturated or filled with water as to be unmanageable and barely able to float, as a ship, etc. **2** Soaked with water.

Wa·ter·loo (wô′tər·lo͞o, wô′tər·lo͞o′) *n.* A decisive defeat, usu. in the phrase **meet one's Waterloo.** [< *Waterloo,* Belgium, scene of Napoleon's final defeat, 1815]

water main A main pipe in a system of pipes for carrying water, esp. one laid underground.

wa·ter·man (wô′tər·mən, wot′ər-) *n. pl.* **·men** (-mən) A boatman or oarsman.

wa·ter·mark (wô′tər·märk′, wot′ər-) *n.* **1** WATERLINE (def. 2). **2** A mark or design made in paper by pressure while the paper is still in a pulpy state; also, the metal pattern which produces these markings. —*v.t.* **1** To impress (paper) with a watermark. **2** To impress (a mark or design) as a watermark.

wa·ter·mel·on (wô′tər·mel′ən, wot′ər-) *n.* **1** A gourd cultivated for its large edible fruit, having a juicy, sweet, red or pink pulp. **2** The fruit.

water mill A mill operated by waterpower.

water moccasin A venomous, brownish pit viper, found along rivers, etc., of the SE U.S.

water nymph *Gk. & Rom. Myth.* A nymph dwelling in a stream, lake, etc.

water of crystallization Water that combines with certain salts to form usu. unstable hydrates of distinct crystalline structure. Also **water of hydration.**

water ouzel Any of various small diving birds related to thrushes.

water pipe **1** A pipe for carrying water. **2** HOOKAH.

water polo A game in which two teams of swimmers attempt to take or throw an inflated ball across each other's goal line.

wa·ter·pow·er (wô′tər·pou′ər, wot′ər-) *n.* The power derived from the kinetic energy of flowing or falling water, used for driving machinery.

wa·ter·proof (wô′tər·pro͞of′, wot′ər-) *adj.* **1** WATERTIGHT. **2** Coated with some substance, as rubber, which prevents the passage of water. —*n.* **1** Waterproof fabric. **2** *Brit.* A raincoat or other waterproof garment. —*v.t.* To render waterproof.

water rat **1** MUSKRAT. **2** Any of various rodents that frequent lakes, streams, etc. **3** *Slang* A waterfront tough or thief.

wa·ter·shed (wô′tər·shed′, wot′ər-) *n.* **1** A ridge of high land that divides two areas drained by different river systems. **2** The whole region from which a river receives its supply of water. **3** A decisive turning point affecting outlook, actions, etc.

wa·ter·side (wô′tər·sīd′, wot′ər-) *n.* The shore of a body of water; the water's edge.

wa·ter-ski (wô′tər·skē′, wot′ər-) *v.i.* **-skied, -ski·ing** To glide over water on skilike runners **(water skis)** while being towed by a motorboat. —**wa′ter-ski′er** *n.*

water snake **1** Any of various harmless North American snakes that live chiefly in water. **2** Any aquatic snake.

wa·ter-soak (wô′tər·sōk′, wot′ər-) *v.t.* To saturate with water.

water softener A substance that removes dissolved minerals from water, as by precipitation, absorption, etc.

water spaniel A breed of spaniel having a water-resistant coat, used for retrieving waterfowl.

wa·ter·spout (wô′tər·spout′, wot′ər-) *n.* **1** A moving, whirling column of spray and mist, resulting from a tornado at sea, on a lake, etc. **2** A pipe for the free discharge of water.

water sprite A nymph, sprite, etc., living in water.

water table The surface marking the upper level of a water-saturated subterranean zone of permeable rock.

wa·ter·tight (wô′tər·tīt′, wot′ər-) *adj.* **1** So closely made that water cannot enter or leak through. **2** That cannot be misunderstood, found illegal or in error, etc.: a *watertight* contract. —**wat′er·tight′ness** *n.*

water tower **1** A tank or tower, used as a reservoir and to maintain pressure in a system of water distribution. **2** A vehicular towerlike structure from which water can be played on a burning building from a great height.

water vapor The vapor of water, esp. below the boiling point, as in the atmosphere.

wa·ter·way (wô′tər·wā′, wot′ər-) *n.* A river, channel, or other stream of water, esp. when navigable by boats and ships.

water wheel A wheel designed to be turned by flowing water. • See UNDERSHOT.

water wings An inflatable device used to keep a beginning swimmer afloat.

wa·ter·works (wô′tər·wûrks′, wot′ər-) *n.pl.* A system of buildings, pipes, pumps, etc. for furnishing a water supply, esp. for a city.

wa·ter·worn (wô′tər·wôrn′, -wōrn′, wot′ər-) *adj.* Worn smooth by running or falling water.

wa·ter·y (wô′tər·ē, wot′ər·ē) *adj.* **1** Of, containing, or like water. **2** Diluted. **3** Overly liquid; thin. **4** Tearful. **5** Weak; vapid; insipid. —**wa′ter·i·ness** *n.*

watt (wot) *n.* A unit of power equivalent to one joule per second, or about 1/746 of a horsepower. [< J. *Watt,* 1736–1819, Scottish engineer]

wat·tage (wot′ij) *n.* An amount of power, esp. electric power, expressed in watts.

watt-hour (wot′our′) *n.* Energy equivalent to one watt acting for one hour.

watt-hr. watt-hour(s).

wat·tle (wot′l) *n.* **1** A framework of poles and twigs woven together, used for walls, fences, etc. **2** The poles and twigs used for this. **3** A fold of skin, often wrinkled and brightly colored, hanging from the throat of a bird or lizard. **4** Any one of various acacias of Australia, Tasmania, and South Africa. —*v.t.* **·tled, ·tling** **1** To weave or twist, as twigs, into a network. **2** To form,, as a fence, by intertwining flexible twigs. **3** To bind together with wattles. [< OE *watul*]

Wattle of turkey

watt·me·ter (wot′mē′tər) *n.* An instrument for measuring electric power in watts.

wave (wāv) *v.* **waved, wav·ing** *v.i.* **1** To move freely back and forth or up and down, as a flag in the wind. **2** To signal by moving something back and forth or up and down. **3** To have an undulating shape or form: Her hair *waves.* —*v.t.* **4** To cause to wave: to *wave* a banner. **5** To flourish, as a weapon. **6** To give a wavy appearance to or form into waves: to *wave* one's hair. **7** To signal by waving something: He *waved* me aside. **8** To express by waving something: to *wave* farewell. —*n.* 1 A ridge or undulation moving on the surface of a liquid. 2 A similar undulation on a freely moving surface: *waves* in the tall grass. 3 A curve or curl in the hair. 4 A curved pattern or shape, as on watered silk. 5 A back-and-forth or up-and-down motion, as with the hand. 6 A more or less prolonged meteorological condition: a heat *wave.* 7 An upsurge of something: a crime *wave;* a *wave* of emotion. 8 A surging movement, as of a mass or group: a *wave* of refugees. 9 *Usu. pl.* A large body of water. 10 *Physics* A periodic disturbance propagated through a medium, characterized by a function of time that defines its frequency, amplitude, phase, and velocity. [< OE *wafian*] —**wav'er** *n.*

Wave (wāv) *n.* A member of the **WAVES,** the women's division of the U.S. Navy. [< *W(omen) A(ppointed for) V(oluntary) E(mergency) S(ervice)*]

wave·form (wāv'fôrm') *n.* 1 The curve produced by recording, as on a graph, the varying dimensions of a wave through successive oscillations. 2 A mathematical formula for such a curve.

wave·length (wāv'length') *n. Physics* The distance, along the line of propagation, between two points of like phase in consecutive cycles of a wave.

wave·let (wāv'lit) *n.* A little wave.

wa·ver (wā'vər) *v.i.* 1 To move one way and the other; flutter. 2 To be uncertain; vacillate. 3 To show signs of falling back or giving way; falter. 4 To flicker; gleam. —*n.* A wavering. [< OE *wafian* to wave] —**wa'ver·er** *n.* —**wa'·ver·ing·ly** *adv.* —**Syn.** 1 oscillate, quiver, shake. 2 hesitate.

wav·y (wā'vē) *adj.* **wav·i·er, wav·i·est** Full of waves or curves, as hair, lines, etc. —**wav'i·ly** *adv.* —**wav'i·ness** *n.*

wax[1] (waks) *n.* 1 BEESWAX. 2 Any of various pliable plant and animal substances that are insoluble in water, that burn in air, or otherwise resemble beeswax. 3 A solid mineral substance resembling wax, as paraffin. 4 SEALING WAX. 5 A waxlike commercial product, used for polishing furniture, floors, etc. —*v.t.* To coat or polish with wax. —*adj.* Made of or pertaining to wax. [< OE *weax*]

wax[2] (waks) *v.i.* **waxed, waxed** (*Archaic* **wax·en**), **wax·ing** 1 To increase in size: said esp. of the moon. 2 To become: to *wax* angry. [< OE *weaxan* grow]

wax bean A pale yellow variety of string bean.

wax·ber·ry (waks'ber'ē) *n. pl.* **·ries** 1 The wax myrtle, or bayberry. 2 Its fruit.

wax·en (wak'sən) *adj.* 1 Consisting of or covered with wax. 2 Pale; pallid: a *waxen* complexion.

wax myrtle Any of various North American shrubs or small trees having fragrant leaves and small berries covered with white wax, often used in making candles.

wax palm Either of two South American palms yielding waxes widely used to make polishes, cosmetics, etc.

wax paper Paper coated with paraffin to render it moistureproof. Also **waxed paper.**

wax·wing (waks'wing') *n.* Any of various crested passerine birds having soft, mainly brown plumage, and red, waxy tips on the wings.

Cedar waxwing

wax·work (waks'wûrk') *n.* 1 Work produced in wax; esp., life-size figures of notable persons. 2 *pl.* An exhibition of such figures. —**wax'work'er** *n.*

wax·y (wak'sē) *adj.* **wax·i·er, wax·i·est** 1 Resembling wax in appearance, consistency, etc. 2 Pale; pallid, as wax. 3 Made of, abounding in, or polished with wax. —**wax'i·ness** *n.*

way (wā) *n.* 1 Direction; route: Which *way* is the city? 2 A path, course, road, etc., leading from one place to another. 3 Space or room to advance or work: Make *way* for the king. 4 Distance in general: a little *way* off. 5 Direction in general: Look the other *way.* 6 Passage from one place to another: on our *way* to Europe. 7 A customary or habitual manner or style of acting or being: Do it her *way.* 8 A plan of action; procedure; method: In what *way* will you accomplish this? 9 Respect; point; particular: He erred in two *ways.* 10 A course of life or experience: the *way* of sin. 11 Desire; wish: to get one's *way.* 12 *Informal* State or condition: to be in a bad *way.* 13 The range of one's experience or observation: An accident threw it in his *way.* 14 *Informal* Neighborhood or locality: out our *way.* 15 *Naut.* a Forward motion; headway. b *pl.* A tilted framework of timbers upon which a ship slides when launched. —**by the way** In passing; incidentally. —**by way of** 1 With the object or purpose of; to serve as: *by way of* introduction. 2 Through; via. —**give way (to)** 1 To yield or submit. 2 To collapse. —**go out of one's** (or **the**) **way** To inconvenience oneself. —**in the way** In a position that impedes or hinders. —**out of the way** 1 In a position so as not to hinder or impede. 2 Out of the usual or convenient location or route. 3 Unusual. 4 Improper; wrong: Has he done anything *out of the way?*—**under way** In motion; making progress. —*adv. Informal* All the distance to: He went *way* to Denver. [< OE *weg*]

way·bill (wā'bil') *n.* A statement listing or giving instructions concerning the shipping of goods.

way·far·er (wā'fâr'ər) *n.* One who travels, esp. on foot. —**way'far'ing** *n., adj.*

way·lay (wā'lā') *v.t.* **·laid, ·lay·ing** 1 To lie in ambush for and attack. 2 To accost on the way. —**way'lay'er** *n.*

way-out (wā'out') *adj. Slang* FAR-OUT.

-ways *suffix of adverbs* In a (specified) manner, direction, or position: *noways, sideways.*

ways and means 1 Means or methods of accomplishing an end or defraying expenses. 2 In legislation, methods of raising funds for the use of the government: also **Ways and Means.**

way·side (wā'sīd') *adj.* Pertaining to or near the side of a road. —*n.* The side or edge of the road or highway.

way station Any station between principal stations, esp. on a railroad.

way train A train stopping at way stations.

way·ward (wā'wərd) *adj.* 1 Willful; headstrong. 2 Not predictable; erratic. [< ME *awei* away + -WARD] —**way'·ward·ly** *adv.* —**way'ward·ness** *n.* —**Syn.** 1 disobedient, perverse, refractory, stubborn. 2 capricious.

WbN west by north.

WbS west by south.

w.c. water closet; without charge.

W.C.T.U. Women's Christian Temperance Union.

we (wē) *pron. pl.* 1 The persons speaking or writing, or a single person writing or speaking when referring to himself and one or more others. 2 A single person denoting himself, as a sovereign, editor, writer, or speaker, when wishing to give his words a formal or impersonal character. [< OE]

weak (wēk) *adj.* 1 Lacking in physical strength, energy, or vigor; feeble. 2 Incapable of resisting stress or supporting weight: a *weak* wall. 3 Lacking in strength of will or stability of character. 4 Not effective, forceful, or convincing: *weak* reasoning. 5 Lacking in power, intensity, etc.: a *weak* voice. 6 Lacking a specified component or components in the usual or proper amount: *weak* tea. 7 Lacking the power or ability to function properly: a *weak* heart. 8 Lacking mental or intellectual capability. 9 Lacking skill, experience, etc.: a *weak* player. 10 Lacking in power, influence, or authority: a *weak* state. 11 Deficient in some specified thing or quality: *weak* in languages. 12 *Gram.* Denoting a verb in English or other Germanic languages that forms its past tense and past participle by adding *d* or *t* rather than by vowel changes. 13 *Phonet.* Unstressed; unaccented, as a syllable or sound. 14 In prosody, indicating a verse ending in which the accent falls on a word or syllable otherwise without stress. 15 Characterized by declining prices: said of the stock market. [< ON *veikr*] —**Syn.** 1 slight, puny, enfeebled, frail.

weak·en (wē'kən) *v.t. & v.i.* To make or become weak or weaker. —**weak'en·er** *n.* —**Syn.** debilitate, enervate, enfeeble, sap.

weak·fish (wēk'fish') *n. pl.* **·fish** or **·fish·es** Any of various marine food fishes, esp. several troutlike species of E U.S. coastal waters.

weak-kneed (wēk′nēd′) *adj.* 1 Weak in the knees. 2 Without resolution, strong purpose, or energy; spineless.
weak·ling (wēk′ling) *n.* A feeble person or animal. —*adj.* Weak.
weak·ly (wēk′lē) *adj.* **·li·er, ·li·est** Sickly; feeble; weak. —*adv.* In a weak manner. —**weak′li·ness** *n.*
weak-mind·ed (wēk′mīn′did) *adj.* 1 Not resolute or firm; indecisive. 2 FEEBLE-MINDED. —**weak′mind′ed·ly** *adv.* —**weak′mind′ed·ness** *n.*
weak·ness (wēk′nis) *n.* 1 The state, condition, or quality of being weak. 2 A characteristic indicating feebleness. 3 A slight failing; a fault. 4 A strong liking or fondness; also, the object of such a liking.
weal[1] (wēl) *n. Archaic* A sound or prosperous condition. [<OE *wela*]
weal[2] (wēl) *n.* A welt, as from a blow. [Var. of WALE]
weald (wēld) *n. Chiefly Brit.* 1 A forest area. 2 An open region; down. [OE, a forest]
wealth (welth) *n.* 1 A large amount of money or property; riches. 2 The state of being rich. 3 Great abundance of anything: a *wealth* of learning. 4 *Econ.* a All material objects which have economic utility. b All property possessing a monetary value. [ME *welthe* < *wele* weal]
wealth·y (wel′thē) *adj.* **wealth·i·er, wealth·i·est** 1 Possessing wealth; affluent. 2 More than sufficient; abounding. —**wealth′i·ly** *adv.* —**wealth′i·ness** *n.* —**Syn.** 1 rich, prosperous, well-to-do, well-off.
wean (wēn) *v.t.* 1 To transfer (the young of any mammal) from dependence on its mother's milk to another form of nourishment. 2 To free from usu. undesirable habits or associations: usu. with *from.* [<OE *wenian* accustom] —**wean′er** *n.*
wean·ling (wēn′ling) *adj.* Freshly weaned. —*n.* A child or animal newly weaned.
weap·on (wep′ən) *n.* 1 Any implement of war or combat, as a sword, gun, etc. 2 Any means that may be used against an adversary. 3 Any defensive organ or part of an animal or plant, as a claw, tooth, thorn, etc. [<OE *wæpen*] —**weap′on·ry** (-rē) *n.*
wear (wâr) *v.* **wore, worn, wear·ing** *v.t.* 1 To have on the person as a garment, ornament, etc. 2 To have on the person habitually: He *wears* a derby. 3 To have in one's aspect; exhibit: He *wears* a scowl. 4 To have as a characteristic: She *wears* her hair short. 5 To display or fly: A ship *wears* its colors. 6 To impair or consume by use or constant action. 7 To cause by scraping, rubbing, etc.: to *wear* a hole in a coat. 8 To bring to a specified condition by wear: to *wear* a sleeve to tatters. 9 To exhaust; weary. —*v.i.* 10 To be impaired or diminished gradually by use, rubbing, etc. 11 To withstand the effects of use, handling, etc.: These shoes *wear* well. 12 To remain sound or interesting over a period of time: a friendship that *wore* well. 13 To become as specified from use or attrition: His patience is *wearing* thin. 14 To pass gradually: with *on* or *away.* 15 To have an unpleasant or exhausting effect. —**wear down** 1 To make or become less through friction, use, etc. 2 To tire out; exhaust. 3 To overcome the resistance of by constant pressure, harassment, etc. —**wear off** To diminish gradually. —**wear out** 1 To make or become worthless by use. 2 To waste or use up gradually. 3 To tire or exhaust. —*n.* 1 The act of wearing, or the state of being worn. 2 Material or articles of dress to be worn: often in combination: *footwear, underwear.* 3 Vogue; fashion. 4 Destruction or impairment from use or time. 5 Capacity to resist use or time; durability. —**wear and tear** Loss or damage from use over a period of time. [<OE *werian*] —**wear′er** *n.*
wear·ing (wâr′ing) *adj.* 1 Fatiguing; exhausting: a *wearing* day. 2 Capable of being, or designed to be, worn. —**wear′ing·ly** *adv.*
wearing apparel Clothing; garments.
wea·ri·some (wir′ē·səm) *adj.* Causing fatigue; tiresome. —**wea′ri·some·ly** *adv.* —**wea′ri·some·ness** *n.* —**Syn.** annoying, irksome, tedious, vexatious.
wea·ry (wir′ē) *adj.* **·ri·er, ·ri·est** 1 Worn out; tired; fatigued. 2 Discontented or bored: usu. with *of: weary* of life. 3 Indicating or characteristic of fatigue: a *weary* sigh. 4 Causing fatigue; wearisome. —*v.t. & v.i.* **·ried, ·ry·ing** To make or become weary. [<OE *wērig*] —**wea′ri·ly** *adv.* —**wea′ri·ness** *n.*
wea·sel (wē′zəl) *n.* 1 Any of certain small, slender, usu. nocturnal carnivorous mammals. 2 A sly or treacherous person. —*v.i.* **·seled, ·sel·ing** *Informal* 1 To fail to fulfill a promise, etc.; renege: with *out.* 2 To speak ambiguously; equivocate. [<OE *wesle*]

Weasel

weath·er (weth′ər) *n.* 1 The general atmospheric condition, as regards temperature, moisture, winds, or related phenomena. 2 Unpleasant atmospheric conditions. —**keep one's weather eye open** *Informal* To be alert. —**under the weather** *Informal* 1 Ailing; ill. 2 Suffering from a hangover. 3 Drunk. —*v.t.* 1 To expose to the action of the weather. 2 To discolor, crumble, or otherwise affect by action of the weather. 3 To pass through and survive, as a crisis. 4 *Naut.* To pass to windward of: to *weather* Cape Fear. —*v.i.* 5 To undergo changes from exposure to the weather. 6 To resist the action of the weather. —*adj.* Facing the wind. [<OE *weder*]
weath·er-beat·en (weth′ər·bēt′n) *adj.* 1 Bearing or showing the effects of exposure to weather. 2 Tanned, wrinkled, etc., by or as if by exposure to weather, as a face.
weath·er·board (weth′ər·bôrd′, -bōrd′) *n.* CLAPBOARD. —*v.t.* To fasten weatherboards on.
weath·er-bound (weth′ər·bound′) *adj.* Detained by unfavorable weather, as a ship.
weath·er·cock (weth′ər·kok′) *n.* 1 A weathervane, properly one in the form of a cock. 2 A fickle person or variable thing.

Weathercock

weath·er·glass (weth′ər·glas′, -gläs′) *n.* An instrument for indicating the weather, esp. a barometer.
weath·er·man (weth′ər·man′) *n. pl.* **·men** (-men′) *n.* A person who reports on daily weather conditions.
weather map *Meteorol.* A map or chart giving weather conditions for a given region and specified time.
weath·er·proof (weth′ər·proof′) *adj.* Capable of withstanding snow, rain, wind, etc., without appreciable deterioration. —*v.t.* To make weatherproof.
weather station A station or office where meteorological observations are made.
weath·er·strip (weth′ər·strip′) *n.* A narrow strip of material to be placed over or in crevices, as at doors and windows, to exclude drafts, rain, etc. Also **weath′er·strip′·ping.** —*v.t.* **·stripped, ·strip·ping** To equip or fit with weatherstrips.
weath·er·vane (weth′ər·vān′) *n.* A vane that indicates the direction in which the wind is blowing.
weath·er·wise (weth′ər·wīz′) *adj.* Experienced in observing or predicting the weather, public opinion, etc.
weath·er·worn (weth′ər·wôrn′, -wōrn′) *adj.* Worn by exposure to the weather.
weave (wēv) *v.* **wove** or *esp. for defs. 7, 8, & 11* **weaved, wo·ven** or *esp. for defs. 7, 8, & 11* **weaved, weav·ing** *v.t.* 1 To make (a fabric) by interlacing threads or yarns, esp. on a loom. 2 To interlace (threads or yarns) into a fabric. 3 To form by interlacing strands, strips, twigs, etc.: to *weave* a basket. 4 To produce by combining details or elements: to *weave* a story. 5 To twist or introduce into: to *weave* ribbons through one's hair. 6 To spin (a web). 7 To make by going from one side to another: to *weave* one's way through a crowd. 8 To direct (a car, etc.) in this manner. —*v.i.* 9 To make cloth, etc., by weaving. 10 To become woven or interlaced. 11 To make one's way by moving from one side to another. —*n.* A particular method, style, or pattern of weaving. [<OE *wefan*]
weav·er (wē′vər) *n.* 1 One who weaves. 2 A person whose job is weaving. 3 WEAVERBIRD.
weav·er·bird (wē′vər·bûrd′) *n.* Any of various finchlike birds of Asia, Africa, and Australia, that weave intricate nests.
web (web) *n.* 1 Fabric being woven on a loom. 2 The net-

work of delicate threads spun by a spider or by certain insect larvae. 3 An artfully contrived trap or snare. 4 Any complex network of interwoven parts, elements, etc.: a *web* of lies; a *web* of highways. 5 *Zool.* A membrane connecting the digits, as in aquatic birds, frogs, etc. 6 The vane of a feather. 7 *Anat.* A membrane or tissue. 8 A plate or sheet, as of metal, connecting the ribs, frames, etc., of a structure. 9 *Archit.* The part of a ribbed vault between the ribs. 10 A large roll of paper, as for use in a web press. —*v.t.* **webbed, web·bing** 1 To provide with a web. 2 To cover or surround with a web; entangle. [<OE]

webbed (webd) *adj.* 1 Having a web. 2 Having the digits united by a membrane.

web·bing (web′ing) *n.* 1 A woven strip of strong fiber, used for safety belts, upholstery, etc. 2 Anything forming a web or weblike structure.

we·ber (vā′bər, wē′bər) *n.* A unit equal to the magnetic flux that, interacting with a single turn of wire, induces a potential difference of one volt as it is uniformly reduced to zero in one second. [< W. E. *Weber,* 1804–91, German physicist]

web·foot (web′fo͝ot′) *n.* 1 A foot with webbed toes. 2 A bird or animal having such feet. —**web′-foot′ed** *adj.*

web press A printing press which is fed from a continuous roll of paper instead of sheets.

wed (wed) *v.* **wed·ded, wed·ded** or **wed, wed·ding** *v.t.* 1 To take as one's husband or wife; marry. 2 To join in wedlock. 3 To unite or join closely: He is *wedded* to his job. —*v.i.* 4 To take a husband or wife; marry. [<OE *weddian* to pledge]

we'd (wēd) Contraction of *we had* or *we would.*

Wed. Wednesday.

wed·ding (wed′ing) *n.* 1 The ceremony of a marriage. 2 The anniversary of a marriage: golden *wedding.* [<OE *weddian* to pledge]

wedge (wej) *n.* 1 A V-shaped piece of metal, wood, etc., used for splitting wood, raising weights, etc. 2 Anything in the form of a wedge. 3 Any action which facilitates policy, entrance, intrusion, etc. 4 An iron golf club with the face at an angle for lofting the ball. —*v.* **wedged, wedg·ing** *v.t.* 1 To force apart with a wedge. 2 To fix in place with a wedge. 3 To crowd or squeeze (something). —*v.i.* 4 To force oneself or itself in like a wedge. [<OE *wecg*]

wedg·ie (wej′ē) *n.* A woman's shoe having a wedge-shaped piece making a solid, flat sole from heel to toe.

Wedg·wood (wej′wo͝od′) *n.* A fine English pottery, characterized by small, white, classical figures in cameo relief against a tinted background. [< J. *Wedgwood,* 1730–95, English potter]

wed·lock (wed′lok) *n.* The state of being married. [<OE *wedd* a pledge + *-lāc,* suffix of nouns of action]

Wednes·day (wenz′dē, -dā) *n.* The fourth day of the week. [<OE *Wōdnesdæg* day of Woden]

wee (wē) *adj.* **we·er, we·est** Very small; tiny. [<OE *wēg* a quantity]

weed[1] (wēd) *n.* 1 Any unwanted or unsightly plant, esp. one that hinders the growth of cultivated plants. 2 *Informal* **a** Tobacco. **b** A cigarette or cigar. **c** Marihuana; also, a marihuana cigarette. 3 A thin, ungainly person. —*v.t.* 1 To pull up and remove weeds from. 2 To remove (a weed): often with *out.* 3 To remove (anything regarded as harmful or undesirable): with *out.* 4 To rid of anything harmful or undesirable. —*v.i.* 5 To remove weeds, etc. [<OE *wēod*] —**weed′er** *n.*

weed[2] (wēd) *n.* 1 *Usu. pl.* Mourning garb, as that worn by widows. 2 A black band, as of crepe, worn by a man on his hat or sleeve as a token of mourning. [<OE *wæd* garment]

weed·y (wē′dē) *adj.* **weed·i·er, weed·i·est** 1 Abounding in weeds. 2 Of or pertaining to a weed or weeds. 3 Gawky; lanky: a *weedy* youth. —**weed′i·ly** *adv.* —**weed′i·ness** *n.*

week (wēk) *n.* 1 A period of seven successive days, esp. one beginning with Sunday. 2 The period within a week devoted to work: a 35-hour *week.* —**week in, week out** Every week. [<OE *wicu, wice*]

week·day (wēk′dā′) *n.* 1 Any day of the week except Sunday. 2 Any day other than those of the weekend.

week·end (wēk′end′) *n.* The time from Friday evening or Saturday to the following Monday morning. —*adj.* Of, for, or on a weekend. —*v.i.* To pass the weekend. —**week′end′er** *n.*

week·ly (wēk′lē) *adj.* 1 Of, pertaining to, or lasting a week. 2 Done or occurring once a week. 3 Reckoned by the week. —*adv.* 1 Once a week. 2 Every week. —*n. pl.* **·lies** A publication issued once a week.

ween (wēn) *v.t.* & *v.i. Archaic* To suppose; guess; fancy. [<OE *wēnan* think]

weep (wēp) *v.* **wept, weep·ing** *v.i.* 1 To manifest grief or other strong emotion by shedding tears. 2 To mourn; lament: with *for.* 3 To give out or shed liquid in drops. —*v.t.* 4 To weep for; mourn. 5 To shed (tears, or drops of other liquid). —*n.* 1 The act of weeping, or a fit of tears. 2 An exhudation of liquid; moisture. [<OE *wēpan*] —**weep′er** *n.* —**Syn.** *v.* 1 cry, sob. 2 bewail, grieve.

weep·ing (wē′ping) *adj.* 1 That weeps. 2 Having branches that curve downward.

weeping willow A willow, originally from China, noted for its long, drooping branches.

Weeping willow

wee·vil (wē′vəl) *n.* Any of numerous small beetles with elongated snoutlike heads, often having larvae destructive to cotton, grain, fruit, etc. [<OE *wifel* a beetle] —**wee′vil·y, wee′vil·ly** *adj.*

weft (weft) *n.* 1 The cross threads in a web of cloth; woof. 2 A woven fabric; web. [<OE]

weigh (wā) *v.t.* 1 To determine the weight of. 2 To balance or hold in the hand so as to estimate weight. 3 To measure (a quantity or quantities of something) according to weight: with *out.* 4 To consider or evaluate carefully: to *weigh* one's words. 5 To raise or hoist: now only in the phrase **weigh anchor.** —*v.i.* 6 To have a specified weight: She *weighs* ninety pounds. 7 To have influence or importance: The girl's testimony *weighed* heavily with the jury. 8 To be burdensome or oppressive: with *on* or *upon:* What *weighs* on your mind? 9 *Naut.* **a** To raise anchor. **b** To begin to sail. —**weigh down** 1 To press or force down by weight or heaviness. 2 To burden or oppress. —**weigh in** To be weighed before a fight or other athletic contest. [<OE *wegan* weigh, carry, lift] —**weigh′er** *n.*

weight (wāt) *n.* 1 The quality of having heaviness. 2 The measure of this quality, expressed indefinitely or in standard units: Its *weight* is ten pounds. 3 A piece of something, usu. metal, used as a standard unit in weighing: a three-pound *weight.* 4 Any unit of heaviness, as a pound, ounce, etc.; also, a system of such units. 5 *Physics* The force of gravity exerted on any object, equal to the mass of the object multiplied by its acceleration due to gravity. 6 Any mass weighing a definite amount: a four-pound *weight* of flour. 7 Any object having heaviness and used to balance things, exert downward force, etc., as a paperweight, a counterbalance in a machine, a dumbbell for exercising, etc. 8 Burden; pressure: the *weight* of responsibility. 9 Influence; importance; consequence: the great *weight* of this decision. 10 The larger or most valuable part: the *weight* of the data is negative. 11 The comparative heaviness of clothes, as appropriate to the season: summer *weight.* —**carry weight** To be important, significant, influential, etc. —**pull one's weight** To do one's share. —**throw one's weight around** *Informal* To use one's importance or influence in an overbearing or improper manner. —*v.t.* 1 To add weight to; make heavy. 2 To oppress or burden. 3 To adulterate or treat (fabrics or other merchandise) with cheap foreign substances. [<OE *wiht, gewiht*]

weight·less (wāt′lis) *adj.* 1 Having little or no heaviness. 2 Subject to little or no gravitational force. —**weight′less·ly** *adv.* —**weight′less·ness** *n.*

weight·y (wā′tē) *adj.* **weight·i·er, weight·i·est** 1 Having great importance; far-reaching; grave: a *weighty* decision.

2 Having power to move the mind; cogent; influential: a *weighty* argument. 3 Burdensome; onerous. 4 Having great weight; heavy. **—weight'i·ly** *adv.* **—weight'i·ness** *n.* — **Syn. 1** momentous, serious, solemn.

weir (wir) *n.* 1 A dam placed in a stream to raise or divert the water. 2 A fence of twigs, rods, etc., in a stream, used to catch fish. [< OE *werian* dam up]

weird (wird) *adj.* 1 Manifesting or concerned with the supernatural; unearthly; uncanny. 2 Odd; bizarre; fantastic. [< OE *wyrd* fate] **—weird'ly** *adv.* **—weird'ness** *n.*

weird·o (wir'dō) *n. pl.* **·os** *Slang* A person who is strange or eccentric. Also **weird'ie, weird'y** (-dē) (*pl.* **·ies**).

welch (welch, welsh) *v.t.* & *v.i. Slang* WELSH. **—welch'er** *n.*

wel·come (wel'kəm) *adj.* 1 Admitted or received gladly and cordially. 2 Producing satisfaction or pleasure; pleasing: *welcome* tidings. 3 Made free to use or enjoy: She is *welcome* to our car. —*n.* The act of bidding or making welcome; a hearty greeting. **—wear out one's welcome** To come so often or to linger so long as no longer to be welcome. —*v.t.* **·comed, ·com·ing** 1 To greet gladly or hospitably. 2 To receive with pleasure: to *welcome* advice. [< OE *wilcuma*] **—wel'come·ly** *adv.* **—wel'come·ness, wel'·com·er** *n.*

weld (weld) *v.t.* 1 To unite, as two pieces of metal, by the application of heat along the area of contact. 2 To bring into close association or connection. —*v.i.* 3 To be welded or capable of being welded. —*n.* The joining of pieces of metal by welding; also, the closed joint so formed. [Alter. of WELL[1]] **—weld'a·ble** *adj.* **—weld'er** *n.*

wel·fare (wel'fâr) *n.* 1 The condition of being happy, healthy, prosperous, etc.; well-being. 2 WELFARE WORK. 3 Money given to those in need; relief. **—on welfare** Receiving welfare (def. 3) from the government. [< ME *wel* well + *fare* a going]

welfare state A state or social system in which the government assumes a large measure of responsibility for the welfare of its members, as regards employment, health insurance, social security, etc.

welfare work Organized efforts by a government or other organization to improve the economic condition of the needy. **—welfare worker**

wel·kin (wel'kin) *n. Archaic* 1 The vault of the sky; the heavens. 2 The air. [< OE *wolcn, wolcen* a cloud]

well[1] (wel) *n.* 1 A hole or shaft sunk into the earth to obtain a fluid, as water, oil, or natural gas. 2 A place where water issues naturally from the ground. 3 A source of continued supply; fount: a *well* of learning. 4 A depression, cavity, or vessel used to hold or collect a liquid: an *inkwell.* 5 A deep vertical opening descending through floors of a building, as for light, ventilation, stairs, etc. —*v.i.* 1 To pour forth or flow up, as water in a spring. —*v.t.* 2 To gush: Her eyes *welled* tears. [< OE *weallan* boil, bubble up]

well[2] (wel) *adv.* **bet·ter, best** 1 Satisfactorily; favorably: Everything goes *well.* 2 In a good or correct manner; expertly: to dance *well.* 3 Suitably; with propriety: I cannot *well* remain here. 4 Agreeably or luxuriously: He lives *well.* 5 Intimately: How *well* do you know him? 6 To a considerable extent or degree: *well* along in years. 7 Completely; thoroughly; fully: *well* aware. 8 Far: He lagged *well* behind us. 9 Kindly; graciously: to speak *well* of someone. **—as well** 1 Also; in addition. 2 With equal effect or consequence: He might just *as well* have sold it. **—as well as** 1 As satisfactorily as. 2 To the same degree as. 3 In addition to. —*adj.* 1 Suitable, fortunate, right, etc.: It is *well* you called first. 2 In good health. 3 Prosperous; comfortable. —*interj.* An exclamation used to express surprise, expectation, indignation, etc., or to preface a remark. [< OE *wel*] **—Syn.** *adv.* 2 excellently. 3 befittingly, properly. 4 comfortably. • *Well* often appears in combination with participles to form modifiers. When used after a verb such as *be, seem,* etc., such a modifier is written as two words: to be *well satisfied.* When placed before a noun, it must be hyphenated: a *well-kept* secret.

we'll (wēl) Contraction of *we shall* or *we will.*

well-ap·point·ed (wel'ə·poin'tid) *adj.* Properly equipped; excellently furnished.

well·a·way (wel'ə·wā') *interj. Archaic* Woe is me! [< OE *wei lā wei*]

well-bal·anced (wel'bal'ənst) *adj.* 1 Evenly balanced, adjusted, or proportioned. 2 Sound mentally; sensible.

well-be·ing (wel'bē'ing) *n.* A condition of health, happiness, or prosperity.

well·born (wel'bôrn') *adj.* Of good family.

well-bred (wel'bred') *adj.* 1 Well brought up; polite. 2 Of good or pure stock: said of animals.

well-dis·posed (wel'dis·pōzd') *adj.* Favorably or kindly disposed or inclined, as to a person, idea, etc.

well-done (wel'dun') *adj.* 1 Performed skillfully or satisfactorily. 2 Thoroughly cooked.

well-fa·vored (wel'fā'vərd) *adj.* Of attractive appearance; comely; handsome.

well-fed (wel'fed') *adj.* 1 Plump; fat. 2 Properly fed.

well-fixed (wel'fikst') *adj. Informal* Affluent; well-to-do.

well-found (wel'found') *adj.* Well equipped.

well-found·ed (wel'foun'did) *adj.* Based on fact or sound thinking: *well-founded* suspicions.

well-groomed (wel'grōōmd') *adj.* 1 Carefully dressed and scrupulously neat. 2 Carefully curried, as a horse.

well-ground·ed (wel'groun'did) *adj.* 1 Adequately schooled in the elements of a subject. 2 WELL-FOUNDED.

well-heeled (wel'hēld') *adj. Slang* Plentifully supplied with money.

well-known (wel'nōn') *adj.* 1 Widely known. 2 Famous. 3 Thoroughly known.

well-man·nered (wel'man'ərd) *adj.* Courteous; polite.

well-mean·ing (wel'mē'ning) *adj.* 1 Having good intentions. 2 Done with or showing good intentions: also **well'·meant'** (-ment').

well-nigh (wel'nī') *adv.* Very nearly; almost.

well-off (wel'ôf', -of') *adj.* 1 In comfortable circumstances; well-to-do. 2 Fortunate.

well-pre·served (wel'pri·zûrvd') *adj.* Not showing many signs of age.

well-read (wel'red') *adj.* Having a wide knowledge of literature or books; having read much.

well-round·ed (wel'roun'did) *adj.* 1 Having a good and balanced variety of elements: a *well-rounded* education. 2 Having many interests, abilities, etc.: a *well-rounded* person. 3 Fully formed: a *well-rounded* figure.

well-spo·ken (wel'spō'kən) *adj.* 1 Speaking fluently, suitably, or courteously. 2 Fitly or excellently said.

well·spring (wel'spring') *n.* 1 The source of a stream, spring, etc. 2 A source of continual supply.

well-thought-of (wel'thôt'uv', -ov') *adj.* In good repute; esteemed; respected.

well-to-do (wel'tə·dōō') *adj.* In prosperous or wealthy circumstances; affluent.

well-turned (wel'tûrnd') *adj.* 1 Gracefully shaped; shapely. 2 Expressed in a graceful or felicitous manner: a *well-turned* phrase.

well-wish·er (wel'wish'ər) *n.* One who wishes well, as to another. **—well'-wish'ing** *adj., n.*

welsh (welsh, welch) *v.t. & v.i. Slang* To fail to pay a debt or fulfill an obligation. [?] **—welsh'er** *n.*

Welsh (welsh, welch) *adj.* Pertaining to Wales, its people, or their language. —*n.* 1 The people of Wales. 2 The Celtic language of Wales.

Welsh·man (welsh'mən, welch'-) *n. pl.* **·men** (-mən) A native or citizen of Wales.

Welsh rabbit Melted cheese cooked with milk, ale, or beer and served hot on toast or crackers. • The form *rarebit* was a later development and is the result of mistaken etymology.

welt (welt) *n.* 1 A raised mark on the skin, resulting from a blow or lashing; wale. 2 A strip of material, covered cord, etc., applied to a seam to cover or strengthen it. 3 In shoemaking, a strip of leather set into the seam between the edges of the upper and the outer sole. —*v.t.* 1 To sew a welt on or in; decorate with a welt. 2 *Informal* To flog severely, so as to raise welts. [ME *welte*]

wel·ter (wel'tər) *v.i.* 1 To roll about; wallow. 2 To lie or be soaked in some fluid, as blood. —*n.* 1 A rolling movement, as of waves. 2 A turmoil; commotion. [< MDu. *welteren*]

wel·ter·weight (wel'tər·wāt') *n.* A boxer or wrestler whose weight is between 136 and 147 pounds. [< earlier *welter* a heavyweight + WEIGHT]

Welt·schmerz (velt′shmerts) *n.* Weariness of life; melancholy. [G, lit., world pain]

wen (wen) *n.* A cyst containing sebaceous matter, occurring on the skin, esp. on the scalp. [< OE *wenn*]

wench (wench) *n. Archaic* **1** A young woman; girl: now a humorous usage. **2** A young peasant woman; also, a female servant. **3** A prostitute; strumpet. [< OE *wencel* a child, servant]

wend (wend) *v.* **wend·ded** (*Archaic* **went**), **wend·ing** *v.t.* **1** To go on (one's way); proceed. —*v.i.* **2** *Archaic* To proceed; go. [< OE *wendan*]

went (went) *p.t.* of GO.

wept (wept) *p.t. & p.p.* of WEEP.

were (wûr, *unstressed* wər) Plural and second person singular past indicative, and past subjunctive singular and plural of BE. [< OE *wære, wæron*]

we're (wir) Contraction of *we are.*

wer·en't (wûrnt, wûr′ənt) Contraction of *were not.*

were·wolf (wir′wo͝olf′, wûr′-) *n. pl.* **·wolves** (-wo͝olvz′) In European folklore, a person changed into a wolf or having power to assume wolf form at will. Also **wer′wolf′**. [< OE *werwulf* man-wolf]

wert (wûrt, *unstressed* wərt) *Archaic* Were: used with *thou.*

west (west) *n.* **1** The general direction in which the sun appears at sunset. **2** The point of the compass at 270°, directly opposite east. **3** Any region lying in this direction. —**the West 1** The countries lying west of Asia and Asia Minor, including Europe and the Western Hemisphere; the Occident. **2** In the U.S.: **a** Formerly, the region west of the Allegheny Mountains. **b** The region west of the Mississippi, esp. the NW part of this region. **3** The noncommunist countries of Europe and the Western Hemisphere. —*adj.* **1** To, toward, facing, or in the west; western. **2** Coming from the west: the *west* wind. —*adv.* In or toward the west; in a westerly direction. [< OE]

west·er·ly (wes′tər·lē) *adj. & adv.* **1** In, toward, or of the west. **2** From the west. —**west′er·li·ness** *n.*

west·ern (wes′tərn) *adj.* **1** Of, in, directed toward, or facing the west. **2** From the west. —*n. Often cap.* A type of fiction or motion picture using cowboy and pioneer life in the western U.S. as its material.

West·ern (wes′tərn) *adj.* **1** Of, from, or characteristic of the West. **2** Belonging or pertaining to the Roman Catholic Church, as distinguished from the Eastern Orthodox Church.

west·ern·er (wes′tər·nər) *n.* **1** One who is native to or dwells in the west. **2** *Usu. cap.* One who is native to or dwells in the western U.S.

Western Hemisphere See HEMISPHERE.

west·ern·ize (wes′tər·nīz) *v.t.* **·ized, ·iz·ing** To make western in characteristics, habits, etc. —**west′ern·i·za′tion** *n.*

Western Roman Empire The part of the Roman Empire W of the Adriatic, which existed as a separate empire from 395 until the fall of Rome in 476.

Western Sa·mo·a (sə·mō′ə) An independent state located in the W part of the islands of Samoa, 1,133 sq. mi., cap. Apia.

West Germany See GERMANY.

West·min·ster Abbey (west′min′stər) A Gothic church in Westminster, London, where English monarchs are crowned and many notable persons are buried.

west-north·west (west′nôrth′west′, *in nautical usage* west′nôr·west′) *n.* The direction midway between west and northwest. —*adj. & adv.* In, toward, or from this direction.

west-south·west (west′south′west′, *in nautical usage* west′sou·west′) *n.* The direction midway between west and southwest. —*adj. & adv.* In, toward, or from this direction.

west·ward (west′wərd) *adj. & adv.* Toward the west. —*n.* A westward direction or region.

west·wards (west′wərdz) *adv.* WESTWARD.

wet (wet) *adj.* **wet·ter, wet·test 1** Moistened, saturated, or covered with water or other liquid. **2** Marked by showers or by heavy rainfall; rainy. **3** Not yet dry: *wet* varnish. **4** Permitting the manufacture and sale of alcoholic beverages: a *wet* county. **5** Preserved or bottled in a liquid. —**all wet** *Slang* Quite wrong; mistaken. —*n.* **1** Water; moisture; wetness. **2** Showery or rainy weather. **3** *Informal* One opposed to prohibition. —*v.t. & v.i.* **wet** or **wet·ted, wet·ting** To make or become wet. [< OE *wæt*] —**wet′ly** *adv.* —**wet′ness, wet′ter** *n.* —**Syn.** *v.* dampen, moisten, soak.

wet·back (wet′bak′) *n. Informal* A Mexican who enters the U.S. illegally, esp. by swimming or wading across the Rio Grande.

wet blanket One who or that which discourages any proceedings.

wet dream *Informal* A male's involuntary expulsion of semen during sleep, usu. accompanying an erotic dream.

weth·er (weth′ər) *n.* A castrated ram. [< OE]

wet·land (wet′land′) *n. Usu. pl.* Swamps, marshes, and other land areas with heavy soil moisture.

wet nurse A woman who is hired to suckle the child of another woman.

wet pack A therapeutic method consisting of wrapping the patient in wet sheets.

wet suit A skin-tight rubber garment worn by divers, surfers, etc., to retain body warmth in cold waters.

we've (wēv) Contraction of *we have.*

wf, w.f. wrong font (printing).

wh, wh., whr, whr., w.-hr. watt-hour(s).

whack (hwak) *v.t. & v.i. Informal* To strike sharply; beat; hit. —*n.* **1** *Informal* A sharp, resounding blow. **2** *Slang* A share; portion. —**have** (or **take**) **a whack at** *Slang* **1** To give a blow to. **2** To have a chance or turn at. —**out of whack** *Slang* Out of order. [?] —**whack′er** *n.*

whack·ing (hwak′ing) *adj. Chiefly Brit. Informal* Strikingly large; whopping.

whale[1] (hwāl) *n.* **1** Any of various very large, air-breathing marine mammals of fishlike form. **2** *Informal* Something extremely good or large: a *whale* of a party. —*v.i.* **whaled, whal·ing** To engage in the hunting of whales. [< OE *hwæl*]

Blue whale

whale[2] (hwāl) *v.t.* **whaled, whal·ing** *Informal* To beat; thrash; flog. [Prob. var. of WALE]

whale·back (hwāl′bak′) *n.* A freight steamer having a rounded bow and main deck, used on the Great Lakes.

whale·boat (hwāl′bōt′) *n.* A long, deep rowboat, sharp at both ends.

whale·bone (hwāl′bōn′) *n.* **1** The horny, pliable substance hanging in plates from the upper jaw of certain whales. **2** A strip of whalebone, used in stiffening corsets, etc.

whal·er (hwā′lər) *n.* A person or a ship engaged in whaling.

whal·ing (hwā′ling) *n.* The industry of capturing whales. —*adj. Slang* Huge; whopping.

wham·my (hwam′ē) *n. pl.* **·mies** *Slang* A jinx; hex: usu. in the phrase **put a** (or **the**) **whammy on.** [< *wham,* informal interjection imit. of the sound of a hard blow]

wharf (hwôrf) *n. pl.* **wharves** (hwôrvz) or **wharfs 1** A structure of masonry or timber erected on the shore of a harbor, river, etc., alongside which vessels may lie to load or unload cargo, passengers, etc. **2** Any pier or dock. —*v.t.* **1** To moor to a wharf. **2** To deposit or store on a wharf. [< OE *hwearf* a dam]

wharf·age (hwôr′fij) *n.* **1** Charge for the use of a wharf. **2** Wharf accommodations for shipping.

wharf rat 1 A rat that inhabits wharves. **2** *Slang* One who loiters about wharves, esp. with criminal intent.

what (hwot, hwut) *pron.* **1** Which specific act, thing, name, value, etc.: *What* is going on? *What* is that? **2** That which: *What* followed is a mystery. **3** How much: *What* will it cost? —**and what not** And so forth. —**but what** But that. —**what have you** What is similar or need not be mentioned. —**what if** Suppose that. —**what's what** *Informal* The actual state of affairs. —**what with** Taking into consideration. —*adj.* **1** Which or which kind of: I know *what* things I want. **2** How surprising, great, etc.: *What* a genius! **3** How much: *What* cash has he? **4** Whatever: Take *what* books you may need. *—adv.* How or how much: *What* do you care? *—interj.* An expression of surprise, annoyance, etc.: *What!* They stole it! [<OE *hwæt*]

what·ev·er (hwot'ev'ər, hwut'-) *pron.* **1** Anything that: Say *whatever* you want to say. **2** No matter what: *Whatever* you cook will be good. **3** *Informal* What: usu. interrogative: *Whatever* are you doing? *—adj.* **1** No matter what or which: *Whatever* things are left, you can keep. **2** Of any kind, amount, etc.: He has no ability *whatever.*

what·not (hwot'not', hwut'-) *n.* An ornamental set of shelves for holding bric-a-brac, etc.

what·so·ev·er (hwot'sō·ev'ər, hwut'-) *pron. & adj.* Whatever: a slightly more formal usage.

wheal (hwēl) *n.* A small raised area or pimple on the skin. [Alter. of WALE]

wheat (hwēt) *n.* **1** Any of a genus of cereal grasses, esp. cultivated species yielding spikes of edible grain. **2** Grains of these species collectively, constituting a staple food usu. ground into flour.

Wheat a. bearded. b. beardless. c. grain: front and back of b.

wheat·en (hwēt'n) *adj.* **1** Made of wheat. **2** Having the pale gold color of ripe wheat.

wheat germ The embryo of the wheat kernel, used as a vitamin source.

whee·dle (hwēd'l) *v.* **·dled, ·dling** *v.t.* **1** To persuade or try to persuade by flattery, cajolery, etc.; coax. **2** To obtain by cajoling or coaxing. *—v.i.* **3** To use flattery or cajolery. [?] **—whee'dler** *n.* **—whee'dling·ly** *adv.*

wheel (hwēl) *n.* **1** A solid disk or a circular rim connected to a hub by spokes or rays capable of rotating on a central axis and used to facilitate movement, as in vehicles, or to act with a rotary motion, as in machines. **2** Anything resembling or suggestive of a wheel. **3** An instrument or device having a wheel or wheels as its distinctive characteristic, as a steering wheel, a potter's wheel, a water wheel, etc. **4** *Informal* A bicycle. **5** An old instrument of torture or execution, consisting of a wheel to which the limbs of the victim were tied and then stretched or broken. **6** A turning or rotating movement; revolution. **7** *Usu. pl.* That which imparts or directs motion or controls activity: the *wheels* of democracy. **8** *Slang* A person of influence or authority: also **big wheel. 9** *pl. Slang* An automobile. **—at** (or **behind**) **the wheel 1** Steering a motor vehicle, motor boat, etc. **2** In charge or in control. *—v.t.* **1** To move or convey on wheels. **2** To cause to turn on or as on an axis; pivot or revolve. **3** To perform with a circular movement. **4** To provide with a wheel or wheels. *—v.i.* **5** To turn on or as on an axis; pivot. **6** To change one's course of action, attitudes, opinions, etc.: often with *about.* **7** To move in a circular or spiral course. **8** To move on wheels. **—wheel and deal** *Slang* To act freely, aggressively, and often unscrupulously, as in the arrangement of a business or political deal. [<OE *hwēol*]

wheel·bar·row (hwēl'bar'ō) *n.* A boxlike vehicle ordinarily with one wheel and two handles, for moving small loads. *—v.t.* To convey in a wheelbarrow.

wheel·base (hwēl'bās') *n.* The distance separating the axles of the front and rear wheels, as an automobile, etc.

wheel·chair (hwēl'châr') *n.* A mobile chair mounted between large wheels, for the use of invalids. Also **wheel chair.**

wheel·er (hwē'lər) *n.* **1** One who wheels. **2** WHEELHORSE (def. 1). **3** Something furnished with a wheel or wheels: a *side-wheeler.*

wheel·er-deal·er (hwē'lər·dē'lər) *n. Slang* One who wheels and deals. **—wheel'er-deal'er·ing** *n.*

wheel·horse (hwēl'hôrs') *n.* **1** A horse harnessed next to the front wheels and behind other horses. **2** A person who works hard and dependably.

wheel·house (hwēl'hous') *n.* PILOTHOUSE.

wheel·wright (hwēl'rīt') *n.* A man whose business is making or repairing wheels.

wheeze (hwēz) *v.t. & v.i.* **wheezed, wheez·ing** To breathe or utter with a husky, whistling sound. *—n.* **1** A wheezing sound. **2** *Informal* A trite joke. [Prob. <ON *hvæsa* hiss] **—wheez'er, wheez'i·ness** *n.* **—wheez'i·ly, wheez'ing·ly** *adv.* **—wheez'y** *adj.* **(·i·er, ·i·est)**

whelk[1] (hwelk) *n.* Any of various large, spiral-shelled, marine snails, some of which are edible. [<OE *weoloc*]

Common whelk

whelk[2] (hwelk) *n.* A pimple or pustule. [<OE *hwelian* suppurate]

whelm (hwelm) *v.t.* **1** To submerge. **2** To overpower; overwhelm. [ME *whelmen*]

whelp (hwelp) *n.* **1** One of the young of a dog, wolf, lion, or certain other carnivores. **2** A dog. **3** A worthless young fellow. *—v.t. & v.i.* To give birth (to): said of certain carnivores. [<OE *hwelp*]

when (hwen) *adv.* **1** At what or which time: *When* did you arrive? **2** Under what circumstances: *When* do I apply the brake? **3** At an earlier time: I knew them *when. —conj.* **1** At which: the time *when* we went on the picnic. **2** At which or what time: They watched till midnight, *when* they fell asleep. **3** As soon as: He laughed *when* he heard it. **4** Although: He walks *when* he might ride. **5** At the time that; while: *when* we were young. **6** If it should happen that: An employee is fired *when* he is caught stealing. **7** After which; then: We had just awakened *when* you called. **8** Considering that: Why bother to ask me *when* you already know the answer? *—pron.* What or which time: since *when;* till *when. —n.* The time; date: to know the *when* and why of something. [<OE *hwanne, hwænne*]

whence (hwens) *adv.* From what place or source: *Whence* does he come? *—conj.* From what or out of which place, source, or cause: asked *whence* these sounds arise. [<OE *hwanne* when]

whence·so·ev·er (hwens'sō·ev'ər) *adv. & conj.* From whatever place, cause, or source.

when·ev·er (hwen'ev'ər) *adv. & conj.* At whatever time.

when·so·ev·er (hwen'sō·ev'ər) *adv. & conj.* WHENEVER.

where (hwâr) *adv.* **1** At or in what place, respect, or situation: *Where* is my book? *Where* am I at fault? **2** To what place or end. *Where* is this getting us? **3** From what place or source: *Where* did you get that hat? *—conj.* **1** At, in, or to which or what place: I know the hotel *where* they are. **2** At, in, or to the place, position, or situation in which: They are living *where* they are happiest. *—pron.* The place in which: from *where* we stood. *—n.* Place; locality. [<OE *hwǣr*]

where·a·bouts (hwâr'ə·bouts') *adv.* Near or at what place; about where. *—n.pl. (construed as sing. or pl.)* The place in which a person or thing is.

where·as (hwâr'az') *conj.* **1** Since the facts are such as they are; seeing that: often used in the preamble of a resolution, etc. **2** While on the contrary; when in truth. *—n. pl.* **·as·es** A clause or item beginning with the word "whereas."

where·at (hwâr'at') *adv. Archaic* At what: *Whereat* are you angry? *—conj.* At which point.

where·by (hwâr'bī') *adv. Archaic* By what; how. *—conj.* By which: a plan *whereby* we will win.

wher·e'er (hwâr'âr') *adj. & conj.* WHEREVER.

where·fore (hwâr'fôr', -fōr') *adv. Archaic* For what reason; why: *Wherefore* didst thou doubt? *—conj.* **1** For which. **2** THEREFORE. *—n.* The cause; reason: the whys and *wherefores.* [<WHERE + FOR]

where·from (hwâr'frum', -from') *adv. & conj.* From which.

where·in (hwâr'in') *adv.* In what way or regard: *Wherein* is the error? *—conj.* In which: a state *wherein* there is discord.

where·of (hwâr'uv', -ov') *adv. & conj.* Of which, whom, or what.

where·on (hwâr'on', -ôn') *adv. Archaic* On what or whom. *—conj.* On which: land *whereon* to build.

where·so·ev·er (hwâr'sō·ev'ər) *adv. & conj.* In, at, or to whatever place; wherever.

where·to (hwâr'tōō') *Archaic adv.* To what place or end. *—conj.* To which or to whom. Also **where'un·to'.**

where·up·on (hwâr'ə·pon', -ə·pôn') *adv. Archaic* Upon

what; whereon. —*conj.* Upon which or whom; in consequence of which; after which: *whereupon* they took in sail.

wher·ev·er (ʰwâr′ev′ər) *adv.* & *conj.* In, at, or to whatever place or situation.

where·with (ʰwâr′wit͟h′, -with′) *adv. Archaic* With what: *Wherewith* shall I do it? —*conj.* With which; by means of which: *wherewith* we abated hunger. —*pron.* That with or by which: used with an infinitive: I have not *wherewith* to do it.

where·with·al (ʰwâr′wit͟h·ôl′, -with-) *n.* The necessary means or resources, esp. money: used with *the.*

wher·ry (ʰwer′ē) *n. pl.* **·ries** 1 A light, fast rowboat built for one person and used for racing or exercise. 2 *Brit.* A very broad, light barge. —*v.t.* & *v.i.* **·ried, ·ry·ing** To transport in or use a wherry. [?]

whet (ʰwet) *v.t.* **whet·ed, whet·ting** 1 To sharpen, as a knife, by friction. 2 To make more keen or eager; excite; stimulate, as the appetite. —*n.* 1 The act of whetting. 2 Something that whets. [<OE *hwettan*] **—whet′ter** *n.*

wheth·er (ʰwet͟h′ər) *conj.* 1 If it be the case that: Tell us *whether* you are going or not. 2 In case; if: *whether* he lived or died, we never heard. 3 Either: He came in first, *whether* by luck or plan. **—whether or no** Regardless; in any case. [<OE *hwæther*]

whet·stone (ʰwet′stōn′) *n.* A fine-grained stone for whetting knives, axes, etc.

whew (ʰwyōō) *interj.* An exclamation of amazement, dismay, relief, etc.

whey (ʰwā) *n.* A clear liquid that separates from the curd when milk is curdled, as in making cheese. [<OE *hwæg*] **—whey′ey, whey′ish** *adj.*

whf. wharf.

which (ʰwich) *pron.* 1 What specific one or ones: *Which* are for sale? 2 The specific one or ones that: I know *which* I bought. 3 The thing, animal, or event designated earlier: used restrictively or nonrestrictively: The flood *which* wiped us out was last year; That car, *which* is not old, no longer runs. 4 *Archaic* The person or persons designated earlier: "Our Father, *which* art in heaven," 5 WHICHEVER: Use *which* you find most convenient. 6 A thing, situation, or fact that: He decided to go, *which* was lucky. —*adj.* 1 What specific one or ones: *Which* play did you see? 2 WHICHEVER: Take *which* one you want. 3 Being the one or ones designated earlier: The clock struck one, at *which* point he left. • See WHO. [<OE *hwelc, hwilc*]

which·ev·er (ʰwich′ev′ər) *pron.* & *adj.* 1 Any one (of two or of several): Select *whichever* (ring) you want. 2 No matter which: *Whichever* (song) you choose, sing it well. Also **which′so·ev′er.**

whiff (ʰwif) *n.* 1 A slight gust or puff of air. 2 A gust or puff of odor: a *whiff* of onions. 3 A sudden expulsion of breath or smoke from the mouth; a puff. —*v.t.* 1 To drive or blow with a whiff or puff. 2 To smoke, as a pipe. —*v.i.* 3 To blow or move in whiffs or puffs. 4 To exhale or inhale whiffs. [Imit.] **—whiff′er** *n.*

whif·fet (ʰwif′it) *n. Informal* 1 A trifling, useless person. 2 A small, snappish dog. [?]

whif·fle (ʰwif′əl) *v.* **·fled, ·fling** *v.i.* 1 To blow with puffs or gusts, as the wind. 2 To vacillate; veer. —*v.t.* 3 To blow or dissipate with a puff. [Freq. of WHIFF] **—whif′fler** *n.*

whif·fle·tree (ʰwif′əl·trē′) *n.* A horizontal crossbar, to the ends of which the traces of a harness are attached. [Var. of WHIPPLETREE]

Whig (ʰwig) *n.* 1 An American colonist who supported the Revolutionary War in the 18th century. 2 A member of an American political party opposed to the Democratic and succeeded by the Republican party in 1856. 3 A member of a political party (later the Liberal party) in England in the 18th and 19th centuries. —*adj.* Belonging to, consisting of, or supported by the Whigs. [Prob. short for *Whiggamore,* one of a body of 17th cent. Scottish insurgents] **—Whig′ger·y, Whig′gism** *n.* **—Whig′gish** *adj.*

while (ʰwīl) *n.* A period of time: a brief *while.* **—between whiles** From time to time. **—the while** At the same time. **—worth (one's) while** Worth one's time, labor, trouble, etc. —*conj.* 1 During the time that. 2 At the same time that; although: *While* he found fault, he also praised. 3 Whereas: This man is short, *while* that one is tall. —*v.t.* **whiled, whil·ing** To cause to pass pleasantly: usu. with *away:* to *while* away the time. [<OE *hwīl*]

whiles (ʰwīlz) *Archaic* or *Regional adv.* Occasionally; at intervals. —*conj.* WHILE.

whi·lom (ʰwī′ləm) *Archaic adj.* FORMER. —*adv.* FORMERLY. [<OE *hwīlum* at times < *hwīl* a while]

whilst (ʰwīlst) *conj. Chiefly Brit.* WHILE.

whim (ʰwim) *n.* A sudden, capricious idea, notion, or desire; fancy. [Short for earlier *whim-wham* a trifle]

whim·per (ʰwim′pər) *v.i.* 1 To cry with plaintive broken sounds. —*v.t.* 2 To utter with or as if with a whimper. —*n.* A low, broken, whining cry. [Imit.] **—whim′per·er** *n.* **—whim′per·ing·ly** *adv.*

whim·si·cal (ʰwim′zi·kəl) *adj.* 1 Capricious; fanciful; unpredictable. 2 Odd; fantastic; quaint. **—whim·si·cal′i·ty** (-kal′ə·tē) (*pl.* **·ties**), **whim′si·cal·ness** *n.* **—whim′si·cal·ly** *adv.*

whim·sy (ʰwim′zē) *n. pl.* **·sies** 1 A whim; caprice. 2 Humor that is somewhat odd, fanciful, or quaint. Also **whim′sey.** [Prob. related to WHIM]

whine (ʰwīn) *v.* **whined, whin·ing** *v.i.* 1 To utter a high, plaintive, nasal sound expressive of grief or distress. 2 To complain in a fretful or childish way. 3 To make a steady, high-pitched sound, as a machine. —*v.t.* 4 To utter with a whine. —*n.* The act or sound of whining. [<OE *hwīnan* whiz] **—whin′er** *n.* **—whin′ing·ly** *adv.* **—whin′y** *adj.*

whin·ny (ʰwin′ē) *v.* **·nied, ·ny·ing** *v.i.* 1 To neigh, esp. in a low or gentle way. —*v.t.* 2 To express with a whinny. —*n. pl.* **·nies** A low, gentle neigh. [<WHINE]

whip (ʰwip) *v.* **whipped, whip·ping** *v.t.* 1 To strike with a lash, rod, strap, etc. 2 To punish by striking thus; flog. 3 To drive or urge with lashes or blows: with *on, up, off,* etc. 4 To strike in the manner of a whip: The wind *whipped* the trees. 5 To beat, as eggs or cream, to a froth. 6 To seize, move, jerk, throw, etc., with a sudden motion: with *away, in, off, out,* etc. 7 In fishing, to make repeated casts upon the surface of (a stream, etc.). 8 To wrap or bind about something. 9 To sew, as a flat seam, with a loose overcast or overhand stitch. 10 *Informal* To defeat; overcome, as in a contest. —*v.i.* 11 To go, move, or turn suddenly and quickly: with *away, in, off, out,* etc. 12 To thrash about in the manner of a whip: pennants *whipping* in the wind. 13 In fishing, to make repeated casts with rod and line. **—whip up** 1 To excite; arouse. 2 *Informal* To prepare quickly, as a meal. —*n.* 1 An instrument consisting of a lash attached to a handle, used for discipline or punishment. 2 A whipping or thrashing motion. 3 A member of a legislative body, as congress or parliament, appointed unofficially to enforce discipline, attendance, etc.: also **party whip.** 4 A dessert containing whipped cream or beaten egg whites, flavoring, sometimes fruit, etc. [ME *wippen*] **—Syn.** *v.* 1 beat, scourge, switch, thrash.

whip·cord (ʰwip′kôrd′) *n.* 1 A strong, hard-twisted cord, used in making whiplashes. 2 A twill fabric with a pronounced diagonal rib.

whip hand 1 The hand in which a person holds the whip while driving. 2 A position or means of advantage.

whip·lash (ʰwip′lash′) *n.* 1 The flexible striking part of a whip. 2 An injury to the neck, due to a sudden snapping back and forth of the head, as in automobile accidents: also **whiplash injury.**

whip·per·snap·per (ʰwip′ər·snap′ər) *n.* A pretentious but insignificant person, esp. a young person. [?]

whip·pet (ʰwip′it) *n.* A swift dog resembling an English greyhound in miniature, used in racing, etc. [?< WHIP]

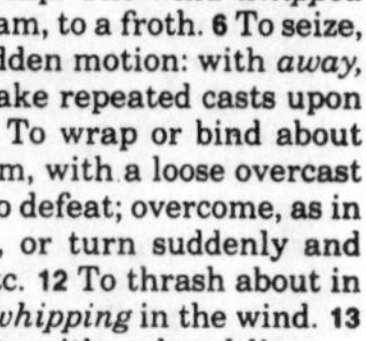

Whippet

whip·ping (ʰwip′ing) *n.* 1 The act of one who or that which whips; esp. a punishment by flogging. 2 Material, as cord or twine, used to whip or bind.

whipping boy Anyone who receives blame deserved by another; scapegoat.

whipping post The fixture to which those sentenced to flogging are secured.

whip·ple·tree (ʰwip′əl·trē′) *n.* WHIFFLETREE.

whip·poor·will (ʰwip′ər·wil) *n.* A small nocturnal bird, allied to the goatsuckers, common in E North America. [Imit.]

whip·saw (ʰwip′sô′) *n.* A thin, narrow, two-man ripsaw. —*v.t.* **·sawed, ·sawed** or **·sawn, ·saw·ing** 1 To saw with a whipsaw. 2 To beat (an opponent) in two ways at the same time.

whip·stitch (ʰwip′stich′) *v.t.* To sew or gather with overcast stitches. —*n.* An overcast stitch.

whip·stock (ʰwip′stok′) *n.* A whip handle.

whir (ʰwûr) *v.t. & v.i.* **whirred, whir·ring** To fly or move with a buzzing sound. —*n.* 1 A whizzing, swishing sound. 2 Confusion; bustle. Also **whirr.** [Prob. < Scand.]

whirl (ʰwûrl) *v.i.* 1 To turn or revolve rapidly, as about a center. 2 To turn away or aside quickly. 3 To move or go swiftly. 4 To have a sensation of spinning: My head *whirls.* —*v.t.* 5 To cause to turn or revolve rapidly. 6 To carry or bear along with a revolving motion. —*n.* 1 A swift rotating or revolving motion. 2 Something whirling. 3 A state of confusion. 4 A round of activities, social events, etc. 5 *Informal* A short drive. 6 *Informal* A try. [Prob. < ON *hvirfla* revolve] —**whirl′er** *n.*

whirl·i·gig (ʰwûr′lə·gig′) *n.* 1 Any toy that spins. 2 A merry-go-round. 3 Anything that moves in a cycle. 4 A whirling motion. 5 Any of certain water beetles that move on the water in swift circles: also **whirligig beetle.** [< WHIRL + GIG]

whirl·pool (ʰwûrl′pōōl′) *n.* 1 An eddy or vortex where water moves in a rapid whirling motion, as from the meeting of two currents. 2 Anything resembling a whirlpool, esp. in movement.

whirl·wind (ʰwûrl′wind′) *n.* 1 A forward-moving column of air, with a rapid circular and upward spiral motion. 2 Anything resembling a whirlwind in movement, energy, or violence. —*adj.* Extremely swift or impetuous: a *whirlwind* courtship.

whish (ʰwish) *v.i.* To make or move with a whizzing sound. —*n.* Such a sound. [Imit.]

whisk (ʰwisk) *v.t.* 1 To brush or sweep off lightly: often with *away* or *off.* 2 To cause to move with a quick sweeping motion. 3 To beat with a quick movement, as eggs, cream, etc. —*v.i.* 4 To move quickly and lightly. —*n.* 1 A light sweeping or whipping movement. 2 A little bunch of straw, feathers, etc. for brushing. 3 A culinary instrument of wire loops for whipping (cream, etc.). [Prob. < Scand.]

whisk·broom (ʰwisk′brōōm′, -brŏŏm′) *n.* A small, short-handled broom for brushing clothing, etc.

whisk·er (ʰwis′kər) *n.* 1 *pl.* The hair of a man's beard, esp. the hair that grows on the cheeks. 2 A hair from the whiskers. 3 One of the long, bristly hairs near the mouth of some animals, as the cat, mouse, etc. [< WHISK] —**whisk′·ered, whisk′er·y** *adj.*

whis·key (ʰwis′kē) *n. pl.* **·keys** or **·kies** 1 An alcoholic liquor obtained by the distillation of a fermented mash of grain, as rye, corn, barley, or wheat. 2 A drink of whiskey. —*adj.* Pertaining to or made of whiskey. Also **whis′ky.** [< Ir. *uisce beathadh,* lit., water of life] • In the U.S. and Ireland, *whiskey* is usu. spelled with an *e.* Scotch and Canadian *whisky,* however, are traditionally spelled without the *e.*

whis·per (ʰwis′pər) *n.* 1 An act or instance of breathy speech with little or no vibration of the vocal chords. 2 An utterance made with such speech. 3 A secret communication; hint; insinuation. 4 Any low, rustling sound. —*v.i.* 1 To speak in a low, breathy way with little or no vibration of the vocal chords. 2 To talk cautiously or furtively; plot or gossip. 3 To make a low, rustling sound, as leaves. —*v.t.* 4 To utter in a whisper. 5 To speak to in a whisper. [< OE *hwisprian*] —**whis′per·er** *n.* —**whis′per·ing·ly** *adv.* —**whis′·per·y** *adj.*

whispering campaign An organized effort to discredit a person, group, cause, etc., by rumors and gossip.

whist (ʰwist) *n.* A game of cards from which bridge developed, played by four persons with a full pack of 52 cards. [Alter. of earlier *whisk*]

whis·tle (ʰwis′əl) *v.* **·tled, ·tling** *v.i.* 1 To make a sound by sending the breath through the teeth or through puckered lips. 2 To make a sharp, shrill sound by forcing air, steam, etc., through a small opening. 3 To make a similar sound by swift passage through the air, as bullets, the wind, etc. 4 To make a shrill cry, as certain animals or birds. 5 To blow or sound a whistle. —*v.t.* 6 To produce (a tune) by whistling. 7 To call, manage, or direct by whistling. —*n.* 1 An instrument for making whistling sounds: a train *whistle;* a toy *whistle.* 2 A whistling sound. 3 The act of whistling. —**wet one's whistle** *Slang* To take a drink. [< OE *hwistlian* a shrill pipe] —**whis′tler** *n.*

whis·tle-stop (ʰwis′əl·stop′) *Informal v.i.* **-stopped, -stop·ping** To make whistle stops, esp. as part of a political campaign.

whistle stop *Informal* 1 A small town, at which formerly a train stopped only on signal. 2 Any of a series of brief stops at small communities during a tour, esp. one made by a political candidate.

whit (ʰwit) *n.* The smallest particle; speck: usu. with a negative: not a *whit* abashed. [< OE *(ænig) wiht* a little amount] —**Syn.** bit, grain, iota, jot, shred.

white (ʰwīt) *adj.* **whit·er, whit·est** 1 Having the color produced by reflection of all the rays of the solar spectrum, as the color of pure snow. 2 Light or comparatively light in color: *white* wine. 3 Bloodless; ashen: *white* with rage. 4 Very fair; blond. 5 Silvery or gray, as with age. 6 Snowy. 7 Wearing white clothing: *white* nuns. 8 Not malicious or harmful: a *white* lie. 9 Innocent; pure. 10 Unmarked by ink or print; blank. 11 Having a light-colored skin; Caucasian. 12 Of, pertaining to, or controlled by Caucasians: the *white* power structure. 13 *Informal* Fair; straightforward; honest. 14 *Music* Of, pertaining to, or being a tonal quality having accuracy of pitch but lacking resonance, color, and warmth. —*n.* 1 A white color. 2 The state or condition of being white; whiteness. 3 The white or light-colored part of something; esp., the albumen of an egg, or the white part of the eyeball. 4 Anything that is white or nearly white, as cloth, white wine, etc. 5 *pl.* A white uniform or outfit: the summer *whites* of the Navy. 6 A Caucasian. —*v.t.* **whit·ed, whit·ing** To make white; whiten. [< OE *hwīt*] —**white′ly** *adv.* —**white′ness** *n.*

white ant TERMITE.

white·bait (ʰwīt′bāt′) *n.* The young of various fishes, esp. of sprat and herring, served as a delicacy.

white birch A North American birch with white bark that peels off in papery sheets.

white·cap (ʰwīt′kap′) *n.* A wave with foam on its crest.

white cedar 1 A strong-scented evergreen tree of the cypress family, having small, scalelike leaves and growing in moist places. 2 Its soft, easily worked wood.

white clover A common variety of clover, with white flowers.

white coal Water power.

white-col·lar (ʰwīt′kol′ər) *adj.* Of, pertaining to, or designating usu. salaried employees, as office personnel, whose work does not often expose their clothes to soil or stain, thus enabling them to wear garments, as white shirts, etc., that are easily stained.

white corpuscle LEUKOCYTE.

whited sepulcher A corrupt or evil person who pretends to be good; hypocrite.

white elephant 1 A rare pale-gray variety of Asian elephant held sacred in E Asia. 2 Anything that is a burden and an expense to maintain.

white feather A symbol of cowardice. —**show the white feather** To show cowardice.

white·fish (ʰwīt′fish′) *n. pl.* **·fish** or **·fish·es** 1 Any of various silvery North American food fishes, living mostly in lakes. 2 Any of various other whitish or silvery fishes.

white flag A white flag or banner used as a signal of surrender.

white gold Gold alloyed with a white metal, usu. nickel and zinc, sometimes palladium, which gives the gold a platinumlike appearance.

white heat 1 The temperature at which metal, etc., becomes white with heat. 2 A state of intense emotion, enthusiasm, etc.

white-hot (ʰwīt′hot′) *adj.* So hot as to glow with white light.

White House, The **1** The official residence of the president of the U.S., at Washington, D.C. **2** The executive branch of the U.S. government.

white lead A poisonous white pigment composed of lead carbonate and hydrated lead oxide.

white lie A harmless, trivial lie.

white matter The whitish portion of the brain and spinal cord that is composed mainly of nerve fibers.

white meat Any light-colored meat, as the breast of chicken, turkey, etc.

whit·en (^{h}wīt′n) *v.t. & v.i.* To make or become white or nearly white. —**whit′en·er** *n.* —**Syn.** blanch, bleach.

white noise Noise in which the average intensity at any frequency between two stated limits is constant.

white oak **1** Any of numerous oaks having gray or whitish bark. **2** The wood of any white oak.

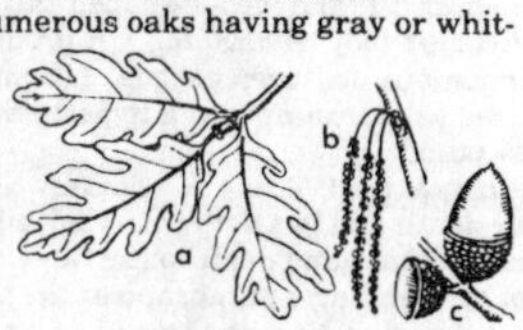

White oak
a. leaves. b. blossom. c. acorn.

white pepper Pepper ground from the white seeds inside black peppercorns.

white pine **1** A pine of E North America, with soft, bluish-green leaves in clusters of five. **2** The light, soft wood of this tree. **3** Any of several related pines.

white poplar A large, rapidly growing tree valued for its ornamental leaves, which are green above and silvery-white below.

white potato The common potato.

White Russian BYELORUSSIAN.

white sauce A cooked sauce of flour, butter, milk, etc.

white slave A woman forced into or held in prostitution. —**white-slave** (^{h}wīt′slāv′) *adj.* —**white slaver** —**white slavery**

white-tailed deer (^{h}wīt′tāld′) A common North American deer, having a tail white on the underside.

white tie **1** A white bow tie, worn with men's formal evening dress. **2** The formal evening dress of men.

white·wash (^{h}wīt′wosh′, -wôsh′) *n.* **1** A mixture of slaked lime and water used for whitening walls, etc. **2** A suppressing or hiding of faults and defects. **3** *Informal* A defeat in which the loser fails to score. —*v.t.* **1** To coat with whitewash. **2** To gloss over; hide. **3** *Informal* In games or sports, to defeat without allowing one's opponent to score. —**white′wash′er** *n.*

whith·er (^{h}with′ər) *adv. Archaic* To what place, condition, end, etc.: *Whither* are we bound? —*conj.* **1** To which place, condition, end, etc.: the village *whither* we went. **2** To whatever place, condition, end, etc.: Go *whither* you will. [< OE *hwider*]

whith·er·so·ev·er (^{h}with′ər·sō·ev′ər) *adv. Archaic* To whatever place.

whit·ing^1 (^{h}wī′ting) *n.* A powdered white chalk used as a pigment, for polishing, etc.

whit·ing^2 (^{h}wī′ting) *n.* **1** A small European food fish related to cod. **2** A silvery-scaled hake. **3** Any of several silvery fishes, esp. the **Carolina whiting,** common on the coast of the S U.S. [< MDu. *wit* white]

Whiting^2

whit·ish (^{h}wī′tish) *adj.* Somewhat white or very light gray. —**whit′ish·ness** *n.*

whit·low (^{h}wit′lō) *n.* An inflammatory, festering lesion at the edge of a fingernail. [< WHITE + FLAW]

Whit·sun (^{h}wit′sən) *adj.* Of, pertaining to, or for Whitsunday or Whitsuntide.

Whit·sun·day (^{h}wit′sun′dē, -dā) *n.* The seventh Sunday after Easter; Pentecost. [< OE *Hwīta Sunnandæg,* lit., white Sunday < the white robes worn by recently baptized persons on that day]

Whit·sun·tide (^{h}wit′sən·tīd′) *n.* The week that begins with Whitsunday. Also **Whitsun Tide.**

whit·tle (^{h}wit′l) *v.* **·tled, ·tling** *v.t.* **1** To cut or shave bits from (wood, a stick, etc.). **2** To make or shape by whittling. **3** To reduce or wear away a little at a time: with *down, off, away,* etc. —*v.i.* **4** To whittle wood. [< OE *thwitan* to cut] —**whit′tler** *n.* —**Syn.** *v.* **1** carve, trim, pare.

whiz (^{h}wiz) *v.* **whizzed, whiz·zing** *v.i.* **1** To make a hissing and humming sound while passing rapidly through the air. **2** To move or pass with such a sound. —*v.t.* **3** To cause to whiz. —*n.* **1** The sound made by whizzing. **2** *Slang* Any person or thing of extraordinary excellence or ability. Also **whizz.** [Imit.] —**whiz′zer** *n.* —**whiz′zing·ly** *adv.*

whiz kid *Slang* A young person who is extraordinarily clever, talented, or successful. [Alter. of *Quiz Kid,* a panel member of a former quiz show made up of children]

who (hōō) *pron. possessive case* **whose;** *objective case* **whom** **1** Which or what person or persons: *Who* is she? They don't know *who* I am. **2** The person or persons that; whoever: *Who* insults my friends insults me. **3** That: used as a relative to introduce a clause: the man *who* mows our lawn. —**who's who** Who the most prominent people are. —**as who should say** As if one should say; so to speak. [< OE *hwa, hwā*] • **who, which, that** *Who* as a relative is usu. applied only to persons, *which* only to animals or to inanimate objects, *that* to persons or things.

WHO World Health Organization.

whoa (^{h}wō) *interj.* Stop! stand still! [Var. of HO]

who·dun·it (hōō·dun′it) *n. Informal* A mystery story, play, etc. [< WHO + DONE + IT]

who·ev·er (hōō·ev′ər) *pron.* **1** Any one without exception; any person who. **2** No matter who.

whole (hōl) *adj.* **1** Containing all the parts necessary to make up a total; entire; complete. **2** Not broken, injured, defective, etc.; sound; intact. **3** Being the full amount, number, duration, etc.: He failed the *whole* class. **4** In or having regained sound health; hale. **5** Having the same parents: a *whole* brother. **6** *Math.* Integral; not mixed or fractional. —**as a whole** Altogether. —**on the whole** Taking all into consideration; in general. —*n.* **1** All the parts or elements making up a thing. **2** A complete unity or system. [< OE *hāl*] —**whole′ness** *n.*

whole·heart·ed (hōl′här′tid) *adj.* Done or undertaken with all earnestness, energy, dedication, etc. —**whole′·heart′ed·ly** *adv.* —**whole′heart′ed·ness** *n.*

whole note *Music* A note whose time value is the same as that of two half notes. • See NOTE.

whole number Any member of the set of numbers {. . . −3, −2, −1, 0, 1, 2, 3 . . .}; an integer.

whole·sale (hōl′sāl′) *n.* The sale of goods in large bulk or quantity, usu. for resale by retailers. —*adj.* **1** Pertaining to or engaged in such selling. **2** Made or done on a large scale or indiscriminately: *wholesale* murder. —*adv.* **1** In bulk or quantity. **2** Extensively or indiscriminately. —*v.t. & v.i.* **·saled, ·sal·ing** To sell (something) in large quantity, usu. for resale by retailers. [< ME *by hole sale* in large quantities] —**whole′sal′er** *n.*

whole·some (hōl′səm) *adj.* **1** Tending to promote health: *wholesome* air or food. **2** Tending to promote mental or moral well-being: a *wholesome* play. **3** Healthy: *wholesome* red cheeks. [< WHOLE + -SOME] —**whole′some·ly** *adv.* —**whole′some·ness** *n.*

whole step An interval consisting of two semitones. Also **whole tone.**

whole-wheat (hōl′^{h}wēt′) *adj.* **1** Made from the entire wheat kernel: *whole-wheat* flour. **2** Made from whole-wheat flour. Also **whole wheat.**

who'll (hōōl) Contraction of *who will* or *who shall.*

whol·ly (hō′lē, hōl′lē) *adv.* **1** Completely; totally. **2** Exclusively; only.

whom (hōōm) *pron.* The objective case of WHO. [< OE *hwam*]

whom·ev·er (hōōm′ev′ər) *pron.* The objective case of WHOEVER.

whom·so·ev·er (hōōm′sō·ev′ər) *pron.* The objective case of WHOSOEVER.

whoop (hōōp, ^{h}wōōp, ^{h}wŏŏp) *v.i.* **1** To utter loud cries, as of excitement, rage, or exultation. **2** To hoot, as an owl. **3** To make a loud, gasping intake of breath. —*v.t.* **4** To utter with a whoop or whoops. **5** To call, urge, chase, etc., with whoops. **—whoop it** (or **things**) **up** *Slang* **1** To celebrate in a noisy, riotous manner. **2** To arouse enthusiasm. —*n.* **1** A shout of excitement, joy, derision, etc. **2** A loud, convulsive intake of breath. **3** An owl's hoot. [Imit.]

whoop·ee (ʰwo͞o′pē, ʰwo͝op′ē) *Slang interj.* An exclamation of joy, excitement, etc. **—make whoopee** To have a noisy, festive time. [< WHOOP]

whooping cough A contagious respiratory disease of bacterial origin chiefly affecting children, marked in later stages by violent coughing.

whooping crane A large white North American crane having a whooplike cry.

whop·per (ʰwop′ər) *n. Informal* **1** Something large or remarkable. **2** An outrageous falsehood.

whop·ping (ʰwop′ing) *adj.* Unusually large, great, or remarkable.

whore (hôr, hōr) *n.* A woman who engages in sexual intercourse promiscuously; esp., a prostitute. —*v.i.* **whored, whor·ing 1** To have illicit sexual intercourse, esp. with a whore. **2** To be or act like a whore. [< OE *hōre*]

whorl (ʰwûrl, ʰwôrl) *n.* **1** The flywheel of a spindle. **2** *Bot.* A set of leaves, etc., distributed in a circle around a stem. **3** *Zool.* A turn of a spiral shell. **4** Any of the convoluted ridges of a fingerprint. [? < WHIRL] **—whorled** *adj.*

Whorl *def. 2*

whor·tle·ber·ry (ʰwûr′təl·ber′ē) *n. pl.* **·ries 1** A European shrub with edible blue-black berries. **2** Its fruit. **3** HUCKLEBERRY. [< OE *horta* whortleberry + BERRY]

whose (ho͞oz) The possessive case of WHO and often of WHICH. [< OE *hwæs*, genitive of *hwā* who]

who·so (ho͞o′sō) *pron. Archaic* WHOEVER.

who·so·ev·er (ho͞o′sō·ev′ər) *pron.* WHOEVER.

why (ʰwī) *adv.* For what cause, purpose, or reason: *Why* did you go? —*conj.* **1** The reason or cause for which: I don't know *why* he went. **2** For or because of which: I know the reason *why* he went. —*n. pl.* **whys** A cause; reason. —*interj.* An exclamation expressing surprise, doubt, etc. [< OE *hwī, hwȳ*]

WI Wisconsin (P.O. abbr.).

W.I. West Indian; West Indies.

wick (wik) *n.* A strand of loosely twisted or woven fibers, as in a candle or lamp, acting by capillary attraction to convey fuel to a flame. [< OE *wēoca*] **—wick′ing** *n.*

wick·ed (wik′id) *adj.* **1** Evil; depraved. **2** Mischievous; roguish. **3** Troublesome; painful: a *wicked* headache. [< OE *wicca* a wizard] **—wick′ed·ly** *adv.* **—wick′ed·ness** *n.* **—Syn. 1** malevolent, sinful, wrong. **2** devilish.

wick·er (wik′ər) *adj.* Made of twigs, osiers, etc. —*n.* **1** A pliant young shoot or rod; twig; osier. **2** WICKERWORK. [Prob. < Scand.]

wick·er·work (wik′ər·wûrk′) *n.* A fabric or texture, as a basket, made of woven twigs, osiers, etc.

wick·et (wik′it) *n.* **1** A small door or gate often within a larger entrance. **2** A small opening in a door. **3** A small sluicegate at the end of a millrace. **4** In cricket: **a** Either of two arrangements of three upright rods set near together. **b** The level playing space between these. **c** A player's turn at bat. **5** In croquet, an arch, usu. of wire, through which one must hit the ball. [< AF *wiket*]

wick·et-keep·er (wik′it·kē′pər) *n.* In cricket, the fielder stationed right behind the wicket.

wide (wīd) *adj.* **wid·er, wid·est 1** Having relatively great extent between sides. **2** Extended far in every direction; spacious: a *wide* expanse. **3** Having a specified degree of width: an inch *wide.* **4** Distant from the desired or proper point, issue, etc.: *wide* of the mark. **5** Having great scope, range, inclusiveness, etc.: a *wide* variety. **6** Loose; ample; roomy: *wide* trousers. **7** Fully open; expanded or extended: *wide* eyes. **8** *Phonet.* Formed with a relatively relaxed tongue and jaw: said of certain vowels. —*n.* In cricket, a ball bowled so as not to be within the batsman's reach. —*adv.* **1** To a great distance; extensively. **2** Far from the mark, issue, etc. **3** To the greatest extent; fully open. [< OE *wīd*] **—wide′ly** *adv.* **—wide′ness** *n.* **—Syn.** *adj.* **2** ample, broad, extensive, vast.

wide-an·gle lens (wīd′ang′gəl) A type of camera lens designed to permit an angle of view wider than that of the ordinary lens.

wide-a·wake (wīd′ə·wāk′) *adj.* **1** Totally awake. **2** Alert.

wide-eyed (wīd′īd′) *adj.* **1** With the eyes wide open. **2** Uninformed or unsophisticated.

wid·en (wīd′n) *v.t. & v.i.* To make or become wide or wider. **—wid′en·er** *n.*

wide-o·pen (wīd′ō′pən) *adj.* **1** Opened wide. **2** *Informal* Remiss in the enforcement of laws which regulate gambling, prostitution, etc.: a *wide-open* city.

wide·spread (wīd′spred′) *adj.* **1** Extending over a large space or territory. **2** Held, believed, indulged in, etc., by many people.

widge·on (wij′ən) *n.* Any of various river ducks having a short bill and wedge-shaped tail. Also **wig·eon.** [?]

wid·get (wij′it) *n. Slang* **1** A product having a unique or ingenious feature; gadget. **2** Something unnamed and used as an example in a hypothetical situation. [Alter. of GADGET]

wid·ow (wid′ō) *n.* **1** A woman who has lost her husband by death and has not remarried. **2** In some card games, an additional hand dealt to the table. **3** *Printing* A short line of type ending a paragraph at the top of a page or column; also, such a line at the end of any paragraph. —*v.t.* To make a widow of. [< OE *widewe*]

wid·ow·er (wid′ō·ər) *n.* A man who has lost his wife by death and has not remarried.

widow's mite A contribution which, although small in amount, is all or even more than the giver can afford.

widow's peak A point of hair growing down from the hairline in the middle of the forehead.

width (width) *n.* **1** Dimension or measurement of an object taken from side to side, or at right angles to the length. **2** Something that has width: a *width* of cloth. [< WIDE]

width·wise (width′wīz) *adv.* In the direction of the width. Also **width′ways′.**

wield (wēld) *v.t.* **1** To use or handle, as a weapon or instrument. **2** To exercise (authority, power, influence, etc.). [Fusion of OE *wealdan* to cause and OE *wildan* to rule] **—wield′er** *n.*

wie·ner (wē′nər) *n.* A kind of smoked sausage, similar to a frankfurter, made of beef and pork. Also **wie·ner·wurst** (wē′nər·wûrst′). [Short for *wienerwurst* < G, Vienna sausage]

wife (wīf) *n. pl.* **wives** (wīvz) **1** A woman joined to a man in lawful wedlock. **2** *Archaic* A woman: now used in combination or in certain phrases: *housewife,* old *wives'* tales. **—take to wife** To marry (a woman). [< OE *wīf*] **—wife′·dom, wife′hood** *n.*

wife·ly (wīf′lē) *adj.* **·li·er, ·li·est 1** Of or like a wife. **2** Suitable to a wife.

wig (wig) *n.* A covering of real or artificial hair for the head. —*v.t.* **wigged, wig·ging 1** To furnish with a wig or wigs. **2** *Brit. Informal* To berate or scold. [Short for PERIWIG]

Barrister's wig

wig·gle (wig′əl) *v.t. & v.i.* **·gled, ·gling** To move or cause to move quickly from side to side; wriggle. —*n.* The act of wiggling. [< MLG *wiggelen*] **—wig′gly** *adj.* **(·gli·er, ·gli·est)**

wig·gler (wig′lər) *n.* **1** One who or that which wiggles. **2** The larva of a mosquito.

wig·wag (wig′wag′) *v.t. & v.i.* **·wagged, ·wag·ging 1** To move briskly back and forth; wag. **2** To send (a message) by hand flags, torches, etc. —*n.* **1** The act of wigwagging. **2** A message sent by wigwagging. [< dial. E *wig* wiggle + WAG[1]] **—wig′wag′ger** *n.*

wig·wam (wig′wom, -wôm) *n.* A dwelling or lodge of certain North American Indians, commonly a rounded or conical framework of poles covered with bark, rush matting, or hides. [< Algon.]

Wigwam

wild (wīld) *adj.* **1** Living or growing in a natural state; not tamed, domesticated, or cultivated: *wild* animals; *wild* flowers. **2** Being in the natural state without civilized inhabitants or cultivation: *wild* prairies. **3** Uncivilized; primitive: the *wild* men of Borneo. **4** Undisciplined; unruly. **5** Morally dissolute; profligate. **6** Violent; turbulent: a *wild* night. **7** Reckless; imprudent: a *wild* speculation. **8** Unusually odd or strange; extravagant; bizarre: a *wild* imagination. **9** Eager and excited: *wild* with delight. **10** Frenzied; crazed: *wild* with fury. **11** Disorderly; disarranged: a *wild* mop of hair. **12** Far from the mark aimed at; erratic: a *wild* pitch. **13** In some card games, having its value arbitrarily determined by the dealer or holder. **14** *Slang* Terrific; great: The party was *wild*. **15** *Slang* Showy; jazzy: a *wild* necktie. —*n. Often pl.* An uninhabited or uncultivated place; wilderness: the *wilds* of Africa. —**the wild 1** The wilderness. **2** The free, natural, wild life. —*adv.* In a wild manner: to run *wild*. [< OE *wilde*] —**wild'ly** *adv.* —**wild'ness** *n.* —**Syn.** *adj.* **3** barbarous, savage. **7** irresponsible, rash. **8** fantastic.

wild boar An Old World hog often hunted as game.

wild carrot A weed from which the cultivated carrot is derived; Queen Anne's lace.

wild·cat (wīld'kat') *n.* **1** Any of various undomesticated felines resembling the domestic cat, but larger and stronger, as the lynx, cougar, etc. **2** An aggressive, quick-tempered person. **3** An unattached locomotive, used on special work, as when sent out to haul a train, etc. **4** A successful oil well drilled in an area previously unproductive. **5** A tricky or unsound business venture, esp. a worthless mine. Also **wild cat.** —*adj.* **1** Unsound; risky; esp. financially. **2** Made, produced, or carried on without official sanction or authorization. **3** Not running on a schedule, as a locomotive. —*v.t. & v.i.* **·cat·ted, ·cat·ting** To drill for oil in (an area not known to be productive). —**wild'cat'·ter** *n.*

wildcat strike A strike unauthorized by regular union procedure.

wilde·beest (wīld'bēst, wil'də-) *n. pl.* **·beests** or **·beest** GNU. [< Du. *wild* wild + *beeste* a beast]

wil·der·ness (wil'dər·nis) *n.* **1** An uncultivated, uninhabited, or barren region. **2** A multitudinous and confusing collection of persons or things. [< OE *wilder* a wild beast + -NESS]

wild·fire (wīld'fīr') *n.* A raging, destructive fire that is hard to extinguish. —**like wildfire** Very quickly; uncontrollably.

wild·flow·er (wīld'flou'ər) *n.* **1** Any uncultivated plant that bears flowers. **2** The flower of such a plant. Also **wild flower.**

wild·fowl (wīld'foul') *n. pl.* **·fowl** or **·fowls** A wild bird, esp. wild duck, pheasant, etc., hunted as game. Also **wild fowl.**

wild-goose chase (wīld'gōōs') Pursuit of the unknown or unattainable.

wild·life (wīld'līf') *n.* Wild animals collectively.

wild oat 1 *Usu. pl.* Any of various uncultivated grasses. **2** *pl.* Indiscretions of youth, usu. in the phrase **sow one's wild oats.**

wild rice 1 A tall aquatic grass of North America. **2** The highly esteemed, edible grain of this plant.

Wild West The w U.S. in its early period of Indian fighting, lawlessness, etc. Also **wild West**

wild·wood (wīld'wŏŏd') *n.* Natural forest land.

wile (wīl) *n.* **1** An act or a means of cunning deception. **2** Any trick or artifice. —*v.t.* **wiled, wil·ing** To lure, beguile, or mislead. —**wile away** To pass (time) pleasantly. [< OE *wīl*] —**Syn.** *n.* **2** machination, maneuver, ruse, stratagem.

wil·ful (wil'fəl) *adj.* WILLFUL.

will[1] (wil) *n.* **1** The power to make conscious, deliberate choices or to control what one does. **2** The act or experience of exercising this power. **3** A specific desire, purpose, choice, etc.: the *will* of the people. **4** Strong determination or purpose: the *will* to succeed. **5** Self-control. **6** Attitude or inclination toward others: ill *will*. **7** *Law* The legal declaration of a person's intentions as to the disposition of his estate after his death. —**at will** As one pleases. —**with a will** Energetically. —*v.* **willed, will·ing** *v.t.* **1** To decide upon; choose. **2** To resolve upon as an action or course. **3** *Law* To bequeath by a will. **4** To control, as a hypnotized person, by the exercise of will. **5** To decree: The king *wills* it. —*v.i.* **6** To wish; desire: as you *will*. [< OE *willa*]

will[2] (wil) *v.* Present *sing. & pl.*: **will** (*Archaic* **thou wilt**); past: **would** (*Archaic* **thou would·est** or **wouldst**) As an auxiliary verb *will* is used with the infinitive without *to*, or elliptically without the infinitive, to express: **1** Futurity: They *will* arrive by dark. **2** Likelihood: You *will* be sorry. **3** Command; order: You *will* leave immediately. **4** Willingness or disposition: Why *will* you not tell the truth? **5** Capability or capacity: The ship *will* survive any storm. **6** Custom or habit: He *will* sit for hours and brood. **7** *Informal* Probability or inference: I expect this *will* be the main street. [< OE *willan*] • See SHALL.

willed (wild) *adj.* Having a will of a given character: used in combination: *weak-willed*.

will·ful (wil'fəl) *adj.* **1** Deliberate; intentional: *willful* disregard of the law. **2** Stubborn; headstrong: a *willful* child. —**will'ful·ly** *adv.* —**will'ful·ness** *n.*

wil·lies (wil'ēz) *n.pl. Slang* Nervousness; jitters: used with *the*. [?]

will·ing (wil'ing) *adj.* **1** Having the mind favorably inclined or disposed. **2** Readily and gladly acting, responding, doing, giving, etc. **3** Readily and gladly offered, done, given, etc. —**will'ing·ly** *adv.* —**will'ing·ness** *n.* —**Syn. 3** accommodating, compliant, obliging.

will-o'-the-wisp (wil'ə·thə·wisp') *n.* IGNIS FATUUS. [Earlier *Will with the wisp*]

wil·low (wil'ō) *n.* **1** Any of a large genus of shrubs and trees having usu. narrow leaves and flexible shoots often used in basketry. **2** The wood of a willow. **3** *Informal* Something made of willow wood, as a cricket bat. —*adj.* Made of willow wood. [< OE *wilige, welig*] • See WEEPING WILLOW.

wil·low·y (wil'ō·ē) *adj.* **·low·i·er, ·low·i·est 1** Tall and graceful. **2** Lithe; flexible; supple. **3** Abounding in willows. —**wil'low·i·ness** *n.*

will·pow·er (wil'pou'ər) *n.* Strength to direct or control one's actions or desires; determination.

wil·ly-nil·ly (wil'ē·nil'ē) *adj.* Being or happening whether one wants it or not. —*adv.* Willingly or unwillingly. [Earlier *will I, nill I* whether I will or not]

wilt[1] (wilt) *v.i.* **1** To lose freshness; droop or become limp. **2** To lose energy and vitality; become faint or languid. **3** To lose courage or spirit. —*v.t.* **4** To cause to wilt. —*n.* **1** The act of wilting or the state of being wilted. **2** A plant disease that causes wilting. [Prob. dial. var. of obs. *welk*]

wilt[2] (wilt) *Archaic* Will: used with *thou*.

Wil·ton (wil'tən) *n.* A kind of carpet having a velvety texture. Also **Wilton carpet, Wilton rug.** [< *Wilton*, England, where first made]

wi·ly (wī'lē) *adj.* **·li·er, ·li·est** Full of or characterized by wiles; sly; cunning. —**wi'li·ly** *adv.* —**wi'li·ness** *n.*

wim·ple (wim'pəl) *n.* A cloth wrapped in folds around the neck close under the chin and over the head, exposing only the face, worn by medieval women and still by certain nuns. —*v.* **·pled, ·pling** *v.t.* **1** To cover or clothe with a wimple. **2** To make or fold into pleats, as a veil. **3** To cause to move with slight undulations; ripple. —*v.i.* **4** To lie in plaits or folds. **5** To ripple. [< OE *wimpel*]

Wimple

win (win) *v.* **won, won, win·ning** *v.i.* **1** To gain a victory; be victorious in a contest, endeavor, etc. **2** To succeed in reaching or attaining a specified end or condition; get: often with *across, over, through*, etc. —*v.t.* **3** To be successful in; gain victory in: to *win* an argument. **4** To gain in competition or contest: to *win* the blue ribbon. **5** To gain by effort, persistence, etc.: to *win* fame. **6** To influence so as to obtain the good will or favor of: often with *over*. **7** To secure the love of; gain in marriage. **8** To succeed in reaching: to *win* the harbor. —**win out** *Informal* To succeed; triumph. —*n. Informal* A victory; success. [< OE *winnan* contend, labor] —**Syn.** *v.* **5** achieve, attain, earn, secure.

wince (wins) *v.i.* **winced, winc·ing** To shrink back; flinch. —*n.* The act of wincing. [< AF *wenchier*] —**winc'er** *n.*

add, āce, câre, pälm; end, ēven; it, īce; odd, ōpen, ôrder; tŏŏk, pōōl; up, bûrn; ə = *a* in *above*, *u* in *focus*; yōō = *u* in *fuse*; oil; pout; check; go; ring; thin; this; zh, *vision*. < derived from; ? origin uncertain or unknown.

winch (winch) *n.* 1 A windlass, particularly one turned by a crank and used for hoisting. 2 A crank with a handle for transmitting motion. [<OE *wince*] —**winch'er** *n.*

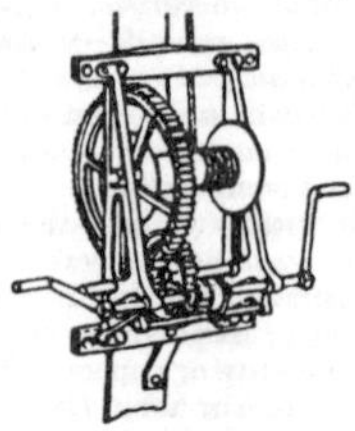
Winch

Win·ches·ter rifle (win'ches·tər) A type of repeating rifle, first produced in 1866: a trade name. Also **Winchester**.

wind¹ (wind) *n.* 1 Any movement of air, esp. a natural horizontal movement. 2 Any powerful or destructive movement of air, as a tornado. 3 The direction from which a wind blows. 4 Air pervaded by a scent, as in hunting. 5 The power of breathing; breath: He lost his *wind*. 6 Idle chatter. 7 Bragging; vanity; conceit. 8 *pl.* The wind instruments of an orchestra; also, the players of these instruments. 9 The gaseous product of indigestion; flatulence. —**break wind** To expel gas through the anus. —**get wind of** To receive a hint or intimation of. —**how the wind blows** (or **lies**, etc.) What is taking place, being decided, etc. —**in the teeth of the wind** Directly against the wind: also **in the wind's eye.** —**in the wind** Impending; afoot. —*v.t.* 1 To follow by scent; to catch a scent of on the wind. 2 To exhaust the breath of, as by racing. 3 To allow to recover breath by resting. 4 To expose to the wind, as in ventilating. [<OE] —**Syn.** *n.* 1 blast, breeze, gale, gust, zephyr.

wind² (wīnd) *v.* **wound** or **wind·ed, wind·ing** *v.t.* 1 To coil (thread, rope, etc.) around some object or fixed core; twine. 2 To encircle or cover with something, as by coiling or wrapping: to *wind* a spool with thread. 3 To renew the motion of, as a clock, by turning a stem, key, etc. 4 To turn in a revolving motion: to *wind* a handle. 5 To cause to turn and twist. 6 To make (one's way) by a turning and twisting course. 7 To introduce carefully or deviously; insinuate: He *wound* himself into my confidence. 8 To raise or hoist, as by means of a capstan or windlass. —*v.i.* 9 To move in a turning, twisting course; meander. 10 To coil or twine about some central object or core. 11 To move in a circular or spiral course. 12 To proceed or gain an end carefully or deviously. —**wind down** To decrease or be decreased gradually; de-escalate: to *wind down* a war. —**wind up** 1 To coil or wind round and round. 2 To excite; arouse. 3 To bring to conclusion or settlement: He *wound up* his affairs. 4 In baseball, to swing the arm preparatory to pitching. 5 To hoist. —*n.* 1 The act of winding, or the condition of being wound. 2 A bend, turn, or twist. [<OE *windan*] —**wind'er** *n.*

wind³ (wīnd, wind) *v.t.* **wind·ed** or **wound, wind·ing** 1 To blow, as a horn; sound. 2 To give (a call or signal), as with a horn. [<WIND¹; infl. by WIND²]

wind·age (win'dij) *n.* 1 The rush of air caused by the rapid passage of an object, as a projectile. 2 Deflection of an object, as a bullet, from its natural course by wind. 3 *Naut.* The surface offered to the wind by a vessel.

wind·bag (wind'bag') *n. Informal* An overly talkative person who says little of significance.

wind·blown (wind'blōn') *adj.* 1 Tossed or blown by the wind. 2 Having a permanent direction of growth as determined by prevailing winds: said of plants and trees.

wind-borne (wind'bôrn', -bōrn') *adj.* Carried or transported by the wind.

wind·break (wind'brāk') *n.* Anything, as a hedge, fence, etc., that protects from or breaks the force of the wind.

wind·break·er (wind'brā'kər) *n.* A sports jacket for outer wear, having a close-fitting or elastic waistband and cuffs. [<*Windbreaker*, a trade name]

wind·bro·ken (wind'brō'kən) *adj.* Having the heaves: said of a horse.

wind·chill factor (wind'chil') 1 A measure of air temperature modified by the chilling effect of wind of a given velocity as felt on the surface of the skin. 2 The effect of wind in reducing perceived air temperature.

wind·ed (win'did) *adj.* 1 Out of breath. 2 Having a specified kind of wind or breath: used in combination: *short-winded.*

wind·fall (wind'fôl') *n.* 1 Something, as ripening fruit, brought down by the wind. 2 A piece of unexpected good fortune.

wind·flow·er (wind'flou'ər) *n.* ANEMONE.

wind gauge An instrument for measuring the velocity of the wind; anemometer.

wind·hov·er (wind'huv'ər) *n. Brit.* KESTREL.

wind·ing (wīn'ding) *n.* 1 The act or condition of one who or that which winds; a turning or coiling. 2 A bend or turn, or a series of them. 3 Something that winds. —*adj.* 1 Turning spirally about an axis or core. 2 Having bends or lateral turns.

wind·ing sheet (wīn'ding) SHROUD (def. 1).

wind instrument (wind) A musical instrument whose sounds are produced by blowing air through it, esp. a portable one, as a flute, oboe, etc.

wind·jam·mer (wind'jam'ər) *n. Naut.* 1 A sailing vessel, as distinguished from a steamship. 2 A member of its crew.

wind·lass (wind'ləs) *n.* Any of several devices for hoisting or hauling, esp. one consisting of a drum turned by means of a crank so that the hoisting rope winds on the drum. [<ON *vinda* wind + *āss* a beam]

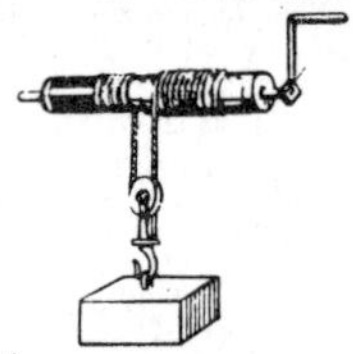
Differential windlass

wind·mill (wind'mil') *n.* 1 A mill having at the top a system of adjustable slats, wings, or sails which, when turned by the wind, transmit power to a pump, millstone, or the like. 2 An imaginary wrong, evil, or foe: usu. in the phrase **tilt at windmills,** an allusion to Don Quixote's combat with windmills, which he mistook for giants. • See VANE.

win·dow (win'dō) *n.* 1 An opening in the wall of a building, etc., to admit light or air, usu. capable of being opened and closed, and including casements or sashes fitted with glass. 2 A windowpane or the sash or framework that encloses it. 3 Anything resembling or suggesting a window, as a transparent patch in certain envelopes. —*v.t.* To provide with a window or windows. [<ON *vindr* wind + *auga* an eye]

window box A box along a window ledge or sill, for growing plants.

window dressing 1 The act or art of arranging merchandise attractively in shop and store windows. 2 Any action, report, etc., designed to make something seem more attractive or plausible than it actually is.

win·dow·pane (win'dō·pān') *n.* A pane of glass for a window.

window seat A seat in the recess of a window.

window shade A flexible covering for the inside of a window, used to regulate light.

win·dow-shop (win'dō·shop') *v.i.* **-shopped, -shop·ping** To look at goods shown in store windows without buying them. —**win'dow-shop'per** *n.*

win·dow·sill (win'dō·sil') *n.* The horizontal ledge at the bottom of a window opening.

wind·pipe (wind'pīp') *n.* TRACHEA.

wind·row (wind'rō') *n.* 1 A long row of hay or grain raked together preparatory to building into cocks. 2 A line of dust, surf, leaves, etc. swept together by wind. —*v.t.* To rake or shape into a windrow. —**wind'row'er** *n.*

wind·screen (wind'skrēn') *n. Brit.* WINDSHIELD.

wind·shear (wind'shir') *n.* A strong, rapid change in wind direction.

wind·shield (wind'shēld') *n.* A transparent screen, as of glass, across and above the dashboard of motor vehicles, power boats, etc., providing protection from the wind.

wind·sock (wind'sok') *n.* A large, conical bag, open at both ends, mounted on a pivot, and used to indicate the direction of the wind. Also **wind sock, wind sleeve.**

Wind·sor (win'zər) Name of the royal family of Great Britain since July 27, 1917.

Windsor chair A wooden chair, typically with a spindle back, slanting legs, and a flat or saddle seat.

Windsor knot A wide knot that can be used to tie a four-in-hand tie.

Windsor tie A wide, soft necktie tied in a loose bow.

wind·storm (wind′stôrm′) *n.* A violent wind, usu. with little or no precipitation.
wind·swept (wind′swept′) *adj.* Exposed to or propelled by the wind.
wind tunnel *Aeron.* A device in which the effects of artificially produced winds, as on airplane wings, can be studied.
wind·up (wīnd′up) *n.* **1** The act of concluding. **2** A conclusion or culmination; end. **3** In baseball, the swing of the arm preparatory to pitching the ball.
wind·ward (wind′wərd) *adj.* **1** Of or toward the direction from which the wind blows. **2** Being on the side exposed to the wind. —*n.* The direction from which the wind blows. —*adv.* In the direction from which the wind blows.
wind·y (win′dē) *adj.* **wind·i·er, wind·i·est 1** Of or abounding in wind; stormy; tempestuous: *windy* weather. **2** Exposed to the wind. **3** Suggestive of wind; boisterous; violent. **4** Flatulent. **5** Boastful, talkative, or pompous. **6** Idle; empty: *windy* talk. —**wind′i·ly** *adv.* —**wind′i·ness** *n.*
wine (wīn) *n.* **1** The fermented juice of the grape, used as an alcoholic beverage and in cooking. **2** The fermented juice of any of several other fruits or vegetables: dandelion *wine.* **3** The color of red wine. —*v.* **wined, win·ing** *v.t.* **1** To entertain or treat with wine. —*v.i.* **2** To drink wine. [< OE *wīn*]
wine·bib·ber (wīn′bib′ər) *n.* A person given to excessive drinking of wine. —**wine′bib′bing** *adj., n.*
wine cellar A storage space for wines; also, the wines stored.
wine-col·ored (wīn′kul′ərd) *adj.* Having the color of red wine.
wine·glass (wīn′glas′, -gläs′) *n.* A small goblet, usu. stemmed, from which to drink wine.
wine·grow·er (wīn′grō′ər) *n.* One who cultivates a vineyard and makes wine. —**wine′grow′ing** *adj., n.*
wine·press (wīn′pres′) *n.* An apparatus or a place where the juice of grapes is expressed. —**wine′press′er** *n.*
win·er·y (wī′nər·ē) *n. pl.* **·er·ies** An establishment where wine is made.
Wine·sap (wīn′sap) *n.* An American variety of red winter apple.
wine·skin (wīn′skin′) *n.* A bag made of the entire skin of an animal, as a goat, used for containing wine.
wing (wing) *n.* **1** An organ of flight; esp. one of a pair of appendages of a bird or bat, adapted for flight. **2** An analogous organ in insects and some other animals. **3** Anything resembling or suggestive of a wing in form or function. **4** *Aeron.* The (or one of the) main supporting surface(s) of an airplane. **5** *Bot.* Any thin, winglike expansion of certain stems, seeds, etc. **6** A vane, as of a windmill. **7** Anything regarded as conferring the swift motion or rapture of flight: on *wings* of song. **8** Flight by or as by wings. **9** *Archit.* A part attached to a side, esp. a projection or extension of a building on the side of the main portion. **10** An annex or separate section of a large building: the surgical *wing* of a hospital. **11** Either of two sides, unseen by the audience, of a proscenium stage; also, a piece of scenery for the side of a stage. **12** Either of two sidepieces on the back of an armchair. **13** A side section of something that shuts or folds, as a screen. **14** A tactical and administrative unit of the U.S. Air Force, larger than a group. **15** *Mil.* Either division of a military force on either side of the center. **16** An analogous formation in certain outdoor games, as hockey or football. **17** Either of two extremist groups or factions in a political organization: the left *wing.* **18** A subsidiary group of a parent organization. **19** *Slang* An arm, esp., in baseball, a pitching or throwing arm. **20** *pl.* The insignia worn by certain qualified aircraft pilots, navigators, etc. —**on** (or **upon**) **the wing 1** In flight. **2** Departing; also, journeying. —**take wing** To fly away. —**under one's wing** Under one's protection. —*v.t.* **1** To pass over or through in flight. **2** To accomplish by flying: the eagle *winged* its way. **3** To enable to fly. **4** To cause to go swiftly; speed. **5** To transport by flight. **6** To provide with wings for flight. **7** To supply with a side body or part. **8** To wound (a bird) in a wing. **9** To disable by a minor wound. —*v.i.* **10** To fly; soar. —**wing it** *Slang* To act, do, arrange, etc., without advance preparation; improvise. [< ON *vængr*]
wing chair A large, upholstered armchair with a high back and side pieces designed as protection from drafts.

Wing chair

winged (wingd, wing′id) *adj.* **1** Having wings. **2** Passing swiftly. **3** Sublime; lofty.
wing·spread (wing′spred′) *n.* The distance between the tips of the fully extended wings, as of a bird, insect, or airplane. Also **wing′span′.**
wink (wingk) *v.i.* **1** To close and open the eye or eyelids quickly. **2** To draw the eyelids of one eye together, as in making a sign. **3** To emit fitful gleams; twinkle. —*v.t.* **4** To close and open (the eye or eyelids) quickly. **5** To move, force, etc., by winking: with *away, off,* etc. **6** To signify or express by winking. —**wink at** To pretend not to see. —*n.* **1** The act of winking. **2** The time necessary for a wink. **3** A twinkle. **4** A hint conveyed by winking. **5** A brief bit (of sleep): I had a *wink* after lunch. —**forty winks** A short nap. [< OE *wincian* close the eyes]
wink·er (wing′kər) *n.* **1** One who winks. **2** *Slang* EYELASH.
win·ner (win′ər) *n.* **1** One who or that which wins. **2** *Informal* Someone or something likely to succeed.
win·ning (win′ing) *adj.* **1** Successful in achievement, esp. in competition. **2** Capable of charming; attractive; winsome. —*n.* **1** The act of one who wins. **2** *Usu. pl.* That which is won, as money in gambling. —**win′ning·ly** *adv.* —**win′ning·ness** *n.*
win·ning·est (win′ing·əst) *adj. Informal* Most often winning: the *winningest* team in baseball.
win·now (win′ō) *v.t.* **1** To separate (grain, etc.) from the chaff. **2** To blow away (the chaff) thus. **3** To separate (what is valuable) or to eliminate (what is valueless): to *winnow* out the good or the bad. **4** To blow upon; cause to flutter. **5** To beat or fan (the air) with the wings. **6** To scatter by blowing; disperse. —*v.i.* **7** To separate grain from chaff. **8** To fly; flap. —*n.* **1** Any device used in winnowing grain. **2** The act of winnowing. [< OE *windwian* < *wind* the wind] —**win′now·er** *n.*
win·o (wī′nō) *n. pl.* **·noes** or **·nos** *Slang* A drunkard who habitually drinks wine, esp. cheap wine. [< WINE]
win·some (win′səm) *adj.* Charming; attractive. [< OE *wyn* joy] —**win′some·ly** *adv.* —**win′some·ness** *n.* —**Syn.** amiable, appealing, engaging, pleasant, winning.
win·ter (win′tər) *n.* **1** The coldest season of the year, extending from the end of autumn to the beginning of spring. **2** A time marked by lack of life, warmth, and cheer. **3** A year as including the winter season: a man of ninety *winters.* —*v.i.* **1** To pass the winter. —*v.t.* **2** To care for, feed, or protect during the winter: to *winter* plants. —*adj.* Pertaining to, suitable for, or characteristic of winter. [< OE] —**win′ter·er** *n.*
win·ter·green (win′tər·grēn) *n.* **1** A small evergreen plant bearing aromatic oval leaves, white, bell-shaped flowers and edible red berries. **2** A colorless, volatile oil extracted from the leaves of this plant or made synthetically, used as a flavor.
win·ter·ize (win′tə·rīz) *v.t.* **·ized, ·iz·ing** To prepare or put in condition for winter, as a motor vehicle, etc.
win·ter·kill (win′tər·kil′) *v.t. & v.i.* To die or kill by exposure to extreme cold: said of plants. —*n.* The act, process, or an instance of winterkilling.
winter solstice See SOLSTICE.
winter wheat Wheat planted before snowfall and harvested the following summer.
win·try (win′trē) *adj.* **·tri·er, ·tri·est** Of or like winter; cold, bleak, cheerless, etc. Also **win′ter·y** (-tər·ē). —**win′tri·ly** *adv.* —**win′tri·ness** *n.*
win·y (wī′nē) *adj.* **win·i·er, win·i·est** Having the taste, color, smell, etc., of wine.
wipe (wīp) *v.t.* **wiped, wip·ing 1** To subject to slight friction or rubbing, usu. with some soft, absorbent material. **2** To remove by rubbing lightly: usu. with *away* or *off.* **3** To

move or draw for the purpose of wiping: He *wiped* his hand across his brow. **4** To apply by wiping. **—wipe out 1** To kill or murder. **2** To destroy utterly; annihilate. **3** In surfing, to be overturned by a wave. *—n.* The act of wiping. [< OE *wīpian*] **—wip′er** *n.*

wire (wīr) *n.* **1** A slender rod, strand, or thread of metal. **2** Something made of wire, as a fence, a cord to conduct an electric current, etc. **3** WIREWORK. **4** A telephone or telegraph cable. **5** The telegraph system as a means of communication. **6** TELEGRAM. **7** The screen of a papermaking machine. **8** A line marking the finish of a race. **—get (in) under the wire** To conclude or achieve something at the very last moment. **—pull wires** *Informal* To use secret or private sources of influence to attain something. *—v.* **wired, wir·ing** *v.t.* **1** To fasten or bind with wire. **2** To furnish or equip with wiring. **3** To telegraph: to *wire* an order. **4** To place on wire, as beads. *—v.i.* **5** To telegraph. [< OE *wīr*] **—wir′er** *n.*

wire gauge 1 A gauge for measuring the diameter of wire. **2** A standard system of sizes for wire.

wire-haired terrier (wīr′hârd′) A fox terrier having a wiry coat. Also **wire′hair′** (-hâr′).

wire·less (wīr′lis) *adj.* **1** Without wire or wires; having no wires. **2** *Brit.* Radio. *—n.* **1** The wireless telegraph or telephone system, or a message transmitted by either. **2** *Brit.* Radio. *—v.t. & v.i. Brit.* To communicate (with) by radio.

Wire·pho·to (wīr′fō′tō) *n. pl.* **·tos** An apparatus and method for transmitting and receiving photographs by wire: a trade name.

wire·pull·er (wīr′po͝ol′ər) *n.* **1** One who pulls wires, as of a puppet. **2** One who uses secret means to control others or gain his own ends; an intriguer. **—wire′pull′ing** *n.*

wire·tap (wīr′tap′) *n.* **1** A device used to make a connection with a telephone or telegraph wire to listen to or record the message transmitted. **2** The act of wiretapping. *—v.* **·tapped, ·tap·ping** *v.t.* **1** To connect a wiretap to. **2** To monitor by the use of a wiretap. *—v.i.* **3** To use a wiretap. **—wire′tap′per** *n.*

wire·work (wīr′wûrk′) *n.* A mesh or netting made of wire.

wir·ing (wīr′ing) *n.* An entire system of wire installed for the distribution of electric power, as for lighting, heating, sound, etc.

wir·y (wīr′ē) *adj.* **wir·i·er, wir·i·est 1** Lean, but tough and sinewy: said of persons. **2** Like wire; stiff; bristly. **—wir′i·ly** *adv.* **—wir′i·ness** *n.*

Wis., Wisc. Wisconsin.

wis·dom (wiz′dəm) *n.* **1** The ability to discern what is true or right and to make sound judgments based on such discernment. **2** Insight or intuition. **3** COMMON SENSE. **4** A high degree of knowledge; learning. **5** An accumulated body of knowledge, as in philosophy, science, etc. [< OE *wīs* wise] **—Syn. 1** sapience, sagacity. **4** enlightenment, erudition.

Wisdom of Solomon A book of the Old Testament Apocrypha, consisting of a hymn in praise of wisdom.

wisdom tooth The last tooth on either side of the upper and lower jaws in man. **—cut one's wisdom teeth** To acquire mature judgment. • See TOOTH.

wise[1] (wīz) *adj.* **wis·er, wis·est 1** Having or showing wisdom (def. 1). **2** Having or showing insight, intuition, common sense, or knowledge. **3** Shrewd; calculating; cunning. **4** *Informal* Aware of: *wise* to his motives. **5** *Slang* Arrogant; fresh: a *wise* guy. **—get wise** *Slang* **1** To learn the true facts about. **2** To become arrogant or fresh. **—wise up** *Slang* To make or become aware, informed, or sophisticated. [< OE *wīs*] **—wise′ly** *adv.* **—wise′ness** *n.*

wise[2] (wīz) *n.* Way of doing; manner; method: chiefly in the phrases **in any wise, in no wise,** etc. [< OE *wīse* manner]

-wise *suffix of adverbs & nouns* **1** In a (specified) way or manner: *nowise, likewise.* **2** In a (specified) direction or position: *lengthwise, clockwise:* often equivalent to *-ways.* **3** *Informal* With reference to: *Moneywise,* the job is worth considering. [< OE *wīse* manner, fashion]

wise·a·cre (wīz′ā′kər) *n.* A person who claims to know everything. [< MDu. *wijsseggher* a soothsayer]

wise·crack (wīz′krak′) *Slang n.* A smart, insolent, or supercilious remark. *—v.i.* To utter a wisecrack. **—wise′·crack′er** *n.*

wish (wish) *n.* **1** A desire or longing, usu. for some definite thing. **2** An expression of such a desire; petition. **3** Something wished for. *—v.t.* **1** To have a desire or longing for; want: We *wish* to be sure. **2** To desire a specified condition or state for (a person or thing): I *wish* this day were over. **3** To invoke upon or for someone: I *wished* him good luck. **4** To bid: to *wish* someone good morning. **5** To request, command, or entreat: I *wish* you would stop yelling. *—v.i.* **6** To have or feel a desire; yearn; long: usu. with *for:* to *wish* for a friend's return. **7** To make or express a wish. **—wish on** *Informal* To impose (something unpleasant or unwanted) on a person. [< OE *wȳscan*] **—wish′er** *n.*

wish·bone (wish′bōn′) *n.* The forked bone situated in front of the sternum in most birds.

wish·ful (wish′fəl) *adj.* Having or indicating a wish or desire. **—wish′ful·ly** *adv.* **—wish′ful·ness** *n.*

wishful thinking A believing that what one wants to be true is true.

wish·y-wash·y (wish′ē·wosh′ē, -wôsh′ē) *adj. Informal* **1** Thin; diluted, as liquor. **2** Lacking in purpose, effectiveness, or strength.

wisp (wisp) *n.* **1** A small bunch, as of hay, straw, or hair. **2** A small bit; a mere indication: a *wisp* of vapor. **3** A slight, delicate thing: a *wisp* of a child. **4** WILL-O'-THE-WISP. [ME *wisp, wips*] **—wisp′y** *adj.* **(·i·er, ·i·est)**

wist (wist) *Archaic p.t. & p.p.* of WIT[2].

wis·te·ri·a (wis·tir′ē·ə, -târ′-) *n.* Any of a genus of woody twining shrubs of the bean family, with pinnate leaves, elongated pods, and showy clusters of blue, purple, or white flowers. Also **wis·tar·i·a** (wis·târ′ē·ə). [< C. *Wistar,* 1761–1818, U.S. anatomist]

Wisteria

wist·ful (wist′fəl) *adj.* **1** Wishful; yearning. **2** Musing; pensive. [Appar. < obs. *wistly* intently] **—wist′ful·ly** *adv.* **—wist′ful·ness** *n.*

wit[1] (wit) *n.* **1** The power of perceiving, reasoning, knowing, etc.; intelligence. **2** *pl.* **a** The mental faculties: to use one's *wits.* **b** Such faculties in relation to their state of balance: out of one's *wits.* **3** Practical intelligence; common sense. **4** The ability to perceive unexpected analogies or incongruities and to express them in an amusing or epigrammatic manner. **5** The ability to make jokes, amusing remarks, etc. **6** A person with wit (defs. 4 & 5). **7** Speech or writing characterized by wit (defs. 4 & 5). **—at one's wits' end** At the limit of one's devices and resources. **—live by one's wits** To make a living by using one's practical intelligence and resourcefulness, often in unscrupulous or fraudulent ways. [< OE]

wit[2] (wit) *v.t. & v.i.* Present indicative: I **wot,** thou **wost,** he, she, it **wot,** we, ye, they **wite(n);** *p.t.* and *p.p.* **wist;** *pr.p.* **wit·ting** *Archaic* To be or become aware (of); learn; know. **—to wit** That is to say; namely. [< OE *witan* know]

witch (wich) *n.* **1** A woman who practices sorcery or has supernatural powers, esp. to work evil. **2** An ugly old woman; a hag. **3** A bewitching or fascinating woman or girl. *—v.t.* **1** To work an evil spell upon; effect by witchcraft. **2** To fascinate or charm. *—v.i.* **3** DOWSE[2]. [< OE *wicce* a witch, fem. of *wicca* a wizard]

witch·craft (wich′kraft′, -kräft′) *n.* **1** Black magic; sorcery. **2** Extraordinary influence or fascination.

witch doctor Among certain primitive peoples, a man skilled in counteracting evil spells.

witch·er·y (wich′ər·ē) *n. pl.* **·er·ies 1** Witchcraft; black magic; sorcery. **2** Power to charm; fascination.

witch hazel 1 Any of a genus of shrubs and small trees with usu. yellow flowers. **2** An extract derived from the bark and dried leaves of a certain witch hazel, used as a mild astringent. [< OE *wice* wych-elm + HAZEL]

witch hunt *Slang* An investigation or harassment of dissenters, often for the undeclared purpose of weakening political opposition.

witch·ing (wich′ing) *adj.* Having the power to enchant; bewitching. **—witch′ing·ly** *adv.*

with (wit͟h, with) *prep.* **1** In the company of: Walk *with* me. **2** Having; bearing: a hat *with* a feather. **3** Characterized or marked by: a man *with* brains. **4** In a manner characterized by; exhibiting: to dance *with* grace. **5** Among, into, near to, etc.: counted *with* the others. **6** In the course of: We forget *with* time. **7** From: to part *with* the past. **8** Against: to struggle *with* an adversary. **9** In the opinion of: That is all right *with* me. **10** Because of: faint *with* hunger. **11** In or under the care, supervision, etc., of: Leave the key *with* the janitor. **12** By means or aid of: to write *with* a pencil. **13** By the use, addition, etc., of: trimmed *with* lace. **14** As an associate, member, etc., of: worked *with* her sister; played *with* an orchestra. **15** In spite of: *With* all his money, he could not buy health. **16** At the same time as: to go to bed *with* the chickens. **17** In the same direction as: to drift *with* the crowd. **18** In regard to; in the case of: I am angry *with* them. **19** Onto; to: Join this tube *with* that one. **20** In proportion to: His fame grew *with* his achievements. **21** In support of: He voted *with* the Left. **22** Of the same opinion as: I'm *with* you there! **23** Having received or been granted: *With* your consent I'll go now. [< OE]

with- *prefix* **1** Against: *withstand.* **2** Back; away: *withhold.* [< OE *with* against]

with·al (wi<u>th</u>·ôl′, with-) *adv.* **1** Besides; in addition. **2** Notwithstanding; nevertheless. —*prep. Archaic* With: used at the end of the clause: a bow to shoot *withal.* [ME *with* + *alle* all]

with·draw (wi<u>th</u>·drô′, with-) *v.* **·drew, ·drawn, ·draw·ing** *v.t.* **1** To draw or take away; remove. **2** To take back, as an assertion or a promise. **3** To keep from use, sale, etc. —*v.i.* **4** To draw back; retreat. **5** To remove oneself; leave, as from an activity.

with·draw·al (wi<u>th</u>·drô′əl, with-) *n.* **1** The act or process of withdrawing. **2** The act or process of overcoming one's addiction to a habit-forming drug.

withdrawal symptom Any of the symptoms caused by the withdrawal of a physically addictive drug from an addict, as tremors, sweating, chills, vomiting, and diarrhea.

with·drawn (wi<u>th</u>·drôn′, with-) *adj.* **1** Not responsive socially or emotionally; introverted. **2** Isolated; remote.

withe (wīth, with, wi<u>th</u>) *n.* A willowy, supple twig, used to bind or wrap. [< OE *withthe*]

with·er (wi<u>th</u>′ər) *v.i.* **1** To become limp or dry, as a plant when deprived of moisture. **2** To waste, as flesh. —*v.t.* **3** To cause to become limp or dry. **4** To abash, as by a scornful glance. [ME *widren*] —**Syn. 1** shrink, shrivel. **4** confuse, shame.

with·ers (wi<u>th</u>′ərz) *n.pl.* The highest part of the back of the horse, ox, etc., between the shoulder blades. [< OE *withre* resistance: so called because this part presses against the harness when a horse is pulling a load]

Withers

with·hold (with·hōld′, wi<u>th</u>-) *v.* **·held, ·hold·ing** *v.t.* **1** To hold back; restrain. **2** To refuse to grant, permit, etc. **3** To deduct (taxes, etc.) from a salary before payment. —*v.i.* **4** To refrain. —**with·hold′er** *n.*

withholding tax That part of an employee's wages or salary which is deducted as an installment on his income tax.

with·in (wi<u>th</u>·in′, with-) *adv.* **1** In the inner part; interiorly. **2** Inside the body, heart, or mind. **3** Indoors. —*prep.* **1** In the inner or interior part or parts of; inside: *within* the house. **2** In the limits, range, or compass of (a specified time, space, or distance): *within* a mile of here; *within* ten minutes' walk. **3** Not exceeding (a specified quantity): Live *within* your means. **4** In the reach, limit, or scope of: *within* my power. [< OE *with* with + *innan* in]

with-it (wi<u>th</u>′it) *adj. Slang* In touch with modern habits, fashions, trends, etc.; up-to-date.

with·out (wi<u>th</u>·out′, with-) *prep.* **1** Not having; lacking: *without* money. **2** In the absence of: We must manage *without* help. **3** Free from: *without* fear. **4** At, on, or to the outside of. **5** Outside of or beyond the limits of: living *without* the pale of civilization. **6** With avoidance of: He listened *without* paying attention. —*adv.* **1** In or on the outer part; externally. **2** OUTDOORS. [< OE *with* with + *ūtan* out]

with·stand (with·stand′, wi<u>th</u>-) *v.* **·stood, ·stand·ing** *v.t.* & *v.i.* To resist, oppose, or endure, esp. successfully. [< OE *with-* against + *standan* stand]

with·y (wi<u>th</u>′ē, with′ē) *n. pl.* **with·ies** WITHE.

wit·less (wit′lis) *adj.* Lacking in wit; foolish. —**wit′less·ly** *adv.* —**wit′less·ness** *n.*

wit·ness (wit′nis) *n.* **1** A person who has seen or knows something and is therefore competent to give evidence concerning it. **2** That which serves as or furnishes evidence or proof. **3** *Law* **a** One who has knowledge of facts relating to a given cause and is subpoenaed to testify. **b** A person who has signed his name to a legal document in order that he may testify to its authenticity. **4** Evidence; testimony. —**bear witness 1** To give evidence; testify. **2** To be evidence. —*v.t.* **1** To see or know by personal experience. **2** To furnish or serve as evidence of. **3** To give testimony to. **4** To be the site or scene of: This spot has *witnessed* many heinous crimes. **5** *Law* To see the execution of (an instrument) and subscribe to its authenticity. —*v.i.* **6** To give evidence; testify. [< OE *witnes* knowledge, testimony] —**wit′ness·er** *n.*

witness stand The platform in a courtroom from which a witness gives evidence.

wit·ted (wit′id) *adj.* Having (a specified kind of) wit: used in combination: *quick-witted.*

wit·ti·cism (wit′ə·siz′əm) *n.* A witty or clever remark. [< WITTY]

wit·ting·ly (wit′ing·lē) *adv.* Designedly; knowingly. [< WIT[2]]

wit·ty (wit′ē) *adj.* **·ti·er, ·ti·est** Having, displaying, or full of wit. [< OE *wittig* wise] —**wit′ti·ly** *adv.* —**wit′ti·ness** *n.*

wive (wīv) *v.t.* & *v.i.* **wived, wiv·ing** *Archaic* To marry (a woman). [< OE *wīf* a wife, woman]

wives (wīvz) *n. pl.* of WIFE.

wiz·ard (wiz′ərd) *n.* **1** A magician or sorcerer. **2** *Informal* A very skillful or clever person. —*adj.* Of or pertaining to wizards. [< OE *wīs* wise]

wiz·ard·ry (wiz′ərd·rē) *n.* The practice or methods of a wizard.

wiz·ened (wiz′ənd) *adj.* Shriveled; dried up. [< OE *wisnian,* dry up, wither]

wk. weak; week; work.

wks. weeks; works.

WL, w.l. water line; wave length.

W. long. west longitude.

WNW, W.N.W., wnw, w.n.w. west-northwest.

WO, W.O. wait order; Warrant Officer.

woad (wōd) *n.* **1** An Old World herb related to mustard. **2** The blue dye obtained from its leaves. [< OE *wād*] —**woad′ed** *adj.*

wob·ble (wob′əl) *v.* **·bled, ·bling** *v.i.* **1** To move or sway unsteadily. **2** To show indecision or unsteadiness; vacillate. —*v.t.* **3** To cause to wobble. —*n.* A wobbling motion. [? < LG *wabbeln*] —**wob′bler** *n.* —**wob′bling·ly** *adv.* —**wob′·bly** *adj.* **(·bli·er, ·bli·est)**

woe (wō) *n.* **1** Overwhelming sorrow; grief. **2** Heavy affliction or calamity; disaster; suffering. —*interj.* Alas! [< OE *wā* misery]

woe·be·gone (wō′bi·gôn′, -gon′) *adj.* Having or exhibiting woe; mournful; sorrowful. —**Syn.** dejected, depressed, lugubrious, melancholy.

woe·ful (wō′fəl) *adj.* **1** Accompanied by or causing woe; direful. **2** Expressive of sorrow; doleful. **3** Paltry; miserable; mean; sorry. —**woe′ful·ly** *adv.* —**woe′ful·ness** *n.*

wok (wok) *n.* A Chinese cooking pan, as of iron, aluminum, or copper, with handles and a rounded bottom, usu. equipped with a separate metal ring to prevent tipping. [< Chinese]

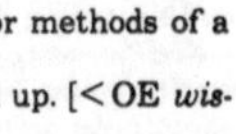

Wok

woke (wōk) *p.t.* of WAKE[1].

wok·en (wō′kən) *Regional & alternative Brit. p.p.* of WAKE[1].

wold (wōld) *n.* An undulating tract of treeless upland. [< OE *wald* a forest]

wolf (wo͝olf) *n. pl.* **wolves** (wo͝olvz) **1** Any of various wild, carnivorous mammals related to the dog. **2** Any ravenous, cruel, or rapacious person. **3** *Slang* A man who zealously and aggressively pursues women. **—cry wolf** To give a false alarm. **—keep the wolf from the door** To avert want or starvation. *—v.t.* To devour ravenously: often with *down.* [< OE *wulf*]

Timber wolf

wolf·ber·ry (wo͝olf′ber′ē) *n. pl.* **·ries** A shrub of the honeysuckle family, with pinkish, bell-shaped flowers and spikes of white berries.

wolf·hound (wo͝olf′hound′) *n.* Either of two breeds of large dogs, the **Russian wolfhound** and the **Irish wolfhound,** formerly trained to hunt wolves.

wolf·ish (wo͝olf′ish) *adj.* Of or like a wolf; rapacious; savage. **—wolf′ish·ly** *adv.* **—wolf′ish·ness** *n.*

wolf·ram (wo͝ol′frəm) *n.* TUNGSTEN. [G]

wolf·ram·ite (wo͝ol′frəm·īt) *n.* A grayish black or brown mineral, an important source of tungsten. [< G *Wolfram* tungsten]

wolfs·bane (wo͝olfs′bān′) *n.* A species of aconite, usu. with yellow flowers. Also **wolf's-bane.**

wol·ver·ine (wo͝ol′və·rēn′) *n.* A rapacious carnivore related to weasels, with stout body and bushy tail. Also **wol′ver·ene′.** [< WOLF]

wolves (wo͝olvz) *n. pl.* of WOLF.

wom·an (wo͝om′ən) *n. pl.* **wom·en** (wim′in) **1** An adult human female. **2** The female part of the human race; women collectively. **3** Womanly character; femininity: usu. with *the.* **4** A female attendant or servant. **5** A paramour or mistress. **6** *Informal* A wife. *—adj.* **1** Of or characteristic of women. **2** Female: a *woman* lawyer. [< OE *wīf* a wife + *mann* a human being] • See LADY.

wom·an·hood (wo͝om′ən·ho͝od) *n.* **1** The state of a woman or of womankind. **2** Women collectively.

wom·an·ish (wo͝om′ən·ish) *adj.* **1** For or characteristic of a woman; womanly. **2** Feminine or effeminate in nature, and according ill with the qualities associated with men. **—wom′an·ish·ly** *adv.* **—wom′an·ish·ness** *n.*

wom·an·ize (wo͝om′ən·īz) *v.* **·ized, ·iz·ing** *v.t.* **1** To make effeminate or womanish. *—v.i.* **2** To have affairs with many women. **—wom′an·iz·er** *n.*

wom·an·kind (wo͝om′ən·kīnd′) *n.* Women collectively.

wom·an·ly (wo͝om′ən·lē) *adj.* Having the qualities natural, suited, or becoming to a woman; feminine. **—wom′an·li·ness** *n.*

womb (wo͞om) *n.* **1** UTERUS. **2** A place where anything is engendered or brought into life. [< OE *wamb, womb* the belly]

wom·bat (wom′bat) *n.* Any of various burrowing Australian marsupials resembling a small bear. [< native Australian name]

Wombat

wom·en (wim′in) *n. pl.* of WOMAN.

wom·en·folk (wim′in·fōk′) *n.pl.* Women collectively: also **wom′·en·folks′.**

won (wun) *p.t. & p.p.* of WIN.

won·der (wun′dər) *n.* **1** A feeling of mingled surprise, admiration, and astonishment. **2** One who or that which causes wonder. *—v.t.* **1** To have a feeling of curiosity or doubt in regard to. *—v.i.* **2** To be affected or filled with wonder; marvel. **3** To be curious or doubtful. *—adj.* Spectacularly successful: a *wonder* drug. [< OE *wundor*] **—won′der·er** *n.* **—won′der·ing·ly** *adv.*

won·der·ful (wun′dər·fəl) *adj.* **1** Of a nature to excite wonder; astonishing. **2** Very good; excellent. **—won′der·ful·ly** *adv.* **—won′der·ful·ness** *n.*

won·der·land (wun′dər·land′) *n.* **1** A realm of imaginary wonders. **2** Any place of unusual beauty, astonishing sights, etc.

won·der·ment (wun′dər·mənt) *n.* **1** The emotion of wonder; surprise. **2** Something wonderful; a marvel.

won·drous (wun′drəs) *adj.* Wonderful; marvelous. *—adv.* Surprisingly. **—won′drous·ly** *adv.* **—won′drous·ness** *n.*

wont (wônt, wōnt) *adj.* Accustomed: He is *wont* to eat late. *—n.* Ordinary manner of doing or acting; habit. [< OE *gewunod,* p.p. of *gewunian* be accustomed]

won't (wōnt) Contraction of *will not.*

wont·ed (wun′tid, wōn′-) *adj.* **1** Commonly used or done; habitual. **2** Habituated; accustomed. **—wont′ed·ness** *n.*

woo (wo͞o) *v.t.* **1** To make love to, esp. so as to marry. **2** To entreat earnestly; beg. **3** To seek. *—v.i.* **4** To pay court; make love. [< OE *wōgian*] **—woo′er** *n.*

wood (wo͝od) *n.* **1** The hard, fibrous material between the pith and bark of a tree or shrub. **2** Trees or shrubs cut for use, as for building, fuel, etc. **3** *Usu. pl.* A large, dense growth of trees; forest. **4** Something made of wood, as a woodwind or certain golf clubs having a wooden head. *—adj.* **1** Made of wood; wooden. **2** Made for burning wood: a *wood* stove. **3** Living or growing in woods. *—v.t.* **1** To furnish with wood for fuel. **2** To plant with trees. *—v.i.* **3** To take on a supply of wood. [< OE *widu, wiodu*]

wood alcohol Methanol, esp. if obtained from wood tar.

wood·bine (wo͝od′bīn) *n.* **1** A climbing European honeysuckle. **2** VIRGINIA CREEPER. [< OE *wudu* wood + *bindan* bind]

wood·block (wo͝od′blok′) *n.* **1** A block of wood. **2** WOODCUT. Also **wood block.**

wood·chuck (wo͝od′chuk) *n.* A hibernating marmot of North America; a groundhog. [Prob. < Algon.; infl. in form by WOOD and CHUCK]

Woodchuck

wood·cock (wo͝od′kok′) *n.* **1** A European game bird related to the snipe. **2** A smaller related North American bird.

wood·craft (wo͝od′kraft′, -kräft′) *n.* **1** Skill in knowing how to survive in the woods by making shelters, hunting game, etc. **2** The act or art of constructing articles of wood. **—wood′crafts′man** (*pl.* **·men**) *n.*

wood·cut (wo͝od′kut′) *n.* **1** A block of wood engraved, as with a design, for making prints. **2** A print made from such a block.

wood·cut·ter (wo͝od′kut′ər) *n.* One who cuts or chops wood. **—wood′cut′ting** *n.*

wood·ed (wo͝od′id) *adj.* Abounding with trees.

wood·en (wo͝od′n) *adj.* **1** Made of wood. **2** Stiff; awkward. **3** Dull; stupid. **—wood′en·ly** *adv.* **—wood′en·ness** *n.*

wood engraving **1** The art of cutting designs on wood for printing. **2** A block of wood with an engraving cut, as with a burin, into a surface that is perpendicular to the direction of the grain. **3** A print from such a block. **—wood engraver**

wood·en·head (wo͝od′n·hed′) *n. Informal* A stupid person; blockhead. **—wood′en·head′ed** *adj.* **—wood′en·head′·ed·ness** *n.*

wood·en·ware (wo͝od′n·wâr′) *n.* Dishes, vessels, bowls, etc., made of wood.

wood·land (wo͝od′lənd, -land′) *n.* Land covered with wood or trees; timberland. *—adj.* (-lənd) Belonging to or dwelling in the woods. **—wood′land′er** *n.*

wood louse Any of numerous small terrestrial flat-bodied crustaceans commonly found under old logs.

wood·note (wo͝od′nōt′ *n.* A simple, artless, or natural song, call, etc., as of a woodland bird.

wood nymph A nymph of the forest.

wood·peck·er (wo͝od′pek′ər) *n.* Any of a large family of birds having stiff tail feathers, strong claws, and a sharp bill for drilling holes in trees in search of wood-boring insects.

Red-headed woodpecker

wood·pile (wo͝od′pīl′) *n.* A pile of wood, esp. of wood cut in sizes for burning.

wood pulp Wood reduced to a pulp, used for making paper.

wood·shed (wo͝od′shed′) *n.* A shed for storing firewood.

woods·man (wo͝odz′mən) *n. pl.* **·men** (-mən) **1** A man who lives or works in the woods. **2** A man skilled in woodcraft.

wood sorrel A creeping perennial woodland plant with cloverlike leaves containing oxalic acid. • See SHAMROCK.

woods·y (wo͝od′zē) *adj.* **woods·i·er, woods·i·est** Of, pertaining to, or like the woods. **—woods′i·ness** *n.*

wood tar A tar produced by the dry distillation of wood.
wood thrush A large, common woodland thrush with reddish brown plumage, having a bell-like song. • See THRUSH[1].
wood turning The shaping of blocks of wood by means of a lathe. —**wood turner**
wood·wind (wŏŏd′wind′) *n.* **1** A musical wind instrument, as the flute, clarinet, bassoon, oboe, or saxophone. **2** *pl.* The woodwinds of an orchestra; also, the players of these instruments.
wood·work (wŏŏd′wûrk′) *n.* Things made of wood, esp. certain interior parts of a house, as moldings, doors, windowsills, etc. —**wood′work′er, wood′work′ing** *n.*
wood·worm (wŏŏd′wûrm′) *n.* A worm or larva dwelling in or that bores in wood.
wood·y (wŏŏd′ē) *adj.* **wood·i·er, wood·i·est 1** Made of or containing wood. **2** Resembling wood. **3** Wooded; abounding with trees. —**wood′i·ness** *n.*
woof[1] (wŏŏf, wōōf) *n.* **1** The threads that are carried back and forth across the warp in a loom. **2** The texture of a fabric. [<OE *ōwef*]
woof[2] (wŏŏf) *n.* A low barking sound or growl, esp. of a dog. —*v.i.* To make such a sound. [Imit.]
woof·er (wŏŏf′ər) *n.* A loudspeaker designed to reproduce sounds of low frequency. [<WOOF[2] + -ER]
wool (wŏŏl) *n.* **1** The soft, durable fiber obtained from the fleece of sheep and some allied animals, as goats, alpacas, etc. **2** Yarn or fabric made of such fibers. **3** Garments made of wool. **4** Something resembling or likened to wool. —**pull the wool over one's eyes** To delude or deceive one. —*adj.* Made of or pertaining to wool or woolen material. [<OE *wull*]
wool·en (wŏŏl′ən) *adj.* **1** Of or pertaining to wool. **2** Made of wool. —*n. Usu. pl.* Cloth or clothing made of wool. Also **wool′en.**
wool·gath·er·ing (wŏŏl′gath′ər·ing) *n.* Idle daydreaming; absent-mindedness. —**wool′gath′er·er** *n.*
wool·grow·er (wŏŏl′grō′ər) *n.* A person who raises sheep for the production of wool. —**wool′grow′ing** *adj.*
wool·ly (wŏŏl′ē) *adj.* **·li·er, ·li·est 1** Consisting of, covered with, or resembling wool. **2** Not clear or sharply detailed; fuzzy. **3** Resembling the roughness and excitement of the early American West, usu. in the phrase **wild and woolly.** —*n. pl.* **·lies** A garment made of wool, esp. woolen underwear. Also **wool′y.** —**wool′li·ness, wool′i·ness** *n.*
wooz·y (wōō′zē) *adj.* **·i·er, ·i·est** *Slang* Befuddled, esp. with drink. [Prob. < *wooze,* var. of OOZE] —**wooz′i·ly** *adv.* —**wooz′i·ness** *n.*
word (wûrd) *n.* **1** A speech sound or combination of sounds which has come to signify and communicate a particular idea or thought, and which functions as the smallest meaningful unit of a language when used in isolation. **2** The letters or characters that stand for such a language unit. **3** *Usu. pl.* Speech; talk: hard to put into *words.* **4** A brief remark or comment. **5** A communication or message: Send him *word.* **6** A command, signal, or direction: Give the *word* to start. **7** A promise: a man of his *word.* **8** Rumor, gossip, or news: What's the latest *word?* **9** A watchword or password. **10** *pl.* The text of a song: *words* and music. **11** *pl.* Language used in anger, rebuke, etc.: They had *words.* —**in a word** In short; briefly. —**eat one's words** To retract what one has said. —**mince words** To be evasive or overly delicate in what one says. —**take one at his word** To believe literally in what another has said and act or respond accordingly. —**word for word** In exactly the same words; verbatim. —*v.t.* To express in a word or words; phrase. —**the Word 1** LOGOS (def. 2). **2** GOSPEL (def. 1). **3** The Scriptures; the Bible. [<OE]
word·age (wûr′dij) *n.* **1** Words collectively. **2** The number of words, as in a novel. **3** VERBIAGE. **4** WORDING.
word·book (wûrd′bŏŏk′) *n.* **1** A collection of words; vocabulary; lexicon; dictionary. **2** An opera libretto.
word·ing (wûr′ding) *n.* The style or arrangement of words; diction; phraseology.
word·less (wûrd′lis) *adj.* Having no words; dumb; silent.
word of mouth Spoken words; speech; oral communication. —**word-of-mouth** (wûrd′uv·mouth′) *adj.*
word order The sequence or arrangement of words in a sentence, phrase, or clause.
word·play (wûrd′plā′) *n.* **1** Clever repartee. **2** A play on words; pun.
word processing The computer-storage editing, transmittal, and reproduction of written information by means of a terminal, printer, memory, software, etc. —**word processor** *n.*
word·y (wûr′dē) *adj.* **word·i·er, word·i·est 1** Expressed in many or too many words; verbose. **2** Of or pertaining to words; verbal. —**word′i·ly** *adv.* —**word′i·ness** *n.* —**Syn. 1** long-winded, prolix, roundabout, redundant.
wore (wôr, wōr) *p.t.* of WEAR.
work (wûrk) *n.* **1** Continued physical or mental exertion or activity directed to some purpose or end; labor; toil. **2** Employment; job: to be out of *work.* **3** One's profession, occupation, business, trade, etc.: What is your *work?* **4** The place where one is employed or occupied professionally: She is at *work.* **5** An undertaking or task, often a part of one's job or occupation: to take *work* home; also, the amount of this that is accomplished or required: a day's *work.* **6** *pl.* A place where something is made, undertaken, etc.: often used in combination: the *oilworks.* **7** The material used or processed in manufacturing something. **8** Something that has been made, created, accomplished, etc., esp.: **a** An engineering structure, as a bridge. **b** A feat or deed: remembered for her good *works.* **c** Needlework or embroidery. **d** A product of the mind and imagination: the *works* of Beethoven. **9** Manner, quality, or style of doing something; workmanship. **10** *pl.* Running gear or machinery: the *works* of a watch. **11** The action of natural forces or the result of such action: the *work* of a storm. **12** *Physics* A transfer of energy between physical systems. —**the works** *Slang* **1** Everything belonging, available, etc. **2** Drastic or vicious treatment: to give someone *the works.* —**shoot the works** *Slang* **1** To risk everything. **2** To make a final, supreme effort. —*v.* **worked** (*Archaic* **wrought**), **work·ing** *v.i.* **1** To perform work; labor; toil. **2** To be employed in some trade or business. **3** To perform a function; operate: The machine *works* well. **4** To prove effective or influential: His stratagem *worked.* **5** To move or progress gradually or with difficulty: He *worked* up in his profession. **6** To become as specified, as by gradual motion: The bolts *worked* loose. **7** To move from nervousness or agitation: His features *worked* with anger. **8** To undergo kneading, hammering, etc.; be shaped: Copper *works* easily. **9** To ferment. —*v.t.* **10** To cause or bring about: to *work* a miracle. **11** To direct the operation of: to *work* a machine. **12** To make or shape by toil or skill. **13** To prepare, as by manipulating, hammering, etc.: to *work* dough. **14** To decorate, as with embroidery or inlaid work. **15** To cause to be productive, as by toil: to *work* a mine. **16** To cause to do work: He *works* his employees too hard. **17** To cause to be as specified, usu. with effort: We *worked* the timber into position. **18** To make or achieve by effort: to *work* one's passage on a ship. **19** To carry on some activity in (an area, etc.); cover: to *work* a sales territory. **20** To solve, as a problem in arithmetic. **21** To cause to move from nervousness or excitement: to *work* one's jaws. **22** To excite; provoke: He *worked* himself into a passion. **23** To influence or manage, as by insidious means; lead. **24** To cause to ferment. **25** *Informal* To practice trickery upon; cheat; swindle. **26** *Informal* To make use of for one's own purposes; use. —**work in** To insert or be inserted. —**work off** To get rid of, as extra flesh by exercise. —**work on** (or **upon**) **1** To try to influence or persuade. **2** To influence or affect. —**work out 1** To make its way out or through. **2** To effect by work or effort; accomplish. **3** To exhaust, as a mine. **4** To discharge, as a debt, by labor rather than by payment of money. **5** To develop; form, as a plan. **6** To solve. **7 a** To prove effective or successful. **b** To result as specified. **8** To exercise, train, etc. —**work over 1** To repeat. **2** *Slang* To treat harshly or cruelly; beat up, torture, etc. —**work up 1** To excite; rouse, as rage or a person to

rage. **2** To form or shape by working; develop: to *work up* a new advertising campaign. **3** To make one's or its way. **4** To cause or bring about. [< OE *weorc*]

-work *combining form* **1** A product made from a (specified) material: *brickwork.* **2** Work of a (given) kind: *piecework.* **3** Work performed in a (specified) place: *housework.*

work·a·ble (wûr′kə·bəl) *adj.* **1** Capable of being worked, developed, etc. **2** Practicable, as a plan. **—work′a·bil′i·ty, work′a·ble·ness** *n.*

work·a·day (wûrk′ə·dā′) *adj.* **1** Of, pertaining to, or suitable for working days; everyday. **2** Commonplace; prosaic.

work·bench (wûrk′bench′) *n.* A bench for work, esp. that of a carpenter, machinist, etc.

work·book (wûrk′bo͝ok′) *n.* **1** A booklet based on a course of study and containing problems and exercises which a student works out directly on the pages. **2** A manual containing operating instructions. **3** A book for recording work performed or planned.

work·day (wûrk′dā′) *n.* **1** Any day, usu. not a Sunday or holiday, on which work is done. **2** The number of hours of one day spent in work. Also **working day.** *—adj.* WORKADAY.

work·er (wûk′kər) *n.* **1** One who or that which performs work. **2** A social insect, as a bee, ant, etc., that is sexually sterile and performs work for the colony. **3** A member of the working class.

work·fare (wûrk′fâr′) *n.* Welfare that is conditional upon assigned work or training by those receiving payments.

work·house (wûrk′hous′) *n.* **1** *Brit.* Formerly, a house for paupers able to work. **2** A prison in which petty offenders are put to work.

work·ing (wûr′king) *adj.* **1** Engaged actively in some employment. **2** That works, or performs its function: This is a *working* model. **3** Sufficient for use or action: They formed a *working* agreement. **4** Of, used in, or occupied by work: a *working* day. **5** Throbbing or twitching, as facial muscles. **—*n.*** **1** The act or operation of any person or thing that works. **2** *Usu. pl.* That part of a mine or quarry where excavation is going on or has gone on.

working capital That part of the finances of a business available for its operation or convertible into cash.

working class People who work for wages, esp. manual and industrial workers. **—work′ing-class′** *adj.*

work·man (wûrk′mən) *n. pl.* **·men** (-men′) **1** A male worker. **2** A man who earns his living by working with his hands or with machines. Also **work·ing·man** (wûr′king·man′).

work·man·like (wûrk′mən·līk) *adj.* Like or befitting a skilled workman; skillfully done. Also **work′man·ly.**

work·man·ship (wûrk′mən·ship) *n.* **1** The art or skill of a workman. **2** The quality of work. **3** The work produced.

work of art **1** A highly artistic product of the fine arts, esp. painting and sculpture. **2** Anything made or done with great beauty or skill.

work·out (wûrk′out′) *n.* **1** Any activity done to increase or maintain skill, physical fitness, etc. **2** Any instance of strenuous activity, disciplined work, etc.

work·room (wûrk′ro͞om, -ro͝om′) *n.* A room where work is performed.

work·shop (wûrk′shop′) *n.* **1** A building or room where any work is carried on; workroom. **2** A seminar or single session for training, discussion, etc., in a specialized field: a writers' *workshop.*

work·ta·ble (wûrk′tā′bəl) *n.* A table with drawers and other conveniences for use while working.

work·week (wûrk′wēk′) *n.* The total number of hours worked in a week; also, the number of required working hours in a week.

world (wûrld) *n.* **1** The earth. **2** The universe. **3** Any celestial body: Are there other inhabited *worlds?* **4** *Often cap.* A part of the earth: the *Old World.* **5** A specific time or period in history: the ancient *world.* **6** A division of existing or created things belonging to the earth; the animal *world.* **7** The human inhabitants of the earth: mankind. **8** A definite class of people having certain interests or activities in common: the scientific *world.* **9** Secular or worldly aims, pleasures, etc., as distinguished from religious or spiritual ones; also, those people who pursue such aims or pleasures. **10** Individual conditions or circumstances of a person's life: His *world* has changed. **11** A large quantity or amount: a *world* of trouble. **—come into the world** To be born. **—for all the world** **1** In every respect. **2** For any reason. **—on top of the world** *Informal* Elated. **—out of this world** *Informal* Exceptionally fine; wonderful. [< OE *weorold*]

world·ly (wûrld′lē) *adj.* **·li·er, ·li·est** **1** Pertaining to the world; mundane; earthly. **2** Devoted to secular, earthly things; not spiritual. **3** Sophisticated; worldly-wise. **—*adv.*** In a worldly manner. **—world′li·ness** *n.*

world·ly-mind·ed (wûrld′lē·mīn′did) *adj.* Absorbed in the things of this world. **—world′ly-mind′ed·ly** *adv.*

world·ly-wise (wûrld′lē·wīz) *adj.* Wise in the ways and affairs of the world; sophisticated.

world power A state or organization whose policies and actions have a worldwide influence.

World Series In baseball, the games played at the finish of the regular season between the champion teams of the two major U.S. leagues. Also **world series.**

World War I The war (1914–18) between the Allies and the Central Powers (Germany, Austria-Hungary, Turkey, and Bulgaria).

World War II The war (1939–45) between the United Nations and the Axis.

world-wea·ry (wûrld′wir′ē) *adj.* **·ri·er, ·ri·est** Weary of life and its conditions. **—world′-wea′ri·ness** *n.*

world·wide (wûrld′wīd′) *adj.* Extended throughout the world.

worm (wûrm) *n.* **1** *Zool.* Any of numerous limbless, elongated, soft-bodied invertebrate animals, including flatworms, roundworms, and annelids. **2** Any small animal resembling a worm, as a caterpillar, maggot, snake, shipworm, etc. **3** Something which suggests the inner, hidden gnawings of a worm: the *worm* of remorse. **4** A despicable or despised person. **5** Something conceived to be like a worm, as the thread of a screw. **6** *pl.* Any disorder due to parasitic worms in the intestines, etc. **—*v.t.*** **1** To move, proceed, insinuate, etc. (oneself or itself) in a wormlike manner: to *worm* one's way. **2** To draw forth by artful means, as a secret: with *out.* **3** To rid of intestinal worms. **—*v.i.*** **4** To move or progress slowly and stealthily. [< OE *wyrm*] **—worm′i·ness** *n.* **—worm′y** *adj.* **(·i·er, ·i·est)**

worm-eat·en (wûrm′ēt′n) *adj.* **1** Eaten or bored through by worms. **2** Worn-out or decayed.

worm gear A gear having teeth shaped so as to mesh with a threaded shaft.

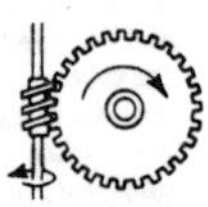

Worm gear

worm·hole (wûrm′hōl′) *n.* The hole made by a worm or a wormlike animal. **—worm′holed′** *adj.*

worm·wood (wûrm′wo͝od′) *n.* **1** Any of various European herbs or small shrubs related to the sagebrush, esp. a species yielding a bitter oil used in making absinthe. **2** Something that embitters or is unpleasant. [< OE *wermōd*]

worn (wôrn, wōrn) *p.p.* of WEAR. **—*adj.*** **1** Affected by wear, use, continuous action, etc.; frayed, damaged, etc. **2** Showing the effects of worry, anxiety, etc. **3** Hackneyed, as a phrase.

worn-out (wôrn′out′, wōrn′-) *adj.* **1** Used until without value or usefulness. **2** Thoroughly tired; exhausted.

wor·ri·some (wûr′i·səm) *adj.* Causing worry or anxiety.

wor·ry (wûr′ē) *v.* **·ried, ·ry·ing** *v.i.* **1** To be uneasy in the mind; feel anxiety. **2** To manage despite trials or difficulties; struggle: with *along* or *through.* **—*v.t.*** **3** To cause to feel uneasy in the mind; trouble. **4** To bother; pester. **5** To bite, pull at, or shake with the teeth. **—*n. pl.*** **·ries** **1** A state of anxiety or uneasiness. **2** Something causing such a state. [< OE *wrygan* strangle] **—wor′ri·er, wor′ri·ment** *n.*

worse (wûrs) Comparative of BAD and ILL. **—*adj.*** **1** Bad or ill in a great degree; inferior. **2** Physically ill in a greater degree. **3** Less favorable, as to conditions, circumstances, etc. **4** More evil, corrupt, etc. **—*n.*** Someone or something worse. **—*adv.*** **1** In a worse manner, way, etc. **2** With greater intensity, severity, etc. [< OE *wyrsa*]

wors·en (wûr′sən) *v.t.* & *v.i.* To make or become worse.

wor·ship (wûr′ship) *n.* **1** Adoration, homage, etc., given to a deity. **2** The rituals, prayers, etc., expressing such adoration or homage. **3** Excessive or ardent admiration or love. 4 The object of such love or admiration. 5 *Chiefly Brit.* A title of honor in addressing certain persons of station. —*v.* **·shiped** or **·shipped, ·ship·ing** or **·ship·ping** *v.t.* 1 To pay an act of worship to; venerate. 2 To have intense or exaggerated admiration or love for. —*v.i.* 3 To perform acts or have sentiments of worship. [< OE *weorthscipe* < *weorth* worthy] **—wor′ship·er, wor′ship·per** *n.* **—Syn.** *v.* 1 exalt, praise. 2 adore, dote on, idolize.

wor·ship·ful (wûr′ship·fəl) *adj.* 1 Feeling or giving great reverence, love, etc. 2 *Chiefly Brit.* Worthy of respect by reason of character or position: applied to certain dignitaries. **—wor′ship·ful·ly** *adv.* **—wor′ship·ful·ness** *n.*

worst (wûrst) Superlative of BAD and ILL. —*adj.* 1 Bad or ill in the highest degree. 2 Least favorable, as to conditions, circumstances, etc. 3 Most evil, corrupt, etc. **—in the worst way** *Informal* Very much. —*n.* Someone or something that is worst. **—at worst** Under the worst possible circumstances or conditions. **—get the worst of it** To be defeated or put at a disadvantage. —*adv.* 1 To the greatest or most extreme degree. 2 To the greatest or most extreme degree of inferiority, badness, etc. —*v.t.* To defeat; vanquish. [< OE *wyrsta*]

wors·ted (wo͝os′tid, wûr′stid) *n.* 1 Woolen yarn spun from long staple, with fibers combed parallel and twisted hard. 2 A tightly woven fabric made from such yarn. —*adj.* Consisting of or made from such yarn. [< *Worsted,* former name of a parish in Norfolk, England]

wort[1] (wûrt) *n.* A plant or herb: usu. in combination: *liverwort.* [< OE *wyrt* a root, a plant]

wort[2] (wûrt) *n.* The unfermented infusion of malt that becomes beer when fermented. [< OE *wyrt* a root, a plant]

worth (wûrth) *n.* 1 Value or excellence of any kind. 2 The market value of something. 3 The amount of something obtainable at a specific sum: two cents' *worth* of candy. 4 Wealth. —*adj.* 1 Equal in value (to); exchangable (for). 2 Deserving (of): not *worth* going. 3 Having wealth or possessions to the value of: He is *worth* a million. **—for all it is worth** To the utmost. **—for all one is worth** With every effort possible. [< OE *weorth*]

worth·less (wûrth′lis) *adj.* Having no worth, usefulness, virtue, etc. **—worth′less·ly** *adv.* **—worth′less·ness** *n.*

worth·while (wûrth′hwīl′) *adj.* Sufficiently important to occupy the time; of enough value to repay the effort. **—worth′while′ness** *n.*

wor·thy (wûr′t͟hē) *adj.* **·thi·er, ·thi·est** 1 Possessing valuable or useful qualities. 2 Having such qualities as to deserve or merit some specified thing: *worthy* of the honor. —*n. pl.* **·thies** A person of eminent worth: sometimes used humorously. **—wor′thi·ly** *adv.* **—wor′thi·ness** *n.*

-worthy *combining form* 1 Meriting or deserving: *trustworthy.* 2 Valuable as; having worth as: *newsworthy.* 3 Fit for: *seaworthy.*

wot (wot) *p.t., first and third person singular,* of WIT[2].

would (wo͝od) *p.t.* of WILL, but used chiefly as an auxiliary to express: 1 Desire: They *would* like to go. 2 Condition: They *would* go if you asked them. 3 Futurity: He said he *would* bring it. 4 Determination: The dog *would* not let go. 5 Custom or habit: He *would* walk there every day. [< OE *wolde,* p.t. of *willan* will]

would-be (wo͝od′bē′) *adj.* Desiring, professing, or intended to be: a *would-be* actress.

would·n't (wo͝od′nt) Contraction of *would not.*

wound[1] (wo͞ond) *n.* 1 A hurt or injury, esp. one in which the skin is torn, cut, etc. 2 A cutting or scraping injury to a tree or plant. 3 Any cause of pain or grief, as to the feelings, honor, etc. —*v.t. & v.i.* 1 To inflict a wound or wounds (upon). 2 To injure the feelings or pride of. [< OE *wund*] **—Syn.** *v.* 2 affront, hurt, offend, pique.

wound[2] (wound) *p.t. & p.p.* of WIND[2].

wove (wōv) *p.t. &* a *p.p.* of WEAVE.

wo·ven (wō′vən) *p.p.* of WEAVE.

wow (wou) *interj. Informal* An exclamation of wonder, surprise, pleasure, etc. —*n. Slang* A person or thing that is extraordinary, successful, etc. —*v.t. Slang* To cause to feel excitement, admiration, etc.

WPA, W.P.A. Works Progress Administration.

wrack (rak) *n.* 1 Ruin; destruction: esp. in the phrase **wrack and ruin.** 2 Marine vegetation cast ashore by the sea, as seaweed. 3 A wrecked vessel; wreckage. —*v.t. & v.i.* To wreck or be wrecked. [Fusion of OE *wræc* punishment, revenge and MDu. *wrak* a wreck]

wraith (rāth) *n.* 1 An apparition of a person seen shortly before or shortly after his or her death. 2 Any specter; ghost. [?]

wran·gle (rang′gəl) *v.* **·gled, ·gling** *v.i.* 1 To argue noisily and angrily. —*v.t.* 2 To argue; debate. 3 To get by stubborn arguing. 4 To herd or round up, as livestock. —*n.* An angry dispute. [ME *wranglen*] **—wran′gler** *n.*

wrap (rap) *v.* **wrapped** or **wrapt, wrap·ping** *v.t.* 1 To surround and cover by something folded or wound about. 2 To fold or wind (a covering) about something. 3 To surround so as to blot out or conceal: a mountain *wrapped* in clouds. 4 To fold or wind. —*v.i.* 5 To be or become twined, coiled, etc.: with *about, around,* etc. **—wrap up** 1 To cover with paper, etc. 2 To put on warm garments. 3 *Informal* To conclude or finish. **—wrapped up in** Involved or absorbed in: *wrapped up in* his music. —*n.* 1 A garment folded about a person. 2 *pl.* Outer garments collectively. 3 A blanket. **—keep under wraps** To keep secret. [ME *wrappen*]

wrap·a·round (rap′ə·round′) *adj.* 1 Made so as to be wrapped around the body and then fastened: a *wraparound* skirt. 2 Designed so as to curve back on each side: a *wraparound* windshield. —*n.* Anything that encircles or curves back on each side.

wrap·per (rap′ər) *n.* 1 A paper enclosing a newspaper, magazine, or similar packet for mailing or otherwise. 2 A woman's dressing gown. 3 One who or that which wraps.

wrap·ping (rap′ing) *n. Often pl.* A covering or something in which an object is wrapped.

wrap-up (rap′up′) *n. Informal* 1 A summary or conclusion: a *wrap-up* of the news. 2 The final event, action, etc., in a connected series.

wrath (rath, räth; *Brit.* rôth) *n.* 1 Violent rage, anger, or fury. 2 An act done in violent rage. [< OE *wrāth* wroth]

wrath·ful (rath′fəl, räth′-) *adj.* 1 Full of wrath; extremely angry. 2 Resulting from or expressing wrath. **—wrath′ful·ly** *adv.* **—wrath′ful·ness** *n.* **—Syn.** 1 furious, apoplectic, mad, raging.

wreak (rēk) *v.t.* 1 To inflict or exact, as vengeance. 2 To give free expression to, as a feeling or passion. [< OE *wrecan* drive, avenge]

wreath (rēth) *n. pl.* **wreaths** (rē͟thz, rēths) 1 A band, as of flowers or leaves, commonly circular, as for a crown, decoration, etc. 2 Any curled or spiral band, as of smoke, snow, etc. [< OE *writha*] **—wreath·y** (rē′thē, -t͟hē) *adj.*

wreathe (rē͟th) *v.* **wreathed, wreath·ing** *v.t.* 1 To form into a wreath, as by twisting or twining. 2 To adorn or encircle with or as with wreaths. 3 To envelop; cover: His face was *wreathed* in smiles. —*v.i.* 4 To take the form of a wreath. 5 To twist, turn, or coil, as masses of cloud.

wreck (rek) *v.t.* 1 To cause the destruction of, as by a collision. 2 To bring ruin, damage, or destruction upon. 3 To tear down, as a building; dismantle. —*v.i.* 4 To suffer destruction; be ruined. 5 To engage in wrecking, as for plunder or salvage. —*n.* 1 The act of wrecking, or the condition of being wrecked. 2 That which has been wrecked or ruined by accident, collision, etc. 3 The broken remnants or remains of something wrecked. 4 SHIPWRECK. 5 The ruined, usu. stranded hulk of a ship that has been wrecked. 6 A person who is ill or under great strain. [< AF *wrec* < Scand.]

wreck·age (rek′ij) *n.* 1 The act of wrecking, or the condition of being wrecked. 2 Broken remnants or fragments from a wreck.

wreck·er (rek′ər) *n.* 1 One who causes destruction of any sort. 2 One employed in tearing down and removing old buildings. 3 A person, train, car, or machine that clears away wrecks. 4 One employed to recover disabled vessels or wrecked cargoes.

wren (ren) *n.* 1 Any of numerous small, active, usu. brown birds having short rounded wings and tail and a thin, curved bill. 2 Any one of numerous similar birds. [<OE *wrenna*]

wrench (rench) *n.* 1 A violent twist. 2 A sprain or violent twist or pull in a part of the body. 3 A sudden surge of emotion, as of sorrow, pity, etc. 4 Any of various gripping tools for turning or twisting bolts, nuts, pipes, etc. —*v.t.* 1 To twist violently; turn suddenly by force. 2 To twist forcibly so as to cause strain or injury; sprain. 3 To cause to suffer. 4 To twist from the proper meaning, intent, or use. —*v.i.* 5 To give a twist or wrench [<OE *wrencan* to wrench]

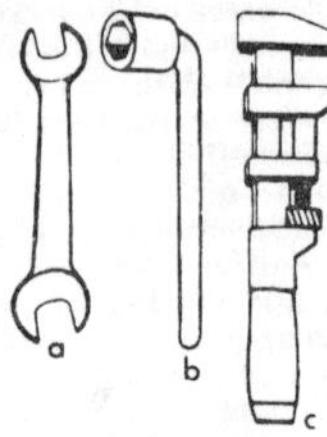

Wrenches *def. 4* a. engineer's. b. offset. c. monkey.

wrest (rest) *v.t.* 1 To pull or force away by violent twisting or wringing; wrench. 2 To turn from the true meaning, intent, etc.; distort. 3 To seize forcibly. 4 To gain or extract by great effort. —*n.* 1 An act of wresting. 2 A key for tuning a piano, harp, etc. [<OE *wræstan*] —**wrest'er** *n.*

wres·tle (res'əl) *v.* **·tled, ·tling** *v.i.* 1 To engage in wrestling. 2 To struggle, as for mastery; contend. —*v.t.* 3 To contend with (someone) in wrestling. 4 To throw (a calf) and hold it down for branding. —*n.* 1 The act or an instance of wrestling. 2 A hard struggle. [<OE *wræstlian*] —**wres'tler** *n.*

wres·tling (res'ling) *n.* A sport or exercise in which each of two unarmed contestants endeavors to throw the other to the ground or force him into a certain fallen position.

wretch (rech) *n.* 1 A vile or contemptible person. 2 A miserable or unhappy person. [<OE *wrecca* an outcast]

wretch·ed (rech'id) *adj.* 1 Sunk in dejection; profoundly unhappy. 2 Causing or characterized by misery, poverty, etc. 3 Unsatisfactory in ability or quality. 4 Despicable; contemptible. —**wretch'ed·ly** *adv.* —**wretch'ed·ness** *n.* —**Syn.** 1 distressed, miserable. 3 bad, paltry, worthless.

wrig·gle (rig'əl) *v.* **·gled, ·gling** *v.i.* 1 To twist in a sinuous manner; squirm; writhe. 2 To proceed as by twisting or crawling. 3 To make one's way by evasive or indirect means. —*v.t.* 4 To cause to wriggle. 5 To make (one's way, etc.) by evasive or sly means. —*n.* The act or motion of one who or that which wriggles. [<MLG *wriggeln*] —**wrig'gly** *adj.*

wrig·gler (rig'lər) *n.* 1 Someone or something that wriggles. 2 A mosquito larva.

wright (rīt) *n.* One who builds or creates something: used in combination: *wheelwright; playwright.* [<OE *wyrhta*]

wring (ring) *v.* **wrung, wring·ing** *v.t.* 1 To squeeze or compress by twisting. 2 To squeeze or press out, as water, by twisting. 3 To acquire by forcible means. 4 To distress: Her plight *wrung* their hearts. 5 To twist violently: to *wring* his neck. —*v.i.* 6 To writhe or squirm with great effort. —*n.* A twisting or wringing. [<OE *wringan*]

wring·er (ring'ər) *n.* 1 One who or that which wrings. 2 A device used to press water out of fabrics after washing.

wrin·kle[1] (ring'kəl) *n.* 1 A small ridge, as on a smooth surface; a crease; fold. 2 A small fold or crease in the skin, usu. produced by age or by excessive exposure to the elements. —*v.* **·kled, ·kling** *v.t.* 1 To make wrinkles in. —*v.i.* 2 To become wrinkled. [<OE *wrincle*] —**wrin'kly** *adj.*

wrin·kle[2] (ring'kəl) *n.* *Informal* A new or ingenious method, device, etc. [Prob. dim. of OE *wrenc* a trick]

wrist (rist) *n.* 1 The part of the arm that lies between the hand and the forearm; the carpus. 2 The part of a glove or garment that covers the wrist. [<OE]

wrist·band (rist'band') *n.* 1 The band of a sleeve that covers the wrist. 2 A band for a wrist watch.

wrist·let (rist'lit) *n.* 1 A flexible band worn on the wrist for support or warmth. 2 A bracelet.

wrist pin *Mech.* A pin attaching a connecting rod to another part.

wrist watch A watch set in a band and worn at the wrist.

writ[1] (rit) *n.* 1 *Law* A written order, issued by a court, and commanding the person to do or not to do some act. 2 That which is written: now chiefly in the phrase **Holy Writ,** the Bible. [<OE *wrītan* write]

writ[2] (rit) *Archaic* or *Regional p.t. & p.p.* of WRITE.

write (rīt) *v.* **wrote** (or *Archaic* **writ**), **writ·ten** (or *Archaic* **writ**), **writ·ing** *v.t.* 1 To trace or inscribe (letters, words, numbers, symbols, etc.) on a surface with pen or pencil. 2 To describe, set down, or signify in writing. 3 To communicate by letter. 4 To communicate with by letter. 5 To produce by writing; be the author or composer of. 6 To draw up; draft: to *write* a check. 7 To cover or fill with writing: to *write* two full pages. 8 To leave marks or evidence of: Anxiety is *written* on his face. 9 To underwrite: to *write* an insurance policy. 10 To store information in computer memory. —*v.i.* 11 To trace or inscribe letters, etc., on a surface, as of paper. 12 To communicate in writing. 13 To be engaged in the occupation of an author. —**write down** 1 To put into writing. 2 To injure or depreciate in writing. —**write in** 1 To insert in writing, as in a document. 2 To cast (a vote) for one not listed on a ballot by inserting his name in writing. —**write off** 1 To cancel or remove (claims, debts, etc.) from an open account. 2 To acknowledge the loss or failure of. —**write out** To write in full or complete form. —**write up** 1 To describe fully in writing. 2 To praise fully or too fully in writing. [<OE *wrītan*] • *Writ,* the archaic past participle of *write,* is now used chiefly in the phrase **writ large,** written or shown on a grand scale: *a name writ large in history.*

write-in (rīt'in) *n.* 1 The act of casting a vote for a candidate not listed on the ballot by writing in his name. 2 The name so written in. —*adj.* Of or pertaining to a write-in.

write-off (rīt'ôf, -of') *n.* 1 A cancellation. 2 An amount canceled or noted as a loss. 3 A person or thing acknowledged to be a failure or a loss.

writ·er (rī'tər) *n.* 1 One who writes. 2 One who engages in literary composition as a profession.

write-up (rīt'up') *n.* A written description or review.

writhe (rīth) *v.* **writhed, writh·ing** *v.t.* 1 To cause to twist or be distorted. —*v.i.* 2 To twist or distort the body, face, or limbs, as in pain. 3 To undergo suffering, as from embarrassment, sorrow, etc. —*n.* An act of writhing. [<OE *wrīthan*] —**writh'er** *n.*

writ·ing (rī'ting) *n.* 1 The act of one who writes. 2 HANDWRITING. 3 Anything written or expressed in letters, esp. a literary production. 4 A written form: put your request in *writing.* 5 The profession or occupation of a writer. —*adj.* 1 Used in or for writing: *writing* paper. 2 That writes.

writ·ten (rit'n) *p.p.* of WRITE.

wrong (rông) *adj.* 1 Not correct; mistaken. 2 Not appropriate: the *wrong* shoes for hiking. 3 Not morally or legally right. 4 Not in accordance with the correct or standard method: the *wrong* way to bake. 5 Not working or operating properly: What is *wrong* with the furnace? 6 Not meant to be seen, used, etc.: the *wrong* side of the fabric. 7 Not intended: a *wrong* turn. —**go wrong** 1 To behave immorrally. 2 To turn out badly; fail. 3 To take a wrong direction, etc. —*adv.* In a wrong direction, place, or manner; erroneously. —*n.* 1 That which is morally or socially wrong or unacceptable. 2 An injury or injustice. —**in the wrong** In error; wrong. —*v.t.* 1 To violate the rights of; inflict injury or injustice upon. 2 To impute evil to unjustly: You *wrong* him. 3 To seduce (a woman). 4 To treat dishonorably. [<Scand.] —**wrong'er, wrong'ness** *n.* —**wrong·ly** *adv.*

wrong·do·er (rông'dōō'ər, rong'-) *n.* One who does wrong. —**wrong'do'ing** *n.*

wrong·ful (rông'fəl) *adj.* 1 Characterized by wrong or injustice; injurious; unjust. 2 Unlawful; illegal. —**wrong'·ful·ly** *adv.* —**wrong'ful·ness** *n.*

wrong-head·ed (rông'hed'id) *adj.* Stubbornly holding to a wrong judgment, opinion, etc. —**wrong'-head'ed·ly** *adv.* —**wrong'-head'ed·ness** *n.*

wrote (rōt) *p.t.* of WRITE.

wroth (rôth) *adj.* Filled with anger; angry. [<OE *wrāth*]

wrought (rôt) *Archaic p.t. & p.p.* of WORK. —*adj.* 1 Beaten or hammered into shape by tools: *wrought* gold. 2 Made delicately or elaborately. 3 Made; fashioned; formed. —**wrought up** Disturbed or excited; agitated. [ME *wrogt,* var. of *worht,* p.p. of *wirchen* work]

wrought iron Strong, malleable, commercially pure iron.

wrung (rung) *p.t. & p.p.* of WRING.

wry (rī) *adj.* **wri·er, wri·est 1** Bent to one side or out of position; contorted; askew. **2** Made by twisting or distorting the features: a *wry* smile. **3** Distorted or warped, as in interpretation or meaning. **4** Somewhat perverse or ironic: *wry* humor. —*v.t.* **wried, wry·ing** To twist; contort. [< OE *wrīgian* move, tend] —**wry′ly** *adv.* —**wry′ness** *n.*

wry·neck (rī′nek′) *n.* **1** A bird allied to the woodpeckers, with the habit of twisting its head and neck. **2** A spasmodic twisting of the neck.

WSW, W.S.W., wsw, w.s.w. west-southwest.

wt, wt. weight.

WV West Virginia (P.O. abbr.).

W.Va. West Virginia.

WY Wyoming (P.O. abbr.).

wy·an·dotte (wī′ən·dot) *n.* One of an American breed of chicken. [< the *Wyandot* Indians, an Iroquoian tribe]

wych-elm (wich′elm′) *n.* **1** A wide-spreading elm with large, dull-green leaves, common in N Europe. **2** Its wood. Also **witch-elm.** [< OE *wice* wych-elm + ELM]

Wyo. Wyoming.

X

X, x (eks) *n. pl.* **X's, x's, Xs, xs** (ek′siz) **1** The 24th letter of the English alphabet. **2** Any spoken sound representing the letter *X* or *x*. **3** In Roman notation, the symbol for 10. **4** An unknown quantity, result, etc. **5** A mark shaped like an X, representing the signature of one who cannot write. **6** A mark used in diagrams, maps, etc., to indicate or point out something. **7** A mark indicating one's answer on a test, one's choice on a ballot, etc. **8** A mark used to indicate a kiss. **9** A mark indicating "times" in multiplication: 4 × 2 = 8. **10** A mark indicating "by" in dimensions: 8½ × 11 inches. **11** Something shaped like an X. —*v.t.* **x-ed** or **x'd, x-ing** or **x'ing 1** To mark with an *x*. **2** To cancel or obliterate with an *x*: usu. with *out*. —*adj.* Shaped like an X.

X Christ; Christian.

xan·thic (zan′thik) *adj.* **1** Having a yellow or yellowish color. **2** Of or pertaining to xanthin or xanthine. [< Gk. *xanthos* yellow]

xan·thin (zan′thin) *n.* A yellow pigment found in plants. Also **xan′tho·phyll** (-thə·fil). [< Gk. *xanthos* yellow]

xan·thine (zan′thēn, -thin) *n.* A white, crystalline, nitrogenous compound, contained in blood, urine, and other animal secretions. [< Gk. *xanthos* yellow]

Xan·thip·pe (zan·tip′ē) The wife of Socrates, renowned as a shrew. —*n.* A shrewish, ill-tempered woman.

xan·thous (zan′thəs) *adj.* Yellow. [< Gk. *xanthos*]

x-ax·is (eks′ak′sis) *n. Math.* A coordinate axis against which the variable *x* is plotted.

X chromosome The sex chromosome that occurs in pairs in the female and is coupled with a Y chromosome in the male of humans and most animals.

X.D., x.d., x-div. ex (without) dividend.

Xe xenon.

xe·bec (zē′bek) *n.* A small, three-masted Mediterranean vessel. [< Ar. *shabbāk*]

xe·non (zē′non) *n.* A heavy, colorless, gaseous element (symbol Xe) occurring in traces in the atmosphere and rarely forming compounds. [< Gk. *xenos* a stranger]

xen·o·pho·bi·a (zen′ə·fō′bē·ə, zē′nə-) *n.* Dislike or fear of strangers or foreigners. [< Gk. *xenos* a stranger + -PHOBIA] —**xen′o·phob′ic** *adj.*

xe·rog·ra·phy (zi·rog′rə·fē) *n.* A method of copying by which a colored powder is distributed by the action of light on an electrically charged plate to form a negative, which is then transferred thermally to a paper or other surface. [< Gk. *xēros* dry + -GRAPHY] —**xe·ro·graph·ic** (zir′ə·graf′ik) *adj.*

xe·roph·i·lous (zi·rof′ə·ləs) *adj.* Thriving under arid conditions: said of plants living in dry regions, as the cactus. [< Gk. *xēros* dry + *philos* loving]

xe·ro·phyte (zir′ə·fīt) *n. Bot.* A plant adapted to arid habitats. [< Gk *xēros* dry + *phyton* plant] —**xe′ro·phyt′ic** (-fit′ik) *adj.*

Xer·ox (zir′oks) *n.* A xerographic copying process: a trade name. —*v.t.* To make or reproduce by Xerox. —*adj.* Of, for, or reproduced by Xeroxing. Also **xer′ox.**

xi (zī, sī; *Gk.* ksē) *n.* The fourteenth letter of the Greek alphabet (Ξ, ξ)

X.I., x.i., x-int. ex (without) interest.

Xmas (kris′məs, eks′məs) *n.* CHRISTMAS. [< *X*, abbr. for *Christ* < Gk. *X*, chi, the first letter of *Christos* Christ + -MAS(s)]

X-ray (eks′rā′) *n.* **1** An electromagnetic radiation having a wavelength shorter than that of ultraviolet light and longer than that of a gamma ray. **2** A photograph made with X-rays. —*adj.* Of, made by, or producing X-rays. —*v.t.* **1** To examine, diagnose, or treat with X-rays. —*v.i.* **2** To use X-rays. Also **X ray.**

x-ref. cross reference.

xy·lem (zī′ləm) *n.* The woody vascular bundles that serve as passageways for water in the roots, stems, and leaves of ferns and seed plants. [< Gk. *xylon* wood]

xy·lo·phone (zī′lə·fōn′) *n.* A musical instrument consisting of an array of wooden bars graduated in length to produce a scale, played by striking the bars with two small mallets. [< Gk. *xylon* wood + *phōnē* sound] —**xy′lo·phon′ist** *n.*

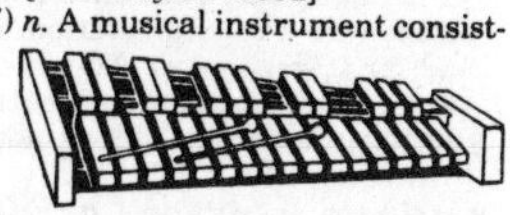

Xylophone

Y

Y, y (wī) *n. pl.* **Y's, y's, Ys, ys** (wīz) **1** The 25th letter of the English alphabet. **2** Any spoken sound representing the letter *Y* or *y*. **3** Something shaped like a Y. —*adj.* Shaped like a Y.

-y[1] *suffix* Being, possessing, or resembling what is expressed in the main element: *stony, rainy.* [< OE *-ig*]

-y[2] *suffix* **1** Quality; condition: *victory.* **2** The place or establishment where something specified happens or is made: *bakery.* **3** The entire group or body of: *soldiery.* [< L *-ia* or < Gk. *-ia, -eia*]

-y[3] *suffix* Little; small: *kitty:* often used to express endearment. [ME *-ie*]

Y (wī) *n. pl.* **Y's** or **Ys 1** YMCA or YWCA. **2** YMHA or YWHA.

Y yttrium.

y. yard(s); year(s).

yacht (yot) *n.* Any of various relatively small sailing or motor-driven ships built or fitted for private pleasure excursions or racing. —*v.i.* To cruise, race, or sail in a yacht. [< Du. *jaghte*, short for *jaghtschip* a pursuit ship]

yacht·ing (yot′ing) *n.* The act, practice, or pastime of sailing in or managing a yacht.

yachts·man (yots′mən) *n. pl.* **-men** (-mən) One who owns or sails a yacht.

---

add, āce, câre, pälm; end, ēven; it, īce; odd, ōpen, ôrder; to͝ok, po͞ol; up, bûrn; ə = *a* in *above*, *u* in *focus;* yo͞o = *u* in *fuse;* oil; pout; check; go; ring; thin; this; zh, *vision.* < derived from; ? origin uncertain or unknown.

ya·hoo (yä′ho͞o, yā′-) *n.* An awkward or crude person; a bumpkin. [< *Yahoo,* one of a race of brutes in Swift's *Gulliver's Travels,* 1726]
Yah·weh (yä′we) In the Old Testament, a name for God. Also **Yah·ve, Yah·veh** (yä′ve). [< Heb. *YHWH*]
yak[1] (yak) *n.* A large, shaggy wild ox of CEN. Asia, often domesticated. [< Tibetan *gyag*]
yak[2] (yak) *Slang v.i.* **yakked, yak·king** To talk or chatter a great deal. —*n.* **1** Persistent chatter or talk. **2** A boisterous laugh. **3** Something, as a joke, causing such a laugh. Also (for *v.* and *n.* def. 1) **yak·e·ty-yak** (yak′ə·tē·yak′). [Imit.] —**yak′ker** *n.*

Yak

yam (yam) *n.* **1** The fleshy, edible, tuberous root of any of a genus of climbing tropical plants. **2** Any of the plants growing this root. **3** A variety of sweet potato. [< Pg. *inhame* < a native w African name]
yam·mer (yam′ər) *v.i. Informal* **1** To complain peevishly; whine; whimper. **2** To howl; roar; shout. —*v.t.* **3** To utter in a complaining or peevish manner. —*n.* The act of yammering. [< OE *geōmrian* to lament]
yang (yang) *n.* In Chinese philosophy, the male principle and element of the universe, source of life and heat and, with yin, co-creator of everything that is. [< Chin.]
yank (yangk) *v.t. & v.i.* To jerk or pull suddenly. —*n.* A sudden sharp pull; jerk. [?]
Yank (yangk) *n. & adj. Informal* YANKEE.
Yan·kee (yang′kē) *n.* **1** A native or citizen of the U.S. **2** A native or inhabitant of the northern U.S. **3** A native or inhabitant of New England. —*adj.* Of, like, or characteristic of Yankees. [?] —**Yan′kee·dom, Yan′kee·ism** *n.*
Yankee Doo·dle (do͞od′l) A song popular in the U.S. from pre-Revolutionary times.
yap (yap) *v.i.* **yapped, yap·ping 1** *Slang* To talk or jabber. **2** To bark or yelp, as a dog. —*n.* **1** A bark or yelp. **2** *Slang* Worthless talk; jabber. **3** *Slang* **a** A crude person. **b** The mouth. [Imit. of a dog's bark]
yard[1] (yärd) *n.* **1** A unit of length equal to 3 feet or 0.914 meter. **2** A long, slender spar set crosswise on a mast and used to support sails. [< OE *gierd* rod, yard measure]
yard[2] (yärd) *n.* **1** A plot of ground enclosed or set apart, as for some specific purpose: often in combination: *barnyard.* **2** The ground or lawn belonging and adjacent to a house, college, university, etc. **3** An enclosure used for building, selling, storing, etc.: often in combination: *shipyard; stockyard.* **4** An enclosure or piece of ground usu. adjacent to a railroad station, used for making up trains and for storage. —*v.t.* To put or collect into or as into a yard. [< OE *geard* an enclosure]
yard·age (yär′dij) *n.* The amount or length of something in yards.
yard·arm (yärd′ärm′) *n.* Either end of the yard of a square sail.
yard goods Fabric sold by the yard; piece goods.
yard·man (yärd′mən) *n. pl.* **·men** (-mən) A man employed in a yard, esp. in a railroad yard.
yard·mas·ter (yärd′mas′tər, -mäs′-) *n.* A railroad official having charge of a yard.
yard·stick (yärd′stik′) *n.* **1** A graduated measuring stick a yard in length. **2** Any measure or standard of comparison; criterion.
yar·mul·ke (yär′məl·kə) *n.* A skullcap traditionally worn by Jewish males in synagogues and often at school and in the home. Also **yar′mel·ke.** [Yiddish]
yarn (yärn) *n.* **1** Any spun fiber, as cotton, wool, or nylon, prepared for use in weaving, knitting, or crotcheting. **2** *Informal* A tale of adventure, often of doubtful truth. —*v.i. Informal* To tell a yarn or yarns. [< OE *gearn*]
yar·row (yar′ō) *n.* Any of a genus of perennial composite plants, esp. a common weed with finely divided, pungent leaves and clusters of small, usu. white flowers. [< OE *gearwe*]
yat·a·ghan (yat′ə·gan, -gən) *n.* A Turkish sword with a double-curved blade and without a handle guard. Also **yat′a·gan.**

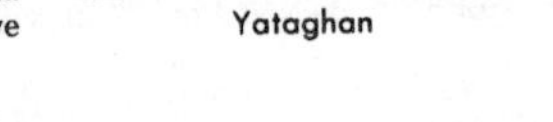
Yataghan

yaw (yô) *v.i.* **1** To move wildly or out of its course, as a ship when struck by a heavy sea. **2** To deviate from a flight path by rotating about a vertical axis: said of spacecraft, projectiles, etc. —*v.t.* **3** To cause to yaw. —*n.* **1** The action of yawing. **2** The amount of deviation in yawing. [?]
yawl (yôl) *n.* **1** A small, fore-and-aft rigged, two-masted sailboat. **2** A ship's small boat; jolly boat. [? < Du *jol*]

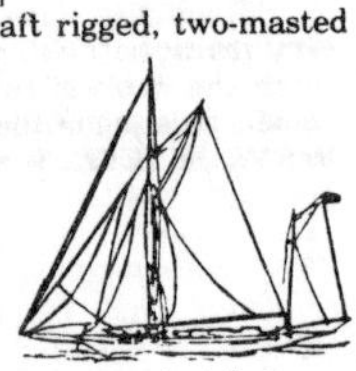
Yawl *def. 1*

yawn (yôn) *v.i.* **1** To open the mouth wide, usu. involuntarily, with a full inhalation, as the result of drowsiness, boredom, etc. **2** To stand wide open: A chasm *yawned* below. —*v.t.* **3** To express or utter with a yawn. —*n.* **1** An act of yawning. **2** A wide opening. [< OE *geonian*] —**yawn′er** *n.*
yawp (yôp) *v.i.* **1** To bark or yelp. **2** *Informal* To talk or shout loudly. —*n.* The act or sound of yawping. [Imit.] —**yawp′er** *n.*
yaws (yôz) *n. pl.* A contagious tropical disease marked by skin lesions. [< Cariban *yáya*]
y-axis (wī′ak′sis) *n. Math.* A coordinate axis along which the variable *y* is plotted.
Yb ytterbium.
Y chromosome The smaller of the unmatched pair of sex chromosomes found in the male of humans and most animals.
y·clept (i·klept′) *adj. Archaic* Called; named. Also **y·cleped′.** [< OE *geclypod,* p.p. of *clypian* call]
yd. yard(s).
ye[1] (t͟hē, yē) *definite article Archaic* The. [< an incorrect transliteration of the Old English thorn, properly transliterated as *th*]
ye[2] (yē) *pron. Archaic* The persons addressed; you. [< OE *gē*]
yea (yā) *adv.* **1** Yes: used in voting orally. **2** *Archaic* Not only so, but more so. **3** *Archaic* In reality; verily: a form of introduction in a sentence. —*n.* **1** An affirmative vote. **2** One who casts such a vote. [< OE *gēa*]
ye·ah (ye′ə) *adv. Informal* Yes.
yean (yēn) *v.t. & v.i.* To bring forth (young), as a goat or sheep. [< OE (assumed) *geēanian*]
yean·ling (yēn′ling) *n.* The young of a goat or sheep. —*adj.* Young; newly born.
year (yir) *n.* **1** The period of time in which the earth completes a revolution around the sun: about 365 days, 5 hours, 49 minutes, and, in the Gregorian calendar, divided into 12 months beginning January 1 and ending December 31. **2** Any period of 12 months. **3** The period of time during which a planet revolves around the sun. **4** Any part of a year devoted to some activity: the school *year.* **5** *pl.* Any extended or past period of time: the *years* before automobiles. **6** *pl.* Length or time of life; age: active for his *years.* [< OE *gēar*]
year·book (yir′bo͝ok′) *n.* A book published annually, usu. presenting information about the previous year.
year·ling (yir′ling) *n.* An animal between one and two years old. —*adj.* Being a year old.
year·long (yir′lông′, -long′) *adj.* Continuing through a year.
year·ly (yir′lē) *adj.* **1** Of a year. **2** Occurring once a year; annual. **3** Continuing for a year: a *yearly* subscription. —*adv.* Once a year; annually.
yearn (yûrn) *v.i.* **1** To desire something earnestly; long: with *for.* **2** To be deeply moved; feel sympathy. [< OE *giernan*] —**yearn′er** *n.* —**Syn. 1** wish, want, covet, hunger, crave, pine for.
yearn·ing (yûr′ning) *n.* A strong emotion of longing or desire, esp. with tenderness.
year-round (yir′round′) *adj.* Continuing, operating, etc., throughout the entire year.
yeast (yēst) *n.* **1** Any of various single-celled fungi that produce ethyl alcohol and carbon dioxide in the process of fermenting carbohydrates. **2** A commercial preparation of certain yeasts, usu. in dry powdery form, used to leaven bread, make beer, etc. **3** Froth or spume. **4** Something causing mental or moral ferment. —*v.i.* To foam; froth. [< OE *gist*]

yeast·y (yēs′tē) *adj.* **yeast·i·er, yeast·i·est** **1** Of or resembling yeast. **2** Causing fermentation. **3** Restless; unsettled. **4** Covered with froth or foam. **5** Light or unsubstantial. —**yeast′i·ness** *n.*

yegg (yeg) *n. Slang* A burglar, esp. one who cracks safes. Also **yegg′man.** [?]

yell (yel) *v.t. & v.i.* **1** To shout; scream. **2** To cheer. —*n.* **1** A sharp, loud cry, as of pain, terror, etc. **2** A rhythmic shout by a group, as in cheering an athletic team. [< OE *giellan*] —**yell′er** *n.*

yel·low (yel′ō) *adj.* **1** Of the color yellow. **2** Changed to a sallow color by age, sickness, etc.: a paper *yellow* with age. **3** Having a yellowish or light brown complexion. **4** Cheaply or offensively sensational: said of newspapers: *yellow* journalism. **5** *Informal* Cowardly; mean; dishonorable. —*n.* **1** The color of ripe lemons or, in the spectrum, the color between green and orange. **2** Any pigment or dyestuff having such a color. **3** The yolk of an egg. —*v.t. & v.i.* To make or become yellow. [< OE *geolu*] —**yel′low·ly** *adv.* —**yel′low·ness** *n.*

yel·low·bird (yel′ō·bûrd′) *n.* Any of various birds with yellow plumage, as the goldfinch.

yellow fever An acute tropical disease caused by a virus transmitted by a mosquito and characterized by jaundice and other symptoms.

yel·low·ham·mer (yel′ō·ham′ər) *n.* **1** A European bunting with bright yellow and black plumage. **2** The flicker or golden-winged woodpecker. [? < OE *geolo* yellow + *amore,* a kind of bird]

yel·low·ish (yel′ō·ish) *adj.* Somewhat yellow.

yellow jack **1** A yellow flag indicating quarantine. **2** YELLOW FEVER.

yellow jacket Any of various social wasps with bright yellow markings.

yellow peril The supposed threat to the West from the power of the peoples of E Asia.

yellow pine **1** Any of various American pines, as the loblolly. **2** Their tough, yellowish wood.

yel·low·wood (yel′ō·wŏŏd′) *n.* Any of various trees having yellow or yellowish wood or yielding a yellow dye.

yel·low·y (yel′ō·ē) *adj.* Yellowish.

yelp (yelp) *v.i.* To utter a sharp or shrill cry. —*v.t.* To express by a yelp or yelps. —*n.* A sharp, shrill cry, as of a dog in distress. [< OE *gielpan* boast] —**yelp′er** *n.*

Yem·en Arab Republic (yem′ən) A country of sw Arabia, 75,000 sq. mi., cap. San'a. —**Yem·e·ni** (yem′ə·nē), **Yem′e·nite** (-nīt) *adj., n.*

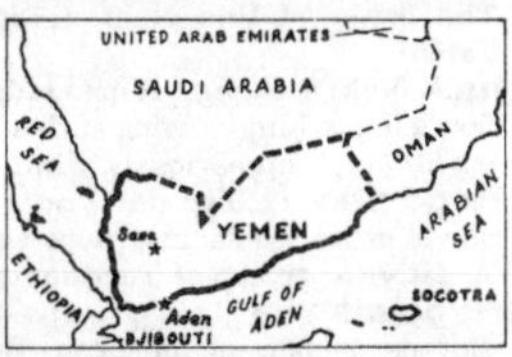

Yemen, People's Democratic Republic of A republic on the s coast of Arabia, 110,000 sq. mi., cap. Madinat ash Sha'b. Also **Southern Yemen.** —**Yem′e·ni, Yem′e·nite** *adj., n.*

yen[1] (yen) *Informal n.* An ardent longing or desire. —*v.i.* **yenned, yen·ning** To yearn; long. [< Chin., opium]

yen[2] (yen) *n.* The basic monetary unit of Japan.

yen·ta (yen′tə) *n.* A female gossip or meddler. Also **yen′·teh.** [Yiddish]

yeo·man (yō′mən) *n. pl.* **·men** (-mən) **1** A petty officer in the U.S. Navy or Coast Guard who performs clerical duties. **2** *Brit.* A farmer, esp. one who cultivates his own farm. **3** YEOMAN OF THE GUARD. **4** *Brit.* One of the attendants of a nobleman or of royalty. [? < OE *geong* young + *mann* a man]

yeo·man·ly (yō′mən·lē) *adj.* **1** Of or pertaining to a yeoman. **2** Brave; rugged. —*adv.* Like a yeoman; bravely.

Yeoman of the (Royal) Guard A member of the ceremonial bodyguard of the English royal household.

yeo·man·ry (yō′mən·rē) *n.* **1** Yeomen, as a group. **2** *Brit.* A home guard of volunteer cavalry, now part of the Territorial Army.

yeoman's service Faithful and useful support or service. Also **yeoman service.**

yep (yep) *adv. Informal* Yes.

yes (yes) *adv.* **1** As you say; truly; just so: a reply of affirmation or consent. **2** Moreover: She is willing, *yes* eager, to go. —*n. pl.* **yes·es** or **yes·ses** A reply in the affirmative. —*v.t. & v.i.* **yessed, yes·sing** To say "yes" (to). [< OE *gēa* yea + *sīe* it may be]

yes-man (yes′man′) *n. pl.* **-men** (men′) *Informal* A person who habitually agrees with the opinions or statements of others, esp. with those of his superiors.

yes·ter·day (yes′tər·dē, -dā′) *n.* **1** The day preceding today. **2** The near past. —*adv.* **1** On the day last past. **2** At a recent time. [< OE *geostran* yesterday + *dæg* day]

yes·ter·year (yes′tər·yir′) *n.* **1** Last year. **2** Recent years; recent past. **3** Time past; a past epoch: the peaceful days of *yesteryear.*

yet (yet) *adv.* **1** In addition; besides. **2** At some future time; eventually: he may *yet* succeed. **3** In continuance of a previous state or condition; still: I can hear him *yet.* **4** At the present time; now: Don't go *yet.* **5** After all the time that has or had elapsed: Are you not ready *yet?* **6** Up to the present time; heretofore: He has never *yet* lied to me. **7** Even: a *yet* hotter day. **8** Nevertheless: They are poor, *yet* happy. **9** As much as; even: He did not believe the reports, nor *yet* the evidence. —**as yet** Up to now. —*conj.* Nevertheless; but: I speak to you peaceably, *yet* you will not listen. [< OE *gīet*]

yew (yōō) *n.* **1** Any of a genus of evergreen trees and shrubs, with narrow, flat, dark green, poisonous leaves and red berrylike cones containing a single seed. **2** The hard, tough wood of the yew. [< OE *ēow, īw*]

Yid·dish (yid′ish) *n.* A language derived from 13th- and 14th-century Middle High German, now spoken primarily by Eastern European Jews and their relatives or descendants in other countries. It contains elements of Hebrew and the Slavic languages. —*adj.* Of, written, or spoken in Yiddish. [< G *jüdisch* Jewish]

yield (yēld) *v.t.* **1** To give forth by a natural process, or as a result of labor or cultivation: The field will *yield* a good crop. **2** To give in return, as for investment; furnish: The bonds *yield* five percent interest. **3** To give up, as to superior power; surrender; relinquish: often with *up:* to *yield* oneself up to one's enemies. **4** To give up one's possession of: to *yield* the right of way . —*v.i.* **5** To provide a return; produce; bear. **6** To give up; submit; surrender. **7** To give way, as to pressure or force. **8** To assent or comply, as under compulsion; consent: We *yielded* to their persuasion. **9** To give place, as through inferiority or weakness: with *to:* We will *yield* to them in nothing. —*n.* The amount yielded; product; result, as of cultivation, investment, etc. [< OE *gieldan* pay] —**yield′er** *n.*

yield·ing (yēl′ding) *adj.* **1** Productive. **2** Flexible; easily bent. **3** Obedient. —**yield′ing·ly** *adv.* —**yield′ing·ness** *n.*

yin (yin) *n.* In Chinese philosophy, the female principle and element of the universe, standing for darkness, cold, and death. [< Chin.]

yip (yip) *n.* A yelp, as of a dog. —*v.i.* **yipped, yip·ping** To yelp. [Imit.]

-yl *suffix Chem.* Used to denote a radical: *ethyl.* [< Gk. *hylē* wood, matter]

YMCA, Y.M.C.A. Young Men's Christian Association.

YMHA, Y.M.H.A. Young Men's Hebrew Association.

yock (yäk) *n. Slang* **1** A loud laugh or guffaw. **2** Something causing such a laugh. [Var. of YAK[2]]

yo·del (yōd′l) *v.t. & v.i.* **·deled** or **·delled, ·del·ing** or **·del·ling** To sing by changing the voice quickly from its low register to a falsetto and back. —*n.* Something yodeled, as a melody or refrain. Also **yo′dle.** [< G *jodeln,* lit., utter the syllable *jo*] —**yo′del·er, yo′del·ler, yo′dler** *n.*

yo·ga (yō′gə) *n.* **1** A Hindu mystical and ascetic discipline, the ultimate purpose of which is to gain spiritual illumination by means of a prescribed series of mental and physical exercises. **2** The exercises, esp. certain physical exercises, based on yoga techniques. [Skt., lit., union] —**yo′gic** (-gik) *adj.*

yo·gi (yō′gē) *n. pl.* **·gis** A person who practices yoga. Also **yo′gin** (-gən, -gin).

yo·gurt (yō'gərt) *n.* A semifluid food made of milk curdled with cultures of bacteria and sometimes flavored with fruit. Also **yo'ghurt.** [<Turk. *yōghurt*]

yoke (yōk) *n.* **1** A curved frame used for coupling draft animals, as oxen, usu. having a bow at each end to receive the neck of the animal. **2** Any of many similar contrivances, as a frame worn on the shoulder to balance pails of milk. **3** A pair of animals joined by a yoke. **4** Something that binds or connects; tie; bond: the *yoke* of marriage. **5** Any of various parts or pieces that connect or hold two things together. **6** Servitude; bondage. **7** A fitted part of a garment designed to support a plaited or gathered part, as at the hips or shoulders. —*v.* **yoked, yok·ing** *v.t.* **1** To attach by means of a yoke, as draft animals. **2** To join with or as with a yoke. —*v.i.* **3** To be joined or linked; unite. [<OE *geoc*]

Yoke *def. 1*

yoke·fel·low (yōk'fel'ō) *n.* A mate or companion, as in labor. Also **yoke'mate'** (-māt').

yo·kel (yō'kəl) *n.* A country bumpkin.[?]

yolk (yōk, yōlk) *n.* **1** The yellow portion of an egg. **2** An oily exudation in unprocessed sheep's wool. [<OE *geolu* yellow] —**yolk'y** *adj.*

Yom Kip·pur (yom kip'ər, yōm, ki·po͞or') The Jewish Day of Atonement, a holiday marked by prayer and fasting, celebrated in late September or in October.

yon (yon) *adj. & adv. Archaic & Regional* YONDER. [<OE *geon*]

yond (yond) *adj. & adv. Archaic & Regional* YONDER. [<OE *geond* across]

yon·der (yon'dər) *adj.* Being at a distance indicated or known. —*adv.* In that place; there. [<OE *geond,* yond]

yoo-hoo (yo͞o'ho͞o') *interj.* A call used to attract the attention of someone

yore (yôr, yōr) *n.* Time long past: in days of *yore.* [<OE *geara* formerly]

York (yôrk) *n.* A royal house of England that reigned from 1461–85.

York·shire pudding (york'shir, -shər) A batter pudding baked in meat drippings.

you (yo͞o) *pron.* **1** The person or persons or the personified thing or things addressed: when used as a subject, always linked with a plural verb. **2** One; anyone: *You* learn by trying. [<OE *ēow,* dat. and acc. pl. of *ge* ye]

you'd (yo͞od) Contraction of *you had* or *you would.*

you'll (yo͞ol) Contraction of *you will* or *you shall.*

young (yung) *adj.* **young·er** (yung'gər), **young·est** (yung'·gist) **1** Being in the early period of life or growth; not old. **2** Not having progressed or developed far; newly formed: The day was *young.* **3** Pertaining to youth or early life. **4** Full of vigor or freshness. **5** Inexperienced; immature. **6** Denoting the younger of two persons having the same name or title; junior. **7** *Geol.* Having the characteristics of an early stage in the geological cycle: said of a river or of certain land forms. —*n.* **1** Young persons as a group. **2** Offspring, esp. of animals. —**with young** Pregnant. [<OE *geong*] —**young'ness** *n.* —**Syn. 4** lively, strong, active, spirited. **5** raw, green, unseasoned, uninitiated.

young·ber·ry (yung'ber'ē) *n. pl.* **·ries** A dark red berry resulting from crossing a blackberry and a dewberry. [<B. M. *Young,* U.S. horticulturist of late 19th c.]

young blood **1** Young people. **2** New, fresh ideas, attitudes, etc.

young·ish (yung'ish) *adj.* Rather young.

young·ling (yung'ling) *n.* **1** A young person, animal, or plant. **2** An inexperienced person. —*adj.* Young. [<OE *geongling*]

young·ster (yung'stər) *n.* A young person, esp. a child.

Young Turk One of a group bent on seizing control of or radically altering an organization, as a political party. [Orig., a member of a 20th c. Turkish revolutionary party]

your (yôr, yo͞or) *pronominal adj.* **1** Of, belonging to or pertaining to you: *your* fate. **2** Used before certain titles: *your* Majesty. [<OE *ēower,* genitive of *gē* ye]

you're (yo͞or, yôr) Contraction of *you are.*

yours (yôrz, yo͞orz) *pron. (construed as sing. or pl.)* The things or persons belonging or pertaining to you: a home as quiet as *yours.* —**of yours** Belonging or relating to you. [ME *youres*]

your·self (yôr·self'; yo͞or-) *pron. pl.* **·selves** (-selvz') **1** The one who is you: used as a reflexive or emphatic form: Try not to hurt *yourself.* **2** Your normal, healthy, etc., condition: You are not *yourself* today. **3** ONESELF: It's best to take care of it *yourself.*

youth (yo͞oth) *n. pl.* **youths** (yo͞oths, yo͞othz) **1** The state or condition of being young. **2** The period when one is young; that part of life between childhood and adulthood. **3** The early period of being or development, as of a movement. **4** A young person, esp. a young man. **5** Young people as a group: the nation's *youth.* [<OE *geoguth*]

youth·ful (yo͞oth'fəl) *adj.* **1** Of, pertaining to, or characteristic of youth. **2** Buoyant; fresh; vigorous. **3** Having youth; being still young. **4** Not far advanced; early; new. **5** *Geol.* Young. —**youth'ful·ly** *adv.* —**youth'ful·ness** *n.*

you've (yo͞ov) Contraction of *you have.*

yowl (youl) *v.i.* To howl; yell. —*n.* A loud, prolonged, wailing cry; a howl. [ME *youlen*]

yo-yo (yō'yō') *n. pl.* **-yos** A wheellike toy with a deep central groove around which is looped a string on which the wheel can be spun in a variety of movements.[?]

yr. year(s); younger; your.

yrs. years; yours.

Y.T. Yukon Territory.

yt·ter·bi·um (i·tûr'bē·əm) *n.* A rare metallic element (symbol Yb) of the lanthanide series. [<*Ytterby,* Sweden]

yt·tri·um (it'rē·əm) *n.* A rare metallic element (symbol Y) similar to and usu. found with ytterbium. [<*Ytterby,* Sweden]

yuc·ca (yuk'ə) *n.* **1** Any of a large genus of liliaceous American plants usu. found in dry, sandy places, having a woody stem which bears a large panicle of white flowers emerging from a crown of sword-shaped leaves. **2** The flower of this plant. [<Sp. *yuca*< Taino]

Yucca

yuck (yuk) *n. Slang* **1** A loud laugh or guffaw. **2** Something causing such a laugh. —*v.i.* To laugh uproariously. [Imit.]

Yu·go·slav (yo͞o'gō·släv') *adj.* Of Yugoslavia or its people: also **Yu'go·slav'ic.** —*n.* A native or citizen of Yugoslavia.

Yu·go·sla·vi·a (yo͞o'gō·slä'vē·ə) *n.* A republic of SE Europe, 98,538 sq. mi., cap. Belgrade. —**Yu'go·sla'vi·an** *adj., n.* • See map at BALKAN STATES.

yuk (yuk) *Slang n. & v.i.* **yukked, yuk·king** YUCK.

Yule (yo͞ol) *n.* Christmas or Christmas time. [<OE *geōl*]

yule log Formerly, a large log, place on the hearth as the foundation of the traditional Christmas Eve fire.

Yule·tide (yo͞ol'tīd') *n.* Christmas time.

yum·my (yum'ē) *Informal adj.* **·mi·er, ·mi·est** Agreeable to the senses, esp. to the taste; delicious. —*n.* Something delicious. [Imit. of the sound made when something is pleasurable to the taste]

yup·pie (yup'ē) *n.pl.* **yup·pies** A young, usually urban, middle-class professional person. [<Y(OUNG) U(RBAN) P(ROFESSIONAL) + -IE]

YWCA, Y.W.C.A. Young Women's Christian Association.

YWHA, Y.W.H.A. Young Women's Hebrew Association.

Z

Z, z (zē, *Brit. & Can.* zed) *n. pl.* **Z's, z's, Zs, zs** (zēz, zedz) **1** The 26th letter of the English alphabet. **2** Any spoken sound representing the letter *Z* or *z*. **3** Something shaped like a Z. —*adj.* Shaped like a Z.

Z., z. zero; zone.

zai·bat·su (zī′bat·sōō′) *n. pl.* **zai·bat·su** The wealthy clique of Japan, representing four or five dominant families. [< Jap. *zai* property + *batsu* family]

Zaire (zīr′, zä·ir′) *n.* A republic of CEN. Africa, 904,754 sq. mi., cap. Kinshasa. • See map at AFRICA.

Zam·bi·a (zam′bē·ə) *n.* An independent member of the Commonwealth of Nations in CEN. Africa, 288,130 sq. mi., cap. Lusaka. • See map at AFRICA.

za·ny (zā′nē) *adj.* **·ni·er, ·ni·est** Absurdly funny; ludicrous. —*n. pl.* **·nies 1** In old comic plays, a clown who absurdly mimics the other performers. **2** Any ludicrous comic or buffoon. **3** A simpleton; fool. [< Ital. *zanni*] —**za′ni·ly** *adv.* —**za′ni·ness** *n.*

zap (zap) *Slang v.t.* **zapped, zap·ping 1** To kill. **2** To attack; hit; clobber. **3** To confront or impress suddenly and forcefully; astound; overwhelm. —*n.* **1** Vigorous effect; punch; vitality. **2** An attack or confrontation.

zeal (zēl) *n.* Ardor, as for a cause; fervor. [< Gk. *zēlos*] —**Syn.** enthusiasm, eagerness, devotion, passion, verve, spirit, heart.

zeal·ot (zel′ət) *n.* One who is zealous, esp. to an immoderate degree; partisan, fanatic, etc. —**zeal′ot·ry** *n.*

zeal·ous (zel′əs) *adj.* Filled with, marked by, or showing zeal; enthusiastic. —**zeal′ous·ly** *adv.* —**zeal′ous·ness** *n.*

ze·bec (zē′bek) *n.* XEBEC. Also **ze′beck.**

ze·bra (zē′brə, *Brit. & Can.* zeb′rə) *n.* Any of various African ponylike mammals having a whitish body with dark stripes. [Pg.] —**ze′brine** (-brēn, -brin), **ze′broid** (-broid) *adj.*

Zebra

ze·bu (zē′byōō) *n.* Any of various breeds of domesticated oxen of Asia and Africa, having a hump on the withers, a large dewlap, and short curved horns. [< Tibetan]

Zech. Zechariah.

zed (zed) *n. Brit. & Can.* The letter *z*. [< Gk. *zēta*]

zeit·geist (tsīt′gīst) *n. Often cap.* The intellectual, moral, and cultural tendencies that characterize any age or epoch. [< G < *Zeit* time + *Geist* spirit]

Zen (zen) *n.* A form of Buddhism that originated in China and became widespread in Japan, that lays particular stress on deep meditation as a means of achieving an abrupt, intuitive, spiritual enlightenment. [< Jap. *zen* meditation]

Zend (zend) *n.* The ancient translation of and commentary on the Avesta. [< Pers., interpretation] —**Zend′ic** *adj.*

Zend-A·ves·ta (zend′ə·ves′tə) *n.* The sacred Zoroastrian writings including the Zend and the Avesta.

ze·nith (zē′nith) *n.* **1** The point of the celestial sphere that is exactly overhead. **2** The highest or culminating point; summit; acme. [< Ar. *samt (ar-rās)* the path (over the head)]

Zeph. Zephaniah.

zeph·yr (zef′ər) *n.* **1** The west wind. **2** Any soft, gentle wind. **3** Worsted or woolen yarn of very light weight: also **zephyr worsted.** [< Gk. *zephyros*]

zep·pe·lin (zep′ə·lin) *n.* A large, cigar-shaped dirigible. [< Count Ferdinand von *Zeppelin*, 1838–1917, German aircraft builder]

ze·ro (zir′ō, zē′rō) *n. pl.* **ze·ros** or **ze·roes 1** The numeral or symbol 0; a cipher. **2** *Math.* The element of a number system that leaves any element unchanged under addition, esp. a real number *0* such that $a + 0 = 0 + a = a$ for any real number *a*. **3** The point on a scale, as of a thermometer, from which measures are counted. **4** The temperature registered at the zero mark on a thermometer. **5** Nothing. **6** The lowest point: Our hopes dropped to *zero*. —*v.t.* **ze·roed, ze·ro·ing** To adjust (instruments) to an arbitrary zero point for synchronized readings. —**zero in 1** To move or bring into a desired position, as an airplane. **2** To adjust the sight of (a gun) or direct (ammunition) toward (a target). —**zero in on 1** To direct gunfire, bombs, etc. toward (a specific target). **2** To concentrate or focus one's energy, attention, efforts, etc., on. —*adj.* **1** Of, at, or being zero. **2** That limits vertical visibility to 50 feet or less: said of a cloud ceiling. **3** That limits horizontal visibility to 165 feet or less: said of conditions on the ground. [< Ar. *ṣifr*] • In popular usage the symbol for zero (0) is often rendered orally as (ō), as if it were the letter O.

zero hour 1 The time set for an attack. **2** Any critical moment.

zest (zest) *n.* **1** Agreeable excitement and keen enjoyment. **2** A quality that imparts such excitement. **3** Any piquant flavoring. [< F *zeste* lemon or orange peel] —**zest′ful, zest′y** *adj.* **(·i·er, ·i·est)** —**zest′ful·ly** *adv.* —**zest′ful·ness** *n.* —**Syn. 1** delight, gusto, relish, pleasure, gratification, savor, thrill, kick.

ze·ta (zā′tə, zē′-) *n.* The sixth letter of the Greek alphabet. (Z,ζ).

Zeus (zōōs) *Gk. Myth.* The supreme deity.

zig·gu·rat (zig′ōō·rat) *n.* Among the Assyrians and Babylonians, a terraced temple tower pyramidal in form, each successive story being smaller than the one below. [< Assyrian *ziqquratu*, orig., a mountain top]

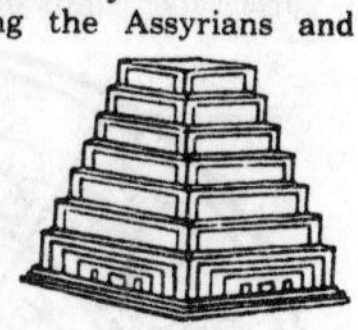
Ziggurat

zig·zag (zig′zag) *n.* **1** One of a series of sharp turns or angles. **2** A path or pattern characterized by such turns or angles going from side to side. —*adj.* Having a series of zigzags. —*adv.* In a zigzag manner. —*v.t. & v.i.* **·zagged, ·zag·ging** To move in zigzags. [< G *zickzack*]

zilch (zilch) *n. Slang* Nothing; zero. [Alter. of ZERO]

zil·lion (zil′yən) *n. Informal* A very large, indeterminate number: a *zillion* things to do before the plane left. [Imit. of *million, trillion*, etc.] —**zil′lionth** *adj.*

zinc (zingk) *n.* A bluish white metallic element (symbol Zn) occurring mostly in combination, extensively used in alloys, as bronze and brass, for galvanizing, and in electric batteries. —*v.t.* **zinced** or **zincked, zinc·ing** or **zinck·ing** To coat or cover with zinc; galvanize. [< G *zink*] —**zinc′ic** (-ik), **zinc′ous** (-əs), **zinck′y, zinc′y, zink′y** *adj.*

zinc ointment A medicated ointment containing zinc oxide.

zinc oxide A white powdery compound, used as a pigment and as a mild antiseptic.

zinc white Zinc oxide used as a pigment.

zing (zing) *Informal n.* **1** A high-pitched buzzing or humming sound. **2** Energy; vitality. —*v.i.* To make a shrill, humming sound.

zin·ni·a (zin′ē·ə, zin′yə) *n.* Any of various cultivated plants having opposite entire leaves and showy, composite flowers. [< J. G. *Zinn*, 1727–59, German botanist]

Zi·on (zī′ən) *n.* **1** A hill in Jerusalem, the site of the Temple of David and his successors. **2** The Jewish people. **3** Any place or community considered to be especially under God's rule, as ancient Israel. **4** The heavenly Jerusalem; heaven. [< Heb. *tsīyōn* a hill]

Zi·on·ism (zī′ən·iz′əm) *n.* A movement for a resettlement of the Jews in Palestine. —**Zi′on·ist** *adj. & n.*

zip (zip) *n.* **1** A sharp, hissing sound, as of a bullet passing through the air. **2** *Informal* Energy; vitality; vim. —*v.* **zipped, zip·ping** *v.t.* **1** To fasten with a zipper: often with *up:* to *zip* up a jacket. **2** To give speed and energy to. —*v.i.* **3** *Informal* To move or act with speed and energy. **4** To move with a sharp, hissing sound. [Imit.]

zip-code (zip′kōd′) *v.t.* **-cod·ed, -cod·ing** *Sometimes cap.* To provide (mail) with a zip code.

zip code (zip) A numerical code devised to identify each postal delivery area in the U.S. Also **ZIP Code, Zip Code.** [< *z(one) i(mprovement) p(lan)*]

zip·per (zip′ər) *n.* A sliding fastener with two rows of interlocking teeth. [< *Zipper,* a trade name]

zip·py (zip′ē) *adj.* **·pi·er, ·pi·est** *Informal* Brisk; energetic.

zir·con (zûr′kon) *n.* **1** An adamantine, variously colored zirconium silicate, used as a gem in certain varieties. **2** A variety of this mineral having an artificially produced lustrous blue appearance. [< Ar. *zarqūn* cinnabar < Pers. *zargūn* golden]

zir·co·ni·um (zûr·kō′nē·əm) *n.* A metallic element (symbol Zr), used in heat-resistant alloys. [< ZIRCON] —**zir·con′·ic** *adj.*

zith·er (zith′ər, zith′-) *n.* A stringed instrument having a flat sounding board and 30 to 40 strings that are played by plucking. Also **zith′ern** (-ərn). [< Gk. *kithara*]

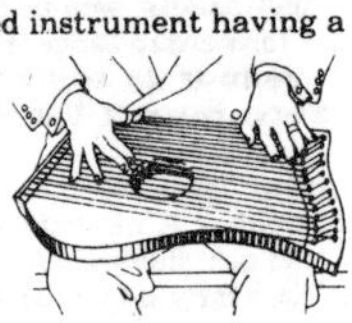

Zither

zlo·ty (zlô′tē) *n. pl.* **·tys** or **·ty** The basic monetary unit of Poland.

Zn zinc.

zo·di·ac (zō′dē·ak) *n.* **1** An imaginary belt encircling the heavens and extending about 8° on each side of the ecliptic, within which are the orbits of the moon, sun, and larger planets. It is divided into twelve parts, called **signs of the zodiac,** which formerly corre-

Signs of the zodiac (reading clockwise):
A. Vernal equinox: Aries, Taurus, Gemini.
B. Summer solstice: Cancer, Leo, Virgo.
C. Autumnal equinox: Libra, Scorpio, Sagittarius.
D. Winter solstice: Capricorn, Aquarius, Pisces.

sponded to twelve constellations. **2** Any complete circuit; round. [< Gk. *(kyklos) zōdiakos* (circle) of animals] —**zo·di·a·cal** (zō·dī′ə·kəl) *adj.*

zom·bie (zom′bē) *n.* **1** In voodoo cults, a snake deity. **2** The supernatural power by which a dead body is believed to be reanimated. **3** A corpse reactivated by such power. **4** *Slang* A person who looks weird or behaves eccentrically, mechanically, etc. **5** A strong cocktail made of several kinds of rum, fruit juices, and liqueurs. Also, esp. for defs. 1, 2, & 3, **zom′bi.** [< West African]

zo·nal (zō′nəl) *adj.* Of, pertaining to, exhibiting, or marked by a zone or zones; having the form of a zone. Also **zo′na·ry** (-nər·ē). —**zon′al·ly** *adv.*

zone (zōn) *n.* **1** One of five divisions of the earth's surface, bounded by parallels of latitude and named for the prevailing climate. These are the **torrid zone,** extending on each side of the equator 23° 27′; the **temperate** or **variable zones,** included between the parallels 23° 27′ and 66° 33′ on both sides of the equator; and the **frigid zones,** within the parallels 66° 33′ and the poles. **2** *Ecol.* A belt or area delimited from others by the character of its plant or animal life, its climate, geological formations, etc. **3** A region, area, belt, etc., distinguished or set off by some special characteristic: a demilitarized *zone;* a residential *zone;* a no-parking *zone.* **4** An area, usu. circular, within which a uniform rate is charged for delivery of goods, telephone calls, etc. **5** In the U.S. postal system: **a** Any of the areas within which a uniform rate is charged for parcel post. **b** Any of the numbered postal districts in a city. **6** *Geom.* A portion of the surface of a sphere enclosed between two parallel planes. —*v.t.* **zoned, zon·ing 1** To divide into zones; esp., to divide (a city, etc.) into zones which are restricted as to types of construction and activity, as residential, industrial, etc. **2** To encircle with a zone or belt. **3** To mark with or as with zones or stripes. [< Gk. *zōnē* a girdle] —**zoned** *adj.*

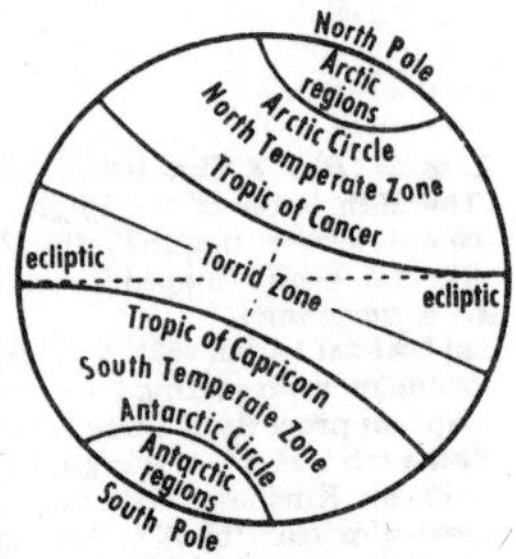

Terrestrial zones

zonk (zongk) *v.t. Slang* To hit, esp. on the head; clobber; brain.

zonked (zongkt) *adj. Slang* Highly intoxicated or stimulated, as by alcohol or a drug: often with *out.* [?]

zoo (zōō) *n. pl.* **zoos** A park or place where wild animals are kept for exhibition. [Short for *zoological garden*]

zoo- *combining form* Animal: *zoology.* [< Gk. *zōion* an animal]

zo·o·ge·o·graph·ic (zō′ə·jē′ə·graf′ik) *adj.* Of, pertaining to, or engaged in zoogeography. Also **zo′o·ge′o·graph′·i·cal.** —**zo′o·ge′o·graph′i·cal·ly** *adv.*

zo·o·ge·og·ra·phy (zō′ə·jē·og′rə·fē) *n.* **1** The systematic study of the distribution of animals and of the factors controlling it. **2** The study of the relations between special animal groups and the land or aquatic areas in which they predominate. —**zo′o·ge·og′ra·pher** *n.*

zo·og·ra·phy (zō·og′rə·fē) *n.* The branch of zoology that describes animals; descriptive zoology. —**zo·og′ra·pher** or **·phist** *n.* —**zo·o·graph·ic** (zō′ə·graf′ik) or **·i·cal** *adj.*

zo·oid (zō′oid) *n.* **1** An entity, usu. very small, capable of movement and independent existence, as a spermatozoon. **2** An individual member of a compound organism, as in a sponge. —*adj.* Having essentially the nature of an animal: also **zo·oi·dal** (zō·oid′l). [< ZO(O)- + -OID]

zool. zoological; zoologist; zoology.

zo·o·log·i·cal (zō′ə·loj′i·kəl) *adj.* **1** Of, pertaining to, or occupied with zoology. **2** Relating to or characteristic of animals. Also **zo′o·log′ic.** —**zo′o·log′i·cal·ly** *adv.*

zoological garden zoo.

zo·ol·o·gy (zō·ol′ə·jē) *n.* **1** The science that treats of animals with reference to their structure, functions, development, nomenclature, and classification. **2** The animal life of a particular area. **3** A scientific treatise on animals. [< ZOO- + -LOGY] —**zo·ol′o·gist** *n.*

zoom (zōōm) *v.i.* **1** To make a low-pitched but loud humming or buzzing sound, esp. when related to speed: The cars *zoomed* down the road. **2** To climb sharply upward, as an airplane. **3** To rise sharply, as prices. **4** To move a motion picture or TV camera rapidly or adjust the focus, as with a zoom lens, to make an image appear to come very close or become more distant: often with *in* or *out.* —*v.t.* **5** To cause to zoom. —*n.* The act of zooming. [Imit.]

zoom lens *Photog.* A lens, used chiefly on television and motion picture cameras, that permits the size of the image to be varied continuously without loss of focus.

zo·o·phyte (zō′ə·fīt) *n.* An invertebrate animal resembling a plant, as a coral or sea anemone. [< ZOO- + Gk. *phyton* plant] **—zo′o·phyt′ic** (-fit′ik) or **·i·cal** *adj.*

zo·o·spore (zō′ə·spôr, -spōr) *n.* A motile, asexual spore of certain fungi and algae, usu. provided with cilia. [< ZOO- + SPORE] **—zo′o·spor′ic** (-spôr′ik, -spor′ik), **zo·os·po·rous** (zō·os′pər·əs) *adj.*

zo·ri (zō′rē) *n.* A flat, thonged sandal of straw or rubber. [< Japanese]

Zo·ro·as·tri·an·ism (zō′rō·as′trē·ən·iz′əm) *n.* The religious system founded in ancient Persia by Zoroaster. It recognizes two creative powers, one good and the other evil, and teaches the final triumph of good over evil.

Zou·ave (zōō·äv′, zwäv) *n.* **1** A member of a unit of the French infantry wearing a brilliant Oriental uniform. **2** A member of any volunteer regiment wearing a similar uniform. [< Ar. *Zouaoua*, a tribal name]

zounds (zoundz) *interj.* An exclamation denoting astonishment. [Short for *God's wounds*]

Zr zirconium.

zuc·chet·to (tsōōk·ket′tō) *n. pl.* **·tos** A skullcap worn by ecclesiastics in the Roman Catholic Church, black for a priest, purple for a bishop, red for a cardinal, white for the pope. [Ital. < *zucchetta*, orig. a small gourd]

zuc·chi·ni (zōō·kē′nē) *n.* An elongated summer squash having a thin green skin. [< Ital. *zucca* a gourd, squash]

Zu·lu (zōō′lōō) *n. pl.* **Zu·lus** or **Zu·lu** **1** A member of a Bantu nation of SE Africa. **2** The Bantu language of the Zulus. *—adj.* Of the Zulus or their language.

Zu·ñi (zōō′nyē) *n. pl.* **·ñi** or **·ñis** **1** A member of a tribe of North American Indians, now living in New Mexico. **2** The language of this tribe.

zwie·back (zwī′bak, zwē′-, swī′-, swē′-, -bäk) *n.* A wheaten bread baked in a loaf and later sliced and toasted. [G, twice baked]

Zwing·li·an (zwing′lē·ən, tsving′-) *adj.* Of or pertaining to Huldreich Zwingli or his doctrines, esp. the doctrine that the Eucharist is simply a symbolic commemoration of the death of Christ. *—n.* A follower of Zwingli. **—Zwing′·li·an·ism** *n.*

zy·gote (zī′gōt, zig′ōt) *n.* **1** The product of the union of two gametes. **2** An individual developing from such a union. [< Gk *zygon* a yoke] **—zy·got·ic** (zī·got′ik) *adj.*

zy·mase (zī′mās) *n.* A mixture of enzymes that promotes fermentation by breaking down glucose and related carbohydrates into alcohol and carbon dioxide. [< Gk. *zymē* leaven]

zy·mol·o·gy (zī·mol′ə·jē) *n.* The science of fermentation. [< Gk. *zymē* leaven + -LOGY] **—zy·mo·log·ic** (zī′mə·loj′ik) or **·i·cal** *adj.* **—zy·mol′o·gist** *n.*

zy·mot·ic (zī·mot′ik) *adj.* Of, pertaining to, or caused by fermentation. [< Gk. *zymōtikos*]

zy·mur·gy (zī′mûr·jē) *n.* The chemistry of fermentation as applied to brewing, making of yeast, and wine making. [< Gk *zymē* leaven + -URGY]